D1287076

COMPLETE TELEVISION, RADIO & CABLE INDUSTRY GUIDE

2018

COMPLETE TELEVISION, RADIO & CABLE INDUSTRY GUIDE

GREY HOUSE PUBLISHING

PUBLISHER:	Leslie Mackenzie
EDITOR:	Richard Gottlieb
EDITORIAL DIRECTOR:	Laura Mars
PRODUCTION MANAGER & COMPOSITION:	Kristen Hayes
EDITORIAL MANAGER:	Stuart Paterson
PRODUCTION ASSISTANTS:	Geoff Graves, Olivia Parsonson, Jael Powell, Sai Rodrigo
MARKETING DIRECTOR:	Jessica Moody

Grey House Publishing, Inc.
4919 Route 22
Amenia, NY 12501
518.789.8700
FAX 845.373.6390
www.greyhouse.com
e-mail: books@greyhouse.com

7th edition published 2018

Publisher's Cataloging-In-Publication Data
(Prepared by The Donohue Group, Inc.)

Names: Gottlieb, Richard, editor. | Grey House Publishing, Inc., publisher.

Title: Complete television, radio & cable industry directory / editor: Richard Gottlieb.

Other Titles: Complete television, radio and cable industry directory

Description: Amenia, NY : Grey House, 2013- | Title varies. | "An earlier version of a similar work was published by Bowker as Broadcasting & Cable Yearbook"—P. vii. | Includes index.

Identifiers: ISBN 9781619251038 (2013 ed.) | ISBN 9781682173886 (2018, 7th ed.)

Subjects: LCSH: Television broadcasting—United States—Directories. | Radio broadcasting—United States—Directories. | Cable television—United States—Directories. | Television broadcasting—Canada—Directories. | Radio broadcasting—Canada—Directories. | Cable television—Canada—Directories.

Classification: LCC HE8689 .C66 | DDC 384.54/097—dc23

Table of Contents

Introduction

The *Complete Television, Radio & Cable Industry Guide* fills the need for current, comprehensive television, radio and cable industry information for both U.S. and Canadian markets, and has consistently done so for more than 80 years. We are pleased to continue to offer authoritative information on this dynamic industry in both print and online formats.

Important Features

Users will find clear separation of U.S. and Canadian material for television, radio and cable. Comprehensive sections include market areas, call letter lists and station profiles. Each station profile separates important elements, such as web sites, ownership, and programming. Key contact names are indented for quick recognition; all television stations include virtual channel as well as digital, and all radio stations include Arbitron's market area.

Users will find clear separation of U.S. and Canadian material for television, radio and cable. Comprehensive sections include market areas, call letter lists and station profiles. Each station profile separates important elements, such as web sites, ownership, and programming. Key contact names are indented for quick recognition; all television stations include virtual channel as well as digital, and all radio stations include Arbitron's market area.

The *Complete Television, Radio & Cable Industry Guide* includes eight major sections, with the "big three"—television, radio and cable—arguably the most detailed and most significant. More than just call letters, however, this directory includes professional services from producers and engineers to equipment manufacturers and legal services, plus those who consult and advocate for this diverse industry.

More than a thousand listings have been updated throughout, with particular attention paid to group owners and major networks. Due to the frequent restructuring typical of this industry, users will find many new and combined listings, such as the recent acquisition of Shaw Media by Corus Entertainment in Canada, making Corus that country's leading media company with 45 specialty television services, including W Network, Oprah Winfrey Network, the Food Network, and Disney.

The front matter of the 2018 edition includes industry statistics: lists of station transactions; top shows; sales of TV receivers and HDTVs and more. A brand new article, "Paradigm Shift: Why Radio Must Adapt to the Rise of Digital," appears at the front of the U.S radio section.

Praise for previous edition:

> *". . . three major sections . . . a few smaller chapters . . . useful chronology of electronic media . . . associations . . . regulatory agencies . . .trade shows . . . awards. . . . [U]seful for major research libraries with specialized media collections serving communications graduate programs. Recommended."*
>
> —*Choice*

> *". . . For libraries serving users in the broadcasting industry or for anyone working in these fields, this is a valuable assemblage of a massive amount of information. . . . Highly recommended."*
>
> —*American Reference Book Annual*

Television

U.S. television starts with statistics that include ranking data. This is followed by detailed listings of national and regional networks, and group owners. TV stations are arranged by DMA (Designated Market Area). These station listings include dozens of technical details direct from the FCC, such as digital and virtual channel numbers, hours of operation, frequency, and antenna height. Corporate information follows—licensee, owner and network—plus names of important decision makers, such as President, Station Manager, Program Director and more.

Following the U.S. stations, are informative lists—TV stations by call letters, by digital and virtual channels, and a list of U.S. stations that broadcast in Spanish. Comprehensive Canadian TV information follows the U.S. sections—including networks, group owners, detailed station listings, and lists by call letters and channels.

Radio

U.S. radio starts with a statistical summary, which is followed by detailed listings of national and regional radio networks, and group owners, all with key contact names. Listings are arranged by state of license, then city within the state. Like the television stations, these listings include dozens of technical details direct from the FCC, such as power, frequency and hours of operation, plus the station's market area. Users will find type of programming and special programming, including hours of news programming, and target audience. Long lists of key contacts follow, assuring you will always be able to reach the right person.

Following the detailed station listings is information on international radio, satellite radio, and call letters listed by AM and FM and frequency. The U.S. radio section ends with detailed programming information—putting each radio station into one or more listening designations, from Adult Contemporary to Vietnamese. This programming index is followed by special programming, where you will find specifics, like which stations in Portland, Oregon offer jazz on Sunday afternoon.

Comprehensive Canadian radio information follows the U.S. sections—including networks, group owners, detailed station listings, lists by call letters and frequency, and programming.

As the radio section of *Directory of Television, Radio & Cable* is the largest, here is where users will notice the most updates—to both US and Canadian listings—with particular focus on the large stations and major markets.

Cable

The cable section starts with a variety of updated statistics on U.S. cable programming, followed by detailed listings of national and regional cable networks, with a separate section on regional cable sports networks. Cable data for Canada follows, with detailed listings of Canadian cable networks. This section also includes industry statistics.

Technical Equipment and Services

In addition to the detailed station listings, the *Complete Television, Radio & Cable Industry Guide* includes current, comprehensive information on those who provide services, materials and equipment to the industry. From major television syndicators to radio news services, from producers to distributors, from equipment manufacturers to cable audio services, this 2018 edition will help you find the product or service you need.

Professional Services and More

This comprehensive directory also includes listings of employment services, technical consultants, legal services, and talent agents. There is a separate section on associations, trade shows and vocational schools and, finally, complete listings for the FCC and other regulatory agencies, as well as Canadian agency information.

This directory is your key to this dynamic industry, all in one place, with valuable profiles, industry statistics, and comprehensive indexes. Find out specifics of any station in the U.S. and Canada, including their audience, how to reach them, what school offers industry training, where to find the latest studio sound board, and how to keep up on the latest industry regulations.

Online Database

For even easier access to this information, the *Compete Television, Radio & Cable Industry Guide* is available by subscription to our online database—G.O.L.D. For more information or a free trial, call 800-562-2139 or visit www.greyhouse.com.

A Chronology of the Electronic Media

From Isaac Newton to YouTube TV's Live Streaming

1666
Sir Isaac Newton performs basic experiments on the spectrum.

1794
Allessandro Volta of Italy invents the voltaic cell, a primitive battery.

1827
George Ohm of Germany shows the relationship between resistance, amperage and voltage. Sir Charles Wheatstone of England invents an acoustic device to amplify sounds that he calls a "microphone."

1844
Samuel F.B. Morse tests the first telegraph with "What hath God wrought?" message sent on link between Washington and Baltimore.

1858
First trans-Atlantic cable completed. President James Buchanan and Queen Victoria exchange greetings.

1867
James Clerk Maxwell of Scotland develops the electromagnetic theory.

1875
George R. Carey of Boston proposes a system that would transmit and receive moving visual images electrically.

1876
Alexander Graham Bell invents the telephone.

1877
Thomas A. Edison applies for a patent on a "phonograph or talking machine."

1878
Sir William Cooke of England passes high voltage through a wire in a sealed glass tube, causing a pinkish glow\Mevidence of cathode rays. It's the first step toward the development of the vacuum tubes.

1884
Paul Nipkow of Germany patents a mechanical, rotating facsimile scanning disk.

1886
Heinrich Hertz of Germany proves that electromagnetic waves can be transmitted through space at the speed of light and can be reflected and refracted.

1895
Wilheim Conrad Roentgen of Germany discovers X-rays.

Guglielmo Marconi sends and receives his first wireless signals across his father's estate at Bologna, Italy.

1896
Marconi applies for British patent for wireless telegraphy. He receives an American patent a year later.

1899
Marconi flashes the first wireless signals across the English Channel.

1900
Constantin Perskyi (France) coins the word television at the International Electricity Congress, part of the 1900 Paris Exhibition.

1901
Marconi at Newfoundland, Canada, receives the first trans-Atlantic signal, the letter "S," transmitted from Poldhu, England.

1906
Dr. Lee de Forest invents the audion, a three-element vacuum tube, having a filament, plate and grid, which leads to the amplification of radio signals.

1909
Nobel Prize awarded to Karl Ferdinand Braun and Guglielmo Marconi for the development of radio

1910
Enrico Caruso and Emmy Destinn, singing backstage at the Metropolitan Opera House in New York, broadcast through the De Forest radiophone and are heard by an operator on the SS Avon at sea and by wireless amateurs in Connecticut.

United States approves an act requiring certain passenger ships to carry wireless equipment and operators.

1912
The Titanic disaster proves the value of wireless at sea; 705 lives saved. Jack Phillips and Harold Bride are the ship's wireless operators.

1920
On August 20, 8MK (later, WWJ) in Detroit, owned by the Detroit News, starts what is later claimed to be regular broadcasting.

The Westinghouse Co.'s KDKA(AM) Pittsburgh broadcasts the Harding-Cox election on returns November 2 as the country's first licensed commercial radio station.

1921
The Dempsey-Carpentier fight is broadcast from Boyle's Thirty Acres in Jersey City through a temporarily installed transmitter at Hoboken, New Jersey. Major J. Andrew White was the announcer. This event gave radio a tremendous boost.

1922
The superheterodyne circuit is demonstrated by its inventor, Edwin H. Armstrong. It dramatically improves AM radio reception.

WEAF(AM) New York broadcasts what is claimed to be the first commercially sponsored program on September 7. The advertiser is the Queensborough Corp., a real estate organization.

WOI(AM) Ames, Iowa, goes on air as the country's first licensed educational station.

1923
Dr. Vladimir K. Zworykin files for a U.S. patent for an all-electronic television system.

A "chain" broadcast features a telephone tie-up between WEAF(AM) New York and WNAC(AM) Boston.

1924
The Republican convention in Cleveland and the Democratic convention in New York are broadcast over networks.

1925
President Calvin Coolidge's inaugural ceremony is broadcast by 24 stations in a transcontinental network.

1926
President Coolidge signs the Dill-White Radio Bill creating the Federal Radio Commission and ending the chaos on the radio dial caused by the wild growth of broadcasting.

National Broadcasting Co. is organized on November 1 with WEAF(AM) and WJZ(AM) in New York as key stations and Merlin Hall Aylesworth as president. Headquarters are at 711 Fifth Ave., New York.

1927
The Columbia Broadcasting System goes on the air with a basic network of 16 stations. Major J. Andrew White is president.

Philo T. Farnsworth applies for a patent on his image dissector television camera tube.

1928
NBC establishes a permanent coast-to-coast radio network.

1929
William S. Paley, 27, is elected president of the Columbia Broadcasting System.

Vladimir Zworykin demonstrates his kinescope or cathode ray television receiver before a meeting of the Institute of Radio Engineers on November 19.

1930
Experimental TV station W2XBS is opened by National Broadcasting Co. in New York.

1931
Experimental television station W2XAB is opened by Columbia Broadcasting System in New York.

The first issue of Broadcasting magazine appears on October 15.

The National Association of Broadcasters reports that more than half of the nation's radio stations are operating without a profit.

1932
CBS, NBC, and New York area stations, notably WOR(AM), go into round-the-clock operations to cover the Lindbergh kidnapping, radio's biggest spot-news reporting job to date.

NBC lifts its ban on recorded programs for its owned-and-operated stations, but continues to bar them from network use.

NBC withdraws prohibitions against price mentions on the air during daytime hours; two months later, both NBC and CBS allow price mentions at nighttime as well.

1933
Associated Press members vote to ban network broadcasts of AP news and to restrict local broadcasts to bulletins to stipulated times with air credit to member newspapers.

The American Newspaper Publishers Association declares radio program schedules are advertising and should be published only if paid for.

CBS assigns publicity director Paul White to organize a nationwide staff to collect news for network broadcast. General Mills agrees to sponsor twice-daily newscasts.

1934
Congress passes the Communication Act, which, among other things, replaces the Federal Radio Commission with the Federal Communications Commission.

1935
RCA announces that it is taking television out of the laboratory for a $1 million field-test program.

1936
A year of TV demonstrations begins in June with the Don Lee Broadcasting System's first public exhibition of cathode ray television in the U.S., using a system developed by Don Lee TV director Harry Lubcke. One month later, RCA demonstrates its system of TV with transmissions from the Empire State Building, and Philco follows with a seven-mile transmission in August.

FM (frequency modulation) broadcasting, a new radio system invented by Major Edwin H. Armstrong, is described at an FCC hearing as static-free, free from fading and cross-talk, having uniformity day and night in all seasons and greater fidelity of reproduction.

A.C. Nielsen, revealing his firm's acquisition of the MIT-developed "Audimeter," proposes a metered tuning method of measuring radio audience size.

1937
WLS(AM) Chicago recording team of Herb Morrison, announcer, and Charles Nehlsen, engineer, on a routine assignment at Lakehurst, New Jersey, records an on-the-spot account of the explosion of the German dirigible Hindenburg. NBC breaks its rigid rule against recordings to put it on the network.

1938
Broadcasting publishes the first facsimile newspaper in a demonstration at the National Association of Broadcasters convention.

1939
After 15 years of litigation, the patent for iconoscope-kinescope tubes, the basis for electronic television, is granted to Dr. Vladimir Zworykin.

A telecast of the opening ceremonies of the New York World's Fair marks the start of a regular daily television schedule by RCA-NBC in New York.

The first baseball game ever televised\MPrinceton vs. Columbia\Mappears on NBC.

1940
The FCC authorizes commercial operation of FM, but puts TV back into the laboratory until the industry reaches an agreement on technical standards.

CBS demonstrates a system of color TV developed by its chief TV engineer, Dr. Peter Goldmark.

1941
Bulova Watch Co., Sun Oil Co., Lever Bros. and Procter & Gamble sign as sponsors of the first commercial telecasts on July 1 over NBC's WNBT(TV) New York (until then W2XBS).

President Roosevelt's broadcast to the nation on December 9, the day after war is declared, has the largest audience in radio history\Mabout 90 million listeners.

1942
The Advertising Council is organized by advertisers, agencies, and media to put the talents and techniques of advertising at the disposal of the government to inspire and instruct the public concerning the war effort.

1943
Edward J. Noble buys the Blue Network from RCA for $8 million in cash. RCA had two networks, NBC Red and NBC Blue.

1944
With the FCC approval of the transfer of owned stations, the Blue Network assumes the name of its holding company, the American Broadcasting Co.

1945
Pooled coverage of the Nazi surrender in May brings the American people full details of the end of the war in Europe. Peace heralds a communications boom: Not only will programming restrictions end, but new station construction, frozen for the duration, will proceed at an explosive pace soon after V-J Day in August.

1946
A telecast of the Louis-Conn heavyweight title fight, sponsored by Gillette Safety Razor Co. on a four-city hookup, reaches an estimated 100,000 viewers and convinces skeptics that television is here to stay.

RCA demonstrates its all-electronic system of color TV.

Bristol-Myers is the first advertiser to sponsor a television network program\MGeographically Speaking\Mwhich debuted October 27 on NBC TV's two-station network.

1947
Radio comedian Fred Allen uses a gag, which NBC had ruled out, about network vice presidents, and is cut off the air while he tells it. The story is front-page news across the country as the sponsor's ad agency demands a rebate for 35 seconds of dead air.

1948
Texaco puts an old-style vaudeville show on NBC TV; the hour-long series stars Milton Berle.

1949
The Academy of Television Arts & Sciences presents the first Emmy Awards at ceremonies televised by KTSL(TV) Los Angeles.

1950
General Foods drops actress Jean Muir, who denies any communist affiliations or sympathies, from the cast of The Aldrich Family (NBC TV) after protests against her appearance by "a number of groups." The Joint Committee Against Communism claims credit for her removal, announcing a drive to "cleanse" radio and television of pro-communist actors, directors, and writers.

The FCC approves CBS's color TV system, effective November 20. The network promises 20 hours of color programming a week within two months. TV set manufacturers are divided, however, over whether to make sets, since the CBS system is incompatible with black-and-white broadcasts. In the meantime, RCA continues work on its color system.

1951
Witness Frank Costello's hands provide TV's picture of the week as he refuses to expose his face to cameras covering New York hearings on organized crime of the Senate Crime Investigation Committee, chaired by Senator Estes Kefauver (D-Tenn.)

Sixteen advertisers sponsor the first commercial color telecast, an hour-long program on a five-station East Coast CBS TV hook-up.

Bing Crosby Enterprises announces the development of a system for recording video and audio programs on magnetic tape. The pictures shown at demonstrations are described as "hazy" but "viewable." A year later the images are described as improved "more than 20-fold."

1952
By rushing equipment across the country, from Bridgeport, Connecticut, to Portland, Oregon, KPTV(TV) Portland goes on the air as the first commercial UHF TV station.

On September 6, 1952, Canadian television was first introduced, in the form of (CBC) CBMF-TV Montreal, followed by CBLT-TV Toronto two days later.

1953
With the end of daylight-saving time, CBS TV and NBC TV inaugurate "hot kinescope" systems to put programs on the air on the West Coast at the same clock hour as in the East.

RCA demonstrates black-and-white and color TV programs recorded on magnetic tape. RCA-NBC Board Chairman David Sarnoff says two years of finishing touches are needed before the system is ready for market.

The FCC approves RCA's compatible (with black-and-white transmission) color TV standards. System supplants the incompatible CBS system.

1954
CBS President Frank Stanton broadcasts the first network editorial, urging that radio and TV be allowed to cover congressional hearings.

1955
A contract between the DuMont TV network and Jackie Gleason Enterprises calls for Gleason's The Honeymooners to be done as a filmed program for CBS TV on Saturday nights.

1956
Ampex Corp. unveils the first practical videotape recorder at the National Association of Radio and Television Broadcasters convention in Chicago. The company takes in $4 million in orders.

1957
Videotape recorders are seen as the solution to the TV networks' daylight-saving time problems.

1958
Subliminal TV messages are put under the spotlight at hearings in Los Angeles and Washington.

The BBDO ad agency converts live commercials to videotape.

1959
Sixty-eight TV stations defy the broadcasters' code of conduct by refusing to drop Preparation H commercials.

The quiz show scandal climaxes when famed Twenty-One prizewinner Charles Van Doren admits to a House committee that he had been provided with answers and strategies in advance. The sad ending to the quiz show era prompts cancellation of big-prize shows and vows by NBC and CBS to end deceptive practices.

1960
A satellite sends weather reports back from a 400-mile-high orbit.

RKO-Zenith plans a $10 million test of an on-air pay TV system in Hartford, Connecticut.

Sam Goldwyn offers a package of movies to television.

The last daytime serial on network radio ends.

The opening Kennedy-Nixon debate attracts the largest TV audience to date.

1961
FCC Chairman Newton Minnow shakes up the National Association of Broadcasters convention with his assessment of TV programming: Although it occasionally shines with programs like Twilight Zone and CBS Reports, it is, more than anything, from sign-on to sign-off "a vast wasteland."

Off-network shows become popular as syndicated fare.

The Ampex "electronic editor" permits inserts and additions to be made in videotape without physical splices.

ABC TV engineers develop a process for the immediate playback of videotape recordings in slow motion.

1962
John Glenn's orbital space flight is seen by 135 million TV viewers.

Telstar, AT&T's orbiting satellite, provides a glamorous debut for global television.

1963
Astronaut Gordon Cooper sends back the first TV pictures from space.

All radio and TV network commercials and entertainment programming are canceled following the assassination of President Kennedy. In the same week, the first trans-Pacific broadcast via satellite previews live TV coverage of the 1964 Olympics in Tokyo.

1964
The government and the tobacco companies each ponder their next move after the surgeon general's report links cigarette smoking and lung cancer. Within weeks, American Tobacco drops sports broadcasts, radio stations begin to ban cigarette ads and CBS TV orders a de-emphasis of cigarette use on programs.

1965
Early Bird, the first commercial communications satellite, goes into stationary orbit, opening trans-Atlantic circuits for TV use.

1966
Fred W. Friendly quits as president of CBS News when his new boss, John Schneider, CBS group vice president for broadcasting, cancels coverage of a Senate hearing on the Vietnam War and runs a rerun of I Love Lucy instead.

Network TV viewers see live close-up pictures of the moon\Msent back by Surveyor I\Mas they come into the Jet Propulsion Laboratory.

1967
ABC Radio introduces a radical plan: four networks instead of one, each tailored to suit different station formats.

President Johnson signs the Public Broadcasting Act into law, establishing the Corporation for Public Broadcasting, federal funding mechanism.

1968
The Children's Television Workshop is created by the Ford Foundation, the Carnegie Corp., and the Office of Education to develop a 26-week series of hour-long color programs for preschool children. Sesame Street is the result.

The U.S. Supreme Court gives the FCC jurisdiction over all cable TV systems.

Pictures taken inside Apollo 7 in flight and sent back to Earth revive public interest in the space program.

NBC TV earns the life-long ire of sports fans when it cuts off the end of a Jets-Raiders game to air its made-for-TV movie Heidi. Viewers miss the Raiders' two-touch-downs-in-nine-seconds defeat of the Jets.

1969
The Corporation for Public Broadcasting plans the creation of the Public Broadcasting Service to distribute programming to noncommercial TV stations.

In the same week that ABC-TV announces its $8 million Monday Night Football deal (games to begin in 1970), Apollo 10 sends back the first color TV pictures of the moon and of Earth from the moon.

The world watches live coverage of Neil Armstrong's walk on the moon.

1970
House and Senate conferees agree on legislation to outlaw cigarette advertising on radio and TV, but change the bill's effective date from January 1, 1971, to January 2, so commercials can appear on New Year's Day football telecasts.

The FCC rules that TV stations in the top 50 markets cannot accept more than three hours of network programming between 7 and 11 p.m., and bars them from domestic syndication and from acquiring subsidiary rights in independently produced programs.

First cable TV networks are introduced.

1971
National Public Radio debuts with a 90-station interconnected lineup.

1972
Judge Benjamin Hooks of Memphis, Tennessee, is nominated to the FCC. He becomes the first black to serve on a federal regulatory agency.

Home Box Office Inc., New York, is formed as a subsidiary of Sterling Communications to provide pay-cable TV systems with live and film programming.

1973
Western Union becomes the first company to receive federal permission to launch a commercial communications satellite in the U.S.

Broadcast media around the world open their coverage of the Senate select committee's investigation of the Watergate scandal.

1974
RCA inaugurates the nation's first domestic satellite communications service, using a Canadian satellite.

More than 110 million viewers watch President Nixon announce his resignation.

1975
Home Box Office, Time Inc.'s pay cable subsidiary, announces that it will inaugurate a satellite delivery network in the fall.

1976
Ampex Corp. and CBS develop the electronic still-store system, which uses a digital recording technique to store 1,500 frames in random mode, each accessible in 100 milliseconds.

Cable network launches include Showtime and Univision.

1977
ABC's eight-day telecast of the miniseries Roots becomes the most watched program in television history, with ratings in the mid-40s and shares in the mid-60s. Eighty million people watch at least some part of the final episode.

Sony unveils its Betamax videocassette in August and later the same month RCA introduces its SelectaVision home videotape recorder.

1978
The U.S. Supreme Court upholds the FCC in the "seven dirty words" case involving Pacifica's WBAI(FM) New York. The ruling says the FCC may regulate and punish for the broadcasting of "indecent material."

1979
Ampex demonstrates its digital videotape recorder at the Society of Motion Picture and Television Engineers conference in San Francisco in February. Sony unveils its version two months later.

Cable network launches include C-SPAN, ESPN, The Movie Channel, and Nickelodeon.

1980
"Who Shot J.R.?" episode of Dallas garners the highest rating for any program in modern TV history, with a 53.3 rating and a 76 share.

Cable network launches include Cable News Network, Black Entertainment Television, the Learning Channel, Bravo, and USA Network.

1981
With five ENG cameras rolling, the shooting of President Reagan becomes history's most heavily covered assassination attempt.

The first U.S. demonstration of high-definition television (HDTV) takes place at the annual convention of the Society of Motion Picture and Television Engineers. The Japanese Broadcasting Corp.'s (NHK) 1,125-line analog system draws raves from engineers and filmmakers.

Cable network launches include MTV: Music Television and the Eternal Word Television Network.

1982
Having reached a settlement with the Justice Department to divest itself of its 23 local telephone companies, communications giant AT&T hopes to lead the country into the "information age." The National Cable Television Association, Congress, and the FCC wonder what the agreement has wrought.

Cable network launches include the Weather Channel and the Playboy Channel.

1983
Reagan appointee Mark Fowler, chairman of the FCC, tells a common carrier conference that the U.S. is heading toward a regulation-free telecommunications marketplace.

In February, the two-and-a-half-hour final episode of CBS's M*A*S*H is the most watched program in TV history, garnering a 60.3 rating and a 77 share.

Cable network launches include the Disney Channel and Country Music Television.

1984
The U.S. Supreme Court rules that home videotaping is legal.

Congress passes the Cable Telecommunications Act of 1984, landmark legislation deregulating cable. Law accelerates the growth of cable.

Cable network launches include the Arts & Entertainment Network (A&E), American Movie Classics, and Lifetime.

1985
Ted Turner makes inquiries at the FCC about a possible takeover of CBS. Later, in March, media company Capital Cities Communications purchases ABC for $3.5 billion. Turner's efforts to acquire CBS fail by the end of July, when a federal judge approves the network's stock buyback plan.

The Advanced Television Services Committee (ATSC) votes in favor of the NHK HDTV standard: 1,125 lines, 60 fields, 2:1 interlace, 5.33:3 ratio. This standard is put forward by the U.S. to the International Radio Consultative Committee (CCIR) for consideration as the international standard. The CCIR adopts the recommendation later in the year.

Having lost his bid to buy CBS, Ted Turner makes a $1.5 billion offer for MGM/UA.

Cable network launches include The Discovery Channel, Home Shopping Network, and VH-1.

1986
MGM and Color Systems Technology sign an agreement for the conversion of 100 of the studio's black-and-white films to color.

Cable network launches include C-SPAN2 and QVC.

1987
Fox Broadcasting Co. introduces its primetime lineup with 108 affiliates in its bid to become the fourth major U.S. commercial television network.

The National Association of Broadcasters and the Association for Maximum Service Television broadcast HDTV over standard TV channels during public demonstrations in Washington.

President Reagan vetoes legislation to write the fairness doctrine into law. The doctrine required broadcast stations to allow opposing views of issues, but critics claimed that it discouraged open debate.

Cable network launches include Movietime (renamed E! Entertainment Television in 1990), The Travel Channel, and Telemundo.

1988
The FCC adopts preliminary ground rules for HDTV. It tentatively decides to require HDTV broadcasts to be compatible with NTSC sets and says it will not make additional spectrum available outside the VHF and UHF bands for HDTV because there is enough already available to accommodate the service.

Cable network launches include Turner Network Television.

1989
Time Inc. and Warner Communications agree to swap stock and merge into what will be world's largest media and entertainment company.

1990
Digital audio broadcasting is demonstrated at the National Association of Broadcasters convention and is heralded as the HDTV of radio.

General Instrument revolutionizes the development of high-definition television by proposing an all-digital system. The video compression system also has implications for satellite transmissions.

Cable network launches include CNBC and The Inspiration Network (INSP).

1991
The U.S. air attack on Iraq begins January 16 with dramatic live coverage from network reporters in Baghdad. CNN is the lone network to maintain contact with its Baghdad reporters through the night.

Free to move around Moscow and ready to commit resources to coverage, television and radio provide gripping details of the short-lived Soviet coup and the collapse of communism in the Soviet Union. During his detention in the Crimea, Soviet President Mikhail Gorbachev keeps track of events by listening to the BBC, Voice of America, and Radio Liberty.

Cable network launches include Court TV, Comedy Central, and Encore.

1992
In March, the Supreme Court let stand an appeals court ruling that struck down the FCC's around-the-clock ban on broadcast indecency as unconstitutional and requiring the commission to establish a safe harbor\Ma part of the day when few children are tuning in and during which radio and TV stations may broadcast without fear of FCC sanctions for indecency.

General Instrument and MIT show the first over-the-air digital HDTV transmission to Washington lawmakers and regulators. The 12-minute transmission of 1,050-line video was broadcast by noncommercial WETA-TV Washington.

The FCC raises the limit on radio stations a single company may own from 12 AM and 12 FM to 30 of each, then backpedals and lowers the caps to 18 each, with no more than two AMs and two FMs in large markets and three stations\Monly two in the same service\Min small markets.

Fox expands its programming lineup to seven nights a week, ending its status as a "weblet" and becoming the fourth full-fledged commercial TV network in the U.S.

The FCC unanimously approves allowing broadcast TV networks to purchase cable systems that serve no more than 10 percent of U.S. homes and up to 50 percent of a particular market's homes.

The FCC tells TV broadcasters they will have five years to begin broadcasting in HDTV once the agency adopts a standard and makes channels available.

Cable network launches include The Cartoon Network and the Sci Fi Channel.

1993
Warner Bros. announces it will launch a fifth broadcast TV network in 1994.

The FCC expands the AM band's upper limit from 1605 kHz to 1705 kHz.

General Instrument, Zenith, AT&T, and the ATRC join forces as the "Grand Alliance" to develop a single HDTV system. Later in the year, the Grand Alliance announces its support of the emerging MPEG-2 digital compression HD system: six-channel, CD-quality Dolby AC-3 music system; 1,920-pixel by 1,080-line interlaced scanning picture; and progressive scanning.

Paramount Communications begins talks with TV stations about forming a fifth broadcast TV network.

Southwestern Bell and Cox Cable form a $4.9-billion partnership.

Cable network launches include ESPN2 and the Television Food Network.

1994
Two companies, Hubbard's United States Satellite Broadcasting and Hughes's DirecTV, begin direct broadcast satellite transmissions to 18-inch home dish antennas from a shared satellite.

Paramount and Viacom merge in a deal worth $9.2 billion, forming the world's most powerful entertainment company. Viacom's Sumner Redstone becomes the new company's chairman. Later in the year, Viacom adds Blockbuster Entertainment to its portfolio.

Cable network launches include FX, Home & Garden TV, the International Film Channel, Starz!, Trio, the Game Show Network, and Turner Classic Movies.

1995
Seagram pays $7 billion for the 80 percent of Hollywood studio MCA Inc. owned by Matsushita Electric Industrial Co. Seagram is controlled by the Bronfman family and is headed by President/CEO Edgar Bronfman Jr.

The Megamedia Age begins when, in the same week, Walt Disney Co. announces it is buying Capital Cities/ABC for $18.5 billion and then Westinghouse Electric Co. releases word of its purchase of CBS Inc. for $5.4 billion.

Time Warner and Turner Broadcasting System agree to merge in an $8 billion stock swap deal.

Live television coverage of the verdict in the O.J. Simpson murder trial sets viewing records when 150 million people watch the jury return a "not guilty" verdict.

Microsoft buys 50 percent stake in NBC's cable channel America's Talking for $250 million. AT's talk format will be dropped and the network will become a news operation after being rechristened MSNBC.

The FCC repeals its Prime Time Access and Fin-Syn rules. These rules restricted the major broadcast networks from owning interest in their own primetime programming.

Cable network launches include CNN/fn, The Golf Channel, Great American Country, the History Channel, and the Outdoor Life Network.

1996
Congress passes\Mand President Clinton signs\Mthe Telecommunications Act of 1996, the first major overhaul of telecommunication legislation since 1934. Its key provisions include: replacing the 12-station TV ownership limit with a national home coverage cap of 35 percent; eliminating the national ownership limits on radio stations and allowing one company to own different numbers of stations locally, depending on the market size; requiring TV sets sold in the U.S. to be equipped with a V-chip to enable blocking of channels based on encoded ratings; deregulating cable rates.

Westinghouse/CBS buys Infinity Broadcasting for $4.9 billion, creating the country's largest radio station group in terms of earnings. The deal results in Westinghouse/CBS owning 83 radio stations in 15 markets.

The FCC releases its first list of proposed digital TV channel assignments for all U.S. analog television stations.

In July, WRAL-HD Raleigh, North Carolina, begins HDTV transmission on channel 32 under an experimental FCC license, making it the first HDTV station to broadcast in the U.S.

The Washington-based Model HDTV Station Project demonstrates live, over-the-air digital TV transmission and reception. A few months later, it bounces digital signals off a satellite and displays them on a receiver.

Cable network launches include Animal Planet, Fox News Channel, MSNBC, the Sundance Channel, and TVLand.

1997
After several starts and stops, the TV industry unveils content-based V-chip ratings to mixed reviews. Recalcitrant NBC maintains it will not implement the new ratings.

Paxson Communications chief Bud Paxson announces plans to launch a new television network, Pax Net, using his 73 owned UHF stations as a base and airing family friendly off-network programming.

ABC Television Network President Preston Padden and Sinclair Broadcasting President David Smith say broadcasters ought to consider using DTV channels for broadcasting multiple channels of conventional TV rather than a single channel of HDTV.

Hearst Corp. (8 TVs) and Argyle Television (6 TVs) join their TV stations and create a new company, Hearst-Argyle Television Inc., that is valued at $1.8 billion.

The FCC gives TV broadcasters a second channel for the delivery of HDTV and other digital services and said that all network affiliates in the top 10 markets have 24 months to start broadcasting a digital signal; those in markets 11-30 have 30 months; all other commercial stations have five years. Noncommercial broadcasters have six.

DTV service provider EchoStar plans to launch two satellites that will give it the ability to provide local broadcast TV signals to about 43 percent of the U.S.

Cable network launches include WE.

1998
The National Association of Broadcasters agrees to support plans by satellite TV providers to retransmit local TV station signals into their markets as long as the satellite services carry all a market's signals.

At 2:17 p.m. on February 27, WFAA-TV Dallas broadcast what it claims is the first non-experimental HDTV signal (in 1080i, 16:9 format). The broadcast began with a half-hour of taped HD programming, followed by a live simulcast of the station's NTSC programming that was upconverted to HDTV. The next month, Sinclair Broadcasting becomes the first TV group owner to broadcast multiple digital channels.

AT&T pays $50 billion for cable system giant Tele-Communications Inc.

Paxson Communications launches its broadcast television network, now called Pax TV, with a lineup of 90 stations covering about 75 percent of U.S. TV homes.

Radio group owner Clear Channel Communications purchases competitor Jacor Communications for $4.4 billion. The deal gives Clear Channel 453 stations in 101 markets. The year's other big deals include: Chancellor Media's purchase of Capstar Broadcasting for $3.9 billion; Hearst-Argyle Television's purchase of Pulitzer Broadcasting for $1.85 billion; Chancellor's purchase of LIN Television for $1.5 billion; and Sinclair Broadcast Group's purchase of Sullivan Broadcasting for $1 billion.

CBS is the first broadcast TV network to air a live HDTV sports event with its Nov. 8 telecast of the New York Jets-Buffalo Bills NFL game. It is carried by CBS stations in New York; Philadelphia; Washington; Cincinnati; Charlotte, North Carolina; Raleigh, North Carolina; and Columbus, Ohio.

Hughes Electronics Corp., parent of DBS provider DirecTV, announces deal to buy rival U.S. Satellite Broadcasting from Hubbard Broadcasting for $1.3 billion. The DBS business now has three providers: DirecTV, EchoStar, and Primestar.

Cable network launches include BBC America, the Biography Channel, Cinemax, Tech TV, and Toon Disney.

1999
Hughes Electronics Corp., parent of DBS provider DirecTV, buys rival Primestar for $1.1 billion plus stock. The DBS business now has two providers: DirecTV and EchoStar.

Paxson Broadcasting sells its 30 percent interest in The Travel Channel to the cable channel's 70 percent owner, Discovery Channel.

MSO Comcast offers $58 billion for MediaOne Group's cable systems. AT&T then comes in with a $69 billion offer that has AT&T swapping and selling Comcast systems with 2 million subscribers for roughly $9 billion. In return, Comcast agrees to withdraw its $58 billion offer.

CBS pays $2.5 billion for syndication giant King World Productions, whose properties include the hit shows Oprah, Wheel of Fortune, and Jeopardy!

FCC votes to allow a broadcaster to own two TV stations in a market under certain conditions and liberalizes its radio/TV cross-ownership restrictions. A flood of station deals follow.

Viacom Inc. buys CBS Corp. for $36 billion, merging Viacom's Paramount Station Group, UPN network, cable networks, and other properties, with those of CBS.

Clear Channel Communications pays $23.5 billion in stock and assumption of debt for the 443 radio stations of AMFM Inc., the country's largest radio broadcaster. Clear Channel will have to divest about 100 stations to comply with FCC and Justice Department regulations. Those spinoffs will bring Clear Channel $4.3 billion.

Legislation takes affect allowing satellite delivery of local television stations in their markets, increasing DBS providers' ability to compete with cable.

2000
America Online Inc. and Time Warner merge in a deal worth $181 billion. The merged company, AOL Time Warner, combines the company that serves the largest number of Internet users with the largest producer of TV shows and movies and cable programming, plus cable systems passing 20 percent of U.S. homes.

Tribune Co. buys Times Mirror Co. for $6.5 billion, acquiring seven daily newspapers and various magazines. The deal will give Tribune co-ownership of TV stations and major daily newspapers in the top three markets and the assets to sell packages of multimedia advertising to clients on national, regional, and local levels.

Harry Pappas, head of Pappas Television, the country's largest privately held TV station group, announces plans to launch Azteca America, the third U.S. Hispanic television network (Univision and Telemundo are the others) in 2001.

Cable network launches include Oxygen.

2001
FCC approves the $5.4-billion sale of Chris-Craft Broadcasting's ten TV stations to Fox Television.

DBS operator EchoStar Communications engineers a $26-billion bid for competitor DirecTV, owned by GM's Hughes Corp. The move follows attempts by Rupert Murdoch's News Corp. to acquire DirecTV. But regulatory reviews keep the deal in limbo.

XM Satellite Radio begins broadcasting a nationwide radio service of 200 channels from two satellites\M"Rock" and "Roll"\Min orbit above the equator. The Washington-based company charges subscribers $9.95 a month for the service. A rival, New York-based Sirius Satellite Radio, plans to launch a similar service later in the year.

The September 11 terrorist attacks on New York and Washington result in around-the-clock news coverage, dropping commercials. It's estimated that the networks lost $200 million-$300 million in the first four days of coverage. Four FM and nine New York TV stations whose antennas were on top of the World Trade Center are knocked off the air and several stations lost employees who had been manning the transmitters in Tower 1. Across the country, broadcasters raised money and arranged blood drives. The fall TV season is delayed, late-night talk/comedy shows are put on hiatus, the Emmy Awards are postponed, and several industry gatherings are canceled.

NBC buys Telemundo, the No. 2 U.S. Spanish-language TV network, for $2.7 billion.

Comcast negotiates $72 billion merger with rival cable operator AT&T Broadband, topping bids by AOL Time Warner and Cox Communications.

Cable network launches include ABC Family, Hallmark Channel, and National Geographic Television.

2002
Sirius Satellite Radio launches its satellite-delivered subscription radio service in four markets in February, then rolls out nationally in July. Sirius follows XM Satellite Radio to become the second U.S. satellite radio programmer.

Prompted by lawsuits from Fox, Viacom, NBC, and Time Warner, a three-judge panel of the federal appeals court in Washington refuses to uphold an FCC rule limiting a TV station group owner's audience reach to 35 percent of U.S. TV households and strikes down a rule barring a cable system from owning TV stations in its market. The court orders the FCC to rewrite or justify the ownership limit rule.

Tom Brokaw of NBC News announces he will step down as evening news anchor after the 2004 presidential election, to be succeeded by NBC's Brian Williams. Brokaw will then focus on in-depth reporting projects.

The Securities and Exchange Commission begins a formal investigation into the accounting practices of cable MSO Adelphia Communications. Five of Adelphia's top executives\Mincluding founder John Rigas and his two sons, Michael and Tim\Mare arrested on fraud charges, alleging that the family used the company as a "personal piggy bank," financing various personal transactions, including $3.1 billion in loans for stock and family businesses.

The FCC mandates that all TV sets must be equipped with digital tuners by 2007 and proposes strong copy-protection measures intended to prevent widespread copying and streaming of content over the Internet.

Lifestyle diva Martha Stewart, whose media empire included TV, magazines, and books, is investigated by the Justice Department for allegedly lying to federal authorities looking into insider trading involving Stewart's sale of ImClone Systems stock the day before it became public that the Food and Drug Administration had denied the company's application to market a new cancer drug.

In October, both the FCC and the Department of Justice reject DBS operator EchoStar Communications' proposed $26-billion purchase of competitor DirecTV, and a revised agreement fails to sway either agency. In December, EchoStar withdrew its merger request from the FCC. Rupert Murdoch's News Corp., whose previous bid for DirecTV had been rebuffed, puts together a new deal.

2003
Rupert Murdoch's News Corp. receives FCC and Justice Department approval of its deal to acquire 34 percent of DBS operator DirecTV's parent company Hughes Electronics for $6.6 billion in cash and stock.

New York City's Metropolitan Television Alliance agrees to place a new broadcast tower for New York-area television stations on top of the Freedom Tower, a 1,776-foot office tower that will be built on the site of the World Trade Center, where the stations' towers were located prior to 9/11. The MTVA comprises all the city's major TV broadcasters. After the terrorist attacks, most of the stations operated from backup facilities atop the Empire State Building. Ground is expected to be broken on the Freedom Tower in the summer of 2004, and broadcasters should begin operating from the tower by 2008.

The FCC releases new media ownership rules in response to a federal appeals court ruling in 2002. Among the changes: raising the national coverage cap for TV groups from 35 percent to 45 percent; allowing ownership of two TV stations (duopoly) in markets with five or more commercial stations; allowing ownership of three TV stations (triopoly) in markets with at least 18 stations; newspaper-TV cross-ownership is permitted in markets with at least four TV stations; radio-TV cross-ownership now include newspapers in the formula\Mowners in markets with nine or more TV stations face no cross-ownership restrictions per se but are limited by individual radio and TV limits applicable to specific markets. TV-duopoly owners would not be permitted to own newspapers in markets with fewer than nine TV stations. In markets with three or fewer TV stations, no cross-ownership of TV, radio, or newspapers is permitted. In markets with four to eight TV stations, an owner may form one of the following combos: (1) A daily newspaper, one TV station, up to one-half the number of radio stations permitted to one owner in that market.

(2) A daily newspaper, the total number of radio stations permitted to one owner there, no TV stations.

(3) Two TV stations and the total number of radio stations permitted there.

Congress quickly reacts with legislation introduced by Rep. John Dingell (D-Mich.), which would restore the 35 percent cap. Other critics of the new rules challenge them in federal court.

Liberty Media pays $7.9 billion for Comcast's 56 percent stake in home shopping giant QVC. With 2002 sales of $4.4 billion, QVC is not just the largest shopping network, it's the second-largest television network of any kind.

A panel of federal appeals court judges in Philadelphia agrees with public advocacy groups and imposes a stay of the FCC's new broadcast-ownership rules scheduled to take effect on September 4. The stay will remain in effect until lawsuits to overturn the new rules are settled. The Philadelphia court then decides to retain the case attacking the new FCC broadcast-ownership limits rather than granting broadcast networks' pleas to transfer it to a court in Washington.

The Bush White House brokered a surprise compromise over media deregulation by agreeing to permanently set the national TV station ownership cap at 39 percent of U.S. television households. That percentage allows Fox and Viacom to retain all their stations. Wielding a threat to veto a catch-all spending bill over a provision that would roll the limit back to 35 percent, aides to President Bush persuaded Senate Appropriations Committee Chairman Ted Stevens (R-Alaska) to back down from the tighter limit. Stevens's action came less than a week after he had persuaded reluctant House leadership to go along with the old level. The compromise splits the difference between the 45 percent limit set by the FCC in June and the previous 35 percent level that rank-and-file lawmakers on both sides of Capitol Hill had been pushing to reinstate. The agreement is part of a spending bill that funds the FCC and many other agencies in fiscal 2004.

After a 36-year run, the California Cable Telecommunications Association's annual Western Cable Show makes its curtain call in December, citing consolidation in the cable industry and economic pressure.

Cable network launches include Spike TV.

2004
NBC gets Federal Trade Commission approval for its $14 billion purchase of Vivendi Universal Entertainment, its last regulatory hurdle. The FCC was not required to review the deal because it involved no station licenses. Among other things, NBC acquires USA Network and the Sci Fi Network. The new entity will be called NBC Universal.

Congress and the FCC react swiftly to the "wardrobe malfunction" that bared Janet Jackson's breast during the MTV-produced half-time entertainment in CBS TV's Super Bowl broadcast. Congress passes legislation that dramatically increases the limits on FCC fines for indecency violations.

Congress and the FCC take the first steps toward punishing stations that air "excessively" violent shows. Under orders from leaders of the House Commerce Committee, FCC Chairman Michael Powell by the end of the year will start investigating whether the commission should restrict onscreen violence. Cable can't count on immunity either. Growing ranks of lawmakers say cable must do more to make sure that children aren't exposed to potentially traumatizing content.

A panel of federal appeals court judges in Philadelphia concludes that the FCC wasn't justified in its June 2003 decision relaxing ownership restrictions in the newspaper, television, and radio industries. The rules, which were blocked from taking effect in September 2003, have been sent back to the FCC for a rewrite. A frustrated FCC Chairman Michael Powell criticized the decision, claiming that it created a "clouded and confused state of media law" and makes it nearly impossible for his agency to design standards for ownership limits.

Cable network launches include TV One.

2005
George W. Bush, on January 20, becomes the first president to have his inauguration covered in HDTV. ABC News deploys 36 HD cameras and four HD production vehicles throughout the parade route to give viewers an unparalleled view of American history.

President Bush chooses FCC commissioner Kevin Martin to be chairman of the agency.

In a King Solomon-like answer to critics that Viacom has become too big to grow, Chairman Sumner Redstone proposes cleaving it in half. The resulting companies would be Viacom and CBS Corp.

Longtime ABC World News Tonight anchor Peter Jennings, 67, died August 7 at his home in Manhattan, four months after being diagnosed with lung cancer.

Following Hurricane Katrina, local TV broadcasters and cable operators in the Gulf Coast area say rebuilding their stations and plants could take several months.

The Disney-ABC Television Group announces that three ABC shows, Desperate Housewives, Lost, and Night Stalker will be available for purchase from the Apple iTunes store for $1.99 an episode. The announcement prompts the other big media companies to begin "repurposing" primetime programming on the Internet. It's soon clear that the Web is the next big TV medium.

2006
In January, PBS dips into the ranks of its member stations and selects Paula Kerger of WNET New York to succeed Pat Mitchell as president of the noncommercial "network."

After battling to be the broadcasting fifth network for 11 years and mostly lackluster years, WB and UPN stun the broadcasting industry in January by deciding to merger into The CW. To fill the vacuum created by the loss of one network, Fox creates My Network Television, a mini network built around telenovelas, a popular Spanish TV format. Both CW and MNT debut in September.

Two years after the Janet Jackson "wardrobe malfunction" at the Super Bowl, broadcasters are still feeling the fallout. In March, the FCC issues another round of fines topped by $3.6 million against CBS affiliates for airing an episode of Without a Trace. A few months later, Congress increases ten-fold the base indecency fine to $325,000 per incident.

Ending a year of speculation, CBS announces in March the hiring of Katie Couric, the popular co-host of NBC's Today Show, to anchor the CBS Evening News. With new set and features, she begins her reign as anchor on September 5. Longtime anchor Dan Rather resigned from the job in March 2005 after botching a 60 Minutes story critical of President Bush's military record. CBS News's Washington Bureau Chief Bob Schieffer anchored the news during the Rather-Couric interregnum.

2007
On January 29 ION Media Networks Inc. changed the name of its TV network from "I" to ION Television.

In 2007 The Sopranos ended an eight-year run on HBO. There was much speculation about the final moments of the finale when the show faded to black.

After years of acquiring stations, on April 20 Clear Channel Communications Inc. entered into an agreement to sell its Television Group. And, as of June 30, the company had entered into definitive agreements to sell 389 radio stations in 77 markets.

2008
On July 25 the FCC approved the merger of Sirius Satellite Radio Inc. and XM Satellite Holdings Inc. On July 29 the two companies announced they had completed their merger, and that the new company would change its name to Sirius XM Radio Inc.

The FCC announced that Wilmington, NC, would be the first market to test the transition to digital television before the nationwide transition to DTV on February 17, 2009. The commercial broadcasters serving the Wilmington market agreed to turn off their analog signals at noon on September 8, 2008. Beginning at noon on September 8 WWAY (ABC), WECT (NBC), WSFX-TV (Fox), WILM-LP (CBS) and W51CW (Trinity Broadcasting) planned to broadcast only digital signals to their viewers in the five North Carolina counties that comprise the Wilmington, NC, market.

2009
The nationwide transition from analog to digital television, scheduled for February 17, 2009, was delayed until June 12, 2009 to allow more time to get ready for the digital transition. The National Telecommunications and Information Administration (NTIA) provided consumers with a TV converter box coupon program to help the consumers make the switch to digital TV. Both the FCC and TV stations across the U.S. made a mighty effort to inform consumers about, and make, the switch. Some TV stations made the switch to digital television early. Notably Hawaii's full-power stations made the switch to digital TV on January 15, 2009. Finally on June 12, 2009 full-power TV stations all over the U.S. became all-digital, when the FCC reported 971 full-power TV stations made the switch.

Later in June 2009 the FCC adopted an order allowing AM radio stations to use FB radio translators to increase their reach within a local community. The FCC action gave AM stations an opportunity to overcome technical problems in their coverage areas.

Walter Cronkite, anchor and managing editor of the CBS Evening News from 1962 to 1981, died on July 17, 2009. A memorial service was held on September 9 at Lincoln Center in New York.

2010
Apple, Inc. introduced the iPad, the first mobile computer tablet to achieve worldwide commercial success. Many manufacturers followed with their own tablet.

2011
"The Oprah Winfrey Show" ends after 25 seasons, and Oprah Winfrey launches OWN - Oprah Winfrey Network.

Satellite TV provider DISH Network acquires Blockbuster LLC.

Axel Technologies releases Fuugo Video 1.0, which aggregates online video content from multiple sources into a single application, and Fuugo TV, a broadcast digital TV application for computer tablets, smart phones, and other portable devices.

Steve Jobs, influential head of Apple, Inc., dies.

2012
Satellite TV provider DISH Network announces its remote access application, which provides the capability of streaming on-demand movies and TV shows to the iPad.

2013
Netflix earns 14 Primetime Emmy Award nominations, becoming the first online-only web television network to be recognized by the Emmys. David Fincher wins Outstanding Directing for a Drama Series for Netflix's *House of Cards*.

2014
President Obama demands that the FCC enforces strong rules in order to defend net neutrality, the principle that Internet service providers treat all internet data equally and not discriminate based on users, content, sites, platforms, applications, types of attached equipment, or modes of communication.

The debate as to whether or not Internet service providers should be permitted to charge certain net organizations for "data-heavy" services (such as Netflix) continues. Net neutrality advocates argue that doing so would sabotage the ideology of a free and equal internet for everyone.
The FCC delayed a decision until 2015 of how it manages the internet.

2015
In January 2015, the FCC concludes its wireless spectrum auction with a total of $44.9 billion raised, over twice as much as the previous 2008 auction. The auction successfully sells spectrum of frequencies between 1700 and 2100 megahertz to wireless carriers.

The FCC passes a net neutrality regulation in a 3-2 vote. Supported by President Obama, the regulation prevents the favoritism of certain technology companies and Internet traffic based on payments made to broadband providers. According to the FCC, net neutrality will ensure fair treatment of all Internet data.

Microsoft launches a Preview Program that enables test users to view live television channels through Xbox One video game consoles.

2016
Authorized by Congress in 2012, the FCC launches the first incentive auction in March 2016. The goal of this two-stage initiative is to encourage broadcasters to offer some of their spectrum usage rights for sale so that they can be resold and relicensed to wireless bidders. In exchange, the sellers are awarded a portion of the funds. The FCC's aim in this undertaking is to keep up with the demand for wireless service, and offer a continued investment in maintaining the television broadcast industry.

The viewership of the first presidential debate between Hillary Clinton and Donald Trump reaches historic highs, with a record 84 million viewers tuning in to watch on television and live-stream. The viewership numbers beat out the Reagan-Carter debate of 1980, which pulled in 80.6 million views. The debate was broadcast across 11 channels, as well as social media sites including Facebook, Twitter, and YouTube. NBC drew in the highest number of watchers among major networks, beating out ABC, CBS, FOX, CNN, and MSNBC.

The course of the 2016 presidential election ushers in a drastic rise in "fake news," with sensationalist headlines being generated and going viral before they can be fact-checked. This phenomenon is far-reaching, impacting not only the hyper-partisan public, but also major news networks like CNN, who air some of these headlines as news. The trend spurs questions into the credibility and reliability of the media and journalism.

PEW Research, in its 2016 State of the News Media report, observes that despite the rise of digital developments, cable and network television continue to grow in revenue. Digital does continue to threaten legacy media, however, as newspapers battle with the rising demand for video content as opposed to print content.

Facebook leads an initiative to fact-check news materials in order to reduce "fake news" content. This was attempted by restricting and flagging stories that lacked sources or which failed verification tests.

2017

ABC makes plans to re-launch Fact Check, a joint venture with MIT's School for Communications and Media, which seeks to research claims made by various groups and individuals in public debates. The aim of the venture is to reduce the spread of misinformation through TV ads, debates, speeches, interviews and news releases.

The FCC issues a Notice of Proposed Rulemaking to authorize broadcasters to utilize ATSC 3.0, the second generation of digital television broadcast standard enabling television stations to improve features such as ultra-high-definition content, datacasting and targeted advertising. This decision followed a petition by America's Public Television Stations and the Communications Technology Association.

YouTube TV is launched, offering live streaming of programs from five major broadcast networks (ABC, CBS, NBC, Fox and The CW) as well as approximately 40 cable channels owned by NBCUniversal, CBS Corporation, 21st Century Fox and The Walt Disney Company.

The FCC and Its Regulatory Authority

The Communications Act. The FCC was created by Congress in the Communications Act for the purpose of "regulating interstate and foreign commerce in communication by wire and radio so as to make available, so far as possible, to all the people of the United States, without discrimination on the basis of race, color, religion, national origin, or sex, a rapid, efficient, Nation-wide, and world-wide wire and radio communications service. . . ." (In this context, the word "radio" covers both broadcast radio and television.) The Communications Act authorizes the FCC to "make such regulations not inconsistent with law as it may deem necessary to prevent interference between stations and to carry out the provisions of [the] Act." It directs us to base our broadcast licensing decisions on the determination of whether those actions will serve the public interest, convenience, and necessity.

How the FCC Adopts Rules. As is the case with most other federal agencies, the FCC generally cannot adopt or change rules without first describing or publishing the proposed rules and seeking comment on them from the public. We release a document called a Notice of Proposed Rule Making, in which we explain the new rules or rule changes that we are proposing and establish a filing deadline for public comment on them. (All such FCC Notices are included in the Commission's Daily Digest and are posted on our website at http://transition.fcc.gov/Daily_Releases/Daily_Digest). After we have had a chance to hear from the public and have considered all comments received, we generally have several options. We can: (1) adopt some or all of the proposed rules, (2) adopt a modified version of some or all of the proposed rules, (3) ask for public comment on additional issues relating to the proposals, or (4) end the rulemaking proceeding without adopting any rules at all. You can find information about how to file comments in our rulemaking proceedings on our Internet website at http://www.fcc.gov/guides/how-comment. The site also provides instructions on how you can file comments electronically. In addition to adopting rules, we also establish broadcast regulatory policies through the individual cases that we decide, such as those involving license renewals, station sales, and complaints about violations of FCC rules.

The FCC and the Media Bureau. The FCC has five Commissioners, each of whom is appointed by the President and confirmed by the Senate. Serving under the Commissioners are a number of Offices and operating Bureaus. One of those is the Media Bureau, which has day-to-day responsibility for developing, recommending, and administering the rules governing the media, including radio and television stations. The FCC's broadcast rules are contained in Title 47 of the Code of Federal Regulations ("CFR"), Parts 73 (broadcast) and 74 (auxiliary broadcast, including low power TV, and translator stations). Our rules of practice and procedure can be found in Title 47 CFR, Part 1. A link to those rules can be found on our website at http://www.fcc.gov/encyclopedia/rules-regulations-title-47. Additional information about the Commission's Offices and Bureaus, including their respective functions, can be found at http://www.fcc.gov/bureaus-offices.

FCC Regulation of Broadcast Radio and Television. The FCC allocates (that is, designates a portion of the broadcast spectrum to) new broadcast stations based upon both the relative needs of various communities for additional broadcast outlets and specified engineering standards designed to prevent interference among stations and to other communications users. As noted above, whenever we review an application – whether to build a new station, modify or renew a license or sell a station – we must determine if its grant would serve the public interest. As discussed earlier, we expect station licensees to be aware of the important problems and issues facing their local communities and to foster public understanding by presenting programming that relates to those local issues. As discussed in this Manual, however, broadcasters – not the FCC or any other government agency – are responsible for selecting the material that they air. By operation of the First Amendment to the U.S. Constitution, and because the Communications Act expressly prohibits the Commission from censoring broadcast matter, our role in overseeing program content is very limited.

We license only individual broadcast stations. We do not license TV or radio networks (such as CBS, NBC, ABC or Fox) or other organizations with which stations have relationships (such as PBS or NPR), except to the extent that those entities may also be station licensees. We also do not regulate information provided over the Internet, nor do we intervene in private disputes involving broadcast stations or their licensees. Instead, we usually defer to the parties, courts, or other agencies to resolve such disputes.

The Licensing of TV and Radio Stations

Commercial and Noncommercial Educational Stations. The FCC licenses FM radio and TV stations as either commercial or noncommercial educational ("NCE"). (All AM radio stations are licensed as commercial facilities.) Commercial stations generally support themselves through the sale of advertising. In contrast, NCE stations generally meet their operating expenses with contributions received from listeners and viewers, and also may receive government funding. In addition, NCE stations may receive contributions from for-profit entities, and are permitted to acknowledge such contributions or underwriting donations with announcements naming and generally describing the contributing party or donor. However, NCE stations may not broadcast commercials or other promotional announcements on behalf of for-profit entities. These limitations on NCE stations are discussed further at page xxiv of this Manual.

Applications to Build New Stations; Length of the License Period. Before a party can build a new TV or radio station, it first must apply to the FCC for a construction permit. The applicant must demonstrate in its application that it is qualified to construct and operate the station as specified in its application and that its proposed facility will not cause objectionable interference to any other station. Once its application has been granted, the applicant is issued a construction permit, which authorizes it to build the station within a specified period of time, usually three years. After the applicant (now considered a "permittee") builds the station, it must file a license application, in which it certifies that it has constructed the station consistent with the technical and other terms specified in its construction permit. Upon grant of that license application, the FCC issues the new license to operate to the permittee (now considered a "licensee"), which authorizes the new licensee to operate for a stated period of time, up to eight years. At the close of this period, the licensee must seek renewal of its station license.

Applications for License Renewal. Licenses expire and renewal applications are due on a staggered basis, based upon the state in which the station is licensed. Before we can renew a station's license, we must first determine whether, during the preceding license term, the licensee has served the public interest; has not committed any serious violations of the Communications Act or the FCC's rules; and has not committed other violations which, taken together, would constitute a pattern of abuse. To assist us in this evaluative process, a station licensee must file a renewal application (FCC Form 303-S), in which it must respond concerning whether:

- it has sent us certain required reports;
- neither it nor its owners have or have had any interest in a broadcast application involved in an FCC proceeding in which character issues were resolved adversely to the applicant or were left unresolved, or were raised in connection with a pending application;
- its ownership is consistent with the Communications Act's restrictions on licensee interests held by foreign governments, foreign corporations, and non-U.S. citizens;
- there has not been an adverse finding or adverse final action against it or its owners by a court or administrative body in a civil or criminal proceeding involving a felony, mass media-related antitrust or unfair competition law, the making of fraudulent statements to a governmental unit, or discrimination;
    - there were no adjudicated violations of the Communications Act or the Commission's rules during the current license term;
    - neither the licensee nor its owners have been denied federal benefits due to drug law violations;
    - its station operation complies with the Commission's radiofrequency ("RF") radiation exposure standards;
- it has, in a timely manner, placed and maintained certain specified materials in its public inspection file (as discussed at pages xxvi-xxviii of this Manual);
- it has not discontinued station operations for more than 12 consecutive months during the preceding license term and is currently broadcasting programming;
- it has filed FCC Form 396, the *Broadcast Equal Employment Opportunity Program Report*; and
- if the application is for renewal of a television license, it has complied with the limitations on commercial matter aired during children's programming and filed the necessary *Children's Television Programming Reports* (FCC Form 398) (as discussed at page xxii of this Manual, https://www.fcc.gov/licensing-databases/forms).

Digital Television. After February 17, 2009, all full-power TV stations are required to stop broadcasting in analog and continue broadcasting only in digital. This is known as the "DTV transition." Because digital is much more efficient than analog, part of the scarce and valuable spectrum that is currently used for analog broadcasting will be used for important new services such as enhanced public safety communications for police, fire departments, and emergency rescue workers. Part of the spectrum will also be made available for advanced wireless services such as wireless broadband.

Digital broadcasting also enables television stations to offer viewers several benefits. For example, stations broadcasting in digital can offer viewers improved picture and sound quality as well as more programming options (referred to as "multicasting") because digital technology gives each television station the ability to broadcast multiple channels at the same time.

Consumers who receive television signals via over-the-air antennas (as opposed to subscribers to pay services like cable and satellite TV) will be able to receive digital signals on their analog sets if they purchase a digital-to-analog converter box that converts the digital signals to analog. Alternatively, if consumers purchase a digital television (a TV with built in digital tuner), they will be able to receive digital broadcast programming. If your TV set receives local broadcast stations through a paid provider such as cable or satellite TV, it is already prepared for the DTV transition.

Regarding consumers who are shopping for new televisions, the Commission's digital tuner rule prohibits the importation or interstate shipment of any device containing an analog tuner unless it also contains a digital tuner. Retailers may continue to sell analog-only devices from existing inventory. However, at the point of sale, retailers must post notices advising consumers that TV sets and equipment such as VCRs that contain only an analog tuner will not be able to receive over-the-air-television signals from full-power broadcast stations after February 17, 2009, without the use of a digital-to-analog converter box.

Television broadcasters must promote public awareness of the DTV transition with an on-air education campaign, providing consumers with information about the transition. They must report their efforts on a quarterly basis by filing FCC Form 388 with the Commission, posting each such Form on their website and placing them in their station public inspection files.

While the February 17, 2009, deadline for ending analog broadcasts does not apply to low-power, Class A, and TV translator stations, these stations will eventually transition to all-digital service. In the meantime, some consumers may continue to receive programming from these stations in analog format after the transition date.

Additional information concerning the DTV transition can be found on the FCC's website, at http://www.fcc.gov/digital-television, or by calling toll free 1-888-CALL-FCC.

Digital Radio. The FCC has also approved digital operation for AM and FM radio broadcast stations (often referred to as "HD Radio"). As with DTV, digital radio substantially improves the quality of the radio signal and allows a station to offer multicasting over several programming streams, as well as certain enhanced services. Unlike the mandatory digital transition deadline for television stations however, radio stations will be able to continue to operate in analog and will have discretion whether also to transmit in digital and, if so, when to begin such operation. In order to receive the digital signals of those stations that choose to so operate, consumers will have to purchase new receivers.

Because digital radio technology allows a radio station to transmit simultaneously in both analog and digital, however, listeners will be able to continue to use their current radios to receive the analog signals of radio stations that transmit both analog and digital signals. Receivers are being marketed that incorporate both modes of reception, with the ability to automatically switch to the analog signal if the digital signal cannot be detected or is lost by the receiver. For additional information about digital radio, see https://www.fcc.gov/encyclopedia/iboc-digital-radio-broadcasting-am-and-fm-radio-broadcast-stations.

Public Participation in the Licensing Process

Renewal Applications. You can submit a protest against a station's license renewal application by filing a formal petition to deny its application, or by sending us an informal objection to the application. Before its license expires, each station licensee must broadcast a series of announcements providing the date its license will expire, the filing date for the renewal application, the date by which formal petitions against it must be filed, and the location of the station's public inspection file that contains the application. Petitions to deny the application must be filed by the end of the first day of the last full calendar month of the expiring license term. (For example, if the license expires on December 31, we must receive any petition at our Washington, D.C. headquarters by the end of the day on December 1.)

Broadcast licenses generally expire on a staggered basis, by state, with most radio licenses next expiring between October 1, 2019 and August 1, 2022, and most television licenses expiring between October 1, 2022 and August 1, 2024, one year after the radio licenses in the same state. A listing of the next expiration dates for radio and television licenses, by state, can be found on the Commission's website at https://www.fcc.gov/media/radio/broadcast-radio-license-renewal and https://www.fcc.gov/media/television/broadcast-television-license-renewal. Before you file a petition to deny an application, you should check our rules and policies to make sure that your petition complies with our procedural requirements. A more complete description of these procedures and requirements can be found on the Commission's website at http://transition/fcc.gov/localism/renew_process_handout.pdf. You can also file an informal objection at any time before we either grant or deny the application. Instructions for filing informal objections can be found on the Commission's website at http://transition.fcc.gov/localism/renew_process_handout.pdf. If you have any specific questions, you may also contact our Broadcast Information Specialist for radio or television, depending on the nature of your inquiry, by calling toll-free, by facsimile, or by sending an e-mail in the manner noted at page xxix of this Manual.

Other Types of Applications. You can also participate in the application process by filing a petition to deny when someone applies for a new station, and when a station is to be sold (technically called an "assignment" of the license), its licensee is to undergo a major transfer of stock or other ownership, or control (technically called a "transfer of control"), or the station proposes major facility changes. The applicant is required to publish a series of notices in the closest local newspaper, containing information similar to that noted above regarding renewal applications, when it files these types of applications. Upon receipt of the application, the FCC will issue a Public Notice and begin a 30-day period during which petitions to deny these applications may be filed. (All FCC Public Notices are included in the Commission's Daily Digest and are posted on our website at http://transition.fcc.gov/Daily_Releases/Daily_Digest). As with renewal applications, you can also file an informal objection to these types of applications, or any other applications, at any time before we either grant or deny the application. Again, if you have any specific questions about our processes or the status of a particular application involving a station, you may contact our Broadcast Information Specialist for radio or television, depending on the nature of your inquiry, by calling toll-free, by facsimile, or by sending an e-mail in the manner noted at pages xxviii of this Manual.

Broadcast Programming: Basic Law and Policy

The FCC and Freedom of Speech. The First Amendment, as well as Section 326 of the Communications Act, prohibits the Commission from censoring broadcast material and from interfering with freedom of expression in broadcasting. The Constitution's protection of free speech includes that of programming that may be objectionable to many viewer or listeners. Thus, the FCC cannot prevent the broadcast of any particular point of view. In this regard, the Commission has observed that "the public interest is best served by permitting free expression of views." However, the right to broadcast material is not absolute. There are some restrictions on the material that a licensee can broadcast. We discuss these restrictions below.

Licensee Discretion. Because the Commission cannot dictate to licensees what programming they may air, each individual radio and TV station licensee generally has discretion to select what its station broadcasts and to otherwise determine how it can best serve its community of license. Licensees are responsible for selecting their entertainment programming, as well as programs concerning local issues, news, public affairs, religion, sports events, and other subjects. As discussed at page xxvii of this Manual, broadcast licensees must periodically make available detailed information about the programming that they air to meet the needs and problems of their communities, which can be found in each station public file. They also decide how their programs will be structured and whether to edit or reschedule material for broadcasting. In light of the First Amendment and Section 326 of the Communications Act, we do not substitute our judgment for that of the licensee, nor do we advise stations on artistic standards, format, grammar, or the quality of their programming. Licensees also have broad discretion regarding commercials, with the exception of those for political candidates during an election and the limitations on advertisements aired during children's programming (we discuss these respective requirements at pages xx and xxii of this Manual).

Criticism, Ridicule, and Humor Concerning Individuals, Groups, and Institutions. The First Amendment's guarantee of freedom of speech similarly protects programming that stereotypes or may otherwise offend people with regard to their religion, race, national background, gender, or other characteristics. It also protects broadcasts that criticize or ridicule established customs and institutions, including the government and its officials. The Commission recognizes that, under our Constitution, people must be free to say things that the majority may abhor, not only what most people may find tolerable or congenial. However, if you are offended by a station's programming, we urge you to make your concerns known to the station licensee, in writing.

Programming Access. In light of their discretion to formulate their programming, station licensees are not required to broadcast everything that is offered or otherwise suggested to them. Except as required by the Communications Act, including the use of stations by candidates for public office (discussed at pages xx of this Manual), licensees have no obligation to allow any particular person or group to participate in a broadcast or to present that person or group's remarks.

Broadcast Programming: Law and Policy on Specific Kinds of Programming

Broadcast Journalism Introduction. As noted above, in light of the fundamental importance of the free flow of information to our democracy, the First Amendment and the Communications Act bar the FCC from telling station licensees how to select material for news programs, or prohibiting the broadcast of an opinion on any subject. We also do not review anyone's qualifications to gather, edit, announce, or comment on the news; these decisions are the station licensee's responsibility. Nevertheless, there are two issues related to broadcast journalism that are subject to Commission regulation: hoaxes and news distortion.

Hoaxes. The broadcast by a station of false information concerning a crime or catastrophe violates the FCC's rules if:

- the station licensee knew that the information was false,
- broadcasting the false information directly causes substantial public harm, and
- it was foreseeable that broadcasting the false information would cause such harm.

In this context, a "crime" is an act or omission that makes the offender subject to criminal punishment by law, and a "catastrophe" is a disaster or an imminent disaster involving violent or sudden events affecting the public. The broadcast must cause direct and actual damage to property or to the health or safety of the general public, or diversion of law enforcement or other public health and safety authorities from their duties, and the public harm must begin immediately. If a station airs a disclaimer before the broadcast that clearly characterizes the program as fiction and the disclaimer is presented in a reasonable manner under the circumstances, the program is presumed not to pose foreseeable public harm.

News Distortion. The Commission often receives complaints concerning broadcast journalism, such as allegations that stations have aired inaccurate or one-sided news reports or comments, covered stories inadequately, or overly dramatized the events that they cover. For the reasons noted above, the Commission generally will not intervene in such cases because it would be inconsistent with the First Amendment to replace the journalistic judgment of licensees with our own. However, as public trustees, broadcast licensees may not intentionally distort the news: the FCC has stated that "rigging or slanting the news is a most heinous act against the public interest." The Commission will investigate a station for news distortion if it receives documented evidence of such rigging or slanting, such as testimony or other documentation, from individuals with direct personal knowledge that a licensee or its management engaged in the intentional falsification of the news. Of particular concern would be evidence of the direction to employees from station management to falsify the news. However, absent such a compelling showing, the Commission will not intervene.

Political Broadcasting: Candidates for Public Office. In recognition of the particular importance of the free flow of information to the public during the electoral process, the Communications Act and the Commission's rules impose specific obligations on broadcasters regarding political speech.

- *Reasonable Access.* The Communications Act requires that broadcast stations provide "reasonable access" to candidates for federal elective office. Such access must be made available during all of a station's normal broadcast schedule, including television prime time and radio drive time. In addition, federal candidates are entitled to purchase all classes of time offered by stations to commercial advertisers, such as preemptible and non- preemptible time. The only exception to the access requirement is for bona fide news programming (as defined below), during which broadcasters may choose not to sell airtime to federal candidates. Broadcast stations have discretion as to whether to sell time to candidates in state and local elections.
- *Equal Opportunities.* The Communications Act requires that, when a station provides airtime to a legally qualified candidate for any public office (federal, state, or local), the station must "afford equal opportunities to all other such candidates for that office." The equal opportunities provision of the Communications Act also provides that the station "shall have no power of censorship over the material broadcast" by the candidate. The law exempts from the equal opportunities requirement appearances by candidates during bona fide news programming, defined as an appearance by a legally qualified candidate on a bona fide newscast, interview, or documentary (if the appearance of the candidate is incidental to the presentation of the subject covered by the documentary) or on–the–spot coverage of a bona fide news event (including debates, political conventions and related incidental activities).

In addition, a station must sell political advertising time to certain candidates during specified periods before a primary or general election at the lowest rate charged for the station's most favored commercial advertiser. Stations must maintain and make available for public inspection, in their public inspection files, a political file containing certain documents and information, discussed at page xxvii of this Manual. For additional information about the political rules, see https://www.fcc.gov/media/policy/political-programming.

Objectionable Programming

Programming Inciting "Imminent Lawless Action." The Supreme Court has held that the government may curtail speech if it is both: (1) intended to incite or produce "imminent lawless action;" and (2) likely to "incite or produce such action." Even when this legal test is met, any review that might lead to a curtailment of speech is generally performed by the appropriate criminal law enforcement authorities, not by the FCC.

Obscene, Indecent, or Profane Programming. Although, for the reasons discussed earlier, the Commission is generally prohibited from regulating broadcast content, the courts have held that the FCC's regulation of obscene and indecent programming is constitutional, because of the compelling societal interests in protecting children from potentially harmful programming and supporting parents' ability to determine the programming to which their children will be exposed at home.

Obscene material is not protected by the First Amendment and cannot be broadcast at any time. To be obscene, the material must have all of the following three characteristics:

- an average person, applying contemporary community standards, must find that the material, as a whole, appeals to the prurient interest;
- the material must depict or describe, in a patently offensive way, sexual conduct specifically defined by applicable law; and
- the material, taken as a whole, must lack serious literary, artistic, political, or scientific value.

Indecent material is protected by the First Amendment, so its broadcast cannot constitutionally be prohibited at all times. However, the courts have upheld Congress' prohibition of the broadcast of indecent material during times of the day in which there is a reasonable risk that children may be in the audience, which the Commission has determined to be between the hours of 6 a.m. and 10 p.m. Indecent programming is defined as "language or material that, in context, depicts or describes, in terms patently offensive as measured by contemporary community standards for the broadcast medium, sexual or excretory organs or activities." Broadcasts that fall within this definition and are aired between 6 a.m. and 10 p.m. may be subject to enforcement action by the FCC.

Profane material also is protected by the First Amendment, so its broadcast cannot be outlawed entirely. The Commission has defined such program matter to include language that is both "so grossly offensive to members of the public who actually hear it as to amount to a nuisance" and is sexual or excretory in nature or derived from such terms. Such material may be the subject of possible Commission enforcement action if it is broadcast within the same time period applicable to indecent programming: between 6 a.m. and 10 p.m.

How to File an Obscenity, Indecency, or Profanity Complaint: In order to allow its staff to make a determination of whether complained-of material is actionable, the Commission requires that complainants provide certain information: (1) the date and time of the alleged broadcast; (2) the call sign, channel or frequency of the station involved; and (3) the details of what was actually said (or depicted) during the alleged indecent, profane, or obscene broadcast. Submission of an audio or video tape, CD, DVD or other recording or transcript of the complained-of material is not required but is helpful, as is specification of the name of the program, the on-air personality, song, or film, and the city and state in which the complainant saw or heard the broadcast.

The fastest and easiest way to file a complaint containing this information is to use the FCC's electronic complaint form, which is available on the FCC's website at https://consumercomplaints.fcc.gov/hc/en-us.

You also may file a complaint about objectionable programming by mailing it to:

Federal Communications Commission
Consumer & Governmental Affairs Bureau
Consumer Inquiries and Complaints Division
445 12th Street, S.W.
Washington, D.C. 20554

If you are submitting an audio or video tape, DVD, CD or other type of media with your complaint, you should send it to the following address to avoid mail processing damage:

Federal Communications Commission
Consumer & Governmental Affairs Bureau
Consumer Inquiries and Complaints Division
9050 Junction Drive
Annapolis Junction, Maryland 20701

You can also electronically file your complaint at fccinfo@fcc.gov. You may also complain by calling the Commission, toll-free, at: 1-888-CALL-FCC (1-888-225-5322)

For additional information on the complaint process for obscene, indecent or profane material, visit http://transition.fcc.gov/eb/oip/.

Violent Programming. Many members of the public have expressed concern about violent television programming and the negative impact such broadcast material may have upon children. In response to these concerns, and at the request of 39 members of the U.S. House of Representatives, the FCC conducted a proceeding seeking public comment on violent programming. In April 2007, the Commission delivered to Congress a Report recommending that the industry voluntarily commit to reducing the amount of such programming viewed by children. The Commission also suggested that Congress consider enacting legislation that would better support parents' efforts to safeguard their children from such objectionable programming. The Commission's Report can be accessed at https://apps.fcc.gov/edocs_public/attachmatch/FCC-07-50A1.pdf.

The V-Chip and TV Program Ratings. In light of the widespread concern about obscene, indecent, profane, violent, or otherwise objectionable programming, in 1996, Congress passed a law to require TV sets with screens 13 inches or larger to be equipped with a "V-Chip" – a device that allows parents to program their sets to block TV programming that carries a certain rating. Since 2000, all such sets manufactured with screens 13 inches or larger must contain the V-Chip technology. This technology, which must be activated by parents, works in conjunction with a voluntary television rating system created and administered by the television industry and others, which enables parents to identify programming containing sexual, violent, or other content that they believe may be harmful to their children. All of the major broadcast networks and most of the major cable networks are encoding their programming with this ratings information to work with the V-Chip. However, some programming, such as news and sporting events, and unedited movies aired on premium cable channels, are not rated. In 2004, the FCC expanded the V-Chip requirement to apply also to devices that do not have a display screen but are used with a TV set, such as a VCR or a digital-to-analog converter box.

For more information about this ratings program, including a description of each ratings category, please see the FCC's V-Chip website at https://www.fcc.gov/consumers/guides/v-chip-putting-restrictions-what-your-children-watch.

Other Broadcasting Content Regulation

Station Identification. Stations must air identification announcements when they sign on and off for the day. They also must broadcast these announcements every hour, as close to the start of the hour as possible, at a natural programming break. TV stations may make these announcements on-screen or by voice only. Official station identification includes the station's call letters, followed by the community specified in its license as the station's location. Between the call letters and its community, the station may insert the name of the licensee, the station's channel number, and/or its frequency. It may also include any additional community or communities, as long as it first names the community to which it is licensed by the FCC. DTV stations also may identify their digital multicast programming streams separately if they wish, and, if so, must follow the format described in the FCC's rules.

Commencing as of a date to be determined, for television stations, twice daily, the station identification will also have to include a notice of the existence, location and accessibility of the station's public file. The notice will have to state that the station's public file is available for inspection and that members of the public can view it at the station's main studio and on its station website. Broadcast of at least one of these announcements will be required between the hours of 6 p.m. and midnight.

Children's Television Programming. Throughout its license term, every TV station must serve the educational and informational needs of children both by means of its overall programming and through programming that is specifically designed to serve those needs. Licensees are eligible for routine staff-level approval of the Children's Television Act portion of their renewal applications if they air at least three hours of "core" children's television programming, per week, or proportionally more if they provide additional free digital programming streams. Core programming is defined as follows:

- *Educational and Informational.* The programming must further the educational and informational needs of children 16 years old and under (this includes their intellectual/cognitive or social/emotional needs).
- *Specifically Designed to Serve Their Needs.* A program is considered "specifically designed to serve the educational and information needs of children" if: (1) that is its significant purpose; (2) it is aired between the hours of 7 a.m. and 10 p.m.; (3) it is a regularly scheduled weekly program; and (4) it is at least 30 minutes in duration.

To ensure that parents and other interested parties are informed of the educational and informational children's programming that their area stations offer, television licensees must identify each program specifically designed to "educate and inform" children by displaying the icon "E/I" throughout the program. In addition, commercial stations must provide information identifying such programs to the publishers of program guides.

During the broadcast of TV programs aimed at children 12 and under, advertising may not exceed 10.5 minutes an hour on weekends and 12 minutes an hour on weekdays.

These rules apply to analog and digital broadcasting. As discussed at page xviii of this Manual, television stations have traditionally operated with analog technology. Television stations, however, are in the process of switching to digital broadcasting, which greatly enhances their capability to serve their communities. Among other things, digital technology permits stations to engage in multicasting, that is, to air more than one stream of programming at the same time. Digital stations that choose to air more than one stream of free, over-the-air video programming must air proportionately more children's educational programming than stations that air only one stream of free, over-the-air video programming.

Each television licensee is required to prepare and place in the public inspection file at the station a quarterly Children's Television Programming Report (FCC Form 398) identifying its core programming. These reports must also be filed electronically with the FCC each quarter and can be viewed on the FCC's website, at https://www.fcc.gov/media/television/childrens-educational-television-reporting-form-398. This requirement of the station's public file is discussed at page xxviii of this Manual.

The FCC has created a children's educational television website to inform parents and other members of the public about the obligation of every television broadcast station to provide educational and informational programming for children. This website provides access to background information about these obligations, as well as information about children's educational programs that are aired on television stations in your area and throughout the country. This website also can help TV stations comply with the children's television requirements. You can access the children's educational television website by going to http://reboot.fcc.gov/parents/.

Station-Conducted Contests. A station that broadcasts or advertises information about a contest that it conducts must fully and accurately disclose the material terms of the contest, and must conduct the contest substantially as announced or advertised. Contest descriptions may not be false, misleading, or deceptive with respect to any material term, including the factors that define the operation of the contest and affect participation, such as entry deadlines, the prizes that can be won, and how winners will be selected. Additional information about the contest rule can be found at http://www.fcc.gov/guides/broadcasting-contests-lotteries-and-solicitation-funds.

Lotteries. Federal law prohibits the broadcast of advertisements for a lottery or information concerning a lottery. A lottery is any game, contest, or promotion that contains the elements of prize, chance, and "consideration" (a legal term that means an act or promise that is made to induce someone into an agreement). For example, casino gambling is generally considered to be a "lottery" subject to the terms of the advertising restriction although, as discussed below, the prohibition is not applied to truthful advertisements for lawful casino gambling. Many types of contests, depending on their particulars, also are covered under this definition.

The statute and FCC rules list a number of exceptions to this prohibition, principally advertisements for: (1) lotteries conducted by a state acting under the authority of state law, when the advertisement or information is broadcast by a radio or TV station licensed to a location in that state or in any other state that conducts such a lottery; (2) gambling conducted by an Indian Tribe under the Indian Gaming Regulatory Act; (3) lotteries authorized or not otherwise prohibited by the state in which they are conducted, and which are conducted by a not-for-profit organization or a governmental organization; and (4) lotteries conducted as a promotional activity by commercial organizations that are clearly occasional and ancillary to the primary business of that organization, as long as the lotteries are authorized or not otherwise prohibited by the state in which they are conducted.

In 1999, the Supreme Court held that the prohibition on broadcasting advertisements for lawful casino gambling could not constitutionally be applied to truthful advertisements broadcast by radio or television stations licensed in states in which such gambling is legal. Relying upon the reasoning in that decision, the FCC and the United States Department of Justice later concluded that the lottery advertising prohibition may not constitutionally be applied to the broadcast of any truthful advertisements for lawful casino gambling, whether or not the state in which the broadcasting station is located permits casino gambling. Additional information about the rule concerning lotteries can be found at http://www.fcc.gov/guides/broadcasting-contests-lotteries-and-solicitation-funds.

Soliciting Funds. No federal law prohibits the broadcast by stations of requests for funds for legal purposes (including appeals by stations for contributions to meet their operating expenses), if the money or other contributions are used for the announced purposes. However, federal law prohibits fraud by wire, radio or television – including situations in which money solicited for one purpose is used for another – and doing so may lead to FCC sanctions, as well as to criminal prosecution by the U.S. Department of Justice. Additional information about fund solicitation can be found at https://www.fcc.gov/consumers/guides/broadcasting-contests-lotteries-and-solicitation-funds.

Broadcast of Telephone Conversations. Before broadcasting a telephone conversation live or recording a telephone conversation for later broadcast, a station must inform any party to the call of its intention to broadcast the conversation. However, that notification is not necessary when the other party knows that the conversation will be broadcast or such knowledge can be reasonably presumed, such as when the party is associated with the station (for example, as an employee or part-time reporter) or originates the call during a program during which the station customarily broadcasts the calls. For additional information on the rule concerning the broadcast of telephone conversations, see http://transition.fcc.gov/eb/broadcast/telphon.html.

Access to Broadcast Material by People With Disabilities

The Communications Act and the Commission's rules require television station licensees to broadcast certain information that makes viewing more accessible to people with disabilities.

Closed Captioning. Closed captioning is a technology designed to provide access to television programming by persons with hearing disabilities by displaying, in text form, the audio portion of a broadcast, as well as descriptions of background noise and sound effects. Closed captioning is hidden as encoded data transmitted within the television signal. A viewer wishing to see the captions must use a set-top decoder or a television with built-in decoder circuitry. All television sets with screens 13 inches or larger manufactured since mid-1993, including digital sets, have built-in decoder circuitry.

As directed by Congress in the Telecommunications Act of 1996, the FCC has adopted rules requiring closed captioning of most, but not all, television programming. The rules require those that distribute television programs directly to home viewers, including broadcast stations, to comply with these rules. The rules also provide certain exemptions from the captioning requirements. Additional information on the closed captioning requirements may be found on the FCC website at https://www.fcc.gov/general/closed-captioning-video-programming-television.

Access to Emergency Information. The FCC also requires television stations to make the local emergency information that they provide to viewers accessible to persons with disabilities. Thus, if emergency information is provided aurally, such information also must be provided in a visual format for persons who are deaf or hard of hearing. The emergency information may be closed captioned or presented through an alternative method of visual presentation. Such methods include open captioning, crawls, or scrolls that appear on the screen. The information provided visually must include critical details regarding the emergency and how to respond. Critical details could include, among other things, specific information regarding the areas that will be affected by the emergency, evacuation orders, detailed descriptions of areas to be evacuated, specific evacuation routes, approved shelters or the way to take shelter in one's home, instructions on how to secure personal property, road closures, and how to obtain relief assistance. Similarly, if the emergency information is presented visually, it must be made accessible. If the emergency information interrupts programming, such as through a crawl, such information must be accompanied with an aural tone to alert persons with visual disabilities that the station is providing this information so that such persons may be alerted to turn to another source, such as a radio, for more information. Additional information concerning this requirement can be found on the FCC website at https://www.fcc.gov/consumers/guides/accessibility-emergency-information-television.

Business Practices and Advertising

Business Practices, Advertising Rates, and Profits. Except for the requirements concerning political advertisements (discussed at page xx of this Manual), the limits on the number of commercials that can be aired during children's programming (see page xxii), and the prohibition of advertisements over noncommercial educational stations (see page xxiv), the Commission does not regulate a licensee's business practices, such as its advertising rates or its profits. Rates charged for broadcast time are matters for private negotiation between sponsors and stations. Further, except for certain classes of political advertisements (see page xx), station licensees have full discretion to accept or reject any advertising.

Employment Discrimination and Equal Employment Opportunity ("EEO"). The FCC requires that all licensees of radio and TV stations afford equal opportunity in employment. We also prohibit employment discrimination on the basis of race, color, religion, national origin, or sex. However, religious stations are permitted to require that some or all of their employees meet a religious qualification.

Our EEO recruitment rules have three prongs. They require all stations that employ five or more full-time employees (defined as those regularly working 30 hours a week or more) to:

- widely distribute information concerning each full-time job vacancy, except for vacancies that need to be filled under demanding or other special circumstances;
- send notices of openings to organizations in the community that are involved in employment if the organization requests such notices; and
- engage in general outreach activities every two years, such as job fairs, internships, and other community events.

Each licensee with five or more full-time employees must maintain records of its recruitment efforts, and create and place in its public file an annual public file report listing specified information about its recruitment efforts. (The requirements for the EEO portion of the public file are discussed at page xxvii of this Manual.) The annual EEO public file report must also be posted on a station's website, if one exists. In addition, television licensees with five or more full-time employees and radio licensees with 11 or more full-time employees must file an FCC Form 397 Broadcast Mid-Term Report. Each licensee, regardless of size, must file an FCC Form 396 EEO Program Report with its license renewal application. Finally, a prospective station licensee must file an FCC Form 396-A Broadcast Model Program Report with its new station or assignment or transfer application. The FCC reviews EEO compliance at the time that it considers the station renewal application, when it reviews Broadcast Mid-Term Reports, when it receives EEO complaints, and during random station audits. A full range of enforcement actions is available for EEO violations, including the imposition of reporting conditions, forfeitures, short-term license renewal, and license revocation.

All EEO forms are electronically filed and are available for public review in CDBS, the FCC's access database (to access these reports, see http://licensing.fcc.gov/prod/cdbs/pubacc/prod/eeo_search.htm). As discussed at page xxvi this Manual, in addition, copies of all FCC EEO audit letters, licensee responses, and FCC rulings must be included in the audited station's public file and are available for public review at the FCC Public Reference Center in Washington, D.C. Additional information concerning the EEO rules is available at https://www.fcc.gov/general/equal-employment-opportunity.

Sponsorship Identification. The sponsorship identification requirements contained in the Communications Act and the Commission's rules generally require that, when money or other consideration for the airing of program material has been received by or promised to a station, its employees or others, the station must broadcast full disclosure of that fact at the time of the airing of the material, and identify who provided or promised to provide the consideration. This requirement is grounded in the principle that members of the public should know who is trying to persuade them with the programming being aired. This disclosure requirement also applies to the broadcast of musical selections for consideration (so-called "payola") and the airing of certain video news releases. In the case of advertisements for commercial products or services, it is sufficient for a station to announce the sponsor's corporate or trade name, or the name of the sponsor's product (where it is clear that the mention of the product constitutes a sponsorship identification). For additional information about the sponsorship identification and payola rules, see https://www.fcc.gov/consumers/guides/fccs-payola-rules.

Underwriting Announcements on Noncommercial Educational Stations. Noncommercial educational stations may acknowledge contributions over the air, but they may not broadcast commercials or otherwise promote the goods and services of for-profit donors or underwriters. Acceptable "enhanced underwriting" acknowledgements of for-profit donors or underwriters may include: (1) logograms and slogans that identify but do not promote; (2) location information; (3) value-neutral descriptions of a product line or service; and (4) brand names, trade names, and product service listings. However, such acknowledgements may not interrupt the station's regular programming. For additional information about the underwriting rules, see https://www.fcc.gov/enforcement/orders/1831.

Loud Commercials. The FCC does not regulate the volume of broadcast programming, including commercials. Surveys and technical studies reveal that the perceived loudness of particular broadcast matter is a subjective judgment that varies with each viewer and listener and is influenced by many factors, such as the material's content and style and the voice and tone of the person speaking. The FCC has found no evidence that stations deliberately raise audio and modulation levels to emphasize commercial messages.

Manually controlling the set's volume level or using the "mute" button with a remote control constitutes the simplest approach to reducing volume levels deemed to be excessive. Many television receivers are equipped with circuits that are designed to stabilize the loudness between programs and commercials. These functions usually must be activated through the receiver's "set up/audio" menu. Should these techniques fail to resolve the problem, you may consider addressing any complaint about broadcast volume levels to the licensee of the station involved. Additional information about loud commercials can be found at http://www.fcc.gov/guides/program-background-noise-and-loud-commercials.

False or Misleading Advertising. The Federal Trade Commission has primary responsibility for determining whether an advertisement is false or deceptive and for taking action against the sponsor. The Food and Drug Administration has primary responsibility for the safety of food and drug products. Depending on the nature of the advertisement, you should contact these agencies regarding advertisements that you believe may be false or misleading. Additional information about false or misleading advertising can be found at https://www.fcc.gov/consumers/guides/complaints-about-broadcast-advertising.

Offensive Advertising. Unless a broadcast advertisement is found to be in violation of a specific law or rule, the government cannot take action against it. However, if you believe that an advertisement is offensive because of the nature of the item advertised, the scheduling of the announcement, or the manner in which the message is presented, you should consider addressing your complaint directly to the station or network involved, providing the date and time of the broadcast and the product or advertiser in question. This will help those involved in the selection of advertising material to become better informed about audience opinion.

Tobacco and Alcohol Advertising. Federal law prohibits the airing of advertising for cigarettes, little cigars, smokeless tobacco, and chewing tobacco on radio, TV, or any other medium of electronic communication under the FCC's jurisdiction. However, the advertising of smoking accessories, cigars, pipes, pipe tobacco, or cigarette-making machines is not prohibited. Congress has not enacted any law prohibiting broadcast advertising of any kind of alcoholic beverage, and the FCC does not have a rule or policy regulating such advertisements.

Subliminal Programming. The Commission sometimes receives complaints regarding the alleged use of subliminal perception techniques in broadcast programming. Subliminal programming is designed to be perceived on a subconscious level only. Regardless of whether it is effective, the broadcast of subliminal material is inconsistent with a station's obligation to serve the public interest because it is designed to be deceptive.

Blanketing Interference

Rules. Some members of the public situated close to a radio station's transmitting antenna may experience impaired reception of other stations. This is called "blanketing" interference. The Commission's rules impose certain obligations on licensees to resolve such interference complaints. Complaints about such interference involving radio stations are handled by the Media Bureau's Audio Division. Blanketing interference is a less common occurrence with television stations than with radio stations due to the location and height of TV transmitting antennas. If this phenomenon does occur with a television station, the Media Bureau's Video Division will handle complaints on a case-by case-basis, subject to the radio guidelines noted below.

At the outset, the policy is designed to provide protection from interference for individuals within a certain distance from a station (in an area known as the station's "blanketing contour") and only involving electronic devices that pick up an over-the-air signal from a broadcast radio or television station. Thus, stations are not required to resolve interference complaints involving the following:

- A complaint from a party located outside of the station's blanketing contour (115 dBu contour for FM stations, 1 V/m contour for AM stations).
- Improperly installed antenna systems.
- Use of high gain antennas or antenna booster amplifiers.
- Mobile receivers, including but not limited to car radios, portable stereos or cellular phones.
- Non-radio frequency ("RF") devices, including but not limited to, tape recorders, CD players, MP3 players or "land-line" telephones.
- Cordless telephones.

For complaints from parties located within the station's blanketing contour involving non-mobile television or radio receivers, a station must resolve the interference complaint at no cost to the complaining party if the party notifies the station of the problem during the first year that the station operates its new or modified facilities. For similar complaints received after the first year of such operation has passed, although the station is not financially responsible for resolving the complaint, it must provide effective technical assistance to the complaining party. These efforts must include the provision of information and assistance sufficiently specific to enable the complaining party to eliminate all blanketing interference and not simply an attempt by the station to correct the problems. Such assistance entails providing specific details about proper corrective measures to resolve the blanketing interference. For example, stations should provide the complaining party with diagrams and descriptions which explain how and where to use radio-frequency chokes, ferrite cores, filters, and/or shielded cable. In addition, effective technical assistance also includes recommending replacement equipment that would work better in high radiofrequency fields. Effective technical assistance does not mean referring the complainant to the equipment manufacturer.

How to Resolve Blanketing Interference Problems. If you believe that you are receiving blanketing or any other type of interference to broadcast reception, we encourage you to first communicate directly, in writing, with the licensee of the station that you believe is causing the interference. If the licensee does not satisfactorily resolve the problem, you can mail, fax, or e-mail a complaint to us as follows:

- For radio stations:
Federal Communications Commission
Audio Division, Media Bureau
445 12th St., S.W., Washington, D.C. 20554

Fax number: (202) 418-1411
E-mail address: radioinfo@fcc.gov

- For TV stations:
Federal Communications Commission
Video Division, Media Bureau
445 12th St., S.W.,
Washington, D.C. 20554
Fax number: (202) 418-2827
E- mail address: tvinfo@fcc.gov

Your complaint should include: (1) your name, address, and phone number; (2) the call letters of each station involved; (3) each location at which the interference occurs; and (4) each specific device receiving the interference. The more specific your complaint is, the easier it is for us and any station involved to identify and resolve the interference problem.

Other Interference Issues
In many cases in which you receive interference on your television set or radio, the source of the problem could be with your equipment, which may not be adequately designed with circuitry or filtering to reject the unwanted signals of nearby transmitters. We recommend that you contact the equipment manufacturer or the store at which the equipment was purchased to attempt to resolve the interference problem. You can find more information about broadcast interference on the Commission's website, at https://www.fcc.gov/consumers/guides/interference-radio-tv-and-telephone-signals.

The Local Public Inspection File
Requirement to Maintain a Public Inspection File. Our rules require that all licensees and permittees of TV and radio stations and applicants for new broadcast stations maintain a file available for public inspection. This file must contain documents relevant to the station's operation and dealings with the community and the FCC. The public inspection file generally must be maintained at the station's main studio. To obtain the location and phone number of a station's main studio, consult your local telephone directory, or call the station's business office. You may also be able to find this information on the station's Internet website, if one exists.

Purpose of the File. Because we do not routinely monitor each station's programming and operations, viewers and listeners are an important source of information about the nature of their area stations' programming, operations, and compliance with their FCC obligations. The documents contained in each station's public inspection file have information about the station that can assist the public in this important monitoring role.

As discussed in this Manual, every station has an obligation to provide news, public affairs, and other programming that specifically treats the important issues facing its community, and to comply with the Communications Act, the Commission's rules, and the terms of its station license. We encourage a continuing dialogue between broadcasters and members of the public to ensure that stations meet their obligations and remain responsive to the needs of the local community. Because you watch and listen to the stations that we license, you can be a valuable and effective advocate to ensure that your area's stations comply with their localism obligation and other FCC requirements.

Viewing the Public Inspection File. Each broadcast licensee, permittee, and applicant must make its station public inspection file available to members of the public at any time during regular business hours. Although you do not need to make an appointment to view the file, making one may be helpful both to the station and to you.

A station that chooses to maintain all or part of its public file on a computer database must provide you a computer terminal if you wish to review the file. As of a date to be determined, television stations will also be required to post most of the content of their public files on their Internet websites, if they have them, or on their state broadcasters association's website, if permitted. Radio stations have not yet been required to post their files on their websites, but may do so if they wish. If you want to view a station's public file over the Internet, you should check its website or contact the station to determine if the file is posted.

You may request copies of materials in the file, which the station must provide to you at a reasonable charge, by visiting the station in person. In addition, if the station's public file is located outside of its community of license (and you live within the station's service area and your request does not involve the station's political file), you may request copies of materials in the file over the telephone. To facilitate telephone requests, we require stations to provide you a copy of the current version of this Manual free of charge if you so request. The Manual can help you identify other documents you may ask to have mailed to you. Stations should assist callers in this process and answer questions you may have about the actual contents of the public file. This information may include, for example, the number of pages and time periods covered by a particular ownership report or children's television programming report, or the types of applications actually maintained in the station's public file and the dates on which they were filed with the FCC. Finally, if you ask a broadcast station for photocopies of material in its public inspection file, the station may require you to pay for those photocopies. Therefore, the station may require a guarantee of payment in advance (such as with a deposit or a credit card). The station must pay the postage for copies requested by telephone. Stations must fulfill requests for copies within a reasonable period of time, which generally should not exceed seven calendar days after the request is made. For additional information on these public file requirements, see http://transition.fcc.gov/eb/broadcast/pif.html.

Contents of the File. The following materials must be maintained in each station public inspection file:

- *The License.* Stations must keep a copy of their current FCC construction permit or license in the public file, together with any material documenting Commission-approved modifications to the authorization. The license or permit reflects the station's authorized technical parameters (such as its frequency, call letters, operating power and transmitter location), as well as any special conditions imposed by the FCC on the station's operation. It also indicates when it was issued and when it will expire.

- *Applications and Related Materials.* The public file must contain copies of all applications involving the station filed with the Commission that are still pending before either the FCC or the courts. These include applications to sell the station or to modify its facilities (for example, to increase power, change the antenna system, or change the transmitter location). If a petition to deny any application was filed, the file must contain a statement to that effect, and the name and address of the petitioning party. Applications must be maintained until "final" FCC action on them, when the action can no longer be appealed or reversed.

  The station must also keep copies of any granted construction permit or assignment or transfer application if its grant required us to waive our rules. Applications that required a waiver, together with any related material, will reflect each particular rule that we waived, and must be maintained as long as any such waiver remains in effect.

  Also, if the FCC renewed the station license for less than a full term, the station must keep that renewal application (FCC Form 303-S) in the file until grant of its next renewal application by final FCC action. We may grant such a short-term renewal when we are concerned about the station's performance over the previous term. These concerns will be reflected in the renewal-related materials in the public file.

- *Citizen Agreements.* Commercial stations must keep copies of any written agreements that they make with local viewers or listeners. These "citizen agreements" may deal with programming, employment, or other issues of community concern. The station must keep these agreements in the public file for as long as they are in effect.
- *Contour Maps.* The public file must contain copies of any station service contour maps or other information submitted with any application filed with the FCC that reflects the station's service contours and/or its main studio and transmitter locations. The Commission's application forms require submission of contour maps only from stations that do not certify that their signals cover their city of license. These documents must stay in the file for as long as they remain current and accurate regarding the station.
- *Material Relating to an FCC Investigation or Complaint.* Stations must keep material relating to any matter that is the subject of an FCC investigation (including EEO audits) or a complaint that the station has violated the Communications Act or FCC rules. The station must keep this material in its file until the FCC notifies it that the material may be discarded. Since the FCC is not involved in disputes regarding matters unrelated to the Communications Act or FCC rules, such as private contractual disputes, stations do not have to retain material relating to such disputes in the public file.
- *Ownership Reports and Related Material.* The public file must contain a copy of the most recent, complete ownership report (FCC Form 323 for commercial stations, FCC Form 323-E for noncommercial educational stations) filed for the station. Among other things, these reports disclose the names of the owners of the station licensee and their ownership interests, list any contracts related to the station that are required to be filed with the FCC, and identify any interests in other broadcast stations held by the station licensee or its owners.
- *List of Contracts Required to be Filed with the FCC.* Stations must keep in the public file either copies of all the contracts that they have to file with the FCC, or an up-to-date list identifying all such contracts. If the station keeps a list and a member of the public asks to see copies of the actual contracts, the station must provide the copies to the requester within seven calendar days. Contracts required to be maintained or listed in the public inspection file include:
  - contracts relating to network service (network affiliation contracts);
  - contracts relating to ownership or control of the licensee or permittee or its stock. Examples include articles of incorporation, bylaws, agreements providing for the assignment of a license or permit or affecting stock ownership or voting rights (stock options, pledges, or proxies), and mortgage or loan agreements that restrict the licensee or permittee's freedom of operation; and
  - management consultant agreements with independent contractors, and contracts relating to the utilization in a management capacity of any person other than an officer, director, or regular employee of the licensee.
- *Political File.* Stations must keep a file which contains "a complete record of a request to purchase broadcast time that: (A) is made by or on behalf of a legally qualified candidate for public office; or (B) communicates a message relating to any political matter of national importance, including: (i) a legally qualified candidate; (ii) any election to federal office; or (iii) a national legislative issue of public importance." The file must identify how the station responded to such requests and, if the request was granted, the charges made, a schedule of time purchased, the times the spots actually aired, the rates charged, and the classes of time purchased. The file also must reflect any free time provided to a candidate. The station must keep the political records in the file for two years after the spot airs. (You can find more information regarding the political broadcasting laws at pages xx of this Manual.)
- *EEO Materials.* As noted earlier, licensees must submit certain forms containing EEO information and include copies in their station public files. Thus, all stations employing five or more full-time employees must put an EEO public file report in their station public file each year. We also require each radio and TV station licensee to file a Form 396 EEO Program Report with its license renewal application and to include the Report in its public file. Those licensees that file a Form 397 Broadcast Mid-Term Report must also include a copy in the public file. These materials must be retained in the file until final action on the station's next license renewal application. A new station applicant or prospective station buyer, if it intends to employ five or more full-time employees, must file a Form 396-A Broadcast EEO Model Program Report with its new station assignment or transfer application and the Report must be included in the public file as a part of the underlying application and retained in the file until the grant of the underlying application becomes final. (You can find more information regarding the EEO rules at pages xxiv of this Manual.)

- *"The Public and Broadcasting."* Stations must keep a copy of the current version of this Manual in the public file and provide a copy, upon request, to any member of the public. As noted above, you can also request a copy from the FCC or access it on our Internet website at https://www.fcc.gov/media/radio/public-and-broadcasting.
- *Letters and E-Mails from the Public.* Commercial stations must keep in their files, for at least three years, written comments, suggestions, and e-mails received from the public regarding their operation. (Noncommercial educational stations are not subject to this requirement.) This obligation is limited to comments, suggestions, and e-mails sent to station management or a publicized station address. Letters need not be placed in the public inspection file when the author has requested that the letter not be made public or when the licensee feels that it should be excluded from public inspection because of the nature of its content (such as defamatory or obscene letters). Moreover, although television stations that post their public file materials on their websites must include e-mails received from the public, they need not post letters from the public, as long as they include hard copies of such letters in their public files, and a notice on their website that the letters can be located in the file. As noted above, all or a part of a station public file may be maintained on a computer database, as long as a computer terminal is made available, at the location of the file, for members of the public who wish to review the file. Accordingly, as an alternative to maintaining hard copies of e-mails in the public file, a station may place the e- mails on a computer database, as long as a terminal is made available at the location of the public file to members of the public who wish to review the file.
- *Quarterly Programming Reports.* Every three months, each broadcast radio and television station licensee must prepare and place in its station public file a list of programs containing its most significant treatment of community issues during the preceding three months ("issues/programs lists"). The list must briefly describe both the issue and the programming during which the issue was discussed, including the date and time that each such program was aired and its title and duration. The licensee must keep these lists in the file until the next grant of the station renewal application has become final. Television stations will be required to file a Standardized Television Disclosure Form instead of these lists once that form is approved and made available. The form, which will also be filed quarterly, will require commercial and noncommercial educational television broadcasters to provide detailed information on the efforts of their station to provide programming responsive to issues facing their communities in a standardized format.
- *Children's Television Programming Reports.* As discussed at pages xxii of this Manual, the Children's Television Act of 1990 and our rules require each TV station to serve the educational and informational needs of children by means of its overall programming and through programming that is specifically designed to serve such needs. Commercial TV stations must make and retain in their files Children's Television Programming Reports (FCC Form 398) identifying the educational and informational programming for children aired by the station. (Noncommercial educational stations are not required to prepare these reports.) The report must include the name of the person at the station responsible for collecting comments on the station's compliance with the Children's Television Act. The station has to prepare these reports each calendar quarter, and it must place them in the public file separate from the file's other material. The licensee must keep these lists in the file until the next grant of the station renewal application has become final. You can also view each station's reports on our website at https://www.fcc.gov/general/parents.
- *Records Regarding Children's Programming Commercial Limits.* As also discussed at page xxii of this Manual, the Children's Television Act of 1990 and our rules limit the type and amount of advertising that may be aired during TV programming directed to children 12 and under. Stations must keep records that substantiate compliance with this limitation in their public files and retain them until the next grant of the station renewal application has become final.
- *Time Brokerage Agreements.* A time brokerage agreement is a type of contract that generally involves a station's sale of blocks of airtime to a third-party broker, who then supplies the programming to fill that time and sells the commercial spot announcements to support the programming. Commercial radio and television stations must keep in their public files a copy of every agreement involving: (1) time brokerage of that station, or (2) time brokerage by any other station owned by the same licensee. These agreements must be maintained in the file for as long as they are in force.
- *Lists of Donors.* Noncommercial educational television and radio stations must keep in their public files a list of donors supporting each specific program. These lists must be retained for two years after the program at issue airs.
- *Local Public Notice Announcements.* As discussed at page xvii of this Manual, when someone files an application to build a new station or to renew, sell, or modify an existing station, we generally require the applicant to make a series of local announcements to inform the public of the application's existence and nature. These announcements are either published in a local newspaper or made over the air on the station, and are intended to give the public an opportunity to comment on the application. A statement certifying compliance with this requirement, including the dates and times that notice was given, must be placed in the public file. The only exception to this public notice requirement is when the proposed station sale is "pro forma" and will not result in a change of ultimate control, or the modification application does not contemplate a "major change" of the station facilities.
- *Must-Carry or Retransmission Consent Election.* The public file for all commercial television stations must also contain documentation of the station's election for carriage over cable and satellite systems. In this regard, there are two ways that a broadcast TV station can choose to be carried over a cable or satellite system: "must-carry" or "retransmission consent." Each is discussed below.
  - *Must carry.* TV stations are generally entitled to be carried on cable television systems in their local markets. A station that chooses to exercise this right receives no compensation from the cable system. Satellite carriers may decide to offer local stations in a designated market area. If they choose to offer one station, then they must carry all the stations in that market that request carriage.

- *Retransmission Consent.* Instead of exercising their "must-carry" rights, commercial TV stations may choose to receive compensation from a cable system or satellite carrier in return for granting permission to the cable system or satellite carrier to carry the station. This option is available only to commercial TV stations. Because it is possible that a station that elects this option may not reach an agreement with the cable system, it may ultimately not be carried by the system.

  Every three years, commercial TV stations must decide whether their relationship with each local cable system and satellite carrier that offers local service will be governed by must-carry or by retransmission consent agreements. Each commercial station must keep a copy of its decision in the public file for the three-year period to which it pertains.

  Noncommercial stations are not entitled to compensation in return for carriage on a cable or satellite system, but they may request mandatory carriage on the system. A noncommercial station making such a request must keep a copy of the request in the public file for the duration of the period to which it applies.

- *DTV Transition Consumer Education Activity Reports.* Each broadcast television station must place in its station public file on a quarterly basis an FCC Form 388 DTV Consumer Education Quarterly Activity Report outlining its efforts during the previous quarter to educate consumers on the transition to digital television. These reports must be maintained in the file for one year. Additional information about the DTV transition can be found at page xviii of this Manual.

Complaints or Comments About a Station

Comments to Stations and Networks. If you feel the need to do so, we encourage you to write directly to station management or to network officials to comment on their broadcast service. These are the people responsible for creating and selecting the station's programs and announcements and determining station operation. Letters to station and network officials keep them informed about audience needs and interests, as well as on public opinion on specific material and practices. Individuals and groups can often resolve problems with stations at the local level.

Comments/Complaints to the FCC. We give full consideration to the broadcast complaints, comments, and other inquiries that we receive. As stated above, we encourage you to first contact the station or network directly about programming and operating issues. If your concerns are not resolved in this manner, with the exception of complaints about obscene, indecent, or profane programming, which should be submitted in the manner described at page xxi of this Manual, and complaints about blanketing interference discussed at page xxv, the best way to provide all the information the FCC needs to process your complaint about other broadcast matters is to complete fully the on-line complaint form, which can be found at http://consumercomplaints.fcc.gov/hc/en-us. You can also call in, e-mail or file your complaint in hard copy with the FCC's Consumer Center in the following manner:

Federal Communications Commission
Consumer & Governmental Affairs Bureau
Consumer Inquiries and Complaints Division
445 12th Street SW
Washington, D.C. 20554
Fax number: 202-418-0232
Telephone number: (888) 225-5322

If you are submitting an audio or video tape, DVD, CD or other type of media with your complaint, you should send it to the following address to avoid mail processing damage:

Federal Communications Commission
Consumer & Governmental Affairs Bureau
Consumer Inquiries and Complaints Division
9050 Junction Drive
Annapolis Junction, Maryland 20701

If you do not use the on-line complaint Form 2000E, your complaint, at a minimum, should indicate: (1) the call letters of the station; (2) the city and state in which the station is located; (3) the name, time, and date of the specific program or advertisement in question, if applicable; (4) the name of anyone contacted at the station, if applicable; and (5) a statement of the problem, as specific as possible, together with an audio or video tape, CD, DVD or other recording or transcript of the program or advertisement that is the subject of your complaint (if possible). Please include your name and address if you would like information on the final disposition of your complaint; you may request confidentiality. We prefer that you submit complaints in writing, although you may submit complaints that are time-sensitive by telephone, especially if they involve safety concerns. Please be aware that we can only act on allegations that a station has violated a provision of the Communications Act or the FCC's rules or policies.

In addition to (or instead of) filing a complaint, you can file a petition to deny or an informal objection to an application that a station licensee has filed, such as a license renewal application. This procedure is discussed at page xviii of this Manual. You may obtain further information on the petition to deny process on the Commission's website, at http://transition.fcc.gov/localism/renew_process_handout.pdf. You may also wish to consider reviewing our rules or contacting an attorney. You can find links to our rules on the Commission website, at https://www.fcc.gov/general/rules-regulations-title-47. As noted earlier, the rules governing broadcast stations are generally found in Part 73 of Title 47 of the Code of Federal Regulations.

Broadcast Information Specialist

We have created contact points at the Commission, accessible via toll-free telephone numbers, by fax, or over the Internet, dedicated to providing information to members of the public regarding how they can become involved in the Commission's processes.

Should you have questions about how do so, including inquiries about our complaint or petitioning procedures or the filing and status of the license renewal, modification or assignment or transfer application for a particular station, you may contact one of our Broadcast Information Specialists, by calling, by facsimile, or by sending an e-mail, as noted below:

- If your question relates to a radio station:
  - Toll-Free: (866) 267-7202
  - Fax: (202) 418-1411
  - E-Mail: radioinfo@fcc.gov
- If your question relates to a television station:
  - Toll-Free: (866) 918-5777
  - Fax: (202) 418-2827
  - E-Mail: tvinfo@fcc.gov

If your question relates to both a radio and a television station or is general in nature, you may contact either specialist.

Glossary of Terms

AM—Amplitude modulation. Also referring to audio service broadcast over 535 khz-1705 khz.

Analog—AA continuous electrical signal that carries information in the form of variable physical values, such as amplitude or frequency modulation.

Basic cable service—Package of programming on cable systems eligible for regulation by local franchising authorities under 1992 Cable Act, including all local broadcast signals and PEG (public, educational and government) access channels.

Cable television—System that transmits original programming, and programming of broadcast television stations, to consumers over wired network.

CC—Closed captioning. Method of transmitting textual information over television channel's vertical blanking interval; transmissions are deciphered with decoders; decoded transmissions appear as text superimposed over television image.

Clear channel—AM radio station allowed to dominate its frequency with up to 50 kw of power; their signals are generally protected for distance of up to 750 miles at night.

Closed circuit—The method of transmission of programs or other material that limits its target audience to a specific group rather than the general public.

Coaxial cable—Cable with several common axis lines under protective sheath used for television signal transmissions.

Common carrier—Telecommunication company that provides communications transmission services to the public.

DAB—Digital audio broadcasting. Modulations for sending digital rather than analog audio signals by either terrestrial or satellite transmitter with audio response up to compact disc quality (20 khz).

DBS—Direct broadcast satellite. High powered satellite authorized to broadcast direct to homes.

Digital—A discontinuous electrical signal that carries information in binary fashion. Data is represented by a specific sequence of off-on electrical pulses.

Directional antenna—An antenna that directs most of its signal strength in a specific direction rather than at equal strength in all directions. Used chiefly in AM radio operation.

Downlink—Earth station used to receive signals from satellites.

Earth station—Equipment used for transmitting or receiving satellite communications.

EDTV—Enhanced-definition television. Proposed intermediate systems for evolution to full HDTV, usually including slightly improved resolution and sound, with a wider (16:9) aspect ratio.

Effective competition—Market status under which cable TV systems are exempt from regulation of basic tier rates by local franchising authorities, as defined in 1992 Cable Act. To claim effective competition, a cable system must compete with at least one other multichannel provider that is available to at least 50\% of an area's households and is subscribed to by more than 15\% of the households.

Encryption—System for scrambling signals to prevent unauthorized reception.

ENG—Electronic news gathering.

ETV—Educational television.

Fiber-optic cable—Wires made of glass fiber used to transmit video, audio, voice or data providing vastly wider bandwidth than standard coaxial cable.

Field—Half of the video information in the frame of a video picture. The NTSC system displays 59.94 fields per second.

FM—Frequency modulation. Also referring to audio service broadcast over 88 mhz-108 mhz.

Footprint—Area on earth within which a satellite's signal can be received.

Frame—A full video picture. The NTSC system displays 29.97 525-line frames per second.

Frequency—The number of cycles a signal is transmitted per second, measured in hertz.

Geostationary orbit—Orbit 22,300 miles above earth's equator where satellites circle earth at same rate earth rotates.

ghz—Gigahertz. One billion hertz (cycles) per second.

HDTV—High-definition television.

Headend—Facility in cable system from which all signals originate. (Local and distant television stations, and satellite programming, are picked up and amplified for retransmission through system.)

Hertz—A measurement of frequency. One cycle per second equals one hertz (hz).

Independent television—Television stations that are not affiliated with networks and that do not use the networks as a primary source of their programming.

Information services—Broad term used to describe full range of audio, video and data transmission services that can be transmitted over the air or by cable.

Interactive—Allowing two-way data flow.

Interlaced scanning—Television transmission technique in which each frame is divided into two fields. NTSC system interleaves odd-numbered lines with even-numbered lines at a transmission rate of 59.94 fields per second.

ITFS—Instructional Television Fixed Service.

khz—Kilohertz. One thousand hertz (cycles) per second.

LED—Light emitting diode. Type of semiconductor that lights up when activated by voltage.

LO—Local origination channel.

MDS—Multipoint distribution service.

mhz—Megahertz. One million hertz (cycles) per second.

Microwave—Frequencies above 1,000 mhz.

MSO—Multiple cable systems operator.

Must carry—Legal requirement that cable operators carry local broadcast signals. Cable systems with 12 or fewer channels must carry at least three broadcast signals; systems with 12 or more channels must carry up to one-third of their capacity; systems with 300 or fewer subscribers are exempt. The 1992 Cable Act requires broadcast station to waive must-carry rights if it chooses to negotiate retransmission compensation (see "Retransmission consent").

NTSC—National Television System Committee. Committee that recommended current American standard color television.

PCM—Pulse code modulation. Conversion of voice signals into digital code.

PPV—Pay-per-view.

Progressive scanning—TV system where video frames are transmitted sequentially, unlike interlaced scanning in which frames are divided into two fields.

PSA—Public service announcement.

PTV—Public television.

Public radio—Radio stations and networks that are operated on a noncommercial basis.

Public television—Television stations and networks that operate as noncommercial ventures.

RCC—Radio common carrier. Common carriers whose major businesses include radio paging and mobile telephone services.

Retransmission consent—Local TV broadcasters' right to negotiate a carriage fee with local cable operators, as provided in 1992 Cable Act.

SCA—Subsidiary communications authorizations. Authorizations granted to FM broadcasters for using subcarriers on their channels for other communications services.

Shortwave—Transmissions on frequencies of 6-25 mhz.

SHF—Super high frequency.

Signal-to-noise ratio—The ratio between the strength of an electronically produced signal to interfering noises in the same bandwidth.

SMATV—Satellite master antenna television.

STV—Subscription television.

Superstation—Local television station whose signal is retransmitted via satellite to cable systems beyond reach of over-the-air signal.

Teletext—A one-way electronic publishing service that can be transmitted over the vertical blanking interval of a standard television signal or the full channel of a television station or cable television system. The major use today is for closed-captioning.

Translator—Broadcast station that rebroadcasts signals of other stations without originating its own programming.

Transponder—Satellite transmitter/receiver that picks up signals transmitted from earth, translates them into new frequencies and amplifies them before retransmitting them back to ground.

UHF—Ultra high frequency band (300 mhz-3,000 mhz), which includes TV channels 14-83.

Uplink—Earth station used for transmitting to satellite.

VHF—Very high frequencies (30 mhz-300 mhz), which include TV channels 2-13 and FM radio.

Videotext—Two-way interactive service that uses either two-way cable or telephone lines to connect a central computer to a television screen.

List of Abbreviations

- ***** ... noncommercial
- **a** ... annual
- **actg** ... acting
- **admin** ... administrative
- **adv** ... advertising
- **affil** ... affiliate
- **affrs** ... affairs
- **AFRTS** ... Armed Forces Radio and TV Service
- **alt** ... alternate
- **ant** ... antenna
- **AOR** ... album-oriented rock
- **AP** ... Associated Press
- **assn** ... association
- **assoc.** ... associate
- **asst** ... assistant
- **atty** ... attorney
- **aur** ... aural
- **aux** ... auxiliary
- **bcst** ... broadcast
- **bcstg** ... broadcasting
- **bcstr** ... broadcaster
- **bd** ... board
- **BET** ... Black Entertainment Television
- **bi-m** ... every two months
- **bk rev** ... book reviews
- **bldg** ... building
- **bor** ... borough
- **btfl** ... beautiful
- **C-SPAN** ... Cable Satellite Public Affairs Network
- **CATV** ... community antenna television
- **CBC** ... Canadian Broadcasting Corp.
- **CEO** ... chief executive officer
- **ch** ... channel
- **CH** ... critical hours
- **chg** ... charge
- **CHR** ... contemporary hit radio
- **chmn** ... chairman
- **circ** ... circulation
- **coml** ... commercial
- **contemp** ... contemporary
- **COO** ... chief operating officer
- **coord** ... coordinator
- **CP** ... construction permit
- **CRTC** ... Canadian Radio-television and Telecommunications Commission
- **C&W** ... country & western
- **D** ... day
- **d** ... daily
- **DA** ... directional antenna
- **dance rev** ... dance reviews
- **DBS** ... direct broadcast satellite
- **dev** ... development
- **dir** ... director
- **div** ... diverse
- **DMA** ... Designated Market Area
- **dups** ... duplicates
- **Eds** ... editors
- **Ed Bd** ... Editorial Board
- **educ** ... educational
- **engr** ... engineer
- **engrg** ... engineering
- **EPG** ... Electronic Program Guide
- **ERP** ... effective radiated power
- **ETV** ... educational television
- **exec** ... executive
- **FCC** ... Federal Communications Commission
- **film rev** ... film reviews
- **fortn** ... fortnightly
- **Fr** ... French
- **g** ... ground
- **gen** ... general
- **Ger** ... German
- **govt** ... government
- **HAAT** ... height above average terrain
- **HBO** ... Home Box Office
- **horiz** ... horizontal polarization
- **hqtrs** ... headquarters
- **ind** ... independent
- **info** ... information
- **instal** ... installation
- **ISBN** ... International Standard Book Number
- **ISSN** ... International Standard Serial Number
- **Illus** ... illustrations
- **Irreg** ... irregular
- **It** ... Italian
- **khz** ... kilohertz
- **kw** ... kilowatts
- **loc** ... local
- **LPTV** ... low power television
- **LS** ... local sunset
- **lstng** ... listening
- **lw** ... long wave
- **m** ... meters
- **MDS** ... Multipoint Distribution Service
- **mdse** ... merchandising
- **mfg** ... manufacturing
- **mgng** ... managing
- **mgr** ... manager
- **mgmt** ... management
- **mhz** ... megahertz
- **mi** ... miles
- **mktg** ... marketing
- **MMDS** ... Multichannel Multipoint Distribution Service
- **mo** ... month
- **mod** ... modification
- **MOR** ... middle of the road
- **MSO** ... multiple system operator
- **Mthy** ... monthly
- **mus** ... music
- **music rev** ... music reviews
- **mw** ... medium wave
- **N** ... night
- **na** ... not available
- **NAB** ... National Association of Broadcasters
- **natl** ... national
- **net** ... network
- **NPR** ... National Public Radio
- **nwspr** ... newspaper
- **off** ... officer
- **opns** ... operations
- **per** ... personnel
- **play rev** ... play reviews (theatre reviews)
- **Pol** ... Polish
- **pop** ... population
- **PR** ... public relations
- **pres** ... president
- **PRI** ... Public Radio International
- **progmg** ... programming
- **progsv** ... progressive
- **prom** ... promotion
- **PSA** ... presunrise authority, public service announcement
- **ptnr** ... partner
- **pub affrs** ... public affairs
- **publ** ... publicity

q .... quarterly
quad .... quadraphonic
record rev .... record reviews
rel .... relations
relg .... religion
rep .... representative
RFE .... Radio Free Europe
rgn .... region
rgnl .... regional
RL .... Radio Liberty
rsch .... research
s-a .... twice annually
s-m .... twice monthly
s-w .... twice weekly
sec .... secretary
sep .... separate
sh .... shares
SH .... specified hours
sls .... sales
SMATV .... satellite master antenna television
Sp .... Spanish
sr .... senior
ST .... shares time
stn .... station
sub .... subscriber
supt .... superintendent
supvr .... supervisor
svcs .... services
sw .... short wave
t .... terrain
tech .... technical
tele rev .... television reviews
3/m .... three times a month
3/y .... three times a year
traf .... traffic
trans .... translators
treas .... treasurer
twp .... township
TWX .... Teletypewriter Exchange
U .... unlimited
UHF .... ultra high frequency
UPI .... United Press International
var .... variety
vert .... vertical polarization
VHF .... very high frequency
video rev .... video reviews
vis .... visual
VOA .... Voice of America
vp .... vice president
w .... watts
wkly .... weekly

TV Households

Every industry needs a measure of the size of its marketplace and the radio and television industries are no exceptions.

A major source of such media market data in the United States is Nielsen Media Research (NMR), and one of the measurements it takes annually is TV Households (TV HH). A home with one operable TV/monitor is a TV HH, and Nielsen is able to extrapolate its "National Universe Estimates" from Census Bureau population data combined with this expression of TV penetration.

With Us from Day One

The advent of broadcast advertising, in July 1941, was coincidental with the dawn of commercial television, and within ten years market research in the new medium was in full swing.

Since the Federal Communications Commission (FCC) allowed those first TV ads—for Sun Oil, Lever Bros., Procter & Gamble and the Bulova Watch Company—reliable audience measurement has been necessary for marketers to target their campaigns. The proliferation of devices for viewing TV content and the continual evolution of consumer behavior have made the task more important—and more challenging—than ever.

Nevertheless, while the reality of "TV Everywhere" has undeniably complicated the work of audience measurement, the use of one rudimentary gauge persists—the number of households with a set, TV HH.

Nielsen Media Research

In the United States, Nielsen Media Research (NMR) is the authoritative source for television audience measurement (TAM). Best-known for its ratings system, which has determined the fates of many television programs, NMR also tracks the number of households in a Designated Market Area (DMA) that own a TV.

Published annually before the start of the new TV season in September, these Universe Estimates, representing potential regional audiences, are used by advertisers to plan effective campaigns.

TV Ownership...

For more than 40 years, almost all households in the United States have owned at least one television. Nielsen estimates that number to be 112.1 million for the 2017-18 season, 2.55 million fewer than the previous season.[1]

Not in decline is the average number of sets per home. According to Nielsen's March 2015 Universe Estimate Report it now stands at 3.03, and more than 80 per cent of TV HH are multi-set homes.

...Is Where One Would Expect

Nielsen Media Research divides the United States into 210 Designated Market Areas (DMAs. See Figure 1). Each market area consists of a number of counties served by the same television and radio stations. Naturally, the largest DMAs are the most heavily populated metropolitan areas in the country.

They are named for the largest city (e.g., New York) or cities (e.g., San Francisco-Oakland-San Jose) in the region, and there is sometimes service overlap with nearby markets.

---

[1] San Francisco Market Drops Two Spots in 2018 Nielsen Rankings (2017, October 9). *TVSpy*. Retrieved December 4, 2017 from http://www.adweek.com/tvspy/san-francisco-market-drops-two-spots-in-2018-nielsen-rankings/195162

This year, all 5 top markets – New York, Los Angeles, Chicago, Philadelphia and Dallas – lost TV homes. San Francisco, number 6 in 2016-17, lost 1.5 percent of TV homes and moves to number 8 as a result. Washington, D.C. moves up from seventh spot to 6; Houston moves to 7 from 8; and Atlanta (9) and Boston (10) round out the top ten.

Figure 1 Designated Market Areas

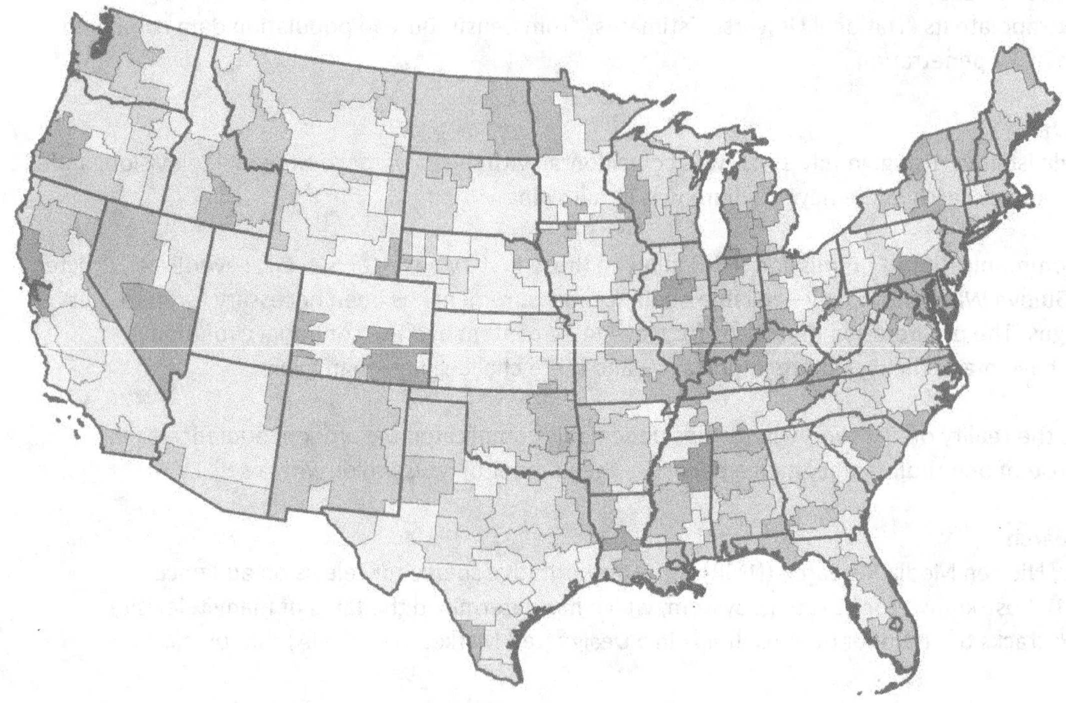

Source "Designated Market Areas, 2013" by 7.11brown licensed under CC BY-SA 3.0

Regional Top Fives[2]

The top 5 market areas in the Northeast (as defined by the Census Bureau) are New York (1), Philadelphia (4), Boston (10), Pittsburgh (24) and Baltimore (26).

In the South, the largest DMAs are Dallas-Ft. Worth (5), Washington, D.C. (6), Houston (7), Atlanta (9), and Tampa-St. Petersburg (13).

Chicago (3) leads the Midwest, followed by Detroit (14), Minneapolis-St. Paul (15), Cleveland-Akron (19) and St. Louis (21).

In the West, the second largest city in the country, Los Angeles, is the number 2 DMA. The other four in the region are San Francisco-Oakland-San Jose (8), Phoenix (11), Seattle-Tacoma (12) and Denver (17).

---

[2] The Nielsen Company. *Local Television Market Universe Estimates*. Retrieved December 4, 2017 from http://www.nielsen.com/content/dam/corporate/us/en/public%20factsheets/tv/2017-18%20TV%20DMA%20Ranks.pdf

55 Years of Station Transactions

YEAR	RADIO ONLY*	GROUPS*	TV ONLY	TOTAL
1954	$10,224,047 (187)	$26,213,323 (18)	$23,906,760 (27)	$60,344,130
1955	27,333,104 (242)	22,351,602 (11)	23,394,660 (29)	$73,079,366
1956	32,563,378 (316)	65,212,055 (24)	17,830,395 (21)	$115,605,828
1957	48,207,470 (357)	47,490,884 (28)	28,489,206 (38)	$124,187,560
1958	49,868,123 (407)	60,872,618 (17)	16,796,285 (23)	$127,537,026
1959	65,544,653 (436)	42,724,727 (15)	15,227,201 (21)	$123,496,581
1960	51,763,285 (345)	24,648,400 (10)	22,930,225 (21)	$99,341,910
1961	55,532,516 (282)	42,103,708 (13)	31,167,943 (24)	$128,804,167
1962	59,912,520 (306)	18,822,745 (8)	23,007,638 (16)	$101,742,903
1963	43,457,584 (305)	25,045,726 (3)	36,799,768 (16)	$105,303,078
1964	52,296,480 (430)	67,185,762 (20)	86,274,494 (36)	$205,756,736
1965	55,933,300 (389)	49,756,993 (15)	29,433,473 (32)	$135,123,766
1966	76,633,762 (367)	28,510,500 (11)	30,574,054 (31)	$135,718,316
1967	59,670,053 (316)	32,086,297 (9)	80,316,223 (30)	$172,072,573
1968	71,310,709 (316)	47,556,634 (9)	33,588,069 (20)	$152,455,412
1969	108,866,538 (343)	35,037,000 (5)	87,794,032 (32)	$231,697,570
1970	86,292,899 (268)	1,038,465 (3)	87,454,078 (19)	$174,785,442
1971	125,501,514 (270)	750,000 (2)	267,296,410 (27)	$393,547,924
1972	114,424,673 (239)	0 (0)	156,905,864 (37)	$271,330,537
1973	160,933,557 (352)	2,812,444 (4)	66,635,144 (25)	$230,381,145
1974	168,998,012 (369)	19,800,000 (5)	118,983,462 (24)	$307,781,474
1975	131,065,860 (363)	0 (0)	128,420,101 (22)	$259,485,961
1976	180,663,820 (413)	1,800,000 (3)	108,459,657 (32)	$290,923,477
1977	161,236,169 (344)	0 (0)	128,635,435 (25)	$289,871,604
1978	331,557,239 (586)	30,450,000 (5)	289,721,159 (51)	$651,728,398
1979	335,597,000 (546)	463,500,000 (52)	317,581,000 (47)	$1,116,678,000
1980	339,634,000 (424)	27,000,000 (3)	534,150,000 (35)	$900,784,000
1981	447,838,060 (625)	78,400,000 (6)	227,950,000 (24)	$754,188,060
1982	470,722,833 (597)	0 (0)	527,675,411 (30)	$998,398,244
1983	621,077,876 (669)	332,000,000 (10)	1,902,701,830 (61)	$2,855,779,706
1984	977,024,266 (782)	234,500,000 (2)	1,252,023,787 (82)	$2,463,548,053
1985	1,414,816,073 (1,558)	962,450,000 (218)	3,290,995,000 (99)	$5,668,261,073
1986	1,490,131,426 (959)	1,993,021,955 (192)	2,709,516,490 (128)	$6,192,669,871
1987	1,236,355,748 (775)	4,610,965,000 (132)	1,661,832,724 (59)	$7,509,153,472
1988	1,841,630,156 (845)	1,326,250,000 (106)	1,779,958,042 (70)	$4,947,838,198
1989	1,148,524,765 (663)	533,599,078 (40)	1,541,055,033 (84)	$3,223,178,876
1990	868,636,700 (1,045)	411,037,150 (60)	696,952,350 (75)	$1,976,626,200
1991	534,694,500 (793)	206,995,500 (61)	273,365,000 (38)	$1,015,055,000
1992	603,192,980 (667)	318,176,050 (24)	124,004,000 (41)	$1,045,373,030
1993	815,450,000 (633)	756,722,000 (NA)	1,728,711,000 (101)	$3,300,883,000
1994	970,400,000 (494)	1,800,000,000 (154)	2,200,000,000 (89)	$4,970,400,000
1995	792,440,000 (524)	2,790,000,000 (213)	4,740,000,000 (112)	$8,322,440,000
1996	2,840,820,000 (671)	12,034,000,000 (345)	10,488,000,000 (99)	$25,362,820,000
1997	2,461,570,000 (630)	14,580,000,000 (329)	6,400,000,000 (108)	$23,441,570,000
1998	1,596,210,000 (589)	14,080,000,000 (271)	7,120,000,000 (90)	$22,796,210,000
1999	1,718,000,000 (382)	26,880,000,000 (196)	4,720,000,000 (86)	$33,318,000,000
2000**	24,900,000,000 (1,794)	0 (0)	8,800,000,000 (154)	$33,700,000,000
2001**	3,800,000,000 (1,000)	0 (0)	4,900,000,000 (108)	$8,700,000,000
2002**	5,594,141,000 (836)	0 (0)	2,529,039,000 (249)	$8,123,180,000
2003**	2,400,000,000 (950)	0 (0)	520,000,000 (97)	$2,920,000,000
2004**	1,897,422,000 (901)	0 (0)	871,923,000 (66)	$2,769,345,000
2005**	2,791,531,000 (895)	0 (0)	2,842,439,000 (86)	$5,633,970,000
2006**	22,871,247,000 (2101)	0 (0)	18,127,686,000 (180)	$40,998,933,000
2007**	1,488,628,000 (1,187)	0 (0)	4,616,018,000 (295)	$6,104,646,000
2008**	642,344,000 (749)	0 (0)	745,511,000 (48)	$1,387,855,000
2009**	345,487,000 (638)		713,490,000 (80)	$1,058,977,000
2010**	339,317,000 (816)		199,288,000 (60)	$538,605,000
2011**	4,275,300,000 (1,067)		1,098,971,000 (49)	$5,374,271,000
2012**	1,082,137 (898)		1,891,012 (95)	$2,973,149
2013**	1,040,135 (887)		8,823,042(290)	$9,863,177
2014**	944,895 (924)		4,615,443 (168)	$5,560,338
2015 YTD**	427,210 (732)		2,828,250 (95)	$3,255,460
2015**	712,000 (785)		669,950 (86)	$1,381,950
2016 YTD**	466,232 (475)		5,271,500 (97)	$5,737,732
2016**	496,540 (576)		5,279,500 (97)	$5,776,040
2017 YTD**	392,907 (662)		4,593,237 (92)	$4,986,144
TOTAL	**$97,205,536,704**	**$85,110,886,616**	**$102,174,850,337**	**$284,491,273,657**

Note: Dollar volume figures represent total considerations reported for all transactions with exception of minority interest transfers in which control of stations did not change hands and stations sold as part of larger company transactions. Although all states have been approved by the FCC, they may not necessarily have reached final closing. Prior to 1978, combined AM-FM facilities were counted as one station in computing total number of stations traded. Now AM-FM combinations are counted as two stations.

*Starting in 1993, the Radio only column includes only stand alone AM and FM deals and the Groups column contains AM-FM combos and all other multiple station deals. In previous years the AM-FM combos were included under Radio only.

**Figures for 2000 to 2017 courtesy of BIA/Kelsey (broadcast.biakelsey.com).

Sales of Television Receivers

Year	Product Category	Units (Thousands)	Dollars (Million)	Average Price
1954	Analog Color TV	5	$2	$400.00
1955	Analog Color TV	20	$10	$500.00
1956	Analog Color TV	100	$46	$460.00
1957	Analog Color TV	85	$37	$435.00
1958	Analog Color TV	80	$34	$425.00
1959	Analog Color TV	90	$37	$411.00
1960	Analog Color TV	120	$47	$392.00
1961	Analog Color TV	147	$56	$381.00
1962	Analog Color TV	438	$154	$352.00
1963	Analog Color TV	747	$258	$345.00
1964	Analog Color TV	1,404	$488	$348.00
1965	Analog Color TV	2,694	$959	$356.00
1966	Analog Color TV	5,012	$1,861	$371.00
1967	Analog Color TV	5,563	$2,015	$362.00
1968	Analog Color TV	6,215	$2,086	$336.00
1969	Analog Color TV	6,191	$2,031	$328.00
1970	Analog Color TV	4,821	$1,684	$349.00
1971	Analog Color TV	6,180	$2,355	$381.00
1972	Analog Color TV	7,555	$2,825	$374.00
1973	Analog Color TV	9,264	$3,097	$334.00
1974	Analog Color TV	7,830	$2,658	$339.00
1975	Analog Color TV	6,485	$2,212	$341.00
1976	Analog Color TV	7,700	$2,688	$349.00
1977	Analog Color TV	9,107	$3,187	$350.00
1978	Analog Color TV	10,236	$3,583	$350.00
1979	Analog Color TV	9,846	$3,545	$360.00
1980	Analog Color TV	10,897	$4,004	$367.00
1981	Analog Color TV	11,157	$4,123	$370.00
1982	Analog Color TV	11,366	$4,141	$364.00
1983	Analog Color TV	13,986	$4,728	$338.00
1984	Analog Color TV	16,083	$5,359	$333.00
1985	Analog Color TV	16,829	$5,522	$328.00
1986	Analog Color TV	18,204	$5,836	$321.00
1987	Analog Color TV	19,330	$6,148	$318.00
1988	Analog Color TV	20,216	$5,907	$292.00
1989	Analog Color TV	21,706	$6,490	$299.00
1990	Analog Color TV	20,384	$6,197	$304.00
1991	Analog Color TV	19,474	$5,979	$307.00
1992	Analog Color TV	21,056	$6,591	$313.00
1993	Analog Color TV	23,005	$7,316	$318.00
1994	Analog Color TV	24,715	$7,225	$292.00
1995	Analog Color TV	23,231	$6,798	$293.00
1996	Analog Color TV	22,384	$6,492	$290.00
1997	Analog Color TV	21,293	$6,036	$283.00
1998	Analog Color TV	22,204	$6,122	$276.00
1999	Analog Color TV	23,218	$6,199	$267.00
2000	Analog Color TV	24,175	$6,140	$254.00
2001	Analog Color TV	21,167	$5,130	$242.00
2002	Analog Color TV	22,469	$5,782	$257.00
2003	Analog Color TV	20,791	$4,756	$229.00
2004	Analog Color TV	19,934	$3,526	$177.00
2005	Analog Color TV	16,934	$2,790	$165.00
2006	Analog Color TV	8,761	$1,000	$114.00
2007	Analog Color TV	1,166	$115	$99.00

1998	Digital TV Sets and Displays	14	$43	$3,147.00
1999	Digital TV Sets and Displays	121	$295	$2,433.00
2000	Digital TV Sets and Displays	625	$1,422	$2,275.00
2001	Digital TV Sets and Displays	1,460	$2,648	$1,812.00
2002	Digital TV Sets and Displays	2,535	$4,280	$1,688.00
2003	Digital TV Sets and Displays	5,532	$8,692	$1,571.00
2004	Digital TV Sets and Displays	8,002	$12,300	$1,537.00
2005	Digital TV Sets and Displays	10,719	$15,043	$1,403.00
2006	Digital TV Sets and Displays	22,366	$22,696	$1,015.00
2007	Digital TV Sets and Displays	24,966	$24,519	$982.00
2008	Digital TV Sets and Displays	31,153	$25,827	$829.00
2009	Digital TV Sets and Displays	34,799	$22,407	$644.00
2010	Digital TV Sets and Displays	34,659	$20,120	$581.00
2011	Digital TV Sets and Displays	33,781	$18,150	$537.00
2012	Digital TV Sets and Displays	40,310	$19,866	$493.00
2013	Digital TV Sets and Displays	39,191	$19,385	$495.00
2014	Digital TV Sets and Displays	37,587	$19,388	$516.00
2015	Digital TV Sets and Displays	40,146	$19,438	$484.00
2016	Digital TV Sets and Displays	40,866	$19,090	$467
2017	Digital TV Sets and Displays	39,562	$19,444	$476
2003	HDTV (720p, 1080i, 1080p)	3,735	$6,253	$1,674
2004	HDTV (720p, 1080i, 1080p)	6,091	$9,212	$1,512
2005	HDTV (720p, 1080i, 1080p)	8,803	$11,547	$1,312
2006	HDTV (720p, 1080i, 1080p)	17,268	$18,410	$1,066
2007	HDTV (720p, 1080i, 1080p)	20,722	$19,439	$938
2008	HDTV (720p, 1080i, 1080p)	26,192	$23,677	$904
2009	HDTV (720p, 1080i, 1080p)	29,662	$21,670	$731
2010	HDTV (720p, 1080i, 1080p)	33,619	$19,600	$583
2011	HDTV (720p, 1080i, 1080p)	33,781	$18,151	$537
2012	HDTV (720p, 1080i, 1080p)	40,310	$19,866	$493
2013	HDTV (720p, 1080i, 1080p)	39,191	$19,385	$495
2014	HDTV (720p, 1080i, 1080p)	37,587	$19,388	$516
2015	HDTV (720p, 1080i, 1080p)	32,824	$11,765	$358
2016	HDTV (720p, 1080i, 1080p)	30,398	$9,058	$298
2017	HDTV (720p, 1080i, 1080p)	24,195	$4,860	$201
2012	4K Ultra HD TV	1	$22	$22,000
2013	4K Ultra HD TV	77	$310	$4,026
2014	4K Ultra HD TV	1,431	$2,238	$1,564
2015	4K Ultra HD TV	7,322	$7,673	$1,048
2016	4K Ultra HD TV	10,488	$10,033	$957
2017	4k Ultra HD TV	16,689	$14,584	$874

Source: Consumer Technology Association U.S. Consumer Technology Sales & Forecasts, July 2017 edition. Reprinted with permission.

Major Broadcast TV Networks

ABC
Mailing Address: 77 West 66th Street, New York, NY 10023
Second Address: 500 S Buena Vista Street, Burbank, CA 91521
(212) 456-7777
Anne Sweeney, Co-Chairman/President
George Bodenheimer, Executive Chairman
John Skipper, President, ESPN Inc
Rebecca Campbell, President, ABC Televisions Stations Group
ABC Daytime:
2300 Riverside Drive, Burbank, CA 91506; Vicki Dummer, EVP, Times Square Studio.
Ownership:
The Walt Disney Company, 500 Buena Vista Street, Burbank, CA 91521-9722; Tel:(818) 560-1000; Website: www.disney.com
Primetime and Late Night
Castle, Dancing with the Stars, Private Practice, The Middle, The Neighbors, Last Resort, Grey's Anatomy, Scandal, Shark Tank, Once Upon a Time, Revenge, 666 Park Avenue, Nashville, Modern Family and Late Night: Jimmy Kimmel Live.

CBS
Mailing Address: CBS Television Network, 51 West 52nd Street, New York, NY 10019
Second Address: 7800 Beverly Blvd, Los Angeles, CA 90036
(212) 975-4321
www.cbs.com
Sumner M Redstone, Chairman
Leslie Moonves, President & CEO
Louis Briskman, EVP/General Counsel
Gil Schwartz, EVP/Chief Communications Officer
Adam Townsend, EVP/Investor Relations
Martin Franks, EVP/Planning and Policy
JospehIanniello, EVP/Chief Financial Officer
Ownership:
CBS Corporation, 51 West 52ns Street, New York, NY 10019-6188; Tel:(212) 975-4321; Website: www.cbscorporation.com; Sumner M Redstone, Executive Chairman; Leslie Moonves, President/CEO.
Primetime:
2 Broke Girls, 48 Hours Mystery, The Amazing Race, The Big Bang Theory, Big Brother, Blue Bloods, Criminal Minds, CSI, Dogs int he City, Elementary, The Good Wife, Hawaii Five-O, How I Met Your Mother, Made in Jersey, The Mentalist, Mike andMolly, NCIS, Person of Interest, Rules of Enagagement, Survivor, Two and a Half Men, Undercover Boss, Unforgettable, Vegas, The Bold and the Beautiful, CBS this Morning, Let's Make a Deal, The Price is Right, The Talk, The Young and the Restless,Late Show with David Letterman, The Late Show with Craig Ferguson.

The CW Television Network
Mailing Address: 4000 Warner Blvd, Burbank, CA 81522
Second Address: 3300 West Olive Street, Burbank, CA 91505
(818) 977-2500 (818) 977-2500; *Fax:* (818) 954-7667
www.cwtv.com
John Maata, COO
Mark Pedowitz, President
Thom Sherman, EVP/Development
Rob Tuck, EVP/National Sales
Rick Haskins, EVP/Marketing and Digital Programming
Dennis Dort, VP Business Affairs
The CW is a joint venture betweeen CBS corporation and Warner Brothers Entertainment, a subsidiary of Time Warner.
Ownership:
CBS Corporation, Warner Bros. Entertainment Inc. (Time Warner)
Programming:
America's Next Top Model, Arrow, Beauty and the Beast, Breaking Pointe, Cult, Emily Owens M.D., Gossip Girl, Hart of Dixie, Nikita, Oh Sit!, One Tree Hill, Remodeled, Supernatural, The Carrie Diaries, The Catalina, The L.A. Complex, The Next,The Vampire Diaries.

FOX Broadcasting Company
10201 West Pico Blvd, Los Angeles, CA 90035
(310) 369-3553
www.fox.com
Peter Rice, Chairman/CEO
Kevin Reilly, Chairman of Entertainment
Joe Early, COO
David Wertheimer, President/Digital
Emiliano Saccone, President/Mundo Fox
Gaude Lydia Paez, VP/Corporate Communications
Keith Rupert Murdoch,Co-Founder
Del Mayberry, Chief Financial Officer
David Wertheimer, President Of Digital
Laural Bernard, Executive Vice President Of Marketing
Jason Clark, Senior VP Of Publicity & Corporate Communications
Ownership:
News Corp., 1211 Avenue of the Americas, New York, NY 10036; Tel: (212) 852-7000; Website: www.newscorp.com
Programming:
American Dad, American Idol, Ben and Kate, Bob's Burgers, Bones, The Choice, The Cleveland Show, Comic Con 2012, Cops, Famiy Guy, Fringe, Glee, Hell's Kitchen, Hotel Hell, Kitchen Nightmares, MasterChef, The Mindy Project, The Mob Doctor,Mobbed, New Girl, Q'Viva: The Chosen, Raising Hope, The Simpsons, So You Think You Can Dance, Take Me Out, Touch, The X Factor.

ION Television
601 Clearwater Park Road, West Palm Beach, FL 33401
(561) 682-4100; *Fax:* (561) 659-4754
www.iontelevision.com/
billwatson@ionmedia.com
Brandon Burgess, Chairman/CEO
William Watson, Vice President/Assistant Secretary
Marc Zand, Programming Acquisitions
Jeffrey Quinn, Commercial Operations
Gordon Lavalette, Finance
Terri Santisiÿ, Administration
Chris Addeo,Marketing
Ownership:
ION Media Networks Inc., 601 Clearwater Park Road, West Palm Beach, FL 33401; Tel: (888) 467-2988.

NBC
Mailing Address: 30 Rockefeller Plaza, Suite 2, New York, NY 10112
Second Address: 100 University City Plaza, Universal City, CA 91608
(818) 840-4444 (212) 664-4444, (212) 664-3700
www.nbc.com
Robert Greenblatt, Chairman, NBC Entertainment
Stephen Burke, CEO and President
Matt Bond, Chairman, Content Distribution
Adam Miller, EVP
Stuart Epstein, EVP/CFO
Kimberley D. Harris, EVP/General Counsel
Anand Kini, CFO
Ownership:
Owned 51% by Comcast Corp. and 49% by General Electric; NBCUniversal, 30 Rockefeller Plaza, New York, NY 10112; Tel: (212) 664-4444; Website: www.nbcuni.com; Comcast Corp, One Comcast Center, Philadelphia, PA 19103; Tel: (215) 286-1700;Website: www.comcast.com.
Primetime:
30 Rock, America's Got Talent, Animal Practice, Chicago Fire. Community Dateline, Go On, Grimm, Guys with Kids, Last Call: Carson, Law & Order SVU, The New Normal, The Office, Parenthood, Parks and Recreation, Revolution, Rock Center withBrian Williams, Tonight Show: Leno Up All Night, The Voice, Whitney.

Regional Broadcast TV Networks

American Public Television
55 Summer Street, Boston, MA 02110
(617) 338-4455; *Fax:* (617) 338-5369
www.aptonline.org
info@aptonline.org
Cynthia A. Fenneman, President and CEO
Rosemary Marbach, Office Manager, Executive Assistant
Eric Luskin, Vice President, Premium Service & Syndication
Chris Funkhouser, VP, Exchange Programming & Multicast Services
Jamie Haines,Vice President, Communications
Gerry Field, Vice President, Technology
David Fournier, Vice President, Finance & Administration
Judy Barlow, Vice President, Business Development
Comprises WETA-TV, WHMM, both Washington, DC; WEDW(TV) Bridgeport, WEDY(TV) New Haven, WEDH(TV) Hartford, WEDN(TV) Norwich, all Connecticut; WCBB(TV) Augusta, WMED-TV Calais, WMEB-TV Orono, WMEM-TV Presque Isle, all Maine; WGBH-TV Boston,WGBX-TV Boston, WGBY-TV Springfield, all Massachusetts; WENH-TV Durham, WEKW-TV Keene, WLED-TV Littleton, all New Hampshire; WNJT-TV Trenton, New Jersey; WSKG(TV) Binghamton, WNED-TV Buffalo, WNET(TV) New York, WLIW-TV Plainview, WXXI(TV) Rochester,WMHT(TV) Schenectady, WCNY-TV Syracuse, WNPE-TV Watertown, all New York; WCET-TV Cincinnati, WVIZ-TV Cleveland, WPTD-TV Dayton, all Ohio; WLVT-TV Bethlehem-Allentown, WPSX-TV Clearfield, WITF-TV Harrisburg, WHYY-TV Philadelphia, WQED(TV) Pittsburgh,WVIA(TV) Scranton-Wilkes Barre, WQLN Erie, all Pennsylvania; WSBE-TV Providence, Rhode Island; WMPT-TV Annapolis, WMPB(TV) Baltimore, WWPB(TV) Hagerstown, WCPB-TV Salisbury, all Maryland. Service virtually all Public Television stations in the U.S.

California Farm Bureau Federation
Div/DBA: California Bountiful TV
Mailing Address: 2300 River Plaza Drive, Sacramento, CA 95833
Second Address: 1127 11th Street, Suite 626, Sacramento, CA 95814
(916) 561-5500; *Fax:* (916) 561-5695
www.californiabountiful.com; www.cfbf.com
cfbf@cfbf.com
Paul Wenger, President
Richard Matteis, Administrator
Marjorie Burghgraef, Manager
Dennis Duncan, Advertising Sales Manager
Joseph M. Peters, Chief Investment Officer
Darlene Licciardo, Executive Assistant/ScholarshipCoordinator
Jamie Johansson, First Vice President
Tony Toso, Second Vice President
Mark Dawson, Secretary/Treasurer
Nancy N. McDonough, General Counsel
Comprises KUVI-TV Bakersfield, KAEF-TV Eureka, KVPT-TV Fresno, KIXE-TV Redding, KRCR-TV Redding, KSBW-TV Salinas, KSBY-TV San Luis Obispo, K26AY Lakeport, KXTV-TV Sacramento, KPXN-TV Los Angeles, KFTY-TV Santa Rosa, KBHAA-TV San Francisco,all California; KYMA(TV) Yuma, Arizona, WAVE-TV Woodland; RFD-TV dish net direct TV.

Kansas Television Network
1500 N West Street, Wichita, KS 67203
(316) 943-4221; *Fax:* (316) 943-5493
www.kake.com
sales@kake.com
Susan Peters, Anchor/Reporter
Chris Stanford, Anchor/Reporter
Deb Farris, Anchor/Reporter
Mike Iuen, Anchor/Reporter
Comprises KLBY-TV Colby, KUPK-TV Garden City, KAKE-TV Wichita, all Kansas. Represented by Katz.

Keloland TV Young Broadcasting of Sioux Falls Inc.
KELO TV Bldg, 501 South Phillips Avenue, Sioux Falls, SD 57105
(605) 336-1100; *Fax:* (605) 334-3447, (605) 336-0202
www.keloland.com
Brittany Larson
Dan Santella
Grant Smith
Jared Ransom
Mike Simundson
Travis Fossing
Comprises KDLO-TV Florence, KPLO-TV Reliance, KELO-TV Sioux Falls, KCLO-TV Rapid City, all South Dakota. Represented by Adam Young Inc.

KSN Television Group
833 N Main Street, Wichita, KS 67203
(316) 265-3333; *Fax:* (316) 292-1195
www.ksn.com
news@ksn.com
Erik Schrader, President and General Manager
Karen Rorke, General Sales Manager
David Bell, Promotions Director
Denise Killian, News Director
Warren Kunkle, Chief Engineer
Angie Collins, Local Sales Manager
Jason Schlitz, DigitalSales Director
Kevin White, Digital Director
Joe Marino, National Sales Manager
Jason Schlitz, Digital Sales Director
Comprises KSNG Garden City, KSNC Great Bend, KSNT Topeka, KSNW Wichita, KSNK Oberlin, all Kansas. Represented by TeleRep. Above TV stns affiliated with NBC Television Network. Owned by SJL of KS.

KWCH-TV, Sunflower Broadcasting Inc.
Div/DBA: (formerly KWCH-TV Schurz Communications Inc.)
2815 E 37th Street North, Wichita, KS 67219
(316) 838-1212, (888) K12-NEWS; *Fax:* (316) 831-6198
www.kwch.com
Marcus Wilkerson, Director Of Sales
Erika Schlup, Promotions Manager
Comprises KBSD-TV Ensign-Dodge City, KBSL-TV Goodland, KBSH-TV Hays, KWCH-TV Wichita-Hutchinson, all Kansas. Represented by HRP.

KX Television
Mailing Address: 1811 North 15th Street, Bismarck, ND 58501
Second Address: 2121 2nd Street SE, Minot, ND 58701

(701) 223-3320; *Fax:* (701) 223-1985
www.myndnow.com
Robbie Romine, VP/General Manager
Tammy Blumhagen, Director of Sales
Tia Streeter, News Director
Rocky Hefty, Chief Engineer
Ross Lytle, Chief Engineer
Tom Schrader, Chief Meteorologist-KXMC/KXMD
Mike Elm, Sports Director
Dorrell Wenninger, Chief Meteorologist-KXMB/KXMA
Comprises KXMB-TV Bismarck, KXMA-TV Dickinson, KXMC-TV Minot, KXMD-TV Williston, all North Dakota.

National Educational Telecommunications Association
Mailing Address: PO Box 50008, Columbia, SC 29250
Second Address: 939 South Stadium Road, Columbia, SC 29201
(803) 799-5517; *Fax:* (803) 771-4831
www.netaonline.org
skip@netaonline.org
Eric Hyyppa, Board Chair
Skip Hinton, President
Greg Tillou, Operations Dir
Gayle Loeber, Programming Director
Anita Sims, Vice President Financeÿÿ
JoAnn Urofsky, Vice Chair
Glen Cerny, Secretary
Jack Galmiche, Treasurer
Ronnie Agnew, Member at large
Shae Hopkins, Past Chair
Comprises Alabama PTV Birmingham, Alabama; KUAC Fairbanks, KYUK Bethel, Alaska; KUAT Tucson, Arizona; Arkansas ETV Conway, Arkansas; KOCE Huntington Beach, KLCS Los Angeles, both California; WBCC Cocoa, WCEU Daytona Beach, WFSU Tallahassee,WGCU Fort Myers, WLRN Miami, WSRE Pensacola, WUFT Gainesville, WUSF Tampa, WXEL West Palm Beach, all Florida; Georgia Public Broadcasting Atlanta, WPBA Atlanta, both Georgia; Idaho PTV Boise, Idaho; WNIT, Elkhart, WYIN Merrillville, both Indiana;Iowa PTV Johnston, Iowa; KOOD Bunker Hill, Kansas; Kentucky ETV Lexington, WKYU Bowling Green, both Kentucky; LA Public Broadcasting Baton Rouge, WLAE New Orleans, both Louisiana; Maryland Public Broadcasting Owings Mills, Maryland; WKAR, E. Lansing,WGVU Grand Rapids, Michigan; Minnesota, Twin Cities PTV St. Paul, Minnesota; Mississippi EB Jackson, Mississippi; KCPT Kansas City, KETC St. Louis, KMOS Warrensburg, KOZK Ozarks Public TV Springfield, all Missouri; Montana PTV Bozeman, Montana;Nebraska ETV Lincoln, Nebraska; KLVX La

Nebraska Television Network (NTV)
Pappas Telecasting, PO Box 220, Kearney, NE 68848
(308) 743-2494; *Fax:* (308) 743-2644
www.nebraska.tv
Vincent F Barresi, General Manager
Tom Long, General Sales Manager
Anita Wragge, Promotion Manager
Matt Weesner, News Director
Krisa Howland, National Sales Manager
Cheryl Alkire, Business Manager
Kent Boughton, Meteorologist
Steve White, Grand Island Reporter
Claire Runions, Traffic Manager
Comprises KTVG(TV) Grand Island; KHGI-TV13, Kearney, Hastings, Grand Island; KWNB-TV North Platte & KSNB-TV Superior and the translators of K02HB, K17CI, K11KV, K12KW, K13OM, K13NP, K13VO, K06EY. Represented by Petry.

North Dakota Television
200 N 4th Street, Bismarck, ND 58501
(701) 255-5757; *Fax:* (701) 255-8220; (701) 255-8244
www.kfyrtv.com
kfyrtv@kfyrtv.com
Dick Heidt, General Manager
Darrell Olsen, General Sales Manager
Jim Sande, Programming Director
Monica Hannan, News Director
Brian Funk, Chief Engineer
Randy Baumgartner, Marketing Consultant
Randy Hoffman, Projects & SalesCoordinator
Wayne Wolff, Creative Services
Lee Ellison, Commercial Photographer
Comprises KFYR-TV Bismarck, KQCD-TV Dickinson, KMOT-TV Minot, KUMV-TV Williston, all North Dakota; KVLY-TV, serving North Dakota, South Dakota & Montana. Represented by Blair.

Wisconsin Educational Communications Board
3319 W Beltline Hwy, Madison, WI 53713-4296
(608) 264-9600; *Fax:* (608) 264-9622
www.ecb.org
Dr. Rolf Wegenke, Chair
Jon Miskowski, News Director
Terry Baun, Engineering Dir
Gene Purcell, Executive Director
Marta Bechtol, Deputy Director
Mike Crane, Director Wisconsinc Public Radio
Comprises WPNE(TV) Green Bay, WHLA-TV La Crosse, WHWC-TV Menomonie/Eau Claire, WLEF-TV Park Falls, WHRM-TV Wausau, all Wisconsin. Affils: Wisconsin: WMVS(TV) Milwaukee; WDSE-TV Duluth, Minnesota.

U.S. TV Group Ownership

ABC Owned Television Stations

77 West 66th St., New York NY 10023
abclocal.go.com
Ownership: Disney-ABC Television Group

TV Stns: 8 TV.
KABC-TV Los Angeles, CA; KFSN-TV Fresno, CA; KGO-TV San Francisco, CA; KTRK-TV Houston, TX; WABC-TV New York, NY; WLS-TV Chicago, IL; WPVI-TV Philadelphia, PA; WTVD-TV Durham, NC

Radio Stns: 28 AM. 3 FM.
KWDZ Salt Lake City, UT; KATL Miles City, MT; KRDY San Antonio, TX; KMIK Tempe, AZ; KMKI Plano, TX; KMKY Oakland, CA; KPHN Kansas City, MO; KQAM Wichita, KS; KIID Sacramento, CA; KMIC Houston, TX; WCOG Greensboro, NC; WDWD Atlanta, GA; WMYM Miami, FL; WFDF Farmington Hills, MI; WGFY Charlotte, NC; WDDY Albany, NY; WHKT Portsmouth, VA; WDYZ Orlando, FL; WKSH Sussex, WI; WDDZ Pittsburgh, PA; WHBE Newburg, KY; WNTT Tazewell, TN; WPMH Portsmouth, VA; WMKI Boston, MA; WQEW New York, NY; WRDZ La Grange, IL; WWJZ Mount Holly, NJ; WWMK Cleveland, OH; KALQ-FM Alamosa, CO; KDIS-FM Little Rock, AR; WRDZ-FM Plainfield, IN

Rebecca Campbell, President

Bahakel Communications Ltd.

1 Television Pl., Charlotte NC 28205
(704) 372-4434; *Fax:* (704) 335-9904
Ownership: Bahakel Communications.

TV Stns: 6 TV.
WBMM Tuskegee, AL; WAKA Selma, AL; WBBJ-TV Jackson, TN; WCCB Charlotte, NC; WFXB Myrtle Beach, SC; WOLO-TV Columbia, SC

Radio Stns: 1 AM. 5 FM.
WDEF Chattanooga, TN; KILO Colorado Springs, CO; KRXP Pueblo West, CO; WDEF-FM Chattanooga, TN; WDOD-FM Chattanooga, TN; WUUQ South Pittsburg, TN

Beverly Poston, President
James Babb, Chief Operating Officer
Amy Liz Pittenger, Vice President
John Hutchinson, Senior VP, Television and Technology
Bob Davis, Director of Engineering and Operations

Bayou City Broadcasting

P.O. Box 131346, The Woodlands TX 77393
(281) 719-9355; *Fax:* (281) 719-9353
www.bayoucitybroadcasting.com

TV Stns: 1 TV.
WEVV-TV Evansville, IN

DuJuan McCoy, Owner, President & CEO

Beach TV Properties Inc.

8317 Front Beach Rd., Suite 23, Panama City FL 32407
(850) 234-2773; *Fax:* (850) 235-1179
www.destinationnetwork.com
toni.davis@tripsmarter.com

TV Stns: 2 TV.
WAWD Fort Walton Beach, FL; WPCT Panama City Beach, FL

Toni Davis, Co-Found/Chief Executive Officer
Jud Colley, Co-Founder/President
Myron Hines, Co-Founder/Director Of Production
Marvin Colley, General Manager
Jeff Blackstone, Broadcast Engineer
Ken Davis, Executive Director

Bell Media Inc.

299 Queen St. W., Toronto ON M5V 2Z5
(416) 384-8000
www.bellmedia.ca
bellmediapr@bellmedia.ca
Ownership: Bell Canada, 100%.

TV Stns: 29 TV.
CFCF-DT Montréal, QC; CFCN-DT-5 Lethbridge, AB; CTV London, ON; CFQC-DT Saskatoon, SK; CFRN-TV-6 Red Deer, AB; CFTO-DT Toronto, ON; CHBX-TV Sault Ste. Marie, ON; CHRO-TV Pembroke, ON; CHWI-DT Wheatley, ON; CICC-TV Yorkton, SK; CICI-TV Sudbury, ON; CIPA-TV Prince Albert, SK; CITO-TV Timmins, ON; CIVT-DT Vancouver, BC; CJCB-TV Halifax, NS; CJCH-DT Halifax, NS; CJDC-TV Dawson Creek, BC; CJOH-DT Ottawa, ON; CKCK-DT Regina, SK; CKCO-DT Kitchener, ON; CKCW-DT Moncton, NB; CKLT-DT Saint John, NB; CKNY-TV North Bay, ON; CKVR-DT Barrie, ON; CKX-TV Brandon, MB; CKY-DT Winnipeg, MB; CIVI-DT Victoria, BC; CHRO-DT-43 Ottawa, ON; CFTK-TV Terrace, BC

Radio Stns: 25 AM. 81 FM.
CFAX Victoria, BC; CFGO Ottawa, ON; CFRA Ottawa, ON; CFRB Toronto, ON; CFRN Edmonton, AB; CFTK Terrace, BC; CFTE Vancouver, BC; CHAM Hamilton, ON; CHUM Toronto, ON; CFRW Winnipeg, MB; CKHJ Fredericton, NB; CJAD Montréal, QC; CJBK London, ON; CJDC Dawson Creek, BC; CJOR Osoyoos, BC; CKFR Kelowna, BC; CKGM Montréal, QC; CKLW Windsor, ON; CKMX Calgary, AB; CKOC Hamilton, ON; CKOR Penticton, BC; CKSL London, ON; CKST Vancouver, BC; CKTB St. Catharines, ON; CKWW Windsor, ON; CFBR-FM Edmonton, AB; CFCA-FM Waterloo, ON; CFEI-FM St-Hyacinthe, QC; CFLY-FM Kingston, ON; CFMG-FM Edmonton, AB; CFWM-FM Winnipeg, MB; CFZZ-FM Saint Jean-Iberville, QC; CHEY-FM Trois Rivieres, QC; CHIK-FM Quebec, QC; CHOM-FM Montréal, QC; CHQM-FM Vancouver, BC; CHRD-FM Drummondville, QC; CHRE-FM St. Catharines, ON; CHRX-FM Fort St. John, BC; CHSU-FM Kelowna, BC; CHTZ-FM St. Catharines, ON; CHUM-FM Toronto, ON; CHVR-FM Pembroke, ON; CJPT-FM Brockville, ON; CIBX-FM Fredericton, NB; CIDR-FM Windsor, ON; CIGB-FM Trois Rivieres, QC; CIKI-FM Rimouski, QC; CILK-FM Kelowna, BC; CIMF-FM Gatineau, QC; CIMO-FM Magog, QC; CIMX-FM Windsor, ON; CIOO-FM Halifax, NS; CIQM-FM London, ON; CITE-FM Montréal, QC; CITE-FM-1 Sherbrooke, QC; CITF-FM Quebec, QC; CJAB-FN Saguenay, QC; CJAT-FM Trail, BC; CJAY-FM Calgary, AB; CJBX-FM London, ON; CJDM-FM Drummondville, QC; CJFM-FM Montréal, QC; CJFW-FM Terrace, BC; CJMG-FM Penticton, BC; CJMJ-FM Ottawa, ON; CJMM-FM Rouyn-Noranda, QC; CJMV-FM Val d'Or, QC; CKFM-FM Toronto, ON; CFXY-FM Fredericton, NB; CKKC-FM Nelson, BC; CKKL-FM Ottawa, ON; CKLH-FM Hamilton, ON; CKLY-FM Kawartha Lakes, ON; CKMF-FM Montréal, QC; CKMM-FM Winnipeg, MB; CKQM-FM Peterborough, ON; CKRX-FM Fort Nelson, BC; CKTF-FM Gatineau, QC; CKTO-FM Truro, NS; CKX-FM Brandon, MB; CKXA-FM Brandon, MB; CHBE-FM Victoria, BC; CJOI-FM Rimouski, QC; CIKX-FM Grand Falls, NB; CFIX-FM Saguenay, QC; CFBT-FM Vancouver, BC; CJCJ-FM Woodstock, NB; CIBK-FM Calgary, AB; CKTY-FM Truro, NS; CFJR-FM Brockville, ON; CFVM-FM Amqui, QC; CICF-FM Vernon, BC; CKBC-FM Bathurst, NB; CKNL-FM Fort St. John, BC; CKTK-FM Kitimat, BC; CKXR-FM Salmon Arm, BC; CKPT-FM Peterborough, ON; CKLC-FM Kingston, ON; CHBD-FM Regina, SK; CJCH-FM Halifax, NS; CKKW-FM Kitchener, ON; CKGR-FM Golden, BC; CHTK-FM Prince Rupert, BC; CKCR-FM Revelstoke, BC; CHOR-FM Summerland, BC

Randy Lennox, President
Stewart Johnston, Media Sales & Marketing
Mike Cosentino, Content & Programming
Wendy Freeman, President, CTV News
Nikki Moffat, Senior Vice-President, Finance
Scott Henderson, Vice-President, Communications
Sonia Brar, Vice-President, Information Technology

Better Life Ministries

8320 W. 66th Ave., Arvada CO 80004
(303) 431-0103

TV Stns: 1 TV.
KTVC Roseburg, OR

Claud Pettit, President

Birach Broadcasting Corp.

21700 Northwestern Hwy., Suite 1190, Tower 14, Southfield MI 48075
(248) 557-3500; *Fax:* (248) 557-2950
www.birach.com
sima@birach.com
Ownership: Sima Birach, 100%.

TV Stns: 1 TV.
KIJR-LP Lucerne Valley, CA

Radio Stns: 22 AM.
KTUV Little Rock, AR; KOLE Port Arthur, TX; KJMU Sand Springs, OK; KXLQ Indianola, IA; WBRD Palmetto, FL; WBVA Bayside, VA; WCAR Livonia, MI; WCXN Claremont, NC; WGOP Pocomoke City, MD; WEW St. Louis, MO; WIJR Highland, IL; WMFN Zeeland, MI; WMJH Rockford, MI; WNWI Oak Lawn, IL; WNZK Dearborn Heights, MI; WPON Walled Lake, MI; WTOR Youngstown, NY; WVAB Virginia Beach, VA; WWCS Canonsburg, PA; WCXI Fenton, MI; WDMV Walkersville, MD; WKGE Johnstown, PA

Sima Birach, President & CEO

Block Communications Inc.

405 Madison Ave., Suite 1200, Toledo OH 43604
(419) 724-6212
www.blockcommunications.com
Ownership: Estate of William Block, Allan Block, John R. Block.

TV Stns: 5 TV.
KTRV-TV Nampa, ID; WAND Decatur, IL; WDRB Louisville, KY; WMYO Salem, IN; WLIO Lima, OH

Allan Block, Chairman
Diana Block, Executive Vice President
Jodi Miehls, Chief Financial Officer
Joe Jensen, Chief Technology Officer

Bonneville International Corporation

55 North 300 West, Salt Lake City UT 84101-3502
(801) 575-7500; *Fax:* (801) 575-5820
www.bonneville.com
Ownership: Deseret Management Corp.

TV Stns: 1 TV.
KSL-TV Salt Lake City, UT

Radio Stns: 5 AM. 8 FM.
KIRO Seattle, WA; KMVP Phoenix, AZ; KTTH Seattle, WA; KSL Salt Lake City, UT; KTAR Phoenix, AZ; KIRO-FM Tacoma, WA; KSWD Los Angeles, CA; KTAR-FM Glendale, AZ; KMVP-FM Phoenix, AZ; KSL-FM Midvale, UT; KRSP-FM Salt Lake City, UT; KSFI Salt Lake City, UT; KYGO-FM Denver, CO

Darrell Brown, President
Kent Nate, SVP & CFO
Mike Dowdle, SVP of Business Affairs & General Counsel
Matthew Sadowski, VP, Human Resources

Bonten Media Group LLC

675 Third Ave., Suite 2521, New York NY 10017
(212) 710-7771; *Fax:* (212) 949-0909
www.bontenmedia.com
invest@bontenmedia.com

TV Stns: 7 TV.
KAEF-TV Arcata, CA; KCFW-TV Kalispell, MT; KECI-TV Missoula, MT; KRCR-TV Redding, CA; KTVM-TV Butte, MT; KTXS-TV Sweetwater, TX; WCYB-TV Bristol, VA

Randall Bongarten, Chairman

Cadillac Telecasting Co.

7669 S. 45 Rd., Cadillac MI 49601
(231) 775-9813; *Fax:* (231) 775-1898
info@fox33.com

TV Stns: 2 TV.
WFQX-TV Cadillac, MI; WFUP Vanderbilt, MI

Alexander Bolea, President

California Oregon Broadcasting Inc.

125 S. Fir St., Medford OR 97501
(541) 779-5555; *Fax:* (541) 779-1151
Ownership: Patricia C. Smullin and Carol Anne Smullin Brown. Other interests: Cable TV: Crestview Cable TV (systems in Oregon).

TV Stns: 3 TV.
KLSR-TV Eugene, OR; KOBI Medford, OR; KOTI Klamath Falls, OR

Patricia Smullin, President

Calipatria Broadcasting Company, LLC

1755 El Camino Del Teatro, La Jolla CA 92037
(202) 331-8800; *Fax:* (202) 331-8330

TV Stns: 1 TV.
KAJB-TV Calipatria, CA

Canadian Broadcasting Corporation (CBC)

205 Wellington St. W, Room 4E301-B, Toronto ON M5V 3G7
(416) 205-3700
www.cbc.ca
tonews@cbc.ca
Ownership: Government of Canada

TV Stns: 27 TV.
CBKT-DT Regina, SK; CBLT-DT Toronto, ON; CBMT-DT Montréal, QC; CBNT-DT Saint John's, NL; CBOFT-DT Ottawa, ON; CBOT-DT Ottawa, ON; CBVT-DT Quebec City, QC; CBWFT-DT Winnipeg, MB; CBWT-DT Winnipeg, MB; CFYK-DT Yellowknife, NT; CJBR-DT Rimouski, QC; CKSH-DT Sherbrooke, QC; CKTM-DT Trois Rivieres, QC; CBAT-DT Fredericton, NB; CBHT-DT Halifax, NS; CBLFT-DT Toronto, ON; CBET-DT Windsor, ON; CBCT-DT Charlottetown, PE; CBFT-DT Montréal, QC; CKTV-DT Saguenay, QC; CBKFT-DT Regina, SK; CBAFT-DT Moncton, NB; CBXFT-DT Edmonton, AB; CBXT-DT Edmonton, AB; CBRT-DT Calgary, AB; CBUFT-DT Vancouver, BC; CBUT-DT Vancouver, BC

Radio Stns: 14 AM. 65 FM.
CBEF Windsor, ON; CBG Gander, NF; CBI Sydney, NS; CBN St. John's, NL; CBT Grand Falls-Windsor, NF; CBY Corner Brook, NF; CFFB Iqaluit, NU; CHAK Inuvik, NT; CJBC Toronto, ON; CBR Calgary, AB; CBX Edmonton, AB; CFPR Prince Rupert, BC; CBU Vancouver, BC; CBW Winnipeg, MB; CBAF-FM Moncton, NB; CBAL-FM Moncton, NB; CBCL-FM London, ON; CBCT-FM Charlottetown, PE; CBD-FM Saint John, NB; CBDQ-FM Labrador City, NL; CBE-FM Windsor, ON; CBF-FM Montréal, QC; CBFX-FM Montréal, QC; CBH-FM Halifax, NS; CBHA-FM Halifax, NS; CBI-FM Sydney, NS; CBJX-FM Chicoutimi, QC; CBK-FM Regina, SK; CBKA-FM La Ronge, SK; CBKF-FM Regina, SK; CBL-FM Toronto, ON; CBLA-FM Toronto, ON; CBM-FM Montréal, QC; CBME-FM Montréal, QC; CBN-FM Saint John's, NL; CBO-FM Ottawa, ON; CBON-FM Timmins, ON; CBOQ-FM Ottawa, ON; CBOX-FM Ottawa, ON; CBQ-FM Thunder Bay, ON; CBQR-FM Rankin Inlet, NU; CBQT-FM

Thunder Bay, ON; CBSI-FM Sept-Iles, QC; CBV-FM Quebec, QC; CBVE-FM Quebec, QC; CBVX-FM Quebec, QC; CBZF-FM Fredericton, NB; CFGB-FM Happy Valley-Goose Bay, NL; CFWH-FM Whitehorse, YT; CJBC-FM Toronto, ON; CBJ-FM Chicoutimi, QC; CJBR-FM Rimouski, QC; CBBX-FM Sudbury, ON; CBBS-FM Sudbury, ON; CBAX-FM Halifax, NS; CBGA-FM Matane, QC; CBAM-FM Moncton, NB; CBEW-FM Windsor, ON; CBK-1-FM Saskatoon, SK; CBLA-FM-2 Paris, ON; CBFX-FM-2 Sherbrooke, QC; CFYK-FM Yellowknife, NT; CBFX-FM-1 Trois Rivieres, QC; CBCX-FM Calgary, AB; CBR-FM Calgary, AB; CBX-FM Edmonton, AB; CHFA-10-FM Edmonton, AB; CBYK-FM Kamloops, BC; CBTK-FM Kelowna, BC; CBYG-FM Prince George, BC; CBU-FM Vancouver, BC; CBUF-FM Vancouver, BC; CBUX-FM Vancouver, BC; CBCV-FM Victoria, BC; CBWK-FM Thompson, MB; CBW-FM Winnipeg, MB; CKSB-10-FM Winnipeg, MB; CKSB-FM St. Boniface, MB; CBAF-FM-5 Halifax, NS

Hubert T. Lacroix, President & CEO
Jennifer McGuire, General Manager and Editor in Chief
Gwen Jones McCauley, Content Sales and Consumer Products
Sally Catto, General Manager, Programming
Lillian Mak, Project Lead, Creative and Promotions
Jeff Vella, Media Engineering Director
Judith Purves, EVP, Chief Financial Officer
Teaghan Hawke, Senior Communication Officer

Capital Community Broadcasting Inc.
360 Egan Dr., Juneau AK 99801-1748
(907) 586-1670; *Fax:* (907) 586-3612

TV Stns: 1 TV.
KTOO-TV Juneau, AK

Radio Stns: 3 FM.
KRNN Juneau, AK; KXLL Juneau, AK; KTOO Juneau, AK

Capitol Broadcasting Co. Inc.
2619 Western Blvd., Raleigh NC 27606
(919) 890-6000; *Fax:* (919) 890-6095
www.capitolbroadcasting.com
webmaster@cbc-raleigh.com
Ownership: Capitol Holding Co. Inc.

TV Stns: 3 TV.
WRAL-TV Raleigh, NC; WRAZ Raleigh, NC; WILM-LD Wilmington, NC

Radio Stns: 1 AM. 6 FM.
WMFD Wilmington, NC; WCMC-FM Holly Springs, NC; WRMR Jacksonville, NC; WKXB Boiling Spring Lakes, NC; WRAL Raleigh, NC; WILT Wilmington, NC; WAZO Southport, NC

James F. Goodmon, President/CEO
Daniel P. McGrath, Vice President/Treasurer
George W. Habel III, Vice President, Radio Networks
James F. Goodmon Jr., Vice President, CBC New Media Group
Angela B. Emerline, Vice President, Human Resources
Jennifer B. Venable, Vice President/General Counsel

CaribeVision Station Group LLC
1401 Brickell Ave., Suite 500, Miami FL 33131
(305) 381-8500; *Fax:* (305) 381-6225

TV Stns: 4 TV.
WIRS Yauco, PR; WJPX San Juan, PR; WJWN-TV San Sebastian, PR; WKPV Ponce, PR

Carlos Barba, CEO

CBS Television Stations Group
51 W 52nd St., New York NY 10019-6188
(212) 975-4321
www.cbscorporation.com
Ownership: CBS Corp., 100%

TV Stns: 29 TV.
KBCW-TV San Francisco, CA; KCAL-TV Los Angeles, CA; KCBS-TV Los Angeles, CA; KCCO-TV Alexandria, MN; KCCW-TV Walker, MN; KCNC-TV Denver, CO; KDKA-TV Pittsburgh, PA; KMAX-TV Sacramento, CA; KOVR-TV Stockton, CA; KPIX-TV San Francisco, CA; KSTW-TV Tacoma, WA; KTVT-TV Fort Worth, TX; KTXA-TV Fort Worth, TX; KYW-TV Philadelphia, PA; WBBM-TV Chicago, IL; WBFS-TV Miami, FL; WBZ-TV Boston, MA; WCBS-TV New York, NY; WCCO-TV Minneapolis, MN; WJZ-TV Baltimore, MD; WKBD-TV Detroit, MI; WLNY-TV Riverhead, NY; WPCW-TV Jeannette, PA; WPSG-TV Philadelphia, PA; WSBK-TV Boston, MA; WTOG-TV St. Petersburg, FL; WUPA Atlanta, GA; WWJ-TV Detroit, MI; WFOR-TV Miami, FL

Leslie Moonves, President & Chief Executive Officer

Chena Broadcasting LLC
3650 Braddock St., Fairbanks AK 99709
(907) 458-1800; *Fax:* (907) 458-1820
www.webcenter11.com

TV Stns: 1 TV.
KTVF Fairbanks, AK

Michael Young, President

Christian Television Corporation Inc.
6922 142nd Ave. N., Largo FL 33771
(727) 535-5622; *Fax:* (727) 531-2497
www.ctnonline.com

TV Stns: 2 TV.
KFXB-TV Dubuque, IA; WCLF Clearwater, FL

Robert D'Andrea, President

Citadel Communications Co. LTD.
99 Pondfield Rd., Bronxville NY 10708
(914) 793-3400; *Fax:* (914) 793-3693
www.citadelltd.com
Ownership: Coronet Communications, Capital Communications, Citadel Comm. LLC.

TV Stns: 2 TV.
KLKN Lincoln, NE; WLNE-TV New Bedford, MA

Philip J. Lombardo, CEO
Ray Cole, President & COO

Commonwealth Broadcasting Corp.
1823 McIntosh Street, Suite 107, Bowling Green KY 42104
(270) 842-4487; *Fax:* (270) 783-8829
www.bowlinggreensam.com

TV Stns: 1 TV.
WABG-TV Greenwood, MS

Radio Stns: 8 AM. 13 FM.
WGRK Jeffersontown, KY; WWKU Plum Springs, KY; WIEL Elizabethtown, KY; WLRS Eminence, KY; WLBN Lebanon, KY; WPKY Princeton, KY; WTCO Campbellsville, KY; WTTL Madisonville, KY; WYSB Springfield, KY; WAVJ Princeton, KY; WCKQ Campbellsville, KY; WGRK-FM Greensburg, KY; WOVO Horse Cave, KY; WWKY Providence, KY; WRZI Hodgenville, KY; WLSK Lebanon, KY; WKMO Lebanon Junction, KY; WPTQ Glasgow, KY; WHHT(FM) Cave City, KY; WTHX Vine Grove, KY; WTTL-FM Madisonville, KY

Derron Steenbergen, General Manager
Greg Bowen, General Sales Mgr

Cordillera Communications Inc.
325 Cedar St., Suite 1001, Saint Paul MN 55105
(651) 379-0050
www.cordillera.tv
Ownership: Evening Post Publishing Co., 100%.

TV Stns: 12 TV.
KATC Lafayette, LA; KBZK Bozeman, MT; KOAA-TV Pueblo, CO; KPAX-TV Missoula, MT; KRIS-TV Corpus Christi, TX; KRTV Great Falls, MT; KSBY San Luis Obispo, CA; KTVH-DT Helena, MT; KTVQ Billings, MT; KVOA Tucson, AZ; KXLF-TV Butte, MT; WLEX-TV Lexington, KY

Terry Hurley, President
Andy Suk, Vice President, Engineering and Technology
Dan Stein, Director of Programming and Operations

Cornerstone TeleVision Inc.
1 Signal Hill Dr., Wall PA 15148-1499
(412) 824-3930; *Fax:* (412) 824-5442
www.ctvn.org
info@ctvn.org
Ownership: Nonprofit.

TV Stns: 3 TV.
WKBS-TV Altoona, PA; WPCB-TV Pittsburgh/Greensburg, PA; W07DP-D Harrisburg, PA

Craig R. Sherwood, Chairman
Donald Black, President & CEO

Corus Entertainment Inc.
Corus Quay, 25 Dockside Dr., Toronto ON M5A 0B5
(416) 479-7000; *Fax:* (416) 479-7006
www.corusent.com
alka.graham@corusent.com
Ownership: JR Shaw and family; Shaw Communications, 39%.

TV Stns: 16 TV.
CFRE-DT Regina, SK; CFSK-DT Saskatoon, SK; CHAN-DT Vancouver, BC; CHBC-DT Kelowna, BC; CHEX-DT Peterborough, ON; CICT-DT Calgary, AB; CIII-DT Toronto, ON; CISA-DT Lethbridge, AB; CITV-DT Edmonton, AB; CKMI-DT-1 Montréal, QC; CKND-DT Winnipeg, MB; CKWS-DT Kingston, ON; CHEX-TV-2 Oshawa, ON; CHNB-DT Saint John, NB; CIHF-DT Halifax, NS; CKWS-DT-1 Brighton, ON

Radio Stns: 10 AM. 29 FM.
CFPL London, ON; CHED Edmonton, AB; CHML Hamilton, ON; CFMJ Richmond Hill, ON; CHQR Calgary, AB; CHQT Edmonton, AB; CJOB Winnipeg, MB; CJOY Guelph, ON; CHMJ Vancouver, BC; CKNW New Westminster, BC; CFHK-FM St. Thomas, ON; CFLG-FM Cornwall, ON; CFMI-FM New Westminster, BC; CFMK-FM Kingston, ON; CFNY-FM Brampton, ON; CFOX-FM Vancouver, BC; CFPL-FM London, ON; CHAY-FM Barrie, ON; CILQ-FM Toronto, ON; CIMJ-FM Guelph, ON; CJXY-FM Burlington, ON; CIQB-FM Barrie, ON; CISN-FM Edmonton, AB; CJDV-FM Kitchener, ON; CJSS-FM Cornwall, ON; CING-FM Hamilton, ON; CKCB-FM Collingwood, ON; CKDK-FM Woodstock, ON; CFGQ-FM Calgary, AB; CKNG-FM Edmonton, AB; CKQB-FM Ottawa, ON; CKRY-FM Calgary, AB; CKWF-FM Peterborough, ON; CJGV-FM Winnipeg, MB; CKBT-FM Kitchener-Waterloo, ON; CKWS-FM Kingston, ON; CJOT-FM Ottawa, ON; CKRU-FM Petersborough, ON; CJKR-FM Winnipeg, MB

Doug Murphy, President & CEO
Barbara Williams, EVP, Chief Operating Officer
Dale Hancocks, EVP, General Counsel
John Gossling, EVP, Chief Financial Officer
Shawn Kelly, EVP, Technology
Cheryl Fullerton, EVP, People & Communications
Colin Bohm, EVP International Development & Corporate Strategy

Cowles Montana Media Co.
W. 999 Riverside Ave., Spokane WA 99201
(509) 459-5520; *Fax:* (509) 459-3815

TV Stns: 4 TV.
KFBB-TV Great Falls, MT; KTMF Missoula, MT; KULR-TV Billings, MT; KWYB Butte, MT

Elizabeth Allison Cowles, President

Cox Television
Box 105357, Atlanta GA 30348-5357
(678) 645-0000; *Fax:* (678) 645-5250
www.coxenterprises.com

TV Stns: 1 TV.
WHIO-TV Dayton, OH

Bruce Baker, President

CP Media LLC
1181 Hwy. 315, Wilkes-Barre PA 18702
(570) 970-5600

TV Stns: 4 TV.
WGFL High Springs, FL; WQMY Williamsport, PA; WOLF-TV Hazleton, PA; WTLH Bainbridge, GA

John Parente, President

Cunningham Broadcasting Corporation
2000 W. 41st St., Baltimore MD 21211
(410) 662-9688; *Fax:* (410) 235-8450

TV Stns: 11 TV.
WMYA-TV Anderson, SC; WDBB Bessemer, AL; WGTQ Sault Ste. Marie, MI; WGTU Traverse City, MI; WNUV Baltimore, MD; WRGT-TV Dayton, OH; WTAT-TV Charleston, SC; WTTE Columbus, OH; WVAH-TV Charleston, WV; WYZZ-TV Bloomington, IL; WBSF Bay City, MI

Robert Simmons, CEO
Jenny Olszewski, General Manager

Dispatch Broadcast Group
770 Twin Rivers Dr., Columbus OH 43215
(614) 460-3700; *Fax:* (614) 460-2809
www.dispatchbroadcast.com
Ownership: Dispatch Printing Company

TV Stns: 2 TV.
WBNS-TV Columbus, OH; WTHR Indianapolis, IN

Radio Stns: 1 AM. 1 FM.
WBNS Columbus, OH; WBNS-FM Columbus, OH

Michael Fiorile, Vice Chairman & CEO
Tani Mann, Vice President

Diversified Communications
121 Free St., Box 7437, Portland ME 04112-7437
(207) 842-5400; *Fax:* (207) 842-5405
www.divbusiness.com
Ownership: Horace A. Hildreth Jr., Josephine H. Detmer. See Cross-Ownership, Sect. A. Cable TV: New England Cablevision Inc.

TV Stns: 2 TV.
WABI-TV Bangor, ME; WCJB-TV Gainesville, FL

David H. Lowell, President
Bill Springer, Executive Vice President
Mary Larkin, Executive Vice President
Mike Lodato, Executive Vice President

Dreamcatcher Broadcasting LLC
2016 Broadway, Santa Monica CA 90404

TV Stns: 3 TV.
WGNT Portsmouth, VA; WNEP Waymart, PA; WTKR Norfolk, VA

Ed Wilson, Manager

Duhamel Broadcasting Enterprises
Box 1760, Rapid City SD 57709

(605) 342-2000; *Fax:* (605) 342-7305
www.kotatv.com
Ownership: William F. Duhamel, 63%; Peter A. and Lois G. Duhamel, 37%.
TV Stns: 4 TV.
KNEP-TV Scottsbluff, NE; KOTA-TV Lead, SD; KOTA-TV Rapid City, SD; KSGW-TV Sheridan, WY
Radio Stns: 1 AM. 1 FM.
KOTA Rapid City, SD; KDDX Spearfish, SD
William Duhamel, President

Eagle Creek Broadcasting LLC
2111 University Park Dr., Suite 650, Okemos MI 48864
(517) 347-4141,
bradybw1@comcast.net
TV Stns: 2 TV.
KVTV Laredo, TX; KZTV Corpus Christi, TX
Brian Brady, CEO

Entravision Communications Corp.
2425 Olympic Blvd., Suite 6000 W., Santa Monica CA 90404
(310) 447-3870; *Fax:* (310) 447-3899
www.entravision.com
Ownership: Walter F. Ulloa, Philip W. Wilkinson, Paul Zevnik, Univision Communications.
TV Stns: 47 TV.
KCBA Salinas, CA; KCEC Denver, CO; KINC Las Vegas, NV; KINT-TV El Paso, TX; KTFN-TV El Paso, TX; KLDO-TV Laredo, TX; KLUZ-TV Albuquerque, NM; KNVO-TV McAllen, TX; KORO-TV Corpus Christi, TX; KPMR-TV Santa Barbara, CA; KREN-TV Reno, NV; KEVC-CD Indio, CA; KUPB-TV Midland, TX; KVYE-TV El Centro, CA; WVEA-TV Venice, FL; WUTH-CD Hartford, CT; WJAL-TV Hagerstown, MD; WVEN-TV Daytona Beach, FL; WUNI-TV Worcester, MA; KVSN-DT Pueblo, CO; KDCU-DT Derby, KS; KTFA-LP Albuquerque, NM; KCRP-CD Corpus Christi, TX; KGHB-CD Pueblo, CO; WHTX-LP Hartford, CT; KETF-CD Laredo, TX; KXOF-CD Laredo, TX; KELV-LD Las Vegas, NV; KNTL-LP Las Vegas, NV; KWWB-LP Las Vegas, NV; KBZO-LP Lubbock, TX; KCWT-CD La Feria, TX; KFXV-LD McAllen, TX; KTFV-CD McAllen, TX; KXFX-CD Brownsville, TX; XHRIO-TDT Matamoros, TX; KDJT-CD Salinas, CA; WVCI-LP Daytona Beach, FL; KVER-CA Indio, CA; KVES-LD Indio, CA; KRNS-CD Reno, NV; KANG-CD San Angelo, TX; KEUS-LD San Angelo, TX; KBNT-CD San Diego, CA; KHAX-LP San Diego, CA; KDTF-LD San Diego, CA; KTCD-LP San Diego, CA
Radio Stns: 11 AM. 37 FM.
KWST El Centro, CA; KSVE El Paso, TX; KBZO Lubbock, TX; KCVR Lodi, CA; KGOL Humble, TX; KMXA Aurora, CO; KRZY Albuquerque, NM; KHRO El Paso, TX; KBMB Black Canyon City, AZ; KMBX Soledad, CA; WLQY Hollywood, FL; KDLD Santa Monica, CA; KYSE El Paso, TX; KDLE Newport Beach, CA; KHHM Sacramento, CA; KFRQ Harlingen, TX; KXSE Davis, CA; KINT-FM El Paso, TX; KJMN Castle Rock, CO; KKPS Brownsville, TX; KLNZ Glendale, AZ; KLOB Thousand Palms, CA; KLOK-FM Greenfield, CA; KSSE Arcadia, CA; KMIX Tracy, CA; KDVA Buckeye, AZ; KMXX Imperial, CA; KOFX El Paso, TX; KRCX-FM Marysville, CA; KRRN Moapa Valley, NV; KRNV-FM Reno, NV; KNTY Shingle Springs, CA; KLYY Riverside, CA; KSSD Fallbrook, CA; KCVR-FM Columbia, CA; KQRT Las Vegas, NV; KVLY Edinburg, TX; KNVO-FM Port Isabel, TX; KSES-FM Seaside, CA; KVVA-FM Apache Junction, AZ; KSSC Ventura, CA; KSEH Brawley, CA; KXPK Evergreen, CO; KTSE-FM Patterson, CA; WNUE-FM Deltona, FL; KAIQ Wolfforth, TX; KPVW Aspen, CO; KPST Coachella, CA
Walter Ulloa, CEO/COO

Esteem Broadcasting
13865 E. Elliott Dr., Marshall IL 62441
(217) 826-6095
TV Stns: 5 TV.
KBVU Eureka, CA; KCVU Paradise, CA; WEMT Greeneville, TN; WFXI Morehead City, NC; WYDO Greenville, NC
David L. Bailey, President

Family Stations Inc.
1350 South Loop Road, Suite 130, Alameda CA 94502
(510) 568-6200; *Fax:* (510) 568-6190
www.familyradio.org
Ownership: Nonprofit corporation.
TV Stns: 1 TV.
WNYJ-TV West Milford, NJ
Radio Stns: 13 AM. 47 FM.
KARR Kirkland, WA; KEBR Rocklin, CA; KECR El Cajon, CA; KEAR San Francisco, CA; KFRN Long Beach, CA; KKAA Aberdeen, SD; KQKD Redfield, SD; KYFR Shenandoah, IA; WFSI Baltimore, MD; WBMD Baltimore, MD; WCTF Vernon, CT; WCUE Cuyahoga Falls, OH; WKDN Philadelphia, PA; KDFR Des Moines, IA; KEAR-FM Sacramento, CA; KEFR Le Grand, CA; KFNO Fresno, CA; KFRB Bakersfield, CA; KFRS Soledad, CA; KHAP Chico, CA; KJVH Longview, WA; KPHF Phoenix, AZ; KPOR Emporia, KS; KPRA Ukiah, CA; KQFE Springfield, OR; KTXB Beaumont, TX; KUFR Salt Lake City, UT; WBFR Birmingham, AL; WEFR Erie, PA; WFBF Buffalo, NY; WFCH Charleston, SC; WFRC Columbus, GA; WFRH Kingston, NY; WFRJ Johnstown, PA; WFRS Smithtown, NY; WJCH Joliet, IL; WMFL Florida City, FL; WMWK Milwaukee, WI; WOTL Toledo, OH; WWFR Stuart, FL; WYTN Youngstown, OH; WFME Mount Kisco, NY; WOFR Schoolcraft, MI; KBFR Bismarck, ND; KEDR(FM) Butte, MT; KAWV Fort Dodge, IA; KPFR Pine Grove, OR; KFRJ China Lake, CA; WFRP Americus, GA; KQFR Rapid City, SD; KFRP Coalinga, CA; KEDR Bay City, TX; KFRW Great Falls, MT; KFRY Pueblo, CO; KFRD Butte, MT; KYOR Newport, OR; WUFR Bedford, PA; WKDN-FM State College, PA; KXFR Socorro, NM; KEAF Fort Smith, AR
Tom Evans, Founder

Fort Myers Broadcasting Co.
2824 Palm Beach Blvd., Fort Myers FL 33916
(239) 334-1111; *Fax:* (239) 334-0744
winktv.com
TV Stns: 1 TV.
WINK-TV Fort Myers, FL
Radio Stns: 2 AM. 2 FM.
WJUA Pine Island Center, FL; WNPL Golden Gate, FL; WTLQ-FM Punta Rassa, FL; WINK-FM Fort Myers, FL
Brian McBride, CEO
Jade McClelland, Radio Operations

Forum Communications Co.
Box 2020, Fargo ND 58107
(701) 235-7311; *Fax:* (701) 241-5406
www.in-forum.com
TV Stns: 4 TV.
KBMY Bismarck, ND; KMCY Minot, ND; WDAY-TV Fargo, ND; WDAZ-TV Devil's Lake, ND
Radio Stns: 1 AM. 1 FM.
WDAY Fargo, ND; WZUU Mattawan, MI
William Marcil, President

Fox Television Stations Inc.
1211 Avenue of the Americas, New York NY 10036
(310) 584-2000
www.21cf.com/Television/Fox_Television_Stations_Group
Ownership: Fox Entertainment Group Inc., 85.2% voting interest. Note: Fox Entertainment Group Inc. is a wholly-owned subsidiary of News Corp.
TV Stns: 32 TV.
KCOP Los Angeles, CA; KDFI Dallas, TX; KDFI Dallas, TX; KFTC Bemidji, MN; KTVU Oakland, CA; KMSP Minneapolis, MN; KRIV Houston, TX; KSAZ Phoenix, AZ; KTBC Austin, TX; KTTV Los Angeles, CA; KTXH Houston, TX; KUTP Phoenix, AZ; WAGA Atlanta, GA; WDCA Washington, DC; WFLD Chicago, IL; WFTC Minneapolis, MN; WMYT Rock Hill, SC; WFXT Boston, MA; WJBK Detroit, MI; WJZY Belmont, NC; WNYW Newburgh, NY; WOFL Orlando, FL; WOGX Ocala, FL; WPWR Gary, IN; WRBW Orlando, FL; WTTG Washington, DC; WTVT Tampa, FL; WTXF-TV Allentown, PA; WUTB Baltimore, MD; WWOR Secaucus, NJ; KICU San Jose, CA; KDFW Dallas, TX
Jack Abernethy, Co-President

Frontier Radio Management Inc.
4311 Wilshire Blvd., Suite 412, Los Angeles CA 90010
(323) 931-1745; *Fax:* (323) 931-0925
TV Stns: 2 TV.
KPVI-DT Pocatello, ID; KXTF Twin Falls, ID
Radio Stns: 3 AM. 10 FM.
KBLU Yuma, AZ; KIXW Apple Valley, CA; KSMX Santa Maria, CA; KSMY Lompoc, CA; KATJ-FM George, CA; KIXA Lucerne Valley, CA; KURQ Grover Beach, CA; KSLY-FM San Luis Obispo, CA; KSTT-FM Los Osos-Baywood Par, CA; KTTI Yuma, AZ; KXFM Santa Maria, CA; KQSR Yuma, AZ; KZXY-FM Apple Valley, CA
Jason Wolff, President

Granite Broadcasting Corp.
767 Third Ave., 34th Fl., New York NY 10017
(212) 826-2530; *Fax:* (212) 826-2858
p.markham@granitetv.com
TV Stns: 9 TV.
KBJR-TV Superior, WI; KOFY-TV San Francisco, CA; WBNG-TV Binghamton, NY; WMYD Detroit, MI; WEEK-TV Peoria, IL; WKBW-TV Buffalo, NY; WISE-TV Fort Wayne, IN; WTVH Syracuse, NY; KRII Chisholm, MN
Peter Markham, Chairman
Duane Lammers, COO

Gray Television Inc.
4370 Peachtree Rd. NE, Suite 400, Atlanta GA 30319
(404) 266-8333
gray.tv
Ownership: Bull Run Corp., Datasouth Computer Corp. and affiliated companies. Other interests: Porta Phone Paging Inc. and Lynqx.
TV Stns: 59 TV.
KAKE Wichita, KS; KALB Alexandria, LA; KBTX Bryan, TX; KEVN Rapid City, SD; KFYR Bismarck, ND; KGIN Grand Island, NE; KGNS Laredo, TX; KGWN Cheyenne, WY; KJCT Grand Junction, CO; KKCO Grand Junction, CO; KKTV Colorado Springs, CO; KLBY Colby, KS; KMOT Minot, ND; KMVT Twin Falls, ID; KNOE Monroe, LA; KNOP North Platte, NE; KOLN Lincoln, NE; KOLO Reno, NV; KOSA Odessa, TX; KQCD Dickinson, ND; KSFY Sioux Falls, SD; KSTF Scottsbluff, NE; KUMV Williston, ND; KUPK Garden City, KS; KVLY Fargo, ND; KWTX Waco, TX; KXII Sherman, TX; WAGM Presque Isle, ME; WBKO Bowling Green, KY; WCTV Thomasville, GA; WEAU Eau Claire, WI; WSWG Valdosta, GA; WHSV Harrisonburg, VA; WIBW Topeka, KS; WIFR Freeport, IL; WILX Onondaga, MI; WITN Washington, NC; WJHG Panama City, FL; WJRT Flint, MI; WKYT Lexington, KY; WMTV Madison, WI; WNDU South Bend, IN; WOWT Omaha, NE; WRDW Augusta, GA; WSAW Wausau, WI; WSAZ Huntington, WV; WTAP Parkersburg, WV; WTOK Meridian, MS; WTVG-TV Toledo, OH; WTVY Dothan, AL; WVLT Knoxville, TN; WYMT Hazard, KY; WCAV Charlottesville, VA; KCWY Casper, WY; KSNB Superior, NE; KSVT Twin Falls, ID; KNPL North Platte, NE; KIIT North Platte, NE; KXIP Paris, TX
Hilton H. Howell Jr., President/Chief Executive Officer
James C. Ryan, Senior Vice President/Chief Financial Officer

Griffin Communications L.L.C.
7401 N. Kelley Ave., Oklahoma City OK 73111
(405) 843-6641; *Fax:* (405) 841-9135
www.griffincommunications.net
TV Stns: 3 TV.
KOTV-DT Tulsa, OK; KQCW-DT Muskogee, OK; KWTV-DT Oklahoma City, OK
Ted Strickland, CFO
David Griffin, President
Dick Dutton, Operations Dir
Joyce Reed, Vice President
Kathy Haney, Vice President
Steve Foerster, Vice President

Hearst Corporation
300 W. 57th St., New York NY 10019
(212) 649-2000
www.hearst.com
contact@hearst.com
Ownership: Hearst Family, 100%.
TV Stns: 31 TV.
KCCI Des Moines, IA; KCRA-TV Sacramento, CA; KCWE Kansas City, MO; KETV Omaha, NE; KHBS Fort Smith, AR; KHOG Fayetteville, AR; KHVO Honolulu, HI; KITV Honolulu, HI; KMAU Wailuku, HI; KMBC Kansas City, MO; KOAT Albuquerque, NM; KOCO Oklahoma City, OK; KQCA Stockton, CA; KSBW Salinas, CA; WAPT Jackson, MS; WBAL Baltimore, MD; WCVB Boston, MA; WESH Daytona Beach, FL; WGAL Lancaster, PA; WISN-TV Milwaukee, WI; WKCF Clermont, FL; WLKY Louisville, KY; WLWT Cincinnati, OH; WMUR-TV Manchester, NH; WNNE Hartford, VT; WPBF Tequesta, FL; WPTZ North Pole, NY; WTAE-TV Pittsburgh, PA; WVTM Birmingham, AL; WXII-TV Winston-Salem, NC; WYFF Greenville, SC
Steven R. Swartz, President/CEO

Hearst Television Inc.
300 W. 57th St., 39th Fl., New York NY 10019
(212) 887-6800; *Fax:* (212) 887-6855
www.hearst.com/broadcasting
Ownership: The Hearst Corp., 100%
TV Stns: 20 TV.
WDSU New Orleans, LA; WMTW Poland Spring, ME; KCCI-TV Des Moines, IA; KCRA-TV Sacramento, CA; KMBC-TV Kansas City, MO; KHBS-TV Rogers, AR; KMBC-TV Kansas City, MO; KOAT-TV Albuquerque, NM; KOCO-TV Oklahoma City, OK; KQCA-TV Sacramento, CA; WAPT-TV Jackson, MS; WBAL-TV Baltimore, MD; WCVB-TV Needham, MA; WDSU-TV New Orleans, LA; WESH-TV New Orleans, LA; WGAL-TV Lancaster, PA; WISN-TV Wilwaukee, WI; WKCF-TV Winter Park, FL; WLKY-TV Louisville, KY; WMTW-TV Westbrook, ME
David Barrett, Chairman/Chief Executive Officer
Jordan Wertlieb, President

Heartland Media LLC
3282 Northside Pkwy. N.W., Atlanta GA 30327
(470) 355-1192
Ownership: Bob Prather.
TV Stns: 5 TV.
KDKF Klamath Falls, OR; KDRV Medford, OR; KEZI Eugene, OR; WKTV Utica, NY; WTVA Tupelo, MS
Bob Prather, CEO

Heritage Broadcasting Co of MI
Box 627, Cadillac MI 49601
(231) 775-3478; *Fax:* (231) 775-3671
www.9and10news.com
Ownership: Heritage Broadcasting Group Inc., 100%.
TV Stns: 2 TV.
WWTV Cadillac, MI; WWUP-TV Sault Ste. Marie, MI
Mario Lacobelli, President
William Kring, VP/General Manager

HITV License Subsidiary Inc.
1100 Wilson Blvd., Suite 3000, Arlington VA 22209
(703) 247-7500; *Fax:* (703) 247-7505
www.mcgcapital.com
Ownership: MCG Capital Corp., 100% of Votes, 97% of equity
TV Stns: 3 TV.
KFVE Honolulu, HI; KGMD-TV Hilo, HI; KGMV Wailuku, HI
Michael McHugh, President

Hoak Media Corporation
500 Crescent Ct., Suite 220, Dallas TX 75201
(972) 960-4848; *Fax:* (972) 960-4899
www.hoakmedia.com
TV Stns: 6 TV.
KAUZ-TV Wichita Falls, TX; KHAS-TV Hastings, NE; KPRY-TV Pierre, SD; KREG-TV Glenwood Springs, CO; KREX-TV Grand Junction, CO; KREY-TV Montrose, CO
Eric Van den Branden, President

Holston Valley Broadcasting Corp.
222 Commerce St., Kingsport TN 37660
(423) 246-9578; *Fax:* (423) 247-9836
www.hvbcgroup.com
Ownership: Glenwood Communications Corp., 100%.
TV Stns: 1 TV.
WKPT-TV Kingsport, TN
Radio Stns: 4 AM. 4 FM.
WKPT Kingsport, TN; WKTP Jonesborough, TN; WUKZ(AM) Marion, VA; WOPI Bristol, TN; WMEV-FM Marion, VA; WRZK Colonial Heights, TN; WVEK-FM Weber City, VA; WTFM Kingsport, TN
George DeVault Jr., President

Howard Stirk Holdings
201 Massachusetts Ave. N.E., Suite C-1, Washington DC 20002
(202) 546-5400
www.hsh.media
contact@hsh.media
Ownership: Armstrong Williams.
TV Stns: 6 TV.
WEYI-TV Saginaw, MI; WLYH-TV Lancaster, PA; WGWG Charleston, SC; WWMB Florence, SC; WGWW Anniston, AL; WSES Tuscaloosa, AL
Armstrong Williams, CEO/COO

Hubbard Broadcasting Inc.
3415 University Ave., St. Paul MN 55114
(651) 646-5555; *Fax:* (651) 642-4103
TV Stns: 13 TV.
KAAL Austin, MN; KOB Albuquerque, NM; KOBF Farmington, NM; KOBR Roswell, NM; KRWF Redwood Falls, MN; KSAX Alexandria, MN; KSTP-TV St. Paul, MN; KSTC-TV Minneapolis, MN; WDIO-DT Duluth, MN; WHEC-TV Rochester, NY; WIRT Hibbing, MN; WNYT Albany, NY; WNYT Pittsfield, MA
Radio Stns: 5 AM. 15 FM.
KSTP St. Paul, MN; WIXK New Richmond, WI; WBQH Silver Spring, MD; WFED Washington, DC; WWFD Frederick, MD; KSTP-FM St. Paul, MN; WTOP-FM Washington, DC; WIL-FM St. Louis, MO; WTMY(FM) Coon Rapids, MN; WARH Granite City, IL; WKRQ Cincinnati, OH; WYGY Fort Thomas, KY; WDRV Chicago, IL; WWDV Zion, IL; WSHE-FM Chicago, IL; WTMX Skokie, IL; WWWT-FM Manassas, VA; WUBE-FM Cincinnati, OH; WXOS East St. Louis, IL; WTLP Braddock Heights, MD
Julia Coyte, Vice President
Robert Hubbard, Vice President
Virginia Morris, Vice President
Stanley Hubbard II, Vice President
Edward Aiken, Vice President
Sue Cook, Vice President
Linda Tremere, Vice President
C. Thomas Newberry, Vice President
Harold Crump, Vice President
Gerald Deeney, SVP/Treasurer/Chief Financial Officer

Independent Communications Inc.
2817 W. 11th St., Sioux Falls SD 57104
(605) 338-0017; *Fax:* (605) 338-7173
fox17@kttw.com
Ownership: Independent Communications Inc.
TV Stns: 2 TV.
KTTM Huron, SD; KTTW Sioux Falls, SD
Ed Hoffman, General Manager

Intermountain West Communications
1500 Foremaster Ln., Las Vegas NV 89101
(702) 642-3333; *Fax:* (702) 657-3152
www.news3lv.com
TV Stns: 4 TV.
KENV-DT Elko, NV; KRNV-DT Reno, NV; KVMY Las Vegas, NV; KYMA-DT Yuma, AZ

ION Media Networks Inc.
601 Clearwater Park Rd., West Palm Beach FL 33401-6233
(561) 659-4100
www.ionmedianetworks.com
ionaffiliates@ionmedia.com
Ownership: Media Holdco L.P., 62.5%; senior lenders from previous rounds of funding, 37.5%.
TV Stns: 62 TV.
KGPX-TV Spokane, WA; KKPX-TV San Jose, CA; KOPX-TV Oklahoma City, OK; KPPX-TV Tolleson, AZ; KPXB-TV Conroe, TX; KPXC-TV Denver, CO; KPXD-TV Arlington, TX; KPXE-TV Kansas City, MO; KPXG-TV Salem, OR; KPXL-TV Uvalde, TX; KPXM-TV St. Cloud, MN; KPXN-TV San Bernardino, CA; KPXO-TV Kaneohe, HI; KPXR-TV Cedar Rapids, IA; KSPX-TV Sacramento, CA; KTPX-TV Okmulgee, OK; KUPX-TV Provo, UT; WBPX-TV Boston, MA; WPXC-TV Brunswick, GA; WCPX-TV Chicago, IL; WEPX-TV Greenville, NC; WFPX-TV Fayetteville, NC; WGPX-TV Burlington, NC; WRBU East St. Louis, IL; WIPX-TV Bloomington, IN; WLPX-TV Charleston, WV; WNPX-TV Cookeville, TN; WOPX-TV Melbourne, FL; WPPX-TV Wilmington, DE; WPXA-TV Rome, GA; WPXD-TV Ann Arbor, MI; WPXE-TV Kenosha, WI; WPXG-TV Boston, MA; WPXH-TV Birmingham, AL; WPXJ-TV Buffalo, NY; WPXK-TV Jellico, TN; WPXL-TV New Orleans, LA; WPXM-TV Miami, FL; WPXN-TV New York, NY; WPXP-TV Lake Worth, FL; WPXQ-TV Block Island, RI; WPXR-TV Roanoke, VA; WPXV-TV Norfolk, VA; WPXW-TV Manassas, VA; WPXX-TV Memphis, TN; WINP-TV Pittsburgh, PA; WQPX-TV Scranton, PA; WRPX-TV Rocky Mount, NC; WSPX-TV Syracuse, NY; WTPX-TV Antigo, WI; WVPX-TV Akron, OH; WWPX-TV Martinsburg, WV; WXPX-TV Bradenton, FL; WYPX-TV Amsterdam, NY; WZPX-TV Battle Creek, MI; WZRB Columbia, SC; WHPX-TV New London, CT; KFPX-TV Newton, IA; WUPX-TV Marquette, MI; WDPX-TV Boston, MA; WPXU-TV Jacksonville, NC; KWPX-TV Bellevue, WA
Brandon Burgess, Chairman/CEO
Stephen Appel, President, Sales & Marketing
Marc Zand, SVP, Business Affairs & Digital Networks

Journal Communications Inc.
333 W. State St., Milwaukee WI 53203
(414) 224-2616; *Fax:* (414) 224-2469
TV Stns: 13 TV.
KGUN-TV Tucson, AZ; KIVI-TV Nampa, ID; KMIR-TV Palm Springs, CA; KMTV-TV Omaha, NE; KNIN-TV Caldwell, ID; KTNV-TV Las Vegas, NV; KWBA-TV Sierra Vista, AZ; WACY-TV Appleton, WI; WFTX-TV Cape Coral, FL; WGBA-TV Green Bay, WI; WSYM-TV Lansing, MI; WTMJ-TV Milwaukee, WI; WTVF Nashville, TN
Radio Stns: 8 AM. 27 FM.
KCID Caldwell, ID; KLIO Wichita, KS; KFFN Tucson, AZ; KGEM Boise, ID; KSGF Springfield, MO; KFAQ Tulsa, OK; KXSP Omaha, NE; WTMJ Milwaukee, WI; KTHI Caldwell, ID; KXBL Henryetta, OK; KEZO-FM Omaha, NE; KFDI-FM Wichita, KS; KRVB Nampa, ID; KTGV Oracle, AZ; KRVI Mount Vernon, MO; KICT-FM Wichita, KS; KJOT Boise, ID; KKCD Omaha, NE; KFXJ Augusta, KS; KSPW Sparta, MO; KMXZ-FM Tucson, AZ; KFTI-FM Newton, KS; KQXR Payette, ID; KSRZ Omaha, NE; KTTS-FM Springfield, MO; KVOO-FM Tulsa, OK; KYQQ Arkansas City, KS; KQTH Tucson, AZ; KSGF-FM Ash Grove, MO; WLWK-FM Milwaukee, WI; WWST Sevierville, TN; WCYQ Oak Ridge, TN; KQCH Omaha, NE; WKHT Knoxville, TN; WNOX Karns, TN
Douglas Kiel, President

KEVN Inc.
2001 Skyline Dr., Rapid City SD 57701
(605) 394-7777
www.blackhillsfox.com
news@blackhillsfox.com
TV Stns: 1 TV.
KIVV-TV Lead, SD
Robert Slocum, CFO
Jack Caudill, New Director
Jamie Zepp, Sports Director

KHQ Inc.
1201 W. Sprague Ave., Spokane WA 99201
(509) 448-6000
www.khq.com
TV Stns: 3 TV.
KHQ-TV Spokane, WA; KNDO Yakima, WA; KNDU Richland, WA
Elizabeth A. Cowles, Chairman

KM Communications Inc.
3654 Jarvis Ave., Skokie IL 60076
(847) 674-0864; *Fax:* (847) 674-9188
www.kmcommunications.com
TV Stns: 3 TV.
KWKB Iowa City, IA; WOCK-CD Chicago, IL; WSKC-CD Atlanta, GA
Radio Stns: 1 AM. 6 FM.
KQMG Independence, IA; KQMG-FM Independence, IA; KWKM St. Johns, AZ; WLCN Atlanta, IL; KTKB Dededo, GU; WMKB Earlville, IL; WDLJ Breese, IL
Myoung Hwa Bae, President

Lake Superior Community Broadcasting Corp.
1390 Bagley St., Alpena MI 49707
(989) 356-3434
TV Stns: 2 TV.
WBKP Calumet, MI; WBUP Ishpeming, MI

Landmark Communications Inc.
112 Berkeley Street, Norfolk VA 23510
(757) 446-2000; *Fax:* (757) 446-2179
Ownership: (Landmark Broadcast Division.)
TV Stns: 1 TV.
KLAS-TV Las Vegas, NV
Frank Batten, Chairman
Decker Anstrom, President

Legacy Broadcasting, LLC
805 Weightman St., Greenwood MS 38930
(662) 822-1655
TV Stns: 4 TV.
KNDB Bismarck, ND; KNDM Minot, ND; KMLU Columbia, LA; KNHL Hastings, NE
Radio Stns: 1 FM.
KYMS Rathdrum, ID
Sherry Nelson, President

LeSEA Broadcasting
LeSEA Broadcasting Corp, South Bend IN 46614
(574) 291-8200; *Fax:* (574) 291-9043
www.lesea.com
TV Stns: 8 TV.
KWHB Tulsa, OK; KETD Castle Rock, CO; KWHE Honolulu, HI; KWHD Hilo, HI; KWHM Wailuku, HI; WHMB-TV Indianapolis, IN; WHME-TV South Bend, IN; WHNO New Orleans, LA
Radio Stns: 3 FM.
WHME South Bend, IN; WHPZ Bremen, IN; WHPD Dowagiac, MI
Peter Sumrall, President/Chief Executive Officer

Liberman Broadcasting Inc.
1845 Empire Ave., Burbank CA 91504
(818) 729-5300; *Fax:* (818) 729-5678
www.lbimedia.com
LBinfo@lbimedia.com
TV Stns: 4 TV.
KPNZ Ogden, UT; KMPX Decatur, TX; KRCA Riverside, CA; KZJL Houston, TX
Radio Stns: 3 AM. 13 FM.
KEYH Houston, TX; KVNR Santa Ana, CA; KZMP University Park, TX; KBOC Bridgeport, TX; KBUA San Fernando, CA; KBUE Long Beach, CA; KNOR Krum, TX; KEBN Garden Grove, CA; KJOJ-FM Freeport, TX; KZMP-FM Pilot Point, TX; KTJM Port Arthur, TX; KWIZ Santa Ana, CA; KRQB San Jacinto, CA; KNTE Bay City, TX; KZZA Muenster, TX; KQQK Beaumont, TX
Jose Liberman, Chairman & President
Lenard Liberman, Executive Vice President
Winter Horton, Cheif Operating Officer
Eduardo Leon, Vice President, Programming

Liberty Media Corp.
12300 Liberty Blvd., Englewood CO 80112
(720) 875-5400
www.libertymedia.com
TV Stns: 2 TV.
WFRV-TV Green Bay, WI; WJMN-TV Escanaba, MI
John Malone, Chairman
Gregory Maffei, CEO

LIN Media
One West Exchange St., Suite 5A, Providence RI 02903
(401) 454-2880; *Fax:* (401) 454-6990
www.linmedia.com

courtney.guertin@linmedia.com
Ownership: Hicks, Muse, Tate & Furst 47%.
TV Stns: 30 TV.
KAII-TV Wailuku, HI; KASA-TV Santa Fe, NM; KBIM-TV Roswell, NM; KHON2 Hilo, HI; KIMT Mason City, IA; KOIN Portland, OR; KREZ-TV Durango, CO; KRQE Albuquerque, NM; KSNC Great Bend, KS; KSNG Garden City, KS; KSNK McCook, NE; KSNT Topeka, KS; KSNW Wichita, KS; KXAN-TV Austin, TX; WALA-TV Mobile, AL; WANE-TV Fort Wayne, IN; WAVY-TV Portsmouth, VA; WDTN Dayton, OH; WIAT Birmingham, AL; WISH-TV Indianapolis, IN; WIVB-TV Buffalo, NY; WJCL Savannah, GA; WKBN-TV Youngstown, OH; WNDY-TV Marion, IN; WNLO Buffalo, NY; WOOD-TV Grand Rapids, MI; WOTV Battle Creek, MI; WNAC-TV Providence, RI; WTHI-TV Terre Haute, IN; WWLP Springfield, MA
Vincent L. Sadusky, President/Chief Executive Officer
Scott M. Blumenthal, EVP, Television
Richard J. Schmaeling, SVP/CFO
Denise M. Parent, SVP, Chief Legal Officer

Local TV LLC
1717 Dixie Hwy., Suite 650, Ft. Wright KY 41011
(859) 448-2700; *Fax:* (859) 331-6014
www.localtvllc.com
TV Stns: 2 TV.
KFCT Fort Collins, CO; KFCT Fort Collins, CO
Bobby Lawrence, CEO
Pam Taylor, CFO

Magnum Communications Inc.
1021 N. Superior Ave., Suite 5, Tomah WI 54660
(608) 742-2544
info@magnumbroadcasting.com
Ownership: David R. Magnum, 100%.
TV Stns: 1 TV.
KQEG-CA La Crescent, MN
Radio Stns: 6 AM. 10 FM.
WBKV West Bend, WI; WDLS Wisconsin Dells, WI; WPDR Portage, WI; WRDB Reedsburg, WI; WRJN Racine, WI; WBOG Tomah, WI; WAUN Kewaunee, WI; WBDL Reedsburg, WI; WBKY Portage, WI; WTMB Tomah, WI; WMBZ West Bend, WI; WDDC Portage, WI; WVTY Racine, WI; WNFM Reedsburg, WI; WNNO Wisconsin Dells, WI; WXYM Tomah, WI
David R. Magnum, President

Malara Broadcast Group Inc.
9257 Bailey Ln., Fairfax VA 22031
(703) 253-2020
TV Stns: 2 TV.
KDLH Duluth, MN; WPTA Fort Wayne, IN

Manship Family
Box 2906, Baton Rouge LA 70821
(225) 387-2222; *Fax:* (225) 336-2246
TV Stns: 2 TV.
KRGV-TV Weslaco, TX; WBRZ-TV Baton Rouge, LA
Richard Manship, President

Mark III Media Inc.
1856 Skyview Dr., Casper WY 82601
(307) 577-5923
Ownership: Julie Jaffe, 35%; Jennifer Lechter, 35%; and Mark R. Nalbone, 30%.
TV Stns: 3 TV.
KGWR-TV Rock Springs, WY; KGWC-TV Casper, WY; KGWL-TV Lander, WY
Julie Jaffe, President

Marshall Broadcasting Group Inc.
8323 S.W. Freeway, Suite 433, Houston TX 77074
(213) 835-1540
Ownership: Pluria Marshall Jr., 100%.
TV Stns: 3 TV.
KLJB Davenport, IA; KMSS-TV Shreveport, LA; KPEJ-TV Odessa, TX
Pluria Marshall Jr., President & CEO

MAX Media L.L.C.
900 Laskin Rd., Virginia Beach VA 23451
(757) 437-9800; *Fax:* (757) 437-0034
www.maxmediallc.com
Ownership: MBG-GG LLC, 42.0345%; MBG Quad-C Investors I Inc., 41.4124%; Aardvarks Also LLC, 6.1967%; Colonnade Max Investors Inc., 4.8671%; Quad-C Max Investors Inc.,4.6799%; MBG Quad-C Investors II Inc., 0.6221%; and Quad-C Max Investors II Inc., 0.1872%.
TV Stns: 3 TV.
WNKY Bowling Green, KY; WMEI Arecibo, PR; WPFO Waterville, ME
Radio Stns: 8 AM. 22 FM.
KGIR Cape Girardeau, MO; KSIM Sikeston, MO; KMAL Malden, MO; KWOC Poplar Bluff, MO; KZIM Cape Girardeau, MO; WCIL Carbondale, IL; WGH Newport News, VA; WJPF Herrin, IL; KCGQ-FM Gordonville, MO; KEZS-FM Cape Girardeau, MO; KGKS Scott City, MO; KJEZ Poplar Bluff, MO; KKLR-FM Poplar Bluff, MO; KLSC Malden, MO; KFCO Bennett, CO; WCIL-FM Carbondale, IL; WVHT Norfolk, VA; WCXL Kill Devil Hills, NC; WVBW Suffolk, VA; WGH-FM Newport News, VA; WFYY Bloomsburg, PA; WOOZ-FM Harrisburg, IL; WXLT Christopher, IL; WWBE Mifflinburg, PA; WCMS-FM Hatteras, NC; WVSP-FM Yorktown, VA; WUEZ Carterville, IL; WYGL-FM Elizabethville, PA; KJHM Strasburg, CO; WVSL-FM Riverside, PA
Aubrey Eugene Loving Jr., Chairman & CEO
John Trinder, President & Chief Operating Officer

McKinnon Broadcasting Co.
4575 Viewridge Ave, San Diego CA 92123
(858) 571-5151; *Fax:* (858) 571-4852
www.kusi.com
Ownership: Michael Dean McKinnon Sr.
TV Stns: 1 TV.
KUSI-TV San Diego, CA
Michael Dean McKinnon Sr., Majority Owner/President/CEO/Chairman

Mel Wheeler Inc.
3934 Electric Rd., Roanoke VA 24018-4513
(540) 989-4591; *Fax:* (540) 774-5667
melwheelerinc.com
Ownership: Leonard E. Wheeler, 35%; Steve Wheeler, 34%; and Clark Wheeler, 31%.
TV Stns: 2 TV.
KPOB-TV Poplar Bluff, MO; WSIL-TV Harrisburg, IL
Radio Stns: 2 AM. 4 FM.
WFIR Roanoke, VA; WVBE Roanoke, VA; WVBE-FM Lynchburg, VA; WSLC-FM Roanoke, VA; WSLQ Roanoke, VA; WXLK Roanoke, VA
Leonard Wheeler, President
Gretchen Cummings, Sec/Treasurer

Meredith Corp.
1716 Locust St, Des Moines IA 50309
(515) 284-3000
www.meredith.com
TV Stns: 13 TV.
KCTV Kansas City, MO; KMOV St. Louis, MO; KPDX Vancouver, WA; KPHO Phoenix, AZ; KPTV Portland, OR; KSMO Kansas City, MO; KTVK Phoenix, AZ; KVVU Henderson, NV; WFSB Hartford, CT; WGCL Atlanta, GA; WHNS Greenville, SC; WNEM Bay City, MI; WSMV Nashville, TN
Paul Karpowicz, President, Local Media Group
Jon Werther, President, National Media Group

Mission Broadcasting Inc.
7650 Chippewa Rd., Suite 305, Brecksville OH 44141
(440) 526-2227; *Fax:* (330) 336-8454,
Ownership: Nancie Smith
TV Stns: 18 TV.
KSAN-TV San Angelo, TX; KAMC Lubbock, TX; KASN Pine Bluff, AR; KCIT Amarillo, TX; KHMT Hardin, MT; KJTL Wichita Falls, TX; KLRT-TV Little Rock, AR; KODE-TV Joplin, MO; KOLR Springfield, MO; KRBC-TV Abilene, TX; KTVE El Dorado, AR; WAWV-TV Terre Haute, IN; WFXP Erie, PA; WTVO Rockford, IL; WTVW Evansville, IN; WUTR Utica, NY; WVNY Burlington, VT; WYOU Scranton, PA
Nancie Smith, Chairman
Dennis Thatcher, President

Morgan Murphy Media
7025 W Raymond Rd, Madison WI 53719
(608) 271-4321; *Fax:* (608) 271-0800
www.morganmurphymedia.com
chris@embtv.com
Ownership: Evening Telegram Co. owns 100% of KVEW(TV), KXLY-AM-FM-TV, KXLY-DT and KAPP(TV). Evening Telegram Co. owns 84.4% of TelevisionWisconsin Inc., with an additional 15.2% of the stn held by Evening Telegram stockholders.
TV Stns: 5 TV.
KAPP-TV Yakima, WA; KVEW Kennewick, WA; KXLY-TV Spokane, WA; WISC-TV Madison, WI; WKBT-TV La Crosse, WI
Radio Stns: 4 AM. 7 FM.
KXLX Airway Heights, WA; KVNI Coeur D'Alene, ID; KXLY-AM Spokane, WA; WPVL-AM Platteville, WI; KEZE Spokane, WA; KHTQ Hayden, ID; KIYX Sageville, IA; KXLY-FM Spokane, WA; KZZU Spokane, WA; WGLR Lancaster, WI; WPVL-FM Platteville, WI
Brian R. Burns, Vice President & COO
Elizabeth Murphy Burns, President & CEO
Glenn R. Krieg, Treasurer & CFO

Morris Multimedia Inc.
27 Abercorn St, Savannah GA 31401
(912) 233-1281; *Fax:* (912) 238-2059
www.morrismultimedia.com
Ownership: Charles H. Morris
TV Stns: 6 TV.
WCBI-DT Columbus, MS; WDEF-TV Chattanooga, TN; WMGT-TV Macon, GA; WTVQ-TV Lexington, KY; WWAY-TV Wilmington, NC; WXXV-TV Gulfport, MS
Charles Morris, President

Mountain Broadcasting Corp.
99 Clinton Rd., West Caldwell NJ 7006
(973) 852-0300; *Fax:* (973) 808-5516
TV Stns: 1 TV.
WMBC-TV Newton, NJ
Radio Stns: 3 AM.
WPWA Chester, PA; WBTK Richmond, VA; WWGB Indian Head, MD
Sun Young Joo, President

Multicultural Capital Trust
c/o 11077 Swansfield Rd., Columbia MD 21044-2724
(202) 350-9658; *Fax:* (703) 991-7120
TV Stns: 1 TV.
WMFP Lawrence, MA

NBCUniversal Owned Television Stations
30 Rockefeller Plaza, New York NY 10112
(212) 664-4444; *Fax:* (212) 664-5830
www.nbcstations.com
Ownership: NBCUniversal
TV Stns: 10 TV.
KNBC Los Angeles, CA; KNSD San Diego, CA; KNTV San Jose, CA; KXAS Fort Worth, TX; WCAU Philadelphia, PA; WMAQ Chicago, IL; WNBC New York, NY; WRC Washington, DC; WTVJ Miami, FL; WVIT New Britain, CT
Valari Dobson Staab, President
Frank Comerford, Chief Revenue Officer/President, Commercial Ops.

NewCap Inc.
8 Basinview Drive, Dartmouth NS B3B 1G4
(902) 468-7557; *Fax:* (902) 468-7558
www.ncc.ca
ncc@ncc.ca
Ownership: Newfoundland Capital Corporation Ltd., 100%.
TV Stns: 2 TV.
CITL-DT Lloydminster, AB; CKSA-DT Lloydminster, AB
Radio Stns: 14 AM. 59 FM.
CFCB Corner Brook, NF; CFCW Camrose, AB; CFSX Stephenville, NF; CHCM Marystown, NF; CHNL Kamloops, BC; CISL Richmond, BC; CJYQ St. John's, NF; CKCM Grand Falls, NF; CKDQ Drumheller, AB; CKGA Gander, NF; CKIM Baie Verte, NF; CKJR Wetaskiwin, AB; CKVO Clarenville, NF; VOCM St. John's, NF; CFCV-FM St. Andrew's, NL; CFLC-FM Churchill Falls, NL; CFLN-FM Goose Bay, NF; CFRQ-FM Dartmouth, NS; CKUL-FM Halifax, NS; CIGM-FM Sudbury, ON; CIGV-FM Penticton, BC; CIRK-FM Edmonton, AB; CIZZ-FM Red Deer, AB; CHBM-FM Toronto, ON; CJMO-FM Moncton, NB; CKBA-FM Athabasca, AB; CKIX-FM St. John's, NL; CKKY-FM Wainwright, AB; CKRA-FM Edmonton, AB; CKRV-FM Kamloops, BC; CKSQ-FM Stettler, AB; CKXX-FM Corner Brook, NL; CKZZ-FM Vancouver, BC; VOCM-FM St. John's, NF; CKXG-FM Grand Falls, NL; CFXJ-FM Toronto, ON; CJXL-FM Moncton, NB; CKGY-FM Red Deer, AB; CKXD-FM Gander, NL; CHNO-FM Sudbury, ON; CFXL-FM Calgary, AB; CIHT-FM Ottawa, ON; CKSA-FM Lloydminster, AB; CJXK-FM Cold Lake, AB; CFXH-FM Hinton, AB; CJPR-FM Blairmore, AB; CKWY-FM Wainwright, AB; CHNI-FM Saint John, NB; CFRK-FM Fredericton, NB; CIXF-FM Brooks, AB; CFCW-FM Camrose, AB; CILV-FM Ottawa, ON; CJKC-FM Kamloops, BC; CFXW-FM Whitecourt, AB; CHTN-FM Charlottetown, PE; CKQK-FM Charlottetown, PE; CHSL-FM Slave Lake, AB; CJEG-FM Bonnyville, AB; CKMP-FM Calgary, AB; CFXE-FM Edson, AB; CHVO-FM Carbonear, NL; CHRK-FM Sydney, NS; CKCH-FM Sydney, NS; CIJK-FM Kentville, NS; CKKO-FM Kelowna, BC; CHLG-FM Vancouver, BC; CKVH-FM High Prairie, AB; CHSP-FM St. Paul, AB; CKWB-FM Westlock, AB; CIBQ-FM Brooks, AB; CIHI-FM Fredericton, NB; CHHI-FM Miramichi, NB; CILB-FM Lac La Biche, AB
Harold R. Steele, Chairman
Robert G. Steele, CEO/COO
Robert G. Steele, President

Newfoundland Broadcasting Co.
446 Logy Bay Rd., St. John's NF A1C 5S2
(709) 722-5015; *Fax:* (709) 726-5107
www.ntv.ca
greetings@ntv.ca

Ownership: G. Scott Stirling, 64.99%; Gregory Stirling, 34.99%; and others, 0.02%.

TV Stns: 1 TV.
CJON-DT St. John's, NF

Radio Stns: 8 FM.
CFOZ-FM Argentia, NF; CKMY-FM Grand Falls, NL; CHOZ-FM St. John's, NF; CIOZ-FM Marystown, NF; CJMY-FM Clarenville, NF; CJOZ-FM Bonavista Bay, NL; CKOZ-FM Corner Brook, NF; CIOS-FM Stephenville, NF

Geoff Stirling, President & CEO
Lindsey Andrews, General Manager
Ernst Rollmann, Station Manager
Lorraine Pope, Sales Director & Program Acquisitions

News-Press & Gazette Co.
825 Edmond St, St. Joseph MO 64502
(816) 271-8500; *Fax:* (816) 271-8695
www.npgco.com
info@npgco.com

TV Stns: 11 TV.
KCOY-TV Santa Maria, CA; KECY-TV El Centro, CA; KESQ-TV Palm Springs, CA; KEYT-TV Santa Barbara, CA; KIDK Idaho Falls, ID; KIFI-TV Idaho Falls, ID; KION-TV Monterey, CA; KMIZ Columbia, MO; KRDO-TV Colorado Springs, CO; KTVZ Bend, OR; KVIA-TV El Paso, TX

Radio Stns: 2 AM. 2 FM.
KESQ Indio, CA; KRDO Colorado Springs, CO; KRDO-FM Security, CO; KUNA-FM La Quinta, CA

David Bradley, Chairman & CEO
Mike Meara, Executive Vice President - Chief Operating Officer

Newsweb Corp.
1645 W Fullerton, Chicago IL 60614
(773) 975-0401; *Fax:* (773) 975-1301
Ownership: Fred Eychaner, 100%.

TV Stns: 1 TV.
KCDO-TV Kimball, NE

Radio Stns: 4 AM. 3 FM.
WAIT Crystal Lake, IL; WNDZ Portage, IN; WSBC Chicago, IL; WCPT-AM Willow Springs, IL; WCPY Arlington Heights, IL; WCPT-FM DeKalb, IL; WCPQ Park Forest, IL

Fred J. Eychaner, President

Nexstar Broadcasting Group Inc.
545 E. John Carpenter Freeway., Suite 700, Irving TX 75062
(972) 373-8800
www.nexstar.tv
Ownership: Shareholders.

TV Stns: 65 TV.
KADN-TV Lafayette, LA; KAMR-TV Amarillo, TX; KARD West Monroe, LA; KASW Phoenix, AZ; KCAU-TV Sioux City, IA; KOZL-TV Springfield, MO; KETK-TV Jacksonville, TX; KNWA-TV Rogers, AR; KFDX-TV Wichita Falls, TX; KREX-TV Grand Junction, CO; KGET-TV Bakersfield, CA; KGPE Fresno, CA; KGCW Burlington, IA; KLBK-TV Lubbock, TX; KLST San Angelo, TX; KMID Midland, TX; KFTA-TV Fort Smith, AR; KQTV St. Joseph, MO; KSEE Fresno, CA; KSNF Joplin, MO; KSVI Billings, MT; KTAB-TV Abilene, TX; KTAL-TV Texarkana, TX; KTSM-TV El Paso, TX; KTVX Salt Lake City, UT; KUCW Ogden, UT; KVEO-TV Brownsville, TX; KWKT-TV Waco, TX; KYLE-TV Bryan, TX; KARZ-TV Little Rock, AR; WBRE-TV Wilkes-Barre, PA; WCIX Springfield, IL; WCIA Champaign, IL; WDHN Dothan, AL; WEHT Evansville, IN; WETM-TV Elmira, NY; WEUX Chippewa Falls, WI; WFFF-TV Burlington, VT; WFFT-TV Fort Wayne, IN; WFXR Roanoke, VA; WFXV Utica, NY; WGMB-TV Baton Rouge, LA; WHAG-TV Hagerstown, MD; WHBF-TV Rock Island, IL; WIVT Binghamton, NY; WSYR-TV Syracuse, NY; WJET-TV Erie, PA; WWCW Lynchburg, VA; WCWJ Jacksonville, FL; WLAX La Crosse, WI; WLMT Memphis, TN; WMBB Panama City, FL; WMBD-TV Peoria, IL; WNTZ-TV Natchez, LA; WOI-DT Ames, IA; WQRF-TV Rockford, IL; WROC-TV Rochester, NY; WTAJ-TV Altoona, PA; WTWO Terre Haute, IN; WWTI Watertown, NY; WZDX Huntsville, AL; KARK-TV Little Rock, AR; WAMY-TV Huntsville, AL; WBRL-CD Baton Rouge, LA; KLAF-LD Lafayette, LA

Perry A. Sook, Chairman, President and CEO
Timonthy Busch, COO

Northwest Broadcasting Inc.
#650, 2111 University Park Dr., Okemos MI 48864
(517) 347-4141; *Fax:* (517) 349-9080
Ownership: LPTV: WBPN-LP Morris, NY; and KCYU-LP Yakima, WA.

TV Stns: 5 TV.
KAYU-TV Spokane, WA; KFFX-TV Pendleton, OR; KMVU-DT Medford, OR; WICZ-TV Binghamton, NY; WSYT Syracuse, NY

Leann Brady, President/Chief Executive Officer

NRJ Holdings LLC
722 S. Denton Tap Road, Suite 130, Coppell TX 75019
(972) 947-3391
Ownership: Ted B. Bartley, 100% votes, 35% of total assets.

TV Stns: 5 TV.
KIKU Honolulu, HI; KSCI Long Beach, CA; KUBE-TV Baytown, TX; WGCB-TV Red Lion, PA; WZME Bridgeport, CT

Ted B. Bartley, President

OTA Broadcasting
3201 Jermantown Road, Suite 380, Fairfax VA 22030-2881
(703) 364-5300
otabroadcasting.com
Ownership: MSDC Management L.P. Group also owns class A TV stn WEBR-CD Manhattan, NY.

TV Stns: 3 TV.
KFFV Seattle, WA; KTLN-TV Novato, CA; KVOS-TV Bellingham, WA

Pappas Telecasting Companies
500 S. Chinowth Rd., Visalia CA 93277
(559) 733-7800; *Fax:* (559) 733-7878
Ownership: Harry J. Pappas.

TV Stns: 8 TV.
KCWK North Las Vegas, NV; KHGI-TV Kearney, NE; KAZA-TV Avalon, CA; KCWI-TV Ames, IA; KSWT Yuma, AZ; KWNB-TV Hayes Center, NE; WCWG Lexington, NC; WLGA Opelika, AL

Radio Stns: 2 AM.
KCWK North Las Vegas, NV; KMPH Modesto, CA

Bruce Yeager, EVP/CFO
Harry J. Pappas, Chairman/CEO
Dennis J. Davis, President/COO

Pollack Broadcasting
5500 Poplar Ave, Suite 1, Memphis TN 38119
(901) 685-3993; *Fax:* (901) 685-3995
pollackcompanies.net
comments@pollackcompanies.net
Ownership: William H. Pollack, 100%.

TV Stns: 2 TV.
KIEM-TV Eureka, CA; KLAX-TV Alexandria, LA

Radio Stns: 6 AM. 3 FM.
KBOA-AM Kennett, MO; KCRV-AM Caruthersville, MO; KMIS-AM Portageville, MO; KSHP North Las Vegas, NV; WBIG Aurora, IL; WRMN Elgin, IL; KBOA-FM Piggott, AR; KCRV-FM Caruthersville, MO; KTMO New Madrid, MO

William Pollack, President

Post-Newsweek Stations Inc.
550 W. Lafayette Blvd., Detroit MI 48226
(313) 223-2260; *Fax:* (313) 223-2263
Ownership: Post-Newsweek Stations is a subsidiary of the publicly traded Washington Post Co.

TV Stns: 5 TV.
KPRC-TV Houston, TX; KSAT-TV San Antonio, TX; WJXT Jacksonville, FL; WKMG-TV Orlando, FL; WPLG Miami, FL

Alan W. Frank, President/CEO

Quincy Media, Inc.
130 S. Fifth St., Quincy IL 62301
(217) 223-5100; *Fax:* (217) 223-5019
www.qni.biz

TV Stns: 12 TV.
KTIV Sioux City, IA; KTTC Rochester, MN; KWWL Waterloo, IA; WAOW Wausau, WI; WGEM-TV Quincy, IL; WKOW Madison, WI; WQOW-DT Eau Claire, WI; WREX-TV Rockford, IL; WSJV Elkhart, IN; WVVA Bluefield, WV; WXOW La Crosse, WI; WYOW Eagle River, WI

Radio Stns: 1 AM. 1 FM.
WGEM Quincy, IL; WGEM-FM Quincy, IL

Thomas Oakley, President

R.H. Drewry Group
Box 708, Lawton OK 73502
(580) 353-0820;; *Fax:* (580) 357-3811
Ownership: R.H. Drewry owns 69% of KSWO-TV. KFDA-TV is a joint venture owned by Lawton Cablevision (50%), KSWD-TV (45%), KSWO(AM) (2 1/2%) and KRHD-AM-FM (2 1/2%). KWAB(TV) and KWES-TV areowned by KSWO Television Inc. (50%) and Lawton Cablevision Inc. (50%). KXXV(TV) is owned by Centrex Television L.P. Cable

TV Stns: 5 TV.
KFDA-TV Amarillo, TX; KSWO-TV Lawton, OK; KWAB-TV Big Spring, TX; KWES-TV Odessa, TX; KXXV Waco, TX

Robert Drewry, President
Larry Patton, General Manager
Bill Drewry, CEO

Ramar Communications II Ltd.
9800 University Ave., Lubbock TX 79423
(806) 748-2404; *Fax:* (806) 748-2470
www.lubbockradioadvertising.com
Ownership: Ray Moran, 51%; Brad Moran, 49%.

TV Stns: 2 TV.
KUPT Hobbs, NM; KJTV Lubbock, TX

Radio Stns: 1 AM. 3 FM.
KJTV Lubbock, TX; KLZK New Deal, TX; KTTU Brownfield, TX; KXTQ Lubbock, TX

Ray Moran, Chairman
Brad Moran, President

Raycom Media Inc.
201 Monroe St., RSA Tower, 20th Fl, Montgomery AL 36104
(334) 206-1400; *Fax:* (334) 206-1555
www.raycommedia.com
Ownership: Raycom Media Inc. Other interests: Raycom Sports, New York, NY; Charlotte, NC; Ft. Lauderdale, FL; Nashville, TN; and Chicago, IL.

TV Stns: 40 TV.
KAIT Jonesboro, AR; KCBD Lubbock, TX; KFVS-TV Cape Girardeau, MO; KHNL/KGMB Honolulu, HI; KHBC-TV Hilo, HI; KHNL Honolulu, HI; KLTV Tyler, TX; KOGG Wailuku, HI; KOLD-TV Tucson, AZ; KPLC Lake Charles, LA; KSLA Shreveport, LA; KTRE Lufkin, TX; KTTU Tucson, AZ; WAFB Baton Rouge, LA; WAFF Huntsville, AL; WALB Albany, GA; WAVE Louisville, KY; WBRC Birmingham, AL; WBTV Charlotte, NC; WCSC-TV Charleston, SC; WDAM-TV Laurel, MS; WDFX-TV Ozark, AL; WECT Wilmington, NC; WFIE Evansville, IN; WFLX West Palm Beach, FL; WIS Columbia, SC; WLBT Jackson, MS; WLOX Biloxi, MS; WMC-TV Memphis, TN; WOIO Shaker Heights, OH; WPGX Panama City, FL; WSFA Montgomery, AL; WTNZ Knoxville, TN; WTOC-TV Savannah, GA; WTOL Toledo, OH; WTVM Columbus, GA; WUAB Lorain, OH; WWBT Richmond, VA; WXIX-TV Newport, KY; WMBF-TV Myrtle Beach, SC

Pat LaPlatney, President & CEO
Susana Schuler, Executive VP, Content & Operations
Sandy Breland, Vice President, Television
Don Richards, Vice President, Television
Jeff Rosser, Vice President, Television
Nick Simonetter, Vice President, Television
Brad Streit, Vice President, Television
Rebecca Bryan, Senior VP, General Counsel
David Burke, VP, Technology
Joe Fiveash, Senior VP, Digital Media Strategy
Wayne Freedman, VP, Sales
Billy Mcdowell, VP, Sales
Ken Reiner, VP, Programming
Warren Spector, Chief Financial Officer
Susan Willower, Vice President, Human Resources

Red River Broadcast Co. L.L.C.
Box 9115, Fargo ND 58106
(701) 277-1515; *Fax:* (701) 277-1830
Ownership: Curtis Squire Inc., 100%. Myron Kunin owns 100% of Curtis Squire Inc.

TV Stns: 6 TV.
KDLT-TV Sioux Falls, SD; KDLV-TV Mitchell, SD; KJRR Jamestown, ND; KNRR Pembina, ND; KQDS-TV Duluth, MN; KVRR Fargo, ND

Ro Grignon, President
Kathy Lau, VP/General Manager

Reiten Television Inc.
Box 1686, Minot ND 58702-1686
(701) 852-2104; *Fax:* (701) 838-9360
www.kxmc.com
dreiten@kxnet.com

TV Stns: 4 TV.
KXMA-TV Dickinson, ND; KXMB-TV Bismarck, ND; KXMC-TV Minot, ND; KXMD-TV Williston, ND

David Reiten, Chairman

RNC MEDIA Inc.
1 Place Ville Marie, Suite 1523, Montréal QC H3B 2B5
(514) 866-8686; *Fax:* (514) 866-8056
www.rncmedia.ca
info@rncmedia.ca
Ownership: Groupe Radio Nord Inc., 100%.

TV Stns: 5 TV.
CFGS-DT Gatineau, QC; CFVS-DT Val-d'Or, QC; CHOT-DT Gatineau, QC; CKRN-DT Rouyn-Noranda, QC; CFEM-DT Rouyn-Noranda, QC

Radio Stns: 11 FM.
CHOA-FM Rouyn-Noranda, QC; CHPR-FM Hawkesbury, ON; CJLA-FM Lachute, QC; CHXX-FM Donnacona, QC; CHGO-FM Val d'Or, QC; CHLX-FM Gatineau, QC; CKVM-FM Ville-Marie, QC; CKLX-FM Montréal, QC; CFTX-FM Gatineau, QC; CHOI-FM Quebec, QC; CJGO-FM La Sarre, QC

Pierre R. Brosseau, Executive Chairman
Raynald BriŠre, Executive Vice President
Robert Ranger, VP Operations, Finance & Administration

Rockfleet Broadcasting Inc.

575 Madison Ave., 10th Fl., New York NY 10022
(212) 605-0401,; *Fax:* (212) 605-0402,
Ownership: Rockfleet Holdings, 100%.

TV Stns: 2 TV.
WJFW-TV Rhinelander, WI; WVII-TV Bangor, ME
R. Joseph Fuchs, President/CEO

Rogers Media

1 Ted Rogers Way, Toronto ON M4Y 3B7
(416) 935-8200; *Fax:* (416) 864-2002
www.rogersmedia.com
lvelazquez@impulsemediasales.com
Ownership: Rogers Media Inc., 100%. Note: Rogers Media Inc. is 100% owned by Rogers Communications Inc.

TV Stns: 11 TV.
CFMT-DT Toronto, ON; CHMI-DT Portage la Prairie, MB; CITY-DT Toronto, ON; CJNT-DT Montréal, QC; CKAL-DT Calgary, AB; CKEM-DT Edmonton, AB; CKVU-DT Vancouver, BC; CJMT-DT Toronto, ON; CHNM-DT Vancouver, BC; CJEO-DT Edmonton, AB; CJCO-DT Calgary, AB

Radio Stns: 8 AM. 48 FM.
CFAC Calgary, AB; CFFR Calgary, AB; CFTR Toronto, ON; CIWW Ottawa, ON; CJCL Toronto, ON; CKAT North Bay, ON; CKGL Kitchener, ON; CKWX Vancouver, BC; CFLT-FM Dartmouth, NS; CFGP-FM Grande Prairie, AB; CKBY-FM Smiths Falls, ON; CFRV-FM Lethbridge, AB; CKSR-FM Chilliwack, BC; CHAS-FM Sault Ste. Marie, ON; CHEZ-FM Ottawa, ON; CHFI-FM Toronto, ON; CHFM-FM Calgary, AB; CHUR-FM North Bay, ON; CHYM-FM Kitchener, ON; CIOC-FM Victoria, BC; CIPN-FM Pender Harbour, BC; CISC-FM Gibsons, BC; CKKS-FM Chilliwack, BC; CISP-FM Pemberton, BC; CISQ-FM Squamish, BC; CJAQ-FM Calgary, AB; CISW-FM Whistler, BC; CITI-FM Winnipeg, MB; CHMN-FM Canmore, AB; CJMX-FM Sudbury, ON; CJQM-FM Sault Ste. Marie, ON; CJQQ-FM Timmins, ON; CJRQ-FM Sudbury, ON; CISS-FM Ottawa, ON; CKER-FM Edmonton, AB; CKFX-FM North Bay, ON; CKIS-FM Toronto, ON; CJAX-FM Vancouver, BC; CHTT-FM Victoria, BC; CFUN-FM Sechelt, BC; CKYX-FM Fort McMurray, AB; CJOK-FM Fort McMurray, AB; CHST-FM London, ON; CJET-FM Smiths Falls, ON; CJRX-FM Lethbridge, AB; CFSR-FM Hope, BC; CIKR-FM Kingston, ON; CKGB-FM Timmins, ON; CKQC-FM Abbotsford, BC; CKY-FM Winnipeg, MB; CIKZ-FM Kitchener, ON; CHDI-FM Edmonton, AB; CHBN-FM Edmonton, AB; CJNI-FM Halifax, NS; CKXC-FM Kingston, ON; CKMH-FM Medicine Hat, AB
Alan Horn, Chairman
Joe Natale, President & CEO
Derek Berghuis, General Management, Operations, Sales

Saga Communications Inc.

73 Kercheval Ave., Suite 201, Grosse Pointe Farms MI 48236
(313) 886-7070; *Fax:* (313) 886-7150
sagacom.com
Ownership: Edward K. Christian, 56.5% of the voting stock.
Other Interests: Illinois Radio Network, Michigan Radio Network, Michigan Farm Radio Network.

TV Stns: 2 TV.
KAVU-TV Victoria, TX; KOAM-TV Pittsburg, KS

Radio Stns: 28 AM. 60 FM.
KGMI Bellingham, WA; KICD Spencer, IA; KBAI Bellingham, WA; KPUG Bellingham, WA; KRNT Des Moines, IA; KPSZ Des Moines, IA; WLFZ Fort Campbell, KY; WBAE Portland, ME; WBCO Bucyrus, OH; WKFN Clarksville, TN; WFEA Manchester, NH; WGAN Portland, ME; WHMQ Greenfield, MA; WHCU Ithaca, NY; WHMP Northampton, MA; WGIN Biddeford, ME; WINA Charlottesville, VA; WJOI Norfolk, VA; WJYI Milwaukee, WI; WZBK Keene, NH; WKBK Keene, NH; WKVT Brattleboro, VT; WHNP East Longmeadow, MA; WTAX Springfield, IL; WNYY Ithaca, NY; WYSE Canton, NC; WZAN Portland, ME; WVAX Charlottesville, VA; KAZR Pella, IA; KEGI Jonesboro, AR; KDXY Lake City, AR; KUQL Ethan, SD; KICD-FM Spencer, IA; KLLT Spencer, IA; KIOA Des Moines, IA; KISM Bellingham, WA; KJBX Cash, AR; KLTI-FM Ames, IA; KMIT Mitchell, SD; KSTZ Des Moines, IA; WAFX Suffolk, VA; WAQY Springfield, MA; WCNR Keswick, VA; WCLZ North Yarmouth, ME; WTMT Weaverville, NC; WCVQ Fort Campbell, KY; WEGI-FM Oak Grove, KY; WDBR Springfield, IL; WFIZ Odessa, NY; WJMR-FM Menomonee Falls, WI; WHAI Greenfield, MA; WLZX Northampton, MA; WYXY(FM) Danville, IL; WIII Cortland, NY; WSNI Keene, NH; WIXY Champaign, IL; WNND Pickerington, OH; WCFF Urbana, IL; WKLH Milwaukee, WI; WKNE Keene, NH; WKVT-FM Brattleboro, VT; WLRW Champaign, IL; WHQG Milwaukee, WI; WMGX Portland, ME; WNOR Norfolk, VA; WPOR Portland, ME; WRSI Turners Falls, MA; WQEL Bucyrus, OH; WMLL Bedford, NH; WQMZ Charlottesville, VA; WQNY Ithaca, NY; WLFZ-FM Springfield, IL; WPVQ Greenfield, MA; WSIG Mount Jackson, VA; WSNY Columbus, OH; WRSY Marlboro, VT; WVVR Hopkinsville, KY; WWWV Charlottesville, VA; WINQ Winchester, NH; WVMX Westerville, OH; WYMG Chatham, IL; WYNZ South Portland, ME; WYXL Ithaca, NY; WQQL Sherman, IL; WZID Manchester, NH; WNNP Richwood, OH; WZZP Hopkinsville, KY; WOXL-FM Biltmore Forest, NC
Edward Christian, President/CEO
Warren Lada, EVP, Operations
Bob Lawrence, VP, Programming
Tom Atkins, Engineering Dir

Sander Media LLC

28150 North Alma School Pkwy., Suite 103, Scottsdale AZ 85262

TV Stns: 3 TV.
KGW Portland, OR; KMSB Tucson, AZ; WHAS-TV Louisville, KY
Jack Sander, Manager

Sarkes Tarzian Inc.

Box 62, Bloomington IN 47402
(812) 332-7251; *Fax:* (812) 331-4575
Ownership: Tom Tarzian; Gray Television Inc.

TV Stns: 2 TV.
KTVN Reno, NV; WRCB-DT Chattanooga, TN

Radio Stns: 1 AM. 3 FM.
WGCL Bloomington, IN; WAJI Fort Wayne, IN; WLDE Fort Wayne, IN; WTTS Bloomington, IN
Tom Tarzian, Chairman
Bob Davis, CFO
Geoff Vargo, President, Radio
Tom Tolar, President, TV

Schurz Communications Inc.

225 W. Colfax Ave., South Bend IN 46626
(574) 287-1001; *Fax:* (574) 287-2257
www.schurz.com
mburdick@schurz.com
Ownership: Franklin D. Schurz Jr., James M. Schurz, Scott C. Schurz and Mary Schurz, trustees.

TV Stns: 6 TV.
KTUU-TV Anchorage, AK; KSCW-DT Wichita, KS; KYTV Springfield, MO; WAGT Augusta, GA; WDBJ Roanoke, VA; WSBT-TV South Bend, IN

Radio Stns: 2 AM. 5 FM.
KBHB Sturgis, SD; WASK Lafayette, IN; KFXS Rapid City, SD; KRCS Sturgis, SD; WASK-FM Battle Ground, IN; WKOA Lafayette, IN; WXXB Delphi, IN
Franklin Schurz Jr., Chairman
Todd Schurz, President
Marcia Burdick, SVP Broadcasting

Sinclair Broadcast Group Inc.

10706 Beaver Dam Rd., Hunt Valley MD 21030
(410) 568-1500
www.sbgi.net
Ownership: David D. Smith; Frederick G. Smith; J. Duncan Smith; Robert E. Smith (major shareholders).

TV Stns: 113 TV.
KAAS-TV Salina, KS; KABB San Antonio, TX; KATU Portland, OR; KATV Little Rock, AR; KBAK-TV Bakersfield, CA; KBOI-TV Boise, ID; KOCW Hoisington, KS; KUNS-TV Bellevue, WA; KUNP La Grande, OR; KBSI Cape Girardeau, MO; KCBY-TV Coos Bay, OR; KDBC-TV El Paso, TX; KDNL-TV St. Louis, MO; KDSM-TV Des Moines, IA; KEPR-TV Pasco, WA; KEYE-TV Austin, TX; KVCW Las Vegas, NV; KFDM Beaumont, TX; KFOX-TV El Paso, TX; KGAN Cedar Rapids, IA; KGBT-TV Harlingen, TX; KHQA-TV Hannibal, MO; KIMA-TV Yakima, WA; KLEW-TV Lewiston, ID; WOAI-TV San Antonio, TX; KMPH-TV Visalia, CA; KFRE-TV Sanger, CA; WUCW Minneapolis, MN; KOCB Oklahoma City, OK; KOKH-TV Oklahoma City, OK; KOMO-TV Seattle, WA; KPIC Roseburg, OR; KPTH Sioux City, IA; KPTM Omaha, NE; KRCG Jefferson City, MO; KRXI-TV Reno, NV; KSAS-TV Wichita, KS; KTUL Tulsa, OK; KTVL Medford, OR; KTVO Kirksville, MO; KMYU St. George, UT; KUTV Salt Lake City, UT; KVAL-TV Eugene, OR; KSNV-DT Las Vegas, NV; KVIH-TV Clovis, NM; KVII-TV Amarillo, TX; WABM Birmingham, AL; WACH Columbia, SC; WBFF Baltimore, MD; WCGV-TV Milwaukee, WI; WCHS-TV Charleston, WV; WCIV Charleston, SC; WPNT Pittsburgh, PA; WDKY-TV Danville, KY; WEAR-TV Pensacola, FL; WFGX Fort Walton Beach, FL; WFXL Albany, GA; WGME-TV Portland, ME; WGXA Macon, GA; WHOI Peoria, IL; WHP-TV Harrisburg, PA; WICD Champaign, IL; WCWF Suring, WI; WJAC-TV Johnstown, PA; WJAR Providence, RI; WJLA-TV Washington, DC; WKEF Dayton, OH; WKRC-TV Cincinnati, OH; WLFL Raleigh, NC; WLOS Asheville, NC; WLUC-TV Marquette, MI; WLUK-TV Green Bay, WI; WCWN Schenectady, NY; WMSN-TV Madison, WI; WNWO-TV Toledo, OH; WNYO-TV Buffalo, NY; WPBN-TV Traverse City, MI; WPDE-TV Florence, SC; WPEC West Palm Beach, FL; WPGH-TV Pittsburgh, PA; WRDC Durham, NC; WRGB Schenectady, NY; WRLH-TV Richmond, VA; WSET-TV Lynchburg, VA; WSMH Flint, MI; WSTM-TV Syracuse, NY; WSYX Columbus, OH; WTGS Hardeeville, SC; WTOM-TV Cheboygan, MI; WTOV-TV Steubenville, OH; WTTO Homewood, AL; WTVC Chattanooga, TN; WTVX Fort Pierce, FL; WTVZ-TV Norfolk, VA; WTWC-TV Tallahassee, FL; WUHF Rochester, NY; WMYV Greensboro, NC; WUTV Buffalo, NY; WUXP-TV Nashville, TN; WVTV Milwaukee, WI; WWMT Kalamazoo, MI; WXLV-TV Winston-Salem, NC; WZTV Nashville, TN; WBMA-LD Birmingham, AL; KBFX-CD Bakersfield, CA; WTCN-CA West Palm Beach, FL; WWHB-CA West Palm Beach, FL; KYUU-LD Boise, ID; WICS Springfield, IL; WSTQ-LP Syracuse, NY; KUNW-CD Yakima, WA; KVVK-CD Kennewick, WA; KORX-CA Walla Walla, WA
David D. Smith, President, CEO & Chairman of the Board
Frederick G. Smith, Vice President
J. Duncan Smith, Vice President, Secretary and Director
Robert E. Smith, Director
Howard E. Friedman, Director
Martin R. Leader, Director

Smith Media License Holdings LLC

1215 Cole St., St. Louis MO 63106
(314) 853-7736
Ownership: Smith Media LLC, 100%.

TV Stns: 3 TV.
KATN Fairbanks, AK; KYUR Anchorage, AK; KJUD Juneau, AK

SomosTV

2601 S. Bayshore Dr., Suite 1250, Miami FL 33133
(786) 220-0280; *Fax:* (305) 858-7188
www.somostv.net
Ownership: SomosTV LLC., 100%.

TV Stns: 2 TV.
VIENDOMOVIES Miami, FL; SEMILLITAS Miami, FL
Luis Villanueva, President & CEO

Southern Broadcast Corp. of Sarasota

1477 10th St., Sarasota FL 34236
(941) 923-8840; *Fax:* (941) 924-3971

TV Stns: 3 TV.
WAAY-TV Huntsville, AL; WTXL-TV Tallahassee, FL; WWSB Sarasota, FL

Spanish Broadcasting System Inc.

2601 South Bayshore Dr., PH 2, Coconut Grove FL 33133
(305) 441-6901; *Fax:* (305) 446-5148
www.spanishbroadcasting.com
Ownership: Raul Alarcon Jr., Jose Grimalt.

TV Stns: 1 TV.
WSBS-TV Key West, FL

Radio Stns: 20 FM.
KXOL-FM Los Angeles, CA; KLAX-FM East Los Angeles, CA; KRZZ San Francisco, CA; WCMQ-FM Hialeah, FL; WODA Bayamon, PR; WEGM San German, PR; WRXD Fajardo, PR; WZET Hormigueros, PR; WIOA San Juan, PR; WIOB Mayaguez, PR; WIOC Ponce, PR; WLEY-FM Aurora, IL; WMEG Guayama, PR; WNOD Mayaguez, PR; WPAT-FM Paterson, NJ; WRMA Fort Lauderdale, FL; WSKQ-FM New York, NY; WXDJ North Miami Beach, FL; WZMT Ponce, PR; WZNT San Juan, PR
Jose Grimalt, EVP
Raul Alarcon, President/CEO

Sunbeam Television Corp.

1401 79th St. Causeway, North Bay Village FL 33141
(305) 751-6692; *Fax:* (305) 795-2715
Ownership: Edmund N. Ansin, 83.09% votes, 80.15% assets; James L. Ansin, 6.3% votes, 7.06% assets; Andrew L. Ansin, 6.3% votes, 7.06% assets; and Andrew L. Ansin, James L. Ansin andStephanie L. Ansin (as trustees for Stephanie L. Ansin), 4.31% votes, 5.73% assets.

TV Stns: 3 TV.
WHDH Boston, MA; WLVI Cambridge, MA; WSVN Miami, FL
Edmund Ansin, President
Deisy Bermudez, Programming Director

Surtsey Media LLC

73 Kercheval Ave., Suite 100, Grosse Pointe Farms MI 48236
(313) 884-7878

TV Stns: 2 TV.
KVCT Victoria, TX; KFJX-DT Pittsburg, KS

Tanana Valley Television Co.

3650 Braddock Street, Suite 2, Fairbanks AK 99701
(907) 452-3697; *Fax:* (907) 456-3428
Ownership: William St. Pierre, 85%.

TV Stns: 1 TV.
KFXF Fairbanks, AK

Radio Stns: 2 FM.

KYSC Fairbanks, AK; KDJF Ester, AK

Tegna Media
7950 Jones Branch Dr., McLean VA 22107-0150
(703) 854-7000
www.tegna.com
Ownership: Tegna Inc., 100%.
TV Stns: 43 TV.
KARE Minneapolis, MN; KBMT Beaumont, TX; KCEN-TV Temple, TX; KENS San Antonio, TX; KHOU Houston, TX; KIDY San Angelo, TX; KIII-TV Corpus Christi, TX; KING-TV Seattle, WA; KYTX Nacogdoches, TX; KNAZ-TV Flagstaff, AZ; KONG Everett, WA; KPNX Mesa, AZ; KREM Spokane, WA; KSDK St. Louis, MO; KSKN Spokane, WA; KTHV Little Rock, AR; KTVB Boise, ID; KTVD Denver, CO; KUSA Denver, CO; KVUE Austin, TX; KXTV Sacramento, CA; WATL Atlanta, GA; WBIR-TV Knoxville, TN; WCNC-TV Charlotte, NC; WCSH Portland, ME; WFAA Dallas, TX; WFMY-TV Greensboro, NC; WGRZ Buffalo, NY; WJXX Orange Park, FL; WKYC Cleveland, OH; WLBZ Bangor, ME; WLTX Columbia, SC; WMAZ-TV Macon, GA; WTLV Jacksonville, FL; WTSP St. Petersburg, FL; WUPL Slidell, LA; WUSA Washington, DC; WVEC Hampton, VA; WWL-TV New Orleans, LA; WXIA-TV Atlanta, GA; WZZM Grand Rapids, MI; KXVA Abilene, TX; KAGS-LD Bryan, TX
Gracia C. Martore, President & CEO
Dave Lougee, President, TEGNA Media
William Behan, Senior Vice President, Labor Relations
Victoria D. Harker, Chief Financial Officer
Kevin Lord, Chief Human Resources Officer

Tele Inter-Rives Lt,e
15, rue de la Chute, RiviŠre-du-Loup QC G5R 5B7
(418) 867-1341; *Fax:* (418) 867-4710
www.teleinterrives.com
nousjoindre@cimt.ca
Ownership: 101885 Canada lt,e., 55.34%; TVA Groupe Inc., 44.66% (See Listing); Marc Simard, 0.97%.
TV Stns: 4 TV.
CHAU-DT Carleton-sur-Mer, QC; CIMT-DT RiviŠre-du-Loup, QC; CKRT-DT RiviŠre-du-Loup, QC; CFTF-DT Rivi,re-du-Loup, QC
Marc Simard, President
Steven Simard, Operations Dir
Cindy Simard, Vice-Chair, Information

Telemundo Station Group
2290 W. 8th Ave., Hialeah FL 33010
(305) 884-8200; *Fax:* (305) 889-7950
www.telemundo.com
Ownership: NBCUniversal
TV Stns: 17 TV.
KBLR Paradise, NV; KDEN Longmont, CO; KHRR Tucson, AZ; KNSO Merced, CA; KSTS San Jose, CA; KTLM Harlingen, TX; KTMD Galveston, TX; KVDA San Antonio, TX; KVEA Corona, CA; KXTX Dallas, TX; WWSI Atlantic City, NJ; WKAQ San Juan, PR; WNJU Linden, NJ; WNEU Merrimack, NH; WSCV Fort Lauderdale, FL; WSNS Chicago, IL; KTAZ Phoenix, AZ

The Curators of the University of Missouri
University of Missouri, 316 University Hall, Columbia MO 65211
(573) 882-2388; *Fax:* (573) 882-0010
www.umsystem.edu
Ownership: (Business Services Division).
TV Stns: 1 TV.
KOMU-TV Columbia, MO
Radio Stns: 7 FM.
KBIA Columbia, MO; KCUR-FM Kansas City, MO; KMNR Rolla, MO; KMST Rolla, MO; KWMU St. Louis, MO; KAUD Mexico, MO; KCIU Columbia, MO
Michael Dunn, General Manager
Martin Siddall, General Manager

The E.W. Scripps Co.
Box 5380, 312 Walnut St., 28th Fl., Cincinnati OH 45202
(513) 977-3000; *Fax:* (513) 977-3728
www.scripps.com
Ownership: The E.W. Scripps Co.
TV Stns: 10 TV.
KJRH-TV Tulsa, OK; KMCI-TV Lawrence, KS; KNXV-TV Phoenix, AZ; KSHB-TV Kansas City, MO; WCPO-TV Cincinnati, OH; WEWS-TV Cleveland, OH; WFTS-TV Tampa, FL; WMAR-TV Baltimore, MD; WPTV-TV West Palm Beach, FL; WXYZ-TV Detroit, MI
Brian G. Lawlor, SVP, Television, The E.W. Scripps Co.

The Jim Pattison Broadcast Group
460 Pemberton Terrace, Kamloops BC V2C 1T5
(250) 372-3322; *Fax:* (250) 374-0445
www.jpbroadcast.com
info@jpbg.ca
Ownership: James A. Pattison, 100%.
TV Stns: 3 TV.
CFJC-TV Kamloops, BC; CHAT-TV Medicine Hat, AB; CKPG-TV Prince George, BC
Radio Stns: 2 AM. 41 FM.
CJNB North Battleford, SK; CKBI Prince Albert, SK; CFMM-FM Prince Albert, SK; CFMY-FM Medicine Hat, AB; CFQX-FM Selkirk, MB; CHIQ-FM Winnipeg, MB; CHLB-FM Lethbridge, AB; CIBW-FM Drayton Valley, AB; CIFM-FM Kamloops, BC; CJJR-FM Vancouver, BC; CKKN-FM Prince George, BC; CKKQ-FM Victoria, BC; CHBZ-FM Cranbrook, BC; CKLR-FM Courtenay, BC; CKLZ-FM Kelowna, BC; CKWV-FM Nanaimo, BC; CJBZ-FM Taber, AB; CHUB-FM Red Deer, AB; CJXX-FM Grande Prairie, AB; CHBW-FM Rocky Mountain House, AB; CJZN-FM Victoria, BC; CHWF-FM Nanaimo, BC; CIBH-FM Parksville, BC; CKBZ-FM Kamloops, BC; CHQX-FM Prince Albert, SK; CKIZ-FM Vernon, BC; CJDR-FM Fernie, BC; CHDR-FM Cranbrook, BC; CKDV-FM Prince George, BC; CFDV-FM Red Deer, AB; CJNS-FM Meadow Lake, SK; CJAV-FM Port Alberni, BC; CHPQ-FM Parksville, BC; CHAT-FM Medicine Hat, AB; CIUP-FM Edmonton, AB; CKCE-FM Calgary, AB; CKQQ-FM Kelowna, BC; CIKT-FM Grande Prairie, AB; CKPK-FM Vancouver, BC; CJHD-FM North Battleford, SK; CKNO-FM Edmonton, AB; CHPK-FM Calgary, AB; CJCQ-FM North Battleford, SK
Rod Schween, President & General Manager
Vanessa Ong, Executive Assistant
Mark Rogers, Vice President, Sales
Ross Winters, Programming Director
Bill Stovold, IT & Engineering Director
Bill Dinicol, Vice President, Finance
Andrew Snook, Digital Director

The Victory Television Network
Box 26207, Little Rock AR 72221
(501) 223-2525
www.vtntv.com
Ownership: Agape Church Inc.
TV Stns: 3 TV.
KVTH-DT Hot Springs, AR; KVTJ-DT Jonesboro, AR; KVTN-DT Pine Bluff, AR
Happy Caldwell, President
Jim Grant, General Manager

Tri-State Christian Television
Box 1010, Marion IL 62959
(618) 997-9333; *Fax:* (618) 997-1859
www.tct.tv
Ownership: Nonprofit corporation. LPTV: WDWO-CA Detroit, MI; and WDYR-CA Dyersburg, TN.
TV Stns: 5 TV.
WINM Angola, IN; WLXI Greensboro, NC; WNYB Jamestown, NY; WTCT Marion, IL; WTLJ Muskegon, MI
Garth Coonce, President
Shane Chaney, CFO

Tribune Broadcasting Co.
435 N. Michigan Ave., Suite 1800, Chicago IL 60611
(312) 222-3333; *Fax:* (312) 329-0611
www.tribune.com
Ownership: The Tribune Employee Stock Ownership Plan as implemented through the Tribune Employee Stock Ownership Trust, Oak Brook, IL, 100%.
TV Stns: 40 TV.
KAUT Oklahoma City, OK; KCPQ Tacoma, WA; KDAF Dallas, TX; KDVR Denver, CO; KFOR Oklahoma City, OK; KFSM Fort Smith, AR; KIAH Houston, TX; KPLR St. Louis, MO; KSTU Salt Lake City, UT; KSWB San Diego, CA; KTLA Los Angeles, CA; KTVI St. Louis, MO; KZJO Seattle, WA; KTXL Sacramento, CA; KRCW Salem, OR; KXNW Eureka Springs, AR; KWGN Denver, CO; WDCW Washington, DC; WSFL Miami, FL; WDAF Kansas City, MO; WGHP High Point, NC; WGN Chicago, IL; WGNO New Orleans, LA; WHNT Huntsville, AL; WHO-DT Des Moines, IA; WITI Milwaukee, WI; WJW Cleveland, OH; WNOL New Orleans, LA; WPHL Philadelphia, PA; WPIX New York, NY; WPMT York, PA; WQAD Moline, IL; WREG-TV Memphis, TN; WTIC-TV Hartford, CT; WTTK Kokomo, IN; WTTV Bloomington, IN; WTVR Richmond, VA; WCCT Waterbury, CT; WXIN Indianapolis, IN; WXMI Battle Creek, MI
Radio Stns: 1 AM.
WGN(AM) Chicago, IL
Larry Wert, President of Broadcast Media

Trinity Broadcasting Network
P.O. Box A, Santa Ana CA 92711
(714) 731-1000
www.tbn.org
Ownership: Nonprofit corporation.
TV Stns: 26 TV.
KAAH-TV Honolulu, HI; KDOR-TV Bartlesville, OK; KDTX-TV Dallas, TX; KNAT-TV Albuquerque, NM; KPAZ-TV Phoenix, AZ; KTAJ-TV St. Joseph, MO; KTBN-TV Santa Ana, CA; KTBO-TV Oklahoma City, OK; KTBW-TV Tacoma, WA; WBUY-TV Holly Springs, MS; WCLJ-TV Bloomington, IN; WDLI-TV Canton, OH; WELF-TV Dalton, GA; WGTW-TV Burlington, NJ; WHFT-TV Miami, FL; WHSG-TV Monroe, GA; WKOI-TV Richmond, IN; WMCF-TV Montgomery, AL; WMPV-TV Mobile, AL; WPGD-TV Hendersonville, TN; WSFJ-TV Newark, OH; WTBY-TV Poughkeepsie, NY; WTJP-TV Gadsden, AL; WWTO-TV La Salle, IL; WRBJ-TV Magee, MS; KPJR-DT Greeley, CO
Paul Crouch, President
Ben Miller, VP Engineering
Janice Crouch, VP Programming
Rod Henke, VP Sales

TVA Group Inc.
1600 Boul de Maisonneuve E, Montréal QC H2L 4P2
(514) 526-9251
groupetva.ca
Ownership: Quebecor Media Inc., 99.97%; public Can, 0.03%.
TV Stns: 6 TV.
CFCM-DT Quebec City, QC; CFER-TV Rimouski, QC; CFTM-DT Montréal, QC; CHEM-DT Trois-Rivieres, QC; CHLT-DT Sherbrooke, QC; CJPM-DT Saguenay, QC
France LauziŠre, President & CEO
Denis Rozon, Vice-President & Chief Financial Officer
Martin Picard, Vice-President, Chief Content Officer
Donald Lizotte, Executive Vice-President, Advertising
Serge Fortin, Vice-President, TVA News
Daniel Boudreau, Vice-President, Information Technology

T,l,-Qu,bec
1000, rue Fullum, Montréal QC H2K 3L7
(514) 521-2424; *Fax:* (514) 873-7464
www.telequebec.tv
info@telequebec.tv
Ownership: Government of Quebec.
TV Stns: 17 TV.
CIVB-DT Rimouski, QC; CIVC-DT Trois Rivieres, QC; CIVF-DT Baie-Trinite, QC; CIVG-DT Sept-Iles, QC; CIVM-DT Montréal, QC; CIVP-DT Chapeau, QC; CIVQ-DT Quebec, QC; CIVS-DT Sherbrooke, QC; CIVV-DT Saguenay, QC; CIVO-DT Gatineau, QC; CIVK-DT Carleton-sur-Mer, QC; CIVK-DT-1 Gascons, QC; CIVK-DT-2 Perce, QC; CIVK-DT-3 Gaspe, QC; CIVB-DT-1 Grand-Fonds, QC; CIVA-DT Val d'Or, QC; CIVA-DT-1 Rouyn-Noranda, QC
Marie Collin, President & CEO
Marie-Pier Mailhot, General Sales Mgr
Virginie Langlois, Programming Officer
Patrice Guay, Technology Manager
Nathalie Blais, Legal Affairs Director

United Communications Corp.
5800 7th Ave., Kenosha WI 53140
(262) 657-1000; *Fax:* (262) 657-6226
www.kenoshanews.com
Ownership: Howard J. Brown, Lucy Brown Minn, Sarah Brown Russ, Amy Brown Tuchler. Note: Group also owns LPTV stn WNYF-CA Watertown, NY.
TV Stns: 2 TV.
KEYC-TV CBS & NEYC FOX Mankato, MN; WWNY-TV Carthage, NY
Howard Brown, President
Kenneth Dowdell, Vice President
Ronald Montemurro, Vice President

Univision Communications Inc.
605 3rd Ave., 12th Fl., New York NY 10158
(212) 455-5200
www.univision.com
Ownership: Broadcasting Media Partners Inc.
TV Stns: 42 TV.
KTFQ-DT Albuquerque, NM; KFTU-DT Douglas, AZ; KFPH-DT Flagstaff, AZ; KDTV-DT San Francisco, CA; KFTV-DT Hanford, CA; KFTR-DT Ontario, CA; KFTH-DT Alvin, TX; KMEX-DT Los Angeles, CA; KFSF-DT Vallejo, CA; KTFF-DT Porterville, CA; KUVI-DT Bakersfield, CA; KUVN-DT Garland, TX; KUVS-DT Modesto, CA; KWEX-DT San Antonio, TX; WFTT-DT Tampa, FL; WOTF-TV Melbourne, FL; WXFT-DT Aurora, IL; WUVG-DT Athens, GA; WFUT-DT Newark, NJ; WUTF-DT Marlborough, MA; WFTY-DT Smithtown, NY; WUVP-DT Vineland, NJ; WUVC-DT Fayetteville, NC; WLTV-DT Miami, FL; WQHS-DT Cleveland, OH; WSTE-DT Ponce, PR; WFDC-DT Arlington, VA; WXTV-DT Paterson, NJ; KUTH-DT Provo, UT; WLII-DT Caguas, PR; WSUR-DT Ponce, PR; KNIC-DT Blanco, TX; KTVW-DT Phoenix, AZ; KXLN-DT Rosenberg, TX; KUVE-DT Green Valley, AZ; KSTR-DT Irving, TX; KAKW-DT Killeen, TX; KTFK-DT Stockton, CA; WGBO-DT Joliet, IL; WAMI-DT Hollywood, FL; KDVT-LP Denver, CO; KTFD-TV Denver, CO
Randy Falco, President & CEO
Tonia O'Connor, President, Content Distribution
Alberto Ciurana, President, Programming and Content

Keith Turner, President of Advertising Sales and Marketing
Isaac Lee, President, Univision News and Digital
Kevin Cuddihy, President, Local Media

V Media Group Inc.
355 Sainte-Catherine O., Bureau 100, Montréal QC H3A 1A5
www.grouperemstar.ca
Ownership: Remstar Group Inc, 45.14%; Fiducie Seismikmax, 9.86%; Investissment Quebec, 15%; F.T.Q., 15%; Caisse de Depot et de Placement du Quebec, 15%.
TV Stns: 5 TV.
CFAP-DT Quebec City, QC; CFJP-DT Montréal, QC; CFKM-DT Trois Rivieres, QC; CFKS-DT Sherbrooke, QC; CFRS-DT Saguenay, QC
Maxime R,millard, Co-President & CEO
Julien R,millard, Co-President

Vaughan Media LLC
c/o Vaughan Acquisition LLC, 14429 Bridgeview Land, Port Charlotte FL 33953
(217) 521-3702; *Fax:* (941) 764-6867
Ownership: Thomas J. Vaughan, 100%.
TV Stns: 3 TV.
KTKA-TV Topeka, KS; WBDT Springfield, OH; WYTV Youngstown, OH
Thomas J. Vaughan, Manager

VCY America Inc.
3434 W. Kilbourn Ave., Milwaukee WI 53208
(414) 935-3000; *Fax:* (414) 935-3015
www.vcyamerica.org
vcy@vcyamerica.org
Ownership: VCY America, Inc.
TV Stns: 1 TV.
WVCY-TV Milwaukee, WI
Radio Stns: 1 AM. 18 FM.
WVCY Oshkosh, WI; KCVS Salina, KS; KVCX Gregory, SD; KVCY Fort Scott, KS; WVCN Baraga, MI; WEGZ Washburn, WI; WJIC Zanesville, OH; WVCF Eau Claire, WI; WVCX Tomah, WI; WVCY-FM Milwaukee, WI; WVCM Iron Mountain, MI; WVFL Fond Du Lac, WI; KVCF Freeman, SD; WVRN Wittenberg, WI; KVFL Pierre, SD; KVCS Spring Valley, MN; KVCH Huron, SD; WQRN Cook, MN; WVCS Owen, WI
Vic Eliason, VP/Gen Mgr
Jim Schneider, Programming Director

Waterman Broadcasting Corp.
Box 7578, Fort Myers FL 33911-7578
(239) 939-2020; *Fax:* (239) 939-7903
www.water.net
Ownership: Bernard Waterman, Edith Waterman.
TV Stns: 2 TV.
WBBH-TV Fort Myers, FL; WVIR-TV Charlottesville, VA
Bernard Waterman, President
Steve Pontius, EVP
Joe Ernest, VP

Weigel Broadcasting Co.
26 N. Halsted St., Chicago IL 60661
(312) 705-2600; *Fax:* (312) 705-2656
www.wciu.com
Ownership: Howard Shapiro Remainder Trust, 51% equity; Norman Shapiro Rem Children's Trust, 10% equity.
TV Stns: 3 TV.
WCIU-TV Chicago, IL; WDJT-TV Milwaukee, WI; WMLW-TV Racine, WI
Norman H. Shapiro, President
Norman Shapiro, President

West Virginia Media Holdings LLC
Box 11848, Charleston WV 25339-1848
(304) 720-6527; *Fax:* (304) 345-7280
TV Stns: 4 TV.
WBOY-TV Clarksburg, WV; WOWK-TV Huntington, WV; WTRF-TV Wheeling, WV; WVNS-TV Lewisburg, WV
Marty Becker, Chairman
Bray Cary, CEO

White Knight Broadcasting
4300 Richmond Rd., Tyler TX 75703
(903) 236-0051
TV Stns: 4 TV.
KFXK-TV Longview, TX; KSHV-TV Shreveport, LA; WVLA-TV Baton Rouge, LA; KZUP-CD Baton Rouge, LA
Drew Balch, Operations Dir
Drew Balch, Programming Director

Wilderness Communications LLC
3501 Northwest Evangeline Thruway, Carencro LA 70520
(337) 896-1600; *Fax:* (337) 896-2695
TV Stns: 2 TV.
KBCA Alexandria, LA; KLWB New Iberia, LA
Radio Stns: 1 AM.
WROD Daytona Beach, FL

Withers Broadcasting Co.
Box 1508, Mount Vernon IL 62864
(618) 242-3500; *Fax:* (618) 242-4444
Ownership: W. Russell Withers Jr., 100%.
TV Stns: 2 TV.
WDTV Weston, WV; WVFX Clarksburg, WV
Radio Stns: 12 AM. 20 FM.
KAPE Cape Girardeau, MO; KOKX Keokuk, IA; KRHW Sikeston, MO; KJXX Jackson, MO; WEBQ Harrisburg, IL; WFRX West Frankfort, IL; WILY Centralia, IL; WMIX Mount Vernon, IL; WMOK Metropolis, IL; WQUL Woodruff, SC; WROY Carmi, IL; WSDR Sterling, IL; KBXB Sikeston, MO; KGMO Cape Girardeau, MO; KOKX-FM Keokuk, IA; KRNQ Keokuk, IA; WDDD-FM Johnston City, IL; WEBQ-FM Eldorado, IL; WGKY Wickliffe, KY; WKIB Anna, IL; WMIX-FM Mount Vernon, IL; WREZ Metropolis, IL; WRUL Carmi, IL; WRXX Centralia, IL; WSSQ Sterling, IL; WTAO-FM Herrin, IL; WYNG Mount Carmel, IL; WVZA Murphysboro, IL; WZZL Reidland, KY; WZZT Morrison, IL; WISH-FM Galatia, IL; WCEZ Carthage, IL
W. Russell Withers, President

Woods Communications Corp.
One WCOV Ave., Montgomery AL 36111
(334) 288-7020
www.wcov.com
TV Stns: 2 TV.
KLCW-TV Wolfforth, TX; WCOV-TV Montgomery, AL
David Woods, President

Word Broadcasting Network Inc.
Box 19229, Louisville KY 40259
(502) 964-3304; *Fax:* (502) 966-9692
www.wbna21.com
TV Stns: 1 TV.
WBNA Louisville, KY
Radio Stns: 3 AM.
WYRM Norfolk, VA; WYMM Jacksonville, FL; WVHI Evansville, IN
Bob Rogers, President
Greg Holt, Operations Dir

Wyomedia Corp.
1856 Skyview Dr., Casper WY 82601
(307) 577-5923; *Fax:* (307) 234-4005
TV Stns: 1 TV.
KLWY Cheyenne, WY
Marvin Gussman, Chairman

Yes TV
1295 N Service Rd., Burlington ON L7R 4X5
(905) 331-7333; *Fax:* (905) 332-7481
www.yestv.com
contactus@yestv.com
Ownership: Crossroads Christian Communications
TV Stns: 3 TV.
CITS-TV Hamilton, ON; CKCS-TV Calgary, AB; CKES-TV Edmonton, AB
Lorna Dueck, CEO
Rob Sheppard, General Manager
Glenn Stewart, Sales Director

Young Broadcasting Inc.
599 Lexington Ave., 47th Fl., New York NY 10022
(212) 754-7070; *Fax:* (212) 758-1229
Ownership: Vincent J. Young, Gabelli Asset Management Inc., New South Capital Management Inc.
TV Stns: 14 TV.
KCLO-TV Rapid City, SD; KDLO-TV Florence, SD; KELO-TV Sioux Falls, SD; KLFY-TV Lafayette, LA; KPLO-TV Reliance, SD; KRON-TV San Francisco, CA; KWQC-TV Davenport, IA; WATE-TV Knoxville, TN; WBAY-TV Green Bay, WI; WCDC-TV Adams, MA; WKRN-TV Nashville, TN; WLNS-TV Lansing, MI; WRIC-TV Petersburg, VA; WTEN Albany, NY
Vincent Young, Chairman
Deborah McDermott, President
James Morgan, CFO/EVP

Zolo Media
63090 Sherman Rd., Bend OR 97703
(541) 749-5151; *Fax:* (866) 996-3232
www.zolomedia.com
info@zolomedia.com
Ownership: BendBroadband.
TV Stns: 2 TV.
KOHD Bend, OR; KBNZ-LD Bend, OR
Julie Brinks, General Manager

ZoomerMedia Ltd.
70 Jefferson Ave., Toronto ON M6K 3H4
(416) 367-5353
www.zoomermedia.ca
d.hamilton@mzmedia.com
Ownership: Olympus Management Limited, 61.77%; Fairfac Financial Holdings Limited, 16.47%; other Canadian Shareholders, 13.31%; MRHD Holdings Ltd., 8.12%; otherNon-Canadian shareholders, 0.30%; and Moses Znaimer, 0.02%.
TV Stns: 2 TV.
CIIT-DT Winnipeg, MB; CHNU-DT Fraser Valley, MB
Radio Stns: 1 AM. 3 FM.
CFZM Toronto, ON; CFMX-FM Cobourg, ON; CFMZ-FM Toronto, ON; CFMO-FM Collingwood, ON
Moses Znaimer, President & CEO
Laas Turnbull, Chief Operating Officer
Beverley Shenken, VP & General Manager, TV Division
Dan Hamilton, Broadcast Sales & General Manager, Radio
David Vickers, Chief Financial Officer
Omri Tintpulver, Chief Digital Officer

Key to TV Listings

Television listings include TV stations in the United States, its territories and Canada. To use the television key, see boldface numbers and corresponding explanations.

(1) WOF-TV-(2) Analog Channel: 17 Digital Channel:53 Analog hrs: 24 2,200 kw vis , 20 kw aur, ant 500t/300g. TL: N36 49 21 W108 47 32 (CP: Ant 750t/550g) **(3)**On air date: Apr 13, 1952.**(4)** Box 100, Dothan, AL 36301. Phone: (909) 555-1000 FAX: (909) 999-9999. Web Site www.wot.tv . **(5)** Licensee: WOF Broadcasting Co. **(6)** Group Owner: Acme Stations (acq 7-20-69; $2 million. **(6a)** FTR 7-29-69). **(7)** Population served: 230,000 **(8)** Natl. Network: CBS. **(9)** Natl. Rep: Jones, Tri-State. Washington Atty: Goltz & Stick. **(10)** News staff: 3; 10 hrs wkly. **(11) Key Personnel:**

Jud Jones .... Pres & Gen Mgr
D. Spark .... Chief Engineer

(1) Station call letters as assigned by the Federal Communications Commission (FCC) or Canadian Radio-television and Telecommunications Commission (CRTC)

(2) Analog channel and digital channels, hours of operation (analog and digital), power, antenna, location and construction permit. WOF-TV operates with 2,200 kilowatts (effective radiated power) visual and 20 kilowatts aural. Its antenna is 500 feet above average terrain and 300 feet above ground. N36 49 21 W108 47 32 refers to the geographical coordinates (latitude and longitude) of the transmitter location, WOF-TV holds a construction permit for an antenna height change to 750 feet above average terrain, 550 feet above ground.

(3) Date station first went on the air (regardless of subsequent ownership changes)

(4) Address and zip code, telephone and fax number, web site and e-mail address.

(5) Licensee name.

(6) Ownership and date of acquisition (if not original owner). If a station has been sold, any available sale information is listed following the acquisition date. WOF-TV is owned by Acme Stations.

(6a) FTR date refers to Broadcasting & Cable magazine's weekly "For the Record" column that appeared in the magazine until June 8, 1998, where station sales were recorded as received from the FCC.

(7) Population served refers to the station's potential market.

(8) Network programming. WOF-TV's national network is CBS.

(9) Representatives and Washington attorney. Sales representatives are listed with the national rep first, then regional.

(10) Number of staff providing local news and number of local news aired weekly.

(11) Key personnel.

An asterisk (*) preceding station call letters indicates noncommercial stations

DMA Cross Reference List

The following cities are in hyphenated markets, but are not the first city given in such a market; i.e., Troy in Albany-Schenectady-Troy, NY. They are listed alphabetically.

Ada, OK	See Sherman-Ada
Akron, OH	See Cleveland-Akron (Canton)
Altoona, PA	See Johnstown-Altoona
Ames, IA	See Des Moines-Ames
Anderson, SC	See Greenville-Spartanburg-Asheville-Anderson
Anniston, AL	See Birmingham (Anniston, Tuscaloosa)
Appleton, WI	See Green Bay-Appleton
Asheville, NC	See Greenville-Spartanburg-Asheville-Anderson
Auburn, ME	See Portland-Auburn
Austin, MN	See Rochester-Mason City-Austin
Battle Creek, MI	See Grand Rapids-Kalamazoo-Battle Creek
Bay City, MI	See Flint-Saginaw-Bay City
Beckley, WV	See Bluefield-Beckley-Oak Hill
Bismarck, ND	See Minot-Bismarck-Dickinson
Bloomington, IL	See Peoria-Bloomington
Bozeman, MT	See Butte-Bozeman
Brownsville, TX	See Harlingen-Weslaco-Brownsville-McAllen
Bryan, TX	See Waco-Temple-Bryan
Cadillac, MI	See Traverse City-Cadillac
Canton, OH	See Cleveland-Akron (Canton)
Cape Girardeau, MO	See Paducah-Cape Girardeau-Harrisburg-Mount Vernon
Daytona Beach, FL	See Orlando-Daytona Beach-Melbourne
Decatur, AL	See Huntsville-Decatur-Florence
Decatur, IL	See Champaign & Springfield-Decatur
Dickinson, ND	See Minot-Bismarck-Dickinson
Dubuque, IA	See Cedar Rapids-Waterloo-Iowa City & Dubuque
Durham, NC	See Raleigh-Durham
Eau Claire, WI	See La Crosse-Eau Claire
El Centro, CA	See Yuma-El Centro
El Dorado, AR	See Monroe-El Dorado
Elkhart, IN	See South Bend-Elkhart
Fayetteville, AR	See Ft. Smith-Fayetteville-Springdale-Rogers
Fayetteville, NC	See Raleigh-Durham (Fayetteville)
Florence, AL	See Huntsville-Decatur-Florence
Florence, SC	See Myrtle Beach-Florence
Ft. Lauderdale, FL	See Miami-Ft. Lauderdale
Ft. Pierce, FL	See West Palm Beach-Ft. Pierce
Ft. Walton Beach, FL	See Mobile-Pensacola (Ft. Walton Beach)
Ft. Worth, TX	See Dallas-Ft. Worth
Greenville, MS	See Greenwood-Greenville
Gulfport, MS	See Biloxi-Gulfport
Hagerstown, MD	See Washington, DC (Hagerstown)
Hannibal, MO	See Quincy-Hannibal-Keokuk
Harrisburg, IL	See Paducah-Cape Girardeau-Harrisburg-Mount Vernon
Hastings, NE	See Lincoln & Hastings-Kearney Plus
High Point, NC	See Greensboro-High Point-Winston Salem
Holyoke, MA	See Springfield-Holyoke
Huntington, WV	See Charleston-Huntington
Hutchinson, KS	See Wichita-Hutchinson Plus
Iowa City, IA	See Cedar Rapids-Waterloo-Iowa City & Dubuque
Jefferson City, MO	See Columbia-Jefferson City
Kalamazoo, MI	See Grand Rapids-Kalamazoo-Battle Creek

Kearney, NE	See Lincoln & Hastings-Kearney Plus
Kennewick, WA	See Yakima-Pasco-Richland-Kennewick
Keokuk, IA	See Quincy-Hannibal-Keokuk
Kirksville, MO	See Ottumwa-Kirksville
Klamath Falls, OR	See Medford-Klamath Falls
Lancaster, PA	See Harrisburg-Lancaster-Lebanon-York
Laurel, MS	See Hattiesburg-Laurel
Lawton, OK	See Wichita Falls & Lawton
Lebanon, PA	See Harrisburg-Lancaster-Lebanon-York
Longview, TX	See Tyler-Longview (Lufkin & Nacogdoches)
Lufkin, TX	See Tyler-Longview (Lufkin & Nacogdoches)
Lynchburg, VA	See Roanoke-Lynchburg
Manchester, NH	See Boston (Manchester)
Mason City, IA	See Rochester-Mason City-Austin
McAllen, TX	See Harlingen-Weslaco-Brownsville-McAllen
Melbourne, FL	See Orlando-Daytona Beach-Melbourne
Midland, TX	See Odessa-Midland
Mitchell, SD	See Sioux Falls (Mitchell)
Modesto, CA	See Sacramento-Stockton-Modesto
Moline, IL	See Davenport-Rock Island-Moline
Montrose, CO	See Grand Junction-Montrose
Nacogdoches, TX	See Tyler-Longview (Lufkin & Nacogdoches)
Naples, FL	See Ft. Myers-Naples
New Bedford, MA	See Providence-New Bedford
New Bern, NC	See Greenville-New Bern-Washington
New Haven, CT	See Hartford & New Haven
Newport News, VA	See Norfolk-Portsmouth-Newport News
Oak Hill, WV	See Bluefield-Beckley-Oak Hill
Oakland, CA	See San Francisco-Oakland-San Jose
Pasco, WA	See Yakima-Pasco-Richland-Kennewick
Pensacola, FL	See Mobile-Pensacola
Petersburg, VA	See Richmond-Petersburg
Pine Bluff, AR	See Little Rock-Pine Bluff
Pittsburg, KS	See Joplin-Pittsburg
Plattsburgh, NY	See Burlington-Plattsburgh
Pocatello, ID	See Idaho Falls-Pocatello
Port Arthur, TX	See Beaumont-Port Arthur
Portsmouth, VA	See Norfolk-Portsmouth-Newport News
Pueblo, CO	See Colorado Springs-Pueblo
Redding, CA	See Chico-Redding
Rhinelander, WI	See Wausau-Rhinelander
Richland, WA	See Yakima-Pasco-Richland-Kennewick
Riverton, WY	See Casper-Riverton
Rock Island, IL	See Davenport-Rock Island-Moline
Rogers, AR	See Ft. Smith-Fayetteville-Springdale-Rogers
Saginaw, MI	See Flint-Saginaw-Bay City
St. Paul, MN	See Minneapolis-St. Paul
St. Petersburg, FL	See Tampa-St. Petersburg-Sarasota
Salinas, CA	See Monterey-Salinas
San Jose, CA	See San Francisco-Oakland-San Jose
San Luis Obispo, CA	See Santa Barbara-Santa Maria-San Luis Obispo
Santa Fe, NM	See Albuquerque-Santa Fe

Santa Maria, CA	See Santa Barbara-Santa Maria-San Luis Obispo
Sarasota, FL	See Tampa-St. Petersburg-Sarasota
Schenectady, NY	See Albany-Schenectady-Troy
Scottsbluff, NE	See Cheyenne-Scottsbluff
Scranton, PA	See Wilkes Barre-Scranton
Selma, AL	See Montgomery (Selma)
Sierra Vista, AZ	See Tucson (Sierra Vista)
Spartanburg, SC	See Greenville-Spartanburg-Asheville-Anderson
Springdale, AR	See Ft. Smith-Fayetteville-Springdale-Rogers
Springfield, IL	See Champaign & Springfield-Decatur
Steubenville, OH	See Wheeling-Steubenville
Stockton, CA	See Sacramento-Stockton-Modesto
Superior, WI	See Duluth-Superior
Sweetwater, TX	See Abilene-Sweetwater
Tacoma, WA	See Seattle-Tacoma
Temple, TX	See Waco-Temple-Bryan
Thomasville, GA	See Tallahassee-Thomasville
Troy, NY	See Albany-Schenectady-Troy
Tupelo, MS	See Columbus-Tupelo-West Point
Tuscaloosa, AL	See Birmingham (Anniston, Tuscaloosa)
Valley City, ND	See Fargo-Valley City
Visalia, CA	See Fresno-Visalia
Washington, NC	See Greenville-New Bern-Washington
Waterloo, IA	See Cedar Rapids-Waterloo-Iowa City & Dubuque
Weslaco, TX	See See Harlingen-Weslaco-Brownsville-McAllen
Weston, WV	See Clarksburg-Weston
West Point, MS	See Columbus-Tupelo-West Point
Winston Salem, NC	See Greensboro-High Point-Winston Salem
York, PA	See Harrisburg-Lancaster-Lebanon-York

TV Stations in the United States

Alabama

Birmingham (Anniston, Tuscaloosa), AL (DMA 45)

WABM *Digital Channel:* 36; *Virtual Channel:* 68; 885 kw; 1332 ft.; N33 29 4 W86 48 25
800 Concourse Pkwy., Suite 200, Birmingham, AL 35244 US
(205) 403-3340; *Fax:* (205) 403-3329
www.wabm68.com
License: Birmingham, Jefferson County, AL held by Birmingham (WABM-TV) Licensee Inc.
Group Owner: Sinclair Broadcast Group Inc.; (acq 2-1-2002).
Nat'l Network: MYTV
David D. Smith, President, CEO & Chairman of the Board

***WBIQ** *Digital Channel:* 10; *Virtual Channel:* 10; 3 kw; 1398 ft.; N33 29 4 W86 48 25
2112 11th Avenue South, Suite 400, Birmingham, AL 35205 US
(205) 328-8756; *Fax:* (205) 251-2192
www.aptv.org
License: Birmingham, Jefferson County, AL held by Alabama ETV Commission
Washington Law Firm: Dow, Lohnes & Albertson, PLLC
Nat'l Network: PBS; *Regional Network:* Alabama Public Television
Ferris W. Stephens, Chairman
Windell Wood, COO
Roy Clem, Executive Director
Dorothy McDonald, Operation Coordinator
Phil Hutcheson, CFO
Ron Manasco, Television Tecnician
Gary Stokes, General Sales Mgr
Roy Clem, ExecutiveDirector
Phil Hutcheson, Chief Legal Counsel/CFO
Mary Davis, Administrative
Paula Drinkard, Executive Assistant
Beverly B. Phillips, Manager of Corporate Support
Tracy Neeley, Personnel Manager

WBMA-LD ; *Virtual Channel:* 40; 15 kw; 1425 ft.; N33 26 28 W86 53 02
800 Concourse Pkwy., Suite 200, Birmingham, AL 35244 US
(205) 403-3340; *Fax:* (205) 403-3329
www.abc3340.com
comments@abc3340.com
License: Birmingham, Jefferson County, AL held by WBMA Licensee LLC
Group Owner: Sinclair Broadcast Group Inc.
David D. Smith, President, CEO and Chairman of the Board
Ron Thomas, Engineering Dir

WBRC *Digital Channel:* 50; *Virtual Channel:* 6; 912 kW; 1385 ft.; N33 29 19 W86 47 58
Mailing Address: PO Box 6, Birmingham, AL 35201 USA
Second Address: 1720 Valley View Dr., Birmingham, AL 35209
(205) 322-6666; *Fax:* (205) 583-4386
www.wbrc.com
editorials@wbrc.com
License: Birmingham, Jefferson County, AL held by WBRC License Subsidiary LLC
Group Owner: Raycom Media Inc.; (acq 3-31-2009; exchange for WTVR-TV Richmond, VA)
Nat'l Network: FOX; *Nat'l Reps:* TeleRep
Size of News Staff: 53; *Hours of Local News Weekly:* news progmg 21 hrs wkly
Collin Gaston, General Manager
Dave Duncan, General Sales Mgr
Wayne Farrell, Programming Director

WCFT-TV *Digital Channel:* 33; *Virtual Channel:* 33; 300 kw; 2162 ft.; N33 28 48 W87 25 50
Mailing Address: PO Box 360039, Birmingham, AL 35236 US
Second Address: 800 Concourse Pkwy., Suite 200, Birmingham, AL 35244
(205) 403-3340, (205) 982-3970; *Fax:* (205) 403-3329, (205) 982-3942
www.abc3340.com
ront@abc3340.com
License: Tuscaloosa, Tuscaloosa County, AL held by TV Alabama Inc.
Group Owner: Allbritton Communications Co.; (acq 1996; $20 million); *Washington Law Firm:* Hogan & Hartson
Nat'l Network: ABC
Mike Murphy, General Manager
Ron Thomas, Director of Engineering

***WCIQ** *Digital Channel:* 7; *Virtual Channel:* 7; 34.8 kw; 1889 ft.; N33 29 6 W85 48 32
2112 11th Avenue South, Suite 400, Birmingham, AL 35205 US
(205) 328-8756, (800) 239-5233; *Fax:* (205) 251-2192
www.aptv.org
License: Mount Cheaha, Talladega County, AL held by Alabama ETV Commission
Washington Law Firm: Dow, Lohnes & Albertson, PLLC
Nat'l Network: PBS; *Regional Network:* Alabama Public Television
Ferris W. Stephens, Chairman
Windell Wood, COO
Dorothy McDonald, Operations Coordinator
Gary Stokes, General Sales Mgr
Roy Clem, Executive Director
Phil Hutcheson, Chief Legal Counsel/CFO
Mary Davis, Administrative
PaulaDrinkard, Executive Assistant III
Mike McKenzie, Public Information Director
Tracy Neeley, Personnel Manager

WDBB *Digital Channel:* 18; *Virtual Channel:* 17; 350 kw; 2215 ft.; N33 28 51 W87 24 3; *Rebroadcasting:* Satellite of WTTO Homewood
800 Concourse Pkwy, Suite 200, Birmingham, AL 35244 US
(205) 403-3340; *Fax:* (205) 403-3329
www.wtto21.com
comments@sbgi.net
License: Bessemer, Jefferson County, AL held by WDBB-TV Inc
Group Owner: Cunningham Broadcasting Corporation; (acq 1-19-95; $1.5 million); *Washington Law Firm:* Fletcher, Heald & Hildreth
Nat'l Network: CW; *Nat'l Reps:* Adam Young; *Wire Services:* NOAA Weather; Weather Wire
Size of News Staff: 20; *Hours of Local News Weekly:* news progmg 15 hrs wkly
Tim Costley, Chief Engineer

WGWW *Digital Channel:* 9; *Virtual Channel:* 40; 15.6 kw; 1,178 ft.; N33 36 24 W86 25 3
2021 Goldencrest Dr., Birmingham, AL 35209 US
(205) 290-4037
www.hsh.media
contact@hsh.media
License: Anniston, Calhoun County, AL held by HSH Birmingham (wCFT) Licensee LLC
Group Owner: Howard Stirk Holdings
Armstrong Williams, CEO/COO

WIAT *Digital Channel:* 30; *Virtual Channel:* 42; 2,163 kw vis, 216 kw aur; ant 1,382t/1,134g; N33 29 02 W86 48 21; *Population Served:* 700,000
Mailing Address: 2075 Golden Crest Dr., Birmingham, AL 35209
Second Address: P.O. Box 59496, Birmingham, AL 35259
(205) 322-4200; *Fax:* (205) 320-2713
www.cbs42.com
ReportIt@cbs42.com
License: Birmingham, Jefferson County, AL held by LIN License Company LLC
Group Owner: LIN Media; (acq 10-6-2006; $35 million with KIMT(TV) Mason City, IA).; *Washington Law Firm:* Dow, Lohnes & Albertson
Nat'l Network: CBS; *Nat'l Reps:* TeleRep
Hours of Local News Weekly: News progmg 6 hrs wkly
Helen Swenson, President & General Manager
Alison Lindsay, Director of Sales
Alex Morrow, Promotions Manager
Rob Martin, News Director
Scott Sarkinson, Chief Engineer
Greg Butler, Operations Director
Greg Butler, ProductionManager
Sebastian Posey, Digital Director

WJSU-TV *Digital Channel:* 9; *Virtual Channel:* 40; 15.6 kw; 1178 ft.; N33 36 24 W86 25 3
P.O. Box 360039, Birmingham, AL 35236 US
(205) 403-3340, (205) 982-3970; *Fax:* (205) 403-3329, (205) 982-3942
www.abc3340.com
ront@abc3340.com
License: Anniston, Calhoun County, AL held by TV Alabama Inc.
Group Owner: Allbritton Communications Co.; (acq 1-24-2000).; *Washington Law Firm:* Haley, Bader & Potts
Nat'l Network: ABC
Size of News Staff: 16; *Hours of Local News Weekly:* news progmg 9 hrs wkly
Mike Murphy, General Manager
Ron Thomas, Director of engineering
Ron Thomas, Director of engineering
Brenda Ladun, Anchor
James Spann, Chief Meterologist
Mike Raita, Sportscaster
Candace White, Reporter
Marissa Mitchell,Anchor/Reporter
Stu McCann, Sports Producer & Reporter

WPXH-TV *Digital Channel:* 45; 225 kw; N33 53 26 W86 13 00; *Population Served:* 1,000,000
2085 Goldencrest Dr., Birmingham, AL 35209 USA
(212) 757-3100; *Fax:* (646) 597-5903
www.television.com
michaelhubner@ionmedia.com
License: Birmingham, AL held by Ion Media License Company, LLC
Group Owner: ION Media Networks; *Washington Law Firm:* Fletcher, Heald & Hildreth
Nat'l Network: ION Television
Hours of Local News Weekly: News progmg 8 hrs wkly
Debra Perry, Operations Dir

WSES *Digital Channel:* 33; *Virtual Channel:* 33; 300 kw; 2,162 ft.; N33 28 48 W87 25 50
2021 Goldencrest Dr., Birmingham, AL 35209 US
(205) 290-4037
www.hsh.media
contact@hsh.media
License: Tuscaloosa, Tuscaloosa County, AL held by HSH Birmingham (wCFT) Licensee LLC
Group Owner: Howard Stirk Holdings
Ron Thomas, Engineering Dir

WTJP-TV *Digital Channel:* 26; *Virtual Channel:* 60; 1000 kw; 1079 ft.; N33 48 53 W86 26 55
Mailing Address: PO Box A, Santa Ana, CA 92711 US
Second Address: P. O. Box 768, Station B, Ottawa, ON K1P 5P8
(714) 731-1000, (888) 731-1000, (714) 832-2950; *Fax:* (256) 543-8623
www.tbn.org
License: Gadsden, Etowah County, AL held by Trinity Christian Center of Santa Ana Inc. dba Trinity Broadcasting Network.
Group Owner: Trinity Broadcasting Network; (acq 5-8-2000).
Nat'l Network: TRINITY BROADCA
Paul Crouch, CEO
Gary Hodges, General Manager
Curtiss Kemp, Chief Engineer
Terry Hickey, Executive Vice President

WTTO *Digital Channel:* 28; *Virtual Channel:* 21; 765 kw; 1402 ft.; N33 29 4 W86 48 25
Mailing Address: 800 Concourse Pkwy., Suite 200, Birmingham, AL 35244 US
Second Address: 10706 Beaver Dam Rd., Hunt Valley, MD 21030
(205) 403-3340; *Fax:* (205) 403-3329
www.wtto21.com
License: Homewood, Jefferson County, AL held by WTTO Licensee LLC
Group Owner: Sinclair Broadcast Group Inc.; *Washington Law Firm:* Arter & Hadden
Nat'l Network: CW; *Nat'l Reps:* Millennium Sales & Marketing
Eric Land, General Manager
Justin Hoekstra, Sales Manager
Lucrecia Rubio, Regional Program Coordinator
Tim Costley, Chief Engineer

WUOA *Digital Channel:* 6; *Virtual Channel:* 23; 26 kw; 1296 ft.; N33 29 2 W86 48 21; *Rebroadcasting:* Rebroadcasts WVUA Tuscaloosa/Northport 100%
Mailing Address: Po Box 870172, Tuscaloosa, AL 35487 US
Second Address: 920 Paul W. Bryant Dr, N323 Bryant-Denny Stadium, Tuscaloosa, AL 35401
(205) 348-7000, (205) 348-0840; *Fax:* (205) 348-7002, (205) 348-8000
www.wvuatv.com
news@wvuatv.com
License: Tuscaloosa, Tuscaloosa County, AL held by The Board of Trustees of the University of Alabama
Nat'l Network: NONE
Scott Spence, Operations Dir
Roy Clem, General Manager
Camille Shotts, General Sales Mgr
Vicki Richardson, Programming Director
Lynn Brooks, News Director
Dave Baughn, Chief Engineer
Dan Bradley, General Sales Manager
PhilipColeman, Anchor
GaryHarris, Sports Director
Danny Salter, Anchor & Producer
Richard Scott, Chief Meterologist
Daniel Sparkman, Assignment Editor

WVTM *Digital Channel:* 13; *Virtual Channel:* 13; 20 kw; 1322 ft.; N33 29 26 W86 47 48
1732 Valley View Dr., Birmingham, AB 35209 USA

(205) 558-7311; (205) 933-1313; *Fax:* (205) 933-7516 (sales)
www.wvtm13.com
License: Birmingham, Jefferson County, AL held by WVTM Hearst Television Inc.
Group Owner: Hearst Television
Nat'l Network: NBC; Me-TV; *Nat'l Reps:* Harrington, Righter & Parsons
Size of News Staff: 70; *Hours of Local News Weekly:* news progmg 24 hrs wkly

Columbus, GA (DMA 127)

***WGIQ** *Digital Channel:* 44; *Virtual Channel:* 43; 925 kw; 860 ft.; N31 43 4 W85 26 3
2112 11th Avenue South, Suite 400, Birmingham, AL 35205 US
(205) 328-8756, (800)-239-5233; *Fax:* (205) 251-2192
www.aptv.org
License: Louisville, Barbour County, AL held by Alabama ETV Commission
Washington Law Firm: Dow, Lohnes & Albertson, PLLC
Nat'l Network: PBS; *Regional Network:* Alabama Public Television
Ferris W. Stephens, Chairman
Windell Wood, COO
Gary Stokes, General Sales Mgr
Roy Clem, Executive Director
Phil Hutcheson, Chief Legal Counsel/CFO
Mary Davis, Administrative
Paula Drinkard, Executive Assistant
Beverly B.Phillips, Manager of Corporate Support
Tracy Neeley, Personnel Manager

WLGA *Digital Channel:* 30; 800 kw; 485.7 meters; N32 19 15.9 W84 47 28.5
1501 13th Ave., Columbus, GA 31901
(706) 257-6703; *Fax:* (334) 749-5768
www.wlgatv.com
License: Opelika, Lee County, AL held by Pappas Telecasting of Opelika L.P. (a Delaware limited partnership).
Group Owner: Pappas Telecasting Companies; (acq 1996; $1.6 million); *Washington Law Firm:* Paul, Hastings, Janofsky & Walker
Harry Pappas, President
Walter Dix, General Manager
Bill Brooks, General Sales Mgr
Mike Carroll, Chief Engineer

Dothan, AL (DMA 173)

WDFX-TV *Digital Channel:* 33; *Virtual Channel:* 34; 15 kw; 495 ft.; N31 12 28 W85 36 49
2221 Ross Clark Circle, Dothan, AL 36301 US
(334) 794-3434, (334) 284-5276; *Fax:* (334) 794-0034
www.dothanconnect.revrocket.us
mmctear@myfox34.tv
License: Ozark, Dale County, AL held by WDFX License Subsidiary, LLC.
Group Owner: Raycom Media Inc.; (acq 10-14-2003; grpsl).; *Ownership:* WDFX,LLC.; *Washington Law Firm:* Covington & Burling
Nat'l Network: FOX; *Nat'l Reps:* Harrington, Righter & Parsons;
Wire Services: AP
Hours of Local News Weekly: 7
Rebecca Jones, Operations Dir
Daryl Heller, General Manager
Erick Steffens, General Sales Mgr
Megan Anderson, Promotions Manager
Denise Holley, News Director
Al Shook, Chief Engineer
Melinda Chaney, Regional Sales Manager

WDHN *Digital Channel:* 21; *Virtual Channel:* 18; 1000 kw; 625 ft.; N31 14 25 W85 18 43
5274 E. State Hwy. 52, Webb, AL 36376 US
(334) 793-1818; *Fax:* (334) 793-2623
www.dothanfirst.com
License: Dothan, Houston County, AL held by Nexstar Broadcasting Inc.
Group Owner: Nexstar Broadcasting Group Inc.; (acq 8-1-2003; $40 million with KARK-TV Little Rock, AR).; *Washington Law Firm:* Fletcher, Heald & Hildreth
Nat'l Network: ABC; *Nat'l Reps:* Millennium Sales & Marketing
Size of News Staff: 8; *Hours of Local News Weekly:* news progmg 7 hrs wkly
Janie Hinson, General Manager
Janie Hinson, General Sales Mgr
Ken Curtis, News Director

WTVY *Digital Channel:* 36; *Virtual Channel:* 4; 100 kw vis, 20 kw aur; 1,670t/1,909g; N30 55 10 W85 44 28; *Population Served:* 230,000
285 N Foster St., Dothan, AL 36303 USA
(334) 792-3195; *Fax:* (334) 793-3947
www.wtvy.com
License: Dothan, Houston County, AL held by Gray Television Licensee Inc.
Group Owner: Gray Television Inc.; (acq 8-29-2002; grpsl).
Nat'l Network: CBS; *Nat'l Reps:* Continental Television Sales;
Wire Services: AP
Size of News Staff: 26; *Hours of Local News Weekly:* news progmg 20.5 hrs wkly
Spencer J. Bienvenu, VP/General Manager
Mark Kirkland, General Sales Mgr
David Killingsworth, Promotions
Kim Allen, News Director
Tom Johnson, Chief Engineer

Huntsville-Decatur (Florence), AL (DMA 79)

WAAY-TV *Digital Channel:* 32; *Virtual Channel:* 31; 468 kw; 1764 ft.; N34 44 12 W86 31 59
1000 Monte Sano Blvd., Huntsville, AL 35801 US
(256) 533-3131, (256) 539-3131; *Fax:* (256) 533-6616
www.waaytv.com
License: Huntsville, Madison County, AL held by WAAY-TV License LLC.
Group Owner: Southern Broadcast Corp. of Sarasota; (acq 1-31-2007; $41.645 million); *Washington Law Firm:* Cohn & Marks
Nat'l Network: ABC
Tracy Slayton, Operations Dir
Art Lanham, General Manager
Ed Groves, Sales Manager
Dave Keller, Programming Director
Susan Bell, Promotions Director
Keith Lowhorne, News Director
Don Roden, Chief Engineer
Robin Dorning, TrafficManager
Rebecca Pugh, Interim News Director
Kimberly Neighbors, Director of New Media
Tracy Slayton, Director of Creative Services
Kim Greene, Human Resources/ Accounting

WAFF *Digital Channel:* 48; *Virtual Channel:* 48; 48 kw; 1890 ft.; N34 42 39 W86 32 7
1414 N. Memorial Parkway, 201 Monroe Street, Huntsville, AL 35801 US
(256) 533-4848; *Fax:* (256) 533-1337
www.waff.com
webmaster@waff.com
License: Huntsville, Madison County, AL held by Raycom America License Subsidiary LLC.
Group Owner: Raycom Media Inc.; (acq 3-16-97; grpsl).; *Washington Law Firm:* Covington & Burling
Nat'l Network: NBC; *Nat'l Reps:* Harrington, Righter & Parsons;
Wire Services: AP
Size of News Staff: 43; *Hours of Local News Weekly:* news progmg 26 hrs wkly
Vanessa Oubre, Operations Director/General Manager
Dale Stafford, General Sales Mgr
Leigh Michal, Programming Director
Becky Shores, Promotions Manager
Adam Henning, News Director
J.T. Harriman, Engineering Dir
Susan Craft, LocalSales Manager
Catherine Young, Traffic Manager
Stephen Gallien, Assistant News Director

WAMY-TV *Digital Channel:* 54; *Virtual Channel:* 54; 2,400 kw vis, 240 kw aur; ant 1,699t/906g; N34 44 12 W86 31 59
1309 N. Memorial Pkwy., Huntsville, AL 35801
(256) 533-5454
www.rocketcitynow.com
License: Huntsville, Madison County, AL held by Nexstar Broadcasting Inc.
Group Owner: Nexstar Broadcasting Group Inc.; (acq 2014)
Nat'l Network: Fox; MyNetworkTV; *Nat'l Reps:* TeleRep
Mark Overstreet, Vice President and General Manager
Dale Stafford, General Sales Mgr
Suzanne Constan, Local Sales Manager
Travasa Buford, Digital Market Manager

***WFIQ** *Digital Channel:* 22; *Virtual Channel:* 36; 418.8 kw; 681 ft.; N34 34 41 W87 47 2
2112 11th Avenue South, Suite 400, Birmingham, AL 35205 US
(205) 328-8756, (800) 239-5233; *Fax:* (205) 251-2192
www.aptv.org
License: Florence, Lauderdale County, AL held by Alabama ETV Commission
Washington Law Firm: Dow, Lohnes & Albertson, PLLC
Nat'l Network: PBS; *Regional Network:* Alabama Public Television
Ferris W. Stephens, Chairman
Windell Wood, COO
Dorothy McDonald, Operations Coordinator
Gary Stokes, General Sales Mgr
Roy Clem, Executive Director
Phil Hutcheson, Chief Legal Counsel/CFO
Mary Davis, Administrative
PaulaDrinkard, Executive Assistant III
Mike McKenzie, Public Information Director
Tracy Neeley, Personnel Manager

WHDF *Digital Channel:* 14; *Virtual Channel:* 15; 1000 kw; 1414 ft.; N35 0 9 W87 8 9
Mailing Address: 200 Galleria Parkway, Suite 1740, Atlanta, GA 30339 US
Second Address: 840 Cypress Mill Rd., Florence, AL 35630
(256) 767-1515;(256) 536-1550; *Fax:* (256) 764-7750
www.thevalleyscw.tv
License: Florence, Lauderdale County, AL held by Huntsville TV L.L.C
Group Owner: Lockwood Broadcast Group
Nat'l Network: CW; *Nat'l Reps:* Blair Television
Louann Thomson, General Manager
Shanda Love, General Sales Mgr
Tim Rovere, Chief Engineer

***WHIQ** *Digital Channel:* 24; *Virtual Channel:* 25; 396 kw; 1110 ft.; N34 44 13 W86 31 45
2112 11th Avenue South, Suite 400, Birmingham, AL 35205 US
(205) 328-8756, (800)-239-5233; *Fax:* (205) 251-2192
www.aptv.org
License: Huntsville, Madison County, AL held by Alabama ETV Commission
Washington Law Firm: Dow, Lohnes & Albertson, PLLC
Nat'l Network: PBS; *Regional Network:* Alabama Public Television
Ferris W. Stephens, Chairman
Windell Wood, COO
Gary Stokes, General Sales Mgr
Roy Clem, Executive Director
Phil Hutcheson, Chief Legal Counsel/CFO
Mary Davis, Administrative
Paula Drinkard, Executive Assistant
Beverly B.Phillips, Manager of Corporate Support
Tracy Neeley, Personnel Manager

WHNT *Digital Channel:* 19; *Virtual Channel:* 19; 250 kw; 1742 ft.; N34 44 19 W86 31 56
200 Holmes Ave., Huntsville, AL 35801 USA
(256) 533-1919; *Fax:* (256) 536-9468
whnt.com
License: Huntsville, Madison County, AL held by WHNT License LLC
Group Owner: Tribune Media; *Washington Law Firm:* Koteen & Naftalin
Nat'l Network: CBS

WZDX *Digital Channel:* 41; *Virtual Channel:* 54; 2,400 kw vis, 240 kw aur; ant 1,699t/906g; N34 44 12 W86 31 59
1309 N. Memorial Pkwy., Huntsville, AL 35801
(256) 533-5454
www.rocketcitynow.com
License: Huntsville, Madison County, AL held by Nexstar Broadcasting Inc.
Group Owner: Nexstar Broadcasting Group Inc.; (acq 2014)
Nat'l Network: Fox; MyNetworkTV; *Nat'l Reps:* TeleRep
Mark Overstreet, Vice President and General Manager
Dale Stafford, General Sales Mgr
Suzanne Constan, Local Sales Manager
Travasa Buford, Digital Market Manager

Mobile, AL-Pensacola (Ft. Walton Beach), FL (DMA 60)

WALA-TV *Digital Channel:* 9; *Virtual Channel:* 10; 29 kw; 1250 ft.; N30 41 17 W87 47 54
950 North Meridian Street, Suite 1200, Indianapolis, IN 46204 US
(251) 434-1010; *Fax:* (251) 434-1073 / 1061
www.fox10tv.com
License: Mobile, Mobile County, AL held by LIN of Alabama LLC.
Group Owner: LIN Media; (acq 11-30-2005; grpsl).; *Washington Law Firm:* Fisher, Wayland, Cooper, Leader & Zaragoza
Nat'l Network: FOX; *Nat'l Reps:* TeleRep
Size of News Staff: 45; *Hours of Local News Weekly:* 23 hrs
Michael Strickler, General Sales Mgr
Kyle Claude, Promotions Manager

Bob Cashen, News Director
Roland Fields, Chief Engineer
Carrie Laughlin, National Sales Manager

***WEIQ** *Digital Channel:* 41; *Virtual Channel:* 42; 464 kw; 590 ft.; N30 39 33 W87 53 33
2112 11th Avenue South, Suite 400, Birmingham, AL 35205 US
(205) 328-8756, (800) 239-5233; *Fax:* (205) 251-2192
www.aptv.org
License: Mobile, Mobile County, AL held by Alabama ETV Commission
Washington Law Firm: Dow, Lohnes & Albertson, PLLC
Nat'l Network: PBS; *Regional Network:* Alabama Public Television
Ferris W. Stephens, Chairman
Windell Wood, COO
Dorothy McDonald, Operations Coordinator
Gary Stokes, General Sales Mgr
Roy Clem, Executive Director
Phil Hutcheson, Chief Legal Counsel/CFO
Mary Davis, Administrative
PaulaDrinkard, Executive Assistant III
Mike McKenzie, Public Information Director
Tracy Neeley, Personnel Manager

WKRG-TV *Digital Channel:* 27; *Virtual Channel:* 5; 1000 kw; 1880 ft.; N30 41 20 W87 49 49
Mailing Address: 555 Broadcast Dr., Mobile, AL 36606 US
Second Address: 1410 N. McKenzie St., Foley, AL 36535
(251) 479-5555, (251) 662-3002, (251) 662-2904, (2; *Fax:* (251) 473-8130, (251) 662-3071, (251) 943-5168
www.wkrg.com
news5@wkrg.com
License: Mobile, Mobile County, AL held by Media General Communications Holdings, LLC
Group Owner: Media General Broadcast Group; (acq 3-27-2000; grpsl).; *Washington Law Firm:* Wiley, Rein & Fielding
Nat'l Network: CBS
Joe Goleniowski, Operations Dir
Mark Bunting, General Sales Mgr
Beverly Hartman, Programming Director
David Mooney, News Director
Keith Brazel, Chief Engineer
Dave Mooney, Closed Captioning Coordinator
Randy Patrick, SportsDirector
Mel Showers, Reporter
Rose Ann Haven, Anchor

WMPV-TV *Digital Channel:* 20; *Virtual Channel:* 21; 700 kw; 1736 ft.; N30 36 40 W87 36 26
Mailing Address: PO Box A, Santa Ana, CA 92711 US
Second Address: P. O. Box 768, Station B, Ottawa, ON K1P 5P8
(334) 272-0045,(819) 770-2333; *Fax:* (334) 277-6635,(819) 770-2338
www.tbn.org
wmpv@tbn.org
License: Mobile, Mobile County, AL held by Trinity Broadcasting Network
Group Owner: Trinity Broadcasting Network; (acq 5-8-2000; grpsl).; *Washington Law Firm:* Fisher, Wayland, Cooper, Leader & Zaragoza
Nat'l Network: TRINITY BROADCA
Linda Dixon, General Manager
LaTrynnda Hollis, Programming Director
Alvin Goins, Chief Engineer
Joseph Mass, Traffic Manager

WPMI-TV *Digital Channel:* 15; *Virtual Channel:* 15; 1000 kw; 1847 ft.; N30 36 40 W87 36 26
Mailing Address: 661 Azalea Road, Mobile, AL 36609 US
Second Address: 10706 Beaver Dam Road, Hunt Valley, MD 21030
(251) 602-1500; *Fax:* (251) 602-1547,(410) 568-1537
www.local15tv.com
local15@local15tv.com
License: Mobile, Mobile County, AL held by Deerfield Media (Mobile) Licensee LLC
Group Owner: Deerfield Media; (acq 3-14-2008; grpsl);
Washington Law Firm: Covington & Burling
Nat'l Network: NBC; *Nat'l Reps:* Millennium Sales & Marketing
Size of News Staff: 50; *Hours of Local News Weekly:* news progmg 5 hrs wkly
Jared Quijas, Operations Dir
Shea Grandquest, General Manager
Ric Phillips, General Sales Mgr
Chuck Reeves, Programming Director
Wes Finley, News Director
Tim Reid, Chief Engineer
Chris Delaporte, General Sales Manager
CareyGolden, Local Sales Manager

Montgomery-Selma, AL (DMA 123)

***WAIQ** *Digital Channel:* 27; *Virtual Channel:* 26; 600 kw; 586 ft.; N32 22 55 W86 17 33
2112 11th Avenue South, Suite 400, Birmingham, AL 35205 US
(205) 328-8756; *Fax:* (205) 251-2192
www.aptv.org
License: Montgomery, Montgomery County, AL held by Alabama ETV Commission
Washington Law Firm: Dow, Lohnes & Albertson, PLLC
Nat'l Network: PBS; *Regional Network:* Alabama Public Television
Ferris W. Stephens, Chairman
Windell Wood, COO
Gary Stokes, General Sales Mgr
Roy Clem, Executive Director
Phil Hutcheson, Chief Legal Counsel/CFO
Mary Davis, Administrative
Paula Drinkard, Executive Assistant
Beverly B.Phillips, Manager of Corporate Support
Tracy Neeley, Personnel Manager

WAKA *Digital Channel:* 42; *Virtual Channel:* 8; 1000 kw; 1627 ft.; N32 8 57 W86 46 43
3251 Harrison Rd., Montgomery, AL 36109 US
(334) 271-8888; *Fax:* (334) 272-6444
www.alabamanews.net
License: Selma, Dallas County, AL held by Alabama Broadcasting Partners.
Group Owner: Bahakel Communications Ltd.; (acq 8-85)
Nat'l Network: CBS; *Wire Services:* AP
Size of News Staff: 22; *Hours of Local News Weekly:* news progmg 9 hrs wkly
Mark Smith, Broadcast Operations Manager
Jesse Grear, Vice President and General Manager
Mark Smith, Station Manager
Steffanie Patterson, National Sales Manager
Mark Smith, Programming Director
Amanda Moyer, Promotions and DigitalDirector
Glenn Halbrooks, News Director
Thomas Mayberry, Chief Engineer
Jim McLean, Creative Services Director
Ricky Baker, Traffic Manager
Laura Ross, Business and Human Resources Manager

WBMM *Digital Channel:* 22; *Virtual Channel:* 22; 65 kw; 1119 ft.; N32 4 5 W85 56 41
3251 Harrison Rd., Montgomery, AL 36109 US
(334) 271-8888; *Fax:* (334) 272-6444
www.alabamanews.net
License: Tuskegee, Macon County, AL held by Alabama Broadcasting Partners.
Group Owner: Bahakel Communications Ltd.; (acq 7-26-2006; $2 million); *Washington Law Firm:* Wiley, Rhein
Nat'l Network: CW; *Nat'l Reps:* Blair Television
Hours of Local News Weekly: 3
Mark Smith, Broadcast Operations Manager
Jesse Grear, Vice President and General Manager
Mark Smith, Station Manager
Steffanie Patterson, National Sales Manager
Mark Smith, Programming Director
Amanda Moyer, Promotions and DigitalDirector
Glenn Halbrooks, News Director
Thomas Mayberry, Chief Engineer
Jim McLean, Creative Services Director
Ricky Baker, Traffic Manager
Laura Ross, Business and Human Resources Manager

WCOV-TV *Digital Channel:* 20; *Virtual Channel:* 20; 460 kw; 1699 ft.; N31 58 28 W86 9 44
One Wcov Avenue, Montgomery, AL 36111 US
(334) 288-7020
www.wcov.com
License: Montgomery, Montgomery County, AL held by Woods Communications Corp.
Group Owner: Woods Communications Corp.; (acq 12-1-85; $4 million; *Washington Law Firm:* Kenkel, Barnard & Edmundson
Nat'l Network: FOX; *Nat'l Reps:* Millennium Sales & Marketing

***WDIQ** *Digital Channel:* 10; *Virtual Channel:* 2; 30 kw; 738 ft.; N31 33 16 W86 23 32
2112 11th Avenue South, Suite 400, Birmingham, AL 35205 US
(205) 328-8756, (800) 239-5233; *Fax:* (205) 251-2192
www.aptv.org
License: Dozier, Crenshaw County, AL held by Alabama ETV Commission
Washington Law Firm: Dow, Lohnes & Albertson, PLLC
Nat'l Network: PBS; *Regional Network:* Alabama Public Television
Ferris W. Stephens, Chairman
Windell Wood, COO
Dorothy McDonald, Operations Coordinator
Gary Stokes, General Sales Mgr
Roy Clem, Executive Director
Phil Hutcheson, Chief Legal Counsel/CFO
Mary Davis, Administrative
PaulaDrinkard, Executive Assistant III
Mike McKenzie, Public Information Director
Tracy Neeley, Personnel Manager

***WIIQ** *Digital Channel:* 19; *Virtual Channel:* 41; 1000 kw; 1067 ft.; N32 21 45 W87 52 30.5
2112 11th Avenue South, Suite 400, Birmingham, AL 35205 US
(205) 328-8756, (800)-239-5233; *Fax:* (205) 251-2192
www.aptv.org
License: Demopolis, Marengo County, AL held by Alabama ETV Commission
Washington Law Firm: Dow, Lohnes & Albertson, PLLC
Nat'l Network: PBS
Ferris W. Stephens, Chairman
Windell Wood, COO
Gary Stokes, General Sales Mgr
Roy Clem, Executive Director
Phil Hutcheson, Chief Legal Counsel/CFO
Mary Davis, Administrative
Paula Drinkard, Executive Assistant
Beverly B.Phillips, Manager of Corporate Support
Tracy Neeley, Personnel Manager

WMCF-TV *Digital Channel:* 46; *Virtual Channel:* 45; 851 kw; 427 ft.; N32 24 13 W86 11 49
Mailing Address: PO Box A, Santa Ana, CA 92711 US
Second Address: P. O. Box 768, Station B, Ottawa, ON K1P 5P8
(334) 272-0045,(819) 770-2333; *Fax:* (334) 277-6635,(819) 770-2338
www.tbn.org
License: Montgomery, Montgomery County, AL held by Christian Center of Santa Ana, Inc.
Group Owner: Trinity Broadcasting Network; (acq 5-8-2000; grpsl).; *Washington Law Firm:* Baraff, Keorner, Olender & Hochberg
Nat'l Network: TRINITY BROADCA
P. Crouch, President
Aaron Motley, General Manager
Larry Dean, Chief Engineer
Rick Hall, Public Affairs Director

WNCF *Digital Channel:* 32; *Virtual Channel:* 32; 35 kw; 1788 ft.; N32 8 30 W86 44 42
3251 Harrison Road, Montgomery, AL 36109 US
(334) 270-3200, (334) 270-2801; *Fax:* (334) 271-6348, (334) 277-1374
www.wncftv.com
License: Montgomery, Montgomery County, AL held by Channel 32 Montgomery L.L.C.
Group Owner: SagamoreHill Broadcasting LLC; (acq 1999; $8 million); *Washington Law Firm:* Wiley, Rein & Fielding
Nat'l Network: ABC; *Nat'l Reps:* Blair Television
Size of News Staff: 2; *Hours of Local News Weekly:* news progmg one hr wkly
Jesse Grear, General Manager
Mitchell Maund, Sales Manager
Lois Crenshaw, Programming Director
Clie Waller, Promotions Manager
Ed Cole, Chief Engineer
Linda Babers, Traffic Manager
Lynn Gilreath, Account Manager
Mike Chase,Account Manager
Louis Cohen, Account Manager

WRJM *Digital Channel:* 48; 2,820 kw vis; ant 1066t/913g; N32 03 37 W85 57 02; *Population Served:* 611,750
Mailing Address: Josie Park Broadcasting Inc., 285 E. Broad St., Ozark, AL 36360
Second Address: 315 S. Three Notch St., Troy, AL 36081
(334) 670-6766; *Fax:* (334) 670-6717
www.wrjm.net
License: Troy, Pike County, AL held by Walter P. Lunsford, Receiver for Josie Park Broadcasting Inc.
Washington Law Firm: Borsari and Assoc, PLC
Nat'l Network: MyNetworkTV
Jack Misell, CEO
Walter Lunsford, Operations Dir
Nicky Vull, Station Manager
Buddy Johnson, General Sales Mgr
Don Hess, Programming Director
Vincent Hodges, Promotions Manager
Boyd Mizell, Operations Manager
Jenny Dykes, PublicAffairs Director
Sonny Strassburger, Regional Sales Manager

WSFA *Digital Channel:* 12; *Virtual Channel:* 12; 31.6 kw; 1962 ft.; N31 58 28 W86 9 44
12 E. Delano Ave., Montgomery, AL 36105 US
(334) 613-8258; *Fax:* (334) 613-8302
www.wsfa.com
closedcaptioning@wsfa.com
License: Montgomery, Montgomery County, AL held by WSFA License Subsidiary LLC.
Group Owner: Raycom Media Inc.; (acq 1-31-2006; grpsl);
Washington Law Firm: Dow, Lohnes & Albertson
Nat'l Network: NBC; *Nat'l Reps:* Harrington, Righter & Parsons
Mark Wilder, Operations Dir
Collin Gaston, VP/ General Manager
Marnie Jackson, General Sales Mgr
Alicia Briscoe, Promotions Manager
Scott Duff, News Director
Morris Pollock, Chief Engineer
Collin Gaston, Regional SalesManager
Valorie Lawson, Anchor
Rich Thomas, Chief Meterologist
Bryan Henry, Reporter
Jeff Shearer, Sports Director

Alaska

Anchorage, AK (DMA 147)

***KAKM** *Digital Channel:* 8; *Virtual Channel:* 7; 50 kw; 787 ft.; N61 25 22 W149 52 20
3877 University Drive, Anchorage, AK 99508-4676 US
(907) 550-8400; *Fax:* (907)550-8401
questions@kakm.org
License: Anchorage, Anchorage County, AK held by Alaska Public Telecommunications Inc
Washington Law Firm: Dow, Lohnes & Albertson
Nat'l Network: PBS
Steve Lindbeck, CEO/General Manager
Mike Martin, President
Constance Huff, FM Operations
Bede Trantina, FM Program Director
Lori Townsend, News Director
Bernie Washington, CFO
Bob Wyatt, CTO
Torrie Allen, Chief Marketing &Development Officer
Mark Wiggin, Vice President
Lauren Blanchett, Treasurer
Susan Fison, Secretary

KDMD *Digital Channel:* 33; *Virtual Channel:* 33; 17.2 kw; 985 ft.; N61 20 10.8 W149 30 48.2
Mailing Address: P. O. Box 255, Evergreen, CO 80439 US
Second Address: 1310 E. 66th Ave., Anchorage, AL
(907) 562-5363; *Fax:* (907) 562-5346
www.kdmd.tv
stationmail@kdmd.tv
License: Anchorage, Anchorage County, AK held by Ketchikan TV LLC
Nat'l Network: IND
David Drucker, CEO
Bill Vanderpoel, President
Andy Tierney, General Manager
Don Nelson, Chief Engineer

KTBY *Digital Channel:* 20; *Virtual Channel:* 4; 234.4 kw; 148 ft.; N61 13 11 W149 53 24
2700 E Tudor Rd, Anchorage, AK 99507 US
(907) 561-1313; *Fax:* (907) 264-5180
www.youralaskalink.com
info@youralaskalink.com
License: Anchorage, Anchorage County, AK held by Coastal Television Broadcasting Company LLC
Nat'l Network: FOX
Hours of Local News Weekly: 4.5
Kirsten Bolton, General Manager
Kyle Keller, Programming Director

KTUU-TV *Digital Channel:* 10; *Virtual Channel:* 2; 50 kw; 787 ft.; N61 25 22 W149 52 20
Mailing Address: 1802 - 136th Place, N.E., Bellevue, WA 98005 US
Second Address: 701 E. Tudor Rd, Suite #220, Anchorage, AK 99503-7488
(907) 762-9202; *Fax:* (907) 561-0874
www.ktuu.com
ktuu@ktuu.com
License: Anchorage, Anchorage County, AK held by Northern Lights Media Inc
Group Owner: Schurz Communications Inc.; 7/1/2008
Nat'l Network: NBC; *Nat'l Reps:* Blair Television; *Wire Services:* AP
Size of News Staff: 40; *Hours of Local News Weekly:* news progmg 19.5 hrs wkly
Andrew MacLeod, President/General Sales Manager
Trent McNelly, Operations
Tracy Sabo, News Director
Leland Verschueren, Chief Engineer
Elisa Fleener, Advertising Director
Nancy Johnson, National Sales Manager
Mike Ross, CoAnchor
Doris Tronstad, Director of Sales
Clinton Bennett, Executive Producer
Abby Hancock, Health Reporter

KTVA *Digital Channel:* 28; *Virtual Channel:* 11; 28.9 kw; 199 ft.; N61 11 33 W149 54 1.1
Mailing Address: 1007 West 32nd Avenue, Anchorage, AK 99503 US
Second Address: 3330 Artic Blvd., Suite 206, Anchorage, AK 99503
(907) 274-1111, (907) 646-2100; *Fax:* (907) 273-3189, (907) 646-2166
www.ktva.com
11news@ktva.com
License: Anchorage, Anchorage County, AK held by Alaska Broadcasting Company Inc
(acq 5-25-2000; grpsl).; *Washington Law Firm:* Wilkinson, Barker, Knauer & Quinn
Nat'l Network: CBS *Regional Reps:* Art Moore
Size of News Staff: 16; *Hours of Local News Weekly:* news progmg 7 hrs wkly
Bush Houston, Operations Dir
Jerry Bever, General Manager
Laurie Bruce, General Sales Mgr
Cyd Terhune, Programming Director
Staci Chil, News Director
Tom Lambert, Chief Engineer
Monica Bouvier, Traffic Manager
Lauren Maxwell,Reporter
Janessa Webb, Weather Dept.
Heather Hintze, Reporter
Brett Shepard, Weather Dept.

KYES-TV *Digital Channel:* 6; 5.9 kw vis, 50 kw aur; ant 820t/160g; N61 20 10 W149 30 49; *Population Served:* 254,479
3700 Woodland Dr., Suite 800, Anchorage, AK 99517
(907) 248-5937; *Fax:* (907) 339-3889
License: Anchorage, Anchorage County, AK held by Fireweed Communications LLC
(acq 12-11-91; $100 & assumption of debt; *Washington Law Firm:* Benjamin Perez
Nat'l Network: MyNetworkTV
Hours of Local News Weekly: News progmg one hr wkly
Jeremy Lansman, President
Roy Nederbrock, Operations Dir
Carol Schatz, General Manager
Lori Erickson, Station Manager
Maryann Spinella, Promotions Manager
Amy Simonson, Traffic Manager

KYUR *Digital Channel:* 12; *Virtual Channel:* 13; 316 kw vis, 31.6 kw aur; ant 781t; N61 25 22 W149 52 20; *Population Served:* 250,000
2700 E. Tudor Rd., Anchorage, AK 99507
(907) 561-1313; *Fax:* (907) 561-1377
www.aksuperstation.com
closedcaptioning@youralaskalink.com
License: Anchorage, Anchorage County, AK held by Smith Media License Holdings LLC.
Group Owner: Smith Media License Holdings LLC; (acq 11-8-2004; grpsl).
Nat'l Network: ABC; CW; *Nat'l Reps:* Continental Television Sales
Scott Centers, General Manager, Director of Sales
Terri Bradley, Programming Director
Nate Kimmell, Promotions Manager
Ty Hardt, News Director
George Heacock, Chief Engineer
Stephanie Lewis, Marketing Coordinator

Fairbanks, AK (DMA 202)

KATN *Digital Channel:* 18; *Virtual Channel:* 2; 28.2 kw vis, 5.5 kw aur; ant 200t/151g; N64 50 42 W147 42 52;
Rebroadcasting: Rebroadcasts KIMO-TV Anchorage 99%.;
Population Served: 84,800
Mailing Address: 516 2nd Ave., Suite 400, Fairbanks, AK 99701
Second Address: 2700 E. Tudor Rd., Anchorage, AK 99507
(907) 452-2125, (877) 304-1313; *Fax:* (907) 561-1377
www.aksuperstation.com
License: Fairbanks, Fairbanks North Star County, AK held by Smith Media License Holdings LLC.
Group Owner: Smith Media License Holdings LLC; (acq 11-8-2004; grpsl).
Nat'l Network: ABC
Hours of Local News Weekly: News progmg 6p - 11p wkly
Sean Bradley, Operations Dir
Scott Centers, General Manager
Jeff Glaser, General Sales Mgr
Terri Bradley, Programming Director
Rita Corwin, Promotions Manager
Lori Tipton, News Director
George Heacock, Engineering Dir
GeorgeHeacock, Chief Engineer
Calli Rabe, Traffic Director
Gerilynne Buonocore, Public Affairs Director
John Thompson, Sports Director
Daniel Hernandez, Chief Photographer
Shannon Riddle, Internet Coordinator

KFXF *Digital Channel:* 7; *Virtual Channel:* 7; 6.1 kw; 879 ft.; N64 55 20 W147 42 55
3650 Bradock Street, Fairbanks, AK 99701 US
(907) 452-3697; *Fax:* (907) 456-3428
www.TVTV.com
License: Fairbanks, Fairbanks North Star County, AK held by Tanana Valley Television Co
Group Owner: Tanana Valley Television Co.; *Washington Law Firm:* Baker & Hostetler
Nat'l Network: FOX
Size of News Staff: 4; *Hours of Local News Weekly:* news progmg 10 hr wkly
Chris Fry, General Manager
Christine Fry, Station Manager
Sam Oxman, News Director
Dave Sala, Chief Engineer
Trent Heineken, Traffic Manager
Brian Virgin, Production Dept.

KJNP-TV *Digital Channel:* 20; 18.66 kw vis, 2.8 kw aur; 1,619t/191g; N64 52 44 W148 03 10; *Population Served:* 8,100
Mailing Address: Box 56359, 2501 Mission Rd., North Pole, AK 99705-1359
Second Address: PO Box 56359, North Pole, AK 99705-1359
(907) 488-2216; *Fax:* (907) 488-5246
www.mosquitonet.com/~kjnp
kjnp@mosquitonet.com
License: North Pole, Fairbanks North Star County, AK held by Evangelistic Alaska Missionary Fellowship
Washington Law Firm: Fletcher, Heald & Hildreth
Yvonne Carriker, President
Richard Olson, Operations Dir
Julie Beaver, Station Manager
Dave Castor, Chief Engineer
Don Nelson, Founder
Gen Nelson, Founder

KTVF *Digital Channel:* 11; *Virtual Channel:* 11; 0.25 kw; 50t/168g; N64 48 43 W147 42 4; *Population Served:* 85,000
3650 Braddock St., Fairbanks, AK 99701
(907) 458-1800; *Fax:* (907) 458-1820
www.webcenter11.com
comments@ktvf11.com
License: Fairbanks, Fairbanks North Star County, AK held by Chena Broadcasting LLC
Group Owner: Chena Broadcasting LLC; (acq 10-13-2011).;
Washington Law Firm: Covington & Burling
Nat'l Network: NBC; *Nat'l Reps:* Blair Television
Size of News Staff: 6; *Hours of Local News Weekly:* news progmg 9 hrs wkly
DeeDee Caciari, General Manager and General Sales Manager
Celia Vissers, Programming Director
Monte Bowen, News Director
David Castor, Engineering Dir
Kimberly Colombero, Web Manager and Art Director
Larry Rhody, National SalesManager
Eric Lohn, Production Manager
Shannon Fett, Sales Account Executive
Jennifer Luke, Sales Account Executive
Nikki Drummond, Sales Account Executive

***KUAC-TV** *Digital Channel:* 9; *Virtual Channel:* 9; 30 kw; 554 ft.; N64 54 42 W147 46 38
312 Tanana Dr., Suite 202, Fairbanks, AK 99775-5620 US
(907) 474-7491; *Fax:* (907) 474-5064
www.kuac.org
comments@kuac.org
License: Fairbanks, Fairbanks North Star County, AK held by University of Alaska
Nat'l Network: PBS

Size of News Staff: 1; *Hours of Local News Weekly:* 2
Patty Dyer-Smith, CFO
Jerry Evans, Operations Dir
Keith Martin, General Manager
Gretchen Gordon, General Sales Mgr
Claudia Clark, Programming Director
Keith Martin, Dir. Of Engineering & Technology
Wanda Peros, Sales
DonnaOlesen, Corporate Support Manager
Patty Dyer-Smith, Director of Finance & Administration
Emily Elterman, TV Traffic Coordinator/Broadcast Technician
Carolyn Hall, Dir. of TV Programming,Traffic & Operations
Jerry Evans, Dir.of FM Programming& Operations

Juneau, AK (DMA 207)

KJUD *Digital Channel:* 11; *Virtual Channel:* 8; 0.14 kw; -951 ft.; N58 18 5 W134 26 26
Mailing Address: 516 2nd Ave., Suite 400, Fairbanks, AK 99701 US
Second Address: 2700 E.Tudor Rd., Anchorage, AK 99507
(907) 561-1313, (907) 586-3145, (877) 304-1313; *Fax:* (907) 561-1377 / (907) 463-3041
www.aksuperstation.com
closedcaptioning@youralaskalink.com
License: Juneau, Juneau County, AK held by Smith Media License Holdings LLC.
Group Owner: Smith Media License Holdings LLC; (acq 11-8-2004; grpsl).; *Washington Law Firm:* Kaye, Scholer, Fierman, Hays & Handler
Nat'l Network: ABC; CW
Size of News Staff: 9; *Hours of Local News Weekly:* news progmg 5 hrs wkly
Scott Centers, General Manager
Jeff Glaser, General Sales Mgr
Terri Bradley, Programming Director
Lori Tipton, News Director
Thomas Howard, Chief Engineer
Calli Rabe, Traffic Director
Daniel Harnandez, Chief Photographer
JohnThompson, Sports Director
Shannon Riddle, Internet Coordinator

KTNL-TV *Digital Channel:* 7; *Virtual Channel:* 13; 0.35 kw; -709 ft.; N57 3 1 W135 20 4
803 Sirstad Street, Sitka, AK 99835 US
(907) 747-5749; *Fax:* (907) 747-8440
License: Sitka, Sitka County, AK held by Ketchikan TV LLC (acq 6-19-2002).; *Washington Law Firm:* Wilkinson, Barker, Knauer L.L.P.
Nat'l Network: CBS
David Drucker, CEO
Bill Vanderpoel, Operations Dir
Charlene Nelson, General Manager
Amanda McMellon, General Sales Mgr
Garrett Leighton, Operations Manager

***KTOO-TV** *Digital Channel:* 10; *Virtual Channel:* 3; 1 kw; -1191 ft.; N58 17 56 W134 24 7; *Rebroadcasting:* Rebroadcasts KUAC-TV Fairbanks 95%.
360 Egan Drive, Juneau, AK 99801 US
(907) 586-1670; *Fax:* (907) 586-3612
www.ktoo.org
ktoo@ktoo.org
License: Juneau, Juneau County, AK held by Capital Community Broadcasting Inc
Group Owner: Capital Community Broadcasting Inc.; *Washington Law Firm:* Schwartz, Woods & Miller
Nat'l Network: PBS
Size of News Staff: 1; *Hours of Local News Weekly:* news progmg one hr wkly
Barbara Sheinberg, Chairman
Bill Legere, President & General Manager
David Waters, Operations Manager
Jim Mahan, Station Manager
Cheryl Levitt, General Sales Mgr
Jeff Brown, Program Director
Rosemarie Alexander, News Director
William Judy, Engineering Dir
Katey Blagden, Administrative Assistant
Christy Ciambor, Development Director
James Mahan, Assistant General Manager for Operations
Mike Sakarias, Operations Manager
John Kelly, Traffic & OperationsAssistant
David Jackson, IT Manager

Ketchikan

KUBD *Digital Channel:* 13; *Virtual Channel:* 4; 0.413 kw; -233 ft.; N55 20 59 W131 40 12
770 Se Summerfield Pl, Corvallis, AK 97333 US
(907) 225-4613; *Fax:* (907) 247-5365
License: Ketchikan, Ketchikan Gateway County, AK held by Ketchikan TV LLC
Nat'l Network: CBS
Jack Gibson, General Manager
Rudy Casillas, Programming Director
Michael Serres, Promotions Manager
Peter Michaels, News Director
David Ross, Chief Engineer

American Samoa

Pago Pago

***KVZK-2** ; 60 kw vis, 6.0 kw aur; 2,000t/400g; N14 16 14 W170 41 12
Mailing Address: Box 2567, Pago Pago, AS 96799 US
Second Address: 1427 Dillingham, Suite 210, Honolulu, HI 96817
(684) 633-4116; *Fax:* (684) 633-2269
www.americansamoa.gov
webmaster@as.gov
License: Pago Pago, American Samoa County, AS held by The Government of American Samoa
Nat'l Network: PBS
Foreign Language Programming
Paolo Sivia, General Manager
Jeff Alwin, Chief Engineer
Fiu J. Saelua, Chief of Staff
Tamailelagi Minnie Tuia, Deputy Chief of Staff
Steven Watson, Legal Counsel
Iu Joseph Pereira, Executive Special Assistant to the Governor
Solomona Aoelua, Executive Special Assistant to the Lt. Governor
Dr. Oreta Mapu-Crichton, Senior Policy Advisor

***KVZK-4** ; 72 kw vis, 7.2 kw aur
Mailing Address: Box 2567, Pago Pago, AS 96799 US
Second Address: 1427 Dillingham, Suite 210, Honolulu, HI 96817
(684) 633-4116; *Fax:* (684) 633-2269
www.americansamoa.gov
webmaster@as.gov
License: Pago Pago, American Samoa County, AS held by The Government of American Samoa
Nat'l Network: ABC; CBS
Sivia Paolo, General Manager
Fiu J. Saelua, Chief of Staff
Tamailelagi Minnie Tuia, Deputy Chief of Staff
Steven Watson, Legal Counsel
Iu Joseph Pereira, Executive Special Assistant to the Governor
Solomona Aoelua, ExecutiveSpecial Assistant to the Lt. Governor
Dr. Oreta Mapu-Crichton, Senior Policy Advisor

***KVZK-5** *Digital Channel:* 5; 72 kw vis, 7.2 kw aur; 2,000t/400g
Mailing Address: Box 2567, Pago Pago, AS 96799 US
Second Address: 1427 Dillingham, Suite 210, Honolulu, HI 96817
(684) 633-4116; *Fax:* (684) 633-2269
www.americansamoa.gov
webmaster@as.gov
License: Pago Pago, American Samoa County, AS held by The Government of American Samoa
Nat'l Network: ABC; CBS
Paolo Sivia, General Manager
Jeff Alwin, Chief Engineer
Fiu J. Saelua, Chief of Staff
Tamailelagi Minnie Tuia, Deputy Chief of Staff
Steven Watson, Legal Counsel
Iu Joseph Pereira, Executive Special Assistant to the Governor
Solomona Aoelua, Executive Special Assistant to the Lt. Governor
Dr. Oreta Mapu-Crichton, Senior Policy Advisor

Arizona

Phoenix

KSAZ ; *Virtual Channel:* 10; 20 kW; N33 20 1 W112 3 32
511 W Adams St., Phoenix, AZ 85003 USA
(602) 257-1234
www.fox10phoenix.com
License: Phoenix, Maricopa County, AZ held by NW Communications of Phoenix Inc.
Group Owner: Fox Television Stations Group
Nat'l Network: FOX

KTAZ *Digital Channel:* 39; *Virtual Channel:* 39; 550 kW; 323 ft.; N33 20 3 W 112 3 38
USA
www.telemundoarizona.com
License: Phoenix, Maricopa County, AZ held by NBC Telemundo License LLC
Group Owner: Telemundo Station Group
Nat'l Network: Telemundo
Luis Silberwasser, President

Phoenix (Prescott), AZ (DMA 12)

***KAET** *Digital Channel:* 8; *Virtual Channel:* 8; 40 kw; 1801 ft.; N33 20 0 W112 3 49
Mailing Address: Arizona State University, P.O. Box 871405, Tempe, AZ 85281 US
Second Address: Stauffer Hall B-Wing, Arizona State Univ., Tempe, AZ 85287
(480) 965-8888; *Fax:* (480) 965-1000
eight@asu.edu
License: Phoenix, Maricopa County, AZ held by Arizona Board of Regents
Washington Law Firm: Covington & Burling
Nat'l Network: PBS
Foreign Language Programming; Size of News Staff: 7; *Hours of Local News Weekly:* news progmg 3 hrs wkly
John Martinez, Operations Dir
Kelly McCullough, General Manager
Nancy Southgate, Associate General Manager
Michael Philipsen, News Director
Gilbert Akroyd, Engineering Dir
John Menzies, Promotions Manager

KASW *Digital Channel:* 49; *Virtual Channel:* 61; 531 kw; 1,631 ft.; N33 20 2 W112 3 44
645 East Missouri Ave., Suite 100, Phoenix, AZ 85012 US
(480) 661-6161
www.yourphx.com
License: Phoenix, Maricopa County, AZ held by Nexstar Broadcasting Inc.
Group Owner: Nexstar Broadcasting Group Inc.
Nat'l Network: CW
Denise McManus, Vice President and General Manager

KAZT-TV *Digital Channel:* 7; *Virtual Channel:* 7; 3.2 kw; 2598 ft.; N34 41 15 W112 7 1
Mailing Address: 3211 Tower Road, Prescott, AZ 86305 US
Second Address: 4343 E. Camelback Road, Suite 130, Phoenix, AZ 85018
(602) 977-7700; *Fax:* (602) 224-2214
www.aztv.com
License: Prescott, Yavapai County, AZ held by KAZT L.L.C (acq 4-1-2002; $7.336 million); *Washington Law Firm:* Shaw Pittman
Nat'l Network: IND; *Nat'l Reps:* Petry Television Inc.; *Wire Services:* AP
Size of News Staff: 6; *Hours of Local News Weekly:* 11
John Ryan, CFO
Dave Ware, General Manager
Richard Howe, Station Manager
Eric Cohen, Programming Director
Cheryl Strong, Traffic Manager

KCFG *Digital Channel:* 32; *Virtual Channel:* 9; 1000 kw; 1116 ft.; N34 58 6 W111 30 29
3654 West Jarvis Avenue, Skokie, IL 60076 US
(928) 526-5234; *Fax:* (928) 526-1172
www.kcfg.net
License: Flagstaff, Coconino County, AZ held by KM Television of Flagstaff L.L.C
Nat'l Network: AMER1
John Banker, General Manager

***KDTP** *Digital Channel:* 11; *Virtual Channel:* 11; 3.2 kw; 177 ft.; N34 55 5 W110 8 25
Mailing Address: 3901 Hwy 121, Bedford, TX 76021 US
Second Address: PO Box 610546, Dallas, TX 75261-0546
(817) 571-1229, (877) 805-2132; *Fax:* (817) 571-7458
www.daystar.com
Partners@Daystar.com
License: Holbrook, Navajo County, AZ held by Community Television Educators Inc
Nat'l Network: IND
Elevra Weigand, Station Manager

KFPH-DT *Digital Channel:* 13; *Virtual Channel:* 13; 33 kw vis; ant 1,555t/239g; N34 58 06 W111 30 34
2158 N. 4th St., Flagstaff, AZ 86004
(928) 527-1300
www.univision.com

License: Flagstaff, Coconino County, AZ held by UniMas Partnership of Flagstaff.
Group Owner: Univision Communications Inc.; (acq 10-2-2001; $19.113 million plus assumption of liabilities with KFTU-TV Douglas).
Nat'l Network: UniMas (Spanish)
Foreign Language Programming
Roberto Yanez, General Manager
Juan Villa, News Director
Gerardo Higginson, Director, Community Empowerment

KMOH-TV *Digital Channel:* 19; *Virtual Channel:* 6; 100 kw vis, 10 kw aur; ant 1,920t; N35 01 57 W114 21 56; *Population Served:* 138,000
2332 Kingman Avenue, Kingman, AZ 22234
928-753-2724; *Fax:* 305-863-5709
License: Kingman, Mohave County, AZ held by Hero Licenseco, LLC
Robert Behar, President
Jerry Albers, Operations Dir
Mara Rankin, General Manager
Loren Blumberg, General Sales Mgr
Charlie Trice, Engineering Dir
Jason Gassner, Account Executive

KNAZ-TV *Digital Channel:* 22; *Virtual Channel:* 2; 283 kw; 1526 ft.; N34 58 6 W111 30 28
Mailing Address: 200 E. Van Buren, Phoenix, AZ 85004 US
Second Address: 307 W. Tormey Dr., NAU School of Communication Bldg. 16, Rm 301, Flagstaff, AZ 86011
(602) 444-1212; *Fax:* (602) 261-6135
www.12news.com
License: Flagstaff, Coconino County, AZ held by Multimedia Holdings Corp.
Group Owner: Tegna Media; (acq 1997; $6.25 million with KMOH-TV Kingman).; *Washington Law Firm:* Dow, Lohnes & Albertson
Nat'l Network: NBC
John Misner, President and General Manager
Mark Casey, News Director

KNXV-TV *Digital Channel:* 15; *Virtual Channel:* 15; 458 kw; 1709 ft.; N33 20 0 W112 3 46
312 Walnut Street, Cincinnati, OH 45202 US
(602) 273-1500; *Fax:* (602) 685-3000
www.abc15.com
news15@abc15.com
License: Phoenix, Maricopa County, AZ held by Scripps Howard Broadcasting Co.
Group Owner: The E. W. Scripps Co.; (acq 1-9-85; $26.6 million); *Washington Law Firm:* Baker & Hostetler
Nat'l Network: ABC; *Nat'l Reps:* Eagle Television Sales
Flor Polanco, Operations Dir
Janice Todd, General Manager
Adam Weyne, General Sales Mgr
Trish Greening, Programming Director
Jim Hart, Promotions Manager
Joe Hengemuehler, News Director
Ryan Steward, Chief Engineer
Craig Fouhy,Sports Commentator
Janet Taylor, Traffic Manager
Bill Bellis, Weather Director
Katie Raml, Anchor
Steve Irvin, Anchor
Paul Calvisi, Sports Commentator

KPAZ-TV *Digital Channel:* 20; *Virtual Channel:* 21; 500 kw; 1604 ft.; N33 20 2.5 W112 3 42
Mailing Address: P. O. Box A, Santa Ana, CA 92711 US
Second Address: P. O. Box 768, Station B, Ottawa, ON K1P 5P8
(714) 731-1000, (888) 731-1000, (714) 832-2950, (8; *Fax:* (602) 267-9427
www.tbn.org
License: Phoenix, Maricopa County, AZ held by Trinity Broadcasting of Arizona Inc.
Group Owner: Trinity Broadcasting Network; (acq 1977).; *Washington Law Firm:* Joseph E. Dunne III
Nat'l Network: TRINITY BROADCA
Oralena Valero, Station Manager
Gary Nichols, Chief Engineer

KPHO *Digital Channel:* 17; *Virtual Channel:* 5; 1000 kW; 1663 ft.; N33 20 2 W112 3 40
5555 N 7th Ave, Phoenix, AZ 85013 USA
(602) 264-1000
www.azfamily.com
License: Phoenix, Maricopa County, AZ held by KPHO Broadcasting Corp.
Group Owner: Meredith Corp.; (acq 6-25-52; grpsl; *Washington Law Firm:* Dow Lohnes
Nat'l Network: CBS; *Nat'l Reps:* Harrington, Righter & Parsons; *Wire Services:* Weather Wire
Size of News Staff: 60; *Hours of Local News Weekly:* news progmg 30.5 hrs wkly

KPNX *Digital Channel:* 12; *Virtual Channel:* 12; 39 kw; 1,821 ft.; N33 20 0 W112 3 48
200 E. Van Buren, Phoenix, AZ 85004 US
(602) 444-1212; *Fax:* (602) 261-6135
www.12news.com
License: Mesa, Maricopa County, AZ held by Multimedia Holdings Corp.
Group Owner: Tegna Media; (acq 6-7-79; grpsl;
Nat'l Network: NBC
Size of News Staff: 70
John Misner, President and General Manager
Mark Casey, Vice President and Station Manager
Dan Mayasich, General Sales Mgr
Heather Gray, Director of Programming and Marketing
Sandra Kotzambasis Johnson, News Director
Michael Mejia,Local Sales Manager

KPPX-TV ; 1000 kw; 1,749t/354g; N33 20 03 W112 03 40
2777 E. Camelback Rd., Suite 101, Phoenix, AZ 85016 USA
(212) 757-3100; *Fax:* (646) 597-5903
www.ionmedianetworks.com
michaelhuber@ionmedia.com
License: Tolleson, AZ held by America 51, LP.
Group Owner: ION Media Networks; (acq 1-2-01; $6.6 million for 51%); *Washington Law Firm:* Skadden, Arps, Slate, Meagher & Flom
Nat'l Network: ION Television
Brandon Burgess, CEO

KTVK *Digital Channel:* 24; *Virtual Channel:* 3; 1,000 kW; 1,644 ft.; N33 20 1 W112 3 48
5555 N 7th Ave, Phoenix, AZ 85013 USA
(602) 207-3304
www.azfamily.com
License: Phoenix, Maricopa County, AZ held by KPHO Broadcasting Corp.
Group Owner: Meredith Corp.; (acq 9-3-99; $315 million cash including 50% of Arizona News Channel).
; *Nat'l Reps:* TeleRep; *Wire Services:* AP
Size of News Staff: 100; *Hours of Local News Weekly:* 48 hrs news progmg wkly

KTVW-DT *Digital Channel:* 33; *Virtual Channel:* 33; 470 kw; 1673 ft.; N33 20 0 W112 3 46
6006 S. 30th St., Phoenix, AZ 85042
(602) 243-3333; *Fax:* (602) 396-4020
www.univision.com
License: Phoenix, Maricopa County, AZ held by KTVW License Partnership G.P.
Group Owner: Univision Communications Inc.
Hours of Local News Weekly: news progmg 10 hrs wkly
Roberto Yanez, General Manager
Juan Villa, News Director
Gerardo Higginson, Director, Community Empowerment

KUTP *Digital Channel:* 26; *Virtual Channel:* 45; 1000 kW; 1696 ft.; N33 20 1 W112 3 32
511 W Adams St., Phoenix, AZ 85003 USA
(602) 257-1234; *Fax:* (602) 262-5109
www.my45.com
License: Phoenix, Maricopa County, AZ held by Fox Television Stations LLC
Group Owner: Fox Television Stations Group; (acq 7-31-2001; grpsl).; *Washington Law Firm:* Wilmer, Cutler & Pickering
Nat'l Network: MyNetworkTV

Tucson (Sierra Vista), AZ (DMA 71)

KFTU-DT *Digital Channel:* 36; *Virtual Channel:* 3; 5 kw vis; ant 30t/180g; N31 28 55 W109 57 32
1111 G Ave., Douglas, AZ 85607
(520) 805-1773
www.univision.com
License: Douglas, Cochise County, AZ held by Univision Partnership of Douglas.
Group Owner: Univision Communications Inc.; (acq 10-2-2001; $19.113 million plus assumption of liabilities with KFPH-TV Flagstaff).
Foreign Language Programming
Roberto Yanez, General Manager
Juan Villa, News Director
Gerardo Higginson, Director, Community Empowerment

KGUN-TV *Digital Channel:* 35; 110 kw vis, 21.94 kw aur; ant 3,739t/220g; N32 24 53 W110 42 58; *Population Served:* 1,050,000
7280 East Rosewood Street, Tucson, AZ 85710
(520) 722-5486; *Fax:* (520) 733-7099, (520) 733-7050
www.kgun9.com
news@kgun9.com
License: Tucson, Pima County, AZ held by Journal Broadcast Corp.
Group Owner: Journal Communications Inc.; (acq 12-5-2005; grpsl); *Washington Law Firm:* Reed Smith LLP
Nat'l Network: ABC; *Nat'l Reps:* MMT; *Wire Services:* NOAA Weather
Size of News Staff: 47; *Hours of Local News Weekly:* news progmg 22 hrs wkly
Kelly Donnell, Operations Dir
Jim Arnold, General Manager & VP
Adam Johnston, General Sales Mgr
Sue Bock, Programming Director
Thor Wasbotten, News Director
Stephen Somerville, Chief Engineer
Kara Quintela, National SalesManager
April Madison, Weather Team
Jason Barr, Sports Department
Charlie Mandala, Purchase Advertising
Ina Ronquillo, Internship Oppurtunities
Steve Swinehart, Commercial Producer

KHRR *Digital Channel:* 40; *Virtual Channel:* 40; 396 kw; 2037 ft.; N32 14 55 W111 6 57
2340 West 8th Avenue, Hialeah, FL 33010 USA
(305) 884-8200 ; *Fax:* (602) 648-3970
www.telemundo.com
License: Tucson, Pima County, AZ held by NBC Telemundo License LLC
Group Owner: Telemundo Station Group; (acq 1-1-2003; $20 million with KDRX-CA Phoenix)
Nat'l Network: Telemundo
Foreign Language Programming; Size of News Staff: 7; *Hours of Local News Weekly:* news progmg 5 hrs wkly
Luis Silberwasser, President

KMSB *Digital Channel:* 25; *Virtual Channel:* 11; 480 kw; 3,684 ft.; N32 42 56 W110 42 50
7831 N. Business Park Dr., Tucson, AZ 85743 US
(520) 770-5442; *Fax:* (520) 629-7185
www.tucsonnewsnow.com
kmsb-questions@tucsonnewsnow.com
License: Tucson, Pima County, AZ held by Sander Operating Co. V LLC dba KMSB Television
Group Owner: Sander Media LLC; *Washington Law Firm:* Wiley, Rein & Fielding
Nat'l Network: Fox; *Nat'l Reps:* TeleRep
Dee Anne Thomas, Local Sales Manager
Jim Watson, National Sales Manager
Kirstin Martin, National Sales Manager

KOLD-TV *Digital Channel:* 32; *Virtual Channel:* 13; 302 kw vis, 3 kw aur; ant 2,040t/187g; N32 14 56 W110 06 58; *Population Served:* 1,100,000
7831 N. Business Park Dr., Tucson, AZ 85743
(520) 744-1313; *Fax:* (520) 744-5233
www.kold.com
dbush@TucsonNewsNow.com
License: Tucson, Pima County, AZ held by KOLD License Subsidiary LLC.
Group Owner: Raycom Media Inc.; (acq 9-12-96); *Washington Law Firm:* Covington & Burling
Nat'l Network: CBS; *Nat'l Reps:* Harrington, Righter & Parsons; *Wire Services:* NWS (National Weather Service); AP
Hours of Local News Weekly: News progmg 27 hrs wkly
Debbie Bush, General Manager
David Rash, General Sales Mgr
Alyson Stogol, Programming Director
Craig Fleming, Promotions Manager
Michelle Germano, News Director
Sonny Reschka, Chief Engineer
Bob Gaff, Operations Manager
BobDuffy, Regional Sales Manager

KTTU *Digital Channel:* 19; *Virtual Channel:* 18; 480 kw; 3,684 ft.; N32 24 56 W110 42 50; *Population Served:* 750,000
7831 N. Business Park Dr., Tucson, AZ 85743 US
(520) 770-5442; *Fax:* (520) 629-7185
www.tucsonnewsnow.com
License: Tucson, Pima County, AZ held by Tucker Operating Co. LLC dba KTTU Television
Group Owner: Raycom Media Inc.; (acq 2-28-2002; $18 million); *Washington Law Firm:* Hogan & Hartson
Nat'l Network: MyNetworkTV; *Nat'l Reps:* TeleRep
Foreign Language Programming
Dee Anne Thomas, Local Sales Manager
Jim Watson, National Sales Manager

***KUAS-TV** *Digital Channel:* 28; *Virtual Channel:* 27; 50 kw; 584 ft.; N32 12 53 W111 0 21

Mailing Address: 1423 E. University Blvd., Tucson, AZ 85721-0067 US
Second Address: PO Box 210067, Tucson, AZ 85721
(520) 621-5828; *Fax:* (520) 621-4122 (news)
www.azpm.org
contactarizonapublicmedia@azpm.org
License: Tucson, Pima County, AZ held by Arizona Board of Regents for Benefit of University of Arizona.
Washington Law Firm: Dow, Lohnes & Albertson
Nat'l Network: PBS
Foreign Language Programming
Christopher Helms, Chair
Jack Gibson, Director & General Manager
Dana Horner, General Sales Mgr
Susie Hernandez, Programming Director
Wendy Erica Werden, Promotions Manager
Peter Michaels, News Director
David Ross, ChiefEngineer
Lili Bell, Traffic Manager
Enrique Aldana, Associate Director of Development
Patricia Callahan, Director of Membership
Frank Fregoso, Chief Broadcast Engineer

***KUAT-TV** *Digital Channel:* 30; *Virtual Channel:* 6; 667.5 kw; 3583 ft.; N32 24 55 W110 42 51
Mailing Address: 1423 E. University Blvd., Tucson, AZ 85721-0067 US
Second Address: PO Box 210067, Tucson, AZ 85721
(520) 621-5828; *Fax:* (520) 621-4122 (news)
www.azpm.org
contactarizonapublicmedia@azpm.org
License: Tucson, Pima County, AZ held by Arizona Board of Regents, University of Arizona
Washington Law Firm: Dow, Lohnes & Albertson
Nat'l Network: PBS
Foreign Language Programming
Christopher Helms, Chair
Jack Gibson, Director & General Manager
Dana Horner, General Sales Mgr
Susie Hernandez, Programming Director
Wendy Erica Werden, Promotions Manager
Peter Michaels, News Director
David Ross, ChiefEngineer
Lili Bell, Traffic Manager
Enrique Aldana, Associate Director of Development
Patricia Callahan, Director of Membership
Frank Fregoso, Chief Broadcast Engineer

KUVE-DT *Digital Channel:* 46; *Virtual Channel:* 46; 172 kw; 3652 ft.; N32 24 54 W110 42 56
2301 N. Forbes Blvd., Suite 103, Tucson, AZ 85745
(520) 204-1246
www.univision.com
License: Green Valley, Pima County, AZ held by Univision Tucson LLC.
Group Owner: Univision Communications Inc.
Roberto Yanez, General Manager
Juan Villa, News Director
Gerardo Higginson, Director, Community Empowerment

KVOA *Digital Channel:* 23; *Virtual Channel:* 4; 405 kw; 3,684 ft.; N32 24 56 W110 42 50; *Population Served:* 1,061,000
Mailing Address: 209 W. Elm St., Tucson, AZ 85705-6538 US
Second Address: P.O. Box 5188, Tucson, AZ 85703
(520) 792-2270; *Fax:* (520) 620-1309
www.kvoa.com
License: Tucson, Pima County, AZ held by KVOA Communications LLC
Group Owner: Cordillera Communications Inc.; (acq 12-31-93; $13.25 million; *Washington Law Firm:* Dow, Lohnes & Albertson
Nat'l Network: NBC; *Nat'l Reps:* HRP
Hours of Local News Weekly: news progmg 27 hrs wkly
Randall K. Smith, Operations Dir
Bill Shaw, President and General Manager
Jeff Green, General Sales Mgr
Dottie Diaz, Programming and Traffic
Cathie Batbie, News Director
Gary Kabrick, Chief Engineer
Linda Tremellin, BusinessManager
Kendra Sewell, Interactive Director

KWBA-TV *Digital Channel:* 44; 5,000 kw vis, 500 kw aur; ant 1,086t; N31 45 33 W110 48 02
7280 E. Rosewood St., Tucson, AZ 85710 US
(520) 722-5486; *Fax:* (520) 733-7050
soundoff@kwba.com
License: Sierra Vista, Cochise County, AZ held by Journal Broadcast Corp.
Group Owner: Journal Communications Inc.; (acq 7-22-2008; $11.885 million); *Washington Law Firm:* Leventhal Senter & Lerman PLLC

Nat'l Network: CW
Julie Brinks, General Manager
Guy Atchley, Anchor
Stella Inger, Anchor
Liz Kotalik, Anchor
Cory Marshall, Anchor
Keaton Thomas, Anchor
Maggie Vaspa, Anchor

Yuma, AZ-El Centro, CA (DMA 167)

KSWT *Digital Channel:* 13; *Virtual Channel:* 13; 50 kw; 1575 ft.; N33 3 18 W114 49 39
Mailing Address: 1301 South 3rd Avenue, Yuma, AZ 85364 US
Second Address: 510 Main Street, Suite 212, El Centro, CA 92243
(928) 782-5113, (928) 783-1300; *Fax:* (928) 783-0866, (928) 782-9411
www.kswt.com
License: Yuma, Yuma County, AZ held by Pappas Arizona License LLC.
Group Owner: Pappas Telecasting Companies; (acq 9-8-2000; $5.375 million); *Washington Law Firm:* Paul, Hastings, Janofsky & Walker
Nat'l Network: CBS AND CW; CW
Size of News Staff: 8; *Hours of Local News Weekly:* news progmg 5 hrs wkly
Julio Bermudez, General Manager
Julie Muhe, Regional/National Sales Manager
Gail Chango, Programming & Traffic Manager
Fred McCarty, Promotions Manager
Steve Nuez, News Director
Doug Melanson, Chief Engineer
Yesi Rios Carlos,Business/ Accounting/ HR Manager
Michael Ochoa, Creative Services Manager
Karen Breit, Sports Director

KYMA-DT ; 2.1 kw; 518t/1,617g; N33 03 10 W114 49 43; *Population Served:* 86,900
1965 S. 4th Ave., Yuma, AZ 85364 US
(928) 782-4944, (928) 782-1111; *Fax:* (928) 782-5401
www.kyma.com
news@kyma.com
License: Yuma, Yuma County, AZ held by Blackhawk Broadcasting LLC
Group Owner: Intermountain West Communications; (acq 6-6-89; $60,000); *Washington Law Firm:* Dow, Lohnes & Albertson
Nat'l Network: NBC
Size of News Staff: 24; *Hours of Local News Weekly:* news progmg 12 hrs wkly
Paul Heebing, General Manager
Matt McCombe, General Sales Mgr
Gail Chango, Programming Director
Ernesto Romero, News Director

Arkansas

Ft. Smith-Fayetteville-Springdale-Rogers, AR (DMA 99)

***KAFT** *Digital Channel:* 9; *Virtual Channel:* 13; 37.9 kw; 1650 ft.; N35 48 53 W94 1 41
Mailing Address: 350 Donaghey, Conway, AR 72032 US
Second Address: 350 S. Donaghey, Conway, AR 72034
(501) 682-2386,(800) 662-2386; *Fax:* (501) 682-4122
www.aetn.org
info@aetn.org
License: Fayetteville, Washington County, AR held by Arkansas Educational Television Commission
Washington Law Firm: Dow, Lohnes & Albertson
Nat'l Network: PBS
DeWayne Wilbur, Operations Dir
Allen Weatherly, Executive Director
Tony Brooks, Deputy Director

KFSM *Digital Channel:* 18; *Virtual Channel:* 5; 100 kw vis, 12.7 kw aur; 1,086t/1,173g; N35 30 43 W94 21 38; *Population Served:* 883,500
318 N 13th St., Fort Smith, AR 72901 USA
(479) 783-3131; *Fax:* (479) 783-3295
5newsonline.com
License: Fort Smith, Sebastian County, AR held by Tribune Broadcasting Fort Smith License LLC
Group Owner: Tribune Media; *Washington Law Firm:* DowLohnes, PLLC
Nat'l Network: CBS; MyNetworkTV; Antenna TV
Size of News Staff: 36; *Hours of Local News Weekly:* news progmg 28 hrs wkly
Van Comer, General Manager
Mark LaCrue, General Sales Mgr
Bill Cummings, News Director
Dan Bishop, Engineering Dept.

KFTA-TV *Digital Channel:* 27; *Virtual Channel:* 24; 600 kw; 1001 ft.; N35 42 36 W94 8 15
609 W. Dickson St., 3rd Floor, Fayetteville, AR 72701 US
(479) 571-5100
www.myfox24.com
License: Fort Smith, Sebastian County, AR held by Nexstar Broadcasting, Inc.
Group Owner: Nexstar Broadcasting Group.; (acq 12-21-2004; $10 million with KNWA-TV Rogers); *Washington Law Firm:* Holland & Knight
Nat'l Network: NBC/FOX; *Nat'l Reps:* TeleRep
Size of News Staff: 45; *Hours of Local News Weekly:* news progmg 20.5 hrs wkly
Lisa Kelsey, General Manager
Sarah Noblin, General Sales Mgr
Jody Birchfield, Promotions Manager

KHBS *Digital Channel:* 21; *Virtual Channel:* 40; 325 kw; 1975 ft.; N35 4 15 W94 40 43
2415 N. Albert Pike, Fort Smith, AR 72904 US
(479) 783-4040; *Fax:* (479) 785-5375
www.4029tv.com
License: Fort Smith, AR held by KHBS Hearst Television Inc.
Group Owner: Hearst Television Inc.; *Washington Law Firm:* Wiley, Rein & Fielding
Nat'l Network: ABC; CW
Size of News Staff: 30; *Hours of Local News Weekly:* news progmg 15 hrs wkly
Deanna J. Luchak, Programming Director

KHOG *Digital Channel:* 15; *Virtual Channel:* 29; 180 kw; 873 ft.; N36 0 57 W94 4 59
2809 Ajax Ave., Suite 200, Rogers, AR 72758 US
(479) 783-4040; *Fax:* (479) 785-5375
www.4029tv.com
news@4029tv.com
License: Fayetteville, AR held by KHBS Hearst Television Inc.
Group Owner: Hearst Television Inc.; (acq 7-16-97; grpsl).; *Washington Law Firm:* Wiley, Rein & Fielding
Nat'l Network: ABC; CW
Deanna J. Luchak, Programming Director

KNWA-TV *Digital Channel:* 50; *Virtual Channel:* 51; 1000 kw; 876 ft.; N36 24 47.8 W93 57 16.8; *Rebroadcasting:* Satellite of KFTA-TV Fort Smith.
609 W. Dickson St., 3rd Floor, Fayetteville, AR 72701 US
(479) 571-5100
www.nwahomepage.com
License: Rogers, Benton County, AR held by Nexstar Broadcasting Inc.
Group Owner: Nexstar Broadcasting Group Inc.; (acq 12-21-2004; $10 million with KFTA-TV Fort Smith).; *Washington Law Firm:* Drinker, Biddle & Reath
Nat'l Network: NBC; *Nat'l Reps:* Blair Television
Size of News Staff: 27; *Hours of Local News Weekly:* 17 hrs news progmg wkly
Lisa Kelsey, General Manager
Sara Noblin, General Sales Mgr
Jody Birchfield, Promotions Manager
Brook Thomas, News Director

KWOG *Digital Channel:* 39; *Virtual Channel:* 57; 35 kw; 374 ft.; N36 11 7 W94 17 49
P.O. Box 6968, Springdale, AR 72766 US
(817) 571-1229; *Fax:* (817) 571-8962
Partners@Daystar.com
License: Springdale, Washington County, AR held by Word of God Fellowship Inc.
Nat'l Network: IND
Marcus Lamb, President
Harvey Rogers, Chief Engineer

Jonesboro, AR (DMA 182)

KAIT *Digital Channel:* 8; *Virtual Channel:* 8; 28.2 kw; 1742 ft.; N35 53 22 W90 56 8
P.O. Box 790, 472 Country Rd. 766, Jonesboro, AR 72401 US
(870) 931-8888; *Fax:* (870) 933-8058 (news),(870) 931-1371(sales)
www.kait8.com
news@kait8.com
License: Jonesboro, Craighead County, AR held by KAIT License Subsidiary LLC.
Group Owner: Raycom Media Inc.; (acq 1-31-2006; grpsl); *Washington Law Firm:* Covington & Burling
Nat'l Network: ABC; *Nat'l Reps:* Harrington, Righter & Parsons; *Wire Services:* Weather Wire; AP

Size of News Staff: 32; *Hours of Local News Weekly:* news progmg 17 hrs wkly
David Rounds, Digital Content Director
Chris Conroy , Vice-President & General Manager
Debra Stephens, General Sales Manager
Debra Stephens, General Sales Manager
Ronnie Weston, Programming Director
Jeremy Shirley, PromotionsManager
Halton Weeks, News Director
Gerald Erickson, Chief Engineer
Ralph Caudill, National Sales Manager
Ronnie Weston, Operations Director
Debi Gann, Traffic Manager

***KTEJ** *Digital Channel:* 20; *Virtual Channel:* 19; 322.9 kw; 1017 ft.; N35 54 14 W90 46 14
Mailing Address: 350 South Donaghey St., Conway, AR 72032 US
Second Address: 350 S. Donaghey, Conway, AR 72034
(501) 682-2386,(800) 662-2386; *Fax:* (501) 682-4122
www.aetn.org
info@aetn.org
License: Jonesboro, Craighead County, AR held by Arkansas Educational Television Commission
Washington Law Firm: Dow, Lohnes & Albertson
Nat'l Network: PBS
Dr. Andrew Fulkerson, Chairman
Allen Weatherly, President
DeWayne Wilbur, Operations Dir
Tony Brooks, Station Manager
Mona Dixon, General Sales Mgr
Allen Weatherly, Executive Director

KVTJ-DT *Digital Channel:* 48; 66.4 kw; 1,023t/1,791g; N35 53 17 W90 56 09
Mailing Address: Box 26207, Little Rock, AR 72221 US
Second Address: 701 Napa Valley Dr., Little Rock, AR 72211
(501) 223-2525; *Fax:* (501) 221-3837
www.vtntv.com
License: Jonesboro, Craighead County, AR held by Agape Church Inc.
Group Owner: The Victory Television Network; (acq 1995).;
Washington Law Firm: Wiley Rein
Jimmie Rushing, Operations Dir
Jim Grant, General Manager
Kim Worden, Programming Director
Andrea Qualls, Promotions Manager
Ron Brown, Engineering Dir
Sharon Case, Traffic Director

Little Rock-Pine Bluff, AR (DMA 57)

KARK-TV *Digital Channel:* 32; *Virtual Channel:* 4; 1000 kw; 1471 ft.; N34 47 57 W92 29 59
1401 W. Capitol Ave., Suite 104, Little Rock, AR 72201 US
(501) 340-4444
www.arkansasmatters.com
License: Little Rock, Pulaski County, AR held by Nexstar Broadcasting Inc.
Group Owner: Nexstar Broadcasting Group Inc.; (acq 3-12-2009; $4 million)
Nat'l Network: MNT
Mike Vaughn, General Manager
Chad Beckham, Director of Sales
Austin Kellerman, News Director

KARZ-TV *Digital Channel:* 44; *Virtual Channel:* 42; 1000 kw; 1471 ft.; N34 47 57 W92 29 59
1401 W. Capitol Ave., Suite 104, Little Rock, AR 72201 US
(501) 340-4444
www.arkansasmatters.com
License: Little Rock, Pulaski County, AR held by Nexstar Broadcasting Inc.
Group Owner: Nexstar Broadcasting Group Inc.; (acq 3-12-2009; $4 million)
Nat'l Network: MNT
Mike Vaughn, General Manager
Chad Beckham, Director of Sales
Austin Kellerman, News Director

KASN *Digital Channel:* 39; 5,000 kw vis, 500 kw aur; ant 2,008t/1,910g; N34 26 31 W92 13 03; *Population Served:* 481,000
1401 W. Capitol Ave., Suite 104, Little Rock, AR 72201 US
(501) 340-4444; *Fax:* (501) 375-1961
License: Pine Bluff, Jefferson County, AR held by Mission Broadcasting Inc.
Group Owner: Mission Broadcasting Inc.; (acq 3-14-2008; grpsl)
Nat'l Network: CW
Joan Hall, Station Manager
Vicki McRae, General Sales Mgr
Ausin Kellerman, News Director

KATV *Digital Channel:* 22; *Virtual Channel:* 7; 1000 kw; 1690 ft.; N34 47 49 W92 29 19.5
P.O. Box 77, Little Rock, AR 72203 US
(501) 324-7777; *Fax:* (501) 324-7852
www.katv.com
newsroom@katv.com
License: Little Rock, Pulaski County, AR held by KATV Licensee LLC
Group Owner: Sinclair Broadcast Group Inc.; (acq 2-14-83; grpsl).; *Washington Law Firm:* Hogan & Hartson
Nat'l Network: ABC
Hours of Local News Weekly: news progmg 31.5 hrs wkly
Mark Rose, General Manager
Rusty Mooney, Engineering Dir

***KEMV** *Digital Channel:* 13; *Virtual Channel:* 6; 12.1 kw; 1398 ft.; N35 48 47 W92 17 24
Mailing Address: 350 South Donaghey, Conway, AR 72032 US
Second Address: 350 South Donaghey, Conway, AR 72034
(501) 450-1727,(501) 682-2386,(800) 662-2386; *Fax:* (501) 682-4122
www.aetn.org
info@aetn.org
License: Mountain View, Stone County, AR held by Arkansas Educational Television Commission
Washington Law Firm: Dow, Lohnes & Albertson
Nat'l Network: PBS
DeWayne Wilbur, Operations Dir
Allen Weatherly, General Manager
Tony Brooks, Station Manager
Mona Dixon, General Sales Mgr
Darbi Blencowe, Viewer Services Coordinator

***KEMV** *Digital Channel:* 13; *Virtual Channel:* 9; 13.85 kw; 1030 ft.; N33 54 26 W93 6 46
Mailing Address: 350 South Donaghey, Conway, AR 72032 US
Second Address: 350 S Donaghey Street, Conway, AR 72034
(501) 450-1727, (501) 682-2386, (800) 662-2386; *Fax:* (501) 682-4122
www.aetn.org
info@aetn.org
License: Arkadelphia, Clark County, AR held by Arkansas Educational Television Commission
Washington Law Firm: Dow, Lohnes & Albertson
Nat'l Network: PBS
DeWayne Wilbur, Operations Dir
Allen Weatherly, General Manager
Tony Brooks, Station Manager
Mona Dixon, General Sales Mgr
Darbi Blencowe, Viewer Services Coordinator
Darbi Blencowe, Viewer Services Coordinator

***KEMV** *Digital Channel:* 7; *Virtual Channel:* 2; 26.73 kw; 1795 ft.; N34 26 31 W92 13 3
Mailing Address: 350 South Donaghey, Conway, AR 72032 US
Second Address: 350 South Donaghey, Conway, AR 72034
(501) 450-1727, (501) 682-2386, (800) 662-2386; *Fax:* (501) 682-4122
www.aetn.org
info@aetn.org
License: Little Rock, Pulaski County, AR held by Arkansas Eucational Television Commission
Washington Law Firm: Dow, Lohnes & Albertson
Nat'l Network: PBS
DeWayne Wilbur, Operations Dir
Allen Weatherly, General Manager
Tony Brooks, Station Manager
Mona Dixon, General Sales Mgr
Darbi Blencowe, Viewer Services Coordinator
Darbi Blencowe, Viewer Services Coordinator

***KKAP** *Digital Channel:* 36; *Virtual Channel:* 36; 50 kw; 1293 ft.; N34 47 56 W92 29 45
#1 Shackleford Drive, Suite 400, Little Rock, AR 72211 US
(817) 571-1229; *Fax:* (817) 571-7458
www.daystart.com
License: Little Rock, Pulaski County, AR held by Educational Broadcasting Corp
Nat'l Network: IND
William Alatini, General Manager
Arnold Torres, Chief Regulatory Officer

KLRT-TV *Digital Channel:* 30; *Virtual Channel:* 16; 1000 kw; 1473 ft.; N34 47 57 W92 29 29
1401 W. Capitol Ave., Suite 104, Little Rock, AR 72201-2940 US
(501) 340-4444; *Fax:* (806) 220-0941
www.fox16.com
news@fox16.com
License: Little Rock, Pulaski County, AR held by Mission Broadcasting Inc.
Group Owner: Mission Broadcasting Inc.; (acq 3-14-2008; grpsl);
Washington Law Firm: Covington & Burling
Nat'l Network: FOX
Nancie Smith, Chairman
Dennis Thatcher, President

KMYA-DT *Digital Channel:* 49; *Virtual Channel:* 49; 1,000 kw vis; ant 600t/571g; N33 16 15 W92 42 14
1 Shackelford Dr., Little Rock, AR 72211
(501) 219-2400; *Fax:* (501) 604-8004
License: Camden, Ouachita County, AR held by KMYA LLC
Ownership: Ellis-Wilson LLC, 100%
Tammy Graham, Operations Dir
Neal Ardman, General Manager
Aaron Rothberg, General Sales Mgr
Chuck Stanely, Chief Engineer

KTHV *Digital Channel:* 12; *Virtual Channel:* 11; 55 kw; 1,702 ft.; N34 47 57 W92 29 59; *Population Served:* 152,483
720 Izard St., Little Rock, AR 72201
(501) 376-1111; *Fax:* (501) 376-3324
www.thv11.com
news@thv11.com
License: Little Rock, Pulaski County, AR held by Cape Publications Inc.
Group Owner: Tegna Media; (acq 11-30-94; $27 million;
Washington Law Firm: Wiley, Rein & Fielding
Nat'l Network: CBS; *Nat'l Reps:* TeleRep
Size of News Staff: 45; *Hours of Local News Weekly:* news progmg 27 hrs wkly
Michael Caplan, President and General Manager
Byron Wilkinson, General Sales Mgr
Dave Parker, News Director
Alison Fletcher, Chief Engineer
Chad Kelley, National Sales Manager

KVTH-DT *Digital Channel:* 26; 780 kw; 941t; N32 22 20 W93 02 47; *Rebroadcasting:* Satellite of KVTN(TV) Pine Bluff.
Mailing Address: Box 26207, Little Rock, AR 72221 US
Second Address: 701 Napa Valley Dr., Little Rock, AR 72211
(501) 223-2525; *Fax:* (501) 221-3837
www.vtntv.com
License: Hot Springs, Garland County, AR held by Agape Church Inc.
Group Owner: The Victory Television Network; (acq 1994).;
Washington Law Firm: Wiley Rein
Jim Grant, General Manager
Kim Worden, Programming Director
Andrea Qualls, Promotions Manager
Ron Brown, Engineering Dir
Sharon Case, Traffic Director

KVTN-DT *Digital Channel:* 24; 725 kw; ant 594t/594g; N34 31 55 W92 02 41
Mailing Address: Box 26207, Little Rock, AR 72221 US
Second Address: 701 Napa Valley Dr., Little Rock, AR 72211
(501) 223-2525; *Fax:* (501) 221-3837
www.vtntv.com
License: Pine Bluff, Jefferson County, AR held by Agape Church Inc.
Group Owner: The Victory Television Network; *Washington Law Firm:* Wiley, Rein
Jim Grant, General Manager
Kim Worden, Programming Director
Andrea Qualls, Promotions Manager
Ron Brown, Engineering Dir
Sharon Case, Traffic Manager

Monroe, LA-El Dorado, AR (DMA 137)

***KETZ** *Digital Channel:* 10; *Virtual Channel:* 12; 16.2 kw; 1765 ft.; N33 4 41 W92 13 30
Mailing Address: 350 S. Donaghey, Conway, AR 72032 US
Second Address: 350 S. Donaghey, Conway, AR 72034
(501) 682-2386, (800) 662-2386; *Fax:* (501) 682-4122
www.aetn.org
info@aetn.org
License: El Dorado, Union County, AR held by Arkansas Educational Television Commission.
Nat'l Network: PBS
Allen Weatherly, General Manager

KTVE *Digital Channel:* 27; *Virtual Channel:* 10; 822.8 kw; 1909 ft.; N33 4 41 W92 13 41
200 Pavilion Rd., West Monroe, LA 71292 US
(318) 323-1972
www.myarklamiss.com
License: El Dorado, Union County, AR held by Mission Broadcasting, Inc.

Group Owner: Mission Broadcasting.; *Washington Law Firm:* Cohn & Marks
Nat'l Network: NBC; *Nat'l Reps:* Continental Television Sales
Size of News Staff: 26; *Hours of Local News Weekly:* news progmg 13 hrs wkly
Brad Singleton, Station Manager
Bob Dowden, General Sales Mgr
John Walten, News Director

Springfield, MO (DMA 75)

KWBM *Digital Channel:* 31; *Virtual Channel:* 31; 191 kw; 1112 ft.; N36 42 18 W93 3 45
C/O Richard Baker, Treas, 2535 Success Drive, Odessa, FL 33556 US
(417) 877-9231; *Fax:* (417) 877-9015
License: Harrison, Boone County, AR held by Word of God Fellowship Inc.
Nat'l Network: DAYSTAR; *Nat'l Reps:* Roslin Television Sales
Regional Reps: Susan Cochran
S. Lanken, General Manager

KXNW *Digital Channel:* 34; *Virtual Channel:* 34; 1,000 kw vis; ant 736t/322g; N36 24 41 W93 57 12
4201 N Shiloh Dr., Suite 169, Fayetteville, AR 72703 USA
(479) 521-1330
5newsonline.com
License: Eureka Springs, Carroll County, AR held by Tribune Broadcasting Fort Smith License LLC
Group Owner: Tribune Media
Nat'l Network: MyNetworkTV; Antenna TV; CBS
Van Comer, General Manager
Mark LaCrue, General Sales Mgr
Bill Cummings, News Director
Dan Bishop, Engineering Dept.

California

Bakersfield, CA (DMA 126)

KBAK-TV *Digital Channel:* 33; *Virtual Channel:* 29; 110 kw; 3701 ft.; N35 27 11 W118 35 25
1901 Westwind Dr., Bakersfield, CA 93301 US
(661) 327-7955; *Fax:* (661) 327-5603
www.bakersfieldnow.com
news@bakersfieldnow.com
License: Bakersfield, Kern County, CA held by Sinclair Bakersfield Licensee LLC
Group Owner: Sinclair Broadcast Group Inc.; *Washington Law Firm:* Brooks, Pierce, McLendon, Humphrey & Leonard
Nat'l Network: CBS; *Nat'l Reps:* Continental Television Sales; *Wire Services:* AP
Size of News Staff: 40; *Hours of Local News Weekly:* news progmg 30.5 hrs wkly
Teresa Burgess, Vice President/General Manager
Cindi Dias, Sales Manager
Yvette Graves, Program Administrator
Tracy Peoples, Director of Promotions and Marketing
Cristi Jessee, News Director
Pete Capra, Chief Engineer

KBFX-CD *Digital Channel:* 29; *Virtual Channel:* 58; 15 kw; 7739 ft.; N35 27 11 W118 35 25
1901 Westwind Dr., Bakersfield, CA 93301 US
(661) 327-7955; *Fax:* (661) 327-5603
www.bakersfieldnow.com
news@bakersfieldnow.com
License: Bakersfield, Kern County, CA held by Sinclair Bakersfield Licensee LLC
Group Owner: Sinclair Broadcast Group Inc.
Nat'l Network: CBS; *Nat'l Reps:* Continental Television Sales; *Wire Services:* AP
Teresa Burgess, Vice President/General Manager
Cindi Dias, Sales Manager
Yvette Graves, Program Administrator
Tracy Peoples, Director of Promotions and Marketing
Cristi Jessee, News Director
Pete Capra, Chief Engineer

KERO-TV *Digital Channel:* 10; *Virtual Channel:* 23; 10.8 kw; 3632 ft.; N35 27 14 W118 35 37
321 21st St, Bakersfield, CA 93301 US
(661) 637-2320, (661) 637-2300; *Fax:* (661) 323-5538.
www.thebakersfieldchannel.com
License: Bakersfield, Kern County, CA held by McGraw-Hill Broadcasting Co.
Group Owner: McGraw-Hill Broadcasting Co.; (acq 3-8-72; grpsl; *Washington Law Firm:* Holland & Knight
Nat'l Network: ABC; *Nat'l Reps:* Harrington, Righter & Parsons
Steve McEvoy, General Manager
Craig Jahelka, Programming Director
Steve Taylor, Promotions Manager
Todd Karli, News Director
Tom Wimberly, Chief Engineer
Lesley Kirk, Edit Director
Maxcine Cole, Traffic Manager

KGET-TV *Digital Channel:* 25; *Virtual Channel:* 17; 135 kw; 1329 ft.; N35 26 17 W118 44 22
2120 L St., Bakersfield, CA 93301 US
(661) 283-1700; *Fax:* (661) 283-1794
www.kerngoldenempire.com
17news@kget.com
License: Bakersfield, Kern County, CA held by Nexstar Broadcasting Inc.
Group Owner: Nexstar Broadcasting; (acq 9-15-2008; grpsl)
Nat'l Network: NBC-CW
Size of News Staff: 33; *Hours of Local News Weekly:* news progmg 27 hrs wkly
Derek Jeffery, General Manager
Adam Chase, General Sales Mgr
Mike Trihey, News Director

KUVI-DT *Digital Channel:* 45; *Virtual Channel:* 45; 5,000 kw vis, 500 kw aur; ant 1,325t/144g; N36 26 20 W118 44 24;
Population Served: 508,000
5801 Truxtun Ave., Bakersfield, CA 93309
(661) 334-2607
www.univision.com
License: Bakersfield, Kern County, CA held by KUVI License Partnership G.P.
Group Owner: Univision Communications Inc.; (acq 2-4-98; $14,010,800).; *Washington Law Firm:* Shaw Pittman
Nat'l Network: MyNetworkTV
Leonardo Ruiz, General Manager and Director of Sales
Kenneth Richter, Chief Engineer

Chico-Redding, CA (DMA 132)

KCVU *Digital Channel:* 20; *Virtual Channel:* 30; 172 kw; 1473 ft.; N39 57 49 W121 42 38
P.O. Box 4159, Modesto, CA 95352 US
(530) 893-1234; *Fax:* (530) 899-5475
www.fox30.com
License: Paradise, Butte County, CA held by Esteem Broadcasting of California LLC
Group Owner: Esteem Broadcasting; *Washington Law Firm:* Fletcher, Heald & Hildreth
Nat'l Network: FOX; *Nat'l Reps:* Millennium Sales & Marketing
Hours of Local News Weekly: News progmg 0 hrs wkly
Doug Holroyd, General Manager
Bert Westhoff, General Sales Mgr
Paula Murphy, Programming Director
Betsy Brewer, Promotions Manager
Ken Rice, Chief Engineer
Glenn Taylor, Regional Sales Manager

KHSL-TV *Digital Channel:* 43; *Virtual Channel:* 12; 235 kw; 1539 ft.; N39 57 29 W121 42 49
3460 Silverbell Road, Chico, CA 95973 US
(530) 342-0141, (530) 343-1212, (530) 893-6554, (5; *Fax:* (530) 342-4905
License: Chico, Butte County, CA held by Catamount Broadcasting of Chico-Redding Inc.
(acq 7-30-98; $10 million); *Ownership:* Catamount Holdings LLC, 100% votes; *Washington Law Firm:* Haley, Bader & Potts
Nat'l Network: CBS; CW; *Nat'l Reps:* Continental Television Sales
Size of News Staff: 34; *Hours of Local News Weekly:* news progmg 20 hrs wkly
Stev Siorenson, Operations Dir
John Stall, General Manager
Keith True, Station Manager/Director of Sales
Chris Sweetin, National/Regional Sales
Andrea Haagenson, Programming
Morgan Schmidt, Promotions Manager
Scott Howard, NewsDirector
Dave Sien, Chief Engineer
Bobby Wadkins, Internet & Digital Sales
Steve Sorensen, Closed Captioning

***KIXE-TV** *Digital Channel:* 9; *Virtual Channel:* 9; 15 kw; 3579 ft.; N40 36 9 W122 39 1
603 North Market St., Redding, CA 96003 US
(530) 243-5493; *Fax:* (530) 243-7443
www.kixe.org
channel9@kixe.org
License: Redding, Shasta County, CA held by Northern California Educational TV Association Inc
Washington Law Firm: Schwartz, Woods & Miller
Nat'l Network: PBS
Hours of Local News Weekly: News progmg one hr wkly
Jack Nehr, Chairman
Myron Tisdel, President
Mike Lampella, Operations Director/General Manager
Anne Kerns, General Sales Mgr
Rob Keenan, Programming Director
Sue Maxey, Engineering Director
Sue Maxey, Chief Engineer
TracyReynolds, Vice-Chairman
Ken Simmon, Traffic Manager
Renee Cooper, CFO
Tom Anderson, IT Engineer
Rosell Herrera, Administrative Asst.
Michelle Slade, Director of Development

KNVN *Digital Channel:* 24; *Virtual Channel:* 24; 321 kw; 1772 ft.; N40 15 31 W122 5 24
The Pinnacle, Suite 875, 3455 Peachtree Rd., N.E., Atlanta, GA 30326 US
(530) 894-6397; *Fax:* (530) 342-2405
news@knvn.com
License: Chico, Butte County, CA held by Chico License L.L.C (acq 6-2000; $9.2 million); *Washington Law Firm:* Leventhal, Senter & Lerman
Nat'l Network: NBC
John Stall, General Manager
Steve Sorenson, Station Manager
Scott Howard, News Director

KRCR-TV *Digital Channel:* 7; *Virtual Channel:* 7; 84 kw; 3593 ft.; N40 36 10 W122 39 0
755 Auditorium Drive, Redding, CA 96001 US
(530) 243-7777, (800) 222-5727; *Fax:* (530) 243-0217, (530) 243-9382
www.krcrtv.com
astewart@krcrtv.com
License: Redding, Shasta County, CA held by BlueStone License Holdings Inc.
Group Owner: Bonten Media Group LLC; (acq 5-31-2007; grpsl)
Nat'l Network: ABC; *Nat'l Reps:* Petry Television Inc.
Size of News Staff: 21; *Hours of Local News Weekly:* news progmg 16 hrs wkly
Andrew Stewart, Vice President/General Manager
Lisa Drafall, Marketing Director/Director of Local Sales Operati
Paula Murphy, Programming Director
Kirstin Moran, Promotions Manager
Jennifer Scarbrough, News Director
Paul Johnson,Chief Engineer
Shannon House, Controller
Stephanie Vatz, Web Manager
Jennifer Scarborough, Anchor
Mike Mangas, Anchor
Kelli Sam, Anchor
Shay Arthur, Anchor

Eureka, CA (DMA 195)

KAEF-TV ; 141 kw vis, 14 kw aur; 1,672t; N40 43 36 W123 58 18
Mailing Address: 755 Auditorium Drive, Redding, CA 96001
Second Address: 540 E Street, Eureka, CA 95501
(530) 243-7777, (800) 222-5727; *Fax:* (530) 243-0217, (530) 243-9382
www.krcrtv.com
License: Arcata, Humboldt County, CA held by BlueStone License Holdings Inc.
Group Owner: Bonten Media Group LLC; (acq 5-31-2007; grpsl); *Washington Law Firm:* Covington & Burling LLP
Nat'l Network: ABC
Size of News Staff: 2; *Hours of Local News Weekly:* news progmg 2 hrs wkly
Andrew Stewart, Vice President/General Manager
Lisa Drafall, Marketing Director/Director of Local Sales Operati
Paula Murphy, Programming Director
Jennifer Scarborough, News Director
Paul Johnson, Chief Engineer
Shannon House,Controller
Stephanie Vatz, Web Manager

KBVU *Digital Channel:* 28; *Virtual Channel:* 29; 50 kw; 1683 ft.; N40 43 39 W123 58 17
P.O. Box 4159, Modesto, CA 95352 US
(707) 442-2999; *Fax:* (707) 441-0111
www.eurekatelevision.tv
engineering@eurekatelevision.tv
License: Eureka, Humboldt County, CA held by Esteem Broadcasting of California LLC

Group Owner: Esteem Broadcasting; acq 7-24-97).; *Washington Law Firm:* Womble, Carlyle, Sandrige & Rice
Nat'l Network: FOX; *Nat'l Reps:* Millennium Sales & Marketing
Chester Smith, CEO
Don Smullin, General Manager
Mark Dare, Chief Engineer

***KEET** *Digital Channel:* 11; *Virtual Channel:* 13; 38.4 kw; 1803 ft.; N40 43 38.9 W123 58 17
Mailing Address: PO Box 13, Eureka, CA 95502 US
Second Address: 7246 Humboldt Hill Rd., Eureka, CA 95503
(707) 445-0813; *Fax:* (707) 445-8977
www.keet.com
License: Eureka, Humboldt County, CA held by Redwood Empire Pub TV Inc
Nat'l Network: PBS
Foreign Language Programming
Ronald Schoenherr, CEO
Seth Frankel, Operations Dir
Karen Barnes, General Sales Mgr
Claire Reynolds, Promotions Manager
Joel Householter, Chief Engineer
Therese Buck, Traffic Manager

KIEM-TV *Digital Channel:* 3; *Virtual Channel:* 3; 12.5 kW; 1591 ft.; N40 43 49 W123 57 11
5650 S Broadway, Eureka, CA 95503 USA
(707) 443-3123; *Fax:* (707) 442-6084
kiem-tv.com
kiemnews@hotmail.com
License: Eureka, Humboldt County, CA held by Pollack/Belz Broadcasting LLC
Group Owner: Pollack Broadcasting; (acq 5-1-96; $3 million)
Size of News Staff: 8
Brenda Brazil, Business Manager
J Warren Hockaday, General Manager
Hank Ingham, General Sales Mgr

KVIQ *Digital Channel:* 17; *Virtual Channel:* 6; 30 kw; 1804 ft.; N40 43 39 W123 58 17
1333 New Hampshire Ave., N.W., Suite 1000, Washington, DC 20036 US
(707) 443-3061; *Fax:* (707) 441-0111
www.kviq.com
License: Eureka, Humboldt County, CA held by Raul Broadcasting Co. of Eureka Inc.
(acq 4-25-2005; $2 million); *Ownership:* Raul Palazuelos, 100%
Nat'l Network: CBS
John Burgess, General Manager
Penny King, Station Manager
Lauren Faucett, Programming Director
Rick St. Charles, Promotions Manager
Deve Silurrbrand, News Director
Jim Mixou, Chief Engineer

Fresno-Visalia, CA (DMA 54)

KAIL *Digital Channel:* 7; 2,510 kw vis, 251 kw aur; ant 1,906t/140g; N37 04 23 W119 15 52; *Population Served:* 1,700,000
1590 Alluvial Ave., Clovis, CA 93611
(559) 299-9753; *Fax:* (559) 299-1523
www.kail.tv
License: Fresno, Fresno County, CA held by Trans-America Broadcasting Corp.
(acq 12-23-66; $236,500; *Washington Law Firm:* Miller & Fields
Nat'l Network: MyNetworkTV
G. Borrego, President
Mike Nicasio, Operations Manager
Charles Williams, General Manager
Dave Hetrick, General Sales Mgr
Robert Jenkins, Programming Director
Angela Bartley, Traffic Manager

KFRE-TV *Digital Channel:* 36; *Virtual Channel:* 59; 360 kw; 1991 ft.; N37 4 37 W119 26 1
5111 E. McKinley Ave., Fresno, CA 93727 US
(559) 255-2600; *Fax:* (559) 255-9626
www.kmph-kfre.com
License: Sanger, Fresno County, CA held by KFRE Licensee LLC
Group Owner: Sinclair Broadcast Group Inc.; (acq 10-1-2013; grpsl); *Ownership:* TTBG Fresno OpCo, LLC; *Washington Law Firm:* Pillsbury Winthrop Shaw Pittman LLP
Nat'l Network: CW
Size of News Staff: 5; *Hours of Local News Weekly:* news progmg 2 hrs wkly
Jack Peck, General Manager
Matt Morse, General Sales Mgr
Mark Hodorowski, Creative Services Director

KFSN-TV *Digital Channel:* 30; *Virtual Channel:* 30; 260 kW; 239 ft.; N37 4 38 W119 26 0
1777 G St., Fresno, CA 93706 USA
(559) 442-1170
abc30.com
kfsndesk@abc.com
License: Fresno, Fresno County, CA held by KFSN Television LLC
Group Owner: ABC Owned Television Stations; *Washington Law Firm:* ABC Legal
Nat'l Network: ABC; *Nat'l Reps:* ABC National Television Sales
Size of News Staff: 50; *Hours of Local News Weekly:* news progmg 30 hrs wkly
Mike Carr, News Director

KFTV-DT *Digital Channel:* 20; *Virtual Channel:* 21; 5,000 kw vis, 605 kw aur; ant 1,984t/216g; N37 04 22 W119 25 50; *Population Served:* 637,000
Mailing Address: 601 West Univision Plaza, Fresno, CA 93704
Second Address: 605 3rd Ave., 12th Fl., New York, NY 10158
(559) 222-2121
www.univision.com
License: Hanford, Kings County, CA held by KFTV License Partnership G.P.
Group Owner: Univision Communications Inc.; (acq 8-87).; *Washington Law Firm:* Shaw Pittman LLP
Nat'l Network: Univision (Spanish)
Foreign Language Programming; Size of News Staff: 58; *Hours of Local News Weekly:* news progmg 7 hrs wkly
Brett Covish, Operations Manager
Angela Navarrete, Station Manager

KGMC *Digital Channel:* 43; *Virtual Channel:* 43; 283 kw; 2106 ft.; N36 44 46 W119 16 57
706 West Herndon Avenue, Fresno, CA 93650-1033 US
(559) 432-4300,(559) 435-7000; *Fax:* (559) 435-3201
www.cocolatv.com
info@cocolatv.com
License: Clovis, Fresno County, CA held by Gary M. Cocola
Group Owner: Cocola Broadcasting Companies LLC; (acq 11-19-92).; *Washington Law Firm:* Dow, Lohnes & Albertson
Nat'l Network: MundoFox
Gary Cocola, CEO
John Her, Operations Dir
Kevin Mosesian, Station Manager
Al Kinney, Chief Engineer

KGPE *Digital Channel:* 34; *Virtual Channel:* 47; 2,500 kw vis; ant 1,958t/226g; N37 04 14 W119 25 31; *Population Served:* 1,453,000
5035 E. McKinley Ave., Fresno, CA 93727 US
(559) 222-2411
www.yourcentralvalley.com
License: Fresno, Fresno County, CA held by Nexstar Broadcasting Inc.
Group Owner: Nexstar Broadcasting; (acq 9-15-2008; grpsl); *Washington Law Firm:* Pillsbury Winthrop Shaw Pittman LLP
Nat'l Network: CBS; *Nat'l Reps:* Continental Television Sales
Size of News Staff: 50; *Hours of Local News Weekly:* news progmg 28hrs wkly
Matthew Rosenfeld, General Manager
Chad McCollum, News Director

KMPH-TV *Digital Channel:* 28; *Virtual Channel:* 26; 219 kw; 2503 ft.; N36 40 2 W118 52 42
5111 E. McKinley Ave., Fresno, CA 93727 US
(559) 255-2600; *Fax:* (559) 255-9626
www.kmph-kfre.com
License: Visalia, Tulare County, CA held by KMPH Licensee LLC
Group Owner: Sinclair Broadcast Group Inc.; (acq 10-1-2013; grpsl); *Ownership:* TTBG Fresno OpCo, LLC; *Washington Law Firm:* Pillsbury Winthrop Shaw Pittman LLC
Nat'l Network: FOX; *Nat'l Reps:* TeleRep
Size of News Staff: 21; *Hours of Local News Weekly:* news progmg 7 hrs wkly
Jack Peck, General Manager
Matt Morse, General Sales Mgr
Mark Hodorowski, Creative Services Director

KNSO *Digital Channel:* 11; *Virtual Channel:* 51; 45 kw; 2041 ft.; N37 4 19 W119 25 49
P.O. Box 4159, Modesto, CA 95352 USA
(559) 252-5101; *Fax:* (559) 252-2747
www.telemundo51fresno.com
License: Merced, Merced County, CA held by NBC Telemundo License LLC
Group Owner: Telemundo Station Group; (acq 4-30-2003; $33 million)
Nat'l Network: Telemundo
Foreign Language Programming
Luis Silberwasser, President

***KNXT** *Digital Channel:* 50; *Virtual Channel:* 49; 185 kw; 2736 ft.; N36 17 14 W118 50 17
1550 N.Fresno St., Fresno, CA 93703 US
(559) 488-7440; *Fax:* (559) 488-7444
www.dioceseoffresno.org
knxt49@hotmail.com
License: Visalia, Tulare County, CA held by Board of Directors Diocese of Fresno Education Corp
Nat'l Network: ETV
Foreign Language Programming
Bishop John Steinback, President
Colin Dougherty, General Manager

KSEE *Digital Channel:* 38; *Virtual Channel:* 24; 1,600 kw vis, 320 kw aur; 2,350t/321g; N36 44 45 W119 16 53; *Population Served:* 165,972
5035 E. McKinley Ave., Fresno, CA 93727 US
(559) 222-2411
www.yourcentralvalley.com
License: Fresno, Fresno County, CA held by Nexstar Broadcasting Inc.
Group Owner: Nexstar Broadcasting Group Inc.; (acq 12-93; $32 million with WTVH(TV) Syracuse, NY; *Washington Law Firm:* Dow Lohnes
Nat'l Network: NBC; *Nat'l Reps:* Continental Television
Matthew Rosenfeld, General Manager
Chad McCollum, News Director

KTFF-DT *Digital Channel:* 48; *Virtual Channel:* 61; 2,510 kw vis, 251 kw aur; 2,638 ft.; N36 17 14 W118 50 17
601 West Univision Plaza, Fresno, CA 93704
(559) 222-2121
www.univision.com
License: Porterville, Tulare County, CA held by UniMas Fresno LLC.
Group Owner: Univision Communications Inc.; (acq 2-7-2003; $35 million)
Nat'l Network: UniMas (Spanish)
Brett Covish, Operations Manager
Angela Navarrete, Station Manager
Jose Elgorriga, Regional VP of Ad Sales
Sandy Sirias, News Director

***KVPT** *Digital Channel:* 40; *Virtual Channel:* 18; 250 kw; 2290 ft.; N36 44 45 W119 16 51
733 L St, Fresno, CA 93721 US
(559) 266-1800; *Fax:* (559) 650-1880
www.kvpt.org
web@kvpt.org
License: Fresno, Fresno County, CA held by Valley Public Television Inc
(acq 11-1-87); *Washington Law Firm:* Fletcher, Heald & Hildreth
Nat'l Network: PBS
Foreign Language Programming; Size of News Staff: 35
Douglas Noll, Chairman
Paula Castadio, CEO
Andrea Bressel, Operations Dir
Eva Torres, General Sales Mgr
Jerry Lee, Programming Director
Jim Page, Promotions Manager
Rodger Hixon, Chief Engineer
Phyllis Brotherton, CFO

Los Angeles (DMA 2)

KABC-TV *Digital Channel:* 7; *Virtual Channel:* 7; 28.7 kW; 451 ft.; N34 13 37 W118 3 58
500 Circle Seven Dr., Glendale, CA 91201 USA
(818) 863-7777
abc7.com
License: Los Angeles, Los Angeles County, CA held by ABC Holding Company Inc.
Group Owner: ABC Owned Television Stations
Nat'l Network: ABC; *Wire Services:* UPI

KAZA-TV *Digital Channel:* 47; *Virtual Channel:* 54; 350 kw; 3073 ft.; N34 13 37 W118 3 57
500 S. Chinowth Road, Visalia, CA 93277 US
(559) 733-7800,(818) 241-5400; *Fax:* (559) 733-7878
License: Avalon, Los Angeles County, CA held by Southern California License LLC.
Group Owner: Pappas Telecasting Companies
Nat'l Network: AZTECA AMERICA
Foreign Language Programming
Fernando Acosta, Operations Dir
Eduardo Urbiola, General Manager
Alberto Ezquerro, General Sales Mgr
Ramon Delgado, Programming Director
Oscar Salcedo, News Director

Bruce Yeager, Chief Operator
Joe Berardi, Chief Engineer
Yolanda Williamson, Traffic Manager

KBEH *Digital Channel:* 24; *Virtual Channel:* 63; 1000 kw; 2867 ft.; N34 12 48 W118 3 41
Mailing Address: 950 Flynn Road, Camarillo, CA 93012 US
Second Address: 5757 W Century Blvd, Suite 490, Los Angeles, CA 90045
(310) 216-0063; *Fax:* (310) 216-0663
www.canal63.com
License: Oxnard, Ventura County, CA held by Hero License Co LLC
4/11/2008; *Washington Law Firm:* Fletcher Heald & Hildreth, PLC
Nat'l Network: MTV TR3S
Bob Behar, President
Mara Rankin, General Manager
Barbara Alvarez, Traffic Director
Charlie Trice, Engineering Dir

KCAL-TV *Digital Channel:* 43; 25 kW; 423 ft.; N34 13 38 W118 4 0
4200 Radford Ave, Studio City, CA 91604 USA
(818) 655-2563, (818) 655-2000; *Fax:* (818) 655-2693
www.kcal.com
kcbscc@cbs.com
License: Los Angeles, CA held by Los Angeles Television Station KCAL LLC
Group Owner: CBS Television Stations Group
Nat'l Network: Independent; CBS; *Nat'l Reps:* Adam Young; *Wire Services:* Conus; World Television News Service

KCBS-TV *Digital Channel:* 43; *Virtual Channel:* 2; 540 kW; 338 ft.; N34 13 38 W118 4 0; *Population Served:* 14,400,000
4200 Radford Ave., Studio City, CA 91604 USA
(818) 655-2000
losangeles.cbslocal.com
License: Los Angeles, Los Angeles County, CA held by CBS Broadcasting Inc.
Group Owner: CBS Television Stations Group; (acq 12-27-50; $3.6 million;
Nat'l Network: CBS
Size of News Staff: 95; *Hours of Local News Weekly:* news progmg 31 hrs wkly

***KCET** *Digital Channel:* 59; *Virtual Channel:* 28; 2,455 kw vis, 245.5 kw au; ant 3,038t/330g; N34 13 26 W118 03 44; *Population Served:* 4,600,000
Mailing Address: 2900 West Alameda Ave., Burbank, CA 91505
Second Address: 2900 W. Alameda Ave., Burbank, CA 91505
(323) 666-6500; *Fax:* (323) 953-5523
www.kcet.org
contact@kcet.org
License: Los Angeles, Los Angeles County, CA held by Community TV of Southern California
Washington Law Firm: Arent, Fox, Kintner, Plotkin & Kahn
Richard Cook, Chair
Mary Mazur, EVP/COO
Al Jerome, President & CEO
Gordon Bell, SVP, Engineering, Operations & I.T.
Palencia Turner, SVP/Chief Development Officer
June M. Baldwin, SVP, General Counsel Corporate & Legal Affairs
Albert Chavez, SVP/CFO
Juan Devis, SVP, Content Development & Production
Ariel Carpenter, Vice President, Communications
Lorraine Hess, VP, Programming and Acquisition

KCOP *Digital Channel:* 13; *Virtual Channel:* 13; 161 kw vis, 32.4 kw aur; ant 2,972t/187g; N34 13 29 W118 03 48; *Population Served:* 149,000
1999 South Bundy Dr., Los Angeles, CA 90025 USA
(310) 584-2000
www.foxla.com/my1
License: Los Angeles, Los Angeles County, CA held by Fox Television Stations LLC
Group Owner: Fox Television Stations Group; (acq 7-31-2001; grpsl).; *Washington Law Firm:* Wilmer, Cutler & Pickering
Nat'l Network: MyNetworkTV

KDOC-TV *Digital Channel:* 32; *Virtual Channel:* 56; 1000 kw; 3114 ft.; N34 13 35 W118 3 58
625 N Grand Ave., Santa Ana, CA 92701 US
(949) 442-9800; *Fax:* (949) 261-5956/(949) 221-4171
www.kdoctv.net
feedback@la56.tv
License: Anaheim, Orange County, CA held by Ellis Communications KDOC Licensee LLC
(acq 2006; $149.5 million); *Washington Law Firm:* Cohn & Marks
Nat'l Network: NONE
Foreign Language Programming

Pat Boone, President
Calvin Brack, Operations Dir
John Manzi, General Manager
Tom Jimenez, General Sales Mgr
John Atkinson, Programming Director
Michelle Merker, Promotions Manager
Roger Knipp, Chief Engineer
Dale Foshee,Regional Sales Manager

KFTR-DT *Digital Channel:* 29; *Virtual Channel:* 46; 2,450 kw vis, 372 kw aur; 3,040t/323g; N34 13 36 W118 03 59
5999 Center Dr., Los Angeles, CA 90045
(310) 348-3600
www.univision.com
License: Ontario, San Bernardino County, CA held by UniMas Los Angeles LLC.
Group Owner: Univision Communications Inc.; (acq 5-21-2001; grpsl).; *Washington Law Firm:* Wiley, Rein & Fielding
Nat'l Network: UniMas (Spanish)
Foreign Language Programming
Beatriz Gomez, Operations Dir
Luis De La Parra, Promotions Manager
Chris Homer, Chief Engineer

KILM *Digital Channel:* 44; *Virtual Channel:* 64; 3,160 kw vis, 627 kw aur; ant 1,699t/203g; N34 36 34 W117 17 11; *Population Served:* 5,000,000
Mailing Address: Box 1468, Victorville, CA 92393-1468
Second Address: 15605 Village Dr., Victorville, CA 92394
(760) 241-6464; *Fax:* (760) 241-0056
www.khiztv.com
License: Barstow, San Bernardino County, CA held by KAZN-TV Licensee LLC.
(acq 11-1-2007; $7.95 million); *Washington Law Firm:* Wilkinson, Barker & Knauer
Size of News Staff: 10; *Hours of Local News Weekly:* news progmg 5 hrs wkly
Arthur Liu, President
Garrett Law, General Manager
Stella Montoya, Programming Director

KJLA *Digital Channel:* 49; *Virtual Channel:* 57; 1000 kw; 3074 ft.; N34 13 35 W118 3 57
Mailing Address: 15304 Sunset Blvd., Suite 204, Pacific Palisades, CA 90272 US
Second Address: 2323 Corinth Ave., West Los Angeles, CA 90064
(310) 943-5288, (800) 588-5788; *Fax:* (310) 943-5299
www.kjla.com
License: Ventura, Ventura County, CA held by KJLA LLC
(acq 11-14-94; *Washington Law Firm:* Thompson Hine & Flory
Nat'l Network: IND
Foreign Language Programming
Ed Safa, CFO
Walter Ulloa, President
Mike Seros, Operations/Production
Francis X. Wilkinson, General Manager
Richard Deanda, General Sales Mgr
Ken Brown, Engineering Director
Daniel Crowe, Executive Vice President
Tim Treadway,Internship Program
Laura Zaragoza, Traffic Manager
Ed Safa, CFO
Daniela nuno, Programming/Traffic Assistant

***KLCS** *Digital Channel:* 41; *Virtual Channel:* 58; 1000 kw; 2958 ft.; N34 13 26 W118 3 45
1061 West Temple Street, Los Angeles, CA 90012 US
(213) 625-6958/(213) 241-4000; *Fax:* (213) 481-1019
www.klcs.org
info@klcs.org
License: Los Angeles, Los Angeles County, CA held by Los Angeles Unified School District
Washington Law Firm: Cohn & Marks
Nat'l Network: PBS
Hours of Local News Weekly: News progmg 5 hrs wkly
Sabrina Fair Thomas, Operations Director/General Manager
Myles Jang, General Sales Mgr
Sabrina Fair Thomas, Programming Director
Alan Popkin, Director of Engineering/Technical Operations
Jorge Briseno, Director of ITV services

KMEX-DT *Digital Channel:* 34; *Virtual Channel:* 34; 1,950 kw vis, 195 kw aur; ant 2,940t/170g; N34 13 36 W118 03 59; *Population Served:* 281,606
5999 Center Dr., Los Angeles, CA 90045
(310) 348-3417
www.univision.com
License: Los Angeles, Los Angeles County, CA held by KMEX License Partnership G.P.
Group Owner: Univision Communications Inc.
Nat'l Network: Univision (Spanish); *Wire Services:* UPI

Foreign Language Programming; Hours of Local News Weekly: news progmg 17 hrs wkly
Luis Patino, Senior Vice President and General Manager
Marco Alejandro Flores, Vice President of News
Antoinette Gill, VP Sales Systems and Procedures

KNBC *Digital Channel:* 36; *Virtual Channel:* 4; 665 kw; 3251 ft.; N34 13 32 W118 3 52
100 Universal City Plaza, Bldg 2120, Universal City, CA 91608 USA
(818) 684-4444; *Fax:* (818) 840-3003
www.nbclosangeles.com
License: Los Angeles, Los Angeles County, CA held by NBC Telemundo License LLC
Group Owner: NBC Owned Television Stations; (acq 6-5-86).
Nat'l Network: NBC; *Nat'l Reps:* NBC TV Stations Sales; *Wire Services:* Reuters; UPI

***KOCE-TV** *Digital Channel:* 48; *Virtual Channel:* 50; 1000 kw; 3114 ft.; N34 13 35 W118 3 57
3080 Bristol Street, Suite 100, Costa Mesa, CA 92626 US
(714) 842-5797; *Fax:* (714) 895-0852
www.pbssocal.org
kmische@koce.org
License: Huntington Beach, Orange County, CA held by KOCE-TV Foundation
(acq 11-1-2004; $25.5 million).; *Washington Law Firm:* Vorys, Sater, Seymour & Pease
Nat'l Network: PBS
Size of News Staff: 4; *Hours of Local News Weekly:* News progmg 12.5 hrs wkly
Jim McCluney, Chairman
Mel Roger, CEO
Carol Schatz, President
Kurt Mische, Operations Dir
Ed Miskevich, Station Manager
Pat Petrick, Programming Director
Mike Taylor, News Director
Gordon Smith, Chief Engineer

KPXN-TV *Digital Channel:* 38; 1000 kw; ant 2,345t; N34 12 46 W118 03 41; *Population Served:* 13,000,000
2600 Olive Ave., Suite 900, Burbank, CA 91505 USA
(212) 757-3100; *Fax:* (646) 597-5903
www.ionmedianetworks.com
michaelhubner@ionmedia.com
License: San Bernardino, CA held by Ion Media Los Angeles License, Inc.
Group Owner: Ion Media Networks
Nat'l Network: ION Television
Aisha Figilis, Operations Dir

KRCA *Digital Channel:* 35; *Virtual Channel:* 62; 1000 kw; 2972 ft.; N34 12 48 W118 3 41
1845 Empire Ave, Burbank, CA 91504 US
(818) 729-5300
www.estrellatv.com
lbiinfo@lbimedia.com
License: Riverside, Riverside County, CA held by KRCA License LLC.
Group Owner: Liberman Broadcasting Inc.; (acq 6-18-90)
Nat'l Network: IND
Foreign Language Programming; Hours of Local News Weekly: 7.5 hours
Winter Horton, General Manager

KSCI *Digital Channel:* 18; *Virtual Channel:* 18; 2,583 kw vis; ant 2,949t/164g; N34 12 47.8 W118 03 41; *Population Served:* 6,000,000
1990 S. Bundy Dr., Suite 850, Los Angeles, CA 90025
(310) 478-1818; *Fax:* (310) 479-8118
info@la18.tv
License: Long Beach, Los Angeles County, CA held by NRJ TV LA OpCo LLP
Group Owner: NRJ Holdings LLC; (acq 8-10-2012); *Washington Law Firm:* Goldberg, Godles, Wiener & Wright
Foreign Language Programming; Size of News Staff: 12; *Hours of Local News Weekly:* news progmg 27 hrs wkly
Dennis J. Davis, CEO/COO
Armando Villalpando, Operations Dir
Larry Potter, General Sales Mgr
Eva McKeown, Programming Director
Alice Lee, Promotions Manager
April Kuan, News Director (Mandarin)
Jeff Kim, News Director(Korean)
Scott Chestnut, Chief Engineer
Bill Welty, Engineering Director

KTBN-TV *Digital Channel:* 33; *Virtual Channel:* 40; 1000 kw; 2871 ft.; N34 13 27 W118 3 44
Mailing Address: PO Box A, Santa Ana, CA 92711 US
Second Address: 2442 Michelle Dr., Tustin, CA 92780

(714) 832-2950; *Fax:* (714) 665-2191
www.tbn.org
comments@tbn.org
License: Santa Ana, Orange County, CA held by Trinity Broadcasting Network.
Group Owner: Trinity Broadcasting Network; (acq 8-2-74; $1,266,400; *Washington Law Firm:* Joseph E. Dunne III
Nat'l Network: TRINITY BROADCA
Paul Crouch, President
Phyllis Smith, General Manager
Mary Jane Allen, Station Manager
Jan Crouch, Promotions Manager
Ken Howerton, Chief Engineer

KTLA *Digital Channel:* 31; *Virtual Channel:* 5; 44.7 kw vis, 6.7 kw aur; 6,176t/473g; N34 13 36 W118 03 56; *Population Served:* 14,443,000
5800 Sunset Blvd., Los Angeles, CA 90028 USA
(323) 460-5500; *Fax:* (323) 460-5243
ktla.com
License: Los Angeles, Los Angeles County, CA held by KTLA LLC
Group Owner: Tribune Media; (acq 12-20-2007; grpsl); *Washington Law Firm:* Dow Lohnes PLLC
Nat'l Network: The CW Network; *Nat'l Reps:* TeleRep; *Wire Services:* Reuters; NWS (National Weather Service)
Hours of Local News Weekly: News progmg 43 hrs wkly

KTTV *Digital Channel:* 11; *Virtual Channel:* 11; 115 kW; 2963 ft.; N34 13 29 W118 3 48
1999 S Bundy Dr., Los Angeles, CA 90025 USA
(310) 584-2000
www.foxla.com
License: Los Angeles, Los Angeles County, CA held by Fox Television Stations LLC
Group Owner: Fox Television Stations Group; (acq 11-14-86; grpsl).
Nat'l Network: FOX
Hours of Local News Weekly: News progmg 25 hrs wkly

***KVCR-DT** *Digital Channel:* 26; 1,318 kw vis, 131.8 kw aur; 3,166t/215g; N30 57 57 W117 17 05; *Population Served:* 17,000,000
701 S. Mt. Vernon Ave., San Bernardino, CA 92410
(909) 384-4444; *Fax:* (909) 885-2116
www.kvcr.org
info@kvcr.org
License: San Bernardino, San Bernardino County, CA held by San Bernardino Community College District
Nat'l Network: PBS
Larry Ciecalone, General Manager
Kenn Couch, Station Manager
Don Leiffer, Programming Director
Lillian Vasquez, Promotions Manager
Ken Vincent, News Director
Thomas Guptill, Chief Engineer
Al Gondos, Producer/Director
PattyLittlejohn, Traffic Manager
Rick Dulock, Program Manager
Ben Holland, Program Director
Yvonne Powers, Development Associate
Lillian Vasquez, Marketing Coordinator

KVEA *Digital Channel:* 39; *Virtual Channel:* 52; 1000 kw; 2989 ft.; N34 12 48 W118 3 41
Mailing Address: 2290 West 8th Avenue, Hialeah, FL 33010 USA
Second Address: 3000 W. Alameda Ave., Burbank, CA 91523
(818) 260-5700; *Fax:* (818) 260-5222
www.telemundo52.com
License: Corona, Riverside County, CA held by NBC Telemundo License LLC
Group Owner: Telemundo Station Group; (acq 4-12-2002; grpsl).
Nat'l Network: Telemundo
Foreign Language Programming
Luis Silberwasser, President

KVMD *Digital Channel:* 23; *Virtual Channel:* 31; 150 kw; 2572 ft.; N34 2 17 W116 48 47
22720 S.E. 410 Street, Enumclaw, WA 98022 US
(949) 365-5710; *Fax:* (949) 365-5709
License: Twentynine Palms, San Bernardino County, CA held by KVMD Licensee Co. LLC
Nat'l Network: IND
Larry Peterson, General Manager
Ken Brown, Chief Engineer
Sherrie Karr, Public Service Director

KVME-TV *Digital Channel:* 20; *Virtual Channel:* 20; 4.2 kw vis; ant 3,031t/30g; N37 24 43 W118 11 06
Mailing Address: Cocola Broadcasting Companies, 706 W. Herndon Ave., Fresno, CA 93650
Second Address: 706 West Herndon Avenue, Fresno, CA 93650-1033
(559) 435-7000; *Fax:* (559) 435-3201
www.cocolatv.com
info@cocolatv.com
License: Bishop, Inyo County, CA held by Bellagio Broadcasting LLC.
Group Owner: Venture Technologies Group LLC
Lawrence Rogow, General Manager

KWHY-TV *Digital Channel:* 42; *Virtual Channel:* 22; 486 kw; 892 meters; N34 13 36 W118 03 59; *Population Served:* 5,000,000
1201 West 5th Street, 9th Floor, Los Angeles, CA 90017
(213) 344-3700; *Fax:* (818) 260-5805
License: Los Angeles, Los Angeles County, CA held by KWHY-22 Broadcasting LLC
Washington Law Firm: Wiley Rein LLP
Nat'l Network: MundoFox; *Wire Services:* Reuters
Foreign Language Programming; Size of News Staff: 6; *Hours of Local News Weekly:* news progmg 12 hrs wkly
Otto Padron, General Manager

KXLA *Digital Channel:* 51; *Virtual Channel:* 44; 1000 kw; 3074 ft.; N34 13 35.3 W118 3 57.7
2323 Corinth Ave., West Los Angeles, CA 90064 US
(310) 478-0055; *Fax:* (310) 478-8070
www.kxlatv.com
cgonzalez@kxlatv.com
License: Rancho Palos Verdes, Los Angeles County, CA held by Rancho Palos Verdes Broadcasters Inc
Nat'l Network: IND
Ron Ulloa, President
Ken Brown, Chief Engineer
Carolina Gonzalez, Traffic Manager

Lucerne Valley

KIJR-LP *Digital Channel:* 47; 9 kw; N33 51 58 W116 26 0
21700 Northwestern Hwy., Suite 1190, Tower 14, Southfield, MI 48075 US
(248) 557-3500; *Fax:* (248) 557-2950
www.birach.com
sima@birach.com
License: Lucerne Valley, San Bernardino County, CA held by Birach Broadcasting Corp.
Group Owner: Birach Broadcasting Corp.
Sima Birach, President

Monterey-Salinas, CA (DMA 125)

KCBA *Digital Channel:* 13; *Virtual Channel:* 35; 19.75 kw; 2362 ft.; N36 45 22 W121 30 6
67 Garden Ct., Monterey, CA 93901 US
(831) 642-4400; *Fax:* (831) 754-1120
www.kcba.com
kmeyenberg@entravision.com
License: Salinas, Monterey County, CA held by Seal Rock Broadcasters LLC
Group Owner: Entravision Communications; *Washington Law Firm:* Rubin, Winston, Diercks, Harris & Cooke
Nat'l Network: FOX
Hours of Local News Weekly: News progmg 10 hrs wkly
Lindsay Nash, National Sales Mgr
Joe Chabala, Promotions Manager
Duane Johnson, Integrated Marketing Solution Consultant
Karla Maciel, Content Manager

KDJT-CD *Digital Channel:* 33; *Virtual Channel:* 33; 8.97 kw; 2431 ft.; N36 45 22.90 W121 30 4.90
67 Garden Ct., Monterey, CA 93940 US
(831) 373-6767; *Fax:* (831) 373-6700
License: Salinas, CA held by Entravision Holdings, LLC
Group Owner: Entravision Communications; *Washington Law Firm:* Rubin, Winston, Diercks, Harris & Cooke
Nat'l Network: FOX
Hours of Local News Weekly: News progmg 10 hrs wkly
Karla Barreto, National Sales Mgr
Victor Ramos, Promotions Manager
Garcia Erandi, News Director
Warren Terriberry, Engineering Dir

KION-TV *Digital Channel:* 32; *Virtual Channel:* 46; 46 kw; 2487 ft.; N36 32 5 W121 37 14
1550 Moffett Street, Salinas, CA 93905 US
(831) 422-3500; *Fax:* (831) 784-6395
www.kion546.com
License: Monterey, Monterey County, CA held by NPG of Monterey-Salinas CA, LLC
Group Owner: News-Press & Gazette Co.; *Washington Law Firm:* Skadden, Arps, Slate, Meagher & Flom LLP
Nat'l Network: CBS; CW; *Wire Services:* UPI
Size of News Staff: 25; *Hours of Local News Weekly:* news progmg 8 hrs wkly
Kristy Santiago, General Sales Mgr

***KQET** *Digital Channel:* 25; 52.5 kw vis; ant 2,198t; N36 45 23 W121 30 05
Mailing Address: c/o KQED, 2601 Mariposa St., San Francisco, CA 94110
Second Address: 50 W. San Fernando St., Ste. 110, San Jose, CA 95113-2415
(415) 864-2000; *Fax:* (415) 553-2333
www.kqed.org
lyoung@kqed.org
License: Watsonville, Santa Cruz County, CA held by KQED Inc.
Nat'l Network: PBS
Kevin E. Martin, SVP/COO
John Boland, President
David Shimada, Dir of Corporate Support/General Sales Manager
Lee Young, Director of Engineering Facilities
Michael Isip, SVP/Chief Content Officer
William L. Lowery, General Counsel& Corporate Secretary
Mitzie Kelley, Chief Financial Officer
Traci A. Eckels, Chief Development Officer
Michael Englehaupt, Chief Technology Officer
Tim Olson, VP, Digital Media & Education

KSBW *Digital Channel:* 8; *Virtual Channel:* 8; 20.6 kw; 2493 ft.; N36 45 23 W121 30 5
238 John St., Salinas, CA 93901 US
(831) 758-8888; *Fax:* (831) 424-3750
www.ksbw.com
License: Salinas, CA held by Hearst Stations Inc.
Group Owner: Hearst Television Inc.; (acq 6-1-98).; *Washington Law Firm:* Brooks, Pierce, McLendon, Humphrey & Leonard
Nat'l Network: NBC; *Nat'l Reps:* Eagle Television Sales
Size of News Staff: 31; *Hours of Local News Weekly:* news progmg 31 hrs wkly
Joseph Heston, President
Jose Camacho, Operations Dir
Wendy Hillan, General Sales Mgr
Karen Pren, Programming Director
Bill Mushrush, Promotions Manager
Britt Govea, Marketing Manager

Palm Springs, CA (DMA 146)

KESQ-TV *Digital Channel:* 42; *Virtual Channel:* 42; 42 kw; 745 ft.; N33 51 58 W116 26 8
31276 Dunham Way, Thousand Palms, CA 92276 US
(760) 773-0342; *Fax:* (760) 773-5107, (760) 343-3512
www.kesq.com
License: Palm Springs, Riverside County, CA held by Gulf-California Broadcast Co.
Group Owner: News-Press & Gazette Co.; (acq 4-24-96; $19.4 million); *Washington Law Firm:* Smithwick & Belendiuk
Nat'l Network: ABC; CW; *Nat'l Reps:* Continental Television Sales; *Wire Services:* News 1; AP
Size of News Staff: 40; *Hours of Local News Weekly:* news progmg 17 hrs wkly
Mike O'Malley, CFO
Bob Allen, President
John Gilhuly, Operations Manager
Mike Stutz, General Manager
Sonia Montano, Programming Director
Kent Kay, Director, Marketing, Promotion & Creative
Bob Smith, News Director

KEVC-CD *Digital Channel:* 36; *Virtual Channel:* 5; 0.349 kw; N33 48 07 W116 13 27
41601 Corporate Way., Palm Desert, CA 92260 US
(760) 341-5837; *Fax:* (760) 341-0951
www.entravision.com
License: Indio, CA held by Entravision Holdings LLC.
Group Owner: Entravision Communications Corp.
Foreign Language Programming
Victor Ramos, Promotions Coordinator

KMIR-TV *Digital Channel:* 46; *Virtual Channel:* 36; 120 kw; 697 ft.; N33 52 0 W116 25 59
72920 Parkview Drive, Palm Desert, CA 92260 US
(760) 568-3636/(760) 340-1623; *Fax:* (760) 568-1176
www.kmir6.com
License: Palm Springs, Riverside County, CA held by Journal Broadcast Corp.
Group Owner: Journal Communications Inc.; (acq 6-11-99; $28.1 million); *Washington Law Firm:* Koteen & Naftalin
Nat'l Network: NBC

Size of News Staff: 30; *Hours of Local News Weekly:* news progmg 27 hrs wkly
Cralg Marrs, Chairman
Lyle Schulze, Operations Dir
Craig Marrs, Vice President/General Manager
Alison Shaw, Sales & Advertising
Mayra Mancilla, Programming Director
David Reese, News Director
Tim Balint, Chief Engineer
SteveSchill, News Commentator
Frank Keller, Operations Manager
Scott Johnson, Regional Sales Manager
Mayra Mancilla, Traffic Manager
Manny dela Rosa, Promotion, Marketing & Community Event

KVER-CA *Digital Channel:* 40; *Virtual Channel:* 4; 0.349 kw; 1768 ft; N33 51 56 W116 25 58
41601 Corporate Way., Palm Desert, CA 92260 US
(760) 341-5837; *Fax:* (760) 341-0951
www.noticias.entravision.com/palm-springs
License: Indio, CA held by Entravision Holdings LLC.
Group Owner: Entravision Communications Corp.
Foreign Language Programming
Leonides Vasquez, Operations Dir
Mercy Castro, Promotions Coordinator
Ricardo Vela, News Director

KVES-LD *Digital Channel:* 40; *Virtual Channel:* 4; 15 kw; 1768 ft; N33 51 56 W116 25 58; *Rebroadcasting:* Rebroadcasts KVER-CA
41601 Corporate Way., Palm Desert, CA 92260 US
(760) 341-5837; *Fax:* (760) 341-0951
License: Indio, CA held by Entravision Holdings LLC.
Group Owner: Entravision Communications Corp.
Foreign Language Programming
Leonides Vasquez, Operations Dir
Mercy Castro, Promotions Coordinator
Ricardo Vela, News Director

Sacramento-Stockton-Modesto, CA (DMA 20)

***KBSV** *Digital Channel:* 15; *Virtual Channel:* 23; 0.421 kw; 1888 ft.; N37 30 28 W121 22 20.2; *Not on Air/Target Date:* unknown
P.O. Box 4116, Modesto, CA 95352 US
(209) 538-4130; *Fax:* (209) 538-2795
KBSV@Aol.com
License: Ceres, Stanislaus County, CA held by Bet-Nahrain
Nat'l Network: ETV
Dr. Sargon Dadesho, President
Shemiran Daniel, Operations Dir

KCRA-TV *Digital Channel:* 35; *Virtual Channel:* 3; 100 kw; 1900 ft.; N38 15 54 W121 29 24
3 Television Cir., Sacramento, CA 95814-0794 US
(916) 446-3333; *Fax:* (916) 441-4050
www.kcra.com
newstips@kcra.com
License: Sacramento, CA held by Hearst Stations Inc.
Group Owner: Hearst Television Inc.; (acq 2-18-99).; *Washington Law Firm:* Koteen & Naftalin
Nat'l Network: NBC; *Nat'l Reps:* Petry Television Inc.
Hours of Local News Weekly: News progmg 55 hrs wkly
Veronica Serrano Padilla, Programming Director
Greg Turner, Engineering Dir

KMAX-TV *Digital Channel:* 21; 850 kW; 1912 ft.; N38 15 54 W121 29 24; *Population Served:* 254,413
2713 KOVR Dr., West Sacramento, CA 95605 USA
(916) 374-1313; *Fax:* (916) 374-1304
gooddaysacramento.cbslocal.com
goodday@kmaxtv.com
License: Sacramento, Sacramento County, CA held by Sacramento Television Stations Inc.
Group Owner: CBS Television Stations Group
Nat'l Network: The CW Network
Foreign Language Programming

KOVR-TV *Digital Channel:* 25; *Virtual Channel:* 13; 1000 kW; 1949 ft.; N38 14 24 W121 30 3
2713 KOVR Dr., West Sacramento, CA 95605 USA
(916) 374-1313; *Fax:* (916) 374-1462
sacramento.cbslocal.com
License: Stockton, San Joaquin County, CA held by Sacramento Television Stations Inc.
Group Owner: CBS Television Stations Group
Nat'l Network: CBS
Size of News Staff: 120; *Hours of Local News Weekly:* news progmg 21 hrs wkly

KQCA *Digital Channel:* 46; *Virtual Channel:* 58; 600 kw; 1903 ft.; N38 15 54 W121 29 24
3 Television Cir., Sacramento, CA 95814-0794 US
(916) 446-3333
www.kcra.com
License: Stockton, CA held by Hearst Stations Inc.
Group Owner: Hearst Television Inc.; (acq 1-24-2000; less than $1 million); *Washington Law Firm:* Skadden, Arps, Slate, Meagher & Flom
Nat'l Network: MNT
Elliot Troshinsky, General Manager
Jerry Brehm, General Sales Mgr
Lori Kesler, Programming Director
Jim Caselli, Promotions Manager
Dan Weiser, News Director
Stefan Hadl, Engineering Dir
Patrick Donnelly, General SalesManager
Gene Robinson, Promotions Manager

KSPX-TV *Digital Channel:* 48; 1000 kw; ant 1,296t/1,300g; N38 15 54 W121 29 24
3352 Mather Field Rd., Rancho Cordova, CA 95670 USA
(916) 368-2929; *Fax:* (646) 597-5903
michaelhubner@ionmedia.com
License: Sacramento, CA held by Ion Media Sacaramento License, Inc.
Group Owner: Ion Media Networks; (acq 5-25-2000; $17.725 million); *Washington Law Firm:* Wiley, Rein & Fielding
Nat'l Network: ION Television
Size of News Staff: 75; *Hours of Local News Weekly:* news progmg 7 hrs wkly
Brandon Burgess, Chairman

KTFK-DT *Digital Channel:* 5; *Virtual Channel:* 64; 850 kw; 1952 ft.; N38 14 24 W121 30 3; *Population Served:* 3,480,000
1710 Arden Way, Sacramento, CA 95815 US
(916) 614-1918; *Fax:* (916) 614-1902
www.univision.com
License: Stockton, San Joaquin County, CA held by UniMas Sacramento LLC.
Group Owner: Univision Communications Inc.
Nat'l Network: UniMas (Spanish)
Steve Stuck, General Manager
Carolina Gore, Director of Community Affairs

KTXL *Digital Channel:* 40; *Virtual Channel:* 40; 1000 kw; 1972 ft.; N38 16 18 W121 30 18
4655 Fruitridge Rd., Sacramento, CA 95820 USA
(916) 733-3109; *Fax:* (916) 739-1079
fox40.com
License: Sacramento, Sacramento County, CA held by KTXL LLC
Group Owner: Tribune Media; (acq 12-20-2007; grpsl); *Washington Law Firm:* Sidley Austin LLP
Nat'l Network: FOX; *Nat'l Reps:* TeleRep
Hours of Local News Weekly: News progmg 29.5 hrs wkly

KUVS-DT *Digital Channel:* 18; *Virtual Channel:* 19; 5,000 kw vis, 560 kw aur; 1,877t/250g; N38 07 07 W120 43 27; *Population Served:* 3,480,000
1710 Arden Way, Sacramento, CA 95815 US
(916) 614-1918; *Fax:* (916) 614-1902
www.univision.com
License: Modesto, Stanislaus County, CA held by KUVS License Partnership G.P.
Group Owner: Univision Communications Inc.; (acq 3-6-97; $40 million); *Washington Law Firm:* Shaw Pittman
Nat'l Network: Univision (Spanish)
Foreign Language Programming; Size of News Staff: 30; *Hours of Local News Weekly:* news progmg 12 hrs wkly
Steve Stuck, General Manager
Tony Martinez, Executive Producer

***KVIE** *Digital Channel:* 9; *Virtual Channel:* 6; 33 kw; 1958 ft.; N38 16 18 W121 30 18
2030 W. El Camino Avenue, Sacramento, CA 95833 US
(916) 929-5843; *Fax:* (916) 929-7215
www.kvie.org
member@kvie.org
License: Sacramento, Sacramento County, CA held by KVIE Inc
Washington Law Firm: Dow, Lohnes & Albertson
Nat'l Network: PBS
James Becksmith, President
Jonathan Breslau, Chief
Walter Cunnigham, Senior Vice President
Jan Tilmon, Programming Director
Michael Wall, Chief Engineer
Kevin Smith-Fagan, Vice President of Development
Michael Sanfor, VicePresident for Content Creation
Karen Dolce, CFO

KXTV *Digital Channel:* 10; *Virtual Channel:* 10; 28.6 kw; 2,008 ft.; N38 14 24 W121 30 3
400 Broadway, Sacramento, CA 95818-2098 US
(916) 441-2345; *Fax:* (916) 321-3384
www.abc10.com
desk@abc10.com
License: Sacramento, Sacramento County, CA held by KXTV LLC
Group Owner: Tegna Media; (acq 1999; swap with KVUE(TV) Austin, TX); *Washington Law Firm:* Wiley, Rein & Fielding
Nat'l Network: ABC; *Nat'l Reps:* Blair Television
Hours of Local News Weekly: news progmg 36 hrs wkly
Maria Barrs, President and General Manager
Jerome Parra, News Director
Ron Adair, Chief Engineer
Dennis Williams, Regional Business Development Director

San Diego, CA (DMA 28)

KBNT-CD *Digital Channel:* 25; *Virtual Channel:* 17; 11.9 kw; 255 ft; N32 41 40 W117 07 17
5770 Ruffin Rd., San Diego, CA 92130 US
(858) 576-1919; *Fax:* (858) 715-1919
www.noticias.entravision.com/san-diego
License: San Diego, CA held by Entravision Holdings LLC.
Group Owner: Entravision Communications Corp.
Foreign Language Programming
Margarita Wilder, CEO/COO
Chip Thomas, National Sales Mgr
Julio Jauregui, Promotions Manager
Lourdes Sandoval, News Director

KDTF-LD *Digital Channel:* 51; *Virtual Channel:* 36; 12.15 kw; 1870 ft; N32 41 47 W116 56 09
5770 Ruffin Rd., San Diego, CA 92130 US
(858) 576-1919; *Fax:* (858) 715-1919
www.noticias.entravision.com/san-diego
License: San Diego, CA held by Entravision Holdings LLC.
Group Owner: Entravision Communications Corp.
Foreign Language Programming
Margarita Wilder, CEO/COO
Chip Thomas, National Sales Mgr
Julio Jauregui, Promotions Manager
Lourdes Sandoval, News Director

KFMB-TV *Digital Channel:* 8; 316 kw vis, 63.2 kw aur; ant 745t/249g; N32 50 17 W117 14 57; *Population Served:* 2,896,000
7677 Engineer Rd., San Diego, CA 92111
(858) 571-8888, (858) 495-8640; *Fax:* (858) 560-0627
www.cbs8.com
License: San Diego, San Diego County, CA held by Midwest Television Inc
(acq 4-17-2007; with KFMB-AM-FM San Diego); *Ownership:* Midwest Television Inc; *Washington Law Firm:* Dow Lohnes
Nat'l Network: CBS; Me-TV 8.2; *Nat'l Reps:* TeleRep; *Wire Services:* UPI
Size of News Staff: 85; *Hours of Local News Weekly:* 24
Elisabeth Kimmel, Owner & President
Pat Nevin, Vice President & General Manager
Adam Weyne, General Sales Mgr
Elyse Sensabaugh, Programming Director
Donna Dube, Promotions Manager
Dean Elwood, News Director
Rich Lochman,Engineering Dir
Rich Lochman, Chief Engineer
Jan Gross, Local Sales Manager
Thelma Presichi, Traffic Manager

KGTV *Digital Channel:* 10; *Virtual Channel:* 10; 20.7 kw; 745 ft.; N32 50 20 W117 14 56
Mailing Address: P.O. Box 85347, San Diego, CA 92186 US
Second Address: 4600 Air Way, San Diego, CA 92102
(619) 237-1010, (619) 237-6383; *Fax:* (619) 527-0369
www.10news.com
linda.blake@10news.com
License: San Diego, San Diego County, CA held by McGraw-Hill Broadcasting Co.
Group Owner: McGraw-Hill Broadcasting Co.; (acq 6-1-72; grpsl; *Washington Law Firm:* DowLohnes, PLLC
Nat'l Network: ABC; *Nat'l Reps:* Harrington, Righter & Parsons
Size of News Staff: 65; *Hours of Local News Weekly:* news progmg 35 hrs wkly
Mike Biltucci, Operations Dir
Jeffrey Block, General Manager
Ken Rycyzn, General Sales Mgr
Jason Maloney, Promotions Manager
John Jorgenson, Closed Caption Supervisor
Andrew Lombard, Chief Engineer
Paul Kaderabek, BusinessManager

Joel Davis, News Director
Allison Ash, News Team
Steve Atkinson, Co-Anchor
Pat Brown, Weather Team
Ben Higgins, Sports team

KHAX-LP *Digital Channel:* 25; *Virtual Channel:* 17; 0.045 kw; 1085 ft; N33 12 53 W117 11 15; *Rebroadcasting:* Rebroadcasts KBNT-CD San Diego
5770 Ruffin Rd., San Diego, CA 92130 US
(858) 576-1919; *Fax:* (858) 715-1919
www.noticias.entravision.com/san-diego
License: San Diego, CA held by Entravision Holdings LLC.
Group Owner: Entravision Communications Corp.
Foreign Language Programming
Margarita Wilder, CEO/COO
Chip Thomas, National Sales Mgr
Julio Jauregui, Promotions Manager
Lourdes Sandoval, News Director

KNSD *Digital Channel:* 40; *Virtual Channel:* 39; 370 kw; 1857 ft.; N32 41 48 W116 56 6
225 Broadway, San Diego, CA 92101 USA
(619) 231-3939; *Fax:* (619) 578-0225
www.nbcsandiego.com
License: San Diego, San Diego County, CA held by Station Venture Operations LP
Group Owner: NBC Owned Television Stations; (acq 3-2-98; with KXAS-TV Fort Worth, TX).; *Washington Law Firm:* Pepper & Corazzini
Nat'l Network: NBC
Foreign Language Programming

***KPBS** *Digital Channel:* 30; *Virtual Channel:* 15; 350 kw; 1862 ft.; N32 41 53 W116 56 3
5200 Campanile Drive, San Diego, CA 92182 US
(619) 594-6983; *Fax:* (619) 594-3812
www.kpbs.org
letters@kpbs.org
License: San Diego, San Diego County, CA held by Board of Trustees, California State University for San Diego State University
Nat'l Network: PUBLIC BROADCAS; *Wire Services:* AP
Doug Myrland, General Manager
Keith York, Programming Director
Nancy Worlie, Promotions Manager
John Decker, News Director
Tammy Carpowich, Director of New Media
Anna Bunge, Traffic Manager

KSWB *Digital Channel:* 19; *Virtual Channel:* 69; 4,790 kw vis, 479 kw aur; 1,950t/151g; N32 41 47 W116 56 07; *Population Served:* 943,500
7191 Engineer Rd., San Diego, CA 92111 USA
(858) 492-9269; *Fax:* (858) 268-0401
fox5sandiego.com
kswbreceptionist@fox5sandiego.com
License: San Diego, San Diego County, CA held by KSWB LLC
Group Owner: Tribune Media; (acq 12-20-2007; grpsl);
Washington Law Firm: Dow Lohnes PLLC
Nat'l Network: FOX; *Nat'l Reps:* TeleRep
Hours of Local News Weekly: News progmg 44.5 hrs wkly

KTCD-LP *Digital Channel:* 51; *Virtual Channel:* 36; 0.012 kw; N33 00 31 W116 58 16; *Rebroadcasting:* Rebroadcasts KBNT-CD San Diego
5770 Ruffin Rd., San Diego, CA 92130 US
(858) 576-1919; *Fax:* (858) 715-1919
License: San Diego, CA held by Entravision Holdings LLC.
Group Owner: Entravision Communications Corp.
Foreign Language Programming
Margarita Wilder, CEO/COO
Chip Thomas, National Sales Mgr
Julio Jauregui, Promotions Manager
Lourdes Sandoval, News Director

KUSI-TV *Digital Channel:* 18; *Virtual Channel:* 51; 355 kW; 1890 ft.; N32 41 51 W116 56 5.7
4575 Viewridge Ave, San Diego, CA 92123 USA
(858) 571-5151
www.kusi.com
sales@kusi.com
License: San Diego, San Diego County, CA held by Channel 51 of San Diego Inc.
Group Owner: McKinnon Broadcasting Co.; (acq 6-29-90;
Washington Law Firm: Cohn & Marks
Nat'l Network: IND
Size of News Staff: 70; *Hours of Local News Weekly:* news progmg 51 hrs wkly
Michael D. McKinnon Sr., CEO/President
Charlie Grisham, General Sales Mgr

XETV-DT *Digital Channel:* 23; 100 kw vis, 50 kw aur; 1,000t/550g; *Population Served:* 920,570
8253 Ronson Rd., San Diego, CA 92111
(858) 279-6666, (866) 700-NEWS; *Fax:* (858) 279-0061
www.sandiego6.com
License: Tijuana, MX held by Radio-Television SA
Washington Law Firm: Leventhal, Senter & Lerman
Nat'l Network: CW
Hours of Local News Weekly: News progmg 20 hrs wkly
Rodrigo Salazar, CFO
Richard Jones, Operations Dir
Chuck Dunning, General Sales Mgr
Judy Albrecht, Promotions Manager
Harry Melkerson, National Sales Manager
Bob Anderson, Operations Director
Lynda DiLorenzo, Regional SalesManager
Scott Dillon, Regional Sales Manager
Marc Bailey, Anchor
CS Keys, Reporter

XEWT-DT *Digital Channel:* 32; 325 kw vis, 32.5 kw aur; 1,000t/200g; N32 30 06 W117 02 23; *Population Served:* 2,200,000
Mailing Address: Box 434537, San Diego, CA 92143
Second Address: 637 Third Ave., Suite B, Chulavista, CA 91910
(800) TELEV 12,(619) 585-9398; *Fax:* (619) 585-9463
www.televisa.com
License: Tijuana, MX held by Televisora de Calimex, SA
Washington Law Firm: Leventhal, Senter & Lerman
Foreign Language Programming; Size of News Staff: 50; *Hours of Local News Weekly:* news progmg 11 hrs wkly
Lourdes Numez, Operations Dir
Ricardo Azcarraga, General Manager

San Francisco-Oakland-San Jose (DMA 6)

KBCW-TV *Digital Channel:* 45; *Virtual Channel:* 44; 1000 kW; 877 ft.; N37 45 19 W122 27 6
855 Battery St., San Francisco, CA 94111 USA
(415) 765-8144
cwsanfrancisco.cbslocal.com
feedback@kbcwtv.com
License: San Francisco, San Francisco County, CA held by San Francisco Television Station KBCW Inc.
Group Owner: CBS Television Stations Group; *Washington Law Firm:* Hogan & Hartson
Nat'l Network: The CW Network
Tom Spitz, Director of Program Operations

KCNS *Digital Channel:* 39; *Virtual Channel:* 38; 1000 kw; 1679 ft.; N37 45 19 W122 27 6
1700 Montgomery Street, Suite 400, San Francisco, CA 94111 US
(415) 217-1355; *Fax:* (415) 352-1800
www.mundofox38.com
rowen@ktnc.com
License: San Francisco, San Francisco County, CA held by NJR TV San Fran License Co. LLC
Group Owner: NRJ Holdings LLC; (acq 2-2-2009)
Nat'l Network: IND
Luis Mendoza, Operations Dir
Andrea Yamazaki, General Manager
Alan Ng, Station Manager

***KCSM-TV** *Digital Channel:* 43; *Virtual Channel:* 60; 500 kw; 1678 ft.; N37 45 19 W122 27 6
1700 West Hillsdale Blvd, San Mateo, CA 94402 US
(650) 574-6586; *Fax:* (650) 524-6975
www.kcsm.org
License: San Mateo, San Mateo County, CA held by San Mateo County Community College District
Washington Law Firm: Tierney & Swift
Nat'l Network: PBS
Foreign Language Programming
Alisa Clancy, Operations Dir
Marilyn Lawrence, General Manager
Shelly Rogers, General Sales Mgr
Michelle Muller, Engineering Dir

KDTV-DT *Digital Channel:* 51; *Virtual Channel:* 14; 3,980 kw vis, 398 kw aur; 2,509t/439g; N37 29 57 W121 52 16; *Population Served:* 1,023,300
50 Fremont St., 41st Fl., San Francisco, CA 94105
(415) 538-6472
www.univision.com
License: San Francisco, San Francisco County, CA held by KDTV License Partnership G.P.
Group Owner: Univision Communications Inc.; *Washington Law Firm:* Fisher, Wayland, Cooper, Leader & Zaragoza
Nat'l Network: Univision (Spanish)

Foreign Language Programming; Size of News Staff: 15; *Hours of Local News Weekly:* news progmg 7 hrs wkly
Marcela Medina, General Manager
Carolina Echeverria, Public Affairs Manager
Maria Rodriguez, Traffic Manager

KEMO-TV *Digital Channel:* 32; 302 kw vis, 60.4 kw aur; ant 3,080t/172g; N38 40 10 W122 37 52; *Population Served:* 1,500,000
533 Mendocino Avenue, Santa Rosa, CA 20036
(707) 526-5050; *Fax:* (707) 526-7429
www.aztecaamericasf.com
License: Santa Rosa, Sonoma County, CA held by High Plains Broadcasting License Co. LLC.
Washington Law Firm: Pillsbury Winthrop Shaw Pittman LLP
Nat'l Network: Azteca America
Hours of Local News Weekly: 0
Richard Starkey, Operations Dir
John Burgess, General Manager
Corinne Flushman, General Sales Mgr
Elizabeth Quinn, News Director

KFSF-DT *Digital Channel:* 34; *Virtual Channel:* 66; 3,470 kw vis, 346 kw aur; ant 1,528t/797g; N37 45 19 W122 27 6;
Population Served: 5,500,000
50 Fremont St., 41st Fl., San Francisco, CA 94105
(415) 538-8076
www.univision.com
License: Vallejo, Solano County, CA held by UniMas San Francisco LLC.
Group Owner: Univision Communications Inc.; (acq 12-18-2001; $39 million)
Nat'l Network: UniMas (Spanish)
Foreign Language Programming
Raul Rodriguez, Vice President and General Manager
Carolina Nunez, News Director
James Van Tassell, Chief Engineer

KGO-TV *Digital Channel:* 7; *Virtual Channel:* 7; 23.8 kW; 951 ft.; N37 45 19 W122 27 6
900 Front St., San Francisco, CA 94111 USA
(415) 954-7777
abc7news.com
License: San Francisco, San Francisco County, CA held by KGO Television Inc.
Group Owner: ABC Owned Television Stations
Nat'l Network: ABC

KKPX-TV ; 1000 kw; 2,667t/223g; N37 41 15 W122 26 01
660 Price Ave., Suite B, Redwood City, CA 94063 USA
(212) 757-3100; *Fax:* (646) 597-5903
www.iontelevision.com
michaelhubner@ionmedia.com
License: San Jose, CA held by Ion Media San Jose License, Inc
Group Owner: Ion Media Networks; *Washington Law Firm:* Joseph E. Dunne III
Nat'l Network: ION Television
Brandon Burgess, Chairman/CEO

***KMTP-TV** *Digital Channel:* 33; *Virtual Channel:* 32; 480 kw; 1696 ft.; N37 45 19 W122 27 6
211 Brannan Street, San Francisco, CA 94107 US
(415) 777-3232; *Fax:* (415) 552-3209
kmtpgm@pacbell.net
License: San Francisco, San Francisco County, CA held by Minority Television Project
Nat'l Network: ETV
Booker Wade Jr., General Manager
Arlene Stevens, Programming Director

KNTV *Digital Channel:* 12; *Virtual Channel:* 11; 103.1 kw; 1236 ft.; N37 41 7 W122 26 1
Mailing Address: 2450 North First St., San Jose, CA 95131 USA
Second Address: 360 3rd St., Suite 103, San Francisco, CA 94107
(408) 432-6221; *Fax:* (408) 432-4425
www.nbcbayarea.com
License: San Jose, Santa Clara County, CA held by NBC Telemundo License LLC
Group Owner: NBC Owned Television Stations; (acq 4-30-2002; $230 million); *Washington Law Firm:* Akin, Gump, Strauss, Hauer & Feld
Nat'l Network: NBC; *Nat'l Reps:* NBC TV Stations Sales
Hours of Local News Weekly: News progmg 20 hrs wkly

KOFY-TV *Digital Channel:* 19; *Virtual Channel:* 20; 3,470 kw vis, 347 kw aur; ant 1,548t/820g; N37 45 19 W122 27 06;
Population Served: 1,200,000
2500 Marin St., San Francisco, CA 94124
(415) 821-2020; *Fax:* (415) 821-1518
kofytv.com

License: San Francisco, San Francisco County, CA held by KBWB License Inc.
Group Owner: Granite Broadcasting Corp.; (acq 7-20-98; $173.75 million)
; *Nat'l Reps:* Katz
Craig Coane, President
Chris Flynn, General Sales Mgr
Warren Holybee, Chief Engineer

KPIX-TV *Digital Channel:* 29; *Virtual Channel:* 5; 500 kW; 486 ft.; N37 45 19 W122 27 6
855 Battery St., San Francisco, CA 94111 USA
(415) 362-5550
sanfrancisco.cbslocal.com
License: San Francisco, San Francisco County, CA held by CBS Broadcasting Inc.
Group Owner: CBS Television Stations Group; *Washington Law Firm:* Wilkes, Artis, Hedrick & Lane
Nat'l Network: CBS; *Nat'l Reps:* CBS TV Stations National Sales; *Wire Services:* Reuters
Size of News Staff: 87; *Hours of Local News Weekly:* news progmg 20 hrs wkly
Tom Spitz, Director of Programming Operations

***KQED** *Digital Channel:* 30; *Virtual Channel:* 9; 710 kw; 1679 ft.; N37 45 19 W122 27 6
Mailing Address: 2601 Mariposa Street, San Franciso, CA 94110 US
Second Address: 50 W San Fernando Street, Suite 110, San Jose, CA 95113-2415
(415) 864-2000; *Fax:* (415) 553-2241
www.kqed.org
checkpleaseBA@kqed.org
License: San Francisco, San Francisco County, CA held by Northern California Public Broadcasting Inc
Washington Law Firm: Arnold & Porter LLP
Nat'l Network: PBS
Size of News Staff: 8; *Hours of Local News Weekly:* news progmg 1/2 hr wkly
Joane Carder, Vice President
Jeff Clarke, CEO
John Boland, President
Donald W. Derheim, Executive Vice President/ Chief Operating Officer
Jo-Anne Wallace, Vice President/General Manager
Traci Eckels, General Sales Mgr
LindaO'Bryon, Programming Director
Michael Isip, TV Content Vice President
Joanne Carder, Vice President - Human Resource & Labor Relations
Tim Olson, Vice President - Digital Media & Education
William L. Lowery, General Counsel/ CorporateSecretary

***KQEH** *Digital Channel:* 50; 661 kw vis, 132 kw aur; 1,922t/137g; N37 29 07 W121 51 57; *Population Served:* 453,000
Mailing Address: 2601 Mariposa St., San Francisco, CA 94110
Second Address: 50 W San Fernando St., Ste. 110, San Jose, CA 95113-2415
(415) 864-2000; *Fax:* (415) 553-2333
www.kqed.org
tv@kqed.org
License: San Jose, Santa Clara County, CA held by KQED Inc.
Nat'l Network: PBS
Donald W. Derheim, Executive VP & COO
John Boland, President
Jo Anne Wallace, VP & General Manager
Lee Young, Director of Engineering
Mitzie Kelly, CFO
Michael Englehaupt, Chief Technology Officer
Traci A. Eckels, ChiefDevelopment Officer
Joanne Carder, VP,Human Resources& Labour Relations
Michael Lupetin, VP,Marketing & Brand
William L. Lowery, General Counsel & Corporate Secretary

***KRCB** *Digital Channel:* 23; *Virtual Channel:* 22; 105 kw; 2068 ft.; N38 20 54.7 W122 34 37.5
5850 Labath Ave., Rohnert Park, CA 94928 US
(707) 584-2000; *Fax:* (707) 585-1363
www.krcb.org
viewer@krcb.org
License: Cotati, Sonoma County, CA held by Rural California Broadcasting Corp
Nat'l Network: PBS
Foreign Language Programming; Size of News Staff: 1
Eric McHenry, Board Chair
Nancy Dobbs, CEO/President
Tom McDonald, TV Traffic/FM Operations
Robin Pressman, FM Program Director
Bruce Robinson, FM News Director
Garry Persitti, Engineering
Larry Stratton, Engineering
MalinalliLopez, Community Engagement Director & Volunteer Manager
Gerry Pacitti, Broadcast Maintenance Engineer
Stan Marvin, TV Program Director
Michelle Olivera, TV Production/Marketing
Amanda Ward, Administrative/Development
Wendy Nicholson, AdminAssistant FM /Marketing

KRON-TV *Digital Channel:* 38; *Virtual Channel:* 4; 1000 kw; 1679 ft.; N37 45 19 W122 27 6
1001 Van Ness Avenue, San Francisco, CA 94109 US
(415) 441-4444; *Fax:* (415) 561-8142
www.kron.com
breakingnews@kron4.com
License: San Francisco, San Francisco County, CA held by Young Broadcasting of San Francisco Inc.
Group Owner: Young Broadcasting Inc.; (acq 6-26-2000; $823 million); *Washington Law Firm:* Brooks, Pierce
Nat'l Network: MNT; *Nat'l Reps:* Adam Young; *Wire Services:* AP
Hours of Local News Weekly: News progmg 53 hrs wkly
Brian Greif, General Manager
Rich DiPilla, General Sales Mgr
Pat Patton, Programming Director
Kevin Adler, Promotions Manager
Aaron Pero, News Director
Craig Porter, Chief Engineer
Mark Sowinski, Sales Manager
Jim Swanson,Local Programming Director
Lori Gravino, Local Sales Manager
Kathy King, Traffic Manager

KSTS *Digital Channel:* 49; *Virtual Channel:* 48; 257 kw; 2257 ft.; N37 29 57 W121 52 16
2450 North First Street, San Jose, CA 95131 USA
(408) 435-8848 / (408) 944-4848; *Fax:* (408) 432-4423
www.telemundoareadelabahia.com
License: San Jose, Santa Clara County, CA held by NBC Telemundo License LLC
Group Owner: Telemundo Station Group; (acq 4-12-2002; grpsl).; *Washington Law Firm:* Hogan & Hartson
Nat'l Network: Telemundo; *Wire Services:* Reuters; UPI
Foreign Language Programming; Size of News Staff: 10; *Hours of Local News Weekly:* news progmg 3 hrs wkly
Luis Silberwasser, President

KTLN-TV *Digital Channel:* 47; *Virtual Channel:* 68; 1000 kw; 1319 ft.; N38 9 0 W122 35 31
100 Pelican Way, Suite E, San Rafael, CA 94901 US
(415) 924-7500, (415) 485-5856; *Fax:* (415) 924-0264, (415) 256-9262
www.ktln.tv
ktln@tln.com
License: Novato, Marin County, CA
Group Owner: OTA Broadcasting; (acq 12-10-98; $500,000)
Nat'l Network: IND
Jerry Rose, CEO
Debbie Fraser, General Manager
Brian Avery, Station Manager
James Nichols, CFO
Matt Kenny, Director of Ministries

KTNC-TV *Digital Channel:* 14; *Virtual Channel:* 42; 47.3 kw; 3091 ft.; N37 52 54 W121 55 5
Mailing Address: 1700 Montgomery St., Suite 400, San Fransisco, CA 94111 US
Second Address: 770 L Street, Suite 950, Scarmento, CA 95814
(415) 398-4242, (916) 492-6046; *Fax:* (415) 352-1800, (916) 492-6047
www.ktnc.com
License: Concord, Contra Costa County, CA held by NRJ TV SF License Co. LLC
Group Owner: NRJ Holdings LLC; (acq 7-1-2013); *Washington Law Firm:* Fletcher, Heald & Hildreth
Nat'l Network: TUVISION
Foreign Language Programming
Harry Pappas, Chairman
Dennis Davis, CEO
Fernando Acosta, General Manager
LeBon Abercrombie, General Sales Mgr
Roberto Pineda, General Sales Manager
Sharon Mendez, National Sales Assistant
Amy Lorenzen, Corporate Dir. OfTraffic
Stella Torres, Accounting Manager
Claudia Estrada, VP of Sales

KTSF *Digital Channel:* 27; *Virtual Channel:* 26; 858 kw; 1323 ft.; N37 41 12 W122 26 3
100 Valley Drive, Brisbane, CA 94005 US
(415) 468-2626; *Fax:* (415) 467-7559
www.ktsf.com
admin@ktsftv.com
License: San Francisco, San Francisco County, CA held by Lincoln Broadcasting Co., a California L.P
Washington Law Firm: Law Office of Michael D. Berg
Nat'l Network: IND; *Wire Services:* Bay City News Service; AP; CNN
Foreign Language Programming; Size of News Staff: 40; *Hours of Local News Weekly:* news progmg 24 hrs wkly
Lillian Howell, Chairman/President
Michael Sherman, General Manager
Victor Marino, Programming Director
Lisa Yokota, Promotions Manager
Rose Shirinian, News Director
Mike Fusaro, Engineering Dir

KTVU *Digital Channel:* 36; *Virtual Channel:* 36; 550 kw; 2251 ft.; N37 29 17 W121 51 59
USA
www.ktvu.com
License: Oakland, Alameda County, CA held by Fox Television Stations LLC
Group Owner: Fox Television Stations Group; *Washington Law Firm:* Leventhal, Senter & Lerman
Nat'l Network: FOX
Size of News Staff: 3; *Hours of Local News Weekly:* news progmg .5 hr wkly

KTVU *Digital Channel:* 44; *Virtual Channel:* 2; 1000 kw; 1680 ft.; N37 45 19 W122 27 6
Two Jack London Square, Oakland, CA 94607 US
(510) 834-1212; *Fax:* (510) 874-0463
www.ktvu.com
newstips@ktvu.com
License: Oakland, Alameda County, CA held by KTVU Partnership.
Group Owner: Cox Media Group; (acq 10-16-63; $12.36 million; *Washington Law Firm:* Dow, Lohnes & Albertson
Nat'l Network: FOX; *Nat'l Reps:* TeleRep; *Wire Services:* Reuters; NWS (National Weather Service)
Jeff Block, Operations Dir
Tim McVay, General Manager
Tom Raponi, General Sales Mgr
Caroline Chang, Programming Director
Ed Chapuis, News Director
Don Thompson, Engineering Dir
Greg Bilte, General Sales Manager
Dan Haass,National Sales Manager
Phil Adams, National Sales Manager
Rosy Chu, Public Affairs Director

San Jose

KICU *Digital Channel:* 36; *Virtual Channel:* 36; 550 kW; N37 29 17 W121 51 59
USA
www.ktvu.com
License: San Jose, Santa Clara County, CA held by Fox Television Stations LLC
Group Owner: Fox Television Stations Group
Nat'l Network: Independent; Fox

Santa Barbara-Santa Maria-San Luis Obispo, CA (DMA 124)

KCOY-TV *Digital Channel:* 19; *Virtual Channel:* 12; 115 kw vis, 22.9 kw aur; 1,940t/140g; N34 54 37 W120 11 08
730 Miramonte Dr, Santa Barbara, CA 93109 US
(805) 925-1200, (805) 928-4748; *Fax:* (805) 349-9965
www.kcoy.com
tracyreiner@kcoy.com
License: Santa Maria, Santa Barbara County, CA held by VistaWest California, LLC
Group Owner: News-Press & Gazette Co.; (acq 5-7-2008; $41 million with KION-TV Monterey); *Washington Law Firm:* Skadden, Arps, Slate, Meagher & Flom LLP
Nat'l Network: CBS; *Nat'l Reps:* Continental Television Sales
Size of News Staff: 42; *Hours of Local News Weekly:* news progmg 28 hrs wkly
Tracy Reiner, Local Sales Manager
Donald Weiting, Promotions Manager
Jimmy Sprague, Chief Engineer

KEYT-TV *Digital Channel:* 27; *Virtual Channel:* 3; 250 kw; 3012 ft.; N34 31 32 W119 57 28
730 Miramonte Dr, Santa Barbara, CA 93109 US
(805) 882-3933; *Fax:* (805) 882-3934
www.keyt.com
keyt@aol.com
License: Santa Barbara, Santa Barbara County, CA held by NPG of California LLC
Group Owner: News-Press & Gazette Co.; (acq 11-8-2004; grpsl).; *Washington Law Firm:* Hogan & Hartson

Nat'l Network: ABC; *Nat'l Reps:* Continental Television Sales; *Wire Services:* AP; CNN
Size of News Staff: 25; *Hours of Local News Weekly:* news progmg 21 hrs wkly
Todd Graham, Operations Manager

KPMR-TV *Digital Channel:* 21; *Virtual Channel:* 38; 1000 kw; 3051 ft.; N34 31 28 W119 57 38
3700 State St., Suite 330, Goleta, CA 93105 US
(805) 685-3800; *Fax:* (805) 685-6892
License: Santa Barbara, Santa Barbara County, CA held by Entravision Holdings LLC.
Group Owner: Entravision Communications Corp.; (acq 11-2-2000; $4.75 million)
Nat'l Network: UNIVISION
Foreign Language Programming
Gabe Quiroz, Senior VP

KSBY *Digital Channel:* 15; *Virtual Channel:* 6; 1000 kw; 1,690 ft.; N35 21 37 W120 39 18
1772 Callie Joaquin, San Luis Obispo, CA 93405 US
(805) 541-6666; *Fax:* (805) 541-5142
www.ksby.com
feedback@ksby.com
License: San Luis Obispo, San Luis Obispo County, CA held by KSBY Communications LLC
Group Owner: Cordillera Communications Inc.; (acq 2-18-2005; $67.75 million); *Washington Law Firm:* Dow Lohnes
Nat'l Network: NBC; CW; *Nat'l Reps:* Harrington, Righter & Parsons; *Wire Services:* AP
Hours of Local News Weekly: news progmg 24.5 hrs wkly
Kathleen Choal, General Manager
William Evans, Director of Sales
Brandon Downing, Director of Marketing
Doug Barden, News Director
Bill Ingram, Chief Engineer
Sarah Johnson, Traffic Manager
Jill Graves, Interactive OperationsSpecialist

Yuma, AZ-El Centro, CA (DMA 167)

KAJB-TV *Digital Channel:* 36; *Virtual Channel:* 54; 1000 kw; 1566 ft.; N33 3 5.3 W114 49 43
1803 N. Imperial Ave., El Centro, CA 92243 US
(760) 482-7777; *Fax:* (760) 482-0099
License: Calipatria, CA held by Entravision Communications Corporation.
Group Owner: Calipatria Broadcasting Company, LLC; *Washington Law Firm:* Thompson, Hine & Flory L
Nat'l Network: UNVISION
Foreign Language Programming; Size of News Staff: 8; *Hours of Local News Weekly:* news progmg 5 hrs wkly
Veronica Avila, Senior VP

KECY-TV *Digital Channel:* 9; *Virtual Channel:* 9; 50 kw; 1568 ft.; N33 3 19 W114 49 44
1965 South 4th Ave, Yuma, AZ 85364 US
(928) 539-9990
dave.miller@kecytv.com
License: El Centro, Imperial County, CA held by Gulf-California Broadcast Co.
Group Owner: News-Press & Gazette Co.; (acq 5-5-2008; $2 million); *Washington Law Firm:* Smithwick & Belendiuk
Nat'l Network: FOX; ABC; *Nat'l Reps:* Millennium Sales & Marketing
Dave Miller, General Manager/National Sales Manager
Becky Estrada, General Sales Mgr
Eric Sawyer, Promotions Manager
Ernesto Romero, News Director

KVYE-TV *Digital Channel:* 22; *Virtual Channel:* 7; 1000 kw; 1566 ft.; N33 3 5.3 W114 49 43
1803 N. Imperial Ave., El Centro, CA 92243 US
(760) 482-7777; *Fax:* (760) 482-0099
www.noticias.entravision.com/el-centro
License: El Centro, Imperial County, CA held by Entravision Holdings LLC.
Group Owner: Entravision Communications Corp.; *Washington Law Firm:* Thompson, Hine & Flory L
Nat'l Network: UNVISION
Foreign Language Programming; Size of News Staff: 8; *Hours of Local News Weekly:* news progmg 5 hrs wkly
Veronica Avila, Senior VP

Colorado

Albuquerque-Santa Fe, NM (DMA 48)

KREZ-TV *Digital Channel:* 15; *Virtual Channel:* 6; 46 kw; 297 ft.; N37 15 46 W107 53 58; *Rebroadcasting:* Satellite of KRQE(TV) Albuquerque, NM
Mailing Address: PO Box 789, Grand Junction, CO 81502 US
Second Address: 158 Bodo Dr., Durango, CO 81303
(970) 259-6666; *Fax:* (970) 247-8472
License: Durango, La Plata County, CO held by LIN of Colorado LLC.
Group Owner: LIN Television Corporation; (acq 11-30-2005; grpsl)
Nat'l Network: CBS; NBC
Bill Anderson, General Manager
Christopher Bartsh, General Manager

***KRMU** *Digital Channel:* 20; *Virtual Channel:* 20; 12.6 kw; 427 ft.; N37 15 46 W107 53 58; *Rebroadcasting:* Rebroadcasts KRMJ-TV Grand Junction 100%.
Mailing Address: 1089 Bannock St, Denver, CO 80204 US
Second Address: 2200 Bonfonte Blvd., Pubelo, CO 81001
(303) 892-6666, (719) 543-8800; *Fax:* (303) 620-5600, (719) 549-2208
www.rmpbs.org
viewer@rmpbs.org
License: Durango, La Plata County, CO held by Rocky Mountain Public Broadcasting Network, Inc.
Permitee: Rocky Moun; Washington Law Firm: Dow, Lohnes & Albertson
Nat'l Network: PBS
Doug Price, President & CEO
Debbie Brennan, Programming Director
Tom Dailey, Engineering Manager
Tom Craig, Chief Engineer
Beth Flambures, CFO
Harris Flambures, COO
Patricia Prevost, Chief Development Officer
Tom Craig, CTO
Cynthia Hessin, Executive Producer
Julie Speer, Executive Producer

Colorado Springs-Pueblo, CO (DMA 88)

KKTV *Digital Channel:* 49; *Virtual Channel:* 11; 550 kw; 2375 ft.; N38 44 42 W104 51 43
520 E Colorado, Colorado Springs, CO 80903 USA
(719) 634-2844; *Fax:* (719) 632-0808
www.kktv.com
news@kktv.com
License: Colorado Springs, El Paso County, CO held by Gray Television Licensee LLC
Group Owner: Gray Television Inc.; (acq 10-25-02; grpsl).
Nat'l Network: CBS; *Nat'l Reps:* Continental Television Sales
Size of News Staff: 42; *Hours of Local News Weekly:* news progmg 27 hrs wkly
Nick Matesi, General Manager
Kerri Blanco, Sales
Becky Tomek, Programming
Liz Haltiwanger, News Director
Christopher Fleming, Chief Engineer

KOAA-TV *Digital Channel:* 42; *Virtual Channel:* 5; 880 kw; 2,165 ft.; N38 44 42 W104 51 39
Mailing Address: 2200 7th Ave., Pueblo, CO 81003 US
Second Address: 5520 Tech Center Dr., Colorado Springs, CO 80919
(719) 544-5781; *Fax:* (719) 295-6677
www.koaa.com
License: Pueblo, Pueblo County, CO held by Sangre De Cristo Communications LLC
Group Owner: Cordillera Communications Inc.; (acq 8-6-76; $4.5 million); *Washington Law Firm:* Dow, Lohnes & Albertson
Nat'l Network: NBC; *Nat'l Reps:* Harrington, Righter & Parsons
Size of News Staff: 23; *Hours of Local News Weekly:* news progmg 7 hrs wkly
Ryan Kercher, Operations Dir
Evan Pappas, General Manager
Steve Chase, Director of Sales
Sydney Rubin, Marketing Director
Kelly Duffy, News Director
Quentin Henry, Chief Engineer
David Randall, Digital News Director
ElaineSheridan, Assignment Manager

KRDO-TV *Digital Channel:* 24; *Virtual Channel:* 13; 200 kw; 2215 ft.; N38 44 45.2 W104 51 37.2
825 Edmond St, St. Joseph, MO 64501 US
(816) 271-8505; *Fax:* (719) 475-0815
www.krdo.com
krdonews@krdo.com
License: Colorado Springs, El Paso County, CO held by Pikes Peak Television Inc.
Group Owner: News-Press & Gazette Co.; (acq 6-26-2006; $45 million with KJCT(TV) Grand Junction).
Nat'l Network: ABC
David Bradley Jr., President
Jerry Killion, Oeprations Manager
Tim Larson, General Manager
Tom Wright, Director, Sales
Tim McSpadden, Promotions Manager
Mike Rausch, News Director
Joe Reed, Chief Engineer

***KTSC** *Digital Channel:* 8; *Virtual Channel:* 8; 22.4 kw; 2362 ft.; N38 44 43 W104 51 39
Mailing Address: 2200 Bonforte Blvd., Pueblo, CO 81001 US
Second Address: 1089 Bannock St., Denver, CO 80204
(719) 543-8800, (719) 630-8800, (303) 892-6666; *Fax:* (719) 549-2208, (303) 620-5600
www.rmpbs.org
ktsc@rmpbs.org
License: Pueblo, Pueblo County, CO held by Rocky Mountain Public Broadcasting Network Inc
Nat'l Network: PBS
Jim Foster, Chairman
Doug Price, CEO/President
Wynona Sullivan, Station Manager
Debbie Brennan, Programming Director
Tiffany Tyson, Promotions Manager
Tom Dailey, Engineering Manager
Ian Hartley, Chief Engineer
Harris Ravine,Chief Operating Officer
Beth Flambures, CFO
Patricia Prevost, Chief Development Officer
Tom Craig, Chief Technology Officer
Elizabeth Mayer, Director of Communications
Michael Reynolds, Director of Production

KVSN-DT *Digital Channel:* 48; *Virtual Channel:* 48; 41 kw; ant 2,280t/271g; N38 44 42 W104 51 39
777 Grant St., Suite 500, Colorado Springs, CO 80203 US
(303) 832-0050; *Fax:* (303) 832-3410
www.noticias.entravision.com/colorado
License: Pueblo, Pueblo County, CO held by Entravision Holdings, LLC.
Group Owner: Entravision Communications Corp.; *Ownership:* Univision (Spanish)
Adrien Seixas, National Sales Mgr
Juan Carlos Gutierrez, News Director
Don Daboub, SVP Integrated Marketing Solutions

KXRM-TV *Digital Channel:* 22; *Virtual Channel:* 21; 51 kw; 2103 ft.; N38 44 43 W104 51 40
560 Wooten Rd., Colorado Springs, CO 80915 US
(719) 596-2100; *Fax:* (719) 591-4180
www.fox21news.com
news@fox21news.com
License: Colorado Springs, El Paso County, CO held by LIN Television Corp.
Group Owner: Media General Broadcast Group; (acq 11-22-2013; grpsl); *Washington Law Firm:* Pillsbury Winthrop Shaw Pittman LLP
Nat'l Network: FOX; *Nat'l Reps:* TeleRep; *Wire Services:* CNN
Size of News Staff: 14; *Hours of Local News Weekly:* News progmg 3.5 hrs wkly
Steve Dant, CEO/COO
Steve Dant, President
James Muller, Promotions Manager
Roger Perales, Chief Engineer
Dan Corken, Vice President and Director of Sales
Joe Cole, Vice President of News Operations

Denver, CO (DMA 17)

***KBDI-TV** *Digital Channel:* 13; *Virtual Channel:* 12; 33.6 kw; 2421 ft.; N39 40 55 W105 29 49
2900 Welton Street, 1st Floor, Denver, CO 80205 US
(303) 296-1212, (800) 727-8812; *Fax:* (303) 296-6650
www.kbdi.org
License: Broomfield, Boulder County, CO held by Colorado Public Television Inc.
Washington Law Firm: Mintz, Levin, Cohn, Ferris, Glovsky & Popeo
Nat'l Network: PBS
Christopher L. Bittman, Chairman
Kim Johnson, President and General Manager
Brad Haug, Programming Director

Shari Bernson, Director of Development
Dominic Dezzutti, Director of Production
Paula Roth, Director of CorporateSupport
Paula DeGroat, Business Manager
Mark Seewald, Director, Technical Services
Pam Osborne, Director, Marketing &Communications

KCDO-TV *Digital Channel:* 23; *Virtual Channel:* 3; 0.24 kW; N41 11 35.4 W103 31 49.2
3001 S Jamaica Ct, Suite 210, Aurora, CO 80014 USA
(303) 925-0303; *Fax:* (303) 925-7461
www.k3colorado.com
info@k3colorado.com
License: Kimball, NE held by Channel 3 TV Company Inc.
Group Owner: Newsweb Corp.; (acq 8-31-99; $240,000);
Ownership: Newsweb Corp.; *Washington Law Firm:* Skadlen, Arps, Slate, Meagher, Flom LLP
Nat'l Network: Independent *Regional Reps:* none
Size of News Staff: 0; *Hours of Local News Weekly:* none
Greg Armstrong, General Manager

KCEC *Digital Channel:* 51; *Virtual Channel:* 50; 900 kw; 763 ft.; N39 43 58 W105 14 8
1907 Mile High Stadium W. Cir., Denver, CO 80204 US
(303) 832-0050; *Fax:* (303) 832-3410
www.noticias.entravision.com/colorado
dddaboub@entravision.com
License: Denver, Denver County, CO held by Entravision Holdings, LLC
Group Owner: Entravision Communications Corp.; (acq 4-25-97)
Nat'l Network: UNIVISION
Foreign Language Programming
Adrien Seixas, National Sales Manager
Juan Carlos Gutierrez, News Director
Don Daboub, SVP Integrated Marketing Solutions
Rafael Medina, Marketing/Communications Dir.

KCNC-TV *Digital Channel:* 4; 1000 kW; 705 ft.; N39 43 51 W105 13 54
1044 Lincoln St., Denver, CO 80203 USA
(303) 861-4444
denver.cbslocal.com
License: Denver, Denver County, CO held by CBS Television Stations Inc.
Group Owner: CBS Television Stations Group
Nat'l Network: CBS; *Nat'l Reps:* CBS TV Stations National Sales;
Wire Services: Conus; PR Newswire; Medialink
Size of News Staff: 90; *Hours of Local News Weekly:* news progmg 28.5 hrs wkly
John Montgomery, Assignment Manager

KDEN *Digital Channel:* 29; 5,000 kw vis; ant 1,066t/964g; N40 05 47 W104 54 04
2851 South Parker Road, Suite 1130, Denver, CO 80014 USA
(303) 338-2390; *Fax:* (303) 832-0777
www.telemundodenver.com
License: Longmont, Boulder County, CO held by NBC Telemundo License LLC
Group Owner: Telemundo Station Group; (acq 7-13-2006; $42 million); *Washington Law Firm:* NBC Legal
Nat'l Network: Telemundo
Foreign Language Programming; Size of News Staff: 1; *Hours of Local News Weekly:* news progmg one hr wkly
Luis Silberwasser, President

KDVR *Digital Channel:* 32; *Virtual Channel:* 31; 1000 kW; 1030 ft.; N39 43 45 W105 14 12
100 East Speer Blvd., Denver, CO 80203 USA
(303) 595-3131
kdvr.com
tips@kdvr.com
License: Denver, Denver County, CO held by Tribune Broadcasting Denver License LLC
Group Owner: Tribune Media; (acq 7-14-2008; grpsl)
Nat'l Network: FOX

KDVT-LP *Digital Channel:* 15; *Virtual Channel:* 14; 200 kw; 1151 ft.; N39 40 17 W105 13 8
1907 Mile High Stadium W. Cir., Denver, CO 80204 US
(303) 832-0050; *Fax:* (303) 832-3410
www.noticias.entravision.com/colorado
dddaboub@entravision.com
License: Denver, CO held by Spanish Television of Denver, Inc.
Group Owner: Univision Communications
Nat'l Network: UNIVISION
Foreign Language Programming
Adrien Seixas, National Sales Manager
Juan Carlos Gutierrez, News Director
Don Daboub, SVP Integrated Marketing Solutions
Rafael Medina, Marketing/Communications Dir.

KETD *Digital Channel:* 46; *Virtual Channel:* 53; 5,000 kw vis, 1,000 kw au; 713t; N39 25 58 W104 39 18; *Population Served:* 1,578,660
Mailing Address: 12999 E. Adam Aircraft, Englewood, CO 46624
Second Address: 1710 Briargate Blvd., Suite 423, Colorado Springs, CO 80920
(719) 228-0651; *Fax:* (303) 792-5303
License: Castle Rock, Douglas County, CO held by LeSea Broadcasting.
Group Owner: Le Sea Broadcasting
Foreign Language Programming
Pete Sumrall, CEO
Dan Smith, General Manager
Ron Vincent, Chief Engineer
Dan Smith, Closed Captioning

KFCT *Digital Channel:* 21; *Virtual Channel:* 22; 50 kw; 764 ft.; N40 38 32 W104 49 5; *Rebroadcasting:* Satellite of KDVR(TV) Denver.
100 E. Speer Blvd., Denver, CO 80203 US
(303) 595-3131, (303) 566-7575, (303) 566-7600; *Fax:* (303) 566-2931
www.kdvr.com
news@denvernewshd.com
License: Fort Collins, Larimer County, CO held by Community Television of Colorado License LLC.
Group Owner: Local TV LLC; (acq 7-14-2008; grpsl)
Nat'l Network: FOX
Dennis Leonard, General Manager
John Strassner, General Sales Mgr
Garrett Sailor, Programming Director
Carolyn Kane, News Director
Rick Wheeler, VP Technology
Jon Bowman, Reporter
Nick Emmons, Anchor
Dave Fraser, ChiefMeterologist
Ken Clark, Traffic Reporter
Nick Griffith, Sports Director

KFCT *Digital Channel:* 21; 1,860 kw vis; ant 840t/705g; N40 38 23 W104 49 05; *Rebroadcasting:* Satellite of KDVR(TV) Denver.
c/o TV Station KDVR, 100 East Speer Blvd, Denver, CO 80203
(303) 595-3131, (303) 566-7575, (303) 566-7600; *Fax:* (303) 566-2931
www.kdvr.com
tips@kdvr.com
License: Fort Collins, Larimer County, CO held by Community Television of Colorado License LLC.
Group Owner: Local TV LLC; (acq 7-14-2008; grpsl)
Nat'l Network: Fox
Dennis Leonard, General Manager
John Strassner, General Sales Mgr
Garrett Sailor, Programming Director
Carolyn Kane, News Director
Rick Wheeler, VP Technology
Nick Griffith, Sports Director
Dave Fraser, Chief Meterologist
KenClark, Traffic Reporter
Jon Bowman, Reporter
Jeremy Hubbard, Anchor

KGHB-CD *Digital Channel:* 27; 15 kw; N38 22 21 W104 33 38
1907 Mile High Stadium W. Cir., Denver, CO 80204 US
(303) 832-0050; *Fax:* (303) 832-3410
www.noticias.entravision.com/colorado
dddaboub@entravision.com
License: Pueblo, CO held by Entravision Holdings, LLC
Group Owner: Entravision Communications
Nat'l Network: UNIVISION
Foreign Language Programming
Adrien Seixas, National Sales Manager
Juan Carlos Gutierrez, News Director
Don Daboub, SVP Integrated Marketing Solutions
Rafael Medina, Marketing/Communications Dir.

KMGH-TV *Digital Channel:* 7; *Virtual Channel:* 7; 54 kw; 1178 ft.; N39 43 51 W105 13 54
123 Speer Boulevard, Denver, CO 80203-3417 US
(303) 832-7777, (303) 832-0162; *Fax:* (303) 832-0119
www.thedenverchannel.com
myreport@thedenverchannel.com
License: Denver, Denver County, CO held by McGraw-Hill Broadcasting Co. Inc.
Group Owner: McGraw-Hill Broadcasting Co.; (acq 6-1-72; grpsl;
Nat'l Network: ABC; *Nat'l Reps:* Harrington, Righter & Parsons
Byron Grandy, Operations Dir
John Curry, General Sales Mgr
Laura Horgis, National Sales Manager
Barry Edmond, Operations Manager

KPJR-DT *Digital Channel:* 38; 1,000 kw vis; ant 1,187t/23g; N40 05 59 W104 54 02; *Not on Air/Target Date:* unknown
PO Box A, Santa Ana, CA 92711
(714) 832-2950, (714) 731-1000, (888) 731-1000; *Fax:* (714) 730-0657
www.tbn.org
License: Greeley, Weld County, CO
Group Owner: Trinity Broadcasting Network; (acq 9-16-2008; $37.5 million for CP)
Paul Crouch, President

KPXC-TV *Digital Channel:* 43; *Virtual Channel:* 59; 1000 kw; 1188 ft.; N40 5 59 W104 54 4
3001 S. Jamaica Crt., Suite 200, Aurora, CO 80014 USA
(303) 751-5959; *Fax:* (303) 751-5993
www.iontelevision.com
michaelhubner@ionmedia.com
License: Denver, CO held by Ion Media Denver License, Inc.
Group Owner: Ion Media Networks; (acq 7-1-96; grpsl).;
Washington Law Firm: Cole, Raywid & Braverman
Nat'l Network: ION
Foreign Language Programming; Hours of Local News Weekly: News progmg 24 hrs wkly
Brandon Burgess, Chairman/CEO

KREG-TV *Digital Channel:* 23; *Virtual Channel:* 3; 16.1 kw; 2530 ft.; N39 25 7 W107 22 6; *Rebroadcasting:* Rebroadcasts KREX-TV Grand Junction
Mailing Address: PO Box 789, Grand Junction, CO 81502 US
Second Address: 345 Hillcrest Dr., Grand Junction, CO 81501
(970) 242-5000; *Fax:* (970) 242-0886
www.krextv.com
closedcaptioning@krextv.com
License: Glenwood Springs, Garfield County, CO held by Hoak Media of Colorado LLC.
Group Owner: Hoak Media Corporation; (acq 10-10-2003; grpsl).;
Washington Law Firm: Gardner, Carton & Douglas
Nat'l Network: CBS; *Nat'l Reps:* Petry Television Inc.
Dave Colvin, Operations Manager
Randy Stone, General Manager
Josh Meuwly, Promotions Director
Jorma Duran, News Director/Evening Anchor,
Dave Colvin, Engineer
Josh Moser, Engineer
Shelley Moore, Business Manager
KevinMcChesney, Account Executive
Greg Rule, Chief Meteorologist
Cori Coffin, Reporter/Weekend Anchor

***KRMA-TV** *Digital Channel:* 18; *Virtual Channel:* 6; 1000 kw; 1263 ft.; N39 40 17 W105 13 6
1089 Bannock St, Broadcasting Network, Denver, CO 80204 US
(303) 892-6666; *Fax:* (303) 620-5600
www.rmpbs.org
viewer@rmpbs.org
License: Denver, Denver County, CO held by Rocky Mountain Public Broadcasting Network Inc.
Washington Law Firm: Dow & Lohnes
Nat'l Network: PBS
Hours of Local News Weekly: News progmg one hr wkly
Jim Foster, Chairman
Scott Long, CFO
Douglas M. Price, President/CEO
Harris Ravine, Chief Operating Officer
Tom Craig, Chief Technology Officer
Donna Sanford, Programming Director
Tom Craig, Chief Engineer

***KRMT** *Digital Channel:* 40; *Virtual Channel:* 41; 74.8 kw; 1129 ft.; N39 35 59 W105 12 35
Mailing Address: 12014 West 64th Ave., Arvada, CO 80004 US
Second Address: 3901 Hwy 121, Bedford, TX 76021
(817) 571-1229; *Fax:* (817) 571-7458
www.daystar.com
Partners@Daystar.com
License: Denver, Denver County, CO held by Word of God Fellowship Inc.
(acq 5-29-97; $1.95 million); *Ownership:* Word Of God Fellowship; *Washington Law Firm:* Hogan & Hartson
Nat'l Network: IND
Foreign Language Programming
Marcus Lamb, CEO
Joni Lamb, President
Kevin Russell, General Manager
Trish Lord, Programming Director
James Barnes, Promotions Manager
Judy Nelson, Office Manager

***KRMZ** *Digital Channel:* 10; *Virtual Channel:* 24; 0.481 kw; 575 ft.; N40 27 43 W106 50 57; *Rebroadcasting:* Rebroadcasts KRMA-TV Denver 100%

P.O. Box 255, Evergreen, CO 80439 US
(303) 892-6666; *Fax:* (303) 620-5600
www.rmpbs.org
viewer@rmpbs.org
License: Steamboat Springs, Routt County, CO held by Rocky Mountain Public Broadcasting Network Inc.
Nat'l Network: PBS; *Regional Network:* Rocky Mountain PBS
Jim Foster, Chairman of the Board
Douglas M. Price, President and CEO
Jim Chavez, Director
Harris Ravine, Chief Operating Officer
Angie Salazar, Station Manager
Suzanne Banning, General Sales Mgr
Donna Sanford, ProgrammingDirector
Andrew Hudson, News Director
Tom Dailey, Engineering Manager
Ian Hartley, Engineering Manager
Cynthia Hessin, Executive Producer
Amanda Mountain, Executive Director

KTFD-TV *Digital Channel:* 15; *Virtual Channel:* 14; 15 kw; N38 22 21 W104 33 38
1907 Mile High Stadium W. Cir., Denver, CO 80204 US
(303) 832-0050; *Fax:* (303) 832-3410
License: Denver, CO held by Spanish Television of Denver, Inc.
Group Owner: Univision Communications
Nat'l Network: UNIVISION
Foreign Language Programming
Adrien Seixas, National Sales Manager
Juan Carlos Gutierrez, News Director
Don Daboub, SVP Integrated Marketing Solutions
Rafael Medina, Marketing/Communications Dir.

KTVD *Digital Channel:* 19; *Virtual Channel:* 20; 1,000 kw; 1,227 ft.; N39 43 51 W105 13 54
500 E. Speer Blvd., Denver, CO 80203-4187 US
(303) 871-9999; *Fax:* (303) 698-4700
www.9news.com
viewerfeedback@9news.com
License: Denver, Denver County, CO held by Multimedia Holdings Corp.
Group Owner: Tegna Media; *Washington Law Firm:* Fletcher, Heald & Hildreth
Nat'l Network: MyNetworkTV
Hours of Local News Weekly: news progmg 20.5 hrs wkly
Mark Cornetta, President and General Manager
Dean Ditmer, Director of Sales
Robbi Gutierrez, Programming Director
Robert Springer, Director of Advertising and Promotion
Patti Dennis, News Director
Scott Gill, Chief Engineer

KUSA *Digital Channel:* 9; *Virtual Channel:* 9; 45 kw; 1,156 ft.; N39 43 50.6 W105 13 53.6; *Population Served:* 3,535,000
500 E. Speer Blvd., Denver, CO 80203-4187 US
(303) 871-9999; *Fax:* (303) 698-4700
www.9news.com
viewerfeedback@9news.com
License: Denver, Denver County, CO held by Multimedia Holdings Corp.
Group Owner: Tegna Media; (acq 6-7-79; grpsl; *Washington Law Firm:* Wiley, Rein & Fielding
Nat'l Network: NBC
Hours of Local News Weekly: news progmg 44.5 hrs wkly
Mark Cornetta, President and General Manager
Dean Ditmer, Director of Sales
Christy Moreno, News Director
Sean Springman, Local Sales Manager

KWGN *Digital Channel:* 34; *Virtual Channel:* 2; 1000 kw; 1102 ft.; N39 43 58 W105 14 8
100 East Speer Blvd., Denver, CO 80203 USA
(303) 595-3131
kwgn.com
tips@kwgn.com
License: Denver, Denver County, CO held by KWGN LLC
Group Owner: Tribune Media; (acq 12-20-2007; grpsl);
Washington Law Firm: Dow Lohnes PLLC
Nat'l Network: The CW Network; *Nat'l Reps:* TeleRep
Size of News Staff: 19; *Hours of Local News Weekly:* News progmg 29.5 hrs wkly

Grand Junction-Montrose, CO (DMA 186)

KJCT *Digital Channel:* 7; *Virtual Channel:* 8; 15 kw; N39 2 55 W108 15 6
2531 Blichmann Ave, Grand Junction, CO 81505 US
(970) 245-8880; *Fax:* (970) 245-8249
www.kjct8.com
stacey.stewart@kjct8.com
License: Grand Junction, Mesa County, CO held by Gray Television Licensee, LLC
Group Owner: Gray Television; (acq 01-02-2007 from News-Press Gazette Co.; $675,000); *Washington Law Firm:* Smithwick & Belendiuk, P.C.
Nat'l Network: ABC; *Nat'l Reps:* Millennium Sales & Marketing;
Wire Services: AP
Size of News Staff: 18; *Hours of Local News Weekly:* news progmg 19.5 wkly
David Bradley Jr., CEO
Stacey (Smith) Stewart, General Manager
Amanda Mayle, News Director
Jay Rademacher, Chief Engineer

KKCO *Digital Channel:* 12; *Virtual Channel:* 11; 5.3 kw; 1483 ft.; N39 4 0 W108 44 45
2531 Blichmann Ave., Grand Junction, CO 81505 USA
(970) 243-1111; *Fax:* (970) 243-1770
www.nbc11news.com
License: Grand Junction, Mesa County, CO held by Gray Television Licensee LLC
Group Owner: Gray Television Inc.; (acq 1-31-2005; $13.5 million with translator K50EZ Montrose).; *Washington Law Firm:* Wood, Maines & Brown, Chartered
Nat'l Network: NBC; *Nat'l Reps:* Millennium Sales & Marketing
Size of News Staff: 35; *Hours of Local News Weekly:* news progmg 28 hrs wkly
Stacey Stewart, General Manager
ReBecca Lintner, Sales Manager
Krista Rhoades, Programming
Brian Wiley, Promotions Manager
Amanda Mayle, News Director
Jay Rademacher, Engineering

KREX-TV *Digital Channel:* 15; *Virtual Channel:* 4; 71.5 kw; 1335 ft.; N39 3 58 W108 44 46
354 Hillcrest Manor., Grand Junction, CO 81501 US
(970) 242-5000
www.krex.com
License: Grand Junction, Mesa County, CO held by Nexstar Broadcasting, Inc.
Group Owner: Nexstar Broadcasting Group; (acq 12-27-2004)
Nat'l Network: FOX
Sandra Zoldowski, General Manager
Jorma Duran, News Director

KREX-TV *Digital Channel:* 2; *Virtual Channel:* 5; 0.8 kw; 91 ft.; N39 5 17 W108 33 58
Mailing Address: PO Box 789, Grand Junction, CO 81502 US
Second Address: 345 Hillcrest Dr., Grand Junction, CO 81501
(970) 242-5000; *Fax:* (970) 242-0886
www.krextv.com
dcolvin@krextv.com
License: Grand Junction, Mesa County, CO held by Hoak Media of Colorado LLC.
Group Owner: Hoak Media Corporation; (acq 11-12-2003; grpsl).
Nat'l Network: CBS; *Nat'l Reps:* Petry Television Inc.
Size of News Staff: 15; *Hours of Local News Weekly:* news progmg 30 hrs wkly
Dave Colvin, Operations Dir
Ron Tillery, General Manager
Josh Meuwly, Promotions Director
Jorma Duran, News Director/Evening Anchor
Jared Kenyon, Engineer
Josh Moser, Engineer
Shelley Moore, Business Manager
Kevin McChesney,Account Executive
Greg Rule, Chief Meteorologist
Cori Coffin, Reporter/Weekend Anchor

KREY-TV *Digital Channel:* 13; *Virtual Channel:* 10; 2.6 kw; 115 ft.; N38 31 2 W107 51 12
345 Hillcrest Manor, Grand Junction, CO 81502 US
(970) 249-9601; *Fax:* (970) 249-9610
kreytv@gwe.net
License: Montrose, Montrose County, CO held by Hoak Media of Colorado LLC.
Group Owner: Hoak Media Corporation; (acq 10-10-2003; grpsl).
Nat'l Network: CBS; NBC
Chris Larum, Station Manager

***KRMJ** *Digital Channel:* 18; *Virtual Channel:* 18; 21 kw; 1342 ft.; N39 3 58 W108 44 43; *Rebroadcasting:* Rebroadcasts KRMA-TV Denver 99.9%.
Mailing Address: Broadcasting Network, 1089 Bannock St, Denver, CO 80217 US
Second Address: 890 Hall Ave, Durango, CO 81501
(970) 245-1818; *Fax:* (303) 620-5600
www.rmpbs.org
viewer@rmpbs.org
License: Grand Junction, Mesa County, CO held by Rocky Mountain Public Broadcasting Network Inc
Washington Law Firm: Dow, Lohnes & Albertson
Nat'l Network: PBS
Jim Foster, Chairman
Scott Long, CFO
Douglas M. Price, President/CEO
Harris Ravine, Chief Operating Officer
Tom Craig, Chief Technology Officer
Tom Craig, Chief Engineer
Cynthia Hessin, Executive Producer
Amanda Mountain,Executive Director

Connecticut

Hartford & New Haven, CT (DMA 30)

WCCT *Digital Channel:* 20; *Virtual Channel:* 20; 2,239 kw vis, 223.9 kw au; ant 1,200t/1,013g; N41 31 04 W73 01 07; *Population Served:* 1,000,000
285 Broad St., Hartford, CT 06115 USA
(860) 723-2166; *Fax:* (860) 723-2111
ct.com
License: Waterbury, New Haven County, CT held by Tribune Broadcasting Hartford LLC
Group Owner: Tribune Media
Nat'l Network: The CW Network; *Nat'l Reps:* MMT
Mark Oxton, Advertising Contact
Dean Maluski, Engineering Dir

WCTX *Digital Channel:* 39; *Virtual Channel:* 59; 170 kw; 988 ft.; N41 25 22 W72 57 6
Mailing Address: 210 Skokie Valley Road, Highland Park, IL 60035 US
Second Address: 8 Elm St., New Haven, CY 6510
(203) 784-8888, (203) 782-5900; *Fax:* (203) 789-2010, (203) 782-5995, (203) 787 9698
www.myzone.tv
wtnh@wtnh.com
License: New Haven, New Haven County, CT held by WTNH Broadcasting Inc.
Group Owner: LIN Media; (acq 3-2002)
Nat'l Network: MY NETWORK; *Nat'l Reps:* Petry Television Inc.
Hours of Local News Weekly: News progmg 8.5 hrs wkly
Jamie Holowaty, Operations Dir
Mark Higgins, VP & General Manager
Roger Hess, General Sales Mgr
Judi Mickmac, Programming Director
Mary Lee Weber, Promotions Manager
Al Carl, News Director
Karen Rorke, Local Sales Manager
RogerMegroz, National Sales Manager
Rich Vedder, Director of Sales
Paul Spingola, Director,Marketing & Digital media
Karen Black, Business/Human Resources
Kierstin Pupkowski, Community Affairs Director

***WEDH** *Digital Channel:* 45; *Virtual Channel:* 24; 490 kw; 1657 ft.; N41 42 13 W72 49 57
1049 Asylum Ave., Hartford, CT 06105 US
(860) 278-5310; *Fax:* (860) 275-7500
www.cpbn.org
wherewelive@wnpr.org
License: Hartford, Hartford County, CT held by Connecticut Public Broadcasting Inc
Washington Law Firm: Schwartz, Woods & Miller
Nat'l Network: PBS
Francisco Borges, Chair
Dean Orton, Chief Operating Officer
Jerry Franklin, President and Chief Executive Officer
Haig Papasian, Operations Dir
Larry Rifkin, Programming Director
Joseph Zareski, Chief Engineer
Meg Sakellarides,CFO
Jeffrey S. Hoffman, Vice Chair
Pamela Pagnani, Secretary
Lisa Di Donato Cambria, Assistant Secretary
Joyce Ahrens, Member of the Board
Tim Bannon, Member of the Board

***WEDN** *Digital Channel:* 9; *Virtual Channel:* 53; 4.2 kw; 630 ft.; N41 31 14 W72 10 3
1049 Asylum Ave., Hartford, CT 06105 US
(860) 278-5310; *Fax:* (860) 275-7402
www.cpbn.org
wherewelive@wnpr.org
License: Norwich, New London County, CT held by Connecticut Public Broadcasting
Nat'l Network: PBS
Francisco Borges, Chair
Dean Orton, Chief Operating Officer
Jerry Franklin, President and Chief Executive Officer

Haig Papasian, Operations Dir
Meg Sakellarides, CFO
Jeffrey S. Hoffman, Vice Chair
Pamela Pagnani, Secretary
LisaDi Donato Cambria, Assistant Secretary
Joyce Ahrens, Member of the Board
Tim Bannon, Member of the Board

***WEDY** *Digital Channel:* 6; *Virtual Channel:* 65; 0.4 kw; 289 ft.; N41 19 42 W72 54 25; *Rebroadcasting:* Rebroadcasts WEDH(TV) Hartford 100%.
1049 Asylum Ave., Hartford, CT 06105 US
(860) 278-5310; *Fax:* (860) 275-7500
www.cpbn.org
wherewelive@wnpr.org
License: New Haven, New Haven County, CT held by Connecticut Public Broadcasting Inc
Nat'l Network: PBS
Francisco Borges, Chair
Dean Orton, Chief Operating Officer
Jerry Franklin, President and Chief Executive Officer
Haig Papasian, Operations Dir
Dean Orton, General Sales Mgr
Larry Rifkin, Programming Director
Joseph Zareski,Chief Engineer
Meg Sakellarides, CFO
Jeffrey S. Hoffman, Vice Chair
Pamela Pagnani, Secretary
Lisa Di Donato Cambria, Assistant Secretary
Joyce Ahrens, Member of the Board
Tim Bannon, Member of the Board

WFSB *Digital Channel:* 33; *Virtual Channel:* 3; 1000 kW; 948 ft.; N41 46 30 W72 48 18
333 Capital Blvd, Rocky Hill, CT 06067 USA
(860) 728-3333; *Fax:* (860) 247-8940
www.wfsb.com
newsdesk3@wfsb.com
License: Hartford, Hartford County, CT held by Meredith Corp.
Group Owner: Meredith Corp.; (acq 9-4-97; $159 million); *Washington Law Firm:* Garvey, Schubert & Barer
Nat'l Network: CBS; *Nat'l Reps:* Harrington, Righter & Parsons
Hours of Local News Weekly: News progmg 36 hrs wkly
Klarn DePalma, VP & General Manager
Bill Whittle, General Sales Mgr
Dana Neves, News Director

WHTX-LP *Digital Channel:* 46; *Virtual Channel:* 18; 217 kw; 901 ft.; N41 42 30 W72 28 34
One Constitution Plaza, 7th Floor, Hartford, CT 06103 US
(860) 278-1818; *Fax:* (860) 278-1811
License: Hartford, Hartford County, CT held by Entravision Holdings LLC.
Group Owner: Entravision Communications Corp.; (acq 1-4-01; $18 million); *Washington Law Firm:* Wiley, Rein & Fielding
Nat'l Network: UniMas (Spanish); TeleFutura (Spanish)
Hours of Local News Weekly: News progmg 5 hrs wkly
Pamela Bias, Operations Dir
Meg Godin, Promotions Manager
Robert Kerrigan, Chief Engineer

WTIC-TV *Digital Channel:* 31; *Virtual Channel:* 61; 495 kw; 1660 ft.; N41 42 13 W72 49 57
285 Broad St., Hartford, CT 06115 USA
(860) 527-6161; *Fax:* (860) 727-0178
fox61.com
newsteam@fox61.com
License: Hartford, Hartford County, CT held by Tribune Broadcasting Hartford LLC
Group Owner: Tribune Media; (acq 12-20-2007; grpsl)
Nat'l Network: FOX; *Nat'l Reps:* TeleRep
Size of News Staff: 31; *Hours of Local News Weekly:* news progmg 6 hrs wkly

WTNH *Digital Channel:* 10; 166 kw vis, 16.6 kw aur; 1,210t/909g; N41 25 23 W72 57 06; *Population Served:* 1,000,000
Mailing Address: 8 Elm St., New Haven, CT 06510
Second Address: One West Exchange Street, Suite 5A, Providence, RI 2903
(203) 784-8888, (203) 782-5900; *Fax:* (203) 789-2010, (203) 787-9698, (203) 782-5995
www.wtnh.com
wtnh@wtnh.com
License: New Haven, New Haven County, CT held by WTNH Broadcasting LLC
Group Owner: LIN Media; (acq 12-94; $120.17 million; *Washington Law Firm:* Lin Legal
Nat'l Network: ABC; *Nat'l Reps:* Petry Television Inc.
Size of News Staff: 77; *Hours of Local News Weekly:* news progmg 32 hrs wkly

Jamie Holowaty, Operations Dir
Mark Higgins, VP/ General Manager
Roger Hess, General Sales Mgr
Judi Mickmac, Programming Director
Mary Lee Weber, Promotions Manager
Al Carl, News Director
Karen Rorke, Local Sales Manager
KarenBlank, Business/HR
Connie Fitch, Public Service Director
Tony Marnaio, Research Director
Paul Spingola, Director, Marketing & Digital Media
Rich vedder, Dir. Of Sales

WUTH-CD *Digital Channel:* 47; *Virtual Channel:* 47; 15 kw; 901 ft.; N41 42 30 W72 28 34
One Constitution Plaza, 7th Floor, Hartford, CT 06103 US
(860) 278-1818; *Fax:* (860) 278-1811
www.noticias.entravision.com/hartford-springfield
License: Hartford, Hartford County, CT held by Entravision Holdings LLC.
Group Owner: Entravision Communications Corp.; (acq 1-4-01; $18 million); *Washington Law Firm:* Wiley, Rein & Fielding
Nat'l Network: UniMas (Spanish); TeleFutura (Spanish)
Hours of Local News Weekly: News progmg 5 hrs wkly
Pamela Bias, Operations Dir
Meg Godin, Promotions Manager
Robert Kerrigan, Chief Engineer

WVIT *Digital Channel:* 35; *Virtual Channel:* 30; 250 kw; 1424 ft.; N41 42 2 W72 49 57
1422 New Britain Ave., West Hartford, CT 06110 USA
(860) 521-3030, (860) 313-6300; *Fax:* (860) 521-4860(news),(860) 521-3110
www.nbcconnecticut.com
License: New Britain, Hartford County, CT held by NBC Telemundo License LLC
Group Owner: NBC Owned Television Stations; (acq 12-07-97; trade).
Nat'l Network: NBC; *Nat'l Reps:* NBC TV Stations Sales

New York (DMA 1)

***WEDW** *Digital Channel:* 49; *Virtual Channel:* 49; 170 kw; 722 ft.; N41 16 44 W73 11 8
1049 Asylum Ave., Hartford, CT 06105 US
(860) 278-5310; *Fax:* (860) 275-7500
www.cpbn.org
wherewelive@wnpr.org
License: Bridgeport, Fairfield County, CT held by Connecticut Public Broadcasting
Nat'l Network: PBS
Francisco Borges, Chair
Dean Orton, Chief Operating Officer
Jerry Franklin, President and Chief Executive Officer
Haig Papasian, Operations Dir
Dean Orton, General Sales Mgr
Larry Rifkin, Programming Director
Joseph Zareski,Chief Engineer
Meg Sakellarides, CFO
Jeffrey S. Hoffman, Vice Chair
Pamela Pagnani, Secretary
Lisa Di Donato Cambria, Assistant Secretary
Joyce Ahrens, Member of the Board
Tim Bannon, Member of the Board

WZME *Digital Channel:* 42; 2.5 kw vis, 2 kw aur; ant 620t/300g; N41 21 43 W73 06 48
7 Wakely St., Seymour, CT 06483
(203) 881-1153; *Fax:* (203) 881-1302
www.wzmetv.com
peter.douglas@wzmetv.com
License: Bridgeport, Fairfield County, CT held by NRJ TV NY License Co. LLC
Group Owner: NRJ Holdings LLC; (acq 3-26-2012); *Washington Law Firm:* Goldberg, Godles, Wiener & Wright
Peter Douglas, General Manager/Chief Engineer
Lee Warpack, Sales Manager
Ron Barnes, Chief Engineer
Kurt Schmied, Office manager

Providence, RI-New Bedford, MA (DMA 52)

WHPX-TV *Digital Channel:* 26; 95 kw; ant 272t; N41 25 4 W72 11 53
3 Shaws Cove, Suite 226, New London, CT 6320 USA
(212) 757-3100; *Fax:* (646) 597-5903
www.iontelevision.com
License: New London, CT held by Ion Media Hartford License, Inc.
Group Owner: Ion Media Networks, Inc; *Washington Law Firm:* Cohn & Marks
Nat'l Network: ION Television
Hours of Local News Weekly: News progmg 5 hrs wkly
Robert Melfi, General Sales Mgr

Delaware

Philadelphia (DMA 4)

***WHYY-TV** *Digital Channel:* 12; 30 kw; 960t/1,148g; N40 02 30 W75 14 24; *Population Served:* 9,297,178
Mailing Address: Independence Mall West, 150 N. 6th Street, Philadelphia, PA 19106
Second Address: 625 Orange Street, Delaware Broadcasting Centre, Wilmington, DE 19801
(215) 351-1200,(302) 888-1200; *Fax:* (215) 351-0398,(302) 575-0346
www.whyy.org
talkback@whyy.org
License: Wilmington, New Castle County, DE held by WHYY Inc
Washington Law Firm: Schwartz, Woods & Miller
Nat'l Network: PBS
Size of News Staff: 10; *Hours of Local News Weekly:* news progmg 1 hr wkly
Gerard W. Sweeney, Chairman
William J. Marrazzo, President & CEO
Kyra G. McGrath, Executive Vice President & COO
Christine Dempsey, Vice President & CCO
Roseann Oleyn, Vice President Institutional Advancement
Chris Satullo, VicePresident of News & Civic Dialogue
William J. Weber, Vice President & CTO
A. William Dana, Vice President & CTO
John Doran, Chief Engineer
Art Ellis, Executive Director of Communications & Management
Jeffrey M. Bundy, Director of MemberRelations

Salisbury, MD (DMA 144)

***WDPB** *Digital Channel:* 44; *Virtual Channel:* 64; 98 kw; 643 ft.; N38 39 15 W75 36 42; *Rebroadcasting:* Satellite of WHYY-TV (Wilmington, DE)
Mailing Address: 625 Orange Street, Wilmington, DE 19801 US
Second Address: 150 N. 6th Street, Philadelphia, PA 19106
(302) 888-1200, (215) 351-1200; *Fax:* (302) 575-0346, (215) 351-0398
www.whyy.org
talkback@whyy.org
License: Seaford, Sussex County, DE held by WHYY Inc (acq 2-28-86); *Washington Law Firm:* Schwartz, Woods & Miller
Nat'l Network: PBS
Size of News Staff: 10; *Hours of Local News Weekly:* news progmg 3 hrs wkly
L. Frederick Sutherland, Chairman of the Board
William Marrazzo, CEO & President
Kyra G. McGrath, Chief Operating Officer/Executive Vice President
Tony Sadowski, Promotions 'n' Games
Kevin Yoshioka, Interim Executive Director ofMember Relations
A. William Dana, Senior Vice President and Chief Financial Officer
Christine Dempsey, Vice President and Chief Content Officer
Art Ellis, Executive Director of Communications and Brand Man
Roseann Oleyn, Vice President,Institutional Advancement
Chris Satullo, Vice President of News and Civic Dialogue

District of Columbia

Washington, DC (Hagerstown, MD) (DMA 7)

WDCA *Digital Channel:* 35; *Virtual Channel:* 20; 500 kW; 745 ft.; N38 57 22 W77 4 59
5151 Wisconsin Ave. NW, Washington, DC 20016 USA
(202) 244-5151
www.my20dc.com
fox5tips@wttg.com
License: Washington, DC County, DC held by Fox Television Stations LLC
Group Owner: Fox Television Stations Group; (acq 11-6-2001; with KTXH(TV) Houston, TX in swap for KBHK-TV San Francisco, CA).; *Washington Law Firm:* Leventhal, Senter & Lerman
Nat'l Network: MyNetworkTV; *Nat'l Reps:* Fox Stations Sales

WDCW *Digital Channel:* 50; *Virtual Channel:* 50; 1000 kW; 830 ft.; N38 57 44 W77 1 36
2121 Wisconsin Ave. NW, Suite 350, Washington, DC 20007 USA
(202) 965-5050
dcw50.com
License: Washington, DC County, DC held by WDCW LLC
Group Owner: Tribune Media; (acq 12-20-2007; grpsl)
Nat'l Network: The CW Network; *Nat'l Reps:* Harrington, Righter & Parsons

***WETA-TV** *Digital Channel:* 27; *Virtual Channel:* 26; 73 kw; 833 ft.; N38 57 1 W77 4 47
3939 Campbell Ave., Arlington, VA 22206 US
(703) 998-2600; *Fax:* (703) 998-3401
www.weta.org
License: Washington, DC County, DC held by Greater Washington Educational Telecommunications Association Inc
Washington Law Firm: Dow, Lohnes & Albertson
Nat'l Network: PBS
Timothy C. Coughlin, Chairman
Sharon Percy Rockefeller, CEO/President
Rick Schneider, Executive Vice President and Chief Operating Offic
Karen Fritz, General Manager
Dalton Delan, Executive Vice President and Chief ProgrammingOff
Vince Forcier, Director of Engineering
Polly Povejsil Heath, Executive Vice President and Chief Financial Offic
Ann Dibble Jordan, Vice Chairman and Secretary, WETA Board of Trustee
Kari Waldack, Assistant Secretary to the Board
CynthiaBaker, Trustee
Marguerite Bateman, Trustee
Karna Small Bodman, Trustee

WFDC-DT *Digital Channel:* 15; *Virtual Channel:* 14; 2,680 kw vis; ant 567t/407g; N38 56 24 W77 04 54
101 Constitution Ave. N.W., Suite L100, Washington, DC 20001
(202) 522-8640
www.univision.com
License: Arlington, Arlington County, VA held by UniMas D.C. LLC.
Group Owner: Univision Communications Inc.; (acq 6-1-2001; $30 million)
Nat'l Network: Univision (Spanish)
Foreign Language Programming
Randy Falco, President
Fred Willard, Chief Engineer
Ron Estrada, Vice President, Corporate Relations

***WHUT-TV** *Digital Channel:* 33; *Virtual Channel:* 32; 100 kw; 833 ft.; N38 57 1 W77 4 47
2600 Fourth Street, N. W., Washington, DC 20059 US
(202) 806-3200; *Fax:* (202) 806-3300
www.whut.org
j_lawson@howard.edu
License: Washington, DC County, DC held by Howard University
Washington Law Firm: Arnold & Porter
Nat'l Network: PBS; *Wire Services:* Bloomberg Financial
Addison Barry Rand, Chairman
Sidney A. Ribeau, President
Harold Burris, Operations Dir
Jennifer Lawson, General Manager
Luma Haj, General Sales Mgr

WJLA-TV *Digital Channel:* 7; *Virtual Channel:* 7; 52 kw; 773 ft.; N38 57 1 W77 4 47
1100 Wilson Blvd., Arlington, VA 22209 US
(703) 236-9552; *Fax:* (703) 236-9541
www.wjla.com
newsdesk@wjla.com
License: Washington, DC County, DC held by ACC Licensee LLC
Group Owner: Sinclair Broadcast Group Inc.; (acq 1-76; grpsl).; *Washington Law Firm:* Dow, Lohnes & Albertson, PLLC
Nat'l Network: ABC
Hours of Local News Weekly: news progmg 30 hrs wkly
Dan Mellon, General Manager
Robert Scutari, General Sales Mgr
Mark Olingy, Director of Engineering and Operations

WPXW-TV *Digital Channel:* 34; 1000 kw; 560t/455g; N38 47 16 W77 19 47
6199 Old Arrington Ln., Fairfax Station, DC 22039 USA
(812) 335-1770; *Fax:* (646) 597-5903
www.iontelevision.com
License: Manassas, VA held by Ion Media Washington License, Inc.
Group Owner: Ion Media Networks; *Washington Law Firm:* Wilmer, Cutler & Pickering
Nat'l Network: Ion Television
Anthony Polcaro, Operations Dir

WRC *Digital Channel:* 48; *Virtual Channel:* 4; 813 kw; 794 ft.; N38 56 24 W77 4 54
4001 Nebraska Ave. NW, Washington, DC 20016 USA
(202) 885-4000, (202) 885-4111, (202) 885-4300; *Fax:* (202) 885-4104
www.nbcwashington.com
License: Washington, DC County, DC held by NBC Telemundo License LLC
Group Owner: NBC Owned Television Stations
Nat'l Network: NBC; *Nat'l Reps:* NBC TV Stations Sales; *Wire Services:* UPI

WTTG *Digital Channel:* 36; *Virtual Channel:* 5; 1000 kw; 745 ft.; N38 57 22 W77 4 59
5151 Wisconsin Ave. NW, Washington, DC 20016 USA
(202) 244-5151
www.fox5dc.com
License: Washington, DC County, DC held by Fox Television Stations LLC
Group Owner: Fox Television Stations Group; (acq 3-86; grpsl).; *Washington Law Firm:* Hogan & Hartson
Nat'l Network: FOX; *Nat'l Reps:* TeleRep

WUSA *Digital Channel:* 9; *Virtual Channel:* 9; 52 kw; 773 ft.; N38 57 1 W77 4 47
4100 Wisconsin Ave. N.W., Washington, DC 20016 US
(202) 895-5999; *Fax:* (202) 895-5964
www.wusa9.com
desk@wusa9.com
License: Washington, DC County, DC held by WUSA-TV Inc.
Group Owner: Tegna Media; (acq 2-18-86).; *Washington Law Firm:* Reed Smith LLP
Nat'l Network: CBS; *Nat'l Reps:* Blair Television
Hours of Local News Weekly: news progmg 39 hrs wkly
Mark Burdett, President and General Manager
Bill Lord, Station Manager and News Director
Greg Sodano, General Sales Mgr
Sue Baldwin, Digital Programming Director
Khalim Piankhi, VP of Community Relations

WWPX-TV *Digital Channel:* 12; 23 kw; ant 984t/200g; N39 27 27 W78 03 52; *Rebroadcasting:* Satellite of WPXW Manassas, Virginia 100%
6199 Old Arrington Ln., Fairfax Station, DC 22039
(212) 757-3100; *Fax:* (646) 597-5903
www.iontelevision.com
License: Martinsburg, WV held by Ion Media Martinsburg License, Inc.
Group Owner: Ion Media Networks; *Washington Law Firm:* Cohn & Marks
Nat'l Network: ION Television
Brandon Burgess, Chairman/CEO

Florida

Ft. Myers-Naples, FL (DMA 61)

WBBH-TV *Digital Channel:* 15; *Virtual Channel:* 20; 1000 kw; 1489 ft.; N26 49 21 W81 45 54
3719 Central Avenue, Fort Myers, FL 33901 US
(239) 939-2020; *Fax:* (239) 939-3244(news);(239) 939-4801
www.nbc-2.com
comments@nbc-2.com
License: Fort Myers, Lee County, FL held by Waterman Broadcasting Corp. of Fla.
Group Owner: Waterman Broadcasting Corp.; *Washington Law Firm:* Cohn & Marks
Nat'l Network: NBC; *Nat'l Reps:* Continental Television Sales
Size of News Staff: 80; *Hours of Local News Weekly:* news progmg 32 hrs wkly
Gerry Poppe, CFO
Bernard Waterman, President
Chris Rhodes, Operations Dir
Bob Beville, General Sales Manager
Deborah Abbott, Programming Director
Darrel Lieze-Adams, Executive News Director
Dan Billings, Dir. Of Engineering &Technical Services
Dan Billings, Chief Engineer
Steven Pontius, Executive Vice President
Evelyn Jewett, Traffic Manager
Laura Mickler, Master Control Supervisor
Bob Hannon, Director of Production
Gerry Poppe, CFO
Harris Segel, Directorof Research

WFTX-TV *Digital Channel:* 35; 4,550 kw vis, 450 kw aur; ant 1,503t/1,450g; N26 47 43 W81 48 04; *Population Served:* 413,000
621 S.W. Pine Island Rd., Cape Coral, FL 33991
(239) 574-3636, (239) 574-4803; *Fax:* (239) 574-2025
www.fox4florida.com
bstruense@jrn.com
License: Cape Coral, Lee County, FL held by Journal Broadcast Corp.
Group Owner: Journal Communications Inc.; (acq 12-5-2005; grpsl).; *Washington Law Firm:* Dow, Lohnes & Albertson
Nat'l Network: Fox
Judy Kenney, Operations Dir
Charlie Henrich, VP/General Manger
Jim Hanning, General Sales Manager
Brent Struense, Promotions Manager
Eric Maze, News Director
Mike Mayne, Chief Engineer
Brent Struense, Director of Marketing
Patrick Nolan, News anchor
Michelle Cunningham, Meterologist
Angela Melvin, Traffic Reporter
Christy Dimond, Reporter/Videojournalist

***WGCU** *Digital Channel:* 30; 1,321 kw vis, 158 kw aur; 963t/992g; N26 48 54 W81 45 44; *Population Served:* 1,217,000
10501 FGCU Blvd. South, Fort Meyers, FL 33965-6565
(239) 590-2300; *Fax:* (239) 590-2310
www.wgcu.org
License: Fort Myers, Lee County, FL held by Board of Trustees, Florida Gulf Coast University (acq 11-16-01).; *Washington Law Firm:* Schwartz Woods Miller
Nat'l Network: PBS
Iris Gerstle, CFO
Barbara Linstrom, Operations Dir
Rick Johnson, General Manager
Toby Cooke, Director of TV Programming
Barbara Steinhoff, Promotions Manager
Amy Tardiff, News Director
Rick Carroll, Engineering Dir
MichaelStepf, Chief Engineer
Muriel Olsen, Administrative Assistant
Terry Brennen, Director of Community Funding
Dwight Esmon, Community Funding
Mike Stepp, Closed captioning
Kimberly Woodle, Director of Development
Pamela James, Membership &Special Events manager

WINK-TV *Digital Channel:* 50; *Virtual Channel:* 11; 1000 kw; 1453 ft; N26 48 01 W81 45 48
2824 Palm Beach Boulevard, Fort Myers, FL 33916 US
(239) 334-1111, (239) 344-5000; *Fax:* (239) 338-4383
www.winknews.com
webmaster@winktv.com
License: Fort Myers, Lee County, FL held by Fort Myers Broadcasting Co.
Group Owner: Fort Myers Broadcasting Co.; *Washington Law Firm:* Leibowitz & Associates
Nat'l Network: CBS; *Nat'l Reps:* Eagle Television Sales
Size of News Staff: 55; *Hours of Local News Weekly:* news progmg 32 hrs wkly
Wayne Simons, Operations Dir
Tom Doerr, News Director
John Demshock, Director, Engineering/IT
Jesse Daniels, National Sales Manager
Roberta Voelker, Local Sales manager
Margaret Delmore, Producer

WRXY-TV *Digital Channel:* 33; *Virtual Channel:* 49; 1000 kw; 1407 ft.; N26 47 8 W81 47 41
Mailing Address: 40000 Horseshoe Rd, Punta Gorda, FL 33982 US
Second Address: 40000 Horseshoe Rd., Punta Gorda, FL 33982
(239) 543-7200; *Fax:* (239) 543-6800
www.ctn10.com
License: Tice, Lee County, FL held by West Coast Christian Television Inc
Nat'l Network: REL
Stevan Speheger, Operations Manager/Chief Engineer
Paul Lodato, General Manager
Stevan Speheger, Chief Engineer
Ivette Lodato, Traffic Manager
Jose Comellas, Master Control Operator
Rick Moreno, Producer & Editor
Diane Moreno,Studio Support Technician
Rodeny Yeargin, Producer & Editor

WXCW *Digital Channel:* 45; *Virtual Channel:* 46; 1000 kw; 1496 ft.; N26 47 8.3 W81 47 45.8
2824 Palm Beach Blvd., Fort Myers, FL 33916 US

(239) 479-5500
www.wxcw.com
License: Naples, Collier County, FL held by Sun Broadcasting Inc.
Group Owner: Sun Broadcasting Inc.; (acq. 9-24-2012; grpsl); *Washington Law Firm:* Dickstein Shapiro Morin & Oshinsky L.L.P.
Nat'l Network: CW; *Nat'l Reps:* Millennium Sales & Marketing
Hours of Local News Weekly: News progmg 13.5 hrs wkly
James W. Schwartzel, President

WZVN-TV *Digital Channel:* 41; *Virtual Channel:* 26; 1000 kw; 1489 ft.; N26 49 21 W81 45 54
3719 Central Ave., Ft. Myers, FL 33901 US
(239) 939-2020, (239) 939-6223; *Fax:* (239) 936-7771
www.abc-7.com
comments@nbc-2.com
License: Naples, Collier County, FL held by Montclair Communications Inc
(acq 10-10-1996; $21.3 million); *Washington Law Firm:* Irwin, Campbell & Tannenwald
Nat'l Network: ABC; *Nat'l Reps:* Continental Television Sales
Size of News Staff: 85; *Hours of Local News Weekly:* news progmg 19.5 hrs wkly
Lara Kunkler, President
Chris Rhodes, Operations Dir
Lara Kunkler, General Manager
Bob Beville, General Sales Manager
Deborah Abbott, Programming Director
Darrel Adams, Executive News dir. & Manager of Marketing/Promot
DanBillings, Dir. Of Engineering & Technical services
Dan Billings, Chief Engineer
Mary Cervenka, HR Manager
Gerry Poppe, CFO
Laura Mickler, Master ControlSupervisor
Bob Hannon, Dir. Of Production
Kevin henry, National Sales Manager
JanAshton, Account Executive

Gainesville, FL (DMA 161)

WCJB-TV *Digital Channel:* 16; 2,818 kw vis, 282 kw aur; ant 1,049t/985g; N29 32 11 W82 24 00; *Population Served:* 370,710
6220 N.W. 43rd St., Gainesville, FL 32653 US
(352) 377-2020, (352) 368-2020; *Fax:* (352) 373-6516
www.wcjb.com
tv20frontdesk@wcjb.com
License: Gainesville, Alachua County, FL held by Diversified Broadcasting Inc.
Group Owner: Diversified Communications; (acq 12-1-76; *Washington Law Firm:* Irwin, Campbell & Tannenwald
Nat'l Network: ABC; CW
Size of News Staff: 35; *Hours of Local News Weekly:* news progmg 17 hrs wkly
Carolyn Barrett, General Manager
Alan Chatman, General Sales Mgr
Sean Kaplan, Promotions Manager
Andrea Crenney, News Director
Steve Ingam, Chief Engineer
Paige Beck, Anchor/Reporter
David Snyder, Anchor/Reporter
Bill Quinlan,Meterologist
Mike Potter, Meterologist
Hubert Mizell, Sports
Chris Price, Sports

WGFL *Digital Channel:* 28; 5,000 kw vis, 53 kw aur; 911t; N29 37 47 W82 34 24; *Population Served:* 400,000
1703 N.W. 80th Blvd., Gainesville, FL 32606
(352) 332-1128; *Fax:* (352) 332-1506
www.mygainesville.tv
info@mygtn.tv, news@mygtn.tv
License: High Springs, Alachua County, FL held by New Age Media of Gainesville License LLC
Group Owner: CP Media LLC; (acq 3-31-2007; grpsl)
Nat'l Network: CBS
Sue Edwards, Operations Dir
Todd Senter, General Manager
Cory Culleton, General Sales Manager
Sue Edwards, Programming & Creative Services Manager
DanEschenfelder, News Director
Terry Blakeney, Chief Engineer
Doris Jones,Business manager
Amy Drew, Traffic manager
Matt Abramson, Production Supervisor
Judi Crown, Business Office Admin. Asst.
Jim Rehrig, Producer/editor
Cassidy Pinkston, Assignment Editor

WNBW-DT *Digital Channel:* 9; *Virtual Channel:* 9; 4.9 kw; 919 ft.; N29 37 47 W82 34 25
1703 NW 80th Blvd, Gainesville, FL 32606 US
(352) 332-1128; *Fax:* (352) 332-1506
License: Gainesville, Alachua County, FL held by MPS Media of Gainesville LLC
Nat'l Network: N/A; *Nat'l Reps:* Petry Television Inc.
Todd Senter, General Manager
Sue Edwards, Programming & Creative Services Dir.
Dan Eschenfelder, News Director
Terry Blakeney, Chief Engineer
Amanda Decker, Anchor
Cassidy Pinkston, general Assignment Editor
Patrick Fleming,Chief videographer
Mayci McLeod, Multi-Media Journalist

WOGX *Digital Channel:* 31; *Virtual Channel:* 51; 500 kw; 850 ft.; N29 21 32 W82 19 43
Mailing Address: 35 Skyline Dr., Lake Mary, FL 32746 US
Second Address: 511 SW North River Point Dr, Stuart, FL 34994
(407) 644-3535, (866) 55-FOX35; *Fax:* (352) 237-5423
www.myfoxorlando.com
clips@tvvideoclips.com
License: Ocala, Marion County, FL held by Fox Television Stations Inc.
Group Owner: Fox Television Stations Inc.; (acq 6-17-2002; with WOFL(TV) Orlando).; *Washington Law Firm:* Skadden, Arps, Slate, Meagher & Flom
Nat'l Network: FOX; *Nat'l Reps:* Fox Stations Sales
Size of News Staff: 35; *Hours of Local News Weekly:* news progmg 7 hrs wkly
Stan Knott, General Manager
John Brown, Anchor
Glenn Richards, Weather & Traffic
Kate Burgess, Reporter

***WUFT** *Digital Channel:* 36; *Virtual Channel:* 5; 1000 kw; 863 ft.; N29 42 34 W82 23 40
1200 Weimer Hall, 1885 Stadium Rd, Po Box 118405, Gainsville, FL 32611 US
(352) 392-5551; *Fax:* (352) 392-5731
www.wuft.org
info@wuft.tv
License: Gainesville, Alachua County, FL held by Board of Trustees, University of Florida
Washington Law Firm: Schwartz, Woods & Miller
Nat'l Network: PBS
Hours of Local News Weekly: News progmg 3 hrs wkly
Larry Bankner, General Manager
Titus Rush, Station Manager
Brent Williams, General Sales Mgr
Rob Carr, Chief Engineer

Jacksonville, FL (DMA 47)

WCWJ *Digital Channel:* 34; *Virtual Channel:* 17; 863 kw; 927 ft.; N30 16 36 W81 33 47
9117 Hogan Rd., Jacksonville, FL 32216 US
(904) 641-1700; *Fax:* (904) 642-7201
www.yourjax.com
License: Jacksonville, Duval County, FL held by Nexstar Broadcasting Inc.
Group Owner: Nexstar Broadcasting Group Inc.; (acq 5-1-2009); *Washington Law Firm:* Drinker Biddle & Reath LLP
Nat'l Network: CW
Marc Hefner, General Manager
Jose Chapa Jr., General Sales Mgr
Mark Marshman, Chief Engineer

WFOX-TV *Digital Channel:* 32; *Virtual Channel:* 30; 1000 kw; 955 ft.; N30 16 51 W81 34 12
1601 W Peachtree St NE, Atlanta, GA 30309 US
(904) 642-3030; *Fax:* (904) 642-5665
www.actionnewsjax.com
web@actionnewsjax.com
License: Jacksonville, Duval County, FL held by Cox Television Jacksonville LLC
Group Owner: Cox Media Group; (acq Dec 2012); *Washington Law Firm:* Cooley
Nat'l Network: FOX 30.1; My Network-MeTV 30.2; Heroes & Icons 30.3; *Nat'l Reps:* Cox Reps; HRP
James D. Zerwekh, Vice President
Jack Potter, General Sales Mgr
Eric Cassella, Programming Director
Bob Longo, News Director
Shane Emery, Engineering Dir
Bill Funke, Director of Sales
Craig Davenport, Creative ServicesDirector
Cindy Neal, Traffic Manager
Karen Buckner, Digital Sales Manager
Lisa Palmer, National Sales Manager
Arleda James, Local Sales Manager

WJAX-TV *Digital Channel:* 19; *Virtual Channel:* 47; 1000 kw; 955 ft.; N30 16 51 W81 34 12
28 Deep Creek Trail, Arden, NC 28704 US
(904) 642-0400; *Fax:* (904) 642-5665
www.actionnewsjax.com
web@actionnewsjax.com
License: Jacksonville, Duval County, FL held by Bayshore Television LLC
Group Owner: Bayshore Television, LLC; *Washington Law Firm:* Law Offices of Jack N. Goodman
Nat'l Network: CBS 47.1; Get TV 47.2; Decades 47.3; *Nat'l Reps:* HRP
James D.Zerwekh, Vice President
David Oshins, General Sales Mgr
Chris Wolf, Director of Programming and Public Affairs
Bob Longo, News Director
Shane Emery, Engineering Dir
Bill Funke, Director of Sales
Lisa Palmer, NationalSales Manager
John Palmer, Local Sales Manager
Karen Buckner, Digital Sales Manager
Cindy Neal, Traffic Manager
Craig Davenport, Creative Services Director

***WJCT** *Digital Channel:* 7; *Virtual Channel:* 7; 18 kw; 991 ft.; N30 16 51 W81 34 12
100 Festival Park Avenue, Jacksonville, FL 32202 US
(904) 353-7770, (904) 358-6360; *Fax:* (904) 358-6331
www.wjct.org
License: Jacksonville, Duval County, FL held by WJCT Inc
Washington Law Firm: Schwartz, Woods & Miller
Nat'l Network: PBS
Foreign Language Programming
Steven Wallace, Chairman
Michael Boylan, CEO/President
Anthony Padgett, Sr. VP of Content & Operations
Jeri Cirillo, General Sales Mgr
Stanley Cleiland, Programming Director
Stephen Jones, Closed Captioning, Producer Content
Donna Starratt, Marketing/Underwriting
Stan Cleiland, VP of Community Relations & Strategic Communicatio

***WJEB-TV** *Digital Channel:* 44; *Virtual Channel:* 59; 1000 kw; 945 ft.; N30 16 34 W81 33 52
3101 Emerson Expressway, Jacksonville, FL 32207 US
(904) 399-8413; *Fax:* (904) 399-8423
www.wjeb.org
License: Jacksonville, Duval County, FL held by Jacksonville Educators Broadcasting Inc
Nat'l Network: TRINITY BROADCA
Colette Snowden, General Manager
Clayton Roney, Engineering Dir
Carolyn Rentrope, Public Affairs Director

WJXT *Digital Channel:* 42; *Virtual Channel:* 4; 976 kw; 965 ft.; N30 16 24 W81 33 13
4 Broadcast Place, Jacksonville, FL 32207 US
(904)-399-4000, (904)-393-9844; *Fax:* (904) 393-9822
www.news4jax.com
dfox@wjxt.com
License: Jacksonville, Duval County, FL held by Post-Newsweek Stations, Fla. Inc.
Group Owner: Post-Newsweek Stations Inc.; (acq 1-28-53; grpsl; *Washington Law Firm:* Covington & Burling
Nat'l Network: IND; *Nat'l Reps:* TeleRep; *Wire Services:* AP; CNN
Size of News Staff: 75; *Hours of Local News Weekly:* 47
Tina Schultz, Operations Dir
Bob Ellis, General Manager
Wayne Reid, General Sales Mgr
Mike Guerrieri, Promotions Manager
Mo Ruddy-Baker, News Director
News Team, George Winterling
Weather Team, Sam Kouvaris
Mary Baer, Newsteam
Joy Purdy, News Anchor
Tarik Minor, News Reporter
Michael Kelly, Sports

WJXX *Digital Channel:* 10; *Virtual Channel:* 25; 29.5 kw; 954 ft.; N30 16 24 W81 33 13
1070 E. Adams St., Jacksonville, FL 32202 US
(904) 354-1212
www.firstcoastnews.com
news@firstcoastnews.com
License: Orange Park, Clay County, FL held by Multimedia Holdings Corp.
Group Owner: Tegna Media; (acq 3-15-00; $81 million)

Nat'l Network: ABC
Hours of Local News Weekly: news progmg 22.5 hrs wkly
Bill Lancaster, Vice President and Station Manager
Mark Overstreet, Director of Sales
Bonnie Solloway, Vice President, Programming and Marketing
Helen Garrard, Promotions Manager
Meagan Harris, News Director
Victor Murphy, ChiefEngineer

WTLV *Digital Channel:* 13; *Virtual Channel:* 12; 53.3 kw; 954 ft.; N30 16 24 W81 33 13
1070 E. Adams St., Jacksonville, FL 32202 US
(904) 354-1212; *Fax:* (904) 353-9010
www.firstcoastnews.com
news@firstcoastnews.com
License: Jacksonville, Duval County, FL held by Multimedia Holdings Corp.
Group Owner: Tegna Media; (acq 5-12-75; $11,401,217;
Washington Law Firm: Reed, Smith, Shaw & McClay
Nat'l Network: NBC; *Nat'l Reps:* Blair Television
Size of News Staff: 54; *Hours of Local News Weekly:* news progmg 29 hrs wkly
Bill Lancaster, Vice President and Station Manager
Mark Overstreet, Director of Sales
Bonnie Solloway, Vice President, Programming and Marketing
Helen Garrard, Promotions Manager
Meagan Harris, News Director
Victor Murphy, ChiefEngineer

Miami

WFOR-TV ; *Virtual Channel:* 4; 100 kW; 620 ft.; N25 58 6.7 W80 13 19.8
8900 NW 18th Terrace, Doral, FL 33172 USA
(305) 591-4444
miami.cbslocal.com
License: Miami, Dade County, FL held by CBS Television Stations Inc.
Group Owner: CBS Television Stations Group
Nat'l Network: CBS

Miami-Ft. Lauderdale, FL (DMA 16)

SEMILLITAS
2601 S. Bayshore Dr., Suite 1250, Miami, FL 33133 USA
(786) 222-0280; *Fax:* (305) 858-7188
www.semillitas.tv
License: Miami, FL held by SomosTV LLC.
Group Owner: SomosTV
Foreign Language Programming
Luis Villanueva, President & CEO

VIENDOMOVIES
2601 S. Bayshore Dr., Suite 1250, Miami, FL 33133 USA
(786) 222-0280; *Fax:* (305) 858-7188
www.viendomovies.com
License: Miami, FL held by SomosTV LLC.
Group Owner: SomosTV
Foreign Language Programming
Luis Villanueva, President & CEO

WAMI-DT *Digital Channel:* 47; *Virtual Channel:* 69; 1000 kw; 974 ft.; N25 59 09 W80 11 37; *Population Served:* 4,600,000
8551 N.W. 30th Terrace, Doral, FL 33122
(305) 487-5550
www.univision.com
License: Hollywood, Broward County, FL held by UniMas Miami LLC.
Group Owner: Univision Communications Inc.
Nat'l Network: UniMas (Spanish)
Bert Delgado, SVP, Production and Technical Operations
Claudia Puig, Senior Vice President and General Manager

***WBEC-TV** *Digital Channel:* 40; *Virtual Channel:* 63; 1000 kw; 935 ft.; N25 59 8.7 W80 11 37.1
6600 SW Nova Dr., Fort Lauderdale, FL 33317 US
(754) 321-1000, (877) TV-BECON; *Fax:* (754) 321-1180
www.becon.tv
License: Boca Raton, Palm Beach County, FL held by The School Board of Broward County, Florida
Nat'l Network: ETV
Chris Bartch, Station Manager
Tom Ford, Programming Director
Andrew Furlong, Engineering Manager
Noel Hyatt, Marketing Coordinator
Eric Powell, Production Manager
Pearl Cook, Print Graphics Manager
Phyllis Schiffer-Simon,Director
Trevor Thomas, School Services manager
Alicia Trotman, Closed Captioning

WBFS-TV *Digital Channel:* 32; *Virtual Channel:* 33; 1000 kW; 973 ft.; N25 58 7 W80 13 20
8900 NW 18th Terrace, Doral, FL 33172 USA
(305) 591-4444
miami.cbslocal.com
License: Miami, Dade County, FL held by Miami Television Station WBFS Inc.
Group Owner: CBS Television Stations Group
Nat'l Network: MyNetworkTV; CBS
Nelly Rubio, Director of Community Relations

WGEN-TV *Digital Channel:* 8; *Virtual Channel:* 8; 7 kw; 183 ft.; N24 33 18 W81 48 5
5420 Mac Donald Avenue, Key West, FL 33040 US
(305) 293-4333; *Fax:* (305) 293-4007
License: Key West, Monroe County, FL held by Sonia Licensed Subsidiary LLC
Nat'l Network: MundoFox
Alberto Monge, Station Manager

WHFT-TV *Digital Channel:* 46; *Virtual Channel:* 45; 1000 kw; 1010 ft.; N25 59 34 W80 10 27
Mailing Address: PO Box A, Santa Ana, CA 92711 US
Second Address: P.O. Box 768, Station B, Ottawa, ON K1P 5P8
(714) 731-1000, (888) 731-1000, (714) 832-2950, (8; *Fax:* (610) 583-1476
www.tbn.org
mrudderow@tbn.org
License: Miami, Dade County, FL held by Trinity Broadcasting of Florida Inc.
Group Owner: Trinity Broadcasting Network; (acq 5-14-80; $10 million); *Washington Law Firm:* Colby M. May
Nat'l Network: TRINITY BROADCA
Foreign Language Programming
Paul Crouch, President
T. Hines, General Manager

***WLRN-TV** *Digital Channel:* 20; *Virtual Channel:* 17; 870 kw; 988 ft.; N25 58 46 W80 11 46
Mailing Address: 172 N.E. 15th St., Miami, FL 33132 US
Second Address: 1 Herald Plaza, Miami, FL 33132
(305) 995-1717, (305) 376-3490; *Fax:* (305) 995-2299
www.wlrn.org
radionews@miamiherald.com
License: Miami, Dade County, FL held by The School Board of Miami-Dade County, FL
Washington Law Firm: Leibowitz & Associates
Nat'l Network: PBS
Mario Barrios, Operations Dir
John LaBonia, General Manager
Bernadette Siy, Station Manager
Ginette Grey, Promotions Manager
Adrienne Kennedy, Special Projects Manager

WLTV-DT *Digital Channel:* 23; *Virtual Channel:* 23; 4,470 kw vis; 974 ft.; N25 58 07 W80 13 20; *Population Served:* 4,600,000
8551 N.W. 30th Terrace, Miami, FL 33122
(305) 487-5550; *Fax:* (305) 702-7114
www.univision.com
License: Miami, Dade County, FL held by WLTV License Partnership G.P.
Group Owner: Univision Communications Inc.; (acq 8-7-88);
Washington Law Firm: Wiley, Rein & Fielding
Nat'l Network: Univision (Spanish)
Foreign Language Programming; Size of News Staff: 70; *Hours of Local News Weekly:* news progmg 17 hrs wkly
Bert Delgado, SVP, Production and Technical Operations
Claudia Puig, Senior Vice President and General Manager
Roberto Vizcon, News Director
Doug Petersen, Engineering Dir
Carlos Espinosa, Managing Editor
Angela Ramos, Director ofCommunity Relations

***WPBT** *Digital Channel:* 18; *Virtual Channel:* 2; 1000 kw; 1014 ft.; N25 57 30 W80 12 44
Mailing Address: PO Box 610002, Miami, FL 33261-0002 US
Second Address: PO Box 610002, Miami, FL 33261-0002
(305) 949-8321; *Fax:* (305) 944-4211
www.channel2.org
channel2@channel2.org
License: Miami, Dade County, FL held by Community Television Foundation of South Florida Inc
Washington Law Firm: Wilmer, Cutler & Pickering
Nat'l Network: PBS
Foreign Language Programming
Jack Lowell, Chairman
Dolores Sukhdeo, President & CEO
Graham Simmons, SVP of Engineering/Operations
Dave Mullins, Promotions Manager
Jody Rafkind, Promotions Manager
Laurie Silvers, Vice Chair
Sandy Batchelor, Director

WPLG *Digital Channel:* 10; *Virtual Channel:* 10; 127.7 kw; 1014 ft.; N25 58 0 W80 12 43
3401 W. Hallandale Beach Blvd., Pembroke Park, FL 33023 US
(954) 364-2500; *Fax:* (954) 364-2935
www.local10.com
License: Miami, Dade County, FL held by Post-Newsweek Stations, Fla. Inc.
Group Owner: Post-Newsweek Stations Inc.; (acq 9-27-69; grpsl;
Washington Law Firm: Covington & Burling
Nat'l Network: ABC; *Nat'l Reps:* MMT
David Boylan, Operations Dir
Paul Wasserman, General Sales Mgr
Melinda Harper, Programming Director
Darren Alline, Chief Engineer
Sharon Harrison, Operations Manager
MJ Acosta, Anchor
Andrea Brody, Sports Team
Trent Aric,Weather Team
Sasha Andrade, Anchor

WPXM-TV *Digital Channel:* 35; 200 kw; N25 59 10 W80 11 36
14901 NE 20th Ave., North Miami, FL 33181 USA
(954) 703-1920; *Fax:* (954) 858-1848
www.iontelevision.com
vieweremail@ionmedia.com
License: Miami, FL held by ION Media License Company, LLC.
Group Owner: ION Media Networks Inc.
Nat'l Network: ION Television
Brandon Burgess, Chairman
Frank Tenore, General Sales Mgr

WSBS-TV *Digital Channel:* 3; *Virtual Channel:* 22; 1 kw; 177 ft.; N24 33 18 W81 48 7
7007 NW 77th Ave., Miami, FL 33166 US
(305) 644-4800; *Fax:* (786) 470-1667
www.mega.tv
info@mega.tv
License: Key West, Monroe County, FL held by WSBS Licensing Inc.
Group Owner: Spanish Broadcasting System Inc.; (acq 2-28-2006; $37.25 million with WSBS-CA Miami).
Nat'l Network: MEGA TV
Foreign Language Programming
Alex Aleman, Operations Dir
Albert Rodriguez, General Manager/General Sales Manager
Andrew Polsky, Advertising Inquiries

WSCV *Digital Channel:* 30; *Virtual Channel:* 51; 1000 kw; 997 ft.; N25 59 9 W80 11 37
15000 SW 27th St., Miramar, FL 33027 USA
(954) 622-7710; *Fax:* (954) 622-6107
www.telemundo51.com
License: Fort Lauderdale, Broward County, FL held by NBC Telemundo License LLC
Group Owner: Telemundo Station Group; (acq 4-12-2002; grpsl).
Nat'l Network: Telemundo
Foreign Language Programming; Size of News Staff: 70; *Hours of Local News Weekly:* news progmg 16 hrs wkly
Luis Silberwasser, President

WSFL *Digital Channel:* 19; *Virtual Channel:* 39; 5,000 kw vis, 500 kw aur; ant 905t/905g; N25 58 07 W80 13 20; *Population Served:* 3,247,000
500 E Broward Blvd., Suite 800, Fort Lauderdale, FL 33394 USA
(954) 627-7300; *Fax:* (954) 355-5200
sflcw.com
License: Miami, Dade County, FL held by WSFL LLC
Group Owner: Tribune Media; (acq 12-20-2007; grpsl)
Nat'l Network: The CW Network; *Nat'l Reps:* TeleRep
Chip Fitzgerald, Sales Manager

WSVN *Digital Channel:* 7; *Virtual Channel:* 7; 158 kw; 1008 ft.; N25 57 49 W80 12 43
1401 79th St. Causeway, Miami, FL 33141 US
(305) 795-2777,(305) 751-6692; *Fax:* (305) 757-2266
www.wsvn.com
newsdesk@wsvn.com
License: Miami, Dade County, FL held by Sunbeam Television Corp
Group Owner: Sunbeam Television Corp.; *Washington Law Firm:* Koteen & Naftalin
Nat'l Network: FOX; *Nat'l Reps:* Harrington, Righter & Parsons
Edmund Ansin, President
Anby Ansin, Operations Dir
Robert Leider, General Manager
Deisy Bermudez, Corporate Dir. Of Programming
Steven Cejas, Executive Producer
Craig Stevens, News anchor

Louis Aguirre, News Reporter
PhilFerro, Wethear Team
Steve Shapiro, Sports Team

WTVJ *Digital Channel:* 31; *Virtual Channel:* 6; 1000 kw; 1020 ft.; N25 58 7 W80 13 20
15000 SW 27th St., Miramar, FL 33027 USA
(954) 622-6000, (954) NBC-6000
www.nbcmiami.com
License: Miami, Dade County, FL held by NBC Telemundo License LLC
Group Owner: NBC Owned Television Stations; (acq 1995).
Nat'l Network: NBC; *Nat'l Reps:* NBC TV Stations Sales; *Wire Services:* NWS (National Weather Service)

Mobile, AL-Pensacola (Ft. Walton Beach), FL (DMA 60)

WAWD *Digital Channel:* 49; *Virtual Channel:* 58; 32 kw; 183 ft.; N30 23 49 W86 30 30.27
8317 Front Beach Rd., Suite 23, Panama City, FL 32407 USA
(850) 234-2773
www.destinationnetwork.com
License: Fort Walton Beach, Okaloosa County, FL held by Beach TV Properties Inc.
Group Owner: Beach TV Properties Inc.; (acq 10-29-99; $175,000); *Washington Law Firm:* Baraff, Koerner, Olender & Hochberg
Nat'l Network: IND

WEAR-TV *Digital Channel:* 17; *Virtual Channel:* 3; 1000 kw; 1900 ft.; N30 36 45 W87 38 43
4990 Mobile Hwy., Pensacola, FL 32506 US
(850) 456-3333
www.weartv.com
news@weartv.com
License: Pensacola, Escambia County, FL held by WEAR Licensee LLC
Group Owner: Sinclair Broadcast Group Inc.; (acq 10-8-97).; *Washington Law Firm:* Shaw Pittman LLP
Nat'l Network: ABC; *Nat'l Reps:* Millennium Sales & Marketing
Size of News Staff: 30; *Hours of Local News Weekly:* news progmg 36 hrs wkly
Terry Cole, General Manager
Deborah Currie, General Sales Mgr
David L. Brown, Chief Engineer

WFGX *Digital Channel:* 50; *Virtual Channel:* 35; 1000 kw; 1912 ft.; N30 36 45 W87 38 42
4990 Mobile Hwy., Pensacola, FL 32506 US
(850) 456-3333; *Fax:* (850) 455-0159
www.wfgxtv.com
License: Fort Walton Beach, Okaloosa County, FL held by WFGX Licensee LLC
Group Owner: Sinclair Broadcast Group Inc.; (acq 3-31-2004; $520,000).; *Washington Law Firm:* Shaw Pittman LLP
Nat'l Network: MYTV
Terry Cole, General Manager
Deborah Currie, General Sales Mgr

WHBR *Digital Channel:* 34; *Virtual Channel:* 33; 1000 kw; 1362 ft.; N30 36 45 W87 38 43
Mailing Address: 6500 Pensacola Blvd, P. O. Box 2633, Pensacola, FL 32505 US
Second Address: 6500 Pensacola Blvd., Pensacola, FL 32505
(850) 473-8633, (800) 533-9427; *Fax:* (850) 473-8631
www.whbr.org
License: Pensacola, Escambia County, FL held by Christian Television of Pensacola/Mobile Inc
(acq 12-16-97).; *Washington Law Firm:* Gammon & Grange
Nat'l Network: IND
Bob D'Andrea, President
Wayne Wetzel, Operations Dir
David Mayo, General Manager

WJTC *Digital Channel:* 45; *Virtual Channel:* 44; 1000 kw; 1499 ft.; N30 35 16 W87 33 13
661 Azalea Road, Mobile, AL 36609 US
(251) 602-1500; *Fax:* (251) 602-1547
www.utv44.com
nbc15@nbc15online.com
License: Pensacola, Escambia County, FL held by Deerfield Media (Mobile) Licensee LLC
Group Owner: Deerfield Media; (acq 3-14-2008; grpsl); *Washington Law Firm:* Covington & Burling
Nat'l Network: IND; *Nat'l Reps:* Millennium Sales & Marketing
Jared Quijas, Operations Dir
Shea Grandquest, General Manager
Chris Delaporte, General Sales Mgr
Chuck Reeves, Programming Director
Kristen Mosley, Promotions Manager
Tim Reid, Chief Engineer

WPAN *Digital Channel:* 40; *Virtual Channel:* 53; 33.5 kw; 719 ft.; N30 24 9 W86 59 35
2425 W. Nine Mile Rd., Suite 1, Pensacola, FL 32534 US
(850) 479-4620; *Fax:* (850) 479-4632
www.wpantv.com
License: Fort Walton Beach, Okaloosa County, FL held by Franklin Media Inc
(acq 5-23-88).; *Washington Law Firm:* Pepper & Corazzini
Nat'l Network: IND
Janna Hoynacki, General Manager
John L. Franklin, Sr., General sales Manager
John Franklin, Jr., Sales/ Marketing
Ed Watts, Media Coordinator
Craig Pippin, Account Executive
Leon Franklin, Sales

***WSRE** *Digital Channel:* 31; *Virtual Channel:* 23; 1000 kw; 1801 ft.; N30 36 40.3 W87 36 26.9
1000 College Blvd., Pensacola, FL 32504 US
(850) 484-1200, (800) 239-9773; *Fax:* (850) 484-1255
www.wsre.org
License: Pensacola, Escambia County, FL held by District Board of Trustees of Pensacola Junior College
Nat'l Network: PBS
Sandy Cesartti Ray, General Manager
Darrel Harrison, Dir, of Engineering/ Broadcast Operations

Orlando-Daytona Beach-Melbourne, FL (DMA 18)

WACX-DT *Digital Channel:* 40; 1,000 kw vis; ant 1,619t/1,591g; N28 35 11.6 W81 04 58.2; *Population Served:* 3,500,000
Mailing Address: Box 608040, Orlando, FL 32860
Second Address: 285 W. Central Pkwy., Suite 1716, Altamonte Springs, FL 32714
(407) 263-4040, (800) 268-8204
www.wacxtv.com
License: Leesburg, Lake County, FL held by Associated Christian Television System Inc
(acq 6-8-83; *Washington Law Firm:* Koerner & Olender
Foreign Language Programming
Claud Bowers, CEO
Carol Gentry, General Sales Mgr
Linda Jarrel, Programming Director

***WDSC-TV** *Digital Channel:* 33; *Virtual Channel:* 15; 708 kw vis, 201.4 kw aur; ant 577t/567g; N29 10 24 W81 09 24; *Population Served:* 3,500,000
Mailing Address: Box 9245, 1200 W. International Speedway Blvd., Daytona Beach, FL 32114 US
Second Address: 1200 W. International Speedway Blvd., Daytona Beach, FL 32114
(800) 638-9238, (386) 506-4415; *Fax:* (386) 506-4427
www.wdsctv.org/
WDSC@daytonastate.edu
License: New Smyrna Beach, Volusia County, FL held by Daytona State College Inc.
(acq 6-30-2002); *Washington Law Firm:* Fletcher, Heald & Hildreth
Bruce Dunn, General Manager
Bill Schwartz, Engineering Dir

***WEFS** *Digital Channel:* 30; *Virtual Channel:* 68; 182 kw; 1611 ft.; N28 36 35 W81 3 35
1519 Clearlake Road, Cocoa, FL 32922 US
(321) 433-7110; *Fax:* (321) 433-7154
www.wbcctv.org
License: Cocoa, Brevard County, FL held by Brevard Community College.
Nat'l Network: PBS
Dr. James Drake, President
Philip T. Wallace, General Manager

WESH *Digital Channel:* 11; *Virtual Channel:* 2; 100 kw vis, 10 kw aur; 1,650t/1,670g; N28 56 17 W81 18 58; *Population Served:* 1,735,900
1021 N. Wymore Rd., Winter Park, FL 32789 US
(407) 645-2222; *Fax:* (407) 539-7812
www.wesh.com
License: Daytona Beach, Volusia County, FL held by Orlando Hearst Television
Group Owner: Hearst Television Inc.; (acq 1999; grpsl).; *Washington Law Firm:* Brooks, Pierce, McLendon, Humphrey & Leonard
Nat'l Network: NBC; *Nat'l Reps:* Eagle Television Sales; *Wire Services:* AP
Size of News Staff: 80; *Hours of Local News Weekly:* 7.5
James Carter, President
Rick Scharf, Operations Dir
James Carter, General Manager

N/A, Station Manager
Rob Halpern, General Sales Mgr
Lenora Boutte, Programming Director
Steve Rifkin, Promotions Manager
Bob Longo, NewsDirector
N/A, Engineering Dir
Richard Monn, Chief Engineer
Justin Jones, National Sales Manager
Brett Connolly, Anchor
Jason Guy, Anchor
Michelle Imperato, Anchor
Meredith McDonough, Anchor
Stewart Moore, Anchor

WFTV *Digital Channel:* 39; *Virtual Channel:* 9; 1000 kw; 1608 ft.; N28 34 7 W81 3 16
Mailing Address: 490 E. South St., Orlando, FL 32801 US
Second Address: 490 E. South St., Orlando, FL 32801
(407) 841-9000, (407) 822-8353, (407) 822-8401, (8; *Fax:* (407) 841-8529, (407) 481-2891, (407) 481-9902
www.wftv.com
captioning.hotline@wftv.com
License: Orlando, Orange County, FL held by WFTV, Inc.
Group Owner: Cox Media Group; (acq 8-85; $185 million)
Nat'l Network: ABC
Size of News Staff: 80; *Hours of Local News Weekly:* news progmg 25 hrs wkly
Shawn Bartelt, Operations Dir
Bill Funke, General Sales Mgr
Bob St. Charles, Promotions Manager
Bob Jordan, News Director
Chip Reif, Operations Manager
Tom Terry, Chief meterologist
Nancy Alvarez, Anchor
Martie Salt, GeneralAssignment Reporter
Racquel Asa, Traffic Reporter
Jamie Holmes, Anchor

WKCF *Digital Channel:* 17; *Virtual Channel:* 18; 1000 kw; 1549 ft.; N28 35 12 W81 4 58
1350 Campus Parkway, Suite 106, Wall, NJ 07753 US
(407) 645-1818; *Fax:* (407) 647-4163
www.wb18.com
License: Clermont, Lake County, FL held by Orlando Hearst Television Inc.
Group Owner: Hearst Television Inc.; (acq 7-7-2006; $217.5 million)
Nat'l Network: CW; *Nat'l Reps:* Harrington, Righter & Parsons
James Carter, President
John Soapes, General Sales Mgr
Steve Rifkin, Promotions Manager
Joe Addalia, Engineering Dir

WKMG-TV *Digital Channel:* 26; *Virtual Channel:* 6; 944 kw; 1693 ft.; N28 36 35 W81 3 35
WKMG-TV Local 6, 4466 N. John Young Parkway, Orlando, FL 32804 US
(407) 521-1200
www.clickorlando.com
License: Orlando, Orange County, FL held by Post-Newsweek Stations Orlando Inc.
Group Owner: Post-Newsweek Stations Inc.; (acq 9-4-97); *Washington Law Firm:* Covington & Burling
Nat'l Network: CBS; *Nat'l Reps:* MMT
Size of News Staff: 80; *Hours of Local News Weekly:* news progmg 24 hrs wkly
Alan Frank, President
Skip Valet, General Manager
Troy Bridges, Weather
Jamie She, Sports
David Pingalore, Sports
Skip Valet, Management
Lisa Bell, Anchor
David Hall, Anchor

***WMFE-TV** *Digital Channel:* 24; 1,350 kw vis; ant 1,246t/1,220g; N28 36 08 W81 05 37; *Population Served:* 1,301,000
12461 Research Parkway, Suite 550, Orlando, FL 32826
(407) 823-1300; *Fax:* (407) 206-2791
www.wucftv.org
wucftv@wucftv.org
License: Orlando, Orange County, FL held by University of Central Florida
Washington Law Firm: Dow Lohnes PLLC
Nat'l Network: PBS
Ana Tangel-Rodriguez, Chairman
Grant J Heston, Operations Dir
Polly Anderson, Executive Director/General Manager
Nancy Zappa, Programming Director
Polly Anderson, Executive Dir.

Bill Doston, Dir. Of Content & Operations
LynnSand, Dir. Of Community Support
Christine Dellert, Dir. Of Communications & Outreach
Jan Klein, Viewer Services Coordinator
Benjamin Jaffe, Production Manager

WOFL *Digital Channel:* 22; *Virtual Channel:* 35; 607 kW; 1473 ft.; N28 36 13 W81 5 11
35 Skyline Dr., Lake Mary, FL 32746 USA
(407) 644-3535
www.fox35orlando.com
License: Orlando, Orange County, FL held by Fox Television Stations LLC
Group Owner: Fox Television Stations Group; (acq 6-17-2002; with WOGX(TV) Ocala).
Nat'l Network: FOX

WOPX-TV *Digital Channel:* 48; 1000 kw; ant 1,548t/1,522g; *Population Served:* 685,000
7091 Grand National Dr., Suite 100, Orlando, FL 32819 USA
(615) 773-6100
www.iontelevision.com
License: Melbourne, FL held by Ion Media Orlando License, Inc.
Group Owner: Ion Media Networks; (acq 12-12-97; $13,161,274).; *Washington Law Firm:* Dow, Lohnes & Albertson
Nat'l Network: Ion Television
Brandon Burgess, Chairman
Conny Fiala, Operations Dir

WOTF-TV *Digital Channel:* 43; *Virtual Channel:* 43; 1,000 kw; 1,049t/1,005g; N28 35 12 W81 04 58
523 Douglas Ave., Orlando, FL 32714 US
(407) 774-2626; *Fax:* (407) 774-3384
www.noticias.entravision.com/orlando
calendarioorlando@entravision.com
License: Melbourne, Brevard County, FL held by UniMas Orlando Inc.
Group Owner: Univision Communications Inc.; (acq 5-21-2001; grpsl).; *Washington Law Firm:* Dow, Lohnes & Albertson
Foreign Language Programming
Cathy Zambrano, Operations Manager

WRBW *Digital Channel:* 41; *Virtual Channel:* 65; 763 kW; 1691 ft.; N28 36 35 W81 3 35
35 Skyline Dr., Lake Mary, FL 32746 USA
(407) 644-3535
www.fox35orlando.com/my65
License: Orlando, Orange County, FL held by Fox Television Stations LLC
Group Owner: Fox Television Stations Group; (acq 7-31-2001; grpsl).
Nat'l Network: MyNetworkTV

WRDQ *Digital Channel:* 27; *Virtual Channel:* 27; 1000 kw; 1608 ft.; N28 34 7 W81 3 16
490 E. South St, Orlando, FL 32801 US
(407) 841-9000, (407) 822-8353; *Fax:* (407) 422-1414
License: Orlando, Orange County, FL held by WFTV, Inc.
Group Owner: Cox Media Group; (acq 2-1-2001).
Nat'l Network: ABC
Shawn Bartelt, General Manager
Mario Mendosa, General Sales Mgr
Bob Jordan, News Director
Nancy Allvarez, Anchor
Tom Terry, Chief Meterologist
Martie Salt, General Assignment Reporter
Racquel Asa, Reporter

***WTGL** *Digital Channel:* 45; 4,680 kw vis, 468 kw aur; ant 934t/1,005g; N28 18 26 W80 54 48; *Population Served:* 3,068,000
31 Skyline Dr., Lake Mary, FL 32746
(407) 215-6745; *Fax:* (407) 215-6789
www.tv45.org
info@tv45.org
License: Cocoa, Brevard County, FL held by Good Life Broadcasting
1982; *Washington Law Firm:* Lerman & Senter
Regional Reps: Ken Mikesell
Foreign Language Programming; Hours of Local News Weekly: 0
Ed Griffis, Operations Dir
Ken Mikesell, General Manager
Eileen Kelly, Programming Director
Michael Flynn, Chief Engineer

WVCI-LP *Digital Channel:* 16; *Virtual Channel:* 16; 9.2 kw; 1,404 ft.; N28 35 35 W81 25 13
523 Douglas Ave., Orlando, FL 32714 US
(407) 774-2626; *Fax:* (407) 774-3384
calendarioorlando@entravision.com
License: Daytona Beach, Volusia County, FL held by Entravision Holdings, LLC.
Group Owner: Entravision Communications Corp.
Nat'l Network: Univision (Spanish)
Foreign Language Programming
Lucy Toledo, Operations Coordinator
Jenny Ash, News Director
Fernando Romero, Dir. of Marketing and Event Sales
Anthony Roman, Production Manager

WVEN-TV *Digital Channel:* 49; *Virtual Channel:* 26; 120 kw; 1,404 ft.; N28 55 16 W81 19 09
523 Douglas Ave., Orlando, FL 32714 US
(407) 774-2626; *Fax:* (407) 774-3384
www.noticias.entravision.com/orlando
calendarioorlando@entravision.com
License: Daytona Beach, Volusia County, FL held by Entravision Holdings LLC.
Group Owner: Entravision Communications Corp.; (acq 9-15-00; $22.55 million)
Nat'l Network: Univision (Spanish)
Foreign Language Programming
Lucy Toledo, Operations Coordinator
Jenny Ash, News Director
Fernando Romero, Dir. of Marketing and Event Sales
Anthony Roman, Production Manager

Panama City, FL (DMA 154)

***WFSG** *Digital Channel:* 38; *Virtual Channel:* 56; 49.2 kw; 449 ft.; N30 22 2 W85 55 28; *Rebroadcasting:* Rebroadcasts WFSU-TV Tallahassee.
Mailing Address: 1600 Red Barber Plaza, Tallahassee, FL 32310 US
Second Address: 402 South Monroe Street, Suite 901, The Capitol Bldg., Tallahassee, FL 32399-1300
(850) 487-3170, (850) 488-1281; *Fax:* (850) 487-3093, (850) 488-4876
www.wfsu.org
mail@wfsu.org, florida@wfsu.org
License: Panama City, Bay County, FL held by Florida State University
(acq 2-28-86).; *Washington Law Firm:* Cohn & Marks
Nat'l Network: PBS
Patrick Keating, General Manager
Caroline Austin, Station Manager
John Kwak, General Sales Mgr
Jannie Whitt, Promotions Manager
Krysta Brown, News Director
Doug Crall, Director Of Engineering
Leo Barfield, Director OfEngineering
Mike Dunn, Director of Production
Sarah Schuetz, Programming/Operations
Denison Graham, Finance Director
Cindy Michaelson, Membership Director
Mike Marshall, Web Programmer
Paul Dam, Production Supervisor

WJHG *Digital Channel:* 18; *Virtual Channel:* 7; 67 kw; 859 ft.; N30 25 59 W85 24 51
8195 Front Beach Rd., Panama City Beach, FL 32407 USA
(850) 234-7777; *Fax:* (850) 233-6647
www.wjhg.com
news@wjhg.com
License: Panama City, Bay County, FL held by Gray Television License LLC
Group Owner: Gray Television Inc.; (acq 6-29-60; $340,000; *Washington Law Firm:* Venable, Baetjer, Howard & Civiletti
Nat'l Network: NBC; The CW Network; *Nat'l Reps:* Continental Television Sales
Jon McKee, Operations Manager
Ulysses Carlini, General Manager
Jennifer Fairbanks, General Sales Mgr
Sean Dixon, Director of Creative Services
Donna Bell, News Director

WMBB *Digital Channel:* 13; *Virtual Channel:* 13; 42 kw; 1424 ft.; N30 21 8 W85 23 28
613 Harrison Ave., Panama City, FL 32401 US
(850) 769-2313
www.wmbb.com
License: Panama City, Bay County, FL held by Nexstar Broadcasting, Inc.
Group Owner: Nexstar Broadcasting Group; (acq 7-15-2008; $60 million with KALB-TV Alexandria, LA); *Washington Law Firm:* Akin Gump Strauss Hauer & Feld LLP
Nat'l Network: ABC; *Nat'l Reps:* Blair Television
Size of News Staff: 24; *Hours of Local News Weekly:* news progmg 143 hrs wkly
Terry Cole, General Manager
George Baker, General Sales Mgr
Heather Kretzer, News Director

WPCT *Digital Channel:* 47; *Virtual Channel:* 46; 132 kw; 194 ft.; N30 10 59 W85 46 42
8317 Front Beach Rd., Suite 23, Panama City Beach, FL 32407 US
(850) 234-2773; *Fax:* (850) 235-1179
www.destinationnetwork.com
toni.davis@tripsmarter.com
License: Panama City Beach, Bay County, FL held by Beach TV Properties Inc.
Group Owner: Beach TV Properties Inc.
Nat'l Network: IND

WPGX *Digital Channel:* 9; *Virtual Channel:* 28; 34 kw vis, 126 kw aur; ant 748t; N30 23 42 W85 32 02; *Population Served:* 250,000
RSA Tower, 20th Floor, 201 Monroe St., Montgomery, AL 36104
(334) 206-1400; *Fax:* (334)206-1555
www.myfox28.com
License: Panama City, Bay County, FL held by WPGX License Subsidiary LLC.
Group Owner: Raycom Media Inc.; (acq 12-15-2003; grpsl)
Nat'l Network: Fox; *Nat'l Reps:* Harrington, Righter & Parsons
Heather Moore, General Manager
Sharon Davlin, General Sales Mgr
Al Shook, Operations Manager

Tallahassee, FL-Thomasville, GA (DMA 107)

***WFSU-TV** *Digital Channel:* 32; *Virtual Channel:* 11; 937.8 kw; 778 ft.; N30 21 31 W84 36 38
Mailing Address: 1600 Red Barber Plaza, Tallahassee, FL 32310 US
Second Address: 402 South Monroe Street, Suite 901, The Capitol Bldg., Tallahassee, FL 32399-1300
(850) 487-3170, (850) 488-1281; *Fax:* (850) 487-3093, (850) 488-4876
www.wfsu.org
License: Tallahassee, Leon County, FL held by Florida State University
Nat'l Network: ETV
Patrick Keating, General Manager
Caroline Austin, Station Manager
John Kwak, General Sales Mgr
Sarah Schuetz, Programming Director
Krysta Brown, News Director
Doug Crall, Director Of Engineering
Leo Barfield, Director OfEngineering
Mike Dunn, Director of Production
Sarah Schuetz, Programming/Operations
Denison Graham, Finance Director
Cindy Michaelson, Membership Director
Michael Plummer, Television Producer
Paul Dam, Production Supervisor

WTWC-TV *Digital Channel:* 40; *Virtual Channel:* 40; 462 kw; 1969 ft.; N30 40 50 W83 58 21
Mailing Address: 8440 Deerlake S., Tallahassee, FL 32312 US
Second Address: 10706 Beaver Dam Rd., Hunt Valley, MD 21030
(850) 893-4140; *Fax:* (850) 893-6974
www.wtwc40.com
License: Tallahassee, Leon County, FL held by WTWC Licensee LLC
Group Owner: Sinclair Broadcast Group Inc.; (acq 1999; grpsl).; *Washington Law Firm:* Dow, Lohnes & Albertson
Nat'l Network: NBC; *Nat'l Reps:* Millennium Sales & Marketing
Size of News Staff: 30; *Hours of Local News Weekly:* news progmg 14 hrs wkly
John Dittmeier, General Manager
Halley Stinchfield, General Sales Mgr
Steve Sheridan, Chief Engineer

WTXL-TV *Digital Channel:* 27; *Virtual Channel:* 27; 1000 kw; 1699 ft.; N30 40 6 W83 58 10
1620 Commerce Blvd., Midway, FL 32343 US
(850) 893-3127, (850) 894-6397; *Fax:* (850) 575-7838
www.wtxl.tv
abc27news@wtxl.tv
License: Tallahassee, Leon County, FL held by WTXL-TV License LLC
Group Owner: Southern Broadcast Corp. of Sarasota; (acq 11-30-2005; $12 million); *Washington Law Firm:* Keck, Mahin & Cate
Nat'l Network: ABC
Size of News Staff: 26; *Hours of Local News Weekly:* news progmg 24 hrs wkly

Gary Wordlaw, General Manager
Marc Stover, General Sales Mgr
Bill Cummings, News Director
David Long, Chief Engineer
Abbey Maurer, Anchor & reporter
Rahman Johnson, Anchor & reporter
Erin Clanahan, Weather team
Brad dalton,Sports Team
Roland Koopman, Contributor

Tampa-St Petersburg (Sarasota), FL (DMA 11)

WCLF *Digital Channel:* 21; *Virtual Channel:* 22; 1000 kw; 1342 ft.; N27 49 10 W82 15 39
Mailing Address: P.O. Box 6922, Clearwater, FL 33758 US
Second Address: 6922 142nd Ave., Largo, FL 33771
(727) 535-5622; *Fax:* (727) 531-2497
www.ctnonline.com
License: Clearwater, Pinellas County, FL held by Christian Television Corporation Inc.
Group Owner: Christian Television Corporation Inc.; (acq 12-16-97).; *Washington Law Firm:* Gammon & Grange
Nat'l Network: IND
Foreign Language Programming
Robert D'Andrea, President
Jennifer Kiser, Director of Operations
Robert D'Andrea, Founder

***WEDU** *Digital Channel:* 13; *Virtual Channel:* 3; 25 kw; 470.9 meters; 27 50'51.5 N 82 15'49.4 W
1300 North Blvd., Tampa, FL 33607-5699 US
(813) 254-9338; *Fax:* (813) 253-0826
www.wedu.org
License: Tampa-St. Petersburg, FL held by Florida West Coast Pub Broadcasting Inc
Ownership: Florida West Coast Public Broadcasting, Inc.; *Washington Law Firm:* Schwartz, Woods & Miller
Nat'l Network: PBS
Foreign Language Programming
Susan Howarth, President and CEO
Frank Wolynski, VP of Engineering
Debra Friedberg , Chief Financial Officer
Jack Conely , Vice President of Content
Allison Hedrick, VP of Communications
Claire O'Connor Solomon, Senior VP ofDevelopment
Larry Jopek, VP of Marketing & Community Partnerships

WFLA-TV *Digital Channel:* 7; *Virtual Channel:* 8; 32 kw; 1526 ft.; N27 50 32 W82 15 45
Mailing Address: P.O. Box 1410, Tampa, FL 33601 US
Second Address: 200 South Parker St., Tampa, FL 33608
(813) 228-8888, (813) 221-5788, (813) 225-2720; *Fax:* (813) 221-5787, (813)225-2770
www.wfla.com
License: Tampa, Hillsborough County, FL held by Media General Communications Inc.
Group Owner: Media General Broadcast Group; (acq 1965; $17.5 million); *Washington Law Firm:* Dow, Lohnes & Albertson
Nat'l Network: NBC; *Nat'l Reps:* Harrington, Righter & Parsons; *Wire Services:* UPI
Michael Pumo, President
Rick McEwen, Operations Dir
Brad Moses, General Manager
Steve Blanchard, General Sales manager
Don North, News Director
Tom Hebel, Marketing Director
Joyce Lueders, Finance Director
Monica Boyer, WebSite Sales & Marketing
Gayle Sierens, Anchor
Steve Andrews, Investigative Reporter
Steve Jerve, Chief Meterologist

WFTS-TV *Digital Channel:* 29; 2.63 kw vis, 260 w aur; 1,546t/1,649g; N27 50 32 W82 15 46
4045 N. Himes Avenue, Tampa, FL 33607
(813) 354-2828, (800) 920-2828, (813) 354-2828, (8; *Fax:* (813) 354-3001, (813) 878-2828
www.abcactionnews.com
License: Tampa, Hillsborough County, FL held by Tampa Bay Television Inc.
Group Owner: The E. W. Scripps Co.; (acq 1-2-86; grpsl).; *Washington Law Firm:* Baker & Hostetler
Nat'l Network: ABC; *Nat'l Reps:* Eagle Television Sales
Rich Pegram, Operations Dir
Sarah Tyrrell, General Sales Mgr
Donna Wilson, Promotions Manager
Jack Winter, Operations Manager
Lisette Campos, Dir. Of Community Affairs
Denis phillips, Chief Meterologist
Tom Korun, SportsAnchor
Ashley Glass, Anchor
Jackie Callaway, Reporter

WFTT-DT *Digital Channel:* 47; *Virtual Channel:* 50; 4,200 kw vis, 420 kw aur; 1,600t/1,580g; N27 50 50 W82 15 50;
Population Served: 1,600,000
2610 W. Hillsborough Ave., Tampa, FL 33614
(813) 998-3648
www.univision.com
License: Tampa, Hillsborough County, FL held by UniMas Tampa LLC.
Group Owner: Univision Communications Inc.; (acq 5-21-2001; grpsl).; *Washington Law Firm:* Wiley, Rein & Fielding
Nat'l Network: UniMas (Spanish)
Foreign Language Programming
Lilly Gonzalez, General Manager
Steve Hess, Chief Engineer
Ivonne Hernandez, Technical Director

WTOG-TV *Digital Channel:* 44; *Virtual Channel:* 44; 550 kW; 1480 ft.; N27 49 46 W82 15 59
365-105th Terrace NE, St. Petersburg, FL 33716 USA
(727) 576-4444
cwtampa.cbslocal.com
wtogmcr@gmail.com
License: St. Petersburg, Pinellas County, FL held by CBS Operations Inc.
Group Owner: CBS Television Stations Group
Nat'l Network: The CW Network; *Nat'l Reps:* TeleRep; *Wire Services:* NWS (National Weather Service)
Stan Gill, Vice President/General Manager
Jim Lange, Chief Engineer

WTSP *Digital Channel:* 10; *Virtual Channel:* 10; 69 kw; 1,565 ft.; N27 49 9.7 W82 15 38.7
11450 Gandy Blvd. N., St. Petersburg, FL 33702 US
(727) 577-1010; *Fax:* (727) 576-6924
www.wtsp.com
tips@wtsp.com
License: St. Petersburg, Pinellas County, FL held by Pacific and Southern LLC
Group Owner: Tegna Media; (acq 12-31-96).; *Washington Law Firm:* Wiley, Rein & Fielding
Nat'l Network: CBS; *Nat'l Reps:* Blair Television
Hours of Local News Weekly: news progmg 28.5 hrs wkly
Lee Griffin, Director of Technology and Operations
Elliott Wiser, President and General Manager
Larry Doyle, Director of Marketing
Michael Mikuliza, Local Sales Manager
Barb Zant, Local Sales Manager

WTTA *Digital Channel:* 32; *Virtual Channel:* 38; 1000 kw; 1531 ft.; N27 50 32 W82 15 45
P.O. Box 1410, Tampa, FL 33601 US
(813) 228-8888; *Fax:* (813) 225-2770
www.wfla.com
License: St. Petersburg, Pinellas County, FL held by LIN Television Corp.
Group Owner: Media General Broadcast Group; *Washington Law Firm:* Shaw Pittman
Nat'l Network: MYTV
Julie Nelson, General Manager

WTVT *Digital Channel:* 12; *Virtual Channel:* 13; 72.3 kW; 1430 ft.; N27 49 8 W82 14 26
3213 W Kennedy Blvd, Tampa, FL 33609 USA
(813) 870-9630; *Fax:* (813) 871-3135
www.fox13news.com
news@wtvt.com
License: Tampa, Hillsborough County, FL held by New World Communications of Tampa Inc.
Group Owner: Fox Television Stations Group; (acq 11-96; grpsl); *Washington Law Firm:* Hogan & Hartson
Nat'l Network: FOX; *Wire Services:* Conus
Size of News Staff: 100; *Hours of Local News Weekly:* news progmg 46 hrs wkly
Renee Swearingen, Programming Coordinator

***WUSF-TV** *Digital Channel:* 34; *Virtual Channel:* 16; 475 kw; 1486 ft.; N27 50 52 W82 15 48
4202 East Fowler Ave., TVB100, Tampa, FL 33620-6870 US
(813) 974-8700, (800) 741-9090; *Fax:* (813) 974-5016
www.wusf.org
info@wusf.org
License: Tampa, Hillsborough County, FL held by University of South Florida
Washington Law Firm: Cohn & Marks
Nat'l Network: PBS
JoAnn Urofsky, General Manager
Tom Dollenmayer, Station Manager
Cathy Coccia, General Sales Mgr
Susan Geiger, Programming Director
Scott Finn, News Director
Dale Goodwin, Engineering
Patrick Morris, Special Projects Manager
Jorge Cunha, Dir. Of Production
Allison Dolcy, Development Specialist

WVEA-TV *Digital Channel:* 25; *Virtual Channel:* 62; 750 kw; 1549 ft.; N27 49 10 W82 15 39
2610 W. Hillsborough Ave., Tampa, FL 33614 US
(813) 872-6262; *Fax:* (813) 998-3600
noticiastampa@entravision.com
License: Venice, Sarasota County, FL held by Entravision Holdings L.L.C.
Group Owner: Entravision Communications Corp.; (acq 1999; $17 million); *Washington Law Firm:* Thompson Hine, LLP
Nat'l Network: UNIVISION; *Wire Services:* AP
Foreign Language Programming; Size of News Staff: 14; *Hours of Local News Weekly:* news progmg 3.5 hrs wkly
Mariana Acosta, Promotions Manager
Jenny Ash, News Director

WWSB *Digital Channel:* 24; *Virtual Channel:* 40; 90 kw; 768 ft.; N27 33 21 W82 21 48
1477 10th St., Sarasota, FL 34236 US
(941) 552-0777, (941) 923-NEWS; *Fax:* (941) 924-3971/ (941) 923-8709
www.mysuncoast.com
License: Sarasota, Sarasota County, FL held by WWSB License LLC
Group Owner: Southern Broadcast Corp. of Sarasota; (acq 3-26-86; $40,500); *Washington Law Firm:* Leibowitz & Associates
Nat'l Network: ABC
Size of News Staff: 45; *Hours of Local News Weekly:* news progmg 21 hrs wkly
Ken Long, CEO
J. Manuel Calvo, President
Jason Wildanstein, Operations Dir
Jeff Benninghoff, VP/ General Manager
Vann Smith, General Sales Manager
Ronda Drago, Programming Coordinator
Steve Sabato, News Director
Jack Dillon,Engineering Dir.
Norm Dempsey, Digital Media dir.
Yvette Perez, Creative Services Dir.
Julie Shaffer, National Sales Manager
Claudia Gutknecht, Traffic Manager
Jill Chandler, Marketing Consultant
Amy Tuten, Marketing Consultant

WXPX-TV *Digital Channel:* 42; 257 kw; N27 49 10 W82 15 39
14444 66th St. N., Clearwatern, FL 33764 USA
(812) 335-1770; *Fax:* (813) 314-5464
www.iontelevision.com
License: Bradenton, FL held by Ion Media License Company, LLC
Group Owner: Ion Media Networks Inc.
Nat'l Network: ION Television
Jon Painter, Chief Engineer

West Palm Beach-Ft. Pierce, FL (DMA 38)

WFGC *Digital Channel:* 49; *Virtual Channel:* 61; 800 kw; 410 ft.; N26 45 47 W80 12 19
1900 South Congress Ave., Suite A, West Palm Beach, FL 33406 US
(561) 642-3361; *Fax:* (561) 967-5961
www.wfgctelevision.com
comments@wfgc.com
License: Palm Beach, Palm Beach County, FL held by Christian TV of Palm Beach County Inc.
(acq 12-16-97).; *Washington Law Firm:* Gammon & Grange
Nat'l Network: IND
Neville Chankersingh, CFO
Wayne Wetzel, President
Mike Gonzalez, General Manager
Chris Mavros, Chief Engineer

WFLX *Digital Channel:* 28; *Virtual Channel:* 29; 630 kw; 1503 ft.; N26 34 37 W80 14 32
1100 Banyan Blvd., West Palm Beach, FL 33401 US
(561) 845-2929, (561) 653-5700; *Fax:* (561) 671-3777
www.wflx.com
fox29news@wflx.com
License: West Palm Beach, Palm Beach County, FL held by WFLX License Subsidiary, LLC
Group Owner: Raycom Media Inc.; (acq 1998).
Nat'l Network: FOX; *Nat'l Reps:* Harrington, Righter & Parsons

John Spinola, Operations Dir
John Heislman, General Sales Mgr
Barb Billens, Program Director
Rachel Leigh, Internet Content Director
Michael Williams, News Team
Roxanne Stein, News Team
John Favole, News Team
Charlie Keegan,News Team
James Wieland, News Team

WPBF *Digital Channel:* 16; *Virtual Channel:* 25; 1000 kw; 1490 ft.; N27 7 17 W80 23 42
959 Eighth Avenue, New York, NY 10019 US
(561) 694-2525; *Fax:* (561) 624-1089
www.wpbf.com
License: Tequesta, Palm Beach County, FL held by Hearst Properties Inc.
Group Owner: Hearst Television Inc.; (acq 8-1-97).
Nat'l Network: ABC; *Nat'l Reps:* Continental Television Sales
Size of News Staff: 48; *Hours of Local News Weekly:* news progmg 25 hrs wkly
Caroline Scollard-Taplett, Operations Dir
Russ Larish, Programming Director

WPEC *Digital Channel:* 13; *Virtual Channel:* 12; 90 kw; 1014 ft.; N26 35 18 W80 12 30
1100 Fairfield Dr., West Palm Beach, FL 33407 US
(561) 844-1212; *Fax:* (561) 881-0712
www.cbs12.com
License: West Palm Beach, Palm Beach County, FL held by WPEC Licensee LLC
Group Owner: Sinclair Broadcast Group Inc.; *Washington Law Firm:* Latham & Watkins
Nat'l Network: CBS; *Nat'l Reps:* TeleRep
Hours of Local News Weekly: news progmg 24 hrs wkly
Carl Pugliese, Operations Manager
Mike McCormick, News Director
Jaime Martinez, Director of Engineering
Mike Rajewski, Sales Manager
Jill Novorro, Sales Manager
James Griffel, Creative Services Director
Josh Brown, Digital SalesManager
Gerry Marcelo, Digital Content Manager
Cynthia Capers, Executive Producer

WPTV-TV *Digital Channel:* 12; 100 kw vis, 20 kw aur; 990t/1,031g; N26 35 20 W80 12 43; *Population Served:* 1,200,000
1100 Banyan Blvd., West Palm Beach, FL 33401
(561) 655-5455, (561) 653-5700; *Fax:* (561) 653-5719 (news)
www.wptv.com
newstips@wptv.com
License: West Palm Beach, Palm Beach County, FL held by Scripps Howard Broadcasting Co.
Group Owner: The E. W. Scripps Co.; (acq 12-27-61; $2 million; *Washington Law Firm:* Baker & Hostetler
Nat'l Network: NBC; *Nat'l Reps:* Harrington, Righter & Parsons; *Wire Services:* Reuters
Size of News Staff: 75; *Hours of Local News Weekly:* news progmg 27 hrs wkly
Richard Boehne, CEO
Steve Wasserman, Operations Dir
Joseph Ne Castro, CFO
Kelly Dunn, Journalist, Anchor
Steve Weagle, Chief Meterologist
Emerson Lotzia, Sports Anchor
Evan Axelbank, Multimedia Journalist, Reporter

WPXP-TV *Digital Channel:* 36; 1,000 kw; 492t; N26 35 20 W80 12 44
14901 NE 20th Ave., North Miami, FL 33181 USA
(954) 703-1920; *Fax:* (954) 858-1848
www.iontelevision.com
License: Lake Worth, FL held by Ion Media West Palm Beach License, Inc.
Group Owner: Ion Media Networks, Inc.
Nat'l Network: Ion Television
Frank Tenore, General Sales Mgr

***WTCE-TV** *Digital Channel:* 38; *Virtual Channel:* 21; 1000 kw; 974 ft.; N27 1 31 W80 10 43
3601 N. 25th St., Fort Pierce, FL 34946 US
(772) 489-2701; *Fax:* (772) 489-6833
License: Fort Pierce, Saint Lucie County, FL held by Jacksonville Educators Broadcasting Inc
Nat'l Network: TRINITY BROADCA
Charles Massi, General Manager

WTCN-CA *Digital Channel:* 43; 15 kw; 974 ft.; N27 01 30 W80 10 42.7
1100 Fairfield Dr., West Palm Beach, FL 33407 US
(561) 681-3434; *Fax:* (561) 684-9193
www.my15wtcn.com
License: West Palm Beach, Palm Beach County, FL held by WTVX Licensee LLC
Group Owner: Sinclair Broadcast Group Inc.
; *Nat'l Reps:* TeleRep
Robert Butterfield, General Manager
Jaime Martinez, Engineering Dir

WTVX *Digital Channel:* 34; *Virtual Channel:* 34; 1000 kw; 1495 ft.; N27 7 19 W80 23 20
1100 Fairfield Dr., West Palm Beach, FL 33407 US
(561) 681-3434; *Fax:* (561) 684-9193
www.cw34.com
License: Fort Pierce, St. Lucie County, FL held by WTVX Licensee LLC
Group Owner: Sinclair Broadcast Group Inc.; (acq 11-21-2007; grpsl); *Washington Law Firm:* Wiley Rein LLP .
Nat'l Network: CW; *Nat'l Reps:* TeleRep
Robert Butterfield, General Manager

WWHB-CA *Digital Channel:* 48; 2.1 kw; 974 ft.; N27 01 30.8 W80 10 42.7
1100 Fairfield Dr., West Palm Beach, FL 33407 US
(561) 681-3434; *Fax:* (561) 684-9193
www.azteca48.com
License: West Palm Beach, Palm Beach County, FL held by WTVX Licensee LLC
Group Owner: Sinclair Broadcast Group Inc.
; *Nat'l Reps:* TeleRep
Robert Butterfield, General Manager
Jaime Martinez, Engineering Dir

***WXEL-TV** *Digital Channel:* 27; *Virtual Channel:* 42; 400 kw; 1444 ft.; N26 34 37 W80 14 32
Mailing Address: 11300 NESecond Avenue, Miami Shores, FL 33161 US
Second Address: 3401 South Congress Ave., Boynton Beach, FL 33426
(561) 737-8000; *Fax:* (561) 369-3067
www.wxel.org
jcarr@wxel.org
License: West Palm Beach, Palm Beach County, FL held by Barry Telecommunications Inc
(acq 4-16-97).; *Washington Law Firm:* Schwartz, Woods & Miller
Nat'l Network: PBS
Jerry Carr, CEO/General Manager
Fred Flaxman, General Sales Mgr
Bernard Henneberg, CFO
Lee Rowand, Promotions Director
Ross Cooper, Sales Director

Georgia

Albany, GA (DMA 152)

***WABW-TV** *Digital Channel:* 6; *Virtual Channel:* 14; 10.5 kw; 1243 ft.; N31 8 5 W84 6 16
260 - 14th Street, N.W., Atlanta, GA 30318 US
(404) 685-2400; *Fax:* (404) 685-2591
www.gpb.org
ask@gpb.org
License: Pelham, Mitchell County, GA held by Georgia Public Telecommunications Commission
Nat'l Network: PBS
Michael H. McDougald, Chairperson
Bonnie Bean, CFO
Teya Ryan, President & Executive Director
Bob Olive, General Manager
Jack Watts, Chief Engineer

***WACS-TV** *Digital Channel:* 8; *Virtual Channel:* 25; 4.7 kw; 1093 ft.; N31 56 15 W84 33 15
260 - 14th Street, N.W., Atlanta, GA 30318 US
(404) 685-2400; *Fax:* (404) 685-2591
www.gpb.org
ask@gpb.org
License: Dawson, Terrell County, GA held by Georgia Public Telecommunications Commission
Washington Law Firm: Arent, Fox, Kintner, Plotkin & Kahn
Nat'l Network: PBS
Michael H. McDougald, Chairperson
Teya Ryan, President & Executive Director
Bob Olive, General Manager

WALB *Digital Channel:* 10; *Virtual Channel:* 10; 22 kw; 974 ft.; N31 19 52 W83 51 43
Mailing Address: 2000 Wade Hampton Blvd., Greenville, SC 29615 US
Second Address: 1709 Stuart Ave., Albany, GA 31707
(229) 446-1010; *Fax:* (229) 446-4000
www.walb.com
walb@walb.com
License: Albany, Dougherty County, GA held by WALB License Subsidiary LLC.
Group Owner: Raycom Media Inc.; (acq 1-31-2006; grpsl)
Nat'l Network: NBC; *Nat'l Reps:* Continental Television Sales
Size of News Staff: 5; *Hours of Local News Weekly:* news progmg 15 hrs wkly
James Wilcox, General Manager
Rick Williams, News Director

WFXL *Digital Channel:* 12; *Virtual Channel:* 31; 60 kw; ant 991t/968g; N31 19 52 W83 51 43; *Population Served:* 385,000
1201 Stuart Ave., Albany, GA 31706
(229) 435-3100; *Fax:* (229) 903-8240
www.wfxl.com
comments@wfxl.com
License: Albany, Dougherty County, GA held by WFXL Licensee LLC
Group Owner: Sinclair Broadcast Group Inc.; (acq 11-22-2013; grpsl); *Washington Law Firm:* Pillsbury Winthrop Shaw Pittman LLP
Nat'l Network: Fox; *Nat'l Reps:* HRP
Size of News Staff: 14; *Hours of Local News Weekly:* news progmg 26 hrs wkly
Pat Coffman, Operations Manager
Deborah Gay, Station Manager
Sandi Lowe, General Sales Mgr
Ben McLeod, Marketing Director
Jenna Huff, News Director
Ken Clubb, Chief Engineer

WSST-TV *Digital Channel:* 51; 91 kw vis; ant 361t/374g; N31 53 35 W83 48 18; *Population Served:* 600,000
Box 917, 112 S. 7th St., Detroit, GA 31015
(229) 273-0001; *Fax:* (229) 273-8894
License: Cordele, Crisp County, GA held by Sunbelt-South Telecommunications Ltd
Washington Law Firm: Law Offices of Scott Cinnamon
Phillip Streetman, Operations Director/General Manager
Sara Howell, General Sales Mgr
Lee Wright, Programming Director
Ricky Smart, Chief Engineer
Barbara Dennis, Traffic Manager

Atlanta (DMA 10)

WAGA *Digital Channel:* 27; *Virtual Channel:* 5; 100 kw vis, 20 kw aur; 1,076t/1,103g; N33 47 51 W84 20 02; *Population Served:* 4,000,000
1551 Briarcliff Rd. NE, Atlanta, GA 30306 USA
(404) 875-5555
www.fox5atlanta.com
License: Atlanta, Fulton County, GA held by New World Communications of Atlanta Inc.
Group Owner: Fox Television Stations Group; (acq 11-96; grpsl).
Nat'l Network: FOX
Hours of Local News Weekly: News progmg 38 hrs wkly
Michael King, Director of Engineering/Operations

***WATC-DT** *Digital Channel:* 41; 398 kw vis, 39.8 kw aur; 423t; N33 48 40 W84 21 51
1862 Enterprise Dr., Norcross, GA 30093
(770) 300-9828; *Fax:* (770) 300-9838
www.watc.tv
License: Atlanta, Gwinnett County, GA held by Community Television Inc
Greg West, President
Patricia Thompson, Vice President
Michael Vallone, Underwriting Manager
Greg West, Programming Director
Greg West, Promotions Manager
Scott Wills, Chief Engineer
Michael Vallone, Underwriting Manager
Jennifer Eichelberger

WATL *Digital Channel:* 25; *Virtual Channel:* 36; 500 kw; 1,089 ft.; N33 48 26 W84 20 22
1 Monroe Pl. N.E., Atlanta, GA 30324 US
(404) 881-3600
www.myatltv.com
License: Atlanta, Fulton County, GA held by Pacific and Southern LLC
Group Owner: Tegna Media; (acq 8-7-2006; $180 million); *Washington Law Firm:* Wiley, Rein & Fielding
Nat'l Network: MyNetworkTV; *Nat'l Reps:* TeleRep
John Deushane, President and General Manager
Tim McNamara, Director of Sales
Jennifer Rigby, News Director

Dave Myer, Digital Sales Manager
Robbin Steed, Community Relations and Sales Marketing

WGCL *Digital Channel:* 19; *Virtual Channel:* 46; 1000 kW; 1079 ft.; N33 48 26 W84 20 22; *Population Served:* 5,725,787
425 14th Street NW, Atlanta, GA 30318 USA
(404) 327-3200; *Fax:* (404) 327-3004
www.cbs46.com
news@cbs46.com
License: Atlanta, Fulton County, GA held by Meredith Corp.
Group Owner: Meredith Corp.; (acq 2-22-99; $370 million swap with KCPQ(TV) Tacoma, WA).; *Washington Law Firm:* Dow, Lohnes & Albertson, PLLC
Nat'l Network: CBS; *Nat'l Reps:* Harrington, Righter & Parsons
Size of News Staff: 80
Mark Pimentel, VP & General Manager
Steve Doerr, News Director
Gary Watkins, Chief Engineer

***WGTV** *Digital Channel:* 8; *Virtual Channel:* 8; 21 kw; 1083 ft.; N33 48 18 W84 8 40
260 - 14th Street, N.W., Atlanta, GA 30318 US
(404) 685-2400; *Fax:* (404) 685-2591
www.gpb.org
ask@gpb.org
License: Athens, Clarke County, GA held by Georgia Public Telecommunications Commission
Washington Law Firm: Arent, Fox, Kintner, Plotkin & Kahn
Nat'l Network: PBS
Michael H. McDougald, Chairperson
Teya Ryan, President & Executive Director

WHSG-TV *Digital Channel:* 44; *Virtual Channel:* 63; 1000 kw; 1018 ft.; N33 48 26 W84 20 22
Mailing Address: PO Box A, Santa Ana, CA 92711 US
Second Address: P.O. Box 768, Station B, Ottawa, ON K1P 5P8
(714) 731-1000, (888) 731-1000, (714) 832-2950, (8; *Fax:* (610) 583-1476
www.tbn.org
mrudderow@tbn.org
License: Monroe, Walton County, GA held by Trinity Broadcasting Network Inc.
Group Owner: Trinity Broadcasting Network; (acq 11-21-89).
Nat'l Network: TRINITY BROADCA
Dorothy Casoria, General Manager

***WPBA** *Digital Channel:* 21; *Virtual Channel:* 30; 55.4 kw; 872 ft.; N33 45 32 W84 20 7
740 Bismark Rd. Ne, Atlanta, GA 30324 US
(678) 686-0321, (678) 686-0345; *Fax:* (678) 686-0356,(678) 686-0336
www.WPBA.org
License: Atlanta, Fulton County, GA held by Board of Education of the City of Atlanta
Washington Law Firm: Schwartz, Woods & Miller
Nat'l Network: PBS
Hours of Local News Weekly: News progmg 1.5 hrs wkly
Milton Clipper, President & CEO
Milton Clipper, General Manager
John Weatherford, COO
Tina Arbes, CFO
Kenneth D. Brown, SVP, Human Resources

WPCH-TV *Digital Channel:* 20; *Virtual Channel:* 17; 1000 kw; 1018 ft.; N33 48 26 W84 20 22
Mailing Address: 425 14th St., NW, Atlanta, GA 30318 US
Second Address: 1050 Techwood Drive, Atlanta, GA 30318
(404) 325-4646; *Fax:* (404) 575-9720
www.peachtreetv.com
information@peachtreetv.com
License: Atlanta, Fulton County, GA held by Superstation Inc.
Nat'l Network: IND
Jonathan Katz, General Manager
Walter Naar, General Sales Mgr
Tracy Underwood, Promotions Manager
Barbara Linebarger, Engineering Dir
Bob Hudson, Traffic Manager

WPXA-TV *Digital Channel:* 51; 1000 kw; 2,021t/787g; N34 18 47 W84 38 55; *Population Served:* 3,900,000
200 Cobb Pkwy. N., Suite 110, Marietta, GA 30062 USA
(770) 919-0575; *Fax:* (770) 919-9621
www.iontelevision.com
License: Rome, GA held by ION Media Atlanta License, Inc.
Group Owner: ION Media Networks Inc.; (acq 7-13-94; $9.5 million); *Washington Law Firm:* Dow, Lohnes & Albertson
Nat'l Network: ION Television
Bob Burgess, Chairman

WSB-TV *Digital Channel:* 39; *Virtual Channel:* 2; 1000 kw; 1037 ft.; N33 45 51 W84 21 42
1601 West Peachtree St., NE, Atlanta, GA 30309 US
(404) 897-7000; *Fax:* (404) 897-6246 (gen mgr)
www.wsbtv.com
License: Atlanta, Fulton County, GA held by Georgia Television Company.
Group Owner: Cox Media Group; *Washington Law Firm:* Dow, Lohnes & Albertson
Nat'l Network: ABC; *Nat'l Reps:* TeleRep
Bill Hoffman, Operations Dir
Deborah Denechaud, General Sales Mgr
Art Rogers, Programming Director
Steve Riley, Promotions Manager
Marian Pittman, News Director
Gary Alexander, Engineering Dir
David Lamothe, OperationsDirector
Jocelyn Dorsey, Public Affairs Director
John Bachman, Anchor
Glenn Burns, Chief meterologist
Zach Klein, Sports Director
Tony Thomas, News Reporter

WSKC-CD *Digital Channel:* 22; 15 kw; 1455.7 ft; N33 58 38 W84 09 23
3654 W. Jarvis Ave., Skokie, IL 60076 US
License: Atlanta, GA held by KM LPTV OF ATLANTA, LLC.
Group Owner: KM Communications Inc.
Myoung Hwa Bae, President

WUPA *Digital Channel:* 43; *Virtual Channel:* 69; 1000 kW; 1152 ft.; N33 48 26 W84 20 22
2700 Northeast Expressway, Building A, Atlanta, GA 30345 USA
(404) 325-6969
cwatlanta.cbslocal.com
License: Atlanta, Fulton County, GA held by Atlanta Television Station WUPA Inc.
Group Owner: CBS Television Stations Group; *Washington Law Firm:* Wiley, Rein & Fielding
Nat'l Network: The CW Network

WUVG-DT *Digital Channel:* 17; *Virtual Channel:* 34; 1,258 kw vis, 125.8 kw aur; 1,351t/1,236g; N34 07 32 W83 51 32; *Population Served:* 750,000
3350 Peachtree Rd., Suite 1250, Atlanta, GA 30326 US
(404) 926-2300; *Fax:* (404) 926-2303
www.univision.com
License: Athens, Clarke County, GA held by Univision Atlanta LLC
Group Owner: Univision Communications Inc.; (acq 6-6-01; grpsl).; *Washington Law Firm:* William M. Barnard
Nat'l Network: Univision (Spanish)
Foreign Language Programming
Gianncarlo Cifuentes, News Director
Mariela J. Romero, Community Affairs Director

WXIA-TV *Digital Channel:* 10; *Virtual Channel:* 11; 80 kw; 994 ft.; N33 45 24 W84 19 55
1 Monroe Pl. N.E., Atlanta, GA 30324 US
(404) 892-1611; *Fax:* (404) 881-0675
www.11alive.com
License: Atlanta, Fulton County, GA held by Pacific and Southern LLC
Group Owner: Tegna Media; (acq 6-7-79; grpsl; *Washington Law Firm:* Reed Smith LLP
Nat'l Network: NBC; *Nat'l Reps:* TeleRep
Hours of Local News Weekly: news progmg 27 hrs wkly
John Deushane, President and General Manager
Tim McNamara, Director of Sales
Jennifer Rigby, News Director
Michael Clifford, Local Sales Manager
Robbin Steed, Community Relations and Sales Marketing

Augusta, GA (DMA 111)

WAGT *Digital Channel:* 30; *Virtual Channel:* 26; 400 kw; 1585 ft.; N33 24 20 W81 50 1
1336 Augusta West Parkway, Augusta, GA 30901 US
(706) 826-0026; *Fax:* (706) 724-4028
www.cwaugusta.com
jrandall@nbc26.tv
License: Augusta, Richmond County, GA held by WAGT Television Inc.
Group Owner: Schurz Communications Inc.; (acq 7-1-80; $5 million); *Washington Law Firm:* Hogan & Hartson
Nat'l Network: NBC/CW; CW; *Nat'l Reps:* Petry Television Inc.
Size of News Staff: 28; *Hours of Local News Weekly:* news progmg 8 hrs wkly
Mike Bell, Station Manager
Mariah Gardner, Promotions Manager
Greg Baldwin, News Director
Dave DeFrehn, Chief Engineer

***WCES-TV** *Digital Channel:* 6; *Virtual Channel:* 20; 7.9 kw; 1409 ft.; N33 15 33 W82 17 9
260 - 14th Street, N.W., Atlanta, GA 30318 US
(404) 685-2400; *Fax:* (404) 685-2491
www.gpb.org
ask@gpb.org
License: Wrens, Jefferson County, GA held by Georgia Public Telecommunications Commission.
Nat'l Network: PBS
Michael H. McDougald, Chairperson
Teya Ryan, President & CEO
Anthony Padgett, Chief Operating Officer
Juanita Rachels, General Manager
Eric Burns, News Director
Elizabeth Laprade, Chief Financial Officer
Robert Brienza, VicePresident-Original Productions & Sports
Robert Butler, Vice President-Engineering
Steve Carey, Vice President-Production
Bert Huffman, Vice President-Development and Marketing
Andrew MacCartney, Director-Education and Digital Media

WFXG *Digital Channel:* 51; *Virtual Channel:* 54
Mailing Address: 3933 Washington Road, Augusta, GA 30907 US
Second Address: Box 204540, Augusta, GA 30917-4540
(706) 650-5400; *Fax:* (706) 650-8411
www.wfxg.com
gtomlinson@wfxg.com
License: Augusta, Richmond County, GA held by Southeastern Media Holdings Inc.
Group Owner: Southeastern Media Holdings Inc.; (acq 12-1-2003; $40 million with WXTX(TV) Columbus).; *Washington Law Firm:* Miller & Fields
Nat'l Network: FOX
Andy Wyatt, VP/General Manger
Jim Laura, General Sales Manager
Becky Maddox, Program coordinator
Gary Williamson, Chief Engineer
Scott Friedline, Web manager/Asst. Chief Engineer
David Harris, Traffic Manager
Mary Hart, DigitalMedia Specialist
Jane Freebern, national sa;es Asst.
Brandon Mullis, Marketing Producer
Waylon cawley, Account Executive

WJBF *Digital Channel:* 42; *Virtual Channel:* 6; 1000 kw; 1663 ft.; N33 24 20.2 W81 50 1.07
Mailing Address: 1336 Augusta West Parkway, Augusta, GA 30909 US
Second Address: P.O. Box 1404, Augusta, GA 30909
(706) 722-6664, (888) 812-9801; *Fax:* (706) 722-0022, (804) 887-7081
www.wjbf.com
License: Augusta, Richmond County, GA held by Media General Operations, Inc.
Group Owner: Media General Broadcast Group; (acq 3-27-2000; grpsl).; *Washington Law Firm:* Dow, Lohnes & Albertson, PLLC
Nat'l Network: ABC
Hours of Local News Weekly: News progmg 22 hrs wky
Mary Gadson, Operations Dir
Bill Stewart, General Manager
Scot Seabolt, General Sales Mgr
Mary Jones, Programming Director
Robert Pippin, Promotions Manager
Mark Rosen, News Director
Cary Hale, Chief Engineer
Roberto Vasquez,Director of Results
Carter Murphy, Local Sales Manager
Michael Schwartz, National Sales Manager
Brad Means, Anchor
George Myers, Chief Meterologist
Matthew Zahn, Sports Director

WRDW *Digital Channel:* 12; *Virtual Channel:* 12; 316 kw vis, 30.2 kw aur; ant 1,590t/1,506g; N33 24 29 W81 50 36; *Population Served:* 604,000
PO Box 1212, Augusta, GA 30903 USA
(803) 278-1212; *Fax:* (803) 442-4561
www.wrdw.com
License: Augusta, Richmond County, GA held by Gray Television Licensee Inc.
Group Owner: Gray Television Inc.
Nat'l Network: CBS; MyNetworkTV; Antenna TV; *Nat'l Reps:* Continental Television Sales
Size of News Staff: 35; *Hours of Local News Weekly:* news progmg 28 hrs wkly
John Ray, President & General Manager
Estelle Parsley, VP, News & Operations
Mark Hodges, Marketing/Promotions
Danalynn McIntyre, News Assignments Manager
Ed Elser, Chief Engineer

Chattanooga, TN (DMA 89)

WELF-TV *Digital Channel:* 16; *Virtual Channel:* 23; 300 kw; 1394 ft.; N34 57 7 W85 22 58
Mailing Address: PO Box A, Santa Ana, CA 92711 US
Second Address: PO Box 768, Station B, Ottawa, ON K1P 5P8
(714) 731-1000, (888) 731-1000; *Fax:* (714) 832-2950
www.tbn.org
welf@tbn.org
License: Dalton, Whitfield County, GA held by Trinity Broadcasting Network
Group Owner: Trinity Broadcasting Network; (acq 5-8-2000; grpsl).
Nat'l Network: TRINITY BROADCA
Onya Richter, Station Manager

***WNGH-TV** *Digital Channel:* 33; *Virtual Channel:* 18; 426 kw; 1762 ft.; N34 45 6 W84 42 54
260 - 14th Street, N.W., Atlanta, GA 30318 US
(404) 685-2400; *Fax:* (404) 685-2491
www.gpb.org
ask@gpb.org
License: Chatsworth, Murray County, GA held by Georgia Public Telecommunications Commission
Washington Law Firm: Arent, Fox, Kintner, Plotkin & Kahn
Nat'l Network: PBS
Michael H. McDougald, Chairperson
Teya Ryan, President & CEO
Anthony Padgett, Chief Operating Officer
Hugh Pearson, Station Manager
Eric Burns, News Director
Elizabeth Laprade, Chief Financial Officer
Robert Brienza, VicePresident-Original Productions & Sports
Robert Butler, Vice President-Engineering
Steve Carey, Vice President-Production
Bert Huffman, Vice President-Development and Marketing
Andrew MacCartney, Director-Education and Digital Media

Columbus, GA (DMA 127)

***WJSP-TV** *Digital Channel:* 23; *Virtual Channel:* 28; 177 kw; 1457 ft.; N32 51 8 W84 42 4
260 - 14th Street, N.W., Atlanta, GA 30318 US
(404) 685-2400; *Fax:* (404) 685-2591
www.gpb.org
ask@gpb.org
License: Columbus, Muscogee County, GA held by Georgia Public Telecommunications Commission
Nat'l Network: PBS
Teya Ryan, President & CEO
Anthony Padgett, COO
Brock Rice, General Sales Manager
Jayne Berklich, Programming
Jayne Hodak, News Director
Robert Butler, VP, Engineering
Alfons Pynenburg, Chief Engineer
Jayne Berklich, Closedcaptioning
Tanya Ott, Vice President-Radio
William Overall, Vice President-Television
Veronica Pemberton-Daniels, Director-Human Resources
Bert Huffman, Vice President-Development and Marketing
Steve Carey, Vice President-Production

WLTZ *Digital Channel:* 35; *Virtual Channel:* 38; 50 kw; 1238 ft.; N32 27 28 W84 53 8
6140 Buena Vista Road, Columbus, GA 31907 US
(706) 561-3838, (706) 507-6397; *Fax:* (706) 561-3880 (sales)
www.wltz.com
wltz@wltz.com
License: Columbus, Muscogee County, GA held by SagamoreHill Broadcasting of Georgia LLC.
Group Owner: SagamoreHill Broadcasting LLC; (acq 8-10-2007; $10.6 million); *Washington Law Firm:* Wiley, Rein & Fielding
Nat'l Network: NBC; *Nat'l Reps:* Blair Television
Louis Wall, President
Drew Rhodes, General Manager
Fred Steppe, General Sales Manager
Jerry Garvin, Chief Engineer
Vince Perry, Production Manager
Della Brown, Traffic Manager
Holly Sutherland, Producer/Director
Dan Lloyd,National Sales Manager
Mike Brooks, Account Executive
Helen Pierson, Master Control

WRBL *Digital Channel:* 15; *Virtual Channel:* 3; 1000 kw; 1663 ft.; N32 19 16 W84 47 28
Mailing Address: 1350 13th Ave., Columbus, GA 31901 US
Second Address: 1350 13th Ave., Columbus, GA 31901
(706) 323-3333,(706) 324-6397; *Fax:* (706) 327-6655,(706) 323-0841
www.wrbl.com
news@wrbl.com
License: Columbus, Muscogee County, GA held by Media General Broadcasting of South Carolina Holdings Inc.
Group Owner: Media General Broadcast Group; (acq 3-27-2000; grpsl).; *Washington Law Firm:* Dow, Lohnes & Albertson
Nat'l Network: CBS; *Nat'l Reps:* MMT
Otis Pickett, Operations Dir
David Hart, VP & General Manager
Kimberly Byrd, General Sales Manage
Debra Bowers, Business Manager
Curtis Holt, Chief Engineer
Phil Scoggins, Anchor
Bob Jeswald, Meteologist
Jonathan Huskey,Sports
Jessi mitchell, Reporter
James Brierton, Web Desk

WTVM *Digital Channel:* 11; *Virtual Channel:* 9; 50 kw; 1663 ft.; N32 19 25 W84 46 46
1909 Wynnton Rd., Columbus, GA 31906 US
(706) 494-5400, (706) 494-5458; *Fax:* (706) 322-7527, (706) 327-0179
www.wtvm.com
License: Columbus, Muscogee County, GA held by WTVM License Subsidiary, LLC
Group Owner: Raycom Media Inc.; (acq 1996; grpsl).; *Washington Law Firm:* Powell, Goldstein, Frazer & Murphy
Nat'l Network: ABC; *Nat'l Reps:* Harrington, Righter & Parsons
Chris Robinson, Operations Manager
Holly Steuart, General Manager
Adelaide Kirk, General Sales Mgr
Darryl Huger, News Director
David Williams, Chief Engineer
Janell Lewis, Asst. News Dir.
Jason Dennis, Anchor
Curtis McCloud,Reporter
Dave Platta, Sports Dir.
Greg Majewski, Weather Team

WXTX *Digital Channel:* 49; *Virtual Channel:* 54; 499.4 kw; 1024 ft.; N32 27 39 W84 52 43
Mailing Address: PO Box 12188, Columbus, GA 31917 US
Second Address: 1909 Wynnton Road, Columbus, GA 31906
(706) 494-5458, (706) 494-5400, (706) 568-2900; *Fax:* (706) 327-0179, (706) 561-5965
www.wxtx.com
programming@wxtx.com
License: Columbus, Muscogee County, GA
Group Owner: American Spirit Media; (acq 12-1-2003; $40 million with WFXG(TV) Augusta).; *Washington Law Firm:* Fisher, Wayland, Cooper, Leader & Zaragoza
Nat'l Network: FOX
Lee Brantley, General Manager
Mark Kirkland, General Sales Mgr
Anne Holmes, News Director
David Williams, Chief Engineer
Semone Doughton, Anchor
Derek Kinkade, Meterologist
Dave Platta, Sports Anchor

Greenville-Spartanburg, SC-Asheville, NC-Anderson, SC (DMA 37)

WUGA-TV *Digital Channel:* 24; 647 kw vis, 129 kw aur; ant 835t/600g; N34 36 44 W83 22 05
802 E. Doyle Street, Toccoa, GA 29304
(706) 886-0032; *Fax:* (706) 886-7033
www.wnegtv.com
License: Toccoa, Stephens County, GA held by UGARF Media Holdings LLC.
(acq 8-18-2008; $1,437,500); *Ownership:* University of Georgia Research Foundation Inc., 100% equity owner; *Washington Law Firm:* Fletcher, Heald & Hildreth
; *Nat'l Reps:* MMT
Size of News Staff: 6; *Hours of Local News Weekly:* news progmg 13 hrs wkly
Michael Castengera, Station Manager
Jim Sanders, General Sales Mgr
Tony Garrison, Promotions Manager
Kevin Moss, Chief Engineer

Jacksonville, FL (DMA 47)

WPXC-TV *Digital Channel:* 24; *Virtual Channel:* 21; 500 kw; 1368 ft.; N30 49 39 W81 44 27
7434 Blythe Island Hwy., Brunswick, GA 31523 USA
(912) 267-0021; *Fax:* (912) 261-9582
www.ionmedianetworks.com
michaelhubner@ionmedia.com
License: Brunswick, GA held by ION Media Brunswick License, Inc.
Group Owner: ION Media Networks Inc.; (acq 12-6-2000; $3.07 million); *Washington Law Firm:* Fleischman & Walsh
Nat'l Network: ION
Joseph Koker, Operations Dir
Nancy O'Connor, General Manager

***WXGA-TV** *Digital Channel:* 8; *Virtual Channel:* 8; 35.3 kw; 1010 ft.; N31 13 17 W82 34 24
260 - 14th Street, N.W., Atlanta, GA 30318 US
(404) 685-2400, (800) 222-6006, (4040 685-4788; *Fax:* (404) 685-2591
www.gpb.org
viewerservices@gpb.org
License: Waycross, Ware County, GA held by Georgia Public Telecommunications Commission
Nat'l Network: PBS
Michael H. McDougald, Chairperson
Teya Ryan, President & Executive Dir.
Bob Olive, General Manager
Janice Paul, Vice-Chairperson

Macon, GA (DMA 121)

WGNM *Digital Channel:* 45; *Virtual Channel:* 64; 1000 kw; 732 ft.; N32 45 51 W83 33 32
Mailing Address: 178 Steven Drive, Macon, GA 31210 US
Second Address: 5962 Zebulon Rd., Suite 364, Macon, GA 31210
(478) 474-8400; *Fax:* (478) 474-4777
www.wgnm.com
wgnm@wgnm.com
License: Macon, Bibb County, GA held by Christian Television Network Inc
(acq 12-31-2003; $3 million); *Washington Law Firm:* Allen & Harold
Nat'l Network: IND
Hours of Local News Weekly: News progmg one hr wkly
Robert D'Andrea, President
Rip Kenley, General Manager
Edie Spradley, Programming Director

WGXA *Digital Channel:* 16; *Virtual Channel:* 24; 1000 kw; 709 ft.; N32 44 58 W83 33 35
599 Martin Luther King Jr. Blvd., Macon, GA 31201 US
(478) 745-2424
www.wgxa.tv
License: Macon, Bibb County, GA held by WGXA Licensee LLC
Group Owner: Sinclair Broadcast Group Inc.; (acq 9-25-2007; $18.8 million); *Washington Law Firm:* Leibowitz & Spencer
Nat'l Network: FOX
Size of News Staff: 17
Marc Nash, Operations/Creative Services
Karen Alston, Sales Manager
Richard Blanton, Chief Engineer

WMAZ-TV *Digital Channel:* 13; *Virtual Channel:* 13; 52.6 kw; 781 ft.; N32 45 10 W83 33 32
1314 Gray Hwy., Macon, GA 31211 US
(478) 752-1313; *Fax:* (478) 752-1331
www.13wmaz.com
eyewitnessnews@13wmaz.com
License: Macon, Bibb County, GA held by Pacific and Southern LLC
Group Owner: Tegna Media; (acq 12-4-95).; *Washington Law Firm:* Wiley, Rein & Fielding
Nat'l Network: CBS
Size of News Staff: 39; *Hours of Local News Weekly:* news progmg 27 hrs wkly
Jeff Dudley, President and General Manager
Frank Shurling, Director of Sales
Angie Czewski, Digital Sales Specialist
Blair Melton, Digital Sales Manager
Maggie Drake, Digital Sales Manager
Cassie Brannen, Account Executive
NinaDamron, Account Executive
Greg Oliver, Account Executive

WMGT-TV *Digital Channel:* 30; *Virtual Channel:* 41; 90.1 kW; 620 ft; N32 45 13 W83 33 46; *Population Served:* 531,000
301 Poplar St, Macon, GA 31201 USA
(478) 745-4141; *Fax:* (478) 742-2626
www.41nbc.com
License: Macon, Bibb County, GA held by Morris Network Inc.
Group Owner: Morris Multimedia Inc.; (acq 11-30-78; $2.8 million; *Washington Law Firm:* McFadden, Evans & Sill

Nat'l Network: NBC; *Nat'l Reps:* Millennium Sales & Marketing
Todd Buccelli, General Manager
Scott Fussell, Chief Engineer
Elizabeth Gantt, Business Manager

***WMUM-TV** *Digital Channel:* 7; *Virtual Channel:* 29; 31 kw; 1088 ft.; N32 28 11 W83 15 17
260 - 14th Street, N.W., Atlanta, GA 30318 US
(404) 685-2400; *Fax:* (404) 685-2491
www.gpb.org
ask@gpb.org
License: Cochran, Bleckley County, GA held by Georgia Public Telecommunications Commission
Nat'l Network: PBS
Michael H. McDougald, Chairperson
Teya Ryan, President & CEO
Anthony Padgett, Chief Operating Officer
Randy Cranford, Station Manager
Eric Burns, News Director
Elizabeth Laprade, Chief Financial Officer
Robert Brienza, VicePresident-Original Productions & Sports
Robert Butler, Vice President-Engineering
Steve Carey, Vice President-Production
Bert Huffman, Vice President-Development and Marketing
Andrew MacCartney, Director-Education and Digital Media

WPGA-TV *Digital Channel:* 32; *Virtual Channel:* 58; 100 kw; 609 ft.; N32 45 4 W83 33 27
1691 Forsyth St., Macon, GA 31201 US
(478) 745-5858; *Fax:* (478) 745-5800
www.wpga.tv
lowell@wpga.tv
License: Perry, Houston County, GA held by Radio Perry Inc
Washington Law Firm: Brown, Nietert & Kaufman
Nat'l Network: ABC
Hours of Local News Weekly: News progmg 3 hrs wkly
Lowell Register, President
Len Register, Operations Manager
Debbie Hart, General Manager
Rick Humphrey, General Sales Manager
Julie Register, TV Promotions/Traffic
Hal Sutton, Chief Engineer
Angie Howell, Business Manager
Janice Register, Vice President
Harold Young, Marketing Consultant
Will Grammer, Video Production
Phil Clark, Radio Manager
Gail Daniels, News

Savannah, GA (DMA 91)

WGSA *Digital Channel:* 35; *Virtual Channel:* 34; 1000 kw; 1145 ft.; N32 2 48 W81 20 27
401 Mall Boulevard, Suite 210B, Savannah, GA 31406-4867 US
(912) 692-8000; *Fax:* (912) 692-0400
www.wgsa.tv
License: Baxley, Appling County, GA held by Southern TV Corp (acq 6-3-98; $3.2 million); *Washington Law Firm:* Irwin, Campbell & Tannenwald
Nat'l Network: CW
Dan Johnson, CEO
Charles Robb, CFO
Jo Johnson, Executive Vice President

WJCL *Digital Channel:* 22; *Virtual Channel:* 22; 350 kw; 1430 ft.; N32 3 29 W81 20 19
The Pinnacle, Suite 875, 3455 Peachtree Rd., N.E., Atlanta, GA 30326 US
(912) 925-0022; *Fax:* (912) 921-2235
www.abc22tv.com
License: Savannah, Chatham County, GA held by LIN Licensing Company LLC .
Group Owner: LIN Media; (acq 10-12-2012; grpsl); *Washington Law Firm:* Wiley Rein LLP
Nat'l Network: ABC; *Nat'l Reps:* Petry Television Inc.
Size of News Staff: 14; *Hours of Local News Weekly:* news progmg 5 hrs wkly
Jason Elkin, CEO
Chris Hays, Operations Dir
Lynn Fairbanks, General Manager

WSAV-TV *Digital Channel:* 39; *Virtual Channel:* 3; 1000 kw; 1450 ft.; N32 3 31 W81 17 55
1430 E. Victory Dr., Savannah, GA 31404 US
(912) 651-0300; *Fax:* (912) 651-0304
www.wsav.com
newsemailalert@wsav.com
License: Savannah, Chatham County, GA held by Media General Communications Holdings, LLC
Group Owner: Media General Broadcast Group; (acq 7-25-97; grpsl).; *Washington Law Firm:* Dow, Lohnes & Albertson
Nat'l Network: NBC; MyNetworkTV
Brad Moses, Operations Dir
Debbi Thompson, General Sales Mgr
Dave Stagnitto, Programming Director
Kevin Brennan, News Director
Tina Tyus-Shaw, Anchor
Ken Slats, Sports Director/ Anchor
Sheila Parker, reporter
Kris Allerd, Chiefmeterologist
Natalie Hendrix, Host

WTOC-TV *Digital Channel:* 11; *Virtual Channel:* 11; 24.4 kw; 1447 ft.; N32 3 14 W81 21 1
Mailing Address: PO Box 8086, Savannah, GA 31412 US
Second Address: 11 News Place, Savannah, GA 31405
(912) 234-1111, (912) 234-6397; *Fax:* (912) 231-9101, (912) 232-4945
www.wtoc.com
closedcaptioning@wtoc.com
License: Savannah, Chatham County, GA held by WTOC License Subsidiary, LLC
Group Owner: Raycom Media Inc.; (acq 4-15-97; grpsl).; *Washington Law Firm:* Covinton & Burling
Nat'l Network: CBS; *Nat'l Reps:* Harrington, Righter & Parsons
Bill Cathcart, VP/ General Manager
William Cathcart, Operations Dir
Scott Dempsey, General Sales Manager
Christine Edwards, Programming Coordinator
Jan Smith, News Director
Lorne Earle, Chief Engineer
Craig Harney, OperationsManager
Joel Kepple, News Operations Manager
Donald Graham, Executive Producer
Jamie Ertle, Assignment Manager
Alicia Briscoe, Marketing director
Robert Roose, IS Manager

***WVAN-TV** *Digital Channel:* 9; *Virtual Channel:* 9; 20 kw; 1274 ft.; N32 8 48 W81 37 5
260 - 14th Street, N.W., Atlanta, GA 30318 US
(404) 685-2400, (800) 222-6006, (4040 685-4788; *Fax:* (404) 685-2591
www.gpb.org
ask@gpb.org
License: Savannah, Chatham County, GA held by Georgia Public Telecommunications Commission
Nat'l Network: PBS
Michael H. McDougald, Chairperson
Teya Ryan, President & Executive Dir.
Bob Olive, General Manager
Janice Paul, Vice-Chairperson

144 (DMA 144)

WMDE *Digital Channel:* 5; 10 kw; 144 m; N38 57 17 W76 05 35
400 North Ashley Drive, Suite 310, Tampa, FL 31636
(813) 579-4491
License: Seaford, Sussex County, DE held by Western Pacific Broadcast LLC
Dale A. West, Vice President

Tallahassee, FL-Thomasville, GA (DMA 107)

WCTV *Digital Channel:* 46; *Virtual Channel:* 6; 1000 kw; 1857 ft.; N30 40 13 W83 56 26
1801 Halstead Blvd., Tallahassee, FL 32309 USA
(850) 893-6666; *Fax:* (850) 383-8410
www.wctv.tv
License: Thomasville, Leon County, GA held by Gray Television Licensee LLC
Group Owner: Gray Television Inc.; *Washington Law Firm:* Wiley-Rein, LLC
Nat'l Network: CBS; MyNetworkTV; *Nat'l Reps:* Continental Television Sales; *Wire Services:* AP; CBS; CNN
Heather Peeples, General Manager
Greg Shelley, Sales
Jeff Schlesser, News Director

WSWG *Digital Channel:* 43; *Virtual Channel:* 44; 50 kw; 830 ft.; N31 10 18 W83 21 57
415 Pine Ave., Suite 100, Albany, GA 31701 USA
(229) 518-2844; *Fax:* (850) 383-8410
www.wctv.tv
License: Valdosta, Lowndes County, GA held by Gray Television Licensee LLC
Group Owner: Gray Television Inc.; (acq 11-10-2005; $3.75 million); *Washington Law Firm:* Robert Bizer
Nat'l Network: CBS; MyNetworkTV; MeTV; The CW Network
Heather Peeples, General Manager
Brenda Holloway, General Sales Mgr
David Doll, Program Manager

WTLH *Digital Channel:* 50; *Virtual Channel:* 49; 665 kw; 1959 ft.; N30 40 51 W83 58 21
950 Commerce Blvd., Midway, FL 32343 US
(850) 576-4990; *Fax:* (850) 576-0200
www.myfoxtallahassee.com
fox49@fox49.com
License: Bainbridge, Decatur County, GA held by New Age Media of Tallahassee License LLC.
Group Owner: CP Media LLC; (acq 3-31-2007; grpsl)
Nat'l Network: FOX; CW; *Nat'l Reps:* Petry Television Inc.
Hours of Local News Weekly: 2.5
John Parente, CEO
Mike Yanuzzi, President
Tyrone Hayes, Operations Manager
Dan Mecca, General Manager
Anna Malcolm, Programming & Promotions Coordinator
Nirmal Singh, Chief Engineer
Doris Jones, Business Manager
Nathan Mears,National Sales Manager
Anna Lewis, Account Executive
Temeka Richardson, Traffic Manager
Wilson Smith, Master Control Operator

Guam

Hagatna

***KGTF** *Digital Channel:* 5; 27.5 kw vis, 5.47 kw aur; ant 297t/196g; N13 26 13 E144 48 17; *Population Served:* 160,000
Mailing Address: Box 21449 GMF, Barrigada, GU 96921
Second Address: 194 Sesame St, Washington Dr., Mangilao, GU 96921
(671) 734-2207,(671) 734-5788; *Fax:* (671) 734-3476
www.kgtf.org
License: Hagatna, Guam County, GU held by Guam Educational Telecommunications Corp
Washington Law Firm: Cohn & Marks
Nat'l Network: PBS
Benny Flores, Operations Dir
Sam Soza, General Manager
Vickey Manglona, Programming Director

Tamuning

KTGM *Digital Channel:* 14; *Virtual Channel:* 14; 12.5 kw; 551 ft.; N13 29 17 E144 49 30
692 N. Marine Drive, Tamuning, GU 96911 US
(671) 477-5700 xt 171; *Fax:* (671) 477-3982
www.abc7guam.com
License: Tamuning, Guam County, GU held by Sorensen Television Systems Inc
(acq 10-26-2005; $500,000); *Washington Law Firm:* Kaye, Scholer LLP
Nat'l Network: ABC
Size of News Staff: 10; *Hours of Local News Weekly:* news progmg 20 hrs wkly
Rex Sorensen, President

Hawaii

Hilo

KGMD-TV *Digital Channel:* 9; *Virtual Channel:* 9; 2 kw; 102 ft.; N19 43 0 W155 8 13
1534 Kapiolani Blvd., Honolulu, HI 96814 US
(808) 973-5462; *Fax:* (808) 941-8153
www.kgmb.com
License: Hilo, Hawaii County, HI held by HITV License Subsidiary Inc.
Group Owner: HITV License Subsidiary Inc.; (acq 5-25-2007; grpsl)
Nat'l Network: CBS; *Nat'l Reps:* Harrington, Righter & Parsons
Rick Blangiardi, President
John Fink, General Manager

KHBC-TV *Digital Channel:* 22; *Virtual Channel:* 2; 8 kw; -558 ft.; N19 43 51 W155 4 11; *Rebroadcasting:* Rebroadcasts KHNL(TV) Honolulu 100%.
400 South Record Street, Dallas, TX 75202 US
(808) 847-3246; *Fax:* (808) 845-3616
www.khnl.com
news8@khnl.com
License: Hilo, Hawaii County, HI held by KHNL/KGMB License Subsidiary LLC

Group Owner: Raycom Media Inc.; (acq 9-2-99; grpsl).;
Washington Law Firm: Covington & Burling
Nat'l Network: NBC; *Nat'l Reps:* TeleRep; *Wire Services:* CNN; NBC
John Fink, Operations Dir
Rick Blangiardi, General Manager

KHON2 *Digital Channel:* 11; *Virtual Channel:* 11; *Rebroadcasting:* Satellite of KHON-TV Honolulu.
Mailing Address: 88 Piikoi Street, Honolulu, HI 96814 US
Second Address: 1110 McCully St., Suite 203, Honolulu, HI 96826
(808) 591-2222; *Fax:* (808) 949-7715
www.khon.com
news@khon2.com
License: Hilo, Hawaii County, HI held by LIN License Company LLC
Group Owner: LIN Media; (acq 11-1-2007; grpsl); *Washington Law Firm:* Wiley Rein LLP
Nat'l Network: FOX; *Nat'l Reps:* Harrington, Righter & Parsons
Size of News Staff: 45; *Hours of Local News Weekly:* news progmg 25 hrs wkly
Joseph McNamara, President
Alexander Rogers, Operations Dir
Kristina Lockwood , General manager
Susii Hearst, General Sales Mgr
Kyle Funasaki, Promotions Manager
Lori Silva, News Director
Bob Vaillancourt, Engineering Dir
Gelene Welch, General Sales Manager

KWHD *Digital Channel:* 23; *Virtual Channel:* 14; 14.9 kw; 108 ft.; N19 43 0 W155 8 13; *Rebroadcasting:* Rebroadcasts KWHE Honolulu 100%.
P. O. Box 12, South Bend, IN 46624 US
(808) 538-1414; *Fax:* (808) 526-0326
kwhe.lesea.com
kwhe@lesea.com
License: Hilo, Hawaii County, HI held by Le Sea Broadcasting of Hawaii Inc.
Group Owner: Le Sea Broadcasting; (acq 10-1-89; $8,277;
Washington Law Firm: Gardner, Carton & Douglas
Nat'l Network: IND
Anthony Hale, CFO
Peter Sumrall, President
T. J. Malievsky, General Manager
Michael Kemmerling, Chief Engineer
David Goebert, Production Manager
Roxanne Viena, Adminstrative Assistant
Tracey Jeremiah, Senior Editor
Darrow Hand,Production Assistant / Editor
Dawn O'Brien, On Air Talent

Honolulu

KHVO *Digital Channel:* 13; *Virtual Channel:* 13; 85 kw; -302 ft.; N19 43 0 W155 8 13; *Rebroadcasting:* Satellite of KITV Honolulu.
801 S. King St., Honolulu, HI 96813 US
(808) 535-0400; *Fax:* (808) 536-8777
www.kitv.com
License: Honolulu, Hawaii County, HI held by KITV, Inc.
Group Owner: Hearst Television Inc.; (acq 7-16-97; grpsl).
Nat'l Network: ABC
Michael Rosenberg, General Manager

Honolulu, HI (DMA 65)

KAAH-TV *Digital Channel:* 27; *Virtual Channel:* 26; 262 kw; 1903 ft.; N21 23 45 W158 5 58; *Rebroadcasting:* Satellite of KTBN-TV Los Angeles (Santa Ana), CA 95%.
Mailing Address: PO Box A, San Ana, CA 92711 US
Second Address: PO Box 768, Station B, Ottawa, ON K1P 5P8
(714) 731-1000, (888) 731-1000, (714) 832-2950; *Fax:* (808) 599-6238
www.tbn.org
tbnkaahtv26@hotmail.com
License: Honolulu, Honolulu County, HI held by Trinity Christian Center of Santa Ana Inc. dba Trinity Broadcasting Network.
Group Owner: Trinity Broadcasting Network; (acq 7-1-2000; grpsl).; *Washington Law Firm:* Colby May
Nat'l Network: TRINITY BROADCA
Cheryl Rzonca, General Manager
Paul Crouch Jr., Executive Vice President

***KALO** *Digital Channel:* 38; *Virtual Channel:* 38; 96.6 kw; 1893 ft.; N21 23 45 W158 5 58; *Rebroadcasting:* Christian programming
P.O. Box 1256, Honolulu, HI 96807 US
(808) 596-4417; *Fax:* (808) 593-2427
www.kalo-tv.com
info@kalo-tv.com
License: Honolulu, Honolulu County, HI held by Pacifica Broadcasting Co
Washington Law Firm: Fletcher, Heald & Hildreth, P.L.C., Harry F. Cole, Esq.
Nat'l Network: IND
Donald Laidlaw, General Manager
Lani Kaaa, Station Manager

KBFD-DT *Digital Channel:* 33; 146 kw vis, 14.6 kw aur; ant 405t/428g; N21 18 49 W157 51 43; *Population Served:* 1,200,000
1188 Bishop Street, Suite PH 1, Honolulu, HI 96813
(808) 521-8066; *Fax:* (808) 521-5233
www.kbfd.com
news@kbfd.com
License: Honolulu, Honolulu County, HI held by Allen Broadcasting Corp
Washington Law Firm: Wilkinson, Barker, Knauer L.L.P.
Size of News Staff: 4; *Hours of Local News Weekly:* news progmg 6 hrs wkly
Kea Sung Chung, CEO
June Ho Chung, Director
Jeff Chung, General Manager
June Ho Chung, Executive Vice President

KFVE *Digital Channel:* 22; 5.9 kw; 12.2 meters above ground; N21 24 03 W158 06 10
420 Waiakamilo Road, Suite 205, Honolulu, HI 96817
(808)- 847-9375; *Fax:* (808)- 847-9315
www.k5thehometeam.com
info@kfve.com
License: Honolulu, Honolulu County, HI held by HITV License Subsidiary Inc.
Group Owner: HITV License Subsidiary Inc.; (acq 12-28-99);
Washington Law Firm: Covington & Burling
Nat'l Network: MyNetworkTV; *Nat'l Reps:* TeleRep; *Wire Services:* CNN
Hours of Local News Weekly: News progmg 7 hrs wkly
John Fink, Operations Dir

***KHET** *Digital Channel:* 11; *Virtual Channel:* 11; 15.7 kw; 2051 ft.; N21 24 3 W158 6 10
Mailing Address: 2350 Dole Street, Honolulu, HI 96822 US
Second Address: P.O Box 11599, Honolulu, HI 96828-0599
(808) 973-1000, (800) 238-4847; *Fax:* (808) 973-1090
www.pbshawaii.org
email@pbshawaii.org
License: Honolulu, Honolulu County, HI held by Hawaii Public Television Foundation
Washington Law Firm: Wilkes, Artis, Hedrick & Lane
Nat'l Network: PBS
Robert Alm, Chairman
Leslie Wilcox, CEO/President
John Nakahira, Engineering Dir
Karen Yamamoto, Sr. Vice President, CFO
Roy Kimura, VP,Creative Services
Roberta Wong Murray, VP,Programming &Communications
Ben Nishimoto, VP,Advancement
Jason Fujimoto, Vice-Chair
Tim Johns, Secretary

KHNL *Digital Channel:* 35; *Virtual Channel:* 13; 25 kw; 2064 ft.; N21 24 3 W158 6 10
420 Waiakamilo Road, Suite 205, Honolulu, HI 96817 US
(808) 847-3246; *Fax:* (808) 845-3616
www.khnl.com
news@hawaiinewsnow.com
License: Honolulu, Honolulu County, HI held by KHNL/KFVE License Subsidiary LLC
Group Owner: Raycom Media Inc.; (acq 9-2-99; grpsl).;
Washington Law Firm: Covington & Burling
Nat'l Network: NBC; *Nat'l Reps:* TeleRep; *Wire Services:* CNN; NBC
Hours of Local News Weekly: News progmg 19.5 hrs wkly
Rick Blangiardi, General Manager

KHNL/KGMB *Digital Channel:* 23; 209 kw vis, 29.5 kw aur; ant -50t/436g; N21 17 46 W157 50 36; *Population Served:* 1,150,000
420 Waiakamilo Road, Suite 205, Honolulu, HI 96817
(808) 973-5462, (808) 847-1112; *Fax:* (808) 973-9354
www.kgmb9.com
news@hawaiinewsnow.com
License: Honolulu, Honolulu County, HI held by KHNL/KGMB License Subsidiary LLC
Group Owner: Raycom Media Inc.; (acq 5-25-2007; grpsl)
Nat'l Network: CBS; *Nat'l Reps:* Harrington, Righter & Parsons
Rick Blangiardi, President

KHON2 *Digital Channel:* 8; *Virtual Channel:* 2; 7.2 kw; 56 ft.; N21 17 39 W157 50 18
Mailing Address: 88 Piikoi Street, Honolulu, HI 96814 US
Second Address: 1110 McCully St., Suite 203, Honolulu, HI 96826
(808) 591-2222; *Fax:* (808) 949-7715
www.khon.com
news@khon2.com
License: Honolulu, Honolulu County, HI held by LIN License Company LLC
Group Owner: LIN Media; (acq 10-12-2013; grpsl)
Nat'l Network: FOX; CW; *Nat'l Reps:* Harrington, Righter & Parsons
Size of News Staff: 45; *Hours of Local News Weekly:* news progmg 25 hrs wkly
Joe McNamara, President
Alexander Rogers, Operations Dir
Susii Hearst, General Sales Mgr
Gelene Welch, Programming Director
Kyle Funasaki, Promotions Manager
Lori Silva, News Director
Bob Vaillancourt, Engineering Dir

KIKU *Digital Channel:* 19; 467 kw vis, 46.7 kw aur; ant 2,040t; N21 23 51 W158 06 01
737 Bishop Street, Honolulu, HI 96813
(808) 847-2021; *Fax:* (808) 841-3326
www.kikutv.com
License: Honolulu, Honolulu County, HI held by NRJ TV Hawaii License Co. LLC
Group Owner: NRJ Holdings LLC; (acq 8-10-2012); *Washington Law Firm:* Goldberg, Godles, Wiener & Wright
; *Nat'l Reps:* Petry Television Inc.
Foreign Language Programming
Phyllis Kihara, General Manager

KITV *Digital Channel:* 40; *Virtual Channel:* 4; 85 kw; 3 ft.; N21 17 37 W157 50 34
801 S. King St., Honolulu, HI 96813 US
(808) 535-0400; *Fax:* (808) 536-8777
www.kitv.com
License: Honolulu, HI held by KITV, Inc.
Group Owner: Hearst Television Inc.; (acq 7-16-97; grpsl).;
Washington Law Firm: Brooks, Pierce, McLendon, Humphrey & Leonard
Nat'l Network: ABC; *Nat'l Reps:* Eagle Television Sales
Size of News Staff: 40; *Hours of Local News Weekly:* news progmg 20 hrs wkly
Michael Rosenberg, General Manager
Jan Dawson, Traffic Manager

KKAI *Digital Channel:* 50; *Virtual Channel:* 50; 19 kw vis; ant 1,115t/107g; N21 19 23 W157 40 53
PO Box 47, Honolulu, HI 96810
(808) 593-5524; *Fax:* (808) 441-0092
www.kkai.tv
License: Kailua, Honolulu County, HI held by Kailua Television LLC
Ownership: Kailua Television LLC; *Washington Law Firm:* Fletcher, Heald & Hildreth
Nat'l Network: RETRO TV
Foreign Language Programming; Hours of Local News Weekly: 14
Dr. Christopher Racine, President
Dr. Christopher Racine, General Manager
Kirt Caldwell, Chief Engineer

KPXO-TV *Digital Channel:* 41; 34 kw; N21 19 37 W157 45 15
875 Waimanu St., Suite 630, Honolulu, HI 96813 USA
(808) 591-1275; *Fax:* (808) 591-1409
www.iontelevision.com
License: Kaneohe, HI held by ION Media Hawaii License, Inc.
Group Owner: ION Media Networks Inc.; (acq 8-12-98; $6.9 million)
Nat'l Network: ION Television
Brandon Burgess, Chairman/CEO
Alex Stroot, Station Manager
Marc Zand, Programming Acquisitions

KUPU *Digital Channel:* 15; *Virtual Channel:* 56; 12 kw; 1224 ft.; N21 19 23 W157 40 53
Post Office Box 143, Honolulu, HI 96810 US
(808) 591-8282; *Fax:* (808) 591-1250
www.kupu.tv
manager@kupu.tv
License: Waimanalo, Honolulu County, HI held by Hawaii Catholic TV Inc.
Washington Law Firm: Fletcher Heal & Hildreth
Nat'l Network: IND

Size of News Staff: 12; *Hours of Local News Weekly:* news progmg 14 hrs wkly
John Fielding, President

***KWBN** *Digital Channel:* 43; *Virtual Channel:* 44; 6.46 kw; 1893 ft.; N21 23 45 W158 5 58
Mailing Address: 3901 Hwy 121, Suite 634, Bedford, TX 76021 US
Second Address: PO Box 610546, Dallas, TX 75261-0546
(817) 571-1229; *Fax:* (817) 571-7458
www.daystar.com
Partners@Daystar.com
License: Honolulu, Honolulu County, HI held by Ho'ona'auao Community Television Inc
Nat'l Network: IND
Marcus D. Lamb, Founder, President and CEO

KWHE *Digital Channel:* 31; *Virtual Channel:* 14; 20.1 kw; 16 ft.; N21 18 49 W157 51 43
1188 Bishop Street, Suite 502, Honolulu, HI 96813 US
(800) 218-1414; *Fax:* (808) 526-0326
kwhe.lesea.com
kwhe@lesea.com
License: Honolulu, Honolulu County, HI held by LeSea Broadcasting Corp.
Group Owner: Le Sea Broadcasting; (acq 8-15-86; $825,000; *Washington Law Firm:* Gardner, Carton & Douglas
Nat'l Network: IND
Anthony Hale, CFO
Peter Sumrall, President
T. J. Malievsky, General Manager
Michael Kemmerling, Chief Engineer
David Goebert, Production Manager
Roxanne Viena, Adminstrative Assistant
Tracey Jeremiah, Senior Editor
Darrow Hand,Production Assistant / Editor
Dawn O'Brien, On Air Talent

Kailua-Kona

KLEI-TV *Digital Channel:* 25; *Virtual Channel:* 6; 52.5 kw vis, 6.7 kw aur; ant 2,910t; N19 42 56 W155 55 00
73-4855 Kanalani Street, Suite 3, Kailua-Kona, HI 96740
(808) 329-8120; *Fax:* (808) 443-0424
www.klei.tv
info@klei.tv
License: Kailua-Kona, Hawaii County, HI held by Pacific Christian Church
(acq 10-1-2011; donation); *Ownership:* Mauna Kea Broadcasting Inc.; *Washington Law Firm:* Fletcher, Heald & Hildreth
Foreign Language Programming; Hours of Local News Weekly: 14 hrs
Dr. Christopher Racine, CEO/COO
Chip Begay, General Manager
Kirk Caldwell, Engineering Dir
Kirk Caldwell, Chief Engineer

Wailuku

KAII-TV *Digital Channel:* 7; *Virtual Channel:* 7; 3.69 kw; 2470 ft.; N20 39 37 W156 21 46; *Rebroadcasting:* Satellite of KHON(TV) Honolulu 100%.
88 Piikoi Street, Honolulu, HI 96814 US
(808) 591-2222; *Fax:* (808) 949-7715
www.khon.com
news@khon.com
License: Wailuku, Maui County, HI held by LIN License Company LLC
Group Owner: LIN Media; (acq 10-12-2012; grpsl); *Washington Law Firm:* Wiley Rein LLP
Nat'l Network: FOX; *Nat'l Reps:* Harrington, Righter & Parsons
Joseph McNamara, President
Alexander Rogers, Operations Dir
Kristina Lockwood, General Manager
Susii Hearst, General Sales Mgr
Gelene Welch, Programming Director
Kyle Funasaki, Promotions Manager
Lori Silva, News Director
BobVaillancourt, Engineering Dir

KGMV *Digital Channel:* 24; *Virtual Channel:* 3; 77 kw; 2477 ft.; N20 39 37 W156 21 46
420 Waiakamilo Road, Suite 205, Honolulu, HI 96817 US
(808) 973-5462, (808) 847-1112; *Fax:* (808) 973-9354
www.kgmb9.com
news@hawaiinewsnow.com
License: Wailuku, Maui County, HI held by HITV License Subsidiary Inc.
Group Owner: HITV License Subsidiary Inc.; (acq 5-25-2007; grpsl)
Nat'l Network: CBS; *Nat'l Reps:* Harrington, Righter & Parsons
Rick Blangiardi, President
John Fink, General Manager

KMAU *Digital Channel:* 12; *Virtual Channel:* 12; 9 kw; 2451 ft.; N20 39 37 W156 21 46; *Rebroadcasting:* Satellite of KITV Honolulu.
801 S. King St., Honolulu, HI 96813 US
(808) 535-0400; *Fax:* (808) 536-8777
www.kitv.com
License: Wailuku, Maui County, HI held by KITV, Inc.
Group Owner: Hearst Television Inc.; (acq 7-16-97; grpsl).
Nat'l Network: ABC
Michael Rosenberg, General Manager

***KMEB** *Digital Channel:* 10; *Virtual Channel:* 10; 21.13 kw; 2451 ft.; N20 39 37 W156 21 46; *Rebroadcasting:* Satellite of *KHET Honolulu.
Mailing Address: 2350 Dole St., Wailuku, HI 96822 US
Second Address: 2350 Dole St., Honolulu, HI 96822
(808) 973-1000; *Fax:* (808) 973-1090
www.pbshawaii.org
email@pbshawaii.org
License: Wailuku, Maui County, HI held by Hawaii Public Television Foundation
Nat'l Network: PBS
Leslie Wilcox, CEO
Ben Nishimoto, Vice President
Tatsu Sasaki, Director
Liberty Peralta, Communication Director
Stephanie Joe, Advancement Assistant
Tara Liu, Club Coordinator

KOGG *Digital Channel:* 16; *Virtual Channel:* 15; 50 kw; 2684 ft.; N20 39 37 W156 21 46; *Rebroadcasting:* 100% rebroadcast satellite of KHNL(TV) Honolulu.
400 South Record Street, Dallas, TX 75202 US
(808) 847-3246; *Fax:* (808) 845-3616
www.khnl.com
news8@khnl.com
License: Wailuku, Maui County, HI held by KHNL/KGMB License Subsidiary LLC
Group Owner: Raycom Media Inc.; (acq 9-2-99; grpsl).; *Washington Law Firm:* Covington & Burling
Nat'l Network: NBC; *Nat'l Reps:* TeleRep; *Wire Services:* CNN; NBC
Hours of Local News Weekly: 19.5 hrs.
John Fink, Operations Dir

KWHM *Digital Channel:* 21; *Virtual Channel:* 21; 23.5 kw; 2477 ft.; N20 39 37 W156 21 46; *Rebroadcasting:* Rebroadcasts KWHE Honolulu 100%
Post Office Box 12, South Bend, IN 46624 US
(808) 538-1414; *Fax:* (808) 526-0326
kwhe.lesea.com
kwhe@lesea.com
License: Wailuku, Maui County, HI held by Le Sea Broadcasting of Hawaii
Group Owner: Le Sea Broadcasting; *Washington Law Firm:* Gardner, Carton & Douglas
Nat'l Network: IND
Anthony Hale, CFO
Peter Sumrall, President
T. J. Malievsky, General Manager
Michael Kemmerling, Chief Engineer
David Goebert, Production Manager
Roxanne Viena, Adminstrative Assistant
Tracey Jeremiah, Senior Editor
Darrow Hand,Production Assistant / Editor
Dawn O'Brien, On Air Talent

Idaho

Boise, ID (DMA 106)

***KAID** *Digital Channel:* 21; 57.2 kw vis, 5.7 kw aur; 2,474t/142g; N43 45 16 W116 05 56; *Population Served:* 157,000
1455 N. Orchard St., Boise, ID 83706-2239
(208) 373-7220, (800) 543-6868; *Fax:* (208) 373-7245
www.idahoptv.org
idptv@idahoptv.org
License: Boise, Ada County, ID held by Idaho State Board of Education
Washington Law Firm: Fletcher, Heald & Hildreth
Nat'l Network: PBS
Size of News Staff: 5; *Hours of Local News Weekly:* news progmg 3 hrs wkly
Peter Morrill, General Manager
Ron Pisaneschi, Programming Director
Megan Griffin, Promotions Manager
Rich Van Genderen, Engineering Dir
Craig Koster, Chief Engineer

KBOI-TV *Digital Channel:* 9; *Virtual Channel:* 2; 25 kw; 2828 ft.; N43 45 21 W116 05 54; *Population Served:* 604,000
140 N. 16th St., Boise, ID 83702
(208) 472-2222
www.kboi2.com
comments@kboi2.com
License: Boise, Ada County, ID held by Sinclair Boise Licensee LLC
Group Owner: Sinclair Broadcast Group Inc.; (acq 7-1-99; grpsl).; *Washington Law Firm:* Shaw Pittman
Nat'l Network: CBS; CW; *Nat'l Reps:* Continental Television Sales
Size of News Staff: 37; *Hours of Local News Weekly:* news progmg 22 hrs wkly
Nicholas Kovach, Production Operations Manager
Valerie Koonce, General Sales Mgr
Sean McBride, Promotions Manager
Fred Lindstrom, Sales Manager

KIVI-TV ; 60.3 kw vis, 12.0 kw aur; ant 2,660t/210g; N43 45 20 W116 05 55; *Population Served:* 580,000
1866 E Chisholm Drive, Nampa, ID 83687
(208) 336-0500; *Fax:* (208) 381-6682
www.kivitv.com
news@idahoonyourside.com
License: Nampa, Canyon County, ID held by Journal Broadcast Corp.
Group Owner: Journal Communications Inc.; (acq 11-15-2001).
Nat'l Network: ABC
Size of News Staff: 45; *Hours of Local News Weekly:* news progmg 19.5 hrs wkly
Bob Rosenthal, Operations Dir
Ken Richie, General Sales Mgr
Brian Perkins, Programming Director
Jason Knose, Promotions Manager
Scott Picken, News Director
Rick Kemp, Engineering Dir
Jeff Hoffert, Chief Engineer
Kevin Eslinger,Chief Photographer
Kendra Martinez, Chief Producer
Norma Petty, Regional Sales Manager

KKJB *Digital Channel:* 39; *Virtual Channel:* 39; 35 kw; 1752 ft.; N43 44 23 W116 8 15
706 West Herndon Avenue, Fresno, CA 93650-1033 US
(208) 331-3900, (559) 435-7000; *Fax:* (559) 435-3201
www.cocolatv.com
info@cocolatv.com
License: Boise, Ada County, ID held by IAM Broadcasting LLC
Washington Law Firm: Fletcher Heald & Hildreth PLC
Nat'l Network: IND
Gary Cocola, CEO
John Her, Operations Dir
Kevin Mosesian, Station Manager
Seth Diviney, General Sales Mgr
Ralph Malerich, Engineering Dir

KNIN-TV *Digital Channel:* 10; *Virtual Channel:* 9; 162 kw vis; ant 2,690t/210g; N43 45 18 W116 05 52
816 W. Bannock St., Suite 402, Boise, ID 93942
(208) 331-0909; *Fax:* (208) 344-0119
www.knin.com
License: Caldwell, Canyon County, ID held by Journal Broadcast Corp.
Group Owner: Journal Communications Inc.; (acq 4-23-2009; $6.6 million); *Washington Law Firm:* Leventhal Senter & Lerman PLLC
Nat'l Network: Fox; *Nat'l Reps:* Blair Television
James Prather, President
Larry Newton, General Manager

KTRV-TV *Digital Channel:* 13; *Virtual Channel:* 12; 17 kw; 2720 ft.; N43 45 18 W116 5 52
1 6th St. N., Nampa, ID 83687 US
(208) 466-1200; *Fax:* (208) 467-6958
License: Nampa, Canyon County, ID held by Idaho Independent Television Inc.
Group Owner: Block Communications Inc.; (acq 4-23-85; $4.9 million; *Washington Law Firm:* Dow, Lohnes & Albertson
Nat'l Network: MyNetworkTV
Size of News Staff: 12; *Hours of Local News Weekly:* news progmg 7 hrs wkly
Ken Hunter, President and General Manager
Larry Polowski, Sales Director
Missy Hughes, Programming Director
Daniel Paixao, Chief Engineer
Dan Widner, Creative Services Director
Joe Mohling, Creative Services Producer

SueGieringer, Creative Services Producer
Mary Van Wyck, Traffic Manager

KTVB *Digital Channel:* 7; *Virtual Channel:* 7; 42.1 kw; 2,644 ft.; N43 45 16 W116 5 56
5407 West Fairview Ave., Boise, ID 83706 US
(208) 375-7277; *Fax:* (208) 375-7770
www.ktvb.com
ktvbnews@ktvb.com
License: Boise, Ada County, ID held by King Broadcasting Co.
Group Owner: Tegna Media; (acq 12-23-2013).; *Washington Law Firm:* Wiley, Rein & Fielding
Nat'l Network: NBC; *Nat'l Reps:* TeleRep
Hours of Local News Weekly: news progmg 27 hrs wkly
I, CEO/COO
Paul Budell, Director of Operations and Creative Services
Doug Armstrong, General Manager
Kristi Edmunds, Director of Sales and Marketing
Kate Morris, News Director
Don Day, Digital Sales and ProductManager
Brad Bond, Local Sales Manager
Logan Tusow, Local Sales Manager
Tom Zito, National Sales Manager

KYUU-LD *Digital Channel:* 28; 8.8 kw; 7364 ft.; N43 45 21 W116 05 54; *Population Served:* 604,000
140 N. 16th St., Boise, ID 83702
(208) 472-2224
www.yourcwtv.com
License: Boise, Ada County, ID held by Sinclair Boise Licensee LLC
Group Owner: Sinclair Broadcast Group Inc.
; *Nat'l Reps:* Continental Television Sales
David D. Smith, President, CEO and Chairman of the Board
Fred Lindstrom, Sales Manager

Idaho Falls-Pocatello, ID (DMA 163)

KFXP *Digital Channel:* 31; *Virtual Channel:* 31; 68.5 kw; 1467 ft.; N42 55 15 W112 20 44
Mailing Address: 103 Entrance Drive, Suite 1, Livingston, ID 77351 US
Second Address: 902 E. Sherman St., Pocatello, ID 83201
(208) 232-6666, (208) 235-3152; *Fax:* (208) 232-6678, (208) 234-3650
www.kpvi.com
swilcox@kpvi.com
License: Pocatello, Bannock County, ID held by Compass Communications of Idaho Inc
Shelley Goings, General Manager
Joe Nielsen, Sales Manager
Scott Larkin, Promotion Director
Todd Blackinton, News Director
Robin Estopinal, Chief Engineer
Loran Whited, Web
Matt Hugie, Assignment Desk
Doug Iverson, Weather
Matt Gittins, Sports

KIDK ; 200 kw; N43 29 51 W112 39 50; *Population Served:* 275,000
1915 N. Yellowstone Hwy, Idaho Falls, ID 83401 US
(208) 528-2145, (208) 525-8888; *Fax:* (208) 529-2443, (208) 522-1930
www.kidk.com
newsdesk@localnews8.com, frontdesk@localnews8.com
License: Idaho Falls, Bonneville County, ID held by VistaWest Media, LLC
Group Owner: News-Press & Gazette & Co; (acq Nov. 29th from Sinclair Broadcast Group); *Washington Law Firm:* Shaw, Pittman
Nat'l Network: CBS; *Nat'l Reps:* Millennium Sales & Marketing
Size of News Staff: 35; *Hours of Local News Weekly:* news progmg 15 hrs wkly
Russ Haack, Operations Director
Monte Young, General Manger
Michael Shiverdecker, Promotions
Curtis Jackson, News Director
Gary Smith, Chief Engineer
Layton Swenson, Internet Sales
Russ Haack, Closed Captioning
Robert Patten,Digital Content Director
Kalvin Pike, Director of Sales

KIFI-TV *Digital Channel:* 8; *Virtual Channel:* 8; 63 kw; 1522 ft.; N43 30 4 W112 39 43
1915 N. Yellowstone Hwy, Idaho Falls, ID 83401 US
(208) 525-8888; *Fax:* (208) 529-2443
www.localnews8.com
License: Idaho Falls, Bonneville County, ID held by NPG of Idaho Inc.
Group Owner: News-Press & Gazette Co.; (acq 6-15-2005; $12.5 million); *Washington Law Firm:* Smithwick & Belendiuk, P.C.
Nat'l Network: ABC; Telemundo (Spanish); CW
Hours of Local News Weekly: news progmg 30 hrs wkly
Russ Haack, Operations Dir
Monte Young, General Manager
Michael Shiverdecker, Promotions Manager
Curtis Jackson, News Director
Gary Smith, Chief Engineer
Layton Swenson, Internet Sales
Russ Haack, Closed Captioning

***KISU-TV** ; *Virtual Channel:* 10; 122 kw vis, 12.2 kw aur; 1,527t/144g; N43 30 02 W112 39 36
Mailing Address: Campus Box 8111, Pocatello, ID 83706
Second Address: 1455 N. Orchard St., Boise, ID 83706-2239
(208) 373-7220, (800) 543-6868; *Fax:* (208) 373-7245
www.idahoptv.org
idptv@idahoptv.org
License: Pocatello, Bannock County, ID held by Idaho State Board of Education
Nat'l Network: PBS
Peter Morrill, General Manager
Ron Pisaneschi, Programming Director
Rich Van Genderen, Engineering Dir
Dave Turnmire, Chief Engineer

KPVI-DT ; 505 kw; 1,530t/619g; N42 55 12 W112 20 44; *Rebroadcasting:* Rebroadcasts: KJWY Jackson Hole, WY; *Population Served:* 309,000
Mailing Address: 902 E. Sherman St., Pocatello, ID 83201 US
Second Address: 956 Lincoln Ave., Idaho Falls, ID 83401
(208) 232-6666; *Fax:* (208) 233-6678
www.kpvi.com
newsroom@kpvi.com
License: Pocatello, ID held by Idaho Broadcast Partners LLC
Group Owner: Frontier Radio Management; (acq 11-15-95).
Nat'l Network: NBC; *Nat'l Reps:* Blair Television; *Wire Services:* AP
Size of News Staff: 23; *Hours of Local News Weekly:* news progmg 17 hrs wkly
Shawn Wilcox, General Manager
Scott Larkin, Promotion Director
Eric Jochim, News Director

Spokane, WA (DMA 73)

KLEW-TV *Digital Channel:* 32; *Virtual Channel:* 3; 133 kw; 1145 ft.; N46 27 27 W117 5 56; *Rebroadcasting:* Satellite of KIMA-TV Yakima Wash.
2626 17th St., Lewiston, ID 83501 US
(208) 746-2636
www.klewtv.com
License: Lewiston, Nez Perce County, ID held by Sinclair Lewiston Licensee LLC
Group Owner: Sinclair Broadcast Group Inc.; (acq 12-4-2001; grpsl).; *Washington Law Firm:* Shaw Pittman
Nat'l Network: CBS; *Nat'l Reps:* Petry Television Inc.; *Wire Services:* AP
Size of News Staff: 4; *Hours of Local News Weekly:* news progmg 12 hrs wkly
Ann Fickenwirth, Operations Administrator
Dan Stellmon, Station Manager
Anna Velasquez, News Director
Marlin Jackson, Chief Engineer
Shawn Clark, Director of Creative Services
Jared Wanegar, Producer/Director
Cory Lenz, AccountExecutive
Laurel Smith, Account Executive
Stacy Larson, Account Executive

***KUID-TV** *Digital Channel:* 12; *Virtual Channel:* 35; 44 kw vis; ant 971t/148g; N46 40 54 W116 58 13; *Population Served:* 151,000
Mailing Address: c/o KAID, 1455 N. Orchard St., Boise, ID 83706 US
Second Address: PO Box 443101, University of Idaho, Moscow, ID 83844-3101
(208) 885-1226; *Fax:* (208) 885-5711
www.idahoptv.org
idptv@idahoptv.org
License: Moscow, Latah County, ID held by State Board of Education, State of Idaho
Washington Law Firm: Fletcher, Heald & Hildreth
Nat'l Network: PBS
Peter Morrill, General Manager
Kris Freeland, Station Manager
Megan Griffin, General Sales Mgr
Ron Pisaneschi, Programming Director
Rich Van Genderen, Engineering Dir
Ken Segota, Chief Engineer

Topeka, KS (DMA 135)

KSQA *Digital Channel:* 12; 5,000 kw vis; ant 738t/26g; N39 03 50 W95 45 49
1155 Connecticut Ave. N.W., Suite 600, Washington, DC 83847
(202) 861-0870; *Fax:* (202) 429-0657
License: Topeka, Shawnee County, KS
James Winston, General Manager

Twin Falls

KSVT *Digital Channel:* 14; 15 kW; N42 43 47 W114 24 52
1100 Blue Lakes Blvd. N, Twin Falls, ID 83301 USA
(208) 733-1100; *Fax:* (208) 733-4649
www.kmvt.com
License: Twin Falls, Twin Falls County, ID held by Gray Television Licensee LLC
Group Owner: Gray Television Inc.
Nat'l Network: FOX; MyNetworkTV
Leslie Flores, Operations Manager
Chris Huston, News Director
Shawn Butler, Chief Engineer

Twin Falls, ID (DMA 191)

***KIPT** *Digital Channel:* 22; 22.4 kw vis; 528t/69g; N42 43 47 W114 24 52; *Rebroadcasting:* Rebroadcasts KAID Boise 100%.
c/o KAID, 1455 N. Orchard St., Boise, ID 83706-2239
(208) 373-7220, (800) 543-6868; *Fax:* (208) 373-7245
www.idahoptv.org
idptv@idahoptv.org
License: Twin Falls, Twin Falls County, ID held by State Board of Education, State of Idaho
Washington Law Firm: Fletcher, Heald & Hildreth
Nat'l Network: PBS
Peter Morrill, General Manager
Ron Pisaneschi, Programming Director
Rich Van Genderen, Engineering Dir
Craig Koster, Chief Engineer

KMVT *Digital Channel:* 11; *Virtual Channel:* 11; 40 kw; 1060 ft.; N42 43 47 W114 24 52
1100 Blue Lakes Blvd. N, Twin Falls, ID 83301 USA
(208) 733-1100; *Fax:* (208) 733-4649
www.kmvt.com
License: Twin Falls, Twin Falls County, ID held by Gray Television Licensee LLC
Group Owner: Gray Television Inc.; *Washington Law Firm:* Schwartz, Woods & Miller
Nat'l Network: CBS; The CW Network; FOX; MyNetworkTV; *Nat'l Reps:* Continental Television Sales; *Wire Services:* AP
Size of News Staff: 14; *Hours of Local News Weekly:* news progmg 10 hrs wkly
Leslie Flores, Operations Manager
Chris Huston, News Director
Shawn Butler, Chief Engineer

KXTF *Digital Channel:* 34; *Virtual Channel:* 35; 49.4 kw; 499 ft.; N42 43 42 W114 24 43
4311 Wilshire Blvd., Suite 408, Los Angeles, CA 90010 US
(323) 964-5300
License: Twin Falls, ID held by Idaho Broadcast Partners
Group Owner: Frontier Radio Management; *Washington Law Firm:* Hamel & Park
Nat'l Network: FOX
Hours of Local News Weekly: News progmg 2 hrs wkly
Bill Fouch, General Manager
Joe Nielsen, Station Manager

Illinois

Champaign & Springfield-Decatur, IL (DMA 86)

WAND *Digital Channel:* 17; *Virtual Channel:* 17; 1000 kw; 1281 ft.; N39 57 8.5 W88 49 56.3
904 South Side Dr., Decatur, IL 62521 US
(217) 424-2500; *Fax:* (217) 422-2583
www.wandtv.com
news@wandtv.com
License: Decatur, Macon County, IL held by WAND(TV) Partnership
Group Owner: Block Communications Inc.; 11/1/2007;
Washington Law Firm: Dow Lohnes
Nat'l Network: NBC

Ricky Joseph, General Manager
Clay Koenig, Vice President and Director of Sales
Rob Comerford, Programming/Production Director
Carol Barnes, Creative Services/Promotions Director
Tai Takahashi, News Director
Frank Brannock, ChiefEngineer

WBUI *Digital Channel:* 22; *Virtual Channel:* 23; 325 kw; 1316 ft.; N39 56 56 W88 50 12
10829 Olive Boulevard, Suite 202, St. Louis, MO 63141 US
(217) 428-2323; *Fax:* (217) 428-6455
www.centralillinoiscw.com
promotions@centralillinoiscw.com
License: Decatur, Macon County, IL held by GOCOM Media of Illinois LLC
Group Owner: GOCOM Media of Illinois LLC; (acq 6-14-99; $13.3 million)
Nat'l Network: CW; *Nat'l Reps:* MMT
Bill Snider, General Manager
Chad Happersett, Station Manager
Allen White, General Sales Mgr
Jim Cloney, Promotions Manager
Scott Washburn, Chief Engineer

WCCU *Digital Channel:* 26; *Virtual Channel:* 27; 507 kw; 374 ft.; N40 18 46 W87 55 0; *Rebroadcasting:* Rebroadcasts WRSP-TV Springfield 100%
712 Killarney St., Urbana, IL 61801 US
(217) 403-9927; *Fax:* (217) 403-1007
License: Urbana, Champaign County, IL held by Springfield Broadcasting Partners.
Group Owner: GOCOM Media of Illinois LLC; (acq 7-20-92).
Nat'l Network: FOX
Peter O'Brien, General Manager
Randy Stone, General Sales Mgr
Jeff Kaufmann, Promotions Manager
Jack Richardson, Chief Engineer

WCIA *Digital Channel:* 48; 100 kw vis, 20 kw aur; 940t/981g; N40 06 23 W88 26 59
509 S. Neil St., Champaign, IL 61820 US
(217) 356-8333; *Fax:* (217) 373-3663, (217) 544-3818, (217) 373-3673
www.illinoishomepage.net
webmaster@wcia.com
License: Champaign, Champaign County, IL held by Nexstar Broadcasting, Inc.
Group Owner: Nexstar Broadcasting Group Inc.; (acq 5-19-2000; grpsl).; *Washington Law Firm:* Covington & Burling
Nat'l Network: CBS
Coby Cooper, VP/General Manager
Dale Stafford, Director of Sales
Angela Smith, Programming Director
Peter Carlson, Promotions Manager
Andy Miller, News Director
Darren Martin, Chief Engineer
Ed Mathias, Production Manager
NancyForeman, Executive producer
Peter Carlson, Creative Services Director
Sam Mauro, Digital Media Manager
Jon Pieczynski, Digital Media Creative Director
Gary Hackler, Local Sales Manager

WCIX *Digital Channel:* 13; 200 kw vis, 20 kw aur; ant 620t/655g; N39 47 27 W89 30 53
509 S. Neil, Champaign, IL 61820 US
(217) 356-8333; *Fax:* (217) 373-3680
www.illinoishomepage.net
License: Springfield, Sangamon County, IL held by Nexstar Broadcasting, Inc.
Group Owner: Nexstar Broadcasting Group Inc.; (acq 5-19-2000; grpsl).; *Washington Law Firm:* Drinker-Biddle-Reath
Nat'l Network: MyNetworkTV; *Nat'l Reps:* Katz Continental
Coby Coopy, General Manager
Andy Miller, News Director

***WEIU-TV** *Digital Channel:* 50; *Virtual Channel:* 51; 255 kw; 479 ft.; N39 34 15 W88 18 25.5
Mailing Address: 1521 Buzzard Hall , Charleston, IL 61920 US
Second Address: Radio & TV Ctr., Eastern Illinois Univ., Charleston, IL 61920
(217) 581-5956,(877) 727-9348; *Fax:* (217) 581-6650
www.weiu.net
weiu@weiu.net
License: Charleston, Coles County, IL held by Eastern Illinois University
Washington Law Firm: Cohn & Marks
Nat'l Network: PBS
Size of News Staff: 25; *Hours of Local News Weekly:* news progmg 3 hrs wkly
Denis Roche, General Manager
Jeff Owens, General Sales Mgr

Linda Kingery, Programming Director
Ke'an Rogers, Promotions Manager
Kelly Runyon, News Director
Kevin Armstrong, Chief Engineer

WICD *Digital Channel:* 41; *Virtual Channel:* 15; 950 kw; ant 1,300t/1,338g; N40 04 11 W87 54 45; *Population Served:* 332,000
250 S. Country Fair Dr., Champaign, IL 61821
(217) 351-8500
License: Champaign, Champaign County, IL held by WICD Licensee LLC
Group Owner: Sinclair Broadcast Group Inc.; (acq 7-2-99; $81 million with WICS(TV) Springfield).; *Washington Law Firm:* Wiley, Rein & Fielding
Nat'l Network: ABC
Size of News Staff: 20; *Hours of Local News Weekly:* news progmg 17 hrs wkly
Scott McBride, General Manager

WICS *Digital Channel:* 42; *Virtual Channel:* 20; 950 kw; 1319 ft.; N39 48 15 W89 27 40
2680 East Cook St., Springfield, IL 62703
(217) 753-5620
www.newschannel20.com
news@wics.com
License: Springfield, Sangamon County, IL held by WICS Licensee LLC
Group Owner: Sinclair Broadcast Group Inc.
Nat'l Network: ABC
Rick Lipps, General Manager

***WILL-TV** *Digital Channel:* 9; *Virtual Channel:* 12; 30 kw; 991 ft.; N40 2 18 W88 40 10
300 North Goodwin Avenue, Urbana, IL 61801 US
(217) 333-7300, (800) 898-1065, (217) 333-4439; *Fax:* (217) 244-2656, (217) 333-7151
www.will.illinois.edu
willamfm@illinois.edu
License: Urbana, Champaign County, IL held by University of Illinois Board of Trustees
Washington Law Firm: Dow, Lohnes & Albertson
Nat'l Network: PBS
Carl Caldwell, Station Manager
David Thiel, Program Director
Rick Finnie, Chief Engineer
Harold (Abe) Nelson, Broadcast Engineer
Mike Pritchard, Radio Operations/Audio Production Manager
Walt Strogoff, Asst. Chief Engineer
JasonCroft, Radio Associate Producers
Paul Defenbaugh, Broadcast operator
David Heckman, Broadcast operator

WRSP-TV *Digital Channel:* 44; *Virtual Channel:* 55; 335 kw; 1362 ft.; N39 47 57 W89 26 46
3003 Old Rochester Road, Springfield, IL 62703 US
(217) 523-8855; *Fax:* (217) 523-4410
License: Springfield, Sangamon County, IL held by GOCOM Media of Illinois LLC
Group Owner: GOCOM Media of Illinois LLC; (acq 7-20-92).;
Ownership: Gocom
Nat'l Network: FOX; *Nat'l Reps:* Continental Television Sales
Hours of Local News Weekly: 3.5
Peter O'Brien, General Manager
Chad Happersett, General Sales Mgr
Jeff Kaufmann, Promotions Manager
Scott Washburn, Chief Engineer

***WSEC** *Digital Channel:* 15; *Virtual Channel:* 14; 75 kw; 968 ft.; N39 36 9 W90 2 47
Mailing Address: P.O.Box 6248, Springfield, IL 62708 US
Second Address: 1475 East Plummer Blvd, Chatham, IL 62629
(217) 483-7887, (800) 232-3605; *Fax:* (217) 483-1112
www.wsec.tv
License: Jacksonville, Morgan County, IL held by West Central Illinois Educational Telecommunication Corp
Washington Law Firm: Dow, Lohnes & Albertson
Nat'l Network: PBS
Jerold Gruebel, President & CEO
Keith Lawson, Opeations Manager
Ed Strong, General Sales Mgr
Stephanie Cole, Dir. Of National Programming & Traffic
Richard Plotkin, Engineeering
Ed Strong, Dir. Of Advancement
Ethan Auby, MasterControl Operator
Norm Brumnaugh, Field Maintainance Engineer
Kayla Green, Membership Coordinator
Becky Cramblit, Producer/ public information
Travis collins, Producer Director/ Image Development

Chicago (DMA 3)

WBBM-TV *Digital Channel:* 12; *Virtual Channel:* 2; 8 kW; 1636 ft.; N41 52 44 W87 38 8
22 West Washington St., Chicago, IL 60602 USA
(312) 899-2222
chicago.cbslocal.com
License: Chicago, Cook County, IL held by CBS Broadcasting Inc.
Group Owner: CBS Television Stations Group
Nat'l Network: CBS; *Nat'l Reps:* CBS TV Stations National Sales;
Wire Services: Reuters
Tom Schnecke, Chief Engineer

WCIU-TV *Digital Channel:* 27; *Virtual Channel:* 26; 550 kw; 1552 ft.; N41 52 44 W87 38 10
26 North Halsted Street, Chicago, IL 60661 US
(312) 705-2600; *Fax:* (312) 705-2656
www.wciu.com
License: Chicago, Cook County, IL held by WCIU-TV L.P.
Group Owner: Weigel Broadcasting Co.; *Washington Law Firm:* Covington & Burling
Nat'l Network: IND; *Nat'l Reps:* Harrington, Righter & Parsons
Norman Shapiro, President
Neal Sabin, President, Digital Networks
John Hendricks, EVP, Sales
Robert Ramsey, General Manager
Molly Kelly, Station Manager
Brad Lesak, General Sales Mgr
Sean Long, Programming Director
Kyle Walker,Chief Engineer
Harvey Moshman, Executive Producer

WCPX-TV *Digital Channel:* 43; 200 kw; ant 1,673t/1,667g; N41 52 44 W87 38 08; *Population Served:* 10,000,000
333 S. Desplaines St., Suite 101, Chicago, IL 60661-8735 USA
(212) 757-3100; *Fax:* (646) 597-5903
www.iontelevision.com
License: Chicago, IL held by Ion Media Chicago License, Inc.
Group Owner: ION Media Networks; *Washington Law Firm:* Dow, Lohnes & Albertson
Nat'l Network: ION Television
Brandon Burgess, Chairman

WFLD *Digital Channel:* 31; *Virtual Channel:* 32; 1000 kW; 1558 ft.; N41 52 44 W87 38 10
205 N Michigan Ave., Chicago, IL 60601 USA
(312) 565-5532
www.fox32chicago.com
License: Chicago, Cook County, IL held by Fox Television Stations LLC
Group Owner: Fox Television Stations Group; (acq 11-14-86; grpsl).
Nat'l Network: FOX; *Nat'l Reps:* Fox Stations Sales
Hours of Local News Weekly: News progmg 35.5 hrs wkly

WGBO-DT *Digital Channel:* 38; *Virtual Channel:* 66; 600 kw; 1,317 ft.; N41 53 56 W87 37 23
541 N. Fairbanks Ct., 11th Fl., Chicago, IL 60611 US
(312) 670-1000; *Fax:* (312) 494-6487
www.univision.com
License: Joliet, Will County, IL held by WGBO License Partnership G.P.
Group Owner: Univision Communications Inc.
Hours of Local News Weekly: news progmg 5 hrs wkly
Doug Levy, Senior Vice President and General Manager
Luisa Echevarria, Community Relations Director

WGN *Digital Channel:* 19; *Virtual Channel:* 9; 50 kw-U, ND1; 1,568 ft AAT; N42 0 42 W88 2 7
2501 West Bradley Place, Chicago, IL 60618-4718 USA
(773) 528-2311
wgntv.com
License: Chicago, IL held by WGN Continental Broadcasting Company LLC
Group Owner: Tribune Media; (acq 12-20-2007; grpsl)
Nat'l Network: The CW Network; *Nat'l Reps:* TeleRep; *Wire Services:* AP
Hours of Local News Weekly: 34.5

WJYS *Digital Channel:* 36; 5,000 kw vis, 300 kw aur; 741; N41 33 10 W87 47 09; *Population Served:* 7,100,000
18600 S. Oak Park Ave., Tinley Park, IL 60477 US
(708) 633-0001; *Fax:* (708) 633-0040
www.wjys.tv
License: Hammond, Lake County, IN held by Jovon Broadcasting Corp
Joseph Stroud, General Manager
Eric Ferguson, Station Manager

WLS-TV *Digital Channel:* 7; *Virtual Channel:* 7; 1000 kW; 1698 ft.; N41 52 44 W87 38 8
190 North State St., Chicago, IL 60601 USA
(312) 750-7777
License: Chicago, Cook County, IL held by WLS Television Inc.
Group Owner: ABC Owned Television Stations
Nat'l Network: ABC; *Wire Services:* PR Newswire; Dow Jones Financial News Services; Sports Wire
Size of News Staff: 151; *Hours of Local News Weekly:* news progmg 8 hrs wkly
Diana Palomar, VP of Community Affairs

WMAQ *Digital Channel:* 29; *Virtual Channel:* 5; 350 kw; 1667 ft.; N41 52 44 W87 38 10
454 N Columbus Dr., Chicago, IL 60611 USA
(312) 836-5555, (800) CH5-NEWS
www.nbcchicago.com
License: Chicago, Cook County, IL held by NBC Telemundo License LLC
Group Owner: NBC Owned Television Stations; (acq 6-5-86).
Nat'l Network: NBC; *Nat'l Reps:* NBC TV Stations Sales

WOCK-CD *Digital Channel:* 4; 300 w; 1455.7 ft; N41 43 29 W91 21 10
3654 W. Jarvis Ave., Skokie, IL 60076 US
License: Chicago, IL held by KM Television of Iowa, LLC.
Group Owner: KM Communications Inc.
Myoung Hwa Bae, President

WSNS ; 4,260 kw vis, 500 kw aur; 1,420t/1,456g; N41 53 56 W87 37 23; *Population Served:* 1,800,000
454 N. Columbus Dr., Chicago, IL 60611 USA
(312) 836-3110; *Fax:* (312) 836-3034
www.telemundochicago.com
License: Chicago, Cook County, IL held by NBC Telemundo License LLC
Group Owner: Telemundo Station Group; (acq 4-12-2002; grpsl).; *Washington Law Firm:* Cohn & Marks
Nat'l Network: Telemundo
Foreign Language Programming; Size of News Staff: 12; *Hours of Local News Weekly:* news progmg 5 hrs wkly
Luis Silberwasser, President

***WTTW** *Digital Channel:* 47; 60.3 kw vis, 12 kw aur; 1,630t/1,710g; N41 52 44 W87 38 10; *Population Served:* 10,000,000
5400 N. St. Louis Ave., Chicago, IL 60625-4698
(773) 583-5000, (773) 279-2103; *Fax:* (773) 583-3046
wttwadsales@wttw.com
License: Chicago, Cook County, IL held by Window to the World Communications Inc
Washington Law Firm: Schwartz, Woods & Miller
Nat'l Network: PBS
Size of News Staff: 15; *Hours of Local News Weekly:* news progmg 5 hrs wkly
Daniel J.Schmidt, CEO & President
Donna Davies, General Sales Mgr
Dan Soles, Programming Director
Reese Marcusson, CFO & EVP
Farrell Frentress, Executive Vice President
Howard Fisher, General Sales Manager
Daniel Soles, SVP &Chief Television Content Officer
Steve Robinson, EVP for Radio & project Development
Anne Gleason, SVP of marketing & Interactive Media

WWTO-TV *Digital Channel:* 10; *Virtual Channel:* 35; 80 kw; 1362 ft.; N41 16 51 W88 56 13
Mailing Address: PO Box A, Santa Ana, CA 92711 US
Second Address: P. O. Box 768, Station B, Ottawa, ON K1P 5P8
(714) 731-1000, (888) 731-1000, (714) 832-2950; *Fax:* (815) 434-2458
www.tbn.org
License: La Salle, LaSalle County, IL held by Trinity Broadcasting Network
Group Owner: Trinity Broadcasting Network; (acq 7-1-2000; grpsl).; *Washington Law Firm:* Joseph E. Dunne III
Nat'l Network: TRINITY BROADCA
Marlene Zepeda, Station Manager
Charlie Boyd, Chief Engineer

WXFT-DT *Digital Channel:* 50; *Virtual Channel:* 60; 5,000 kw vis, 500 kw aur; 1,600t/1,621g; N41 52 44 W87 38 08
541 N. Fairbanks Ct., 11th Fl., Chicago, IL 60611 US
(312) 670-1000; *Fax:* (312) 494-6487
www.univision.com
License: Aurora, Kane County, IL held by UniMas Chicago LLC.
Group Owner: Univision Communications Inc.; (acq 5-21-2001; grpsl).; *Washington Law Firm:* Wiley, Rein & Fielding
Nat'l Network: UniMas (Spanish); *Wire Services:* City News Bureau
Doug Levy, Senior Vice President and General Manager
Luisa Echevarria, Community Relations Director

***WYCC** ; *Virtual Channel:* 20; 2,421 kw vis, 242.1 kw au; 1,239t/1,110g; N41 53 56 W87 37 23
6258 S Union Ave., Chicago, IL 60621
(773) 224-3300, (773) 487-3757; *Fax:* (773) 581-2071
www.wycc.org
info@wycc.org
License: Chicago, Cook County, IL held by College Dist. #508, County of Cook
(acq 11-3-81).; *Washington Law Firm:* Dow, Lohnes & Albertson
Nat'l Network: PBS
Foreign Language Programming
Phyllis Stevens, Operations Dir
Arthur Wood, General Manager
Jill Ittersagen, General Sales Mgr
Cynthia Syperek, Programming Director
James Kirwan, Promotions Manager
Mark Jahnke, Engineering Dir

Davenport, IA-Rock Island-Moline, IL (DMA 101)

WHBF-TV *Digital Channel:* 4; *Virtual Channel:* 4; 33.7 kw; 1,342 ft.; N41 32 49 W90 28 35
231 18th St., Rock Island, IL 61201 US
(309) 786-5315; *Fax:* (309) 788-4975
www.ourquadcities.com
License: Rock Island, Rock Island County, IL held by Nexstar Broadcasting Inc.
Group Owner: Nexstar Broadcasting Group Inc.; (acq 9-16-2013).; *Washington Law Firm:* Latham & Watkins
Nat'l Network: CBS; *Nat'l Reps:* Continental Television Sales
Size of News Staff: 22; *Hours of Local News Weekly:* news progmg 7 hrs wkly
J.D. Walls, Director of Broadcast Operations
Marshall Porter, General Manager
Angie Salas, General Sales Mgr
Patty Gilbert, Promotions Manager
Heather Stevenson, News Director
Ron Schmidt, Chief Engineer
Brad Hoffman, Local SalesManager
Courtney Booth, Digital Media Manager
Mike Turner, Director of Sales
Michelle Peterson, Account Executive
Trisha Stepanek, Account Executive
Jon Popham, Account Executive

WQAD *Digital Channel:* 38; *Virtual Channel:* 8; 1000 kw; 1096 ft.; N41 18 44 W90 22 46
3003 Park 16th St., Moline, IL 61265 USA
(309) 764-8888; *Fax:* (309) 764-7181
wqad.com
news@wqad.com
License: Moline, Rock Island County, IL held by WQAD License LLC
Group Owner: Tribune Media
Nat'l Network: ABC; Antenna TV; MyNetworkTV
Size of News Staff: 75; *Hours of Local News Weekly:* news progmg 22.5 hrs wkly
Dan Englund, Local Sales Manager
Alan Baker, News Director

***WQPT-TV** *Digital Channel:* 23; *Virtual Channel:* 24; 80 kw; 883 ft.; N41 18 44 W90 22 45
3300 River Drive, Moline, IL 61265 US
(309) 764-2400,(877) 413-2424; *Fax:* (309) 764-2410
www.wqpt.org
License: Moline, Rock Island County, IL held by Black Hawk College
Washington Law Firm: Drinker, Biddle & Reath
Nat'l Network: ETV
Foreign Language Programming; Hours of Local News Weekly: 0
Richard Diamond, Traffic/Operations Coordinator
Mary Pruess, General Manager
Dawn Schmit, Business Manager
Lora Adams, Director of Marketing
Jerry Myers, Program Manager
Terry Wynn, Engineering Dir
Lora Adams, Dir. OfMarketing
Jamie Lange, Chief Development Officer
Dawn Schmit, Business Manager
Bea Brasel, Special Events & Volunteer Coordinator
Ana Kehoe, Dir. Of Education
Candace Eastman, Membership Coordinator

Paducah, KY-Cape Girardeau, MO-Harrisburg-Mount Vernon, IL (DMA 83)

WPXS *Digital Channel:* 21; *Virtual Channel:* 13; 350 kw; 299 ft.; N38 41 19 W89 33 38
231 Bradley Place, Suite 204, Palm Beach, FL 33480 US
(618) 822-6900; *Fax:* (618) 822-6526
www.melissadata.com
wpxs@mvn.net
License: Mount Vernon, Jefferson County, IL held by WPXS Inc.
Nat'l Network: IND
Dee Rose, Station Manager

WSIL-TV *Digital Channel:* 34; *Virtual Channel:* 3; 1000 kw; 955 ft.; N37 36 50 W88 52 20
1416 Country Aire Dr., Carterville, IL 62918 US
(618) 985-2333; *Fax:* (618) 985-3709, (618) 985-6482
www.wsiltv.com
License: Harrisburg, Saline County, IL held by WSIL TV Inc.
Group Owner: Mel Wheeler Inc.; (acq 5-12-83; grpsl; *Washington Law Firm:* Brooks, Pierce, McLendon, Humprey & Leonard
Nat'l Network: ABC; *Nat'l Reps:* Continental Television Sales
Steve Wheeler, President
Dave Cisco, General Sales Mgr
Mike Snuffer, News Director

***WSIU-TV** *Digital Channel:* 8; *Virtual Channel:* 8; 53 kw vis; ant 890t/861g; N38 06 11 W89 14 40; *Rebroadcasting:* Rebroadcasts WUSI-TV Olney 99%.; *Population Served:* 326,000
Suite 1003, 1100 Lincoln Dr., Carbondale, IL 62901-4306
(618) 453-4343, (866) 496-5561; *Fax:* (618) 453-6186, (618) 453-6246
www.wsiu.org
License: Carbondale, Jackson County, IL held by Board of Trustees of Southern Illinois University
Washington Law Firm: Cohn & Marks
Nat'l Network: PBS; *Wire Services:* AP
Size of News Staff: 1; *Hours of Local News Weekly:* news progmg 2 hrs wkly
Greg Petrovich, CEO
Delores Kerstein, CFO
Renee Dillard, Aasociate Director/Marketing
Trina Thomas, Programming Director
Monica Tichenor, Promotions Manager
Vacant, Engineering Dir
Vacant, Chief Engineer

WTCT *Digital Channel:* 17; *Virtual Channel:* 27; 2,600 kw vis, 260 kw aur; 775t/500g; N37 33 26 W89 01 24
Mailing Address: Box 1010, 11717 Rt. 37 N., Marion, IL 62959
Second Address: PO Box 1220, Fort Erie, ON L2A 5Y2
(618) 997-4700, (800) 232-9855; *Fax:* (618) 993-9778
www.tct.tv
today@tct.tv, ask@tct.tv
License: Marion, Williamson County, IL held by Tri-State Christian TV.
Group Owner: Tri-State Christian Television; (acq 5-29-84; $1.2 million)
Garth W. Coone, President & Founder
Peggy Carter, Station Manager
Todd Creamer, Chief Engineer
Tina coonce, VP & Co-Founder

Peoria-Bloomington, IL (DMA 118)

WAOE *Digital Channel:* 39; *Virtual Channel:* 59; 26 kw; 696 ft.; N40 37 46 W89 32 53
124 Monterey Road #304, South Pasadena, CA 91030 US
(309) 674-5900; *Fax:* (309) 674-5959
www.my59.tv
License: Peoria, Peoria County, IL held by Four Seasons Peoria LLC
Nat'l Network: MY NETWORK TV
Mark DeSantis, Operations Dir
Sara Horn, Station Manager
Pete Russell, General Sales Mgr
Tim Campbell, Promotions Manager
Jim Garrott, News Director

WEEK-TV *Digital Channel:* 25; *Virtual Channel:* 25; 246 kw; 694 ft.; N40 37 45.9 W89 32 52.6
2907 SpringfieldRd., East Peoria, IL 61611 US
(309) 698-2525; *Fax:* (309) 698-9663 (sales),(309) 698-3737 (news)
www.cinewsnow.com
news25@week.com
License: Peoria, Peoria County, IL held by WEEK-TV License Inc.

Group Owner: Granite Broadcasting Corp.; (acq 10-31-88; $33 million); *Washington Law Firm:* Akin, Gump, Strauss, Hauer & Feld
Nat'l Network: NBC
Size of News Staff: 26; *Hours of Local News Weekly:* news progmg 16 hrs wkly
Mark DeSantis, General Manager
Dennis Riley, Chief Engineer
Eric Greene, Anchor
Alyssa Donovan, Reporter
Jim Mattson, Sports Director
Sandy Gallant, Weather Team
Anna Yee, Sports Team
Mark Welp, News Team

WHOI *Digital Channel:* 19; *Virtual Channel:* 19; 195 kw; 666 ft.; N40 39 11 W89 35 14
2907 Springfield Rd., East Peoria, IL 61611 US
(309) 698-2525
www.cinewsnow.com
License: Peoria, Peoria County, IL held by WHOI Licensee LLC
Group Owner: Sinclair Broadcast Group Inc.; (acq 11-22-2013; $22 million); *Washington Law Firm:* Pillsbury Winthrop Shaw Pittman LLP
Nat'l Network: ABC; CW; *Nat'l Reps:* Harrington, Righter & Parsons
Hours of Local News Weekly: news progmg 7 hrs wkly
Mark DeSantis, General Manager

WMBD-TV *Digital Channel:* 30; *Virtual Channel:* 31; 800 kw; 633 ft.; N40 38 6 W89 32 19
3131 N. University, Peoria, IL 61604 US
(309) 688-3131; *Fax:* (309) 686-8650, (309) 686-8658
License: Peoria, Peoria County, IL held by Nexstar Broadcasting, Inc.
Group Owner: Nexstar Broadcasting Group Inc.; (acq 1999); *Washington Law Firm:* Covington & Burling
Nat'l Network: CBS
Rick Moll, News Director/Operations
Richard Engberg, VP & General manager
Nik Adams, Director of Sales & National Sales
Sandy Deshutter, Himan Resource/Programming
John Kim, Marketing/Dircetor of Promotions
Herman Marvel, ChiefEngineer
Nancy Linebaugh, Local Sales Manager
Blake Long, Managing Editor
Debbie Bart, Sales Team
Sandy DeSutter, Human Resources/FCC Concerns/Programming
Thom Parker, Chief Photographer
Ryan Campen, Sales Team

***WTVP** *Digital Channel:* 46; *Virtual Channel:* 47; 190 kw; 709 ft.; N40 37 44 W89 34 12
Mailing Address: 101 State St., Peoria, IL 61602-1547 US
Second Address: PO Box 1347, Peoria, IL 61654-1347
(309) 677-4747, (309) 495-0547; *Fax:* (309) 677-4730
www.wtvp.org
License: Peoria, Peoria County, IL held by Illinois Valley Public Telecommunication Corp
Washington Law Firm: Dow, Lohnes PLLC
Nat'l Network: PBS
Chet Tomczyk, CEO & President
Jackie Luebcke, Operations Manager
Linda Miller, VP of Programming
Stacey Tomczyk, Promotion Director
Bill Porter, Chief Engineer
Ben Bier, Traffic Manager
Jennifer Davis, Development Dir.
MarkLasswell, IT Dir./ Web Master
Jerry Dubose, Technical specialist
William baker, Executive Producer
Tracy Simmons, Studio Supervisor

WYZZ-TV *Digital Channel:* 28; *Virtual Channel:* 43; 1000 kw; 961 ft.; N40 38 45 W89 10 45
3131 N. University, Peoria, IL 61604 US
(309) 688-3131
www.centralillinoisproud.com
License: Bloomington, McLean County, IL held by Peoria (WYZZ-TV) Licensee Inc.
Group Owner: Cunningham Broadasting Corporation; (acq 11-22-2013; $22 millio); *Washington Law Firm:* Pillsbury Winthrop Shaw Pittmann LLP
Nat'l Network: FOX; *Nat'l Reps:* Harrington, Righter & Parsons

Quincy, IL-Hannibal, MO-Keokuk, IA (DMA 170)

WGEM-TV *Digital Channel:* 10; *Virtual Channel:* 10; 26 kw; 781 ft.; N39 57 4 W91 19 53
513 Hampshire Street, Quincy, IL 62301 US
(217) 228-6600, (217) 221-3415; *Fax:* (217) 228-6670, (217) 223-5019
wgem.com
License: Quincy, Adams County, IL held by Quincy Broadcasting Co.
Group Owner: Quincy Newspapers Inc.; *Washington Law Firm:* Wilkinson, Barker, Knauer & Quinn
Nat'l Network: NBC; CW; Fox; *Nat'l Reps:* Petry Television Inc.;
Wire Services: AP
Size of News Staff: 20; *Hours of Local News Weekly:* News progmg 20 hrs wkly
Ralph Oakley, CEO
Carlos Fernandez, VP & General Manager
Amy Carothers, General Sales Manager
Terri Stutheit, Programming Manager
Chad Mahoney, News Director
Jim Lawrence, Director of Operations & Engineering
Brent Clingingsmith,Director of Operations & Engineering
Brian Shoemaker, Internet Director
Don Morehead, National Sales Manager
Alisa Elkins, Radio Sales Manager
Wendy Gunn, Local Sales Manager
Shawn Dickerman, Creative Services Manager
Greg Haubrich, RadioOpeartions Manager

***WMEC** *Digital Channel:* 21; 24.15 kw vis, 2.42 kw aur; 519t/535g; N40 25 40 W90 40 58; *Population Served:* 915,000
Box 6248, Springfield, IL 62708
(217) 483-7887, (800) 232-3605; *Fax:* (217) 483-1112
www.wmec.tv
License: Macomb, McDonough County, IL held by West Central Illinois Educational Telecommunications Corp
Washington Law Firm: Dow, Lohnes & Albertson
Nat'l Network: PBS
Dr. Jerold Gruebel, CEO & President
Keith Lawson, Operations Engineer
Ed Strong, General Sales Mgr
Richard Plotkin, Engineering
Stephanie Cole, Dir. Of National Programming & Traffic
Dr. Ed Strong, Dir. Of Advancement
Ethan Auby,Master Control Operator
John Deemer, Field Maintainance Engineer
Becky Cramblit, Producer/ Public Information
Travis Collins, Producer Dir./ Image Development

***WQEC** *Digital Channel:* 34; *Virtual Channel:* 27; 58.6 kw; 502 ft.; N39 58 41 W91 18 32
PO Box 6248, Springfield, IL 62708 US
(217) 483-7887,(800) 232-3605; *Fax:* (217) 483-1112
www.wqec.tv
License: Quincy, Adams County, IL held by West Central Illinois Educational Telecommunications Corp
Washington Law Firm: Dow, Lohnes & Albertson
Nat'l Network: PBS
Jerold Gruebel, President & CEO
Richard Plotkin, Operations & Engineering Coordinator
Ed Strong, General Sales Mgr
Stephanie Cole, Dir. Of National Programming & Traffic
Ed Strong, Dir. Of Advancement
Matthew Martin, Master Controloperator
Norm Brumbaugh, Field Maintainance Engineer
Becky Cramblit, Producer/ Public information
Keith Lawson, Operations Engineer
Travis Collins, Producer Dir./ Imge development

WTJR *Digital Channel:* 32; *Virtual Channel:* 16; 1000 kw; 1010 ft.; N39 58 19 W91 19 40
222 N. 6th St., Quincy, IL 62301 US
(217) 228-1616
www.wtjr.org
tv16@wtjr.org
License: Quincy, Adams County, IL held by Christian Television Network Inc
Nat'l Network: N/A
A. Donette Douglas, Station Manager
James A. Wilson, Engineer
Karen White, Administrative asst.
Nick Fasnacht, Master Control Operator
Don Russell, Production Asst.

Rockford, IL (DMA 138)

WIFR *Digital Channel:* 41; *Virtual Channel:* 23; 100 kw; 577 ft.; N42 17 48 W89 10 15
2523 North Meridian Rd., Rockford, IL 61101 USA
(815) 987-5300; *Fax:* (815) 965-0981
www.wifr.com
talkto23@wifr.com
License: Freeport, Winnebago County, IL held by Gray Television Licensee LLC
Group Owner: Gray Television Inc.; *Washington Law Firm:* Covington & Burling
Nat'l Network: CBS; *Nat'l Reps:* Continental Television Sales
Size of News Staff: 19; *Hours of Local News Weekly:* news progmg 19 hrs wkly
Jeff Clark, Operations Manager
Tim Myers, General Manager
Nella Hoskinson, Sales
Dave Smith, News Director

WQRF-TV *Digital Channel:* 42; *Virtual Channel:* 39; 900 kw; 486 ft.; N42 17 14 W89 10 15
1917 N. Meridian Rd., Rockford, IL 61101 US
(815) 963-5413; *Fax:* (815) 963-6113
www.mystateline.com
License: Rockford, Winnebago County, IL held by Nexstar Broadcasting, Inc.
Group Owner: Nexstar Broadcasting Group Inc.; (acq 12-31-03; grpsl).; *Washington Law Firm:* Arter & Hadden
Nat'l Network: FOX
Kelly Lattimer, VP & General Manager
Scott Picken, News Director

WREX-TV *Digital Channel:* 13; 316 kw vis, 39.8 kw aur; 710t/652g; N42 17 50 W89 14 24; *Population Served:* 452,000
Mailing Address: Box 530, Rockford, IL 61105
Second Address: 10322 Auburn Rd., Rockford, IL 61103
(815) 335-2213, (815) 335-7796; *Fax:* (815) 335-7230, (815) 335-2055
www.wrex.com
License: Rockford, Winnebago County, IL held by WREX Television LLC.
Group Owner: Quincy Newspapers Inc.; (acq 5-22-2001; grpsl).; *Washington Law Firm:* Wilkinson, Barker & Knauer
Nat'l Network: NBC; CW; *Nat'l Reps:* Blair Television
John Chadwick, Operations Dir
John Chadwick, VP & General Manager
Jeff Glass, General Sales Manager
Trista Truesdale, Programming Director
Josh Morgan, News director
Peter Gungel, Chief Engineer
Kim Carney, National SalesManager
Samantha Jeffreys, Internet Director
Trista Truesdale, Administrative Asst.
Shawn Fagan, Account Executive
Tina Ryan, Account Executive

WTVO *Digital Channel:* 16; *Virtual Channel:* 17; 196 kw; 659 ft.; N42 17 14 W89 10 15
1917 N. Meridian Rd., Rockford, IL 61101 US
(815) 963-5413; *Fax:* (815) 963-6113
www.mystateline.com
License: Rockford, Winnebago County, IL held by Mission Broadcasting Inc.
Group Owner: Mission Broadcasting Inc.; (acq 1-4-2005; $20,750,000).; *Washington Law Firm:* Wiley, Rein & Fielding
Nat'l Network: ABC; MyNetworkTV
Size of News Staff: 16; *Hours of Local News Weekly:* news progmg 7 hrs wkly
Eileen Boucek, Station Manager
Kelly Lattimer, Dir. of Sales
Scott Picken, News Director

St. Louis, MO (DMA 21)

WRBU *Digital Channel:* 47; *Virtual Channel:* 46; 109.4 kw; 1043 ft.; N38 23 18 W90 29 16
150 Cattle Lndg., Meredith, NH 03253 USA
(401) 338-0565
www.iontelevision.com
License: East St. Louis, IL held by Broadcast Trust.
Group Owner: Ion Media Networks; *Washington Law Firm:* Dow, Lohnes & Albertson
Size of News Staff: 4
Bonni Burns, General Manager

Terre Haute, IN (DMA 155)

***WUSI-TV** *Digital Channel:* 19; *Virtual Channel:* 16; 46 kw; 931 ft.; N38 50 19 W88 7 47; *Rebroadcasting:* Rebroadcasts WSIU-TV Carbondale 100%.
Mailing Address: 1100 Lincoln Dr.-Suite 1003, SIU mailcode 6602, Carbondale, IL 62901-4306 US
Second Address: 1100 Lincoln Dr.-Suite 1003, SIU mailcode 6602, Carbondale, IL 62901-4306

(618) 453-4343, (866) 498-5561; *Fax:* (618) 453-6186, (618) 453-6159
www.wsiu.org
License: Olney, Richland County, IL held by Board of Trustees, Southern Illinois University.
Washington Law Firm: Cohn & Marks
Nat'l Network: ETV; *Wire Services:* AP
Delores Kerstein, CFO
Trina Thomas, Programming Director
Terry Harvey, Engineering Dir

Indiana

Chicago (DMA 3)

WPWR *Digital Channel:* 51; *Virtual Channel:* 50; 1000 kW; 1716 ft.; N41 52 44 W87 38 10
205 N Michigan Ave., Chicago, IL 60601 USA
(312) 565-5532
www.fox32chicago.com
License: Gary, Lake County, IN held by Fox Television Stations LLC
Group Owner: Fox Television Stations Group; (acq 8-21-2002; $425 million)
Nat'l Network: MyNetworkTV; *Nat'l Reps:* Fox Stations Sales

***WYIN** *Digital Channel:* 17; *Virtual Channel:* 56; 300 kw; 951 ft.; N41 20 56 W87 24 2
8625 Indiana Place, Merrillville, IN 46410 US
(219) 756-5656; *Fax:* (219) 755-4312
www.lakeshoreptv.com
news@lakeshoreptv.com
License: Gary, Lake County, IN held by Northwest Indiana Public Broadcasting Inc
Washington Law Firm: Schwartz, Woods & Miller
Nat'l Network: PBS
Bonita Neff, Chair
Thomas Carroll, CEO
James Muhammad, President & CEO
Carrie Kuck, Program Manager
Jerry Howard, News Director
Bob Liptack, Chief Engineer
Paul Nelson, Production Manager
Wende Burbridge, Dir. OfDevelopment
Roger Wexelberg, VP of Development & Public Relations
Travis Buchan, Interim VP of Radio Operations
Mary Lewis, VP of Administration

Dayton, OH (DMA 64)

WKOI-TV *Digital Channel:* 39; *Virtual Channel:* 43; 500 kw; 909 ft.; N39 30 44 W84 38 9
Mailing Address: P.O. Box A, Santa Ana, CA 92711 US
Second Address: PO Box 768, Station B, Ottawa, ON K1P 5P8
(714) 731-1000, (888) 731-1000, (714) 832-2950, (8; *Fax:* (819) 770-2338
www.tbn.org
License: Richmond, Wayne County, IN held by Trinity Broadcasting of Indiana, Inc.
Group Owner: Trinity Broadcasting Network; (acq 9-81).;
Washington Law Firm: Gammon & Grange
Nat'l Network: TRINITY BROADCA
Mark Crouch, General Manager

Evansville, IN (DMA 103)

WEHT *Digital Channel:* 7; *Virtual Channel:* 25; 12.5 kw; 1037 ft.; N37 51 56 W87 34 4
800 Marywood Dr., Henderson, KY 42420-2431 US
(270) 826-9566
www.nexstar.tv
License: Evansville, Vanderburgh County, IN held by Nexstar Broadcasting, Inc.
Group Owner: Nexstar Broadcasting Group; (acq 1-15-2003).;
Washington Law Firm: Wiley, Rein & Fielding
Nat'l Network: ABC
Curt Molander, General Manager
Brent Butler, Dir. of Sales

WEVV-TV *Digital Channel:* 45; *Virtual Channel:* 44; 340 kw; 1017 ft; N37 53 17 W87 32 37
477 Carpenter St, Evansville, IN 47708 US
(812) 464-4444; *Fax:* (812) 465-4559
44news.wevv.com
news@wevv.com
License: Evansville, Vanderburgh County, IN held by BCBE License Subsidiary, LLC
Group Owner: Bayou City Broadcasting; (acq 2015; $26.85 million from Nexstar Broadcasting); *Washington Law Firm:* Leventhal, Senter & Lerman
Nat'l Network: CBS; Fox; MyNetworkTV
Size of News Staff: 30; *Hours of Local News Weekly:* news progmg 9 hrs wkly
Jeff Fisher, General Manager
Nicole Neidlinger, Director, Sales
Warren Korff, News Director
Glenn Edwards, Chief Engineer

WFIE *Digital Channel:* 46; 2,510 kw vis; ant 1,017t/905g; N37 53 14 W87 31 07; *Population Served:* 290,000
Mailing Address: Box 1414, Evansville, IN 47701 US
Second Address: 1115 Mt. Auburn Rd., Evansville, IN 47720
(812) 426-1414, (812) 425-3026; *Fax:* (812) 426-1945
www.14news.com
License: Evansville, Vanderburgh County, IN held by WFIE License Subsidiary LLC.
Group Owner: Raycom Media Inc.; (acq 1-31-2006; grpsl);
Washington Law Firm: Dow, Lohnes & Albertson
Nat'l Network: NBC
Size of News Staff: 35
Nick Ulmer , General Manager
Nick Ulmer, General Manager
Jay Hiett, General Sales manager
Kirk Williams, Director/Children's Programming
Brandon Ridge, Marketing & Promotions
Scott Galloway, News Director
Bobby Barnett, ChiefEngineer
Marie Young, Traffic Director
Mike Jerstad, Creative Services Director
Maria Hillenbrand, Assistant to GM
Andy Overton, Assignment editor
Brook Arnold, Local Sales Manager
Drew Bush, Marketing Producer

***WKMA-TV** *Digital Channel:* 42; 617 kw vis, 61.7 kw aur; 1,040t/998g; N37 11 25 W87 30 47
600 Cooper Drive, Lexington, KY 40502 US
(859) 258-7000, (800) 432-0951; *Fax:* (859) 258-7399
www.ket.org
help@ket.org
License: Madisonville, Hopkins County, KY held by Kentucky Authority for Educational TV
Nat'l Network: PBS; *Regional Network:* Kentucky Educational Television
Mike Brower, Operations Dir
Malcolm Wall, Station Manager
Craig Cornwell, Senior Director, Programming
Tim Bischoff, Promotions Manager
Shae Hopkins, Executive Director
Tim Bischoff, Senior Director, Marketing and OnlineContent
Mike Brower, Senior Director, Production Operations
Nancy Carpenter, Senior Director, Education
Fred Engel, Senior Director, Technology
Linda Hume, Senior Director, Finance and Administration

***WNIN** *Digital Channel:* 9; 282 kw vis, 56.2 kw aur; 570t/570g; N38 01 27 W87 21 43; *Population Served:* 138,764
405 Carpenter St., Evansville, IN 47708
(812) 423-2973; *Fax:* (812) 428-7548
www.wnin.org
info@wnin.org
License: Evansville, Vanderburgh County, IN held by WNIN Tri-State Public Media, Inc
(acq 9-12-73).; *Washington Law Firm:* Dow, Lohnes PLLC
Nat'l Network: PBS
David Dial, President
Bonnie Rheinhardt, Operations Dir
Tonya Wolf, General Sales Mgr
Don Hollingsworth, Chief Engineer

WTVW *Digital Channel:* 28; 316 kw vis, 63.2 kw aur; 1,013t/880g; N38 01 27 W87 21 43; *Population Served:* 686,500
800 Marywood Dr., Henderson, KY 42420 US
(812) 424-7777; *Fax:* (270) 827-0561
www.tristatehomepage.com
License: Evansville, Vanderburgh County, IN held by Mission Broadcasting Inc.
Group Owner: Mission Broadcasting; (acq 10-30-2003; grpsl).;
Washington Law Firm: Arter & Hadden
Nat'l Network: CW; *Nat'l Reps:* Blair Television
Hours of Local News Weekly: News progmg 22.5 hrs wkly
Pam Miller, Station Manager
Brent Butler, Dir. of Sales

Ft. Wayne, IN (DMA 110)

WANE-TV *Digital Channel:* 31; *Virtual Channel:* 15; 1000 kw; 761 ft.; N41 5 38 W85 10 48
Mailing Address: 200 Crescent Court, Suite 1600, Dallas, TX 75201 US
Second Address: 2915 W. State Blvd., Fort Wayne, IN 46808
(260) 481-1515; *Fax:* (260) 481-1429
www.wane.com
License: Fort Wayne, Allen County, IN held by Indiana Broadcasting L.L.C.
Group Owner: LIN Television Corporation; (acq 11-14-94;
Nat'l Network: CBS; *Nat'l Reps:* Blair Television; *Wire Services:* CNN; CBS; NWS (National Weather Ser; NOAA Weather Wire Service
Size of News Staff: 35; *Hours of Local News Weekly:* news progmg 22 hrs wkly
Jim Riecken, Operations Dir
Alan Riebe, General Manager
Mike Luckett, General Sales Mgr
Nancy Applegate, Programming Director
Jerry Grider, Promotions Manager
Ted Linn, News Director
Jeff Kracium, Engineering Dir
Tom Antisdel,Local Sales Manager
April McCampbell, Public Affairs Director
Alyssa Ivanson, Anchor & Health Reporter
Gina Glaros, Anchor/Reporter
Nicholas Ferreri, Anchor/Reporter
Greg Shoup, Anchor/Reporter

WFFT-TV *Digital Channel:* 36; *Virtual Channel:* 55; 600 kw vis, 38 kw aur; 780t/805g; N41 06 33 W85 11 44; *Population Served:* 1,855,000
3707 Hillegas Rd., Fort Wayne, IN 46808 US
(260) 471-5555; *Fax:* (260) 484-4331
www.fortwaynehomepage.net
License: Fort Wayne, Allen County, IN held by Nexstar Broadcasting, Inc.
Group Owner: Nexstar Broadcasting Group; (acq 12-31-2003; grpsl); *Washington Law Firm:* Drinker, Biddle & Reath
; *Nat'l Reps:* Blair Television
Bill Ritchhart, General Manager
Dan Ball, News Director

***WFWA** *Digital Channel:* 40; *Virtual Channel:* 39; 90 kw; 725 ft.; N41 6 13 W85 11 28
2501 East Coliseum Boulevard, Fort Wayne, IN 46805-1562 US
(260) 484-8839, (260) 484-8839, (888) 484-8839; *Fax:* (260) 482-3632
www.wfwa.org
info@wfwa.org
License: Fort Wayne, Allen County, IN held by Fort Wayne Public Television
Washington Law Firm: Wiley Rein LLP
Nat'l Network: PBS
Randall S. Steiner, Chairman
Bruce R. Haines, President/General Manager
Todd Grimes, Operations Manager
Kris Hensler, Programming Director
Mark Ryan, Creative Services Manager
Matt Kyle, Engineering Manager
Rich Bienz,Administration
Rick Welling, Vice president
Gail Waymire, Finance Manager
Tom Theard, HR Director
Lisa Rysiawa, Broadcast Traffic Coordinator
Deb Farmer, Corporate Development Account Executive

WINM *Digital Channel:* 12; *Virtual Channel:* 63; 16.5 kw; 433 ft.; N41 27 15 W84 48 10
Mailing Address: 11717 Rt. 37, Marion, IL 62959 US
Second Address: P.O. Box 1010, Marion, IL 62959
(618) 997-4700; *Fax:* (618) 993-9778
www.tct.tv
winm@tct.tv
License: Angola, Steuben County, IN held by Tri-State Christian TV.
Group Owner: Tri-State Christian Television; (acq 1-24-91; $400,000;
Nat'l Network: IND
Garth W. Coonce, President
Leo Vogt, Station Manager

WISE-TV *Digital Channel:* 19; 594 kw vis, 59 kw aur; ant 770t/793g; N41 05 40 W85 10 36; *Population Served:* 222,480
3401 Butler Rd., Fort Wayne, IN 46808
(260) 483-0584, (260) 483-8111; *Fax:* (260) 483-2568, (260) 484-8240

www.indianasnewscenter.com
newsroom@incnow.tv
License: Fort Wayne, Allen County, IN held by WISE-TV License LLC.
Group Owner: Granite Broadcasting Corp.; (acq 3-8-2005; $44.2 million); *Washington Law Firm:* Dow Lohnes PLLC
Nat'l Network: NBC; MyNetwork TV
Size of News Staff: 32; *Hours of Local News Weekly:* news progmg 14 hrs wkly
Jerry Giesler, President
Jim Turcovsky, Operations Dir
Dan Hoffman, General Sales Mgr
Bill Schneider, Programming Director
Tad Frank, Promotions Manager
Peter Neumann, News Director
Bret Angel, Engineering Dir
Debbie Sand,Business Manager
Melissa Long, Anchor
Rachel Martin, Multimedia Journalist
Curtis Smith, Chief Meterologist
Eric DeFreeuw, Reporter

WPTA *Digital Channel:* 24; *Virtual Channel:* 21; 335 kw; 736 ft.; N41 6 7.9 W85 11 4.9
3401 Butler Rd., Ft.Wayne, IN 46808-3811 US
(260) 483-0584, (260) 483-8111; *Fax:* (260) 483-2568, (260) 484-8240
www.indianasnewscenter.com
License: Fort Wayne, Allen County, IN held by Malara Broadcast Group of Fort Wayne License LLC.
Group Owner: Malara Broadcast Group Inc.; (acq 12-8-2004; $45.9 million); *Washington Law Firm:* Akin, Gump, Strauss, Hauer & Feld
Nat'l Network: ABC
Size of News Staff: 31; *Hours of Local News Weekly:* news progmg 31 hrs wkly
Anthony Malara, CEO
Jerry Giesler, President
Doug Barrow, Station Manager
Dan Hoffman, General Sales Mgr
Tad Frank, Promotions Manager
Peter Neumann, News Director
Melissa Long, Anchor
Katie Law, Weather Specialist
StephanieParkinson, Multimedia journalist
Linda Jackson, Anchor/ Producer

Indianapolis, IN (DMA 27)

WCLJ-TV *Digital Channel:* 42; *Virtual Channel:* 42; 850 kw; 1030 ft.; N39 24 12 W86 8 50
PO Box A, Santa Ana, CA 92711 US
(714) 731-1000, (888) 731-1000; *Fax:* (714) 832-2950
www.tbn.org
License: Bloomington, Monroe County, IN held by Trinity Broadcasting of Indiana Inc.
Group Owner: Trinity Broadcasting Network
Nat'l Network: TRINITY BROADCA
Mark Crouch, General Manager
Ken Harl, Chief Engineer

***WDTI** *Digital Channel:* 44; *Virtual Channel:* 69; 28 kw; 961 ft.; N39 53 40 W86 12 21
Mailing Address: 3901 Hwy 121, Bedford, TX 76021 US
Second Address: PO Box 610546, Dallas, TX 75261-0546
(817) 571-1229, (877) 805-2132; *Fax:* (817) 571-7458
www.daystar.com/schedules.htm
License: Indianapolis, Marion County, IN held by Indianapolis Community Television Inc
(acq 8-2-2004; $4 million); *Washington Law Firm:* Koerner & Olender
Nat'l Network: IND
Marcus Lamb, President

***WFYI** *Digital Channel:* 21; 1,135 kw vis, 114 kw aur; 847t/867g; N39 53 59 W86 12 01; *Population Served:* 792,500
1630 N. Meridian St., Indianapolis, IN 46202
(317) 636-2020; *Fax:* (317) 283-6645
www.wfyi.org
sjensen@wfyi.org
License: Indianapolis, Marion County, IN held by Metropolitan Indianapolis Public Broadcasting, Inc.
Nat'l Network: PBS
Anna S. White, Chairman
Lloyd Wright, CEO/President
Bryan Spetter, CFO, VP - Finance
Lloyd Wright, General Manager
Kristina Uland, General Sales Mgr
Steve Jensen, VP of Engineering
Jeanelle Adamak, Executive Vice President
AlanCloe, Executive Vice President
Rena Barraclogh, VP of Communications
Kristina Uland, VP - Development
Clayton Taylor, VP - Television Production
Judy Muessig, VP of Organizational Relations

WHMB-TV *Digital Channel:* 20; 2,090 kw vis, 209 kw aur; 991t/1,007g; N39 53 39 W86 12 19; *Population Served:* 2,700,000
10511 Greenfield Avenue, Noblesville, IN 46060
(317) 773-5050, (800) 365-3732, (317) 773-3909, (3; *Fax:* (317) 776-4051
www.whmbtv.com
kpasson@lesea.com
License: Indianapolis, Marion County, IN held by LeSea Broadcasting of Indianapolis Inc.
Group Owner: Le Sea Broadcasting; (acq 8-15-72; $354,618; *Washington Law Firm:* Gardner, Carton & Douglas
Hours of Local News Weekly: News progmg one hr wkly
Brian Coyne, CFO
Pete Sumrall, President
Keith Passon, General Manager
DeWayne Roberts, Chief Engineer
Susane McAlister, Executive Producer
J.R. Brestin, Master Control Operator
Jeff Elliott, Production Manager
Karen King,Office Manager
Dave West, Producer/Director
Rob McGreevy, Senior Editor

***WIPB** *Digital Channel:* 23; *Virtual Channel:* 49; 250 kw; 807 ft.; N40 5 37 W85 23 32
1111 North McKinley Avenue, Ball State University, Muncie, IN 47306 US
(765) 285-1249, (800) 252-9472; *Fax:* (765) 285-5548
www.bsu.edu/wipb
wipb@bsu.edu
License: Muncie, Delaware County, IN held by Ball State University
(acq 10-31-71; $125,000; *Washington Law Firm:* Schwartz, Woods & Miller
Nat'l Network: PBS
Foreign Language Programming
Alice J. Van Dyke, General Manager
Susan Bunner, Program Director
Bob Rickner, Chief Engineer
Angela Rapp, Marketing Manager

WIPX-TV *Digital Channel:* 27; 165 kw; ant 1,053t/2,300g; N39 24 13 W86 08 40; *Population Served:* 825,000
2441 Production Dr., Suite 104, Indianapolis, IN 46241 USA
(317) 486-0633; *Fax:* (317) 486-0298
www.iontelevision.com
License: Bloomington, IN held by ION Media Indianapolis License, Inc.
Group Owner: ION Media Networks Inc.; (acq 2-18-2000; grpsl).; *Washington Law Firm:* Fisher, Wayland, Cooper, Leader & Zaragoza
Nat'l Network: ION Television
Brandon Burgess, Chairman/CEO

WISH-TV *Digital Channel:* 9; *Virtual Channel:* 8; 22.8 kw; 932 ft.; N39 53 25 W86 12 20
1950 N. Meridian St., Indianapolis, IN 46202 US
(317) 923-8888, (317) 874-0304, (317) 931-2222, (3; *Fax:* (317) 926-1144, (317) 926-2242
www.wishtv.com
newsdesk@wishtv.com
License: Indianapolis, Marion County, IN held by Indiana Broadcasting L.L.C.
Group Owner: LIN Television Corporation; (acq 11-14-94; *Washington Law Firm:* Covington & Burling
Nat'l Network: CBS; *Nat'l Reps:* Petry Television Inc.; *Wire Services:* AP
Jeff White, President
Tina Cosby, Operations Dir
Julie Zoumbaris, General Sales Mgr
Lance Carwile, Programming Director
Scott Hainey, Promotions Manager
Patti McGettigan, News Director
Terry Van Bibber, Engineering Dir
JasonCrundwell, Internet Director
Marilyn Fernandez, Office Administrator
Becky Hardy, Production Manager
Debby Knox, Anchor
Drew Blair, Reporter
Robb Ellis, Meterologist

WNDY-TV *Digital Channel:* 32; *Virtual Channel:* 23; 1000 kw; 889 ft.; N40 8 56 W85 56 7
1950 N. Meridian St., Indianapolis, IN 46202 US
(317) 923-8888, (317) 931-2222; *Fax:* (317) 926-1144 (sales), (317) 931-2242
www.indytv.com
caption@wishtv.com
License: Marion, Grant County, IN held by Indiana Broadcasting LLC.
Group Owner: LIN Television Corporation; (acq 3-31-2005; $85 million with WWHO(TV) Chillicothe, OH).; *Washington Law Firm:* Covington & Burling
Nat'l Network: MYNETWORK; *Nat'l Reps:* Blair Television
Jeff White, President
Tina Cosby, Operations Dir
Marilyn Fernandez, General Manager
Julie Zoumbaris, General Sales Mgr
Lance Carwile, Programming Director
Scott Hainey, Promotions Manager
Patti McGettigan, News Director
TerryVanBibber, Engineering Dir
Jason Crundwell, Internet Director
Becky Hardy, Production Manager

WRTV *Digital Channel:* 25; *Virtual Channel:* 6; 1000 kw; 965 ft.; N39 53 56.5 W86 12 3.7
1330 N. Meridian Street, Indianapolis, IN 46202-2364 US
(317) 635-9788,(317) 269-1440; *Fax:* (317) 269-1400, (317) 269-1445
www.theindychannel.com
newstips@theindychannel.com
License: Indianapolis, Marion County, IN held by McGraw-Hill Broadcasting Co. Inc.
Group Owner: McGraw-Hill Broadcasting Co.; (acq 6-1-72).; *Washington Law Firm:* Holland & Knight
Nat'l Network: ABC; *Nat'l Reps:* Harrington, Righter & Parsons
Larry Blackerby, General Manager
Sally Kohn, General Sales Mgr
Paul Montgomery, Promotions Manager
Terri Cope-Walton, News director
Brian Vetor, Chief Engineer
Todd Connor, News Team
Norman Cox, News Team
Ashley Brown, WeatherTeam
Kevin Gregory, Weather Team
Lauren Casey, Traffic Reporter
Brad Brown, Sports Team

WTHR *Digital Channel:* 13; *Virtual Channel:* 13; 42.1 kw; 981 ft.; N39 55 43 W86 10 55
Mailing Address: 1000 North Meridian St., Indianapolis, IN 46204 US
Second Address: 1000 N. Meridian St., Indianapolis, IN 46204
(317) 636-1313; *Fax:* (317) 636-3717,(317) 632-6720
www.wthr.com
newsdesk@wthr.com
License: Indianapolis, Marion County, IN held by VideoIndiana Inc.
Group Owner: Dispatch Broadcast Group; (acq 10-1-75; $17.65 million; *Washington Law Firm:* Sidley & Austin
Nat'l Network: NBC
Larry Delia, President & General Manager
Jim Tellus, President
Tim Warner, General Sales Mgr
Jeff Dutton, Promotions Manager
Roger Bishop, Chief Engineer
Dave Calabro, Sports team
Sean Ash, Weather Team
Jeremy Brilliant,Reporter
Angela Clain, News anchor

***WTIU** *Digital Channel:* 14; *Virtual Channel:* 30; 224 kw; 725 ft.; N39 8 31 W86 29 43
1229 E. 7th St., Bloomington, IN 47405 US
(812) 855-1357; *Fax:* (812) 855-5900
www.wtiu.indiana.edu
License: Bloomington, Monroe County, IN held by Trustees of Indiana University.
Ownership: Trustees of IU; *Washington Law Firm:* Crowell & Moring
Nat'l Network: PBS
Size of News Staff: 5; *Hours of Local News Weekly:* 3 hours plus online
Perry Metz, CEO
Brad Howard, Operations Dir
Phil Meyer, Station Manager
Brent Molnar, Program Manager
Ann Wesley, Promotions Manager
Ann Shea, News Director
Marianne Woodruff, Corporate Underwriting
Eva Zogorski, Membership
Mary Ducette, Outreach Coordinator
Gabrielle sloan, Traffic Manager

Donna Stroup, CFO
Marianne Woodruff, Corporate Development Manager

WTTK *Digital Channel:* 29; *Virtual Channel:* 29; 550 kw; 984 ft.; N39 53 20 W86 12 7; *Rebroadcasting:* Satellite of Bloomington WTTV(TV)
6910 Network Pl., Indianapolis, IN 46278 USA
cbs4indy.com
License: Kokomo, Howard County, IN held by Tribune Broadcasting Indianapolis LLC
Group Owner: Tribune Media
Nat'l Network: CBS; *Nat'l Reps:* TeleRep
Brad Norris, Master Control Manager

WTTV *Digital Channel:* 48; *Virtual Channel:* 4; 870 kw; 1043 ft.; N39 24 27 W86 8 52
6910 Network Pl., Indianapolis, IN 46278 USA
(317) 632-5900; *Fax:* (317) 715-2677
cbs4indy.com
news4@cbs4indy.com
License: Bloomington, Monroe County, IN held by Tribune Broadcasting Indianapolis LLC
Group Owner: Tribune Media; (acq 12-20-2007; grpsl);
Washington Law Firm: Dow Lohnes PLLC
Nat'l Network: CBS; *Nat'l Reps:* TeleRep
Brad Norris, Master Control Manager

WXIN *Digital Channel:* 45; *Virtual Channel:* 59; 1000 kw; 984 ft.; N39 53 20 W86 12 7
6910 Network Pl., Indianapolis, IN 46278 USA
(317) 687-6584; *Fax:* (317) 715-2677
fox59.com
fox59news@fox59.com
License: Indianapolis, Marion County, IN held by Tribune Broadcasting Indianapolis LLC
Group Owner: Tribune Media; (acq 12-20-2007; grpsl);
Washington Law Firm: Dow Lohnes PLLC
Nat'l Network: FOX; *Nat'l Reps:* TeleRep
Hours of Local News Weekly: News progmg 19 hrs wkly
Amanda Rakes, Digital Manager

Lafayette, IN (DMA 187)

WLFI-TV *Digital Channel:* 11; *Virtual Channel:* 18; 30 kw; 702 ft.; N40 23 20 W86 36 46
2605 Yeager Rd., West Lafayette, IN 47906 US
(765) 463-1800, (765) 313-1028; *Fax:* (765) 463-7979, (765) 237-5001
www.wlfi.com
License: Lafayette, Tippecanoe County, IN held by Primeland LLC
Group Owner: LIN Media; (acq 4-1-2000; in exchange for 67% of WAND(TV) Decatur, IL).
Nat'l Network: CBS; *Nat'l Reps:* Petry Television Inc.; *Wire Services:* UPI
Size of News Staff: 30; *Hours of Local News Weekly:* news progmg 22 hrs wkly
Baron Brendel, Operations Dir
Tom Combs, Station Manager
Jenny Olszewski, General Sales Mgr
Rick Thedwall, Programming Director
Kurt Lahrman, Promotions Manager
Chris Morisse, News Director
Mark Brooks, Chief Engineer
JeffSmith, Anchor
Dan Klein, Multi-platform Journalist
Chad Evans, Chief meterologist
Rob Hughes, Sports Director

Louisville, KY (DMA 49)

WMYO *Digital Channel:* 51; *Virtual Channel:* 58; 1000 kw; 1281 ft.; N38 21 0 W85 50 57
624 W. Muhammad Ali Blvd., Louisville, KY 40203 US
(502) 584-6441; *Fax:* (502) 485-7004
www.wmyo.com
License: Salem, Washington County, IN held by Independence Television Co.
Group Owner: Block Communications Inc.; (acq 3-30-2001).;
Washington Law Firm: Dow, Lohnes & Albertson
Nat'l Network: MYNETWORKTV; *Nat'l Reps:* TeleRep
Harry Beam, Director, Programming and Operations
Ray Foushee, Director of Marketing, Research and Publicity
Gary Schroder, Chief Engineer
Rick Burrice, Local Sales Manager
Shahara Ross, National Sales Manager
LaVerne Pike, NationalSales Coordinator
Lindsey Braun, Account Exeuctive
Glenn Davis, Account Executive
Bailey Wilson, Account Manager

South Bend-Elkhart, IN (DMA 96)

WHME-TV *Digital Channel:* 48; *Virtual Channel:* 46; 300 kw; 968 ft.; N41 35 43 W86 9 38
61300 S. Ironwood Road, South Bend, IN 46614 US
(574) 291-8200; *Fax:* (574) 291-9043
www.whme.com
License: South Bend, Saint Joseph County, IN held by Le Sea Broadcasting of South Bend, Inc.
Group Owner: Le Sea Broadcasting; (acq 6-10-77; $496,000);
Washington Law Firm: Gardner, Carton & Douglas
Nat'l Network: IND
Mike Swinehart, Operations Dir
Peter Sumrall, General Manager
Anna Riblet, Sales Manager
Wes Hylton, Chief Engineer
Jennifer Eash, Senior Account Executive
Jeff Castello, Senior Account Executive
Mike Pooler, Senior AccountExecutive
Ron Bedward, Senior Account Executive
Sharl Luzney, Account Executive

WNDU *Digital Channel:* 42; *Virtual Channel:* 16; 800 kw; 1023 ft.; N41 36 20 W86 12 46
54516 State Road 933, South Bend, IN 46637 USA
(574) 284-3000; *Fax:* (574) 284-3009
www.wndu.com
newscenter16@wndu.com
License: South Bend, Saint Joseph County, IN held by Gray Television Licensee LLC
Group Owner: Gray Television Inc.; (acq 3-6-2006; $85 million)
Nat'l Network: NBC

***WNIT** *Digital Channel:* 35; 708 kw vis, 77 kw aur; 530t/500g; N41 36 59 W86 11 43; *Population Served:* 478,000
Mailing Address: PO Box 7034, South Bend, IN 46634-7034
Second Address: 300 West Jefferson Blvd., South Bend, IN 46601
(574) 675-9648; *Fax:* (574) 289-3441
www.wnit.org
wnit@wnit.org
License: South Bend, Saint Joseph County, IN held by Michiana Public Broadcasting Corp
Washington Law Firm: Dow, Lohnes & Albertson
Nat'l Network: PBS
Amy Cassidy, CFO
Greg Giczi, President & General Manager
Brian Hoover, Dir. Of Broadcast Operations
Diane Marlow, Programming Director
Diane Marlow, Traffic & Content Specialist
Brenda Bowyer, Sr. Producer/ Director
AngelHernandez, VP of Production
Cindy McCraner, Development Department Manager
Steven Funk, Associate General Manager & VP of Development
Mike kauffman, Engineering supervisor

WSBT-TV *Digital Channel:* 22; *Virtual Channel:* 22; 266 kw; 1091 ft.; N41 37 0 W86 13 1
1301 E. Douglas Rd., Mishawaka, IN 46545 US
(574) 247-7861; *Fax:* (574) 288-6630
www.wsbt.com
wsbtnews@wsbt.com
License: South Bend, Saint Joseph County, IN held by WSBT Inc.
Group Owner: Schurz Communications Inc.; *Washington Law Firm:* Wilmer Hale
Nat'l Network: CBS; *Nat'l Reps:* Harrington, Righter & Parsons
Size of News Staff: 34; *Hours of Local News Weekly:* news progmg 22 hrs wkly
John Mann, President
Bob Johnson, Operations Dir
Beth Young, General Sales Mgr
Michelle Jewell, Programming Coordinator
Scott Leiter, Promotions Manager
Meg Sauer, News Director
C. Eugene Hale, Chief Engineer
Rhonda Malone,Human Resources
Chris Dautel, Vice President, Finance
Jason overholt, Digital Content Manager
Jennifer copeland, News Team
Paul Emmick, Weather Team
Pete Byrne, Sports Team

WSJV *Digital Channel:* 28; *Virtual Channel:* 28; 311 kw; 1099 ft.; N41 36 58 W86 11 38
58096 County Rd 7 S, Elkhart, IN 46517 US
(574) 679-9758; *Fax:* (574) 294-1267
www.fox28.com
fox28@fox28.com
License: Elkhart, Elkhart County, IN held by WSJV Television Inc.
Group Owner: Quincy Newspapers Inc.; (acq 3-31-75; $3.2 million; *Washington Law Firm:* Wilkinson, Barker, Knauer & Quinn
Nat'l Network: FOX
Size of News Staff: 22; *Hours of Local News Weekly:* news progmg 16 hrs wkly
Ed Kral, Station Manager
Heather Stewart, Programming/ Aministrative Asst.
Adam Bull, Chief Engineer
Resa Toeller, Creative Services
Adam Ziegler, Internet Dir.

Terre Haute, IN (DMA 155)

WAWV-TV *Digital Channel:* 39; 2,140 kw vis, 214 kw aur; ant 976t/1,004g; N39 13 58 W87 23 49; *Population Served:* 70,286
PO Box 9268, Terre Haute, IN 47808 US
(812) 238-3838; *Fax:* (812) 696-2755
www.mywabashvalley.com
License: Terre Haute, Vigo County, IN held by Mission Broadcasting Inc.
Group Owner: Mission Broadcasting Inc.
Nat'l Network: ABC
Hours of Local News Weekly: News progmg 2 hrs wkly
Lois Mathis, Station Manager
Deana Reece, News Director

WTHI-TV *Digital Channel:* 10; 316 kw vis, 31.6 kw aur; ant 960t/993g; N39 14 36 W87 23 07; *Population Served:* 164,800
Mailing Address: 800 Ohio St., Terre Haute, IN 47807
Second Address: 800 Ohio St., Terre Haute, IN 47807
(812) 232-9481, (800) 589-8810, (812) 232-4953; *Fax:* (812) 232-8953, (812) 232-3694
www.wthitv.com
news10@wthitv.com
License: Terre Haute, Vigo County, IN held by Indiana Broadcasting LLC.
Group Owner: LIN Television Corporation; (acq 11-30-2005; grpsl).
Nat'l Network: CBS (10.1); FOX (10.2); *Nat'l Reps:* Petry Television Inc.
Rod Garvin, Operations Dir.
Todd Weber, VP/ General Manager
Nick Telezyn, General Sales Manager
Rod Garvin, Programming Manager
David Shearer, Promotions/ Creative Services dir.
Susan Dinkel, News Director/ Anchor
Jeff Tucker,Chief Engineer
Ruth Nasser, Digital Sales Director
Sean Dempsey, Graphics Dir.
Scott Arnold, Digital Director/ Webmaster
Michael Delaunois, Local Sales manager
Jay Kirk, Production Manager
Myranda Gott, Producer/ Promotions Dept.

WTWO *Digital Channel:* 36; 100 kw vis, 19.5 kw aur; 950t/999g; N39 14 33 W87 23 29; *Population Served:* 162,320
Box 9268, Terre Haute, IN 47808 US
(812) 696-2121; *Fax:* (812) 696-2755
www.mywabashvalley.com
License: Terre Haute, Vigo County, IN held by Nexstar Broadcasting Inc.
Group Owner: Nexstar Broadcasting Group Inc.; (acq 2-14-97; with KQTV(TV) Saint Joseph, MO); *Washington Law Firm:* Drinker, Biddle & Reath LLP
Nat'l Network: NBC
Size of News Staff: 25; *Hours of Local News Weekly:* news progmg 20 hrs wkly
Timothy Sturgess, General Manager
Deana Reece, News Director

***WVUT** *Digital Channel:* 22; *Virtual Channel:* 22; 57 kw; 538 ft.; N38 39 6 W87 28 37
1002 North First Street, Vincennes, IN 47591 US
(812) 888-4345; *Fax:* (812) 882-2237
www.vubroadcasting.org
wvut@vinu.edu
License: Vincennes, Knox County, IN held by Board of Trustees for the Vincennes Univ
(acq 9-16-76; *Washington Law Firm:* Fletcher, Heald & Hildreth
Nat'l Network: PBS; *Wire Services:* UPI
Size of News Staff: 4; *Hours of Local News Weekly:* news progmg 5 hrs wkly

Jill Ballinger, Operations Dir
Al Rerko, General Manager
Sharon Keifer, Programming Director

Iowa

Cedar Rapids-Waterloo-Iowa City & Dubuque, IA (DMA 90)

KCRG-TV *Digital Channel:* 9; *Virtual Channel:* 9; 30.4 kw; 1991 ft.; N42 18 59 W91 51 31
Mailing Address: PO Box 816, Cedar Rapids, IA 52406 US
Second Address: 501 2nd Ave SE, Cedar Rapids, IA 52401
(319) 365-9999, (319)398-8422; *Fax:* (319) 368-8505, (319) 339-3148
www.kcrg.com
online@kcrg.com
License: Cedar Rapids, Linn County, IA held by Cedar Rapids TV Co.
(acq 8-12-54; $101,500; *Ownership:* The Gazette Co., 100%;
Washington Law Firm: Wiley, Rein & Fielding
Nat'l Network: ABC
Joseph Hladky III, CEO
John Phelan III, General Manager
John Phelan, Station Manager
Tom Hurn, Senior Manager - Local Sales
Kevin Schrader, Programming Director
Adam Carros, News Director
Kirk Schroeder, Chief Engineer
ShannonBooth, Product Director
Steve Lake, Sr. Manager, National Sales
Kaj O'Mara, KCRG-TV9 Meteorologist
Amy Thuente, Care & Community Support
Kevin Schrader, Director, Broadcast Technical Operations/Programmi

KFPX-TV ; 1000 kw; 466t; N41 49 5 W93 12 35; *Population Served:* 442,400
4570 114th St., Urbandaleids, IA 50322 USA
(319) 378-1260; *Fax:* (319) 378-0076
www.iontelevision.com
michaelhubner@ionmedia.com
License: Newton, IA held by Ion Media Des Moines License, Inc.
Group Owner: ION Media Networks Inc.; (acq 7-15-97; $5 million)
Brandon Burgess, Chairman/CEO
Vikki Steele, Station Manager

KFXA *Digital Channel:* 27; *Virtual Channel:* 28; 1000 kw; 1473 ft.; N42 5 25 W92 5 13
600 Old Marion Road. NE, Cedar Rapids, IA 52402 US
(800) 642-6140; *Fax:* (319) 395-987
www.kfxa.tv
License: Cedar Rapids, IA held by Second Generation of Iowa Ltd
Nat'l Network: FOX
Size of News Staff: 6; *Hours of Local News Weekly:* news progmg 13.5 hrs wkly
Larry Blum, President
Greg Stuart, Operations Dir

KGAN *Digital Channel:* 29; *Virtual Channel:* 2; 850 kw; ant 1,450t/1,355g; N42 18 59 W91 51 30; *Population Served:* 117,040
Mailing Address: 600 Old Marion Rd. N.E., Cedar Rapids, IA 52402
Second Address: 10706 Beaver Dam Rd., Hunt Valley, MD 21030
(800) 642-6140; *Fax:* (319) 395-0987
www.cbs2iowa.com
news@cbs2iowa.com
License: Cedar Rapids, Linn County, IA held by KGAN Licensee LLC
Group Owner: Sinclair Broadcast Group Inc.; (acq 1999; grpsl).;
Washington Law Firm: Shaw Pittman
Nat'l Network: CBS; *Nat'l Reps:* Millennium Sales & Marketing;
Wire Services: AP; CBS
Size of News Staff: 35; *Hours of Local News Weekly:* news progmg 12 hrs wkly
Glen Callanan, General Manager
Steve Rohrer, General Sales Mgr
David Bell, Promotions Manager
Corey Miller, Engineering Dir

***KRIN** *Digital Channel:* 35; *Virtual Channel:* 32; 250 kw; 1916 ft.; N42 18 59 W91 51 31
Mailing Address: 6450 Corporate Drive, PO Box 6450, Johnston, IA 50131-6450 US
Second Address: 6535 Corporate Drive, PO Box 6400, Johnston, IA 50131-6450
(515) 242-3100 / (800) 532-1290
www.iptv.org
friends@iptv.org
License: Waterloo, Black Hawk County, IA held by Iowa Public Broadcasting Board
Washington Law Firm: Dow, Lohnes PLLC
Nat'l Network: PBS
Brent Siegrist, Vice President
Betty J Furgerson, CEO/COO
Gary Steinke, President
Molly M. Phillips, Executive Director/General Manager
Justin Beaupre, Director of Programming and Production
William T. Hayes, Director ofEngineering and Technology
Kristen L. Gray, Director of Communications
Terry Rinehart, Director of Educational Services
Kristine K. Houston, Director of Administration and Finance

KWKB ; 1,000 kw; 1455.7 ft; N41 43 29 W91 21 10
3654 W. Jarvis Ave., Skokie, IL 60076 US
(319) 643-5952; *Fax:* (319) 643-3124
www.kwkb.tv
kwkbtransfer@gmail.com
License: Iowa City, IA held by KM Television of Iowa, LLC.
Group Owner: KM Communications Inc.
Dawn Neal, Business Administrator
Trish Wethington, Traffic Mgr

KWWF *Digital Channel:* 22; *Virtual Channel:* 22; 11.85 kw; 1084 ft.; N42 17 17.33 W91 52 53.86
Mailing Address: 224 Amberglow Place, Cary, NC 27513 US
Second Address: 501 Sycamore St., Suite 710, Waterloo, IA 50703
(319) 287-5841
License: Waterloo, Black Hawk County, IA held by Waterloo Television Group LLC
Nat'l Network: RTN
Ken Musgrave, Operations Dir
Jason Effinger, General Manager
Bob Bunch, General Sales Mgr

KWWL *Digital Channel:* 7; *Virtual Channel:* 7; 49 kw; 1972 ft.; N42 24 2 W91 50 36
500 E. 4th St., Waterloo, IA 50603-1200 US
(319) 291-1200, (3190 291-1240, (800) 947-7746, (3; *Fax:* (319) 291-1233
www.kwwl.com
License: Waterloo, Black Hawk County, IA held by KWWL Television Inc.
Group Owner: Quincy Newspapers Inc.; (acq 7-1-2006; $63 million); *Washington Law Firm:* Covington & Burling
Nat'l Network: NBC; *Nat'l Reps:* Petry Television Inc.; *Wire Services:* AP
Size of News Staff: 35; *Hours of Local News Weekly:* news progmg 22 hrs wkly
Jeremy Ott, Operations Manager
Jim McKernan, General Manager
Kim Leer, Station Manager
John Huff, General Sales Manager
Chris Hussey, Promotions Manager
Dan Schillinger, News Director
Dan Whealy, Chief Engineer
Don Morehead,National Sales Manager
Shelly Davis, Local Sales Manager
Sandy Youngblut, Human Resources
Amie Steffan, Internet Director
Chris Hussey, Marketing& Community Relations Manager
Josette Bates, Master Control Supervisor

Davenport, IA-Rock Island-Moline, IL (DMA 101)

KGCW *Digital Channel:* 41; *Virtual Channel:* 26; 54.3 kw vis, 5.43 kw aur; ant 315t; N41 8 8 W90 48 30; *Population Served:* 590,000
231 18th St., Rock Island, IL 61201
(309) 786-5441
www.ourquadcities.com
License: Burlington, Des Moines County, IA held by Nexstar Broadcasting Inc.
Group Owner: Nexstar Broadcasting Group Inc.; *Washington Law Firm:* Wilkinson, Barker, Knauer & Quinn
Nat'l Network: CW; *Nat'l Reps:* TeleRep
Marshall Porter, General Manager
Angie Salas, Director of Sales
Michael Lopez, News Director

KLJB *Digital Channel:* 49; *Virtual Channel:* 18; 3,000 kw vis, 300 kw aur; ant 1,010t/993g; N41 18 44 W90 22 45; *Population Served:* 737,000
231 18th St., Rock Island, IL 61201
(309) 786-5441
www.ourquadcities.com
License: Davenport, Scott County, IA held by Marshall Broadcasting Group Inc.
Group Owner: Marshall Broadcasting Group Inc.; *Washington Law Firm:* Wilkinson, Barker, Knauer & Quinn
Nat'l Network: Fox; *Nat'l Reps:* TeleRep
Hours of Local News Weekly: News progmg 3.5 hrs wkly
Deborah Cram, Station Manager
Mike Turner, Director of Sales

KWQC-TV *Digital Channel:* 36; *Virtual Channel:* 6; 1000 kw; 1079 ft.; N41 18 44 W90 22 46
805 Brady Street, Davenport, IA 52803 US
(563) 383-7000; *Fax:* (563) 383-7129
www.kwqc.com
License: Davenport, Scott County, IA held by Young Broadcasting of Davenport, Inc., Debtor-in-possession
Group Owner: Young Broadcasting Inc.; (acq 4-15-96; $55 million); *Washington Law Firm:* Wiley, rein & Fielding
Nat'l Network: NBC; *Nat'l Reps:* Adam Young
Ken Freedman, Vice President & General Manager
John Mann, General Sales Manager
Joydene Koresko, Programming Director
Michelle Makelbust, Promotions Manager
Beth Marsoun, News Director
Doug Bierman, Chief Engineer
Sue O'Malley,Business Manager
Joydene Koresko, Office Administrator
Jeff Glass, Local Sales Manager
Angie McClimon, Digital Sales Manager
Eric VanWinkle, Creative Services Director
Sharon DeRycke, Anchor

Des Moines-Ames, IA (DMA 69)

KCCI *Digital Channel:* 8; *Virtual Channel:* 8; 28.3 kw; 1959 ft.; N41 48 35 W93 37 16
Box 1800, Raleigh, NC 27602 US
(919) 839-0300
www.kcci.com
License: Des Moines, IA held by Hearst Properties Inc.
Group Owner: Hearst Television Inc.; (acq 1999; grpsl).;
Washington Law Firm: Brooks, Pierce, McLendon, Humprey & Leonard, LLP
Nat'l Network: CBS; *Nat'l Reps:* Eagle Television Sales
Size of News Staff: 50; *Hours of Local News Weekly:* news progmg 30 hrs wkly
Bob Day, Operations Dir
Sue Knudson, Programming Director

KCWI-TV *Digital Channel:* 23; 5,000 kw vis; ant 2,011t; N41 49 47 W93 36 56
500 SW 7th Street, Suite 300, Des Moines, IA 50390
(515) 283-2323; *Fax:* (515) 289-4323
License: Ames, Story County, IA held by KPWB License LLC.
Group Owner: Pappas Telecasting Companies
Nat'l Network: CW
Ted Stephens, General Manager
Larry Schuler, Chief Engineer
Tony Hoffman, Local Sales Manager

***KDIN-TV** *Digital Channel:* 11; *Virtual Channel:* 11; 22.5 kw; 1969 ft.; N41 48 33 W93 36 53
Mailing Address: 6450 Corporate Drive, P.O. Box 6450, Johnston, IA 50131-6450 US
Second Address: 6450 Corporate Drive, Johnston, IA 50131-6450
(515) 725-9700, (800) 532-1290
www.iptv.org
publicinformation@iptv.org
License: Des Moines, Polk County, IA held by Iowa Public Broadcasting Board
Washington Law Firm: Dow, Lohnes PLLC
Nat'l Network: PBS
Molly M. Phillips, General Manager
Bill Hayes, Engineering Dir
Justin Beaupre, Director,Programming & Production
Terry Rinehart, Director,Educational services
Kristen L.Gray, Director,Communications
William T. Hayes,Director,Engineering & technology
Kristine K. Houton, Director,Administration & Finance

KDSM-TV *Digital Channel:* 16; *Virtual Channel:* 17; 1000 kw; 2008 ft.; N41 49 48 W93 36 54
4023 Fleur Dr., Des Moines, IA 50321 US
(515) 287-1717; *Fax:* (515) 287-0064
www.kdsm17.com
License: Des Moines, Polk County, IA held by KDSM Licensee LLC

Group Owner: Sinclair Broadcast Group Inc.; *Washington Law Firm:* Dow, Lohnes & Albertson
Nat'l Network: FOX; *Nat'l Reps:* Millennium Sales & Marketing
Size of News Staff: 7; *Hours of Local News Weekly:* news progmg 4 hrs wkly
Mike Wilson, General Manager
Anthony Bonanno, General Sales Mgr
Roni Dixon, Programming Coordinator
Doug Hammond, Chief Engineer

***KTIN** *Digital Channel:* 25; *Virtual Channel:* 21; 600 kw; 1165 ft.; N42 49 3 W94 24 41
Mailing Address: 6450 Corporate Drive, PO Box 6450, Johnston, IA 50131 US
Second Address: 6450 Corporate Dr., Johnston, IA 50131
(515) 242-3100, (800) 532-1290
www.iptv.org
public_information@iptv.org
License: Fort Dodge, Webster County, IA held by Iowa Public Broadcasting Board
Washington Law Firm: Dow, Lohnes PLLC
Nat'l Network: PBS
Gary Steinke, President
Molly M. Phillips, Executive Director and General Manager
Justin Beaupr, Programming Director
William T. Hayes, Director of Engineering and Technology
Kristine K. Houston, Director of Administration andFinance
Kristen L. Gray, Director of Communications
Terry Rinehart, Director of Educational Services
Justin Beaupr, Production Director

Omaha, NE (DMA 74)

***KHIN** *Digital Channel:* 35; *Virtual Channel:* 36; 600 kw; 1558 ft.; N41 20 40 W95 15 21
Mailing Address: P.O.Box 6450, Johnston, IA 50131 US
Second Address: 6450 Corporate Drive, Johnston, IA 50131
(515) 242-3100
www.iptv.org
public_information@iptv.org
License: Red Oak, Montgomery County, IA held by Iowa Public Broadcasting Board
Washington Law Firm: Dow, Lohnes PLLC
Nat'l Network: PBS
Daniel Miller, General Manager
Bill Hayes, Engineering Dir

Ottumwa, IA-Kirksville, MO (DMA 200)

KYOU-TV *Digital Channel:* 15; *Virtual Channel:* 15; 249 kw; 1181 ft.; N41 11 42 W91 57 15
13906 Gold Circle, Suite 201, Omaha, NE 68144 US
(641) 684-5415; *Fax:* (641) 682-5173
www.kyoutv.com
reception@kyoutv.com
License: Ottumwa, Wapello County, IA held by Ottumwa Media Holdings LLC
Group Owner: American Spirit Media; (acq 12-15-2003; $4 million); *Washington Law Firm:* Covington & Burling
Nat'l Network: FOX; *Nat'l Reps:* MMT
Dianne Little, General Manager
Phil Benjamin, Chief Engineer

Rochester, MN-Mason City, IA-Austin, MN (DMA 153)

KIMT *Digital Channel:* 42; *Virtual Channel:* 3; 800 kw; 1519 ft.; N43 28 32 W92 42 29
112 North Pennsylvania Avenue, Mason City, IA 50401 US
(641) 423-2540; *Fax:* (641) 423-9309
www.kimt.com
news@kimt.com
License: Mason City, Cerro Gordo County, IA held by LIN License Company LLC
Group Owner: LIN Media; (acq 10-12-2012; grpsl); *Washington Law Firm:* Paul Hastings LLP
Nat'l Network: CBS; *Nat'l Reps:* Harrington, Righter & Parsons
Size of News Staff: 21; *Hours of Local News Weekly:* news progmg 19 hrs wkly
Steve Martinson, President & General Manager
Michael Fitzgerald, General Sales Mgr
Jerome Risting, Programming Director
Jerome Risting, Promotions Manager
John Murray, News Director
Larry Eckblad, Chief Engineer
Wayne Kohlhaas,Sales

***KYIN** *Digital Channel:* 18; *Virtual Channel:* 24; 533 kw; 1471 ft.; N43 28 32 W92 42 29
Mailing Address: 6450 Corporate Drive, PO Box 6450, Johnston, IA 50131 US
Second Address: 6450 Corporate Dr., Johnston, IA 50131
(515) 242-3100, (800) 532-1290
www.iptv.org
License: Mason City, Cerro Gordo County, IA held by Iowa Public Broadcasting Board
Washington Law Firm: Dow, Lohnes PLLC
Nat'l Network: PBS
Gary Steinke, President
Molly M. Phillips, Executive Director and General Manager
Justin Beaupr, Programming Director
William T. Hayes, Director of Engineering and Technology
Kristine K. Houston, Director of Administration andFinance
Kristen L. Gray, Director of Communications
Terry Rinehart, Director of Educational Services
Justin Beaupr, Production Director

Sioux City, IA (DMA 149)

KCAU-TV *Digital Channel:* 9; *Virtual Channel:* 9; 43.9 kw; 2,021 ft.; N42 35 11 W96 13 56; *Population Served:* 166,000
625 Douglas, Sioux City, IA 51101 US
(712) 277-2345; *Fax:* (712) 277-4298
www.siouxlandmatters.com
jcurry@kcautv.com
License: Sioux City, Woodbury County, IA held by Nexstar Broadcasting Inc.
Group Owner: Nexstar Broadcasting Group Inc.; (acq 9-16-2013).; *Washington Law Firm:* Latham & Watkins
Nat'l Network: ABC
John Curry, General Manager
Dan Marsh, General Sales Mgr
Jennifer McReynolds, Local Sales Manager
Aaron Thiele, Digital Media Manager
Angie Galles, Account Executive
Pat O'Connor, Account Executive
Pat Rooney, AccountExecutive
Natalie Payne, Account Executive

KMEG *Digital Channel:* 39; *Virtual Channel:* 14; 1000 kw; 2005 ft.; N42 35 12 W96 13 19
Mailing Address: P.O. Box 3103, Sioux City, IA 51102 US
Second Address: 100 Gold Circle, Dakota Dunes, SD 57049
(712) 277-3554; *Fax:* (712) 255-5250
www.siouxlandnews.com
sscollard@siouxlandnews.com
License: Sioux City, Woodbury County, IA held by Waitt Broadcasting Inc.
(acq 6-23-98; $12.25 million); *Ownership:* Waitt Media Inc., 100% of total assets; *Washington Law Firm:* Wilkinson, Barker, Knauer & Quinn
Nat'l Network: CBS; *Nat'l Reps:* Harrington, Righter & Parsons
Steve Scollard, General Manager
Kathan Jager, General Sales Manager
Ed Bok, Chief Engineer
Jill Foley, Local Sales Manager
Kathan Jager, National Sales Manager

KPTH *Digital Channel:* 49; *Virtual Channel:* 44; 1000 kw; 1926 ft.; N42 35 12 W96 13 18
100 Gold Circle, North Sioux City, SD 57049 US
(712) 277-3554; *Fax:* (712) 255-5250
www.siouxlandnews.com
news@siouxlandnews.com
License: Sioux City, Woodbury County, IA held by KPTH Licensee LLC
Group Owner: Sinclair Broadcast Group Inc.
Nat'l Network: FOX; MyNetworkTV; *Nat'l Reps:* Harrington, Righter & Parsons
Steve Scollard, General Manager
Kathan Jager, General Sales Mgr
Jill Foley, Local Sales Manager

KTIV *Digital Channel:* 41; *Virtual Channel:* 4; 873 kw; 1998 ft.; 42 35'11.8 N 96 13'19.7 W
2929 Signal Hill Dr., Sioux City, IA 51108 US
(712) 239-4100; *Fax:* (712) 239-2621
www.ktiv.com
ktivreception@ktiv.com
License: Sioux City, Woodbury County, IA held by KTIV Television Inc.
Group Owner: Quincy Media, Inc.; (acq 11-20-89).; *Washington Law Firm:* Wilkinson, Barker, Knauer & Quinn
Nat'l Network: NBC; CW; MeTV; *Nat'l Reps:* Blair Television
Hours of Local News Weekly: News progmg 19.5 hrs wkly
Ralph Oakley, CEO/COO
Jerry Watson, Regional VP and General Manager
Bridget Breen, Station Manager
Adrian Wisner, General Sales Mgr
David Washburn, Programming and Marketing Director
Keith Bliven, News Director
Andy Benz, ChiefEngineer
Brooke Hensley, Local Sales Manager

Kansas

Joplin, MO-Pittsburg, KS (DMA 151)

KOAM-TV *Digital Channel:* 7; *Virtual Channel:* 7; 14.8 kw; 1102 ft.; N37 13 15 W94 42 25
Mailing Address: Box 659, Pittsburg, KS 66762 US
Second Address: 2950 N.E. Hwy. 69, Pittsburg, KS 66762-0659
(417) 624-0233; *Fax:* (417) 624-3115, sls & admin
www.koamtv.com
news@koamtv.com
License: Pittsburg, Crawford County, KS held by Saga Quad States Communications LLC.
Group Owner: Saga Communications Inc.; (acq 10-12-94; $8.55 million)
Nat'l Network: CBS; *Nat'l Reps:* Continental Television Sales
Hours of Local News Weekly: News progmg 19 hrs wkly
Danny Thomas, President
Vance Lewis, Promotions Manager
Kristi Spencer, News Director
Larry White, Chief Engineer
Jordan Aubey, Anchor
Tawnya Bach, News Anchor
Rudy Harper, Reporter
Jacob Lenard, Reporter
Dowe Quick,Executive Producer
Kelly Reid, Reporter

Topeka, KS (DMA 135)

KSNT *Digital Channel:* 27; *Virtual Channel:* 27; 77.9 kw; 1050 ft.; N39 5 34 W95 47 4
Mailing Address: P.O. Box 2700, Topeka, KS 66601 US
Second Address: 6835 N.W. Hwy. 24, Topeka, KS 66618
(785) 582-4000; *Fax:* (785) 582-5283,(785) 582-4783
www.ksnt.com
27news@ksnt.com
License: Topeka, Shawnee County, KS held by LIN License Company LLC
Group Owner: LIN Media; (acq 10-12-2012; grpsl); *Washington Law Firm:* Paul Hastings LLP
Nat'l Network: NBC; CW; *Nat'l Reps:* Harrington, Righter & Parsons; *Wire Services:* AP
Size of News Staff: 30; *Hours of Local News Weekly:* news progmg 25 hrs wkly
Jean Turnbough, General Manager
Nate Hill, News Director
Charlie Good, Chief Engineer
Matt Broxterman, Regional Sales Manager

KTKA-TV *Digital Channel:* 49; *Virtual Channel:* 49; 89.1 kw; 1480 ft.; N39 1 34 W95 55 1
Mailing Address: 6835 NW Hwy 24, Topeka, KS 66618 US
Second Address: 6835 NW Hwy 24, Topeka, KS 66618
(785) 582-4000, (785) 582-5100; *Fax:* (785) 582-4783
www.ktka.com
49email@ktka.tv
License: Topeka, Shawnee County, KS held by Free State Communications LLC.
Group Owner: Vaughan Media LLC; (acq 8-29-2005; $6.2 million); *Ownership:* Free State Communications, LLC; *Washington Law Firm:* Cohn & Marks
Nat'l Network: ABC; CW; *Nat'l Reps:* Millennium Sales & Marketing; *Wire Services:* AP
Size of News Staff: 21; *Hours of Local News Weekly:* news progmg 15 hrs wkly
Jean Turnbough, General Manager
Christy Gurney, Programming Director
Tracy Smith, Digital & Promotions Director
Nate Hill, News Director
Jeff Groves, Chief Engineer
Alex Wiebel, Sports Director
Matt Miller, Chief Meterologist
Johnny Faith, Director of Sales
Joshua N. Pila, Senior Counsel

***KTWU** *Digital Channel:* 11; *Virtual Channel:* 11; 38 kw; 991 ft.; N39 3 50 W95 45 49
1700 College, Topeka, KS 66621-1100 US
(785) 670-1111; *Fax:* (785) 670-1112
www.ktwu.org
ktwu-press@lists.washburn.edu
License: Topeka, Shawnee County, KS held by Washburn University of Topeka

Nat'l Network: PBS
Eugene Williams, General Manager/CEO
Dave Kendall, Operations Dir
Cindy Barry, General Sales Mgr
Val VanDerSluis, Program Director
Kevin Goodman, Promotion/Marketing Director
Duane Loyd, Chief Engineer
Doug Barrington,Development/Ed Services Director
Dave Kendall, Production Manager

WIBW *Digital Channel:* 13; *Virtual Channel:* 13; 42 kw; 1355 ft.; N39 0 22 W96 2 57
631 SW Commerce Place, Topeka, KS 66615 USA
(785) 272-6397
www.wibw.com
feedback@wibw.com
License: Topeka, Shawnee County, KS held by Gray Television Licensee LLC
Group Owner: Gray Television Inc.; *Washington Law Firm:* Wiley Rein LLP
Nat'l Network: CBS; MyNetworkTV; *Nat'l Reps:* Continental Television Sales
Size of News Staff: 26; *Hours of Local News Weekly:* news progmg 30.5 hrs wkly
Shane McMurdo, Engineering

Wichita-Hutchinson Plus, KS (DMA 66)

KAAS-TV *Digital Channel:* 17; *Virtual Channel:* 18; 65 kw; 1030 ft.; N39 6 16 W97 23 15; *Rebroadcasting:* Satellite of KSAS-TV Wichita.
316 N. West St., Wichita, KS 67203 US
(316) 942-2424; *Fax:* (316) 942-8927
www.foxkansas.com
tgdisis@foxkansas.com
License: Salina, Saline County, KS held by KSAS Licensee LLC
Group Owner: Sinclair Broadcast Group; (acq 3-14-2008; grpsl);
Washington Law Firm: Covington & Burling
Nat'l Network: FOX
Chuck Reid, General Manager
Tom Gdisis, Station Manager
Jason Wilson, General Sales Mgr
Michelle Cleaton, Programming Director
Mike Haden, Promotion Coordinator
Jerome Biggars, Chief Engineer
Ken Whitney, ProductionManagerager
Jake McCabe, Local Sales Manager
Denice Petty, Traffic Coordinator

KAKE *Digital Channel:* 10; *Virtual Channel:* 10; 316 kw vis, 44.7 kw aur; 1,030t/1,079g; N37 46 54 W97 31 10; *Population Served:* 300,000
1500 N West St., Wichita, KS 67203-1323 USA
(316) 943-4221; *Fax:* (316) 943-5493
www.kake.com
License: Wichita, Sedgwick County, KS held by Gray Television Licensee LLC
Group Owner: Gray Television Inc.; *Washington Law Firm:* Covington & Burling
Nat'l Network: ABC; Me-TV; *Nat'l Reps:* Continental Television Sales
Size of News Staff: 40; *Hours of Local News Weekly:* news progmg 16 hrs wkly

***KDCK** *Digital Channel:* 21; *Virtual Channel:* 21; 8.423 kw; 325 ft.; N37 49 33 W100 10 40
604 Elm Street, Po Box 9, Bunker Hill, KS 67626 US
(785) 483-6990; *Fax:* (785) 483-4605
www.shptv.org
shptv@shptv.org
License: Dodge City, Ford County, KS held by Smoky Hills Public Television
Washington Law Firm: Dow, Lohnes PLLC
Nat'l Network: PBS
Michael Quade, General Manager & CEO
Terry Cutler, Operations/Engineering Director
Terry Cutler, Director of Engineering
Jarrod Brantley, Traffic Director
Leona Breeden, Director, Educational Services
Kelli King, Director, Finance& Administration
Callie Kolacny, Marketing Director
Malinda Walker, Director of Membership
Aaron Roe, IT Engineer

KDCU-DT *Digital Channel:* 31; *Virtual Channel:* 31; 1,000 kw; ant 905t/909g; N37 48 01 W97 31 29
2815 E. 37th St. N., Wichita, KS 67219 US
(316) 831-6020; *Fax:* (316) 831-6190
feedback@kwch.com
License: Derby, Sedgwick County, KS held by Entravision Holdings, LLC
Group Owner: Entravision Communications Corp.
Tim Vanderzwaag, National Sales Mgr
Laverne Goering, Dir. of Programming/Operations

KLBY *Digital Channel:* 17; *Virtual Channel:* 4; 625 kw; 732 ft.; N39 15 9 W101 21 9; *Rebroadcasting:* Satellite of KAKE-TV Wichita.
1500 North West Street, Wichita, KS 67203-1323 US
(316) 943-4221; *Fax:* (316) 945-0599
www.kake.com
KAKE@kake.com
License: Colby, Thomas County, KS held by Gray Television Licensee Inc.
Group Owner: Gray Television Inc.; (acq 8-29-2002; grpsl).;
Washington Law Firm: Covington & Burling
Nat'l Network: ABC; ME-TV
Size of News Staff: 0
Dan Wall, Vice President/General Manager/Station Manager
Patrick Myers, Operations Dir
George Brown, General Sales Mgr
Bryan Frye, Programming Director/Promotions Manager
Michael Sipes, News Director
Dale Morrell, EngineeringDir
Dale Morrell, Chief Engineer

KMTW *Digital Channel:* 35; *Virtual Channel:* 36; 1000 kw; 1017 ft.; N37 56 23 W97 30 42
316 N. West Street, Wichita, KS 67203 US
(316) 942-2424; *Fax:* (316) 942-8927
www.mytvwichita.com
License: Hutchinson, Reno County, KS held by Mercury Broadcasting Co. Inc.
(acq 7-1-2001).; *Ownership:* Van H. Archer III, 100%;
Washington Law Firm: Fletcher, Heald & Hildreth
Nat'l Network: MYTV; *Nat'l Reps:* Millennium Sales & Marketing
Jeff McClausland, General Manager
Chuck Reid, General Sales Mgr
Michelle Cleaton, Programming Director
Mike Haden, Promotion Coordinator
David Caruso, Chief Engineer
Kari Barrett, National Sales Manager
Ken Whitney, ProductionManager
Denice Petty, Traffic Manager

KOCW *Digital Channel:* 14; *Virtual Channel:* 14; 40 kw; 535 ft.; N38 37 53 W98 50 52; *Rebroadcasting:* Satellite of KSAS-TV Wichita 100%.
316 N. West St., Wichita, KS 67203 US
(316) 942-2424; *Fax:* (316) 942-8927
www.foxkansas.com
tgdisis@foxkansas.com
License: Hoisington, Barton County, KS held by KSAS Licensee LLC
Group Owner: Sinclair Broadcast Group; (acq 3-14-2008; grpsl);
Washington Law Firm: Covington & Burling
Nat'l Network: FOX
Chuck Reid, General Manager
Tom Gdisis, Station Manager
Jason Wilson, General Sales Mgr
Michelle Cleaton, Programming Director
Mike Haden, Promotion Coordinator
Jerome Biggars, Chief Engineer
Ken Whitney, Production Manager
Denice Petty, Traffic Coordinator
Jake McCabe, Local Sales Manager

***KOOD** *Digital Channel:* 16; *Virtual Channel:* 9; 496 kw; 997 ft.; N38 46 16 W98 44 16
P. O. Box 9, Bunker Hill, KS 67626 US
(785) 483-6990; *Fax:* (785) 483-4605
www.shptv.org
shptv@shptv.org
License: Hays, Ellis County, KS held by Smoky Hills Public Television Corp
Washington Law Firm: Dow, Lohnes & Albertson
Nat'l Network: PBS
Foreign Language Programming
Randall Weller, Chair
Lynn Meredith, CEO
Mary-Pat Waymaster, Operations Dir
Michael Quade, General Manager
Jayne Heller, General Sales Mgr
Glenna Letsch, Programming Director
Jane Habiger, Promotions Manager
Tery Cutler,Engineering Dir
Aaron Roe, Chief Engineer
Leona Breeden, Director of Educational Services

***KPTS** *Digital Channel:* 29; 32 kw; 785; N38 03 21 W97 46 35; *Population Served:* 120,250
320 W. 21st St. N., Wichita, KS 67203-2499
(316) 838-3090, (800) 794-8498; *Fax:* (316) 838-8586
www.kpts.org
tv8@kpts.org
License: Hutchinson, Reno County, KS held by Kansas Public Telecommunications Service Inc
(acq 1979).; *Washington Law Firm:* Dow, Lohnes PLLC
Nat'l Network: PBS
Michele Gors, President/Chief Executive Officer
Michelle Gors, President
Dave McClintock, Director of Operations
Chris Freshour, General Sales Mgr
David Brewer, Programming Director
Bob Locke, Chief Engineer
Pat Moyer, ContentDirector
Richard Hess, Continuity Director
Carolyn Potter, Director of Administration
Justin Rupert, Producer Director
Phil Searle, Producer Director
Steve Downey, Account Executive

KSAS-TV *Digital Channel:* 26; *Virtual Channel:* 24; 350 kw; 994 ft.; N37 46 40 W97 30 37
316 N. West St., Wichita, KS 67203 US
(316) 942-2424; *Fax:* (316) 942-8927
www.foxkansas.com
tgdisis@foxkansas.com
License: Wichita, Sedgwick County, KS held by KSAS Licensee LLC
Group Owner: Sinclair Broadcast Group Inc.; (acq 3-14-2008; grpsl); *Washington Law Firm:* Covington & Burling
Nat'l Network: FOX; *Nat'l Reps:* Millennium Sales & Marketing
Chuck Reid, General Manager
Tom Gdisis, Station Manager
Jason Wilson, General Sales Mgr
Michelle Cleaton, Programming Director
Mike Haden, Promotion Coordinator
Jerome Biggars, Chief Engineer
Ken Whitney, Production Manager
Jake McCabe, Local Sales Manager

KSCW-DT *Digital Channel:* 19; 1,000 kw vis; ant 1,381t/1,320g; N38 03 38 W97 45 49; *Population Served:* 443,690
2815 E. 37th N, Wichita, KS 67219 US
(316) 303-0700; *Fax:* (316) 303-0160 (sales; traffic),(316) 303-9807
www.kansascw.com
License: Wichita, Sedgwick County, KS held by Sunflower Broadcasting Inc.
Group Owner: Schurz Communications Inc.; (acq 7-20-2007; $6.8 million)
Nat'l Network: CW
Joan Barrett, President
Marty Heffner, Operations Dir
Marcus Wilkerson, General Sales Mgr
Lisa Bryce, Programming Director
Shawn Hilferty, Promotions Manager

KSNC *Digital Channel:* 22; *Virtual Channel:* 2; 500 kw; 932 ft.; N38 25 54 W98 46 18
833 North Main, Wichita, KS 67203 US
(316) 265-3333; *Fax:* (316) 292-1197
www.ksn.com
ksnc@ksn.com
License: Great Bend, Barton County, KS held by LIN License Company LLC
Group Owner: LIN Media; (acq 10-12-2012; grpsl)
Nat'l Network: NBC; *Nat'l Reps:* TeleRep
Al Buck, General Manager
Dan Shurtz, General Sales Mgr
Betty Erickson, Programming Director
Gregg Cox, Promotions Manager
Jason Kravarik, News Director
Warren Kunkle, Chief Engineer
Kevin White, New Media Manager
Darren Dedo,New Media Manager
Mark Davidson, New Media Manager
Katie Tauba, New Media Manager
Craig Andres, New Media Manager
Chris Arnold, New Media Manager

KSNG *Digital Channel:* 11; *Virtual Channel:* 11; 56.8 kw; 784 ft.; N37 46 40 W100 52 8
833 North Main, Wichita, KS 67203 US
(316) 265-3333; *Fax:* (316) 292-1197
www.ksn.com

License: Garden City, Finney County, KS held by LIN License Company LLC
Group Owner: LIN Media; (acq 10-12-2012; grpsl); *Washington Law Firm:* Paul Hastings LLP
Nat'l Network: NBC; *Nat'l Reps:* TeleRep
Al Buck, General Manager
Dan Shurtz, General Sales Mgr
Betty Erickson, Programming Director
Gregg Cox, Promotions Manager
Jason Kravarik, News Director
Warren Kunkle, Chief Engineer
Kevin White, New Media Manager
Darren Dedo,New Media Manager
Mark Davidson, New Media Manager
Katie Tauba, New Media Manager
Craig Andres, New Media Manager
Chris Arnold, New Media Manager

KSNW *Digital Channel:* 45; *Virtual Channel:* 3; 891 kw; 1024 ft.; N37 46 26 W97 30 51
833 North Main, Wichita, KS 67203 US
(316) 265-3333; *Fax:* (316) 292-1197
www.ksn.com
news@ksn.com
License: Wichita, Sedgwick County, KS held by LIN License Company LLC
Group Owner: LIN Media; (acq 10-12-2012; grpsl); *Washington Law Firm:* Paul Hastings LLP
Nat'l Network: NBC; *Nat'l Reps:* TeleRep
Al Buch, General Manager
Dan Shurtz, General Sales Mgr
Betty Erickson, Programming Director
Greg Cox, Promotions Manager
Jason Kravarik, News Director
Warren Kunkle, Chief Engineer
Kevin White, New Media Manager
Darren Dedo,New Media Manager
Mark Davidson, New Media Manager
Katie Tauba, New Media Manager
Craig Andres, New Media Manager
Chris Arnold, New Media Manager

***KSWK** *Digital Channel:* 8; *Virtual Channel:* 3; 33 kw; 502 ft.; N37 49 40 W101 6 35
Mailing Address: 604 Elm Street, Bunker Hill, KS 67626 US
Second Address: PO Box 9, Bunker Hill, KS 67626
(785) 483-6990; *Fax:* (785) 483-4605
www.shptv.org
shptv@shptv.org
License: Lakin, Kearny County, KS held by Smoky Hills Public Television Corp
Washington Law Firm: Dow, Lohnes PLLC
Nat'l Network: PBS
Randall Weller, Chair
Lynn Meredith, CEO
Sheila Frahm, President
Mary-Pat Waymaster, Operations Dir
Michael Quade, General Manager/CEO
Jayne Heller, General Sales Mgr
Callie Kolacny, Marketing Manager
Terry Cutler, Director ofEngineering
Brian Pert, Director of Engineering
Leona Breeden, Director of Educational Services
Michael Freeland, Marketing Director
Mary Pat Waymaster, Director of Content
Malinda Walker, Director of Membership
Kelli King, Director ofFinance and Administration
Les Kinderknecht, Senior Producer/Director

KUPK *Digital Channel:* 18; 225 kw vis, 45 kw aur; ant 870t/881g; N37 39 01 W100 40 06; *Rebroadcasting:* Satellite of KAKE-TV Wichita.; *Population Served:* 435,000
2900 E. Schulman Ave., Garden City, KS 67846
(818) 688-1541
www.kake.com
License: Garden City, Finney County, KS held by Gray Television Licensee Inc.
Group Owner: Gray Television Inc.; (acq 8-29-2002; grpsl).; *Washington Law Firm:* Covington & Burling
Nat'l Network: ABC
Size of News Staff: 2; *Hours of Local News Weekly:* news progmg 7 hrs wkly
Bryce Baker, General Manager

***KWKS** *Digital Channel:* 19; *Virtual Channel:* 19; 464 kw; 1257 ft.; N39 14 31 W101 21 38
604 Elm St., PO Box 9, Bunker Hill, KS 67626 US
(785) 483-6990; *Fax:* (785) 483-4605
www.shptv.org
License: Colby, Thomas County, KS held by Smoky Hills Public Television Corp.
Washington Law Firm: Dow, Lohnes, LLC
Nat'l Network: PBS
Michel Quade, General Manager & CEO
Terry Cutler, Dir. Of Engineering
Glenna Letsch, Traffic Dir.
Kelli King, Dir. Of Finance & Administration
Callie Kolancy, Marketing Dir.
Mary Pat Waymaster, Dir. Of Content
Malina Walker, Dir.Of Membership
Rodrigo lopez, Producer/Director

Kentucky

Bowling Green, KY (DMA 181)

WBKO *Digital Channel:* 13; 22 kw vis; ant 723t/543g; N37 03 49 W86 26 07; *Population Served:* 67,300
2727 Russellville Rd., Bowling Green, KY 42101-3976
(270) 781-1313; *Fax:* (270) 781-1814
www.wbko.com
License: Bowling Green, Warren County, KY held by Gray Television Licensee LLC
Group Owner: Gray Television Inc.; *Washington Law Firm:* Covington & Burling
Nat'l Network: ABC; *Nat'l Reps:* Continental Television Sales
Size of News Staff: 22; *Hours of Local News Weekly:* news progmg 17 hrs wkly
Rick McCue, General Manager
Brad Odil, VP Sales/Station Manager
Barbara Powell, Programming Director
Cliff Cothern, Promotions/Marketing Director
Henry Chu, News Director
Wilburn England, Chief Engineer

***WKGB-TV** *Digital Channel:* 48; *Virtual Channel:* 53; 54.8 kw; 768 ft.; N37 5 22 W86 38 5
600 Cooper Drive, Lexington, KY 40502 US
(859) 258-7000, (800) 432-0951; *Fax:* (859) 258-7399
www.ket.org
help@ket.org
License: Bowling Green, Warren County, KY held by Kentucky Authority for Educational TV
Nat'l Network: PBS
Mike Brower, Operations Dir
Malcolm Wall, Station Manager
Craig Cornwell, Senior Director, Programming
Tim Bischoff, Promotions Manager
Shae Hopkins, Executive Director
Tim Bischoff, Senior Director, Marketing and OnlineContent
Mike Brower, Senior Director, Production Operations
Nancy Carpenter, Senior Director, Education
Fred Engel, Senior Director, Technology
Linda Hume, Senior Director, Finance and Administration

***WKYU-TV** *Digital Channel:* 18; *Virtual Channel:* 24; 61 kw; 580 ft.; N37 3 49 W86 26 7
1906 College Heights Blvd, Bowling Green, KY 42101-3576 US
(270) 745-0111; *Fax:* (270) 745-2084
www.wkyu.org
License: Bowling Green, Warren County, KY held by Western Kentucky University
Washington Law Firm: Leventhal, Senter & Lerman
Nat'l Network: PBS
Size of News Staff: 1; *Hours of Local News Weekly:* news progmg one hr wkly
Gary Ransdell, President
Jack Hanes, General Manager
Linda Gerossky, Station Manager

WNKY *Digital Channel:* 16; *Virtual Channel:* 40; 120 kw; 582 ft.; N37 2 3.8 W86 10 40.9
325 Emmett Ave., Suite N, Bowling Green, KY 42101 US
(270) 781-2140; *Fax:* (270) 842-7140
www.wnky.com
wnky@wnky.com
License: Bowling Green, Warren County, KY held by MMK License LLC
Group Owner: MAX Media L.L.C.; (acq 3-1-2003; $7 million); *Washington Law Firm:* Williams & Mullen, P.C.
Nat'l Network: NBC; CBS; *Nat'l Reps:* Millennium Sales & Marketing
Linda Gray, President/General Manager
Julie Milam, General Sales Mgr
Richard Smith, Chief Engineer
Christi Hull, Business Manager
Kathy Werner, Traffic Manager
Atlee McHeffey, Digital Manager

Charleston-Huntington, WV (DMA 70)

***WKAS** *Digital Channel:* 26; *Virtual Channel:* 25; 61.3 kw; 449 ft.; N38 27 44 W82 37 12
600 Cooper Drive, Lexington, KY 40502 US
(859) 258-7000, (800) 432-0951; *Fax:* (859) 258-7399
www.ket.org
help@ket.org
License: Ashland, Boyd County, KY held by Kentucky Authority for Educational TV
Nat'l Network: PBS; *Regional Network:* Kentucky Educational Television
Mike Brower, Operations Dir
Malcolm Wall, Station Manager
Craig Cornwell, Senior Director, Programming
Tim Bischoff, Promotions Manager
Shae Hopkins, Executive Director, CEO
Tim Bischoff, Senior Director, Marketing and OnlineContent
Mike Brower, Senior Director, Production Operations
Nancy Carpenter, Senior Director, Education
Fred Engel, Senior Director, Technology
Linda Hume, Senior Director, Finance and Administration

Cincinnati, OH (DMA 36)

***WCVN-TV** *Digital Channel:* 24; *Virtual Channel:* 54; 53.5 kw; 384 ft.; N39 1 50 W84 30 23
600 Cooper Dr., Lexington, KY 40502 US
(859) 258-7000, (800) 432-0951; *Fax:* (859) 258-7399
www.ket.org
help@ket.org
License: Covington, Kenton County, KY held by Kentucky Authority for Educational TV
Nat'l Network: PBS; *Regional Network:* Kentucky Educational Television
Shae Hopkins, Executive Director and CEO
Mike Brower, Senior Director, Production Operations
Craig Cornwell, Senior Director, Programming
Tim Bischoff, Promotions Manager
Michele Ripley, President, Commonwealth Fund for KET
TimBischoff, Senior Director, Marketing and Online Content
Julie Schmidt, Senior Director, External Affairs
Nancy Carpenter, Senior Director, Education
Fred Engel, Senior Director, Technology
Linda Hume, Senior Director, Finance andAdministration

***WKON** *Digital Channel:* 44; *Virtual Channel:* 52; 49.7 kw; 702 ft.; N38 31 31 W84 48 39
600 Cooper Drive, Lexington, KY 40502 US
(859) 258-7000, (800) 432-0951; *Fax:* (859) 258-7399
www.ket.org
help@ket.org
License: Owenton, Owen County, KY held by Kentucky Authority for Educational TV
Nat'l Network: PBS; *Regional Network:* Kentucky Educational Television
Mike Brower, Operations Dir
Malcolm Wall, Station Manager
Craig Cornwell, Senior Director, Programming
Tim Bischoff, Promotions Manager
Shae Hopkins, Executive Director
Tim Bischoff, Senior Director, Marketing and OnlineContent
Mike Brower, Senior Director, Production Operations
Nancy Carpenter, Senior Director, Education
Fred Engel, Senior Director, Technology
Linda Hume, Senior Director, Finance and Administration

WXIX-TV *Digital Channel:* 29; 4,680 kw vis, 468 kw aur; 1,004t/984g; N39 07 19 W84 32 52; *Population Served:* 1,946,000
19 Broadcast Plaza, 635 W. 7th St., Cincinnati, OH 45203
(513) 421-1919; *Fax:* (513) 421-2829
www.fox19.com
fox19@fox19.com
License: Newport, Campbell County, KY held by wxix License Subsidiary, LLC
Group Owner: Raycom Media Inc.; (acq 1998; $45 million; grpsl).; *Washington Law Firm:* Covington & Burling
Nat'l Network: Fox; *Nat'l Reps:* TeleRep
Size of News Staff: 57; *Hours of Local News Weekly:* news progmg 46.5 hrs wkly
Paul McTear, CEO
Rick Oliver, Operations Dir
Bill Lanesey, General Manager
Branden Frantz, General Sales Mgr
Rick Oliver, Programming Director
Kevin Goryl, Creative Services Director
Kevin Roach, News Director
Jim Gilbert,Chief Engineer

Amy Goetz, National Sales Manager
Chris Plennert, Regional Sales Manager

Evansville, IN (DMA 103)

***WKOH** *Digital Channel:* 30; *Virtual Channel:* 31; 63.3 kw; 407 ft.; N37 51 7 W87 19 44
600 Cooper Drive, Lexington, KY 40502 US
(859) 258-7000, (800) 432-0951; *Fax:* (606) 258-7399
www.ket.org
help@ket.org
License: Owensboro, Daviess County, KY held by Kentucky Authority for Educational TV
Washington Law Firm: Kenkel, Barnard & Edmundson
Nat'l Network: PBS; *Regional Network:* Kentucky Educational Television
Mike Brower, Operations Dir
Malcolm Wall, Station Manager
Craig Cornwell, Senior Director, Programming
Tim Bischoff, Promotions Manager
Shae Hopkins, Executive Director
Tim Bischoff, Senior Director, Marketing and OnlineContent
Mike Brower, Senior Director, Production Operations
Nancy Carpenter, Senior Director, Education
Fred Engel, Senior Director, Technology
Linda Hume, Senior Director, Finance and Administration

Knoxville, TN (DMA 62)

WAGV *Digital Channel:* 51; *Virtual Channel:* 44; 550 kw; 1893 ft.; N36 48 0 W83 22 36; *Rebroadcasting:* Satellite of WLFG(TV) Grundy, VA.
Mailing Address: P.O. Box 151, Vansant, VA 24656 US
Second Address: PO Box 1867, Abingdon, VA 24212
(276) 676-3806, (888) 275-9534; *Fax:* (276) 676-3572
www.livingfaithtv.com
info@livingfaithtv.com
License: Harlan, Harlan County, KY held by Living Faith Ministries Inc
Nat'l Network: IND
Michael Smith, CEO
Lisa Smith, CFO
Sheila Stanley, Account VP

Lexington, KY (DMA 63)

WDKY-TV *Digital Channel:* 31; *Virtual Channel:* 56; 1000 kw; 1155 ft.; N37 52 51 W84 19 16
836 Euclid Ave., Suite 201, Lexington, KY 40502 US
(859) 269-5656; *Fax:* (859) 269-3774
www.foxlexington.com
License: Danville, Boyle County, KY held by WDKY Licensee LLC
Group Owner: Sinclair Broadcast Group Inc.; (acq 1996; $63 million with KOCB(TV) Oklahoma City, OK).; *Washington Law Firm:* Fisher, Wayland, Cooper, Leader & Zaragoza
Nat'l Network: FOX; *Nat'l Reps:* Millennium Sales & Marketing
Hours of Local News Weekly: news progmg 7 hrs wkly
Ronna Corrente, General Manager
Kevin Neumann, Regional Sales Manager
Dave Kollar, Chief Engineer

***WKHA** *Digital Channel:* 16; *Virtual Channel:* 35; 53.2 kw; 1211 ft.; N37 11 35 W83 11 17
600 Cooper Drive, Lexington, KY 40502 US
(859) 258-7000, (800) 432-0951; *Fax:* (859) 258-7399
www.ket.org
help@ket.org
License: Hazard, Perry County, KY held by Kentucky Authority for Educational TV
Nat'l Network: PBS; *Regional Network:* Kentucky Educational Television
Mike Brower, Operations Dir
Malcolm Wall, Station Manager
Craig Cornwell, Senior Director, Programming
Tim Bischoff, Promotions Manager
Shae Hopkins, Executive Director
Tim Bischoff, Senior Director, Marketing and OnlineContent
Mike Brower, Senior Director, Production Operations
Nancy Carpenter, Senior Director, Education
Fred Engel, Senior Director, Technology
Linda Hume, Senior Director, Finance and Administration

***WKLE** *Digital Channel:* 42; *Virtual Channel:* 46; 45.8 kw; 845 ft.; N37 52 45 W84 19 33
600 Cooper Drive, Lexington, KY 40502 US
(859) 258-7000, (800) 432-0951; *Fax:* (859) 258-7399
www.ket.org
help@ket.org
License: Lexington, Fayette County, KY held by Kentucky Authority for Educational TV
Washington Law Firm: Kenkel, Barnard & Edmundson
Nat'l Network: PBS; *Regional Network:* Kentucky Educational Television
Malcolm Wall, Station Manager
Craig Cornwell, Senior Director, Programming
Shae Hopkins, Executive Director
Tim Bischoff, Senior Director, Marketing and Online Content
Mike Brower, Senior Director, Production Operations
NancyCarpenter, Senior Director, Education
Fred Engel, Senior Director, Technology
Linda Hume, Senior Director, Finance and Administration

***WKMR** *Digital Channel:* 15; *Virtual Channel:* 38; 51.4 kw; 948 ft.; N38 10 38 W83 24 17
600 Cooper Drive, Lexington, KY 40502 US
(859) 258-7000, (800) 432-0951; *Fax:* (859) 258-7399
www.ket.org
help@ket.org
License: Morehead, Rowan County, KY held by Kentucky Authority for Educational TV
Nat'l Network: PBS; *Regional Network:* Kentucky Educational Television
Mike Brower, Operations Dir
Malcolm Wall, Station Manager
Craig Cornwell, Senior Director, Programming
Tim Bischoff, Promotions Manager
Shae Hopkins, Executive Director
Tim Bischoff, Senior Director, Marketing and OnlineContent
Mike Brower, Senior Director, Production Operations
Nancy Carpenter, Senior Director, Education
Fred Engel, Senior Director, Technology
Linda Hume, Senior Director, Finance and Administration

***WKSO-TV** *Digital Channel:* 14; *Virtual Channel:* 29; 53.3 kw; 1407 ft.; N37 10 3 W84 49 30
600 Cooper Dr., Lexington, KY 40502 US
(859) 258-7000, (800) 432-0951; *Fax:* (606) 258-7399
www.ket.org
help@ket.org
License: Somerset, Casey County, KY held by Kentucky Authority for Educational TV
Nat'l Network: PBS; *Regional Network:* Kentucky Educational Television
Mike Brower, Operations Dir
Malcolm Wall, Station Manager
Craig Cornwell, Senior Director, Programming
Tim Bischoff, Promotions Manager
Shae Hopkins, Executive Director
Tim Bischoff, Senior Director, Marketing and OnlineContent
Mike Brower, Senior Director, Production Operations
Nancy Carpenter, Senior Director, Education
Fred Engel, Senior Director, Technology
Linda Hume, Senior Director, Finance and Administration

WKYT *Digital Channel:* 36; *Virtual Channel:* 27; 1,510 kw vis, 151 kw aur; ant 984t/992g; N38 02 22 W84 24 11; *Population Served:* 871,000
2851 Winchester Rd., Lexington, KY 40509
(859) 299-0411
www.wkyt.com
newstip@wkyt.com
License: Lexington, Fayette County, KY held by Gray Television Licensee LLC
Group Owner: Gray Television Inc.; (acq 1-21-76; *Washington Law Firm:* Venable, Baetjer, Howard & Civiletti
Nat'l Network: CBS; *Nat'l Reps:* Harrington, Righter & Parsons; *Wire Services:* AP
Size of News Staff: 50; *Hours of Local News Weekly:* news progmg 43 hrs wkly
Mike Kanarek, Operations
Chris Mossman, General Manager
Kevin Kidd, Broadcast Sales
Kellen Dargle, Promotions
Robert Thomas, News Director

WLEX-TV *Digital Channel:* 39; *Virtual Channel:* 18; 475 kw; 938 ft.; N38 2 3 W84 23 39
Mailing Address: P.O. Box 1457, Lexington, KY 40588-1457 US
Second Address: 1065A Russell Cave Rd., Lexington, KY 40505
(859) 259-1818; *Fax:* (859) 254-2217
www.lex18.com
news@lex18.com
License: Lexington, Fayette County, KY held by WLEX Communications LLC
Group Owner: Cordillera Communications Inc.; (acq 7-8-99; $99.1 million); *Washington Law Firm:* Dow, Lohnes PLLC
Nat'l Network: NBC; Me-TV
Pat Dalbey, General Manager
Chris Fedele, Director of Sales
Trish Simkins, Creative Services Director
Gail Branham, Local Sales Manager

WLJC-TV *Digital Channel:* 7; *Virtual Channel:* 65; 185 kw; 1055 ft.; N37 36 47 W83 40 18
P.O. Box Y, 219 WLJC Drive, Beattyville, KY 41311 US
(606) 464-3600; *Fax:* (606) 464-5021
www.wljc.com
wljc@wljc.com
License: Beattyville, Lee County, KY held by Hour of Harvest Inc
Washington Law Firm: Fletcher, Heald & Hildreth
Nat'l Network: REL; *Nat'l Reps:* Rgnl Reps
Margaret Drake, President
Rachel Bogale, Operations Dir
Jonathan Drake, General Manager
Kim Mitchell, General Sales Mgr
Allan Mulford, Chief Engineer
Margaret Drake, Host

WTVQ-TV *Digital Channel:* 27; *Virtual Channel:* 36; 487 kW; 935 ft; N38 02 03 W84 23 39; *Population Served:* 1,981,200
6940 Man O'War Blvd, Lexington, KY 40509 USA
(859) 204-3636; *Fax:* (859) 293-5002
www.wtvq.com
news36@wtvq.com
License: Lexington, Fayette County, KY held by WTVQ-TV, LLC
Group Owner: Morris Multimedia Inc.; (acq 5-13-2008; $16.5 million); *Washington Law Firm:* Fletcher, Heald & Hildreth
Nat'l Network: ABC; My Netwrok TV; Antenna TV; *Nat'l Reps:* Telerep; *Wire Services:* UPI
Size of News Staff: 25; *Hours of Local News Weekly:* news progmg 27 hrs wkly

WYMT *Digital Channel:* 12; *Virtual Channel:* 57; 50 kw; 1304 ft.; N37 11 38 W83 10 52
199 Black Gold Blvd., Hazard, KY 41701 USA
(606) 436-5757
www.wkyt.com/wymt/home
newstip@wymtnews.com
License: Hazard, Perry County, KY held by Gray Television Licensee LLC
Group Owner: Gray Television Inc.; (acq 9-2-94).
Nat'l Network: CBS; *Nat'l Reps:* Harrington, Righter & Parsons
Size of News Staff: 15
Neil Middleton, General Manager
Morrison Stepp, Sales Manager
Kelly Allen, Promotions
Steven Hensley, News Director
Phil Hayes, Chief Engineer

Louisville, KY (DMA 49)

WAVE *Digital Channel:* 47; *Virtual Channel:* 3; 1000 kw; 1286 ft.; N38 22 8 W85 49 48
Mailing Address: PO Box 32970, Louisville, KY 40232 US
Second Address: 725 S. Floyd St., Louisville, KY 40203
(502) 585-2201, (502) 561-4150; *Fax:* (502) 561-4115, (502) 561-4105
www.wave3.com
newsrelease@wave3.com
License: Louisville, Jefferson County, KY held by WAVE License Subsidiary LLC.
Group Owner: Raycom Media Inc.; (acq 1-31-2006; grpsl);
Washington Law Firm: Covington & Burling
Nat'l Network: NBC; *Nat'l Reps:* Harrington, Righter & Parsons
Steve Langford, General Manager
Nick Ulmer, Station Manager
Dan Foos, Programming Director
Bob Mack, Promotions Manager
Jim Sears, Chief Engineer
Shannon Cogan, Anchor
Scott Reynolds, Anchor
Theo Keith, Reporter
RogerDunaway, Photojournalist
Kevin Harned, Chief Meterologist
Kent Taylor, SportsStaff

WBKI-TV *Digital Channel:* 19; *Virtual Channel:* 34; 1000 kw; 1119 ft.; N37 31 51 W85 26 45
624 W. Muhammad Ali Blvd, Louisville, KY 40203 US
(502) 809-3400; *Fax:* (502) 589-5559
www.wbki.tv/
Feedback@wbki.tv
License: Campbellsville, Taylor County, KY held by WBKISLG LLC.
(acq 6-9-2000); *Ownership:* Cascade Broadcasting Group L.L.C., 100%; *Washington Law Firm:* Shaw Pittman

Nat'l Network: CW; *Nat'l Reps:* Harrington, Righter & Parsons
Lynn Martin, President
Craig Hoffman, Operations Dir
Bill Lane, General Manager
Trevor Crouch, Station Administrator
Tom Vickery, Local Sales Manager
Harry Beam, Director of Programming & Operations
Joshua Hawkins, PromotionsCoordinator
David Smith, Chief Engineer
Steve Ballard, CFO
David Callan, Director of Production
Libby Wilcoxson, Traffic Manager
Kim Bauerla, Director of Human Resources
Joseph Phelps, Creative Services Poducer
Phillip Pennington,Editor/Producer - Creative Services

WBNA *Digital Channel:* 8; *Virtual Channel:* 21; 27 kw; 656 ft.; N38 1 59 W85 45 17
Mailing Address: P. O. Box 19859, Louisville, KY 40259 US
Second Address: 3701 Fern Valley Rd., Louisville, KY 40219
(502) 964-2121
License: Louisville, Jefferson County, KY held by Word Broadcasting Network Inc.
Group Owner: Word Broadcasting Network Inc.; *Washington Law Firm:* Pepper & Corazzini
Nat'l Network: ION
Tom Fawbush, General Manager
Calvin Bader, Chief Engineer

WDRB *Digital Channel:* 49; *Virtual Channel:* 41; 1000 kw; 1281 ft.; N38 21 0 W85 50 57
624 W. Muhammad Ali Blvd., Louisville, KY 40203 US
(502) 584-6441; *Fax:* (502) 584-7004
www.wdrb.com
news@wdrb.com
License: Louisville, Jefferson County, KY held by Independence Television Co.
Group Owner: Block Communications Inc.; (acq 3-84; $10 million; *Washington Law Firm:* Dow, Lohnes & Albertson
Nat'l Network: FOX; *Nat'l Reps:* TeleRep
Size of News Staff: 45; *Hours of Local News Weekly:* news progmg 56.5 hrs wkly
Harry Beam, Director, Programming and Operations
Marti Hazel, Vice President and Director of Sales
Ray Foushee, Director of Marketing, Research and Publicity
Rick Burrice, Local Sales Manager
Shahara Ross, National Sales Manager
LaVerne Pike, National Sales Coordinator
Lindsey Braun, Account Executive
Glenn Davis, Account Executive
Bailey Wilson, Account Manager

WHAS-TV *Digital Channel:* 11; *Virtual Channel:* 11; 16.4 kw; 1,286 ft.; N38 21 23 W85 50 52
502 West Chestnut, Louisville, KY 40202 US
(502) 582-7711; *Fax:* (502) 582-7279
www.whas11.com
assign@whas11.com
License: Louisville, Jefferson County, KY held by Sander Operating Co. I LLC dba WHAS Television
Group Owner: Sander Media LLC; (acq 12-23-2013).;
Washington Law Firm: Covington & Burling
Nat'l Network: ABC
Hours of Local News Weekly: news progmg 39.5 hrs wkly
Linda Danna, President and General Manager
Brian Ahladas, Director of Sales
Kirk Szesny, Director of Marketing and Creative Services
David Seals, News Director
Bill Brown, Chief Engineer

***WKMJ-TV** *Digital Channel:* 38; 1,170 kw vis, 230 kw aur; 835t/550g; N38 22 02 W85 49 53
600 Cooper Drive, Lexington, KY 40502 US
(859) 258-7000, (800) 432-0951; *Fax:* (859) 258-7399
www.ket.org
help@ket.org
License: Louisville, Jefferson County, KY held by Kentucky Authority for Educational TV
Nat'l Network: PBS; *Regional Network:* Kentucky Educational Television
Mike Brower, Operations Dir
Malcolm Wall, Station Manager
Craig Cornwell, Senior Director, Programming
Tim Bischoff, Promotions Manager
Shae Hopkins, Executive Director
Tim Bischoff, Senior Director, Marketing and OnlineContent
Mike Brower, Senior Director, Production Operations
Nancy Carpenter, Senior Director, Education
Fred Engel, Senior Director, Technology
Linda Hume, Senior Director, Finance and Administration

***WKPC-TV** *Digital Channel:* 17; *Virtual Channel:* 15; 60.3 kw; 778 ft.; N38 22 1 W85 49 54
600 Cooper Drive, Lexington, KY 40502 US
(859) 258-7000, (800) 432-0951; *Fax:* (859) 258-7399
www.ket.org
help@ket.org
License: Louisville, Jefferson County, KY held by Kentucky Authority for Educational Television
Washington Law Firm: Schwartz, Woods & Miller
Nat'l Network: PBS; *Regional Network:* Kentucky Educational Television
Mike Brower, Operations Dir
Malcolm Wall, Station Manager
Craig Cornwell, Senior Director, Programming
Tim Bischoff, Promotions Manager
Shae Hopkins, Executive Director
Tim Bischoff, Senior Director, Marketing and OnlineContent
Mike Brower, Senior Director, Production Operations
Nancy Carpenter, Senior Director, Education
Fred Engel, Senior Director, Technology
Linda Hume, Senior Director, Finance and Administration

***WKZT-TV** *Digital Channel:* 43; *Virtual Channel:* 23; 61 kw; 584 ft.; N37 40 55 W85 50 31
600 Cooper Dr., Lexington, KY 40502 US
(859) 258-7000, (800) 432-0951; *Fax:* (859) 258-7399
www.ket.org
help@ket.org
License: Elizabethtown, Hardin County, KY held by Kentucky Authority for Educational TV
Nat'l Network: PBS; *Regional Network:* Kentucky Educational Television
Mike Brower, Operations Dir
Malcolm Wall, Station Manager
Craig Cornwell, Senior Director, Programming
Tim Bischoff, Promotions Manager
Shae Hopkins, Executive Director
Tim Bischoff, Senior Director, Marketing and OnlineContent
Mike Brower, Senior Director, Production Operations
Nancy Carpenter, Senior Director, Education
Fred Engel, Senior Director, Technology
Linda Hume, Senior Director, Finance and Administration

WLKY *Digital Channel:* 26; *Virtual Channel:* 32; 4,300 kw vis, 430 kw aur; 1,260t/989g; N38 22 10 W85 50 02
1918 Mellwood Ave., Louisville, KY 40206-1035
(502) 893-3671,(502) 893-7300,(502) 571-7332; *Fax:* (502) 897-2384,(502) 896-0725
www.wlky.com
License: Louisville, Jefferson County, KY held by Hearst Properties Inc.
Group Owner: Hearst Television Inc.; (acq 3-18-99; grpsl);
Washington Law Firm: Brooks, Pierce, McLendon, Humphrey & Leonard
Nat'l Network: CBS; *Wire Services:* UPI
Hours of Local News Weekly: News progmg 37.5 hrs wkly
Glenn Haygood, President
Glenn Haygood, General Manager
Greg Baird, General Sales Mgr
Debbie Roberson, Program Coordinator
Michael Neelly, News Director
Bill Greep, Engineering Dir

Paducah, KY-Cape Girardeau, MO-Harrisburg-Mount Vernon, IL (DMA 83)

WDKA *Digital Channel:* 49; *Virtual Channel:* 49; 1000 kw; 1073 ft.; N37 23 42 W88 56 23
806 Enterprise, Cape Giradeau, MO 63703 US
(573) 334-1223; *Fax:* (573) 334-1208
www.mywdka.com
closedcaptioning@mywdka.com
License: Paducah, McCracken County, KY held by WDKA Acquisition Corp
Nat'l Network: MYTV
Rob Chronister, Operations Dir
Tom Tipton, General Manager
Jennifer Chronister, General Sales Mgr
Alan Muster, Programming Director
Chuck Moffitt, Promotions Manager
Chris Girard, Chief Engineer
Glenn Ralston, National SalesManager

***WKMU** *Digital Channel:* 36; *Virtual Channel:* 21; 56.9 kw; 614 ft.; N36 41 34 W88 32 11
600 Cooper Drive, Lexington, KY 40502 US
(859) 258-7000, (800) 432-0951; *Fax:* (859) 258-7399
www.ket.org
help@ket.org
License: Murray, Calloway County, KY held by Kentucky Authority for Educational TV
Nat'l Network: PBS; *Regional Network:* Kentucky Educational Television
Mike Brower, Operations Dir
Malcolm Wall, Station Manager
Craig Cornwell, Senior Director, Programming
Tim Bischoff, Promotions Manager
Shae Hopkins, Executive Director
Tim Bischoff, Senior Director, Marketing and OnlineContent
Mike Brower, Senior Director, Production Operations
Nancy Carpenter, Senior Director, Education
Fred Engel, Senior Director, Technology
Linda Hume, Senior Director, Finance and Administration

***WKPD** *Digital Channel:* 41; *Virtual Channel:* 29; 55.7 kw; 469 ft.; N37 5 39 W88 40 20
600 Cooper Drive, Lexington, KY 40502 US
(859) 258-7000, (800) 432-0951; *Fax:* (859) 258-7399
www.ket.org
help@ket.org
License: Paducah, McCracken County, KY held by Kentucky Authority for Educational TV
(acq 2-28-78).; *Washington Law Firm:* Kenkel, Barnard & Edmundson
Nat'l Network: PBS; *Regional Network:* Kentucky Educational Television
Mike Brower, Operations Dir
Malcolm Wall, Station Manager
Craig Cornwell, Senior Director, Programming
Tim Bischoff, Promotions Manager
Shae Hopkins, Executive Director
Tim Bischoff, Senior Director, Marketing and OnlineContent
Mike Brower, Senior Director, Production Operations
Nancy Carpenter, Senior Director, Education
Fred Engel, Senior Director, Technology
Linda Hume, Senior Director, Finance and Administration

WPSD-TV *Digital Channel:* 32; *Virtual Channel:* 6; 906 kw; 1614 ft.; N37 11 31 W88 58 53
Mailing Address: 100 Television Lane, Paducah, KY 42003 US
Second Address: 100 Television Ln., Paducah, KY 42003
(270) 415-1900, (270) 415-2001; *Fax:* (270) 415-1981,(270) 415-1995
www.wpsdlocal6.com
newstip@wpsdlocal6.com
License: Paducah, McCracken County, KY held by WPSD-TV LLC
(acq 12-3-01).; *Washington Law Firm:* Covington & Burling
Nat'l Network: NBC; *Nat'l Reps:* Continental Television Sales
Size of News Staff: 49; *Hours of Local News Weekly:* news progmg 23 hrs wkly
Richard Paxton, President
Bill Evans, Operations Dir
David Jernigan, General Sales Mgr
Cathy Crecelius, Promotions Manager
Griff Potter, News Director
Joey Gill, Chief Engineer
Mark Hall, Operations Manager
Carolyn Fox,Regional Sales Manager

Louisiana

Alexandria, LA (DMA 179)

KALB *Digital Channel:* 35; *Virtual Channel:* 5; 820 kw; 1578 ft.; N31 2 15 W92 29 45
605 Washington St., Alexandria, LA 71301 USA
(318) 445-2456
www.kalb.com
news@kalb.com
License: Alexandria, Rapides County, LA held by Gray Television Licensee LLC
Group Owner: Gray Television Inc.; *Washington Law Firm:* Akin Gump Strauss Hauer & Feld LLP
Nat'l Network: NBC; CBS
Phillip Taylor, Operations Manager
Michele Godard, General Manager
Herbert Bruce, General Sales Mgr
Vernilla Brooks, Programming Manager
Mark Klein, Promotions Manager
Keith Weiss, News Director

KBCA *Digital Channel:* 41; *Virtual Channel:* 41; 1000 kw; 993 ft.; N30 54 17 W92 37 28
1107 Marie Antoinette, Lafayette, LA 70506 US
(337) 896-1600; *Fax:* (337) 896-2695
License: Alexandria, Rapides County, LA held by Wilderness Communications LLC.

Group Owner: Wilderness Communications LLC; (acq 4-1-2006); *Washington Law Firm:* Fletcher, Heald & Hildreth
Nat'l Network: CW; *Nat'l Reps:* Roslin Television Sales
Charles Chatelain, President
Eddie Blanchard, General Manager
John Rockweiler, Sales Manager

KLAX-TV *Digital Channel:* 31; *Virtual Channel:* 31; 200 kW; 1093 ft.; N31 33 55 W92 33 0
1811 England Dr, Alexandria, LA 71303 USA
(318) 473-0031
klax-tv.com
License: Alexandria, Rapides County, LA held by Pollack/Belz Communication Co. Inc.
Group Owner: Pollack Broadcasting Co.; (acq 6-3-88; $1.1 million); *Washington Law Firm:* Wood, Maines & Brown
Nat'l Network: ABC
Size of News Staff: 4; *Hours of Local News Weekly:* news progmg 5.5 hrs wkly

***KLPA-TV** *Digital Channel:* 26; *Virtual Channel:* 25; 500 kw; 1355 ft.; N31 33 56.4 W92 32 50.5
7733 Perkins Rd, Baton Rouge, LA 70810 US
(225) 767-5660, (800) 272-8161, (800)-973-7246; *Fax:* (225) 767-4288
www.lpb.org
bawilliams@lpb.org
License: Alexandria, Rapides County, LA held by Louisiana Educational Television Authority
Washington Law Firm: Schwartz, Woods & Miller
Nat'l Network: PBS
Beth Courtney, CEO/President
William Woodside Jr, Operations
Steve Graziano, General Manager
Jason Viso, Programming Director
Bob Neese, Promotions Manager
Randy Ward, Engineering Director
Bill Belson, Chief Administrativeofficer
Candace Morgan, Human Resources Director
Ken Miller, Production Manager
Joanne Gaudet, Director,Business
John Tooraen, IT& Web Manager
C.C. Copeland, Asst Director of Engineering-Operations

Baton Rouge, LA (DMA 93)

KZUP-CD *Digital Channel:* 20; *Virtual Channel:* 20; 1000 kw; N30 19 35 W91 16 36; *Population Served:* 773,400
10000 Perkins Rd., Baton Rouge, LA 70810 US
(225) 768-2980; *Fax:* (225) 768-9284
www.brproud.com
License: Baton Rouge, LA held by Knight Broadcasting of Baton Rouge License Corp.
Group Owner: White Knight Holdings Inc.; (acq 1996; $23.975 million); *Washington Law Firm:* Pillsbury, Winthrop, Shaw & Pittman LLP
Nat'l Network: NBC
Size of News Staff: 3; *Hours of Local News Weekly:* news progmg 6 hrs wkly
Drew Balch, Station Manager

WAFB *Digital Channel:* 9; *Virtual Channel:* 9; 5.57 kw; 1677 ft.; N30 21 58 W91 12 47
Mailing Address: Rsa Tower, 20th Floor, 201 Monroe Street, Montgomery, AL 36104 US
Second Address: 844 Government Stree, Baton Rouge, LA 70802
(225) 383-9999; *Fax:* (225) 379-7891,TWX: 510-993-3406
www.wafb.com
news@wafb.com
License: Baton Rouge, East Baton Rouge County, LA held by WAFB License Subsidiary LLC.
Group Owner: Raycom Media Inc.; (acq 12-31-96; grpsl).; *Washington Law Firm:* Covington & Burling
Nat'l Network: CBS; *Nat'l Reps:* Harrington, Righter & Parsons
Sandy Breland, General Manager
Vicki Kellum, General Sales Mgr
Brent Ledet, Promotions Manager
Robb Hays, News Director
Dale Russell, Chief Engineer
Ellen Salmon, Regional Sales Manager
Tommy Doherty, National Sales Manager
Ellen Salmon, Local Sales Manager
Robert Bienvenu, Internet Sales Director
Brent Ledet, Creative Services Director
Amber Stegall, Digital Content Director

WBRL-CD *Digital Channel:* 21; *Virtual Channel:* 21; 3,871 kw vis; ant 1,164t; N30 19 35 W91 16 36; *Population Served:* 710,500
10000 Perkins Rd., Baton Rouge, LA 70810 US
(225) 766-3233
www.brproud.com
License: Baton Rouge, East Baton Rouge County, LA held by Nexstar Broadcasting, Inc.
Group Owner: Nexstar Broadcasting Group; (acq 2-13-95; *Washington Law Firm:* Fletcher, Heald & Hildreth
Nat'l Network: Fox
Jim Baronet, General Manager
Gary Wordlaw, News Director

WBRZ-TV *Digital Channel:* 13; *Virtual Channel:* 2; 30 kW; 1624 ft; N30 17 49 W91 11 37; *Rebroadcasting:* DTV 2.2-News, DTV 2.3-Weather; *Population Served:* 723,000
PO Box 2906, Baton Rouge, LA 70821
(225) 387-2222; *Fax:* (225) 336-2246
www.wbrz.com
License: Baton Rouge, East Baton Rouge County, LA held by Louisiana Television Broadcasting LLC
Group Owner: Manship Family; (acq 1958; $548,000).; *Washington Law Firm:* Pillsbury
Nat'l Network: ABC; *Nat'l Reps:* Petry Television Inc.
Size of News Staff: 62; *Hours of Local News Weekly:* 30.5
Rocky Daboval, General Manager

WGMB-TV *Digital Channel:* 45; 3,871 kw vis; ant 1,164t; N30 19 35 W91 16 36; *Population Served:* 710,500
10000 Perkins Rd., Baton Rouge, LA 70810 US
(225) 766-3233
www.brproud.com
License: Baton Rouge, East Baton Rouge County, LA held by Nexstar Broadcasting, Inc.
Group Owner: Nexstar Broadcasting Group; (acq 2-13-95; *Washington Law Firm:* Fletcher, Heald & Hildreth
Nat'l Network: Fox
Jim Baronet, General Manager
Gary Wordlaw, News Director

***WLPB-TV** *Digital Channel:* 25; *Virtual Channel:* 27; 355 kw; 1013 ft.; N30 22 22 W91 12 16
7733 Perkins Rd, Baton Rouge, LA 70810 US
(225) 767-5660,(800) 272-8161; *Fax:* (225) 767-4299
beta.lpb.org/index.php/
License: Baton Rouge, East Baton Rouge County, LA held by Louisiana Educational Television Authority
Washington Law Firm: Schwartz, Woods & Miller
Nat'l Network: PBS
Foreign Language Programming; Size of News Staff: 3; *Hours of Local News Weekly:* news progmg one hr wkly
Beth Courtney, President & CEO
Bob Graziano, General Manager
Jason Viso, Director of Programming
Bob Neese, Promotions Manager
Randy Ward, Engineering Dir
Bill Belsom, Chief Administrative Offier
Joanne Gaudet, Director,Business
Donna LaFleur, Production Director
Nancy R. Tooraen, Educational Technology Specialist
Christina Melton, Special Projects Producer
Tika Laudun, Senior Producer

WVLA-TV *Digital Channel:* 34; 1000 kw; N30 19 35 W91 16 36; *Population Served:* 773,400
10000 Perkins Rd., Baton Rouge, LA 70810 US
(225) 768-2980; *Fax:* (225) 768-9284
www.brproud.com
License: Baton Rouge, LA held by Knight Broadcasting of Baton Rouge License Corp.
Group Owner: White Knight Holdings Inc.; (acq 1996; $23.975 million); *Washington Law Firm:* Pillsbury, Winthrop, Shaw & Pittman LLP
Nat'l Network: NBC
Size of News Staff: 3; *Hours of Local News Weekly:* news progmg 6 hrs wkly
Drew Balch, Station Manager

Lafayette, LA (DMA 120)

KADN-TV *Digital Channel:* 16; 2,630 kw vis, 231 kw aur; ant 1,181t/1,282g; N30 21 44 W92 12 53; *Population Served:* 650,000
1500 Eraste Landry Rd., Lafayette, LA 70506 US
(337) 237-1500
www.kadn.com
contactus@kadn.com
License: Lafayette, Lafayette County, LA held by Nexstar Broadcasting, Inc.
Group Owner: Nexstar Broadcasting Group.; (acq 12-9-2004; $13,125,000).; *Washington Law Firm:* Fletcher, Heald & Hildreth
Nat'l Network: Fox
Foreign Language Programming
Tom Poehler, General Manager
Sean Trcalek, General Sales Mgr

KATC *Digital Channel:* 28; *Virtual Channel:* 3; 1000 kw; 1,762 ft.; N30 19 25 W92 17 24
1103 Eraste Landry Rd., Lafayette, LA 70506 US
(337) 235-3333; *Fax:* (225) 791-8810
www.katc.com
recep@katctv.com
License: Lafayette, Lafayette County, LA held by KATC Communications Inc.
Group Owner: Cordillera Communications Inc.; (acq 1995; $24.5 million); *Washington Law Firm:* Dow, Lohnes
Nat'l Network: ABC; *Nat'l Reps:* Continental Television Sales;
Wire Services: AP; CNN
Size of News Staff: 45; *Hours of Local News Weekly:* news progmg 19.5 hrs wkly
Andrew D. Shenkan, General Manager
Mike Zikmund, National/Regional Sales Manager
Arte Richard, Marketing Director
Letitia Walker, News Director
Don Mouton, Chief Engineer
Kelly Garrett, Online Director

KLAF-LD *Digital Channel:* 46; 2,630 kw vis, 231 kw aur; ant 1,181t/1,282g; N30 21 44 W92 12 53; *Population Served:* 650,000
1500 Eraste Landry Rd., Lafayette, LA 70506 US
(337) 237-1500
www.cajunfirst.com
contactus@kadn.com
License: Lafayette, Lafayette County, LA held by Nexstar Broadcasting, Inc.
Group Owner: Nexstar Broadcasting Group.; (acq 12-9-2004; $13,125,000).; *Washington Law Firm:* Fletcher, Heald & Hildreth
Nat'l Network: Fox
Foreign Language Programming
Tom Poehler, General Manager
Sean Trcalek, General Sales Mgr

KLFY-TV *Digital Channel:* 10; *Virtual Channel:* 10; 20.3 kw; 1729 ft.; N30 19 19 W92 16 59
Mailing Address: PO Box 90665, Lafayette, LA 70509 US
Second Address: 1808 Eraste Landry Rd, Lafayette, LA 70509
(337) 981-4823, (337) 981-4844; *Fax:* (337) 984-8323, (337) 981-6533
www.klfy.com
tip10@klfy.com
License: Lafayette, Lafayette County, LA held by Young Broadcasting of Louisiana Inc.
Group Owner: Young Broadcasting Inc.; (acq 5-28-88; $51 million; *Washington Law Firm:* Brooks, Pierce
Nat'l Network: CBS; *Nat'l Reps:* Adam Young
Foreign Language Programming; Size of News Staff: 24; *Hours of Local News Weekly:* news progmg 14 hrs wkly
Nanette Lavergne, Operations Director/Station Manager
Mike Barras, General Manager
Spencer Bienvenu, General Sales Mgr
Chris Cook, Marketing & Promotions Director
Dwight Dugas, News Director
Rodney Evans, Chief Engineer
CarolynChretien, Traffic Manager
Brett Judice, Production Manager
Devin Bayliss, Webmaster

***KLPA-TV** *Digital Channel:* 23; *Virtual Channel:* 24; 50 kw; 1520 ft.; N30 19 19 W92 16 58
7733 Perkins Rd, Baton Rouge, LA 70810 US
(225) 767-5660, (800) 272-8161, (800)-973-7246; *Fax:* (225) 767-4288
www.lpb.org
bawilliams@lpb.org
License: Lafayette, Lafayette County, LA held by Louisiana Educational Television Authority
Washington Law Firm: Schwartz, Woods & Miller
Nat'l Network: PBS
Beth Courtney, CEO/President
William Woodside Jr, Operations
Steve Graziano, General Manager
Jason Viso, Programming Director
Bob Neese, Promotions Manager
Randy Ward, Engineering Director
Bill Belson, Chief Administrativeofficer
Candace Morgan, Human Resources Director
Ken Miller, Production Manager
Joanne Gaudet, Director,Business
John Tooraen, IT& Web Manager
C.C. Copeland, Asst Director of Engineering-Operations

KLWB *Digital Channel:* 50; *Virtual Channel:* 50; 1000 kw; 995 ft.; N30 20 32 W91 57 46

516 St. Landry Street, Lafayette, LA 70506 US
(337) 896-1600; *Fax:* (337) 896-2695
License: New Iberia, Iberia County, LA held by Wilderness Communications LLC.
Group Owner: Wilderness Communications LLC; (acq 8-1-2006).; *Washington Law Firm:* Fletcher, Heald & Hildreth
Nat'l Network: CW; *Nat'l Reps:* Roslin Television Sales
Eddie Blanchard, General Manager
Dave Pierce, General Sales Mgr
Layla Mouton, Programming Director

Lake Charles, LA (DMA 174)

***KLPA-TV** *Digital Channel:* 20; *Virtual Channel:* 18; 131.4 kw; 981 ft.; N30 23 46 W93 0 3
7733 Perkins Rd, Baton Rouge, LA 70810 US
(225) 767-5660, (800) 272-8161, (800)-973-7246; *Fax:* (225) 767-4288
www.lpb.org
bawilliams@lpb.org
License: Lake Charles, Calcasieu County, LA held by Louisiana Educational Television Authority
Washington Law Firm: Schwartz, Woods & Miller
Nat'l Network: PBS
Beth Courtney, CEO/President
William Woodside Jr, Operations
Steve Graziano, General Manager
Jason Viso, Programming Director
Bob Neese, Promotions Manager
Randy Ward, Engineering Director
Bill Belson, Chief Administrativeofficer
Candace Morgan, Human Resources Director
Ken Miller, Production Manager
Joanne Gaudet, Director,Business
John Tooraen, IT& Web Manager
C.C. Copeland, Asst Director of Engineering-Operations

KPLC *Digital Channel:* 7; *Virtual Channel:* 7; 62 kw; 1480 ft.; N30 23 46 W93 0 3
Mailing Address: P.O. Box 1490, Lake Charles, LA 70601 US
Second Address: 320 Division St., Lake Charles, LA 70602
(337) 439-9071; *Fax:* (337) 437-7600
www.kplctv.com
jserra@kplctv.com
License: Lake Charles, Calcasieu County, LA held by KPLC License Subsidiary LLC.
Group Owner: Raycom Media Inc.; (acq 1-31-2006; grpsl);
Washington Law Firm: Covington & Burling LP
Nat'l Network: NBC; *Nat'l Reps:* Harrington, Righter & Parsons
Size of News Staff: 37
Dianna Mayo, Operations Dir
Jim Serra, General Manager
John Ware, General Sales Mgr
Agnes DeRouen, Programming Director
Scott Flannagan, News Director
Frank Brucks, Chief Engineer
Veronica Bilbo, EEO Coordinator
RobinDaugereau, Programming Director
Mari Wilson, Public Service Director
Bridget Courtney, Traffic Manager
John Bridges, Anchor
Britney Glaser, Anchor

KVHP *Digital Channel:* 30; *Virtual Channel:* 29; 1000 kw; 1033 ft.; N30 17 26 W93 34 35
129 West Prien Lake Road, Lake Charles, LA 70601 US
(337) 474-1316, (337) 477-1041; *Fax:* (337) 477-6795
www.watchfox.com
License: Lake Charles, Calcasieu County, LA held by National Communications Inc
(acq 10-3-96).; *Washington Law Firm:* Baraff, Koerner, Olender & Hochberg
Nat'l Network: FOX
Size of News Staff: 20; *Hours of Local News Weekly:* news progmg 9 hrs wkly
Carol Kalna, Operations Dir
Madelyn Bonnot, General Manager
Gary Mutchler, General Sales Mgr
Kim Anderson, Programming Director
Crystal Miller, Promotions Manager
Mark Ewing, Chief Engineer
Madelyn Bennet, General SalesManager
Paul Imbragulio, National Sales Manager
Mary Stevens, National Sales Manager
Robin Killmer, Traffic Manager

Monroe, LA-El Dorado, AR (DMA 137)

KAQY *Digital Channel:* 11; *Virtual Channel:* 11; 12.3 kw; 1699 ft.; N32 11 50 W92 4 14
Mailing Address: P.O. Box 2738, Monroe, LA 71207 US
Second Address: 3100 Sterlington Rd., Monroe, LA 71203
(318) 325-3011; *Fax:* (318) 327-7519
www.abc11.com
License: Columbia, Caldwell County, LA held by Monroe Broadcasting Inc
Nat'l Network: ABC
Joe Currie, General Manager
Carolyn Clampit, General Sales Mgr
Doug Ginn, Programming Director
Mike Halbrook, Promotions Manager
Pat O'Brien, Chief Engineer

KARD *Digital Channel:* 36; *Virtual Channel:* 14; 1000 kw; 1709 ft.; N32 5 42 W92 10 34
200 Pavilion Rd., West Monroe, LA 71292 US
(318) 323-1972
www.myarklamiss.com
License: West Monroe, Ouachita County, LA held by Nexstar Broadcasting, Inc.
Group Owner: Nexstar Broadcasting Group Inc.; (acq 12-31-03; grpsl).; *Washington Law Firm:* Arter & Hadden
Nat'l Network: FOX; *Nat'l Reps:* Continental Television Sales
Size of News Staff: 24; *Hours of Local News Weekly:* 22
Randy Stone, General Manager
Susie Cumpton, General Sales Mgr
John Walton, News Director

***KLPA-TV** *Digital Channel:* 13; *Virtual Channel:* 13; 17.2 kw; 1785 ft.; N32 11 50 W92 4 14
7733 Perkins Rd, Baton Rouge, LA 70810 US
(225) 767-5660, (800) 272-8161, (800)-973-7246; *Fax:* (225) 767-4288
www.lpb.org
bawilliams@lpb.org
License: Monroe, Ouachita County, LA held by Louisiana Educational Television Authority
Washington Law Firm: Schwartz, Woods & Miller
Nat'l Network: PBS
Beth Courtney, CEO/President
William Woodside Jr, Operations
Steve Graziano, General Manager
Jason Viso, Programming Director
Bob Neese, Promotions Manager
Randy Ward, Engineering Director
Bill Belson, Chief Administrativeofficer
Candace Morgan, Human Resources Director
Ken Miller, Production Manager
Joanne Gaudet, Director,Business
John Tooraen, IT& Web Manager
C.C. Copeland, Asst Director of Engineering-Operations

KMCT-TV *Digital Channel:* 38; *Virtual Channel:* 39; 14 kw; 472 ft.; N32 30 21 W92 8 55
701 Parkwood Dr, West Monroe, LA 71291 US
(318) 322-1399; *Fax:* (318) 323-3783
License: West Monroe, Ouachita County, LA held by Louisiana Christian Broadcasting Inc.
(acq 7-13-2004).; *Washington Law Firm:* Hardy, Chautin & Balkin
Nat'l Network: IND
Hours of Local News Weekly: News progmg 6 hrs wkly
Mike Reed, President
David Thompson, Chief Engineer

KMLU *Digital Channel:* 11; *Virtual Channel:* 11; 12.3 kw; 1699 ft.; N32 11 50 W92 4 14
805 Weightman St., Greenwood, MS 38930 US
(662) 822-1655
License: Columbia, LA held by Parker Broadcasting of Louisiana License, LLC
Group Owner: Legacy Broadcasting, LLC
Sherry Nelson, President

KNOE *Digital Channel:* 8; *Virtual Channel:* 8; 22.3 kw; 1890 ft.; N32 11 50 W92 4 14
1400 Oliver Rd., Monroe, LA 71201 USA
(318) 388-8888
www.knoe.com
news@knoe.com
License: Monroe, Ouachita County, LA held by Gray Television Licensee LLC
Group Owner: Gray Television Inc.; *Washington Law Firm:* Cohn & Marks
Nat'l Network: CBS; *Nat'l Reps:* Blair Television; *Wire Services:* CBS; AP; CNN
Size of News Staff: 28; *Hours of Local News Weekly:* news progmg 22 hrs wkly
Randy Minter, General Sales Mgr
Bob Walters, News Director

New Orleans, LA (DMA 50)

KGLA-AM *Digital Channel:* 42; 1,000 kw vis; ant 964t/964g; N29 58 41 W89 56 26
Box 50790, New Orleans, LA 70150
(504) 913-1540; *Fax:* (504) 340-4737
License: Hammond, Tangipahoa County, LA held by Mayavision Inc.
Nat'l Network: Telemundo (Spanish)
Foreign Language Programming
Ernesto Schweikert III, President

WDSU *Digital Channel:* 43; *Virtual Channel:* 6; 1000 kw; 938 ft.; N29 56 59 W89 57 28
846 Howard Avenue , New Orleans, LA 70113 US
(504) 679-0600; *Fax:* (504) 679-0745
www.wdsu.com
License: New Orleans, Orleans County, LA held by New Orleans Hearst Television Inc.
Group Owner: Hearst Television Inc.; (acq 1999; grpsl);
Washington Law Firm: Brooks, Pierce, McLendon, Humphrey & Leonard
Nat'l Network: NBC; *Nat'l Reps:* Eagle Television Sales; *Wire Services:* AP
Size of News Staff: 60; *Hours of Local News Weekly:* news progmg 32 hrs. wkly
Joel Vilmenay, President
Wendy Walters, General Sales Mgr
Joy Maurice, Programming Director
Joseph Schiltz, Promotions Manager
Johnathan Shelley, News Director
Chet Guillot, Chief Engineer
Frank Raterman, General SalesManager
Greg Turner, Research Director
Camille Whitworth, News Team
Scott Walker, News Team
Randi Rousseau, News Team
Sula Kim, News Team

WGNO *Digital Channel:* 26; *Virtual Channel:* 26; 1000 kw; 938 ft.; N29 56 59 W89 57 28
One Galleria Blvd., Suite 850, Metairie, LA 70001 USA
(504) 525-3838; *Fax:* (504) 569-0908
wgno.com
news@wgno.com
License: New Orleans, Orleans County, LA held by Tribune Television New Orleans Inc.
Group Owner: Tribune Media; (acq 12-20-2007; grpsl);
Washington Law Firm: Dow Lohnes PLLC
Nat'l Network: ABC; *Nat'l Reps:* TeleRep
John Cruse, General Manager
Rocky Daigle, Sales Manager
Rick Erbach, News Director
Rick Barber, Chief Engineer

WHNO *Digital Channel:* 21; *Virtual Channel:* 20; 300 kw; 833 ft.; N29 55 11 W90 1 29
839 St. Charles Avenue, Suite 309, New Orleans, LA 70130 US
(504) 681-0120, (800)-365-3732; *Fax:* (504) 681-0180
www.whno.com
whno@lesea.com
License: New Orleans, Orleans County, LA held by Le Sea Broadcasting Corp.
Group Owner: Le Sea Broadcasting
Nat'l Network: IND
Hours of Local News Weekly: News progmg 10 hrs wkly
Dean Powery, General Manager
David Vasquez, General Sales Mgr
Steve Warnecke, Programming Director
Bob Lawrence, Chief Engineer
Ivan Hinson, Senior Account Manager
Sue Bosio, Traffic Manager
Jennifer Nero, Office Manager/Asst. toGM
Adam Bandera, Production Coordinator
John Collins, Master Control Operator
Alex Michael, Account Manager

***WLAE-TV** *Digital Channel:* 31; *Virtual Channel:* 32; 200 kw; 899 ft.; N29 58 57 W89 57 9
3330 N. Causeway Blvd, Suite 345, Metairie, LA 70002 US
(504) 830-3700; *Fax:* (504) 840-9838
www.pbs.org/wlae
License: New Orleans, Orleans County, LA held by Educational Broadcasting Foundation Inc
Washington Law Firm: Marmet & McCombs

Nat'l Network: PBS
Foreign Language Programming
Ron Yager, General Manager
Barbara Wick, Programming Director

WNOL *Digital Channel:* 15; *Virtual Channel:* 38; 775 kw; 938 ft.; N29 56 59 W89 57 28
One Galleria Blvd., Suite 850, Metairie, LA 70001 USA
(504) 525-3838; *Fax:* (504) 569-0908
wgno.com
wnoltv@tribunemedia.com
License: New Orleans, Orleans County, LA held by Tribune Television New Orleans Inc.
Group Owner: Tribune Media
Nat'l Network: The CW Network; *Nat'l Reps:* MMT
John Cruse, General Manager
Larry Nuss, Sales Manager
Rick Erbach, News Director
Rick Barber, Chief Engineer

WPXL-TV *Digital Channel:* 49; 1000 kw; ant 945t/948g; N29 55 13 W90 01 28
3900 Veterans Memorial Blvd., Suite 202, Metairie, LA 70002 USA
(812) 335-1770; *Fax:* (504) 887-1518
www.iontelevision.com
License: New Orleans, LA held by Ion Media New Orleans License, Inc.
Group Owner: ION Media Networks Inc.
Ami Jenkins, Station Manager

WUPL *Digital Channel:* 24; *Virtual Channel:* 54; 1,000 kw; 892 ft.; N29 55 11 W90 1 29
1024 N. Rampart St., New Orleans, LA 70116 US
(504) 529-6298
www.wupltv.com
License: Slidell, St. Tammany County, LA held by Belo TV Inc.
Group Owner: Tegna Media
Nat'l Network: MyNetworkTV
Tod Smith, President and General Manager
Lourdes Keiffer, Local Sales Manager

WVUE-DT *Digital Channel:* 29; 316 kw vis, 31.6 kw aur; ant 990t/1,046g; N29 57 14 W89 56 58; *Population Served:* 1,648,000
1025 S. Jefferson Davis Pkwy., New Orleans, LA 70125
(504) 486-6161, (504) 483-1503; *Fax:* (504) 483-1543
www.fox8live.com
fox8news@fox8tv.net
License: New Orleans, Orleans County, LA held by Louisiana Media Co. LLC.
(acq 7-18-2008; $41 million); *Ownership:* Benson Football L.L.C.
Nat'l Network: Fox; *Nat'l Reps:* Harrington, Righter & Parsons
Size of News Staff: 54; *Hours of Local News Weekly:* news progmg 21 hrs wkly
Patrice Gunter, CFO
Joe Cook, General Manager
Johnny Faith, General Sales Mgr
Heidi Hoffmeister, Programming Dir.
Kelly Donnell, Promotions Manager
Mimi Strawn, News Director
Michelle Kehoe Ogden, National Sales Manager
ScottWilson, Regional Sales Manager
Wes cook, Interactive Manager
Jessica Burlet, Interactive Producer
Bebe Francis, Sales Dir.
Laura Burgmeyer, National/ Local Sales Asst.

WWL-TV *Digital Channel:* 36; *Virtual Channel:* 4; 1,000 kw; 1,020 ft.; N29 54 22 W90 2 22
1024 North Rampart St., New Orleans, LA 70116 US
(504) 529-6298; *Fax:* (604) 529-6473
www.wwltv.com
pressrelease@wwltv.com
License: New Orleans, Orleans County, LA held by WWL-TV Inc.
Group Owner: Tegna Media; (acq 12-23-2013).; *Washington Law Firm:* Holland & Knight
Nat'l Network: CBS; *Nat'l Reps:* TeleRep
Hours of Local News Weekly: news progmg 35 hrs wkly
Tod Smith, President and General Manager
Weezie Porter, Local Sales Manager
Josh Meza, Marketing Director
Keith Esparros, Executive News Director
Robert Gass, Chief Engineer

***WYES-TV** *Digital Channel:* 11; *Virtual Channel:* 12; 104 kw; 1004 ft.; N29 57 13 W89 56 58
Mailing Address: 916 Navarre Ave., New Orleans, LA 70124 US
Second Address: PO Box 24026, New Orleans, LA 70184
(504) 486-5511; *Fax:* (504) 840-9954
www.wyes.org
info@wyes.org
License: New Orleans, Orleans County, LA held by Greater New Orleans Educational TV Foundation
Washington Law Firm: Schwartz, Woods & Miller
Nat'l Network: PBS
Marc Leunissen, Chair
Randall Feldman, CEO
Allan Pizzato, President
Fred Barrett, Chief Engineer
Katie Crosby, Vice Chair
Larry Katz, Secretary
Cleland Powell, Treasurer
Harold Block, Trustee

Shreveport, LA (DMA 82)

***KLPA-TV** *Digital Channel:* 24; *Virtual Channel:* 24; 350 kw; 1070 ft.; N32 40 39.6 W93 55 30.1
7733 Perkins Rd, Baton Rouge, LA 70810 US
(225) 767-5660, (800) 272-8161, (800)-973-7246; *Fax:* (225) 767-4288
www.lpb.org
bawilliams@lpb.org
License: Shreveport, Caddo County, LA held by Louisiana Education Television Authority
Washington Law Firm: Schwartz, Woods & Miller
Nat'l Network: PBS
Beth Courtney, CEO/President
William Woodside Jr, Operations
Ken Miller, General Manager
Jason Viso, Programming Director
Bob Neese, Promotions Manager
Randy Ward, Engineering Director
Bill Belson, Chief Administrativeofficer
Candace Morgan, Human Resources Director
Ken Miller, Production Manager
Joanne Gaudet, Director,Business
John Tooraen, IT& Web Manager
C.C. Copeland, Asst Director of Engineering-Operations

KMSS-TV *Digital Channel:* 34; *Virtual Channel:* 33; 4,570 kw vis, 457 kw aur; 1,813t/1,781g; N32 05 51 W102 17 21
3150 N. Market St., Shreveport, LA 71137
(318) 629-6000; *Fax:* (318) 629-6001
www.arklatexhomepage.com
License: Shreveport, Caddo County, LA held by Marshall Broadcasting Group Inc.
Group Owner: Marshall Broadcasting Group Inc.; (acq 2015); *Washington Law Firm:* Fletcher, Heald & Hildreth, PLC
Nat'l Network: Fox
Van Greer, General Manager
Van Greer, General Sales Mgr

KPXJ *Digital Channel:* 21; *Virtual Channel:* 21; 1000 kw; 1647 ft.; N32 41 8 W93 56 0
Mailing Address: 601 Clearwater Park Road, West Palm Beach, FL 33401 US
Second Address: 312 E. Kings Hwy, Shreveport, LA 71104
(318) 861-5800; *Fax:* (318) 219-4680
License: Minden, Webster County, LA held by Minden Television Co. LLC
(acq 5-7-2004; $10 million); *Washington Law Firm:* Garvey, Schubert & Barer
Nat'l Network: CW
Lauren Wray Ostendorff, President
George Sirven, General Manager

KSHV-TV *Digital Channel:* 44; 500 kw; 662t; N32 39 57 W93 55 58; *Population Served:* 410,000
3150 N. Market St., Shreveport, LA 71107 US
(318) 629-7127; *Fax:* (318) 629-7158
www.arklatexhomepage.com
awillie@kmsstv.com
License: Shreveport, LA held by White Knight Broadcasting of Shreveport License Corp.
Group Owner: White Knight Holdings Inc.; (acq 1995; $3.8 million); *Washington Law Firm:* Pillsbury, Winthrop, Shaw Pittman, LLC
Nat'l Network: MyNetworkTV
Ray Willie, Station Manager

KSLA *Digital Channel:* 17; 316 kw vis, 40.7 kw aur; 1,800t/1,800g; N32 40 29 W93 55 59; *Population Served:* 461,600
1812 Fairfield Ave., Shreveport, LA 71101
(318) 222-1212; *Fax:* (318) 677-6703
www.ksla.com
ksla@ksla.com
License: Shreveport, Caddo County, LA held by KSLA License Subsidiary LLC.
Group Owner: Raycom Media Inc.; (acq 9-1-96; grpsl).
Nat'l Network: CBS; *Nat'l Reps:* TeleRep; *Wire Services:* AP
Size of News Staff: 32
James Smith, VP/General Manager/Operations Director
John Clark, General Sales Mgr
Barbara Bennett, Promotions Manager
Jayne Ruben, News Director
Ted Small, Chief Engineer
Delena Leary, Public Service Director

KTBS-TV *Digital Channel:* 28; *Virtual Channel:* 3; 1000 kw; 1847 ft.; N32 41 8 W93 56 0
Mailing Address: PO Box 44227, Shreveport, LA 71104 US
Second Address: 312 E. Kings Hwy., Shreveport, LA 71104
(318) 861-5800, (318) 861-5880; *Fax:* (318) 219-4680
www.ktbs.com
License: Shreveport, Caddo County, LA held by KTBS Inc
Washington Law Firm: Fletcher, Heald & Hildreth
Nat'l Network: ABC; *Wire Services:* AP
Lauren Wray Ostendorff, President
George Sirven, General Manager/Station Manager
Linda Howard, General Sales Mgr
Bernadette Collier, Programming Director
Cheryl May, Promotions Manager
Randy Bain, News Director
Dale Cassidy,Chief Engineer
Katharyn DeVille, Marketing/Production
Jan Elkins, Community Affairs
Gerry May, Anchor
Rick Rowe, Multimedia Journalists
Joe Haynes, Meterologist
Paul Crane, Sports Anchor

Maine

Albuquerque-Santa Fe, NM (DMA 48)

KOAT-TV *Digital Channel:* 7
3801 Carlisle Blvd. NE, Albuquerque, NM 87107
(505) 884-7777
www.koat.com
License: Albuquerque, NM held by Hearst Properties Inc.
Group Owner: Hearst Television Inc.; *Washington Law Firm:* Brooks, Pierce, McLendon, Humphrey & Leonard LLP
Nat'l Network: ABC; *Nat'l Reps:* Eagle Television Sales; *Wire Services:* AP
Hours of Local News Weekly: News progmg 25.5 hrs wkly

Baltimore, MD (DMA 26)

WBAL-TV *Digital Channel:* 11
3800 Hooper Ave., Baltimore, MD 21211 USA
(800) 977-WBAL
www.wbaltv.com
License: Baltimore, MD held by Hearst Properties Inc.
Group Owner: Hearst Television Inc.; *Washington Law Firm:* Brooks, Pierce, McLendon, Humphrey & Leonard LLP
Nat'l Network: ABC; *Nat'l Reps:* Eagle Television Sales; *Wire Services:* AP
Hours of Local News Weekly: News progmg 25.5 hrs wkly

Bangor, ME (DMA 156)

WABI-TV *Digital Channel:* 13; *Virtual Channel:* 5; 12 kw; 1284 ft.; N44 42 11.7 W69 4 46.8
35 Hildreth Street, Bangor, ME 04401 US
(207) 947-8321; *Fax:* (207) 941-9378
www.wabi.tv
wabi@wabi.tv
License: Bangor, Penobscot County, ME held by Community Broadcasting Service.
Group Owner: Diversified Communications; (acq 10-7-53; $125,000; *Washington Law Firm:* Irwin, Campbell & Tannenwald
Nat'l Network: CBS/CW; CW; *Nat'l Reps:* Continental Television Sales; *Wire Services:* AP
Size of News Staff: 30; *Hours of Local News Weekly:* news progmg 25 hrs wkly
Michael Young, Operations Dir
Tom Gass, General Sales Mgr
Steve Hiltz, Programming Director
Paul Saliwanchik, Promotions Manager
Jim Morris, News Director
Dale Carter, Chief Engineer
Keith Allen, Operations Manager
Jon Small,Assistant News Director
Caitlin Burchill, Anchor
Joy Hollowell, Anchor
Tania Morales, Reporter
Erica Stapleton, Reporter

WLBZ *Digital Channel:* 2; *Virtual Channel:* 2; 3 kw; 630 ft.; N44 44 10 W68 40 17
329 Mount Hope Ave., Bangor, ME 04401 US
(207) 942-4821
www.wlbz2.com
newscenter@wlbz2.com
License: Bangor, Penobscot County, ME held by Pacific and Southern LLC
Group Owner: Tegna Media; (acq 1998; $110 million with WCSH(TV) Portland).; *Washington Law Firm:* Wiley, Rein & Fielding
Nat'l Network: NBC
Size of News Staff: 22; *Hours of Local News Weekly:* news progmg 33 hrs wkly
Judy Horan, President and General Manager
Bud Cushman, Local Sales Manager
Mike Marshall, Vice President, Programming and Marketing
Jeff Pierce, Creative Services and Marketing Supervisor
Joe Whalen, Regional Sales Manager

***WMEB-TV** *Digital Channel:* 9; *Virtual Channel:* 12; 15 kw; 1230 ft.; N44 42 11 W69 4 47
Mailing Address: 63 Texas Avenue, Bangor, ME 04401 US
Second Address: 1450 Lisbon Street, Lewiston, ME 04240
(800) 884-1717,(207) 783-9101; *Fax:* (207) 783-5193,(207) 942-2857
www.mpbn.net
License: Orono, Penobscot County, ME held by Maine Public Broadcasting Corp
(acq 6-23-92; *Washington Law Firm:* Dow, Lohnes PLLC
Nat'l Network: PBS
Foreign Language Programming
Mark Vogelzang, President/CEO
Jim Dowe, General Manager
Charles Beck, V.P., Dir. of Radio & Television
Jeff Pierce, Promotions Manager
Keith Shortall, Director of News and Public Affairs
Gil Maxwell, V.P. Technology/ChiefTechnology Officer
Charles Beck, V.P., Dir. of Radio & Television
Jennifer Foley, V.P. Development:Philanthropic Giving
Clare Hannan, V.P. of Administration & CFO
Lisa Toner, Human Resource Director

***WMED-TV** *Digital Channel:* 10; *Virtual Channel:* 13; 3.5 kw; 436 ft.; N45 1 45 W67 19 25
Mailing Address: 1450 Libson St., Lewiston, ME 04240 US
Second Address: 65 Texas Ave, Bangor, ME 04401
(800) 884-1717, (207) 783-9101; *Fax:* (207) 783-5193, (207) 942-2857
comments@mpbn.net
License: Calais, Washington County, ME held by Maine Public Broadcasting Corp
(acq 6-23-92; *Washington Law Firm:* Dow, Lohnes PLLC
Nat'l Network: PBS
Foreign Language Programming
Mark Vogelzang, CEO & President
Jim Dowe, General Manager
Charles Beck, Programming Director
Jeff Pierce, Promotions Manager
Keith Shortall, News & Public Affairs Director
Gil Maxwell, Chief Engineer
Clare E. Hannan, VP ofAdministration & CFO
Gil Maxwell, VP Technology/ Chief Technology Officer
Lisa Toner, Dir. Of Human Resources
Cory Morrissey, Dir. Of marketing, Public relations & Corporate Su
Jennifer Foley, VP Development: Philanthropic Giving
CharlesBeck, VP, Dir. Of Radio & Television

WVII-TV *Digital Channel:* 7; *Virtual Channel:* 7; 14 kw; 751 ft.; N44 45 35 W68 34 1
371 Target Indust. Cir., Bangor, ME 04401 US
(207) 945-6457, (207) 945-3122; *Fax:* (207) 942-0511
www.wvii.com
news@foxbangor.com
License: Bangor, Penobscot County, ME held by Bangor Communications LLC.
Group Owner: Rockfleet Broadcasting Inc.; *Washington Law Firm:* Mullin, Rhyne, Emmons & Topel
Nat'l Network: ABC; Fox; *Nat'l Reps:* Continental Television Sales
Size of News Staff: 15; *Hours of Local News Weekly:* news progmg 6 hrs wkly
Mike Palmer, Operations Dir
Michael Palmer, VP& General Manager
Keryn Smith, Sales
Stacey Kinney, Programming
Gene Hardin, Promotions Manager
George Thomas, News Director
Mike Staples, Engineering Dir
Steve Brant, EngineeringDir
Sue Lovell, Regional Sales Manager
Gene Hardin, Public Service

Des Moines-Ames, IA (DMA 69)

KCCI-TV *Digital Channel:* 8; 316 kw vis; ant 1,994t/1,630g; N43 50 44 W70 45 43
888 9th St., Des Moines, IA 50309
(515) 247-8888
www.kcci.com
License: Des Moines, IA held by Hearst Properties Inc.
Group Owner: Hearst Television Inc.; (acq 5-11-2004; $37.5 million); *Washington Law Firm:* Brooks, Pierce, McLendon, Humphrey & Leonard LLP
Nat'l Network: ABC; *Nat'l Reps:* Eagle Television Sales; *Wire Services:* AP
Hours of Local News Weekly: News progmg 25.5 hrs wkly
David J. Barrett, President
David W. Abel, General Manager
Micahel Grant, General Sales Mgr
Gloria Shallcross, Programming Director
Matt Earl, Promotions Manager
Amy Beveridge, News Director
Greg Roehr, Engineering Dir
JackConnor, Chief Engineer
John Gregory
Donna Rideout
Leianne M. Gervais

Ft. Smith-Fayetteville-Springdale-Rogers, AR (DMA 99)

KHBS-TV *Digital Channel:* 7
2809 Ajax Avenue, 200, Rogers, AR 72758
(479) 631-4029
www.4029tv.com
news@4029tv.com
License: Rogers, AR held by Hearst Properties Inc.
Group Owner: Hearst Television Inc.; *Washington Law Firm:* Brooks, Pierce, McLendon, Humphrey & Leonard LLP
Nat'l Network: ABC; *Nat'l Reps:* Eagle Television Sales; *Wire Services:* AP
Hours of Local News Weekly: News progmg 25.5 hrs wkly

Greensboro-High Point-Winston Salem, NC (DMA 46)

WCVB-TV *Digital Channel:* 5
5 TV Place, Needham, MA 02494 USA
(781) 449-0400
www.wcvb.com
License: Needham, MA held by Hearst Properties Inc.
Group Owner: Hearst Television Inc.; *Washington Law Firm:* Brooks, Pierce, McLendon, Humphrey & Leonard LLP
Nat'l Network: ABC; *Nat'l Reps:* Eagle Television Sales; *Wire Services:* AP
Hours of Local News Weekly: News progmg 25.5 hrs wkly

Harrisburg-Lancaster-Lebanon-York, PA (DMA 43)

WGAL-TV *Digital Channel:* 8
1300 Columbia Avenue, Lancaster, PA 17603 USA
www.wgal.com
llwarner@hearst.com
License: Lancaster, PA held by Hearst Properties Inc.
Group Owner: Hearst Television Inc.; *Washington Law Firm:* Brooks, Pierce, McLendon, Humphrey & Leonard LLP
Nat'l Network: ABC; *Nat'l Reps:* Eagle Television Sales; *Wire Services:* AP
Hours of Local News Weekly: News progmg 25.5 hrs wkly
Laura Warner, Programming
Nancy Tulli, General Sales Manager
Ben Warntz, Local Sales Manager

WISN-TV *Digital Channel:* 12
P.O. Box 402, Milwaukee, WI 53201 USA
(414) 342-8812
www.wisn.com
webstaff@wisn.com
License: Wilwaukee, WI held by Hearst Properties Inc.
Group Owner: Hearst Television Inc.; *Washington Law Firm:* Brooks, Pierce, McLendon, Humphrey & Leonard LLP
Nat'l Network: ABC; *Nat'l Reps:* Eagle Television Sales; *Wire Services:* AP
Hours of Local News Weekly: News progmg 25.5 hrs wkly
Laura Warner, Programming
Nancy Tulli, General Sales Manager
Ben Warntz, Local Sales Manager

Jacksonville, FL (DMA 47)

WAPT-TV *Digital Channel:* 16
7616 Channel 16 Way, Jackson, MS 39209 USA
(601) 922-1607
www.wapt.com
License: Jackson, MS held by Hearst Properties Inc.
Group Owner: Hearst Television Inc.; *Washington Law Firm:* Brooks, Pierce, McLendon, Humphrey & Leonard LLP
Nat'l Network: ABC; *Nat'l Reps:* Eagle Television Sales; *Wire Services:* AP
Hours of Local News Weekly: News progmg 25.5 hrs wkly

WKCF-TV *Digital Channel:* 22
1021 N. Wymore Road, Winter Park, FL 32789 USA
(407) 645-2222
www.wesh.com
License: Winter Park, FL held by Hearst Properties Inc.
Group Owner: Hearst Television Inc.; *Washington Law Firm:* Brooks, Pierce, McLendon, Humphrey & Leonard LLP
Nat'l Network: ABC; *Nat'l Reps:* Eagle Television Sales; *Wire Services:* AP
Hours of Local News Weekly: News progmg 25.5 hrs wkly
Laura Warner, Programming
Nancy Tulli, General Sales Manager
Ben Warntz, Local Sales Manager

WLKY-TV *Digital Channel:* 22
1918 Mellwood Ave., Louisville, KY 40206 USA
(407) 645-2222
www.wlky.com
License: Louisville, KY held by Hearst Properties Inc.
Group Owner: Hearst Television Inc.; *Washington Law Firm:* Brooks, Pierce, McLendon, Humphrey & Leonard LLP
Nat'l Network: ABC; *Nat'l Reps:* Eagle Television Sales; *Wire Services:* AP
Hours of Local News Weekly: News progmg 25.5 hrs wkly
Laura Warner, Programming
Nancy Tulli, General Sales Manager
Ben Warntz, Local Sales Manager

Kansas City, MO (DMA 33)

KMBC-TV *Digital Channel:* 9
6455 Winchester Ave., Kansas City, MO 64133
(816) 221-9999
www.kmbc.com
news@kmbc.com
License: Kansas City, MO held by Hearst Properties Inc.
Group Owner: Hearst Television Inc.; *Washington Law Firm:* Brooks, Pierce, McLendon, Humphrey & Leonard LLP
Nat'l Network: ABC; *Nat'l Reps:* Eagle Television Sales; *Wire Services:* AP
Hours of Local News Weekly: News progmg 25.5 hrs wkly

KMBC-TV *Digital Channel:* 9
6455 Winchester Ave., Kansas City, MO 64133
(816) 221-9999
www.kmbc.com
news@kmbc.com
License: Kansas City, MO held by Hearst Properties Inc.
Group Owner: Hearst Television Inc.; *Washington Law Firm:* Brooks, Pierce, McLendon, Humphrey & Leonard LLP
Nat'l Network: ABC; *Nat'l Reps:* Eagle Television Sales; *Wire Services:* AP
Hours of Local News Weekly: News progmg 25.5 hrs wkly

New Orleans, LA (DMA 50)

WDSU-TV *Digital Channel:* 6
846 Howard Avenue, New Orleans, LA 70113 USA
(504) 679-0600
www.wdsu.com
License: New Orleans, LA held by Hearst Properties Inc.
Group Owner: Hearst Television Inc.; *Washington Law Firm:* Brooks, Pierce, McLendon, Humphrey & Leonard LLP
Nat'l Network: ABC; *Nat'l Reps:* Eagle Television Sales; *Wire Services:* AP
Hours of Local News Weekly: News progmg 25.5 hrs wkly

Oklahoma City, OK (DMA 41)

KOCO-TV *Digital Channel:* 5
1300 East Britton Road, Oklahoma City, OK 73131 USA
(405) 478-3000
www.koco.com
License: Oklahoma City, OK held by Hearst Properties Inc.

Group Owner: Hearst Television Inc.; *Washington Law Firm:* Brooks, Pierce, McLendon, Humphrey & Leonard LLP
Nat'l Network: ABC; *Nat'l Reps:* Eagle Television Sales; *Wire Services:* AP
Hours of Local News Weekly: News progmg 25.5 hrs wkly

Orlando-Daytona Beach-Melbourne, FL (DMA 18)

WESH-TV *Digital Channel:* 2
, Daytona Beach, FL USA
www.wesh.com
License: New Orleans, LA held by Hearst Properties Inc.
Group Owner: Hearst Television Inc.; *Washington Law Firm:* Brooks, Pierce, McLendon, Humphrey & Leonard LLP
Nat'l Network: ABC; *Nat'l Reps:* Eagle Television Sales; *Wire Services:* AP
Hours of Local News Weekly: News progmg 25.5 hrs wkly

Portland-Auburn, ME (DMA 81)

***WCBB** *Digital Channel:* 10; *Virtual Channel:* 10; 30 kw; 997 ft.; N44 9 15 W70 0 37
Mailing Address: 1450 Lisbon St., Lewiston, ME 04240 US
Second Address: 63 Texas Avenue, Bangor, ME 04401
(800) 884-1717,(207) 783-9101; *Fax:* (207) 783-5193,(207) 942-2857
www.mpbn.net
comments@mpbn.net
License: Augusta, Kennebec County, ME held by Maine Public Broadcasting Corp
(acq 6-23-92; *Washington Law Firm:* Dow, Lohnes PLLC
Nat'l Network: PBS
Foreign Language Programming
Mark Vogelzang, President/CEO
Jim Dowe, General Manager
Charles Beck, V.P., Dir. of Radio & Television
Jeff Pierce, Promotions Manager
Keith Shortall, News & Public Affairs Director
Gil Maxwell, V.P. Technology/Chief TechnologyOfficer
Charles Beck, V.P., Dir. of Radio & Television
Jennifer Foley, V.P. Development:Philanthropic Giving
Clare Hannan, V.P. of Administration & CFO
Lisa Toner, Human Resource Director
Cory Morrissey, Director of Maketing

WCSH *Digital Channel:* 44; *Virtual Channel:* 6; 1,000 kw; 1,929 ft.; N43 51 30 W70 42 41
1 Congress Sq., Portland, ME 04101 US
(207) 828-6666; *Fax:* (207) 828-6620
www.wcsh6.com
newscenter@wcsh6.com
License: Portland, Cumberland County, ME held by Pacific and Southern LLC
Group Owner: Tegna Media; (acq 1-98).; *Washington Law Firm:* Wiley, Rein & Fielding
Nat'l Network: NBC
Steve Carter, President and General Manager
Brian Cliffe, Director of Sales
Mike Marshall, Program Manager
Mike Redding, News Director

WGME-TV *Digital Channel:* 38; *Virtual Channel:* 13; 1000 kw; 1526 ft.; N43 55 28 W70 29 28
81 Northpoint Dr., Portland, ME 04103 US
(207) 797-1313; *Fax:* (207) 878-7482
www.wgme.com
License: Portland, Cumberland County, ME held by WGME Licensee LLC
Group Owner: Sinclair Broadcast Group Inc.; (acq 5-3-99; grpsl).; *Washington Law Firm:* Dow, Lohnes PLLC
Nat'l Network: CBS
Size of News Staff: 55; *Hours of Local News Weekly:* news progmg 25 hrs wkly
Tom Humpage, General Manager
Erik Snell, Promotions
Kathleen Reynolds, News Director
Craig Clark, Chief Engineer
Jim Linsky, Production
Mike Mayo, Digital Sales

***WMEA-TV** *Digital Channel:* 45; *Virtual Channel:* 26; 50 kw; 758 ft.; N43 25 0 W70 48 17
Mailing Address: 63 Texas Avenue, Bangor, ME 04401 US
Second Address: 1450 Lisbon Street, Lewiston, ME 04240
(207) 783-9101; *Fax:* (207) 942-2857,(207) 783-5193
www.mpbn.net
comments@mpbn.net
License: Biddeford, York County, ME held by Maine Public Broadcastig Corp
(acq 6-23-92; *Washington Law Firm:* Dow, Lohnes PLLC
Nat'l Network: PBS
Mark Vogelzang, President/CEO
Charles Beck, V.P., Dir. of Radio & Television
Keith Shortall, Director of News and Public Affairs
Gil Maxwell, V.P. Technology/Chief Technology Officer
Charles Beck, V.P., Dir. of Radio & Television
Jennifer Foley, V.P. Development:Philanthropic Giving
Clare Hannan, V.P. of Administration & CFO
Lisa Toner, Human Resource Director

WMTW *Digital Channel:* 8; 316 kw vis; ant 1,994t/1,630g; N43 50 44 W70 45 43
99 Danville Corner Rd, Auburn, ME 04210
(207) 782-1800, (800) 248-6397; *Fax:* (207) 783-7371,(207) 782-2165
www.wmtw.com
wmtw@wmtw.com
License: Poland Spring, Androscoggin County, ME held by Hearst Properties Inc.
Group Owner: Hearst Television Inc.; (acq 5-11-2004; $37.5 million); *Washington Law Firm:* Brooks, Pierce, McLendon, Humphrey & Leonard LLP
Nat'l Network: ABC; *Nat'l Reps:* Eagle Television Sales; *Wire Services:* AP
Hours of Local News Weekly: News progmg 25.5 hrs wkly
David J. Barrett, President
David W. Abel, General Manager
Micahel Grant, General Sales Mgr
Gloria Shallcross, Programming Director
Matt Earl, Promotions Manager
Amy Beveridge, News Director
Greg Roehr, Engineering Dir
JackConnor, Chief Engineer
John Gregory
Donna Rideout
Leianne M. Gervais

WMTW-TV *Digital Channel:* 22
4 Ledgeview Dr., Westbrook, ME 04092 USA
(207) 782-1800
www.wmtw.com
License: Westbrook, ME held by Hearst Properties Inc.
Group Owner: Hearst Television Inc.; *Washington Law Firm:* Brooks, Pierce, McLendon, Humphrey & Leonard LLP
Nat'l Network: ABC; *Nat'l Reps:* Eagle Television Sales; *Wire Services:* AP
Hours of Local News Weekly: News progmg 25.5 hrs wkly
Laura Warner, Programming
Nancy Tulli, General Sales Manager
Ben Warntz, Local Sales Manager

WPFO *Digital Channel:* 23; *Virtual Channel:* 23; 390 kw; 1,086 ft.; N44 09 15 W70 00 37; *Population Served:* 400,000
81 Northport Dr., Portland, ME 04103 US
(207) 347-7318; *Fax:* (207) 347-7330
www.myfoxmaine.com
License: Waterville, Kennebec County, ME held by CMCG Portland License LLC.
Group Owner: MAX Media L.L.C.; (acq 4-7-2003; $10 million with WVIF(TV) Christiansted, VI); *Washington Law Firm:* Williams Mullen & Garvey, Schubert & Barer
Nat'l Network: Fox; *Nat'l Reps:* TeleRep
Size of News Staff: 1; *Hours of Local News Weekly:* news progmg 18.5 hrs wkly
Tom MacArthur, General Manager
Rob Barry, National Sales Manager
Jennifer Flint, Promotions Manager
Dave Cox, Chief Engineer
Ann Gagne, Business Manager
Eric Turner, Local Sales Manager
Amie Marzen, Producer

WPME *Digital Channel:* 35; *Virtual Channel:* 35; 14.35 kw; 912 ft.; N43 51 6 W70 19 40
4 Ledgeview Drive, Westbrook, ME 4092 US
(207) 774-0051; *Fax:* (207) 774-6849
www.ourmaine.com
comments@ourmaine.com
License: Lewiston, Androscoggin County, ME held by Cottonwood Communications Portland LLC
(acq 3-31-2007; $4 million); *Ownership:* Daniel D. Davenport III, 100%; *Washington Law Firm:* Fletcher, Heald & Hildreth
Nat'l Network: MYTV; *Nat'l Reps:* Petry Television Inc.
Jeff McDonald, Operations Dir
Jeff Christenbury, Station Manager
Douglas Finck, General Sales Mgr
Cory Culleton, Local Sales Manager

WPXT *Digital Channel:* 43; *Virtual Channel:* 51; 137.4 kw; 833 ft.; N43 51 6 W70 19 40
4 Ledgeview Drive, Westbrook, ME 4092 US
(207) 774-0051,(877) 353-7634; *Fax:* (207) 774-6849
www.ourmaine.com
wpxt@ourmaine.com
License: Portland, Cumberland County, ME held by Ironwood Communications Portland LLC
(acq 3-31-2007; grpsl); *Ownership:* David J. Joseph, 100% of votes; *Washington Law Firm:* Fletcher, Heald & Hildreth
Nat'l Network: CW; *Nat'l Reps:* Petry Television Inc.
Emily Lamoureux, Operations Dir
Douglas Finck, General Manager
Jeff Christenbury, Programming Director
John Marshall, Promotions Manager
Jim Ledger, Chief Engineer
Chet Cook, IT Manager
Cory Culleton, Regional Sales Manager
JenParadis, Traffic/Operations Manager

Presque Isle, ME (DMA 206)

WAGM *Digital Channel:* 8; *Virtual Channel:* 8; 10 kw; 1148 ft.; N46 33 4 W67 48 34
12 Brewer Rd., Presque Isle, ME 04769 USA
(207) 764-4461; *Fax:* (207) 764-5329
www.wagmtv.com
License: Presque Isle, Aroostook County, ME held by Gray Television Licensee LLC
Group Owner: Gray Television Inc.; *Washington Law Firm:* Holland & Knight
Nat'l Network: FOX; *Nat'l Reps:* Continental Television Sales; *Wire Services:* AP
Size of News Staff: 12; *Hours of Local News Weekly:* news progmg 14 hrs wkly
Kelly Landeen, VP/General Manager/General Sales Manager
Rebecca Penney, Promotions Director
Kelly O'Mara, News Director
Chris Spinney, Chief Engineer

***WMEM-TV** *Digital Channel:* 10; *Virtual Channel:* 10; 14.5 kw; 1158 ft.; N46 33 6 W67 48 38
107 N. Franklin St., Saginaw, MI 48607 US
(989) 755-2111, (989) 758-2044, (989) 758-2040,(98; *Fax:* (989) 758-2111
www.wnem.com
edie.adams@wnem.com
License: Presque Isle, Aroostook County, ME held by Maine Public Broadcasting Network
(acq 6-23-92; *Washington Law Firm:* Dow, Lohnes PLLC
Nat'l Network: PBS
Foreign Language Programming
P. James Dowe, CEO
Sam Merrill, Journalist
Katie O'Mara, Reporter
Craig McMorris, News Team
Ted Phaeton, Meterologist
Jason Fielder, Sports Team

Sacramento-Stockton-Modesto, CA (DMA 20)

KCRA-TV *Digital Channel:* 3
3 Television Circle, Sacramento, CA 95814
(916) 446-3333
www.kcra.com
engineering@kcra.com
License: Sacramento, CA held by Hearst Properties Inc.
Group Owner: Hearst Television Inc.; *Washington Law Firm:* Brooks, Pierce, McLendon, Humphrey & Leonard LLP
Nat'l Network: ABC; *Nat'l Reps:* Eagle Television Sales; *Wire Services:* AP
Hours of Local News Weekly: News progmg 25.5 hrs wkly

KQCA-TV *Digital Channel:* 3
3 Television Circle, Sacramento, CA 95814 USA
(916) 446-3333
www.kcra.com
License: Sacramento, CA held by Hearst Properties Inc.
Group Owner: Hearst Television Inc.; *Washington Law Firm:* Brooks, Pierce, McLendon, Humphrey & Leonard LLP
Nat'l Network: ABC; *Nat'l Reps:* Eagle Television Sales; *Wire Services:* AP
Hours of Local News Weekly: News progmg 25.5 hrs wkly

Maryland

Baltimore, MD (DMA 26)

WBAL *Digital Channel:* 59; *Virtual Channel:* 11; 316 kw vis, 31.6 kw aur; 1,000t/998g; N39 20 05 W76 39 03; *Population Served:* 905,759

3800 Hooper Ave., Baltimore, MD 21211
(410) 467-3000; *Fax:* (410) 338-6526
www.wbaltv.com
License: Baltimore, MD held by WBAL Hearst Television Inc.
Group Owner: Hearst Television Inc.; *Washington Law Firm:* Brooks, Pierce, McLendon, Humphrey & Leonard
Nat'l Network: NBC; *Nat'l Reps:* Eagle Television Sales; *Wire Services:* UPI
Size of News Staff: 63; *Hours of Local News Weekly:* news progmg 24 hrs wkly
Wanda Draper, Programming Director
Michelle Butt, News Director

WBFF *Digital Channel:* 46; *Virtual Channel:* 45; 655 kw; 1223 ft.; N39 20 10 W76 38 59
2000 W. 41st St., Baltimore, MD 21211 US
(410) 467-4545; *Fax:* (410) 467-5093
www.foxbaltimore.com
news@foxbaltimore.com
License: Baltimore, Baltimore County, MD held by Chesapeake Television Licensee LLC
Group Owner: Sinclair Broadcast Group Inc.; (acq 9-10-90; grpsl; *Washington Law Firm:* Shaw Pittman
Nat'l Network: FOX; *Nat'l Reps:* TeleRep
Hours of Local News Weekly: news progmg 42 hrs wkly
William Fanshawe, General Manager
Peter Ferraro, Promotion Director

WJZ-TV *Digital Channel:* 13; *Virtual Channel:* 13; 33.8 kW; 922 ft.; N39 20 5 W76 39 3
3725 Malden Ave., Baltimore, MD 21211 USA
(410) 466-0013
baltimore.cbslocal.com
License: Baltimore, Baltimore County, MD held by CBS Television Licenses LLC
Group Owner: CBS Television Stations Group; *Washington Law Firm:* Wilkes, Artis, Hedrick & Lane
Nat'l Network: CBS; *Wire Services:* UPI
Susan Otradovec, Public Affairs Manager

WMAR-TV *Digital Channel:* 38; *Virtual Channel:* 2; 1000 kw; 1024 ft.; N39 20 5 W76 39 3
6400 York Rd., 28th Floor, Baltimore, MD 21212 US
(410) 377-2222; *Fax:* (410) 377-0493
www.abc2news.com
newsroom@wmar.com
License: Baltimore, Baltimore County, MD held by Scripps Howard Broadcasting Co.
Group Owner: The E. W. Scripps Co.; (acq 1991; $125 million; *Washington Law Firm:* Baker & Hostetler
Nat'l Network: ABC; *Nat'l Reps:* Harrington, Righter & Parsons; *Wire Services:* AP
Bill Hooper, VP & General Manager
Andrew Kinkead, Sales Director
Darlene Dorman, Programming Dircector
Maria Mager, Promotions Manager
Kelly Groft, News Director
Paul Wilkinson, Engineering Director
Rob Brockmeyer, ProductionManager
Karen Nichols, Digital Sales Manager
Alex Shaw, Creative Services & Commuity Affairs
David Carberry, Local Sales Manager

***WMPB** *Digital Channel:* 29; *Virtual Channel:* 67; 42.6 kw; 1014 ft.; N39 26 50 W76 46 48
11767 Owings Mills Blvd, Owing Mills, MD 21117 US
(410) 356-5600, (800) 223-3678; *Fax:* (410) 581-6579
www.mpt.org
comments@mpt.org, jmann@mpt.org
License: Baltimore, Baltimore County, MD held by Maryland Public Broadcasting Commission
Washington Law Firm: Schwartz, Woods & Miller
Nat'l Network: PBS
Robert Shuman, President
Kirby Storms, General Manager
George Beneman, Programming Director
Larry Unger, Executive Vice President/Chief

***WMPT** *Digital Channel:* 42; *Virtual Channel:* 22; 516 kw; 951 ft.; N39 0 36 W76 36 33; *Rebroadcasting:* Rebroadcasts WMPB(TV) Baltimore 100%.
11767 Owings Mills Blvd, Owings Mills, MD 21117 US
(410) 356-5600, (800) 223-3678; *Fax:* (410) 581-6579
www.mpt.org
License: Annapolis, Anne Arundel County, MD held by Maryland Public Broadcasting Commission
Washington Law Firm: Schwartz, Woods & Miller
Nat'l Network: PBS
Robert Shuman, President
Kirby Storms, General Manager
George Beneman, Programming Director
Larry Unger, Executive Vice President/Chief

WNUV *Digital Channel:* 40; *Virtual Channel:* 54; 845 kw; 1223 ft.; N39 20 10 W76 38 59
Mailing Address: 2000 West 41st St, Baltimore, MD 21211 US
Second Address: 10706 Beaver Dam Road, Hunt Valley, MD 21030
(410) 467-4545; *Fax:* (410) 467-5093
www.cwbaltimore.com
news@foxbaltimore.com
License: Baltimore, Baltimore County, MD held by Baltimore (WNUV-TV) Licensee Inc.
Group Owner: Cunningham Broadcasting Corporation; (acq 1-9-2002).; *Washington Law Firm:* Arter & Hadden
Nat'l Network: CW
William Fanshawe, General Manager
Billy Robbins, General Sales Mgr
Jennifer Furbay, Programming Director
Sharon Wylie, Public Affairs Manager

WUTB *Digital Channel:* 41; *Virtual Channel:* 24; 290 kw; 1027 ft.; N39 17 15 W76 45 38
2000 W 41st Street, Baltimore, MD 21211 US
(410) 358-2400; *Fax:* (410) 764-7232
wttg-hr@foxtv.com
License: Baltimore, Baltimore County, MD held by Fox Television Stations Inc.
Group Owner: Fox Television Stations Inc.; (acq 7-31-2001; grpsl).; *Washington Law Firm:* Law Offices of Hogan & Hartson
Nat'l Network: MY NETWORK; *Nat'l Reps:* Fox Stations Sales
Alan Sawyer, Operations Dir
Brock Abernathy, General Sales Mgr
Dan Carlin, Programming Director
Michael O'Toole, Promotions Manager
Duane Myers, Chief Engineer
Martha Palmer, National Sales Manager
Eduardo Zuniga, TrafficManager

Pittsburgh, PA (DMA 23)

***WGPT** *Digital Channel:* 36; *Virtual Channel:* 36; 100 kw; 935 ft.; N39 24 14 W79 17 37; *Rebroadcasting:* Rebroadcasts WMPB(TV) Baltimore 100%.
11767 Owings Mills Boulevard , Owings Mills, MD 21117 US
(410) 356-5600, (800)-223-3678; *Fax:* (410) 581-6579
www.mpt.org
comments@mpt.org
License: Oakland, Garrett County, MD held by Maryland Public Broadcasting Commission
Washington Law Firm: Schwartz, Woods & Miller
Nat'l Network: PBS
Larry D. Unger, President, CEO
Kirby Storms, General Manager
George Beneman, Programming Director
Gail Porter Long, Senior Vice President, Chief Education Officer
Steven J. Schupak, Senior Vice President, Chief Content Officer
Martin G. Jacobs, Vice President, Chief Financial Officer
Colette Colclough, Vice President, Human Resources
Zvi Shoubin, Managing Director, Program Services
Harry Vaughn, Managing Director, Production Operations

Salisbury, MD (DMA 144)

WBOC-TV *Digital Channel:* 21; *Virtual Channel:* 16; 740 kw; 915 ft.; N38 30 17 W75 38 37
Mailing Address: 1729 N.Salisbury Blvd., Salisbury, MD 21801 US
Second Address: 1839 S. Dupont Highway, Dover, DE 19901
(410) 749-1111, (302) 734-9262; *Fax:* (410) 742-1616, (410) 742-5190, (302) 734-3674
www.wboc.com
wboc@wboc.com
License: Salisbury, Wicomico County, MD held by WBOC Inc (acq 9-80; $8 million); *Washington Law Firm:* Covington & Burling
Nat'l Network: CBS AND FOX; Fox
Size of News Staff: 40; *Hours of Local News Weekly:* news progmg 31 hrs wkly
Craig Jahelka, Operations Dir
K. Jahelka, Station Manager
David Speicher, General Sales Mgr
Mary Borger, Promotions Manager
John Dearing, News Director
Danny Panicella, Chief Engineer
Steve Bach, Regional Sales Manager
BobBachman, Regional Sales Manager

***WCPB** *Digital Channel:* 28; *Virtual Channel:* 28; 132 kw; 509 ft.; N38 23 9 W75 35 33; *Rebroadcasting:* Rebroadcasts WMPB(TV) Baltimore 100%.
11767 Owings Mills Blvd, Owings Mills, MD 21117 US
(410) 356-5600, (800) 223-3678; *Fax:* (410) 998-3717
www.mpt.org
License: Salisbury, Wicomico County, MD held by Maryland Public Broadcasting Commission
Washington Law Firm: Schwartz, Woods & Miller
Nat'l Network: PBS
Larry D. Unger, President & CEO
Harry Vaughn , Managing Director, Production Operations
Zvi Shoubin, Managing Director, Program Services
Steven J. Schupak , Senior Vice President, Chief Content Officer
Gail Porter Long , Senior VicePresident, Chief Education Officer
George R. Beneman II , Vice President, Chief Technology Officer
Martin G. Jacobs, Vice President, Chief Financial Officer
Colette Colclough, Vice President, Human Resources
Andrew H. Levine, GeneralCounsel

WMDT *Digital Channel:* 53; *Virtual Channel:* 47; 350 KW ERP Digital; TFU-20GTH-R C170SP; N38 30 06 W76 44 09;
Population Served: 248,969
Mailing Address: 202 Downtown Plaza, Salisbury, MD 21801
Second Address: 202 Downtown Plaza, Salisbury, MD 21801
(410) 742-4747; *Fax:* (410) 742-5767
www.wmdt.com
wmdt@wmdt.com
License: Salisbury, Wicomico County, MD held by Delmarva Broadcast Service LLC.
(acq 1982); *Washington Law Firm:* Fletcher, Heath, Hildreth
Nat'l Network: ABC; CW
Size of News Staff: 23; *Hours of Local News Weekly:* news progmg 23 hrs wkly
Freddie Mitchell, News Operations/Promotions Manager
Kathleen McLain, General Manager
Phil Bankert, Sales Manager
Kathleen McLain, Programming Director
Sarah Truitt, News Director
Bill Hoctor, Chief Engineer
Lindsy Adkins,Business Manager
John Ebert, Creative Services Manager
Emily Lampa, Senior Anchor
Kody Leibowitz, Reporter
Stephen Shiveley, Meterologist
Jarred Hill, Reporeter/Producer

Washington, DC (Hagerstown, MD) (DMA 7)

***WFPT** *Digital Channel:* 28; *Virtual Channel:* 62; 41.2 kw; 518 ft.; N39 15 37 W77 18 44; *Rebroadcasting:* Rebroadcasts WMPB(TV) Baltimore 100%.
11767 Owings Mills Boulevard, Owings Mills, MD 21117 US
(410) 356-5600, (800)-223-3678; *Fax:* (410) 581-6579, (410)-998-3717
www.mpt.org
comments@mpt.org
License: Frederick, Frederick County, MD held by Maryland Public Broadcasting Commission
Washington Law Firm: Schwartz, Woods & Miller
Nat'l Network: PBS
Robert Shuman, President
Kirby Storms, General Manager
George Beneman, Programming Director
Larry Unger, Executive Vice President/Chief

WHAG-TV *Digital Channel:* 26; *Virtual Channel:* 25; 575 kw; 1234 ft.; N39 39 45 W77 57 54
13 E. Washington St., Hagerstown, MD 21740 US
(301) 797-4400; *Fax:* (301) 733-1735
www.your4state.com
License: Hagerstown, Washington County, MD held by Nexstar Broadcasting Inc.
Group Owner: Nexstar Broadcasting Group Inc.; (acq 12-31-2003; grpsl).; *Washington Law Firm:* Drinker Biddle & Reath L.L.P.
Nat'l Network: NBC; *Nat'l Reps:* Continental Television Sales
Hours of Local News Weekly: News progmg 20 hrs wkly
Hugh Breslin, General Manager

WJAL-TV *Digital Channel:* 39; *Virtual Channel:* 68; 105 kw; 1220 ft.; N39 53 25 W77 58 4
262 Swamp Fox Rd., Suite 190, Hagerstown, PA 17201 US
(717) 375-4000; *Fax:* (717) 375-4052
sullom@entravision.com
License: Hagerstown, MD held by Entravision Holdings, LLC.
Group Owner: Entravision Communications Corp.; *Washington Law Firm:* Leventhal, Senter & Lerman
Nat'l Network: UNIVISION
Hours of Local News Weekly: 5 hrs local news wkly

Donna Jeter, Operations Dir
Jason Green, Programming/Traffic
Brian Wilhide, Engineering Dir

***WWPB** *Digital Channel:* 44; *Virtual Channel:* 31; 500 kw; 1211 ft.; N39 39 4 W77 58 15; *Rebroadcasting:* Rebroadcasts WMPB(TV) Baltimore 100%.
11767 Owings Mills Blvd, Owings Mills, MD 21117 US
(410) 356-5600, (800) 223-3678; *Fax:* (410) 581-6579
www.mpt.org
comments@mpt.org
License: Hagerstown, Washington County, MD held by Maryland Public Broadcasting Commission
Washington Law Firm: Schwartz, Woods & Miller
Nat'l Network: PBS
Robert Shuman, President
Kirby Storms, General Manager
George Beneman, Programming Director
Larry Unger, Executive Vice President/Chief

Massachusetts

Albany-Schenectady-Troy, NY (DMA 59)

WNYT *Digital Channel:* 13; *Virtual Channel:* 51; 12.69 kw; 988 ft.; N42 38 13 W73 59 45
715 N. Pearl St., Albany, NY 12204 US
(800) 999-9698; *Fax:* (518) 434-0659
www.my4albany.com
newstips@wnyt.com
License: Pittsfield, Berkshire County, MA held by WNYT-TV LLC
Group Owner: Hubbard Broadcasting; (acq 7-15-2013; $2.3 million); *Washington Law Firm:* Holland & Knight LLP
Nat'l Network: MY NETWORK TV
Stephen P. Baboulis, VP/General Manager
David Palmer, Chief Engineer
Carla Clark, Business Manager
Alisha Siligato, Programming Director
progmg dir, Promotions Manager

Boston (Manchester, NH) (DMA 9)

WBPX-TV *Digital Channel:* 32; 300 kw; ant 1,184t/1,175g; N42 18 27 W71 13 27; *Population Served:* 6,366,400
1120 Soldiers Field Rd., Boston, MA 2134 USA
(617) 787-6868; *Fax:* (617) 787-4114
www.iontelevision.com
License: Boston, MA held by ION Media Boston License, Inc.
Group Owner: ION Media Networks Inc.
Nat'l Network: ION Television
Hours of Local News Weekly: News progmg 20 hrs wkly
Brandon Burgess, Chairman

WBZ-TV *Digital Channel:* 30; *Virtual Channel:* 4; 825 kW; 1270 ft.; N42 18 37 W71 14 14
1170 Soldiers Field Rd., Boston, MA 02134 USA
(617) 787-7000
boston.cbslocal.com
License: Boston, Suffolk County, MA held by CBS Television Licenses LLC
Group Owner: CBS Television Stations Group; *Washington Law Firm:* Wilkes, Artis, Hedrick & Lane
Nat'l Network: CBS; *Nat'l Reps:* CBS TV Stations National Sales
Foreign Language Programming; Size of News Staff: 81; *Hours of Local News Weekly:* news progmg 20 hrs wkly
Paul Pabis, Director of Broadcast Operations & Engineering

WCVB *Digital Channel:* 20; *Virtual Channel:* 5; 625 kw; 1280 ft.; N42 18 37 W71 14 14
888 Seventh Ave., New York, NY 10106 US
(781) 449-0400; *Fax:* (800) 441-1948
www.wcvb.com
License: Boston, Suffolk County, MA held by WCVB Hearst Television Inc.
Group Owner: Hearst Television Inc.; (acq 7-16-97; grpsl)
Nat'l Network: ABC; *Nat'l Reps:* Eagle Television Sales; *Wire Services:* AP
Foreign Language Programming; Hours of Local News Weekly: News progmg 30 hrs wkly
Ro Dooley Webster, Programming Director

WDPX-TV *Digital Channel:* 40; 300 kw; ant 1,128t/259g; N42 18 27 W71 13 27; *Rebroadcasting:* Satellite of WBPX Boston.
1120 Soldiers Field Rd., Boston, MA 2134 USA
(812) 335-1770; *Fax:* (617) 787-4114
www.iontelevision.com
License: Boston, MA held by ION Media Boston License, Inc.
Group Owner: ION Media Networks Inc.
Brandon Burgess, Chairman

WFXT *Digital Channel:* 31; *Virtual Channel:* 25; 780 kw; 1191 ft.; N42 18 10 W71 13 7
Mailing Address: 25 Fox Drive, P.O. Box 9125, Dedham, MA 02027-2563 US
Second Address: PO Box 900, Beverly Hills, CA 90213
(781) 467-2525, (781) 467-1300, (781) 467-1499; *Fax:* (781) 467-7213
www.myfoxboston.com
License: Boston, Suffolk County, MA held by Fox Television Stations Inc.
Group Owner: Fox Television Stations Inc.; (acq 7-95;
Nat'l Network: FOX
Size of News Staff: 70; *Hours of Local News Weekly:* news progmg 7 hrs wkly
Greg Kelly, VP & General Manager
Marc Fauci, VP & General Sales Manager
Tricia Maloney, Programming Director
Paul McGonagle, VP & News Director
Bill Holbrook, VP of Engineering
Rosa Wong, VP Finance
Lowell Briggs, VP CreativeServices
Gary LaPlante, Asst. News Director
Marguerite Kerr, Director of Human Resources
Debby Pellerin, Traffic Manager
Tricia Maloney, Director of Research & Programming

***WGBH** *Digital Channel:* 19; 98 kw; 650 ft.; N42 12 42 W71 6 51
One Guest Street, Boston, MA 02135 US
(617) 300-5400; *Fax:* (617) 300-1013
www.wgbh.org
feedback@wgbh.org
License: Boston, Suffolk County, MA held by WGBH Educational Foundation
Washington Law Firm: Covington & Burling
Nat'l Network: PBS
Foreign Language Programming
Amos B. Hostetter, Jr., Chair
Benjamin Godley, Chief Operating Officer and EVP
Jonathan C. Abbott, President & CEO
David Bernstein, Vice President & General Manager, WGBH Enterprises
John Bredar, Vice President for NationalProgramming
Jeanne M. Hopkins, VP, Communications & Government Relations
Susan L. Kantrowitz, Vice President and General Counsel
Winifred Lenihan, Vice President for Development
Vinay Mehra, CFO, VP for Finance & Administration
Frances M.Sullivan, VP - Human Resources
Phil Redo, General Manager for Radio

***WGBH-TV** *Digital Channel:* 19; *Virtual Channel:* 2; 700 kw; 1227 ft.; N42 18 37 W71 14 14
One Guest Street, Boston, MA 02135 US
(617) 300-5400; *Fax:* (617) 300-1026
www.wgbh.org
feedback@wgbh.org
License: Boston, Suffolk County, MA held by WGBH Educational Foundation
Washington Law Firm: Covington & Burling
Nat'l Network: PBS
Foreign Language Programming
Amos B. Hostetter, Jr., Chair
Benjamin Godley, Chief Operating Officer and EVP
Jonathan C. Abbott, President & CEO
Marita Rivero, Operations Dir
David Bernstein, Vice President & General Manager, WGBH Enterprises
John Bredar, VicePresident for National Programming
Jeanne M. Hopkins, VP, Communications & Government Relations
Susan L. Kantrowitz, Vice President and General Counsel
Winifred Lenihan, Vice President for Development
Vinay Mehra, CFO, VP for Finance &Administration
Frances M. Sullivan, VP - Human Resources
Phil Redo, General Manager for Radio

WHDH *Digital Channel:* 42; 1,000 kw; 944 ft.; N42 18 41 W71 13 00; *Population Served:* 5,330,400
7 Bulfinch Place, Boston, MA 02114 US
(617) 725-0777, (617) 248-5504; *Fax:* (617) 723-6117, (617) 227-1513
www.whdh.com
station_management@whdh.com
License: Boston, Suffolk County, MA held by WHDH-TV
Group Owner: Sunbeam Television Corp.; *Washington Law Firm:* Holland & Knight
Nat'l Network: NBC; *Nat'l Reps:* TeleRep
Chris Wayland, General Manager
Robert Burns, General Sales Mgr
Joan McCready, Programming Director
Linda Miele, News Director
James E. Shultis, Director of Engineering

WLVI *Digital Channel:* 41; 690 kw; ant 1,186t/1,201g; N42 18 12 W71 13 08; *Population Served:* 641,071
7 Bulfinch Pl., Boston, MA 02114
(617) 248-5413, (617) 248-5504; *Fax:* (617) 227-1513
www.whdh.com/category/264877/cw56
station_management@whdh.com
License: Cambridge, Middlesex County, MA held by WHDH-TV
Group Owner: Sunbeam Television Corp.; (acq 12-19-2006; $113.7 million); *Washington Law Firm:* Holland & Knight
Nat'l Network: CW; *Nat'l Reps:* TeleRep
Size of News Staff: 44; *Hours of Local News Weekly:* news progmg 7 hrs wkly
Chris Wayland, General Manager
Robert Burns, General Sales Mgr
Joan McCready, Programming Director
Linda Miele, News Director
James E. Shultis, Dir. Of Engineering

WMFP *Digital Channel:* 18; *Virtual Channel:* 62; 1000 kw; 949 ft.; N42 18 27 W71 13 27
11 Lakeland Park Dr., Peabody, MA 01960 US
(978) 717-5633; *Fax:* (978) 717-5635
www.wmfp-tv.com
wmfptv@yahoo.com
License: Lawrence, Essex County, MA held by MTB Boston Licensee LLC.
Group Owner: Multicultural Capital Trust; (acq 2-2-2009);
Washington Law Firm: Sciarrino & Shubert PLLC
Nat'l Network: IND
Steve Marra, Operations Manager
Bill Desmond, General Manager/Chief Engineer/Station Manager
Lee Warpack, Sales Manager
Bill Desmond, Chief Engineer

WPXG-TV *Digital Channel:* 33; 300 kw; ant 1,128t/259g; N42 18 27 W71 13 27; *Rebroadcasting:* Satellite of WBPX Boston.
1120 Soldiers Field Rd., Boston, MA 2134 USA
(812) 335-1770; *Fax:* (617) 787-4114
www.iontelevision.com
License: Boston, MA held by ION Media Boston License, Inc.
Group Owner: ION Media Networks Inc.
Brandon Burgess, Chairman

WSBK-TV *Digital Channel:* 39; 135 kW; 1270 ft.; N42 18 37 W71 14 14; *Population Served:* 2,140,000
1170 Soldiers Field Rd., Boston, MA 02134 USA
(617) 787-7000
boston.cbslocal.com
License: Boston, Suffolk County, MA held by CBS Television Licenses LLC
Group Owner: CBS Television Stations Group
Nat'l Network: MyNetworkTV; CBS
Hours of Local News Weekly: News progmg 4 hrs wkly

WUNI-TV *Digital Channel:* 29; *Virtual Channel:* 27; 270 kw; 1535 ft.; N42 20 8.8 W71 42 55
33 Fourth Ave., Needham, MA 02494 US
(781) 433-2727; *Fax:* (781) 433-2702
www.wunitv.com
smcgavick@entravision.com
License: Worcester, Worcester County, MA held by Entravision Holdings, LLC.
Group Owner: Entravision Communications Corp.; (acq 1-4-01; $47.5 million); *Washington Law Firm:* Thompson Hine LLP
Nat'l Network: UNIVISION; *Wire Services:* AP
Foreign Language Programming; Size of News Staff: 13; *Hours of Local News Weekly:* news progmg 3 hrs wkly
Pamela Bias, Operations Mgr
Scott McGavick, Director of Sales
Meg Godin, Promotions Manager
Sara Suarez, News Director
Robert Kerrigan, Chief Engineer

WUTF-DT *Digital Channel:* 27; *Virtual Channel:* 66; 3,311 kw vis; ant 1,168t/1,227g; N42 23 02 W71 29 37; *Population Served:* 2,200,000
71 Parmenter Rd., Hudson, MA 01749
(978) 562-0660
www.univision.com
License: Marlborough, Middlesex County, MA held by UniMas Boston LLC.
Group Owner: Univision Communications Inc.; (acq 5-21-2001; grpsl).
Nat'l Network: UniMas (Spanish)

Foreign Language Programming
Randy Falco, President

WWDP *Digital Channel:* 10; *Virtual Channel:* 46; 5 kw; 466 ft.; N42 0 38 W71 2 42
6740 Shady oak Rd., Eden Praire, MN 55344 US
(952) 943-6000, (800) 676-5523, (800) 884-2212; *Fax:* (952) 943-6566
www.shopnbc.com
License: Norwell, Plymouth County, MA held by Norwell Television LLC
Nat'l Network: N/A
Jon Stoltz, Operations Dir

***WYDN** *Digital Channel:* 47; *Virtual Channel:* 48; 365 kw; 712 ft.; N42 18 27 W71 13 27
Mailing Address: 3901 Hwy 121, Bedford, TX 76021 US
Second Address: PO Box 610546, Dallas, TX 75261-0546
(817) 571-1229, (877) 805-2132; *Fax:* (817) 571-7458
www.daystar.com
comments@daystar.com
License: Worcester, Worcester County, MA held by Educational Public TV Corp
Nat'l Network: IND
Arnold Toraz, General Manager

Providence, RI-New Bedford, MA (DMA 52)

WLNE-TV *Digital Channel:* 49; *Virtual Channel:* 6; 350 kw; 932 ft.; N41 51 54 W71 17 15; *Population Served:* 1,437,000
10 Orms St., Providence, RI 02904 US
(401) 453-8000; *Fax:* (401) 331-4399
www.abc6.com
License: New Bedford, Bristol County, MA held by Citadel Communications LLC
Group Owner: Citadel Communications Co. LTD.; (acq 3-22-2011; $4 million); *Ownership:* Global Broadcasting LLC, 100%; *Washington Law Firm:* Latham & Watkins
Nat'l Network: ABC; *Nat'l Reps:* TeleRep
John Methia, Director of Broadcast Operations
Chris Tzianabos, Vice President/General Manager
Cindy Walsh, Local Sales Manager
Judy Shoemaker, Promotions Manager
Nicole Moye, News Director
Mike Tullie, National Sales Manager
Sherri Leo, Account Development and Management
Bill Lancaster, Account Executive
Caitriona Crawford, Account Executive
Susan Gazerro, Account Executive

WLWC *Digital Channel:* 22; *Virtual Channel:* 28; 350 kw; 666 ft.; N41 46 39 W70 55 41
630 Fifth Avenue, 27th Floor, New York, NY 10111 US
(401) 351-8828; *Fax:* (401) 351-0222
License: New Bedford, Bristol County, MA held by OTA Broadcasting (PVD) LLC
Group Owner: OTA Broadcasting; (acq 11-21-2007; grpsl);
Washington Law Firm: Wilkinson Barker Knauer LLP
Nat'l Network: CW; *Nat'l Reps:* TeleRep
Tina Castano, General Manager
Joe Mulvey, General Sales Mgr

Springfield-Holyoke, MA (DMA 114)

***WGBY-TV** *Digital Channel:* 22; *Virtual Channel:* 57; 50 kw; 1004 ft.; N42 14 29 W72 38 56
44 Hampden Street, Springfield, MA 01103 US
(413) 781-2801, (800) 781-9429; *Fax:* (413) 731-5093, (413) 731-7163
www.wgby.org
feedback@wgby.org
License: Springfield, Hampden County, MA held by WGBH Educational Foundation
Washington Law Firm: Covington & Burling
Nat'l Network: PBS
Geoffrey Post, Chairman
Jonathan Abbott, CEO/President
Russell J. Peotter, General Manager
Lynn Page, Programming Director
Charley Rose, Promotions Manager
Ray Miller, Chief Engineer
Chris Schwantner, Interim Chief TechnologyEngineer
Timothy Suffish, Vice-Chair
Karen Burkinshaw, Treasurer
Arlene Rodriguez, Secretary
Patricia A. Churchfield, Director of Human Resources
Gary Czelusniak, Director of Marketing

WGGB-TV *Digital Channel:* 40; *Virtual Channel:* 40; 460 kw; 1063 ft.; N42 14 30 W72 38 57
1300 Liberty St., Springfield, MA 01104 US
(413) 733-4040, (413) 733-8840; *Fax:* (413) 781-5733
www.wggb.com
newstips@wggb.com
License: Springfield, Hampden County, MA held by Gormally Broadcasting Licenses LLC
(acq 11-1-2007; $21.15 million); *Ownership:* Gormally Broadcasting LLC, 100%
Nat'l Network: ABC; Fox; *Nat'l Reps:* Millennium Sales & Marketing *Regional Reps:* Millennium
Dean Davidson, Operations Dir
Dave Kaufman, General Manager
Gerry Dunn, General Sales Mgr
Carol Moran, Programming Director
David Baer, News Director
Dwight Mayhew, Director of Engineering
Jason Brusa, Production Manager

WWLP *Digital Channel:* 11; *Virtual Channel:* 22; 4,170 kw vis, 417 kw aur; 877t/530g; N42 05 05 W72 42 14
Mailing Address: One Broadcast Ctr., Chicopee, MA 01013
Second Address: One Broadcast Ctr., Chicopee, MA 01013
(413) 377-2200; *Fax:* (413) 377-2261
www.wwlp.com
reportit@wwlp.com
License: Springfield, Hampden County, MA held by WWLP Broadcasting L.L.C.
Group Owner: LIN Television Corporation; (acq 10-20-2000; about $128 million); *Washington Law Firm:* Covington & Burling
Nat'l Network: NBC; *Nat'l Reps:* Petry; *Wire Services:* AP
William Pepin, General Manager
John Baran, Station Manager
Lowell McLane, Director of Sales
Anna Giza, Promotions Manager
Michael Garreffi, News Director
Dave Cote, Chief Engineer
Joshua N. Pila, Senior Counsel
Sy Becker,General assignment Reporter
Kaitlin Goslee, Multimedia journalist
Christine Lee, Correspondent

Michigan

Alpena, MI (DMA 208)

WBKB-TV *Digital Channel:* 11; *Virtual Channel:* 11; 20 kw; 662 ft.; N44 42 11 W83 31 26
1390 N. Bagley Street, Alpena, MI 49707 US
(989) 356-3434; *Fax:* (989) 356-4188
www.wbkb11.com
License: Alpena, Alpena County, MI held by Thunder Bay Broadcasting Corp
Washington Law Firm: Cohn & Marks
Nat'l Network: CBS; Fox; *Nat'l Reps:* Millennium Sales & Marketing; *Wire Services:* UPI
Size of News Staff: 6; *Hours of Local News Weekly:* news progmg 5.5 hrs wkly
Stephen Marks, President
Adam Claibon, Meteorologist
Cher Allen, General Manager
Robert Race, Promotions Manager
Mark Nowak, Chief Engineer
Barb Bowen, Regional sales
Kim Rabeau, Local Sales
Travis Kozek, Sports
Adam Claibon,Meterologist
Kelsey Fabian, News
Velena Jones, News

***WCML** *Digital Channel:* 24; *Virtual Channel:* 6; 300 kw vis, 15.1 kw aur; ant 1,289t/1,148g; N45 08 18 W84 09 45;
Rebroadcasting: Satellite of WCMU-TV Mt. Pleasant.
Central Michigan Univ., 1999 E. Campus Dr., Mt. Pleasant, MI 48859 US
(989) 774-3105, (800) 727-9268; *Fax:* (989) 774-4427
www.wcmu.org
grant1eb@cmich.edu
License: Alpena, Alpena County, MI held by Central Michigan University
Washington Law Firm: Dow, Lohnes & Albertson
Nat'l Network: PBS
Kim Walters, Director, Development and Business Operations
Ed Grant, General Manager
Rick Schudiske, Station Manager
Kurt Wilson, General Sales Mgr
Linda Dielman, Program/Outreach Manager
David Nicholas, News Director
WayneHenderson, Director of Technical Services
Shannon Peak, Assistant Manager/Business Operations
Kurt Wilson, Director, Corporate Support / Major Gifts
Tom Ball , Marketing Representative
Patricia Link, Marketing Representative
MichaelJohnson, Marketing Representative
Stacy Earl, Fundraising Coordinator

Detroit (DMA 13)

WADL *Digital Channel:* 39; *Virtual Channel:* 38; 1000 kw; 558 ft.; N42 33 15 W82 53 15
35000 Adell Drive, Mt. Clemens, MI 48043 US
(586) 790-3838; *Fax:* (586) 790-3841
www.wadldetroit.com
License: Mount Clemens, Macomb County, MI held by Adell Broadcasting Corp
Nat'l Network: IND; *Nat'l Reps:* Blair Television
Kevin Adell, CEO
Lewis Gibbs, President
Fredrica Crowe, General Sales Mgr
Jamie Harrington, Programming Director
Tom Ponsart, Chief Engineer
Evelyn Brown, Traffic Manager

WJBK *Digital Channel:* 7; *Virtual Channel:* 2; 15 kW; 1030 ft.; N42 27 38 W83 12 50
16550 West Nine Mile Rd., Southfield, MI 48037-2000 USA
(248) 557-2000
www.fox2detroit.com
fox2newsdesk@foxtv.com
License: Detroit, Wayne County, MI held by New World Communications of Detroit Inc.
Group Owner: Fox Television Stations Group; (acq 1-22-97; grpsl).
Nat'l Network: FOX; *Wire Services:* Reuters
Size of News Staff: 140; *Hours of Local News Weekly:* news progmg 36 hrs wkly
Sheila Bruce, Advertising Contact

WKBD-TV *Digital Channel:* 14; 180 kW; 942 ft.; N42 29 1 W83 18 44; *Population Served:* 5,521,787
26905 W 11 Mile Rd., Southfield, MI 48033 USA
(248) 355-7000
cwdetroit.cbslocal.com
License: Detroit, Wayne County, MI held by Detroit Television Station WKBD Inc.
Group Owner: CBS Television Stations Group
Nat'l Network: The CW Network; *Nat'l Reps:* TeleRep
Kris Kelly, Community Affairs Manager

WMYD *Digital Channel:* 21; *Virtual Channel:* 20; 500 kw; 1063 ft.; N42 26 53 W83 10 23
20777 W. Ten Mile Rd., Southfield, MI 48075 US
(248) 827-7777; *Fax:* (800) 825-0770
www.wxyz.com/tv20detroit
License: Detroit, Wayne County, MI held by WXON License Inc.
Group Owner: Granite Broadcasting Corp.; (acq 1-31-97; $175 million); *Washington Law Firm:* Akin, Gump, Strauss, Hauer & Feld
Nat'l Network: MYTV
David Bangura, General Manager
Dan Riley, Chief Engineer
Denny Vinchook, National Sales Manager
Stephen Clark, Anchor
Dave Rexroth, Meterologist
Keenan Smith, Meterologist
Chris Edwards, Meterologist
Hally Vogel,Meterologist

WPXD-TV *Digital Channel:* 31; 345 kw; ant 1,080t/1,044g; N42 29 0 W83 18 43
26935 West 11 Mile Rd., Southfield, MI 48033 USA
(812) 335-1770; *Fax:* (734) 973-7906
www.iontelevision.com
License: Ann Arbor, MI held by Ion Media License Company, LLC
Group Owner: ION Media Networks Inc.; *Washington Law Firm:* Verner, Liipfert, Bernhard, McPherson & Hand
Nat'l Network: ION Television
Brandon Burgess, Chairman

***WTVS** *Digital Channel:* 43; 2,200 kw vis, 200 kw aur; 961t/1,020g; N42 29 01 W83 18 44; *Population Served:* 4,500,000
(dba/Detroit Public Television)
Riley Broadcast Ctr, 1 Clover Ct, Wixom, MI 48393-2247
(248) 305-3900, (313) 872-7500; *Fax:* (248) 305-3980
www.dptv.org
email@dptv.org
License: Detroit, Wayne County, MI held by Detroit Educational Television Foundation
Ownership: Detroit Educational Television Foundation;
Washington Law Firm: Schwartz, Woods & Miller

Nat'l Network: PBS *Regional Reps:* Karole White
Charles Ciuni, Chairman
Rich Homberg, CEO & President
Jeff Forster, Productions & Operations
Daniel Gaitens, Programming Director
John Mark, Chief Engineer
John Wenzel, CFO
Dan Alpert, Sr Vice PresidentDevelopment/Communications
Jeff Forster, Sr Vice President Production/Station Enterprises
Georgeann Herbert, Sr Vice President Content/Engagement
Tina Woods, Executive Asst. to the President, CFO & General Ma

WWJ-TV *Digital Channel:* 44; *Virtual Channel:* 62; 425 kW; 1053 ft.; N42 26 53 W83 10 23
26905 W 11 Mile Rd., Southfield, MI 48033 USA
(248) 355-7000; *Fax:* (248) 355-7044
detroit.cbslocal.com
License: Detroit, Wayne County, MI held by CBS Broadcasting Inc.
Group Owner: CBS Television Stations Group; *Washington Law Firm:* Hogan & Hartson
Nat'l Network: CBS; *Nat'l Reps:* CBS TV Stations National Sales
Tom Canedo, General Manager

WXYZ-TV *Digital Channel:* 41; *Virtual Channel:* 7; 1000 kw; 1001 ft.; N42 28 14 W83 15 1
20777 West Ten Mile Road, Southfield, MI 48075-1086 US
(248) 827-7777, (800) 825-0770, (248) 827-9407; *Fax:* (248) 827-9444
www.wxyz.com
wxyzdesk@wxyz.com
License: Detroit, Wayne County, MI held by Channel 7 of Detroit Inc.
Group Owner: The E. W. Scripps Co.; (acq 1-2-86; grpsl);
Washington Law Firm: Baker & Hostetler
Nat'l Network: ABC; *Nat'l Reps:* Eagle Television Sales; *Wire Services:* Reuters
Robert Silva, Operations Dir
Mike Murri, General Sales Mgr
Gary Schlaff, Programming Director
Andrea Parquet-Taylor, News Director
Ray Thurber, Engineering Dir
Steve Kopicki, National Sales Manager
Mike MacLean, Regional SalesManager
Stephen Clark, Anchor
Dave rexroth, Chief meterologist
Alerandra Bahou, Digital Reporter
Tom Leyden, Sports Dir.

Flint-Saginaw-Bay City, MI (DMA 72)

WBSF *Digital Channel:* 46; *Virtual Channel:* 46; 70 kw; 1004 ft; N43 28 26.80 W83 50 44.90
3463 West Pierson Rd, Flint, MI 48504 US
(810) 687-1000; *Fax:* (810) 687-4925
www.thecw46.com
comments@nbc25news.com
License: Bay City, MI held by Flint (WBSF-TV) Licensee Inc.
Group Owner: Cunningham Broadcasting Corporation; (acq 11-22-2013); *Washington Law Firm:* Pillsbury Winthrop Shaw Pittman LLP
Nat'l Network: CW; *Nat'l Reps:* HRP; *Wire Services:* AP

***WCMU-TV** *Digital Channel:* 26; *Virtual Channel:* 14; 450 kw vis; ant 981t/941g; N43 45 11 W85 12 40; *Population Served:* 151,000
Central Michigan Univ., 1999 E. Campus Dr., Mount Pleasant, MI 48859 US
(989) 774-3105, (800) 727-9268; *Fax:* (989) 774-4427
www.wcmu.org
grant1eb@cmich.edu
License: Mount Pleasant, Isabella County, MI held by Central Michigan University
Washington Law Firm: Dow, Lohnes & Albertson
Nat'l Network: PBS
Kim Walters, Director, Development and Business Operations
Ed Grant, General Manager
Rick Schudiske, Station Manager
Kurt Wilson, General Sales Mgr
Linda Dielman, Program/Outreach Manager
David Nicholas, News Director
WayneHenderson, Director of Technical Services
Shannon Peak, Assistant Manager/Business Operations
Kurt Wilson, Director, Corporate Support / Major Gifts
Tom Ball , Marketing Representative
Patricia Link, Marketing Representative
MichaelJohnson, Marketing Representative
Stacy Earl, Fundraising Coordinator

***WDCQ-TV** *Digital Channel:* 15; *Virtual Channel:* 35; 200 kw; 1014 ft.; N43 32 33 W83 39 37
1961 Delta Rd., University Center, MI 48710 US
(877) 472-7677, (989) 686-9362; *Fax:* (989) 686-0155
www.deltabroadcasting.org
wdcq@delta.edu
License: Bad Axe, Huron County, MI held by Delta College
Washington Law Firm: Cohn & Marks
Nat'l Network: PBS
Jean Goodnow, CEO
Barry Baker, General Manager
Joseph Yezak, Program manager
Tom Garnett, Chief Engineer
Chas Eldridge, Website Contact
Pamela Clark, Executive Director of Institutional Advancement
Thomas Bennett, ChiefTechnologist

WEYI-TV *Digital Channel:* 30; *Virtual Channel:* 25; 193 kw; 1,168 ft.; N43 13 01 W83 43 17; *Population Served:* 104,868
2225 W. Willard Rd., Clio, MI 48420 US
(810) 687-1000; *Fax:* (810) 687-4925
www.nbc25news.com
comments@nbc25news.com
License: Saginaw, Saginaw County, MI held by HSH Flint (WEYI) Licensee LLC
Group Owner: Howard Stirk Holdings; (acq 11-22-2013; grpsl);
Washington Law Firm: Pillsbury Winthrop Shaw Pittman LLP
Nat'l Network: NBC; *Nat'l Reps:* HRP; *Wire Services:* AP
Hours of Local News Weekly: News progmg 19.5 hrs wkly
Pam Bishop, Programming Director
Jeff Reinarz, Creative Services and Promotions Manager
Kathy Reynolds, News Director
Mark Olson, Chief Engineer
Jim Joly, Director of National Digital Sales
Greg Siegel, Vice President, NationalSales

***WFUM** *Digital Channel:* 28; 17.5 kw; 489 ft.; N42 53 57 W83 27 42
303 E. Kearsley St., Flint, MI 48502 US
(810) 762-3028, (800) 728-9386; *Fax:* (810) 233-6017
www.michigantelevision.org
information@michigantelevision.org
License: Flint, Genesee County, MI held by Board of Regents, University of Michigan
Washington Law Firm: Dow, Lohnes PLLC
Nat'l Network: PBS
Steve Schram, General Manager
Jennifer White, Station Manager
Wayne Henderson, Chief Engineer
Rick Schudiske, Asst. General manager

WJRT *Digital Channel:* 12; *Virtual Channel:* 12; 30 kW; 963 ft.; N43 13 49 W84 3 32
3121 Davenport Ave., Saginaw, MI 48602 USA
(810) 233-3130
abc12.com
abc12news@abc12.com
License: Flint, Genesee County, MI held by Gray Television Licensee LLC
Group Owner: Gray Television Inc.
Nat'l Network: ABC
Size of News Staff: 49; *Hours of Local News Weekly:* news progmg 34 hrs wkly
Pete Veto, President & General Manager
Brock Rice, General Sales Mgr
Jayne Berklich, Programming Director
Jayne Hodak, News Director

WNEM *Digital Channel:* 22; *Virtual Channel:* 5; 1000 kW; 902 ft.; N43 28 14 W83 50 36; *Population Served:* 1,251,000
107 N Franklin St, Saginaw, MI 48607
(989) 755-8191; *Fax:* (989) 758-2111
www.wnem.com
wnem@wnem.com
License: Bay City, Bay County, MI held by Meredith Corp.
Group Owner: Meredith Corp.; (acq 4-16-69; $11.5 million;
Washington Law Firm: Haley, Bader & Potts
Nat'l Network: CBS; MyNetworkTV; *Nat'l Reps:* TeleRep
Jeff Guilbert, General Sales Mgr
Ian Rubin, News Director
Garth Sims, Chief Engineer
Karen Frey, Creative Services Director

WSMH *Digital Channel:* 16; *Virtual Channel:* 66; 245 kw; 1199 ft.; N43 13 31 W84 4 33
G-3463 W. Pierson Rd., Flint, MI 48504 US
(810) 785-8866; *Fax:* (810) 785-8963
www.wsmh.com
promotions@wsmh.com
License: Flint, Genesee County, MI held by WSMH Licensee LLC
Group Owner: Sinclair Broadcast Group Inc.; (acq 2-28-96; $33 million)
Nat'l Network: FOX; *Nat'l Reps:* Millennium Sales & Marketing
Hours of Local News Weekly: news progmg 7 hrs wkly
Andrew Massimino, Sales Manager

Grand Rapids-Kalamazoo-Battle Creek, MI (DMA 44)

***WGVK** *Digital Channel:* 5; *Virtual Channel:* 52; 10 kw; 554 ft.; N42 18 23 W85 39 25; *Rebroadcasting:* Rebroadcasts WGVU-TV Grand Rapids 100%.
301 Fulton St. W, Grand Rapids, MI 49504-6492 US
(616) 331-6666, (800) 442-2771; *Fax:* (616) 331-6625
www.wgvu.org
wgvu@gvsu.edu
License: Kalamazoo, Kalamazoo County, MI held by Grand Valley State University
Washington Law Firm: Mark Van Bergh
Nat'l Network: PBS
Size of News Staff: 15; *Hours of Local News Weekly:* news progmg one hr wkly
Michael T. Walenta, General Manager
Gary Hunt, General Sales Mgr
Carrie Corbin, Programming Director
Patrick Center, News Director
Robert Lumbert, Engineering Dir
Ken Kolbe, Asst General Manager
Scott VanderWerf, Music Critic
Ed Spier, Traffic Manager

***WGVU-TV** *Digital Channel:* 11; *Virtual Channel:* 35; 41.5 kw; 853 ft.; N42 57 34.9 W85 53 44.9
301 West Fulton Street, Grand Rapids, MI 49504-6492 US
(616) 331-6666, (800) 442-2771; *Fax:* (616) 331-6625
www.wgvu.org
wgvu@gvsu.edu
License: Grand Rapids, Kent County, MI held by Grand Valley State University
Washington Law Firm: Mark Van Bergh
Nat'l Network: PBS
Michael T. Walenta, General Manager
Gary Hunt, General Sales Mgr
Carrie Corbin, Programming Director
Robert Lumbert, Engineering Dir
Ken Kolbe, Asst General Manager
Scott VanderWerf, Music Critic
Ed Spier, Traffic Manager

WLLA *Digital Channel:* 45; *Virtual Channel:* 64; 440 kw; 1085 ft.; N42 33 52 W85 27 31
Mailing Address: PO Box 3157, Kalamazoo, MI 49003 US
Second Address: 7048 E. Kilgore Rd, Kalamazoo, MI 49003
(269) 345-6421; *Fax:* (269) 345-5665
License: Kalamazoo, Kalamazoo County, MI held by Christian Faith Broadcast, Inc.
Group Owner: Christian Faith Broadcasting Inc.; (acq 1-13-86; $35,000;
Nat'l Network: IND
Richard Hawkins, General Manager
Barb Hawkins, Programming Director
Jacob Potter, Promotions Manager

WOOD-TV *Digital Channel:* 7; *Virtual Channel:* 8; 30 kw; 945 ft.; N42 41 14 W85 30 34
Mailing Address: 4 Richmond Square, Suite 200, Providence, RI 02906 US
Second Address: 120 College Ave. S.E., Grand Rapids, MI 49503
(616) 456-8888; *Fax:* (616) 456-5755 (news)
www.woodtv.com
woodtv@woodtv.com
License: Grand Rapids, Kent County, MI held by Wood License Co. LLC.
Group Owner: LIN Television Corporation; (acq 6-30-99).;
Washington Law Firm: Covington & Burling
Nat'l Network: NBC
Diane Kniowski, President
Eva Cooper, Operations Dir
Barb Klap, General Sales Mgr
Craig Cole, Programming Director
Kurtis Kaechele, Promotions Manager
Ken Selvig, Chief Engineer
Dani Carlson, Reporter
Eva Aguirre Cooper,Community Affairs
Jack Doles, Sports Director
Matt Kirkwood, Meterologist
Henry Erb, Investigator
Susan Shaw, Anchor

WOTV *Digital Channel:* 20; *Virtual Channel:* 41; 270 kw; 1020 ft.; N42 34 15 W85 28 7
Mailing Address: 120 College Ave. SE, Grand Rapids, MI 49503 US
Second Address: 120 College Ave. S.E., Grand Rapids, MI 49503
(616) 456-8888, (616) 771-9633; *Fax:* (616) 456-9169
www.wotv.com
License: Battle Creek, Calhoun County, MI held by Wood License Co. LLC
Group Owner: LIN Television Corporation; (acq 12-6-2001; $2.25 million); *Washington Law Firm:* Covington & Burling
Nat'l Network: ABC
Size of News Staff: 25; *Hours of Local News Weekly:* news progmg 13 hrs wkly
Diane Kniowski, President
Ann Young, General Sales Mgr
Craig Cole, Programming Director
Molly Kelly, Promotions Manager
Patti McGethgain, News Director
Dave Morse, Chief Engineer
Swaina Noble, National Sales Manager
EthanBeute, Promotions Manager

WTLJ *Digital Channel:* 24; *Virtual Channel:* 54; 310 kw; 928 ft.; N42 57 25 W85 54 7
Mailing Address: Box 1010, 11717 Rt. 37 N., Marion, IL 62959 US
Second Address: PO Box 1220, Fort Erie, ON L2A 5Y2
(618) 997-4700, (800) 232-9855; *Fax:* (618) 993-9778
www.tct.tv
License: Muskegon, Muskegon County, MI held by TCT of Michigan Inc.
Group Owner: Tri-State Christian Television; (acq 1-15-92; $1.5 million;
Nat'l Network: IND
Vic Van Deventer, General Manager
Frank Ayre, Chief Engineer

WWMT *Digital Channel:* 8; *Virtual Channel:* 3; 25 kw; 843 ft.; N42 37 56 W85 32 16
590 W. Maple St., Kalamazoo, MI 49008 US
(800) 875-3333
www.wwmt.com
desk@wwmt.com
License: Kalamazoo, Kalamazoo County, MI held by WWMT Licensee LLC
Group Owner: Sinclair Broadcast Group Inc.; (acq 4-2-2012); *Washington Law Firm:* Akin, Gump, Strauss, Hauer & Feld
Nat'l Network: CBS; CW; *Nat'l Reps:* TeleRep
Hours of Local News Weekly: news progmg 31 hrs wkly
James Lutton, Vice President and General Manager
Steve Koles, News Director
Jim Steffey, Engineering Dir
Bill Bradley, Director of Sales
Mark Bishop, Marketing Director

WXMI *Digital Channel:* 17; *Virtual Channel:* 17; 725 kw; 1004 ft.; N42 41 15 W85 31 57
3117 Plaza Dr. NE, Grand Rapids, MI 49525 USA
(616) 364-8722; *Fax:* (616) 364-8506
fox17online.com
License: Battle Creek, Kent County, MI held by WXMI LLC
Group Owner: Tribune Media
Nat'l Network: FOX; *Nat'l Reps:* Harrington, Righter & Parsons
Size of News Staff: 30; *Hours of Local News Weekly:* news progmg 4 hrs wkly
Stephanie Gonda, General Sales Mgr
Bob Brenzing, Digital Manager

WZPX-TV *Digital Channel:* 44; 212 kw; 1,058t; N42 40 45 W85 03 57; *Population Served:* 4,500,000
2610 Horizon Dr., Suite E, Grand Rapids, MI 49546 USA
(812) 335-1770; *Fax:* (616) 493-2677
www.iontelevision.com
License: Battle Creek, MI held by ION Media Battle Creek License, Inc.
Group Owner: ION Media Networks Inc.
Brandon Burgess, Chairman

WZZM *Digital Channel:* 13; *Virtual Channel:* 13; 24.5 kw; 1,064 ft.; N43 18 35 W85 54 45; *Population Served:* 635,000
645 Three Mile, Grand Rapids, MI 49544 US
(616) 785-1313; *Fax:* (616) 785-1301
www.wzzm13.com
management@wzzm13.com
License: Grand Rapids, Kent County, MI held by Combined Communications of Oklahoma LLC
Group Owner: Tegna Media; (acq 1-27-97; grpsl).
Nat'l Network: ABC; *Nat'l Reps:* TeleRep; *Wire Services:* AP
Hours of Local News Weekly: news progmg 31 hrs wkly
Janet Mason, President and General Manager
Jay Lowe, Operations Supervisor
Kim Krause, Vice President of Sales and Marketing
Chuck Mikowski, Programming Director
Taz Painter, News Director
Catherine Behrendt, Programming andCommunity Director

Indianapolis, IN (DMA 27)

WUPX-TV *Digital Channel:* 27; 1.7 kw; ant 1,053t/2,300g; N46 30 52 W87 29 07; *Population Served:* 825,000
2166 McCausey Ridge Rd., Frenchburg, KY 40322 USA
(317) 486-0633; *Fax:* (317) 486-0298
www.iontelevision.com
License: Marquette, MI held by Board of Trustees of Northern Michigan University
Group Owner: ION Media Networks Inc.; *Washington Law Firm:* Fisher, Wayland, Cooper, Leader & Zaragoza
Nat'l Network: ION Television
Brandon Burgess, Chairman/CEO

Lansing, MI (DMA 113)

WHTV *Digital Channel:* 34; *Virtual Channel:* 18; 13.6 kw; 863 ft.; N42 41 19 W84 22 35
600 W Saint Joseph Street, Suite 47, Lansing, MI 48933 US
(517) 372-9497, (517) 367-2194; *Fax:* (517) 372-9499, (517) 372-5065
info@my18.tv
License: Jackson, Jackson County, MI held by Spartan-TV LLC
Nat'l Network: MY NETWORK TV
Kristine Melser, Station Manager
Corey Cummings, Chief Engineer

WILX *Digital Channel:* 10; *Virtual Channel:* 10; 30 kw; 979 ft.; N42 26 33 W84 34 21
500 American Rd., Lansing, MI 48911 USA
(517) 393-0110
www.wilx.com
newstips@wilx.com
License: Onondaga, Ingham County, MI held by Gray Television Licensee LLC
Group Owner: Gray Television Inc.; (acq 8-29-2002; grpsl).
Nat'l Network: NBC; *Nat'l Reps:* Continental Television Sales
Size of News Staff: 45
Tom Dolata, Operations/Production Manager
Michael King, VP/General Manager
Debbie Petersmark, General Sales Mgr
Kevin Ragan, News Director
Mike Winsky, Chief Engineer

***WKAR-TV** *Digital Channel:* 40; *Virtual Channel:* 23; 425 kw; 969 ft.; N42 42 7 W84 24 48
404 Wilson Rd. Room 212, Communication Arts & Sciences Bldg., Michigan State Universi, East Lansing, MI 48824 US
(517) 884-4700; *Fax:* (517) 432-3858
www.wkar.org
License: East Lansing, Ingham County, MI held by Michigan State University
Washington Law Firm: Schwartz, Woods & Miller
Nat'l Network: PBS
De Anne Hamilton, General Manager
Susi Elkins, TV Station Manager
Cindy Herfindahl, General Sales Mgr
Jeanie Croope, Promotions Manager
Gary Blievernicht, Engineering Dir
Susan Goodrich, Director of Business Operations
Al Martin,Host, Sports
Jeanie Croope, TV Host & Communicaions Manager
Peter Whorf, Radio Station Manager
Brad Walker, Host & Producer

WLAJ *Digital Channel:* 51; *Virtual Channel:* 53; 900 kw; 984 ft.; N42 25 13 W84 31 25
2820 East Saginaw Street, Lansing, MI 48912 US
(517) 372-8282,(517) 372-1300; *Fax:* (517) 372-1507
www.wlaj.com
newstips@wlns.com
License: Lansing, Ingham County, MI held by WLAJ-TV LLC
Group Owner: Shield Media LLC; (acq 6-22-98; $170 million with WWMT(TV) Kalamazoo).
Nat'l Network: ABC; CW
Size of News Staff: 10; *Hours of Local News Weekly:* news progmg 5 hrs wkly
Jim Wareham, Operations Dir
Susan Angel, General Sales Mgr
Jim Fordyce, News Director
Mike Winsky, Chief Engineer

WLNS-TV *Digital Channel:* 36; *Virtual Channel:* 6; 984 kw; 945 ft.; N42 41 19 W84 22 35
2820 East Saginaw Street, Lansing, MI 48912 US
(517) 372-8282, (517) 372-1300; *Fax:* (517) 372-1507
www.wlns.com
License: Lansing, Ingham County, MI held by Young Broadcasting of Lansing, Inc., Debtor-in-possession
Group Owner: Young Broadcasting Inc.; (acq 9-15-86; $72 million; *Washington Law Firm:* Wiley, Rein & Fielding
Nat'l Network: CBS
Gene Shanahan, Operations Dir
Don Carmichael, General Manager
Doug Powers, Station Manager
Steve South, General Sales Manager
Teresa Morton, Programming Director
Jam Sardar, News Director
Cory Cumming, Chief Engineer
Bob Serre,National Sales manager
Susan Angel, Local Sales Manager
Peter Clay, Digital sales Manager
Brooke Noback, Account executive
Anna Walz, Sales Asst.
Ryan Armbrustmacher, Digital Account Executive

WSYM-TV *Digital Channel:* 38; *Virtual Channel:* 47; 933 kw; 922 ft.; N42 28 3 W84 39 6
600 W. Saint Joseph St., Suite 47, Milwaukee, WI 48933 US
(517) 484-7747, (517) 484-8847; *Fax:* (517) 484-3144
www.fox47news.com
newstips@fox47news.com
License: Lansing, Ingham County, MI held by Journal Broadcast Corp.
Group Owner: Journal Communications Inc.; (acq 11-9-85; *Washington Law Firm:* Crowell & Moring
Nat'l Network: FOX; *Nat'l Reps:* Harrington, Righter & Parsons
Size of News Staff: 22; *Hours of Local News Weekly:* news progmg 10 hrs wkly
Gary Baxter, VP/General Manager/Operations Director
Jami Anderson, National Sales Manager
Joe Antonelli, General Sales Manager
Kip Bohne, Production & Promotion
Joe Antonelli, Sales & Advertising/ Local Sales Manager
Jane Sugiyama,Web Content Producer
Stephanie Miller, Digital Media Manager
Stefanie Pohl, Web Content Producer
Jami Anderson, National Sales Manager
Amy Garcia, Administrative Asst.

Marquette, MI (DMA 180)

WBKP *Digital Channel:* 5; *Virtual Channel:* 5; 6.4 kw; 988 ft.; N47 2 11 W88 41 43
1122 Calumet Ave #5, Calumet, MI 49913 US
(906) 204-2436; *Fax:* (906) 204-2433
License: Calumet, Houghton County, MI held by Lake Superior Community Broadcasting Corp.
Group Owner: Lake Superior Community Broadcasting Corp.; (acq 1-15-2004; $500,000 with WBUP(TV) Ishpeming)
Nat'l Network: CW TELEVISION N
Size of News Staff: 7; *Hours of Local News Weekly:* news progmg 10 hrs wkly
Cher Allen, General Manager
Tim Thompson, General Sales Mgr
Burns Severson, Promotions Manager
Gerry Heyn, Chief Engineer

WBUP *Digital Channel:* 10; *Virtual Channel:* 10; 4.8 kw; 344 ft.; N46 21 10 W87 51 15
1705 Ash St., Ste. 5, Ishpeming, MI 49849 US
(906) 204-2436; *Fax:* (906) 204 2433
www.tv5and10.com
news@abc10up.com
License: Ishpeming, Marquette County, MI held by Lake Superior Community Broadcasting Corp.
Group Owner: Lake Superior Community Broadcasting Corp.; (acq 1-15-2004; $500,000 with WBKP(TV) Calumet).;
Washington Law Firm: Latham and Watkins
Nat'l Network: ABC
Cher Allen, General Manager
Cynthia Thompson, News dir./ Station Manager
Tim Thompson, General Sales Mgr
Burns Severson, Promotions Manager
Gerry Heyn, Chief Engineer
Mike Hoey, Sr. News Reporter
Jerry Taylor, Sports Dir.
JeffLaMay, PhotoJournalist
Molly Smerika, Multi-Media Journalist
William Burns, Multi-Media Journalist

WJMN-TV *Digital Channel:* 48; *Virtual Channel:* 3; 1000 kw; 1165 ft.; N46 8 5 W86 56 55; *Rebroadcasting:* Satellite of WFRV-TV Green Bay, WI.
600 New Hampshire Ave, NW, Ste 1200, Washington, DC 20037 US
(920) 437-5411,(906) 226-3023 (sales); *Fax:* (920) 437-5769 (news)
www.marquettehomepage.com
License: Escanaba, Delta County, MI held by WFRV and WJMN Television Station Inc.
Group Owner: Liberty Media Corp.; (acq 4-16-2007; with WFRV-TV Green Bay, WI)
Nat'l Network: CBS; *Nat'l Reps:* TeleRep
R. Perry Kidder, President
Dale Mitchell, Operations Dir
Jackie Stewart, General Sales Mgr
Jaci Haakonson, Programming Director
Kristen Kent, Promotions Manager
H. Lee Hitter, News Director
Mike Smith, National Sales Manager
Erin Davisson, News Commentator
Kit Overlock, Regional Sales Manager
Jill Harkoff, Traffic Manager

WLUC-TV *Digital Channel:* 35; *Virtual Channel:* 6; 63 kw; ant 978t/1,018g; N46 20 11 W87 50 55; *Population Served:* 292,600
177 U.S. 41 E., Negaunee, MI 49866
(906) 475-4161; *Fax:* (906) 475-4824
www.uppermichiganssource.com
tv6@wluctv6.com
License: Marquette, Marquette County, MI held by WLUC Licensee LLC
Group Owner: Sinclair Broadcast Group Inc.; (acq 11-22-2013; grpsl); *Washington Law Firm:* Pillsbury Winthrop Shaw Pittman LLP
Nat'l Network: NBC; *Nat'l Reps:* Harrington, Righter & Parsons; *Wire Services:* AP
Foreign Language Programming; Size of News Staff: 17; *Hours of Local News Weekly:* news progmg 16 hrs wkly
Jeffrey Collins, Operations Manager
Rob Jamros, General Manager
Rick Rhoades, Local Sales Manager
Steve Asplund, News Director
Daniel DiLoreto, Digital Sales Manager
Nick Terbrack, Producer

***WNMU** *Digital Channel:* 33; 316 kw vis, 63.1 kw aur; 1,090t/1,000g; N46 21 09 W87 51 32; *Population Served:* 250,000
1401 Presque Isle Ave., Marquette, MI 49855
(800) 227-9668, (800) 227-1300; *Fax:* (906) 227-2905
www.nmu.edu/wnmutv
esmith@nmu.edu
License: Marquette, Marquette County, MI held by Board of Control of Northern Michigan University
Washington Law Firm: Cohn & Marks
Nat'l Network: PBS; *Wire Services:* UPI
Hours of Local News Weekly: News progmg one hr wkly
Eric Smith, General Manager & Engineering
Bruce Turner, Station Manager
Melinda Stamp, Web Designer
Bob Thomson, Producer/ Director
Bill Hart, Media Meet Producer & Host
Marianne Eyer, Membership & Volunteer upervisor

WZMQ *Digital Channel:* 19; *Virtual Channel:* 19; 31 kw; 577 ft.; N46 30 8 W87 38 52
PO Box 416, Marquette, MI 49855 US
(906) 360-8848, (906) 362-TV4U; *Fax:* (920) 785-0480
www.wzmqtv.com
License: Marquette, Marquette County, MI held by MMMRC, LLC (acq 4-15-2009); *Ownership:* MMMRC, LLC
Nat'l Network: FOX
Paul Belschner, President
Danny Hood, General Manager

Traverse City-Cadillac, MI (DMA 119)

***WCMV** *Digital Channel:* 17; *Virtual Channel:* 27; 338 kw; 1289 ft.; N44 44 53 W85 4 8; *Rebroadcasting:* Rebroadcasts WCMU(TV) Mt. Pleasant 100%.
Central Michigan Univ., 1999 E. Campus Dr., Mt. Pleasant, MI 48859 US
(989) 774-3105, (800) 727-9268; *Fax:* (989) 774-4427
www.wcmu.org
grant1eb@cmich.edu
License: Cadillac, Wexford County, MI held by Central Michigan University
Washington Law Firm: Dow, Lohnes & Albertson
Nat'l Network: PBS
Kim Walters, Director, Development and Business Operations
Edward Grant, General Manager
Linda Dielman, Program/Outreach Manager
David Nicholas, News Director
Wayne Henderson, Director of Technical Services
Shannon Peak, AssistantManager/Business Operations
Kurt Wilson, Director, Corporate Support / Major Gifts
Tom Ball , Marketing Representative
Patricia Link, Marketing Representative
Michael Johnson, Marketing Representative
Stacy Earl, FundraisingCoordinator

***WCMW** *Digital Channel:* 21; *Virtual Channel:* 21; 50 kw vis; ant 305t/277g; N44 03 57 W86 19 58; *Rebroadcasting:* Satellite of WCMU-TV Mt. Pleasant
Central Michigan Univ., 1999 E. Campus Dr., Mt. Pleasant, MI 48859 US
(989) 774-3105, (800) 727-9268; *Fax:* (989) 774-4427
www.wcmu.org
License: Manistee, Manistee County, MI held by Central Michigan University
Washington Law Firm: Dow, Lohnes & Albertson
Nat'l Network: PBS
Kim Walters, Director, Development and Business Operations
Ed Grant, General Manager
Rick Schudiske, Station Manager
Kurt Wilson, General Sales Mgr
Linda Dielman, Program/Outreach Manager
David Nicholas, News Director
WayneHenderson, Director of Technical Services
Shannon Peak, Assistant Manager/Business Operations
Kurt Wilson, Director, Corporate Support / Major Gifts
Tom Ball , Marketing Representative
Patricia Link, Marketing Representative
MichaelJohnson, Marketing Representative
Stacy Earl, Fundraising Coordinator

WFQX-TV *Digital Channel:* 32; *Virtual Channel:* 33; 200 kw; 1385 ft.; N44 8 12 W85 20 33
Mailing Address: PO Box 282, Cadillac, MI 49601 US
Second Address: 7669 S. 45 Rd., Cadillac, MI 49601
(231) 775-9813; *Fax:* (231) 775-3671
www.mifox32.com
info@mifox32.com
License: Cadillac, Wexford County, MI held by Cadillac Telecasting Co.
Group Owner: Cadillac Telecasting Co.; (acq 10-31-2007; $11 million with WFUP(TV) Vanderbilt); *Washington Law Firm:* Womble, Carlyle, Sandridge & Rice PLLC
Nat'l Network: FOX
Hours of Local News Weekly: News progmg 3 hrs wkly
William Kring, General Manager
Tom O'Hare, Chief meterologist
Marisa McKay, General Assignment Reporter
Jeff Blakeman, Photojournalist
Jared smith, Sports Director
Adam Bartelmay, News anchor
Kalin Franks, Reporter & webproducer

WFUP *Digital Channel:* 45; *Virtual Channel:* 45; 108 kw; 1063 ft.; N45 10 12 W84 45 4; *Rebroadcasting:* Satellite of WFQX-TV Cadillac
Mailing Address: 7669 South 45 Road, Cadillac, MI 49601 US
Second Address: 7669 S. 45 Rd., Cadillac, MI 49601
(231) 775-9813; *Fax:* (231) 775-3671
www.fox33.com
info@fox33.com
License: Vanderbilt, Otsego County, MI held by Cadillac Telecasting Co.
Group Owner: Cadillac Telecasting Co.; (acq 10-31-2007; $11 million with WFQX-TV Cadillac); *Washington Law Firm:* Womble, Carlyle, Sandridge & Rice PLLC
Nat'l Network: FOX
Size of News Staff: 5; *Hours of Local News Weekly:* news progmg 3 hrs wkly
William Kring, General Manager

WGTQ *Digital Channel:* 8; *Virtual Channel:* 8; 15 kw; 945 ft.; N46 3 8 W84 6 38; *Rebroadcasting:* Satellite of WGTU(TV) Traverse City, rebroadcast 100%.
8513 East Traverse Hwy, Traverse City, MI 49684 US
(800)-968-7770; *Fax:* (231) 947-0354
www.upnorthlive.com
rwerly@upnorthlive.com
License: Sault Ste. Marie, Chippewa County, MI held by Traverse City (WGTU-TV) Licensee Inc.
Group Owner: Cunningham Broadcasting Corporation; (acq 11-22-2013; with WGTU(TV) Traverse City); *Washington Law Firm:* Pillsbury Winthrop Shaw Pittman LLP
Nat'l Network: ABC

WGTU *Digital Channel:* 29; *Virtual Channel:* 29; 68.4 kw; 1289 ft.; N44 44 53 W85 4 8
8513 East Traverse Hwy, Traverse City, MI 49684 US
(800)-968-7770; *Fax:* (231) 947-0354
www.upnorthlive.com
License: Traverse City, Grand Traverse County, MI held by Traverse City (WGTU-TV) Licensee Inc.
Group Owner: Cunninham Broadcasting Corporation; (acq 11-22-2013; with WGTQ(TV) Sault Ste. Marie); *Washington Law Firm:* Pillsbury Winthrop Shaw Pittman LLP
Nat'l Network: ABC
Kevin Dunaway, News Director

WPBN-TV *Digital Channel:* 47; *Virtual Channel:* 7; 500 kw; 1289 ft.; N44 44 53 W85 4 8
8513 East Traverse Hwy., Traverse City, MI 49684 US
(800) 968-7770; *Fax:* (231) 947-0354
www.upnorthlive.com
rwerly@upnorthlive.com
License: Traverse City, Grand Traverse County, MI held by WPBN Licensee LLC
Group Owner: Sincalir Broadcast Group Inc.; (acq 11-22-2013; grpsl); *Washington Law Firm:* Pillsbury Winthrop Shaw Pittman LLP
Nat'l Network: NBC; *Nat'l Reps:* Harrington, Righter & Parsons
Jill Saarela, General Manager
Betsy Bard, Director of Sales
Patrick Livingston, News Director
Jim Joly, Director of National Digital Sales
Greg Siegel, Vice President, National Sales

WTOM-TV *Digital Channel:* 35; *Virtual Channel:* 4; 78 kw; 551 ft.; N45 39 1 W84 20 37; *Rebroadcasting:* Satellite of WPBN-TV Traverse City
8513 East Traverse Hwy., Traverse City, MI 49684 US
(800) 968-7770; *Fax:* (231) 947-0354
www.upnorthlive.com
rwerly@upnorthlive.com
License: Cheboygan, Cheboygan County, MI held by WPBN Licensee LLC
Group Owner: Sinclair Broadcast Group Inc.; (acq 11-22-2013; grpsl); *Washington Law Firm:* Pillsbury Winthrop Shaw Pittman LLP
Nat'l Network: NBC
Jill Saarela, General Manager
Patrick Livingston, News Director
Jim Joly, Director of National Digital Sales
Greg Siegel, Vice President, National Sales

WWTV *Digital Channel:* 9; *Virtual Channel:* 9; 45 kw; 1631 ft.; N44 8 12 W85 20 33; *Rebroadcasting:* Satellite of WWUP-TV Sault Ste. Marie.
P. O. Box 627, Cadillac, MI 49601 US
(231) 775-3478, (800) 782-7910, (800) STAR-910; *Fax:* (231) 775-3671
www.9and10news.com
info@9and10news.com
License: Cadillac, Wexford County, MI held by Heritage Broadcasting Co. of Michigan.
Group Owner: Heritage Broadcasting Co of MI; (acq 3-3-89; grpsl; *Ownership:* .; *Washington Law Firm:* Wamble Carlyle
Nat'l Network: CBS; *Wire Services:* UPI
William Kring, General Manager
Sherri Magiera, Programming Director
Tessia Klix, Promotions Manager
Kevin Dunaway, News Director
Lowell Shore, Chief Engineer
Tom O'Hare, Chief Meterologist
Adam Bartelmay, Anchor
jared Smith,Sports dir.
Jared Barraco, Photojournalist
Marisa McKay, Reporter

WWUP-TV *Digital Channel:* 10; *Virtual Channel:* 10; 25 kw; 1214 ft.; N46 3 36 W84 5 57; *Rebroadcasting:* Satellite of WWTV-TV Cadillac
P.O. Box 627, Cadillac, MI 49601 US
(231) 775-3478, (800) 782-7910, (800) STAR-910; *Fax:* (231) 775-3671
www.9and10news.com
info@9and10news.com
License: Sault Ste. Marie, Chippewa County, MI held by Heritage Broadcasting Co. of Michigan.
Group Owner: Heritage Broadcasting Co of MI; (acq 3-3-89; grpsl; *Washington Law Firm:* Wamble Carlyle
Nat'l Network: CBS
William Kring, General Manager
Sherri Magiera, Programming Director
Tessia Klix, Promotions Manager
Kevin Dunaway, News Director
Lowell Shore, Chief Engineer

Tom O'Hare, Chief Meterologist
Adam Bartelmay, Anchor
jared Smith,Sports dir.
Jared Barraco, Photojournalist
Marisa McKay, Reporter

Minnesota

Duluth, MN-Superior, WI (DMA 142)

KCWV *Digital Channel:* 27; *Virtual Channel:* 27; 40 kw; 679 ft.; N46 47 7 W92 7 15; *Not on Air/Target Date:* unknown
US
(901) 375-9324
License: Duluth, Saint Louis County, MN held by George S. Flinn III
Terry Elaqua, President
George Flinn III, General Manager
Julie Fruecht, Traffic Manager

KDLH *Digital Channel:* 33; *Virtual Channel:* 3; 381 kw; 1023 ft.; N46 47 21.3 W92 6 50.7
425 West Superior Street, Duluth, MN 55802 US
(218) 733-0303; *Fax:* (218) 720-9699
License: Duluth, Saint Louis County, MN held by Malara Broadcast Group of Duluth Licensee LLC.
Group Owner: Malara Broadcast Group Inc.; (acq 3-14-2005; $10.8 million); *Washington Law Firm:* Wolf Bloch
Nat'l Network: CBS; CW; *Nat'l Reps:* Harrington, Righter & Parsons
Size of News Staff: 17; *Hours of Local News Weekly:* news progmg 12 hrs wkly
Anthony Malara, President
Kelli Latuska, Station Manager
Carl Keller, General Sales Mgr
Nate Stoltman, Promotions Manager
Barbara Reyelts, News Director
Larry Erickson, Engineering Dir
Todd Wentworth, General Sales Manager
JoeBiondi, Local Sales Manager
Mary Rhodes, Traffic Manager

KQDS-TV *Digital Channel:* 17; *Virtual Channel:* 21; 1000 kw; 981 ft.; N46 47 37 W92 7 3
2001 London Rd., Duluth, MN 55812 US
(218) 728-8930; *Fax:* (877) 573-7369
www.fox21online.com
License: Duluth, Saint Louis County, MN held by KQDS Acquisition Corp.
Group Owner: Red River Broadcast Co. L.L.C.; (acq 10-21-98; grpsl).
Nat'l Network: FOX; *Nat'l Reps:* Harrington, Righter & Parsons; *Wire Services:* AP
Size of News Staff: 20; *Hours of Local News Weekly:* news progmg 2.5 hrs wkly
Ro Grignon, President
Kathy Lau, Operations Dir
Dave Hileman, General Manager
Julie Moravchik, News Director
Greg Chandler, Sports Director
Eric Gullickson, Weekend Sports Anchor / Reporter
Jason Sydejko, Chief Meteorologist
Diane Alexander, Anchor / Producer / Reporter

KRII *Digital Channel:* 11; *Virtual Channel:* 11; 63 kw; 657 ft.; N47 51 39 W92 56 46; *Rebroadcasting:* Satellite of KBJR-TV Superior, WI.
C/O Granite B/C Corp, 767 Third Ave, 28th Fl, New York, NY 10017 US
(218) 720-9600; *Fax:* (218) 720-9660
www.news6.tv
License: Chisholm, St. Louis County, MN held by Channel 11 License Inc.
Group Owner: Granite Broadcasting Corp.; (acq 5-9-2001; grpsl).
Nat'l Network: NBC
Dustin DeSanto, Chief Director/ News Operations Manager
Kelli Latuska, Station Manager
Vincent Nelson, General Sales Mgr
Barb Wentworth, Programming Director
Chris Hussey, Promotions Manager
Derrick Hinds, News Director
LarryErickson, Engineering Dir

WDIO-DT *Digital Channel:* 10; 316 kw vis, 105 kw aur; 987t/836g; N46 47 13 W92 07 17; *Population Served:* 176,000
Mailing Address: Box 16897, Duluth, MN 55816-0897 US
Second Address: 10 Observation Rd., Duluth, MN 55811-3506
(218) 727-6864, (800) 477-1013; *Fax:* (218) 727-4415
www.wdio.com
news@wdio.com
License: Duluth, Saint Louis County, MN held by WDIO-TV L.L.C.
Group Owner: Hubbard Broadcasting Inc.; (acq 12-87; grpsl).;
Washington Law Firm: Fletcher, Heald & Hildreth
Nat'l Network: ABC
Size of News Staff: 18; *Hours of Local News Weekly:* news progmg 9 hrs wkly
George Couture, General Manager
Deb Messer, General Sales Mgr
Dave Poirier, Programming Director
Jeff Laumdergan, Promotions Manager
Steve Goodspeed, News Director
Mike Hatlestad, Chief Engineer

***WDSE** *Digital Channel:* 8; *Virtual Channel:* 8; 34 kw; 968 ft.; N46 47 30 W92 7 21
632 Niagara Court, Duluth, MN 55811 US
(888) 563-9373; *Fax:* (218) 788-2832
www.wdse.org
email@wdse.org
License: Duluth, Saint Louis County, MN held by Duluth-Superior Area Educ TV Corp
Washington Law Firm: Arnold & Porter
Nat'l Network: PBS
Allen Harmon, General Manager
Cheryl Leeper, General Sales Mgr
Juli Kellner, Director of Programming and Production
Brita Edgerton, Promotions Manager
Larry Erickson, Director of Engineering and Operations
Rex Greenwell, ChiefEngineer

WIRT *Digital Channel:* 13; 125 kw vis, 21.6 kw aur; 670t/476g; N47 22 52 W92 57 18; *Rebroadcasting:* Satellite of WDIO-TV Duluth.
Mailing Address: P.O. Box 16897, Duluth, MN 55816-0897
Second Address: 10 Observation Road, Duluth, MN 55811
(218) 727-6864, (800) 477-1013; *Fax:* (218) 727-4415, (218) 727-2318
www.wdio.com
news@wdio.com
License: Hibbing, Saint Louis County, MN held by WDIO-TV L.L.C.
Group Owner: Hubbard Broadcasting Inc.; (acq 12-87; grpsl).
Nat'l Network: ABC
George Couture, General Manager
Deb Messer, General Sales Mgr
Dave Poirier, Programming Director
Jeff Laumdergan, Promotions Manager
Steve Goodspeed, News Director
Mike Hatlestad, Chief Engineer
Justin Liles, ChiefMeterologist
Dan Williamson, Sports Director
Alan Hoglund, Reporter/Producer
Darren Danielson, News Anchor
Maarja Anderson, News Anchor
Laurie Stribling, News Anchor

La Crescent

KQEG-CA ; 15 kw; N43 44 53.10 W91 17 50.50
505 King St., La Crosse, WI 54601 US
(608) 784-0876
www.kqegtv.com
License: La Crescent, MN held by Magnum Radio, Inc.
Group Owner: Magnum Radio, Inc.
Richard Wilson, Station Manager

Mankato, MN (DMA 199)

KEYC-TV CBS & NEYC FOX *Digital Channel:* 12; *Virtual Channel:* 12; 316 kw vis, 63 kw aur; 1,045t/1,116g; N43 56 14 W94 24 41; *Population Served:* 352,000
Mailing Address: Box 128, Mankato, MN 56002
Second Address: 1570 Lookout Dr., N. Mankato, MN 56003
(507) 625-7905; *Fax:* (507) 625-5745
keyc@keyc.com
License: Mankato, Blue Earth County, MN held by United Communications Corp.
Group Owner: United Communications Corp.; (acq 10-14-77; $5 million); *Washington Law Firm:* Wood, Maines & Nolan
Nat'l Network: CBS; Fox; *Nat'l Reps:* Continental Television Sales; *Wire Services:* AP; CBS; NWS (National Weather Service); Bloomberg Financial; NWS (National Weather Service)
Size of News Staff: 19; *Hours of Local News Weekly:* news progmg 13 hrs wkly
Dennis Wahlstrom, Operations Dir
John Ginther, General Sales Mgr
Sue Briggs, Programming Director
Dan Ruiter, News Director
Terry Rudenick, Chief Engineer
Sharon Freitag, Business Manager
Jan Ellanson, Operations Manager
JeffPoole, Production Manager
Perry Dyke, Sports Commentator
Mark Tarello, Weather Director

Minneapolis-St. Paul, MN (DMA 15)

KARE *Digital Channel:* 11; *Virtual Channel:* 11; 45.3 kw; 1,493 ft.; N45 03 44 W93 08 21; *Population Served:* 2,500,000
8811 Olson Memorial Hwy., Minneapolis, MN 55427 US
(763) 546-1111; *Fax:* (763) 546-8772
www.kare11.com
License: Minneapolis, Hennepin County, MN held by Multimedia Holdings Corp.
Group Owner: Tegna Media; (acq 4-13-83; $75 million;
Nat'l Network: NBC
Hours of Local News Weekly: news progmg 30 hrs wkly
John Remes, President and General Manager
David Crawford, General Sales Mgr
Jane Helmke, News Director
Jeff Phillips, VP Technology and Operations

***KAWB** *Digital Channel:* 28; *Virtual Channel:* 22; 137.5 kw; 745 ft.; N46 25 21 W94 27 41
Mailing Address: 1500 Birchmont Drive, NE #9, Bemidji, MN 56601 US
Second Address: 422 NW 3rd Street, Brainerd, MN 56401
(218) 751-3407; (800) 292-0922; *Fax:* (218) 751-3142
www.lakelandptv.org
news@lptv.org
License: Brainerd, Crow Wing County, MN held by Northern Minnesota Public TV Inc
Washington Law Firm: Dow, Lohnes PLLC
Nat'l Network: PBS
Hours of Local News Weekly: News progmg 2.5 hrs wkly
Jess Skala, Traffic/Operations Manager
Bill Sanford, Genral Manager
Dan Hegstad, KAWB Station Manager/ Underwriting Sales
Jeff Hanks, Program/Production Manager
Dennis Weimann, New Director
Tom Lembrick, Chief Engineer
GlennMclean, Development Director
Tim McMohan, Broadcast Engineer/Computer Services
Jackie Hanson, Manager of Accounting Services

***KAWE** *Digital Channel:* 9; *Virtual Channel:* 9; 27 kw; 1098 ft.; N47 42 3 W94 29 14
Mailing Address: 1500 Birchmont Drive, NE #9, Bemidji, MN 56601 US
Second Address: 422 NW 3rd Street, Brainerd, MN 56401
(218) 751-3407, (800) 292-0922; *Fax:* (218) 751-3142
www.lakelandptv.org
news@lptv.org
License: Bemidji, Beltrami County, MN held by Northern Minnesota Public TV Inc
Washington Law Firm: Dow, Lohnes PLLC
Nat'l Network: PBS
Size of News Staff: 7; *Hours of Local News Weekly:* news progmg 2.5 hrs wkly
Travis Annette, President
Jess Skala, Traffic/Operations Manager
Bill Sanford, Genral Manager
Sharon Pugh, General Sales Mgr
Jeff Hanks, Program/Production Manager
Dennis Weimann, New Director
Tom Lembrick, Chief Engineer
TimMcMohan, Broadcast Engineer/Computer Services
Jackie Hanson, Manager of Accounting Services

KCCO-TV *Digital Channel:* 7; *Virtual Channel:* 7; 29 kW; 1061 ft.; N45 41 10 W95 8 3; *Rebroadcasting:* WCCO (Minneapolis)
90 S 11th St., Minneapolis, MN 55403 USA
(612) 339-4444; *Fax:* (612) 330-2627
minnesota.cbslocal.com
License: Alexandria, Douglas County, MN held by CBS Broadcasting Inc.
Group Owner: CBS Television Stations Group; *Washington Law Firm:* Rosenman & Colin
Nat'l Network: CBS; *Nat'l Reps:* CBS TV Stations National Sales; *Wire Services:* NOAA Weather
Gary Kroger, Director of Engineering

KCCW-TV *Digital Channel:* 12; *Virtual Channel:* 12; 59 kW; 940 ft.; N46 56 5 W94 27 19; *Rebroadcasting:* WCCO (Minneapolis)
90 S 11th St., Minneapolis, MN 55403 USA
(612) 339-4444
minnesota.cbslocal.com

License: Walker, Cass County, MN held by CBS Broadcasting Inc.
Group Owner: CBS Television Stations Group; *Washington Law Firm:* Rosenman & Colin
Nat'l Network: CBS
Gary Kroger, Director of Engineering

KFTC *Digital Channel:* 26; *Virtual Channel:* 26; 4.5 kW; 512 ft.; N47 33 21 W94 48 4; *Rebroadcasting:* Satellite of Minneapolis WFTC(TV); *Not on Air/Target Date:* 2000
11358 Viking Dr., Eden Prairie, MN 55344 USA
(952) 946-5767
www.fox29.com
fox9news@foxtv.com
License: Bemidji, Beltrami County, MN held by Fox Television Stations LLC
Group Owner: Fox Television Stations Group; (acq 9-21-2001; grpsl).
Nat'l Network: MyNetworkTV

KMSP *Digital Channel:* 9; *Virtual Channel:* 9; 30 kW; 1421 ft.; N45 3 30 W93 7 27
11358 Viking Dr., Eden Prairie, MN 55344 USA
(952) 946-5767
www.fox9.com
fox9news@foxtv.com
License: Minneapolis, Hennepin County, MN held by Fox Television Stations LLC
Group Owner: Fox Television Stations Group; (acq 7-31-2001; grpsl).
Nat'l Network: FOX; *Wire Services:* AP
Size of News Staff: 64; *Hours of Local News Weekly:* news progmg 19.5 hrs wkly
Jason Sirek, Advertising Contact

KPXM-TV *Digital Channel:* 40; 1000 kw; 1,469t/1,498g; N45 23 00 W93 42 30; *Population Served:* 1,100,000
22601 176th St. NW, Big Lake, MN 55309 USA
(763) 263-8666; *Fax:* (763) 263-6600
www.iontelevision.com
License: St. Cloud, MN held by Ion Media Minneapolis License, Inc.
Group Owner: ION Media Networks Inc.; *Washington Law Firm:* Mullin, Rhyne, Emmons & Topel
Nat'l Network: ION Television
Brandon Burgess, Chairman/CEO
Stephen Appel, Sales
Marc Zand, Programming Acquisitions

KRWF *Digital Channel:* 27; *Virtual Channel:* 43; 58 kw; 495 ft.; N44 29 3 W95 29 27
Mailing Address: 3415 University Ave.West, St. Paul, MN 55114 US
Second Address: 415 Fillmore St., Alexandria, MN 56308
(320) 763-5729; *Fax:* (320) 763-4627
www.ksax.com
ksax@ksax.com
License: Redwood Falls, Redwood County, MN held by KSAX-TV Inc.
Group Owner: Hubbard Broadcasting Inc.; *Washington Law Firm:* Holland & Knight
Nat'l Network: ABC; *Wire Services:* AP
Robert Hubbard, General Manager
Edward Smith, Station Manager

KSAX *Digital Channel:* 42; *Virtual Channel:* 42; 80 kw; 1168 ft.; N45 41 59 W95 10 35
Mailing Address: 3415 University Ave.West, St. Paul, MN 55114 US
Second Address: 415 Fillmore St., Alexandria, MN 56308
(320) 763-5729; *Fax:* (320) 763-4627
www.ksax.com
License: Alexandria, Douglas County, MN held by KSAX-TV Inc.
Group Owner: Hubbard Broadcasting Inc.; *Washington Law Firm:* Holland & Knight
Nat'l Network: ABC; *Nat'l Reps:* Petry Television Inc.; *Wire Services:* AP
Melissa Mathews, Operations Dir
Robert Hubbard, General Manager
Edward Smith, Station Manager
Bill Lunn, Anchor
Tom Durian, Anchor
Jessica Melissa, Anchor
Chris Egent, Anchor
Joe Augustine, Reporter
Brandi Powell, Reporter

KSTC-TV *Digital Channel:* 45; *Virtual Channel:* 45; 1000 kw; 1404 ft.; N45 3 45 W93 8 21
Mailing Address: 1080 W County Rd E, Shoreview, MN 55126 US
Second Address: 3415 University Avenue, Saint Paul, MN 55114
(651) 645-4500; *Fax:* (651) 523-7320
www.kstc45.com
License: Minneapolis, Hennepin County, MN held by KSTC.TV LLC.
Group Owner: Hubbard Broadcasting Inc.; (acq 4-24-2000).; *Washington Law Firm:* Holland & Knight LLP
Nat'l Network: IND
Minica Doyle, Dir. Of Operations
Susan Wenz, Station Manager
Mary Jo Ferguson, General Sales Manager
Michael Smith, Programming Director
Joe Johnston, Promotions Manager
Christopher Berg, News Director
Ed Smith, Director ofEngineering
Dick Rice, Chief Engineer
Joe Johnston, Director of Marketing

KSTP-TV *Digital Channel:* 35; *Virtual Channel:* 5; 755 kw; 1421 ft.; N45 3 44 W93 8 21
3415 University Avenue, St. Paul, MN 55114-2099 US
(651) 646-5555; *Fax:* (651) 642-4409
www.kstp.com
gennewstips@kstp.com
License: St. Paul, Ramsey County, MN held by KSTP-TV LLC.
Group Owner: Hubbard Broadcasting Inc.; *Washington Law Firm:* Holland and Knight
Nat'l Network: ABC; *Nat'l Reps:* Petry Television Inc.; *Wire Services:* AP
Hours of Local News Weekly: 37 hrs weekly
Robert Hubbard, President
Monica Doyle, Operations Dir
Ray Mirabella, General Sales Mgr
Michael Smith, Programming Director
Paul Gaulke, Promotions Manager
Lindsay Radford, News Director
Dick Rice, Chief Engineer
Dixie Hansen,Business Manager
Anne Wittenborg, Assistant News Director

***KTCA-TV** *Digital Channel:* 34; *Virtual Channel:* 2; 662 kw; 1349 ft.; N45 3 30 W93 7 27
172 East 4th Street, St. Paul, MN 55101 US
(651) 222-1717; *Fax:* (651) 229-1282
www.tpt.org
viewerservices@tpt.org
License: St. Paul, Ramsey County, MN held by Twin Cities Public TV Inc
Nat'l Network: PBS
R. Kirk Weidner, Chairman
Jim Pagliarini, President & CEO
Stephen Usery, Promotions Manager
Bruce Jacobs, Chief Engineer
Terry O'Reilly, Chief Content Officer
Jenny Masters-Wolfe, Senior Vice President of Human Resources andOrgan
Jenn Schmidt, Senior Vice President of Finance and Business Admi
Allen Giles, Senior Vice President, Legal & General Counsel
Heather Stevenson, Senior Vice President, Revenue
Judy Diaz, President, Next Avenue

***KTCI-TV** *Digital Channel:* 23; *Virtual Channel:* 17; 325 kw; 1349 ft.; N45 3 30 W93 7 27
172 East 4th Street, St Paul, MN 55101 US
(651) 222-1717; *Fax:* (651) 229-1282
www.tpt.org
viewerservices@tpt.org
License: St. Paul, Ramsey County, MN held by Twin Cities Public Television Inc
Nat'l Network: PBS
R. Kirk Weidner, Chairman
Jim Pagliarini, President & CEO
Stephen Usery, Promotions Manager
Bruce Jacobs, Chief Engineer
Terry O'Reilly, Chief Content Officer
Jenny Masters-Wolfe, Senior Vice President of Human Resources andOrgan
Jenn Schmidt, Senior Vice President of Finance and Business Admi
Allen Giles, Senior Vice President, Legal & General Counsel
Heather Stevenson, Senior Vice President, Revenue
Judy Diaz, President, Next Avenue

***KWCM-TV** *Digital Channel:* 10; *Virtual Channel:* 10; 50 kw; 1250 ft.; N45 10 3 W96 0 2
120 West Schleiman Avenue, Appleton, MN 56208 US
(800) 726-3178; *Fax:* (320) 289-2634
www.pioneer.org
yourtv@pioneer.org
License: Appleton, Swift County, MN held by West Central Minnesota Educational TV Co
Washington Law Firm: Fletcher, Heald & Hildreth
Nat'l Network: PBS
James D. Massee, Chairperson
Janet Suckow, Operations Dir
Les Heen, General Manager
Jon Panzer, Engineering Director/Station Manager
Shirley Schwarz, Programming Director
Jon Panzer, Engineering Director/Station Manager
TimBakken, Production Director
Matthew Moe, Director of Finance
Robert Rakow, Broadcast Operations Director
Dana Johnson, Executive Producer
Janet Suckow, Membership Director
Jeanette Pfaff, Project Director / Office Manager

WCCO-TV *Digital Channel:* 32; *Virtual Channel:* 4; 1000 kW; 1335 ft.; N45 3 44 W93 8 21
90 S 11th St., Minneapolis, MN 55403 USA
(612) 339-4444; *Fax:* (612) 330-2627
minnesota.cbslocal.com
License: Minneapolis, Hennepin County, MN held by CBS Broadcasting Inc.
Group Owner: CBS Television Stations Group
Nat'l Network: CBS; *Nat'l Reps:* CBS TV Stations National Sales; *Wire Services:* WU; Reuters
Size of News Staff: 75; *Hours of Local News Weekly:* news progmg 23 hrs wkly
Gary Kroger, Director of Engineering

WFTC *Digital Channel:* 29; *Virtual Channel:* 29; 1000 kw; 1276 ft.; N45 3 30 W93 7 27
Mailing Address: 200 Concord Plaza, Suite 600, San Antonio, TX 78216 US
Second Address: 11358 Viking Drive, Eden Praire, MN 55344
(952) 944-9999; *Fax:* (952) 942-0455, (952) 995-1830
www.my29tv.com
License: Minneapolis, Hennepin County, MN held by Fox Television Stations Inc.
Group Owner: Fox Television Stations Inc.; (acq 10-1-2001; grpsl).
Nat'l Network: MY NETWORK; *Wire Services:* AP
Hours of Local News Weekly: News progmg 3.5 hrs wkly
Carol Rueppel, General Manager
Sheila Oliver, General Sales Mgr
Bill Dallman, News Director
Marc Majerus, VP Engineering
Marc Majerus, Chief Engineer

WUCW *Digital Channel:* 22; *Virtual Channel:* 23; 1000 kw; 1345 ft.; N45 3 44 W93 8 21
1640 Como Ave., St. Paul, MN 55108 US
(651) 646-2300; *Fax:* (651) 646-1220
www.thecw23.com
License: Minneapolis, Hennepin County, MN held by KLGT Licensee LLC
Group Owner: Sinclair Broadcast Group Inc.; (acq 3-16-98; $52.5 million)
Nat'l Network: CW
Joe Tracy, General Manager
Tom Burke, Regional Sales Manager

Rochester, MN-Mason City, IA-Austin, MN (DMA 153)

KAAL *Digital Channel:* 36; *Virtual Channel:* 6; 620 kw; 1070 ft.; N43 38 34 W92 31 35
Mailing Address: 2720 Superior Drive NW, Suite 101, Rochester, MN 55901 US
Second Address: 1701 10th Pl. N.E., Austin, MN 55912
(507) 437-6666, (507) 288-7555; *Fax:* (507) 433-9560, (507) 285-0038
www.kaaltv.com
License: Austin, Mower County, MN held by KAAL-TV LLC.
Group Owner: Hubbard Broadcasting Inc.; (acq 12-13-00; $9.5 million); *Washington Law Firm:* Schwartz, Woods & Miller
Nat'l Network: ABC
Size of News Staff: 18; *Hours of Local News Weekly:* news progmg 11 hrs wkly
Deb Nerud, Operations Dir
David Harbert, General Manager
Bill Klein, General Sales Mgr
Sheryl Barlow, Programming Director
Heather Holmes, Promotions Manager
David Springer, NewsDirector
Wendell Nelson, Chief Engineer
JanThompson, Programming Director
Harlan Carlson, Traffic Manager
Chris Kuball, Weather
Dan Conradt, Reporter
Betsy Singer, Anchor
Caleb Ostrander, Sports

***KSMQ-TV** *Digital Channel:* 20; *Virtual Channel:* 15; 319.2 kw; 993 ft.; N43 38 34 W92 31 35
2000 8th Ave. NW, Austin, MN 55912 US
(507) 433-0678; *Fax:* (507) 433-0670
www.ksmq.org
ksmq@ksmq.org
License: Austin, Mower County, MN held by KSMQ Public Service Media, Inc
(acq 5-27-2005); *Washington Law Firm:* Schwartz, Woods & Miller
Nat'l Network: PBS
Roger Boughton, Chairman
Eric Olson, President & CEO
Randy Kher, Executive Vice President/Treasurer/Chief Financial
Mary Davenport, General Manager
Suzi Stone, Programming Director
Timothy Gassmann, Chief Engineer
David Hagen,Account Manager
Michele Hoeper, Promotions Coordinator/Traffic Specialist

KTTC *Digital Channel:* 10; *Virtual Channel:* 10; 43.1 kw; 1250 ft.; N43 34 15 W92 25 37
6301 Bandel Road NW, Rochester, MN 55901 US
(507) 288-4444; *Fax:* (507) 288-6324,(507) 288-6278 (news)
www.kttc.com
License: Rochester, Olmsted County, MN held by KTTC Television, Inc.
Group Owner: Quincy Newspapers Inc.; (acq 7-1-76; $4.25 million); *Washington Law Firm:* Wilkinson, Barker, Knauer & Quinn
Nat'l Network: NBC; CW; *Nat'l Reps:* Blair Television; *Wire Services:* AP; CNN; NBC
Size of News Staff: 15; *Hours of Local News Weekly:* news progmg 11 hrs wkly
Jerry Watson, Regional VP Quincy/General Manager KTTC
Elizabeth Dahlen, Station Manager
Peggy Dalland, Local Sales Manager
Vickie Broughton, Programming/Traffic
Rita Duda, Promotions Manager
Noel Sederstrom, News Director
TimMorgan, Chief Engineer
Brendan Ford, Production Manager
Pat Lund, Sports Director
Dave Osborn, Creative Services

KXLT-TV *Digital Channel:* 46; *Virtual Channel:* 47; 220 kw; 1125 ft.; N43 38 34 W92 31 35
5727 Tokay Boulevard, Madison, WI 53719 US
(507) 252-4747; *Fax:* (507) 252-5050
www.myfox47.com
comments@fox47kxlt.com
License: Rochester, Olmsted County, MN held by SagamoreHill of Minnesota Licenses LLC
(acq 3-31-2005; $2.05 million); *Washington Law Firm:* Rosenman & colin
Nat'l Network: FOX
Hours of Local News Weekly: News progmg 7 hrs wkly
Louis Wall, General Manager
Kristopher Lake, General Sales Mgr
Danika Stagemeyer, Programming Director
Rita Duda, Promotions Manager
Tim Morgan, Engineering Dir
Mary McGuire, Anchor/Reporter/Producer
Randy Brook,Anchor/Reporter/Producer
Nicholas Quallich, Anchor/Reporter/Producer
Ted Schmidt, Anchor/Reporter/Producer
Nicole Goodrich, Reporter/Producer
Eric Lear, Weekend Sports Anchor

Sioux Falls (Mitchell), SD (DMA 109)

***KSMN** *Digital Channel:* 15; *Virtual Channel:* 20; 200 kw; 952 ft.; N43 53 52 W95 56 50; *Rebroadcasting:* Rebroadcasts KWCM-TV Appleton 100%
120 W. Schlieman, Appleton, MN 56208 US
(800) 726-3178; *Fax:* (320) 289-2634
www.pioneer.org
yourtv@pioneer.org
License: Worthington, Nobles County, MN held by West Central Minnesota Educational TV Co
Nat'l Network: PBS
Jonathan Miller, On Air Operator
Les Heen, General Manager
Shirley Schwarz, Programming Director
Janet Suckow, News Director
Jon Panzer, Engineering Director/Station Manager
Todd Johnson, Chief Engineer
Greg Bader, MaintenanceSupervisor
Chris Meinert, Corporate Support Rep

Mississippi

Biloxi-Gulfport, MS (DMA 157)

WLOX *Digital Channel:* 39; *Virtual Channel:* 13; 715 kw; 1201 ft.; N30 43 22 W89 5 28
208 DeBuys Rd., Biloxi, MS 39531 US
(228) 896-1313, (228) 896-0791; *Fax:* (228) 896-0749, (228) 896-2596
www.wlox.com
License: Biloxi, Harrison County, MS held by WLOX License Subsidiary LLC.
Group Owner: Raycom Media Inc.; (acq 1-31-2006; grpsl); *Washington Law Firm:* Covington & Burling
Nat'l Network: ABC; *Wire Services:* AP
Size of News Staff: 44; *Hours of Local News Weekly:* news progmg 18 hrs wkly
Leon Long, Operations Dir
Dave Vincent, Station Manager
Linda Sherman, General Sales Mgr
Darlene Duffano, Programming Director
Brad Kessie, News Director
John Armstrong, Chief Engineer
Roger Garrett, Operations Manager
DonMoore, Regional Sales Manager
Mike Reader, Chief Meterologist
Jeff Lawson, Anchor
A.J. Giardina, Sportscaster
Michelle Lady, Broadcast Jornalism

***WMAH-TV** *Digital Channel:* 16; *Virtual Channel:* 19; 540 kw; 1556 ft.; N30 45 18 W88 56 44
3825 Ridgewood Road, Jackson, MS 39211 US
(601) 432-6565; *Fax:* (601) 432-6654 / (601) 432-6311
www.mpbonline.org
mpbinfo@mpbonline.org
License: Biloxi, Harrison County, MS held by Mississippi Authority for Educational TV
Washington Law Firm: Schwartz, Woods & Miller
Nat'l Network: PBS; *Regional Network:* Mississippi Educational Broadcasting
Robert J. Sawyer, Chairman
Cy Vance, Operations Dir
Dr. Judy Lewis, General Manager
Shirley Mixon, Programming Director
Teresa Collier, Director of News and Public Affairs
Ronnie Agnew, Executive Director
Paul Moore, DeputyAdministrator
Nikki McCelleis, Deputy Executive Director for Education
Margaret McPhillips, Public Relations Director
Cy Vance, Director for Technical Services
Cindy Neal, Human Resource Director

WXXV-TV *Digital Channel:* 25; *Virtual Channel:* 25; 190 kW; 1,496 ft; N30 44 49 W89 03 30; *Population Served:* 128,150
14351 Hwy 49 North, Gulfport, MS 39503 USA
(228) 832-2525; *Fax:* (228) 314-9223
License: Gulfport, Harrison County, MS held by Morris Network of Mississippi, Inc.
Group Owner: Morris Multimedia Inc.; (acq 5-22-97; $17.475 million); *Washington Law Firm:* Fletcher, Heald & Hildroth
Nat'l Network: FOX; NBC; CW; *Nat'l Reps:* Millennium Sales & Marketing

Columbus-Tupelo-West Point, MS (DMA 133)

WCBI-DT *Digital Channel:* 27; *Virtual Channel:* 4; 599 kW; 1,916 ft; N33 45 6 W88 52 40; *Population Served:* 165,000
201 5th Street South, Columbus, MS 39701 USA
(662) 327-4444; *Fax:* (662) 329-1004
www.wcbi.com
License: Columbus, Lowndes County, MS held by WCBI-TV, LLC
Group Owner: Morris Multimedia Inc.; (acq 12-31-03; $20 million); *Washington Law Firm:* Fletcher, Heald & Hildreth
Nat'l Network: CBS; CW; MyNetworkTV; *Wire Services:* Weather Wire
Derek Rogers, General Manager
Bert Sparks, General Sales Mgr
Robert Davidson, News Director
Chris Horton, Engineering Dir

WLOV-TV *Digital Channel:* 16; *Virtual Channel:* 27; 390 kw; 1670 ft.; N33 47 39.6 W89 5 15.8
Mailing Address: 1828 L Street, NW, Suite 1111, Washington, DC 20036 US
Second Address: Post Office Box 680, Tupelo, MI 38802-0680
(662) 842-2227,(662) 494-8327; *Fax:* (662) 844-7061
www.wlov.com
manager@wlov.com
License: West Point, Clay County, MS held by Lingard Broadcasting Corp
(acq 4-12-94).; *Ownership:* John R. Lingard; *Washington Law Firm:* Robert E. Levine, Esq.
Nat'l Network: FOX; *Nat'l Reps:* Continental Television Sales; *Wire Services:* FNS
Hours of Local News Weekly: 5.5 hrs
Matthew M. Dee, President
Jennifer Dennington, General Manager
Marty Davis, Chief Engineer

***WMAB-TV** *Digital Channel:* 10; *Virtual Channel:* 2; 8 kw; 1145 ft.; N33 21 14 W89 9 0
3825 Ridgewood Road, Jackson, MS 39211 US
(601) 432-6565; *Fax:* (601) 432-6654
www.mpbonline.org
mpbinfo@mpbonline.org
License: Mississippi State, Choctaw County, MS held by Mississippi Authority for Educational TV
Washington Law Firm: Schwartz, Woods & Miller
Nat'l Network: PBS
Size of News Staff: 4
Robert J. Sawyer, Chairman
Cy Vance, Operations Dir
Dr. Judy Lewis, Station Manager
Shirley Mixon, Programming Director
Mari Irby, Promotions Manager
Teresa Collier, Director of News and Public Affairs
Ronnie Agnew, ExecutiveDirector
Paul Moore, Deputy Administrator
Nikki McCelleis, Deputy Executive Director for Education
Margaret McPhillips, Public Relations Director
Cy Vance, Director for Technical Services
Cindy Neal, Human Resource Director

***WMAE-TV** *Digital Channel:* 12; *Virtual Channel:* 12; 31 kw; 732 ft.; N34 40 0 W88 45 5
3825 Ridgewood Road, Jackson, MS 39211 US
(601) 432-6565; *Fax:* (601) 432-6654,(601) 432-6311
www.mpbonline.org
mpbinfo@mpbonline.org
License: Booneville, Prentiss County, MS held by Mississippi Authority for Educational TV
Washington Law Firm: Schwartz, Woods & Miller
Nat'l Network: PBS; *Regional Network:* Mississippi Educational Broadcasting
Robert J. Sawyer, Chairman
Dr. Judy Lewis, General Manager
Shirley Mixon, Programming Director
Teresa Collier, Director of News and Public Affairs
Ronnie Agnew, Executive Director
Paul Moore, Deputy Administrator
Nikki McCelleis,Deputy Executive Director for Education
Margaret McPhillips, Public Relations Director
Cy Vance, Director for Technical Services
Cindy Neal, Human Resource Director

WTVA *Digital Channel:* 8; 16 kw; 1,800t/1,561g; N33 47 40 W89 05 16
Mailing Address: P.O. Box 350, Tupelo, MS 38802 US
Second Address: 1359 Beech Springs Rd., Saltillo, MS 38866
(662) 842-7620; *Fax:* (662) 844-7061
www.wtva.com
License: Tupelo, Lee County, MS held by Mississippi TV License Company LLC
Group Owner: Heartland Media LLC; *Washington Law Firm:* Garvey, Schubert & Barer
Nat'l Network: NBC; *Nat'l Reps:* Continental Television Sales; *Wire Services:* AP; NBC
Size of News Staff: 22; *Hours of Local News Weekly:* news progmg 17 hrs wkly
Dan Modisett, General Manager
Jay Richer, General Sales Mgr
Emily Mowers, Marketing and Creative Services Director
David Beech, News Director
Danny Walker, Local Sales Manager
Blakely Young, Digital Sales Manager
Sunny Grimes,Regional Account Manager
Renee Cameron-Anderson, Account Executive
Don Borel, Account Executive
Janay Shells, Account Executive

Greenwood-Greenville, MS (DMA 193)

WABG-TV *Digital Channel:* 32; *Virtual Channel:* 6; 1000 kw; 1877 ft.; N33 22 23 W90 32 25
849 Washington Ave., Greenville, MS 38701 US

(662) 332-0949, (800) 898-0968, (662) 332-2614; *Fax:* (662) 344-1814, (662) 378-2958
www.wabg.com
License: Greenwood, Leflore County, MS held by Commonwealth Broadcasting Group, Inc.
Group Owner: Commonwealth Broadcasting Corp.
Nat'l Network: ABC; Fox; *Nat'l Reps:* Continental Television Sales
Size of News Staff: 16; *Hours of Local News Weekly:* news progmg 13 hrs wkly
Charles Harker, President
Sherry Nelson, General Manager
Sarah Zepponi, General Sales Mgr
Donnie Reid, Programming Director
Pam Chatman, News Director
Mike Sands, Anchor/Sports
Tanya Carter, Anchor

WMAI *Digital Channel:* 31; *Not on Air/Target Date:* unknown
3825 Ridgewood Rd, Jackson, MS 39211 US
(601) 432-6565; *Fax:* (610) 432-6392
www.mpbonline.org
mpbinfo@mpbonline.org
License: Cleveland, Bolivar County, MS held by Mississippi Authority for Educational Television
; *Regional Network:* Mississippi Educational Broadcasting
Robert J. Sawyer, Chairman
Marie Antoon, General Manager
Shirley Mixon, Programming Director
Teresa Collier, Director of News and Public Affairs
Ronnie Agnew, Executive Director
Paul Moore, Deputy Administrator
Nikki McCelleis,Deputy Executive Director for Education
Margaret McPhillips, Public Relations Director
Cy Vance, Director for Technical Services
Cindy Neal, Human Resource Director

***WMAO-TV** *Digital Channel:* 25; *Virtual Channel:* 23; 815 kw; 1041 ft.; N33 22 34 W90 32 32
3825 Ridgewood Road, Jackson, MS 39211 US
(601) 432-6565; *Fax:* (601) 432-6654,(601) 432-6311
www.mpbonline.org
mpbinfo@mpbonline.org
License: Greenwood, Leflore County, MS held by Mississippi Authority for Educational TV
Washington Law Firm: Schwartz, Woods & Miller
Nat'l Network: PBS; *Regional Network:* Mississippi Educational Broadcasting
Robert J. Sawyer, Chairman
Cy Vance, Operations Dir
Dr. Judy Lewis, General Manager
Shirley Mixon, Programming Director
Teresa Collier, Director of News and Public Affairs
Ronnie Agnew, Executive Director
Paul Moore, DeputyAdministrator
Nikki McCelleis, Deputy Executive Director for Education
Margaret McPhillips, Public Relations Director
Cy Vance, Director for Technical Services
Cindy Neal, Human Resource Director

WXVT *Digital Channel:* 15; *Virtual Channel:* 15; 330 kw; 883 ft.; N33 39 26 W90 42 18
3015 E. Reed Road, Greenville, MS 38703 US
(662) 334-1500; *Fax:* (662) 378-8122
www.wxvt.com
License: Greenville, Washington County, MS held by H3 Communications LLC
Ownership: Christopher Harker, 33.3%; Timothy Harker, 33.3%; Jamie Harker, 33.3%
Nat'l Network: CBS
Darren Lehrmann, General Manager
Larry Cazavan, General Sales Mgr
Carolyn Byars, Programming Director
Stephen Ross, Promotions Manager
Earl Phelps, News Director
Paul Serio, Chief Engineer

Hattiesburg-Laurel, MS (DMA 168)

WDAM-TV *Digital Channel:* 7; *Virtual Channel:* 7; 75 kw; 509 ft.; N31 27 12 W89 17 5
Mailing Address: 2362 U.S. Hwy 11, Moselle, MS 39459 US
Second Address: PO Box 16269, Hattiesburg, MS 39404
(601) 544-4730, (800) 844-9326, (800) 844-0730; *Fax:* (601) 584-9302
www.wdam.com
info@wdam.com
License: Laurel, Jones County, MS held by WDAM License Subsidiary Inc.
Group Owner: Raycom Media Inc.; (acq 9-24-96; grpsl).;
Washington Law Firm: Covington & Burling
Nat'l Network: NBC; *Nat'l Reps:* Harrington, Righter & Parsons
Size of News Staff: 26; *Hours of Local News Weekly:* news progmg 20 hrs wkly
Jim Cameron, Operations Dir
Joe Sciortino, General Manager
Ted Palmer, General Sales Mgr
Betty Young, Programming Director
Pam McGovern, Promotions Manager
Nick Ortego, News Director
Jim Wilkinson, Chief Engineer
AustinSimmons, Sports
Daniel Brown, Sports
Nick Lilja, Senior Weatherman
Miranda Beard, Asst. News Director
Steven Williams, Anchor
Rex Thompson, Weather

WHLT *Digital Channel:* 22; *Virtual Channel:* 22; 1000 kw; 797 ft.; N31 24 20 W89 14 13
5912 Hwy., 49, Suite A, Hattiesburg, MS 39401 US
(601) 545-2077; *Fax:* (601) 545-3589
www.cbs22thehub.com
License: Hattiesburg, Forrest County, MS held by Media General Broadcasting Inc.
Group Owner: Media General Broadcast Group; (acq 7-25-97; grpsl).
Nat'l Network: CBS; *Nat'l Reps:* MMT
Jimmy Cromwell, General Manager
Wally Babbidge, Station Manager
Aime Spears, General Sales Manager
Jackie McDonald, Programming Director
Gary Wolverton, Promotions Manager
Gary Wright, Chief Engineer
Jasmine Cooper, CommercialProduction
Katie Townsend, Brand Manager
Sheena Thompson, Sales Assistant
Cheryl Jacks, Traffic & Sales Assistant
Donesha Aldridge, News team
Dawn Webb, Traffic & Sales Assistant

Jackson, MS (DMA 95)

WAPT *Digital Channel:* 21; *Virtual Channel:* 16; 1000 kw; 1089 ft.; N32 16 41 W90 17 40
888 Seventh Ave., New York, NY 10106 US
(601) 922-1607; *Fax:* (601) 922-1663
www.wapt.com
License: Jackson, MS held by WAPT Hearst Television Inc.
Group Owner: Hearst Television Inc.; (acq 7-16-97; grpsl).
Nat'l Network: ABC
Size of News Staff: 26; *Hours of Local News Weekly:* news progmg 14 hrs wkly
Stuart Kellogg, General Manager

WDBD *Digital Channel:* 40; *Virtual Channel:* 40; 981.2 kw; 1962 ft.; N32 12 49.4 W90 22 56.2
715 South Jefferson Street, Jackson, MS 39201 US
(601) 948-3333, (601) 983-3731; *Fax:* (601) 355-7830
www.msnewsnow.com
License: Jackson, Hinds County, MS held by WDBD License Subsidiary LLC
Group Owner: American Spirit Media LLC; *Washington Law Firm:* Fisher, Wayland, Cooper, Leader & Zaragoza
Nat'l Network: FOX; *Nat'l Reps:* Millennium Sales & Marketing
Bonnie Alaimo, Operations Dir
Marc Jaromin, General Manager
Will Hammond, General Sales Mgr
Mike Ingalls, News Director
Mark Wade, Chief Engineer
Maggie Wade, Weekday Anchor
Howard Ballou, Weekday Anchor
Marsha Thompson,Weekday Anchor
Ashley Garner, Reporter
Jessica Bowman, Reporter
Dave Roberts, Weather

WJTV *Digital Channel:* 12; *Virtual Channel:* 12; 316 kw vis, 63.1 kw aur; 1,630t/1,615g; N32 14 26 W90 24 15; *Population Served:* 477,300
1820 TV Rd., Jackson, MS 39204
(601) 372-6311; *Fax:* (601) 372-8798
www.wjtv.com
wcromwell@wjtv.com
License: Jackson, Hinds County, MS held by Media General Broadcasting Inc.
Group Owner: Media General Broadcast Group; (acq 7-25-97; grpsl); *Washington Law Firm:* Dow Lohnes LLC
Nat'l Network: CBS; *Nat'l Reps:* HRP
Size of News Staff: 34; *Hours of Local News Weekly:* news progmg 21 hrs wkly
William Cromwell, Operations Dir
Wm James Cromwell, General Manager
Al Evans, General Sales Mgr
Jackie McDonald, Programming Director
Rick Russell, Promotions Manager
Jason Stevens, News Director
Steve Schrader, ChiefEngineer
Stephen Patton, Promotions Director
Brett Kenyon, Brand Manager
Ross Reardon, Director of Revenue
Stephanie Dumeyer, National Sales manager
Jeff Inman, Local Sales manager
Melanie Christopher, News team

WLBT *Digital Channel:* 30; *Virtual Channel:* 3; 535 kw; 2047 ft.; N32 12 49 W90 22 56
715 South Jefferson Street, Jackson, MI 39201 US
(601) 948-3333, (601) 960-4426; *Fax:* (601) 355-7830
www.wlbt.com
news@wlbt.com
License: Jackson, Hinds County, MS held by WLBT License Subsidiary, LLC
Group Owner: Raycom Media Inc.; (acq 1-13-2006; grpsl).;
Washington Law Firm: Dow, Lohnes & Albertson
Nat'l Network: NBC; *Nat'l Reps:* Continental Television Sales;
Wire Services: AP
Dan Modisett, VP & General Manager
Frankie Thomas, General Sales Mgr
Teresa White, Programming Director
Dennis Smith, News Director
Curtis McKnight, Chief Engineer
Brandon Artiles, Anchor
Jessica Bowman, Reporter
Dave Roberts,Chief Meterologist
Rob Jay, Sports Anchor

WLOO *Digital Channel:* 41; *Virtual Channel:* 35; 981 kw; 1962 ft.; N32 12 49.4 W90 22 56.2
Mailing Address: Fisher, Wayland, Cooper, 2001 Penn Ave, NW, Washington, DC 20006 US
Second Address: One Great Place, Jackson, MS 39209
(601) 922-1234; *Fax:* (601) 922-0268
www.gomiss.com
License: Vicksburg, Warren County, MS held by Tougaloo College
Nat'l Network: MY NETWORK
Tracy Day, Operations Dir
Marc Jaromin, General Manager
Will Hammond, General Sales Mgr
Mike Ingalls, News Director
Mark Wade, Chief Engineer

***WMAU-TV** *Digital Channel:* 18; *Virtual Channel:* 17; 682 kw; 1115 ft.; N31 22 22 W90 45 4
3825 Ridgewood Road, Jackson, MS 39211 US
(601) 432-6565; *Fax:* (610) 432-6654 / (601) 432-6311
www.mpbonline.org
mpbinfo@mpbonline.org
License: Bude, Franklin County, MS held by Mississippi Authority for Educational TV
Washington Law Firm: Schwartz, Woods & Miller
Nat'l Network: PBS; *Regional Network:* Mississippi Educational Broadcasting
Robert J. Sawyer, Chairman
Judith Lewis, General Manager
Shirley Mixon, Programming Director
Teresa Collier, Director of News and Public Affairs
Ronnie Agnew, Executive Director
Paul Moore, Deputy Administrator
Nikki McCelleis,Deputy Executive Director for Education
Margaret McPhillips, Public Relations Director
Cy Vance, Director for Technical Services
Cindy Neal, Human Resource Director

***WMPN-TV** *Digital Channel:* 20; *Virtual Channel:* 29; 400 kw; 1581 ft.; N32 11 29 W90 24 22
3825 Ridgewood Road, Jackson, MS 39211 US
(601) 432-6565; *Fax:* (601) 432-6654,(601) 432-6311
www.mpbonline.org
mpbinfo@mpbonline.org
License: Jackson, Hinds County, MS held by Mississippi Authority for Educational TV
Washington Law Firm: Schwartz, Woods & Miller
Nat'l Network: PBS
Cy Vance, Operations Dir
Dr. Judy Lewis, General Manager
Shirley Mixon, Programming Dir.
Teresa Collier, News & Public Affairs Dir.
Ronnie Agnew, Executive Director

Margaret McPhillips, Public Relations Director
Cindy Neal, HRDirector
Cy Vance, Dir. Of Technical Services
Scott Colwell, Dir. Of Production
Paul Moore, Deputy Administrator

WNTZ-TV *Digital Channel:* 49; 1,170 kw vis, 117 kw aur; ant 843t/848g; N31 30 33 W91 24 19
4615 Parliament Dr., Suite 202, Alexandria, LA 71303 US
(318) 443-4700
www.fox48tv.com
License: Natchez, Adams County, LA held by Nexstar Broadcasting, Inc.
Group Owner: Nexstar Broadcasting Group; (acq 6-22-98);
Washington Law Firm: Shaw Pittman L.L.P.
Nat'l Network: Fox; MyNetworkTV; *Nat'l Reps:* Millennium Sales & Marketing
Aleece Way, Dir. of Sales

WRBJ-TV *Digital Channel:* 34; *Virtual Channel:* 34; 968 kw; 374.6 meters; N32 07 18 W89 32 52
745 N. State St., Jackson, MS 0
(601) 974-5700; *Fax:* (601) 974-5711
www.tbn.org
License: Magee, Simpson County, MS held by Trinity Christian Center of Santa Ana Inc.
Group Owner: Trinity Broadcasting Network; *Washington Law Firm:* Fletcher, Heald & Hildreth
; *Nat'l Reps:* Harrington, Righter & Parsons
Gregory McCoy, Operations Dir
Monica Johnson, Programming Director
Tambra Cooper, Promotions Manager
Charles Flowers, Chief Engineer
Terrill Weiss, General Sales Manager

Memphis, TN (DMA 51)

WBUY-TV *Digital Channel:* 41; *Virtual Channel:* 40; 1000 kw; 1040 ft.; N35 16 33 W89 46 38
Mailing Address: P. O. Box A, Santa Ana, CA 92711 US
Second Address: P.O.Box 768, Station B, Ottawa, ON K1P 5P8
(714) 731-1000; *Fax:* (819) 770-2338
www.tbn.org
wbuy@tbn.org
License: Holly Springs, Marshall County, MS held by Trinity Broadcasting Network.
Group Owner: Trinity Broadcasting Network; (acq 5-8-2000; grpsl).
Nat'l Network: TRINITY BROADCA
Tamela Calvin, Station Manager
Cliff Pickell, Programming Director
Douglas Puryear, Chief Engineer

***WMAV-TV** *Digital Channel:* 36; *Virtual Channel:* 18; 272.5 kw; 1399 ft.; N34 17 28 W89 42 21
3825 Ridgewood Road, Jackson, MS 39211 US
(601) 432-6565; *Fax:* (601) 432-6654,(601) 432-6311
www.mpbonline.org
mpbinfo@mpbonline.org
License: Oxford, Lafayette County, MS held by Mississippi Authority for Educational TV
Nat'l Network: PBS
Size of News Staff: 4
Robert J. Sawyer, Chairman
Cy Vance, Operations Dir
Dr. Judy Lewis, General Manager
Shirley Mixon, Programming Director
Teresa Collier, Director of News and Public Affairs
Ronnie Agnew, Executive Director
Paul Moore, DeputyAdministrator
Nikki McCelleis, Deputy Executive Director for Education
Margaret McPhillips, Public Relations Director
Cy Vance, Director for Technical Services
Cindy Neal, Human Resource Director

Meridian, MS (DMA 190)

WGBC *Digital Channel:* 31; *Virtual Channel:* 30; 828 kw; 542 ft.; N32 19 39.5 W88 41 30.8
1151 Crestview Cr., Meridian, MS 39301 US
(601) 485-3030; *Fax:* (601) 693-9889
www.wgbctv.com
License: Meridian, Lauderdale County, MS held by WGBC-TV, LLC
1/23/2008; *Ownership:* Michael Reed; *Washington Law Firm:* Akin Gump Strauss Hauer & Feld
Nat'l Network: NBC; NBC; *Nat'l Reps:* Millennium Sales & Marketing
Mike Reed, CEO/President
Susan Ross, Sales Manager
Lucky Lisenbe, Programming
Tim Garrett, Promotions
Preston Rainer, Chief Engineer
Mark Hill, Chief Engineer
Virgil Reed, Creative Services Manager/Your Morning
Carol Lisenbe,Business Manager
Angie Denney, Your morning Report
Leah Mays, Promotions & Marketing Director

***WMAW-TV** *Digital Channel:* 44; *Virtual Channel:* 14; 880 kw; 1211 ft.; N32 8 18 W89 5 36
3825 Ridgewood Road, Jackson, MS 39211 US
(601) 432-6565; *Fax:* (601) 432-6654,(601) 432-6311
www.mpbonline.org
mpbinfo@mpbonline.org
License: Meridian, Lauderdale County, MS held by Mississippi Authority for Educational TV
Washington Law Firm: Schwartz, Woods & Miller
Nat'l Network: PBS; *Regional Network:* Mississippi Educational Broadcasting
Size of News Staff: 4
Robert J. Sawyer, Chairman
Dr. Judy Lewis, General Manager
Shirley Mixon, Programming Director
Teresa Collier, Director of News and Public Affairs
Ronnie Agnew, Executive Director
Paul Moore, Deputy Administrator
Nikki McCelleis,Deputy Executive Director for Education
Margaret McPhillips, Public Relations Director
Cy Vance, Director for Technical Services
Cindy Neal, Human Resource Director

WMDN *Digital Channel:* 24; *Virtual Channel:* 24; 616 kw; 597 ft.; N32 19 40 W88 41 31
1151 Crestview Cr., Meridian, MS 39301 US
(601) 485-3030; *Fax:* (601) 693-9889
www.wmdntv.com
administration@wmdn.net
License: Meridian, Lauderdale County, MS held by Meridian Media LLC.
(acq 1-23-2008; $5.8 million); *Ownership:* Sharlyn Threadgill, 50%; and Wade Threadgill, 50%; *Washington Law Firm:* Fletcher, Heald & Hildreth
Nat'l Network: CBS; *Nat'l Reps:* Millennium Sales & Marketing
Mike Reed, President & CEO
Susan Ross, General Manager
Mike Reed, Station Manager
Susan Ross, Sales Manager
Lucky Lisenbe, Programming
Tim Garrett, Promotions
Clyde Walker, Chief Engineer
Virgil Reed, Creative ServicesManager
Carol Lisenbe, Business Manager
Angie Denney, Your Morning Report

WTOK *Digital Channel:* 11; *Virtual Channel:* 11; 90 kw; 525 ft.; N32 19 38 W88 41 28
815 23rd Ave., Meridian, MS 39301 USA
(601) 693-1441; *Fax:* (601) 483-3266
www.wtok.com
wtok@wtok.com
License: Meridian, Lauderdale County, MS held by Gray Television Licensee LLC
Group Owner: Gray Television Inc.; (acq 8-29-2002; grpsl).;
Washington Law Firm: Wiley, Rein & Fielding, LLP
Nat'l Network: ABC; MyNetworkTV; The CW Network; Jewelry Television; *Nat'l Reps:* Continental Television Sales; *Wire Services:* AP
Size of News Staff: 15; *Hours of Local News Weekly:* news progmg 15 hrs wkly
Tim Walker, General Manager
Jim Briggs, General Sales Mgr
Julie Walker, Promotions Manager
John Johnson, News Director
Brad LeBrun, Chief Engineer

Missouri

Cedar Rapids-Waterloo-Iowa City & Dubuque, IA (DMA 90)

KFXB-TV *Digital Channel:* 43; 646 kw vis, 64.6 kw aur; ant 841t; N42 31 05 W90 37 16; *Population Served:* 90,000
744 Main Street, Dubuque, IA 52001
(563) 690-1704; *Fax:* (563) 557-9383
www.kfxb.net
ctnofiowa@mchsi.com
License: Dubuque, Dubuque County, IA held by Christian Television Network of Iowa Inc.
Group Owner: Christian Television Corporation Inc.; (acq 8-2-2004).
Thomas Bond, General Manager
Tamie Cook, Business Manager
Jason Heim, Chief Engineer
Tamie Cook, Office/Manager
Neil Cook, Master Control operator

***KIIN** *Digital Channel:* 12; 316 kw vis, 31.6 kw aur; 1,440t/1,449g; N41 43 14 W91 20 29
Mailing Address: Box 6450, Iowa Public TV, Johnston, IA 50131-6450
Second Address: 6450 Corporate Drive, Johnston, IA 50131-6450
(515) 242-3100, (800) 532-1290
www.iptv.org
public_information@iptv.org
License: Iowa City, Johnson County, IA held by Iowa Public Broadcasting Board
Washington Law Firm: Dow, Lohnes PLLC
Nat'l Network: PBS
Gary Steinke, President
Molly M. Phillips, General Manger & Executive Director
Justin Beaupre, Director, Programming & Production
Bill Hayes, Engineering Dir
Kristine K. Houston, Director, Administration & Finance
William T. Hayes,Director, Engineering & Technology
Kristine L. Gray, Director, Communications
Terry Rinehart, Director of Educational Services
Brent Siegrist, Vice President

KPXR-TV ; 500 kw; 466t; N42 17 17 W91 52 54; *Population Served:* 442,400
1957 Blairs Ferry Rd. NE., Cedar Rapids, IA 52402-5819 USA
(319) 378-1260; *Fax:* (319) 378-0076
www.iontelevision.com
vieweremail@ionmedia.com
License: Cedar Rapids, IA held by Ion Media License Company, LLC
Group Owner: ION Media Networks Inc.; (acq 7-15-97; $5 million)
Brandon Burgess, Chairman/CEO
Vikki Steele, Operations Mgr

Columbia-Jefferson City, MO (DMA 136)

KMIZ *Digital Channel:* 17; *Virtual Channel:* 17; 120 kw; 1142 ft.; N38 46 29 W92 33 22.3
501 Business Loop, 70 East, Columbia, MO 65201 US
(573) 449-0917, (573) 449-1700; *Fax:* (573) 875-7078
www.abc17news.com
news@kmiz.com
License: Columbia, Boone County, MO held by NPG of Missouri, LLC
Group Owner: News-Press & Gazette Co.; (acq 10-21-03).;
Washington Law Firm: Covington & Burling
Nat'l Network: ABC; MyNetworkTV; Fox; *Nat'l Reps:* Petry Television Inc.; *Wire Services:* AP
Size of News Staff: 12; *Hours of Local News Weekly:* news progmg 19 hrs wkly

KNLJ *Digital Channel:* 20; *Virtual Channel:* 25; 1000 kw; 1037 ft.; N38 42 15 W92 5 21
Mailing Address: 311 W.Dunklin, Jefferson City, MO 65101 US
Second Address: 9810 State Rd. AE, New Bloomfield, MO 65603
(573) 896-5105; *Fax:* (573) 896-4376
www.knlj.tv
traffic@knlj.tv
License: Jefferson City, Cole County, MO held by New Life Evangelistic Center Inc
Washington Law Firm: John H. Midlen Jr
Nat'l Network: REL
Larry Rice, General Manager
Vickie A.Davenport, Station Manager
Charles Hale, General Sales Mgr
James Shackleford, Programming Director
Shawn Baker, Chief Engineer

KOMU-TV *Digital Channel:* 8; *Virtual Channel:* 8; 13.6 kw; 794 ft.; N38 53 17 W92 15 48
5550 Hwy 63 South, Columbia, MO 65201 US
(573) 882-8888; *Fax:* (573) 884-8888
www.komu.com
garrettm@missouri.edu
License: Columbia, Boone County, MO held by The Curators of the University of Missouri.
Group Owner: The Curators of the University of Missouri;
Washington Law Firm: Shaw Pittman
Nat'l Network: NBC; CW; *Nat'l Reps:* Millennium Sales & Marketing

Size of News Staff: 23; *Hours of Local News Weekly:* news progmg 20 hrs wkly
Martin Siddall, General Manager
Tom Dugan, General Sales Mgr
Matt Garrett, Promotions Manager
Stacey Woelfel, News Director
Chris Swisher, Chief Engineer
John Parker, National Sales Manager
Angie Bailey, Anchor
Brittany Pieper,Anchor
Jim Reik, Anchor
Megan Judy, Anchor
Eric Aldrich, Anchor

KRCG *Digital Channel:* 12; *Virtual Channel:* 13; 15.1 kw; 1010 ft.; N38 41 30 W92 5 44
10188 Old Hwy. 54 N., New Bloomfield, MO 65063 US
(573) 896-5144; *Fax:* (573) 896-5193
www.krcgtv.com
news@krcg.com
License: Jefferson City, Cole County, MO held by KRCG Licensee LLC
Group Owner: Sinclair Broadcast Group Inc.; (acq 11-22-2013; grpsl); *Washington Law Firm:* Pillsbury Winthrop Shaw Pittman LLP
Nat'l Network: CBS
Size of News Staff: 14; *Hours of Local News Weekly:* news progmg 14 hrs wkly
Beth Worsham, General Manager
Lori Ehlert, General Sales Mgr
Jim Joly, Director of National Digital Sales
Greg Siegel, Vice President, National Sales

Davenport, IA-Rock Island-Moline, IL (DMA 101)

***KQIN** ; 6.76 kw vis, 676 w aur; 213t; N41 31 58 W90 34 40; *Rebroadcasting:* Satellite of *WQPT-TV Moline IL 100%.
3561 60th Street, Moline, IA 61265
(309) 764-2400, (877) 413-2424; *Fax:* (309) 764-2410
www.wqpt.org
wqpt@bhc.edu
License: Davenport, Scott County, IA held by Iowa Public Broadcasting Board
Richard Diamond, Traffic/Operations Coordinator
Mary Pruess, General Manager
Lora Adams, General Sales Mgr
Jerry Myers, Programming Director
Lora Adams, Promotions Manager
Steve Ellis, Chief Engineer
Ana Kehoe, Director ofEducation
Dawn Schmit, Business Manager
Amanda Bergeson, Office Support Associate
Jamie Lange, Chief Development Officer

Des Moines-Ames, IA (DMA 69)

WHO-DT *Digital Channel:* 13; 316 kw vis, 47.9 kw aur; ant 1,970t/2,000g; N41 48 33 W93 36 53; *Population Served:* 500,000
1801 Grand Ave., Des Moines, IA 50309 USA
(515) 242-3500
whotv.com
License: Des Moines, Polk County, IA held by WHO License LLC
Group Owner: Tribune Media; *Washington Law Firm:* Covington & Burling
Nat'l Network: NBC; *Nat'l Reps:* Millennium Sales & Marketing
Size of News Staff: 50; *Hours of Local News Weekly:* news progmg 30 hrs wkly
Dale R. Woods, General Manager
Angela Skinner, General Sales Mgr
Tim Gardner, Promotion/Community Events
Rod Petersen, News Director
Brad Olk, Chief Engineer

WOI-DT *Digital Channel:* 5; *Virtual Channel:* 5; 13.9 kw; 1,857 ft.; N41 48 33 W93 36 53; *Population Served:* 559,700
3903 Westown Pkwy., West Des Moines, IA 50266
(515) 457-9645; *Fax:* (515) 457-1025
www.weareiowa.com
License: Ames, Story County, IA held by Nexstar Broadcasting Inc.
Group Owner: Nexstar Broadcasting Group Inc.; (acq 9-16-2013).; *Washington Law Firm:* Latham & Watkins
Nat'l Network: ABC; *Nat'l Reps:* Continental Television Sales; *Wire Services:* AP
Size of News Staff: 25; *Hours of Local News Weekly:* news progmg 15 hrs wkly
Randy Shelton, Director of Broadcast Operations
Jon Skorburg, Vice President/General Manager
Kelly Beeck, Local Sales Manager
Doug Sawyer, Promotions Manager
April Samp, News Director
John Franz, Chief Engineer
Teresa Fuquey,Business Manager
Holly Cihota, Account Executive
Rachel Heinrichs, Account Executive
Amber Sexton, Account Executive
Chelsea Eggers, Account Executive
Tom Woody, Account Executive

Joplin, MO-Pittsburg, KS (DMA 151)

KFJX-DT ; 5,000 kw vis; ant 1,112t/1,069g; N37 18 46 W94 48 59; *Population Served:* 350,000
Box 659, 2950 NE Hwy 69, Pittsburg, KS 66762-0659
(417) 782-1414, (620) 230-0565; *Fax:* (417) 624-3115, (417) 624-3158
www.fox14tv.com
ddishman@fox14tv.com
License: Pittsburg, Crawford County, KS held by Surtsey Media LLC
Group Owner: Surtsey Media LLC; (acq 3-7-2003).
Nat'l Network: Fox
Size of News Staff: 4; *Hours of Local News Weekly:* news progmg 3 hrs wkly
Steve Holinsworth, Operations manager
Darren Dishman, General Manager
Darren Prather, General Sales Manager
Vance Lewis, Promotions Manager
Kristi Spencer, News dir.
Bill Vickery, Chief Engineer
Debbie Auman, Business manager
Alan Bybee, IT Dir.
jill Nelson, Traffic Manager
Chris Wilson, Web Producer
Dale Switzer, Creative Services Dir.

KODE-TV *Digital Channel:* 43; *Virtual Channel:* 12; 1000 kw; 881 ft.; N37 4 37 W94 32 15
Mailing Address: PO Box 1393, Joplin, MO 64802 US
Second Address: 1928 W. 13th St., Joplin, MO 64801
(417) 623-7260; *Fax:* (417) 623-3736
www.fourstateshomepage.com
License: Joplin, Jasper County, MO held by Mission Broadcasting Inc.
Group Owner: Mission Broadcasting; (acq 2-27-2002; $6 million); *Washington Law Firm:* Cohn
Nat'l Network: ABC
Size of News Staff: 18; *Hours of Local News Weekly:* news progmg 16 hrs wkly
Shirley Morton, Station Manager
Bill May, Dir. of Sales
Leisha Beard, News Director

***KOZJ** *Digital Channel:* 25; *Virtual Channel:* 26; 55 kw vis; ant 922t/850g; N37 04 37 W94 32 15; *Rebroadcasting:* Satellite of *KOZK Springfield.
Mailing Address: 901 S. National, Springfield, MO 65897
Second Address: 403 S. Main St., Joplin, MO 64801
(417) 836-3500,(866) 684-5695; *Fax:* (417) 836-3569
www.optv.org
mail@optv.org
License: Joplin, Jasper County, MO held by Board of Governors of Southwest Missouri State University
(acq 4-25-2001; $1.3 million assumption of debt with KOZK(TV) Springfield).; *Washington Law Firm:* Dow, Lohns PLLC
Nat'l Network: PBS
Tammy Wiley, General Manager
Norma Scott, General Sales Mgr
Tom Carter, Programming Director
Rebecca Scott, Promotions Manager
Brent Moore, Chief Engineer

KSNF *Digital Channel:* 46; *Virtual Channel:* 16; 175 kw; 1057 ft.; N37 4 33 W94 33 16
Mailing Address: PO Box 1393, Joplin, MO 64802 US
Second Address: 1502 Cleveland, Joplin, MO 64801
(417) 781-2345; *Fax:* (417) 782-2417
www.fourstateshomepage.com
License: Joplin, Jasper County, MO held by Nexstar Broadcasting Group Inc.
Group Owner: Nexstar Broadcasting Group Inc.; (acq 11-6-97; grpsl).; *Washington Law Firm:* Arter & Hadden
Nat'l Network: NBC
John Hoffman, General Manager
Bill May, Dir. of Sales
Leisha Beard, News Director

Kansas City, MO (DMA 33)

***KCPT** *Digital Channel:* 18; *Virtual Channel:* 19; 1000 kw; 1165 ft.; N39 4 59 W94 28 49
125 East 31st Street, Kansas City, MO 64108 US
(816) 756-3580, (888) 203-1747; *Fax:* (816) 931-2500
www.kcpt.org
customer_service@kcpt.org
License: Kansas City, Jackson County, MO held by Public TV 19 Inc
(acq 1-1-72; $22,226; *Washington Law Firm:* Arter & Hadden
Nat'l Network: PBS
Karen Zecy, Chairman
Kliff Kuehl, CEO/President
Karen Button, CFO
Jeff Evans, CTO
Michael Murphy, Chief Content Officer
Michael Zeller, Chief Development Officer
Shane Guiter, VP,Digital Media Services
William Coughlin,Treasurer

KCTV *Digital Channel:* 24; *Virtual Channel:* 5; 1000 kW; 1129 ft.; N39 4 14 W94 34 57
4500 Shawnee Mission Pkwy, Fairway, KS 66205 USA
(913) 677-5555; *Fax:* (913) 677-7243
www.kctv5.com
kctv5@kctv5.com
License: Kansas City, Clay County, MO held by Meredith Corp.
Group Owner: Meredith Corp.; (acq 10-1-53; $2 million)
Nat'l Network: CBS; *Nat'l Reps:* TeleRep
Mike Sulzman, Engineering Dir

KCWE *Digital Channel:* 31; *Virtual Channel:* 29; 1000 kw; 1089 ft.; N39 5 1 W94 30 57
6455 Winchester Ave., Kansas City, MO 64133 US
(816) 221-9999; *Fax:* (816) 760-9149
www.KCWE.com
License: Kansas City, MO held by Hearst Stations Inc.
Group Owner: Hearst Television Inc.; (acq 8-15-2006; $10.96 million)
Nat'l Network: CW; *Nat'l Reps:* Harrington, Righter & Parsons
Hours of Local News Weekly: 10
Karen King, Programming Director

KMBC *Digital Channel:* 29; *Virtual Channel:* 9; 1000 kw; 1175 ft.; N39 5 1 W94 30 57
6455 Winchester Ave., Kansas City, MO 64133 US
(816) 221-9999; *Fax:* (816) 760-9245
www.kmbc.com
License: Kansas City, MO held by KMBC Hearst Television Inc.
Group Owner: Hearst Television Inc.; (acq 7-16-97; grpsl).; *Washington Law Firm:* Brooks, Pierce, McLendon, Humphrey & Leonard
Nat'l Network: ABC; *Nat'l Reps:* Eagle Television Sales; *Wire Services:* AP; CNN; ABC
Size of News Staff: 55; *Hours of Local News Weekly:* 28 hrs wkly
Karen King, Programming Director

KMCI-TV *Digital Channel:* 36; 5,000 kw vis, 494 kw aur; ant 1,069t/1,128g; N38 58 42 W94 32 01; *Population Served:* 2,182,000
4720 Oak St., Kansas City, MO 64112
(816) 753-4141; *Fax:* (816) 932-4122
www.38thespot.com
comments@38thespot.com
License: Lawrence, Douglas County, KS held by Scripps Howard Broadcasting Co.
Group Owner: The E. W. Scripps Co.; (acq 2-3-2000).
; *Nat'l Reps:* Harrington, Righter & Parsons
Craig Allison, Operations Dir
Alan Fuchsman, General Sales Mgr
Dana Boyd, Programming Director
Randy Thurman, Promotions Manager
Peggy Phillip, News Director
Jay Nix, Chief Engineer

***KMOS-TV** *Digital Channel:* 15; *Virtual Channel:* 6; 322 kw vis; ant 1,978t/1,965g; N38 37 36 W92 52 03; *Population Served:* 1,500,000
University of Central Missouri, Wood 11, Warrensburg, MO 64093
(660) 543-4155, (800) 753-3436; *Fax:* (660) 543-8863
www.kmos.org
kmos@kmos.org
License: Sedalia, Pettis County, MO held by Central Missouri State University
(acq 6-6-78; $1,000); *Washington Law Firm:* Shaw Pittman
Nat'l Network: PBS

Josh Tomlinson, Operations Dir
Rosemary Olas, General Manager
Mark Pearce, General Sales Mgr
Michael O'Keefe, Programming Director
John Long, Chief Engineer
Sarah Bailey, Finance Manager
Dorothy McGrath, Product AffairsDirector

KPXE-TV *Digital Channel:* 51; 1000 kw; 1,119t/1,164g; N39 01 19 W94 30 50; *Population Served:* 750,000
4220 Shawnee Mission Pkwy., Suite 110-B, Fairway, MO 66205 USA
(816) 924-5050; *Fax:* (816) 931-1818
www.iontelevision.com
vieweremail@ionmedia.com
License: Kansas City, MO held by Ion Media Kansas City License, Inc.
Group Owner: ION Media Networks Inc.; (acq 3-3-97; $16.4 million); *Washington Law Firm:* Wiley, Rein & Fielding
Nat'l Network: ION Television
Foreign Language Programming
Brandon Burgess, Chairman/CEO
Frank Barajas, General Manager
Alex Stroot, Station Manager
Stephen Appel, Sales
Marc Zand, Programming Acquisitions

KSHB-TV *Digital Channel:* 42; *Virtual Channel:* 41; 730 kw; 1062 ft.; N38 58 42 W94 32 1
Mailing Address: P. O. Box 5610, 28th Floor, Cincinnati, OH 45201 US
Second Address: 4720 Oak Street, Kansas City, MO 64112
(816) 753-4141; *Fax:* (816) 932-4145
www.nbcactionnews.com
programming@nbcactionnews.com
License: Kansas City, Jackson County, MO held by Scripps Howard Broadcasting Co.
Group Owner: The E. W. Scripps Co.; (acq 10-28-77;
Nat'l Network: NBC; *Nat'l Reps:* Harrington, Righter & Parsons
Size of News Staff: 75; *Hours of Local News Weekly:* news progmg 32 hrs wkly
Craig Allison, Operations Dir
John McKenna, General Sales Mgr
Dana Boyd, Programming Director
Dominick Nardo, Promotions Manager
Debbie Bush, News Director
Jay Nix, Chief Engineer
Lisa Benson, Reporter
Garrette Haake,Reporter
Sarah Hollenbeck, Reporter
Mitch Weber, Reporter
Lexi Sutter, Reporter
Syed Shabbir, Reporter

KSMO *Digital Channel:* 32; *Virtual Channel:* 62; 750 kW; 1175 ft.; N39 5 26 W94 28 19
4500 Shawnee Mission Pkwy, Fairway, KS 66205 USA
(913) 677-5555; *Fax:* (913) 677-7243
www.myksmotv.com
ksmo@myKSMOtv.com
License: Kansas City, Jackson County, MO held by Meredith Corp.
Group Owner: Meredith Corp.; (acq 9-29-2005; $26.8 million)
Nat'l Network: MYTV; *Nat'l Reps:* Millennium Sales & Marketing
Brett Akagi, News Operations Manager
Mike Sulzman, Director of Engineering

WDAF *Digital Channel:* 34; *Virtual Channel:* 4; 1000 kw; 1138 ft.; N39 4 21 W94 35 45
3030 Summit, Kansas City, MO 64108 USA
(816) 753-4567; *Fax:* (816) 931-3984
fox4kc.com
License: Kansas City, Jackson County, MO held by WDAF License Inc.
Group Owner: Tribune Media; (acq 1-23-97; grpsl).
Nat'l Network: FOX; *Nat'l Reps:* Fox Stations Sales
Size of News Staff: 115; *Hours of Local News Weekly:* news progmg 49 hrs wkly

Ottumwa, IA-Kirksville, MO (DMA 200)

KTVO *Digital Channel:* 33; *Virtual Channel:* 3; 87 kw; 951 ft.; N40 31 47 W92 26 29
15518 US Hwy. 63 N., Kirksville, MO 63501 US
(660) 627-3333; *Fax:* (660) 627-1885
www.ktvo.com
comments@ktvo.com
License: Kirksville, Adair County, MO held by KTVO Licensee LLC
Group Owner: Sinclair Broadcast Group Inc.; (acq 11-22-2013; grpsl); *Washington Law Firm:* Pillsbury Winthrop Shaw Pittman LLP
Nat'l Network: ABC; *Nat'l Reps:* Harrington, Righter & Parsons
Size of News Staff: 16; *Hours of Local News Weekly:* news progmg 14 hrs wkly
Marlene Speas, News Director
Mike Graves, Chief Engineer
Jim Joly, Director of National Digital Sales
Greg Siegel, Vice President, National Sales

Paducah, KY-Cape Girardeau, MO-Harrisburg-Mount Vernon, IL (DMA 83)

KBSI *Digital Channel:* 22; *Virtual Channel:* 23; 705 kw; 1781 ft.; N37 24 23 W89 33 44
806 Enterprise St., Cape Girardeau, MO 63703 US
(573) 334-1223
www.kbsi23.com
License: Cape Girardeau, Cape Girardeau County, MO held by KBSI Licensee L.P.
Group Owner: Sinclair Broadcast Group Inc.; (acq 1998; grpsl).
Nat'l Network: FOX; *Nat'l Reps:* Millennium Sales & Marketing
Rob Chronister, Operations Dir
Ed Groves, General Manager
Brad Zaruba, General Sales Mgr
Chuck Moffitt, Promotions Manager
Chris Girard, Engineering Dir
Glenn Ralston, Sales Manager
Brandy McIntire, Account Executive
Jill Frey,Account Executive
Tammy Kell, Account Executive
LaVar Sinks, Account Executive
Laura Poole, Account Executive

KFVS-TV *Digital Channel:* 12; *Virtual Channel:* 12; 6.8 kw; 1998 ft.; N37 25 46 W89 30 14
Mailing Address: 500 E. Plaza Dr., Suite #2, Carterville, IL 62918 US
Second Address: 310 Broadway, PO Box 100, Cape Girardeau, MO 63701
(573) 335-1212, (800) 455-KFVS; *Fax:* (573) 335-6303, (573) 335-7723
www.kfvs12.com
news@kfvs12.com
License: Cape Girardeau, Cape Girardeau County, MO held by Kfvs Licensing Subsidiary LLC
Group Owner: Raycom Media Inc.; (acq 4-97; grpsl).;
Washington Law Firm: Covington & Burling
Nat'l Network: CBS; *Nat'l Reps:* Harrington, Righter & Parsons
Size of News Staff: 45; *Hours of Local News Weekly:* news progmg 28 hrs wkly
Mike Wunderlich, Operations Dir
Tim Ingram, General Manager
Dave Thomason, Director of Sales
Kathy Cowan, Program Director
Paul Keener, Promotions Manager
Mark Little, News Director
Arnold Killian, Chief Engineer
Brad Zaruba,National Sales Manager
Dan Timpe, Promotions Director
Karen Wade, Regional Sales Manager
Paul Keener, Director of Marketing
Alycia Reitenbach, Producer
Christy Russell, Digital Content Manager

KPOB-TV *Digital Channel:* 15; *Virtual Channel:* 15; 34.5 kw; 604 ft.; N36 48 4 W90 27 6; *Rebroadcasting:* Satellite of WSIL-TV Harrisburg IL.
1416 Country Aire Drive, Suite 101, Carterville, IL 62918 US
(618) 985-2333; *Fax:* (618) 985-3709, (618) 985-6482
www.wsiltv.com
License: Poplar Bluff, Butler County, MO held by Mel Wheeler Inc.
Group Owner: Mel Wheeler Inc.; (acq 5-12-83; $6.6 million;
Washington Law Firm: Brooks, Pierce, McLendon, Humphrey & Leonard
Nat'l Network: ABC
Steve Wheeler, General Manager
Pat Victoria, Chief Engineer

Quincy, IL-Hannibal, MO-Keokuk, IA (DMA 170)

KHQA-TV *Digital Channel:* 7; *Virtual Channel:* 7; 13.6 kw; 889 ft.; N39 58 22 W91 19 54
301 South 36th St., Quincy, IL 62301 US
(217) 222-6200; *Fax:* (217) 224-4909
www.khqa.com
news7@khqa.com
License: Hannibal, Marion County, MO held by KHQA Licensee LLC
Group Owner: Sinclair Broadcast Group Inc.; (acq 11-22-2013; grpsl); *Washington Law Firm:* Pillsbury Winthrop Shaw Pittman LLP
Nat'l Network: CBS; ABC; *Nat'l Reps:* Telerep
Size of News Staff: 20 (FTE); *Hours of Local News Weekly:* news progmg 17.5 hrs wkly
Steve Harris, Operations Manager
Sharon Rachal, Director of Sales
Matthew Gerstner, Chief Engineer
Jim Joly, Director of National Digital Sales
Greg Siegel, Vice President, National Sales

Sioux City, IA (DMA 149)

***KSIN-TV** *Digital Channel:* 28; 4,070 kw vis, 407 kw aur; 1070; N42 30 53 W96 18 13
Mailing Address: 6450 Corporate Drive, P.O. Box 6450, Johnston, IA 50131-6450
Second Address: 6450 Corporate Dr., Joohnston, IA 50131
(515) 242-3100
www.iptv.org
public_information@iptv.org
License: Sioux City, Woodbury County, IA held by Iowa Public Broadcasting Board
Washington Law Firm: Dow, Lohnes PLLC
Nat'l Network: PBS
Molly M. Phillips, Executive Director and General Manager
Daniel Miller, General Manager
Justin Beaupr, Director of Programming and Production
William T. Hayes, Director of Engineering and Technology
Kristine K. Houston, Director ofAdministration and Finance
Kristen L. Gray, Director of Communications

Springfield, MO (DMA 75)

KOLR *Digital Channel:* 52; 316 kw vis, 31.6 kw aur; 2,070t/1,887g; N37 13 08 W92 56 56; *Population Served:* 1,472,000
2650 E. Division, Springfield, MO 65803 US
(417) 862-2727; *Fax:* (417) 862-6439
www.ozarksfirst.com
License: Springfield, Greene County, MO held by Mission Broadcasting Inc.
Group Owner: Mission Broadcasting Inc.; (acq 12-17-2003).
Nat'l Network: CBS
Size of News Staff: 30; *Hours of Local News Weekly:* news progmg 22 hrs wkly
Jeff Gamble, General Sales Mgr
Chuck Maulden, News Director

***KOZK** *Digital Channel:* 23; *Virtual Channel:* 21; 100 kw vis; ant 2,024t/1,925g; N37 10 11 W92 56 30; *Population Served:* 650,000
901 S. National, Springfield, MO 65897
(417) 836-3500,(866) 684-5695; *Fax:* (417) 863-3569
www.optv.org
mail@optv.org
License: Springfield, Greene County, MO held by Board of Governors of Missouri State University
Washington Law Firm: Dow, Lohnes PLLC
Nat'l Network: PBS
Tammy Wiley, General Manager
Barb McMeekin, General Sales Mgr
Tom Carter, Programming Director
Brent Moore, Chief Engineer
Rachel Knight, Assistant To General Manager

KOZL-TV *Digital Channel:* 28; *Virtual Channel:* 27; 5,000 kw vis, 500 kw aur; ant 1,694t/1,569g; N37 13 08 W92 56 56;
Population Served: 890,000
2650 E. Division, Springfield, MO 65803 US
(417) 862-2727; *Fax:* (417) 862-6439
www.ozarksfirst.com
License: Springfield, Greene County, MO held by Nexstar Broadcasting Inc.
Group Owner: Nexstar Broadcasting Group Inc.; (acq 12-31-2003; grpsl)
Hours of Local News Weekly: News progmg 12 hrs wkly
Leo Henning, General Manager
Jeff Gamble, General Sales Mgr
Chuck Maulden, News Director

KRBK ; *Virtual Channel:* 49; 5,000 kw vis; ant 1,519t/1,375g; N37 49 10 W92 44 52; *Not on Air/Target Date:* unknown
1701 S. Enterprise, Springfield, MO 65804
(417) 522-0020
www.foxkrbk.com

License: Osage Beach, Camden County, MO
Nat'l Network: Fox
Edward Koplar, President
Bret Falcetto, Dir. Of Operations/ Engineering
Craig Carnesi, General Sales Manager
Chris Iller, Dir. Of Marketing & promotions
Cindy Montoya, Traffic Dir.
James Kerr, Production Dir.
Amber Karnes,Internet Content Supervisor
Danielle Hellon, Sales Asst.
David koeller, Meterologist

KSPR *Digital Channel:* 19; *Virtual Channel:* 33; 1000 kw; 1886 ft.; N37 10 26 W92 56 27
Mailing Address: 7621 Little Avenue, Suite 506, Charlotte, NC 28266 US
Second Address: 999 W. Sunshine Street, Springfield, MO 65807
(417) 831-1333; *Fax:* (417) 831-9358
www.kspr.com
news@kspr.com
License: Springfield, Greene County, MO held by Perkin Media LLC.
(acq 2007; $20.629 million); *Ownership:* William N. Perkin, 100%; *Washington Law Firm:* Sciarrino and Associates PLLC
Nat'l Network: ABC
Size of News Staff: 21; *Hours of Local News Weekly:* news progmg 9 hrs wkly
Brad Belote, News Director
Neal Evans, Chief Engineer

KYTV *Digital Channel:* 44; *Virtual Channel:* 3; 967 kw; 2060 ft.; N37 10 26 W92 56 27
Mailing Address: 999 West Sunshine Street, Springfield, MO 65807 US
Second Address: PO Box 3500, Springfield, MO 65808
(417) 268-3000, (417) 268-3200; *Fax:* (417) 268-3100
www.ky3.com
License: Springfield, Greene County, MO held by KY-3 Inc.
Group Owner: Schurz Communications Inc.; (acq 2-19-87; $50.8 million); *Washington Law Firm:* Wilmer Hale
Nat'l Network: NBC; CW; *Nat'l Reps:* Harrington, Righter & Parsons
Size of News Staff: 40; *Hours of Local News Weekly:* news progmg 24 hrs wkly
Mike Scott, General Manager
Mary Chalender, General Sales Mgr
Trenna Underhill, Programming Director
Dan McGrane, Promotions Manager
Scott Brady, News Director
Kirk Lemons, Chief Engineer
Steve Grant, News Team
Lisa Rose, NewsTeam
Emily Wood, News Team
Paul Edler, News Team
Maria Neider, News Team
Paula Morehouse, News Team

St. Joseph, MO (DMA 201)

KQTV *Digital Channel:* 7; *Virtual Channel:* 2; 40 kw; 587 ft.; N39 46 12 W94 47 53
Mailing Address: PO Box 8369, St. Joseph, MO 64508 US
Second Address: 40th & Faraon St., St. Joseph, MO 64506
(816) 364-2222; *Fax:* (816) 364-3787
www.stjoechannel.com
License: St. Joseph, Buchanan County, MO held by Nexstar Broadcasting Inc.
Group Owner: Nexstar Broadcasting Group Inc.; (acq 2-14-97; with WTWO(TV) Terre Haute, IN).; *Washington Law Firm:* Drinker, Biddle & Reath
Nat'l Network: ABC; *Nat'l Reps:* Blair Television; Petry Television Inc.
Size of News Staff: 18; *Hours of Local News Weekly:* news progmg 16 hrs wkly
Heather Shearin, General Manager
Dirk Allsbury, Local Sales Manager
Bridget Blevins, News Director

KTAJ-TV *Digital Channel:* 21; *Virtual Channel:* 16; 1000 kw; 1036 ft.; N39 1 20 W94 30 49
Mailing Address: 4410-B, South 40th St., St. Joseph, MO 64503 US
Second Address: PO Box A, Santa Ana, CA 92711
(714) 731-1000, (888) 731-1000; *Fax:* (816) 364-6729
www.tbn.org
ktaj@tbn.org
License: St. Joseph, Buchanan County, MO held by Trinity Christian Center of Santa Ana Inc. dba Trinity Broadcasting Network.
Group Owner: Trinity Broadcasting Network; (acq 5-8-2000; grpsl).
Nat'l Network: TRINITY BROADCA
Paul Crouch, President
Jan Crouch, Operations Dir
Julie Cluck, Station Manager
Jeff Landers, Engineering Dir
Andrae Hannon, Public Affairs Director

St. Louis, MO (DMA 21)

KDNL-TV *Digital Channel:* 31; *Virtual Channel:* 30; 1000 kw; 1052 ft.; N38 34 50 W90 19 45
1215 Cole St., St. Louis, MO 63106 US
(314) 436-3030; *Fax:* (314) 259-5709
www.abcstlouis.com
info@abcstlouis.com
License: St. Louis, St. Louis County, MO held by KDNL Licensee LLC
Group Owner: Sinclair Broadcast Group Inc.; (acq 5-30-96); *Washington Law Firm:* Shaw, Pittman
Nat'l Network: ABC; *Nat'l Reps:* Millennium Sales & Marketing
Tom Tipton, General Manager
Mike Held, Local Sales Manager

***KETC** *Digital Channel:* 39; *Virtual Channel:* 9; 142.5 kw; 1064 ft.; N38 28 55.8 W90 23 52.6
3655 Olive Street, St. Louis, MO 63108 US
(314) 512-9000; *Fax:* (314) 512-9005
www.ketc.org
letters@ketc.org
License: St. Louis, Saint Louis City County, MO held by St. Louis Regional Educational and Public Television Commission
Washington Law Firm: Dow, Lohnes & Albertson
Nat'l Network: ETV
Jeffery M. McDonnell, Chairman
John (Jack) Galmiche III, CEO/President
Patricia Kistler, VP, Programming
Patrick Murphy, Promotions Manager
Chrys Marlow, VP,Engineering & Operations
Amy Shaw, Senior VP,Community Engagement
DickSkalski, COO,CFO,Senior VP
Patrick Murphy, Production Vice President
Dan Shasserre, VP,Development
Patrick J. Sly, Vice Chairman,Executive VP
Steven N. Frank, Treasurer

KMOV *Digital Channel:* 24; *Virtual Channel:* 4; 412 kW; 872 ft.; N38 31 47 W90 17 58
One Memorial Dr, St. Louis, MO 63102 USA
(314) 621-4444; *Fax:* (314) 444-6307
www.kmov.com
License: St. Louis, MO held by Meredith Corp.
Group Owner: Meredith Corp.; (acq 6-02-97; grpsl); *Washington Law Firm:* Wiley, Rein & Fielding
Nat'l Network: CBS; *Nat'l Reps:* TeleRep
Size of News Staff: 70; *Hours of Local News Weekly:* news progmg 29 hrs wkly
Mike Murphy, General Manager

KNLC *Digital Channel:* 14; *Virtual Channel:* 24; 900 kw; 1300 ft.; N38 21 40 W90 32 55
Mailing Address: 1411 Locust Street, St. Louis, MO 63103 US
Second Address: 1411 Locust St., St. Louis, MO 63188
(314) 436-2424; *Fax:* (314) 436-2434
www.knlc.tv
judy@knlc.tv
License: St. Louis, Saint Louis City County, MO held by New Life Evangelistic Center Inc
Washington Law Firm: Midlen & Guillot
Nat'l Network: NONE
Larry Rice, President
Ray Redlich, Operations Dir
Judy Redlich, General Sales Mgr
Victor Anderson, Programming Director
Jim Barnes, Chief Engineer

KPLR *Digital Channel:* 26; *Virtual Channel:* 11; 1000 kw; 945 ft.; N38 34 24 W90 19 30
2250 Ball Dr., St. Louis, MO 63146 USA
(314) 213-7831
kplr11.com
License: St. Louis, Saint Louis City County, MO held by KPLR Inc.
Group Owner: Tribune Media; (acq 12-20-2007; grpsl)
Nat'l Network: The CW Network; *Nat'l Reps:* TeleRep
Hours of Local News Weekly: News progmg 4 hrs wkly

KSDK *Digital Channel:* 35; *Virtual Channel:* 5; 838 kw; 1,112 ft.; N38 34 5 W90 19 55
1000 Market St., St. Louis, MO 63101 US
(314) 421-5055; *Fax:* (314) 425-5348
www.ksdk.com
comments@ksdk.com
License: St. Louis, Saint Louis City County, MO held by Multimedia KSDK LLC
Group Owner: Tegna Media; (acq 11-30-95; grpsl).; *Washington Law Firm:* Wiley, Rein & Fielding
Nat'l Network: NBC; *Nat'l Reps:* Blair Television
Marv Danielski, President and General Manager
Alicia Elsner, Director of Sales
Rebecca Rahm, Director of Operations and Programming
Jeff Winget, Promotions Manager
Karin Movesian, News Director
Dave Hummert, Chief Engineer

KTVI *Digital Channel:* 43; *Virtual Channel:* 2; 1000 kw; 1106 ft.; N38 32 7 W90 22 23
2250 Ball Dr., St. Louis, MO 63146 USA
(314) 213-7831
fox2now.com
License: St. Louis, Saint Louis City County, MO held by KTVI License LLC
Group Owner: Tribune Media; (acq 7-14-2008; grpsl);
Washington Law Firm: Dow Lohnes PLLC
Nat'l Network: FOX
Hours of Local News Weekly: News progmg 37.5 hrs wkly
Spencer Koch, Operations Dir
Kurt Krueger, General Sales Mgr
Elaine Claspill, Programming Director
Kathryn Collett, Promotions Manager
Ernie Dachel, Chief Engineer
Cindy Solomon, National Sales Manager
Steve Mills, Regional SalesManager

Montana

Billings, MT (DMA 166)

KHMT *Digital Channel:* 22; 1,000 kw vis; ant 812t/368g; N45 44 24 W108 08 18; *Population Served:* 150,000
445 S. 24th St. W., Billings, MT 59102 US
(406) 652-4743; *Fax:* (406) 652-6963
www.yourbigsky.com
License: Hardin, Big Horn County, MT held by Mission Broadcasting Inc.
Group Owner: Mission Broadcasting Inc.; (acq 12-30-2003).; *Washington Law Firm:* Drinker, Biddle & Reath L.L.P.
Nat'l Network: Fox
Bill Burckhard, Station Manager

KSVI *Digital Channel:* 18; *Virtual Channel:* 6; 1000 kw; 746 ft.; N45 48 26 W108 20 25
445 S. 24th St. W., Billings, MT 59102 US
(406) 652-4743; *Fax:* (406) 652-6963
www.yourbigsky.com
License: Billings, Yellowstone County, MT held by Nexstar Broadcasting Inc.
Group Owner: Nexstar Broadcasting Group Inc.; (acq 12-31-2003; grpsl); *Washington Law Firm:* Drinker, Biddle & Reath L.L.P.
Nat'l Network: ABC

KTVQ *Digital Channel:* 10; *Virtual Channel:* 2; 26.1 kw; 591 ft.; N45 46 1 W108 27 26
3203 3rd Ave. N., Billings, MT 59101 US
(406) 252-5611; *Fax:* (406) 252-9938
www.ktvq.com
License: Billings, Yellowstone County, MT held by KTVQ Communications LLC
Group Owner: Cordillera Communications Inc.; (acq 1994; $8.5 million); *Washington Law Firm:* Dow, Lohnes & Albertson
Nat'l Network: CBS; CW; *Nat'l Reps:* Harrington, Righter & Parsons; *Wire Services:* AP
Size of News Staff: 21; *Hours of Local News Weekly:* news progmg 17 hrs wkly
Tim Keating, Director of Regional/National Sales
Pam Hofferber, Programming Director
Jon Stepanek, News Director
John Webber, Chief Engineer

KULR-TV *Digital Channel:* 11; *Virtual Channel:* 8; 16 kw; 627 ft.; N45 45 35 W108 27 14; *Rebroadcasting:* Rebroadcasts KYUS(TV) Miles City.
2045 Overland Ave., Billings, MT 59102 US
(406) 656-8000; *Fax:* (406) 655-2688
www.kulr8.com
news@kulr.com
License: Billings, Yellowstone County, MT held by Cowles Montana Media Co.

Group Owner: Cowles Montana Media Co.; (acq 10-1-2013).
Nat'l Network: NBC; *Wire Services:* AP
Size of News Staff: 24; *Hours of Local News Weekly:* news progmg 20 hrs wkly
Doug Miles, General Manager
Tim White, General Sales Mgr
Scott Warder, Promotions Manager
Emily Nantz, News Director
Peter Davies, Chief Engineer

Butte-Bozeman, MT (DMA 185)

KBZK *Digital Channel:* 13; *Virtual Channel:* 7; 18.9 kw; 889 ft.; N45 40 24 W110 52 2
Mailing Address: 90 Television Way, Bozeman, MT 59718 US
Second Address: 1003 S. Montana St., Butte, MT 59701
(406) 922-2400; *Fax:* (406) 586-4135
www.kbzk.com
newstips@kbzk.com
License: Bozeman, Gallatin County, MT held by KCTZ Communications Inc.
Group Owner: Cordillera Communications Inc.; (acq 12-93).;
Washington Law Firm: Dow, Lohnes & Albertson
Nat'l Network: CBS; CW; *Wire Services:* AP
Size of News Staff: 3
Terry Hurley, President
Jon Saunders, General Manager
Kristin Morgan, Sales and Marketing Coordinator
Pam Hofferber, Programming Director
John Sherer, News Director
Mike Warner, Chief Engineer

KTVM-TV *Digital Channel:* 33; 100 kw vis, 10 kw aur; ant 1,940t/213g; N46 00 29 W112 26 30; *Population Served:* 59,300
Mailing Address: 201 S. Wallace, Suite A5, Bozeman, MT 59715 US
Second Address: PO Box 1618, Bozeman, MT 59771
(406) 586-0296; *Fax:* (406) 586-0554
www.nbcmontana.com/ktvm
news@ktvm.com
License: Butte, Silver Bow County, MT held by BlueStone License Holdings Inc.
Group Owner: Bonten Media Group LLC; (acq 5-31-2007; grpsl);
Washington Law Firm: Covington & Burling LLP
Nat'l Network: NBC; *Nat'l Reps:* Continental Television Sales
Richard Reingold, General Manager
Swan Beck, Station Manager
Scott Bruce, General Sales Mgr
Louise Kingston, Promotion
Chris Grogan, News Director
Charlie Cannaliato, Chief Engineer
Dennis O'Brien, Market Controller
EricJochim, Executive Producer

***KUSM-TV** *Digital Channel:* 8; 44 kw vis; ant 817t/305g; N45 40 24 W110 52 02; *Population Served:* 46,000
Mailing Address: Box 173340, Visual Communications, Bldg. 183, Montana State Univ., Bozeman, MT 59717-3340
Second Address: Visual Communications Bldg. 183, Montana Stata University, Bozeman, MT 59717
(406) 243-4101, (866) 832-0829; *Fax:* (406) 243-3299, (406) 994-6545
www.montanapbs.org
kusm@montanapbs.org
License: Bozeman, Gallatin County, MT held by Montana State University
Nat'l Network: PBS
William Marcus, General Manager
Lisa Titus, General Sales Mgr
Aaron Pruitt, Programming Director
Amy Colson, Promotions Manager
Dean Lawver, Engineering Dir
Linda Talbott, Associate Director
Saxon Holbrook, Technical Director
Ivy Wells, Systems Administrator
Gus Chambers, Producers
Ray Ekness, Producers
Tim Martins, Engineer

KWYB *Digital Channel:* 19; *Virtual Channel:* 18; 110.7 kw; 1,920 ft.; N46 0 24 W112 26 30
3825 Harrison Ave., Suite B, Butte, MT 59701 US
(406) 782-7185; *Fax:* (406) 723-9269
www.abcfoxmontana.com
abcfoxmt@abcfoxmontana.com
License: Butte, Silver Bow County, MT held by Cowles Montana Media Co.
Group Owner: Cowles Montana Media Co.; (acq 10-1-2013).;
Washington Law Firm: Reddy, Begley & McCormick
Nat'l Network: ABC
Tom Ciprari, Station Manager/Operations Director
Craig Toomey, General Sales Mgr
Linda Julius, Program Manager
Andrea Lutz, News Director
Larry O'Donnell, Chief Engineer
Paula Bauer, Business Manager
Bob Nicklay, Local SalesManager
Sharikay Austin, Traffic Manager

KXLF-TV *Digital Channel:* 5; *Virtual Channel:* 4; 10 kw; 1,929 ft.; N46 00 27 W112 26 30; *Population Served:* 134,400
1003 S. Montana St., Butte, MT 59701 US
(406) 496-8400; *Fax:* (406) 782-8906
www.kxlf.com
newstips@kxlf.com
License: Butte, Silver Bow County, MT held by KXLF Communications LLC
Group Owner: Cordillera Communications Inc.; (acq 12-15-86; grpsl; *Washington Law Firm:* Dow, Lohnes & Albertson
Nat'l Network: CBS; CW; *Nat'l Reps:* Harrington, Righter & Parsons; *Wire Services:* AP
Size of News Staff: 6+; *Hours of Local News Weekly:* news progmg 20 hrs wkly
Jon Saunders, General Manager
Pam Hofferber, Programming Director
Mike Warner, Chief Engineer

Glendive, MT (DMA 210)

KXGN-TV *Digital Channel:* 5; *Virtual Channel:* 5; 1 kw; 500 ft.; N47 2 39 W104 40 52.5
210 South Douglas, Glendive, MT 59330 US
(406) 377-3377, (406) 377-3378; *Fax:* (406) 365-2181
www.kxgn.com
kxgnkdzn@midrivers.com
License: Glendive, Dawson County, MT held by Glendive Broadcasting Corp.
Ownership: Stephen A. Marks.; *Washington Law Firm:* Davis Wright Tremaine LLP
Nat'l Network: CBS/NBC; NBC; *Wire Services:* UPI
Stephen Marks, President
Paul Sturlaugson, General Sales Mgr
Andrew Sturlaugson, Programming Director
Mike Huseby, Chief Engineer
Tonya Bruner, Traffic Manager

Great Falls, MT (DMA 192)

KFBB-TV *Digital Channel:* 8; *Virtual Channel:* 5; 31 kw; 470 ft.; N47 32 08 W111 17 02; *Population Served:* 161,800
Mailing Address: P.O. Box 1139, Great Falls, MT 59403 US
Second Address: 3200 Old Havre Hwy., Black Eagle, MT 59414
(406) 453-4377; *Fax:* (406) 727-9703
www.kfbb.com
License: Great Falls, Cascade County, MT held by Cowles Montana Media Co.
Group Owner: Cowles Montana Media Co.; (acq 10-1-2013).;
Washington Law Firm: Baker & Hostetler
Nat'l Network: ABC; Fox; *Wire Services:* Direct Line Weather Wire
Size of News Staff: 6; *Hours of Local News Weekly:* news progmg 6 hrs wkly
Keith Teske, Station Manager/Director of Sales
Linda Julius, Programming Manager
Deyja Charles, News Director
Sam Nishoff, Chief Engineer
Sharikay Austin, Traffic Manager

KRTV *Digital Channel:* 7; *Virtual Channel:* 3; 28.5 kw; 504 ft.; N47 32 7.7 W111 17 2.6
Mailing Address: P.O. Box 2989, Great Falls, MT 59403 US
Second Address: 3300 Old Havre Hwy., Black Eagle, MT 59414
(406) 791-5400
www.krtv.com
krtvnews@krtv.com
License: Great Falls, Cascade County, MT held by KRTV Communications LLC
Group Owner: Cordillera Communications Inc.; (6-86).;
Washington Law Firm: Dow, Lohnes & Albertson
Nat'l Network: CBS; CW; *Nat'l Reps:* Harrington, Righter & Parsons; *Wire Services:* AP; CNN
Size of News Staff: 15; *Hours of Local News Weekly:* news progmg 15 hrs wkly
Jon Saunders, General Manager
Heath Heggem, Station Manager
Roxie Rattray, Programming Director
Jerry Howard, News Director

KTGF *Digital Channel:* 45; *Virtual Channel:* 16
PO Box 7393, Helena, MT 59604 US
(406) 502-1500; *Fax:* (406) 454-3484
FamilyTV@Gmail.com
License: Great Falls, Cascade County, MT held by Destiny Licenses LLC.
(acq 11-24-2004; $3 million with translator K47DP Lewistown);
Ownership: Destiny Communications LLC, 100%; *Washington Law Firm:* Garvey, Schubert & Barer
Nat'l Network: IND
Darnell Washington, CEO
Andrea Dean, Station Manager
Jennifer Rimmel, Programming Director

***KUFM-TV** *Digital Channel:* 21; *Virtual Channel:* 21; 23.4 kw; 501 ft.; N47 32 9.2 W111 17 2.1
32 Campus Dr., University of Montana, Missoula, MT 59812 US
(406) 243-3299; *Fax:* (406) 994-6545
www.montanapbs.org
License: Great Falls, Cascade County, MT held by Board of Regents of the Montana University System
Eric Hyppa, General Manager of Montana PBS
Nancy Ockford, Business& Finance Manager
Josh Winterrowd, IT Manager
Crystal Leach, Dir. Of Deveolopment
dean Lawver, Dir. Of Technology
Saxon Holbrook, Technical Dir.

Helena, MT (DMA 205)

KMTF *Digital Channel:* 29; *Virtual Channel:* 10; 43.4 kw; 2287 ft.; N46 49 35 W111 42 33
100 W.Lyndale Avenue, Suite B, Helena, MT 59601 US
(406) 457-1010; *Fax:* (406) 457-2758
www.cwhelena.com
cw10@surewest.net
License: Helena, Lewis and Clark County, MT held by Rocky Mountain Broadcasting Co
Nat'l Network: CW
Jon Gibson, General Manager
Paul Albertson, Station Manager
Carmen Sharps, Sales Manager

KTVH-DT *Digital Channel:* 12; *Virtual Channel:* 12; 17.5 kw vis; 2,202 ft.; N46 49 29.6 W111 42 12.6; *Population Served:* 140,000
100 W. Lyndale Ave., Suite A, Helena, MT 59601 US
(406) 457-1212
www.ktvh.com
news@ktvh.com
License: Helena, MT held by KRTV Communications LLC
Group Owner: Cordillera Communications Inc.; (acq 11-3-2015).;
Washington Law Firm: Gerald S. Rourke
Nat'l Network: NBC
Size of News Staff: 8; *Hours of Local News Weekly:* news progmg 7 hrs wkly
Nick Hessler, General Manager

Kalispell

***KUKL-TV** *Digital Channel:* 46; 23.4 kw; 830 m; N48 0 48.2 W114 21 54.5
Visual Communications Bldg 183, Montana State University, Bozeman, MT 59717
(406) 994-3437; *Fax:* (406) 756-0317
www.montanapbs.org
info@montanapbs.org
License: Kalispell, Flathead County, MT held by Board of Regents of the Montana University System
Angela McLean, Chair
Todd Buchanan, Vice Chair

Missoula, MT (DMA 164)

KCFW-TV *Digital Channel:* 9; *Virtual Channel:* 9; 2.5 kw; 2789 ft.; N48 0 48 W114 21 55
Mailing Address: 340 West Main Street, Missoula, MT 59802 US
Second Address: PO Box 5268, Missoula, MT 59806
(406) 721-2063, (406) 721-5642; *Fax:* (406) 752-8002
www.nbcmontana.com
news@kcfw.com
License: Kalispell, Flathead County, MT held by BlueStone License Holdings Inc.
Group Owner: Bonten Media Group LLC; (acq 5-31-2007; grpsl);
Washington Law Firm: Covington & Burling LLP
Nat'l Network: NBC
Size of News Staff: 5; *Hours of Local News Weekly:* news progmg 6 hrs wkly
Richard Reingold, General Manager
Wade Muehlhof, Station Manager

Tamy Wagner, Sales Manager
Louise Kingston, Marketing/Promotions
Chris Grogan, News Director
Robert Owen, Engineering Dir
Rob Owen, Engineering Dir
Cyndy Koures,Executive Producer
William Miller, Web Manager
Scott Ashleman, Production Manager
Dennis O'Brien, Market Controller
Steve Fetveit, Anchor
Kevin Maki, Reporter

KECI-TV *Digital Channel:* 13; *Virtual Channel:* 13; 41.3 kw; 2001 ft.; N47 1 4 W114 0 47
Mailing Address: 340 West Main Street, Missoula, MT 59802 US
Second Address: Box 5268, Missoula, MT 59806
(406) 721-2063, (406) 721-5642; *Fax:* (406) 721-2083/(406) 549-6507
www.nbcmontana.com
License: Missoula, Missoula County, MT held by BlueStone License Holdings Inc.
Group Owner: Bonten Media Group LLC; (acq 5-31-2007; grpsl); *Washington Law Firm:* Covington & Burling LLP
Nat'l Network: NBC; *Nat'l Reps:* Continental Television Sales
Hours of Local News Weekly: News progmg 14 hrs wkly
Richard Reingold, General Manager
Tamy Wagner, Sales Manager
Jean Zosel, Promotions Manager
Chris Grogan, News Director
Robert Owen, Engineering Dir
Rob Owen, Engineering Dir
Louise Kingston, Marketing/Promotion
William Miller,Web Manager
Cyndy Koures, Executive Producer
Scott Ashleman, Production Manager
Mark Heyka, Chief Meteorologist
Cyndy Koures, Executive Producer

KPAX-TV *Digital Channel:* 7; *Virtual Channel:* 8; 22.5 kw; 2,144 ft.; N47 1 6 W114 0 41
1049 W. Central Ave., Missoula, MT 59801 US
(406) 542-4400; *Fax:* (406) 543-7111
www.kpax.com
news@kpax.com
License: Missoula, Missoula County, MT held by KPAX Communications LLC
Group Owner: Cordillera Communications Inc.; *Washington Law Firm:* Dow, Lohnes & Albertson
Nat'l Network: CBS; CW
Hours of Local News Weekly: news progmg 15 hrs wkly
Bob Hermes, General Manager
Jim McLean, General Sales Mgr
Tammy Engle, Programming Director
James Rafferty, Promotions Manager
Joel Lundstad, News Director
Larry Arbaugh, Chief Engineer
Derek Buerkle, Sports Director

KTMF *Digital Channel:* 23; *Virtual Channel:* 23; 92.6 kw; 2,106 ft.; N47 1 10 W114 0 46; *Rebroadcasting:* Rebroadcasts KTMF(LP) Kalispell 90%.
2200 Stephens Ave., Missoula, MT 59801 US
(406) 542-8900; *Fax:* (406) 728-4800
www.abcfoxmontana.com
abcfoxmt@abcfoxmontana.com
License: Missoula, Missoula County, MT held by Cowles Montana Media Co.
Group Owner: Cowles Montana Media Co.; (acq 10-1-2013).; *Washington Law Firm:* Reddy, Begley & McCormick
Nat'l Network: ABC; Fox
Tom Ciprari, Station Manager/Operations Director
Craig Toomey, General Sales Mgr
Linda Julius, Program Manager
Andrea Lutz, News Director
Larry O'Donnell, Chief Engineer
Paula Bauer, Business Manager
Bob Nicklay, Local SalesManager
Sharikay Austin, Traffic Manager

***KUFM-TV** *Digital Channel:* 11; *Virtual Channel:* 11; 125 kw vis; 2,116t/259g; Missoula, MT; *Rebroadcasting:* Rebroadcasts KUSM(TV) Bozeman 85%.
Mailing Address: PARTV 180, 32 Campus Dr., Univ. of Montana, Missoula, MT 59812
Second Address: Visual Communications Bldg. 183, Montana Stata University, Bozeman, MT 59717
(406) 243-4101, (866) 832-0829; *Fax:* (406) 243-3299, (406) 994-6545
www.montanapbs.org
kufm@montanapbs.org
License: Missoula, Missoula County, MT held by The University of Montana
Nat'l Network: PBS
Size of News Staff: 1; *Hours of Local News Weekly:* 0
Daniel Dauterive, Operations Director
William Marcus, General Manager
Drew Jenkins, General Sales Mgr
Saxon Holbrook, Engineering Dir
Jeff Croonenberghs, Chief Engineer
Linda Talbott, Associate Director
Saxon Holbrook, TechnicalDirector
Ivy Wells, Systems Administrator
Gus Chambers, Producers
Ray Ekness, Producers
Tim Martins, Engineer

Nebraska

Cheyenne, WY-Scottsbluff, NE (DMA 198)

KNEP-TV *Digital Channel:* 7; *Virtual Channel:* 4; 32 kw; 1558 ft.; N41 50 28 W103 4 27
Mailing Address: PO Box 1760, Rapid City, SD 57709 US
Second Address: 1523 First Avenue, Scottsbluff, NE 69361
(308) 632-3071; *Fax:* (308) 632-3596
www.nbcneb.com/scottsbluff/home
License: Scottsbluff, Scotts Bluff County, NE held by Duhamel Broadcasting Enterprises.
Group Owner: Duhamel Broadcasting Enterprises; *Washington Law Firm:* Fisher, Wayland, Cooper, Leader & Zaragoza
Nat'l Network: ABC
Size of News Staff: 6; *Hours of Local News Weekly:* news progmg 2 hrs wkly
Patrick Maag, General Manager
Doug Loos, Programming Director
Jerry Dishong, News Director
Teddy Johnson, Chief Engineer
Brandon Marshall, Territory News Team
Anndrea Anderson, Territory News Team
Ryan Murphy, News Team
KennaNash, Territory News Team
Jerry Dishong, News & Weather
John Clanton, Reporting & Anchoring

KSTF *Digital Channel:* 29; *Virtual Channel:* 10; 2.7 kw; 764 ft.; N41 59 58 W103 39 55
3385 N 10th St., Gering, NE 69341 USA
(308) 632-7535
www.kgwn.tv
License: Scottsbluff, Scotts Bluff County, NE held by Gray Television Licensee LLC
Group Owner: Gray Television Inc.; *Washington Law Firm:* Dow, Lohnes & Albertson
Nat'l Network: CBS
Size of News Staff: 6; *Hours of Local News Weekly:* news progmg 8 hrs wkly
Tregg White, General Manager
Barbara Parenti, Programming Director
Jeremy Downing, News Director
Tony Schaefer, Engineering Dir

***KTNE-TV** *Digital Channel:* 13; *Virtual Channel:* 13; 27 kw; 1529 ft.; N41 50 27 W103 3 18; *Rebroadcasting:* Satellite of *KUON-TV Lincoln.
1800 North 33rd Street, Lincoln, NE 68503 US
(800) 868-1868; *Fax:* (402) 472-1785
www.netnebraska.org
customerservice@netNebraska.org
License: Alliance, Box Butte County, NE held by Nebraska Educational Telecommunications Commission
Washington Law Firm: Dow, Lohnes & Albertson
Nat'l Network: PBS; *Regional Network:* National Educational Telecommunications Association
Joe Turco, Operations Dir
Rod Bates, General Manager
Michael Winkle, General Sales Mgr
David Feingold, Programming Director
Terry Dugas, Programming & Promotion

Lincoln & Hastings-Kearney, NE (DMA 105)

KGIN *Digital Channel:* 11; *Virtual Channel:* 11; 25 kw; 1032 ft.; N40 35 14 W98 48 10
123 N Locust St., Grand Island, NE 68802 USA
(308) 382-6100
www.1011now.com
kgin@1011now.com
License: Grand Island, Hall County, NE held by Gray Television Licensee LLC
Group Owner: Gray Television Inc.; (acq 7-30-98; grpsl).; *Washington Law Firm:* Pepper & Corazzini
Nat'l Network: CBS; *Nat'l Reps:* Continental Television Sales
Troy Frankforter, Operations Dir

KHAS-TV *Digital Channel:* 5; *Virtual Channel:* 5; 45 kw; 712 ft.; N40 39 6 W98 23 4
Mailing Address: P.O. Box 578, Hastings, NE 68902 US
Second Address: 6475 Osborne Dr. W, Hastings, NE 68901
(402) 463-1321; *Fax:* (402) 463-6551
www.khastv.com
License: Hastings, Adams County, NE held by Hoak Media of Nebraska License LLC.
Group Owner: Hoak Media Corporation; (acq 11-7-2005; with KNOP-TV North Platte).; *Washington Law Firm:* Fletcher, Heald & Hildreth
Nat'l Network: NBC; *Wire Services:* Skycom
Alan Uerling, Operations Manger
Ulysses Carlini, General manager
Connie Caldwell, General Sales Mgr
Jackie Arkerman, Programming Director
Jackie Ackerman, Promotions Manager
Jack Bowe, News Director
Connie Cardwell, SalesRepresentative
Marcia Hogan, National Sales Manger
Ken Maddox, Local Sales Manager
Chris Schukei, Morning Anchor/Assistant news Director
Ginger ten Bensel, Reporter
Ed Littler, Sports Director

KHGI-TV *Digital Channel:* 13; *Virtual Channel:* 13; 19.8 kw; 1115 ft.; N40 39 28 W98 52 4
Mailing Address: P.O. Box 220, Kearney, NE 68848 US
Second Address: 1078 25th Road, Axtell, NE 68924
(308) 743-2494, (308) 384-1313; *Fax:* (308) 743-2644
www.nebraska.tv
License: Kearney, Buffalo County, NE held by Pappas Telecasting of Central Nebraska L.P. (DE limited partnership).
Group Owner: Pappas Telecasting Companies; (acq 7-1-96; grpsl).
Nat'l Network: ABC; *Nat'l Reps:* Harrington, Righter & Parsons
Size of News Staff: 26; *Hours of Local News Weekly:* news progmg 17.5 hrs wkly
Vincent F. Barresi, General Manager
Dallas Nau, General Sales Manager
Scott Swenson, Programming Director
Anita Wragge, Promotions Manager
Matt Weesner, News Director
Jerry Fuehrer, Chief Engineer
Claire Runions, TrafficManager
Cheryl Alkire, Business Manager
Kent Boughton, Meterologist
Andrea Hay, Asst. News Director
Seth Denney, Anchor
Krisa Howland, National Sales Manager

***KHNE-TV** *Digital Channel:* 28; *Virtual Channel:* 29; 200 kw; 1201 ft.; N40 46 20 W98 5 21; *Rebroadcasting:* Satellite of *KUON-TV Lincoln.
Mailing Address: P.O. Box 83111, Lincoln, NE 88501 US
Second Address: 1800 North 33rd Street, Lincoln, NE 68503
(402) 472-3611, (800) 868-1868; *Fax:* (402) 472-1785
www.netnebraska.org
customerservice@netNebraska.org
License: Hastings, Adams County, NE held by Nebraska Educational Telecommunications Commission
Washington Law Firm: Dow, Lohnes & Albertson
Nat'l Network: PBS; *Regional Network:* National Educational Telecommunications Association
Size of News Staff: 3
Joe Turco, Operations Dir
Rod Bates, General Manager
Michael Winkle, General Sales Mgr
David Feingold, Programming Director
Terry Dugas, Programming & Promotion

KLKN *Digital Channel:* 8; *Virtual Channel:* 8; 25.9 kw; 1,434 ft.; N40 52 59 W97 18 19
3240 S. 10th St., Lincoln, NE 68502 US
(402) 434-8000; *Fax:* (402) 436-2236
www.klkntv.com
8@klkntv.com
License: Lincoln, Lancaster County, NE held by Citadel Communications Co. LLC
Group Owner: Citadel Communications Co. LTD.; (acq 11-15-86; *Washington Law Firm:* Latham & Watkins
Nat'l Network: ABC; *Nat'l Reps:* Millennium Sales & Marketing; *Wire Services:* AP
Size of News Staff: 22; *Hours of Local News Weekly:* news progmg 22 hrs wkly

Roger Moody, General Manager
Kay Wunderlich, National Sales Manager
Jeff Swanson, Program Manager
Nick Kumpula, Promotion/Public Service
Mark Haggar, News Director
Dan Ackerman, Chief Engineer
Steve Anderson, Business Manager
Peg Schoen, Local Sales Manager
Lanise Barber, Traffic Manager

***KLNE-TV** *Digital Channel:* 26; *Virtual Channel:* 3; 375 kw; 1086 ft.; N40 23 5 W99 27 30; *Rebroadcasting:* Satellite of *KUON-TV Lincoln.
Mailing Address: P. O. Box 83111, Lincoln, NE 88501 US
Second Address: 1800 N.33rd St., Lincoln, NE 68503
(800) 698-3426, (402) 470-6304; *Fax:* (402) 472-1785
www.netnebraska.org
tdugas@unlnotes.unl.edu
License: Lexington, Dawson County, NE held by Nebraska Educational Telecommunications Commission
Washington Law Firm: Dow, Lohnes & Albertson
Nat'l Network: PBS; *Regional Network:* National Educational Telecommunications Association
Joe Turco, Operations Dir
Rod Bates, General Manager
Michael Winkle, General Sales Mgr
David Feingold, Programming Director
Terry Dugas, Promotions Manager

***KMNE-TV** *Digital Channel:* 7; *Virtual Channel:* 7; 27 kw; 1486 ft.; N42 20 5 W99 29 2; *Rebroadcasting:* Satellite of *KUON-TV Lincoln.
1800 North 33rd St, Lincoln, NE 68503 US
(800) 868-1868; *Fax:* (402) 472-1785
www.netnebraska.org
customerservice@netNebraska.org
License: Bassett, Rock County, NE held by Nebraska Educational Telecommunications Commission
Washington Law Firm: Dow, Lohnes & Albertson
Nat'l Network: PBS; *Regional Network:* National Educational Telecommunications Association
Margaret Hornady-David, Chairman
Joe Turco, Operations Dir
Rod Bates, General Manager
Michael Winkle, General Sales Mgr
David Feingold, Programming Director
Terry Dugas, Promotions Manager
Carroll Russell, Vice Chair
MarkLeonard, Secretary/Treasurer
Randy Hansen, Assistant Secretary/Treasurer

KNHL *Digital Channel:* 51; *Virtual Channel:* 51; 45 kw; 711 ft.; N40 39 6 W98 23 44
805 Weightman St., Greenwood, MS 38930 US
(662) 822-1655
License: Hastings, NE held by Hoak Media of Hastings, LLC
Group Owner: Legacy Broadcasting, LLC
Sherry Nelson, President

KOLN *Digital Channel:* 10; *Virtual Channel:* 10; 28 kw; 1489 ft.; N40 48 11 W97 10 52
840 North 40th, Lincoln, NE 68503 USA
(402) 467-4321
www.1011now.com
info@1011now.com
License: Lincoln, Lancaster County, NE held by Gray Television Licensee LLC
Group Owner: Gray Television Inc.; (acq 7-30-98; grpsl).;
Washington Law Firm: Holland & Knight, LLP
Nat'l Network: CBS; *Nat'l Reps:* Continental Television Sales; *Wire Services:* AP
Troy Frankforter, Operations Manager

KTVG-TV *Digital Channel:* 19; 3,890 kw vis, 21.9 kw aur; 610t/270g; N40 43 44 W98 34 13
Mailing Address: Box 220, Kearney, NE 68848 US
Second Address: 1078 25th Rd., Axtell, NE 68924
(308) 734-2494; *Fax:* (308) 743-2644
www.nebraska.tv
comments@nebraska.tv
License: Grand Island, Hall County, NE held by Hill Broadcasting Inc
Nat'l Network: Fox; *Nat'l Reps:* Harrington, Righter & Parsons
Vince Barresi, General Manager
Dalla Nau, General Sales Manager
Scott Swenson, Programming Director
Anita Wragge, Promotion Manager
Mark Baumert, News Director
Jerry Fuehrer, Chief Engineer
Claire Runions, Traffic Manager
Cheryl Alkire, Business Manager
Andrea Hay, Assistant News Director
Krisa Howland, National Sales Manager

***KUON-TV** *Digital Channel:* 12; *Virtual Channel:* 12; 75 kw; 830 ft.; N41 8 18 W96 27 20
1800 North 33rd Street, Lincoln, NE 68503 US
(402) 472-3611; *Fax:* (402) 472-1785
www.netnebraska.org
customerservice@netNebraska.org
License: Lincoln, Lancaster County, NE held by University of Nebraska
(acq 7-28-54; *Washington Law Firm:* Dow, Lohnes & Albertson
Nat'l Network: PBS; *Regional Network:* National Educational Telecommunications Association
Size of News Staff: 3; *Hours of Local News Weekly:* 30 min. wkly
Joe Turco, Operations Dir
Rod Bates, General Manager
Michael Winkle, General Sales Mgr
David Feingold, Programming Director
Terry Dugas, Programming & Promotion

KWNB-TV *Digital Channel:* 6; *Virtual Channel:* 6; 11.9 kw; 725 ft.; N40 37 32 W101 1 45; *Rebroadcasting:* Rebroadcasts KHGI-TV, Kearney, 100%.
Mailing Address: P.O. Box 220, Kearney, NE 68840 US
Second Address: 1078 25th Rd., Axtell, NE 68924
(308) 743-2794; *Fax:* (308) 743-2644
www.nebraska.tv
comments@nebraska.tv
License: Hayes Center, Hayes County, NE held by Pappas Telecasting of Central Nebraska L.P. (DE limited partnership).
Group Owner: Pappas Telecasting Companies; (acq 7-1-96; grpsl).
Nat'l Network: ABC; *Nat'l Reps:* Harrington, Righter & Parsons
Size of News Staff: 26; *Hours of Local News Weekly:* news progmg 17.5 hrs wkly
Vince Barresi, General Manager
Dalla Nau, General Sales Manager
Scott Swensen, Programming Director
Anita Wragge, Promotion Manager
Mark Baumert, News Director
Jerry Fuehrer, Chief Engineer
Claire Runions, Traffic Manager
Cheryl Alkire, Business Manager
Andrea Hay, Assistant News Director
Krisa Howland, National Sales Manager

North Platte

KIIT *Digital Channel:* 11; .084 kW; N41 12 13 W100 43 58 NE USA
License: North Platte, Lincoln County, NE held by Gray Television Licensee LLC
Group Owner: Gray Television Inc.
Nat'l Network: FOX

KNPL *Digital Channel:* 25; 10 kW; N41 5 6 W100 45 28
400 N Dewey St., North Platte, NE 69101 USA
1011np.com
knpl@1011now.com
License: North Platte, Lincoln County, NE held by Gray Television Licensee LLC
Group Owner: Gray Television Inc.
Nat'l Network: CBS

North Platte, NE (DMA 209)

KNOP *Digital Channel:* 2; *Virtual Channel:* 2; 16 kw; 643 ft.; N41 12 13 W100 43 58
402 S Dewey, North Platte, NE 69101 USA
(308) 532-2222
www.knopnews2.com
License: North Platte, Lincoln County, NE held by Gray Television Licensee LLC
Group Owner: Gray Television Inc.; *Washington Law Firm:* Fletcher, Heald & Hildreth
Nat'l Network: NBC; *Nat'l Reps:* Blair Television; *Wire Services:* AP
Size of News Staff: 10; *Hours of Local News Weekly:* news progmg 15 hrs wkly
Rob Mandeville, General Sales Mgr
Jacque Harms, News Director

***KPNE-TV** *Digital Channel:* 9; *Virtual Channel:* 9; 85 kw; 1096 ft.; N41 1 22 W101 9 14; *Rebroadcasting:* Satellite of *KUON-TV Lincoln.
1800 North 33rd Street, PO Box 83111, Lincoln, NE 68503 US
(402) 472-3611, (800) 868-1868; *Fax:* (402) 472-1785
www.netnebraska.org
customerservice@netnebraska.org
License: North Platte, Lincoln County, NE held by Nebraska Educational Telecommunications Commission
Washington Law Firm: Dow, Lohnes & Albertson
Nat'l Network: PBS; *Regional Network:* National Educational Telecommunications Association
Margaret Hornady-David, Chair
Joe Turco, Operations Dir
Rod Bates, General Manager
Michael Winkle, General Sales Mgr
David Feingold, Programming Director
Mark Leonard, Secretary/Treasurer
Randy Hansen, AssistantSecretary/Treasurer
Terry Dugas, Programming & Promotion

Omaha, NE (DMA 74)

***KBIN-TV** *Digital Channel:* 33; 575 kw vis, 57.5 kw aur; ant 317t/163g; N41 15 14 W95 50 07
Mailing Address: Box 6450, Iowa Public TV, Johnston, IA 50131-6450
Second Address: 6535 Corporate Drive, PO Box 6450, Johnston, IA 50131-6400
(515) 725-9700, (800) 532-1290; *Fax:* (515) 242-4112
www.iptv.org
friends@iptv.org
License: Council Bluffs, Pottawattamie County, IA held by Iowa Public Broadcasting Board
Washington Law Firm: Dow, Lohnes PLLC
Nat'l Network: PBS
Molly M. Phillips, Executive Director and General Manager
Justin Beaupr,, Director of Programming and Production
William T. Hayes, Director of Engineering and Technology
Kristine K. Houston, Director of Administration and Finance
Kristen L. Gray, Director of Communications
Terry Rinehart, Director of Educational Services

KETV *Digital Channel:* 20; *Virtual Channel:* 7; 700 kw; 1299 ft.; N41 18 32 W96 1 33
2665 Douglas St., Omaha, NE 68131 US
(402) 522-7777; *Fax:* (402) 978-8931
www.ketv.com
news@ketv.com
License: Omaha, NE held by KETV Hearst Television Inc.
Group Owner: Hearst Television Inc.; (acq 3-18-99; grpsl)
Nat'l Network: ABC; *Nat'l Reps:* Eagle Television Sales; *Wire Services:* AP
Hours of Local News Weekly: News progmg 28 hrs wkly
Linda Hood, Programming Director

KMTV-TV *Digital Channel:* 45; 100 kw vis, 20 kw aur; ant 1,371t/1,409g; N41 18 25 W96 01 37; *Population Served:* 357,800
10714 Mockingbird Dr., Omaha, NE 68127
(402) 592-3333
www.action3news.com
kmtvsuggestions@jrn.com
License: Omaha, Douglas County, NE held by Journal Broadcast Corp.
Group Owner: Journal Communications Inc.; (acq 3-27-2007)
Nat'l Network: CBS
Hours of Local News Weekly: News progmg 23 hrs wkly
Chris Sehring, General Manager
Eric Hanneman, General Sales Mgr
Renee Rich, Programming Director
Willie Garrett, Promotions Manager
Ken Dudzik, News Director
Brady Pedersen, Engineering Dir
Scott Krayenhagen, Chief Engineer
Willie Garrett, Director of Marketing

KPTM *Digital Channel:* 43; *Virtual Channel:* 42; 700 kw; 1558 ft.; N41 4 14 W96 13 33
4625 Farnam St., Omaha, NE 68132 US
(402) 558-4200; *Fax:* (402) 554-4290
www.fox42kptm.com
contact@fox42kptm.com
License: Omaha, Douglas County, NE held by KPTM Licensee LLC
Group Owner: Sinclair Broadcast Group Inc.; (acq 10-1-2013; grpsl); *Washington Law Firm:* Pillsbury Winthrop Shaw Pittman LLP
Nat'l Network: FOX; MyNetworkTV; *Nat'l Reps:* TeleRep; *Wire Services:* FNS
Size of News Staff: 20; *Hours of Local News Weekly:* news progmg 7 hrs wkly
Patrick Kelly, Operations Supervisor
Jeff Miller, General Manager

KXVO *Digital Channel:* 38; *Virtual Channel:* 15; 490 kw; 1558 ft.; N41 4 16 W96 13 31

4625 Farnam St., Omaha, NE 68132 US
(402) 558-4200; *Fax:* (402) 554-4279
www.kxvo.com
License: Omaha, Douglas County, NE held by Mitts Telecasting Co. LLC
(acq 6-13-2000; $972,000); *Washington Law Firm:* Dow Lohnes PLLC
Nat'l Network: CW; *Nat'l Reps:* TeleRep
Thomas F. Mitts, President
Chris McDade, Operations Dir
Jeff Miller, General Sales Mgr
John King, Programming Director
Sam Lawson, Promotions Manager
Ed Bok, Chief Engineer
Tim Moan, Regional Sales Manager

***KYNE-TV** *Digital Channel:* 17; *Virtual Channel:* 26; 200 kw; 384 ft.; N41 15 28 W96 0 32; *Rebroadcasting:* Satellite of *KUON-TV Lincoln.
1800 North 33rd, Lincoln, NE 68503 US
(402) 472-3611; *Fax:* (402) 472-1785
www.netnebraska.org
customerservice@netNebraska.org
License: Omaha, Douglas County, NE held by Nebraska Educational Telecommunications Commission
Washington Law Firm: Dow, Lohnes & Albertson
Nat'l Network: PBS; *Regional Network:* National Educational Telecommunications Association
Size of News Staff: 3; *Hours of Local News Weekly:* 30 min. wkly
Joe Turco, Operations Dir
Rod Bates, General Manager
Michael Winkle, General Sales Mgr
David Feingold, Programming Director
Terry Dugas, Programming & Promotion

WOWT *Digital Channel:* 22; *Virtual Channel:* 6; 1000 kw; 1371 ft.; N41 18 40 W96 1 37
3501 Farnam St., Omaha, NE 68131 USA
(402) 346-6666; *Fax:* (402) 233-7881
www.wowt.com
sixonline@wowt.com
License: Omaha, Douglas County, NE held by Gray Television Licensee LLC
Group Owner: Gray Television Inc.; (acq 10-2002; grpsl).; *Washington Law Firm:* Fletcher, Heald & Hildreth
Nat'l Network: NBC; *Nat'l Reps:* Continental Television Sales
Size of News Staff: 52; *Hours of Local News Weekly:* news progmg 37 hrs wkly
Joel Helzer, General Sales Mgr

Sioux City, IA (DMA 149)

***KXNE-TV** *Digital Channel:* 19; *Virtual Channel:* 19; 475 kw; 1056 ft.; N42 14 15 W97 16 41; *Rebroadcasting:* Satellite of *KUON-TV Lincoln.
1800 North 33rd Street, Lincoln, NE 68503 US
(402) 472-3611; *Fax:* (402) 472-1785
www.netnebraska.org
customerservice@netNebraska.org
License: Norfolk, Madison County, NE held by Nebraska Educational Telecommunications Commission.
Washington Law Firm: Dow, Lohnes & Albertson
Nat'l Network: PBS; *Regional Network:* National Educational Telecommunications Association
Size of News Staff: 3; *Hours of Local News Weekly:* 30 min.wkly
Joe Turco, Operations Dir
Rod Bates, General Manager
Michael Winkle, General Sales Mgr
David Feingold, Programming Director
Terry Dugas, Programming & Promotion

Sioux Falls (Mitchell), SD (DMA 109)

***KRNE-TV** *Digital Channel:* 12; *Virtual Channel:* 12; 75 kw; 1056 ft.; N42 40 37 W101 42 39; *Rebroadcasting:* Satellite of KUON-TV Lincoln.
Mailing Address: 1800 North 33rd., Lincoln, NE 68501 US
Second Address: 1800 North 33rd Street, Lincoln, NE 68503
(402) 472-3611; *Fax:* (402) 472-1785
www.netnebraska.org
customerservice@netNebraska.org
License: Merriman, Cherry County, NE held by Nebraska Educational Telecommunications Commission
Washington Law Firm: Dow, Lohnes & Albertson
Nat'l Network: PBS; *Regional Network:* National Educational Telecommunications Association
Michael Winkle, Operations
Mark Leonard, General Manager
Debbie Hamlett, Marketing Director
David Feingold, Programming Director
Terry Dugas, Programming & Promotion

Superior

KSNB *Digital Channel:* 4; *Virtual Channel:* 4; .225 kW; N40 1 30 W98 4 38
6475 Osborne Dr. W, Hastings, NE 68902 USA
www.nbcneb.com
License: Superior, Nuckolls County, NE held by Gray Television Licensee LLC
Group Owner: Gray Television Inc.
Nat'l Network: ABC; FOX
Susan Ramsett, General Manager
Alan Uerling, Station Manager
Abby Richter, Local Sales Manager
Stephanie Hedrick, News Director

Wichita-Hutchinson Plus, KS (DMA 66)

KSNK *Digital Channel:* 12; *Virtual Channel:* 8; 10.4 kw; 715 ft.; N39 49 48 W100 42 4
833 North Main Street, P.O. Box 333, Wichita, KS 67201 US
(316) 265-3333; *Fax:* (316) 292-1197
www.ksn.com
License: McCook, Red Willow County, NE held by LIN License Company LLC
Group Owner: LIN Media; (acq 10-12-2012; grpsl); *Washington Law Firm:* Paul Hastings LLP
Nat'l Network: NBC; *Nat'l Reps:* TeleRep
Al Buch, General Manager
Dan Shurtz, General Sales Mgr
Betty Erickson, Programming Director
Gregg Cox, Promotions Manager
Jason Kravarik, News Director
Warren Kunkle, Chief Engineer
Kevin White, New Media Manager
Darren Dedo,New Media Manager
Mark Davidson, New Media Manager
Katie Tauba, New Media Manager
Craig Andres, New Media Manager
Chris Arnold, New Media Manager

Nevada

Las Vegas, NV (DMA 40)

KBLR *Digital Channel:* 40; *Virtual Channel:* 39; 1000 kw; 1191 ft.; N36 0 36 W115 0 20
450 Fremont Street, Suite 310, Las Vegas, NV 89101 USA
(702) 388-3200; *Fax:* (702) 258-0556
www.telemundolasvegas.com
License: Paradise, Clark County, NV held by Telemundo Las Vegas License LLC
Group Owner: Telemundo Station Group; (acq 1993; $1.5 million); *Washington Law Firm:* KMZ Rosenman
Nat'l Network: Telemundo
Foreign Language Programming; Size of News Staff: 8; *Hours of Local News Weekly:* news progmg 2 hrs wkly
Luis Silberwasser, President

KELV-LD *Digital Channel:* 15; *Virtual Channel:* 27; 15 kw; 1872 ft.; N35 56 46 W115 02 34
500 Pilor Rd., Suite D, Las Vegas, NV 89119 US
(702) 434-0015; *Fax:* (702) 434-0527
www.noticias.entravision.com/las-vegas
asignacionesnv@entravision.com
License: Las Vegas, Clark County, NV held by Entravision Holdings LLC.
Group Owner: Entravision Communications Corp.; *Washington Law Firm:* Thompson Hine L.L.P.
Nat'l Network: UNIVISION
Hours of Local News Weekly: News progmg 5 hrs wkly
Jose Monreal, Operations Dir
Fabian Saldivar, Promotions Manager
John Garcia, Engineering Dir

KINC *Digital Channel:* 16; *Virtual Channel:* 15; 1000 kw; 1872 ft.; N35 56 45 W115 2 37
500 Pilor Rd., Suite D, Las Vegas, NV 89119 US
(702) 434-0015; *Fax:* (702) 434-0527
www.noticias.entravision.com/las-vegas
asignacionesnv@entravision.com
License: Las Vegas, Clark County, NV held by Entravision Holdings LLC.
Group Owner: Entravision Communications Corp.; *Washington Law Firm:* Thompson Hine L.L.P.
Nat'l Network: UNIVISION
Foreign Language Programming; Hours of Local News Weekly: News progmg 5 hrs wkly
Jose Monreal, Operations Dir
Fabian Saldivar, Promotions Manager
John Garcia, Engineering Dir

KLAS-TV *Digital Channel:* 7; *Virtual Channel:* 8; 30.1 kw; 1998 ft.; N35 56 44 W115 2 33
3228 Channel 8 Dr., Las Vegas, NV 89109 US
(702) 792-8888
www.lasvegasnow.com
License: Las Vegas, Clark County, NV held by KLAS Inc., a Nevada Corp.
Group Owner: Landmark Communications Inc.; (acq 7-1-78; $8 million).; *Washington Law Firm:* Wiley, Rein Fielding, LLP
Nat'l Network: CBS; *Nat'l Reps:* Continental Television Sales
Lisa Howfield, General Manager
Linda Bonnici, General Sales Mgr
Terri Foley, News Director

***KLVX** *Digital Channel:* 11; *Virtual Channel:* 10; 105 kw; 1206 ft.; N36 0 27 W115 0 24
4210 Channel 10 Dr., Las Vegas, NV 89119 US
(702) 799-1010; *Fax:* (702) 799-5586
License: Las Vegas, Clark County, NV held by Clark County School District Board of Trustees
Washington Law Firm: Wiley, Rein & Fielding
Nat'l Network: ETV; *Wire Services:* Accu-Weather
Barbara Mirman, Operations Dir
Tom Axtell, General Manager
Cyndy Robbins, Programming Director
Lee Solonche, Distance Learning Manager
Martin Vodovoz, TV Technical Manager

KMCC *Digital Channel:* 32; *Virtual Channel:* 34; 1000 kw; 1991 ft.; N35 39 7 W114 18 42
455 Capitol Mall, Suite 604, Sacramento, CA 95814 US
(702) 699-9520; *Fax:* (702) 298-3495
License: Laughlin, Clark County, NV held by Mojave Broadcasting Co
Washington Law Firm: Wiley, Rein & Fielding
Nat'l Network: RTN; *Nat'l Reps:* Blair Television
Bruce Clark, General Manager

KNTL-LP *Digital Channel:* 47; 15 kw; 1872 ft.; N35 56 46 W115 02 34
500 Pilor Rd., Suite D, Las Vegas, NV 89119 US
(702) 434-0015; *Fax:* (702) 434-0527
www.noticias.entravision.com/las-vegas
asignacionesnv@entravision.com
License: Las Vegas, Clark County, NV held by Entravision Holdings LLC.
Group Owner: Entravision Communications Corp.; *Washington Law Firm:* Thompson Hine L.L.P.
Nat'l Network: UNIVISION
Hours of Local News Weekly: News progmg 5 hrs wkly
Jose Monreal, Operations Dir
Fabian Saldivar, Promotions Manager
John Garcia, Engineering Dir

KSNV-DT *Digital Channel:* 22; *Virtual Channel:* 3; 630 kw; ant 1,263t/226g; N36 00 28 W115 00 24; *Population Served:* 1,101,000
1500 Foremaster Ln., Las Vegas, NV 89101
(702) 657-3128; *Fax:* (702) 657-3152
www.news3lv.com
License: Las Vegas, NV held by KUPN Licensee LLC
Group Owner: Sinclair Broadcast Group Inc.; *Washington Law Firm:* Dow, Lohnes & Albertson
Nat'l Network: NBC
Size of News Staff: 55; *Hours of Local News Weekly:* news progmg 29 hrs wkly
Audra Swain, General Manager
Jeff Finkel, Director of Sales
Pam Sewell, Programming Director
Willie Garrett, Dir. Of Promotions
Mark Neerman, News Director
Shawn Dyke, Production Mgr

KTNV-TV *Digital Channel:* 12; 316 kw vis, 31.6 kw aur; 2,001t/259g; N35 56 43 W115 02 32; *Population Served:* 1,564,000
3355 S. Valley View Blvd., Las Vegas, NV 89102 US
(702) 876-1313; *Fax:* (702) 876-2237
www.ktnv.com
desk@ktnv.com
License: Las Vegas, Clark County, NV held by Journal Broadcast Corp.
Group Owner: Journal Communications Inc.; (acq 6-29-79); *Washington Law Firm:* Crowell & Moring
Nat'l Network: ABC; *Nat'l Reps:* Petry Television Inc.

Size of News Staff: 60; *Hours of Local News Weekly:* news progmg 22 hrs wkly
Jim Prather, Executive Vice President & General Manager
Thomas Porterfield, Station Manager/General Sales Manager
Roselia Hernandez, Programming
Jim Koonce, Promotions Manager
Karin Movesian, News Director
Greg Rogers, Production &Engineering
Vicki Nelms, Local Sales Manager
Loretta Seitz, Traffic Manager
Loretta Seitz, Traffic Manager

KVCW *Digital Channel:* 29; *Virtual Channel:* 33; 1000 kw; 1256 ft.; N36 0 28 W115 0 24
3830 South Jones Blvd., Las Vegas, NV 89103 US
(702) 382-2121; *Fax:* (702) 952-4676
www.cwlasvegas.com
License: Las Vegas, Clark County, NV held by Channel 33 Inc.
Group Owner: Sinclair Broadcast Group Inc.; (acq 2-23-2000; $33 million for stock).; *Washington Law Firm:* Fletcher, Heald & Hildreth
Nat'l Network: CW
Audra Swain, General Manager
Jeff Finkel, General Sales Mgr
Roni Dixon, Programming Coordinator
Mike Brown, Director of Engineering and Operations

KVMY *Digital Channel:* 22; *Virtual Channel:* 21; 27.7 kw; 1256 ft.; N36 0 28 W115 0 24
3830 S. Jones Blvd., Las Vegas, NV 89103 US
(702) 382-2121; *Fax:* (702) 952-4676
www.mylvtv.com
License: Las Vegas, Clark County, NV held by Southern Nevada Communications LLC
Group Owner: Intermountain West Communications; (acq 5-30-97; $87 million); *Washington Law Firm:* Dow, Lohnes & Albertson
Nat'l Network: MYTV
Roni Dixon, Programming Coordinator

KVVU *Digital Channel:* 9; *Virtual Channel:* 5; 86 kW; 1263 ft.; N36 0 26 W115 0 25
25 TV5 Dr, Henderson, NV 89014 USA
(702) 435-5555; *Fax:* (702) 451-4220
www.fox5vegas.com
License: Henderson, Clark County, NV held by KVVU Broadcasting Corp.
Group Owner: Meredith Corp.; (acq 5-85; $36 million);
Washington Law Firm: Haley, Bader & Potts
Nat'l Network: FOX; *Nat'l Reps:* TeleRep
Todd Brown, General Manager
Michael Korr, General Sales Mgr

KWWB-LP *Digital Channel:* 45; 15 kw; 1872 ft.; N35 56 46 W115 02 34
500 Pilor Rd., Suite D, Las Vegas, NV 89119 US
(702) 434-0015; *Fax:* (702) 434-0527
asignacionesnv@entravision.com
License: Las Vegas, Clark County, NV held by Entravision Holdings LLC.
Group Owner: Entravision Communications Corp.; *Washington Law Firm:* Thompson Hine L.L.P.
Nat'l Network: UNIVISION
Hours of Local News Weekly: News progmg 5 hrs wkly
Jose Monreal, Operations Dir
Fabian Saldivar, Promotions Manager
John Garcia, Engineering Dir

New York (DMA 1)

KVNV *Digital Channel:* 3; *Virtual Channel:* 3; 7.09 kw; 338.4 meters; N40 45 22 W73 59 12
63 West Parish Road, Concord, NH 03303 US
(732) 245-4705
License: Middletown Township, Monmouth County, NJ held by PMCM TV LLC
Group Owner: PMCM TV LLC; (acq 11-12-2008; $200,000)
Richard T. Morena, General Manager

Reno, NV (DMA 112)

***KNPB** *Digital Channel:* 15; *Virtual Channel:* 5; 32.3 kw; 490 ft.; N39 35 2 W119 47 55
1670 North Virginia Street, Reno, NV 89503 US
(775) 784-4555; *Fax:* (775) 784-1438
www.knpb.org
info@knpb.org
License: Reno, Washoe County, NV held by Channel 5 Public Broadcasting Inc
Washington Law Firm: Schwartz, Woods & Miller
Nat'l Network: PBS
Kurt Mische, CEO/President
Barbara Harmon, Programming Director
Tony Manfredi, Promotions Manager
Pat Miller, VP Programming/Promotions
Fred Ihlow, VP Technology
Donna Amato, Production Resource Coordinator
Ben Asnis, AssociateProducer
Brent Boynton, News Director

KOLO *Digital Channel:* 8; *Virtual Channel:* 8; 15 kw; 2,929t/119g; N39 18 49 W119 53 00; *Population Served:* 432,400
4850 Ampere Dr., Reno, NV 89502 USA
(775) 858-8888; *Fax:* (775) 858-8855
www.kolotv.com
License: Reno, Washoe County, NV held by Gray Television Licensee LLC
Group Owner: Gray Television Inc.; *Washington Law Firm:* Wiley Rein LL
Nat'l Network: ABC; *Nat'l Reps:* Millennium Sales & Marketing
Hours of Local News Weekly: News progmg 22 hrs wkly
Matt Eldredge, President
Matt Eldredge, General Manager
Laura Newman, General Sales Mgr
Doug Tepe, Promotions Manager
Stanton Tang, News Director

KREN-TV *Digital Channel:* 26; *Virtual Channel:* 27; 1000 kw; 2940 ft.; N39 18 47 W119 52 59
300 S. Wells Ave., Suite 12, Reno, NV 89502 US
(775) 333-1017; *Fax:* (775) 333-9046
vcody@entravision.com
License: Reno, Washoe County, NV held by Entravision Holdings LLC.
Group Owner: Entravision Communications Corp.; (acq 4-1-2009; $4 million); *Washington Law Firm:* Thompson Hine LLP
Nat'l Network: CW; *Nat'l Reps:* Harrington, Righter & Parsons
Nellie Elmore, Operations Dir
Lori Warren, National Sales Mgr
Cesar Perez, Promotions Dir.
Anya Arechiga, News Director

KRNS-CD *Digital Channel:* 46; *Virtual Channel:* 26; 93.9 kw; 2890 ft.; N39 18 47 W119 52 59
300 S. Wells Ave., Suite 12, Reno, NV 89502 US
(775) 333-1017; *Fax:* (775) 333-9046
www.yourcwtv.com/partners/reno
vcody@entravision.com
License: Reno, Washoe County, NV held by Entravision Holdings LLC.
Group Owner: Entravision Communications Corp.; (acq 4-1-2009; $4 million); *Washington Law Firm:* Thompson Hine LLP
Nat'l Network: CW; *Nat'l Reps:* Harrington, Righter & Parsons
Nellie Elmore, Operations Dir
Lori Warren, National Sales Mgr
Cesar Perez, Promotions Dir.
Anya Arechiga, News Director

KRNV-DT *Digital Channel:* 7; 16.1 kw; 420t/92g; N39 35 03 W119 48 06; *Population Served:* 172,863
1790 Vassar St., Reno, NV 89502
(775) 322-4444; *Fax:* (775) 785-1208
www.mynews4.com
License: Reno, NV held by Sierra Communications LLC
Group Owner: Intermountain West Communications; (acq 9-13-89).; *Washington Law Firm:* Gerald S. Rourke
Nat'l Network: NBC
Size of News Staff: 26
Nick Stathes, Operations Dir
Amie Chapman, General Manager
Kelly Buda, Director of Sales
Jason Goodwin, News Director

KRXI-TV *Digital Channel:* 44; *Virtual Channel:* 11; 950 kw; 2743 ft.; N39 35 23 W119 55 37
4920 Brookside Ct., Reno, NV 89502 US
(775) 856-1100
www.foxreno.com
newsroom@foxreno.com
License: Reno, Washoe County, NV held by KRXI Licensee LLC
Group Owner: Sinclair Broadcast Group Inc.; *Washington Law Firm:* Dow, Lohnes & Albertson
Nat'l Network: FOX; *Nat'l Reps:* TeleRep
Steve Cummings, General Manager

KRXI *Digital Channel:* 20; *Virtual Channel:* 21; 53 kw; 577 ft.; N39 35 3 W119 47 51
4920 Brookside Court, Reno, NV 89502 US
(775) 856-1100; *Fax:* (775) 856-2100
www.foxreno.com
newsroom@foxreno.com
License: Reno, Washoe County, NV held by Broadcast Development Corp.
(acq 2-28-94).; *Washington Law Firm:* Bryan Cave
Nat'l Network: MYTV; *Nat'l Reps:* TeleRep
Peter Grimm, Operations Dir
Ray Stofer, General Sales Mgr
Ray Stofer, Chief of Operations

KTVN *Digital Channel:* 13; *Virtual Channel:* 2; 16.1 kw; 2874 ft.; N39 18 57 W119 53 2
Mailing Address: P.O. Box 7220, Reno, NV 89510 US
Second Address: 4925 Energy Way, Reno, NV 89502
(775) 858-2222; *Fax:* (775) 861-4298
www.ktvn.com
ktvn@ktvn.com
License: Reno, Washoe County, NV held by Sarkes Tarzian Inc.
Group Owner: Sarkes Tarzian Inc.; (acq 8-13-80; $12.5 million);
Washington Law Firm: Lerman Senter PLLC
Nat'l Network: CBS
Size of News Staff: 31; *Hours of Local News Weekly:* news progmg 23.5 hrs wkly
Tom Tarzian, Chairman
Bob Davis, CFO
Tom Tolar, President
John Richardson, General Sales Manager
Pat Hall, Programming Director
Ann Burns, Promotions Manager
Jason Pasco, News Director
Jack Antonio, Chief Engineer
SharonFacque, National Sales Manager
Wendy Damonte, News Team
Mike Alger, News Team
Jack Sutton, News Team
Jennifer Burton, News Team
Jeff Martinez, News Team

Salt Lake City, UT (DMA 34)

KENV-DT ; 1.5 kw; N40 41 52 W115 54 13;
Rebroadcasting: Rebroadcasts KRNV-DT Reno.; *Population Served:* 37,000
1025 Chilton Cir., Elko, NV 89801
(775) 777-8500; *Fax:* (775) 777-7758
www.kenvtv.com
news@kentv.com
License: Elko, Elko County, NV held by Ruby Mountain Broadcasting LLC
Group Owner: Intermountain West Communications; (acq 11-8-96).
Nat'l Network: NBC
Lori Gilbert, News Director
Troy Edler, Creative Services
James Burns, Productions

Yakima-Pasco-Richland-Kennewick, WA (DMA 122)

KCWK *Digital Channel:* 9; ant 577t
424 E. Yakima Ave., Suite 110, Yakima, WA 98901 US
(509) 575-0999; *Fax:* (509) 575-9562
License: North Las Vegas, NV held by KAZW License LLC.
Group Owner: Pappas Telecasting Companies; (acq 11-7-2002; $3 million)
Nat'l Network: CW
Robert Powers, Operations Dir
Mike Dunlop, General Sales Mgr

New Hampshire

Boston (Manchester, NH) (DMA 9)

WBIN-TV *Digital Channel:* 50; 4,790 kw vis, 479 kw aur; ant 699t; N42 44 07 W71 23 36; *Population Served:* 5,200,000
11 A Street, Derry, NH 03038
(603) 845-1000; *Fax:* (603) 434-8627
www.wbintv.com
info@wbintv.com
License: Derry, Rockingham County, NH held by WBIN Inc. 5-17-2011; *Ownership:* Carlisle One Media, Inc., 100%
Nat'l Network: Independent; *Nat'l Reps:* Petry Television Inc.;
Wire Services: AP
Hours of Local News Weekly: 0
Bill Binnie, President
Gerry McGavick, General Manager
Alvin Turner, General Sales Mgr
Matt Houseman, Assistant Programming Director/VP, Public

Affairs
Richard Zach, Chief Engineer
Angela Bianchi, Traffic Manager
Steven Pomeroy,Office Manager
Kristina Letourneau, Local Sales Manager
Brian O'Keefe, National Sales Manager
Al Kaprielian, Weather
Stephen Reardon, Executive Producer

***WEKW-TV** *Digital Channel:* 49; *Virtual Channel:* 52; 43 kw; 1083 ft.; N43 2 0 W72 22 4
268 Mast Road, Durham, NH 03824 US
(603) 868-1100; *Fax:* (603) 868-7552
www.nhptv.org
themailbox@nhptv.org
License: Keene, Cheshire County, NH held by University of New Hampshire
Washington Law Firm: Schwartz, Woods & Miller
Nat'l Network: PBS
Jeffrey Gilbert, Board Chair
Peter A. Frid, CEO/President/General Manager
Dennis Malloy, General Sales Mgr
James T. McKim, Program Manager
Brian Shepperd, Chief Engineer
Ronald L. Abramson, Esq., Board Secretary
William A.Barker, Board Member
Colleen T. Chen, Board Member
Marjorie Chiafery, Board Member
Katharine Eneguess, Board Member
Marilyn Higgins Forest, Board Member

***WENH-TV** *Digital Channel:* 11; *Virtual Channel:* 11; 30 kw; 998 ft.; N43 10 33 W71 12 29
268 Mast Road, Durham, NH 03824 US
(603) 868-1100; *Fax:* (603) 868-7552
www.nhptv.org
themailbox@nhptv.org
License: Durham, Strafford County, NH held by University of New Hampshire
Washington Law Firm: Schwartz, Woods & Miller
Nat'l Network: PBS
Hours of Local News Weekly: News progmg 2 hrs wkly
Jeffrey Gilbert, Board Chair
Peter A. Frid, CEO/General Manager
James T. McKim, Program Manager
Brian Shepperd, Chief Engineer
Ronald L. Abramson, Esq., Board Secretary
William A. Barker, Board Member
Colleen T. Chen, BoardMember
Marjorie Chiafery, Board Member
Katharine Eneguess, Board Member
Marilyn Higgins Forest, Board Member

WMUR-TV *Digital Channel:* 9; 282 kw vis, 33.5 kw aur; 1,030t/227g; N42 58 59 W71 35 19; *Population Served:* 1,100,000
100 S. Commercial St., Manchester, NH 03101
(603) 669-9999; *Fax:* (603) 641-9005 (admin)
www.wmur.com
storyideas@wmur.com
License: Manchester, Hillsborough County, NH held by Hearst Properties Inc.
Group Owner: Hearst Television Inc.; (acq 3-28-01; $185 million); *Washington Law Firm:* Brooks, Pierce, McLendon, Humphrey & Leonard
Nat'l Network: ABC; *Regional Network:* MeTV; *Nat'l Reps:* Eagle Television Sales; *Wire Services:* AP
Size of News Staff: 54; *Hours of Local News Weekly:* news progmg 29 hrs wkly
Jeff Bartlett, President
Jeff Bartlett, General Manager
David Parker, General Sales Mgr
Betsey Braun, Programming Director
Alex Jasiukowicz, Promotions Manager
Alisha McDevitt, News Director
Roger Rosendahl, Chief Engineer
AhniMalachi, Public Service Manager
Patrick McCarthy, Business Manager

WNEU *Digital Channel:* 34; *Virtual Channel:* 60; 80 kw; 961 ft.; N42 59 2 W71 35 20
300 Sevilla Avenue, Suite 211, Coral Gables, FL 33134 USA
(603) 647-6060
www.telemundoboston.com
License: Merrimack, Hillsborough County, NH held by NBC Telemundo License LLC
Group Owner: Telemundo Station Group; (acq 10-22-2002; $26 million); *Washington Law Firm:* Davis Wright Tremaine L.L.P.
Nat'l Network: Telemundo
Foreign Language Programming
Luis Silberwasser, President

Portland-Auburn, ME (DMA 81)

***WLED-TV** *Digital Channel:* 48; *Virtual Channel:* 49; 45 kw; 1273 ft.; N44 21 10 W71 44 15; *Rebroadcasting:* Rebroadcasts *WENH Durham 100%.
268 Mast Rd., Durham, NH 03824 US
(603) 868-1100; *Fax:* (603) 868-7552
www.nhptv.org
themailbox@nhptv.org
License: Littleton, Grafton County, NH held by University of New Hampshire
Washington Law Firm: Schwartz, Woods & Miller
Nat'l Network: PBS; *Regional Network:* New Hampshire Public Television
Jeffrey Gilbert, Chairman
Peter Frid, General Manager
Dennis Malloy, General Sales Mgr
Brian Shepperd, Chief Engineer
Jeff Morris, Advertising Manager
Mark Collin, Sr.VP, CFO & Treasurer

New Jersey

New York (DMA 1)

WFUT-DT *Digital Channel:* 30; *Virtual Channel:* 68; 2,630 kw vis; 1,440t/1,430g; N40 44 54 W73 59 10; *Rebroadcasting:* Rebroadcasts WFTY, Smithtown, NY, 100%.
500 Frank W. Burr Blvd., Suite 19, Teaneck, NJ 07666
(201) 287-4042
www.univision.com
License: Newark, Essex County, NJ held by Univision New York LLC
Group Owner: Univision Communications Inc.; (acq 5-21-2001; grpsl).; *Washington Law Firm:* Shaw, Pittman
Foreign Language Programming
Ramon Pineda, General Manager
Morris Marotta, Business Manager

WMBC-TV *Digital Channel:* 18; 2,190 kw vis, 109 kw aur; 731t; N41 00 36 W74 35 39; *Population Served:* 13,000,000
99 Clinton Rd., West Caldwell, NJ 07006
(973) 852-0300; *Fax:* (973) 808-5516
www.wmbctv.com
cc@wmbctv.com
License: Newton, Sussex County, NJ held by Mountain Broadcasting Corp.
Group Owner: Mountain Broadcasting Corp.; *Washington Law Firm:* Fleischman & Walsh
Foreign Language Programming; Size of News Staff: 8; *Hours of Local News Weekly:* news progmg 5 hrs wkly
Victor Joo, General Manager
Hansen Lau, News Director
Joon Joo, Chief Engineer

***WNET** *Digital Channel:* 13; *Virtual Channel:* 13; 9.3 kw; 1329 ft.; N40 44 54 W73 59 10
825 8th Ave., New York, NY 10019 US
(212) 560-1313,(212) 560-3506; *Fax:* (212) 560-2793
www.thirteen.org
programming@thirteen.org
License: Newark, Essex County, NJ held by Educational Broadcasting Corp
(acq 1970); *Washington Law Firm:* Leventhal, Senter & Lerman
Nat'l Network: PBS
Hours of Local News Weekly: News progmg 5 hrs wkly
Neal Shapiro, CEO

***WNJB** *Digital Channel:* 8; *Virtual Channel:* 58; 40.82 kw; 715 ft.; N40 37 17 W74 30 15; *Rebroadcasting:* Satellite of *WNJT(TV) Trenton.
Mailing Address: PO Box 5776, Englewood, NJ 07631 US
Second Address: 825 8th Ave., New York, NY 10019
(212) 560-3506; *Fax:* (212) 560-2793
www.njn.net
closedcaptioning@thirteen.org
License: New Brunswick, Middlesex County, NJ held by New Jersey Public Broadcasting Authority
Washington Law Firm: Schwartz, Woods & Miller
Nat'l Network: PBS; *Regional Network:* New Jersey Network
Hours of Local News Weekly: News progmg 2 hrs wkly
Josh Weston, Chairman
John Servidio, General Manager
Janice Selinger, Station Manager
Frank Graybill, Managing Director of Engineering & IT

***WNJN** *Digital Channel:* 51; *Virtual Channel:* 50; 200 kw; 764 ft.; N40 51 53 W74 12 3; *Rebroadcasting:* Satellite of *WNJT Trenton.
Mailing Address: PO Box 5776, Englewood, NJ 07631 US
Second Address: 825 8th Ave., New York, NY 10019
(212) 560-3506; *Fax:* (212) 560-2793
www.njn.net
closedcaptioning@thirteen.org
License: Montclair, Essex County, NJ held by New Jersey Public Broadcasting Authority
Washington Law Firm: Schwartz, Woods & Miller
Nat'l Network: PBS; *Regional Network:* New Jersey Network
Hours of Local News Weekly: News progmg 3 hrs wkly
Josh Weston, Chairman
John Servidio, General Manager
Janice Selinger, Station Manager
Frank Graybill, Managing Director of Engineering & IT

WNJU *Digital Channel:* 36; *Virtual Channel:* 47; 650 kw; 733 ft.; N40 48 8 W74 14 48
2200 Fletcher Ave, Fort Lee, NJ 7024 USA
(877) 478-3536, (877) 47TELEMUNDO; *Fax:* (201) 969-4120
www.telemundo47.com
License: Linden, Union County, NJ held by NBC Telemundo License LLC
Group Owner: Telemundo Station Group; (acq 4-12-2002; grpsl).; *Washington Law Firm:* Hogan & Hartson
Nat'l Network: Telemundo
Foreign Language Programming
Luis Silberwasser, President

***WNYJ-TV** *Digital Channel:* 29; *Virtual Channel:* 66; 200 kw; 548 ft.; N40 47 18 W74 15 19
289 Mount Pleasant Avenue, West Orange, NJ 07052 US
(973) 736-3600; *Fax:* (973) 736-4832
www.wfme.net
License: West Milford, Passaic County, NJ held by FSINJ License Co. LLC
Group Owner: Family Stations Inc.
Harold Camping, General Manager
Charles Menut, General Sales Mgr
Charlie Menut, Chief Engineer
Artie Merkel, Assistant Engineer
Igor Ipince, Board Operator
Vinnie Gallini, WFME Electrical Engineer

WWOR *Digital Channel:* 38; *Virtual Channel:* 9; 15 kW; N40 57 38.6 W73 55 22.5
9 Broadcast Plaza, Secaucus, NJ 07095 USA
(201) 348-0009; *Fax:* (201) 330-3486
www.my9nj.com
License: Secaucus, Hudson County, NJ held by Fox Television Stations LLC
Group Owner: Fox Television Stations Group; a(cq 7-31-2001; grpsl).
Nat'l Network: MyNetworkTV; *Wire Services:* Conus
Size of News Staff: 70; *Hours of Local News Weekly:* news progmg 7 hrs wkly

WXTV-DT *Digital Channel:* 40; *Virtual Channel:* 41; 2,340 kw vis, 234 kw aur; ant 1,381t; N40 44 54 W73 59 10; *Population Served:* 3,600,000
500 Frank W. Burr Blvd., Suite 19, Teaneck, NJ 07666
(201) 287-4042; *Fax:* (201) 287-9428
www.univision.com
License: Paterson, Passaic County, NJ held by WXTV License Partnership G.P.
Group Owner: Univision Communications Inc.; (acq 1986; grpsl).; *Washington Law Firm:* Shaw, Pittman
Nat'l Network: Univision (Spanish)
Foreign Language Programming; Hours of Local News Weekly: news progmg 17 hrs wkly
Ramon Pineda, General Manager
Morris Marotta, Business Manager

Philadelphia (DMA 4)

WACP *Digital Channel:* 4; 10 kw; 256 m; N39 44 05 W74 50 29
207 Bogden Boulevard , Suite A, Millville, NJ 8332
(855) 461-2835; *Fax:* (813) 579-4474
feedback@wacp.com
License: Atlantic City, Atlantic County, NJ held by Western Pacific Broadcast LLC
Dale A. West, Vice President
Greg Kraft, Chief Operator
Natasha Jenkins, Compliance & Administration
Suzanna Lupia, Public Relations

WGTW-TV *Digital Channel:* 27; *Virtual Channel:* 48; 160 kw; 1161 ft.; N40 2 30 W75 14 11
Mailing Address: P.O. Box A, Santa Ana, CA 92711 US
Second Address: P.O. Box 768, Station B, Ottawa, ON K1P 5P8

(714) 731-1000, (888) 731-1000, (714) 832-2950, (8; *Fax:* (610) 583-1476
www.tbn.org
mrudderow@tbn.org
License: Burlington, Burlington County, NJ held by Trinity Christian Center of Santa Ana Inc.
Group Owner: Trinity Broadcasting Network; (acq 10-1-2004; $7 million plus assumption of $41 million in debt).
Nat'l Network: TRINITY BROADCA
Dennis Pritchett, Operations Dir
Al Box, General Manager
Mark Rudderow, Public Relations

WMCN-TV *Digital Channel:* 44; *Virtual Channel:* 44; 200 kw; 696 ft.; N39 43 41 W74 50 39
100 Dobbs Lane, Suite 112, Cherry Hill, NJ 08034 US
(609) 569-7280; *Fax:* (609) 569-7295
www.wmcn.tv
License: Atlantic City, Atlantic County, NJ held by Lenfest Broadcasting L.L.C
(acq 7-19-2000; $9 million); *Washington Law Firm:* Wiley, Rein & Fielding
Nat'l Network: IND
H. Chase Lenfest, CEO
Jon Gorchow, President
Mark Chesterton, Operations manager
Steve Cass, General Sales Mgr
Vojislav Radosavljevic, Chief Engineer
bruce Hanby, Traffic Coordinator
Mike Golla, Traffic Coordinator
AndreaEisenberg, Sales Manager
Justin LeFevre, Excutive Producer

WMGM-TV *Digital Channel:* 36; *Virtual Channel:* 40; 205 kw; 415 ft.; N39 7 28 W74 45 56
1601 New Road, Linwood, NJ 08221 US
(609) 927-4440,(609) 926-0300; *Fax:* (609) 926-8875
www.nbc40.net
License: Wildwood, Cape May County, NJ held by Univision Local Media, Inc.
Group Owner: Univision Communications; (acq 2004; grpsl)
Nat'l Network: NBC; *Wire Services:* AP
Hours of Local News Weekly: News progmg 8 hrs wkly
Arthur Benjamin, CFO
Chesley Maddox-Dorsey, President
Roger Powe, General Sales Manager & General Manager
Julie Mulhall, Promotions & Programming
Harvey Cox, News Director
Alyson Scofield, Production Manager
Dan Skeldon, ChiefMeterologist
Pete Thompson, Sports Director
Megan Wolf, Executive Producer
Pat Carragher, Assignment Editor
Ryan Parmer, Producer

***WNJS** *Digital Channel:* 22; *Virtual Channel:* 23; 197 kw; 866 ft.; N39 43 41 W74 50 39; *Rebroadcasting:* Satellite of *WNJT Trenton.
Mailing Address: PO Box 5776, Englewood, NJ 07631 US
Second Address: 825 8th Ave., New York, NY 10019
(212) 560-3506; *Fax:* (212) 560-2793
www.njn.net
closedcaptioning@thirteen.org
License: Camden, Camden County, NJ held by New Jersey Public Broadcasting Authority
Washington Law Firm: Schwartz, Woods & Miller
Nat'l Network: PBS; *Regional Network:* New Jersey Network
Hours of Local News Weekly: News progmg 2 hrs wkly
Josh Weston, Chairman
John Servidio, General Manager
Janice Selinger, Station Manager
Frank Graybill, Managing Director of Engineering & IT

***WNJT** *Digital Channel:* 43; *Virtual Channel:* 52; 59.4 kw; 873 ft.; N40 16 58 W74 41 11
Mailing Address: PO Box 5776, Englewood, NJ 07631 US
Second Address: 825 8th Ave., New York, NY 10019
(212) 560-3506; *Fax:* (212) 560-2793
www.njn.net
closedcaptioning@thirteen.org
License: Trenton, Mercer County, NJ held by New Jersey Public Broadcasting Authority
Washington Law Firm: Schwartz, Woods & Miller
Nat'l Network: PBS; *Regional Network:* New Jersey Network
Hours of Local News Weekly: News progmg 10 hrs wkly
Josh Weston, Chairman
John Blair, Operations Dir
John Servidio, General Manager
Andre Butts, Programming Director
Joanne Ruscio, Promotions Manager
Michael Aron, News Director
Frank Graybill, Managing Director of Engineering &IT

WUVP-DT *Digital Channel:* 29; *Virtual Channel:* 65; 4,070 kw vis, 407 kw aur; ant 1,299t/1,220g; N40 02 30 W75 14 11
Mailing Address: 4449 N. Delsea Dr., Newfield, NJ 08344 US
Second Address: #1100, 1608 Walnut St., Philadelphia, PA 19103
(856) 691-6565; *Fax:* (856) 690-3558
www.univision.com
License: Vineland, Cumberland County, NJ held by Univision Philadelphia LLC.
Group Owner: Univision Communications Inc.; (acq 8-21-2001; grpsl)
Nat'l Network: Univision (Spanish)
Foreign Language Programming
John Duffin, Sales Manager
Jose Irizarry, News Director and Community Relations Manager
John Skelnik, Chief Engineer

WWSI *Digital Channel:* 49; 5,000 kw vis, 500 kw aur; ant 972t/970g; N39 37 53 W74 21 12
Mailing Address: 1341 N. Delaware Ave., Suite 408, Philadelphia, PA 19119 USA
Second Address: One S. New York Ave., Atlantic City, NJ 8401
(215) 634-8862,(609) 449-0049; *Fax:* (215) 425-2683,(609) 441-9559
www.telemundo62.com
License: Atlantic City, Atlantic County, NJ held by NBC Telemundo License LLC
Group Owner: Telemundo Station Group; (acq 5-14-2002).
Nat'l Network: Telemundo *Regional Reps:* Telemundo Philadelphia
Foreign Language Programming; Size of News Staff: 4; *Hours of Local News Weekly:* news progmg 3 hrs wkly
Luis Silberwasser, President

New Mexico

Albuquerque-Santa Fe, NM (DMA 48)

KASA-TV *Digital Channel:* 27; 28.2 kw vis, 2.82 kw aur; 1,968t/178g; N35 46 50 W106 31 35; *Population Served:* 1,664,000
13 Broadcast Plaza S.W., Albuquerque, NM 75202
(505) 243-2285; *Fax:* (505) 248-1464
www.kasa.com
newsdesk@krqe.com
License: Santa Fe, Santa Fe County, NM held by LIN of New Mexico LLC
Group Owner: LIN Media; (acq 2007)
Nat'l Network: Fox; *Nat'l Reps:* TeleRep
Hours of Local News Weekly: News progmg 7 hrs wkly
Bill Anderson, General Manager
Jim Giudicessi, General Sales Mgr
Pat Gonzales, Programming Director
Parker Harms, Promotions Manager
Ian Munro, News Director
Frank Lilley, Engineering Dir
Yolanda Tyner-Ward, Local SalesManager
Don Pierce, Program Director

KASY-TV *Digital Channel:* 45; *Virtual Channel:* 50; 245 kw; 4222 ft.; N35 12 48 W106 27 0
PO Box 3757, Lubbock, TX 79452 US
(505) 797-1919; *Fax:* (505) 938-4401
www.my50.tv
License: Albuquerque, Bernalillo County, NM held by KASY-TV Licensee LLC
Group Owner: Tamer Media LLC; (acq 6-18-99; $25.4 million);
Washington Law Firm: Leventhal, Senter & Lerman
Nat'l Network: CW
Stan Gill, General Manager
Rosalie Drake, General Sales Mgr
Chris Iller, Promotions Manager
Scott Stokes, Chief Engineer

***KAZQ** *Digital Channel:* 17; *Virtual Channel:* 32; 65.6 kw; 4091 ft.; N35 12 51 W106 27 1
4501 Montgomery Boulevard NE, Albuquerque, NM 87109 US
(505) 884-8355
www.kazq32.org
info@kazq32.org
License: Albuquerque, Bernalillo County, NM held by Alpha-Omega Broadcasting of Albuquerque Inc
Ownership: Non-Profit Corporation; *Washington Law Firm:* Donald C. Martin
Nat'l Network: ETV
Foreign Language Programming
Raymond Franks, President
Ruth Franks, Operations Manager
Howard Holley, Production Manager
Isaac Milleson, Lead Editor/Website Developer
Steven Minor, Master Control, Traffic
Howard Holley, Production Manager
Brenda Gallegos,Administrative Assistant

KBIM-TV *Digital Channel:* 10; *Virtual Channel:* 10; 24.32 kw; 2001 ft.; N33 3 20 W103 49 12; *Rebroadcasting:* Rebroadcasts KRQE(TV) Albuquerque 90%.
Mailing Address: Bx 910, Roswell, NM 88202 US
Second Address: 214 N. Main St., Roswell, NM 88202
(575) 622-2120, (800) 289-5246; *Fax:* (505) 623-6606
www.kbimtv.com
License: Roswell, Chaves County, NM held by LIN of New Mexico LLC
Group Owner: LIN Media; (acq 11-30-2005; grpsl).; *Washington Law Firm:* Reed, Smith, Shaw & McClay
Nat'l Network: CBS
Size of News Staff: 11; *Hours of Local News Weekly:* news progmg 6 hrs wkly
Marcus Damberger, Operations Dir
Gene Munsey, General Manager
Joshua Pila, Station Manager
Pat Gonzales, Programming Director

KCHF *Digital Channel:* 10; *Virtual Channel:* 11; 30 kw; 1995 ft.; N35 46 49 W106 31 34
Mailing Address: P.O.Box 4338, Albuquerque, NM 87106 US
Second Address: 27556 I 25 &. Frontage Rd., Santa Fe, NM 87508
(505) 345-1991 (radio),(505) 473-1111; *Fax:* (505) 345-5669
kchftv.org
info@kchftv.org
License: Santa Fe, Santa Fe County, NM held by Son Broadcasting Inc
Washington Law Firm: Gammon & Grange
Nat'l Network: IND
Foreign Language Programming
Belarmino Gonzalez, CEO
Annette Garcia, General Manager
Mary Kay Gonzales, Programming Director
Rob Ramseyer, Chief Engineer

KLUZ-TV *Digital Channel:* 42; *Virtual Channel:* 41; 321 kw; 4140 ft.; N35 12 41 W106 26 58
2725 F. Broadbent Pkwy. NE., Albuquerque, NM 87107 US
(505) 342-4141; *Fax:* (505) 344-8714
www.noticias.entravision.com
rmather@entravision.com
License: Albuquerque, Bernalillo County, NM held by Entravision Holdings LLC.
Group Owner: Entravision Communications Corp.; (acq 3-21-99).
Nat'l Network: UNIVISION
Foreign Language Programming; Size of News Staff: 10; *Hours of Local News Weekly:* news progmg 1/2 hr wkly
Carlos Fourzan, General Manager
Esmeralda Ruiz, National Sales Mgr
Francisco Gutierrez, Promotions Manager
Rafael Henriquez, News Director

KNAT-TV *Digital Channel:* 24; *Virtual Channel:* 23; 320 kw; 4081 ft.; N35 12 54 W106 27 2
1510 Corrs Road, N.W., Albuquerque, NM 87105 US
(505) 836-6585; *Fax:* (505) 831-8725
www.tbn.org
cmansfield@tbn.org
License: Albuquerque, Bernalillo County, NM held by Trinity Broadcasting Network
Group Owner: Trinity Broadcasting Network; (acq 5-8-2000; grpsl).; *Washington Law Firm:* Joseph E. Dunne III
Nat'l Network: TRINITY BROADCA
Foreign Language Programming
Cynthia Mansfield, General Manager

***KNMD-TV** *Digital Channel:* 8; *Virtual Channel:* 9; 5.14 kw; 4180 ft.; N35 12 44 W106 26 57
1130 University Blvd NE, Albuquerque, NM 87102 US
(505) 277-2121, (505) 277-2922, (800) 328-5663
www.knmetv.org
memberservices@nmpbs.org
License: Santa Fe, Santa Fe County, NM held by The Regents of the University of New Mexico.
Washington Law Firm: Dow, Lohnes & Albertson, LLC
Nat'l Network: PBS
Polly Anderson, CEO
Franz Joachim, General Manager
Chad Davis, Programming Director
Jim Gale, Dir. Of Engineering
Dan Zilch, Dir. Of Engineering
Karen Mann, Director, Finance & Admin

Kevin McDonald, Prooduction Manager
StevenCampbell, IT Manager
michael Kamins, Executive producer
Theresa Spencer, Development Dir.
Karen Mann, Dir. Of Finanace & Administration

***KNME-TV** *Digital Channel:* 35; *Virtual Channel:* 5; 250 kw; 4222 ft.; N35 12 49 W106 27 1
1130 University Blvd.Ne, Albuquerque, NM 87102 US
(505) 277-2121
www.knmetv.org
License: Albuquerque, Bernalillo County, NM held by Regents of University of New Mexico and Board of Education, Albuquerque
Washington Law Firm: Dow, Lohnes & Albertson
Nat'l Network: PBS
Karen Mann, CFO
Franz Joachim, General Manager
Chad Davis, Programming Director
Jim Gale, Engineering Dir
Joanne Bachmann, Associate General Manager
Theresa Spencer, Director of Development
Michael Kamins

KOAT *Digital Channel:* 7; *Virtual Channel:* 7; 26.5 kw; 4239 ft.; N35 12 53 W106 27 1
3801 Carlisle Blvd. NE., Albuquerque, NM 87107 US
(505) 884-7777
www.koat.com
License: Albuquerque, NM held by KOAT Hearst Television Inc
Group Owner: Hearst Television Inc.; (acq 3-18-99; grpsl).; *Washington Law Firm:* Brooks, Pierce, McLendon, Humphrey & Leonard
Nat'l Network: ABC
Teri Hernandez, Operations Dir
Gary Williams, Chief Engineer

KOB *Digital Channel:* 26; 270kW; ant 4,198t/178g; N35 12 42 W106 26 57; *Population Served:* 568,700
Mailing Address: 4 Broadcast Plaza SW, Albuquerque, NM 87104
Second Address: 4 Broadcast Plaza S.W., Albuquerque, NM 87104
(505) 243-4411; *Fax:* (505) 764-2456
www.kob.com
kobtv@kob.com
License: Albuquerque, Bernalillo County, NM held by KOB-TV L.L.C.
Group Owner: Hubbard Broadcasting Inc.; (acq 3-15-57; grpsl; *Washington Law Firm:* Fletcher, Heald & Hildreth
Nat'l Network: NBC; *Wire Services:* AP
Hours of Local News Weekly: News progmg 29 hrs wkly
Mike Burgess, Operations Dir
Charlie Blanco, General Manager
Susan Connor, Station Manager
Jeff Finkel, General Sales Mgr
Nora Nieto, Programming Director
Dusty Deane, Promotions Manager
Wayne Koontz, Chief Engineer
Joan Lucas,Public Affairs Director
Elena Hernandez, Research Director
Jackie Gregory, Traffic Manager

KOBF *Digital Channel:* 12; *Virtual Channel:* 12; 30 kw; 410 ft.; N36 41 43 W108 13 14; *Rebroadcasting:* Satelite of KOB-TV Albuquerque
Mailing Address: 825 W. Broadway, Farmington, NM 87401 US
Second Address: 825 W. Broadway, Farmington, NM 87401
(505) 326-1141; *Fax:* (505) 327-5196
www.kob.com
License: Farmington, San Juan County, NM held by KOB-TV L.L.C.
Group Owner: Hubbard Broadcasting Inc.; (acq 9-19-83; $2.35 million; *Washington Law Firm:* Fletcher, Heald & Hildreth
Nat'l Network: NBC
Size of News Staff: 6; *Hours of Local News Weekly:* news progmg 4 hrs wkly
Don Baughan, Operations Dir

KOBR *Digital Channel:* 8; *Virtual Channel:* 8; 40 kw; 1749 ft.; N33 22 31 W103 46 12; *Rebroadcasting:* Rebroadcasts KOB-TV Albuquerque 90%.
124 E. 4th Street, Roswell, NM 88201 US
(575) 625-8888; *Fax:* (575) 625-8866
www.kob.com
kobtv@kob.com
License: Roswell, Chaves County, NM held by Stanley S. Hubbard Revocable Trust.
Group Owner: Hubbard Broadcasting Inc.; (acq 8-10-2001).; *Washington Law Firm:* Fletcher, Heald & Hildreth
Nat'l Network: NBC
Size of News Staff: 4
Stanley Hubbard, President
Charlie Blanco, General Manager
Nora Nieto, Programming Director
Dusty Deane, Promotions Manager
Wayne Koontz, Chief Engineer

KRPV-DT *Digital Channel:* 27; 50 kw vis; ant 399t/269g; N33 23 50 W104 22 34; *Population Served:* 272,826
Mailing Address: 12706 W. Highway 80 East, Odessa, TX 79765
Second Address: PO Box 61000, Midland, TX 79711-1000
(800) 707-0420, (432) 563-0420; *Fax:* (432) 563-1736
www.godslearningchannel.com
info@glc.us.com
License: Roswell, Chaves County, NM held by Prime Time Christian Broadcasting
Foreign Language Programming
Al Cooper, CEO
Tommy Cooper, Operations Dir
Al Cooper, Founder
Tommie Cooper, Founder

KRQE *Digital Channel:* 13; *Virtual Channel:* 13; 21.5 kw; 4222 ft.; N35 12 40 W106 26 57
13 Broadcast Place S.W., Albuquerque, NM 87104 US
(505) 243-2285, (800) 283-4227; *Fax:* (505) 248-1464, (505) 842-8483, (505) 764-5261
www.krqe.com
newsdesk@krqe.com
License: Albuquerque, Bernalillo County, NM held by LIN License Compnany LLC
Group Owner: LIN Media; (acq 11-30-2005; grpsl).; *Washington Law Firm:* Reed, Smith, Shaw & McClay
Nat'l Network: CBS; *Nat'l Reps:* Harrington, Righter & Parsons; *Wire Services:* CBS
Size of News Staff: 65; *Hours of Local News Weekly:* news progmg 24 hrs wkly
Gina Galindo, Operations Dir
Bill Anderson, General Manager
Dino Damelio, General Sales Mgr
Don Pierce, Programming Director
Parker Harms, Promotions Manager
Ian Munro, News Director
Frank Lilley, Engineering Dir
Frank Montoya,Local Sales Manager
Marilyn Painter, Research Director
Pat Gonzales, Traffic Manager

KRWB-TV *Digital Channel:* 21; *Virtual Channel:* 21; 1000 kw; 420 ft.; N33 6 1 W104 15 15
5925 Cromo, El Paso, TX 79912 US
(505) 797-1919; *Fax:* (505) 938-4401
License: Roswell, Chaves County, NM held by KASY-TV Licensee LLC
Group Owner: Tamer Media LLC; (acq 1-7-2004)
Nat'l Network: CW
Stan Gill, General Manager
Rosalie Drake, General Sales Mgr
Chris Iller, Promotions Manager
Larry Oliver, Chief Engineer

KTFA-LP *Digital Channel:* 41; *Virtual Channel:* 48; 147.1 kw; 4140 ft.; N35 12 41 W106 26 56
2725 F. Broadbent Pkwy. NE., Albuquerque, NM 87107 US
(505) 342-4141; *Fax:* (505) 344-8714
www.noticias.entravision.com
rmather@entravision.com
License: Albuquerque, Bernalillo County, NM held by Entravision Holdings LLC.
Group Owner: Entravision Communications Corp.; (acq 3-21-99).
Nat'l Network: UNIVISION
Foreign Language Programming; Size of News Staff: 10; *Hours of Local News Weekly:* news progmg 1/2 hr wkly
Carlos Fourzan, General Manager
Esmeralda Ruiz, National Sales Mgr
Francisco Gutierrez, Promotions Manager
Rafael Henriquez, News Director

KTFQ-DT *Digital Channel:* 22; *Virtual Channel:* 14; 1,000 kw vis; ant 1,233t/1,046g; N35 24 44 W106 43 32
2725 F. Broadbent Pkwy. NE., Albuquerque, NM 87107 US
(505) 341-6102
www.noticias.entravision.com
License: Albuquerque, Bernalillo County, NM held by UniMas Albuquerque LLC.
Group Owner: Univision Communications, Inc.; (acq 5-30-2003; $20 million)
Nat'l Network: UniMas (Spanish)
Foreign Language Programming
Randy Falco, President

KUPT *Digital Channel:* 29; *Virtual Channel:* 29; 50 kw; 515 ft.; N32 43 28 W103 5 46
9800 University Ave., Lubbock, TX 79423 US
(806) 745-3434; *Fax:* (806) 748-1949
www.mylubbocktv.com
License: Hobbs, Lea County, NM held by Ramar Communications, Inc.
Group Owner: Ramar Communications, Ltd.; *Washington Law Firm:* Leventhal, Senter & Lerman
Brad Moran, General Manager
Chris Torres, Programming Director

KWBQ *Digital Channel:* 29; *Virtual Channel:* 19; 245 kw; 4229 ft.; N35 12 44 W106 26 57
4100 Hawkins, N.E., Albuquerque, NM 87109 US
(505) 797-1919; *Fax:* (505) 344-1145
www.newmexicoscw.tv
License: Santa Fe, Santa Fe County, NM held by KASY-TV Licensee LLC
Group Owner: Tamer Media LLC
Nat'l Network: CW
Stan Gill, General Manager
Dan Marchese, General Sales Mgr
Chris Iller, Promotions Manager
Larry Oliver, Chief Engineer

Amarillo, TX (DMA 131)

***KENW** ; *Virtual Channel:* 3; 100 kw vis, 20 kw aur; 1,150t/1,085g; N33 33 19 W103 39 03; *Population Served:* 400,000
52 Broadcast Ctr., ENMU, 1500 S. Ave. K, Portales, NM 88130
(575) 562-2112; *Fax:* (575) 562-2590
www.kenw.org
License: Portales, Roosevelt County, NM held by Regents of Eastern New Mexico University
Washington Law Firm: Dow, Lohnes & Albertson, PLLC
Nat'l Network: PBS; NETA; APT; *Wire Services:* AP
Foreign Language Programming; Size of News Staff: 2; *Hours of Local News Weekly:* news progmg 3 hrs wkly
Ronnie Birdsong, Vice President
Steven Gamble, President
Orlando Ortega, Operations Dir
Duane Ryan, General Manager
Rena Garrett, General Sales Mgr
Jenifer Baca, Programming Director
Rena Garrett, Promotions Manager
JanetBresenham, News Director
Jeff Burmeister, Engineering Dir
Don Criss, Public Affairs Director
Richard Rivera, Producer/Director/Sports
Jacob Workman, Producer/Director

KVIH-TV *Digital Channel:* 12; *Virtual Channel:* 12; 5 kw; 669 ft.; N34 11 34 W103 16 44; *Rebroadcasting:* Satellite of KVII-TV Amarillo, TX
1 Broadcast Center, Amarillo, TX 79101 US
(806) 373-1787; *Fax:* (806) 371-7329
www.abc7amarillo.com
pronews7@kvii.com
License: Clovis, Curry County, NM held by KVII Licensee LLC
Group Owner: Sinclair Broadcast Group Inc.; (acq 2-28-2013; grpsl); *Washington Law Firm:* Wiley, Rein & Fielding
Nat'l Network: CBS
Laura Wolf, General Manager
Ryan Hazelwood, News Director

El Paso (Las Cruces, NM), TX (DMA 92)

***KRWG-TV** *Digital Channel:* 23; *Virtual Channel:* 22; 200 kw; 673 ft.; N32 17 33 W106 41 51
Mailing Address: P.O. Box 30001 Msc:Tv22, Las Cruces, NM 88003 US
Second Address: 2915 McFie Cir., Rm. 100, Las Cruces, NM 88003
(575) 646-2222; *Fax:* (575) 646-1924
www.krwg-tv.org
krwgtv@nmsu.edu
License: Las Cruces, Dona Ana County, NM held by Regents of New Mexico State University
Washington Law Firm: Dow, Lohnes & Albertson
Nat'l Network: PBS; *Wire Services:* AP
Foreign Language Programming; Hours of Local News Weekly: News progmg 3 hrs wkly
J.D. Jarvis, Operations Dir
Anthony Casaus, General Sales Mgr
William Saggerson, Chief Engineer
Glen Cerny, Director of Broadcasting

KTDO *Digital Channel:* 47; *Virtual Channel:* 48; 200 kw; 1821 ft.; N31 48 19 W106 28 59

400 Putman Building, 215 North Main Street, Davenport, IA 52801 US
(915) 591-9595; *Fax:* (915) 591-9896
www.telemundo.com
License: Las Cruces, Dona Ana County, NM held by ZGS El Paso Televison LP
Group Owner: ZGS Communications; (acq 9-13-2004; $11.8 million); *Washington Law Firm:* Reed, Smith, Shaw & McClay
Nat'l Network: TELEMUNDO
Foreign Language Programming
Lorena Caltamon, General Manager
Monic Diaz, Programming Director
Phillip Cortez, Promotions Manager
Elios Ventanilla, Chief Engineer

New York

Albany-Schenectady-Troy, NY (DMA 59)

WCDC-TV *Digital Channel:* 36; 538 kw vis, 53 kw aur; 3,688t/248g; N42 38 14 W73 10 07; *Rebroadcasting:* Satellite of WTEN-TV Albany
341 Northern Blvd., Albany, NY 12204 US
(518) 436-4822, (800)-888-WTEN; *Fax:* (518) 426-4792, (518) 436-7557, (518) 465-6166
www.news10.com
news@news10.com
License: Adams, Berkshire County, MA held by Young Broadcasting of Albany, Inc., Debtor-in-possession
Group Owner: Young Broadcasting Inc.; (acq 10-11-89; grpsl; *Washington Law Firm:* Wiley, Rein & Fielding
Nat'l Network: ABC
Size of News Staff: 37; *Hours of Local News Weekly:* news progmg 15 hrs wkly
Michael Sechrist, General Manager
Christina Burke, Programming Coordinator
Elisa Streeter, News Team
Lydia Kulbida, News Team
Steve Caporizzo, Weather Team
Steve Teeling, Weather Team
Liana Bonavita, Sports Team

WCWN *Digital Channel:* 43; *Virtual Channel:* 45; 600 kw; 1398 ft.; N42 37 31 W74 0 38
Mailing Address: 1400 Balltown Rd., Schenectady, NY 12309 US
Second Address: 10706 Beaver Dam Rd., Hunt Valley, MD 21030
(518) 381-4900; *Fax:* (518) 381-3734
www.cwalbany.com
License: Schenectady, Schenectady County, NY held by WCWN Licensee LLC
Group Owner: Sinclair Broadcast Group Inc.; (acq 12-5-2006; $17 million)
Nat'l Network: CW
Vincent Nelson, General Manager

***WMHT** *Digital Channel:* 34; *Virtual Channel:* 17; 325 kw; 1398 ft.; N42 37 31 W74 0 38
4 Global View, Troy, NY 12180-8368 US
(518) 880-3400; *Fax:* (518) 880-3409
www.wmht.org
email@wmht.org
License: Schenectady, Schenectady County, NY held by WMHT Educational Telecommunications
Washington Law Firm: Schwartz, Woods & Miller
Nat'l Network: PBS
Robert Altman, CEO & President
Julie Raskin, VP of Finance & Accounting
Valerie Belden, Executive Asst. to the President & Volunteer Coord
Kathy Beam, Dir. Of Corporate Support
Tony Grocki, Producer/ Director
Dominick Figliomeni,Production manager
Jayne Robinson, TV Traffic Operations Manager

WNYT *Digital Channel:* 12; *Virtual Channel:* 13; 15 kw; 1427 ft.; N42 37 31 W74 0 38
715 N. Pearl St., Albany, NY 12204 US
(518) 436-4791, (518) 207-4700, (800) 999-WNYT; *Fax:* (518) 434-0659
www.wnyt.com
License: Albany, Albany County, NY held by WNYT-TV LLC.
Group Owner: Hubbard Broadcasting Inc.; (acq 9-19-96).
Nat'l Network: NBC; *Nat'l Reps:* Petry Television Inc.
Hours of Local News Weekly: News progmg 27 hrs wkly
Steve Robbins, Dir. Of Operations & Web Services
Stephen P. Baboulis, General Manager
Tony McManus, General Sales Mgr
Maryann Ryan, Programming Director
Eric Hoppel, News Director
Richard Klein, Engineering Dir
Rich Klein,Engineering Dir
Carla Clark, Business Manager
Tony McManus, Sales Director
Maryann Ryan, Dir. Of Public Affairs, Programming & Special Prom

WRGB *Digital Channel:* 6; *Virtual Channel:* 6; 30.2 kw; 1286 ft.; N42 37 31 W74 0 38
Mailing Address: 1400 Balltown Rd., Schenectady, NY 12309 US
Second Address: 10706 Beaver Dam Rd., Hunt Valley, MD 21030
(518) 346-6666
www.cbs6albany.com
news@cbs6albany.com
License: Schenectady, Schenectady County, NY held by WRGB Licensee LLC
Group Owner: Sinclair Broadcast Group Inc.; acq 3-4-86; *Washington Law Firm:* Latham & Watkins
Nat'l Network: CBS; *Nat'l Reps:* TeleRep; *Wire Services:* AP
Hours of Local News Weekly: news progmg 31.5 hrs wkly
Peter Brancato, News Operations Manager
Vincent Nelson, General Manager
Tim Pennings, Promotion Director
Stephen Richards, News Director
Terry Beacham, Engineering Dir
Robert Hewitt, National Sales Manager

WTEN *Digital Channel:* 26; *Virtual Channel:* 10; 700 kw; 1398 ft.; N42 37 31 W74 0 38
341 Northern Blvd., Albany, NY 12204 US
(518) 436-4822; *Fax:* (518) 462-6065
www.wten.com
news@news10.com
License: Albany, Albany County, NY held by Young Broadcasting of Albany, Inc., Debtor-in-possession
Group Owner: Young Broadcasting Inc.; (acq 10-11-89; grpsl).; *Washington Law Firm:* Wiley, Rein & Fielding
Nat'l Network: ABC
Size of News Staff: 50; *Hours of Local News Weekly:* news progmg 22 hrs wkly
Michael Sechrist, General Manager
Ron Romines, General Sales Mgr
Chris Terwilliger, Programming Director
Skeeter Lansing, Chief Engineer
Steve Caporizzo, Weather Team
Elisa Streeter, News Team
Mark Baker, News Team

WXXA-TV *Digital Channel:* 7; *Virtual Channel:* 23; 10 kw; 1424 ft.; N42 37 31 W74 0 38
341 Northern Blvd, Albany, NY 12204 US
(518) 862-2323,(518) 862-0995; *Fax:* (518) 862-0865,(518) 862-0930
www.fox23news.com
news@fox23news.com
License: Albany, Albany County, NY held by WXXA-TV LLC
Group Owner: Shield Media LLC; (acq 3-14-2008; grpsl);
Washington Law Firm: Covington & Burling
Nat'l Network: FOX; *Nat'l Reps:* Millennium Sales & Marketing
Size of News Staff: 70; *Hours of Local News Weekly:* news progmg 23.5 hrs wkly
Sandy DiPasquale, CEO
Bill Sally, General Manager
Todd Kuhn, General Sales Mgr
Paul Pelliccia, Programming Director
Gene Ross, News Director
Sargent Cathrall, Chief Engineer
Steve Kimatian, Executive Vice President

WYPX-TV *Digital Channel:* 50; 450 kw vis; ant 679t/675g; N42 59 04 W74 10 54
1 Charles Blvd., Guilderland, NY 12084 USA
(518) 464-0143; *Fax:* (518) 464-0633
www.iontelevision.com
License: Amsterdam, NY held by Ion Media Albany License, Inc.
Group Owner: ION Media Networks Inc.; (acq 6-1-96; $2.5 million)
Nat'l Network: ION Television
Brandon Burgess, CEO

Binghamton, NY (DMA 160)

WBNG-TV *Digital Channel:* 7; 166 kw vis, 18.2 kw aur; ant 1,210t/785g; N42 02 33 W75 57 06; *Population Served:* 154,400
560 Columbia Dr., Johnson City, NY 13790
(607) 729-8812; *Fax:* (607) 797-6211
www.wbng.com
wbng@wbngtv.com
License: Binghamton, Broome County, NY held by WBNG License Inc.
Group Owner: Granite Broadcasting Corp.; (acq 7-26-2006; $45 million); *Washington Law Firm:* Latham & Watkins
Nat'l Network: CBS; CW; *Nat'l Reps:* Continental Television Sales; *Wire Services:* AP
Hours of Local News Weekly: News progmg 30 hrs wkly
Greg Catlin, General Manager
Bob Krummunecker, Station Manager
Bob Krummunecker, General Sales Mgr
Kate Garger, Programming Director
Christina Rockhill, Promotions Manager
Candace Chapman, News Director
Chris Ball, ChiefEngineer
Janet Heatherman, Traffic Supervisor

WICZ-TV *Digital Channel:* 8; *Virtual Channel:* 40; 7.9 kw; 371 meters; 42 3'23 N 75 56'38.7 W
4600 Vestal Pkwy., Vestal, NY 13850 US
(607) 770-4040; *Fax:* (607) 798-7950
www.wicz.com
wgordon@wicz.com
License: Binghamton, Broome County, NY held by Stainless Broadcasting Company
Group Owner: Northwest Broadcasting Inc.; (acq 7-15-97; $16 million cash-out merger with KTVZ(TV) Bend, OR); *Washington Law Firm:* Leventhal, Senter & Lerman
Nat'l Network: FOX
Size of News Staff: 13; *Hours of Local News Weekly:* news progmg 2 hrs wkly
John Leet, General Manager
Wayne Gordon, General and National Sales Manager
Vernon Rowlands, Programming Director
Mike Melnyk, Chief Engineer
Keith Krech, Traffic
Rosemary Gaeta, Business Administration
Jeff Horn, InternetManager

WIVT *Digital Channel:* 34; *Virtual Channel:* 34; 345 kw; 912 ft.; N42 3 39 W75 56 36
203 Ingraham Hill Rd., Binghamton, NY 20036 US
(607) 771-3434
www.binghamtonhomepage.com
License: Binghamton, Broome County, NY held by Nexstar Broadcasting Inc.
Group Owner: Nexstar Broadcasting Group Inc.; (acq 3-14-2008; grpsl)
Nat'l Network: NBC; *Nat'l Reps:* Millennium Sales & Marketing
John Birchall, General Manager
Maura Burtis, Dir. of Sales
Jim Ehmke, News Director

***WSKG-TV** *Digital Channel:* 42; *Virtual Channel:* 46; 50 kw; 1339 ft.; N42 3 40 W75 56 45
Mailing Address: PO Box 3000, Binghamton, NY 13902 US
Second Address: 601 Gates Road, Vestal, NY 13850
(607) 729-0100, (607) 729-0200; *Fax:* (607) 729-7328
www.wskg.org
mail@wskg.org
License: Binghamton, Broome County, NY held by WSKG Public Telecommunications Council
Washington Law Firm: Dow, Lohnes & Albertson
Nat'l Network: PBS
Lawrence Kiley, Chairman
Brian Sickora, President & CEO
Erik Jensen, Operations Dir
Katherine Fitzgerald, Vice Chairman
Aiden Hannan, Secretary/ Treasurer

Buffalo, NY (DMA 53)

WBBZ-TV *Digital Channel:* 7; 15.5 kw vis; ant 1,348t/963g; N42 38 15 W78 37 12; *Not on Air/Target Date:* 10/1/2009 ; *Station Currently Dark*; *Population Served:* 500,000
4545 Transit Rd., Suite 750, Williamsville, NY 14221
(716) 630-9229; *Fax:* (716) 630-9233
www.wbbz.tv
info@wbbz.tv
License: Springville, Erie County, NY held by Word of God Fellowship, Inc.
Marcus Lamb, President
Mark Ewart, VP, Operations & Engineering
Bob Koshinski, VP/ Genearl manager
Al Green, General Sales Manager
Diane Breen, Program & Sales Coordinator
John Disciullo, Promotion & Production Dir.
AndySmyczynski, Technical Director
Patti Forbes, Traffic Manager
Joe Maulucci, Creative Director

Anthony Christy, Account Manager
Katie Burden, Production asst.

WGRZ *Digital Channel:* 33; *Virtual Channel:* 2; 480 kw; 968 ft.; N42 43 07 W78 33 47; *Population Served:* 1,325,500
259 Delaware Ave., Buffalo, NY 14202 US
(716) 849-2222; *Fax:* (716) 849-7602
www.wgrz.com
webmaster@wgrz.com
License: Buffalo, Erie County, NY held by Multimedia Entertainment LLC
Group Owner: Tegna Media; (acq 1-27-97; grpsl).
Nat'l Network: NBC; *Wire Services:* Newsweek; CNBC; NBC; UPI
Hours of Local News Weekly: news progmg 33.5 hrs wkly
Jim Toellner, President and General Manager
Julie Mecklenberg, Local Sales Manager
Colleen Nossavage, Programming Director
Dan Meyers, Marketing and Promotions Director
Jeff Woodard, News Director
Mark Manders, Director ofSales
Jon May, Research Director
Matt Phifer, Digital Media Executive
Samantha Schlein, Digital Media Specialist

WIVB-TV *Digital Channel:* 39; *Virtual Channel:* 4; 790 kw; 1368 ft.; N42 39 33 W78 37 33
200 Crescent Court, Suite 1600, Dallas, TX 75201 US
(716) 874-4410; *Fax:* (716) 879-4896
www.wivb.com
License: Buffalo, Erie County, NY held by WIVB Broadcasting LLC
Group Owner: LIN Media; (acq 12-16-97).; *Washington Law Firm:* Covington & Burling
Nat'l Network: CBS
Chris Musial, CEO
Diane Breen, Programming Director
Dan Meyers, Promotions Manager
Dennis Majewicz, Chief Engineer

WKBW-TV *Digital Channel:* 38; *Virtual Channel:* 7; 358 kw; 1420 ft.; N42 38 14.8 W78 37 11.9
7 Broadcast Plaza, Buffalo, NY 14202 US
(716) 845-6100, (716) 840-7873; *Fax:* (710) 522-1846, (716) 840-7820
www.wkbw.com
License: Buffalo, Erie County, NY held by Granite Broadcasting Corp.
Group Owner: Granite Broadcasting Corp.; (acq 1995; $13.42 million); *Washington Law Firm:* Akin, Gump, Strauss, Haver & Feld
Nat'l Network: ABC; *Nat'l Reps:* TeleRep
William Ransom, General Manager
Mike Anger, Chief Engineer
Keith Radford, News Team
Jeff Russo, Sports Team
Mike Randall, Weather Team
Shawn Stepner, Sports
Andy Parker, Weather
Matthew Bove, News Team

***WNED-TV** *Digital Channel:* 43; *Virtual Channel:* 17; 156 kw; 1076 ft.; N43 1 48 W78 55 15
PO Box 1263, Buffalo, NY 14240-1263 USA
(716) 845-7000; *Fax:* (716) 845-7036
www.wned.org/television
License: Buffalo, Erie County, NY held by Western NY Public Broadcasting Association
Washington Law Firm: Schwartz, Woods & Miller
Nat'l Network: PBS
Foreign Language Programming
Donald K. Boswell, President & CEO
Sylvia Bennett, SVP, Development & Corporate Communications
Ron Santora, VP, Broadcasting/Station Manager
Joseph Puma, VP, Engineering & Technology

WNLO *Digital Channel:* 32; *Virtual Channel:* 23; 1000 kw; 994 ft.; N43 1 48 W78 55 15
2077 Elmwood Avenue, Buffalo, NY 14207 US
(716) 876-7333, (800) 794-3687; *Fax:* (716) 874-8173
www.cw23.com
License: Buffalo, Erie County, NY held by WIVB Broadcasting LLC
Group Owner: LIN Media; (acq 6-6-2001; $26.2 million); *Washington Law Firm:* Covington & Burling
Nat'l Network: CW
Chris Musial, CEO
Diane Breen, Programming Director
Dan Meyers, Promotions Manager
Dennis Majewicz, Chief Engineer

WNYB *Digital Channel:* 26; *Virtual Channel:* 26; 243 kw; 1519 ft.; N42 23 36 W79 13 44
5775 Big Tree Road, Orchard Park, NY 14217 US
(716) 662-2659; *Fax:* (716) 667-2499
www.tct-net.org
wnyb@tct.tv
License: Jamestown, Chautauqua County, NY held by Faith Broadcasting Network Inc.
Group Owner: Tri-State Christian Television; (acq 5-7-2002).
Nat'l Network: IND
Loren Speery, General Manager

WNYO-TV *Digital Channel:* 49; *Virtual Channel:* 49; 198 kw; 1234 ft.; N42 46 58 W78 27 28
Mailing Address: 699 Hertel Ave., Suite 100, Buffalo, NY 14207 US
Second Address: 10706 Beaver Dam Rd., Hunt Valley, MD 21030
(716) 447-3200; *Fax:* (716) 875-4919
www.mytvbuffalo.com
License: Buffalo, Erie County, NY held by New York Television Inc.
Group Owner: Sinclair Broadcast Group Inc.; (acq 1-25-2002; $51.5 million for stock).
Nat'l Network: MYTV; *Nat'l Reps:* Millennium Sales & Marketing
Nick Magnini, General Manager
Mary Beth Marble, General Sales Mgr
Jose Chapa, Director of Sales

WPXJ-TV *Digital Channel:* 23; *Virtual Channel:* 51; 455 kw; 906 ft.; N42 53 42 W78 0 56
726 Exchange St., Suite 819, Buffalo, NY 14210 USA
(716) 852-1818; *Fax:* (716) 852-8288
www.iontelevision.com
michaelhubner@ionmedia.com
License: Buffalo, NY held by ION Media Buffalo License, Inc.
Group Owner: ION Media Networks Inc.; (acq 7-15-97; $3 million)
Nat'l Network: ION
Brandon Burgess, Chairman/CEO

WUTV *Digital Channel:* 14; *Virtual Channel:* 29; 1000 kw; 983 ft.; N43 1 32 W78 55 43
Mailing Address: 699 Hertel Ave., Suite 100, Buffalo, NY 14207 US
Second Address: 10706 Beaver Dam Rd., Hunt Valley, MD 21030
(716) 477-3200; *Fax:* (716) 875-4919
www.wutv29.com
License: Buffalo, Erie County, NY held by WUTV Licensee LLC
Group Owner: Sinclair Broadcast Group Inc.; (acq 12-10-01; grpsl).; *Washington Law Firm:* Arter & Hadden
Nat'l Network: FOX; *Nat'l Reps:* Millennium Sales & Marketing
Nick Magnini, General Manager
Mary Beth Marble, General Sales Mgr
Jose Chapa, Director of Sales

Burlington, VT-Plattsburgh, NY (DMA 97)

***WCFE-TV** *Digital Channel:* 38; *Virtual Channel:* 57; 55 kw; 2418 ft.; N44 41 43 W73 53 0
One Sesame Street, Plattsburgh, NY 12901 US
(518) 563-9770, (800) 836-5700; *Fax:* (518) 561-1928
www.mountainlake.org
mlpbs@mountainlake.org
License: Plattsburgh, Clinton County, NY held by Mountain Lake Public Telecommunications Council
Washington Law Firm: Dow, Lohnes & Albertson
Nat'l Network: PBS
Hours of Local News Weekly: 30 minutes
Jacqueline Kelleher, BoardChair
Alice Recore, President & CEO
Zachary Kowalczyk, Operations Dir
Paul King, Director of Programming & On Air Fundraising
Rhonda Santos, Promotions Manager
Charlie Zarbo, Director of Engineering
Janine Scherline, Director of Fundraising & Business Development
Dan Swinton, Director of Production & Content
Jane Owens, Director of Outreach & Education
Dr. James Liszka, 1st Vice Chair
Charlotte Brimstein, 2nd Vice Chair
Jim Holmes,Treasurer

WPTZ *Digital Channel:* 14; *Virtual Channel:* 5; 25.1 kw vis, 4.3 kw aur; ant 1,991t/978g; N44 34 26 W73 40 29
Mailing Address: 5 Television Dr., Plattsburgh, NY 12901
Second Address: 553 Roosevelt Highway, Colchester, VT 05446
(518) 561-5555, (802) 655-0027, (802) 655-5455; *Fax:* (518) 561-5940, (802) 655-5451
www.wptz.com
License: North Pole, Lake Placid County, NY held by Hearst Stations Inc.
Group Owner: Hearst Television Inc.; (acq 6-1-98).
Nat'l Network: NBC
Size of News Staff: 31; *Hours of Local News Weekly:* news progmg 23 hrs wkly
Paul Sands, General Manager
Luke Commare, General Sales Mgr
Susan Acklen, Promotions Manager
Sinan Sadar, News Director
William Harp, Chief Engineer
Courtney Kabot, Anchor
Laura Lareau, Traffic Manager
Ashley Allen,Reporter
Ken Drake, Sports Team
Gib Brown, Weather town
Sally Kidd, Washington Bureau

Elmira (Corning), NY (DMA 175)

WENY-TV *Digital Channel:* 36; *Virtual Channel:* 36; 75 kw; 1122 ft.; N42 8 31 W77 4 40
474 Old Ithaca Rd., Horseheads, NY 14845 US
(607) 739-3636, (607) 739-1412; *Fax:* (607) 796-6171
www.weny.com
License: Elmira, Chemung County, NY held by Lilly Broadcasting L.L.C
(acq 10-17-99; $4.8 million); *Washington Law Firm:* Cordon & Kelly
Nat'l Network: ABC; CW; CBS
Hours of Local News Weekly: News progmg 10 hrs wkly
Kevin Lilly, CEO
Brian Lilly, Operations Dir
Peter Veto, General Manager
Sharon Ewsuk, General Sales Mgr
Dan Beach, Programming Director
Bruce Hauver, Promotions Manager
Renata Stiehl, News Director
Jennifer Sheahen, Anchor/Ex.Producer
Joe Veres, Chief Meterologist
Andy Malnoske, Sports Director
Asha McKenzie, News Reporter
Lauren Adams, Washington,DC Bureau
Jacqueline Policastro, Washington,DC Bureau

WETM-TV *Digital Channel:* 18; *Virtual Channel:* 18; 45 kw; 1234 ft.; N42 6 22 W76 52 17
101 E. Water St., Elmira, NY 14901 US
(607) 733-5518
www.mytwintiers.com
License: Elmira, Chemung County, NY held by Nexstar Broadcasting Inc.
Group Owner: Nexstar Broadcasting Group Inc.; (acq 3-14-2008; grpsl); *Washington Law Firm:* Covington & Burling
Nat'l Network: NBC
Size of News Staff: 21; *Hours of Local News Weekly:* news progmg 14 hrs wkly
Steve Luccarelli, General Sales Mgr
Robert Rockstroh, News Director
Don Hunt, Chief Engineer

***WSKA** *Digital Channel:* 30; *Virtual Channel:* 30; 25 kw; 1096 ft.; N42 8 29.73 W77 4 39.11; *Rebroadcasting:* rebroadcast of WSKG(TV) Binghamton
Mailing Address: P.O. Box 3000, Binghamton, NY 13902 US
Second Address: 601 Gates Road, Suite 4, Vestal, NY 13850
(607) 729-0100, (607) 729-0200; *Fax:* (607) 729-7328
www.wskg.org
License: Corning, Steuben County, NY held by WSKG Public Telecommunications Council
Nat'l Network: PBS
Brian Sickora, President & CEO
Brian Sickora, General Manager
Dave Fulton, Dir. Of Engineering & IT
Caroline Basso, Dir. Of Development & marketing
Teresa Peltier, Manager of Digital Content
Judy Ghosin, Dir. Of Finance & HR
KateCook, Radio Operations & programming Coordinator
Erik Jensen, Community Engagement Dir.
Eric Adler, Broadcast Engineer

WYDC *Digital Channel:* 48; *Virtual Channel:* 48; 7.6 kw; 1096 ft.; N42 8 30 W77 4 39
33 E. Market St., Corning, NY 148830 US
(607) 937-5000; *Fax:* (607) 937-4019, (607) 937-4269
www.wydctv.com
info@wydctv.com

License: Corning, Steuben County, NY held by WYDC Inc (acq 11-19-97; $1.75 million); *Washington Law Firm:* Drinker Biddle & Reath LLP
Nat'l Network: FOX
Bill Christian, CEO
Bill Christian, General Manager
Mary Reed, Station Manager
Jennifer mattison, Programming
Shylah Davies, Traffic Manager
Sharon Casles, Marketing Consultant
Josh Rampulla, Master Control
Ali Kingsbury,Marketing Consultant
David Scott, Production Manager

New York (DMA 1)

WABC-TV *Digital Channel:* 7; 11 kW; 972 ft.; N40 45 22 W73 59 12
7 Lincoln Sq., New York, NY 10023 USA
(917) 260-7000
abc7ny.com
License: New York, New York County, NY held by American Broadcasting Companies Inc.
Group Owner: ABC Owned Television Stations
Nat'l Network: ABC; *Nat'l Reps:* ABC National Television Sales
Evelyn del Cerro, Operations Manager

WCBS-TV *Digital Channel:* 33; *Virtual Channel:* 2; 284 kW; 1296 ft.; N40 44 54 W73 59 10
524 W 57th St., New York, NY 10019 USA
(212) 975-4321
newyork.cbslocal.com
License: New York, New York County, NY held by CBS Broadcasting Inc.
Group Owner: CBS Television Stations Group
Nat'l Network: CBS; *Nat'l Reps:* CBS TV Stations National Sales
Joel Goldberg, Senior Vice President

WFTY-DT *Digital Channel:* 23; *Virtual Channel:* 67; 2,630 kw vis, 263 kw aur; 720t/678g; N40 53 23 W72 57 13; *Population Served:* 3,000,000
607 Middle Country Rd., Middle Island, NY 11953
(201) 287-4042; *Fax:* (201) 287-9428
www.univision.com
License: Smithtown, Suffolk County, NY held by Univision New York LLC.
Group Owner: Univision Communications Inc.; (acq 5-21-2001; grpsl).; *Washington Law Firm:* Wiley, Rein & Fielding
Nat'l Network: UniMas (Spanish)
Foreign Language Programming; Hours of Local News Weekly: news progmg 4 hrs wkly
Randy Falco, President
David Marinace, Chief Engineer
Maria D. Lopez, Programming and Cable Supervisor

***WLIW** *Digital Channel:* 21; *Virtual Channel:* 21; 89.9 kw; 364 ft.; N40 47 19 W73 27 9
825 Eigth Avenue, New York, NY 10019 US
(21) 560-8021; *Fax:* (516) 692-7629
www.wliw.org
programming@wliw.org
License: Garden City, Nassau County, NY held by Educational Broadcasting Corp
(acq 1-31-2003); *Washington Law Firm:* Schwartz, Woods & Miller
Nat'l Network: PBS; *Wire Services:* UPI
Neal Shapiro, President
John Servidio, General Manager

WLNY-TV *Digital Channel:* 47; 1000 kW; 620 ft.; N40 53 50 W72 54 56; *Population Served:* 4,200,000
270 S Service Rd., Melville, NY 11747 USA
(631) 777-8855
www.cbsnewyork.com
License: Riverhead, Suffolk County, NY held by CBS LITV LLC
Group Owner: CBS Television Stations Group; *Washington Law Firm:* Cohn & Marks
Nat'l Network: Independent; CBS
Hours of Local News Weekly: News progmg 2 hrs wkly

WNBC *Digital Channel:* 28; *Virtual Channel:* 4; 200.2 kw; 1302 ft.; N40 44 54 W73 59 10
30 Rockefeller Plaza, 7th Fl., New York, NY 10112 USA
(212) 664-4444, (866) 639-7244; *Fax:* (212) 664-2994 (news)
www.nbcnewyork.com
License: New York, New York County, NY held by NBC Telemundo License LLC
Group Owner: NBC Owned Television Stations; (acq 6-5-86; grpsl).
Nat'l Network: NBC

***WNYE-TV** *Digital Channel:* 24; *Virtual Channel:* 25; 151 kw; 1016 ft.; N40 45 22 W73 59 12
112 Tillary Street, Brooklyn, NY 11201 US
(212) 669-7400; *Fax:* (212) 669-8448
www.nyc.gov/tv
License: New York, New York County, NY held by New York City Dept. of Info Technology & Telecommunications
Washington Law Firm: Arnold & Porter
Nat'l Network: ETV
Foreign Language Programming
Katherine Oliver, General Manager
Diane Petzke, Programming Director
Chang Kim, Chief Engineer
Marybeth Ihle, Press
Allie Kleva, Marketing
Jorge Hernandez, Marketing
Milly Perez, Radio Scheduling
Teence O'Driscoll, TechncalOerations & ClosedCationing Issues
Jacob Glickman, leasetime Access

WNYW *Digital Channel:* 44; *Virtual Channel:* 5; 990 kW; 1204 ft.; N41 29 19.5 W73 56 52.5
USA
www.fox5ny.com
License: Newburgh, Orange County, NY held by Fox Television Stations LLC
Group Owner: Fox Television Stations Group; (acq 11-14-86; grpsl).
Nat'l Network: FOX

WPIX *Digital Channel:* 11; *Virtual Channel:* 11; 7.5 kW; 1329 ft.; N40 44 54 W73 59 10
220 East 42nd St., New York, NY 10017 USA
(212) 210-2411
pix11.com
news@pix11.com
License: New York, New York County, NY held by WPIX LLC
Group Owner: Tribune Media; (acq 12-20-2007; grpsl);
Washington Law Firm: Dow Lohnes PLLC
Nat'l Network: The CW Network; *Wire Services:* AP
Hours of Local News Weekly: News progmg 19.5 hrs wkly
Debbie Presser, General Sales Mgr

WPXN-TV *Digital Channel:* 31; *Virtual Channel:* 31; 100 kw; 1181 ft.; N40 44 54 W73 59 08
810 Seventh Ave., New York, NY 10019 USA
(212) 757-3100; *Fax:* (212) 956-2661
www.iontelevision.com
License: New York, NY held by ION Media License Company, LLC.
Group Owner: ION Media Networks Inc.; (acq 3-4-98; $257.5 million)
Nat'l Network: ION
Mildred Diaz, Operations Dir

WRNN-TV *Digital Channel:* 48; *Virtual Channel:* 48; 950 kw; 1240 ft.; N41 29 18 W73 56 56
Mailing Address: 800 Westchester Ave., Suite S-640, Rye Brook, NY 10573 US
Second Address: 9465 Wilshire Blvd., Suite 300, Beverly Hills, CA 90210
(914) 417-2700; *Fax:* (914) 696-0279
www.rnntv.com
comments@rnntv.com
License: Kingston, Ulster County, NY held by WRNN License Co. LLC
(acq 7-31-2001).; *Washington Law Firm:* Baker & Hostetler
Nat'l Network: IND
Size of News Staff: 9; *Hours of Local News Weekly:* news progmg 82 hrs wkly
Richard E. French, Jr., CEO & President
Richard French, General Manager
Jerry Andrews, News director
Christian J. French, COO
Edward Van Saders, CFO
Richard French III, President of News & Programming

WTBY-TV *Digital Channel:* 27; *Virtual Channel:* 54; 1000 kw; 1174 ft.; N41 29 20 W73 56 53
Mailing Address: PO Box A, Santa Ana, CA 92711 US
Second Address: P. O. Box 768, Station B, Ottawa, ON K1P 5P8
(714) 731-1000, (888) 731-1000, (714) 832-2950; *Fax:* (845) 896-4614
www.tbn.org
wtby@tbn.org
License: Poughkeepsie, Dutchess County, NY held by Trinity Broadcasting of N.Y. Inc.
Group Owner: Trinity Broadcasting Network; (acq 7-13-82; $2.97 million; *Washington Law Firm:* Joseph E. Dunne III
Nat'l Network: TRINITY BROADCA
Paul Crouch, President
Maria Idoni, Operations Dir
Chris Elia, General Manager
Paul Swartzendruber, Chief Engineer

Rochester, NY (DMA 76)

WHAM-TV *Digital Channel:* 13; *Virtual Channel:* 13; 316 kw vis, 47.9 kw aur; ant 500t/363.5g; N43 08 07 W77 35 03; *Population Served:* 393,630
Mailing Address: 4225 West Henrietta Road, Rochester, NY 20036
Second Address: 10706 Beaver Dam Road, Hunt Valley, MD 21030
(585) 334-8700; *Fax:* (585) 359-1570
13wham.com
License: Rochester, Monroe County, NY held by Deerfield Media (Rochester) Licensee LLC
Group Owner: Deerfield Media; (acq 3-14-2008; grpsl);
Washington Law Firm: Covington & Burling
Nat'l Network: ABC; CW; *Nat'l Reps:* Millennium Sales & Marketing; *Wire Services:* AP; CNN; Bloomberg News
Size of News Staff: 52; *Hours of Local News Weekly:* news progmg 24 hrs wkly
Craig Heslor, Production Manager
Chuck Samuels, General Manager
David DiProsa, Director of Sales
Kevin Kalvitis, Promotions Manager
Marilynn Garbarino, Local Sales Manager
Mark Zeger, National Sales Manager
Allison Watts,Director of Digital Media

WHEC-TV *Digital Channel:* 10; *Virtual Channel:* 10; 18.1 kw; 502 ft.; N43 8 8 W77 35 2
191 E. Avenue, Rochester, NY 14604 US
(585) 546-5670, (585) 546-5750; *Fax:* (585) 546-5688, (585) 454-7433
caption@whec.com
License: Rochester, Monroe County, NY held by WHEC-TV LLC.
Group Owner: Hubbard Broadcasting Inc.; (acq 9-19-96).;
Washington Law Firm: Arent, Fox, Kintner, Plotkin & Kahn
Nat'l Network: NBC; *Nat'l Reps:* Petry Television Inc.
Hours of Local News Weekly: News progmg 22 hrs wkly
Sherron Sheridan, Operations Dir
Arnold Klinsky, General Manager
Lauren Burruto, General Sales Mgr
Lynette Baker, Programming Director
John Walsh, Director of Engineering
Janet Lomax, News anchor
Josh Nichols, Meterologist
Justin Granit, Sports Anchor/Reporter
Scott Kilbury, News Anchor
Lia Lando, News Anchor
Brett Davidsen, News Anchor

WROC-TV *Digital Channel:* 45; *Virtual Channel:* 8; 1000 kw; 401 ft.; N43 8 8 W77 35 2
201 Humboldt St., Rochester, NY 14610 US
(585) 287-8000; *Fax:* (585) 288-6999
www.rochesterfirst.com
License: Rochester, Monroe County, NY held by Nexstar Broadcasting Inc.
Group Owner: Nexstar Broadcasting Group Inc.; (acq 12-9-99; $46 million)
Nat'l Network: CBS
Size of News Staff: 40; *Hours of Local News Weekly:* news progmg 14 hrs wkly
Louis A. Gattozzi, General Manager
Connie Howard, News Director

WUHF *Digital Channel:* 28; *Virtual Channel:* 31; 320 kw; 528 ft.; N43 8 5 W77 35 7
4225 West Henrietta Rd., Rochester, NY 14623 US
(585) 321-2290; *Fax:* (585) 359-1570
www.foxrochester.com
License: Rochester, Monroe County, NY held by WUHF Licensee LLC
Group Owner: Sinclair Broadcast Group Inc.; (acq 4-12-2002; for assumption liabilities).; *Washington Law Firm:* Pillsbury, Winthrop & Shaw Pittman
Nat'l Network: FOX
Hours of Local News Weekly: news progmg 3.5 hrs wkly
Charles Samuels, General Manager
Craig Heslor, Production Manager

***WXXI-TV** *Digital Channel:* 16; *Virtual Channel:* 21; 180 kw; 427 ft.; N43 8 7 W77 35 3
Mailing Address: PO Box 21, 280 State St., Rochester, NY 14601 US
Second Address: 280 State St., Rochester, NY 14614

(585) 258-0200; *Fax:* (585) 258-0335
www.wxxi.org
License: Rochester, Monroe County, NY held by WXXI Public Broadcasting Council
Washington Law Firm: Schwartz, Woods & Miller
Nat'l Network: PBS
Foreign Language Programming; Size of News Staff: 4; *Hours of Local News Weekly:* news progmg 2 hrs wkly
Norm Silverstein, CEO
Carole Edelman, Operations Dir
Robert Owens, Programming Director
Kent Hatfield, Engineering Dir
Susan Rogers, COO

Syracuse, NY (DMA 85)

***WCNY-TV** *Digital Channel:* 25; *Virtual Channel:* 24; 97 kw; 1289 ft.; N42 56 42 W76 7 7
Mailing Address: 415 Fayette St., Syracuse, NY 13204 US
Second Address: P.O. Box 2400, Syracuse, NY 13220-2400
(315) 453-2424; *Fax:* (315) 451-8824
www.wcny.org
wcny-online@wcny.org
License: Syracuse, Onondaga County, NY held by Public Broadcasting Council of Central New York
Washington Law Firm: Dow, Lohnes & Albertson
Nat'l Network: PBS
Jeffrey Scheer, Chairman
Robert J. Daino, President & CEO
John Duffy, Operations Dir
Brian Damm, Promotions Manager
Shiu-Kai Chin, Vice Chairman
James Burns, Treasurer
Jason Wallace, Assistant Treasurer
Jessica Cohen,Secretary
Evelyn Carter, Member of the Board
Robert A. Dracker, Member of the Board

WNYI *Digital Channel:* 20; *Virtual Channel:* 52; 110 kw; 778 ft.; N42 45 30 W76 2 47
Mailing Address: 4811 Jenkins Rd., Vernon, NY 13476 US
Second Address: 401 W. Kirkpatrick St., Syracuse, NY 13204
(501) 219-2400
License: Ithaca, Tompkins County, NY held by Word of God Fellowship Inc.
Nat'l Network: DAYSTAR
Greg Fess, General Manager

WNYS-TV *Digital Channel:* 44; *Virtual Channel:* 43; 680 kw; 1460 ft.; N42 52 50 W76 12 0
1000 James St., Syracuse, NY 13203 US
(315) 472-6800; *Fax:* (315) 471-8889
www.my43.tv
License: Syracuse, Onondaga County, NY held by RKM Media Inc
(acq 7-2-96).; *Washington Law Firm:* Fletcher, Heald & Hildreth
Nat'l Network: MYTV
Mike Asiedu, Operations Dir
Don O'Connor, General Manager
Ed Kampf, General Sales Manager
Linda Deeb, Programming
Lleslie Baycura, Promotions
Vinny Lopez, Engineering- Tech Support
Roy Taylor, Chief Engineer
Ed Kampf, LocalSales Manager
Joan Lescenski, Traffic Manager
Andrew Brazil, Commercial Production
Candie Sullivan, Sales Asst.
Tom Blanden, Account Executive
Katie Blake, Account Executive

WSPX-TV *Digital Channel:* 15; *Virtual Channel:* 56; 49 kw; 1243 ft.; N43 18 18 W76 3 0
6508-B Basile Rowe, East Syracuse, NY 13057 USA
(812) 335-1770; *Fax:* (315) 414-0482
www.iontelevision.com
License: Syracuse, NY held by Ion Media Syracuse License, Inc.
Group Owner: ION Media Networks Inc.; (acq 4-29-99).
Nat'l Network: ION
Brandon Burgess, Chairman/CEO

WSTM-TV *Digital Channel:* 24; *Virtual Channel:* 3; 210 kw; 1289 ft.; N42 56 41.8 W76 7 7.6
1030 James St., Syracuse, NY 13203 US
(315) 477-9400; *Fax:* (315) 477-9675
www.cnycentral.com
news@cnycentral.com
License: Syracuse, Onondaga County, NY held by WSTQ Licensee LLC
Group Owner: Sinclair Broadcast Group Inc.; *Washington Law Firm:* Covington & Burling
Nat'l Network: NBC; *Nat'l Reps:* TeleRep
Size of News Staff: 45; *Hours of Local News Weekly:* news progmg 27.5 hrs wkly
Amy Collins, General Manager
Rae Fulkerson, News Director

WSTQ-LP *Digital Channel:* 14; 9.8 kw; 668 ft.; N43 03 30 W76 10 0
1030 James St., Syracuse, NY 13203 US
(315) 477-9400; *Fax:* (315) 477-9675
www.cnycentral.com
news@cnycentral.com
License: Syracuse, Onondaga County, NY held by WSTQ Licensee LLC
Group Owner: Sinclair Broadcast Group Inc.
Nat'l Network: CW; *Nat'l Reps:* TeleRep
Amy Collins, General Manager
Rae Fulkerson, News Director

WSYR-TV *Digital Channel:* 17; *Virtual Channel:* 9; 105 kw; 1319 ft.; N42 56 42 W76 1 28
5904 Bridge St., East Syracuse, NY 13057 US
(315) 446-9999
www.localsyr.com
License: Syracuse, Onondaga County, NY held by Nexstar Broadcasting Inc.
Group Owner: Nexstar Broadcasting Group Inc.; (acq 3-14-2008; grpsl)
Nat'l Network: ABC; *Nat'l Reps:* Millennium Sales & Marketing
Size of News Staff: 55; *Hours of Local News Weekly:* news progmg 22.5 hrs wkly
Bill Evans, General Manager
Phil Rankin, News Director

WSYT *Digital Channel:* 19; *Virtual Channel:* 68; 621 kw; 1460 ft.; N42 52 50 W76 12 0
1000 James St., Syracuse, NY 13203 US
(315) 472-6800; *Fax:* (315) 471-8889
www.foxsyracuse.com
doconnor@foxsyracuse.com
License: Syracuse, Onondaga County, NY held by Bristlecone Broadcasting LLC
Group Owner: Northwest Broadcasting Inc.; (acq 7-7-98; grpsl).
Nat'l Network: FOX
Hours of Local News Weekly: News progmg 3.5 hrs wkly
Don O'Connor, General Manager
Ed Kampf, General Sales Mgr
Leslie Baycura, Promotions and Programming
Vinny Lopez, Engineering and Tech Support
Kyrsten Bellen, National Sales Manager
Nikki Tabone, National Sales Coordinator
AndrewBrazil, Commercial Production

WTVH *Digital Channel:* 47; *Virtual Channel:* 5; 500 kw; 952 ft.; N42 57 18.8 W76 6 34.3
Mailing Address: 1030 James St., Syracuse, NY 13203 US
Second Address: 980 James Street, Syracuse, NY 13203
(315) 477-9400; *Fax:* (315) 477-9675
www.cnycentral.com
news@cnycentral.com
License: Syracuse, Onondaga County, NY held by WTVH License Inc.
Group Owner: Granite Broadcasting Corp.; *Washington Law Firm:* Akin, Gump, Strauss, Hauer & Feld
Nat'l Network: CBS; *Nat'l Reps:* Harrington, Righter & Parsons
Size of News Staff: 42; *Hours of Local News Weekly:* news progmg 24 hrs wkly
Chris Geiger, CEO & President
Tom Stemmler, Operations Dir
Amy Collins, General Sales Mgr
Mary Baker, Programming Director
Dean Walters, Promotions Manager
Rae Fulkerson, News Director
Tom Stemmler, Engineering Dir
Kevin Tubbs,Chief Engineer
Terri Endries, Local Sales Manager
Pam Sanson, Traffic Manager
Matt Mulcahy, News Team
Niko Tamurian, Sports Team
Wayne Mahar, Weather Team
Megan Coleman, News Team

Utica, NY (DMA 171)

WFXV *Digital Channel:* 27; *Virtual Channel:* 33; 1000 kw; 692 ft.; N43 8 43 W75 10 35
5956 Smith Hill Rd., Utica, NY 13503 US
(315) 797-5220; *Fax:* (315) 797-5409
www.cnyhomepage.com
License: Utica, Oneida County, NY held by Nexstar Broadcasting, Inc.
Group Owner: Nexstar Broadcasting Group Inc.; (acq 12-31-03; grpsl).; *Washington Law Firm:* Arter & Hadden
Nat'l Network: FOX
Steve Ventura, VP & General Manager
Stephen J. Ventura, Dir. of Sales
Don Dudley, News Director

WKTV *Digital Channel:* 29; *Virtual Channel:* 2; 708 kw; 1,319 ft.; N43 6 9 W74 56 27
5936 Smith Hill Rd., Utica, NY 13502 US
(315) 793-3477; *Fax:* (315) 793-3499
www.wktv.com
License: Utica, Oneida County, NY held by WKTV Licensee LLC
Group Owner: Heartland Media LLC; (acq 10-22-2013).;
Washington Law Firm: Dow, Lohnes & Albertson, PLLC
Nat'l Network: NBC; CW; *Nat'l Reps:* Continental Television Sales
Hours of Local News Weekly: news progmg 31.5 hrs wkly
David E. Streeter, Operations Manager
Steve McMurray, General Manager
Daphne Berle, General Sales Manager
Jeremy Ryan, News Director
Tom McNicholl, Engineering Dir
Michelle Liddy, Director of Digital Sales
Cindy McNicholl, ArtDirector

WUTR *Digital Channel:* 30; *Virtual Channel:* 20; 50 kw; 745 ft.; N43 8 43 W75 10 35
5956 Smith Hill Rd., Utica, NY 13503 US
(315) 797-5220; *Fax:* (315) 797-5409
www.cnyhomepage.com
License: Utica, Oneida County, NY held by Mission Broadcasting Inc.
Group Owner: Mission Broadcasting Inc.; (acq 4-1-2004; $3.725 million)
Nat'l Network: ABC
Diane Siembab, Station Manager
Stephen J. Ventura, Dir. of Sales
Don Dudley, News Director

Watertown, NY (DMA 178)

***WGTV** *Digital Channel:* 41; 59 kw vis; ant 1,212t/914g; N43 51 46 W75 43 39; *Population Served:* 151,000
Mailing Address: 1056 Arsenal St., Watertown, NY 13601
Second Address: PO Box 45, Gananoque, ON K7G 2T6
(315) 782-3142, (315) 782-8600; *Fax:* (315) 782-2491
www.wpbstv.org
lbrown@wpbstv.org
License: Watertown, Jefferson County, NY held by St. Lawrence Valley ETV Council
Washington Law Firm: Schwartz, Woods & Miller
Nat'l Network: PBS
Jack J. Boak, Chairman
Lynn Brown, President & General Manager
Lynn Brown, General Sales Mgr
Joline Furgison, Program Manager
David Glenn, Engineering
Timothy Ames, Engineering
Deborah Jones, IT & Content Manager
Tracy Duflo,Dir. Of Production
Bonnie Eppolito, Dir. Of Development
Kraig Everard, Dir. Of Corporate Support
Roque Murray, Producer/Director
Andrew Lacky, Brand Manager

***WPBS-DT** *Digital Channel:* 23; 60.5 kw vis; ant 794t/725g; N44 29 29 W74 51 27; *Rebroadcasting:* Rebroadcasts WPBS-TV Watertown 100%; *Population Served:* 220,000
Mailing Address: 1056 Arsenal St., Watertown, NY 13601
Second Address: PO Box 45, Gananoque, ON K7G 2T6
(315) 782-3142, (315) 782-8600; *Fax:* (315) 782-2491
www.wpbstv.org
License: Norwood, Jefferson County, NY held by St. Lawrence Valley ETV Council
Washington Law Firm: Schwartz, Woods & Miller
Nat'l Network: PBS
Carole McCoy, Chairman
Art Rees, Vice Chair
Lynn Brown, President & General Manager
Lynn Brown, General Sales Mgr
Joline Furgison, Program Manager
Timothy Ames, Chief Engineer
Deborah Jones, IT & Content Manager
Tracy Duflo,Dir. Of Production
Bonnie Eppolito, Dir. Of Development

Kraig Everard, Dir. Of Corporate Support
Roque Murray, Producer/Director
Andrew Lacky, Brand Manager

WWNY-TV *Digital Channel:* 7; 316 kw vis, 47 kw aur42kw; ant 718t/572g; N43 57 16 W75 43 45; *Population Served:* 107,406
120 Arcade St., Watertown, NY 13601
(315) 788-3800; *Fax:* (315) 782-7468,(315) 788-3787
www.wwnytv.net
wwny@wwnytv.net
License: Carthage, Jefferson County, NY held by United Communications Corp.
Group Owner: United Communications Corp.; (acq 12-5-81; $8.1 million; *Washington Law Firm:* Wood, Maines & Brown, Chartered
Nat'l Network: CBS
Size of News Staff: 16; *Hours of Local News Weekly:* news progmg 19 hrs wkly
John Seymour, Operations Dir
Cathy Pircsuk, General Manager
Patrick Powers, General Sales Mgr
Jim Corbin, Programming Director
Jeff Shannon, Promotions Manager
Scott Atkinson, News Director
Jim Felton, Chief Engineer
JohnKubis, Chief Weathercaster
Jeff nelson, Anchor
Candace Dunkley, News journalist
Cindy Habeeb, Health Repoter

WWTI *Digital Channel:* 21; *Virtual Channel:* 50; 25 kw; 1086 ft.; N43 52 47 W75 43 12
1222 Arsenal St., Watertown, NY 13601 US
(315) 785-8850
www.informnny.com
License: Watertown, Jefferson County, NY held by Nexstar Broadcasting Inc.
Group Owner: Nexstar Broadcasting Group Inc.; (acq 3-14-2008; grpsl)
Nat'l Network: ABC; CW; *Nat'l Reps:* Millennium Sales & Marketing; *Wire Services:* AP
Size of News Staff: 10; *Hours of Local News Weekly:* news progmg 5 hrs wkly
David Males, General Mgr/Dir. of Sales
Mark Mason, News Director

North Carolina

Charlotte, NC (DMA 22)

WAXN-TV *Digital Channel:* 50; *Virtual Channel:* 64; 150 kw; 1194 ft.; N35 15 41 W80 43 38
222 Commerce Street, Kingsport, TN 37660 US
(704) 338-9999; *Fax:* (704) 371-3131
www.wsoctv.com
License: Kannapolis, Cabarrus County, NC held by WSOC-TV Holdings Inc.
Group Owner: Cox Media Group; (acq 1-31-2000); *Washington Law Firm:* Dow, Lohnes & Albertson
Nat'l Network: IND; *Nat'l Reps:* TeleRep
Dave Siegler, Operations Dir
Kay Hall, Programming Director
Sally Ganz, Promotions Manager
Robin Whitmeyer, News Director
Ted Hand, Engineering Dir
Patricia Marsden, Research Director
Kierstin Boujlil, Traffic Manager

WBTV *Digital Channel:* 23; *Virtual Channel:* 3; 1000 kw; 1854 ft.; N35 21 51 W81 11 13
One Julian Price Pl, Charlotte, NC 28208 US
(704) 374-3500, (704) 374-3698; *Fax:* (704) 374-3614
www.wbtv.com
assignmentdesk@wbtv.com
License: Charlotte, Mecklenburg County, NC held by WBTV License Subsidiary LLC.
Group Owner: Raycom Media Inc.; (acq 3-31-2008; grpsl);
Washington Law Firm: Wiley, Rein & Fielding
Nat'l Network: CBS; *Nat'l Reps:* Petry Television Inc.; *Wire Services:* UPI
Don Shaw, Operations Dir
Nick Simonette, General Manager
Shelly Hill, Promotions Manager
Mike Gurthie, Chief Engineer
Molly Grantham, WBTV Anchor
Ashton Pellom, WBTV Reporter
Paul Cameron, WBTV Anchor
Ron Lee, WBTV Reporter
Delano Little, Sports Team
Tonya Rivens, Traffic Team

WCCB *Digital Channel:* 27; *Virtual Channel:* 18; 1000 kw; 1207 ft.; N35 16 1 W80 44 5
1 Television Pl., Charlotte, NC 28205 US
(704) 372-4434; *Fax:* (704) 335-9904
www.wccbcharlotte.com
newsdesk@wccbcharlotte.com
License: Charlotte, Mecklenburg County, NC held by North Carolina Broadcasting Partners.
Group Owner: Bahakel Communications Ltd.
Nat'l Network: CW
Size of News Staff: 1; *Hours of Local News Weekly:* news progmg 29.5 hrs wkly
Jim White, Station Manager
Gaston Bates, General Sales Mgr
Rick Aydlett, Chief Engineer
Elaine Cox, Local Sales Manager
Chris Gray, National Sales Manager
Andy Madewell, Creative/Media Services Director
Larissa Fontana, DigitalSales Specialist

WCNC-TV *Digital Channel:* 22; *Virtual Channel:* 36; 791 kw; 1,893 ft.; N35 20 49 W81 10 15
1001 Wood Ridge Center Dr., Charlotte, NC 28217-1901 US
(704) 329-3636; *Fax:* (704) 357-4986
www.wcnc.com
news@wcnc.com
License: Charlotte, Mecklenburg County, NC held by WCNC-TV Inc.
Group Owner: Tegna Media; (acq 12-23-2013).; *Washington Law Firm:* Wiley, Rein & Fielding
Nat'l Network: NBC; *Nat'l Reps:* Harrington, Righter & Parsons
Hours of Local News Weekly: news progmg 38 hrs wkly
Deborah Collura, President and General Manager
Luanne Stuart, Creative Services Director
Matt King, News Director
Steve Kiser, Director of Technology

WHKY-TV *Digital Channel:* 40; *Virtual Channel:* 14; 600 kw; 597 ft.; N35 43 59 W81 19 51
Mailing Address: P.O. Box 1059, Hickory, NC 28603-1059 US
Second Address: 526 Main Avenue S.E., Hickory, NC 28602
(828) 322-1290, (828) 327-9459, (828) 485-5555; *Fax:* (828) 322-8256
www.whky.com
whky@whky.com
License: Hickory, Catawba County, NC held by Long Communications LLC
(acq 12-31-2001; with WHKY(AM) Hickory).; *Washington Law Firm:* Hardy & Carey
Nat'l Network: IND
Size of News Staff: 4; *Hours of Local News Weekly:* news progmg 5 hrs wkly
Thomas Long, General Manager
Jeff Long, Station Manager
Patty Guthrie, General Sales Mgr
Heather Isenhour, Programming Director
Jim Karas, News Director

WJZY *Digital Channel:* 47; *Virtual Channel:* 46; 1000 kW; 1816 ft.; N35 21 44 W81 9 19
3501 Performance Rd., Charlotte, NC 28214 USA
(704) 944-3300
www.fox46charlotte.com
newstips@myfoxcarolinas.com
License: Belmont, Gaston County, NC held by Fox Television Stations LLC
Group Owner: Fox Television Stations Group; (acq 11-87; $1.581 million); *Washington Law Firm:* Fletcher, Heald & Hildreth
Nat'l Network: FOX; *Nat'l Reps:* Millennium Sales & Marketing
Don Travis, Local Sales Manager

WSOC-TV *Digital Channel:* 34; *Virtual Channel:* 9; 1000 kw; 1142 ft.; N35 15 41 W80 43 38
Mailing Address: 3773 Howard Hughes Parkway, Suite 300n, Las Vegas, NV 89109 US
Second Address: 1901 N. Tryon St., Charlotte, NC 28206
(704) 338-9999; *Fax:* (704) 335-4961
www.wsoctv.com
elaine.farias@wsoc-tv.com
License: Charlotte, Mecklenburg County, NC held by WSOC-TV Holdings Inc.
Group Owner: Cox Media Group; (acq 4-13-59; grpsl;
Washington Law Firm: Dow, Lohnes & Albertson
Nat'l Network: ABC; *Nat'l Reps:* TeleRep
Dave Siegler, Operations Dir
Joe Pomilla, General Manager
Kay Hall, Programming Director
Sally Ganz, Promotions Manager
Mark Becker, Anchors & Reporters
Jim bradley, Anchors & Reporters
Steve Udelson, Weather Team
TiffanyWright, Sports Team

***WTVI** *Digital Channel:* 11; *Virtual Channel:* 42; 2.57 kw; 1191 ft.; N35 17 14 W80 41 45
PO Box 35009, Charlotte, NC 28235 US
(704) 372-2442; *Fax:* (704) 335-1358
www.wtvi.org
License: Charlotte, Mecklenburg County, NC held by Charlotte-Mecklenburg Public Broadcasting Authority
Washington Law Firm: Schwartz, Woods & Miller
Nat'l Network: PBS
Elsie Garner, CEO
Regina Berry, Dir. Of Operations/Programming
Amy Burkett, Dir. & General Manager
Tom Green, Chief Engineer
David Rhew, Asst. General Manager
Rick Fitts, Dir. Of Production
Donna Chavis, Carolina BusinessReview
Jay Ahuja, Underwriting
Fatima Acurio-Gonzalez, Membership

***WUNE-TV** *Digital Channel:* 17; *Virtual Channel:* 17; 100 kw; 1791 ft.; N36 3 50 W81 50 33
Mailing Address: 10 TW Alexander Dr., Research Triangle Park, NC 27709-4900 US
Second Address: 10 TW Alexander Dr., Research Triangle Park, NC 27709-4900
(919) 549-7000; *Fax:* (919) 549-7201
www.unctv.org
viewer@unctv.org
License: Linville, Avery County, NC held by University of North Carolina
Washington Law Firm: Schwartz, Woods & Miller
Nat'l Network: PBS
Tom Howe, General Manager

***WUNG-TV** *Digital Channel:* 44; *Virtual Channel:* 58; 160 kw; 1378 ft.; N35 21 30 W80 36 37
Mailing Address: 10 TW Alexander Dr., Research Triangle Park, NC 27709-4900 US
Second Address: 10 TW Alexander Dr, Research Triangle Park, NC 27709-4900
(919) 549-7000; *Fax:* (919) 549-7201
www.unctv.org
viewer@unctv.org
License: Concord, Cabarrus County, NC held by University of North Carolina
Washington Law Firm: Schwartz, Woods & Miller
Nat'l Network: PBS
Tom Howe, General Manager

Greensboro-High Point-Winston Salem, NC (DMA 46)

WCWG *Digital Channel:* 19; *Virtual Channel:* 20; 800 kw; 1890 ft.; N35 52 2 W79 49 26
Mailing Address: 500 S. Chinowth Rd., Visalia, CA 93277 US
Second Address: 2-A Pai Park, Greensboro, NC 27409
(336) 307-4900; *Fax:* (336) 307-4950
License: Lexington, Davidson County, NC held by WCWG License, LLC
Group Owner: Pappas Telecasting Companies; (acq 1995; $4 million); *Washington Law Firm:* Paul, Hastings, Janofsky & Walker LLP
Nat'l Network: CW; *Nat'l Reps:* TeleRep
John Bailie, General Manager
Lynn Bailie, General Sales Mgr
Cheronda Jones, Programming Director
Chris Balash, Promotions Manager
Lindsay Bold, Chief Engineer

WFMY-TV *Digital Channel:* 51; *Virtual Channel:* 2; 1,000 kw; 1,866 ft.; N35 52 13 W79 50 25
1615 Phillips Ave., Greensboro, NC 27405 US
(336) 379-9369; *Fax:* (336) 230-0971
www.wfmynews2.com
news@wfmy.com
License: Greensboro, Guilford County, NC held by WFMY Television LLC
Group Owner: Tegna Media; (acq 2-1-88).
Nat'l Network: CBS; *Nat'l Reps:* TeleRep; *Wire Services:* CBS; AP
Hours of Local News Weekly: news progmg 38 hrs wkly
Larry Audas, President and General Manager
Dan Scutari, Director of Sales
David Reeve, Director of Marketing
Bob Clinkingbeard, News Director
Grant Gilmore, Chief Meteorologist

WGHP *Digital Channel:* 35; *Virtual Channel:* 8; 300 kw vis; ant 1,305t/1,217g; N35 48 46 W79 50 29; *Population Served:* 533,300
2005 Francis St., High Point, NC 27263 USA
(336) 841-8888
myfox8.com
License: High Point, Guilford County, NC held by WGHP License LLC
Group Owner: Tribune Media
Nat'l Network: FOX; *Nat'l Reps:* Katz/Millennium; *Wire Services:* AP
Size of News Staff: 75; *Hours of Local News Weekly:* 46.5
Jim Himes, General Manager
Ben Oldham, General Sales Mgr
Kevin Daniels, VP, News
Bob Ladka, VP, Finance
Zack Greer, VP, Engineering & Operations
Stephanie Doyle, Executive Producer, Digital & Social Media

WGPX-TV *Digital Channel:* 14; 95 kw; 840t/500g; N36 14 54 W79 39 21
1114 N. O'Henry Blvd., Greensboro, NC 27405 USA
(336) 272-9227; *Fax:* (336) 272-9298
www.iontelevision.com
License: Burlington, Alamance County, NC held by Ion Media Greensboro License, Inc.
Group Owner: Ion Media Networks; *Washington Law Firm:* Baraff, Koerner, Olender & Hochberg
Nat'l Network: ION Television
Dana Lambert, Station Manager

WLXI *Digital Channel:* 43; 501 kw vis, 50 kw aur; 573t/499g; N36 08 58 W80 03 21; *Population Served:* 2,500,000
Mailing Address: 11717 Rt. 37, PO Box 1010, Marion, IL 62959
Second Address: P.O. Box 1220, Fort Erie, ON L2A 5Y2
(618) 997-4700, (800) 232-9855; *Fax:* (618) 993-9778
www.tct.tv
today@tct.tv
License: Greensboro, Guilford County, NC held by Radiant Life Ministries Inc.
Group Owner: Tri-State Christian Television; (acq 10-7-91; $1.9 million; *Washington Law Firm:* Joseph E. Dunne III
Garth W. Coonce, President
Larry Patton, General Manager
Gil Couch, Chief Engineer
Tina Coone, Co-Founder & Vice-President

WMYV *Digital Channel:* 33; *Virtual Channel:* 48; 700 kw; 1886 ft.; N35 52 3 W79 49 26
Mailing Address: 3500 Myer Lee Dr., Winston-Salem, NC 27101 US
Second Address: 10706 Beaver Dam Rd., Hunt Valley, MD 21030
(336) 722-4545; *Fax:* (336) 723-8217
www.my48.tv
License: Greensboro, Guilford County, NC held by WUPN Licensee LLC
Group Owner: Sinclair Broadcast Group Inc.; (acq 1-9-2002; $50,000 and cancellation of debt).; *Washington Law Firm:* Arter & Hadden
Nat'l Network: MYTV; *Nat'l Reps:* Millennium Sales & Marketing
Hours of Local News Weekly: news progmg 7 hrs wkly
Greg Conner, General Manager
Matt Bowman, General Sales Mgr
Jeanette Pruitt, Programming Director
Jim Hartline, Engineering Dir

***WUNL-TV** *Digital Channel:* 32; *Virtual Channel:* 26; 575 kw; 1637 ft.; N36 22 31 W80 22 18
Mailing Address: 10 TW Alexander Dr., Research Triangle Park, NC 27709-4900 US
Second Address: 10 TW Alexander Dr., Research Triangle Park, NC 27709-4900
(919) 549-7000; *Fax:* (919) 549-7201
www.unctv.org
viewer@unctv.org
License: Winston-Salem, Forsyth County, NC held by University of North Carolina
Washington Law Firm: Schwartz, Woods & Miller
Nat'l Network: PBS
Tom Howe, General Manager

WXII-TV *Digital Channel:* 31; *Virtual Channel:* 12; 815 kw; 1877 ft.; N36 22 31 W80 22 26
700 Coliseum Drive, Winston-Salem, NC 27106 US
(336) 721-9944; *Fax:* (336)721-0856
www.wxii12.com
License: Winston-Salem, Forsyth County, NC held by WXII Hearst Television Inc.
Group Owner: Hearst Television Inc.; (acq 3-18-99; grpsl).; *Washington Law Firm:* Brooks, Pierce, McLendon, Humphrey & Leonard
Nat'l Network: NBC
Henry Price, General Manager
Mark Strand, Promotions Manager
Barry Klaus, News Director
John Norvell, Chief Engineer

WXLV-TV *Digital Channel:* 29; *Virtual Channel:* 45; 990 kw; 1890 ft.; N35 52 3 W79 49 26
Mailing Address: 3500 Myer Lee Dr., Winston-Salem, NC 27101 US
Second Address: 10706 Beaver Dam Rd., Hunt Valley, MD 21030
(336) 722-4545; *Fax:* (336) 723-8217
www.abc45.com
License: Winston-Salem, Forsyth County, NC held by WXLV Licensee LLC
Group Owner: Sinclair Broadcast Group Inc.; (acq 12-10-01; grpsl).; *Washington Law Firm:* Arter & Hadden
Nat'l Network: ABC
Hours of Local News Weekly: news progmg 2.5 hrs wkly
Greg Conner, General Manager
Matt Bowman, General Sales Mgr
Jeanette Pruitt, Programming Director
Jim Hartline, Engineering Dir

Greenville-New Bern-Washington, NC (DMA 100)

WCTI-TV *Digital Channel:* 12; *Virtual Channel:* 12; 32.8 kw; 1932 ft.; N35 6 15 W77 20 12
225 Glenburnie Drive, New Bern, NC 28560 US
(252) 638-1212; *Fax:* (252) 637-4141
news@wcti12.com
License: New Bern, Craven County, NC held by Newport License Holdings Inc.
(acq 6-15-2004; $4 million); *Ownership:* Bonten Media Group, LLC; *Washington Law Firm:* Koteen & Naftalin
Nat'l Network: ABC; *Nat'l Reps:* Continental Television Sales
Eric Hardtle, Operation Manager
Lyle R. Schulze, VP & General Manager
Joe Carriere, National Sales Manager
Carolyn Stevens, Programming Director
Scott Nichols, News Director
Ken Hughes, Chief Engineer
Lisa Leonard, SalesManager
Josephine Brinkley, Controller
Chris Yu , Website Manager
Wes Goforth, News Anchor
Valentina Wilson, News Anchor
Brian North, News Anchor

WEPX-TV *Digital Channel:* 51; 271 kw; N35 24 9 W77 25 10
1301 S. Glenburnie Rd., New Bern, NC 28562 USA
(888) 467-2988; *Fax:* (561) 659-4754
www.iontelevision.com
License: Greenville, NC held by Ion Media Greenville License, Inc.
Group Owner: ION Media Networks Inc.
Nat'l Network: ION Television
Brandon Burgess, Chairman/CEO

WFXI *Digital Channel:* 8; *Virtual Channel:* 8; 22.4 kw; 812 ft.; N34 53 1 W76 30 22
7621 Little Avenue, Suite 506, Charlotte, NC 28266 US
(252) 638-1212; *Fax:* (252) 637-4141
www.fox8fox14.com
License: Morehead City, Carteret County, NC held by Esteem Broadcasting of North Carolina LLC.
Group Owner: Esteem Broadcasting; (acq 12-31-2007; $5.885 million wtih WYDO(TV) Greenville); *Washington Law Firm:* Cohn & Marks
Nat'l Network: FOX
Hours of Local News Weekly: News progmg 4 hrs wkly
David Bailey, President
Erick Hardtle, Operations Dir
Lisa Leonard, Station Manager
Joe Carriere, General Sales Mgr
Carolyn Stevens, Programming Director
Walt Young, Promotions Manager
Shane Moreland, News Director
Ken Hughes,Chief Engineer
Charlotte Cohen, General Sales Manager

WITN *Digital Channel:* 32; *Virtual Channel:* 7; 795 kW; 605/597 meters; N35 21 55 W77 23 38; *Population Served:* 1,388,000
203 West Main St., Washington, NC 27889 USA
(252) 439-7777
www.witn.com
License: Washington, Beaufort County, NC held by Gray Television Licensee LLC
Group Owner: Gray Television Inc.; *Washington Law Firm:* Wiley Rein LLP
Nat'l Network: NBC; MyNetworkTV; Me-TV; *Nat'l Reps:* Self-repped; *Wire Services:* AP
Size of News Staff: 28; *Hours of Local News Weekly:* news progmg 28.5 hrs wkly
Michael Riddle, Operations Manager
Mark Gentner, General Manager
Ron Henslee, Sales Manager
Stephanie Shoop, News Director

WNCT-TV *Digital Channel:* 10; *Virtual Channel:* 9; 35 kw; 1886 ft.; N35 21 55 W77 23 38
3221 S. Evans At., Greenville, NC 27834 US
(252) 355-8500, (252) 355-8542; *Fax:* (252) 355-8568
www.wnct.com
newsdesk@wnct.com
License: Greenville, Pitt County, NC held by Media General Broadcasting Inc.
Group Owner: Media General Broadcast Group; (acq 3-21-97; grpsl).; *Washington Law Firm:* Dow, Lohnes & Albertson
Nat'l Network: CBS; CW; *Nat'l Reps:* Harrington, Righter & Parsons
Vickie Jones, General Manager
Johnny Lewis, Sales Manager
Ingrid Johansen, News Director
Bertie Cartwright, Chief Engineer
William A. Morrisette, Business Manager
Marc Morriston, Marketing
Wade Poorman, Production Manager
AmieHudspeth, Asst. News Diretcor
George Crocker, Online Producer

***WUND-TV** *Digital Channel:* 20; *Virtual Channel:* 2; 543 kw; 1601 ft.; N35 54 0 W76 20 45
Mailing Address: 10 TW Alexander Dr., Research Triangle Pk, NC 27709-4900 US
Second Address: 10 TW Alexander Dr., Research Triangle Park, NC 27709-4900
(919) 549-7000; *Fax:* (919) 549-7201
www.unctv.org
viewer@unctv.org
License: Edenton, Tyrrell County, NC held by University of North Carolina
Nat'l Network: PBS
Tom Howe, General Manager

***WUNK-TV** *Digital Channel:* 23; *Virtual Channel:* 25; 1000 kw; 1152 ft.; N35 33 10 W77 36 6
Mailing Address: 10 T.W. Alexander Drive, Research Triangle Park, NC 27709-4900 US
Second Address: 10 TW Alexander Dr., Research Triangle Park, NC 27709-4900
(919) 549-7000; *Fax:* (919) 549-7201
www.unctv.org
viewer@unctv.org
License: Greenville, Pitt County, NC held by University of North Carolina
Washington Law Firm: Schwartz, Woods & Miller
Nat'l Network: PBS
Size of News Staff: 15; *Hours of Local News Weekly:* news progmg 3 hrs wkly
Tom Howe, General Manager

***WUNM-TV** *Digital Channel:* 19; *Virtual Channel:* 19; 100 kw; 1841 ft.; N35 6 15 W77 20 12
Mailing Address: 10 T.W. Alexander Drive, Research Triangle Park, NC 27709-4900 US
Second Address: 10 TW Alexander Dr, Research Triangle Park, NC 27709-4900
(919) 549-7000; *Fax:* (919) 549-7201
www.unctv.org
viewer@unctv.org
License: Jacksonville, Onslow County, NC held by University of North Carolina
Washington Law Firm: Schwartz, Woods & Miller
Nat'l Network: PBS
Tom Howe, General Manager

WYDO *Digital Channel:* 47; *Virtual Channel:* 14; 200 kw; 1778 ft.; N35 6 15 W77 20 12; *Rebroadcasting:* Satellite of WFXI Morehead City 100%.
7621 Little Avenue, Suite 506, Charlotte, NC 28266 US
(252) 638-1212; *Fax:* (252) 637-4141
www.fox8fox14.com
License: Greenville, Pitt County, NC held by Esteem Broadcasting of North Carolina LLC.

Group Owner: Esteem Broadcasting; (acq 12-31-2007; $5.885 million with WFXXI(TV) Morehead City); *Washington Law Firm:* Wilkinson, Barker, Knauer & Quinn
Nat'l Network: FOX
Lisa Leonard, Station Manager
Shane Moreland, News Director
Ken Hughes, Chief Engineer

Greenville-Spartanburg, SC-Asheville, NC-Anderson, SC (DMA 37)

WLOS *Digital Channel:* 13; *Virtual Channel:* 13; 50 kw; 2787 ft.; N35 25 32 W82 45 25
110 Technology Dr., Asheville, NC 28803 US
(828) 684-1340; *Fax:* (828) 651-4612
www.wlos.com
comments@wlos.com
License: Asheville, Buncombe County, NC held by WLOS Licensee LLC
Group Owner: Sinclair Broadcast Group Inc.; (acq 6-96).; *Washington Law Firm:* Dow, Lohnes & Albertson
Nat'l Network: ABC; *Nat'l Reps:* Harrington, Righter & Parsons
Size of News Staff: 57; *Hours of Local News Weekly:* news progmg 33 hrs wkly
Jack Connors, General Manager
Joe Fishleigh, Director of Sales
Guy Chancey, Promotions Manager
Julie Fries, News Director
Rollin Tompkins, Chief Engineer

***WUNF-TV** *Digital Channel:* 25; *Virtual Channel:* 33; 185 kw; 2615 ft.; N35 25 32 W82 45 25
Mailing Address: 10 TW Alexander Dr., Research Triangle Pk, NC 27709-4900 US
Second Address: 10 TW Alexander Dr., Research Triangle Park, NC 27709-4900
(919) 549-7000; *Fax:* (919) 549-7201
www.unctv.org
viewer@unctv.org
License: Asheville, Buncombe County, NC held by University of North Carolina
Washington Law Firm: Schwartz, Woods & Miller
Nat'l Network: PBS
Tom Howe, General Manager

***WUNW** *Digital Channel:* 27; 50 kw; ant 1,555t/68g; N35 34 06 W82 54 25
Mailing Address: Box 14900, Research Triangle Park, NC 33040
Second Address: 10 TW Alexander Dr, Research Triangle Park, NC 27709
(919) 549-7000; *Fax:* (919) 549-7201
www.unctv.org
viewer@unctv.org
License: Canton, Haywood County, NC held by University of North Carolina
Tom Howe, General Manager

WYCW *Digital Channel:* 45; *Virtual Channel:* 62; 1000 kw; 1821 ft.; N35 13 20 W82 32 58
Mailing Address: 250 International Dr., Spartanburg, SC 29303 US
Second Address: 250 International Dr., Spartanburg, NC 29303
(864) 576-7777; *Fax:* (864) 587-5430
www.carolinascw.com
webmaster@carolinascw.com
License: Asheville, Buncombe County, NC held by Media General Broadcasting of South Carolina Holdings Inc.
Group Owner: Media General Broadcast Group; (acq 1-15-2002; $4.5 million); *Washington Law Firm:* Dow, Lohnes & Albertson
Nat'l Network: CW
Jim Zimmerman, President
Jim Conschafter, Operations Dir
Phil Lane, General Manager
Randy Ingram, Station Manager
Jimmy Lizer, Operations Manager

Jacksonville

WPXU-TV *Digital Channel:* 35; 600 kw; *Rebroadcasting:* Rebroacasts WEPX-TV Greenville 100%.
1301 S. Glenburnie Rd., New Bern, NC 28562 USA
(888) 467-2988; *Fax:* (561) 659-4754
www.iontelevision.com
License: Jacksonville, NC held by Ion Media Jacksonville License, Inc.
Group Owner: ION Media Networks Inc.
Nat'l Network: ION Television
Brandon Burgess, Chairman/CEO

Myrtle Beach-Florence, SC (DMA 102)

***WUNU** *Digital Channel:* 31; *Virtual Channel:* 31; 175 kw; 1047 ft.; N34 47 50 W79 2 42
Mailing Address: 10 TW Alexander Dr., Research Triangle Park, NC 27709-4900 US
Second Address: 10 TW Alexander Dr., Research Triangle Park, NC 27709-4900
(919) 549-7000; *Fax:* (919) 549-7201
www.unctv.org
License: Lumberton, Robeson County, NC held by University of North Carolina
Washington Law Firm: Schwartz, Woods & Miller
Nat'l Network: PBS
Tom Howe, General Manager

Norfolk-Portsmouth-Newport News, VA (DMA 42)

WSKY-TV *Digital Channel:* 9; 100 kw vis; ant 1,030t/1,023g; N36 08 08 W75 49 28; *Population Served:* 1,278,000
220 Salters Creek Rd., Hampton, VA 23661
(757) 382-0004; *Fax:* (757) 382-0365
www.4hamptonroads.com
programming@wsky4.com
License: Manteo, Dare County, NC held by Sky Television LLC (acq 8-19-2002).; *Washington Law Firm:* Leventhal, Senter and Lerman
Glenn Holterhaus, CEO
Tom Powers, Dir. Of Operations
John Cochrane, General Manager
Ed Marlowe, Promotions Manager
Jacquelyn Smullen, CFO
Tom Powers, Operations Vice President
Melissa Haithcock, Account Executive
Kathy yevak,Local Sales Manager

Raleigh-Durham (Fayetteville), NC (DMA 27)

WFPX-TV *Digital Channel:* 36; 1000 kw; 846t/855g; N34 53 05 W79 04 29; *Population Served:* 275,000
3209 Gresham Lake Rd., Suite 151, Raleigh, NC 27615 USA
(910) 843-3884; *Fax:* (910) 843-2873
www.iontelevision.com
License: Fayetteville, NC held by ION Media License Company, LLC
Group Owner: ION Media Networks, Inc.; *Washington Law Firm:* Baraff, Koerner, Olender & Hochberg
Nat'l Network: ION Television
Brandon Burgess, Chairman/CEO

WLFL *Digital Channel:* 27; *Virtual Channel:* 22; 725 kw; 2001 ft.; N35 40 28 W78 31 40
Mailing Address: 3012 Highwoods Blvd., Suite 101, Raleigh, NC 27604 US
Second Address: 10706 Beaver Dam Rd., Hunt Valley, MD 21030
(919) 872-2854; *Fax:* (919) 878-6588
www.raleighcw.com
License: Raleigh, Wake County, NC held by WLFL Licensee LLC
Group Owner: Sinclair Broadcast Group Inc.; *Washington Law Firm:* Shaw, Pittman
Nat'l Network: CW; *Nat'l Reps:* Millennium Sales & Marketing
Size of News Staff: 36; *Hours of Local News Weekly:* news progmg 7 hrs wkly
John Hummel, General Manager
Kim Rivenbark, Promotions Manager
Gary Todd, Engineering Dir

WNCN *Digital Channel:* 17; *Virtual Channel:* 17; 291 kw; 2005 ft.; N35 40 29 W78 31 40
1205 Front St., Raleigh, NC 27609 USA
(919) 836-1717; *Fax:* (919) 836-1687
wncn.com
License: Goldsboro, Wayne County, NC held by Media General Communications Holdings LLC
Group Owner: Media General Inc.; (acq 6-26-2006; grpsl).
Nat'l Network: NBC; *Nat'l Reps:* Harrington, Righter & Parsons
Hours of Local News Weekly: News progmg 30 hrs wkly
Carey Adams, Operations Dir
Doug Hamilton, General Manager
Chris Wilbur, General Sales Mgr
Russell Mizelle, Chief Engineer

WRAL-TV *Digital Channel:* 48; *Virtual Channel:* 5; 1000 kw; 2,064 ft.; N35 40 29 W78 31 40
Mailing Address: P.O. Box 12000, Raleigh, NC 27605 US
Second Address: 2619 Western Blvd., Raleigh, NC 27606
(919) 821-8555; *Fax:* (919) 821-8541
www.wral.com
License: Raleigh, Wake County, NC held by Capitol Broadcasting Co. Inc.
Group Owner: Capitol Broadcasting Co. Inc.; *Washington Law Firm:* Holland & Knight
Nat'l Network: CBS; *Nat'l Reps:* TeleRep; *Wire Services:* NWS (National Weather Service); AP
Size of News Staff: 100; *Hours of Local News Weekly:* news progmg 33 hrs wkly
Leesa Moore, Operations Manager
Steve Hammel, Vice President/General Manager
Jim Rothschild, Station Manager
Laura Stillman, Local Sales Manager
Steve Tanner, Programming Coordinator
Jay Yovanovich, Promotions Manager
Rick Gall,News Director
Peter Sockett, Chief Engineer
Dan Straub, National Sales Manager
Melissa Haefele, Traffic Manager
Shelly Leslie, Creative Director
Chris Coles, Maintenance Coordinator
Marian Bell, Sales Marketing Director
Jeff Suss,Research Director

WRAZ *Digital Channel:* 49; *Virtual Channel:* 50; 1000 kw; 2,015 ft.; N35 40 29 W78 31 40
2619 Western Blvd., Raleigh, NC 27606 US
(919) 595-5050; *Fax:* (919) 595-5028
www.fox50.com
License: Raleigh, Wake County, NC held by WRAZ-TV Inc.
Group Owner: Capitol Broadcasting Co. Inc.; (acq 2000; $1 million); *Washington Law Firm:* Holland & Knight
Nat'l Network: FOX; *Nat'l Reps:* TeleRep
Chris Downey, Operations Dir
Niel Sollod, Local Sales Manager
Joanne Stanley, Programming Director
Kevin Kolbe, Creative Services Director
Jim Gamble, Chief Engineer

WRDC *Digital Channel:* 28; *Virtual Channel:* 28; 725 kw; 1919 ft.; N35 40 35 W78 32 8
Mailing Address: 3012 Highwoods Blvd., Suite 101, Raleigh, NC 27604 US
Second Address: 10706 Beaver Dam Rd., Hunt Valley, MD 21030
(919) 872-2854; *Fax:* (919) 878-6588
www.myrdctv.com
License: Durham, Durham County, NC held by Raleigh (WRDC-TV) Licensee Inc.
Group Owner: Sinclair Broadcast Group Inc.; (acq 11-15-01; $2.3 million in stock).; *Washington Law Firm:* Fisher, Wayland, Cooper, Leader & Zaragoza
Nat'l Network: MYTV; *Nat'l Reps:* Millennium Sales & Marketing
John Hummel, General Manager
Kim Rivenbark, Promotions Manager
Gary Todd, Engineering Dir

WRPX-TV *Digital Channel:* 15; 180 kw; N36 06 11 W78 11 29; *Population Served:* 352,154
3209 Gresham Lake Rd., Suite 151, Raleigh, NC 27615 USA
(919) 827-4800; *Fax:* (919) 876-1415
www.iontelevision.com
License: Rocky Mount, NC held by Ion Media Raleigh License, Inc.
Group Owner: ION Media Networks Inc.; *Washington Law Firm:* Mitchell, Fielstra & Assoc
Nat'l Network: ION Television
Brandon Burgess, Chairman

WTVD-TV *Digital Channel:* 11; *Virtual Channel:* 11; 45 kW; 1965 ft.; N35 40 5 W78 31 59
411 Liberty St., Durham, NC 27701 USA
(919) 683-1111
abc11.com
License: Durham, Durham County, NC held by WTVD Television LLC
Group Owner: ABC Owned Television Stations; *Washington Law Firm:* Wilmer, Cutler & Pickering
Nat'l Network: ABC

***WUNC-TV** *Digital Channel:* 25; *Virtual Channel:* 4; 1000 kw; 1522 ft.; N35 51 59 W79 10 0
Mailing Address: 10 TW Alexander Dr., Research Triangle Pk, NC 27709-4900 US
Second Address: 10 TW Alexander Dr., Research Triangle Park, NC 27709-4900
(919) 549-7000; *Fax:* (919) 549-7201
www.unctv.org
viewer@unctv.org
License: Chapel Hill, Durham County, NC held by University of North Carolina

Washington Law Firm: Schwartz, Woods & Miller
Nat'l Network: PBS
Tom Howe, General Manager

***WUNP-TV** *Digital Channel:* 36; *Virtual Channel:* 36; 125 kw; 1207 ft.; N36 17 27 W77 50 11
Mailing Address: 10 T.W. Alexander Drive, Research Triangle Park, NC 27709-4900 US
Second Address: 10 T W Alexander Dr., Research Triangle Park, NC 27709-4900
(919) 549-7000; *Fax:* (919) 549-7201
www.unctv.org
viewer@unctv.org
License: Roanoke Rapids, Halifax County, NC held by University of North Carolina
Washington Law Firm: Schwartz, Woods & Miller
Nat'l Network: PBS
Tom Howe, General Manager

WUVC-DT *Digital Channel:* 38; *Virtual Channel:* 40; 5,000 kw vis, 500 kw aur; ant 1,842t/1,749g; N35 30 44 W78 58 41;
Population Served: 947,750
Mailing Address: 4505 Falls of the Neuse Rd., Suite 660, Raleigh, NC 27609 US
Second Address: 230 Donaldson St., Fayetteville, NC 28301
(910) 872-7440; *Fax:* (910) 323-3924
www.univision.com
License: Fayetteville, Cumberland County, NC held by WUVC License Partnership G.P.
Group Owner: Univision Communications Inc.; (acq 3-31-2003).;
Washington Law Firm: Brooks, Pierce, McLendon, Humphrey & Leonard
Nat'l Network: Univision (Spanish)
Foreign Language Programming
Randy Falco, President
Jeff Lamb, Chief Engineer

Wilmington, NC (DMA 130)

WECT *Digital Channel:* 44; *Virtual Channel:* 6; 710 kw; 1936 ft.; N34 7 53 W78 11 17
322 Shipyard Blvd, Wilmington, NC 28412 US
(910) 791-8070, (910) 791-6681; *Fax:* (910) 392-1509, (910) 350-6790
www.wect.com
License: Wilmington, New Hanover County, NC held by Raycom America License Subsidiary LLC.
Group Owner: Raycom Media Inc.; (acq 9-12-96; grpsl)
Nat'l Network: NBC; *Nat'l Reps:* Harrington, Righter & Parsons
Regional Reps: Covington & Burling
Will Tapper, News Operations Manager
Gary McNair, Vice President and General Manager
Mark Mendenhall, General Sales Mgr
Donna Lanier, Programming Director
Dave Toma, Promotions Manager
Scott Saxton, News Director
Dan Ullmer,Chief Engineer
Tom Cheatham, News Production Supervisor
Justin West, Assistant News Director
Heather Setzler, Executive Producer and Theater/Arts Reporter
Debra Worley, Digital Content Manager
Ryan Koresko, Chief Photographer
ChrisWinger, Director

WILM-LD *Digital Channel:* 40; *Virtual Channel:* 10; 15 kw; N34 19 16 W78 13 43
3333-G Wrightsville Ave., Wilmington, NC 28403 US
(919) 798-0000; *Fax:* (910) 798-0001
www.wilm-tv.com
contact@wilm-tv.com
License: Wilmington, New Hanover County, NC held by WILM Inc.
Group Owner: Capitol Broadcasting Co. Inc.
Nat'l Network: CBS; *Nat'l Reps:* TeleRep
Constance Henley Knox, General Manager

WSFX-TV *Digital Channel:* 30; *Virtual Channel:* 26; 170.6 kw; 1936 ft.; N34 7 53 W78 11 17
322 Shipyard Blvd., Wilmington, NC 28412 US
(910) 343-8826; *Fax:* (910) 202-0493
www.wsfx.com
tpostema@wsfx.com
License: Wilmington, New Hanover County, NC
Group Owner: American Spirit Media; (acq 9-22-2003; $14 million); *Washington Law Firm:* Baraff, Koerner, Olender & Hochberg
Nat'l Network: FOX; *Nat'l Reps:* MMT
Size of News Staff: 6; *Hours of Local News Weekly:* news progmg 3 hrs wkly
Tom Postema, General Manager
Kimberly Herring, Traffic & Programming Manager
Herschel Howie, Promotions Manager
Bob Bonner, News Director
Dan Ullmer, Chief Engineer
Chrissy Coor, Local Sales Manager
Connie Petway, National/ LocalSales Asst.
Johnny Williams, Sr. Account Executive
Debra Worley, Digital Content Manager
Chelsey Ferrell, Account Executive
Bob Bonner, News anchor

***WUNJ-TV** *Digital Channel:* 29; *Virtual Channel:* 39; 1000 kw; 974 ft.; N34 19 16 W78 13 43
Mailing Address: 10 T.W. Alexander Drive, Research Triangle Park, NC 27709-4900 US
Second Address: 10 TW Alexander Dr., Research Triangle Park, NC 27709-4900
(919) 549-7000; *Fax:* (919) 549-7201
www.unctv.org
viewer@unctv.org
License: Wilmington, New Hanover County, NC held by University of North Carolina
Washington Law Firm: Schwartz, Woods & Miller
Nat'l Network: PBS
Tom Howe, General Manager

WWAY-TV *Digital Channel:* 24; *Virtual Channel:* 32; 652 kW; 1,935 ft; N34 07 54 W78 11 16; *Population Served:* 120,284
615 N Front St, Wilmington, NC 28401 USA
(910) 762-8581; *Fax:* (910) 762-8367
www.wwaytv3.com
newsroom@wwaytv3.com
License: Wilmington, New Hanover County, NC held by WWAY-TV, LLC
Group Owner: Morris Multimedia Inc.; (acq 1-31-2006; grpsl)
Nat'l Network: ABC

North Dakota

Fargo-Valley City, ND (DMA 116)

***KCGE-DT** *Digital Channel:* 16; 105 kw vis; ant 720t/720g; N47 58 38 W96 36 18; *Rebroadcasting:* Satellite of KFME(TV) Fargo, ND
207 N. 5th St., Fargo, ND 58102
(701) 241-6900, (800) 359-6900, (800) 366-6888; *Fax:* (701) 239-7650
www.prairiepublic.org
info@prairiepublic.org
License: Crookston, Polk County, MN held by Prairie Public Broadcasting Inc
Nat'l Network: PBS
John Harris, President & CEO
John Peterson, Operations manager
Steve Wennblom, Program Manager
Jack Anderson, Dir. Of Engineering
John Gast, Finance Dir.
Ann Clark, Development Dir.
Pauline Holmlund, HR
RussellFord-Dunker,Business Development Manager
Barbara gravel, Production Manager
Marie Offutt, Communications Manager

***KFME** *Digital Channel:* 13; *Virtual Channel:* 13; 56.2 kw; 1122 ft.; N47 0 45 W97 11 41
Mailing Address: P.O. Box 3240, Fargo, ND 58108 US
Second Address: 207 N 5th Street, Fargo, ND 58102
(701) 241-6900, (800) 359-6900; *Fax:* (701) 239-7650
www.prairiepublic.org
info@prairiepublic.org
License: Fargo, Cass County, ND held by Prairie Public Broadcasting Inc
Washington Law Firm: Dow, Lohnes & Albertson
Nat'l Network: PBS; *Regional Network:* Prairie Public Television
John Harris, CEO/President
John Peterson, Operations
Ann Clark, General Sales Mgr
Steve Wennblom, Program Manager
Jack Anderson, Engineering Director
Ann Clark, Director of Development
Troy Davis, Membership Manger
BarbaraGravel, Production Manager
Kristin Lindbery, Executive Assistant
Marie Offutt, Communications Manager
Beth Bradley, Business Development Representative

***KGFE** *Digital Channel:* 15; *Virtual Channel:* 2; 22.6 kw; 611 ft.; N47 58 38 W96 36 18; *Rebroadcasting:* Satellite of *KFME Fargo.
Mailing Address: P.O. Box 3240, Fargo, ND 58108 US
Second Address: 207 Norht 5th Street, Fargo, ND 58102
(701) 241-6900, (800) 359-6900; *Fax:* (701) 239-7650
www.prairiepublic.org
info@prairiepublic.org
License: Grand Forks, Grand Forks County, ND held by Prairie Public Broadcasting Inc
Washington Law Firm: Dow, Lohnes & Albertson
Nat'l Network: PBS
John Harris, CEO/President
John Peterson, Operations Manager
Steve Wennblom, Programming Director
Dave Thompson, News Director
Jack Anderson, Director of Engineering
Ann Clark, Director of Development
Troy Davis, MembershipManager
John Gast, Director of Finance
Kristin lindbery, Executive Assistant
Russell Ford Dunker, Business Development Manager
Mike Olsen, Host

***KJRE** *Digital Channel:* 20; *Virtual Channel:* 19; 72.3 kw; 533 ft.; N46 17 56 W98 51 56; *Rebroadcasting:* Satellite of *KFME(TV) Fargo.
Mailing Address: Post Office Box 3240, Fargo, ND 58108 US
Second Address: 207 North 5th Street, Fargo, ND 58102
(701) 241-6900; *Fax:* (701) 239-7650
info@prairiepublic.org
License: Ellendale, Dickey County, ND held by Prairie Public Broadcasting Inc
Washington Law Firm: Dow, Lohnes & Albertson
Nat'l Network: PBS
John Harris, CEO
Steve Wennblom, Programming Director

KJRR *Digital Channel:* 7; *Virtual Channel:* 7; 21.3 kw; 443 ft.; N46 55 27 W98 46 19; *Rebroadcasting:* Satellite of KVRR(TV) Fargo
1108 Pebble Lake Rd., Fergus Falls, ND 58106 US
(218) 739-3331, (800) 332-7142; *Fax:* (701) 277-1830
www.kvrr.com
news@kvrr.com
License: Jamestown, Stutsman County, ND held by Red River Broadcast Co. L.L.C.
Group Owner: Red River Broadcast Co. L.L.C.; *Washington Law Firm:* Crowell & Moring
Nat'l Network: FOX
Kathy Lau, General Manager
Ed Beiswenger, General Sales Mgr
Jim Shaw, News Director/Assignment Editor/Political Analyst
Darren Bjerke, Chief Engineer
Rob Kupec, Chief Meterologist
Jim Nelson, Sports Anchor
Aaron Boerner,Reporter/Producer
John Hanson, News photographer
Greg Master, Weekend Weather Forecaster
TJ Nelson, News Anchor/Producer/Reporter

***KMDE** *Digital Channel:* 25; *Virtual Channel:* 25; 134 kw; 802 ft.; N48 3 47.8 W99 20 8.7; *Rebroadcasting:* Satellite of KFME Fargo.
207 N. 5th St., Fargo, ND 58102 US
(701) 241-6900, (800) 359-6900, (800) 366-6888; *Fax:* (701) 239-7650
www.prairiepublic.org
info@prairiepublic.org
License: Devils Lake, Ramsey County, ND held by Prairie Public Broadcasting Inc
Nat'l Network: PBS
John Harris, President & CEO
John Peterson, Operations manager
Steve Wennblom, Program Manager
John Gast, Finance Dir.
Ann Clark, Development Dir.
Pauline Holmlund, HR
RussellFord-Dunker, Business Development Manager
Barbaragravel, Production Manager
Marie Offutt, Communications Manager

KNRR *Digital Channel:* 12; *Virtual Channel:* 12; 4.44 kw; 1401 ft.; N48 59 44 W97 24 28; *Rebroadcasting:* Satellite of KVRR(TV) Fargo
P.O. Box 9115, Fargo, ND 58106 US
(701) 277-1515; *Fax:* (701) 277-1830
www.kvrr.com
License: Pembina, Pembina County, ND held by Red River Broadcast Co. L.L.C.
Group Owner: Red River Broadcast Co. L.L.C.; *Washington Law Firm:* Crowell & Moring
Nat'l Network: FOX

Kathy Lau, General Manager
Ed Beiswenger, General Sales Mgr
Jim Shaw, News Director
Darren Bjerke, Chief Engineer
Randy Vangrud, Account Executive
Kayla Straabe, Account Executive
Dan O'Rourke, Account Executive
Milt Rost,National Sales
Sam Humann, Account Executive
Travis McLaurin, Account Executive

KRDK-DT *Digital Channel:* 38; *Virtual Channel:* 4; 382 kw; 1880 ft.; N47 16 45 W97 20 26
Mailing Address: 1350 21st Ave. S., Fargo, ND 58103 US
Second Address: 600 DeMers Ave., Grand Forks, ND 58201
(701) 282-0444, (701) 772-3481; *Fax:* (701) 232-0493, (701) 772-4070
www.kx4.com
License: Valley City, Barnes County, ND held by Parker Broadcasting of Dakota LLC.
(acq 1-3-2007); *Washington Law Firm:* Cohn & Marks
Nat'l Network: CBS; *Nat'l Reps:* Continental Television Sales
Size of News Staff: 20; *Hours of Local News Weekly:* news progmg 10 hrs wkly
Sean Kelly, Operations Manager
Jim Wareham, President/General Manager
Ron Westrick, General Sales Manager
Jeff Petrik, Programming Director
Wendy Bernier, Promotions Director
Ike Walker, News Director
Ron Barr, Chief Engineer
Lynette Samuelson, Business manager
Shauna Wimer, National Sales Manager
Dan Ness, Account Executive
Mike Morkan, Anchor
Lisa Budeau, Reporter
Christina Craig, Reporter

KVLY *Digital Channel:* 44; 304 kw vis, 45.7 kw aur; 2,000t/2,063g; N47 20 36 W97 17 17; *Population Served:* 577,000
1350 21st Ave. S, Fargo, ND 58103 USA
(701) 772-3481; *Fax:* (701) 772-4070
www.valleynewslive.com
mail@valleynewslive.com
License: Fargo, Cass County, ND held by Gray Television Licensee LLC
Group Owner: Gray Television Inc.; *Washington Law Firm:* Wyrick, Robbins, Yates & Pontin
Nat'l Network: NBC; *Nat'l Reps:* Blair Television; *Wire Services:* AP
Size of News Staff: 36; *Hours of Local News Weekly:* news progmg 16 hrs wkly
Ron Westrick, General Sales Mgr
Ike Walker, News Director

KVRR *Digital Channel:* 19; *Virtual Channel:* 15; 1000 kw; 1243 ft.; N46 40 29 W96 13 40
P.O. Box 9115, Fargo, ND 58106 US
(701) 277-1515; *Fax:* (701) 277-1830
www.kvrr.com
Engineering@kvrr.com
License: Fargo, Cass County, ND held by Red River Broadcast Co L.L.C.
Group Owner: Red River Broadcast Co. L.L.C.; *Washington Law Firm:* Crowell & Moring
Nat'l Network: FOX
Kathy Lau, General Manager
Ed Beiswenger, Sales Manager
Jim Shaw, News Director/Assignment Editor/ Political Analyst
Darren Bjerke, Chief Engineer
Randy Vangrud, Account Executive
Kayla Straabe, Account Executive
Dan O'Rourke,Account Executive
Milt Rost, National Sales
Sam Humann, Account Executive
Travis McLaurin, Account Executive

WDAY-TV *Digital Channel:* 21; *Virtual Channel:* 6; 100 kw vis, 11.4 kw aur; ant 1,150t/1,206g; N47 00 43 W97 11 58;
Population Served: 214,200
301 8th St S., Fargo, ND 58103 US
(701) 237-6500; *Fax:* (701) 241-5368
www.wday.com
License: Fargo, Cass County, ND held by Forum Communications Co.
Group Owner: Forum Communications Co.; (acq 7-20-60; $900,000;
Nat'l Network: ABC; CW
Sue Eider, Television Operations Manager
Mark Prather, General Manager
Carol Anhorn, National Sales Manager
Jeremy Ness, News Production Director
Dave Johnson, Chief Engineer
Lori Becker, Operations Manager of Traffic
MariOssenfort, Director of Broadcast
Bri Bachmeier, Producer
Mike Erickson, Chief Photographer
Kerstin Kealy, Anchor/Producer
Dana Mogck, Anchor/Producer

WDAZ-TV *Digital Channel:* 8; *Virtual Channel:* 8; 19 kw; 1480 ft.; N48 8 18 W97 59 35; *Rebroadcasting:* Satellite of WDAY-TV Fargo.
2220 South Washington, Grand Forks, ND US
(701) 775-2511; *Fax:* (701) 746-8565
www.wdaz.com
License: Devil's Lake, Ramsey County, ND held by Forum Communications Co.
Group Owner: Forum Communications Co.; *Washington Law Firm:* Holland & Knight
Nat'l Network: ABC
Robert Kerr, General Manager
Rob Horken, Station Manager
Josh Rohrer, General Sales Manager
Julie Moravchik, News Director
Jeff Awes, Chief Engineer
Dom Izzo, Sports Director
Phil Neumann, Asst. Sports Director
Amanda Kennedy,Web Producer
Carissa Hunter, Web Producer
Amanda Kennedy, Web Producer
Ryan Moen, WDAZ Account Executive

Minot-Bismarck-Dickinson, ND (DMA 140)

***KBME-TV** *Digital Channel:* 22; *Virtual Channel:* 3; 97.3 kw; 1286 ft.; N46 35 23 W100 48 2; *Rebroadcasting:* Satellite of KFME-TV Fargo, ND
Mailing Address: P.O. Box 3240, Fargo, ND 58108 US
Second Address: 207 N. 5th St., Fargo, ND 58102
(701) 241-6900, (800) 359-6900; *Fax:* (701) 239-7650
www.prairiepublic.org
License: Bismarck, Burleigh County, ND held by Prairie Public Broadcasting Inc
Washington Law Firm: Dow, Lohnes & Albertson
Nat'l Network: PBS
John Harris, CEO/President
John Peterson, Operations Manager
Ann Clark, General Sales Mgr
Steve Wennblom, Program Manager
Dave Thompson, Radio News Director
Jack Anderson, Engineering Director
Marie Offutt, CommunicationsManager
Pauline Holmlund, Human Resources
Kristin Lindbery, Executive assistant
Ann Clark, Director of Development
Troy Davis, Membership Manager
Barbara Gravel, Production Manager

KBMY *Digital Channel:* 16; 75 kw; 950t/649g; N46 35 11 W100 48 20
1811 N. 15th St., Bismarck, ND 58502
(701) 223-1700; *Fax:* (701) 258-0886
www.abc17.tv
abc@abc17.tv
License: Bismarck, Burleigh County, ND held by KBMY-KMCY LLC.
Group Owner: Forum Communications Co.; *Washington Law Firm:* Marmet & McCombs
Nat'l Network: ABC
Mark Prather, General Manager
Tony Kruckenberg, Chief Engineer

***KDSE** *Digital Channel:* 9; *Virtual Channel:* 9; 30.3 kw; 782 ft.; N46 43 35 W102 54 57; *Rebroadcasting:* Satellite of KFME(TV) Fargo.
P. O. Box 3240, Fargo, ND 58108 US
(701) 241-6900; *Fax:* (701) 239-7650
info@prairiepublic.org
License: Dickinson, Stark County, ND held by Prairie Public Broadcasting Inc
Washington Law Firm: Dow, Lohnes & Albertson
Nat'l Network: PBS
John Harris, CEO
Steve Wennblom, Programming Director

KFYR *Digital Channel:* 31; *Virtual Channel:* 5; 500 kw; 1276 ft.; N46 36 20 W100 48 22
200 N 4th St., Bismarck, ND 58501 USA
(701) 255-5757; *Fax:* (701) 255-8220
www.kfyrtv.com
kfyrtv@kfyrtv.com
License: Bismarck, Burleigh County, ND held by Gray Television Licensee LLC
Group Owner: Gray Television Inc.; *Washington Law Firm:* Hogan & Hartson
Nat'l Network: NBC; FOX
Size of News Staff: 29; *Hours of Local News Weekly:* news progmg 24 hrs wkly
Barry Schumaier, General Manager
Jim Sande, Programming Director
Richard Farley, Chief Engineer

KMCY *Digital Channel:* 14; 40kw; 2,720t/649g; N48 03 13 W101 23 05
2121 2nd ST SE, Minot, ND 58701
(701) 838-6614
www.abc14.tv
License: Minot, Ward County, ND held by KBMY-KMCY LLC.
Group Owner: Forum Communications Co.
Nat'l Network: ABC
Mark Prather, General Manager
Anton Kruckenberg, Chief Engineer

KMOT *Digital Channel:* 10; *Virtual Channel:* 10; 7.69 kw; 679 ft.; N48 12 56 W101 19 5
1800 SW 16th St., Minot, ND 58701 USA
(701) 852-4101; *Fax:* (701) 838-8195
www.kfyrtv.com
news@kmot.com
License: Minot, Ward County, ND held by Gray Television Licensee LLC
Group Owner: Gray Television Inc.; *Washington Law Firm:* Hogan & Hartson
Nat'l Network: NBC; FOX; Me-TV
Jim Sande, Programming Director
Nicole DesRosier, News Director
Richard Farley, Chief Engineer

KNDB *Digital Channel:* 26; *Virtual Channel:* 26; 50 kw; 984 ft.; N46 35 23 W100 47 39
805 Weightman St., Greenwood, MS 38930 US
(662) 822-1655
License: Bismarck, Burleigh County, ND held by Legacy Broadcasting. LLC
Group Owner: Legacy Broadcasting, LLC
Nat'l Network: FOX
Sherry Nelson, President

KNDM *Digital Channel:* 24; *Virtual Channel:* 24; 50 kw; 784 ft.; N48 3 14 W101 26 3; *Rebroadcasting:* Satellite of KNDB-TV Bismarck, ND
805 Weightman St., Greenwood, MS 38930 US
(662) 822-1655
License: Minot, Ward County, ND held by Legacy Broadcasting, LLC
Group Owner: Legacy Broadcasting, LLC
Sherry Nelson, President

KQCD *Digital Channel:* 7; *Virtual Channel:* 7; 11.3 kw; 673 ft.; N46 56 53 W102 59 25; *Rebroadcasting:* Satellite of Bismarck KFYR(TV)
373 21st St. E, Dickinson, ND 58601 USA
(701) 483-7777; *Fax:* (701) 483-8231
www.kfyrtv.com
kqcd@kqcd.com
License: Dickinson, Stark County, ND held by Gray Television Licensee LLC
Group Owner: Gray Television Inc.; *Washington Law Firm:* Hogan & Hartson
Nat'l Network: NBC
Jim Sande, Programming Director
Richard Farley, Chief Engineer

***KSRE** *Digital Channel:* 40; *Virtual Channel:* 6; 146 kw; 818 ft.; N48 3 2 W101 23 25; *Rebroadcasting:* Satellite of KFME Fargo.
207 North 5th Street, Fargo, ND 58102 US
(701) 241-6900; *Fax:* (701) 239-7650
www.prairiepublic.org
info@prairiepublic.org
License: Minot, Ward County, ND held by Prairie Public Broadcasting
Washington Law Firm: Dow, Lohnes & Albertson
Nat'l Network: PBS
John Harris, President/CEO
John Peterson, Operations Manager
Steve Wennblom, Programming Director
Jack Anderson, Director of Engineering
Mark Antonishin, Business Development Representative
Troy Davis, Membership Manager

KUMV *Digital Channel:* 8; *Virtual Channel:* 8; 6 kw; 1050 ft.; N48 8 2 W103 51 36; *Rebroadcasting:* Satellite of Minot KMOT(TV)
Mailing Address: PO Box 1287, Williston, ND 58801 USA
Second Address: 602 Main St., Willinston, ND 58801
(701) 572-4676; *Fax:* (701) 572-0118
www.kfyrtv.com
kumv@kumv.com
License: Williston, Williams County, ND held by Gray Television Licensee LLC
Group Owner: Gray Television Inc.
Nat'l Network: NBC
Size of News Staff: 2; *Hours of Local News Weekly:* news progmg 6 hrs wkly
Darrell Olsen, General Manager
Jim Sande, Programming Director
Richard Farley, Chief Engineer

***KWSE** *Digital Channel:* 11; *Virtual Channel:* 4; 84.9 kw; 912 ft.; N48 8 30 W103 53 34; *Rebroadcasting:* Satellite of KFME(TV) Fargo.
Mailing Address: 207 N 5th Street, Fargo, ND 58102 US
Second Address: PO Box 3240, Fargo, ND 58108
(701) 241-6900; *Fax:* (701) 239-7650
www.prairiepublic.org
info@prairiepublic.org
License: Williston, Williams County, ND held by Prairie Public Broadcasting Inc
Washington Law Firm: Dow, Lohnes & Albertson
Nat'l Network: PBS
John Harris, President & CEO
John Peterson, Operations Manager
Steve Wennblom, Program Manager
Dave Thompson, News Director
Jack Anderson, Director of Engineering
Ann Clark, Director of Development
Bob Dambach, Director ofTelevision
Troy Davis, Membership Manager
Barbara Gravel, Production Manager
John Gast, Director of Finance

KXMA-TV *Digital Channel:* 19; *Virtual Channel:* 2; 150 kw; 712 ft.; N46 43 35 W102 54 57
Box 1617 1811 N 15th St., Bismark, ND 58501 US
(701) 223-9197; *Fax:* (701) 223-3320
www.kxnet.com
treiten@kxnet.com
License: Dickinson, Stark County, ND held by Reiten Television Inc.
Group Owner: Reiten Television Inc.; (acq 12-4-84; $362,500);
Washington Law Firm: Fisher, Wayland, Cooper, Leader & Zaragoza
Nat'l Network: CBS
Mark Enderle, Operations Dir
Tim Reiten, General Manager
Julie Bernhardt, National Regional Sales Manager
Jim Olson, News Director
Rocky Hefty, Chief Engineer
Kathleen Reiten, Public Service Director
Tia Streeter, SportsDirector
Tammy Blumhagen, Corporate Sales Manager
Bonnie Campo, Anchor/Reporter
Jennifer Kleen, Anchor/Reporter
Tim Olson, Weather Anchor

KXMB-TV *Digital Channel:* 12; *Virtual Channel:* 12; 19.1 kw; 1458 ft.; N46 35 23 W100 48 20
Box 1617 1811 N 15th St., Bismark, ND 58501 US
(701) 223-9197; *Fax:* (701) 223-3320
www.kxnet.com
treiten@kxnet.com
License: Bismarck, Burleigh County, ND held by Reiten Television Inc.
Group Owner: Reiten Television Inc.; (acq 1-27-71; $1.2 million);
Washington Law Firm: Fisher, Wayland, Cooper, Leader & Zaragoza
Nat'l Network: CBS
Size of News Staff: 11; *Hours of Local News Weekly:* news progmg 9 hrs wkly
Janean Rambaugh, Operations Dir
Tim Reiten, General Manager
Julie Bernhardt, National Regional Sales Manager
Jim Olson, News Director
Rocky Hefty, Chief Engineer
Kathleen Reiten, Public Service Director
Tia Streeter, SportsDirector
Tammy Blumhagen, Corporate Sales Manager
Bonnie Campo, Anchor/Reporter
Jennifer Kleen, Anchor/Reporter
Tim Olson, Weather Anchor

KXMC-TV *Digital Channel:* 13; *Virtual Channel:* 13; 16.1 kw; 1096 ft.; N48 3 0 W101 20 32
Mailing Address: 2121 2nd St SE, Minot, ND 58701 US
Second Address: 2121 2nd St. SE, Minot, ND 58701
(701) 852-2104; *Fax:* (701) 838-9360
www.kxnet.com
treiten@kxnet.com
License: Minot, Ward County, ND held by Reiten Television Inc.
Group Owner: Reiten Television Inc.; (acq 7-31-74; *Washington Law Firm:* Davis Wright Tremaine
Nat'l Network: CBS; *Nat'l Reps:* Continental Television Sales
Size of News Staff: 10; *Hours of Local News Weekly:* news progmg 9 hrs wkly
Tim Reiten, General Manager
Julie Bernhardt, National Regional Sales Manager
Jim Olson, News Director
Rocky Hefty, Chief Engineer
Kathleen Reiten, Public Service Director
Tia Streeter, Sports Director
Tammy Blumhagen, CorporateSales Manager
Bonnie Campo, Anchor/Reporter
Jennifer Kleen, Anchor/Reporter
Tim Olson, Weather Anchor

KXMD-TV *Digital Channel:* 14; *Virtual Channel:* 11; 100 kw; 843 ft.; N48 8 30 W103 53 34
Mailing Address: Box 1802 13th Ave. West, Williston, ND 58801 US
Second Address: 1802 13th Ave. W., Williston, NC 58801
(701) 572-2345; *Fax:* (701) 572-0658
www.kxnet.com
treiten@kxnet.com
License: Williston, Williams County, ND held by Reiten Television Inc.
Group Owner: Reiten Television Inc.; *Washington Law Firm:* Fisher, Wayland, Cooper, Leader & Zaragoza
Nat'l Network: CBS
Tim Reiten, General Manager
Julie Bernhardt, National Regional Sales Manager
Jim Olson, News Director
Rocky Hefty, Chief Engineer
Kathleen Reiten, Public Service Director
Tia Streeter, Sports Director
Tammy Blumhagen, CorporateSales Manager
Bonnie Campo, Anchor/Reporter
Jennifer Kleen, Anchor/Reporter
Tim Olson, Weather Anchor

Ohio

Charleston-Huntington, WV (DMA 70)

***WOUB-TV** *Digital Channel:* 27; 1,000 kw vis, 100 kw aur; 800t/856g; N39 18 50 W82 08 54; *Population Served:* 151,000
35 S. College St., Athens, OH 45701
(740) 593-1771, (800) 456-0244; *Fax:* (740) 593-0240
www.woub.org
woub@woub.org
License: Athens, Athens County, OH held by Ohio University
Washington Law Firm: Dow, Lohnes & Albertson
Nat'l Network: PBS; *Regional Network:* Ohio Educ. Telecommunications
Size of News Staff: 3; *Hours of Local News Weekly:* news progmg 3 hrs wkly
Sue Cyran, Dir. Of Business Operations
Thomas Hodson, Director and General Manager
Loring Lovett, General Sales Mgr
Joan Butcher, Dir. Of Program Srvices/Chief to Staff
Tim Sharp, News Director
Ted Ross, Engineering Dir.
SteveSkidmore, CTO
Mark Brewer, Chief Content Officer
Jeannie Jeffers, Development Director
Jeffery Harmison, broadcast IT Supervisor
Tim Myers, Dir. Of Digital Delivery
Rusty Smith, Dir. ofRadio

***WPBO** *Digital Channel:* 43; *Virtual Channel:* 42; 50 kw; 1253 ft.; N38 45 42 W83 3 41; *Rebroadcasting:* Rebroadcasts WOSU-TV Columbus 100%.
2400 Olentangy River Rd, Columbus, OH 43210-1027 US
(614) 292-9678, (614) 292-9678; *Fax:* (614) 292-7625, (614) 292-0513
www.wosu.org
info@wosu.org
License: Portsmouth, Scioto County, OH held by The Ohio State University
Washington Law Firm: Dow, Lohnes & Albertson
Nat'l Network: PBS
Foreign Language Programming
Karen Olstad, COO
Mary Alice Akins, Sr. Dir. Of Operations
Tom Rieland, General Manager
Stacia Hehentz, Station Manager
Doug Partusch, General Sales Mgr
Stacia Hentz, TV program Dir.
Michael Thompson, News & Public AffairsDir.
Brent Davis, Sr. Dir. Of Content
Meredith Hart, Dir. Of Marketing & Communications
David Carwile, Dir. Of Planning & Initiatives
Christine Sadic, Manager of Underwriting
Amy Milbourne, Dir. Of Advancement
Nick Houser, Digital MediaDirector

WQCW *Digital Channel:* 17; *Virtual Channel:* 30; 1000 kw; 1299 ft.; N38 30 21 W82 12 33
Mailing Address: 1732 Dunraven, Knoxville, TN 37922 US
Second Address: 400 Capitol St., Charleston, WV 25301
(740) 353-3391; *Fax:* (740) 353-3372
www.tristatescw.com
License: Portsmouth, Scioto County, OH held by Mountain TV L.L.C.
Group Owner: Lockwood Broadcast Group; (acq 7-11-2002).
Nat'l Network: CW
Dave Hanna, President
William White, General Manager
Vince Wardell, General Sales Mgr

Cincinnati, OH (DMA 36)

***WCET** *Digital Channel:* 34; *Virtual Channel:* 48; 400 kw; 1070 ft.; N39 7 27 W84 31 18
1223 Central Parkway, Cincinnati, OH 45214-2812 US
(513) 381-4033; *Fax:* (513) 381-7520
www.cetconnect.org
comments@cetconnect.org
License: Cincinnati, Hamilton County, OH held by Greater Cincinnati TV Educational Foundation
Washington Law Firm: Dow, Lohnes & Albertson
Nat'l Network: PBS
Al Leland, Chairman
David Fogarty, Ex-Officio
Ricardo Ang, Operations Dir
Sherry Sargeant, General Sales Mgr
Brian Snape, Promotions Manager
Neal Schmidt, Chief Engineer
Steve Black, Vice Chair
Troy Snider, Treasurer
SusieWoodhull, Secretary
Barbara Bushman, Trustee
Mark Casella, Trustee
Terry Foy, Trustee

WCPO-TV *Digital Channel:* 22; *Virtual Channel:* 9; 880 kw; 984 ft.; N39 7 30 W84 29 56
1720 Gilbert Ave., Cincinnati, OH 45202 US
(513) 721-9900, (513) 852-4026, (513) 852-4049; *Fax:* (513) 721-7717, (513) 852-4068, (513) 852-4066
www.wcpo.com
newsdesk@wcpo.com
License: Cincinnati, Hamilton County, OH held by Scripps Howard Broadcasting Co.
Group Owner: The E. W. Scripps Co.; *Washington Law Firm:* Baker & Hostetler
Nat'l Network: ABC; *Wire Services:* UPI
Size of News Staff: 70; *Hours of Local News Weekly:* news progmg 24 hrs wkly
Bill Fee, General Manager
Bill Fee, Programming Director
Joe Martinelli, Engineering Dir
Katherine Nero, Anchor
Steve Raleigh, Chief Meterologist,Weather Team
John Matarese, Reporter
John Popovich, Sports
Kareem Elgazzar,Digital Reporters
Maxim Alter, Web Editor

WKRC-TV *Digital Channel:* 12; *Virtual Channel:* 12; 15.55 kw; 1001 ft.; N39 6 59 W84 30 7
Mailing Address: 1906 Highland Ave., Cincinnati, OH 45219 US
Second Address: 10706 Beaver Dam Rd., Hunt Valley, MD 21030
(513) 763-5500; *Fax:* (513) 421-3820
www.local12.com
local12@local12.com
License: Cincinnati, Hamilton County, OH held by WKRC Licensee LLC
Group Owner: Sinclair Broadcast Group Inc.; (acq 3-14-2008; grpsl); *Washington Law Firm:* Covington & Burling
Nat'l Network: CBS; CW; *Nat'l Reps:* TeleRep; *Wire Services:* AP

Hours of Local News Weekly: news progmg 35 hrs wkly
Jon Lawhead, General Manager
Dale Thomas, Local Sales Manager
Kurt Thelen, Engineering Dir

WLWT *Digital Channel:* 35; *Virtual Channel:* 5; 1000 kw; 1019 ft.; N39 7 27 W84 31 18
888 Seventh Avenue, New York, NY 10106 US
(513) 412-5000; *Fax:* (513) 412-6121 (news)
www.wlwt.com
newsdesk@wlwt.com
License: Cincinnati, Hamilton County, OH held by Ohio/Oklahoma Hearst Television Inc.
Group Owner: Hearst Television Inc.; (acq 7-16-97; grpsl).; *Washington Law Firm:* Brooks, Pierce, McLendon, Humphrey & Leonard
Nat'l Network: NBC; *Nat'l Reps:* Eagle Television Sales
Tracy Ahlers, CFO
Richard J. Dyer, President
Mark Diangela, General Sales Mgr
Pete Salkowski, Promotions Manager
Stacy Owens, News Director
Paul Nowakowski, Chief Engineer

***WPTO** *Digital Channel:* 28; *Virtual Channel:* 14; 400 kw; 881 ft.; N39 7 19 W84 32 52
110 S.Jefferson Street, Dayton, OH 45402 US
(937) 220-1600; *Fax:* (937) 220-1642
www.thinktv.org
comments@thinktv.org
License: Oxford, Butler County, OH held by Greater Dayton Public Television Inc
(acq 1975).; *Washington Law Firm:* Dow, Lohnes & Albertson
Nat'l Network: PBS; *Regional Network:* Ohio Educ. Telecommunications
Size of News Staff: 1; *Hours of Local News Weekly:* news progmg one hr wkly
Suzanne O'Brien, CFO
David Fogarty, President
Kitty Lensman, Station Manager
Ed Valles, General Sales Mgr
Gloria Skurski, Programming Director
Kitty Lensman, Promotions Manager
George MacKnight, Engineering/Technical
GeorgeHopstetter, Engineering Manager
Jim Wiener, Dir. Of Broadcast Services
Sue Brinson, Promotions Manager
Kay High, Auction Inquiries
Greg Schell, Corporate Support/ Program Underwriting
Sue Brinson, Communications Manager

WSTR-TV *Digital Channel:* 33; *Virtual Channel:* 64; 360 kw; 1106 ft.; N39 12 1 W84 31 22
10706 Beaver Dam, Cockeysville, MD 21030 US
(513) 641-4400; *Fax:* (513) 242-2633
www.my64.tv
License: Cincinnati, Hamilton County, OH held by Deerfield Media (Cincinnati) Licensee LLC
Group Owner: Deerfield Media; (acq 1996; $11 million);
Washington Law Firm: Cole, Raywid & Braverman
Nat'l Network: MYTV; *Nat'l Reps:* Millennium Sales & Marketing
Jon Lawhead, General Manager
Joe Marino, General Sales Mgr
Rick White, Programming Director
Pete Ferraro, Promotions Manager
Terry Roberts, Engineering Dir
Stefan Schellhas, General Sales Manager
Ashly Richards, ResearchDirector
Laurel Adams, Traffic Manager

Cleveland-Akron (Canton), OH (DMA 19)

WBNX-TV *Digital Channel:* 30; *Virtual Channel:* 55; 1000 kw; 1087 ft.; N41 23 2 W81 41 44
2690 State Road, Cuyahoga Falls, OH 44223 US
(330) 922-5500, (440) 843-5555; *Fax:* (330) 929-2410, (440) 842-5597
www.wbnx.com
License: Akron, Summit County, OH held by Winston Broadcasting Network Inc
(acq 5-20-87; *Washington Law Firm:* Irwin, Campbell & Tannenwald
Nat'l Network: CW; *Nat'l Reps:* Adam Young
Lou Spangler, President
Dave Armstrong, Operations Dir
Eddie Brown, General Manager
Eddie Brown, General Sales Mgr
Colleen Metheney, Programming Director
Duane Sullivan, Promotions Manager
Don Richardson, Chief Engineer
PattyArmstrong, Research Director
Colleen Metheney, Traffic & Billing Manager
Lori Bruch, LSM
Dave Armstrong, Production Manager
Russell Lephew, senior Art Director
Julie Wertheimer, Public Service Director

WDLI-TV *Digital Channel:* 49; *Virtual Channel:* 17; 900 kw; 958 ft.; N41 3 20 W81 35 38
PO Box A, Santa Ana, CA 92711 US
(714) 731-1000, (888) 731-1000; *Fax:* (714) 832-2950
www.tbn.org
wdli@tbn.org
License: Canton, Stark County, OH held by Trinity Broadcasting Network.
Group Owner: Trinity Broadcasting Network; (acq 4-15-86; $4.5 million; *Washington Law Firm:* Joseph E. Dunne III
Nat'l Network: TRINITY BROADCA
Joanne Mann, Station Manager

***WEAO** *Digital Channel:* 50; 250 kW; 1,047t/923g; N40 04 58 W81 38 00; *Rebroadcasting:* Rebroadcasts WNEO(TV) Alliance 100%; *Population Served:* 3,920,000
P.O. Box 5191, 1750 Campus Center Dr., Kent, OH 44240-5191 US
(330) 677-4549, (800) 554-4549; *Fax:* (330) 678-0688
www.westernreservepublicmedia.org
web@WesternReservePublicMedia.org
License: Akron, Summit County, OH held by Northeastern Educational TV of Ohio Inc
Washington Law Firm: Dow, Lohnes & Albertson
Nat'l Network: PBS
Hours of Local News Weekly: News progmg one hr wkly
Dr. Bryan DePoy, Chairperson
Trina Cutter, President and Chief Executive Officer
Don Freeman, Programming Director
Lisa Martinez, Vice President of Marketing and Development
Eileen Korey, Vice-Chairperson
Dr. Mark S. Auburn,Secretary
Eugenia C. Atkinson, Executive Committee
Iris E. Harvey, Executive Committee
David M. Hunter , Executive Committee
Renee S. Pipitone , Executive Committee

WEWS-TV *Digital Channel:* 15; 93.3 kw vis, 10 kw aur; 1,020t/851g; N41 22 27 W81 43 06; *Population Served:* 1,463,900
3001 Euclid Ave., Cleveland, OH 44115 US
(216) 431-5555; *Fax:* (216) 431-3666, (216) 431-3640, (216) 431-4290
www.newsnet5.com
License: Cleveland, Cuyahoga County, OH held by Scripps Howard Broadcasting Co.
Group Owner: The E. W. Scripps Co.; *Washington Law Firm:* Baker & Hostetler
Nat'l Network: ABC; *Nat'l Reps:* Eagle Television Sales; *Wire Services:* Reuters
Hours of Local News Weekly: News progmg 22 hrs wkly
Victoria Regan, General Manager
Brian Archer, Multimedia Journalist
Dave Arnold, Multimedia Journalist
Tracy Carloss, Anchor and reporter
Mark Johnson, Chief meterologist
Josh Boose, Anchor & Reporter
Danita Harris, Anchor

WGGN-TV *Digital Channel:* 42; *Virtual Channel:* 52; 450 kw; 928 ft.; N41 4 30 W82 27 5
3809 Maple Ave., PO Box 247, Castalia, OH 44824 US
(419) 684-5311, (419) 684-5375; *Fax:* (419) 684-5378
www.cfbroadcast.net
License: Sandusky, Erie County, OH held by Christian Faith Broadcasting Inc.
Group Owner: Christian Faith Broadcasting Inc.; *Washington Law Firm:* Joseph E. Dunne III
Nat'l Network: TBN
Shelby Gillam, President
Rusty Yost, General Manager
Roy Billman, Programming Director

WJW *Digital Channel:* 8; *Virtual Channel:* 8; 11 kw; 1122 ft.; N41 21 48 W81 42 58
5800 South Marginal Rd., Cleveland, OH 44103 USA
(216) 432-4240; *Fax:* (216) 391-9559
fox8.com
License: Cleveland, Cuyahoga County, OH held by WJW License LLC
Group Owner: Tribune Media; (acq 7-14-2008; grpsl)
Nat'l Network: FOX

WKYC *Digital Channel:* 17; *Virtual Channel:* 3; 868 kw; 1,008 ft.; N41 23 10 W81 41 21; *Population Served:* 2,800,000
1333 Lakeside Ave., Cleveland, OH 44114 USA
(216) 344-3333; *Fax:* (216) 344-3314
www.wkyc.com
news@wkyc.com
License: Cleveland, Cuyahoga County, OH held by WKYC-TV LLC
Group Owner: Tegna Media; (acq 12-4-95; grpsl).
Nat'l Network: NBC
Micki Byrnes, President and General Manager
Mac Mahaffee, Director of Digital Media Marketing
Brennan Donnellan, News Director
Cory Jackson, Local Sales Manager
Mike Albrecht, Local Sales Manager
Justin Gutschmidt, Digital SalesManager
Monique Jackson, Director of Brand Strategy

WMFD-TV *Digital Channel:* 12; *Virtual Channel:* 68; 14 kw; 591 ft.; N40 45 50 W82 37 4
2900 Park Avenue West, Mansfield, OH 44906 US
(419) 529-5900; *Fax:* (419) 529-2319
www.wmfd.com
comments@wmfd.com
License: Mansfield, Richland County, OH held by Mid-State Television Inc
(acq 5-31-92; *Washington Law Firm:* Fletcher, Heald & Hildreth
Nat'l Network: IND; *Wire Services:* AP; CNN
Size of News Staff: 12; *Hours of Local News Weekly:* news progmg 36 hrs wkly
Gunther Meisse, President
Robert Meisse, Station Manager

WOIO *Digital Channel:* 10; *Virtual Channel:* 19; 3.5 kw; 997 ft.; N41 23 15 W81 41 43
1717 E. 12thSt., Cleveland, OH 44114 US
(216) 771-1943, (800) 929-0132, (216) 367-7216; *Fax:* (216) 515-7152
www.woio.com
License: Shaker Heights, Cuyahoga County, OH held by WOIO License Subsidiary, LLC
Group Owner: Raycom Media Inc.; (acq 8-13-98).; *Washington Law Firm:* Covington & Burling
Nat'l Network: CBS; *Nat'l Reps:* TeleRep
Jim Stunek, Operations Dir
Bill Applegate, VP & General Manager
Renee Morley, General Sales Manager
Lisa McManus, Programming
Rob Boenau, Promotions Manager
Dan Salamone, News Director
Bob Maupin, Chief Engineer
Todd Galloway,Research Director
Karen Bizjak, Business Manager
Jim Stunek, Production Manager
Rob boenau, Marketing Director
Jean niznik, Traffic
Tony Zarrella, Sports

WQHS-DT *Digital Channel:* 34; *Virtual Channel:* 61; 525 kw vis, 200 kw aur; ant 1,160t/1,029g; N41 22 58 W81 42 07; *Population Served:* 3,500,000
2861 W. Ridgewood Dr., Parma, OH 44134
(440) 888-0061
www.univision.com
License: Cleveland, Cuyahoga County, OH held by Univision Cleveland LLC.
Group Owner: Univision Communications Inc.; (acq 5-21-2001; grpsl).; *Washington Law Firm:* Wiley, Rein & Fielding
Nat'l Network: Univision (Spanish); *Wire Services:* UPI
Foreign Language Programming
Randy Falco, President

WUAB *Digital Channel:* 28; *Virtual Channel:* 43; 200 kw; 1106 ft.; N41 22 45 W81 43 12
1717 East 12th Street, Cleveland, OH 44114 US
(216) 771-1943, (800) 929-0132, (216) 367-7216; *Fax:* (216) 515-7152
www.cle43.com
License: Lorain, Lorain County, OH held by WOIO License Subsidiary, LLC
Group Owner: Raycom Media Inc.; (acq 3-2-00).; *Washington Law Firm:* Covington & Burling
Nat'l Network: MNT; *Nat'l Reps:* TeleRep; *Wire Services:* Reuters
Jim Stunek, Operations Dir
Bill Applegate, VP/ General Manager
Renee Morley, General Sales manager
Lisa McManus, Programming Director
Dan Salamone, News Director
Bob Maupin, Chief Engineer
Todd Galloway, Research Director
RobBoenau, Marketing Dir.
Jim Stunek, Production Manager

Tony Zarrella, Sports
Jeff Tanchak, Weather Team

***WVIZ** *Digital Channel:* 26; *Virtual Channel:* 25; 150 kw; 1105 ft.; N41 23 10 W81 41 21
1375 Euclid Ave., Cleveland, OH 44115-1835 US
(216) 916-6100, (877) 399-3307, (216) 916-6301; *Fax:* (216) 916-6123
www.wviz.org
License: Cleveland, Cuyahoga County, OH held by Ideastream
Nat'l Network: PBS
Jerry Wareham, CEO & President
Bob Stern, Station Manager
Kent Geist, General Sales Mgr
David Kanzeg, Programming Dir.
Maureen Paschke, Promotions Manager
John Phillips, CFO
Kit Jensen, COO
Jane Temple, Promotions Director
Mark Smukler, Station Manager
Tom furnas, Sr. Director, Technology
Mark Smukler, Sr. Director, Content

WVPX-TV *Digital Channel:* 23; 1,000 kw; N41 03 53 W81 34 59; *Population Served:* 1,500,000
26650 Renaissance Pkwy., Suite 1A, Warrensville Heights, OH 44128 USA
(216) 344-3333; *Fax:* (216) 344-7430
www.iontelevision.com
License: Akron, OH held by ION Media Akron License, Inc.
Group Owner: ION Media Networks Inc.; *Washington Law Firm:* Dow, Lohnes & Albertson
Nat'l Network: ION Television
Brandon Burgess, Chairman

Columbus, OH (DMA 32)

WBNS-TV *Digital Channel:* 21; *Virtual Channel:* 10; 1000 kw; 915 ft.; N39 58 16 W83 1 40
770 Twin Rivers Drive, Columbus, OH 43215 US
(614) 460-3700, (614) 280-6309; *Fax:* (614) 460-2826
www.10tv.com
License: Columbus, Franklin County, OH held by WBNS TV Inc.
Group Owner: Dispatch Broadcast Group; *Washington Law Firm:* Sidley & Austin
Nat'l Network: CBS
Size of News Staff: 80; *Hours of Local News Weekly:* news progmg 31 hrs wkly
John Cardenas, President
Frank Wilson, Operations Dir
John Cardenas, General Manager
Chuck Devendra, General Sales Mgr
Elbert Tucker, News Director
Pat Ingram, Director of Engineering
Mike Berry, 10TV Productions
Angela Pace,Director of Community Affairs
Chuck DeVendra, Director of Sales
Angela Pace, Public Affairs Director
Patty Williams, Finance director
Carol Triplett, Traffic Manager

WCMH-TV *Digital Channel:* 14; *Virtual Channel:* 4; 902 kw; 866 ft.; N39 58 16 W83 1 40
3165 Olentangy River Road, Columbus, OH 43202 USA
(614) 263-4444, (614)263-5555; *Fax:* (614) 447-9107, (614) 263-0166
nbc4i.com
License: Columbus, Franklin County, OH held by Media General Communications Holdings Inc.
Group Owner: Media General Inc.; (acq 6-26-2006; grpsl).
Nat'l Network: NBC; *Nat'l Reps:* MMT
Size of News Staff: 60; *Hours of Local News Weekly:* news progmg 31.5 hrs wkly
Jennifer Kiser, Operations Dir
Ken Freedman, Vice President & General Manager
Chuck DeVendra, General Sales Mgr

***WOSU-TV** *Digital Channel:* 38; *Virtual Channel:* 34; 503 kw; 1079 ft.; N40 9 33 W82 55 23
2400 Olentangy River Rd, Columbus, OH 43210-1027 US
(614) 292-9678, (614) 247-2475; *Fax:* (614) 292-7625, (614) 292-0513
www.wosu.org
info@wosu.org
License: Columbus, Franklin County, OH held by The Ohio State University
Washington Law Firm: Dow, Lohnes & Albertson
Nat'l Network: PBS
Karen Olstad, COO
Mary Alice Akins, Sr. Dir. Of Operations
Tom Rieland, General Manager
Stacia Hehentz, Station Manager
Doug Partusch, General Sales Mgr
Stacia Hentz, TV Program Dir.
Michael Thompson, News & Public AffairsDir.
Tom Lahr, Chief Engineer
Brent Davis, Sr. Dir. Of Content
Meredith Hart, Dir. Of Marketing & Communications
David Carwile, Dir. Of Planning & Initiatives
Christine Sadic, Manager of Underwriting
Amy Milbourne, Dir. Of Advancement
Nick Houser, Digital Media Director

WSFJ-TV *Digital Channel:* 24; *Virtual Channel:* 51; 724 kw vis, 72.4 kw aur; ant 439t/279g; N40 04 44 W82 41 42;
Population Served: 1,935,300
Mailing Address: PO Box A, Santa Ana, CA 92711
Second Address: P. O. Box 768, Station B, Ottawa, ON K1P 5P8
(714) 731-1000, (888) 731-1000, (714) 832-2950; *Fax:* (740) 548-3815
www.tbn.org
lbell@tbn.org
License: Newark, Licking County, OH held by Trinity Christian Center of Santa Ana, Inc.
Group Owner: Trinity Broadcasting Network; 1-Oct-08;
Washington Law Firm: Colby M. May, Esq., P.C.
Size of News Staff: 1
Art Ratliff, Operations Dir
Linda Bell, Station Manager/Programming Director
Tim Geist, Chief Engineer

WSYX *Digital Channel:* 48; *Virtual Channel:* 6; 1000 kw; 938 ft.; N39 56 14 W83 1 16
Mailing Address: 1261 Dublin Rd., Columbus, OH 43215 US
Second Address: 10706 Beaver Dam Rd., Hunt Valley, MD 21030
(614) 481-6666; *Fax:* (614) 481-6624
www.abc6onyourside.com
news@wsyx6.com
License: Columbus, Franklin County, OH held by WSYX Licensee Inc.
Group Owner: Sinclair Broadcast Group Inc.; (acq 1998; $228 million)
Nat'l Network: ABC; *Nat'l Reps:* Millennium Sales & Marketing
Tony D'Angelo, General Manager
Lorie Luthman, General Sales Mgr
Mike Hansen, Promotions Manager
Jeffrey J. Kinzinger, Digital Sales Manager

WTTE *Digital Channel:* 36; *Virtual Channel:* 28; 1000 kw; 889 ft.; N39 56 14 W83 1 16
Mailing Address: 1261 Dublin Rd., Columbus, OH 43215 US
Second Address: 2000 West 41st St, Baltimore, MD 21211
(614) 481-6666; *Fax:* (614) 481-6624
www.myfox28columbus.com
news@wsyx6.com
License: Columbus, Franklin County, OH held by Columbus (WTTE-TV) Licensee Inc.
Group Owner: Cunningham Broadcasting Corporation; (acq 1-9-2002).
Nat'l Network: FOX; *Nat'l Reps:* Millennium Sales & Marketing
Tony D'Angelo, General Manager
James (Jimmy) Grilli, General Sales Mgr
Ron Taylor, Chief Engineer

WWHO *Digital Channel:* 46; 1,000 kw; 328 meters; N39 35 20 W83 06 44
1160 Dublin Rd., Suite 400, Columbus, OH 20005
(614) 485-5300; *Fax:* (614) 485-5339
License: Chillicothe, Ross County, OH held by Mahan Media Inc. (acq 2-16-2012; $7 million); *Washington Law Firm:* Pillsbury Winthrop Shaw Pittman LLP
Nat'l Network: CW
Ellen Daly, Station Manager

Dayton, OH (DMA 64)

WBDT *Digital Channel:* 26; *Virtual Channel:* 26; 770 kw; 1145 ft.; N39 43 28 W84 15 18
10829 Olive Boulevard, Suite 202, St. Louis, MO 63141 US
(937) 384-9226; *Fax:* (937) 384-7392
daytonscw.com
License: Springfield, Clark County, OH held by WBDT Television LLC
Group Owner: Vaughan Media LLC; (acq 6-14-99; grpsl)
Nat'l Network: CW; *Nat'l Reps:* Harrington, Righter & Parsons
Hours of Local News Weekly: 4
Gregg Abbott, Operations Dir
John Hannon, General Manager
Melanie Simon, General Sales Mgr
Shasta Scarberry, Promotions Manager
Al Schmidt, Chief Engineer
Bonnie Meyers, Business Manager
Billie Sue Adkins, National SalesManager
Brian Mercer, Research & Sales Marketing Director

WDTN *Digital Channel:* 50; *Virtual Channel:* 2; 1000 kw; 1060 ft.; N39 43 7 W84 15 22
4595 S. Dixie Dr., Dayton, OH 45439 US
(937) 293-2101; *Fax:* (937) 296-7147
www.wdtn.com
newstips@wdtn.com
License: Dayton, Montgomery County, OH held by WDTN Broadcasting LLC
Group Owner: LIN Media; (acq 11-8-2002; grpsl).
Nat'l Network: NBC; *Nat'l Reps:* Blair Television
Sharon Howard, Operations Dir
Lisa Barhorst, General Manager
Patrick Donnelly, General Sales Mgr
Jason Doyle, Promotions Manager
Steve Diorio, News Director
Jim Atkinson, Chief Engineer
Shawn MacIntyre, National Sales Manager
Janice Barney, Traffic Manager
Mark Allan, Anchor
Katie Ussin, Anchor
Marsha Bonhart, Anchor
John Seibel, Anchor

WHIO-TV *Digital Channel:* 41; *Virtual Channel:* 7; 1000 kw; 1142 ft.; N39 44 2 W84 14 53
1611 S. Main Street, Dayton, OH 45409 US
(937) 259-2111; *Fax:* (937) 259-2168
www.whiotv.com
Jeremy.Ratliff@coxinc.com
License: Dayton, Montgomery County, OH held by Miami Valley Broadcasting Corp.
Group Owner: Cox Television; *Washington Law Firm:* Dow, Lohnes & Albertson
Nat'l Network: CBS; *Nat'l Reps:* TeleRep
Harry Delaney, Operations Dir
Rob Rohr, General Manager
James Cosby, General Sales Mgr
Jeremy Ratliff, Program Director
Tony Getts, Promotions Manager
David Bennallack, News Director
Chuck Eastman, Operations Manager
JuliaWallace, Market VP
Caryn Golden, Managing Editor
Becky Grimes, Special Projects
Tony Getts, Creative Service Director
James Cosby, VP of Broadcast Sales

WKEF *Digital Channel:* 51; *Virtual Channel:* 22; 515 kw; 1152 ft.; N39 43 28 W84 15 18
2245 Corporate Pl., Miamisburg, OH 45342 US
(937) 263-4500; *Fax:* (937) 268-5265
www.abc22now.com
comments@abc22now.com
License: Dayton, Montgomery County, OH held by WKEF Licensee L.P.
Group Owner: Sinclair Broadcast Group Inc.; (acq 7-7-98; grpsl)
Nat'l Network: NBC
Hours of Local News Weekly: news progmg 17 hrs wkly
Lisa Barhorst, General Manager

***WPTD** *Digital Channel:* 16; *Virtual Channel:* 16; 163 kw; 1129 ft.; N39 43 16 W84 15 0
110 S. Jefferson Street, Dayton, OH 45402 US
(937) 220-1600; *Fax:* (937) 220-1642
www.thinktv.org
comments@thinktv.org
License: Dayton, Montgomery County, OH held by Greater Dayton Public TV Inc
Washington Law Firm: Dow, Lohnes & Albertson
Nat'l Network: PBS; *Regional Network:* Ohio Educ. Telecommunications
Size of News Staff: 1; *Hours of Local News Weekly:* news progmg one hr wkly
David Fogarty, President
Kitty Lensman, Station Manager
Ed Valles, General Sales Mgr
Gloria Skurski, Programming Director
Kitty Lensman, Promotions Manager
George MacKnight, Engineering/Technical
George Hopstetter, EngineeringManager
Jim Wiener, Dir. Of Broadcast Services
Sue Brinson, Promotions Manager
Kay High, Auction Inquiries
Greg Schell, Corporate Support/ Program Underwriting
Sue Brinson, Communications Manager

WRGT-TV *Digital Channel:* 30; *Virtual Channel:* 45; 498 kw; 1152 ft; N39 43 28 W84 15 18
2245 Corporate Pl, Miamisburg, OH 45342 US
(937) 263-4500; *Fax:* (937) 268-5265
www.fox45now.com
comments@fox45now.com
License: Dayton, Montgomery County, OH held by WRGT Licensee, LLC
Group Owner: Cunningham Broadcasting Corporation; (acq 11-15-2001; grpsl).
Nat'l Network: Fox; MyNetworkTV
Hours of Local News Weekly: News progmg 16 hrs wkly
Lisa Barhorst, General Manager

Lima, OH (DMA 189)

WLIO *Digital Channel:* 8; *Virtual Channel:* 35; 27.5 kw; 486 ft.; N40 44 51 W84 7 54.5
1424 Rice Ave., Lima, OH 45805 US
(419) 228-8835; *Fax:* (419) 229-7091
www.hometownstations.com
License: Lima, Allen County, OH held by Lima Communications Corp.
Group Owner: Block Communications Inc.; (acq 2-1-72; $1.5 million); *Washington Law Firm:* Dow, Lohnes & Albertson
Nat'l Network: NBC
Size of News Staff: 17; *Hours of Local News Weekly:* news progmg 24 hrs wkly
Kevin Creamer, General Manager
Kylie Miller, Programming Director
Dan McCormick, Promotions Director
Jeff Fitzgerald, News Director
Fred Vobbe, Chief Engineer
Terry Johns, Production Manager
Sonia Haggerty, Traffic Manager

WTLW *Digital Channel:* 44; *Virtual Channel:* 44; 165 kw; 679 ft.; N40 45 47 W84 10 59
1844 Baty Rd., Lima, OH 45805 US
(419) 339-4444; *Fax:* (419) 339-1736
www.wtlw.com
kbowers@wtlw.com
License: Lima, Allen County, OH held by American Christian Television Services Inc
Washington Law Firm: Wiley, Rein & Fielding
Nat'l Network: IND
Kevin Bowers, CEO
Kevin Bowers, President & General Manager
Kelli Getz, Traffic/Operations
Victoria Kaufaman, General Sales Manager
Jeff Klingler, Chief Engineer
Ron Mighell, Founder
Wayne Getz, Production Manager
Andy Lynch,Sports Director
Nathan Warnecke, Master Control Operator
Doug Dewese, Account Executive

Toledo, OH (DMA 78)

***WBGU-TV** *Digital Channel:* 27; *Virtual Channel:* 27; 153 kw; 1050 ft.; N41 8 12 W83 54 24
245 Troup Street, Bowling Green, OH 43403 US
(419) 372-2700, (888) 892-0010; *Fax:* (419) 372-7048
www.wbgu.org
License: Bowling Green, Wood County, OH held by Bowling Green State University
(acq 11-17-76; *Washington Law Firm:* Cohn & Marks
Nat'l Network: PBS; *Regional Network:* Ohio Educ. Telecommunications
Patrick Fitzgerald, General Manager
Ron Gargasz, Programming Director
Deb Boyce, Promotions Manager
Al Bowe, Chief Engineer
Mike Fitzpatrick, Asst Programming Manager

***WGTE-TV** *Digital Channel:* 29; *Virtual Channel:* 30; 49.5 kw; 1029 ft.; N41 39 26 W83 25 55
Mailing Address: 1270 S. Detroit Ave., P.O. Box 30, Toledo, OH 43614 US
Second Address: P.O. Box 30, Toledo, OH 43614
(419) 380-4600, (419) 380-4613, (419) 380-4747; *Fax:* (419) 380-4710
www.wgte.org
License: Toledo, Lucas County, OH held by Public Broadcasting Foundation of N.W. Ohio
Washington Law Firm: Schwartz, Woods & Miller
Nat'l Network: PBS; *Regional Network:* Ohio Educ. Telecommunications
Daniel T. Anderson, Chairman
Marlon P. Kiser, CEO/President
Barbara Heslop, Operations Dir
Kelly Repka, General Sales Mgr
Darren LaShelle, Programming Director
Jen Homier, Promotions Manager
Dan Niedzwiecki, Dir. OfEngineering
Ron Harrison, CFO
Lindsey Eberly, Director of Major Gifts and Planned Giving
Darren LaShelle, Dir. Of Content & Creative Services
Charlene Patten, Dir. Of Educational Resource Center
Jennifer L. Hildebrand, Vice-Chairperson
Daniel T. Anderson, Chairperson

WLMB *Digital Channel:* 5; *Virtual Channel:* 40; 10 kw; 509 ft.; N41 44 41 W84 1 6
825 Capital Commons Dr., Toledo, OH 43615 US
(419) 720-9562, (800) 218-5740, (419) 720-9562; *Fax:* (419) 720-9563
www.wlmb.com
info@wlmb.com
License: Toledo, Lucas County, OH held by Dominion Broadcasting Inc
Washington Law Firm: Wiley, Rein & Fielding
Nat'l Network: IND
Gary Tipping, Chairman
Jamey Schmitz, President & CEO
Jeff Millslagle, Sr. VP of Operations
Jamey Schmitz, General Manager
Curt MIller, General Sales Mgr
Jeff Millslagle, Programming Director
Dale Dutridge, Sr. Engineer
EricJingst, Sr. Engineer
Bryan Croninger, VP of Production
Joshua Dyer, VP of Commercial Production
Shawn Rames, Sr. VP of Business Affairs
Dan Rogers, Vice-Chairman
Dave Draper, Secretary & Treasurer
Ron Mighell, Founder/Board Member

WNWO-TV *Digital Channel:* 49; *Virtual Channel:* 24; 105 kw; 1342 ft.; N41 40 3 W83 21 22
300 S. Byrne Rd., Toledo, OH 43615 US
(419) 535-0024; *Fax:* (419) 535-0664
www.nbc24.com
news@wnwo.com
License: Toledo, Lucas County, OH held by WNWO Licensee LLC
Group Owner: Sinclair Broadcast Group Inc.; (acq 11-25-2013; grpsl)
Nat'l Network: NBC; *Nat'l Reps:* TeleRep
Hours of Local News Weekly: news progmg 22 hrs wkly
John Nizamis, General Manager
Rich Stewart, Programming Director
Jim Blue, News Director
Jim Joly, Director of National Digital Sales
Greg Siegel, Vice President, National Sales

WTOL *Digital Channel:* 11; *Virtual Channel:* 11; 16.9 kw; 1001 ft.; N41 40 22 W83 22 47
730 North Summit St., Toledo, OH 43604 US
(419) 248-1111, (419) 248-1100, (419) 248-1135; *Fax:* (419) 248-1177, (419) 244-7104
www.wtol.com
news@toledonewsnow.com
License: Toledo, Lucas County, OH held by WTOL License Subsidiary LLC.
Group Owner: Raycom Media Inc.; (acq 1-31-2006; grpsl);
Washington Law Firm: Dow, Lohnes & Albertson
Nat'l Network: CBS; *Nat'l Reps:* Harrington, Righter & Parsons
Size of News Staff: 50; *Hours of Local News Weekly:* news progmg 25 hrs wkly
Bob Chirdon, General Manager
Linda Blackburn, General Sales Mgr
Andi Roman, News Director
Steve Crum, Chief Engineer
Nancy Bright, National Sales Manager
Chrys Peterson, Anchor
Robert shiels, Weather team
Dan Cummins, SportsTeam

WTVG-TV *Digital Channel:* 13; *Virtual Channel:* 13; 16.7 kW; 1012 ft.; N41 41 0 W83 24 49
4247 Dorr St., Toledo, OH 43607 USA
(419) 531-1313; *Fax:* (419) 531-1399
13abc.com
wtvg.news@13abc.com
License: Toledo, Lucas County, OH held by Gray Television Licensee LLC
Group Owner: Gray Television Inc.; *Washington Law Firm:* Koteen & Naftalin
Nat'l Network: ABC; The CW Network
Size of News Staff: 30; *Hours of Local News Weekly:* news progmg 10 hrs wkly
Tamara Rost, Director of Programming & Promotion
Todd Albrecht, National Sales

WUPW *Digital Channel:* 46; 110 kw; 356 meters; N41 39 22 W83 26 41
Four SeaGate, Toledo, OH 33703
(419) 244-3600; *Fax:* (419) 244-8842
www.foxtoledo.com
news@foxtoledo.com
License: Toledo, Lucas County, OH held by WUPW License Sunsidiary LLC
Group Owner: American Spirit Media; (acq 11-8-2002; grpsl).;
Washington Law Firm: Fletcher, Heald & Hildreth PLC
Nat'l Network: Fox; *Nat'l Reps:* Blair Television
Size of News Staff: 5; *Hours of Local News Weekly:* news progmg 5 hrs wkly
Gary Yoder, General Manager
Brian Lorenzen, General Sales Mgr
Cathy Stoner, Programming Director
Betsy Russell, Promotions Manager
Steve France, News Director
Steve Pietras, Engineering Dir

Wheeling, WV- Steubenville, OH (DMA 158)

***WOUC-TV** *Digital Channel:* 35; 759 kw vis; ant 1,263t/1,174g; N40 05 32 W81 17 19; *Rebroadcasting:* Rebroadcasts WOUB-TV Athens 100%.
35 S. College St., Athens, OH 45701
(740) 593-1771, (800) 456-0244; *Fax:* (740) 593-0240
www.woub.org
woub@woub.org
License: Cambridge, Guernsey County, OH held by Ohio University
(acq 12-10-75; *Washington Law Firm:* Cohn & Marks
Nat'l Network: PBS; *Regional Network:* Ohio Educ. Telecommunications
Sue Cyran, Dir. Of Business Operations
Thomas Hodson, Director and General Manager
Loring Lovett, General Sales Mgr
Joan Butcher, Dir. Of Program Srvices/Chief to Staff
Tim Sharp, News Director
Ted Ross, Engineering Dir.
SteveSkidmore, CTO
Mark Brewer, Chief Content Officer
Jeannie Jeffers, Development Director
Jeffery Harmison, broadcast IT Supervisor
Tim Myers, Dir. Of Digital Delivery
Rusty Smith, Dir. ofRadio

WTOV-TV *Digital Channel:* 9; *Virtual Channel:* 9; 30 kw; 925 ft.; N40 20 33 W80 37 14
9 Red Donley Plaza, Steubenville, OH 43952 US
(740) 282-9999; *Fax:* (740) 282-0439
www.wtov9.com
station@wtov.com
License: Steubenville, Jefferson County, OH held by WTOV Licensee LLC
Group Owner: Sinclair Broadcast Group Inc.; (acq 9-22-2000; $58 million); *Washington Law Firm:* Dow,Lohnes & Albertson
Nat'l Network: NBC; *Nat'l Reps:* TeleRep; *Wire Services:* AP
Size of News Staff: 28; *Hours of Local News Weekly:* news progmg 22 hrs wkly
Tim McCoy, General Manager
Tom Pleva, General Sales Mgr
Cory Bayle, Promotions Manager
Don Sloan, News Director
Don Fogle, Chief Engineer

Youngstown, OH (DMA 115)

WFMJ-TV *Digital Channel:* 20; *Virtual Channel:* 21; 460 kw; 968 ft.; N41 4 48 W80 38 25
Mailing Address: 101 West Boardman Street, Youngstown, OH 44503 US
Second Address: PO Box 689, Youngstown, OH 44501-0689
(330) 744-8821, (800) 4TV-WFMJ, (330) 399-5208; *Fax:* (330) 742-2472, (330) 744-1746
www.wfmj.com
License: Youngstown, Mahoning County, OH held by WFMJ Television Inc
(acq 7-14-93; *Ownership:* NPM Inc.; *Washington Law Firm:* Fisher, Wayland, Cooper, Leader & Zaragoza
Nat'l Network: NBC; CW; *Nat'l Reps:* Petry Television Inc.
Regional Reps: OAB; *Wire Services:* AP

Size of News Staff: 30; *Hours of Local News Weekly:* news progmg 20 hrs wkly
John Grdic, Operations Director/General Sales Manager
Jack Stevenson, Promotions Manager
Mona Alexander, News Director
Bob Flis, Chief Engineer
Larry Bell, Chief Photographer
Kathie Brickman, National Sales Manager
Amy Williams,Traffic manager
Charlie Weisel, Asst. Chief Engineer
Madonna Pinkard, Community Relations Director

WKBN-TV *Digital Channel:* 41; *Virtual Channel:* 27; 650 kw; 1444 ft.; N41 3 23.2 W80 38 43.7
7621 Little Avenue, Suite 506, Charlotte, NC 28266 US
(330) 782-1144
www.wkbn.com
License: Youngstown, Mahoning County, OH held by LIN License Company LLC
Group Owner: LIN Media; (acq 10-12-2012; grpsl); *Washington Law Firm:* Paul Hastings LLP
Nat'l Network: CBS; *Nat'l Reps:* Continental Television Sales
Size of News Staff: 50; *Hours of Local News Weekly:* news progmg 25 hrs wkly
John Amann, Operations Dir
David Coy, General Manager
Jill Duffy, General Sales Mgr
Phyllis Rappach, Programming Director
Gary Coursen, News Director
Thomas Zocolo, Chief Engineer
Nikki Manuel, Regional Sales Manager
RyanAllison, Sports Director
Don Guthrie, Weather Director

***WNEO** *Digital Channel:* 45; 500 kW; 830t/770g; N40 54 23 W80 54 40; *Population Served:* 450,000
Box 5191, 1750 Campus Center Dr, Kent, OH 44240-5191
(330) 677-4549, (800) 554-4589; *Fax:* (330) 678-0688
www.westernreservepublicmedia.org
questions@westernreservepublicmedia.org
License: Alliance, Stark County, OH held by Northeastern Educational TV of Ohio Inc
Washington Law Firm: Dow, Lohnes & Albertson
Nat'l Network: PBS
Hours of Local News Weekly: News progmg one hr wkly
Trina Cutter, President and Chief Executive Officer
Anthony Dennis, Operations Manager
Bill O'Neil, Station Manager
Don Freeman, Programming Director
Lisa Martinez, Vice President of Marketing and Development

WYTV *Digital Channel:* 36; *Virtual Channel:* 33; 1000 kw; 581 ft.; N41 3 43 W80 38 7
3930 Sunset Blvd., Youngstown, OH 44512 US
(330) 782-1144, (330) 788-2456; *Fax:* (330) 782-3504, (330) 782-5261
www.wytv.com
License: Youngstown, Mahoning County, OH
Group Owner: Vaughan Media LLC; (acq 8-15-2007);
Washington Law Firm: Drinker Biddle & Reath LLP
Nat'l Network: ABC; MyNetworkTV
Size of News Staff: 26; *Hours of Local News Weekly:* news progmg 20 hrs wkly
Dave Coy, General Manager
Nikki Manuel, General Sales Mgr
Cheryl Huston, Programming Director
John Amann, Promotions Manager
Bill Castrovince, News Director
Tom Zocolo, Chief Engineer
Stan Boney, Weather Director
Amy Radinovic,Host
Damon Maloney, Anchor & Videojournalist
Jon Scott, Sports Team

Zanesville, OH (DMA 204)

WHIZ-TV *Digital Channel:* 40; *Virtual Channel:* 18; 620 kw; 554 ft.; N39 55 42 W81 59 7
629 Downard Road, Zanesville, OH 43701 US
(740) 452-5431, (740) 450-1240, (740) 450-0927; *Fax:* (740) 452-6553, (740) 452-2994, (740) 452-5675
www.whiznews.com
slauka@whiznews.com
License: Zanesville, Muskingum County, OH held by Southeastern Ohio TV System
Washington Law Firm: Leventhal, Senter & Lerman
Nat'l Network: NBC
Size of News Staff: 14; *Hours of Local News Weekly:* news progmg 10 hrs wkly
N.J. Littick, Chairman
H.C. Littick, President
Doug Pickrell, General Sales Mgr
Brian Wagner, Programming Director
George Hiotis, News Director
J. T. Raymond, Sports Commentator
Carolyn Rider, Traffic Manager
Wesley Sass,Weather Director
Doug Pickrell, Director of TV Sales
Tom Strock, Sr. Account Executive
Erika Brooks, News Team

Oklahoma

Oklahoma City, OK (DMA 41)

KAUT *Digital Channel:* 40; *Virtual Channel:* 43; 1000 kw; 1433 ft.; N35 35 51.89 W97 29 22.06
444 E Britton Road, Oklahoma City, OK 73114 USA
kfor.com/category/freedom-43
License: Oklahoma City, Oklahoma County, OK held by Tribune Broadcasting Oklahoma City License LLC
Group Owner: Tribune Media
Nat'l Network: Independent; NBC

***KETA-TV** *Digital Channel:* 13; 50 kw; 1,525t/1,578g; N35 32 58 W97 29 50; *Population Served:* 1,300,000
Box 14190, 7403 N. Kelley Avenue, Oklahoma City, OK 73113
(405) 848-8501; *Fax:* (405) 841-9216
programming@keta.com
License: Oklahoma City, Oklahoma County, OK held by Oklahoma Educational TV Authority
Washington Law Firm: DowLohnes
Nat'l Network: PBS
Size of News Staff: 8; *Hours of Local News Weekly:* news progmg 3 hrs wkly
Janette Thornbrue, Operations Dir
Bill Thrash, Station Manager
Mark Norman, Programming Director
Ashley Barcum, Promotions Manager
Bob Sands, News Director
Earle Conners, Engineering Dir
Richard Ladd, Chief Engineer
JohnMcCarroll, Executive Director

KFOR *Digital Channel:* 27; *Virtual Channel:* 4; 60 kw; 1,540t/1,602g; N35 34 07 W97 29 20; *Population Served:* 2,177,200
444 E Britton Rd., Oklahoma City, OK 73114 USA
(405) 424-4444; *Fax:* (405) 478-6228
kfor.com
License: Oklahoma City, Oklahoma County, OK held by Tribune Broadcasting Oklahoma City License LLC
Group Owner: Tribune Media; *Washington Law Firm:* Dow Lohnes
Nat'l Network: NBC; *Nat'l Reps:* Millennium Sales & Marketing;
Wire Services: AP
Size of News Staff: 70; *Hours of Local News Weekly:* news progmg 38 hrs wkly

KOCB *Digital Channel:* 33; *Virtual Channel:* 34; 900 kw; 1501 ft.; N35 32 58 W97 29 18
Mailing Address: 1228 E. Wilshire Blvd., Oklahoma City, OK 73111 US
Second Address: 10706 Beaver Dam Rd., Hunt Valley, MD 21030
(405) 843-2525; *Fax:* (405) 478-4343
www.cwokc.com
License: Oklahoma City, Oklahoma County, OK held by KOCB Licensee LLC
Group Owner: Sinclair Broadcast Group Inc.; (acq 1996; $63 million with WDKY-TV Danville, KY).
Nat'l Network: CW; *Nat'l Reps:* Harrington, Righter & Parsons
John Rossi, General Manager
Steve Bottkol, Director of Engineering and Operations
Gerry Klingbeil, Regional Sales Manager

KOCM *Digital Channel:* 46; *Virtual Channel:* 46; 50 kw; 1365 ft.; N35 35 52 W97 29 22
Mailing Address: 3901 Hwy 121, Bedford, TX 76021 US
Second Address: PO Box 610546, Dallas, TX 75261-0546
(817) 571-1229, (877) 805-2132; *Fax:* (817) 571-7458
www.daystar.com
comments@daystar.com
License: Norman, Cleveland County, OK held by Word of God Fellowship Inc.
Nat'l Network: IND
Joni Show, General Manager

KOCO *Digital Channel:* 7; *Virtual Channel:* 5; 65.7 kw; 1,519t/1,562g; N35 33 45 W97 29 24; *Population Served:* 663,200
1300 E. Britton Rd., Oklahoma City, OK 73131 US
(405) 478-3000
www.koco.com
License: Oklahoma City, OK held by Ohio/Oklahoma Hearst Television Inc.
Group Owner: Hearst Television Inc.; (acq 7-16-97; grpsl).;
Washington Law Firm: Brooks, Pierce, McLendon
Nat'l Network: ABC; *Nat'l Reps:* HRP Television Sales; *Wire Services:* NWS (National Weather Ser; AP
Size of News Staff: 55; *Hours of Local News Weekly:* 30 hrs news progrg wkly
Jennifer Payne, Programming Director
David Evans, Chief Engineer

KOKH-TV *Digital Channel:* 24; *Virtual Channel:* 25; 1000 kw; 1561 ft.; N35 32 58 W97 29 18
1228 E. Wilshire Blvd., Oklahoma City, OK 73111 US
(405) 843-2525; *Fax:* (405) 478-4343
www.okcfox.com
news@okcfox.com
License: Oklahoma City, Oklahoma County, OK held by KOKH Licensee LLC
Group Owner: Sinclair Broadcast Group Inc.; (acq 1998; grpsl).
Nat'l Network: FOX; *Nat'l Reps:* Harrington, Righter & Parsons
John Rossi, General Manager
Steve Bottkol, Director of Engineering and Operations
Gerry Klingbeil, Regional Sales Manager

KOPX-TV *Digital Channel:* 50; 200 kw; 787t; N35 34 52 W97 29 23
13424 Railway Dr., Oklahoma City, OK 73114 USA
(405) 478-9562; *Fax:* (405) 751- 6867
www.iontelevision.com
License: Oklahoma City, OK held by Ion Media Oklahoma City License, Inc.
Group Owner: ION Media Networks Inc.; *Washington Law Firm:* Dow, Lohnes and Albertson PLLC
Nat'l Network: ION Television
Brandon Burgess, Chairman/CEO

KSBI *Digital Channel:* 51; *Virtual Channel:* 52; 1000 kw; 1502 ft.; N35 35 52 W97 29 22
Mailing Address: P.O. Box 26128, Oklahoma City, OK 73126 US
Second Address: 9802 N. Morgan Rd, Yukon, OK 73099
(405) 470-0993; *Fax:* (405) 470-8309
www.ksbitv.com
info@ksbitv.com
License: Oklahoma City, Oklahoma County, OK held by Family Broadcasting Group Inc
Washington Law Firm: Booth, Freret, Imlay & Tepper
Nat'l Network: IND
Brady Brus, CEO
Vince Orza, President
Jerry Hart, Vice-President of Operations
Lee Redick, General Sales Mgr
Lori Peters, Programming Director
Drew Stone, Engineering Dir
Cody Blount, Chief Engineer
Staci McCart, HumanResources/CPA
Angela Graham, Traffic

KTBO-TV *Digital Channel:* 15; *Virtual Channel:* 14; 700 kw; 1175 ft.; N35 34 35 W97 29 9
PO Box A, Santa Ana, CA 92711 US
(714) 832-2950; *Fax:* (714) 665-2191
www.tbn.org
comments@tbn.org
License: Oklahoma City, Oklahoma County, OK held by Trinity Broadcasting of Oklahoma City Inc.
Group Owner: Trinity Broadcasting Network; *Washington Law Firm:* Joseph E. Dunne III
Nat'l Network: TRINITY BROADCA
Paul Crouch, President
Phyllis Smith, General Manager
Mary Jane Allen, Station Manager
Jan Crouch, Promotions Manager
Ken Howerton, Chief Engineer

KTUZ-TV30 *Digital Channel:* 29; *Virtual Channel:* 30; 1000 kw; 1555 ft.; N35 33 36 W97 29 7
5101 S. Shields, Oklahoma City, OK 73129 US
(405) 616-9900; *Fax:* (405) 616-5511
www.ktuztv.com
License: Shawnee, Pottawatomie County, OK held by Oklahoma Land Company LLC.
Nat'l Network: TELEMUNDO
Foreign Language Programming

Armando Rubio, General Manager
Chris Fusselman, General Sales Mgr

KUOK *Digital Channel:* 35; *Virtual Channel:* 35; 8 kw; 646 ft.; N36 16 6 W99 26 56
1 Shackle Ford Dr, Suite 400, Little Rock, AR 72211 US
(405) 616-5500; *Fax:* (405) 616-5511
www.TylerMedia.com
Lee.R@TylerMedia.com
License: Woodward, Woodward County, OK held by Oklahoma Land Company, LLC
7/1/2009; *Ownership:* Tyler Broadcasting Corporation
Foreign Language Programming
Ty Tyler, General Manager
Lee Redick, General Sales Mgr

***KWET** *Digital Channel:* 8; 30 kw; ant 994t/958g; N35 35 36 W99 40 01; *Population Served:* 647,390
Mailing Address: 7403 N. Kelley Ave., Oklahoma City, OK 73111 US
Second Address: PO Box 14190, Oklahoma City, OK 73113
(405) 848-8501, (800) 879-6382; *Fax:* (405) 841-9216
www.oeta.tv
License: Cheyenne, Roger Mills County, OK held by Oklahoma Educational TV Authority
Washington Law Firm: DowLohnes
Nat'l Network: PBS
Dr Jim Utterback, Chair
Janette Thorton, Operations Dir
Bill Thrash, Station Manager
Holly Emig, Programming Director
Ashley Barcum, Promotions Manager
Dick Pryor, News Director
Mark Norton, Engineering Dir
Richard Ladd, ChiefEngineer
Dan Skiedel, Executive Director

KWTV-DT *Digital Channel:* 39; 316 kw vis, 33.9 kw aur; ant 1,525t/1,537g; N35 32 68 W97 29 50; *Population Served:* 582,000
7401 N. Kelley Ave., Oklahoma City, OK 73111
(405) 843-6641; *Fax:* (405) 841-9926
www.news9.com
License: Oklahoma City, Oklahoma County, OK held by Griffin Television OKC, LLC
Group Owner: Griffin Communications L.L.C.; (acq 7-1-98).;
Washington Law Firm: Holland & Knight
Nat'l Network: CBS; *Nat'l Reps:* TeleRep; *Wire Services:* CBS; CNN
Size of News Staff: 80; *Hours of Local News Weekly:* news progmg 33 hrs wkly
Rob Krier, COO
Wade Deaver, General Sales Mgr
Kim Eubank, Programming Director
Jenny Monroe, News Director
Julie Cameron, Engineering Dir
Linda Mason, Traffic Manager

Sherman, TX-Ada, OK (DMA 162)

KTEN *Digital Channel:* 26; *Virtual Channel:* 10; 1000 kw; 1398 ft.; N34 21 34 W96 33 34
P.O. Box 549, Hampton, VA 23669 US
(903) 337-4000; *Fax:* (908) 465-1207,(903) 465-1368
www.kten.com
10news@kten.com
License: Ada, Pontotoc County, OK held by Lockwood Broadcast Group
Washington Law Firm: Brooks, Pierce, McLendon, Humprey & Leonard
Nat'l Network: NBC; CW; *Nat'l Reps:* Continental Television Sales; *Wire Services:* AP
Size of News Staff: 25; *Hours of Local News Weekly:* news progmg 36 hrs wkly
Anthony Maisel, General Manager
Brian Capaldo, Station Manager
David MacMullen, General Sales Mgr
Kris Anderson, Chief Engineer
Tom Crespo, Anchor
Meredith Saldana, Anchor
Markie Martin, Reporter
Meredith Yeomans, Reporter
Kathleen Jordan, Reporter
Rick Springer, Executive Producers

Tulsa, OK (DMA 58)

KDOR-TV *Digital Channel:* 17; *Virtual Channel:* 17; 1000 kw; 1043 ft.; N36 30 59 W95 46 10
Mailing Address: P. O. Box A, Santa Ana, CA 92711 US
Second Address: PO Box 768, Station B, Ottawa, ON K1P 5P8
(714) 731-1000, (888) 731-1000, (819) 770-2333; *Fax:* (819) 770-2338
www.tbn.org
kdor@tbn.org
License: Bartlesville, Washington County, OK held by Trinity Broadcasting Network
Group Owner: Trinity Broadcasting Network; (acq 5-8-2000; grpsl).
Nat'l Network: TRINITY BROADCA
Paul Crouch, CEO
Craig Nelson, General Manager

KGEB *Digital Channel:* 49; *Virtual Channel:* 53; 1,770 kw vis, 177 kw aur; 597t/672g; N36 02 39 W95 57 11
7777 S. Lewis Ave., Tulsa, OK 74101 US
(918) 488-5300; *Fax:* (918) 495-7388
www.kgeb.net
kgeb@oru.edu
License: Tulsa, Tulsa County, OK held by University Broadcasting Inc
Walter Richardson, General Manager
Amy Calvert, General Sales Mgr
Christi Vanover, Programming Director

KJRH-TV *Digital Channel:* 56; *Virtual Channel:* 2; 100 kw vis, 10 kw aur; ant 1,828t; N36 01 15 W95 40 32; *Population Served:* 1,143,000
3701 S. Peoria Ave., Tulsa, OK 74105
(918) 743-2222; *Fax:* (918) 748-1438, (918) 748-1436
www.kjrh.com
news@kjrh.com
License: Tulsa, Tulsa County, OK held by Scripps Howard Broadcasting Co.
Group Owner: The E. W. Scripps Co.; (acq 1-1-71; $7.8 million);
Washington Law Firm: Baker & Hostetler
Nat'l Network: NBC; *Nat'l Reps:* Eagle Television Sales
Size of News Staff: 50; *Hours of Local News Weekly:* news progmg 26.5 hrs wkly
Ken Lowe, CEO
Donna Wilson, VP/General Manager
Joe Brunnhuber, Sales Director
Karen Framel, Research Director
Susan D'Astoli, News Director
Dale Vennes, Chief Engineer
Samantha Knowlton, creative Services/Community RelationsDirector
Al Jerkens, Sports Director
Tracy Hardison, Traffic Manager
Brett Anthony, Chief Meterologist
Cara Palmer, Business Manager
Linda Gibby, Human Resources Manager

KMYT-TV *Digital Channel:* 42; *Virtual Channel:* 41; 900 kw; 1250 ft.; N36 1 36 W95 40 44
115 East Travis, Suite 1427, San Antonio, TX 78205 US
(918) 388-5100; *Fax:* (918) 493-5739
License: Tulsa, Tulsa County, OK held by Cox Television Tulsa LLC
Group Owner: Cox Media Group; (acq 3-14-2008; grpsl);
Washington Law Firm: Covington & Burling
Nat'l Network: MYNETWORK TV; *Nat'l Reps:* Millennium Sales & Marketing
Sandy DiPasquale, President
Holly Allen, Operations Dir
Jim Hanning, General Sales Mgr
Chooi Ning, Programming Director
Amber Musselman, Promotions Manager
Brian Egan, Chief Engineer
Stephanie Spry, Local Sales Manager
KariBarrett, National Sales Manager
Joan King, Traffic Manager

***KOED-TV** *Digital Channel:* 11; *Virtual Channel:* 11; 47 kw; 1709 ft.; N36 1 15 W95 40 32
Mailing Address: P.O. Box 14190, Oklahoma City, OK 73113 US
Second Address: 7403 N. Kelley Avenue, Oklahoma City, OK 73113
(405) 848-8501,(800)879-6382; *Fax:* (405) 841-9252
www.oeta.tv
membership@oeta.tv
License: Tulsa, Tulsa County, OK held by Oklahoma Educational TV Authority
Washington Law Firm: DowLohnes
Nat'l Network: PBS
Size of News Staff: 7; *Hours of Local News Weekly:* 3
Bill Thrash, Station Manager
Mark Norman, Programming Director
Liz Exon, News Director
Roger Newton, Chief Engineer
John McCarroll, Executive Director

***KOET** *Digital Channel:* 31; *Virtual Channel:* 3; 1000 kw; 1195 ft.; N35 11 1 W95 20 19
Mailing Address: P.O. Box 14190, Oklahoma City, OK 73113 US
Second Address: 7403 N. Kelley Avenue, Oklahoma City, OK 73113
(405) 848-8501,(800)879-6382; *Fax:* (405) 841-9252
www.oeta.tv
membership@oeta.tv
License: Eufaula, Oklahoma County, OK held by Oklahoma Educational Television Authority
Washington Law Firm: DowLohnes
Nat'l Network: PBS
Mike Palmer, Operations Dir
Bill Thrash, Station Manager
Mark Norman, Programming Director
Ashley Barcum, Promotions Manager
Bob Sands, News Director
Earle Connors, Engineering Dir
Richard Ladd, Chief Engineer
John McCarroll,Executive Director

KOKI-TV *Digital Channel:* 22; *Virtual Channel:* 23; 1000 kw; 1312 ft.; N36 1 36 W95 40 44
200 Concord Plaza, Suite 600, San Antonio, TX 78216 US
(918) 491-0023; *Fax:* (918) 491-6650
www.fox23.com
License: Tulsa, Tulsa County, OK held by Cox Television Tulsa LLC
Group Owner: Cox Media Group; (acq 3-14-2008; grpsl);
Washington Law Firm: Covington & Burling
Nat'l Network: FOX
Size of News Staff: 38; *Hours of Local News Weekly:* news progmg 7 hrs wkly
Sandy DiPasquale, President
Craig Millar, Operations Dir
Greg Blite, General Manager
Chooi Ning, Programming Director
Deedra Determan, Promotions Manager
Suzanne Nadell, News Director
Brian Egan, Chief Engineer
Jim Hanning,National Sales Manager
Jennifer Calvert, Traffic Manager

KOTV-DT *Digital Channel:* 45; 100 kw vis, 50 kw aur; ant 1,885t/1,849g; N36 01 15 W95 40 32; *Population Served:* 1,893,300
Mailing Address: 303 N.Boston Ave, Tulsa, OK 74103
Second Address: 302 S. Frankfort, Tulsa, OK 74120
(918) 732-6000; *Fax:* (918) 732-6185
www.newson6.com
License: Tulsa, Tulsa County, OK held by Griffin Licensing L.L.C.
Group Owner: Griffin Communications L.L.C.; (acq 12-6-2000; $82 million); *Washington Law Firm:* Dow, Lohnes & Albertson
Nat'l Network: CBS; *Nat'l Reps:* TeleRep
Size of News Staff: 40
Ted Strickland, CFO
John Quesnel, Operations Dir
John Trook, General Sales Mgr
Christy Sheppler, Programming Director
Ron Harig, News Director
Gerald Weaver, Chief Engineer
Rob Krier, COO
Cheryl Sutton, Business Director
Donita Quesnel, Public Service Director
Travis Meyer, Weather Director

KQCW-DT *Digital Channel:* 20; 5,000 kw vis; ant 823t/777g; N35 45 08 W95 48 15
Mailing Address: Box 6, Tulsa, OK 74101
Second Address: 303 N.Boston Ave., Tulsa, OK 74103
(918) 732-6000; *Fax:* (918) 732-6016
www.tulsacw.com
License: Muskogee, Muskogee County, OK held by Griffin Licensing L.L.C.
Group Owner: Griffin Communications L.L.C.; (acq 12-9-2005; $14.5 million)
Nat'l Network: CW
Rob Krier, COO
John Quesnel, Operations Dir
John Trook, General Sales Mgr
Ron Harig, News director
Gerald Weaver, Chief Engineer
Donita Quesnel, Public Affairs Director

***KRSC-TV** *Digital Channel:* 36; *Virtual Channel:* 35; 2,750 kw vis; 840t; N36 24 05 W95 36 33
RSU Public Television, 1701 W. Will Rogers Blvd., Claremore, OK 74017

(800) 823-7210; *Fax:* (918) 343-7952
www.rsupublictv.org
krsc-tv@rsu.edu
License: Claremore, Rogers County, OK held by Board of Regents of Oklahoma Colleges
Washington Law Firm: Schwartz, Woods & Miller
Foreign Language Programming
Dale McKinney, Operations Dir
Dan Schiedel, General Manager
Jennifer Sterling, Programming Director
Jim Mertins, Chief Engineer
OPEN, Traf Coordinator

KTPX-TV *Digital Channel:* 28; 1,000 kw; 1,770t; N35 50 02 W96 07 28; *Population Served:* 887,000
5800 E. Skelly Dr., Suite 101, Tulsa, OK 74135 USA
(918) 664-1044; *Fax:* (918) 664-4913
www.iontelevision.com
License: Okmulgee, OK held by Ion Media Tulsa License, Inc.
Group Owner: ION Media Networks Inc.; (acq 8-21-98; $404,000 for 51% of stock).
Nat'l Network: ION Television
Brandon Burgess, Chairman/CEO

KTUL *Digital Channel:* 10; *Virtual Channel:* 8; 15 kw; 1896 ft.; N35 58 8 W95 36 55
3333 S. 29th West Ave., Tulsa, OK 74101 US
(918) 445-8888; *Fax:* (918) 445-9354
www.ktul.com
aequince@sbgtv.com
License: Tulsa, Tulsa County, OK held by KTUL Licensee LLC
Group Owner: Sinclair Broadcast Group Inc.; (acq 7-29-2013; grpsl); *Washington Law Firm:* Hogan & Hartson
Nat'l Network: ABC; *Wire Services:* AP
Size of News Staff: 50; *Hours of Local News Weekly:* news progmg 24 hrs wkly
Roger Herring, Director of Broadcast Operations
Pat Baldwin, General Manager
John Trook, Director of Sales
Alexander Quince, News Director
Jim Joly, Director of National Digital Sales
Greg Siegel, Vice President, National Sales

KWHB *Digital Channel:* 47; *Virtual Channel:* 47; 50 kw; 1509 ft.; N36 1 15 W95 40 32
8835 S. Memorial, Tulsa, OK 74133 US
(918) 254-4701; *Fax:* (918) 254-5614
www.lesea.com
License: Tulsa, Tulsa County, OK held by LeSea Broadcasting.
Group Owner: Le Sea Broadcasting; (acq 5-14-86; $3.4 million;
Washington Law Firm: John Fiorini
Nat'l Network: IND
Peter Sumrall, CEO
Dan Smith, General Manager
Keith Krebbs, Station Manager
Susan Smith, Office Manager
Ben Stephens, Production Coordinator
Billy Bentley, Account Executive
Anita Repp, Account Excutive
Ed Short, AccountExecutive

Wichita Falls, TX & Lawton, OK (DMA 148)

KSWO-TV *Digital Channel:* 11; *Virtual Channel:* 7; 316 kw vis, 63.1 kw aur; 1,050t/1,059g; N34 12 55 W98 43 13; *Population Served:* 300,000
Mailing Address: 1401 SE 60th Street, Lawton, OK 73501 US
Second Address: 1401 SE 60th Street, Lawton, OK 73502
(580) 355-7000; *Fax:* (580) 357-3811, (580) 355-0059, (580) 355-0982
www.kswo.com
lpatton@kswo.com
License: Lawton, Comanche County, OK held by KSWO TV Inc.
Group Owner: R.H. Drewry Group
Nat'l Network: ABC
Larry Patton, General Manager
Cindy Coleman, General Sales Mgr
Todd Young, Promotions Manager
David Bradley, Executive News Director
Nathan Bowers, Chief Engineer
Kyle Weatherly, Sports Director

Oregon

Bend, OR (DMA 188)

KBNZ-LD *Digital Channel:* 7; 3 kw; N44 4 38.8 W121 19 56.6
63090 Sherman Rd., Bend, OR 97703 US
(541) 749-5151; *Fax:* (866) 996-3232
License: Bend, Deschutes County, OR held by TDS Broadcasting LLC
Group Owner: Zolo Media; (acq 2010).
Nat'l Network: CBS
Julie Brinks, General Manager
Sean Levitt, National Sales Manager
Greg Fair, Programming Director
Michele O'Hara, Creative Services and Marketing
Josh Burke, Chief Engineer
Juliane Reed, Local Sales Manager
Michele Lepore,Traffic Supervisor

***KOAB-TV** *Digital Channel:* 11; *Virtual Channel:* 3; 90 kw; 804 ft.; N44 4 41 W121 19 57
7140 Sw Macadam Avenue, Portland, OR 97219 US
(503) 244-9900; (800) 241-8123; *Fax:* (503) 293-1919
www.opb.org
membercenter@opb.org
License: Bend, Deschutes County, OR held by Oregon Public Broadcasting
(acq 9-20-93; grpsl; *Washington Law Firm:* Schwartz, Woods & Miller
Nat'l Network: PBS
Steve Bass, CEO
Dan Metziga, General Sales Mgr
Mary Gardner, Programming Director
Keith Mobley, Chairman
Jim Huston, Vice Chairman

KOHD *Digital Channel:* 18; *Virtual Channel:* 51; 84.1 kw; 725 ft.; N44 4 40.5 W121 19 56.8
63090 Sherman Rd., Bend, OR 97703 US
(541) 749-5151; *Fax:* (866) 996-3232
www.kohd.com
License: Bend, Deschutes County, OR held by TDS Broadcasting LLC
Group Owner: Zolo Media; (acq 7-26-2013).
Nat'l Network: ABC
Julie Brinks, General Manager
Sean Levitt, National Sales Manager
Greg Fair, Programming Director
Michele O'Hara, Creative Services and Marketing
Josh Burke, Chief Engineer
Juliane Reed, Local Sales Manager
Michele Lepore,Traffic Supervisor

KTVZ *Digital Channel:* 21; *Virtual Channel:* 21; 131.8 kw; 646 ft.; N44 4 40 W121 19 49
62990 O.B. Riley Rd., Bend, OR 07701 US
(541) 383-2121; *Fax:* (541) 382-1616
www.ktvz.com
stories@ktvz.com
License: Bend, Deschutes County, OR held by NPG of Oregon Inc.
Group Owner: News-Press & Gazette Co.; (acq 4-17-2002; $18.9 million)
Nat'l Network: NBC; CW; Fox; Telemundo (Spanish); *Nat'l Reps:* Continental Television Sales
Foreign Language Programming; Size of News Staff: 19; *Hours of Local News Weekly:* news progmg 20 hrs wkly
Nic Moye, News Director
Daniel Bay, Chief Engineer

Eugene, OR (DMA 117)

KCBY-TV *Digital Channel:* 11; *Virtual Channel:* 11; 5 kw; 630 ft.; N43 23 26 W124 7 46
Mailing Address: P.O. Box 1156, Coos Bay, OR 97420 US
Second Address: 3451 Broadway, North Bend, OR 97459
(541) 269-1111
www.kcby.com
nwnews@kcby.com
License: Coos Bay, Coos County, OR held by Sinclair Eugene Licensee LLC
Group Owner: Sinclair Broadcast Group Inc.; (acq 8-8-2013; grpsl); *Washington Law Firm:* Dow, Lohnes & Albertson
Nat'l Network: CBS
Size of News Staff: 4
Cameron Derrick, Station Manager
Steve Murray, General Sales Mgr

***KEPB-TV** *Digital Channel:* 29; *Virtual Channel:* 28; 100 kw; 1322 ft.; N44 0 7 W123 6 53
7140 Sw Macadam Avenue, Portland, OR 97219 US
(503) 244-9900; (800) 241-8123; *Fax:* (503) 293-1919, (503) 293-4877
www.opb.org
membercenter@opb.org
License: Eugene, Lane County, OR held by Oregon Public Broadcasting.
Nat'l Network: PBS
Keith Mobley, Chairman
Steven M. Bass, CEO/President
Lynne Clendenin, Vp, Programming
Mike Foti, VP, Engineering
Jan Heskiss, CFO
Morgan Holm, Senior VP, Chief Content Officer
Dan Metziga, Senior VP, Development
Linda Hoffman,Treasurer
Jim Huston, Vice-Chairman
Mary Gardner, Director,TV Programming

KEZI *Digital Channel:* 9; *Virtual Channel:* 9; 43.9 kw; 1,750 ft.; N44 06 56.5 W122 59 56.7; *Population Served:* 279,240
Mailing Address: P.O. Box 7009, Springfield, OR 97475 US
Second Address: 2975 Chad Dr., Eugene, OR 97408
(541) 485-5611; *Fax:* (541) 686-8004
www.kezi.com
newsdesk@kezi.com
License: Eugene, Lane County, OR held by Oregon TV License Company LLC
Group Owner: Heartland Media LLC; (acq 3-5-2014).
Nat'l Network: ABC
Size of News Staff: 28; *Hours of Local News Weekly:* news program 22 hrs wkly
Mike Boring, General Manager
Dan O'Brien, General Sales Mgr

KLSR-TV *Digital Channel:* 31; *Virtual Channel:* 34; 88 kw; 1,220 ft.; N44 0 4 W123 6 45
2940 Chad Dr., Eugene, OR 97408 US
(541) 683-3434; *Fax:* (541) 683-8016
www.oregonsfox.com
info@oregonsfox.com
License: Eugene, Lane County, OR held by California Oregon Broadcasting Inc.
Group Owner: California Oregon Broadcasting Inc.; (acq 9-1-94; $2.65 million; *Washington Law Firm:* Fletcher, Heald & Hildreth
Nat'l Network: FOX
Patricia Smullin, President
Mark Metzger, Vice President and General Manager
Alaina Burgess, National Sales Manager
Sandra Belmont, Programming Director
Nick Brown, Creative Services Director
Justin Atkin, Chief Engineer
KathyWofford, Business Manager
Jeannie Crane, Traffic Manager
Chris Breen, Local Sales Executive
David Fenley, Local Sales Executive
Marc Belmont, Local Sales Executive

KMCB *Digital Channel:* 22; *Virtual Channel:* 23; 10 kw; 587 ft.; N43 23 39 W124 7 56; *Rebroadcasting:* Satellite of KMTR(TV) Eugene.
1333 New Hampshire Ave., N.W., Suite 1000, Washington, DC 20036 US
(541) 746-1600; *Fax:* (541) 747-0866
www.kmtr.com
kmtpgm@pacbell.net
License: Coos Bay, Coos County, OR held by KMTR Television LLC
Group Owner: Roberts Media LLC; (acq 3-14-2008; grpsl);
Washington Law Firm: Covington & Burling
Nat'l Network: NBC; *Nat'l Reps:* Millennium Sales & Marketing
Regional Reps: Blair.; *Wire Services:* AP
Hours of Local News Weekly: News progmg 22 hrs wkly
Kurt Thelen, Operations Dir
Sky Muller, Anchor
Ty Steele, Anchor
Kelli Warner, Anchor
Joel Porter, Anchor

KMTR *Digital Channel:* 17; *Virtual Channel:* 16; 70 kw; 1552 ft.; N44 6 57 W122 59 57
1333 New Hampshire Ave., N.W., Suite 1000, Washington, DC 20036 US
(541) 746-1600; *Fax:* (541) 747-0866
www.kmtr.com
License: Eugene, Lane County, OR held by KMTR Television LLC
Group Owner: Roberts Media LLC; (acq 3-14-2008; grpsl);
Washington Law Firm: Covington & Burling
Nat'l Network: NBC; *Nat'l Reps:* Millennium Sales & Marketing
Regional Reps: Blair.; *Wire Services:* AP
Size of News Staff: 22; *Hours of Local News Weekly:* news progmg 15 hrs wkly
Kurt Thelen, Operations Dir
Sky Muller, Anchor
Ty Steele, Anchor

Kelli Warner, Anchor
Joel Porter, Anchor

***KOAC-TV** *Digital Channel:* 7; *Virtual Channel:* 7; 18.1 kw; 1171 ft.; N44 38 25 W123 16 25
7140 Sw Macadam Avenue, Portland, OR 97219 US
(503) 244-9900; (800) 241-8123; *Fax:* (503) 293-1919
www.opb.org
membercenter@opb.org
License: Corvallis, Benton County, OR held by Oregon Public Broadcasting
(acq 1993; grpsl; *Washington Law Firm:* Schwartz, Woods & Miller
Nat'l Network: PBS; *Wire Services:* UPI
Steve Bass, CEO
Mary Gardner, Programming Director
Morgan Holm, News Director
Don McKay, Chief Engineer
Keith Mobley, Chairman
Jim Huston, Vice Chairman

KPIC *Digital Channel:* 19; *Virtual Channel:* 4; 50 kw; 958 ft.; N43 14 8 W123 19 18; *Rebroadcasting:* Satellite of KVAL-TV Eugene.
655 W. Umpqua, Roseburg, OR 97470 US
(541) 672-4481
www.kpic.com
kpic4news@kpic.com
License: Roseburg, Douglas County, OR held by South West Oregon TV Broadcasting Corp.
Group Owner: Sinclair Broadcast Group Inc.; (acq 8-8-2013; grpsl).; *Washington Law Firm:* Dow, Lohnes & Albertson
Nat'l Network: CBS
Size of News Staff: 4; *Hours of Local News Weekly:* news progmg 14 hrs wkly
Connie Williamson, Station Manager
Steve Murray, General Sales Mgr
Mike Hill, Chief Engineer

KTCW *Digital Channel:* 45; *Virtual Channel:* 46; 12 kw; 358 ft.; N43 12 22 W123 21 56; *Rebroadcasting:* Satellite of KMTR Eugene.
1333 New Hampshire Ave., N.W., Suite 1000, Washington, DC 20036 US
(541) 746-1600; *Fax:* (541) 747-0866
www.kmtr.com
kmtpgm@pacbell.net
License: Roseburg, Douglas County, OR held by KMTR Television LLC
Group Owner: Roberts Media LLC; (acq 3-14-2008; grpsl);
Washington Law Firm: Covington & Burling
Nat'l Network: NBC; *Wire Services:* AP
Hours of Local News Weekly: News progmg 22 hrs wkly
Kurt Thelen, Operations Dir
Sky Muller, Anchor
Ty Steele, Anchor
Kelli Warner, Anchor
Joel Porter, Anchor

KTVC *Digital Channel:* 18; *Virtual Channel:* 36; 50 kw; 698 ft.; N43 14 9 W123 19 16; *Station Currently Dark*
PO Box 766, Grants Pass, OR 97528 US
(541) 474-3089; *Fax:* (541) 474-9409
www.blbn.org
kbln@betterlifetv.tv
License: Roseburg, Douglas County, OR held by Better Life Television, Inc.
Group Owner: Better Life Ministries; (acq 4/16/09)
Nat'l Network: RTN
Robert Heisler, President
Ron Davis, General Manager/ Secretary
Marta Davis, Station Manager
William Whitt, Chief Engineer
Denise Bradford, Accountant
Dennis Kamberg, Production Manager
Char, Gallimore, Development Director
KipBradford, Assistant to the General Manager
Douglas Garcia, Creative Director

KVAL-TV *Digital Channel:* 13; *Virtual Channel:* 13; 30.64 kw; 1447 ft.; N44 0 7 W123 6 53
4575 Blanton Rd., Eugene, OR 97405 US
(541) 342-4961
www.kval.com
kvalnews@kval.com
License: Eugene, Lane County, OR held by Sinclair Eugene Licensee LLC
Group Owner: Sinclair Broadcast Group Inc.; (acq 8-8-2013; grpsl).; *Washington Law Firm:* Pillsbury, Winthrop & Pittman
Nat'l Network: CBS *Regional Reps:* Petry
Hours of Local News Weekly: news progmg 17 hrs wkly

Steve Murray, General Sales Mgr
Dino Francois, Promotions/Marketing Director
Chris Wright, Producer

Medford-Klamath Falls, OR (DMA 139)

KBLN-TV *Digital Channel:* 30; *Virtual Channel:* 30; 2 kw; 2146 ft.; N42 22 56 W123 16 29
Mailing Address: 10255 Sw Arctic Drive, Beaverton, OR 97005 US
Second Address: PO Box 766, Grants Pass, OR 97528
(541) 474-3089, (877) 741-2588; *Fax:* (541) 474-9409
www.betterlifetv.tv
kbln@betterlifetv.tv
License: Grants Pass, Josephine County, OR held by Better Life Television Inc
Nat'l Network: 3 ANGLS
Marta Davis, General Manager
Ron Davis, Station Manager

KDKF *Digital Channel:* 29; *Virtual Channel:* 31; 4.87 kw; 2,136 ft.; N42 5 50 W121 37 59; *Rebroadcasting:* Satellite of KDRV(TV) Medford, OR.
Mailing Address: P.O. Box 4220, Medford, OR 97501 US
Second Address: 231 East Main St., Klamath Falls, OR 97601
(541) 883-3131; *Fax:* (541) 883-8931
www.kdrv.com
programming@kdrv.com
License: Klamath Falls, Klamath County, OR held by Oregon TV License Company LLC
Group Owner: Heartland Media LLC; (acq 3-5-2014).;
Washington Law Firm: Fletcher, Heald & Hildreth
Nat'l Network: ABC
Size of News Staff: 20; *Hours of Local News Weekly:* news progmg 12 hrs wkly
Mark Hatfield, General Manager
Catherine Hatfield, General Sales Mgr
Ashley Hall, News Director
Rick Carrara, Chief Engineer
Brian May, Sales

KDRV *Digital Channel:* 12; *Virtual Channel:* 12; 16.9 kw; 2700 ft.; N42 41 30 W123 13 44
Mailing Address: P.O. Box 4220, Medford, OR 97501 US
Second Address: 1090 Knutson Ave., Medford, OR 97504
(541) 773-1212; *Fax:* (541) 779-9261
www.kdrv.com
programming@kdrv.com
License: Medford, Jackson County, OR held by Oregon TV License Company LLC
Group Owner: Heartland Media LLC; (acq 3-5-2014).;
Washington Law Firm: Fisher, Wayland, Cooper, Leader & Zaragoza
Nat'l Network: ABC; *Nat'l Reps:* Millennium Sales & Marketing;
Wire Services: AP
Size of News Staff: 12; *Hours of Local News Weekly:* news progmg 20 hrs wkly
Mark Hatfield, General Manager
Catherine Hatfield, General Sales Mgr
Ashley Hall, News Director
Rick Carrara, Chief Engineer
Brian May, Sales

KMVU-DT *Digital Channel:* 26; 110 kw vis; ant 1,444t/113g; N42 17 54 W122 44 53; *Population Served:* 410,000
820 Crater Lake Ave., Suite 105, Medford, OR 97504
(541) 772-2600; *Fax:* (541) 772-7364
www.fox26medford.com
reception@kmvu-tv.com
License: Medford, Jackson County, OR held by Broadcasting Licenses L.P.
Group Owner: Northwest Broadcasting Inc.; *Washington Law Firm:* Leventhal, Senter & Lerman
Nat'l Network: Fox; *Nat'l Reps:* Continental Television Sales
Jon Rand, COO
Brian Brady, President
Dave Olmsted, General Manager
John Flores, General Sales Manager
Brian Henning, Chief Engineer
Becky Torrison, Account Executive
Theresa Zwan, Account Executive
Tom Carnes, AccountExecutive
Kimberlee Cannizzaro, Account Executive
Tami Kinsey, Sales Coordinator

KOBI *Digital Channel:* 5; *Virtual Channel:* 5; 6.35 kw; 2,700 ft.; N42 41 49 W123 13 39
125 S. Fir St., Medford, OR 97501 US
(541) 779-5555; *Fax:* (541) 779-5564
www.kobi5.com
comments@kobi5.com
License: Medford, Jackson County, OR held by California Oregon Broadcasting Inc.
Group Owner: California Oregon Broadcasting Inc.; *Washington Law Firm:* Wiley, Rein & Fielding
Nat'l Network: NBC; *Nat'l Reps:* Blair Television
Patricia Smullin, President
Robert Wise, Vice President and General Manager
Connie Eaton, Sales Manager
Donna Rodriguez, Programming Director
Scott Gee, Creative Services/Promotion
Craig Smullin, News Director
Steve Aase, ChiefEngineer

KOTI *Digital Channel:* 13; *Virtual Channel:* 2; 9 kw; 2,162 ft.; N42 5 48 W121 37 57; *Rebroadcasting:* Rebroadcasts KOBI Medford 90%.
125 S. Fir St., Medford, OR 97501 US
(541) 779-5555; *Fax:* (541) 779-5564
www.kobi5.com
comments@kobi5.com
License: Klamath Falls, Klamath County, OR held by California Oregon Broadcasting Inc.
Group Owner: California Oregon Broadcasting Inc.; *Ownership:* Patricia Smullin; *Washington Law Firm:* Wiley, Rein & Fielding
Nat'l Network: NBC; *Wire Services:* NBC
Size of News Staff: 2
Patricia Smullin, President
Robert Wise, Vice President and General Manager
Connie Eaton, Sales Manager
Donna Rodriguez, Programming Director
Scott Gee, Creative Services/Promotion
Craig Smullin, News Director
Steve Aase, ChiefEngineer

***KSYS** *Digital Channel:* 8; *Virtual Channel:* 8; 16.9 kw; 2684 ft.; N42 41 32 W123 13 45
Mailing Address: 28 South Fir Street, Suite 200, Medford, OR 97501 US
Second Address: PO Box 4688, Medford, OR 97501
(541) 779-0808, (800) 888-1847; *Fax:* (541) 779-2178
www.soptv.org
License: Medford, Jackson County, OR held by Southern Oregon Public Television Inc
Nat'l Network: PBS
Foreign Language Programming
Mark Stanislawski, CEO/ President
Tom Werner, Programming Director
Joyce Laidlaw, Administration Manager
Brad Fay, Director of Content & Services
Jeff LeBeau, Production Manager & Producer
Jan Abramsson, Producer & Director
Robert Mead, Director of Corporate Support
Linda Pinkham, Communications Manager

KTVL *Digital Channel:* 10; *Virtual Channel:* 10; 9 kw; 3,310t/151g; N42 04 55 W122 43 09; *Population Served:* 402,000
1440 Rossanley Dr., Medford, OR 97501 US
(541) 773-7373; *Fax:* (541) 779-0451
www.ktvl.com
License: Medford, Jackson County, OR held by KTVL Licensee LLC
Group Owner: Sinclair Broadcast Group Inc.; (acq 11-2-2011);
Washington Law Firm: Latham & Watkins
Nat'l Network: CBS; CW; *Nat'l Reps:* TeleRep
Hours of Local News Weekly: news progmg 16 hrs wkly
Kingsley Kelley, General Manager
Jack McCauley, General Sales Mgr
Chad Hypes, News Director
Carl Randall, Chief Engineer
Mike Gantenbein, Creative Services Director
Jim Underhill, Accounting Manager

***SOPTV** *Digital Channel:* 33; *Virtual Channel:* 22; 9.6 kw; 2129 ft.; N42 5 50 W121 37 59; *Rebroadcasting:* Satellite of KSYS(TV) Medford 100%.
Mailing Address: 34 South Fir Street, Medford, OR 97501 US
Second Address: 28 South Fir Street, Suite 200, Medford, OR 97501
(541) 779-0808, (800) 888-1847; *Fax:* (541) 779-2178
www.soptv.org
License: Klamath Falls, Klamath County, OR held by Southern Oregon Public Television Inc
Nat'l Network: PBS
Dick Robertson, Chairman
Mark Stanislawski, CEO/President
Tom Werner, Programming Director

Fred Willms, Treasurer
David Groff, Secretary

Portland, OR (DMA 25)

KATU *Digital Channel:* 43; *Virtual Channel:* 2; 1000 kw; 1719 ft.; N45 30 57 W122 43 59
Mailing Address: P.O. Box 2, Portland, OR 97207 US
Second Address: 2135 N.E. Sandy Blvd., Portland, OR 97232
(503) 231-4222
www.katu.com
custserv@katu.com
License: Portland, Multnomah County, OR held by Sinclair Portland Licensee LLC
Group Owner: Sinclair Broadcast Group Inc.; (acq 8-8-2013; grpsl).; *Washington Law Firm:* Fisher, Wayland, Cooper, Leader & Zaragoza
Nat'l Network: ABC; *Nat'l Reps:* TeleRep
Hours of Local News Weekly: news progmg 33.5 hrs wkly
John Tamerlano, General Manager

KGW *Digital Channel:* 8; *Virtual Channel:* 8; 45 kw; 1,719 ft.; N45 31 21 W122 44 45
1501 S.W. Jefferson St., Portland, OR 97201 US
(503) 226-5000; *Fax:* (503) 226-4448
www.kgw.com
License: Portland, Multnomah County, OR held by Sander Operating Co. III LLC dba KGW Television
Group Owner: Sander Media LLC; *Washington Law Firm:* Wiley, Rein & Fielding
Nat'l Network: NBC; *Nat'l Reps:* Blair Television; *Wire Services:* UPI
Hours of Local News Weekly: News progmg 35 hrs wkly
Josy Ansley, Operations Dir
DJ Wilson, General Manager
Brenda Buratti, Programming Director
Doug Dougherty, News Operations Manager
David Boyd, Director of Technology

***KNMT** ; 2,690 kw vis, 269 kw aur; 1,519t/2,535g; N45 30 58 W122 43 59
432 N.E. 74th Ave., Portland, OR 97213
(503) 252-0792; *Fax:* (503) 256-4205
www.nmtv.org
License: Portland, Multnomah County, OR held by National Minority TV Inc
Jane Duff, President
Dr. Paul Crouch, Operations Dir
Adolfo Carbajal, Station Manager
Steven Hendrix, Chief Engineer
Bonnie Gaulding, Public Affairs Director

KOIN *Digital Channel:* 40; *Virtual Channel:* 6; 1000 kw; 1717 ft.; N45 30 58 W122 43 58
222 S.W. Columbia Street, Portland, OR 97201 US
(503) 464-0600; *Fax:* (503) 464-0655
www.koin.com
koin@koin.com
License: Portland, Multnomah County, OR held by LIN License Company LLC
Group Owner: LIN Media; (acq 10-12-2013; grpsl)
Nat'l Network: CBS
Hours of Local News Weekly: News progmg 27 hrs wkly
Durwood Werner, CFO
Tim Perry, General Manager
Nicole Meyers, Programming Director
Rodger O'Connor, Promotions Manager
Lynn Heider, News Director
David Bird, Engineering Dir
Carl Gonzales, Traffic Manager
Jeff Gianola,Anchor
Dan Tilkin, Anchor
Mike Murad, Anchor
Tim Becker, Reporter
Ken Boddie, Anchor

***KOPB-TV** *Digital Channel:* 10; *Virtual Channel:* 10; 46 kw; 1719 ft.; N45 31 21 W122 44 45
7140 Sw Macadam Avenue, Portland, OR 97219 US
(503) 244-9900; (800) 241-8123; *Fax:* (503) 293-1919
www.opb.org
membercenter@opb.org
License: Portland, Multnomah County, OR held by Oregon Public Broadcasting
(acq 9-20-93; grpsl; *Washington Law Firm:* Schwartz, Woods & Miller
Nat'l Network: PBS
Steve Bass, CEO
Steve Bass, President
Dan Metziga, General Sales Mgr
Mary Gardner, Programming Director
Keith Mobley, Chairman
Jim Huston, Vice Chairman

KPTV *Digital Channel:* 12; *Virtual Channel:* 12; 24.5 kW; 1736 ft.; N45 31 18 W122 44 57
14975 NW Greenbrier Pkwy, Beaverton, OR 97006 USA
(503) 906-1249; *Fax:* (503) 548-6920
www.kptv.com
License: Portland, Multnomah County, OR held by KPTV-KPDX Broadcasting Corp.
Group Owner: Meredith Corp.; (acq 6-17-2002; swap).;
Washington Law Firm: Dow, Lohnes & Albertson
Nat'l Network: FOX; *Nat'l Reps:* TeleRep; *Wire Services:* AP
Hours of Local News Weekly: News progmg 42.5 hrs wkly
Adrienne Roark, General Manager
Denise Daniels, General Sales Mgr
Corey Hanson, News Director

KPXG-TV *Digital Channel:* 22; 745 kw; 1,187t/945g; N45 31 21 W122 44 45
811 SW. Naito Pkwy, Suite 100, Portland, OR 97204 USA
(503) 222-2221; *Fax:* (503) 222-4613
www.iontelevision.com
License: Salem, OR held by Ion Media Portland License, Inc.
Group Owner: ION Media Networks Inc.
Brandon Burgess, Chairman/CEO

KRCW *Digital Channel:* 33; *Virtual Channel:* 32; 750 kw; 1717 ft.; N45 30 58 W122 43 58
10255 SW Arctic Dr., Beaverton, OR 97005 USA
(503) 644-3232; *Fax:* (503) 626-3576
portlandscw32.com
License: Salem, Marion County, OR held by KRCW LLC
Group Owner: Tribune Media; (acq 12-20-2007; grpsl);
Washington Law Firm: Dow Lohnes PLLC
Nat'l Network: The CW Network; *Nat'l Reps:* TeleRep
Hours of Local News Weekly: News progmg 3.5 hrs wkly

***KTVR** *Digital Channel:* 13; *Virtual Channel:* 13; 16.1 kw; 2543 ft.; N45 18 33 W117 43 54
7140 Sw Macadam Avenue, Portland, OR 97219 US
(503) 244-9900; *Fax:* (503) 293-1919
www.opb.org
membercenter@opb.org
License: La Grande, Union County, OR held by Oregon Public Broadcasting
(acq 1993; grpsl; *Washington Law Firm:* Schwartz, Woods & Miller
Nat'l Network: PBS
Keith Mobley, Chairman
Steve Bass, CEO/President
Tom Doggett, Programming Director
Morgan Holm, News Director
Don McKay, Chief Engineer
Jim Huston, Vice Chair
Morgan Holm, Senior VP and Chief Content Officer
Dan Metziga, SeniorVP, Development
Lynne Clendenin, VP, Programming
Dave Davis, VP, TV Production
Mike Foti, VP, Engineering

KUNP *Digital Channel:* 16; *Virtual Channel:* 16; 18.95 kw; 2536 ft.; N45 18 33 W117 43 54
2153 N.E. Sandy Blvd., Portland, OR 97232 US
(503) 231-4222
www.kunptv.com
noticias@kunptv.com
License: La Grande, Union County, OR held by Sinclair Lagrande Licensee LLC
Group Owner: Sinclair Broadcast Group Inc.; (acq 8-8-2013)
Nat'l Network: UNIVISION
Foreign Language Programming
David Smith, General Sales Mgr
Evelin Hernandez, Program Coordinator
Mauricio Valadrian, Creative Services Director
LaRae Babb, Traffic Director
Ivan Garcia, News Producer
Oswaldo Bernal, Account Executive
Suzan Khouri, AccountExecutive
Ana Spain, Account Executive

Yakima-Pasco-Richland-Kennewick, WA (DMA 122)

KFFX-TV *Digital Channel:* 11; *Virtual Channel:* 11; 60 kw; 1549 ft.; N45 44 51 W118 2 11
Mailing Address: 105 Cedar Green Lane, Berkeley Heights, NJ 07922 US
Second Address: 4600 S Regal Street, Spokane, WA 99223
(509) 735-1700; *Fax:* (509) 735-1004
www.fox11tricities.com
License: Pendleton, Umatilla County, OR held by Mountain Licenses L.P.
Group Owner: Northwest Broadcasting Inc.; (acq 1-14-2003; $239,659 for CP); *Washington Law Firm:* Leventhal, Senter & Lerman
Nat'l Network: FOX; *Nat'l Reps:* Millennium Sales & Marketing
Brian Brady, CEO
Rick Andrycha, Operations Dir
Jon Rand, General Manager
Glenn Rousch, Station Manager
Lynn Creager, General Sales Mgr
Robin Lennell, Programming Director
Jennifer Ranney, Promotions Manager
Ron Sweatte, ChiefEngineer
Bill Quarles, CFO
Lonnie Eaton, Regional Sales Manager

Pennsylvania

Erie, PA (DMA 150)

WFXP *Digital Channel:* 22; 882 kw vis, 82 kw aur; 889t/697g; N42 02 31 W80 03 57; *Population Served:* 412,700
8455 Peach St., Erie, PA 16509 US
(814) 864-2400; *Fax:* (814) 864-5393
www.yourerie.com
License: Erie, Erie County, PA held by Mission Broadcasting Inc.
Group Owner: Mission Broadcasting Inc.; (acq 10-22-98).;
Washington Law Firm: Arter & Hadden
Nat'l Network: Fox
Hours of Local News Weekly: News progmg 3.5 hrs wkly
Barb Behr, Station Manager
Steve Freifeld, General Sales Mgr
Lou Baxter, News Director

WICU-TV *Digital Channel:* 12; *Virtual Channel:* 12; 5.4 kw; 1006 ft.; N42 3 50 W80 0 21
3514 State Street, Erie, PA 16508 US
(814) 454-5201, (800)-454-8812; *Fax:* (814) 455-0703
www.wicu12.com
License: Erie, Erie County, PA held by SJL of Pennsylvania License Subsidiary LLC
(acq 8-96; $11 million); *Washington Law Firm:* Latham & Watkins
Nat'l Network: NBC
Size of News Staff: 20; *Hours of Local News Weekly:* news progmg 22 hrs wkly
Brian Lilly, General Manager
Doug Beers, General Sales Mgr
Paula Randolph, Programming Director
Julie Eisenman, News Director
John Wilkosz, Chief Engineer

WJET-TV *Digital Channel:* 24; *Virtual Channel:* 24; 523 kw; 997 ft.; N42 2 25 W80 4 9
8455 Peach St., Erie, PA 16509 US
(814) 864-2400; *Fax:* (814) 868-3041
www.yourerie.com
License: Erie, Erie County, PA held by Nexstar Broadcasting Group
Group Owner: Nexstar Broadcasting Group Inc.; (acq 12-16-97; $18.5 million); *Washington Law Firm:* Drinker, Riddle & Reath
Nat'l Network: ABC
Hours of Local News Weekly: News progmg 3.5 hrs wkly
Stephen Freifeld, General Manager
Lou Baxter, News Director
Phil Kowalczyk, Chief Engineer

***WQLN** *Digital Channel:* 50; *Virtual Channel:* 54; 39.1 kw; 888 ft.; N42 2 34 W80 3 56
8425 Peach St, Erie, PA 16509 US
(814) 864-3001,(800) 727-8854; *Fax:* (814) 864-4077
www.wqln.org
wqln@wqln.org
License: Erie, Erie County, PA held by Public Broadcasting of Northwest Pennsylvania, Inc
Washington Law Firm: Dow, Lohnes & Albertson
Nat'l Network: PBS; *Regional Network:* Pennsylvania Public Television Network
Dwight Miller, President

WSEE-TV *Digital Channel:* 16; 1,170 kw vis, 117 kw aur; 941t/741g; N42 02 20 W80 03 45; *Population Served:* 500,000
3514 State St., Erie, PA 16508
(814) 454-5201; *Fax:* (814) 455-0703
www.wsee.tv
License: Erie, Erie County, PA held by Lilly Broadcasting of Pennslvania License Subsidiary LLC
(acq 11-28-02;. $10 million); *Washington Law Firm:* Lathan & Watkins
Nat'l Network: CBS; CW

Size of News Staff: 25; *Hours of Local News Weekly:* news progmg 14 hrs wkly
Kevin Lilly, President
John Christenson, General Manager
Doug Beers, General Sales Mgr
Michael Wolf, Programming Director
Bill Cummings, News director
John Wilkosz, Chief Engineer
Katie Keenan, Asst. News Dir. & AssignmentEditor/ Community Eve
Paula Randolph, Traffic
Justin Jarrett, IT
Matt Filippi, Sales Supervisor
Adam Snow, Chief Videographer

Harrisburg-Lancaster-Lebanon-York, PA (DMA 43)

***W07DP-D** *Digital Channel:* 7; *Virtual Channel:* 35; 0.3 kw ERP; 221m; 40 18 19 N Latitude, 77 00 28 W Longitude
One Signal Hill Drive, Wall, PA 15148-1499
(800) 820-4808, (412) 824-3930, (888) 665-4483; *Fax:* (412) 824-5442, (412) 824-9523
www.ctvn.org
License: Harrisburg, Dauphin County, PA held by Cornerstone Television Inc.
Group Owner: Cornerstone TeleVision Inc.; *Washington Law Firm:* Pillsbury, Winthrop & Shaw Pittman

WGAL *Digital Channel:* 8; *Virtual Channel:* 8; 32.2 kw; 1375 ft.; N40 2 4 W76 37 8
Mailing Address: 888 - 7th Avenue, New York, NY 10106 US
Second Address: 1300 Columbia Avenue, Lancaster, PA 17603
(717) 393-5851; *Fax:* (717) 295-7457
www.wgal.com
License: Lancaster, Lancaster County, PA held by WGAl Hearst Television Inc.
Group Owner: Hearst Television Inc.; (acq 1999; grpsl).; *Washington Law Firm:* Brooks, Pierce
Nat'l Network: NBC; *Nat'l Reps:* Eagle Television Sales
Size of News Staff: 53; *Hours of Local News Weekly:* news progmg 29 hrs wkly
Paul Quinn, President
Bob Good, Operations Dir
Nancy Tulli, General Sales Manager
Laura Warner, Programming
John Baldwin, Promotions Manager
Dan O'Donnell, News Director
Paul Ladrow, National Sales Manager
Neil Parker, LocalSales Manager
Elizabeth Montijo, Creative Services Director

WGCB-TV *Digital Channel:* 30; 617 kw vis, 114 kw aur; 581t/375g; N39 54 18 W76 35 00; *Population Served:* 740,000
P.O. Box 349, 2900 Windsor Rd, Red Lion, PA 17356
(717) 246-1681; *Fax:* (717) 244-9316
www.family49.com
info@family49.com
License: Red Lion, York County, PA held by NRJ TV RL License Co. LLC
Group Owner: NRJ Holdings LLC; 12/1/12; *Washington Law Firm:* Booth, Freret, Imlay and Tepper
Nat'l Network: MeTV
John Peeling, Operations Dir
Lou Castriota, Sr., GM/General Sales Manager/Programming Director
John McLaughlin, Chief Engineer
George Montgomery, Creative Services Director
Brian George, Chief Operator & General Manager

WHP-TV *Digital Channel:* 21; *Virtual Channel:* 21; 750 kw; 1211 ft.; N40 20 43 W76 52 9
3300 North 6th St., Harrisburg, PA 17110 US
(717) 238-2100; *Fax:* (717) 238-4903
www.local21news.com
news@local21news.com
License: Harrisburg, Dauphin County, PA held by WHP Licensee LLC
Group Owner: Sinclair Broadcast Group Inc.; (acq 3-14-2008; grpsl)
Nat'l Network: CBS
Size of News Staff: 23; *Hours of Local News Weekly:* news progmg 22 hrs wkly
Bill Bradley, General Manager
Scott Beaver, General Sales Mgr
Rob Hershey, Chief Engineer
Stu Brenner, National Sales Manager

WHTM-TV *Digital Channel:* 10; *Virtual Channel:* 27; 16.2 kw; 1021 ft.; N40 18 58 W76 57 1
3235 Hoffman Street, Harrisburg, PA 17110 US
(717) 236-2727; *Fax:* (717) 232-5272
www.abc27.com
tfalk@abc27.com
License: Harrisburg, Dauphin County, PA held by Harrisburg Television Inc.
Group Owner: Allbritton Communications Co.; (acq 1996; $113 million)
Nat'l Network: ABC
Size of News Staff: 46; *Hours of Local News Weekly:* news progmg 27 hrs wkly
Joe Lewin, President
Sharon Chambers, Operations Dir
Rob Saylor, General Sales Mgr
Betty Fish, Promotions Manager
Dennis Fisher, News Director
Jan Strock, Chief Engineer
Patti Jarvis, Human Resources
Paul Roda, National SalesManager
Tishia Falk, Asst. to the General manager
Al Gnoza, News Team
Alex Hoff, News Team
Ryan Coyle, News Team

***WITF-TV** *Digital Channel:* 36; *Virtual Channel:* 33; 50 kw; 1348 ft.; N40 20 44 W76 52 7
4801 Lindle Rd., Harrisburg, PA 17111 US
(717) 704-3000, (800) 366-9483; *Fax:* (717) 704-3659
www.witf.org
customerservice@witf.org
License: Harrisburg, Dauphin County, PA held by WITF Inc
Washington Law Firm: Dow, Lohnes & Albertson
Nat'l Network: PBS
Justin Weber, Chairman
Kathleen Pavelko, CEO/President
Michael Greenwald, Operations Dir
Darren Smith, General Manager, SVP - Sales
Bob Rich, General Sales Mgr
Craig Cohen, Programming Director
Gregory Poland, CFO, Sr. VP
Ronald Kain, Senior VP, CTO
Cara Williams Fry, Sr. VP, Chief Content Officer
Mark Duncan, Sr. VP, Chief Development Officer
Ronald Hetrick, Sr. VP, Chief Human Resources & Operational Performance
Donna Andrews, Assistant to the President

WLYH-TV *Digital Channel:* 23; *Virtual Channel:* 15; 500 kw; 1250 ft.; N40 15 45 W76 27 51
374 S, Butler Road, Lebanon, PA 17042 US
(717) 273-4697 ; *Fax:* (717) 270-0901
www.cw15.com
License: Lancaster, Lancaster County, PA
Nat'l Network: CW
Holly Stuart, General Manager
Scott Beaver, General Sales Mgr
Taylor Miller, Programming Director
Rob Hershey, Engineering Dir
Stuart Brenner, National Sales Manager

WPMT *Digital Channel:* 47; *Virtual Channel:* 43; 933 kw; 1263 ft.; N40 1 41 W76 36 0
2005 S Queen St., York, PA 17403 USA
fox43.com
wpmt@fox43.com
License: York, York County, PA held by WPMT LLC
Group Owner: Tribune Media
Nat'l Network: FOX; *Nat'l Reps:* TeleRep
Size of News Staff: 45; *Hours of Local News Weekly:* news progmg 17 hrs wkly
Sandy Hawk, Administative Asst./Program Coordinator

Johnstown-Altoona, PA (DMA 104)

WATM-TV *Digital Channel:* 24; *Virtual Channel:* 23; 1000 kw; 1020 ft.; N40 34 6 W78 26 38
1450 Scalp Avenue, Johnstown, PA 15904 US
(814) 266-8088,(814) 949-8823(sales); *Fax:* (814) 266-7749
www.abc23.com
License: Altoona, Blair County, PA held by Palm Television LP (acq 8-17-99; $12.5 million); *Washington Law Firm:* Dow, Lohnes & Albertson
Nat'l Network: ABC; *Wire Services:* AP
Brian Durham, CFO
Frank Quitoni, President/ General Manager
Jim Pastore, Regional/National Sales Manager
Jill Ream, Production Mgr/Programming Coordinator
Jill Brazill, Promotion Manager
Dan Owens, Chief Engineer
ShawnGlass-Lucas, Local Sales Manager
Bill Creager, Local Sales Manager
Brenda Pentz, Traffic Manager
TJ Coursen, Local Sales Manager

WJAC-TV *Digital Channel:* 34; *Virtual Channel:* 6; 1000 kw; 1266 ft.; N40 22 17 W78 58 56
49 Old Hickory Lane, Johnstown, PA 15905 US
(814) 255-7600; *Fax:* (814) 255-3958
www.wjactv.com
news@wjactv.com
License: Johnstown, Cambria County, PA held by WJAC Licensee LLC
Group Owner: Sinclair Broadcast Group Inc.; (acq 9-22-2000); *Washington Law Firm:* Dow, Lohnes & Albertson
Nat'l Network: NBC
Size of News Staff: 38; *Hours of Local News Weekly:* news progmg 25 hrs wkly
James Doty, General Manager

WKBS-TV ; *Virtual Channel:* 47; 1,510 kw vis, 151 kw aur; 1,010t/184g; N40 34 12 W78 26 26
One Signal Hill Drive, Wall, PA 15148-1499
(800) 820-4808, (412) 824-3930, (888) 665-4483, (4; *Fax:* (412) 824-5442, (412) 824-9523
www.ctvn.org
info@ctvn.org, focus4@ctvn.org
License: Altoona, Blair County, PA held by Cornerstone Television Inc.
Group Owner: Cornerstone TeleVision Inc.; *Washington Law Firm:* Pillsbury, Winthrop & Shaw Pittman
Rev. Gary Mitrik, Chairman
Tom Scott, CFO
Donald Black, President/CEO
Steve Johnson, Operations Dir
Tom McGough, General Sales Mgr
Tom Hollis, Programming Director
Tom Scott, CFO & Treasurer of the Board
Laurie Hamby, ExecutiveAsst. & Secretary

***WPSU-TV** *Digital Channel:* 15; *Virtual Channel:* 3; 810 kw; 1354 ft.; N41 7 20 W78 26 29.8
238 Outreach Building, 100 Innovation Blvd., University Park, PA 16802 US
(814) 865-3333, (800) 543-8242; *Fax:* (814) 863-9786
wpsu.org
License: Clearfield, Clearfield County, PA held by The Pennsylvania State University
Washington Law Firm: Paul, Hastings, Janofsky & Walker
Nat'l Network: PBS; *Regional Network:* Pennsylvania Public Television Network; *Wire Services:* AP
Jo Lash, Chairman
Kate Domico, Operations Dir
Ted Krichels, General Manager
Tom Yourchak, General Sales Mgr
Greg Petersen, Promotions Manager
Russ Rockwell, Chief Engineer
Ashear Barr, Advertising Director
Tom Keiter, CreativeServices Director
Annie Doncsecz, Finance Director
Amy Kelley, Traffic Manager

WTAJ-TV *Digital Channel:* 32; *Virtual Channel:* 10; 883 kw; 1001 ft.; N40 34 1 W78 26 30
5000 6th Ave., Altoona, PA 16602 US
(814) 942-1010; *Fax:* (814) 946-8746
www.wearecentralpa.com
License: Altoona, Blair County, PA held by Nexstar Broadcasting Inc.
Group Owner: Nexstar Broadcasting Group Inc.; (acq 12-29-2006; $56 million with WLYH-TV Lancaster); *Washington Law Firm:* Latham & Watkins
Nat'l Network: CBS; *Wire Services:* AP
Size of News Staff: 39; *Hours of Local News Weekly:* news progmg 29 hrs wkly
Phil Dubrow, VP/General Manager
Chris Miller, News Director

WWCP-TV *Digital Channel:* 8; *Virtual Channel:* 8; 9.3 kw; 1207 ft.; N40 10 53 W79 9 5
Mailing Address: 1450 Scalp Avenue, Johnstown, PA 15904 US
Second Address: 141 W. Beaver Ave., State College, PA 16801
(814) 266-8088, (814) 237-2300; *Fax:* (814) 266-7749, (814) 237-3545
www.fox8tv.com
fquitoni@fox8tv.com
License: Johnstown, Cambria County, PA held by Peak Media of Pennsylvania Licensee LLC
Washington Law Firm: Dow, Lohnes & Albertson
Nat'l Network: FOX; *Wire Services:* AP
Frank Quitoni, President & General Manager
Jill Ream, Production Manager/ Programming Coordinator
Jill Brazill, Promotion Manager
Dan Owens, Chief Engineer

Brenda Pentz, Traffic Manager
Brian Durham, CFO
Jim Pastore, Regional/National Sales Manager
Bill creager, Local Sales Manager
TJ Coursen, Local Sales Manager

Philadelphia (DMA 4)

KYW-TV *Digital Channel:* 26; *Virtual Channel:* 3; 790 kW; 1201 ft.; N40 2 33 W75 14 33; *Population Served:* 1,688,210
1555 Hamilton St., Philadelphia, PA 19130 USA
(215) 977-5333; *Fax:* (215) 977-5658
philadelphia.cbslocal.com
License: Philadelphia, Philadelphia County, PA held by CBS Broadcasting Inc.
Group Owner: CBS Television Stations Group
Nat'l Network: CBS; *Nat'l Reps:* CBS TV Stations National Sales
Perry Casciato, Programming Director

WBPH-TV *Digital Channel:* 9; *Virtual Channel:* 60; 80.6 kw; 991 ft.; N40 34 1.5 W75 26 4.8
813 N. Fenwick Street, Allentown, PA 18109 US
(610) 433-4400; *Fax:* (610) 433-8251
www.wbph.org
info@wbph.org
License: Bethlehem, Northampton County, PA held by Sonshine Family TV Inc
Nat'l Network: IND
Pat Huber, CEO

WCAU *Digital Channel:* 34; *Virtual Channel:* 10; 700 kw; 1313 ft.; N40 2 30 W75 14 11
10 Monument Rd., Bala Cynwyd, PA 19004 USA
(610) 668-5510, (610) 668-5705; *Fax:* (610) 668-7039
www.nbcphiladelphia.com
License: Philadelphia, Philadelphia County, PA held by NBC Telemundo License LLC
Group Owner: NBC Owned Television Stations; (acq 9-10-95).
Nat'l Network: NBC; *Nat'l Reps:* NBC TV Stations Sales; *Wire Services:* UPI; AP
Size of News Staff: 110; *Hours of Local News Weekly:* news progmg 21 hrs wkly

WFMZ-TV *Digital Channel:* 46; *Virtual Channel:* 69; 800 kw; 1086 ft.; N40 33 52 W75 26 24
Mailing Address: 300 East Rock Road, Allentown, PA 18103-7599 US
Second Address: 225 Court Street, Reading, PA 19601
(610) 791-1111, (610) 372-6969, (800) 577-6970; *Fax:* (610) 791-9994, (610) 372-7269
www.WFMZ.com
news@wfmz.com
License: Allentown, Lehigh County, PA held by Maranatha Broadcasting Co
Washington Law Firm: Bentley Law Offices
Nat'l Network: IND; *Wire Services:* AP; Accu-Weather; PR Newswire
Size of News Staff: 120; *Hours of Local News Weekly:* news progmg 32 hrs wkly
Richard Dean, Chairman
Mike Kulp, CFO
Barry Fisher, President
Brad Rinehart, General Manager
Kevin Arndt, General Sales Mgr
Charles Gale, News Director

***WLVT-TV** *Digital Channel:* 39; *Virtual Channel:* 39; 52 kw; 968 ft.; N40 33 52 W75 26 24
839 Sesame St., Bethelem, PA 18015 US
(610) 867-4677; *Fax:* (610) 867-3544
www.wlvt.org
License: Allentown, Lehigh County, PA held by Lehigh Valley Public Telecommunications Corp
Washington Law Firm: Dow, Lohnes
Nat'l Network: PBS; *Regional Network:* Pennsylvania Public Television Network
Foreign Language Programming
Jamie Musselman, Chairman
Tim Fallon, CEO
David Smith, Chief Engineer
Charles Stinner, Vice-Chairman

WPHL *Digital Channel:* 17; *Virtual Channel:* 17; 645 kW; 1063 ft.; N40 2 30 W75 14 23
5001 Wynnefield Ave., Philadelphia, PA 19131 USA
(215) 878-1700
phl17.com
feedback@phl17.com
License: Philadelphia, Philadelphia County, PA held by WPHL LLC
Group Owner: Tribune Media; (acq 12-20-2007; grpsl);
Washington Law Firm: Dow Lohnes PLLC
Nat'l Network: MyNetworkTV; *Nat'l Reps:* TeleRep

WPPX-TV *Digital Channel:* 31; 200 kw; ant 958t/951g; N40 02 30 W75 14 11; *Population Served:* 2,700,000
3901 B. Main St., Suite 301, Philadelphia, PA 19127 USA
(215) 482-4770; *Fax:* (215) 482-4777
www.iontelevision.com
License: Wilmington, DE held by ION Media Philadelphia License Inc.
Group Owner: ION Media Networks Inc.
Nat'l Network: ION Television
Brandon Burgess, Chairman/CEO

WPSG-TV *Digital Channel:* 32; *Virtual Channel:* 57; 800 kW; 1234 ft.; N40 2 30 W75 14 11
1555 Hamilton St., Philadelphia, PA 19130 USA
(215) 977-5710; *Fax:* (215) 977-5658
cwphilly.cbslocal.com
License: Philadelphia, Philadelphia County, PA held by Philadelphia Television Station WPSG, Inc.
Group Owner: CBS Television Stations Group; *Washington Law Firm:* Fisher, Wayland, Cooper, Leader & Zaragoza
Nat'l Network: The CW Network
Perry Casciato, Programming Director

WPVI-TV *Digital Channel:* 6; *Virtual Channel:* 6; 34 kW; 1052 ft.; N40 2 33 W75 14 33
4100 City Ave., Philadelphia, PA 19131 USA
(215) 878-9700; *Fax:* (215) 581-4530
6abc.com
License: Philadelphia, Philadelphia County, PA held by ABC Inc.
Group Owner: ABC Owned Television Stations; *Washington Law Firm:* Wilmer, Cutler & Pickering
Nat'l Network: ABC
Diane Hamlet, Creative Services Coordinator
Tim Gianettino, VP & National Sales Manager
Dirk Ohley, VP & Local Sales Manager

WTVE *Digital Channel:* 25; *Virtual Channel:* 51; 126 kw; 1241 ft.; N40 2 29.56 W75 14 12.89
1729 North 11th Street, Reading, PA 19604 US
(610) 921-9181; *Fax:* (610) 921-9139
www.wtve.com
jmclaughlin@wtve.com
License: Reading, Berks County, PA held by WRNN-TV Associates LP.
(acq 5-12-2008; $13.5 million); *Washington Law Firm:* Covington & Burling
Nat'l Network: IND
George Mattmiller, General Manager
Lee Wapack, Sales Manager
Danny Kischel, Programming Director
john McLaughlin, Chief Engineer
Christine Adams, Office manager

WTXF-TV *Digital Channel:* 42; *Virtual Channel:* 29; 620 kW; 1125 ft.; N40 2 26 W75 14 19
330 Market St., Phildaelphia, PA 19106 USA
(215) 925-2929; *Fax:* (215) 982-5494
www.fox29.com
fox29.programming@foxtv.com
License: Allentown, Lehigh County, PA held by Fox Television Stations LLC
Group Owner: Fox Television Stations Group; (acq 1995; $200 million)
Nat'l Network: FOX
Hours of Local News Weekly: News progmg 36.5 hrs wkly

***WYBE** *Digital Channel:* 35; *Virtual Channel:* 35; 450 kw; 1234 ft.; N40 2 30 W75 14 11
441 N. 5th St., Phildaelphia, PA 19123 US
(215) 483-3900; *Fax:* (215) 483-6908
www.mindtv.org
nwebb@mindtv.org
License: Philadelphia, Philadelphia County, PA held by Independence Public Media of Philadelphia Inc
Washington Law Firm: Drinker, Biddle & Reath L.L.P.
Nat'l Network: ETV
Foreign Language Programming
Rene Degeorge Smith, Chair
Howard Blumenthal, CEO
Joni Helton, Programming Director
Frank Lordi, Treasurer

Pittsburgh, PA (DMA 23)

KDKA-TV *Digital Channel:* 25; *Virtual Channel:* 2; 1000 kW; 656 ft.; N40 29 38 W80 1 9
420 Fort Duquesne Blvd., Suite 100, Pittsburgh, PA 15222 USA
(412) 575-2200; *Fax:* (412) 578-2871
pittsburgh.cbslocal.com
newsdesk@kdka.com
License: Pittsburgh, Allegheny County, PA held by CBS Broadcasting Inc.
Group Owner: CBS Television Stations Group; *Washington Law Firm:* Wilkes, Artis, Hedrick & Lane
Nat'l Network: CBS; *Nat'l Reps:* CBS TV Stations National Sales
Mike Karas, Director of Programming

WINP-TV *Digital Channel:* 38; 500 kw; ant 705t/601g; N40 26 46 W79 57 51
285 Kappa Dr., Suite 130, Pittsburgh, PA 15238 USA
(412) 622-1370; *Fax:* (412) 622-1488
www.iontelevision.com
License: Pittsburgh, PA held by Ion Media of Scranton, Inc.
Group Owner: Ion Media Networks; *Washington Law Firm:* Schwartz, Woods & Miller
Nat'l Network: ION Television
Brandon Burgess, Chairman/CEO

WPCB-TV *Digital Channel:* 40; Kw ERP vis; SWR SWCSD160l/50; N40 23 34 W79 46 54; *Rebroadcasting:* Top 6 owned and operated stations + 80+ affiliated stations nationwide via satellite
1 Signal Hill Drive, Wall, PA 15148-1499
(412) 824-3930; *Fax:* (412) 824-9523
www.ctvn.org
info@ctvn.org
License: Pittsburgh/Greensburg, Westmoreland County, PA held by Cornerstone Television Inc.
Group Owner: Cornerstone TeleVision Inc.; (acq 7-78).;
Washington Law Firm: Shaw Pittman
Pastor Gary Mitrick, Chairman of the Board
Don Black, President/Chief Executive Officer
Steve Johnson, Operations Dir
Tom McGough, General Sales Mgr
Tom Hollis, Programming Director
Roger Wilson, Chief Engineer
Crystal Bynum,Marketing Coordinator

WPCW-TV *Digital Channel:* 11; *Virtual Channel:* 19; 30 kW; 486 ft.; N40 29 38 W80 1 9
420 Fort Duquesne Blvd., Suite 100, Pittsburgh, PA 15222 USA
(412) 575-2200; *Fax:* (412) 578-2871
cwpittsburgh.cbslocal.com
feedback@wpcwtv.com
License: Jeannette, Westmoreland County, PA held by Pittsburgh Television Station WPCW Inc.
Group Owner: CBS Television Stations Group
Nat'l Network: The CW Network
Jack Rosenberger, Local Sales Manager
Mike Karas, Director of Programming

WPGH-TV *Digital Channel:* 43; *Virtual Channel:* 53; 1000 kw; 993 ft.; N40 29 43 W80 0 18
Mailing Address: 750 Ivory Ave., Pittsburgh, PA 15214 US
Second Address: 10706 Beaver Dam Rd., Hunt Valley, MD 21030
(412) 931-5300; *Fax:* (412) 931-4284
www.wpgh53.com
License: Pittsburgh, Allegheny County, PA held by WPGH Licensee LLC
Group Owner: Sinclair Broadcast Group Inc.; (acq 8-30-91; $55 million; *Washington Law Firm:* Pillsbury, Winthrop & Pittman
Nat'l Network: FOX; *Nat'l Reps:* Millennium Sales & Marketing
Jim Lapiana, General Manager

WPNT *Digital Channel:* 42; *Virtual Channel:* 22; 1000 kw; 1033 ft.; N40 29 43 W80 0 17
750 Ivory Ave., Pittsburgh, PA 15214 US
(412) 931-5300; *Fax:* (412) 931-4284
www.22thepoint.com
License: Pittsburgh, Allegheny County, PA held by WCWB Licensee LLC
Group Owner: Sinclair Broadcast Group Inc.; (acq 12-10-2001; $17.808 million); *Washington Law Firm:* Pillsbury, Winthrop & Pittman
Nat'l Network: MYTV; *Nat'l Reps:* Millennium Sales & Marketing
Jim Lapiana, General Manager

WPXI *Digital Channel:* 48; *Virtual Channel:* 11; 1000 kw; 948 ft.; N40 27 48 W80 0 16
4145 Evergreen Rd., Pittsburgh, PA 15214 US
(412) 237-1100; *Fax:* (412) 237-4900
www.wpxi.com
webstaff@wpxi.com
License: Pittsburgh, Allegheny County, PA held by WPXI-TV Holdings Inc.
Group Owner: Cox Media Group; (acq 1-1-65; $20.5 million;
Washington Law Firm: Dow, Lohnes & Albertson
Nat'l Network: NBC; *Nat'l Reps:* TeleRep

Ann Glausser, CFO
Ray Carter, General Manager
Paul Curran, General Sales Mgr
Mark Barash, Programming Director
Karen Lah, Promotions Manager
Corrie Harding, News Director
Annette Parks, Engineering Dir
Darryl Griffin, NationalSales Manager
Joe Arena, News Anchor
Stephen Cropper, Meterologist
Alby Oxenreiter, Sports
Timyka Artist, General Assignment Reporter
Renee Kaminski, News Reporter

***WQED** *Digital Channel:* 13; *Virtual Channel:* 13; 25 kw; 689 ft.; N40 26 46 W79 57 51
4802 Fifth Avenue, Pittsburgh, PA 15213 US
(412) 622-1370; *Fax:* (412) 622-1488,(412) 622-1427
www.wqed.org
viewers@wqed.org
License: Pittsburgh, Allegheny County, PA held by WQED Multimedia
Washington Law Firm: Schwartz, Woods & Miller
Nat'l Network: PBS; *Wire Services:* Reuters
Debra L. Caplan, Chairman
Deborah L. Acklin, President & CEO
Debbie Acklin, General Manager
Lilli Mosco, VP of Development & Membership
Carolie Bailey, CFO & Treasurer
Darryl Ford williams, VP of content
Carole A. Bailey,Treasurer
Jacquelyn Thomas, Secretary

WTAE-TV *Digital Channel:* 51; *Virtual Channel:* 4; 1000 kw; 896 ft.; N40 16 49 W79 48 11
888 Seventh Avenue, New York, NY 10106 US
(412) 242-4300; *Fax:* (412) 244-4595
www.wtae.com
License: Pittsburgh, Allegheny County, PA held by WTAE Hearst Television Inc.
Group Owner: Hearst Television Inc.; (acq 7-16-97; grpsl).;
Washington Law Firm: Brooks, Pierce, McLendon, Humphrey & Leonard
Nat'l Network: ABC; *Nat'l Reps:* Eagle Television Sales
Size of News Staff: 70; *Hours of Local News Weekly:* news progmg 32 hrs wkly
Bob Bee, General Sales Mgr
Luanne Russell, Programming Director
Leslie Wojdowski, Promotions Manager

Wilkes Barre-Scranton, PA (DMA 56)

WBRE-TV *Digital Channel:* 11; *Virtual Channel:* 28; 30 kw; 1545 ft.; N41 10 58 W75 52 26
Mailing Address: PO Box 28, Wilkes-Barre, PA 18773 US
Second Address: 62 S. Franklin St., Wilkes-Barre, PA 18701
(570) 823-2828; *Fax:* (570) 823-4523
www.pahomepage.com
License: Wilkes-Barre, Luzerne County, PA held by Nexstar Broadcasting Inc.
Group Owner: Nexstar Broadcasting Group Inc.; (acq 11-14-97; $47 million); *Washington Law Firm:* Drinker, Biddle & Reath, LLP
Nat'l Network: NBC; *Nat'l Reps:* Continental Television Sales
Size of News Staff: 68; *Hours of Local News Weekly:* news progmg 24 hrs wkly
Bob Bee, General Manager
Jim Depury, News Director

WNEP *Digital Channel:* 22; *Virtual Channel:* 16; 500 kw; 1696 ft.; N41 10 57 W75 52 15
16 Montage Mountain Rd., Moosic, PA 18507 USA
(570) 346-7474; *Fax:* (570) 347-0359
wnep.com
License: Waymart, Wayne County, PA held by Local TV Pennsylvania License LLC
Group Owner: Dreamcatcher Broadcasting LLC; *Washington Law Firm:* Covington & Burling
Nat'l Network: ABC; *Nat'l Reps:* Millennium Sales & Marketing; *Wire Services:* AP; PR Newswire
Size of News Staff: 64; *Hours of Local News Weekly:* news progmg 36 hrs wkly

WOLF-TV *Digital Channel:* 45; *Virtual Channel:* 56; 420 kw; 1601 ft.; N41 11 0 W75 52 10
1181 Highway 315, Plains, PA 18702 US
(570) 970-5600; *Fax:* (570) 970-5601
www.myfoxnepa.com
myfoxnepa@fox56.com
License: Hazleton, Luzerne County, PA held by New Age Media of Pennsylvania License LLC.
Group Owner: CP Media LLC; (acq 3-31-2007; grpsl);
Washington Law Firm: Leventhal Senter & Lerman PLLC
Nat'l Network: FOX *Regional Reps:* Petry
Hours of Local News Weekly: News progmg 6.5 hrs wkly
Michael Yanuzzi, President
Jon Cadman, General Manager
Bob Spager, General Sales Manager
Melissa Schwartz, Programming
Maria Stalter, National Sales Manager
Jeffery Nelson, Webmaster
Steve Phillips, Creative Services Manager

WQMY *Digital Channel:* 29; *Virtual Channel:* 53; 50 kw; 797 ft.; N41 12 1 W77 7 13
1181 Highway 315, Plains, PA 18702 US
(570) 970-5600; *Fax:* (570) 970-5601
www.myfoxnepa.com
myfoxnepa@fox56.com
License: Williamsport, Lycoming County, PA held by New Age Media of Pennsylvania License LLC.
Group Owner: CP Media LLC; (acq 3-31-2007; grpsl);
Washington Law Firm: Leventhal Senter & Lerman PLLC
Nat'l Network: MYTV
Jon Cadmon, General Sales Manager
Bob Spager, General Sales Manager
Melissa Schwartz, Programming
Maria Stalter, Regional Sales Manager
Steve Phillips, Creative Services Manager
Jeffery Nelson, Webmaster

WQPX-TV *Digital Channel:* 32; 528 kw; ant 1,220t/377g; N41 26 06 W75 43 35
409 Lackawanna Ave., Suite 700, Scranton, PA 18503 USA
(570) 344-6400; *Fax:* (570) 344-3303
www.iontelevision.com
License: Scranton, PA held by Ion Media Scranton License, Inc.
Group Owner: ION Media Networks Inc.; *Washington Law Firm:* Schwartz, Woods & Miller
Nat'l Network: ION Television
Brandon Burgess, Chairman/CEO

WSWB *Digital Channel:* 31; *Virtual Channel:* 38; 100 kw; 1155 ft.; N41 26 9 W75 43 46
1181 Hwy. 315, Plains, PA 18702 US
(570) 970-5600; *Fax:* (570) 970-5601,(570) 970-5605
www.myfoxnepa.com
License: Scranton, Lackawanna County, PA held by MPS Media of Scranton License LLC.
(acq 3-31-2007; $3.044 million with WTLF(TV) Tallahassee, FL);
Ownership: Eugene J. Brown, 100% votes
Nat'l Network: CW
Michael Yanuzzi, President
Aldo Cardoni, Operations Dir
Jon Cadman, General Manager
Bob Spager, General Sales Manager
Melissa Schwartz, Programming
Steve Phillips, Promotions Manager
Rich Chofey, Chief Engineer
Maria Stalter,National Sales Manager
Lisa Miller, Traffic Manager
Jeffery Nelson, Webmaster
Steve Phillips, Creative Services Manager

***WVIA-TV** *Digital Channel:* 41; *Virtual Channel:* 44; 365 kw; 1673 ft.; N41 10 55.3 W75 52 16.3
100 WVIA Way, Pittston, PA 18640 US
(570) 826-6144, (570) 344-1244; *Fax:* (570) 655-1180
www.wvia.org
License: Scranton, Lackawanna County, PA held by Northeastern Pennsylvania Educational TV Association
Washington Law Firm: Dow, Lohnes & Albertson
Nat'l Network: PBS
Bill Kelly, CEO & President
Thomas Curra, Operations Dir
Joe Glynn, VP of Engineering
Mark Ruddy, VP of Engineering
Lynn Volk, CFO
Ron Prislupski, VP of Corporate & Business Development
George Thomas, VP of Membership
BenPayavis II, VP of Studios & Production
Doug Cook, VP of Distribution & Promotion
Kathryn Davies, Sr. producer

WYOU *Digital Channel:* 13; *Virtual Channel:* 22; 30 kw; 1545 ft.; N41 10 58 W75 52 26
62 S. Franklin St., Wilkes-Barre, PA 18701 US
(570) 961-2222; *Fax:* (570) 823-4523
www.pahomepage.com
License: Scranton, Lackawanna County, PA held by Mission Broadcasting Inc.
Group Owner: Mission Broadcasting Inc.; (acq 1-5-98; $21 million); *Washington Law Firm:* Drinker, Biddle & Reath LLP
Nat'l Network: CBS; *Nat'l Reps:* Blair Television
Hours of Local News Weekly: News progmg 19.5 hrs wkly
Gina Schreiber, Station Manager
Jim Depury, News Director

Puerto Rico

Aguada

WQHA *Digital Channel:* 50; *Virtual Channel:* 50; 50 kw; 1125 ft.; N18 19 7 W67 10 48
Post Office Box 847, Mayaguez, PR 0681 US
(787) 750-4090; *Fax:* (787) 701-4245
www.ncntelevision.com
conciliofav@hotmail.com
License: Aguada, Aguada County, PR held by Concilio Mision Cristiana Fuente de Agua Viva
Nat'l Network: IND
Otoniel Font, General Manager
Edwin Rodriguez, General Sales Mgr
Josue Salgado, Programming Director

Aguadilla

WOLE-DT ; 47 kw; 661 meters; 18 09'0 N 66 59'0 W
111 Bo Palmar Rd., Auguadilla, PR 00603
(787) 997-1200; *Fax:* (787) 891-3380
www.wole12.com
recepcion@wole12.com
License: Aguadilla, Aguadilla County, PR held by Western Broadcasting Corp. of Puerto Rico
Foreign Language Programming
Glorianne Muniz, Sales Director
Doel Oriol, Chief Engineer

Arecibo

WCCV-TV *Digital Channel:* 46; *Virtual Channel:* 54; 50 kw; 1969 ft.; N18 14 6 W66 45 36
P.O. Box 949, Camuy, PR 00627 US
(787) 262-5400, (787) 898-5410; *Fax:* (787) 262-0541
License: Arecibo, Arecibo County, PR held by Asociacion Evan. Cristo Viene Inc
Washington Law Firm: Fletcher, Heald & Hildreth, P.L.C.
Nat'l Network: IND
Marcos Plaud, General Manager

WMEI *Digital Channel:* 14; *Virtual Channel:* 14; 315 kw; 2,733 ft.; N18 9 17.1 W66 33 16.4; *Not on Air/Target Date:* unknown
1095 Wilson St., San Juan, PR 00907 US
(787) 723-0060; *Fax:* (787) 725-0091
www.maxmediallc.com
License: Arecibo, Arecibo County, PR held by CMCG Puerto Rico License LLC.
Group Owner: MAX Media L.L.C.; (acq 7-17-2006; $4.25 million)
Nat'l Network: IND
Aubrey Eugene Loving Jr., Chairman & CEO
John Trinder, President & Chief Operating Officer
Dick Lamb, Radio Operations Director
Enid Catarineu, Administrative Assistant

Bayamon

WDWL *Digital Channel:* 30; *Virtual Channel:* 36; 100 kw; 1027 ft.; N18 16 49 W66 6 35
P.O. Box 50615, Levitown Station, PR 0950 US
(787) 795-8113, (787) 795-8115, (787) 795-8181; *Fax:* (787) 795-8140
www.teleadoracion.com
info@teleadoracion.com
License: Bayamon, Bayamon County, PR held by Bayamon Christian Network.
Nat'l Network: TBN ENLACE
Jesus Velez, President
Zoraida Jostinano, General Manager
David Baez, Chief Engineer

Caguas

WLII-DT *Digital Channel:* 11; *Virtual Channel:* 11; 48 kw; 1004 ft.; N18 16 52 W66 06 43.3
64 Carazo St., Guaynabo, PR 00969
(787) 300-5000
www.univision.com
License: Caguas, PR held by WLII/WSUR License Partnership G.P.
Group Owner: Univision Communications Inc.
Foreign Language Programming
Jaime Bauza, General Manager
Carlos Pagan, General Sales Mgr

Andres Diaz, Chief Engineer
Maxi Paglia, Senior Content Director

***WUJA** *Digital Channel:* 48; *Virtual Channel:* 58; 50 kw; 1024 ft.; N18 16 48 W66 6 33
Post Office Box 4039, Carolina, PR 0628 US
(787) 625-5858; *Fax:* (787) 701-4245
www.wuja.org
License: Caguas, Caguas County, PR held by Caguas Educational TV Inc
Nat'l Network: ETV
Otoniel Font, General Manager

Fajardo

***WMTJ** *Digital Channel:* 16; *Virtual Channel:* 40; 140 kw; 2796 ft.; N18 18 35 W65 47 43
Mailing Address: P. O. Box 21345, Rio Piedras, PR 0928 US
Second Address: 1395 Isidoro Colon St., San Juan, PR 928
(787) 766-2600; *Fax:* (787) 250-8546
www.suagm.edu/sitv
License: Fajardo, Fajardo County, PR held by Sistema Universitario Ana G. Mendez, Inc.
Washington Law Firm: Dow, Lohnes & Albertson
Nat'l Network: PBS
Foreign Language Programming
Margarita Millan, Operations Dir

Mayaguez

***WIPM-TV** *Digital Channel:* 35; *Virtual Channel:* 3; 620 kw; 2211 ft.; N18 9 0 W66 59 0; *Rebroadcasting:* WIPR (San Juan) 100%
P.O. Box 190909, Hato Rey, PR 0919 US
(787) 834-0164; *Fax:* (787) 832-9139
www.tutv.puertorico.pr
tutvwebmaster@tutv.puertorico.pr
License: Mayaguez, Mayaguez County, PR held by Puerto Rico Public Broadcasting Corp
Washington Law Firm: Steptoe & Johnson
Nat'l Network: ETV
Victor Morales, Operations Dir
E. Feliciano, General Manager
Diane Ramos, General Sales Mgr
Jorge Gonzalez, Chief Engineer

WNJX-TV *Digital Channel:* 23; *Virtual Channel:* 4; 400 kw; 2274 ft.; N18 9 0 W66 59 0; *Rebroadcasting:* Rebroadcasts WAPA-TV San Juan 100%
Carribean Plaza, Mendez, Viga #69, Suite 303, Mayaguez, PR 0680 US
(787) 792-4444; *Fax:* (787) 782-4420
www.wapa.tv
License: Mayaguez, Mayaguez County, PR held by Televicentro of Puerto Rico, L.L.C.
Group Owner: Hemisphere Media Group Inc.; (acq 3-20-2007; grpsl)
Nat'l Network: IND
Foreign Language Programming
Joe Ramos, General Manager
Jonathan Garcia, General Sales Mgr
Jimmy Artega, Programming Director
Enrique Cruz, News Director
Jose Guerra, Chief Engineer
Aurora Tirado, Traffic Manager

WORA-TV *Digital Channel:* 29; 100 kw vis, 20 kw aur; 2,001t/241g; N18 09 02 W66 59 20
Carr 102 Km 5.2 Bo. Guanajibo, Mayaguez, PR 00680
(787) 831-5555/(787) 721-4054; *Fax:* (787) 833-0075/(787) 724-1554
www.woratv.com
gvega@woratv.com
License: Mayaguez, Mayaguez County, PR held by Telecinco Inc
Washington Law Firm: Drinker Biddle & Reath LLP
Foreign Language Programming
Jose Vizcarronda, President
Alejandro Luciano, Engineering Director
Lilliam Rodriguez, Sales Department
Fred Toledo, Chief Engineer
Aixa Benejan, Traffic Manager

Ponce

WKPV *Digital Channel:* 19; *Virtual Channel:* 20; 700 kw; 883 ft.; N18 4 49 W66 44 53; *Rebroadcasting:* Satellite of WJPX(TV) San Juan
601clearwater Park Rd, West Palm Beach, FL 33401 US
(787) 792-4760,(787) 705-4153; *Fax:* (787) 782-7825
www.caribevision.com
edwn.pujols@wapa-tv.com
License: Ponce, Ponce County, PR held by S & E Network Inc.
Group Owner: CaribeVision Station Group LLC; (acq 9-20-2007; grpsl)
Nat'l Network: MundoFox
Joe Ramos, General Manager

***WQTO** *Digital Channel:* 25; *Virtual Channel:* 26; 800 kw; 1017 ft.; N18 4 48 W66 44 56; *Rebroadcasting:* Satellite of WMTJ Fajardo
Mailing Address: P.O. Box E, Rio Piedras, PR 0928 US
Second Address: 1395 Isidoro Colon St., San Juan, PR 928
(787) 766-2600; *Fax:* (787) 250-8546
www.suagm.edu/sitv
License: Ponce, Ponce County, PR held by Sistema Universitario Ana G. Mendez, Inc
Washington Law Firm: Dow, Lohnes & Albertson
Nat'l Network: PBS
Margarita Millan, Operations Dir

WSTE-DT *Digital Channel:* 7; *Virtual Channel:* 7; 3.2 kw vis; ant 289t/220g; N18 02 52 W66 39 16
64 Carazo St., Guaynabo, PR 00969
(787) 300-5000
www.univision.com
License: Ponce, Ponce County, PR held by WLII/WSUR License Partnership G.P.
Group Owner: Univision Communications Inc.; (acq 11-30-2007; $15.5 million)
Foreign Language Programming
Jaime Bauza, General Manager
Carlos Pagan, General Sales Mgr
Andres Diaz, Chief Engineer
Maxi Paglia, Senior Content Director

WSUR-DT *Digital Channel:* 9; *Virtual Channel:* 9; 21.6 kw; 2812 ft.; N18 10 9 W66 34 36
Mailing Address: Calle Lolita Tizol #47, Ponce, PR 00730
Second Address: 64 Carazo St., Guaynabo, PR 00960
(787) 300-5000
www.univision.com
License: Ponce, Ponce County, PR held by WLII/WSUR License Partnership G.P.
Group Owner: Univision Communications Inc.
Foreign Language Programming
Jaime Bauza, General Manager
Carlos Pagan, General Sales Mgr
Andres Diaz, Chief Engineer
Maxi Paglia, Senior Content Director
Sheryll Perez, Director, Communications and Community Empowerment

WTIN-TV *Digital Channel:* 15; 1070 kw vis, 10 kw aur; ant 2,824t/53g; N18 10 11 W66 34 38; *Rebroadcasting:* Rebroadcasts WAPA-TV San Juan 100%
Box 362050, San Juan, PR 00936-2050
(787) 792-4444; *Fax:* (787) 782-4420
www.wapa.tv
License: Ponce, Ponce County, PR held by Televicentro of Puerto Rico LLC.
Group Owner: Hemisphere Media Group Inc.; (acq 5-6-2004; $5 million); *Washington Law Firm:* Lerman Senter PLLC
Jimmy Artega, Programming Director
Jose Guerra, Chief Engineer

San Juan

WAPA-TV *Digital Channel:* 27; *Virtual Channel:* 4; 1000 kw; 2605 ft.; N18 6 42 W66 3 5
300 Crescent Court, Suite 600, Dallas, TX 75201 US
(787) 792-4444; *Fax:* (787) 782-4420
www.wapa.tv
info@wapa.tv
License: San Juan, San Juan County, PR held by Televicentro of Puerto Rico L.L.C.
Group Owner: Hemisphere Media Group Inc.; (acq 3-30-2007; grpsl); *Washington Law Firm:* Fletcher, Heald & Hildreth
Nat'l Network: IND
Foreign Language Programming; Size of News Staff: 29; *Hours of Local News Weekly:* news progmg 20 hrs wkly
Joe Ramos, General Manager
Jonathan Garcia, General Sales Mgr
Jimmy Artega, Programming Director
Enrique Cruz, News Director
Jose Guerra, Chief Engineer
Aurora Tirado, Traffic Manager

***WIPR-TV** *Digital Channel:* 43; *Virtual Channel:* 6; 791 kw; 2546 ft.; N18 6 42 W66 3 5
P.O. Box 190909, Hato Rey, PR 0919 US
(787) 766-0505; *Fax:* (787) 753-9846
License: San Juan, San Juan County, PR held by Puerto Rico Public Broadcasting Corp
Washington Law Firm: Steven Huffines
Nat'l Network: PBS
Foreign Language Programming
Pedro Rua, Operations Dir
Ray Cruz, General Manager
Jocelyn Lamas, General Sales Mgr
Evangeline Vazquez, Programming Director
Jorge Gonzalez, Chief Engineer
Victor Morales, Operations Vice President

WJPX *Digital Channel:* 21; *Virtual Channel:* 24; 1000 kw; 1850 ft.; N18 16 45 W65 51 14
601 Clearwater Park Rd, West Palm Beach, FL 33401 US
(787) 792-4444,(787) 706-4153; *Fax:* (787) 782-7825
www.caribevision.com
edwin.pujols@wapa-tv.com
License: San Juan, San Juan County, PR held by S&E Network Inc.
Group Owner: CaribeVision Station Group LLC; (acq 9-20-2007; grpsl); *Washington Law Firm:* Dow, Lohnes & Albertson
Nat'l Network: MundoFox
Joe Ramos, General Manager
Edwin Pujols, Station Manager
Jonathan Garcia, General Sales Mgr
Margarita Millan, Programming Director
Enrique Cruz, News Director
Jose Guerra, Chief Engineer
Aurora Tirado, Traffic Manager

WKAQ *Digital Channel:* 28; *Virtual Channel:* 2; 925 kw; 2802 ft.; N18 6 55 W66 3 11
Mailing Address: 2290 West 8th Avenue, Hialeah, FL 33010 USA
Second Address: 383 Roosevelt Ave., Hato Rey, PR 919
(787) 758-2222,(787) 641-2222
www.telemundopr.com
License: San Juan, San Juan County, PR held by Telemundo of Puerto Rico
Group Owner: Telemundo Station Group; (acq 4-10-2002; grpsl).; *Washington Law Firm:* Hogan & Hartson
Nat'l Network: Telemundo
Foreign Language Programming; Size of News Staff: 40; *Hours of Local News Weekly:* news progmg 10 hrs wkly
Luis Silberwasser, President

San Sebastian

WJWN-TV *Digital Channel:* 39; *Virtual Channel:* 38; 700 kw; 2057 ft.; N18 9 0 W66 59 0; *Rebroadcasting:* Satellite of WJPX(TV) San Juan
P. O. Box 10001, El Commandate, Canovanas, PR 0729 US
(787) 792-4444; *Fax:* (787) 782-7825
www.caribevision.com
edwin.pujols@wapa-tv.com
License: San Sebastian, San Sebastian County, PR held by S&E Network Inc.
Group Owner: CaribeVision Station Group LLC; (acq 9-20-2007; grpsl)
Nat'l Network: MundoFox
Joe Ramos, General Manager

Yauco

WIRS *Digital Channel:* 41; *Virtual Channel:* 42; 185 kw; 2730 ft.; N18 10 10 W66 34 36; *Rebroadcasting:* Satellite of WJPX(TV) San Juan
Post Office Box 635, Bayamon, PR 0621 US
(787) 799-1480
License: Yauco, Yauco County, PR held by CaribeVision Station Group LLC.
Group Owner: CaribeVision Station Group LLC; (acq 9-20-2007; grpsl)
Nat'l Network: MundoFox
Myriam Rodriguez, General Manager

Rhode Island

Providence, RI-New Bedford, MA (DMA 52)

WJAR *Digital Channel:* 51; *Virtual Channel:* 10; 1000 kw; 1004 ft.; N41 51 55 W71 17 14.5
23 Kenney Dr., Cranston, RI 02920 USA
(401) 455-9100; *Fax:* (401) 455-9140
www.turnto10.com
vvetters@wjar.com
License: Providence, Providence County, RI held by WJAR Licensee LLC
Group Owner: Sinclair Broadcast Group; (acq 12-19-2014; grpsl).
Nat'l Network: NBC; Me-TV; *Nat'l Reps:* Harrington, Righter & Parsons
Foreign Language Programming
Mark McMillen, Chief Engineer

WNAC-TV *Digital Channel:* 12; *Virtual Channel:* 64; 30 kw; 1001 ft.; N41 52 36 W71 16 57
25 Catamore Blvd., East Providence, RI 02914 US
(401) 438-7200, (401) 438-3310; *Fax:* (401) 435-3625
www.foxprovidence.com
desk@wpri.com
License: Providence, Providence County, RI held by WNAC LLC
Nat'l Network: FOX; *Nat'l Reps:* Blair Television
Jay Howell, President
Patrick Wholey, General Sales Mgr
Pam Brennan, Programming Director
Susan Tracy-Durant, Promotions Manager
Joe Abouzeid, News Director
William Hague, Chief Engineer
John Macek, Local Sales Manager
RyanMachado, Regional Sales Manager

WNAC-TV *Digital Channel:* 13; *Virtual Channel:* 12; 30 kw; 1001 ft.; N41 52 36 W71 16 57
25 Catamore Blvd, East Providence, RI 2914 US
(401) 438-7200; *Fax:* (401) 434-3761,(401) 435-3625
www.wpri.com
License: Providence, Providence County, RI held by TVL Broadcasting of Rhode Island LLC
Group Owner: LIN Media; (acq 11-8-2002; grpsl).
Nat'l Network: CBS; *Nat'l Reps:* Blair Television
Jay Howell, President
Patrick Wholey, General Sales Mgr
Pam Brennan, Programming Director
Susan Tracy-Durant, Promotions Manager
William Hague, Chief Engineer
Patti St. Pierre, National Sales Manager

WPXQ-TV *Digital Channel:* 17; 1000 kw; ant 272t; N41 29 41 W71 47 05
3 Shaws Cove, Suite 226, New London, CT 6320 USA
(812) 335-1770
www.iontelevision.com
License: Block Island, RI held by Ocean State Television, LLC
Group Owner: Ion Media Networks; *Washington Law Firm:* Cohn & Marks
Nat'l Network: ION Television
Hours of Local News Weekly: News progmg 5 hrs wkly
Robert Melfi, General Sales Mgr

***WSBE-TV** *Digital Channel:* 21; *Virtual Channel:* 36; 50 kw; 879 ft.; N41 51 54 W71 17 15
50 Park Lane, Providence, RI 02907-3124 US
(401) 222-3636; *Fax:* (401) 222-3407
www.ripbs.org
info@ripbs.org
License: Providence, Providence County, RI held by Rhode Island Public Telecommunications Authority
Washington Law Firm: Schwartz, Woods & Miller
Nat'l Network: PBS
David Piccerelli, CFO
Robert Fish, President
Janet Zwolinski, General Sales Mgr
Kathryn Larsen, Program Director
Gunnar Rieger, Chief Engineer
Jodi mesolella, Dir. Of membership

South Carolina

Augusta, GA (DMA 111)

***WEBA-TV** *Digital Channel:* 33; *Virtual Channel:* 14; 427 kw; 792 ft.; N33 11 15 W81 23 50
1041 George Rogers Boulevard, Columbia, SC 29201 US
(803) 737-3200; *Fax:* (803) 737-3495
www.scetv.org
csr@scetv.org
License: Allendale, Allendale County, SC held by South Carolina ETV Commission
Nat'l Network: PBS
Linda O'Bryon, President and Chief Executive Officer
Shari Hutchinson, General Manager
John Crockett, Vice President of Engineering
Kerry Feduk, Vice President of Content
Kim Parris, Director of Financial Operations and ChiefFinanci
Bobbi Kennedy, Special Projects Director for the Office of the Pr
Mark Whittington, Director of Administration/HR
Dean Byrd, Director of Education
Don Godish, Managers, Broadcast Community Operations

Charleston, SC (DMA 94)

WCBD-TV *Digital Channel:* 50; *Virtual Channel:* 2; 1000 kw; 1906 ft.; N32 56 24 W79 41 45
210 W. Coleman Blvd, Mt. Pleasant, SC 29464 US
(843) 884-2222, (843) 216-4875; *Fax:* (843) 881-3410
www.counton2.com
news@wcbd.com
License: Charleston, Charleston County, SC held by Media General Broadcasting Inc.
Group Owner: Media General Broadcast Group; (acq 3-1-83; $8 million; *Washington Law Firm:* Cohn & Marks
Nat'l Network: NBC; CW; *Nat'l Reps:* Harrington, Righter & Parsons
Size of News Staff: 29; *Hours of Local News Weekly:* news progmg 17 hrs wkly
Rick Lipps, General Manager
Patrick J. Ryal, General Sales Mgr
Lowell Beckner, Chief Engineer
Rob Fowler, Chief Meterologist
Raymond Owens, Digital Journalist
Brendan Clark, Sports Anchor/Reporter
Octavia Mitchell, Anchor
Joshmarthers, Meterologist
Haley Hernandez, Anchor/Digital Journalist

WCIV *Digital Channel:* 36; *Virtual Channel:* 36; 1000 kw; 1913 ft.; N32 56 24 W79 41 45
888 Allbritton Blvd., Mount Pleasant, SC 29464 US
(843) 881-4444; *Fax:* (843) 849-2507
www.abcnews4.com
desk@abcnews4.com
License: Charleston, Charleston County, SC held by WWMP Licensee L.P.
Group Owner: Sinclair Broadcast Group Inc.; *Washington Law Firm:* Hogan & Hartson
Nat'l Network: ABC; *Wire Services:* Conus
Size of News Staff: 32; *Hours of Local News Weekly:* news progmg 12 hrs wkly
Brian Farmer, General Sales Mgr
Cathy Hobbs, News Director
Erin Bassily, Local Sales Manager
Ben Barna, Digital Sales Executive
Aubrey Dougherty, Account Executive
Lindsey McCoy , Account Executive
Elizabeth Rawl , AccountExecutive
Catherine Griffin, Account Executive

WCSC-TV *Digital Channel:* 47; *Virtual Channel:* 5; 1000 kw; 1709 ft.; N32 55 28 W79 41 58
2126 Charlie Hall Blvd., Charleston, SC 29414 US
(843) 402-5555; *Fax:* (843) 402-5744
www.live5news.com
License: Charleston, Charleston County, SC held by WCSC License Subsidiary LLC.
Group Owner: Raycom Media Inc.; (acq 3-31-2008; grpsl)
Nat'l Network: CBS
Size of News Staff: 44; *Hours of Local News Weekly:* news progmg 21 hrs wkly
Rita O'Neill, General Manager
John Cochran, General Sales Manager
Amanda Curry, Promotions Manager
James Warner, News Director
Mike Miller, Chief Engineer
Debi Chard, News anchor
Andy Pruitt, Sports Team
Bill Walsh, WeatherTeam
Sujata Jain, Reporter
Brad Miller, Weather Team
Corey Davis, Reporter

WGWG *Digital Channel:* 34; *Virtual Channel:* 4; 630 kw; 1914 ft.; N32 55 28 W79 41 58
888 Allbritton Blvd., Mount Pleasant, SC 29464 US
(843) 881-4444; *Fax:* (843) 849-2507
www.hsh.media
contact@hsh.media
License: Charleston, Charleston County, SC held by HSH Charleston (WCIV) Licensee Inc.
Group Owner: Howard Stirk Holdings
Lauren Raycroft, Programming Coordinator

***WITV** *Digital Channel:* 7; *Virtual Channel:* 7; 20 kw; 1844 ft.; N32 55 28 W79 41 58
Mailing Address: 1041 George Rogers Boulevard, Columbia, SC 29201-4761 US
Second Address: 1041 George Rogers Boulevard, Columbia, SC 29201
(803) 737-3200, (803) 737-3500; *Fax:* (803) 737-3417
www.myetv.org
csr@scetv.org
License: Charleston, Charleston County, SC held by South Carolina Educational TV Commission
Washington Law Firm: Dow, Lohnes & Albertson
Nat'l Network: PBS
Linda O'Bryon, CEO/President
Shari Hutchinson, General Manager,ETV Radio
John Crockett, VP, Engineering
Bobbi Kennedy, CFO/Director of Financial Operations
Mark Whittington, Director of Administration/HR
Kerry Feduk, VP ofContent
Don Godish, Manager,Broadcast Community Operations
Bobbi Kennedy, Special Projects Director for the Office of the Pr
Tara Thomas, Technical Difficulties & Outages

WTAT-TV *Digital Channel:* 24; *Virtual Channel:* 24; 1000 kw; 1914 ft.; N32 56 24 W79 41 45
4301 Arco Lane, Charleston, SC 29418 US
(843) 744-2424; *Fax:* (843) 554-9649
www.foxcharleston.com
emails@foxcharleston.com
License: Charleston, Charleston County, SC held by WTAT Licensee LLC.
Group Owner: Cunningham Broadcasting Corporation; (acq 11-15-2001; grpsl).; *Washington Law Firm:* Arter & Hadden
Nat'l Network: FOX
Hours of Local News Weekly: News progmg 3.5 hrs wkly
Michael Kordek, Director, Engineering & Operations

Charlotte, NC (DMA 22)

WMYT *Digital Channel:* 39; *Virtual Channel:* 55; 225 kW; 1873 ft.; N35 21 44 W81 9 19
3501 Performance Rd., Charlotte, NC 28214 USA
(704) 944-3300
www.wmyt12.com
newstips@myfoxcarolinas.com
License: Rock Hill, York County, SC held by Fox Television Stations LLC
Group Owner: Fox Television Stations Group; (acq 2—2000; $4.5 million)
Nat'l Network: MyNetworkTV; *Nat'l Reps:* Millennium Sales & Marketing
Don Travis, Local Sales Manager

***WNSC-TV** *Digital Channel:* 15; *Virtual Channel:* 30; 403 kw; 694 ft.; N34 50 23 W81 1 7
Mailing Address: 1101 George Rogers Blvd., Columbia, SC 29201-4761 US
Second Address: 1041 George Rogers Blvd., Columbia, SC 29201
(803) 737-3200; *Fax:* (803) 324-0580,(803) 737-3270
www.myetv.org
mail@myetv.org
License: Rock Hill, York County, SC held by S.C. Educ TV Commission
Nat'l Network: PBS
Linda O'Bryon, President & CEO
Tim Coghill, Operations Dir
Gary Stevens, Chief Engineer
David Beverley, Education Technology
Bonnie Hite, Facility Rental
Glenn Rawls, Media Inquiries
Dean Byrd, Education Division
Judy Bynum,ETV & ETV Radio Fundraising
Jean Pinkston, Festival/ On-Air Fundraising

Columbia, SC (DMA 77)

WACH *Digital Channel:* 48; *Virtual Channel:* 57; 520 kw; 1522 ft.; N34 6 58 W80 45 51
1400 Pickens St., Suite 600, Columbia, SC 29201 US
(803) 252-5757; *Fax:* (803) 212-7309
www.wach.com
viewercomments@wach.com
License: Columbia, Richland County, SC held by WACH Licensee LLC
Group Owner: Sinclair Broadcast Group Inc.; (acq 2-28-2013; grpsl); *Washington Law Firm:* Covington & Burling
Nat'l Network: FOX; *Nat'l Reps:* TeleRep
Hours of Local News Weekly: news progmg 26 hrs wkly
Allison Aldridge, General Manager
John Farmer, General Sales Mgr
Reese Barkley, Program Manager
Huger Darryl, News Director

WIS *Digital Channel:* 10; *Virtual Channel:* 10; 57 kw; 1578 ft.; N34 7 29 W80 45 23
Mailing Address: 1111 Bull Street, Columbia, SC 29201 US
Second Address: Box 367, Columbia, SC 29202
(803) 799-1010, (803) 758-1261; *Fax:* (803) 758-1155, (803) 758-1278
www.wistv.com
License: Columbia, Richland County, SC held by WIS License Subsidiary LLC.
Group Owner: Raycom Media Inc.; (acq 1-31-2006; grpsl);
Washington Law Firm: Covington & Burling LLP
Nat'l Network: NBC; *Nat'l Reps:* Harrington, Righter & Parsons
Hours of Local News Weekly: News progmg 26.5 hrs wkly
- Donita Todd, Operations Director/General Manager
- Scott Sanders, General Sales Manager
- Barry Ahrendt, Promotions Manager
- Bryan Queen, News Director
- Emir Hadziahmetovic, Chief Engineer
- Quentin Kenney, Regional Business Manager
- Shana Till, Asst. News Director
- Randy Johnson, News Assignment Manager
- Jason Old, Digital Content Director
- Jim Hays, Marketing Director
- Joyce Murphy, Traffic Supervisor

WKTC *Digital Channel:* 39; *Virtual Channel:* 63; 500 kw; 1283 ft.; N34 6 58 W80 45 51
15 South Main Street, Sumter, SC 29150 US
(803) 419-6363; *Fax:* (803) 419-6399
www.wktctv.com
mail@wktctv.com
License: Sumter, Sumter County, SC held by WBHQ Columbia LLC.
Washington Law Firm: Pillsbury, Withrop, Shaw Pittman
Nat'l Network: MYTV
- Stefanie Rein, General Manager

WLTX *Digital Channel:* 17; *Virtual Channel:* 19; 1,000 kw; 1,640 ft.; N34 05 49 W80 45 51; *Population Served:* 1,013,410
6027 Garners Ferry Rd., Columbia, SC 29209-1304 US
(803) 776-3600; *Fax:* (803) 695-3714
www.wltx.com
news19@wltx.com
License: Columbia, Richland County, SC held by Pacific and Southern LLC
Group Owner: Tegna Media; (acq 4-29-98; $87.5 million)
Nat'l Network: CBS; *Nat'l Reps:* TeleRep; *Wire Services:* AP
Hours of Local News Weekly: news progmg 31.5 hrs wkly
- Rich O'Dell, General Manager
- Tim Weaver, General Sales Mgr
- Courtney McCallum, Marketing Director
- Marybeth Jacoby, News Director
- Andy Peeler, Manager of Technology
- Keely Richardson, Business Manager

WOLO-TV *Digital Channel:* 8; *Virtual Channel:* 25; 43.7 kw; 1736 ft.; N34 6 58 W80 45 51
5807 Shakespeare Rd., Columbia, SC 29223 US
(803) 754-7525
www.abccolumbia.com
eyewitnessnews@wolo.com
License: Columbia, Richland County, SC held by South Carolina Broadcasting Partners.
Group Owner: Bahakel Communications Ltd.; (acq 7-20-92)
Nat'l Network: ABC; *Wire Services:* AP
Hours of Local News Weekly: news progmg 18.5 hrs wkly
- Chris Bailey, General Manager
- Dave Aiken, Station Manager
- Chris Bailey, General Sales Mgr
- Dave Aiken, Program Manager
- Crysty Vaughan, News Director
- Shelley Magee, Local Sales Manager
- Marty White, Business Manager

***WRJA-TV** *Digital Channel:* 28; *Virtual Channel:* 27; 98.4 kw; 1194 ft.; N33 52 51 W80 16 15
1041 George Rogers Boulevard, Columbia, SC 29201-4761 US
(803) 737-3200; (803) 737-3545; *Fax:* (803) 775-1059,(803) 737-3270
www.myetv.org
mail@myetv.org
License: Sumter, Sumter County, SC held by South Carolina Educational TV Commission
Nat'l Network: PBS
Foreign Language Programming
- Shari Hutchinson, General Manager
- John Crockett, VP of Engineering
- Kerry Feduk, VP of Content
- Mark Whittington, Dir. Of Administration
- Brad Livingston, Dir. Of Financial Operations & CFO
- Dean Byrd, Dir. Of Education
- BobbiLivingston, Special Projects Dir. For the Office of the Presid
- Dean Byrd, Dir. Of Education

***WRLK-TV** *Digital Channel:* 32; *Virtual Channel:* 35; 250 kw; 1035 ft.; N34 7 6 W80 56 13
Mailing Address: 1041 George Rogers Boulevard, Columbia, SC 29201-4761 US
Second Address: 1101 George Rogers Blvd., Columbia, SC 29201-4761
(803) 737-3200; (803) 737-3545; *Fax:* (803) 737-3417,(803) 737-3270
www.myetv.org
License: Columbia, Richland County, SC held by South Carolina Educational TV Commission
Washington Law Firm: Dow, Lohnes & Albertson
Nat'l Network: PBS
- Linda O'Bryon, CEO & President
- Shari Hutchinson, General Manager
- John Crockett, VP of Engineering
- Kerry Feduk, VP of Content
- Mark Whittington, Dir. Of Administration
- Brad Livingston, Dir. Of Financial Operations & CFO
- Dean Byrd, Dir. Of Education
- Bobbi Livingston, Special Projects Dir. For the Office of the Presid
- Dean Byrd, Dir. Of Education

WZRB *Digital Channel:* 47; *Virtual Channel:* 47; 240 kw; 630 ft.; N34 2 38 W80 59 51
150 Cattle Lndg., Meredith, NH 03523 USA
(401) 338-0565
www.iontelevision.com
License: Columbia, SC held by Broadcast Trust.
Group Owner: Ion Media Networks; *Washington Law Firm:* Dow, Lohnes & Albertson
- Brian Payne, Operations Dir

Greenville-Spartanburg, SC-Asheville, NC-Anderson, SC (DMA 37)

WGGS-TV *Digital Channel:* 16; *Virtual Channel:* 16; 175 kw; 1181 ft.; N34 56 26 W82 24 41
Mailing Address: 3409 Rutherford Road, Taylors, SC 29687 US
Second Address: 3409 Rutherford Rd. Ext, Taylors, SC 29687
(864) 244-1616, (800) 849-3683; *Fax:* (864) 292-8481
www.dovebroadcasting.com
License: Greenville, Greenville County, SC held by Carolina Christian Broadcasting Inc
Washington Law Firm: Hardy & Chautin
Nat'l Network: IND
- James Thompson, President
- Joanne Thompson, Operations Dir
- Billy Rainey, General Sales Mgr
- Derek Myers, Programming Director
- Pete Littlefield, Chief Engineer
- Dante Thompson, National Sales Manager
- Kym MacKinnon, ProgrammingDirector
- Tob Tolbert, Web Support

WHNS *Digital Channel:* 17; *Virtual Channel:* 21; 364 kW; 2490 ft.; N35 10 56 W82 40 55
21 Interstate Ct, Greenville, SC 29615 USA
(864) 288-2100; *Fax:* (864) 297-0728
www.foxcarolina.com
foxcarolinanews@foxcarolina.com
License: Greenville, Greenville County, SC held by Meredith Corp.
Group Owner: Meredith Corp.; (acq 7-1-97; grpsl); *Washington Law Firm:* Dow, Lohnes & Albertson
Nat'l Network: FOX; *Nat'l Reps:* TeleRep
Size of News Staff: 45; *Hours of Local News Weekly:* news progmg 27 hrs wkly
- Derrick Jefferson, Local Sales Manager
- Kelly Boan, News Director
- Bob Munyon, Chief Engineer
- Leigh Champion, Accounting Manager
- Robert Dwyer, Creative Services Director
- Amanda Shaw, Digital Content Manager

WMYA-TV *Digital Channel:* 14; *Virtual Channel:* 40; 360 kw; 940 ft.; N34 38 51 W82 16 13
Mailing Address: 33 Villa Rd, Greenville, SC 29615 US
Second Address: 110 Technology Dr, Asheville, NC 28803
(828) 684-1340; *Fax:* (828) 651-4612
www.my40.tv
comments@wlos.com
License: Anderson, Anderson County, SC held by Anderson (WFBC-TV) Licensee Inc.
Group Owner: Cunningham Broadcasting Corporation; (acq 1-7-2002).
Nat'l Network: FOX; MyNetworkTV
- Jack Connors, General Manager
- Guy Chancey, Regional Promotions Manager

***WNEH** *Digital Channel:* 18; *Virtual Channel:* 38; 106.7 kw; 754 ft.; N34 22 19 W82 10 5
Mailing Address: 1041 George Rogers Boulevard, Columbia, SC 29201-4761 US
Second Address: 1101 George Rogers Blvd., Columbia, SC 29201
(803) 737-3200,(803) 737-3545; *Fax:* (803) 737-3270
www.myetv.org
mail@myetv.org
License: Greenwood, Greenwood County, SC held by South Carolina Educational TV Commission
Nat'l Network: PBS
- Linda O'Bryon, CEO & President
- Shari Hutchinson, General Manager
- John Crockett, VP of Engineering
- Kerry Feduk, VP of Content
- Mark Whittington, Dir. Of Administration
- Brad Livingston, Dir. Of Financial Operations & CFO
- Dean Byrd,Dir. Of Education
- Bobbi Livingston, Special Projects Dir. For the Office of the Presid
- Dean Byrd, Dir. Of Education

***WNTV** *Digital Channel:* 9; *Virtual Channel:* 29; 102.3 kw; 1239 ft.; N34 56 29 W82 24 38
Mailing Address: 1101 George Rogers Blvd., Columbia, SC 29201-4761 US
Second Address: 1041 George Rogers Blvd., Columbia, SC 29201
(803) 737-3200; *Fax:* (803) 737-3495
www.scetv.org
csr@scetv.org
License: Greenville, Greenville County, SC held by South Carolina ETV Commission
Nat'l Network: PBS
- Linda O'Bryon, President & CEO
- L.W. Griffin Jr., Engineering Dir
- David Beverley, Education Technology
- Bonnie Hite, Facility Rental
- Glenn Rawls, Media Inquiries
- Dean Byrd, Education Division
- Judy Bynum, ETV & ETV RadioFundraising
- Jean Pinkston, Festival/ On-Air Fundraising

***WRET-TV** *Digital Channel:* 43; *Virtual Channel:* 49; 106.2 kw; 991 ft.; N34 53 11 W81 49 16; *Rebroadcasting:* Satellite of WNTV Greenville.
Mailing Address: 800 University Way, Columbia, SC 29303 US
Second Address: PO Box 4069, Spartanburg, SC 29305
(864) 503-9371; *Fax:* (864) 503-3615
www.wret.org
wrichard@scetv.org
License: Spartanburg, Spartanburg County, SC held by South Carolina Educational TV Commission
Washington Law Firm: Dow, Lohnes & Albertson
Nat'l Network: PBS
- William Richardson, Operations Manager
- Gary Stevens, Engineering Manager
- William I.Richardson, Regional Studio Manager

WSPA-TV *Digital Channel:* 7; *Virtual Channel:* 7; 25.7 kw; 2188 ft/667m HAAT; N35 10 12 W82 17 27; *Population Served:* 784,300
250 International Drive, Spartanburg, SC 29303
(864) 576-7777, (800) 207-6397; *Fax:* (864) 587-5430
www.wspa.com
webmaster@wspa.com
License: Spartanburg, Spartanburg County, SC held by Media General Communications Holdings, LLC
Group Owner: Media General Broadcast Group; (acq 3-27-2000; grpsl).; *Washington Law Firm:* Dow, Lohnes
Nat'l Network: CBS; *Wire Services:* UPI
Size of News Staff: 51; *Hours of Local News Weekly:* news progmg 26.5 hrs wkly
- Bob Romine, General Manager
- Beth Worsham, General Sales Mgr
- Ross Lytle, Promotions Manager
- Dan Cates, News Director
- Bob Richardson, Chief Engineer
- Jimmy Lizer, Operations Manager

WYFF *Digital Channel:* 36; *Virtual Channel:* 4; 1000 kw; 1955 ft.; N35 6 43 W82 36 24
Mailing Address: 888 Seventh Avenue, New York, NY 10106 US
Second Address: 505 Rutherford St., Greenville, SC 29609

(864) 242-4404; *Fax:* (864) 240-5329
www.wyff4.com
License: Greenville, Greenville County, SC held by WYFF Hearst Television Inc.
Group Owner: Hearst Television Inc.; (acq 3-18-99; grpsl).; *Washington Law Firm:* Brooks, Pierce, McLendon, Humphrey & Leonard
Nat'l Network: NBC; *Nat'l Reps:* Eagle Television Sales; *Wire Services:* AP
Size of News Staff: 55; *Hours of Local News Weekly:* news progmg 30 hrs wkly
Michael Hayes, President
Doug Durkee, Operations Dir
John Humphries, General Sales Mgr
Cathy Petroupoulos, Programming Director
Marsa Jarrett, Promotions Manager
Justin Antoniotte, News Director
Steve Eaton, Local SalesManager
Blake Bridges, National Sales Manager
Danny Ross, Program/Production Manager

Myrtle Beach-Florence, SC (DMA 102)

WBTW *Digital Channel:* 13; *Virtual Channel:* 13; 31.6 kw; 1962 ft.; N34 22 4 W79 19 21
Mailing Address: 310 S. Dargan Street, Florence, SC 29506 US
Second Address: 310 s. Dargan St., Florence, SC 29506
(843) 317-6397; *Fax:* (843) 317-1410
www.scnow.com
news@scnow.com
License: Florence, Florence County, SC held by Media General Communications Inc.
Group Owner: Media General Broadcast Group; (acq 3-27-2000; grpsl).
Nat'l Network: CBS; *Nat'l Reps:* Harrington, Righter & Parsons
Size of News Staff: 14; *Hours of Local News Weekly:* news progmg 78 hrs wkly
Michael Caplan, Operations Dir
Brian Lang, General Sales Mgr
Sandra Sellers, Programming Director
Chuck Spruill, Promotions Manager
David Halt, News Director
Scott Johnson, Chief Engineer
Don Luehrs, Chief Meteorologist
KathrynSmith, HR Administrator
John Russell, Multimedia Journalist
Sam Bundy, Sports editor
Kimberly Ginfrida, Content Manager
Sarah Thibodeaux, Digital sales manager

WFXB *Digital Channel:* 18; *Virtual Channel:* 43; 1000 kw; 1506 ft.; N34 11 19 W79 11 0
Mailing Address: 3364 Huger St., Myrtle Beach, SC 29577 US
Second Address: #18D, 181 E. Evans St., Florence, SC 29506
(843) 828-4300; *Fax:* (843) 828-4343
www.wfxb.com
License: Myrtle Beach, Horry County, SC held by Springfield Broadcasting Partners.
Group Owner: Bahakel Communications Ltd.; (acq 8-18-2006; $19.5 million); *Washington Law Firm:* Fisher, Wayland, Cooper, Leader & Zaragoza
Nat'l Network: FOX; *Nat'l Reps:* Millennium Sales & Marketing
Size of News Staff: 50; *Hours of Local News Weekly:* news progmg 2.5 hrs wkly
Alan Ball, Operations Manager
Rigby Wilson, General Manager/VP
Steve Albright, Programming Director
Dave Milligan, Promotions Director
Doug Carter, Chief Engineer
Linda Todd, Business Manager
Carolyn Allaire, Traffic Manager
Brian Richardson, Local Sales Manager
Lee Camp, Local Sales Manager
Lauren Pogulis, Producer
Kaylin Bergeson, Producer

***WHMC** *Digital Channel:* 9; *Virtual Channel:* 23; 31.8 kw; 753 ft.; N33 56 58 W79 6 31
1041 George Rogers Boulevard, Columbia, SC 29201-4761 US
(803) 737-3200; *Fax:* (803) 737-3495
www.scetv.org
csr@scetv.org
License: Conway, Horry County, SC held by South Carolina Educational TV Commission.
Nat'l Network: PBS
Linda O'Bryon, President and Chief Executive Officer
John Crockett, Vice President of Engineering
Kerry Feduk, Vice President of Content
Kim Parris, Director of Financial Operations & CFO
Shari Hutchinson, General Manager, ETVRadio
Mark Whittington, Director of Administration/HR
Dean Byrd, Director of Education

***WJPM-TV** *Digital Channel:* 45; *Virtual Channel:* 33; 108.9 kw; 795 ft.; N34 16 48 W79 44 35
1041 George Rogers Boulevard, Columbia, SC 29201-4761 US
(803) 737-3200; *Fax:* (803) 737-3495
www.scetv.org
csr@scetv.org
License: Florence, Florence County, SC held by South Carolina ETV Commission
Nat'l Network: PBS
Linda O'Bryon, President and Chief Executive Officer
John Crockett, Vice President of Engineering
Kerry Feduk, Vice President of Content
Brad Livingston, Director of Financial Operations and CFO
Shari Hutchinson, General Manager, ETVRadio
Mark Whittington, Director of Administration/HR
Dean Byrd, Director of Education
Bobbi Kennedy, Special Projects Dir. - Office of the President

WMBF-TV *Digital Channel:* 32; *Virtual Channel:* 32; 530 kw; 600 ft.; N33 43 50 W79 4 32
918 Frontage Rd. E, Myrtle Beach, SC 29577 US
(843) 839-9623, (843) 839-9623; *Fax:* (843) 839-9625
www.wmbfnews.com
news@wmbfnews.com
License: Myrtle Beach, Horry County, SC held by Raycom TV Broadcasting Inc.
Group Owner: Raycom Media Inc.; (acq 1-31-2006; grpsl);
Washington Law Firm: Covington & Burling
Nat'l Network: N/A; *Nat'l Reps:* TeleRep; *Wire Services:* AP
Size of News Staff: 52; *Hours of Local News Weekly:* news progmg 30.5 hrs wkly
Ted Fortenberry, Operations Dir
Eileen Russo, General Sales Mgr
Sarah Miles, News Director
Paula Caruso, News anchors
Jamie Arnold, Meterologist
ken Baker, Video Journalist
Joe Murano, Sports Dir.
Catherine Franklin, ExecutiveProducer
Drew Hansen, NewsOperations Manager

WPDE-TV *Digital Channel:* 16; *Virtual Channel:* 15; 421 kw; 1969 ft.; N34 22 2 W79 19 49
10 University Blvd., Conway, SC 29526 US
(843) 234-9733; *Fax:* (843) 234-9739
www.wpde.com
abc15news@wpde.com
License: Florence, Florence County, SC held by WPDE Licensee LLC
Group Owner: Sinclair Broadcast Group Inc.; *Washington Law Firm:* Covington & Burling LLP
Nat'l Network: ABC
William Huggins, General Manager
Leigh Vaters, General Sales Mgr

WWMB *Digital Channel:* 21; *Virtual Channel:* 21; 400 kw; 1,906 ft.; N34 22 2 W79 19 49
10 University Blvd., Conway, SC 29576 US
(843) 234-9733; *Fax:* (843) 234-9739
www.hsh.media
contact@hsh.media
License: Florence, Florence County, SC held by HSH Myrtle Beach (WWMB) Licensee LLC
Group Owner: Howard Stirk Holdings; (acq 11-22-2013)
Nat'l Network: CW
William Huggins, General Manager
Leigh Vaters, General Sales Mgr
Debbie Yost, Programming Director
Marty Shelley, Promotions Manager
Mark Olson, Chief Engineer
Jim Joly, Director of National Digital Sales
Greg Siegel, VicePresident, National Sales

Savannah, GA (DMA 91)

***WJWJ-TV** *Digital Channel:* 44; *Virtual Channel:* 16; 440 kw; 1196 ft.; N32 42 42 W80 40 54
Mailing Address: 1041 George Rogers Boulevard, Columbia, SC 29201-4761 US
Second Address: 925 Ribaut Rd., Beaufort, SC 29902
(803) 737-3200; *Fax:* (803) 737-3495
www.scetv.org
csr@scetv.org
License: Beaufort, Beaufort County, SC held by South Carolina ETV Commission
Nat'l Network: PBS
Linda O'Bryon, President and Chief Executive Officer
Scott Johnson, Operations Dir
John Crockett, Vice President of Engineering
Mike Milburn, Chief Engineer
Kerry Feduk, Vice President of Content
Brad Livingston, Director ofFinancial Operations and CFO
Shari Hutchinson, General Manager, ETV Radio
Mark Whittington, Director of Administration/HR
Dean Byrd, Director of Education
Bobbi Kennedy, Special Projects Dir. - Office of the President

WTGS *Digital Channel:* 28; *Virtual Channel:* 28; 1000 kw; 1493 ft.; N32 2 45 W81 20 27
Mailing Address: 1375 Chatham Pkwy., Savannah, GA 31405 US
Second Address: 10706 Beaver Dam Rd., Hunt Valley, MD 21030
(912) 436-3928
www.foxsavannah.com
License: Hardeeville, Jasper County, SC held by WTGS Licensee LLC
Group Owner: Sinclair Broadcast Group Inc.; (acq 12-19-2014);
Washington Law Firm: Drinker Biddle & Reath LLP
Nat'l Network: FOX
Hours of Local News Weekly: news progmg 5 hrs wkly
Timothy Walsh, General Sales Mgr
Jason Lewis, Promotions Manager

South Dakota

Minot-Bismarck-Dickinson, ND (DMA 140)

***KPSD-TV** *Digital Channel:* 13; *Virtual Channel:* 13; 27 kw; 1693 ft.; N45 3 14 W102 15 47
Mailing Address: Cherry & Dakota Streets, Box 5000, Vermillion, SD 57069 US
Second Address: 555 N. Dakota St., Vermillion, SD 57069
(605) 677-5861,(800) 456-0766; *Fax:* (605) 677-5010
www.sdpb.org
programming@sdpb.org
License: Eagle Butte, Roberts County, SD held by South Dakota Board of Directors for Educational Telecommunications
Washington Law Firm: Cohn & Marks
Nat'l Network: PBS
Julie Andersen, President
Terry Spencer, General Sales Mgr
Bob Bosse, Programming Director
Julie Andersen, Executive Director
Larry Rohrer, Director of Content
Bob Bosse, Director of Television
Joe Tlustos, Director of Radio

***KQSD-TV** *Digital Channel:* 11; *Virtual Channel:* 11; 33.72 kw; 1026 ft.; N45 16 38 W99 59 10
Mailing Address: 555 N. Dakota Street, PO Box 5000, Vermillion, SD 57069 US
Second Address: 555 N. Dakota St., PO Box 5000, Vermillion, SD 57069
(605) 677-6451, (800) 456-0766, (800) 456-0766, (8; *Fax:* (605) 677-5010, (605) 677-3164
www.sdpb.org
admin@sdpb.org
License: Lowry, Walworth County, SD held by South Dakota Board of Directors for Educational Telecommunications
Washington Law Firm: Cohn & Marks
Nat'l Network: PBS
Julie Andersen, President
Craig Jensen, Operations Dir
Terry Spencer, General Sales Mgr
Bob Bosse, Programming Director
Fritz Miller, Director of Marketing
Julie Andersen, Executive Director
Larry Rohrer, Director of Content
Bob Bosse, Director of Television
Joe Tlustos, Director of Radio
Kent Osborne, Director of Education and Online Services
SeVern Ashes, Director of Engineering and Operations

Rapid City, SD (DMA 172)

***KBHE-TV** *Digital Channel:* 26; *Virtual Channel:* 9; 79.06 kw; 629 ft.; N44 3 8 W103 14 34
555 N. Dakota Street, Box 5000, Vermillion, SD 57069 US
(605) 394-2551, (800) 46-0766; *Fax:* (605) 677-5010, (605) 677-3164
www.sdpb.org
admin@sdpb.org
License: Rapid City, Pennington County, SD held by South Dakota Board of Directors for Educational Telecommunications

Nat'l Network: PBS
Terry Spencer, General Sales Mgr
Severn Ashes, Chief Engineer
Fritz Miller, Director of Marketing
Kent Osborne, Director of Education and Online Services
Julie Andersen, Executive Director
Larry Rohrer, Director of Content
BobBosse, Director of Television
Joe Tlustos, Director of Radio

KCLO-TV *Digital Channel:* 16; *Virtual Channel:* 15; 150 kw; 505 ft.; N44 4 13 W103 15 1; *Rebroadcasting:* Satellite of KELO-TV Sioux Falls 99%
501 South Phillips Avenue, Sioux Falls, SD 57105 US
(605) 336-1100, (800) 888-5356; *Fax:* (605) 334-3447, (605) 336.0202
www.keloland.com
kelotv@keloland.com
License: Rapid City, Pennington County, SD held by Young Broadcasting of Rapid City Inc.
Group Owner: Young Broadcasting Inc.; (acq 1996; grpsl).; *Washington Law Firm:* Brooks, Pierce, McLendon, Humphrey & Leonard
Nat'l Network: CBS; *Nat'l Reps:* Adam Young
Karen Floyd, Programming Director
Paul Farmer, Promotions Manager
Beth Jensen, News Director
Paul Myrick, Chief Engineer

KEVN *Digital Channel:* 7; *Virtual Channel:* 7; 43.5 kw; 669 ft.; N44 4 0 W103 15 1
2001 Skyline Dr., Rapid City, SD 57701 USA
(605) 394-7777
www.blackhillsfox.com
License: Rapid City, Pennington County, SD held by Gray Television Licensee LLC
Group Owner: Gray Television Inc.; *Washington Law Firm:* Law Offices of Covington & Burling
Nat'l Network: FOX; *Nat'l Reps:* Millennium Sales & Marketing; *Wire Services:* AP
Size of News Staff: 14; *Hours of Local News Weekly:* news progmg 9 hrs wkly
Chris Gross, General Manager
Jack Caudill, News Director

KIVV-TV *Digital Channel:* 5; *Virtual Channel:* 5; 9.2 kw; 1841 ft.; N44 19 30 W103 50 14; *Rebroadcasting:* Satellite of KEVN-TV Rapid City.
2001 Skyline Dr., Rapid City, SD 57701 US
(605) 394-7777
www.blackhillsfox.com
chrisg@blackhillsfox.com
License: Lead, Lawrence County, SD held by KEVN Inc.
Group Owner: KEVN Inc.; 10/29/1998; *Washington Law Firm:* Law Offices of Covington & Burling
Nat'l Network: FOX; *Nat'l Reps:* Millennium Sales & Marketing; *Wire Services:* AP
Size of News Staff: 14; *Hours of Local News Weekly:* news progmg 9 hrs wkly
Jack Caudill, News Director
Zach Nugent, Weekend Anchor & Weekday Reporter
Taylor Nicolaisen, Chief meterologist
Cory Coppock, Weekend Sports Anchor
Jaleesa Irizarry, General Assignment Reporter
Al Van Zee, Reporter &Photographer
Tessa Thomas, Reporter

KNBN *Digital Channel:* 21; *Virtual Channel:* 21; 50 kw; 692 ft.; N44 5 33 W103 14 53
Mailing Address: 2424 Plaza Dr., Rapid City, SD 57702 US
Second Address: 2424 S. Plaza Dr., Rapid City, SD 57701
(605) 355-0024; *Fax:* (605) 355-9274
www.newscenter1.tv
License: Rapid City, Pennington County, SD held by Rapid Broadcasting Co.
Ownership: James F. Simpson, 10.5%; Scott Barbour, 9.1%; Leeann Rieman, 9.1%; Frank Simpson, 8.3%; Clark D. Moyle, 8.1%; Gilbert D. Moyle III, 8.1%; W.R. Barbour, 6.1%; William F. Turner, 3.2%; Suzanne M. Gabrielson, 2.4%;Charles H. Lien, 2.4%; and David M. Simpson, 1.3%
Nat'l Network: NBC
Hours of Local News Weekly: News progmg 11 hrs wkly
Jim Simpson, Operations Dir
Mark Walter, Operations Manager

KOTA-TV *Digital Channel:* 10; *Virtual Channel:* 11; 34.8 kw; 1890 ft.; N44 19 36 W103 50 12; *Rebroadcasting:* Satellite of KOTA-TV Rapid City.
Mailing Address: PO Box 2480, Rapid City, SD 57709 US
Second Address: 1523 1st Avenue, Scottsbluff, NE 69361
(605) 342-2000; *Fax:* (605) 721-5730
www.kotatv.com
kotanews@kotatv.com
License: Lead, Lawrence County, SD held by Duhamel Broadcasting Enterprises.
Group Owner: Duhamel Broadcasting Enterprises; *Washington Law Firm:* Pillsbury Law
Nat'l Network: ABC; *Nat'l Reps:* Continental Television Sales
William Duhamel, President
Monte Loos, Operations Dir
Steve Duffy, General Sales Mgr
Doug Loos, Programming Director
John Petersen, News Director
Dan Black, Engineering Dir
Gerry Fenske, Regional Sales Manager
Helene Duhamel,News Anchor & Health Cast Reporter
Alicia Garcia, Anchor & Consumer Reports Producer
Mike Modrick, Chief Meterologist
Vic Quick, Sports Director
Cindy Davis, Assistant News Director & Assignment Editor

KOTA-TV *Digital Channel:* 2; *Virtual Channel:* 3; 18.2 kw; 673 ft.; N44 4 8 W103 15 3
Mailing Address: P. O. Box 1760, Rapid City, SD 57709 US
Second Address: 518 St. Joseph St., Rapid City, SD 57701
(605) 342-2000; *Fax:* (605) 342-7305
www.kotatv.com
License: Rapid City, Pennington County, SD held by Duhamel Broadcasting Enterprises.
Group Owner: Duhamel Broadcasting Enterprises; *Washington Law Firm:* Pillsbury Law
Nat'l Network: ABC; *Nat'l Reps:* Continental Television Sales; *Wire Services:* AP
Hours of Local News Weekly: News progmg 9 hrs wkly
William Duhamel, President
Monte Loos, Operations Dir
Steve Duffy, General Sales Mgr
Doug Loos, Programming Director
John Peterson, News Director
Dan Black, Engineering Dir
Gerry Fenske, Regional Sales Manager
Helene Duhamel,News Anchor
Alexa Block, Reporter
Patt Dobs, Reporter

***KZSD-TV** *Digital Channel:* 8; *Virtual Channel:* 8; 44.7 kw; 873 ft.; N43 25 59 W101 33 16
Mailing Address: 555 N. Dakota St., Box 5000, Vermillion, SD 57069 US
Second Address: 555 N. Dakota St., Vermillion, SD 57069-5000
(605) 677-5861; *Fax:* (605) 677-5010
www.sdpb.org
programming@sdpb.org
License: Martin, Bennett County, SD held by South Dakota Board of Directors for Educational Telecommunications
Washington Law Firm: Cohn & Marks
Nat'l Network: PBS
Julie Andersen, President
Owen DeJong, Operations Director
Terry Spencer, General Sales Mgr
Susan Hanson, Programming Director
Carol Robertson, Promotions Manager
Cara Hetland, News Director
Severn Ashes, Engineering Director
Julie Andersen, Executive Director
Larry Rohrer, Director of Content
Bob Bosse, Director of Television
Joe Tlustos, Director of Radio
Fritz Miller, Director of Marketing

Sioux Falls (Mitchell), SD (DMA 109)

***KCSD-TV** *Digital Channel:* 24; *Virtual Channel:* 23; 80.9 kw; 246 ft.; N43 34 28 W96 39 19
Mailing Address: 555 N. Dakota Street, PO Box 5000, Vermillion, SD 57069 US
Second Address: 555 N. Dakota St., Vermillion, SD 57069
(605) 677-5861, (800) 456-0766; *Fax:* (605) 677-5010, (605) 677 3164
www.sdpb.org
programming@sdpb.org
License: Sioux Falls, Minnehaha County, SD held by South Dakota Board of Directors for Educational Telecommunications
Washington Law Firm: Cohn & Marks
Nat'l Network: PBS
Fritz Miller, Director of Marketing
Craig Jensen, Operations Dir
Terry Spencer, General Sales Mgr
Bob Bosse, Programming Director
Fritz Miller, Promotions Manager
SeVern Ashes, Director of Engineering and Operations
JulieAndersen, Executive Director
Larry Rohrer, Director of Content
Bob Bosse, Director of Television
Joe Tlustos, Director of Radio
Kent Osborne, Director of Education and Online Services
Fritz Miller, Director of Marketing

KDLO-TV *Digital Channel:* 3; *Virtual Channel:* 3; 14.4 kw; 1684 ft.; N44 57 56 W97 35 22; *Rebroadcasting:* Satellite of KELO-TV Sioux Falls 100%.
Mailing Address: 599 Lexington Avenue, 47th Floor, New York, NY 10022 US
Second Address: 501 S. Phillips Ave., Sioux Falls, SD 57105
(605) 336-1100, (800) 888-5356; *Fax:* (605) 334-3447
www.keloland.com
kelotv@keloland.com
License: Florence, Clark County, SD held by Young Broadcasting of Sioux Falls Inc.
Group Owner: Young Broadcasting Inc.; (acq 6-1-96; grpsl).; *Washington Law Firm:* Brooks, Pierce, McLendon, Humphrey & Leonard
Nat'l Network: CBS; *Nat'l Reps:* Adam Young
Karen Floyd, Programming Director
Paul Farmer, Promotions Manager
Beth Jensen, News Director
Paul Myrick, Chief Engineer

KDLT-TV *Digital Channel:* 47; *Virtual Channel:* 46; 1000 kw; 1995 ft.; N43 30 18 W96 33 22
Mailing Address: P.O. Box 9115, Fargo, ND 58106 US
Second Address: 3600 S. Westport Ave., Sioux Falls, SD 57106-6344
(605) 361-5555, (800) 727-5358; *Fax:* (605) 361-7017,(605) 361-3982
www.kdlt.com
news@kdlt.com
License: Sioux Falls, Minnehaha County, SD held by Red River Broadcast Co. L.L.C.
Group Owner: Red River Broadcast Co. L.L.C.; *Washington Law Firm:* Holland and Knight
Nat'l Network: NBC; *Nat'l Reps:* Harrington, Righter & Parsons; *Wire Services:* AP
Size of News Staff: 25; *Hours of Local News Weekly:* news progmg 19 hrs wkly
Myron Kunin, CEO
Ro Grignon, President
Kathy Lau, Operations Dir
Mari Ossenfort, General Manager
Stacey Torvik, Programming Director
Amanda Sievert, Promotions Manager
Paul Heinert, News director
Donald Sturzenbecher, ChiefEngineer
Susan Endres, Operations Manager
Tom Hanson, Anchor
Brandon Spinner, Chief Meterologist
Mark Ovenden, Sports Director
Kenny Bass, Assignment Editor
Jeff Rusack, Reporter

KDLV-TV *Digital Channel:* 26; *Virtual Channel:* 5; 1000 kw; 1033 ft.; N43 45 33 W98 24 44; *Rebroadcasting:* Satellite of KDLT-TV Sioux Falls.
Mailing Address: P.O. Box 9115, Fargo, ND 58106 US
Second Address: 3600 S. Westport Ave., Sioux Falls, SD 57106-6344
(605) 361-5555, (800) 727-5358; *Fax:* (605) 361-7017, (605) 361-3982
www.kdlt.com
news@kdlt.com
License: Mitchell, Davison County, SD held by Red River Broadcast Co. L.L.C.
Group Owner: Red River Broadcast Co. L.L.C.; (acq 8-26-94; $4 million); *Washington Law Firm:* Holland & Knight
Nat'l Network: NBC; *Nat'l Reps:* Harrington, Righter & Parsons
Foreign Language Programming; Size of News Staff: 25; *Hours of Local News Weekly:* news progmg 20 hrs wkly
Myron Kunin, CEO
Ro Grignon, President
Kathy Lau, Operations Dir
Mari Ossenfort, General Manager
Stacey Torvik, Programming Director
Amanda Sievert, Promotions Manager
Paul Heinert, News director
Donald Sturzenbecher, ChiefEngineer
Susan Endres, Operations Manager
Tom Hanson, Anchor
Brandon Spinner, Chief Meterologist
Mark Ovenden, Sports Director
Kenny Bass, Assignment Editor
Jeff Rusack, Reporter

***KDSD-TV** *Digital Channel:* 17; *Virtual Channel:* 16; 37.82 kw; 1145 ft.; N45 29 54 W97 40 28
Mailing Address: PO Box 5000, Vermillion, SD 57069 US
Second Address: 555 North Dakota Street, Vermillion, SD 57069
(800) 456-0766, (800) 333-0789; *Fax:* (605) 677-5010, (605) 677-3164
www.sdpb.org
Fritz.Miller@state.sd.us
License: Aberdeen, Brown County, SD held by South Dakota Board of Directors for Educational Telecommunications
Washington Law Firm: Cohn & Marks
Nat'l Network: PBS
Craig Jensen, Operations Dir
Terry Spencer, General Sales Mgr
Bob Bosse, Director of Television
Fritz Miller, Director of Marketing
SeVern Ashes, Director of Engineering and Operations
Julie Andersen, Executive Director
KentOsborne, Director of Education and Online Services
Joe Tlustos, Director of Radio
Larry Rohrer, Director of Content

KELO-TV *Digital Channel:* 11; *Virtual Channel:* 11; 30 kw; 2001 ft.; N43 31 7 W96 32 5
501 South Phillips Ave., Sioux Falls, SD 57104 US
(605) 336-1100, (800) 888-5356; *Fax:* (605) 334-3447(sales),(605) 357-5530
www.keloland.com
kelotv@keloland.com
License: Sioux Falls, Minnehaha County, SD held by Young Broadcasting of Sioux Falls Inc.
Group Owner: Young Broadcasting Inc.; (acq 6-1-96; grpsl).;
Washington Law Firm: Brooks, Pierce, McLendon, Humphrey & Leonard
Nat'l Network: CBS; MyNetworkTV; *Nat'l Reps:* Adam Young
Jay Huizenga, General Manager
Karen Floyd, Programming Director
Paul Farmer, Promotions Manager
Beth Jensen, News Director
Paul Myrick, Chief Engineer

***KESD-TV** *Digital Channel:* 8; *Virtual Channel:* 8; 15 kw; 751 ft.; N44 20 16 W97 13 42
Mailing Address: Box 5000, Vermittion, SD 57069 US
Second Address: 555 North Dakota Street, Vermillion, SD 57069
(605) 677-5861, (800) 456-0766; *Fax:* (605) 677-5010
www.sdpb.org
programming@sdpb.org
License: Brookings, Brookings County, SD held by South Dakota Board of Directors for Educational Telecommunications
Washington Law Firm: Cohn & Marks
Nat'l Network: PBS
Julie Andersen, President
Terry Spencer, General Sales Mgr

KPLO-TV *Digital Channel:* 13; *Virtual Channel:* 6; 40 kw; 1043 ft.; N43 57 57 W99 36 11; *Rebroadcasting:* Satellite of KELO-TV Sioux Falls 100%.
501 South Philiphs Avenue, Sioux Falls, SD 57105 US
(605) 336-1100,(800) 888-5356; *Fax:* (605) 334-3447
www.keloland.com
kelotv@keloland.com
License: Reliance, Lyman County, SD held by Young Broadcasting of Sioux Falls Inc.
Group Owner: Young Broadcasting Inc.; (acq 6-1-96; grpsl).;
Washington Law Firm: Brooks, Pierce, McLendon, Humphrey & Leonard
Nat'l Network: CBS; *Nat'l Reps:* Adam Young
Karen Floyd, Programming Director
Paul Farmer, Promotions Manager
Beth Jensen, News Director
Paul Myrick, Chief Engineer

KPRY-TV *Digital Channel:* 19; *Virtual Channel:* 4; 311 kw; 1138 ft.; N44 3 7 W100 5 3; *Rebroadcasting:* Rebroadcasts KSFY-TV Sioux Falls
300 N. Dakota Ave., Suite 100, Sioux Falls, SD 57104 US
(605) 336-1300, (800) 955-5739; *Fax:* (605) 336-7936, (605) 336-3468 (sales)
www.ksfy.com
ksfy@ksfy.com
License: Pierre, Hughes County, SD held by Hoak Media of Dakota License LLC.
Group Owner: Hoak Media Corporation; (acq 1-3-2007; grpsl);
Washington Law Firm: Arent, Fox, Kintner, Plotkin & Kahn
Nat'l Network: ABC
Size of News Staff: 45; *Hours of Local News Weekly:* news progmg 15 hrs wkly
Jim Berman, President/General Manager
Jeff Morlan, Operations Manager
Kelly Manning, General Manager
Michael Cornette, General Sales Manager
Kevin King, News Director
Mike Borszich, Chief Engineer
Jeff Bonk, Dir. of CreativeServices
Kristen Boyle, Business Manager
Mara Walter, Account Executive
Leah Jones, Account Executive
Beth Knutson, Account Executive
Ryan Bolger, Account Executive

KSFY *Digital Channel:* 13; *Virtual Channel:* 13; 22.7 kw; 2001 ft.; N43 31 7 W96 32 5
300 N Dakota Ave., Suite 100, Sioux Falls, SD 57104 USA
(605) 336-1300; *Fax:* (605) 336-7936
www.ksfy.com
License: Sioux Falls, Minnehaha County, SD held by Gray Television Licensee LLC
Group Owner: Gray Television Inc.
Nat'l Network: ABC; *Nat'l Reps:* TeleRep
Size of News Staff: 30; *Hours of Local News Weekly:* news progmg 15 hrs wkly
Jim Berman, President/General Manager
Michael Cornette, General Sales Mgr
Kevin King, News Director
Mike Borszich, Chief Engineer

***KTSD-TV** *Digital Channel:* 10; *Virtual Channel:* 10; 54.7 kw; 1600 ft.; N43 58 5 W99 35 40
Mailing Address: 555 N. Dakota St., Box 5000, Vermillion, SD 57069 US
Second Address: 555 N. Dakota St., Vermillion, SD 57069-5000
(605) 677-5861,(800) 456-0766; *Fax:* (605) 677-5010
www.sdpb.org
programming@sdpb.org
License: Pierre, Hughes County, SD held by South Dakota Board of Directors for Educational Telecommunications
Washington Law Firm: Cohn & Marks
Nat'l Network: PBS
Owen DeJong, Operations Director
Terry Spencer, General Sales Mgr
Susan Hanson, Programming Director
Cara Hetland, News Director
SeVern Ashes, Engineering Director
Julie Andersen, Executive Director
Joe Tlustos, RadioDirector
Steve Zwemke, Programming Assistant

KTTM *Digital Channel:* 12; *Virtual Channel:* 12; 12.6 kw; 843 ft.; N44 11 39 W98 19 5; *Rebroadcasting:* Satellite of KTTW(TV) Sioux Falls 100%
Mailing Address: 2817 W 11th St., Sioux Falls, SD 57104 US
Second Address: 2817 W. 11th St., Sioux Falls, SD 57104
(605) 338-0017; *Fax:* (605) 338-7173
www.kttw.com
yourcomments@foxnews.com
License: Huron, Beadle County, SD held by Independent Communications Inc
Group Owner: Independent Communications Inc.
Nat'l Network: FOX; *Nat'l Reps:* Continental Television Sales
Ed Hoffman, General Manager
Stacey Sieverding, Sales Manager
Judy Buie, Programming Director
Adam Veurink, Promotion Manager
John Bennett, Engineering
Jon Yirka, Chief Engineer
Stacey Sieverding, Sales Manager
Scott Nelson,Marketing Specialist
. Rodney Bergeson, Production
Corey Thompson, Master Control
Stacey Ratkiewicz, Sales Executives
Gina Reiser, Sales Executives

KTTW *Digital Channel:* 7; *Virtual Channel:* 17; 7.5 kw; 714 ft.; N43 30 19 W96 34 19
Mailing Address: 2817 W 11th St., Sioux Falls, SD 57104 US
Second Address: 2817 W. 11th St., Sioux Falls, SD 57104
(605) 338-0017; *Fax:* (605) 338-7173
www.kttw.com
yourcomments@foxnews.com
License: Sioux Falls, Minnehaha County, SD held by Independent Communications Inc
Group Owner: Independent Communications Inc.; (acq 3-9-88).;
Washington Law Firm: Reddy, Begley & McCormick
Nat'l Network: FOX; *Nat'l Reps:* Continental Television Sales
Ed Hoffman, General Manager
Stacey Sieverding, Sales Manager
Judy Buie, Programming Director
John Bennett, Engineering
Stacey Sieverding, Sales Manager
Scott Nelson, Marketing Specialist
Rodney Bergeson, Production
CoreyThompson, Master Control
Stacey Ratkiewicz, Sales Executives
Gina Reiser, Sales Executives

***KUSD-TV** *Digital Channel:* 34; *Virtual Channel:* 2; 277 kw; 768 ft.; N43 3 1 W96 47 1
Mailing Address: 555 N. Dakota St., Box 5000, Vermillion, SD 57069 US
Second Address: 555 N. Dakota St., Vermillion, SD 57069
(605) 677-5861; *Fax:* (605) 677-5010
www.sdpb.org
programming@sdpb.org
License: Vermillion, Clay County, SD held by South Dakota Board of Directors for Educational Telecommunications
Washington Law Firm: Cohn & Marks
Nat'l Network: PBS
Owen DeJong, Operations Director
Terry Spencer, General Sales Mgr
Susan Hanson, Programming Director
Cara Hetland, News Director
SeVern Ashes, Engineering Director
Julie Andersen, Executive Director
Larry Rohrer, Director ofContent
Bob Bosse, Director of Television
Joe Tlustos, Director of Radio
Fritz Miller, Director of Marketing

Tennessee

Chattanooga, TN (DMA 89)

WDEF-TV *Digital Channel:* 82; *Virtual Channel:* 12; 26 kW; 1,260 ft; N35 08 06 W85 19 25; *Population Served:* 884,000
3300 Broad St, Chattanooga, TN 37408 USA
(423) 785-1200; *Fax:* (423) 785-1271
www.wdef.com
License: Chattanooga, Hamilton County, TN held by WDEF-TV, Inc.
Group Owner: Morris Multimedia Inc.; (acq 10-13-2006; $23 million); *Washington Law Firm:* Fletcher, Heald & Hildreth, P.L.C.
Nat'l Network: CBS; Bounce TV; *Nat'l Reps:* Millennium
Size of News Staff: 23; *Hours of Local News Weekly:* news progmg 26 hrs wkly
Phil Cox, General Manager
Tommy Youngblood, General Sales Mgr
Dutch Terry, News Director
Rick McClain, Chief Engineer
Mike Newberry, Business Manager

WDSI-TV *Digital Channel:* 40; *Virtual Channel:* 61; 84 kw; 1148 ft.; N35 12 34 W85 16 39
1101 East Main St., Chattanooga, TN 37408 US
(423) 265-0061; *Fax:* (423) 265-3636
www.myfoxchattanooga.com
comments@fox61tv.com
License: Chattanooga, Hamilton County, TN held by New Age Media of Tennessee License LLC.
(acq 3-31-2007; *Ownership:* Sedgwick Media LLC, 65%; Dallas Media LLC, 33.64%; Michael Yanuzzi, 1.36%; *Washington Law Firm:* Leventhal Senter & Lerman PLLC
Nat'l Network: FOX; MyNetworkTV
Hours of Local News Weekly: 3.5
Patrick Notley, Operations Dir
Tracye McCarthy, General Manager
Nathan Mears, General Sales Mgr
Jenny Giddens, Programming Director
Rebecca Sims, Promotions Manager
Latricia Thomas, News Director
Patrick Motley, ChiefEngineer
Tonetta Jones, Traffic Manager

WFLI-TV *Digital Channel:* 42; *Virtual Channel:* 53; 500 kw; 1093 ft.; N35 12 34 W85 16 39
1101 E. Main St., Chattanooga, TN 37408 US
(423) 265-0061, (423) 386-2362; *Fax:* (423) 265-3636, (423) 265-0062
License: Cleveland, Bradley County, TN held by MPS Media of Tennessee License LLC
(acq 4-1-2008; $6.8 million); *Ownership:* Eugene J. Brown, 100%; *Washington Law Firm:* Fletcher, Heald & Hildreth
Nat'l Network: CW; *Nat'l Reps:* MMT
Tracye McCarthy, General Manager
Kellye Dillard, Business Manager

WRCB-DT *Digital Channel:* 13; 111 kw; DCBR-C3SP-4H/10H-1; N35 09 40 W85 18 52; *Population Served:* 900,000
900 Whitehall Rd., Chattanooga, TN 37405

(423) 267-5412; *Fax:* (423) 267-6840,(423) 756-3148
www.wrcbtv.com
ttolar@wrcbtv.com
License: Chattanooga, Hamilton County, TN held by Sarkes Tarzian Inc.
Group Owner: Sarkes Tarzian Inc.; (acq 10-82; $16 million; *Washington Law Firm:* Lerman, Senter
Nat'l Network: NBC (3.1); Antenna TV (3.2); *Nat'l Reps:* Continental Television Sales; *Wire Services:* AP
Hours of Local News Weekly: News progmg 24.5 hrs wkly

Tom Tarzian, Chairman
Bob Davis, CFO
Tom Tolar, President/General Manager
Doug Loveridge, Operations Dir
Ralph Flynn, General Sales Mgr
Pam Teaque, Programming Director
Ronnie Minton, Promotions Manager
Derrall Stalvey, NewsDirector
Dan Sommers, Chief Engineer
Pam Teague, Controller/Program Director

***WTCI** *Digital Channel:* 29; *Virtual Channel:* 45; 200 kw; 1102 ft.; N35 12 26 W85 16 52
7540 Bonnyshire Dr., Chattanooga, TN 37416 US
(423) 702-7800; *Fax:* (423) 702-7823
www.wtcitv.org
captioning@wtcitv.org
License: Chattanooga, Hamilton County, TN held by The Greater Chattanooga Public Television Corporation
(acq 7-84).; *Washington Law Firm:* Dow, Lohnes & Albertson
Nat'l Network: PBS

Paul Grove, President & CEO
Peter DeLynn, SVP of Production & Operations
Richard Johnson, Vice President of Development
Ann Cater, Director of Corporate Support
Bryan Fuqua, Vice President, Technical Services
Pam Carpenter,Director of Traffic
Jennifer Crutchfield, Dir. Of Public Relations
Angela Ballard, Chief Learning Officer
Susan Cates, VP of Business & Finance
Bryan Fuqua, VP, Technical Services
Ann Cater, Dir. Of Corporate support
Jens Christensen, VPof Development

WTVC *Digital Channel:* 9; *Virtual Channel:* 9; 45 kw; ant 1,056t/246g; N35 09 38 W85 19 06; *Population Served:* 350,000
Mailing Address: 4279 Benton Dr., Chattanooga, TN 37406
Second Address: 10706 Beaver Dam Rd., Hunt Valley, MD 21030
(423) 756-5500; *Fax:* (423) 757-7401
www.newschannel9.com
producers@newschannel9.com
License: Chattanooga, Hamilton County, TN held by WTVC Licensee LLC
Group Owner: Sinclair Broadcast Group Inc.; (acq 11-2-2013; grpsl); *Washington Law Firm:* Latham & Watkins
Nat'l Network: ABC; *Nat'l Reps:* TeleRep; *Wire Services:* AP; CNN; ABC
Size of News Staff: 40; *Hours of Local News Weekly:* news progmg 24 hrs wkly

Mike Costa, General Manager
Margie Scott, Program Coordinator
Angie Beal, Promotions Coordinator
Tom Henderson, News Director
Dennis Brown, Chief Engineer
Angela Bryant, Local Sales Manager
Gina Johnson, Digital Sales Manager
Bill Lenzi, Marketing and Creative Services
Dan Lehr, Interactive Content Producer
Katie Bandy, Business Manager

Jackson, TN (DMA 176)

WATN-TV *Digital Channel:* 39; *Virtual Channel:* 16; 392 kw; 971 ft.; N35 47 22 W89 6 14
1725 Shelby Oaks Dr. N., Suite 101, Memphis, TN 38134 US
(901) 323-2430
www.localmemphis.com
License: Jackson, Madison County, TN held by Nexstar Broadcasting Inc.
Group Owner: Nexstar Broadcasting Group Inc.; (acq 3-14-2008;. grpsl)
Nat'l Network: FOX

Joseph Denk, General Manager
Lisa Lovell, News Director

WBBJ-TV *Digital Channel:* 43; *Virtual Channel:* 7; 316 kw vis, 31.6 kw aur; ant 1,060t/1,065g; N35 38 15 W88 41 33; *Population Served:* 198,150
346 Muse St., Jackson, TN 38301
(731) 424-4515; *Fax:* (731) 424-9299
www.wbbjtv.com
License: Jackson, Madison County, TN held by Tennessee Broadcasting Partners
Group Owner: Bahakel Communications Ltd.; (acq 7-20-92)
Nat'l Network: ABC

Mark Brooks, General Manager
Kirk Newcom, Sales Manager
Wayne Thing, Program Manager
Craig Faulkner, Account Executive
Meredith Fuller, Account Executive
Shelby Kee, Accont Executive
Kathy Kitzman, Account Executive
LeathaMcCroskey, Account Executive
Tracey Pelham, Account Executive

***WLJT-DT** ; 316 kw vis, 63.1 kw aur; 640t/496g; N35 45 12 W88 36 10; *Population Served:* 211,000
Mailing Address: Box 966, Martin, TN 38237
Second Address: 210 Hurt St., Martin, TN 38238
(731) 881-7561; *Fax:* (731) 881-7566
www.wljt.org
wljt@wljt.org
License: Lexington, Henderson County, TN held by West Tennessee Public Television Council Inc
Nat'l Network: PBS

Monica Cochran, CEO & General Manager
Bud Grimes, President
Katrina C. Cobb, Dir. of Broadcast Operations
Shorri Puckett, General Sales Mgr
Robbie Green, Promotions Manager
Kenneth Robinson, Dir. Of Engineering
Monica Shumake,CFO
Maxine Knoll, Traffic Operations Associate
Bill Brundige, Business Manager
Sandra Holliman, Administrative Asst.
Sue Lasky, Education & Outreach Director
Darrell Conner, Director of Production

Knoxville, TN (DMA 62)

WATE-TV *Digital Channel:* 26; *Virtual Channel:* 6; 930 kw; 1736 ft.; N36 0 13 W83 56 34
Mailing Address: 599 Lexington Avenue, 47th Floor, New York, NY 10022 US
Second Address: 1306 N. Broadway NE, Knoxville, TN 37917
(865) 637-6666, (865) 637-6397, (865) 470-9283; *Fax:* (865) 525-4091, (865) 523-3561, (865) 5210-6611
www.wate.com
newsroom@wate.com
License: Knoxville, Knox County, TN held by Young Broadcasting of Knoxville
Group Owner: Young Broadcasting Inc.; (acq 11-14-94; grpsl; *Nat'l Network:* ABC; Live Well; *Nat'l Reps:* Cox Reps g
Size of News Staff: 50; *Hours of Local News Weekly:* news progmg 24 hrs wkly

Tom McCoy, Operations Dir
Dan Phillips, General Manager
Tony Kahl, General Sales Mgr
Melanie Morris, Programming Director
Jamie Foster, News Director
Steve Martin, Chief Engineer
Sarah Burton, Sales Manager

WBIR-TV *Digital Channel:* 10; *Virtual Channel:* 10; 40.9 kw; 1,791 ft.; N36 0 19 W83 56 23
1513 Bill Williams Ave., Knoxville, TN 37917-3851 US
(865) 637-1010; *Fax:* (865) 522-7341
www.wbir.com
License: Knoxville, Knox County, TN held by Gannett Pacific LLC
Group Owner: Tegna Media; (acq 12-4-95; grpsl).; *Washington Law Firm:* Wiley, Rein & Fielding
Nat'l Network: NBC
Size of News Staff: 50; *Hours of Local News Weekly:* news progmg 24 hrs wkly

Jeff Lee, President and General Manager
Beth Weissfeld, General Sales Mgr
Andrew Coleman Smith, Image Promotions Producer
Martha Jennings, News Director
Christopher Casteel, Digital Sales Manager

WBXX-TV *Digital Channel:* 20; 562kw; ant 157t; N35 56 12 W85 00 46; *Population Served:* 1,000,000
10427 Cogdill Rd., Suite 100, Knoxville, TN 37932
(865) 777-9220; *Fax:* (865) 777-9221
www.wbxx.tv
License: Crossville, Cumberland County, TN held by Knoxville TV LLC
Group Owner: Lockwood Broadcasting Group; (acq 8-28-97; $13.2 million); *Washington Law Firm:* Dickstein Shapiro Morin & Oshinsky L.L.P.
Nat'l Network: CW; *Nat'l Reps:* Harrington, Righter & Parsons

Dan Phillippi, Operations Dir
Neal Davis, General Manager
Doug Koontz, General Sales Manager
Anna Robins, Programming Director
Tom Theilmann, Chief Engineer
Mike Baxter, Creative Services Producer
Andy Nuchlos, AccountExecutive
Liz Schutt, Local Sales Manager
Tania Monhollan, Office Manager
Ashley Brody-Suggs, Account Executive
Brian Case, Account Executive

WKNX-TV *Digital Channel:* 7; *Virtual Channel:* 7; 55 kw; 1253 ft.; N36 0 36 W83 55 57
6215 Kingston Pike, Suite A, Knoxville, TN 37919 US
(865) 329-8777; *Fax:* (817) 571-0239
www.wmaktv.com
License: Knoxville, Knox County, TN held by WMAK TV LLC
Group Owner: Lockwood Broadcast Group; *Washington Law Firm:* Fletcher, Heald & Hildreth
Nat'l Network: IND

David A. Hanna, President

***WKOP-TV** *Digital Channel:* 17; *Virtual Channel:* 15; 100 kw; 1809 ft.; N35 59 44 W83 57 23
1611 E. Magnolia Avenue, Knoxville, TN 37917 US
(865) 595-0220; *Fax:* (865) 595-0300
www.etptv.org
License: Knoxville, Knox County, TN held by East Tennessee Public Communications Corp
Nat'l Network: PBS

Teresa James, President
Frank Miller, Operations Dir
Kelly Hodges, General Sales Mgr
Bob Hutchinson, Programming Director
Katharine Seaton, Promotions Manager
Curtis Allin, Chief Engineer
Russ Manning, Public Affairs Director

WPXK-TV *Digital Channel:* 23; 18 kw; ant 1,007t; N36 11 53 W84 13 50; *Population Served:* 490,000
9000 Executive Park Dr. Bldg D, Suite 210, Knoxville, TN 37923 USA
(865) 531-4037; *Fax:* (865) 531-4760
www.iontelevision.com
License: Jellico, TN held by ION Media Knoxville License, Inc.
Group Owner: ION Media Networks Inc.
Nat'l Network: ION Television

Brandon Burgess, CEO/Chairman

WTNZ *Digital Channel:* 34; *Virtual Channel:* 43; 460 kw; 1736 ft.; N36 0 13 W83 56 34
9000 Executive Park Dr., Building D Suite 300, Knoxville, TN 37923 US
(865) 693-4343; *Fax:* (865) 691-6904, (865) 691-6770, (865) 691-7527
wtnzfox43.com
publicfile@wtnzfox43.com
License: Knoxville, Knox County, TN held by Raycom America License Subsidiary LLC.
Group Owner: Raycom Media Inc.; (acq 1996; grpsl).; *Washington Law Firm:* Covington & Burling
Nat'l Network: FOX; *Nat'l Reps:* TeleRep
Hours of Local News Weekly: 7 hrs weekly

Paul McTear, CEO
John Hayes, Operations Dir
Kelvin Mize, General Manager
Sara Foster, Sales Manager
Brad Butzbach, Chief Engineer
Wayne Daugherty, COO
Scott Key, Traffic Dept.
Holly Romero, Marketing Director
Fred Lohman,Business Manager
Susan Smith, Business Office Coordinator

WVLR *Digital Channel:* 48; *Virtual Channel:* 48; 1000 kw; 1411 ft.; N36 15 30 W83 37 43
1724 South Hills Dr., Knoxville, TN 37920 US
(865) 932-4803; *Fax:* (865) 932-4102
MariaTV48@comcast.net
License: Tazewell, Claiborne County, TN held by Volunteer Christian Television Inc.
Nat'l Network: REL

Theron Woodward, General Manager
Tom Evenson, Chief Engineer

WVLT *Digital Channel:* 30; *Virtual Channel:* 8; 870 kw; 1809 ft.; N35 59 44 W83 57 23

6450 Papermill Dr., Knoxville, TN 37919 USA
(865) 450-8888
www.local8now.com
License: Knoxville, Knox County, TN held by Gray Television Licensee LLC
Group Owner: Gray Television Inc.; (acq 1996; $165 million with WCTV(TV) Thomasville, GA).
Nat'l Network: CBS; MyNetworkTV; *Nat'l Reps:* Continental Television Sales
Size of News Staff: 38; *Hours of Local News Weekly:* news progmg 24.5 hrs wkly
Les Phillips, VP of Broadcast Operations
Chris Baker, General Manager
Jasmine Hardin, VP of Sales
Marty Parham, VP of Programming
Tony Bernhardt, VP of News & Operations
Doug Stallard, Chief Engineer

Memphis, TN (DMA 51)

WHBQ-TV *Digital Channel:* 13; *Virtual Channel:* 13; 95 kw; 308 meters; 35 10'29 N 89 50'43 W
485 S Highland St., Memphis, TN 38111 US
(901) 320-1313
www.fox13memphis.com
news@fox13memphis.com
License: Memphis, Shelby County, TN held by Fox 13
Group Owner: Cox Media Group; (acq 7-5-95; $80 million)
Nat'l Network: FOX; *Nat'l Reps:* Fox Stations Sales
Size of News Staff: 55; *Hours of Local News Weekly:* news progmg 54 hrs wkly
Paul Briggs, VP and General Manager
Omesh Somaru, Sales Director
Tim Doyle, Promotions Manager
Patti McGettigan, News Director
Ben Rainwater, Digital Content Manager
Jeff Klayman, Local Sales Manager

***WKNO** *Digital Channel:* 29; 316 kw vis, 56.2 kw aur; ant 1,079t/1,113g; N35 09 17 W89 49 20; *Population Served:* 1,600,000
7151 Cherry Farms Road, Cordova, TN 38016
(901) 458-2521, (901) 729-8735; *Fax:* (901) 729-8178
www.wkno.org
License: Memphis, Shelby County, TN held by Mid-South Public Communications Foundation
Washington Law Firm: Schwartz, Woods & Miller
Nat'l Network: PBS
Michael LaBonia, CEO
Russ Abernathy, Director of Television and Technology
Charles McLarty, Director of Radio, Dev. & Communications
Scott Davidson, Director of Finance and Administration

WLMT *Digital Channel:* 31; *Virtual Channel:* 30; 871 kw; 1115 ft.; N35 16 33 W89 46 38
1725 Shelby Oaks Dr. N., Suite 101, Memphis, TN 38134 US
(901) 323-2430
www.localmemphis.com
License: Memphis, Shelby County, TN held by Nexstar Broadcasting Inc.
Group Owner: Nexstar Broadcasting Group Inc.; (acq 3-14-2008; grpsl); *Washington Law Firm:* Covington & Burling
Nat'l Network: CW
Joseph Denk, General Manager
Lisa Lovell, News Director

WMC-TV *Digital Channel:* 5; *Virtual Channel:* 5; 34.5 kw; 1010 ft.; N35 10 9 W89 53 10
1960 Union Dr., Memphis, TN 38104 US
(901) 726-0555, (901) 726-0416; *Fax:* (901) 278-7633
www.wmctv.com
License: Memphis, Shelby County, TN held by WMC License Subsidiary, LLC.
Group Owner: Raycom Media Inc.; (acq 1997; grpsl).; *Washington Law Firm:* Goldberg, Godles, Wiener & Wright
Nat'l Network: NBC; *Nat'l Reps:* TeleRep
Clint Moore, Operations Manager
Lee Meredith, VP & General manager
Don Fisher, General Sales Manager
Chris Conroy, Promotions Manager
Tammy Phillips, News Director
Tim Seymour, Local Sales Manager
Andrea Starr, Internet SalesManager
Kelsey Jacobson, Digital content Director
Jeremy Jones, Special Projects Producer
Chris Conroy, Director of Marketing

WPXX-TV *Digital Channel:* 51; *Virtual Channel:* 50; 1000 kw; 978 ft.; N35 12 41 W89 48 54
3145 Brother Blvd., Bartlett, TN 38133 USA
(901) 821-8593; *Fax:* (901) 821-8331
www.iontelevision.com
License: Memphis, Shelby County, TN held by ION Media Memphis License, Inc.
Group Owner: ION Media Networks Inc.
Nat'l Network: ION
Brandon Burgess, Chairman/CEO

WREG-TV *Digital Channel:* 28; *Virtual Channel:* 3; 906 kw; 1027 ft.; N35 10 52 W89 49 56
803 Channel 3 Dr., Memphis, TN 38103 USA
(901) 543-2333
wreg.com
License: Memphis, Shelby County, TN held by WREG License LLC
Group Owner: Tribune Media; *Washington Law Firm:* Koteen & Naftalin
Nat'l Network: CBS; *Nat'l Reps:* Eagle Television Sales; *Wire Services:* New York Times News Service
Size of News Staff: 50

Nashville, TN (DMA 29)

***WCTE** *Digital Channel:* 22; *Virtual Channel:* 22; 200 kw; 1394 ft.; N36 10 26 W85 20 37
Mailing Address: P.O. Box 2040, Cookeville, TN 38502 US
Second Address: 1151 Stadium Dr., Suite 104, Cookeville, TN 38501
(931) 528-2222, (800) 282-9238; *Fax:* (931) 372-6284
www.wcte.org
info@wcte.org
License: Cookeville, Putnam County, TN held by Upper Cumberland Broadcast Council
Nat'l Network: PBS
Becky Magura, President & CEO
Craig LeFevre, Operations Manager/FCC Compliance
Avery Owens, Director of Advancement
Lindsey Sasser, Programming Director
Ralph Welch, Director of Engineering & Technology
Randall Jackson, BroadcastEngineer
Rick Wells, Senior Producer/Director
Craig Gray, Business Development Producer
Mary Boring, Special Projects/Executive asst. to CEO
Seth Stanger, Sales & Develpoment Asst.
Desiree Duncan, Director of Content

WHTN *Digital Channel:* 38; *Virtual Channel:* 39; 1000 kw; 820 ft.; N36 4 58 W86 25 52
9582 Lebanon Road, Mt. Juliet, TN 37122 US
(615) 754-0039; *Fax:* (615) 754-0047
www.ctntv.org
License: Murfreesboro, Rutherford County, TN held by Christian Television Network Inc
Washington Law Firm: Gammon & Grange
Nat'l Network: IND
Foreign Language Programming; Size of News Staff: 1; *Hours of Local News Weekly:* news progmg 2 hrs wkly
Monica Schmelter, Station Manager

WKRN-TV *Digital Channel:* 27; *Virtual Channel:* 2; 1,000 kw; 1,350t/942g; N36 02 50 W86 49 48; *Population Served:* 1,844,000
441 Murfreesboro Rd., Nashville, TN 37210
(615) 369-7222, (615) 369-7329; *Fax:* (615) 369-7329
www.wkrn.com
License: Nashville, Davidson County, TN held by WKRN G.P.
Group Owner: Young Broadcasting LLC; (acq 7-1-89; $42 million;
Washington Law Firm: Brooks Pierce
Nat'l Network: ABC; *Nat'l Reps:* Cox Reps
Size of News Staff: 65; *Hours of Local News Weekly:* news progmg 33 hrs wkly
Dirk Mooth, News Operations Manager
Stan Knott, General manager
Matthew Zelkind, Station Manager & News director
Steve Watt, General Sales Manager
Michelle Dube, Program & Community Affairs Director
Mike Tarrolly, PromotionsManager
Matthew Zelkind, Station Manager & News director
Dave Parker, Chief Engineer
Barry Cunningham, Business Manager
Jamie Camp, Local Sales Manager
Mike Tarrolly, Marketing Director
Heather Pelat, Web Manager
Alison Coe, Asst. NewsDirector

WNAB *Digital Channel:* 23; *Virtual Channel:* 58; 350 kw; 1204 ft.; N36 15 50 W86 47 39
Mailing Address: 631 Mainstream Dr., Nashville, TN 37228 US
Second Address: 10706 Beaver Dam Road, Hunt Valley, MD 21030
(615) 259-5617, (615) 259-5645; *Fax:* (615) 259-5684
www.cw58.tv
closedcaptioning@mytv30web.com
License: Nashville, Davidson County, TN held by Nashville License Holdings LLC
Nat'l Network: CW
Michael Jones, CFO
Michael Lambert, President
Mark Dillion, Station Manager
DeJuan Buford, General Sales Mgr
Michael Hook, Programming Director
Lee Scott, Promotions Manager
Dale Bukowski, National Sales Manager
PattyDaugherty, Traffic Manager

***WNPT** *Digital Channel:* 8; *Virtual Channel:* 8; 17.65 kw; 1280 ft.; N36 2 49 W86 49 49
161 Rains Avenue, Nashville, TN 37203-5330 US
(615) 259-9325; *Fax:* (615) 248-6120
www.wnpt.org
tv8@wnpt.net
License: Nashville, Davidson County, TN held by Nashville Public Television Inc
Washington Law Firm: Schwartz, Woods & Miller
Nat'l Network: PBS
Richard F. Warren, Chairman
Beth Curley, CEO/President
Kevin Crane, Vice President of Content and Technology
Justin Harvey, Programming Director
Dale Baker, Sr. Director of Engineering
Robert V. Dale, Treasurer
Frank E. Gordon,Secretary
Scott E. Becker, Director
Charles W. Cook, Emeritus
Jennifer R. Frist, Director
Jeff W. Gregg, Director

WNPX-TV *Digital Channel:* 36; 733 kw; 869t/623g; N36 16 04 W86 47 44; *Population Served:* 2,474,000
1281 N. Mt. Juliet Rd., Suite L, Mt. Juliet, TN 37122 USA
(615) 773-6100
www.iontelevision.com
License: Cookeville, TN held by ION Media License Company, LLC
Group Owner: ION Media Networks Inc.
Nat'l Network: ION Television
Brandon Burgess, Chairman/CEO

WPGD-TV *Digital Channel:* 33; *Virtual Channel:* 50; 1000 kw; 1352 ft.; N36 16 5 W86 47 45
Mailing Address: PO Box A, Santa Ana, CA 92711 US
Second Address: P. O. Box 768, Station B, Ottawa, ON K1P 5P8
(714) 731-1000, (888) 731-1000, (714) 832-2950; *Fax:* (615) 822-1642
www.tbn.org
License: Hendersonville, Sumner County, TN held by Trinity Broadcasting Network
Group Owner: Trinity Broadcasting Network; (acq 7-2000; grpsl)
Nat'l Network: TRINITY BROADCA
Russell Hall, General Manager
Allen Partlow, Chief Engineer

WSMV *Digital Channel:* 10; *Virtual Channel:* 4; 42.4 kW; 1361 ft.; N36 8 27 W86 51 56
5700 Knob Rd, Nashville, TN 37209 USA
(615) 353-4444
www.wsmv.com
news@wsmv.com
License: Nashville, Davidson County, TN held by Meredith Corp.
Group Owner: Meredith Corp.; (acq 11-1-94; $159 million;
Washington Law Firm: Wilmer, Cutler & Pickering
Nat'l Network: NBC; *Nat'l Reps:* TeleRep
Paul Scott, General Sales Mgr
Brian Hallett, Promotions Manager
Denise Eck, News Director

WTVF *Digital Channel:* 25; *Virtual Channel:* 5; 1000 kw; 428 meters; N36 16 05 W86 47 16; *Population Served:* 2,268,000
474 James Robertson Pkwy., Nashville, TN 37219
(615) 244-5000; *Fax:* (615) 248-5353,TWX: 810-371-1168
www.newschannel5.com
news@newschannel5.com
License: Nashville, Davidson County, TN held by NewsChannel 5 Network LP.
Group Owner: Journal Communications Inc.; (acq 9-12-91; $46 million; *Washington Law Firm:* Hogan & Hartson
Nat'l Network: CBS
Hours of Local News Weekly: News progmg 24 hrs wkly

Debbie Turner, General Manager
Mark Binda, Programming Director
Mike Cutler, News Director

WUXP-TV *Digital Channel:* 21; *Virtual Channel:* 30; 1000 kw; 1355 ft.; N36 15 50 W86 47 39
631 Mainstream Dr., Nashville, TN 37228 US
(615) 259-5617; *Fax:* (615) 259-5684
www.mytv30web.com
itate@fox17.com
License: Nashville, Davidson County, TN held by WUXP Licensee LLC
Group Owner: Sinclair Broadcast Group Inc.; (acq 12-10-2001; $2.829 million); *Washington Law Firm:* Arter & Hadden
Nat'l Network: MYTV
Noreen Parker, General Manager
Mark Dillon, Station Manager
Greg Pollard, Local Sales Manager
Toni Fitzgerald, Sales Manager
David Holt, Promotional Producer

WZTV *Digital Channel:* 15; *Virtual Channel:* 17; 1000 kw; 1348 ft.; N36 15 50 W86 47 39
Mailing Address: 631 Mainstream Dr., Nashville, TN 37228 US
Second Address: 10706 Beaver Dam Rd., Hunt Valley, MD 21030
(615) 259-5617; *Fax:* (615) 259-5684
www.fox17.com
news@fox17.com
License: Nashville, Davidson County, TN held by WZTV Licensee LLC
Group Owner: Sinclair Broadcast Group Inc.; (acq 12-10-01; grpsl).; *Washington Law Firm:* Arter & Hadden
Nat'l Network: FOX
Size of News Staff: 9; *Hours of Local News Weekly:* news progmg 7 hrs wkly
Noreen Parker, General Manager
Mark Dillon, Station Manager
Greg Pollard, Local Sales Manager
Toni Fitzgerald, Sales Manager
Scott Walls, Promotions Producer

Tri-Cities, TN-VA (DMA 98)

WEMT *Digital Channel:* 38; *Virtual Channel:* 39; 1000 kw; 2365 ft.; N36 26 58 W82 6 29
Mailing Address: 900 Laskin Road, Virginia Beach, VA 23451 US
Second Address: 3206 Hanover Rd., Johnson City, TN 37602-3489
(423) 283-3900; *Fax:* (423) 283-4938
www.wemt39.com
License: Greeneville, Greene County, TN held by Esteem License Holdings Inc.
Group Owner: Esteem Broadcasting; (acq 5-31-2007; for stock); *Washington Law Firm:* Shaw, Pittman
Nat'l Network: FOX
Leesa Wilcher, General Manager
Rebecca Berry, Programming Director
Jim Hartline, Chief Engineer
Amy McClary, Regional Sales Manager

WJHL-TV *Digital Channel:* 11; *Virtual Channel:* 11; 34.5 kw; 2323 ft.; N36 25 55 W82 8 15
320 Bob Morrison Blvd, Bristol, VA 24201 US
(276) 669-2181; *Fax:* (423) 434-4537
www.tricities.com
features@bristolnews.com
License: Johnson City, Washington County, TN held by Media General Communications Holdings, LLC
Group Owner: Media General Broadcast Group; (acq 3-21-97; grpsl).; *Washington Law Firm:* Dow, Lohnes and Albertson
Nat'l Network: CBS; *Nat'l Reps:* Harrington, Righter & Parsons
Jack Dempsey, General Manager
Lisa Wilcher, General Sales Mgr
Amanda Adams, Promotions Manager
Neal Boling, News Director
Mike Moore, Chief Engineer
Kenny Hawkins, Sports Commentator
Mark Reynolds, Weather Director

WKPT-TV *Digital Channel:* 19; *Virtual Channel:* 19; 200 kw; ant 2,320t/225g; N36 25 54 W82 08 15; *Population Served:* 1,000,000
222 Commerce St., Kingsport, TN 37660
(423) 246-9578, (423) 246-6122; *Fax:* (423) 246-4249
www.wkpttv.com
viewermail@hvbcgroup.com
License: Kingsport, Sullivan County, TN held by Holston Valley Broadcasting Corp.
Group Owner: Glenwood Communications Corp.; *Ownership:* Glenwood Communications Corp, 100%.; *Washington Law Firm:* Dennis J. Kelly
Nat'l Network: ABC; *Nat'l Reps:* Harrington, Righter & Parsons
George DeVault Jr, President
Fred Falin, VP/TV Programming & Operations
George Devault Jr, General Manager
Lamar Reid, General Sales Mgr
Jerreese Rockwell, Promotions Manager
Jim Bailey, News Director
George Devault, EngineeringDir
Bob Haywood, VP/Local Sales Manager
Bette Lawson, VP/Treasurer

Texas

Abilene-Sweetwater, TX (DMA 165)

KPCB-DT ; 464 kw vis; 443t; N32 46 52 W100 53 52
Mailing Address: Box 61000, Midland, TX 79711-1000
Second Address: 12706 W. Highway 80 East, Odessa, TX 79765
(800) 707-0420, (432) 563-0420; *Fax:* (432) 563-1736
www.godslearningchannel.com
info@ptcbglc.com
License: Snyder, Scurry County, TX held by Prime Time Christian Broadcasting Inc
Jeff Tveit, General Manager
Al Cooper, Founder
Tommie Cooper, Founder

KRBC-TV *Digital Channel:* 29; *Virtual Channel:* 9; 1000 kw; 846 ft.; N32 16 38 W99 35 51
4510 S. 14th St., Abilene, TX 79605 US
(325) 692-4242; *Fax:* (325) 692-8265
www.bigcountryhomepage.com
License: Abilene, Taylor County, TX held by Mission Broadcasting Inc.
Group Owner: Mission Broadcasting Inc.; (acq 6-13-2003; $10 million with KSAN-TV San Angelo); *Washington Law Firm:* Hogan & Hartson
Nat'l Network: NBC
Albert Gutierrez, General Manager
Marian Zett, Station Manager
Sari David, General Sales Mgr
Megan Dobbs, News Director

KTAB-TV *Digital Channel:* 24; *Virtual Channel:* 32; 1,000 ERP; 261 m HAAT; N32 16 35 W99 35 39; *Population Served:* 330,000
4510 S. 14th St., Abilene, TX 79605 US
(325) 695-2777; *Fax:* (325) 695-9922
www.bigcountryhomepage.com
License: Abilene, Taylor County, TX held by Nexstar Broadcasting Inc.
Group Owner: Nexstar Broadcasting Group Inc.; (acq 8-15-99; $16.7 million)
Nat'l Network: CBS
Size of News Staff: 32; *Hours of Local News Weekly:* news progmg 21.5 hr wkly
Albert Gutierrez, General Manager
Sari David, General Sales Mgr
Megan Dobbs, News Director

KTXS-TV *Digital Channel:* 20; *Virtual Channel:* 12; 530 kw; 1319 ft.; N32 24 48 W100 6 25
Mailing Address: Box 2997, Abilene, TX 79604 US
Second Address: 4420 N. Clack, Abilene, TX 79601
(325) 677-2281, (32) 672-5987; *Fax:* (325) 676-9231, (325) 672-5307
www.ktxs.com
License: Sweetwater, Nolan County, TX held by BlueStone License Holdings Inc.
Group Owner: Bonten Media Group LLC; (acq 5-31-2007; grpsl)
Nat'l Network: ABC & CW (DIGIT; CW
Jackie Rutledge, Operations Dir
Bud Brown, VP & General Manager
Jorge Montoya, General Sales Mgr
Maria Jefer, Programming
Roger Ingram, Promotion Producer
Jason Goodwin, News Director
John Mark Woodard, Engineer
Adam McKinney,Engineer
David Caldwell, Creative Services Manager
Nikki Caudle, Technical Director
Brad Bullington, National Sales Manager
Lynn Wilkinson, Business Development Manager
Joe Fry, Assignments Editor
Doug Myres, Internet Content Director

KXVA *Digital Channel:* 15; *Virtual Channel:* 15; 31 kw; 981 ft.; N32 16 31 W99 35 23; *Rebroadcasting:* Rebroadcasts KIDY(TV) San Angelo 98%.; *Population Served:* 364,000
Mailing Address: 500 Chestnut St., Suite 804, Abilene, TX 79602 US
Second Address: 5 S. Chadbourne, San Angelo, TX 76903
(325) 672-5606; *Fax:* (325) 655-8461
www.myfoxzone.com
License: Abilene, Taylor County, TX held by LSB Broadcasting Inc.
Group Owner: Tegna Media; (acq 12-28-2004).; *Washington Law Firm:* Fletcher, Heard and Hildreth0
Nat'l Network: Fox; *Nat'l Reps:* Millennium Sales & Marketing
Justin Riggan, President and General Manager
Glenn Edwards, Chief Engineer

Amarillo, TX (DMA 131)

***KACV-TV** *Digital Channel:* 9; 5 kw; 481.7 meters AGL; N35 20 33 W101 49 21; *Population Served:* 400,000
Mailing Address: Box 447, Amarillo, TX 79178
Second Address: 2408 S. Jackson, Amarillo, TX 79178
(806) 371-5222; *Fax:* (806) 371-5258
www.kacvtv.org
kacvtv@actx.edu
License: Amarillo, Potter County, TX held by Amarillo Junior College District.
Washington Law Firm: Cohn & Marks LLP
Nat'l Network: PBS
Jackie Smith, Operations Dir
Linda Pitner, General Manager
Lynne Groom, General Sales Mgr
Lee Proctor, Engineering Dir
Melissa Treiber, Outreach Coordinator

KAMR-TV *Digital Channel:* 19; *Virtual Channel:* 4; 400 kw; 1493 ft.; N35 20 33 W101 49 21
1015 S. Fillmore, Amarillo, TX 79101 US
(806) 383-3321; *Fax:* (806) 381-2943
www.myhighplains.com
License: Amarillo, Potter County, TX held by Nexstar Broadcasting, Inc.
Group Owner: Nexstar Broadcasting Group Inc.; (acq 12-31-03; grpsl).; *Washington Law Firm:* Arter & Hadden
Nat'l Network: NBC
Brandy Sanchez, General Manager
Stuart Stallard, Dir. of Sales
Ny Lynn Nichols, News Director

KCIT *Digital Channel:* 15; *Virtual Channel:* 14; 925 kw; 1522 ft.; N35 20 33 W101 49 21
Mailing Address: PO Box 1414, Amarillo, TX 79105 US
Second Address: 1015 S. Fillmore St., Amarillo, TX 79101
(806) 374-1414; *Fax:* (806) 381-2943
www.myhighplains.com
License: Amarillo, Potter County, TX held by Mission Broadcasting Inc.
Group Owner: Mission Broadcasting Inc.; (acq 1999; $28.5 million with KJTL(TV) Wichita Falls).; *Washington Law Firm:* Drinker Biddle & Reath L.L.P.
Nat'l Network: FOX; *Nat'l Reps:* Blair Television
Hours of Local News Weekly: News progmg 3 hrs wkly
Wesley Wilson, Station Manager
Stuart Stallard, Dir. of Sales
Ny Lynn Nichols, News Director

KEYU *Digital Channel:* 31; *Virtual Channel:* 31; 700 kw; 1002 ft.; N35 20 33 W101 49 20
Mailing Address: #1 Shackleford Drive, Suite 400, Little Rock, AR 72211 US
Second Address: PO Box 10, Amarillo, TX 79105
(806) 359-8900; *Fax:* (806) 352-8912
www.univision-amarillo.com
License: Borger, Hutchinson County, TX held by Midessa Broadcasting L.P.
Group Owner: Equity Media Holdings Corp.
Nat'l Network: UNIVISION
Foreign Language Programming
Brent McClure, General Manager

KFDA-TV *Digital Channel:* 10; *Virtual Channel:* 10; 62 kw; 1529 ft.; N35 17 34 W101 50 42
Mailing Address: P.O. Box 10, Amarillo, TX 79105 US
Second Address: 7900 Broadway, Amarillo, TX 79108
(806) 383-1010,(806) 383-6397; *Fax:* (806) 381-9859
www.newschannel10.com
newsroom@newschannel10.com
License: Amarillo, Potter County, TX held by Panhandle Telecasting Co.

Group Owner: R.H. Drewry Group; (acq 10-4-76; $3 million;
Washington Law Firm: Shaw Pittman
Nat'l Network: CBS; *Wire Services:* AP
Size of News Staff: 32; *Hours of Local News Weekly:* news progmg 19.5 hrs wkly
Bill Drewry, President
Larry Patton, Operations Dir
Brent McClure, General Manager
Joyce Austin, General Sales Mgr
Tony Smitherman, Promotions Manager
Richard Fulkerson, Operations Manager
Robert Drewry, President
BrentMcClure, Vice President

KPTF-DT *Digital Channel:* 18; 5,000 kw vis; ant 331t; N34 21 48 W103 13 05
Mailing Address: Box 61000, Midland, TX 79711-1000
Second Address: 12706 W. Highway 80 E, Odessa, TX 79765
(432) 563-0420, (800) 572-4242, (866) 846-5200; *Fax:* (432) 563-1736
www.GLC.US.com
info@glc.us.com
License: Farwell, Parmer County, TX held by Prime Time Christian Broadcasting Inc
Al Cooper, President/General Manager
Al Cooper, Founder
Tommie Cooper, Founder

KVII-TV *Digital Channel:* 7; *Virtual Channel:* 7; 21.9 kw; 1703 ft.; N35 22 30 W101 52 56
1 Broadcast Center, Amarillo, TX 79101 US
(806) 373-1787; *Fax:* (806) 371-7329
www.abc7amarillo.com
pronews7@kvii.com
License: Amarillo, Potter County, TX held by KVII Licensee LLC
Group Owner: Sinclair Broadcast Group Inc.; (acq 2-28-2013; grpsl); *Washington Law Firm:* Wiley, Rein & Fielding
Nat'l Network: ABC
Foreign Language Programming; Hours of Local News Weekly: news progmg 36 hrs wkly
Laura Wolf, General Manager
Byron Williams, Local Sales Manager
Ryan Hazelwood, News Director
Michelle Cook, Business Manager

Austin, TX (DMA 39)

KAKW-DT *Digital Channel:* 13; *Virtual Channel:* 62; 39 kw; 1814 ft.; N30 43 34 W97 59 23
2233 W. North Loop, Austin, TX 78756
(512) 453-8899; *Fax:* (512) 533-2874
www.univision.com
License: Killeen, Bell County, TX held by KAKW License Partnership L.P.
Group Owner: Univision Communications Inc.
Hours of Local News Weekly: news progmg 5 hrs wkly
Randy Falco, President
Fely Garcia, Community Relations Manager

KBVO *Digital Channel:* 27; 700 kw; 1297 ft.; N30 19 33 W97 47 58
908 W. Martin Luther King, Jr., Blvd., Austin, TX 78701 US
(512) 476-3636, (512) 703-5255; *Fax:* (512) 476-1520, (401)454-6990
www.kxan.com
License: Llano, Travis County, TX held by KXAN LLC
Group Owner: LIN Media; (acq 11-14-94; *Washington Law Firm:* Covington & Burling
Nat'l Network: NBC
Size of News Staff: 60; *Hours of Local News Weekly:* news progmg 22 hrs wkly
Eric Lassberg, VP/ General Manager
Deirdre Conley, Promotions Dir.
Chad Cross, News Director
Mark Dunhan, Chief Engineer
Denise Daniels, Dir. Of Sales
Devin Walker, Regional Digital Media Dir.

KEYE-TV *Digital Channel:* 43; *Virtual Channel:* 42; 1000 kw; 1296 ft.; N30 19 18 W97 48 11
Mailing Address: 10700 Metric Blvd., Austin, TX 78758 US
Second Address: 10706 Beaver Dam Rd., Hunt Valley, MR 21030
(512) 835-0042; *Fax:* (512) 837-6753
www.keyetv.com
webteam@keyetv.com
License: Austin, Travis County, TX held by KEYE Licensee LLC
Group Owner: Sinclair Broadcast Group Inc.; (acq 11-21-2007; grpsl); *Washington Law Firm:* Wiley Rein LLP
Nat'l Network: CBS; *Nat'l Reps:* TeleRep
Size of News Staff: 50; *Hours of Local News Weekly:* news progmg 20 hrs wkly
Amy Villarreal, General Manager
Todd Ricke, Director of Sales
Gerald Weaver, Engineering Dir
Jim Joly, Director of National Digital Sales
Greg Siegel, Vice President, National Sales

***KLRU** *Digital Channel:* 22; *Virtual Channel:* 18; 700 kw; 1173 ft.; N30 19 19 W97 48 12
Mailing Address: PO Box 7158, Austin, TX 78713-7158 US
Second Address: 2504-B Whitis Ave., Austin, TX 78712
(512) 471-4811; *Fax:* (512) 475-9090
www.klru.org
info@klru.org
License: Austin, Travis County, TX held by Capital of Texas Public Telecomm
Washington Law Firm: Cohn & Marks
Nat'l Network: PBS
Gabriel Ornelas, Chairman
Bill Stotesbery, CEO/General Manager
Karin Morrison, Operations Dir
Lori Holliday, General Sales Mgr
Maury Sullivan, Promotions Manager
David Kuipers, Chief Engineer
Pat Wertz, CFO
Dick Peterson,Executive Vice President
Ed Bailey, VP, Sales
Maury Sullivan, Sr. VP,Community Management
Pamela Cosel, Chair Elect

KNVA *Digital Channel:* 49; *Virtual Channel:* 54; 500 kw; 1299 ft.; N30 19 33 W97 47 58
Mailing Address: P.O. Box 684647, Austin, TX 78768 US
Second Address: 908 W. Martin Luther King Blvd., Austin, TX 78701
(512) 478-5400; *Fax:* (512) 476-1520
www.thecwaustin.com
License: Austin, Travis County, TX held by 54 Broadcasting Inc
Nat'l Network: CW
Korey Wisland, Operations Dir
Eric Lassberg, General Manager
Devin Walker, Station Manager
Denise Daniels, General Sales Mgr
Chadd Cross, Program Director
Deirdre Conley, Promotions Manager
Devin Walker, News Director
MarkDunham, Chief Engineer
Tom Michel, Local Sales Manager
Bryan Hastings, National Sales Manager
Amy Coplen, Regional Sales Manager

KTBC *Digital Channel:* 7; *Virtual Channel:* 7; 98.6 kW; 1257 ft.; N30 18 35 W97 47 34
119 East 10th St., Austin, TX 78701 USA
(512) 476-7777; *Fax:* (512) 495-7001
www.fox7austin.com
news@fox7.com
License: Austin, Travis County, TX held by NW Communications of Austin Inc.
Group Owner: Fox Television Stations Group; (acq 1-97)
Nat'l Network: FOX
Size of News Staff: 54; *Hours of Local News Weekly:* news progmg 24 hrs wkly

KVUE *Digital Channel:* 33; *Virtual Channel:* 24; 1,000 kw; 1,234 ft.; N30 19 18 W97 48 11
3201 Steck Ave., Austin, TX 78757 US
(512) 459-6521; *Fax:* (512) 533-2233
www.kvue.com
news@kvue.com
License: Austin, Travis County, TX held by KVUE Television Inc.
Group Owner: Tegna Media; (acq 12-23-2013)
Nat'l Network: ABC; *Nat'l Reps:* Harrington, Righter & Parsons
Hours of Local News Weekly: news progmg 29.5 hrs wkly
Patti C. Smith, President and General Manager

KXAN-TV *Digital Channel:* 21; *Virtual Channel:* 36; 700 kw; 1297 ft.; N30 19 33 W97 47 58
Mailing Address: 200 Crescent Court, Suite 1600, Dallas, TX 75201 US
Second Address: 908 W. Martin Luther King, Jr. Blvd., Austin, TX 78701
(512) 476-3636, (512) 703-5255; *Fax:* (512) 476-1520
www.kxan.com
License: Austin, Travis County, TX held by KXAN LLC
Group Owner: LIN Media; (acq 11-14-94; *Washington Law Firm:* Covington & Burling
Nat'l Network: NBC
Size of News Staff: 60; *Hours of Local News Weekly:* news progmg 22 hrs wkly
Eric Lassberg, VP,General Manger
Denise Daniels, General Sales Mgr
Laura Franklin, Programming Director
Deirdre Conley, Promotions Director
Chad Cross, News Director
Mark Dunham, Engineering Dir
Mark Dunham, Engineering Dir
Todd Krauss, Local Sales Manager
Amy Coplen, Regional Sales Manager
Jamie Aragon, Traffic and Program Director
Jim Spencer, Weather Director
Korey Wisland, Production Manager
Denise Daniels, Director of Sales

Beaumont-Port Arthur, TX (DMA 141)

KBMT *Digital Channel:* 12; *Virtual Channel:* 12; 18.2 kw; 1,001 ft.; N30 11 26 W93 53 8
525 Interstate 10 S., Beaumont, TX 77708 US
(409) 833-7512; *Fax:* (409) 981-1564
www.12newsnow.com
12news@kbmt12.com
License: Beaumont, Jefferson County, TX held by LSB Broadcasting Inc.
Group Owner: Tegna Media; (acq 7-8-2014).; *Washington Law Firm:* Cohn & Marks
Nat'l Network: ABC; NBC
Size of News Staff: 26; *Hours of Local News Weekly:* news progmg 13 hrs wkly
Bruce Cummings, General Manager
Don Davis, General Sales Mgr
Paul Bergen, News Director
Mark Cormier, Chief Engineer

KBTV-TV *Digital Channel:* 40; *Virtual Channel:* 4; 1000 kw; 829 ft.; N30 9 20 W93 59 10
6155 Eastex Fwy, Ste. 300, Beaumont, TX 77706 US
(409) 840-4444; *Fax:* (409) 892-4632, (409) 899-4632
www.kbtv4.tv
webteam@fox4beaumont.com
License: Port Arthur, Jefferson County, TX held by Deerfield Media (Port Arthur) Licensee LLC
Group Owner: Deerfield Media; (acq 11-6-97; grpsl).;
Washington Law Firm: Drinker, Biddle & Roth
Nat'l Network: NBC; *Nat'l Reps:* Blair Television; *Wire Services:* AP
Perry Sook, CEO
Scott Price, Operations Manager
Chris Puritt, General Manager
Jimbo Davis, Local Sales Manager
Barbara Nixon, Programming Manager
Paul Bergen, News Director
Don Dobbs, Chief Engineer
Lori Perkins, Digital SalesManager
Margie Redkey, Traffic/Sales Asst.
Susan E. Domozych, Senior Paralegal

KFDM *Digital Channel:* 25; *Virtual Channel:* 6; 350 kw; 960t/1,031g; N30 08 24 W93 58 44; *Population Served:* 163,500
Mailing Address: 2955 I-10 E., Beaumont, TX 77702
Second Address: 10706 Beaver Dam Rd., Hunt Valley, MD 21030
(409) 892-6622; *Fax:* (409) 899-4639
www.kfdm.com
License: Beaumont, Jefferson County, TX held by KFDM Licensee LLC
Group Owner: Sinclair Broadcast Group Inc.; (acq 11-2-2011; grpsl); *Washington Law Firm:* Latham & Watkins
Nat'l Network: CBS; CW; *Nat'l Reps:* TeleRep
Paula Hayward, General Manager
Barbara Nixon, Programming Director
Scott Lawrence, News Director
Don Dobbs, Chief Engineer

***KITU-TV** *Digital Channel:* 33; *Virtual Channel:* 34; 1,000 kw vis; ant 1,023t/1,027g; N30 10 41 W93 54 26
Mailing Address: 11221 Interstate 10, P.O. Box 158 , Orange, TX 77630
Second Address: 10902 S. Wilcrest, Houston, TX 77099
(281) 561-5828; *Fax:* (281) 561-9793
www.communityedtv.org
License: Beaumont, Jefferson County, TX held by Community Educational Television Inc
Dr. Reginald Cherry, President
Sandy Aulquist, Operations Manager
Wayne Ozio, Station Manager
Wayne Ozio, Chief Engineer

Corpus Christi, TX (DMA 128)

KCRP-CD *Digital Channel:* 41; *Virtual Channel:* 41; 15 kw; 334.6 ft; N27 47 45.9 W97 23 47
102 N. Mesquite St., Corpus Christi, TX 78401 US
(361) 883-2823; *Fax:* (361) 883-2931
asaenz@entravision.com
License: Corpus Christi, Nueces County, TX held by Entravision Holdings LLC.
Group Owner: Entravision Communications Corp.; (acq 3-17-98; $1.336 million); *Washington Law Firm:* Mullin, Rhyne, Emmons & Topel
Nat'l Network: UNIVISION
Anita Saenz-Carvalho, General Manager
Claire Arredondo-Lemons, Interactive Sales Manager
Nelly Guzman Posada, News Director
Tino Burriola, Chief Engineer

***KEDT** *Digital Channel:* 23; *Virtual Channel:* 16; 50 kw; 896 ft.; N27 39 20 W97 33 55
4455 S.Padre Isl.Dr.St38, Corpus Christi, TX 78411 US
(361) 855-2213; *Fax:* (361) 855-3877
www.kedt.org
License: Corpus Christi, Nueces County, TX held by South Texas Public Broadcasting System
Washington Law Firm: Schwartz, Woods & Miller
Nat'l Network: PBS
Steve Hipes, Chairman
Norma Camarillo, CFO
Don Dunlap, President/General Manager
Myra Lombardo, Operations Dir
Molly Goodwin, General Sales Mgr
Sylvia Coronado, Programming Director
Johanna Zwernemann, Asst Music Director
Robert Chabot, Music Director
Cody Blount, Operations Director
Diane DeCou, Vice-Chair
Andy Heines, Secretary
Jim Johnston, Treasurer

KIII-TV *Digital Channel:* 8; *Virtual Channel:* 3; 160 kw; 883 ft.; N27 39 30 W97 36 4
5002 S. Padre Island Dr., Corpus Christi, TX 78411 US
(361) 986-8300; *Fax:* (361) 986-8507
www.kiiitv.com
info@kiiitv.com
License: Corpus Christi, Nueces County, TX held by LSB Broadcasting Inc.
Group Owner: Tegna Media; (acq 7-8-2014).; *Washington Law Firm:* Cohn & Marks
Nat'l Network: ABC; *Nat'l Reps:* Continental Television Sales
Foreign Language Programming; Size of News Staff: 30; *Hours of Local News Weekly:* news progmg 17.5 hrs wkly
Scott Jones, Operations Manager
Dan Robbins, General Manager
Larry Hogue, Regional Sales Manager
Richard Longoria, News Director
Moe Strout, Chief Engineer

KORO-TV *Digital Channel:* 27; *Virtual Channel:* 28; 1000 kw; 943 ft.; N27 42 27.9 W97 37 59
102 N. Mesquite St., Corpus Christi, TX 78401 US
(361) 883-2823; *Fax:* (361) 883-2931
www.noticias.entravision.com/corpus_christi
asaenz@entravision.com
License: Corpus Christi, Nueces County, TX held by Entravision Holdings LLC.
Group Owner: Entravision Communications Corp.; (acq 3-17-98; $1.336 million); *Washington Law Firm:* Mullin, Rhyne, Emmons & Topel
Nat'l Network: UNIVISION
Foreign Language Programming; Size of News Staff: 5; *Hours of Local News Weekly:* news progmg 5 hrs wkly
Anita Saenz-Carvalho, General Manager
Claire Arredondo-Lemons, Interactive Sales Manager
Nelly Guzman Posada, News Director
Tino Burriola, Chief Engineer

KRIS-TV *Digital Channel:* 13; *Virtual Channel:* 6; 46.1 kw; 786 ft.; N27 44 29 W97 36 9
301 Artesian St., Corpus Christi, TX 78401 US
(361) 886-6100; *Fax:* (361) 884-6666
www.kristv.com
License: Corpus Christi, Nueces County, TX held by KRIS Communications LLC
Group Owner: Cordillera Communications Inc.; *Washington Law Firm:* Nixon, Hargrave, Devans & Doyle
Nat'l Network: NBC; CW
Size of News Staff: 31; *Hours of Local News Weekly:* news progmg 14 hrs wkly
Greg McAlister, General Manager
Angelle Croman, Director of Sales
Paul Alexander, News Director
Steve West, Chief Engineer
Kristen Darden, Internet Director
Billy Brotherton, National Sales Manager
Veronica Coronado, TrafficManager
Anthony Gloria, IT Manager
Ben Lloyd, Online Content Manager

KUQI *Digital Channel:* 38; *Virtual Channel:* 38; 50 kw; 810 ft.; N27 45 31.8 W97 36 26.3; *Not on Air/Target Date:* unknown
7228 Canyon Run, El Paso, TX 79912 US
(3610 600-3800; *Fax:* (361) 882-1973
License: Corpus Christi, Nueces County, TX
Nat'l Network: FOX
Lee W. Shubert, Court-Appointed Rece
Dallas Stevens, Sales dept.

KZTV *Digital Channel:* 10; *Virtual Channel:* 10; 39 kw; 951 ft.; N27 42 27.9 W97 37 59
P.O. Box Tv-10, Corpus Christi, TX 78403 US
(361) 883-7070; *Fax:* (361) 882-8553
www.kztv10.com
License: Corpus Christi, Nueces County, TX held by Eagle Creek of Corpus Christi LLC.
Group Owner: Eagle Creek Broadcasting LLC; (acq 6-13-2002; grpsl)
Nat'l Network: CBS
Size of News Staff: 18
Billy Brotherton, General Manager
Norman Barron, General Sales Mgr
Hollis Grizzard, News Director
Steve West, Chief Engineer
Anthony Gloria, IT Manager
Veronica Coronado, Traffic Manager
Andrew Lesh, Internet Content Manager
Don Grubaugh, Local Sales Manager
Lee Sausley, News Anchor
Arlene Warden, Internet Sales Director

Dallas

KDFW *Digital Channel:* 35; *Virtual Channel:* 4; 153 kW; N32 35 17 W96 58 34
400 N Griffin St., Dallas, TX 75202 USA
(214) 720-4444; *Fax:* (214) 720-3263
www.fox4news.com
kdfw@kdfwfox4.com
License: Dallas, TX held by NW Communications of Texas Inc.
Group Owner: Fox Television Stations Group

Dallas-Ft. Worth (DMA 5)

KDAF *Digital Channel:* 32; *Virtual Channel:* 33; 780 kw; 1762 ft.; N32 32 35 W96 57 32
8001 John W. Carpenter Freeway, Dallas, TX 75247 USA
(214) 252-9233; *Fax:* (214) 252-3379
cw33.com
newstips@cw33.com
License: Dallas, Dallas County, TX held by KDAF LLC
Group Owner: Tribune Media; (acq 12-20-2007; grpsl);
Washington Law Firm: Dow Lohnes PLLC
Nat'l Network: The CW Network; *Nat'l Reps:* TeleRep
Size of News Staff: 40; *Hours of Local News Weekly:* news progmg 6 hrs wkly

KDFI *Digital Channel:* 36; *Virtual Channel:* 27; 1000 kW; 1624 ft.; N32 32 36 W96 57 32
400 North Griffin St., Dallas, TX 75202 USA
(214) 720-4444; *Fax:* (214) 720-3263
www.fox4news.com/kdfi-my27
kdfw@kdfwfox4.com
License: Dallas, Dallas County, TX held by NW Communications of Texas Inc.
Group Owner: Fox Television Stations Group; (acq 2-18-00; $6.2 million)
Nat'l Network: MyNetworkTV; *Nat'l Reps:* Fox Stations Sales

KDFI *Digital Channel:* 35; *Virtual Channel:* 4; 1000 kw; 1673 ft.; N32 35 6 W96 58 41
400 North Griffin Street, Dallas, TX 75202 US
(214) 720-4444; *Fax:* (214) 720-3263, (214) 720-3333
www.myfoxdfw.com
kdfw@kdfwfox4.com
License: Dallas, Dallas County, TX held by KDFW License Inc.
Group Owner: Fox Television Stations Inc.; (acq 1-97; grpsl).
Nat'l Network: FOX
Hours of Local News Weekly: News progmg 50 hrs wkly
Kathy Saunders, Operations Dir
Dennis Welsh, General Sales Mgr
Andy Alexander, Programming Director
John Kukla, Promotions Manager
Maria Barrs, News Director
Jeff Gurley, General Sales Manager
Stacy Garland, National SalesManager
Jennifer Owen, National Sales Manager
TBA, Promotions Manager

***KDTN** *Digital Channel:* 43; *Virtual Channel:* 2; 1000 kw; 1621 ft.; N32 32 35 W96 57 32
Mailing Address: PO box 610546, Dallas, TX 75261-0546 US
Second Address: 3901 Hwy 121, Bedford, TX 76021
(817) 571-1229; *Fax:* (817) 571-7458
www.daystar.com
Partners@Daystar.com
License: Denton, Denton County, TX held by Community Television Educators of DFW Inc
Nat'l Network: IND
Marcus Lamb, CEO
Arnold Torres, General Manager
Jennette Hawkins, Programming Director

KDTX-TV *Digital Channel:* 45; *Virtual Channel:* 58; 1000 kw; 1621 ft.; N32 32 36 W96 57 32
Mailing Address: PO Box 768, Station B, Ottawa, ON K1P 5P8 US
Second Address: PO Box A, Santa Ana, CA 92711
(714) 731-1000, (888) 731-1000, (714) 832-2950, (8; *Fax:* (819) 770-2338
www.tbn.org
License: Dallas, Dallas County, TX held by Trinity Broadcasting of Texas Inc.
Group Owner: Trinity Broadcasting Network; (acq 7-86; $1.6 million;
Nat'l Network: TRINITY BROADCA
Paul Crouch, President
Jennye Gardner, Operations Dir
Steve Fjordbak, General Manager
Corrie Hickey, Public Affairs Director
Jim Forman, Chief Engineer

***KERA-TV** *Digital Channel:* 14; *Virtual Channel:* 13; 474 kw; 1640 ft.; N32 34 43 W96 57 12
3000 Harry Hines Blvd., Dallas, TX 75201 US
(214) 871-1390, (972) 263-3151; *Fax:* (214) 754-0635
www.kera.org
License: Dallas, Dallas County, TX held by North Texas Public Broadcasting Inc
Washington Law Firm: Schwartz, Woods & Miller
Nat'l Network: PBS
Mary Anne Alhadeff, CEO/President
Daniel Slentz, Operations Dir
Mary Anne Alhadeff, General Manager
Bill Young, Vp, Programming
Bill Leftwich, CFO
Sylvia Komatsu, Executive VP,Chief Content Officer
Deborah Johnson, ExecutiveVP,Development & Marketing
Millie Adan-Garza, VP,Corporate Sponsorship
Jeff Ramirez, VP, Radio
Deanna Collingwood, VP,Grants & Foundation

KFWD *Digital Channel:* 9; *Virtual Channel:* 52; 13 kw; 1791 ft.; N32 35 19 W96 58 5
3000 West Story Road, Irving, TX 75038 US
(214) 977-6780; *Fax:* (214) 977-6544
License: Fort Worth, Tarrant County, TX held by HIC Broadcast Inc
Washington Law Firm: Dow, Lohnes & Albertson
Nat'l Network: MundoFox
Wayne Casa, General Manager
Tony Montes, Station Manager
Steve Brooks, General Sales Mgr
Sandra Ventura, Programming Director
Don Guemmer, Chief Engineer

KMPX *Digital Channel:* 30; *Virtual Channel:* 29; 1000 kw; 1785 ft.; N32 35 19 W96 58 5
2410 Gateway Dr, Irving, TX 75063 US
(972) 652-2900
www.estrellatv.com
dallasinfo@lbimedia.com
License: Decatur, Wise County, TX held by Liberman Television of Dallas License LLC.
Group Owner: Liberman Broadcasting Inc.; (acq 1-12-2004; $37 million)
Nat'l Network: IND
Lenard Liberman, President

KPXD-TV ; 1,000 kw vis; 1,181t; N32 35 25 W96 58 23
600 Six Flags Dr., Suite 652, Arlington, TX 76011 USA
(817) 654-6467
www.iontelevision.com

License: Arlington, Tarrant County, TX held by Ion Media Dallas License, Inc.
Group Owner: ION Media Networks Inc.
Nat'l Network: ION Television
Brandon Burgess, Chairman/CEO

KSTR-DT *Digital Channel:* 48; *Virtual Channel:* 49; 1000 kw; 1755 ft.; N32 32 35 W96 57 32
2323 Bryan St., Suite 1900, Dallas, TX 75201
(214) 758-2335
www.univision.com
License: Irving, Dallas County, TX held by UniMas Dallas LLC.
Group Owner: Univision Communications Inc.
Nat'l Network: UniMas
Randy Falco, President
Grace Olivares, Community Affairs Director

KTVT-TV *Digital Channel:* 19; *Virtual Channel:* 11; 1000 kW; 1604 ft.; N32 32 36 W96 57 32
5233 Bridge St., Fort Worth, TX 76103 USA
(817) 451-1111
dfw.cbslocal.com
cbs11@ktvt.com
License: Fort Worth, Tarrant County, TX held by CBS Stations Group of Texas LLC
Group Owner: CBS Television Stations Group; *Washington Law Firm:* Leventhal, Senter & Lerman
Nat'l Network: CBS
Size of News Staff: 100; *Hours of Local News Weekly:* news progmg 27 hrs wkly
Ken Foote, Programming Director

KTXA-TV *Digital Channel:* 29; *Virtual Channel:* 21; 255 kW; 1300 ft.; N32 32 35 W96 57 32
5233 Bridge St., Fort Worth, TX 76103 USA
(817) 451-1111
dfw.cbslocal.com
cbs11@ktvt.com
License: Fort Worth, Tarrant County, TX held by Television Station KTXA Inc.
Group Owner: CBS Television Stations Group; *Washington Law Firm:* Leventhal, Senter & Lerman
Nat'l Network: Independent; CBS
Ken Foote, Programming Director

KTXD-TV *Digital Channel:* 46; *Virtual Channel:* 47; 600 kw; 1627 ft.; N32 32 36 W96 57 32
Mailing Address: C/O Gammon & Grange, 8280 Greensboro Dr, 7th, McLean, VA 22102 US
Second Address: 1058 Country Rd., Greenville, TX 75404
(903) 455-8847; *Fax:* (903) 455-8891
License: Greenville, Hunt County, TX held by KTXD License Co. LLC
Group Owner: London Broadcasting Co. Inc.; (acq 4-1-92; $50,000 for CP;
Nat'l Network: IND
Mike Simons, General Manager

KUVN-DT ; 5,000 kw vis, 1,000 kw aur; 1,142t; N32 35 21 W96 58 12
2323 Bryan St., Suite 1900, Dallas, TX 75201-2646 US
(214) 758-2300; *Fax:* (214) 758-2350
www.univision.com
License: Garland, Dallas County, TX held by KUVN License Partnership L.P.
Group Owner: Univision Communications Inc.; (acq 5-88; $5.2 million)
Nat'l Network: Univision (Spanish)
Foreign Language Programming; Size of News Staff: 22; *Hours of Local News Weekly:* news progmg 10 hrs wkly
Becky Munoz Diaz, Vice President and General Manager
Felicitas Cadena, Community Affairs Manager

KXAS *Digital Channel:* 41; *Virtual Channel:* 5; 891 kw; 1660 ft.; N32 35 7 W96 58 6
Mailing Address: C/O Nbc, Inc., 11th Flr., 1299 Pennsylvania Ave., N.W., Washington, DC 20004 US
Second Address: PO Box 1780, Fort Worth, TX 76101-1780
(800) 232-KXAS, (800) 654-KXAS; *Fax:* (817) 654-6362
www.nbcdfw.com
License: Fort Worth, Tarrant County, TX held by Station Venture Operations LP
Group Owner: NBC Owned Television Stations
Nat'l Network: NBC; *Nat'l Reps:* NBC TV Stations Sales
Hours of Local News Weekly: News progmg 37 hrs wkly

KXTX *Digital Channel:* 40; *Virtual Channel:* 39; 1000 kw; 1621 ft.; N32 35 7 W96 58 6
3100 Mckinnon, 8th Floor, Dallas, TX 75235 USA
(214) 521-3900, (877) 266-8325; *Fax:* (214) 303-5156
www.telemundodallas.com
License: Dallas, Dallas County, TX held by NBC Telemundo License LLC
Group Owner: Telemundo Station Group; (acq 4-12-2002; grpsl).; *Washington Law Firm:* Fisher, Wayland, Cooper, Leader & Zaragoza
Nat'l Network: Telemundo; *Nat'l Reps:* Harrington, Righter & Parsons
Foreign Language Programming
Luis Silberwasser, President

WFAA *Digital Channel:* 8; *Virtual Channel:* 8; 55 kw; 1,673 ft.; N32 35 06 W96 58 41; *Population Served:* 3,591,600
Communications Ctr., 606 Young St., Dallas, TX 75202-4870 US
(214) 748-9631; *Fax:* (214) 977-6590
www.wfaa.com
License: Dallas, Dallas County, TX held by WFAA-TV Inc.
Group Owner: Tegna Media; (acq 12-23-2013); *Washington Law Firm:* Wiley, Rein & Fielding
Nat'l Network: ABC; *Nat'l Reps:* TeleRep; *Wire Services:* Reuters; NWS (National Weather Service)
Size of News Staff: 85; *Hours of Local News Weekly:* news progmg 28 hrs wkly
Mike Devlin, President and General Manager
Nicki Harkrider-Probey, Sales Director
Carolyn Mungo, Executive News Director
Jim Glass, Director of Creative Services and Digital Media

El Paso (Las Cruces, NM), TX (DMA 92)

***KCOS** *Digital Channel:* 13; *Virtual Channel:* 13; 42 kw; 850 ft.; N31 47 15 W106 28 47
Mailing Address: P.O. Box 26668, El Paso, TX 79926 US
Second Address: 9050 Viscount Blvd., Suite A440, El Paso, TX 79925
(915) 590-1313; *Fax:* (915) 594-5394
www.kcostv.org
cbrush@kcostv.org
License: El Paso, El Paso County, TX held by El Paso Public Television Foundation
Washington Law Firm: Cohn & Marks
Nat'l Network: PBS
Dr. Ernst E. Roberts II, Chairman
Craig Brush, CEO
Emily Martin Loya, General Manager
Trashelta Tyler, Director, Traffic & Programming
David Echaniz, Engineering Director
Rodrigo Velarde, Director, Production Assistant
LeticiaAlderete, Director, Production Services
Michael Northcutt, Business Manager
Marty Escandon, Executive Assistant
Debra McDowell, Web Developer

KDBC-TV *Digital Channel:* 18; *Virtual Channel:* 4; 413.9 kw; 1532 ft.; N31 47 46 W106 28 57
Mailing Address: 200 S. Alto Mesa St., El Paso, TX 79912 US
Second Address: Las Cruces Bureau, 110 Idaho Ave., Suite A, Las Cruces, NM 88005
(915) 833-8585; *Fax:* (915) 833-8973
www.cbs4local.com
License: El Paso, El Paso County, TX held by KDBC Licensee LLC
Group Owner: Sinclair Broadcast Group Inc.; *Washington Law Firm:* Fletcher, Heald & Hildreth, P.L.C.
Nat'l Network: CBS; MyNetworkTV; *Nat'l Reps:* Harrington, Righter & Parsons
Size of News Staff: 22; *Hours of Local News Weekly:* news progmg 12 hrs wkly
Kevin Hayes, General Manager
Matthew Kaplowitz, Director of Sales
Nichole Villalobos, Programming Director
Shauna Ziegler, News Director
Cheri Dorsey, Local Sales Manager
Josh Padilla, Creative Services
David Ramirez, CreativeServices
Don Bohac, Creative Services

KFOX-TV *Digital Channel:* 15; *Virtual Channel:* 14; 1000 kw; 1975 ft.; N31 48 55 W106 29 20
Mailing Address: 200 S. Alto Mesa St., El Paso, TX 79912 US
Second Address: Las Cruces Bureau, 110 Idaho Ave., Suite A, Las Cruces, NM 88005
(915) 833-8585; *Fax:* (915) 833-8973
www.kfoxtv.com
webmaster@kfoxtv.com
License: El Paso, El Paso County, TX held by KFOX Licensee LLC
Group Owner: Sinclair Broadcast Group Inc.; (acq 1996; $20.855 million); *Washington Law Firm:* Dow, Lohnes & Albertson
Nat'l Network: FOX; *Nat'l Reps:* TeleRep
Size of News Staff: 23; *Hours of Local News Weekly:* news progmg 26 hrs wkly
Kevin Hayes, General Manager
Nichole Villalobos, Programming Director
Cheri Dorsey, Sales
Cristina Perales, Sales
Patrick Williams, Sales

KINT-TV *Digital Channel:* 25; *Virtual Channel:* 26; 1000 kw; 1441 ft.; N31 47 46 W106 28 57
5426 N. Mesa, El Paso, TX 79912 US
(915) 581-1126; *Fax:* (915) 581-1393
www.noticias.entravision.com/el-paso
License: El Paso, El Paso County, TX held by Entravision Communications Co. LLC.
Group Owner: Entravision Communications Corp.; (acq 6-4-97; grpsl).; *Washington Law Firm:* Thompson, Hine & Flory L
Nat'l Network: UNIVISION
Foreign Language Programming; Size of News Staff: 14; *Hours of Local News Weekly:* news progmg 10 hrs wkly
David Candelaria, General Manager
Diana DeLara, General Sales Mgr
Nidia Holguin, Programming Director
Abel Rodriguez, Promotions Director
Zoltan Csanyi, News Director
Alfredo Durand, Chief Engineer
David Candelaria, ExecutiveVP
James Valdez, Sales,Local
Nora Sandoval, Sales,National

***KSCE** *Digital Channel:* 39; *Virtual Channel:* 38; 150 kw; 1827 ft.; N31 48 19 W106 28 59
2201 E. Wyoming Ave., El Paso, TX 79903 US
(915) 532-8588; *Fax:* (915) 585-8841
www.kscetv.com
ksce@aol.com
License: El Paso, El Paso County, TX held by Channel 38 Christian Television
Ownership: Channel 38 Christian Television; *Washington Law Firm:* James L. Oyster
Nat'l Network: ETV
Foreign Language Programming
Grace Rendall, Vice President/Operations Director/General Manager
Angel Conger, General Sales Mgr
Mark Stephenson, Engineering Technician
Owen Smith, Engineering Technician
Eddie Hernandez, Production Manager
Alex Carrillo,Editor/Producer
Rene Cadena, Graphics, Editor/Producer
Shaun Frankland, IT/Web Manager
Angel Conger, Traffic Manager
Jerry Escalante, Supervisor, Help Ministry

KTFN-TV *Digital Channel:* 51; *Virtual Channel:* 65; 250 kw; 1722 ft.; N31 48 19 W106 29 0.8
5426 N. Mesa, El Paso, TX 79912 US
(915) 581-1126; *Fax:* (915) 581-1393
jwoods@entravision.com
License: El Paso, El Paso County, TX held by Entravision Holdings LLC.
Group Owner: Entravision Communications Corp.; (acq 12-10-01; $18 million)
Nat'l Network: UniMas
Foreign Language Programming
Joseph M. Woods, General Sales Mgr
Joe Garcia, Promotions Manager
Uriel Posada, News Director

KTSM-TV *Digital Channel:* 9; *Virtual Channel:* 9; 34 kw; 1893 ft.; N31 48 18 W106 28 57.6
801 N. Oregon St., El Paso, TX 79902 US
(915) 532-5421
www.ktsm.com
License: El Paso, El Paso County, TX held by Nexstar Broadcasting, Inc.
Group Owner: Nexstar Broadcasting Group; (acq 7-25-97; $30.5 million for stock with KTSM-AM-FM).; *Washington Law Firm:* Fletcher, Heald & Hildreth
Nat'l Network: NBC; *Nat'l Reps:* Millennium Sales & Marketing; *Wire Services:* AP
Size of News Staff: 33; *Hours of Local News Weekly:* news progmg 19.5 hrs wkly
David Candelaria, General Manager
Neil Henderson, Director of Sales
Veronika Placencia, News Director

KVIA-TV *Digital Channel:* 17; *Virtual Channel:* 7; 463 kw; N31 48 18 W106 28 58
4140 Rio Bravo St, El Paso, TX 79902 US

(915) 496-7777; *Fax:* (915) 532-0505
www.kvia.com
kvia@kvia.com
License: El Paso, El Paso County, TX held by NPG of Texas L.P.
Group Owner: News-Press & Gazette Co.; (acq 12-9-94; $19.9 million); *Washington Law Firm:* Robert Thompson
Nat'l Network: ABC; CW
Size of News Staff: 30; *Hours of Local News Weekly:* news progmg 31.5 hrs wkly
David Bradley, CEO
Brian Bradley, President
Chris Swann, Operations Manager
Kevin Lovell, General Manager
Mark Niethamer, Promotions Manager
Brenda DeAnda-Swann, News Director
Dan Overstreet, National Sales Manager

XHIJ-DT *Digital Channel:* 45; 240 kw vis, 60 kw aur; 1,200t/150g
5925 Cromo Dr., El Paso, TX 79912
(915) 585-6344, (915) 929-2886; *Fax:* (915) 585-6333
www.canal44.com
License: Ciudad Juarez, MX held by Arnoldo Cabada De la O
Nat'l Network: Telemundo (Spanish)
Foreign Language Programming; Size of News Staff: 20; *Hours of Local News Weekly:* news progmg 15 hrs wkly
Sergio Cavada, General Manager

Harlingen-Weslaco-Brownsville-McAllen, TX (DMA 84)

KGBT-TV *Digital Channel:* 31; *Virtual Channel:* 4; 1000 kw; 1207 ft.; N26 8 56 W97 49 18
9201 W. Expressway 83, Harlingen, TX 78552 US
(956) 366-4444; *Fax:* (956) 366-4494
www.valleycentral.com
listens@valleycentral.com
License: Harlingen, Cameron County, TX held by KGBT Licensee LLC
Group Owner: Sinclair Broadcast Group Inc.; (acq 2-28-2013; grpsl); *Washington Law Firm:* Dow, Lohnes & Albertson
Nat'l Network: CBS
Foreign Language Programming; Size of News Staff: 29; *Hours of Local News Weekly:* news progmg 22 hrs wkly
Colleen Willis, General Sales Mgr
Zoltan Csanyi-Salcedo, News Director
Victor Medellin, Engineering Dir
Roni Martinez, Executive Producer
Linda Guerrero Deicla, Accounting Manager

***KLUJ-TV** *Digital Channel:* 34; *Virtual Channel:* 44; 45 kw; 928 ft.; N26 13 0 W97 46 48
10902 S. Wilcrest, Houston, TX 77099 US
(281) 561-5828; *Fax:* (281) 561-9793
www.communityedtv.org
klujtv@asbglobal.net
License: Harlingen, Cameron County, TX held by Community Educational TV Inc
(acq 4-84).; *Washington Law Firm:* Joseph E. Dunne III
Nat'l Network: TRINITY BROADCA
Foreign Language Programming
Sandy Hulquist, Operations Manager
Margie Gonzales, General Manager/VP
Corrie Hickey, Public Affairs Director

***KMBH** *Digital Channel:* 38; *Virtual Channel:* 60; 1000 kw; 1134 ft.; N26 7 14 W97 49 18
Mailing Address: P.O. Box 2147, Harlingen, TX 78551 US
Second Address: 1701 Tennessee St., Harlingen, TX 78551
(956) 421-4111, (800) 433-2522; *Fax:* (956) 421-4150
www.kmbh.org
License: Harlingen, Cameron County, TX held by RGV Educational Broadcasting Inc
Washington Law Firm: Thelen Reid & Priest LLP
Nat'l Network: PBS
Foreign Language Programming
Bishop Daniel, Chairman
Robert Gutierrez, President/CEO
Andy Hagen, Vice President
Chris Maley, Program Director
Javier Guerra, Chief Engineer
Nick Rice, Underwriting Manager/Radio Manager
Monsignor Gustavo Barrera, AssistantSecretary
Richard Walker, Treasurer
Martha Ybarra, Broadcast Traffic Coordinator
Ismael Herrera, TV Production Manager
Juan Pablo Ramirez, Chief Operator/IT Systems Administrator

KNVO-TV *Digital Channel:* 49; *Virtual Channel:* 48; 1000 kw; 937 ft.; N26 5 18 W98 3 45
801 N. Jackson Rd., McAllen, TX 78501 US
(956) 687-4848; *Fax:* (956) 687-7784
License: McAllen, Hidalgo County, TX held by Entravision Holdings LLC.
Group Owner: Entravision Communications Corp.; *Washington Law Firm:* Schwartz, Woods & Miller
Nat'l Network: UNIVISION
Foreign Language Programming
Elizabeth Gonzales, Operations Manager
Alex Duran, Radio Program Director
Monica Quintanilla, Promotions Director
Joe Medrano, News Director

KRGV-TV *Digital Channel:* 13; *Virtual Channel:* 5; 57 kW; 1456 ft.; N26 6 2 W97 50 21
PO Box 5, Weslaco, TX 78599 USA
(956) 968-5555; *Fax:* (956) 973-5016
www.krgv.com
License: Weslaco, Hidalgo County, TX held by Mobile Video Tapes Inc.
Group Owner: Manship Family; (acq 1-28-64; grpsl; *Washington Law Firm:* Pillsbury
Nat'l Network: ABC; *Nat'l Reps:* Blair Television; *Wire Services:* AP
Size of News Staff: 40; *Hours of Local News Weekly:* news progmg 24.5 hrs wkly
John Kittleman, General Manager
Robert Ledesma, General Sales Mgr
Ginger Walker, Director of Programming & Traffic
Jenny Martinez, News Director
Michael Leal, Chief Engineer

KTFV-CD *Digital Channel:* 48; *Virtual Channel:* 32; 2 kw; 472 ft.; N26 5 18 W98 3 44
801 N. Jackson Rd., McAllen, TX 78501 US
(956) 687-4848; *Fax:* (956) 687-7784
License: McAllen, TX held by Entravision Holdings LLC.
Group Owner: Entravision Communications Corp.; *Washington Law Firm:* Schwartz, Woods & Miller
Nat'l Network: UNIVISION
Foreign Language Programming
Elizabeth Gonzales, Operations Manager
Alex Duran, Radio Program Director
Monica Quintanilla, Promotions Director
Joe Medrano, News Director

KTLM *Digital Channel:* 40; *Virtual Channel:* 40; 355 kw; 1893 ft.; N26 31 1 W98 39 7
USA
(956) 686-0040; *Fax:* (956) 686-0770
www.telemundo40.com
License: Harlingen, Cameron County, TX held by NBC Telemundo License LLC
Group Owner: Telemundo Station Group; (acq 8-12-2005; $3.15 million)
Nat'l Network: Telemundo
Foreign Language Programming; Size of News Staff: 12; *Hours of Local News Weekly:* news progmg 8 hrs wkly
Luis Silberwasser, President

KVEO-TV *Digital Channel:* 24; 2,570 kw vis, 1,000 kw aur; ant 1,460t/1,454g; N26 05 59 W97 50 16; *Population Served:* 700,000
394 N. Expressway, Brownsville, TX 78521 US
(956) 544-2323
www.kveo.com
License: Brownsville, Cameron County, TX held by Nexstar Broadcasting, Inc.
Group Owner: Nexstar Broadcasting Group; (acq 2-13-95; *Washington Law Firm:* Dow, Lohnes
Nat'l Network: NBC; *Wire Services:* AP
William Jorn, General Manager
Mona Leveck, Director of Sales
Jon McCall, News Director

KXFX-CD *Digital Channel:* 20; *Virtual Channel:* 67; 0.5 kw; 462 ft.; N25 57 49 W97 31 12
801 N. Jackson Rd., McAllen, TX 78501 US
(956) 687-4848; *Fax:* (956) 687-7784
License: Brownsville, TX held by Entravision Holdings LLC.
Group Owner: Entravision Communications Corp.; *Washington Law Firm:* Schwartz, Woods & Miller
Nat'l Network: UNIVISION
Elizabeth Gonzales, Operations Manager
Alex Duran, Radio Program Director
Monica Quintanilla, Promotions Director
Joe Medrano, News Director

XHRIO-TDT *Digital Channel:* 26; *Virtual Channel:* 2; 250 kw; 1040 ft.; N25 56 28 W97 50 49
801 N. Jackson Rd., McAllen, TX 78501 US
(956) 687-4848; *Fax:* (956) 687-7784
License: Matamoros, TX held by TVNorte, S.A. de C.V.
Group Owner: Entravision Communications Corp.; *Washington Law Firm:* Schwartz, Woods & Miller
Nat'l Network: UNIVISION
Elizabeth Gonzales, Operations Manager
Alex Duran, Radio Program Director
Monica Quintanilla, Promotions Director
Joe Medrano, News Director

Houston (DMA 8)

***KETH-TV** *Digital Channel:* 24; *Virtual Channel:* 14; 1000 kw; 1903 ft.; N29 34 15 W95 30 37
PO Box 721582, Houston, TX 77059 US
(281) 561-5828; *Fax:* (281) 561-9793
www.communityedtv.org
License: Houston, Harris County, TX held by Community Educational Television Inc
Nat'l Network: TRINITY BROADCA
Hours of Local News Weekly: News progmg 3 hrs wkly
Laura Hanks, Operations Dir
Rod Harty, Chief Engineer

KFTH-DT *Digital Channel:* 36; *Virtual Channel:* 67; 5,000 kw vis, 500 kw aur; ant 1,781t/1,155g; N29 34 15 W95 30 37
5100 S.W. Freeway, Houston, TX 77056
(713) 662-4545
www.univision.com
License: Alvin, Brazoria County, TX held by UniMas Houston LLC.
Group Owner: Univision Communications Inc.; (acq 5-21-2001; grpsl).
Nat'l Network: UniMas
Foreign Language Programming
Angela Navarrete, General Manager and Director of Sales
Grace Olivares, Community Affairs Director

KHOU *Digital Channel:* 11; *Virtual Channel:* 11; 60 kw; 1,946 ft.; N29 33 40 W95 30 04; *Population Served:* 5,000,000
1945 Allen Pkwy., Houston, TX 77019 US
(713) 526-1111; *Fax:* (713) 521-4326
www.khou.com
assignments@khou.com
License: Houston, Harris County, TX held by KHOU-TV Inc.
Group Owner: Tegna Media; (acq 1984; grpsl;
Nat'l Network: CBS; *Nat'l Reps:* TeleRep; *Wire Services:* Reuters
Hours of Local News Weekly: news progmg 28 hrs wkly
Susan McEldoon, President and General Manager
Lori Clark, Director of Local Sales

KIAH *Digital Channel:* 38; *Virtual Channel:* 39; 1000 kw; 1909 ft.; N29 34 6 W95 29 57
7700 Westpark Dr., Houston, TX 77063 USA
(713) 781-3939
cw39.com
License: Houston, Harris County, TX held by KIAH LLC
Group Owner: Tribune Media; (acq 12-20-2007; grpsl);
Washington Law Firm: Dow Lohnes PLLC
Nat'l Network: The CW Network; *Nat'l Reps:* Harrington, Righter & Parsons
Size of News Staff: 34; *Hours of Local News Weekly:* news progmg 4 hrs wkly
Peggy Nan Moore, Engineering Dir

***KLTJ** *Digital Channel:* 23; *Virtual Channel:* 22; 350 kw; 1900 ft.; N29 34 15 W95 30 37
Mailing Address: 3901 Hwy 121, Bedford, TX 70201 US
Second Address: PO Box 610546, Dallas, TX 75261-0546
(877)805-2132, (817) 571-1229; *Fax:* (817) 571-7458
www.daystar.com
contactus@daystar.com
License: Galveston, Galveston County, TX held by Word of God Fellowship Inc. aka Community TV Educators
Nat'l Network: IND
Foreign Language Programming
Marcus D. Lamb, CEO/President
Nathan Williams, General Manager
Arnold Torres, Chief Regulatory Officer

KPRC-TV *Digital Channel:* 35; *Virtual Channel:* 2; 1000 kw; 1919 ft.; N29 34 6 W95 29 57
Mailing Address: 8181 Southwest Freeway, Houston, TX 77074 US
Second Address: PO Box 2222, Houston, TX 77252-2222
(713) 778-4910, (713) 222-6397; *Fax:* (713) 771-4930
www.click2houston.com
License: Houston, Harris County, TX held by Post-Newsweek Stations Inc.
Group Owner: Post-Newsweek Stations Inc.; (acq 4-22-94;
Washington Law Firm: Covington & Burling
Nat'l Network: NBC; *Nat'l Reps:* MMT; *Wire Services:* AP

Size of News Staff: 80; *Hours of Local News Weekly:* news progmg 34 hrs wkly
Deborah Collura, Vice President
Tammy Dean, Operations Dir
Jerry Martin, Vice President/General Manager
Ben Oldham, General Sales Mgr
Mr. Skip Valet, News Director
Dale Werner, Chief Engineer
Eric Braate, Executive Producer

KPXB-TV *Digital Channel:* 32; 1,000 kw vis; 1,775t/1,200g; N29 34 15 W95 30 37; *Population Served:* 3,050,000
4124 McHard Rd., Missouri City, TX 77489 USA
(281) 820-4900; *Fax:* (281) 820-3916
www.iontelevision.com
License: Conroe, TX held by Ion Media Houston License, Inc.
Group Owner: ION Media Networks Inc.; (acq 1995; $7.9 million); *Washington Law Firm:* Pepper & Corazzini
Nat'l Network: ION Television
Brandon Burgess, Chairman/CEO

KRIV *Digital Channel:* 26; *Virtual Channel:* 26; 800 kW; 1962 ft.; N29 34 28 W95 29 37
4261 Southwest Freeway, Houston, TX 77027 USA
(713) 479-2600; *Fax:* (713) 479-2859
www.fox26houston.com
License: Houston, Harris County, TX held by Fox Television Stations LLC
Group Owner: Fox Television Stations Group; *Washington Law Firm:* Molly Pauker
Nat'l Network: FOX; *Nat'l Reps:* Fox Stations Sales; *Wire Services:* AP

KTMD *Digital Channel:* 48; *Virtual Channel:* 47; 1000 kw; 1959 ft.; N29 34 15 W95 30 37
1235 North Loop West, Suite 125, Houston, Tx 77008 USA
(713) 974-4848; *Fax:* (713) 782-5575
www.telemundohouston.com
License: Galveston, Galveston County, TX held by NBC Telemundo License LLC
Group Owner: Telemundo Station Group; (acq 4-12-2002; grpsl).; *Washington Law Firm:* Hogan & Hartson
Nat'l Network: Telemundo
Foreign Language Programming; Size of News Staff: 14; *Hours of Local News Weekly:* news progmg 7 hrs wkly
Luis Silberwasser, President

KTRK-TV *Digital Channel:* 13; *Virtual Channel:* 13; 32.4 kW; 1912 ft.; N29 34 27 W95 29 37
3310 Bissonnet, Houston, TX 77005 USA
(713) 666-0713; *Fax:* (713) 663-4648
abc13.com
License: Houston, Harris County, TX held by KTRK Television Inc.
Group Owner: ABC Owned Television Stations
Nat'l Network: ABC; *Wire Services:* TWX

KTXH *Digital Channel:* 19; *Virtual Channel:* 20; 1000 kW; 1955 ft.; N29 33 44 W95 30 35
4261 Southwest Freeway, Houston, TX 77027 USA
(713) 479-2801; *Fax:* (713) 479-2859
www.fox26houston.com/my20-houston
License: Houston, Harris County, TX held by Fox Television Stations LLC
Group Owner: Fox Television Stations Group; (acq 11-6-2001; with WDCA(TV) Washington, DC in swap for KBHK-TV San Francisco, CA).
Nat'l Network: MyNetworkTV

KUBE-TV *Digital Channel:* 53; *Virtual Channel:* 57; 1,000 kw; 580 meters; N29 34 15 W95 30 37
2620 Fountain View, Ste.322, Houston, TX 55344
(713) 467-5757; *Fax:* (713) 783-4157
License: Baytown, Liberty County, TX held by NRJ TV Houston License Co. LLC
Group Owner: NRJ Holdings LLC; (acq 7-7-99; $28 million)
Foreign Language Programming
Harry Pappas, CEO
Emilio Nicolas Jr., General Manager
Emilio Nicolas, Station Manager

***KUHT** *Digital Channel:* 8; *Virtual Channel:* 8; 64.6 kw; 1857 ft.; N29 34 28 W95 29 37
4343 Elgin, Houston, TX 77004 US
(713) 748-8888,(800) 364-8300; *Fax:* (713) 743-8867
www.houstonpbs.org
License: Houston, Harris County, TX held by University of Houston System, Board of Regents
Washington Law Firm: Dow, Lohnes & Albertson
Nat'l Network: PBS
Foreign Language Programming
Steve Pyndus, Operations Dir
Lisa Trapani Shumate, Executive Director & General Manager
Jack Neal, Station Manager
Christina Ordonez-Campos, Director of Finance
Karen Mapp, Financial Coordinator
Dacia Clay, Content Producer
CapellaTucker, Director of Content
Joycelyn Moris, Director of Advancement
Josh Adams, Director of Technology

KXLN-DT *Digital Channel:* 45; *Virtual Channel:* 45; 1000 kw; 1949 ft.; N29 33 44 95 30 35
5100 S.W. Freeway, Houston, TX 77056
(713) 662-4545; *Fax:* (713) 965-2604
www.univision.com
License: Rosenberg, Fort Bend County, TX held by KXLN License Partnership L.P.
Group Owner: Univision Communications Inc.
Hours of Local News Weekly: news progmg 17 hrs wkly
Randy Falco, President
Grace Olivares, Community Affairs Director

KYAZ *Digital Channel:* 52; *Virtual Channel:* 51; 2,290 kw vis; ant 1,640t/1,624g; N29 33 40 W95 30 04
8440 Westpark, Houston, TX 77063
(713) 974-5151; *Fax:* (713) 974-5188
www.knws51.com
License: Katy, Harris County, TX held by Johnson Broadcasting Inc
Washington Law Firm: Smithwick & Belendiuk
Nat'l Network: Azteca America
Douglas Johnson, President
Chris Bourne, Operations Dir
Jack Dabbah, General Manager

KZJL *Digital Channel:* 44; *Virtual Channel:* 61; 1000 kw; 1513 ft.; N29 33 44 W95 30 35
3000 Bering Dr, Houston, TX 77057 US
(713) 315-3400
www.estrellatv.com/inicio
houstoninfo@lbimedia.com
License: Houston, Harris County, TX held by KZJL License LLC.
Group Owner: Liberman Broadcasting Inc.; (acq 1-10-2001; $57 million)
Nat'l Network: IND
Winter Horton, General Manager
Nicole Burri, Vice President Network Sales

La Feria

KCWT-CD *Digital Channel:* 23; *Virtual Channel:* 21; 15 kw; N26 08 28 W97 50 04
801 N. Jackson Rd., McAllen, TX 78501 US
(956) 687-4848; *Fax:* (956) 687-7784
www.yourcwtv.com
info@yourcwtv.com
License: La Feria, TX held by Entravision Holdings LLC.
Group Owner: Entravision Communications Corp.

Laredo, TX (DMA 184)

KETF-CD *Digital Channel:* 31; 15 kw; 433 ft.; N27 39 53 W99 36 25
222 Bob Bullock Loop., Laredo, TX 78043 US
(956) 727-0027; *Fax:* (956) 727-2673
telena@entravision.com
License: Laredo, Webb County, TX held by Entravision Holdings LLC.
Group Owner: Entravision Communications Corp.; (acq 7-30-97; $6.2 million); *Washington Law Firm:* Martin E. Firestone
Nat'l Network: UNIVISION
Foreign Language Programming
Daniel Martinez, General Sales Mgr
Angel Covarrubias, News Director

KGNS *Digital Channel:* 8; *Virtual Channel:* 8; 20 kw; 1024 ft.; N27 40 21 W99 39 51
120 W Del Mar Blvd., Laredo, TX 78041 USA
(956) 727-8888; *Fax:* (956) 267-8649
www.kgns.tv
email8@kgns.tv
License: Laredo, Webb County, TX held by Gray Television Licensee LLC
Group Owner: Gray Television Inc.; (acq 9-28-2004; $14.4 million); *Washington Law Firm:* Wiley, Rein & Fielding, LLP
Nat'l Network: NBC; ABC; Telemundo; *Nat'l Reps:* Continental Television Sales
Foreign Language Programming; Size of News Staff: 26; *Hours of Local News Weekly:* news progmg 17 hrs wkly
Luis Villareal, General Manager
Juan Cue, Sales Manager
Jerry Garza, News Director
David York, Chief Engineer

KLDO-TV *Digital Channel:* 19; 50 kw; 433 ft.; N27 39 53 W99 36 25
222 Bob Bullock Loop., Laredo, TX 78043 US
(956) 727-0027; *Fax:* (956) 727-2673
www.noticias.entravision.com/laredo
telena@entravision.com
License: Laredo, Webb County, TX held by Entravision Holdings LLC.
Group Owner: Entravision Communications Corp.; (acq 7-30-97; $6.2 million); *Washington Law Firm:* Martin E. Firestone
Nat'l Network: UNIVISION
Foreign Language Programming
Daniel Martinez, General Sales Mgr
Angel Covarrubias, News Director

KVTV *Digital Channel:* 13; *Virtual Channel:* 13; 3 kw; 932 ft.; N27 31 12 W99 31 19
P.O. Box 2039, Laredo, TX 78044 US
(956) 727-1300; *Fax:* (956) 712-0185
www.kvtv13laredo.com
License: Laredo, Webb County, TX held by Eagle Creek of Laredo LLC.
Group Owner: Eagle Creek Broadcasting LLC; (acq 6-13-2002; grpsl).
Nat'l Network: FOX
Dale Remy, General Manager
Joe Herrera, General Sales Mgr
Carol Rostohar, Promotions Manager
Kent Harrell, News Director
George Sanders, Chief Engineer

KXOF-CD *Digital Channel:* 39; 3.2 kw; N27 31 12 W99 31 19
222 Bob Bullock Loop., Laredo, TX 78043 US
(956) 727-0027; *Fax:* (956) 727-7723
www.mylaredofox.com
telena@entravision.com
License: Laredo, TX held by Entravision Holdings LLC.
Group Owner: Entravision Communications Corp.; (acq 7-30-97; $6.2 million); *Washington Law Firm:* Martin E. Firestone
Nat'l Network: UNIVISION
Terry Elena Ordaz, General Manager
Jeannette Puig, General Sales Mgr

Lubbock

KBZO-LP *Digital Channel:* 51; *Virtual Channel:* 51; 60 kw
6502 Caprock Dr., Lubbock, TX 79412 US
(806) 763-6051; *Fax:* (806) 748-0216
License: Lubbock, TX held by Entravision Holdings LLC.
Group Owner: Entravision Communications Corp.
Leticia Flores, General Manager
Isla Islas, Promotions Manager

Lubbock, TX (DMA 145)

KAMC *Digital Channel:* 27; *Virtual Channel:* 28; 1000 kw; 720 ft.; N33 31 33 W101 52 7
7403 S. University Ave., Lubbock, TX 79423 US
(806) 745-2828; *Fax:* (806) 748-1080
www.everythinglubbock.com
License: Lubbock, Lubbock County, TX held by Mission Broadcasting Inc.
Group Owner: Mission Broadcasting Inc.; (acq 12-17-2003).; *Washington Law Firm:* Bryan Cave
Nat'l Network: ABC
Size of News Staff: 26; *Hours of Local News Weekly:* news progmg 39 hrs wkly
George Damron, General Manager
Cindy Gilstrap, General Sales Mgr
Russ Poteet, News Director

KCBD *Digital Channel:* 11; *Virtual Channel:* 11; 41 kw; 761 ft.; N33 32 32 W101 50 14
5600 Ave. A, Lubbock, TX 79404 US
(806) 744-1414; *Fax:* (806) 749-1111, (806) 744-2118, (806) 744-0449
www.kcbd.com
11listens@kcbd.com
License: Lubbock, Lubbock County, TX held by KCBD License Subsidiary LLC.
Group Owner: Raycom Media Inc.; (acq 1-31-2006; grpsl); *Washington Law Firm:* Dow, Lohnes & Albertson
Nat'l Network: NBC
Brent McClure, Operations Dir
Dan Jackson, General Manager
Beverly McBeth, General Sales Mgr
Peggy Sullivan, Programming Director

Benji Snead, News Director
Ricky Price, Chief Engineer
Josh Young, Marketing manager
MicheleDoggett, Traffic Manager
Danny Kochis, Internet Director
Pete Christy, Sports Director
Abner Euresti, Anchor/Managing Editor
Sharon Maines, Anchor/Reporter

KJTV *Digital Channel:* 35; *Virtual Channel:* 34; 1000 kw; 899 ft.; N33 30 8 W101 52 20
9800 University Ave., Lubbock, TX 79423 US
(806) 745-3434
www.fox34.com
License: Lubbock, Lubbock County, TX held by Ramar Communications, Inc.
Group Owner: Ramar Communications, Ltd.; *Washington Law Firm:* Leventhal, Senter & Lerman
Nat'l Network: FOX
Size of News Staff: 20; *Hours of Local News Weekly:* news progmg 7 hrs wkly
Brad Moran, General Manager
Chris Torres, Programming Director

KLBK-TV *Digital Channel:* 40; *Virtual Channel:* 13; 1000 kw; 720 ft.; N33 31 33 W101 52 7
7403 University Ave., Lubbock, TX 79423 US
(806) 745-2345; *Fax:* (806) 748-2250
www.everythinglubbock.com
License: Lubbock, Lubbock County, TX held by Nexstar Broadcasting Inc
Group Owner: Nexstar Broadcasting Group Inc.; (acq 12-31-03; grpsl).; *Washington Law Firm:* Arter & Hadden
Nat'l Network: CBS
Size of News Staff: 47; *Hours of Local News Weekly:* news progmg 27 hrs wkly
Eric Thomas, General Manager
Cindy Gilstrap, General Sales Mgr
Russ Poteet, News Director

KLCW-TV *Digital Channel:* 43; *Virtual Channel:* 22; 179 kw vis; ant 923t; N33 30 08 W101 52 20
9800 University Ave., Lubbock, TX 79423
(806) 745-3434
www.fox34.com
news@fox34news.com
License: Wolfforth, Lubbock County, TX held by Woods Communications Corp.
Group Owner: Woods Communications Corp.
Nat'l Network: CW; *Nat'l Reps:* Millennium
Jeff Klotzman, News Director
Audra Coffman, Web Content Producer

KPTB-DT ; 214 kw vis; 272t; N33 33 12 W101 49 13
Mailing Address: PO Box 61000, Midland, TX 79711-1000
Second Address: 12706 W. Highway 80 East, Odessa, TX 79765
(800) 707-0420 (806) 846-5200; *Fax:* (432) 563-1736
www.godslearningchannel.com
info@glc.us.com
License: Lubbock, Lubbock County, TX held by Prime Time Christian Broadcasting Inc
Jeff Tveit, General Manager
Jeff Cooper, Station Manager
Al Cooper, Founder
Tommie Cooper

***KTTZ-TV** *Digital Channel:* 39; *Virtual Channel:* 5; 100 kw vis, 25 kw aur; 440t/817g; N33 34 55 W101 53 25; *Population Served:* 375,000
Mailing Address: Box 42161, Lubbock, TX 79409
Second Address: 17th & Indiana Ave., Lubbock, TX 79409
(806) 742-2209; *Fax:* (806) 742-1274
License: Lubbock, Lubbock County, TX held by Texas Tech University
Washington Law Firm: Cohn & Marks
Nat'l Network: PBS
Pat Cates, General Manager
Robert Giovannetti, Interim General Manager

McAllen

KFXV-LD *Digital Channel:* 20; *Virtual Channel:* 67; 15 kw; N26 08 28 W97 50 04
801 N. Jackson Rd., McAllen, TX 78501 US
(956) 687-4848; *Fax:* (956) 661-6082
www.foxrio2.com
dsalvarado@entravision.com
License: McAllen, TX held by Entravision Holdings LLC.
Group Owner: Entravision Communications Corp.
Monica Quintanilla, Promotions Manager
Angel Cobarrubias, News Director

Odessa-Midland, TX (DMA 143)

KMID *Digital Channel:* 26; *Virtual Channel:* 2; 1000 kw; 902 ft.; N32 5 51 W102 17 21
Mailing Address: PO Drawer 60230, Midland, TX 79711 US
Second Address: 3200 LaForce Blvd., Midland, TX 79711
(432) 563-2222; *Fax:* (432) 563-5819
www.yourbasin.com
License: Midland, Midland County, TX held by Nexstar Broadcasting Inc.
Group Owner: Nexstar Broadcasting Group Inc.; (acq 7-31-2000; $10 million); *Washington Law Firm:* Cohn & Marks
Nat'l Network: ABC; *Regional Network:* Alabama Public Television; *Nat'l Reps:* Blair Television
Size of News Staff: 23; *Hours of Local News Weekly:* news progmg 17 hrs wkly
Kyle King, General Manager
Heather Trevino, General Sales Mgr
Jay Reynolds, News Director

KMLM-DT *Digital Channel:* 42; 1,120 kw vis, 112 kw aur; ant 479t/473g; N32 02 53 W102 17 44; *Population Served:* 245,000
Mailing Address: Box 61000, Midland, TX 79711-1000
Second Address: 12706 W. Highway 80 E., Odessa, TX 79765
(800) 707-0420 (432) 563-0420; *Fax:* (432) 563-1736
www.GLC.US.com
info@glc.us.com
License: Odessa, Ector County, TX held by Prime Time Christian Broadcasting Inc
Foreign Language Programming
Matt Montgomery, Chief Engineer
Al Cooper, Founder
Tommie Cooper, Founder

KOSA *Digital Channel:* 7; *Virtual Channel:* 7; 48 kw; 741 ft.; N31 51 50 W102 34 41
TX USA
www.cbs7.com
License: Odessa, Ector County, TX held by Gray Television Licensee LLC
Group Owner: Gray Television Inc.; *Washington Law Firm:* Covington Burling
Nat'l Network: CBS; *Nat'l Reps:* Continental Television Sales
Size of News Staff: 22; *Hours of Local News Weekly:* news progmg 22 hrs wkly

***KPBT-TV** *Digital Channel:* 38; *Virtual Channel:* 36; 513 kw vis, 51.3 kw aur; ant 289t/306g; N31 51 59 W102 22 50; *Population Served:* 350,000
Mailing Address: Box 8940, Midland, TX 79708
Second Address: 201 West University, Odessa, TX 79764
(432) 563-5728; *Fax:* (432) 563-5731
www.kpbt.org
basinpbs@basinpbs.org
License: Odessa, Ector County, TX held by Permian Basin Public Telecommunications Inc
Nat'l Network: PBS
John James, Chairman
Daphne Dowdy, General Manager
Amy Lynch, Programming Director
Domingo Machuca, Chief Engineer

KPEJ-TV *Digital Channel:* 23; *Virtual Channel:* 24; 2,880 kw vis; ant 1,099t/1,102g; N32 05 51 W102 17 21; *Population Served:* 133,600
3200 LaForce Blvd., Midland, TX 79711
(432) 580-0024
www.yourbasin.com
License: Odessa, Ector County, TX held by Marshall Broadcasting Group Inc.
Group Owner: Marshall Broadcasting Group Inc.; (acq 2015); *Washington Law Firm:* Dow Lohnes PLLC
Nat'l Network: Fox; *Nat'l Reps:* Millennium Sales & Marketing
Debbie Holtzclaw, Station Manager
Jay Reynolds, News Director

KUPB-TV *Digital Channel:* 18; *Virtual Channel:* 18; 1000 kw; 922 ft.; N31 50 19 W102 31 59
Mailing Address: PO Box 61907, Mixland, TX 79711 US
Second Address: 10313 Younger Rd., Midland, TX 79706
(432) 563-1826; *Fax:* (432) 563-0215
www.noticias.entravision.com
univision18@entravision.com
License: Midland, Midland County, TX held by Entravision Holdings LLC.
Group Owner: Entravision Communications Corp.; *Washington Law Firm:* Thompson, Hine & Flory L
Nat'l Network: UNIVISION
Foreign Language Programming
Letticia Martinez, Senior vP
Sarah Taccone, National Sales Mgr

KWAB-TV *Digital Channel:* 33; *Virtual Channel:* 4; 33.5 kw; 273 ft.; N32 16 55 W101 29 34
Mailing Address: 11320 West County Road 127, Midland, TX 79711 US
Second Address: PO Box 60150, Midland, TX 79711
(432) 567-9999; *Fax:* (432) 567-9994
www.newswest9.com
publicfile@kwes.com
License: Big Spring, Howard County, TX held by Midessa Television Co
Group Owner: R.H. Drewry Group; (acq 9-9-91; $4.85 million with KWES-TV Odessa;
Nat'l Network: NBC
Josh Young, General Manager
Kevin Southern, Chief Engineer
Ronnie Marley, Digital Content Manager

KWES-TV *Digital Channel:* 9; *Virtual Channel:* 9
Mailing Address: 11320 West County Road 127, Midland, TX 79711 US
Second Address: PO Box 60150, Midland, TX 79711
(432) 567-9999; *Fax:* (432) 567-9992
www.newswest9.com
License: Odessa, Ector County, TX held by Midessa Television Co.
Group Owner: R.H. Drewry Group; (acq 10-31-91; $4.85 million with KWAB(TV) Big Spring;
Nat'l Network: NBC
Josh Young, General Manager
Kevin Southern, Chief Engineer
Mac Douglas, General Manager
Carlos Fernandez, News Director

KWWT *Digital Channel:* 30; *Virtual Channel:* 30; 50 kw; 482 ft.; N32 2 52.5 W102 17 44
1146 19th St NW, Suite 200, Washington, DC 20036 US
(432) 272-7514; *Fax:* (432) 614-4054
www.cwtv.com
License: Odessa, Ector County, TX held by WinStar Odessa Inc.
Nat'l Network: CW
James Primm, General Manager
Jayne Faltus, Station Manager
Doug Faltus, Chief Engineer

Paris

KXIP *Digital Channel:* 24; 15 kW; N33 38 54 W95 36 12;
Rebroadcasting: Satellite of Sherman KXII(TV)
Mailing Address: 4201 Texoma Pkwy., Sherman, TX 75090 USA
Second Address: 2624 S Commerce, Ardmore, OK 73402
(903) 892-8123; *Fax:* (903) 893-7858
www.kxii.com
news12@kxii.com
License: Paris, Lamar County, TX held by Gray Television Licensee LLC
Group Owner: Gray Television Inc.
Nat'l Network: CBS; MyNetworkTV; FOX
Todd Bates, Sales
Stephen Woodall, Promotions
Dennis Kite, Chief Engineer

San Angelo, TX (DMA 196)

KANG-CD ; 11.3 kw; N31 29 47 W100 28 40
40 W. Twohig, Suite 101, San Angelo, TX 76903 US
(325) 482-9277; *Fax:* (325) 481-3272
www.noticias.entravision.com/san-angelo
lmartinez@entravision.com
License: San Angelo, TX held by Entravision Holdings LLC.
Group Owner: Entravision Communications Corp.; *Washington Law Firm:* Thompson, Hine & Flory L
Nat'l Network: UNIVISION
Foreign Language Programming
Letticia Martinez, Senior vP

KEUS-LD ; 12.4 kw; N31 29 46 W100 28 40
40 W. Twohig, Suite 101, San Angelo, TX 76903 US
(325) 482-9277; *Fax:* (325) 481-3272
lmartinez@entravision.com
License: San Angelo, TX held by Entravision Holdings LLC.
Group Owner: Entravision Communications Corp.; *Washington Law Firm:* Thompson, Hine & Flory L
Nat'l Network: UNIVISION
Foreign Language Programming
Letticia Martinez, Senior vP

KIDY *Digital Channel:* 19; *Virtual Channel:* 6; 3.7 kw; 433 ft.; N31 35 21 W100 31 0

5 S. Chadbourne, San Angelo, TX 76903 US
(325) 655-6006; *Fax:* (325) 655-8461
www.myfoxzone.com
License: San Angelo, Tom Green County, TX held by LSB Broadcasting Inc.
Group Owner: Tegna Media; *Washington Law Firm:* Fletcher, Heald & Hildreth
Nat'l Network: Fox; *Nat'l Reps:* Millennium Sales & Marketing
Size of News Staff: 2; *Hours of Local News Weekly:* news progmg 2.5 hrs wkly
Justin Riggan, President and General Manager
Glenn Edwards, Chief Engineer

KLST *Digital Channel:* 11; *Virtual Channel:* 8; 18.8 kw; 1425 ft.; N31 22 1 W100 2 48
2800 Armstrong St., San Angelo, TX 76903 US
(325) 949-8800
www.conchovalleyhomepage.com
License: San Angelo, Tom Green County, TX held by Nexstar Broadcasting Inc.
Group Owner: Nexstar Broadcasting Group Inc.; (acq 9-2-2004; $12 million); *Washington Law Firm:* Skadden, Arps, Slate, Meagher & Flom
Nat'l Network: CBS
Size of News Staff: 12; *Hours of Local News Weekly:* news progmg 17 hrs wkly
Tom Stovall, VP/General Manager
Terry Hucks, Dir. of Sales
David Wagner, News Director

KSAN-TV ; *Virtual Channel:* 3; 17.8 kw vis, 3.5 kw aur; 600t/469g; N31 37 22 W100 26 14
2800 Armstrong St., San Angelo, TX 76903 US
(325) 949-8800
www.conchovalleyhomepage.com
License: San Angelo, Tom Green County, TX held by Mission Broadcasting Inc.
Group Owner: Mission Broadcasting Inc.; (acq 6-13-2003; $10 million with KRBC-TV Abilene).; *Washington Law Firm:* Kenkel, Barnard & Edmundson
Nat'l Network: NBC; *Nat'l Reps:* Blair Television
Sherri Scott, Station Manager
Terry Hucks, Dir. of Sales
David Wagner, News Director

San Antonio

KVDA ; 1000 kW; 1361 ft.; N29 17 38 W98 15 30 USA
www.telemundosanantonio.com
License: San Antonio, TX held by NBC Telemundo License LLC
Group Owner: Telemundo Station Group
Nat'l Network: Telemundo
Luis Silberwasser, President

San Antonio, TX (DMA 31)

KABB *Digital Channel:* 30; *Virtual Channel:* 29; 1000 kw; 1447 ft.; N29 17 28 W98 16 12
4335 N.W. Loop 410, San Antonio, TX 78229 US
(210) 366-1129; *Fax:* (210) 377-4758
www.foxsanantonio.com
kabbtv@kabb.com
License: San Antonio, Bexar County, TX held by KABB Licensee LLC
Group Owner: Sinclair Broadcast Group Inc.; *Washington Law Firm:* Shaw, Pittman
Nat'l Network: FOX; *Nat'l Reps:* Millennium Sales & Marketing
Size of News Staff: 35; *Hours of Local News Weekly:* news progmg 7 hrs wkly
Dean Radia, General Manager
David Ostmo, Regional Director of Operations
Pam Simpson, General Sales Mgr
Grace Jones, Programming Director
Robyn Keeny, Promotions Manager
Keith McMahan, News Director
Mike Guerrero, EngineeringDir
Robert Canales, Director of Sales
Heathre Ray, Director of Sales Promotions
Jimmy Cola, National Sales Manager
Max Nombrano, Digital Sales Manager

KCWX *Digital Channel:* 5; *Virtual Channel:* 2; 100 kw vis, 10 kw aur; 1,355t/1,017g; N30 08 13 W98 36 35
5400 Fredericksburg Rd., San Antonio, TX 78229
(210) 366-0000, (210) 366-2002; *Fax:* (210) 348-9142,(210) 377-8779
www.kens5.com
webmaster@kens5.com
License: Fredericksburg, Gillespie County, TX held by Corridor Television L.L.P
Nat'l Network: MyNetworkTV; *Nat'l Reps:* TeleRep
Robert McGann, General Manager
Boots Walker, General Sales Mgr
Rich Barton, Engineering Dir
Robert G. McGann, News Team
Sarah Lucero, News Team
Jeff Goldblatt, News Team
Deborah Knapp, News Team
Bill Taylor, News Team
SarahForgany, News Team

KENS *Digital Channel:* 55; *Virtual Channel:* 5; 1,000 kw; 1,447 ft.; N29 16 10 W98 15 55; *Population Served:* 700,000
5400 Fredericksburg Rd., San Antonio, TX 78229 US
(210) 366-5000; *Fax:* (210) 377-8790
www.kens5.com
webmaster@kens5.com
License: San Antonio, Bexar County, TX held by KENS-TV Inc.
Group Owner: Tegna Media; *Washington Law Firm:* Wiley, Rein & Fielding
Nat'l Network: CBS; *Nat'l Reps:* TeleRep; *Wire Services:* NWS (National Weather Service)
Size of News Staff: 55; *Hours of Local News Weekly:* news progmg 31.5 hrs wkly
Tom Cury, President and General Manager
Marty Schack, Director of Sales
Jack Acosta, News Director
Rich Barton, Director of Technology

***KHCE-TV** *Digital Channel:* 16; *Virtual Channel:* 23; 850 kw; 1076 ft.; N29 17 24 W98 15 20
Mailing Address: Box 691246, San Antonio, TX 78269 US
Second Address: 15533 Capitol Port, San Antonio, TX 78249
(210) 479-0123; *Fax:* (210) 492-5679
www.khce.org
License: San Antonio, Bexar County, TX held by San Antonio Community Educational TV Inc
Nat'l Network: TRINITY BROADCA
Paul Crouch, President
Dr. Cherry, Operations Dir
Laura Hanks, General Manager
Dorcas Rogers, Station Manager
Jessica Mathews, Programming Director
Mike Bundrant, Engineering Dir
Corrie Hickey, Public Affairs Director

***KLRN** *Digital Channel:* 9; *Virtual Channel:* 9; 28 kw; 938 ft.; N29 19 38 W98 21 17
Mailing Address: PO Box 9, San Antonio, TX 78291-0009 US
Second Address: 501 Broadway, San Antonio, TX 78291-0009
(210) 270-9000, (800) 627-8193; *Fax:* (210) 270-9078
www.klrn.org
info@klrn.org
License: San Antonio, Bexar County, TX held by Alamo Public Telecommunications Council
(acq 8-11-89).; *Washington Law Firm:* Cohn & Marks
Nat'l Network: PBS
Mike Novak, Chairman
Mario A.Vazquez, CEO/President
Patrick Lopez, Operations Dir
Joanne Winik, General Manager
Cynthia Shields, General Sales Mgr
Peter Gonzalez, VP, Engineering
Julie Coan, Senior Vice President & ChiefOperating Officer
Patrick Lopez, Executive Vice President & CFO
Katrina Kehoe, VP, Marketing & Communications
Cynthia Shields, VP, Institutional Advancement
Kathy Babb, Marketing Manager
John Costello, VP, Events & Volunteers

KMYS *Digital Channel:* 32; 5,000 kw vis, 500 kw aur; ant 1,758t; N29 36 37 W98 53 35; *Population Served:* 1,500,000
4335 N.W. Loop 410, San Antonio, TX 15235
(210) 366-1129; *Fax:* (210) 377-4758
www.kmys.tv
kmys@kmys.tv
License: Kerrville, Kerr County, TX held by Deerfield Media (San Antonio) Licensee LLC
Group Owner: Deerfield Media; (acq 12-10-01; grpsl).; *Washington Law Firm:* Shaw, Pittman
Nat'l Network: CW
Dean Radla, General Sales Mgr
Jessica Aguilar, Promotions Manager
Gwen Frames, Local Sales Manager
Jimmy Cola, National Sales Manager

KNIC-DT *Digital Channel:* 18; *Virtual Channel:* 17; 1000 kw; 656 ft.; N29 41 48 W98 30 45
12451 Network Blvd., Suite 140, San Antonio, TX 78249 US
(210) 610-4171
www.univision.com
License: Blanco, Blanco County, TX held by UniMas Partnership San Antonio
Group Owner: Univision Communications Inc.
David Loving, General Manager

KPXL-TV ; 228 kw; 1,837t; N29 37 11 W99 02 55
6100 Bandera Rd., Suite 304, San Antonio, TX 78238 USA
(210) 682-2626; *Fax:* (210) 682-3155
www.iontelevision.com
License: Uvalde, TX held by Ion Media San Antonio License, Inc.
Group Owner: ION Media Networks Inc.; (acq 6-24-99; $5 million for remaining 51%).
Nat'l Network: ION Television
Brandon Burgess, Chairman/CEO

KSAT-TV *Digital Channel:* 12; *Virtual Channel:* 12; 22.2 kw; 1493 ft.; N29 16 11 W98 15 31
1408 N. St Mary's Street, San Antonio, TX 78215 US
(210) 351-1200; *Fax:* (210) 351-1310
www.ksat.com
contactus@ksat.com
License: San Antonio, Bexar County, TX held by Post-Newsweek Stations Inc.
Group Owner: Post-Newsweek Stations Inc.; (acq 2-28-94; *Washington Law Firm:* Covington & Burling
Nat'l Network: ABC; *Nat'l Reps:* MMT
Hours of Local News Weekly: News progmg 21 hrs wkly
James Joslyn, Operations Dir

KWEX-DT *Digital Channel:* 41; *Virtual Channel:* 41; 832 kw vis, 83.2 kw aur; ant 500t/604g; N29 17 38 W98 15 31;
Population Served: 2,478,680
12451 Network Blvd., Suite 140, San Antonio, TX 78249 US
(210) 242-7444; *Fax:* (210) 227-0469
www.univision.com
License: San Antonio, Bexar County, TX held by KWEX License Partnership L.P.
Group Owner: Univision Communications Inc.; (acq 7-86; grpsl).; *Washington Law Firm:* Fisher, Wayland, Cooper, Leader & Zaragoza
Nat'l Network: Univision (Spanish)
Foreign Language Programming; Hours of Local News Weekly: news progmg 7 hrs wkly
David Loving, General Manager

WOAI-TV *Digital Channel:* 48; *Virtual Channel:* 4; 905 kw; 1499 ft.; N29 16 11 W98 15 55
4335 N.W. Loop 410, San Antonio, TX 78229 US
(210) 226-4444; *Fax:* (210) 224-9898
www.news4sanantonio.com
webteam@news4sanantonio.com
License: San Antonio, Bexar County, TX held by WOAI Licensee LLC
Group Owner: Sinclair Broadcast Group Inc.; (acq 12-1-2012; grpsl); *Washington Law Firm:* Pillsbury Winthrop Shaw Pittman LLP
Nat'l Network: NBC
Size of News Staff: 68; *Hours of Local News Weekly:* news progmg 24.5 hrs wkly
Todd Schliewen, Local Sales Manager
Carolyn Mastin, Programming Director
April Young, TV News Producer

Sherman, TX-Ada, OK (DMA 162)

KXII *Digital Channel:* 12; *Virtual Channel:* 12; 36 kw; 1790 ft.; N34 1 58 W96 48 0
4201 Texoma Pkwy., Sherman, TX 75090 USA
(903) 892-8123; *Fax:* (903) 893-7858
www.kxii.com
news12@kxii.com
License: Sherman, Grayson County, TX held by Gray Television Licensee LLC
Group Owner: Gray Television Inc.; (acq 6-29-99; $41.5 million); *Washington Law Firm:* Wiley Rein, LLP
Nat'l Network: CBS; MyNetworkTV; FOX; *Nat'l Reps:* Millennium Sales & Marketing; *Wire Services:* AP; CNN; CBS
Hours of Local News Weekly: News progmg 20 hrs wkly
Todd Bates, Sales
Stephen Woodall, Promotions
Dennis Kite, Chief Engineer

Shreveport, LA (DMA 82)

KTAL-TV *Digital Channel:* 15; *Virtual Channel:* 6; 1000 kw; 1490 ft.; N32 54 11 W94 0 20
Mailing Address: PO Box 7428, Shreveport, LA 71137 US
Second Address: 3150 N. Market, Shreveport, LA 71107
(318) 629-6000; *Fax:* (318) 629-6001
www.arklatexhomepage.com

License: Texarkana, Bowie County, TX held by Nexstar Broadcasting, Inc.
Group Owner: Nexstar Broadcasting Group Inc.; (acq 9-11-2000; $35.25 million); *Washington Law Firm:* Covington & Burling
Nat'l Network: NBC
Mark McKay, General Manager
Glynn Duncan, General Sales Mgr

Tyler-Longview (Lufkin & Nacogdoches), TX (DMA 108)

KCEB *Digital Channel:* 51; *Virtual Channel:* 54; 500 kw; 1243 ft.; N32 15 36 W94 57 2
14141 Sw Freeway, Suite 6200, Sugar Land, TX 77478 US
(337) 896-1600; *Fax:* (337) 896-2695
License: Longview, Gregg County, TX held by KCEB License Company LLC
Group Owner: London Broadcasting Co. Inc.; (acq 11-24-2003).; *Washington Law Firm:* Fletcher, Heald & Hildreth
Nat'l Network: CW
Eddie Blanchard, General Manager

KETK-TV *Digital Channel:* 22; *Virtual Channel:* 56; 1000 kw; 1505 ft.; N32 3 40 W95 18 50
4300 Richmond Rd., Tyler, TX 75703 US
(903) 581-5656; *Fax:* (903) 561-1648
www.ketknbc.com
License: Jacksonville, Cherokee County, TX held by Nexstar Broadcasting, Inc.
Group Owner: Nexstar Broadcasting Group; (acq 11-12-2004; $38 million); *Washington Law Firm:* Dow, Lohnes
Nat'l Network: NBC; *Nat'l Reps:* Millennium Sales & Marketing
Size of News Staff: 37; *Hours of Local News Weekly:* news progmg 25 hrs wkly
Dave Tillery, General Manager
Suzanne Calhoun, Dir. of Sales
Neal Barton, News Director

KFXK-TV *Digital Channel:* 31; *Virtual Channel:* 51; 1000 kw; ant 1,249t/1,199g; N32 15 35 W94 57 02
4300 Richmond Rd., Tyler, TX 75703 US
(903) 581-5656; *Fax:* (903) 561-1648
www.myeasttex.com
dtrent@myeasttex.com
License: Longview, TX held by Warwick Communications Inc.
Group Owner: White Knight Broadcasting
Nat'l Network: Fox
Drew Balch, Station Manager

KLTV *Digital Channel:* 7; *Virtual Channel:* 7; 66 kw; 984 ft.; N32 32 23 W95 13 11
105 W Ferguson, Tyler, TX 75702 US
(903) 597-5588; *Fax:* (903) 510-7777
www.kltv.com
License: Tyler, Smith County, TX held by Civco Inc.
Group Owner: Raycom Media Inc.; (acq 1-13-2006; grpsl).; *Washington Law Firm:* Covington & Burling
Nat'l Network: ABC
Pat Stacey, Vice President & General Manager
Stephen Bryan, Local Sales Manager
Stephen Rainwater, Digital Sales Manager
John Kelbe, Regional National Sales Manager
Misty Wages, General Sales Manager
Kenny Boles, News Director
Steve Magee, Director Of Technology
Butch Adair, Chief Engineer
Mary Ryan, National Sales Manager
Hazel Kennedy, Traffic Manager
Mark Scirto, Weather Director
Mark Scirto, Chief Meterologist
Ryan Peterson, Sports Director
MichaelThompson, Executive Producer

KTRE *Digital Channel:* 9; *Virtual Channel:* 9; 23.5 kw; 669 ft.; N31 25 9 W94 48 3
Mailing Address: 358 TV Road, Pollok, TX 75969 US
Second Address: 358 TV Rd., Pollok, TX 75969
(936) 853-8639; *Fax:* (936) 853-3084
www.ktre.com
dlorenz@ktre.com
License: Lufkin, Angelina County, TX held by Raycom Media, Inc.
Group Owner: Raycom Media Inc.; (acq 1-13-2006; grpsl).; *Washington Law Firm:* Covington & Burling
Nat'l Network: ABC
Foreign Language Programming; Size of News Staff: 15; *Hours of Local News Weekly:* news progmg 20 hrs wkly
Paul McTear, CEO
Artie Bedard, Operations Dir
Melissa Thurber, CFO
Wayne Dougherty, Executive Vice President

KYTX *Digital Channel:* 18; *Virtual Channel:* 19; 640 kw; 1,499 ft.; N31 54 20 W95 5 5
2211 ESE Loop 323, Tyler, TX 75701 US
(903) 581-2211; *Fax:* (903) 581-5769
www.cbs19.tv
news@cbs19.tv
License: Nacogdoches, Nacogdoches County, TX held by LSB Broadcasting Inc.
Group Owner: Tegna Media; (acq 7-8-2014).; *Washington Law Firm:* William Mullen
Nat'l Network: CBS; *Nat'l Reps:* Blair Television; *Wire Services:* AP
Size of News Staff: 25; *Hours of Local News Weekly:* news progmg 19 hrs wkly
John Gaston, General Manager
Chris Nesbit, General Sales Mgr
Mark Allen, Promotions Manager
Jennifer Dodd, News Director
J.C. Johnson, Chief Engineer
Holly Austin-Carroll, Local Sales Manager
Judy Oglesby, Community RelationsDirector
Brandi Ishmael, Business Manager
Connie Jobe, Traffic Manager
Kevin Meyer, Director of Creative Services
Steve Jackson, News Assignment Manager

Victoria, TX (DMA 203)

KAVU-TV *Digital Channel:* 15; *Virtual Channel:* 25; 900 kw; 1024 ft.; N28 50 42 W97 7 33
3808 N. Navarro St., Victoria, TX 77901 US
(361) 575-2500; *Fax:* (361) 575-2255
www.crossroadstoday.com
jpryor@kavutv.com
License: Victoria, Victoria County, TX held by Saga Broadcasting LLC.
Group Owner: Saga Communications Inc.; (acq 10-20-98; $11.875 million; with KNAL(AM) Victoria).; *Washington Law Firm:* Smithwick & Belendiuk, P.C
Nat'l Network: ABC; *Nat'l Reps:* Continental Television Sales
Regional Reps: Katz Continental; *Wire Services:* AP
Size of News Staff: 15; *Hours of Local News Weekly:* news progmg 29 hrs wkly
Jeff Pryor, General Manager
Mike Halbrook, Promotions
Jennifer Dodd, News Director
Michael Wall, Business Manager
Howard Esse, Creative Services
John Garcia, Technical/IT

KVCT *Digital Channel:* 11; *Virtual Channel:* 19; 11.35 kw; 951 ft.; N28 50 42 W97 7 33
Mailing Address: 943 Lincoln Road, Grosse Pointe, MI 48230 US
Second Address: 3808 N. Navarro St., Victoria, TX 77901
(361) 575-2500; *Fax:* (361) 575-2255
License: Victoria, Victoria County, TX held by Surtsey Media LLC
Group Owner: Surtsey Media LLC; (acq 4-26-99).; *Washington Law Firm:* Fletcher, Heald & Hildreth, P.L.C.
Nat'l Network: FOX; *Nat'l Reps:* Continental Television Sales; *Wire Services:* AP
Hours of Local News Weekly: News progmg 2.5 hrs wkly
John Garcia, Operations Dir
Jeff Pryor, General Manager
Rebecca Sarlls, Programming Director
Mike Halbrook, Promotions
Jennifer Dodd, News Director
Kevin John, Engineering
Kevin John, Chief Engineer
Phil Stevens, InteractiveMedia
Todd Long, Public Affairs Director
Jennifer Rosales, Traffic Manager
Michael Wall, Business manager
Howard Esse, Creative Services
John Garcia, Technical/IT

Waco-Temple-Bryan, TX (DMA 87)

KAGS-LD *Digital Channel:* 23; 2.1 kw; N30 41 18 W96 25 35
2800 S. Texas Ave., Suite 110, Bryan, TX 77802 US
(979) 703-8404; *Fax:* (979) 703-8409
www.kagstv.com
License: Bryan, Brazos County, TX held by LSB Broadcasting Inc.
Group Owner: Tegna Media
Nat'l Network: NBC
Roby Somerford, General Manager
Jan Shuler, Programming Director
Luke Simons, News Director
Cody Blount, Chief Engineer

***KAMU-TV** *Digital Channel:* 12; *Virtual Channel:* 15; 3.2 kw; 344 ft.; N30 37 47 W96 20 33
Mailing Address: Houston St. at John David Crow St, College Station, TX 77843-4244 US
Second Address: Texas A&M University, 4244 TAMU, College Station, TX 77843-4244
(979) 845-5611; *Fax:* (979) 845-1643
www.kamu.tamu.edu
License: College Station, Brazos County, TX held by Texas A&M University
Nat'l Network: PBS
John Prihoda, Operations Dir
Rodney Zent, General Manager
Penny Zent, FM-radio Station Manager
Elaine Hoyak, General Sales Mgr
Jon Bennett, TV Station Manager & Program Director
Wayne Pecena, Engineering Dir
Ken Nelson,Engineering Dir
Sherill Simpson, Traffic Manager
B. Howard Johnson, Web Administrator

KBTX *Digital Channel:* 50; *Virtual Channel:* 3; 1000 kw; 1664 ft.; N30 33 16 W96 1 51
4141 E 29th St., Bryan, TX 77802 USA
(979) 846-7777; *Fax:* (979) 846-1490
www.kbtx.com
news@kbtx.com
License: Bryan, Brazos County, TX held by Gray Television Licensee Inc.
Group Owner: Gray Television Inc.
Nat'l Network: CBS; The CW Network; *Nat'l Reps:* Millennium Sales & Marketing; *Wire Services:* AP
Size of News Staff: 30; *Hours of Local News Weekly:* news progmg 19 hrs. wkly
Mike Wright, General Manager
Lori Bruffett, Station Manager
Lauren Ghinelli, National/Regional Sales
Zac Reynolds, Promotions Director
Josh Gorbutt, News Director

KCEN-TV *Digital Channel:* 9; *Virtual Channel:* 6; 25 kw; 1,729 ft.; N31 16 24 W97 13 14
Mailing Address: P.O. Box 6103, Temple, TX 76503 US
Second Address: 314 Interstate Hwy. 35 S., Eddy, TX 76513
(254) 859-5481; *Fax:* (254) 859-4004
www.kcentv.com
comments@kcentv.com
License: Temple, Bell County, TX held by LSB Broadcasting Inc.
Group Owner: Tegna Media; (acq 7-8-2014).; *Washington Law Firm:* Wiley Rein LLP
Nat'l Network: NBC; *Nat'l Reps:* Petry Television Inc.; *Wire Services:* AP
Size of News Staff: 33; *Hours of Local News Weekly:* news progmg 21.5 hrs wkly
Gayle Kiger, Vice President and General Manager
Mike Stanford, Director of Marketing
Cody Blount, Director of Operations and Technology

***KDYW** *Digital Channel:* 20; *Virtual Channel:* 34; 79.4 kw vis, 7.9 kw aur; 508t/446g; N31 30 31 W97 10 03; *Population Served:* 100,000
Mailing Address: One Bear Pl. #97296, Waco, TX 76798-7296
Second Address: 2100 River Street, Waco, TX 76706
(254) 710-3472; *Fax:* (254) 710-3874
www.kwbu.org
Carla@KWBU.org
License: Waco, McLennan County, TX held by Brazos Valley Public Broadcasting Foundation
(acq 12-6-93; $80,000; *Washington Law Firm:* Cohn & Marks
Nat'l Network: PBS; *Regional Network:* National Educational Telecommunications Association
Cynthia Jackson, Chairman
Joe Riley, President & CEO
Brodie Bashaw, Station Manager/ Host, Morning Edition
Ashley Kortis, General Sales Mgr
Clare Paul, Promotions Manager
Derek Smith, News Director
Tony Poole, Chief Engineer
Carla Hervey, Business Affairs Manager
Dave Ulman, Director of Development
Loretta Howard, Membership Manager
Ryland Barton, News Reporter/Host, All Things Considered
Charles S. Madden, Professor of Marketing

***KNCT** *Digital Channel:* 46; 479 kw vis, 67.6 kw aur; 1,261t/1,126g; N30 59 12 W97 37 47
Mailing Address: Box 1800, Killeen, TX 76540
Second Address: KNCT/ Central Texas College, 6200 W. Centex Expwy., Killeen, TX 76549-4199

(254) 526-1176; *Fax:* (254) 526-1850
www.knct.org
knct@knct.org
License: Belton, Bell County, TX held by Central Texas College
Nat'l Network: PBS; Create
Size of News Staff: 1; *Hours of Local News Weekly:* news progmg one hr wkly
Max Rudolph, General Manager
Steve Benger, Programming Director
Sean Greenthaner, Promotions Manager
Steve Sulzer, Engineering Dir
Christian Wohlfahrt, Production Manager
Laury Sisko, Traffic Coordinator

KWKT-TV *Digital Channel:* 44; *Virtual Channel:* 44; 4,170 kw vis, 417 kw aur; ant 1,811t/1,673g; N31 18 52 W97 19 37
8803 Woodway Dr., Waco, TX 76712 US
(254) 776-3844
www.kwkt.com
License: Waco, McLennan County, TX held by Nexstar Broadcasting, Inc.
Group Owner: Nexstar Broadcasting Group; (acq 10-31-90; grpsl; *Washington Law Firm:* Fletcher, Heald & Hildreth
Nat'l Network: Fox; MyNetworkTV; *Nat'l Reps:* Millennium Sales & Marketing
Duane Sartor, General Manager
Debora Fowler, Director of Sales
Neal Barton, News Director

KWTX *Digital Channel:* 10; *Virtual Channel:* 10; 39 kw; 1821 ft.; N31 19 19 W97 19 2
6700 American Plaza, Waco, TX 76712 USA
(254) 776-1330; *Fax:* (254) 751-1088
www.kwtx.com
news@kwtx.com
License: Waco, McLennan County, TX held by Gray Television Licensee LLC
Group Owner: Gray Television Inc.; *Washington Law Firm:* Wiley Rein
Nat'l Network: CBS; The CW Network; *Nat'l Reps:* Millennium Sales & Marketing
Size of News Staff: 30; *Hours of Local News Weekly:* news progmg 20 hrs wkly
Mike Wright, VP/General Manager
Robert Lepping, General Sales Mgr
Mike Lauber, News Director
Larry Brown, Chief Engineer

KXXV *Digital Channel:* 26; *Virtual Channel:* 25; 1000 kw; 1842 ft.; N31 20 16 W97 18 36; *Rebroadcasting:* ABC, Telemundo, Weather Now(Local Weather)
Mailing Address: 1909 S. New Road, Waco, TX 76711 US
Second Address: 1909 S. New Rd., Waco, TX 76711
(254) 754-2525, (254) 757-2525; *Fax:* (254) 752-1002
www.kxxv.com
news25@kxxv.com
License: Waco, McLennan County, TX held by Centex Television L.P.
Group Owner: R.H. Drewry Group; (acq 1994).
Nat'l Network: ABC; Telemundo (Spanish)
Size of News Staff: 18; *Hours of Local News Weekly:* news progmg 14.5 hrs wkly
Mike Lee, Operations Dir
Darlene Mahler, National Sales Manager
Dani Fox, Programming Director
Dennis Kinney, News Director
Randy Lee, Chief Engineer
Bruce Gietzen, Anchor
Ann Harder, Anchor
Bruce Gietzen, News Anchor
LeeSmall, Sports Director,Anchor & reporter
Matt Hines, Chief Meteorologist
Conley Isom, Chief Meteorologist

KYLE-TV *Digital Channel:* 28; *Virtual Channel:* 28; 50 kw vis; ant 722t/640g; N30 41 18 W96 25 35; *Rebroadcasting:* Satellite of KWKT(TV) Waco.; *Population Served:* 200,000
2402 Broadmoor Dr., Suite B-101, Bryan, TX 77802 US
(979) 774-1800
www.mycentx.com
License: Bryan, Brazos County, TX held by Nexstar Broadcasting, Inc.
Group Owner: Nexstar Broadcasting Group; (acq 1996; $1.1 million); *Washington Law Firm:* Gardner, Carton & Douglas
Nat'l Network: Fox; MyNetworkTV
Duane Sartor, General Manager
Debora Fowler, Director of Sales
Neal Barton, News Director

Wichita Falls, TX & Lawton, OK (DMA 148)

KAUZ-TV *Digital Channel:* 22; *Virtual Channel:* 6; 433 kw; 1020 ft.; N33 54 4 W98 32 21
Mailing Address: P.O. Box 2130, Wichita Falls, TX 76307 US
Second Address: 3601 Seymour Highway, Wichita Falls, TX 76309
(940) 322-6957, (940) 322 1146; *Fax:* (940) 761-2354
www.newschannel6now.com
nbowers@kauz.com
License: Wichita Falls, Wichita County, TX held by Hoak Media of Wichita Falls L.P.
Group Owner: Hoak Media Corporation; (acq 11-5-2003; $8.2 million); *Washington Law Firm:* Covington & Burling
Nat'l Network: CBS; CW; *Nat'l Reps:* Harrington, Righter & Parsons; *Wire Services:* CBS
Size of News Staff: 20; *Hours of Local News Weekly:* news progmg 15 hrs wkly
Chris Horgen, News
Ashley Fitzwater, News
Ken Johnson, Weather
John Cameron, Weather
Adam Ostrow, Sports
Terry Fox, Sports

KFDX-TV *Digital Channel:* 28; *Virtual Channel:* 3; 1000 kw; 884 ft.; N33 53 23 W98 33 30
4500 Seymour Hwy., Wichita Falls, TX 76309 US
(940) 691-0003; *Fax:* (940) 691-0330
www.texomashomepage.com
License: Wichita Falls, Wichita County, TX held by Nexstar Broadcasting Inc.
Group Owner: Nexstar Broadcasting Group Inc.; (acq 11-6-97; grpsl).; *Washington Law Firm:* Arter & Hadden
Nat'l Network: NBC
Size of News Staff: 24; *Hours of Local News Weekly:* news progmg 19.5 hrs wkly
Wayne Reed, General Manager
Britt Milstead, General Sales Mgr
Doug Bilyeu, News Director

KJTL *Digital Channel:* 15; *Virtual Channel:* 18; 1000 kw; 863 ft.; N34 12 5 W98 43 45
4500 Seymour Hwy., Wichita Falls, TX 76309 US
(940) 691-1808; *Fax:* (940) 691-5766
www.texomashomepage.com
License: Wichita Falls, Wichita County, TX held by Mission Broadcasting Inc.
Group Owner: Mission Broadcasting Inc.; (acq 1999; $28.5 million with KCIT(TV) Amarillo); *Washington Law Firm:* Spector & Goldberg
Nat'l Network: FOX
Stephanie Reed, Station Manager
Britt Milstead, General Sales Mgr

Utah

Salt Lake City, UT (DMA 34)

***KBYU-TV** *Digital Channel:* 44; *Virtual Channel:* 11; 346 kw; 4124 ft.; N40 39 33 W112 12 7
Brigham Young University, Provo, UT 84602 US
(801) 422-8450, (800) 298-5298; *Fax:* (801) 422-8478
www.kbyu.org
License: Provo, Utah County, UT held by Brigham Young University
Washington Law Firm: Wilkinson, Barker, Knauer & Quinn
Nat'l Network: PBS
Foreign Language Programming; Size of News Staff: 3; *Hours of Local News Weekly:* news progmg 3 hrs wkly
Derek Marquis, General Manager
Bart Chidester, Production Supervisor
Wendy Thomas, Programming Director
Jim Bell, Promotions Manager
Wesley Sims, News Director
Brian Leifson, Chief Engineer

KCSG *Digital Channel:* 14; *Virtual Channel:* 4; 25 kw; 1263 ft.; N37 38 22 W113 2 0
Mailing Address: 158 West 1600 South, Suite 200, St. George, UT 84770 US
Second Address: 158 W 1600 S #200, Suite 200, St. George, UT 84770
(435) 634-7500; *Fax:* (435) 674-2774
www.kcsg.com
info@kcsg.com
License: Cedar City, Iron County, UT held by Southwest Media LLC
(acq 7-30-2002; $450,000); *Washington Law Firm:* Garvey, Schubert & Barer
Nat'l Network: IND
Ed Merrifield, General Manager

KJZZ-TV *Digital Channel:* 46; *Virtual Channel:* 14; 200 kw; 4154 ft.; N40 39 33 W112 12 7
Mailing Address: 5181 Amelia Earhart Dr., Salt Lake City, UT 84123 US
Second Address: 301 W. South Temple, Salt Lake City, UT 84101
(801) 537-1414, (801) 238-6304; *Fax:* (801) 238-6414, (801) 238-6305
www.kjzz.com
bquigley@kjzz.com
License: Salt Lake City, Salt Lake County, UT held by Larry H. Miller Communications Corp
(acq 2-12-93; *Washington Law Firm:* Fleischman & Walsh
Nat'l Network: MYTV; *Nat'l Reps:* Blair Television
Randy Wright, Operations Dir
Jeremy Castro, General Manager
Marc Lowry, General Sales Mgr
Jeremy Castro, Programming
Eric Schulz, Promotions Manager
Mike Grover, Chief Engineer
Bob Gauld, National Sales Manager
Dean Paynter,Production Director
Charla Hastings, Traffic Manager
Bob Quigley, Closed Captioning
Marc Lowy, Sales

KMYU *Digital Channel:* 9; *Virtual Channel:* 12; 3.2 kw; ant 138t; N37 03 48 W113 34 23
299 S. Main St., Suite 150, Salt Lake City, UT 84111
(801) 839-1234; *Fax:* (801) 839-1101
www.kmyu.tv
License: St. George, Washington County, UT held by KUTV Licensee LLC
Group Owner: Sinclair Broadcast Group Inc.; (acq 11-21-2007; grpsl)
Nat'l Network: MyNetworkTV; *Nat'l Reps:* TeleRep
Kent Crawford, General Manager
Wade Nielsen, Sales Manager

KPNZ *Digital Channel:* 24; *Virtual Channel:* 24; 450 kw; 4032 ft.; N40 39 33 W112 12 7
150 North Wright Brothers Dr, Salt Lake City, UT 84116 US
; *Fax:* (801) 519-2424
www.estrellatv.com
kpnzinfo@kpnz24.tv
License: Ogden, Weber County, UT held by KRCA License LLC.
Group Owner: Liberman Broadcasting Inc.; (acq 11-30-2007; $10 million)
Nat'l Network: IND
Lenard Liberman, President

KSL-TV *Digital Channel:* 38; *Virtual Channel:* 5; 546 kw; 4,157 ft.; N40 39 33 W112 12 7
5 Triad Center, 55 N. 3rd W., Salt Lake City, UT 84180 US
(801) 575-5555; *Fax:* (801) 575-5560
www.ksl.com
License: Salt Lake City, Salt Lake County, UT held by Bonneville International Corporation
Group Owner: Bonneville International Corporation; *Washington Law Firm:* Wilkinson, Barker, Knauer & Quinn
Nat'l Network: NBC; *Nat'l Reps:* Eagle Television Sales; *Wire Services:* UPI
Foreign Language Programming; Size of News Staff: 65; *Hours of Local News Weekly:* news progmg 21 hrs wkly
Tanya Vea, Vice President and General Manager
Alan Blackburn, Advertising

KSTU *Digital Channel:* 28; *Virtual Channel:* 13; 350 kw; 3970 ft.; N40 39 33 W112 12 8
5020 Amelia Earhart Dr., Salt Lake City, UT 84116 USA
(801) 536-1313
fox13now.com
news@fox13now.com
License: Salt Lake City, Salt Lake County, UT held by KSTU License LLC
Group Owner: Tribune Media
Nat'l Network: FOX; *Nat'l Reps:* Fox Stations Sales
Hours of Local News Weekly: News progmg 34 hrs wkly

KTMW *Digital Channel:* 20; *Virtual Channel:* 20
Company, Llc, 530 East First S, #204, Salt Lake City, UT 84102 US
(801) 973-8820; *Fax:* (801) 973-7145
www.tv20.tv
License: Salt Lake City, Salt Lake County, UT held by Alpha & Omega Communications LLC

(acq 7-31-2003; $1.5 million); *Washington Law Firm:* Wood, Maines & Nolan, Chartered
Nat'l Network: IND; *Nat'l Reps:* Apex Media Sales Inc.
Pat Openhaw, President
Anthon Jeppesan, Operations Dir
Dennis Ermel, General Manager
Michelle Ermel, Promotions Manager
Dennis Silver, Chief Engineer

KTVX *Digital Channel:* 40; *Virtual Channel:* 4; 475.7 kw; 4121 ft.; N40 39 33 W112 12 7; *Population Served:* 1,000,000
2175 W. 1700 S., Salt Lake City, UT 84104 US
(801) 975-4444; *Fax:* (801) 924-8099
www.good4utah.com
License: Salt Lake City, Salt Lake County, UT held by Nexstar Broadcasting Inc.
Group Owner: Nexstar Broadcasting Group Inc.; (acq 3-14-2008; grpsl)
Nat'l Network: ABC
Size of News Staff: 50; *Hours of Local News Weekly:* 28 Hours
Perry Sook, CEO/President

KUCW *Digital Channel:* 48; *Virtual Channel:* 30; 200 kw; 4124 ft.; N40 39 33 W112 12 7
2175 W. 1700 S., Salt Lake City, UT 84104 US
(801) 975-4444
License: Ogden, Weber County, UT held by Nexstar Broadcasting Inc.
Group Owner: Nexstar Broadcasting Group Inc.; (acq 9-15-2008; grpsl)
Nat'l Network: CW; *Nat'l Reps:* MMT
Richard Doutre' Jones, General Manager
George Severson, News Director

***KUED** *Digital Channel:* 42; *Virtual Channel:* 7; 239 kw; 4154 ft.; N40 39 33 W112 12 7
101 S. Wasatch Drive, Salt Lake City, UT 84112 US
(801) 581-7777; *Fax:* (801) 585-5096
www.kued.org
webmaster@kued.org
License: Salt Lake City, Salt Lake County, UT held by University of Utah
Nat'l Network: PBS
Foreign Language Programming
Bruce Jensen, Chair
Larry Smith, General Manager
Rebecca Davis, Assistant General Manager
Bruce Jensen, Vice-Chair
Kate Jones, Staff Support
Shane Smith, Creative Services
Mark Thomas, Web Developer
Alice Gear Webber,Development Dir.

***KUEN** *Digital Channel:* 36; *Virtual Channel:* 9; 200 kw; 4121 ft.; N40 39 33 W112 12 7
101 Wasatch Drive, Salt Lake City, UT 84112 US
(801) 581-2999, (800) 866-5852; *Fax:* (801) 585-6105
www.uen.org
resources@uen.org
License: Ogden, Weber County, UT held by Utah State Board of Regents
Nat'l Network: PBS
Foreign Language Programming
Mike Petersen, General Manager
Kyel Anderson, Programming Director
Phil Titus, Chief Engineer
Lisa Kuhn, CFO
Karen Krier, Web Services manager
Don Mahaffey, Field Operation manager
Byan peterson, Enterprise Systems & SoftwareDevelopment Manager
James Stewart, Director
Kevin Quire, Manager

***KUEW** *Digital Channel:* 18; *Virtual Channel:* 18; 1.62 kw; 218 ft.; N37 3 50 W113 34 20; *Rebroadcasting:* Rebroadcasts KUED-TV Salt Lake City 100%
Philip Titus, 101 Wasatch Blvd, Salt Lake City, UT 84112 US
(801) 581-2999; *Fax:* (801) 585-6105
www.kued.com
webmaster@kued.org
License: St. George, Washington County, UT held by University of Utah.
Nat'l Network: PBS
Bruce Jensen, Chair
Larry Smith, General Manager
Phil Titus, Chief Engineer

KUPX-TV *Digital Channel:* 29; 530 kw; 2,308t; N40 39 12 W112 12 06; *Population Served:* 800,000
466-C Lawndale Dr., Salt Lake City, UT 84115 USA
(801) 474-0016; *Fax:* (646) 597-5903
www.iontelevision.com
michaelhubner@ionmedia.com
License: Provo, Utah County, UT held by Ion Media Salt Lake City License, Inc.
Group Owner: ION Media Networks Inc.
Nat'l Network: ION Television
Brandon Burgess, Chairman/CEO

KUTF *Digital Channel:* 12; *Virtual Channel:* 12; 22.3 kw; 2264 ft.; N41 47 3 W112 13 55
1772 North 600 West, Logan, UT 84341 US
(501) 219-2400; *Fax:* (501) 716-3502
License: Logan, Cache County, UT held by Word of God Fellowship Inc.
Nat'l Network: DAYSTAR
Doug Cryle, Operations Dir

KUTH-DT *Digital Channel:* 32; *Virtual Channel:* 32; 3,072 kw vis; ant 2,663t/125g; N40 16 45 W111 56 00
5140 W. Amelia Earhart Dr., Suite C & D, Salt Lake City, UT 84116
(801) 715-3240
www.univision.com
License: Provo, Utah County, UT held by Univision Salt Lake City LLC.
Group Owner: Univision Communications Inc.
Nat'l Network: Univision (Spanish)
Foreign Language Programming; Hours of Local News Weekly: news progmg 5 hrs wkly
Leonardo Ruiz, General Manager

KUTV *Digital Channel:* 34; *Virtual Channel:* 2; 423 kw; 4157 ft.; N40 39 33 W112 12 7
299 South Main St., Suite 150, Salt Lake City, UT 84111 USA
(801) 839-1234; *Fax:* (801) 839-1235
www.kutv.com
newsdesk@kutv2.com
License: Salt Lake City, Salt Lake County, UT held by KUTV Licensee LLC
Group Owner: Sinclair Broadcast Group; *Washington Law Firm:* Wiley Rein LLP
Nat'l Network: CBS; *Nat'l Reps:* TeleRep
Size of News Staff: 73; *Hours of Local News Weekly:* news progmg 36.5 hrs wkly

Vermont

Burlington, VT-Plattsburgh, NY (DMA 97)

WCAX-TV *Digital Channel:* 22; 38 kw vis, 7.25 kw aur; ant 2,739t; N44 31 36 W72 48 57; *Population Served:* 550,000
Mailing Address: Box 4508, Burlington, VT 05406-4508
Second Address: 30 Joy Dr, S. Burlington, VT 5403
(802) 652-6300; *Fax:* (802) 652-6319
www.wcax.com
channel3@wcax.com
License: Burlington, Chittenden County, VT held by Mount Mansfield TV Inc
Washington Law Firm: Wilmer/Hace
Nat'l Network: CBS; *Nat'l Reps:* Harrington, Righter & Parsons
Size of News Staff: 35; *Hours of Local News Weekly:* news progmg 15 hrs wkly
Peter Martin, President/General Manager/Programming Director
Phil Scharf, Operations Dir
Bruce Grindle, General Sales Mgr
Anson Tebbits, News Director
Tim Thayer, Chief Engineer
Alex Martin, New Media Director
Meredith Neary,Public Service Director
Mike McCune, Sports Director
Brenda Bouvier, Traffic Manager
Sharon Myer, Weather Director
Phil Scharf, Closed Captioning Issues

***WETK** *Digital Channel:* 32; *Virtual Channel:* 33; 90 kw; 2723 ft.; N44 31 32 W72 48 51
Mailing Address: 204 Ethan Allen Avenue, Colchester, VT 05446 US
Second Address: PO Box 11110, Station Centre Ville, Montreal, QC H3C 5E3
(802) 655-4800, (800) 639-7811
www.vpt.org
view@vpt.org
License: Burlington, Chittenden County, VT held by Vermont ETV Inc
(acq 11-6-89).; *Washington Law Firm:* Covington & Burling
Nat'l Network: PBS; *Regional Network:* Vermont Public Television
Rob Hofmann, Chairman
John King, CEO/President
Lee Ann Lee, General Sales Mgr
Bruce Bouchard, Board Member
Patricia Sabalis, Board Member
Jeremy Schrauf, Board Member
Lorilee A. Lawton, Board Member
David Taplin, BoardMember
Lisa M. Ventriss, Board Member

WFFF-TV *Digital Channel:* 43; *Virtual Channel:* 44; 5,000 kw vis; ant 1,738t; N44 31 32 W72 48 54
298 Mountain View Dr., Colchester, VT 05446 US
(802) 660-9333; *Fax:* (802) 660-8673
www.fox44now.com
License: Burlington, Chittenden County, VT held by Nexstar Broadcasting Inc.
Group Owner: Nexstar Broadcasting Group Inc.; (acq 11-15-2004; grpsl).
Nat'l Network: Fox; CW; *Nat'l Reps:* Continental Television Sales; *Wire Services:* AP; CNN
Size of News Staff: 30; *Hours of Local News Weekly:* 24.5
Roger Hess, General Manager
JoAnn Cyr, Director of Sales
Jolene Green, News Director

WNNE *Digital Channel:* 25; 2,240 kw vis, 2.24 kw aur; ant 2,220t/149g; N43 26 38 W72 27 17; *Population Served:* 133,000
Box 1310, White River Junction, VT 5001
(802) 295-3100; *Fax:* (802) 655-5451
www.wnne.com
License: Hartford, Windsor County, VT held by Hearst Stations Inc.
Group Owner: Hearst Television Inc.
Nat'l Network: NBC
Paul Sands, General Manager

***WVER** *Digital Channel:* 9; *Virtual Channel:* 28; 15 kw; 1263 ft.; N43 39 31 W73 6 25; *Rebroadcasting:* Satellite of WETK(TV) Burlington.
Mailing Address: 204 Ethan Allen Avenue, Colchester, VT 05446 US
Second Address: PO Box 11110, Station Centre Ville, Montreal, QC H3C 5E3
(802) 655-4800, (800) 639-7811
www.vpt.org
License: Rutland, Rutland County, VT held by Vermont ETV Inc
Washington Law Firm: Covington & Burling
Nat'l Network: PBS; *Regional Network:* Vermont Public Television
Jim Wyant, Chairman
John King, CEO & President
Lee Ann Lee, General Sales Mgr
Kelly Luoma, Programming Director
Jeff Vande Griek, Promotions Manager
Rob Belle-Isle, Engineering Dir
Andrea Bergeron, CFO
Peter Shea, SalesDirector
George Hauenstein, Chief Development Officer
Elizabeth Metraux, Cgief Communications & Public Relations officer
Joe Tymecki, CTO

WVNY *Digital Channel:* 13; *Virtual Channel:* 22; 1,000 kw vis, 100 kw aur; 2,739t/310g; N44 31 40 W72 48 58
298 Mountain View Dr., Colchester, VT 05446 US
(802) 660-9333
www.abc22.com
License: Burlington, Chittenden County, VT held by Mission Broadcasting Inc.
Group Owner: Mission Broadcasting Inc.
Nat'l Network: ABC; *Nat'l Reps:* Continental Television Sales
Greg Towne, Station Manager
JoAnn Cyr, Director of Sales
Jolene Green, News Director

***WVTA** *Digital Channel:* 24; *Virtual Channel:* 41; 55.7 kw; 2270 ft.; N43 26 14.7 W72 27 7.7; *Rebroadcasting:* Satellite of *WETK Burlington.
Mailing Address: 204 Ethan Allen Avenue, Colchester, VT 05446 US
Second Address: PO Box 11110, Station Centre Ville, Montreal, QC H3C 5E3
(802) 655-4800, (800) 639-7811
www.vpt.org
view@vpt.org
License: Windsor, Windsor County, VT held by Vermont ETV Inc
Washington Law Firm: Covington & Burling
Nat'l Network: PBS; *Regional Network:* Vermont Public Television
John King, CEO & President
Joseph Merone, Operations Dir

Lee Ann Lee, General Sales Mgr
Kelly Luoma, Programming Director
Jeff Vande Griek, Promotions Manager
Rob Belle-Isle, Engineering Dir
Peter Shea, Sales Director
GeorgeHauenstein, Chief Development Officer
Elizabeth Metraux, Cgief Communications & Public Relations officer
Joe Tymecki, CTO

***WVTB** *Digital Channel:* 18; *Virtual Channel:* 20; 67 kw; 1936 ft.; N44 34 16 W71 53 39; *Rebroadcasting:* Satellite of WETK(TV) Burlington
Mailing Address: 204 Ethan Allen Avenue, Colchester, VT 05446 US
Second Address: PO Box 11110, Station Centre Ville, Montreal, QC H3C 5E3
(802) 655-4800, (800) 639-7811
www.vpt.org
view@vpt.org
License: St. Johnsbury, Caledonia County, VT held by Vermont ETV Inc
Washington Law Firm: Covington & Burling
Nat'l Network: PBS; *Regional Network:* Vermont Public Television
John King, CEO & President
Lee Ann Lee, General Sales Mgr
George Hauenstein, Chief Development Officer
Elizabeth Metraux, Cgief Communications & Public Relations officer
Joe Tymecki, CTO

Virgin Islands

Charlotte Amalie

***WTJX-TV** *Digital Channel:* 44; 28.8 kw vis, 2.9 kw aur; ant 1,479t; N18 21 26 W64 56 50; *Population Served:* 110,000
Mailing Address: Box 7879, St. Thomas, VI 00801
Second Address: PO Box 808, St. Croix, VI 821
(340) 774-6255, (340) 718-3339; *Fax:* (340) 774-7092, (340) 718-4555
www.wtjx.org
opotter@wtjx.org
License: Charlotte Amalie, VI held by Virgin Islands Public Television System
Washington Law Firm: Schwartz, Woods & Miller
Nat'l Network: PBS
Raul Carrillo, Chairman
Osbert E Potter, CEO
Tanya Marie Singh, COO
Yvette Delaubanque, Director, Development/Funding
Jose Raul Carrillo, Board Chair
Robert Dickinson, Chief Engineer
James AD Francis, Treasurer
Eugene Peterson,Secretary

WVXF *Digital Channel:* 17; *Virtual Channel:* 17; 4.2 kw; 1490 ft.; N18 21 26 W64 56 50
Mailing Address: 100 Dobbs Lane, Suite 112, Cherry Hill, NJ 8034 US
Second Address: Metro Office Park Calle#1 Lote#6, Suite 203, Guaynabo, PR 00968-1705
(323) 957-8701, (800) 275-6437, (787) 793-0348; *Fax:* (323) 933-4953, (787) 793-0371,(609) 569-7295
www.lkkgroup.com
License: Charlotte Amalie, VI held by Storefront Television (acq 9-30-2004; $600,000); *Washington Law Firm:* Dow, Lohnes & Albertson
Nat'l Network: CBS
Keith Bass, General Manager

WZVI *Digital Channel:* 43; *Virtual Channel:* 43; 1.4 kw; 92 ft.; N18 20 43 W64 55 45; *Rebroadcasting:* WSVI (Christiansted) 100%
Mailing Address: C/O Thomas J. Dougherty, Jr., 1301 K St., NW Ste.900 East, Washington, DC 20005 US
Second Address: Barren Spot, Village Mall, downstairs, Kingshill, VI 851
(340) 778-5008; *Fax:* (340) 778-5011
www.wsvi.tv
channel8@wsvitv.com
License: Charlotte Amalie, VI held by Marri Broadcasting LP.
Nat'l Network: ABC
David Lampel, President
Glen Dratte, General Manager
Chester Benjamin, Chief Engineer

Christiansted

WCVI-TV *Digital Channel:* 23; *Virtual Channel:* 39; 0.659 kw; 407 ft.; N17 44 53 W64 43 40
PO B. 24027, St. Croix, VI 00824 US
(340) 718-9927; *Fax:* (340) 718-0712
www.wcvi.tv
License: Christiansted, Saint Croix County, VI held by Virgin Blue Inc.
Nat'l Network: CW
Victor Gold, General Manager
Marty Adamshick, Programming Director

WSVI *Digital Channel:* 20; *Virtual Channel:* 8; 1.1 kw; 951 ft.; N17 45 21 W64 47 56
Mailing Address: PO Box 8, Abc, Christiansted, VI 0823 US
Second Address: Barren Spot, Village Mall, downstairs, Kingshill, VI 851
(340) 778-5008; *Fax:* (340) 778-5011
www.wsvi.tv
channel8@wsvitv.com
License: Christiansted, Saint Croix County, VI held by Alpha Broadcasting Corp.
Washington Law Firm: Marmet & McCombs
Nat'l Network: ABC; *Nat'l Reps:* Roslin
Foreign Language Programming
David Lampel, CEO
Glen Dratte, General Manager
Chester Benjamin, Chief Engineer

Virginia

Charlottesville, VA (DMA 183)

WCAV *Digital Channel:* 19; *Virtual Channel:* 19; 155 kw; 1068 ft.; N37 59 3 W78 28 52
999 2nd St. SE, Charlottesville, VA 22902 USA
(434) 242-1919; *Fax:* (434) 220-0398
www.newsplex.com
License: Charlottesville, Albemarle County, VA held by Gray Television Licensee LLC
Group Owner: Gray Television Inc.; (acq 5-28-2004; $1 million for CP).
Nat'l Network: CBS
Jorma Tuomisto, Operations Dir
Jay Barton, VP/General Manager
Eric Krebs, General Sales Mgr
Joey Kinsley, Promotions & Marketing Director
Val Thompson, News Director

***WHTJ** *Digital Channel:* 46; *Virtual Channel:* 41; 165 kw; 1088 ft.; N37 58 59 W78 29 2; *Rebroadcasting:* Rebroadcasts WCVE-TV Richmond.
23 Sesame Street, North Chesterfield, VA 23235 US
(804) 320-1301, (800) 476-2357, (800) 476-8440; *Fax:* (804) 320-8729
www.ideastations.org
License: Charlottesville, Charlottesville City County, VA held by Commonwealth Public Broadcsting Corp
Washington Law Firm: Wiley, Rein & Fielding
Nat'l Network: PBS
Cynthia Bailey, Chairman
A. Curtis Monk, CEO/President
John Felton, General Manager
Lisa Tait, General Sales Mgr
Gwynne Brown, Production Services
Marshall Lloyd, Website Inquiries
Janet Campbell, Closed Captioning
WayneFarrar, News Inquiries
Michael Bisceglia, Vice-Chair

WVIR-TV *Digital Channel:* 32; *Virtual Channel:* 29; 1000 kw; 1207 ft.; N37 59 2 W78 28 53
503 E. Market St., Charlottesville, VA 22902 US
(434) 220-2900; *Fax:* (434) 220-2904
www.nbc29.com
newsdesk@nbc29.com
License: Charlottesville, Charlottesville City County, VA held by Virginia Broadcasting Corp.
Group Owner: Waterman Broadcasting Corp.; *Washington Law Firm:* Fletcher, Heald, & Hildreth
Nat'l Network: NBC/CW; CW; *Nat'l Reps:* Continental Television Sales; *Wire Services:* AP
Size of News Staff: 50; *Hours of Local News Weekly:* news progmg 32 hrs wkly
Harold Wright, Operations Dir
Jim Fernald, General Sales Mgr
Ralph Tobias, Promotions Manager
Neal Bennett, News Director
Bob Jenkins, Chief Engineer

Harrisonburg, VA (DMA 177)

WHSV *Digital Channel:* 49; *Virtual Channel:* 3; 832 kw vis, 432 kw aur; ant 2,130t/337g; N38 36 05 W78 37 57; *Population Served:* 350,000
50 N Main St., Harrisonburg, VA 22802 USA
(540) 433-9191; *Fax:* (540) 433-4028
www.whsv.com
whsv@whsv.com
License: Harrisonburg, Rockingham County, VA held by Gray Television Licensee LLC
Group Owner: Gray Television Inc.; (acq 8-29-2002; grpsl).;
Washington Law Firm: Wiley, Rein LLP
Nat'l Network: ABC
Size of News Staff: 18; *Hours of Local News Weekly:* news progmg 16 hrs wkly
Tim Merritt, Sales

***WVPT** *Digital Channel:* 11; *Virtual Channel:* 51; 10 kw; 2231 ft.; N38 9 54 W79 18 51
847 MLK, Jr. Way, Harrisonburg, VA 22801-3063 US
(540) 434-5391, (8000 345-9878; *Fax:* (540) 434-7084
www.wvpt.net
wvptcomments@wvpt.net
License: Staunton, Staunton City County, VA held by Shenandoah Valley ETV Corp
Washington Law Firm: Covington & Burling
Nat'l Network: PBS
Neal Menefee, Chairman
Tony Mancari, COO
David Mullins, President & General Manager
Tony Mancari, Chief Operating Office
George Lilly, Creative Services Manager
John Harper, Studio Supervisor
George Lily, Creative ServicesManager
Michael Hawkins, Corporate Support Representative, Harrisonburg
Anne Jolly, Corporate Support Representative, Charlottesville
Donna McCurdy, Vice-Chairman
Phillip Stone, Treasurer

Norfolk-Portsmouth-Newport News, VA (DMA 42)

WAVY-TV *Digital Channel:* 31; *Virtual Channel:* 10; 1000 kw; 919 ft.; N36 49 14 W76 30 41
Mailing Address: 200 Crescent Court, Suite 200, Dallas, TX 75201 US
Second Address: 300 WAVY St., Portsmouth, VA 23704
(757) 393-1010; *Fax:* (757) 399-7628
www.wavy.com
newsdesk@wavy.com
License: Portsmouth, Portsmouth City County, VA held by LIN License Company LLC
Group Owner: LIN Media; (acq 12-16-97; grpsl).; *Washington Law Firm:* Covington & Burling
Nat'l Network: NBC; *Nat'l Reps:* Petry Television Inc.; *Wire Services:* AP
Size of News Staff: 80; *Hours of Local News Weekly:* news progmg 31 hrs wkly
Doug Davis, President
John Cochran, General Sales Mgr
Eather White, Programming Director
Judy Triska, Promotions Manager
Mark Johnson, Engineering Dir
Joshua N. Pila, Senior Counsel

WGNT *Digital Channel:* 50; *Virtual Channel:* 27; 800 kw; 866 ft.; N36 48 43 W76 27 45
720 Boush St., Norfolk, VA 23510 USA
(757) 446-1000
wgnt.com
License: Portsmouth, Portsmouth City County, VA held by Local TV Virginia License LLC
Group Owner: Dreamcatcher Broadcasting LLC
Nat'l Network: The CW Network; *Nat'l Reps:* Harrington, Righter & Parsons
Cindi Dove, Director of Sales

***WHRO-TV** *Digital Channel:* 16; *Virtual Channel:* 15; 2,630 kw vis, 263 kw aur; 964t/964g; N36 48 32 W76 30 13; *Not on Air/Target Date:* DTV on Air 2/5/2001 ; *Population Served:* 707,750
5200 Hampton Boulevard, Norfolk, VA 23508
(757) 889-9400; *Fax:* (757) 489-0007
www.whro.org
info@whro.org
License: Hampton-Norfolk, Hampton City County, VA held by Hampton Roads Educ. Telecommunications Association Inc
Washington Law Firm: Dow-Lohnes

Nat'l Network: PBS
Size of News Staff: 2; *Hours of Local News Weekly:* news progmg 1 hr wkly
Bert Schmidt, CEO/President
Doug Weiss, VP of Operations
Virginia Thumm, VP/Development
Dwight Davis, Program Director
Bobbie Fisher, Promotions Manager
Chris Gunnufsen, Engineering & IT
Tom Morehouse, CFO/ VP of Finance
Heather Mazzoni, Content Officer
Brian Callahan, Chief Education Officer
Mark Burnett, Dir. Of Production & Media Services
Jenie Hill, Dir. of Traffic
Jan Johnson, Development Officer

WPXV-TV *Digital Channel:* 46; 1,000 kw vis; ant 508t; N36 48 31 W76 30 13
3702 C Nansemond Pkwy., Suffolk, VA 23435 USA
(212) 757-3100; *Fax:* (646) 597-5903
www.iontelevision.com
michaelhubner@ionmedia.com
License: Norfolk, VA held by ION Media License Company, LLC.
Group Owner: ION Media Networks Inc.; (acq 12-18-97; $14.75 million)
Nat'l Network: ION Television
Brandon Burgess, Chairman

WTKR *Digital Channel:* 40; *Virtual Channel:* 3; 950 kw; 1237 ft.; N36 48 31 W76 30 13
720 Boush St., Norfolk, VA 23510 USA
(757) 446-1000
wtkr.com
License: Norfolk, Norfolk City County, VA held by Local TV Virginia License LLC
Group Owner: Dreamcatcher Broadcasting LLC; *Washington Law Firm:* Reed, Smith, Shaw & McClay
Nat'l Network: CBS
Cindi Dove, Director of Sales

WTPC-TV *Digital Channel:* 7; 5,000 kw vis; ant 1,017t/1,014g; N36 48 31 W76 30 12
PO Box A, Santa Ana, CA 92711
(714) 832-2950, (714) 731-1000, (888) 731-1000
www.tbn.org
whrepa@tbn.org
License: Virginia Beach, Virginia Beach County, VA held by Copeland Channel 21 LLC
J. R. Brestin, Station Manager
Mike Cochran, Engineering Dir

WTVZ-TV *Digital Channel:* 33; *Virtual Channel:* 33; 960 kw; 1232 ft.; N36 48 31 W76 30 13
Mailing Address: 900 Granby St., Norfolk, VA 23510 US
Second Address: 10706 Beaver Dam Rd., Hunt Valley, MD 21030
(757) 622-3333; *Fax:* (757) 623-1541
www.mytvz.com
License: Norfolk, VA held by WTVZ Licensee LLC
Group Owner: Sinclair Broadcast Group Inc.; (acq 2-9-95; $47 million); *Washington Law Firm:* Gardner, Carton & Douglas
Nat'l Network: MYTV
Jeff McCallister, General Manager
Keith Chapman, Local Sales Manager
Bonnie Pihlcrantz, Marketing and Research Director
Julie R. Mantos, Account Executive
Kelley Vickers, Account Executive
Sheri Ainsley, Account Executive
JoAnneLindholm, Account Executive

WVBT *Digital Channel:* 29; *Virtual Channel:* 43; 1000 kw; 791 ft.; N36 49 14 W76 30 41
Mailing Address: 243 Wythe Street, Portsmouth, VA 23704 US
Second Address: One West Exchange Street, Suite 5A, Providence, RI 2903
(757) 393-4343; *Fax:* (757) 673-5300
www.fox43tv.com
doug.davis@wavy.com
License: Virginia Beach, Virginia Beach County, VA held by WAVY Broadcasting LLC.
Group Owner: LIN Media; (acq 1-9-2002; $4.25 million)
Nat'l Network: FOX; *Nat'l Reps:* Petry Television Inc.
Doug Davis, General Manager
John Cochrane, General Sales Mgr
Nick Hasenecz, Local Sales Director
Jane Plante, Local Sales Director
Andrew Hilton, National Sales Director
Eileen Baggett, National Sales Director

WVEC *Digital Channel:* 13; *Virtual Channel:* 13; 35 kw; 1,191 ft.; N36 48 59 W76 28 06; *Population Served:* 1,253,200
613 Woodis Ave., Norfolk, VA 23510-1017 US
(757) 625-1313; *Fax:* (757) 628-6533
www.13newsnow.com
news@wvec.com
License: Hampton, Hampton City County, VA held by WVEC Television Inc.
Group Owner: Tegna Media; (acq 12-23-2013).
Nat'l Network: ABC; *Nat'l Reps:* TeleRep; *Wire Services:* Reuters
Size of News Staff: 65; *Hours of Local News Weekly:* news progmg 24 hrs wkly
Kari Jacobs, President and General Manager
Eric Nichols, Director of Sales
Ed Tudor, Marketing/Programming/Community Relations
Doug Wieder, News Director
Keith O'Malley, Chief Engineer
Charlie Mirkle, Local Sales Manager
DaraKalvort, Local Sales Manager
Karen CF Vachon, National Sales Manager
Scott Cash, Sports Director
Christopher Collette, Digital/Mobile/Social Media Content

Richmond-Petersburg, VA (DMA 55)

***WCVE-TV** *Digital Channel:* 42; *Virtual Channel:* 23; 160 kw; 1136 ft.; N37 30 44 W77 36 4
23 Sesame Street, Richmond, VA 23235 US
(804) 320-1301, (800) 476-2357; *Fax:* (804) 320-8729
www.ideastations.org
info@ideastations.org
License: Richmond, Richmond City County, VA held by Commonwealth Public Broadcasting Corp
Washington Law Firm: Wiley, Rein & Fielding
Nat'l Network: PBS
Curtis Monk, President
Lisa Tait, General Sales Mgr
John Felton, Programming Director
Marshall Lloyd, Website Inquiries
Lanny Fields, Business Sponsors
Wayne Farrar, News Inquiries
Gwynne Brown, Production Services
JanetCampbell, Closed Captioning
Sharon Johnson, Day Sponsorship Information

***WCVE-TV** *Digital Channel:* 44; *Virtual Channel:* 57; 112 kw; 1076 ft.; N37 30 45 W77 36 5
23 Sesame Street, Richmond, VA 23235 US
(804) 320-1301, (800) 476-2357; *Fax:* (804) 320-8729
www.ideastations.org
info@ideastations.org
License: Richmond, Richmond City County, VA held by Commonwealth Public Broadcasting Corporation
Washington Law Firm: Wiley, Rein & Fielding
Nat'l Network: PBS
Curtis Monk, President
Lisa Tait, General Sales Mgr
John Felton, Programming Director
Marshall Lloyd, Website Inquiries
Lanny Fields, Business Sponsors
Wayne Farrar, News Inquiries
Gwynne Brown, Production Services
JanetCampbell, Closed Captioning
Sharon Johnson, Day Sponsorship Information

WRIC-TV *Digital Channel:* 22; *Virtual Channel:* 8; 850 kw; 1077 ft.; N37 30 45 W77 36 6
301 Arboretum Place, Richmond, VA 23236-3464 US
(804) 330-8888, (804) 330-8888, (804) 330-8814; *Fax:* (804) 330-8881, (804) 330-8883
www.wric.com
news@wric.com
License: Petersburg, Chesterfield County, VA held by Young Broadcasting of Richmond Inc.
Group Owner: Young Broadcasting Inc.; (acq 11-14-94; grpsl; *Washington Law Firm:* Brooks, Pierce, McLendon, Humphrey & Leonard
Nat'l Network: ABC; *Nat'l Reps:* Adam Young
Viki regan, General manager
Matthew Zelkird, Station Manager
David Weems, General Sales Manager
Bill Blank, Programming Manager
Steve Bays, Promotion Director
Kelly Woodard, News Director
Darrell Cheney, Chief Engineer
DonnaVilliott, Business Manager
Mike Laffey, Production Manager
Jim Vernier, Loca Sales Manager
Dixon Johnston, Creative Services Director

WRLH-TV *Digital Channel:* 26; *Virtual Channel:* 35; 800 kw; 1075 ft.; N37 30 45 W77 36 5
1925 Westmoreland St., Richmond, VA 23230 US
(804) 358-3535; *Fax:* (804) 358-1495
www.foxrichmond.com
newsroom@nbc12.com
License: Richmond, Henrico County, VA held by WRLH Licensee LLC
Group Owner: Sinclair Broadcast Group Inc.; (acq 12-10-01; grpsl).; *Washington Law Firm:* Arter & Hadden
Nat'l Network: FOX; MyNetworkTV
Size of News Staff: 15; *Hours of Local News Weekly:* news progmg 3 hrs wkly
Tim Perry, General Manager
Doug Pasquinelli, Local Sales Manager
Mark Bartholomew, Promotions Manager
Steve Hardy, Chief Engineer
Donna Brady, Accounting Manager
Jay Endicott, Production Manager
Virginia Kenney, CommunityRelations Manager

WTVR *Digital Channel:* 25; *Virtual Channel:* 6; 410 kw; 1138 ft.; N37 30 45 W77 36 5
3301 W Broad St., Richmond, VA 23230 USA
(804) 254-3600; *Fax:* (804) 254-3697
wtvr.com
newstips@wtvr.com
License: Richmond, Richmond City County, VA held by WTVR License LLC
Group Owner: Tribune Media; *Washington Law Firm:* Dow Lohnes PLLC
Nat'l Network: CBS; *Nat'l Reps:* TeleRep; *Wire Services:* AP
Stephen Hayes, General Manager
Dee Davies, General Sales Mgr
Shannon Sivils, Promotions Director
Sheryl Barnhouse, News Director
Roger Katchen, Chief Engineer

WUPV *Digital Channel:* 47; *Virtual Channel:* 65; 1,000 kw ERP; 219m/153m AGL; N37 44 31 W77 15 15; *Population Served:* 1,362,000
5710 Midlothian Turnpike, Richmond, VA 23225
804-230-1212; *Fax:* 804-230-7059
www.cwrichmond.tv
programming@cwrichmond.tv
License: Ashland, Hanover County, VA held by WUPV License Subsidiary LLC
Group Owner: American Spirit Media; April 2011
Nat'l Network: CW (Ch 65.1); Bounce TV (Ch 65.2); *Nat'l Reps:* TeleRep
Size of News Staff: 30; *Hours of Local News Weekly:* 2.5
Rosalie Drake, General Manager
Rosalie Drake, General Sales Mgr
Blake Peddicord, Program Coordinator
Nancy Kent Smith, News Director
Bruce Tinoco, Engineering Dir
Rob Whitley, Chief Engineer
Chris Thomas, News anchor

WWBT *Digital Channel:* 12; *Virtual Channel:* 12; 26 kw; 794 ft.; N37 30 23 W77 30 12
Mailing Address: 5710 Midlothian Turnpike, Richmond, VA 23225 US
Second Address: PO Box 12, Richmond, VA 23218
(804) 230-1212; *Fax:* (804) 230-2793
www.nbc12.com
newsroom@nbc12.com
License: Richmond, Richmond City County, VA held by WWBT License Subsidiary LLC.
Group Owner: Raycom Media Inc.; (acq 3-31-2008; grpsl); *Washington Law Firm:* Covington & Burling
Nat'l Network: NBC
Donald S. Richards, Operations Dir
Kym Grinnage, VP/ General Manager
M. Kym Grinnage, General Sales Mgr
Nancy Kent, News Director
Curt Autry, Reporter & Anchor
Kelly Avellino, Multimedia Journalist
Matt Boyce, Special projectsProducer & Photojournalist
Ray Daudani, Dir. Of New Media
Jim Duncan, Chief meterologist
Jessica Jaglois, General Assignment Reporter

Roanoke-Lynchburg, VA (DMA 67)

***WBRA-TV** *Digital Channel:* 3; *Virtual Channel:* 15; 7.25 kw; 2028 ft.; N37 11 46 W80 9 17
Mailing Address: 1215 McNeil Dr. S.W., Roanoke, VA 24015 US
Second Address: Blue Ridge PBS, 1215 McNeil Dr. S.W., Roanoke, VA 24015
(540) 344-0991, (888) 332-7788; *Fax:* (540) 344-2148
www.blueridgepbs.org
info@blueridgepbs.org

License: Roanoke, Roanoke City County, VA held by Blue Ridge Public Television Inc
Nat'l Network: PBS
Dr. Jack Lewis, Chairman
Will Anderson, VP/COO
James Baum, President
Will Anderson, VP/Chief Operating Officer
Sherry Spradlin, Programming/Closed Captioning
David Spruell, Engineering
Erwin Roman, Chief Engineer
Deborah Stone,Corporate Support
Carol Jennings, Production
Rita Thurman, Human Resource
Rose Martin, Ed.D., Corporate Support
Marsha Combs, Vice-Chair
Brenda Collins, Secretay-Treasurer

WDBJ *Digital Channel:* 18; *Virtual Channel:* 7; 675 kw; 1988 ft.; N37 11 42 W80 9 23
2807 Hershberger Rd., Roanoke, VA 24017 US
(540) 344-7000, (800) 777-9325; *Fax:* (540) 344-5097
www.wdbj7.com
news@wdbj7.com
License: Roanoke, Roanoke City County, VA held by WDBJ Television Inc.
Group Owner: Schurz Communications Inc.; (acq 11-1-69; $8.2 million; *Washington Law Firm:* Wilmer Cutler Pickering Hale and Dorr
Nat'l Network: CBS; MyNetworkTV; *Nat'l Reps:* Harrington, Righter & Parsons; *Wire Services:* UPI; AP
Size of News Staff: 48; *Hours of Local News Weekly:* news progmg 18 hrs wkly
Jeffrey A. Marks, President/General Manager
Kelly Zuber, Operations Dir
Lolly Quigley, General Sales Mgr
Mike Bell, Programming Director
Kelly Zuber, News Director
Alan Novitsky, Engineering Dir
Brian Boush, National SalesManager
Marilyn Brock, Treasurer/Business Manager
Tim Saunders, Bureau Chief
Orlando Salinas, Bureau Chief
Justin Ward, Bureau Chief
Lindsey Anderson, News Team

WFXR *Digital Channel:* 17; *Virtual Channel:* 27; 2,690 kw vis, 269 kw aur; ant 1,991t/200g; N37 11 47 W80 09 15; *Population Served:* 206,000
2618 Colonial Ave. SW., Roanoke, VA 24015 US
www.virginiafirst.com
License: Roanoke, Roanoke County, VA held by Nexstar Broadcasting Inc.
Group Owner: Nexstar Broadcasting Group Inc.; (acq 2014); *Washington Law Firm:* Birch, Horton, Bittner & Cherot
Nat'l Network: Fox; CW
Size of News Staff: 2; *Hours of Local News Weekly:* news progmg 27 hrs wkly
Arika Zink, General Manager
Ralph Claussen, General Sales Mgr

WPXR-TV *Digital Channel:* 36; 700 kw vis; ant 2,043t/180g; N37 11 37 W80 09 25; *Population Served:* 369,000
401 3rd St. SW, Roanoke, VA 24011 USA
(540) 857-0038; *Fax:* (540) 345-8568
www.iontelevision.com
michaelhubner@ionmedia.com
License: Roanoke, VA held by ION Media License Company, LLC
Group Owner: ION Media Networks Inc.; (acq 10-28-97).
Nat'l Network: ION Television
Brandon Burgess, Chairman

WSET-TV *Digital Channel:* 13; *Virtual Channel:* 13; 28.7 kw; 2,050t/1,240g; N37 18 54 W79 38 06; *Population Served:* 1,023,000
2320 Langhorne Rd., Lynchburg, VA 24501
(434) 528-1313; *Fax:* (434) 847-0458
www.wset.com
comments@wset.com
License: Lynchburg, Campbell County, VA held by WSET Licensee LLC
Group Owner: Sinclair Broadcast Group Inc.; (acq 7-29-2013; grpsl); *Washington Law Firm:* Sidley, Austin, LLP
Nat'l Network: ABC; RTV; WeatherNation; *Nat'l Reps:* Continental Television Sales; *Wire Services:* AP; ABC
Size of News Staff: 41; *Hours of Local News Weekly:* news progmg 18 hrs wkly
K.C. Spiron, Director of Operations and Engineering
George Kayes, General Manager
Leesa Wilcher, General Sales Mgr
John Crumpler, Promotional Marketing Coordinator
Len Stevens, News Director
Willis Little, Chief Engineer
D.H.Powell, Local Sales Manager
Mark Allen, Local Sales Manager
Anita Grandeo, Digital Sales Manager
Rhonda Cantrell, Sales and Marketing Coordinator
Nancy Johnson, National Sales Coordinator

WSLS-TV *Digital Channel:* 30; *Virtual Channel:* 10; 1000 kw; 1942 ft.; N37 12 3 W80 8 54
PO Box 10, Roanoke, VA 24022-0010 US
(540) 981-9110,540-981-9126; *Fax:* (540) 343-3157/(540)343-2059
www.wsls.com
news@wsls.com
License: Roanoke, Roanoke City County, VA held by Media General Broadcasting Inc.
Group Owner: Media General Broadcast Group; (acq 3-21-97; grpsl).; *Washington Law Firm:* Wiley, Rein & Fielding
Nat'l Network: NBC
Size of News Staff: 33; *Hours of Local News Weekly:* news progmg 15 hrs wkly
Kathy Mohn, Operations Dir
Bill Norris, General Sales Manager
Daniel Coyle, Promotions Manager
Melissa Stacy, News director
Scott Martin, National Sales Manager
Robert Kerry, Operations Vice President

WWCW *Digital Channel:* 20; *Virtual Channel:* 21; 916 kw; 1641 ft.; N37 19 14 W79 37 58
2618 Colonial Ave. S.W., Roanoke, VA 24015 US
(540) 344-2127
www.virginiafirst.com
License: Lynchburg, VA held by Nexstar Broadcasting Inc.
Group Owner: Nexstar Broadcasting Group Inc.; (acq 2014); *Washington Law Firm:* Birch, Horton, Bittner & Cherot
Nat'l Network: FOX; CW
Size of News Staff: 2; *Hours of Local News Weekly:* news progmg one hr wkly
Arika Zink, General Manager
Ralph Claussen, General Sales Mgr

Tri-Cities, TN-VA (DMA 98)

WCYB-TV *Digital Channel:* 5; *Virtual Channel:* 5; 29.9 kw; 2438 ft.; N36 26 58 W82 6 29
101 Lee Street, Bristol, VA 24201 US
(276) 821-9296, (276) 645-1555; *Fax:* (276) 645-1519
www.wcyb.com
License: Bristol, Washington County, VA held by BlueStone License Holdings Inc.
Group Owner: Bonten Media Group LLC; (acq 5-31-2007; grpsl); *Washington Law Firm:* Covington & Burling LLP
Nat'l Network: NBC & CW (DIGIT; CW; Fox
Conie McCully, CFO
Jack D. Dempsey, General Manager & VP
Jerry Witt, Station Manager
Candy Crigger, Director of Sales
Cris Aguilar, Program manager
Tony Venable, Promotions Manager
Ken Smith, News Director
Tom Cupp, ChiefEngineer
Bill Rambo, New Media Manager
Tammy Vaughan, Market Controller
Cris Aguilar, Traffic Manager
Terry Radnocozi, Asst. News Director
Preston Ayres, News Team
Samantha Kozsey, News Team

WLFG *Digital Channel:* 49; *Virtual Channel:* 68; 1000 kw; 2172 ft.; N36 49 47 W82 4 45
Mailing Address: PO Box 1867, Abingdon, VA 24212 US
Second Address: 8594 Hidden Valley Rd, Abingdon, VA 24210
(888) 275-9534,(276) 676-3806; *Fax:* (276) 676-3572
www.livingfaithtv.com
shelia@livingfaithtv.com
License: Grundy, Buchanan County, VA held by Living Faith Ministries Inc
Nat'l Network: REL
Michael Smith, CEO
Lisa Smith, Operations Dir
Wayne Price, Engineering Dir
Sue Howington, Traffic Manager

***WMSY-TV** *Digital Channel:* 42; *Virtual Channel:* 52; 100 kw; 1470 ft.; N36 54 7 W81 32 32
Mailing Address: P. O. Box 13246, Roanoke, VA 24032 US
Second Address: 1215 McNeil Dr. S. W., Roanoke, VA 24015
(540) 344-0991, (888) 332-7788; *Fax:* (540) 344-2148
www.blueridgepbs.com
info@blueridgepbs.org
License: Marion, Smyth County, VA held by Blue Ridge Public Television Inc
Nat'l Network: PBS
Greg Feldman, Chairman
Will Anderson, VP/ COO
William Anderson, Operations Dir
Kate Foreman, General Sales Mgr
Sherry Spradlin, Programming/ Closed Captioning
David Spruell, Engineering
Anita Sims, CFO
Carol Jennings,Production
Deborah Stone, Corporate Support
TRitaThurman, HR
Suzanna Cory, Membership
Rose Martin, Corporate Support

***WSBN-TV** *Digital Channel:* 32; *Virtual Channel:* 47; 100 kw; 1939 ft.; N36 53 53 W82 37 21
Mailing Address: 1215 McNeil Dr. S.W., Roanoke, VA 24015 US
Second Address: 1215 McNeil Dr. S.W., Roanoke, VA 24015
(540) 344-0991, (888) 332-7728; *Fax:* (540) 344-2148
www.blueridgepbs.org
info@blueridgepbs.org
License: Norton, Wise County, VA held by Blue Ridge Public Television Inc
Nat'l Network: PBS
Javk Lewis, Chairman
Will Anderson, VP/ COO
Barbara Spencer, Operations Dir
Kate Foreman, General Sales Mgr
Sherry Spradlin, Programming/ Closed Captioning
David Spruell, Engineering
Rita Thurman, Engineering
Carol Jennings,Production
Deborah Stone, Corporate Support
Suzanna Cory, Membership
Robin Woolbirght, Corporate Support Manager
Rose Martin, Corporate Support
Marsha Combs, Vice Chairman

Washington, DC (Hagerstown, MD) (DMA 7)

***WNVC** *Digital Channel:* 24; *Virtual Channel:* 30; 160 kw; 725 ft.; N38 52 28 W77 13 24
8101 A. Lee Highway, Falls Church, VA 22042 US
(703) 770-7100
www.mhznetworks.org
viewerservices@mhznetworks.org
License: Fairfax, Fairfax County, VA held by Commonwealth Public Broadcasting Corp.
(acq 6-4-2004); *Washington Law Firm:* Wiley, Rein & Fielding
Nat'l Network: ETV
Fred Thomas, General Manager

***WNVT** *Digital Channel:* 30; *Virtual Channel:* 53; 160 kw; 751 ft.; N38 37 43 W77 26 21
8101 A. Lee Highway, Falls Church, VA 22042 US
(703) 770-7100
www.mhznetworks.org
viewerservices@mhznetworks.org
License: Goldvein, Fairfax County, VA held by Commonweath Public Broadcasting Corp
(acq 6-4-2004); *Washington Law Firm:* Wiley, Rein & Fielding
Nat'l Network: ETV
Fred Thomas, General Manager

***WVPY** *Digital Channel:* 21; 50 KW; ant 1,309t/89g; N38 57 36 W78 19 52; *Rebroadcasting:* Rebroadcasts WVPT Staunton 100%.; *Population Served:* 345,000
c/o WVPT, 847 MLK, Jr. Way, Harrisonburg, VA 22801
(540) 434-5391; *Fax:* (540) 434-7084
www.wvpt.net
License: Front Royal, Warren County, VA held by Shenandoah Valley Educational TV Corp
Washington Law Firm: Covington & Burling
Nat'l Network: PBS
Tony Mancari, COO
David Mullins, President/General Manager
George Lilly, Promotions Manager
John Harper, Engineering Dir

Washington

Portland, OR (DMA 25)

KPDX *Digital Channel:* 30; *Virtual Channel:* 49; 741 kW; 1732 ft.; N45 31 18 W122 44 57
14975 NW Greenbrier Pkwy, Beaverton, OR 97006-5731 USA
(503) 906-1249; *Fax:* (503) 548-6920
www.kptv.com
License: Vancouver, Clark County, WA held by KPTV-KPDX Broadcasting Corp.
Group Owner: Meredith Corp.; (acq 7-1-97; grpsl); *Washington Law Firm:* Dow, Lohnes & Albertson
Nat'l Network: MyNetworkTV; *Nat'l Reps:* TeleRep; *Wire Services:* AP
Adrienne Roark, General Manager
Denise Daniels, General Sales Mgr
Jamie Holmes, Programming Director
Corey Hanson, News Director

Seattle-Tacoma, WA (DMA 14)

KBCB *Digital Channel:* 19; *Virtual Channel:* 24; 165 kw; 2484 ft.; N48 40 46 W122 50 31; *Rebroadcasting:* ShopNBC
Mailing Address: 4164 Meridian St., Ste. 102, Bellingham, WA 98226 US
Second Address: 4164 MeridianSt., Suite 102, Bellingham, WA 98226
(360) 647-8842; *Fax:* (360) 647-9204
www.kbcbtv.com
License: Bellingham, Whatcom County, WA held by World Television of Washington LLC
Washington Law Firm: Wiley, Rein & Fielding
Nat'l Network: IND
Hours of Local News Weekly: News progmg 4 hrs wkly
Garry Spire, CEO
Paul Koplin, President
Brian Holton, Operations Dir
Andy Wilcoxson, Station Manager
Dewi Cashion, CFO

***KBTC-TV** *Digital Channel:* 27; *Virtual Channel:* 28; 100 kw; 771 ft.; N47 16 44 W122 30 42
2320 S. 19th St., Tacoma, WA 98405 US
(253) 680-7700, (888) 596-KBTC; *Fax:* (253) 680-7725
www.kbtc.org
kbtcproductions@kbtc.org
License: Tacoma, Pierce County, WA held by Bates Technical College
Nat'l Network: PBS
Brad Berger, President
Ed Ulman, Executive Director/General Manager
Phil Kane, Programming Director
Darin Gerchak, Director of Engineering
Sherri Stanton, Director of Development
Vicki Valdez, KBTC Financial Officer
Phil Kane,Manager of Programming and On-Air Promotion
Michael Peters, Creative Services Manager
Adrienne Loska, Manager of On-Air Fundraising
Brent Mason, Manager of Individual Giving

***KCKA** *Digital Channel:* 19; *Virtual Channel:* 15; 187 kw; 1138 ft.; N46 33 16 W123 3 26; *Rebroadcasting:* Rebroadcasts KBTC(TV) Tacoma.
2320 S. 19th St., Tacoma, WA 98405 US
(253) 680-7700, (888) 596-KBTC; *Fax:* (253) 680-7725
www.kbtc.org
kbtcproductions@kbtc.org
License: Centralia, Lewis County, WA held by Bates Technical College
(acq 11-29-91; *Washington Law Firm:* Akin, Gump, Strauss, Hauer & Feld
Nat'l Network: PBS
Ed Ulman, Executive Director/General Manager
Phil Kane, Programming & Promotions Manager
Darin Gerchak, Engineering Director
Darin Gerchak, Chief Engineer
Vicki Valdez, CFO
Michael Peters, Creative Services Manager
Brent Mason,Individual Giving Manager
Adrienne Loska, On-Air Fundraising Manager

KCPQ *Digital Channel:* 22; *Virtual Channel:* 13; 15 kW; 2001 ft.; N47 32 53 W122 48 22
1813 Westlake Ave. N, Seattle, WA 98109 USA
(206) 674-1313; *Fax:* (206) 674-1550
q13fox.com
tips@q13fox.com
License: Tacoma, Pierce County, WA held by Tribune Broadcasting Seattle LLC
Group Owner: Tribune Media; (acq 12-20-2007; grpsl).; *Ownership:* Tribune; *Washington Law Firm:* Sidley & Austin
Nat'l Network: FOX; *Nat'l Reps:* TeleRep; *Wire Services:* SportsTicker
Size of News Staff: 44; *Hours of Local News Weekly:* news progmg 21 hrs wkly
Adam Bischoff, General Sales Mgr
Sheri Liguori, Program Coordinator

***KCTS-TV** *Digital Channel:* 9; *Virtual Channel:* 9; 21.7 kw; 817 ft.; N47 36 58 W122 18 28
401 Mercer Street, Seattle, WA 98109 US
(206) 728-6463; *Fax:* (206) 443-6691
viewer@KCTS9.org
License: Seattle, King County, WA held by KCTS Television (acq 7-15-87).; *Washington Law Firm:* Dow, Lohnes & Albertson
Nat'l Network: PBS
Robert 'Rob' Dunlop, President & CEO
Randy Brinson, General Manager
Cliff Anderson, Engineering Dir
Amy Jolley, Legal Affairs Manager
Ray Kugler, Production Manager
April M. Collier, Vice President of Development
Tom Cohen, VicePresident of Content
Carlos Espinoza, VP, Marketing and Communications
Jabran Soubeih, Exe Director of Engineering & Technical Planning

KFFV *Digital Channel:* 44; 2,000 kw vis; ant 2,283t; N47 30 17 W121 58 06; *Population Served:* 3,000,000
9825 Willows Rd. NE., Suite 140, Redmond, WA 98032
(425) 497-1515; *Fax:* (425) 497-1616
www.npitv.com
License: Seattle, King County, WA
Group Owner: OTA Broadcasting; acq 12-24-92; *Ownership:* Dr Kenneth & Charlene Casey
Nat'l Network: Azteca America (Spanish)
Foreign Language Programming
Charlene Casey, CFO
Dr. Kenneth Casey, President

KING-TV *Digital Channel:* 48; *Virtual Channel:* 5; 960 kw; 784 ft.; N47 37 55 W122 20 59; *Population Served:* 3,848,400
333 Dexter Ave. N., Seattle, WA 98109 US
(206) 448-5555; *Fax:* (206) 448-3195
www.king5.com
License: Seattle, King County, WA held by King Broadcasting Co.
Group Owner: Tegna Media; *Washington Law Firm:* Wiley Rein
Nat'l Network: NBC; *Nat'l Reps:* TeleRep
Jim Rose, Vice President and Station Manager
Rick Swanson, Programming Director
Mark Ginther, News Director
Kathy Palmer, Chief Engineer

KIRO-TV *Digital Channel:* 39; *Virtual Channel:* 7; 1000 kw; 843 ft.; N47 38 1 W122 21 20
Mailing Address: 3773 Howard Hughes Parkway, Suite 300n, Las Vegas, NV 89109 US
Second Address: 2807 3rd Ave., Seattle, WA 98121
(206) 728-7777; *Fax:* (206) 728-8230
www.kirotv.com
scook@kirotv.com
License: Seattle, King County, WA held by KIRO-TV Inc.
Group Owner: Cox Media Group; (acq 4-16-97); *Washington Law Firm:* Dow, Lohnes & Alberterson, PLLC
Nat'l Network: CBS; *Nat'l Reps:* Harrington, Righter & Parsons
Size of News Staff: 115; *Hours of Local News Weekly:* news progmg 46 hrs wkly
Eric Lerner, General Manager
Kristin Reese, General Sales Mgr
Therese Weiler, Programming Director
Todd Mokhtari, News Director
John Walters, Engineering Dir
Pat Otis, Chief Engineer
Sandy Zogg, General Sales Manager
DaveBlakely, National Sales Manager
Holly Grambihler, Regional Sales Manager
Amy Clancy, Anchor & Reporter
Alison Burns, Reporters
Sam Argier, Weather Team

KOMO-TV *Digital Channel:* 38; *Virtual Channel:* 4; 1000 kw; 850 ft.; N47 37 55 W122 21 9
Mailing Address: 140 4th Ave. N., Seattle, WA 98109 US
Second Address: 10706 Beaver Dam Rd., Hunt Valley, MD 21030
(206) 404-4000; *Fax:* (206) 404-4422
www.komonews.com
tips@komo4news.com
License: Seattle, King County, WA held by Sinclair Seattle Licensee LLC
Group Owner: Sinclair Broadcast Group Inc.; (acq 8-8-2013; grpsl).; *Washington Law Firm:* Shaw Pittman
Nat'l Network: ABC; *Nat'l Reps:* Blair Television
Hours of Local News Weekly: news progmg 38 hrs wkly
Janene Drafs, General Manager
Ted Davis, General Sales Mgr
Holly Gauntt, News Director
Lee Wood, Chief Engineer
Scott Altus, Director of Creative Services and Marketing
Patty Dean, National Sales Manager
Troy Hill, Local SalesManager
Jacqueline Brackett, Local Sales Manager

KONG *Digital Channel:* 31; *Virtual Channel:* 16; 679 kw; 721 ft.; N47 37 55 W122 20 59
333 Dexter Ave. N., Seattle, WA 98109 US
(206) 448-5555; *Fax:* (206) 448-3167
www.king5.com
License: Everett, Snohomish County, WA held by KONG-TV Inc.
Group Owner: Tegna Media; *Washington Law Firm:* Thompson, Hine & Flory L
Hours of Local News Weekly: news progmg 22 hrs wkly
Jim Rose, Vice President and Station Manager
Rick Swanson, Programming Director
Mark Ginther, News Director

KSTW-TV *Digital Channel:* 11; *Virtual Channel:* 11; 100 kW; 610 ft.; N47 36 56 W122 18 29
1000 Dexter Ave. N, Suite 205, Seattle, WA 98109 USA
(206) 441-1111; *Fax:* (206) 861-8915
cwseattle.cbslocal.com
cw11@kstwtv.com
License: Tacoma, Pierce County, WA held by The CW Television Stations Inc.
Group Owner: CBS Television Stations Group
Nat'l Network: The CW Network
Bruno Cohen, President
Mark Boe, General Manager
Tom Spitz, Director of Program Operations
Ron Diotte, Chief Engineer

KTBW-TV *Digital Channel:* 14; *Virtual Channel:* 20; 90 kw; 1552 ft.; N47 32 50 W122 47 40
PO Box A, Santa Ana, CA 92711 US
(253) 927-7720,(253) 874-7420; *Fax:* (253) 874-7432
www.tbn.org
comments@tbn.org
License: Tacoma, Pierce County, WA held by Trinity Broadcasting of Washington.
Group Owner: Trinity Broadcasting Network
Nat'l Network: TRINITY BROADCA
Paul Crouch, President
Phyllis Smith, General Manager
Mary Jane Allen, Station Manager
Jan Crouch, Promotions Manager
Ken Howerton, Chief Engineer

KUNS-TV *Digital Channel:* 50; *Virtual Channel:* 51; 1000 kw; 800.5 ft.; N47 37 55 W122 21 9
140 4th Ave. N., Seattle, WA 98109 US
(206) 404-4877
www.kunstv.com
info@kunstv.com
License: Bellevue, King County, WA held by Sinclair Seattle Licensee LLC
Group Owner: Sinclair Broadcast Group Inc.; (acq 8-8-2013; grpsl)
Nat'l Network: UNIVISION
Foreign Language Programming
Janine Drafs, Vice President and General Manager
Houman Aliabadi, Sales Manager
Carmen Redd, Programming Manager
Holly Gauntt, News Director
Jefe Ingeniero, Chief Engineer
Teresa Jones, Sales
Ivan Rodriguez, Sales
Jose LuisGonzalez, Executive Producer

KVOS-TV *Digital Channel:* 35; *Virtual Channel:* 12; 580 kw; 2621 ft.; N48 40 50 W122 50 22
Mailing Address: 3111 Newmarket Street, Suite 108, Bellingham, WA 98226 US
Second Address: 3223 3rd Ave. South, Suite 200, Seattle, WA 98134
(360) 671-1212,(604) 681-1212 (sales); *Fax:* (360) 647-0824
metvnetwork.com
License: Bellingham, Whatcom County, WA
Group Owner: OTA Broadcasting; (acq 3-14-2008; grpsl);
Washington Law Firm: Covington & Burling
Nat'l Network: IND; *Nat'l Reps:* Airtime TV

Size of News Staff: 10; *Hours of Local News Weekly:* news progmg one hr wkly
Gary Nielsen, President
Dave Kerrigan, Operations Dir
Yvette Perez, Promotions Manager
Kathleen Choal, News Director

***KWDK** *Digital Channel:* 42; *Virtual Channel:* 56; 144 kw; 2280 ft.; N47 30 17 W121 58 6
Mailing Address: 3901 Hwy 121, Bedford, TX 76021 US
Second Address: PO Box 610546, Dallas, TX 75261-0546
(817) 571-1229; *Fax:* (817) 571-7458
www.daystar.com
Partners@Daystar.com
License: Tacoma, Pierce County, WA held by Puget Sound Educational TV Inc
Nat'l Network: REL
Marcus D. Lamb, Founder, President and CEO
Janet Suckow, Operations Dir
Jon Panzer, Station Manager
Shirley Schwarz, Programming Director

KWPX-TV *Digital Channel:* 33; 400 kw; N47 30 17 W121 58 06
8112-C 304th Ave. SE., Box 426, Preston, WA 98050 USA
(509) 340-3400; *Fax:* (509) 340-3417
www.iontelevision.com
michaelhubner@ionmedia.com
License: Bellevue, WA held by Ion Media License Company, LLC
Group Owner: ION Media Networks Inc.
Brandon Burgess, Chairman/CEO

KZJO *Digital Channel:* 25; *Virtual Channel:* 22; 5,000 kw vis, 501 kw aur; ant 890t/639g; N47 36 57 W122 18 26; *Population Served:* 3,516,000
1813 Westlake Ave. N, Seattle, WA 98109 USA
(206) 674-1313
joeswall.com
joeswallinfo@tribunemedia.com
License: Seattle, King County, WA held by Tribune Broadcasting Seattle LLC
Group Owner: Tribune Media; (acq 12-20-2007; grpsl);
Washington Law Firm: Dow Lohnes PLLC
Nat'l Network: MyNetworkTV; *Nat'l Reps:* TeleRep
Julie Ferkingstad, Program Coordinator

Spokane, WA (DMA 73)

KAYU-TV *Digital Channel:* 28; *Virtual Channel:* 28; 445 kw; 1972 ft.; N47 34 44 W117 17 46
4600 S. Regal Street, Spokane, WA 99223 US
(509) 448-2828; *Fax:* 509-448-3815
www.myfoxspokane.com
License: Spokane, Spokane County, WA held by Mountain Licenses L.P.
Group Owner: Northwest Broadcasting Inc.; (acq 1996; $6.44 million); *Washington Law Firm:* Leventhal, Senter and Lerman
Nat'l Network: FOX; *Nat'l Reps:* Millennium Sales & Marketing; *Wire Services:* AP
Hours of Local News Weekly: News progmg 8 hrs wkly
David Lockhert, Sales Manager
Ron Sweatte, Director of Engineering
Lynn Stryker, National Sales Manager
Gordy Cummings, Regional Sales Manager
Tom Holcomb, Local Sales Manager

***KCDT** ; *Virtual Channel:* 26; 12.3 kw vis, 1.2 kw aur; 1,525t; N47 43 54 W116 43 47; *Rebroadcasting:* Rebroadcasts KUID Moscow 100%.
Mailing Address: c/o KAID, 1455 N. Orchard St., Boise, ID 83706-2239
Second Address: Box 443101, University of Idaho, Moscow, ID 83844-3101
(208) 373-7220, (800) 543-6868
www.idahoptv.org
idptv@idahoptv.org
License: Coeur d'Alene, Kootenai County, ID held by State Board of Education, State of Idaho
Washington Law Firm: Fletcher, Heald & Hildreth
Nat'l Network: PBS
Peter Morrill, General Manager
Kris Freeland, Station Manager
Megan Griffin, General Sales Mgr
Ron Pisaneschi, Programming Director
Rich Van Genderen, Engineering Dir
Ken Segota, Chief Engineer

KGPX-TV *Digital Channel:* 34; 104 kw; ant 1,476t/535g; N47 35 57 W117 18 00
1201 W. Sprague Ave., Spokane, WA 99201 USA
(509) 340-3400; *Fax:* (509) 340-3417
www.iontelevision.com
License: Spokane, Spokane County, WA held by Ion Media Spokane License, Inc.
Group Owner: ION Media Networks Inc.
Brandon Burgess, Chairman/CEO

KHQ-TV *Digital Channel:* 15; *Virtual Channel:* 6; 1000 kw; 2142 ft.; N47 34 52 W117 17 47
Mailing Address: 1201 W. Sprague Ave., Spokane, WA 99201 USA
Second Address: P.O. Box 600, Spokane, WA 99210
(509) 448-6000
www.khq.com
q6news@khq.com
License: Spokane, Spokane County, WA held by KHQ Inc.
Group Owner: KHQ Inc.; *Washington Law Firm:* Skadden, Arps
Nat'l Network: NBC; *Nat'l Reps:* Blair Television
Size of News Staff: 52; *Hours of Local News Weekly:* news progmg 26 hrs wkly
Madison Callan, Producer

KQUP *Digital Channel:* 24; *Virtual Channel:* 24
1146 - 19th Street, N.W., Suite 200, Washington, DC 20036 US
(509) 924-5787; *Fax:* (509) 924-5789
License: Pullman, Whitman County, WA held by Word of God Fellowship Inc.
Nat'l Network: DAYSTAR
Rod Hall, General Manager

KREM *Digital Channel:* 20; *Virtual Channel:* 2; 893 kw; 2,103 ft.; N47 35 41 W117 17 53; *Population Served:* 174,500
4103 S. Regal St., Spokane, WA 99223 US
(509) 448-2000; *Fax:* (509) 448-6397
www.krem.com
newsdesk@krem.com
License: Spokane, Spokane County, WA held by King Broadcasting Co.
Group Owner: Tegna Media; (acq 12-23-2013); *Washington Law Firm:* Covington & Burling
Nat'l Network: CBS
Size of News Staff: 36; *Hours of Local News Weekly:* news progmg 17 hrs wkly
R.J. Merritt, General Manager
Diane Daugherty, Director of Sales
Christine Werfelmann, Program Coordinator
Dan Weig, Creative Services Director
Boyd Lundberg, Chief Engineer
Trinity Spencer, Assignment Manager
DJ Talarico, LocalSales Manager

KSKN *Digital Channel:* 36; *Virtual Channel:* 22; 1,000 kw; 2,041 ft.; N47 35 41 W117 17 53
4103 S. Regal St., Spokane, WA 99223 US
(509) 448-2000; *Fax:* (509) 448-6397
www.spokanescw22.com
License: Spokane, Spokane County, WA held by KSKN Television Inc.
Group Owner: Tegna Media; (acq 12-23-2013)
Nat'l Network: CW
Size of News Staff: 5; *Hours of Local News Weekly:* news progmg 6 hrs wkly
R.J. Merritt, General Manager
Diane Daugherty, Director of Sales
Christine Werfelmann, Program Coordinator
Dan Weig, Creative Services Director
Boyd Lundberg, Chief Engineer
Trinity Spencer, Assignment Manager
DJ Talarico, LocalSales Manager

***KSPS-TV** *Digital Channel:* 7; *Virtual Channel:* 7; 45.1 kw; 1831 ft.; N47 34 34 W117 17 58
3911 S Regal St., Spokane, WA 99223 US
(509) 354-7800; *Fax:* (509) 354-7757
www.ksps.org
ksps@ksps.org
License: Spokane, Spokane County, WA held by Spokane School District No. 81
Washington Law Firm: Garvey, Schubert & Barer
Nat'l Network: PBS
Lynn Veltrie, Operations Manager
Gary Stokes, General Manager
Patty Starkey, General Sales Mgr
Cary Balzer, Programming Director
Kerry Faggiano, Promotions Manager
Director of Development, Scott Tindall
Director of Membership

***KWSU-TV** *Digital Channel:* 10; *Virtual Channel:* 10; 6.2 kw; 1339 ft.; N46 51 43 W117 10 26
PO Box 642530, Pullman, WA 99164 US
(509) 335-6588; *Fax:* (509) 335-3772
www.kwsu.org
kwsutv@wsu.edu
License: Pullman, Whitman County, WA held by Washington State University
Washington Law Firm: Dow, Lohnes & Albertson
Nat'l Network: PBS
Sarah McDaniel, Operations Dir
Thomas Hungate, TV Manager
Linda Pasch, TV Account Manager
Don Peters, Project Manager
Kari Watkins, Production Coordinator

KXLY-TV *Digital Channel:* 13; *Virtual Channel:* 4; 46 kW; 3071 ft; N47 55 18 W117 6 52
500 W Boone, Spokane, WA 99201 USA
(509) 324-4000; *Fax:* (509) 328-5274
www.kxly.com
info@kxly.com
License: Spokane, Spokane County, WA held by Spokane Television, Inc.
Group Owner: Morgan Murphy Media; (acq 1-17-63; grpsl;
Washington Law Firm: Rini, Coran, PC
Nat'l Network: ABC; MyNetworkTV; *Nat'l Reps:* Continental Television Sales; *Wire Services:* AP
Hours of Local News Weekly: News progmg 19 hrs wkly

Yakima-Pasco-Richland-Kennewick, WA (DMA 114)

KAPP-TV *Digital Channel:* 14; *Virtual Channel:* 35; 160 kW; 942 ft; N46 31 56.4 W120 30 46.5
PO Box 1749 , Yakima, WA 98907 USA
(509) 453-0351; *Fax:* (509) 453-3623
www.yaktrinews.com
License: Yakima, Yakima County, WA held by Apple Valley Broadcasting Inc.
Group Owner: Morgan Murphy Media; *Washington Law Firm:* Manatt, Phelps & Phillips
Nat'l Network: ABC; MyNetworkTV
Size of News Staff: 11; *Hours of Local News Weekly:* 3
Brian Paul, General Manager
Suzanne Snyder, National Sales Manager
Shelley Ransier, General Sales Mgr
Mike Gonzalez, News Director
Neil Bennett, Chief Engineer

KEPR-TV *Digital Channel:* 18; *Virtual Channel:* 19; 83 kw; 1204 ft.; N46 5 51 W119 11 29
2807 W. Lewis St., Pasco, WA 99301 US
(509) 547-0547
www.keprtv.com
newsroom@keprtv.com
License: Pasco, Franklin County, WA held by Sinclair Yakima Licensee LLC
Group Owner: Sinclair Broadcast Group Inc.; (acq 8-8-2013; grpsl).; *Washington Law Firm:* Winthrope, Shaw, Pittman, LLP
Nat'l Network: CBS; CW; *Wire Services:* CBS; Pacifica Network News
Size of News Staff: 12; *Hours of Local News Weekly:* news progmg 17 hrs wkly
Cris Headley, Operations Administrator
David Praga, General Manager
John Mazza, Chief Engineer
Owen Mansfield, Creative Services Director
Randy Muszynski, Account Executive
Andrew Paye, Account Executive
Mary Mosman, AccountExecutive

KIMA-TV *Digital Channel:* 33; *Virtual Channel:* 29; 100 kw; 958 ft.; N46 31 58 W120 30 33
2801 Terrace Heights Dr., Yakima, WA 98901 US
(509) 575-0029
www.kimatv.com
tips@kimatv.com
License: Yakima, Yakima County, WA held by Sinclair Yakima Licensee LLC
Group Owner: Sinclair Broadcast Group Inc.; (acq 8-8-2013; grpsl); *Washington Law Firm:* Shaw Pittman
Nat'l Network: CBS; CW; *Nat'l Reps:* Petry Television Inc.; *Wire Services:* CBS; CNN; AP
Size of News Staff: 24; *Hours of Local News Weekly:* news progmg 15 hrs wkly
David Praga, General Manager
Bob Berry, Station Manager
Steve Crow, National Sales Manager
Dane Pierone, Promotions
Scott Stovall, News Director
Cliff Grady, Chief Engineer
Reed Hansen, Creative Services
Alan Sillence, SportsDirector

KNDO *Digital Channel:* 26; *Virtual Channel:* 25; 150 kw; 873 ft.; N46 6 12 W119 7 51.7
216 W. Yakima Ave., Yakima, WA 98902 US
(509) 225-2323; *Fax:* (509) 225-2330
www.nbcrightnow.com
news@kndo.com
License: Yakima, Yakima County, WA held by KHQ Inc.
Group Owner: KHQ Inc.; (acq 6-17-99; $22.25 million with KNDU(TV) Richland).
Nat'l Network: NBC
Size of News Staff: 9; *Hours of Local News Weekly:* news progmg 27 hrs wkly

KNDU *Digital Channel:* 26; *Virtual Channel:* 25; 150 kw; 1319 ft.; N46 6 12 W119 7 49; *Rebroadcasting:* Satellite of KNDO(TV) Yakima 94%.
3312 W. Kennewick Ave., Kennewick, WA 99336 US
(509)737-6725; *Fax:* (509) 737-6749
www.nbcrightnow.com
news@kndu.com
License: Richland, Benton County, WA held by KHQ Inc.
Group Owner: KHQ Inc.; (acq 6-17-99; $22.25 million with KNDO(TV) Yakima).; *Washington Law Firm:* Hogan & Hartson
Nat'l Network: NBC
Size of News Staff: 20; *Hours of Local News Weekly:* news progmg 22.5 hrs wkly

KORX-CA *Digital Channel:* 16; 1 kw; 3907 ft.; N46 59 3.9 W118 10 7.9
2807 W. Lewis St., Pasco, WA 93301 US
(509) 547-0547
www.kunwtv.com
kunwtv@kunwtv.com
License: Walla Walla, Walla Walla County, WA held by Sinclair Kennewick Licensee LLC
Group Owner: Sinclair Broadcast Group Inc.; (acq 8-8-2013; grpsl)
Nat'l Network: UNIVISION
Bob Berry, General Manager
Jon Snider, Director of Creative Services
Abigail Camilo, Producer

***KTNW** *Digital Channel:* 38; *Virtual Channel:* 31; 47.6 kw; 1184 ft.; N46 6 12 W119 7 40
P.O. Box 642530, Pullman, WA 99164-2530 US
(509) 335-6588, (800) 922-4220; *Fax:* (509) 335-3772
www.kwsu.org
License: Richland, Benton County, WA held by Washington State University
Washington Law Firm: Dow, Lohnes & Albertson
Nat'l Network: PBS
Sarah McDaniel, Operations Dir
Kari Watkins, Programming Director

KUNW-CD *Digital Channel:* 30; 15 kw; 2144 ft.; N46 31 58 W120 30 33
2801 Terrace Heights Dr., Yakima, WA 98901 US
(509) 575-0029
www.kunwtv.com
kunwtv@kunwtv.com
License: Yakima, Yakima County, WA held by Sinclair Kennewick Licensee LLC
Group Owner: Sinclair Broadcast Group Inc.; (acq 8-8-2013; grpsl)
Nat'l Network: UNIVISION; *Nat'l Reps:* Petry Television Inc.; *Wire Services:* CBS; CNN; AP
Bob Berry, General Manager
Jon Snider, Director of Creative Services
Abigail Camilo, Producer

KVEW *Digital Channel:* 44; *Virtual Channel:* 42; 160 kW; 1325 ft; N46 06 11.4 W119 08 0.6; *Rebroadcasting:* Satellite of KAPP Yakima.
601 N Edison, Kennewick, WA 99336 USA
(509) 735-8369; *Fax:* (509) 735-1836
www.yaktrinews.com
License: Kennewick, Benton County, WA held by Apple Valley Broadcasting Inc.
Group Owner: Morgan Murphy Media
Nat'l Network: ABC; MyNetworkTV
Brian Paul, General Manager
Suzanne Snyder, National Sales Manager
Shelley Ransier, General Sales Mgr
Mike Gonzalez, News Director
Neil Bennett, Chief Engineer

KVVK-CD *Digital Channel:* 15; 15 kw; 2324 ft.; N46 5 51 W119 11 29
2807 W. Lewis St., Pasco, WA 93301 US
(509) 547-0547
www.kunwtv.com
kunwtv@kunwtv.com
License: Kennewick, Benton County, WA held by Sinclair Kennewick Licensee LLC
Group Owner: Sinclair Broadcast Group Inc.; (acq 8-8-2013; grpsl)
Nat'l Network: UNIVISION
Bob Berry, General Manager
Jon Snider, Director of Creative Services
Abigail Camilo, Producer

***KYVE** *Digital Channel:* 21; *Virtual Channel:* 47; 50 kw; 919 ft.; N46 31 58 W120 30 33
12 South 2nd Street, Yakima, WA 98902 US
(509) 452-4700; *Fax:* (509) 452-4704
www.kyve.org
License: Yakima, Yakima County, WA held by KCTS Television (acq 8-1-94; *Washington Law Firm:* Schwartz, Woods & Miller
Nat'l Network: PBS
Bill Mohler, CEO
Mark Leonard, General Manager
Rod Venable, Station Manager
Brenda Setterlund, General Sales Mgr
Chris Splawn, Programming Director
Ken Messer, Station Manager

West Virginia

Bluefield-Beckley-Oak Hill, WV (DMA 159)

WLFB *Digital Channel:* 40; *Virtual Channel:* 40; 1000 kw; 1309 ft.; N37 13 12 W81 15 20; *Rebroadcasting:* Satellite of WLFG(TV) Grundy, VA.
Mailing Address: PO Box 1867, Abingdon, VA 24212 US
Second Address: 8594 Hidden Valley Rd., Abingdon, VA 24210
(888) 275-9534,(276) 676-3806; *Fax:* (276) 676-3572
www.livingfaithtv.com
shelia@livingfaithtv.com
License: Bluefield, Mercer County, WV held by Living Faith Ministries Inc
Nat'l Network: IND
Michael Smith, CEO

WOAY-TV *Digital Channel:* 50; *Virtual Channel:* 4; 660 KW; 656 ft.; N37 57 26 W81 9 3; *Population Served:* 150,000
PO Box 3001, 7113 Legends Highway, Oak Hill, WV 25901 US
(304) 469-3361; *Fax:* (304) 465-1420
www.woay.com
news@woay.com
License: Oak Hill, Fayette County, WV held by Thomas Broadcasting Co
Ownership: Thomas Broadcasting Co.; *Washington Law Firm:* Fletcher, Heald & Hildreth
Nat'l Network: ABC; *Nat'l Reps:* Continental Television Sales
Size of News Staff: 15; *Hours of Local News Weekly:* 15
Robert Thomas III, President
Al Marra, General Manager
Joetta Kelly-Oliver, General Sales Mgr
Al Marra, Programming Director
Keith Conner, News Director
Bob Gauther, Engineering Dir
Jennifer Peake, Traffic Manager
RobertRussell Thomas, Jr., Founder

***WSWP-TV** *Digital Channel:* 10; *Virtual Channel:* 9; 24 kw; 1043 ft.; N37 53 46 W80 59 21
600 Capitol Street, Charleston, WV 25301 US
(304) 556-4900, (888) 596-9729; *Fax:* (304) 556-4982
www.wvpubcast.org
audienceservices@wvpubcast.org
License: Grandview, Raleigh County, WV held by West Virginia Educational Broadcasting Authority
Nat'l Network: PBS
Hours of Local News Weekly: News progmg 5 hrs wkly
Dennis Atkins, CEO
Bill Acker, Operations Dir
Mike Meador, Station Manager
Marilyn DiVita, General Sales Mgr

WVNS-TV *Digital Channel:* 8; *Virtual Channel:* 59; 3.68 kw; 1893 ft.; N37 46 22 W80 42 25
Mailing Address: 141 Old Cline Rd., Ghent, WV 25843 US
Second Address: 141 Old Cline Rd., Ghent, WV 25843
(304) 929-6420, (304) 787-6420; *Fax:* (304) 787-2440
www.cbs59.com
news@wvnstv.com
License: Lewisburg, Greenbrier County, WV held by West Virginia Media Holdings LLC
Group Owner: West Virginia Media Holdings LLC; (acq 1-9-2003).; *Washington Law Firm:* Borsari & Paxson
Nat'l Network: CBS; Fox; *Nat'l Reps:* Petry Television Inc.
Marstow Becker, Chairman
Bray Cary, CEO
Chris Leister, Operations Dir
Mark Ford, General Sales Manager
Mark Durham, News Director
Ken McCrimmon, Chief Engineer
Charlie Dusic, CFO
Valerie Sullivan, Executive Producer
SpencerAdkins, Chief Meterologist
Sarah Pisciuneri, News Team
Don Thorn, News Team

WVVA *Digital Channel:* 46; *Virtual Channel:* 6; 1000 kw; 1220 ft.; N37 15 20.7 W81 10 54
Mailing Address: 3052 Big Laurel Highway, Bluefield, WV 24701 US
Second Address: 101 Main St., Beckley, WV 25801
(304) 325-5487, (304) 253-0006; *Fax:* (304) 327-5586
www.wvva.com
fbrady@wvva.com
License: Bluefield, Mercer County, WV held by WVVA TV Inc.
Group Owner: Quincy Newspapers Inc.; (acq 5-1-79; $8 million);
Washington Law Firm: Wilkinson, Barker, Knauer & Quinn
Nat'l Network: NBC; CW; *Nat'l Reps:* Blair Television
Size of News Staff: 20; *Hours of Local News Weekly:* news progmg 27 hrs wkly
Ralph Oakley, CEO
Frank Brady, Operations Dir
Frank Brady, General Manager
Charity Holman, General Sales Mgr
Brad Suiter, Promotions Director
Elisabeth Shaffer, News Director
Danny Via, Engineering Dir
Danny Via, EngineeringDir
Yvonne Moses, Regional Sales Manager
Frank brady, Jr., National Sales Manager
Audrey Sluss, Business Manager
Allen Roberts, Internet dir.
charity Holman, Local Sales Manager

Charleston-Huntington, WV (DMA 70)

WCHS-TV *Digital Channel:* 41; *Virtual Channel:* 8; 475 kw; 1687 ft.; N38 24 28 W81 54 13
1301 Piedmont Rd., Charleston, WV 25301 US
(304) 346-5358; *Fax:* (304) 346-4765
www.wchstv.com
news@wchstv.com
License: Charleston, Kanawha County, WV held by WCHS Licensee LLC
Group Owner: Sinclair Broadcast Group Inc.; (acq 10-8-97).; *Washington Law Firm:* Fisher, Wayland, Cooper, Leader & Zaragoza
Nat'l Network: ABC
Size of News Staff: 37; *Hours of Local News Weekly:* 19.5 hrs news progmg wkly
Harold Cooper, General Manager
Matt Snyder, News Director
Sherri Allen, Traffic Manager

***WKPI-TV** *Digital Channel:* 24; 468 kw vis, 93.3 kw aur; 1,410t/153g; N37 17 06 W82 31 29
600 Cooper Drive, Lexington, KY 40502 US
(859) 258-7000, (800) 432-0951; *Fax:* (859) 258-7399
www.ket.org
help@ket.org
License: Pikeville, Pike County, KY held by Kentucky Authority for Educational TV
Nat'l Network: PBS; *Regional Network:* Kentucky Educational Television
Mike Brower, Operations Dir
Malcolm Wall, Station Manager
Craig Cornwell, Senior Director, Programming
Tim Bischoff, Promotions Manager
Shae Hopkins, Executive Director
Tim Bischoff, Senior Director, Marketing and OnlineContent
Mike Brower, Senior Director, Production Operations
Nancy Carpenter, Senior Director, Education
Fred Engel, Senior Director, Technology
Linda Hume, Senior Director, Finance and Administration

WLPX-TV *Digital Channel:* 39; 1,000 kw; ant 1,207t/968g; N38 28 12 W81 46 35
600-C Prestige Park Dr., Hurricane, WV 25526 USA
(304) 760-1029; *Fax:* (304) 760-1036
www.iontelevision.com
michaelhubner@ionmedia.com

License: Charleston, Kanawha County, WV held by ION Media Charleston License, Inc.
Group Owner: ION Media Networks Inc.; (acq 10-28-98; $8.25 million); *Washington Law Firm:* Dow Lohnes
Nat'l Network: ION Television
Brandon Burgess, Chairman & CEO
Joseph Koker, President
Tony Polcaro, Operations Dir
Joseph Koker, Stations
Marc Zand, Programming Acquisitions
David Glenn, Engineering
Gene Monday, Chief Engineer
Chris Addeo, SVP,Marketing
Terri Santisi, Administration
Jeff Quinn, Finance
Douglas Holloway, Distribution
Russell Frederickson, On-Air Services
Stephen Appel, Sales

WOWK-TV *Digital Channel:* 13; *Virtual Channel:* 13; 12.5 kw; 1358 ft.; N38 30 20 W82 12 32
PO Box 11848, Charleston, WV 25339-1848 US
(304) 343-1313; *Fax:* (304) 343-6138
www.wowktv.com
bgalloway@wvmh.com
License: Huntington, Cabell County, WV held by West Virginia Media Holdings LLC
Group Owner: West Virginia Media Holdings LLC; (acq 4-8-2002; $40.5 million); *Washington Law Firm:* Cohn & Marks LLP
Nat'l Network: CBS; *Nat'l Reps:* Petry Television Inc.
Mike Sechrist, General Manager
Ken White, News Director

***WPBY-TV** *Digital Channel:* 34; *Virtual Channel:* 33; 2,371 kw vis, 105 kw aur; 1,243t; N38 29 41 W82 12 03; *Population Served:* 300,000
600 Capitol St., Charleston, WV 25301
(304) 556-4900, (888) 596-9729; *Fax:* (304) 284-1454,(304) 556-4982
www.wvpubcast.org
audienceservices@wvpubcast.org
License: Charleston, Kanawha County, WV held by West Virginia Educational Broadcasting Authority
Nat'l Network: PBS
Willima File III, Chairman
Tammy Threadley, CEO
Dennis Adkins, General Manager
Jane Siers Wright, General Sales Mgr
Craig Lanburg, Programming Director
Shawn Patterson, Promotions Manager
Beth Vorhees, News Director
CraigLanham, Programming Director

WSAZ *Digital Channel:* 23; *Virtual Channel:* 3; 724 kw; 1203 ft.; N38 30 36 W82 13 10
Mailing Address: 645 Fifth Ave., Huntington, WV 25701 USA
Second Address: 111 Columbia Ave., Charleston, WV 25302
(304) 697-4780; *Fax:* (304) 690-3061
www.wsaz.com
news@wsaz.com
License: Huntington, Cabell County, WV held by Gray Television Licensee LLC
Group Owner: Gray Television Inc.; (acq 11-30-2005; $186 million)
Nat'l Network: NBC
Jeff Perry, Operations Manager
Matt Jaquint, General Manager
Matt Moran, General Sales Mgr
Rob Serey, Marketing & Promotions Manager
Dan Fabrizio, News Director
Aaron Withrow, Manager of Engineering

WVAH-TV *Digital Channel:* 19; *Virtual Channel:* 11; 475 kw; 1687 ft.; N38 24 28 W81 54 13
1301 Piedmont Rd., Charleston, WV 25301 US
(304) 346-5358; *Fax:* (304) 346-4765
www.wvah.com
news@wvah.com
License: Charleston, Kanawha County, WV held by WVAH Licensee LLC
Group Owner: Cunningham Broadcasting Corporation; (acq 11-15-2001; grpsl).; *Washington Law Firm:* Arter & Hadden
Nat'l Network: FOX
Size of News Staff: 38; *Hours of Local News Weekly:* news progmg 7 hrs wkly
Mark Turner, General Manager
Chris Swope, News Director

Clarksburg-Weston, WV (DMA 168)

WBOY-TV *Digital Channel:* 12; *Virtual Channel:* 12; 12.25 kw; 860 ft.; N39 17 6 W80 19 46
Mailing Address: 904 West Pike Street, Clarksburg, WV 26301 US
Second Address: 904 West Pike Street, Clarksburg, WV 26301
(304) 623-3311; *Fax:* (304) 624-6152
www.wboy.com
License: Clarksburg, Harrison County, WV held by West Virginia Media Holdings LLC
Group Owner: West Virginia Media Holdings LLC; (acq 10-25-2001; $20 million); *Washington Law Firm:* Cohn & Marks LLP
Nat'l Network: NBC; ABC; *Nat'l Reps:* Petry Television Inc.; *Wire Services:* AP
Size of News Staff: 24; *Hours of Local News Weekly:* news progmg 24 hrs wkly
Marty Becker, Chairman
Bray Cary, CEO
Larry Cottrill, General Manager
Jim Dodrill, General Sales Manager
Gary McNair, Programming Director
Aaron Williams, News Director
Bob Hardman, Chief Engineer
Charlie Dusic, CFO
VirginiaRichison, Traffic Manager
Jason Parrish, Chief Meterologist
Stacy Moniot, Anchor/Reporter
Matt Hauswirth, Sports Reporter
Geoff Coyle, Multimedia journalist

WDTV *Digital Channel:* 5; *Virtual Channel:* 5; 10 kw; 787 ft.; N39 18 2 W80 20 37
Mailing Address: P. O. Box 1508, Mount Vernon, IL 62864 US
Second Address: 5 Television Dr., Bridgeport, WV 26330
(304) 848-5000; *Fax:* (304) 842-7501
www.wdtv.com
news@wdtv.com
License: Weston, Lewis County, WV held by Withers Broadcasting Company of West Virginia
Group Owner: Withers Broadcasting Co.; (acq 5-8-73; $600,000; *Washington Law Firm:* Gardner, Carton & Douglas
Nat'l Network: CBS
Size of News Staff: 21; *Hours of Local News Weekly:* news progmg 18.5 hrs wkly
W. Russell Withers Jr., President
John Breen, Operations Dir
Tim DeFazio, General Manager
Nate Smail, News Director
Kristin Keeling, Anchor/Producer
Lindsay Watson, Anchor/Producer
Joe Brocato, Sports Director
Ben Eshenbaugh,Sports Reporter
Ken Meehan, Chief Meterologist
Pierce Legeion, Meterologist

WVFX *Digital Channel:* 10; *Virtual Channel:* 46; 30 kw; 771 ft.; N39 18 2 W80 20 37
Mailing Address: 5 Television Dr., Bridgeport, WV 26330 US
Second Address: 5 Television Dr., Bridgeport, WV 26330
(304) 848-5000; *Fax:* (304) 842-7501
www.wdtv.com
wdtv@wdtv.com
License: Clarksburg, Harrison County, WV held by Withers Broadcasting Co. of Clarksburg LLC
Group Owner: Withers Broadcasting Co.; (acq 5-6-2008; $5 million); *Washington Law Firm:* Law Office of Dennis J. Kelly
Nat'l Network: FOX; CW
W. Russell Withers Jr., President
John Breen, Operations Dir
Tim DeFazio, General Manager
Nate Smail, News Director/ Anchor
Kristin Keeling, Anchor/ Producer
Lindsey watson, Reporter
Joe Brocato, Sports Director
Ken Meehan,Chief Meterologist

Parkersburg, WV (DMA 194)

WTAP *Digital Channel:* 49; *Virtual Channel:* 15; 315 kw; 645 ft.; N39 21 0 W81 33 56
One Television Plaza, Parkersburg, WV 26101 USA
(304) 485-4588
www.thenewscenter.tv
news@thenewscenter.tv
License: Parkersburg, Wood County, WV held by Gray Television Licensee LLC
Group Owner: Gray Television Inc.; (acq 8-29-2002; grpsl).; *Washington Law Firm:* Covington & Burling
Nat'l Network: NBC; Jewelry Television; *Nat'l Reps:* Continental Television Sales; *Wire Services:* AP; CNN
Size of News Staff: 15; *Hours of Local News Weekly:* news progmg 24 hrs wkly
Roger Sheppard, VP/Station Manager
Ken Long, General Sales Mgr
Dirk Kreiss, Programming & Promotions Director
Phillip Hickman, News Director
Kevin Buskirk, Engineering Dir

Pittsburgh, PA (DMA 23)

***WNPB-TV** *Digital Channel:* 33; *Virtual Channel:* 24; 92 kw; 1498 ft.; N39 41 44.7 W79 45 44.8
600 Capitol Street, Charleston, WV 25301 US
(304) 556-4900, (888) 596-9729; *Fax:* (304) 556-4982
www.wvpubcast.org
audienceservices@wvpubcast.org
License: Morgantown, Monongalia County, WV held by West Virginia Educational Broadcasting Authority
(acq 7-1-83).; *Washington Law Firm:* Wilkinson, Barker, Knauer & Quinn
Nat'l Network: PBS
Size of News Staff: 2; *Hours of Local News Weekly:* news progmg one hr wkly
Scott Finn, Executive Director and CEO
Bill Acker, Operations Dir
Jack Wells, Station Manager
Marilyn DiVita, General Sales Mgr
Jack Wells, Engineering Dir
Mike Meador, CFO

Wheeling, WV- Steubenville, OH (DMA 158)

WTRF-TV *Digital Channel:* 7; *Virtual Channel:* 7; 25.4 kw; 961 ft.; N40 3 41 W80 45 8
96 16th St., Wheeling, WV 26003 US
(304) 232-7777; *Fax:* (304) 232-5822
www.wtrf.com
License: Wheeling, Ohio County, WV held by West Virginia Media Holdings LLC
Group Owner: West Virginia Media Holdings LLC; (acq 3-12-2002; grpsl).; *Washington Law Firm:* Edmundson & Edmundson
Nat'l Network: CBS; Fox; ABC; *Nat'l Reps:* Petry Television Inc.
Size of News Staff: 25; *Hours of Local News Weekly:* news progmg 28 hrs wkly
Roger Lyons, General Manager
Mike Allodi, General Sales Mgr
M.J. Coss, Programming Director
Jessica Nixon, Promotions Manager
Brenda Danehart, News Director
Brad Stanford, Chief Engineer
Dave Walker, Chief Meterologist

Wisconsin

Duluth, MN-Superior, WI (DMA 142)

KBJR-TV *Digital Channel:* 19; *Virtual Channel:* 6; 384 kw; 1023 ft.; N46 47 21.3 W92 6 50.7
230 East Superior Street, Duluth, MN 55802 US
(218) 720-9600; *Fax:* (218) 720-9699
www.northlandnewscenter.com
news6@kbjr.com
License: Superior, Douglas County, WI held by KBJR License Inc.
Group Owner: Granite Broadcasting Corp.; (acq 11-1-88; $12.8 million; *Washington Law Firm:* Akin, Gump, Strauss, Hauer & Feld
Nat'l Network: NBC; MyNetworkTV
Size of News Staff: 80; *Hours of Local News Weekly:* news progmg 10 hrs wkly
Robert Wilmers, General Manager
David Jensch, Station Manager

Green Bay-Appleton, WI (DMA 68)

WACY-TV *Digital Channel:* 27; 1,070 kw vis, 107 kw aur; 1,220t/1,026g; N44 21 32 W87 58 58
1391 North Rd., Green Bay, WI 54313-5723
(920) 494-2626, (920) 733-3232; *Fax:* (920) 490-7071
www.mynew32.com
wglover@journalbroadcastgroup.com

License: Appleton, Outagamie County, WI held by Journal Broadcast Corp
Group Owner: Journal Communications; *Washington Law Firm:* Lerman Senter PLLC
Nat'l Network: MyNetworkTV
Warren Glover, General Manager
Joe Poss, General Sales Mgr

WBAY-TV *Digital Channel:* 23; *Virtual Channel:* 2; 1000 kw; 1220 ft.; N44 24 35 W88 0 6
115 S.Jefferson St., Green Bay, WI 54301 US
(920) 432-3331,(800) 242-8090; *Fax:* (920) 432-1190 (news)
www.wbay.com
wbay@wbay.com
License: Green Bay, Brown County, WI held by Young Broadcasting of Green Bay Inc., Debtor-in-possession
Group Owner: Young Broadcasting Inc.; (acq 8-24-94; grpsl; *Washington Law Firm:* Brooks, Pierce, McClendon & Humphry
Nat'l Network: ABC; *Nat'l Reps:* Adam Young
Size of News Staff: 100; *Hours of Local News Weekly:* news progmg 19 hrs wkly
Dick Millhiser, Operations Manager
Don Carmichael, General Manager
Melissa Feldman, Station Business Manager
Steve Lavin, General Sales Manager
Dick Millhiser, Programming Manager
Tom McCarey, News Director
Dale Mitchell, ChiefEngineer
Lori Meyers, Traffic Supervisor
Vickie Frank, Trade Show Director
Ted Miller, Web Producer
Rhonda Roberts, Web Producer

WCWF *Digital Channel:* 21; *Virtual Channel:* 14; 800 kw; 613t/544g; N44 20 1 W87 58 56; *Population Served:* 1,035,000
787 Lombardi Ave., Green Bay, WI 54304
(920) 494-8711; *Fax:* (920) 494-8782
www.cw14online.com
jeff.bartel@wluk.com
License: Suring, Oconto County, WI held by WCWF Licensee LLC
Group Owner: Sinclair Broadcast Group Inc.; (acq 8-20-2014; grpsl).; *Washington Law Firm:* Dickstein, Shapiro, Morin & Oshinsky LLP
Nat'l Network: CW; *Nat'l Reps:* Millennium Sales & Marketing
Jay Zollar, General Manager
Kathy Silk, Sales Manager
Jeff Bartel, Promotions Manager

WFRV-TV *Digital Channel:* 39; *Virtual Channel:* 5; 1000 kw; 1194 ft.; N44 20 1 W87 58 56
1181 E. Mason St., Green Bay, WI 54301 US
(920) 437-5411
www.wearegreenbay.com
License: Green Bay, Brown County, WI held by Nexstar Broadcasting Group, Inc.
Group Owner: Nexstar Broadcasting, Inc.; (acq 4-16-2007; with WJMN-TV Escanaba, MI)
Nat'l Network: CBS; *Nat'l Reps:* Millinimum
Hours of Local News Weekly: News progmg 31 hrs wkly
Mike Smith, General Sales Mgr
Kevin Osgood, News Director

WGBA-TV *Digital Channel:* 41; 5,000 kw vis, 500 kw aur; ant 1,181t/982g; N44 21 30 W87 58 48; *Population Served:* 1,930,100
Mailing Address: 1391 North Road, Green Bay, WI 54313
Second Address: 720 E. Capitol Dr., Milwaukee, WI 53212
(920) 494-2626, (800) 800-6619, (414) 332-9611; *Fax:* (920) 490-2500, (920) 490-9550, (920) 494-7071, (4
www.nbc26.com
comments@nbc26.com
License: Green Bay, Brown County, WI held by Journal Broadcast Corp.
Group Owner: Journal Communications Inc.; (acq 10-7-2004; $43.25 million); *Washington Law Firm:* Shaw Pittman
Nat'l Network: NBC; *Nat'l Reps:* Petry Television Inc.; *Wire Services:* AP
Size of News Staff: 33; *Hours of Local News Weekly:* news progmg 16 hrs wkly
Peter Marquardt, General Manager
Joe Poss, General Sales Mgr
Dave Driessen, Chief Engineer
Stacy Engebreston, News team
Cameron Moreland, News Team
Warren Glover, Public File Assistance
Alex Hagan, Anchor/Reporter
Brooke Hafs,Anchor/Reporter
Megan Lowry, Anchor/Reporter

WLUK-TV *Digital Channel:* 11; *Virtual Channel:* 11; 40 kw; ant 1,260t/1,159g; N44 24 32 W87 59 31; *Population Served:* 1,049,000
787 Lombardi Ave., Green Bay, WI 54304
(920) 494-8711; *Fax:* (920) 494-9109
www.fox11online.com
wlukwebteam@wluk.com
License: Green Bay, Brown County, WI held by WLUK Licensee LLC
Group Owner: Sinclair Broadcast Group Inc.; (acq 8-20-2014; grpsl).
Nat'l Network: Fox; *Nat'l Reps:* Petry Television; *Wire Services:* AP
Size of News Staff: 55; *Hours of Local News Weekly:* news progmg 38 hrs wkly
Jay Zollar, General Manager
Kathy Silk, Sales Manager
Juli Buehler, News Director
Mike Nipps, Engineering Dir
Dan Spangler, Creative Services Director
Katie Grandaw, Producer
Brian Kerhin, Assignment Manager

***WPNE** *Digital Channel:* 42; 97 kw; 938 ft.; N44 24 35 W88 0 6; *Rebroadcasting:* Rebroadcasts WHA-TV Madison 100%
821 University Ave., Madison, WI 53706 US
(800) 422-9707, (608) 265-2302; *Fax:* (608) 263-9763
www.wpt.org
comments@wpt.org
License: Green Bay, Brown County, WI held by State of Wisconsin-Educational Communications Board
Washington Law Firm: Dow, Lohnes & Albertson
Nat'l Network: PBS
James Steinbach, Operations Dir
Jon Miskowski, General Sales Mgr
Mike Edgette, Operations Manager
Deborah Allen Schultz, Finance Manager

La Crosse-Eau Claire, WI (DMA 129)

WEAU *Digital Channel:* 38; *Virtual Channel:* 13; 316 kw vis, 37 kw aur; ant 1,990t/2,000g; N44 39 51 W90 57 41; *Population Served:* 224,000
Mailing Address: PO Box 47, Eau Claire, WI 54702 USA
Second Address: 1907 S Hastings Way, Eau Claire, WI 54701
(715) 835-1313; *Fax:* (715) 832-0246
www.weau.com
info@weau.com
License: Eau Claire, Eau Claire County, WI held by Gray Television Licensee LLC
Group Owner: Gray Television Inc.; (acq 8-1-98; grpsl).;
Washington Law Firm: Pepper & Corazzini
Nat'l Network: NBC; *Nat'l Reps:* Continental Television Sales;
Wire Services: Medialink
Hours of Local News Weekly: News progmg 34 hrs wkly
Kathy Wright, Sales Manager
Andrew Fefer, News Director

WEUX *Digital Channel:* 49; *Virtual Channel:* 48; 1000 kw; 732 ft.; N44 57 24 W91 40 3
1035 Interchange Pl., La Crosse, WI 54603 US
(608) 781-0025
www.wiproud.com
License: Chippewa Falls, Chippewa County, WI held by Nexstar Broadcasting Inc.
Group Owner: Nexstar Broadcasting Group Inc.; (acq 2014)
Nat'l Network: FOX; *Nat'l Reps:* TeleRep
Judson Beck, Vice President and General Manager
Steve Roth, Director of Sales
Mike Lopez, News Director

***WHLA-TV** *Digital Channel:* 30; *Virtual Channel:* 31; 307.5 kw; 1131 ft.; N43 48 17 W91 22 6
3319 West Beltline Hwy., Madison, WI 53713 US
(608) 264-9600 / (507) 895-2026; *Fax:* (608) 264-9622
www.ecb.org
License: La Crosse, La Crosse County, WI held by State of Wisconsin-Educational Communications Board
Washington Law Firm: Dow, Lohnes & Albertson
Nat'l Network: PBS
Rolf Wegenke, Chair
Mike Edgette, Operations Dir
James Steinbach, General Manager
Jon Miskowski, General Sales Mgr
Irene Ekleberry, Programming Director
Michael Bridgeman, Promotions Manager
Kathy Bissen, News Director
TerryBaun, Chief Engineer
Mary Clare Sorenson, Advertising Director
Gene Purcell, Executive Director
Marta Bechtol, Deputy Director
Mike Crane, Director, Wisconsin Public Radio
James Steinbach, Director, Wisconsin Public Television

WKBT-TV *Digital Channel:* 8; *Virtual Channel:* 8; 25.7 kW; 1525 ft; N44 05 28 W91 20 17
141 South 6th St, La Crosse, WI 54601 USA
(608) 782-4678; *Fax:* (608) 782-4674
www.news8000.com
news8@wkbt.com
License: La Crosse, La Crosse County, WI held by QueenB Television, LLC
Group Owner: Morgan Murphy Media; (acq 3-31-2000; $22 million).
Nat'l Network: CBS; MyNetworkTV; *Nat'l Reps:* Harrington, Righter & Parsons
Anne Paape, Station Manager
Anne Paape, News Director

WLAX *Digital Channel:* 17; *Virtual Channel:* 25; 852 kw; 975 ft.; N43 48 16.14 W91 22 19.29
1305 Interchange Pl., Lacrosse, WI 54603 US 54603
(608) 781-0025
www.wiproud.com
License: La Crosse, La Crosse County, WI held by Nexstar Broadcasting Inc.
Group Owner: Nexstar Broadcasting Group Inc.; (acq 2014)
Nat'l Network: FOX; *Nat'l Reps:* TeleRep
Hours of Local News Weekly: news progmg 3.5 hrs wkly
Judson Beck, Vice President and General Manager
Steve Roth, Director of Sales

WQOW-DT *Digital Channel:* 15; 407 kw vis, 40.7 kw aur; 741t/507g; N44 57 49 W91 40 05; *Population Served:* 214,000
5545 Hwy. 93, Eau Claire, WI 54701
(715) 835-1881, (715) 831-1824, (800) 594-6721; *Fax:* (715) 835-8009,(217) 223-5019
www.wqow.com
news@wqow.com
License: Eau Claire, Eau Claire County, WI held by WXOW-WQOW Television Inc.
Group Owner: Quincy Newspapers Inc.; (acq 6-1-2001; grpsl).;
Washington Law Firm: Wilkinson, Barker, Knauer LLP
Nat'l Network: ABC; CW; *Nat'l Reps:* Petry Television Inc.
Size of News Staff: 16; *Hours of Local News Weekly:* news progmg 18 hrs wkly
Ralph Oakley, President
Lisa Patrow, Dir. Of News & Operations
Dave Booth, General Manager
Mark Golden, General Sales Mgr
Todd Zschernitz, Engineering
Edward Woloszyn, Sales
Bob Bradovich, Sports Director
Bridget Kurtenbach,Internet Director

WXOW *Digital Channel:* 48; *Virtual Channel:* 19; 631 kw vis, 63 kw aur; ant 1,138t/790g; N43 48 23 W91 22 02; *Population Served:* 1,542,600
Mailing Address: 3705 County Hwy. 25, La Crescent, MN 55947
Second Address: 3705 County Hwy. 25, La Crescent, MN 55947
(507) 895-9969, (507) 895-1919, (507) 895-1900; *Fax:* (507) 895-8124
www.wxow.com
aedesk@wxow.com
License: La Crosse, La Crosse County, WI held by WXOW-WQOW Television Inc.
Group Owner: Quincy Newspapers Inc.; (acq 6-1-2001).;
Washington Law Firm: Wilkinson, Barker & Knauer, L.L.P.
Nat'l Network: ABC; CW; This TV; *Nat'l Reps:* Millenium; *Wire Services:* AP
Size of News Staff: 24; *Hours of Local News Weekly:* news progmg 19 hrs wkly
David Booth, General Manager
Brian Schumacher, General Sales Manager
Deb Simonis, Programming Dir.
Jacob Anderson, Marketing & promotions Manager
Sean Dwyer, News Director
Dan Rasmussen, Chief Engineer
Theresa Wopat,Administrative asst.
Kevin Millard, Internet Dir.
Todd Rastall, Master Control Supervisor
Scott hackworth, News Anchor
Dave Solie, General Assignment Reporter
Dan Breeden, Chief Meterologist

Madison, WI (DMA 80)

WBUW *Digital Channel:* 32; *Virtual Channel:* 57; 200 kw; 1270 ft.; N43 3 3 W89 29 13
P.O. Box 5726, Rockford, IL 61125 US

(608) 270-5700; *Fax:* (608) 270-5717
License: Janesville, Rock County, WI held by Byrne Acquisition Group LLC
Washington Law Firm: Dickstein, Shapiro, Morin & Oshinsky LLP
Nat'l Network: CW; *Nat'l Reps:* MMT
John B. Byrne, President
Tom Keeler, General Manager
Sharon Weiler, General Sales Mgr
Christopher Hawbaker, Promotions Manager
Emmy Fink, News Director
Tom Allen, CFO
Doug Gealy, COO
Eric Krieghoff, National Sales Manager

***WHA-TV** *Digital Channel:* 20; *Virtual Channel:* 21; 140 kw; 1486 ft.; N43 3 21 W89 32 6
821 University Avenue, Madison, WI 53706 US
(800) 422-9707; *Fax:* (608) 263-9763
www.wpt.org
comments@wpt.org
License: Madison, Dane County, WI held by University of Wisconsin Board of Regents
Washington Law Firm: Dow, Lohnes & Albertson
Nat'l Network: PBS
Rolf Wegenke, Chair
James Steinbach, Operations Dir
Jon Miskowski, General Sales Mgr
Garry Denny, Programming Director
Chad Myers, Chief Engineer
Mike Edgette, Operations Manager
Deborah Allen Schultz, Finanace Manager
KathyBissen, Director of Production
Lynne Blinkenberg, Director of Community Outreach
Malcolm Brett, Director of Broadcasting and Media Innovations
Michael Harryman, Communications Director

WISC-TV *Digital Channel:* 11; *Virtual Channel:* 3; 10.2 kW; 1539 ft; N43 03 21 W89 32 06; *Population Served:* 385,000
7025 Raymond Rd, Madison, WI 53719 USA
(608) 271-4321; *Fax:* (608) 271-0800
www.channel3000.com
License: Madison, Dane County, WI held by Television Wisconsin, Inc.
Group Owner: Morgan Murphy Media; *Washington Law Firm:* Rini Coran, PC
Nat'l Network: CBS; MyNetworkTV; *Nat'l Reps:* Harrington, Righter & Parsons
Size of News Staff: 34; *Hours of Local News Weekly:* news progmg 22 hrs wkly
Tom Keeler, General Manager
Steve Scadden, General Sales Mgr
Colin Benedict, News Director

WKOW *Digital Channel:* 27; 1,000 kw vis, 100 kw aur; 1,250t/1,182g; N43 03 09 W89 28 42; *Population Served:* 214,800
5727 Tokay Blvd., Madison, WI 53719
(608) 274-1234, (608) 273-2727; *Fax:* (608) 274-9514
www.wkowtv.com
closedcaption@wkowtv.com
License: Madison, Dane County, WI held by WKOW Television Inc.
Group Owner: Quincy Newspapers Inc.; (acq 5-22-2001; grpsl).;
Washington Law Firm: Rosenman & Colin
Nat'l Network: ABC
Size of News Staff: 28; *Hours of Local News Weekly:* news progmg 22 hrs wkly
Bob Goessling, Director of Programming & Operations
Tom Allen, VP/General manager
Bruce Briney, General Sales Manager
Anna Engelhart, Program Manager
Joe Radske, News Director
Brandy Dreasler, Engineering Director
Keith Triller,National Sales manager
Jill Genter, Manager og Marketing & Community Relations
Javki Witkowski, Internet Director
Dani Maxwell, Co-Anchor & ExecutiveProducer
Jennifer Kliese, Multimedia Journalist
Lance Veeser, Sports Director

WMSN-TV *Digital Channel:* 49; *Virtual Channel:* 47; 310 kw; 1476 ft.; N43 3 21 W89 32 6
Mailing Address: 7847 Big Sky Dr., Madison, WI 53719 US
Second Address: 10706 Beaver Dam Rd., Hunt Valley, MD 21030
(608) 833-0047; *Fax:* (608) 833-5055
www.fox47.com
feedback@fox47.com
License: Madison, Dane County, WI held by WMSN Licensee LLC
Group Owner: Sinclair Broadcast Group Inc.; (acq 12-10-01; grpsl).
Nat'l Network: FOX
Kerry Johnson, General Manager
Linda Hart, Creative Services Manager

WMTV *Digital Channel:* 19; *Virtual Channel:* 15; 155 kw; 1361 ft.; N43 3 3 W89 29 13
615 Forward Dr., Madison, WI 53711 USA
(608) 274-1515; *Fax:* (608) 271-5193
www.nbc15.com
news@nbc15.com
License: Madison, Dane County, WI held by Gray Television Licensee LLC
Group Owner: Gray Television Inc.; (acq 8-29-2002; grpsl).;
Washington Law Firm: Covington & Burling
Nat'l Network: NBC; *Wire Services:* AP; CNN
Size of News Staff: 36; *Hours of Local News Weekly:* news progmg 19 hrs wkly
Becki Noel, General Sales Mgr

Milwaukee, WI (DMA 35)

***MPTV** *Digital Channel:* 8; *Virtual Channel:* 10; 25 kw; 1161 ft.; N43 5 46 W87 54 15
1036 North 8th Street, Milwaukee, WI 53233 US
(414) 271-1036; *Fax:* (414) 297-6771
www.mptv.org
info@mptv.org, tvviewe@matc.edu
License: Milwaukee, Milwaukee County, WI held by Milwaukee Area Technical College District Board
Washington Law Firm: Dow, Lohnes & Albertson
Nat'l Network: PBS
Tom Dvorak, Operations Dir
Ellis Bromberg, General Manager
David Felland, Chief Engineer
Dan Jones, Producer
Debbie O'Connor-Callahan, Publicist

***MPTV** *Digital Channel:* 35; *Virtual Channel:* 36; 500 kw; 1164 ft.; N43 5 46 W87 54 15
1036 North 8th Street, Milwaukee, WI 53233 US
(414) 271-1036; *Fax:* (414) 297-6771
www.mptv.org
License: Milwaukee, Milwaukee County, WI held by Milwaukee Area Technical College District Board
Washington Law Firm: Dow, Lohnes & Albertson
Nat'l Network: PBS
Foreign Language Programming
Tom Dvorak, Operations Dir
Ellis Bromberg, General Manager
David Felland, Chief Engineer
Dan Jones, Producer
Debbie O'Connor-Callahan, Publicist

WCGV-TV *Digital Channel:* 25; *Virtual Channel:* 24; 1000 kw; 1116 ft.; N43 5 46 W87 54 15
11520 W. Calumet Rd., Milwaukee, WI 53224 US
(414) 815-4100; *Fax:* (414) 815-4102
www.my24Milwaukee.com
info@my24milwaukee.com
License: Milwaukee, Milwaukee County, WI held by WCGV Licensee LLC
Group Owner: Sinclair Broadcast Group Inc.; (acq 5-23-94; grpsl;
Nat'l Network: MYTV; *Nat'l Reps:* Millennium Sales & Marketing
Terry Gaughan, General Manager
Rob Krieghoff, Local Sales Manager
Julie Ford-Moody, Regional Controller

WDJT-TV *Digital Channel:* 46; *Virtual Channel:* 58; 1000 kw; 1056 ft.; N43 6 42 W87 55 50
809 S. 60th St., Milwaukee, WI 53214 US
(414) 777-5800, (414) 607-8140; *Fax:* (414) 777-5802
www.cbs58.com
newsdesk@cbs58.com
License: Milwaukee, Milwaukee County, WI held by WDJT-TV L.P.
Group Owner: Weigel Broadcasting Co.; *Washington Law Firm:* Cohn & Marks
Nat'l Network: CBS; *Nat'l Reps:* Harrington, Righter & Parsons
Norman Shapiro, President
Jim Hall, General Manager
Marty Schack, General Sales Mgr
Grant Uitti, News Director
Dan Dyer, Chief Engineer
Paul Piaskoski, Anchor
Carlos Vergara, Anchor/Reporter
Bill Walsh, Anchor/Reporter
LilaCarrera, Reporter
Mark McGinnis, Chief Meterologist
Kevin Holden, Sports Anchor/Reporter

WISN-TV *Digital Channel:* 34; *Virtual Channel:* 12; 1000 kw; 993 ft.; N43 6 42 W87 55 42
C/O Brooks, Pierce, Et. Al., P.O. Box 1800, Raleigh, NC 27602 US
(414) 342-8812; *Fax:* (414) 342-4486
www.wisn.com
License: Milwaukee, Milwaukee County, WI held by WISN Hearst Television Inc.
Group Owner: Hearst Television Inc.; *Washington Law Firm:* Peper, Martin, Jensen, Maichel & Hetlage
Nat'l Network: ABC; *Nat'l Reps:* Continental Television Sales;
Wire Services: News 1
Jan Wade, General Manager
Pete Monfre, General Sales Mgr
Dean Maytag, Programming Director
Lori Waldon, News Director
Tony Coleman, Chief Engineer
Sue Samuelson, Traffic Manager

WITI *Digital Channel:* 33; *Virtual Channel:* 6; 1000 kw; 997 ft.; N43 5 26 W87 53 50
9001 N Green Bay Rd., Milwaukee, WI 53209 USA
(414) 355-6666; *Fax:* (414) 586-2141
fox6now.com
fox6news@fox6now.com
License: Milwaukee, Milwaukee County, WI held by WITI License LLC
Group Owner: Tribune Media; *Washington Law Firm:* Dow Lohnes PLLC
Nat'l Network: FOX; *Nat'l Reps:* Millennium Sales & Marketing;
Wire Services: CNN
Hours of Local News Weekly: 43
Chuck Steinmetz, Operations Dir
Mike Neale, General Sales Mgr
Bob O'Neil, Local Sales Manager
Stu Swaziek, National Sales Manager
Julie Beck, Digital Sales Manager

WMLW-TV *Digital Channel:* 48; 500 kw; 300 m; N43 06 42 W87 55 50
809 S. 60th Street, Milwaukee, WI 53214
(414) 777-5800; *Fax:* (414) 777-5802
www.wmlw.com
License: Racine, Racine County, WI held by TV-49 Inc
Group Owner: Weigel Broadcasting Co.; (acq 4-21-2008; $6.5 million); *Washington Law Firm:* Cohn & Marks
; *Nat'l Reps:* Harrington, Righter & Parsons
Norman Shapiro, President
Jim Hall, General Manager
Marty Schack, General Sales Mgr
Dan Dyer, Chief Engineer

WPXE-TV *Digital Channel:* 40; 830 kw vis; ant 449t/349g; N43 05 45 W87 54 15
6161 N. Flint Rd., Suite F, Glendale, WI 53209 USA
(414) 247-0117; *Fax:* (414) 247-1302
www.iontelevision.com
License: Kenosha, WI held by Ion Media Milwaukee License, Inc.
Group Owner: ION Media Networks Inc.; (acq 2-18-00; grpsl).;
Washington Law Firm: Gardner, Carton & Douglas
Nat'l Network: ION Television
Brandon Burgess, Chairman/CEO

WTMJ-TV *Digital Channel:* 28; *Virtual Channel:* 4; 1000 kw; 894 ft.; N43 5 29 W87 54 7
Mailing Address: P.O. Box 693, 720 East Capitol Dr., Milwaukee, WI 53212 US
Second Address: 2025 N. Summit Ave, Ste 107, Milwaukee, WI 53202
(414) 967-5444,(414) 277-0606; *Fax:* (414) 967-5378,(414) 277-0630
www.todaystmj4.com
tmj4feedback@todaystmj4.com
License: Milwaukee, Milwaukee County, WI held by Journal Broadcast Corp.
Group Owner: Journal Communications Inc.; *Washington Law Firm:* Hogan & Hartson
Nat'l Network: NBC
Steve Wexler, EVP of Television & Radio Operations
Steve Wexler, General Manager
Mark LeGrand, General Sales Manager
Brenda Serio, Programming Dir.
Sean O'Flaherty, News Director
Tony Lucas, Engineering
Ron Adair, ChiefEngineer
Mike O'Brien, Local Sales Manager

Tim McCormack, Traffic Manager
James Conigliaro, interactive

WVCY-TV *Digital Channel:* 22; 1070 kw, 30.3 DBK; 301.4 meters agl; N43 05 15 W87 54 12
3434 W. Kilbourn Ave., Milwaukee, WI 53208
(8000 729-9829; *Fax:* (414) 935-3015
www.vcyamerica.org
vcy@vcyamerica.org
License: Milwaukee, Milwaukee County, WI held by VCY America Inc.
Group Owner: VCY America Inc.; *Ownership:* VCY America, Inc.; *Washington Law Firm:* Wiley Rein LLP
Dr. Randall Melchert, President
Vic Eliason, General Manager
Jim Schneider, Programming Director
Andy Eliason, Chief Engineer
Jim Cronin, Operations Manager

WVTV *Digital Channel:* 18; *Virtual Channel:* 18; 745 kw; ant 1,008t/1,101g; N43 05 44 W87 54 17; *Population Served:* 1,826,000
11520 W. Calumet Rd., Milwaukee, WI 53224
(414) 815-4100; *Fax:* (414) 815-4102
www.cw18milwaukee.com
info@cw18milwaukee.com
License: Milwaukee, Milwaukee County, WI held by WVTV Licensee Inc.
Group Owner: Sinclair Broadcast Group Inc.; (acq 2-1-2002).
Nat'l Network: CW; *Nat'l Reps:* Millennium Sales & Marketing
Paul Rudolph, Operations Manager
Terry Gaughan, General Manager
Nate Harbison, Regional Sales Manager
Jason Van Acker, Promotion Manager
Deanne Monaghan, Director of Sales
Linda Chase, Integrated Marketing Executive
Amanda Drake,Integrated Marketing Executive
Kara Volpintesta, Integrated Marketing Executive
Emmet Light, Integrated Marketing Executive
Carolyn Mendez, Integrated Marketing Executive

WWRS-TV *Digital Channel:* 43; *Virtual Channel:* 52; 300 kw; 610 ft.; N43 26 11 W88 31 34
Mailing Address: PO Box A, Santa Ana, CA 92711 US
Second Address: P. O. Box 768, Station B, Ottawa, ON K1P 5P8
(714) 731-1000, (888) 731-1000, (714) 832-2950; *Fax:* (920) 387-9053
www.tbn.org
dcalhoun@tbn.org
License: Mayville, Dodge County, WI held by National Minority T.V. Inc
(acq 2-16-99; $3,300,000); *Washington Law Firm:* Shaw Pittman
Nat'l Network: TRINITY BROADCA
Dinah Calhoun, General Manager

Minneapolis-St. Paul, MN (DMA 15)

***WHWC-TV** *Digital Channel:* 27; *Virtual Channel:* 28; 291 kw; 1148 ft.; N45 2 49 W91 51 47; *Rebroadcasting:* Rebroadcasts WHA-TV Madison 100%
821 University Avenue, Madison, WI 53706 US
(800) 422-9707; *Fax:* (608) 263-9763
www.wpt.org
comments@wpt.org
License: Menomonie, Dunn County, WI held by State of Wisconsin-Educational Communications Board
Washington Law Firm: Dow, Lohnes & Albertson
Nat'l Network: PBS
Rolf Wegenke, Chair
Mike Edgette, Operations Dir
Jon Miskowski, General Sales Mgr
Garry Denny, Programming Director
Michael Bridgeman, Promotions Manager
Chad Myers, Chief Engineer
Kathy Bissen, Director of Production
DeborahAllen Schultz, Finance Manager
Kathy Bissen, Director of Production
Lynne Blinkenberg, Director of Community Outreach
Malcolm Brett, Director of Broadcasting and Media Innovations
Michael Harryman, Communications Director

Wausau-Rhinelander, WI (DMA 134)

WAOW *Digital Channel:* 9; 316 kw vis, 31.6 kw aur; ant 1,210t/647g; N44 55 14 W89 41 31; *Population Served:* 533,000
1908 Grand Ave., Wausau, WI 53719 US
(715) 842-2251; *Fax:* (715) 848-0195,(715) 842-7808
www.waow.com
License: Wausau, Marathon County, WI held by WAOW-WYOW Television Inc.
Group Owner: Quincy Newspapers Inc.; (acq 5-22-2001; grpsl).; *Washington Law Firm:* Wilkinson, Baker & Knauer, LLP
Nat'l Network: ABC; CW; *Nat'l Reps:* Petry Television Inc.; *Wire Services:* AP; CNN
Size of News Staff: 26; *Hours of Local News Weekly:* news progmg 15.5 hrs wkl
Ralph Oakley, CEO
Laurin Jorstad, Operations Dir
Randy Winters, Station Manager
Tricia Schairer, Programming Director
Mark Oliver, Promotions Manager
Randy Winter, News Director
Russ Crass, Chief Engineer

***WHRM-TV** *Digital Channel:* 24; *Virtual Channel:* 20; 172 kw; 1270 ft.; N44 55 14 W89 41 28
3319 West Beltline Hwy., Madison, WI 53713 US
(608) 264-9600; *Fax:* (608) 264-9622
www.ecb.org
gene.purcell@ecb.org
License: Wausau, Marathon County, WI held by State of Wisconsin-Educational Communications Board
Washington Law Firm: Dow, Lohnes & Albertson
Nat'l Network: PBS
Rolf Wegenke, Chair
Mike Edgette, Operations Dir
James Steinbach, General Manager
Jon Miskowski, General Sales Mgr
Irene Ekleberry, Programming Director
Michael Bridgeman, Promotions Manager
Kathy Bissen, News Director
TerryBaun, Chief Engineer
Mary Clare Sorenson, Advertising Director
Gene Purcell, Executive Director
Marta Bechtol, Deputy Director
Mike Crane, Director, Wisconsin Public Radio
James Steinbach, Director, Wisconsin Public Television

WJFW-TV *Digital Channel:* 16; *Virtual Channel:* 12; 269 kw; 1188 ft.; N45 40 3 W89 12 29
3217 Country Road G, Rhinelander, WI 54501 US
(715) 365-8812, (715) 365-4701; *Fax:* (715) 365-8810
www.wjfw.com
License: Rhinelander, Oneida County, WI held by Northland Television LLC.
Group Owner: Rockfleet Broadcasting Inc.; *Washington Law Firm:* Wiley, Rein & Fielding
Nat'l Network: NBC; *Nat'l Reps:* Blair Television
Size of News Staff: 13; *Hours of Local News Weekly:* news progmg 18.5 hrs wkly
Gil Buettner, General Manager
Charlotte Berens, General Sales Mgr
John Quarderer, News Director
Greg Buzzell, Dir. Of Engineering/Chief Engineer
Greg Buzzell, Dir. Of Engineering/Chief Engineer
Angela Barr, Traffic Manager
BenMeyer, Executive producer
Joe Dufek, Sports Director
Lyndsey Stemm, Anchor, Producer, Reporter

***WLEF-TV** *Digital Channel:* 36; *Virtual Channel:* 36; 277 kw; 1460 ft.; N45 56 43 W90 16 22; *Rebroadcasting:* Rebroadcasts WHA-TV Madison 100%
821 University Avenue, Madison, WI 53706 US
(800) 422-9707,(608) 265-2302; *Fax:* (608) 263-9763
www.wpt.org
comments@wpt.org
License: Park Falls, Price County, WI held by State of Wisconsin-Educational Communications Board
Washington Law Firm: Dow, Lohnes & Albertson
Nat'l Network: PBS
Rolf Wegenke, Chair
Mike Edgette, Operations Dir
Jon Miskowski, General Sales Mgr
Garry Denny, Programming Director
Michael Bridgeman, Promotions Manager
Chad Myers, Chief Engineer
Kathy Bissen, Director of Production
DeborahAllen Schultz, Finanace Manager
Kathy Bissen, Director of Production
Lynne Blinkenberg, Director of Community Outreach
Malcolm Brett, Director of Broadcasting and Media Innovations
Michael Harryman, Communications Director

WSAW *Digital Channel:* 7; *Virtual Channel:* 7; 72 kw; 1224 ft.; N44 55 14 W89 41 28
1114 Grand Ave., Wausau, WI 54403 USA
(715) 845-4211; *Fax:* (715) 845-2649
www.wsaw.com
news@wsaw.com
License: Wausau, Marathon County, WI held by Gray Television Licensee LLC
Group Owner: Gray Television Inc.
Nat'l Network: CBS; MyNetworkTV; Jewelry Television; *Nat'l Reps:* Continental Television Sales; *Wire Services:* AP
Size of News Staff: 21; *Hours of Local News Weekly:* news progmg 15 hrs wkly
Al Lancaster, VP/General Manager
Scott Stilley, Promotions Manager
Jessica Laszewski, News Director
Bill Deloney, Chief Engineer

WTPX-TV *Digital Channel:* 46; 50 kw; ant 918t; N45 03 21 W89 27 57
6161 N. Flint Rd., Suite F, Glendale, WI 53209 USA
(812) 335-1770; *Fax:* (561) 659-4754
www.iontelevision.com
License: Antigo, Langlade County, WI held by Ion Media Wausau License, Inc.
Group Owner: ION Media Networks Inc.; (acq 4-18-2000; $887,500 for CP).
Nat'l Network: ION Television
Brandon Burgess, Chairman/CEO

WYOW *Digital Channel:* 28; *Virtual Channel:* 34; 70 kw; 472 ft.; N45 46 30 W89 14 55; *Rebroadcasting:* Rebroadcasts WAOW-TV Wausau 100%
Mailing Address: 1908 Grand Ave., Wasau, WI 54403 US
Second Address: P.O. Box 909, Quincy, IL 62306
(715) 842-2251, (715) 842-9293, (800) 236-9269; *Fax:* (715) 848-0195, (715) 842-7808, (715) 849-2999
www.waow.com
License: Eagle River, Vilas County, WI held by WAOW-WYOW Television Inc.
Group Owner: Quincy Newspapers Inc.; (acq 5-22-2001; grpsl).; *Washington Law Firm:* Wilkinson, Barker & Knauer, LLP.
Nat'l Network: ABC; CW; *Nat'l Reps:* Petry Television Inc.; *Wire Services:* AP; CNN
Ralph Oakley, CEO
Laurin Jorstad, General Manager
Carol Kellum, General Sales Mgr
Tricia Schairer, Programming Director
Mark Oliver, Promotions Manager
Randy Winter, News Director
Brady Dreasler, Engineering Dir.
Russ Crass,Chief Engineer
Tim Atterberg, Regional Sales Manager
Melissa Langbehn, Anchor
Nate Barrett, Content producer& Multimedia Journalist
Justin Loew, Meterologist
Lauren Magiera, Sports Team
Bryon Graff, Executive Producer

Wyoming

Casper

KCWY *Digital Channel:* 12; *Virtual Channel:* 13; 3.2 kW; N42 44 37 W106 18 24
141 Progress Circle, PO Box 1540, Mills, WY 82644 USA
(307) 577-0013
www.kcwy13.com
License: Casper, Natrona County, WY held by Gray Television Licensee LLC
Group Owner: Gray Television Inc.
Nat'l Network: NBC; The CW Network
Jim Beck, Station Manager
Jim Beck, Local Sales Manager
John Ehrhart, News Director
Mark Hildebrand, Chief Engineer

Casper-Riverton, WY (DMA 197)

KGWC-TV *Digital Channel:* 14; *Virtual Channel:* 14; 53.3 kw; 1844 ft.; N42 44 26 W106 21 34
1856 Skyview Dr., Casper, WY 82601 US
(307) 577-5923
License: Casper, Natrona County, WY held by Mark III Media Inc.
Group Owner: Mark III Media Inc.; (acq 5-31-2006; grpsl).; *Washington Law Firm:* Covington & Burling
Nat'l Network: CBS
Mark Nalbone, General Manager

KGWL-TV *Digital Channel:* 7; *Virtual Channel:* 5; 14.3 kw; 370 ft.; N42 53 43 W108 43 34; *Rebroadcasting:* Satellite of KGWC-TV Casper.

1856 Skyview Dr., Casper, WY 82601 US
(307) 577-5923
License: Lander, Fremont County, WY held by Mark III Media Inc.
Group Owner: Mark III Media Inc.; (acq 5-31-2006; grpsl).;
Washington Law Firm: Covington & Burling
Nat'l Network: CBS
Mark Nalbone, General Manager

KGWR-TV *Digital Channel:* 13; *Virtual Channel:* 13; 14.2 kw; 1624 ft.; N41 26 21 W109 6 42; *Rebroadcasting:* Satellite of KGWC-TV Casper.
1856 Skyview Dr., Casper, WY 82601 US
(307) 577-5923
License: Rock Springs, Sweetwater County, WY held by Mark III Media Inc.
Group Owner: Mark III Media Inc.; (acq 5-31-2006; grpsl).;
Washington Law Firm: Covington & Burling
Nat'l Network: CBS
Mark Nalbone, General Manager

***KPTW** *Digital Channel:* 8; *Virtual Channel:* 6; 2.3 kw; 1864 ft.; N42 44 26 W106 21 34; *Rebroadcasting:* Satellite of KCWC-TV Lander 100%
2660 Peck Avenue, Riverton, WY 82501 US
(307) 856-6944; *Fax:* (307) 856-3893
License: Casper, Natrona County, WY held by Central Wyoming College.
Nat'l Network: PBS; *Regional Network:* Wyoming Public Television
Ruby Calvert, General Manager
Suze Kanack, Programming Director
Jennifer Amend, Promotions Manager
Robert Spain, Dir. Of Engineering
Bob Spain, Chief Engineer
Kyle Nicholoff, Production Services manger
Richard Ager, Publicaffairs Producer
Joel Kindle, Master Control Operations Manager
lonny Fairfield, broadcast Technician
Lara Miller, Administrative Asst.
Lee haines, Executive Dir.

KTWO-TV *Digital Channel:* 17; *Virtual Channel:* 2; 52.9 kw; 1837 ft.; N42 44 26 W106 21 34
1896 Skyview Drive, Casper, WY 82601 US
(307) 237-3711; *Fax:* (307) 234-9866
www.k2tv.com
info@k2tv.com
License: Casper, Natrona County, WY held by Silverton Broadcasting Co. LLC
(acq 5-31-2006; $1.2 million); *Ownership:* Barry Silverton, 100%
Nat'l Network: ABC; *Nat'l Reps:* Millennium Sales & Marketing
Size of News Staff: 23; *Hours of Local News Weekly:* news progmg 19.5 hrs wkly
Kristi Lockard, General Manager
Mick Birge, Station Manager
Tina Nalbone, General Sales Mgr
Amie Miller, News Director

Cheyenne, WY-Scottsbluff, NE (DMA 198)

KATV *Digital Channel:* 11; *Virtual Channel:* 33; 16 kw; 2133 ft.; N40 32 47 W105 11 50
401 Main Street, Little Rock, AR 72201 US
(501) 324-7760; *Fax:* (501) 324-7852
www.katv.com
License: Cheyenne, Laramie County, WY held by Casa En Denver Inc.
Ownership: Casa Media Partners LLC, 100%
Nat'l Network: Mundo Fox; *Nat'l Reps:* Millennium Sales & Marketing
Size of News Staff: 17; *Hours of Local News Weekly:* news progmg 15 hrs wkly
Barbara Laurence, Director
Barry Schumaier, General Sales Mgr
Jim Sande, Programming Director
LuWanna Lawrence, Promotions Manager
Monica Hannan, News Director
Brian Funk, Chief Engineer

KGWN *Digital Channel:* 30; *Virtual Channel:* 5; 459 kw; 531 ft.; N41 6 1 W105 0 23
2923 E Lincolnway, Cheyenne, WY 82001 USA
(307) 634-7755
www.kgwn.tv
License: Cheyenne, Laramie County, WY held by Gray Television Licensee LLC
Group Owner: Gray Television Inc.; *Washington Law Firm:* Dow, Lohnes & Albertson
Nat'l Network: CBS; *Nat'l Reps:* Continental Television Sales
Size of News Staff: 16; *Hours of Local News Weekly:* news progmg 15 hrs wkly
Tregg White, General Manager
Barbara Parenti, Programming Director
Jeremy Downing, News Director
Tony Schaefer, Engineering Dir

KLWY *Digital Channel:* 27; *Virtual Channel:* 27; 169 kw; 761 ft.; N41 2 55 W104 53 28
1856 Skyview Dr., Casper, WY 82601 US
(307) 577-5923
www.foxflash.com
License: Cheyenne, Laramie County, WY held by Wyomedia Corp
Group Owner: Wyomedia Corp.; (acq 12-4-91; $100,000;
Nat'l Network: FOX
Mark Nalbone, General Manager

Philadelphia (DMA 4)

KJWP *Digital Channel:* 2; *Virtual Channel:* 2; 9.36 kw; 310.8 meters; N40 02 30 W75 14 11
63 West Parish Road, Concord, NH 03301 US
(732) 245-4705; *Fax:* (307) 733-4834
License: Wilmington, New Castle County, DE held by PMCM TV LLC
Group Owner: PMCM TV TV LLC; (acq 6-12-2009; $1 million)
Richard T. Morena, General Manager

Rapid City, SD (DMA 172)

KSGW-TV *Digital Channel:* 13; 50.0 kW; 16.99 DBK; ant 1,220t; N44 37 20 W107 06 57; *Population Served:* 241,224
518 St Joseph St, Rapid City, SD 57709
(605) 342-2000; *Fax:* (605) 342-7305
www.kotatv.com
KOTACalendar@kotatv.com
License: Sheridan, Sheridan County, WY held by Duhamel Broadcasting Enterprises.
Group Owner: Duhamel Broadcasting Enterprises; *Washington Law Firm:* Pillsbury Law
Nat'l Network: ABC; *Nat'l Reps:* Continental Television Sales;
Wire Services: AP
Hours of Local News Weekly: News progmg 8 hrs wkly
William Duhamel, President
Monte Loos, Operations Dir
Steve Duffy, General Sales Mgr
Doug Loos, Programming Director
John Petersen, News Director
Dan Black, Engineering Dir
Dan Duff, Chief Engineer
Gerry Fenske, Regional SalesManager

U.S. Television Stations by Call Letters

KAAH-TV Honolulu, Hawaii
KAAL Austin, Minnesota
KAAS-TV Salina, Kansas
KABB San Antonio, Texas
KABC-TV Los Angeles, California
KACV-TV Amarillo, Texas
KADN-TV Lafayette, Louisiana
KAEF-TV Arcata, California
KAET Phoenix, Arizona
KAFT Fayetteville, Arkansas
KAGS-LD Bryan, Texas
KAID Boise, Idaho
KAII-TV Wailuku, Hawaii
KAIL Fresno, California
KAIT Jonesboro, Arkansas
KAJB-TV Calipatria, California
KAKE Wichita, Kansas
KAKM Anchorage, Alaska
KAKW-DT Killeen, Texas
KALB Alexandria, Louisiana
KALO Honolulu, Hawaii
KAMC Lubbock, Texas
KAMR-TV Amarillo, Texas
KAMU-TV College Station, Texas
KANG-CD San Angelo, Texas
KAPP-TV Yakima, Washington
KAQY Columbia, Louisiana
KARD West Monroe, Louisiana
KARE Minneapolis, Minnesota
KARK-TV Little Rock, Arkansas
KARZ-TV Little Rock, Arkansas
KASA-TV Santa Fe, New Mexico
KASN Pine Bluff, Arkansas
KASW Phoenix, Arizona
KASY-TV Albuquerque, New Mexico
KATC Lafayette, Louisiana
KATN Fairbanks, Alaska
KATU Portland, Oregon
KATV Little Rock, Arkansas
KATV Cheyenne, Wyoming
KAUT Oklahoma City, Oklahoma
KAUZ-TV Wichita Falls, Texas
KAVU-TV Victoria, Texas
KAWB Brainerd, Minnesota
KAWE Bemidji, Minnesota
KAYU-TV Spokane, Washington
KAZA-TV Avalon, California
KAZQ Albuquerque, New Mexico
KAZT-TV Prescott, Arizona
KBAK-TV Bakersfield, California
KBCA Alexandria, Louisiana
KBCB Bellingham, Washington
KBCW-TV San Francisco, California
KBDI-TV Broomfield, Colorado
KBEH Oxnard, California
KBFD-DT Honolulu, Hawaii
KBFX-CD Bakersfield, California
KBHE-TV Rapid City, South Dakota
KBIM-TV Roswell, New Mexico
KBIN-TV Council Bluffs, Nebraska
KBJR-TV Superior, Wisconsin
KBLN-TV Grants Pass, Oregon
KBLR Paradise, Nevada
KBME-TV Bismarck, North Dakota
KBMT Beaumont, Texas
KBMY Bismarck, North Dakota
KBNT-CD San Diego, California
KBNZ-LD Bend, Oregon
KBOI-TV Boise, Idaho
KBSI Cape Girardeau, Missouri
KBSV Ceres, California
KBTC-TV Tacoma, Washington
KBTV-TV Port Arthur, Texas
KBTX Bryan, Texas
KBVO Llano, Texas
KBVU Eureka, California
KBYU-TV Provo, Utah
KBZK Bozeman, Montana
KBZO-LP Lubbock, Texas
KCAL-TV Los Angeles, California
KCAU-TV Sioux City, Iowa
KCBA Salinas, California
KCBD Lubbock, Texas
KCBS-TV Los Angeles, California
KCBY-TV Coos Bay, Oregon
KCCI Des Moines, Iowa
KCCI-TV Des Moines, Maine
KCCO-TV Alexandria, Minnesota
KCCW-TV Walker, Minnesota
KCDO-TV Kimball, Colorado
KCDT Coeur d'Alene, Washington
KCEB Longview, Texas
KCEC Denver, Colorado
KCEN-TV Temple, Texas
KCET Los Angeles, California
KCFG Flagstaff, Arizona
KCFW-TV Kalispell, Montana
KCGE-DT Crookston, North Dakota
KCHF Santa Fe, New Mexico
KCIT Amarillo, Texas
KCKA Centralia, Washington
KCLO-TV Rapid City, South Dakota
KCNC-TV Denver, Colorado
KCNS San Francisco, California
KCOP Los Angeles, California
KCOS El Paso, Texas
KCOY-TV Santa Maria, California
KCPQ Tacoma, Washington
KCPT Kansas City, Missouri
KCRA-TV Sacramento, California
KCRA-TV Sacramento, Maine
KCRG-TV Cedar Rapids, Iowa
KCRP-CD Corpus Christi, Texas
KCSD-TV Sioux Falls, South Dakota
KCSG Cedar City, Utah
KCSM-TV San Mateo, California
KCTS-TV Seattle, Washington
KCTV Kansas City, Missouri
KCVU Paradise, California
KCWE Kansas City, Missouri
KCWI-TV Ames, Iowa
KCWK North Las Vegas, Nevada
KCWT-CD La Feria, Texas
KCWV Duluth, Minnesota
KCWX Fredericksburg, Texas
KCWY Casper, Wyoming
KDAF Dallas, Texas
KDBC-TV El Paso, Texas
KDCK Dodge City, Kansas
KDCU-DT Derby, Kansas
KDEN Longmont, Colorado
KDFI Dallas, Texas
KDFI Dallas, Texas
KDFW Dallas, Texas
KDIN-TV Des Moines, Iowa
KDJT-CD Salinas, California
KDKA-TV Pittsburgh, Pennsylvania
KDKF Klamath Falls, Oregon
KDLH Duluth, Minnesota
KDLO-TV Florence, South Dakota
KDLT-TV Sioux Falls, South Dakota
KDLV-TV Mitchell, South Dakota
KDMD Anchorage, Alaska
KDNL-TV St. Louis, Missouri
KDOC-TV Anaheim, California
KDOR-TV Bartlesville, Oklahoma
KDRV Medford, Oregon
KDSD-TV Aberdeen, South Dakota
KDSE Dickinson, North Dakota
KDSM-TV Des Moines, Iowa
KDTF-LD San Diego, California
KDTN Denton, Texas
KDTP Holbrook, Arizona
KDTV-DT San Francisco, California
KDTX-TV Dallas, Texas
KDVR Denver, Colorado
KDVT-LP Denver, Colorado
KDYW Waco, Texas
KECI-TV Missoula, Montana
KECY-TV El Centro, California
KEDT Corpus Christi, Texas
KEET Eureka, California
KELO-TV Sioux Falls, South Dakota
KELV-LD Las Vegas, Nevada
KEMO-TV Santa Rosa, California
KEMV Mountain View, Arkansas
KEMV Arkadelphia, Arkansas
KEMV Little Rock, Arkansas
KENS San Antonio, Texas
KENV-DT Elko, Nevada
KENW Portales, New Mexico
KEPB-TV Eugene, Oregon
KEPR-TV Pasco, Washington
KERA-TV Dallas, Texas
KERO-TV Bakersfield, California
KESD-TV Brookings, South Dakota
KESQ-TV Palm Springs, California
KETA-TV Oklahoma City, Oklahoma
KETC St. Louis, Missouri
KETD Castle Rock, Colorado
KETF-CD Laredo, Texas
KETH-TV Houston, Texas
KETK-TV Jacksonville, Texas
KETV Omaha, Nebraska
KETZ El Dorado, Arkansas
KEUS-LD San Angelo, Texas
KEVC-CD Indio, California
KEVN Rapid City, South Dakota
KEYC-TV CBS & NEYC FOX Mankato, Minnesota
KEYE-TV Austin, Texas
KEYT-TV Santa Barbara, California
KEYU Borger, Texas
KEZI Eugene, Oregon
KFBB-TV Great Falls, Montana
KFCT Fort Collins, Colorado
KFCT Fort Collins, Colorado
KFDA-TV Amarillo, Texas
KFDM Beaumont, Texas
KFDX-TV Wichita Falls, Texas
KFFV Seattle, Washington
KFFX-TV Pendleton, Oregon
KFJX-DT Pittsburg, Missouri
KFMB-TV San Diego, California
KFME Fargo, North Dakota
KFOR Oklahoma City, Oklahoma
KFOX-TV El Paso, Texas
KFPH-DT Flagstaff, Arizona
KFPX-TV Newton, Iowa
KFRE-TV Sanger, California
KFSF-DT Vallejo, California
KFSM Fort Smith, Arkansas
KFSN-TV Fresno, California
KFTA-TV Fort Smith, Arkansas
KFTC Bemidji, Minnesota
KFTH-DT Alvin, Texas
KFTR-DT Ontario, California
KFTU-DT Douglas, Arizona
KFTV-DT Hanford, California
KFVE Honolulu, Hawaii
KFVS-TV Cape Girardeau, Missouri
KFWD Fort Worth, Texas
KFXA Cedar Rapids, Iowa
KFXB-TV Dubuque, Missouri
KFXF Fairbanks, Alaska
KFXK-TV Longview, Texas
KFXP Pocatello, Idaho
KFXV-LD McAllen, Texas
KFYR Bismarck, North Dakota
KGAN Cedar Rapids, Iowa
KGBT-TV Harlingen, Texas
KGCW Burlington, Iowa
KGEB Tulsa, Oklahoma
KGET-TV Bakersfield, California
KGFE Grand Forks, North Dakota
KGHB-CD Pueblo, Colorado
KGIN Grand Island, Nebraska
KGLA-AM Hammond, Louisiana
KGMC Clovis, California
KGMD-TV Hilo, Hawaii
KGMV Wailuku, Hawaii
KGNS Laredo, Texas
KGO-TV San Francisco, California
KGPE Fresno, California
KGPX-TV Spokane, Washington
KGTF Hagatna, Guam
KGTV San Diego, California
KGUN-TV Tucson, Arizona
KGW Portland, Oregon
KGWC-TV Casper, Wyoming
KGWL-TV Lander, Wyoming
KGWN Cheyenne, Wyoming
KGWR-TV Rock Springs, Wyoming
KHAS-TV Hastings, Nebraska
KHAX-LP San Diego, California
KHBC-TV Hilo, Hawaii
KHBS Fort Smith, Arkansas
KHBS-TV Rogers, Maine
KHCE-TV San Antonio, Texas
KHET Honolulu, Hawaii
KHGI-TV Kearney, Nebraska
KHIN Red Oak, Iowa
KHMT Hardin, Montana
KHNE-TV Hastings, Nebraska
KHNL Honolulu, Hawaii
KHNL/KGMB Honolulu, Hawaii
KHOG Fayetteville, Arkansas
KHON2 Hilo, Hawaii
KHON2 Honolulu, Hawaii
KHOU Houston, Texas
KHQ-TV Spokane, Washington

KHQA-TV Hannibal, Missouri
KHRR Tucson, Arizona
KHSL-TV Chico, California
KHVO Honolulu, Hawaii
KIAH Houston, Texas
KICU San Jose, California
KIDK Idaho Falls, Idaho
KIDY San Angelo, Texas
KIEM-TV Eureka, California
KIFI-TV Idaho Falls, Idaho
KIII-TV Corpus Christi, Texas
KIIN Iowa City, Missouri
KIIT North Platte, Nebraska
KIJR-LP Lucerne Valley, California
KIKU Honolulu, Hawaii
KILM Barstow, California
KIMA-TV Yakima, Washington
KIMT Mason City, Iowa
KINC Las Vegas, Nevada
KING-TV Seattle, Washington
KINT-TV El Paso, Texas
KION-TV Monterey, California
KIPT Twin Falls, Idaho
KIRO-TV Seattle, Washington
KISU-TV Pocatello, Idaho
KITU-TV Beaumont, Texas
KITV Honolulu, Hawaii
KIVI-TV Nampa, Idaho
KIVV-TV Lead, South Dakota
KIXE-TV Redding, California
KJCT Grand Junction, Colorado
KJLA Ventura, California
KJNP-TV North Pole, Alaska
KJRE Ellendale, North Dakota
KJRH-TV Tulsa, Oklahoma
KJRR Jamestown, North Dakota
KJTL Wichita Falls, Texas
KJTV Lubbock, Texas
KJUD Juneau, Alaska
KJWP Wilmington, Wyoming
KJZZ-TV Salt Lake City, Utah
KKAI Kailua, Hawaii
KKAP Little Rock, Arkansas
KKCO Grand Junction, Colorado
KKJB Boise, Idaho
KKPX-TV San Jose, California
KKTV Colorado Springs, Colorado
KLAF-LD Lafayette, Louisiana
KLAS-TV Las Vegas, Nevada
KLAX-TV Alexandria, Louisiana
KLBK-TV Lubbock, Texas
KLBY Colby, Kansas
KLCS Los Angeles, California
KLCW-TV Wolfforth, Texas
KLDO-TV Laredo, Texas
KLEI-TV Kailua-Kona, Hawaii
KLEW-TV Lewiston, Idaho
KLFY-TV Lafayette, Louisiana
KLJB Davenport, Iowa
KLKN Lincoln, Nebraska
KLNE-TV Lexington, Nebraska
KLPA-TV Alexandria, Louisiana
KLPA-TV Lafayette, Louisiana
KLPA-TV Lake Charles, Louisiana
KLPA-TV Monroe, Louisiana
KLPA-TV Shreveport, Louisiana
KLRN San Antonio, Texas
KLRT-TV Little Rock, Arkansas
KLRU Austin, Texas
KLSR-TV Eugene, Oregon
KLST San Angelo, Texas
KLTJ Galveston, Texas
KLTV Tyler, Texas
KLUJ-TV Harlingen, Texas
KLUZ-TV Albuquerque, New Mexico
KLVX Las Vegas, Nevada
KLWB New Iberia, Louisiana
KLWY Cheyenne, Wyoming
KMAU Wailuku, Hawaii
KMAX-TV Sacramento, California
KMBC Kansas City, Missouri
KMBC-TV Kansas City, Maine
KMBC-TV Kansas City, Maine
KMBH Harlingen, Texas
KMCB Coos Bay, Oregon
KMCC Laughlin, Nevada
KMCI-TV Lawrence, Missouri
KMCT-TV West Monroe, Louisiana
KMCY Minot, North Dakota
KMDE Devils Lake, North Dakota
KMEB Wailuku, Hawaii
KMEG Sioux City, Iowa
KMEX-DT Los Angeles, California
KMGH-TV Denver, Colorado
KMID Midland, Texas
KMIR-TV Palm Springs, California
KMIZ Columbia, Missouri
KMLM-DT Odessa, Texas
KMLU Columbia, Louisiana
KMNE-TV Bassett, Nebraska
KMOH-TV Kingman, Arizona
KMOS-TV Sedalia, Missouri
KMOT Minot, North Dakota
KMOV St. Louis, Missouri
KMPH-TV Visalia, California
KMPX Decatur, Texas
KMSB Tucson, Arizona
KMSP Minneapolis, Minnesota
KMSS-TV Shreveport, Louisiana
KMTF Helena, Montana
KMTP-TV San Francisco, California
KMTR Eugene, Oregon
KMTV-TV Omaha, Nebraska
KMTW Hutchinson, Kansas
KMVT Twin Falls, Idaho
KMVU-DT Medford, Oregon
KMYA-DT Camden, Arkansas
KMYS Kerrville, Texas
KMYT-TV Tulsa, Oklahoma
KMYU St. George, Utah
KNAT-TV Albuquerque, New Mexico
KNAZ-TV Flagstaff, Arizona
KNBC Los Angeles, California
KNBN Rapid City, South Dakota
KNCT Belton, Texas
KNDB Bismarck, North Dakota
KNDM Minot, North Dakota
KNDO Yakima, Washington
KNDU Richland, Washington
KNEP-TV Scottsbluff, Nebraska
KNHL Hastings, Nebraska
KNIC-DT Blanco, Texas
KNIN-TV Caldwell, Idaho
KNLC St. Louis, Missouri
KNLJ Jefferson City, Missouri
KNMD-TV Santa Fe, New Mexico
KNME-TV Albuquerque, New Mexico
KNMT Portland, Oregon
KNOE Monroe, Louisiana
KNOP North Platte, Nebraska
KNPB Reno, Nevada
KNPL North Platte, Nebraska
KNRR Pembina, North Dakota
KNSD San Diego, California
KNSO Merced, California
KNTL-LP Las Vegas, Nevada
KNTV San Jose, California
KNVA Austin, Texas
KNVN Chico, California
KNVO-TV McAllen, Texas
KNWA-TV Rogers, Arkansas
KNXT Visalia, California
KNXV-TV Phoenix, Arizona
KOAA-TV Pueblo, Colorado
KOAB-TV Bend, Oregon
KOAC-TV Corvallis, Oregon
KOAM-TV Pittsburg, Kansas
KOAT Albuquerque, New Mexico
KOAT-TV Albuquerque, Maine
KOB Albuquerque, New Mexico
KOBF Farmington, New Mexico
KOBI Medford, Oregon
KOBR Roswell, New Mexico
KOCB Oklahoma City, Oklahoma
KOCE-TV Huntington Beach, California
KOCM Norman, Oklahoma
KOCO Oklahoma City, Oklahoma
KOCO-TV Oklahoma City, Maine
KOCW Hoisington, Kansas
KODE-TV Joplin, Missouri
KOED-TV Tulsa, Oklahoma
KOET Eufaula, Oklahoma
KOFY-TV San Francisco, California
KOGG Wailuku, Hawaii
KOHD Bend, Oregon
KOIN Portland, Oregon
KOKH-TV Oklahoma City, Oklahoma
KOKI-TV Tulsa, Oklahoma
KOLD-TV Tucson, Arizona
KOLN Lincoln, Nebraska
KOLO Reno, Nevada
KOLR Springfield, Missouri
KOMO-TV Seattle, Washington
KOMU-TV Columbia, Missouri
KONG Everett, Washington
KOOD Hays, Kansas
KOPB-TV Portland, Oregon
KOPX-TV Oklahoma City, Oklahoma
KORO-TV Corpus Christi, Texas
KORX-CA Walla Walla, Washington
KOSA Odessa, Texas
KOTA-TV Lead, South Dakota
KOTA-TV Rapid City, South Dakota
KOTI Klamath Falls, Oregon
KOTV-DT Tulsa, Oklahoma
KOVR-TV Stockton, California
KOZJ Joplin, Missouri
KOZK Springfield, Missouri
KOZL-TV Springfield, Missouri
KPAX-TV Missoula, Montana
KPAZ-TV Phoenix, Arizona
KPBS San Diego, California
KPBT-TV Odessa, Texas
KPCB-DT Snyder, Texas
KPDX Vancouver, Washington
KPEJ-TV Odessa, Texas
KPHO Phoenix, Arizona
KPIC Roseburg, Oregon
KPIX-TV San Francisco, California
KPJR-DT Greeley, Colorado
KPLC Lake Charles, Louisiana
KPLO-TV Reliance, South Dakota
KPLR St. Louis, Missouri
KPMR-TV Santa Barbara, California
KPNE-TV North Platte, Nebraska
KPNX Mesa, Arizona
KPNZ Ogden, Utah
KPOB-TV Poplar Bluff, Missouri
KPPX-TV Tolleson, Arizona
KPRC-TV Houston, Texas
KPRY-TV Pierre, South Dakota
KPSD-TV Eagle Butte, South Dakota
KPTB-DT Lubbock, Texas
KPTF-DT Farwell, Texas
KPTH Sioux City, Iowa
KPTM Omaha, Nebraska
KPTS Hutchinson, Kansas
KPTV Portland, Oregon
KPTW Casper, Wyoming
KPVI-DT Pocatello, Idaho
KPXB-TV Conroe, Texas
KPXC-TV Denver, Colorado
KPXD-TV Arlington, Texas
KPXE-TV Kansas City, Missouri
KPXG-TV Salem, Oregon
KPXJ Minden, Louisiana
KPXL-TV Uvalde, Texas
KPXM-TV St. Cloud, Minnesota
KPXN-TV San Bernardino, California
KPXO-TV Kaneohe, Hawaii
KPXR-TV Cedar Rapids, Missouri
KQCA Stockton, California
KQCA-TV Sacramento, Maine
KQCD Dickinson, North Dakota
KQCW-DT Muskogee, Oklahoma
KQDS-TV Duluth, Minnesota
KQED San Francisco, California
KQEG-CA La Crescent, Minnesota
KQEH San Jose, California
KQET Watsonville, California
KQIN Davenport, Missouri
KQSD-TV Lowry, South Dakota
KQTV St. Joseph, Missouri
KQUP Pullman, Washington
KRBC-TV Abilene, Texas
KRBK Osage Beach, Missouri
KRCA Riverside, California
KRCB Cotati, California
KRCG Jefferson City, Missouri
KRCR-TV Redding, California
KRCW Salem, Oregon
KRDK-DT Valley City, North Dakota
KRDO-TV Colorado Springs, Colorado
KREG-TV Glenwood Springs, Colorado
KREM Spokane, Washington
KREN-TV Reno, Nevada
KREX-TV Grand Junction, Colorado
KREX-TV Grand Junction, Colorado
KREY-TV Montrose, Colorado
KREZ-TV Durango, Colorado
KRGV-TV Weslaco, Texas
KRII Chisholm, Minnesota
KRIN Waterloo, Iowa

KRIS-TV Corpus Christi, Texas
KRIV Houston, Texas
KRMA-TV Denver, Colorado
KRMJ Grand Junction, Colorado
KRMT Denver, Colorado
KRMU Durango, Colorado
KRMZ Steamboat Springs, Colorado
KRNE-TV Merriman, Nebraska
KRNS-CD Reno, Nevada
KRNV-DT Reno, Nevada
KRON-TV San Francisco, California
KRPV-DT Roswell, New Mexico
KRQE Albuquerque, New Mexico
KRSC-TV Claremore, Oklahoma
KRTV Great Falls, Montana
KRWB-TV Roswell, New Mexico
KRWF Redwood Falls, Minnesota
KRWG-TV Las Cruces, New Mexico
KRXI-TV Reno, Nevada
KRXIÿ Reno, Nevada
KSAN-TV San Angelo, Texas
KSAS-TV Wichita, Kansas
KSAT-TV San Antonio, Texas
KSAX Alexandria, Minnesota
KSAZ Phoenix, Arizona
KSBI Oklahoma City, Oklahoma
KSBW Salinas, California
KSBY San Luis Obispo, California
KSCE El Paso, Texas
KSCI Long Beach, California
KSCW-DT Wichita, Kansas
KSDK St. Louis, Missouri
KSEE Fresno, California
KSFY Sioux Falls, South Dakota
KSGW-TV Sheridan, Wyoming
KSHB-TV Kansas City, Missouri
KSHV-TV Shreveport, Louisiana
KSIN-TV Sioux City, Missouri
KSKN Spokane, Washington
KSL-TV Salt Lake City, Utah
KSLA Shreveport, Louisiana
KSMN Worthington, Minnesota
KSMO Kansas City, Missouri
KSMQ-TV Austin, Minnesota
KSNB Superior, Nebraska
KSNC Great Bend, Kansas
KSNF Joplin, Missouri
KSNG Garden City, Kansas
KSNK McCook, Nebraska
KSNT Topeka, Kansas
KSNV-DT Las Vegas, Nevada
KSNW Wichita, Kansas
KSPR Springfield, Missouri
KSPS-TV Spokane, Washington
KSPX-TV Sacramento, California
KSQA Topeka, Idaho
KSRE Minot, North Dakota
KSTC-TV Minneapolis, Minnesota
KSTF Scottsbluff, Nebraska
KSTP-TV St. Paul, Minnesota
KSTR-DT Irving, Texas
KSTS San Jose, California
KSTU Salt Lake City, Utah
KSTW-TV Tacoma, Washington
KSVI Billings, Montana
KSVT Twin Falls, Idaho
KSWB San Diego, California
KSWK Lakin, Kansas
KSWO-TV Lawton, Oklahoma
KSWT Yuma, Arizona
KSYS Medford, Oregon
KTAB-TV Abilene, Texas
KTAJ-TV St. Joseph, Missouri
KTAL-TV Texarkana, Texas
KTAZ Phoenix, Arizona
KTBC Austin, Texas
KTBN-TV Santa Ana, California
KTBO-TV Oklahoma City, Oklahoma
KTBS-TV Shreveport, Louisiana
KTBW-TV Tacoma, Washington
KTBY Anchorage, Alaska
KTCA-TV St. Paul, Minnesota
KTCD-LP San Diego, California
KTCI-TV St. Paul, Minnesota
KTCW Roseburg, Oregon
KTDO Las Cruces, New Mexico
KTEJ Jonesboro, Arkansas
KTEN Ada, Oklahoma
KTFA-LP Albuquerque, New Mexico
KTFD-TV Denver, Colorado
KTFF-DT Porterville, California
KTFK-DT Stockton, California
KTFN-TV El Paso, Texas
KTFQ-DT Albuquerque, New Mexico
KTFV-CD McAllen, Texas
KTGF Great Falls, Montana
KTGM Tamuning, Guam
KTHV Little Rock, Arkansas
KTIN Fort Dodge, Iowa
KTIV Sioux City, Iowa
KTKA-TV Topeka, Kansas
KTLA Los Angeles, California
KTLM Harlingen, Texas
KTLN-TV Novato, California
KTMD Galveston, Texas
KTMF Missoula, Montana
KTMW Salt Lake City, Utah
KTNC-TV Concord, California
KTNE-TV Alliance, Nebraska
KTNL-TV Sitka, Alaska
KTNV-TV Las Vegas, Nevada
KTNW Richland, Washington
KTOO-TV Juneau, Alaska
KTPX-TV Okmulgee, Oklahoma
KTRE Lufkin, Texas
KTRK-TV Houston, Texas
KTRV-TV Nampa, Idaho
KTSC Pueblo, Colorado
KTSD-TV Pierre, South Dakota
KTSF San Francisco, California
KTSM-TV El Paso, Texas
KTTC Rochester, Minnesota
KTTM Huron, South Dakota
KTTU Tucson, Arizona
KTTV Los Angeles, California
KTTW Sioux Falls, South Dakota
KTTZ-TV Lubbock, Texas
KTUL Tulsa, Oklahoma
KTUU-TV Anchorage, Alaska
KTUZ-TV30 Shawnee, Oklahoma
KTVA Anchorage, Alaska
KTVB Boise, Idaho
KTVC Roseburg, Oregon
KTVD Denver, Colorado
KTVE El Dorado, Arkansas
KTVF Fairbanks, Alaska
KTVG-TV Grand Island, Nebraska
KTVH-DT Helena, Montana
KTVI St. Louis, Missouri
KTVK Phoenix, Arizona
KTVL Medford, Oregon
KTVM-TV Butte, Montana
KTVN Reno, Nevada
KTVO Kirksville, Missouri
KTVQ Billings, Montana
KTVR La Grande, Oregon
KTVT-TV Fort Worth, Texas
KTVU Oakland, California
KTVU Oakland, California
KTVW-DT Phoenix, Arizona
KTVX Salt Lake City, Utah
KTVZ Bend, Oregon
KTWO-TV Casper, Wyoming
KTWU Topeka, Kansas
KTXA-TV Fort Worth, Texas
KTXD-TV Greenville, Texas
KTXH Houston, Texas
KTXL Sacramento, California
KTXS-TV Sweetwater, Texas
KUAC-TV Fairbanks, Alaska
KUAS-TV Tucson, Arizona
KUAT-TV Tucson, Arizona
KUBD Ketchikan, Alaska
KUBE-TV Baytown, Texas
KUCW Ogden, Utah
KUED Salt Lake City, Utah
KUEN Ogden, Utah
KUEW St. George, Utah
KUFM-TV Missoula, Montana
KUFM-TV Great Falls, Montana
KUHT Houston, Texas
KUID-TV Moscow, Idaho
KUKL-TV Kalispell, Montana
KULR-TV Billings, Montana
KUMV Williston, North Dakota
KUNP La Grande, Oregon
KUNS-TV Bellevue, Washington
KUNW-CD Yakima, Washington
KUOK Woodward, Oklahoma
KUON-TV Lincoln, Nebraska
KUPB-TV Midland, Texas
KUPK Garden City, Kansas
KUPT Hobbs, New Mexico
KUPU Waimanalo, Hawaii
KUPX-TV Provo, Utah
KUQI Corpus Christi, Texas
KUSA Denver, Colorado
KUSD-TV Vermillion, South Dakota
KUSI-TV San Diego, California
KUSM-TV Bozeman, Montana
KUTF Logan, Utah
KUTH-DT Provo, Utah
KUTP Phoenix, Arizona
KUTV Salt Lake City, Utah
KUVE-DT Green Valley, Arizona
KUVI-DT Bakersfield, California
KUVN-DT Garland, Texas
KUVS-DT Modesto, California
KVAL-TV Eugene, Oregon
KVCR-DT San Bernardino, California
KVCT Victoria, Texas
KVCW Las Vegas, Nevada
KVDA San Antonio, Texas
KVEA Corona, California
KVEO-TV Brownsville, Texas
KVER-CA Indio, California
KVES-LD Indio, California
KVEW Kennewick, Washington
KVHP Lake Charles, Louisiana
KVIA-TV El Paso, Texas
KVIE Sacramento, California
KVIH-TV Clovis, New Mexico
KVII-TV Amarillo, Texas
KVIQ Eureka, California
KVLY Fargo, North Dakota
KVMD Twentynine Palms, California
KVME-TV Bishop, California
KVMY Las Vegas, Nevada
KVNV Middletown Township, Nevada
KVOA Tucson, Arizona
KVOS-TV Bellingham, Washington
KVPT Fresno, California
KVRR Fargo, North Dakota
KVSN-DT Pueblo, Colorado
KVTH-DT Hot Springs, Arkansas
KVTJ-DT Jonesboro, Arkansas
KVTN-DT Pine Bluff, Arkansas
KVTV Laredo, Texas
KVUE Austin, Texas
KVVK-CD Kennewick, Washington
KVVU Henderson, Nevada
KVYE-TV El Centro, California
KVZK-2 Pago Pago, American Samoa
KVZK-4 Pago Pago, American Samoa
KVZK-5 Pago Pago, American Samoa
KWAB-TV Big Spring, Texas
KWBA-TV Sierra Vista, Arizona
KWBM Harrison, Arkansas
KWBN Honolulu, Hawaii
KWBQ Santa Fe, New Mexico
KWCM-TV Appleton, Minnesota
KWDK Tacoma, Washington
KWES-TV Odessa, Texas
KWET Cheyenne, Oklahoma
KWEX-DT San Antonio, Texas
KWGN Denver, Colorado
KWHB Tulsa, Oklahoma
KWHD Hilo, Hawaii
KWHE Honolulu, Hawaii
KWHM Wailuku, Hawaii
KWHY-TV Los Angeles, California
KWKB Iowa City, Iowa
KWKS Colby, Kansas
KWKT-TV Waco, Texas
KWNB-TV Hayes Center, Nebraska
KWOG Springdale, Arkansas
KWPX-TV Bellevue, Washington
KWQC-TV Davenport, Iowa
KWSE Williston, North Dakota
KWSU-TV Pullman, Washington
KWTV-DT Oklahoma City, Oklahoma
KWTX Waco, Texas
KWWB-LP Las Vegas, Nevada
KWWF Waterloo, Iowa
KWWL Waterloo, Iowa
KWWT Odessa, Texas
KWYB Butte, Montana
KXAN-TV Austin, Texas
KXAS Fort Worth, Texas
KXFX-CD Brownsville, Texas
KXGN-TV Glendive, Montana
KXII Sherman, Texas
KXIP Paris, Texas

KXLA Rancho Palos Verdes, California
KXLF-TV Butte, Montana
KXLN-DT Rosenberg, Texas
KXLT-TV Rochester, Minnesota
KXLY-TV Spokane, Washington
KXMA-TV Dickinson, North Dakota
KXMB-TV Bismarck, North Dakota
KXMC-TV Minot, North Dakota
KXMD-TV Williston, North Dakota
KXNE-TV Norfolk, Nebraska
KXNW Eureka Springs, Arkansas
KXOF-CD Laredo, Texas
KXRM-TV Colorado Springs, Colorado
KXTF Twin Falls, Idaho
KXTV Sacramento, California
KXTX Dallas, Texas
KXVA Abilene, Texas
KXVO Omaha, Nebraska
KXXV Waco, Texas
KYAZ Katy, Texas
KYES-TV Anchorage, Alaska
KYIN Mason City, Iowa
KYLE-TV Bryan, Texas
KYMA-DT Yuma, Arizona
KYNE-TV Omaha, Nebraska
KYOU-TV Ottumwa, Iowa
KYTV Springfield, Missouri
KYTX Nacogdoches, Texas
KYUR Anchorage, Alaska
KYUU-LD Boise, Idaho
KYVE Yakima, Washington
KYW-TV Philadelphia, Pennsylvania
KZJL Houston, Texas
KZJO Seattle, Washington
KZSD-TV Martin, South Dakota
KZTV Corpus Christi, Texas
KZUP-CD Baton Rouge, Louisiana
MPTVÿ Milwaukee, Wisconsin
MPTVÿ Milwaukee, Wisconsin
SEMILLITAS Miami, Florida
SOPTV Klamath Falls, Oregon
VIENDOMOVIES Miami, Florida
W07DP-D Harrisburg, Pennsylvania
WAAY-TV Huntsville, Alabama
WABC-TV New York, New York
WABG-TV Greenwood, Mississippi
WABI-TV Bangor, Maine
WABM Birmingham, Alabama
WABW-TV Pelham, Georgia
WACH Columbia, South Carolina
WACP Atlantic City, New Jersey
WACS-TV Dawson, Georgia
WACX-DT Leesburg, Florida
WACY-TV Appleton, Wisconsin
WADL Mount Clemens, Michigan
WAFB Baton Rouge, Louisiana
WAFF Huntsville, Alabama
WAGA Atlanta, Georgia
WAGM Presque Isle, Maine
WAGT Augusta, Georgia
WAGV Harlan, Kentucky
WAIQ Montgomery, Alabama
WAKA Selma, Alabama
WALA-TV Mobile, Alabama
WALB Albany, Georgia
WAMI-DT Hollywood, Florida
WAMY-TV Huntsville, Alabama
WAND Decatur, Illinois
WANE-TV Fort Wayne, Indiana
WAOE Peoria, Illinois
WAOW Wausau, Wisconsin
WAPA-TV San Juan, Puerto Rico
WAPT Jackson, Mississippi
WAPT-TV Jackson, Maine
WATC-DT Atlanta, Georgia
WATE-TV Knoxville, Tennessee
WATL Atlanta, Georgia
WATM-TV Altoona, Pennsylvania
WATN-TV Jackson, Tennessee
WAVE Louisville, Kentucky
WAVY-TV Portsmouth, Virginia
WAWD Fort Walton Beach, Florida
WAWV-TV Terre Haute, Indiana
WAXN-TV Kannapolis, North Carolina
WBAL Baltimore, Maryland
WBAL-TV Baltimore, Maine
WBAY-TV Green Bay, Wisconsin
WBBH-TV Fort Myers, Florida
WBBJ-TV Jackson, Tennessee
WBBM-TV Chicago, Illinois
WBBZ-TV Springville, New York
WBDT Springfield, Ohio
WBEC-TV Boca Raton, Florida
WBFF Baltimore, Maryland
WBFS-TV Miami, Florida
WBGU-TV Bowling Green, Ohio
WBIN-TV Derry, New Hampshire
WBIQ Birmingham, Alabama
WBIR-TV Knoxville, Tennessee
WBKB-TV Alpena, Michigan
WBKI-TV Campbellsville, Kentucky
WBKO Bowling Green, Kentucky
WBKP Calumet, Michigan
WBMA-LD Birmingham, Alabama
WBMM Tuskegee, Alabama
WBNA Louisville, Kentucky
WBNG-TV Binghamton, New York
WBNS-TV Columbus, Ohio
WBNX-TV Akron, Ohio
WBOC-TV Salisbury, Maryland
WBOY-TV Clarksburg, West Virginia
WBPH-TV Bethlehem, Pennsylvania
WBPX-TV Boston, Massachusetts
WBRA-TV Roanoke, Virginia
WBRC Birmingham, Alabama
WBRE-TV Wilkes-Barre, Pennsylvania
WBRL-CD Baton Rouge, Louisiana
WBRZ-TV Baton Rouge, Louisiana
WBSF Bay City, Michigan
WBTV Charlotte, North Carolina
WBTW Florence, South Carolina
WBUI Decatur, Illinois
WBUP Ishpeming, Michigan
WBUW Janesville, Wisconsin
WBUY-TV Holly Springs, Mississippi
WBXX-TV Crossville, Tennessee
WBZ-TV Boston, Massachusetts
WCAU Philadelphia, Pennsylvania
WCAV Charlottesville, Virginia
WCAX-TV Burlington, Vermont
WCBB Augusta, Maine
WCBD-TV Charleston, South Carolina
WCBI-DT Columbus, Mississippi
WCBS-TV New York, New York
WCCB Charlotte, North Carolina
WCCO-TV Minneapolis, Minnesota
WCCT Waterbury, Connecticut
WCCU Urbana, Illinois
WCCV-TV Arecibo, Puerto Rico
WCDC-TV Adams, New York
WCES-TV Wrens, Georgia
WCET Cincinnati, Ohio
WCFE-TV Plattsburgh, New York
WCFT-TV Tuscaloosa, Alabama
WCGV-TV Milwaukee, Wisconsin
WCHS-TV Charleston, West Virginia
WCIA Champaign, Illinois
WCIQ Mount Cheaha, Alabama
WCIU-TV Chicago, Illinois
WCIV Charleston, South Carolina
WCIX Springfield, Illinois
WCJB-TV Gainesville, Florida
WCLF Clearwater, Florida
WCLJ-TV Bloomington, Indiana
WCMH-TV Columbus, Ohio
WCML Alpena, Michigan
WCMU-TV Mount Pleasant, Michigan
WCMV Cadillac, Michigan
WCMW Manistee, Michigan
WCNC-TV Charlotte, North Carolina
WCNY-TV Syracuse, New York
WCOV-TV Montgomery, Alabama
WCPB Salisbury, Maryland
WCPO-TV Cincinnati, Ohio
WCPX-TV Chicago, Illinois
WCSC-TV Charleston, South Carolina
WCSH Portland, Maine
WCTE Cookeville, Tennessee
WCTI-TV New Bern, North Carolina
WCTV Thomasville, Georgia
WCTX New Haven, Connecticut
WCVB Boston, Massachusetts
WCVB-TV Needham, Maine
WCVE-TV Richmond, Virginia
WCVE-TV Richmond, Virginia
WCVI-TV Christiansted, Virgin Islands
WCVN-TV Covington, Kentucky
WCWF Suring, Wisconsin
WCWG Lexington, North Carolina
WCWJ Jacksonville, Florida
WCWN Schenectady, New York
WCYB-TV Bristol, Virginia
WDAF Kansas City, Missouri
WDAM-TV Laurel, Mississippi
WDAY-TV Fargo, North Dakota
WDAZ-TV Devil's Lake, North Dakota
WDBB Bessemer, Alabama
WDBD Jackson, Mississippi
WDBJ Roanoke, Virginia
WDCA Washington, District of Columbia
WDCQ-TV Bad Axe, Michigan
WDCW Washington, District of Columbia
WDEF-TV Chattanooga, Tennessee
WDFX-TV Ozark, Alabama
WDHN Dothan, Alabama
WDIO-DT Duluth, Minnesota
WDIQ Dozier, Alabama
WDJT-TV Milwaukee, Wisconsin
WDKA Paducah, Kentucky
WDKY-TV Danville, Kentucky
WDLI-TV Canton, Ohio
WDPB Seaford, Delaware
WDPX-TV Boston, Massachusetts
WDRB Louisville, Kentucky
WDSC-TV New Smyrna Beach, Florida
WDSE Duluth, Minnesota
WDSI-TV Chattanooga, Tennessee
WDSU New Orleans, Louisiana
WDSU-TV New Orleans, Maine
WDTI Indianapolis, Indiana
WDTN Dayton, Ohio
WDTV Weston, West Virginia
WDWL Bayamon, Puerto Rico
WEAO Akron, Ohio
WEAR-TV Pensacola, Florida
WEAU Eau Claire, Wisconsin
WEBA-TV Allendale, South Carolina
WECT Wilmington, North Carolina
WEDH Hartford, Connecticut
WEDN Norwich, Connecticut
WEDU Tampa-St. Petersburg, Florida
WEDW Bridgeport, Connecticut
WEDY New Haven, Connecticut
WEEK-TV Peoria, Illinois
WEFS Cocoa, Florida
WEHT Evansville, Indiana
WEIQ Mobile, Alabama
WEIU-TV Charleston, Illinois
WEKW-TV Keene, New Hampshire
WELF-TV Dalton, Georgia
WEMT Greeneville, Tennessee
WENH-TV Durham, New Hampshire
WENY-TV Elmira, New York
WEPX-TV Greenville, North Carolina
WESH Daytona Beach, Florida
WESH-TV New Orleans, Maine
WETA-TV Washington, District of Columbia
WETK Burlington, Vermont
WETM-TV Elmira, New York
WEUX Chippewa Falls, Wisconsin
WEVV-TV Evansville, Indiana
WEWS-TV Cleveland, Ohio
WEYI-TV Saginaw, Michigan
WFAA Dallas, Texas
WFDC-DT Arlington, District of Columbia
WFFF-TV Burlington, Vermont
WFFT-TV Fort Wayne, Indiana
WFGC Palm Beach, Florida
WFGX Fort Walton Beach, Florida
WFIE Evansville, Indiana
WFIQ Florence, Alabama
WFLA-TV Tampa, Florida
WFLD Chicago, Illinois
WFLI-TV Cleveland, Tennessee
WFLX West Palm Beach, Florida
WFMJ-TV Youngstown, Ohio
WFMY-TV Greensboro, North Carolina
WFMZ-TV Allentown, Pennsylvania
WFOR-TV Miami, Florida
WFOX-TV Jacksonville, Florida
WFPT Frederick, Maryland
WFPX-TV Fayetteville, North Carolina
WFQX-TV Cadillac, Michigan
WFRV-TV Green Bay, Wisconsin
WFSB Hartford, Connecticut
WFSG Panama City, Florida
WFSU-TV Tallahassee, Florida
WFTC Minneapolis, Minnesota
WFTS-TV Tampa, Florida
WFTT-DT Tampa, Florida
WFTV Orlando, Florida
WFTX-TV Cape Coral, Florida
WFTY-DT Smithtown, New York

WFUM Flint, Michigan
WFUP Vanderbilt, Michigan
WFUT-DT Newark, New Jersey
WFWA Fort Wayne, Indiana
WFXB Myrtle Beach, South Carolina
WFXG Augusta, Georgia
WFXI Morehead City, North Carolina
WFXL Albany, Georgia
WFXP Erie, Pennsylvania
WFXR Roanoke, Virginia
WFXT Boston, Massachusetts
WFXV Utica, New York
WFYI Indianapolis, Indiana
WGAL Lancaster, Pennsylvania
WGAL-TV Lancaster, Maine
WGBA-TV Green Bay, Wisconsin
WGBC Meridian, Mississippi
WGBH Boston, Massachusetts
WGBH-TV Boston, Massachusetts
WGBO-DT Joliet, Illinois
WGBY-TV Springfield, Massachusetts
WGCB-TV Red Lion, Pennsylvania
WGCL Atlanta, Georgia
WGCU Fort Myers, Florida
WGEM-TV Quincy, Illinois
WGEN-TV Key West, Florida
WGFL High Springs, Florida
WGGB-TV Springfield, Massachusetts
WGGN-TV Sandusky, Ohio
WGGS-TV Greenville, South Carolina
WGHP High Point, North Carolina
WGIQ Louisville, Alabama
WGMB-TV Baton Rouge, Louisiana
WGME-TV Portland, Maine
WGN Chicago, Illinois
WGNM Macon, Georgia
WGNO New Orleans, Louisiana
WGNT Portsmouth, Virginia
WGPT Oakland, Maryland
WGPX-TV Burlington, North Carolina
WGRZ Buffalo, New York
WGSA Baxley, Georgia
WGTE-TV Toledo, Ohio
WGTQ Sault Ste. Marie, Michigan
WGTU Traverse City, Michigan
WGTV Athens, Georgia
WGTV Watertown, New York
WGTW-TV Burlington, New Jersey
WGVK Kalamazoo, Michigan
WGVU-TV Grand Rapids, Michigan
WGWG Charleston, South Carolina
WGWW Anniston, Alabama
WGXA Macon, Georgia
WHA-TV Madison, Wisconsin
WHAG-TV Hagerstown, Maryland
WHAM-TV Rochester, New York
WHAS-TV Louisville, Kentucky
WHBF-TV Rock Island, Illinois
WHBQ-TV Memphis, Tennessee
WHBR Pensacola, Florida
WHDF Florence, Alabama
WHDH Boston, Massachusetts
WHEC-TV Rochester, New York
WHFT-TV Miami, Florida
WHIO-TV Dayton, Ohio
WHIQ Huntsville, Alabama
WHIZ-TV Zanesville, Ohio
WHKY-TV Hickory, North Carolina
WHLA-TV La Crosse, Wisconsin
WHLT Hattiesburg, Mississippi
WHMB-TV Indianapolis, Indiana
WHMC Conway, South Carolina
WHME-TV South Bend, Indiana
WHNO New Orleans, Louisiana
WHNS Greenville, South Carolina
WHNT Huntsville, Alabama
WHO-DT Des Moines, Missouri
WHOI Peoria, Illinois
WHP-TV Harrisburg, Pennsylvania
WHPX-TV New London, Connecticut
WHRM-TV Wausau, Wisconsin
WHRO-TV Hampton-Norfolk, Virginia
WHSG-TV Monroe, Georgia
WHSV Harrisonburg, Virginia
WHTJ Charlottesville, Virginia
WHTM-TV Harrisburg, Pennsylvania
WHTN Murfreesboro, Tennessee
WHTV Jackson, Michigan
WHTX-LP Hartford, Connecticut
WHUT-TV Washington, District of Columbia
WHWC-TV Menomonie, Wisconsin
WHYY-TV Wilmington, Delaware
WIAT Birmingham, Alabama
WIBW Topeka, Kansas
WICD Champaign, Illinois
WICS Springfield, Illinois
WICU-TV Erie, Pennsylvania
WICZ-TV Binghamton, New York
WIFR Freeport, Illinois
WIIQ Demopolis, Alabama
WILL-TV Urbana, Illinois
WILM-LD Wilmington, North Carolina
WILX Onondaga, Michigan
WINK-TV Fort Myers, Florida
WINM Angola, Indiana
WINP-TV Pittsburgh, Pennsylvania
WIPB Muncie, Indiana
WIPM-TV Mayaguez, Puerto Rico
WIPR-TV San Juan, Puerto Rico
WIPX-TV Bloomington, Indiana
WIRS Yauco, Puerto Rico
WIRT Hibbing, Minnesota
WIS Columbia, South Carolina
WISC-TV Madison, Wisconsin
WISE-TV Fort Wayne, Indiana
WISH-TV Indianapolis, Indiana
WISN-TV Milwaukee, Wisconsin
WISN-TV Wilwaukee, Maine
WITF-TV Harrisburg, Pennsylvania
WITI Milwaukee, Wisconsin
WITN Washington, North Carolina
WITV Charleston, South Carolina
WIVB-TV Buffalo, New York
WIVT Binghamton, New York
WJAC-TV Johnstown, Pennsylvania
WJAL-TV Hagerstown, Maryland
WJAR Providence, Rhode Island
WJAX-TV Jacksonville, Florida
WJBF Augusta, Georgia
WJBK Detroit, Michigan
WJCL Savannah, Georgia
WJCT Jacksonville, Florida
WJEB-TV Jacksonville, Florida
WJET-TV Erie, Pennsylvania
WJFW-TV Rhinelander, Wisconsin
WJHG Panama City, Florida
WJHL-TV Johnson City, Tennessee
WJLA-TV Washington, District of Columbia
WJMN-TV Escanaba, Michigan
WJPM-TV Florence, South Carolina
WJPX San Juan, Puerto Rico
WJRT Flint, Michigan
WJSP-TV Columbus, Georgia
WJSU-TV Anniston, Alabama
WJTC Pensacola, Florida
WJTV Jackson, Mississippi
WJW Cleveland, Ohio
WJWJ-TV Beaufort, South Carolina
WJWN-TV San Sebastian, Puerto Rico
WJXT Jacksonville, Florida
WJXX Orange Park, Florida
WJYS Hammond, Illinois
WJZ-TV Baltimore, Maryland
WJZY Belmont, North Carolina
WKAQ San Juan, Puerto Rico
WKAR-TV East Lansing, Michigan
WKAS Ashland, Kentucky
WKBD-TV Detroit, Michigan
WKBN-TV Youngstown, Ohio
WKBS-TV Altoona, Pennsylvania
WKBT-TV La Crosse, Wisconsin
WKBW-TV Buffalo, New York
WKCF Clermont, Florida
WKCF-TV Winter Park, Maine
WKEF Dayton, Ohio
WKGB-TV Bowling Green, Kentucky
WKHA Hazard, Kentucky
WKLE Lexington, Kentucky
WKMA-TV Madisonville, Indiana
WKMG-TV Orlando, Florida
WKMJ-TV Louisville, Kentucky
WKMR Morehead, Kentucky
WKMU Murray, Kentucky
WKNO Memphis, Tennessee
WKNX-TV Knoxville, Tennessee
WKOH Owensboro, Kentucky
WKOI-TV Richmond, Indiana
WKON Owenton, Kentucky
WKOP-TV Knoxville, Tennessee
WKOW Madison, Wisconsin
WKPC-TV Louisville, Kentucky
WKPD Paducah, Kentucky
WKPI-TV Pikeville, West Virginia
WKPT-TV Kingsport, Tennessee
WKPV Ponce, Puerto Rico
WKRC-TV Cincinnati, Ohio
WKRG-TV Mobile, Alabama
WKRN-TV Nashville, Tennessee
WKSO-TV Somerset, Kentucky
WKTC Sumter, South Carolina
WKTV Utica, New York
WKYC Cleveland, Ohio
WKYT Lexington, Kentucky
WKYU-TV Bowling Green, Kentucky
WKZT-TV Elizabethtown, Kentucky
WLAE-TV New Orleans, Louisiana
WLAJ Lansing, Michigan
WLAX La Crosse, Wisconsin
WLBT Jackson, Mississippi
WLBZ Bangor, Maine
WLED-TV Littleton, New Hampshire
WLEF-TV Park Falls, Wisconsin
WLEX-TV Lexington, Kentucky
WLFB Bluefield, West Virginia
WLFG Grundy, Virginia
WLFI-TV Lafayette, Indiana
WLFL Raleigh, North Carolina
WLGA Opelika, Alabama
WLII-DT Caguas, Puerto Rico
WLIO Lima, Ohio
WLIW Garden City, New York
WLJC-TV Beattyville, Kentucky
WLJT-DT Lexington, Tennessee
WLKY Louisville, Kentucky
WLKY-TV Louisville, Maine
WLLA Kalamazoo, Michigan
WLMB Toledo, Ohio
WLMT Memphis, Tennessee
WLNE-TV New Bedford, Massachusetts
WLNS-TV Lansing, Michigan
WLNY-TV Riverhead, New York
WLOO Vicksburg, Mississippi
WLOS Asheville, North Carolina
WLOV-TV West Point, Mississippi
WLOX Biloxi, Mississippi
WLPB-TV Baton Rouge, Louisiana
WLPX-TV Charleston, West Virginia
WLRN-TV Miami, Florida
WLS-TV Chicago, Illinois
WLTV-DT Miami, Florida
WLTX Columbia, South Carolina
WLTZ Columbus, Georgia
WLUC-TV Marquette, Michigan
WLUK-TV Green Bay, Wisconsin
WLVI Cambridge, Massachusetts
WLVT-TV Allentown, Pennsylvania
WLWC New Bedford, Massachusetts
WLWT Cincinnati, Ohio
WLXI Greensboro, North Carolina
WLYH-TV Lancaster, Pennsylvania
WMAB-TV Mississippi State, Mississippi
WMAE-TV Booneville, Mississippi
WMAH-TV Biloxi, Mississippi
WMAI Cleveland, Mississippi
WMAO-TV Greenwood, Mississippi
WMAQ Chicago, Illinois
WMAR-TV Baltimore, Maryland
WMAU-TV Bude, Mississippi
WMAV-TV Oxford, Mississippi
WMAW-TV Meridian, Mississippi
WMAZ-TV Macon, Georgia
WMBB Panama City, Florida
WMBC-TV Newton, New Jersey
WMBD-TV Peoria, Illinois
WMBF-TV Myrtle Beach, South Carolina
WMC-TV Memphis, Tennessee
WMCF-TV Montgomery, Alabama
WMCN-TV Atlantic City, New Jersey
WMDE Seaford, Georgia
WMDN Meridian, Mississippi
WMDT Salisbury, Maryland
WMEA-TV Biddeford, Maine
WMEB-TV Orono, Maine
WMEC Macomb, Illinois
WMED-TV Calais, Maine
WMEI Arecibo, Puerto Rico
WMEM-TV Presque Isle, Maine
WMFD-TV Mansfield, Ohio
WMFE-TV Orlando, Florida
WMFP Lawrence, Massachusetts
WMGM-TV Wildwood, New Jersey
WMGT-TV Macon, Georgia
WMHT Schenectady, New York

WMLW-TV Racine, Wisconsin
WMPB Baltimore, Maryland
WMPN-TV Jackson, Mississippi
WMPT Annapolis, Maryland
WMPV-TV Mobile, Alabama
WMSN-TV Madison, Wisconsin
WMSY-TV Marion, Virginia
WMTJ Fajardo, Puerto Rico
WMTV Madison, Wisconsin
WMTW Poland Spring, Maine
WMTW-TV Westbrook, Maine
WMUM-TV Cochran, Georgia
WMUR-TV Manchester, New Hampshire
WMYA-TV Anderson, South Carolina
WMYD Detroit, Michigan
WMYO Salem, Indiana
WMYT Rock Hill, South Carolina
WMYV Greensboro, North Carolina
WNAB Nashville, Tennessee
WNAC-TV Providence, Rhode Island
WNAC-TV Providence, Rhode Island
WNBC New York, New York
WNBW-DT Gainesville, Florida
WNCF Montgomery, Alabama
WNCN Goldsboro, North Carolina
WNCT-TV Greenville, North Carolina
WNDU South Bend, Indiana
WNDY-TV Marion, Indiana
WNED-TV Buffalo, New York
WNEH Greenwood, South Carolina
WNEM Bay City, Michigan
WNEO Alliance, Ohio
WNEP Waymart, Pennsylvania
WNET Newark, New Jersey
WNEU Merrimack, New Hampshire
WNGH-TV Chatsworth, Georgia
WNIN Evansville, Indiana
WNIT South Bend, Indiana
WNJB New Brunswick, New Jersey
WNJN Montclair, New Jersey
WNJS Camden, New Jersey
WNJT Trenton, New Jersey
WNJU Linden, New Jersey
WNJX-TV Mayaguez, Puerto Rico
WNKY Bowling Green, Kentucky
WNLO Buffalo, New York
WNMU Marquette, Michigan
WNNE Hartford, Vermont
WNOL New Orleans, Louisiana
WNPB-TV Morgantown, West Virginia
WNPT Nashville, Tennessee
WNPX-TV Cookeville, Tennessee
WNSC-TV Rock Hill, South Carolina
WNTV Greenville, South Carolina
WNTZ-TV Natchez, Mississippi
WNUV Baltimore, Maryland
WNVC Fairfax, Virginia
WNVT Goldvein, Virginia
WNWO-TV Toledo, Ohio
WNYB Jamestown, New York
WNYE-TV New York, New York
WNYI Ithaca, New York
WNYJ-TV West Milford, New Jersey
WNYO-TV Buffalo, New York
WNYS-TV Syracuse, New York
WNYT Albany, New York
WNYT Pittsfield, Massachusetts
WNYW Newburgh, New York
WOAI-TV San Antonio, Texas
WOAY-TV Oak Hill, West Virginia
WOCK-CD Chicago, Illinois
WOFL Orlando, Florida
WOGX Ocala, Florida
WOI-DT Ames, Missouri
WOIO Shaker Heights, Ohio
WOLE-DT Aguadilla, Puerto Rico
WOLF-TV Hazleton, Pennsylvania
WOLO-TV Columbia, South Carolina
WOOD-TV Grand Rapids, Michigan
WOPX-TV Melbourne, Florida
WORA-TV Mayaguez, Puerto Rico
WOSU-TV Columbus, Ohio
WOTF-TV Melbourne, Florida
WOTV Battle Creek, Michigan
WOUB-TV Athens, Ohio
WOUC-TV Cambridge, Ohio
WOWK-TV Huntington, West Virginia
WOWT Omaha, Nebraska
WPAN Fort Walton Beach, Florida
WPBA Atlanta, Georgia
WPBF Tequesta, Florida
WPBN-TV Traverse City, Michigan
WPBO Portsmouth, Ohio
WPBS-DT Norwood, New York
WPBT Miami, Florida
WPBY-TV Charleston, West Virginia
WPCB-TV Pittsburgh/Greensburg, Pennsylvania
WPCH-TV Atlanta, Georgia
WPCT Panama City Beach, Florida
WPCW-TV Jeannette, Pennsylvania
WPDE-TV Florence, South Carolina
WPEC West Palm Beach, Florida
WPFO Waterville, Maine
WPGA-TV Perry, Georgia
WPGD-TV Hendersonville, Tennessee
WPGH-TV Pittsburgh, Pennsylvania
WPGX Panama City, Florida
WPHL Philadelphia, Pennsylvania
WPIX New York, New York
WPLG Miami, Florida
WPME Lewiston, Maine
WPMI-TV Mobile, Alabama
WPMT York, Pennsylvania
WPNE Green Bay, Wisconsin
WPNT Pittsburgh, Pennsylvania
WPPX-TV Wilmington, Pennsylvania
WPSD-TV Paducah, Kentucky
WPSG-TV Philadelphia, Pennsylvania
WPSU-TV Clearfield, Pennsylvania
WPTA Fort Wayne, Indiana
WPTD Dayton, Ohio
WPTO Oxford, Ohio
WPTV-TV West Palm Beach, Florida
WPTZ North Pole, New York
WPVI-TV Philadelphia, Pennsylvania
WPWR Gary, Indiana
WPXA-TV Rome, Georgia
WPXC-TV Brunswick, Georgia
WPXD-TV Ann Arbor, Michigan
WPXE-TV Kenosha, Wisconsin
WPXG-TV Boston, Massachusetts
WPXH-TV Birmingham, Alabama
WPXI Pittsburgh, Pennsylvania
WPXJ-TV Buffalo, New York
WPXK-TV Jellico, Tennessee
WPXL-TV New Orleans, Louisiana
WPXM-TV Miami, Florida
WPXN-TV New York, New York
WPXP-TV Lake Worth, Florida
WPXQ-TV Block Island, Rhode Island
WPXR-TV Roanoke, Virginia
WPXS Mount Vernon, Illinois
WPXT Portland, Maine
WPXU-TV Jacksonville, North Carolina
WPXV-TV Norfolk, Virginia
WPXW-TV Manassas, District of Columbia
WPXX-TV Memphis, Tennessee
WQAD Moline, Illinois
WQCW Portsmouth, Ohio
WQEC Quincy, Illinois
WQED Pittsburgh, Pennsylvania
WQHA Aguada, Puerto Rico
WQHS-DT Cleveland, Ohio
WQLN Erie, Pennsylvania
WQMY Williamsport, Pennsylvania
WQOW-DT Eau Claire, Wisconsin
WQPT-TV Moline, Illinois
WQPX-TV Scranton, Pennsylvania
WQRF-TV Rockford, Illinois
WQTO Ponce, Puerto Rico
WRAL-TV Raleigh, North Carolina
WRAZ Raleigh, North Carolina
WRBJ-TV Magee, Mississippi
WRBL Columbus, Georgia
WRBU East St. Louis, Illinois
WRBW Orlando, Florida
WRC Washington, District of Columbia
WRCB-DT Chattanooga, Tennessee
WRDC Durham, North Carolina
WRDQ Orlando, Florida
WRDW Augusta, Georgia
WREG-TV Memphis, Tennessee
WRET-TV Spartanburg, South Carolina
WREX-TV Rockford, Illinois
WRGB Schenectady, New York
WRGT-TV Dayton, Ohio
WRIC-TV Petersburg, Virginia
WRJA-TV Sumter, South Carolina
WRJM Troy, Alabama
WRLH-TV Richmond, Virginia
WRLK-TV Columbia, South Carolina
WRNN-TV Kingston, New York
WROC-TV Rochester, New York
WRPX-TV Rocky Mount, North Carolina
WRSP-TV Springfield, Illinois
WRTV Indianapolis, Indiana
WRXY-TV Tice, Florida
WSAV-TV Savannah, Georgia
WSAW Wausau, Wisconsin
WSAZ Huntington, West Virginia
WSB-TV Atlanta, Georgia
WSBE-TV Providence, Rhode Island
WSBK-TV Boston, Massachusetts
WSBN-TV Norton, Virginia
WSBS-TV Key West, Florida
WSBT-TV South Bend, Indiana
WSCV Fort Lauderdale, Florida
WSEC Jacksonville, Illinois
WSEE-TV Erie, Pennsylvania
WSES Tuscaloosa, Alabama
WSET-TV Lynchburg, Virginia
WSFA Montgomery, Alabama
WSFJ-TV Newark, Ohio
WSFL Miami, Florida
WSFX-TV Wilmington, North Carolina
WSIL-TV Harrisburg, Illinois
WSIU-TV Carbondale, Illinois
WSJV Elkhart, Indiana
WSKA Corning, New York
WSKC-CD Atlanta, Georgia
WSKG-TV Binghamton, New York
WSKY-TV Manteo, North Carolina
WSLS-TV Roanoke, Virginia
WSMH Flint, Michigan
WSMV Nashville, Tennessee
WSNS Chicago, Illinois
WSOC-TV Charlotte, North Carolina
WSPA-TV Spartanburg, South Carolina
WSPX-TV Syracuse, New York
WSRE Pensacola, Florida
WSST-TV Cordele, Georgia
WSTE-DT Ponce, Puerto Rico
WSTM-TV Syracuse, New York
WSTQ-LP Syracuse, New York
WSTR-TV Cincinnati, Ohio
WSUR-DT Ponce, Puerto Rico
WSVI Christiansted, Virgin Islands
WSVN Miami, Florida
WSWB Scranton, Pennsylvania
WSWG Valdosta, Georgia
WSWP-TV Grandview, West Virginia
WSYM-TV Lansing, Michigan
WSYR-TV Syracuse, New York
WSYT Syracuse, New York
WSYX Columbus, Ohio
WTAE-TV Pittsburgh, Pennsylvania
WTAJ-TV Altoona, Pennsylvania
WTAP Parkersburg, West Virginia
WTAT-TV Charleston, South Carolina
WTBY-TV Poughkeepsie, New York
WTCE-TV Fort Pierce, Florida
WTCI Chattanooga, Tennessee
WTCN-CA West Palm Beach, Florida
WTCT Marion, Illinois
WTEN Albany, New York
WTGL Cocoa, Florida
WTGS Hardeeville, South Carolina
WTHI-TV Terre Haute, Indiana
WTHR Indianapolis, Indiana
WTIC-TV Hartford, Connecticut
WTIN-TV Ponce, Puerto Rico
WTIU Bloomington, Indiana
WTJP-TV Gadsden, Alabama
WTJR Quincy, Illinois
WTJX-TV Charlotte Amalie, Virgin Islands
WTKR Norfolk, Virginia
WTLH Bainbridge, Georgia
WTLJ Muskegon, Michigan
WTLV Jacksonville, Florida
WTLW Lima, Ohio
WTMJ-TV Milwaukee, Wisconsin
WTNH New Haven, Connecticut
WTNZ Knoxville, Tennessee
WTOC-TV Savannah, Georgia
WTOG-TV St. Petersburg, Florida
WTOK Meridian, Mississippi
WTOL Toledo, Ohio
WTOM-TV Cheboygan, Michigan
WTOV-TV Steubenville, Ohio
WTPC-TV Virginia Beach, Virginia
WTPX-TV Antigo, Wisconsin
WTRF-TV Wheeling, West Virginia
WTSP St. Petersburg, Florida

WTTA St. Petersburg, Florida
WTTE Columbus, Ohio
WTTG Washington, District of Columbia
WTTK Kokomo, Indiana
WTTO Homewood, Alabama
WTTV Bloomington, Indiana
WTTW Chicago, Illinois
WTVA Tupelo, Mississippi
WTVC Chattanooga, Tennessee
WTVD-TV Durham, North Carolina
WTVE Reading, Pennsylvania
WTVF Nashville, Tennessee
WTVG-TV Toledo, Ohio
WTVH Syracuse, New York
WTVI Charlotte, North Carolina
WTVJ Miami, Florida
WTVM Columbus, Georgia
WTVO Rockford, Illinois
WTVP Peoria, Illinois
WTVQ-TV Lexington, Kentucky
WTVR Richmond, Virginia
WTVS Detroit, Michigan
WTVT Tampa, Florida
WTVW Evansville, Indiana
WTVX Fort Pierce, Florida
WTVY Dothan, Alabama
WTVZ-TV Norfolk, Virginia
WTWC-TV Tallahassee, Florida
WTWO Terre Haute, Indiana
WTXF-TV Allentown, Pennsylvania
WTXL-TV Tallahassee, Florida
WUAB Lorain, Ohio
WUCW Minneapolis, Minnesota
WUFT Gainesville, Florida
WUGA-TV Toccoa, Georgia
WUHF Rochester, New York
WUJA Caguas, Puerto Rico
WUNC-TV Chapel Hill, North Carolina
WUND-TV Edenton, North Carolina
WUNE-TV Linville, North Carolina
WUNF-TV Asheville, North Carolina
WUNG-TV Concord, North Carolina
WUNI-TV Worcester, Massachusetts
WUNJ-TV Wilmington, North Carolina
WUNK-TV Greenville, North Carolina
WUNL-TV Winston-Salem, North Carolina
WUNM-TV Jacksonville, North Carolina
WUNP-TV Roanoke Rapids, North Carolina
WUNU Lumberton, North Carolina
WUNW Canton, North Carolina
WUOA Tuscaloosa, Alabama
WUPA Atlanta, Georgia
WUPL Slidell, Louisiana
WUPV Ashland, Virginia
WUPW Toledo, Ohio
WUPX-TV Marquette, Michigan
WUSA Washington, District of Columbia
WUSF-TV Tampa, Florida
WUSI-TV Olney, Illinois
WUTB Baltimore, Maryland
WUTF-DT Marlborough, Massachusetts
WUTH-CD Hartford, Connecticut
WUTR Utica, New York
WUTV Buffalo, New York
WUVC-DT Fayetteville, North Carolina
WUVG-DT Athens, Georgia
WUVP-DT Vineland, New Jersey
WUXP-TV Nashville, Tennessee
WVAH-TV Charleston, West Virginia
WVAN-TV Savannah, Georgia
WVBT Virginia Beach, Virginia
WVCI-LP Daytona Beach, Florida
WVCY-TV Milwaukee, Wisconsin
WVEA-TV Venice, Florida
WVEC Hampton, Virginia
WVEN-TV Daytona Beach, Florida
WVER Rutland, Vermont
WVFX Clarksburg, West Virginia
WVIA-TV Scranton, Pennsylvania
WVII-TV Bangor, Maine
WVIR-TV Charlottesville, Virginia
WVIT New Britain, Connecticut
WVIZ Cleveland, Ohio
WVLA-TV Baton Rouge, Louisiana
WVLR Tazewell, Tennessee
WVLT Knoxville, Tennessee
WVNS-TV Lewisburg, West Virginia
WVNY Burlington, Vermont
WVPT Staunton, Virginia
WVPX-TV Akron, Ohio
WVPY Front Royal, Virginia
WVTA Windsor, Vermont
WVTB St. Johnsbury, Vermont
WVTM Birmingham, Alabama
WVTV Milwaukee, Wisconsin
WVUE-DT New Orleans, Louisiana
WVUT Vincennes, Indiana
WVVA Bluefield, West Virginia
WVXF Charlotte Amalie, Virgin Islands
WWAY-TV Wilmington, North Carolina
WWBT Richmond, Virginia
WWCP-TV Johnstown, Pennsylvania
WWCW Lynchburg, Virginia
WWDP Norwell, Massachusetts
WWHB-CA West Palm Beach, Florida
WWHO Chillicothe, Ohio
WWJ-TV Detroit, Michigan
WWL-TV New Orleans, Louisiana
WWLP Springfield, Massachusetts
WWMB Florence, South Carolina
WWMT Kalamazoo, Michigan
WWNY-TV Carthage, New York
WWOR Secaucus, New Jersey
WWPB Hagerstown, Maryland
WWPX-TV Martinsburg, District of Columbia
WWRS-TV Mayville, Wisconsin
WWSB Sarasota, Florida
WWSI Atlantic City, New Jersey
WWTI Watertown, New York
WWTO-TV La Salle, Illinois
WWTV Cadillac, Michigan
WWUP-TV Sault Ste. Marie, Michigan
WXCW Naples, Florida
WXEL-TV West Palm Beach, Florida
WXFT-DT Aurora, Illinois
WXGA-TV Waycross, Georgia
WXIA-TV Atlanta, Georgia
WXII-TV Winston-Salem, North Carolina
WXIN Indianapolis, Indiana
WXIX-TV Newport, Kentucky
WXLV-TV Winston-Salem, North Carolina
WXMI Battle Creek, Michigan
WXOW La Crosse, Wisconsin
WXPX-TV Bradenton, Florida
WXTV-DT Paterson, New Jersey
WXTX Columbus, Georgia
WXVT Greenville, Mississippi
WXXA-TV Albany, New York
WXXI-TV Rochester, New York
WXXV-TV Gulfport, Mississippi
WXYZ-TV Detroit, Michigan
WYBE Philadelphia, Pennsylvania
WYCC Chicago, Illinois
WYCW Asheville, North Carolina
WYDC Corning, New York
WYDN Worcester, Massachusetts
WYDO Greenville, North Carolina
WYES-TV New Orleans, Louisiana
WYFF Greenville, South Carolina
WYIN Gary, Indiana
WYMT Hazard, Kentucky
WYOU Scranton, Pennsylvania
WYOW Eagle River, Wisconsin
WYPX-TV Amsterdam, New York
WYTV Youngstown, Ohio
WYZZ-TV Bloomington, Illinois
WZDX Huntsville, Alabama
WZME Bridgeport, Connecticut
WZMQ Marquette, Michigan
WZPX-TV Battle Creek, Michigan
WZRB Columbia, South Carolina
WZTV Nashville, Tennessee
WZVI Charlotte Amalie, Virgin Islands
WZVN-TV Naples, Florida
WZZM Grand Rapids, Michigan
XETV-DT Tijuana, California
XEWT-DT Tijuana, California
XHIJ-DT Ciudad Juarez, Texas
XHRIO-TDT Matamoros, Texas

U.S. Television Stations by Analog Channel

Channel 2

KATN Fairbanks, Alaska
KATU Portland, Oregon
KBOI-TV Boise, Idaho
KCBS-TV Los Angeles, California
KCWX Fredericksburg, Texas
KDKA-TV Pittsburgh, Pennsylvania
KDTN Denton, Texas
KEMV Little Rock, Arkansas
KGAN Cedar Rapids, Iowa
KGFE Grand Forks, North Dakota
KHBC-TV Hilo, Hawaii
KHON2 Honolulu, Hawaii
KJRH-TV Tulsa, Oklahoma
KJWP Wilmington, Wyoming
KMID Midland, Texas
KNAZ-TV Flagstaff, Arizona
KNOP North Platte, Nebraska
KOTI Klamath Falls, Oregon
KPRC-TV Houston, Texas
KQTV St. Joseph, Missouri
KREM Spokane, Washington
KSNC Great Bend, Kansas
KTCA-TV St. Paul, Minnesota
KTUU-TV Anchorage, Alaska
KTVI St. Louis, Missouri
KTVN Reno, Nevada
KTVQ Billings, Montana
KTVU Oakland, California
KTWO-TV Casper, Wyoming
KUSD-TV Vermillion, South Dakota
KUTV Salt Lake City, Utah
KWGN Denver, Colorado
KXMA-TV Dickinson, North Dakota
WBAY-TV Green Bay, Wisconsin
WBBM-TV Chicago, Illinois
WBRZ-TV Baton Rouge, Louisiana
WCBD-TV Charleston, South Carolina
WCBS-TV New York, New York
WDIQ Dozier, Alabama
WDTN Dayton, Ohio
WESH Daytona Beach, Florida
WFMY-TV Greensboro, North Carolina
WGBH-TV Boston, Massachusetts
WGRZ Buffalo, New York
WJBK Detroit, Michigan
WKAQ San Juan, Puerto Rico
WKRN-TV Nashville, Tennessee
WKTV Utica, New York
WLBZ Bangor, Maine
WMAB-TV Mississippi State, Mississippi
WMAR-TV Baltimore, Maryland
WPBT Miami, Florida
WSB-TV Atlanta, Georgia
WUND-TV Edenton, North Carolina
XHRIO-TDT Matamoros, Texas

Channel 3

KATC Lafayette, Louisiana
KBME-TV Bismarck, North Dakota
KBTX Bryan, Texas
KCDO-TV Kimball, Colorado
KCRA-TV Sacramento, California
KDLH Duluth, Minnesota
KDLO-TV Florence, South Dakota
KENW Portales, New Mexico
KEYT-TV Santa Barbara, California
KFDX-TV Wichita Falls, Texas
KFTU-DT Douglas, Arizona
KGMV Wailuku, Hawaii
KIEM-TV Eureka, California
KIII-TV Corpus Christi, Texas
KIMT Mason City, Iowa
KLEW-TV Lewiston, Idaho
KLNE-TV Lexington, Nebraska
KOAB-TV Bend, Oregon
KOET Eufaula, Oklahoma
KOTA-TV Rapid City, South Dakota
KREG-TV Glenwood Springs, Colorado
KRTV Great Falls, Montana
KSAN-TV San Angelo, Texas
KSNV-DT Las Vegas, Nevada
KSNW Wichita, Kansas
KSWK Lakin, Kansas
KTBS-TV Shreveport, Louisiana
KTOO-TV Juneau, Alaska
KTVK Phoenix, Arizona
KTVO Kirksville, Missouri
KVNV Middletown Township, Nevada
KYTV Springfield, Missouri
KYW-TV Philadelphia, Pennsylvania
WAVE Louisville, Kentucky
WBTV Charlotte, North Carolina
WEAR-TV Pensacola, Florida
WEDU Tampa-St. Petersburg, Florida
WFSB Hartford, Connecticut
WHSV Harrisonburg, Virginia
WIPM-TV Mayaguez, Puerto Rico
WISC-TV Madison, Wisconsin
WJMN-TV Escanaba, Michigan
WKYC Cleveland, Ohio
WLBT Jackson, Mississippi
WPSU-TV Clearfield, Pennsylvania
WRBL Columbus, Georgia
WREG-TV Memphis, Tennessee
WSAV-TV Savannah, Georgia
WSAZ Huntington, West Virginia
WSIL-TV Harrisburg, Illinois
WSTM-TV Syracuse, New York
WTKR Norfolk, Virginia
WWMT Kalamazoo, Michigan

Channel 4

KAMR-TV Amarillo, Texas
KARK-TV Little Rock, Arkansas
KBTV-TV Port Arthur, Texas
KCSG Cedar City, Utah
KDBC-TV El Paso, Texas
KDFI Dallas, Texas
KDFW Dallas, Texas
KFOR Oklahoma City, Oklahoma
KGBT-TV Harlingen, Texas
KITV Honolulu, Hawaii
KLBY Colby, Kansas
KMOV St. Louis, Missouri
KNBC Los Angeles, California
KNEP-TV Scottsbluff, Nebraska
KOMO-TV Seattle, Washington
KPIC Roseburg, Oregon
KPRY-TV Pierre, South Dakota
KRDK-DT Valley City, North Dakota
KREX-TV Grand Junction, Colorado
KRON-TV San Francisco, California
KSNB Superior, Nebraska
KTBY Anchorage, Alaska
KTIV Sioux City, Iowa
KTVX Salt Lake City, Utah
KUBD Ketchikan, Alaska
KVER-CA Indio, California
KVES-LD Indio, California
KVOA Tucson, Arizona
KWAB-TV Big Spring, Texas
KWSE Williston, North Dakota
KXLF-TV Butte, Montana
KXLY-TV Spokane, Washington
WAPA-TV San Juan, Puerto Rico
WBZ-TV Boston, Massachusetts
WCBI-DT Columbus, Mississippi
WCCO-TV Minneapolis, Minnesota
WCMH-TV Columbus, Ohio
WDAF Kansas City, Missouri
WFOR-TV Miami, Florida
WGWG Charleston, South Carolina
WHBF-TV Rock Island, Illinois
WIVB-TV Buffalo, New York
WJXT Jacksonville, Florida
WNBC New York, New York
WNJX-TV Mayaguez, Puerto Rico
WOAI-TV San Antonio, Texas
WOAY-TV Oak Hill, West Virginia
WRC Washington, District of Columbia
WSMV Nashville, Tennessee
WTAE-TV Pittsburgh, Pennsylvania
WTMJ-TV Milwaukee, Wisconsin
WTOM-TV Cheboygan, Michigan
WTTV Bloomington, Indiana
WTVY Dothan, Alabama
WUNC-TV Chapel Hill, North Carolina
WWL-TV New Orleans, Louisiana
WYFF Greenville, South Carolina

Channel 5

KALB Alexandria, Louisiana
KCTV Kansas City, Missouri
KDLV-TV Mitchell, South Dakota
KENS San Antonio, Texas
KEVC-CD Indio, California
KFBB-TV Great Falls, Montana
KFSM Fort Smith, Arkansas
KFYR Bismarck, North Dakota
KGWL-TV Lander, Wyoming
KGWN Cheyenne, Wyoming
KHAS-TV Hastings, Nebraska
KING-TV Seattle, Washington
KIVV-TV Lead, South Dakota
KNME-TV Albuquerque, New Mexico
KNPB Reno, Nevada
KOAA-TV Pueblo, Colorado
KOBI Medford, Oregon
KOCO Oklahoma City, Oklahoma
KPHO Phoenix, Arizona
KPIX-TV San Francisco, California
KREX-TV Grand Junction, Colorado
KRGV-TV Weslaco, Texas
KSDK St. Louis, Missouri
KSL-TV Salt Lake City, Utah
KSTP-TV St. Paul, Minnesota
KTLA Los Angeles, California
KTTZ-TV Lubbock, Texas
KVVU Henderson, Nevada
KXAS Fort Worth, Texas
KXGN-TV Glendive, Montana
WABI-TV Bangor, Maine
WAGA Atlanta, Georgia
WBKP Calumet, Michigan
WCSC-TV Charleston, South Carolina
WCVB Boston, Massachusetts
WCYB-TV Bristol, Virginia
WDTV Weston, West Virginia
WFRV-TV Green Bay, Wisconsin
WKRG-TV Mobile, Alabama
WLWT Cincinnati, Ohio
WMAQ Chicago, Illinois
WMC-TV Memphis, Tennessee
WNEM Bay City, Michigan
WNYW Newburgh, New York
WOI-DT Ames, Missouri
WPTZ North Pole, New York
WRAL-TV Raleigh, North Carolina
WTTG Washington, District of Columbia
WTVF Nashville, Tennessee
WTVH Syracuse, New York
WUFT Gainesville, Florida

Channel 6

KAAL Austin, Minnesota
KAUZ-TV Wichita Falls, Texas
KBJR-TV Superior, Wisconsin
KCEN-TV Temple, Texas
KEMV Mountain View, Arkansas
KFDM Beaumont, Texas
KHQ-TV Spokane, Washington
KIDY San Angelo, Texas
KLEI-TV Kailua-Kona, Hawaii
KMOH-TV Kingman, Arizona
KMOS-TV Sedalia, Missouri
KOIN Portland, Oregon
KPLO-TV Reliance, South Dakota
KPTW Casper, Wyoming
KREZ-TV Durango, Colorado
KRIS-TV Corpus Christi, Texas
KRMA-TV Denver, Colorado
KSBY San Luis Obispo, California
KSRE Minot, North Dakota
KSVI Billings, Montana
KTAL-TV Texarkana, Texas
KUAT-TV Tucson, Arizona
KVIE Sacramento, California
KVIQ Eureka, California
KWNB-TV Hayes Center, Nebraska
KWQC-TV Davenport, Iowa
WABG-TV Greenwood, Mississippi
WATE-TV Knoxville, Tennessee
WBRC Birmingham, Alabama
WCML Alpena, Michigan
WCSH Portland, Maine
WCTV Thomasville, Georgia
WDAY-TV Fargo, North Dakota
WDSU New Orleans, Louisiana
WECT Wilmington, North Carolina
WIPR-TV San Juan, Puerto Rico
WITI Milwaukee, Wisconsin
WJAC-TV Johnstown, Pennsylvania
WJBF Augusta, Georgia
WKMG-TV Orlando, Florida
WLNE-TV New Bedford, Massachusetts

WLNS-TV Lansing, Michigan
WLUC-TV Marquette, Michigan
WOWT Omaha, Nebraska
WPSD-TV Paducah, Kentucky
WPVI-TV Philadelphia, Pennsylvania
WRGB Schenectady, New York
WRTV Indianapolis, Indiana
WSYX Columbus, Ohio
WTVJ Miami, Florida
WTVR Richmond, Virginia
WVVA Bluefield, West Virginia

Channel 7

KABC-TV Los Angeles, California
KAII-TV Wailuku, Hawaii
KAKM Anchorage, Alaska
KATV Little Rock, Arkansas
KAZT-TV Prescott, Arizona
KBZK Bozeman, Montana
KCCO-TV Alexandria, Minnesota
KETV Omaha, Nebraska
KEVN Rapid City, South Dakota
KFXF Fairbanks, Alaska
KGO-TV San Francisco, California
KHQA-TV Hannibal, Missouri
KIRO-TV Seattle, Washington
KJRR Jamestown, North Dakota
KLTV Tyler, Texas
KMGH-TV Denver, Colorado
KMNE-TV Bassett, Nebraska
KOAC-TV Corvallis, Oregon
KOAM-TV Pittsburg, Kansas
KOAT Albuquerque, New Mexico
KOSA Odessa, Texas
KPLC Lake Charles, Louisiana
KQCD Dickinson, North Dakota
KRCR-TV Redding, California
KSPS-TV Spokane, Washington
KSWO-TV Lawton, Oklahoma
KTBC Austin, Texas
KTVB Boise, Idaho
KUED Salt Lake City, Utah
KVIA-TV El Paso, Texas
KVII-TV Amarillo, Texas
KVYE-TV El Centro, California
KWWL Waterloo, Iowa
WBBJ-TV Jackson, Tennessee
WCIQ Mount Cheaha, Alabama
WDAM-TV Laurel, Mississippi
WDBJ Roanoke, Virginia
WHIO-TV Dayton, Ohio
WITN Washington, North Carolina
WITV Charleston, South Carolina
WJCT Jacksonville, Florida
WJHG Panama City, Florida
WJLA-TV Washington, District of Columbia
WKBW-TV Buffalo, New York
WKNX-TV Knoxville, Tennessee
WLS-TV Chicago, Illinois
WPBN-TV Traverse City, Michigan
WSAW Wausau, Wisconsin
WSPA-TV Spartanburg, South Carolina
WSTE-DT Ponce, Puerto Rico
WSVN Miami, Florida
WTRF-TV Wheeling, West Virginia
WVII-TV Bangor, Maine
WXYZ-TV Detroit, Michigan

Channel 8

KAET Phoenix, Arizona
KAIT Jonesboro, Arkansas
KCCI Des Moines, Iowa
KESD-TV Brookings, South Dakota
KGNS Laredo, Texas
KGW Portland, Oregon
KIFI-TV Idaho Falls, Idaho
KJCT Grand Junction, Colorado
KJUD Juneau, Alaska
KLAS-TV Las Vegas, Nevada
KLKN Lincoln, Nebraska
KLST San Angelo, Texas
KNOE Monroe, Louisiana
KOBR Roswell, New Mexico
KOLO Reno, Nevada
KOMU-TV Columbia, Missouri
KPAX-TV Missoula, Montana
KSBW Salinas, California
KSNK McCook, Nebraska
KSYS Medford, Oregon
KTSC Pueblo, Colorado
KTUL Tulsa, Oklahoma
KUHT Houston, Texas
KULR-TV Billings, Montana
KUMV Williston, North Dakota
KZSD-TV Martin, South Dakota
WAGM Presque Isle, Maine
WAKA Selma, Alabama
WCHS-TV Charleston, West Virginia
WDAZ-TV Devil's Lake, North Dakota
WDSE Duluth, Minnesota
WFAA Dallas, Texas
WFLA-TV Tampa, Florida
WFXI Morehead City, North Carolina
WGAL Lancaster, Pennsylvania
WGEN-TV Key West, Florida
WGHP High Point, North Carolina
WGTQ Sault Ste. Marie, Michigan
WGTV Athens, Georgia
WISH-TV Indianapolis, Indiana
WJW Cleveland, Ohio
WKBT-TV La Crosse, Wisconsin
WNPT Nashville, Tennessee
WOOD-TV Grand Rapids, Michigan
WQAD Moline, Illinois
WRIC-TV Petersburg, Virginia
WROC-TV Rochester, New York
WSIU-TV Carbondale, Illinois
WSVI Christiansted, Virgin Islands
WVLT Knoxville, Tennessee
WWCP-TV Johnstown, Pennsylvania
WXGA-TV Waycross, Georgia

Channel 9

KAWE Bemidji, Minnesota
KBHE-TV Rapid City, South Dakota
KCAU-TV Sioux City, Iowa
KCFG Flagstaff, Arizona
KCFW-TV Kalispell, Montana
KCRG-TV Cedar Rapids, Iowa
KCTS-TV Seattle, Washington
KDSE Dickinson, North Dakota
KECY-TV El Centro, California
KEMV Arkadelphia, Arkansas
KETC St. Louis, Missouri
KEZI Eugene, Oregon
KGMD-TV Hilo, Hawaii
KIXE-TV Redding, California
KLRN San Antonio, Texas
KMBC Kansas City, Missouri
KMSP Minneapolis, Minnesota
KNIN-TV Caldwell, Idaho
KNMD-TV Santa Fe, New Mexico
KOOD Hays, Kansas
KPNE-TV North Platte, Nebraska
KQED San Francisco, California
KRBC-TV Abilene, Texas
KTRE Lufkin, Texas
KTSM-TV El Paso, Texas
KUAC-TV Fairbanks, Alaska
KUEN Ogden, Utah
KUSA Denver, Colorado
KWES-TV Odessa, Texas
WAFB Baton Rouge, Louisiana
WCPO-TV Cincinnati, Ohio
WFTV Orlando, Florida
WGN Chicago, Illinois
WNBW-DT Gainesville, Florida
WNCT-TV Greenville, North Carolina
WSOC-TV Charlotte, North Carolina
WSUR-DT Ponce, Puerto Rico
WSWP-TV Grandview, West Virginia
WSYR-TV Syracuse, New York
WTOV-TV Steubenville, Ohio
WTVC Chattanooga, Tennessee
WTVM Columbus, Georgia
WUSA Washington, District of Columbia
WVAN-TV Savannah, Georgia
WWOR Secaucus, New Jersey
WWTV Cadillac, Michigan

Channel 10

KAKE Wichita, Kansas
KBIM-TV Roswell, New Mexico
KFDA-TV Amarillo, Texas
KGTV San Diego, California
KISU-TV Pocatello, Idaho
KLFY-TV Lafayette, Louisiana
KLVX Las Vegas, Nevada
KMEB Wailuku, Hawaii
KMOT Minot, North Dakota
KMTF Helena, Montana
KOLN Lincoln, Nebraska
KOPB-TV Portland, Oregon
KREY-TV Montrose, Colorado
KSAZ Phoenix, Arizona
KSTF Scottsbluff, Nebraska
KTEN Ada, Oklahoma
KTSD-TV Pierre, South Dakota
KTTC Rochester, Minnesota
KTVE El Dorado, Arkansas
KTVL Medford, Oregon
KWCM-TV Appleton, Minnesota
KWSU-TV Pullman, Washington
KWTX Waco, Texas
KXTV Sacramento, California
KZTV Corpus Christi, Texas
MPTVÿ Milwaukee, Wisconsin
WALA-TV Mobile, Alabama
WALB Albany, Georgia
WAVY-TV Portsmouth, Virginia
WBIQ Birmingham, Alabama
WBIR-TV Knoxville, Tennessee
WBNS-TV Columbus, Ohio
WBUP Ishpeming, Michigan
WCAU Philadelphia, Pennsylvania
WCBB Augusta, Maine
WGEM-TV Quincy, Illinois
WHEC-TV Rochester, New York
WILM-LD Wilmington, North Carolina
WILX Onondaga, Michigan
WIS Columbia, South Carolina
WJAR Providence, Rhode Island
WMEM-TV Presque Isle, Maine
WPLG Miami, Florida
WSLS-TV Roanoke, Virginia
WTAJ-TV Altoona, Pennsylvania
WTEN Albany, New York
WTSP St. Petersburg, Florida
WWUP-TV Sault Ste. Marie, Michigan

Channel 11

KAQY Columbia, Louisiana
KARE Minneapolis, Minnesota
KBYU-TV Provo, Utah
KCBD Lubbock, Texas
KCBY-TV Coos Bay, Oregon
KCHF Santa Fe, New Mexico
KDIN-TV Des Moines, Iowa
KDTP Holbrook, Arizona
KELO-TV Sioux Falls, South Dakota
KFFX-TV Pendleton, Oregon
KGIN Grand Island, Nebraska
KHET Honolulu, Hawaii
KHON2 Hilo, Hawaii
KHOU Houston, Texas
KKCO Grand Junction, Colorado
KKTV Colorado Springs, Colorado
KMLU Columbia, Louisiana
KMSB Tucson, Arizona
KMVT Twin Falls, Idaho
KNTV San Jose, California
KOED-TV Tulsa, Oklahoma
KOTA-TV Lead, South Dakota
KPLR St. Louis, Missouri
KQSD-TV Lowry, South Dakota
KRII Chisholm, Minnesota
KRXI-TV Reno, Nevada
KSNG Garden City, Kansas
KSTW-TV Tacoma, Washington
KTHV Little Rock, Arkansas
KTTV Los Angeles, California
KTVA Anchorage, Alaska
KTVF Fairbanks, Alaska
KTVT-TV Fort Worth, Texas
KTWU Topeka, Kansas
KUFM-TV Missoula, Montana
KXMD-TV Williston, North Dakota
WBAL Baltimore, Maryland
WBKB-TV Alpena, Michigan
WENH-TV Durham, New Hampshire
WFSU-TV Tallahassee, Florida
WHAS-TV Louisville, Kentucky
WINK-TV Fort Myers, Florida
WJHL-TV Johnson City, Tennessee
WLII-DT Caguas, Puerto Rico
WLUK-TV Green Bay, Wisconsin
WPIX New York, New York
WPXI Pittsburgh, Pennsylvania
WTOC-TV Savannah, Georgia
WTOK Meridian, Mississippi

WTOL Toledo, Ohio
WTVD-TV Durham, North Carolina
WVAH-TV Charleston, West Virginia
WXIA-TV Atlanta, Georgia

Channel 12

KBDI-TV Broomfield, Colorado
KBMT Beaumont, Texas
KCCW-TV Walker, Minnesota
KCOY-TV Santa Maria, California
KDRV Medford, Oregon
KETZ El Dorado, Arkansas
KEYC-TV CBS & NEYC FOX Mankato, Minnesota
KFVS-TV Cape Girardeau, Missouri
KHSL-TV Chico, California
KMAU Wailuku, Hawaii
KMYU St. George, Utah
KNRR Pembina, North Dakota
KOBF Farmington, New Mexico
KODE-TV Joplin, Missouri
KPNX Mesa, Arizona
KPTV Portland, Oregon
KRNE-TV Merriman, Nebraska
KSAT-TV San Antonio, Texas
KTRV-TV Nampa, Idaho
KTTM Huron, South Dakota
KTVH-DT Helena, Montana
KTXS-TV Sweetwater, Texas
KUON-TV Lincoln, Nebraska
KUTF Logan, Utah
KVIH-TV Clovis, New Mexico
KVOS-TV Bellingham, Washington
KXII Sherman, Texas
KXMB-TV Bismarck, North Dakota
WBOY-TV Clarksburg, West Virginia
WCTI-TV New Bern, North Carolina
WDEF-TV Chattanooga, Tennessee
WICU-TV Erie, Pennsylvania
WILL-TV Urbana, Illinois
WISN-TV Milwaukee, Wisconsin
WJFW-TV Rhinelander, Wisconsin
WJRT Flint, Michigan
WJTV Jackson, Mississippi
WKRC-TV Cincinnati, Ohio
WMAE-TV Booneville, Mississippi
WMEB-TV Orono, Maine
WNAC-TV Providence, Rhode Island
WPEC West Palm Beach, Florida
WRDW Augusta, Georgia
WSFA Montgomery, Alabama
WTLV Jacksonville, Florida
WWBT Richmond, Virginia
WXII-TV Winston-Salem, North Carolina
WYES-TV New Orleans, Louisiana

Channel 13

KAFT Fayetteville, Arkansas
KCOP Los Angeles, California
KCOS El Paso, Texas
KCPQ Tacoma, Washington
KCWY Casper, Wyoming
KECI-TV Missoula, Montana
KEET Eureka, California
KERA-TV Dallas, Texas
KFME Fargo, North Dakota
KFPH-DT Flagstaff, Arizona
KGWR-TV Rock Springs, Wyoming
KHGI-TV Kearney, Nebraska
KHNL Honolulu, Hawaii
KHVO Honolulu, Hawaii
KLBK-TV Lubbock, Texas
KLPA-TV Monroe, Louisiana
KOLD-TV Tucson, Arizona
KOVR-TV Stockton, California
KPSD-TV Eagle Butte, South Dakota
KRCG Jefferson City, Missouri
KRDO-TV Colorado Springs, Colorado
KRQE Albuquerque, New Mexico
KSFY Sioux Falls, South Dakota
KSTU Salt Lake City, Utah
KSWT Yuma, Arizona
KTNE-TV Alliance, Nebraska
KTNL-TV Sitka, Alaska
KTRK-TV Houston, Texas
KTVR La Grande, Oregon
KVAL-TV Eugene, Oregon
KVTV Laredo, Texas
KXMC-TV Minot, North Dakota
KYUR Anchorage, Alaska
WBTW Florence, South Carolina
WEAU Eau Claire, Wisconsin
WGME-TV Portland, Maine
WHAM-TV Rochester, New York
WHBQ-TV Memphis, Tennessee
WIBW Topeka, Kansas
WJZ-TV Baltimore, Maryland
WLOS Asheville, North Carolina
WLOX Biloxi, Mississippi
WMAZ-TV Macon, Georgia
WMBB Panama City, Florida
WMED-TV Calais, Maine
WNET Newark, New Jersey
WNYT Albany, New York
WOWK-TV Huntington, West Virginia
WPXS Mount Vernon, Illinois
WQED Pittsburgh, Pennsylvania
WSET-TV Lynchburg, Virginia
WTHR Indianapolis, Indiana
WTVG-TV Toledo, Ohio
WTVT Tampa, Florida
WVEC Hampton, Virginia
WVTM Birmingham, Alabama
WZZM Grand Rapids, Michigan

Channel 14

KARD West Monroe, Louisiana
KCIT Amarillo, Texas
KDTV-DT San Francisco, California
KDVT-LP Denver, Colorado
KETH-TV Houston, Texas
KFOX-TV El Paso, Texas
KGWC-TV Casper, Wyoming
KJZZ-TV Salt Lake City, Utah
KMEG Sioux City, Iowa
KOCW Hoisington, Kansas
KTBO-TV Oklahoma City, Oklahoma
KTFD-TV Denver, Colorado
KTFQ-DT Albuquerque, New Mexico
KTGM Tamuning, Guam
KWHD Hilo, Hawaii
KWHE Honolulu, Hawaii
WABW-TV Pelham, Georgia
WCMU-TV Mount Pleasant, Michigan
WCWF Suring, Wisconsin
WEBA-TV Allendale, South Carolina
WFDC-DT Arlington, District of Columbia
WHKY-TV Hickory, North Carolina
WMAW-TV Meridian, Mississippi
WMEI Arecibo, Puerto Rico
WPTO Oxford, Ohio
WSEC Jacksonville, Illinois
WYDO Greenville, North Carolina

Channel 15

KAMU-TV College Station, Texas
KCKA Centralia, Washington
KCLO-TV Rapid City, South Dakota
KINC Las Vegas, Nevada
KNXV-TV Phoenix, Arizona
KOGG Wailuku, Hawaii
KPBS San Diego, California
KPOB-TV Poplar Bluff, Missouri
KSMQ-TV Austin, Minnesota
KVRR Fargo, North Dakota
KXVA Abilene, Texas
KXVO Omaha, Nebraska
KYOU-TV Ottumwa, Iowa
WANE-TV Fort Wayne, Indiana
WBRA-TV Roanoke, Virginia
WDSC-TV New Smyrna Beach, Florida
WHDF Florence, Alabama
WHRO-TV Hampton-Norfolk, Virginia
WICD Champaign, Illinois
WKOP-TV Knoxville, Tennessee
WKPC-TV Louisville, Kentucky
WLYH-TV Lancaster, Pennsylvania
WMTV Madison, Wisconsin
WPDE-TV Florence, South Carolina
WPMI-TV Mobile, Alabama
WTAP Parkersburg, West Virginia
WXVT Greenville, Mississippi

Channel 16

KDSD-TV Aberdeen, South Dakota
KEDT Corpus Christi, Texas
KLRT-TV Little Rock, Arkansas
KMTR Eugene, Oregon
KONG Everett, Washington
KSNF Joplin, Missouri
KTAJ-TV St. Joseph, Missouri
KTGF Great Falls, Montana
KUNP La Grande, Oregon
WAPT Jackson, Mississippi
WATN-TV Jackson, Tennessee
WBOC-TV Salisbury, Maryland
WGGS-TV Greenville, South Carolina
WJWJ-TV Beaufort, South Carolina
WNDU South Bend, Indiana
WNEP Waymart, Pennsylvania
WPTD Dayton, Ohio
WTJR Quincy, Illinois
WUSF-TV Tampa, Florida
WUSI-TV Olney, Illinois
WVCI-LP Daytona Beach, Florida

Channel 17

KBNT-CD San Diego, California
KDOR-TV Bartlesville, Oklahoma
KDSM-TV Des Moines, Iowa
KGET-TV Bakersfield, California
KHAX-LP San Diego, California
KMIZ Columbia, Missouri
KNIC-DT Blanco, Texas
KTCI-TV St. Paul, Minnesota
KTTW Sioux Falls, South Dakota
WAND Decatur, Illinois
WCWJ Jacksonville, Florida
WDBB Bessemer, Alabama
WDLI-TV Canton, Ohio
WLRN-TV Miami, Florida
WMAU-TV Bude, Mississippi
WMHT Schenectady, New York
WNCN Goldsboro, North Carolina
WNED-TV Buffalo, New York
WPCH-TV Atlanta, Georgia
WPHL Philadelphia, Pennsylvania
WTVO Rockford, Illinois
WUNE-TV Linville, North Carolina
WVXF Charlotte Amalie, Virgin Islands
WXMI Battle Creek, Michigan
WZTV Nashville, Tennessee

Channel 18

KAAS-TV Salina, Kansas
KJTL Wichita Falls, Texas
KLJB Davenport, Iowa
KLPA-TV Lake Charles, Louisiana
KLRU Austin, Texas
KRMJ Grand Junction, Colorado
KSCI Long Beach, California
KTTU Tucson, Arizona
KUEW St. George, Utah
KUPB-TV Midland, Texas
KVPT Fresno, California
KWYB Butte, Montana
WCCB Charlotte, North Carolina
WDHN Dothan, Alabama
WETM-TV Elmira, New York
WHIZ-TV Zanesville, Ohio
WHTV Jackson, Michigan
WHTX-LP Hartford, Connecticut
WKCF Clermont, Florida
WLEX-TV Lexington, Kentucky
WLFI-TV Lafayette, Indiana
WMAV-TV Oxford, Mississippi
WNGH-TV Chatsworth, Georgia
WVTV Milwaukee, Wisconsin

Channel 19

KCPT Kansas City, Missouri
KEPR-TV Pasco, Washington
KJRE Ellendale, North Dakota
KTEJ Jonesboro, Arkansas
KUVS-DT Modesto, California
KVCT Victoria, Texas
KWBQ Santa Fe, New Mexico
KWKS Colby, Kansas
KXNE-TV Norfolk, Nebraska
KYTX Nacogdoches, Texas
WCAV Charlottesville, Virginia
WHNT Huntsville, Alabama
WHOI Peoria, Illinois
WKPT-TV Kingsport, Tennessee
WLTX Columbia, South Carolina
WMAH-TV Biloxi, Mississippi
WOIO Shaker Heights, Ohio
WPCW-TV Jeannette, Pennsylvania
WUNM-TV Jacksonville, North Carolina
WXOW La Crosse, Wisconsin
WZMQ Marquette, Michigan

Channel 20

KOFY-TV San Francisco, California
KRMU Durango, Colorado
KSMN Worthington, Minnesota
KTBW-TV Tacoma, Washington
KTMW Salt Lake City, Utah
KTVD Denver, Colorado
KTXH Houston, Texas
KVME-TV Bishop, California
KZUP-CD Baton Rouge, Louisiana
WBBH-TV Fort Myers, Florida
WCCT Waterbury, Connecticut
WCES-TV Wrens, Georgia
WCOV-TV Montgomery, Alabama
WCWG Lexington, North Carolina
WDCA Washington, District of Columbia
WHNO New Orleans, Louisiana
WHRM-TV Wausau, Wisconsin
WICS Springfield, Illinois
WKPV Ponce, Puerto Rico
WMYD Detroit, Michigan
WUTR Utica, New York
WVTB St. Johnsbury, Vermont
WYCC Chicago, Illinois

Channel 21

KCWT-CD La Feria, Texas
KDCK Dodge City, Kansas
KFTV-DT Hanford, California
KNBN Rapid City, South Dakota
KOZK Springfield, Missouri
KPAZ-TV Phoenix, Arizona
KPXJ Minden, Louisiana
KQDS-TV Duluth, Minnesota
KRWB-TV Roswell, New Mexico
KRXIÿ Reno, Nevada
KTIN Fort Dodge, Iowa
KTVZ Bend, Oregon
KTXA-TV Fort Worth, Texas
KUFM-TV Great Falls, Montana
KVMY Las Vegas, Nevada
KWHM Wailuku, Hawaii
KXRM-TV Colorado Springs, Colorado
WBNA Louisville, Kentucky
WBRL-CD Baton Rouge, Louisiana
WCMW Manistee, Michigan
WFMJ-TV Youngstown, Ohio
WHA-TV Madison, Wisconsin
WHNS Greenville, South Carolina
WHP-TV Harrisburg, Pennsylvania
WKMU Murray, Kentucky
WLIW Garden City, New York
WMPV-TV Mobile, Alabama
WPTA Fort Wayne, Indiana
WPXC-TV Brunswick, Georgia
WTCE-TV Fort Pierce, Florida
WTTO Homewood, Alabama
WWCW Lynchburg, Virginia
WWMB Florence, South Carolina
WXXI-TV Rochester, New York

Channel 22

KAWB Brainerd, Minnesota
KFCT Fort Collins, Colorado
KLCW-TV Wolfforth, Texas
KLTJ Galveston, Texas
KRCB Cotati, California
KRWG-TV Las Cruces, New Mexico
KSKN Spokane, Washington
KWHY-TV Los Angeles, California
KWWF Waterloo, Iowa
KZJO Seattle, Washington
SOPTV Klamath Falls, Oregon
WBMM Tuskegee, Alabama
WCLF Clearwater, Florida
WCTE Cookeville, Tennessee
WHLT Hattiesburg, Mississippi
WJCL Savannah, Georgia
WKEF Dayton, Ohio
WLFL Raleigh, North Carolina
WMPT Annapolis, Maryland
WPNT Pittsburgh, Pennsylvania
WSBS-TV Key West, Florida
WSBT-TV South Bend, Indiana
WVNY Burlington, Vermont
WVUT Vincennes, Indiana
WWLP Springfield, Massachusetts
WYOU Scranton, Pennsylvania

Channel 23

KBSI Cape Girardeau, Missouri
KBSV Ceres, California
KCSD-TV Sioux Falls, South Dakota
KERO-TV Bakersfield, California
KHCE-TV San Antonio, Texas
KMCB Coos Bay, Oregon
KNAT-TV Albuquerque, New Mexico
KOKI-TV Tulsa, Oklahoma
KTMF Missoula, Montana
WATM-TV Altoona, Pennsylvania
WBUI Decatur, Illinois
WCVE-TV Richmond, Virginia
WELF-TV Dalton, Georgia
WHMC Conway, South Carolina
WIFR Freeport, Illinois
WKAR-TV East Lansing, Michigan
WKZT-TV Elizabethtown, Kentucky
WLTV-DT Miami, Florida
WMAO-TV Greenwood, Mississippi
WNDY-TV Marion, Indiana
WNJS Camden, New Jersey
WNLO Buffalo, New York
WPFO Waterville, Maine
WSRE Pensacola, Florida
WUCW Minneapolis, Minnesota
WUOA Tuscaloosa, Alabama
WXXA-TV Albany, New York

Channel 24

KBCB Bellingham, Washington
KFTA-TV Fort Smith, Arkansas
KLPA-TV Lafayette, Louisiana
KLPA-TV Shreveport, Louisiana
KNDM Minot, North Dakota
KNLC St. Louis, Missouri
KNVN Chico, California
KPEJ-TV Odessa, Texas
KPNZ Ogden, Utah
KQUP Pullman, Washington
KRMZ Steamboat Springs, Colorado
KSAS-TV Wichita, Kansas
KSEE Fresno, California
KVUE Austin, Texas
KYIN Mason City, Iowa
WCGV-TV Milwaukee, Wisconsin
WCNY-TV Syracuse, New York
WEDH Hartford, Connecticut
WGXA Macon, Georgia
WJET-TV Erie, Pennsylvania
WJPX San Juan, Puerto Rico
WKYU-TV Bowling Green, Kentucky
WMDN Meridian, Mississippi
WNPB-TV Morgantown, West Virginia
WNWO-TV Toledo, Ohio
WQPT-TV Moline, Illinois
WTAT-TV Charleston, South Carolina
WUTB Baltimore, Maryland

Channel 25

KAVU-TV Victoria, Texas
KLPA-TV Alexandria, Louisiana
KMDE Devils Lake, North Dakota
KNDO Yakima, Washington
KNDU Richland, Washington
KNLJ Jefferson City, Missouri
KOKH-TV Oklahoma City, Oklahoma
KXXV Waco, Texas
WACS-TV Dawson, Georgia
WEEK-TV Peoria, Illinois
WEHT Evansville, Indiana
WEYI-TV Saginaw, Michigan
WFXT Boston, Massachusetts
WHAG-TV Hagerstown, Maryland
WHIQ Huntsville, Alabama
WJXX Orange Park, Florida
WKAS Ashland, Kentucky
WLAX La Crosse, Wisconsin
WNYE-TV New York, New York
WOLO-TV Columbia, South Carolina
WPBF Tequesta, Florida
WUNK-TV Greenville, North Carolina
WVIZ Cleveland, Ohio
WXXV-TV Gulfport, Mississippi

Channel 26

KAAH-TV Honolulu, Hawaii
KCDT Coeur d'Alene, Washington
KFTC Bemidji, Minnesota
KGCW Burlington, Iowa
KINT-TV El Paso, Texas
KMPH-TV Visalia, California
KNDB Bismarck, North Dakota
KOZJ Joplin, Missouri
KRIV Houston, Texas
KRNS-CD Reno, Nevada
KTSF San Francisco, California
KYNE-TV Omaha, Nebraska
WAGT Augusta, Georgia
WAIQ Montgomery, Alabama
WBDT Springfield, Ohio
WCIU-TV Chicago, Illinois
WETA-TV Washington, District of Columbia
WGNO New Orleans, Louisiana
WMEA-TV Biddeford, Maine
WNYB Jamestown, New York
WQTO Ponce, Puerto Rico
WSFX-TV Wilmington, North Carolina
WUNL-TV Winston-Salem, North Carolina
WVEN-TV Daytona Beach, Florida
WZVN-TV Naples, Florida

Channel 27

KCWV Duluth, Minnesota
KDFI Dallas, Texas
KELV-LD Las Vegas, Nevada
KLWY Cheyenne, Wyoming
KOZL-TV Springfield, Missouri
KREN-TV Reno, Nevada
KSNT Topeka, Kansas
KUAS-TV Tucson, Arizona
WBGU-TV Bowling Green, Ohio
WCCU Urbana, Illinois
WCMV Cadillac, Michigan
WFXR Roanoke, Virginia
WGNT Portsmouth, Virginia
WHTM-TV Harrisburg, Pennsylvania
WKBN-TV Youngstown, Ohio
WKYT Lexington, Kentucky
WLOV-TV West Point, Mississippi
WLPB-TV Baton Rouge, Louisiana
WQEC Quincy, Illinois
WRDQ Orlando, Florida
WRJA-TV Sumter, South Carolina
WTCT Marion, Illinois
WTXL-TV Tallahassee, Florida
WUNI-TV Worcester, Massachusetts

Channel 28

KAMC Lubbock, Texas
KAYU-TV Spokane, Washington
KBTC-TV Tacoma, Washington
KCET Los Angeles, California
KEPB-TV Eugene, Oregon
KFXA Cedar Rapids, Iowa
KORO-TV Corpus Christi, Texas
KYLE-TV Bryan, Texas
WBRE-TV Wilkes-Barre, Pennsylvania
WCPB Salisbury, Maryland
WHWC-TV Menomonie, Wisconsin
WJSP-TV Columbus, Georgia
WLWC New Bedford, Massachusetts
WPGX Panama City, Florida
WRDC Durham, North Carolina
WSJV Elkhart, Indiana
WTGS Hardeeville, South Carolina
WTTE Columbus, Ohio
WVER Rutland, Vermont

Channel 29

KABB San Antonio, Texas
KBAK-TV Bakersfield, California
KBVU Eureka, California
KCWE Kansas City, Missouri
KHNE-TV Hastings, Nebraska
KHOG Fayetteville, Arkansas
KIMA-TV Yakima, Washington
KMPX Decatur, Texas
KUPT Hobbs, New Mexico
KVHP Lake Charles, Louisiana
WFLX West Palm Beach, Florida
WFTC Minneapolis, Minnesota
WGTU Traverse City, Michigan
WKPD Paducah, Kentucky
WKSO-TV Somerset, Kentucky
WMPN-TV Jackson, Mississippi
WMUM-TV Cochran, Georgia
WNTV Greenville, South Carolina
WTTK Kokomo, Indiana
WTXF-TV Allentown, Pennsylvania

WUTV Buffalo, New York
WVIR-TV Charlottesville, Virginia

Channel 30

KBLN-TV Grants Pass, Oregon
KCVU Paradise, California
KDNL-TV St. Louis, Missouri
KFSN-TV Fresno, California
KTUZ-TV30 Shawnee, Oklahoma
KUCW Ogden, Utah
KWWT Odessa, Texas
WFOX-TV Jacksonville, Florida
WGBC Meridian, Mississippi
WGTE-TV Toledo, Ohio
WLMT Memphis, Tennessee
WNSC-TV Rock Hill, South Carolina
WNVC Fairfax, Virginia
WPBA Atlanta, Georgia
WQCW Portsmouth, Ohio
WSKA Corning, New York
WTIU Bloomington, Indiana
WUXP-TV Nashville, Tennessee
WVIT New Britain, Connecticut

Channel 31

KDCU-DT Derby, Kansas
KDKF Klamath Falls, Oregon
KDVR Denver, Colorado
KEYU Borger, Texas
KFXP Pocatello, Idaho
KLAX-TV Alexandria, Louisiana
KTNW Richland, Washington
KVMD Twentynine Palms, California
KWBM Harrison, Arkansas
WAAY-TV Huntsville, Alabama
WFXL Albany, Georgia
WHLA-TV La Crosse, Wisconsin
WKOH Owensboro, Kentucky
WMBD-TV Peoria, Illinois
WPXN-TV New York, New York
WUHF Rochester, New York
WUNU Lumberton, North Carolina
WWPB Hagerstown, Maryland

Channel 32

KAZQ Albuquerque, New Mexico
KMTP-TV San Francisco, California
KRCW Salem, Oregon
KRIN Waterloo, Iowa
KTAB-TV Abilene, Texas
KTFV-CD McAllen, Texas
KUTH-DT Provo, Utah
WFLD Chicago, Illinois
WHUT-TV Washington, District of Columbia
WLAE-TV New Orleans, Louisiana
WLKY Louisville, Kentucky
WMBF-TV Myrtle Beach, South Carolina
WNCF Montgomery, Alabama
WWAY-TV Wilmington, North Carolina

Channel 33

KATV Cheyenne, Wyoming
KDAF Dallas, Texas
KDJT-CD Salinas, California
KDMD Anchorage, Alaska
KMSS-TV Shreveport, Louisiana
KSPR Springfield, Missouri
KTVW-DT Phoenix, Arizona
KVCW Las Vegas, Nevada
WBFS-TV Miami, Florida
WCFT-TV Tuscaloosa, Alabama
WETK Burlington, Vermont
WFQX-TV Cadillac, Michigan
WFXV Utica, New York
WHBR Pensacola, Florida
WITF-TV Harrisburg, Pennsylvania
WJPM-TV Florence, South Carolina
WPBY-TV Charleston, West Virginia
WSES Tuscaloosa, Alabama
WTVZ-TV Norfolk, Virginia
WUNF-TV Asheville, North Carolina
WYTV Youngstown, Ohio

Channel 34

KDYW Waco, Texas
KITU-TV Beaumont, Texas
KJTV Lubbock, Texas
KLSR-TV Eugene, Oregon
KMCC Laughlin, Nevada
KMEX-DT Los Angeles, California
KOCB Oklahoma City, Oklahoma
KXNW Eureka Springs, Arkansas
WBKI-TV Campbellsville, Kentucky
WDFX-TV Ozark, Alabama
WGSA Baxley, Georgia
WIVT Binghamton, New York
WOSU-TV Columbus, Ohio
WRBJ-TV Magee, Mississippi
WTVX Fort Pierce, Florida
WUVG-DT Athens, Georgia
WYOW Eagle River, Wisconsin

Channel 35

KAPP-TV Yakima, Washington
KCBA Salinas, California
KRSC-TV Claremore, Oklahoma
KUID-TV Moscow, Idaho
KUOK Woodward, Oklahoma
KXTF Twin Falls, Idaho
W07DP-D Harrisburg, Pennsylvania
WDCQ-TV Bad Axe, Michigan
WFGX Fort Walton Beach, Florida
WGVU-TV Grand Rapids, Michigan
WKHA Hazard, Kentucky
WLIO Lima, Ohio
WLOO Vicksburg, Mississippi
WOFL Orlando, Florida
WPME Lewiston, Maine
WRLH-TV Richmond, Virginia
WRLK-TV Columbia, South Carolina
WWTO-TV La Salle, Illinois
WYBE Philadelphia, Pennsylvania

Channel 36

KDTF-LD San Diego, California
KHIN Red Oak, Iowa
KICU San Jose, California
KKAP Little Rock, Arkansas
KMIR-TV Palm Springs, California
KMTW Hutchinson, Kansas
KPBT-TV Odessa, Texas
KTCD-LP San Diego, California
KTVC Roseburg, Oregon
KTVU Oakland, California
KXAN-TV Austin, Texas
MPTVÿ Milwaukee, Wisconsin
WATL Atlanta, Georgia
WCIV Charleston, South Carolina
WCNC-TV Charlotte, North Carolina
WDWL Bayamon, Puerto Rico
WENY-TV Elmira, New York
WFIQ Florence, Alabama
WGPT Oakland, Maryland
WLEF-TV Park Falls, Wisconsin
WSBE-TV Providence, Rhode Island
WTVQ-TV Lexington, Kentucky
WUNP-TV Roanoke Rapids, North Carolina

Channel 38

KALO Honolulu, Hawaii
KCNS San Francisco, California
KPMR-TV Santa Barbara, California
KSCE El Paso, Texas
KUQI Corpus Christi, Texas
WADL Mount Clemens, Michigan
WJWN-TV San Sebastian, Puerto Rico
WKMR Morehead, Kentucky
WLTZ Columbus, Georgia
WNEH Greenwood, South Carolina
WNOL New Orleans, Louisiana
WSWB Scranton, Pennsylvania
WTTA St. Petersburg, Florida

Channel 39

KBLR Paradise, Nevada
KIAH Houston, Texas
KKJB Boise, Idaho
KMCT-TV West Monroe, Louisiana
KNSD San Diego, California
KTAZ Phoenix, Arizona
KXTX Dallas, Texas
WCVI-TV Christiansted, Virgin Islands
WEMT Greeneville, Tennessee
WFWA Fort Wayne, Indiana
WHTN Murfreesboro, Tennessee
WLVT-TV Allentown, Pennsylvania
WQRF-TV Rockford, Illinois
WSFL Miami, Florida
WUNJ-TV Wilmington, North Carolina

Channel 40

KHBS Fort Smith, Arkansas
KHRR Tucson, Arizona
KTBN-TV Santa Ana, California
KTLM Harlingen, Texas
KTXL Sacramento, California
WBMA-LD Birmingham, Alabama
WBUY-TV Holly Springs, Mississippi
WDBD Jackson, Mississippi
WGGB-TV Springfield, Massachusetts
WGWW Anniston, Alabama
WICZ-TV Binghamton, New York
WJSU-TV Anniston, Alabama
WLFB Bluefield, West Virginia
WLMB Toledo, Ohio
WMGM-TV Wildwood, New Jersey
WMTJ Fajardo, Puerto Rico
WMYA-TV Anderson, South Carolina
WNKY Bowling Green, Kentucky
WTWC-TV Tallahassee, Florida
WUVC-DT Fayetteville, North Carolina
WWSB Sarasota, Florida

Channel 41

KBCA Alexandria, Louisiana
KCRP-CD Corpus Christi, Texas
KLUZ-TV Albuquerque, New Mexico
KMYT-TV Tulsa, Oklahoma
KRMT Denver, Colorado
KSHB-TV Kansas City, Missouri
KWEX-DT San Antonio, Texas
WDRB Louisville, Kentucky
WHTJ Charlottesville, Virginia
WIIQ Demopolis, Alabama
WMGT-TV Macon, Georgia
WOTV Battle Creek, Michigan
WVTA Windsor, Vermont
WXTV-DT Paterson, New Jersey

Channel 42

KARZ-TV Little Rock, Arkansas
KESQ-TV Palm Springs, California
KEYE-TV Austin, Texas
KPTM Omaha, Nebraska
KSAX Alexandria, Minnesota
KTNC-TV Concord, California
KVEW Kennewick, Washington
WCLJ-TV Bloomington, Indiana
WEIQ Mobile, Alabama
WIAT Birmingham, Alabama
WIRS Yauco, Puerto Rico
WPBO Portsmouth, Ohio
WTVI Charlotte, North Carolina
WXEL-TV West Palm Beach, Florida

Channel 43

KAUT Oklahoma City, Oklahoma
KGMC Clovis, California
KRWF Redwood Falls, Minnesota
WFXB Myrtle Beach, South Carolina
WGIQ Louisville, Alabama
WKOI-TV Richmond, Indiana
WNYS-TV Syracuse, New York
WOTF-TV Melbourne, Florida
WPMT York, Pennsylvania
WTNZ Knoxville, Tennessee
WUAB Lorain, Ohio
WVBT Virginia Beach, Virginia
WYZZ-TV Bloomington, Illinois
WZVI Charlotte Amalie, Virgin Islands

Channel 44

KBCW-TV San Francisco, California
KLUJ-TV Harlingen, Texas
KPTH Sioux City, Iowa
KWBN Honolulu, Hawaii
KWKT-TV Waco, Texas
KXLA Rancho Palos Verdes, California
WAGV Harlan, Kentucky
WEVV-TV Evansville, Indiana
WFFF-TV Burlington, Vermont
WJTC Pensacola, Florida
WMCN-TV Atlantic City, New Jersey
WSWG Valdosta, Georgia
WTLW Lima, Ohio
WTOG-TV St. Petersburg, Florida
WVIA-TV Scranton, Pennsylvania

Channel 45

KSTC-TV Minneapolis, Minnesota
KUTP Phoenix, Arizona
KUVI-DT Bakersfield, California
KXLN-DT Rosenberg, Texas
WBFF Baltimore, Maryland
WCWN Schenectady, New York
WFUP Vanderbilt, Michigan
WHFT-TV Miami, Florida
WMCF-TV Montgomery, Alabama
WRGT-TV Dayton, Ohio
WTCI Chattanooga, Tennessee
WXLV-TV Winston-Salem, North Carolina

Channel 46

KDLT-TV Sioux Falls, South Dakota
KFTR-DT Ontario, California
KION-TV Monterey, California
KOCM Norman, Oklahoma
KTCW Roseburg, Oregon
KUVE-DT Green Valley, Arizona
WBSF Bay City, Michigan
WGCL Atlanta, Georgia
WHME-TV South Bend, Indiana
WJZY Belmont, North Carolina
WKLE Lexington, Kentucky
WPCT Panama City Beach, Florida
WRBU East St. Louis, Illinois
WSKG-TV Binghamton, New York
WVFX Clarksburg, West Virginia
WWDP Norwell, Massachusetts
WXCW Naples, Florida

Channel 47

KGPE Fresno, California
KTMD Galveston, Texas
KTXD-TV Greenville, Texas
KWHB Tulsa, Oklahoma
KXLT-TV Rochester, Minnesota
KYVE Yakima, Washington
WJAX-TV Jacksonville, Florida
WKBS-TV Altoona, Pennsylvania
WMDT Salisbury, Maryland
WMSN-TV Madison, Wisconsin
WNJU Linden, New Jersey
WSBN-TV Norton, Virginia
WSYM-TV Lansing, Michigan
WTVP Peoria, Illinois
WUTH-CD Hartford, Connecticut
WZRB Columbia, South Carolina

Channel 48

KNVO-TV McAllen, Texas
KSTS San Jose, California
KTDO Las Cruces, New Mexico
KTFA-LP Albuquerque, New Mexico
KVSN-DT Pueblo, Colorado
WAFF Huntsville, Alabama
WCET Cincinnati, Ohio
WEUX Chippewa Falls, Wisconsin
WGTW-TV Burlington, New Jersey
WMYV Greensboro, North Carolina
WRNN-TV Kingston, New York
WVLR Tazewell, Tennessee
WYDC Corning, New York
WYDN Worcester, Massachusetts

Channel 49

KMYA-DT Camden, Arkansas
KNXT Visalia, California
KPDX Vancouver, Washington
KRBK Osage Beach, Missouri
KSTR-DT Irving, Texas
KTKA-TV Topeka, Kansas
WDKA Paducah, Kentucky
WEDW Bridgeport, Connecticut
WIPB Muncie, Indiana
WLED-TV Littleton, New Hampshire
WNYO-TV Buffalo, New York
WRET-TV Spartanburg, South Carolina
WRXY-TV Tice, Florida
WTLH Bainbridge, Georgia

Channel 50

KASY-TV Albuquerque, New Mexico
KCEC Denver, Colorado
KKAI Kailua, Hawaii
KLWB New Iberia, Louisiana
KOCE-TV Huntington Beach, California
WDCW Washington, District of Columbia
WFTT-DT Tampa, Florida
WNJN Montclair, New Jersey
WPGD-TV Hendersonville, Tennessee
WPWR Gary, Indiana
WPXX-TV Memphis, Tennessee
WQHA Aguada, Puerto Rico
WRAZ Raleigh, North Carolina
WWTI Watertown, New York

Channel 51

KBZO-LP Lubbock, Texas
KFXK-TV Longview, Texas
KNHL Hastings, Nebraska
KNSO Merced, California
KNWA-TV Rogers, Arkansas
KOHD Bend, Oregon
KUNS-TV Bellevue, Washington
KUSI-TV San Diego, California
KYAZ Katy, Texas
WEIU-TV Charleston, Illinois
WNYT Pittsfield, Massachusetts
WOGX Ocala, Florida
WPXJ-TV Buffalo, New York
WPXT Portland, Maine
WSCV Fort Lauderdale, Florida
WSFJ-TV Newark, Ohio
WTVE Reading, Pennsylvania
WVPT Staunton, Virginia

Channel 52

KFWD Fort Worth, Texas
KSBI Oklahoma City, Oklahoma
KVEA Corona, California
WEKW-TV Keene, New Hampshire
WGGN-TV Sandusky, Ohio
WGVK Kalamazoo, Michigan
WKON Owenton, Kentucky
WMSY-TV Marion, Virginia
WNJT Trenton, New Jersey
WNYI Ithaca, New York
WWRS-TV Mayville, Wisconsin

Channel 53

KETD Castle Rock, Colorado
KGEB Tulsa, Oklahoma
WEDN Norwich, Connecticut
WFLI-TV Cleveland, Tennessee
WKGB-TV Bowling Green, Kentucky
WLAJ Lansing, Michigan
WNVT Goldvein, Virginia
WPAN Fort Walton Beach, Florida
WPGH-TV Pittsburgh, Pennsylvania
WQMY Williamsport, Pennsylvania

Channel 54

KAJB-TV Calipatria, California
KAZA-TV Avalon, California
KCEB Longview, Texas
KNVA Austin, Texas
WAMY-TV Huntsville, Alabama
WCCV-TV Arecibo, Puerto Rico
WCVN-TV Covington, Kentucky
WFXG Augusta, Georgia
WNUV Baltimore, Maryland
WQLN Erie, Pennsylvania
WTBY-TV Poughkeepsie, New York
WTLJ Muskegon, Michigan
WUPL Slidell, Louisiana
WXTX Columbus, Georgia
WZDX Huntsville, Alabama

Channel 55

WBNX-TV Akron, Ohio
WFFT-TV Fort Wayne, Indiana
WMYT Rock Hill, South Carolina
WRSP-TV Springfield, Illinois

Channel 56

KDOC-TV Anaheim, California
KETK-TV Jacksonville, Texas
KUPU Waimanalo, Hawaii
KWDK Tacoma, Washington
WDKY-TV Danville, Kentucky
WFSG Panama City, Florida
WOLF-TV Hazleton, Pennsylvania
WSPX-TV Syracuse, New York
WYIN Gary, Indiana

Channel 57

KJLA Ventura, California
KUBE-TV Baytown, Texas
KWOG Springdale, Arkansas
WACH Columbia, South Carolina
WBUW Janesville, Wisconsin
WCFE-TV Plattsburgh, New York
WCVE-TV Richmond, Virginia
WGBY-TV Springfield, Massachusetts
WPSG-TV Philadelphia, Pennsylvania
WYMT Hazard, Kentucky

Channel 58

KBFX-CD Bakersfield, California
KDTX-TV Dallas, Texas
KLCS Los Angeles, California
KQCA Stockton, California
WAWD Fort Walton Beach, Florida
WDJT-TV Milwaukee, Wisconsin
WMYO Salem, Indiana
WNAB Nashville, Tennessee
WNJB New Brunswick, New Jersey
WPGA-TV Perry, Georgia
WUJA Caguas, Puerto Rico
WUNG-TV Concord, North Carolina

Channel 59

KFRE-TV Sanger, California
KPXC-TV Denver, Colorado
WAOE Peoria, Illinois
WCTX New Haven, Connecticut
WJEB-TV Jacksonville, Florida
WVNS-TV Lewisburg, West Virginia
WXIN Indianapolis, Indiana

Channel 60

KCSM-TV San Mateo, California
KMBH Harlingen, Texas
WBPH-TV Bethlehem, Pennsylvania
WNEU Merrimack, New Hampshire
WTJP-TV Gadsden, Alabama
WXFT-DT Aurora, Illinois

Channel 61

KASW Phoenix, Arizona
KTFF-DT Porterville, California
KZJL Houston, Texas
WDSI-TV Chattanooga, Tennessee
WFGC Palm Beach, Florida
WQHS-DT Cleveland, Ohio
WTIC-TV Hartford, Connecticut

Channel 62

KAKW-DT Killeen, Texas
KRCA Riverside, California
KSMO Kansas City, Missouri
WFPT Frederick, Maryland
WMFP Lawrence, Massachusetts
WVEA-TV Venice, Florida
WWJ-TV Detroit, Michigan
WYCW Asheville, North Carolina

Channel 63

KBEH Oxnard, California
WBEC-TV Boca Raton, Florida
WHSG-TV Monroe, Georgia
WINM Angola, Indiana
WKTC Sumter, South Carolina

Channel 64

KILM Barstow, California
KTFK-DT Stockton, California
WAXN-TV Kannapolis, North Carolina
WDPB Seaford, Delaware
WGNM Macon, Georgia
WLLA Kalamazoo, Michigan
WNAC-TV Providence, Rhode Island
WSTR-TV Cincinnati, Ohio

Channel 65

KTFN-TV El Paso, Texas
WEDY New Haven, Connecticut
WLJC-TV Beattyville, Kentucky
WRBW Orlando, Florida
WUPV Ashland, Virginia
WUVP-DT Vineland, New Jersey

Channel 66

KFSF-DT Vallejo, California
WGBO-DT Joliet, Illinois
WNYJ-TV West Milford, New Jersey
WSMH Flint, Michigan
WUTF-DT Marlborough, Massachusetts

Channel 67

KFTH-DT Alvin, Texas
KFXV-LD McAllen, Texas
KXFX-CD Brownsville, Texas
WFTY-DT Smithtown, New York
WMPB Baltimore, Maryland

Channel 68

KTLN-TV Novato, California
WABM Birmingham, Alabama
WEFS Cocoa, Florida
WFUT-DT Newark, New Jersey
WJAL-TV Hagerstown, Maryland
WLFG Grundy, Virginia
WMFD-TV Mansfield, Ohio
WSYT Syracuse, New York

Channel 69

KSWB San Diego, California
WAMI-DT Hollywood, Florida
WDTI Indianapolis, Indiana
WFMZ-TV Allentown, Pennsylvania
WUPA Atlanta, Georgia

U.S. Television Stations by Digital Channel

Channel 2

KJWP Wilmington, Wyoming
KNOP North Platte, Nebraska
KOTA-TV Rapid City, South Dakota
KREX-TV Grand Junction, Colorado
WLBZ Bangor, Maine
WESH-TV New Orleans, Maine

Channel 3

KVNV Middletown Township, Nevada
KDLO-TV Florence, South Dakota
KIEM-TV Eureka, California
WBRA-TV Roanoke, Virginia
WSBS-TV Key West, Florida
KCRA-TV Sacramento, Maine
KQCA-TV Sacramento, Maine

Channel 4

KCNC-TV Denver, Colorado
WHBF-TV Rock Island, Illinois
WACP Atlantic City, New Jersey
WOCK-CD Chicago, Illinois
KSNB Superior, Nebraska

Channel 5

KCWX Fredericksburg, Texas
KGTF Hagatna, Guam
KHAS-TV Hastings, Nebraska
KIVV-TV Lead, South Dakota
KOBI Medford, Oregon
KVZK-5 Pago Pago, American Samoa
KXGN-TV Glendive, Montana
KXLF-TV Butte, Montana
WBKP Calumet, Michigan
WCYB-TV Bristol, Virginia
WDTV Weston, West Virginia
WGVK Kalamazoo, Michigan
WLMB Toledo, Ohio
WMC-TV Memphis, Tennessee
WOI-DT Ames, Missouri
WMDE Seaford, Georgia
KTFK-DT Stockton, California
KOCO-TV Oklahoma City, Maine
WCVB-TV Needham, Maine

Channel 6

KWNB-TV Hayes Center, Nebraska
KYES-TV Anchorage, Alaska
WABW-TV Pelham, Georgia
WCES-TV Wrens, Georgia
WEDY New Haven, Connecticut
WUOA Tuscaloosa, Alabama
WPVI-TV Philadelphia, Pennsylvania
WRGB Schenectady, New York
WDSU-TV New Orleans, Maine

Channel 7

KABC-TV Los Angeles, California
KAII-TV Wailuku, Hawaii
KAIL Fresno, California
KCCO-TV Alexandria, Minnesota
KNEP-TV Scottsbluff, Nebraska
KEMV Little Rock, Arkansas
KEVN Rapid City, South Dakota
KFXF Fairbanks, Alaska
KGO-TV San Francisco, California
KHQA-TV Hannibal, Missouri
KJCT Grand Junction, Colorado
KJRR Jamestown, North Dakota
KLAS-TV Las Vegas, Nevada
KLTV Tyler, Texas
KMGH-TV Denver, Colorado
KMNE-TV Bassett, Nebraska
KOAC-TV Corvallis, Oregon
KOAM-TV Pittsburg, Kansas
KOAT Albuquerque, New Mexico
KOCO Oklahoma City, Oklahoma
KOSA Odessa, Texas
KPAX-TV Missoula, Montana
KPLC Lake Charles, Louisiana
KQCD Dickinson, North Dakota
KQTV St. Joseph, Missouri
KRCR-TV Redding, California
KRNV-DT Reno, Nevada
KRTV Great Falls, Montana
KSPS-TV Spokane, Washington
KTBC Austin, Texas
KTNL-TV Sitka, Alaska
KTTW Sioux Falls, South Dakota
KTVB Boise, Idaho
KAZT-TV Prescott, Arizona
KVII-TV Amarillo, Texas
KWWL Waterloo, Iowa
WABC-TV New York, New York
WBNG-TV Binghamton, New York
WCIQ Mount Cheaha, Alabama
WDAM-TV Laurel, Mississippi
WMUM-TV Cochran, Georgia
WEHT Evansville, Indiana
WFLA-TV Tampa, Florida
WITV Charleston, South Carolina
WJBK Detroit, Michigan
WJCT Jacksonville, Florida
WJLA-TV Washington, District of Columbia
WLJC-TV Beattyville, Kentucky
WLS-TV Chicago, Illinois
WBBZ-TV Springville, New York
WOOD-TV Grand Rapids, Michigan
WSAW Wausau, Wisconsin
WSPA-TV Spartanburg, South Carolina
WSTE-DT Ponce, Puerto Rico
WSVN Miami, Florida
WTRF-TV Wheeling, West Virginia
WVII-TV Bangor, Maine
WWNY-TV Carthage, New York
WXXA-TV Albany, New York
WKNX-TV Knoxville, Tennessee
WTPC-TV Virginia Beach, Virginia
KGWL-TV Lander, Wyoming
KBNZ-LD Bend, Oregon
W07DP-D Harrisburg, Pennsylvania
KHBS-TV Rogers, Maine
KOAT-TV Albuquerque, Maine

Channel 8

KAET Phoenix, Arizona
KAIT Jonesboro, Arkansas
KAKM Anchorage, Alaska
KCCI Des Moines, Iowa
KESD-TV Brookings, South Dakota
KFBB-TV Great Falls, Montana
KFMB-TV San Diego, California
KGNS Laredo, Texas
KGW Portland, Oregon
KHON2 Honolulu, Hawaii
KIFI-TV Idaho Falls, Idaho
KIII-TV Corpus Christi, Texas
KLKN Lincoln, Nebraska
KNOE Monroe, Louisiana
KOBR Roswell, New Mexico
KOLO Reno, Nevada
KOMU-TV Columbia, Missouri
KSBW Salinas, California
KSWK Lakin, Kansas
KSYS Medford, Oregon
KTSC Pueblo, Colorado
KUHT Houston, Texas
KUMV Williston, North Dakota
KUSM-TV Bozeman, Montana
KWET Cheyenne, Oklahoma
KZSD-TV Martin, South Dakota
WACS-TV Dawson, Georgia
WAGM Presque Isle, Maine
WBNA Louisville, Kentucky
WDAZ-TV Devil's Lake, North Dakota
WNPT Nashville, Tennessee
WDSE Duluth, Minnesota
WFAA Dallas, Texas
WFXI Morehead City, North Carolina
WGAL Lancaster, Pennsylvania
WGTQ Sault Ste. Marie, Michigan
WGTV Athens, Georgia
WICZ-TV Binghamton, New York
WJW Cleveland, Ohio
WKBT-TV La Crosse, Wisconsin
WLIO Lima, Ohio
WMTW Poland Spring, Maine
MPTVÿ Milwaukee, Wisconsin
WNJB New Brunswick, New Jersey
WOLO-TV Columbia, South Carolina
WSIU-TV Carbondale, Illinois
WTVA Tupelo, Mississippi
WVNS-TV Lewisburg, West Virginia
WWCP-TV Johnstown, Pennsylvania
WGEN-TV Key West, Florida
WWMT Kalamazoo, Michigan
WXGA-TV Waycross, Georgia
KNMD-TV Santa Fe, New Mexico
KPTW Casper, Wyoming
KCCI-TV Des Moines, Maine
WGAL-TV Lancaster, Maine

Channel 9

KACV-TV Amarillo, Texas
KAFT Fayetteville, Arkansas
KAWE Bemidji, Minnesota
KBOI-TV Boise, Idaho
KCWK North Las Vegas, Nevada
KCAU-TV Sioux City, Iowa
KCEN-TV Temple, Texas
KCFW-TV Kalispell, Montana
KCRG-TV Cedar Rapids, Iowa
KCTS-TV Seattle, Washington
KDSE Dickinson, North Dakota
KECY-TV El Centro, California
KEZI Eugene, Oregon
KFWD Fort Worth, Texas
KGMD-TV Hilo, Hawaii
KIXE-TV Redding, California
KLRN San Antonio, Texas
KMSP Minneapolis, Minnesota
KPNE-TV North Platte, Nebraska
KTRE Lufkin, Texas
KTSM-TV El Paso, Texas
KUAC-TV Fairbanks, Alaska
KUSA Denver, Colorado
KMYU St. George, Utah
KVIE Sacramento, California
KVVU Henderson, Nevada
KWES-TV Odessa, Texas
WAFB Baton Rouge, Louisiana
WALA-TV Mobile, Alabama
WAOW Wausau, Wisconsin
WBPH-TV Bethlehem, Pennsylvania
WEDN Norwich, Connecticut
WHMC Conway, South Carolina
WILL-TV Urbana, Illinois
WISH-TV Indianapolis, Indiana
WJSU-TV Anniston, Alabama
WMEB-TV Orono, Maine
WMUR-TV Manchester, New Hampshire
WNIN Evansville, Indiana
WNTV Greenville, South Carolina
WPGX Panama City, Florida
WTOV-TV Steubenville, Ohio
WTVC Chattanooga, Tennessee
WUSA Washington, District of Columbia
WVAN-TV Savannah, Georgia
WVER Rutland, Vermont
WWTV Cadillac, Michigan
WSKY-TV Manteo, North Carolina
WNBW-DT Gainesville, Florida
WSUR-DT Ponce, Puerto Rico
WGWW Anniston, Alabama
KMBC-TV Kansas City, Maine
KMBC-TV Kansas City, Maine

Channel 10

KAKE Wichita, Kansas
KBIM-TV Roswell, New Mexico
KCHF Santa Fe, New Mexico
KERO-TV Bakersfield, California
KFDA-TV Amarillo, Texas
KGTV San Diego, California
KOTA-TV Lead, South Dakota
KLFY-TV Lafayette, Louisiana
KMEB Wailuku, Hawaii
KMOT Minot, North Dakota
KNIN-TV Caldwell, Idaho
KOLN Lincoln, Nebraska
KOPB-TV Portland, Oregon
KRMZ Steamboat Springs, Colorado
KTOO-TV Juneau, Alaska
KTSD-TV Pierre, South Dakota
KTTC Rochester, Minnesota
KTUL Tulsa, Oklahoma
KTUU-TV Anchorage, Alaska
KTVL Medford, Oregon
KTVQ Billings, Montana
KWCM-TV Appleton, Minnesota
KWSU-TV Pullman, Washington
KWTX Waco, Texas
KXTV Sacramento, California
KZTV Corpus Christi, Texas
WALB Albany, Georgia

WBIQ Birmingham, Alabama
WBIR-TV Knoxville, Tennessee
WCBB Augusta, Maine
WDIO-DT Duluth, Minnesota
WDIQ Dozier, Alabama
WGEM-TV Quincy, Illinois
WHEC-TV Rochester, New York
WHTM-TV Harrisburg, Pennsylvania
WILX Onondaga, Michigan
WIS Columbia, South Carolina
WJXX Orange Park, Florida
WMAB-TV Mississippi State, Mississippi
WMED-TV Calais, Maine
WMEM-TV Presque Isle, Maine
WNCT-TV Greenville, North Carolina
WOIO Shaker Heights, Ohio
WPLG Miami, Florida
WSMV Nashville, Tennessee
WSWP-TV Grandview, West Virginia
WTHI-TV Terre Haute, Indiana
WTNH New Haven, Connecticut
WTSP St. Petersburg, Florida
WVFX Clarksburg, West Virginia
WWDP Norwell, Massachusetts
WWTO-TV La Salle, Illinois
WWUP-TV Sault Ste. Marie, Michigan
WXIA-TV Atlanta, Georgia
WBUP Ishpeming, Michigan
KETZ El Dorado, Arkansas

Channel 11

KAQY Columbia, Louisiana
KARE Minneapolis, Minnesota
KCBD Lubbock, Texas
KCBY-TV Coos Bay, Oregon
KDIN-TV Des Moines, Iowa
KEET Eureka, California
KELO-TV Sioux Falls, South Dakota
KFFX-TV Pendleton, Oregon
KGIN Grand Island, Nebraska
KHON2 Hilo, Hawaii
KHET Honolulu, Hawaii
KHOU Houston, Texas
KJUD Juneau, Alaska
KATV Cheyenne, Wyoming
KLST San Angelo, Texas
KLVX Las Vegas, Nevada
KMVT Twin Falls, Idaho
KNSO Merced, California
KOAB-TV Bend, Oregon
KOED-TV Tulsa, Oklahoma
KQSD-TV Lowry, South Dakota
KSNG Garden City, Kansas
KSTW-TV Tacoma, Washington
KSWO-TV Lawton, Oklahoma
KTTV Los Angeles, California
KTVF Fairbanks, Alaska
KTWU Topeka, Kansas
KUFM-TV Missoula, Montana
KULR-TV Billings, Montana
KVCT Victoria, Texas
KWSE Williston, North Dakota
WBKB-TV Alpena, Michigan
WBRE-TV Wilkes-Barre, Pennsylvania
WENH-TV Durham, New Hampshire
WESH Daytona Beach, Florida
WGVU-TV Grand Rapids, Michigan
WHAS-TV Louisville, Kentucky
WISC-TV Madison, Wisconsin
WJHL-TV Johnson City, Tennessee
WLFI-TV Lafayette, Indiana
WLUK-TV Green Bay, Wisconsin
WPCW-TV Jeannette, Pennsylvania
WPIX New York, New York
WTOC-TV Savannah, Georgia
WTOK Meridian, Mississippi
WTOL Toledo, Ohio
WTVD-TV Durham, North Carolina
WTVI Charlotte, North Carolina
WTVM Columbus, Georgia
WVPT Staunton, Virginia
WWLP Springfield, Massachusetts
WYES-TV New Orleans, Louisiana
KDTP Holbrook, Arizona
KRII Chisholm, Minnesota
WLII-DT Caguas, Puerto Rico
KMLU Columbia, Louisiana
KIIT North Platte, Nebraska
WBAL-TV Baltimore, Maine

Channel 12

KAMU-TV College Station, Texas
KBMT Beaumont, Texas
KCCW-TV Walker, Minnesota
KDRV Medford, Oregon
KEYC-TV CBS & NEYC FOX Mankato, Minnesota
KFVS-TV Cape Girardeau, Missouri
KIIN Iowa City, Missouri
KYUR Anchorage, Alaska
KKCO Grand Junction, Colorado
KMAU Wailuku, Hawaii
KNRR Pembina, North Dakota
KNTV San Jose, California
KOBF Farmington, New Mexico
KPNX Mesa, Arizona
KPTV Portland, Oregon
KRCG Jefferson City, Missouri
KRNE-TV Merriman, Nebraska
KSAT-TV San Antonio, Texas
KSNK McCook, Nebraska
KTHV Little Rock, Arkansas
KTNV-TV Las Vegas, Nevada
KTTM Huron, South Dakota
KTVH-DT Helena, Montana
KUID-TV Moscow, Idaho
KUON-TV Lincoln, Nebraska
KVIH-TV Clovis, New Mexico
KXII Sherman, Texas
KXMB-TV Bismarck, North Dakota
WBBM-TV Chicago, Illinois
WBOY-TV Clarksburg, West Virginia
WCTI-TV New Bern, North Carolina
WFXL Albany, Georgia
WHYY-TV Wilmington, Delaware
WICU-TV Erie, Pennsylvania
WINM Angola, Indiana
WJRT Flint, Michigan
WJTV Jackson, Mississippi
WKRC-TV Cincinnati, Ohio
WMAE-TV Booneville, Mississippi
WMFD-TV Mansfield, Ohio
WNAC-TV Providence, Rhode Island
WNYT Albany, New York
WPTV-TV West Palm Beach, Florida
WRDW Augusta, Georgia
WSFA Montgomery, Alabama
WTVT Tampa, Florida
WWBT Richmond, Virginia
WWPX-TV Martinsburg, District of Columbia
WYMT Hazard, Kentucky
KUTF Logan, Utah
KSQA Topeka, Idaho
KCWY Casper, Wyoming
WISN-TV Wilwaukee, Maine

Channel 13

KBDI-TV Broomfield, Colorado
KFPH-DT Flagstaff, Arizona
KCBA Salinas, California
KCOP Los Angeles, California
KCOS El Paso, Texas
KBZK Bozeman, Montana
KECI-TV Missoula, Montana
KEMV Mountain View, Arkansas
KETA-TV Oklahoma City, Oklahoma
KEMV Arkadelphia, Arkansas
KFME Fargo, North Dakota
KGWR-TV Rock Springs, Wyoming
KHGI-TV Kearney, Nebraska
KHVO Honolulu, Hawaii
KLPA-TV Monroe, Louisiana
KOTI Klamath Falls, Oregon
KPLO-TV Reliance, South Dakota
KPSD-TV Eagle Butte, South Dakota
KREY-TV Montrose, Colorado
KRGV-TV Weslaco, Texas
KRIS-TV Corpus Christi, Texas
KRQE Albuquerque, New Mexico
KSFY Sioux Falls, South Dakota
KSGW-TV Sheridan, Wyoming
KSWT Yuma, Arizona
KTNE-TV Alliance, Nebraska
KTRK-TV Houston, Texas
KTRV-TV Nampa, Idaho
KTVN Reno, Nevada
KTVR La Grande, Oregon
KUBD Ketchikan, Alaska
KVAL-TV Eugene, Oregon
KVTV Laredo, Texas
KXLY-TV Spokane, Washington
KXMC-TV Minot, North Dakota
WABI-TV Bangor, Maine
WBKO Bowling Green, Kentucky
WBRZ-TV Baton Rouge, Louisiana
WBTW Florence, South Carolina
WCIX Springfield, Illinois
WEDU Tampa-St. Petersburg, Florida
WHBQ-TV Memphis, Tennessee
WHO-DT Des Moines, Missouri
WIBW Topeka, Kansas
WIRT Hibbing, Minnesota
WJZ-TV Baltimore, Maryland
WLOS Asheville, North Carolina
WMAZ-TV Macon, Georgia
WMBB Panama City, Florida
WNET Newark, New Jersey
WHAM-TV Rochester, New York
WOWK-TV Huntington, West Virginia
WPEC West Palm Beach, Florida
WNAC-TV Providence, Rhode Island
WQED Pittsburgh, Pennsylvania
WRCB-DT Chattanooga, Tennessee
WREX-TV Rockford, Illinois
WSET-TV Lynchburg, Virginia
WTHR Indianapolis, Indiana
WTLV Jacksonville, Florida
WTVG-TV Toledo, Ohio
WVEC Hampton, Virginia
WVNY Burlington, Vermont
WVTM Birmingham, Alabama
WYOU Scranton, Pennsylvania
WZZM Grand Rapids, Michigan
WNYT Pittsfield, Massachusetts
KAKW-DT Killeen, Texas

Channel 14

KAPP-TV Yakima, Washington
KOCW Hoisington, Kansas
KCSG Cedar City, Utah
KERA-TV Dallas, Texas
KMCY Minot, North Dakota
KNLC St. Louis, Missouri
KTBW-TV Tacoma, Washington
KTGM Tamuning, Guam
KTNC-TV Concord, California
KXMD-TV Williston, North Dakota
WMYA-TV Anderson, South Carolina
WCMH-TV Columbus, Ohio
WGPX-TV Burlington, North Carolina
WHDF Florence, Alabama
WKBD-TV Detroit, Michigan
WKSO-TV Somerset, Kentucky
WMEI Arecibo, Puerto Rico
WPTZ North Pole, New York
WTIU Bloomington, Indiana
WUTV Buffalo, New York
WSTQ-LP Syracuse, New York
KGWC-TV Casper, Wyoming
KSVT Twin Falls, Idaho

Channel 15

KAVU-TV Victoria, Texas
KBSV Ceres, California
KCIT Amarillo, Texas
KFOX-TV El Paso, Texas
KREX-TV Grand Junction, Colorado
KGFE Grand Forks, North Dakota
KHOG Fayetteville, Arkansas
KHQ-TV Spokane, Washington
KJTL Wichita Falls, Texas
KMOS-TV Sedalia, Missouri
KNPB Reno, Nevada
KNXV-TV Phoenix, Arizona
KPOB-TV Poplar Bluff, Missouri
KREZ-TV Durango, Colorado
KSBY San Luis Obispo, California
KSMN Worthington, Minnesota
KTAL-TV Texarkana, Texas
KTBO-TV Oklahoma City, Oklahoma
KYOU-TV Ottumwa, Iowa
WBBH-TV Fort Myers, Florida
WDCQ-TV Bad Axe, Michigan
WEWS-TV Cleveland, Ohio
WKMR Morehead, Kentucky
WNOL New Orleans, Louisiana
WNSC-TV Rock Hill, South Carolina
WPMI-TV Mobile, Alabama
WPSU-TV Clearfield, Pennsylvania
WQOW-DT Eau Claire, Wisconsin
WRBL Columbus, Georgia

WRPX-TV Rocky Mount, North Carolina
WSEC Jacksonville, Illinois
WSPX-TV Syracuse, New York
WTIN-TV Ponce, Puerto Rico
WFDC-DT Arlington, District of Columbia
WXVT Greenville, Mississippi
WZTV Nashville, Tennessee
KXVA Abilene, Texas
KUPU Waimanalo, Hawaii
KVVK-CD Kennewick, Washington
KDVT-LP Denver, Colorado
KTFD-TV Denver, Colorado
KELV-LD Las Vegas, Nevada

Channel 16

KADN-TV Lafayette, Louisiana
KBMY Bismarck, North Dakota
KUNP La Grande, Oregon
KCLO-TV Rapid City, South Dakota
KDSM-TV Des Moines, Iowa
KHCE-TV San Antonio, Texas
KINC Las Vegas, Nevada
KOGG Wailuku, Hawaii
KOOD Hays, Kansas
WCJB-TV Gainesville, Florida
WELF-TV Dalton, Georgia
WGGS-TV Greenville, South Carolina
WGXA Macon, Georgia
WHRO-TV Hampton-Norfolk, Virginia
WJFW-TV Rhinelander, Wisconsin
WKHA Hazard, Kentucky
WNKY Bowling Green, Kentucky
WLOV-TV West Point, Mississippi
WMAH-TV Biloxi, Mississippi
WMTJ Fajardo, Puerto Rico
WPBF Tequesta, Florida
WPDE-TV Florence, South Carolina
WPTD Dayton, Ohio
WSEE-TV Erie, Pennsylvania
WSMH Flint, Michigan
WTVO Rockford, Illinois
WXXI-TV Rochester, New York
KCGE-DT Crookston, North Dakota
KORX-CA Walla Walla, Washington
WVCI-LP Daytona Beach, Florida
WAPT-TV Jackson, Maine

Channel 17

KAAS-TV Salina, Kansas
KAZQ Albuquerque, New Mexico
KDOR-TV Bartlesville, Oklahoma
KDSD-TV Aberdeen, South Dakota
KLBY Colby, Kansas
KMIZ Columbia, Missouri
KMTR Eugene, Oregon
KPHO Phoenix, Arizona
KQDS-TV Duluth, Minnesota
KSLA Shreveport, Louisiana
KTWO-TV Casper, Wyoming
KVIA-TV El Paso, Texas
KVIQ Eureka, California
KYNE-TV Omaha, Nebraska
WAND Decatur, Illinois
WCMV Cadillac, Michigan
WEAR-TV Pensacola, Florida
WFXR Roanoke, Virginia
WQCW Portsmouth, Ohio
WHNS Greenville, South Carolina
WUVG-DT Athens, Georgia
WSYR-TV Syracuse, New York
WKCF Clermont, Florida
WKOP-TV Knoxville, Tennessee
WKPC-TV Louisville, Kentucky
WKYC Cleveland, Ohio
WLAX La Crosse, Wisconsin
WLTX Columbia, South Carolina
WNCN Goldsboro, North Carolina
WPHL Philadelphia, Pennsylvania
WPXQ-TV Block Island, Rhode Island
WTCT Marion, Illinois
WUNE-TV Linville, North Carolina
WVXF Charlotte Amalie, Virgin Islands
WXMI Battle Creek, Michigan
WYIN Gary, Indiana

Channel 18

KATN Fairbanks, Alaska
KPTF-DT Farwell, Texas
KCPT Kansas City, Missouri
KDBC-TV El Paso, Texas
KEPR-TV Pasco, Washington
KFSM Fort Smith, Arkansas
KYTX Nacogdoches, Texas
KRMA-TV Denver, Colorado
KRMJ Grand Junction, Colorado
KSCI Long Beach, California
KSVI Billings, Montana
KTVC Roseburg, Oregon
KUEW St. George, Utah
KUPB-TV Midland, Texas
KUPK Garden City, Kansas
KUSI-TV San Diego, California
KUVS-DT Modesto, California
KYIN Mason City, Iowa
WDBB Bessemer, Alabama
WDBJ Roanoke, Virginia
WETM-TV Elmira, New York
WFXB Myrtle Beach, South Carolina
WJHG Panama City, Florida
WKYU-TV Bowling Green, Kentucky
WMAU-TV Bude, Mississippi
WMBC-TV Newton, New Jersey
WMFP Lawrence, Massachusetts
WNEH Greenwood, South Carolina
WPBT Miami, Florida
WVTB St. Johnsbury, Vermont
WVTV Milwaukee, Wisconsin
KOHD Bend, Oregon
KNIC-DT Blanco, Texas

Channel 19

KAMR-TV Amarillo, Texas
KBCB Bellingham, Washington
KBJR-TV Superior, Wisconsin
KOFY-TV San Francisco, California
KCKA Centralia, Washington
KCOY-TV Santa Maria, California
KIDY San Angelo, Texas
KIKU Honolulu, Hawaii
KLDO-TV Laredo, Texas
KMOH-TV Kingman, Arizona
KPIC Roseburg, Oregon
KPRY-TV Pierre, South Dakota
KSPR Springfield, Missouri
KSWB San Diego, California
KTTU Tucson, Arizona
KTVD Denver, Colorado
KTVG-TV Grand Island, Nebraska
KTVT-TV Fort Worth, Texas
KTXH Houston, Texas
KVRR Fargo, North Dakota
KSCW-DT Wichita, Kansas
KWYB Butte, Montana
KXMA-TV Dickinson, North Dakota
KXNE-TV Norfolk, Nebraska
WCWG Lexington, North Carolina
WSFL Miami, Florida
WGBH-TV Boston, Massachusetts
WGBH Boston, Massachusetts
WGN Chicago, Illinois
WGCL Atlanta, Georgia
WBKI-TV Campbellsville, Kentucky
WHNT Huntsville, Alabama
WHOI Peoria, Illinois
WIIQ Demopolis, Alabama
WISE-TV Fort Wayne, Indiana
WKPT-TV Kingsport, Tennessee
WKPV Ponce, Puerto Rico
WMTV Madison, Wisconsin
WSYT Syracuse, New York
WJAX-TV Jacksonville, Florida
WUNM-TV Jacksonville, North Carolina
WUSI-TV Olney, Illinois
WVAH-TV Charleston, West Virginia
WZMQ Marquette, Michigan
WCAV Charlottesville, Virginia
KWKS Colby, Kansas

Channel 20

KRXIÿ Reno, Nevada
KDYW Waco, Texas
KCVU Paradise, California
KETV Omaha, Nebraska
KFTV-DT Hanford, California
KJNP-TV North Pole, Alaska
KJRE Ellendale, North Dakota
KLPA-TV Lake Charles, Louisiana
KNLJ Jefferson City, Missouri
KPAZ-TV Phoenix, Arizona
KREM Spokane, Washington
KSMQ-TV Austin, Minnesota
KTBY Anchorage, Alaska
KTEJ Jonesboro, Arkansas
KTMW Salt Lake City, Utah
KTXS-TV Sweetwater, Texas
KQCW-DT Muskogee, Oklahoma
WBXX-TV Crossville, Tennessee
WCOV-TV Montgomery, Alabama
WCVB Boston, Massachusetts
WFMJ-TV Youngstown, Ohio
WHA-TV Madison, Wisconsin
WHMB-TV Indianapolis, Indiana
WWCW Lynchburg, Virginia
WLRN-TV Miami, Florida
WMPN-TV Jackson, Mississippi
WMPV-TV Mobile, Alabama
WOTV Battle Creek, Michigan
WSVI Christiansted, Virgin Islands
WPCH-TV Atlanta, Georgia
WCCT Waterbury, Connecticut
WUND-TV Edenton, North Carolina
KRMU Durango, Colorado
WNYI Ithaca, New York
KVME-TV Bishop, California
KFXV-LD McAllen, Texas
KXFX-CD Brownsville, Texas
KZUP-CD Baton Rouge, Louisiana

Channel 21

KAID Boise, Idaho
KDCK Dodge City, Kansas
KFCT Fort Collins, Colorado
KHBS Fort Smith, Arkansas
KMAX-TV Sacramento, California
KPMR-TV Santa Barbara, California
KPXJ Minden, Louisiana
KTAJ-TV St. Joseph, Missouri
KTVZ Bend, Oregon
KWHM Wailuku, Hawaii
KXAN-TV Austin, Texas
KYVE Yakima, Washington
WAPT Jackson, Mississippi
WBNS-TV Columbus, Ohio
WBOC-TV Salisbury, Maryland
WCLF Clearwater, Florida
WCMW Manistee, Michigan
WDAY-TV Fargo, North Dakota
WDHN Dothan, Alabama
WMYD Detroit, Michigan
WFYI Indianapolis, Indiana
WHNO New Orleans, Louisiana
WHP-TV Harrisburg, Pennsylvania
WCWF Suring, Wisconsin
WJPX San Juan, Puerto Rico
WLIW Garden City, New York
WMEC Macomb, Illinois
WPBA Atlanta, Georgia
WPXS Mount Vernon, Illinois
WSBE-TV Providence, Rhode Island
WUXP-TV Nashville, Tennessee
WVPY Front Royal, Virginia
WWMB Florence, South Carolina
WWTI Watertown, New York
KNBN Rapid City, South Dakota
KRWB-TV Roswell, New Mexico
KUFM-TV Great Falls, Montana
KFCT Fort Collins, Colorado
WBRL-CD Baton Rouge, Louisiana

Channel 22

KTFQ-DT Albuquerque, New Mexico
KATV Little Rock, Arkansas
KAUZ-TV Wichita Falls, Texas
KBME-TV Bismarck, North Dakota
WBMM Tuskegee, Alabama
KBSI Cape Girardeau, Missouri
KCPQ Tacoma, Washington
KETK-TV Jacksonville, Texas
KFVE Honolulu, Hawaii
KHBC-TV Hilo, Hawaii
KHMT Hardin, Montana
KIPT Twin Falls, Idaho
KLRU Austin, Texas
KMCB Coos Bay, Oregon
WUCW Minneapolis, Minnesota
KNAZ-TV Flagstaff, Arizona
KOKI-TV Tulsa, Oklahoma
KPXG-TV Salem, Oregon
KSNC Great Bend, Kansas
KSNV-DT Las Vegas, Nevada

KVMY Las Vegas, Nevada
KVYE-TV El Centro, California
KXRM-TV Colorado Springs, Colorado
WBUI Decatur, Illinois
WCAX-TV Burlington, Vermont
WCNC-TV Charlotte, North Carolina
WCPO-TV Cincinnati, Ohio
WCTE Cookeville, Tennessee
WFIQ Florence, Alabama
WFXP Erie, Pennsylvania
WGBY-TV Springfield, Massachusetts
WHLT Hattiesburg, Mississippi
WJCL Savannah, Georgia
WLWC New Bedford, Massachusetts
WNEM Bay City, Michigan
WNEP Waymart, Pennsylvania
WNJS Camden, New Jersey
WOFL Orlando, Florida
WOWT Omaha, Nebraska
WRIC-TV Petersburg, Virginia
WSBT-TV South Bend, Indiana
WVCY-TV Milwaukee, Wisconsin
WVUT Vincennes, Indiana
KWWF Waterloo, Iowa
WSKC-CD Atlanta, Georgia
WKCF-TV Winter Park, Maine
WLKY-TV Louisville, Maine
WMTW-TV Westbrook, Maine

Channel 23

KEDT Corpus Christi, Texas
KHNL/KGMB Honolulu, Hawaii
KLPA-TV Lafayette, Louisiana
KLTJ Galveston, Texas
KOZK Springfield, Missouri
KPEJ-TV Odessa, Texas
KCWI-TV Ames, Iowa
KRCB Cotati, California
KREG-TV Glenwood Springs, Colorado
KRWG-TV Las Cruces, New Mexico
KTCI-TV St. Paul, Minnesota
KTMF Missoula, Montana
KCDO-TV Kimball, Colorado
KVMD Twentynine Palms, California
KVOA Tucson, Arizona
KWHD Hilo, Hawaii
WBAY-TV Green Bay, Wisconsin
WBTV Charlotte, North Carolina
WCVI-TV Christiansted, Virgin Islands
WFTY-DT Smithtown, New York
WIPB Muncie, Indiana
WJSP-TV Columbus, Georgia
WLTV-DT Miami, Florida
WLYH-TV Lancaster, Pennsylvania
WPFO Waterville, Maine
WNAB Nashville, Tennessee
WNJX-TV Mayaguez, Puerto Rico
WPBS-DT Norwood, New York
WPXJ-TV Buffalo, New York
WPXK-TV Jellico, Tennessee
WQPT-TV Moline, Illinois
WSAZ Huntington, West Virginia
WUNK-TV Greenville, North Carolina
WVPX-TV Akron, Ohio
XETV-DT Tijuana, California
KAGS-LD Bryan, Texas
KCWT-CD La Feria, Texas

Channel 24

KBEH Oxnard, California
KPNZ Ogden, Utah
KQUP Pullman, Washington
KCSD-TV Sioux Falls, South Dakota
KCTV Kansas City, Missouri
KETH-TV Houston, Texas
KGMV Wailuku, Hawaii
KLPA-TV Shreveport, Louisiana
KMOV St. Louis, Missouri
KNAT-TV Albuquerque, New Mexico
KNVN Chico, California
KOKH-TV Oklahoma City, Oklahoma
KRDO-TV Colorado Springs, Colorado
KTAB-TV Abilene, Texas
KTVK Phoenix, Arizona
KVEO-TV Brownsville, Texas
KVTN-DT Pine Bluff, Arkansas
KNDM Minot, North Dakota
WATM-TV Altoona, Pennsylvania
WPXC-TV Brunswick, Georgia
WCML Alpena, Michigan
WCVN-TV Covington, Kentucky
WHIQ Huntsville, Alabama
WHRM-TV Wausau, Wisconsin
WJET-TV Erie, Pennsylvania
WKPI-TV Pikeville, West Virginia
WMDN Meridian, Mississippi
WMFE-TV Orlando, Florida
WUGA-TV Toccoa, Georgia
WNVC Fairfax, Virginia
WNYE-TV New York, New York
WPTA Fort Wayne, Indiana
WSFJ-TV Newark, Ohio
WSTM-TV Syracuse, New York
WTAT-TV Charleston, South Carolina
WTLJ Muskegon, Michigan
WUPL Slidell, Louisiana
WVTA Windsor, Vermont
WWAY-TV Wilmington, North Carolina
WWSB Sarasota, Florida
KXIP Paris, Texas

Channel 25

KQET Watsonville, California
KDKA-TV Pittsburgh, Pennsylvania
KFDM Beaumont, Texas
KGET-TV Bakersfield, California
KINT-TV El Paso, Texas
KLEI-TV Kailua-Kona, Hawaii
KMSB Tucson, Arizona
KOVR-TV Stockton, California
KOZJ Joplin, Missouri
KTIN Fort Dodge, Iowa
KZJO Seattle, Washington
WATL Atlanta, Georgia
WVEA-TV Venice, Florida
WCGV-TV Milwaukee, Wisconsin
WCNY-TV Syracuse, New York
WEEK-TV Peoria, Illinois
WLPB-TV Baton Rouge, Louisiana
WMAO-TV Greenwood, Mississippi
WNNE Hartford, Vermont
WQTO Ponce, Puerto Rico
WRTV Indianapolis, Indiana
WTVE Reading, Pennsylvania
WTVF Nashville, Tennessee
WTVR Richmond, Virginia
WUNC-TV Chapel Hill, North Carolina
WUNF-TV Asheville, North Carolina
WXXV-TV Gulfport, Mississippi
KMDE Devils Lake, North Dakota
KBNT-CD San Diego, California
KHAX-LP San Diego, California
KNPL North Platte, Nebraska

Channel 26

KBHE-TV Rapid City, South Dakota
KDLV-TV Mitchell, South Dakota
KFTC Bemidji, Minnesota
KLNE-TV Lexington, Nebraska
KLPA-TV Alexandria, Louisiana
KMID Midland, Texas
KMVU-DT Medford, Oregon
KNDO Yakima, Washington
KNDU Richland, Washington
KNDB Bismarck, North Dakota
KOB Albuquerque, New Mexico
KPLR St. Louis, Missouri
KREN-TV Reno, Nevada
KRIV Houston, Texas
KSAS-TV Wichita, Kansas
KTEN Ada, Oklahoma
KUTP Phoenix, Arizona
KVCR-DT San Bernardino, California
KVTH-DT Hot Springs, Arkansas
KXXV Waco, Texas
KYW-TV Philadelphia, Pennsylvania
WATE-TV Knoxville, Tennessee
WBDT Springfield, Ohio
WCCU Urbana, Illinois
WCMU-TV Mount Pleasant, Michigan
WGNO New Orleans, Louisiana
WHAG-TV Hagerstown, Maryland
WKAS Ashland, Kentucky
WKMG-TV Orlando, Florida
WLKY Louisville, Kentucky
WNYB Jamestown, New York
WRLH-TV Richmond, Virginia
WTEN Albany, New York
WTJP-TV Gadsden, Alabama
WVIZ Cleveland, Ohio
WHPX-TV New London, Connecticut
XHRIO-TDT Matamoros, Texas

Channel 27

KAAH-TV Honolulu, Hawaii
KAMC Lubbock, Texas
KASA-TV Santa Fe, New Mexico
KBTC-TV Tacoma, Washington
KEYT-TV Santa Barbara, California
KFOR Oklahoma City, Oklahoma
KFXA Cedar Rapids, Iowa
KLWY Cheyenne, Wyoming
KORO-TV Corpus Christi, Texas
KFTA-TV Fort Smith, Arkansas
KRPV-DT Roswell, New Mexico
KRWF Redwood Falls, Minnesota
KSNT Topeka, Kansas
KTSF San Francisco, California
KTVE El Dorado, Arkansas
WACY-TV Appleton, Wisconsin
WAGA Atlanta, Georgia
WAIQ Montgomery, Alabama
WAPA-TV San Juan, Puerto Rico
WBGU-TV Bowling Green, Ohio
WCBI-DT Columbus, Mississippi
WCCB Charlotte, North Carolina
WCIU-TV Chicago, Illinois
WETA-TV Washington, District of Columbia
WFXV Utica, New York
WGTW-TV Burlington, New Jersey
WUTF-DT Marlborough, Massachusetts
WHWC-TV Menomonie, Wisconsin
WIPX-TV Bloomington, Indiana
WKOW Madison, Wisconsin
WKRG-TV Mobile, Alabama
WKRN-TV Nashville, Tennessee
WLFL Raleigh, North Carolina
WOUB-TV Athens, Ohio
WRDQ Orlando, Florida
WTBY-TV Poughkeepsie, New York
WTVQ-TV Lexington, Kentucky
WTXL-TV Tallahassee, Florida
WXEL-TV West Palm Beach, Florida
KCWV Duluth, Minnesota
WUNW Canton, North Carolina
KBVO Llano, Texas
WUPX-TV Marquette, Michigan
KGHB-CD Pueblo, Colorado

Channel 28

KATC Lafayette, Louisiana
KAWB Brainerd, Minnesota
KAYU-TV Spokane, Washington
KBVU Eureka, California
KOZL-TV Springfield, Missouri
KFDX-TV Wichita Falls, Texas
KHNE-TV Hastings, Nebraska
KMPH-TV Visalia, California
KSIN-TV Sioux City, Missouri
KSTU Salt Lake City, Utah
KTBS-TV Shreveport, Louisiana
KTPX-TV Okmulgee, Oklahoma
KTVA Anchorage, Alaska
KUAS-TV Tucson, Arizona
KYLE-TV Bryan, Texas
WCPB Salisbury, Maryland
WFLX West Palm Beach, Florida
WFPT Frederick, Maryland
WFUM Flint, Michigan
WGFL High Springs, Florida
WKAQ San Juan, Puerto Rico
WNBC New York, New York
WPTO Oxford, Ohio
WRDC Durham, North Carolina
WREG-TV Memphis, Tennessee
WRJA-TV Sumter, South Carolina
WSJV Elkhart, Indiana
WTGS Hardeeville, South Carolina
WTMJ-TV Milwaukee, Wisconsin
WTTO Homewood, Alabama
WTVW Evansville, Indiana
WUAB Lorain, Ohio
WUHF Rochester, New York
WYOW Eagle River, Wisconsin
WYZZ-TV Bloomington, Illinois
KYUU-LD Boise, Idaho

Channel 29

KTUZ-TV30 Shawnee, Oklahoma
KDEN Longmont, Colorado

KDKF Klamath Falls, Oregon
KEPB-TV Eugene, Oregon
KVCW Las Vegas, Nevada
KGAN Cedar Rapids, Iowa
KUPT Hobbs, New Mexico
KFTR-DT Ontario, California
KMBC Kansas City, Missouri
KMTF Helena, Montana
KPIX-TV San Francisco, California
KPTS Hutchinson, Kansas
KRBC-TV Abilene, Texas
KSTF Scottsbluff, Nebraska
KTXA-TV Fort Worth, Texas
KUPX-TV Provo, Utah
KWBQ Santa Fe, New Mexico
WNYJ-TV West Milford, New Jersey
WFTC Minneapolis, Minnesota
WFTS-TV Tampa, Florida
WGTE-TV Toledo, Ohio
WGTU Traverse City, Michigan
WUVP-DT Vineland, New Jersey
WQMY Williamsport, Pennsylvania
WKNO Memphis, Tennessee
WKTV Utica, New York
WMAQ Chicago, Illinois
WMPB Baltimore, Maryland
WORA-TV Mayaguez, Puerto Rico
WTCI Chattanooga, Tennessee
WTTK Kokomo, Indiana
WUNI-TV Worcester, Massachusetts
WUNJ-TV Wilmington, North Carolina
WVBT Virginia Beach, Virginia
WVUE-DT New Orleans, Louisiana
WXIX-TV Newport, Kentucky
WXLV-TV Winston-Salem, North Carolina
KBFX-CD Bakersfield, California

Channel 30

KABB San Antonio, Texas
KFSN-TV Fresno, California
KGWN Cheyenne, Wyoming
KLRT-TV Little Rock, Arkansas
KMPX Decatur, Texas
KPBS San Diego, California
KPDX Vancouver, Washington
KWWT Odessa, Texas
KQED San Francisco, California
KUAT-TV Tucson, Arizona
KVHP Lake Charles, Louisiana
WAGT Augusta, Georgia
WEFS Cocoa, Florida
WBNX-TV Akron, Ohio
WBZ-TV Boston, Massachusetts
WDWL Bayamon, Puerto Rico
WEYI-TV Saginaw, Michigan
WGCB-TV Red Lion, Pennsylvania
WGCU Fort Myers, Florida
WHLA-TV La Crosse, Wisconsin
WFUT-DT Newark, New Jersey
WIAT Birmingham, Alabama
WKOH Owensboro, Kentucky
WLBT Jackson, Mississippi
WMBD-TV Peoria, Illinois
WMGT-TV Macon, Georgia
WNVT Goldvein, Virginia
WRGT-TV Dayton, Ohio
WSCV Fort Lauderdale, Florida
WSFX-TV Wilmington, North Carolina
WSLS-TV Roanoke, Virginia
WLGA Opelika, Alabama
WUTR Utica, New York
WVLT Knoxville, Tennessee
KBLN-TV Grants Pass, Oregon
WSKA Corning, New York
KUNW-CD Yakima, Washington

Channel 31

KEYU Borger, Texas
KCWE Kansas City, Missouri
KDNL-TV St. Louis, Missouri
KFXK-TV Longview, Texas
KFXP Pocatello, Idaho
KFYR Bismarck, North Dakota
KGBT-TV Harlingen, Texas
KLAX-TV Alexandria, Louisiana
KLSR-TV Eugene, Oregon
KOET Eufaula, Oklahoma
KONG Everett, Washington
KTLA Los Angeles, California
KWBM Harrison, Arkansas
KWHE Honolulu, Hawaii
WANE-TV Fort Wayne, Indiana
WAVY-TV Portsmouth, Virginia
WDKY-TV Danville, Kentucky
WFLD Chicago, Illinois
WFXT Boston, Massachusetts
WGBC Meridian, Mississippi
WLAE-TV New Orleans, Louisiana
WLMT Memphis, Tennessee
WMAI Cleveland, Mississippi
WOGX Ocala, Florida
WPPX-TV Wilmington, Pennsylvania
WPXD-TV Ann Arbor, Michigan
WPXN-TV New York, New York
WSRE Pensacola, Florida
WSWB Scranton, Pennsylvania
WTIC-TV Hartford, Connecticut
WTVJ Miami, Florida
WUNU Lumberton, North Carolina
WXII-TV Winston-Salem, North Carolina
KDCU-DT Derby, Kansas
KETF-CD Laredo, Texas

Channel 32

KCFG Flagstaff, Arizona
KDAF Dallas, Texas
KDOC-TV Anaheim, California
KDVR Denver, Colorado
KEMO-TV Santa Rosa, California
KION-TV Monterey, California
KLEW-TV Lewiston, Idaho
KMCC Laughlin, Nevada
KOLD-TV Tucson, Arizona
KPXB-TV Conroe, Texas
KMYS Kerrville, Texas
KSMO Kansas City, Missouri
WAAY-TV Huntsville, Alabama
WABG-TV Greenwood, Mississippi
WFOX-TV Jacksonville, Florida
WBFS-TV Miami, Florida
WBPX-TV Boston, Massachusetts
WCCO-TV Minneapolis, Minnesota
WETK Burlington, Vermont
WFSU-TV Tallahassee, Florida
WFQX-TV Cadillac, Michigan
WBUW Janesville, Wisconsin
WITN Washington, North Carolina
WNCF Montgomery, Alabama
WNDY-TV Marion, Indiana
WNLO Buffalo, New York
WPGA-TV Perry, Georgia
WPSD-TV Paducah, Kentucky
WPSG-TV Philadelphia, Pennsylvania
WQPX-TV Scranton, Pennsylvania
WRLK-TV Columbia, South Carolina
WSBN-TV Norton, Virginia
WTAJ-TV Altoona, Pennsylvania
WTJR Quincy, Illinois
WTTA St. Petersburg, Florida
WUNL-TV Winston-Salem, North Carolina
WVIR-TV Charlottesville, Virginia
XEWT-DT Tijuana, California
KUTH-DT Provo, Utah
WMBF-TV Myrtle Beach, South Carolina
KARK-TV Little Rock, Arkansas

Channel 33

KBAK-TV Bakersfield, California
KBFD-DT Honolulu, Hawaii
KBIN-TV Council Bluffs, Nebraska
KDLH Duluth, Minnesota
KDMD Anchorage, Alaska
SOPTV Klamath Falls, Oregon
KIMA-TV Yakima, Washington
KITU-TV Beaumont, Texas
KMTP-TV San Francisco, California
KOCB Oklahoma City, Oklahoma
KTBN-TV Santa Ana, California
KTVM-TV Butte, Montana
KTVO Kirksville, Missouri
KVUE Austin, Texas
KWAB-TV Big Spring, Texas
KRCW Salem, Oregon
WCBS-TV New York, New York
WDSC-TV New Smyrna Beach, Florida
WCFT-TV Tuscaloosa, Alabama
WNGH-TV Chatsworth, Georgia
WDFX-TV Ozark, Alabama
WEBA-TV Allendale, South Carolina
WFSB Hartford, Connecticut
WGRZ Buffalo, New York
WHUT-TV Washington, District of Columbia
WITI Milwaukee, Wisconsin
WNMU Marquette, Michigan
WNPB-TV Morgantown, West Virginia
WPGD-TV Hendersonville, Tennessee
WPXG-TV Boston, Massachusetts
WRXY-TV Tice, Florida
WSTR-TV Cincinnati, Ohio
WTVZ-TV Norfolk, Virginia
WMYV Greensboro, North Carolina
KTVW-DT Phoenix, Arizona
KWPX-TV Bellevue, Washington
WSES Tuscaloosa, Alabama
KDJT-CD Salinas, California

Channel 34

KGPX-TV Spokane, Washington
KGPE Fresno, California
KLUJ-TV Harlingen, Texas
KMEX-DT Los Angeles, California
KMSS-TV Shreveport, Louisiana
KFSF-DT Vallejo, California
KTCA-TV St. Paul, Minnesota
KUSD-TV Vermillion, South Dakota
KUTV Salt Lake City, Utah
KXNW Eureka Springs, Arkansas
KWGN Denver, Colorado
KXTF Twin Falls, Idaho
WCAU Philadelphia, Pennsylvania
WCET Cincinnati, Ohio
WDAF Kansas City, Missouri
WHBR Pensacola, Florida
WHTV Jackson, Michigan
WISN-TV Milwaukee, Wisconsin
WIVT Binghamton, New York
WJAC-TV Johnstown, Pennsylvania
WCWJ Jacksonville, Florida
WMHT Schenectady, New York
WGWG Charleston, South Carolina
WPBY-TV Charleston, West Virginia
WNEU Merrimack, New Hampshire
WPXW-TV Manassas, District of Columbia
WQEC Quincy, Illinois
WQHS-DT Cleveland, Ohio
WSIL-TV Harrisburg, Illinois
WSOC-TV Charlotte, North Carolina
WTNZ Knoxville, Tennessee
WTVX Fort Pierce, Florida
WUSF-TV Tampa, Florida
WVLA-TV Baton Rouge, Louisiana
WRBJ-TV Magee, Mississippi

Channel 35

KALB Alexandria, Louisiana
KCRA-TV Sacramento, California
KDFI Dallas, Texas
KGUN-TV Tucson, Arizona
KHIN Red Oak, Iowa
KHNL Honolulu, Hawaii
KJTV Lubbock, Texas
KNME-TV Albuquerque, New Mexico
KPRC-TV Houston, Texas
KRCA Riverside, California
KRIN Waterloo, Iowa
KMTW Hutchinson, Kansas
KSDK St. Louis, Missouri
KSTP-TV St. Paul, Minnesota
KVOS-TV Bellingham, Washington
WDCA Washington, District of Columbia
WFTX-TV Cape Coral, Florida
WGHP High Point, North Carolina
WGSA Baxley, Georgia
WIPM-TV Mayaguez, Puerto Rico
WLTZ Columbus, Georgia
WLUC-TV Marquette, Michigan
WLWT Cincinnati, Ohio
MPTVÿ Milwaukee, Wisconsin
WNIT South Bend, Indiana
WOUC-TV Cambridge, Ohio
WPME Lewiston, Maine
WPXM-TV Miami, Florida
WTOM-TV Cheboygan, Michigan
WVIT New Britain, Connecticut
WYBE Philadelphia, Pennsylvania
KUOK Woodward, Oklahoma
WPXU-TV Jacksonville, North Carolina
KDFW Dallas, Texas

Channel 36

KAAL Austin, Minnesota
KARD West Monroe, Louisiana
KFTU-DT Douglas, Arizona
KDFI Dallas, Texas
KFTH-DT Alvin, Texas
KTVU Oakland, California
KKAP Little Rock, Arkansas
KMCI-TV Lawrence, Missouri
KFRE-TV Sanger, California
KNBC Los Angeles, California
KRSC-TV Claremore, Oklahoma
KSKN Spokane, Washington
KEVC-CD Indio, California
KUEN Ogden, Utah
KWQC-TV Davenport, Iowa
WABM Birmingham, Alabama
WCDC-TV Adams, New York
WCIV Charleston, South Carolina
WENY-TV Elmira, New York
WFFT-TV Fort Wayne, Indiana
WFPX-TV Fayetteville, North Carolina
WGPT Oakland, Maryland
WITF-TV Harrisburg, Pennsylvania
WJYS Hammond, Illinois
WKMU Murray, Kentucky
WKYT Lexington, Kentucky
WLEF-TV Park Falls, Wisconsin
WLNS-TV Lansing, Michigan
WMAV-TV Oxford, Mississippi
WMGM-TV Wildwood, New Jersey
WNJU Linden, New Jersey
WNPX-TV Cookeville, Tennessee
WPXP-TV Lake Worth, Florida
WPXR-TV Roanoke, Virginia
WTTE Columbus, Ohio
WTTG Washington, District of Columbia
WTVY Dothan, Alabama
WTWO Terre Haute, Indiana
WUFT Gainesville, Florida
WUNP-TV Roanoke Rapids, North Carolina
WWL-TV New Orleans, Louisiana
WYFF Greenville, South Carolina
WYTV Youngstown, Ohio
KAJB-TV Calipatria, California
KICU San Jose, California

Channel 38

KALO Honolulu, Hawaii
KIAH Houston, Texas
KMBH Harlingen, Texas
KMCT-TV West Monroe, Louisiana
KPBT-TV Odessa, Texas
KOMO-TV Seattle, Washington
KPXN-TV San Bernardino, California
KRON-TV San Francisco, California
KSEE Fresno, California
KSL-TV Salt Lake City, Utah
KTNW Richland, Washington
KRDK-DT Valley City, North Dakota
KXVO Omaha, Nebraska
WCFE-TV Plattsburgh, New York
WEAU Eau Claire, Wisconsin
WEMT Greeneville, Tennessee
WFSG Panama City, Florida
WGME-TV Portland, Maine
WHTN Murfreesboro, Tennessee
WKBW-TV Buffalo, New York
WUVC-DT Fayetteville, North Carolina
WKMJ-TV Louisville, Kentucky
WMAR-TV Baltimore, Maryland
WOSU-TV Columbus, Ohio
WQAD Moline, Illinois
WINP-TV Pittsburgh, Pennsylvania
WSYM-TV Lansing, Michigan
WTCE-TV Fort Pierce, Florida
WWOR Secaucus, New Jersey
KUQI Corpus Christi, Texas
KPJR-DT Greeley, Colorado
WGBO-DT Joliet, Illinois

Channel 39

KASN Pine Bluff, Arkansas
KCNS San Francisco, California
KETC St. Louis, Missouri
KIRO-TV Seattle, Washington
KMEG Sioux City, Iowa
KWOG Springdale, Arkansas
KSCE El Paso, Texas
KTTZ-TV Lubbock, Texas
KVEA Corona, California
KWTV-DT Oklahoma City, Oklahoma
WADL Mount Clemens, Michigan
WAOE Peoria, Illinois
WAWV-TV Terre Haute, Indiana
WCTX New Haven, Connecticut
WFRV-TV Green Bay, Wisconsin
WFTV Orlando, Florida
WMYT Rock Hill, South Carolina
WIVB-TV Buffalo, New York
WJAL-TV Hagerstown, Maryland
WJWN-TV San Sebastian, Puerto Rico
WKOI-TV Richmond, Indiana
WLEX-TV Lexington, Kentucky
WLOX Biloxi, Mississippi
WLPX-TV Charleston, West Virginia
WLVT-TV Allentown, Pennsylvania
WATN-TV Jackson, Tennessee
WKTC Sumter, South Carolina
WSAV-TV Savannah, Georgia
WSB-TV Atlanta, Georgia
WSBK-TV Boston, Massachusetts
KKJB Boise, Idaho
KXOF-CD Laredo, Texas
KTAZ Phoenix, Arizona

Channel 40

KAUT Oklahoma City, Oklahoma
KBLR Paradise, Nevada
KBTV-TV Port Arthur, Texas
KHRR Tucson, Arizona
KITV Honolulu, Hawaii
KLBK-TV Lubbock, Texas
KNSD San Diego, California
KOIN Portland, Oregon
KPXM-TV St. Cloud, Minnesota
KRMT Denver, Colorado
KSRE Minot, North Dakota
KTLM Harlingen, Texas
KTVX Salt Lake City, Utah
KTXL Sacramento, California
KVPT Fresno, California
KXTX Dallas, Texas
WACX-DT Leesburg, Florida
WDBD Jackson, Mississippi
WDSI-TV Chattanooga, Tennessee
WFWA Fort Wayne, Indiana
WGGB-TV Springfield, Massachusetts
WHIZ-TV Zanesville, Ohio
WHKY-TV Hickory, North Carolina
WKAR-TV East Lansing, Michigan
WLFB Bluefield, West Virginia
WNUV Baltimore, Maryland
WPAN Fort Walton Beach, Florida
WPCB-TV Pittsburgh/Greensburg, Pennsylvania
WBEC-TV Boca Raton, Florida
WPXE-TV Kenosha, Wisconsin
WTKR Norfolk, Virginia
WTWC-TV Tallahassee, Florida
WXTV-DT Paterson, New Jersey
WDPX-TV Boston, Massachusetts
KVER-CA Indio, California
KVES-LD Indio, California
WILM-LD Wilmington, North Carolina

Channel 41

KGCW Burlington, Iowa
KLCS Los Angeles, California
KPXO-TV Kaneohe, Hawaii
KTIV Sioux City, Iowa
KWEX-DT San Antonio, Texas
KXAS Fort Worth, Texas
WATC-DT Atlanta, Georgia
WBUY-TV Holly Springs, Mississippi
WCHS-TV Charleston, West Virginia
WEIQ Mobile, Alabama
WGBA-TV Green Bay, Wisconsin
WHIO-TV Dayton, Ohio
WICD Champaign, Illinois
WIFR Freeport, Illinois
WIRS Yauco, Puerto Rico
WKBN-TV Youngstown, Ohio
WKPD Paducah, Kentucky
WLVI Cambridge, Massachusetts
WGTV Watertown, New York
WRBW Orlando, Florida
WUTB Baltimore, Maryland
WVIA-TV Scranton, Pennsylvania
WXYZ-TV Detroit, Michigan
WZDX Huntsville, Alabama
WZVN-TV Naples, Florida
KBCA Alexandria, Louisiana
WLOO Vicksburg, Mississippi
KTFA-LP Albuquerque, New Mexico
KCRP-CD Corpus Christi, Texas

Channel 42

KESQ-TV Palm Springs, California
KIMT Mason City, Iowa
KLUZ-TV Albuquerque, New Mexico
KMLM-DT Odessa, Texas
KOAA-TV Pueblo, Colorado
KSAX Alexandria, Minnesota
KSHB-TV Kansas City, Missouri
KMYT-TV Tulsa, Oklahoma
KUED Salt Lake City, Utah
KWDK Tacoma, Washington
KWHY-TV Los Angeles, California
WAKA Selma, Alabama
WCLJ-TV Bloomington, Indiana
WCVE-TV Richmond, Virginia
WPNT Pittsburgh, Pennsylvania
WFLI-TV Cleveland, Tennessee
WGGN-TV Sandusky, Ohio
WHDH Boston, Massachusetts
WJBF Augusta, Georgia
WJXT Jacksonville, Florida
WKLE Lexington, Kentucky
WKMA-TV Madisonville, Indiana
WMPT Annapolis, Maryland
WMSY-TV Marion, Virginia
WNDU South Bend, Indiana
WPNE Green Bay, Wisconsin
WQRF-TV Rockford, Illinois
WZME Bridgeport, Connecticut
WSKG-TV Binghamton, New York
WTXF-TV Allentown, Pennsylvania
WXPX-TV Bradenton, Florida
KGLA-AM Hammond, Louisiana
WICS Springfield, Illinois

Channel 43

KATU Portland, Oregon
KLCW-TV Wolfforth, Texas
KCAL-TV Los Angeles, California
KCBS-TV Los Angeles, California
KCSM-TV San Mateo, California
KDTN Denton, Texas
KEYE-TV Austin, Texas
KFXB-TV Dubuque, Missouri
KGMC Clovis, California
KHSL-TV Chico, California
KODE-TV Joplin, Missouri
KPTM Omaha, Nebraska
KPXC-TV Denver, Colorado
KTVI St. Louis, Missouri
KWBN Honolulu, Hawaii
WBBJ-TV Jackson, Tennessee
WOTF-TV Melbourne, Florida
WCPX-TV Chicago, Illinois
WDSU New Orleans, Louisiana
WFFF-TV Burlington, Vermont
WSWG Valdosta, Georgia
WIPR-TV San Juan, Puerto Rico
WKZT-TV Elizabethtown, Kentucky
WLXI Greensboro, North Carolina
WCWN Schenectady, New York
WNED-TV Buffalo, New York
WNJT Trenton, New Jersey
WPBO Portsmouth, Ohio
WPGH-TV Pittsburgh, Pennsylvania
WPXT Portland, Maine
WRET-TV Spartanburg, South Carolina
WTVS Detroit, Michigan
WUPA Atlanta, Georgia
WWRS-TV Mayville, Wisconsin
WZVI Charlotte Amalie, Virgin Islands
WTCN-CA West Palm Beach, Florida

Channel 44

KBYU-TV Provo, Utah
KFFV Seattle, Washington
KILM Barstow, California
KRXI-TV Reno, Nevada
KSHV-TV Shreveport, Louisiana
KTVU Oakland, California
KVEW Kennewick, Washington
KVLY Fargo, North Dakota
KWBA-TV Sierra Vista, Arizona
KWKT-TV Waco, Texas

KARZ-TV Little Rock, Arkansas
KYTV Springfield, Missouri
KZJL Houston, Texas
WCSH Portland, Maine
WCVE-TV Richmond, Virginia
WDPB Seaford, Delaware
WECT Wilmington, North Carolina
WGIQ Louisville, Alabama
WHSG-TV Monroe, Georgia
WJEB-TV Jacksonville, Florida
WJWJ-TV Beaufort, South Carolina
WKON Owenton, Kentucky
WMAW-TV Meridian, Mississippi
WNYS-TV Syracuse, New York
WNYW Newburgh, New York
WRSP-TV Springfield, Illinois
WDTI Indianapolis, Indiana
WTJX-TV Charlotte Amalie, Virgin Islands
WTLW Lima, Ohio
WTOG-TV St. Petersburg, Florida
WUNG-TV Concord, North Carolina
WMCN-TV Atlantic City, New Jersey
WWJ-TV Detroit, Michigan
WWPB Hagerstown, Maryland
WZPX-TV Battle Creek, Michigan

Channel 45

KASY-TV Albuquerque, New Mexico
KBCW-TV San Francisco, California
KDTX-TV Dallas, Texas
KMTV-TV Omaha, Nebraska
KTCW Roseburg, Oregon
KOTV-DT Tulsa, Oklahoma
KSNW Wichita, Kansas
KTGF Great Falls, Montana
KUVI-DT Bakersfield, California
KSTC-TV Minneapolis, Minnesota
WYCW Asheville, North Carolina
WEDH Hartford, Connecticut
WEVV-TV Evansville, Indiana
WFUP Vanderbilt, Michigan
WGMB-TV Baton Rouge, Louisiana
WGNM Macon, Georgia
WJPM-TV Florence, South Carolina
WJTC Pensacola, Florida
WLLA Kalamazoo, Michigan
WMEA-TV Biddeford, Maine
WNEO Alliance, Ohio
WOLF-TV Hazleton, Pennsylvania
WPXH-TV Birmingham, Alabama
WROC-TV Rochester, New York
WTGL Cocoa, Florida
WXCW Naples, Florida
WXIN Indianapolis, Indiana
XHIJ-DT Ciudad Juarez, Texas
KXLN-DT Rosenberg, Texas
KWWB-LP Las Vegas, Nevada

Channel 46

KJZZ-TV Salt Lake City, Utah
KMIR-TV Palm Springs, California
KNCT Belton, Texas
KQCA Stockton, California
KSNF Joplin, Missouri
KTXD-TV Greenville, Texas
KETD Castle Rock, Colorado
KXLT-TV Rochester, Minnesota
WBFF Baltimore, Maryland
WCCV-TV Arecibo, Puerto Rico
WCTV Thomasville, Georgia
WDJT-TV Milwaukee, Wisconsin
WFIE Evansville, Indiana
WFMZ-TV Allentown, Pennsylvania
WHFT-TV Miami, Florida
WHTJ Charlottesville, Virginia
WMCF-TV Montgomery, Alabama
WPXV-TV Norfolk, Virginia
WTPX-TV Antigo, Wisconsin
WTVP Peoria, Illinois
WUPW Toledo, Ohio
WVVA Bluefield, West Virginia
WWHO Chillicothe, Ohio
KOCM Norman, Oklahoma
WBSF Bay City, Michigan
KUKL-TV Kalispell, Montana
KUVE-DT Green Valley, Arizona
WHTX-LP Hartford, Connecticut
KRNS-CD Reno, Nevada

KLAF-LD Lafayette, Louisiana

Channel 47

KDLT-TV Sioux Falls, South Dakota
KAZA-TV Avalon, California
KTDO Las Cruces, New Mexico
KTLN-TV Novato, California
KWHB Tulsa, Oklahoma
WAVE Louisville, Kentucky
WFTT-DT Tampa, Florida
WCSC-TV Charleston, South Carolina
WUTH-CD Hartford, Connecticut
WRBU East St. Louis, Illinois
WJZY Belmont, North Carolina
WLNY-TV Riverhead, New York
WPBN-TV Traverse City, Michigan
WPCT Panama City Beach, Florida
WPMT York, Pennsylvania
WTTW Chicago, Illinois
WTVH Syracuse, New York
WUPV Ashland, Virginia
WYDN Worcester, Massachusetts
WYDO Greenville, North Carolina
WZRB Columbia, South Carolina
WAMI-DT Hollywood, Florida
KIJR-LP Lucerne Valley, California
KNTL-LP Las Vegas, Nevada

Channel 48

KING-TV Seattle, Washington
WOAI-TV San Antonio, Texas
KOCE-TV Huntington Beach, California
KTFF-DT Porterville, California
KSPX-TV Sacramento, California
KTMD Galveston, Texas
KUCW Ogden, Utah
KVTJ-DT Jonesboro, Arkansas
WACH Columbia, South Carolina
WAFF Huntsville, Alabama
WCIA Champaign, Illinois
WHME-TV South Bend, Indiana
WMLW-TV Racine, Wisconsin
WJMN-TV Escanaba, Michigan
WKGB-TV Bowling Green, Kentucky
WLED-TV Littleton, New Hampshire
WOPX-TV Melbourne, Florida
WPXI Pittsburgh, Pennsylvania
WRAL-TV Raleigh, North Carolina
WRC Washington, District of Columbia
WRJM Troy, Alabama
WRNN-TV Kingston, New York
WSYX Columbus, Ohio
WTTV Bloomington, Indiana
WUJA Caguas, Puerto Rico
WXOW La Crosse, Wisconsin
WYDC Corning, New York
WVLR Tazewell, Tennessee
KVSN-DT Pueblo, Colorado
WWHB-CA West Palm Beach, Florida
KSTR-DT Irving, Texas
KTFV-CD McAllen, Texas

Channel 49

KASW Phoenix, Arizona
KJLA Ventura, California
KKTV Colorado Springs, Colorado
KMYA-DT Camden, Arkansas
KLJB Davenport, Iowa
KNVA Austin, Texas
KNVO-TV McAllen, Texas
KPTH Sioux City, Iowa
KSTS San Jose, California
KTKA-TV Topeka, Kansas
KGEB Tulsa, Oklahoma
WWSI Atlantic City, New Jersey
WAWD Fort Walton Beach, Florida
WDKA Paducah, Kentucky
WDLI-TV Canton, Ohio
WDRB Louisville, Kentucky
WEDW Bridgeport, Connecticut
WEKW-TV Keene, New Hampshire
WEUX Chippewa Falls, Wisconsin
WFGC Palm Beach, Florida
WHSV Harrisonburg, Virginia
WLFG Grundy, Virginia
WLNE-TV New Bedford, Massachusetts
WMSN-TV Madison, Wisconsin
WVEN-TV Daytona Beach, Florida

WNTZ-TV Natchez, Mississippi
WNWO-TV Toledo, Ohio
WNYO-TV Buffalo, New York
WPXL-TV New Orleans, Louisiana
WRAZ Raleigh, North Carolina
WTAP Parkersburg, West Virginia
WXTX Columbus, Georgia

Channel 50

KUNS-TV Bellevue, Washington
KBTX Bryan, Texas
KNWA-TV Rogers, Arkansas
KNXT Visalia, California
KOPX-TV Oklahoma City, Oklahoma
KQEH San Jose, California
WAXN-TV Kannapolis, North Carolina
WDCW Washington, District of Columbia
WBRC Birmingham, Alabama
WCBD-TV Charleston, South Carolina
WDTN Dayton, Ohio
WEAO Akron, Ohio
WXFT-DT Aurora, Illinois
WEIU-TV Charleston, Illinois
WFGX Fort Walton Beach, Florida
WGNT Portsmouth, Virginia
WINK-TV Fort Myers, Florida
WBIN-TV Derry, New Hampshire
WOAY-TV Oak Hill, West Virginia
WQHA Aguada, Puerto Rico
WQLN Erie, Pennsylvania
WTLH Bainbridge, Georgia
WYPX-TV Amsterdam, New York
KKAI Kailua, Hawaii
KLWB New Iberia, Louisiana

Channel 51

KCEC Denver, Colorado
KDTV-DT San Francisco, California
KTFN-TV El Paso, Texas
KPXE-TV Kansas City, Missouri
KXLA Rancho Palos Verdes, California
KSBI Oklahoma City, Oklahoma
WAGV Harlan, Kentucky
WEPX-TV Greenville, North Carolina
WFMY-TV Greensboro, North Carolina
WMYO Salem, Indiana
WFXG Augusta, Georgia
WJAR Providence, Rhode Island
WKEF Dayton, Ohio
WLAJ Lansing, Michigan
WNJN Montclair, New Jersey
WPWR Gary, Indiana
WPXA-TV Rome, Georgia
WPXX-TV Memphis, Tennessee
WSST-TV Cordele, Georgia
WTAE-TV Pittsburgh, Pennsylvania
KCEB Longview, Texas
KBZO-LP Lubbock, Texas
KDTF-LD San Diego, California
KTCD-LP San Diego, California
KNHL Hastings, Nebraska

Channel 52

KYAZ Katy, Texas
KOLR Springfield, Missouri

Channel 53

KUBE-TV Baytown, Texas
WMDT Salisbury, Maryland

Channel 54

WAMY-TV Huntsville, Alabama

Channel 55

KENS San Antonio, Texas

Channel 56

KJRH-TV Tulsa, Oklahoma

Channel 59

KCET Los Angeles, California
WBAL Baltimore, Maryland

Channel 82

WDEF-TV Chattanooga, Tennessee

U.S. Spanish-Language Television Stations

Arizona

Phoenix (Prescott), AZ
KAET Phoenix (*Analog ch* 8, *Digital ch* 8)
KFPH-DT Flagstaff (*Analog ch* 13, *Digital ch* 13)

Tucson (Sierra Vista), AZ
KFTU-DT Douglas (*Analog ch* 3, *Digital ch* 36)
KHRR Tucson (*Analog ch* 40, *Digital ch* 40)
KTTU Tucson (*Analog ch* 18, *Digital ch* 19)
KUAS-TV Tucson (*Analog ch* 27, *Digital ch* 28)
KUAT-TV Tucson (*Analog ch* 6, *Digital ch* 30)

California

Fresno-Visalia, CA
KFTV-DT Hanford (*Analog ch* 21, *Digital ch* 20)
KNSO Merced (*Analog ch* 51, *Digital ch* 11)
KNXT Visalia (*Analog ch* 49, *Digital ch* 50)
KVPT Fresno (*Analog ch* 18, *Digital ch* 40)

Los Angeles
KAZA-TV Avalon (*Analog ch* 54, *Digital ch* 47)
KFTR-DT Ontario (*Analog ch* 46, *Digital ch* 29)
KJLA Ventura (*Analog ch* 57, *Digital ch* 49)
KMEX-DT Los Angeles (*Analog ch* 34, *Digital ch* 34)
KRCA Riverside (*Analog ch* 62, *Digital ch* 35)
KVEA Corona (*Analog ch* 52, *Digital ch* 39)
KWHY-TV Los Angeles (*Analog ch* 22, *Digital ch* 42)

Palm Springs, CA
KEVC-CD Indio (*Analog ch* 5, *Digital ch* 36)
KVER-CA Indio (*Analog ch* 4, *Digital ch* 40)
KVES-LD Indio (*Analog ch* 4, *Digital ch* 40)

Sacramento-Stockton-Modest
KMAX-TV Sacramento (*Digital ch* 21)
KUVS-DT Modesto (*Analog ch* 19, *Digital ch* 18)

San Diego, CA
KBNT-CD San Diego (*Analog ch* 17, *Digital ch* 25)
KDTF-LD San Diego (*Analog ch* 36, *Digital ch* 51)
KHAX-LP San Diego (*Analog ch* 17, *Digital ch* 25)
KNSD San Diego (*Analog ch* 39, *Digital ch* 40)
KTCD-LP San Diego (*Analog ch* 36, *Digital ch* 51)
XEWT-DT Tijuana (*Digital ch* 32)

San Francisco-Oakland-San
KCSM-TV San Mateo (*Analog ch* 60, *Digital ch* 43)
KDTV-DT San Francisco (*Analog ch* 14, *Digital ch* 51)
KFSF-DT Vallejo (*Analog ch* 66, *Digital ch* 34)
KRCB Cotati (*Analog ch* 22, *Digital ch* 23)
KSTS San Jose (*Analog ch* 48, *Digital ch* 49)
KTNC-TV Concord (*Analog ch* 42, *Digital ch* 14)

Santa Barbara-Santa Maria-
KPMR-TV Santa Barbara (*Analog ch* 38, *Digital ch* 21)

Yuma, AZ-El Centro, CA
KAJB-TV Calipatria (*Analog ch* 54, *Digital ch* 36)
KVYE-TV El Centro (*Analog ch* 7, *Digital ch* 22)

Colorado

Denver, CO
KCEC Denver (*Analog ch* 50, *Digital ch* 51)
KDEN Longmont (*Digital ch* 29)
KDVT-LP Denver (*Analog ch* 14, *Digital ch* 15)
KETD Castle Rock (*Analog ch* 53, *Digital ch* 46)
KGHB-CD Pueblo (*Digital ch* 27)
KRMT Denver (*Analog ch* 41, *Digital ch* 40)
KTFD-TV Denver (*Analog ch* 14, *Digital ch* 15)

District of Columbia

Washington, DC
WFDC-DT Arlington (*Analog ch* 14, *Digital ch* 15)

Florida

Miami-Ft. Lauderdale, FL
WHFT-TV Miami (*Analog ch* 45, *Digital ch* 46)
WLTV-DT Miami (*Analog ch* 23, *Digital ch* 23)
WSBS-TV Key West (*Analog ch* 22, *Digital ch* 3)
WSCV Fort Lauderdale (*Analog ch* 51, *Digital ch* 30)

Orlando-Daytona Beach-Melb
WACX-DT Leesburg (*Digital ch* 40)
WOTF-TV Melbourne (*Analog ch* 43, *Digital ch* 43)
WVCI-LP Daytona Beach (*Analog ch* 16, *Digital ch* 16)
WVEN-TV Daytona Beach (*Analog ch* 26, *Digital ch* 49)

Tampa-St Petersburg (Saras
WCLF Clearwater (*Analog ch* 22, *Digital ch* 21)
WFTT-DT Tampa (*Analog ch* 50, *Digital ch* 47)
WVEA-TV Venice (*Analog ch* 62, *Digital ch* 25)

Georgia

Atlanta
WUVG-DT Athens (*Analog ch* 34, *Digital ch* 17)

Hawaii

Honolulu, HI
KKAI Kailua (*Analog ch* 50, *Digital ch* 50)

Kailua-Kona
KLEI-TV Kailua-Kona (*Analog ch* 6, *Digital ch* 25)

Illinois

Chicago
WSNS Chicago (*Analog ch* 44, *Digital ch* 45)
WYCC Chicago (*Analog ch* 20)

Kansas

Wichita-Hutchinson Plus, Kansas
KOOD Hays (*Analog ch* 9, *Digital ch* 16)

Louisiana

New Orleans, LA
KGLA-AM Hammond (*Digital ch* 42)
WLAE-TV New Orleans (*Analog ch* 32, *Digital ch* 31)

Maine

Bangor, ME
WMEB-TV Orono (*Analog ch* 12, *Digital ch* 9)
WMED-TV Calais (*Analog ch* 13, *Digital ch* 10)

Portland-Auburn, ME
WCBB Augusta (*Analog ch* 10, *Digital ch* 10)

Presque Isle, ME
WMEM-TV Presque Isle (*Analog ch* 10, *Digital ch* 10)

Massachusetts

Boston (Manchester, NH)
WBZ-TV Boston (*Analog ch* 4, *Digital ch* 30)
WCVB Boston (*Analog ch* 5, *Digital ch* 20)
WUNI-TV Worcester (*Analog ch* 27, *Digital ch* 29)
WUTF-DT Marlborough (*Analog ch* 66, *Digital ch* 27)

Missouri

Kansas City, MO
KPXE-TV Kansas City (*Digital ch* 51)

Nevada

Las Vegas, NV
KBLR Paradise (*Analog ch* 39, *Digital ch* 40)
KINC Las Vegas (*Analog ch* 15, *Digital ch* 16)

New Hampshire

Boston (Manchester, NH)
WNEU Merrimack (*Analog ch* 60, *Digital ch* 34)

New Jersey

New York
WFUT-DT Newark (*Analog ch* 68, *Digital ch* 30)
WMBC-TV Newton (*Digital ch* 18)
WNJU Linden (*Analog ch* 47, *Digital ch* 36)
WXTV-DT Paterson (*Analog ch* 41, *Digital ch* 40)

Philadelphia
WUVP-DT Vineland (*Analog ch* 65, *Digital ch* 29)
WWSI Atlantic City (*Digital ch* 49)

New Mexico

Albuquerque-Santa Fe, NM
KAZQ Albuquerque (*Analog ch* 32, *Digital ch* 17)
KCHF Santa Fe (*Analog ch* 11, *Digital ch* 10)
KLUZ-TV Albuquerque (*Analog ch* 41, *Digital ch* 42)
KNAT-TV Albuquerque (*Analog ch* 23, *Digital ch* 24)
KRPV-DT Roswell (*Digital ch* 27)
KTFA-LP Albuquerque (*Analog ch* 48, *Digital ch* 41)
KTFQ-DT Albuquerque (*Analog ch* 14, *Digital ch* 22)

Amarillo, TX
KENW Portales (*Analog ch* 3)

El Paso (Las Cruces, NM),
KRWG-TV Las Cruces (*Analog ch* 22, *Digital ch* 23)
KTDO Las Cruces (*Analog ch* 48, *Digital ch* 47)

New York

New York
WFTY-DT Smithtown (*Analog ch* 67, *Digital ch* 23)

North Carolina

Raleigh-Durham (Fayettevil
WUVC-DT Fayetteville (*Analog ch* 40, *Digital ch* 38)

Ohio

Cleveland-Akron (Canton),
WQHS-DT Cleveland (*Analog ch* 61, *Digital ch* 34)

Oklahoma

Oklahoma City, OK
KTUZ-TV30 Shawnee (*Analog ch* 30, *Digital ch* 29)
KUOK Woodward (*Analog ch* 35, *Digital ch* 35)

Tulsa, OK
KRSC-TV Claremore (*Analog ch* 35, *Digital ch* 36)

Oregon

Portland, OR
KUNP La Grande (*Analog ch* 16, *Digital ch* 16)

Pennsylvania

Philadelphia
WLVT-TV Allentown (*Analog ch* 39, *Digital ch* 39)
WYBE Philadelphia (*Analog ch* 35, *Digital ch* 35)

Rhode Island

Providence, RI-New Bedford
WJAR Providence (*Analog ch* 10, *Digital ch* 51)

South Dakota

Sioux Falls (Mitchell), SD
KDLV-TV Mitchell (*Analog ch* 5, *Digital ch* 26)

Tennessee

Nashville, TN
WHTN Murfreesboro (*Analog ch* 39, *Digital ch* 38)

Texas

Amarillo, TX
KEYU Borger (*Analog ch* 31, *Digital ch* 31)
KVII-TV Amarillo (*Analog ch* 7, *Digital ch* 7)

Corpus Christi, TX
KIII-TV Corpus Christi (*Analog ch* 3, *Digital ch* 8)
KORO-TV Corpus Christi (*Analog ch* 28, *Digital ch* 27)

Dallas-Ft. Worth
KUVN-DT Garland (*Digital ch* 23)
KXTX Dallas (*Analog ch* 39, *Digital ch* 40)

El Paso (Las Cruces, NM), TX
KINT-TV El Paso (*Analog ch* 26, *Digital ch* 25)
KSCE El Paso (*Analog ch* 38, *Digital ch* 39)
KTFN-TV El Paso (*Analog ch* 65, *Digital ch* 51)
XHIJ-DT Ciudad Juarez (*Digital ch* 45)

Harlingen-Weslaco-Brownsvi
KGBT-TV Harlingen (*Analog ch* 4, *Digital ch* 31)
KLUJ-TV Harlingen (*Analog ch* 44, *Digital ch* 34)
KMBH Harlingen (*Analog ch* 60, *Digital ch* 38)
KNVO-TV McAllen (*Analog ch* 48, *Digital ch* 49)
KTFV-CD McAllen (*Analog ch* 32, *Digital ch* 48)
KTLM Harlingen (*Analog ch* 40, *Digital ch* 40)

Houston
KFTH-DT Alvin (*Analog ch* 67, *Digital ch* 36)
KLTJ Galveston (*Analog ch* 22, *Digital ch* 23)
KTMD Galveston (*Analog ch* 47, *Digital ch* 48)
KUBE-TV Baytown (*Analog ch* 57, *Digital ch* 53)
KUHT Houston (*Analog ch* 8, *Digital ch* 8)

Laredo, TX
KETF-CD Laredo (*Digital ch* 31)
KGNS Laredo (*Analog ch* 8, *Digital ch* 8)
KLDO-TV Laredo (*Digital ch* 19)

Odessa-Midland, TX
KMLM-DT Odessa (*Digital ch* 42)
KUPB-TV Midland (*Analog ch* 18, *Digital ch* 18)

San Angelo, TX
KANG-LP San Angelo (*Digital ch* 31)
KEUS-LD San Angelo (*Digital ch* 41)

San Antonio, TX
KWEX-DT San Antonio (*Analog ch* 41, *Digital ch* 41)

Tyler-Longview (Lufkin & N
KTRE Lufkin (*Analog ch* 9, *Digital ch* 9)

Utah

Salt Lake City, UT
KBYU-TV Provo (*Analog ch* 11, *Digital ch* 44)
KSL-TV Salt Lake City (*Analog ch* 5, *Digital ch* 38)
KUEN Ogden (*Analog ch* 9, *Digital ch* 36)
KUTH-DT Provo (*Analog ch* 32, *Digital ch* 32)

Washington

Seattle-Tacoma, WA
KFFV Seattle (*Digital ch* 44)
KUNS-TV Bellevue (*Analog ch* 51, *Digital ch* 50)

Wisconsin

Milwaukee, WI
MPTVÿ Milwaukee (*Analog ch* 36, *Digital ch* 35)

Puerto Rico

Aguadilla
WOLE-DT Aguadilla (*Analog ch* 12, *Digital ch* 12)

Caguas
WLII-DT Caguas (*Analog ch* 11, *Digital ch* 11)

Fajardo
WMTJ Fajardo (*Analog ch* 40, *Digital ch* 16)

Mayaguez
WNJX-TV Mayaguez (*Analog ch* 4, *Digital ch* 23)
WORA-TV Mayaguez (*Digital ch* 29)

Ponce
WSTE-DT Ponce (*Analog ch* 7, *Digital ch* 7)
WSUR-DT Ponce (*Analog ch* 9, *Digital ch* 9)

San Juan
WAPA-TV San Juan (*Analog ch* 4, *Digital ch* 27)
WIPR-TV San Juan (*Analog ch* 6, *Digital ch* 43)
WKAQ San Juan (*Analog ch* 2, *Digital ch* 28)

Virgin Islands

Christiansted
WSVI Christiansted (*Analog ch* 8, *Digital ch* 20)

Canadian Radio-television and Telecommunications Commission | Conseil de la radiodiffusion et des télécommunications canadiennes

Canada

Communications Monitoring Report 2017

Canadians continue to watch TV

- Traditional TV viewing time remained relatively stable, decreasing by 0.6 hours from 2015 to 2016. Canadians (aged 2 and over) watched, on average, 26.6 hours of traditional television per week during the 2015-2016 broadcast year, compared to 27.2 hours in 2014-2015, and 28.2 hours in 2011-2012.
- Internet TV viewing continued to increase in 2016. Weekly users 18 years of age and older watched 6.4 hours of Internet TV on a weekly basis, compared to 1.5 hours in 2008.
- IPTV service revenues continued their rapid growth. IPTV service providers reported revenues of approximately $1.8 billion in 2016, up $232 million or 15% from 2015.

Source: *Executive Summary - Canadians continue to watch TV*, Communications Monitoring Report 2017, Canadian Radio-television and Telecommunications Commission, https://crtc.gc.ca/eng/publications/reports/PolicyMonitoring/2017/cmr2017.pdf, p. 32. Reproduced with the permission of the Canadian Radio-television and Telecommunications Commission on behalf of Her Majesty the Queen in Right of Canada, 2017.

Table 4.2.11 Average number of hours Canadians watched traditional television each week, by age group

Age group	Average number of hours watching traditional television (Weekly)					Growth (%) 2014-15 to 2015-16
	2011-12	2012-13	2013-14	2014-15	2015-16	
All persons 2+	28.2	27.9	27.4	27.2	26.6	-2.2
Children 2-11	22.2	21.6	20.6	21.4	20.3	-5.1
Teens 12–17	22.7	21	19.9	18.8	16.4	-12.8
18–34	22.8	21.9	20.6	19.7	18.5	-6.1
35–49	24.8	24.7	24	23.6	22.1	-6.4
50-64	33.1	33.2	33.4	33	32.9	-0.3
65+	41.9	41.5	41.8	42	42.8	1.9

Source: Numeris

This table shows the national average of weekly viewing hours by age group. It does not include digital media.

Average weekly viewing declined across all age groups except for the 65+ age group which saw little movement over the same timeframe.

Source: *Table 4.2.11 Average number of hours Canadians watched tradition television each week, by age group*, Communications Monitoring Report 2017, Canadian Radio-television and Telecommunications Commission, https://crtc.gc.ca/eng/publications/reports/PolicyMonitoring/2017/cmr2017.pdf, p. 157. Reproduced with the permission of the Canadian Radio-television and Telecommunications Commission on behalf of Her Majesty the Queen in Right of Canada, 2017.

4.2 Television programming sector

$7.3 billion

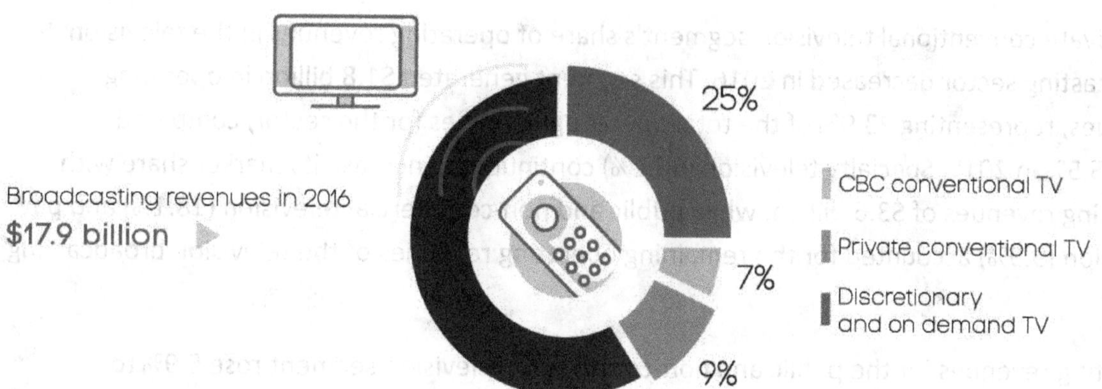

Television programming revenues	Viewing	Private conventional television revenues	CBC conventional television revenues	Discretionary and on demand TV revenues
$7.3 B	**26.6 HRS**	**$1.7 B**	**$1.2 B**	**$4.4 B**
Increase of 1.7% from 2015	Canadians (2+) watch TV each week	Decrease of 4.5% from 2015	Increase of 7.0% from 2015	Increase of 2.9% from 2015

Source: *4.2 Television programming sector*, Communications Monitoring Report 2017, Canadian Radio-television and Telecommunications Commission, https://crtc.gc.ca/eng/publications/reports/PolicyMonitoring/2017/cmr2017.pdf, p. 133. Reproduced with the permission of the Canadian Radio-television and Telecommunications Commission on behalf of Her Majesty the Queen in Right of Canada, 2017.

Total operating revenues for the Canadian television broadcasting sector rose 0.9% from 2015 to $7.5 billion in 2016. Profits before interest and taxes increased 15.9%, from $732.8 million in 2015 to $849.0 million in 2016.

These gains were the result of an increase in subscription revenues of $68.3 million, from $2.920 billion in 2015 to $2.988 billion in 2016. Public and private subsidies increased 5.8%, from $892.9 million to $944.8 million. These increases more than offset the 0.9% decrease in air time sales and a 7.5% decline in other revenue.

The private conventional television segment's share of operating revenues in the television broadcasting sector decreased in 2016. This segment generated $1.8 billion in operating revenues, representing 23.9% of the total operating revenues for the sector, compared with 25.5% in 2015. Specialty television (48.2%) continued to increase its market share with operating revenues of $3.6 billion, while public and non-commercial television (18.1%) and pay television (9.9%) accounted for the remaining operating revenues of the television broadcasting sector.

Operating revenues for the public and non-commercial television segment rose 5.9% to $1.4 billion in 2016. Advertising sales for this segment increased 20.3% to $279.4 million in 2016, compared with $232.3 million in 2015.

Operating expenses for the public and non-commercial television segment increased 2.2%, from $1.29 billion in 2015 to $1.32 billion in 2016, as a result of programming expenses and sales and promotion expenses. In 2016, this segment posted $824.5 million in programming expenses, compared with $770.0 million in 2015. Sales and promotion rose from $121.0 million in 2015 to $135.5 million in 2016. This segment saw a surplus of $36.2 million in 2016. The segment's gross profit margin was 2.7%.

With a 2.7% increase in its operating revenues, the specialty television segment saw a 4.5% increase in its profits before interest and taxes in 2016, bringing the profit margin to 25.7%. Operating expenses were up 2.2% to $2.7 billion, mainly due to a $75.5 million rise in programming expenses.

The pay television segment generated a $292.0 million profit before interest and taxes in 2016, bringing the gross profit margin to 0.04%.

Revenue from air time sales continue to fall

Air time sales, the main component of revenue, fell 0.9% to $3.2 billion in 2016, continuing a downward trend that began in 2012. In 2016, the private television segment saw air time sales decrease 5.4%, while the pay television segment experienced a 41.1% drop. Air time sales for the public and non-commercial television segment increased 20.3%, while sales in the specialty television segment rose 1.7%.

The decline in air time sales in the television broadcasting sector in 2016 was slightly offset by an increase in subscription revenues, which rose 2.3% from 2015 to $3.0 billion in 2016.

The private conventional television sector accounted for 52% of the market share of air time sales in 2016. By comparison, the market share of advertising sales was 39.3% for the specialty television segment and 8.8% for the public and non-commercial television segment.

Private conventional television posts losses in all provinces

Total operating revenues for the Canadian private conventional television segment decreased 5.4% to $1.8 billion in 2016. Operating expenses fell 6.5% to $1.9 billion, leading to losses of $114.0 million and a profit margin before interest and taxes of negative 6.4%.

In the Atlantic provinces, the losses amounted to $16.3 million in 2016, compared with $14.8 million in 2015. A 4.1% decrease in operating revenues, combined with a 1.5% decline in operating expenses, explains these losses.

In Quebec, losses before interest and taxes were $9.8 million in 2016, compared with losses of $11.7 million the previous year. This slight improvement in 2016 is explained by a 2.6% decrease in operating revenues, to $363.7 million, and a 3.0% decline in operating expenses, to $373.6 million.

In Ontario, operating revenues fell 6.8% to $809.7 million in 2016, compared with $868.8 million in 2015. Operating expenses declined 8.2% to $851.9 million, resulting in losses of $42.1 million.

Private conventional television stations in Western Canada recorded losses before interest and taxes of $45.8 million in 2016, compared with $57.4 million in 2015. This improvement is due to operating expenses that fell 6.6% to $591.2 million and operating revenues that saw a 5.3% decline to $545.4 million.

Source: *The Daily – Television broadcasting, 2016*. Statistics Canada. Released 2017-06-20. http://www.statcan.gc.ca/daily-quotidien/170620/dq170620e-eng.htm

Major Broadcast Networks in Canada

Alberta

Bear Creek Broadcasting

81716-108 Street, Suite 104, Grande Prarie, AB T8V 4C7
Canada
(780) 882-6612; *Fax:* (780) 882-6708
www.q99live.com
events@q99live.com
Ken Trulen, General Manager
Barb Shannon, Marketing Manager
Paul Oulette, Programming Director
Brittany Meen, Promotions Director
Sheena Roszell, News Director
Shannon Wallace, Traffic Manager
Justin Alloway, CreativeDirector

The Miracle Channel Association

450-31 Street North, Lethbridge, AB T1H 3Z3 Canada
(403) 380-3399; *Fax:* (403) 380-7490
www.miraclechannel.ca
info@miraclechannel.ca
Services Offered: Miracle Channel reaches people with the hope of Christ through contemporary, life-giving and life-changing programs from leading ministries as well as documentaries, talk shows, music videos, movies, Canadian news,and live programs.
Leon Fontaine, CEO

Aboriginal Multi-Media Society

13425-146 Street, Edmonton, AB T5L 4S8 Canada
(780) 455-2700; *Fax:* (780) 455-7639
www.ammsa.com
letters@ammsa.com
Services Offered: The Aboriginal Multi-Media Society is an independent Aboriginal communications organization committed to facilitating the exchange of information reflecting Aboriginal culture to a growing and diverse audience.AMMSA is dedicated to providing objective, mature and balanced coverage of news, information and entertainment relevant to Aboriginal issues and peoples while maintaining profound respect for the values, principles and traditions of Aboriginalpeople.
Paul Macedo, CEO/Publisher/Founder
Bert Crowfoot, General Manager
Paul Macedo, Marketing Director
Deborah Steel, News Director

British Columbia

The Jim Pattison Broadcast Group

460 Pemberton Terrace, Suite 1800, Kamloops, BC V2C 1T5
Canada
(250) 372-3322; *Fax:* (250) 374-0445
www.jimpattison.com/media/broadcast-group
info@jpbroadcast.com
Jim A Pattison, Chairman & CEO
William R Fatt, CEO/COO
Glen Clark, President
Nick Desmarais, Managing Director, Legal Services
Michael J Korenberg, Deputy Chairman&Managing Director
David Bell, Managing Director, CorporateFinance
Ryan Barrington-Foote, Managing Director, Accounting
David Cobb, Managing Director, Corporate Development
Breedon Grauer, Manager, Corporate Relations

Mainstream Broadcasting Corporation

100-1200 West 73rd Street, Vancouver, BC V5B 2S2 Canada
(604) 263-1320; *Fax:* (604) 261-0310
www.am1320.com
adm@am1320.com
Services Offered: Mainstream Broadcasting Corporation is a British Columbia media company owned and operated by local Vancouver resident and businessman, James Ho. Mainstream began its broadcasting service in 1973 as OverseasChinese Voice (OCV). In 1993, OCV programming was incorporated into the multicultural AM radio station of CHMB AM1320, serving the needs of Vancouver's multicultural community.
Victor Qin, Manager
Kat Lai Li Jiayu, General Sales Mgr
Harry Lee Shaoming, Programming Director
Andy Cheung Zhang Yi Liang, News Director
Victor Qin, Manager
Kay Lai, Sales & Marketing Manager

New Brunswick

Radio Beausejour Inc

51 Cornwall, PO Box 5001, Shediac, NB E4P 8T8 Canada
(506) 532-0080; *Fax:* (506) 532-0120
www.cjse.ca
cjse@cjse.ca
Services Offered: After eight years in development, Radio Beausejour began broadcasting July 26, 1994. Located in southeastern New Brunswick, at the heart of the seaside town of Shediac and near the Greater Moncton Radio Beausejourserves a large Acadian community.
Gilles Arsenault, CEO/COO
Patricia Bourque-Chevarie, Director General And Finance Officer
Marcel Parker-Gallant, Director Of Programming
John Richard, Advertising Representative
Diane Richard, Host
Roger Boudreau, Host
JasonOuellette, Chief Information Officer
Normand Cormier, Head Of Music

Newfoundland

Okalakatiget Society

PO Box 160, Nain, NL A0P 1L0 Canada
(709) 922-2187; *Fax:* (709) 922-2293
www.oksociety.com
Services Offered: The OKalaKatiget Society provides Inuktitut and English language programming to Inuit in the Northern Labrador and Lake Melville region. This aboriginal language programming is designed to strengthen our culturethrough language retention.
Carol Gear, President
Morris Prokop, Executive Director
Joanna Dicker, Sr Radio Producer
Sarah Abel, Sr Television Producer
Justine Obed, VP

VOWR 800 Radio Broadcasting

PO Box 26006, St John's, NL A1E 0A5 Canada
(709) 579-9233
www.vowr.org
vowr@vowr.org
Services Offered: VOWR is the only radio station owned by The United Church of Canada and has been broadcasting from the same location (Patrick Street and Hamilton Avenue) since 1924. The station began as an outreach ministry ofWesley United Church and was the 'child' of Rev. Dr. J.G. Joyce. Operated solely by volunteers, our station broadcasts 24 hours a day, 365 days a year - They are never off the air!
Marvin Barnes, Chairman
John Tessier, Station Manager
Trevor Pike, Technical Advisor
Glenn Tilley, Vice Chairperson
Doreen Whalen, Secretary
Trevor Pike, Technical Advisor

Ontario

Inuit Broadcasting Corporation

Mailing Address: 331 Cooper Street, Suite 301, Ottawa, ON K2P 0G5 Canada
Second Address: PO Box 700, Iqaluit, NU XOA OHO
(613) 235-1892, (867) 979-6231; *Fax:* (613) 230-8824, (867) 979-5853
www.inuitbroadcasting.ca
Services Offered: The Inuit Broadcasting Corporation provides a window to the Arctic by producing award winning television programming by Inuit, for Inuit. IBC is indeed, Nunavut's public producer. IBC does not produce the regularfare of TV sitcoms and talk shows. Instead, IBC producers make programming about one of the richest and enduring cultures in our nation, the Inuit of Canada, in the language Inuit speak.Inuktitut. We produce shows about our kids, our musicians, ourpoliticians, our humour, our issues, etc. No one else can make these shows for us!
Okalik Eegeesiak, President
Malakie Kilabuk, Director of Operations
Monica Ell, Director of Programming
Debbie Brisebois, Executive Director
Noah Papatsie, Executive Producer
Janett Brummel, Director of Finance
Joseph Kaviok,Vice-President
Ammie Kipsigak, Secretary/Treasurer
Joseph Niptanatiak, Board Member

Shaw Media

121 Bloor Street East, Toronto, ON M4W 3M5 Canada
(416) 967-1174, (877) 345-9195; *Fax:* (416) 967-2854
shawmedia.ca
Services Offered: Shaw Media operates Global Television and 18 of the country's most popular specialty channels, including HGTV Canada, Mystery TV, National Geographic Channel, Showcase, History, Food Network Canada and TVtropolis,plus more than 20 online properties.
Paul Robertson, Group VP/Brodcasting/President Shaw Media
Paul Burns, VP/Online Experience
Troy Reeb, Senior Vice President, Global News & Station Opera
Errol Da Re, SVP/Sales
Greg Treffry, VP, Business Development & Media DigitalStrategy
Barbara Williams, VP/Engineering and Broadcast Systems
Michael French, VP/Finance
Dervla Kelly, Head of Corporate Commun. & Network Publication
Christine Shipton, SVP/Content
Amanda Ploughman, Vice President, Marketing
DanMarkou, VP, Human Resource
Shawn Kelly, Vice President, Media Technology

Bay Shore Broadcasting Inc

Mailing Address: PO Box 280, Owen Sound, ON N4K 5P5 Canada
Second Address: 270 Ninth Street East, Owen Sound, ON N4K 5P5
(519) 376-2030; *Fax:* (519) 371-4242
bayshorebroadcasting.ca
info@bayshorebroadcasting.ca
Services Offered: Bayshore Broadcasting Corporation, which began in Owen Sound, Ontario, is an independent private broadcaster operating seven radio stations in Grey, Bruce, Huron and Simcoe Counties in Southern Ontario.
Jim Bichard, News Director
Peter Jackson, Assistant News Director
Marianne McLeod, News Director
Manny Paiva, News Manager
Fred Wallace, Sports Director

Blackburn Radio Inc.

700 Richmond Street, Unit 102, London, ON N6A 5C7 Canada
(519) 679-8680; *Fax:* (519) 679-5321
www.blackburnradio.com/
Ownership: Cogent Investments Inc., 90.91%; Richard Costley-White Family Trust, 0.09%
Services Offered: Blackburn Radio Inc. is a family-owned broadcasting company with 13 radio stations serving Southwestern and Midwestern Ontario. The company operates 14 radio stations in Wingham, Sarnia, London, Chatham, Leamingtonand Windsor.
Richare Costley White, CEO & President

Ontario Educational Communications Authority

Mailing Address: Box 200, Station Q, Toronto, ON M4T 2T1 Canada
Second Address: 2180 Yonge Street, Toronto, ON M4S 2B9
(416) 484-2665; *Fax:* (416) 484-2600
ww3.tvo.org
asktvo@tvo.org
Services Offered: TVO's vision is to empower people to be engaged citizens of Ontario through educational media.
Lisa De Wilde, CEO
Paul Ginis, Director/Sales/Media
Jim Marchbank, Board of Directors
Toby Jenkins, Board of Directors

Corus Entertainment Inc

Mailing Address: 25 Dockside Drive, Toronto, ON M5A 0B5 Canada
Second Address: 200 Barclay Parade SW, Suite 300, Calgary, AB T2P 4R5
(416) 479-7000, (403) 716-6500; *Fax:* (416) 479-7006, (403) 444-4240
www.corusent.com
Services Offered: Corus Entertainment is one of Canada's most successful integrated media and entertainment companies. Founded by JR Shaw, the company was built from the media assets originally owned by Shaw Communications, and spunoff as a separate, publicly-traded company in 1999. Since then, the Company's asset base has grown substantially through strategic acquisitions and a strong operating discipline.
Heather Shaw, Executive Chair
Doug Murphy, President/CEO
Judy Adman, Vice President, Finance
Scott Dyer, EVP/Strategic Planning CTO
Gary Maavara, EVP/General Counsel
Kathleen McNair, EVP/Human Resources
Tom Peddie, Executive VPand CFO

Wawatay Native Communications Society

16 Fifth Avenue, Box 1180, Sioux Lookout, ON P8T 1B7 Canada
(807) 737-2951, (800) 243-9059; *Fax:* (807) 737-3224
www.wawatay.on.ca
jamesb@wawatay.on.ca

Services Offered: Wawatay Native Communications Society serves the communication needs of First Nations people and communities of Nishnawbe Aski Nation. It does this through the distribution of a bi-weekly newspaper, daily radioprogramming, television production services and a multimedia website that seeks to preserve and enhance indigenous languages and cultures of Aboriginal people in northern Ontario.

James Brohm, CEO & Sales Administrator
Mike Metatawabin, President
Micah Winter, Vice President
Nick Day, Director
Trish Kakegamic, Finance Clerk
Mike Hunter, Elder & Member
Mark Kakekagumick, Client Services Clerk
LennyCarpenter, Publisher/Editor

Distribution Access (Access Learning)
2 Pardee Avenue, Suite 102, Toronto, ON M6K 3H5 Canada
(416) 363-6765; *Fax:* (416) 363-7834
www.accesslearning.com
Services Offered: DISTRIBUTION ACCESS is Canada's leading provider of the world's best educational video programs and multi media content. With a library of over 15,000 titles, DISTRIBUTION ACCESS serves over 16,000 Canadianeducational institutions - elementary, secondary, post-secondary, libraries - Canadian learners of all ages in their homes and educational and broadcasting organizations around the world.

Dr. Ronald Keast, Chairman
Doug Connolly, President & Chief Operating Officer
Marijke Daye, National Marketing & Manager, Operations
Bill McGowan, Director Sales/Acquisitions
Ross Mayot, Director
Moses Znaimer, Director
PeterPalframan, Secretary/Treasurer
Greg Abrams, Director, Access Digital Media

Pineridge Broadcasting
Mailing Address: PO Box 520, Cobourg, ON K9A 4L3 Canada
Second Address: 360 George Street North, Unit 1, Peterborough, ON K9H 7E7
(905) 372-5401, (705) 876-7773; *Fax:* (905) 372-6280, (705) 876-1917
www.pineridgemedia.ca

Don Conway, President
Joel Scott, Operations Manager
Dave Hughes, General Sales Mgr
Charlie Toner, Chief Engineer
Jennifer Daignault, Peterborough Sales Manager
Jay Owen, Digital Services Manager

CTV
Mailing Address: PO Box 9, Station O, Toronto, ON M4A 2M9 Canada
Second Address: 299 Queen Street West, Toronto, ON M5V 2Z5
(416) 384-5000; (800) 668-0060; (866) 690-6179; *Fax:* (416) 332-5022
www.ctv.ca
ctvsupport@insinc.com

Rick Brace, President/Specialty Channels
Mary Ann Turcke, President/ Bel Media
Phil King, President/CTV Programming/Sports
Mike Cosentino, SVP Programming/CTV Networks
Wendy Freeman, President, CTV News
Scott Henderson,VP/Communications
Domenic Vivolo, Exec VP/Content Sales&Dist Marketing
Christian Roy, Vice President, Network
Sonia Brar, Vice President, IT

Canadian Broadcasting Corp (CBC)
PO Box 500, Station A, Toronto, ON M5W 1E6 Canada
(866) 306-4636
www.cbc.ca
Services Offered: The Canadian Broadcasting Corp. (CBC) is a publicly owned corporation established by the Broadcasting Act (1936) of the Canadian Parliament to provide the natl bcstg svc in Canada in the two official languagesEnglish and French. Under this legislation, the CBC is subject to regulations of the Canadian Radio-Television & Telecommunications Commission (CRTC).

Hubert T. Lacroix, President & CEO
Kristine Stewart, EVP English Services
Judith Purves, Chief Financial Officer
William B Chambers, VP/Brand, Communications & Corporate Affairs
Heather Conway, Executive VP, English Services
SylvieGadoury, VP/Legal Services & General Counsel
Josee Girard, VP/People And Culture
Steven Guiton, VP/Technology&Chief Regulatory Officer
Louis Lalande, Executive VP/French Services

Global Television Network/Shaw Media
121 Bloor Street, Toronto, ON M4W 3M5 Canada
(877) 307-1999
www.globaltv.com
Services Offered: Shaw Media operates Global Television and 18 of the country's most popular specialty channels, including HGTV Canada, Mystery TV, National Geographic Channel, Showcase, History, Food Network Canada and TVtropolis,plus more than 20 online properties.

Paul Robertson, President/Group VP
Paul Burns, VP Online Experience
Carol Darling, Vice President
Troy Reeb, Sr VP/Global News & Station Mgr
Errol Da Re, VP/Sales
Michael French, VP/Finance
Shawn Kelly, VP/Media Technology
Dervla Kelly, VP/Marketing & Communications
Barbara Williams, Exec VP Broadcasting, President Shaw Media

TVA Group Inc
1600 de Maisonneuve Boulevard, Montréal, QC H2L 4P2 Canada
(514) 526-9251; *Fax:* (514) 598-6086
www.tva.ca

David Thompson, Chairman
Richard H. King, EVP/COO
James C. Smith, President and Chief Executive Officer
Stephane Bello, EVP/CFO
Gus Carlson, EVP/Chief Communications Officer
James T. Powell, EVP/Chief Technology Officer
BrianPeccarelli, Tax & Accounting
Andrew Rashbass, Chief Executive, Reuters
Brian Scanlon, EVP/Chief Strategy Officer

Québec

Groupe TVA Incorporated
1600 Boul De Maisonneuve East, Montréal, QC H2L 4P2 Canada
(514) 526-9251
www.tva.canoe.ca
Services Offered: TVA., A subsidiary of Québecor Media inc., Is a communications company that operates in two business segments: television and publishing. In television, the company is active in the creation, production anddistribution of entertainment, information and public affairs, distribution of audiovisual products, commercial production and teleshopping. It operates largest private network of French-language television in North America, in addition to operatingeleven specialized services.

Pierre Dion, President/CEO
Jocelyn Poirier, President
Daniel Boudreau, VP/Operations
Denis Rozon, VP/CFO
Frances Lauziere, VP/Programming
Edith Perreault, VP/Sales/Marketing

RNC Media
1 Place Ville Marie, Suite 1523, Montréal, QC H3B 2B5 Canada
(514) 866-8686; *Fax:* (514) 866-8056
www.rncmedia.ca
Services Offered: Since 1948, RNC MEDIA offers guests advertisers, listeners and viewers, advertising, production and quality programming. Faithful to its origins which is now one of the largest broadcasting companies in Québec, RNCMEDIA continues to invest in its mission with a passion to communicate. Today the company has 16 radio stations, five television stations in major regions of Québec.

Pierre Brosseau, Chairman/CEO
Raynald Briere, President, COO & Chief Of Exploitation
Robert Ranger, VP/Operations
Yves Bombardier, VP/Programming
Jean-Yves Gourd, Board Member
Pierre Parent, Board Member
Claude Beaudoin, BoardMember
Fernand Belisle
Rejean F Nadeau, VP Of Finance And Administration

Radio Canada International
1400 Rene-Levesque Blvd East, Montréal, QC H2L 2M2 Canada
(866) 218-0208, (514) 597-7094; *Fax:* (514) 597-7621
www.rcinet.ca
info@rcinet.ca
Services Offered: RCI is CBC/Radio-Canada's multilingual service, providing audiences with an opportunity to discover and, above all, to understand and gain insight into the reality of Canadian society, along with its cultural anddemocratic values.

Helene Parent, Director
Soleiman, Editor-in-Chief
Lynn Desjardins, Producer

Saskatchewan

Harvard Broadcasting
2060 Halifax Street, Regina, SK S4P 1T7 Canada
(403) 670-0210; *Fax:* (403) 670-0518
www.harvardbroadcasting.com
ccowie@harvardbroadcasting.com
Services Offered: Originally opening its doors in 1926, 620 CKRM has almost as long a history as The Hill Companies in Saskatchewan. Currently, 620 CKRM the Source has been the official Saskatchewan Roughrider broadcast rights holdersince 1983. Under their current agreement, Harvard Broadcasting will have 620 CKRM as the Rider Play-by Play voice until the year 2015.

Cam Cowie, Vice President/ COO
Gary Brasil, National Sales Manager
Christian Hall, National Program Manager
Helene Kolada, Accounting & Finance Manager
Bonnie Day, Interactive Producer
Alison Clemmensen, Payroll/HR Administrator

Missinipi Broadcasting
Mailing Address: 712 Finlayson Street, La Ronge, SK S0J 1L0 Canada
Second Address: 27-11th Street West, 2nd Floor, Prince Albert, SK S6V 3A8
(306) 425-4003, (866) 922-4566; *Fax:* (306) 425-3123 306) 922-6969
www.mbcradio.com
Services Offered: MBC Network Radio currently airs 24 hours of programming daily, 7 days a week, from studios located in La Ronge Saskatchewan. It reaches an ever expanding listening audience of over 100,000 people in dozens ofcommunities and offers programming featuring interviews, information, education, (and music) in the Cree, Dene and English languages. MBC maintains a grass roots connection in it's programming via phone-in shows and on-location broadcasts.

William Dumais, Chairman
Mike Bouvier, Vice Chairperson
Deborah Charles, President/CEO
Dallas Hicks, Director of Operations
Darrell Prokopie, Sales & Marketing Manager
Kelly Provost, News Director
Keith Kratchmer, Controller
Fabian Ratt, Creative/Traffic Assistant
Annamarie Giesbrecht, Traffic/Sales Assistant
Kent Worth, Sales Representative
James Toung, Sales Representative
Susie Charles, Receptionist

Rawlco Radio Broadcasting
Mailing Address: 715 Saskatchewan Crescent West, Saskatoon, SK S7M 5V7 Canada
Second Address: 210-2401 Saskatchewan Drive, Regina, SK S4P 4HB
(306) 525-0000, (306) 934-2222
www.rawlco.com
kwerner@rawlco.com
Services Offered: No one loves being in radio more than we do at Rawlco Radio! We're a private, family owned radio company and we're debt free - something that's increasingly rare.. We work really hard every day to provide trulygreat radio stations to our listeners and clients in the communities we serve. Rawlco has 15 stations - 12 in Saskatchewan and 3 in Alberta. You'll find links on this site to all of them. Check us out! If you're interested in working for, or with, apassionate, fun-loving, enthusiastic bunch of radio people, you're at the right place.

Tom Newton, VP/General Manager
Kristy Werner, VP/General Manager
Kent Newson, VP/General Manager Calgary
Sandee Reed, Sales Manager
Angela Hill, Program Director
Nicole Kelly, Promotions Director
Janelle Cignac, PromotionsCoordinator
Vanessa Thomas, Promotions Coordinator
Angela Hill, Website News Editor
Sadie Swanson, Website Administrator

Yukon Territory

Mid Arctic Technology Services
200-4201 4th Avenue, Whitehorse, YT Y1A 1K1 Canada
(867) 668-6024, (888) 668-6024; *Fax:* (867) 668-6612
www.midarctic.com/
Services Offered: NNBY reaffirms and maintains First Nation culture, spiritual beliefs, language, traditional values, land and animals. NNBY works for present and future generations, looking seven generations into the future. Whilewe focus on First Nations, NNBY is for all people. NNBY protects traditional knowledge, empowers First Nations people, supports self determination of First Nations, and facilitates the development of

a respectful relationship between First Nations and other people. Culture also includes stories and customs, improving quality of life, and fosters the development of positive social and economic partnerships.

Stanley James Jr, Chairman
Chris May, President
Dennis Gerard, General Manager/Engineering Director
Marion Telep, Director/Finance
Mike, Service Manager
Jessie Peter, Vice Chairman
Marion Telep, Director/Finance

TV Group Ownership in Canada

Bell Media Inc.
299 Queen St. W., Toronto ON M5V 2Z5
(416) 384-8000
www.bellmedia.ca
bellmediapr@bellmedia.ca
Ownership: Bell Canada, 100%.

Canadian Broadcasting Corporation (CBC)
205 Wellington St. W, Room 4E301-B, Toronto ON M5V 3G7
(416) 205-3700
www.cbc.ca
tonews@cbc.ca
Ownership: Government of Canada

Corus Entertainment Inc.
Corus Quay, 25 Dockside Dr., Toronto ON M5A 0B5
(416) 479-7000; *Fax:*(416) 479-7006
www.corusent.com
alka.graham@corusent.com
Ownership: JR Shaw and family; Shaw Communications, 39%.

NewCap Inc.
8 Basinview Drive, Dartmouth NS B3B 1G4
(902) 468-7557; *Fax:*(902) 468-7558
www.ncc.ca
ncc@ncc.ca
Ownership: Newfoundland Capital Corporation Ltd., 100%.

Newfoundland Broadcasting Co.
446 Logy Bay Rd., St. John's NF A1C 5S2
(709) 722-5015; *Fax:*(709) 726-5107
www.ntv.ca
greetings@ntv.ca
Ownership: G. Scott Stirling, 64.99%; Gregory Stirling, 34.99%; and others, 0.02%.

RNC MEDIA Inc.
1 Place Ville Marie, Suite 1523, Montréal QC H3B 2B5
(514) 866-8686; *Fax:*(514) 866-8056
www.rncmedia.ca
info@rncmedia.ca
Ownership: Groupe Radio Nord Inc., 100%.

Rogers Media
1 Ted Rogers Way, Toronto ON M4Y 3B7
(416) 935-8200; *Fax:*(416) 864-2002
www.rogersmedia.com
lvelazquez@impulsemediasales.com
Ownership: Rogers Media Inc., 100%. Note: Rogers Media Inc. is 100% owned by Rogers Communications Inc.

Tele Inter-Rives Ltée
15, rue de la Chute, Rivière-du-Loup QC G5R 5B7
(418) 867-1341; *Fax:*(418) 867-4710
www.teleinterrives.com
nousjoindre@cimt.ca
Ownership: 101885 Canada Ltée., 55.34%; TVA Groupe Inc., 44.66% (See Listing); Marc Simard, 0.97%.

The Jim Pattison Broadcast Group
460 Pemberton Terrace, Kamloops BC V2C 1T5
(250) 372-3322; *Fax:*(250) 374-0445
www.jpbroadcast.com
info@jpbg.ca
Ownership: James A. Pattison, 100%.

TVA Group Inc.
1600 Boul de Maisonneuve E, Montréal QC H2L 4P2
(514) 526-9251
groupetva.ca
Ownership: Quebecor Media Inc., 99.97%; public Can, 0.03%.

Télé-Québec
1000, rue Fullum, Montréal QC H2K 3L7
(514) 521-2424; *Fax:*(514) 873-7464
www.telequebec.tv
info@telequebec.tv
Ownership: Government of Quebec.

V Media Group Inc.
355 Sainte-Catherine O., Bureau 100, Montréal QC H3A 1A5
www.grouperemstar.ca
Ownership: Remstar Group Inc, 45.14%; Fiducie Seismikmax, 9.86%; Investissment Quebec, 15%; F.T.Q., 15%; Caisse de Depot et de Placement du Quebec, 15%.

Yes TV
1295 N Service Rd., Burlington ON L7R 4X5
(905) 331-7333; *Fax:*(905) 332-7481
www.yestv.com
contactus@yestv.com
Ownership: Crossroads Christian Communications

ZoomerMedia Ltd.
70 Jefferson Ave., Toronto ON M6K 3H4
(416) 367-5353
www.zoomermedia.ca
d.hamilton@mzmedia.com
Ownership: Olympus Management Limited, 61.77%; Fairfac Financial Holdings Limited, 16.47%; other Canadian Shareholders, 13.31%; MRHD Holdings Ltd., 8.12%; otherNon-Canadian shareholders, 0.30%; and Moses Znaimer, 0.02%.

TV Stations in Canada

Alberta

Calgary

CBRT-DT *Analog Channel:* 9; *Digital Channel:* 21; 23.5 kw; 276.3 meters; 51 3'53 N 114 12'51 W
1000 Veteran's Pl. N.W., Unit 105, Calgary, AB T3B 5Y7 Canada
(403) 521-6340
www.cbc.ca
jaclyn.doll@cbc.ca
License: Calgary, AB held by CBC Television
Group Owner: CBC
Hours of Local News Weekly: 11+ hrs news progmg wkly
Jaclyn Doll, Broadcast Sales
Suzanne Waddell, Communications Manager

Edmonton

CBXFT-DT *Analog Channel:* 11; *Digital Channel:* 47; 15.18 kw; 166.5 meters
123 Cdmonton City Centre, 10062-102 Ave., Edmonton, AB T5J 2Y8 Canada
(888) 680-2432
ici.radio-canada.ca/alberta
tom.shipman@cbc.ca
License: Edmonton, AB held by Ici Radio-Canada Télé
Group Owner: CBC
Hours of Local News Weekly: 12 hrs news progmg wkly
Tom Shipman, Senior Sales Manager
Paul Moore, Executive Producer
Jessica Chan, Communications Manager

CBXT-DT *Analog Channel:* 5; *Digital Channel:* 42; 131.71 kw; 233.1 meters
123 Edmonton City Centre, 10062-102 Ave., Edmonton, AB T5J 2Y8 Canada
(780) 468-2300
www.cbc.ca
tom.shipman@cbc.ca
License: Edmonton, AB held by CBC Television
Group Owner: CBC
Hours of Local News Weekly: news progmg 12 hrs wkly
Tom Shipman, Senior Sales Manager
Paul Moore, Executive Producer
Jessica Chan, Communications Manager

Vancouver

CBUFT-DT *Analog Channel:* 26; *Digital Channel:* 26; 27.52 kw; 615.4 meters
700 Hamilton St., Vancouver, BC V6B 4A2 Canada
(604) 662-6000
www.cbc.ca
tom.shipman@cbc.ca
License: Vancouver, BC held by Ici Radio-Canada Télé
Group Owner: CBC
Hours of Local News Weekly: 11 hrs wkly news
Tom Shipman, Associate Director
Cathy Hunt, Business Development Manager

CBUT-DT *Analog Channel:* 2; *Digital Channel:* 43; 103.34 kw; 615.4 meters; 49 21'13 N 122 57'24 W
700 Hamilton St., Vancouver, BC V6B 4A2 Canada
(604) 662-6000
www.cbc.ca
tom.shipman@cbc.ca
License: Vancouver, BC held by CBC Television
Group Owner: CBC
Size of News Staff: 9; *Hours of Local News Weekly:* 8.5 hrs wkly news
Tom Shipman, Associate Director
Cathy Hunt, Business Development Manager

CFCN-DT *Analog Hrs:* 24; *Digital Channel:* 29; *Digital Hrs:* 24; 120 kw; ant 623t/380g; N52 03 37 W114 10 13
80 Patina Rise SW., Calgary, AB T3H 2W4 Canada
(403) 240-5600; *Fax:* (403) 317-2420
www.calgary.ctv.ca
hilary.whyte@bellmedia.ca
License: Calgary, AB held by Bell Media Inc.
Group Owner: CTV Inc.
Nat'l Network: CTV
Lloyd Lewis, General Manager
Hilary Whyte, General Sales Manager

CICT-DT *Digital Channel:* 41; 50 kw; 378 meters;
Rebroadcasting: Rebroadcast CISA-TV Lethbridge 90%.
222 23rd St. N.E., Calgary, AB T2E 7N2 Canada
(403) 235-7777; *Fax:* (403) 248-3842
globalnews.ca/pages/about-global-calgary
doung.young@corusent.com
License: Calgary, AB held by Global Television Network
Group Owner: Corus Entertainment Inc.
Size of News Staff: 50; *Hours of Local News Weekly:* news progmg 46.5 hrs wkly
Doug Young, General Sales Mgr
Nikki Harris, Promotions Manager
Sarah Offin, Digital Journalist

CJCO-DT *Analog Channel:* 38; *Digital Channel:* 38; 25 kw; 371 meters; 51 3 53 N 114 12 51 W
535 7 Ave. S.W., Calgary, AB T2P 0Y4 Canada
(416) 764-3005
www.omnitv.ca
License: Calgary, AB held by Rogers Media Inc.
Group Owner: Rogers Media Inc.
Jake Dheer, Senior Manager

CKAL-DT *Analog Channel:* 5; *Digital Channel:* 49; 100 kw; 378 m
535 7th Ave. S.W., Calgary, AB T2P 0Y4 Canada
(403) 508-2222
www.citytv.com
info@cityline.tv
License: Calgary, AB held by Rogers Media Inc.
Group Owner: Rogers Media Inc.; (acq 10-31-2007; grpsl)
Hours of Local News Weekly: news progmg 15 hrs wkly
Jennifer Pauley Baier, Senior Producer, Breakfast Television

CKCS-TV *Analog Channel:* 32; 36 kw; N51 03 00 W114 05 00
839 - 5 Avenue SW., Suite 100B, Calgaryton, ON T2P 3C8 Canada
(403) 263-3191; *Fax:* (403) 263-3705
www.yestv.com
contactus@yestv.com
License: Calgary, AB held by Yes TV
Group Owner: Yes TV
Nat'l Reps: Airtime TV
Byron Winsor, COO
Robert Melnichuk, Operations Dir
Glenn Stewart, Director of Sales
Rob Sheppard, Programming Director
Natalie Faith, Promotions Manager
Katee Duarte, Social Media Lead

Cardston

CFSO-TV 20 w; N49 10 40 W113 19 36
Box 1238, Cardston, AB T0K 0K0 Canada
(403) 653-3792; *Fax:* (403) 653-3792
www.channel32.ca
channel32@mac.com
License: Cardston, AB held by Logan McCarthy
Logan McCarthy, Station Manager

Edmonton

CFRN-DT *Digital Channel:* 12; 16 kw; 228.1 m; N53 23 06 W113 12 48 *Population Served:* 1,200,000
18520 Stony Plain Rd., Edmonton, AB T5S 1A8 Canada
(780) 483-3311; *Fax:* (780) 484-4426
www.edmonton.ctvnews.ca
cfrn@ctv.ca
License: Edmonton, AB held by Bell Media Inc.
Group Owner: CTV Inc.; (acq 1998).
Nat'l Network: CTV
Hours of Local News Weekly: News progmg 12 hrs wkly
Lloyd Lewis, General Manager
David Fisher, Promotions Manager

CITV-DT *Digital Channel:* 13; 25 kw; 53 22'57 113 12'59 W
5325 Allard Way, Edmonton, AB T6H 5B8 Canada
(780) 436-1250; *Fax:* (780) 989-4686
www.globalnews.ca
gisele.sowa@corusent.com
License: Edmonton, Canada County, AB held by Global Television Network
Group Owner: Corus Entertainment Inc.; (acq 2-6-91)
Size of News Staff: 33; *Hours of Local News Weekly:* news progmg 43 hrs wkly
Tim Spelliscy, Station Manager
Gisele Sowa, General Sales Mgr
Kerry Powell, Managing Editor
Deb Zinck, Executive Producer
Eve Noga, Creative Services Manager
Rhonda Halarewich, Marketing Manager

CJEO-DT *Analog Channel:* 56; *Digital Channel:* 44; 58 kw; 294 meters; 53 31 54.7 N 113 46 52.2 W
10212 Jasper Ave., Edmonton, AB T5J 5A3 Canada
(416) 764-3005
www.omnitv.ca
License: Edmonton, AB held by Rogers Media Inc.
Group Owner: Rogers Media Inc.
Jake Dheer, Senior Manager

CKEM-DT *Analog Channel:* 51; *Digital Channel:* 17; 107 kw; 294 meters
5915 Gateway Blvd, Edmonton, AB T5J 5A3 Canada
(780) 424-2222
www.citytv.com
info@cityline.tv
License: Edmonton, AB held by Rogers Media Inc.
Group Owner: Rogers Media Inc.; (acq 10-31-2007; grpsl)
Hours of Local News Weekly: news progmg 24 hrs wkly
Lance Corbett, Sr Manager, Advertising and Promotions
Alison Smith, Promotions Producer
Stanley Papulkas, Executive Producer

CKES-TV 34 kw vis
5330 Calgary Trail, Edmontonon, ON T6H 4J8 Canada
(780) 433-3118; *Fax:* (780) 433-3248
www.yestv.com
contactus@yestv.com
License: Edmonton, AB held by Yes TV
Group Owner: Yes TV
Nat'l Reps: Airtime TV
Glenn Stewart, Director of Sales
Rob Sheppard, Programming Director
Katee Duarte, Social Media Lead

Lethbridge

CFCN-DT-5 *Digital Channel:* 13; 47 kw vis, 7.34 kw aur; ant 564t; N49 43 59 W112 57 36
80 Patina Rise SW., Calgary, AB T3H 2W4 Canada
(403) 317-2400; *Fax:* (403) 317-2420
www.calgary.ctv.ca
hilary.whyte@bellmedia.ca
License: Lethbridge, AB held by Bell Media Inc.
Group Owner: Bell Media Inc.
Nat'l Network: CTV
Len Perry, General Manager
Hilary Whyte, General Sales Manager

CISA-DT *Digital Channel:* 7; 19.7 kw; 201.4 m; 49 46 47 N 112 52'18 W
28th St. N., Suite 1401, Lethbridge, AB T1H 6H9 Canada
(403) 329-2903
globalnews.ca/lethbridge
viewercontactlethbridge@globalnews.ca
License: Lethbridge, AB held by Global Television Network
Group Owner: Corus Entertainment Inc.; (acq 9-1-2000; grpsl)
Size of News Staff: 19; *Hours of Local News Weekly:* news progmg 7.5 hrs wkly
Liam Nixon, Anchor & News Manager
Christina Succi, Digital Journalist

CJIL-DT *Digital Channel:* 17; 31.6 kw vis
Box 1566, 450 31st St. N., Lethbridge, AB T1H 3Z3 Canada
(403) 380-3399; *Fax:* (403)380-7490
www.miraclechannel.ca
License: Lethbridge, AB held by Miracle Channel
Leon Fontaine, CEO
Gord Klussen, General Manager
Len Whyte, Chief Engineer

Lloydminster

CITL-DT *Digital Channel:* 4; 9.1 kw; 220.6 m
5026 - 50th St., Lloydminster, AB T9V 1P3 Canada
(780) 875-3321; *Fax:* (780) 875-4704
www.citltv.ca
tvnews@newcap.ca
License: Lloydminster, AB held by NewCap Inc.
Group Owner: NewCap Inc.; (acq 12-22-2004; C$6,304,000 with CKSA-TV Lloydminster).
Nat'l Network: CTV
Chad Tabish, General Manager
Jane Hoskins, Sales Manager
Bob Cameron, Program Manager
Stacey Commer, News Director
Raymond Green, Chief Engineer
Chris MacBurnie, Television Creative Supervisor

CKSA-DT *Digital Channel:* 2; 8.1 kw; 220.6 m
5026 50th St., Lloydminster, AB T9V 1P3 Canada
(780) 875-3321; *Fax:* (780) 875-4704
www.cksatv.ca
tvnews@newcap.ca
License: Lloydminster, AB held by NewCap Inc.

Group Owner: NewCap Inc.; (acq 12-22-2004; C$6,304,000 with CITL-TV Lloydminster).
Nat'l Network: CBC
Chad Tabish, General Manager
Jane Hoskins, Sales Manager
Bob Cameron, Program Manager
Stacey Commer, News Director
Raymond Green, Chief Engineer
Chris MacBurnie, Television Creative Supervisor

Medicine Hat

CHAT-TV *Analog Channel:* 6; 58 kw vis, 5.8 kw aur; 700t/559g
10 Boundary Rd. S.E., Redcliff, AB T0J 2P0 Canada
(403) 548-8282; *Fax:* (403) 548-8270
www.chattelevision.ca
chatnews@jpbg.com
License: Medicine Hat, AB held by Jim Pattison Broadcast Group Ltd. (the general partner) and Jim Pattison Industries Ltd. (the limited partner) carrying on business as Jim Pattison Broadcast Group L.P.
Group Owner: The Jim Pattison Broadcast Group; (acq 12-21-2000; grpsl).
Nat'l Reps: Airtime TV
Hours of Local News Weekly: news progmg 15 hrs wkly
Tim Weinberger, General Sales Mgr
Curtis Cruickshank, Creative Director
John Cartwright, Marketing Consultant
Lisa Finkbeiner, Marketing Consultant
Rita Profeta, Marketing Consultant
Sandy Clemis, Marketing Consultant

Red Deer

CFRN-TV-6 *Analog Channel:* 8; 22 kw vis, 2.2 kw aur; ant 882t/588g; N52 19 10 W113 40 37
18520 Stony Plain Rd., Edmonton, AB T5S 1A8 Canada
(780) 483-3311
www.edmonton.ctvnews.ca
License: Red Deer, AB held by Bell Media Inc.
Group Owner: Bell Media Inc.
Nat'l Network: CTV
Lloyd Lewis, General Manager

British Columbia

Abbotsford

CFEG-TV 50 w vis; N49 03 07 W122 20 29
2719 Clearbrook Rd., Abbotsford, BC V2T 2Y9 Canada
(604) 850-6607; *Fax:* (604) 852-2720
office@clearbrookmbchurch.ca
License: Abbotsford, BC held by Clearbrook Mennonite Brethren Church.
Len Perry, General Manager

Dawson Creek

CJDC-TV 9.5 kw; ant 1,500t/500g
102 Ave., Suite 901, Dawson Creek, BC V1G 2B6 Canada
(250) 782-3341; *Fax:* (250) 782-3154
www.cjdctv.com
terry.shepherd@bellmedia.ca
License: Dawson Creek, BC held by Bell Media Radio G.P.
Group Owner: Bell Media Inc.; (acq 10-29-2007; grpsl)
Size of News Staff: 4; *Hours of Local News Weekly:* news progmg 10 hrs wkly
Terry Shepherd, General Manager
Amy Titley, Sales Supervisor
Jeremy Keefe, News Director

Fraser Valley

CHNU-DT *Digital Channel:* 47; 17 kw vis *Population Served:* 2,200,000
5668 192 St., Suite 204, Surrey, BC V3S 2V7 Canada
(604) 576-6880, (866) 669-8810; *Fax:* (604) 576-6895
www.joytv10.ca
License: Fraser Valley, BC held by Christian Channel Inc.
Group Owner: ZoomerMedia Ltd.
Terry Mahoney, General Manager
Gary Milne, General Sales Mgr
Karen Corbeil, Promotions Manager

Kamloops

CFJC-TV *Analog Channel:* 4; 4.4 kw vis, 2.4 kw aur; 501t/114g *Population Served:* 200,000
460 Pemberton Terrace, Kamloops, BC V2C 1T5 Canada
(250) 372-3322; *Fax:* (250) 374-0445
www.cfjctv.com
License: Kamloops, BC held by Jim Pattison Broadcast Group Ltd. (the general partner) and Jim Pattison Industries Ltd. (the limited partner) carrying on business as Jim Pattison Broadcast Group L.P.
Group Owner: The Jim Pattison Broadcast Group; (acq 1987).
Size of News Staff: 8; *Hours of Local News Weekly:* news progmg 14 hrs wkly
Bruce Uptigrove, General Sales Mgr
Doug Collins, News Director
Tim Gaudet, Account Manager
Petrina Dumais, Account Manager
Randy Mistal, Account Manager

Kelowna

CHBC-DT *Digital Channel:* 27; 23.3 kw; 509.6 m; N49 58'2 N 119 31'50 W *Population Served:* 360,000
342 Leon Ave., Kelowna, BC V1Y 6J2 Canada
(250) 762-4535; *Fax:* (250) 868-0662
www.globalnews.ca
okanagan@globalnews.ca
License: Kelowna, BC held by Global Television Network
Group Owner: Corus Entertainment Inc.
Size of News Staff: 31; *Hours of Local News Weekly:* news progmg 15.5 hrs wkly
Derek Hinchliffe, Station Manager & News Director
Megan Turcato, Reporter

Prince George

CKPG-TV *Analog Channel:* 2; 778 w vis, 389 w aur
1810 3rd Ave., 2nd Fl., Prince George, BC V2M 1G4 Canada
(250) 564-8861; *Fax:* (250) 562-8768
www.ckpg.com
License: Prince George, BC held by Jim Pattison Broadcast Group LP. (the general partner) and Jim Pattison Industries Ltd. (the limited partner) carrying on business as Jim Pattison Broadcast Group L.P.
Group Owner: The Jim Pattison Broadcast Group; (acq 12-21-2000; grpsl).
Nat'l Reps: Airtime TV
Hours of Local News Weekly: news progmg 12.5 hrs wkly
Mike Clotildes, General Manager
Kelli Moorhead, General Sales Mgr
Kharah Black, Promotions Director
Dave Barry, News Director
Brenda Clotildes, CKPG Production Manager

Valemount

CHVC-TV 10 kw vis
Box 922, Valemount, BC V0E 2Z0 Canada
(250) 566-8288; *Fax:* (250) 566-4645
www.vctv.ca
tv@vctv.ca
License: Valemount, BC held by The Valemount Entertainment Society
Penni Osadchuk, General Manager

Vancouver

CHAN-DT *Digital Channel:* 22; *Digital Hrs:* 24; 40 kw; ant 2,315t/250g; N49 21 29 W122 57 09
7850 Enterprise St., Burnaby, BC V5A 1V7 Canada
(604) 420-2288; *Fax:* (604) 422-6466
www.globalnews.ca
globalbcsalesteam@corusent.com
License: Vancouver, BC held by Corus Entertainment Inc.
Group Owner: Corus Entertainment Inc.
Nat'l Network: Global
Size of News Staff: 34; *Hours of Local News Weekly:* 47.5 hrs of news wkly
Jill Krop, News Director

CHNM-DT *Analog Channel:* 42; *Digital Channel:* 20; 8.3 kw; 670 metres
180 West 2nd Ave., Vancouver, BC V5Y 3T9 Canada
(604) 876-1344
www.omnitv.ca
License: Vancouver, BC held by Rogers Media Inc.
Group Owner: Rogers Media Inc.; (acq 4-30-2008; C$61,291,913)
Hours of Local News Weekly: news progmg 12.5 hrs wkly
Jake Dheer, Senior Manager
Bob Wilson, Account Executive

CIVT-DT *Analog Channel:* 9; *Digital Channel:* 32; 33 kw; 740.3 meters; N49 21 29 W122 57 09 *Population Served:* 2,500,000
969 Robson St., Suite 500, Vancouver, BC V6Z 1X5 Canada
(604) 608-2868; *Fax:* (604) 608-2698
www.bc.ctvnews.ca
License: Vancouver, BC held by Bell Media Inc.
Group Owner: Bell Media Inc.; *Ownership:* Bell Media
Nat'l Network: CTV *Regional Network:* CTV Two Vancouver Island
Hours of Local News Weekly: 24/7
Les Staff, News Director
Charles Wright, Senior Director

CKVU-DT *Analog Channel:* 10; *Digital Channel:* 33; 8.3 kw; 670 metres; 49 21 13 N 122 57 24 W
180 West 2nd Ave., Vancouver, BC V5Y 3T9 Canada
(604) 876-1344
www.citytv.com
manuel.fonseca@rci.rogers.com
License: Vancouver, BC held by Rogers Media Inc.
Group Owner: Rogers Media Inc.; (acq 10-31-2007; grpsl)
Hours of Local News Weekly: news progmg 17.5 hrs wkly
Manuel Fonseca, Programming Director
Steve Scarrow, Regional Creative Director
Susan Lee, Coordinating Producer

Victoria

CHEK-DT *Analog Hrs:* 24; *Digital Channel:* 49; 100 kw vis, 10 kw aur; 1,628t/380g
780 Kings Road, Victoria, BC V8T 5A2 Canada
(250)480-3700, (866) 639-7241; *Fax:* (250) 384-7766
www.cheknews.ca
info@cheknews.ca
License: Victoria, BC held by CHEK Media Group
Ownership: CHEK Media Group
John Pollard, President/General Manager
Bill Pollock, Programming/Engineering Director
Tanya Smith, Promotions Manager
Rob Germain, News Director

CIVI-DT *Digital Channel:* 23; 12 kw vis
1420 Broad St., Victoria, BC V8W 2B1 Canada
(250) 381-2484; *Fax:* (250) 381-2485
vancouverisland.ctvnews.ca
islandcontactus@ctv.ca
License: Victoria, Canada County, BC held by Bell Media Inc.
Group Owner: Bell Media Inc.
Heather Kim, News Director

Manitoba

Brandon

CKX-TV *Analog Channel:* 5 *Analog Hrs:* 6 AM-2 AM; 44 kw vis, 27 kw aur; ant 511t/525g
2940 Victoria Ave., Brandon, MB R7B 3Y3 Canada
(204) 728-1150; *Fax:* (204) 727-2505
License: Brandon, MB
Group Owner: Bell Media Inc.
Size of News Staff: 20; *Hours of Local News Weekly:* news progmg 15 hrs wkly
Alan Cruise, General Manager
Brian Atkinson, Station Manager

Fraser Valley

CHNU-DT *Digital Channel:* 44
5668 192 St., Suite 204, Surrey, BC V3S 2V7 Canada
(604) 576-6880; *Fax:* (604) 576-6895
www.joytv.ca
audience@joytv.ca
License: Fraser Valley, MB held by Christian Channel Inc.
Group Owner: ZoomerMedia Ltd.; (acq 6-30-2008; C$6,247,908 with CHNU-TV Fraser Valley, BC)
Dan Hamilton, VP Sales, Broadcast and General Manager

Mafeking

CBWYT *Analog Channel:* 2 *Analog Hrs:* 24; 4 kw vis; 370g
Mailing Address: 541 Portage Avenue, Winnipeg, MB R3C 2H1 Canada
Second Address: 541 Portage Ave., Winnipeg, MB R3B 2G1
(204) 788-3222; *Fax:* (866) 220-6045
www.cbc.ca/manitoba
License: Mafeking, MB held by CBC
Nat'l Network: CBC
Remi Racine, Chairman
Hubert T. Lacroix, President/CEO
John Bertrand, Director
Jason Perring, Broadcast Sales
Leona Johnson, Promotions Manager
Maryse Bertrand, VP, Real Estate, Legal Services & General Counsel
William B.Chambers, VP, Brand, Communications and Corporate Affairs
Steven Guiton, VP, Technology & Chief Regulatory Officer

Louis Lalande, Executive Vice-President, French Services
Suzanne Morris, Vice-President and Chief Financial Officer
RoulaZaarour, Vice-President, People and Culture

Portage la Prairie

CHMI-DT *Analog Channel:* 13; *Digital Channel:* 13; 8.3 kw; 324.3 metres
8 Forks Market Rd., Winnipeg, MB R3C 4Y3 Canada
(204) 947-9613
www.citytv.com
info@cityline.tv
License: Portage la Prairie, MB held by Rogers Media Inc.
Group Owner: Rogers Media Inc.; (acq 10-31-2007; grpsl)
Size of News Staff: 35; *Hours of Local News Weekly:* news progmg 14 hrs wkly
Steve Urias, Account Manager

Winnipeg

CBWFT-DT *Analog Channel:* 3; *Digital Channel:* 51; 7.6 kw; 138.9 meters; 49 53'43 N 97 08'17 W
541 Portage Ave., Winnipeg, MB R3C 2H1 Canada
(204) 788-3262
ici.radio-canada.ca
manitoba@radio-canada.ca
License: Winnipeg, MB held by Ici Radio-Canada Télé
Group Owner: CBC
Nat'l Network: Radio Canada
Hours of Local News Weekly: 12+ hrs wkly
Hubert T. Lacroix, President and CEO
Philippe Vrignon, Programming Director
Marc Pichette, PR and Television Promotion Director

CBWT-DT *Analog Channel:* 6; *Digital Channel:* 27; 42 kw; 138.6 meters; 49 53'43 N 97 08'17 W
541 Portage Ave., Winnipeg, MB R3C 2H1 Canada
(204) 788-3114
www.cbc.ca/manitoba
jason.perring@cbc.ca
License: Winnipeg, MB held by CBC Television
Group Owner: CBC
Hours of Local News Weekly: news 10.4 hrs wkly
John Bertrand, Senior Managing Director
Jason Perring, Broadcast and Digital Sales Manager
Michelle Gazze, Senior Communications Officer
Lucille Brunette, Administration

CIIT-DT *Digital Channel:* 35
64 Jefferson Ave., Toronto, ON M6K 3Y4 Canada
(416) 368-3194; *Fax:* (416) 368-9774
www.hopetelevision.ca
License: Winnipeg, MB held by Christian Channel Inc.
Group Owner: ZoomerMedia Ltd.; (acq 6-30-2008; C$6,247,908 with CHNU-TV Fraser Valley, BC)
Dan Hamilton, VP Sales, Broadcast and General Manager

CKND-DT *Digital Channel:* 40; 25.1 kw; 131.2 m
201 Portage Ave., Suite 30, Winnipeg, MB R3B 3K6 Canada
(204) 233-3304; *Fax:* (204) 233-5615
www.globalnews.ca
winnipeg@globalnews.ca
License: Winnipeg, MB held by Global Television Network
Group Owner: Corus Entertainment Inc.
Size of News Staff: 13; *Hours of Local News Weekly:* news progmg 24.5 hrs wkly
Brent Williamson, Station Manager & News Director
Riley Martin, Web Producer

CKY-DT *Digital Channel:* 7; 325 kw vis, 65 kw aur; ant 1,000g
345 Graham Ave., Suite 400, Winnipeg, MB R3C 5S6 Canada
(204) 788-3300; *Fax:* (204) 943-3112
www.winnipeg.ctvnews.ca
winnipegnews@ctv.ca
License: Winnipeg, MB held by Bell Media Inc.
Group Owner: Bell Media Inc.
Nat'l Network: CTV
Ken Peron, Operations Mgr
Jeff Bollenbach, General Manager
Anne Skrynsky, Sales Mgr
Diane Kashton, Promotions Manager
Karen Mitchell, News Director

New Brunswick

Fredericton

CBAT-DT *Analog Channel:* 4; *Digital Channel:* 31; 7.36 kw; 102.8 meters; 45 28'39 N 66 13'59 W
1160 Regent St., Fredericton, NB E3B 5G4 Canada
(506) 451-4000
www.cbc.ca/news/canada/new-brunswick
darrow.macintyre@cbc.ca
License: Fredericton, NB held by CBC Television
Group Owner: CBC
Darrow MacIntyre, Executive Producer
Karissa Donkin, Associate Producer

Moncton

CBAFT-DT *Analog Channel:* 11; *Digital Channel:* 11; 17.65 kw; 227.5 meters; 46 8'37 N 64 54'8 W
165 Main St., Suite 15, Moncton, NB E1C 1B8 Canada
(514) 853-6666
www.cbc.radio-canada.ca
infoacadie@radio-canada.ca
License: Moncton, NB held by Ici Radio-Canada Télé
Group Owner: CBC
Hubert T. Lacroix, President and CEO
Judith Purves, EVP and Chief Financial Officer

CKCW-DT *Digital Channel:* 29; 56 kw vis, 9.2 kw aur
Mailing Address: Box 1653, Halifax, NS B3J 2Z4 Canada
Second Address: 191 Halifax St., Moncton, NB E1C 9R7
(902) 453-4000
www.atlantic.ctvnews.ca
atlanticnews@bellmedia.ca
License: Moncton, NB held by Bell Media Inc.
Group Owner: Bell Media Inc.
Glenn McLanders, Station Manager
Glenn McLanders, General Sales Mgr
Steve Murphy, News Director

Saint John

CHNB-DT *Digital Channel:* 12; 6 kw; 354.0 m; 45 28 40 N 66 14 0 W
1 Germain St., Saint John, NB E2L 4V1 Canada
(800) 833-0592
www.globalnews.ca
halifax@globalnews.ca
License: Saint John, NB held by Global Television Network
Group Owner: Corus Entertainment Inc.
Nat'l Network: Global
Sean Previl, Web Producer
Alexander Quon, Web Producer

CKLT-DT *Digital Channel:* 9; 7.6 kw vis; 1,361t/241g
Box 1653, Halifax, NS B3J 2Z4 Canada
(902) 453-4000
www.atlantic.ctvnews.ca
atlanticnews@bellmedia.ca
License: Saint John, NB held by Bell Media Inc.
Group Owner: Bell Media Inc.
Glenn McLanders, Station Manager
Glenn McLanders, General Sales Mgr
Steve Murphy, News Director

St. Andrews

CHCT-TV 480 w vis; N45 04 54 W67 03 34 *Population Served:* 20,000
24 Reed Ave., Unit 2, St. Andrews, NB E5B 1A1 Canada
(506) 529-8826; *Fax:* (506) 529-2601
www.chct.ca
news@chco.tv
License: St. Andrews, Charlotte County, NB held by St. Andrews Community Channel
Size of News Staff: 2; *Hours of Local News Weekly:* 5
David Welch, Chairman
Patrick Watt, Operations Dir

Newfoundland

Saint John's

CBNT-DT *Analog Channel:* 8; *Digital Channel:* 8; 14.54 kw; 252.9 meters; 47 31'59 N 52 47'26 W
PO Box 12010, Station A, St. John's, NL A1B 3T8 Canada
(709) 576-5225; *Fax:* (709) 576-5011
www.cbc.ca/nl
victoria.king@cbc.ca
License: Saint John's, NL held by CBC
Group Owner: CBC
Nat'l Network: CBC Television
Hours of Local News Weekly: 10.05 hrs news wkly
Victoria King, Senior Manager
Peter Gullage, Executive Producer

St. John's

CJON-DT *Digital Channel:* 21; 128.4 kw; 254.6 m; N47 31 36 W52 42 50 *Population Served:* 575,000
Mailing Address: P.O. Box 2020, St. John's, NF A1C 5S2 Canada
Second Address: 446 Logy Bay Rd., St. John's, NF
(709) 722-5015; *Fax:* (709) 726-5107
www.ntv.ca
greetings@ntv.ca
License: St. John's, NF held by Newfoundland Broadcasting Co. Ltd.
Group Owner: Newfoundland Broadcasting Co. Ltd.; *Washington Law Firm:* Johnston & Buchan
Nat'l Network: CTV; *Wire Services:* BN Wire
Size of News Staff: 12; *Hours of Local News Weekly:* news progmg 11 hrs wkly
Lindsey Andrews, Acting General Manager
Glen Carter, Co-Host, NTV Evening Newshour
Lynn Burry, Senior Producer and Co-Host, NTV Evening Newshour
Toni Marie Wiseman, Host, NTV News First Edition
Eddie Sheerr, Chief Meteorologist
Jodi Cooke, Co-Host, NTV Sunday Evening Newshour
Larry Jay, Co-Host, NTV Sunday Evening Newshour

Northwest Territories

Yellowknife

CFYK-DT *Analog Channel:* 8; *Digital Channel:* 8; 2.4 kw; 62.5 meters
5002 Forrest Dr., Yellowknife, NT X1A 2A9 Canada
(867) 920-5465
www.cbc.ca/north
cbcnorth@cbc.ca
License: Yellowknife, NT held by CBC
Group Owner: CBC
Nat'l Network: CBC North
Janice Stein, Managing Director
Catherine Pigott, Producer
Mervin Brass, Managing Editor

Nova Scotia

Halifax

CBHT-DT *Analog Channel:* 3; *Digital Channel:* 39; 157.54 kw; 266.5 meters; 44 39'3 N 63 39'26 W
6940 Mumford Rd., Suite 100, Halifax, NS B3L 0B7 Canada
(902) 420-4100; *Fax:* (902) 420-4137
www.cbc.ca/ns
john.channing@cbc.ca
License: Halifax, NS held by CBC
Group Owner: CBC
Nat'l Network: CBC Television
John Channing, Broadcast Sales
Ken MacIntosh, Executive Producer, News and Current Affairs

CIHF-DT *Digital Channel:* 8; 1 kw; 241.0 m
2110 Gottingen St., Halifax, NS B3K 3B3 Canada
(902) 481-7400
www.globalnews.ca
montreal@globalnews.ca
License: Halifax, NS held by Global Television Network
Group Owner: Corus Entertainment Inc.
Nat'l Network: Global
Jim Haskins, Station Manager

CJCB-TV *Analog Channel:* 4 *Analog Hrs:* 24; 180 kw
Mailing Address: Box 1653, Halifax, NS B3J 2Z4 Canada
Second Address: 191 Halifax St., Moncton, NB E1C 9R7
(902) 453-4000
www.atlantic.ctvnews.ca
atlanticnews@bellmedia.ca
License: Halifax, NS held by Bell Media Inc.
Group Owner: Bell Media Inc.
Nat'l Network: CTV
Glenn McLanders, Station Manager
Glenn McLanders, General Sales Mgr
Steve Murphy, News Director

CJCH-DT *Digital Channel:* 48; 100 kw vis, 10 kw aur; ant 821t/575g; N44 39 03 W63 39 28
Mailing Address: P.O. Box 1653, Halifax, NS B3J 2Z4 Canada
Second Address: 2885 Robie St., Halifax, NS B3K 5Z4
(902) 453-4000; *Fax:* (902) 454-3302
www.ctv.ca
atlanticnews@bellmedia.ca
License: Halifax, NS held by Bell Media Canada Radio 2013 Partnership

Group Owner: Bell Media Inc.
Michael Elgie, Operations Dir
Ian MacArthur, General Sales Mgr
Renee Fournier, Promotions Manager
Jay Witherbee, News Director
Gary Robertson, Chief Engineer

Isle Madame

CIMC-TV *Analog Hrs:* 24; 450 w vis
Mailing Address: Box 87, Arichat, NS B0E 1A0 Canada
Second Address: 17 Conney's Lane, Arichat, NS B0E 1A0
(902) 226-1928; *Fax:* (902) 226-1331
www.telile.tv
telile@telile.tv
License: Isle Madame, NS held by Telile:Isle Madame Community Television Association/Association Television Communautaire de l'Ile Madame
Gloria Hill, General Manager
Rhonda LeBlanc, Community Programmer
Cora LeBlanc, Business Manager
Angele Richard, Administrative Asst.

Ontario

Barrie

CKVR-DT *Digital Channel:* 10; 11 kw; 332.3 m; N44 21 05 W79 41 55 *Population Served:* 6,000,000
33 Beacon Rd., Barrie, ON L4N 9J9 Canada
(705) 734-3300, (800) 461-5820; *Fax:* (705) 733-0302
www.barrie.ctvnews.ca
barrieinbox@ctv.ca
License: Barrie, ON held by Bell Media Inc.
Group Owner: Bell Media Inc.
Size of News Staff: 30; *Hours of Local News Weekly:* news progmg 10 hrs wkly
Tom Fitz-Gerald, General Sales Mgr
Michael Whyte, Promotions Manager
Ruth Anderson, News Director
Michelle Wilson, Business/HR Manager

Brighton

CKWS-DT-1 *Analog Hrs:* 24
170 Queen St., Kingston, ON K7K 1B2 Canada
(613) 544-2340; *Fax:* (613) 544-5508
www.ckwstv.com
peter.mayhew@corusent.com
License: Brighton, ON held by 591987 B.C. Ltd.
Group Owner: Corus Entertainment Inc.
Nat'l Network: CBC
Hours of Local News Weekly: news progmg 12 hrs wkly
Peter Mayhew, General Sales Mgr
Jay Westman, News and TV Operations Manager

Hamilton

CHCH-DT *Digital Channel:* 11; 6.1 kw; 358 m
Box 2230, Stn. A, 163 Jackson St. W., Hamilton, ON L8N 3A6 Canada
(905) 522-1101; *Fax:* (905)523-8011
www.chtv.ca
License: Hamilton, ON held by 2190015 Ontario Inc.
Ownership: 2185220 Ontario Ltd., 30% of the voting shares.
Nat'l Network: Global
Patrick O'Hara, General Manager

CITS-TV *Digital Channel:* 36; 20 kww; 335 m
1295 N. Service Rd., Burlington, ON L7R 4M2 Canada
(905) 331-7333; *Fax:* (905) 332-6005
www.yestv.com
contactus@yestv.com
License: Hamilton, ON held by Yes TV
Group Owner: Yes TV
Fred Vanstone, President
Glenn Stewart, Director of Sales
Rob Sheppard, Programming Director
Chris Somerville, Promotions Manager
David Storey, Engineering Dir

Kenora

CJBN-TV 177 kw vis, 35 kw aur; 200g
Mailing Address: 102 10th Street, Keewatin, ON Canada
Second Address: 104 Tenth St., Keewatin, ON P9N 3X8
(807) 547-2852; *Fax:* (807) 547-2348
darrylm@norcomcable.ca
License: Kenora, ON held by Shaw Cablesystems G.P.
Nat'l Network: CTV
Size of News Staff: 2; *Hours of Local News Weekly:* news progmg one hr wkly
Darryl Michaluk, Station Manager

Kingston

CKWS-DT *Analog Hrs:* 24; *Digital Channel:* 11; 9.4 kw; 312.5 meters; 44 9'59 N 76 25 28 W
170 Queen St., Kingston, ON K7K 1B2 Canada
(613) 544-2340; *Fax:* (613) 544-5508
www.ckwstv.com
peter.mayhew@corusent.com
License: Kingston, ON held by 591987 B.C. Ltd.
Group Owner: Corus Entertainment Inc.; (acq 3-24-2000; grpsl).
Nat'l Network: CBC
Hours of Local News Weekly: news progmg 28 hrs wkly
Peter Mayhew, General Sales Mgr
Jay Westman, News and TV Operations Manager

Kitchener

CKCO-DT *Digital Channel:* 13; 325 kw vis, 32.5 kw aur; 954t/653g; N43 24 15 W80 38 05 *Population Served:* 2,000,000
864 King St. W., Kitchener, ON N2G 1E8 Canada
(519) 578-1314; *Fax:* (519) 743-0730
www.kitchener.ctvnews.ca
viewermail@kitchener.ctv.ca
License: Kitchener, ON held by Bell Media Inc.
Group Owner: Bell Media Inc.; (acq 8-31-97).
Nat'l Network: CTV
Foreign Language Programming
Ivan Fecan, CEO
Dennis Watson, Operations Dir
Cameron Crassweller, General Sales Mgr
Janet Taylor, Promotions Manager
Andy LeBlanc, News Director
Dave Melse, Chief Engineer
Dave MacNeill, Operations Director

Leamington

CFTV-DT *Digital Channel:* 34; 587 w; 27 meters
223 Talbot St. W., Leamington, ON N8H 1N8 Canada
(519) 326-4000
www.cftv.ca
info@cftv.ca
License: Leamington, ON held by Southshore Broadcasting Inc
Tony Vidal, President
Ted Mastronardi, Operations Dir

London

CTV *Digital Channel:* 10; 325 kw vis, 43.2 kw aur; 1,000t/975g *Population Served:* 500,000
Mailing Address: PO Box 9, Station O, Toronto, ON M4A 2M9 Canada
Second Address: 299 Queen St. W, Toronto, ON M5V 2Z5
(416) 384-5000, (800) 668-0060, (866) 690-6179; *Fax:* (800) 461-1542
www.ctv.ca
ctvsupport@insinc.com
License: London, Middlesex County, ON held by Bell Media Inc.
Group Owner: Bell Media Inc.; (acq 1997)
Don Mumford, Station Manager
Jim Kippen, Chief Engineer

North Bay

CKNY-TV *Analog Channel:* 10 *Analog Hrs:* 20; 132.6 kw; 607t/1,165g *Population Served:* 156,000
245 Oak St., North Bay, ON P1B 8P8 Canada
(705) 476-3111, (877) 303-6288; *Fax:* (705) 495-4474
www.northernontario.ctvnews.ca
newsforthenorth@ctv.ca
License: North Bay, ON held by Bell Media Inc.
Group Owner: Bell Media Inc.
Hours of Local News Weekly: News progmg 10 hrs wkly
Scott Lund, General Manager
Ron Driscoll, General Sales Mgr

Oshawa

CHEX-TV-2 *Analog Channel:* 22 *Analog Hrs:* 20; 5.5 kw; 133.5 m; 43 57 16 N 78 48 22 W
10 Simcoe St. N., Oshawa, ON L1G 4R8 Canada
(905) 259-9424
www.channel12.ca
brenda.obrien@corusent.com
License: Oshawa, ON held by 591987 B.C. Ltd.
Group Owner: Corus Entertainment Inc.; (acq 3-24-2000; grpsl).
Nat'l Network: CBC
Brenda O'Brien, General Sales Mgr
Jay Westman, News & TV Operations Manager
Roger Cole, Chief Engineer
Joe McLoughlin, Creative Services Director
Sue Korytko, Office Administration
Heather Pearce, Traffic

Ottawa

CBOFT-DT *Digital Channel:* 33; 282 kw; ant 1,394t/702g
Mailing Address: Box 6000, Station centre-ville, Montreal, ON H3C 3A8 Canada
Second Address: P.O. Box 3220, Station C, Ottawa, ON K1Y 1E4
(514) 597-6000; *Fax:* (866) 306-4636
www.radio-canada.ca
License: Ottawa, ON held by CBC
Nat'l Network: Radio Canada
R,mi Racine, Chairman
Hubert T. Lacroix, President/CEO
Richard Simoens, General Manager
Maryse Bertrand, Vice-President, Real Estate, Legal Services and Ge
William B. Chambers, Vice-President, Brand, Communications and Corporat
Steven Guiton, Vice-President Technology and Chief Regulatory Off
Louis Lalande, Executive Vice-President
Suzanne Morris, Vice-President and Chief Financial Officer
Roula Zaarour, Vice-President, People and Culture

CBOT-DT *Digital Channel:* 25; 214.8 kw; 426.4 meters
Mailing Address: PO Box 500, Station A, Toronto, ON M5W 1E6 Canada
Second Address: Ottawa Broadcast Centre, 181 Queen St., Ottawa, ON K1P 1K9
(866) 306-4636; *Fax:* (866) 220-6045
www.cbc.ca
License: Ottawa, ON held by CBC
Nat'l Network: CBC
Remi Racine, Chairman
Hubert T. Lacroix, President/CEO
Rob Renaud, General Sales Mgr
Maryse Bertrand, VP, Real Estate, Legal Services & General Counsel
William B. Chambers, VP, Brand, Communications and Corporate Affairs
StevenGuiton, VP, Technology & Chief Regulatory Officer
Louis Lalande, Executive Vice-President, French Services
Suzanne Morris, Vice-President and Chief Financial Officer
Roula Zaarour, Vice-President, People and Culture

CHRO-DT-43 *Digital Channel:* 43; 282 kw vis; N45 13 01 W75 33 51
87 George St., Ottawa, ON K1N 9H7 Canada
(613) 224-1313; *Fax:* (888) 770-2192
www.ottawa.ctvnews.ca
ctvottawa@ctv.ca
License: Ottawa, ON held by Bell Media Inc.
Group Owner: Bell Media Inc.
Richard Gray, Operations Dir
Peter Angione, News Director

CJOH-DT *Analog Channel:* 13; 19 kw; 373.4 m; N45 30 11 W75 51 02 *Population Served:* 2,000,000
87 George St., Ottawa, ON K1N 9H7 Canada
(613) 224-1313; *Fax:* (888) 770-2192
www.ottawa.ctv.ca
ctvottawa@ctv.ca
License: Ottawa, ON held by Bell Media Inc.
Group Owner: Bell Media Inc.
Nat'l Reps: Canadian Broadcast Sales
Richard Gray, General Manager
Peter Angione, News Director
John Ruttle, Producer
Kim Closs, Traffic Manager

Pembroke

CHRO-TV *Analog Channel:* 5 *Analog Hrs:* 24; 100 kw vis, 10 kw aur; 496t/520g; N45 50 02 W77 09 50 *Population Served:* 1,000,000
87 George St., Ottawa, ON K1N 9H7 Canada
(613) 224-1313; *Fax:* (888) 770-2192
www.ottawa.ctvnews.ca
ctvottawa@ctv.ca
License: Pembroke, ON held by Bell Media Inc.
Group Owner: Bell Media Inc.; (acq 1997)
Hours of Local News Weekly: News progmg 30 hrs wkly
Richard Gray, General Manager
Peter Angione, News Director
Robert Edgley, Chief Engineer

Peterborough

CHEX-DT *Digital Channel:* 12; 20 kw; 316.5 meters; 44 19 42 N 78 17'58 W
743 Monaghan Rd., Peterborough, ON K9J 5K2 Canada
(705) 742-0451; *Fax:* (705) 742-7274
www.chextv.com
brenda.obrien@corusent.com
License: Peterborough, ON held by 591987 B.C. Ltd.
Group Owner: Corus Entertainment Inc.; (acq 3-24-2000; grpsl).
Nat'l Network: CBC *Nat'l Reps:* TeleRep
Hours of Local News Weekly: news progmg 16 hrs wkly
Brenda O'Brien, General Sales Mgr
Jay Westman, News & TV Operations Manager
Roger Cole, Chief Engineer
Denise Drumm, Sales Administration
Joe McLoughlin, Creative Services Director
Paul Dinsdale, Master Control Supervisor

Sault Ste. Marie

CHBX-TV *Analog Channel:* 2 *Analog Hrs:* 6 AM-2 AM; 100 kw vis, 10 kw aur; 600t/500g *Population Served:* 104,000
119 East St., Sault Ste. Marie, ON P6A 3C7 Canada
(705) 759-8232; *Fax:* (705) 759-7783
www.northernontario.ctvnews.ca
newsforthenorth@ctv.ca
License: Sault Ste. Marie, ON held by Bell Media Inc.
Group Owner: Bell Media Inc.
Nat'l Reps: Canadian Broadcast Sales
Scott Lund, General Manager
Brett Lund, General Sales Mgr

Sudbury

CICI-TV *Analog Channel:* 5; 100 kw vis, 10 kw aur; 1,057t/975g
699 Frood Rd., Sudbury, ON P3C 5A3 Canada
(705) 674-8301, (866)389-6288; *Fax:* (705) 674-2706
www.northernontario.ctvnews.ca
newsforthenorth@ctv.ca
License: Sudbury, ON held by Bell Media Inc.
Group Owner: Bell Media Inc.
Size of News Staff: 15; *Hours of Local News Weekly:* news progmg 10 hrs wkly
Scott Lund, General Manager
Marett McCulloch, General Sales Mgr
John Eddy, Operations Manager

Thunder Bay

CHFD-DT *Digital Channel:* 4; 1.2 kw; 366.2 m; N48 31 30 W89 06 50 *Population Served:* 160,000
87 North Hill St, Thunder Bay, ON P7A 5V6 Canada
(807) 346-2600; *Fax:* (807) 345-9923
globalthunderbay.tbtv.com
tbtv@tbtv.com
License: Thunder Bay, Thunder Bay County, ON held by Thunder Bay Electronics Ltd
Nat'l Network: Global *Nat'l Reps:* CanWest Media Sales; *Wire Services:* CNW Broadcast
D. Caron, CFO
H.F. Dougall, President
A. Snell, Operations Dir
K. Harris, General Sales Mgr
P. Bentz, Programming Director
S. Lockwood, National Sales Director

CKPR-DT *Digital Channel:* 2; 1.2 kw; 366.2 m; N48 31 30 W89 06 50 *Population Served:* 160,000
87 North Hill St., Thunder Bay, ON P7A 5V6 Canada
(807) 346-2600; *Fax:* (807) 345-9923
www.ckprthunderbay.com
tbt@tbtv.com
License: Thunder Bay, Thunder Bay County, ON held by Thunder Bay Electronics Ltd
Nat'l Network: CBC *Nat'l Reps:* CanWest Media Sales
Hours of Local News Weekly: News progmg 11 hrs wkly
H.F. Dougall, President
D. Caron, Operations Dir
K. Harris, General Sales Mgr
P. Bentz, Programming Director
S. Lockwood, National Sales Director
A. Snell, Operations Director

Timmins

CITO-TV *Analog Channel:* 3; 100 kw vis, 10 kw aur; 544t/499g *Population Served:* 132,900
681 Pine St. N., Timmins, ON P4N 7L6 Canada
(705) 264-4211, (800) 797-6288; *Fax:* (705) 264-3266
www.northernontario.ctvnews.ca
newsforthenorth@ctv.ca
License: Timmins, ON held by Bell Media Inc.
Group Owner: Bell Media Inc.
Scott Lund, General Manager
Jason Laneville, General Sales Mgr

Toronto

CBLFT-DT *Digital Channel:* 25
250 Front St. W, Toronto, ON M5V 3G5 Canada
(416) 205-3311
www.radio-canada.ca
License: Toronto, ON

CBLT-DT *Digital Channel:* 20; 77 kw vis, 7 kw aur; ant 444t/541g
Mailing Address: PO Box 500, Station A, Toronto, ON M5W 1E6 Canada
Second Address: 205 Wellington St. W., Toronto, ON M5V 3G7
(416) 205-5808, (416) 205-2500; *Fax:* (416) 205-3888
www.cbc.ca
License: Toronto, ON held by CBC
Nat'l Network: CBC
Size of News Staff: 45; *Hours of Local News Weekly:* news progmg 10 hrs wkly
Remi Racine, Chairman
Hubert T. Lacroix, President/CEO
Maryse Bertrand, VP, Real Estate, Legal Services & General Counsel
William B. Chambers, VP, Brand, Communications and Corporate Affairs
Steven Guiton, VP, Technology & ChiefRegulatory Officer
Louis Lalande, Executive Vice-President, French Services
Suzanne Morris, Vice-President and Chief Financial Officer
Roula Zaarour, Vice-President, People and Culture

CFMT-DT *Digital Channel:* 47; *Digital Hrs:* 24; 807 kw vis, 80.7 kw aur; ant 1,600t/1,427g
33 Dundas St. E., Toronto, ON M5B 1C6 Canada
(416) 764-3005
www.omnitv.ca
License: Toronto, ON held by Rogers Broadcasting Ltd.
Group Owner: Rogers Broadcasting Ltd.
Foreign Language Programming
Guy Laurence, President
Sandro Belfiglio, Local Ad Sales Manager

CFTO-DT *Digital Channel:* 9; 10.2 kw; ant 1815t/1614g; N43 38 33 W79 23 15
Mailing Address: Box 9, Station O, Scarborough, ON M4A 2M9 Canada
Second Address: 9 Channel Nine Crt., Scarborough, ON M1S 4B5
(416) 332-5000; *Fax:* (416) 332-5022
www.toronto.ctvnews.ca
License: Toronto, ON held by Bell Media Inc.
Group Owner: Bell Media Inc.
Joanne MacDonald, Vice President
Lisa Beaton, General Manager

CICA-TV *Digital Channel:* 18; 2.4 kw; 316 m
Mailing Address: TVO Box 200, Station Q, Toronto, ON M4T 2T1 Canada
Second Address: 2180 Yonge St., Toronto, ON M4S 2B9
(416) 484-2600; *Fax:* (416) 484-4234
www.tvo.org
asktvo@tvo.org
License: Toronto, ON held by Ontario Educational Communications Authority
Lisa de Wilde, CEO

CIII-DT *Digital Channel:* 41; 100 kw; 503 m; 43 38'33N 79 23 14 W
81 Barber Greene Rd., Toronto, ON M3C 2A2 Canada
(416) 446-5460; *Fax:* (416) 446-5447
www.globalnews.ca
viewercontacttoronto@globalnews.ca
License: Toronto, ON held by Global Television Network
Group Owner: Corus Entertainment Inc.
Size of News Staff: 29; *Hours of Local News Weekly:* news progmg 28 hrs wkly
Mackay Taggart, News Director
Simon Ostler, Managing Editor
Kieron O'Dea, Producer

CITY-DT *Digital Channel:* 44; 280 kw vis, 28 kw aur; 1,690t/1,780g *Population Served:* 4,000,000
33 Dundas St. E., Toronto, ON M5B 1B8 Canada
(416) 599-2489
www.citytv.com
License: Toronto, ON held by Rogers Broadcasting Ltd.
Group Owner: Rogers Broadcasting Ltd.; (acq 10-31-2007; grpsl)
Hours of Local News Weekly: News progmg 25 hrs wkly
David Boorne, Operations Manager

CJMT-DT *Digital Channel:* 40; *Digital Hrs:* 24; 19.5 kw
33 Dundas St. E., Toronto, ON M5B 1C6 Canada
(416) 764-3005
www.omnitv.ca
License: Toronto, ON held by Rogers Broadcasting Ltd.
Group Owner: Rogers Broadcasting Ltd.
Hours of Local News Weekly: news progmg 5 hrs wkly
Guy Laurence, President
Sandro Belfiglio, Local Ad Sales Manager

Wheatley

CHWI-DT *Digital Channel:* 16; 183 kw vis *Station Currently Dark*
1149 Goyeau Street, Windsor, ON N9A 1H9 Canada
(519) 977-7432, (800) 267-3107; *Fax:* (519) 977-0564
windsor.ctvnews.ca
windsorcontact@ctv.ca
License: Wheatley, Middlesex County, ON
Group Owner: Bell Media Inc.; (acq 1997)
Don Mumford, Regional Vice-President
Tom Fitz-Gerald, Regional Sales Manager - CTV Barrie/Kitchener/Lond
Dan Appleby, News Director - CTV Windsor
Don Mumford, Regional Vice-President - Radio and TV Operations
John Lewis, AssignmentEditor - CTV Windsor
Mandi Fields, Community Relations
Tom Fitz-Gerald, Regional Sales Manager - CTV Barrie/Kitchener/Lond
Mark Schembri, Regional Manager - Engineering and IT - Radio and
John Cordiner, Regional Manager - Promotion andDigital Media - C

Windsor

CBET-DT *Digital Channel:* 9; 13.03 kw; 186.1 m
825 Riverside Drive W, Windsor, ON N9A 5K9 Canada
(519) 255-3411, (519) 255-3411, 519) 255-3456
www.cbc.ca/windsor
License: Windsor, ON
Remi Racine, Chairman
Hubert T. Lacroix, President/CEO
Maryse Bertrand, VP, Real Estate, Legal Services & General Counsel
William B. Chambers, VP, Brand, Communications and Corporate Affairs
Steven Guiton, VP, Technology & ChiefRegulatory Officer
Louis Lalande, Executive Vice-President, French Services
Suzanne Morris, Vice-President and Chief Financial Officer
Roula Zaarour, Vice-President, People and Culture

Prince Edward Island

Charlottetown

CBCT-DT *Digital Channel:* 13; 13.03 kw; 268.8 m; N46 12 44 W63 20 30
Mailing Address: 430 University Ave., Windsor, ON N9A 5K9 Canada
Second Address: P.O. Box 500, Station A, Toronto, ON M5W 1E6
(519) 255-3411, (519) 255-3411
www.cbc.ca
License: Charlottetown, PE
Group Owner: Canadian Broadcasting Corporation
Remi Racine, Chairman
Hubert T. Lacroix, President/CEO
Maryse Bertrand, VP, Real Estate, Legal Services & General Counsel
William B. Chambers, VP, Brand, Communications and Corporate Affairs
Steven Guiton, VP, Technology & ChiefRegulatory Officer
Louis Lalande, Executive Vice-President, French Services
Suzanne Morris, Vice-President and Chief Financial Officer
Roula Zaarour, Vice-President, People and Culture

Québec

Baie-Trinite

CIVF-DT *Digital Channel:* 12; 62 kw vis; 2,001t; N49 23 28 W67 28 18
1000, rue Fullum, Montreal, QC H2K 3L7 Canada

(514) 521-2424; *Fax:* (514) 873-7464
www.teleQuébec.tv
info@teleQuébec.tv
License: Baie-Trinite, QC held by Societe de telediffusion du Québec.
Group Owner: Tele-Québec
Marie Collin, President

Carleton-sur-Mer

CHAU-DT *Digital Channel:* 5; 9.85 kw; N44 08 08 W66 06 58
349, boulevard Perron, Carleton-sur-Mer, QC G0C 1J0 Canada
(418) 364-3344; *Fax:* (418) 364-7168
www.chau.teleinterrives.com
nousjoindre@chautva.com
License: Carleton-sur-Mer, QC held by CHAU-TV Communications lt,e.
Group Owner: Tele Inter-Rives lt,e.; (acq 1-5-01).
Nat'l Network: TVA
Foreign Language Programming
Pierre Harvey, General Manager

CIVK-DT *Digital Channel:* 15; 140 kw; 459 meters; N48 08 W66 06 58
436, boul Perron, Carleton-sur-Mer, QC G0C 1J0 Canada
(418) 364-7025; *Fax:* (418) 364-7641
www.teleQuébec.tv
info@teleQuébec.tv
License: Carleton-sur-Mer, QC held by Societe de telediffusion du Québec.
Group Owner: Tele-Québec
Marie Collin, President
Caroline Bujold, Coordinator

Chapeau

CIVP-DT *Digital Channel:* 23; 8.65 kw vis; N45 55 29 W77 04 23
1000, rue Fullum, Montreal, QC H2K 3L7 Canada
(514) 521-2424; *Fax:* (514) 864-1970
www.teleQuébec.tv
info@teleQuébec.tv
License: Chapeau, QC held by Societe de telediffusion du Québec.
Group Owner: Tele-Québec
Marie Collin, President

Gascons

CIVK-DT-1 *Digital Channel:* 32; 180 kw; 200.9 meters; N48 12 41 W64 52 14
436, boul Perron, Carleton-sur-Mer, QC G0C 1J0 Canada
(418) 364-7025; *Fax:* (418) 364-7641
www.teleQuébec.tv
info@teleQuébec.tv
License: Gascons, QC held by Societe de telediffusion du Québec.
Group Owner: Tele-Québec
Marie Collin, President
Caroline Bujold, Coordinator, Carleton-sur-Mer

Gaspe

CIVK-DT-3 *Digital Channel:* 35; 0.55 kw; 424.5 meters; N48 50 01 W64 15 24
436, boul Perron, Carleton-sur-Mer, QC G0C 1J0 Canada
(418) 364-7025; *Fax:* (418) 364-7641
www.teleQuébec.tv
info@teleQuébec.tv
License: Gaspe, QC held by Societe de telediffusion du Québec.
Group Owner: Tele-Québec
Marie Collin, President
Caroline Bujold, Coordinator, Carleton-sur-Mer

Gatineau

CFGS-DT *Digital Channel:* 34; 54.9 kw; 358 m
171-A, rue Jean-Proulx, Gatineau, QC J8Z 1W5 Canada
(819) 770-1040; *Fax:* (819) 770-0272
www.vgatineau.ca
License: Gatineau, QC held by RNC MEDIA Inc.
Group Owner: RNC MEDIA Inc.
Nat'l Network: Quatre Saisons *Nat'l Reps:* Canadian Broadcast Sales
Pierre R. Brosseau, Chairman
Raynald Briere, CEO/COO
Raynald Briere, President

CHOT-DT *Digital Channel:* 40; 46.5 kw; 358 m
171-A, rue Jean-Proulx, Gatineau, QC J8Z 1W5 Canada
(819) 770-1040; *Fax:* (819) 770-0272
www.tvagatineau.ca
License: Gatineau, QC held by RNC MEDIA Inc.
Group Owner: RNC MEDIA Inc.
Nat'l Network: TVA
Pierre R. Brosseau, Chairman
Raynald Briere, CEO/COO
Raynald Briere, President

CIVO-DT *Digital Channel:* 30; 300.2 kw; 358 meters; N45 30 09 W75 50 59
Edifice Joe-Montferrand, #7.100, 170, rue de l'Hotel-de-Ville, Gatineau, QC J8X 4C2 Canada
(819) 772-3471; *Fax:* (819) 772-3473
www.teleQuébec.tv
info@teleQuébec.tv
License: Gatineau, QC held by Societe de telediffusion du Québec.
Group Owner: Tele-Québec
Marie Collin, President
Francois Desrochers, Coordinator

Grand-Fonds

CIVB-DT-1 *Analog Hrs:* 24; *Digital Channel:* 31; 95 kw; 508 meters; N47 46 47 W70 09 08
79, rue de L'Eveche est, Rimouski, QC G5L 1X7 Canada
(418) 727-3743; *Fax:* (418) 727-3814
www.teleQuébec.tv
info@teleQuébec.tv
License: Grand-Fonds, QC held by Societe de telediffusion du Québec.
Group Owner: Tele-Québec
Marie Collin, President
Diane Dube, Coordinator

Montr,al

CBFT-DT *Digital Channel:* 19; 250 kw; 300 m; N45 30 19 W73 35 29
1400 Rene-Levesque Blvd E., Montreal, QC H2L 2M2 Canada
(514) 597-6000
www.radio-canada.ca
License: Montr,al, QC
Group Owner: Canadian Broadcasting Corporation

CBMT-DT *Digital Channel:* 21; 100 kw vis, 15 kw aur; ant 820t/167g
Mailing Address: Box 6000, Montreal, ON H3C 3A8 Canada
Second Address: PO Box 18800, Québec City, QC QC G1K
(514) 597-6000; *Fax:* (514) 597-6354
www.cbc.ca/montreal
License: Montr,al, QC held by CBC
Nat'l Network: CBC
Remi Racine, Chairman
Hubert T. Lacroix, President/CEO
Rob Renaud, General Manager
Kenny King, General Sales Mgr
Hugh Brodie, Promotions Manager
Mary-Jo Barr, English Services
Maryse Bertrand, VP, Real Estate, Legal Services &General Counsel
William B. Chambers, VP, Brand, Communications and Corporate Affairs
Steven Guiton, VP, Technology & Chief Regulatory Officer
Louis Lalande, Executive Vice-President, French Services
Suzanne Morris, Vice-President and ChiefFinancial Officer
Roula Zaarour, Vice-President, People and Culture

CFCF-DT *Digital Channel:* 12; 10.6 kw; 299.6 m
CTV Television Inc., 1205 Papineau Ave., Montreal, QC H2K 4R2 Canada
(514) 273-6311; *Fax:* (514) 273-1973
www.montreal.ctvnews.ca
License: Montr,al, QC held by Bell Media Inc.
Group Owner: Bell Media Inc.
Louis Douville, General Manager
Jed Kahane, News Director
Barry Wilson, Executive Producer

CFHD-DT *Digital Channel:* 47; 2.7 kw; 196 meters; N45 30 12 W73 35 47
9525 Avenue Christophe-Colomb, Montr,al,
(514) 312-4747
www.icitelevision.ca
License: Montr,al, QC held by 4517466 Canada Inc.

CFHD-DT *Digital Channel:* 47; 2.7 kw; 196 meters; N45 30 12 W73 35 47
9525 Avenue Christophe-Colomb, Montr,al, QC H2M 2E3 Canada
(514) 312-4747
www.icitelevision.ca
License: Montr,al, QC held by 4517466 Canada Ind.

CFJP-DT *Digital Channel:* 35; 697 kw vis, 70 kw aur; ant 900t/335g; N45 35 20 W73 35 32
85 rue St-Paul West, Montr,al, QC H2X 3V4 Canada
(514) 390-6100; *Fax:* (514) 390-6056
www.vtele.ca
License: Montr,al, QC held by V Interactions Inc.
Group Owner: Remstar Broadcasting Inc.; (acq 6-26-2008; grpsl)
Foreign Language Programming; Size of News Staff: 51; *Hours of Local News Weekly:* news progmg 12 hrs wkly
Maxime R,millard, CEO/COO
Marie Eve Berlinger, Head of Digital Content

CFTM-DT *Digital Channel:* 10; 365 kw vis, 65 kw aur; ant 325t/1,068g
1600, boul de Maisonneuve est, Montr,al, QC H2L 4P2 Canada
(514) 526-9251; *Fax:* (514) 599-5502
www.tva.canoe.com
License: Montr,al, QC held by Groupe TVA Inc.
Group Owner: Groupe TVA Inc.
Nat'l Network: TVA
Julie Tremblay, President

CFTU-DT *Analog Hrs:* 24; *Digital Channel:* 29; 910w; 196.4 meters
4750 Ave. Henri-Julien, Bureau 100, local 0058, Montr,al, QC Canada
(514) 841-2626; *Fax:* (514) 284-9363
License: Montr,al, QC held by Canal Savoir
Michel Umbriaco, President
Guy Massicotte, Operations Dir
Sylvie Godbout, General Manager

CIVM-DT *Digital Channel:* 26; 126.6 kw; 398.1 m *Population Served:* 7,000,000
1000, rue Fullum, Montr,al, QC H2K 3L7 Canada
(514) 521-2424; *Fax:* (514) 864-1979
www.teleQuébec.tv
info@teleQuébec.tv
License: Montr,al, QC held by Societe de telediffusion du Québec.
Group Owner: Tele-Québec
Size of News Staff: 25; *Hours of Local News Weekly:* news progmg 5 hrs wkly
Marie Collin, President
Veronique Labonte, Coordinator

CJNT-DT *Digital Channel:* 49; 11 kw vis
1200, McGill College Ave., 8th Fl., Montr,al, QC H3B 4G7 Canada
(416) 764-3003
www.citytv.com
License: Montr,al, QC held by Rogers Broadcasting Ltd.
Group Owner: Rogers Broadcasting Ltd.
Hours of Local News Weekly: news progmg 17 hrs wkly
Guy Laurence, President

CKMI-DT-1 *Digital Channel:* 15; 8 kw; 298 m
1010 St. Catherine St. W., Montr,al, QC H3B 5L1 Canada
(514) 521-4323; *Fax:* (514) 590-4060
www.globalnews.ca
License: Montr,al, QC held by Global Television Network
Group Owner: Corus Entertainment Inc.
Hours of Local News Weekly: news progmg 25 hrs wkly
Suzanne Lapalme, Regional Sales Director
Karen MacDonald, News Director

Perce

CIVK-DT-2 *Digital Channel:* 40; 0.6 kw; 405.4 meters; N48 31 38 W64 14 37
436, boul Perron, Carleton-sur-Mer, QC G0C 1J0 Canada
(418) 364-7025; *Fax:* (418) 364-7641
www.teleQuébec.tv
info@teleQuébec.tv
License: Perce, QC held by Societe de telediffusion du Québec.
Group Owner: Tele-Québec
Marie Collin, President
Caroline Bujold, Coordinator, Carleton-sur-Mer

Québec

CIVQ-DT *Digital Channel:* 15; 1,298 kw vis, 259 kw aur; 628t/576g; N46 48 27 W71 13 02
270, Chemin Sainte-Foy, Québec, QC G1R 1T3 Canada
(418) 643-5303; *Fax:* (418) 646-1233
www.teleQuébec.tv
info@teleQuébec.tv

License: Québec, QC held by Societe de telediffusion du Québec.
Group Owner: Tele-Québec
Marie Collin, President
Marie-Claude Paradis, Coordinator

Québec City

CBVT-DT *Digital Channel:* 25; 126.1 kw; 515.4 m
Mailing Address: P.O. Box 500, Station A, Toronto, ON M5W 1E6 Canada
Second Address: PO BOX 4600, Vancouver, BC V6B 4A2
(866) 306-4636; *Fax:* (866) 220-6045
www.cbc.ca
License: Québec City, QC held by CBC
Nat'l Network: Radio Canada
Remi Racine, Chairman
Hubert T. Lacroix, President/CEO
Louise Cordeau, General Manager
Maryse Bertrand, VP, Real Estate, Legal Services & General Counsel
William B. Chambers, VP, Brand, Communications and Corporate Affairs
StevenGuiton, VP, Technology & Chief Regulatory Officer
Louis Lalande, Executive Vice-President, French Services
Suzanne Morris, Vice-President and Chief Financial Officer
Roula Zaarour, Vice-President, People and Culture

CFAP-DT *Digital Channel:* 39; 98 kw; N46 48 27 W71 13 02
330 St-Vallier Est., Bureau 335, Qu,bec, QC G1K 9C5 Canada
(418) 624-2222; *Fax:* (418) 624-8930
www.vtele.ca
License: Québec City, QC held by V Interactions Inc.
Group Owner: Remstar Broadcasting Inc.; (acq 6-26-2008; grpsl)
Nat'l Network: Quatre Saisons
Foreign Language Programming; Size of News Staff: 29; *Hours of Local News Weekly:* news progmg 10 hrs wkly
Renaud Francoeur, General Manager
Joel Godin, General Sales Mgr
Denise Delisle, Engineering Manager
Pierre Martineau, Public Affairs Director

CFCM-DT *Digital Channel:* 17; 12.5 kw; 384t
1000, av Myrand, Québec City, QC G1V 2W3 Canada
(418) 688-9330; *Fax:* (418) 688-0413
www.tva.canoe.ca
administrationQuébec@tva.ca
License: Québec City, QC held by Groupe TVA Inc.
Group Owner: Groupe TVA Inc.
Hours of Local News Weekly: news progmg 5 hrs wkly
Nathalie Langevin, General Manager
Nathalie Langevin, Director of Sales
Robert Plouffe, News Director

Rimouski

CFER-TV *Analog Channel:* 11; 325 kw vis, 32.5 kw aur; 1,420t/289g
465, boul Sainte-Anne, Rimouski, QC G5M 1G1 Canada
(418) 722-6011; *Fax:* (418) 724-7810, (418) 723-0857
www.tva.canoe.com
License: Rimouski, QC held by Groupe TVA Inc.
Group Owner: Groupe TVA Inc.
Nat'l Network: TVA
Claude Auger, General Manager
Michel Nadeau, News Director

CIVB-DT *Analog Hrs:* 24; *Digital Channel:* 22; 136 kw; 460.5 meters; N48 28 02 W68 12 53
79, rue de L'Eveche est, Rimouski, QC G5L 1X7 Canada
(418) 727-3743; *Fax:* (418) 727-3814
www.teleQuébec.tv
info@teleQuébec.tv
License: Rimouski, QC held by Societe de telediffusion du Québec.
Group Owner: Tele-Québec
Marie Collin, President
Diane Dube, Coordinator

CJBR-DT *Digital Channel:* 45; 110.22 kw; 283.4 m
Mailing Address: 273 St. Jeans Baptiste W., Rimouski, QC G5L 4J8 Canada
Second Address: PO Box 6000, Stn. Downtown, Montreal, QC H3C 3A8
(418) 723-2217,(418) 723-4730; *Fax:* (418) 743-6126
www.radio-canada.ca
License: Rimouski, QC held by CBC
Nat'l Network: CBC
R,mi Racine, Chairman
Hubert T. Lacroix, President/CEO
Bernard Lepage, General Manager
Maryse Bertrand, Vice-President, Real Estate, Legal Services and Ge
William B. Chambers, Vice-President, Brand, Communications and Corporat
Steven Guiton, Vice-President Technology and Chief Regulatory Off
Louis Lalande, Executive Vice-President
Suzanne Morris, Vice-President and Chief Financial Officer
Roula Zaarour, Vice-President, People and Culture

Rivi,re-du-Loup

CFTF-DT *Digital Channel:* 29; 44 kw vis; ant 1,086t; N47 35 03 W69 22 08 *Population Served:* 600,000
103 rue des ▯quipements, Rivi,res-du-Loup, QC G5R 5W7 Canada
(418) 862-2909; *Fax:* (418) 862-8147
nouvelles@cftf.ca
License: Rivi,re-du-Loup, QC held by Television MBS Inc.
Group Owner: Tele Inter-Rives Ltee.
Foreign Language Programming
Marc Simard, President
Michel Belanger, Operations Dir
Catherine Simard, General Manager
Nancy Fortin, Promotions Vice President
Yves Belanger, Sales Director
Ginette Dumant, VP, Sales

RiviŠre-du-Loup

CIMT-DT *Digital Channel:* 9; 27.5 kw, 2.7 kw aur; ant 1,178t/200g; N47 35 03 W69 22 08
15, rue de la Chute, RiviŠre-du-Loup, QC G5R 5B7 Canada
(418) 867-1341; *Fax:* (418) 867-4710
www.cimt.teleinterrives.com
nousjoindre@cimt.ca
License: RiviŠre-du-Loup, QC held by Tele Inter-Rives Ltee.
Group Owner: Tele Inter-Rives Ltee.
Nat'l Network: TVA
Foreign Language Programming
Marc Simard, General Manager

CKRT-DT *Digital Channel:* 7; 7 kw; 345.1 meters; N47 35 03 W69 22 10
15 rue de la Chute, RiviŠre-du-Loup, QC G5R 5B7 Canada
(418) 867-1341; *Fax:* (418) 867-4710
www.cimt.teleinterrives.com
License: RiviŠre-du-Loup, QC held by CKRT-TV lt,e.
Group Owner: Tele Inter-Rives lt,e.
Nat'l Network: Radio Canada
Foreign Language Programming
Marc Simard, General Manager

Rouyn-Noranda

CFEM-DT *Digital Channel:* 13; 22 kw; 219.6 m
380, rue Murdoch, Rouyn-Noranda, QC J9X 1G5 Canada
(819) 762-0741; *Fax:* (819) 762-6331
www.tvaabitibi.ca
License: Rouyn-Noranda, QC held by RNC MEDIA Inc.
Group Owner: RNC MEDIA Inc.
Pierre R. Brosseau, Chairman
Raynald Briere, CEO/COO
Raynald Briere, President
Nancy Deschenes, General Manager

CIVA-DT-1 *Digital Channel:* 8; 19 kw; 219.6 meters; N48 15 52 W79 02 38
#201, 689, 3e av, Val d'Or, QC J9P 1S7 Canada
(819) 874-5132; *Fax:* (819) 824-2431
www.teleQuébec.tv
info@teleQuébec.tv
License: Rouyn-Noranda, QC held by Societe de telediffusion du Québec.
Group Owner: Tele-Québec
Marie Collin, President
Josee Lacoste, Coordinator, Val d'Or

CKRN-DT *Digital Channel:* 9; 9.096 kw; 219.6 m
380, rue Murdoch, Rouyn-Noranda, QC J9X 1G5 Canada
(819) 762-0741; *Fax:* (819) 762-6331
www.tvaabitibi.ca
License: Rouyn-Noranda, QC held by RNC MEDIA Inc.
Group Owner: RNC MEDIA Inc.
Nat'l Network: Radio Canada
Pierre R. Brosseau, Chairman
Raynald Briere, CEO/COO
Raynald Briere, President
Nancy Deschenes, General Manager

Saguenay

CFRS-DT *Digital Channel:* 13; 4.344 kw; 593.8 m
Population Served: 300,000
2303 rue Sir Wilfred Laurier, JonquiŠre, QC G7X 5Z2 Canada
(418) 542-4551; *Fax:* (418) 542-7217
www.vtele.ca
License: Saguenay, QC held by V Interactions Inc.
Group Owner: Remstar Broadcasting Inc.; (acq 6-26-2008; grpsl)
Nat'l Network: Quatre Saisons
Foreign Language Programming
Maxime R,millard, CEO/COO

CIVV-DT *Digital Channel:* 8; 84.9 kw; 593.8 meters; N48 36 04 W70 49 46
3788, rue de la Fabrique, Pavillon Joseph-Angers, Saguenay, QC G7X 3P4 Canada
(418) 695-8152; *Fax:* (418) 695-8155
www.teleQuébec.tv
info@teleQuébec.tv
License: Saguenay, QC held by Societe de telediffusion du Québec.
Group Owner: Tele-Québec
Nat'l Network: TeleFutura (Spanish)
Marie Collin, President
Jocelyn Robert, Coordinator

CJPM-DT *Digital Channel:* 46; 89.3 kw; 107.4 m
1, rue Mont Ste-Claire, Chicoutimi, QC G7H 5G3 Canada
(418) 549-2576; *Fax:* (418) 549-1130
www.tva.canoe.ca
License: Saguenay, QC held by Groupe TVA Inc.
Group Owner: Groupe TVA Inc.
Nat'l Network: TVA
Hours of Local News Weekly: News progmg 6 hrs wkly
Myriam Donaldson, News Director
Martine Lafleur, Sales Coordinator
Lucie Gagnon, Sales Coordinator

CKTV-DT *Digital Channel:* 12; 3.1 kw; 581.1 m
500 rue des Sagueneens, Chicoutimi, QC G7H 6N4 Canada
(418) 696-6600; *Fax:* (418) 696-6689
www.radio-canada.ca/saguenay-lac-saint-jean
License: Saguenay, QC
Nat'l Network: Radio Canada

Sept-Iles

CIVG-DT *Analog Hrs:* 16; *Digital Channel:* 9; 246 kw vis, 49.2 kw aur; 943t/500g
410, rue Evangeline, Sept-Iles, QC G4R 2N5 Canada
(418) 964-8240; *Fax:* (418) 964-8923
www.teleQuébec.tv
info@teleQuébec.tv
License: Sept-Iles, QC held by Societe de telediffusion du Québec.
Group Owner: Tele-Québec
Marie Collin, President
Virginie Lamontagne, Coordinator

Sherbrooke

CFKS-DT *Digital Channel:* 30; 4.63 kw; 591.19 m; N45 18 43 W72 14 32
3720 Industrial Blvd., Sherbrooke, QC J1L 1Z9 Canada
(819) 565-9232; *Fax:* (819) 822-4205
www.vtele.ca
License: Sherbrooke, QC held by V Interactions Inc.
Group Owner: Remstar Broadcasting Inc.; (acq 6-26-2008; grpsl)
Foreign Language Programming
Maxime R,millard, CEO/COO

CHLT-DT *Digital Channel:* 7; 2.369 kw; 588.1 m
3330, rue King ouest, Sherbrooke, QC J1L 1C9 Canada
(819) 565-7777; *Fax:* (819) 565-4650
www.tva.canoe.ca
License: Sherbrooke, QC held by Groupe TVA Inc.
Group Owner: Groupe TVA Inc.; (acq 7-9-90).
Nat'l Network: TVA
Sarah Beaulieu, General Manager
Bernard Couture, Promotions Manager
Michel Gagnon, News Director

CIVS-DT *Digital Channel:* 24; 475 kw vis, 47.5 kw aur; 2,000t/90g
#1000, 3330, rue King ouest, Sherbrooke, QC J1L 1C9 Canada
(819) 820-3436; *Fax:* (819(820-3449
www.teleQuébec.tv
info@teleQuébec.tv
License: Sherbrooke, QC held by Societe de telediffusion du Québec.
Group Owner: Tele-Québec

Marie Collin, President
Pascal-Gilles Gervais, Coordinator

CKSH-DT *Digital Channel:* 9; 11.16 kw
Mailing Address: 1335 King St. W., Sherbrooke, QC J1J 2B8 Canada
Second Address: 1400, boul., Rene-Levesque, Montreal, QC H2L 2M2
(819) 620-0000; *Fax:* (819) 348-1326
www.radio-canada.ca
License: Sherbrooke, QC held by Canadian Broadcasting Corp.
Nat'l Network: Radio Canada
R,mi Racine, Chairman
Hubert T. Lacroix, President/CEO
Stephane Laberge, General Manager
Maryse Bertrand, Vice-President, Real Estate, Legal Services and Ge
William B. Chambers, Vice-President, Brand, Communications and Corporat
Steven Guiton, Vice-President Technology and Chief Regulatory Off
Louis Lalande, Executive Vice-President
Suzanne Morris, Vice-President and Chief Financial Officer
Roula Zaarour, Vice-President, People and Culture

Trois Rivieres

CFKM-DT *Digital Channel:* 34; 9.4 kw; ant 1,073t/1,071g; N46 29 27 W72 39 00
926 Notre Dame Center, Trois-Rivieres, QC G9A 4W8 Canada
(819) 377-6053; *Fax:* (819) 377-5442
www.vtele.ca
License: Trois Rivieres, QC held by V Interactions Inc.
Group Owner: Remstar Broadcasting Inc.; (acq 6-26-2008; grpsl)
Nat'l Network: Quatre Saisons
Foreign Language Programming
Maxime R,millard, CEO/COO

CIVC-DT *Analog Hrs:* 16; *Digital Channel:* 45; 290 kw; 398.1 meters; N46 29 27 W72 39 00
100, rue Laviolette, RC 20, Trois Rivieres, QC G9A 5S9 Canada
(819) 371-6752; *Fax:* (819) 371-6684
www.teleQuébec.tv
info@teleQuébec.tv
License: Trois Rivieres, QC held by Societe de telediffusion du Québec.
Group Owner: Tele-Québec
Marie Collin, President
Marie-Josee Desjardins, Coordinator

CKTM-DT *Digital Channel:* 28; 164.4 kw vis, 65 kw aur; ant 1,660t/1,085g; N46 29 27 W72 39 00
4141 boul.St-Jean, Trois-Rivieres, QC G9B 2M8 Canada
(819) 377-4413; *Fax:* (819) 377-5239
License: Trois Rivieres, QC held by Canadian Broadcasting Corp.
Nat'l Network: CBC
Hubert Lacroix, President

Trois-Rivieres

CHEM-DT *Digital Channel:* 8; 325 kw vis, 32.5 kw aur; 946t/698g
C.P. 170, Succursale C, Montr,al, QC H2L 4P6 Canada
(514) 598-2869; *Fax:* (514) 598-6073
www.tvanouvelles.ca
License: Trois-Rivieres, QC held by Groupe TVA Inc.
Group Owner: Groupe TVA Inc.; (acq 7-9-90).
Nat'l Network: TVA
Julie Tremblay, President

Val d'Or

CIVA-DT *Digital Channel:* 12; 22 kw; 201.1 meters; N48 25 17 W77 50 49
#201, 689, 3e av, Val d'Or, QC J9P 1S7 Canada
(819) 874-5132; *Fax:* (819) 824-2431
www.teleQuébec.tv
info@teleQuébec.tv
License: Val d'Or, QC held by Societe de telediffusion du Québec.
Group Owner: Tele-Québec
Marie Collin, President
Josee Lacoste, Coordinator

Val-d'Or

CFVS-DT *Digital Channel:* 15; 133.3 kw; 182.9 m
380, rue Murdoch, Rouyn-Noranda, QC J9X 1G5 Canada
(819) 762-0741; *Fax:* (819) 762-6331
www.vabitibi.ca
nouvelles@rncmedia.ca
License: Val-d'Or, QC held by RNC MEDIA INC.
Group Owner: RNC MEDIA Inc.
Pierre R. Brosseau, Chairman
Raynald Briere, CEO/COO
Raynald Briere, President
Nancy Deschenes, General Manager

Saskatchewan

Prince Albert

CIPA-TV *Analog Channel:* 9 *Analog Hrs:* 24; 325 kw vis, 32.5 kw aur; 711t/460g
216 First Ave. N., Saskatoon, SK S7K 3W3 Canada
(306) 665-8600; *Fax:* (306) 665-0450
www.saskatoon.ctvnews.ca
cfqcnews@ctv.ca
License: Prince Albert, SK held by Bell Media Inc.
Group Owner: Bell Media Inc.; (acq 8-1-86).
Nat'l Network: CTV
Size of News Staff: 5
David Fisher, General Manager
Teena Monteleone, News Director

Regina

CBKFT-DT *Digital Channel:* 13; 27.1 kw; 183.7 m; N50 28 58 W104 30 20
Mailing Address: PO Box 3220, Station C, Ottawa, ON K1Y 1E4 Canada
Second Address: PO Box 6000, Station Centre Ville, Montreal, QC H3C 3A8
(514) 597-6000, (866) 306-4636; *Fax:* (306) 347-9493
www.cbc.radio-canada.ca
License: Regina, SK held by Canadian Broadcasting Corporation
Group Owner: Canadian Broadcasting Corporaton
Remi Racine, Chairman
Hubert T. Lacroix, President/CEO
Maryse Bertrand, VP, Real Estate, Legal Services & General Counsel
William B. Chambers, VP, Brand, Communications and Corporate Affairs
Steven Guiton, VP, Technology & ChiefRegulatory Officer
Louis Lalande, Executive Vice-President, French Services
Suzanne Morris, Vice-President and Chief Financial Officer
Roula Zaarour, Vice-President, People and Culture

CBKT-DT *Digital Channel:* 9; 33.6 kw; 207.2 m
Mailing Address: Box 540, Regina, SK S4P 4A1 Canada
Second Address: 2440 Broad Street, Regina, SK S4P 4A1
(306) 347-9540; *Fax:* (306) 347-9616
www.cbc.ca/sask
SaskNews@cbc.ca
License: Regina, SK held by CBC
Nat'l Network: CBC
Remi Racine, Chairman
Hubert T. Lacroix, President/CEO
Jill Spelliscy, General Manager
Jason Perring, General Sales Mgr
Shawna Kelly, Promotions Manager
Bob Rankin, News Director
Maryse Bertrand, VP, Real Estate, Legal Services &General Counsel
William B. Chambers, VP, Brand, Communications and Corporate Affairs
Steven Guiton, VP, Technology & Chief Regulatory Officer
Louis Lalande, Executive Vice-President, French Services
Suzanne Morris, Vice-President and ChiefFinancial Officer
Roula Zaarour, Vice-President, People and Culture

CFRE-DT *Analog Channel:* 11; *Digital Channel:* 11; 146 kw vis; 984t *Population Served:* 320,000
370 Hoffer Dr., Regina, SK S4N 7A4 Canada
(306) 775-4000; *Fax:* (306) 721-4817
www.globalnews.ca
mitch.bozak@corusent.com
License: Regina, SK held by Global Television Network
Group Owner: Corus Entertainment Inc.
Size of News Staff: 16; *Hours of Local News Weekly:* news progmg 24.5 hrs wkly
Mitch Bozak, Station and Sales Manager
Lyndon Bray, Promotions Manager
Michael Fulmes, News Director
Rob Crone, Marketing Consultant

CKCK-DT *Digital Channel:* 8; 23 kw vis, 10 kw aur; 588t/670g; N50 26 52 W104 30 00
#1 Highway E., Box 2000, Regina, SK S4P 3E5 Canada
(306) 569-2000; *Fax:* (306) 522-0090
www.regina.ctvnews.ca
ckck@ctv.ca
License: Regina, SK held by Bell Media Inc.
Group Owner: Bell Media Inc.
Nat'l Network: CTV
Hours of Local News Weekly: 15.5 hrs local news wkly
Dennis Dunlop, General Manager
Teena Monteleone, News Director

Saskatoon

CFQC-DT *Digital Channel:* 8; 8 kw; 267.9 m; N52 07 51 W106 39 49 *Population Served:* 333,400
216 First Ave. N., Saskatoon, SK S7K 3W3 Canada
(306)665-8600; *Fax:* (306)665-0450
www.saskatoon.ctvnews.ca
cfqcnews@ctv.ca
License: Saskatoon, SK held by Bell Media Inc.
Group Owner: Bell Media Inc.; (acq 1972).
Nat'l Network: CTV
David Fisher, General Manager
Teena Monteleone, News Director
Dale Leibrecht, Chief Engineer
Geoff Bradley, Promotions Manager

CFSK-DT *Analog Channel:* 4; *Digital Channel:* 42; 54 kw vis, 5.4 kw aur; 455t/219g *Population Served:* 290,000
218 Robin Cres., Saskatoon, SK S7L 7C3 Canada
(306) 665-6969; *Fax:* (306) 665-6069
www.globalnews.ca
License: Saskatoon, SK held by Global Television Network
Group Owner: Corus Entertainment Inc.
Nat'l Network: Global
Size of News Staff: 17; *Hours of Local News Weekly:* news progmg 24.5 hrs wkly
Lisa Ford, Station Manager and News Director
Mitch Bozak, General Sales Mgr
Meagan Laycock, Promotions Manager
Charlene Priel, Marketing Consultant
Doug Lett, Morning News Producer

Yorkton

CICC-TV *Analog Channel:* 10 *Analog Hrs:* 24; 56 kw vis, 18 kw aur
#1 Highway East, Box 2000, Regina, SK S4P 3E5 Canada
(306) 569-2000; *Fax:* (306) 782-7212, (306) 522-0090
www.regina.ctvnews.ca
License: Yorkton, SK held by Bell Media Inc.
Group Owner: Bell Media Inc.
Nat'l Network: CTV
Darrell Romuld, Reporter

Canadian Television Stations by Call Letters

CBAFT-DT Moncton, New Brunswick
CBAT-DT Fredericton, New Brunswick
CBCT-DT Charlottetown, Prince Edward Island
CBET-DT Windsor, Ontario
CBFT-DT Montréal, Québec
CBHT-DT Halifax, Nova Scotia
CBKFT-DT Regina, Saskatchewan
CBKT-DT Regina, Saskatchewan
CBLFT-DT Toronto, Ontario
CBLT-DT Toronto, Ontario
CBMT-DT Montréal, Québec
CBNT-DT Saint John's, Newfoundland
CBOFT-DT Ottawa, Ontario
CBOT-DT Ottawa, Ontario
CBRT-DT Calgary, Alberta
CBUFT-DT Vancouver, British Columbia
CBUT-DT Vancouver, British Columbia
CBVT-DT Québec City, Québec
CBWFT-DT Winnipeg, Manitoba
CBWT-DT Winnipeg, Manitoba
CBWYT Mafeking, Manitoba
CBXFT-DT Edmonton, Alberta
CBXT-DT Edmonton, Alberta
CFAP-DT Québec City, Québec
CFCF-DT Montréal, Québec
CFCM-DT Québec City, Québec
CFCN-DT Calgary, Alberta
CFCN-DT-5 Lethbridge, Alberta
CFEG-TV Abbotsford, British Columbia
CFEM-DT Rouyn-Noranda, Québec
CFER-TV Rimouski, Québec
CFGS-DT Gatineau, Québec
CFHD-DT Montréal, Québec
CFHD-DT Montréal, Québec
CFJC-TV Kamloops, British Columbia
CFJP-DT Montréal, Québec
CFKM-DT Trois-Rivières, Québec
CFKS-DT Sherbrooke, Québec
CFMT-DT Toronto, Ontario
CFQC-DT Saskatoon, Saskatchewan
CFRE-DT Regina, Saskatchewan
CFRN-DT Edmonton, Alberta
CFRN-TV-6 Red Deer, Alberta
CFRS-DT Saguenay, Québec
CFSK-DT Saskatoon, Saskatchewan
CFSO-TV Cardston, Alberta
CFTF-DT Rivière-du-Loup, Québec
CFTM-DT Montréal, Québec
CFTO-DT Toronto, Ontario
CFTU-DT Montréal, Québec
CFTV-DT Leamington, Ontario
CFVS-DT Val-d'Or, Québec
CFYK-DT Yellowknife, Northwest Territories
CHAN-DT Vancouver, British Columbia
CHAT-TV Medicine Hat, Alberta
CHAU-DT Carleton-sur-Mer, Québec
CHBC-DT Kelowna, British Columbia
CHBX-TV Sault Ste. Marie, Ontario
CHCH-DT Hamilton, Ontario
CHEK-DT Victoria, British Columbia
CHEM-DT Trois-Rivieres, Québec
CHEX-DT Peterborough, Ontario
CHEX-TV-2 Oshawa, Ontario
CHFD-DT Thunder Bay, Ontario
CHLT-DT Sherbrooke, Québec
CHMI-DT Portage la Prairie, Manitoba
CHNB-DT Saint John, New Brunswick
CHNM-DT Vancouver, British Columbia
CHNU-DT Fraser Valley, British Columbia
CHNU-DT Fraser Valley, Manitoba
CHOT-DT Gatineau, Québec
CHRO-DT-43 Ottawa, Ontario
CHRO-TV Pembroke, Ontario
CHVC-TV Valemount, British Columbia
CHWI-DT Wheatley, Ontario
CICA-TV Toronto, Ontario
CICC-TV Yorkton, Saskatchewan
CICI-TV Sudbury, Ontario
CICT-DT Calgary, Alberta
CIHF-DT Halifax, Nova Scotia
CIII-DT Toronto, Ontario
CIIT-DT Winnipeg, Manitoba
CIMC-TV Isle Madame, Nova Scotia
CIMT-DT Rivière-du-Loup, Québec
CIPA-TV Prince Albert, Saskatchewan
CISA-DT Lethbridge, Alberta
CITL-DT Lloydminster, Alberta
CITO-TV Timmins, Ontario
CITS-TV Hamilton, Ontario
CITV-DT Edmonton, Alberta
CITY-DT Toronto, Ontario
CIVA-DT Val d'Or, Québec
CIVA-DT-1 Rouyn-Noranda, Québec
CIVB-DT Rimouski, Québec
CIVB-DT-1 Grand-Fonds, Québec
CIVC-DT Trois-Rivières, Québec
CIVF-DT Baie-Trinite, Québec
CIVG-DT Sept-Îles, Québec
CIVI-DT Victoria, British Columbia
CIVK-DT Carleton-sur-Mer, Québec
CIVK-DT-1 Gascons, Québec
CIVK-DT-2 Perce, Québec
CIVK-DT-3 Gaspe, Québec
CIVM-DT Montréal, Québec
CIVO-DT Gatineau, Québec
CIVP-DT Chapeau, Québec
CIVQ-DT Québec, Québec
CIVS-DT Sherbrooke, Québec
CIVT-DT Vancouver, British Columbia
CIVV-DT Saguenay, Québec
CJBN-TV Kenora, Ontario
CJBR-DT Rimouski, Québec
CJCB-TV Halifax, Nova Scotia
CJCH-DT Halifax, Nova Scotia
CJCO-DT Calgary, Alberta
CJDC-TV Dawson Creek, British Columbia
CJEO-DT Edmonton, Alberta
CJIL-DT Lethbridge, Alberta
CJMT-DT Toronto, Ontario
CJNT-DT Montréal, Québec
CJOH-DT Ottawa, Ontario
CJON-DT St. John's, Newfoundland
CJPM-DT Saguenay, Québec
CKAL-DT Calgary, Alberta
CKCK-DT Regina, Saskatchewan
CKCO-DT Kitchener, Ontario
CKCS-TV Calgary, Alberta
CKCW-DT Moncton, New Brunswick
CKEM-DT Edmonton, Alberta
CKES-TV Edmonton, Alberta
CKLT-DT Saint John, New Brunswick
CKMI-DT-1 Montréal, Québec
CKND-DT Winnipeg, Manitoba
CKNY-TV North Bay, Ontario
CKPG-TV Prince George, British Columbia
CKPR-DT Thunder Bay, Ontario
CKRN-DT Rouyn-Noranda, Québec
CKRT-DT Rivière-du-Loup, Québec
CKSA-DT Lloydminster, Alberta
CKSH-DT Sherbrooke, Québec
CKTM-DT Trois-Rivières, Québec
CKTV-DT Saguenay, Québec
CKVR-DT Barrie, Ontario
CKVU-DT Vancouver, British Columbia
CKWS-DT Kingston, Ontario
CKWS-DT-1 Brighton, Ontario
CKX-TV Brandon, Manitoba
CKY-DT Winnipeg, Manitoba
CTV London, Ontario

Canadian Television Stations by Analog Channel

Channel 2

CBUT-DT Vancouver, British Columbia
CBWYT Mafeking, Manitoba
CHBX-TV Sault Ste. Marie, Ontario
CKPG-TV Prince George, British Columbia

Channel 3

CBHT-DT Halifax, Nova Scotia
CBWFT-DT Winnipeg, Manitoba
CITO-TV Timmins, Ontario

Channel 4

CBAT-DT Fredericton, New Brunswick
CFJC-TV Kamloops, British Columbia
CFSK-DT Saskatoon, Saskatchewan
CJCB-TV Halifax, Nova Scotia

Channel 5

CBXT-DT Edmonton, Alberta
CHRO-TV Pembroke, Ontario
CICI-TV Sudbury, Ontario
CJDC-TV Dawson Creek, British Columbia
CKAL-DT Calgary, Alberta
CKX-TV Brandon, Manitoba

Channel 6

CBWT-DT Winnipeg, Manitoba
CHAT-TV Medicine Hat, Alberta

Channel 7

CHVC-TV Valemount, British Columbia

Channel 8

CBNT-DT Saint John's, Newfoundland
CFRN-TV-6 Red Deer, Alberta
CFYK-DT Yellowknife, Northwest Territories

Channel 9

CBRT-DT Calgary, Alberta
CIPA-TV Prince Albert, Saskatchewan
CIVT-DT Vancouver, British Columbia

Channel 10

CICC-TV Yorkton, Saskatchewan
CIMC-TV Isle Madame, Nova Scotia
CKNY-TV North Bay, Ontario
CKVU-DT Vancouver, British Columbia

Channel 11

CBAFT-DT Moncton, New Brunswick
CBXFT-DT Edmonton, Alberta
CFER-TV Rimouski, Québec
CFRE-DT Regina, Saskatchewan
CKWS-DT-1 Brighton, Ontario

Channel 13

CHMI-DT Portage la Prairie, Manitoba
CJOH-DT Ottawa, Ontario

Channel 22

CHEX-TV-2 Oshawa, Ontario

Channel 26

CBUFT-DT Vancouver, British Columbia

Channel 32

CFSO-TV Cardston, Alberta
CKCS-TV Calgary, Alberta

Channel 38

CJCO-DT Calgary, Alberta

Channel 42

CHNM-DT Vancouver, British Columbia

Channel 45

CKES-TV Edmonton, Alberta

Channel 51

CKEM-DT Edmonton, Alberta

Channel 56

CJEO-DT Edmonton, Alberta

Canadian Television Stations by Digital Channel

Channel 2
CKPR-DT Thunder Bay, Ontario
CKSA-DT Lloydminster, Alberta

Channel 4
CHFD-DT Thunder Bay, Ontario
CITL-DT Lloydminster, Alberta
CFSO-TV Cardston, Alberta

Channel 5
CHAU-DT Carleton-sur-Mer, Québec

Channel 7
CHLT-DT Sherbrooke, Québec
CISA-DT Lethbridge, Alberta
CKRT-DT Rivière-du-Loup, Québec
CKY-DT Winnipeg, Manitoba

Channel 8
CBNT-DT Saint John's, Newfoundland
CFQC-DT Saskatoon, Saskatchewan
CFYK-DT Yellowknife, Northwest Territories
CHEM-DT Trois-Rivières, Québec
CIVV-DT Saguenay, Québec
CKCK-DT Regina, Saskatchewan
CIHF-DT Halifax, Nova Scotia
CIVA-DT-1 Rouyn-Noranda, Québec

Channel 9
CBKT-DT Regina, Saskatchewan
CFTO-DT Toronto, Ontario
CIMT-DT Rivière-du-Loup, Québec
CIVG-DT Sept-Îles, Québec
CKLT-DT Saint John, New Brunswick
CKRN-DT Rouyn-Noranda, Québec
CKSH-DT Sherbrooke, Québec
CBET-DT Windsor, Ontario

Channel 10
CTV London, Ontario
CFTM-DT Montréal, Québec
CKVR-DT Barrie, Ontario

Channel 11
CFRE-DT Regina, Saskatchewan
CHCH-DT Hamilton, Ontario
CKWS-DT Kingston, Ontario
CBAFT-DT Moncton, New Brunswick

Channel 12
CFCF-DT Montreal, Québec
CFRN-DT Edmonton, Alberta
CHEX-DT Peterborough, Ontario
CIVF-DT Baie-Trinite, Québec
CKTV-DT Saguenay, Québec
CHNB-DT Saint John, New Brunswick
CIVA-DT Val d'Or, Québec

Channel 13
CFCN-DT-5 Lethbridge, Alberta
CFRS-DT Saguenay, Québec
CHMI-DT Portage la Prairie, Manitoba
CITV-DT Edmonton, Alberta
CJBN-TV Kenora, Ontario
CKCO-DT Kitchener, Ontario
CBCT-DT Charlottetown, Prince Edward Island
CBKFT-DT Regina, Saskatchewan
CFEM-DT Rouyn-Noranda, Québec

Channel 15
CFVS-DT Val-d'Or, Québec
CIVQ-DT Québec, Québec
CKMI-DT-1 Montréal, Québec
CIVK-DT Carleton-sur-Mer, Québec

Channel 16
CHWI-DT Wheatley, Ontario

Channel 17
CFCM-DT Québec City, Québec
CJIL-DT Lethbridge, Alberta
CKEM-DT Edmonton, Alberta

Channel 18
CICA-TV Toronto, Ontario

Channel 19
CFEG-TV Abbotsford, British Columbia
CBFT-DT Montréal, Québec

Channel 20
CBLT-DT Toronto, Ontario
CHNM-DT Vancouver, British Columbia

Channel 21
CBMT-DT Montréal, Québec
CJON-DT St. John's, Newfoundland
CBRT-DT Calgary, Alberta

Channel 22
CHAN-DT Vancouver, British Columbia
CIVB-DT Rimouski, Québec

Channel 23
CIVP-DT Chapeau, Québec
CIVI-DT Victoria, British Columbia

Channel 24
CIVS-DT Sherbrooke, Québec

Channel 25
CBOT-DT Ottawa, Ontario
CBVT-DT Québec City, Québec
CBLFT-DT Toronto, Ontario

Channel 26
CIVM-DT Montréal, Québec
CBUFT-DT Vancouver, British Columbia

Channel 27
CBWT-DT Winnipeg, Manitoba
CHBC-DT Kelowna, British Columbia

Channel 28
CKTM-DT Trois-Rivières, Québec

Channel 29
CFCN-DT Calgary, Alberta
CFTU-DT Montréal, Québec
CKCW-DT Moncton, New Brunswick
CFTF-DT Rivière-du-Loup, Québec

Channel 30
CFKS-DT Sherbrooke, Québec
CKES-TV Edmonton, Alberta
CKWS-DT-1 Brighton, Ontario
CIVO-DT Gatineau, Québec

Channel 31
CJDC-TV Dawson Creek, British Columbia
CBAT-DT Fredericton, New Brunswick
CIVB-DT-1 Grand-Fonds, Québec

Channel 32
CIVT-DT Vancouver, British Columbia
CHVC-TV Valemount, British Columbia
CIVK-DT-1 Gascons, Québec

Channel 33
CBOFT-DT Ottawa, Ontario
CKVU-DT Vancouver, British Columbia

Channel 34
CFGS-DT Gatineau, Québec
CFKM-DT Trois-Rivières, Québec
CFTV-DT Leamington, Ontario

Channel 35
CFJP-DT Montréal, Québec
CIIT-DT Winnipeg, Manitoba
CIVK-DT-3 Gaspe, Québec

Channel 36
CITS-TV Hamilton, Ontario

Channel 38
CJCO-DT Calgary, Alberta

Channel 39
CFAP-DT Québec City, Québec
CBHT-DT Halifax, Nova Scotia

Channel 40
CHOT-DT Gatineau, Québec
CKND-DT Winnipeg, Manitoba
CJMT-DT Toronto, Ontario
CIVK-DT-2 Perce, Québec

Channel 41
CICT-DT Calgary, Alberta
CIII-DT Toronto, Ontario

Channel 42
CFSK-DT Saskatoon, Saskatchewan
CBXT-DT Edmonton, Alberta

Channel 43
CHRO-DT-43 Ottawa, Ontario
CBUT-DT Vancouver, British Columbia

Channel 44
CITY-DT Toronto, Ontario
CJEO-DT Edmonton, Alberta
CHNU-DT Fraser Valley, Manitoba

Channel 45
CIVC-DT Trois-Rivières, Québec
CJBR-DT Rimouski, Québec

Channel 46
CJPM-DT Saguenay, Québec

Channel 47
CFMT-DT Toronto, Ontario
CHNU-DT Fraser Valley, British Columbia
CFHD-DT Montréal, Québec
CFHD-DT Montréal, Québec
CBXFT-DT Edmonton, Alberta

Channel 48
CJCH-DT Halifax, Nova Scotia

Channel 49
CHEK-DT Victoria, British Columbia
CJNT-DT Montréal, Québec
CKAL-DT Calgary, Alberta

Channel 51
CBWFT-DT Winnipeg, Manitoba

Channel 63
CIMC-TV Isle Madame, Nova Scotia

As with television, the largest markets for radio are urban centers. And as with television, audience measurement is used by stations to set advertising rates and by advertisers to plan campaigns.

Of the nearly 600 markets identified by Nielsen Audio, New York, Los Angeles, Chicago, San Francisco, Dallas-Ft. Worth, Houston-Galveston, Washington, DC, Atlanta, Philadelphia and Boston make up the top ten.[1]

These metropolitan areas have a combined population (age 12+) of more than 70 million. The total population of the top 25 markets is 112 million, or almost 36 per cent of the total US population.

Audience estimates such as these – projections based on the latest census data – are one "currency" of radio advertising. Another is the detailed listener data provided by Nielsen's "diarykeepers" and Portable People Meter (PPM) "panelists."

Four times a year, Nielsen employs a random sample of the population to track its listening activity for a period of one week. Participants are known as diarykeepers and the information they record in paper diaries is mailed to the company for processing. Panelists, by contrast, agree to wear a PPM for a term of one to two years and the data gathering is passive rather than active.

Electronic measurement was developed by Nielsen in response to criticism of the perceived failings of the old, paper-based method. Now in use in 48 cities, the pager-sized device panelists wear gathers subaudible codes from radio broadcasts and the results are then used by advertisers and radio stations to buy and sell airtime.

[1] The Nielsen Company. *Radio Market Survey Population, Rankings & Information*, Fall 2017

Sales of Home and Clock Radios

Year	Product Category	Units (Thousands)	Dollars (Million)	Average Price
1922	Home and Clock Radios	100		
1923	Home and Clock Radios	500		
1924	Home and Clock Radios	1,500		
1925	Home and Clock Radios	2,000		
1926	Home and Clock Radios	1,750		
1927	Home and Clock Radios	2,350		
1928	Home and Clock Radios	3,281		
1929	Home and Clock Radios	4,435		
1930	Home and Clock Radios	3,793		
1931	Home and Clock Radios	3,312		
1932	Home and Clock Radios	2,477		
1933	Home and Clock Radios	3,082		
1934	Home and Clock Radios	3,304		
1935	Home and Clock Radios	4,375		
1936	Home and Clock Radios	6,746		
1937	Home and Clock Radios	6,631		
1938	Home and Clock Radios	5,823		
1939	Home and Clock Radios	8,900		
1940	Home and Clock Radios	8,900		
1941	Home and Clock Radios	9,650		
1942	Home and Clock Radios	3,400		
1943	Home and Clock Radios	589		
1946	Home and Clock Radios	12,113		
1947	Home and Clock Radios	14,972		
1948	Home and Clock Radios	10,325		
1949	Home and Clock Radios	5,127		
1950	Home and Clock Radios	9,218	$184	$20.00
1951	Home and Clock Radios	6,445	$129	$20.00
1952	Home and Clock Radios	7,232	$137	$19.00
1953	Home and Clock Radios	7,283	$138	$19.00
1954	Home and Clock Radios	6,119	$116	$19.00
1955	Home and Clock Radios	7,327	$139	$19.00
1956	Home and Clock Radios	8,951	$170	$19.00
1957	Home and Clock Radios	9,952	$189	$19.00
1958	Home and Clock Radios	10,797	$209	$19.00
1959	Home and Clock Radios	15,772	$304	$19.00
1960	Home and Clock Radios	18,031	$326	$18.00
1961	Home and Clock Radios	23,654	$388	$16.00
1962	Home and Clock Radios	24,781	$434	$18.00
1963	Home and Clock Radios	23,602	$405	$17.00
1964	Home and Clock Radios	23,558	$389	$17.00
1965	Home and Clock Radios	31,689	$486	$15.00
1966	Home and Clock Radios	34,779	$555	$16.00
1967	Home and Clock Radios	31,684	$507	$16.00
1968	Home and Clock Radios	34,332	$562	$16.00
1969	Home and Clock Radios	39,414	$629	$16.00
1970	Home and Clock Radios	34,049	$531	$16.00
1971	Home and Clock Radios	34,105	$487	$14.00
1972	Home and Clock Radios	42,149	$606	$14.00
1973	Home and Clock Radios	36,968	$572	$15.00
1974	Home and Clock Radios	33,076	$559	$17.00
1975	Home and Clock Radios	25,434	$369	$15.00

1976	Home and Clock Radios	28,198	$367	$13.00
1977	Home and Clock Radios	41,430	$523	$13.00
1978	Home and Clock Radios	31,760	$449	$14.00
1979	Home and Clock Radios	27,684	$437	$16.00
1980	Home and Clock Radios	28,062	$468	$17.00
1981	Home and Clock Radios	29,415	$501	$17.00
1982	Home and Clock Radios	32,663	$530	$16.00
1983	Home and Clock Radios	39,496	$564	$14.00
1984	Home and Clock Radios	46,456	$661	$14.00
1985	Home and Clock Radios	21,575	$379	$18.00
1986	Home and Clock Radios	25,364	$408	$16.00
1987	Home and Clock Radios	28,110	$409	$15.00
1988	Home and Clock Radios	23,623	$377	$16.00
1989	Home and Clock Radios	25,254	$379	$15.00
1990	Home and Clock Radios	21,585	$360	$17.00
1991	Home and Clock Radios	18,530	$311	$17.00
1992	Home and Clock Radios	21,553	$324	$15.00
1993	Home and Clock Radios	19,697	$307	$16.00
1994	Home and Clock Radios	18,325	$306	$17.00
1995	Home and Clock Radios	17,051	$284	$17.00
1996	Home and Clock Radios	17,581	$291	$17.00
1997	Home and Clock Radios	17,664	$301	$17.00
1998	Home and Clock Radios	18,734	$334	$18.00
1999	Home and Clock Radios	19,899	$348	$17.00
2000	Home and Clock Radios	19,976	$351	$18.00
2001	Home and Clock Radios	18,200	$326	$18.00
2002	Home and Clock Radios	16,194	$300	$19.00
2003	Home and Clock Radios	16,535	$318	$19.00
2004	Home and Clock Radios	9,983	$232	$23.00
2005	Home and Clock Radios	9,066	$202	$22.00
2006	Home and Clock Radios	9,059	$158	$17.00
2007	Home and Clock Radios	13,320	$290	$22.00
2008	Home and Clock Radios	9,692	$178	$18.00
2009	Home and Clock Radios	15,282	$342	$22.00
2010	Home and Clock Radios	12,469	$310	$25.00
2011	Home and Clock Radios	9,523	$254	$27.00
2012	Home and Clock Radios	8,819	$235	$27.00
2013	Home and Clock Radios	7,957	$203	$26.00
2014	Home and Clock Radios	7,863	$203	$25.85
2015	Home and Clock Radios	7,529	$196	$26.25
2016	Home and Clock Radios	7,004	$185	$26.06
2017	Home and Clock Radios	6,944	$184	$26

Source: Consumer Technology Association U.S. Consumer Technology Sales & Forecasts, July 2017 edition. Reprinted with permission.

PARADIGM SHIFT: WHY RADIO MUST ADAPT TO THE RISE OF DIGITAL

By LARRY S. MILLER
Director, Steinhardt Music Business Program,
New York University

August 30, 2017

II. INTRODUCTION

1. Radio has been historically resilient when confronted with new competitive technology. When faced with new competition in the form of television, radio adapted and became portable, capitalizing on the invention of the transistor and an increased focus on local content.

2. However, that resilience is weakening.[1] Radio, and music radio in particular, is now falling behind as audiences have begun to move on and listen to music on Spotify, Pandora, YouTube and other digital services via smartphones at listening locations and times of day that have been radio's exclusive province for nearly a century: in the car and during drive time. Car manufacturers are transitioning vehicles to be digitally compatible. Many models now come with built-in Bluetooth technology and other easy ways to integrate hand-held mobile devices, enabling drivers to listen to digital services, while other newer models are "connected cars" with built-in support for these digital services. These advances are essentially turning the car into an interactive, digital, mobile media device. Radio is facing competition of virtually unlimited choice, exactly where it has enjoyed a virtual monopoly since the first commercially successful car radio was first introduced in 1930.[2]

3. AM/FM radio had been able to wait out the digital disruption that has already affected every other form of media. Now radio is the latest industry facing massive disruption from the digital age. To survive, radio must innovate, learn from other media and take control of its path to maintain its unique position with advertisers, audiences and other stakeholders into the third decade of this century and beyond.

4. The structure of this white paper is as follows: In section III, we look at how the relationship between radio and record labels has changed in recent years. In section IV, we examine current research on the rapidly developing connected car and smart speaker markets. In section V, we discuss the shortcomings of the ratings system and how radio is failing to grow spot revenue while at the same time losing "favoriteness" among younger listeners. We'll also reveal illuminating new insights from MusicWatch on teen listening. A summary follows in section VI.

---

[1] Madalena Oliveira, Gryna Stachyra, and Guy Starkey, Radio: The Resilient Medium: Papers From the Third Conference of the Ecrea Radio Research Section (2014).

[2] Justin Berkowitz, *The History of Car Radios*, CAR AND DRIVER (Oct. 2010), http://www.caranddriver.com/features/the-history-of-car-radios, retrieved 8-18-17.

III. THE CHANGING RELATIONSHIP BETWEEN RADIO AND RECORD LABELS

5. Radio has great reach, and most of what's on radio is music.[3] Music stations comprise about three-quarters of American commercial radio stations, and music drives about three-quarters of radio's over-the-air advertising revenues.

6. In the past, radio along with television, print and in-store play exposed fans to new music. However, the music industry is now less dependent on radio as a source of music discovery and exposure. As the music market accelerates its transition from a sales model to a streaming-driven access model, radio's contribution to music business revenue in the form of driving record sales in all formats has declined significantly.

> "However, the music industry is now less dependent on radio as a source of music discovery and exposure."

7. Streaming now provides record labels the majority of their revenue, as well as directly impacting the Billboard Hot 100 chart.[4] Radio is now less of a tastemaker and more of a validator of the biggest hits often discovered on streaming music platforms. Younger music fans are not turning to radio first for music discovery, and the music industry is responding.

> "Radio is now less of a tastemaker and more of a validator of the biggest hits often discovered on streaming music platforms."

8. The addition of streaming data to the Billboard Hot 100 chart, which both reflects and drives hit radio playlists, means that streaming is now playing an important part in determining which songs are played on radio rather than the other way around, reducing its status as a taste-making tool. In fact, streaming now accounts for 20-30% of the data that comprises the Hot 100, with sales at 35-45% and airplay at 30-40%.[5] Streaming data was first added to the Billboard Hot 100 singles chart in 2007, when nascent streaming services like AOL Music and Yahoo Music were available in the U.S. After Spotify's arrival in 2011, Billboard launched the On-Demand Songs chart and

---

[3] BIA/Kelsey's database covers both Nielsen-rated and non-rated markets and delivers information on 25,000 commercial and non-commercial radio stations. BIA/Kelsey's data is drawn from its access to stations, ownership groups, and industry resources.

[4] Gary Trust, *Ask Billboard: How Does The Hot 100 Work?*, Billboard (Sep. 9, 2013), http://www.billboard.com/articles/columns/ask-billboard/5740625/ask-billboard-how-does-the-hot-100-work.

[5] *Id.*

added Spotify, Rhapsody and others into the mix. The chart fed directly into the Hot 100 and was supplemented by the more comprehensive Streaming Songs chart in 2013, which added music video plays from YouTube and Vevo to the formula. [6] Immediately following the new rules, Baauer's "Harlem Shake" jumped to #1 on the Hot 100 driven by more than 100 million first-week views. [7] "From then on, radio would have to compete with the Internet as the primary motor of pop stardom." Pandora data was added to the Billboard formula in January 2017, immediately moving nine songs up the Hot 100 rankings by at least five places and breaking Callum Scott's "Dancing on My Own" onto the chart for the first time.

9. 2016 marked a tipping point for the music industry, with streaming overtaking sales as the single highest source of revenue in the U.S. Streaming accounted for 51% of all U.S. music industry revenue, up 68% from 2015 to $3.9 billion. It's an astonishing turnaround, with streaming accounting for just 9% of revenue in 2011, only five years prior. In addition, 2016 marked the first double-digit revenue growth (11.4%) in the U.S. recorded music industry since 1998, driven primarily by a 114% increase in revenue from paid subscription streaming services to $2.5 billion.

> **"Streaming accounted for 51% of all U.S. music industry revenue."**

FIGURE 1[8]

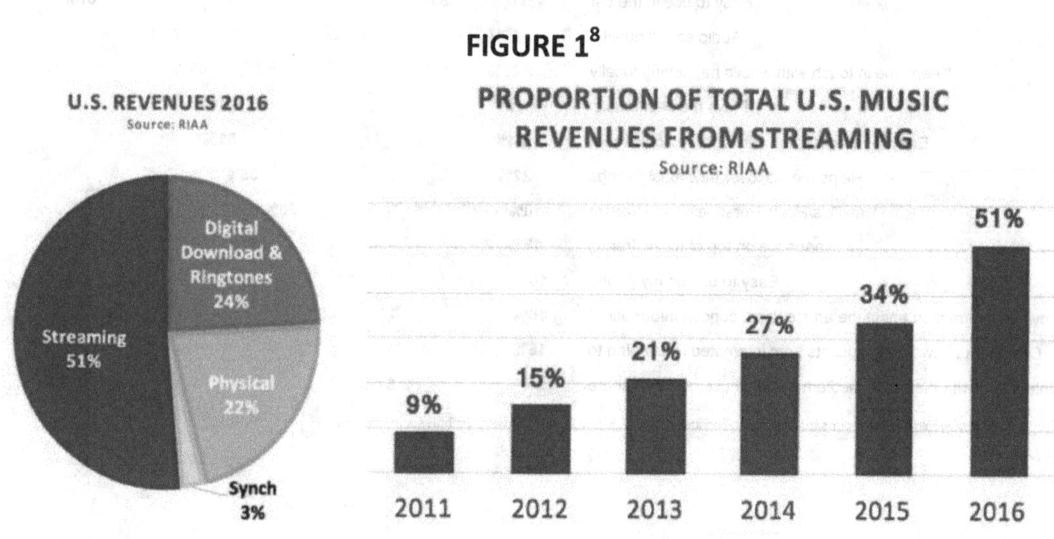

[6] Chris Molanphy, *How Streaming Services Are Remaking The Pop Charts*, NPR MUSIC (Jun. 5, 2015), http://www.npr.org/sections/therecord/2015/06/05/412037432/how-streaming-services-are-remaking-the-pop-charts.

[7] *Id.*

[8] *Id.*

10. Until now, AM/FM radio has remained the dominant force in U.S. music listening, and when the numbers are seen in aggregate, radio listening arguably remains relatively stable. But competition for audience and attention is mounting. Edison Research's "Share of Ear" report for Q2 2017 shows that AM/FM radio is responsible for over half (51%) of all time spent listening to music in the U.S. among listeners 18 and older, with owned music at 12%, YouTube music videos at 8%, Pandora at 6% (paid and ad-supported), SiriusXM at 6% (paid and ad-supported), TV music channels at 5%, Spotify at 4% (paid and ad-supported), and podcasts at 3%.[9]

11. Importantly, radio's audience is increasingly dissatisfied with the medium. Music Watch's Music Monitor survey from January 2017 benchmarked AM/FM radio against streaming services regarding feature satisfaction. While AM/FM radio scored highly on ease of use in the car, with 53% of respondents saying they were "very satisfied," the next highest rating was audio sound quality with only 27%.

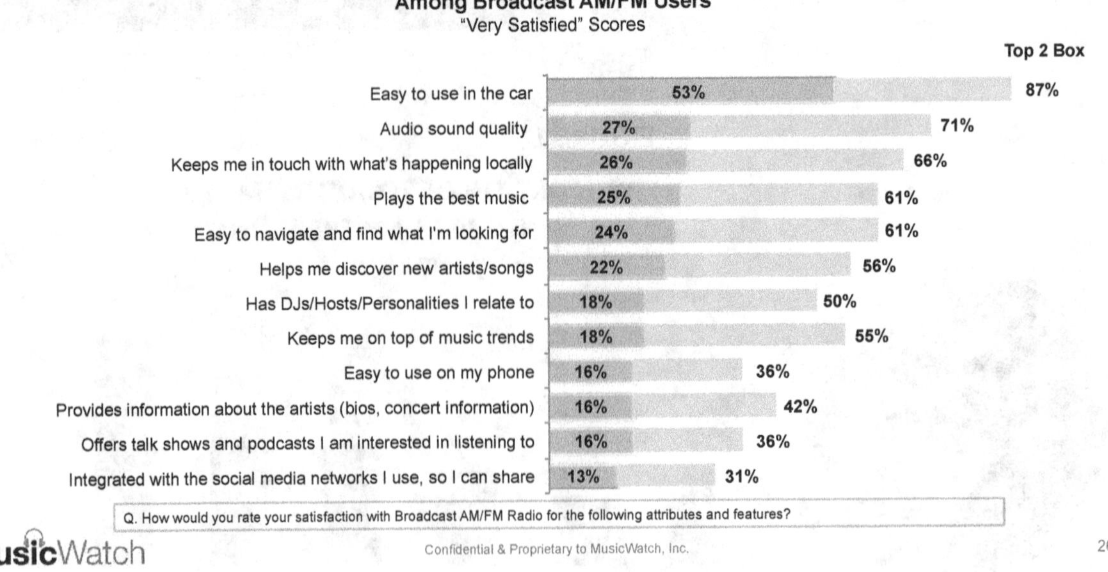

12. Further, scores were low for features where broadcast radio would be expected to score well, such as keeping listeners in touch with what is happening locally (26%), helping

[9] Insights @ Westwood, *Everyone's Listening: AM/FM Radio: The Centerpiece of American Audio,* WESTWOOD ONE, http://westwoodone.com/BLOG/ArtMID/8027/ArticleID/83.

listeners discover new artists and songs (22%), and having DJs/personalities/hosts that the audience relates to (18%). In addition, broadcast radio's top feature satisfaction rating, ease of use in the car, was bested by both Spotify Premium, with 66% saying they were "very satisfied," and Pandora One, with 75%.[10]

13. When examining radio use by the Generation Z, under-18 audience, the numbers drop even more dramatically. As we discuss in section V(c) of this paper, self-reported listening to AM/FM radio among teens 13+ declined by almost 50 percentage points between 2005 and 2016. Radio is being out-innovated by digital competitors.

> **"...listening to AM/FM radio among teens 13+ declined by almost 50 percentage points between 2005 and 2016."**

14. Streaming services like Spotify have ascended in their importance to record labels as a vehicle for exposing fans to new music and changing the calculus of label promotion efforts. Historically, labels' promotional focus was nearly exclusively on music radio. Currently, the traditional ROI on radio spins to sales is arguably less compelling to labels than streaming, where music discovery, consumption and monetization are integrated in one place.[11] "Previously, in the era of the traditional customer journey, we generated discovery for 8 to 12 weeks (allowing customers to discover new music by promoting through intermediaries such as TV, radio and press), and then the purchase or 'consumption' of music would come afterwards," wrote Samuel Potts, Head of Radio at Columbia Records UK. "In a world led by music-streaming, we are directly monetizing both discovery and consumption at the same time. We are monetizing the public's engagement with music and the currency of that engagement is a 'play' on a streaming service."[12]

15. Leading music industry analyst Mark Mulligan of Midia Research said "The power of music discovery used to lie in the hands of the radio DJ, now it lies in the hands of the playlist curator. And because streaming has melded discovery and consumption into a single whole, that means their power is becoming absolute."[13]

---

[10] MusicWatch, Music Monitor survey (Jan. 2017) (unpublished survey) (on file with author).

[11] Samuel Potts, *Record Labels Need a Change of Culture in the 'Dashboard Era' of the Music Industry*, CUEPOINT (Jul. 11, 2016), https://medium.com/cuepoint/record-labels-need-a-change-of-culture-in-the-dashboard-era-of-the-music-industry-585e91f6de99.

[12] *Id.*

[13] Mark Mulligan, *After the Album: How Playlists are Re-Defining Listening*, MUSIC INDUSTRY BLOG (Apr. 26, 2016), https://musicindustryblog.wordpress.com/2016/04/26/after-the-album-how-playlists-are-re-defining-listening/.

16. Of course, "listening" is a form of "consumption," even when the person listens to AM/FM radio. Indeed, the heaviest radio listeners actually generate less revenue for music companies by buying a physical CD or vinyl album, paid download or stream – than light listeners. According to the MusicWatch Annual Music Study 2016, the most frequent radio listeners are 20-30% *less* valuable to the music industry per capita than the less frequent listener. For example, those who listen more than once per week spend $64 on recorded music and premium subscriptions; the less frequent, $80. This same dynamic holds true for music "products," too – CDs, vinyl albums and permanent downloads, at $20 and $28 respectively. While radio consumption can translate into revenue for labels and digital music services, that revenue doesn't come from obvious sources – heavy listeners – and that spending pattern doesn't generate confidence in radio as the primary promotional tool for all genres of music.

> **"...the most frequent radio listeners are 20-30% *less* valuable to the music industry per capita..."**

FIGURE 2[14]

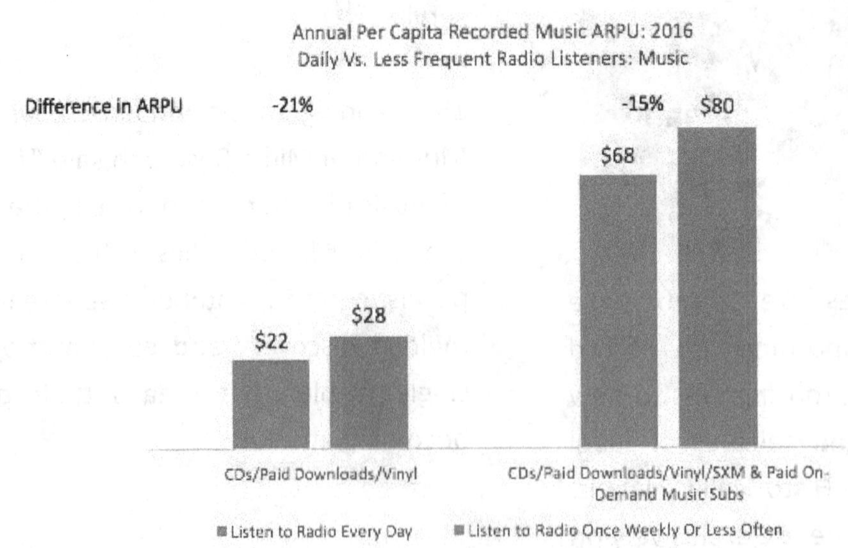

Source: MusicWatch Annual Music Study 2016

[14] MusicWatch, Annual Music Study (2016) (unpublished survey) (on file with author).

17. The spin-to-sales conversion rate for radio is extremely low, according to David Touve, Director of the University of Virginia's iLab and founder of music industry economics publication *Rockonomic*, calculating it at between .01% and .02%.[15]

18. And, of course, American radio does not contribute any direct revenue to the recorded music industry. U.S. radio is not required to pay royalties for the use of master recordings, an exemption unique in the developed nations with advanced intellectual property protection, and one that has been defended by the radio industry for its "promotional value." It is beyond the scope of this paper to quantify whatever promotional value radio may provide (see Phoenix Center Study, "Promotional Effects and the Determination of Royalty Rates for Music").[16] But it is indisputable that radio's role in the promotion of music is dramatically lower than it may have been five or ten years ago, especially among younger, active music consumers.

19. Music discovery as a whole is moving away from AM/FM radio and toward YouTube, Spotify and Pandora, especially among younger listeners. According to data from Edison Research and Triton Digital's *Infinite Dial 2017* webinar, AM/FM radio remained a top source for keeping up-to-date with music with 19% of all respondents citing it, second only to friends/family with 22%.[17] However, this was a dramatic decline from the previous year, when 28% cited AM/FM radio. In the same report, Spotify saw the biggest increase (more than doubling from 4% to 10%). YouTube (14% to 15%) and Pandora (7% to 9%) also gained. Among new music fans making up 49% of the key age 12+ demographic (those who said keeping up-to-date with music is important to them), YouTube overtook AM/FM radio for the first time. Digging deeper into the younger generation (12-24 year olds) who find music discovery important, AM/FM radio (50%) becomes even less influential, trailing YouTube (80%), Spotify (59%), and Pandora (53%).[18] This Infinite Dial insight indicates how musically-engaged young people who drive a tremendous amount of music discovery and consumption are moving away from radio at a significant rate.

20. Accordingly, many record labels are implementing promotion strategies that eschew radio and go directly to fans via streaming and social media. 300 Entertainment is among these labels, having achieved great success with hip-hop group

---

[15] David Touve, *0.02%: the possible Sales-to-Spins conversion rate of US Radio,* ROCKONOMIC (May 12, 2015), https://rockonomic.com/0-02-the-possible-sales-to-spins-conversion-rate-of-us-radio-4712e72b24c3.

[16] http://www.phoenix-center.org/PolicyBulletin/PCPB39Final.pdf

[17] *Music Discovery Competition Heats Up*, INSIDE RADIO (Mar. 10, 2017), http://www.insideradio.com/free/music-discovery-competition-heats-up/article_2f246156-0561-11e7-b485-1fc08f73ac31.html.

[18] *Id.*

Migos. After signing with 300 in 2014, the group doubled and then tripled their online imprint in just months thanks to the label's social media tools and partnership with Twitter. They grew their fan base for three years through extensive touring and a steady stream of new music via singles, mixtapes and albums. In January 2017, Migos topped the Billboard Hot 100 chart for the first time with their single "Bad and Boujee" and followed up with their second album, *Culture*, which debuted at #1 on the Billboard 200 chart without relying on radio play.[19] One need only look at today's radio trade advertisements to see streaming's impact on radio playlists, with labels promoting artists across radio formats, ranging from veteran alternative rock band Foo Fighters to hip-hop act Logic to pop singer Sigrid to country stars Dan+Shay touting their streaming figures in a bid to gain radio airplay for their latest tracks (*See Exhibit A*).

21. In June 2016, the GRAMMY® Awards changed their rules of eligibility, which previously required music to be made commercially available for sale. Now, music can be eligible for GRAMMY® nominations so long as the music appears on at least one major streaming service, such as Spotify or Apple Music.[20]

22. Music is most of what's on radio and drives tremendous value in terms of ad sales and EBITDA for the radio industry, however the value record labels and artists get from radio is declining. Streaming is already the largest source of revenue in recorded music, and where the earliest music discovery happens. Radio programmers today are influenced by traction demonstrated by artists and songs performing well on streaming services. Record companies understand this very well.

23. Music fans today have many choices for access to music and are becoming increasingly dissatisfied with AM/FM radio's traditional service offering.

24. It's never been clearer. Radio has to innovate now to remain relevant as a source of music discovery.

[19] Bansky Gonzalez, How Young Thug Became The Prototype For The Streaming Era Star, UPROXX (Jun. 28, 2017), http://uproxx.com/realtalk/young-thug-prototype-streaming-era-star/.

[20] The 2017 GRAMMY® telecast then saw Chance the Rapper's streaming-only *Coloring Book* album win three GRAMMYs®.

IV. FALLING FURTHER BEHIND IN THE CAR AND HOME

25. Previously, radio was insulated from disruption by its stranglehold on in-car listening. According to the U.S. Department of Transportation, the typical car in the U.S. was 11.6 years old in 2016. This explains why radio hasn't faced its disruption event yet: when it comes to in-car listening, you're talking about technology that, on average, pre-dates the iPhone.

26. However, drivers are buying new cars at a faster rate than ever, with U.S. vehicle sales hitting 17.55 million in 2016, topping the previous record of 17.47 million in 2015 for a seventh consecutive year of sales gains. [21] These vehicles come with more installed options for commercial-free satellite radio, hands-free connection to mobile devices, and installed digital music services in connected cars. The car is ceasing to be AM/FM radio's exclusive, walled garden of captive audiences and limited choices.

27. The internet and the mobile phone were the first "in-home" challenges to radio, which responded to disruptive new technology in the form of cell phones with entertainment apps by fighting to force the inclusion of FM chips in cell phones. However, activation is a device manufacturer and carrier option, and so far, the nation's largest carrier, Verizon, has withheld support while Apple has only recently allowed a downloadable NextRadio app in the App Store.[22] AT&T, Sprint, and T-Mobile are activating chips in Android phones, but this initiative smacks of protectionism; as if buggy whips were being forced by regulation into the trunk of every new car in the early days of the automobile. Consumers didn't demand FM receivers in their smart phones – that was the result of the broadcast lobby. Mexico recently mandated smartphone manufacturers to activate their FM chips, but "The rest of the world is not likely to follow suit...because there are too many forces arrayed against requiring FM chip activation on smartphones – especially carriers with a vested interest in consumers paying for streaming audio rather than listening free," according to NextRadio President Paul Brenner. [23] Time will tell whether carriers activate FM chips

[21] Associated Press, *2016 U.S. auto sales set a new record high, led by SUVs*, LA TIMES (Jan. 4, 2017), http://www.latimes.com/business/autos/la-fi-hy-auto-sales-20170104-story.html.

[22] Paul McLane, *NextRadio Takes a Bite of Apple With Streaming*, RADIOWORLD (Aug. 1, 2017), http://www.radioworld.com/news-and-business/0002/nextradio-supports-streaming-including-on-apple/340116.

[23] James Careless, Will Other Countries Follow Mexico in Chip Madate? http://www.radioworld.com/news-and-business/0002/mexico-mandates-fm-chip-activation/340110

across the board – and whether consumers will notice or care.[24]

28. Meanwhile, smart speakers present a much different challenge to radio, because smart speakers don't have, and likely never will have, an FM chip at all. While it's possible to listen to AM/FM simulcasts on smart speakers, the lack of real investment in simulcasting has led to a subpar listening experience.[25]

29. Thus, it's no surprise that early adopters of these devices, including the Amazon Echo and Google Home, tend to prefer digital services like Spotify and Pandora. Further, the technology titans offering these devices already have their own music services with well-developed playlists, delivering an even more refined listening experience to users, commercial-free and free for Amazon Prime members for a curated selection, and $3.99 per month for tens of millions of songs on Alexa via Amazon Music Unlimited.[26]

A. The Connected Car

30. Radio believes the power of its strong, local brands will insulate it from digital competition. However, this may not be the case in the car as the dashboard reconfigures around connectivity with advanced digital services. The car is currently the number one location for listening to radio, and automotive is the number one revenue category for radio. As such, the connected car and its multiple audio offerings may be the greatest threat to AM/FM radio broadcasting, with 75% of new cars expected to be connected by 2020.[27]

31. The interfaces controlling in-car media systems are becoming more standardized thanks to Apple CarPlay and Android Auto, which mimic drivers' smartphone displays in-dash and come pre-installed across manufacturers, resulting in a more consistent user experience.[28] Virtually every car manufacturer has made significant and potentially transformative investments in this space.

32. Car companies recognize the value in capturing user data and providing new telematics and entertainment offerings. Ford's incoming CEO Jim Hackett previously ran the company's Smart Mobility unit and has no qualms about investing in advanced

---

[24] April Glaser, *Your Phone Has An FM Chip, So Why Can't You Listen To The Radio?*, WIRED (Jul. 9, 2016), https://www.wired.com/2016/07/phones-fm-chips-radio-smartphone/.

[25] Why are Radio Station Simulcasts Failing to Compete on Phones? May 1, 2015. http://www.infinitedial.com/blog/2015/5/1/jsm3bi0o001wfew7mf897p57xwschi

[26] AMAZON MUSIC, https://www.amazon.com/b?node=15451028011.

[27] *Understanding the Connected Car: An Introduction for Radio Broadcasters (Webinar Recording)*, JACOBS MEDIA STRATEGIES, http://jacobsmedia.com/webinar-understanding-connected-car-an-introduction-radio-broadcasters/.

[28] *Id.*

digital services. In May, Hackett said "inside of our industrial businesses will be digital

> "My message is evolve or die."
> *-Scott Burnell, Ford*

businesses, businesses that today have (financial ratios) a dozen times more than ours (manufacturing business)."[29]

33. Scott Burnell, global lead of business development and partner management for Ford, said the company is moving forward with a new vision of the car dashboard that includes AM/FM radio but also provides easy access to a variety of digital services via mobile phones. To that end, Ford has abandoned its proprietary Sync dashboard platform in favor of support for both Apple CarPlay and Android Auto. He urged radio broadcasters to embrace a new vision for their content that moves away from the one-to-many nature of broadcast and toward a more communicative experience in line with how Millennials and other younger generations consume content.[30] "My message is evolve or die," said Burnell.[31]

34. U.S. drivers appear to be on board with Burnell's sentiments. According to McKinsey & Company data, drivers are increasingly more loyal to their phones than they are to their cars. In 2015, 37% of drivers responding to a McKinsey survey said they would switch to another auto manufacturer if it were the only one offering full access to apps, data, and media in their vehicles. It's a marked change from 2014, where only 20% said they would switch manufacturers for better media access.[32] This is an incentive for auto manufacturers to provide drivers with more ways to connect their phones to their dashboards, which will likely cannibalize radio's in-car dominance as time goes on.

35. Furthermore, drivers are now more interested in in-car technology vs. driving performance of the vehicle when making automobile purchase decisions. In a recent Accenture study in which drivers were asked to state their preferences between in-car technology and driving performance, the most-selected answers favored a preference for better technology. Driving performance alone was the least chosen option. And when asked about importance of services for passengers (partner, children etc.), streaming music was the top answer with 63% of respondents; even higher than surfing the internet via a monitor in the car.

---

[29] Ian Thibodeau, *Ford CEO: Income from connected cars to boost earnings*, DETROIT NEWS (May 23, 2017), http://www.detroitnews.com/story/business/autos/mobility/2017/05/23/ford-hackett-connected-cars/102079706/.

[30] Scott Burnell, *Ford Wants Radio Along For Ride In Future*, INSIDE RADIO (Jul. 19, 2017), http://www.insideradio.com/free/ford-wants-radio-along-for-ride-in-future/article_b5eff1b6-6c52-11e7-8647-978502935a7c.html.

[31] *Id.*

[32] *Understanding the Connected Car: An Introduction for Radio Broadcasters* (Webinar Recording), JACOBS MEDIA STRATEGIES, http://jacobsmedia.com/webinar-understanding-connected-car-an-introduction-radio-broadcasters/.

36. So car companies realize that music is a point of differentiation. Tesla, for example, is rumoured to be in talks with major labels to license a proprietary in-car music service for its Model 3 vehicle.[33] Such a service would provide Tesla with two new revenue streams: one for the music subscription and the other for the usage data from its drivers. "The expectation in the auto industry is that car-related data could be a huge future business with double-digit margins (building and selling vehicles yields at best 10% in good times for most carmakers) and low capital costs." A very real possibility exists for the in-car dashboard to be the stage of a new content battle in which radio might find it difficult to maintain positioning.

37. Radio finds itself relegated to a physical position further and further removed – several clicks away -- from the center of the dashboard, notwithstanding limited use of single-station apps. As shown in Figure 3 in-car media screens allowing access to everything from Spotify to Pandora to iTunes are becoming the centerpiece for new models from virtually every manufacturer. AM/FM radio controls are often found below this screen, rendering them less prominent and less accessible than in the past.

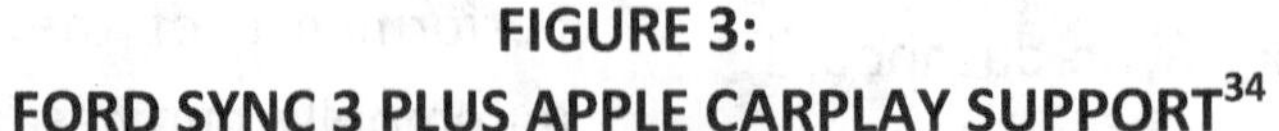

FIGURE 3:
FORD SYNC 3 PLUS APPLE CARPLAY SUPPORT[34]

[33] Johana Bhuiyan and Peter Kafka, *Tesla is talking to the music labels about creating its own streaming service*, RECODE (Jun. 22, 2017), https://www.recode.net/2017/6/22/15855346/tesla-elon-musk-streaming-music-service.

[34] *Id.*

B. The Smart Speaker

38. eMarketer estimates 35 million smart audio devices are already in use.[35] According to Edison Research's Infinite Dial 2017, 7% of Americans aged 12 and up now own a smart speaker, including both Amazon Alexa and Google Home.[36] Edison's Smart Audio Report, which examined smart speaker owners aged 18 and up, found that nearly three-quarters of owners (70%) said they are listening to more audio since they got the speaker – all kinds of audio. This included 65% more listening to music, 28% more listening to news/talk, 20% more listening to podcasts, and 18% more listening to audiobooks. An overwhelming 90% said they bought a smart speaker to listen to music, and 62% also said they purchased a smart speaker to "hear better music than on AM/FM radio."[37] AM/FM radio was also far down the list of use cases cited by smart speaker owners, with only 38% saying they regularly listen to AM/FM music radio on their device and 32% saying the same of AM/FM news/talk.[38]

39. Radio believes that the smart speaker will reverse the decline in the number of radios in households.[39] According to Fred Jacobs of Jacobs Media Strategies, "Most [millennials] don't have a working radio where they live, so they listen to 'radio' on their smartphones, tablets, and laptops."[40] Now, we can add smart speakers to that list. But the Edison report shows that pureplay digital services have a big head start on the smart speaker platform.

40. Part of this issue is that, radio has not meaningfully invested in new programming or advanced digital services for smart speakers. With apologies to Curtis Mayfield, the smart speaker train is leaving the station, and it is time for radio broadcasters to get on board. AM/FM radio broadcasters need to develop a compelling digital presence in order to participate in the smart speaker revolution, but so far, there are few signs that they are doing so.

41. Ironically, broadcasters are uniquely positioned to take advantage of the smart

---

[35] *Alexa, Say What?! Voice-Enabled Speaker Usage to Grow Nearly 130% This Year*, EMARKETER (May 8, 2017), https://www.emarketer.com/Article/Alexa-Say-What-Voice-Enabled-Speaker-Usage-Grow-Nearly-130-This-Year/1015812.

[36] http://nationalpublicmedia.com/wp-content/uploads/2017/06/The-Smart-Audio-Report-from-NPR-and-Edison-Research-2017.pdf

[37] *Id.*

[38] *Id.*

[39] *Smart Speakers Are Bringing Radio Back Into Living Rooms.*, INSIDE RADIO (June 22, 2017), http://www.insideradio.com/smart-speakers-are-bringing-radio-back-into-living-rooms/article_277c3a50-5714-11e7-b545-233001632826.html.

[40] Fred Jacobs, *10 Lessons We Learned From "The Millennial Research Project"*, JACOBS MEDIA STRATEGIES (Aug. 17, 2017), http://jacobsmedia.com/10-lessons-learned-millennial-research-project/?utm_source=Jacobs+Media+Strategies+Blog&utm_campaign=bf962b5ef0-Blog_Daily_FullInfo&utm_medium=email&utm_term=0_5007ff924d-bf962b5ef0-179838909.

speaker revolution. As Glenn Peoples of Pandora wrote, "The quick ascent of the VA [voice-activated] smart speaker is causing companies to re-think how a person engages with music in a voice-only environment. What happens when people aren't scrolling through an MP3 collection, choosing from one of dozens or hundreds of playlists, or picking a CD to play on the home stereo? Recalling something specific can be tough."[41] This is where radio has the potential to shine: With established brands in local markets associated with certain genres and formats, radio stations could earn a key place in the smart speaker market by building out their digital presence.

42. But it won't be easy. In addition to addressing the technical issues associated with streaming, they'll need to adapt to the particular ways that consumers engage with smart speakers, and, importantly, to find a way to stand out. Local stations may find that their brands are confusingly similar (or identical) to the brands of other markets. And, listeners in smaller markets may decide they prefer the out-of-market options offered by big-market taste-making stations like New York's Z100 or LA's Kiss FM. Simply put, broadcasters will have to rely on more than their place on the dial to gain listeners; they'll need a robust digital presence that users can identify with their voice.

"Local stations may find that their brands are confusingly similar (or identical) to the brands of other markets."

43. Moreover, there is a significant risk that radio's delay in entering the smart speaker market will mean missing out on the chance to shape consumer behavior. Amazon made waves in August 2017 when it added functionality to Alexa that allows it to play music for specific activities, such as running or meditation.[42] It does so by connecting the command to a playlist created by Amazon's editors, with over 500 activities supported and the ability to supplement them with a genre (i.e. rock music for a dinner party).[43] In that vein, users can also ask Alexa to play music from specific genres, such as '90s pop, alternative rock, and more.[44] According to Amazon, these controls were designed around data gathered from the way Alexa users were requesting songs,[45] and as this

[41] *How Music And The Smart Speaker Will Help Each Other Succeed*, HYPEBOT, http://www.hypebot.com/hypebot/2017/08/how-music-and-the-smart-speaker-will-help-each-other-succeed.html.

[42] Chaim Gartenberg, *Amazon's Alexa can now play music for 'hooking up' and 'baby-making'*, THE VERGE (Aug. 3, 2017), https://www.theverge.com/2017/8/3/16090228/amazon-alexa-music-specific-activities-working-out-cooking-meditation.

[43] Sarah Perez, *Alexa can now find and play music with over 500 'activity phrases'*, TECH CRUNCH (Aug. 4, 2017), https://techcrunch.com/2017/08/04/alexa-can-now-find-and-play-music-for-over-500-activities/.

[44] *Help & Customer Service: Listen to Music*, AMAZON (Aug. 18, 2017, 1:28pm), https://www.amazon.com/gp/help/customer/display.html?nodeId=201601830.

[45] Sarah Perez, *Alexa can now find and play music with over 500 'activity phrases'*, TECH CRUNCH (Aug. 4, 2017),

method takes hold, it stands to reason that someone looking for music to accompany almost any activity will ask for that playlist or activity directly, rather than a local broadcast radio station.[46]

44. Broadcasters are uniquely positioned to build on their existing customer relationships and brand identities in the new smart speaker market. But if they don't act, they will quickly lose whatever advantage they may have. If radio broadcasters aim to maintain relevance if not dominance of listenership on new and rapidly evolving platforms like the connected car and smart speakers, they will have to out-innovate and out-compete digital-born disruptors for hearts, minds and ears in a way they haven't since the birth of their industry.

https://techcrunch.com/2017/08/04/alexa-can-now-find-and-play-music-for-over-500-activities/.

[46] Chaim Gartenberg, *Amazon's Alexa can now play music for 'hooking up' and 'baby-making'*, THE VERGE (Aug. 3, 2017), https://www.theverge.com/2017/8/3/16090228/amazon-alexa-music-specific-activities-working-out-cooking-meditation.

V. TO THE BARRICADES: LOSING LOCAL FAVOR AND FLAVOR

A. Radio's Local Advertising Problem

45. Radio has long converted audience reach and engagement to local advertising revenue. However, indications are that radio's favor with local advertisers and local audiences is declining, as mobile and digital options are better able to deliver accurately within local markets, with clearer ROI. [47]

46. Indeed, radio's reach might not be as large as it seems, as the standards for measurement of radio station ratings pale in comparison to the transparent and detailed audience segments delivered by digital. For example, Nielsen's ratings system does not take into account the actual granular measurement of radio listeners. "A P1 [those listeners in the top quintile of reported listenership] can be someone who listens to a station for just a handful of quarter-hours throughout the week. Or it can be someone who tunes in to a favorite station six hours a day. A P1 is a P1. Except when they're not," wrote Fred Jacobs. [48] Ratings can be manipulated to serve the narrative of those measuring them. "How many times have you heard someone say (or maybe you've said it yourself) that even though the numbers look bad, we have a good feeling about the format, a personality, a contest, or anything else? And so you end up acting against the cold, hard message the data is trying to deliver," wrote Jacobs. [49] This is not what brand marketers want to hear when defending an ad buy to their CEO or CFO."

47. The Personal People Meter (PPM) has now been collecting radio measurement data in top markets for over a decade. The PPM, a portable, pager-like electronic device, picks up encoded identifiers buried in broadcast audio signals. Fred Jacobs said in a blog post reflecting on 10 years of PPM use, "The great PPM hope was that listening and engagement would increase, accompanied by positive reactions from the ad community, leading to more sales and ultimately, greater credibility and respect for a medium that had fallen behind in the measurement game. Sadly, none of that happened."[50]

48. Like Arbitron before it, Nielsen has been challenged to recruit a radio measurement sample frame that mirrors the measured market. Historically, Nielsen and Arbitron relied on random-digit dialing to

[47] Alison Weissbrot, *Why Digital Hasn't Killed the Radio Star*, AD EXCHANGER (Jan. 6, 2017), https://adexchanger.com/digital-audio-radio/digital-hasnt-killed-radio-star/.

[48] Fred Jacobs, *Are Polls as Wrong as The Ratings?* JACOBS MEDIA STRATEGY (Nov. 11, 2016), http://jacobsmedia.com/are-polls-as-wrong-as-the-ratings/.

[49] *Id.*

[50] Fred Jacobs, *PPM Turns 10 – Celebration or Regret?* JACOBS MEDIA STRATEGY (Feb. 22, 2017), http://jacobsmedia.com/ppm-radio-ratings/.

landlines for survey recruitment. Today, more than half of American households no longer have a landline and rely exclusively on cell phones. This has serious ramifications for accurate measurement of younger demographic groups that, along with people who rent their homes are even less likely to have a landline than the average household. Nielsen has responded by attempting to recruit participants in person, a costlier and more time-consuming approach as the number of panelists recruited by unsolicited home visits has increased to 25%.[51]

49. Too-small sample sizes in smaller markets are typically addressed by overweighting, particularly in ethnic and young male households, which tend to be particularly difficult to recruit. This often leads to instability in audience estimates across rating periods when one diary can have an outsized influence on a station's ratings.[52]

50. "I just delivered a research project for a broadcaster in a relatively small market. The study contained the opinions of 600 people," wrote consultant Mark Ramsay in "The Unfortunate Farce of Radio Ratings." "Do you know how long it takes Nielsen to recruit a sample in this market as large as the sample in my research project? Two years. That's right. The sample sizes in markets like this one – and markets like yours – are almost laughably small."[53] In fact, Nielsen is said to have deployed only 800 PPMs to cover the entire Kansas City, MO, metro area, which contains around 2 million people.[54] "The more your clients understand about the intricacies of the ratings system, the more likely they are to be appalled – particularly in the presence of precise metrics from online radio players like Pandora and Spotify and digital natives like Google and Facebook," wrote Ramsay. "When I can go through Facebook's ad creation process and arrive at a specific number of consumers who will be impacted by my messaging with no estimates or random guesses required, what is the long-term effect of this on attitudes about media measurement?"[55]

51. Outside the roughly top 50 markets measured by PPM, radio is still measured by the paper and ink diary system in use for over 60 years, representing approximately half the country. Here too, sample size is a persistent issue. Former national radio sales executive and now consultant Gerry

[51] *Cell-Only Homes Now Top Landline Homes – A Nielson Challenge.*, Inside Radio (May 11, 2017), http://www.insideradio.com/cell-only-homes-now-top-landline-homes-a-nielsen-challenge/article_fb4060a4-361d-11e7-a77f-874d5fa0b0fc.html.

[52] *Why Nielsen Comes Up Short In Radio Measurement.*, Inside Radio (Dec. 11, 2016), http://www.insideradio.com/why-nielsen-comes-up-short-in-radio-measurement/article_5136c95e-c002-11e6-a72a-675bf13ae312.html.

[53] Hearne Christopher Jr., *Hearne: The Farce & Folly of Radio Ratings*, KC Confidential (Oct. 27, 2016), http://www.kcconfidential.com/2016/10/27/hearne-the-farce-folly-of-radio-ratings/.

[54] *Id.*

[55] *Id.*

Boehme said "Radio is being terribly short-changed by a system that is totally incapable of measuring current broadcast channels, much less streaming and podcasting."[56]

> **"Radio is being terribly short-changed by a system that is totally incapable of measuring current broadcast channels, much less streaming and podcasting." –*Gerry Boheme***

52. Underscoring this audience measurement failure, Nielsen's radio rating system, dependent on Portable People Meters (PPMs), may be responsible for killing off an entire format of radio that wasn't suited for the device. Although PPMs pick up inaudible audio signals hidden under radio broadcasts and ostensibly providing a more accurate accounting of which radio stations people are hearing on a regular basis, smooth jazz suffered tremendously under this system, as its soft sound left little room for the PPMs' audio signal to hide behind without becoming audible. As such, 16 smooth jazz stations switched to noisier formats such as rock and sports immediately after the PPMs were introduced in 2013, and as of April 2015, the total number of jazz stations had dropped from 159 to 101.[57]

53. PPMs have also opened up new opportunities for radio stations to game the ratings. A new technology known as Voltair is now available for stations to purchase for $15,000 from equipment manufacturer 25-Seven, improving the encoding process to make their signal more discoverable to PPMs.[58] "According to one radio-company executive I talked to whose company has used Voltair since February, it really works — spurring ratings increases in certain demographics by 20 percent to 80 percent," wrote Carl Bialik of FiveThirtyEight.[59] As this technology has not been adopted as an industry standard, it currently creates a ratings imbalance between the bigger stations that can afford Voltair and the smaller stations that cannot.

54. Spot radio revenue has been flat at roughly $15 billion since 2010. Digital radio revenues, which include online streaming of radio signals, crossed $1 billion for the first time in 2015 and is expected to grow faster than on-air revenue. But revenue accruing to radio from off-air events exceeded $2 billion for the first time in 2015.[60]

---

[56] *Id.*

[57] Carl Bialik, *Did Nielsen Kill the Radio Star?* FIVETHIRTYEIGHT (June 30, 2015), https://fivethirtyeight.com/features/did-nielsen-kill-the-radio-star/.

[58] *Id.*

[59] *Id.*

[60] Paul McLane, *U.S. Radio Revenue: $17.4 Billion, Down 1% Last Year*, RADIO WORLD (Mar. 3, 2016), http://www.radioworld.com/business-and-law/0009/us-radio-revenue-174-billion-down-1-last-year/336865.

55. Radio is also losing its dominance in local advertising spend. According to BIA/Kelsey's U.S. Local Advertising forecast 2016, radio ad revenues were at $15.4 billion in 2016, good enough to place it within the Top 5 for the year. However, 2017 is a different story. In BIA/Kelsey's forecast for this year, radio was replaced in the Top 5 by mobile, which brought in $16 billion.[61] "We are on the precipice of different advertising channels taking lead positions in the local advertising marketplace," said BIA Chief Economist Mark Fratrik. "Although national and local businesses still utilize a mix of digital and traditional advertising platforms, the opportunities afforded by mobile, social and video advertising are incredibly valuable due to their measurability, adoption by consumers and enhancements by technologies such as beacons and data attribution that blend extraordinarily well with today's mobile consumer."[62]

"We are on the precipice of different advertising channels taking lead positions in the local advertising marketplace."
-Mark Fratrik, BIA

56. Mobile's ascendance is also seen in the 2016 IAB Advertising Revenue Report, up 77% from 2015 to $36.6 billion. Mobile advertising accounted for over half (51%) of the record-breaking $72.5 billion total spent on internet advertising, which was up 22% from 2015. Digital audio also earned enough internet ad spend to be measured by the IAB for the first time, bringing in $1.1 billion.[63] The upward trend for digital advertising appears to be continuing into 2017, with total spend hitting $19.6 billion in Q1 2017, the highest Q1 earnings on record.[64] Radio, perhaps the first mobile medium, is not remotely keeping up with the pace of innovation or revenue growth in competing mobile services.

B. Radio's Losing "Favoriteness" Among Listeners

57. While radio's reach is high, time spent listening to radio is fracturing.

58. Steve Goldstein, CEO of Amplifi Media and former EVP and Group Program Director of radio broadcaster Saga Communications wrote, "In 2007, radio's TSL was around 20 hours. Today it hovers at 14 hours, and it is even lower among Millennials. While radio

---

[61] *U.S. Local Ad Revs to Exceed $174 Billion In 2021 Says BIA/Kelsey; Mobile Replaces Radio in Top 5*, ALL ACCESS (Jul. 12, 2017), https://www.allaccess.com/net-news/archive/story/167471/u-s-local-ad-revs-to-exceed-174-billion-in-2021-sa.

[62] *Id.*

[63] *Mobile Captures More Than Half of All U.S. Internet Advertising Revenue For The First Time Ever, Total Digital Ad Spend Hits a Landmark $72.5 Billion in 2016*, IAB (Apr. 26, 2017), https://www.iab.com/news/internet-advertising-revenue-first-time-ever-total-digital-ad-spend-hits-landmark-72-5-billion-2016/.

[64] *Digital Advertising Revenues Hit $19.6 Billion in Q1 2017, Climbing 23% Year-Over-Year, According to IAB*, IAB (Jun. 14, 2017), https://www.iab.com/news/ad-revenues-hit-19-6b/.

continues to have remarkable reach, time spent listening is shifting to other platforms. The move to mobile and on-demand is rapid. Radio needs to decide whether it is in the transmitter business or the audio business. The audience is already voting."[65]

"In 2007, radio's TSL was around 20 hours. Today it hovers at 14 hours..."

59. Radio's historical "favoriteness," or the amount of people who consider radio to be their favorite medium for listening to music, declined significantly beginning with the rise of digital downloads by 2007.[66]

60. "The trends are clear and from this long-range perspective broadcast radio may have missed its opportunity to take advantage of the available technology to transition listeners seeking different ways to consume music. According to a recent Bridge Ratings study, creation of alternative pure-play internet radio stations by broadcasters could have and can still capture listening that has funnelled to internet radio."[67]

61. The study also shows the change in broadcast radio "favoriteness" between 2001 when Bridge Ratings started these studies. By their estimates, broadcast radio has thus far seen a 33% attrition of "favoriteness." 30% of the attrition has been attributed to on-line music streaming, which includes internet on-demand services like Spotify and YouTube. Internet Radio accounted for 15% attrition. This includes non-interactive services like Pandora and AM/FM simulcasts. Less than 2% of the attrition can be attributed to AM/FM simulcast streams.[68]

62. Perhaps most importantly, radio is rapidly losing its audience of the future. The trend line is most pronounced among the youngest respondents to the Bridge Ratings survey, 18-34 year old adults, "few of which had a favorite (radio station) they could name."[69]

"...18-34 year old adults, "few of which had a favorite (radio station) they could name.""

[65] *Let's Click "Pause" And Celebrate International Podcast Day*, AMPLIFI MEDIA (Sep. 30, 2016), http://www.amplifimedia.com/blogstein/?offset=1475579873783
.

[66] *Radio's New Media Gauntlet – 2017*, BRIDGE RATINGS (Aug. 24, 2017 at 8:37 pm), http://www.bridgeratings.com/the-new-media-gauntlet-2017.

[67] *Id.*

[68] *Id.*

[69] *Id.*

63. Few radio stations sell advertising specifically targeted for teens, which may account for the lack of teen audience studies by the trend analysts. But today's teens are tomorrow's 18-34's and 25-54's, and we thought it might be instructive to examine how today's teens discover and consume music while they are still forming their media consumption habits and brand allegiances. The numbers are dramatic, but not surprising.

C. New Insights on Teen Listening

64. The rising "Gen Z" demographic is showing little interest in traditional media, having grown up in an on-demand environment as true digital natives. These individuals, defined as those born in 1995 or later, are projected to account for 40% of all consumers in the U.S. market by 2020.[70] They currently make up 25% of the U.S. population, according to the U.S. Census Bureau, making them a larger group than either Baby Boomers or Millennials.[71]

65. Teens have even more opportunity to engage with music than their post-Baby Boomer, Generation X parents. It is not only streaming that supplements radio, as teens also actively use search and social media tools and apps such as Musical.ly, Shazam and blogs to stay on top of music trends. Radio, though still important, is being challenged by these platforms as a source of music discovery.

66. We begin with new MusicWatch data on the overall percentage of teens that said they had listened to music on AM/FM radio in the past three months.[72]

67. This research shows that the percentage fell from the mid-70% range a decade ago in Q3 2007 to 56% by as long ago as Q4 2013, a 20 percentage-point decline. As teens continue to be presented with more digital options and grow increasingly literate in using online music services, we can expect this number to drop even further.

---

[70] Giselle Abramovich, *15 Mind-Blowing Stats About Generation Z*, CMO (Jun. 12, 2015), http://www.cmo.com/features/articles/2015/6/11/15-mind-blowing-stats-about-generation-z.html#gs.Kk1xlBM.

[71] Kathryn Dill, *7 Things Employers Should Know About The Gen Z Workforce*, FORBES (Nov. 6, 2015), https://www.forbes.com/sites/kathryndill/2015/11/06/7-things-employers-should-know-about-the-gen-z-workforce/#4e13ff1dfad7.

[72] MusicWatch's Music Acquisition Monitor was a tracking survey which ran quarterly between 2007 and 2012, and semi-annually between 2013 and 2014. The study measured participation in various music activities including purchase of CDs and downloads, participation in piracy, streaming services used and time spent listening to music. Music Acquisition Monitor was an online survey fielded to ~5000 respondents aged 13 and older, and was weighted and projected to the US internet population. MusicWatch's Monitor Study examines consumer usage of, and satisfaction with, a variety of audio options, including specific streaming services. The Monitor is conducted semi-annually to a sample of 3,000 music listeners aged 13 and older.

FIGURE 4[73]

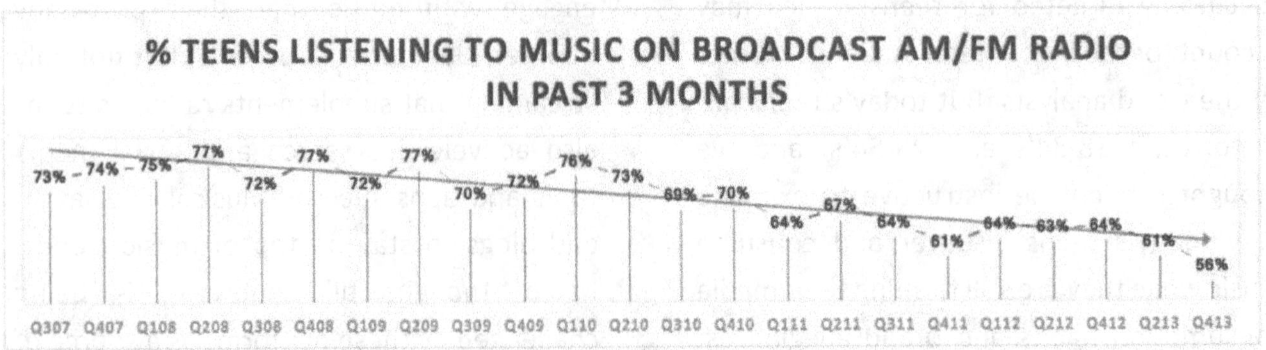

Source: MusicWatch MusicAcquisitionMonitor Q3 2007-Q4 2013. Based on online survey to ~5000 respondents per wave and projected to internet using population 13 and older. Study was quarterly between 2007 and 2011; semi-annual from 2012 forward.

MusicWatch

Not surprisingly, while teen music listenership on broadcast AM/FM was falling, the proportion of teens who listened to music on free non-interactive digital radio was on the rise. By Q4 2016 the same proportion of teens (58%) listened to music on AM/FM as online radio. It's a remarkable transition, as online radio accounted for only 30% of teen listening in Q3 2007, compared to 73% for AM/FM. As today's teens age into 18-34's and beyond, broadcast radio could fall even further behind pureplay options among the audience demographic groups most sought after by stations and most highly valued by advertisers.

[73] MusicWatch, MusAcquisitionMonitor survey Q3 2007 – Q4 2017 (2017) (unpublished survey) (on file with author).

FIGURE 5[74]

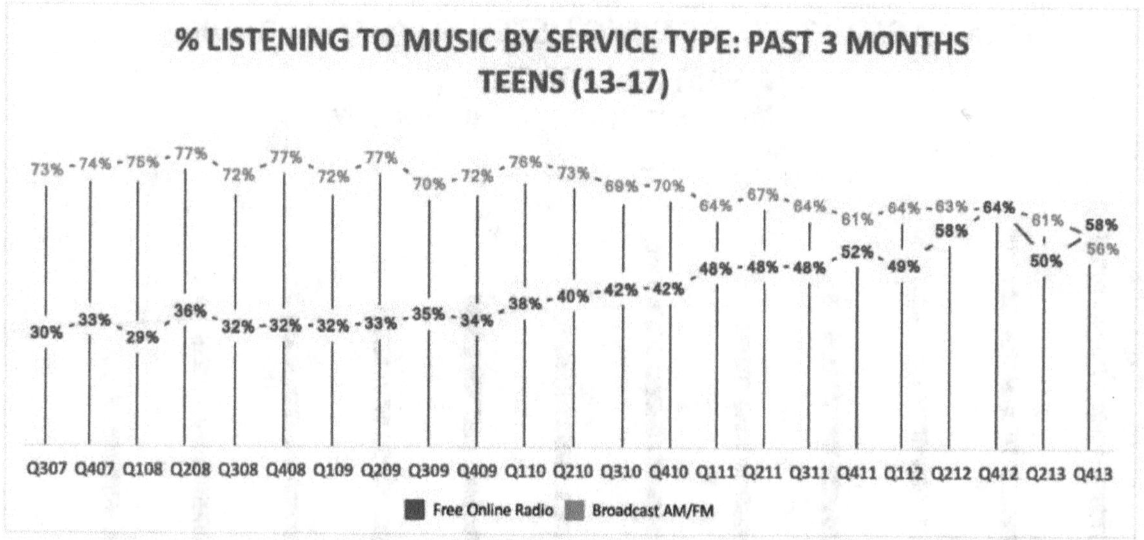

Source: MusicWatch MusicAcquisitionMonitor Q3 2007-Q4 2013. Based on online survey to ~5000 respondents per wave and projected to internet using population 13 and older. Study was quarterly between 2007 and 2011; semi-annual from 2012 forward.

68. MusicWatch also evaluated data going back more than a decade for past-year listening to AM/FM radio among teens. In 2005, nearly 90% of teens reported that they had listened to AM/FM radio in the past year. That dipped somewhat from 2006-2008, the years that saw peak iTunes usage and increasing use of streaming platforms. Although radio engagement fell during the years that Pandora and YouTube were ramping up, a healthy majority of teens were still listening to AM/FM radio, with 2008's 69% figure being the then-lowest percentage. However, once Spotify entered the U.S. market in 2011 and it along with Apple Music, and other premium on-demand services gained traction starting in 2014, many teens abandoned AM/FM radio. While teen listenership had remained relatively stable from 2009 to 2014, with increases in 2010 and 2012, it dropped sharply in 2015, reaching its then-lowest level of 68%, before plummeting further in 2016, dropping over 10 percentage points to 56%.

[74] *Id.*

FIGURE 6[75]

TEENS AGED 13-17: % SAYING LISTEN TO AM/FM RADIO PAST 12 MONTHS

(SOURCE: MUSICWATCH ANNUAL MUSIC STUDY)

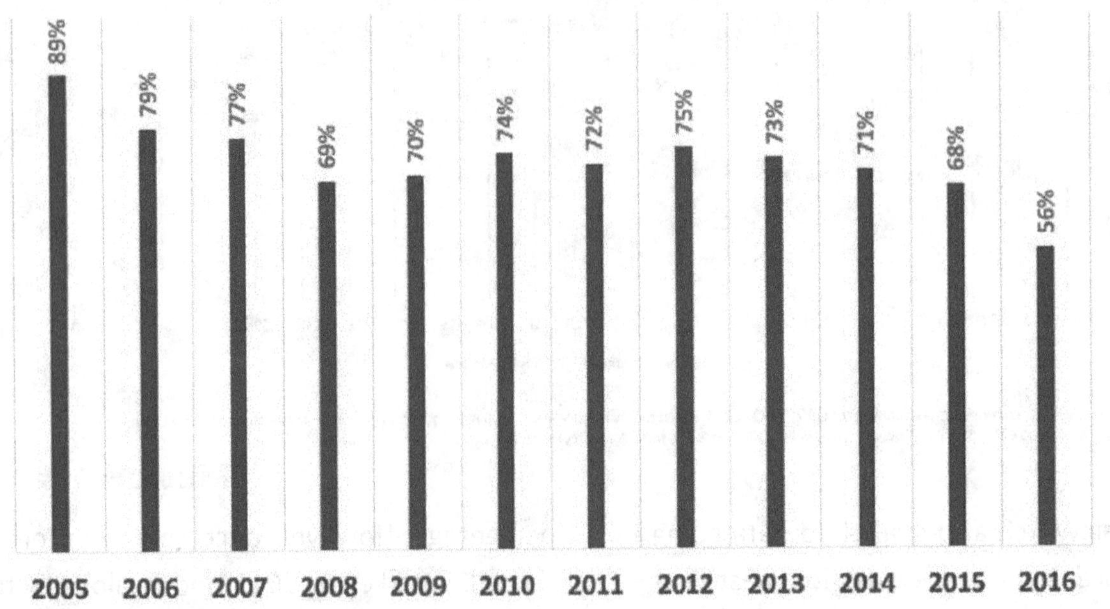

Source: MusicWatch Annual Music Study. Online sample of ~5,000 respondents representing the internet population 13 and older. Prior to 2013, respondents were asked about "Listening to AM/FM Radio." As of 2014 respondents were asked specifically about music on broadcast AM/FM, news/talk/sports on broadcast AM/FM and music on digital audio AM/FM stations.

MusicWatch

69. How teens listen to any music is important. However, the time that teens actually invest listening to specific platforms is a better indicator of the health and prospects for those platforms. According to MusicWatch, teens' average weekly share of AM/FM listening hours was only 13%, far lower than streaming at 44% (See Figure 7 below). These streaming figures include both pure-play music streaming services like Spotify and Apple Music and sites such as YouTube or Vevo that host music videos. While a significant percentage of teens still listen to broadcast radio, they are far more engaged with streaming options that give them some form of control over what they hear.

> **"...MusicWatch's research shows, many teens are abandoning radio.**

---

[75] *Id.*

SHARE OF MUSIC TSL: 2016 AVERAGE MONTH: TEENS (13-17)

FIGURE 7[76]

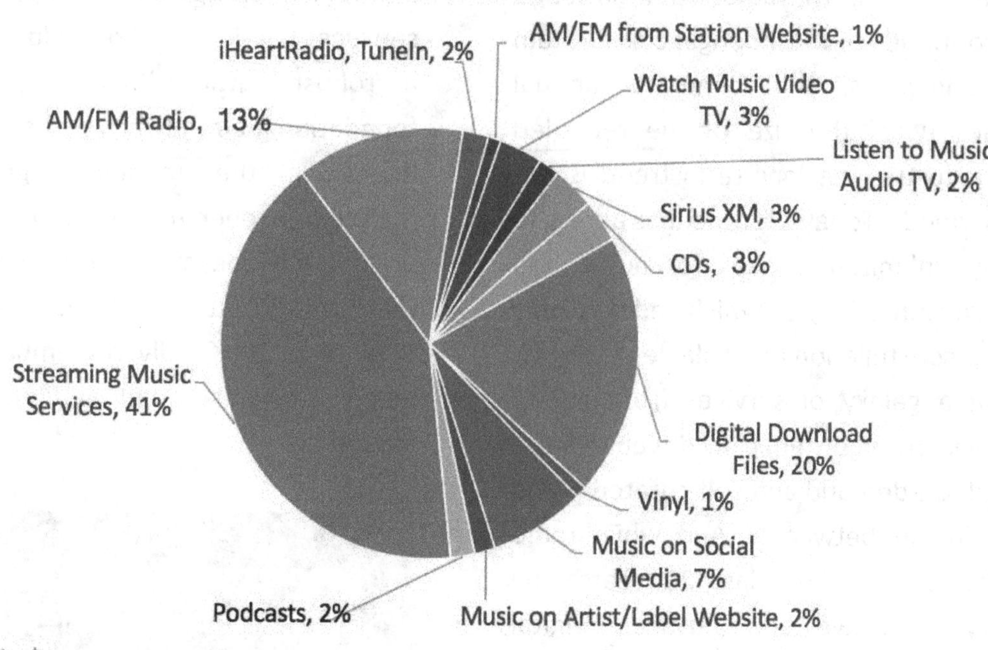

70. In the past, radio could rely on new generations of in-demo listeners to replenish and grow its audiences. However, with the advent of music and video streaming, connected devices, and an app economy, this reliance is being challenged. As MusicWatch's research shows, many teens are abandoning radio. Some of them are completely bypassing the medium, with the number who listened both in the past three months and over the past year in decline. Even more concerning is the share of time teens spend listening to AM/FM radio, which pales in comparison to streaming. It's worth noting that teens do not spend the same amount of time commuting in cars as their parents, but when they do enter the workforce, it will likely be in cars that are much better natively enabled for streaming.

[76] *Id.*

VI. SUMMARY

71. Music is the lifeblood of the radio industry. It represents the vast majority of all content on AM/FM radio. And although radio continues to reach, engage and retain large audiences and generate annual revenues twice the size of the recorded music industry, the long-term trend is not radio's friend. Today's listener has access to virtually unlimited choices for audio and music consumption, of which radio is only one of a constellation of available platforms offering a galaxy of services from linear, lean-back and algorithmically driven to lean-forward, on-demand and self-curated – and everything in between. And while radio consolidated over the last 20 years, the industry under-invested in advanced digital music services and failed to anticipate the emergence and scale of new competitors.

72. The car provided a Maginot Line of defense for radio, insulating it from competition through the early years of the digital transition. But the explosion of smartphones in the last decade and the proliferation and growth of music and audio apps and pureplay digital services have weakened AM/FM radio's dominance of in-car listening, especially among younger audiences.

73. What are the conditions for sustainability and growth? Unfortunately, it's easy to describe and hard to do. But unless the industry is set to make peace with a long and inevitable decline, radio needs to invest in strong and compelling digital services. If it does, radio can look forward to a robust future built on the strong foundation it already has in the marketplace leveraging the medium's great reach, habitual listenership, local presence and brands. If it doesn't, radio risks becoming a thing of the past, like the wax cylinder or 78 RPM record – fondly remembered but no longer relevant to an audience that has moved on.

"…radio needs to invest in strong and compelling digital services. If it does, radio can look forward to a robust future built on the strong foundation it already has in the marketplace leveraging the medium's great reach, habitual listenership, local presence and brands."

National Radio Networks

ABC Radio Networks
444 Madison Avenue, New York, NY 10022
(212) 735-1700
www.abcradio.com
Lewis Dickey, Chairman
Jonathan Pinch, Co-COO/EVP
John Dickey, Co-COO/EVP
Richard Denning, SVP/Secretary/General Counsel
Joseph Hannan, SVP/Treasurer/CFO
Linda Hill, Corporate Controller/Chief Accounting Officer
East Region, ABC Inc
47 West 66th Street, New York, NY 10023; Tel: (212) 456-7777; Departments: ABC News Radio, Engineering, Network Programming, International; Executives: John Mohoney, EVP/Programming; Chris Berry, VP News Radio.
West Region, ABC Inc
13725 Montfort Drive, Dallas, TX 75240; Tel: (972) 991-9200; Departments: Affiliate marketing West, Entertainment Programming, Marketing and Promotion, 24 Hour Formats, Advertising/Sales, Engineering, Finance, MIS, Research; Executives: JamesRobinson, President; Michael Connolly, SVP/Advertising; Kevin Miller, SVP/Business Development.

American Urban Radio Networks
432 Park Avenue, South, 14th Floor, New York, NY 10016
(212) 883-2100
www.aurn.com
Howard Elsen, President
Andy Anderson, VP Sales/Eastern Region
Michelle Pearson, Executive Sales
Basil Murrain, VP Promotions
Barry Feldman, VP Research
Sharita Manickham, Marketing Manager
Programming Headquarters
960 Penn Ave., 4th Floor, Pittsburgh, PA 15222; Tel: (412) 456-4000
Atlanta Office
2424 Old Rex Morrow Road, Ellenwood, GA 30294; Tel: (732) 309-0301; Contact: Tanya Forret Hall, Executive Sales Director.
Chicago Office
180 North Stetson, Suite 3500, Chicago, IL 60601; Tel: (312) 558-9090; Contact: Stephen Bates, Executive Sales Director.
Detroit Office
1133 Whittier Road, Grosse Pointe, MI 48230; Tel: (313) 885-4243; Contact: J.D. Mackay, Executive Sales Director.

AP Broadcast
1100 13th Street, Suite 700, Washington, DC 20005
(800) 527-7234
www.apbroadcast.com
James Williams, VP/Director Global Broadcast
Greg Groce, Director Business Operations
Brad Kalbfeld, Managing Editor
Roger Lockhart, Director Marketing Communications
Lee Perryman, Deputy Director
John Phillips, Director FinancialPlanning

CBS Radio
1515 Broadway Avenue, New York, NY 10036
(212) 846-3939
www.cbsradio.com
Anton Guitano, COO
Dan Mason, President/CEO
Scott Herman, EVP Operations
Micheal Weiss, President of Sales
Ezra Kucharz, President of Digital Media
Jo Ann Haller, VP/General Counsel

CNN Radio Networks
One CNN Center NW, Atlanta, GA 30303
(404) 827-1700
Robert Garcia, Principle Executive
Harley Hotchkiss, Director Operations
Richard Benson, Executive Producer
Bureaus
Atlanta, Boston, Chicago, Denver, Dallas, Los Angeles, Miami, New York, San Francisco, Seattle, Washington DC, Baghdad, Buenos Aires, Dubai, Frankfurt, Hong Kong, Istanbul, Jakarta, Jerusalem, Lagos, London, Madrid, Mexico City, Moscow,Nairobi, New Delhi, Paris, Rome, Tokyo, Seoul, Sidney.

Eastern Region Public Radio
PO Box 615, Kensington, MD 20895
(301) 961-0252
Glenn Gleixner, Chairman
James Muhammad, Vice Chairman
Georgette Bronfman, Executive Director
Lafontaine Oliver, General Manager

Jones Radio Network
8200 South Akron Street, Suite 103, Centennial, CO 80112
(800) 609-5663
Glenn Jones, Chairman
Phil Barry, General Manager/VP
Frank De Santis, General Manager/VP
James LaMarca, EVP/COO
Amy Bolton, VP/General Manager News
Patrick Crocker, Sales/Marketing

KEDA Radio
1246 W Laurel Street, San Antonio, TX 78201
(210) 226-5254
www.kedaradio.com
kedakid@aol.com
Manuel G, Davila, Sr., Founder, deceased
Comprises three stns in Texas, three affiliates. Represented by Caballero Spanish Media.

National Public Radio
635 Massachusetts Avenue NW, Washington, DC 20001
(202) 513-2000; *Fax:* (202) 513-3329
www.npr.org
Gary Knell, President
Antoine Van Agtmael, Chief Investment Officer
Zach Brand, VP Digital Media
Jeff Perkins, Chief People Officer
Margaret Smith, SVP/News
Mike Starling, Executive Director

Public Radio International
401 Second Avenue, Minneapolis, MN 55401
(612) 338-5000
www.pri.org
Peter Darrow, Chairman
Linda Larson, Vice Chair
Alisa Miller, President
Stewart Vanderwilt, Secretary
Lawrence Wilkinson, Treasurer
Sharon Ferraro, VP/Resource Development
Michael Skoler, VP Interactive Media
Julie Yager, VPBrand Management

Super Radio Network
24 Boston Post Road West, Marlborough, MA 01752
(508) 620-0006; *Fax:* (952) 556-9375
mixes@superadio.com
Rich O'Brien, SVP/Programming
Joan Brooks, Business Manager
Dianne Cook, Business Manager
Headquarters New York
112 West 34th Street, Suite 1401, New York, NY 10120; Tel: (212) 714-1000; Executives: Jack Bryant, COO; Eric Faison, VP; Barbara DeLaleu, Affiliation Rep.

United Press International
1133 19th Street NW, Washington, DC 20036
(202) 898-8000; *Fax:* (202) 898-8048
www.upi.com
Sayla Seng, COO
Nicholas Chiaia, President
John Hendel, Executive Editor

The Wall Street Radio Network
1155 Avenue of the Americas, 8th Floor, New York, NY 10036
(212) 659-1208; *Fax:* (212) 659-1908
www.wsjradio.com
wsjradio@dowjones.com
Nancy Abramson, Executive Director
Susan O'Connell, Senior Director
Susan Moran, Sales Director
Jean Rodier, New Media Manager

WFMT Radio Network
5400 North St Louis Avenue, Chicago, IL 60625
(773) 279-2000
www.wfmt.com
Daniel Schmidt, President/CEO
Greg Cameron, COO
Reese Marcusson, EVP/CFO
Steve Robinson, EVP Radio
Anne Gleason, VP Marketing

Regional Radio Networks

Alaska Public Radio Network
3877 University Drive, Anchorage, AK 99508-4676
(907) 550-8400; *Fax:* (907) 550-8401
www.alaskapublic.org/
Ed Ulman, CEO/General Manager
Bernie Washington, CFO
Jessica Stugelmayer, Director of Marketing & Promotions
Lori Townsend, News Director
Bede Trantina, FM Program Director
Bob Wyatt, Chief Technology Officer
Satellite-delivered news/info programs to 26 member stn across Alaska from state-of-the-art studios, hqtr in Anchorage.
Washington, DC News Bureau
2801 Quebec St. N.W., Suite 505, Washington, DC 20008-1227
(202) 488-1961
Joel Southern, Capitol Bureau Chief
Juneau Alaska News Bureau
530 Park St, Juneau, AK 99801-1065
(907) 586-6948
Dave Donaldson, State Capitol Bureau Chief

American Ag Network
PO Box 9439, Fargo, ND 58106-9439
(701) 237-5000; *Fax:* (701) 280-0861
americanagnetwork.com
americanagnetwork@gmail.com
Mark Swendsen, President/Sales Manager
Steve Carlson, Operations Dir
Rusty Halvorson, Farm Director
Katie Miller, Farm Broadcaster
Lance Knudson, Sales Representative
Mark Swartzell, News Director
Steve Carlson,Operations/Affiliate Relations/Sports
Comprises 40 stns: 16 in South Dakota, 22 in North Dakota & 2 in Montana.
2501 13th Ave., Suite 201, Fargo, ND 58103-3601
(701) 237-5000; *Fax:* (701) 280-0816
Steve Carlson, Opns Mgr
Box 13919, Grand Forks, ND 58208-3919
(701) 775-3910; *Fax:* (701) 775-3932
Lance Knudson, Sls Mgr

Beasley Broadcast Group
3033 Riviera Drive, Suite 200, Naples, FL 34103 USA
(239) 263-5000; *Fax:* (239) 263-8191
www.bbgi.com
email@bbgi.com
Ownership: George G. Beasley.
George Beasley, Chairman/Chief Executive Officer
B. Caroline Beasley, Executive Vice President/Chief Financial Officer
Bruce Beasley, President/Chief Operating Officer
Brian E. Beasley, Vice President of Operations
Tim Huston,General Sales Manager
Justin Chase, VP, Programming
Michael Cooney, VP, Chief Technology Officer
Joyce Fitch, Esq., General Counsel
Shaun Greening, VP Financial Reporting
Denyse Smith Mesnik, VP, Corporate Communications
Kimberley R.Sonneborn, VP, Digital Production
Radio stns 44: 27 FMs & 17 AMs in 11 large, mid-sized markets.

Brownfield Network
Div/DBA: (A division of Learfield Communications Inc.)
505 Hobbs Road, Jefferson City, MO 65109
(573) 893-5700; (573) 893-7200; (573) 893-8255; *Fax:* (573) 893-8094
www.brownfieldnetwork.com
cyoung@BrownfieldNetwork.com
Bruce Beasley, President
Joyce Steinman, General Sales Mgr
Comprises 280 stns in Illinois, Iowa, Missouri, Nebraska, Indiana, South Dakota & Wisconsin. Represented by In-House.

California News Radio
Div/DBA: skyview networks
14605 N Airport Drive, Suite 370, Scottsdale, AZ 85260
(480) 503-8700, (866) 858-6397, (877) 503-8910; *Fax:* (480) 998-5751
www.skyviewsatellite.com
Ken Thiele, President
Jeanne-Marie Condo, General Manager
Comprises 26 stns in California.

CMS Station Brokerage, Inc.
1439 Denniston St., Pittsburgh, PA 15217 USA
(412) 421-2600; *Fax:* (412) 421-6001
www.cmsstationbrokerage.com
roger.rafson@genmediapartners.com
Roger Rafson, President
Shirley Brown, Office Manager
Offers media brokerage services. CMS Station Brokerage helps radio station owners sell their radio stations to qualified buyers and helps buyers find radio stations which make sense to meet their objectives. CMS Station Brokerage alsospecializes in providing radio brokerage services for broadcasters in small and medium sized markets across the United States and Canada.

Commercial Media Sales
1439 Denniston Street, Pittsburgh, PA 15217
(412) 421-2600; *Fax:* (412) 421-6001
www.cmsradio.com
rafson@cmsradio.com
Roger Rafson, Founder
Comprises three stns in Pennsylvania. Represented by Commercial Media Sales.

Compu-Weather Inc.
2566 Rt 52, Forensic Services Division, Hopewell Junction, NY 12533
(800) 825-4445, (845) 227-8500; *Fax:* (845) 227-8400
www.compuweather.com
sales@compuweather.com
Jeff Wimmer, President
Patti Robertson, Forensic Account Executive

CRN International, Inc.
One Circular Avenue, Hamden, CT 06514
(203) 288-2002; *Fax:* (203) 281-3291
www.crnradio.com
hr@crnradio.com
S. Richard Kalt, President
Steve Wakeen, Operations Dir
Rob O'Mara, Managing Director, Strategy & Development
Jim Alkon, Marketing Director
Stragtegy & execution, retail mktg, lifestyle progmg, promotions, digital media & other non-traditional communication tactics, small business, collaborative mktg, weather-triggered media placement, Ethnic, Just -In-Time Marketing.
Branch Office: Minneapolis, MN,

Florida News Network
2500 Maitland Center Parkway, Suite 407, Maitland, FL 32751
(888) 407-4376; *Fax:* (407) 916-7425
www.fnnonline.net
Jim Poling, Director of Opeartions
Rick Green, General Manager
Pat Byrd, Sales Manager
Al Spry, Affiliate Relations
Susan Patterson, Regional Account Manager
Lori Stout, Regional Account Manager
Comprises 58 stns in Florida. Represented by StateNets Inc.

Florida Public Radio Network
1600 Red Barber Plaza, Tallahassee, FL 32310
(850) 487-3170; (850) 487-3086; *Fax:* (850) 487-3093
www.wfsu.org
mail@wfsu.org
Carolina Austin, Operations Dir
Patrick Keating, General Manager
Tom Flanigan, News Director
Denison Graham, Finance Director
Sherri Leggett, Accounting Supervisor
Leah Gigi, Accounting Specialist
Teresa Bryan, FinancialAssociate
Lydell Rawls
Serves 13 FM public radio stns in Florida.

Georgia News Network
1819 Peachtree Road, Suite 700, Atlanta, GA 30309
(404) 607-9045, (800) 776-4638; *Fax:* (404) 367-6404
www.georgianewsnetwork.com
robmaynard@clearchannel.com
John Clark, Programming/ Operations/ Affiliate Relations
Linda Kent, General Sales Mgr
Matt Cook, News Director
Doug Nodine, Anchor
Comprises 108 stns in Georgia. Represented by StateNts.

Hawkeye Network
505 Hobbs Road, Jefferson City, MO 65109
(573) 893-7200; *Fax:* (573) 893-8076; (573) 893-2321
www.learfield.com
Marc Jenkins, Chief Operating Officer
Greg Brown, President/Chief Executive Officer
Sarah Stieferman, VP Operations Controller
Bob Agramonte, General Manager
Roy Seinfeld, Executive VP National Sales
Keith Sampson, ProgrammingDirector
John Raleigh, Chief Legal Officer
Andy Rawlings, Executive VP/Chief Revenue Officer
Tom Stevens, Vice President
Matt Hupfeld, Chief Financial Officer
Comprises 50 stns in Iowa. Sports Network.

Hispanic Communications Network
50 F Street, NW, 8th Floor, Washington, DC 20001
(202) 637-8800; *Fax:* (202) 637-8801
www.hcnmedia.com
Jeff Kline, Founder & Chairman
Carlos Alcazar, CEO & President
Mercy Padillo, Business Development
Veronica Diaz, Director, Project Management & Operations
Alison Rodden, VP, Client Engagement & Business Dev.
David Castro,Director, Media Production & Programming CS
Mercy Padilla, Dir. Of Affiliate & Media Relations
Cresta Archuletta, Client Engagement Associate
National-All 50 states & Puerto Rico: 200 radio stns.

Hometown Radio Network
6505 Rockside Road, Suite 200, Cleveland, OH 44131
(216) 781-0035; *Fax:* (216) 781-7508
www.regionalreps.com
info@regionalreps.com
Stuart J. Sharpe, President
Douglas L. Trostler, VP/Sales
Kevin Bennett, Regional Manager/ Southeast
Linley A. Grande, Regional Manager/ Chicago
Emily R. Powers, Corporate Administrator
Jeffery T. Slivka, VP, Finance &Operations
Shayna N. Sharpe, VP, Business
Comprises over 1000 affils in Delaware, Florida, Georgia, Iowa, Illinois, Indiana, Kansas, Kentucky, Maryland, Nebraska, North Carolina, Ohio, Oklahoma, Pennsylvania, South Carolina, Virginia, & West Virginia. Represented by: Rgnl Reps Corp.

Illinois Radio Network
3501 E Sangamon Avenue, Springfield, IL 62702
(312) 943-6363; (217) 753-5400; *Fax:* (312) 943-5109
www.illinoisradionetwork.com
newsirn@sbcglobal.net
Charlie Ferguson, President & General Manager
Alex Degman, News Director
Dale Barnes, Marketing Consultant
Jennifer Wernsing, Traffic Manager
John Gregory, Reporter
Dave Dahl, Reporter
Jason Goch, Sports Director
A statewide satellite-delivered net providing news, sports, business & special progmg. IRN 67 affils. Representative: StateNets.

ION Radio Network
Box 1223, Airport Road, Morristown, NJ 07960
(973) 983-8222; *Fax:* (973) 983-1390
www.ionweather.com
Stephen Pellettiere, President
stephen Pellettiere, Meterologist
Comprises 10 stns, four in New Jersey, four in New York, one in Pennsylvania & one in Connecticut.

Kansas Agriculture Network
1210 SW Executive Drive, Topeka, KS 66615
(785) 272-3456; *Fax:* (785) 272-7282
www.radionetworks.com
dan.johnson@morris.com
Comprises 30 stns in Kansas. Represented by Learfield Radio.

Kansas Information Network
1210 SW Executive Drive, Topeka, KS 66615
(785) 272-3456; *Fax:* (785) 228-7282
www.radionetworks.com
dan.johnson@morris.com
Comprises 32 stns in Kansas. Represented by StateNets.

KEDA Radio
1246 W Laurel St, San Antonio, TX 78201
(210) 226-5254
www.kedaradio.com
Richard Cruz, Sales
Melisa Gatica-Garza, Sales
Belinda Aguilar, Secretary
Olga Rivera Jackson, DiscJockey
Mark weber, DiscJockey
Canada's only 24-hour national specialty service dedicated to the world of showbiz news and information. Programming includes in-depth specials and events, detailed behind-the scene features on major movies, exclusive interviews with theworld's biggest celebrities and extensive live coverage of award shows, premieres and galas.

Kentucky News Network (KNN)
Div/DBA: (A subsidiary of Clear Channel Radio Inc.)
4000 # 1 Radio Drive, Louisville, KY 40218
(502) 479-2248; *Fax:* (502) 479-2231
www.kentuckynewsnetwork.com
nathanbutler@clearchannel.com
Mark S Williams
Comprises 87 stns in Kentucky. Represented by StatesNets. Live via satellite.

Learfield
Div/DBA: (A division of Learfield Communications Inc.)
505 Hobbs Road, Jefferson City, MO 65109
(573) 893-7200; *Fax:* (573) 893-2321
www.learfield.com
Marc Jenkins, Chief Operating Officer
Clyde G. Lear, President
Aaron Worsham, Operations Dir
Bob Agramonte, Chief Business Development Officer
Keith Sampson, Programming Director
Gary Sobba, Sr Vice President
Phil Atkinson, VP OfIT
Time Cline, Sr Vice President
Roger Gardner, Executive VP/Chief Culture&Communications Officer
Matt Hupfeld, Chief Financial Officer
Comprises 55 stns in Missouri.

Linder Farm Network
255 Cedardale Drive, Owatonna, MN 55060
(507) 444-9224; *Fax:* (507) 444-9080
www.linderfarmnetwork.com
farm@linderradio.com
Lynn Ketelsen, General Manager
Jeff Stewart, General Sales Mgr
Lynn Ketelsen, Farm Dir.
Linda Brekke, Farm Editor
Jeff Stewart, Ag Marketing Specialist
Matt Ketelsen
Comprises 22 stns in Minnesota. Represented by Katz Radio.

Louisiana Radio Network
10500 Coursey Blvd, Suite 104, Baton Rouge, LA 70816 US
(225) 291-2727; *Fax:* (225) 297-7539
www.louisianaradionetwork.com
jim@louisianaradionetwork.com
Jim Engster, President
Dawn Dicharry, Operations Manager
Neal Gladner, Vice President of Sales & Marketing
Jeff Palermo, News Director
Carolyn Roche, Controller
Robert Stewart, Editor
Joe Gallinaro, Graphic Designer
NealGladner, VP, Sales & Marketing
Don Molino, Affiliate Relations Director & Sr. Farm Broad.
Michelle Southern, Assistant News Director
Comprises 84 stns in Louisiana. Represented by news net: State Nets, Agri-News Network: McGavren Guild.

Michigan Farm Radio Network
325 South Walnut, Lansing, MI 48933
(517) 484-4888; *Fax:* (517) 484-5015
www.mfrn.com
Dennis Mellott, President & General Manager
Ryan Hermes, Affiliate Relations Dir.
Nicole Heslip, Agri-News Reporter
Rob Buttery, Agri-News Editor
Comprises 21 Michigan, affils. Represented by J.L. Farmakis.

Michigan Radio Network
325 South Walnut Street, Lansing, MI 48933
(517) 484-4888; *Fax:* (517) 484-1389
www.michiganradionetwork.com
news@mrnradionet.com
Dennis Mellott, President / General Manager
Dennis Krolik, Operations Dir
Kirsten Buys, General Manager
Rob Baykian, News Director
Ryan Hermes, Director of Affiliate Relations
Dale Barnes, Sales Director
Chris Lepley, SportsDirector
Tim Skubick, Capitol Correspondent
Bill Thompson, Audio News Editor
A statewide satellite-delivered net providing news, sports, business & special progmg. MRN 55 affils. Representative: StateNets.

Mid-America Ag Network
1632 S Maize Road, Wichita, KS 67209
(316) 721-8484; *Fax:* (316) 721-8276
www.midamericaagnetwork.com
Greg Steckline, President
Rick Betzen, General Manager
Craig Mead, News Director
Rick Betzen, Sales
Jeff Strahl, Sales
Comprises 33 stns in Colorado, Kansas & Nebraska.. Represented by Torbet Radio.

Midwestern Broadcsting Company
Div/DBA: (Formerly Paul Bunyan Network)
300 E Front Street, Suite 450, Traverse City, MI 49684
(231) 929-HITS (4487), (231) 946-6211; *Fax:* (231) 929-3988
www.z93hits.com/midwestern-broadcasting
RonPritchard@Z93Hits.com
Ross Biederman, President
Chris Warren, General Manager
Chris Davis, Marketing Director
Ron Pritchard, Programming Director
Courtney Rehmer, News Director
Jordan Anderson, Production Manager
Comprises 10 stns in Michigan. Represented by Katz Radio.

Mississippi Agri Network
6311 Ridgewood Road, Jackson, MS 39211
(601) 957-1700, (888) 808-8637; *Fax:* (601) 956-5228
www.supertalk.fm/
feedback@supertalk.fm
Stacy Long, General Sales Mgr
Comprises 35 affils in Mississippi. Represented by McGavren/Guild.

Mississippi News Network
6311 Ridgewood Road, Jackson, MS 39211
(601) 957-1700, (888) 808-8637; *Fax:* (601) 956-5228
www.supertalk.fm/
newsms@supertalk.fm
Stacy Long, General Sales Mgr
Comprises 82 affils in Mississippi. Represented by StateNets.

Mississippi State Basketball Network
6311 Ridgewood Road, Jackson, MS 39211
(601) 957-1700; (888) 808-8637; *Fax:* (601) 956-5228
www.supertalk.fm/
feedback@supertalk.fm
Kim Dillon, Promotions Manager
Comprises 28 affils in Mississippi & one in Tennessee.

Mississippi State Football Network
6311 Ridgewood Road, Jackson, MS 39211
(601) 957-1700, (888) 808-8637; *Fax:* (601) 956-5228
www.supertalk.fm/
feedback@supertalk.fm
Steve Davenport, CEO/COO
Steve Davenport, President
Comprises 30 affils in Mississippi & one in Alabama. Represented by Kim Dillon.

Missourinet
Div/DBA: (A division of Learfield Communications Inc.)
505 Hobbs Road, Jefferson City, MO 65109
(573) 893-2829; *Fax:* (573) 893-8094
www.missourinet.com
info@missourinet.com
Bob Priddy, News Director
Bill Pollock, Sports Dir.
Mike Lear, Anchor/Reporter
Jessica Machetta, Anchor/Reporter
Laurie Bonnot, Advertising
Steve Houser, Advertising
K.C. Riedl, Advertising
Serves Missouri, 50-60 affils.

Mountain News Network
50 Vashell Way, Suite 400, Orinda, CA 94563
(925) 254-4456, (650) 747-0605, (831) 423-0396; *Fax:* (925) 254-6135
www.mnn.net
news@mnn.net
Neil Wiley, Webmaster
Comprises 1,537 stns nationwide.

National Educational Telecommunications Association
Mailing Address: Box 50008, Columbia, SC 29250
Second Address: 939 S Stadium Road, Columbia, SC 29201
(803) 799-5517; *Fax:* (803) 771-4831; (803) 779-5553
www.netaonline.org
skip@netaonline.org
Anita Sims, VP, Finance & Business Development
Skip Hinton, President
Greg Tillou, Director Of Operations
Gayle Loeber, Director Of Programming
Anita Sims, VP, finance & business Development
John Chambers, Education Center
DavidCrouch, Administration
Tinia Milhouse, Conference Services
Ninety-five members in 45 states & the U.S. Virgin Islands.

North Carolina News Network
3012 Highwood Blvd, Suite 201, Raleigh, NC 27604
(919) 878-1724; *Fax:* (919) 890-6146
www.ncnn.com
newsroom@ncnn.com
David Stuckey, General Sales Manager
Brian Freeman, News Director/Affiliate Relations
Allen Sherrill, Chief Engineer
Bruce Ferrell, Assis. News Director/Managing Editor
Scott Briggaman, Anchor/Reporter
George Douglas, AffiliateManager
Patrick Johnson, Sports Anchor/Reporter
Josh Zach, Anchor/ Reporter
Joseph Cupolo III, Account Executive
Comprises 75 stns in North Carolina. Represented by StateNets.

NRG Media, LLC
Mailing Address: 5011 Capitol Avenue, Omaha, NE 68132
Second Address: 2875 Mount Vernon Rd Se, Cedar Rapids, IA 52403
(608) 756-0747, (800) 242-0107; *Fax:* (920) 563-0315
www.lite1073.com
jvriezen@nrgmedia.com
Chuck DuCoty, COO
Mary Quass, CEO/President
Gary Douglas Lundberg, Operations Manager
James Vriezen, General Manager
Shane Sparks, Sales Manager
Jeff Winfield, Programming Director
George Nicholas, Engineering Dir
Eric Stone,Morning Host
Polly Peterson, Midday Host
Jason Ryan, afternoon Host
Comprises 55 radio stns in Illinois, Iowa, Nebraska & Wisconsin.

Radio Iowa
Div/DBA: (A division of Learfield Communications Inc.)
2700 Grand Avenue, Suite 103, Des Moines, IA 50312
(515) 282-1984; *Fax:* (515) 282-1879
www.radioiowa.com
Clyde G. Lear, President
Jennifer Shaefer, General Sales Mgr
O. Kay Henderson, News Director
Jennifer Simpson, Advertising
Todd Kimm, Sports Director
Dar Danielson, Anchor/Reporter
Matt Kelley, Anchor/Reporter
Pat Curtis,Anchor/Reporter
Comprises 66 affils in Iowa.

Radio Pennsylvania Network
Div/DBA: (A Division of WITF Inc.)
4801 Lindle Road, Harrisburg, PA 17111
(800) 735-8400; *Fax:* (717) 704-3678
www.radiopa.com
dsmith@topflightmedia.com
Darren Smith, General Manager
Brad Christman, News Director
Paula Barton, Affiliate Relations
Christie Zdanowicz, Traffic Manager
Bcsts state news, sports & features to affils in Pennsylvania. Comprises 80 stns. Represented by NASRN.

Saga Communications, Inc,
73 Kercheval Avenue, Suite 201, Grosse Pointe Farms, MI 48236
(313) 886-7070; *Fax:* (313) 886-7150
www.sagacom.com/
echristian@sagacom.com
Sam Bush, Chief Financial Officer/Treasurer/Sr VP
Edward Christian, President & CEO
Warren Lada, Executive Vice President/Operations
Ann Karrick, Programming Coordinator
Tom Atkins, Director of Engineering
Sam Bush, Senior VicePresident, CFO, Treasurer
Marcia Lobaito, Senior Vice President/Dir. Business Affairs
Cathy Bobinski, Senior Vice President, Chief Accounting Officer, C
Tracy Cleeton, Director, IT
Matt Nystrom, Saga Interactive Operations Director

Southeast AgNet
5053 NW Hwy 225 A, Ocala, FL 34482
(352) 671-1909; *Fax:* (352) 671-1364
www.southeastagnet.com
office@southeastagnet.com
Gary Cooper, Founder/ President
Elayna Rexrode, VP of Operations
Robin Loftin, Co-Owner / Publisher
Sabrina Hill-Wilcox, Farm News Director
Daniel Lee, Radio/Web Production
Randall Weiseman, Network Program Director
TracyCallies, Interim Editor
Brayanna Bullard, News Producer
Marc Stockwell, Senior Account Executive
Nicholle Saylor, Account Executive
Marc Hook, Graphic Designer
Tange Sigal, Bookkeeper
Ernie Neff, Editor/Broadcaster
Stns interconnected via Internet. Comprises 65 affils in Florida, Georgia & the Alabama rgn.

Southern Farm Network
Div/DBA: (Curtis Media Group)
3012 Highwoods Blvd, Suite 200, Raleigh, NC 27604
(919) 790-9392; *Fax:* (919) 790-8369
www.sfntoday.com
info@sfntoday.com
Don Curtis, Chairman & Chief Executive Officer
David Stuckey, Sr VP/General Manager
Terry Ratliff, Station Manager
Bill Whitley, General Sales Manager
Lisa McKay, VP Programming
Rhonda Garrison, Ag News Director
Howard Hollar,Controller
Tammy O'Dell, Director Of Sales
Trip Savery, Executive Vice President
Comprises 20 affils in North Carolina & South Carolina.

Super Talk Mississippi
6311 Ridgewood Road, Jackson, MS 39211
(601) 957-1700, (888) 808-8637; *Fax:* (601) 956-5228
www.supertalk.fm/
feedback@supertalk.fm
Comprises 30 affils in Mississippi & one in Tennessee. Represented by Kim Dillon.

TeleSouth Communications,Inc
6311 Ridgewood Road, Jackson, MS 39211
(601) 957-1700; *Fax:* (601) 956-5228
www.telesouth.com
sdavenport@telesouth.com
Steve Davenport, Owner/CEO
Kim Dillon, President/COO
John Winfield, Executive VP, Operations
Larry Tate, VP, Sales
David Day, Program Director
Chris Davis, News Director
Houston McDavitt, Director of Engineering
Tanya Taylor,Executive Vice-President CFO
Angie Cockerill, Accounting
Brent Lape, Multimedia Director
Jared Bounds, Social Media Coordinator
Comprises 30 affils in Mississippi & one in Tennessee. Represented by Kim Dillon.

Tennessee Agri-Net
Div/DBA: (Subsidiary of Clear Channel Communications Inc.)
55 Music Square West, Nashville, TN 37203
(615) 664-2400; *Fax:* (615) 687-9797
www.tennesseeradionetwork.com
craighahn@clearchannel.com
Chris Romer, Operations
Dan Zuleger, Sales
Dan Eidem, News Director
Nathan Butler, Director, Affiliate Relations
Comprises 48 stns in Tennessee.

Tennessee Radio Network
Div/DBA: (A subsidiary of Clear Channel Broadcasting Inc.)
55 Music Square W, Nashville, TN 37203
(615) 664-2400; *Fax:* (615) 687-9797
www.tennesseeradionetwork.com
craighahn@clearchannel.com
Chris Romer, Operations
Dan Zuleger, Sales
Tom English, Promotions Manager
Dan Eidem, News Director
Nathan Butler, Director, Affiliate Relations
Comprises 74 stns in Tennessee. Representative Nathan Butler (Loisville, KY location) affil rel dir.

Texas State Network
4131 N Central Expwy, Suite 1000, Dallas, TX 75204
(214) 525-7000; *Fax:* (214) 525-7371
www.tsnradio.com
pwdavis@cbs.com
Brian Purdy, Operations Dir
Jerry Bobo, General Manager
Dan Bell, General Sales Mgr
Julis Graw, News Director
Raul Jaurequi
P W Davis
Provides newscasts, sportscasts, agriculture reports, longform programs to 165 stns in Texas & the Texas Rangers Radio

Network. The oldest & largest state radio net owned by CBS Radio. Represented by StateNets.
502 E. 11th St, Suite 320, Austin, TX 78701-2658
(512) 474-5275; *Fax:* 512 476 9232
Candy Schmidt, Regional Sales Director

University of Mississippi Football Network
6311 Ridgewood Road, Jackson, MS 39211
(601) 957-1700, (888) 808-8637; *Fax:* (601) 956-5228
www.supertalk.fm/
feedback@supertalk.fm
Steve Davenport, President
Comprises 30 affils in Mississippi & one in Tennessee. Represented by Tim Fritts.

Univision Radio
3102 Oak Lawn Avenue, Suite 215, Dallas, TX 75219
(214) 525-7700; *Fax:* (214) 525-7750
www.univision.com
Ownership: Univision Communications Inc., 100% (see listing under TV Group Ownership, Section B)
Alan F. Horn, President
Comprises 72 stns, 18 in California, four in Florida, five in Illinois, three in Nevada, three in New York, 26 in Texas & five in Arizona, four in New Mexico, four in Puerto Rico.

Vox Communications
Div/DBA: (formerly Berkshire Broadcasting Co. Inc.)
466 Curran Highway, North Adams, MA 01247
(413) 663-6567; *Fax:* (413) 662-2143
www.wnaw.com
wnaw@wnaw.com
Bob Heck, Sales Manager
Melanie Gageant, Marketing Consultant
Bob Heck, Sales Manager
Comprises 6 stns in Berkshire County, MA.

West Virginia MetroNews Network
1111 Virginia Street East, Charleston, WV 25301
(304) 346-7055; *Fax:* (304) 296-3876
www.wvmetronews.com
jparsons@wvradio.com
Dale B. Miller, President
Hoppy Kercheval, Operations Dir
Kyle Wiggs, Sports Anchor
Jeff Jenkins, Head Of News Division
Garrett Cullen
Fred Persinger
Travis Jones
Comprises West Virginia News, 58 stns in West Virginia & Mountaineer Sports Network, 72 stns in West Virginia.
1111 Virginia St. E., Charleston, WV 25301-2406
(304) 342-8131

Western Agri-Radio Networks Inc.
on 17 Radio Station Affiliations Cable Systems
Div/DBA: (dba California Agri-Radio Network & Southwest Agr
680 W 20th Street, Yuma, AZ 85364
(928) 782-1440, (800) 944-6077; (928) 920-6116; *Fax:* (928) 782-1474
www.westernagri-radio.net/
ggatley@sprynet.com
Transponder: Fed by MP3 off website
George G. Gatley, President & Director
Chris Gatley, Secretary And Traffic Director
Fifteen radio stns in California, two in Arizona & one in Texas. Represented by J.L. Famakis.
Southwest Agri-Radio Network
1700 S. 1st Ave, Suite 214, Yuma, AZ 85364-5745
(800) 944-6077; *Fax:* (520) 782-1474
www.home.com/sprynet/ggatley
ggatley@sprynet.com
California Agri-Radio Network
1700 S. 1st Ave, Suite 214, Yuma, AZ 85364-5745
(800) 944-6077, (520) 782-1440; *Fax:* (520) 782-1474
www.home.com/sprynet/ggatley
ggatley@sprynet.com

WGN Radio
435 N Michigan Avenue, Suite 720, Chicago, IL 60611
(312) 981-7200, (312) 222-3879; *Fax:* (312) 222-4180
www.wgnradio.com
comments@wgnradio.com

Wisconsin Radio Network
Div/DBA: A Division of Learfield Communications
222 State Street, Suite 403, Madison, WI 53703-2273
(608) 251-3900; (608) 848-2770; *Fax:* (608) 251-7233
www.wrn.com
info@wrn.com
Joyce Steinman, General Sales Mgr
Bob Hague, News Director
Jill Makovec, Advertising
Jackie Johnson
Bill Scott
Andrew Beckett
Statewide satellite-delivered net providing Wisconsin news & sports.

WRTI-FM
1509 Cecil B Moore Avenue, 3rd Floor, Philadelphia, PA 19121
(215) 204-2300, (866) 809-9784; *Fax:* (215) 204-7027
www.wrti.org
Tobias Poole, Operations Dir
David S. Conant, General Manager
William Johnson, Station Manager
Patty Prevost, General Sales Mgr
Jack Moore, Programming Director
Jeffrey DePolo, Engineering Dir
Edward Brown, Technology Manager
Jane Kelly, Director Of Development
Jessica Schultz, Digital Content Manager/Editor
Joe Patti, Production Manager
Kristine Plegaria, Office Manager
Comprises four stns in Pennsylvania, one in New Jersey & one in Delaware.

Yancey AG Network
Box 1000, Oklahoma City, OK 73101
(405) 858-10297
www.aghub.net
ashliacker@clearchannel.com
Ben Buckland, Station Manager
Ron Hays, Programming Director
A satellite delivered Agsource providing affil radio stns with agricultural markets, news & weather. Represents 17 stns.

Radio Group Ownership

ABC Owned Television Stations
77 West 66th St., New York NY 10023
abclocal.go.com
Ownership: Disney-ABC Television Group
Radio Stns: 28 AM. 3 FM.
KWDZ Salt Lake City, UT; KATL Miles City, MT; KRDY San Antonio, TX; KMIK Tempe, AZ; KMKI Plano, TX; KMKY Oakland, CA; KPHN Kansas City, MO; KQAM Wichita, KS; KIID Sacramento, CA; KMIC Houston, TX; WCOG Greensboro, NC; WDWD Atlanta, GA; WMYM Miami, FL; WFDF Farmington Hills, MI; WGFY Charlotte, NC; WDDY Albany, NY; WHKT Portsmouth, VA; WDYZ Orlando, FL; WKSH Sussex, WI; WDDZ Pittsburgh, PA; WHBE Newburg, KY; WNTT Tazewell, TN; WPMH Portsmouth, VA; WMKI Boston, MA; WQEW New York, NY; WRDZ La Grange, IL; WWJZ Mount Holly, NJ; WWMK Cleveland, OH; KALQ-FM Alamosa, CO; KDIS-FM Little Rock, AR; WRDZ-FM Plainfield, IN
TV Stns: 8 TV.
KABC-TV Los Angeles, CA; KFSN-TV Fresno, CA; KGO-TV San Francisco, CA; KTRK-TV Houston, TX; WABC-TV New York, NY; WLS-TV Chicago, IL; WPVI-TV Philadelphia, PA; WTVD-TV Durham, NC
Rebecca Campbell, President

Absolute Broadcasting LLC
30 Temple Dr., Litchfield NH 3052
(603) 883-9900
Radio Stns: 3 AM.
WGAM Manchester, NH; WGHM Nashua, NH; WSMN Nashua, NH

Acadia Broadcasting Ltd.
58 King St., 3rd Floor, Saint John NB E2L 1G4
(506) 648-2100
www.acadiabroadcastinglimited.ca
info@radioabl.ca
Ownership: Black-Tip Investments Ltd., 50%; Rosa Rugosa Investments Ltd., 50%.
Radio Stns: 13 FM.
CHSJ-FM Saint John, NB; CHWV-FM Saint John, NB; CHTD-FM Saint Stephen, NB; CKBW-FM Bridgewater, NS; CFOB-FM Fort Frances, ON; CJUK-FM Thunder Bay, ON; CJRL-FM Kenora, ON; CKNI-FM Moncton, NB; CKDR-FM Dryden, ON; CKDR-2-FM Sioux Lookout, ON; CKDR-5-FM Red Lake, ON; CJHK-FM Bridgewater, NS; CKTG-FM Thunder Bay, ON
Chris Pearson, President
Troy Wallace, General Sales Mgr
Brian Mclain, News Director

Access.1 Communications Corp.
11 Penn Plaza, 16th Fl., New York NY 10001
(212) 714-1000; *Fax:*(212) 714-1563
Radio Stns: 1 FM.
KSYR Benton, LA
Sydney Small, CEO

Ace Radio Corp.
2801 Via Fortuna Dr., Suite 675, Austin TX 78746
Radio Stns: 5 FM.
KQLP Leupp, AZ; KCOO Dunkerton, IA; WTPO New Albany, MS; KQMX Lost Hills, CA; WZHL New Augusta, MS

Ackley Media Group
P.O. Box 302179, St. Thomas VI 00803
(340) 776-1000; *Fax:*(340) 776-5357
www.amg.vi
Radio Stns: 1 AM. 2 FM.
WVWI Charlotte Amalie, VI; WVJZ Charlotte Amalie, VI; WWKS Cruz Bay, VI
Gordon Ackley, President

ACM JCE IV B LLC.
426 S. River Rd., Tryon NC 28782
(828) 859-6982
Radio Stns: 4 AM.
KBXD Dallas, TX; WFTL West Palm Beach, FL; WFLL Fort Lauderdale, FL; WMEN Royal Palm Beach, FL
Mark Jorgenson, President

Ad Astra Per Aspera Broadcasting Inc.
10 E. 5th Ave., Hutchinson KS 67501
(620) 665-5758; *Fax:*(620) 665-5758
www.adastraradio.com
ksku@adastra.kscoxmail.com
Radio Stns: 4 FM.
KSKU Sterling, KS; KNZS Arlington, KS; KXKU Lyons, KS; KWHK Hutchinson, KS
Cliff Shank, President
Michael Hill, Operations Dir

Adams Radio Group
16233 Kenyon Avenue South, Suite 220, Lakeville MN 55044
(952) 232-0588; *Fax:*(612) 437-4520
www.adamsradiogroup.com
Radio Stns: 10 AM. 17 FM.
KSNM Las Cruces, NM; KOMO Seattle, WA; KVI Seattle, WA; WLYV-AM Laurel, DE; WJWK Seaford, DE; WJWL Georgetown, DE; WAKE-AM Georgetown, DE; KWML-AM Georgetown, DE; KSNM-FM Georgetown, DE; WLYV-AM Georgetown, DE; KGRT-FM Las Cruces, NM; KPLZ-FM Seattle, WA; WGBG Seaford, DE; WJKI Bethany Beach, DE; WKHI Fruitland, MD; WXSH Pocomoke City, MD; WLJE Valparaiso, IN; WOCQ Berlin, MD; WZEB Ocean View, DE; WZBH Georgetown, DE; KIKF Cascade, MT; W245CA Pocomoke City, MD; WXKE-FM Pocomoke City, MD; WLJE-FM Georgetown, DE; WZVN-FM Georgetown, DE; WXRD-FM Georgetown, DE; KWML Georgetown, DE
Ron Stone, President & CEO
Sharon Bordwell, Corporate Controller

Adelman Broadcasting Inc.
731 N. Balsam St., Ridgecrest CA 93555
(760) 371-1700; *Fax:*(760) 371-1824
www.adelmanbroadcasting.com
contact@adelmanbroadcasting.com
Radio Stns: 1 AM. 3 FM.
KLOA Ridgecrest, CA; KGBB Edwards, CA; KLOA Ridgecrest, CA; KRAJ Johannesburg, CA
Robert Adelman, President

Adonai Radio Group
2448 E. 81st St., Suite 5500, Tulsa OK 74137
(918) 492-2660; *Fax:*(918) 492-8840
www.kxoj.com
Radio Stns: 2 AM. 6 FM.
KBIX Muskogee, OK; KYAL Sapulpa, OK; KEMX Locust Grove, OK; KEOJ Caney, KS; KCXR Taft, OK; KYAL-FM Muskogee, OK; KTFR Chelsea, OK; KXOJ-FM Sapulpa, OK
Michael Stephens, President

Air South Radio Inc.
1241 Cliff Gookin Boulevard, Tupelo MS 38801
(662) 842-7625; *Fax:*(662) 842-9568
Ownership: Olvie E. Sisk; Kathern Sisk.
Radio Stns: 3 FM.
WCNA Potts Camp, MS; WFTA Fulton, MS; WLZA Eupora, MS
Olvie E. Sisk, President, Director and Manager
Ivous T. Sisk, Director, Secretary and Treasurer

Alaska Broadcast Communications Inc.
3161 Channel Dr., Suite 2, Juneau AK 99801
(907) 586-3630; *Fax:*(907) 463-3685
www.taku105.com
Radio Stns: 4 AM. 3 FM.
KIFW Sitka, AK; KJNO Juneau, AK; KTKN Ketchikan, AK; KXXJ Juneau, AK; KGTW Ketchikan, AK; KSBZ Sitka, AK; KTKU Juneau, AK
Richard Burns, CEO

Alaska Integrated Media
4700 Business Park Blvd., Building E, Suite 44-A, Anchorage AK 99503
(907) 522-1018; *Fax:*(907) 522-1027
Radio Stns: 2 AM. 2 FM.
KOAN Anchorage, AK; KVNT Eagle River, AK; KZND Houston, AK; KMVN Anchorage, AK

Alex Media Inc.
25 E. 86th St., New York NY 10028
(917) 535-0419
Ownership: Alexander Berger, 51%; Darryl Delawder, 24.5%; Evan Carb, 24.5%.
Radio Stns: 4 FM.
WZFL Islamorada, FL; KAFZ Ash Fork, AZ; KPUT Mona, UT; KHNO Huntington, OR
Alexander Berger, President

Alexandra Communications Inc.
1600 Gray Lynn Dr., Walla Walla WA 99362
(509) 527-1000; *Fax:*(509) 529-5534
Radio Stns: 2 AM. 4 FM.
KTIL(AM) Netarts, OR; KUJ Walla Walla, WA; KDEP Garibaldi, OR; KZIU-FM Weston, OR; KLKY Stanfield, OR; KTIL-FM Bay City, OR

Allegheny Mountain Network Stations
9836 Browns Creek Road, Dunmore WV 24934
(304) 799-6004; *Fax:*(304) 799-7444
amnet@aol.com
Ownership: Cary H. Simpson.
Radio Stns: 3 AM. 3 FM.
WFRM Coudersport, PA; WNBT Wellsboro, PA; WTRN Tyrone, PA; WEEO-FM McConnellsburg, PA; WNBQ Mansfield, PA; WNBT-FM Wellsboro, PA
Richard Hise, Managing Director
Sue Fertig, Resource Director
Cary H. Simpson, President
Erin Will, Station Coordinator
John Simpson, General Manager

Alpha Media LLC
1211 S.W. 5th Ave., Suite 750, Portland OR 97204
(503) 517-6000; *Fax:*(503) 517-6401
www.alphamediausa.com
Ownership: Larry Wilson.
Radio Stns: 37 AM. 98 FM.
KABI Abilene, KS; KNWZ Coachella, CA; KNWQ Palm Springs, CA; KCUL Marshall, TX; KFQD Anchorage, AK; KWOK Aberdeen, WA; KGNC Amarillo, TX; KHAR Anchorage, AK; KKRT Wenatchee, WA; KNZR Bakersfield, CA; KOKA Shreveport, LA; KNWH Yucca Valley, CA; KSAH Universal City, TX; KSAL Salina, KS; KTUB Centerville, UT; KTSA San Antonio, TX; KWIQ Moses Lake North, WA; KXTG Portland, OR; KXRO Aberdeen, WA; KZDC San Antonio, TX; WCHA Chambersburg, PA; WHHW Hilton Head Island, SC; WHAG Halfway, MD; WHIS Bluefield, WV; WIBW Topeka, KS; WING Dayton, OH; WIRL Peoria, IL; WJNT Pearl, MS; WKEZ Bluefield, WV; WJQS Jackson, MS; WMBD Peoria, IL; WOAD Jackson, MS; WOIC Columbia, SC; WXBD Biloxi, MS; WNTX Fredericksburg, VA; WTNI Biloxi, MS; KUFO Portland, OR; KDUT Randolph, UT; KBLS North Fort Riley, KS; KLEY-FM Jourdanton, TX; KBRJ Anchorage, AK; KCLB-FM Coachella, CA; KCUL-FM Marshall, TX; KBTT Haughton, LA; KEAG Anchorage, AK; KKDV Walnut Creek, CA; KXXK Hoquiam, WA; KGNC-FM Amarillo, TX; KHTN Planada, CA; KINK Portland, OR; KKBB Bakersfield, CA; KKIQ Livermore, CA; KKRV Wenatchee, WA; KKUS Tyler, TX; KKUU Indio, CA; KTFM Floresville, TX; KBTE Tulia, TX; KOYE Frankston, TX; KLLL-FM Lubbock, TX; KLLY Oildale, CA; KMMX Tahoka, TX; KMXS Anchorage, AK; KONE Lubbock, TX; KOOI Jacksonville, TX; KBMG Evanston, WY; KXGL Amarillo, TX; KNZR-FM Shafter, CA; KDKS-FM Blanchard, LA; KSAJ-FM Abilene, KS; KLKL Minden, LA; KTAL-FM Texarkana, TX; KJXK San Antonio, TX; KTPK Topeka, KS; KUBB Mariposa, CA; KUIC Vacaville, CA; KUPL Portland, OR; KWLN Wilson Creek, WA; KWHL Anchorage, AK; KWIQ-FM Moses Lake, WA; KYEZ Salina, KS; KCLZ Twentynine Palms, CA; KYKX Longview, TX; KXGT Carrington, ND; KDGL Yucca Valley, CA; KSAL-FM Salina, KS; WARQ Columbia, SC; WQCM Greencastle, PA; WCPR-FM D'Iberville, MS; WDJX Louisville, KY; WFLS-FM Fredericksburg, VA; WFXH-FM Hilton Head Island, SC; WGCO Midway, GA; WGTZ Eaton, OH; WGZB-FM Lanesville, IN; WHAJ Bluefield, WV; WHKX Bluefield, VA; WHQX Gary, WV; WHXT Orangeburg, SC; WIBW-FM Topeka, KS; WIKZ Chambersburg, PA; WDHT Urbana, OH; WWLB Ettrick, VA; WJMI Jackson, MS; WKOY-FM Princeton, WV; WCLI-FM Enon, OH; WKXI-FM Magee, MS; WRWN Port Royal, SC; WGBL Gulfport, MS; WXMA Louisville, KY; WMFX St. Andrews, SC; WMJM Jeffersontown, KY; WPBG Peoria, IL; WDLD Halfway, MD; WSCZ Winnsboro, SC; WROU-FM West Carrollton, OH; WARV-FM Petersburg, VA; WSWT Peoria, IL; WNGY Morton, IL; WWDM Sumter, SC; WWUZ Bowling Green, VA; WUBB Bluffton, SC; WXCL Pekin, IL; WGHL Shepherdsville, KY; WBBT-FM Powhatan, VA; WXYK Gulfport, MS; KSAH-FM Pearsall, TX; KHHL Karnes City, TX; WLFV Midlothian, VA; KAYO Wasilla, AK; WRKS Pickens, MS; WQBB Pascagoula, MS; KBFF Portland, OR; KXL-FM Portland, OR; WVBX Spotsylvania, VA; KDUX-FM Hoquiam, WA
Larry Wilson, Chairman
Bob Proffitt, President & CEO
Donna Heffner, Chief Financial Officer

Altus FM, Inc.
PO Box 1077, Altus OK 73522
(580) 482-1555; *Fax:*(580) 482-8353
Ownership: Paul Wilmes, 46%; Scott Wilmes, 44%; Gayle Ledbetter, 10%.
Radio Stns: 3 FM.
KEYB Altus, OK; KKRE Hollis, OK; KJOK Hollis, OK
Paul Wilmes, President
Gayle Ledbetter, General Manager

American Family Radio
P.O. Box 3206, Tupelo MS 38803
(662) 844-8888; *Fax:*(662) 842-6791
www.afr.net
faq@afa.net

RADIO - U.S.

Ownership: American Family Association, a nonprofit organization.

Radio Stns: 152 FM.

KAKA Salina, KS; KANX Sheridan, AR; KAOG Jonesboro, AR; KAOW Fort Smith, AR; KAPI Ruston, LA; KAPM Alexandria, LA; KAQD Abilene, TX; KSJY St. Martinville, LA; KAQF Clovis, NM; KARG Poteau, OK; KARH Forrest City, AR; KAUF Kennett, MO; KAVK Many, LA; KAVW Amarillo, TX; KAFR Conroe, TX; KAVO Pampa, TX; KAXR Arkansas City, KS; KAXV Bastrop, LA; KAYA Hubbard, NE; KAYB Sunnyside, WA; KAYC Durant, OK; KAYK Victoria, TX; KAYM Weatherford, OK; KAYP Burlington, IA; KBAH Plainview, TX; KBAN DeRidder, LA; KBCM Blytheville, AR; KBCX Big Spring, TX; KBDA Great Bend, KS; KBDE Temple, TX; KBDO Des Arc, AR; KBGM Park Hills, MO; KBJQ Bronson, KS; KBMH Holbrook, AZ; KBMJ Heber Springs, AR; KBMM Odessa, TX; KBNV Fayetteville, AR; KBPG Montevideo, MN; KBUZ Topeka, KS; KCFN Wichita, KS; KRBW Ottawa, KS; KVRS Lawton, OK; WAAE New Bern, NC; WAEF Cordele, GA; WAFR Tupelo, MS; WAII Hattiesburg, MS; WAJS Tupelo, MS; WAKD Sheffield, AL; WALN Carrollton, AL; WAMP Jackson, TN; WAOY Gulfport, MS; WAPD Campbellsville, KY; WAPO Mount Vernon, IL; WAQB Tupelo, MS; WAQG Ozark, AL; WAQL McComb, MS; WAQU Selma, AL; WARN Culpeper, VA; WASM Natchez, MS; WASW Waycross, GA; WATI Vincennes, IN; WATP Laurel, MS; WATU Port Gibson, MS; WAUI Shelby, OH; WAUM Duck Hill, MS; WAUO Hohenwald, TN; WAUV Ripley, TN; WAVI Oxford, MS; WAWH Dublin, GA; WAWI Lawrenceburg, TN; WAWJ Marion, IL; WAWN Franklin, PA; WAXG Mount Sterling, KY; WAXR Geneseo, IL; WAXU Troy, AL; WAZD Savannah, TN; WBEL Cairo, IL; WBHZ Elkins, WV; WBIA Shelbyville, TN; WBIE Delphos, OH; WBJV Steubenville, OH; WBJY Americus, GA; WBKG Macon, GA; WBKU Ahoskie, NC; WBMK Morehead, KY; WDFX Cleveland, MS; WGCF Paducah, KY; WIGH Jackson, TN; WJZB Starkville, MS; WMSB Byhalia, MS; WTRM Winchester, VA; KBPW Hampton, AR; KBQC Independence, KS; KQPD Ardmore, OK; KXRT Idabel, OK; KCKT Crockett, TX; WMCQ Muskegon, MI; KYLC Lake Charles, LA; WPRG Columbia, MS; WPAS Pascagoula, MS; WPWV Princeton, WV; KANL Baker, OR; WVDA Valdosta, GA; KZFT Fannett, TX; WXBE Beaufort, NC; WQVI Madison, MS; WSQH Decatur, MS; WJJE Delaware, OH; WQSG Lafayette, IN; WSLE Salem, IL; WYTF Indianola, MS; WYAZ Yazoo City, MS; WCSO Columbus, MS; WRAE Raeford, NC; KPAQ Plaquemine, LA; KASD Rapid City, SD; KTXG Greenville, TX; KIAD Dubuque, IA; WRIH Richmond, VA; KAKO Ada, OK; KAFH Great Falls, MT; KMEO Mertzon, TX; KMSL Mansfield, LA; KWVI Waverly, IA; WJKA Jacksonville, NC; KATG Elkhart, TX; WEFI Effingham, IL; KLGS College Station, TX; KNLL Nashville, AR; KDVI Devils Lake, ND; KTDA Dalhart, TX; KHYS Hays, KS; KDLI Del Rio, TX; WDLL Dillon, SC; WPRH Paris, TN; KJTW Jamestown, ND; KOBH Hobbs, NM; WRYN Hickory, NC; WWGV Grove City, OH; KJSB Jonesboro, AR; KGLL Gillette, WY; KVHR Van Horn, TX; KEEA Aberdeen, SD; KKNL Valentine, NE; KAWN Winslow, AZ; KMLL Marysville, KS; KSNB Norton, KS; KEJA Cale, AR; KPKO Pecos, TX; WGBQ Lynchburg, TN; WJGS Norwood, GA; WQST Forest, MS

Tim Wildmon, President
Donald Wildmon, Founder
Buddy Smith, Sr VP
Ed Vitagliano, Exec VP
Randy Sharp, Director Of Special Projects
Meeke Addison, Director Of Communications
Abraham Hamilton III, General Counsel

American General Media
1400 Easton Dr, Suite 144, Bakersfield CA 93309
(661) 328-1410; *Fax:*(661) 328-0873
www.americangeneralmedia.com
management@americangeneralmedia.com

Radio Stns: 5 AM. 18 FM.

KARS Belen, NM; KERN Wasco-Greenacres, CA; KGEO Bakersfield, CA; KSMA Santa Maria, CA; KVEC San Luis Obispo, CA; KABG Los Alamos, NM; KAGM Los Alamos, NM; KBOX Lompoc, CA; KKXX-FM Shafter, CA; KKAL Paso Robles, CA; KGFM Bakersfield, CA; KSTT Atascadero, CA; KISV Bakersfield, CA; KKJG San Luis Obispo, CA; KLVO Belen, NM; KHFM Santa Fe, NM; KPAT Orcutt, CA; KRQK Lompoc, CA; KSNI-FM Santa Maria, CA; KEBT Lost Hills, CA; KDLW Los Lunas, NM; KZOZ San Luis Obispo, CA; KERN Wasco-Greenacres, CA

Anthony Brandon, Chairman
Rogers Brandon, President
Margaret Nuanez, Chief Financial Officer
Otis Warren, National Sales Manager - Bakersfield

American Media Investments Inc.
1162 E. Hwy. 126, Pittsburg KS 66762
(620) 231-7200

Radio Stns: 4 AM. 7 FM.

KBTN Neosho, MO; KCAR Clarksville, TX; KKTK Texarkana, TX; KQYX Galena, KS; KCAR-FM Baxter Springs, KS; KBTN-FM Neosho, MO; KEWL-FM New Boston, TX; KGAP Clarksville, TX; KPGG Ashdown, AR; KMOQ Columbus, KS; KJML(FM) Columbus, KS

O. Gene Bicknell, CEO

Americom Broadcasting
961 Matley Lane, Suite 120, Reno NV 89502
(775) 829-1964; *Fax:*(775) 825-3183

Radio Stns: 2 AM. 4 FM.

KSGG Reno, NV; KBZZ Sparks, NV; KLCA Tahoe City, CA; KODS Carnelian Bay, CA; KRNO Incline Village, NV; KOLC Carson City, NV

Tom Quinn, President
Lori Heeren, Vice President and General Manager
Heather Forcier, National Regional Sales Director
Carrie Carano, Local Sales Manager
Teresa Estabrook, Local Sales Manager
Lori Songe, Internet Content Manager

Amistad Communications Inc.
7480 Greenwood Rd., Shreveport LA 71119
(318) 938-1885; *Fax:*(318) 425-7507

Radio Stns: 1 AM. 1 FM.

KSYB Shreveport, LA; KBEF Gibsland, LA

Anaheim Broadcasting Corp.
1940 Orange Tree Lane, Suite 200, Redlands CA 92374
(909) 793-3554; *Fax:*(909) 798-6627

Ownership: Tim Sullivan.

Radio Stns: 2 FM.

KCAL-FM Redlands, CA; KOLA San Bernardino, CA

Tim Sullivan, President
Jeff Parke, General Manager
Glenn Watson, National Sales Manager
Doug Fleniken, Sales Manager
Curtis Parcell, Sales Manager
Lisha Voss, Business Manager
Tony Nordbeck, Senior Account Executive
Robert Topping, Senior Account Executive
Rod Landon, Senior Account Executive

Anderson Radio Broadcasting Inc.
36581 North Reservoir Rd., Polson MT 59860
(406) 883-5255, ; *Fax:*(406) 883-4441,
www.andersonbroadcasting.com

Radio Stns: 1 AM. 6 FM.

KERR Polson, MT; KKMT Ronan, MT; KIBG Bigfork, MT; KZXT Eureka, MT; KZJZ St. Regis, MT; KYWL Evergreen, MT; KQRK Pablo, MT

Apex Broadcasting Inc.
2294 Clements Ferry Rd., Charleston SC 29492-1100
(843) 972-1100; *Fax:*(843) 972-1200
www.apexbroadcasting.com

Radio Stns: 9 FM.

WVSC Port Royal, SC; WLHH Ridgeland, SC; WXST Hollywood, SC; WAVF Hanahan, SC; WECQ Destin, FL; WMXZ Isle of Palms, SC; WCKN Hollywood, SC; WZLB Santa Rosa Beach, FL; WHWY Holt, FL

David Abel, General Manager
LaDonna Andrews, General Sales Mgr
Linda Mixon, Business Manager

Arkansas County Broadcasters Inc.
Box 789, Wynne AR 72396-0789
(870) 238-8141; *Fax:*(870) 238-5997

Radio Stns: 1 AM. 3 FM.

KWAK Stuttgart, AR; KOTN(FM) Gould, AR; KDEW-FM De Witt, AR; KWAK-FM Stuttgart, AR

Arklatex LLC
615 W. Olive, Texarkana TX 75501
(903) 793-4671; *Fax:*(903) 792-4261

Radio Stns: 2 AM. 3 FM.

KCMC Texarkana, TX; KTFS Texarkana, TX; KFYX(FM) Texarkana, AR; KBYB Hope, AR; KTOY Texarkana, AR

Alex Rain, Operations Dir
Mike Simpson, General Manager

ARKLATEX Radio Inc.
1513 S. Fourth St., Nashville AR 71852
(870) 845-3601; *Fax:*(870) 845-3680
www.southwestarkansasradio.com
gm@southwestarkansasradio.com

Radio Stns: 1 AM. 2 FM.

KBHC Nashville, AR; KMTB Murfreesboro, AR; KNAS Nashville, AR

Jay Bunyard, President

Armada Media Corp.
1 W. Second St., 2nd Fl., Fond du Lac WI 54935-4908
(920) 906-9900; *Fax:*(920) 906-9800
www.armadamedia.com

Radio Stns: 11 AM. 20 FM.

KBRL McCook, NE; KDIO Ortonville, MN; KGIM Aberdeen, SD; KMSD Mibank, SD; KOAQ Terrytown, NE; KODY North Platte, NE; KOLT Scottsbluff, NE; KSDN Aberdeen, SD; KUVR Holdrege, NE; WAGN Menominee, MI; WMAM Marinette, WI; KOZY-FM Bridgeport, NE; KBFO Aberdeen, SD; KBWS-FM Sisseton, SD; KFNF Oberlin, KS; KGIM-FM Redfield, SD; KICX-FM McCook, NE; KSTH Holyoke, CO; KPHR Ortonville, MN; KSDN-FM Aberdeen, SD; KXNP North Platte, NE; WHYB Menominee, MI; WLST Marinette, WI; WSFQ Peshtigo, WI; KHAQ Maxwell, NE; KADL Imperial, NE; KJBL Julesburg, CO; KHYY Minatare, NE; KETT Mitchell, NE; KRNP Sutherland, NE; KQHK McCook, NE

Terry Shockley, Chairman
Chris Bernier, CEO
John Larson, Operations Dir

Arnold Broadcasting Inc.
Box 753, Lamar CO 81052
(719) 336-4227

Radio Stns: 1 AM. 3 FM.

KSTC Sterling, CO; KNEC Yuma, CO; KNNG Sterling, CO; KECK Eckley, CO

Bill Arnold, President

Artistic Media Partners Inc.
5520 E. 75th St., Indianapolis IN 46250
(317) 594-0600; *Fax:*(317) 594-9567
www.artisticradio.com
artradio@aol.com

Ownership: Arthur A. Angotti.

Radio Stns: 2 AM. 8 FM.

WSHY Lafayette, IN; WDND South Bend, IN; WAZY-FM Lafayette, IN; WBWB Bloomington, IN; WSHP Attica, IN; WHCC Ellettsville, IN; WSMM New Carlisle, IN; WBPE Brookston, IN; WNDV-FM South Bend, IN; WSSM(FM) Goshen, IN

Arthur Angotti, President/Chief Executive Officer
Arthur Angotti III, Senior Vice President

Asian American Broadcasting LLC
7980 36th Ave. N., Minneapolis MN 55427
(763) 544-0114

Ownership: Kongsue Xiong; Xeng Xiong.

Radio Stns: 1 AM.

KFXN Minneapolis, MN

Kongsue Xiong, CEO
Xeng Xiong, Vice President and General Manager

Astor Broadcast Group
1835 Aston Ave., Carlsbad CA 92008
(760) 729-1000; *Fax:*(760) 476-9604

Radio Stns: 3 AM.

KCEO Vista, CA; KSPA Ontario, CA; KFSD Escondido, CA

Peri Corso, General Manager

Atlantic Broadcasting
1601 New Rd., Linwood NJ 08221-1116
(609) 653-1400; *Fax:*(609) 601-0450

Radio Stns: 1 FM.

CJFX-FM Antigonish, NS

Brett DeNafo, CEO

Atlantic Coast Radio L.L.C.
779 Warren Ave., Portland ME 04103
(207) 773-9695; *Fax:*(207) 761-4406
atlanticcoastradio.com

Radio Stns: 2 AM. 3 FM.

WRED Westbrook, ME; WLOB Portland, ME; WJJB-FM Gray, ME; WPEI Saco, ME; WPPI Topsham, ME

J.J. Jeffrey, President

Attraction Radio Inc.
200-5455, avenue De Gasp,, Montr,al QC H2T 3B3
(514) 846-1228; *Fax:*(514) 846-1227
www.attractionradio.ca
info@attractionradio.ca

Ownership: Canada Inc., 55%; Investissment Quebec, 19.75%; F.T.Q., 19.13%.; Others, 6.12%.

Radio Stns: 9 FM.

CFJO-FM Thetford Mines, QC; CJLM-FM Joliette, QC; CKLD-FM Thetford Mines, QC; CKYQ-FM Plessisville, QC; CHEQ-FM Sainte-Marie, QC; CFDA-FM Victoriaville, QC; CJIT-FM Lac Megantic, QC; CKRS-FM Saguenay, QC; CKGS-FM La Baie, QC

Sylvain Chamberland, President
Carl Vaillancourt, VP Sales & Business Development

Marc Thibault, VP Finance & Administration
Stefanie Machabee Primeau, Executive Coordinator
Andreanne Lamothe, Reporter, Radio Attraction Info

AVC Communications Inc.
Box 338, Cambridge OH 43725
(740) 432-5605; *Fax:*(740) 432-1991
www.yourradioplace.com
Radio Stns: 2 FM.
WCMJ Cambridge, OH; WILE-FM Byesville, OH
Grant Hafley, President
David Wilson, Operations Dir
Joel Losego, General Manager

Azteca Broadcasting Corp.
323 E. San Joaquin St., Tulare CA 93274
(559) 686-1370; *Fax:*(559) 685-1394
Radio Stns: 3 AM. 1 FM.
KGEN Tulare, CA; KSVN Ogden, UT; KXEQ Reno, NV; KGEN-FM Hanford, CA

B&M Broadcasting LLC
410 New Bridge St., Suite 3B, Jacksonville NC 28450
(910) 346-2248
941thebeach.com
wsme1120@yahoo.com
Radio Stns: 2 AM.
WLSG Wilmington, NC; WSME Camp Lejeune, NC
Ashley Moseley, General Manager

Backyard Broadcasting LLC
1685 Four Mile Dr, Williamsport PA 17701
(570) 323-8200; *Fax:*(570) 323-5075
dfarr@backyardbroadcasting.com
Radio Stns: 1 AM. 5 FM.
WWPA Williamsport, PA; WCXR Lewisburg, PA; WBZD Muncy, PA; WILQ Williamsport, PA; WZXR South Williamsport, PA; WLMY Williamsport, PA
Dan Farr, President

Bahakel Communications Ltd.
1 Television Pl., Charlotte NC 28205
(704) 372-4434; *Fax:*(704) 335-9904
Ownership: Bahakel Communications.
Radio Stns: 1 AM. 5 FM.
WDEF Chattanooga, TN; KILO Colorado Springs, CO; KRXP Pueblo West, CO; WDEF-FM Chattanooga, TN; WDOD-FM Chattanooga, TN; WUUQ South Pittsburg, TN
TV Stns: 6 TV.
WBMM Tuskegee, AL; WAKA Selma, AL; WBBJ-TV Jackson, TN; WCCB Charlotte, NC; WFXB Myrtle Beach, SC; WOLO-TV Columbia, SC
Beverly Poston, President
James Babb, Chief Operating Officer
Amy Liz Pittenger, Vice President
John Hutchinson, Senior VP, Television and Technology
Bob Davis, Director of Engineering and Operations

Baker Family Stations
P.O. Box 889, Blacksburg VA 24063
(540) 951-9791; *Fax:*(540) 961-2021
Ownership: Virginia L. Baker; Edward A. Baker; Vanessa Baker Pavlik.
Radio Stns: 8 AM. 5 FM.
WBGS Point Pleasant, WV; WKEX Blacksburg, VA; WKGM Smithfield, VA; WKNV Fairlawn, VA; WKTR Earlysville, VA; WLGN Logan, OH; WMPO Middleport-Pomeroy, OH; WODY Fieldale, VA; WBNN-FM Dillwyn, VA; WCEF Ripley, WV; WKNA Logan, OH; WTGR Union City, OH; WZFM Narrows, VA
Edward A. Baker, President
Virginia L. Baker, Treasurer

Baldridge-Dumas Communications Inc.
605 San Antonio Ave., Many LA 71449
(318) 256-5924; *Fax:*(318) 256-0950
www.bdcradio.com
Radio Stns: 6 FM.
KDBH-FM Natchitoches, LA; KTEZ Zwolle, LA; KVCL-FM Winnfield, LA; KZBL Natchitoches, LA; KTHP Hemphill, TX; KBDV Leesville, LA
Tedd Dumas, President
Rhonda Benson, General Manager

Barry P. Lunderville Stns
195 Main St., Lancaster NH 3584
(603) 788-3636; *Fax:*(603) 788-3536
Radio Stns: 4 AM. 2 FM.
WLTN Littleton, NH; WMOU Berlin, NH; WKDR Berlin, NH; WGAM(AM) Manchester, NH; WLTN-FM Lisbon, NH; WXXS Lancaster, NH

Bayshore Broadcasting Corp.
P.O. Box 280, Owen Sound ON N4K 5P5
(519) 376-2030; *Fax:*(519) 371-4242
www.bayshorebroadcasting.ca
info@bayshorebroadcasting.ca
Ownership: C. Douglas Caldwell, 100%.
Radio Stns: 1 AM. 7 FM.
CFOS Owen Sound, ON; CIXK-FM Owen Sound, ON; CKYC-FM Owen Sound, ON; CFPS-FM Port Elgin, ON; CHGB-FM Wasaga Beach, ON; CHWC-FM Goderich, ON; CFDC-FM Shelburne, ON; CISO-FM Orillia, ON
Ross Kentner, General Manager
Rob Wiltshire, Sales & Marketing Manager

Beacon Broadcasting Inc.
Box 1789, Warren OH 44482-1790
(330) 394-7700; *Fax:*(330) 394-7701
Radio Stns: 1 AM. 1 FM.
WLOA Farrell, PA; WRTK Paxton, IL

Beasley Broadcast Group Inc.
3033 Riviera Dr., Suite 200, Naples FL 34103
(239) 263-5000; *Fax:*(239) 263-8191
www.bbgi.com
Ownership: George G. Beasley.
Radio Stns: 22 AM. 51 FM.
KDWN Las Vegas, NV; WAEC Atlanta, GA; WRDW Augusta, GA; WAZZ Fayetteville, NC; WBCN Charlotte, NC; WBT Charlotte, NC; WCTC New Brunswick, NJ; WFNZ Charlotte, NC; WGAC Augusta, GA; WHSR Pompano Beach, FL; WMTR Morristown, NJ; WNCT Greenville, NC; WHFS Seffner, FL; WRCA Watertown, MA; WSBR Boca Raton, FL; WTEL Philadelphia, PA; WTMR Camden, NJ; WJBX North Fort Myers, FL; WWDB Philadelphia, PA; WWNN Pompano Beach, FL; WWTR Bridgewater, NJ; WWWE Hapeville, GA; KOAS Dolan Springs, AZ; KCYE Boulder City, NV; KKLZ Las Vegas, NV; KVGS Meadview, AZ; WGUS-FM New Ellenton, SC; WBAV-FM Gastonia, NC; WBOS Brookline, MA; WBT-FM Chester, SC; WGAC-FM Harlem, GA; WKLB-FM Waltham, MA; WCSX Birmingham, MI; WDHA-FM Dover, NJ; WFLB Laurinburg, NC; WDRR Martinez, GA; WIKS New Bern, NC; WJBR-FM Wilmington, DE; WWCN Fort Myers Beach, FL; WJRZ-FM Manahawkin, NJ; WJPT Fort Myers, FL; WKML Lumberton, NC; WKXC-FM Aiken, SC; WLLD Lakeland, FL; WLNK Charlotte, NC; WMGQ New Brunswick, NJ; WMGV Newport, NC; WMJX Boston, MA; WMMR Philadelphia, PA; WNCT-FM Greenville, NC; WNKS Charlotte, NC; WPEG Concord, NC; WPEN-FM Burlington, NJ; WQYK-FM St. Petersburg, FL; WRAT Point Pleasant, NJ; WRBQ-FM Tampa, FL; WCHZ-FM Warrenton, GA; WRIF Detroit, MI; WROR-FM Framingham, MA; WRXK-FM Bonita Springs, FL; WSFL-FM New Bern, NC; WBQT Boston, MA; WHHD Clearwater, SC; WSOC-FM Charlotte, NC; WKQC Charlotte, NC; WUKS St. Pauls, NC; WMGC-FM Detroit, MI; WXKB Cape Coral, FL; WXNR Grifton, NC; WBEN-FM Philadelphia, PA; WYUU Safety Harbor, FL; WZFX Whiteville, NC; WBRN Holmes Beach, FL
George Beasley, Chairman & CEO
Bruce Beasley, President & Chief Operating Officer
Caroline Beasley, Executive Vice President & Chief Financial Officer
Brian Beasley, Vice President of Operations
Joe B. Cox, Director
Mark S. Fowler, Director
Herbert W. McCord, Director
Allen B. Shaw, Vice Chairman of the Board of Directors

Bee Broadcasting Inc.
2432 Hwy 2 E., Box 5409, Kalispell MT 59903
(406) 755-8700; *Fax:*(406) 755-8770
www.beebroadcasting.com
Ownership: Benny Bee Sr.
Radio Stns: 2 AM. 3 FM.
KJJR Whitefish, MT; KSAM Whitefish, MT; KBBZ Kalispell, MT; KDBR Kalispell, MT; KHNK Columbia Falls, MT
Benny Bee Sr., President

Bell Media Inc.
299 Queen St. W., Toronto ON M5V 2Z5
(416) 384-8000
www.bellmedia.ca
bellmediapr@bellmedia.ca
Ownership: Bell Canada, 100%.
Radio Stns: 25 AM. 81 FM.
CFAX Victoria, BC; CFGO Ottawa, ON; CFRA Ottawa, ON; CFRB Toronto, ON; CFRN Edmonton, AB; CFTK Terrace, BC; CFTE Vancouver, BC; CHAM Hamilton, ON; CHUM Toronto, ON; CFRW Winnipeg, MB; CKHJ Fredericton, NB; CJAD Montr,al, QC; CJBK London, ON; CJDC Dawson Creek, BC; CJOR Osoyoos, BC; CKFR Kelowna, BC; CKGM Montr,al, QC; CKLW Windsor, ON; CKMX Calgary, AB; CKOC Hamilton, ON; CKOR Penticton, BC; CKSL London, ON; CKST Vancouver, BC; CKTB St. Catharines, ON; CKWW Windsor, ON; CFBR-FM Edmonton, AB; CFCA-FM Waterloo, ON; CFEI-FM St-Hyacinthe, QC; CFLY-FM Kingston, ON; CFMG-FM Edmonton, AB; CFWM-FM Winnipeg, MB; CFZZ-FM Saint Jean-Iberville, QC; CHEY-FM Trois Rivieres, QC; CHIK-FM Quebec, QC; CHOM-FM Montr,al, QC; CHQM-FM Vancouver, BC; CHRD-FM Drummondville, QC; CHRE-FM St. Catharines, ON; CHRX-FM Fort St. John, BC; CHSU-FM Kelowna, BC; CHTZ-FM St. Catharines, ON; CHUM-FM Toronto, ON; CHVR-FM Pembroke, ON; CJPT-FM Brockville, ON; CIBX-FM Fredericton, NB; CIDR-FM Windsor, ON; CIGB-FM Trois Rivieres, QC; CIKI-FM Rimouski, QC; CILK-FM Kelowna, BC; CIMF-FM Gatineau, QC; CIMO-FM Magog, QC; CIMX-FM Windsor, ON; CIOO-FM Halifax, NS; CIQM-FM London, ON; CITE-FM Montr,al, QC; CITE-FM-1 Sherbrooke, QC; CITF-FM Quebec, QC; CJAB-FN Saguenay, QC; CJAT-FM Trail, BC; CJAY-FM Calgary, AB; CJBX-FM London, ON; CJDM-FM Drummondville, QC; CJFM-FM Montr,al, QC; CJFW-FM Terrace, BC; CJMG-FM Penticton, BC; CJMJ-FM Ottawa, ON; CJMM-FM Rouyn-Noranda, QC; CJMV-FM Val d'Or, QC; CKFM-FM Toronto, ON; CFXY-FM Fredericton, NB; CKKC-FM Nelson, BC; CKKL-FM Ottawa, ON; CKLH-FM Hamilton, ON; CKLY-FM Kawartha Lakes, ON; CKMF-FM Montr,al, QC; CKMM-FM Winnipeg, MB; CKQM-FM Peterborough, ON; CKRX-FM Fort Nelson, BC; CKTF-FM Gatineau, QC; CKTO-FM Truro, NS; CKX-FM Brandon, MB; CKXA-FM Brandon, MB; CHBE-FM Victoria, BC; CJOI-FM Rimouski, QC; CIKX-FM Grand Falls, NB; CFIX-FM Saguenay, QC; CFBT-FM Vancouver, BC; CJCJ-FM Woodstock, NB; CIBK-FM Calgary, AB; CKTY-FM Truro, NS; CFJR-FM Brockville, ON; CFVM-FM Amqui, QC; CICF-FM Vernon, BC; CKBC-FM Bathurst, NB; CKNL-FM Fort St. John, BC; CKTK-FM Kitimat, BC; CKXR-FM Salmon Arm, BC; CKPT-FM Peterborough, ON; CKLC-FM Kingston, ON; CHBD-FM Regina, SK; CJCH-FM Halifax, NS; CKKW-FM Kitchener, ON; CKGR-FM Golden, BC; CHTK-FM Prince Rupert, BC; CKCR-FM Revelstoke, BC; CHOR-FM Summerland, BC
TV Stns: 29 TV.
CFCF-DT Montr,al, QC; CFCN-DT-5 Lethbridge, AB; CTV London, ON; CFQC-DT Saskatoon, SK; CFRN-TV-6 Red Deer, AB; CFTO-DT Toronto, ON; CHBX-TV Sault Ste. Marie, ON; CHRO-TV Pembroke, ON; CHWI-DT Wheatley, ON; CICC-TV Yorkton, SK; CICI-TV Sudbury, ON; CIPA-TV Prince Albert, SK; CITO-TV Timmins, ON; CIVT-DT Vancouver, BC; CJCB-TV Halifax, NS; CJCH-DT Halifax, NS; CJDC-TV Dawson Creek, BC; CJOH-DT Ottawa, ON; CKCK-DT Regina, SK; CKCO-DT Kitchener, ON; CKCW-DT Moncton, NB; CKLT-DT Saint John, NB; CKNY-TV North Bay, ON; CKVR-DT Barrie, ON; CKX-TV Brandon, MB; CKY-DT Winnipeg, MB; CIVI-DT Victoria, BC; CHRO-DT-43 Ottawa, ON; CFTK-TV Terrace, BC
Randy Lennox, President
Stewart Johnston, Media Sales & Marketing
Mike Cosentino, Content & Programming
Wendy Freeman, President, CTV News
Nikki Moffat, Senior Vice-President, Finance
Scott Henderson, Vice-President, Communications
Sonia Brar, Vice-President, Information Technology

Bennie E. Hewett Stns
Box 907670, Gainesville GA 30501-0911
(770) 519-0082; *Fax:*(770) 536-4103
Ownership: Bennie Hewett.
Radio Stns: 1 AM. 2 FM.
WRJX Jackson, AL; WBMH Grove Hill, AL; WHOD Jackson, AL
Bennie E. Hewett, President

Benton-Weatherford Broadcasting Inc. of Tennessee
110 India Rd., Paris TN 38242
(731) 644-9455; *Fax:*(731) 644-9421
wmuf@bellsouth.net
Radio Stns: 2 AM. 2 FM.
WHDM McKenzie, TN; WRQR(AM) Paris, TN; WLZK Paris, TN; WMUF Henry, TN
Gary Benton, President

Berkshire Broadcasting Corp.
98 Mill Plain Rd., Danbury CT 06811
(203) 744-4800; *Fax:*(203) 778-4655
www.98q.com www.wlad.com
Radio Stns: 2 AM. 1 FM.
WLAD Danbury, CT; WAXB Ridgefield, CT; WDAQ Danbury, CT
Irv Goldstein, Exec. VP

Bernard Radio LLC
745 Fifth Ave., 18th Fl., New York NY 10151
(646) 720-9100
Radio Stns: 4 AM. 1 FM.
KFCD Farmersville, TX; WGFT Campbell, OH; WVKO Columbus, OH; KHSE Wylie, TX; WVKO-FM Johnstown, OH

Best Broadcast Group
107 S. Main St., Brookfield MO 64628
(660) 258-3383; *Fax:*(660) 258-7307
www.bestbroadcastgroup.com
gm@bestbroadcastgroup.com
Radio Stns: 2 AM. 3 FM.
KLTI Macon, MO; KFMZ Brookfield, MO; KMCR Montgomery City, MO; KZBK Brookfield, MO; KZZT Moberly, MO
Dale Palmer, General Manager

Bethesda Christian Broadcasting
Box 168, Rapid City SD 57709
(719) 481-0100; *Fax:*(719) 481-4649
www.bcbradio.org
Ownership: Nonprofit bd of directors.
Radio Stns: 5 FM.
KTPT Rapid City, SD; KSLT Spearfish, SD; WPFF Sturgeon Bay, WI; WNLI Sturgeon Bay, WI; KLMP Rapid City, SD
Mark Pluimer, President

Bible Broadcasting Network
P.O. Box 7300, Charlotte NC 28241-7300
(704) 523-5555; *Fax:*(704) 522-1967
www.bbnradio.org
bbn@bbnmedia.org
Ownership: Nonprofit, non-stock corporation.
Radio Stns: 4 AM. 40 FM.
KYFI St. Louis, MO; WYBY Cortland, NY; WYFN Nashville, TN; WYFQ Charlotte, NC; KYFJ New Iberia, LA; KWFJ Roy, WA; KYFL Monroe, LA; KYFO-FM Ogden, UT; KYFP Palestine, TX; KYFS San Antonio, TX; KYFW Wichita, KS; WYBP Fort Lauderdale, FL; WYBK Chattanooga, TN; WHPE-FM High Point, NC; WYFZ Belleview, FL; WYFA Waynesboro, GA; WYFB Gainesville, FL; WYFC Clinton, TN; WYFD Decatur, AL; WYFE Tarpon Springs, FL; WYFG Gaffney, SC; WYFH North Charleston, SC; WYFI Norfolk, VA; WYFJ Ashland, VA; WYFK Columbus, GA; WYFL Henderson, NC; WYFO Lakeland, FL; WYFP Harpswell, ME; WYFQ-FM Wadesboro, NC; WYFS Savannah, GA; WYFT Luray, VA; WYFU Masontown, PA; WYFV Cayce, SC; WYFW Winder, GA; WYBX Key West, FL; WYBV Wakarusa, IN; KYFB Denison, TX; WYBA Coldwater, MI; WYBH Fayetteville, NC; WYFY Cambridge, OH; WYBW Key Colony Beach, FL; KYFG Omaha, NE; WYBQ Leesport, PA; KYFQ Tacoma, WA
Lowell Davey, President
Jason Padgett, Operations Manager

Bicoastal Media L.L.C.
140 N. Main St., Lakeport CA 94953
(707) 263-6113; *Fax:*(707) 263-6191
www.bicoastalmedia.com
Radio Stns: 17 AM. 26 FM.
KACI The Dalles, OR; KATA Eureka, CA; KBAM Longview, WA; KBBR Coos Bay, OR; KEDO Longview, WA; KEJO Albany, OR; KELA Centralia-Chehalis, WA; KGOE Eureka, CA; KIHR Hood River, OR; KLOO Albany, OR; KMED Medford, OR; KPNW Eugene, OR; KPOD Crescent City, CA; KTHH Albany, OR; KUKI Ukiah, CA; KWRO Coquille, OR; KXBX Ukiah, CA; KACI-FM The Dalles, OR; KOOS North Bend, OR; KBDN Bandon, OR; KCGB-FM Columbia River, OR; KDUK-FM Eugene, OR; KFLY Eugene, OR; KFMI Eureka, CA; KKHB Eureka, CA; KIFS Medford, OR; KLDZ Medford, OR; KLOO-FM Albany, OR; KNTI Lakeport, CA; KODZ Eugene, OR; KTEE North Bend, OR; KPOD-FM Crescent City, CA; KQPM Ukiah, CA; KJMX Coos Bay, OR; KRED Eureka, CA; KRKT-FM Albany, OR; KRQT Longview, WA; KRWQ Gold Hill, OR; KSHR-FM Coquille, OR; KUKI-FM Ukiah, CA; KLYK Kelso, WA; KMSW The Dalles, OR; KMNT Chehalis, WA
Mike Wilson, President & COO
Kevin Mostyn, VP & CTO

Big League Broadcasting LLC
3350 Peachtree Rd., Suite 1610, Atlanta GA 30326-1040
(404) 467-1877; *Fax:*(404) 231-5923
Radio Stns: 2 AM. 1 FM.
KFNS Wood River, IL; KQQZ Fairview Heights, IL; KFNS-FM Troy, MO

Big River Broadcasting Corp.
624 Sam Phillips St., Florence AL 35630
(256) 764-8121; *Fax:*(256) 764-8169
www.kix96country.com
sbrook@bigriverbroadcasting.com
Radio Stns: 1 AM. 2 FM.
WSBM Florence, AL; WQLT-FM Florence, AL; WXFL Florence, AL
Sharon Brook, General Sales Mgr

Birach Broadcasting Corp.
21700 Northwestern Hwy., Suite 1190, Tower 14, Southfield MI 48075
(248) 557-3500; *Fax:*(248) 557-2950
www.birach.com
sima@birach.com
Ownership: Sima Birach, 100%.
Radio Stns: 22 AM.
KTUV Little Rock, AR; KOLE Port Arthur, TX; KJMU Sand Springs, OK; KXLQ Indianola, IA; WBRD Palmetto, FL; WBVA Bayside, VA; WCAR Livonia, MI; WCXN Claremont, NC; WGOP Pocomoke City, MD; WEW St. Louis, MO; WIJR Highland, IL; WMFN Zeeland, MI; WMJH Rockford, MI; WNWI Oak Lawn, IL; WNZK Dearborn Heights, MI; WPON Walled Lake, MI; WTOR Youngstown, NY; WVAB Virginia Beach, VA; WWCS Canonsburg, PA; WCXI Fenton, MI; WDMV Walkersville, MD; WKGE Johnstown, PA
TV Stns: 1 TV.
KIJR-LP Lucerne Valley, CA
Sima Birach, President & CEO

Birch Broadcasting Corp.
11971 Glenmore Dr., Coral Springs FL 33071-7806
(954) 323-8531
Radio Stns: 1 AM. 3 FM.
WSHV South Hill, VA; WLUS-FM Clarksville, VA; WWHK Concord, NH; WKSK-FM South Hill, VA

Black Crow Media Group LLC
1711 Ellis Dr., Valdosta GA 31601
(229) 244-8642
mymixvaldosta.com
mymixvaldosta@gmail.com
Radio Stns: 3 AM. 10 FM.
WLOR Huntsville, AL; WQHL Live Oak, FL; WVLD Valdosta, GA; WAHR Huntsville, AL; WCJX Five Points, FL; WKAA Willacoochee, GA; WVGA Lakeland, GA; WRTT-FM Huntsville, AL; WQHL-FM Live Oak, FL; WQPW Valdosta, GA; WSTI-FM Quitman, GA; WWRQ-FM Valdosta, GA; WXHT Madison, FL
Mike Linn, CEO

Black Diamond Broadcasting
, Sault Ste. Marie MI
(231) 922-4981
blackdiamondbroadcasting.com
nlmckee@blackdiamondbroadcasting.com
Radio Stns: 1 AM. 4 FM.
WCBY Cheboygan, MI; WGFM Cheboygan, MI; WGFN Glen Arbor, MI; WWMK Onaway, MI; WMKC Indian River, MI
Mike Chires, CEO/COO
Norm Mckee, CFO

Black Media Works Inc.
1150 W. King St., Cocoa FL 32922
(321) 632-1000; *Fax:*(321) 636-0000
Radio Stns: 3 FM.
KAYT Jena, LA; WJFP Fort Pierce, FL; WJCB Clewiston, FL
Kimberly Holman Kassis, President

Blakeney Communications Inc.
Box 6408, 4580 Hwy. 15 N., Laurel MS 39441
(601) 649-0095; *Fax:*(601) 649-8199
www.pinebeltradio.com
blakeneycommunications@pinebeltradio.com
Radio Stns: 4 FM.
WBBN Taylorsville, MS; WKZW Sandersville, MS; WXHB Richton, MS; WXRR Hattiesburg, MS
Larry Blakeney, President/CEO
Debbie Blakeney, General Manager

Bliss Communications Inc.
Box 5001, One S. Parker Dr., Janesville WI 53547-5001
(608) 754-3311; *Fax:*(608) 754-8038
www.blissnet.net
sbliss@gazetteextra.com
Ownership: Bliss Communications, Inc
Radio Stns: 2 AM. 4 FM.
WCLO Janesville, WI; WRJN Janesville, WI; WJVL Janesville, WI; WEZY Janesville, WI; WIBD Janesville, WI; WBWI Janesville, WI
Sidney Bliss, President/CEO

Blount Broadcasting Corporation
216 Hannum St., Alcoa TN 37701
(865) 724-1100
wkvl.com
info@wkvl.com
Radio Stns: 3 AM.
WGAP Maryville, TN; WKVL Knoxville, TN; WLOD Loudon, TN

Blount Communications Group
8 Lawrence Rd., Derry NH 03038
(603) 434-9302
www.lifechangingradio.com
Ownership: William A. Blount; Deborah C. Blount.
Radio Stns: 5 AM. 2 FM.
WARV Warwick, RI; WDER Derry, NH; WSDK Bloomfield, CT; WFIF Milford, CT; WVNE Leicester, MA; WBCI Bath, ME; WDER-FM Peterborough, NH
William Blount, President
Deborah Blount, Executive Vice President
David Young, Vice President

Blue Ridge Radio Inc.
312 Robin Rd., Mount Airy NC 27030
(336) 786-4498; *Fax:*(336) 789-7792
Radio Stns: 3 AM. 1 FM.
WPAQ Mount Airy, NC; WSYD Mount Airy, NC; WWWJ Galax, VA; WBRF Galax, VA
Earlene Epperson, President
Ralph Epperson, Operations Dir
John Mullins, Chief Engineer

Blueberry Broadcasting LLC
Box 2600, Kennebunkport ME 4046
(207) 967-8094
Radio Stns: 3 AM. 12 FM.
WAEI Bangor, ME; WFAU Gardiner, ME; WVOM Rockland, ME; WABK Gardiner, ME; WBAK Belfast, ME; WTQX Boothbay Harbor, ME; WQSK Madison, ME; WVQM Augusta, ME; WKSQ Ellsworth, ME; WBFE Bar Harbor, ME; WBKA Bar Harbor, ME; WQSS Camden, ME; WTOS-FM Skowhegan, ME; WVOM-FM Howland, ME; WBFB Bangor, ME
Louis Vitali, CEO

BMG Billings, LLC
222 N. 32nd St., 10th Fl., Billings MT 59101
(406) 238-1000; *Fax:*(406) 238-1038
Ownership: Peter J. Benedetti, 85.1% votes, 58.8% equity; Richard G. Maynard, 10.6% votes, 29.4% equity; Paul C. Benedetti, 2.6% votes, 7.1% equity; Barry R. Remington, 1.7% votes, 4.7%equity.
Radio Stns: 2 FM.
KRSQ Laurel, MT; KEWF Billings, MT
Pete Benedetti, Owner

Bold Gold Media Group LP
575 Grove St., Honesdale PA 18431
(570) 253-1616; *Fax:*(570) 253-6297
www.boldgoldmedia.com
mstanton@boldgoldmedia.com
Radio Stns: 6 AM. 6 FM.
WICK Scranton, PA; WCDL Carbondale, PA; WBWX(AM) Berwick, PA; WVOS Liberty, NY; WPSN Honesdale, PA; WYCK Plains, PA; WTRW(FM) Carbondale, PA; WDNH-FM Honesdale, PA; WSUL Monticello, NY; WWRR Scranton, PA; WDNB Jeffersonville, NY; WYCY Hawley, PA
Vince Benedetto, Founder/President
Michael G. Staton, General Manager

Bonneville International Corporation
55 North 300 West, Salt Lake City UT 84101-3502
(801) 575-7500; *Fax:*(801) 575-5820
www.bonneville.com
Ownership: Deseret Management Corp.
Radio Stns: 5 AM. 8 FM.
KIRO Seattle, WA; KMVP Phoenix, AZ; KTTH Seattle, WA; KSL Salt Lake City, UT; KTAR Phoenix, AZ; KIRO-FM Tacoma, WA; KSWD Los Angeles, CA; KTAR-FM Glendale, AZ; KMVP-FM Phoenix, AZ; KSL-FM Midvale, UT; KRSP-FM Salt Lake City, UT; KSFI Salt Lake City, UT; KYGO-FM Denver, CO
TV Stns: 1 TV.
KSL-TV Salt Lake City, UT
Darrell Brown, President
Kent Nate, SVP & CFO
Mike Dowdle, SVP of Business Affairs & General Counsel
Matthew Sadowski, VP, Human Resources

Border Media Partners LLC
201 Main St., Suite 2001, Fort Worth TX 76102
(817) 335-5999; *Fax:*(817) 335-1197
www.bmpradio.com
Radio Stns: 5 AM. 6 FM.
KLGO Austin, TX; KLNT Laredo, TX; KSOX Raymondville, TX; KURV Edinburg, TX; KVJY Pharr, TX; KBDR Mirando City, TX; KESO South Padre Island, TX; KBUC Raymondville, TX; KUTX Leander, TX; KNEX Laredo, TX; KZSP South Padre Island, TX

Bott Radio Network
10550 Barkley St., Suite 100, Overland Park KS 66212

(913) 642-7770; *Fax:*(913) 642-1319
www.bottradionetwork.com
comments@bottradionetwork.com
Ownership: Richard P. Bott Sr.
Radio Stns: 12 AM. 25 FM.
KCCV Overland Park, KS; KJRG Newton, KS; KLEX Lexington, MO; KMOZ Rolla, MO; KOFC Fayetteville, AR; KQCV Oklahoma City, OK; KSIV Clayton, MO; WCRT Donelson, TN; WCRV Collierville, TN; WFCV Fort Wayne, IN; KBCV Hollister, MO; KJCV Jackson, WY; KSCV Springfield, MO; KCVN Cozad, NE; KARF Independence, KS; KAYH Fayetteville, AR; KAYX Richmond, MO; KTAA Big Sandy, TX; KMCV High Point, MO; KBMP Enterprise, KS; KCCV-FM Olathe, KS; KCIV Mount Bullion, CA; KCRL Sunrise Beach, MO; KCVT Silver Lake, KS; KCVW Kingman, KS; KLCV Lincoln, NE; KLTE Kirksville, MO; KQCV-FM Shawnee, OK; KSIV-FM St. Louis, MO; KTFC Sioux City, IA; KTFG Sioux Rapids, IA; KJCV-FM Country Club, MO; KKCV Rozel, KS; KCGR Oran, MO; KYLF Adrian, MO; WFCV-FM Bluffton, IN; KFCV Dixon, MO
Richard Bott Sr., President & CEO
Tom Holdeman, Chief Financial Officer
Richard Bott II, Executive Vice President

Bravo Mic Communications LLC
101 Perkins Dr., Las Cruces NM 88005
(505) 527-1111; *Fax:*(505) 527-1100
Radio Stns: 1 AM. 3 FM.
KOBE Las Cruces, NM; KMVR Mesilla Park, NM; KXPZ Las Cruces, NM; KVLC Hatch, NM

Brazos Valley Communications Ltd.
1240 E. Villa Maria Rd., Bryan TX 77802
(979) 776-1240; *Fax:*(979) 776-0123
brazosradio.com
Ownership: Brazos Valley Communications GP LLC, 100% votes, 10% equity; Tommy R. Vascocu, 24% equity.
Radio Stns: 1 AM. 4 FM.
KTAM Bryan, TX; KJXJ Franklin, TX; KAPN Caldwell, TX; KORA-FM Bryan, TX; KBXT Wixon Valley, TX
Chris Kiske, VP/gen mgr

Brewer Broadcasting Corp.
1305 Carter St., Chattanooga TN 37402
(423) 265-9494; *Fax:*(423) 266-2335
www.brewermediagroup.com
Ownership: Brewer Media Group, 100%.
Radio Stns: 1 AM. 5 FM.
WHON Centerville, IN; WPLZ Ooltewah, TN; WALV-FM Lakesite, TN; WJTT Red Bank, TN; WMPZ Harrison, TN; WQLK Richmond, IN
James L. Brewer Sr., Chairman
Jim Brewer II, President
Keith Landecker, Operations Manager
Kira Headlee, Controller

Bristol Broadcasting Co. Inc.
Box 1389, Bristol VA 24203
(276) 669-8112; *Fax:*(276) 669-0541
Ownership: Lisa Nininger Hale, 100%.
Radio Stns: 8 AM. 11 FM.
WDXR Paducah, KY; WNGO Mayfield, KY; WKYX Paducah, KY; WPAD Paducah, KY; WBES Charleston, WV; WVTS Dunbar, WV; WFHG Bristol, VA; WVTS(AM) Charleston, WV; WFHG-FM Bluff City, TN; WTZR Elizabethton, TN; WVTS-FM Dunbar, WV; WLLE Mayfield, KY; WDDJ Paducah, KY; WKYX-FM Golconda, IL; WAEZ Greeneville, TN; WQQR Clinton, KY; WKYQ Paducah, KY; WLNQ-FM Newport, TN; WXBQ-FM Bristol, VA
W.L. Nininger, President/General Manager

Broadcast Communications Inc.
Box 990, Greensburg PA 15601
(724) 853-7000
Radio Stns: 4 AM. 3 FM.
WANB Waynesburg, PA; WKFB Jeannette, PA; WKHB Irwin, PA; WMSG Oakland, MD; WKVE Mount Pleasant, PA; WKHJ Mountain Lake Park, MD; WWHQ Oakland, MD
Robert Stevens, President
Ashley Stevens, Operations Dir

Broadcast South LLC
1931 Ga. Hwy. 32 East, Douglas GA 31533
(912) 389-0995; *Fax:*(912) 383-8552
Radio Stns: 3 AM. 4 FM.
WBHB Fitzgerald, GA; WDMG Douglas, GA; WHJD Hazlehurst, GA; WDMG-FM Ambrose, GA; WKZZ Tifton, GA; WRDO Fitzgerald, GA; WVOH-FM Nicholls, GA
John Higgs, President

Brooke Communications Inc.
1445 W. Harvard Ave., Roseburg OR 97471
(541) 672-6641; *Fax:*(541) 673-7598
Radio Stns: 2 AM. 3 FM.
KQEN Roseburg, OR; KSKR Roseburg, OR; KSKR-FM Sutherlin, OR; KKMX Tri City, OR; KRSB-FM Roseburg, OR
Rachelle Carter, National Sales Dir.
Ashley Smith, Promotions Manager
Kyle Bailey, News Director

Brothers Broadcasting Corp.
560 W. Amsler Rd., Box D, Rensselaer IN 47978
(219) 866-4104
Ownership: John Balvich, 100%.
Radio Stns: 1 FM.
WIBN Earl Park, IN
John Balvich, General Manager

Bryan Broadcasting Corp.
2700 Earl Rudder Fwy., Suite 5000, College Station TX 77845
(979) 695-9595; *Fax:*(979) 695-1933
www.bryanbroadcasting.com
radio@bryanbroadcasting.com
Ownership: William R. Hicks, 89%; Ben D. Downs, 11%.
Radio Stns: 4 AM. 3 FM.
KAGC Bryan, TX; WTAW College Station, TX; KWBC College Station, TX; KZNE College Station, TX; KNDE College Station, TX; KPWJ Kurten, TX; WTAW-FM Buffalo, TX
William R. Hicks, President
Ben Downs, Vice President and General Manager

BS&T Wireless, Inc.
PO Box 1099, Santa Monica CA 90406-1099
(239) 263-7700
Radio Stns: 2 FM.
KGHT El Jebel, CO; KTND Aspen, CO
Lerman Senter, President

Buck Owens Productions Inc.
3223 Sillect, Bakersfield CA 93308
(661) 326-1011; *Fax:*(661) 328-7503
Ownership: Buck Owens Revocable Trust II (Michael Owens and Melvin L. Owens Jr., co-trustees), 100%.
Radio Stns: 1 AM. 2 FM.
KUZZ Bakersfield, CA; KCWR Bakersfield, CA; KUZZ-FM Bakersfield, CA

Buddy Tucker Association Inc.
Box 63, Mobile AL 36601
(386) 738-1348; *Fax:*(251) 432-1396
Radio Stns: 3 AM.
WTOF Bay Minette, AL; WMOB Mobile, AL; WYND Deland, FL

Burbach Broadcasting Group
5 Rosemar Circle, Parkersburg WV 26104
(304) 485-4565; *Fax:*(304) 424-6955
www.resultsradiowv.com
Ownership: Estate of John L. Laubach Jr., Nicholas A. Galli, chmn/pres.
Radio Stns: 3 AM. 6 FM.
WADC Parkersburg, WV; WXKX Clarksburg, WV; WVNT Parkersburg, WV; WOBG-FM Salem, WV; WRZZ Parkersburg, WV; WGYE Mannington, WV; WGIE Clarksburg, WV; WXIL Elizabeth, WV; WGGE Parkersburg, WV
Nicholas Galli, President
Thomas Bayer, Vice President

Burt Broadcasting Inc.
Box 1848, Alamogordo NM 88311-1414
(505) 434-1414; *Fax:*(505) 434-2213
Radio Stns: 1 AM. 3 FM.
KINN Alamogordo, NM; KYEE Alamogordo, NM; KZZX Alamogordo, NM; KQEL Alamogordo, NM
Bill Burt, General Manager

BusinessTalkRadio.Net Inc.
Box 4826, Greenwich CT 06831-9998
(203) 323-7300; *Fax:*(203) 323-7302
businesstalkradio.net
Radio Stns: 3 AM.
KNIH Paradise, NV; WXBR Brockton, MA; WGCH Greenwich, CT
Michael Metter, CEO

Butler County Radio Network Inc.
112 Hollywood Dr., Suite 203, Butler PA 16001
(724) 287-5778; *Fax:*(724) 282-9188
www.insidebutlercounty.com
frontdesk@bcrnetwork.com
Radio Stns: 2 AM. 1 FM.
WBUT Butler, PA; WISR Butler, PA; WLER-FM Butler, PA
Scott Briggs, Operations Dir
Vicki Hinterberger, General Manager
Ron Willison, Programming Director
Bill Davis, News Director

Calvary Chapel of Albuquerque
4001 Osuna Rd NE, Albuquerque NM 87109
(505) 344-0880; *Fax:*(505) 345-9140
www.calvaryabq.org
Radio Stns: 2 FM.
KKCJ Cannon Afb, NM; KPKJ Mentmore, NM

Calvary Chapel of Susanville
P.O. Box 1316, Susanville CA 96130
(530) 257-4833
www.ccsusanville.com
Radio Stns: 1 FM.
KWLK Westwood, CA

Calvary Evangelistic Mission Inc.
Box 367000, San Juan PR 00936-7000
(787) 724-1190; *Fax:*(787) 722-5395
radio@therockradio.org
Radio Stns: 3 AM.
WBMJ San Juan, PR; WCGB Juana Diaz, PR; WIVV Island of Vieques, PR
Nila Luttrell, CFO
Ruth Lutterall, President
Janet Luttrell, General Manager

Calvary Radio Network
150 West Lincolnway, Suite 2001, Valparaiso IN 46383
(219) 548-5800
www.calvaryradionetwork.com
info@calvaryradionetwork.com
Radio Stns: 13 FM.
WQKO Howe, IN; WHLP Hanna, IN; WJWD Marshall, WI; WJCO Montpelier, IN; WJCY Cicero, IN; WJCZ Milford, IL; WOJC Crothersville, IN; WCJL Morgantown, IN; WMJC Richland, MI; WTZI Rosemont, IL; WVWG Seelyville, IN; WTZY Wonder Lake, IL; WJCI Huntington, IN

Cameron Broadcasting Inc.
1615 Orange Tree Ln., Suite 102, Redlands CA 92374
(909) 793-2233; *Fax:*(909) 798-6984
kflg947.com; lucky98fm.com; theknack107.com
Radio Stns: 3 AM. 3 FM.
KAAA Kingman, AZ; KZZZ Bullhead City, AZ; KFLG Bullhead City, AZ; KLUK Needles, CA; KFLG-FM Big River, CA; KNKK Needles, CA
William Jaeger, CEO
Don Jaeger, Operations Dir

Canadian Broadcasting Corporation (CBC)
205 Wellington St. W, Room 4E301-B, Toronto ON M5V 3G7
(416) 205-3700
www.cbc.ca
tonews@cbc.ca
Ownership: Government of Canada
Radio Stns: 14 AM. 65 FM.
CBEF Windsor, ON; CBG Gander, NF; CBI Sydney, NS; CBN St. John's, NL; CBT Grand Falls-Windsor, NF; CBY Corner Brook, NF; CFFB Iqaluit, NU; CHAK Inuvik, NT; CJBC Toronto, ON; CBR Calgary, AB; CBX Edmonton, AB; CFPR Prince Rupert, BC; CBU Vancouver, BC; CBW Winnipeg, MB; CBAF-FM Moncton, NB; CBAL-FM Moncton, NB; CBCL-FM London, ON; CBCT-FM Charlottetown, PE; CBD-FM Saint John, NB; CBDQ-FM Labrador City, NL; CBE-FM Windsor, ON; CBF-FM Montr,al, QC; CBFX-FM Montr,al, QC; CBH-FM Halifax, NS; CBHA-FM Halifax, NS; CBI-FM Sydney, NS; CBJX-FM Chicoutimi, QC; CBK-FM Regina, SK; CBKA-FM La Ronge, SK; CBKF-FM Regina, SK; CBL-FM Toronto, ON; CBLA-FM Toronto, ON; CBM-FM Montr,al, QC; CBME-FM Montr,al, QC; CBN-FM Saint John's, NL; CBO-FM Ottawa, ON; CBON-FM Timmins, ON; CBOQ-FM Ottawa, ON; CBOX-FM Ottawa, ON; CBQ-FM Thunder Bay, ON; CBQR-FM Rankin Inlet, NU; CBQT-FM Thunder Bay, ON; CBSI-FM Sept-Iles, QC; CBV-FM Quebec, QC; CBVE-FM Quebec, QC; CBVX-FM Quebec, QC; CBZF-FM Fredericton, NB; CFGB-FM Happy Valley-Goose Bay, NL; CFWH-FM Whitehorse, YT; CJBC-FM Toronto, ON; CBJ-FM Chicoutimi, QC; CJBR-FM Rimouski, QC; CBBX-FM Sudbury, ON; CBBS-FM Sudbury, ON; CBAX-FM Halifax, NS; CBGA-FM Matane, QC; CBAM-FM Moncton, NB; CBEW-FM Windsor, ON; CBK-1-FM Saskatoon, SK; CBLA-FM-2 Paris, ON; CBFX-FM-2 Sherbrooke, QC; CFYK-FM Yellowknife, NT; CBFX-FM-1 Trois Rivieres, QC; CBCX-FM Calgary, AB; CBR-FM Calgary, AB; CBX-FM Edmonton, AB; CHFA-10-FM Edmonton, AB; CBYK-FM Kamloops, BC; CBTK-FM Kelowna, BC; CBYG-FM Prince George, BC; CBU-FM Vancouver, BC; CBUF-FM Vancouver, BC; CBUX-FM Vancouver, BC; CBCV-FM Victoria, BC; CBWK-FM Thompson, MB; CBW-FM Winnipeg, MB;

CKSB-10-FM Winnipeg, MB; CKSB-FM St. Boniface, MB; CBAF-FM-5 Halifax, NS

TV Stns: 27 TV.
CBKT-DT Regina, SK; CBLT-DT Toronto, ON; CBMT-DT Montr,al, QC; CBNT-DT Saint John's, NL; CBOFT-DT Ottawa, ON; CBOT-DT Ottawa, ON; CBVT-DT Quebec City, QC; CBWFT-DT Winnipeg, MB; CBWT-DT Winnipeg, MB; CFYK-DT Yellowknife, NT; CJBR-DT Rimouski, QC; CKSH-DT Sherbrooke, QC; CKTM-DT Trois Rivieres, QC; CBAT-DT Fredericton, NB; CBHT-DT Halifax, NS; CBLFT-DT Toronto, ON; CBET-DT Windsor, ON; CBCT-DT Charlottetown, PE; CBFT-DT Montr,al, QC; CKTV-DT Saguenay, QC; CBKFT-DT Regina, SK; CBAFT-DT Moncton, NB; CBXFT-DT Edmonton, AB; CBXT-DT Edmonton, AB; CBRT-DT Calgary, AB; CBUFT-DT Vancouver, BC; CBUT-DT Vancouver, BC

Hubert T. Lacroix, President & CEO
Jennifer McGuire, General Manager and Editor in Chief
Gwen Jones McCauley, Content Sales and Consumer Products
Sally Catto, General Manager, Programming
Lillian Mak, Project Lead, Creative and Promotions
Jeff Vella, Media Engineering Director
Judith Purves, EVP, Chief Financial Officer
Teaghan Hawke, Senior Communication Officer

Canfin Enterprises Inc.
Box 3498, Abilene TX 79604
(325) 672-5442; *Fax:*(325) 672-6128
radioabilene.com

Radio Stns: 2 AM. 1 FM.
KZQQ Abilene, TX; KWKC Abilene, TX; KKHR Abilene, TX

Canxus Broadcasting Corp.
152 E. Green Ridge Rd., Caribou ME 04736-3737
(207) 473-7513; *Fax:*(207) 472-3221
www.channelxradio.com

Radio Stns: 3 FM.
WCXU Caribou, ME; WCXX Madawaska, ME; WCXV Van Buren, ME

Capital Community Broadcasting Inc.
360 Egan Dr., Juneau AK 99801-1748
(907) 586-1670; *Fax:*(907) 586-3612

Radio Stns: 3 FM.
KRNN Juneau, AK; KXLL Juneau, AK; KTOO Juneau, AK

TV Stns: 1 TV.
KTOO-TV Juneau, AK

Capital Media Corp.
30 Park Ave., Cohoes NY 12047-3330
(518) 237-1330; *Fax:*(518) 235-4468
www.aliveradionetwork.com
events@aliveradionetwork.com

Radio Stns: 1 AM. 4 FM.
WHAZ Troy, NY; WBAR-FM Lake Luzerne, NY; WMNV Rupert, VT; WMYY Schoharie, NY; WHAZ-FM Hoosick Falls, NY

Paul Lotters, President
Steve Klob, Operations Dir
Aaron Lucrezio, Production Director

Capitol Broadcasting Co. Inc.
2619 Western Blvd., Raleigh NC 27606
(919) 890-6000; *Fax:*(919) 890-6095
www.capitolbroadcasting.com
webmaster@cbc-raleigh.com
Ownership: Capitol Holding Co. Inc.

Radio Stns: 1 AM. 6 FM.
WMFD Wilmington, NC; WCMC-FM Holly Springs, NC; WRMR Jacksonville, NC; WKXB Boiling Spring Lakes, NC; WRAL Raleigh, NC; WILT Wilmington, NC; WAZO Southport, NC

TV Stns: 3 TV.
WRAL-TV Raleigh, NC; WRAZ Raleigh, NC; WILM-LD Wilmington, NC

James F. Goodmon, President/CEO
Daniel P. McGrath, Vice President/Treasurer
George W. Habel III, Vice President, Radio Networks
James F. Goodmon Jr., Vice President, CBC New Media Group
Angela B. Emerline, Vice President, Human Resources
Jennifer B. Venable, Vice President/General Counsel

Capps Broadcast Group
2003 N.W. 56th Dr., Pendleton OR 97801
(541) 276-1511; *Fax:*(541) 276-1480

Radio Stns: 3 AM. 2 FM.
KTEL Walla Walla, WA; KTIX Pendleton, OR; KUMA Pendleton, OR; KUMA-FM Pilot Rock, OR; KWHT Pendleton, OR

Randy McKone, General Manager

CapSan Media LLC
277 Bendix Rd., Suite 411, Virginia Beach VA 23452
(757) 497-1415; *Fax:*(757) 497-2560

Radio Stns: 4 FM.
WFMZ Hertford, NC; WZPR Nags Head, NC; WVOD Manteo, NC; WYND-FM Hatteras, NC

Carlson Communications International
3606 S. 500 W., Salt Lake City UT 84115
(801) 262-5624; *Fax:*(801) 266-1510

Radio Stns: 3 AM. 2 FM.
KDYL South Salt Lake, UT; KTSN Elko, NV; KCPX Spanish Valley, UT; KCYN Moab, UT; KRJC Elko, NV

Ralph J. Carlson, President

Carolina Christian Radio
3305 Burnt Mill Dr., Wilmington NC 28403
(910) 763-2452; *Fax:*(910) 763-6578
carolinachristianradio.org
info@carolinachristianradio.com

Radio Stns: 1 AM. 3 FM.
WWIL Wilmington, NC; WDVV Wilmington, NC; WWIL-FM Wilmington, NC; WZDG Scotts Hill, NC

Carroll Broadcasting Co.
1119 E. Plaza Dr., Carroll IA 51401
(712) 792-4321
www.1380kcim.com

Radio Stns: 1 AM. 2 FM.
KCIM Carroll, IA; KIKD Lake City, IA; KKRL Carroll, IA

Mary Collison, CEO/COO
John Ryan, Operations Dir
Deb Lupardus, General Sales Mgr

Carroll Enterprises Inc.
Box 549, Tawas City MI 48764
(989) 362-3417; *Fax:*(989) 362-4544
www.carrollenterprises.com

Radio Stns: 1 AM. 3 FM.
WIOS Tawas City-East Tawas, MI; WKJC-FM Tawas City, MI; WKJZ Hillman, MI; WQLB Tawas City, MI

John Carroll Jr., General Manager

Carter Broadcast Group Inc.
11131 Colorado Ave., Kansas City MO 64137
(816) 763-2040; *Fax:*(816) 966-1055
www.kprs.com

Radio Stns: 1 AM. 1 FM.
KPRT Kansas City, MO; KPRS Kansas City, MO

Todd Fries, General Sales Mgr
Myron Fears, Programming Director
Rich McCauley, Promotions Manager
Mark Leaver, Chief Engineer

Catholic Radio Network Inc.
201 N. Industrial Park Rd., Excelsior Springs MO 64024-1736
(816) 630-1090

Radio Stns: 4 AM. 1 FM.
KEXS Excelsior Springs, MO; KFEL Pueblo, CO; KPIO Loveland, CO; KAHS El Dorado, KS; KEXS-FM Ravenwood, MO

James O'Laughlin, President

CBS Radio
1515 Broadway, 46th Fl., New York NY 10036
(212) 846-3939
www.cbsradio.com
Ownership: CBS Corp., 100%. Note: CBS Corp. also owns the CBS Television Stations Group (see listing under TV Group Ownership, Section B)

Radio Stns: 29 AM. 87 FM.
KCBS San Francisco, CA; KDKA Pittsburgh, PA; KHTK Sacramento, CA; KIKK Pasadena, TX; KILT Houston, TX; KMOX St. Louis, MO; KFNQ Seattle, WA; KNX Los Angeles, CA; KRLD Dallas, TX; KXST North Las Vegas, NV; KRAK Hesperia, CA; KXNT North Las Vegas, NV; KZDG San Francisco, CA; KYW Philadelphia, PA; WAOK Atlanta, GA; WBBM Chicago, IL; WBZ Boston, MA; WCBS New York, NY; WCCO Minneapolis, MN; WFAN New York, NY; WINS New York, NY; WJZ Baltimore, MD; WSCR Chicago, IL; WJFK Morningside, MD; WPHT Philadelphia, PA; WQAM Miami, FL; WTIC Hartford, CT; WWJ Detroit, MI; WXYT Detroit, MI; KCBS-FM Los Angeles, CA; KFRC San Francisco, CA; KEZK St. Louis, MO; KEZN Palm Desert, CA; KMVQ San Francisco, CA; KFRG San Bernardino, CA; KVFG Victorville, CA; KHMX Houston, TX; KKHH Houston, TX; KILT-FM Houston, TX; KITS San Francisco, CA; KLLC San Francisco, CA; KLOL Houston, TX; KLUC Las Vegas, NV; KLUV Dallas, TX; KMLE Chandler, AZ; KMPS Seattle, WA; KMXB Henderson, NV; KXNT-FM Henderson, NV; KNCI Sacramento, CA; KMVK Fort Worth, TX; KOOL Phoenix, AZ; KEGY San Diego, CA; KJKK Dallas, TX; KROQ Pasadena, CA; KRTH Los Angeles, CA; KSFM Woodland, CA; KTWV Los Angeles, CA; KVIL Highland Park-Dallas, TX; KXFG Menifee, CA; KXTE Pahrump, NV; KJAQ Seattle, WA; KYKY St. Louis, MO; KYMX Sacramento, CA; KRLD-FM Dallas, TX; KYXY San Diego, CA; KZOK Seattle, WA; KZON Phoenix, AZ; KZZO Sacramento, CA; WIAD Bethesda, MD; WBBM-FM Chicago, IL; WBMX Boston, MA; KDKA-FM Pittsburgh, PA; WCBS-FM New York, NY; WCFS Elmwood Park, IL; WDOK Cleveland, OH; WDSY Pittsburgh, PA; WLZL Annapolis, MD; WNEW Bowie, MD; WIP Philadelphia, PA; WJFK-FM Manassas, VA; WJMK Chicago, IL; WKIS Boca Raton, FL; WXYT-FM Detroit, MI; WLIF Baltimore, MD; KMNB Minneapolis, MN; WNCX Cleveland, OH; WOCL Deland, FL; WODS Boston, MA; WOGL Philadelphia, PA; WOMC Detroit, MI; WOMX Orlando, FL; WPGC Morningside, MD; WPOW Miami, FL; WQAL Cleveland, OH; WFAN-FM New York, NY; WJZ-FM Catonsville, MD; WRCH New Britain, CT; WTIC-FM Hartford, CT; WUSN Chicago, IL; WVEE Atlanta, GA; WDZH Detroit, MI; WWMX Baltimore, MD; KZJK St. Louis Park, MN; WXRT Chicago, IL; WXTU Philadelphia, PA; WYCD Detroit, MI; WZGC Atlanta, GA; WKRK-FM Cleveland Heights, OH; WZLX Boston, MA; WZMX Hartford, CT; WBZZ New Kensington, PA; WBZ-FM Boston, MA; KXQQ Henderson, NV; KAMP Los Angeles, CA; WBMP New York, NY; WZMP Philadelphia, PA

Andre Fernandez, President
Scott Herman, Chief Operating Officer
Adam Wiener, EVP & General Manager
Chris Oliviero, EVP Programming
Jo Ann Haller, Sr. VP
Bob Philips, Sr. VP & Director Of Sales
Jeff Schultz, Senior Vice President
Stacey Benson, Senior Vice President Finance
Kenetta Bailey, Sr. VP Marketing

CDO Broadcasting Inc.
Radio Stns: 1 AM. 1 FM.
WCDO Sidney, NY; WCDO-FM Sidney, NY

Cenla Broadcasting Co. Inc.
1115 Texas Ave., Alexandria LA 71301
(318) 445-1234; *Fax:*(318) 473-1960
www.cenlabroadcasting.com

Radio Stns: 2 AM. 4 FM.
KDBS Alexandria, LA; KSYL Alexandria, LA; KKST Oakdale, LA; KQID-FM Alexandria, LA; KRRV-FM Alexandria, LA; KZMZ Alexandria, LA

Taylor Thompson, President

Center Broadcasting Co. Inc.
307 San Augustine St., Center TX 75935
(936) 598-3304; *Fax:*(936) 598-9537
www.cbc-radio.com
programdirector@cbc-radio.com

Radio Stns: 1 AM. 2 FM.
KDET Center, TX; KXXE-FM San Augustine, TX; KQBB Center, TX

Justine Mott, News Director
Lori Alvis, Sales
Jessie Jacobs, Programming Director

Central Wisconsin Broadcasting Inc.
Box 387, 1201 E. Division St., Neillsville WI 54456
(715) 743-3333; *Fax:*(715) 743-2288
1075therock.com
1075therock@tds.net

Radio Stns: 1 AM. 2 FM.
WCCN Neillsville, WI; WCCN-FM Neillsville, WI; WPKG Neillsville, WI

J. Kevin Grap, General Manager

Centro Cristiano Vida Abundante
3401 W. Holland Ave., Fresno CA 93722
(559) 222-0900; *Fax:*(559) 222-1573
www.ccvapr.com

Radio Stns: 1 AM.
KIRV Fresno, CA

Tony Donato, General Mgr/Operations Mgr

Cessna Communications Inc.
Box 1, Bedford PA 15522
(814) 623-1000; *Fax:*(814) 623-9692
www.bedfordcountyradio.com
info@bedfordcountyradio.com
Ownership: Jay B. Cessna; John H. Cessna.

Radio Stns: 2 AM. 2 FM.
WAYC Bedford, PA; WBFD Bedford, PA; WAYC Bedford, PA; WBVE Bedford, PA

Jay Cessna, President
John H. Cessna, Operations Dir

Charles W. Dowdy, Debtor-In-Possession
PO Box 30, Magnolia MS 39652
(601) 783-6600
Radio Stns: 2 AM. 6 FM.
WAPF McComb, MS; WAKK McComb, MS; WAKH McComb, MS; WAZA Liberty, MS; WTGG Amite, LA; WJSH Folsom, LA; WKJN Centreville, MS; WFCG Tylertown, MS
C. Wayne Dowdy, President

Cherry Creek Radio LLC
501 S. Cherry St., Suite 480, Denver CO 80246
(303) 468-6500; *Fax:*(303) 468-6555
www.cherrycreekradio.com
jschwartz@cherrycreekradio.com
Radio Stns: 20 AM. 36 FM.
KBLL Helena, MT; KBLJ La Junta, CO; KCAP Helena, MT; KCOM Comanche, TX; KDXU St. George, UT; KEYZ Williston, ND; KGRZ Missoula, MT; KROP Brawley, CA; KLMR Lamar, CO; KMON Great Falls, MT; KONA Kennewick-Richland-P, WA; KHKR Washington, UT; KSTV Stephenville, TX; KSUB Cedar City, UT; KTAN Sierra Vista, AZ; KUBC Montrose, CO; KZNW Wenatchee, WA; KXTL Butte, MT; KYLT Missoula, MT; KOWL South Lake Tahoe, CA; KAAR Butte, MT; KTHN La Junta, CO; KBLL-FM Helena, MT; KSNN-FM Ridgway, CO; KCIN Cedar City, UT; KXFF Colorado City, AZ; KGGL Missoula, MT; KBMI-FM East Helena, MT; KKXK Montrose, CO; KVVR Dutton, MT; KMBR Butte, MT; KMON-FM Great Falls, MT; KONA-FM Kennewick, WA; KREC Brian Head, UT; KRLT South Lake Tahoe, CA; KLMR-FM Lamar, CO; KIYK Saint George, UT; KXBN Cedar City, UT; KSTV-FM Dublin, TX; KTHC Sidney, MT; KWCD Bisbee, AZ; KWWW-FM Quincy, WA; KAAP Rock Island, WA; KXDR Pinesdale, MT; KYOX Comanche, TX; KYSN East Wenatchee, WA; KURL(FM) Billings, MT; KYYZ Williston, ND; KZHR Dayton, WA; KZMK Sierra Vista, AZ; KZMT Helena, MT; KZOQ-FM Missoula, MT; KWWX Cashmere, WA; KXDR(FM) Pinesdale, MT; KOYT(FM) Alberton, MT; KOYT(FM) Montana City, MT
Joe Schwartz, CEO
Dennis Goodman, Operations Dir
Dan Gittings, General Sales Mgr

Chesapeake-Portsmouth Broadcasting Corp.
2202 Jolliff Rd., Chesapeake VA 23321
(757) 488-1010
Radio Stns: 4 AM.
WBOB(AM) Jacksonville, FL; WLES Bon Air, VA; WLVA Lynchburg, VA; WTJZ Newport News, VA

Christian Broadcasting System Ltd.
5210 S. Saginaw St., Flint MI 48507
(810) 694-4146; *Fax:*(810) 694-0661
cbsat.net
graham.parker@cbslradio.com
Radio Stns: 5 AM. 5 FM.
WCVX Florence, KY; WCGW Nicholasville, KY; WLCM Holt, MI; WSNL Flint, MI; WGRI Cincinnati, OH; KAFC Anchorage, AK; KATB Anchorage, AK; WJIV Cherry Valley, NY; WJMM-FM Keene, KY; WVKY Shelbyville, KY
John Yinger, General Sales Mgr
Graham Parker, Programming Director
Antoniette Parson, Business Manager

Christian Listening Network Inc.
996 Helen St., Fayetteville NC 28303
(910) 864-5028; *Fax:*(910) 864-6270
Radio Stns: 1 FM.
WCLN-FM Clinton, NC

Christian Ministries of the Valley
2720 W. Business Hwy 83, Weslaco TX 78596
(956) 968-7777
Radio Stns: 1 AM. 1 FM.
KXTO Reno, NV; KBIC Raymondville, TX
Enrique Garza, General Manager

Christian Voice of Central Ohio Inc.
Box 793, New Albany OH 43054
(614) 855-9171; *Fax:*(614) 855-9280
Radio Stns: 2 FM.
WCVO Gahanna, OH; WZCP Chillicothe, OH
Drenda Keesee, Chairman
Dan Baughman, President

Churchill Communications LLC
871 Country Club Rd., Eugene OR 97401
(541) 344-5500; *Fax:*(541) 485-2550
Radio Stns: 3 AM.
KLZS Eugene, OR; KXPD Tigard, OR; KXOR Junction City, OR

Clarion County Broadcasting Corp.
1168 Greenville Pike, Clarion PA 16214-0688
(814) 226-4500; *Fax:*(814) 226-5898
clarionradio@comcast.net
Radio Stns: 2 AM. 2 FM.
WKQW Oil City, PA; WWCH Clarion, PA; WCCR Clarion, PA; WKQW-FM Oil City, PA
William S. Hearst, President

Clarke Broadcasting Corp.
342 S. Washington St., Sonora CA 95370
(209) 533-1450; *Fax:*(209) 533-9520
www.mymotherlode.com
news@clarkebroadcasting.com
Radio Stns: 1 AM. 2 FM.
KVML Sonora, CA; KKBN Twain Harte, CA; KZSQ-FM Sonora, CA
H. Randolph Holder Jr., President & CEO

Claro Communications Ltd.
11737 Nelon Dr., Corpus Christi TX 78410
(361) 774-4354; *Fax:*(361) 241-7945
Radio Stns: 3 AM. 4 FM.
KBRN Boerne, TX; KROB Robstown, TX; KOPY Alice, TX; KMZZ Bishop, TX; KOPY-FM Alice, TX; KUKA San Diego, TX; KGGB Yorktown, TX

Classic Communications Inc.
Box 1600, Woodward OK 73802-1600
(580) 256-1450; *Fax:*(580) 254-9102
Radio Stns: 1 AM. 2 FM.
KSIW Woodward, OK; KWDQ Woodward, OK; KWFX Woodward, OK
Sherre House, President
Bret Brewer, Operations Dir

Clear Sky Radio Inc.
220 3rd Ave. S., Suite 400, Lethbridge AB T1J 0G9
(403) 388-2910
www.clearskyradio.com
info@clearskyradio.com
Ownership: Paul Larsen.
Radio Stns: 4 FM.
CKBD-FM Lethbridge, AB; CJOC-FM Lethbridge, AB; CJCY-FM Medicine Hat, AB; CFSM-FM Cranbrook, BC
Paul Larsen, President & Co-Owner
Peter Deys, General Manager
Trent Fujita, General Sales Mgr
Scott McGregor, Programming Director
Pat Siedlecki, Corporate News Director
Matthew Finnie, Producer

Coast Radio Group, Inc.
10250 Lorraine Rd., Gulfport MS 39503
228-896-5500
Radio Stns: 1 FM.
KDLC Dulac, LA

Coastal Broadcasting Systems Inc.
3208 Pacific Ave., Wildwood NJ 8260
(609) 522-1987; *Fax:*(609) 522-3666
Radio Stns: 1 AM. 2 FM.
KANE New Iberia, LA; WJSE North Cape May, NJ; WCZT Villas, NJ
Bill Huf, President

Cochise Broadcasting LLC
Box 11060, Jackson WY 83002
(703) 812-0482
Radio Stns: 2 AM. 7 FM.
KCUZ Clifton, AZ; KOMJ Omaha, NE; KCDQ Douglas, AZ; KFMM Thatcher, AZ; KKYZ Sierra Vista, AZ; KWYX Casper, WY; KWXR Reliance, WY; KXZK Vail, AZ; KZXK Doney Park, AZ

Cohan Radio Group Inc.
3750 US 27N, Suite 1, Sebring FL 33870
(863) 382-9999; *Fax:*(863) 382-1982
www.cohanradiogroup.com
Ownership: Peter Coughlin.
Radio Stns: 3 AM. 2 FM.
WITS Sebring, FL; WJCM Sebring, FL; WWTK Lake Placid, FL; WWLL Sebring, FL; WWOJ Avon Park, FL
Peter Coughlin, President/GM

College Creek Media LLC
980 N. Michigan Ave., Suite 1875, Chicago IL 60611
(312) 204-9900
Radio Stns: 6 FM.
KADQ-FM Evanston, WY; KQPI Aberdeen, ID; KINX Fairfield, MT; KXJO St. Maries, ID; KHSK Allen, NE; KPAU Center, CO

Combined Communications
63088 NE 18th St., Bend OR 97701
(541) 382-5263; *Fax:*(541) 388-0456
www.combinedcommunications.com
Radio Stns: 1 AM. 3 FM.
KBND Bend, OR; KLRR Redmond, OR; KTWS Bend, OR; KMTK Bend, OR

Combined Media Group Inc.
Box 789, Wynne AR 72396
(870) 238-8141; *Fax:*(870) 238-5997
Radio Stns: 2 AM.
KPOC Pocahontas, AR; KRLW Walnut Ridge, AR
Tim Scott, General Manager

Commonwealth Broadcasting Corp.
1823 McIntosh Street, Suite 107, Bowling Green KY 42104
(270) 842-4487; *Fax:*(270) 783-8829
www.bowlinggreensam.com
Radio Stns: 8 AM. 13 FM.
WGRK Jeffersontown, KY; WWKU Plum Springs, KY; WIEL Elizabethtown, KY; WLRS Eminence, KY; WLBN Lebanon, KY; WPKY Princeton, KY; WTCO Campbellsville, KY; WTTL Madisonville, KY; WYSB Springfield, KY; WAVJ Princeton, KY; WCKQ Campbellsville, KY; WGRK-FM Greensburg, KY; WOVO Horse Cave, KY; WWKY Providence, KY; WRZI Hodgenville, KY; WLSK Lebanon, KY; WKMO Lebanon Junction, KY; WPTQ Glasgow, KY; WHHT(FM) Cave City, KY; WTHX Vine Grove, KY; WTTL-FM Madisonville, KY
TV Stns: 1 TV.
WABG-TV Greenwood, MS
Derron Steenbergen, General Manager
Greg Bowen, General Sales Mgr

Communications Capital Managers LLC
1111 Michigan Ave., Suite 301, East Lansing MI 48823-1096
(517) 351-3333; *Fax:*(517) 351-4481
Radio Stns: 2 AM. 2 FM.
KRUS Ruston, LA; WUBR Baton Rouge, LA; KPCH Ruston, LA; KXKZ Ruston, LA
Deb Grugen, CFO
Michael Oesterle, CEO

Communicom Broadcasting LLC
220 Josephine St., Suite 200, Denver CO 80206
(303) 759-8481
Radio Stns: 2 AM.
KXEG Phoenix, AZ; KXXT Tolleson, AZ

Community Broadcasters LLC
300 First Ave, Suite 204, Needham MA 02494
(781) 247-0730; *Fax:*(617) 597-9996
www.commbroadcasters.com
Radio Stns: 11 AM. 19 FM.
WATN Watertown, NY; WDKD Kingstree, SC; WDXY Sumter, SC; WRCE Watkins Glen, NY; WHDL Olean, NY; WHYM Lake City, SC; WOLH Florence, SC; WWHM Sumter, SC; WSLB Ogdensburg, NY; WWLZ Horseheads, NY; WTQS Cameron, SC; WGFG Branchville, SC; WLFK Gouverneur, NY; WIBZ Wedgefield, SC; WWBD Sumter, SC; WQKI-FM Orangeburg, SC; WSIM Lamar, SC; WLJI Summerton, SC; WNGZ Montour Falls, NY; WNKI Corning, NY; WEFX Henderson, NY; WQTK Ogdensburg, NY; WPDT Coward, SC; WPGI Horseheads, NY; WPIG Olean, NY; WSPX Bowman, SC; WTOJ Carthage, NY; WWKT-FM Kingstree, SC; WBDR Copenhagen, NY; WOTT Calcium, NY
Bruce J. Mittman, General Partner, COO
Jim Leven, General Partner, President & CEO
Stephen Ciaccio, Director, Digital & Sports
Peter Henderson, Chief Controller

Conner Media Corp.
702 Hartness Rd., Statesville NC 28677
(704) 878-9004
Radio Stns: 3 AM. 2 FM.
WEGG Rose Hill, NC; WJNC Jacksonville, NC; WAVQ Jacksonville, NC; WZUP La Grange, NC; WSTK Aurora, NC
Ronald Benfield, President

Connoisseur Media LLC
136 Main St., Suite 202, Westport CT 06880-3304
(203) 227-1978; *Fax:*(203) 227-2373
www.connoisseurmedia.com
Radio Stns: 16 AM. 24 FM.
KBLG Billings, MT; KYYA Billings, MT; WALK Patchogue, NY; WNJE Trenton, NJ; WDRC Hartford, CT; WEEX Easton, PA; WFNN Erie, PA; WHLI Hempstead, NY; WCHR Flemington, NJ;

WJET Erie, PA; WMMW Meriden, CT; WSNG Torrington, CT; WTKZ Allentown, PA; WVPO Stroudsburg, PA; WWCO Waterbury, CT; WBYN Lehighton, PA; KRZN Billings, MT; KWMY Joliet, MT; KBBX-FM Nebraska City, NE; KRKX Billings, MT; KIBB Haven, KS; WBZO Bay Shore, NY; WDRC-FM Hartford, CT; WFOX Norwalk, CT; WEZN-FM Bridgeport, CT; WXBB Erie, PA; WIHN Normal, IL; WKJY Hempstead, NY; WWSK Smithtown, NY; WPST Trenton, NJ; WODE-FM Easton, PA; WPLR New Haven, CT; WRKT North East, PA; WRTS Erie, PA; WSBG Stroudsburg, PA; WWYY Belvidere, NJ; WTWF Fairview, PA; WBBE Heyworth, IL; KPLN Lockwood, MT; KXMZ Box Elder, SD

Jeffrey Warshaw, CEO
Michael Driscoll, President

Convergent Broadcasting LP
826 S. Padre Island Drive, Corpus Christi TX 78416
(361) 814-3800; *Fax:*(361) 855-3770

Radio Stns: 2 FM.
KKPN Rockport, TX; KPUS Gregory, TX
Bruce Danziger, President
John Hiatt, Operations Dir

Coon Valley Communications Inc.
2260 141st Dr., Perry IA 50220
(507) 643-0065

Radio Stns: 1 AM. 1 FM.
KDLS Perry, IA; KKRF Stuart, IA

Core Communicators Broadcasting LLC
1570 Northside Dr., Bldg. 200, Suite B, Atlanta GA 30318
(240) 605-7820
Ownership: Steve Hegwood.

Radio Stns: 2 FM.
WMRG Albany, GA; WIPK-FM Calhoun
Steve Hegwood, President & CEO

Corus Entertainment Inc.
Corus Quay, 25 Dockside Dr., Toronto ON M5A 0B5
(416) 479-7000; *Fax:*(416) 479-7006
www.corusent.com
alka.graham@corusent.com
Ownership: JR Shaw and family; Shaw Communications, 39%.

Radio Stns: 10 AM. 29 FM.
CFPL London, ON; CHED Edmonton, AB; CHML Hamilton, ON; CFMJ Richmond Hill, ON; CHQR Calgary, AB; CHQT Edmonton, AB; CJOB Winnipeg, MB; CJOY Guelph, ON; CHMJ Vancouver, BC; CKNW New Westminster, BC; CFHK-FM St. Thomas, ON; CFLG-FM Cornwall, ON; CFMI-FM New Westminster, BC; CFMK-FM Kingston, ON; CFNY-FM Brampton, ON; CFOX-FM Vancouver, BC; CFPL-FM London, ON; CHAY-FM Barrie, ON; CILQ-FM Toronto, ON; CIMJ-FM Guelph, ON; CJXY-FM Burlington, ON; CIQB-FM Barrie, ON; CISN-FM Edmonton, AB; CJDV-FM Kitchener, ON; CJSS-FM Cornwall, ON; CING-FM Hamilton, ON; CKCB-FM Collingwood, ON; CKDK-FM Woodstock, ON; CFGQ-FM Calgary, AB; CKNG-FM Edmonton, AB; CKQB-FM Ottawa, ON; CKRY-FM Calgary, AB; CKWF-FM Peterborough, ON; CJGV-FM Winnipeg, MB; CKBT-FM Kitchener-Waterloo, ON; CKWS-FM Kingston, ON; CJOT-FM Ottawa, ON; CKRU-FM Petersborough, ON; CJKR-FM Winnipeg, MB

TV Stns: 16 TV.
CFRE-DT Regina, SK; CFSK-DT Saskatoon, SK; CHAN-DT Vancouver, BC; CHBC-DT Kelowna, BC; CHEX-DT Peterborough, ON; CICT-DT Calgary, AB; CIII-DT Toronto, ON; CISA-DT Lethbridge, AB; CITV-DT Edmonton, AB; CKMI-DT-1 Montr,al, QC; CKND-DT Winnipeg, MB; CKWS-DT Kingston, ON; CHEX-TV-2 Oshawa, ON; CHNB-DT Saint John, NB; CIHF-DT Halifax, NS; CKWS-DT-1 Brighton, ON
Doug Murphy, President & CEO
Barbara Williams, EVP, Chief Operating Officer
Dale Hancocks, EVP, General Counsel
John Gossling, EVP, Chief Financial Officer
Shawn Kelly, EVP, Technology
Cheryl Fullerton, EVP, People & Communications
Colin Bohm, EVP International Development & Corporate Strategy

Coshocton Broadcasting Co.
114 N. Sixth St., Coshocton OH 43812
(740) 622-1560; *Fax:*(740) 622-7940
Ownership: Bruce Wallace, 100%.

Radio Stns: 1 AM. 1 FM.
WTNS Coshocton, OH; WKLM Millersburg, OH
Bruce Wallace, President/General Manager

Costa-Eagle Radio Ventures L.P.
462 Merrimack St., Methuen MA 1844
(978) 686-9966

Radio Stns: 4 AM.
WNNW Lawrence, MA; WCEC Haverhill, MA; WMVX Salem, NH; WCCM Methuen, MA

Country Mountain Airwaves LLC
1491 W. Thatcher Blvd., Safford AZ 85546-3306
(928) 428-2217

Radio Stns: 1 AM. 3 FM.
KRVZ Springerville, AZ; KQAZ Springerville, AZ; KTHQ Eagar, AZ; KJIK Duncan, AZ

Covenant Network
4424 Hampton Ave., St. Louis MO 63109
(314) 752-7000; *Fax:*(314) 752-7702
www.covenantnet.net

Radio Stns: 5 AM. 3 FM.
KHOJ St. Charles, MO; WCKW Garyville, LA; WIHM Taylorville, IL; WRMS Beardstown, IL; WRYT Edwardsville, IL; KBKC Moberly, MO; WHOJ Terre Haute, IN; WOLG Carlinville, IL
John Anthony Holman, President

Cox Radio Inc.
6205 Peachtree Dunwoody Rd., Atlanta GA 30328
(678) 645-0000; *Fax:*(678) 645-5002
www.coxmediagroup.com
Ownership: Cox Enterprises Inc., 100%. Note: Cox Enterprises Inc. also owns 100% of Cox Media Group (see listing). Privately Owned by Cox family.

Radio Stns: 10 AM. 48 FM.
KKYX San Antonio, TX; KONO San Antonio, TX; WDBO Orlando, FL; WGAU Athens, GA; WGBB Freeport, NY; WHIO Dayton, OH; WOKV(AM) Jacksonville, FL; WRFC Athens, GA; WSB Atlanta, GA; WSTC Stamford, CT; KTKX Terrell Hills, TX; KCYY San Antonio, TX; KISS-FM San Antonio, TX; KKBQ-FM Pasadena, TX; KGLK Lake Jackson, TX; KTHT Cleveland, TX; KONO-FM Helotes, TX; KRAV-FM Tulsa, OK; KRMG-FM Sand Springs, OK; KSMG San Antonio, TX; KGLK Lake Jackson, TX; WAPE-FM Jacksonville, FL; WBAB Babylon, NY; WEZI Ponte Vedra Beach, FL; WCFB Orlando, FL; WXGL St. Petersburg, FL; WDUV New Port Richey, FL; WEDR Miami, FL; WPOI St. Petersburg, FL; WFLC Miami, FL; WSRV Gainesville, GA; WOKV-FM Atlantic Beach, FL; WGMG Crawford, GA; WHFM Southampton, NY; WHKO Dayton, OH; WHPT Sarasota, FL; WHQT Coral Gables, FL; WDBO(FM) Orlando, FL; WALR-FM Palmetto, GA; WKLV-FM Port Chester, NY; WJGL Jacksonville, FL; WMMO Orlando, FL; WXXJ Jacksonville, FL; WSB(FM) Clemson, GA; WXKT Maysville, GA; WPYO Maitland, FL; WSB-FM Atlanta, GA; WNGC Arcade, GA; WSUN-FM Holiday, FL; WFEZ(FM) Miami, FL; WWKA Orlando, FL; WWRM Tampa, FL; WPUP Watkinsville, GA; WZLR Xenia, OH; KISS-FM San Antonio, TX; KWEN Sand Springs, OK; KJSR Sand Springs, OK; WBLI Patchogue, NY
James C. Kennedy, Chariman Cox Enterprises
John Dyer, President & CEO Cox Enterprises
Bill Hoffman, President, Cox Media Group
Kim Guthrie, EVP of Radio

Crain Media Group LLC
200 S. Commerce, Suite 702, Little Rock AR 72201
(501) 537-0720; *Fax:*(501) 537-0722

Radio Stns: 2 AM. 7 FM.
KAWW Heber Springs, AR; KWCK Searcy, AR; KEAZ Kensett, AR; KOLL Lonoke, AR; KCNY Greenbrier, AR; KHTE-FM England, AR; KKSP Bryant, AR; KWCK-FM Searcy, AR; KSMD Pangburn, AR
Paul Coates, General Manager
Phil Weaver, General Manager

Cram Communications LLC
401 W. Kirkpatrick St., Syracuse NY 13204
(315) 468-0908

Radio Stns: 2 AM.
WSIV E. Syracuse, NY; WOSW Fulton, NY
Craig Fox, President

Crawford Broadcasting Co.
2821 South Parker Road, Suite 1205, Aurora CO 80014
(303) 481-1800; *Fax:*(303) 433-1555
www.crawfordbroadcasting.com
info@crawfordbroadcasting.com
Ownership: Donald B. Crawford is sole owner of all the stns except WMUZ(FM), WRDT(AM), WEXL(AM), KJSL(AM) and KSTL(AM).WMUZ(FM), WRDT(AM), WEXL(AM), KJSL(AM) and KSTL(AM) are owned by Donald B. Crawford and Dean A. Crawford.

Radio Stns: 14 AM. 11 FM.
KLDC Denver, CO; KBRT Avalon, CA; KCBC Manteca, CA; KKPZ Portland, OR; KLVZ Brighton, CO; KLTT Commerce City, CO; KLZ Denver, CO; KAAM Garland, TX; KSTL St. Louis, MO; WDCX Rochester, NY; WYDE Birmingham, AL; WEXL Royal Oak, MI; WRDT Monroe, MI; WXJC Cordova, AL; WDCD-FM Clifton Park, NY; WDCX-FM Buffalo, NY; WLGZ-FM Webster, NY; WDJC-FM Birmingham, AL; WMUZ Detroit, MI; WYRB Genoa, IL; WYDE-FM Cullman, AL; WYCA Crete, IL; WSRB Lansing, IL; WPWX Hammond, IL; WXJC-FM Cordova, AL
Donald Crawford, President/CEO

CRISTA Broadcasting
19303 Fremont Ave. N., Seattle WA 98133
(206) 546-7350; *Fax:*(206) 546-7372
www.cristamedia.com
heidi@praise1065.com
Ownership: CRISTA Ministries.

Radio Stns: 1 AM. 3 FM.
KCIS Edmonds, WA; KCMS Edmonds, WA; KFMK Round Rock, TX; KWPZ Lynden, WA
Bob Lonac, President & CEO
Stan Mak, Vice President and General Manager

Criswell Communications
Box 619000, Dallas TX 75261-9000
(817) 792-3800; *Fax:*(817) 277-9929
www.kcbi.org
kcbi@kcbi.org

Radio Stns: 1 AM. 3 FM.
KCRN San Angelo, TX; KCBI Dallas, TX; KCRN-FM San Angelo, TX; KSYE Frederick, OK
Dr. Jerry Johnson, President
Ronald Harris, EVP

CSN International
P.O. Box 391, Twin Falls ID 83303
(800) 357-4226; *Fax:*(208) 736-1958
www.csnradio.com

Radio Stns: 3 AM. 28 FM.
KMHI Mountain Home, ID; WSFW Seneca Falls, NY; WWYC Toledo, OH; KAWZ Twin Falls, ID; KBLD Kennewick, WA; KTBJ Festus, MO; WIFF Windsor, NY; WWUN-FM Friar's Point, MS; KHJC Lihue, HI; KDJC Baker, OR; KJCC Carnegie, OK; KJCH Coos Bay, OR; KVJC Globe, AZ; WUJC St. Marks, FL; WSMA Scituate, MA; KJFT Arlee, MT; KWRC Hermosa, SD; KPIJ Junction City, OR; KNMA Tularosa, NM; KGSF Hunstville, AR; KKJA Redmond, OR; KVIR Bullhead City, AZ; WGWS St. Mary's City, MD; KGFJ Belt, MT; KQDL Hines, OR; KNGW Juneau, AK; KLWL Chillicothe, MO; KOGJ Kenai, AK; KIMW Heflin, LA; KAWS Marsing, ID; KGNR John Day, OR
Charles W. Smith, President
Mike Stocklin, Operations Dir
Joe Jennings, Programming Director
Kelly Carlson, Engineering Dir

CTC Media Group Inc.
Box 353, Royal Oak MD 21662
(410) 745-5958
www.ctc-media.com
mail@ctc-media.com

Radio Stns: 3 AM.
WNOS New Bern, NC; WWNB New Bern, NC; WECU Winterville, NC
Lee Afflerbach, CEO
Mike Afflerbach, Operations Dir

Cumulus Media Inc.
3280 Peachtree Road NW, Suite 2300, Atlanta GA 30305
(404) 949-0700; *Fax:*(404) 949-0740
www.cumulus.com
Ownership: Cumulus Media Inc., 25% (See Listing); Bain Funds, 25%; Blackstone Funds, 25%; and THLee Funds, 25%.

Radio Stns: 69 AM. 180 FM.
KAAY Little Rock, AR; KABC Los Angeles, CA; KESP Modesto, CA; KARN Little Rock, AR; KKAT Salt Lake City, UT; KBGG Des Moines, IA; KBOI Boise, ID; KCUB Tucson, AZ; KFNZ Salt Lake City, UT; KGO San Francisco, CA; KNML Albuquerque, NM; KKOB Albuquerque, NM; KKOH Reno, NV; KLIF Dallas, TX; KPZK Little Rock, AR; KMJ Fresno, CA; KNBR San Francisco, CA; KNEK Washington, LA; KTBL Los Ranchos, NM; KSFO San Francisco, CA; KTCK Dallas, TX; KTCT San Francisco, CA; KTIK Nampa, ID; KTUC Tucson, AZ; KCSF Colorado Springs, CO; KVOR Colorado Springs, CO; KJQS Murray, UT; WABC New York City, NY; WAPI Birmingham, AL; WARM Scranton, PA; WBAP Fort Worth, TX; WLBY Saline, MI; WDUZ Green Bay, WI; WXSM Blountville, TN; WGOW Chattanooga, TN; WHLD Niagara Falls, NY; WIBR Baton Rouge, LA; WIOV Reading, PA; WISW Columbia, SC; WJBC Bloomington, IL; WJCW Johnson City, TN; WJOX Birmingham, AL; WJR Detroit, MI; WGOC Kingsport, TN; WKY Oklahoma City, OK; WLS Chicago, IL; WMAL Washington, DC; WHLL Springfield, MA; WLTI New Castle, IN; WBBF Buffalo, NY; WNML Knoxville, TN; WSKO Syracuse, NY; WKLQ Whitehall, MI; WPRO Providence, RI; WRIE Erie, PA; WSBA York, PA; WPRV Providence, RI; WXLM Groton, CT; WGLD Manchester Township, PA; WTKA Ann

Arbor, MI; WTMA Charleston, SC; WTRX Flint, MI; WODJ Big Rapids, MI; WVEL Pekin, IL; WVNN Athens, AL; KWPN Moore, OK; WXOK Port Allen, LA; WJRW Grand Rapids, MI; WTOD Hartsville, SC; KATM Modesto, CA; KATT Oklahoma City, OK; KBEE Salt Lake City, UT; KBER Ogden, UT; KBUL Carson City, NV; KCHZ Ottawa, KS; KDJK Mariposa, CA; KFFG Los Altos, CA; KFOG San Francisco, CA; KGGO Des Moines, IA; KHKI Des Moines, IA; KHKK Modesto, CA; KHOP Oakdale, CA; KHYT Tucson, AZ; KIIM Tucson, AZ; KIPR Pine Bluff, AR; KIZN Boise, ID; KJJY West Des Moines, IA; KJOY Stockton, CA; KENZ Provo, UT; KKFM Colorado Springs, CO; KKGL Nampa, ID; KKMG Pueblo, CO; KKND Port Sulphur, LA; KKOB Albuquerque, NM; KLIF Haltom City, TX; KLAL Wrightsville, AR; KLOS Los Angeles, CA; KTCK Flower Mound, TX; KKND Belle Chasse, LA; KMGV Fresno, CA; KNEK Washington, LA; KNEV Reno, NV; KSZR Oro Valley, AZ; KPLX Fort Worth, TX; KQFC Boise, ID; KQRS Golden Valley, MN; KQXL New Roads, LA; KRBE Houston, TX; KATC Colorado Springs, CO; KWQW Boone, IA; KMJ Fresno, CA; KRRQ Lafayette, LA; KRST Albuquerque, NM; KSAN San Mateo, CA; KSCS Fort Worth, TX; KSKS Fresno, CA; KSMB Lafayette, LA; KKPK Colorado Springs, CO; KDRF Albuquerque, NM; WKIM Munford, TN; KURB Little Rock, AR; KARN-FM Sheridan, AR; KWYE Fresno, CA; KWIN Lodi, CA; KWNN Lodi, CA; KXKC New Iberia, LA; KNRQ Harrisburg, OR; KXXR Minneapolis, MN; KYIS Oklahoma City, OK; KENZ Provo, UT; WGVX Lakeville, MN; WRXP Cambridge, MN; WGVZ Eden Prairie, MN; KWYL South Lake Tahoe, CA; WABD Mobile, AL; WAQX Manlius, NY; WARM York, PA; WELJ Montauk, NY; WZPW Peoria, IL; WBHT Mountain Top, PA; WBNQ Bloomington, IL; WBWN LeRoy, IL; WRQQ Hammond, LA; WRKN LaPlace, LA; WSJR Dallas, PA; WCTO Easton, PA; WHTS Coopersville, MI; WDRQ Detroit, MI; WEDG Buffalo, NY; WEMX Kentwood, LA; WFBE Flint, MI; WNSH Newark, NJ; WFMS Fishers, IN; WFYR Elmwood, IL; WGFX Gallatin, TN; WGKX Memphis, TN; WJJK Noblesville, IN; WGLO Pekin, IL; WGOW Soddy-Daisy, TN; WGRF Buffalo, NY; WRWM Lawrence, IN; WGRR Hamilton, OH; WNNX College Park, GA; WHNN Bay City, MI; WHTT Buffalo, NY; WILZ Saginaw, MI; WIOG Bay City, MI; WIOV Ephrata, PA; WWWW-FM Ann Arbor, MI; WIVK Knoxville, TN; WJBQ Portland, ME; WQHZ Erie, PA; WMAL Woodbridge, VA; WKDF Nashville, TN; WKHX Marietta, GA; WTNR Holland, MI; WKOS Kingsport, TN; WKQX Chicago, IL; WKQZ Midland, MI; WZRH Picayune, MS; WLAV Grand Rapids, MI; WLCS North Muskegon, MI; WJEZ Dwight, IL; WLEV Allentown, PA; WXTL Syracuse, NY; WOMG Lexington, SC; WJQX Helena, AL; WMAS Enfield, CT; WMDH New Castle, IN; WMEZ Pensacola, FL; WMGL Ravenel, SC; WMGS Wilkes-Barre, PA; WMXS Montgomery, AL; WNKT Eastover, SC; WJBC Pontiac, IL; WNNK Harrisburg, PA; WWWQ Atlanta, GA; WNML Friendsville, TN; WNTQ Syracuse, NY; WOGB Reedsville, WI; WOGT East Ridge, TN; WLXC Columbia, SC; WORC Webster, MA; WPCK Denmark, WI; WPLJ New York, NY; WDVD Detroit, MI; WPRO Providence, RI; WQLH Green Bay, WI; WQUT Johnson City, TN; WQXA York, PA; WUHT Birmingham, AL; WRBO Como, MS; WZCY Hershey, PA; WRQX Washington, DC; WRRM Cincinnati, OH; WVIB Holton, MI; WOKI Oliver Springs, TN; WSOX Red Lion, PA; WXMX Millington, TN; WSSX Charleston, SC; WIWF Charleston, SC; WTCB Orangeburg, SC; WMOS Stonington, CT; WIXO Peoria, IL; WWFX Southbridge, MA; WWKI Kokomo, IN; WWKX Woonsocket, RI; WWLI Providence, RI; WWWZ Summerville, SC; WBHD Olyphant, PA; WBSX Hazleton, PA; WXBM-FM Milton, FL; WLS Chicago, IL; WEAN Wakefield-Peacedale, RI; WXKC Erie, PA; WXLO Fitchburg, MA; WXTA Edinboro, PA; WDUZ-FM Brillion, WI; WYAY Gainesville, GA; WYFM Sharon, PA; WFTK Lebanon, OH; WJOX Birmingham, AL; WZRR Birmingham, AL; WZYP Athens, AL; WLAW Newaygo, MI; WDLT Saraland, AL; KRMW Cedarville, AR; KTIK New Plymouth, ID; WBBL Greenville, MI

Mary G. Berner, Chief Executive Officer
Joseph P. Hannan, SVP, Treasurer & CFO
Richard S. Denning, SVP, Secretary & General Counsel

Curtis Media Group
3012 Highwoods Blvd., Raleigh NC 27604
(919) 876-0674; *Fax:*(919) 790-8369
www.curtismedia.com
Ownership: Donald W. Curtis.
Radio Stns: 13 AM. 11 FM.
WATA Boone, NC; WCLY Raleigh, NC; WDNC Durham, NC; WECR Newland, NC; WFMC Goldsboro, NC; WGBR Goldsboro, NC; WMFR High Point, NC; WPCM Burlington-Graham, NC; WPTF Raleigh, NC; WFNL Raleigh, NC; WSML Graham, NC; WXIT Blowing Rock, NC; WYRN Louisburg, NC; WMMY Boone, NC; WBBB Raleigh, NC; WECR-FM Beech Mountain, NC; WWPL Smithfield, NC; WPLW Hillsborough, NC; WBZJ Goldsboro, NC; WYMY Burlington, NC; WQDR-FM Raleigh, NC; WKIX-FM Raleigh, NC; WEQR Walnut Creek, NC; WZJS Banner Elk, NC

Donald Curtis, Chairman/Chief Executive Officer
Philip Zachary, President/Chief Operating Officer
Adam Maisano, Vice President/Director of Sales
Allen Sherrill, Engineering Dir

Dailey Corp.
Box 10, New Martinsviille WV 26155
(304) 455-1111; *Fax:*(304) 455-1170
Radio Stns: 1 AM. 1 FM.
WETZ New Martinsville, WV; WYMJ New Martinsville, WV
Calvin Dailey Jr., President

Dakota Communications Ltd.
Box 364, Pierre SD 57501
(605) 224-5434; *Fax:*(605) 224-5444
ddb@eaglecarver.com
Radio Stns: 1 AM. 3 FM.
KOKK Huron, SD; KZKK Huron, SD; KXLG Milbank, SD; KJRV Wessington Springs, SD
Linda Marcus, General Manager

Darby Advertising Inc.
Box 1766, Gaylord MI 49734
(989) 732-2341; *Fax:*(989) 732-6202
Radio Stns: 3 FM.
WMJZ-FM Gaylord, MI; WUPN Paradise, MI; WWSS Tuscarora Township, MI
Kent Smith, President

Davidson Media Group LLC
709 Peninsula Dr., Davidson NC 28036-7200
(704) 987-3585; *Fax:*(704) 987-3586
Radio Stns: 30 AM. 4 FM.
KDTD Kansas City, KS; KMNV St. Paul, MN; KCZZ Mission, KS; WACM West Springfield, MA; WVXX Norfolk, VA; WCVG Covington, KY; WPYR Baton Rouge, LA; WFNO Norco, LA; WVNZ Richmond, VA; WLLV Louisville, KY; KMNQ Brooklyn Park, MN; WLOU Louisville, KY; WMDB Nashville, TN; WDRJ Inkster, MI; WNOW Mint Hill, NC; WNVL Nashville, TN; WNTS Beech Grove, IN; WXCT Southington, CT; WOLI Spartanburg, SC; WREJ Richmond, VA; WSGH Lewisville, NC; WSPR Springfield, MA; WRJD Durham, NC; WEMG Camden, NJ; WTIK Durham, NC; WTUV Louisville, KY; WTOB Winston-Salem, NC; WLEE Richmond, VA; WWBG Greensboro, NC; WTOX Glen Allen, VA; WKKB Middletown, RI; WOLI-FM Easley, SC; WSTS Fairmont, NC; WTUV-FM Eminence, KY
Russ Jones, Operations Dir

Davis Broadcasting Inc.
2203 Wynnton Rd., Columbus GA 31906
(706) 576-3565; *Fax:*(706) 576-3683
gdavisjr@dbicolumbus.com
Ownership: Gregory A. Davis, 76%.
Radio Stns: 3 AM. 5 FM.
WCHK Canton, GA; WIOL Columbus, GA; WOKS Columbus, GA; WKZJ Eufaula, AL; WIOL-FM Waverly Hall, GA; WLKQ-FM Buford, GA; WEAM-FM Buena Vista, GA; WNSY Talking Rock, GA
Gregory Davis, President/CEO

DCBroadcasting Inc.
Box 1009, Jasper IN 47547
(812) 634-9232; *Fax:*(812) 482-3696
www.dcbroadcasting.com
Radio Stns: 1 AM. 3 FM.
WXGO Madison, IN; WAXL Santa Claus, IN; WBDC Huntingburg, IN; WORX-FM Madison, IN
Paul Knies, President

Debut Broadcasting Corp. Inc.
1209 16th Ave. S., Suite 200, Nashville TN 37212
(615) 301-0001; *Fax:*(615) 301-0002
Radio Stns: 3 FM.
WLTM Greenville, MS; WBBV Vicksburg, MS; WIQQ Leland, MS

Dee Rivers Radio Group
GRAM Corp., 43 Sherman Hill Rd. #204, Woodbury CT 6798
(203) 263-1900; *Fax:*(203) 263-1969
Radio Stns: 1 AM. 2 FM.
WGUN Valdosta, GA; WAAC Valdosta, GA; WGOV-FM Valdosta, GA
Georgia Salva, CEO

Deer Creek Broadcasting LLC
2225 First Ave., Napa CA 94558
(707) 226-2309
Radio Stns: 1 AM. 3 FM.
KPAY Chico, CA; KHSL-FM Paradise, CA; KMXI Chico, CA; KHHZ Gridley, CA

Delmarva Broadcasting Co.
Box 7492, 2727 Shipley Rd., Wilmington DE 19803
(302) 478-2700; *Fax:*(302) 478-0100
www.delmarvabroadcasting.com
Ownership: Steinman
Radio Stns: 3 AM. 8 FM.
WDEL Wilmington, DE; WICO Salisbury, MD; WYUS Milford, DE; WAFL Milford, DE; WKTT Salisbury, MD; WAVD Ocean Pines, MD; WSTW Wilmington, DE; WXCY Havre De Grace, MD; WXDE Lewes, DE; WNCL Milford, DE; WICO-FM Pocomoke City, MD
Julian Booker, President/Chief Executive Officer

Delmarva Educational Association
7235 Bonneval Rd., Jacksonville FL 32256
(904) 460-1010
www.thesalemcentre.com/Delmarva
Radio Stns: 2 AM. 2 FM.
WNTW Chester, VA; WZNZ Atlantic Beach, FL; WWIP Chesapeake, VA; WMUV Brunswick, GA
Nancy Epperson, President

Delta Media Corp.
3501 NW Evangeline Thruway, Carencro LA 70520
(337) 896-1600
www.deltamediacorp.com
Ownership: Charles Chatelain, 100%.
Radio Stns: 3 AM. 5 FM.
KFXZ Lafayette, LA; KSLO Opelousas, LA; KVOL Lafayette, LA; KYMK-FM Maurice, LA; KOGM Opelousas, LA; KFXZ-FM Opelousas, LA; KSLO Simmesport, LA; KLWB Carencro, LA
Charles Chatelain, CEO/COO
Chuck Wood, General Manager

Dickey Broadcasting Co.
3535 Piedmont Rd., Bldg. 14, Suite 1200, Atlanta GA 30305
(404) 688-0068; *Fax:*(404) 995-4045
www.680thefan.com
Radio Stns: 3 AM.
WIFN Atlanta, GA; WCNN North Atlanta, GA; WFOM Marietta, GA
David Dickey, CEO

Dierking Communications Inc.
937 Jayhawk Rd., Marysville KS 66508
(785) 562-2361; *Fax:*(785) 562-2188
www.dierkingcommunications.com
Radio Stns: 2 AM. 4 FM.
KNDY Marysville, KS; KQNK Norton, KS; KDNS Downs, KS; KNDY-FM Marysville, KS; KQNK-FM Norton, KS; KZDY Cawker City, KS
Bruce Dierking, General Manager

Digital Radio Broadcasting Inc.
135 White Bridge Rd., Middletown NY 10940
(845) 355-4001; *Fax:*(845) 355-4002
Radio Stns: 3 AM.
WYNY(AM) Ontario, NY; WYNY(AM) Milford, PA; WYNY(AM) Milford, PA
Charles Williamson, President

Digity LLC
701 Northpoint Pkwy., 5th Floor, West Palm Beach FL 33407
(561) 616-4777
Radio Stns: 17 AM. 30 FM.
KATE Albert Lea, MN; KAUS Austin, MN; KBRK Brookings, SD; KFOR Lincoln, NE; KGLO Mason City, IA; KJAM Madison, SD; KJJQ Volga, SD; KJSK Columbus, NE; KLGR Redwood Falls, MN; KLMS Lincoln, NE; KQAD Luverne, MN; KRIB Mason City, IA; KSDR Watertown, SD; KTTT Columbus, NE; KVFD Fort Dodge, IA; KWAT Watertown, SD; KWMT Fort Dodge, IA; KAUS-FM Austin, MN; KDBX Clear Lake, SD; KBRK-FM Brookings, SD; KCPI Albert Lea, MN; KDLO-FM Watertown, SD; KEEZ-FM Mankato, MN; KIAI Mason City, IA; KIAQ Clarion, IA; KFRX Lincoln, NE; KIXX Watertown, SD; KJAM-FM Madison, SD; KKEZ Fort Dodge, IA; KIBZ Crete, NE; KKOT Columbus, NE; KKQQ Volga, SD; KKSD Milbank, SD; KLIR Columbus, NE; KLSS-FM Mason City, IA; KRBI-FM St. Peter, MN; KSDR-FM Watertown, SD; KTGL Beatrice, NE; KTLB Twin Lakes, IA; KZLB Fort Dodge, IA; KYSM-FM Mankato, MN; KYTC Northwood, IA; KZEN Central City, NE; KZKX Seward, NE; WCCQ Crest Hill, IL; KMKO-FM Lake Crystal, MN; KXFT Manson, IA

Dimes Media Corporation
795 Buckley Rd., Suite 2, San Luis Obispo CA 93401
(805) 786-2570
www.953thebeach.com
Radio Stns: 1 AM. 3 FM.
KYNS San Luis Obispo, CA; KWWV Santa Margarita, CA; KXTZ Pismo Beach, CA; KXDZ Templeton, CA
Martha Fahnoe, President
Eric Fahnoe, Promotions Manager

Disney Channels Worldwide
500 S Buena Vista St., Burbank CA 91521
(818) 560-1000
www.disneyabcpress.com/disneyabctv/about-us/disney-channels
Ownership: Disney-ABC Television Group
Radio Stns: 6 AM.
KDDZ Arvada, CO; KDIZ Golden Valley, MN; KDZR Lake Oswego, OR; KDIS Pasadena, CA; WSDZ Belleville, IL; WWMI St. Petersburg, FL
Gary Marsh, President & Chief Creative Officer
Sean Cocchia, EVP, Business Operations & General Manager
Rita Ferro, EVP, Disney Media Sales & Marketing

Dispatch Broadcast Group
770 Twin Rivers Dr., Columbus OH 43215
(614) 460-3700; *Fax:*(614) 460-2809
www.dispatchbroadcast.com
Ownership: Dispatch Printing Company
Radio Stns: 1 AM. 1 FM.
WBNS Columbus, OH; WBNS-FM Columbus, OH
TV Stns: 2 TV.
WBNS-TV Columbus, OH; WTHR Indianapolis, IN
Michael Fiorile, Vice Chairman & CEO
Tani Mann, Vice President

DLC Media, Inc.
800 W. National Hwy., Washington IN 475001
www.wamwamfm.com
Radio Stns: 4 AM. 7 FM.
WAKO Lawrenceville, IL; WAMW-AM Washington, IN; WAMB Brazil, IN; WFNF Brazil, IN; WAKO-FM Lawrenceville, IL; WAMW-FM Washington, IN; WAXI Rockville, IN; WFML Vincennes, IN; WFNB Brazil, IN; WVGO Terre Haute, IN; WZJK West Terre Haute, IN
Dave Crooks, President/CEO
Andy Morrison, Operations Dir
Chad Schaefer, General Sales Mgr
Shelley L. Crooks, Promotions Manager
Dave Foster, News Director
Lisa Gray, Traffic Director

DMC Broadcasting Inc.
5542 NDCBU, Taos NM 87571-6122
(505) 758-4491; *Fax:*(505) 758-4452
Radio Stns: 1 AM. 3 FM.
KVOT Taos, NM; KXMT Taos, NM; KKTC Angel Fire, NM; KKIT Taos, NM

Dos Costas Communications Corp.
1818 S. Australian Ave., Suite 102, West Palm Beach FL 33409
(561) 655-6615
Radio Stns: 3 FM.
KDUC Barstow, CA; KDUQ Ludlow, CA; KXXZ Barstow, CA
Roland Ulloa, President
Jime Garza, Operations Dir

Dowdy & Dowdy Partnership
5921 W. Main St., Houma LA 70360
985-274-0017
Radio Stns: 1 FM.
WZKX Bay St. Louis, MS

Dr. Pepper Pepsi-Cola Bottling Co. of Dyersburg
35 Radio Rd., Dyersburg TN 38025-0100
(731) 285-1339; *Fax:*(731) 287-0100
Radio Stns: 1 AM. 2 FM.
WTRO Dyersburg, TN; WASL Dyersburg, TN; WTNV Tiptonville, TN

DreamCatcher Communications Inc.
334 Recreation Park Rd., Flemingsburg KY 41041
(606) 849-4433; *Fax:*(606) 845-9533
Ownership: Donald Bowles, 50%; Venita Bowles, 50%.
Radio Stns: 1 AM. 2 FM.
WFLE Flemingsburg, KY; WFLE-FM Flemingsburg, KY; WRAC Georgetown, OH
Don Bowles, CEO

Duhamel Broadcasting Enterprises
Box 1760, Rapid City SD 57709
(605) 342-2000; *Fax:*(605) 342-7305
www.kotatv.com
Ownership: William F. Duhamel, 63%; Peter A. and Lois G. Duhamel, 37%.
Radio Stns: 1 AM. 1 FM.
KOTA Rapid City, SD; KDDX Spearfish, SD
TV Stns: 4 TV.
KNEP-TV Scottsbluff, NE; KOTA-TV Lead, SD; KOTA-TV Rapid City, SD; KSGW-TV Sheridan, WY
William Duhamel, President

Durham Radio Inc.
1200 Airport Blvd., Unit 207, Oshawa ON L1J 8P5
(905) 571-0949; *Fax:*(905) 571-1150
powerofradio.ca
Ownership: Douglas Kirk, 82.61%; Mary L. Kirk, 10.85%; Others (Can.), 6.54%.
Radio Stns: 1 AM. 3 FM.
CKDO Oshawa, ON; CJKX-FM Ajax, ON; CKGE-FM Oshawa, ON; CHKX-FM Hamilton, ON
Doug Kirk, President
Steve Kassay, Vice-President, Programming & Operations
Steve Macaulay, Vice-President, Sales
April Galenzoski, Promotions Coordinator
Samantha Paterson, News Director

Eagle Bluff Enterprises
932 County Rd. 448, Poplar Bluff MO 63901
(573) 686-3700
www.foxradionetwork.com
Radio Stns: 1 AM. 3 FM.
KDFN Doniphan, MO; KAHR Poplar Bluff, MO; KFEB Campbell, MO; KOEA Doniphan, MO
Steven Fuch, President

Eagle Communications Group
2703 Hall St., Suite 15, Hays KS 67601
(785) 625-4000
www.eaglecom.net
Ownership: Eagle Communications Inc. Employee Stock Ownership Trust.
Radio Stns: 9 AM. 18 FM.
KAYS Hays, KS; KCOW Alliance, NE; KFEQ St. Joseph, MO; KINA Salina, KS; KJCK Junction City, KS; KOOQ North Platte, NE; KESJ St. Joseph, MO; KVGB Great Bend, KS; KWBW Hutchinson, KS; KAAQ Alliance, NE; KBGL Larned, KS; KHMY Pratt, KS; KELN North Platte, NE; KFIX Plainville, KS; KHAZ Hays, KS; KHOK Hoisington, KS; KHUT Hutchinson, KS; KJCK-FM Junction City, KS; KJLS Hays, KS; KKJO-FM St. Joseph, MO; KKQY Hill City, KS; KQLA Ogden, KS; KSJQ Savannah, MO; KSKG Salina, KS; KVGB-FM Great Bend, KS; KNPQ Hershey, NE; KCNB Chadron, NE
Gary Shorman, President/CEO

Eagle's Nest Inc.
6855 HWY 431, Roanoke AL 36274
(334) 863-4139; *Fax:*(334) 863-2540
www.eagle1023.com
eaglenestinc@gmx.com
Ownership: Jim Vice, 51%; Kay Vice, 49%.
Radio Stns: 2 AM. 1 FM.
WLWE Roanoke, AL; WLAG La Grange, GA; WELR-FM Roanoke, AL
Jim Vice, President

Earls Broadcasting Co.
202 Courtney St., Branson MO 65616
(417) 334-6003; *Fax:*(417) 334-7141
www.mykomc.com
Ownership: Charles Earls, Scottie Earls, Scott Earls.
Radio Stns: 2 AM. 3 FM.
KHOZ Harrison, AR; KOMC Branson, MO; KHBZ Harrison, AR; KOMC-FM Kimberling City, MO; KRZK Branson, MO
Charles Earls, CEO
Scott Earls, President
Scottie Earls, General Manager

East Arkansas Broadcasters Inc.
Box 789, Wynne AR 72396
(870) 238-8141; *Fax:*(870) 238-5997
Radio Stns: 5 AM. 9 FM.
KBRI Brinkley, AR; KCAB Dardanelle, AR; KNEA Jonesboro, AR; KVOM Morrilton, AR; KWYN Wynne, AR; KCJC Dardanelle, AR; KFIN Jonesboro, AR; KIYS Walnut Ridge, AR; KWHF Harrisburg, AR; KCON Atkins, AR; KTRQ Colt, AR; KVOM-FM Morrilton, AR; KWKK Russellville, AR; KWYN-FM Wynne, AR

East Carolina Radio Group
2422 S. Wrightsville Ave., Nags Head NC 27959
(252) 449-8331; *Fax:*(252) 449-8354
www.ecri.net
Radio Stns: 3 AM. 4 FM.
WCNC Elizabeth City, NC; WOBX Wanchese, NC; WZBO Edenton, NC; WERX-FM Columbia, NC; WKJX Elizabeth City, NC; WOBR-FM Wanchese, NC; WRSF Columbia, NC
Rick Loesch, President

East Kentucky Broadcasting Corp.
PO Box 2200, 1240 Radio Dr., Pikeville KY 41501
(606) 437-4051; *Fax:*(606) 432-2809
www.ekbradio.com
Radio Stns: 5 AM. 4 FM.
WEKB Elkhorn City, KY; WBTH Williamson, WV; WLSI Pikeville, KY; WPKE Pikeville, KY; WPRT Prestonsburg, KY; WDHR Pikeville, KY; WPKE-FM Coal Run, KY; WXCC Williamson, WV; WZLK Virgie, KY
Walter E. May, Owner/CEO
Cindy May Johnson, President/General Manager
John Roberts, Director of Sales
Walt May, Vice President/Programming Director

East Tennessee Radio Group III L.P.
112 Jordan Dr., Chattanooga TN 47421
(423) 485-8987
Radio Stns: 2 AM. 1 FM.
WBAC Cleveland, TN; WDNT Dayton, TN; WAYA-FM Ridgeville, SC

East Tennessee Radio Group L.P.
112 Jordan Dr., Chattanooga TN 37421
(423) 485-8987
Radio Stns: 2 FM.
WSEV-FM Gatlinburg, TN; WPFT Pigeon Forge, TN

East Texas Broadcasting Inc.
1798 US Hwy. 67 W., PO Box 990, Mount Pleasant TX 75456
(903) 572-8726; *Fax:*(903) 572-7232
www.easttexasradio.com
bud@easttexasradio.com
Radio Stns: 2 AM. 6 FM.
KIMP Mount Pleasant, TX; KPLT Paris, TX; KALK Winfield, TX; KBUS Paris, TX; KOYN Paris, TX; KPLT-FM Paris, TX; KSCH Sulphur Springs, TX; KSCN Pittsburg, TX
Bud Kitchens, President/General Manager

Edwards Communications L.C.
125 Eagles Nest Dr., Seneca SC 29678
(864) 882-3272; *Fax:*(864) 882-3718
www.edwgroupinc.com
Radio Stns: 3 AM. 5 FM.
KVOW Riverton, WY; WHAK Rogers City, MI; WKYO Caro, MI; KTAK Riverton, WY; WWTH Oscoda, MI; WHAK-FM Rogers City, MI; WHSB Alpena, MI; WIDL Cass City, MI
Jerry Edwards, President
Steve Edwards Jr., Operations Dir

Effect Radio
P.O. Box 271, Twin Falls ID 83303
(800) 357-4226
www.effectradio.com
Radio Stns: 1 AM. 2 FM.
WTZE Tazewell, VA; KEFX Twin Falls, ID; KEFS North Powder, OR
Jon Gibson, Programming Director

Electronic Applications Radio Service Inc.
15 Wood St., Greenfield IN 46140
(317) 467-1062
Radio Stns: 1 AM. 3 FM.
WRFM Muncie, IN; WYJZ Fearsville, KY; WBOO Morganfield, KY; WHUZ(FM) Cole, IN
Patrick Diemer, President

Elkhorn Media Group
PO Box 1426, Pikeville KY 41651
(606) 226-1476
www.myeasternoregon.com
elkhornmedia@gmail.com
Radio Stns: 3 FM.
KCMB Baker City, OR; KWRL La Grande, OR; KVBL La Grande, OR
Randy McKone, President
Kelly Workman, Operations Mgr
Tori Brock Gandy, General Sales Mgr

Ely Radio LLC
5010 Spencer, Las Vegas NV 89119
(702) 740-5588
Radio Stns: 2 AM. 1 FM.
KELY Ely, NV; KWNA Winnemucca, NV; KWNA-FM Winnemucca, NV

Elyria-Lorain Broadcasting Co.
538 Broad St., Box 4006, Elyria OH 44036
(440) 322-3761; *Fax:*(440) 284-3189
Radio Stns: 2 AM. 2 FM.
WEOL Elyria, OH; WLKR Norwalk, OH; WKFM Huron, OH; WLKR Norwalk, OH

Lonnie Gronek, Operations Dir

Emerald Wave Media

718 E. Chapel St., Santa Maria CA 93454
(805) 928-4334; *Fax:*(805) 349-2765

Radio Stns: 1 AM. 2 FM.
KTAP Santa Maria, CA; KIDI-FM Lompoc, CA; KRTO Guadalupe, CA

EMF Broadcasting

P.O. Box 2098, Omaha NE 68103-2098
(800) 434-8400
www.emfbroadcasting.com
Ownership: Educational Media Foundation, 100%. Educational Media is a nonprofit, nonstock corporation, governed by a seven-member board of directors.

Radio Stns: 2 AM. 286 FM.
WNWT Rossford, OH; DWKEL Myrtle Beach, SC; KKLV Orem, UT; KALR Hot Springs, AR; KDKL Coalinga, CA; KDRH King City, CA; KLVK Fountain Hills, AZ; KWLU Chester, CA; KKRD Enid, OK; KMLR Gonzales, TX; KLXV Glenwood Springs, CO; KLVB Citrus Heights, CA; KKLM Corpus Christi, TX; KFLV Wilber, NE; KARO Nyssa, OR; KJBR Marked Tree, AR; KLFV Grand Junction, CO; KLVP Aloha, OR; KKVO Altus, OK; KYLA(FM) Fountain Valley, CA; KXLV Amarillo, TX; KPOS Fouke, AR; KLOV Winchester, OR; KLRD Yucaipa, CA; KSBC Nile, WA; KLRQ Clinton, MO; KSRI Santa Cruz, CA; KLVA Maricopa, AZ; KLVH San Luis Obispo, CA; KLVC Magalia, CA; KLVG Garberville, CA; KLVJ Julian, CA; KLVN Livingston, CA; KZRI Sandy, OR; KLVR Middletown, CA; KLVS Livermore, CA; KLVU Sweet Home, OR; KLVY Fairmead, CA; KILV Castana, IA; KYGA Goleta, CA; KKLC Fall River Mills, CA; KMLV Ralston, NE; KOBC Joplin, MO; KJLV Hoxie, AR; KSSL Post, TX; KOKF Edmond, OK; KXAI Refugio, TX; KLXA Alexandria, LA; KOAR Beebe, AR; KLRJ Aberdeen, SD; KYKV Selah, WA; KQLV(FM) Bosque Farms, NM; KYLR Hutto, TX; KKLQ Harwood, ND; KYAR Lorena, TX; KLRO Hot Springs, AR; KIKL Lafayette, LA; KLCF Truth or Consequence, NM; KZKL Wichita Falls, TX; KTLI El Dorado, KS; KZLO Kilgore, TX; KTSL Medical Lake, WA; KRKL Walla Walla, WA; KLAG Alamogordo, NM; KZAR McQueeney, TX; KLMK Marvell, AR; KLDV Morrison, CO; KKLY El Paso, TX; KZLV Lytle, TX; KXRD Victorville, CA; KXRI Amarillo, TX; KKLU Lubbock, TX; KYXA Homer, LA; KYLV Oklahoma City, OK; KYDA Azle, TX; WYKV Ravena, NY; WAUQ Charles City, VA; WKIV Westerly, RI; WKVV Searsport, ME; WCVJ Jefferson, OH; WARX Lewiston, ME; WKEL Webster, NY; WKHL West Lafayette, IN; WAKL Flint, MI; WKVZ Dexter, ME; WNGA Clermont, GA; WLAI Wilmore, KY; WLKU Rock Island, IL; WJKL Glendale Heights, IL; WJLR Seymour, IN; WORI Harrison, OH; WVKV Nashville, GA; WKVP Camden, NJ; WZKV Dyersburg, TN; WLVZ Collins, MS; WLKP Belpre, OH; WHKU Proctorville, OH; WKVC North Myrtle Beach, SC; WKVN Morganfield, KY; WMXK Morristown, TN; WKVK Semora, NC; WBKL Clinton, LA; WQRP Dayton, OH; WKVU Utica, NY; WOKR Remsen, NY; WBGI-FM Moundsville, WV; WYDA Troy, OH; WKDL-FM Brockport, NY; WXKY-FM Stanford, KY; WKVO Georgetown, KY; WHKV Sylvester, GA; WGKV Pulaski, NY; WYPA Cherry Hill, NJ; WTKL North Dartmouth, MA; WARA New Washington, IN; WDKL Grafton, WV; WTLG Starke, FL; WLKB Bay City, MI; WJLV Jackson, MS; WIKL(FM) Elwood, IN; WJAI Pearl, MS; WLKV Ripley, WV; WUTQ-FM Utica, NY; WWLT Manchester, KY; WMSO Quitman, MS; WKVF Bartlett, TN; WYKL Crestline, OH; WNHI Farmington, NH; WEKV South Webster, OH; WKVW Marmet, WV; WKGV Swansboro, NC; WYAI Scotia, NY; WKWV Watertown, NY; KLVW Odessa, TX; WLKA Tafton, PA; WNKL Wauseon, OH; KHRI Hollister, CA; WCLR Arlington Heights, IL; KXPC Welches, OR; KWBI Great Bend, KS; KMKL North Branch, MN; KWKL Grandfield, OK; KAIS(FM) Tracy, CA; KAKV El Dorado, AR; KKRI Pocola, OK; WTRK Freeland, MI; KWRI Bartlesville, OK; WLVE Mukwonago, WI; KGBM Randsburg, CA; KSRD St. Joseph, MO; KHKL Laytonville, CA; WSRI Sugar Grove, IL; WKVH Monticello, FL; KLFS Van Buren, AR; KLWV Chugwater, WY; KARQ San Andreas, CA; KJKL Selma, OR; KQKL Selma, CA; KBIL Park City, MT; KLRV Billings, MT; KTKL Stigler, OK; KGCL Jordan Valley, OR; KLWC Casper, WY; KGCO Fort Collins, CO; KARA Williams, CA; KKLP La Pine, OR; KULV Ukiah, CA; KAIZ Mesquite, NV; KKRO Red Bluff, CA; KVLB Bend, OR; KARU Cache, OK; KKLW Willmar, MN; KLRI Rigby, ID; KAKL Anchorage, AK; KNKL North Ogden, UT; KHCO Hayden, CO; KLBV Steamboat Springs, CO; KKLT Texarkana, AR; WTAI Union City, TN; KLNB Grand Island, NE; KARJ Kuna, ID; KAIP Wapello, IA; KLJV Scottsbluff, NE; KKLJ Klamath Falls, OR; KKLG Newton, IA; WIKV Plymouth, IN; KAGT Abilene, TX; KGRI Lebanon, OR; KAIA Bloomfield, MO; KFRI West Odessa, TX; KHLV Helena, MT; WDKV Fond Du Lac, WI; WKVY Somerset, KY; WZRI Spring Lake, NC; KLZV Brush, CO; KLRW Byrne, TX; KBMK Bismarck, ND; WQRA Greencastle, IN; WGCN Nashville, GA; WLRK Greenville, MS; KYRA Thousand Oaks, CA; KNRI Bismarck, ND; KQRI Bosque Farms, NM; KGCD Wray, CO; WARW Dorsey, IL; KDRE Sterling, CO; KAER Mesquite, NV; KLKM Kalispell, MT; KZAI Superior, AZ; KLRH Sparks, NV; KAIK Tillamook, OR; KLON Rockaway Beach, OR; KWAO Ocean Park, WA; WQKV Warsaw, IN; KRLU Roswell, NM; KELU Clovis, NM; KLRY Gypsum, CO; KLOY Astoria, OR; KAIB Shafter, CA; KAIH Lake Havasu City, AZ; KQAI Roswell, NM; KVLK Milan, NM; KNAR San Angelo, TX; KGFA Great Falls, MT; KAIC Tucson, AZ; KAIX Cheyenne, WY; KITA Iota, LA; WNKV Norco, LA; KYAI McKee, KY; KDRI Grants, NM; KLBZ Bozeman, MT; KLLR Dripping Springs, TX; WOAR South Vienna, OH; WXKV Selmer, TN; WPAI Nanty Glo, PA; KMLT Jackson, WY; KRLR Sulphur, LA; WKMY Winchendon, MA; KAIW Laramie, WY; KRNZ Gonzales, TX; KQLR Whitehall, MT; KBLV Tehachapi, CA; KLUW East Wenatchee, WA; KLRM Melbourne, AR; KZLU Inyokern, CA; KDAI Scottsbluff, NE; KGCM Belgrade, MT; KAIO Idaho Falls, ID; KAIG Dodge City, KS; WKMV Muncie, IN; KGGA Gallup, NM; KLLU Gallup, NM; WKIW Ironwood, MI; KLUU Jamestown, ND; KSFS Sioux Falls, SD; WLVU Belle Meade, TN; KHAI Wahiawa, HI; KKWV Aransas Pass, TX; WQAI Thomson, GA; KVRA Sisters, OR; WPRZ-FM Brandy Station, VA; KMKV Paia, HI; KRLP Fairmont, MN; KGLV Manhattan, KS; KGKV Garberville, CA; KVLP Tucumcari, NM; KVLZ Sheridan, WY; KRLE Oberlin, KS; KRLH Hereford, TX; KCAI Lodi, CA; KKLB Ruidoso, NM; KLOF Gillette, WY; KLKI Dolan Springs, AZ; KIFR Alice, TX; KGCN Roswell, NM; KRKA Severance, CO; KPGA Morton, TX; WCKU Clarksburg, WV; WZKL Woodstock, IL; KLKV Hunt, TX; KAKI Juneau, AK; KYZA Adelanto, CA; WKYV Colonial Heights, VA; WVLO Cridersville, OH; WTCF Wardensville, WV; KVLR Elgin, TX; KYKA Meadow Lakes, AK; WLVM Chickasaw, AL

Darrell Chambliss, Chairman
Mike Novak, President & CEO

Emmanuel Communications Inc.

P.O. Box 20027, Worcester MA 01602
(508) 767-1230
www.1230radio.com
info@1230radio.com
Ownership: Raymond Lauring.

Radio Stns: 1 AM.
WNEB Worcester, MA

Raymond Lauring, President
Cindy R. Dorsey, General Manager
Mark Lauring, Treasurer

Emmis Communications

One EMMIS Plaza, 40 Monument Circle, Suite 700, Indianapolis IN 46204
317-266-0100; *Fax:*317-631-3750
www.emmis.com
IR@emmis.com
Ownership: Jeffrey H. Smulyan, approximately 61% votes.

Radio Stns: 3 AM. 17 FM.
KLBJ Austin, TX; WFNI Indianapolis, IN; WLIB New York, NY; KBPA San Marcos, TX; KNOU St. Louis, MO; KLBJ-FM Austin, TX; KGSR Cedar Park, TX; KPNT Collinsville, IL; KPWR Los Angeles, CA; KROX-FM Buda, TX; KSHE Crestwood, MO; KFTK Florissant, MO; KMVN Palmer, AK; WBLS New York, NY; WLHK Shelbyville, IN; WIBC Indianapolis, IN; WQHT New York, NY; WEPN-FM New York, NY; WYXB Indianapolis, IN; KLZT Bastrop, TX

Jeff Smulyan, Chairman & CEO
Patrick Walsh, President & COO

Empire Broadcasting Corp.

100 Saratoga Village Blvd., Suite 21, Ballston Spa NY 12020
(518) 899-3000; *Fax:*(518) 899-3057
www.empirebroadcasting.net
Ownership: Robert Kieve, 100%.

Radio Stns: 4 AM. 2 FM.
KLIV San Jose, CA; WUAM Watervliet, NY; WABY Watervliet, NY; WPTR Schenectady, NY; KRTY Los Gatos, CA; WJKE Stillwater, NY

Robert Kieve, President

Emporia's Radio Stations Inc.

Box 968, Emporia KS 66801
(620) 342-1400; *Fax:*(620) 342-0804
Ownership: Steve Sauder, 100%.

Radio Stns: 1 AM. 2 FM.
KVOE Emporia, KS; KFFX Emporia, KS; KVOE-FM Emporia, KS

Lee Schroeder, General Manager
Susan Grother, Business Manager

Entercom Communications Corp.

401 City Ave., Suite 809, Bala-Cynwyd PA 19004
(610) 660-5610; *Fax:*(610) 660-5620
www.entercom.com
Ownership: Joseph M. Field.

Radio Stns: 32 AM. 92 FM.
KEPN Lakewood, CO; KIFM West Sacramento, CA; KEZW Aurora, CO; KNSS Wichita, KS; KMTT Vancouver, WA; KJCE Rollingwood, TX; KMBZ Kansas City, MO; KFH Wichita, KS; KFXX Portland, OR; WAXY South Miami, FL; WBEN Buffalo, NY; KCSP Kansas City, MO; WEAL Greensboro, NC; WEEI Boston, MA; WROC Rochester, NY; WBZU Scranton, PA; WGR Buffalo, NY; WILK Wilkes-Barre, PA; WKZN West Hazleton, PA; WMC Memphis, TN; WXNT Indianapolis, IN; WPET Greensboro, NC; WQXI Atlanta, GA; KYYS Kansas City, KS; WRKO Boston, MA; WWWL New Orleans, LA; WORD Spartanburg, SC; WWKB Buffalo, NY; WWL New Orleans, LA; WVEI Worcester, MA; WWWS Buffalo, NY; WYRD Greenville, SC; KALC Denver, CO; KAMX Luling, TX; KFH-FM Clearwater, KS; KUDL Sacramento, CA; KBLX-FM Berkeley, CA; KBZT San Diego, CA; WDAF-FM Mission, KS; KKFN Longmont, CO; KDFC Angwin, CA; KDGS Wichita, KS; KDND Sacramento, CA; KESN Allen, TX; KEYN-FM Wichita, KS; KSOQ-FM Escondido, CA; KGON Portland, OR; KIFM San Diego, CA; KISW Seattle, WA; KQMT Denver, CO; KKMJ-FM Austin, TX; KYCH-FM Portland, OR; KHTP Tacoma, WA; KNDD Seattle, WA; KNRK Camas, WA; KOIT San Francisco, CA; KOSI Denver, CO; KKWF Seattle, WA; KQKS Lakewood, CO; KQRC-FM Leavenworth, KS; KRSK Molalla, OR; KRXQ Sacramento, CA; KSEG Sacramento, CA; KSON San Diego, CA; KADO(FM) Fair Oaks, CA; KMBZ-FM Kansas City, KS; KWJJ-FM Portland, OR; KUDL Sacramento, CA; KFBZ Haysville, KS; KRBZ Kansas City, MO; KZPT Kansas City, MO; KGMZ(FM) San Francisco, CA; WAAF Westborough, MA; WBZA Rochester, NY; WWEI Easthampton, MA; WBEE-FM Rochester, NY; WAAF Brockton, MA; WCMF-FM Rochester, NY; WYRD-FM Simpsonville, SC; WSSP Milwaukee, WI; WEZB New Orleans, LA; WGGI Benton, PA; WGGY Scranton, PA; WSMB Harbor Beach, MI; WJMH Reidsville, NC; WKRF Tobyhanna, PA; WKRZ Freeland, PA; WKSE Niagara Falls, NY; WSMW Greensboro, NC; WKTK Crystal River, FL; WLMG New Orleans, LA; WWL-FM Kenner, LA; WLYF Miami, FL; WMC-FM Memphis, TN; WMFS-FM Bartlett, TN; WMMM-FM Verona, WI; WPAW Winston-Salem, NC; WMXJ Pompano Beach, FL; WMYX-FM Milwaukee, WI; WLKK Wethersfield Twnshp, NY; WNVZ Norfolk, VA; WKQK Germantown, TN; WOLX-FM Baraboo, WI; WPTE Virginia Beach, VA; WPXY-FM Rochester, NY; WQMG Greensboro, NC; WEEI(FM) Lawrence, MA; WROQ Anderson, SC; WRVR Memphis, TN; WHBS Pittston, PA; WSKY-FM Micanopy, FL; WSPA-FM Spartanburg, SC; WSTR Smyrna, GA; WKBU New Orleans, LA; WNTR Indianapolis, IN; WTPT Forest City, NC; WVKL Norfolk, VA; WWDE-FM Hampton, VA; WILK-FM Avoca, PA; WEEI-FM Lawrence, MA; WXSS Wauwatosa, WI; WMHX Waunakee, WI; WZPL Greenfield, IN; WAXY-FM Miramar, FL

David Field, President & CEO
Steve Fisher, Executive VP & CEO
Weezie Kramer, COO
Pat Paxton, President Of Programming
Deborah Kane, President Of Sales
Michael Doyle, Regional President
Andrew Sutor, Senior VP & General Counsel
Ruth Gaviria, Chief Marketing Officer

Entravision Communications Corp.

2425 Olympic Blvd., Suite 6000 W., Santa Monica CA 90404
(310) 447-3870; *Fax:*(310) 447-3899
www.entravision.com
Ownership: Walter F. Ulloa, Philip W. Wilkinson, Paul Zevnik, Univision Communications.

Radio Stns: 11 AM. 37 FM.
KWST El Centro, CA; KSVE El Paso, TX; KBZO Lubbock, TX; KCVR Lodi, CA; KGOL Humble, TX; KMXA Aurora, CO; KRZY Albuquerque, NM; KHRO El Paso, TX; KBMB Black Canyon City, AZ; KMBX Soledad, CA; WLQY Hollywood, FL; KDLD Santa Monica, CA; KYSE El Paso, TX; KDLE Newport Beach, CA; KHHM Sacramento, CA; KFRQ Harlingen, TX; KXSE Davis, CA; KINT-FM El Paso, TX; KJMN Castle Rock, CO; KKPS Brownsville, TX; KLNZ Glendale, AZ; KLOB Thousand Palms, CA; KLOK-FM Greenfield, CA; KSSE Arcadia, CA; KMIX Tracy, CA; KDVA Buckeye, AZ; KMXX Imperial, CA; KOFX El Paso, TX; KRCX-FM Marysville, CA; KRRN Moapa Valley, NV; KRNV-FM Reno, NV; KNTY Shingle Springs, CA; KLYY Riverside, CA; KSSD Fallbrook, CA; KCVR-FM Columbia, CA; KQRT Las Vegas, NV; KVLY Edinburg, TX; KNVO-FM Port Isabel, TX; KSES-FM Seaside, CA; KVVA-FM Apache Junction, AZ; KSSC Ventura, CA; KSEH Brawley, CA; KXPK Evergreen, CO; KTSE-FM Patterson, CA; WNUE-FM Deltona, FL; KAIQ Wolfforth, TX; KPVW Aspen, CO; KPST Coachella, CA

TV Stns: 47 TV.
KCBA Salinas, CA; KCEC Denver, CO; KINC Las Vegas, NV; KINT-TV El Paso, TX; KTFN-TV El Paso, TX; KLDO-TV Laredo, TX; KLUZ-TV Albuquerque, NM; KNVO-TV McAllen, TX; KORO-TV Corpus Christi, TX; KPMR-TV Santa Barbara, CA; KREN-TV Reno, NV; KEVC-CD Indio, CA; KUPB-TV Midland, TX; KVYE-TV El Centro, CA; WVEA-TV Venice, FL; WUTH-CD Hartford, CT; WJAL-TV Hagerstown, MD; WVEN-TV Daytona

Beach, FL; WUNI-TV Worcester, MA; KVSN-DT Pueblo, CO; KDCU-DT Derby, KS; KTFA-LP Albuquerque, NM; KCRP-CD Corpus Christi, TX; KGHB-CD Pueblo, CO; WHTX-LP Hartford, CT; KETF-CD Laredo, TX; KXOF-CD Laredo, TX; KELV-LD Las Vegas, NV; KNTL-LP Las Vegas, NV; KWWB-LP Las Vegas, NV; KBZO-LP Lubbock, TX; KCWT-CD La Feria, TX; KFXV-LD McAllen, TX; KTFV-CD McAllen, TX; KXFX-CD Brownsville, TX; XHRIO-TDT Matamoros, TX; KDJT-CD Salinas, CA; WVCI-LP Daytona Beach, FL; KVER-CA Indio, CA; KVES-LD Indio, CA; KRNS-CD Reno, NV; KANG-CD San Angelo, TX; KEUS-LD San Angelo, TX; KBNT-CD San Diego, CA; KHAX-LP San Diego, CA; KDTF-LD San Diego, CA; KTCD-LP San Diego, CA

Walter Ulloa, CEO/COO

Equity Communications LP
8025 Black Horse Pike, Suite 100-102, W. Atlantic City NJ 08232
(609) 484-8444; *Fax:*(609) 646-6331
951wayv.com
gfisher@equitycommunications.net

Radio Stns: 2 AM. 7 FM.
WCMC Wildwood, NJ; WMID Atlantic City, NJ; WAYV Atlantic City, NJ; WEZW Wildwood Crest, NJ; WGBZ Cape May, NJ; WZBZ Pleasantville, NJ; WTTH Margate City, NJ; WAIV Cape May Court House, NJ; WZXL Wildwood, NJ

Gary Fisher, President
Rob Garcia, Programming Director
Shannon Wray, Promotions Manager

ESPN Inc.
ESPN Plaza, Bristol CT 06010
(888) 549-3776
espn.go.com

Ownership: The Walt Disney Company (80%), Hearst Corporation (20%)

Radio Stns: 3 AM.
KSPN Los Angeles, CA; WEPN New York, NY; WMVP Chicago, IL

George Bodenheimer, Executive Chairman
John Skipper, President

Eureka Broadcasting Co. Inc.
1101 Marsh Rd., Eureka CA 95501
(707) 442-5744
www.eurekaradio.com

Ownership: Barbara Papstein, 50%; Hugo Papstein, 28%; and Brian Papstein, 22%.

Radio Stns: 3 AM. 3 FM.
KWSW Eureka, CA; KURY Brookings, OR; KEJY Eureka, CA; KEKA-FM Eureka, CA; KURY-FM Brookings, OR; KINS-FM Blue Lake, CA

Hugo Papstein, President

Evangel Ministries Inc.
1909 W. 2nd, Appleton WI 54914
(920) 749-9456; *Fax:*(920) 749-0474
www.thefamily.net

Radio Stns: 3 FM.
WEMI Appleton, WI; WEMY Green Bay, WI; WGNV Milladore, WI

Paul Comeron, Executive Director

Evanov Communications Inc.
5312 Dundas St. W, Etobicoke ON M9B 1B3
(416) 213-1035; *Fax:*(416) 233-8617
www.evanovradio.com
info@evanovradio.com

Ownership: William Evanov, 74.26%; Paul Evanov, 25%; And The Bill Evanov Family Trust, 0.74%.

Radio Stns: 5 AM. 13 FM.
CFMB Montr,al, QC; CIAO Brampton, ON; CKJS Winnipeg, MB; CKPC Brantford, ON; CHRF Montr,al, QC; CIDC-FM Orangeville, ON; CKDX-FM Newmarket, ON; CKPC-FM Brantford, ON; CFJL-FM Winnipeg, MB; CKHZ-FM Halifax, NS; CJWL-FM Ottawa, ON; CIRR-FM Toronto, ON; CKHK-FM Hawkesbury, ON; CKHY-FM Halifax, NS; CHWE-FM Winnepeg, MB; CHRC-FM Clarence-Rockland, ON; CHSV-FM Hudson/Saint-Lazare, QC; CJGB-FM Meaford, ON

Bill Evanov, President & CEO
Paul Evanov, Vice-President
Adam Robinson, IT & Engineering Director

Expression Production Group LLC
P.O. Box 7773, Huntington WV 25701
(304) 529-2517

Ownership: Kevin West.

Radio Stns: 1 AM. 2 FM.
WONS Cannonsburg, KY; WOKE Garrison, KY; WZAQ Louisa, KY

Stephanie Skragg, President & CEO

Pam Lemley, Director of Commerce
Matt Murray, Account Executive

F W Robbert Broadcasting Co. Inc.
2730 Loumor Ave., Metairie LA 70001
(504) 831-6941
www.wwcr.com

Ownership: Fred P. Westenberger, 51%; Chris P. Westenberger, 9.75%; Fritz N. Westenberger, 9.75%; Lisa M. Westenberger, 9.75%; Eric M. Westenberger, 9.75%; George McClintock, 10%.

Radio Stns: 3 AM.
WMQM Lakeland, TN; WNQM Nashville, TN; WVOG New Orleans, LA

Fred P. Westenberger, President
Eric Westenberger, General Manager

Faith Communications Corp.
2201 S. 6th St., Las Vegas NV 89104
(702) 731-5452; *Fax:*(702) 731-1992
www.sosradio.net

Radio Stns: 1 AM. 6 FM.
KANN Roy, UT; KCIR Twin Falls, ID; KHMS Victorville, CA; KSOS Las Vegas, NV; KMZL Missoula, MT; KMZO Hamilton, MT; KSQS Ririe, ID

Brad Staley, President

Family Life Communications Inc.
Box 35300, Tucson AZ 85740
(520) 742-6976; *Fax:*(520) 742-6979
www.flr.org

Ownership: All stns are owned by Family Life Communications Inc. A nonprofit, noncommercial Christian organization. No individual stockholders.

Radio Stns: 4 AM. 14 FM.
KFLB Odessa, TX; KFLT Tucson, AZ; WUFL Sterling Heights, MI; WUNN Mason, MI; KAMY Lubbock, TX; KFLB-FM Stanton, TX; KFLQ Albuquerque, NM; KFLR-FM Phoenix, AZ; KJTA Flagstaff, AZ; KJTY Topeka, KS; KWFL Roswell, NM; WJBP Red Bank, TN; WJTF Panama City, FL; WJTG Fort Valley, GA; WJTY Lancaster, WI; WUFN Albion, MI; WUGN Midland, MI; KFLT-FM Tucson, AZ

Randy Carlson, President
Evan Carlson, Vice President Of Ministry
Alonzo Willians, Vice President Of Operations
Rod Robinson, Vice President Of Development
Mack Piotrowski, Controller

Family Life Network
Box 506, Bath NY 14810
(607) 776-4151
www.fln.org

Radio Stns: 20 FM.
WCID Friendship, NY; WCIH Elmira, NY; WCII Spencer, NY; WCIY Canandaigua, NY; WCOG-FM Galeton, PA; WCOT Jamestown, NY; WCOU Attica, NY; WCOH-FM Du Bois, PA; WCOV-FM Clyde, NY; WCIT-FM Trout Run, PA; WCOF Arcade, NY; WCIG Dallas, PA; WCIM Shenandoah, PA; WCOP Farmington Township, PA; WCIJ Unadilla, NY; WCOM-FM Silver Creek, NY; WCGF Cambridge Springs, PA; WCIS Laporte, PA; WCIN-FM Tunkhannock, PA; WCGM Wattsburg, PA

Rick Snavely, CEO/COO

Family Stations Inc.
1350 South Loop Road, Suite 130, Alameda CA 94502
(510) 568-6200; *Fax:*(510) 568-6190
www.familyradio.org

Ownership: Nonprofit corporation.

Radio Stns: 13 AM. 47 FM.
KARR Kirkland, WA; KEBR Rocklin, CA; KECR El Cajon, CA; KEAR San Francisco, CA; KFRN Long Beach, CA; KKAA Aberdeen, SD; KQKD Redfield, SD; KYFR Shenandoah, IA; WFSI Baltimore, MD; WBMD Baltimore, MD; WCTF Vernon, CT; WCUE Cuyahoga Falls, OH; WKDN Philadelphia, PA; KDFR Des Moines, IA; KEAR-FM Sacramento, CA; KEFR Le Grand, CA; KFNO Fresno, CA; KFRB Bakersfield, CA; KFRS Soledad, CA; KHAP Chico, CA; KJVH Longview, WA; KPHF Phoenix, AZ; KPOR Emporia, KS; KPRA Ukiah, CA; KQFE Springfield, OR; KTXB Beaumont, TX; KUFR Salt Lake City, UT; WBFR Birmingham, AL; WEFR Erie, PA; WFBF Buffalo, NY; WFCH Charleston, SC; WFRC Columbus, GA; WFRH Kingston, NY; WFRJ Johnstown, PA; WFRS Smithtown, NY; WJCH Joliet, IL; WMFL Florida City, FL; WMWK Milwaukee, WI; WOTL Toledo, OH; WWFR Stuart, FL; WYTN Youngstown, OH; WFME Mount Kisco, NY; WOFR Schoolcraft, MI; KBFR Bismarck, ND; KEDR(FM) Butte, MT; KAWV Fort Dodge, IA; KPFR Pine Grove, OR; KFRJ China Lake, CA; WFRP Americus, GA; KQFR Rapid City, SD; KFRP Coalinga, CA; KEDR Bay City, TX; KFRW Great Falls, MT; KFRY Pueblo, CO; KFRD Butte, MT; KYOR Newport, OR; WUFR Bedford, PA; WKDN-FM State College, PA; KXFR Socorro, NM; KEAF Fort Smith, AR

TV Stns: 1 TV.
WNYJ-TV West Milford, NJ

Tom Evans, Founder

Family Worship Center Church Inc.
Box 262550, Baton Rouge LA 70826
(225) 768-3224
www.jsm.org

Radio Stns: 3 AM. 23 FM.
KNHD Camden, AR; KMFS Guthrie, OK; WJYM Bowling Green, OH; KJSM-FM Augusta, AR; KBDD Winfield, KS; KDJR De Soto, MO; KNRB Atlanta, TX; KTOC-FM Jonesboro, LA; KUUZ Lake Village, AR; WAWF Kankakee, IL; WAYB-FM Graysville, TN; WJCA Albion, NY; WBMF Crete, IL; WJFM Baton Rouge, LA; WJNS-FM Bentonia, MS; WQUA Citronelle, AL; WTGY Charleston, MS; WWGN Ottawa, IL; KSSW Nashville, AR; KPSH Coachella, CA; KAJT Ada, OK; KNFA Grand Island, NE; KSSO Norman, OK; WFFL Panama City, FL; KCKR Church Point, LA; KNBE Beatrice, NE

Jimmy Swaggart, President
David Whitelaw, Operations Dir

Federated Media
245 Edison Rd., Suite 250, Mishawaka IN 46545
(574) 295-2500; *Fax:*(574) 294-4014
www.federatedmedia.com

Radio Stns: 4 AM. 7 FM.
WKJG Fort Wayne, IN; WOWO Niles, MI; WOWO Fort Wayne, IN; WTRC Elkhart, IN; WRSW Niles, MI; WBYR Woodburn, IN; WBYT Elkhart, IN; WOWO-FM Fort Wayne, IN; WLEG Ligonier, IN; WMEE Fort Wayne, IN; WQHK-FM Huntertown, IN

John F. Dille, President
Jeffrey P. Laderer, Secretary/Treasurer

Finger Lakes Radio Group
3568 Lenox Rd., Geneva NY 14456
(315) 781-7000; *Fax:*(315) 781-7700
www.flradiogroup.com
abishop@flradiogroup.com

Radio Stns: 2 AM. 3 FM.
WAUB Auburn, NY; WFLR Dundee, NY; WFLK Geneva, NY; WNYR Waterloo, NY; WLLW Seneca Falls, NY

Alan Bishop, President

First Broadcasting Operating Inc.
8300 Douglas Ave., Suite 730, Dallas TX 75225
(214) 855-0002; *Fax:*(214) 855-5145
www.firstbroadcasting.com

Radio Stns: 1 AM. 1 FM.
KREL Colorado Springs, CO; KMCQ Covington, WA

Hal Rose, COO
Gary Lawrence, President
Neil Read, CFO

First Media Radio LLC
306 Port St., Easton MD 21601
(410) 822-3301; *Fax:*(410) 822-0576

Radio Stns: 5 AM. 13 FM.
WCPA Clearfield, PA; WREL Lexington, VA; WRMT Rocky Mount, NC; WSMY Weldon, NC; WWDR Murfreesboro, NC; WWDW Alberta, VA; WCEI-FM Easton, MD; WDLZ Murfreesboro, NC; WPWZ Pinetops, NC; WTRG Gaston, NC; WOWQ Du Bois, PA; WPTM Roanoke Rapids, NC; WQYX Clearfield, PA; WWZW Buena Vista, VA; WDWG Rocky Mount, NC; WZAX Nashville, NC; WYTT Emporia, VA; WZDB Sykesville, PA

Alex Kolobielski, President/CEO

First Natchez Radio Group
2 O'Ferrall St., Natchez MS 39120
(601) 442-4895; *Fax:*(601) 446-8260
listenupyall.com

Radio Stns: 1 AM. 3 FM.
WNAT Natchez, MS; KZKR Jonesville, LA; WQNZ Natchez, MS; WKSO Natchez, MS

Margaret Perkins, President
Josh Wells, Technical Operations Manager
Rene Adams, General Sales Mgr
Andrew Duhl, Programming Director

Flint Media Inc.
Box 7425, Bainbridge GA 39818-7425
(229) 416-6021; *Fax:*(229) 246-9995

Radio Stns: 1 AM. 2 FM.
WSEM Donalsonville, GA; WGMK Donalsonville, GA; WBGE Bainbridge, GA

Florida Keys Media LLC
93351 Overseas Hwy., Tavernier FL 33070
(305) 852-9085; *Fax:*(305) 852-2304

Radio Stns: 7 FM.
WAIL Key West, FL; WCNK Key West, FL; WCTH Plantation Key, FL; WEOW Key West, FL; WFKZ Plantation Key, FL; WAVK Marathon, FL; WWUS Big Pine Key, FL

FM Idaho Co., LLC
5660 Franklin Road, Suite 200, Nampa ID 83687
(208) 465-9966; *Fax:*(208) 465-2922
www.impactradiogroup.com
darrell@impactradiogroup.com
Radio Stns: 4 FM.
KWYD Parma, ID; KINF Gooding, ID; KSRV-FM Ontario, OR; KQBL Emmett, ID
Darrell Calton, General Manager
Mark Broz, General Sales Mgr

Focus Radio Communications
2305 Holmes Ave. NW., Huntsville AL 35816
(256) 533-1450; *Fax:*(256) 551-9865
www.wtkiradio.com
info@wtkiradio.com
Radio Stns: 2 AM. 2 FM.
WTKI Huntsville, AL; WEKI Decatur, AL; WTKI Huntsville, AL; WEKI Decatur, AL
Fred Holland, General Manager

Foothills Radio Group LLC
827 S. Fairview Dr., Lenoir NC 28645
(828) 758-1033; *Fax:*(828) 757-3300
www.gofoothills.com
al@gofoothills.com
Radio Stns: 2 AM. 1 FM.
WJRI Lenoir, NC; WKGX Lenoir, NC; WKVS Lenoir, NC
Al Bunch, President

Forcht Broadcasting
290 Witlo Road, Somerset KY 40701
(606) 678-8151
www.forchtbroadcasting.com
amstroud@forchtbroadcasting.com
Ownership: Terry E. Forcht.
Radio Stns: 8 AM. 10 FM.
WAIN Columbia, KY; WCVL Crawfordsville, IN; WFTG London, KY; WHOP Hopkinsville, KY; WSIP Paintsville, KY; WTCW Whitesburg, KY; WTLO Somerset, KY; WVLN Olney, IL; WAIN-FM Columbia, KY; WHOP-FM Hopkinsville, KY; WIKK Newton, IL; WIMC Crawfordsville, IN; WSEI Olney, IL; WSIP-FM Paintsville, KY; WCDQ Crawfordsville, IN; WXKQ-FM Whitesburg, KY; WANV Annville, KY; WYKY Science Hill, KY
Terry Forcht, President/CEO

Forever Broadcasting
1 Forever Dr., Hollidaysburg PA 16648
(814) 941-9800; *Fax:*(814) 943-2754
www.foreverradio.com
Ownership: Kerby Confer; Donald Alt; Carol Logan; Lynn A. Deppen.
Radio Stns: 12 AM. 20 FM.
WFBG Altoona, PA; WFRA Franklin, PA; WHUN Huntingdon, PA; WJST New Castle, PA; WQWK State College, PA; WMGW Meadville, PA; WNTJ Johnstown, PA; WRSC State College, PA; WTIV Titusville, PA; WVAM Altoona, PA; WKST New Castle, PA; WLLI Somerset, PA; WALY Bellwood, PA; WXMJ Cambridge Springs, PA; WBUS Boalsburg, PA; WFGY Altoona, PA; WHMJ Franklin, PA; WJHT Johnstown, PA; WFGE State College, PA; WWGY Grove City, PA; WFGI-FM Johnstown, PA; WUZZ Saegertown, PA; WKYE Johnstown, PA; WRKY-FM Hollidaysburg, PA; WGYI Oil City, PA; WWOT Altoona, PA; WRKW Ebensburg, PA; WCCL Central City, PA; WMAJ-FM Centre Hall, PA; WGYY Meadville, PA; WUUZ Cooperstown, PA; WRSC-FM State College, PA
Lynn Deppen, President
Mike Sherry, Vice President of Sales
Charles Lavera, Interactive Promotions Coordinator
Shannon Harbaugh, Corporate Controller
Patty Fye, Corporate Human Resources
Christopher Nebgen, Web Development Specialist

Fort Bend Broadcasting Co.
1610 Woodstead Ct., Suite 350, Spring TX 77380-3414
(281) 298-6797; *Fax:*(281) 298-8707
Radio Stns: 1 AM. 6 FM.
WARD Petoskey, MI; KLTR Brenham, TX; KULM-FM Columbus, TX; KHTZ Ganado, TX; WOUF Beulah, MI; WLDR-FM Traverse City, MI; WCUZ Bear Lake, MI
Roy Henderson, President

Fort Myers Broadcasting Co.
2824 Palm Beach Blvd., Fort Myers FL 33916
(239) 334-1111; *Fax:*(239) 334-0744
winktv.com
Radio Stns: 2 AM. 2 FM.
WJUA Pine Island Center, FL; WNPL Golden Gate, FL; WTLQ-FM Punta Rassa, FL; WINK-FM Fort Myers, FL
TV Stns: 1 TV.
WINK-TV Fort Myers, FL
Brian McBride, CEO
Jade McClelland, Radio Operations

Forum Communications Co.
Box 2020, Fargo ND 58107
(701) 235-7311; *Fax:*(701) 241-5406
www.in-forum.com
Radio Stns: 1 AM. 1 FM.
WDAY Fargo, ND; WZUU Mattawan, MI
TV Stns: 4 TV.
KBMY Bismarck, ND; KMCY Minot, ND; WDAY-TV Fargo, ND; WDAZ-TV Devil's Lake, ND
William Marcil, President

Foster Communications Co. Inc.
Box 2191, San Angelo TX 76902-2191
(325) 949-2112; *Fax:*(325) 944-0851
www.fostercommunications.us
Radio Stns: 1 AM. 3 FM.
KKSA San Angelo, TX; KIXY-FM San Angelo, TX; KWFR San Angelo, TX; KCLL San Angelo, TX
Fred Key, President
Jay Michaels, Operations Dir
Doug Smith, General Sales Mgr

Four Corners Broadcasting LLC.
190 Turner Dr., Suite G, Durango CO 81303
(970) 259-4444; *Fax:*(970) 247-1005
www.radiodurango.com
fcb@frontier.net
Ownership: Four Corners Communications LLC., Fordstone, Inc.
Radio Stns: 1 AM. 3 FM.
KIUP Durango, CO; KIQX Durango, CO; KRSJ Durango, CO; KKDC Dolores, CO
Kim Emanual, General Sales Mgr
Ed Lacy, Programming Director
Ryan Baker, Chief Engineer
Ward Holmes, Regional Manager
Kristin Dills, Business Manager

4-K Radio Inc.
2560 Snake River Ave., Lewiston ID 83501
(208) 743-2502; *Fax:*(208) 743-1995
www.koze.com
radiorip@aol.com
Ownership: Eugene Hamblin Trust; Michael R. Ripley.
Radio Stns: 2 AM. 2 FM.
KORT Grangeville, ID; KOZE Lewiston, ID; KORT-FM Grangeville, ID; KOZE-FM Lewiston, ID
Michael Ripley, President

Freedom Communications of Connecticut Inc.
330 Main St., Hartford CT 6106
(860) 524-0001; *Fax:*(860) 548-1922
mssm2115@msn.com
Radio Stns: 1 AM.
WLAT New Britain, CT
Stephen Brisker, Chairman

Freeland Broadcasting Stations
Box 387, Benton KY 42025
(270) 527-3102; *Fax:*(270) 527-5606
Radio Stns: 2 AM. 3 FM.
WCBL Benton, KY; WWDX Huntingdon, TN; WCBL-FM Grand Rivers, KY; WCCK Calvert City, KY; WEIO(FM) Huntingdon, TN

Fresh Life Radio
120 - 2nd St East, Kalispell MT 59901
(406) 257-3339
www.freshliferadio.com
info@freshliferadio.com
Radio Stns: 1 FM.
KYWH Lockwood, MT

Frontier Radio Management Inc.
4311 Wilshire Blvd., Suite 412, Los Angeles CA 90010
(323) 931-1745; *Fax:*(323) 931-0925
Radio Stns: 3 AM. 10 FM.
KBLU Yuma, AZ; KIXW Apple Valley, CA; KSMX Santa Maria, CA; KSMY Lompoc, CA; KATJ-FM George, CA; KIXA Lucerne Valley, CA; KURQ Grover Beach, CA; KSLY-FM San Luis Obispo, CA; KSTT-FM Los Osos-Baywood Par, CA; KTTI Yuma, AZ; KXFM Santa Maria, CA; KQSR Yuma, AZ; KZXY-FM Apple Valley, CA
TV Stns: 2 TV.
KPVI-DT Pocatello, ID; KXTF Twin Falls, ID
Jason Wolff, President

Fuchs Radio L.L.C.
Box 311, Hobart OK 73651
(580) 726-5656; *Fax:*(580) 726-2222
Radio Stns: 1 AM. 3 FM.
KTJS Hobart, OK; KHIM Mangum, OK; KJCM Snyder, OK; KTIJ Elk City, OK

G2 Media Group LLC
333 S. Kerr Blvd., Sallisaw OK 74955
(918) 790-4444; *Fax:*(918) 790-1052
Ownership: Darren F. Girdner.
Radio Stns: 1 AM. 1 FM.
KFSW Fort Smith, AR; KXMX Muldrow, OK
Darren F. Girdner, Founder

Galaxy Communications L.P.
235 Walton St., Syracuse NY 13202
(315) 472-9111; *Fax:*(315) 472-1888
www.galaxycommunications.com
Radio Stns: 6 AM. 8 FM.
WIXT Little Falls, NY; WRNY Rome, NY; WSCP Sandy Creek-Pulaski, NY; WSGO Oswego, NY; WTLA North Syracuse, NY; WTLB Utica, NY; WKLL Frankfort, NY; WKRH Minetto, NY; WKRL-FM North Syracuse, NY; WOUR Utica, NY; WZUN Phoenix, NY; WUMX Rome, NY; WTKV Oswego, NY; WTKW Bridgeport, NY
Ed Levine, President & CEO
Carrie Wojtaszek, General Manager
Steve Vasick, Director of Sales
Michael Lucarelli, Chief Financial Officer
Tami Grashof, Utica Director of Sales
Pam Levine, Event Director

Galesburg Broadcasting Co.
154 E. Simmons St., Galesburg IL 61401
(309) 342-5131; *Fax:*(309) 342-0840
www.galesburgradio.com
Radio Stns: 1 AM. 3 FM.
WGIL Galesburg, IL; WAAG Galesburg, IL; WKAY Knoxville, IL; WLSR Galesburg, IL
John Pritchard, President
Roger Lundeen, General Manager

Gamma Broadcasting LLC
275 Grove St., Bldg 2-400, Newton MA 02466
(617) 663-4938
Radio Stns: 4 AM. 2 FM.
WBEC Pittsfield, MA; WNAW North Adams, MA; WSBS Great Barrington, MA; WUPE Pittsfield, MA; WUPE-FM North Adams, MA; WBEC-FM Pittsfield, MA

Gateway Radio Works Inc.
22 W. Main St., Mount Sterling KY 40353
(859)-498-5608; *Fax:*(859)-498-7930
www.gatewayradio.net
Radio Stns: 1 AM. 3 FM.
WMST Mount Sterling, KY; WKCA Salt Lick, KY; WIVY Morehead, KY; WKYN Mount Sterling, KY
Hays McMakin, CEO/President

GCC Bend LLC
969 SW Colorado Ave., Bend OR 97702
(541) 388-3300
www.magic100fm.com www.power94.fm
Ownership: Gross Holdings L.P., 100%.
Radio Stns: 1 AM. 3 FM.
KICE Bend, OR; KMGX Bend, OR; KSJJ Redmond, OR; KXIX Sunriver, OR
Dana Horner, COO

Genesis Communications Inc.
2110 Powers Ferry Rd., Suite 198, Atlanta GA 30339
(678) 324-0170; *Fax:*(678) 324-0174
www.radiogenesis.com
ceo@radiogenesis.com
Ownership: Bruce C. Maduri, J. Donald Childress.
Radio Stns: 6 AM.
WAMT Pine Castle Sky Lake, FL; WIXC Titusville, FL; WHOO Kissimmee, FL; WMGG Egypt Lake, FL; WHBO Pinellas Park, FL; WWBA Largo, FL
Bruce C. Maduri, President/CEO
J Donald Childress, VP

Georgia Eagle Media Inc.
1350 Radio Loop Rd., Warner Robins GA 31088
(478) 923-3416; *Fax:*(478) 923-3236

Radio Stns: 1 AM. 2 FM.
WDXQ Cochran, GA; WMCD Claxton, GA; WCEH-FM Pinehurst, GA

Georgia-Carolina Radiocasting Companies
Drawer E, 233 Big A Rd, Toccoa GA 30577
(706) 297-7264; *Fax:*(706) 297-7266
www.gacaradio.com
sutton@gacaradio.com

Radio Stns: 4 AM. 5 FM.
WFSC Franklin, NC; WNEG Toccoa, GA; WSNW Seneca, SC; WSGC Elberton, GA; WSGC-FM Tignall, GA; WGOG Walhalla, SC; WRBN Clayton, GA; WNCC Franklin, NC; WLHR-FM Lavonia, GA

Douglas M. (Art) Sutton Jr., Chairman
M. Terry Carter, President
Tonya Burgess, Operations Dir

Geos Communications
Box 701, Tunkhannock PA 18657
(570) 836-4200; *Fax:*(570) 928-2100

Radio Stns: 3 AM. 3 FM.
WAZL Hazleton, PA; WZMF(AM) Nanticoke, PA; WGMF Tunkhannock, PA; WVYS Ridgebury, PA; WDYS Dushore, PA; WVYS-FM2 Towanda, PA

Kevin Fitzgerald, President

GHB Radio Group
1776 Briarcliff Rd. N.E., Suite A, Atlanta GA 30306-2106
(404) 875-1110; *Fax:*(404) 875-1186
Ownership: George H. Buck Jr.

Radio Stns: 11 AM. 1 FM.
WEGO(AM) Winston-Salem, NC; WAVO Rock Hill, SC; WCGC Belmont, NC; WHVN Charlotte, NC; WAME Statesville, NC; WMGY Montgomery, AL; WNAP Norristown, PA; WSVM Valdese, NC; WQNO New Orleans, LA; WBLO Thomasville, NC; WYZE Atlanta, GA; WOLS Waxhaw, NC

Jacob Bogan, COO
George Buck Jr., President

Gleason Radio Group
555 Center St., Auburn ME 04210
(207) 748-5868; *Fax:*(207) 784-4700
www.gleasonmedia.com
dick@gleasonmedia.com
Ownership: Richard D. Gleason, 100%.

Radio Stns: 3 AM. 2 FM.
WKTQ South Paris, ME; WTME Rumford, ME; WEZR Lewiston, ME; WOXO-FM Norway, ME; WTBM Mexico, ME

Richard Gleason, President/General Manager

Gleiser Communications LLC
1001 ESE Loop 323, Suite 455, Tyler TX 75701
(903) 593-2519; *Fax:*(903) 597-4141
www.gleisercom.com
Ownership: Broadcasting Partners Holdings, LP, Paul L. Gleiser.

Radio Stns: 2 AM. 2 FM.
KTBB Tyler, TX; KYZS Tyler, TX; KTBB Troup, TX; KRWR Tyler, TX

Paul Gleiser, CEO

Glory Communications Inc.
PO Box 951, Columbia SC 29202
(803) 939-9530; *Fax:*(803) 939-9469
www.columbiainspiration.com

Radio Stns: 1 AM. 1 FM.
WGCV Cayce, SC; WFMV South Congaree, SC

Alex Snipe, CEO

Goforth Media Inc.
P.O.Box 1328, Mobile AL 36633
(251) 473-8488
www.goforth.org
wilbur@goforth.org

Radio Stns: 2 AM. 1 FM.
WBHY Mobile, AL; WLPR-AM Mobile, AL; WBHY-FM Mobile, AL

Wilbur Goforth, President/General Manager
Robert Barber, Vice President/Station Manager
Charlie Smith, Director of Development
Kenny Fowler, Music Director

Gold Coast Broadcasting LLC
2284 South Victoria Ave, Suite 2G, Ventura CA 93003
(805) 289-1400,
goldcoastbroadcasting.com

Radio Stns: 3 AM. 3 FM.
KKZZ Port Hueneme, CA; KVTA Ventura, CA; KUNX Santa Paula, CA; KCAQ Camarillo, CA; KFYV Ojai, CA; KOCP Oxnard, CA

John Hearne, Chairman
Miles Sexton, President

Golden West Broadcasting Ltd.
201-125 Centre Ave., Altona MB R0G 0B0
(204) 324-6464; *Fax:*1-(888)-765-703
www.goldenwestradio.com
help@goldenwestradio.com
Ownership: Elmer Hildebrand Ltd., 53.98%; Airwave Investments Ltd., 26.74%; and others, 19.28%.

Radio Stns: 12 AM. 24 FM.
CFAM Altona, MB; CFRY Portage La Prairie, MB; CFSL Weyburn, SK; CFYM Kindersley, SK; CHAB Moose Jaw, SK; CHRB High River, AB; CHSM Steinbach, MB; CJRB Boissevain, MB; CJSL Estevan, SK; CJSN Shaunavon, SK; CJYM Rosetown, SK; CKSW Swift Current, SK; CILT-FM Steinbach, MB; CIMG-FM Swift Current, SK; CJEL-FM Winkler, MB; CHVN-FM Winnipeg, MB; CILG-FM Moose Jaw, SK; CHSN-FM Estevan, SK; CKCL-FM Winnipeg, MB; CKUV-FM High River, AB; CJPG-FM Portage la Prairie, MB; CKVX-FM Kindersley, SK; CKFI-FM Swift Current, SK; CKQV-FM Vermilion Bay, ON; CKRC-FM Weyburn, SK; CFIT-FM Airdrie, AB; CJAW-FM Moose Jaw, SK; CFXO-FM High River, AB; CKSE-FM Estevan, SK; CHBO-FM Humboldt, SK; CHWY-FM Weyburn, SK; CJXR-FM Steinbach, MB; CKMW-FM Winkler-Morden, MB; CKFT-FM Fort Saskatchewan, AB; CHOO-FM Drumheller, AB; CHPO-FM Portage La Prairie, MB

Elmer Hildebrand, CEO
Lyndon Friesen, President
Ron Zuke, Station Manager
Darrell Friesen, General Sales Mgr
Corney Unger, IT Coordinator
Richard Kroeker, Vice President

Good Karma Broadcasting L.L.C.
310 W. Wisconsin Ave., Milwaukee WI 53203
(414) 209-3100
goodkarmabrands.com

Radio Stns: 5 AM. 4 FM.
WWGK Cleveland, OH; WBEV Beaver Dam, WI; WKNR Cleveland, OH; WTTN Columbus, WI; WAUK Jackson, WI; WWHG Evansville/Rockten, WI; WTLX Monona, WI; WXRO Beaver Dam, WI; WUUB Jupiter, FL

Craig Karmazin, CEO/COO
Steve Paitziner, President
Keith Williams, General Manager
Warren Jorgensen, Chief Engineer
Rick Armon, Operations Director
Tim Calligan, VP/Chief of Staff

Good News Communications Inc.
3222 S. Richey Ave., Tucson AZ 85713
(520) 790-2440; *Fax:*(520) 790-2937

Radio Stns: 4 AM.
KAPR Douglas, AZ; KGMS Tucson, AZ; KNXN Sierra Vista, AZ; KVOI Cortaro, AZ

Douglas Martin, President
Mary Martin, Operations Dir

Good News Media Inc.
Box 1400, Traverse City MI 49685-1400
(231) 946-1400; *Fax:*(231) 946-3959
www.wljn.com

Radio Stns: 2 AM. 1 FM.
WLJW Cadillac, MI; WLJN Elmwood Township, MI; WLJN-FM Traverse City, MI

Doug Knorr, President

Good News Network
P.O. Box 510, Appling GA 30802
(800) 926-4669
www.gnnradio.org
brian@gnnradio.org

Radio Stns: 1 AM. 12 FM.
WQRX Valley Head, AL; WNNG-FM Unadilla, GA; WGPH Vidalia, GA; WLGP Jacksonville, NC; WLPF Ocilla, GA; WPMA Greensboro, GA; WPWB Byron, GA; WWGF Donalsonville, GA; WZIQ Smithville, GA; WTHP Gibson, GA; WSJA York, AL; WHBJ Barnwell, SC; WGHJ Fair Bluff, NC

Clarence Barinowski, President
Dolly Martin, Programming Director

GoodRadio.TV
777 S. Flagler Dr., Suite 800, West Palm Beach FL 33401
(561) 515-6142
goodradio.tv
info@goodradio.tv

Radio Stns: 12 AM. 12 FM.
KAAN Bethany, MO; KBNN Lebanon, MO; KCOB Newton, IA; KDKD Clinton, MO; KGRN Grinnell, IA; KJFF Festus, MO; KJPW Waynesville, MO; KMCD Fairfield, IA; KMRN Cameron, MO; KIIK Waynesville, MO; KREI Farmington, MO; KWIX Moberly, MO; KAAN-FM Bethany, MO; KCOB-FM Newton, IA; KDKD-FM Clinton, MO; KKFD-FM Fairfield, IA; KIRK Macon, MO; KJEL Lebanon, MO; KOZQ-FM Waynesville, MO; KKWK Cameron, MO; KRES Moberly, MO; KRTI Grinnell, IA; KTJJ Farmington, MO; KTCM Madison, MO

Dean Goodman, CEO

Gore-Overgaard Broadcasting Inc.
11310 E. Arabian Park Dr., Scottsdale AZ 85259
(480) 797-2002

Radio Stns: 1 AM.
KBIF Fresno, CA

Cordell J. Overgaard, President

Grace Broadcasting Services Inc.
25 Stonebrook Pl., Suite G, #322, Jackson TN 38305
(731) 663-3931; *Fax:*(731) 663-9804
www.gracebroadcasting.com

Radio Stns: 3 AM. 4 FM.
WDTM Selmer, TN; WMAK Lobelville, TN; WTNE Trenton, TN; WDVW(FM) Humboldt, TN; WSIB Selmer, TN; WWGM Alamo, TN; WOPC Linden, TN

Graham Newspapers Inc.
620 Oak St., Graham TX 76450
(940) 549-1330; *Fax:*(940) 549-8628

Radio Stns: 2 AM. 2 FM.
KROO Breckenridge, TX; KSWA Graham, TX; KLXK Breckenridge, TX; KWKQ Graham, TX

Joe Graham, General Manager

Great Eastern Radio LLC
35 S. Main St., Suite 300, Hanover NH 3755
(603) 643-4007

Radio Stns: 3 AM. 13 FM.
WSNO Barre, VT; WTSL Hanover, NH; WTSV Claremont, NH; WZEI Meredith, NH; WEEY Swanzey, NH; WGXL Hanover, NH; WHDQ Claremont, NH; WLKZ Wolfeboro, NH; WTHK Wilmington, VT; WWOD Woodstock, VT; WRFK Barre, VT; WTPL Hillsboro, NH; WKKN Westminster, VT; WWFY Berlin, VT; KIXX Lebanon, NH; WFYX Walpole, NH

Great Lakes Radio Inc.
3060 US 41 W., Marquette MI 49855
(906) 228-6800
www.greatlakesradio.org

Radio Stns: 1 AM. 3 FM.
WQXO Munising, MI; WFXD Marquette, MI; WRUP Palmer, MI; WKQS-FM Negaunee, MI

Todd Noordyk, President

Great Plains Media Inc.
Box 1628, Cape Girardeau MO 63702-1628
(573) 651-0707

Radio Stns: 3 AM. 7 FM.
KLWN Lawrence, KS; WHUB Cookeville, TN; WPTN Cookeville, TN; KMXN Osage City, KS; KKSW Lawrence, KS; WKSW Cookeville, TN; WGSQ Cookeville, TN; WRPW Colfax, IL; WZIM(FM) Lexington, IL; WIBL(FM) Fairbury, IL

Jerome Zimmer, President

Greeley Broadcasting Corp.
1020 9th St., Suite 201, Greeley CO 80631
(970) 356-1452; *Fax:*(970) 356-8522

Radio Stns: 1 AM. 1 FM.
KGRE Greeley, CO; KFVR-FM Beulah, CO

Ricardo Salazar, President

Grenax Broadcasting LLC
10337 Carriage Club Dr., Lone Tree CO 80124
(303) 790-4015

Radio Stns: 4 FM.
KBTK(FM) Kachina Village, AZ; KSED Sedona, AZ; KWMX Williams, AZ; WCFX Clare, MI

Greg Dinetz, President

Guaranty Broadcasting Co. of Baton Rouge LLC
929 Government St., Suite B, Baton Rouge LA 70802-6034
(225) 388-9898; *Fax:*(225) 344-3077
owen.weber@gbcradio.com
Ownership: Guaranty Broadcasting Company LLC, 100%.

Radio Stns: 5 FM.
KNXX Donaldsonville, LA; WNXX Jackson, LA; WDGL Baton Rouge, LA; WBRP Baker, LA; WTGE Baton Rouge, LA
Owen Weber, VP

Guyann Corp.
Box 1930, Flagstaff AZ 86002
(928) 774-5231; *Fax:*(928) 779-2988
www.kaff.com
Ownership: Richard D. Guest, 50%; Pamela Flaherty, 50%. Note: Richard D. Guest and Pamela Flaherty are co-special administrators.
Radio Stns: 2 AM. 4 FM.
KAFF Flagstaff, AZ; KNOT Prescott, AZ; KAFF-FM Flagstaff, AZ; KMGN Flagstaff, AZ; KTMG Prescott, AZ; KFSZ Munds Park, AZ

Hall Communications Inc.
Box 2038, 404 W. Lime St., Lakeland FL 33806
(863) 682-8184; *Fax:*(863) 683-2409
www.hallradio.com
Ownership: Bonnie Hall Rowbotham.
Radio Stns: 8 AM. 12 FM.
WLKW West Warwick, RI; WICH Norwich, CT; WILI Willimantic, CT; WJOY Burlington, VT; WLKF Lakeland, FL; WLPA Lancaster, PA; WNBH New Bedford, MA; WONN Lakeland, FL; WBTZ Plattsburgh, NY; WCTK New Bedford, MA; WCTY Norwich, CT; WILI-FM Willimantic, CT; WIZN Vergennes, VT; WKOL Plattsburgh, NY; WNLC East Lyme, CT; WOKO Burlington, VT; WPCV Winter Haven, FL; WROZ Lancaster, PA; WKNL New London, CT; WWRZ Fort Meade, FL
Bonnie Rowbotham, Chairman
Arthur Rowbotham, President
Bill Baldwin, EVP

Harvard Broadcasting Inc.
1900 Rose St., Regina SK S4P 0A9
(306) 546-6200; *Fax:*(306) 781-7338
www.harvardbroadcasting.com
gbrasil@harvardbroadcasting.com
Ownership: Paul James Hill, 90.91%; Paul James Hill Family Trust, 9.09%.
Radio Stns: 2 AM. 10 FM.
CKRM Regina, SK; CJGX Yorkton, SK; CFWF-FM Regina, SK; CHMX-FM Regina, SK; CFEX-FM Calgary, AB; CFWD-FM Saskatoon, SK; CFVR-FM Fort McMurray, AB; CHFT-FM Fort McMurray, AB; CKEA-FM Edmonton, AB; CKRI-FM Red Deer, AB; CJNW-FM Edmonton, AB; CFGW-FM Yorkton, SK
Cam Cowie, Vice-President and COO
Gary Brasil, National Sales Manager
Christian Hall, National Program Manager
Helene Kolada, Accounting & Finance Manager

Haugo Broadcasting Inc.
3601 Canyon Lake Dr., Suite 1, Rapid City SD 57702
(605) 343-0888; *Fax:*(605) 342-3075
www.951ksky.com
studio@951ksky.com
Ownership: Houston Haugo, 100%.
Radio Stns: 1 AM. 2 FM.
KTOQ Rapid City, SD; KIQK Rapid City, SD; KSQY Deadwood, SD
Houston Haugo, CEO/COO

He's Alive Inc.
Box 540, Grantsville MD 21536
(301) 895-3292; *Fax:*(301) 895-3293
Ownership: Non-stock, nonprofit organization.
Radio Stns: 4 FM.
WAIJ Grantsville, MD; WLIC Frostburg, MD; WPCL Northern Cambria, PA; WRIJ Masontown, PA
Dewayne Johnson, President

Heartland Christian Broadcasters Inc.
Box 433, International Falls MN 56649
(218) 285-7398; *Fax:*(218) 285-7419
Radio Stns: 3 FM.
KBHW International Falls, MN; KXBR International Falls, MN; KADU Hibbing, MN

Heartland Communications Group LLC
2320 Ellis Ave., Ashland WI 54806
(715) 682-2727; *Fax:*(715) 292-2619
www.heartlandcomm.com
Radio Stns: 2 AM. 4 FM.
WATW Ashland, WI; WERL Eagle River, WI; WBSZ Ashland, WI; WJJH Ashland, WI; WNXR Iron River, WI; WRJO Eagle River, WI
Thomas L. Bookey, President/CEO

Hi-Favor Broadcasting LLC
136 S. Oak Knoll Ave., Pasadena CA 91101
(626) 356-4230; *Fax:*(626) 795-9185
Radio Stns: 3 AM.
KEZY San Bernardino, CA; KLTX Long Beach, CA; KSDO San Diego, CA

Hi-Line Radio Fellowship
PO Box 2426, Havre MT 59501
(800) 442-9222
www.ynop.org
Radio Stns: 1 FM.
KJCG Missoula, MT
Roger Lonnquist, Network General Manager
Ron Huckeby, Chief Engineer

High Desert Broadcasting LLC
570 E. Ave. Q9, Palmdale CA 93550
(661) 947-3107; *Fax:*(661) 272-5688
www.highdesertbroadcasting.com
Radio Stns: 2 AM. 4 FM.
KOSS Lancaster, CA; KUTY Palmdale, CA; KMVE California City, CA; KGMX Lancaster, CA; KKZQ Tehachapi, CA; KQAV Rosamond, CA
Miles Sexton, President

Hispanic Target Media Inc.
c/o Leventhal Senter & Lerman PLLC, 2000 K St. N.W., Suite 600, Washington DC 20006-1809
(202) 429-8970; *Fax:*(202) 293-7783
Radio Stns: 4 FM.
KJJS Zapata, TX; KGWT George West, TX; KAJP Carrizo Springs, TX; KALN Dexter, NM
Francisco San Millan, President

Holladay Broadcasting of Louisiana LLC
Box 4808, Monroe LA 71211
(318) 398-1618
Radio Stns: 3 AM. 5 FM.
KRJO Monroe, LA; KBYO Tallulah, LA; KMLB Monroe, LA; KLSM Tallulah, LA; KJLO-FM Monroe, LA; KJMG Bastrop, LA; KLIP Monroe, LA; KRVV Bastrop, LA
Robert Holladay, Member

Holston Valley Broadcasting Corp.
222 Commerce St., Kingsport TN 37660
(423) 246-9578; *Fax:*(423) 247-9836
www.hvbcgroup.com
Ownership: Glenwood Communications Corp., 100%.
Radio Stns: 4 AM. 4 FM.
WKPT Kingsport, TN; WKTP Jonesborough, TN; WUKZ(AM) Marion, VA; WOPI Bristol, TN; WMEV-FM Marion, VA; WRZK Colonial Heights, TN; WVEK-FM Weber City, VA; WTFM Kingsport, TN
TV Stns: 1 TV.
WKPT-TV Kingsport, TN
George DeVault Jr., President

Holy Family Communications
6325 Sheridan Dr., Williamsville NY 14221
(716) 839-6117; *Fax:*(716) 839-0400
www.wlof.net
Radio Stns: 2 AM. 1 FM.
WQOR Olyphant, PA; WHIC Rochester, NY; WLOF Elma, NY
James Wright, President

Hoosier Broadcasting Corp.
3500 DePauw Blvd., Suite 2085, Indianapolis IN 46268-6103
(317) 870-8400; *Fax:*(317) 870-8404
Radio Stns: 3 FM.
WIRE Lebanon, IN; WSPM Cloverdale, IN; WCNB Dayton, IN
William Poorman, President

Hope Christian Church of Marlton
55 East Main St, Marlton NJ 08053
(856) 983-1662
www.hopefm.net
info@hopefm.net
Radio Stns: 1 FM.
WWFP Brigantine, NJ
Pastor Bill Luebkemann, President

Horizon Broadcasting Group, LLC
854 N.E. 4th St., Bend OR 97701
(541) 383-3825; *Fax:*(541) 383-3403
www.horizonbroadcasting.com
Radio Stns: 1 AM. 3 FM.
KRCO Prineville, OR; KLTW-FM Prineville, OR; KWPK-FM Sisters, OR; KQAK Bend, OR
Dave Clemens, Operations Dir
Keith Shipman, General Manager
Kenn Brown, General Sales Mgr
Heather Roberts, Promotions Manager

Horizon Christian Fellowship
356 Broad St, Fitchburg MA 01420
(978) 665-9956; *Fax:*(978) 696-0610
renewfm.org
info@renewfm.org
Radio Stns: 1 AM. 3 FM.
WFGL Fitchburg, MA; WRYP Wellfleet, MA; WJWT Gardner, MA; WWDL Plainfield, IN

Horne Radio Group
517 Watt Rd., Knoxville TN 37922
(865) 675-4105
www.myi105.com
Radio Stns: 2 AM. 2 FM.
WDEH Sweetwater, TN; WMTY Farragut, TN; WMTY-FM Sweetwater, TN; WFIV-FM Loudon, TN

Houston Christian Broadcasters Inc.
2424 South Blvd., Houston TX 77098-5110
(888) 777-5200
www.khcb.org
email@khcb.org
Radio Stns: 2 AM. 15 FM.
KHCB League City, TX; KHCH Huntsville, TX; KANJ Giddings, TX; KKER Kerrville, TX; KHCP Paris, TX; KHTA Wake Village, TX; KHCB-FM Houston, TX; KHBW Brownwood, TX; KHKV Kerrville, TX; KHMD Mansfield, LA; KHIB Bastrop, TX; KHCL Arcadia, LA; KHCJ Jefferson, TX; KHVT Bloomington, TX; KHML Madisonville, TX; KBLC Fredericksburg, TX; KHPO Port O'Connor, TX
Bruce E. Munsterman, President

HRN Broadcasting Inc.
Box 430, Lincolnton NC 28093
(704) 735-8071; *Fax:*(704) 732-9567
www.hrnb.com
Radio Stns: 5 AM.
WOHS Shelby, NC; WCSL Cherryville, NC; WLON Lincolnton, NC; WZGV Cramerton, NC; WZGM Black Mountain, NC

Hubbard Broadcasting Inc.
3415 University Ave., St. Paul MN 55114
(651) 646-5555; *Fax:*(651) 642-4103
Radio Stns: 5 AM. 15 FM.
KSTP St. Paul, MN; WIXK New Richmond, WI; WBQH Silver Spring, MD; WFED Washington, DC; WWFD Frederick, MD; KSTP-FM St. Paul, MN; WTOP-FM Washington, DC; WIL-FM St. Louis, MO; WTMY(FM) Coon Rapids, MN; WARH Granite City, IL; WKRQ Cincinnati, OH; WYGY Fort Thomas, KY; WDRV Chicago, IL; WWDV Zion, IL; WSHE-FM Chicago, IL; WTMX Skokie, IL; WWWT-FM Manassas, VA; WUBE-FM Cincinnati, OH; WXOS East St. Louis, IL; WTLP Braddock Heights, MD
TV Stns: 13 TV.
KAAL Austin, MN; KOB Albuquerque, NM; KOBF Farmington, NM; KOBR Roswell, NM; KRWF Redwood Falls, MN; KSAX Alexandria, MN; KSTP-TV St. Paul, MN; KSTC-TV Minneapolis, MN; WDIO-DT Duluth, MN; WHEC-TV Rochester, NY; WIRT Hibbing, MN; WNYT Albany, NY; WNYT Pittsfield, MA
Julia Coyte, Vice President
Robert Hubbard, Vice President
Virginia Morris, Vice President
Stanley Hubbard II, Vice President
Edward Aiken, Vice President
Sue Cook, Vice President
Linda Tremere, Vice President
C. Thomas Newberry, Vice President
Harold Crump, Vice President
Gerald Deeney, SVP/Treasurer/Chief Financial Officer

Hunt County Radio LLC
1517 Wolfe City Dr., Greenville TX 75401
(214) 693-4289
Radio Stns: 1 AM. 1 FM.
KGVL Greenville, TX; KIKT Greenville, TX
Jean McCoy, Programming Director

Huth Broadcasting
Box 669, Marysville CA 95901
(530) 742-5555; *Fax:*(530) 741-3758
Radio Stns: 5 AM.
KBLF Red Bluff, CA; KNTF Oroville, CA; KMYC Marysville, CA; KOBO Yuba City, CA; KRAC Quincy, CA

Hutton Broadcasting LLC
915 Orchid Point Way, Vero Beach FL 32963-9518
(772) 559-3790
Radio Stns: 2 AM. 5 FM.

KVSF Santa Fe, NM; KTRC Santa Fe, NM; KBAC Las Vegas, NM; KQBA Los Alamos, NM; KLBU Pecos, NM; KLBU Santa Fe, NM; KVSF-FM Pecos, NM
Jennifer Owens Hutton, President
Scott Hutton, General Manager

ICA Radio Ltd.

700 N. Grant St., 6th Fl., Odessa TX 79761
(432) 580-5672; *Fax:*(432) 580-9102
Ownership: ICA Broadcasting L.L.C., sole gen ptnr, 100% votes. Note: ICA Broadcasting L.L.C. also owns KOSA-TV Odessa, TX.
Radio Stns: 1 AM. 4 FM.
KCRS Midland, TX; KCHX Midland, TX; KCRS-FM Midland, TX; KFZX Gardendale, TX; KMRK-FM Odessa, TX
Barry Marks, President

Icicle Broadcasting Inc.

PO Box 2675, Wenatchee WA 98807
(509) 548-1011
Radio Stns: 1 AM. 3 FM.
KOZI Chelan, WA; KOHO Leavenworth, WA; KOZI-FM Chelan, WA; KZAL Manson, WA
Elliott Salmon, General Manager

Icon Broadcasting Inc.

443 Hwy. 42 W., Ahoskie NC 27910
(252) 332-7993
www.iconbroadcasting.com
Ownership: Charles D. Marsh, 50%; Mark Tarte, 25%; Don Wendelken, 25%.
Radio Stns: 1 FM.
WQDK Gatesville, NC

Idaho Wireless Corp.

Box 97, Pocatello ID 83204
(208) 234-1290; *Fax:*(208) 234-9451
Radio Stns: 2 AM. 3 FM.
KOUU Pocatello, ID; KSEI Pocatello, ID; KMGI Pocatello, ID; KORR American Falls, ID; KZBQ Pocatello, ID
Paul Anderson, General Manager

iHeartMedia

200 E. Basse Rd., San Antonio TX 78209
(210) 822-2828
www.iheartmedia.com
Ownership: iHeartMedia Inc., 100%.
Radio Stns: 244 AM. 603 FM.
KABQ Albuquerque, NM; KHTY Bakersfield, CA; KAKC Tulsa, OK; KQNT Spokane, WA; KASI Ames, IA; KATZ St. Louis, MO; KBME Houston, TX; KBMR Bismarck, ND; KCBL Fresno, CA; KCJB Minot, ND; KTDD San Bernardino, CA; KIIX Fort Collins, CO; KCQL Aztec, NM; KCSJ Pueblo, CO; KXNO Des Moines, IA; KGHM Midwest City, OK; KENI Anchorage, AK; KPOJ Portland, OR; KEX Portland, OR; KFAB Omaha, NE; KFBK Sacramento, CA; KFI Los Angeles, CA; KFIV Modesto, CA; KGME Phoenix, AZ; KFYR Bismarck, ND; KCCY Pueblo, CO; KFYI Phoenix, AZ; KGMY Springfield, MO; KTSM El Paso, TX; KHHO Tacoma, WA; KBFP Bakersfield, CA; KHOW Denver, CO; KHVH Honolulu, HI; KFBX Fairbanks, AK; KCOL Wellington, CO; KIKI Honolulu, HI; KWSX Stockton, CA; KJR Seattle, WA; KKDD San Bernardino, CA; KKSF Oakland, CA; KKXL Grand Forks, ND; KLAC Los Angeles, CA; KLTC Dickinson, ND; KFXR Dallas, TX; KLVI Beaumont, TX; KMNS Sioux City, IA; KNEW Oakland, CA; KNRS Salt Lake City, UT; KNST Tucson, AZ; KOA Denver, CO; KOGA Ogallala, NE; KOGO San Diego, CA; KOY Phoenix, AZ; KLSD San Diego, CA; KPRC Houston, TX; KTBZ Tulsa, OK; KVNS Brownsville, TX; KRDU Dinuba, CA; KKTX Corpus Christi, TX; KRZR Visalia, CA; KSSK Honolulu, HI; KSTE Rancho Cordova, CA; KTKR San Antonio, TX; KKZN Thornton, CO; KMJM Cedar Rapids, IA; KTOK Oklahoma City, OK; KTRH Houston, TX; KHEY El Paso, TX; KION Salinas, CA; KTZN Anchorage, AK; KTZR Tucson, AZ; KZFS Spokane, WA; KUNO Corpus Christi, TX; KVET Austin, TX; KFAN Rochester, MN; KWHN Fort Smith, AR; KWSL Sioux City, IA; KWTX Waco, TX; KXEW South Tucson, AZ; KXIC Iowa City, IA; KXMR Bismarck, ND; KTLK Minneapolis, MN; WAAX Gadsden, AL; WACT Tuscaloosa, AL; WAEB Allentown, PA; WDDV Venice, FL; WAVZ New Haven, CT; WAXE Vero Beach, FL; WBBD Wheeling, WV; WYNF Augusta, GA; WBEX Chillicothe, OH; WBHP Huntsville, AL; WBIZ Eau Claire, WI; WJNO West Palm Beach, FL; WCAO Baltimore, MD; WCCF Punta Gorda, FL; WCHI Chillicothe, OH; WCHO Washington Ct House, OH; WTKS Savannah, GA; WSAI Cincinnati, OH; WCOH Newnan, GA; WCOS Columbia, SC; WCWA Toledo, OH; WHNZ Tampa, FL; WDAK Columbus, GA; WDFN Detroit, MI; WDIA Memphis, TN; WDIZ Panama City, FL; WDOV Dover, DE; WDSC Dillon, SC; WELI New Haven, CT; WJIP Ellenville, NY; WENE Endicott, NY; WERC Birmingham, AL; WLFJ Greenville, SC; WYTS Columbus, OH; WFLA Tampa, FL; WFOR Hattiesburg, MS; WGRB Chicago, IL; WGIG Brunswick, GA; WPKX Rochester, NH; WGIR Manchester, NH; WGST Atlanta, GA; WGVL Greenville, SC; WGY Schenectady, NY; WHAM Rochester, NY; WHAS Louisville, KY; WMXF Waynesville, NC; WHEN Syracuse, NY; WHJJ Providence, RI; WHLO Akron, OH; WHO Des Moines, IA; WHOS Decatur, AL; WHP Harrisburg, PA; WVON Berwyn, IL; WHTK Rochester, NY; WHUC Hudson, NY; WHYN Springfield, MA; WIBA Madison, WI; WILM Wilmington, DE; WIMA Lima, OH; WKCI Waynesboro, VA; WINR Binghamton, NY; WINZ Miami, FL; WIOD Miami, FL; WISN Milwaukee, WI; WIZE Springfield, OH; WJBO Baton Rouge, LA; WWTX Wilmington, DE; WJDX Jackson, MS; WJDY Salisbury, MD; WWRK Florence, SC; WBZT West Palm Beach, FL; WJYZ Albany, GA; WSAN Allentown, PA; WKBN Youngstown, OH; WKCY Harrisonburg, VA; WKDW Staunton, VA; WVHU Huntington, WV; WSFE Burnside, KY; WKII Solana, FL; WKIP Poughkeepsie, NY; WKJK Louisville, KY; WXKS Newton, MA; WKRC Cincinnati, OH; WLAC Nashville, TN; WLAN Lancaster, PA; WLAP Lexington, KY; WIHB Macon, GA; WFXN Moline, IL; WHNK Parkersburg, WV; WLW Cincinnati, OH; WMAN Mansfield, OH; WMEQ Menomonie, WI; WMMB Melbourne, FL; WMMV Cocoa, FL; WBGA Brunswick, GA; WMRE Charlestown, WV; WMRN Marion, OH; WMT Cedar Rapids, IA; WKBZ Muskegon, MI; WVCC Hogansville, GA; WMYF Portsmouth, NH; WNCO Ashland, OH; WNDE Indianapolis, IN; WTLY Tallahassee, FL; WNTM Mobile, AL; WFXJ Jacksonville, FL; WOAI San Antonio, TX; WOC Davenport, IA; WODT New Orleans, LA; WOKY Milwaukee, WI; WONE Dayton, OH; WONW Defiance, OH; WOOD Grand Rapids, MI; WOR New York, NY; WJMX Darlington, SC; WHAL Phenix City/Columbus, AL; WPOP Hartford, CT; WFLF Pine Hills, FL; WRAK Williamsport, PA; WRAW Reading, PA; WREC Memphis, TN; WRKK Hughesville, PA; WPLA Dry Branch, GA; WRNL Richmond, VA; WNIO Youngstown, OH; WRVA Richmond, VA; WDAE St. Petersburg, FL; WCKY Cincinnati, OH; WVOC Columbia, SC; WSFC Somerset, KY; WLRO Denham Springs, LA; WSOK Savannah, GA; WSDV Sarasota, FL; WSPD Toledo, OH; WSRW Hillsboro, OH; WSYR Syracuse, NY; WTAG Worcester, MA; WTAM Cleveland, OH; WTCR Kenova, WV; WTGM Salisbury, MD; WTKG Grand Rapids, MI; WWTF Georgetown, KY; WTLM Opelika, AL; WARF Akron, OH; WOFX Troy, NY; WTSO Madison, WI; WTVN Columbus, OH; WPEK Fairview, NC; WTKT Harrisburg, PA; WKRD Louisville, KY; WWNC Asheville, NC; WYGM Orlando, FL; WBGG Pittsburgh, PA; WWVA Wheeling, WV; WKOX Everett, MA; WYLD New Orleans, LA; WLTP Marietta, OH; WZMG Pepperell, AL; KEIB Los Angeles, CA; KFNY Riverside, CA; WZTA Vero Beach, FL; WPCH West Point, GA; KAGG Madisonville, TX; KAJA San Antonio, TX; KAKQ-FM Fairbanks, AK; KHGE Fresno, CA; KASE-FM Austin, TX; KASH-FM Anchorage, AK; KAZX Kirtland, NM; KXJM Banks, OR; KBCO Boulder, CO; KBFM Edinburg, TX; KBFX Anchorage, AK; KBIG Los Angeles, CA; KBKS-FM Tacoma, WA; KNFX-FM Bryan, TX; KBOS-FM Tulare, CA; KBPI Denver, CO; KCAD Dickinson, ND; KCYZ Ames, IA; KCCY-FM Pueblo, CO; KCDA Post Falls, ID; KBGO Waco, TX; KCQQ Davenport, IA; KDAG Farmington, NM; KHKN Maumelle, AR; KDMX Dallas, TX; KDON-FM Salinas, CA; KDWB-FM Richfield, MN; KDZA-FM Pueblo, CO; KEEY-FM St. Paul, MN; KISO Omaha, NE; KEGL Fort Worth, TX; KESZ Phoenix, AZ; KEZA Fayetteville, AR; KALZ Fowler, CA; KFMQ Gallup, NM; KFSO-FM Visalia, CA; KFXR-FM Chinle, AZ; KGB-FM San Diego, CA; KGBX-FM Nixa, MO; KFBK-FM Pollock Pines, CA; KGGI Riverside, CA; KGLI Sioux City, IA; KSME Greeley, CO; KGLX Gallup, NM; KYWD Green Valley, AZ; KSWF Aurora, MO; KGOR Omaha, NE; KGOT Anchorage, AK; KHEY-FM El Paso, TX; KHFI-FM Georgetown, TX; KPTT Denver, CO; KHKS Denton, TX; KHTS-FM El Cajon, CA; KHYL Auburn, CA; KIAK-FM Fairbanks, AK; KXBG Cheyenne, WY; KIIS-FM Los Angeles, CA; KIIZ-FM Killeen, TX; KIOC Orange, TX; KIOI San Francisco, CA; KIOZ San Diego, CA; KISC Spokane, WA; KZHT Salt Lake City, UT; KISQ San Francisco, CA; KIZZ Minot, ND; KBEB Sacramento, CA; KIGL Seligman, MO; KJKJ Grand Forks, ND; KJMS Olive Branch, MS; KMYI San Diego, CA; KJR-FM Seattle, WA; KJSN Modesto, CA; KJYO Oklahoma City, OK; KRRL Los Angeles, CA; KKBW Eatonville, WA; KKCW Beaverton, OR; KBFP-FM Delano, CA; KKDM Des Moines, IA; KKED Fairbanks, AK; KKFG Bloomfield, NM; KKIX Fayetteville, AR; KLTH Lake Oswego, OR; KKLI Widefield, CO; KDNN Honolulu, HI; KMRQ Riverbank, CA; KKMY Orange, TX; KTHR Wichita, KS; KKRQ Iowa City, IA; KQBT Houston, TX; KKRZ Portland, OR; KKYS Bryan, TX; KKZX Spokane, WA; KTBZ-FM Houston, TX; KLFX Nolanville, TX; KLOU St. Louis, MO; KTEG Santa Fe, NM; KMAG Fort Smith, AR; KMCX-FM Ogallala, NE; KMEL San Francisco, CA; KMFX-FM Lake City, MN; KBWX Columbia, IL; KMJX Conway, AR; KYNW Centralia, WA; KMOD-FM Tulsa, OK; KIZS Collinsville, OK; KSSX Carlsbad, CA; KMXA-FM Minot, ND; KDRB Des Moines, IA; KMXF Lowell, AR; KMXG Clinton, IA; KKBD Sallisaw, OK; KMXP Phoenix, AZ; KMXR Corpus Christi, TX; KNCN Sinton, TX; KIIX-FM Opportunity, WA; KNIX-FM Phoenix, AZ; KTBT Broken Arrow, OK; KOCN Pacific Grove, CA; KODA Houston, TX; KODJ Salt Lake City, UT; KOGA-FM Ogallala, NE; KOHT Marana, AZ; KOLZ Cheyenne, WY; KPHT Rocky Ford, CO; KOSO Patterson, CA; KVVS Rosamond, CA; KOST Los Angeles, CA; KAAZ-FM Spanish Fork, UT; KPAW Fort Collins, CO; KPEK Albuquerque, NM; KPEZ Austin, TX; KPRR El Paso, TX; KIBT Fountain, CO; KDJE Jacksonville, AR; KQDY Bismarck, ND; KQHT Crookston, MN; KTGX Owasso, OK; KQOD Stockton, CA; KPLV Las Vegas, NV; KQQL Anoka, MN; KBRU Oklahoma City, OK; KQXT-FM San Antonio, TX; KRAB Greenacres, CA; KRBB Wichita, KS; KRCH Rochester, MN; KRFX Denver, CO; KTOM-FM Marina, CA; KRQQ Tucson, AZ; KRVE Brusly, LA; KRYS-FM Corpus Christi, TX; KZCH Derby, KS; KSAB Robstown, TX; KSD St. Louis, MO; KSEZ Sioux City, IA; KSFT-FM South Sioux City, NE; KRPT Devine, TX; KSLZ St. Louis, MO; KDFO Delano, CA; KSNE-FM Las Vegas, NV; KSNR Fisher, MN; KSOF Dinuba, CA; KSSK-FM Waipahu, HI; KSSN Little Rock, AR; KSSS Bismarck, ND; KLQT Corrales, NM; KTCL Wheat Ridge, CO; KTCZ-FM Minneapolis, MN; KBQI Albuquerque, NM; KTEX Mercedes, TX; KCOL-FM Groves, TX; KHKZ San Benito, TX; KQXX-FM Mission, TX; KFFF Bennington, NE; KPRC-FM Salinas, CA; KTOZ-FM Pleasant Hope, MO; KSRY Tehachapi, CA; KTRA-FM Farmington, NM; KTSM-FM El Paso, TX; KTST Oklahoma City, OK; KDGE Fort Worth-Dallas, TX; KUBE Seattle, WA; KUCD Pearl City, HI; KVDU Houma, LA; KJMY Bountiful, UT; KUUL East Moline, IL; KVET-FM Austin, TX; KVJM Hearne, TX; KVUU Pueblo, CO; KMIY Tucson, AZ; KWNR Henderson, NV; KWTX-FM Waco, TX; KXKT Glenwood, IA; KQJK Roseville, CA; KXTC Thoreau, NM; KXUS Springfield, MO; KXXM San Antonio, TX; KXXY-FM Oklahoma City, OK; KYKR Beaumont, TX; KYLD San Francisco, CA; KYMG Anchorage, AK; KYOT-FM Phoenix, AZ; KYSR Los Angeles, CA; KDXA Ankeny, IA; KYYX Minot, ND; KYYY Bismarck, ND; KZBB Poteau, OK; KZEP-FM San Antonio, TX; KZPR Minot, ND; KZPS Dallas, TX; KZRR Albuquerque, NM; KZRX Dickinson, ND; KZSN Hutchinson, KS; KZZP Mesa, AZ; WACL Elkton, VA; WACO-FM Waco, TX; WWKZ Okolona, MS; WAEB-FM Allentown, PA; WAEV Savannah, GA; WBFA Fort Mitchell, AL; WMTX Tampa, FL; WAMX Milton, WV; WAMZ Louisville, KY; WASH Washington, DC; WATQ Chetek, WI; WAXQ New York, NY; WAZR Woodstock, VA; WCZR Vero Beach, FL; WNCD Youngstown, OH; WBBI Endwell, NY; WBBQ-FM Augusta, GA; WBBS Fulton, NY; WBCT Grand Rapids, MI; WAGH Smiths, AL; WYNR Waycross, GA; WBGG-FM Fort Lauderdale, FL; WBIG-FM Washington, DC; WBIZ-FM Eau Claire, WI; WZRX-FM Fort Shawnee, OH; WBUL-FM Lexington, KY; WBVB Coal Grove, OH; WFKS Melbourne, FL; WBWZ New Paltz, NY; WXXF Loudonville, OH; WCHO-FM Washington Ct House, OH; WCIB Falmouth, MA; WCJM-FM West Point, GA; WCKT Lehigh Acres, FL; WCKY-FM Pemberville, OH; WCOD-FM Hyannis, MA; WCOL-FM Columbus, OH; WCTQ Sarasota, FL; WCTW Catskill, NY; WBFX Grand Rapids, MI; WCVU Solana, FL; WDAR-FM Darlington, SC; WDAS-FM Philadelphia, PA; WDCG Durham, NC; WLTQ-FM Venice, FL; WDFM Defiance, OH; WMRN-FM Marion, OH; WDMX Vienna, WV; WDRM Decatur, AL; WRDX Smyrna, DE; WDVE Pittsburgh, PA; WBUV Moss Point, MS; WLQB Ocean Isle Beach, NC; WEBN Cincinnati, OH; WVKF Shadyside, OH; WEGR Arlington, TN; WEGW Wheeling, WV; WEGX Dillon, SC; WEND Salisbury, NC; WERZ Exeter, NH; WESC-FM Greenville, SC; WESE Baldwyn, MS; WEZL Charleston, SC; WFBQ Indianapolis, IN; WKKJ Chillicothe, OH; WFLZ-FM Tampa, FL; WMKS Clemmons, NC; WBWL Lynn, MA; WFQX Front Royal, VA; WFSY Panama City, FL; WGAR-FM Cleveland, OH; WGCI-FM Chicago, IL; WGIR-FM Manchester, NH; WFXN-FM Galion, OH; WGMZ Glencoe, AL; WRZE Kingstree, SC; WRDA-FM Canton, GA; WGSY Phenix City, AL; WGTR Bucksport, SC; WHCN Hartford, CT; WHCY Blairstown, NJ; WHEB Portsmouth, NH; WHJY Providence, RI; WKDD Munroe Falls, OH; WNRW Salem, IN; WHRK Memphis, TN; WGY-FM Albany, NY; WVBZ High Point, NC; WHTZ Newark, NJ; WHYI-FM Fort Lauderdale, FL; WHYN-FM Springfield, MA; WIBA-FM Sauk City, WI; WIBB-FM Fort Valley, GA; WIKX Charlotte Harbor, FL; WIMT Lima, OH; WIOQ Philadelphia, PA; WIOT Toledo, OH; WBLJ-FM Shamokin, PA; WVOR Canandaigua, NY; WNOH Windsor, VA; WHOF North Canton, OH; WJIZ-FM Albany, GA; WPGB Pittsburgh, PA; WISX Philadelphia, PA; WJKX Ellisville, MS; WJLB Detroit, MI; WJMN Boston, MA; WIHT Washington, DC; WJMX-FM Cheraw, SC; WJRR Cocoa Beach, FL; WUBT Russellville, KY; WFLA-FM Midway, FL; WMXY Youngstown, OH; WKCI-FM Hamden, CT; WKCY-FM Harrisonburg, VA; WAKS Akron, OH; WKEE-FM Huntington, WV; WKFS Milford, OH; WKGB-FM Conklin, NY; WKGR Wellington, FL; WKGS Irondequoit, NY; WODC Ashville, OH; WKKR Auburn, AL; WKKT Statesville, NC; WKKV-FM Racine, WI; WWPW Atlanta, GA; WKNN-FM Pascagoula, MS; WKQI Detroit, MI; WKQQ Winchester, KY; WKSB Williamsport, PA; WKSF Old Fort, NC; WKSJ-FM Mobile, AL; WKSS Hartford-Meriden, CT; WHLH Jackson, MS; WKTU Lake Success, NY; WKWK-FM Wheeling, WV; WLAN-FM Lancaster, PA; WLDI Juno Beach, FL; WJJX Appomattox, VA; WLIT-FM Chicago, IL; WLKT Lexington-Fayette, KY; WLLK-FM Somerset, KY; WLLR-FM Davenport, IA; WRXR-FM Rossville, GA; WLND Signal Mountain, TN; WFMF Baton Rouge, LA; WRNW Milwaukee, WI; WLTW New York, NY; WLTY Cayce, SC;

WMIA-FM Miami Beach, FL; WLVH Hardeeville, SC; WLKO Hickory, NC; WXXM Sun Prairie, WI; WMAG High Point, NC; WNBL South Bristol Township, NY; WWMG Millbrook, AL; WMEQ-FM Menomonie, WI; WZLD Petal, MS; WMGF Mount Dora, FL; WGEX Bainbridge, GA; WMIL-FM Waukesha, WI; WMJI Cleveland, OH; WMJJ Birmingham, AL; WMJY Biloxi, MS; WRDG Peachtree City, GA; WMAD Cross Plains, WI; WMLX St. Marys, OH; WMMS Cleveland, OH; WMMX Dayton, OH; WZCB Dublin, OH; WMRR Muskegon Heights, MI; WBNW-FM Endicott, NY; WMSI-FM Jackson, MS; WOOD-FM Muskegon, MI; WHLK Cleveland, OH; WMXA Opelika, AL; WMXC Mobile, AL; WMXD Detroit, MI; WQNQ Fletcher, NC; WMXL Lexington, KY; WMXW Vestal, NY; WMYI Hendersonville, NC; WBYL Salladasburg, PA; WMZQ-FM Washington, DC; WBBG Niles, OH; WNCI Columbus, OH; WNCO-FM Ashland, OH; WNDH Napoleon, OH; WNIC Dearborn, MI; WNNJ Newton, NJ; WNOE-FM New Orleans, LA; WNOK Columbia, SC; WNRQ Nashville, TN; WNSL Laurel, MS; WEBG Chicago, IL; WNUS Belpre, OH; WAIO Honeoye Falls, NY; WOBB Tifton, GA; WZFT Baltimore, MD; WOLL Hobe Sound, FL; WOLT Indianapolis, IN; WOLZ Fort Myers, FL; WSRW-FM Grand Rapids, MI; WKZP Bethany Beach, DE; WZJZ Port Charlotte, FL; WHAL-FM Horn Lake, MS; WOVK Wheeling, WV; WDXB Jasper, AL; WOWI Norfolk, VA; WPAP Panama City, FL; WFLF-FM Parker, FL; WUBL Atlanta, GA; WUCS Windsor Locks, CT; WJBT Callahan, FL; WMIB Fort Lauderdale, FL; WPOC Baltimore, MD; WPYX Albany, NY; WQBZ Fort Valley, GA; WQEN Trussville, AL; WQHQ Ocean City-Salisbury, MD; WQIK-FM Jacksonville, FL; WJDX-FM Kosciusko, MS; WHLW Luverne, AL; WQMF Jeffersonville, IN; WQNS Waynesville, NC; WBTT Naples Park, FL; WQOL Vero Beach, FL; WQRB Bloomer, WI; WTFX-FM Clarksville, IN; WQSO Rochester, NH; WQUE-FM New Orleans, LA; WQYZ Ocean Springs, MS; WRBT Harrisburg, PA; WRBV Warner Robins, GA; WBTJ Richmond, VA; WJJS Roanoke, VA; WTKK Knightdale, NC; WDSD Dover, DE; WRFQ Mount Pleasant, SC; WRFX Kannapolis, NC; WRFY-FM Reading, PA; WRKH Mobile, AL; WRLX West Palm Beach, FL; WIHB-FM Gray, GA; WRNO-FM New Orleans, LA; WRNQ Poughkeepsie, NY; WRNX Amherst, MA; WROV-FM Martinsville, VA; KFXN-FM Minneapolis, MN; WRQK-FM Canton, OH; WNCB Cary, NC; WRTR Brookwood, AL; WRVB Marietta, OH; WRVE Schenectady, NY; WRVF Toledo, OH; WRVQ Richmond, VA; WRVV Harrisburg, PA; WRVW Lebanon, TN; WRWD-FM Highland, NY; WRXL Richmond, VA; WKSP Aiken, SC; WEII Dennis, MA; WRZX Greenville, OH; WSBY-FM Salisbury, MD; WQBT Savannah, GA; WKEQ Somerset, KY; WRUM Orlando, FL; WEBZ Mexico Beach, FL; WMUS Muskegon, MI; WSIX-FM Nashville, TN; WSNE-FM Taunton, MA; WSNX-FM Muskegon, MI; WSOL-FM Brunswick, GA; WVRZ Mount Carmel, PA; WZTF Scranton, SC; WSRS Worcester, MA; WSRZ-FM Coral Cove, FL; WSSL-FM Gray Court, SC; WSCC-FM Goose Creek, SC; WBTP Clearwater, FL; WSTH-FM Alexander City, AL; WSTZ-FM Vicksburg, MS; WSUS Franklin, NJ; WSVO Staunton, VA; WHBT-FM Moyock, NC; WSWR Shelby, OH; WTAK-FM Hartselle, AL; WFUS Gulfport, FL; WTCR-FM Huntington, WV; WLGX Louisville, KY; WZCR Hudson, NY; WRWB-FM Ellenville, NY; WWPR-FM New York, NY; WTKS-FM Cocoa Beach, FL; WTKX-FM Pensacola, FL; WPKF Poughkeepsie, NY; WTNT-FM Tallahassee, FL; WAKZ Sharpsville, PA; WTQR Winston-Salem, NC; WRDU Wake Forest, NC; WTRY-FM Rotterdam, NY; WTUE Dayton, OH; WTVR-FM Richmond, VA; WTXT Fayette, AL; WTBU York Center, ME; WKSC-FM Chicago, IL; WUSL Philadelphia, PA; WUSQ-FM Winchester, VA; WFFX Hattiesburg, MS; WUSY Cleveland, TN; WPRW-FM Martinez, GA; WVAZ Oak Park, IL; WVKS Toledo, OH; WQRV Meridianville, AL; WDVI Rochester, NY; WVRK Columbus, GA; WVRT Mill Hall, PA; WMAX-FM Holland, MI; WWBB Providence, RI; WMAN-FM Fredericktown, OH; WWDC Washington, DC; WWFG Ocean City, MD; WWHT Syracuse, NY; WHKF Harrisburg, PA; WZZR Riviera Beach, FL; WHQC Shelby, NC; WRXZ Briarcliff Acres, SC; WQGA Waycross, GA; WWSW-FM Pittsburgh, PA; WWXM Garden City, SC; WWYZ Waterbury, CT; WSEK Burnside, KY; WKKF Ballston Spa, NY; WXDX-FM Pittsburgh, PA; WZDA Beavercreek, OH; WXKS-FM Medford, MA; WPTI Eden, NC; WXSR Quincy, FL; WXTB Clearwater, FL; WXTK West Yarmouth, MA; WKSI-FM Stephens City, VA; WXXL Tavares, FL; WQSR Baltimore, MD; WBZY Bowdon, GA; WYHT Mansfield, OH; WYKZ Beaufort, SC; WYLD-FM New Orleans, LA; WYNA Calabash, NC; WTZB Englewood, FL; WYNK-FM Baton Rouge, LA; WHFX Darien, GA; WYNT Caledonia, OH; WRFF Philadelphia, PA; WYYD Amherst, VA; WYYY Syracuse, NY; WBWR Hilliard, OH; WZBQ Carrollton, AL; WZEE Madison, WI; WZHT Troy, AL; WMGP Hogansville, GA; WSCG Augusta, GA; WZOM Defiance, OH; WMGE Miami Beach, FL; WRIT-FM Milwaukee, WI; WZZO Bethlehem, PA; WAVW Stuart, FL; KMYT Temecula, CA; WDTW-FM Detroit, MI; KTMQ Temecula, CA; WBKS Columbus Grove, OH; WMRZ Dawson, GA; WGMY Thomasville, GA; KKSY-FM Cedar Rapids, IA; WXBT West Columbia, SC; WERC-FM Hoover, AL; KFBT Hanford, CA; KOSF San Francisco, CA; WKSL Neptune Beach, FL; WWJK Green Cove Springs, FL; WLRQ-FM Cocoa, FL; WRGV Pensacola, FL; KHJZ Honolulu, HI; WUBG Plainfield, IN; KOSY-FM Anamosa, IA; WSYR Solvay, NY; WQLX Chillicothe, OH; WCHD Kettering, OH; WKST-FM Pittsburgh, PA; WCOS-FM Columbia, SC; WMOV-FM Norfolk, VA

Bob Pittman, Chairman & CEO
Richard J. Bressler, President, COO & Chief Financial Officer
Wendy Goldberg, Executive Vice President
Robert H. Walls, Jr., Executive Vice President
Gayle Troberman, Executive Vice President

IHR Educational Broadcasting
Box 180, Tahoma CA 96142
(530) 584-5700; *Fax:*(530) 584-5705
www.ihradio.org
info@ihradio.org

Radio Stns: 10 AM. 2 FM.
KAHI Auburn, CA; KIHM Reno, NV; KJOP Lemoore, CA; KHJ Los Angeles, CA; KSFB San Francisco, CA; KSMH West Sacramento, CA; KJPG Frazier Park, CA; KWG Stockton, CA; KIHP Mesa, AZ; KIHH Eureka, CA; KXXQ Milan, NM; KPJP Greenville, CA

Illinois Bible Institute Inc.
Box 140, Carlinville IL 62626
(217) 854-4600; *Fax:*(217) 854-4610
www.wibi.org

Radio Stns: 8 FM.
WBGL Champaign, IL; WBMV Mount Vernon, IL; WCIC Pekin, IL; WCRT-FM Terre Haute, IN; WIBI Carlinville, IL; WTSG Carlinville, IL; WPRC Sheffield, IL; WZGL Charleston, IL
Richard Whitworth, Director

Impact Radio LLC
59750 Constantine Rd., Three Rivers MI 49093-9303
(269) 278-1815; *Fax:*(269) 273-7975
drumsey@wlkm.com

Radio Stns: 2 AM. 2 FM.
WRCI Three Rivers, MI; WQCT Bryan, OH; WBNO-FM Bryan, OH; WLKM-FM Three Rivers, MI
Dennis Rumsey, President

Independence Media Holdings LLC
8226 Douglas Ave., Suite 627, Dallas TX 75225
(469) 619-1001

Radio Stns: 1 AM. 5 FM.
WOCN Miami, FL; WHPI Glasford, IL; WPIA Eureka, IL; WWCT Bartonville, IL; WZPN Farmington, IL; WWKN Morgantown, KY

Information Communications Corp.
Box 2061, Bristol TN 37621-2061
(423) 878-6279; *Fax:*(423) 878-6520

Radio Stns: 3 AM.
WABN Abingdon, VA; WHGG Kingsport, TN; WPWT Colonial Heights, TN
Dr. Kenneth C. Hill, CEO

Ingstad Brothers Broadcasting LLC
Box 1248, Minnetonka MN 55345
(952) 938-0575; *Fax:*(952) 938-2295

Radio Stns: 2 AM. 2 FM.
KCHK New Prague, MN; KNUJ New Ulm, MN; KCHK-FM New Prague, MN; KNUJ-FM Sleepy Eye, MN

Ingstad Radio Washington LLC
1020 25th St. South, Fargo ND 58103
(701) 277-4200
Ownership: James D. Ingstad, 100%.

Radio Stns: 4 AM. 8 FM.
KALE Richland, WA; KTCR Yakima, WA; KJOX Kennewick, WA; KBBO Selah, WA; KARY-FM Grandview, WA; KEGX Richland, WA; KHHK Yakima, WA; KIOK Richland, WA; KKSR Walla Walla, WA; KRSE Yakima, WA; KUJ-FM Burbank, WA; KXDD Yakima, WA

Inland Northwest Broadcasting
805 Stewart Ave., Lewiston ID 83501
(208) 743-1551
www.inlandnwbroadcasting.com
rprasil@idavend.com

Radio Stns: 4 AM. 5 FM.
KCLX Colfax, WA; KMAX Colfax, WA; KRLC Lewiston-Clarkston, ID; KRPL Moscow, ID; KMOK Lewiston, ID; KRAO-FM Colfax, WA; KVTY Lewiston, ID; KZFN Moscow, ID; KZZL-FM Pullman, WA
Shad Spreiter, Moscow Operations Manager
Kelly Wayne, Lewiston Operations Manager
Kevin Keenan, General Sales Mgr

Inner Banks Media LLC
408 W. Arlington Blvd., Suite 101-B, Greenville NC 27834
(252) 355-8822

Radio Stns: 4 FM.
WTIB Williamston, NC; WRHD Farmville, NC; WNBU(FM) Oriental, NC; WRHT Morehead City, NC

Inner City Broadcasting
3 Park Ave., 41st Fl., New York NY 10016
(212) 447-1000; *Fax:*(212) 447-5197
www.wbls.com
info@wbls.com

Radio Stns: 1 FM.
WZMJ Batesburg, SC
Percy Sutton, Chairman/Chief Executive Officer
Hal Jackson, President
Charlie Morgan, SVP & Market Manager
Patricia Robinson, Director Of Operations
Koren Vaughan, Director Of Marketing
Bethany Kent, Promotions Director

Inter-Island Communications Inc.
1868 Halsey Dr., Piti GU 96915
(671) 477-7108; *Fax:*(671) 477-6411

Radio Stns: 2 AM. 4 FM.
KCNM Saipan, MP; KTWG Agana, GU; KNUT Tamuning, GU; KSTO Agana, GU; KZMI Garapan-Saipan, MP; KISH Agana, GU
Edward Poppe Jr., President

International Broadcasting Corp.
1554 Bori St., San Juan PR 00927-6113
(787) 274-1800; *Fax:*(787) 281-9758

Radio Stns: 7 AM. 1 FM.
WIBS Guayama, PR; WDNO Quebradillas, PR; WEKO Morovis, PR; WRSJ Bayamon, PR; WTIL Mayaguez, PR; WXRF Guayama, PR; WGIT Canovanas, PR; WVOZ-FM Carolina, PR
Pedro Callazo, President
Margarita Nazario, General Manager

Iorio Broadcasting Inc.
1316 7th Ave., Beaver Falls PA 15010
(724) 846-4100; *Fax:*(724) 843-7771

Radio Stns: 2 AM.
WBVP Beaver Falls, PA; WMBA Ambridge, PA
Frank Iorio, President

Iowa State University
2111 Grand Ave., Suite 100, Des Moines IA 50312-5393
(515) 725-1700
www.iowapublicradio.org
info@iowapublicradio.org

Radio Stns: 1 AM.
WOI Ames, IA
Douglas West, Treasurer

J&V Communications Inc.
222 Hazard St., Orlando FL 32804-3030
(407) 841-8282; *Fax:*(407) 841-8250
www.wprd.com
wprd1440@hotmail.com

Radio Stns: 4 AM.
WOTS Kissimmee, FL; WPRD Winter Park, FL; WSDO Sanford, FL; WTJV Deland, FL
John Torrado, President
Jocelyn Torrado, Operations Dir
Hector L. Reyes, General Manager

J-Systems Franchising Corp.
Hotel Traylor, 1444 Hamilton St., Allentown PA 18102
(610) 435-5913; *Fax:*(610) 435-8918
www.wmgh.com
wmgh@ptd.net
Ownership: Harold G. Fulmer III, 100%.

Radio Stns: 1 AM. 1 FM.
WLSH Lansford, PA; WMGH-FM Tamaqua, PA
Harold Fulmer III, President

J. & J. Fritz Media Ltd.
Box 311, Fredericksburg TX 78624
(830) 997-2197; *Fax:*(830) 997-2198
www.texasrebelradio.com
txradio@ktc.com

Radio Stns: 1 AM. 3 FM.
KNAF Fredericksburg, TX; KEEP Bandera, TX; KFAN-FM Johnson City, TX; KNAF-FM Fredericksburg, TX
Jayson Fritz, General Manager
Jan Fritz, General Sales Mgr

J.R. Livesay Group
Box 322, Mattoon IL 61938-0322

RADIO - U.S.

(217) 234-6464; *Fax:*(217) 234-6019
Ownership: J.R. Livesay II owns 50% of WLBH-AM-FM. Shirley L. Herrington owns 35% of WLBH-AM-FM.
Radio Stns: 1 AM. 1 FM.
WLBH Mattoon, IL; WLBH-FM Mattoon, IL
J.R. Livesay, Chairman
Shirley Herrington, CFO

Jabar Communications Inc.
5081 Rivers Ave., North Charleston SC 29406
(843) 554-1063; *Fax:*(843) 554-1088
jabarcommunications.com
traffic@jabarcommunications.com
Radio Stns: 2 AM.
WAZS Summerville, SC; WZJY Mount Pleasant, SC
Thomas Daniel, President

Jackson County Broadcasting Inc.
Box 667, 295 E. Main St., Jackson OH 45640
(740) 286-3023; *Fax:*(740) 286-6679
jmossbarger@jbiradio.com
Ownership: Alan Stockmeister
Radio Stns: 1 AM. 2 FM.
WYPC Wellston, OH; WCJO Jackson, OH; WKOV-FM Wellston, OH
Jerry Mossbarger, General Manager

Jackson Radio Works Inc.
1700 Glenshire Dr., Jackson MI 49201
(517) 787-9546; *Fax:*(517) 787-7517
www.wkhm.com
bgoldsen@wkhm.com
Ownership: Bruce & Susan Goldsen, 100%
Radio Stns: 2 AM. 1 FM.
WIBM Jackson, MI; WKHM Jackson, MI; WKHM-FM Brooklyn, MI
Bruce Goldsen, President
Susan Goldsen, VP of Sales/Marketing

Jacobs Media Corp.
PO Box 10, Gainesville GA 30503
(770) 532-9921; *Fax:*(770) 532-0506
jay.jacobs@jacobsmedia.net
Ownership: John W. Jacobs, III
Radio Stns: 2 AM. 1 FM.
WDUN Gainesville, GA; WGGA Gainesville, GA; WDUN-FM Clarkesville, GA
John W. Jacobs III, President & CEO
Elizabeth J. Carswell, Secretary

JER Licenses LLC
194 McGee Rd., Versailles KY 40383
(859) 879-0818
Radio Stns: 3 FM.
WDTX Rothschild, WI; KXZT Newell, SD; KXZS Wall, SD

JMD, Inc.
PO Box 2639, Gulfport MS 39503
Radio Stns: 1 FM.
WZNF Lumberton, MS

Jodesha Broadcasting Inc.
1520 Simpson Ave., Aberdeen WA 98520
(360) 533-3000; *Fax:*(360) 532-1456
www.jodesha.com
info@jodesha.com
Radio Stns: 1 AM. 3 FM.
KBKW Aberdeen, WA; KJET Raymond, WA; KSWW Ocean Shores, WA; KANY Montesano, WA
Gabrielle Jordan, General Manager
Bill Wolfenbarger, General Sales Mgr

Johnson Enterprises Inc.
338 S. KLEY Dr., Wellington KS 67152
(620) 326-3341; *Fax:*(620) 326-8512
www.kleyam.com
Ownership: E. Gordon Johnson, Susan G. Johnson.
Radio Stns: 2 AM. 1 FM.
KKLE Winfield, KS; KLEY Wellington, KS; KWME Wellington, KS
E. Gordon Johnson, President

Journal Communications Inc.
333 W. State St., Milwaukee WI 53203
(414) 224-2616; *Fax:*(414) 224-2469
Radio Stns: 8 AM. 27 FM.
KCID Caldwell, ID; KLIO Wichita, KS; KFFN Tucson, AZ; KGEM Boise, ID; KSGF Springfield, MO; KFAQ Tulsa, OK; KXSP Omaha, NE; WTMJ Milwaukee, WI; KTHI Caldwell, ID; KXBL Henryetta, OK; KEZO-FM Omaha, NE; KFDI-FM Wichita, KS; KRVB Nampa, ID; KTGV Oracle, AZ; KRVI Mount Vernon, MO; KICT-FM Wichita, KS; KJOT Boise, ID; KKCD Omaha, NE; KFXJ Augusta, KS; KSPW Sparta, MO; KMXZ-FM Tucson, AZ; KFTI-FM Newton, KS; KQXR Payette, ID; KSRZ Omaha, NE; KTTS-FM Springfield, MO; KVOO-FM Tulsa, OK; KYQQ Arkansas City, KS; KQTH Tucson, AZ; KSGF-FM Ash Grove, MO; WLWK-FM Milwaukee, WI; WWST Sevierville, TN; WCYQ Oak Ridge, TN; KQCH Omaha, NE; WKHT Knoxville, TN; WNOX Karns, TN
TV Stns: 13 TV.
KGUN-TV Tucson, AZ; KIVI-TV Nampa, ID; KMIR-TV Palm Springs, CA; KMTV-TV Omaha, NE; KNIN-TV Caldwell, ID; KTNV-TV Las Vegas, NV; KWBA-TV Sierra Vista, AZ; WACY-TV Appleton, WI; WFTX-TV Cape Coral, FL; WGBA-TV Green Bay, WI; WSYM-TV Lansing, MI; WTMJ-TV Milwaukee, WI; WTVF Nashville, TN
Douglas Kiel, President

JVC Broadcasting
3075 Veterans Memorial Hwy., Suite 201, Ronkonkoma NY 11779
(631) 648-2500; *Fax:*(631) 648-2510
www.jvcbroadcasting.com
Ownership: Northwood Ventures LLC.
Radio Stns: 2 AM. 10 FM.
WSWN Belle Glade, FL; WSVU North Palm Beach, FL; WBGF Belle Glade, FL; WBON Westhampton, NY; WJVC Center Moriches, NY; WMFQ Ocala, FL; WRCN-FM Riverhead, NY; WTRS Dunnellon, FL; WYGC High Springs, FL; WPTY Calverton-Roanoke, NY; WXJZ Gainesville, FL; WOTW Windermere, FL
John Caracciolo, President & CEO
Victor Canales, Vice President

JWC Broadcasting
259 S. Willow Ave., Cookeville TN 38501
(931) 528-6064; *Fax:*(931) 520-1590
Radio Stns: 1 AM. 3 FM.
WATX Algood, TN; WBXE Baxter, TN; WKXD-FM Monterey, TN; WLQK Livingston, TN
Joel Wilmoth, President

Kaspar Broadcasting Group
1401 W. Barner St., Frankfort IN 46041
(765) 659-3338; *Fax:*(765) 659-3338
Radio Stns: 2 AM. 2 FM.
KWRE Warrenton, MO; WILO Frankfort, IN; KFAV Warrenton, MO; WSHW Frankfort, IN
Vern Kaspar, CEO
Russ Kaspar, Operations Dir

KCD Enterprises Inc.
1200 S.E. Frank Phillips Blvd., Bartlesville OK 74003
(918) 336-1001; *Fax:*(918) 336-3939
www.bartlesvilleradio.com
radio@bartlesvilleradio.com
Radio Stns: 2 AM. 2 FM.
KPGM Pawhuska, OK; KWON Bartlesville, OK; KRIG-FM Nowata, OK; KYFM Bartlesville, OK
Kevin Potter, President

KD Radio Inc.
733 E. Roosevelt Ave., Grants NM 87020
(505) 285-5598; *Fax:*(505) 285-5575
Ownership: Derek Underhill, 100%.
Radio Stns: 2 AM. 1 FM.
KDSK Los Ranchos De Albuquerque, NM; KMIN Grants, NM; KDSK-FM Grants, NM
Derek Underhill, President

KEA Radio Inc.
P.O. Box 966, Fort Payne AL 35967
(256) 845-7721
www.wkeafm.com
Radio Stns: 2 FM.
WKEA-FM Scottsboro, AL; WMXN-FM Stevenson, AL
Ronald Livengood, President/General Manager
Danny Lee, Operations Dir
Charis Wise, Traffic Manager
David Kennamer, Chief Engineer
Jennifer Livengood, Assistant Manager

Kemp Communications Inc.
3800 Howard Hughes Pkwy., Wells Fargo Tower, 17th Fl., Las Vegas NV 89169
(702) 385-6000; *Fax:*(702) 385-6001
Radio Stns: 1 AM. 4 FM.
KMZQ Las Vegas, NV; KVEG Mesquite, NV; KMZQ-FM Payson, AZ; KVGQ Overton, NV; KVGG Salome, AZ
Will Kemp, President

KERM Inc.
113 E. New Hope, Rogers AR 72758
(479) 633-0790; *Fax:*(479) 631-9711
www.kurm.net
Ownership: Kermit Womack, 100%
Radio Stns: 2 AM. 2 FM.
KARV Russellville, AR; KURM Rogers, AR; KARV-FM Ola, AR; KURM-FM Gravette, AR

Keyhole Broadcasting LLC
305 S. Garner Lake Rd., Gillette WY 82716
(307) 687-1003; *Fax:*(307) 687-1006
Radio Stns: 3 FM.
KQOL Sleepy Hollow, WY; KGCC Gillette, WY; KXXL Moorcroft, WY
Kevin Clements, President

Keymarket Communications LLC
1 Forever Dr., Hollidaysburg PA 16648
(814) 941-9800
www.froggyland.com
Radio Stns: 2 AM. 6 FM.
WOHI East Liverpool, OH; WOMP Bellaire, OH; WOGG Oliver, PA; WOGI Moon Township, PA; WKPL Ellwood City, PA; WRQY-FM Bellaire, OH; WPKL Uniontown, PA; WUKL Bethlehem, WV
Gerald Getz, CEO

KGHL Radio, LLC
222 N. 32nd St., 10th Fl., Billings MT 59101
Radio Stns: 1 AM.
KGHL Billings, MT

KHWY, Inc. Highway Radio
1611 East Main St, P.O. Box 1668, Barstow CA 92312
(760) 256-0326; *Fax:*(760) 256-9507
www.highwayradio.com
Radio Stns: 7 FM.
KHWY Essex, CA; KHYZ Mountain Pass, CA; KIXF Baker, CA; KIXW-FM Lenwood, CA; KRXV Yermo, CA; KHDR Lenwood, CA; KHRQ Baker, CA
Kirk Anderson, President/COO
John Gregg, Operations Dir
Heidi Gable, General Sales Mgr
Sean McNeill, Engineering Dir

Kindred Communications Inc.
555 5th Avenue, Suite K, Huntington WV 25701
(304) 523-8401; *Fax:*(304) 523-4848
www.kindredcom.net
Radio Stns: 2 AM. 4 FM.
WCMI Ashland, KY; WRVC Huntington, WV; WDGG Ashland, KY; WCMI-FM Catlettsburg, KY; WXBW Gallipolis, OH; WMGA Kenova, WV
Mike Kirtner, General Manager

Kirkman Broadcasting Inc.
60 Markfield Dr., Charleston SC 29403
(843) 763-6631
www.kirkmanbroadcasting.com
Radio Stns: 4 AM. 2 FM.
WJKB Moncks Corner, SC; WQNT Charleston, SC; WQSC Charleston, SC; WTMZ Dorchester Terrace-Brentwood, SC; WJNI Ladson, SC; WWIK McClellanville, SC
Rick Howze, General Sales Mgr

KM Communications Inc.
3654 Jarvis Ave., Skokie IL 60076
(847) 674-0864; *Fax:*(847) 674-9188
www.kmcommunications.com
Radio Stns: 1 AM. 6 FM.
KQMG Independence, IA; KQMG-FM Independence, IA; KWKM St. Johns, AZ; WLCN Atlanta, IL; KTKB Dededo, GU; WMKB Earlville, IL; WDLJ Breese, IL
TV Stns: 3 TV.
KWKB Iowa City, IA; WOCK-CD Chicago, IL; WSKC-CD Atlanta, GA
Myoung Hwa Bae, President

Knight Broadcasting Inc.
1693 Mission Dr., Solvang CA 93463
(805) 688-8386; *Fax:*(805) 688-2271
Radio Stns: 1 AM. 2 FM.
KUHL Santa Maria, CA; KRAZ Santa Ynez, CA; KSYV Solvang, CA

KNZA Inc.
1828 S. Hwy. 73, Hiawatha KS 66434

(785) 547-3461; *Fax:*(785) 547-9900
www.knzafm.com
Ownership: Greg Buser, 51%; Robert Hilton, 45%; Doug Weinberg, 4%.
Radio Stns: 2 AM. 4 FM.
KAIR Atchison, KS; KTNC Falls City, NE; KAIR-FM Horton, KS; KLZA-FM Falls City, NE; KMZA-FM Seneca, KS; KNZA-FM Hiawatha, KS
LJ Trant, Programming Director

Kona Coast Radio LLC
87 Jasper Lake Rd., Loveland CO 80537
(970) 669-9200
vicmichael@aol.com
Radio Stns: 1 AM. 3 FM.
KQSC Santa Barbara, CA; KKHI Kihei, HI; KVAM Goodland, KS; KNIT Humboldt, NE

KOOR Communications Inc.
P.O. Box 2295, New London NH 03257
(603) 448-0500; *Fax:*(603) 448-6601
www.wntk.com
admin@wntk.com
Radio Stns: 3 AM. 1 FM.
WCFR Springfield, VT; WCNL Newport, NH; WUVR Lebanon, NH; WNTK-FM New London, NH
Robert Vinikoor, General Manager

Koser Radio Group
1859 21st Ave., Rice Lake WI 54868
(715) 234-2131; *Fax:*(715) 234-6942
www.wjmcradio.com
info@wjmcradio.com
Radio Stns: 2 AM. 1 FM.
WAQE Rice Lake, WI; WJMC Rice Lake, WI; WJMC-FM Rice Lake, WI
Thomas A. Koser, President

KSPD Inc.
1440 S. Weideman Ave., Boise ID 83709
(208) 377-3790; *Fax:*(208) 377-3792
www.myfamilyradio.com
info@myfamilyradio.com
Radio Stns: 1 AM. 2 FM.
KSPD Boise, ID; KBXL Caldwell, ID; KDZY McCall, ID
David Schafer, General Manager
Lee Schafer, General Manager

KSRM Inc.
40960 K. Beach Rd., Kenai AK 99611
(907) 283-5811; *Fax:*(907) 283-9177
www.radiokenai.com
info@radiokenai.com
Radio Stns: 2 AM. 3 FM.
KSLD Soldotna, AK; KSRM Soldotna, AK; KKIS-FM Soldotna, AK; KWHQ-FM Kenai, AK; KFSE Kasilof, AK
John Davis, President
Cherie Curry, General Manager

KTLO LLC
P.O. Box 2010, Mountain Home AR 72654
(870) 425-3101; *Fax:*(870) 424-4314
www.ktlo.com
Ownership: Mountain Lakes Broadcasting Corp., 92%.
Radio Stns: 1 AM. 3 FM.
KTLO Mountain Home, AR; KCTT-FM Yellville, AR; KBOD Gainesville, MO; KTLO-FM Mountain Home, AR
Bobby Dean Knight, President

Kuiper Stns
Box 1808, Grand Rapids MI 49501
(616) 451-9387; *Fax:*(616) 451-8460
Ownership: William E. Kuiper Sr.
Radio Stns: 2 AM.
WFUR Grand Rapids, MI; WKPR Kalamazoo, MI
William Kuiper Sr., President/General Manager

KUTE Inc.
Box 737, Ignacio CO 81137-0737
(970) 563-0255; *Fax:*(970) 563-0399
Radio Stns: 6 FM.
KSUT Ignacio, CO; KUTE Ignacio, CO; KUUT Farmington, NM; KPGS Pagosa Springs, CO; KUSW Flora Vista, NM; KDNG Durango, CO

KZLZ LLC
204 E. 4th St., North Little Rock AR 72114
(501) 375-9131; *Fax:*(520) 325-3495
Radio Stns: 1 AM. 2 FM.
KHIL Willcox, AZ; KWCX-FM Tanque Verde, AZ; KZLZ Casas Adobes, AZ

L M Communications Inc.
401 W. Main St., Suite 301, Lexington KY 40507
(859) 233-1515; *Fax:*(859) 233-1517
www.lmcomm.com
jmac@lmcomm.com
Radio Stns: 4 AM. 8 FM.
WJYP St. Albans, WV; WLXG Lexington, KY; WMON Montgomery, WV; WSCW South Charleston, WV; WBTF Midway, KY; WCDA Versailles, KY; WCOO Kiawah Island, SC; WGKS Paris, KY; WMXE South Charleston, WV; WKLC-FM St. Albans, WV; WBVX Carlisle, KY; WYBB Folly Beach, SC
Lynn M. Martin, President & CEO
Pam Mccarty, Business Manager
Craig Olive, General Manager
Cathryn W. Gibson, VP Public Relations & Business Development
Don Trail, Director Of Sales
Charlie Cohn, General Manager South Carolina
Dotsy Klei, General Manager West Virginia

La Crosse Radio Group
P.O. Box 2017, La Crosse WI 54602
(608) 782-8335; *Fax:*(608) 782-8340
www.lacrosseradiogroup.net
Ownership: Howard G. Bill, 45%; TCOM Inc., 45%; and Patrick H. Smith, 10%.
Radio Stns: 1 AM. 4 FM.
WLFN La Crosse, WI; KQEG La Crescent, MN; WKBH-FM West Salem, WI; WLXR-FM La Crosse, WI; WQCC La Crosse, WI
Pat Smith, General Manager
Erik Sjolander, Sales Manager
Heidi Hanse, Promotions Director
Caroline Grosvold, Business Manager
JoAnn Steffes, HR Director
Laurie Lane, Traffic Director
Lois Losby, Public Service
Isaac Wenzel, Director of Interactive Media

La Favorita Radio Network
4043 Greer Rd, Hughson CA 95326
(209) 883-8760; *Fax:*(209) 883-8769
www.lafavorita.net
ngomez@lafavorita.net
Radio Stns: 5 AM. 3 FM.
KLOC Turlock, CA; KAFY Bakersfield, CA; WAOS Austell, GA; WLBA Gainesville, GA; WXEM Buford, GA; KBYN Arnold, CA; KCFA Arnold, CA; KNTO Chowchilla, CA
Samuel Zamarron, CEO
Graciela Zamarron, Operations Dir
Nelson Gomez, General Manager

La Promesa Foundation
1406 E. Garden Ln., Midland TX 79702
(432) 682-1485; *Fax:*(432) 682-5230
www.grnonline.com
Radio Stns: 3 AM. 4 FM.
KWMF Pleasanton, TX; KLPF Midland, TX; KSHJ Houston, TX; KBKN Lamesa, TX; KBMD Marble Falls, TX; KJMA Floresville, TX; KVDG Midland, TX

La Salle County Broadcasting Corp.
1 Broadcast Ln., Oglesby IL 61348
(815) 223-3100
www.lcbcradio.com
programdirector@classichits1039wlpo.com
Radio Stns: 1 AM. 2 FM.
WLPO Lasalle, IL; WAJK La Salle, IL; WLWF Marseilles, IL
Peter Miller, President
Joyce McCullough, General Manager
Mark Lippert, General Sales Mgr
John Spencer, Programming Director
Jeremy Aitkens, News Director
Steve Vogler, Chief Engineer
Beck Roberts, Office Manager
Tricia Salata, Traffic Director

Lake Michigan Broadcasting Inc.
13999 S. W. Bayshore Dr., Traverse City MI 49684
(231) 947-3220
Radio Stns: 1 AM.
WMTE Manistee, MI
Lynn Barewolf, President

Lake Region Radio Works
Box 882, Devils Lake ND 58301
(701) 662-7563; *Fax:*(701) 662-2222
www.lrradioworks.com
kzzyfm@gondtc.com
Radio Stns: 1 AM. 2 FM.
KDLR Devils Lake, ND; KDVL Devils Lake, ND; KZZY Devils Lake, ND
Curtis Teigen, Operations Dir

Lakes Radio Inc.
524 Ludington St., Suite 300, Escanaba MI 49829-3900
(906) 789-9700
www.radioresultsnetwork.com
Radio Stns: 2 AM. 3 FM.
WCHT Escanaba, MI; WTIQ Manistique, MI; WCMM Gulliver, MI; WGKL Gladstone, MI; WGLQ Escanaba, MI
Rick Duerson, VP/General Manager

Lakeway Broadcasting
PO Box 430, Jefferson City TN 37760
(865) 475-3825
Radio Stns: 1 AM. 1 FM.
WJFC Jefferson City, TN; WNRX Jefferson City, TN

Langer Broadcasting Group LLC
94 St. Rose St., Boston MA 02130
(617) 522-4889
Radio Stns: 3 AM.
WQOM Natick, MA; WSRO Ashland, MA; WZBR Coral Springs, FL
Alexander G. Langer, Managing Member

Larche Communications Inc.
355 Cranston Cres., Midland ON L4R 4L3
(705) 720-1991; *Fax:*(705) 526-3060
larchecom.com
lyoung@larche.com
Ownership: Paul Larche, 100%.
Radio Stns: 4 FM.
CICX-FM Orillia, ON; CICZ-FM Midland, ON; CICS-FM Sudbury, ON; CJOS-FM Owen Sound, ON
Paul Larche, President
Mick Weaver, General Manager, Sudbury
Linda Young, Sales Director
Ted Roop, Programming Director
Mora Austin, Vice President
Shelley Barry, Creative Director
Marilyn Wideman, Controller

Larry H. Miller Communications Corporation
301 W.S. Temple, Salt Lake City UT 84101
(801) 325-2570
lhm.com
frank.zang@lhmse.com
Radio Stns: 1 AM.
KZNS Salt Lake City, UT
Gail Miller, Chairman
Clark Whitworth, CEO/COO
Steve Starks, President
Frank Zang, Sr. VP of Communications Sports/Entertainment

Last Frontier Mediactive LLC
819 1st Ave, Suite A, Fairbanks AK 99701-4449
(907) 451-5910; *Fax:*(907) 451-5999
Ownership: Robert J. Ingstad, 50%; Tor H. Ingstad, 50%.
Radio Stns: 1 AM. 4 FM.
KCBF Fairbanks, AK; KTDZ College, AK; KWLF Fairbanks, AK; KXLR Fairbanks, AK; KWDD(FM) Fairbanks, AK
Perry Walley, General Manager

Latino Communications LLC
600 Grant St., Suite 600, Denver CO 80203
(303) 733-5266; *Fax:*(303) 733-5242
kbno@kbno.net
Radio Stns: 3 AM.
KAVA Pueblo, CO; KBNO Denver, CO; KXRE Manitou Springs, CO
Zee Ferrufino, CEO

Laurel Media Inc.
14902 Boot Jack Rd., P.O. Box O, Ridgway PA 15853
(814) 772-9700; *Fax:*(814) 772-9750
Ownership: Dennis Heindl.
Radio Stns: 1 AM. 2 FM.
WKBI St. Marys, PA; WKBI-FM St. Marys, PA; WDDH St. Marys, PA
Dennis Heindl, President

Lazer Broadcasting Corp.
200 S. A St., 4th Fl., Oxnard CA 93030
(805) 240-2070
www.radiolazer.com
Radio Stns: 4 AM. 15 FM.

KCAL(AM) Redlands, CA; KZER Santa Barbara, CA; KOXR Oxnard, CA; KSBQ Santa Maria, CA; KSRT Cloverdale, CA; KBTW Lenwood, CA; KLMM Oceano, CA; KLUN Paso Robles, CA; KXSM Hollister, CA; KLJR-FM Santa Paula, CA; KXZM Felton, CA; KSRN Kings Beach, CA; KGAM(FM) Merced, CA; KJOR Windsor, CA; KSSB Calipatria, CA; KXRS Hemet, CA; KXSB Big Bear Lake, CA; KXTT Maricopa, CA; KEAL Taft, CA
Alfredo Plascencia, CEO/COO
Joshua Mednick, Operations Dir
Sean O'Neil, General Manager
Mark Spellman, General Sales Mgr

Leatherstocking Media Group Inc.
5035 Forest Ave., Oneida NY 13421
(315) 363-1253
Ownership: James V. Johnson.
Radio Stns: 3 AM. 2 FM.
WFBL Syracuse, NY; WSEN Baldwinsville, NY; WMCR Oneida, NY; WMCR-FM Oneida, NY; WSEN-FM Baldwinsville, NY
James V. Johnson, President

Leclerc Communication Inc.
815 Blvd. Lebourgneuf, Suite 505, Ville de Qu,bec QC G2J 0C1
(418) 688-0919; *Fax:*(418) 682-8430
www.leclerccommunication.ca
nicolas.leclerc@leclerccommunication.ca
Ownership: Jacques Leclerc, 99.7% of voting shares.
Radio Stns: 2 FM.
CFEL-FM Levis, QC; CJEC-FM Quebec, QC
Jean-Fran‡ois Leclerc, General Manager
Pierre-Luc Gilbert, General Sales Mgr
Steven Croatto, Assistant Programming Director
Charles Pineault, Promotions Manager
Audrey Rodrigue, Executive Assistant
John Pedulla, Musical Leadership

Lee Family Broadcasting Inc.
3219 Laurelwood Dr., Twin Falls ID 83301
(208) 733-2974
kimlee@leeradio.net
Ownership: Kim Lee, 100%.
Radio Stns: 3 AM. 4 FM.
KART Jerome, ID; KBAR Burley, ID; KXTA Rupert, ID; KKMV Rupert, ID; KZDX Burley, ID; KXTA-2 Gooding, ID; KEDJ Jerome, ID
Kim Lee, President

Legacy Broadcasting, LLC
805 Weightman St., Greenwood MS 38930
(662) 822-1655
Radio Stns: 1 FM.
KYMS Rathdrum, ID
TV Stns: 4 TV.
KNDB Bismarck, ND; KNDM Minot, ND; KMLU Columbia, LA; KNHL Hastings, NE
Sherry Nelson, President

Legacy Communications LLC
3205 W. North Front St., Grand Island NE 68803-4024
(308) 381-0206
Radio Stns: 5 FM.
KIOD McCook, NE; KRGY Aurora, NE; KSWN McCook, NE; KZMC McCook, NE; KZTL Paxton, NE

Legend Communications L.L.C.
6805 Douglas Legum Dr., Suite 100, Elkridge MD 21075
(410) 799-1740; *Fax:*(410) 799-1705
www.patcomm.com
Radio Stns: 5 AM. 9 FM.
KBBS Buffalo, WY; KIML Gillette, WY; KODI Cody, WY; KWOR Worland, WY; KZMQ Ten Sleep, WY; KAML-FM Gillette, WY; KGWY Gillette, WY; KKLX Worland, WY; KLGT Buffalo, WY; KTAG Cody, WY; KZMQ-FM Greybull, WY; KCGL Powell, WY; KZZS Story, WY; KDDV-FM Wright, WY
Jason R. James, Vice President

Leighton Broadcasting Inc.
Box 1458, St. Cloud MN 56302
(320) 251-1450; *Fax:*(320) 251-8952
www.1047kcld.com
Ownership: Thomas H. Graham, trustee, Leighton Children's LP Trust, 27.3%; Thomas H. Graham, trustee, Leighton Grandchildren's LP Trust, 25.7%.
Radio Stns: 3 AM. 8 FM.
KDLM Detroit Lakes, MN; KNOX Grand Forks, ND; KNSI St. Cloud, MN; KBOT Pelican Rapids, MN; KCLD-FM St. Cloud, MN; KCML St. Joseph, MN; KGFK East Grand Forks, MN; KZGF Grand Forks, ND; KYCK Crookston, MN; KZLT-FM East Grand Forks, MN; KZPK Paynesville, MN
John Sowada, President

Dennis Niess, VP
Al Leighton, Chairman/Chief Executive Officer

Leisure Interactive, LLC.
1855 W Katella Ave., Suite #200, Orange CA 92867
(714) 288-8688
Ownership: Bob Elliot, 100%.
Radio Stns: 1 AM. 2 FM.
WABJ Adrian, MI; WBZV Hudson, MI; WQTE Adrian, MI
Bob Elliot, President
Moneca Morton, General Sales Manager

LeSEA Broadcasting
LeSEA Broadcasting Corp, South Bend IN 46614
(574) 291-8200; *Fax:*(574) 291-9043
www.lesea.com
Radio Stns: 3 FM.
WHME South Bend, IN; WHPZ Bremen, IN; WHPD Dowagiac, MI
TV Stns: 8 TV.
KWHB Tulsa, OK; KETD Castle Rock, CO; KWHE Honolulu, HI; KWHD Hilo, HI; KWHM Wailuku, HI; WHMB-TV Indianapolis, IN; WHME-TV South Bend, IN; WHNO New Orleans, LA
Peter Sumrall, President/Chief Executive Officer

Liberman Broadcasting Inc.
1845 Empire Ave., Burbank CA 91504
(818) 729-5300; *Fax:*(818) 729-5678
www.lbimedia.com
LBIinfo@lbimedia.com
Radio Stns: 3 AM. 13 FM.
KEYH Houston, TX; KVNR Santa Ana, CA; KZMP University Park, TX; KBOC Bridgeport, TX; KBUA San Fernando, CA; KBUE Long Beach, CA; KNOR Krum, TX; KEBN Garden Grove, CA; KJOJ-FM Freeport, TX; KZMP-FM Pilot Point, TX; KTJM Port Arthur, TX; KWIZ Santa Ana, CA; KRQB San Jacinto, CA; KNTE Bay City, TX; KZZA Muenster, TX; KQQK Beaumont, TX
TV Stns: 4 TV.
KPNZ Ogden, UT; KMPX Decatur, TX; KRCA Riverside, CA; KZJL Houston, TX
Jose Liberman, Chairman & President
Lenard Liberman, Executive Vice President
Winter Horton, Cheif Operating Officer
Eduardo Leon, Vice President, Programming

Liberty University, Inc.
1971 University Blvd, Lynchburg VA 24515
(434) 582-2000
www.liberty.edu
Radio Stns: 8 FM.
WVRD Zebulon, NC; WVRH Norlina, NC; WRVL Lynchburg, VA; WVRP Roanoke Rapids, NC; WVRL Elizabeth City, NC; WVRA Enfield, NC; WVRI Clifton Forge, VA; WQLU Lynchburg, VA
Chris Wygal, Operations Manager & Host
Barry Armstrong, General Manager
Mike Weston, Programming Director
Pattie Silverthorn, Marketing & Promotions Director
Mark Edwards, Production Director

Liggett Communications LLC.
808 Huron Ave., Port Huron MI 48060
(810) 982-9000; *Fax:*(810) 987-9380
Radio Stns: 3 AM. 2 FM.
WHLS Port Huron, MI; WHLX Marine City, MI; WPHM Port Huron, MI; WBTI Lexington, MI; WSAQ Port Huron, MI
Robert Liggett, President

Linder Broadcasting Group
59346 Madison Ave., Mankato MN 56001
(507) 345-4537; *Fax:*(507) 345-5364
www.katoinfo.com
Ownership: Donald Linder, John Linder.
Radio Stns: 6 AM. 14 FM.
KBIZ Ottumwa, IA; KLEE Ottumwa, IA; KMHL Marshall, MN; KRUE Waseca, MN; KTOE Mankato, MN; KFSP Mankato, MN; KARL Tracy, MN; KARZ Marshall, MN; KDOG North Mankato, MN; KKSI Eddyville, IA; KOLV Olivia, MN; KOTM-FM Ottumwa, IA; KOWZ-FM Blooming Prairie, MN; KRKN Eldon, IA; KRRW St. James, MN; KRUE Waseca, MN; KTWA Ottumwa, IA; KXAC St. James, MN; KATO-FM New Ulm, MN; KXLP Eagle Lake, MN
John Linder, President

Little Falls Radio Corp.
25801 Nacre St. N.W., St. Francis MN 55070
(763) 862-9909
www.fallsradio.com
Radio Stns: 1 AM. 2 FM.
KLTF Little Falls, MN; KFML Little Falls, MN; WYRQ-FM Little Falls, MN

Living Proof Inc.
P.O. Box 637, Bishop CA 93515
(866) 466-5989
www.kwtw.org
recep@kwtw.org
Radio Stns: 1 FM.
KJCU Fort Bragg, CA

LKCM Radio Group L.P.
115 W. 3rd St., Fort Worth TX 76102
(817) 332-0959; *Fax:*(817) 332-4630
Radio Stns: 1 AM. 9 FM.
KVSO Ardmore, OK; KKAJ-FM Davis, OK; KTFW-FM Glen Rose, TX; KYBE Frederick, OK; KYNZ Lone Grove, OK; KFWR Jacksboro, TX; KRVA-FM Campbell, TX; KRVF Kerens, TX; KTRX Dickson, OK; KOME-FM Meridian, TX
Gerry Schlegel, President

Local Voice Media
4732 Longhill Rd., Suite 2201, Williamsburg VA 23188
(757) 565-1079
localvoicemedia.com
Radio Stns: 2 FM.
WWNU Irmo, SC; WWNQ Forest Acres, SC
Thomas G. Davis, President

Local Voice Media Group
4732 Longhill Rd., Suite 2201, Williamsburg VA 23188
(757) 565-1079
localvoicemedia.com
Radio Stns: 5 FM.
WUIN Oak Island, NC; WUDE Bolivia, NC; WBQK West Point, VA; WTYD Deltaville, VA; WNTB Topsail Beach, NC
Thomas G. Davis, President

Locally Owned Radio LLC
21361 Hwy. 30, Twin Falls ID 83301
(208) 735-8300; *Fax:*(208) 733-4196
www.locallyownedradio.com
Radio Stns: 1 AM. 4 FM.
KTFI Wendell, ID; KIKX Ketchum, ID; KTPZ Hazelton, ID; KIRQ Twin Falls, ID; KYUN Hailey, ID
Stephanie Johnson, President
Jerry Fender, Operations Dir
Larry Johnson, General Manager

Long Island Radio Broadcasting LLC
Box 157, Water Mill NY 11976
(631) 267-7800; *Fax:*(631) 267-1018
Ownership: Cherry Creek Radio LLC, 98.26% votes, 95.44% of total assets (see listing).
Radio Stns: 4 FM.
WBEA Southold, NY; WBAZ Bridgehampton, NY; WEHN East Hampton, NY; WEHM Manorville, NY
Barbara King, Business Manager

Longport Media LLC
1601 New Rd., Linwood NJ 08221
(609) 653-1400
Ownership: George Miller; Louis Katz; Roy Goldberg.
Radio Stns: 3 AM. 3 FM.
WBSS(AM) Pleasantville, NJ; WOND Pleasantville, NJ; WBSS Pleasantville, NJ; WWAC Ocean City, NJ; WMGM Atlantic City, NJ; WTKU-FM Petersburg, NJ
Dave Coskey, President
Joe Croce, VP of Sales
Paul Kelly, VP of Broadcast Operations

Lost Coast Communications Inc.
Box 25, Ferndale CA 95536
(707) 786-5104; *Fax:*(707) 786-5100
www.khum.com www.kslg.com
Radio Stns: 4 FM.
KSLG-FM Hydesville, CA; KHUM Cutten, CA; KWPT Fortuna, CA; KXGO Arcata, CA
Patrick Cleary, President

Lotus Communications Corp.
3301 Barham Blvd., Suite 200, Los Angeles CA 90068
(323) 512-2225; *Fax:*(323) 512-2224
www.lotuscorp.com
hq@lotuscorp.com
Radio Stns: 12 AM. 17 FM.
KBAD Las Vegas, NV; KCHJ Delano, CA; KENO Las Vegas, NV; KGST Fresno, CA; KHIT Reno, NV; KPLY Reno, NV; KTKT Tucson, AZ; KIRN Simi Valley, CA; KWAC Bakersfield, CA; KWKW Los Angeles, CA; KWKU Pomona, CA; KWWN Las Vegas, NV; KDOT Reno, NV; KFMA Green Valley, AZ; KWID Las Vegas, NV; KUUB Sun Valley, NV; KPSL-FM Bakersfield,

CA; KVMX Bakersfield, CA; KKBZ Auberry, CA; KLPX Tucson, AZ; KHIT-FM Madera, CA; KOMP Las Vegas, NV; KLBN Fresno, CA; KOZZ-FM Reno, NV; KSEQ Visalia, CA; KIWI McFarland, CA; KXPT Las Vegas, NV; KCMT Oro Valley, AZ; KLPX Tucsun, AZ
Howard Kalmenson, President
Jerry Roy, SVP
Bill Shriftman, SVP

Lovcom Inc.
Box 5086, Sheridan WY 82801
(307) 672-7421; *Fax:*(307) 672-2933
www.sheridanmedia.com
info@sheridanmedia.com
Ownership: W.K. Love and family.
Radio Stns: 2 AM. 4 FM.
KROE Sheridan, WY; KWYO Sheridan, WY; KYTI Sheridan, WY; KZWY Sheridan, WY; KLQQ Clearmont, WY; KZWY-HD Clearmont, WY
Kim Love, Owner
Jim Schellinger, Sales Manager
Bob Grammens, General Manager
Leslie Stratmoen, News Director

M.B. Communications
481 Hamilton St., Geneva NY 14456
(315) 781-1101, ; *Fax:*(315) 781-6666,
www.k1017.com
k1017@fltg.net
Ownership: Russ Kimble, 100%.
Radio Stns: 1 AM.
WYLF Penn Yan, NY
Russell Kimble, President
Deborah Kimble, VP

MacDonald Broadcasting
2000 Whittier St, PO Box 1776, Saginaw MI 48601-2271
(989) 752-8161; *Fax:*(989) 752-8102
www.98fmkcq.com
Radio Stns: 3 AM. 5 FM.
WILS Lansing, MI; WSAM Saginaw, MI; WXLA Dimondale, MI; WMJO Essexville, MI; WHZZ Lansing, MI; WKCQ Saginaw, MI; WQHH DeWitt, MI; WSAG Linwood, MI
Kenneth MacDonald Jr., CEO
Duane Alverson, President

MacDonald Garber Broadcasting Co.
2095 US 131, Petoskey MI 49770
(231) 347-8713; *Fax:*(231) 347-9920
macdonaldgarberbroadcasting.com
Radio Stns: 3 AM. 3 FM.
WATT Cadillac, MI; WMBN Petoskey, MI; WMKT Charlevoix, MI; WKHQ-FM Charlevoix, MI; WLXT Petoskey, MI; WLXV Cadillac, MI
Trish Garber, President

Madison Media Partners LLC
P.O. Box 158, Fitzgerald GA 31750
(912) 381-9395
Ownership: Vernon E. Egli, 50%; Victor M. Vickers, 50%.
Radio Stns: 1 FM.
WOHA Ashtabula, OH

Magnum Broadcasting Inc.
Box 436, State College PA 16804
(814) 272-1320; *Fax:*(814) 272-3291
Radio Stns: 2 AM. 2 FM.
WBLF Bellefonte, PA; WPHB Philipsburg, PA; WQCK(FM) Philipsburg, PA; WQKK(FM) Renovo, PA
Diana Albright, General Manager

Magnum Communications Inc.
1021 N. Superior Ave., Suite 5, Tomah WI 54660
(608) 742-2544
info@magnumbroadcasting.com
Ownership: David R. Magnum, 100%.
Radio Stns: 6 AM. 10 FM.
WBKV West Bend, WI; WDLS Wisconsin Dells, WI; WPDR Portage, WI; WRDB Reedsburg, WI; WRJN Racine, WI; WBOG Tomah, WI; WAUN Kewaunee, WI; WBDL Reedsburg, WI; WBKY Portage, WI; WTMB Tomah, WI; WMBZ West Bend, WI; WDDC Portage, WI; WVTY Racine, WI; WNFM Reedsburg, WI; WNNO Wisconsin Dells, WI; WXYM Tomah, WI
TV Stns: 1 TV.
KQEG-CA La Crescent, MN
David R. Magnum, President

Mahalo Broadcasting L.L.C.
6890 E. Sunrise Dr., Box 120-40, Tucson AZ 85750
(407) 488-2098
Radio Stns: 2 AM. 2 FM.
KHNU Hilo, HI; KHNU(AM) Hilo, HI; KKOA Volcano, HI; KBGX Keaau, HI

Malkan Interactive Communications
2117 Leopard St, Corpus Christi TX 78408
(361) 883-3516; *Fax:*(361) 882-9767
Radio Stns: 1 AM. 2 FM.
KEYS Corpus Christi, TX; KKBA Kingsville, TX; KZFM Corpus Christi, TX
Rodney Brown, General Manager
Daniel Luna, Promotions and Events Director

Manhattan Broadcasting Co. Inc.
2414 Casement Rd., Manhattan KS 66502
(785) 776-1350; *Fax:*(785) 539-1000
1350kman.com
dave@1350kman.com
Radio Stns: 1 AM. 4 FM.
KMAN Manhattan, KS; KXBZ Manhattan, KS; KACZ Riley, KS; KMKF Manhattan, KS; KBLS North Fort Riley, KS
Corey Reeves, General Manager
Andrea Besthorn, General Sales Mgr
Dave Lewis, Programming Director
Cathy Dawes, News Director
John Kurtz, Sports Director

Mapleton Communications LLC
1601 E. 57th Ave., Spokane WA 99223
(509) 448-1000
Radio Stns: 9 AM. 28 FM.
KBRE Merced, CA; KNRO Redding, CA; KCMX Phoenix, OR; KEYF Dishman, WA; KGA Spokane, WA; KSFN Piedmont, CA; KJRB Spokane, WA; KQMS Redding, CA; KYOS Merced, CA; KABX-FM Merced, CA; KZBD Spokane, WA; KAKT Phoenix, OR; KALF Red Bluff, CA; KKHK Carmel, CA; KBOY-FM Medford, OR; KCDU Carmel, CA; KCMX-FM Ashland, OR; KNNW Columbia, LA; KDRK-FM Spokane, WA; KEYF-FM Cheney, WA; KFMF Chico, CA; KBOQ Seaside, CA; KBRE Atwater, CA; KLOQ-FM Winton, CA; KHIP Gonzales, CA; KNNN(FM) Shasta Lake City, CA; KPYG Cayucos, CA; KPIG-FM Freedom, CA; KQPT Colusa, CA; KRDG Shingletown, CA; KRRX Burney, CA; KSHA Redding, CA; KTMT-FM Medford, OR; KWAV Monterey, CA; KBBD Spokane, WA; KZAP Paradise, CA; KBLO Corcoran, CA
Jim Shea, President/CEO

Marion R. Williams Stns
210 S. Philip Rd., P.O. Box 213, Niles MI 49120
(269) 683-4343
www.wsmkradio.com
Radio Stns: 2 AM. 1 FM.
WONG Canton, MS; WSTT Thomasville, GA; WSMK Buchanan, MI
Marion Williams, President

Maritime Broadcasting
90 Lovett Lake Ct., Halifax NS B3S 0H6
(902) 425-1225; *Fax:*(902) 423-2093
www.mbsradio.com
mail@mbsradio.com
Ownership: Robert L. Pace, 100%.
Radio Stns: 7 AM. 16 FM.
CFAB Windsor, NS; CFBC Saint John, NB; CJCB Sydney, NS; CJCW Sussex, NB; CKAD Middleton, NS; CKDY Digby, NS; CKNB Campbellton, NB; CFQM-FM Moncton, NB; CHFX-FM Halifax, NS; CHLQ-FM Charlottetown, PE; CIOK-FM Saint John, NB; CJYC-FM Saint John, NB; CKPE-FM Sydney, NS; CKEN-FM Kentville, NS; CHOY-FM Moncton, NB; CKCW-FM Moncton, NB; CJRW-FM Summerside, PE; CFAN-FM Miramichi, NB; CKWM-FM Kentville, NS; CFCY-FM Charlottetown, PE; CHNS-FM Halifax, NS; CHER-FM Sydney, NS; CKDH-FM Amherst, NS
Robert Pace, Owner
David Pace, Vice-President, Buildings & Operations
Ashley MacDonald, Sales Director

Mark Media Group
Box 607, Burnsville NC 28714
(828) 682-6221; *Fax:*(828) 682-0998
www.wkyk.com
mmg@wkyk.com
Radio Stns: 3 AM.
WKYK Burnsville, NC; WTOE Spruce Pine, NC; WTZQ Hendersonville, NC
J. Ardell Sink, Chairman
Remelle Sink, CFO
Michael Sink, President

MarMac Communications LLC
7515 Blythe Island Hwy., Brunswick GA 31523
(912) 264-6251; *Fax:*(912) 264-9991
Radio Stns: 4 AM.
WFNS Blackshear, GA; WSFN Brunswick, GA; WSEG Savannah, GA; WWGA(AM) Waycross, GA

Mars Hill Network
4044 Makyes Rd, Syracuse NY 13215
(800) 677-1881
www.marshillnetwork.org
info@marshillnetwork.org
Ownership: Not-for-profit corporation. Note: Group also has a radio net, 14 translators.
Radio Stns: 5 FM.
WMHI Cape Vincent, NY; WMHN Webster, NY; WMHR Syracuse, NY; WMHQ Malone, NY; WMHU Cold Brook, NY
Wayne Taylor, General Manager
Mike Dwinell, Chief Engineer

Martin Broadcasting Inc.
15307 Falcon Ridge Dr, Humble TX 77396
(281) 441-3665
Radio Stns: 5 AM.
KANI Wharton, TX; KYOK Conroe, TX; KCHL San Antonio, TX; KRMY Killeen, TX; KZZB Beaumont, TX
Eugene Martin, Principal

Martz Communications Group
86 Porter Rd, Malone NY 12953
(518) 483-1100; *Fax:*(518) 483-1382
radioworksbest.com
Ownership: Tim Martz; Slaight Communications
Radio Stns: 2 AM. 3 FM.
WICY Malone, NY; WAMO Wilkinsburg, PA; WVNV Malone, NY; WYUL Chateaugay, NY; WSNN Potsdam, NY
Tim Martz, CEO/COO

Matinee Radio LLC
2801 Via Fortuna, Suite 675, Austin TX 78746
(512) 329-5843; *Fax:*(512) 329-5847
Radio Stns: 2 FM.
KTXO Goldsmith, TX; KRTS Marfa, TX

MAX Media L.L.C.
900 Laskin Rd., Virginia Beach VA 23451
(757) 437-9800; *Fax:*(757) 437-0034
www.maxmediallc.com
Ownership: MBG-GG LLC, 42.0345%; MBG Quad-C Investors I Inc., 41.4124%; Aardvarks Also LLC, 6.1967%; Colonnade Max Investors Inc., 4.8671%; Quad-C Max Investors Inc., 4.6799%; MBG Quad-C Investors II Inc., 0.6221%; and Quad-C Max Investors II Inc., 0.1872%.
Radio Stns: 8 AM. 22 FM.
KGIR Cape Girardeau, MO; KSIM Sikeston, MO; KMAL Malden, MO; KWOC Poplar Bluff, MO; KZIM Cape Girardeau, MO; WCIL Carbondale, IL; WGH Newport News, VA; WJPF Herrin, IL; KCGQ-FM Gordonville, MO; KEZS-FM Cape Girardeau, MO; KGKS Scott City, MO; KJEZ Poplar Bluff, MO; KKLR-FM Poplar Bluff, MO; KLSC Malden, MO; KFCO Bennett, CO; WCIL-FM Carbondale, IL; WVHT Norfolk, VA; WCXL Kill Devil Hills, NC; WVBW Suffolk, VA; WGH-FM Newport News, VA; WFYY Bloomsburg, PA; WOOZ-FM Harrisburg, IL; WXLT Christopher, IL; WWBE Mifflinburg, PA; WCMS-FM Hatteras, NC; WVSP-FM Yorktown, VA; WUEZ Carterville, IL; WYGL-FM Elizabethville, PA; KJHM Strasburg, CO; WVSL-FM Riverside, PA
TV Stns: 3 TV.
WNKY Bowling Green, KY; WMEI Arecibo, PR; WPFO Waterville, ME
Aubrey Eugene Loving Jr., Chairman & CEO
John Trinder, President & Chief Operating Officer

MBC Grand Broadcasting Inc.
1360 E. Sherwood Dr., Grand Junction CO 81501
(970) 254-2100
www.961kstr.com
Radio Stns: 3 AM. 4 FM.
KGLN Glenwood Springs, CO; KNZZ Grand Junction, CO; KTMM Grand Junction, CO; KMOZ-FM Grand Junction, CO; KMGJ Grand Junction, CO; KKVT Grand Junction, CO; KSTR-FM Montrose, CO
Richard C. Dean, CEO
David G. Hinson, President
Michael Kulp, Chief Financial Officer

McKenzie River Broadcasting Company, Inc.
925 Country Club Rd., Suite 200, Eugene OR 97401
(541) 484-9400; *Fax:*(541) 344-9424
Radio Stns: 3 FM.

KEUG Veneta, OR; KKNU Springfield-Eugene, OR; KMGE Eugene, OR
John Q. Tilson III, President
Renate R. Tilson, Operations Dir

McMurray Communications Inc.
3335 W. 8th St., Thatcher AZ 85552
(928) 428-1230; *Fax:*(928) 428-1311
www.mysouthernaz.com
traffic@mcmurrayradio.com
Radio Stns: 1 AM. 2 FM.
KATO Safford, AZ; KWRQ Clifton, AZ; KXKQ Safford, AZ
Harry McMurray, CEO
Reed Richins, Operations Dir
Davis Nathan, General Sales Mgr

Media Logic LLC
Box 430, Fort Morgan CO 80701-0430
(970) 867-5674; *Fax:*(970) 542-1023
Radio Stns: 2 AM. 2 FM.
KFTM Fort Morgan, CO; KRDZ Wray, CO; KATR-FM Wray, CO; KSRX Sterling, CO
Wayne Johnson, General Manager

Media One Group
147 Bell St., Suite 200, Chagrin Falls OH 44022
(440) 893-8114
Radio Stns: 2 AM. 3 FM.
WJTN Jamestown, NY; WKSN Jamestown, NY; WHUG Jamestown, NY; WQFX-FM Russell, PA; WWSE Jamestown, NY

Media Power Group Inc.
100 Gran Bulevar Paseos, Suite 403A, San Juan PR 926
(787) 292-1700; *Fax:*(787) 292-1717
wskn1320@yahoo.com
Radio Stns: 4 AM.
WKFE Yauco, PR; WDEP Ponce, PR; WLEY Cayey, PR; WSKN San Juan, PR
Eduardo Albino Rivero, President
Ismael Nieves, Operations Dir

Media Professionals, Inc
PO Box 230, Houston MO 65483
(417) 217-1404
Radio Stns: 1 AM. 1 FM.
KBTC Houston, MO; KUNQ Houston, MO

Mel Wheeler Inc.
3934 Electric Rd., Roanoke VA 24018-4513
(540) 989-4591; *Fax:*(540) 774-5667
melwheelerinc.com
Ownership: Leonard E. Wheeler, 35%; Steve Wheeler, 34%; and Clark Wheeler, 31%.
Radio Stns: 2 AM. 4 FM.
WFIR Roanoke, VA; WVBE Roanoke, VA; WVBE-FM Lynchburg, VA; WSLC-FM Roanoke, VA; WSLQ Roanoke, VA; WXLK Roanoke, VA
TV Stns: 2 TV.
KPOB-TV Poplar Bluff, MO; WSIL-TV Harrisburg, IL
Leonard Wheeler, President
Gretchen Cummings, Sec/Treasurer

Melia Communications Inc.
1065 S Range, Colby KS 67701
(785) 462-3305; *Fax:*(785) 462-3307
www.nwksradio.com
sacha@rockingmradio.com
Radio Stns: 1 AM. 3 FM.
KLOE Goodland, KS; KKCI Goodland, KS; KRDQ Colby, KS; KWGB Colby, KS
Chelsea Kinnett, Operations Dir
Sacha Sanguinetti, General Manager
Will Sterrett, News Director

Memphis First Ventures, LP
3710 Rawlins St., Suite 150, Dallas TX 75219
(214) 273-6440
Radio Stns: 1 AM.
WUMY Turrell, AR
Terry Unkefer, CEO/COO
Ronald Unkefer, President

Mentor Partners Inc.
18720 16 Mile Rd., Big Rapids MI 49307
(231) 796-7000; *Fax:*(231) 796-7951
Radio Stns: 1 AM. 2 FM.
WBRN Big Rapids, MI; WWBR Big Rapids, MI; WYBR Big Rapids, MI

Metro Radio Inc.
2251 Hunter Mill Rd., Vienna VA 22181
(703) 938-1016; *Fax:*(703) 331-4706
www.metroradioinc.com
Radio Stns: 3 AM.
WKCW Warrenton, VA; WKDV Manassas, VA; WKDL Warrenton, VA
Bruce Houston, President

Meyer Communications Inc.
3000 E Chestnut Expy, Springfield MO 65802
(417) 862-3751; *Fax:*(417) 869-7675
radiospringfield.com
Ownership: Kenneth E. Meyer, 100%.
Radio Stns: 2 AM. 3 FM.
KBFL-AM Springfield, MO; KWTO-AM Springfield, MO; KBFL-FM Buffalo, MO; KTXR Springfield, MO; KWTO-FM Springfield, MO
Kenneth Meyer, President

Michael Radio Group
1063 W Hwy. 34, Apt. F, Loveland CO 80537-9424
(307) 778-9318
Radio Stns: 4 FM.
KYOY Hillsdale, WY; KGRK Glenrock, WY; KHAN Medicine Bow, WY; KLLM(FM) Rawlins, WY

Mid-America Radio Group Inc.
60 N Wayne St, Martinsville IN 46151
(765) 349-1485; *Fax:*(765) 342-3569
mid-americaradio@scican.net
Ownership: David Keister, principal owner.
Radio Stns: 2 AM. 6 FM.
WJOT Wabash, IN; WMYJ Martinsville, IN; WCBK-FM Martinsville, IN; WHZR Royal Center, IN; WJOT-FM Wabash, IN; WCLS Spencer, IN; WVNI Nashville, IN; WMYJ-FM Bloomfield, IN
David C. Keister, President

Mid-West Family Broadcasting
730 Rayovac Dr, Madison WI 53711
(608) 273-1000; *Fax:*(608) 273-3588
midwestfamilybroadcasting.com
Ownership: Philip Fisher, Richard T. Record, Thomas A. Walker.
Radio Stns: 11 AM. 32 FM.
WAYY Eau Claire, WI; WEAQ Chippewa Falls, WI; WHIT Madison, WI; WIZM-AM La Crosse, WI; WKTY La Crosse, WI; WMAY Springfield, IL; WNTA Rockford, IL; WSBT South Bend, IN; WSJM-AM Benton Harbor, MI; WLMV Madison, WI; WOZN Madison, WI; KOSP Ozark, MO; KKLH Marshfield, MO; KQYB Spring Grove, MN; KCLH Caledonia, MN; WAXX Eau Claire, WI; WSJM-FM Benton Harbor, MI; WCXT Hartford, MI; WECL Elk Mound, WI; WIAL Eau Claire, WI; WIRX St. Joseph, MI; WISM Altoona, WI; WIZM-FM La Crosse, WI; WJJO Watertown, WI; WRTB Winnebago, IL; WLCE Petersburg, IL; WMGN Madison, WI; WNNS Springfield, IL; WNSN South Bend, IN; WQLZ Petersburg, IL; WRQT La Crosse, WI; WGFB Rockton, IL; WWQM-FM Middleton, WI; WXRX Belvidere, IL; WYTZ Bridgman, MI; WZOC Plymouth, IN; WCSY South Haven, MI; WJQM De Forest, WI; KQRA Brookline, MO; WOZN-FM Mount Horeb, WI; W263BJ Loves Park, IL; WUSW Taylorville, IL; WQLQ Benton Harbor, MI
Thomas Walker, President
Jason McCutchin, CFO
Richard Record, Director

Midwest Communications Inc.
904 Grand Ave, Wausau WI 54403
(715) 842-1437; *Fax:*(715) 842-7061
mwcradio.com
Ownership: Duey E. Wright, 100% votes, 10% equity; Wright Family Irrevocable Trust of 2010, 90% equity.
Radio Stns: 21 AM. 50 FM.
KDAL-AM Duluth, MN; KFGO Fargo, ND; KWSN Sioux Falls, SD; WIBQ Terre Haute, IN; WDSM Superior, WI; WTAQ-AM Green Bay, WI; WHBL Sheboygan, WI; WHTC Holland, MI; WBOW Terre Haute, IN; WKZO Kalamazoo, MI; WMFG-AM Hibbing, MN; WNFL-AM Green Bay, WI; WNMT Nashwauk, MN; WNWN-AM Portage, MI; WRIG Schofield, WI; WSAU-AM Wausau, WI; WTVB-AM Coldwater, MI; WDUL Superior, WI; KNFL Fargo, ND; WQLR Kalamazoo, MI; KELO-AM Sioux Falls, SD; KDAL-FM Duluth, MN; KTWB Sioux Falls, SD; KRWK Fargo, ND; KQDS Duluth, MN; KRRO Sioux Falls, SD; KQSF Dell Rapids, SD; KTCO Duluth, MN; KELO-FM Sioux Falls, SD; KVOX-FM Moorhead, MN; WABX Evansville, IN; WBFM Sheboygan, WI; WDEZ Wausau, WI; WEVE Eveleth, MN; WYVN Saugatuck, MI; WZOX Portage, MI; WIFC Wausau, WI; WIKY Evansville, IN; WIMZ Knoxville, TN; WIXX Green Bay, WI; WSAU-FM Rudolph, WI; WLFW Chandler, IN; WJXA Nashville, TN; WJXB Knoxville, TN; WJXQ Charlotte, MI; WMFG-FM Hibbing, MN; WMGI Terre Haute, IN; WNCY Neenah-Menasha, WI; WNFN Millersville, TN; WNWN-FM Coldwater, MI; WOZZ Mosinee, WI; WGEE-FM New London, WI; WVFM Kalamazoo, MI; WCJK Murfreesboro, TN; WYDR Neenah-Menasha, WI; WSTO Owensboro, KY; WTBX Hibbing, MN; WDKE Coleraine, MN; WTHI-FM Terre Haute, IN; WUSZ Virginia, MN; WLMI Grand Ledge, MI; WQTX St. Johns, MI; WHBZ Sheboygan Falls, WI; WWVR Paris, IL; WXER Plymouth, WI; WWDK Jackson, MI; KMJO Hope, ND; KDKE Superior, WI; KOYY Fargo, ND; WDKW Maryville, TN; WDWQ Terre Haute, IN
Michael Wright, Chief Operating Officer
Duke Wright, President & Chief Executive Officer
Peter Tanz, Senior Vice President
Jeff Wright, Chief Sales Officer
Jeff McCarthy, Vice President, Programming
Tim Laes
Mary Kay Wright, Chief Marketing Officer
Paul Rahmlow, Chief Financial Officer

Midwestern Broadcasting Co.
300 E. Front St., Suite 450, Traverse City MI 49684
(231) 946-6211; *Fax:*(231) 946-1914
www.midwesternbroadcasting.com
Ownership: Ross Biederman, 52.5%; William Kiker Estate, 16.25%; William McClay, 15%.
Radio Stns: 2 AM. 8 FM.
WCCW Traverse City, MI; WTCM Traverse City, MI; WZTK Alpena, MI; WATZ-FM Alpena, MI; WBCM Boyne City, MI; WCCW-FM Traverse City, MI; WJZQ Cadillac, MI; WTCM-FM Traverse City, MI; WRGZ Rogers City, MI; WCZW Charlevoix, MI
Ross Biederman, President
Chris Warren, Business Manager

Mildred R Porter
4400 Clear Creek Pkwy., Northport AL 35475
(205) 345-4787; *Fax:*(205) 345-4790
Ownership: Mildred Porter, 100%.
Radio Stns: 1 FM.
WQZZ Boligee, AL
Mildred R. Porter, President

Millcreek Broadcasting L.L.C.
980 N. Michigan Ave., Suite 1880, Chicago IL 60611
(312) 204-9900; *Fax:*(312) 587-9466
Radio Stns: 3 FM.
KAUU Manti, UT; KUDD Roy, UT; KUDE Nephi, UT
Bruce Buzil, President
Christopher Devine, President

Miller Media Group
918 East Park Street, P.O. Box 169, Taylorville IL 62568-0169
(217) 824-3395; *Fax:*(217) 824-3301
www.randyradio.com/corp
Radio Stns: 2 AM. 6 FM.
WHOW Clinton, IL; WTIM Assumption, IL; WEZC Clinton, IL; WMKR Pana, IL; WRAN Taylorville, IL; WTIM Taylorville, IL; WTIM Taylorville, IL; WSVZ Tower Hill, IL
Randal J. Miller, President

Milner Broadcasting Enterprises LLC
292 N. Convent, Bourbonnais IL 60914
(815) 933-9287; *Fax:*(815) 933-8696
Radio Stns: 1 FM.
WIVR Kentland, IN
Timothy Milner, President

Milwaukee Radio Alliance L.L.C.
N72 W12922 Good Hope Rd., Menomonee Falls WI 53051-4441
(414) 771-1021
www.milwaukeeradio.com
cheng@milwaukeeradio.com
Radio Stns: 1 AM. 2 FM.
WZTI Greenfield, WI; WLDB Milwaukee, WI; WLUM-FM Milwaukee, WI
Willie Davis, Chairman
William Lynette, President
Tom Cheng, General Sales Mgr

Minn-Iowa Christian Broadcasting Inc.
Box 72, Blue Earth MN 56013
(507) 526-3233; *Fax:*(507) 526-3235
www.kjly.com
kjly@kjly.com
Radio Stns: 5 FM.
KJCY St. Ansgar, IA; KJLY Blue Earth, MN; KJYL Eagle Grove, IA; KJIA Spirit Lake, IA; KJWR Windom, MN
Matt Dorfner, Station Manager

Mississippi Broadcasters L.L.C.
Box 1699, Meridian MS 39302
(601) 693-2661; *Fax:*(601) 483-0826
Radio Stns: 4 FM.
WJXM De Kalb, MS; WMLV Butler, AL; WALT-FM Meridian, MS; WZKS Union, MS
Clay Holladay, General Manager

Missouri River Christian Broadcasting Inc.
Box 187, Washington MO 63090
(636) 239-0400; *Fax:*(636) 293-4448
www.goodnewsvoice.org
Radio Stns: 3 FM.
KGNA-FM Arnold, MO; KGNN-FM Cuba, MO; KGNV Washington, MO
J.C. Goggan, General Manager

Mitten Media, LLC
4225 E. Burt Lake Rd., Chemboygan MI 49721
(231) 290-1107; *Fax:*(607) 749-2374
Radio Stns: 1 FM.
WMTE-FM Manistee, MI
Todd Mohr, President

Momentum Broadcasting LP
700 E. Mineral King Ave., Visalia CA 93277
(559) 553-1500; *Fax:*(559) 627-1496
www.momentumbroadcasting.com
Ownership: Don Groppetti.
Radio Stns: 2 FM.
KIOO Porterville, CA; KJUG-FM Tulare, CA
Don Groppetti, Managing General Partner
Amy Kehrmeyer-Moore, Senior Account Executive
Rachel Otis-Leija, Account Executive
Rochelle Daly, Account Exeuctive
Mark Cole, Account Executive

Monarch Broadcasting Inc.
212 W. Cypress St., Altus OK 73521
(580) 482-1450; *Fax:*(580) 482-3420
www.kwhw.com
Radio Stns: 1 AM. 1 FM.
KWHW Altus, OK; KQTZ Hobart, OK
Matthew Ward, President

Monticello Media LLC
3948 S. Third St., Suite 191, Jacksonville Beach FL 32250
(904) 285-3239
Radio Stns: 2 AM. 4 FM.
WCHV Charlottesville, VA; WKAV Charlottesville, VA; WCYK-FM Staunton, VA; WCHV-FM Charlottesville, VA; WZGN Crozet, VA; WHTE-FM Ruckersville, VA
George Reed, President

Montrose Broadcasting Corp.
9 Locust St, Montrose PA 18801
(570) 278-2811; *Fax:*(570) 278-1442
www.wpel.org
Ownership: Non Profit Non Stock Corporation.
Radio Stns: 3 FM.
WBGM New Berlin, PA; WPEL Montrose, PA; WPGM Danville, PA
Lawrence H. Souder, President

Moody Radio
820 N LaSalle Blvd, Chicago IL 60610
(312) 329-4300
www.moodyradio.org
Radio Stns: 4 AM. 34 FM.
WDLM-AM East Moline, IL; WFCN Nashville, TN; WGNR-AM Anderson, IN; WMBI-AM Chicago, IL; KMBN Las Cruces, NM; KMBI Spokane, WA; KMLW Moses Lake, WA; KSPL Kalispell, MT; WCRF Cleveland, OH; WFCM-FM Murfreesboro, TN; WFOF Covington, IN; WGNB Zeeland, MI; WGNR-FM Anderson, IN; WHPL West Lafayette, IN; WIWC Kokomo, IN; WJSO Pikeville, KY; WKES Lakeland, FL; WKZM Sarasota, FL; WMBI-FM Chicago, IL; WMBU Forest, MS; WMBV Dixons Mills, AL; WMBW Chattanooga, TN; WMKW Crossville, TN; WRMB Boynton Beach, FL; WSOR Naples, FL; WVMN New Castle, PA; WVMS Sandusky, OH; WHGN Crystal River, FL; WVME Meadville, PA; WMBL Mitchell, IN; WVML Millersburg, OH; WMFT Tuscaloosa, AL; WRNF Selma, AL; KMWY Jackson, WY; K204CE Clifton, AZ; K216FX Mena, AR; K220EO Hilo, HI; WVMU Ashtabula, OH
Collin G. Lambert, VP, Broadcasting
Doug Hastings, General Manager
Dan Craig, Programming Director
Pierre Chestang, Regional Manager, Southern Region
Ray Hashley, Regional Manager, Northern Region
Elsa Mazon, Manager, Radio Moody (Spanish)

Moon Broadcasting
1200 W. Venice Blvd., Los Angeles CA 90006
(213) 745-6224; *Fax:*(213) 745-7577
Radio Stns: 3 AM. 7 FM.
KIQQ Barstow, CA; KTNS Oakhurst, CA; KZXR Prosser, WA; KAAT Oakhurst, CA; KAEH Beaumont, CA; KIQQ-FM Newberry Springs, CA; KMNA Mabton, WA; KMQA East Porterville, CA; KLES Prosser, WA; KMEN Mendota, CA
Abel DeLuna, President

Morgan County Industries Inc.
129 College St., West Liberty KY 41472
Radio Stns: 3 AM. 4 FM.
WLKS West Liberty, KY; WMOR Morehead, KY; WRLV Salyersville, KY; WCBJ Campton, KY; WLKS-FM West Liberty, KY; WMOR-FM Morehead, KY; WRLV-FM Salyersville, KY
Paul Lyons, Chief Engineer

Morgan Murphy Media
7025 W Raymond Rd, Madison WI 53719
(608) 271-4321; *Fax:*(608) 271-0800
www.morganmurphymedia.com
chris@embtv.com
Ownership: Evening Telegram Co. owns 100% of KVEW(TV), KXLY-AM-FM-TV, KXLY-DT and KAPP(TV). Evening Telegram Co. owns 84.4% of TelevisionWisconsin Inc., with an additional 15.2% of the stn held by Evening Telegram stockholders.
Radio Stns: 4 AM. 7 FM.
KXLX Airway Heights, WA; KVNI Coeur D'Alene, ID; KXLY-AM Spokane, WA; WPVL-AM Platteville, WI; KEZE Spokane, WA; KHTQ Hayden, ID; KIYX Sageville, IA; KXLY-FM Spokane, WA; KZZU Spokane, WA; WGLR Lancaster, WI; WPVL-FM Platteville, WI
TV Stns: 5 TV.
KAPP-TV Yakima, WA; KVEW Kennewick, WA; KXLY-TV Spokane, WA; WISC-TV Madison, WI; WKBT-TV La Crosse, WI
Brian R. Burns, Vice President & COO
Elizabeth Murphy Burns, President & CEO
Glenn R. Krieg, Treasurer & CFO

Mortenson Broadcasting Co.
501 Darby Creek Rd, Lexington KY 40509
(859) 245-1000; *Fax:*(859) 245-1600
mortensonradio.com
Ownership: Jack Mortenson, 100%.
Radio Stns: 5 AM. 1 FM.
KGGN Gladstone, MO; KGGR Dallas, TX; KHVN Fort Worth, TX; KKGM Fort Worth, TX; KRVA Cockrell Hill, TX; WEMM Huntington, WV
Jack Mortenson, President

Mount Wilson FM Broadcasters Inc.
1500 Cotter Avenue, Los Angeles CA 90025
(310) 478-5540
www.mountwilsoninc.com
reception@mountwilsoninc.com
Radio Stns: 1 AM.
KIDD Monterey, CA
Saul Levine, President

Mountain Broadcasting Corp.
99 Clinton Rd., West Caldwell NJ 7006
(973) 852-0300; *Fax:*(973) 808-5516
Radio Stns: 3 AM.
WPWA Chester, PA; WBTK Richmond, VA; WWGB Indian Head, MD
TV Stns: 1 TV.
WMBC-TV Newton, NJ
Sun Young Joo, President

Mountain Communications
Box 211, Saranac Lake NY 12983-0211
(518) 891-1544; *Fax:*(518) 891-1545
Radio Stns: 2 AM. 3 FM.
WIRD Lake Placid, NY; WNBZ Saranac Lake, NY; WLPW Lake Placid, NY; WRGR Tupper Lake, NY; WYZY Saranac, NY
Ted Morgan, President

Mountain Dog Media
254 Winnebago Dr., Fond du Lac WI 54935
(920) 921-1071; *Fax:*(920) 921-0757
Radio Stns: 2 AM. 1 FM.
KFIZ Fond Du Lac, WI; WCLB Sheboygan, WI; WFON Fond Du Lac, WI
Randy Hopper, President

Mountain Wireless Inc.
PO Box 274, North Marshfield MA 02059
(207) 474-5171
Radio Stns: 1 AM. 2 FM.
WSKW Skowhegan, ME; WCTB Fairfield, ME; WFMX Skowhegan, ME
Alan W. Anderson, President

Mt. Rushmore Broadcasting Inc.
218 N. Wolcott, Casper WY 82601-1923
(307) 265-1984; *Fax:*(307) 266-3295
Ownership: Jan Charles Gray, 100%.
Radio Stns: 4 AM. 7 FM.
KFCR Custer, SD; KRAL Rawlins, WY; KVOC Casper, WY; KZMX Hot Springs, SD; KASS Casper, WY; KAWK Custer, SD; KHOC Casper, WY; KIQZ Rawlins, WY; KMLD Casper, WY; KQLT Casper, WY; KZMX-FM Hot Springs, SD
Jan Gray, CEO

Mt. Washington Radio & Gramophone L.L.C.
Box 2008, Conway NH 03818
(603) 356-8870; *Fax:*(603) 356-8875
Ownership: Greg Frizzell, 51%; Frizzell Family Revocable Trust, 49%.
Radio Stns: 2 FM.
WVMJ Conway, NH; WMWV Conway, NH
Greg Frizzell, General Manager

MTD Inc.
1086 Mechem, Ruidoso NM 88346
(505) 258-9922
mymtdradio.com
sales@mtdradio.com
Radio Stns: 1 AM. 4 FM.
KRUI Ruidoso Downs, NM; KWMW Maljamar, NM; KIDX Ruidoso, NM; KNMB Cloudcroft, NM; KTUM Tatum, NM
Bruce Rimbo, President
Timothy Keithley, General Manager
Tim Keithley, VP of Marketing
Greg Widener, Radio Coordinator
Lori Estrada, Sr. Account Executive & Air Personality
Beth Schueler, Accpimt Execitive
Jason Adams, Regional Manager, Music Director & Air Personality
Teresa Jones, Account Executive

MTS Broadcasting
2 Bay St., Cambridge MD 21613
(410) 228-4800
www.mtslive.com
news@mtslive.com
Radio Stns: 1 AM. 3 FM.
WCEM Cambridge, MD; WAAI Hurlock, MD; WCEM-FM Cambridge, MD; WTDK Federalsburg, MD
Shane Walker, Operations Mgr
Troy Hill, General Manager
Beverly Jones, Business Mgr

Muirfield Broadcasting Inc.
200 Short Rd., Southern Pines NC 28387
(910) 692-2107; *Fax:*(910) 692-6849
Radio Stns: 1 AM. 1 FM.
WIOZ Pinehurst, NC; WIOZ Southern Pines, NC
Walker Morris, President

MultiCultural Radio Broadcasting Inc.
27 William St., 11th Floor, New York NY 10005
(212) 966-1059; *Fax:*(212) 625-2894
www.mrbi.net
Ownership: Arthur S. Liu.
Radio Stns: 39 AM.
KMNY Hurst, TX; KALI West Covina, CA; KARI Blaine, WA; KATD Pittsburg, CA; KAZN Pasadena, CA; KBLA Santa Monica, CA; KVRI Blaine, WA; KCHN Brookshire, TX; KDFT Ferris, TX; KEST San Francisco, CA; KWRU Fresno, CA; KIQI San Francisco, CA; KLIB Roseville, CA; KAHZ Pomona, CA; KMRB San Gabriel, CA; KSJX San Jose, CA; KNSN San Diego, CA; KFSG Roseville, CA; KXPA Bellevue, WA; KXYZ Houston, TX; KYPA Los Angeles, CA; WATB Decatur, GA; WEXY Wilton Manors, FL; WGFS Covington, GA; WHWH Princeton, NJ; WLXE Rockville, MD; WJDM Elizabeth, NJ; WFBR Glen Burnie, MD; WKDM New York, NY; WLYN Lynn, MA; WNMA Miami Springs, FL; WNSW Newark, NJ; WNYG Medford, NY; WPAT Paterson, NJ; WAZN Watertown, MA; WTTM Lindenwold, NJ; WWRU Jersey City, NJ; WZHF Arlington, VA; WZRC New York, NY
Arthur S. Liu, President

Munbilla Broadcasting Properties Ltd.
5526 Hwy. 281 N., Marble Falls TX 78654
(830) 693-5551; *Fax:*(830) 693-5107
Radio Stns: 2 FM.
KHLB Mason, TX; KYRT Hunt, TX

Duane Fox, General Manager
Sabrina Preiss, Programming Director
Bill Woleben, Chief Engineer

Muzzy Broadcasting L.L.C.

500 Division St., Stevens Point WI 54481
(715) 341-9800; *Fax:*(715) 341-0000
Ownership: Richard L. Muzzy.

Radio Stns: 2 AM. 2 FM.
WPTW Piqua, OH; WPCN Stevens Point, WI; WKQH Marathon, WI; WSPT Stevens Point, WI
Richard Muzzy, President

MY Broadcasting Corp.

Box 961, Renfrew ON K7V 4H4
(613) 432-6936; *Fax:*(877) 840-6936
www.mybroadcastingcorp.com
jeffd@mbcmedia.ca
Ownership: Andrew Dickson Family Trust, 35.05%; Jon Pole Family Trust, 35.05%; and Blackburn Radio Inc., 29.9%.

Radio Stns: 14 FM.
CHCD-FM Simcoe, ON; CJMB-FM Peterborough, ON; CHMY-FM Renfrew, ON; CIMY-FM Pembroke, ON; CIYN-FM Kincardine, ON; CJMI-FM Strathroy, ON; CKYM-FM Napanee, ON; CJGM-FM Gananoque, ON; CIMA-FM Alliston, ON; CHMY-FM-1 Arnprior, ON; CIYM-FM Brighton, ON; CKMO-FM Orangeville, ON; CKXM-FM Exeter, ON; CKZM-FM St. Thomas, ON
Jon Pole, President
Joel Scott, Operations & Programming
Jeff Degraw, Vice-President, Sales
D'Arcy Magee, Group Program Director
Cindy Clyne, Group News Director
Andrew Dickson, Vice-President
Marg Tubman, Administration Director

MyTown Media, LLC.

412 N. Locust St., Pittsburg KS 67202
(620) 232-5993
www.mytown-media.com

Radio Stns: 1 AM. 4 FM.
KKOY Chanute, KS; KHST Lamar, MO; KKOY-FM Chanute, KS; KSNP Burlington, KS; KWXD Asbury, MO
Bill Wachter, President

Neuhoff Family L.P.

1501 N. Washington, Danville IL 61832
(217) 442-1700, ; *Fax:*(217) 431-1489
neuhoffmedia.com
mhulvey@cooketech.net
Ownership: Neuhoff Corp., North Palm Beach, FL, 100% of votes.

Radio Stns: 4 AM. 8 FM.
WDAN Danville, IL; WDZ Decatur, IL; WFMB Springfield, IL; WSOY Decatur, IL; WCVS-FM Virden, IL; WCZQ Monticello, IL; WDNL Danville, IL; WDZQ Decatur, IL; WFMB-FM Springfield, IL; WRHK Danville, IL; WSOY-FM Decatur, IL; WXAJ Hillsboro, IL
Geoff Neuhoff, President
Mike Hulvey, General Manager

Nevada County Broadcasters Inc.

1255 E. Main St., Suite A, Grass Valley CA 95945
(530) 272-3424; *Fax:*(530) 272-2872
www.knco.com
knco@nccn.com

Radio Stns: 2 AM. 1 FM.
KNCO Grass Valley, CA; KUBA Yuba City, CA; KNCO-FM Grass Valley, CA
Bob Breck, CEO

New Media Broadcasters Inc.

2210 31st St. N., Havre MT 59501-8003
(406) 265-7841; *Fax:*(406) 265-8855
nmb@nmbi.com

Radio Stns: 1 AM. 2 FM.
KOJM Havre, MT; KPQX Havre, MT; KRYK Chinook, MT
C. David Leeds, President
Cynthia H. Leeds, Operations Dir

New West Broadcasting Corp.

1145 Kilauea Ave., Hilo HI 96720
(808) 935-5461; *Fax:*(808) 935-7761

Radio Stns: 1 AM. 2 FM.
KPUA Hilo, HI; KAOY Kealakekua, HI; KNWB Hilo, HI

New WRRD

1224 E. Brady St., Milwaukee WI 53202
(844) 967-2789

Radio Stns: 1 AM.
WRRD Waukesha, WI
Mike Crute, President

New York Public Radio

160 Varick St., New York NY 10013
(646) 829-4400
www.wnyc.org

Radio Stns: 1 AM. 5 FM.
WNYC New York, NY; WQXR-FM Newark, NJ; WQXW Ossining, NY; WNJT-FM Trenton, NJ; WNYC-FM New York, NY; WNJO Toms River, NJ
Laura R. Walker, President & CEO
Tom Bartunek, Vice President, Planning and Special Projects
Dean Cappello, Executive Vice President and Chief Content Officer
Thomas Hjelm, Executive Vice President and Chief Digital Officer
Margaret Pomeroy Hunt, Chief Development Officer
Michele Rusnak, Chief Financial Officer

NewCap Inc.

8 Basinview Drive, Dartmouth NS B3B 1G4
(902) 468-7557; *Fax:*(902) 468-7558
www.ncc.ca
ncc@ncc.ca
Ownership: Newfoundland Capital Corporation Ltd., 100%.

Radio Stns: 14 AM. 59 FM.
CFCB Corner Brook, NF; CFCW Camrose, AB; CFSX Stephenville, NF; CHCM Marystown, NF; CHNL Kamloops, BC; CISL Richmond, BC; CJYQ St. John's, NF; CKCM Grand Falls, NF; CKDQ Drumheller, AB; CKGA Gander, NF; CKIM Baie Verte, NF; CKJR Wetaskiwin, AB; CKVO Clarenville, NF; VOCM St. John's, NF; CFCV-FM St. Andrew's, NL; CFLC-FM Churchill Falls, NL; CFLN-FM Goose Bay, NF; CFRQ-FM Dartmouth, NS; CKUL-FM Halifax, NS; CIGM-FM Sudbury, ON; CIGV-FM Penticton, BC; CIRK-FM Edmonton, AB; CIZZ-FM Red Deer, AB; CHBM-FM Toronto, ON; CJMO-FM Moncton, NB; CKBA-FM Athabasca, AB; CKIX-FM St. John's, NL; CKKY-FM Wainwright, AB; CKRA-FM Edmonton, AB; CKRV-FM Kamloops, BC; CKSQ-FM Stettler, AB; CKXX-FM Corner Brook, NL; CKZZ-FM Vancouver, BC; VOCM-FM St. John's, NF; CKXG-FM Grand Falls, NL; CFXJ-FM Toronto, ON; CJXL-FM Moncton, NB; CKGY-FM Red Deer, AB; CKXD-FM Gander, NL; CHNO-FM Sudbury, ON; CFXL-FM Calgary, AB; CIHT-FM Ottawa, ON; CKSA-FM Lloydminster, AB; CJXK-FM Cold Lake, AB; CFXH-FM Hinton, AB; CJPR-FM Blairmore, AB; CKWY-FM Wainwright, AB; CHNI-FM Saint John, NB; CFRK-FM Fredericton, NB; CIXF-FM Brooks, AB; CFCW-FM Camrose, AB; CILV-FM Ottawa, ON; CJKC-FM Kamloops, BC; CFXW-FM Whitecourt, AB; CHTN-FM Charlottetown, PE; CKQK-FM Charlottetown, PE; CHSL-FM Slave Lake, AB; CJEG-FM Bonnyville, AB; CKMP-FM Calgary, AB; CFXE-FM Edson, AB; CHVO-FM Carbonear, NL; CHRK-FM Sydney, NS; CKCH-FM Sydney, NS; CIJK-FM Kentville, NS; CKKO-FM Kelowna, BC; CHLG-FM Vancouver, BC; CKVH-FM High Prairie, AB; CHSP-FM St. Paul, AB; CKWB-FM Westlock, AB; CIBQ-FM Brooks, AB; CIHI-FM Fredericton, NB; CHHI-FM Miramichi, NB; CILB-FM Lac La Biche, AB

TV Stns: 2 TV.
CITL-DT Lloydminster, AB; CKSA-DT Lloydminster, AB
Harold R. Steele, Chairman
Robert G. Steele, CEO/COO
Robert G. Steele, President

Newfoundland Broadcasting Co.

446 Logy Bay Rd., St. John's NF A1C 5S2
(709) 722-5015; *Fax:*(709) 726-5107
www.ntv.ca
greetings@ntv.ca
Ownership: G. Scott Stirling, 64.99%; Gregory Stirling, 34.99%; and others, 0.02%.

Radio Stns: 8 FM.
CFOZ-FM Argentia, NF; CKMY-FM Grand Falls, NL; CHOZ-FM St. John's, NF; CIOZ-FM Marystown, NF; CJMY-FM Clarenville, NF; CJOZ-FM Bonavista Bay, NL; CKOZ-FM Corner Brook, NF; CIOS-FM Stephenville, NF

TV Stns: 1 TV.
CJON-DT St. John's, NF
Geoff Stirling, President & CEO
Lindsey Andrews, General Manager
Ernst Rollmann, Station Manager
Lorraine Pope, Sales Director & Program Acquisitions

News-Press & Gazette Co.

825 Edmond St, St. Joseph MO 64502
(816) 271-8500; *Fax:*(816) 271-8695
www.npgco.com
info@npgco.com

Radio Stns: 2 AM. 2 FM.
KESQ Indio, CA; KRDO Colorado Springs, CO; KRDO-FM Security, CO; KUNA-FM La Quinta, CA

TV Stns: 11 TV.
KCOY-TV Santa Maria, CA; KECY-TV El Centro, CA; KESQ-TV Palm Springs, CA; KEYT-TV Santa Barbara, CA; KIDK Idaho Falls, ID; KIFI-TV Idaho Falls, ID; KION-TV Monterey, CA; KMIZ Columbia, MO; KRDO-TV Colorado Springs, CO; KTVZ Bend, OR; KVIA-TV El Paso, TX
David Bradley, Chairman & CEO
Mike Meara, Executive Vice President - Chief Operating Officer

Newsweb Corp.

1645 W Fullerton, Chicago IL 60614
(773) 975-0401; *Fax:*(773) 975-1301
Ownership: Fred Eychaner, 100%.

Radio Stns: 4 AM. 3 FM.
WAIT Crystal Lake, IL; WNDZ Portage, IN; WSBC Chicago, IL; WCPT-AM Willow Springs, IL; WCPY Arlington Heights, IL; WCPT-FM DeKalb, IL; WCPQ Park Forest, IL

TV Stns: 1 TV.
KCDO-TV Kimball, NE
Fred J. Eychaner, President

NextMedia Group Inc.

6312 S. Fiddler's Green Cir., Suite 360E, Englewood CO 80111
(303) 694-9118; *Fax:*(303) 694-4940
Ownership: NextMedia Investors LLC, 100% of votes.

Radio Stns: 8 AM. 22 FM.
WANG Havelock, NC; WHBC Canton, OH; WJOL Joliet, IL; WKRS Waukegan, IL; WRNN Myrtle Beach, SC; WLIP Kenosha, WI; WRNS Kinston, NC; WSGW Saginaw, MI; KLAK Tom Bean, TX; KMAD-FM Whitesboro, TX; KMKT Bells, TX; WLVG Havelock, NC; WQZL Belhaven, NC; WKZQ-FM Forestbrook, SC; WRXQ Coal City, IL; WCEN-FM Hemlock, MI; WERO Washington, NC; WHBC-FM Canton, OH; WMYB Myrtle Beach, SC; WERV-FM Aurora, IL; WSSR Joliet, IL; WRNN-FM Socastee, SC; WQSL Jacksonville, NC; WRNS-FM Kinston, NC; WSGW-FM Carrollton, MI; WTLZ Saginaw, MI; WXLC Waukegan, IL; WXQR-FM Jacksonville, NC; WYAV Myrtle Beach, SC; WZSR Woodstock, IL
Steven Dinetz, CEO
Skip Weller, President

Nicolet Broadcasting

30 N 18th Ave, Suite 8, Sturgeon Bay WI 54235
(920) 746-9430; *Fax:*(920) 746-9433
www.doorcountydailynews.com
wbdk@doorcountydailynews.com
Ownership: Roger Utnehmer.

Radio Stns: 4 FM.
WBDK Algoma, WI; WRKU Forestville, WI; WRLU Algoma, WI; WSBW Ephraim, WI

Noalmark Broadcasting Corp.

202 W. 19th St., El Dorado AR 71730
(870) 862-7777; *Fax:*(870) 862-0203
Ownership: William C. Nolan Jr., 65%; Edwin B. Alderson Jr., 35%.

Radio Stns: 6 AM. 12 FM.
KZHS Hot Springs, AR; KBIM Roswell, NM; KELD El Dorado, AR; KVMA Magnolia, AR; KBHS Hot Springs, AR; KYKK Humble City, NM; KAGL El Dorado, AR; KBIM-FM Roswell, NM; KMRX El Dorado, AR; KMLK El Dorado, AR; KIXV(FM) Malvern, AR; KIXB El Dorado, AR; KIXN Hobbs, NM; KELD-FM Hampton, AR; KLAZ Hot Springs, AR; KPER Hobbs, NM; KPZA-FM Jal, NM; KVMZ Waldo, AR
William Nolan, President
Edwin Alderson, Executive Vice President
Paul Starr, Vice President
Anna Canterbury, Secretary/Treasurer

Norsan Consulting and Management Inc.

Box 2148, Tucker GA 30085
(770) 414-5026

Radio Stns: 9 AM. 1 FM.
WCEO Columbia, SC; WEWC Callahan, FL; WFAY Fayetteville, NC; WGSP Charlotte, NC; WVOJ Fernandina Beach, FL; WKGN Knoxville, TN; WSOS St. Augustine Beach, FL; WXNC Monroe, NC; WNNR Jacksonville, FL; WGSP-FM Pageland, SC

North American Broadcasting Co. Inc.

1458 Dublin Rd., Columbus OH 43215
(614) 481-7800

Radio Stns: 1 AM. 2 FM.
WMNI Columbus, OH; WRKZ Columbus, OH; WJKR Worthington, OH
Norma Mnich, Chairman
Matthew Mnich, CEO
Steve Wilson, Senior Sales/Marketing

Eric McGuire, Digital Brand Manager

North Cascades Broadcasting Inc.
PO Box 151, Omak WA 98841
(509) 826-0100; *Fax:*(509) 826-3929
www.komw.net
Ownership: John and Becki Andrist.
Radio Stns: 1 AM. 1 FM.
KOMW Omak, WA; KZBE Omak, WA
John Andrist, Station Manager

North Georgia Radio Group L.P.
112 Jordan Dr., Chattanooga TN 37421
(423) 425-8987
Radio Stns: 2 AM. 2 FM.
WBLJ Dalton, GA; WDAL Dalton, GA; WOCE Ringgold, GA; WYYU Dalton, GA

Northeast Broadcasting Company Inc.
288 S. River Rd., Bedford NH 03110
(603) 668-9999; *Fax:*(603) 668-6470
www.nebcast.com
Ownership: Steven A. Silberberg, Ed Flanagan.
Radio Stns: 9 AM. 25 FM.
KHAT Laramie, WY; WTUB Lake City, FL; WTWK Plattsburgh, NY; WFAD Middlebury, VT; WGAW Gardner, MA; WCAT Burlington, VT; WSKI Montpelier, VT; WRSA St. Albans, VT; KJMP Pierce, CO; KIMX Nunn, CO; WFNX Athol, MA; WWMP Waterbury, VT; WNCS Montpelier, VT; WRJT Royalton, VT; WIFY Addison, VT; WDOT Danville, VT; WXRV Andover, MA; KVUW Wendover, NV; KVRG Victor, ID; KRVQ-FM Lake Isabella, CA; KTED Evansville, WY; KDAD Bar Nunn, WY; KZQL Mills, WY; KWHO Lovell, WY; KRQU Laramie, WY; KANT Guernsey, WY; KAZY Cheyenne, WY; KRAN Warren Afb, WY; KROW Cody, WY; WNYN-FM Whitefield, NH; KTUG Hudson, WY; KHAD Upton, WY; KKAR Wamsutter, WY; KBEN-FM Cowley, WY
Steven Silberberg, CEO
Edward Flanagan, VP

Northeast Colorado Broadcasting LLC
220 State St., Suite 106, Fort Morgan CO 80701
(970) 867-7271; *Fax:*(970) 867-2676
Radio Stns: 1 AM. 2 FM.
KSIR Brush, CO; KPMX Sterling, CO; KPRB Brush, CO
Alec Creighton, General Manager

Northeast Communications Corp.
110 Babbit Rd., Franklin NH 03235
(603) 934-2500; *Fax:*(603) 934-2933
www.mix941fm.com
Ownership: Jeff Fisher, 44.5%; Chris Fisher, 17.5%; and Phil Fisher, 16.5%.
Radio Stns: 2 AM. 1 FM.
WFTN Franklin, NH; WPNH Plymouth, NH; WSCY Moultonborough, NH
Jeff Fisher, President
Cathy Keyser, Operations Manager
Fred Caruso, Programming Diretor
Rick Ganley, Programming Director

Northeast Oklahoma Broadcast Network Inc.
1 W. 3rd St., Grove OK 74344
(918) 786-2211; *Fax:*(918) 786-2284
Radio Stns: 1 AM. 2 FM.
KVIS Miami, OK; KGLC Miami, OK; KESA Eureka Springs, AR
Larry Hestand, President

Northern Christian Radio, Inc.
P.O. Box 695, Gaylord MI 49734
(800) 545-8857
promisefm.com
info@thepromisefm.com
Radio Stns: 4 FM.
WHST Tawas City, MI; WOLW Cadillac, MI; WPHN Gaylord, MI; WTHN Sault Ste. Marie, MI
Pat Scott, Executive Director
Fred Young, Programming Director
Dawn Summerland, Donor Relations

Northwestern College & Radio
3003 Snelling Ave. N., St. Paul MN 55113-1598
(651) 631-5000; *Fax:*(651) 631-5086
www.nwc.edu
Ownership: Non-profit organization. Northwestern College, St. Paul, is the owner and operator of the 15 radio licenses.
Radio Stns: 5 AM. 10 FM.
KFNW West Fargo, ND; KNWC Sioux Falls, SD; KNWS Waterloo, IA; KTIS Minneapolis, MN; WNWC Sun Prairie, WI; KDNI Duluth, MN; KDNW Duluth, MN; KFNW-FM Fargo, ND; KNWI Osceola, IA; KJNW Kansas City, MO; KNWM Madrid, IA; KFNL Kindred, ND; KTIS-FM Minneapolis, MN; WNWC-FM Madison, WI; WSMR Sarasota, FL
Dr. Alan Cureton, President
Dr. Paul Virts, SVP

NRC Broadcasting Inc.
1201 Eighteenth St., Suite 250, Denver CO 80202
(303) 675-4698; *Fax:*(303) 296-7030
www.nrcbroadcasting.com
Radio Stns: 10 FM.
KDSP(FM) Greenwood Village, CO; KQZR Hayden, CO; KFMU-FM Oak Creek, CO; KIDN-FM Burns, CO; KJAC Timnath, CO; KKCH Glenwood Springs, CO; KNFO Basalt, CO; KSMT Breckenridge, CO; KSPN-FM Aspen, CO; KTUN New Castle, CO
Tim Brown, Chairman
Dave Rogers, CFO
Ray Skibitsky, President

NRG Media LLC
2875 Mount Vernon Rd. S.E., Cedar Rapids IA 52403
(319) 862-0300; *Fax:*(319) 286-9383
www.nrgmedia.com
Radio Stns: 12 AM. 25 FM.
KAYL Storm Lake, IA; KGFW Kearney, NE; KLGA Algona, IA; KLIN Lincoln, NE; KQWC Webster City, IA; KWBG Boone, IA; WCMY Ottawa, IL; WFAW Fort Atkinson, WI; WIXN Dixon, IL; WJBD Salem, IL; WLKD Minocqua, WI; WOBT Rhinelander, WI; KAYL-FM Storm Lake, IA; KBBK Lincoln, NE; KFGE Milford, NE; KHBT Humboldt, IA; KKIA Ida Grove, IA; KLNC Lincoln, NE; KLGA-FM Algona, IA; KQKY Kearney, NE; KQWC-FM Webster City, IA; KRNY Kearney, NE; KROR Hastings, NE; KSYZ-FM Grand Island, NE; WGLX-FM Wisconsin Rapids, WI; WHDG Rhinelander, WI; WRCV Dixon, IL; WJBD-FM Salem, IL; WKCH Whitewater, WI; WYTE Marshfield, WI; WMQA-FM Minocqua, WI; WRHN Rhinelander, WI; WRKX Ottawa, IL; WRLO-FM Antigo, WI; WSEY Oregon, IL; WSJY Fort Atkinson, WI; WBCV Wausau, WI
Norman W. Waitt Jr., Chairman
Mary Quass, CEO

Ohana Media Group LLC
Box 99827, Seattle WA 98139-0827
(425) 891-1200
www.ohanamediagroup.com
info@ohanamediagroup.com
Ownership: Trila Bumstead, 100%.
Radio Stns: 1 AM. 6 FM.
KAST Astoria, OR; KVAS-FM Ilwaco, WA; KFAT Anchorage, AK; KDBZ Anchorage, AK; KBBO-FM Houston, AK; KCRX-FM Seaside, OR; KXLW Houston, AK
Trila Bumstead, President/CEO
Bill Sigmar, COO
Tom Oakes, VP of Programming

Olivet Nazarene University
One University Ave, Bourbonnais IL 60914
(815) 939-5011
www.olivet.edu
Radio Stns: 1 FM.
WTMK Wanatah, IN

Omni Broadcasting Co.
502 Beltrami Ave. N.W., Bemidji MN 56601-3010
(218) 444-1500; *Fax:*(218) 759-0345
Ownership: Louis H. Buron Jr., Mary Campbell, G. Michael Boen.
Radio Stns: 5 AM. 11 FM.
KBUN Bemidji, MN; KLIZ Brainerd, MN; KNSP Staples, MN; KVBR Brainerd, MN; KWAD Wadena, MN; KBHP Bemidji, MN; KBLB Nisswa, MN; KUAL-FM Brainerd, MN; KIKV-FM Sauk Centre, MN; KKWS Wadena, MN; KKZY Bemidji, MN; KLIZ-FM Brainerd, MN; KLLZ-FM Walker, MN; KULO Alexandria, MN; WJJY-FM Brainerd, MN; WQXJ Blackduck, MN
Mary Campbell, VP/CFO
Louis Buron Jr., President/CEO

One Ten Broadcast Group Inc.
2 E. Main St., Shawnee OK 74801
(405) 878-0077
Radio Stns: 1 AM. 2 FM.
KWSH Wewoka, OK; KIRC Seminole, OK; KSLE Wewoka, OK
Linda Jones, President

1TV.Com Inc.
Box 1416, Los Altos CA 94023
(650) 520-6002
Radio Stns: 2 AM. 2 FM.
KBSZ Apache Junction, AZ; KJAA Globe, AZ; KIKO Miami, AZ; KIKO-FM Claypool, AZ
John Low, President

Opus Broadcasting Systems Inc.
511 Rossanley Dr., Medford OR 97501
(541) 772-0322; *Fax:*(541) 772-4233
Radio Stns: 2 AM. 3 FM.
KEZX Medford, OR; KRTA Medford, OR; KCNA Cave Junction, OR; KROG Grants Pass, OR; KRVC Hornbrook, CA
Dean Flock, General Manager
Brian Fraser, General Sales Mgr

Opus Media Holdings LLC
950 Third Ave., 19th Fl., New York NY 10022
(212) 634-3376
Radio Stns: 9 FM.
KEZP Bunkie, LA; KBKK Ball, LA; KLAA-FM Tioga, LA; KXRR Monroe, LA; KMYY Rayville, LA; KZRZ West Monroe, LA; WWOF(FM) Tallahassee, FL; WHTF Havana, FL; WQTL Tallahassee, FL
Richard Linhart, Chairman
James Shea, CEO

Ouachita Broadcasting Inc.
Box 1450, Mena AR 71953
(479) 394-1450
Radio Stns: 1 AM. 3 FM.
KENA Fort Smith, AR; KILX Hatfield, AR; KQOR Mena, AR; KENA-FM Mena, AR
Jay Bunyard, President
Teresa Bunyard, Operations Dir

Our Three Sons Broadcasting LLP.
Box 307, Rock Hill SC 29731
(803) 324-1340; *Fax:*(803) 324-2860
www.wrhi.com
Ownership: Allan M. Miller, mgng ptnr; Manning Kimmel, ptnr.
Radio Stns: 1 AM. 1 FM.
WRHI Rock Hill, SC; WVSZ Chesterfield, SC
Allan Miller, Managing Partner
Manning Kimmel, Managing Partner

Ozark Media Inc.
555 Marshall Dr., St. Robert MO 65584
(573) 336-5535; *Fax:*(573) 336-7619
Radio Stns: 3 FM.
KELE-FM Mountain Grove, MO; KFLW St. Robert, MO; KOZX Cabool, MO
Dalton Wright, President

Pacific Cascade Communications Corp.
1139 Hartnell Ave., Redding CA 96002-2113
(530) 222-4455; *Fax:*(530) 222-4484
Radio Stns: 2 AM. 3 FM.
KGRV Winston, OR; KVIP Redding, CA; KVIP-FM Redding, CA; KMWR Brookings, OR; KNDZ McKinleyville, CA
Phil Morrow, Operations Dir

Pacific Empire Radio Corp.
403 Capital St., Lewiston ID 83501
(208) 743-6564
www.pacempire.com
benb@pacempire.com
Ownership: AIA Services Corp.; Connie Taylor; R. John Taylor.
Radio Stns: 3 AM. 7 FM.
KBKR Baker, OR; KCLK Asotin, WA; KLBM La Grande, OR; KATW Lewiston, ID; KCLK-FM Clarkston, WA; KKBC-FM Baker, OR; KUBQ La Grande, OR; KVAB Clarkston, WA; KRJT Elgin, OR; KQZB Troy, ID
Kurt Luchs, President & CEO
Ben Bonfield, General Manager

Pacific Radio Group Inc.
311 Ano St., Kahului HI 96732
(808) 877-5566; *Fax:*(808) 871-0666
www.pacificradiogroup.com
bergson@pacificradiogroup.com
Radio Stns: 3 AM. 10 FM.
KHLO Hilo, HI; KKON Kealakekua, HI; KMVI Kahului, HI; KAGB Waimea, HI; KAPA Hilo, HI; KKBG Hilo, HI; KLEO Kahaluu, HI; KLUA Kailua Kona, HI; KJMD Pukalani, HI; KJKS Kahului, HI; KPOA Lahaina, HI; KPVS Hilo, HI; KLHI-FM Kahului, HI
Chuck Bergson, CEO
Robert Van Dine, General Manager
L.E. Johnson, CFO

Pacific West Broadcasting Inc.
906 SW. Alder, PO Box 1430, Newport OR 97365
(541) 265-2266; *Fax:*(541) 265-6397
ybcradio.com
info@ybcradio.com

Radio Stns: 1 AM. 2 FM.
KBCH Lincoln City, OR; KNCU Newport, OR; KCRF-FM Lincoln City, OR
David Miller, President

Pacifica Foundation Inc.
1925 Martin Luther King Jr. Way, Berkeley CA 94704
(510) 849-2590
www.pacifica.org
Ownership: (dba Pacific Radio).
Radio Stns: 6 FM.
KPFA Berkeley, CA; KPFB Berkeley, CA; KPFK Los Angeles, CA; KPFT Houston, TX; WBAI New York, NY; WPFW Washington, DC
Dan Coughlin, Executive Director

Palm Beach Broadcasting
701 Northpoint Pkwy., Suite 500, West Palm Beach FL 33407
(561) 868-1100
Radio Stns: 3 FM.
WEAT West Palm Beach, FL; WIRK Indiantown, FL; WMBX Jensen Beach, FL

Pamal Broadcasting Ltd.
6 Johnson Rd., Latham NY 12110
(518) 786-6600; *Fax:*(518) 786-6610
www.pamal.com
Ownership: James Morrell, owner.
Radio Stns: 7 AM. 15 FM.
WBNR Beacon, NY; WENU South Glen Falls, NY; WIZR Johnstown, NY; WMML Glens Falls, NY; WROW Albany, NY; WSYB Rutland, VT; WPNI Amherst, MA; WAJZ Voorheesville, NY; WJEN Killington, VT; WNYQ Hudson Falls, NY; WFLY Troy, NY; WFFG-FM Corinth, NY; WHUD Peekskill, NY; WDVT Rutland, VT; WJJR Rutland, VT; WKLI-FM Albany, NY; WBPM Saugerties, NY; WSPK Poughkeepsie, NY; WYJB Albany, NY; WXPK Briarcliff Manor, NY; WZMR Altamont, NY; WZRT Rutland, VT
Michael Dufort, CFO
Debbie Grembowicz, General Manager
Dave Lobb, Regional Vice President
Clay Ashworth, Market Manager
Jason Finkelberg, Market Mangaer
Dan Austin, Market Manager

Pamplin Broadcasting
6605 S.E. Lake Rd., Portland OR 97222
(503) 684-0360
portlandtribune.com
mgarber@commnewspapers.com
Radio Stns: 2 AM.
KPAM Troutdale, OR; KKOV Vancouver, WA
Mark Garber, President

Pappas Telecasting Companies
500 S. Chinowth Rd., Visalia CA 93277
(559) 733-7800; *Fax:*(559) 733-7878
Ownership: Harry J. Pappas.
Radio Stns: 2 AM.
KCWK North Las Vegas, NV; KMPH Modesto, CA
TV Stns: 8 TV.
KCWK North Las Vegas, NV; KHGI-TV Kearney, NE; KAZA-TV Avalon, CA; KCWI-TV Ames, IA; KSWT Yuma, AZ; KWNB-TV Hayes Center, NE; WCWG Lexington, NC; WLGA Opelika, AL
Bruce Yeager, EVP/CFO
Harry J. Pappas, Chairman/CEO
Dennis J. Davis, President/COO

Paradis Broadcasting of Alexandria Inc.
1312 Broadway, Alexandria MN 56308
(320) 763-3131
www.voiceofalexandria.com
thefolks@kxra.com
Radio Stns: 1 AM. 2 FM.
KXRA Alexandria, MN; KXRZ Alexandria, MN; KXRA-FM Alexandria, MN
Brett Paradis, General Manager

Paragon Communications Inc.
220 S. Pioneer Rd., Elk City OK 73644
(580) 225-9696
www.kecofm.com
Radio Stns: 3 FM.
KADS Elk City, OK; KECO Elk City, OK; KXOO Elk City, OK

Payne Radio Group
1600 W. Jackson, Hugo OK 74743
(580) 326-2555; *Fax:*(580) 326-2623
www.k955.com
will@payneradiogroup.com
Radio Stns: 1 AM. 7 FM.
KTLQ Tahlequah, OK; KEOK Tahlequah, OK; KTFX-FM Warner, OK; KTNT Eufaula, OK; KDOE Antlers, OK; KITX Hugo, OK; KYHD Valliant, OK; KQIK Haileyville, OK
William Payne, President

Pearson Broadcasting
9530 Midlothian Pike, Richmond VA 23235
(804) 521-0603; *Fax:*(804) 674-8938
Ownership: Max H. Pearson, 100%.
Radio Stns: 3 FM.
KBCN-FM Marshall, AR; KERX Paris, AR; KTTG Mena, AR
Max Pearson, President
Bruce Hale, VP

Pecos Valley Broadcasting Co.
317 W. Quay Ave., Artesia NM 88210
(505) 746-2751; *Fax:*(505) 748-3748
Radio Stns: 1 AM. 3 FM.
KSVP Artesia, NM; KPZE-FM Carlsbad, NM; KEND Roswell, NM; KTZA Artesia, NM
Sam Beard, President
David Ruckman, Operations Dir
Gene Dow, General Manager

Peg Broadcasting Crossville LLC
961 Miller Ave., Crossville TN 38555
(931) 707-1102; *Fax:*(931) 707-1220
Radio Stns: 6 AM. 4 FM.
WAEW Crossville, TN; WAKI McMinnville, TN; WBMC McMinnville, TN; WCSV Crossville, TN; WSMT Sparta, TN; WTZX Sparta, TN; WOWF Crossville, TN; WOWC Morrison, TN; WTRZ Spencer, TN; WPBX Crossville, TN

Peggy Sue Broadcasting Corp.
Box 838, Richlands VA 24641
(276) 964-4066; *Fax:*(276) 963-4927
Radio Stns: 1 AM. 2 FM.
WNRG Grundy, VA; WMJD Grundy, VA; WRIC-FM Richlands, VA

Pembrook Pines Media Group
1705 Lake St., Elmira NY 14901
(607) 733-5626; *Fax:*(607) 733-5627
Ownership: Robert J. Pfuntner, 100%. Company also owns Pembrook Pines Media agency.
Radio Stns: 5 AM. 7 FM.
WABH Bath, NY; WEHH Elmira Hts-Horsehds, NY; WELM Elmira, NY; WGGO Salamanca, NY; WOEN Olean, NY; WLVY Elmira, NY; WMXO Olean, NY; WOKN Southport, NY; WQRS Salamanca, NY; WZKZ Alfred, NY; WQRW Wellsville, NY; WZKZ(FM) Alfred, NY
Robert Pfuntner, President/CEO
Donna, Office Manager

Penfold Communications, Inc.
3232 West Macarthur Blvd, Santa Ana CA 92704
(714) 825-9663
Radio Stns: 9 FM.
KDKR Decatur, TX; KKRS Davenport, WA; KTWD Wallace, ID; KRTM Banning, CA; KYJC Commerce, TX; WJIK Fulton, AL; WKJA Brunswick, OH; WTPG Whitehouse, OH; WIGW Eustis, FL

Peninsula Communications Inc.
Box 109, Homer AK 99603
(907) 235-6000; *Fax:*(907) 235-6683
kwavefm@xyz.net
Ownership: David F. Becker, 50%; Eileen L. Becker, 50%.
Radio Stns: 2 AM. 3 FM.
KGTL Homer, AK; KGTL(AM) Homer, AK; KPEN-FM Soldotna, AK; KWVV-FM Homer, AK; KXBA Nikiski, AK
David Becker, General Manager
Tim White, Operations
Dave Webb, Production Manager

Perry Publishing & Broadcasting Co.
1457 N.E. 23rd St., Oklahoma City OK 73111
(405) 425-4100
www.perrybroadcasting.net
Radio Stns: 4 AM. 9 FM.
KGTO Tulsa, OK; KPNS Duncan, OK; KXCA Lawton, OK; WTHB Augusta, GA; KACO Apache, OK; KDDQ Comanche, OK; KJMM Bixby, OK; KJMZ Cache, OK; KVSP Anadarko, OK; WAEG Evans, GA; WAKB Hephzibah, GA; WTHB-FM Wrens, GA; WFXA-FM Augusta, GA
Russell Perry, CEO

Pharis Broadcasting Inc.
321 N. Greenwood, Fort Smith AR 72902
(479) 242-1047
www.kfpwam.com
Radio Stns: 2 AM. 3 FM.
KHGG Van Buren, AR; KFPW Fort Smith, AR; KQBK Booneville, AR; KFPW-FM Barling, AR; KHGG-FM Waldron, AR
William Pharis, CEO
Karen Pharis, General Manager

Phillips Broadcasting Inc.
100 Fisher Dr., Trinidad CO 81082
(719) 846-3355; *Fax:*(719) 846-4711
kcrt@adelphia.net
Radio Stns: 1 AM. 2 FM.
KCRT Trinidad, CO; KBKZ Raton, NM; KCRT-FM Trinidad, CO
David Phillips, President

Phoenix Media Communications Group
126 Brookline Ave., Boston MA 2215
(617) 536-5390; *Fax:*(617) 859-8201
www.thephoenix.com
Radio Stns: 1 AM. 1 FM.
WWSF Sanford, ME; WXEX-FM Sanford, ME
Stephen Mindich, CEO
Barry Morris, President

Piedmont Communications Inc.
Box 271, Orange VA 22960
(540) 672-1000; *Fax:*(540) 672-0282
Radio Stns: 2 AM. 2 FM.
WCVA Culpeper, VA; WVCV Orange, VA; WJMA Culpeper, VA; WOJL Louisa, VA

Pilgrim Communications Inc.
3402 C St. NE., Suite 101, Auburn WA 98002
(253) 887-8464; *Fax:*(253) 887-8661
www.pilgrimcommunicationsinc.com
Radio Stns: 3 AM. 2 FM.
KSKE Buena Vista, CO; KRCN Longmont, CO; KVLE Vail, CO; KVLE-FM Gunnison, CO; WFDM-FM Franklin, IN
Mick Whitecotton, President
Rick Johnson, Operations Dir

Pillar of Fire Inc.
Box 9058, Weston Canal Rd., Zarephath NJ 08890
(732) 469-0991; *Fax:*(732) 469-2115
www.star991fm.com
info@star991fm.com
Ownership: No stockholders; non-profit corporation.
Radio Stns: 1 AM. 2 FM.
KPOF Denver, CO; WAKW Cincinnati, OH; WAWZ Zarephath, NJ
Robert Dallenbach, Network President
Scott Taylor, Station Manager

Pines Broadcasting Inc.
1255 N. Myrtle St., Warren AR 71671
(870) 226-2653; *Fax:*(870) 226-3039
Radio Stns: 1 AM. 3 FM.
KHBM Monticello, AR; KGPQ Monticello, AR; KHBM-FM Monticello, AR; KXSA-FM Dermott, AR
Jimmy Sledge, President

Pittman Broadcasting Services LLC
307 S. Jefferson Ave., Covington LA 70433
(985) 892-3661
Radio Stns: 1 AM. 1 FM.
WOMN Franklinton, LA; WUUU Franklinton, LA
Marcus Pittman, President

Plant Broadcasting
114 Kent Rd., Tifton GA 31794
(229) 382-1340; *Fax:*(229) 386-8658
www.plantbroadcasting.com
Radio Stns: 1 AM. 2 FM.
WTIF Tifton, GA; WFFM Ashburn, GA; WTIF-FM Omega, GA
Nettie Hatcher, General Manager
David Nelson, Human Resources

Platte River Radio Inc.
Box 130, Kearney NE 68848
(308) 236-9900; *Fax:*(308) 234-6781
Radio Stns: 3 AM. 2 FM.
KHAS Hastings, NE; KICS Hastings, NE; KXPN Kearney, NE; KLIQ Hastings, NE; KKPR-FM Kearney, NE

PMB Broadcasting LLC
1820 Wynnton Rd., Columbus GA 31904
(706) 327-1217; *Fax:*(706) 596-4600
www.pmbbroadcasting.com

Radio Stns: 1 AM. 3 FM.
WRCG Columbus, GA; WCGQ Columbus, GA; WKCN Fort Benning South, GA; WRLD Valley, AL
Dave Arwood, Operations Dir
Helen Neal, Dir. of Sales

Point Broadcasting Company
2319 Alameda Ave., Suite 1-D, Ventura CA 93003
(805) 654-0414
pointbroadcastingllc.com
Radio Stns: 1 FM.
KSPE-FM Ellwood, CA
John Hearne, Chairman

Pollack Broadcasting
5500 Poplar Ave, Suite 1, Memphis TN 38119
(901) 685-3993; *Fax:*(901) 685-3995
pollackcompanies.net
comments@pollackcompanies.net
Ownership: William H. Pollack, 100%.
Radio Stns: 6 AM. 3 FM.
KBOA-AM Kennett, MO; KCRV-AM Caruthersville, MO; KMIS-AM Portageville, MO; KSHP North Las Vegas, NV; WBIG Aurora, IL; WRMN Elgin, IL; KBOA-FM Piggott, AR; KCRV-FM Caruthersville, MO; KTMO New Madrid, MO
TV Stns: 2 TV.
KIEM-TV Eureka, CA; KLAX-TV Alexandria, LA
William Pollack, President

Polnet Communications Ltd.
3656 W. Belmont Ave., Chicago IL 60618
(773) 588-6300; *Fax:*(773) 588-0834
www.pclradio.com
Ownership: Walter Kotaba, 100%.
Radio Stns: 7 AM.
WPJX Zion, IL; WEEF Deerfield, IL; WKTA Evanston, IL; WLIM Patchogue, NY; WNVR Vernon Hills, IL; WRKL New City, NY; WRXB St. Petersburg Beach, FL
Walter Kotaba, President

Porter County Broadcasting Corp.
2755 Sager Rd., Valparaiso IN 46383
(219) 462-8125
Radio Stns: 1 AM. 1 FM.
WAKE Valparaiso, IN; WXRD Crown Point, IN

Positive Alternative Radio Inc.
Box 889, Blacksburg VA 24063
(540) 552-4282; *Fax:*(540) 951-5282
www.parfm.com
Radio Stns: 22 FM.
WCQR-FM Kingsport, TN; WJYA Emporia, VA; WJYJ Fredericksburg, VA; WOKD-FM Danville, VA; WPAR Salem, VA; WPCN(FM) Point Pleasant, WV; WPER Culpeper, VA; WPIB Bluefield, WV; WPIM Martinsville, VA; WPIN-FM Dublin, VA; WPIR Hickory, NC; WPVA Waynesboro, VA; WRXT Roanoke, VA; WTJY Asheboro, NC; WTTX-FM Appomattox, VA; WXRI Winston-Salem, NC; WOKG Galax, VA; WHRX Nassawadox, VA; WRFE Chesterfield, SC; WPJY Blennerhassett, WV; WPJW Hurricane, WV; WKAO Ashland, KY
Edward Baker, President

Powell Broadcasting Co. L.L.C.
Box 788, Baton Rouge LA 70821-0788
(225) 922-4662; *Fax:*(225) 922-4544
Ownership: The Powell Group L.L.C., 100%.
Radio Stns: 2 AM. 8 FM.
KLEM Le Mars, IA; KSCJ Sioux City, IA; KKYY Whiting, IA; KKMA Le Mars, IA; KSUX Winnebago, NE; KQNU(FM) Onawa, IA; WASJ Panama City Beach, FL; WPFM-FM Panama City, FL; WRBA Springfield, FL; WKNK(FM) Callaway, FL
Thomas J. Spies, COO
Nanette Noland, President

Prairie Radio Communications
205 N. Second St., Dekalb IL 60115
(815) 517-0845
www.prcmedia.net
Radio Stns: 5 AM. 5 FM.
KCLN Clinton, IA; KWPC Muscatine, IA; WAIK Galesburg, IL; WBYS Canton, IL; WRAM Monmouth, IL; KMCS Muscatine, IA; KMCN Clinton, IA; WCDD Canton, IL; WMOI Monmouth, IL; WSLD Whitewater, WI
Vanessa Wetterling, President/CEO

Premier Broadcasters
1133 Kresky, Centralia WA 98531
(360) 736-1355; *Fax:*(360) 736-4761
www.live95.com
Ownership: Rod Etherton.
Radio Stns: 1 AM. 3 FM.
KITI Chehalis-Centralia, WA; KITI-FM Winlock, WA; KRXY Shelton, WA; KRZY-FM Santa Fe, NM
Rod Etherton, President

Prescott Valley Broadcasting Co. Inc.
Box 26523, Prescott Valley AZ 86312
(928) 445-8289; *Fax:*(928) 442-0448
Radio Stns: 1 AM. 3 FM.
KQNA Prescott Valley, AZ; KDDL Chino Valley, AZ; KPPV Prescott Valley, AZ; KPKR Parker, AZ

Press Communications L.L.C.
1329 Campus Pkwy., Suite 106, Wall NJ 07753-6815
(732) 751-1119; *Fax:*(732) 751-1726
Radio Stns: 1 AM. 4 FM.
WHTG Eatontown, NJ; WBBO(FM) Ocean Acres, NJ; WBHX Tuckerton, NJ; WKMK Eatontown, NJ; WWZY Long Branch, NJ

Prieto Broadcasting Inc.
Box 48122, Doraville GA 30362
(770) 825-0095; *Fax:*(770) 246-0054
Radio Stns: 2 AM.
WETC Wendell-Zebulon, NC; WFTD Marietta, GA
Filiberto Prieto, CEO
Franco Vera, General Sales Mgr

Priority Communications
2307 Pennsylvania Ave., Weirton WV 26062
(304) 723-1444; *Fax:*(304) 723-1688
www.prioritycommunications.net
sunny106@penn.com
Radio Stns: 2 AM. 2 FM.
WCED Du Bois, PA; WEIR Weirton, WV; WCDK Cadiz, OH; WDSN Reynoldsville, PA
Jay Philippone, President

Priority Radio Inc.
Box 5204, Wilmington DE 19808-5204
(302) 731-7270; *Fax:*(302) 738-3090
www.thereachfm.com
Radio Stns: 1 AM. 4 FM.
WSRY Elkton, MD; WXHL-FM Christiana, DE; WVBH Beach Haven West, NJ; KXRL Cherry Valley, AR; WXHM Middletown, DE

Pritchard Broadcasting Corp.
610 N. 4th St., Suite 300, Burlington IA 52601
(319) 752-5402; *Fax:*(319) 752-4715
www.kbur.com
johnp@burlingtonradio.com
Radio Stns: 2 AM. 4 FM.
KBKB Fort Madison, IA; KBUR Burlington, IA; KDMG Burlington, IA; KKMI Burlington, IA; WQKQ Carthage, IL; KHDK New London, IA
Joe Bates, Operations Dir
John Pritchard, General Manager
Chet Young, General Sales Mgr
Steve Hexom, Programming Director
Rob Sussman, News Director

Programmers Broadcasting Inc.
Box 28, Bottineau ND 58318-0028
(701) 228-5151; *Fax:*(701) 228-2483
Radio Stns: 3 FM.
KBTO Bottineau, ND; KWGO Burlington, ND; KTZU Velva, ND

Progressive Broadcasting System Inc.
P.O. Box 307, Elkhart IN 46515
(574) 875-5166
www.wfrn.com
comments@wfrn.com
Radio Stns: 1 AM. 2 FM.
WCMR Elkhart, IN; WFRI Winamac, IN; WFRN-FM Elkhart, IN
Ed Moore, President

Prophecy Media Group LLC
6401 Cobbs Dr., Waco TX 76710
(254) 772-6104
Ownership: William W. McCutchen III.
Radio Stns: 2 FM.
KWPW Robinson, TX; KWOW Clifton, TX
William McCutchen, President

Public Reality Radio
3777 - 44th St SE, Grand Rapids MI 49512
(616) 656-1680; *Fax:*(616) 656-2158
www.publicrealityradio.org
info@publicrealityradio.org
Radio Stns: 1 AM. 2 FM.
WPRR Ada, MI; WPJC Pontiac, IL; WPRR-FM Clyde Township, MI
Robert Goodrich, President
Darren Gibson, Programming Director

Qantum Communications Corp.
1266 E. Main St., 6th Fl., Stamford CT 6902
(203) 388-0048
Radio Stns: 1 AM. 2 FM.
WPLV West Point, GA; WBGA St. Simons Island, GA; WWAV Santa Rosa Beach, FL
Michael Mangan, CFO
Frank Osborn, President

Quarnstrom Media Group LLC
1104 Cloquet Ave., Cloquet MN 55720
(218) 879-4534; *Fax:*(218) 879-1962
Ownership: Alan & Linda Quarnstrom, 100%.
Radio Stns: 3 AM. 4 FM.
KCUE Red Wing, MN; WCMP Pine City, MN; WKLK Cloquet, MN; WMOZ Moose Lake, MN; KWNG Red Wing, MN; WCMP-FM Pine City, MN; WKLK-FM Cloquet, MN
Alan Quarnstrom, President
Don Welch, VP

Quincy Media, Inc.
130 S. Fifth St., Quincy IL 62301
(217) 223-5100; *Fax:*(217) 223-5019
www.qni.biz
Radio Stns: 1 AM. 1 FM.
WGEM Quincy, IL; WGEM-FM Quincy, IL
TV Stns: 12 TV.
KTIV Sioux City, IA; KTTC Rochester, MN; KWWL Waterloo, IA; WAOW Wausau, WI; WGEM-TV Quincy, IL; WKOW Madison, WI; WQOW-DT Eau Claire, WI; WREX-TV Rockford, IL; WSJV Elkhart, IN; WVVA Bluefield, WV; WXOW La Crosse, WI; WYOW Eagle River, WI
Thomas Oakley, President

Quinte Broadcasting Ltd.
10 South Front St., Box 488, Belleville ON K8N 5B2
(613) 969-5555; *Fax:*(613) 969-8122
www.quintenews.com
billmorton@mix97.com
Ownership: Herbert M. Morton, 66.67%; Joyce Mulock, 33.33%.
Radio Stns: 1 AM. 2 FM.
CJBQ Belleville, ON; CIGL-FM Belleville, ON; CJTN-FM Trenton, ON
Bill Morton, CEO/COO
Jody Brooker, General Sales Mgr

RAAD Broadcasting Corp
Hc 71 Box, Bayamono PR 00956
(787) 269-1000
www.lax.fm
Radio Stns: 2 FM.
WXLX Lajas, PR; WXYX Bayamon, PR
Roberto Davila, President

Radio Billings, LLC
222 N. 32nd St., 10th Fl., Billings MT 59101
(406) 238-1098
Radio Stns: 2 FM.
KYSX Billings, MT; KRPM Billings, MT
Terry Strickland, General Manager
Kyle McCoy, Programming Director

Radio Cleveland Inc.
Drawer 780, Cleveland MS 38732
(662) 843-4091; *Fax:*(662) 843-9805
wcld@tecinfo.com
Ownership: Homer Sledge Jr., pres, 37.1/5%; Kevin W. Cox, treas, 37.1/2%; Clint L. Webster, gen mgr, 37.1/2%.
Radio Stns: 1 AM. 2 FM.
WCLD Cleveland, MS; WAID Clarksdale, MS; WMJW Rosedale, MS
Clint Webster, General Manager

Radio Dubuque Inc.
Box 659, Dubuque IA 52004
(563) 690-0800; *Fax:*(563) 588-5688
Radio Stns: 1 AM. 3 FM.
KDTH Dubuque, IA; KATF Dubuque, IA; KGRR Epworth, IA; WVRE Dickeyville, WI
Thomas Parsley, General Manager

Radio Fargo-Moorhead Inc.
Box 9439, Fargo ND 58106-9439
(701) 277-4200
Radio Stns: 2 AM. 4 FM.

KBMW Breckenridge, MN; KQWB West Fargo, ND; KBVB Barnesville, MN; KQWB-FM Breckenridge, MN; KPFX Fargo, ND; KLTA-FM Moorhead, MN

Radio Free Ministries, Inc.
radiofreeministries.com
Radio Stns: 1 FM.
KRSS Tarkio, MO

Radio Greeneville Inc.
Box 278, 1004 Arnold Rd., Greeneville TN 37744
(423) 638-4147; *Fax:*(423) 638-1979
www.greeneville.com\wgrv
wgrv@greeneville.com
Radio Stns: 2 AM. 1 FM.
WGRV Greeneville, TN; WSMG Greeneville, TN; WIKQ Tusculum, TN
Ronnie Metcalfe, President

Radio La Grande
1010 Vermont Ave. N.W., Suite 100, Washington DC 20005
(202) 638-1959; *Fax:*(202) 393-7464
radiolagrande.net
Radio Stns: 7 AM.
WGSB Mebane, NC; WLLY Wilson, NC; WLNR Kinston, NC; WREV Reidsville, NC; WRTG Garner, NC; WLLQ Chapel Hill, NC; WSRP Jacksonville, NC
Ronald Metcalfe, President

Radio Maria Inc.
601 Washington St., Alexandria LA 71301
(318) 561-6145; *Fax:*(318) 449-9954
www.radiomaria.us
info.usa@radiomaria.org
Radio Stns: 4 AM. 3 FM.
KDEI Port Arthur, TX; KJMJ Alexandria, LA; KNIR New Iberia, LA; WULM Springfield, OH; KBIO Natchitoches, LA; KOJO Lake Charles, LA; WHJM Anna, OH

Radio One Inc.
1010 Wayne Ave., 14th Floor, Silver Spring MD 20910
(301) 306-1111; *Fax:*(301) 306-9426
www.radio-one.com
Ownership: Alfred C. Liggins, 39.4% of voting shares; Catherine L. Hughes, 16.7% of voting shares.
Radio Stns: 11 AM. 44 FM.
WCHB Taylor, MI; WJMO Cleveland, OH; WTPS Petersburg, VA; WILD Boston, MA; WERE Cleveland Heights, OH; WOL Washington, DC; WOLB Baltimore, MD; WTLC Indianapolis, IN; WDBZ Cincinnati, OH; WWIN Baltimore, MD; WYCB Washington, DC; KBFB Dallas, TX; KBXX Houston, TX; KSOC Gainesville, TX; KMJQ Houston, TX; KROI Seabrook, TX; WQNC Harrisburg, NC; WOSF Gaffney, SC; WAMJ Roswell, GA; WPZE Mableton, GA; WHOK-FM Circleville, OH; WTLC-FM Greenwood, IN; WPZS Harrisburg, NC; WCDX Mechanicsville, VA; WCKX Columbus, OH; WXMG London, OH; WPZR Mount Clemens, MI; WDMK Detroit, MI; WENZ Cleveland, OH; WERQ-FM Baltimore, MD; WFUN-FM Bethalto, IL; WFXC Durham, NC; WFXK Bunn, NC; WGPR Detroit, MI; WHHH Indianapolis, IN; WZOH-FM Lancaster, OH; WUMJ Fayetteville, GA; WOSL Norwood, OH; WIZF Erlanger, KY; WKJS Richmond, VA; WPZZ Crewe, VA; WKYS Washington, DC; WMMJ Bethesda, MD; WNNL Fuquay-Varina, NC; WHTA Hampton, GA; WPPZ-FM Jenkintown, PA; WPHI-FM Pennsauken, NJ; WKJM Petersburg, VA; WQOK Carrboro, NC; WRNB Media, PA; WWIN-FM Glen Burnie, MD; WPRS-FM Waldorf, MD; WHHL Hazelwood, MO; WNOW Speedway, IN; WZAK Cleveland, OH
Catherine Hughes, Chairman
Alfred Liggins, President/CEO

Radio Palouse Inc.
Box 1, Pullman WA 99163
(509) 332-6551; *Fax:*(509) 332-5151
khtr@aol.com
Radio Stns: 1 AM.
KQQQ Pullman, WA
Bill Weed, General Manager

Radio Partners LLC
Box 719, Beaver Falls PA 15010
(724) 846-4100; *Fax:*(724) 843-7771
kibcoradio.com
Radio Stns: 1 AM. 2 FM.
WNAE Warren, PA; WKNB Clarendon, PA; WRRN Warren, PA
Dave Whipple, General Sales Mgr

Radio Rancho, LLC
5660 E. Franklin Rd., Suite 305, Nampa ID 83687
(208) 713-7269
Radio Stns: 2 FM.
KQTA Homedale, ID; KPDA Mountain Home, ID
Kevin Terry, Owner

Radio Vermont Group Inc.
9 Stowe St., P.O. Box 550, Waterbury VT 05676
(802) 244-7321; *Fax:*(802) 244-1771
wdevradio.com
ksquier@radiovermont.com
Radio Stns: 1 AM. 4 FM.
WDEV Waterbury, VT; WCVT Stowe, VT; WDEV-FM Warren, VT; WEXP Brandon, VT; WLVB Morrisville, VT
Ken Squier, President
Charlotte Strasser, Operations Dir
Steve Cormier, Station Manager

Radio Works Inc.
111 Westwood Dr., De Queen AR 71832
(870) 642-3637
Radio Stns: 3 FM.
KAMD-FM Camden, AR; KCXY East Camden, AR; KMGC Camden, AR

Radioactive LLC
1717 Dixie Hwy., Suite 650, Fort Wright KY 41011
(859) 331-9100
Radio Stns: 16 FM.
WUPF Powers, MI; WUPG Republic, MI; WUPZ Chocolay Township, MI; WUPT Gwinn, MI; WKFC North Corbin, KY; WPBK Crab Orchard, KY; KMML Cimarron, KS; KRMR Hays, KS; KDJM Lindsborg, KS; WZXP Au Sable, NY; WRAX Lake Isabella, MI; KYME Rockford, IA; KEWS(FM) Sac City, IA; WNMR Dannemora, NY; WBLH Black River, NY; WPLB Plattsburgh West, NY
Randy Michaels, CEO/COO

RadioJones LLC
Box 5356, Atlanta GA 31107-5356
(404) 432-1450
www.radiojones.com
dj@radiojones.com
Radio Stns: 2 AM. 2 FM.
WJAT Swainsboro, GA; WXRS Swainsboro, GA; WEDB East Dublin, GA; WXRS-FM Portal, GA
Dennis Jones, President

RadioStar Inc.
781 Bolsana Dr., Laguna Beach CA 92651-4124
(915) 715-9770
Radio Stns: 4 FM.
WSJK(FM) Tuscola, IL; WGKC Mahomet, IL; WQQB Rantoul, IL; WJEK(FM) Rantoul, IL
Jim Glassman, President

Rama Communications Inc.
3765 N. John Young Pkwy., Orlando FL 32804
(407) 291-1395
Radio Stns: 3 AM.
WRFV Valdosta, GA; WQBQ Leesburg, FL; WMEL Cocoa Beach, FL
Shanti Persaud, President

Ramar Communications II Ltd.
9800 University Ave., Lubbock TX 79423
(806) 748-2404; *Fax:*(806) 748-2470
www.lubbockradioadvertising.com
Ownership: Ray Moran, 51%; Brad Moran, 49%.
Radio Stns: 1 AM. 3 FM.
KJTV Lubbock, TX; KLZK New Deal, TX; KTTU Brownfield, TX; KXTQ Lubbock, TX
TV Stns: 2 TV.
KUPT Hobbs, NM; KJTV Lubbock, TX
Ray Moran, Chairman
Brad Moran, President

Randy Sheffield-Wayne Bishop
700 W. 23rd St., Panama City Beach FL 32405
(850) 235-2195; *Fax:*(850) 235-2795
www.beach951.com
Ownership: Randy Sheffield and Wayne Bishop, 100%.
Radio Stns: 1 FM.
WBPC Ebro, FL
Randy Sheffield, President

Rawlco Radio Ltd.
715 Saskatchewan Cres. W, Saskatoon SK S7M 5V7
(306) 934-2222; *Fax:*(306) 477-0002
www.rawlco.com
kwerner@rawlco.com
Ownership: Gordon S. Rawlinson, 100%.
Radio Stns: 2 AM. 5 FM.
CKOM Saskatoon, SK; CJME Regina, SK; CFMC-FM Saskatoon, SK; CIZL-FM Regina, SK; CJDJ-FM Saskatoon, SK; CKCK-FM Regina, SK; CHUP-FM Calgary, AB
Gordon Rawlinson, CEO
Pam Leyland, President
Kristy Werner, VP & General Manager of Rawlco Saskatoon
Christine Thille, General Sales Mgr
Bret Donnelly, Senior Advertising Consultant

Red Rock Radio Corp.
501 Lake Ave. S., Suite 200, Duluth MN 55802
(218) 728-9500
www.redrockradio.org
Radio Stns: 4 AM. 12 FM.
KGHS International Falls, MN; KKIN Aitkin, MN; KRBT Eveleth, MN; WHSM Hayward, WI; KAOD Babbitt, MN; KBAJ Deer River, MN; KGPZ Coleraine, MN; KKIN-FM Aitkin, MN; KSDM International Falls, MN; KFGI Crosby, MN; KZIO Two Harbors, MN; WXCX Siren, WI; WHSM-FM Hayward, WI; WWAX Hermantown, MN; WLMX-FM Balsam Lake, WI; WXXZ Grand Marais, MN
Romeo Grignon, CEO/COO
Shawn Skramstad, President

Red Zebra Holdings LLC
21300 Redskin Park Dr., Ashburn VA 20147
(703) 726-7015
www.espn980.com
Radio Stns: 5 AM. 3 FM.
WXTG Hampton, VA; WTNT Alexandria, VA; WWRC Washington, DC; WTEM Washington, DC; WXGI Richmond, VA; WXTG-FM Virginia Beach, VA; WWXT Prince Frederick, MD; WWXX Warrenton, VA

Redwood Empire Broadcasters
Box 100, Santa Rosa CA 95402
(707) 528-4434; *Fax:*(707) 284-9114
Ownership: Gordon D. Zlot Revocable Trust, 98% of assets; Gordon D. Zlot trustee, 98% votes.
Radio Stns: 3 FM.
KJZY Sebastopol, CA; KZST Santa Rosa, CA; KTRY(FM) Cazadero, CA
Gordon D. Zlot, President

Regional Media, A Virden Broadcasting Corporation
1020 Lincoln Rd, Bettendorf IA 52722
(563) 345-6454
www.regionalmedia.info
Radio Stns: 1 AM. 7 FM.
WKEI Kewanee, IL; WJRE Galva, IL; WJEQ Macomb, IL; KQCJ Cambridge, IL; WKAI Macomb, IL; WLMD Bushnell, IL; WMQZ Colchester, IL; WNLF Macomb, IL
Fletcher M. Ford, President & CEO
Jason Gilbraith, Vice President - Macomb/Kewanee/Quad Cities
Sean Patrick Kernan, Corporate Program Director

Regional Radio Group LLC
128 Glen St., Glens Falls NY 12801
(518) 761-9890; *Fax:*(518) 761-9893
www.radiowins.com
Radio Stns: 1 AM. 2 FM.
WWSC Glens Falls, NY; WCKM-FM Lake George, NY; WCQL Queensbury, NY
Clay Ashworth, General Manager

Reier Broadcasting Co. Inc.
Box 20, Bozeman MT 59718
(406) 587-9999; *Fax:*(406) 587-5855
Radio Stns: 2 AM. 3 FM.
KBOZ Bozeman, MT; KOBB Bozeman, MT; KOBB-FM Bozeman, MT; KOZB Livingston, MT; KBOZ-FM Bozeman, MT

Relevant Radio
PO Box 10707, Green Bay WI 54307-0707
(800) 342-0306; *Fax:*(920) 469-3023
www.relevantradio.com
info@relevantradio.com
Radio Stns: 9 AM. 4 FM.
KIXL Del Valle, TX; WAUR Sandwich, IL; WDVM Eau Claire, WI; WHFA Poynette, WI; WJOK Kaukauna, WI; WKBH Holmen, WI; WLOL Minneapolis, MN; WNTD Chicago, IL; WWCA Gary, IN; WPJP Port Washington, WI; WOVM Appleton, WI; WMMA Nekoosa, WI; WYNW Birnamwood, WI
Mark Follett, CEO

Renda Broadcasting Corp.
900 Parish Street, 4th Fl, Pittsburgh PA 15220

(412) 875-1800; *Fax:*(412) 875-1801
Ownership: S.F. Renda, 100%.
Radio Stns: 4 AM. 13 FM.
WCCS Homer City, PA; WDAD Indiana, PA; WECZ Punxsutawney, PA; WJAS Pittsburgh, PA; KHTT Muskogee, OK; WJGO Tice, FL; WKQL Brookville, PA; WEJZ Jacksonville, FL; WGNE-FM Middleburg, FL; WGUF Marco, FL; WLCY Blairsville, PA; WQMU Indiana, PA; WSGL Naples, FL; WSHH Pittsburgh, PA; WSOS-FM Fruit Cove, FL; WWGR Fort Myers, FL; WMUV Brunswick, GA
Anthony Renda, President
Maryann Kelly, VP/Controller
Alan Serena, VP Operations
Judy Reich, VP Sales

Results Broadcasting
1456 E. Green Bay St., Shawano WI 54166
(715) 524-2194; *Fax:*(715) 524-9980
Radio Stns: 3 AM. 8 FM.
WATK Antigo, WI; WOTE Clintonville, WI; WTCH Shawano, WI; WACD Antigo, WI; WCYE Three Lakes, WI; WJMQ Clintonville, WI; WJNR-FM Iron Mountain, MI; WOBE Crystal Falls, MI; WOWN Shawano, WI; WHTO Iron Mountain, MI; WHOH Rhinelander, WI
Bruce Grassman, President

Revolution Broadcast Company of the West
2125 Sidney Baker North, Kerrville TX 78028
(830) 896-1230; *Fax:*(830) 792-4142
Radio Stns: 2 AM. 4 FM.
KERV Kerrville, TX; KMBL Junction, TX; KHOS-FM Sonora, TX; KOOK Junction, TX; KRVL Kerrville, TX; KYXX Ozona, TX
David Greenwald, President

Reynolds Radio Inc.
212 Old Grand Blvd., Suite B100, Tyler TX 75703
(903) 581-5259
theblaze.fm
Radio Stns: 3 FM.
KBLZ Winona, TX; KAPW White Oak, TX; KAZE Ore City, TX
Ken Reynolds, President
Chris Reynolds, Operations Dir

Rhattigan Broadcasting (Texas) LP
Box 1420, Plainview TX 79073
(806) 853-9147; *Fax:*(815) 346-2084
Radio Stns: 5 AM. 7 FM.
KBST Big Spring, TX; KEPS Eagle Pass, TX; KVOP Plainview, TX; KREW Plainview, TX; KGWU Uvalde, TX; KBST-FM Big Spring, TX; KBTS Big Spring, TX; KINL Eagle Pass, TX; KKYN-FM Plainview, TX; KUVA Uvalde, TX; KRIA Plainview, TX; KVOU-FM Uvalde, TX

Rich Broadcasting LLC
1401 E. Stillwood Dr., Salt Lake City UT 84117
(801) 277-6139; *Fax:*(801) 294-5145
richbroadcasting.com
Ownership: Richard O. Mecham, 38.4%; Trevor Larsen, 9.6%; Mark Nelson, 8%.
Radio Stns: 4 AM. 15 FM.
KID Idaho Falls, ID; KRXK Rexburg, ID; KSGT Jackson, WY; KWIK Pocatello, ID; KJAX Jackson, WY; KQEZ(FM) Shelley, ID; KECH-FM Sun Valley, ID; KGTM Rexburg, ID; KID-FM Idaho Falls, ID; KLLP Chubbuck, ID; KMTN Jackson, WY; KPKY Pocatello, ID; KSKI-FM Sun Valley, ID; KOUW(FM) Island Park, ID; KZJH Jackson, WY; KYZK Sun Valley, ID; KCHQ Driggs, ID; KEGE Pocatello, ID; KZKY(FM) Ucon, ID
Richard O. Mecham, Manager

Rincon Broadcasting LLC
414 E. Cota St., Santa Barbara CA 93101
(805) 879-8300; *Fax:*(805) 879-8430
www.rinconbroadcasting.com
Ownership: Point Broadcasting Co., 95%.
Radio Stns: 1 AM. 3 FM.
KTMS Santa Barbara, CA; KIST-FM Carpinteria, CA; KSBL Isla Vista, CA; KTYD Santa Barbara, CA

Riverbend Communications LLC
2880 N. 55th W., Idaho Falls ID 83402
(208) 528-6635
Radio Stns: 2 AM. 4 FM.
KBLI Blackfoot, ID; KBLY Idaho Falls, ID; KCVI Blackfoot, ID; KFTZ Idaho Falls, ID; KLCE Blackfoot, ID; KTHK Idaho Falls, ID

Riviera Broadcast Group LLC
3333 Sierra Oaks Dr., Sacramento CA 95864-5738
(916) 768-8049; *Fax:*(480) 247-5123
www.rivierabroadcast.com
Radio Stns: 2 FM.
KKFR Mayer, AZ; KEXX(FM) Gilbert, AZ
Chris Maguire, CFO
Tim Pohlman, President

RNC MEDIA Inc.
1 Place Ville Marie, Suite 1523, Montr,al QC H3B 2B5
(514) 866-8686; *Fax:*(514) 866-8056
www.rncmedia.ca
info@rncmedia.ca
Ownership: Groupe Radio Nord Inc., 100%.
Radio Stns: 11 FM.
CHOA-FM Rouyn-Noranda, QC; CHPR-FM Hawkesbury, ON; CJLA-FM Lachute, QC; CHXX-FM Donnacona, QC; CHGO-FM Val d'Or, QC; CHLX-FM Gatineau, QC; CKVM-FM Ville-Marie, QC; CKLX-FM Montr,al, QC; CFTX-FM Gatineau, QC; CHOI-FM Quebec, QC; CJGO-FM La Sarre, QC
TV Stns: 5 TV.
CFGS-DT Gatineau, QC; CFVS-DT Val-d'Or, QC; CHOT-DT Gatineau, QC; CKRN-DT Rouyn-Noranda, QC; CFEM-DT Rouyn-Noranda, QC
Pierre R. Brosseau, Executive Chairman
Raynald BriŠre, Executive Vice President
Robert Ranger, VP Operations, Finance & Administration

RNC Media Saguenay-Lac-St-Jean
345, Rue des Saguen,ens, Ville de Saguenay QC G7H 6K9
(418) 543-8912
www.rncmedia.ca
info@rncmedia.ca
Ownership: RNC Media Inc., 75% (See Listing); 9150-2898 Quebec inc., 25%.
Radio Stns: 5 FM.
CHVD-FM Dolbeau-Mistassini, QC; CKYK-FM Alma, QC; CHRL-FM Roberval, QC; CKXO-FM Chibougamau, QC; CFGT-FM Alma, QC
Marc-Andre Levesque, President

Robert Ingstad Broadcast Properties
Box 994, Valley City ND 58072
(701) 845-1490; *Fax:*(701) 845-1245
Ownership: the estate of Robert E. Ingstad, Janice M. Ingstad, Robert J. Ingstad and Todd M. Ingstad.
Radio Stns: 8 AM. 13 FM.
KBUF Holcomb, KS; KDAK Carrington, ND; KDDR Oakes, ND; KGFX Pierre, SD; KOLY Mobridge, SD; KOVC Valley City, ND; KQDJ Jamestown, ND; KULY Ulysses, KS; KFXX-FM Hugoton, KS; KGFX-FM Pierre, SD; KKJQ Garden City, KS; KMLO Lowry, SD; KPLO-FM Reliance, SD; KQZZ Devils Lake, ND; KSKL Scott City, KS; KWKR Leoti, KS; KSSA Ingalls, KS; KYNU Jamestown, ND; KSKZ Copeland, KS; KRVX Wimbledon, ND; KJBI Fort Pierre, SD

Roberts Broadcasting Co.
1408 N. Kingshighway Blvd., St. Louis MO 63113
(314) 367-4600
www.thebeatofthecapital.com
Ownership: St. Louis/Denver LLC.
Radio Stns: 1 FM.
WRBJ Brandon, MS
Michael Roberts, CEO
Steven Roberts, President

Robinson Corporation
WI
(608) 326-2411; *Fax:*(608) 326-2412
www.wqpcradio.com
wqpcwpre@mwt.net
Radio Stns: 2 AM. 3 FM.
WPRE Prairie Du Chien, WI; WVRQ Viroqua, WI; WQPC Prairie Du Chien, WI; WVRQ-FM Viroqua, WI; WKPO Soldiers Grove, WI
David Robinson, President
Jeff Robinson, General Manager

Rocking M Radio Inc.
4806 Vue du Lac Place, Suite B, Manhattan KS 66503
(785) 565-0406; *Fax:*(785) 565-0437
www.rockingmradio.com
Radio Stns: 5 AM. 8 FM.
KGNO Dodge City, KS; KNNS Larned, KS; KMMM Pratt, KS; KXXX Colby, KS; KSMM Liberal, KS; KERP Ingalls, KS; KSOB Larned, KS; KZUH Minneapolis, KS; KAHE Dodge City, KS; KVOB Lindsborg, KS; KZRD Dodge City, KS; KSMM-FM Liberal, KS; KZRS Great Bend, KS
Monte Miller, President
Christopher Miller, Operations Dir
Doris Miller, Tresurer/Secretary

Rodgers Broadcasting Corp.
Box 1646, Richmond IN 47374
(765) 962-6533; *Fax:*(765) 966-1499
Ownership: David Rodgers, 100%.
Radio Stns: 2 AM. 2 FM.
WBML Macon, GA; WLPK Connersville, IN; WIFE-FM Rushville, IN; WZZY Winchester, IN
David Rodgers, President

Rogers Media
1 Ted Rogers Way, Toronto ON M4Y 3B7
(416) 935-8200; *Fax:*(416) 864-2002
www.rogersmedia.com
lvelazquez@impulsemediasales.com
Ownership: Rogers Media Inc., 100%. Note: Rogers Media Inc. is 100% owned by Rogers Communications Inc.
Radio Stns: 8 AM. 48 FM.
CFAC Calgary, AB; CFFR Calgary, AB; CFTR Toronto, ON; CIWW Ottawa, ON; CJCL Toronto, ON; CKAT North Bay, ON; CKGL Kitchener, ON; CKWX Vancouver, BC; CFLT-FM Dartmouth, NS; CFGP-FM Grande Prairie, AB; CKBY-FM Smiths Falls, ON; CFRV-FM Lethbridge, AB; CKSR-FM Chilliwack, BC; CHAS-FM Sault Ste. Marie, ON; CHEZ-FM Ottawa, ON; CHFI-FM Toronto, ON; CHFM-FM Calgary, AB; CHUR-FM North Bay, ON; CHYM-FM Kitchener, ON; CIOC-FM Victoria, BC; CIPN-FM Pender Harbour, BC; CISC-FM Gibsons, BC; CKKS-FM Chilliwack, BC; CISP-FM Pemberton, BC; CISQ-FM Squamish, BC; CJAQ-FM Calgary, AB; CISW-FM Whistler, BC; CITI-FM Winnipeg, MB; CHMN-FM Canmore, AB; CJMX-FM Sudbury, ON; CJQM-FM Sault Ste. Marie, ON; CJQQ-FM Timmins, ON; CJRQ-FM Sudbury, ON; CISS-FM Ottawa, ON; CKER-FM Edmonton, AB; CKFX-FM North Bay, ON; CKIS-FM Toronto, ON; CJAX-FM Vancouver, BC; CHTT-FM Victoria, BC; CFUN-FM Sechelt, BC; CKYX-FM Fort McMurray, AB; CJOK-FM Fort McMurray, AB; CHST-FM London, ON; CJET-FM Smiths Falls, ON; CJRX-FM Lethbridge, AB; CFSR-FM Hope, BC; CIKR-FM Kingston, ON; CKGB-FM Timmins, ON; CKQC-FM Abbotsford, BC; CKY-FM Winnipeg, MB; CIKZ-FM Kitchener, ON; CHDI-FM Edmonton, AB; CHBN-FM Edmonton, AB; CJNI-FM Halifax, NS; CKXC-FM Kingston, ON; CKMH-FM Medicine Hat, AB
TV Stns: 11 TV.
CFMT-DT Toronto, ON; CHMI-DT Portage la Prairie, MB; CITY-DT Toronto, ON; CJNT-DT Montr,al, QC; CKAL-DT Calgary, AB; CKEM-DT Edmonton, AB; CKVU-DT Vancouver, BC; CJMT-DT Toronto, ON; CHNM-DT Vancouver, BC; CJEO-DT Edmonton, AB; CJCO-DT Calgary, AB
Alan Horn, Chairman
Joe Natale, President & CEO
Derek Berghuis, General Management, Operations, Sales

Rooney Moon Broadcasting Inc.
208 E. Grand Ave., Clovis NM 88101
(505) 763-4649; *Fax:*(505) 763-1693
www.bettermix.com
info.rmb@yucca.net
Radio Stns: 1 AM. 3 FM.
KSEL Portales, NM; KSEL-FM Portales, NM; KSMX-FM Clovis, NM; KRMQ-FM Clovis, NM
Steve Rooney, President

Roser Communications Network Inc.
185 Genessee St., Suite 1600, Utica NY 13501
(315) 734-9245; *Fax:*(315) 624-9245
Ownership: Kenneth F. Roser, 100%.
Radio Stns: 1 AM. 5 FM.
WRCK Remsen, NY; WBGK Newport Village, NY; WVTL Amsterdam, NY; WBUG-FM Fort Plain, NY; WSKU Little Falls, NY; WSKS Whitesboro, NY
Ken Roser, President

Roswell Radio Inc./Quay Broadcasters Inc.
Box 670, Roswell NM 88202
(505) 622-6450; *Fax:*(505) 622-9041
Radio Stns: 2 AM. 4 FM.
KBCQ Roswell, NM; KTNM Tucumcari, NM; KBCQ-FM Roswell, NM; KMOU Roswell, NM; KQAY-FM Tucumcari, NM; KSFX Roswell, NM
John Dunn, President

RR Broadcasting
2100 E. Tahquitz Canyon Way, Palm Springs CA 92262
(760) 325-2582; *Fax:*(760) 322-3562
Radio Stns: 2 AM. 3 FM.
KPSI Palm Springs, CA; KPTR Palm Springs, CA; KDES-FM Cathedral City, CA; KGAM Merced, CA; KPSI-FM Palm Springs, CA
Mike Keane, General Manager

Rubber City Radio Group Inc.
1795 W. Market St., Akron OH 44313

(330) 869-9800; *Fax:*(330) 864-6799
www.wqmx.com
Ownership: Morton L. Mandel, 52%; Barbara A. Mandel, trustee under The Living Trust Between Thomas Mandel and Barbara Mandel FTB Thomas Mandel, 48%.
Radio Stns: 1 AM. 3 FM.
WAKR Akron, OH; WNWV Elyria, OH; WONE-FM Akron, OH; WQMX Medina, OH
Thomas A. Mandel, President/Treasurer/General Manager
Nick Anthony, Vice President

Ruby Radio Corp.
1750 Manzanita, Suite 1, Elko NV 89801
(775) 777-1196; *Fax:*(775) 777-9587
Radio Stns: 3 FM.
KHIX Carlin, NV; KZBI Elko, NV; KBGZ Spring Creek, NV
Ken Sutherland, President

RZ Radio LLC
352 E. Ave. K-4, Lancaster CA 93535
(661) 942-1121
Ownership: Saul Rosenzweig.
Radio Stns: 2 AM. 1 FM.
KTPI Mojave, CA; KAVL Lancaster, CA; KTPI-FM Mojave, CA
Saul Rosenzweig, President

Saga Communications Inc.
73 Kercheval Ave., Suite 201, Grosse Pointe Farms MI 48236
(313) 886-7070; *Fax:*(313) 886-7150
sagacom.com
Ownership: Edward K. Christian, 56.5% of the voting stock. Other Interests: Illinois Radio Network, Michigan Radio Network, Michigan Farm Radio Network.
Radio Stns: 28 AM. 60 FM.
KGMI Bellingham, WA; KICD Spencer, IA; KBAI Bellingham, WA; KPUG Bellingham, WA; KRNT Des Moines, IA; KPSZ Des Moines, IA; WLFZ Fort Campbell, KY; WBAE Portland, ME; WBCO Bucyrus, OH; WKFN Clarksville, TN; WFEA Manchester, NH; WGAN Portland, ME; WHMQ Greenfield, MA; WHCU Ithaca, NY; WHMP Northampton, MA; WGIN Biddeford, ME; WINA Charlottesville, VA; WJOI Norfolk, VA; WJYI Milwaukee, WI; WZBK Keene, NH; WKBK Keene, NH; WKVT Brattleboro, VT; WHNP East Longmeadow, MA; WTAX Springfield, IL; WNYY Ithaca, NY; WYSE Canton, NC; WZAN Portland, ME; WVAX Charlottesville, VA; KAZR Pella, IA; KEGI Jonesboro, AR; KDXY Lake City, AR; KUQL Ethan, SD; KICD-FM Spencer, IA; KLLT Spencer, IA; KIOA Des Moines, IA; KISM Bellingham, WA; KJBX Cash, AR; KLTI-FM Ames, IA; KMIT Mitchell, SD; KSTZ Des Moines, IA; WAFX Suffolk, VA; WAQY Springfield, MA; WCNR Keswick, VA; WCLZ North Yarmouth, ME; WTMT Weaverville, NC; WCVQ Fort Campbell, KY; WEGI-FM Oak Grove, KY; WDBR Springfield, IL; WFIZ Odessa, NY; WJMR-FM Menomonee Falls, WI; WHAI Greenfield, MA; WLZX Northampton, MA; WYXY(FM) Danville, IL; WIII Cortland, NY; WSNI Keene, NH; WIXY Champaign, IL; WNND Pickerington, OH; WCFF Urbana, IL; WKLH Milwaukee, WI; WKNE Keene, NH; WKVT-FM Brattleboro, VT; WLRW Champaign, IL; WHQG Milwaukee, WI; WMGX Portland, ME; WNOR Norfolk, VA; WPOR Portland, ME; WRSI Turners Falls, MA; WQEL Bucyrus, OH; WMLL Bedford, NH; WQMZ Charlottesville, VA; WQNY Ithaca, NY; WLFZ-FM Springfield, IL; WPVQ Greenfield, MA; WSIG Mount Jackson, VA; WSNY Columbus, OH; WRSY Marlboro, VT; WVVR Hopkinsville, KY; WWWV Charlottesville, VA; WINQ Winchester, NH; WVMX Westerville, OH; WYMG Chatham, IL; WYNZ South Portland, ME; WYXL Ithaca, NY; WQQL Sherman, IL; WZID Manchester, NH; WNNP Richwood, OH; WZZP Hopkinsville, KY; WOXL-FM Biltmore Forest, NC
TV Stns: 2 TV.
KAVU-TV Victoria, TX; KOAM-TV Pittsburg, KS
Edward Christian, President/CEO
Warren Lada, EVP, Operations
Bob Lawrence, VP, Programming
Tom Atkins, Engineering Dir

Salem Media Group
4880 Santa Rosa Rd., Camarillo CA 93012
(805) 987-0400
salemmedia.com
info@salem.cc
Radio Stns: 66 AM. 29 FM.
KHCM Honolulu, HI; KNTS Seattle, WA; KOTK Omaha, NE; KBJD Denver, CO; KDOW Palo Alto, CA; KCBQ San Diego, CA; KCRO Omaha, NE; KNTH Houston, TX; KFAX San Francisco, CA; KPXQ Glendale, AZ; KFIA Carmichael, CA; KGNW Burien-Seattle, WA; KGU Honolulu, HI; KRLA Glendale, CA; KZNT Colorado Springs, CO; KKMO Tacoma, WA; KKMS Richfield, MN; KKOL Seattle, WA; KLFE Seattle, WA; KLUP Terrell Hills, TX; KNUS Denver, CO; KPDQ Portland, OR; KPRZ San Marcos-Poway, CA; KKNT Phoenix, AZ; KHNR Honolulu, HI; KRKS Denver, CO; KSLR San Antonio, TX; KTIE San Bernardino, CA; KTKZ Sacramento, CA; KTNO University Park, TX; KYCR Golden Valley, MN; KXFN Saint Louis, MO; WAVA Arlington, VA; WGKA Atlanta, GA; WEZE Boston, MA; WFIA Louisville, KY; WFIL Philadelphia, PA; WAFS Atlanta, GA; WGUL Dunedin, FL; WHIM Coral Gables, FL; WHK Cleveland, OH; WTBN Pinellas Park, FL; WIND Chicago, IL; WKAT North Miami, FL; WHKW Cleveland, OH; WLSS Sarasota, FL; WGTK Louisville, KY; WLQV Detroit, MI; WLTA Alpharetta, GA; WMCA New York, NY; WWDJ Boston, MA; WNIV Atlanta, GA; WORL Altamonte Springs, FL; WPIT Pittsburgh, PA; WDTK Detroit, MI; WHKZ Warren, OH; WRFD Columbus-Worthington, OH; WROL Boston, MA; WYLL Chicago, IL; WTWD Plant City, FL; WTLN Orlando, FL; WHIM(AM) Coral Gables, FL; WNYM Hackensack, NJ; WWTC Minneapolis, MN; WZAZ Jacksonville, FL; WNTP Philadelphia, PA; KAIM-FM Honolulu, HI; KRYP Gladstone, OR; KBIQ Manitou Springs, CO; KDAR Oxnard, CA; KGBI-FM Omaha, NE; KGFT Pueblo, CO; KKOL-FM Aiea, HI; KFIS Scappoose, OR; KKLA-FM Los Angeles, CA; KSAC-FM Dunnigan, CA; KHUI Alamosa, CO; KPDQ-FM Portland, OR; KHCM-FM Honolulu, HI; KPXI Overton, TX; KWRD-FM Highland Village, TX; KRKS-FM Lafayette, CO; KKHT-FM Lumberton, TX; KLTY Arlington, TX; KKFS Lincoln, CA; KFSH-FM La Mirada, CA; WFSH-FM Athens, GA; WAVA-FM Arlington, VA; WBOZ Woodbury, TN; WFHM-FM Cleveland, OH; WFIA-FM New Albany, IN; WORD-FM Pittsburgh, PA; WFFH Smyrna, TN; WTOH Upper Arlington, OH; WFFI Kingston Springs, TN
Stuart W. Epperson, Chairman
Edward G. Atsinger III, CEO/COO
Evan D. Masyr, EVP & Chief Financial Officer

San Luis Valley Broadcasting Inc.
Box 631, Monte Vista CO 81144
(719) 852-3581; *Fax:*(719) 852-3583
Radio Stns: 1 AM. 2 FM.
KSLV Monte Vista, CO; KYDN Monte Vista, CO; KSLV-FM Del Norte, CO

Sand Hill Media Corp.
Box 570, Logan UT 84323
(435) 752-1390
Radio Stns: 1 AM. 3 FM.
KSPZ Ammon, ID; KSNA Idaho Falls, ID; KUPI-FM Rexburg, ID; KQEO Idaho Falls, ID

Sandab Communications L.P. II
737 W. Main St., Hyannis MA 02601
(508) 771-1224; *Fax:*(508) 775-2605
www.ccb-media.com
sales@capecodbroadcasting.com
Radio Stns: 4 FM.
WFCC-FM Chatham, MA; WOCN-FM Orleans, MA; WKPE-FM South Yarmouth, MA; WQRC Barnstable, MA
Wayne White, Operations Dir
Maureen Quail, Business Manager
Melinda Baker, General Sales Mgr
Jerry McKenna, Programming Director
Anthony Pepe, Promotions Manager
Matt Pitta, News Director
Skip Comeau, Engineering Dir
Steve Hall, Chief Engineer
Rachel Simon, Engineer
Brian Barth, Director of Digital
Elaine Twomey, Traffic Director
Gregory D. Bone, General Partner

Sandusky Radio
515 Park Ave., Apt. 4A, New York NY 10022
(212) 355-3074; *Fax:*(212) 355-3075
Ownership: Alice S. White trust. All 100% owned by the White and Rau families
Radio Stns: 4 AM. 6 FM.
KDUS Tempe, AZ; KIXI Mercer Island/Seattl, WA; KAZG Scottsdale, AZ; KKNW Seattle, WA; KDKB Mesa, AZ; KQMV Bellevue, WA; KRWM Bremerton, WA; KSLX-FM Scottsdale, AZ; KUPD Tempe, AZ; KLCK-FM Seattle, WA
Norman Rau, President
Peter Vogt, CFO
David Rau, Chairman/CEO

Sanpete County Broadcasting Co.
Box 40, Manti UT 84642
(435) 835-7301; *Fax:*(435) 835-2250
Radio Stns: 1 AM. 2 FM.
KMTI Manti, UT; KUTC Mount Pleasant, UT; KMXD Monroe, UT

Sarkes Tarzian Inc.
Box 62, Bloomington IN 47402
(812) 332-7251; *Fax:*(812) 331-4575
Ownership: Tom Tarzian; Gray Television Inc.
Radio Stns: 1 AM. 3 FM.
WGCL Bloomington, IN; WAJI Fort Wayne, IN; WLDE Fort Wayne, IN; WTTS Bloomington, IN
TV Stns: 2 TV.
KTVN Reno, NV; WRCB-DT Chattanooga, TN
Tom Tarzian, Chairman
Bob Davis, CFO
Geoff Vargo, President, Radio
Tom Tolar, President, TV

Saskatoon Media Group
366 3rd Ave. S., Saskatoon SK S7K 1M5
(306) 244-1975; *Fax:*(306) 665-8484
www.saskatoonmediagroup.com
tim@saskatoonmediagroup.com
Ownership: Elmer Hildebrand
Radio Stns: 1 AM. 2 FM.
CJWW Saskatoon, SK; CKBL-FM Saskatoon, SK; CJMK-FM Saskatoon, SK
Vic Dubois, General Manager
Tim Kostuik, General Sales Mgr
Shannon Harnett, Advertising Consultant

Schurz Communications Inc.
225 W. Colfax Ave., South Bend IN 46626
(574) 287-1001; *Fax:*(574) 287-2257
www.schurz.com
mburdick@schurz.com
Ownership: Franklin D. Schurz Jr., James M. Schurz, Scott C. Schurz and Mary Schurz, trustees.
Radio Stns: 2 AM. 5 FM.
KBHB Sturgis, SD; WASK Lafayette, IN; KFXS Rapid City, SD; KRCS Sturgis, SD; WASK-FM Battle Ground, IN; WKOA Lafayette, IN; WXXB Delphi, IN
TV Stns: 6 TV.
KTUU-TV Anchorage, AK; KSCW-DT Wichita, KS; KYTV Springfield, MO; WAGT Augusta, GA; WDBJ Roanoke, VA; WSBT-TV South Bend, IN
Franklin Schurz Jr., Chairman
Todd Schurz, President
Marcia Burdick, SVP Broadcasting

Scott Communications Inc.
Box 1150, Selma AL 36702-1150
(334) 875-9360; *Fax:*(334) 875-1340
Radio Stns: 1 AM. 1 FM.
WJAM Selma, AL; WALX Orrville, AL

Seattle Streaming Radio LLC
Box 1471, Evergreen CO 80437
(303) 688-5162; *Fax:*(303) 660-4930
Radio Stns: 4 AM.
KBRO Bremerton, WA; KLDY Lacey, WA; KNTB Lakewood, WA; WKIZ Key West, FL

Seehafer Broadcasting Corp.
Box 1385, Manitowoc WI 54221-1385
(920) 682-0351; *Fax:*(920) 682-1008
Radio Stns: 4 AM. 3 FM.
WDLB Marshfield, WI; WFHR Wisconsin Rapids, WI; WOMT Manitowoc, WI; WXCO Wausau, WI; WOSQ Spencer, WI; WQTC-FM Manitowoc, WI; WLJY Nekoosa, WI
Don Seehafer, President
Mark Seehafer, Operations Dir

Service Broadcasting Group LLC
621 N.W. 6th St., Grand Prairie TX 75050-5555
(972) 263-9911; *Fax:*(972) 558-0010
www.k104fm.com
Radio Stns: 1 AM. 2 FM.
KKDA Grand Prairie, TX; KKDA Dallas, TX; KRNB Decatur, TX
Hymen Childs, President

Seward County Broadcasting Co.
1410 N. Western, Liberal KS 67901
(620) 624-3891; *Fax:*(620) 624-7885
www.kscb.net
sales@kscb.net
Ownership: Jack Landon, Robert Larrabee, Stuart Melchert.
Radio Stns: 1 AM. 2 FM.
KSCB Liberal, KS; KLDG Liberal, KS; KSCB-FM Liberal, KS
Stuart Melchert, General Manager

Shamrock Communications Inc.
149 Penn Ave., Scranton PA 18503
(570) 348-9103; *Fax:*(570) 348-9109
www.timesshamrockcommunications.com
Ownership: Edward J. Lynett Jr., 25% of Votes; George V. Lynett, 25% of Votes; William R. Lynett, 25% of Votes; Cecilia Haggerty, 12.5% of Votes; JamesJ. Haggerty, 12.5% of Votes, .

Shamrock Communications Owns 50% of The Milwaukee Radio Alliance LLC (See Listing).

Radio Stns: 4 FM.
KTSO Glenpool, OK; KMYZ-FM Pryor, OK; WZBA Westminster, MD; KWNZ Lovelock, NV
Jim Loftus, COO
William Lynett, President

Sheila Callahan and Friends Inc.
Box 309, Missoula MT 59806-0309
(406) 542-1025; *Fax:*(406) 721-1036

Radio Stns: 4 FM.
KMSO Missoula, MT; KMTZ Three Forks, MT; KDXT Lolo, MT; KHDV Darby, MT
Max Murphy, CFO
Sheila Callahan, President

SIGA Broadcasting Corp.
1302 N. Shepherd Dr., Houston TX 77008
(713) 868-5559; *Fax:*(713) 868-9631
www.sigabroadcasting.com
sigabroadcasting@gmail.com

Radio Stns: 6 AM.
KAML Kenedy-Karnes City, TX; KHFX Cleburne, TX; KFJZ Fort Worth, TX; KGBC Galveston, TX; KLVL Pasadena, TX; KTMR Converse, TX

Silver Dove Broadcasting
50 Millies Place, Studio A, Dahlonega GA 30533
(706) 482-0525
www.talkradioamerica.net
wcdg887@windstream.net

Radio Stns: 1 FM.
WCDG Dahlonega, GA
Ken Alcorn, Marketing Director

Simmons Broadcasting Inc.
1403 Third St., Langdon ND 58249
(701) 256-1080; *Fax:*(701) 256-1081
kndkkicksbs@utma.com

Radio Stns: 1 AM. 3 FM.
KNDK Langdon, ND; KAOC Cavalier, ND; KYTZ Walhalla, ND; KNDK-FM Langdon, ND

Sinclair Communications Inc.
999 Waterside Dr., Suite 500, Norfolk VA 23510
(757) 640-8500; *Fax:*(757) 640-8552
www.sinclairstations.com
Ownership: John L. Sinclair, chmn; Robert Sinclair, J. David Sinclair, Ann Adams. Note: Group also manages KNOB(FM) Healdsburg, CA.

Radio Stns: 2 AM. 6 FM.
WNIS Norfolk, VA; WTAR Norfolk, VA; KSXY Forestville, CA; KXTS Geyserville, CA; KRSH Healdsburg, CA; WNOB Chesapeake, VA; WROX-FM Exmore, VA; WUSH Poquoson, VA
John Sinclair, Chairman
J. David Sinclair, President
Robert L. Sinclair, Secretary

SkyWest Media L.L.C.
Box 36148, Tucson AZ 85740
(520) 797-4434

Radio Stns: 1 AM. 5 FM.
KNFT Bayard, NM; KNFT-FM Bayard, NM; KSCQ Silver City, NM; KFMR Ballard, UT; KRZX Redlands, CO; KXML Fairfield, ID

Smoke and Mirrors LLC
Number 10 Media Center Dr., Lake Havasu City AZ 86403
(928) 855-1051; *Fax:*(928) 855-7996

Radio Stns: 4 FM.
KFTT Bagdad, AZ; KRRK Desert Hills, AZ; KVAL Cal-Nev-Ari, NV; KVYL Mohave Valley, AZ

Somar Communications Inc.
28095 Three Notch Rd., Suite 2-B, Mechanicsville MD 20659
(301) 870-5550; *Fax:*(301) 884-0280
www.star983.com

Radio Stns: 2 AM. 3 FM.
WKIK La Plata, MD; WPTX Lexington Park, MD; WKIK-FM California, MD; WMDM Lexington Park, MD; WSMD-FM Mechanicsville, MD
Roy Robertson, CEO

Sorensen Pacific Broadcasting Inc.
111 W. Chanlan Santo Papa, Suite 800, Hagatna GU 96910
(671) 477-5700; *Fax:*(671) 477-3982
comments@radiopacific.com
Ownership: Rex W. Sorensen, 97.6%.

Radio Stns: 1 AM. 4 FM.
KGUM Hagatna, GU; KGUM-FM Dededo, GU; KPXP Garapan-Saipan, MP; KRSI Garapan-Saipan, MP; KZGZ Hagatna, GU
Jay Shedd, President & COO
Rex Sorensen, Chairman/CEO

Sorenson Broadcasting Corp.
2804 S. Ridgeview Way, Sioux Falls SD 57105
(605) 334-1117; *Fax:*(605) 338-0326
sorenson@sbcradio.com
Ownership: Dean P. Sorenson, 100%. Note: WZGA(FM) Helen, GA is licensed to Sorenson Southeast Radio LLC, a separate entity also owned 100% by Dean Sorenson.

Radio Stns: 4 AM. 7 FM.
KCCR Pierre, SD; KORN Mitchell, SD; KSOU Sioux Center, IA; KYNT Yankton, SD; KIHK Rock Valley, IA; KKYA Yankton, SD; KLXS-FM Pierre, SD; KQRN Mitchell, SD; KSOU-FM Sioux Center, IA; KUOO Spirit Lake, IA; KUQQ Milford, IA
Dean Sorenson, President

South Central Communications Corp.
Box 3848, Evansville IN 47736
(812) 463-7950; *Fax:*(812) 463-7915
www.southcentralcommunications.net
Ownership: John D. Engelbrecht, 80%, J.P. Engelbrecht, 20%.

Radio Stns: 1 AM. 2 FM.
WEOA Evansville, IN; WEJK Boonville, IN; WVRX Maryville, TN
John D. Engelbrecht, President
J.P. Engelbrecht, VP

South Texas FM Investments LLC
Box 880, Roma TX 78584
(956) 487-8015

Radio Stns: 1 FM.
KZAM Pleasant Valley, TX

Southeast Kansas Independent Living Resource Center Inc.
202 E. Centennial Ave., Suite 2B, Pittsburg KS 66762
(620) 232-9912; *Fax:*(620) 232-9915

Radio Stns: 2 AM. 1 FM.
KLKC Parsons, KS; KSEK Pittsburg, KS; KSEK-FM Girard, KS
Shari Coatney, President

Southeastern Oklahoma Radio LLC
Box 1011, Hartshorne OK 74547
(918) 297-2501

Radio Stns: 2 AM. 2 FM.
KNED McAlester, OK; KTMC McAlester, OK; KMCO Wilburton, OK; KTMC-FM McAlester, OK

Southern Broadcasting Companies Inc.
1010 Tower Pl., Bogart GA 30622
(706) 369-7301; *Fax:*(706) 353-1967
www.magic1021.com
Ownership: Paul C. Stone.

Radio Stns: 2 AM. 3 FM.
WLOV Washington, GA; WRGA Rome, GA; WMGZ Eatonton, GA; WQTU Rome, GA; WSRM Coosa, GA
Paul Stone, President
Traci Long, General Manager

Southern Communications Corp.
306 S. Kanawaha St., Beckley WV 25801
(304) 253-7000; *Fax:*(304) 255-1044
www.103cir.com
Ownership: R. Shane Southern, 50.4%; Karen L. Martin, 24.8%; and Kristin E. Wallace, 24.8%.

Radio Stns: 3 AM. 4 FM.
WBKW(AM) Beckley, WV; WMTD Hinton, WV; WWNR Beckley, WV; WAXS Oak Hill, WV; WCIR-FM Beckley, WV; WMTD-FM Hinton, WV; WTNJ Mount Hope, WV
R. Shane Southern, President
Jay Quesenberry, General Manager

Southern Stone Communications
126 West Intl. Speedway Blvd., Daytona Beach FL 32114
(386) 255-9300
www.daytonaradio.com

Radio Stns: 1 AM. 3 FM.
WNDB Daytona Beach, FL; WHOG-FM Ormond-By-The-Sea, FL; WKRO-FM Port Orange, FL; WVYB Holly Hill, FL
Paul C. Stone, CEO/COO

Southern Wabash Communications Corp.
435 37th Ave. N., Nashville TN 37209
(615) 844-1039; *Fax:*(615) 777-2284
www.wnsr.com

Radio Stns: 2 AM. 2 FM.
WMGC Murfreesboro, TN; WNSR Brentwood, TN; WNTC Drakesboro, KY; WSJD Princeton, IN
Ted Johnson, President

Southwest Florida Radio Broadcasting, LLC
1956 Main St., Sarasota FL 34236
(941) 955-9387
www.wtmyradio.com

Radio Stns: 1 AM.
WTMY Sarasota, FL

Sovereign Communications
1411 Ashmun St., Sault Ste. Marie MI 49783
(906) 774-4321
www.wznl.net

Radio Stns: 7 AM. 10 FM.
WDBC Escanaba, MI; WDMJ Marquette, MI; WIAN Ishpeming, MI; WKNW Sault Sainte Marie, MI; WMIQ Iron Mountain, MI; WNBY Newberry, MI; WSOO Sault Ste. Marie, MI; WIMK Iron Mountain, MI; WJPD Ishpeming, MI; WNBY-FM Newberry, MI; WNGE Negaunee, MI; WSUE Sault Ste. Marie, MI; WUPK Marquette, MI; WYKX Escanaba, MI; WYSS Sault Ste. Marie, MI; WZNL Norway, MI; WMKD Pickford, MI
William C. Gleich, CEO/COO
Tim Sabean, President

Spanish Broadcasting System Inc.
2601 South Bayshore Dr., PH 2, Coconut Grove FL 33133
(305) 441-6901; *Fax:*(305) 446-5148
www.spanishbroadcasting.com
Ownership: Raul Alarcon Jr., Jose Grimalt.

Radio Stns: 20 FM.
KXOL-FM Los Angeles, CA; KLAX-FM East Los Angeles, CA; KRZZ San Francisco, CA; WCMQ-FM Hialeah, FL; WODA Bayamon, PR; WEGM San German, PR; WRXD Fajardo, PR; WZET Hormigueros, PR; WIOA San Juan, PR; WIOB Mayaguez, PR; WIOC Ponce, PR; WLEY-FM Aurora, IL; WMEG Guayama, PR; WNOD Mayaguez, PR; WPAT-FM Paterson, NJ; WRMA Fort Lauderdale, FL; WSKQ-FM New York, NY; WXDJ North Miami Beach, FL; WZMT Ponce, PR; WZNT San Juan, PR

TV Stns: 1 TV.
WSBS-TV Key West, FL
Jose Grimalt, EVP
Raul Alarcon, President/CEO

Spanish Peaks Broadcasting Inc.
3702 Sunridge Dr., Park City UT 84098-4618
(801) 560-9595

Radio Stns: 3 FM.
KKVU Stevensville, MT; KYJK Missoula, MT; KDTR Florence, MT

Sparta-Tomah Broadcasting Co. Inc.
113 W. Oak St., Sparta WI 54656
(608) 269-3307; *Fax:*(608) 269-5170

Radio Stns: 1 AM. 2 FM.
WKLJ Sparta, WI; WCOW-FM Sparta, WI; WFBZ Trempealeau, WI
William R. Hoffman, General Manager

Spectrum Radio Group LLC
8519 Rapley Preserve Circle, Potomac MD 20854
(301) 802-1250; *Fax:*(301) 365-4399

Radio Stns: 2 AM. 2 FM.
WMMN Fairmont, WV; WTCS Fairmont, WV; WRLF Fairmont, WV; WZST Westover, WV

Spirit Catholic Radio
13326 A St., Omaha NE 68144
(402) 571-0200; *Fax:*(402) 571-0833
www.spiritcatholicradio.com
Ownership: Nonprofit corporation.

Radio Stns: 1 FM.
KVSS Papillion, NE
Bruce McGregor, Programming Director
Kelly Miller, Marketing and Promotions Manager
Mark Voris, Chief Engineer
Jim Carroll, Executive Director
Bernie Schaefer, Development Director
Mary Jorgensen, Director of Underwriting
Matt Willkom, Program Producer

Spotlight Broadcasting LLC
Box 8888, Metairie LA 70011
(504) 309-7260; *Fax:*(504) 309-7262
www.kmrc1430.com

Radio Stns: 3 AM.
KAGY Port Sulphur, LA; KMRC Morgan City, LA; WABL Amite, LA
Patrick Andras, President

St. Gabriel Communications
P.O. Box 838, Des Moines IA 50304
(515) 223-1150
Radio Stns: 1 FM.
KIHS Adel, IA

St. Paul Radio Co.
P.O. Box 3744, Charleston WV 25337
(304) 342-8131
Radio Stns: 2 AM.
WMUX Hurricane, WV; WLUX Dunbar, WV
Mark Sadd, President
Jim Blankenship, Director
Joe Deegan, Director
Paul Howard, Director
Mike Kawash, Director
Tony Marks, Director

Stanford Communications Inc.
P.O. Box 458, Amory MS 38821
(662) 256-9726; *Fax:*(662) 256-9725
www.fm95radio.com
fm95@fm95radio.com
Radio Stns: 2 AM. 1 FM.
WAMY Amory, MS; WWZQ Aberdeen, MS; WAFM Amory, MS
Ed Stanford, President
Teresa Stanford, Operations Dir

Star Broadcasting Inc.
21 Miracle Strip Pkwy., Fort Walton Beach FL 32548
(850) 244-1400; *Fax:*(850) 243-1471
Radio Stns: 2 AM. 1 FM.
WEDM(AM) Fort Walton Beach, FL; WEVG Evergreen, AL; WTKE-FM Niceville, FL

Star Radio Network
102 S. Fifth St., Crockett TX 75835
(936) 544-2171
Ownership: Leon Hunt, 100%.
Radio Stns: 3 AM. 4 FM.
KTKC Springhill, LA; KIVY Crockett, TX; KMVL Madisonville, TX; KIVY-FM Crockett, TX; KJVC Mansfield, LA; KMVL-FM Madisonville, TX; KTKC Springhill, LA
Leon Hunt, President

STARadio Corp.
329 Maine St., Quincy IL 62301-3928
(217) 224-4102; *Fax:*(217) 224-4133
Ownership: Lisa Parrish, 31%
Radio Stns: 4 AM. 7 FM.
KQDI Great Falls, MT; KXGF Great Falls, MT; WKAN Kankakee, IL; WTAD Quincy, IL; KGRC Hannibal, MO; KQDI-FM Highwood, MT; KZZK New London, MO; WQCY Quincy, IL; WCOY Quincy, IL; WYKT Wilmington, IL; WXNU St. Anne, IL
Howard A. Doss, President

Starlight Broadcasting Co.
1101 Oregon Ave, Burns, Oregon WA 97720
(270) 298-3268; *Fax:*(270) 298-9326
www.starlightbroadcasting.com
Radio Stns: 1 FM.
WKYA Greenville, KY
Andy Anderson, President/CEO

Steckline Communications Inc.
1632 S. Maize Rd., Wichita KS 67209
(316) 721-8484; *Fax:*(316) 721-8276
www.maanradio.com
Radio Stns: 3 AM.
KYUL Scott City, KS; KIUL Garden City, KS; KGSO Wichita, KS
Greg Steckline, President

Stephens Family L.P.
Box 1250, Sapulpa OK 74067
(918) 492-2660
Radio Stns: 3 AM. 10 FM.
WMSA Massena, NY; WTNY Watertown, NY; WNER Watertown, NY; WVLF Norwood, NY; WCIZ-FM Watertown, NY; WFRY-FM Watertown, NY; WYSX Morristown, NY; WFKL Fairport, NY; WRCD Canton, NY; WRMM-FM Rochester, NY; WNCQ-FM Canton, NY; WPAC Ogdensburg, NY; WZNE Brighton, NY
Michael Stephens, President

Studstill Media
3905 Progress Blvd., Peru IL 61354
(815) 224-2100; *Fax:*(815) 224-2066
www.studstillmedia.com
Ownership: Owen L. Studstill; Lamar Studstill; Cole C. Studstill.
Radio Stns: 1 AM. 6 FM.
WSPL Streator, IL; WIVQ Spring Valley, IL; WALS Oglesby, IL; WGLC Mendota, IL; WBZG Peru, IL; WSTQ Streator, IL; WYYS Streator, IL
Cole Studstill, Manager of Programming

Sudbury Services Inc.
Box 989, Blytheville AR 72316
(870) 762-2093; *Fax:*(870) 763-8459
www.thundercountry963.com
Ownership: Harold L. Sudbury Jr., Lydia Sudbury Langston, LaNeal Sudbury Salter. Cable TV: Blytheville TV Cable Co., Blytheville, AR.
Radio Stns: 5 AM. 5 FM.
KLCN Blytheville, AR; KNBY Newport, AR; KOSE Wilson, AR; KTPA Prescott, AR; KXAR Hope, AR; KAMJ Gosnell, AR; KHLS Blytheville, AR; KHPA Hope, AR; KOKR Newport, AR; KQMJ(FM) Osceola, AR
Harold Sudbury, President

Summit City Radio Group
2000 Lower Huntington Rd., Fort Wayne IN 46819
(260) 747-1511; *Fax:*(260) 747-3999
Radio Stns: 1 AM. 3 FM.
WGL Fort Wayne, IN; WNHT Churubusco, IN; WGL-FM Huntington, IN; WXKE Fort Wayne, IN
Lloyd B. Roach, President

Summit Media Broadcasting LLC
180 Main St., Sutton WV 26601
(304) 765-7373; *Fax:*(304) 765-7836
www.summitmediaradio.com
Radio Stns: 6 AM. 21 FM.
KPRP Honolulu, HI; KKNE Waipahu, HI; WAGG Birmingham, AL; WENN Birmingham, AL; WSGB Sutton, WV; WVAR Richwood, WV; KCCN-FM Honolulu, HI; KINE-FM Honolulu, HI; KRTR-FM Kailua, HI; KPHW Kaneohe, HI; WAFD Webster Springs, WV; WBHJ Midfield, AL; WBHK Warrior, AL; WDBS Sutton, WV; WHTI(FM) Lakeside, VA; WJMZ-FM Anderson, SC; WKHK Colonial Heights, VA; WKLR Fort Lee, VA; WRKA Louisville, KY; WURV(FM) Richmond, VA; WBPT Homewood, AL; WHZT Williamston, SC; WQNU Lyndon, KY; WSFR Corydon, IN; WVEZ St. Matthews, KY; WZZK-FM Birmingham, AL; WKQV Cowen, WV
Carl Parmer, Chairman/CEO
David R. DuBose, Executive Vice President/COO

Sumter Broadcasting Co. Inc.
239 Ezzard St., Lawrenceville GA 30046
(229) 924-1390,
www.americusradio.com
Radio Stns: 1 AM. 2 FM.
WISK Lawrenceville, GA; WDEC-FM Americus, GA; WISK-FM Americus, GA
Steve Lashley, General Sales Mgr

Sun Mountain Inc.
9045 Hobble Creek, Billings MT 59101
(406) 665-2828; *Fax:*(406) 665-2131
www.bigskyradio.net
Radio Stns: 3 AM.
KBSR Laurel, MT; KHDN Hardin, MT; KYLW Lockwood, MT

Sun Valley Radio Inc.
810 W. 200 North, Logan UT 84321
(435) 752-1390; *Fax:*(435) 752-1392
Ownership: M. Kent Frandsen, owner.
Radio Stns: 2 AM. 4 FM.
KLGN Logan, UT; KVNU Logan, UT; KGNT Smithfield, UT; KKEX Preston, ID; KZHK St. George, UT; KLZX Weston, ID
M. Kent Frandsen, President

Sunbelt Broadcasting Corp.
37 S. High School Ave., Columbia MS 39429
(601) 736-2616; *Fax:*(601) 736-2617
www.wcjufm.com
wcju@wcjufm.com
Radio Stns: 2 FM.
WCJU-FM Prentiss, MS; WJDR Prentiss, MS
Tommy McDaniel, President

Sunburst Media-Louisiana LLC
300 Crescent Ct., Suite 850, Dallas TX 75201
(214) 661-3100
Radio Stns: 1 AM. 3 FM.
KJIN Houma, LA; KXMG Jean Lafitte, LA; KCIL Gray, LA; KXOR-FM Thibodaux, LA

Sunbury Broadcasting Corp.
Box 1070, Sunbury PA 17801
(570) 286-5838; *Fax:*(570) 743-7837
www.wqkx.com
Radio Stns: 2 AM. 3 FM.
WKOK Sunbury, PA; WMLP Milton, PA; WEGH Northumberland, PA; WQKX Sunbury, PA; WVLY-FM Milton, PA
Roger Haddon Jr., CEO

Sunrise Broadcasting Corp.
Box 2307, Newburgh NY 12550
(845) 561-2131; *Fax:*(845) 561-2138
www.wgnyfm.com
Ownership: CVC Capital Corp.
Radio Stns: 1 AM. 1 FM.
WGNY Newburgh, NY; WJGK(FM) Newburgh, NY
J. Klebe, President

Superior Communications
3302 N. Van Dyke, Imlay City MI 48444
(810) 724-2638; *Fax:*(877) 850-0881
www.positivehits.com
Radio Stns: 8 FM.
WEJC White Star, MI; WLGH Leroy Township, MI; WTLI Bear Creek Township, MI; WAIR Lake City, MI; WHYT Goodland Township, MI; WSLI Belding, MI; WTAC Burton, MI; WSIS Riverside, MI
Edward Czelada, President

Sweet Home Ashtabula LLC
Second Generation Place, 3209 Prospect, Cleveland OH 44115
(216) 426-1500; *Fax:*(216) 588-1558
Radio Stns: 1 AM. 4 FM.
WFUN Ashtabula, OH; WREO-FM Ashtabula, OH; WZOO-FM Edgewood, OH; WFXJ-FM North Kingsville, OH; WYBL Ashtabula, OH
James Embrescia, President

Talking Stick Communications LLC
421 S. Second St., Elkhart IN 46514
(574) 258-5483
Radio Stns: 1 AM. 3 FM.
WRSW Warsaw, IN; WAWC Syracuse, IN; WRBR-FM South Bend, IN; WRSW-FM Warsaw, IN
Alec Dille, President

Talley Radio Stations
Box 10, Litchfield IL 62056
(217) 324-5921; *Fax:*(217) 532-2431
wsmiradio.com
wsmi@wsmiradio.com
Ownership: Hayward L. Talley, Emma C. Talley.
Radio Stns: 1 AM. 2 FM.
WSMI Litchfield, IL; WAOX Staunton, IL; WSMI-FM Litchfield, IL
Hayward Talley, President
Brian Talley, SVP

Tallgrass Broadcasting LLC
1174 Hunters Ridge East, Hoffman Estates IL 60192-4540
(847) 289-8018; *Fax:*(847) 289-1423
Radio Stns: 3 AM. 6 FM.
KICA Clovis, NM; KIND Independence, KS; KMUL Farwell, TX; KOSG Pawhuska, OK; KICA-FM Farwell, TX; KBIK Independence, KS; KKYC Clovis, NM; KMUL-FM Muleshoe, TX; KIND-FM Elk City, KS

Tama Broadcasting Inc.
5207 Washington Blvd., Tampa FL 33619
(813) 620-1300; *Fax:*(813) 628-0713
www.wtmp.com
Radio Stns: 1 AM. 7 FM.
WTMP Egypt Lake, FL; WTHG Hinesville, GA; WSSJ Rincon, GA; WTMP-FM Dade City, FL; WFJO Jacksonville Beach, FL; WSGA Hinesville, GA; WJGM(FM) Baldwin, FL; WJSJ Fernandina Beach, FL
Glenn Cherry, CEO

Tanana Valley Television Co.
3650 Braddock Street, Suite 2, Fairbanks AK 99701
(907) 452-3697; *Fax:*(907) 456-3428
Ownership: William St. Pierre, 85%.
Radio Stns: 2 FM.
KYSC Fairbanks, AK; KDJF Ester, AK
TV Stns: 1 TV.
KFXF Fairbanks, AK

Taylor University Broadcasting
236 West Reade Ave, Upland IN 46989
(765) 998-5134; *Fax:*(765) 998-4925
www.taylor.edu
Radio Stns: 4 FM.

WBCJ Spencerville, OH; WBCL Fort Wayne, IN; WBCY Archbold, OH; WCVM Bronson, MI
Ross McCampbell, Executive Director
Scott Tsuleff, Program Director
Ken Church, Promotions Coordinator
Larry Bower, News Director

Team Radio LLC
Box 2509, Ponca City OK 74602
(580) 765-2485; *Fax:*(580) 767-1103
www.eteamradio.com
Radio Stns: 2 AM. 3 FM.
KOKB Blackwell, OK; KOKP Perry, OK; KLOR-FM Ponca City, OK; KOSB Perry, OK; KPNC Ponca City, OK
Bill Coleman, General Manager

Tejas Broadcasting Ltd. LLP
1227 W. Magnolia Ave., Suite 300, Fort Worth TX 76104-4400
(817) 920-7599
Radio Stns: 1 AM. 7 FM.
KTNZ Amarillo, TX; KBZD Amarillo, TX; KGRW Friona, TX; KMJR Odem, TX; KLTG Corpus Christi, TX; KQFX Borger, TX; KLHB Portland, TX; KKNM Bovina, TX
Jim Anderson, CEO

TeleSouth Communications Inc.
6311 Ridgewood Rd., Jackson MS 39211
(601) 957-1700; *Fax:*(601) 956-5228
telesouth.com
Radio Stns: 2 AM. 11 FM.
WKCU Corinth, MS; WOEG Hazlehurst, MS; WDXO Hazlehurst, MS; WFMM Sumrall, MS; WFMN Flora, MS; WLAU Heidelberg, MS; WTNM Water Valley, MS; WQLJ Oxford, MS; WRQO Monticello, MS; WTCD Indianola, MS; WXRZ Corinth, MS; WYMX Greenwood, MS; WBZL(FM) Greenwood, MS
Stephen Davenport, CEO
Kim Dillon, President
Larry Tate, General Sales Mgr
Will East, Programming Director
Houston McDavitt, Chief Engineer
Dawn Dugle, Creative Director
Tanya Taylor, EVP, CFO
Camie Martin, Content Director

Texas Christian University
Box 298020, Moudy Bldg., Fort Worth TX 76129
(817) 257-7631; *Fax:*(817) 257-7637
www.ktcu.tcu.edu
Radio Stns: 1 FM.
KTCU Fort Worth, TX
Russell Scott, Station Manager

Texoma Broadcasting Inc.
1418 N. 1st Ave., Durant OK 74701
(580) 924-3100
Ownership: Allen Wheeler, 50%; Gerald Todd Tidwell, 40%; Gerald Winston Tidwell, 10%.
Radio Stns: 1 AM. 2 FM.
KSEO Durant, OK; KLBC Durant, OK; KBBC Tishomingo, OK
Gerald Todd Tidwell, President

The Chickasaw Nation
Box 609, Ada OK 74821-0609
(580) 332-1212; *Fax:*(580) 332-0128
www.chickasaw.net
Radio Stns: 1 AM. 5 FM.
KADA Ada, OK; KADA-FM Ada, OK; KXFC Coalgate, OK; KCNP Ada, OK; KTLS-FM Holdenville, OK; KYKC Byng, OK

The Cromwell Group Inc.
P.O. Box 150846, Nashville TN 37215
(615) 361-7560; *Fax:*(615) 366-4313
www.cromwellradio.com
Ownership: Bayard H. Walters, 100%.
Radio Stns: 9 AM. 21 FM.
WCRA Effingham, IL; WQZQ Goodlettsville, TN; WKCM Hawesville, KY; WPMB Vandalia, IL; WPRT Pegram, TN; WTCJ Tell City, IN; WVJS Owensboro, KY; WPRT-HD2 Philpot, TN; WCRA Effingham, IL; WBIO Philpot, KY; WCBH Casey, IL; WCRC Effingham, IL; WEJT Shelbyville, IL; WHQQ Neoga, IL; WKRV Vandalia, IL; WLME Lewisport, KY; WMCI Neoga, IL; WWGO Charleston, IL; WXCM Whitesville, KY; WZUS Macon, IL; WYDS Decatur, IL; WZNX Sullivan, IL; WBUZ La Vergne, TN; WCJZ Cannelton, IN; WQZQ-FM Goodlettsville, TN; WPRT-FM Pegram, TN; WYDS-HD2 Decatur, IL; WWGO-HD2 Casey, IL; WCRA-FM Effingham, IL; WJKG Effingham, IL
Bayard Walters, President
Janice Russell, Administrative Director
Andrea Kramer, Business Manager
Dorothy Black, Controller

The Curators of the University of Missouri
University of Missouri, 316 University Hall, Columbia MO 65211
(573) 882-2388; *Fax:*(573) 882-0010
www.umsystem.edu
Ownership: (Business Services Division).
Radio Stns: 7 FM.
KBIA Columbia, MO; KCUR-FM Kansas City, MO; KMNR Rolla, MO; KMST Rolla, MO; KWMU St. Louis, MO; KAUD Mexico, MO; KCIU Columbia, MO
TV Stns: 1 TV.
KOMU-TV Columbia, MO
Michael Dunn, General Manager
Martin Siddall, General Manager

The Findlay Publishing Co.
701 W. Sandusky St., Findlay OH 45840
(419) 422-5151; *Fax:*(419) 422-2937
daveglass@findlayoh.com
Radio Stns: 2 AM. 6 FM.
WCSI Columbus, IN; WFIN Findlay, OH; WWWY North Vernon, IN; WKKG Columbus, IN; WKXA-FM Findlay, OH; WBUK Ottawa, OH; WRBI Batesville, IN; WINN Columbus, IN
Karl Heminger, President

The Jim Pattison Broadcast Group
460 Pemberton Terrace, Kamloops BC V2C 1T5
(250) 372-3322; *Fax:*(250) 374-0445
www.jpbroadcast.com
info@jpbg.ca
Ownership: James A. Pattison, 100%.
Radio Stns: 2 AM. 41 FM.
CJNB North Battleford, SK; CKBI Prince Albert, SK; CFMM-FM Prince Albert, SK; CFMY-FM Medicine Hat, AB; CFQX-FM Selkirk, MB; CHIQ-FM Winnipeg, MB; CHLB-FM Lethbridge, AB; CIBW-FM Drayton Valley, AB; CIFM-FM Kamloops, BC; CJJR-FM Vancouver, BC; CKKN-FM Prince George, BC; CKKQ-FM Victoria, BC; CHBZ-FM Cranbrook, BC; CKLR-FM Courtenay, BC; CKLZ-FM Kelowna, BC; CKWV-FM Nanaimo, BC; CJBZ-FM Taber, AB; CHUB-FM Red Deer, AB; CJXX-FM Grande Prairie, AB; CHBW-FM Rocky Mountain House, AB; CJZN-FM Victoria, BC; CHWF-FM Nanaimo, BC; CIBH-FM Parksville, BC; CKBZ-FM Kamloops, BC; CHQX-FM Prince Albert, SK; CKIZ-FM Vernon, BC; CJDR-FM Fernie, BC; CHDR-FM Cranbrook, BC; CKDV-FM Prince George, BC; CFDV-FM Red Deer, AB; CJNS-FM Meadow Lake, SK; CJAV-FM Port Alberni, BC; CHPQ-FM Parksville, BC; CHAT-FM Medicine Hat, AB; CIUP-FM Edmonton, AB; CKCE-FM Calgary, AB; CKQQ-FM Kelowna, BC; CIKT-FM Grande Prairie, AB; CKPK-FM Vancouver, BC; CJHD-FM North Battleford, SK; CKNO-FM Edmonton, AB; CHPK-FM Calgary, AB; CJCQ-FM North Battleford, SK
TV Stns: 3 TV.
CFJC-TV Kamloops, BC; CHAT-TV Medicine Hat, AB; CKPG-TV Prince George, BC
Rod Schween, President & General Manager
Vanessa Ong, Executive Assistant
Mark Rogers, Vice President, Sales
Ross Winters, Programming Director
Bill Stovold, IT & Engineering Director
Bill Dinicol, Vice President, Finance
Andrew Snook, Digital Director

The Last Bastion
700 Wellington Hills Rd., Little Rock AR 72211
(501) 401-0200; *Fax:*(501) 401-0374
Radio Stns: 3 FM.
KPZK Cabot, AR; KOKY Sherwood, AR; KINB Kingfisher, OK

The Original Company Inc.
522 Busseron St., PO Box 242, Vincennes IN 47591
(812) 882-6060; *Fax:*(812) 882-7770
www.originalcompany.com
marklange@originalcompany.com
Ownership: Mark R. Lange, 50%; Saundra K. Lange, 50%.
Radio Stns: 4 AM. 11 FM.
WAOV Vincennes, IN; WFIW Fairfield, IL; WRCY Mt. Vernon, IN; WTAY Robinson, IL; WYFX Mount Vernon, IN; WFIW Fairfield, IL; WBTO Petersburg, IN; WOKZ Fairfield, IL; WQTY Linton, IN; WREB Greencastle, IN; WTYE Robinson, IL; WUZR Bicknell, IN; WWBL Washington, IN; WZDM Vincennes, IN; WJPS Boonville, IN
Mark Lange, President

The Presence Radio Network
PO Box 10660, Portland ME 04104
(207) 689-9939
www.thepresence.fm
info@thepresence.fm
Radio Stns: 4 FM.
WXTP North Windham, ME; WTBP Bath, ME; WWTP Augusta, ME; WXBP Augusta, ME
Craig Foster, President
Eric Marenghi, Operations Mgr
Richard A. Hyatt, Engineering Consultant
Cynthia Nickless, Executive Director

The Radio Group
Box 1319, Columbia LA 71418
(318) 649-7959; *Fax:*(318) 649-5874
radiotom1@yahoo.com
Ownership: Tom D. Gay, 100%.
Radio Stns: 5 FM.
KAPB-FM Marksville, LA; KFNV-FM Ferriday, LA; KJNA-FM Jena, LA; KMAR-FM Winnsboro, LA; KWTG Vidalia, LA
Tom Gay, General Manager

The Result Radio Group
Box 767, Winona MN 55987-0767
(507) 452-4000; *Fax:*(507) 452-9494
winonaradio.com
Ownership: Jerry Papenfuss.
Radio Stns: 6 AM. 8 FM.
KAGE Winona, MN; KBEW Blue Earth, MN; KBRF Fergus Falls, MN; KDOM Windom, MN; KJJK Fergus Falls, MN; KWNO Winona, MN; KAGE-FM Winona, MN; KBEW-FM Blue Earth, MN; KDOM-FM Windom, MN; KHME Winona, MN; KJJK-FM Fergus Falls, MN; KPRW Perham, MN; KWNO-FM Rushford, MN; KZCR Fergus Falls, MN
Jerry Papenfuss, Owner

The Wireless Group Inc.
Box 198, 42 South Washington Avenue, Second Floor, Brownsville TN 38012
(731) 772-3700
www.brownsvilleradio.com
Ownership: Carlton Veirs, pres, 50%; Lyle Reid, 50%. (See also Cross-Ownership, Sect. A.)
Radio Stns: 1 AM. 1 FM.
WNWS Brownsville, TN; WNWS-FM Jackson, TN
Rita Hathcock, Operations Manager
Carlton Veirs, General Manager
Leigh Turnage, Sales Manager
Drew Magruder, Program Manager
Joyce Moore, Sales Account Executive
Ivory T. Ellison, Gospel Program Manager

The Zone Corp.
PO Box 1929, Bangor ME 04402
(207) 990-2800; *Fax:*(207) 990-2444
www.zoneradio.com
Ownership: Stephen King, 100%.
Radio Stns: 1 AM. 2 FM.
WZON Bangor, ME; WKIT Brewer, ME; WZLO Dover-Foxcroft, ME
Stephen King, President
Tabitha King, Vice President

Thomas Media
111 W. Main St., Jackson TN 38301
(731) 427-9616
www.facebook.com/pages/Thomas-Media/166138450079364
Radio Stns: 4 FM.
WFKX Henderson, TN; WHHM-FM Henderson, TN; WWYN McKenzie, TN; WZDQ Humboldt, TN

3 Daughters Media Inc.
c/o Brooks, Pierce, et al, Box 1800, Raleigh NC 27602
(919) 839-0300
Radio Stns: 6 AM. 1 FM.
KSOP South Salt Lake, UT; WGMN Roanoke, VA; WDYN Rossville, GA; WMNA Gretna, VA; WVGM Lynchburg, VA; WBLT Bedford, VA; WMNA-FM Gretna, VA

Three Eagles Communications
7600 County Rd. 120, Salida CO 81201
(719) 539-2575; *Fax:*(719) 539-4851
www.threeeagles.com
gbuchanan@threeeagles.com
Ownership: Gary Buchanan, 100%.
Radio Stns: 1 AM. 3 FM.
KVRH Salida, CO; KBVC Buena Vista, CO; KVRH-FM Salida, CO; KWUZ Poncha Springs, CO
Gary Buchanan, President/COO

3 Point Media
980 N. Michigan Ave., Suite 1880, Chicago IL 60611
(312) 204-9900; *Fax:*(312) 587-9466
Radio Stns: 4 FM.

KCUA Naples, UT; KNIV Lyman, WY; KMGR Delta, UT; KZNSFM) Coalville, UT

Three Rivers Media Corp.
Box 1247, Wytheville VA 24382
(276) 228-3185; *Fax:*(276) 228-9261
3 Rivers Media.net
wyve.wxbx@wiredog.com
Radio Stns: 2 AM. 1 FM.
WLOY Rural Retreat, VA; WYVE Wytheville, VA; WXBX Rural Retreat, VA
Gary W. Hagerich, COO

Thunderbolt Broadcasting Co.
1410 N. Lindell St., Martin TN 38237
(731) 587-9526; *Fax:*(731) 587-5079
www.thunderboltradio.com
Ownership: Paul Freeman Tinkle, trustee of the Paul Freeman Tinkle Revocable Trust, 40.42%; Jimmy C. Smith, 23.75%; Thomas L. Moore Jr., 19.16%; and Fred C.Stoker, 16.67%.
Radio Stns: 1 AM. 4 FM.
WCMT Martin, TN; WCDZ Dresden, TN; WCMT Martin, TN; WQAK Union City, TN; KYTN Union City, TN
Paul Tinkle, President

Tiger Communications Inc.
2514 S. College St., Suite 104, Auburn AL 36832
(334) 821-6078
Ownership: Thomas Hayley, 100%.
Radio Stns: 4 AM. 2 FM.
WAUD Auburn, AL; WACQ Tuskegee, AL; WRLA West Point, GA; WTRP LaGrange, GA; WQNR Tallassee, AL; WTGZ Union Springs, AL
Thomas Hayley, President

Toccoa Foundation
179 Cross Creek Dr., Toccoa GA 30577
(709) 491-4457
Radio Stns: 1 FM.
WHTD Tallulah Falls, GA

Tom Ingstad Broadcasting Group
148 E Highway 28, Morris MN 56267
(952) 938-0575; *Fax:*(952) 938-2295
Radio Stns: 4 AM. 4 FM.
KDMA Montevideo, MN; KDUZ Hutchinson, MN; KKAQ Thief River Falls, MN; KMRS Morris, MN; KRVY-FM Starbuck, MN; KARP-FM Dassel, MN; KKRC Granite Falls, MN; KMGM Montevideo, MN
Tom Ingstad, President/CEO
Janice Ingstad, Chairperson
Tim Ost, General Manager
Tanea Clocksene, General Manager
Lynn Lambrecht, Sales Manager
Jamie Dickerman, Program Director
Max Thomas, Program Director
Erin Tombarge, Marketing Specialist
Steve Urness, News Director
Steve Linzmeier, Sports Director

Tomlinson-Leis Communications LP
Box 3649, 800 W. Palestine Ave., Palestine TX 75802
(903) 729-6077
www.tlcmedia.org
Radio Stns: 1 AM. 2 FM.
KNET Palestine, TX; KKHA Markham, TX; KYYK Palestine, TX
Edward Tomlinson II, Chairman
Kent Burkhart, CEO/COO

Top O' Texas Educational Broadcasting Foundation
PO Box 8088, Amarillo TX 79114
(806) 359-8855; *Fax:*(806) 354-2039
www.kingdomkeysradio.org
Radio Stns: 7 FM.
KIJN-FM Farwell, TX; KJRT Amarillo, TX; KPDR Wheeler, TX; KUHC Clayton, NM; KJDR Guymon, OK; KVED Vernon, TX; KWAS Borger, TX

Touch Canada Broadcasting LP.
5316 Calgary Trail NW., Edmonton AB T6H 4J8
(780) 466-4930; *Fax:*(780) 469-5335
www.shinefm.com
105.9@shinefm.com
Ownership: Charles R. Allard, 100%.
Radio Stns: 2 AM. 3 FM.
CJCA Edmonton, AB; CJLI Calgary, AB; CJSI-FM Calgary, AB; CJRY-FM Edmonton, AB; CKRD-FM Red Deer, AB
Charles Allard, President
Carol Henders, General Sales Mgr
Marco Auriti, Chief Engineer

Tower Investment Trust Inc.
819 S. Federal Hwy., Suite 106, Stuart FL 34994-2952
(772) 215-1634
Radio Stns: 4 FM.
KTTY New Boston, TX; KLOW Reno, TX; KXXN Iowa Park, TX; WBNK Pine Knoll Shores, NC
Bill Brothers, President
Gary Hess, Operations Dir

Town and Country Broadcasting Inc.
486 W. 2nd St., Xenia OH 45385-3610
(937) 372-3531; *Fax:*(937) 372-3508
Radio Stns: 3 AM.
WBZI Xenia, OH; WEDI Eaton, OH; WKFI Wilmington, OH

Townsend Broadcasting Enterprise
100 Water St., Suite A, Camden AL 36726
(256) 497-2840
Ownership: Townsend Broadcasting Enterprise, 100%.
Radio Stns: 2 FM.
WVPL Dozier, AL; WQLS Camden, AL
Timothy Townsend, President

Townsquare Media
240 Greenwich Ave., Greenwich CT 06830
(203) 861-0900
www.townsquaremedia.com
adrian.soyars@townsquaremedia.com
Ownership: Oaktree Capital Management, 47%; The Madison Square Garden Company, 12%.
Radio Stns: 71 AM. 199 FM.
KYYW Abilene, TX; KBUL Billings, MT; KEEL Shreveport, LA; KEXO Grand Junction, CO; KEZJ Twin Falls, ID; KIDO Nampa, ID; KFYO Lubbock, TX; KGAB Orchard Valley, WY; KGKL San Angelo, TX; KSLI Abilene, TX; KGVO Missoula, MT; KHMO Hannibal, MO; KFXD Boise, ID; KIXZ Amarillo, TX; KJEF Jennings, LA; KJOC Davenport, IA; KKAM Lubbock, TX; KKTL Casper, WY; KOSY Texarkana, AR; KLCL Lake Charles, LA; KMPT East Missoula, MT; KLIX Twin Falls, ID; KLXX Bismarck-Mandan, ND; KLYQ Hamilton, MT; KMMS Bozeman, MT; KMND Midland, TX; KOWB Laramie, WY; WLIQ Quincy, IL; KPEL Lafayette, LA; KPRK Livingston, MT; KRIL Odessa, TX; KROD El Paso, TX; KROF Abbeville, LA; KSEN Shelby, MT; KSFA Nacogdoches, TX; KSIS Sedalia, MO; KSKY Balch Springs, TX; KSOO Sioux Falls, SD; KTEM Temple, TX; KTWO Casper, WY; KWFS Wichita Falls, TX; KWKH Shreveport, LA; KXRB Sioux Falls, SD; KXSS Waite Park, MN; WADB(AM) Asbury Park, NJ; WALL Middletown, NY; WBSM New Bedford, MA; WCHN Norwich, NY; WDBQ Dubuque, IA; WDEA Ellsworth, ME; WDLA Walton, NY; WDOS Oneonta, NY; WEBC Duluth, MN; WEOK Poughkeepsie, NY; WJZN Augusta, ME; WFNT Flint, MI; WPGG Atlantic City, NJ; WGBF Evansville, IN; WIBX Utica, NY; WJIM Lansing, MI; WJON St. Cloud, MN; WKNY Kingston, NY; WYOS Binghamton, NY; WLCO Lapeer, MI; WNBF Binghamton, NY; WNWZ Grand Rapids, MI; WOBM Lakewood Township, NJ; WOMI Owensboro, KY; WTSK Tuscaloosa, AL; WTVL Waterville, ME; WVFN East Lansing, MI; KACL Bismarck, ND; KAFX-FM Diboll, TX; KSAS-FM Caldwell, ID; KMJI Ashdown, AR; KATP Amarillo, TX; KZBT Midland, TX; KMHK Billings, MT; KBKL Grand Junction, CO; KBAZ Hamilton, MT; KMXJ-FM Amarillo, TX; KBYZ Bismarck, ND; KCGY Laramie, WY; KCIX Garden City, ID; KQBR Lubbock, TX; KNRX Sterling City, TX; KCTR-FM Billings, MT; KEAN-FM Abilene, TX; KEKB Fruita, CO; KELI San Angelo, TX; KEYJ-FM Abilene, TX; KFMX-FM Lubbock, TX; KPEL-FM Breaux Bridge, LA; KBAT Monahans, TX; KGKL-FM San Angelo, TX; KNGT Lake Charles, LA; KICK-FM Palmyra, MO; KIKN-FM Salem, SD; KISX Whitehouse, TX; KXKS-FM Shreveport, LA; KIXS Victoria, TX; KHLA Jennings, LA; KKBR Billings, MT; KKCB Duluth, MN; KKCL Lorenzo, TX; KKCN Ballinger, TX; KKCT Bismarck, ND; KOEL-FM Cedar Falls, IA; KKLS-FM Sioux Falls, SD; KGEE Pecos, TX; KKNN Delta, CO; KZRV Sartell, MN; KKTX-FM Kilgore, TX; KKYR-FM Texarkana, TX; KLAQ El Paso, TX; KLAW Lawton, OK; KLDJ Duluth, MN; KLEN Cheyenne, WY; KLIX-FM Twin Falls, ID; KAWO Boise, ID; KLTD Temple, TX; KLUB Bloomington, TX; KLYV Dubuque, IA; KLZZ Waite Park, MN; KMDL Kaplan, LA; KMHK Billings, MT; KRNK Casper, WY; KXSS-FM Amarillo, TX; KMMS-FM Bozeman, MT; KIGN Burns, WY; KMXC Sioux Falls, SD; KMXK Cold Spring, MN; KMXY Grand Junction, CO; KNIN-FM Wichita Falls, TX; KPRF Amarillo, TX; KNUE Tyler, TX; KODM Odessa, TX; KOOC(FM) Belton, TX; KSSM Copperas Cove, TX; KULL Abilene, TX; KFTE Abbeville, LA; KPWW Hooks, TX; KDBL(FM) Toppenish, WA; KJMH Lake Charles, LA; KENR Superior, MT; KTSR De Quincy, LA; KARS-FM Laramie, WY; KKPL Cheyenne, WY; KRRY Canton, MO; KRUF Shreveport, LA; KRVK Vista West, WY; KHXT Erath, LA; KISN Belgrade, MT; KSDL Sedalia, MO; KSII El Paso, TX; KTBQ Nacogdoches, TX; KTDY Lafayette, LA; KBZS Wichita Falls, TX; KTRR Loveland, CO; KTRS-FM Casper, WY; KTUX Carthage, TX; KTYL-FM Tyler, TX; KUAD-FM Windsor, CO; KMWX Abilene, TX; KBMX Proctor, MN; KVKI-FM Shreveport, LA; KVLL-FM Wells, TX; KQVT Victoria, TX; KVRW Lawton, OK; KWFS-FM Wichita Falls, TX; KWYY Midwest, WY; KXGE Dubuque, IA; KXKX Knob Noster, MO; KXLT-FM Eagle, ID; KYBB Canton, SD; KYGL Texarkana, AR; KYKS Lufkin, TX; KYSS-FM Missoula, MT; KUSJ Harker Heights, TX; KZCD Lawton, OK; KZII-FM Lubbock, TX; KZIN-FM Shelby, MT; WTMM-FM Mechanicville, NY; WBKR Owensboro, KY; WBKT Norwich, NY; WBLK Depew, NY; WBLM Portland, ME; WKXP Kingston, NY; WBPW Presque Isle, ME; WBCK-FM Battle Creek, MI; WBZN Old Town, ME; WCHR-FM Manahawkin, NJ; WCRZ Flint, MI; WCYY Biddeford, ME; WCZX Hyde Park, NY; WDBQ-FM Galena, IL; WDHI Delhi, NY; WDKS Newburgh, IN; WDLA-FM Walton, NY; WRRB Arlington, NY; WEBB Waterville, ME; WSJO Egg Harbor City, NJ; WEZQ Bangor, ME; WFFN Coaling, AL; WFGR Grand Rapids, MI; WFHN Fairhaven, MA; WFMK Lansing, MI; WFPG Atlantic City, NJ; WFRG-FM Utica, NY; WGBF-FM Henderson, KY; WGNA-FM Albany, NY; WGRD-FM Grand Rapids, MI; WHOM Mount Washington, NH; WHWK Binghamton, NY; WITL Lansing, MI; WIYN Deposit, NY; WJIM Lansing, MI; WJLK Asbury Park, NJ; WJOD Asbury, IA; WJYE Buffalo, NY; WKDQ Henderson, KY; WKXW Trenton, NJ; WKXZ Norwich, NY; WBUF Buffalo, NY; WLHT-FM Grand Rapids, MI; WLZW Utica, NY; WMME-FM Augusta, ME; WMMQ Lansing, MI; WQSH Malta, NY; WOBM-FM Toms River, NJ; WODZ-FM Rome, NY; WOKQ Dover, NH; WOZI Presque Isle, ME; WPDA Jeffersonville, NY; WPDH Poughkeepsie, NY; WPKQ North Conway, NH; WPUR Atlantic City, NJ; WQBJ Cobleskill, NY; WQBK-FM Rensselaer, NY; WQCB Brewer, ME; WQHR Presque Isle, ME; WRRV Middletown, NY; WQUS Lapeer, MI; WSRK Oneonta, NY; WBEI Reform, AL; WTRV Walker, MI; WTUG-FM Northport, AL; WWBN Tuscola, MI; WWJO St. Cloud, MN; WBXX Marshall, MI; WSHK Kittery, ME; WSAK Hampton, NH; WJLT Evansville, IN; WWYL Chenango Bridge, NY; WYRK Buffalo, NY; WZAD Wurtsboro, NY; WZOZ Oneonta, NY; KXLB Livingston, MT; WRCL Frankenmuth, MI; WDGM Greensboro, AL; KZMY Bozeman, MT; KRQN Vinton, IA; KMAX-FM Wellington, CO; KUSB Hazelton, ND; KDEZ Brandon, SD; KSOO-FM Lennox, SD; KGVO-FM Frenchtown, MT; WTBD-FM Delhi, NY; KCHH Worden, MT; WENJ Millville, NJ
Steven Price, Chairman
Dhruv Prasad, Co-Cheif Executive Officer
Adrian Soyars, Digital Sales Manager
Michael Josephs, EVP, Business Development and Aquisitions
Stuart Rosenstein, EVP and Chief Financial Officer
Scott Schatz, EVP, Operations and Technology

Tri-County Broadcasting Inc.
Box 366, Sauk Rapids MN 56379
(320) 252-6200; *Fax:*(320) 252-9367
Radio Stns: 2 AM. 1 FM.
WBHR Sauk Rapids, MN; WVAL Sauk Rapids, MN; WHMH-FM Sauk Rapids, MN

Tribune Broadcasting Co.
435 N. Michigan Ave., Suite 1800, Chicago IL 60611
(312) 222-3333; *Fax:*(312) 329-0611
www.tribune.com
Ownership: The Tribune Employee Stock Ownership Plan as implemented through the Tribune Employee Stock Ownership Trust, Oak Brook, IL, 100%.
Radio Stns: 1 AM.
WGN(AM) Chicago, IL
TV Stns: 40 TV.
KAUT Oklahoma City, OK; KCPQ Tacoma, WA; KDAF Dallas, TX; KDVR Denver, CO; KFOR Oklahoma City, OK; KFSM Fort Smith, AR; KIAH Houston, TX; KPLR St. Louis, MO; KSTU Salt Lake City, UT; KSWB San Diego, CA; KTLA Los Angeles, CA; KTVI St. Louis, MO; KZJO Seattle, WA; KTXL Sacramento, CA; KRCW Salem, OR; KXNW Eureka Springs, AR; KWGN Denver, CO; WDCW Washington, DC; WSFL Miami, FL; WDAF Kansas City, MO; WGHP High Point, NC; WGN Chicago, IL; WGNO New Orleans, LA; WHNT Huntsville, AL; WHO-DT Des Moines, IA; WITI Milwaukee, WI; WJW Cleveland, OH; WNOL New Orleans, LA; WPHL Philadelphia, PA; WPIX New York, NY; WPMT York, PA; WQAD Moline, IL; WREG-TV Memphis, TN; WTIC-TV Hartford, CT; WTTK Kokomo, IN; WTTV Bloomington, IN; WTVR Richmond, VA; WCCT Waterbury, CT; WXIN Indianapolis, IN; WXMI Battle Creek, MI
Larry Wert, President of Broadcast Media

Truth Broadcasting Corp.
4405 Providence Ln., Suite D, Winston-Salem NC 27106
(336) 759-0363; *Fax:*(336) 759-0366
www.truthnetwork.com
info@truthnetwork.com
Radio Stns: 5 AM.
WCRU Dallas, NC; WDRU Creedmore, NC; WKEW Greensboro, NC; WPOL Winston-Salem, NC; WTRU Kernersville, NC

Stuart Epperson, President

Tune In Broadcasting LLC
1721 Black River Rd., Rome NY 13440
(315) 335-2795
Ownership: Coreen Frisch.
Radio Stns: 1 AM.
WKAL Rome, NY
Ron Frisch, President

2510 Licenses LLC
100 Ryan Ct., Suite 98, Pittsburgh PA 15205
(412) 489-1001; *Fax:*(412) 489-1002
Radio Stns: 5 FM.
KFFB Fairfield Bay, AR; WEMR Pleasant Gap, PA; WBHV-FM State College, PA; WOWY University Park, PA; WLKH Somerset, PA

Tyler Media Broadcasting Corp.
5101 S. Shields Blvd., Oklahoma City OK 73129
(405) 616-5500; *Fax:*(405) 616-5505
www.tylermedia.com
Radio Stns: 2 AM. 7 FM.
KOKC Oklahoma City, OK; KEBC Del City, OK; KTUZ-FM Okarche, OK; KJKE Newcastle, OK; KMGL Oklahoma City, OK; KOMA Oklahoma City, OK; KRXO-FM Oklahoma City, OK; K225BN Oklahoma City, OK; K243BJ Oklahoma City, OK
Ty Tyler, President

UB Louisville
6721 W. 121st St., Overland Park KS 66209
(913) 344-1500
Radio Stns: 1 FM.
WLCL Sellersburg, IN

United Ministries
300 E. Rock Rd., Allentown PA 18103
(970) 254-5565; *Fax:*(970) 254-5550
Radio Stns: 2 AM.
KDTA Delta, CO; KJOL Grand Junction, CO

United States CP LLC
1311 Swanner Court, High Point NC 27262
(336) 307-3828
Ownership: W. Philip Robinson, 100% voting interest, 9.9% ownership interest.
Radio Stns: 1 AM. 6 FM.
KCBR Monument, CO; KNKN(FM) Pueblo, CO; KRKY-FM Estes Park, CO; KRMX Marlin, TX; KRYE Olney Springs, CO; KXCL Rock Creek Park, CO; WKHF(FM) Lynchburg, VA

Unity Broadcasting LLC.
3765 N. John Young Pkwy., Orlando FL 32804
(407) 291-1395
Radio Stns: 4 AM.
WKIQ Eustis, FL; WNTF Bithlo, FL; WLAA Winter Garden, FL; WOKB Winter Garden, FL
Shanti Persaud, President

Universal Broadcasting of New York Inc.
Corporate Offices, WTHE Radio 260 E. 2nd St., Mineola NY 11501
(516) 742-1520; *Fax:*(516) 742-2878
www.wthe1520am.com
nygospelradio@aol.com
Ownership: Howard Warshaw and Miriam Warshaw.
Radio Stns: 2 AM.
WTHE Mineola, NY; WVNJ Oakland, NJ
Miriam Warshaw, President
Howard Warshaw, VP

Univision Radio
605 3rd Ave., 12th Fl., New York NY 10158
(212) 455-5200
www.univision.com
Ownership: Univision Communications Inc., 100% (see listing under TV Group Ownership, Section B).
Radio Stns: 15 AM. 53 FM.
KAMA El Paso, TX; KQBU El Paso, TX; KCOR San Antonio, TX; KFLC Benbrook, TX; KGBT Harlingen, TX; KLAT Houston, TX; KLSQ Whitney, NV; KTNQ Los Angeles, CA; WADO New York, NY; WYEL Mayaguez, PR; WAQI Miami, FL; WUKQ Ponce, PR; WKAQ San Juan, PR; WRTO Chicago, IL; WQBA Miami, FL; KRCD Inglewood, CA; KLJA Georgetown, TX; KLLE North Fork, CA; KVVF Santa Clara, CA; KBNA-FM El Paso, TX; KBRG San Jose, CA; KBBT Schertz, TX; KKMR Arizona City, AZ; KJFA-FM Santa Fe, NM; KQMR Globe, AZ; KFZO Lewisville, TX; KESS Benbrook, TX; KOMR Sun City, AZ; KGBT-FM McAllen, TX; KDXX Denton, TX; KHOT-FM Paradise Valley, AZ; KIOT Los Lunas, NM; KISF Las Vegas, NV; KBTQ Harlingen, TX; KVVZ San Rafael, CA; KKSS Santa Fe, NM; KLNV San Diego, CA; KLQV San Diego, CA; KLTN Houston, TX; KLNO Fort Worth, TX; KLVE Los Angeles, CA; KRDA Hanford, CA; KHOV-FM Wickenburg, AZ; KAMA-FM Deer Park, TX; KQBU-FM Port Arthur, TX; KRGT Indian Springs, NV; KLQB Taylor, TX; KOVE-FM Galveston, TX; KMYO Comfort, TX; KROM San Antonio, TX; KKRG Albuquerque, NM; KRCV West Covina, CA; KSCA Glendale, CA; KSOL San Francisco, CA; KXTN-FM San Antonio, TX; KOND Clovis, CA; KSQL Santa Cruz, CA; WAMR-FM Miami, FL; WVIX Lemont, IL; WKAQ-FM San Juan, PR; WQBU-FM Garden City, NY; WOJO Evanston, IL; WXNY-FM New York, NY; WRTO-FM Goulds, FL; WUKQ-FM Mayaguez, PR; WVIV-FM Highland Park, IL; WPPN Des Plaines, IL; KAJZ Llano, TX
Randy Falco, President & CEO
Tonia O'Connor, President, Content Distribution
Alberto Ciurana, President, Programming and Content
Keith Turner, President of Advertising Sales and Marketing

Uno Radio Group
P.O. Box 363222, San Juan PR 00936-3222
(787) 474-0630; *Fax:*(787) 758-1410
www.unoradio.com
Ownership: Jesus M. Soto.
Radio Stns: 6 AM. 7 FM.
WCMN Arecibo, PR; WNEL Caguas, PR; WORA Mayaguez, PR; WPRP Ponce, PR; WUNO San Juan, PR; WLEO Ponce, PR; WCMN-FM Arecibo, PR; WFID Rio Piedras, PR; WIVA-FM Aguadilla, PR; WMIO Cabo Rojo, PR; WFDT Aguada, PR; WPRM-FM San Juan, PR; WRIO Ponce, PR
Jesus Soto, CEO
Luis Soto, President
Vicente Belgodere, Sales
Ray Cruz, Vice President of Programming
Luis Gonzalez, Vice President of Finance

Urban One Broadcasting Network LLC
414 S.W. 140th Terrace, Newberry FL 32669
(352) 328-6232
Ownership: William Johnson.
Radio Stns: 1 FM.
WURB Cross City, FL
William Johnson, President

Urban Radio Licenses LLC
273 Azalea Rd., Suite 1-308, Mobile AL 36609
(251) 343-4900; *Fax:*(251) 343-4905
www.urbanradio.fm
info@urbanradio.fm
Radio Stns: 4 AM. 9 FM.
WLAY Muscle Shoals, AL; WKMQ Tupelo, MS; WTUP Tupelo, MS; WVNA Tuscumbia, AL; WAJV Brooksville, MS; WBVV Guntown, MS; WIMX Gibsonburg, OH; WMXV St. Joseph, TN; WJZE Oak Harbor, OH; WLAY-FM Littleville, AL; WVNA-FM Muscle Shoals, AL; WMSU Starkville, MS; WACR-FM Columbus Afb, MS

US Stations LLC
125 Corporate Terr., Hot Springs AR 71913
(501) 525-9700; *Fax:*(501) 525-9739
Radio Stns: 1 AM. 4 FM.
KZNG Hot Springs, AR; KHTO(FM) Hot Springs, AR; KQUS-FM Hot Springs, AR; KLBL Pearcy, AR; KLXQ Mountain Pine, AR
Charles Shinn
Craig Dale
Gary Terrell

Vazquez Broadcasting Corp.
580 W. Clark Rd., Ypsilanti MI 48198
(734) 484-1480
Ownership: Baudelio Vazquez.
Radio Stns: 1 AM.
WSDS Salem Township, MI
Jose Luis Vazquez, President
Alex Resendez, General Manager and Program Director

VCY America Inc.
3434 W. Kilbourn Ave., Milwaukee WI 53208
(414) 935-3000; *Fax:*(414) 935-3015
www.vcyamerica.org
vcy@vcyamerica.org
Ownership: VCY America, Inc.
Radio Stns: 1 AM. 18 FM.
WVCY Oshkosh, WI; KCVS Salina, KS; KVCX Gregory, SD; KVCY Fort Scott, KS; WVCN Baraga, MI; WEGZ Washburn, WI; WJIC Zanesville, OH; WVCF Eau Claire, WI; WVCX Tomah, WI; WVCY-FM Milwaukee, WI; WVCM Iron Mountain, MI; WVFL Fond Du Lac, WI; KVCF Freeman, SD; WVRN Wittenberg, WI; KVFL Pierre, SD; KVCS Spring Valley, MN; KVCH Huron, SD; WQRN Cook, MN; WVCS Owen, WI
TV Stns: 1 TV.
WVCY-TV Milwaukee, WI
Vic Eliason, VP/Gen Mgr
Jim Schneider, Programming Director

Vermont Broadcast Associates Inc.
Box 97, Lyndonville VT 05851
(802) 626-9800; *Fax:*(802) 626-8500
Ownership: Bruce A. James, 100%.
Radio Stns: 2 AM. 6 FM.
WIKE Newport, VT; WSTJ St. Johnsbury, VT; WGMT Lyndon, VT; WKXH St. Johnsbury, VT; WMOO Derby Center, VT; WMTK Littleton, NH; WQJQ Barton, VT; WJJZ Irasberg, VT
Bruce A. James, President

Vernal Enterprises Inc.
Box 1032, Indiana PA 15701-1032
(724) 543-1380; *Fax:*(724) 543-1140
Radio Stns: 1 AM.
WNCC Barnesboro, PA

Vernon R Baldwin Inc.
8686 Michael Lane, Fairfield OH 45014-3015
(513) 829-8686
Ownership: Baldwin Broadcasting Inc., 100%.
Radio Stns: 2 AM. 3 FM.
WCNW Fairfield, OH; WMOH Hamilton, OH; WNLT Delhi Hills, OH; WKLN Wilmington, OH; WVRB Wilmore, KY
Marcella Baldwin, President

Vero Beach Broadcasters LLC
1235 16th St., Vero Beach FL 32960
(772) 794-7748; *Fax:*(772) 562-4747
www.937wgyl.com
Radio Stns: 1 AM. 3 FM.
WTTB Vero Beach, FL; WGYL Vero Beach, FL; WOSN Indian River Shores, FL; WJKD Vero Beach, FL
Jim Davis, General Manager
Karen Franke, Station Manager
John Anthony, Programming Director
Miguel Santiesteban, Promotions Manager

VerStandig Broadcasting
4850 Connecticut Ave. N.W., Suite 103, Washington DC 20008
(202) 244-1422; *Fax:*(202) 362-4149
Ownership: John VerStandig, 1996 VerStandig Children's Trust, M. Belmont VerStandig Trust.
Radio Stns: 3 AM. 5 FM.
WHBG Harrisonburg, VA; WCBG Waynesboro, PA; WSVA Harrisonburg, VA; WTGD Bridgewater, VA; WBHB-FM Waynesboro, PA; WJDV Broadway, VA; WQPO Harrisonburg, VA; WAYZ Hagerstown, MD
John VerStandig, CEO

Victoria RadioWorks Ltd.
8023 Vantage Dr., Suite 840, San Antonio TX 78230
(210) 340-7080; *Fax:*(210) 341-1777
Radio Stns: 2 AM. 3 FM.
KVNN Victoria, TX; KNAL Victoria, TX; KBAR-FM Victoria, TX; KITE Port Lavaca, TX; KVIC Victoria, TX
John Barger, President
Cindy Cox, General Manager

Vidalia Communications Corp.
Box 900, Hwy 280 W., Vidalia GA 30474
(912) 537-9202; *Fax:*(912) 537-4477
www.southeastgeorgiatoday.com
zfowler@vidaliacommunications.com
Radio Stns: 1 AM. 2 FM.
WVOP Vidalia, GA; WTCQ Vidalia, GA; WYUM Mount Vernon, GA
Zack Fowler, General Manager
John Koon, General Sales Mgr
Dick Boekeloo, Chief Engineer
Dorothy Davis, Office Manager

Viper Communications Inc.
PO Box 225, Osage Beach MO 65065
(573) 348-2772; *Fax:*(573) 348-2779
www.krmsradio.com
Radio Stns: 2 AM. 1 FM.
KRMS Osage Beach, MO; WENG Englewood, FL; KMYK Osage Beach, MO
Dennis Klautzer, Co-Owner
Ken Kuenzie, Co-Owner

Visionary Related Entertainment L.L.C.
Box 1437, Wailuku HI 96793
(808) 244-9145; *Fax:*(808) 244-8247
www.kaoi.net

kaoi@kaoi.net
Ownership: Visionary Related Entertainment Inc., 50.1% of votes, 40.58% of total assets; Frontier Radio Investors L.L.C., 49.9% of votes, 59.42% of totalassets.
Radio Stns: 1 AM. 4 FM.
KAOI Kihei, HI; KAOI-FM Wailuku, HI; KDLX Makawao, HI; KNUQ Paauilo, HI; KHEI-FM Kihei, HI
John Detz, President
James McKeon, VP

Vista Radio Ltd.
201-910 Fitzgerald Ave., Courtenay BC V9N 2R5
(250) 338-1133
www.vistaradio.ca
apersaud@vistaradio.ca
Ownership: Westerkirk Capital Inc.
Radio Stns: 6 AM. 42 FM.
CFBV Smithers, BC; CFLD Burns Lake, BC; CFNI Port Hardy, BC; CIVH Vanderhoof, BC; CKBX 100 Mile House, BC; CKWL Williams Lake, BC; CFBG-FM Bracebridge, ON; CFBK-FM Huntsville, ON; CFCP-FM Comox Valley, BC; CFFM-FM Williams Lake, BC; CIRX-FM Prince George, BC; CJCD-FM Yellowknife, NT; CJCS-FM Stratford, ON; CFLZ-FM Fort Erie, ON; CKLP-FM Parry Sound, ON; CKNR-FM Elliot Lake, ON; CKQR-FM Castlegar, BC; CFIF-FM Iroquois Falls, ON; CHMS-FM Bancroft, ON; CKLM-FM Lloydminster, AB; CJSU-FM Duncan, BC; CKAP-FM Kapuskasing, ON; CJED-FM Niagara Falls, ON; CHMT-FM Timmins, ON; CHGK-FM Stratford, ON; CJCI-FM Prince George, BC; CFSF-FM Sturgeon Falls, ON; CHPB-FM Cochrane, ON; CKGF-FM Grand Forks, BC; CJLT-FM Medicine Hat, AB; CKCQ-FM Quesnel, BC; CFXN-FM North Bay, ON; CHNV-FM Nelson, BC; CKAY-FM Gibsons, BC; CFZN-FM Haliburton, ON; CFNA-FM Bonnyville, AB; CFRI-FM Grande Prairie, AB; CJFB-FM Bolton, ON; CJJM-FM Espanola, ON; CFPW-FM Powell River, BC; CIQC-FM Campbell River, BC; CKVV-FM Kemptville, ON; CHBY-FM Barry's Bay, ON; CFGM-FM Caledon, ON; CKPP-FM Prescott, ON; CIRX-FM-1 Vanderhoof, BC; CKCV-FM Creston, BC; CFFM-FM-2 Quesnel, BC
Geoff Poulton, President
Andy Boyd, Chief Financial Officer
Sean Matheson, General Manager, NTR Sales Division
Lisa Walker, Regional & National Sales Director
Murray Brookshaw, National Director of Programming
Darren Fowler, Engineering Director

Vox AM/FM LLC
70 Walnut St., Suite 411, Wellesley MA 2481
(781) 239-8018; *Fax:*(781) 239-8007
voxmedia@aol.com
Radio Stns: 2 AM. 5 FM.
WEAV Plattsburgh, NY; WCVR(AM) Randolph, VT; WCPV Essex, NY; WVXR Randolph, VT; WEZF Burlington, VT; WVTK Port Henry, NY; WXZO Willsboro, NY

W&B Broadcasting Inc
519 N. Miles St., Suite 3, Elizabethtown KY 42701
(270) 766-1035
Ownership: William Walters, 100%.
Radio Stns: 1 AM. 1 FM.
WAKY Radcliff, KY; WAKY Radcliff, KY
Bill Walters, President

Wagenvoord Advertising Group Inc.
2360 N.E. Coachman Rd., Clearwater FL 33765
(727) 726-8247; *Fax:*(727) 799-8866
www.tantalk1340.com
Radio Stns: 3 AM.
WDCF Dade City, FL; WTAN Clearwater, FL; WZHR Zephyrhills, FL
Lola Wagenvoord, General Manager

Wagon Wheel Broadcasting LLC
201 N. Union St., Suite 340, Alexandria VA 22314
(703) 519-3703; *Fax:*(703) 519-9756
Radio Stns: 3 FM.
WIKI Carrollton, KY; WSCH Aurora, IN; WXCH Columbus, IN

Wagonwheel Communications Corp.
40 Shoshone Ave., Green River WY 82935
(307) 875-6666; *Fax:*(303) 875-5847
www.theradionetwork.net
Radio Stns: 1 AM. 3 FM.
KUGR Green River, WY; KFRZ Green River, WY; KYCS Rock Springs, WY; KZWB Green River, WY

Walking by Faith Ministries Inc.
336 Rodenberg Ave., Biloxi MS 39531-3444
(228) 374-9739
Radio Stns: 3 AM.
WAML Laurel, MS; WQFX Gulfport, MS; WMLC Monticello, MS
James Black, President

Waller Broadcasting
Box 1648, Jacksonville TX 75766
(903) 586-2527; *Fax:*(903) 586-1394
Radio Stns: 1 AM. 4 FM.
KEBE Jacksonville, TX; KZQX Tatum, TX; KFRO-FM Gilmer, TX; KLJT Jacksonville, TX; KMPA Pittsburg, TX
Dudley Waller, CEO
Dave Moreland, Operations Dir

Wallingford Broadcasting Co.
128 Big Hill Ave., Richmond KY 40475
(859) 623-1386; *Fax:*(859) 623-1341
www.wcyofm.com
Radio Stns: 3 AM. 2 FM.
WEKY Richmond, KY; WIRV Irvine, KY; WKXO Berea, KY; WCYO Irvine, KY; WLFX Berea, KY
Kelly Wallingford, CEO

Walton Stns
Box 776, Kermit TX 79745
(432) 586-3366; *Fax:*(432) 586-3958
Ownership: John B. Walton, 100%.
Radio Stns: 2 AM. 1 FM.
KBUY Ruidoso, NM; KWES Ruidoso, NM; KWES-FM Ruidoso, NM
John Walton, President
Harold Oakes, General Manager

WAMC/Northeast Public Radio
318 Central Ave., Albany NY 12206
(518) 465-5233; *Fax:*(518) 432-6974
www.wamc.org
mail@wamc.org
Ownership: Non-stock educ corporation.
Radio Stns: 2 AM. 9 FM.
WAMC Albany, NY; WUTI Utica, NY; WAMC-FM Albany, NY; WAMK Kingston, NY; WAMQ Great Barrington, MA; WANC Ticonderoga, NY; WCAN Canajoharie, NY; WCEL Plattsburgh, NY; WOSR Middletown, NY; WRUN Remsen, NY; WWES Mount Kisco, NY
Alan Chartock, President/CEO
David Galletly, SVP/CFO

WAY Media Inc.
Box 64500, Colorado Springs CO 80962
(719) 533-0300
www.wayfm.com
Ownership: Robert D. Augsburg, 12.5%; Joe Battaglia, 12.5%; John Scaggs, 12.5%; Felice Augsburg, 12.5%; Kurt Leander, 12.5%; Dusty Black, 12.5%; Neal Joseph, 12.5%; Nancy Overfield-Delmar, 12.5%.
Radio Stns: 17 FM.
KYWA Wichita, KS; WAYF West Palm Beach, FL; WAYJ Naples, FL; WAYM Spring Hill, TN; WAYP Marianna, FL; WSYI Valley Station, KY; WAY New Johnsonville, TN; WAYQ Clarksville, TN; WAYH Harvest, AL; WAYT Thomasville, GA; WAYD Auburn, KY; KXWA Centennial, CO; KBWA Brush, CO; KJWA Trinidad, CO; KRWA Rye, CO; WAYU Steele, AL; *KFWA(FM) Weldona, CO
Robert D. Augsburg, President
Lloyd Parker, COO

Wendlee Broadcasting
600 Fisk St., Brownwood TX 76801
(325) 646-3535; *Fax:*(325) 646-5347
Wendleebroadcasting.com
Ownership: Ray L. Boazman, 50%; Donald Rex Tackett, 50%.
Radio Stns: 1 AM. 2 FM.
KSTA Coleman, TX; KXYL-FM Coleman, TX; KQBZ Brownwood, TX
Rex Tackett, President

WENK of Union City Inc.
1729 Nailling Dr., Union City TN 38261
(731) 885-1240; *Fax:*(731) 885-3405
thailey@wenkwtpr.com
Ownership: Bill Latimer; Robert Kirkland; Robert Terrell Jr.
Radio Stns: 2 AM. 3 FM.
WENK Union City, TN; WTPR Paris, TN; WAKQ Paris, TN; WTPR-FM McKinnon, TN; WWKF Fulton, KY
Bill Latimer, Chairman
Terry Hailey, President

West Alabama Radio Inc.
Box 938, Demopolis AL 36732
(334) 289-9850; *Fax:*(334) 289-9811
Radio Stns: 2 FM.
WINL Linden, AL; WZNJ Demopolis, AL

West Virginia Radio Corp.
1251 Earl L. Core Rd., Morgantown WV 26505
(304) 296-0029; *Fax:*(304) 296-3876
Ownership: Greer Industries, Inc.
Radio Stns: 10 AM. 22 FM.
WAJR Morgantown, WV; WBUC Buckhannon, WV; WKAZ Charleston, WV; WCHS Charleston, WV; WDNE Elkins, WV; WEPM Martinsburg, WV; WJLS Beckley, WV; WKLP Keyser, WV; WCMD Cumberland, MD; WSWW Charleston, WV; WBRB Buckhannon, WV; WBTQ Buckhannon, WV; WDNE-FM Elkins, WV; WDZN Midland, MD; WELK Elkins, WV; WWLW Clarksburg, WV; WJLS-FM Beckley, WV; WKAZ-FM Miami, WV; WKKW Fairmont, WV; WLTF Martinsburg, WV; WKWS Charleston, WV; WQZK-FM Keyser, WV; WRVZ Pocatalico, WV; WFBY Weston, WV; WVAF Charleston, WV; WVAQ Morgantown, WV; WFGM-FM Barrackville, WV; WICL Williamsport, MD; WDYK Ridgeley, WV; WAJR-FM Salem, WV; WVMD Romney, WV; WSWW-FM Craigsville, WV
Harvey Kercheval, Operations VP
Dale Miller, President/CEO
Joe Parsons, Vice President/ General Manager

West Virginia-Virginia Holding Co. LLC
18385 Coal Heritage Rd., Welch WV 24801
(304) 436-2131
Ownership: Bob Spencer; Rick Lambert.
Radio Stns: 1 AM. 2 FM.
WAMN Green Valley, WV; WKQB Pocahontas, VA; WKQR Mullens, WV
Bob Spencer, Manager

Westburg Media Capital LP
530 9th Ave., Kirkland WA 98033
(425) 893-9230
Radio Stns: 2 AM. 2 FM.
KDEB(AM) Estes Park, CO; KRSY Alamogordo, NM; KNMZ Alamogordo, NM; KRSY-FM La Luz, NM

Western Inspirational Broadcasters Inc
PO Box 21888, Carson City NV 89721
(800) 541-5647
www.pilgrimradio.com
info@pilgrimradio.com
Radio Stns: 6 FM.
KPMD Evanston, WY; KNIS Carson City, NV; KLMT Billings, MT; KDNR South Greeley, WY; KTME Reliance, WY; KCSP Casper, WY
Tom Hesse, General Manager

Western Slope Communications LLC
751 Horizon Ct., Suite 225, Grand Junction CO 81506
(970) 241-6460; *Fax:*(970) 241-6452
wscradio.net
kelcie@wscradio.net
Radio Stns: 2 AM. 2 FM.
KAVP Colona, CO; KRGS Rifle, CO; KZKS Rifle, CO; KRVG Glenwood Springs, CO
Cyrene Jagger, Station Manager
Louis Stark, Programming Director
Kelcie Zobel, Business Manager/PSA Coordinator

Western Wyoming Radio
PO Box 1210, Afton WY 83110
(307) 885-5778
Ownership: Western Wyoming Radio, 100%.
Radio Stns: 1 AM. 1 FM.
KRSV Afton, WY; KRSV Afton, WY

Weston Entertainment L.P.
112 E. Pecan St., Suite 1212, San Antonio TX 78205
(386) 423-3289
Radio Stns: 1 AM. 2 FM.
KVRP Stamford, TX; KBPC Crockett, TX; KVRP-FM Haskell, TX
Dennis W. Goodman, Station Manager

Wheeler Broadcasting Inc.
Box K, Grand Coulee WA 99133-0841
(509) 633-2020; *Fax:*(509) 633-1014
Radio Stns: 1 AM. 2 FM.
KEYG Grand Coulee, WA; KEYG-FM Grand Coulee, WA; KXAA Cle Elum, WA
Verl Wheeler, CEO
Mark Wheeler, Operations Dir

White Mountain Radio
1838 W. Commerce Dr., Suite A, Lakeside AZ 85929
(928) 368-8100; *Fax:*(928) 368-8108
Radio Stns: 2 AM. 3 FM.

KDJI Holbrook, AZ; KVWM Show Low, AZ; KRFM Show Low, AZ; KSNX Show Low, AZ; KZUA Holbrook, AZ
F. Lewis Robertson, COO
Henry A. Ash, President

Wilderness Communications LLC
3501 Northwest Evangeline Thruway, Carencro LA 70520
(337) 896-1600; *Fax:*(337) 896-2695
Radio Stns: 1 AM.
WROD Daytona Beach, FL
TV Stns: 2 TV.
KBCA Alexandria, LA; KLWB New Iberia, LA

Wilkins Communications Network Inc.
P.O. Box 444, Spartanburg SC 29304
(864) 585-1885; *Fax:*(864) 597-0687
www.wilkinsradio.com
Ownership: Robert Wilkins; LuAnn Wilkins.
Radio Stns: 22 AM. 5 FM.
KCNW Fairway, KS; KERI Bakersfield, CA; KIOU Shreveport, LA; KKIM Albuquerque, NM; KLNG Council Bluffs, IA; KWDF Ball, LA; KXKS Albuquerque, NM; WASG Daphne, AL; WBRI Indianapolis, IN; WBXR Hazel Green, AL; WCPC Houston, MS; WDZY Colonial Heights, VA; WELP Easley, SC; WFAM Augusta, GA; WITK Pittston, PA; WIJD Prichard, AL; WLMR Chattanooga, TN; WNVY Cantonment, FL; WWNL Pittsburgh, PA; WYYC York, PA; WSKY Asheville, NC; WVTJ Pensacola, FL; WIJD Prichard, AL; WDZY Colonial Heights, VA; WASG Daphne, AL; WIJD Prichard, AL; KWDF Ball, LA
Robert Wilkins, CEO
LuAnn Wilkins, Senior Vice President
Janet Stevens, Director, Corporate Administration and Programming
Julie Ziegler, Chief Financial Officer
Greg Garrett, Senior Director, Operations
Jacob Wilkins, Corporate Vice President

Wilks Broadcast Group LLC
100 North Point Center East, Suite 310, Alpharetta GA 30022
(770) 754-3211; *Fax:*(678) 893-0123
info@wilksbroadcasting.com
Radio Stns: 15 FM.
KBEQ-FM Kansas City, MO; KWOF Broomfield, CO; KFKF-FM Kansas City, KS; KFRR Woodlake, CA; KIMN Denver, CO; KJFX Fresno, CA; KMXV Kansas City, MO; KURK Reno, NV; KMXW Sparks, NV; KCKC Kansas City, MO; KWFP Sparks, NV; KTHX-FM Dayton, NV; KJZN San Joaquin, CA; KXKL-FM Denver, CO; WLVQ Columbus, OH
Jeff Wilks, CEO
Jeff Sanders, President
Stephen Bradshaw, CFO
Lee Killian, Executive Vice President

William W. McCutchen III Stns
1551 Queens Rd., Los Angeles CA 90069
(323) 656-0796
Radio Stns: 2 FM.
KQDR Savoy, TX; KMDR McKinleyville, CA

Williams Communications Inc.
801 Noble St, 8th Fl., Suite 30, Anniston AL 36201
(256) 236-1880; *Fax:*(256) 236-4480
whmabig95.com
whmabig95@cableone.net
Radio Stns: 3 AM. 4 FM.
WHMA Anniston, AL; WLTG Panama City, FL; WZZX Lineville, AL; WHMA-FM Hobson City, AL; WFXO Ashland, AL; WKLS Southside, AL; WFCT Apalachicola, FL
Walton Williams Jr., President

Willis Broadcasting Corp.
645 Church St., Suite 400, Norfolk VA 23510
(757) 622-4600; *Fax:*(757) 624-6515
Radio Stns: 6 AM. 2 FM.
KLPL(AM) Lake Providence, LA; WCPK Chesapeake, VA; WGPL Portsmouth, VA; WGRM Greenwood, MS; WPCE Portsmouth, VA; WTJH East Point, GA; WBXB Edenton, NC; WGRM-FM Greenwood, MS
Levi Willis, President

Wilson Broadcasting Inc.
4106 Ross Clark Circle., Dothan AL 36303
(334) 671-1753; *Fax:*(334) 677-6923
www.wjjn.net
Radio Stns: 1 AM. 2 FM.
WAGF Dothan, AL; WAGF-FM Dothan, AL; WJJN Columbia, AL
James R. Wilson, CEO/President
Jimmy Doctrie, Operations Mgr
Alvin Harvey, General Manager
Jamar M. Wilson, Programming Director

Winton Road Broadcasting Co. LLC
Box 2700, Bakersfield CA 93303
(661) 328-0118; *Fax:*(661) 328-1648
Radio Stns: 3 AM. 3 FM.
KDGO Durango, CO; KENN Farmington, NM; KVFC Cortez, CO; KISZ-FM Cortez, CO; KPTE Durango, CO; KRWN Farmington, NM
Rogers Brandon, President

Withers Broadcasting Co.
Box 1508, Mount Vernon IL 62864
(618) 242-3500; *Fax:*(618) 242-4444
Ownership: W. Russell Withers Jr., 100%.
Radio Stns: 12 AM. 20 FM.
KAPE Cape Girardeau, MO; KOKX Keokuk, IA; KRHW Sikeston, MO; KJXX Jackson, MO; WEBQ Harrisburg, IL; WFRX West Frankfort, IL; WILY Centralia, IL; WMIX Mount Vernon, IL; WMOK Metropolis, IL; WQUL Woodruff, SC; WROY Carmi, IL; WSDR Sterling, IL; KBXB Sikeston, MO; KGMO Cape Girardeau, MO; KOKX-FM Keokuk, IA; KRNQ Keokuk, IA; WDDD-FM Johnston City, IL; WEBQ-FM Eldorado, IL; WGKY Wickliffe, KY; WKIB Anna, IL; WMIX-FM Mount Vernon, IL; WREZ Metropolis, IL; WRUL Carmi, IL; WRXX Centralia, IL; WSSQ Sterling, IL; WTAO-FM Herrin, IL; WYNG Mount Carmel, IL; WVZA Murphysboro, IL; WZZL Reidland, KY; WZZT Morrison, IL; WISH-FM Galatia, IL; WCEZ Carthage, IL
TV Stns: 2 TV.
WDTV Weston, WV; WVFX Clarksburg, WV
W. Russell Withers, President

WJAG Inc.
Box 789, Norfolk NE 68702-0789
(402) 371-0780; *Fax:*(402) 371-6303
Ownership: E.F. Huse Jr., 51%; Mary E. Olsen Revocable Trust, Doug Oldaker, trustee, 45%.
Radio Stns: 1 AM. 2 FM.
WJAG Norfolk, NE; KQKX Norfolk, NE; KEXL Pierce, NE
Bradley S. Hughes, EVP

WOLF Radio Inc.
401 W. Kirkpatrick St., Syracuse NY 13204
(315) 472-0222; *Fax:*(315) 478-7745
Radio Stns: 2 AM. 2 FM.
WMBO Auburn, NY; WOLF Syracuse, NY; WMVN Sylvan Beach, NY; WWLF-FM Oswego, NY
Craig Fox, President

Wolfhouse Radio Group Inc.
548 E. Alisal St., Salinas CA 93905
(831) 757-1910; *Fax:*(831) 757-8015
Radio Stns: 1 AM. 3 FM.
KTGE Salinas, CA; KMJV Soledad, CA; KRAY-FM Salinas, CA; KEXA King City, CA
Hector Villalobos, President

Woodrow Michael Warren Stns
P.O. Box 106, Alturas CA 96101
(530) 233-4842; *Fax:*(530) 233-4173
Radio Stns: 2 FM.
KALT-FM Alturas, CA; KLCR Lakeview, OR
Woodrow Warren, President
Matt Warren, Operations Dir
Mike Warren, General Manager

Woodward Communications Inc.
Box 688, Dubuque IA 52004-0688
(563) 588-5687; *Fax:*(563) 588-5739
www.wcinet.com
Ownership: Woodward Communications Inc. Employee Stock Ownership Trust, 60%
Radio Stns: 4 AM. 7 FM.
KWLO Waterloo, IA; KXEL Waterloo, IA; WHBY Kimberly, WI; WSCO Appleton, WI; KFMW Waterloo, IA; KOKZ Waterloo, IA; WAPL Appleton, WI; WKZG Seymour, WI; WZOR Mishicot, WI; WKSZ De Pere, WI; WKZY Chilton, WI
Tom Woodward, President

Wooster Republican Printing Co.
212 E. Liberty St., Wooster OH 44691
(330) 264-3511; *Fax:*(330) 263-5013
www.dixcom.com
Ownership: (dba Dix Communications).
Radio Stns: 3 AM. 6 FM.
WFRB Frostburg, MD; WKVX Wooster, OH; WTBO Cumberland, MD; WFRB-FM Frostburg, MD; WKGO Cumberland, MD; WNDD Silver Springs, FL; WNDT Alachua, FL; WOGK Ocala, FL; WQKT Wooster, OH
Dale Gerber, CFO
G. Charles Dix, VP
Robert Dix, TV Division Chairman

Word Broadcasting Network Inc.
Box 19229, Louisville KY 40259
(502) 964-3304; *Fax:*(502) 966-9692
www.wbna21.com
Radio Stns: 3 AM.
WYRM Norfolk, VA; WYMM Jacksonville, FL; WVHI Evansville, IN
TV Stns: 1 TV.
WBNA Louisville, KY
Bob Rogers, President
Greg Holt, Operations Dir

Word Radio Educational Foundation
P.O. Box 398, New Durham NH 03855
(603) 859-9170; *Fax:*(603) 859-8172
www.communityliferadio.org
Radio Stns: 4 FM.
WMTP Conway, NH; WSEW Sanford, ME; WRKJ Westbrook, ME; WMEK Kennebunkport, ME
Ronald R. Malone, President

World Radio Link Inc.
Box 5429, Twin Falls ID 83303-5429
(208) 733-3551
Radio Stns: 2 FM.
WSIZ-FM Jacksonville, GA; KXRV Cannon Ball, ND
Earl Williamson, President

World Radio Network Inc.
Box 3765, McAllen TX 78502-3765
(956) 787-9788; *Fax:*(956) 787-9783
www.wrn-rcm.org
Ownership: Non-profit corporation. Note: World Radio Network Inc. is affiliated with World Radio Missionary Fellowship Inc., which operates international sw missionary stnHCJB in Quito, Ecuador.
Radio Stns: 8 FM.
KBNJ Corpus Christi, TX; KBNL Laredo, TX; KBNR Brownsville, TX; KRMB Bisbee, AZ; KRUC Las Cruces, NM; KVER El Paso, TX; KVMV Mc Allen, TX; KYRM Yuma, AZ
Ted Haney, President
Glenn Lafitte, Director

WRD Entertainment Inc.
Box 2077, Batesville AR 72503
(870) 793-4196; *Fax:*(870) 793-5222
Radio Stns: 2 AM. 4 FM.
KAAB Batesville, AR; KBTA Batesville, AR; KBTA-FM Batesville, AR; KWOZ Mountain View, AR; KZLE Batesville, AR; KKIK Horseshoe Bend, AR
John Grace, President
Gary Bridgman, General Manager

Wright Broadcasting Systems
Box 587, Weatherford OK 73096
(580) 772-5939; *Fax:*(580) 772-1590
www.wrightwradio.com
traffic@wrightradio.com
Ownership: G. Harold Wright, 100%.
Radio Stns: 2 AM. 2 FM.
KCLI Clinton, OK; KWEY Weatherford, OK; KCLI-FM Cordell, OK; KWEY-FM Clinton, OK
G. Harold Wright, President

Wynne Enterprises LLC
1338 Oregon Ave., Klamath Falls OR 97601
(541) 882-4656; *Fax:*(541) 884-2845
www.klamathradio.com
kflskkrb@aol.com
Ownership: Robert Wynne, Floyd Wynne, Barbara Wynne.
Radio Stns: 1 AM. 2 FM.
KFLS Klamath Falls, OR; KFLS-FM Tulelake, CA; KKRB Klamath Falls, OR
Floyd Wynne, VP
Robert Wynne, President/CEO

WZOE Inc.
Box 69, Princeton IL 61356
(815) 875-8014
www.wzoe.com
Radio Stns: 1 AM. 2 FM.
WZOE Princeton, IL; WRVY-FM Henry, IL; WZOE-FM Princeton, IL
Steve Samet, President

Yavapai Broadcasting Corp.
3405 E. Hwy. 89-A, Suite A, Cottonwood AZ 86326

(928) 634-2286; *Fax:*(928) 634-2295
www.myradioplace.com

Radio Stns: 2 AM. 3 FM.
KVNA Flagstaff, AZ; KYBC Cottonwood, AZ; KQST Sedona, AZ; KVRD-FM Cottonwood, AZ; KKLD Cottonwood, AZ
Grant Hafley, President
David Kessel, General Manager

ZGS Communications

2000 North 14th Street, Suite 400, Arlington VA 22201
(703) 528-5656; *Fax:*(703) 526-0878
www.zgsgroup.com
info@zgsgroup.com

Radio Stns: 1 AM.
WILC Laurel, MD
Julissa Marenco, President

Zia Broadcasting Co.

Box 1907, Clovis NM 88102-1907
(505) 763-4401; *Fax:*(505) 769-2564
kclv@allsups.com

Ownership: Allsup's Convenience Stores Inc., 100%.

Radio Stns: 3 AM. 3 FM.
KACT Andrews, TX; KCLV Clovis, NM; KQTY Borger, TX; KACT-FM Andrews, TX; KCLV-FM Clovis, NM; KQTY-FM Borger, TX
Lonnie Alsup, President
Rick Keefer, General Manager

Zimmer Radio Inc.

3215 Lemone Industrial Blvd, Ste 200, Columbia MO 65201
(573) 875-1099; *Fax:*(573) 875-2439
www.zimmercommunications.com
contact@zimmercreative.com

Ownership: James L. Zimmer Revocable Trust U/A/D May 24, 2005 (James L. Zimmer, Sole Trustee), 100%.

Radio Stns: 2 AM. 6 FM.
KZRG Joplin, MO; KZYM Joplin, MO; KATI California, MO; KCLR-FM Boonville, MO; KIXQ Joplin, MO; KJMK Webb City, MO; KSYN Joplin, MO; KXDG Webb City, MO
James Zimmer, President

Zoe Communications Inc.

Box 190, Hwy 63 S, Shell Lake WI 54871
(715) 468-9500; *Fax:*(715) 468-9505
www.zoestations.com

Radio Stns: 1 AM. 2 FM.
WCSW Shell Lake, WI; WDMO Baldwin, WI; WPLT Sarona, WI
Mike Oberg, President

ZoomerMedia Ltd.

70 Jefferson Ave., Toronto ON M6K 3H4
(416) 367-5353
www.zoomermedia.ca
d.hamilton@mzmedia.com

Ownership: Olympus Management Limited, 61.77%; Fairfax Financial Holdings Limited, 16.47%; other Canadian Shareholders, 13.31%; MRHD Holdings Ltd., 8.12%; otherNon-Canadian shareholders, 0.30%; and Moses Znaimer, 0.02%.

Radio Stns: 1 AM. 3 FM.
CFZM Toronto, ON; CFMX-FM Cobourg, ON; CFMZ-FM Toronto, ON; CFMO-FM Collingwood, ON

TV Stns: 2 TV.
CIIT-DT Winnipeg, MB; CHNU-DT Fraser Valley, MB
Moses Znaimer, President & CEO
Laas Turnbull, Chief Operating Officer
Beverley Shenken, VP & General Manager, TV Division
Dan Hamilton, Broadcast Sales & General Manager, Radio
David Vickers, Chief Financial Officer
Omri Tintpulver, Chief Digital Officer

Key to Radio Listings

Radio listings include Radio stations in the United States, its territories and Canada.
To use the radio key, see boldface numbers and corresponding explanations.

(1) KSDS(FM) **(2)** On air date: n/a **(3)** Frequency: 88.3 mhz **(3a)** KSDS broadcasts in stereo. **(3b)** KSDS broadcasts 24 hours a day. **(4)** 1313 Park Blvd. , San Diego, CA 92108; Phone: (619) 292-2000 FAX: (619) 388-3928. Web Site: www.jazz88.org . **(5)** Licensee: San Diego, San Diego County, CA held by San Diego Community College District. **(5a)** FTR: unavailable **(6)** Population served: 696,679. **(7)** Network: NPR; Arbitration Metro Market: San Diego, CA; Hrs of News Programming: 7 hrs weekly; Number of News Employees: 1; Target Audience: 25-65 plus, affluent professional adults. **(8) Key Personnel:**
Joseph Kocherhams .... Executive Director
Mark DeBoskey .... Station Manager
Ann Bauer .... General Sales Manger
Claudia Russell .... Programming Director .
(9) KSDS frequency is 88.3 mhz, with 22 kilowatts of radiated power and an antenna height of 246 ft above average terrain, KSDS broadcasts in stereo (see (3a)). **(10)** Programming: Jazz format. **(11)** Co-Ownership: No.

(1) Station call letters as assigned by the Federal Communications Commission (FCC) or Canadian Radio-television and Telecommunications Commission (CRTC)

(1a) Station call letters for co-owned FM station.

(2) Date station first went on the air (regardless of subsequent owner changes).

(3) Frequency in kilohertz.

(4) Address and zip code, telephone, fax, web site and email address.

(5) Licensee name and ate of acquisition (if not original owner). If the licensee is a group owner-company with several boradcast properties – is so identified, as a group owner of which the licensee is a subsidiary. Details on group owners are listed in section A. If the station has been sol and the sale information is available, it is recorded after the acquisition date, ie. Acp. Date; purchase price; FTR date.

(5a) FTR date. FTR refers to the Broadcasting & Cable magazine's weekly For the Record column that appeared in the magazine until June 8, 1998, where station sales were recorded as received from the FCC.

(6) Population served refers to the station's potential market.

(7) Network, representative and programming.

(8) Key personnel.

(9) Frequency, kilowatts of effective radiated power, antenna height, and broadcasting.

(10) Programming and format.

(11) Co-ownership.

An asterisk (*) preceding station call letters indicates noncommercial stations

Radio Stations in the United States

Alabama

Abbeville

***WIZB**
02-02-1968; 94.3 MHz FM; *Hrs Open:* 24; 19.5 kw; 371 ft.; N31 26 19 W85 17 22
Mailing Address: Post Ofc Box 126, Headland, AL 36345 US
Second Address: 2563 Montgomery Hwy., Dothan, AL 36303
(334) 699-5672; *Fax:* (334) 699-5034
www.hisradio943.com
License: Abbeville, Henry County, AL held by Radio Training Network, Inc.
Arbitron Metro Market: Dothan, AL; *Format:* Christian; *Hrs. of News Programming:* News progmg 3 hrs wkly; *Target Audience:* 25-49; women; *Adv. Rates:* 28; 26; 25; 18
Jim Campbell, CEO
Earl Kelley, General Manager
Russell Brooks, Programming Director
Johanna Antes, Director of Support
Melinda McKenna, Office Manager
Neal Riddle, Engineering Dir

Addison

WQAH-FM
01-01-1996; 105.7 MHz FM; *Hrs Open:* 24; 6 kw; 328 ft.; N34 18 19 W87 4 24
Mailing Address: 2231 Burningtree Drive, Decatur, AL 35603 US
Second Address: 219 Chestnut St, Hartelle, AL 35640
(256) 773-2563; *Fax:* (256) 773-6915
www.wqah.com
info@WQAH.com
License: Addison, Winston County, AL held by Abercrombie Broadcasting FM Inc.
Arbitron Metro Market: Addison, FL; *Format:* Country
Alvin Abercrombie, President
Carol Lynn, General Manager
Keith Abercrombie, Engineering Dir
Mark Donovan, Disc Jockey

Alabaster

WQCR
09-28-1981; 1500 kHz AM; *Hrs Open:* Sunrise-sunset
PO Bo X 584, Alabaster, AL 35007 US
(508) 771-1224; *Fax:* (508) 775-2605
www.wqrc.com
joelrivera1500am@yahoo.com
License: Alabaster, AL held by Rivera Communications LLC
Arbitron Metro Market: Birmingham, AL
Maria Esparza, Operations Dir
Joel Rivera, General Manager
Israel deJesus, Programming Director

Albertville

WAVU
01-01-1947; 630 kHz AM; *Hrs Open:* 24; 1 kw-D, 28 w-N; N34 14 19 W86 09 59
Mailing Address: Box 190, Albertville, AL 35950
Second Address: 3770 US Hwy. 431, Albertville, AL 35951
(256) 878-8575; *Fax:* (256) 878-1051
License: Albertville, Marshall County, AL held by Sand Mountain Broadcasting Service Inc.
Nat'l Network: AP Radio; *Wire Services:* AP
Population Served: 25,000; *No. News Employees:* 1; *Target Audience:* 35 plus.; *Adv. Rates:* 10; 8; 9; 3
Pat Courington Jr., President
Tommy Lee, General Manager
Ted McCreless, General Sales Mgr
Dale Stallings, Programming Director
Al Taylor, News Director

WQSB
01-01-1948; 105.1 MHz FM; *Hrs Open:* 24; 2.7 kw; 1001 ft.; N34 9 27 W86 2 44
Mailing Address: P.O Box 190, Albertville, AL 35950 US
Second Address: 3770 US Hwy. 431, Albertville, AL 35951
(256) 878-8575; *Fax:* (256) 878-1051
www.wqsb.com
wqsb@aol.com
License: Albertville, Marshall County, AL held by Sand Mountain Broadcasting Service Inc.
Wire Services: AP
Format: Country; *No. News Employees:* 1; *Target Audience:* 25-54.; *Adv. Rates:* 68; 58; 63; 20
Pat Courington Jr., President
Tommy Lee, General Manager
Ted McCreless, General Sales Mgr
Barry Galloway, Programming Director
Dale Stallings, Music Director
Al Taylor, News Director

WWGC
04-01-1982; 1090 kHz AM; *Hrs Open:* 6 AM-7:15 PM
P.O. Box 863, Albertville, AL 35950 US
(256) 878-8333; *Fax:* (256) 878-7999
wwgc1090@yahoo.com
License: Albertville, AL held by Jeff Beck Media Group, LLC
Arbitron Metro Market: Albertville, AL; *Format:* Spanish
Jeff Beck, President/General Manager
Joel Arriga, Programming Director

Alexander City

WBNM
05-31-1947; 1050 kHz AM; *Hrs Open:* 24
908 Opelika Road, Auburn, AL 36830 US
(256) 215-7296
License: Alexander City, AL held by William and Margaret Neeck, Co-Trustees
Group Owner: Cumulus Media
Nat'l Network: ABC; *Regional Network:* Alabama Radio Net.
Format: Gospel, Sports; *Adv. Rates:* 7; 5; 7; 5
Ralph Turpen, President

WSTH-FM
09-30-1949; 106.1 MHz FM; *Hrs Open:* 24; 86 kw; 1047 ft.; N32 45 30 W85 28 20
Mailing Address: P.O. Box 1640, Columbus, GA 31994 US
Second Address: 1501 13th Ave., Columbus, GA 31901
(706) 576-3000; *Fax:* (706) 576-3010
www.mysouth1061.com
License: Alexander City, Tallapoosa County, AL held by CC Licenses LLC.
Group Owner: iHeartMedia; (acq 5-9-2003; $2.73 million with WDAK(AM) Columbus, GA).
Nat'l Network: ABC
Arbitron Metro Market: Columbus, GA; *Format:* Country; *No. News Employees:* 1; *Target Audience:* General.
Jennifer Newman, General Manager
Chuck Thompson, Sales Manager
Paul Laseter, Programming Director

***WJHO**
01-01-2008; 89.7 MHz FM; 10.5 kw vert; 492 ft.; N33 12 30 W85 59 31
US
(334) 705-8004; *Fax:* (334) 705-8006
License: Alexander City, Tallapoosa County, AL held by Jimmy Jarrell Communications Foundation Inc.
Arbitron Metro Market: Alexander City, AL; *Format:* Gospel
Jimmy Jarrell, President
Joe May, Programming Director

Andalusia

WAAO-FM
08-24-1987; 93.7 FM; *Hrs Open:* 24; 23 kw; 328 ft.; 31 20'27 N 86 28'02.00 W
121 E 3 Notch St., Andalusia, AL 36420 US
(334) 222-1166; *Fax:* (334) 222-1167
www.waao.com
waao@waao.com
License: Andalusia, Covington County, AL held by Three Notch Communications
Group Owner: Three Notch Communications
Arbitron Metro Market: McAllen-Brownsville-Harlingen TX;
Format: Country
Blaine Wilson, General Manager and Sales
Amos Josey, Operation Manager and Program Director
Andrea Wilson, Billing and Account Receivables

***WSTF**
03-01-1996; 91.5 MHz FM; 20.5 kw; 361 ft.; N31 26 20 W86 30 48
P.O. Box 210789, Montgomery, AL 36121 US
(334) 271-8900; *Fax:* (334) 260-8962
www.faithradio.org
mail@faithradio.org
License: Andalusia, Covington County, AL held by Faith Broadcasting Inc.
Format: Adult Contemp, Religious
Russell Dean, General Manager
Billy Irvin, General Sales Mgr

***WDWZ**
89.3 MHz FM; 700 w; 108 m; N31 17 47.9 W86 30 09.6
828 20th St. SW, Lanett, AL
(706)518-3911
License: Andalusia, Covington County, AL held by B. Jordan Communications Corp.
Ben Jordan, President

Anniston

WFZX
08-01-1954; 1490 kHz AM; *Hrs Open:* 24; 1 kw-U; N33 41 15 W85 49 49
1913 Barry Street, Suite B, Oxford, AL 36203
(256) 741-6088; *Fax:* (256) 741-6080
www.wtdrthunder.com
License: Anniston, Calhoun County, AL
Wire Services: AP
Population Served: 22,959; *Arbitron Metro Market:* Anniston, Al; *Format:* Country; *No. News Employees:* 1; *Adv. Rates:* 18; 16; 17; 14
Jeff Beck, President
Grady Sapp, Operations & Program Director
Grady Sapp, General Manager
Shannon Wheeles, General Sales Mgr

WDNG
07-01-1957; 1450 kHz AM; *Hrs Open:* 24; 1 kw-U, ND1; N33 40 1 W85 50 56
1115 Leighton Avenue, Anniston, AL 36201 US
(256) 236-8291; *Fax:* (256) 236-8292
License: Anniston, AL held by WDNG Inc.
Nat'l Network: CBS
Arbitron Metro Market: Anniston, AL; *Format:* News, News/Talk, 86; *Target Audience:* General.
Charlene Gossett, President
Pamela Bates, Operations Dir

***WGRW**
07-01-1999; 90.7 MHz FM; *Hrs Open:* 24; 3 kw vert; 328 ft.; N33 46 41 W85 56 38
Mailing Address: P.O. Box 2555, Anniston, AL 36202 US
Second Address: 4265 Hill St., Anniston, AL 36206
(256) 238-9990; *Fax:* (256) 237-1102
www.graceradio.com
jon@graceradio.com
License: Anniston, Calhoun County, AL held by Word Works Inc.
Nat'l Network: Moody
Format: Christian
Aaron Acker, President
Jon Holder, General Manager

WHMA
01-01-1938; 1390 kHz AM; *Hrs Open:* 24; 5 kw-D, DAN; 1 kw-N, DAN; N33 42 31 W85 51 14
801 Noble Street, Suite 30, Anniston, AL 36201 US
(256) 236-1274; *Fax:* (256) 231-9414
www.whmabig95.com
texbig95@cableone.net
License: Anniston, AL held by Williams Communications Inc.
Group Owner: Williams Communications Inc.; acq 8-12-2003; $275,000).
Format: Gospel; *Hrs. of News Programming:* news progmg 12 hrs wkly; *No. News Employees:* 1; *Target Audience:* 25-54; those with upscale, mobile, discretionary incomes
Eva Gibson, General Manager
Tex Carter, Programming/Sales Director

Arab

WAFN-FM
11-05-1979; 92.7 MHz FM; *Hrs Open:* 24; 1.15 kw; 663 ft.; N34 20 40.6 W86 26 23.3
P.O. Box 1297, Arab, MO 35016 US
(256) 586-9300; *Fax:* (256) 586-9301
www.fun927.com
funhouse@fun927.com
License: Arab, Marshall County, AL held by Fun Media Group Inc.
Nat'l Network: CNN Radio
Arbitron Metro Market: Arab, AL; *Format:* Oldies; *Hrs. of News Programming:* news progmg 3 hrs wkly; *No. News Employees:* 1; *Target Audience:* 18-54.
Susan McKenney, President
Michael St. John, Operations Dir
Suan McKenney, General Sales Mgr

WRAB
10-25-1961; 1380 kHz AM; *Hrs Open:* 6am-6pm; 1 kw-D, ND1; 0.049 kw-N, ND1; N34 20 6 W86 28 7
Mailing Address: P.O. Box 625, Arab, AL 35016 US
Second Address: 619 S. Brindlee Mountain Pkwy., Arab, AL 35016
(256) 586-4123; *Fax:* (256) 586-4124
License: Arab, AL held by Reed Broadcasting LLC
Wire Services: AP

Format: Country, Gospel, 74; *Hrs. of News Programming:* news progmg 12 hrs. wkly; *No. News Employees:* 1; *Adv. Rates:* 8; 6.50; 6.50; na
Ed Reed, President
Archie Anderson, General Manager

Ashland

WFXO
12-20-1959; 98.3 MHz FM; *Hrs Open:* 24; 1.7 kw; Ant 617 ft; N33 18 30 W85 50 58
801 Noble St. 8th Fl., Suite 30, Anniston, AL 35150
(256) 236-1880; *Fax:* (256) 231-9414
rock983.com
License: Ashland, Clay County, AL held by Williams Communications Inc.
Group Owner: Williams Communications Inc.; (acq 8-16-2001)
Nat'l Network: ABC
No. News Employees: 1; *Target Audience:* 25-54.
Eva Gibson, General Manager

WCKF
12-17-2007; 100.7 MHz FM; 1.9 kw; Ant 590 ft; N33 19 14.2 W85 51 39.2
518 Mountain View Road, Ashland, AL 36251
(256) 354-1444; *Fax:* (256) 254-1445
License: Ashland, Clay County, AL held by Alabama 810 LLC.
Nat'l Network: Fox; *Regional Network:* Alabama Radio Net.
Hrs. of News Programming: news progmg 5 hrs wkly; *No. News Employees:* 1
E. Gradick, Engineer/Owner
Leslie Gradick, General Manager/Owner
Teresa Goodman, Station Manager
Alicia Hamburger, General Sales Mgr
Teresa Goodman, Programming Director
Andy Evans, Promotions Manager
Wes Leadbetter, NewsDirector

Athens

WKAC
09-01-1964; 1080 kHz AM; *Hrs Open:* Sunrise-sunset; 2.5 kw-C, NDD; 5 kw-D, NDD; N34 50 13 W86 58 28
Mailing Address: P.O. Box 1083, Athens, AL 35612 US
Second Address: 19245 Hwy. 127, Athens, AL 35614
(256) 232-6827; *Fax:* (256) 232-6828
www.wkac1080.com
wkac@companet.net
License: Athens, AL held by Limestone Broadcasting Co.
Nat'l Network: CNN Radio
Arbitron Metro Market: Huntsville, AL; *Format:* Oldies *Special Programming:* Farm 5 hrs; *Hrs. of News Programming:* News progmg 6 hrs wkly; *Target Audience:* 25-54; adults mid/upper income, blue/white collar *Adv.Rates:* 10; 8; 10; n/a
Joyce Casey, President
Keith Casey, General Manager
Kirk Harvey, Programming Director
Joyce Casey, News Director

WVNN
11-08-1948; 770 kHz AM; *Hrs Open:* 24; 7 kw-D, 0.25 kw-N
1717 US Highway 72 E., Athens, AL 35611-4413 US
(256) 830-8300; *Fax:* (256) 232-6842
www.wvnn.com
programdirector@wvnn.com
License: Athens, AL held by Cumulus Licensing LLC.
Group Owner: Cumulus Media Inc.; (acq 7-21-2003; grpsl)
Arbitron Metro Market: Huntsville, AL; *Format:* News/Talk; *Target Audience:* 25-64.
Matt Tobin, VP of Sale

WZYP
10-01-1958; 104.3 MHz FM; *Hrs Open:* 24; 100 kw; 1115 ft.; N34 49 6 W86 44 16
1717 Hwy 72 E., Athens, AL 35611 US
(256) 830-8300
www.wzyp.com
steve.smith@cumulus.com
License: Athens, AL held by Cumulus Licensing LLC
Group Owner: Cumulus Media Inc.
Arbitron Metro Market: Athens, AL; *Format:* Contemporary Hits/Top 40; *Target Audience:* 18-49.
Steve Smith, Programming Director
Jeff Lyons, Promotions Manager
Matt Tobin, VP of Sales

Attalla

WKXX
08-31-1991; 102.9 MHz FM; *Hrs Open:* 24; 1.1 kw; 702 ft.; N33 58 28 W86 12 24
Mailing Address: 100 Spurlock Street, Rainbow City, AL 35906 US
Second Address: Box 8405, Gadsden, AL 35902
(256) 442-3944; *Fax:* (256) 442-7287
www.wkxx.com
tommylee@wasc.com
License: Attalla, Etowah County, AL held by Broadcast Media L.L.C.
Wire Services: AP
Format: Adult Contemp; *Hrs. of News Programming:* news progmg 2 hrs wkly; *No. News Employees:* 1; *Target Audience:* 18-49.; *Adv. Rates:* 35; 20; 25; 18
Pat Courington, CEO
Tommy Lee, General Manager
Ted McReless, General Sales Mgr
Shane Wilson, Programming Director

Auburn

WAUD
12-22-1947; 1230 kHz AM; *Hrs Open:* 24; 1 kw-D, ND1; 1 kw-N, ND1; N32 37 40 W85 27 37
2514 S. College St., Suite 104, Auburn, AL 36830 US
(334) 887-3401; *Fax:* (334) 826-9599
License: Auburn, Lee County, AL held by Tiger Communications Inc.
Group Owner: Tiger Communications Inc.; (acq 2-26-98)
Nat'l Network: CBS Radio; *Regional Network:* Alabama Radio Net; *Nat'l Reps:* Rgnl Reps
Arbitron Metro Market: Auburn, AL; *Format:* Sports; *Hrs. of News Programming:* news progmg 7 hrs wkly; *No. News Employees:* 1; *Target Audience:* 25 plus.; *Adv. Rates:* 12; 10; 10; 8
Bill Bailey, General Manager

*WEGL
04-25-1971; 91.1 MHz FM; *Hrs Open:* 24; 3 kw; 213 ft.; N32 36 11 W85 29 12
Samford Hall, Auburn, AL 36849 US
(334) 844-4114; *Fax:* (334) 844-4118
wegl.auburn.edu
greendm@auburn.edu
License: Auburn, Lee County, AL held by Board of Trustees Auburn University.
Arbitron Metro Market: Auburn, AL; *Format:* Alternative *Special Programming:* Various specialty shows; *Hrs. of News Programming:* news progmg 6 hrs wkly; *No. News Employees:* 1; *Target Audience:* Collegestudents.
Elizabeth Kent, General Manager
Natalie Stevenson, Station Manager
Rachel Warfield, Programming Director
Kasey Langley, Promotions Manager
Chandler White, Music Director
Dafni Greene, Faculty Advisor
Kasey Langley, StationManager

WKKR
07-08-1968; 97.7 MHz FM; *Hrs Open:* 24; 3.1 kw; 453 ft.; N32 33 54 W85 22 13
915 Veterans Parkway, Opelika, AL 36801 US
(334) 745-4657; *Fax:* (334) 749-1520
www.kickerfm.com
License: Auburn, Lee County, AL held by AMFM Radio Licenses LLC.
Group Owner: iHeartMedia; (acq 2014)
Format: Country; *Hrs. of News Programming:* news progmg 7 hrs wkly; *No. News Employees:* 2; *Target Audience:* 25-54.
Van Riggs, Senior Vice President of Programming

Bay Minette

WTOF
01-01-1958; 1110 kHz AM; 2.5 kw-C, ND2; 10 kw-D, ND2; N30 52 10 W87 46 9
2p.O. Box 63, Mobile, AL 36601 US
(435) 649-9004; *Fax:* (435) 645-9063
License: Bay Minette, AL held by Buddy Tucker Association Inc.
Group Owner: Buddy Tucker Association Inc.; (acq 1-16-2007; $300,000)
Arbitron Metro Market: Sioux Falls SD
Theodore D. Tucker, General Manager

WNSP
10-01-1964; 105.5 MHz FM; *Hrs Open:* 24; 5.3 kw; 348 ft.; N30 49 34 W87 51 52
1100 Dolphin Street, Mobile, AL 36604 US
(251) 438-5460; *Fax:* (251) 438-5462
www.wnsp.com
wnsp@wnsp.com
License: Bay Minette, Baldwin County, AL held by Dot Com+ L.L.C.
Arbitron Metro Market: Mobile, AL; *Format:* Sports; *Target Audience:* 18-49.
Ken Johnson, President
Clint Crouch, Operations Dir
Ken Johnson, General Manager
Kenny Johnson, General Sales Mgr
Chip Ramsey, Programming Director
Ryan Foster, Promotions Manager

Bessemer

WZGX
06-01-1950; 1450 kHz AM; 1 kw-U, ND1; N33 25 23 W86 57 17
P.O. Box 368, Bessemer, AL 35020 US
(205) 428-0146; *Fax:* (205) 426-3178
License: Bessemer, AL held by Bessemer Radio Inc.
Arbitron Metro Market: Birmingham, AL
Joel Garcia, General Manager
Jerry Lopez, Programming Director

*WSJL
01-01-2008; 88.1 MHz FM; 0.01 kw horiz, 15 kw vert; 492 ft.; N33 28 51 W87 24 3
516 S Fourth Street, Las Vegas, NV 89101 US
(817) 641-3495
License: Bessemer, Tuscaloosa County, AL held by Mary V. Harris Foundation.
Arbitron Metro Market: Tuscaloosa, AL
Linda De Romanett, President

Birmingham

WAGG
01-01-1927; 610 kHz AM; 5 kw-D, DAN; 1 kw-N, DAN; N33 29 40 W86 52 30
2700 Corporate Drive, Suite 115, Birmingham, AL 35242 US
(205) 322-2987; *Fax:* (205) 322-2390
david.dubose@coxradio.com
License: Birmingham, AL held by SM-WAGG LLC
Group Owner: SummitMedia LLC
Nat'l Network: ABC; *Nat'l Reps:* Christal; *Wire Services:* AP
Arbitron Metro Market: Birmingham, AL; *Format:* Gospel; *Hrs. of News Programming:* news progmg 5 hrs wkly; *No. News Employees:* 2; *Target Audience:* 45 plus.; *Adv. Rates:* 200; 75; 100; 25
David DuBose, General Manager
Paul Bankston, General Sales Mgr
Jay Bryant, Programming Director
Kori White, Promotions Manager

WAPI
01-01-1922; 1070 kHz AM; *Hrs Open:* 24; 50 kw-D, DAN; 5 kw-N, DAN; N33 33 7 W86 54 40
244 Goodwin Crest Dr., Suite 300, Birmingham, AL 35209 US
(205) 945-4646; *Fax:* (205) 945-3999
www.1070wapi.com
License: Birmingham, AL held by Radio License Holding CBC, LLC
Group Owner: Cumulus Media Inc.
Nat'l Reps: Christal
Arbitron Metro Market: Birmingham, AL; *Format:* News/Talk; *Target Audience:* 35 plus.
Hertisene Riley, General Sales Mgr
Matt Murphy, Programming Director
Laurence Salvary, Promotions Manager

WATV
05-20-1946; 900 kHz AM; *Hrs Open:* 24 hrs
3025 Ensley Ave, Birmingham, AL 35208 US
(205) 780-2014; *Fax:* (205) 780-4034
www.900goldwatv.com/
rjanuary@watv900.com
License: Birmingham, AL held by McL/McM Alabama LLC.
Group Owner: Sheridan Broadcasting Corp.; (acq 10-12-2004; $1.5 million)
Nat'l Network: American Urban; *Nat'l Reps:* Interep
Arbitron Metro Market: Birmingham, AL; *Format:* Black, Oldies, 74; *Target Audience:* 18 plus.
Ron Davenport, President
Ron January, Operations Dir

WAYE
08-01-1972; 1220 kHz AM; *Hrs Open:* 24 hours; 1 kw-D, ND1; 0.075 kw-N, ND1; N33 28 39 W86 50 57
P.O. Box 19123, Birmingham, AL 35219 US
(205) 942-1776; *Fax:* (360) 423-1554
License: Birmingham, AL held by Birmingham Christian Radio, Inc
Group Owner: Richardson Broadcasting Corp.
Arbitron Metro Market: Rainier OR; *Format:* Adult Contemp
Gary Richardson, President/CEO
Willamena Richardson, Sales/General Manager

***WBFR**
01-01-1988; 89.5 MHz FM; 0.1 kw vert; 673 ft.; N33 29 2 W86 48 35
Mailing Address: US
Second Address: 290 Hegenberger Rd., Oakland, CA 94621
1-(800)-543-1495; *Fax:* (916) 641-8238 (510) 633-7983
www.familyradio.com
familyradio@familyradio.org
License: Birmingham, Jefferson County, AL held by Family Stations Inc.
Group Owner: Family Stations Inc.
Arbitron Metro Market: Oakland, CA; *Format:* Christian, Religious
Tom Evans, General Manager

***WBHM**
12-01-1976; 90.3 MHz FM; *Hrs Open:* 24; 32 kw; 1214 ft.; N33 29 19 W86 47 58 *Rebroadcasts:* Rebroadcasts WSGN(FM) Gadsden 100%
1028 7th Avenue South, Birmingham, AL 35294 US
(205) 934-2606; *Fax:* (205) 934-5075
www.wbhm.org
info@wbhm.org
License: Birmingham, Jefferson County, AL held by Board of Trustees, University of Alabama.
Nat'l Network: NPR; PRI; *Wire Services:* AP
Arbitron Metro Market: Birmingham, AL; *Format:* News *Special Programming:* New age 6 hrs wkly; *Hrs. of News Programming:* news progmg 74 hrs wkly; *No. News Employees:* 3; *Target Audience:* General.
Scott E. Hanley, General Manager
Michael Krall, Programming Director
Audrey Atkins, Marketing Manager
Mary Hendley, Development Director

WYDE
03-25-1953; 1260 kHz AM; 5 kw-D, ND2; 0.041 kw-N, ND2; N34 04 56 W86 54 15
120 Summit Parkway, Suite 200, Birmingham, AL 35209 US
(205) 879-3324; *Fax:* (205) 802-4555
www.101wyde.com
thejunction@wdjconline.com
License: Birmingham, AL held by Kimtron Inc.
Group Owner: Crawford Broadcasting Co.; (acq 1994)
Nat'l Reps: McGavren Guild
Arbitron Metro Market: Birmingham, AL; *Format:* News, News/Talk, 86
Laura Scotti, General Manager
Chris Mileski, Programming Director
Melodye Grubb, News Director
Todd Dixon, Chief Engineer

WDJC-FM
04-22-1968; 93.7 MHz FM; 99 kw; 1007 ft.; N33 44 3 W86 88 1
120 Summit Parkway, Suite 200, Birmingham, AL 35209 US
(205) 879-3324; *Fax:* (205) 802-4555
www.wdjconline.com
thejunction@wdjconline.com
License: Birmingham, Jefferson County, AL held by Kimtron Inc.
Group Owner: Crawford Broadcasting Co.
Arbitron Metro Market: Birmingham, AL; *Format:* Christian, Religious; *Target Audience:* 25-60; conservative middle income
Laura Scotti, General Manager
Chris Mileski, Programming Director

WERC
05-25-1925; 960 kHz AM
600 Beacon Parkway West, Birmingham, AL 35209 US
(205) 439-9600; *Fax:* (205) 439-8390
www.wercfm.com
License: Birmingham, AL held by Capstar TX LLC
Group Owner: iHeartMedia
Arbitron Metro Market: Birmingham, AL; *Format:* News, News/Talk, 86; *Target Audience:* Adults.
Cynthia Collins, General Sales Mgr
John Mountz, Programming Director
Lacey Walker, Promotions Director
Kevin Klein, Senior Vice President of Sales

WENN
01-01-1950; 1320 kHz AM; 5 kw-D, ND2; 0.111 kw-N, ND2; N33 33 41 W86 51 37
2700 Corporate Drive, Suite 115, Birmingham, AL 35242 US
(205) 916-1100; *Fax:* (205) 290-1061
www.wzzk.com
David.Walls@coxradio.com
License: Birmingham, AL held by SM-WENN LLC
Group Owner: SummitMedia LLC
Arbitron Metro Market: Birmingham, AL
David Dubose, General Manager
David Walls, General Sales Mgr
Paul Orr, Programming Director
Justin Ragland, Promotions Manager
Paul Bankston, National Sales Manager
Kelsey Dollar, Internet Manager

WJOX
10-15-1947; 690 kHz AM; 50 kw-D, 500 w-N, DA-N; N33 26 56 W86 55 18
244 Goodwin Crest Dr., Suite 300, Birmingham, AL 35209 US
(205) 945-4646; *Fax:* (205) 945-3999
www.wjoxam.com
ryan@joxfm.com
License: Birmingham, AL held by Radio License Holding CBC, LLC
Group Owner: Cumulus Media Inc.; (acq 4-26-2001; grpsl)
Wire Services: SportsTicker
Population Served: 375,900; *Arbitron Metro Market:* Birmingham, AL; *Format:* Sports; *Target Audience:* 25-54.
Reade Taylor, General Sales Mgr
Ryan Haney, Programming Director
Laurence Salvary, Promotions Manager

***WJSR**
08-11-1977; 91.1 MHz FM; *Hrs Open:* 24; 0.23 kw; 194 ft.; N33 39 7 W86 42 20
2601 Carson Road, Birmingham, AL 35215 US
(565) 927-4232; *Fax:* (256) 927-6503
www.angelfire.com
License: Birmingham, Jefferson County, AL held by Bakre Enterprises, Inc.
Arbitron Metro Market: Birmingham, AL; *Format:* Classic Rock; *Hrs. of News Programming:* News progmg 4 hrs wkly; *Target Audience:* 24-49; college population
Ray Edwards, General Manager

***WLJR**
01-01-1998; 88.5 MHz FM; *Hrs Open:* 24; 0 kw horiz, 0.37 kw vert; 600 ft.; N33 23 51 W86 39 41
2200 Briarwood Way, Birmingham, AL 35243 US
(205) 776-5270; *Fax:* (205) 824-8419
www.wljr.org
wljr@briarwood.org
License: Birmingham, Jefferson County, AL held by Briarwood Presbyterian Church.
Nat'l Network: Moody
Arbitron Metro Market: Birmingham, AL; *Format:* Variety/Diverse, Religious; *Hrs. of News Programming:* News progmg 10 hrs wkly; *Target Audience:* General; upper middle class
John Scruggs, General Manager

WMJJ
06-01-1961; 96.5 MHz FM; 100 kw; 1027 ft.; N33 26 38 W86 52 47
600 Beacon Parkway West, Suite 400, Birmingham, AL 35209 US
(205) 439-9600; *Fax:* (205) 439-8390
www.magic96.com
License: Birmingham, Jefferson County, AL held by Capstar TX LLC
Group Owner: iHeartMedia; (acq 8-30-00; grpsl)
Arbitron Metro Market: Birmingham, AL; *Format:* Adult Contemp; *Target Audience:* 25-54.
Ray Quinn, Regional Market Manager
Cyndi Collins, General Sales Mgr
Tom Hanrahan, Programming Director
Bob Newberry, Chief Engineer
Kevin Klein, Senior Vice President of Sales

WUHT
09-15-1969; 107.7 MHz FM; *Hrs Open:* 24; 42 kw; 1345 ft.; N33 29 4 W86 48 25
244 Goodwin Crest Dr., Suite 300, Birmingham, AL 35209 US
(205) 945-4646; *Fax:* (205) 945-3999
www.hot1077radio.com
ken.johnson@cumulus.com
License: Birmingham, AL held by Radio License Holding CBC, LLC
Group Owner: Cumulus Media Inc.
Arbitron Metro Market: Birmingham, AL; *Format:* Adult Contemp, Urban Contemporary; *Target Audience:* 18-34.
Ken Johnson, Operations Mgr/Program Dir
Hertisene Riley, General Sales Mgr

***WVSU-FM**
04-06-1967; 91.1 MHz FM; *Hrs Open:* 17; 500 w vert; Ant 413 ft; N33 27 47 W86 46 08
Samford Univ., Birmingham, AL 35209
(205) 726-2877; *Fax:* (205) 726-4032
www.samford.edu/wvsu
wvsu@samford.edu
License: Birmingham, Jefferson County, AL held by Samford University.
Population Served: 212,413; *Arbitron Metro Market:* Birmingham, AL; *Hrs. of News Programming:* News progmg one hr wkly; *Target Audience:* General.
Andy Parrish, General Manager

WJOX
01-01-1947; 94.5 MHz FM; 100 kw; 1014 ft.; N33 27 45 W86 50 59
244 Goodwin Crest Dr., Suite 300, Birmingham, AL 35209 US
(205) 945-4646; *Fax:* (205) 945-3999
www.joxfm.com
ryan@joxfm.com
License: Birmingham, AL held by Radio License Holding CBC, LLC
Group Owner: Cumulus Media Inc.
Arbitron Metro Market: Birmingham, AL; *Format:* Sports
Ryan Haney, Operations Mgr/Program Dir
Reade Taylor, General Sales Mgr
Laurence Salvary, Promotions/Marketing

WZRR
12-01-1975; 99.5 MHz FM; 100 kw; 1014 ft.; N33 27 45 W86 50 59
244 Goodwin Crest Dr., Suite 300, Homewood, AL 35209 US
(205) 945-4646
www.995nashicon.com
hertisene.riley@cumulus.com
License: Birmingham, AL held by Radio License Holding CBC, LLC
Group Owner: Cumulus Media Inc.
Arbitron Metro Market: Birmingham, AL; *Format:* Country
Peter Z, Programming Director

WZZK-FM
01-01-1948; 104.7 MHz FM; *Hrs Open:* 24; 97.8 kw; 1325 ft.; N33 29 4 W86 48 25
2700 Corporate Drive, Suite 115, Birmingham, AL 35242 US
(205) 916-1100; *Fax:* (205) 290-1061
www.wzzk.com
License: Birmingham, Jefferson County, AL held by SM-WZZK LLC
Group Owner: SummitMedia LLC
Arbitron Metro Market: Birmingham, AL; *Format:* Country; *Hrs. of News Programming:* news progmg 10 hrs wkly; *No. News Employees:* 2; *Target Audience:* 25-54.
David Dubose, General Manager
David Walls, General Sales Mgr
Paul Orr, Programming Director
Justin Ragland, Promotions Manager
Paul Bankston, National Sales Manager
Kelsey Dollar, Internet Manager

Boaz

WBSA
10-01-1959; 1300 kHz AM; 1 kw-D, ND1; 0.037 kw-N, ND1; N34 12 50 W86 9 10
1525 Wills Road, Boaz, AL 35957 US
(256) 593-4264; *Fax:* (256) 593-4265
www.wbsaam.com
1300@wbsaam.com
License: Boaz, AL held by Watkins Broadcasting Inc.
Arbitron Metro Market: Boaz, Al; *Format:* Gospel; *Target Audience:* General.; *Adv. Rates:* 7; 7; 7
Roger Watkins, General Manager
Dale Johnson, Programming Director

Boligee

WQZZ
107.3 MHz FM; 113 watts
440 Clear Creek Pkwy., Northport, AL 35475 US
(205) 345-4787; *Fax:* (205) 345-4790
License: Boligee, AL held by Porter, Mildred R
Group Owner: Porter, Mildred R
Format: Adult Contemp
Mildred R. Porter, President

Brantley

WEZZ
12-06-1982; 920 kHz AM; 5 kw-D, ND1; 0.048 kw-N, ND1; N31 29 40 W87 21 29
1016 C South Alabama Ave, Monroeville, AL 36460 US
(205) 618-2020
License: Brantley, AL held by Brantley Broadcast Associates LLC
Arbitron Metro Market: Brantley, AL
Wendy Smith, General Manager

Brewton

WEBJ
08-01-1947; 1240 kHz AM; *Hrs Open:* 6 AM-8 PM; 1 kw-U, ND1; N31 6 35 W87 3 36
301 Downing Street, Brewton, AL 36426 US
(251) 867-5717; *Fax:* (251) 867-5718
info@webj.com
License: Brewton, AL held by Brewton Broadcasting Inc.
Arbitron Metro Market: Brewton, AL; *Format:* Oldies; *Hrs. of News Programming:* news progmg 20 hrs wkly; *No. News Employees:* 1; *Target Audience:* 21 plus; 60% female, 40% male
Jan Dunaway, General Manager

WKNU
08-19-1974; 106.3 MHz FM; *Hrs Open:* 24; 3.8 kw; 417 ft.; N31 6 42 W87 1 17
Mailing Address: P.O. Box 468, Brewton, AL 36427 US
Second Address: 2832 Ridge Rd., Brewton, AL 36426
(251) 867-4824; *Fax:* (251) 867-7003
www.wnku.org
wknubroadcasting@bellsouth.net
License: Brewton, Escambia County, AL held by WKNU Radio Inc.
Format: Country *Special Programming:* Gospel 2 hrs, relg 2 hrs wkly; *Hrs. of News Programming:* News progmg 8 hrs wkly; *Target Audience:* General.; *Adv. Rates:* 10; 10; 10; 10
Jack Floyd, President

***WOWB**
01-01-1998; 90.9 MHz FM; 45 kw; Ant 502 ft; N31 18 13 W87 02 50
Mailing Address: Box 347, Brewton, AL 36502
Second Address: 42676 Hwy. 31, Brewton, AL 36427
(251) 809-1915; *Fax:* (251) 809-1916
info@wowradio.org
License: Brewton, Escambia County, AL held by Gateway Public Radio

Dale Riddick, General Manager
Debra Johnson, Station Manager

Bridgeport

WVOV
09-19-1961; 1480 kHz AM; *Hrs Open:* 24; 1 kw-D, ND1; 0.039 kw-N, ND1; N34 56 34 W85 42 26
1237 County Road 295, Higdon, AL 35979 US
(256) 495-2500; *Fax:* (914) 730-9820
www.wgnq.net
License: Bridgeport, AL held by Partners Media Investments LLC
Nat'l Network: Salem Radio Network; *Regional Network:* Alabama Radio Net.
Format: Christian, Talk; *Adv. Rates:* 3; 3; 3; N/A

Brookwood

WRTR
06-01-1966; 105.9 MHz FM; *Hrs Open:* 24; 25 kw; 269 ft.; N33 14 17 W87 29 6
3900 11th Avenue S., Tuscaloosa, AL 35401 US
(205) 344-4589; *Fax:* (205) 366-9774
www.talkradio1059.com
License: Brookwood, Tuscaloosa County, AL held by Capstar TX LLC
Group Owner: iHeartMedia
Nat'l Network: USA
Arbitron Metro Market: Tuscaloosa, AL; *Format:* News, News/Talk, 86; *Target Audience:* 25 plus.
Todd Robbins, Senior Vice President of Programming
Jackie Toye, Senior Vice President of Sales
Tom Canterbury, Promotions Director
Justin Barnett, Digital Manager

Brundidge

WTBF-FM
10-01-1997; 94.7 MHz FM; *Hrs Open:* 24; 14.5 kw; 433 ft.; N31 40 38 W85 56 43
67 Court Square, Troy, AL 36081 US
(334) 566-0300; *Fax:* (334) 566-5689
wtbf947970@gmail.com
License: Brundidge, Pike County, AL held by Troy Broadcasting Corp.
Nat'l Network: Moody; *Regional Network:* Alabama Radio Net.; *Wire Services:* National Weather Network
Format: Oldies; *Hrs. of News Programming:* News progmg 20 hrs wkly; *Target Audience:* 28-60.; *Adv. Rates:* 25; 10; 25; 5
Doc Kirby, Operations Dir
Jim Roling, General Manager

Butler

***WMLV**
11-20-1978; 93.5 MHz FM; 32 kw; 610 ft.; N32 9 26 W88 29 17
P. O. Box 566, Butler, AL 36904 US
(601) 693-2661; *Fax:* (601) 483-0826
www.klove.com
License: Butler, Choctaw County, AL held by Mississippi Broadcasters L.L.C.
Group Owner: Mississippi Broadcasters L.L.C.; (acq 10-30-2002; $771,500)
Format: Adult Contemp
Scott Stevens, Operations Dir
Clay Holladay, Station Manager

Camden

***WQLS**
01-01-2012; 90.5 MHz FM; 0.4 kw; N31 57 34 W87 16 04
100 Water St., Suite A, Camden, AL 36726 US
(256) 497-2840
License: Camden, AL held by Townsend Broadcasting Enterprise
Group Owner: Townsend Broadcasting Enterprise
Format: Gospel
Timothy Townsend, President

Carrollton

***WALN**
01-01-1997; 89.3 MHz FM; *Hrs Open:* 24; 9.5 kw vert; 699 ft.; N33 13 6 W88 5 46
P.O. Box 3206, Tupelo, MS 38803 US
(662) 844-8888; *Fax:* (662) 842-6791
www.afr.net
faq@afa.net
License: Carrollton, Pickens County, AL held by American Family Association.
Group Owner: American Family Radio
Arbitron Metro Market: Carrollton, AL; *Format:* Christian, Religious
Tim Wildmon, President
Donald Wildmon, Founder
Buddy Smith, Sr VP
Ed Vitagliano, Executive VP
Randy Sahrp, Director Of Special Projects
Meeke Addison, Director Of Communications
Abraham Hamilton III, General Counsel & PublicPolicy Analyst

WZBQ
02-01-1970; 94.1 MHz FM; 98 kw; 1007 ft.; N33 13 7 W88 5 47
3900 11th Avenue South, Suite 1400, Tuscaloosa, AL 35401 US
(205) 344-4589; *Fax:* (205) 752-9774
www.941zbq.com
info@941zbq.com
License: Carrollton, 00ckens County, AL held by Capstar TX LLC
Group Owner: iHeartMedia; (acq 8-30-2000; grpsl)
Arbitron Metro Market: Tuscaloosa, AL; *Format:* Contemporary Hits/Top 40; *Target Audience:* 18-49.
Todd Robbins, Senior Vice President of Programming
Jackie Toye, Senior Vice President of Sales
Tom Canterbury, Promotions Director
Justin Barnett, Digital Manager

Centre

WLYG
11-09-1962; 1560 kHz AM; *Hrs Open:* 6 AM-sunset; 1 kw-D; N34 07 41 W85 38 27
Box 2, Centre, AL 35960
(256) 927-4027; *Fax:* (205) 295-1238
www.joychristian.com
License: Centre, Cherokee County, AL held by Joy Christian Communications Inc.
Group Owner: Joy Christian Communications Inc.; (acq 12-1-2003)
Regional Network: Tenn. Radio Net.
Population Served: 245,000 *Special Programming:* Farm one hr wkly; *Hrs. of News Programming:* news progmg 7 hrs wkly; *No. News Employees:* 1; *Target Audience:* 25-55; working middle class, rural
Ed Smith, President
Marie Smith, Operations Dir

WEIS
09-30-1961; 990 kHz AM; *Hrs Open:* 24
P.O. Box 297, Centre, AL 35960 US
(256) 927-4232; *Fax:* (256) 927-6503
License: Centre, AL held by Baker Enterprises Inc.
Arbitron Metro Market: Centre, AL; *Format:* Country, Gospel; *Hrs. of News Programming:* news progmg 10 hrs wkly; *No. News Employees:* 1; *Target Audience:* General.; *Adv. Rates:* 10; 8; 10; 6
Jerry Baker, General Manager
Nolen Sanford, Sports Director
Phil Baker, Engineering Director

Centreville

WBIB
12-14-1964; 1110 kHz AM; *Hrs Open:* Sunrise-sunset; 1 kw-D, NDD; N32 58 1 W87 9 1
P.O. Box 216, Centerville, AL 35042 US
(205) 926-6286; *Fax:* (205) 926-6288
www.wbibradio.com
wbibradio@att.net
License: Centreville, AL held by James DeLoach
Nat'l Reps: Keystone (unwired net)
Arbitron Metro Market: Centreville,AL; *Format:* Country, Gospel; *Target Audience:* Adults.; *Adv. Rates:* 10; 7; 10; na
Bo DeLoach, President
Horrace Cruchfield, General Manager
Kim DeLoach, Vice President

Chickasaw

WLVM
01-01-1980; 98.3 MHz FM; 40 kw; 167 meters; N30 35 05 W88 15 57
5700 West Oaks Boulevard, Rocklin, CA 95765 US
(916) 251-1600; *Fax:* (916) 251-1650
www.klove.com
License: Chickasaw, AL held by Educational Media Foundation
Group Owner: EMF Broadcasting

Mike Novak, President

Citronelle

***WQUA**
06-25-1989; 102.1 MHz FM; *Hrs Open:* 24; 15 kw; 427 ft.; N31 5 4 W88 23 51
Mailing Address: 5321 Albert Evans Rd, Wilmer, AL 36587 US
Second Address: 8919 World Ministry Ave., Baton Rouge, LA 70810
(225) 768-8300; *Fax:* (225) 768-3729
www.jsm.org
kawikfish@yahoo.com
License: Citronelle, Mobile County, AL held by Family Worship Center Church Inc.
Group Owner: Family Worship Center Church Inc.; (acq 8-25-2005; $1.25 million)
Arbitron Metro Market: Mobile, AL; *Format:* Christian
David Whitelaw, COO
Jimmy Swaggart, President

Coaling

WFFN
06-22-1987; 95.3 MHz FM
142 Skyland Blvd., Tuscaloosa, AL 35504
(205) 339-4953; *Fax:* (205) 349-1715
www.953thebear.com
monk.monk@townsquaremedia.com
License: Coaling, Tuscaloosa County, AL
Group Owner: Townsquare Media; (acq 7-12-2005; grpsl).
Population Served: 1,684; *Arbitron Metro Market:* Coaling, AL; *Target Audience:* 25-54
Greg Thomas, Operations Dir
Todd Livingston, General Manager
Tammy Boyd, Director of Sales
Meg Summers, Promotions Manager
Monk, Program Director

Columbia

WJJN
09-01-1992; 92.1 MHz FM; 2.55 kw; 499 ft.; N31 10 25 W85 12 49
4106 Ross Clark Circle, Dothan, AL 36303 US
(334) 671-1753; *Fax:* (334) 677-6923
www.wjjn.net
License: Columbia, Houston County, AL held by Wilson Broadcasting Co, Inc.
Group Owner: Wilson Broadcasting Co, Inc.
Arbitron Metro Market: Dothan, AL; *Format:* Urban Contemporary
James R. Wilson, CEO/President
Jimmy Doctrie, Operations Mgr
Alvin Harvey, General Manager
Jamar M. Wilson, Programming Director

Columbiana

*WQEM
01-01-2000; 101.5 MHz FM; 1.8 kw; 607 ft.; N33 13 45 W86 42 56
1137 10th Place South, Birmingham, AL 35205 US
(205) 323-1516; *Fax:* (205) 323-2747 (Phone/Fax)
www.gleniris.net
License: Columbiana, Shelby County, AL held by Glen Iris Baptist School
Arbitron Metro Market: Birmingham, AL; *Format:* Gospel
Chris Lamb, Chairman

Coosada

WACV
93.1 MHz FM; 3.1 kw; 464 ft.; N32 28 41 W86 24 28
4101-A Wall Street, Montgomery, AL 36106 US
(334) 244-0961; *Fax:* (334) 279-9563
www.newstalk931.com
License: Coosada, AL held by Liberty Aquisitions 825 LC
Format: News, News/Talk, 86
Rick Peters, President
Terry Barber, General Manager/Vice President
Jay Scott, Programming Director
Susan Ashworth, Promotions Director
Tom Jones, Chief Engineer

Cordova

WXJC
04-01-1953; 92.5 kHz AM
120 Summit ParkwayFl, Suite 200, Homewood, AL 35209 US
(205) 879-3324; *Fax:* (205) 941-1095
www.850wxjc.com
thejunction@wdjconline.com
License: Cordova, Walker County, AL held by Kimtron Inc.
Group Owner: Crawford Broadcasting Co.; (acq 11-12-99)
Nat'l Network: USA
Arbitron Metro Market: Birmingham, AL; *Format:* Religious, Christian, 86; *Target Audience:* Under 12.
Laura Scotti, General Manager
Laura Scotti, General Sales Mgr
Chris Mileski, Programming Director
Melodye Grubb, News Director
Todd Dixon, Chief Engineer

WXJC-FM
01-01-1997; 92.5 MHz FM; *Hrs Open:* 24; 2.2 kw; 548 ft.; N33 38 55 W87 9 19
120 Summit Parkway, Suite 200, Birmingham, AL 35209 US
(205) 879-3324; *Fax:* (205) 941-1095
License: Cordova, Walker County, AL held by Kimtron Inc.
Group Owner: Crawford Broadcasting Co.; (acq 7-15-2004; $1.15 million)
Arbitron Metro Market: Birmingham, AL; *Format:* Gospel, Religious, 20
Laura Scotti, General Manager
Jennifer Paepcke, General Sales Mgr
Melodye Grubb, Office Manager
Todd Dixon, Chief Engineer

Cullman

WMCJ & WMCJ
03-25-1950; 1460 kHz AM; *Hrs Open:* 24; 5 kw-D, DAN; 0.5 kw-N, DAN; N34 10 44 W86 51 58
1707 Warnke Road NW, Cullman, AL 35055 US
(256) 734-3271; *Fax:* (256) 734-3622
License: Cullman, AL held by Walton E. Williams III
Format: Gospel
Walt Williams, General Manager
Josh Kraft, Programming Director

WKUL
09-01-1967; 92.1 MHz FM; 6 kw; 328 ft; N34 11 41 W86 43 52
Box 803, 214 1st Ave. S.E., Cullman, AL 35033
(256) 734-0183; *Fax:* (256) 739-2999
www.wkul.com
License: Cullman, Cullman County, AL held by Jonathan Christian Corp.
Population Served: 1,200,000 *Special Programming:* Farm 15 hrs wkly; *Hrs. of News Programming:* news progmg 20 hrs wkly; *No. News Employees:* 1; *Target Audience:* 25-54.; *Adv. Rates:* 28; 22; 28; 18
Ron Mosley, President
Ron Mosley Jr., Operations/Program Director
Grant Smith, News Director

WYDE-FM
08-06-1949; 101.1 MHz FM; *Hrs Open:* 24; 100 kw; 1345 ft.; N34 4 56 W86 54 15
120 Summit Parkway, Suite 200, Birmingham, AL 35209 US
(205) 879-3324; *Fax:* (205) 802-4555
thejunction@wdjconline.com
License: Cullman, Cullman County, AL held by Kimtron Inc.
Group Owner: Crawford Broadcasting Co.; (acq 6-14-2002; $8.5 million)
Arbitron Metro Market: Birmingham, AL; *Format:* Adult Contemp
Steve Armstrong, General Manager
Jennifer Paepcke, General Sales Mgr
Melodye Grubb, Traffic Director
Todd Dexon, Chief Engineer

WFMH
10-01-1946; 1340 kHz AM; *Hrs Open:* 24
1707 Warnke Road, N.W., Cullman, AL 35055 US
(256) 734-3271; *Fax:* (256) 734-3622
wfmh@adelphia.net
License: Cullman, AL held by Walton E. Williams III
Nat'l Reps: Keystone (unwired net)
Arbitron Metro Market: Cullman, AL; *Format:* News, News/Talk, 84, Talk; *Hrs. of News Programming:* News progmg 18 hrs wkly; *Target Audience:* 25-54; middle & upper income adults; *Adv. Rates:* 6; 6; 6; 4
Walt Williams, General Manager
Susan Hackney, Programming Director

Daphne

WASG
11-12-1981; 540 kHz AM; *Hrs Open:* 24; 2.5 kw; N30 44 44 W88 05 40
273 Azalea Rd., Suite 403, Two Office Park, Mobile, AL 36609 US
(251) 340-0442
www.wilkinsradio.com
denise@wilkinsradio.com
License: Daphne, AL held by Alabama Radio Corp.
Group Owner: Wilkins Communications Network Inc.
Arbitron Metro Market: Mobile, AL; *Format:* Gospel, Talk
Scot Chestnut, Station Manager

WAVH
05-15-1993; 106.5 MHz FM; *Hrs Open:* 24; 50 kw; 449 ft.; N30 44 44 W88 5 40
900 Western America Drive, Suite 106, Mobile, AL 36609 US
(251) 344-1065
www.fmtalk1065.com
License: Daphne, Baldwin County, AL held by Bigler Broadcasting LLC
Nat'l Reps: McGavren Guild
Arbitron Metro Market: Oakland ME; *Format:* Christian, Country; *Hrs. of News Programming:* News progmg one hr wkly
Sean Sullivan, Operations Dir
Wayne Gardner, General Manager
Roger Jackson, Programming Director

WASG
11-12-1981; 106.1 Hz FM; *Hrs Open:* 24; 2.5 kw; N30 44 44 W88 05 40
273 Azalea Rd., Suite 403, Two Office Park, Mobile, AL 36609 US
(251) 340-0442
www.wilkinsradio.com
denise@wilkinsradio.com
License: Daphne, AL held by Alabama Radio Corp.
Group Owner: Wilkins Communications Network Inc.
Arbitron Metro Market: Mobile, AL; *Format:* Gospel, Talk
Scot Chestnut, Station Manager

Decatur

WDRM
09-01-1951; 102.1 MHz FM; *Hrs Open:* 24; 100 kw; 981 ft.; N34 47 36 W86 37 51
26869 Peoples Road, Madison, AL 35756 US
(256) 309-2400; *Fax:* (256) 350-2653
www.wdrm.com
info@wdrm.com
License: Decatur, Morgan County, AL held by Capstar TX LLC
Group Owner: iHeartMedia
Arbitron Metro Market: Decatur, AL; *Format:* Country
Carmelita Palmer, Market President
Erich West, Senior Vice President of Programming
Stuart Langston, Production Director
Beth Ridgeway, Digital Content Director

WHOS
10-01-1948; 800 kHz AM; *Hrs Open:* 24; 1 kw-D, ND1; 0.215 kw-N, ND1; N34 35 55 W87 0 24
Mailing Address: 600 Congress Ave., Suite 1400, Austin, TX 78701 US
Second Address: 26869 Peoples Rd., Madison, AL 35756
(256) 353-1750; *Fax:* (256) 350-2653
www.wbhpam.com
License: Decatur, AL held by Capstar TX LLC
Group Owner: iHeartMedia; (acq 7-18-2000; grpsl)
Arbitron Metro Market: Huntsville, AL; *Format:* News, News/Talk, 86; *No. News Employees:* 3; *Target Audience:* 25-54.
Carmelita Palmer, Market President
Stuart Langston, Programming Director
Kevin Younkin, Sales and Marketing Consultant

*WYFD
05-07-1975; 91.7 MHz FM; *Hrs Open:* 24; 9 kw; 787 ft.; N34 47 53 W86 38 24
P.O. Box 7300, Charlotte, NC 28241 US
(800) 888-7077
www.bbnradio.org
bbn@bbnmedia.org
License: Decatur, Morgan County, AL held by Bible Broadcasting Network Inc.
Group Owner: Bible Broadcasting Network; acq 10-19-90; $75,000;
Arbitron Metro Market: Decatur, AL; *Format:* Christian
Lowell Davey, President
Jason Padgett, Operations Manager

WWTM
05-01-1935; 1400 kHz AM; 1 kw-U, ND1; N34 36 44 W86 59 28
1209 Danville Road, Decatur, GA 35601 US
(256) 353-1400; *Fax:* (256) 353-0363
espn1400.info
License: Decatur, AL held by R & B Communications Inc.
Nat'l Network: ESPN Radio
Arbitron Metro Market: Decature, AL; *Format:* Sports; *Target Audience:* 25-54.
Joe Burns, General Manager

WEKI
01-01-1953; 1490 kHz AM; 1000 watts; N34 35 14 W86 59 13
Mailing Address: 2305 Holmes Ave. NW., Huntsville, AL 35816 US
Second Address: 2305 Holmes Ave. NW, Huntsville, AL 35816
(256) 533-1450; *Fax:* (256) 551-9865
www.wekiradio.com
License: Decatur, AL held by FRC of Alabama, LLC.
Group Owner: Focus Radio Communications
Format: Talk, Sports
Fred Holland, General Manager

WEKI
01-01-1953; 94.7 MHz FM; 1000 watts; N34 35 14 W86 59 13
Mailing Address: 2305 Holmes Ave. NW., Huntsville, AL 35816 US
Second Address: 2305 Holmes Ave. NW, Huntsville, AL 35816
(256) 533-1450; *Fax:* (256) 551-9865
www.wekiradio.com
License: Decatur, AL held by FRC of Alabama, LLC.
Group Owner: Focus Radio Communications
Format: Talk, Sports
Fred Holland, General Manager

Demopolis

WZNJ
01-01-1975; 106.5 MHz FM; 25 kw; 305 ft.; N32 30 8 W87 49 7
1028 Highway 80, Demopolis, AL 36732 US
(334) 289-1106
www.znj1065.com
License: Demopolis, Marengo County, AL held by Westburg Broadcasting, Alabama, LLC
Group Owner: Westburg Broadcasting
Nat'l Network: Westwood One; USA
Arbitron Metro Market: Demopolis, AL; *Format:* Oldies, Sports; *Target Audience:* 18-49.
Morgan Dowdy, CEO
Mike Reynolds, President
Buddy Baylor, General Manager
Beth Hancock
Sarah James

*WMWI
88.7 MHz FM; 0.1 kw; 157 ft.; N32 30 43 W87 51 0
US
(205) 929-1609
License: Demopolis, Marengo County, AL held by Miles College.
Arbitron Metro Market: Demopolis, AL
Kenneth Jones, General Manager

Dixons Mills

*WMBV
08-15-1988; 91.9 MHz FM; *Hrs Open:* 24; 62 kW; 614 ft.; N32 7 45 W87 44 16

5710 Watermelon Rd, Suite 316, Northport, AL 35473 USA
www.moodyradiosouth.fm
License: Dixons Mills, Marengo County, AL held by The Moody Bible Institute of Chicago
Group Owner: Moody Radio; (acq 3-31-88)
Nat'l Network: Moody
Arbitron Metro Market: Demopolis, AL; *Format:* Christian *Special Programming:* Financial 3 hrs, children 3 hrs, sports one hr wkl; *Hrs. of News Programming:* News progmg 10 hrs wkly; *Target Audience:* 35-55; general

Dora

WCOC
04-01-1982; 1010 kHz AM; 5 kw-D, ND1; 0.041 kw-N, ND1; N33 48 4 W87 6 42
P. O. Box 460, Dora, AL 35062 US
(619) 929-9186
License: Dora, AL held by Azteca Communications of Alabama Inc.
Arbitron Metro Market: Birmingham, AL
Patricia Perez, General Manager

Dothan

WAGF
09-29-1932; 1320 kHz AM
4106 Ross Clark Circle., Dothan, AL 36303 US
(334) 671-1753; *Fax:* (334) 677-6923
www.wjjn.net
License: Dothan, AL held by Wilson Broadcasting Inc.
Group Owner: Wilson Broadcasting Inc.; acq 8-13-92; $60,000;
Arbitron Metro Market: Dothan, AL; *Format:* Talk, Urban Contemporary
James R. Wilson, CEO/President
Jimmy Doctrie, Operations Mgr
Alvin Harvey, General Manager
Jamar M. Wilson, Programming Director

WAGF-FM
01-01-1991; 101.3 MHz FM; *Hrs Open:* 24; 1.15 kw; 535 ft.; N31 12 4 W85 20 4
4106 Ross Clark Circle., Dothan, AL 36303 US
(334) 671-1753; *Fax:* (334) 677-6923
www.wjjn.net
License: Dothan, Houston County, AL held by Wilson Broadcasting Inc.
Group Owner: Wilson Broadcasting Inc.
Nat'l Network: Jones Radio Networks; *Regional Network:* Alabama Radio Net; *Nat'l Reps:* Rgnl Reps
Arbitron Metro Market: Dothan, AL; *Format:* Urban Contemporary, Blues, 44, Sports, Oldies; *Target Audience:* 25-54; female; *Adv. Rates:* 20; 18; 20; 12
James R. Wilson, CEO/President
Jimmy Doctrie, Operations Mgr
Alvin Harvey, General Manager
Jamar M. Wilson, Programming Director

WESP
09-01-1989; 102.5 MHz FM; *Hrs Open:* 24; 16.5 kw; 404 ft.; N31 15 48 W85 18 24
285 North Foster Street, Charles Woods Building, 8th Floor, Dothan, AL 36303 US
(334) 699-0047; *Fax:* (334) 712-0374
1025theq.com
george@wiregrassradio.com
License: Dothan, Houston County, AL held by Alabama Media LLC
Group Owner: Alabama Media LLC; (acq 1999; $1.4 million)
Nat'l Reps: McGavren Guild
Arbitron Metro Market: Dothan, AL; *Target Audience:* 25-54; men
George Francis, General Manager

*WGTF
09-01-1988; 89.5 MHz FM; *Hrs Open:* 24; 19 kw; 210 ft.; N31 14 2 W85 26 2
107 Wanda Court, Dothan, AL 36303 US
(334) 794-4770; *Fax:* (334) 794-4770
www.bbnradio.org
wgtf@bbnradio.org
License: Dothan, Houston County, AL held by Dothan Community Educational Radio Inc.
Nat'l Network: Bible Bcstg Net
Arbitron Metro Market: Dothan, AL; *Format:* Religious
Raymond Brown, General Manager

WCNF
07-03-1995; 700 kHz AM; *Hrs Open:* Sunrise-sunset; 1.6 kw-D; N31 26 19 W85 17 22
3385 Reeves St., Dothan, AL 31820
(502) 776-1240
License: Dothan, Houston County, AL held by Dothan Broadcasting LLC
Arbitron Metro Market: Dothan, AL
Argie Dale Sr., General Manager

WOOF
02-17-1947; 560 kHz AM; 5 kw-D, ND2; 0.118 kw-N, ND2; N31 13 5 W85 21 10
Mailing Address: P. O. Box 1427, Dothan, AL 36301 US
Second Address: 2518 Columbia Hwy., Dothan, AL 36303
(334) 792-1149; *Fax:* (334) 677-4612
www.woofradio.com/ballindex.html
woof@ala.net
License: Dothan, AL held by WOOF Inc.
Arbitron Metro Market: Dothan, AL *TV Affiliate:* Sports; *Format:* Black, Gospel

WOOF-FM
09-18-1964; 99.7 MHz FM; 100 kw; 981 ft.; N31 15 7 W85 17 12
Mailing Address: P. O. Box 1427, Dothan, AL 36301 US
Second Address: 2518 Columbia Hwy., Dothan, AL 36303
(334) 792-1149; *Fax:* (334) 677-4612
www.997wooffm.com
woof@ala.net
License: Dothan, Houston County, AL held by WOOF Inc.
Nat'l Reps: Christal
Arbitron Metro Market: Dothan, AL *TV Affiliate:* Adult contemp *Special Programming:* news progmg 3 hrs wkly; *Hrs. of News Programming:* 2; *No. News Employees:* 25-54; women 18-49 domina
Hal Edwards, General Manager

*WRWA
12-01-1985; 88.7 MHz FM; *Hrs Open:* 6 AM-midnight; 50 kw; 469 ft.; N31 12 30 W85 36 51 *Rebroadcasts:* Rebroadcasts WTSU(FM) Troy 100%
University Ave, Troy, AL 36082 US
(334) 670-3268; *Fax:* (334) 670-3934
www.troypublicradio.org/
wtsu@troy.edu
License: Dothan, Houston County, AL held by Troy State University.
Nat'l Network: NPR; PRI
Arbitron Metro Market: Dothan, AL; *Format:* News *Special Programming:* Children one hr wkly; *Hrs. of News Programming:* News progmg 25 hrs wkly; *Target Audience:* General.
Joanne Jacobs, Development Manager
Fred Azbell, Programming Director
John Brunson, Chief Engineer

WTVY-FM
09-20-1968; 95.5 MHz FM; *Hrs Open:* 24; 100 kw; 1060 ft.; N31 15 16 W85 15 39
Mailing Address: P.O. Box 2088, Dothan, AL 36302 US
Second Address: 285 N. Foster, 8th Fl., Dothan, AL 36303
(334) 792-0047; *Fax:* (334) 712-9346
www.955wtvy.com
melody@trpdothan.com
License: Dothan, Houston County, AL held by Gulf South Communications Inc.
Group Owner: Gulf South Communications Inc.; (acq 7-27-2001)
Nat'l Reps: Christal
Arbitron Metro Market: Dothan, AL; *Format:* Country *Special Programming:* Farm 5 hrs, gospel 4 hrs, religion 3 hrs wkly; *Hrs. of News Programming:* News progmg 5 hrs wkly; *Target Audience:* 25-54. *Adv. Rates:* 35; 32; 32; 15
Melody Lee, General Manager/Sales Manager

*WVOB
12-08-1988; 91.3 MHz FM; *Hrs Open:* 24; 2.5 kw; 328 ft.; N31 10 57 W85 24 21
Mailing Address: P.O. Box 1944, Dothan, AL 36302 US
Second Address: 2573 Hodgesville Rd., Dothan, AL 36301
(334) 671-9862; *Fax:* (334) 793-4344
www.gospel91.com
wvob913fm@bethanybc.edu
License: Dothan, Houston County, AL held by Bethany Divinity College & Seminary Inc.
Nat'l Network: USA
Arbitron Metro Market: Dothan, AL; *Format:* Gospel; *Hrs. of News Programming:* news progmg 6 hrs wkly; *No. News Employees:* 1; *Target Audience:* General; college students & relg community
Dr. H. D. Shuemake, CEO
Keithy Brady, Operations Manager
Dr.H.D.Shuemake, Manager
Dr. Samuel Shuemake, Station Manager
Sylvia Green, Programming Director

WWNT
04-30-1947; 1450 kHz AM; 1 kw-U, ND1; N31 13 10 W85 22 14
1733 Columbia Hwy, Dothan, AL 36303 US
(334) 671-0075; *Fax:* (334) 671-0091
www.wwntradio.com
License: Dothan, AL held by WWNT LLC
Nat'l Network: USA
Arbitron Metro Market: Dothan, AL; *Format:* News, Talk; *No. News Employees:* 2; *Target Audience:* 25-54 men; 25-54 males
Larry Williams, General Manager

*WDYF
01-01-2004; 90.3 MHz FM; 9.2 kw; 561 ft.; N31 19 29 W85 36 6
Mailing Address: Post Office Box 210789, Montgomery, AL 36121 US
Second Address: 381 Mendel Parkway, Montgomery, AL 36117
(334) 271-8900; *Fax:* (334) 260-8962
www.faithradio.org
mail@faithradio.org
License: Dothan, Houston County, AL held by Faith Broadcasting Inc.
Arbitron Metro Market: Montgomery, AL; *Format:* Adult Contemp, Religious
Mark Williams, President
Andrew Leuthold, Operations Dir
Russell Dean, General Manager
Bob Crittenden, Programming Director
Wiely Boswell, Chief Engineer
Bob Crittenden, Director of Special Projects
Billy Irvin, Director ofMinistry Relation
Jeremy Smith, Operations Manager
Donna Spears, Office Manger
Ramona Henson, Graphic Design Coordinator
Beth Garland, Bookkeeper

Dozier

*WVPL
12-01-2011; 90.5 MHz FM; 0.3 kw; 243 ft.; N31 25 38 W86 21 21
100 Water St., Suite A, Camden, AL 36726 US
(256) 497-2840
License: Dozier, Crenshaw County, AL held by Townsend Broadcasting Enterprise
Group Owner: Townsend Broadcasting Enterprise
Format: Religious
Timothy Townsend, President

Eirmingham

*WGIB
01-01-1983; 91.9 MHz FM; *Hrs Open:* 24; 3.5 kw; 873 ft.; N33 24 59 W86 36 28
1137 10th Place South, Birmingham, AL 35256 US
(205) 323-1516; *Fax:* (205) 323-2747
www.gleniris.net
nmills@gleniris.net
License: Eirmingham, Jefferson County, AL held by Glen Iris Baptist School
Arbitron Metro Market: Birmingham, AL; *Format:* Christian
Chris Lamb, Chairman
Dan Ratje, Operations Dir

Elba

WELB
11-16-1958; 1350 kHz AM; *Hrs Open:* 11; 1 kw-D, ND1; 0.044 kw-N, ND1; N31 27 10 W86 4 0
100 N Main St, Enterprise, AL 36330 US
(334) 897-2216(334) 897-2217; *Fax:* (334) 897-3694
welbam1350@yahoo.com
License: Elba, AL
Arbitron Metro Market: Elba, AL; *Format:* Country *Special Programming:* Gospel 12 hrs wkly; *Hrs. of News Programming:* News progmg 6 hrs wkly; *Target Audience:* General.
Rhett S. Snellgrove, President

WVVL
10-01-1986; 101.1 MHz FM; *Hrs Open:* 19; 0.64 kw; 682 ft.; N31 24 41 W85 57 32
1800 Neil Grantham Drive, Elba, AL 36323 US
(334) 347-5621; *Fax:* (334) 347-5631
www.weevil101.com
wvvl@weevil101.com
License: Elba, Coffee County, AL
Arbitron Metro Market: Enterprise, AL; *Format:* Country
Doug Holderfielf, General Manager

Enterprise

WDJR
07-01-1968; 96.9 MHz FM; 100 kw; 1037 ft.; N30 55 19 W85 44 41
Box 9663, Dothan, AL 36304 US

(334) 712-9233; *Fax:* (334) 712-0374
www.mix969.net
ron@wdjr.com
License: Enterprise, Coffee County, AL held by Gulf South Communications Inc.
Group Owner: Gulf South Communications Inc.; (acq 7-9-92; $700,000;
Nat'l Reps: McGavren Guild
Arbitron Metro Market: Dothan, AL; *Format:* Country
Misty Huff, Operations Dir
Ron Eubanks, General Manager
Bill Moody, General Sales Mgr
Brett Mason, Programming Director
April Granger, News Director

WKMX

11-27-1974; 106.7 MHz FM; *Hrs Open:* 24; 100 kw; 1070 ft.; N31 24 41 W85 57 32
P. O. Box 840, Enterprise, AL 36330 US
(334) 792-0047; *Fax:* (334) 712-9346
www.wkmx.com
info@wkmx.com
License: Enterprise, Coffee County, AL held by Gulf South Communications Inc.
Group Owner: Gulf South Communications Inc.; (acq 9-3-2004; $4.5 million)
Arbitron Metro Market: Dothan, AL; *Format:* Contemporary Hits/Top 40; *Hrs. of News Programming:* News progmg 2 hrs wkly; *Target Audience:* Females; 18-49
Doc Thompson, Operations Dir
Dan Bradley, General Manager
Richard Reinhardt, General Sales Mgr
John Houston, Promotions Manager
Sue Hughes, General Manager
Chris Green, General Sales Manager
Amie Pollard, National SalesManager
Richard Reomjardt, Operations Manager

Equality

*WBNB

91.3 MHz FM; kw
Po Box 25051, Greenville, SC 29616 US
(334) 430-4296
License: Equality, Coosa County, AL held by LIFE Network
Arbitron Metro Market: Equality, AL
Liz McClure, Marketing Director
Rodney Baucom, Program Director

Eufaula

WYDK

03-16-1992; 97.9 MHz FM; *Hrs Open:* 24; 6 kw; Ant 328 ft; N31 56 04 W85 12 27
Mailing Address:
Second Address: 1347 S. Eufaula Ave., Eufaula, AL 36027
(334) 272-4532
License: Eufaula, Barbour County, AL held by Big Fish Broadcasting LLC
Nat'l Network: Jones Radio Networks
Target Audience: 24 plus.; *Adv. Rates:* 9; 6; 8; 5
Clyde Earnest, General Manager
Pam Sharp, General Sales Mgr
John Crumpton, Programming Director
Terry Harper, Engineering Dir

WKZJ

01-01-1969; 92.7 MHz FM; 39 kw; 551 ft.; N32 7 58 W85 4 13
Mailing Address: P O Box 2127, Columus, GA 31902 US
Second Address: 2203 Wynnton Rd., Columbus, GA 31907
(706) 576-3565; *Fax:* (706) 576-3683
www.k927.com
License: Eufaula, Barbour County, AL held by Davis Broadcasting Inc.
Group Owner: Davis Broadcasting Inc.; (acq 7-20-2004; $2.7 million).
Arbitron Metro Market: Columbus, GA; *Format:* Adult Contemp; *Hrs. of News Programming:* news progmg 6 hrs wkly; *No. News Employees:* 2
Gregory Davis, President
Cheryl Davis, Operations Dir
Angela Verdejo, General Sales Mgr
Carl Conner, Programming Director
Bernie Corcoran, Operations Manager

WNRA

01-01-1948; 1240 kHz AM; 1 kw-U; N31 54 30 W85 09 51
Box 1419, Eufaula, AL 30143
(334) 616-0097; *Fax:* (334) 687-3600
lake98fm@gmail.com
License: Eufaula, Barbour County, AL held by Big Fish Broacasting LLC

Population Served: 20,000 *Special Programming:* Farm 2 hrs, Black 3 hrs wkly; *Target Audience:* 25-54; adults; *Adv. Rates:* 6.50; 4.50; 5.50; 4.50
Jeffrey Roper, President

Eutaw

WWPG

08-01-1990; 104.3 MHz FM; *Hrs Open:* 24; 2.3 kw; 370 ft; N32 54 16 W87 50 09
Mailing Address: Box 70427, Tuscaloosa, AL 35407
Second Address: 601 Greensboro Ave., Suite 507, Tuscaloosa, AL 35401
(205) 345-4787; *Fax:* (205) 345-4790
jwlawson@bellsouth.net
License: Eutaw, Greene County, AL held by Jim Lawson Communications Inc.
Arbitron Metro Market: Tuscaloosa, AL
Jim Lawson, General Manager

Eva

WRJL-FM

01-01-1996; 99.9 MHz FM; *Hrs Open:* 24; 25 kw; 318 ft.; N34 18 43 W86 43 54
Rt. 2, Box 27, Eva, AL 35621 US
(256) 796-8000; *Fax:* (256) 796-8515
License: Eva, Morgan County, AL held by Rojo Inc.
Format: Gospel
Jo French, General Manager
Amy Holland, Programming Director

Evergreen

WEVG

07-01-1957; 1470 kHz AM; *Hrs Open:* 24; 1 kw-D; N31 26 29 W86 56 08
Mailing Address: Box 705, Evergreen, AL 36561
Second Address: Hwy. 31 S, Evergreen, AL 36401
(251) 578-2780; *Fax:* (251) 578-5399
License: Evergreen, Conecuh County, AL held by Star Broadcasting Inc.
Group Owner: Star Broadcasting Inc.; (acq 4-13-2004; $2.75 million with co-located FM).
Population Served: 20,000 *Hrs. of News Programming:* news progmg 20 hrs wkly; *No. News Employees:* 3; *Target Audience:* 34-64.
Luther Upton, General Manager

Fairfield

WJLD(AM)

01-01-1942; 1400 kHz AM; *Hrs Open:* 24; 1 kw-U; N33 28 36 W86 53 01
Mailing Address: Box 19123, Birmingham, AL 35219-9123
Second Address: 1449 Spaulding Ishkooda Rd., Birmingham, AL 35211-5059
(205) 942-1776; *Fax:* (205) 942-4814
www.wjldfm.com
License: Fairfield, Jefferson County, AL held by Richardson Broadcasting Corp.
Nat'l Network: American Urban; CNN Radio
Population Served: 900,000; *Arbitron Metro Market:* Birmingham, AL; *Format:* Blues, Gospel, 86 *Special Programming:* ""Morning Talk"" 6-8AM M-F; *Hrs. of News Programming:* TOH 6A-9P; *Target Audience:* 35+;majority Black, adult, blue and white collar working class; *Adv. Rates:* 35; 15; 10
Gary Richardson, President
Bob Friedman, Operations Dir
Willamena Richardson, VP/GM
David Austin, Sales/Marketing Manager

Fairhope

WABF

08-12-1961; 1220 kHz AM; *Hrs Open:* 24
Mailing Address: P.O. Box 679, Orange Beach, AL 36561 US
Second Address: 460 S. Section St., Fairhope, AL 36533
(608) 273-1000; *Fax:* (608) 271-8182
www.q106.com
License: Fairhope, AL held by Gulf Coast Broadcasting Co. Inc.
Nat'l Network: CBS Radio
Arbitron Metro Market: Redding CA; *Format:* Country; *Target Audience:* 25-54; general; *Adv. Rates:* 11;10;11;8
Lori Dubose, General Manager
John Rhodes, General Sales Mgr

WXQW

04-22-1965; 660 kHz AM; *Hrs Open:* 24; 10 kw-D, DAN; 0.85 kw-N, DAN; N30 35 51 W87 52 57 *Rebroadcasts:* Simulcast with WGOK(AM(Mobile 100%
2800 Dauphin Rd, Suite 104, Mobile, AL 36606 US

(251) 652-2000; *Fax:* (251) 652-2007
www.gospel900.com
License: Fairhope, AL held by Cumulus Licensing Corp.
Group Owner: Cumulus Media Inc.; (acq 10-18-99; grpsl)
Arbitron Metro Market: Mobile, AL; *Format:* Gospel; *Target Audience:* 18-54; Black adults
Angel Taylor, VP/Marketing Manager
Felicia Allbritton, Programming Director

WZEW

08-28-1966; 92.1 MHz FM; *Hrs Open:* 24; 20.5 kw; 363 ft.; N30 31 23 W88 6 32
1100 Dauphin St, Mobile, AL 36604 US
(251) 433-9236; *Fax:* (251) 438-5462
www.92zew.net
License: Fairhope, Baldwin County, AL held by Dot Com Plus LLC
Arbitron Metro Market: Mobile, AL; *Format:* Alternative, Blues *Special Programming:* Jazz 6 hrs wkly; *Hrs. of News Programming:* news progmg 6 hrs wkly; *No. News Employees:* 1; *Target Audience:* 25-44.
Tim Camp, General Manager
Lee Camp, Web Manager
Gene Murrell, Programming Director

Fayette

WLDX

09-03-1949; 990 kHz AM; 1 kw-D, ND1; 0.042 kw-N, ND1; N33 41 6 W87 49 16
733 Columbus Street East, Fayette, AL 35555 US
(205) 932-3318; *Fax:* (205) 932-3318
www.wldx.com
wldx@wldx.com
License: Fayette, AL held by Dean Broadcasting Inc.
Format: Country; *Target Audience:* 25-55; middle-income adults
J. Wiley Dean, President
Jill Dean, Operations Dir
Steve Dean, Vice President
Joe Redker, Programming Director

WTXT

01-29-1977; 98.1 MHz FM; *Hrs Open:* 24; 100 kw; 906 ft.; N33 19 17 W87 46 29
3900 11th Avenue South, Tuscaloosa, AL 35401 US
(205) 344-4589; *Fax:* (205) 366-9774
www.98txt.com
License: Fayette, Fayette County, AL held by Capstar TX LLC
Group Owner: iHeartMedia; (acq 8-30-00; grpsl).
Nat'l Network: ABC; *Nat'l Reps:* Christal; *Wire Services:* Direct Line Weather Wire
Arbitron Metro Market: Tuscaloosa, AL; *Format:* Country; *No. News Employees:* 1; *Target Audience:* 25-54.
Todd Robbins, Senior Vice President of Programming
Jackie Toye, Senior Vice President of Sales
Tom Canterbury, Promotions Director
Justin Barnett, Digital Manager

Five Points

*WJBE-FM

88.5 MHz FM; 0 kw horiz, 0.5 kw vert; 200 ft.; N33 57 51 W87 12 34
US
(205) 295-2055
License: Five Points, Chambers County, AL held by Big South Community Broadcasting Inc.
Arbitron Metro Market: Five Points, AL
Brett Elmore, President

Florala

WKWL

11-03-1979; 1230 kHz AM; *Hrs Open:* 6 AM-6 PM; 1 kw-U, ND1; N31 0 20 W86 19 53
Mailing Address: P.O. Box 158, South 6th St, Florala, AL 36442 US
Second Address: 427 S Sixth St, Florala, AL 36442
(334) 858-6162; *Fax:* (334) 858-6162
wkwl.ezstream.com
wkwl@alaweb.com
License: Florala, AL held by Florala Broadcasting Co. Inc.
Nat'l Network: USA
Format: Christian, Country, 44 *Special Programming:* Farm one hr, relg 12 hrs wkly; *Hrs. of News Programming:* news progmg 15 hrs wkly; *No. News Employees:* 1; *Target Audience:* 5 plus; general
Robert Williamson, President

Florence

WBCF
01-01-1946; 1240 kHz AM; *Hrs Open:* 24; 1 kw-U, ND1; N34 47 1 W87 42 15
Mailing Address: 525 E. Tennessee St, Florence, AL 35631 US
Second Address: 525 E. Tennessee St., Florence, AL 35630
(800) 877-5600; *Fax:* (916) 251-1650
www.klove.com
License: Florence, AL held by BCB Inc.
Nat'l Network: Westwood One; Fox News Radio; CBS Radio; ABC; Talk Radio Network
Arbitron Metro Market: Ely NV; *Format:* Christian
Mike Novak, President

***WFIX**
03-20-1988; 91.3 MHz FM; *Hrs Open:* 12am-12am; 100 kw; 869 ft.; N34 40 24 W87 42 56
2806 West Mall Drive, Florence, AL 35630 US
(256) 760-9191; *Fax:* (256) 764-9154
www.wfix.net
wfix@wfix.net
License: Florence, Lauderdale County, AL held by Tri-State Inspirational Broadcasting Inc.
Nat'l Network: USA
Arbitron Metro Market: Florence, AL; *Format:* Adult Contemp, Christian *Special Programming:* Friday & Saturday Night Youth Shows; *Hrs. of News Programming:* News progmg 2 hrs wkly; *Target Audience:* 25-54; upscalefamily oriented women & men
Mark Allen Pyle, General Manager

WQLT-FM
08-08-1962; 107.3 MHz FM; *Hrs Open:* 24; 93 kw; 1017 ft.; N34 40 24 W87 42 56
624 Sam Phillips St., Florence, AL 35630 US
(256) 764-8121; *Fax:* (256) 764-8169
www.wqlt.com
sbrook@bigriverbroadcasting.com
License: Florence, Lauderdale County, AL held by Big River Broadcasting Corp.
Group Owner: Big River Broadcasting Corp.
Arbitron Metro Market: Florence-Muscle Shoals, AL; *Format:* Adult Contemp; *Target Audience:* 25-54.
Sharon Brook, General Sales Mgr

WSBM
03-29-1946; 1340 kHz AM; *Hrs Open:* 24; 1 kw-U, ND1; N34 47 50 W87 39 54
624 Sam Phillips St., Florence, AL 35630 US
(256) 764-8121; *Fax:* (256) 764-8169
License: Florence, AL held by Big River Broadcasting Corp.
Group Owner: Big River Broadcasting Corp.
Nat'l Network: Fox Sports
Arbitron Metro Market: Florence-Muscle; *Format:* Sports
Fletch Brown, Operations Dir

WXFL
02-01-1992; 96.1 MHz FM; *Hrs Open:* 24; 20.5 kw; 781 ft.; N34 54 17 W87 24 2
624 Sam Phillips St., Florence, AL 35630 US
(256) 764-8121; *Fax:* (256) 764-8169
www.kix96country.com
License: Florence, AL held by Big River Broadcasting Corp.
Group Owner: Big River Broadcasting Corp.
Arbitron Metro Market: Florence, AL; *Format:* Country; *Target Audience:* 18-49; general
Sharon Brook, General Sales Mgr

Foley

WHEP
05-31-1953; 1310 kHz AM; *Hrs Open:* 24
Mailing Address: P. O. Box 1747, Foley, AL 36536 US
Second Address: 20109 Hadley Rd., Foley, AL 36535
(251) 943-7131; *Fax:* (251) 943-7031
www.whep1310.com
whepsports@yahoo.com
License: Foley, AL held by Stewart Broadcasting Co. Inc.
Nat'l Network: CNN Radio; Talk Radio Network; Westwood One;
Regional Network: Alabama Radio Net.
Arbitron Metro Market: Mobile, AL; *Format:* Adult Contemp, News, 62, Sports, Talk *Special Programming:* Farm 2 hrs wkly; *No. News Employees:* 2; *Target Audience:* 25 plus.; *Adv. Rates:* 8.75; 8.75; 8.75; na
Clark Stewart, President

Fort Deposit

WKXN
07-18-1977; 95.7 MHz FM; *Hrs Open:* 24; 4 kw; 226 ft.; N31 50 43 W86 38 56 *Rebroadcasts:* Simulcasts WKXK(FM) Pine Hill 100%
Mailing Address: US
Second Address: 563 Manningham Rd., Greenville, AL 36037
(334) 382-6555; *Fax:* (334) 382-7770
www.wkxn.com
License: Fort Deposit, Butler County, AL held by Autaugaville Radio Inc.
Format: Blues
Roscoe Miller, General Manager
Chelli Flores, General Sales Mgr

Fort Mitchell

WBFA
01-01-1988; 98.3 MHz FM; 6 kw; 328 ft.; N32 21 48 W85 3 6
1501 13th Ave., Columbus, GA 31901 US
(706) 576-3000; *Fax:* (706) 576-3010
www.thebeatcolumbus.com
License: Fort Mitchell, Russell County, AL held by Aloha Station Trust LLC
Group Owner: iHeartMedia; (acq 2-21-2002; grpsl)
Arbitron Metro Market: Columbus, GA; *Format:* Urban Contemporary *Special Programming:* Relg 6 hrs wkly
Jennifer Newman, General Manager
Chuck Thompson, Sales Manager
Derrick Greene, Programming Director

Fort Payne

WFPA
12-01-1949; 1400 kHz AM; *Hrs Open:* 24; 1 kw-U, ND1; N34 26 21 W85 42 9
1210 Johnson St E, Fort Payne, AL 35967 US
(256) 845-7721; *Fax:* (256) 845-6593
www.1400wfpa.com
wfpa@1400wfpa.com
License: Fort Payne, AL held by J.A.R. Services LLC
Nat'l Network: CBS Radio; Premiere Radio Networks; Talk Radio Network; Jones Radio Networks
Arbitron Metro Market: Huntsville, AL; *Format:* News, News/Talk, 86; *Hrs. of News Programming:* news progmg 15 hrs wkly; *No. News Employees:* 1; *Target Audience:* 25-59; women/men; *Adv. Rates:* 10;10;10;10
Mike Wallace, General Manager
Tim Dobson, Chief Engineer

WZOB
07-02-1950; 1250 kHz AM; *Hrs Open:* 24 hrs; 5 kw-D, ND1; 0.122 kw-N, ND1; N34 26 23 W85 45 12
P. O. Box 967, Dublin, GA 31021 US
(256) 845-2810; *Fax:* (256) 845-7521
wzobam@windjammer.net
License: Fort Payne, AL held by Central Broadcasting Co. Inc.
Regional Reps: Dora-Clayton.; *Wire Services:* NOAA Weather
Arbitron Metro Market: Fort Payne, AL; *Format:* Country *Special Programming:* Farm 2 hrs, gospel 5 hrs, relg 5 hrs wkly; *No. News Employees:* 1
Mike Kirby, President
Doris Hobbs, Station Manager

Fort Rucker

WLDA
10-05-1968; 103.9 MHz FM; *Hrs Open:* 24; 25 kw; Ant 292 ft; N31 26 25 W85 33 49
285 N. Foster St., Dothan, AL 36302
(334) 792-0047; *Fax:* (334) 712-9346
License: Fort Rucker, Dale County, AL held by Magic Broadcasting Alabama Licensing LLC.
Group Owner: Magic Broadcasting LLC; (acq 8-1-2002; $750,000 with co-located AM)
Nat'l Network: Moody
Arbitron Metro Market: Dothan, AL *Special Programming:* Gospel 8 hrs, jazz 4 hrs, oldies 6 hrs wkly; *Hrs. of News Programming:* news progmg 15 hrs wkly; *No. News Employees:* 1
Greg Kamishlian, General Manager
Chris Green, General Sales Mgr
John Houston, Programming Director
Steve Youngblood, Chief Engineer

Fruithurst

WCKS
05-09-1994; 102.7 MHz FM; 1.65 kw; 630 ft.; N33 37 24 W85 20 14
2225 Victory Church Road, Bowdon, GA 30174 US
(770) 834-5477; *Fax:* (770) 830-1027
www.gradickcommunications.com
cworthington@newstalk1330.com
License: Fruithurst, Cleburne County, AL held by WCKS LLC.
Arbitron Metro Market: Atlanta, GA; *Format:* Adult Contemp; *Target Audience:* 25-44.
Linda Bearden, Promotions Director

Fulton

***WJIK**
89.3 MHz FM; 2.1 kw; 545 ft.; N31 53 28 W87 42 45
P.O. Box 890820, Temecula, CA 92589 US
(855) 500-3759
wjik.krtmradio.org
License: Fulton, Clarke County, AL held by Penfold Communications, Inc.
Group Owner: Penfold Communications, Inc.
Arbitron Metro Market: Fulton, AL; *Format:* Christian, Religious

Gadsden

WAAX
10-18-1947; 570 kHz AM; 5 kw-D, DAN; 0.5 kw-N, DAN; N33 58 45 W86 0 9 *Rebroadcasts:* Rebroadcasts WERC(AM) Birmingham 80%
6510 Whorton Bend Rd., Gadsden, AL 35901 US
(256) 543-9229; *Fax:* (256) 543-8777
www.waax570.com
License: Gadsden, AL held by Capstar TX LLC
Group Owner: iHeartMedia; (acq 8-30-2000; grpsl).
Arbitron Metro Market: Gadsden, AL; *Format:* News, News/Talk, 86; *Adv. Rates:* 50; 40; 25; 10
John Mountz, Programming Director
Pam Gaylor, Traffic Manager
Richard Spavins, Chief Engineer
Colin Peterson, Digital Director
Kevin Moore, Producer
Wayne Ball, Account Executive
Rachel Hyatt, Account Executive
Ed Hyde, ITManager

WTDR
05-26-1947; 1350 kHz AM; *Hrs Open:* 24; 5 kw-D, 1 kw-N, DA-N; N34 01 03 W86 05 15
Mailing Address: Box 1350, Gadsden, AL 35901
Second Address: 750 Walnut St., Gadsden, AL 35901
(256) 546-1611; *Fax:* (256) 547-9062
License: Gadsden, Etowah County, AL held by The DR Group LLC
Population Served: 100,000 *Adv. Rates:* 13; 13; 13; 10
Dave Hedrick, General Manager

WMGJ
09-11-1985; 1240 kHz AM; 1 kw-U, ND1; N34 0 4 W86 1 48
P. O. Box 408, Gadsden, AL 35902 US
(256) 546-4434; *Fax:* (256) 546-9645
www.wmgj.com
floyddonald@aol.com
License: Gadsden, AL held by Floyd L. Donald Broadcasting Co. Inc.
Nat'l Reps: Roslin
Arbitron Metro Market: GADSDEN, AL; *Format:* Urban Contemporary
Floyd Donald, General Manager

***WSGN**
02-11-1975; 91.5 MHz FM; *Hrs Open:* 24; 6.3 kw vert; 522 ft.; N34 4 29 W86 1 11 *Rebroadcasts:* Rebroadcasts WBHM(FM) Birmingham 80%
1001 George Wallace Dr., P.O. Box 27, Gadsden, AL 35902 US
(256) 549-8200
www.gadsdenstate.edu
License: Gadsden, Etowah County, AL held by Gadsden State Community College.
Format: News *Special Programming:* Folk 2 hrs, new age 10 hrs wkly; *Hrs. of News Programming:* News progmg 34 hrs wkly; *Target Audience:* General.
Dr. Renee Culverhouse, President
Scott E. Hanley, General Manager
Michael Krall, Programming Director
Audrey Atkins, Marketing Manager
Dan Carsen, Education Reporter

***WTBB**
07-20-1999; 89.9 MHz FM; *Hrs Open:* 24; 4.8 kw; Ant 515 ft; N34 06 03 W85 59 37 *Rebroadcasts:* Rebroadcasts WTBJ(FM) Oxford 100%
Trinity Christian Academy, 1500 Airport Rd., Oxford, AL 36203
(256) 831-3333; *Fax:* (256) 831-5895
www.trinityoxford.org
truth@trinityoxford.org
License: Gadsden, Etowah County, AL held by Trinity Christian Academy.
Population Served: 500,000 *Special Programming:* Sp one hr wkly
Dr. C.O. Grinstead, General Manager

Gardendale

WEZZ-FM
01-01-1998; 97.3 MHz FM; 6.2 kw; 1,325 ft; N33 29 04 W86 48 25
2700 Corporate Drive, Suite 115, Birmingham, AL 35242 US
(205) 322-2987; *Fax:* (205) 322-2390
www.easy973.com
License: Gardendale, AL held by SM-WZNN LLC
Group Owner: SummitMedia LLC

David DuBose, General Manager

Geneva

WGEA
03-17-1953; 1150 kHz AM; 1 kw-D, ND1; 0.035 kw-N, ND1; N31 1 21 W85 52 16
Mailing Address: 409 East Broad Street, Ozark, AL 36360 US
Second Address: 420 Riverside Ave., Geneva, AL 36340
(334) 293-8987; *Fax:* (334) 774-6450
www.wgea.us
yell@wgea.us
License: Geneva, AL held by Shelley Broadcasting Co.
Arbitron Metro Market: Dothan, AL; *Format:* Country, Gospel, 60, News/Talk, Talk; *Target Audience:* 30 plus.
Jack Mizell, President
Doc Parker, General Manager

Georgiana

WFXX
01-01-1999; 107.7 MHz FM; *Hrs Open:* 24; 42 kw; 535 ft.; N31 27 8 W86 37 7
108 Stanfield St, Greenville, AL 36037 US
(334) 222-2222; *Fax:* (334) 427-8888
www.fox107.com
wfxx@alaweb.com
License: Georgiana, Butler County, AL held by Star Broadcasting Inc.
Format: Adult Contemp
Jim Walker, General Manager
Billy Bimbo, Sales Manager
Kim Herman, Traffic Director

Glencoe

WGMZ
10-11-1993; 93.1 MHz FM; *Hrs Open:* 24; 1.65 kw; 620 ft.; N33 57 16 W85 51 40
Mailing Address: 600 Congress Avenue, Suite 1400, Austin, TX 78701 US
Second Address: 6510 Whorton Bend Road, Gadsden, AL 35901
(256) 549-0931; *Fax:* (256) 543-8777
www.wgmz.com
License: Glencoe, Etowah County, AL held by Capstar TX LLC
Group Owner: iHeartMedia; (acq 8-30-00; grpsl).
Format: Oldies; *No. News Employees:* 1; *Target Audience:* 35 plus.
Jason Mack, Programming Director
Pam Gaylor, Traffic Manager
Richard Spavins, Chief Engineer
Colin Peterson, Digital Director
Kevin Moore, Producer
Wayne Ball, Account Executive
Rachel Hyatt, Account Executive
Ed Hyde, ITManager

Goodwater

WKGA
04-04-1990; 97.5 MHz FM; *Hrs Open:* 24; 5.1 kw; 354 ft.; N33 1 42 W85 59 23
Mailing Address: 1009 Cherokee Rd, Alexander City, AL 35010 US
Second Address: 1051 Tallapoosa St., Alexander City, AL 35011
(256) 234-6977; *Fax:* (256) 234-6976
License: Goodwater, Coosa County, AL held by Lake Broadcasting Inc.
Format: Country
John Kennedy, President
Jeremy Jeffcoat, General Manager

***WFAZ**
91.1 MHz FM; 700 w; Ant 220 ft; N33 07 01 W86 07 01
182 So College St, Auburn, AL 36849
(334) 844-4114
License: Goodwater, Coosa County, AL held by Auburn University Board Of Trustees
Chris Adler, Station Manager

Goshen

WAOQ
06-03-1999; 100.3 MHz FM; *Hrs Open:* 24; 6 kw; 328 ft.; N31 42 26 W86 13 12
P.O. Box 83, Clanton, AL 35045 US
(334) 335-2877; *Fax:* (205) 755- 3329
www.waoq.com
office@waoq.com
License: Goshen, Crenshaw County, AL held by Alatron Corp. Inc.
Arbitron Metro Market: Brantley, Al; *Format:* Country *Special Programming:* Gospel 14 hrs wkly; *Hrs. of News Programming:* News progmg 14 hrs wkly
Robert Williams, President
Christopher Johnson, General Manager
Ken Lyons, Station Manager

Greensboro

WDGM
03-03-2002; 99.1 MHz FM; *Hrs Open:* 24; 25 kw; Ant 328 ft; N32 49 46 W87 40 19
142 Skyland Boulevard East, Tuscaloosa, AL 35476
(205) 339-4953; *Fax:* (205) 349-1715
www.991wdgm.com
todd.livingston@townsquaremedia.com
License: Greensboro, Hale County, AL
Group Owner: Townsquare Media; (acq 7-12-2005; grpsl).
Nat'l Network: ESPN Radio; *Nat'l Reps:* Roslin
Population Served: 91,605; *Arbitron Metro Market:* Tuscaloosa, AL; *Target Audience:* 25 plus; male & female
Todd Livingston, General Manager
Meg Summers, Promotions Manager
Tammy Boyd, Director of Sales
Benjamin George, Program Director

Greenville

WGYV
08-18-1948; 1380 kHz AM; 1 kw-D, NDD; N31 50 1 W86 36 7
PO Box 585, Greenville, AL 36037 US
(334) 382-5444; *Fax:* (334) 382-5444
www.wgyv.com
wgyv@alaweb.com
License: Greenville, AL held by Robert John Williamson
Format: News, News/Talk, 64, Talk *Special Programming:* Black 6 hrs wkly; *Target Audience:* 25-54; general; *Adv. Rates:* 6.95; 6.95; 6.95; na
Robert Williamson, General Manager
Bob Luman, Chief Engineer

WQZX
08-19-1985; 94.3 MHz FM; *Hrs Open:* 24; 3.9 kw; 410 ft.; N31 54 40 W86 36 19
205 West Commerce Street, Greenville, AL 36037 US
(334) 382-6633; *Fax:* (334) 382-6634
www.q94.net
q94@q94.net
License: Greenville, Butler County, AL held by Haynes Broadcasting Inc.
Nat'l Network: ABC
Format: Country
Kyle Haynes, General Manager/Operations, Sales Manager
Mark Ritchie, Programming Director
Kim Herman, Traffic Manager

Grove Hill

WBMH
05-01-1999; 106.1 MHz FM; 12 kw; 472 ft.; N31 43 30 W87 54 58
Mailing Address: 324 Bradford Street, NW, Gainesville, GA 30501 US
Second Address: 4428 N College Ave, Jackson, AL 36545
(251) 246-4431; *Fax:* (251) 246-1980
bama1061@yahoo.com
License: Grove Hill, Clarke County, AL held by Capital Assets Inc.
Group Owner: Bennie E. Hewett Stns
Format: Country
Paul McVay, Operations Dir
Gabriel Puello, Station Manager

Guntersville

WGSV
04-16-1950; 1270 kHz AM; 1 kw-D, NDD; 0.124 kw-N, ND1; N34 18 31 W86 17 44
Mailing Address: P. O. Box 220, Guntersville, AL 35970 US
Second Address: 2301 Thomas Ave., Guntersville, AL
(256) 582-8131; *Fax:* (256) 582-4347
www.wgsv.com
License: Guntersville, AL held by Guntersville Broadcasting Co. Inc.
Nat'l Network: ABC
Format: News, News/Talk, 86
Lavell Jackson, President
Kerry Jackson, Operations Dir

***WJIA**
09-01-1995; 88.5 MHz FM; 2.2 kw vert; 427 ft.; N34 25 33 W86 18 25
5025 Spring Creek Drive, Guntersville, AL 35976 US
(256) 505-0885; *Fax:* (256) 505-0886
License: Guntersville, Marshall County, AL held by Lake City Educational Broadcasting Inc.
Format: Christian
Stan Broadus, President
Kerry Rich, Station Manager

WTWX-FM
08-01-1969; 95.9 MHz FM; 10.5 kw; 515 ft.; N34 20 14 W86 16 46
Mailing Address: P. O. Box 220, Guntersville, AL 35976 US
Second Address: 2301 Thomas Ave., Guntersville, AL
(256) 582-4946; *Fax:* (256) 582-4347
www.wtwx.com
wtwx@wtwx.com
License: Guntersville, Marshall County, AL held by Guntersville Broadcasting Co., Inc.
Nat'l Network: ABC
Arbitron Metro Market: Huntsville, AL; *Format:* Country
Lavell Jackson, President
Kerry Jackson, General Manager

Gurley

WHRP
06-08-1995; 94.1 MHz FM; *Hrs Open:* 24; 0.71 kw; 945 ft.; N34 40 50 W86 30 55
1717 Highway 72 East, Athens, AL 35611 US
(256) 830-8300; *Fax:* (256) 232-6842
www.whrpfm.com
toni.terrell@cumulus.com
License: Gurley, Madison County, AL held by Cumulus Licensing LLC.
Group Owner: Cumulus Media Inc.; (acq 4-4-2006; $3.3 million with WVNN-FM Trinity)
Nat'l Reps: Katz Radio
Arbitron Metro Market: Huntsville, AL; *Format:* Urban Contemporary; *Hrs. of News Programming:* 4 hrs per wk
John Walker, General Manager/Vice President
Matt Tobin, General Sales Mgr
Toni Terrell, Programming Director
Tara Harrison, Promotions Manager
Chuck Miller, Engineering Dir

Hackleburg

WFMH-FM
01-01-1996; 95.5 MHz FM; *Hrs Open:* 24; 4.1 kw; 400 ft.; N34 18 38 W87 56 13
1707 Warnke Road, N.W., Cullman, AL 35055 US
(205) 935-3730; *Fax:* (205) 935-3734
www.big955.com
License: Hackleburg, Marion County, AL held by Williams Communications.
Group Owner: TNT Inc.; (acq 8-18-2004; $2.45 million with WFMH(AM) Cullman).
Wire Services: AP
Format: Country; *Hrs. of News Programming:* News progmg 15 hrs wkly; *Target Audience:* 35-64.
Walt Williams, General Manager

Haleyville

WWWH
04-01-1949; 1230 kHz AM; *Hrs Open:* 24; 1 kw-U; N34 14 00 W87 37 32
Drawer 370, 807 Hwy. 13 N., Haleyville, AL 35565
(205) 486-2277,(205) 486-2278; *Fax:* (205) 486-3905
License: Haleyville, Winston County, AL held by Haleyville Broadcasting Co. Inc.
Nat'l Reps: Rgnl Reps
Population Served: 87,000 *Special Programming:* Farm 3 hrs wkly; *Hrs. of News Programming:* news progmg 36 hrs wkly; *No. News Employees:* 1; *Target Audience:* 25-55; professionals
Terry Slatton, General Manager
Debby Aderholt, General Sales Mgr
Robert Wakefield, Programming Director

Sherron Hayes, News Director
Larry Gardner, Public Affairs Director
Aubrey Haynes, Sales VP

WWWH-FM
07-14-1979; 92.7 MHz FM; 3.9 kw; Ant 240 ft; N34 14 00 W87 37 32
Mailing Address: Drawer 370, Haleyville, AL 35565
Second Address: 807 Hwy. 13 N., Haleyville, AL 35565
(205) 486-2277,(205) 486-2278; *Fax:* (205) 486-3905
wjbb@southnet.net
License: Haleyville, Winston County, AL held by Haleyville Broadcasting Co. Inc.
Population Served: 118,000 *Target Audience:* 24-55.
Terry Slatton, President
Andy Marbutt, Operations Dir
Aubrey Haynes, General Sales Mgr
Keith Page, Programming Director
Sherron Hayes, News Director
Misty Sawyer, Disc Jockey

Hamilton

WERH
08-24-1950; 970 kHz AM; 5 kw-D, NDD; N34 7 1 W87 59 29
P.O. Box 1119, Hamilton, AL 35570 US
(205) 921-3481; *Fax:* (205) 921-7187
werh@sonet.net
License: Hamilton, AL held by Kate F. Fite.
Arbitron Metro Market: Hamilton, AL; *Format:* Country, Gospel
Special Programming: Farm; *Target Audience:* General.; *Adv. Rates:* 6; 6; 6; 6
James Fowler, General Manager
Geraldine Miller, General Sales Manager/Traffic Manager
Bryan Williams, Programming Director

WERH-FM
04-01-1968; 92.1 MHz FM; *Hrs Open:* 24; 3 kw; 121 ft.; N34 7 1 W87 59 29
P.O. Box 1119, Hamilton, AL 35570 US
(205) 921-3481; *Fax:* (205) 921-7187
License: Hamilton, Marion County, AL
Arbitron Metro Market: Hamilton, AL; *Format:* Classic Rock; *Adv. Rates:* Same as AM
Geraldine Miller, General Manager/Traffic Manager

Hanceville

WQHC
04-01-1986; 1170 kHz AM; *Hrs Open:* Sunrise-sunset
P.O. Box 483, Pleasant Grove, AL 35127 US
(205) 744-5127
www.queenofheavenradio.com
jack@queenofheavenradio.com
License: Hanceville, AL held by Queen of Heaven Catholic Radio Inc.
Arbitron Metro Market: Hanceville, AL; *Format:* Gospel
Jack Williams, General Manager

Hartford

WDBT
09-12-1969; 93.7 MHz FM; *Hrs Open:* 24; 100 kw; Ant 853 ft; N31 02 42 W85 57 33
285 E. Broad St., Ozark, AL 36360
(334) 774-7673; *Fax:* (334) 774-6450
License: Hartford, Geneva County, AL held by Gulf South Communications Inc.
Group Owner: Gulf South Communications Inc.; (acq 2-6-2008)
Nat'l Network: ABC; Westwood One; *Nat'l Reps:* Rgnl Reps
Population Served: 790,000; *Arbitron Metro Market:* Dothan, AL; *Target Audience:* 30 plus.; *Adv. Rates:* 40; 35; 30; 25
Robert Holladay, President

Hartselle

WTAK-FM
08-01-1992; 106.1 MHz FM; *Hrs Open:* 24; 5.4 kw; 725 ft.; N34 27 45 W86 38 36
26869 Peoples Road, Madison, AL 35756 US
(256) 353-1750; *Fax:* (256) 350-2653
www.wtak.com
info@wtak.com
License: Hartselle, Morgan County, AL held by Capstar TX LLC
Group Owner: iHeartMedia; (acq 8-30-00; grpsl)
Arbitron Metro Market: Huntsville, AL; *Format:* Classic Rock
Carmelita Palmer, Market President
Erich West, Senior Vice President of Programming
Beth Ridgeway, Digital Content Director

WYAM
10-01-1956; 890 kHz AM; *Hrs Open:* 12; 2.5 kw-D, NDD; N34 34 0 W86 54 46
1301 Central Parkway SW, Decatur, AL 35601 US
(256) 355-4567; *Fax:* (256) 351-1234
wileywg@acninc.net
License: Hartselle, AL held by Decatur Communications Properties LLC
Arbitron Metro Market: Huntsville, AL; *Format:* Spanish; *Hrs. of News Programming:* news progmg 6 hrs wkly; *No. News Employees:* 2; *Target Audience:* 18-60; General
William Wiley, President
Adam Rudell, Sales Manager

Harvest

***WAYH**
01-01-2003; 88.1 MHz FM; *Hrs Open:* 24; 3.5 kw; 669 ft.; N34 49 8 W86 44 19
9582 Madison Boulevard, Suite 8, Madison, AL 35758 US
(256) 837-9293; *Fax:* (256) 772-6731
www.wayh.wayfm.com
supportservices@wayfm.com
License: Harvest, Madison County, AL held by WAY-FM Media Group Inc.
Group Owner: WAY-FM Media Group Inc.
Arbitron Metro Market: Harvest, AL; *Format:* Christian; *Target Audience:* 18-34; youth & young adults
Lloyd Parker, COO
Bob Augsburg, President
Claire Decleene, Operations Dir
Thom Ewing, General Manager
Tonya Hayes, General Sales Mgr
Traci Hite, Promotions Manager
Linda Cashin, Administrative Service Manager

Hazel Green

WBXR
12-11-1970; 1140 kHz AM; *Hrs Open:* Sunrise-sunset; 7.5 kw-C, DAD; 15 kw-D, DAD; N34 57 11 W86 38 46
2926-D Huntsville Hwy, Fayetteville, TN 37334 US
(931) 433-7017
www.wilkinsradio.com
denise@wilkinsradio.com
License: Hazel Green, AL held by New England Communications Inc.
Group Owner: Wilkins Communications Network Inc.; (acq 9-16-97; $150,000).
Nat'l Network: Salem Radio Network
Arbitron Metro Market: Fayetteville, TN; *Format:* Christian, Talk; *Target Audience:* 35 plus.; *Adv. Rates:* 35; 35, 35, 35
Matthew Gonzalez, Station Manager

Headland

WECB
09-01-1992; 105.3 MHz FM; *Hrs Open:* 24; 11.5 kw; Ant 485 ft; N31 15 48 W85 18 24
P.O. Box 889, Dothan, AL 36302
(334) 699-0047; *Fax:* (334) 712-0374
www.b1053.com
License: Headland, Henry County, AL held by Alabama Media LLC
Group Owner: Alabama Media LLC
Arbitron Metro Market: Dothan, AL; *No. News Employees:* 7
Tim Shelton, Operations Director/Program Director
George Francis, General Manager
Tim Shelton, News Director

Heflin

***WPIL**
01-01-2003; 91.7 MHz FM; 1.3 kw; 85 ft.; N33 36 55 W85 32 41
321 Freeman Circle, Norcross, GA 30071 US
(256) 463-4226; *Fax:* (256) 463-4232
www.wpilfm.com
License: Heflin, Cleburne County, AL held by Jimmy Jarrell Communications Foundation Inc.
Arbitron Metro Market: Heflin, AL; *Format:* Country, Gospel
Jimmy Jarrell, President
Robert Jarrell, General Manager
Dale Hamilton, Programer
Jean Hemby, Accounts Executive Manager

***WKNG-FM**
05-01-2005; 89.1 MHz FM; 0.25 kw; 719 ft.; N33 33 18 W85 27 25
1 Golf Course Road, Tallapoosa, GA 30176 US
(770) 574-0891; *Fax:* (770) 574-0892
www.rejoice891.com
License: Heflin, Cleburne County, AL held by Covenant Communications Inc.
Arbitron Metro Market: Heflin, AL; *Format:* Gospel
Steven Gradick, President

Helena

WJQX
07-15-1991; 100.5 MHz FM; *Hrs Open:* 24; 69 kw; Ant 912 ft; N33 05 42 W87 15 16
244 Goodwin Crest Dr., Suite 300, Birmingham, AL 35209 US
(205) 945-4646; *Fax:* (205) 945-3999
www.jox2fm.com
License: Helena, AL held by Radio License Holding CBC, LLC
Group Owner: Cumulus Media Inc.; (acq 7-12-2005; grpsl)
Arbitron Metro Market: Tuscaloosa, AL; *Format:* Sports
Ryan Headey, Operations Dir
Reade Taylor, General Sales Mgr
Laurence Salvary, Promotions Manager

Hobson City

WHMA-FM
10-04-1984; 95.5 MHz FM; *Hrs Open:* 24; 0.53 kw; 1089 ft.; N33 37 38 W85 53 25
P.O. Box 2552, Anniston, AL 36202 US
(256) 236-1274; *Fax:* (256) 236-9414
www.whmabig95.com
texbig95@cableone.net
License: Hobson City, Calhoun County, AL held by Williams Communications Inc.
Group Owner: Williams Communications Inc.; (acq 8-2-2002; $2.88 million with WZZX(AM) Lineville).
Arbitron Metro Market: Hobson City, AL; *Format:* Country *Special Programming:* Black 6 hrs wkly; *Target Audience:* 18-54.
Tex Carter, General Manager
Tex Carter, Programming Director

WHOG
04-15-1991; 1120 kHz AM; *Hrs Open:* Sunrise-sunset; 0.5 kW; N33 36 50 W85 51 19
1330 Noble St, Suite 25, Anniston, AL 36201
(256) 236-6484; *Fax:* (256) 236-6484
hog1120@aol.com
License: Hobson City, Calhoun County, AL held by Hobson City Broadcasting Co.
Nat'l Reps: Dora-Clayton
Population Served: 75,000 *Format:* Adult Contemp, Urban Contemporary; *Target Audience:* General.
Mark Timothy, Operations Dir
Mark Hogan, General Manager
Mark Hogan, General Sales Mgr
Mark Timothy, Programming Director
Mark Timothy, Promotions Manager
Chris Hogan, Chief Engineer

Holly Pond

WRSA-FM
11-23-1965; 96.9 MHz FM; *Hrs Open:* 24; 100 kw; 1,010 ft; N34 29 19 W86 37 08
8402 Memorial Pkwy SW, Huntsville, AL 35754
(256) 885-9797; *Fax:* (256) 885-9796
www.lite969.com
License: Holly Pond, Cullman County, AL held by NCA Inc.
Nat'l Reps: Local Focus
Population Served: 500,000; *Arbitron Metro Market:* Huntsville, AL; *Hrs. of News Programming:* news progmg one hr wkly; *No. News Employees:* 1; *Target Audience:* Women 25-54
Penny Nielsen, President/CEO
Nate Adams, Sales Manager
John Malone, Programming Director
Abby Kay, Promotions Director
Don Roden, Chief Engineer
Shellie Erskine, Traffic Director

Homewood

WBPT
06-01-1959; 106.9 MHz FM; 97 kw; 1325 ft.; N33 29 4 W86 48 25
2700 Corporate Drive, Suite 115, Birmingham, AL 35242 US
(205) 916-1100; *Fax:* (205) 290-1061
http://www.birminghamseagle.com/
License: Homewood, Jefferson County, AL held by SM-WBPT LLC
Group Owner: SummitMedia LLC
Nat'l Reps: Katz Radio
Arbitron Metro Market: Birmingham, AL *TV Affiliate:* Classic hits *Special Programming:* news progmg 15 hrs wkly; *Hrs. of News Programming:* 1; *No. News Employees:* 25-54; affluent baby boom

Mike Dubose, General Manager
Program Director, Justin Ragland
Justin Ragland, Promotions Director
Traffic Manager

Hoover

WERC-FM
01-01-1993; 105.5 MHz FM; 29.5 kw
600 Beacon Parkway West, Birmingham, AL 35209 US
(205) 439-9600; *Fax:* (205) 439-8390
www.wercfm.com
License: Hoover, AL held by Capstar TX LLC
Group Owner: iHeartMedia
Arbitron Metro Market: Birmingham, AL; *Format:* News, News/Talk, 86; *Target Audience:* Adults.
Cynthia Collins, General Sales Mgr
John Mountz, Programming Director
Lacey Walker, Promotions Director
Kevin Klein, Senior Vice President of Sales

Huntsville

WAHR
07-28-1959; 99.1 MHz FM; 100 kw; 984 ft.; N34 47 53 W86 38 24
1555 The Boardwalk, Suite 1, Huntsville, AL 35816 US
(256) 536-1568
www.mystar991.com
k.daniels@radiohuntsville.com
License: Huntsville, Madison County, AL held by BCA Radio LLC.
Group Owner: Black Crow Media Group LLC; (acq 11-15-2001; grpsl).
Arbitron Metro Market: Huntsville, AL; *Format:* Adult Contemp; *Target Audience:* 25-55.
Leeann Foster, Production Director
Kevin Daniels, General Manager
Laura Orand, Director of Sales
Buzz Stephens, Programming Director
Marsha Seymour, Promotions Manager
Don Phelps, News Director
Nick Emmons, Engineering Dir
Stephanie Smith, Traffic Manager
Kim Lee, Business Manager

WBHP
05-23-1937; 1230 kHz AM; 1 kw-U, ND1; N34 43 9 W86 35 42
Mailing Address: 600 Congress Ave., Suite 1400, Austin, TX 78701 US
Second Address: 266869 Peoples Rd., Madison, AL 35758
(256) 309-2400; *Fax:* (256) 350-2653
www.wbhpam.com
License: Huntsville, AL held by Capstar TX LLC
Group Owner: iHeartMedia; (acq 8-30-00; grpsl).
Arbitron Metro Market: Madison, AL; *Format:* News, News/Talk, 86; *Target Audience:* General.
Carmelita Palmer, Market President
Stuart Langston, Programming Director
Kevin Younkin, Sales and Marketing Consultant
Beth Ridgeway, Digital Content Director

WDJL
10-01-1968; 1000 kHz AM; *Hrs Open:* Sunrise-sunset
3400 Bluespring Road, Suite A3, Huntsville, AL 35810 US
(256) 852-1223; *Fax:* (256) 852-1900
www.love1000am.com
License: Huntsville, AL held by James K. Sharp dba 5th Avenue Broadcasting.
Nat'l Network: Westwood One
Arbitron Metro Market: Huntsville, AL; *Format:* Gospel *Special Programming:* Gospel comedy 6 hrs wkly; *Target Audience:* 35-65; upscale decision makers that enjoy hits of the 40s, 50s & 60s
Dorothy Sandifer, President/CEO
Dorothy Sandifer and Antonio Acklin, Programming Director

WHIY
03-20-1958; 1600 kHz AM; 5 kw-D, DAN; 0.5 kw-N, DAN; N34 45 32 W86 38 35
P. O. Box 920, Huntsville, AL 35804 US
(256) 837-9387; *Fax:* (256) 837-9404
www.whiyam.com
hundley@103weup.com
License: Huntsville, AL held by Hundley Batts Sr. & Virginia Caples.
Arbitron Metro Market: Huntsville, AL; *Format:* Blues; *Target Audience:* 25-65.
Hundley Batts Sr., President
Hundley Batts Sr., General Manager
Steve Murry, Programming Director

*WJAB
05-09-1991; 90.9 MHz FM; *Hrs Open:* 24; 100 kw; 335 ft.; N34 47 9 W86 34 0
Mailing Address: PO Box 174, Normal, AL 35762 US
Second Address: 3409 Meridian St., Huntsville, AL 35811
(256) 372-5795; *Fax:* (256) 372-5907
www2.aamu.edu/wjab
License: Huntsville, Madison County, AL held by Board of Trustees Alabama A&M University.
Nat'l Network: NPR; PRI; *Wire Services:* AP
Arbitron Metro Market: Huntsville, AL; *Format:* Blues, Jazz
Special Programming: Black 3 hrs, oldies 8 hrs, reggae 4 hrs, Latin one; *No. News Employees:* 1
Michael Burns, Operations Dir
Elizabeth Sloan-Ragland, General Manager
Erica Fox Colman, News Director
Michael Morns, Chief Engineer
Elizabeth Sloan-Ragland, Director of Telecommunication
Rita Hayes, Traffic Manager
Lois Watkins,Production Manager
Jerome Foster, Producer

WLOR
06-01-1948; 1550 kHz AM; *Hrs Open:* 24
1555 The Boardwalk, Suite 1, Huntsville, AL 35816 US
www.981thebeat.com
License: Huntsville, AL held by BCA Radio LLC.
Group Owner: Black Crow Media Group LLC; (acq 11-15-2001; grpsl)
Nat'l Network: ABC
Arbitron Metro Market: Huntsville, AL; *Format:* Oldies; *Hrs. of News Programming:* news progmg one hr wkly; *No. News Employees:* 1; *Target Audience:* General.; *Adv. Rates:* 25; 20; 10; 10
Ed Gaines, Programming Director

*WLRH
10-13-1976; 89.3 MHz FM; *Hrs Open:* 24; 100 kw; 810 ft.; N34 37 41 W86 30 59
UAH Campus, John Wright Drive, Huntsville, AL 35899 US
(256) 895-9574; *Fax:* (256) 830-4577
www.wlrh.org
License: Huntsville, Madison County, AL held by Alabama ETV Commission.
Nat'l Network: PRI; NPR
Arbitron Metro Market: Huntsville, AL; *Format:* News; *Hrs. of News Programming:* news progmg 40 hrs wkly; *No. News Employees:* 1; *Target Audience:* General.
Brett Tannehill, General Manager
Joe Cook, Programming Director
Brian Monie, Corporate Support Manager

WRTT-FM
10-06-1960; 95.1 MHz FM; *Hrs Open:* 24; 12 kw; 909 ft.; N34 47 53 W86 38 24
1555 The Boardwalk, Suite 1, Huntsville, AL 35816 US
(256) 536-1568
www.therocket951.com
k.daniels@radiohuntsville.com
License: Huntsville, Madison County, AL held by BCA Radio LLC.
Group Owner: Black Crow Media Group LLC; (acq 11-15-2001; grpsl).
Arbitron Metro Market: Huntsville, AL; *Format:* Rock/AOR *Special Programming:* Relg; *No. News Employees:* 1; *Target Audience:* 24-54; male
Leeann Foster, Production Director
Kevin Daniels, General Manager
Laura Orand, Director of Sales
Jimbo Wood, Programming Director
Marsha Seymour, Promotions Manager
Nick Emmons, Engineering Dir
Kim Lee, Business Manager
Stephanie Smith, Traffic Director

*WJOU
12-01-1978; 90.1 MHz FM; 25 kw; 230 ft.; N34 45 28 W86 39 44
Oakwood Road, NW, Huntsville, AL 35806 US
(256) 722-9990; *Fax:* (256) 837-7918
www.wocg.org
wjou@oakwood.eduÿ
License: Huntsville, Madison County, AL held by Oakwood College.
Nat'l Network: USA
Arbitron Metro Market: Huntsville, AL *TV Affiliate:* Relg *Special Programming:* News progmg 14 hrs wkly; *No. News Employees:* 34-55; families with inte
Victoria Miller, General Manager

WTKI
11-26-1946; 1450 kHz AM; *Hrs Open:* 24; 1 kw-U, ND1; N34 43 30 W86 36 15
2305 Holmes Ave. NW, Huntsville, AL 35816 US
(256) 533-1450; *Fax:* (256) 551-9865
www.wtkiradio.com
info@wtkiradio.com
License: Huntsville, AL held by FRC of Alabama, LLC.
Group Owner: Focus Radio Communications
Arbitron Metro Market: Huntsville, AL; *Format:* Sports, Talk
Dan Baughman, General Manager

WEUP
01-01-2001; 1700 kHz AM
2609 Jordan Lane NW, Huntsville, AL 35816 US
(256) 837-9387; *Fax:* (256) 837-9404
www.weupam.com
hundley@103weup.com
License: Huntsville, AL held by Hundley Batts Sr. & Virginia Caples.
Arbitron Metro Market: Huntsville, AL; *Format:* Gospel
Hundley Batts, General Manager
Steve Murry, Programming Director

WTKI
11-26-1946; 92.9 MHz FM; *Hrs Open:* 24; 1 kw-U, ND1; N34 43 30 W86 36 15
2305 Holmes Ave. NW., Huntsville, AL 35816 US
(256) 533-1450; *Fax:* (256) 551-9865
www.wtkiradio.com
info@wtkiradio.com
License: Huntsville, AL held by FRC of Alabama, LLC.
Group Owner: Focus Radio Communications
Arbitron Metro Market: Huntsville, AL; *Format:* Sports, Talk
Dan Baughman, General Manager

Irondale

WQOH
12-05-1960; 1480 kHz AM; *Hrs Open:* 24
P.O. Box 482, Pleasant Grove, AL 35127 US
(205) 744-4456
www.queenofheavenradio.com
jack@queenofheavenradio.com
License: Irondale, AL held by Queen of Heaven Gatholic Radio Inc.
Nat'l Network: EWTN Radio
Arbitron Metro Market: Birmingham, AL; *Format:* Christian
Marc Corsini, President

Jackson

WRJX
06-01-1950; 1230 kHz AM; *Hrs Open:* 5 AM-midnight; 1 kw-U, ND1; N31 32 38 W87 52 30
Mailing Address: 311 Green St, NESte 211, Gainesville, GA 30501 US
Second Address: 4428 College Ave., Jackson, AL 36545
(251) 246-4431; *Fax:* (251) 246-1980
radiocenter@starband.com
License: Jackson, AL held by Capital Assets Inc.
Group Owner: Bennie E. Hewett Stns
Format: Black, Gospel; *No. News Employees:* 1; *Target Audience:* 25-54; business minded, baby-boomers
Wes Yoakam, General Manager
Gabriel Puello, Station Manager/Sales Director
Wendy Metzger, Programming Director

WHOD
08-01-1964; 94.5 MHz FM; *Hrs Open:* 5 AM-midnight; 30 kw; 640 ft.; N31 28 59 W87 47 27
Mailing Address: 324 Bradford Street NW, Gainesville, GA 30501 US
Second Address: 4428 College Ave., Jackson, AL 36545
(251) 246-4431; *Fax:* (251) 246-1980
License: Jackson, Clarke County, AL
Group Owner: Bennie E. Hewett Stns
Nat'l Network: ABC
Format: Adult Contemp; *Hrs. of News Programming:* news progmg 2 hrs wkly; *No. News Employees:* 1
Wes Yoakam, General Manager
Gabriel Puello, Station Manager/Sales Director
Wes Metzger, Programming Director

Jacksonville

*WLJS-FM
09-29-1975; 91.9 MHz FM; 0.61 kw; 1024 ft.; N33 50 12 W85 43 59
700 North Pelham Road, Jacksonville, AL 36265 US
(256) 782-5300; *Fax:* (256) 782-5645
programdirectorwljs@gmail.com

RADIO - U.S.

License: Jacksonville, Calhoun County, AL held by Board of Trustees-Jacksonville State University.
Nat'l Network: NPR
Format: Variety/Diverse *Special Programming:* Relg 3 hrs wkly; *Target Audience:* 18-34; college, young adult
Mike Stedham, Manager of Student Media

WCKA
01-01-1986; 810 kHz AM; *Hrs Open:* 24; 50 kw-D, DA2; 0.5 kw-N, DA2; N33 50 58 W85 45 46
Mailing Address: 3 River Street, White Springs, FL 32096 US
Second Address: 188 Broadcast Blvd., Jacksonville, AL 36265
(256) 237-0810; *Fax:* (256) 782-2489
License: Jacksonville, AL held by Alabama 810 LLC
Nat'l Network: USA; *Regional Network:* Alabama Radio Net.
Arbitron Metro Market: Calhoun, AL; *Format:* Country *Special Programming:* Gospel 2 hrs wkly; *Hrs. of News Programming:* news progmg 15 hrs wkly; *No. News Employees:* 2; *Target Audience:* 25 plus; adults *Adv. Rates:* 25; 25; 25; 15
L.E. Gradick, General Manager
Ann Johnson, Programming Director
Wesley Leadbetter, News Director

Jasper

WJLX
03-01-1957; 1240 kHz AM; *Hrs Open:* 24; 1 kw-U, ND1; N33 48 54 W87 16 19
1499 North Airport Road, Jasper, AL 35504 US
(205) 221-2222
License: Jasper, AL held by Wal Win LLC
Arbitron Metro Market: Birmingham, AL; *Format:* Gospel
Brett Elmore, General Manager

WDXB
03-28-1962; 102.5 MHz FM; 79 kw; 2,096 ft; N33 28 51 W87 24 03
600 Beacon Pkwy. W., Suite 400, Birmingham, AL 35209 US
(205) 439-9600; *Fax:* (205) 439-8390
www.1025thebull.com
License: Jasper, Walker County, AL held by Capstar TX LLC
Group Owner: iHeartMedia; (acq 8-30-00; grpsl).
Population Served: 400,000; *Arbitron Metro Market:* Birmingham, AL; *Format:* Country
Ray Quinn, Regional Market President
Cynthia Collins, General Sales Mgr
Tom Hanrahan, Programming Director
Ellen Leffel, Promotions Director
Bob Newberry, Chief Engineer
Kevin Klein, Senior Vice President of Sales

WIXI
11-02-1946; 1360 kHz AM; *Hrs Open:* 14
PO Box 19123, Birmingham, AL 35219 US
(205) 942-1776; *Fax:* (205) 384-3462
wjld@bellsouth.net
License: Jasper, AL held by Richardson Broadcasting Corporation
Arbitron Metro Market: Jasper, AL; *Format:* Christian, Gospel *Special Programming:* Gospel 6 hrs wkly; *Hrs. of News Programming:* News progmg 4 hrs wkly; *Target Audience:* General.; *Adv. Rates:* 6; 6; 6; 3
Gary Richardson, President
Willamena Richardson, General Manager/Sales Manager
Gary Richardson, Programming Director

Jemison

WHPH
05-15-1953; 97.7 MHz FM; *Hrs Open:* 24; 13 kw; 459 ft.; N32 58 55 W86 51 2
P.O. Box 787, Pelham, AL 35124 US
(205) 949-4584
www.977thepeach.com
977thepeach@gmail.com
License: Jemison, Chilton County, AL held by Great South Wireless LLC.
Arbitron Metro Market: Jemison, AL; *Format:* Oldies
Mike Self, General Manager

***WPJN**
89.3 MHz FM; 500 w; Ant 187 ft; N33 00 25 W86 44 03
908 Opelika Rd., Auburn, AL
(334) 821-0744; *Fax:* (334) 821-4031
License: Jemison, Chilton County, AL held by Chad Wilbank

Chad Wilbank, President

Langdale

***WEBT**
01-17-1986; 91.5 MHz FM; 0.38 kw; 85 ft.; N32 48 15 W85 10 43
2615 64th Blvd, Valley, AL 36854 US
(334) 756-6923; *Fax:* (334) 756-8430
License: Langdale, Chambers County, AL held by Langdale Educational Broadcasting Foundation.
Format: Gospel *Special Programming:* Southern gospel; *Target Audience:* General.
Tim Foster, Station Manager

Level Plains

WIRB
1490 kHz AM
US
(334) 894-5047; *Fax:* (334) 894-6684
www.myspace.com
License: Level Plains, AL held by Virgle Leon Strickland, individually.
Arbitron Metro Market: Level Plains, AL; *Format:* Gospel
Virgle Strickland, General Manager

Lexington

WJHX
02-20-1981; 620 kHz AM; 5 kw-D, ND1; 0.099 kw-N, ND1; N34 58 37 W87 22 10
17967 Brownsferry Road, Athens, AL 35611 US
(256) 353-5959
License: Lexington, AL held by BAR Broadcasting Inc.

Pedro Zamora, President
Moises Gomez, General Manager

Linden

WINL
04-01-1991; 98.5 MHz FM; *Hrs Open:* 24; 100 kw; 817 ft.; N32 7 34 W87 44 2
1226 Jefferson Road, Demopolis, AL 36732 US
(334) 289-9850; *Fax:* (334) 289-9811
www.bestcountryaround.com
License: Linden, Marengo County, AL held by West Alabama Communications Inc.
Group Owner: West Alabama Radio Inc.; (acq 2-12-2001; $1.28 million)
Nat'l Network: ABC; *Nat'l Reps:* Dora-Clayton
Format: Country *Special Programming:* Gospel 5 hrs, farm 10 hrs wkly; *Target Audience:* 25-54.
Amy Douglas, General Manager

Lineville

WZZX
01-01-1967; 780 kHz AM
P.O. Box 2522, Anniston, AL 36202 US
(256) 236-1274; *Fax:* (256) 236-4480
License: Lineville, AL held by Williams Communications Inc.
Group Owner: Williams Communications Inc.; (acq 7-25-2002; $2.88 million).
Arbitron Metro Market: Anniston, AL; *Format:* Country
Tex Carter, General Manager
Tex Carter, Programming Director

WZEV
90.5 MHz FM; 500 w; 31 m; N33 18 22 W85 44 42
828 20th St. SW, Lanett, AL
(706) 518-3911
License: Lineville, Clay County, AL held by B. Jordan Communications Corp.

Benjamin Ray Jordan, President

Lisman

WHSL
01-01-1997; 107.7 MHz FM; 6 kw; Ant 328 ft; N32 05 27 W88 13 57
909 W. Pushmataha St., Butler, AL 39604
(205) 459-3222; *Fax:* (205) 459-4140
License: Lisman, Choctaw County, AL held by Leap of Faith, LLC

Joshua Coyle, General Manager

Littleville

WLAY-FM
09-12-1986; 103.5 MHz FM; *Hrs Open:* 24; 3.3 kw; 386 ft.; N34 40 27 W87 42 48
509 N. Main Street, Tuscumbia, AL 35674 US
(256) 383-2525
License: Littleville, Colbert County, AL held by Urban Radio Licenses LLC.
Group Owner: Urban Radio Licenses LLC; (acq 5-13-2005; grpsl)
Arbitron Metro Market: Florence-Muscle Shoals, AL; *Format:* Oldies; *No. News Employees:* 1; *Target Audience:* 18-49.
Kevin Wagner, CEO
Derrick Robinson, Director of Sales
Wes Adams, Programming Director
Donna Johnson, Business Manager
Rob Green, Chief Engineer

Luverne

WHLW
01-01-1997; 104.3 MHz FM; 13.5 kw; 1831 ft.; N31 58 28 W86 9 44
203 Gunn Road, Montgomery, AL 36117 US
(334) 274-6464; *Fax:* (334) 274-6465
www.1043hallelujahfm.com
License: Luverne, Crenshaw County, AL held by Capstar TX LLC
Group Owner: iHeartMedia; (acq 8-30-2000; grpsl).
Arbitron Metro Market: Montgomery, AL; *Format:* Gospel; *Target Audience:* 18-49.
Becky Sweeney, Market President
John Long, Programming Director
Kimberly Brown, Promotions Director/Online Content Director
Kimberly Parker, Business Manager

Madison

WUMP
03-29-1983; 730 kHz AM; *Hrs Open:* 24; 1 kw-D, ND1; 0.129 kw-N, ND1; N34 41 46 W86 44 19
1717 Highway 72 East, Athens, AL 35611 US
(256) 830-8300; *Fax:* (256) 232-6842
www.730ump.com
jason.marks@cumulus.comÿ
License: Madison, AL held by Cumulus Licensing LLC.
Group Owner: Cumulus Media Inc.; (acq 7-21-2003; grpsl).
Nat'l Network: ESPN Radio; *Nat'l Reps:* Katz Radio
Arbitron Metro Market: Athens, AL; *Format:* Sports *Special Programming:* Univ. of Alabama Sports; *Target Audience:* 18-54; males
Matt Tobin, General Manager
Dale Jackson, Programming Director
Aaron Hurd, Promotions Manager
Audrey Raines, News Director

Marion

WJUS
12-08-1951; 1310 kHz AM
P.O. Box 930, Marion, AL 36756 US
(334) 683-2043; *Fax:* (334) 872-2329
www.partybluesandoldies.com
License: Marion, AL held by Marion Radio Inc.
Format: Urban Contemporary
Rev. Glenn King, General Manager

WNPT-FM
12-19-1990; 102.9 MHz FM; *Hrs Open:* 24; 24 kw; 663 ft.; N32 49 46 W87 25 46
645 Church Street, Suite 400, Norfolk, VA 23510 US
(205) 758-5523; *Fax:* (205) 752-9696
wtbc@dbtech.net
License: Marion, Perry County, AL held by John Sisty Enterprises Inc.
Arbitron Metro Market: Marion, AL; *Format:* Country
John Sisty, President
Nancy Wilson, General Sales Mgr
Jay Bronson, Programming Director

Meridianville

WQRV
05-02-1962; 100.3 MHz FM; *Hrs Open:* 24; 8.5 kw; 981 ft.; N34 47 36 W86 37 51
26869 Peoples Road, Madison, AL 35756 US
(256) 309-2400; *Fax:* (256) 389-1912
www.1003theriver.com
License: Meridianville, Colbert County, AL held by CC Licenses LLC.
Group Owner: iHeartMedia; (acq 12-19-2000; grpsl)
Arbitron Metro Market: Meridianville, AL; *Format:* Oldies; *Hrs. of News Programming:* news progmg 60 hrs wkly; *No. News Employees:* 2; *Target Audience:* 18-34.
Carmelita Palmer, Market President
Erich West, Programming Director
Stuart Langston, Production
Beth Ridgeway, Digital Content Director

Midfield

WBHJ
01-01-1952; 95.7 MHz FM; *Hrs Open:* 24; 12 kw; 1004 ft.; N33 27 37 W86 51 7
2700 Corporate Drive, Suite 115, Birmingham, Al 35242 US
(205) 322-2987; *Fax:* (205) 322-2390
www.957jamz.com
maryk@957jamz.com
License: Midfield, Jefferson County, AL held by SM-WBHJ LLC
Group Owner: SummitMedia LLC
Nat'l Network: Westwood One; *Nat'l Reps:* Christal
Arbitron Metro Market: Birmingham, AL; *Format:* Blues; *Hrs. of News Programming:* news progmg one hr wkly; *No. News Employees:* 1; *Target Audience:* 18-34; upscale baby boomers; *Adv. Rates:* 250; 150; 200; 125
David DuBose, General Manager/Vice President
Paul Bankston, National Sales Manager
Mary Kay Schmitt, Programming Director
Deanna Reed, Promotions Manager
Linda McNeal, Local Sales Manager
Lil Home, Music Director

Millbrook

WWMG
08-01-1993; 97.1 MHz FM; *Hrs Open:* 24; 5.4 kw; 702 ft.; N32 20 6 W86 17 16
203 Gunn Road, Montgomery, AL 36117 US
(334) 274-6464; *Fax:* (334) 274-6467
www.mymagic97.com
License: Millbrook, Elmore County, AL held by Capstar TX LLC
Group Owner: iHeartMedia; (acq 8-30-2000; grpsl).
Nat'l Network: American Urban; Westwood One
Arbitron Metro Market: Montgomery, AL; *Format:* Urban Contemporary; *Target Audience:* 25-54.
Becky Sweeney, Market President
Chris Coleman, Senior Vice President of Programming
Kimberly Brown, Promotions/Online Content Director
Kimberly Parker, Business Manager

Mobile

WTKD
11-01-1948; 1480 kHz AM; *Hrs Open:* 24; 5 kw-D, DAN; 4.4 kw-N, DAN; N30 43 11 W88 4 16
Mailing Address: P.O. Box 2148, Moblie, AL 36652 US
Second Address: 1551 Springhill Ave., Mobile, AL 36604
(434) 534-6100; *Fax:* (434) 534-6101
www.espninva.com
wblt@inbox.com
License: Mobile, AL held by WABB-FM Inc.
Nat'l Reps: Christal
Arbitron Metro Market: Eugene-Springfield OR; *Format:* Sports
Gary Burns, President
Devin Taylor, Operations Dir

WABD
02-05-1973; 97.5 MHz FM; *Hrs Open:* 24; 100 kw; Ant 1,551 ft; N30 41 20 W87 49 49
2800 Dauphin St., Suite 104, Mobile, AL 36606 US
(251) 652-2073
www.975wabd.com
License: Mobile, AL held by Cumulus Licensing LLC
Group Owner: Cumulus Media Inc.
Nat'l Reps: Christal
Population Served: 1,092,100; *Arbitron Metro Market:* Mobile, AL; *Format:* Contemporary Hits/Top 40
Laura English, Local Sales Mgr
Hayden Green, Interim Program Director
Amberly Harris, Promotions Manager
Angel Taylor Brown, VP/Market Mgr

WBHY
12-09-1943; 840 kHz AM; 10 kw-D, NDD; N30 45 50 W88 6 36
Mailing Address: P.O. Box 1328, Mobile, AL 36633 US
Second Address: 6530 Spanish Fort Blvd., Suite B, Spanish Fort, AL 36527
(251) 473-8488; *Fax:* (251) 300-3149
www.goforth.org
License: Mobile, Mobile County, AL held by Goforth Media Inc.
Group Owner: Goforth Media Inc.; (Acq 4-11-86)
Regional Network: Salem Radio Network
Arbitron Metro Market: Mobile, AL; *Format:* Christian; *Target Audience:* 34-64; Christian
Wilbur Goforth, President/GM
Robert Barber, Station Manager/VP
Brad Arnold, Chief Engineer
Kenny Fowler, Music Director
Charlotte Bouzigard, Marketing & Sales

*WBHY-FM
03-20-1992; 88.5 MHz FM; 33 kw; 624 ft; N30 40 55 W87 49 41
Mailing Address: P.O. Box 1328, Mobile, AL 36633
Second Address: 6530 Spanish Fort Blvd., Suite B, Spanish Fort, AL 36527
(251) 473-8488; *Fax:* (251) 300-3149
www.goforth.org
power88.5@goforth.org
License: Mobile, Mobile County, AL held by Goforth Media Inc.
Group Owner: Goforth Media Inc.; (acq 6-27-90)
Arbitron Metro Market: Mobile, AL; *Format:* Christian; *Hrs. of News Programming:* News progmg 7 hrs wkly; *Target Audience:* 18-34; Religious
Wilbur Goforth, President/GM
Robert Barber, Station Manager/VP
Brad Arnold, Chief Engineer
Kenny Fowler, Music Director
Charlotte Bouzigard, Marketing & Sales

WBLX-FM
04-01-1976; 92.9 MHz FM; 98 kw; 1708 ft.; N30 36 45 W87 38 43
One Independence Plaza, 280 Highway 35, Red Bank, NJ 07701 US
(251)471-9393; *Fax:* (251)652-2007
www.thebigstation93blx.com
chuck.sullivan@cumulus.com
License: Mobile, Mobile County, AL
Group Owner: Cumulus Media Inc.
Nat'l Network: ABC; *Nat'l Reps:* Katz Radio
Arbitron Metro Market: Mobile, AL; *Format:* Urban Contemporary; *Target Audience:* 12 plus; primarily Black women, 18-34
Angel Taylor-Brown, VP/Market Manager
Angela Reynolds, General Sales Mgr
Jay Nyce, Programming Director
Amberly Harris, Promotions Manager
Angela Adams, Traffic Manager

WGOK
11-21-1958; 900 kHz AM
1 Office Park, Suite 215, Mobile, AL 36609 US
(251) 652-2000; *Fax:* (251) 652-2001
www.gospel900.com
License: Mobile, AL held by Cumulus Licensing Corp.
Group Owner: Cumulus Media Inc.; (acq 10-18-99; $6 million with WYOK(FM) Atmore)
Nat'l Reps: Roslin
Arbitron Metro Market: Mobile, AL; *Format:* Gospel; *Target Audience:* 18-54; Black adults
Angela Taylor-Brown, VP/Market Manager
Amberly Harris, Promotions Director
Angela Reynolds, Director of Sales
Felicia Albritton, Programming Director
Angela Adams, Traffic Manager

*WHIL-FM
09-05-1979; 91.3 MHz FM; *Hrs Open:* 24; 100 kw; 1066 ft.; N30 41 20 W87 49 49
Mailing Address: PO Box 870370, Tuscaloosa, AL 35487 US
Second Address: AL
(205) 348-6644
whil@whil.org
License: Mobile, Mobile County, AL held by Spring Hill College.
Nat'l Network: PRI; NPR
Arbitron Metro Market: Mobile, AL; *Format:* Classical; *Hrs. of News Programming:* News progmg 40 hrs wkly; *No. News Employees:* 2; *Target Audience:* 35 plus.
Elizabeth Brock, Executive Director
Brian Poellnitz, Operations Manager
Kathy Henslee, Development Director
Barbara Charnetski, Underwriting Manager
Pat Duggins, News Director

WKSJ-FM
04-12-1971; 94.9 MHz FM; 98 kw; 1708 ft.; N30 36 45 W87 38 43
555 Broadcast Drive, Mobile, AL 36606 US
(251) 450-0100; *Fax:* (251) 479-3418
www.95ksj.com
License: Mobile, Mobile County, AL held by CC Licenses LLC.
Group Owner: iHeartMedia; (acq 11-21-97; grpsl)
Regional Reps: David Coppock
Arbitron Metro Market: Mobile, AL; *Format:* Country; *Hrs. of News Programming:* news progmg 25 hrs wkly; *No. News Employees:* 2; *Target Audience:* 25-54; mid level to high class country music listeners; *Adv. Rates:* 115; 105; 110; 60
Ronnie Bloodworth, General Sales Mgr
Bill Black, Programming Director
Brett Mouron, Digital Content Director

WNGL
02-07-1930; 1410 kHz AM; *Hrs Open:* 24; 5 kw-U, DA-N; N30 40 52 W88 00 02
399 S. Section Street, Fairhope, AL 36532
(251) 626-1090; *Fax:* (251) 626-1099
License: Mobile, Mobile County, AL held by WLVV Inc.
Group Owner: Archangel Comminications Inc.; (acq 4-14-99; $263,750)
Nat'l Network: American Urban; *Nat'l Reps:* Katz Radio
Arbitron Metro Market: Mobile, AL; *Target Audience:* 18-44; Black
John K. Fahn, General Manager

WMOB
01-25-1961; 1360 kHz AM; *Hrs Open:* 24; 5 kw-D, DA2; 0.212 kw-N, DA2; N30 41 26 W88 1 33
Mailing Address: 316 East Taylor Road, Deland, FL 32724 US
Second Address: 200 Addsco Rd. Causeway, Mobile, AL 36601
(716) 748-0815
www.buddytuckerassociation.org
License: Mobile, AL held by Buddy Tucker Association Inc.
Group Owner: Buddy Tucker Association Inc.; (acq 4-84; $395,000;
Arbitron Metro Market: Mobile, AL; *Format:* Talk, Religious
Theodore Tucker, President
LeVaughn Tucker, Operations Dir
Buddy Tucker, General Manager
Don Tucker, Operations Manager

WMXC
10-16-1947; 99.9 MHz FM; 94 kw; 1755 ft.; N30 41 20 W87 49 49
555 Broadcast Drive, Floor 3, Mobile, AL 36606 US
(251) 450-0100; *Fax:* (251) 479-3418
www.litemix.com
License: Mobile, Mobile County, AL held by CC Licenses LLC
Group Owner: iHeartMedia
Arbitron Metro Market: Mobile, AL; *Format:* Light Rock; *Target Audience:* 25-54.
Ronnie Bloodworth, General Sales Mgr
Mason LaFayette, Programming Director
Brett Mouron, Digital Content Director

WNTM
01-01-1946; 710 kHz AM
555 Broadcast Drive, Mobile, AL 36606 US
(251) 450-0100; *Fax:* (251) 479-3418
www.newsradio710.com
License: Mobile, AL held by CC Licenses LLC.
Group Owner: iHeartMedia; (acq 11-21-97; grpsl)
Nat'l Network: CBS
Arbitron Metro Market: Mobile, AL; *Format:* News, News/Talk, 84, Talk; *Target Audience:* 25 plus.
Steve Powers, Regional Programming Manager
Ronnie Bloodworth, General Sales Mgr
Dan Mason, Programming Director
Brett Mouron, Digital Content Director

WRKH
12-05-1964; 96.1 MHz FM; *Hrs Open:* 24; 73 kw; 1755 ft.; N30 41 20 W87 49 49
555 Broadcast Drive, Mobile, AL 36606 US
(251) 450-0100; *Fax:* (251) 479-3418
www.961therocket.com
License: Mobile, Mobile County, AL held by CC Licenses LLC.
Group Owner: iHeartMedia; (acq 11-21-97; grpsl)
Nat'l Reps: D & R Radio
Arbitron Metro Market: Mobile, AL; *Format:* Classic Rock; *Hrs. of News Programming:* news progmg 2 hrs wkly; *No. News Employees:* 2; *Target Audience:* 25-49; front edge baby boomers; *Adv. Rates:* 100; 85; 90; 45
Ronnie Bloodworth, General Sales Mgr
Brett Ballard, Programming Director
Brett Mouron, Digital Content Director

*WLPR-AM
960 MHz AM; 6 kw-D, ND2; 0.032 kw-N, ND2; N30 45 50 W88 06 36
Mailing Address: P.O. Box 1328, Mobile, AL 36633
Second Address: 6530 Spanish Fort Blvd., Suite B, Spanish Fort, AL 36527
(251) 473-8488; *Fax:* (251) 300-3149
www.goforth.org
License: Mobile, Mobile County, AL held by Goforth Media Inc.
Group Owner: Goforth Media Inc.; (acq 7-7-1994)
Regional Network: Salem Radio Network
Arbitron Metro Market: Mobile, AL; *Format:* Gospel
Wilbur Goforth, President/GM
Robert Barber, Station Manager/VP
Brad Arnold, Chief Engineer

Kenny Fowler, Music Director
Charlotte Bouzigard, Marketing & Sales

Monroeville

WMFC
12-01-1965; 99.3 MHz FM; *Hrs Open:* 5 AM-midnight; 30 kw; 308 ft.; N31 30 51 W87 17 55
P.O. Box 645, Monroeville, AL 36461 US
(251) 575-3281; *Fax:* (251) 575-3280
License: Monroeville, Monroe County, AL held by Monroe Broadcasting Co. Inc.
Nat'l Network: Jones Radio Networks; *Regional Network:* Alabama Radio Net.
Arbitron Metro Market: Monroeville, AL; *Format:* Oldies; *Target Audience:* General.
David Stewart, President/GM
Kevin Peterson, Programming Director
Gerald Wilson, Chief Engineer

Montgomery

WGMP
01-16-1939; 1170 kHz AM; *Hrs Open:* 24; 10 kw-D, 1 kw-N, DA-2; N32 27 16 W86 17 21
4101 A Wall Street, Montgomery, AL 36121
(334) 244-0961; *Fax:* (334) 279-9563
www.1049thegump.com
License: Montgomery, Montgomery County, AL held by Bluewater Broadcasting Co. LLC
Nat'l Network: CBS
Population Served: 250,000; *Arbitron Metro Market:* Montgomery, AL *Special Programming:* Farm 5 hrs wkly; *No. News Employees:* 1; *Target Audience:* 25 plus.
Terry Barber, General Manager/Vice President
Rick Peters, Programming Director

WBAM-FM
01-01-1961; 98.9 MHz FM; *Hrs Open:* 24; 100 kw; 981 ft.; N31 58 28 W86 11 31
4740 Radio Road, Montgomery, AL 36116 US
(419) 423-3285
www.wtkc897.com
wtkc89.7@sbcglobal.net
License: Montgomery, Montgomery County, AL held by Bluewater Broadcasting Co. LLC
Nat'l Reps: Christal
Arbitron Metro Market: Findlay OH; *Format:* Christian, Talk
Juan Salinas, General Manager
Richard Lugo, Programming Director

WLWI
04-30-1930; 1440 kHz AM; 5 kw-D, DAN; 1 kw-N, DAN; N32 18 24 W86 16 35
One Office Park Circle, Suite 300, Birmingham, AL 35223 US
(334) 240-9274; *Fax:* (334) 240-9211
www.cumulus.com
whhv@whhvradio.com
License: Montgomery, AL held by Cumulus Licensing Corp.
Group Owner: Cumulus Media Inc.
Nat'l Network: CNN Radio
Arbitron Metro Market: Montgomery, AL; *Format:* News, News/Talk, 86; *No. News Employees:* 1; *Target Audience:* 18 plus.
Kevin Waltman, Vice President
Matt Ward, General Sales Mgr
Bill Dollar, Programming Director
Bill Hardin, Promotions Manager

WHHY-FM
01-09-1962; 101.9 MHz FM; 100 kw; 1096 ft.; N32 24 13 W86 11 47
One Office Park Circle, Suite 300, Birmingham, AL 35223 US
(334) 240-9274; *Fax:* (334) 240-9219
www.y102montgomery.com
License: Montgomery, Montgomery County, AL held by Cumulus Licensing Corp.
Group Owner: Cumulus Media Inc.; (acq 3-12-01; grpsl)
Nat'l Reps: McGavren Guild
Arbitron Metro Market: Montgomery, AL; *Format:* Contemporary Hits/Top 40, Variety/Diverse; *Hrs. of News Programming:* News progmg one hr wkly; *Target Audience:* 18-40.
Kevin Waltman, Vice President/Market Manager
Matt Ward, General Sales Mgr
Bill Hardin, Promotions Manager
Herb Connellan, Chief Engineer

*WLBF
04-04-1984; 89.1 MHz FM; *Hrs Open:* 24; 100 kw; 538 ft.; N32 24 13 W86 11 50
Mailing Address: P.O. Box 210789, Montgomery, AL 36121 US
Second Address: 381 Mendel Parkway, Montgomery, AL 36117
(334) 271-8900; *Fax:* (334) 260-8962
www.faithradio.org
mail@faithradio.org
License: Montgomery, Montgomery County, AL held by Faith Broadcasting Inc.
Nat'l Network: Moody; USA
Arbitron Metro Market: Montgomery, AL; *Format:* Adult Contemp, Religious; *Hrs. of News Programming:* News progmg 14 hrs wkly; *Target Audience:* General.
Russell Dean, General Manager
Gary Hundley, General Sales Mgr
Donna Spears, News Director

WLWI-FM
07-15-1969; 92.3 MHz FM; 100 kw; 1096 ft.; N32 24 13 W86 11 47
111 East Kilborn Avenue, Suite 2700, Milwaukee, WI 53202 US
(334) 240-9274; *Fax:* (334) 240-9219
www.wlwi.com
bill.dollar@cumulus.com
License: Montgomery, Montgomery County, AL held by Cumulus Licensing Corp.
Group Owner: Cumulus Media Inc.
Nat'l Network: CNN Radio
Arbitron Metro Market: Montgomery, AL; *Format:* Country *Special Programming:* Gospel 4 hrs wkly; *No. News Employees:* 1; *Target Audience:* 25-54.
Matt Ward, General Manager
Bill Dollar, Programming Director
Bill Hardin, Promotions Manager
Herb Connellan, Chief Engineer

WMGY
06-01-1946; 800 kHz AM; *Hrs Open:* 6 AM-midnight; 1 kw-D, ND2; 0.143 kw-N, ND2; N32 24 48 W86 17 25
2305 Upper Wetumpka Rd, Montgomery, AL 36107 US
(334) 834-3710; *Fax:* (334) 834-3711
www.wmgyradio.com
License: Montgomery, AL held by WMGY Radio Inc.
Group Owner: GHB Radio Group; (acq 7-75)
Nat'l Network: USA
Arbitron Metro Market: Montgomery, AL; *Format:* Gospel *Special Programming:* Black 15 hrs, sports 6 hrs wkly; *Hrs. of News Programming:* News progmg 7 hrs wkly; *Target Audience:* 35 plus.; *Adv. Rates:* 6; 6; 6;5
Dane Harris, General Manager

WMSP
01-01-1953; 740 kHz AM
111 East Kilborn Avenue, Suite 2700, Milwaukee, WI 53202 US
(334) 240-9274; *Fax:* (334) 240-9219
www.sportsradio740.com
License: Montgomery, AL held by Cumulus Licensing Corp.
Group Owner: Cumulus Media Inc.; (acq 12-12-98; grpsl)
Nat'l Network: ESPN Radio
Arbitron Metro Market: Montgomery, AL; *Format:* Sports; *Target Audience:* Adults 18 plus.
Matt Ward, General Manager
Bob Wooddy, Programming Director
Herb Connellan, Chief Engineer
Bill Hardin, Promotions Director

WMXS
07-09-1961; 103.3 MHz FM; 100 kw; 1096 ft.; N32 24 13 W86 11 47
1 Commerce St., Montgomery, AL 36104 US
(334) 240-9274; *Fax:* (334) 240-9219
www.mix103.com
jamie.thompson@cumulus.com
License: Montgomery, AL held by Cumulus Licensing LLC
Group Owner: Cumulus Media Inc.
Nat'l Network: CNN Radio
Arbitron Metro Market: Montgomery, AL; *Format:* Adult Contemp
Jamie Thompson, Programming Director

WNZZ
05-08-1953; 950 kHz AM; 1 kw-U, DA-N; N32 26 23 W86 15 49
One Commerce St., Suite 300, Montgomery, AL 53202
(334) 240-9274; *Fax:* (334) 240-9219
www.cumulus.com
License: Montgomery, Montgomery County, AL held by Volt Radio LLC
Group Owner: Cumulus Media Inc.; (acq 12-12-98; grpsl)
Population Served: 133,386; *Arbitron Metro Market:* Montgomery, AL; *No. News Employees:* 1
Bill Jones, Operations Dir
Bernie Barker, General Manager
Bob Wooddy, Programming Director
Herb Connellan, Chief Engineer
Bill Hardin, Promotions Director

WQKS-FM
12-01-1990; 96.1 MHz FM; *Hrs Open:* 24; 0.9 kw; 820 ft.; N32 22 3 W86 15 42
P.O. Box 210723, Montgomery, AL 36121 US
(334) 244-0961; *Fax:* (334) 279-9563
License: Montgomery, Montgomery County, AL held by Bluewater Broadcasting Co. LLC
Nat'l Network: ABC
Arbitron Metro Market: Montgomery, AL; *Format:* Oldies; *Hrs. of News Programming:* News progmg one hr wkly; *Target Audience:* 25-54.
Rick Peters, President/Programming Director
Terry Barber, General Manager
Susan Ashworth, Promotions Director
Traffic Director, News Director
Tom Jones, Chief Engineer

*WVAS
06-15-1984; 90.7 MHz FM; *Hrs Open:* 24 (M-F); 24 (S, Su); 80 kw; 348 ft.; N32 21 58 W86 17 40
P.O. Box 271, Montgomery, AL 36101 US
(334) 229-4708; *Fax:* (334) 269-4995
www.wvasfm.org
License: Montgomery, Montgomery County, AL held by Alabama State University.
Nat'l Network: NPR; *Wire Services:* AP
Arbitron Metro Market: Montgomery, AL; *Format:* Jazz *Special Programming:* Gospel 5 hrs, Blues 9 hrs, news/talk 7 hrs wkly; *Hrs. of News Programming:* news progmg 5 hrs wkly; *No. News Employees:* 5 *TargetAudience:* General; African-American community
John Knight Jr., General Manager
Candy Capel, Station Manager
Mel Marshall, Programming Director
Shedd Johnson, News Director
Jay Holcey, Music Director
Temeki Tolbert, Program Assistant
Marcus Hyles, Senior News Correspondent

WXVI
05-01-1947; 1600 kHz AM; *Hrs Open:* 24; 5 kw-D, DA2; 1 kw-N, DA2; N32 23 40 W86 17 21
207 Montgomery Street, Suite 1025, Montgomery, AL 36104 US
(334) 263-4141; *Fax:* (334) 263-9191
License: Montgomery, AL held by New Life Ministries Inc.
Nat'l Network: American Urban; *Nat'l Reps:* Roslin
Arbitron Metro Market: Montgomery, AL; *Format:* Christian; *Target Audience:* 35 plus; urban; *Adv. Rates:* 25; 17; 25; 12
Terry Ellison, CEO
Glenda Perkins, Programming Director
Gwen Pierce, Traffic Manager

Montgomery-Troy

*WTSU
03-01-1977; 89.9 MHz FM; *Hrs Open:* 24; 100 kw; 755 ft.; N32 3 40 W86 1 19 *Rebroadcasts:* Rebroadcasts WTJB(FM) Columbus 100%
University Ave, Tv Dept, Troy, AL 36082 US
(800) 800-6616; *Fax:* (334) 670-3934
publicradio@troy.edu
License: Montgomery-Troy, Montgomery County, AL held by Troy State University.
Nat'l Network: NPR; PRI
Arbitron Metro Market: Montgomery, AL; *Format:* Classical, News *Special Programming:* Children one hr wkly; *Hrs. of News Programming:* News progmg 25 hrs wkly; *Target Audience:* General.
Kyle Gassiott, Operations Dir
Buddy Johnson, General Manager
Fred Azbell, Programming Director
John Brunson, Chief Engineer
Robert Barner, Production Coordinator
Wade Giddens, Broadcast Engineer
Ann Hart, Program Assistant
Joshua Yohn, Digital Media Web Manager

Moody

WURL
10-01-1984; 760 kHz AM; 1 kw-D, NDD; N33 35 13 W86 28 18
2999 Radio Park, Moody, AL 35004 US
(205) 699-9875; *Fax:* (205) 640-4379
www.wurlradio.com
wurlradio@aol.com
License: Moody, AL held by Bill Davison Evangelistic Assn.
Nat'l Network: USA
Arbitron Metro Market: Moody, AL; *Format:* Gospel; *Target Audience:* General.
William Davison Sr., President

Moulton

WEUV
12-11-1963; 1190 kHz AM; 2.5 kw-D, NDD; N34 28 55 W87 18 4
P.O. Box 920, Huntsville, AL 35804 US
(256) 974-0681
License: Moulton, AL held by Hundley Batts Sr. and Virginia Caples
Format: Black, Gospel; *Target Audience:* General.
Hundley Batts, General Manager
Steve Murry, Programming Director

WEUP-FM
09-01-1991; 103.1 MHz FM; *Hrs Open:* 20; 11.5 kw; 492 ft.; N34 27 8 W87 6 20
P.O. Box 920, Huntsville, AL 35804 US
(256) 837-9387; *Fax:* (256) 837-9404
103weup.com
License: Moulton, Lawrence County, AL held by Hundley Batts Sr. and Virginia Caples
Nat'l Network: USA; *Nat'l Reps:* Rgnl Reps; *Wire Services:* NOAA Weather
Arbitron Metro Market: Moulton, AL; *Format:* Adult Contemp
Special Programming: Relg one hr wkly; *No. News Employees:* 1; *Target Audience:* 21-55.
Hundley Batts, General Manager
Big Ant, Programming Director

Moundville

WKUA
88.5 MHz FM; 5500 w; 272 ft; N33 04 00 W87 42 01
1900 Crestwood Boulevard, Suite 11, Birmingham, AL 35210
License: Moundville, AL
Group Owner: TBTA Ministries

Kenneth Layton, General Manager

Muscle Shoals

WLAY
01-15-1933; 1450 kHz AM
509 North Main Street, Tuscumbia, AL 35764 US
(256) 383-2525; *Fax:* (256) 389-1912
www.wlay1035.com
donnajohnson@clearchannel.com
License: Muscle Shoals, AL held by Urban Radio Licenses LLC.
Group Owner: Urban Radio Licenses LLC; (acq 5-13-2005; grpsl).
Format: Sports; *Target Audience:* 18-54.
Kevin Wagner, CEO
Derrick Robinson, Director of Sales
Donna Johnson, Business Manager
Wed Adams, Programming Director

WVNA-FM
10-28-1964; 105.5 MHz FM; 4.4 kw; 387 ft.; N34 40 27 W87 42 48
509 North Main Street, Tuscumbia, AL 35674 US
(256) 383-2525; *Fax:* (256) 389- 1912
www.wlay1035.com
License: Muscle Shoals, Sheffield County, AL
Group Owner: Urban Radio Licenses LLC
Format: Classic Rock
Kevin Wagner, CEO
Derrick Robinson, Sales Manager
T.C. Kincaid, Programming Director
Donna Johnson, Business Manager

***WQPR**
11-01-1987; 88.7 MHz FM; *Hrs Open:* 24; 20 kw; 429 ft.; N34 34 41 W87 47 2 *Rebroadcasts:* Rebroadcasts WUAL-FM Tuscaloosa 95%
Box 870370, #17 Bryce La, Tuscaloosa, AL 35487 US
(205) 348-6644; *Fax:* (205) 348-6648
www.apr.org
License: Muscle Shoals, Sheffield County, AL held by Board of Trustees University of Alabama.
Nat'l Network: PRI; NPR
Format: Jazz, News *Special Programming:* Bluegrass, blues, folk 5 hrs, new age 19 hrs wkly; *Hrs. of News Programming:* news progmg 5 hrs wkly; *No. News Employees:* 1
Brian Poellnitz, Operations Manager
Elizabeth Brock, General Manager
Kathy Henslee, Development Director
David Duff, Music Director

New Hope

WHVK
01-01-2007; 103.5 MHz FM; 0.29 kw; 1473 ft.; N34 38 11 W86 30 42
PO Box 2098, Omaha, NE 68103-2098 US
(256) 489-9498; *Fax:* (256) 489-5035
License: New Hope, Madison County, AL held by Educational Media Foundation
Arbitron Metro Market: New Hope, AL; *Format:* Urban Contemporary
Mike Novak, President/CEO

New Market

WWFF-FM
07-01-1962; 93.3 MHz FM; *Hrs Open:* 24; 14.5 kw; 914 ft.; N34 47 37 W86 37 51
1717 Highway 72 East, Athens, AL 35611 US
(256) 830-8300; *Fax:* (256) 232-6842
www.wolf933.com
License: New Market, Madison County, AL held by Cumulus Licensing LLC.
Group Owner: Cumulus Media Inc.; (acq 7-21-2003; grpsl)
Nat'l Reps: Katz Radio
Arbitron Metro Market: Huntsville, AL; *Format:* Country; *No. News Employees:* 3; *Target Audience:* Adult; 25-54
John Walker, General Manager/Vice President
Matt Tobin, General Sales Mgr
Steve Smith, Programming Director
Tara Harrison, Promotions Manager
Chuck Miller, Chief Engineer

Northport

WTUG-FM
03-01-1979; 92.9 MHz FM; *Hrs Open:* 24; 100 kw; Ant 980 ft; N33 03 15 W87 32 57
142 Skyland Blvd., Tuscaloosa, AL 35405
(205) 345-7200; *Fax:* (205) 349-1715
www.wtug.com
License: Northport, Tuscaloosa County, AL
Group Owner: Townsquare Media
Population Served: 91,605; *Arbitron Metro Market:* Tuscaloosa, AL; *Target Audience:* 25-54.
Greg Thomas, Operations Dir
Todd Livingston, General Manager
Tammy Boyd, Sales Director
Charles Anthony, Programming Director
Meg Summers, Promotions Manager
Jade Nicole, Community Affairs Director

Oneonta

WCRL
07-29-1952; 1570 kHz AM; 2.5 kw-D, ND2; 0.064 kw-N, ND2; N33 57 16 W86 28 20
908 2nd Avenue E., Oneonta, AL 35121 US
(205) 274-9530; *Fax:* (205) 625-5433
www.wcrlradio.com
License: Oneonta, AL held by Our Town Radio Inc.
Nat'l Network: Jones Radio Networks
Arbitron Metro Market: Oneonta, AL; *Format:* Spanish; *Adv. Rates:* 8; 7; 8; 6
Mark S. Sims, President

WZZN
07-12-1968; 97.7 MHz FM; 3.2 kw; Ant 367 ft; N33 56 48 W86 29 06
108 Woodson Street, Hunstville, AL 35801
License: Oneonta, Blount County, AL held by Great South Wireless, LLC
Population Served: 200,000; *Arbitron Metro Market:* Birmingham, AL *Special Programming:* Atlanta Braves baseball; *Adv. Rates:* $8; $7; $8; $6
Joan Reynolds, CEO
Mike Self, Station Manager

Opelika

WANI
06-03-1940; 1400 kHz AM; *Hrs Open:* 24; 1 kw-U; N32 38 13 W85 24 23
Mailing Address: Box 950, Auburn, AL 36831
Second Address: 197 E. University Dr., Auburn, AL 36830
(334) 826-2929; *Fax:* (334) 826-9151
www.wani1400.com
aburcham@aunetwork.com
License: Opelika, Lee County, AL held by Auburn Network Inc.
Nat'l Network: ABC; Fox News Radio; Business Talk Radio; Radio America; Talk Radio Network; *Wire Services:* AP
Population Served: 120,000; *No. News Employees:* 1
Mike Hubbard, President/CEO
Andy Burcham, General Manager
Ann Bergman, General Sales Mgr
Julie Burns, News Director
Rich Perkins, Traffic Manager

WMXA
07-01-1991; 96.7 MHz FM; *Hrs Open:* 24; 3.5 kw; 430 ft.; N32 33 54 W85 22 13
915 Veterans Parkway, Opelika, AL 36801 US
(334) 745-4656; *Fax:* (334) 749-1520
www.mix967online.com
mix97online@gmail.com
License: Opelika, Lee County, AL held by AMFM Radio Licenses LLC
Group Owner: iHeartMedia
Arbitron Metro Market: Opelika, AL; *Format:* Adult Contemp; *Hrs. of News Programming:* news progmg 2 hrs wkly; *No. News Employees:* 1; *Target Audience:* 18-49.
Van Riggs, Senior Vice President of Programming

WTLM
08-12-1968; 1520 kHz AM; *Hrs Open:* Sunrise-sunset
915 Veterans Parkway, Opelika, AL 36801 US
(334) 745-4656; *Fax:* (334) 749-1520
License: Opelika, AL held by AMFM Radio Licenses LLC.
Group Owner: iHeartMedia; (acq 2014).
Arbitron Metro Market: Opelika, AL; *Format:* Country; *No. News Employees:* 1; *Target Audience:* 35 plus.
Van Riggs, Senior Vice President of Programming

Opp

WAMI
12-12-1952; 860 kHz AM; 1 kw-D, 47 w-N; N31 18 54 W86 15 45
Box 40, Opp, AL 36467
(334) 493-3588; *Fax:* (334) 493-4182
wami@oppcatv.com
License: Opp, Covington County, AL held by Opp Broadcasting Co. Inc.
Population Served: 150,000 *Special Programming:* 24 hours; *No. News Employees:* 3; *Target Audience:* 25-65; agricultural & garment industry workers; *Adv. Rates:* 9; 8; 8; 8
Harry Phillips, General Manager/General Sales Manager
Virginia Phillips, Programming Director

WAMI-FM
11-09-1973; 102.3 MHz FM; 3.4 kw; 230 ft; N31 18 54 W86 15 45
Mailing Address: Box 40, Opp, AL 36467
Second Address: 1807 N. Main, Opp, AL 36467
(334) 493-3588; *Fax:* (334) 493-4182
wami@oppcatv.com
License: Opp, Covington County, AL held by OPP Broadcasting Co, Inc
Population Served: 175,000 *Hrs. of News Programming:* 9 hours; *No. News Employees:* 3; *Adv. Rates:* Same as AM
Harry Phillips, General Manager
Harry Phillips, General Sales Mgr
Virginia Phillips, Programming Director

***WJIF**
01-01-1986; 91.9 MHz FM; 0.38 kw; 164 ft.; N31 15 50 W86 13 26
700 Hwy 52, Opp, AL 36467 US
(334) 493-4947; *Fax:* (334) 493-4947
License: Opp, Covington County, AL held by Opp Educational Broadcasting Foundation.
Format: Gospel
Heywood Nyland, General Manager

WOPP
09-19-1980; 1290 kHz AM; 2.5 kw-D, DA2; 0.5 kw-N, DA2; N31 17 27 W86 13 51
1101 Cameron Road, Opp, AL 36467 US
(334) 493-4545; *Fax:* (334) 493-4546
www.wopp.com
License: Opp, AL held by E & R Broadcasting Inc.
Nat'l Network: Salem Radio Network *Regional Reps:* Rgnl Reps.
TV Affiliate: Country; *Format:* Black, Gospel *Special Programming:* news progmg 16 hrs wkly; *Hrs. of News Programming:* 1; *No. News Employees:* 19-58; progsv & highly lo; *Adv. Rates:* 10; 9; 10; 9
Robert Booth, General Manager
Ronnie Booth, Chief Engineer
Rachel Booth, Traffic Manager

Orange Beach

WCSN-FM
07-02-1996; 105.7 MHz FM; *Hrs Open:* 24; 5 kw; 246 ft.; N30 17 45 W87 33 42
Mailing Address: Post Office Box 679, Orange Beach, AL 36561 US
Second Address: 2421 E. Second St., Gulf Shores, AL 36542

(251) 967-1057; *Fax:* (251) 967-1050
www.sunny105.com
sunny105@gulftel.com
License: Orange Beach, Baldwin County, AL held by Gulf Coast Broadcasting Co. Inc.
Arbitron Metro Market: Mobile, AL; *Format:* Adult Contemp; *Target Audience:* 25-54; upscale
R. Lee Hagan, President
Kathryn Hagan, General Manager
Don Brown, General Sales Mgr

Orrville

WALX
12-12-1973; 100.9 MHz FM; 50 kw; 492 ft.; N32 21 40 W86 52 28
273 Persimmon Tree Rd., Selma, AL 36701 US
(334) 875-9360; *Fax:* (334) 875-1340
License: Orrville, Dallas County, AL held by Scott Communications Inc.
Group Owner: Scott Communications Inc.
Arbitron Metro Market: Orrville, AL; *Format:* Adult Contemp; *Target Audience:* 18-40.
Paul Alexander, General Manager

Oxford

WVOK
04-01-1956; 1580 kHz AM; *Hrs Open:* 24; 2.5 kw-D, ND1; 0.0218 kw-N, ND1; N33 35 27 W85 49 54; N33 26 55 W86 3 54
Mailing Address: P. O. Box 3770, Oxford, AL 36203 US
Second Address: 1215 Church St., Oxford, AL 36203
(256) 835-1580; *Fax:* (256) 831-1500
License: Oxford, AL held by Woodard Broadcasting Co.
Nat'l Network: ABC
Format: Oldies; *Target Audience:* 25-54.; *Adv. Rates:* 20; 12; 12; 8
Jimmy E. Woodward, President
Steve Stevens, Operations Dir
Chuck Woodard, General Manager

***WTBJ**
05-29-1994; 91.3 MHz FM; *Hrs Open:* 24; 0.17 kw; 1578 ft.; N33 29 7 W85 48 33
1500 Airport Road, Oxford, AL 36203 US
(256) 831-3333; *Fax:* (256) 831-5895
www.trinityoxford.org
truth@trinityoxford.org
License: Oxford, Calhoun County, AL held by Trinity Christian Academy.
Format: Religious *Special Programming:* Sp one hr wkly; *Target Audience:* General.
Dr. C.O. Grinstead, General Manager

WVOK-FM
02-19-1990; 97.9 MHz FM; *Hrs Open:* 24; 510 w; Ant 1,109 ft; N33 37 20 W85 52 19
Mailing Address: PO Box 3770, Oxford, AL 36203
Second Address: 1215 Church St., Oxford, AL 36203
(256) 835-1500; *Fax:* (256) 831-1500
www.979wvok.com
production@979wvok.com
License: Oxford, Calhoun County, AL
Population Served: 40,000
Jimmy E. Woodard, President
Steve Stevens, Operations Dir
Chuck Woodward, General Manager
Timmy Woodard, Sales Manager
Jock Burgess, Programming Director

Ozark

***WAQG**
06-01-1998; 91.7 MHz FM; 5 kw; 377 ft.; N31 26 25 W85 33 49
P.O. Box 3206, Tupelo, MS 38803 US
(601) 844-8888; *Fax:* (601) 842-6791
www.afr.net
faq@afa.net
License: Ozark, Dale County, AL held by American Family Association.
Group Owner: American Family Radio
Arbitron Metro Market: Ozark, AL; *Format:* Christian, Religious
Tim Wildmon, President
Donald Wildmon, Founder
Buddy Smith, Sr VP
Ed Vitagliano, Exec VP
Randy Sharp, Director Of Special Projects
Meeke Addison, Director Od Communications
Abraham Hamilton III, General Counsel

WOAB
07-09-1967; 104.9 MHz FM; 6 kw; 269 ft.; N31 27 19 W85 40 58
982 West Highway 27, Ozark, AL 36360 US
(334) 774-5600; *Fax:* (334) 774-1148
License: Ozark, Dale County, AL held by Ozark Broadcasting Corp.
Arbitron Metro Market: Dothan, AL *TV Affiliate:* Hits of the 40s, 50s & 60s

WOZK
05-03-1953; 900 kHz AM; 1 kw-D, ND1; 0.07 kw-N, ND1; N31 27 19 W85 40 58
982 West Highway 27, Ozark, AL 36360 US
(334) 774-5600; *Fax:* (334) 774-1148
wozk@alaweb.com
License: Ozark, AL held by Ozark Broadcasting Corp.
Arbitron Metro Market: Dothan, AL; *Format:* Adult Contemp; *Adv. Rates:* 7; 7; 7; 7
John Stein, General Manager

Pell City

WFHK
01-07-1956; 1430 kHz AM; *Hrs Open:* 6 AM-6 PM; 5 kw-D, NDD; N33 35 10 W86 19 35
Talladega Shopping Ctr. Brzwy, Suite A, Talladegta, AL 35161 US
(205) 338-1430; *Fax:* (205) 814-1430
License: Pell City, AL held by Stocks Broadcasting Inc.
Regional Network: Alaska Pub.
Arbitron Metro Market: Pell City, AL; *Format:* Country; *Adv. Rates:* 7.25; 6.25; 6.25; na
John Simpson, General Manager

Pepperell

WZMG
10-01-1979; 910 kHz AM; *Hrs Open:* 24; 0.65 kw-D, ND1; 0.056 kw-N, ND1; N32 39 26 W85 25 27
915 Veterans Parkway, Opelika, AL 36801 US
(334) 745-4656; *Fax:* (334) 749-1520
www.intouch910am.com
License: Pepperell, AL held by AMFM Radio Licenses LLC.
Group Owner: iHeartMedia; (acq 2014).
Nat'l Network: ABC
Arbitron Metro Market: Pepperell, AL; *Format:* Urban Contemporary; *Target Audience:* 25-54; African Americans; *Adv. Rates:* 18;15;17;10
Van Riggs, Senior Vice President of Programming

Phenix City

WGSY
03-04-1971; 100.1 MHz FM; *Hrs Open:* 24; 6 kw; 328 ft.; N32 30 42 W85 0 41
1501 13th Avenue, Columbus, GA 31901 US
(706) 576-3000; *Fax:* (706) 576-3010
www.sunny100.com
License: Phenix City, Russell County, AL held by CC Licenses LLC.
Group Owner: iHeartMedia; (acq 2-21-2002; grpsl).
Nat'l Reps: McGavren Guild
Arbitron Metro Market: Columbus, GA; *Format:* Adult Contemp; *Target Audience:* 25-54; women
Jennifer Newman, General Manager
Chuck Thompson, Sales Manager
Brian Thomas, Programming Director

Phenix City/Columbus

WHAL
01-01-1951; 1460 kHz AM; 4 kw-D, ND1; 0.14 kw-N, ND1; N32 25 58 W84 57 2
1501 13th Ave., Columbus, GA 31901 US
(706) 576-3000; *Fax:* (706) 576-3010
License: Phenix City/Columbus, AL held by CC Licenses LLC.
Group Owner: iHeartMedia; (acq 2-21-2002; grpsl).
Nat'l Reps: McGavren Guild
Arbitron Metro Market: Columbus, GA; *Format:* Country; *Target Audience:* 25 plus.
Jennifer Newman, Market President

Piedmont

***WJCK**
04-01-1994; 88.3 MHz FM; *Hrs Open:* 24; 2.7 kw vert; 968 ft.; N33 50 12 W85 43 59
P.O. Box 1000, 779 South Erwin Street, Cartersville, GA 30120 US
(256)447-6008; *Fax:* 770-387-2856
www.ibn.org
jo@ibn.org
License: Piedmont, Calhoun County, AL held by Immanuel Broadcasting Network
Format: Religious
Patrick Miller, CFO
Ed Tuten, President
Neil Hopper, General Manager
Jo Kirk, Station Manager
Howard Tuten, Programming Director

WPID
06-01-1953; 1280 kHz AM; *Hrs Open:* 6 AM-10 PM; 1 kw-D, ND1; 0.084 kw-N, ND1; N33 55 50 W85 35 0
P.O. Box 227, Piedmont, AL 36272 US
(256) 447-9096; *Fax:* (256) 447-6669
License: Piedmont, AL held by Piedmont Radio Co.
Format: Adult Contemp, Oldies; *Hrs. of News Programming:* News progmg 2 hrs wkly; *Target Audience:* 25-55.
Andy Kennedy, Operations Dir
Jimmy Kennedy, General Manager

Pike Road

WTXK
04-01-1968; 1210 kHz AM; 10 kw-D, 3 w-N, 5 kw-CH; N31 28 40 W85 41 07
1359 Carmichael Way, Montgomery, AL 36106
(334) 517-1210; *Fax:* (334) 356-9776
License: Pike Road, Dale County, AL held by Frontdoor Broadcasting LLC
Arbitron Metro Market: Dothan, AL; *Target Audience:* 25-64.
Allan Stroh, CEO
Ray Dodson, Sales Manager

Pine Hill

WKXK
01-01-2000; 96.7 MHz FM; 41 kw; 535 ft.; N32 4 24 W87 35 27
Rebroadcasts: Simulcast of WKXN(FM) Greenville 100%
Mailing Address: Manningham Road At I-65, P. O. Box 369, Greenville, AL 36037 US
Second Address: 563 Manningham Rd., Greenville, AL 36037
(334) 382-6555; *Fax:* (334) 382-7770
www.wkxn.com
wkxn@alaweb.com
License: Pine Hill, Wilcox County, AL held by Autaugaville Radio Inc.
Format: Blues, Gospel
Roscoe Miller, General Manager
Bob Luman, Chief Engineer
Chelli Merrett, Business Manager

Pine Level

WVRV
01-01-2008; 97.5 MHz FM; 6 kw; Ant 328 ft; N31 58 32 W85 58 27
1359 Carmichael Way, Montgomery, AL
(334) 239-9750; *Fax:* (334) 356-9776
www.wvrvfmtheriver.com
License: Pine Level, Montgomery County, AL held by Back Door Broadcasting LLC.

Allan Stroh, President
Mike Alan, Operations Dir
Ann Collister, General Manager
Ann Collister, General Sales Mgr
Mike Alan, Programming Director
Terry Harper, Engineering Dir

Prattville

WIQR
03-01-1969; 1410 kHz AM; 5 kw-D, DA2; 1 kw-N, DA2; N32 25 23 W86 26 21
319 17th Street North, Birmingham, AL 35203 US
(334) 358-0410
wiqr@hotmail.com
License: Prattville, AL held by Star Power Communications Corp.
Regional Reps: Alabama Net.
Arbitron Metro Market: Montgomery, AL; *Format:* Sports; *Target Audience:* General.
Greg Meadows, General Manager

WXFX
08-01-1977; 95.1 MHz FM; *Hrs Open:* 24; 5.4 kw; 333.8 meters; N32 28 01 W86 24 15
1 Commerce St., Suite 300, Montgomery, AL 35223
(334) 240-9274; *Fax:* (334) 240-9219
www.wxfx.com
License: Prattville, Montgomery County, AL held by Cumulus Licensing Corp.
Group Owner: Cumulus Media Inc.; (acq 3-12-01; grpsl)
Nat'l Network: CNN Radio; Motor Racing Net; *Regional Network:* Alabama Radio Net; *Nat'l Reps:* Katz Radio

Population Served: 280,000; *Arbitron Metro Market:* Montgomery, AL; *No. News Employees:* 1; *Target Audience:* 25-54; upscale adults, two paycheck households
Bill Jones, Operations Dir
Kevin Waltman, General Manager
Matt Ward, General Sales Mgr
Rick Hendrick, Programming Director
Larry Wilkins, Chief Engineer

Priceville

WKZD
08-01-1986; 1310 kHz AM; *Hrs Open:* Sunrise-sunset
Mailing Address: 1431 Hwy 31 N, Hartselle, AL 35640 US
Second Address: 303 2nd Ave. S.E., Decatur, AL 35601
(256) 773-4114; *Fax:* (256) 773-6915
License: Priceville, AL held by Abercrombie Broadcasting AM Inc.
Arbitron Metro Market: Huntsville, AL; *Format:* Oldies; *Target Audience:* 25-65.
Percy Yarbrough, General Manager

Prichard

WIJD
06-13-1966; 1270 kHz AM; *Hrs Open:* 24; 5 kw-D, ND1; 0.103 kw-N, ND1; N30 44 44 W88 5 40
273 Azalea Road, Suite 403, Two Office Park, Mobile, AL 36609 US
(251) 340-0442
www.wilkinsradio.com
denise@wilkinsradio.com
License: Prichard, AL held by Mobile Bay Corp.
Group Owner: Wilkins Communications Network Inc.; (acq 7-18-2006; $450,000)
Arbitron Metro Market: Mobile, AL; *Format:* Christian, Talk; *Target Audience:* 35 plus.
Scot Chestnut, Station Manager

WLPR
12-31-1986; 960 kHz AM; *Hrs Open:* 24
P.O. Box 1328, Mobile, AL 36633 US
(251) 473-8488
www.goforth.org
License: Prichard, AL held by Goforth Media Inc.
Nat'l Network: Salem Radio Network; *Nat'l Reps:* Salem
Arbitron Metro Market: Mobile, AL; *Format:* Gospel; *Hrs. of News Programming:* News progmg 6 hrs wkly; *Target Audience:* 35 plus.
James A. Muhammad, President
Carrie Kuck, Director, Programming/Membership
Bob Liptack, Chief Engineer
Wende Burbridge, Director, Development
Roger Wexelberg, VP, Development/Public Relations

WIJD
01-01-2012; 95.7 MHz FM; *Hrs Open:* 24; 5 kw-D, ND1; 0.103 kw-N, ND1
273 Azalea Road, Suite 403, Two Office Park, Mobile, AL 36609 US
(251) 340-0442
www.wilkinsradio.com
denise@wilkinsradio.com
License: Prichard, AL held by Mobile Bay Corp.
Group Owner: Wilkins Communications Network Inc.; (acq 7-18-2006; $450,000)
Arbitron Metro Market: Mobile, AL; *Format:* Christian, Talk; *Target Audience:* 35 plus.
Scot Chestnut, Station Manager

WIJD
06-13-1966; 97.9 kHz FM; *Hrs Open:* 24; 5 kw-D, ND1; 0.103 kw-N, ND1; N30 44 44 W88 5 40
273 Azalea Road, Suite 403, Two Office Park, Mobile, AL 36609 US
(251) 340-0442
www.wilkinsradio.com
denise@wilkinsradio.com
License: Prichard, AL held by Mobile Bay Corp.
Group Owner: Wilkins Communications Network Inc.; (acq 7-18-2006; $450,000)
Arbitron Metro Market: Mobile, AL; *Format:* Christian, Talk; *Target Audience:* 35 plus.
Scot Chestnut, Station Manager

Rainbow City

WGAD
01-01-1926; 930 kHz AM; *Hrs Open:* 17; 5 kw-D, 500 w-N, DA-2; N33 59 09 W86 02 15
Mailing Address: Box 930, Gadsden, AL 35902
Second Address: 750 Walnut St, Gadsen, AL 35901
(256) 546-1611; *Fax:* (256) 547-9062
www.wgad.com
License: Rainbow City, Etowah County, AL held by Coosa River Communications Inc.
Nat'l Network: ABC
Population Served: 200,000 *Hrs. of News Programming:* News progmg 16 hrs wkly; *Target Audience:* 25 plus; general; *Adv. Rates:* 15; 12; 15; 12
Neil Mitchem, President
David Ford, General Manager

Rainsville

WVSM
05-16-1967; 1500 kHz AM; *Hrs Open:* Sunrise-sunset; 1 kw-C, NDD; 1 kw-D, NDD; N34 29 56 W85 50 34
P.O. Box 339, Rainsville, AL 35986 US
(256) 638-2137
www.wvsmam.com
wvsm@farmerstel.com
License: Rainsville, AL held by Sand Mountain Advertising Co. Inc.
Arbitron Metro Market: Rainsville, AL; *Format:* Gospel; *Hrs. of News Programming:* news progmg 9 hrs wkly; *No. News Employees:* 3; *Target Audience:* General.; *Adv. Rates:* 15; 15
Mark Huber, President
Kayron Guffey, Operations Dir
Annie Ruth Huber, General Sales Mgr
Jesse Finley, Disc Jockey
Ann Spears, Disc Jockey

Red Bay

WRMG
06-29-1968; 1430 kHz AM; 1 kw-D, NDD; N34 24 51 W88 8 11
PO Box 656, Red Bay, AL 35582 US
(256) 356-4458
License: Red Bay, AL held by Jack W. Ivy Sr.
Format: Country, Gospel
Jack Ivy Sr., President

Reform

WBEI
05-07-1991; 101.7 MHz FM; *Hrs Open:* 24; 22.5 kw; Ant 725 ft; N33 13 48 W87 50 50
142 Skyland Blvd., Tuscaloosa, AL 35405
(205) 345-7200; *Fax:* (205) 349-1715
www.b1017online.com
todd.livingston@townsquaremedia.com
License: Reform, Pickens County, AL
Group Owner: Townsquare Media; (acq 7-21-2012; grpsl).
Population Served: 91,605; *Arbitron Metro Market:* Tuscaloosa, AL; *Target Audience:* 18-49
Todd Livingston, Market Manager
Julie Salter, General Sales Mgr
Greg Thomas, Programming Director
Meg Summers, Promotions Manager

Repton

WPPG
10-01-2002; 101.1 MHz FM; *Hrs Open:* 24; 3.1 kw; 459 ft.; N31 26 45 W87 16 59
866 West Front Street, Greenville, AL 36401 US
(251) 575-7601; *Fax:* (251) 575-7703
fun101@frontiernet.net
License: Repton, Conecuh County, AL held by Wolff Broadcasting Corp.
Arbitron Metro Market: Repton, AL; *Format:* Classic Rock
Wendy Smith, General Manager
Robert Williams, Chief Engineer

Roanoke

WLWE
04-01-1954; 1360 kHz AM; 1 kw-D, ND2; 0.054 kw-N, ND2; N33 9 45 W85 22 30
P.O. Box 709, Roanoke, AL 36274 US
(334) 863-4139; *Fax:* (334) 863-2540
www.eagle1023.com
WELR@Eagle1023.com
License: Roanoke, AL held by Eagle's Nest Inc.
Group Owner: Eagle's Nest Inc.; acq 10-15-88)
Nat'l Network: ESPN Radio
Arbitron Metro Market: Roanoke, AL.; *Format:* Sports
Jim Vice, President/CEO
Kay Vice, Operations Dir
Coleman Vice, General Sales Mgr
Don Strength, Program Director
Al Haynes, News Director

WELR-FM
02-14-1969; 102.3 MHz FM; *Hrs Open:* 24; 8.9 kw; 545 ft.; N33 2 39 W85 20 15
P.O. Box 709, Roanoke, AL 36274 US
(334) 863-4139; *Fax:* (334) 863-2540
www.eagle1023.com
WELR@Eagle1023.com
License: Roanoke, Randolph County, AL held by Eagle's Nest Inc.
Group Owner: Eagle's Nest Inc.; (acq 1988)
Arbitron Metro Market: Roanoke, AL.; *Format:* Country; *No. News Employees:* 2
Kay Vice, Operations Dir
Jim Vice, General Manager/CEO
Coleman Vice, General Sales Mgr
Don Strength, Programming Director
Al Haynes, News Director

Robertsdale

WDXZ
03-01-1985; 1000 kHz AM; *Hrs Open:* 6 am-6 pm; 1 kw-D; N30 32 10 W87 42 55
Box 578, Robertsdale, AL 36561
(251) 947-2346; *Fax:* (251) 947-2347
License: Robertsdale, Baldwin County, AL held by Great American Radio Network Inc.
Population Served: 40,000; *Arbitron Metro Market:* Mobile, AL *Special Programming:* Religion 6 hrs wkly; *Hrs. of News Programming:* news progmg 2 hrs wkly; *No. News Employees:* 1; *Target Audience:* 45 plus;upscale
R. Lee Hagen, President

Rogersville

WYTK
01-01-1994; 93.9 MHz FM; *Hrs Open:* 24; 2.25 kw; 531 ft.; N34 51 52 W87 23 43
113 N. Seminary Street, Florence, AL 35630 US
(256) 764-9390; *Fax:* (256) 764-7760
www.939thescore.com
thescore@939thescore.com
License: Rogersville, Lauderdale County, AL held by Valley Broadcasting Inc.
Arbitron Metro Market: Florence-Muscle Shoals, AL; *Format:* Sports; *Hrs. of News Programming:* sports news progmg 28 hrs wkly; *Target Audience:* 25-54; male; *Adv. Rates:* 22; 18; 20; 16
Greg Thornton, President
Al Mann, Operations Dir
J.D. Byars, General Sales Mgr
Mike Greenberg, News Reporter and Sports Commentator
Mike Golic, News Reporter and Sports Commentator
Tim Brando, Sports Commentator
Harold Bugg,Sports Commentator
Brett Beaird, Sports Commentator
Paul Finebaum, Sports Commentator

Russellville

WGOL
05-29-1949; 920 kHz AM; *Hrs Open:* 16; 1 kw-D, ND1; 0.04 kw-N, ND1; N34 30 50 W87 42 55
113 Washington Avenue Northwest, Russellville, AL 35653 US
(256) 332-0214; *Fax:* (256) 332-7430
www.wgolam.com
License: Russellville, AL held by Pilati Investments Corp.
Regional Network: Alaska Pub.
Format: Country *Special Programming:* Black gospel 4 hrs, relg 10 hrs wkly; *Hrs. of News Programming:* News progmg 9 hrs wkly; *Target Audience:* 25-60.
John Pilati, General Manager
John Pilati, Station Manager
Thomas Foster, Programming Director
Christopher Arthur, Chief Engineer
Buddy Matthues, Sales & Assistant Operator

WKAX
04-03-1974; 1500 kHz AM; 1 kw-D, NDD; N34 31 42 W87 42 41
112 Washington Avenue, Russellville, AL 35653 US
(256) 332-6103; *Fax:* (256) 332-7430
License: Russellville, AL held by Pilati Investments Corp.
Format: Gospel *Special Programming:* Black 4 hrs wkly; *Target Audience:* 21-54.; *Adv. Rates:* 6; 6; 6; na
John Pilati, General Manager

Saraland

WDLT-FM
05-19-1966; 104.1 MHz FM; *Hrs Open:* 24; 98 kw; 508 meters; N30 36 45 W87 38 42
2800 Dauphin St., #104, Mobile, AL 36606-2400

(251) 652-2000; *Fax:* (251) 652-2001
mobile.prog@cumulus.com
License: Saraland, Escambia County, AL held by Cumulus Licensing Corp.
Group Owner: Cumulus Media Inc.; (acq 10-18-99; grpsl)
Population Served: 954,300; *Arbitron Metro Market:* Mobile, AL; *Format:* Adult Contemp; *Hrs. of News Programming:* news progmg 5 hrs wkly; *No. News Employees:* 1; *Target Audience:* 25-40.
Angel Taylor, Regional VP/Sales Manager
Catherine Barlow, Program/Music Director
Vinny Duncan, Promotions/Marketing Director
Chuck Sullivan, Regional VP/Market Manager

WDLT
05-19-1966; 104.1 MHz FM; 98 kw; 1708 ft; N30 36 45 W87 38 42
2800 Dauphin St., Suite 104, Mobile, AL 36606 US
(251) 652-2007
www.1041wdlt.com
License: Saraland, AL held by Cumulus Licensing LLC.
Group Owner: Cumulus Media Networks
Format: Urban Contemporary, Blues
Angel Taylor-Brown, VP/Market Manager
Laure English, Local Sales Mgr
Cathe B, Program Director/Music Director
Amberly Harris, Promotions Manager

Scottsboro

WKEA-FM
11-03-1965; 98.3 MHz FM; *Hrs Open:* 24; 11 kw; 492 ft.; N34 32 0 W85 55 20
P.O. Box 966, Port Payne, AL 35967 USA
(256) 845-7721
www.wkeafm.com
ron@wkeafm.com
License: Scottsboro, Jackson County, AL held by KEA Radio Inc.
Group Owner: KEA Radio Inc.
Format: Country *Special Programming:* Farm one hr, relg 4 hrs wkly; *Hrs. of News Programming:* news progmg 2 hrs wkly; *No. News Employees:* 1; *Target Audience:* 25-54.

WWIC
06-13-1950; 1050 kHz AM; *Hrs Open:* 24; 1 kw-D, ND1; 0.1 kw-N, ND1; N34 40 23 W86 3 11
815 West Willow St., Scottsboro, AL 35768 US
(256) 259-1050; *Fax:* (256) 575-2411
www.wwicradio.com
wwic@scottsboro.org
License: Scottsboro, AL held by Scottsboro Broadcasting Co. Inc.
Nat'l Network: ABC; *Regional Network:* Alabama Radio Net.
Arbitron Metro Market: Jackson County, AL; *Format:* Country, Sports; *Adv. Rates:* 7.62; 6.24; 6.79; 6.24
Greg Bell, President
Lisa Manning, Director of Sales & Promotions

WZCT
06-11-1952; 1330 kHz AM; *Hrs Open:* 24; 5 kw-D, ND1; 0.038 kw-N, ND1; N34 42 7 W86 0 15
111 East Willow Street, Scottsboro, AL 35768 US
(256) 574-1330; *Fax:* (256) 218-3013
License: Scottsboro, AL held by Bonner and Carlile Enterprises.
Nat'l Network: Reach Satellite; USA
Arbitron Metro Market: Scottsboro, AL; *Format:* Gospel *Special Programming:* Sports 19 hrs wkly; *Hrs. of News Programming:* News progmg 14 hrs wkly; *Target Audience:* 25 plus.; *Adv. Rates:* 108; 96; 108; 96
Rob Carlile, Station Manager

Selma

***WAPR**
05-05-1996; 88.3 MHz FM; 53 kw vert; 1401 ft.; N32 8 30 W86 44 43 *Rebroadcasts:* Rebroadcasts WUAL-FM Tuscaloosa 100%
The Univ. of Alabama, Box 870150, 166 Reese Phifer Hall, Tuscaloosa, AL 35487 US
(205) 348-6644; *Fax:* (205) 348-6648
www.apr.org
apr@apr.org
License: Selma, Dallas County, AL held by Ua-Asu-Tsu Educational Radio Corp.
Nat'l Network: NPR; PRI
Arbitron Metro Market: Selma, AL.; *Format:* Jazz, News
Brian Poellnitz, Operations Dir
Elizabeth Brock, Station Manager
Pat Duggins, News Director
David Duff, Music Director
Kathy Henslee, Development Director
Barbara Charnetski, Director of Corporate Sponsorship

***WAQU**
03-01-1998; 91.1 MHz FM; 21.5 kw; 335 ft.; N32 24 17 W87 25 32
P.O. Box 3206, Tupelo, MS 38803 US
(662) 844-8888; *Fax:* (662) 842-6791
www.afr.net
faq@afa.net
License: Selma, Dallas County, AL held by American Family Association.
Group Owner: American Family Radio
Arbitron Metro Market: Selma, AL; *Format:* Christian, Religious
Tim Wildmon, President
Donald Wildmon, Founder
Buddy Smith, Sr VP
Ed Vitagliano, Exec VP
Randy Sharp, Director Of Special Projects
Meeke Addison, Director Of Communications
Abraham Hamilton III, General Counsel

WHBB
11-11-1935; 1490 kHz AM; *Hrs Open:* 24; 1 kw-U, ND1; N32 26 2 W87 0 40
Mailing Address: 505 Lauderdale Street, PO Box 1055, Selma, AL 36706 US
Second Address: 505 Lauderdale St., Selma, AL 36701
(334) 875-3350; *Fax:* (334) 874-6959
www.wdxx.com
License: Selma, AL held by Broadsouth Communications Inc.
Nat'l Reps: Rgnl Reps
Format: News, News/Talk, 86 *Special Programming:* Black 18 hrs, farm 10 hrs wkly; *Hrs. of News Programming:* news progmg 13 hrs wkly; *No. News Employees:* 1; *Target Audience:* 25-54.; *Adv. Rates:* 26; 20; 22;10
Mike Reynolds, General Manager
Evelyn Ogle, General Sales Mgr
George Henry, Programming Director

WJAM
12-19-1946; 1340 kHz AM; 1 kw-U, ND1; N32 25 31 W86 59 47
273 Persimmon Tree Rd, Selma, AL 36701 US
(334) 875-9360; *Fax:* (334) 875-1340
License: Selma, AL held by Scott Communications Inc.
Group Owner: Scott Communications Inc.; (acq 12-30-2005; $29,500 for 47.2% of stock with co-located FM)
Arbitron Metro Market: Selma, AL; *Format:* Adult Contemp; *Target Audience:* 25-49.
Scott Alexander, President

***WRNF**
01-01-2007; 89.5 MHz FM; 6 kW; 328 ft.; N32 32 50 W86 55 33
5710 Watermelon Rd, Suite 316, Northport, AL 35473 USA
www.moodyradiosouth.fm
License: Selma, Dallas County, AL held by The Moody Bible Institute of Chicago
Group Owner: Moody Radio
Arbitron Metro Market: Selma, AL; *Format:* Religious

Sheffield

***WAKD**
01-01-1996; 89.9 MHz FM; 7.4 kw vert; 236 ft.; N34 50 11 W87 37 20
P.O. Box 3206, Tupelo, MS 38803 US
(662) 844-8888; *Fax:* (662) 842-6791
www.afr.net
faq@afa.net
License: Sheffield, Colbert County, AL held by American Family Association.
Group Owner: American Family Radio
Arbitron Metro Market: Shoals, AL; *Format:* Christian, Religious
Tim Wildmon, President
Donald Wildmon, Founder
Buddy Smith, Sr VP
Ed Vitagliano, Executive VP
Randy Sharp, Director Of Special Projects
Meeke Addison, Director Of Communications
Abraham Hamilton III, General Sounsel & PublicPolicy Analyst

WBTG
11-06-1963; 1290 kHz AM; *Hrs Open:* 24; 1 kw-D, ND1; 0.079 kw-N, ND1; N34 46 27 W87 40 14
Mailing Address: P. O. Box 518, Sheffield, AL 35660 US
Second Address: 1605 Gospel Rd., Sheffield, AL 35660
(256) 381-6800; *Fax:* (256) 381-6801
www.wbtgradio.com
announcements@wbtgradio.com
License: Sheffield, AL held by Slatton & Associates.
Nat'l Network: Salem Radio Network; *Regional Network:* Ill. Radio Net.
Arbitron Metro Market: Sheffield, Al; *Format:* Sports; *Target Audience:* 25 up; conservative, mainstream family audience
Paul Slatton, President
Josey Traywick, Programming Director
Angela Green, News Director
Kathy Harroway, Office Manager

WBTG-FM
07-02-1969; 106.3 MHz FM; *Hrs Open:* 24; 6 kw; 682 ft.; N34 41 34 W87 47 49
Mailing Address: P.O. Box 518, Sheffield, AL 35660 US
Second Address: 1605 Gospel Rd., Sheffield, AL 35660
(256) 381-6800; *Fax:* (256) 381-6801
www.wbtgradio.com
announcements@wbtgradio.com
License: Sheffield, Colbert County, AL
Arbitron Metro Market: Sheffield, Al; *Format:* Sports; *Hrs. of News Programming:* News progmg 12 hrs wkly
Paul Slatton, General Manager

Shorter

WMRK-FM
08-01-1994; 107.9 MHz FM; 25 kw; 328 ft.; N32 21 9 W86 3 6
Mailing Address: 273 Persimmon Tree Rd, Selma, AL 36701 US
Second Address: 273 Persimmon Tree Rd, Selma, AL 36701
(334) 244-0961; *Fax:* (334) 279-9563
www.newstalk1079.com
tbarber@bluewaterbroadcasting.com
License: Shorter, Perry County, AL
Format: Urban Contemporary
Rick Peters, CEO/COO
Terry Barber, General Manager
Lanier Harris, General Sales Mgr
Susan Ashworth, Promotions Director
Mary Brazell, Traffic Director
Tom Jones, Chief Engineer
Jay Scott, Production Director

Slocomb

WJRL-FM
01-01-1991; 100.5 MHz FM; *Hrs Open:* 24; 16.5 kw; 408 ft.; N31 11 0 W85 24 23
285 North Foster Street, 8th Floor, Dothan, AL 36303 US
(334) 792-0049; *Fax:* (334) 712-9346
casualmusic@aol.com
License: Slocomb, Dale County, AL held by Alabama Media LLC
Group Owner: Alabama Media LLC
Arbitron Metro Market: Dothan, AL; *Format:* Adult Contemp; *No. News Employees:* 1; *Target Audience:* 25-54; upscale baby boomers, acitive duty & retired military; *Adv. Rates:* 15; 12; 12; 9
Georgia Edminston, President
Cliff Hawthorne, Programming Director

Smiths

WAGH
01-01-1998; 101.3 MHz FM; 18 kw; 354 ft.; N32 25 35 W85 8 20
1501 13th Avenue, Columbus, GA 31901 US
(706) 576-3000; *Fax:* (706) 576-3010
www.mymagic101.com
License: Smiths, Lee County, AL held by CC Licenses LLC.
Group Owner: iHeartMedia; (acq 2-21-2002; grpsl)
Arbitron Metro Market: Columbus, GA; *Format:* Adult Contemp; *Target Audience:* 25-54; working Black adults
Jennifer Newman, General Manager
Chuck Thompson, Sales Manager
Derrick Greene, Programming Director

Southside

WKLS
10-10-1992; 105.9 MHz FM; *Hrs Open:* 24; 1.6 kw; 196 meters; N34 12 51 W85 46 20
801 Nobel St., Fl. 8, Anniston, AL 35203
(888) 983-1059; *Fax:* (256) 236-4480
www.y-106.com
License: Southside, Cherokee County, AL held by Williams Communications Inc.
Group Owner: Williams Communications Inc.; (acq 6-99; $380,000)
Nat'l Network: Motor Racing Net; PRI
Population Served: 440,000 *Hrs. of News Programming:* News progmg one hr wkly; *Target Audience:* 25-54.
Walt Williams, President/General Manager
Tex Carter, Sales Director
Tex Carter, Programming Director
Eva Gibson, Business Manager

St. Florian

WWFA
102.7 MHz FM; 10 kw; 463 ft.; N34 45 28 W87 30 6
1905 C Florence Boulevard, Florence, AL 35630 US
(256) 349-2041; *Fax:* (256) 349-2088
www.1027kiss.fm
License: St. Florian, Lauderdale County, AL held by George S. Flinn Jr.
Arbitron Metro Market: Saint Florian, AL; *Format:* Adult Contemp, Contemporary Hits/Top 40
George Flinn Jr., General Manager

Steele

***WAYU**
91.1 MHz FM; 0.15 kw vert; 755 ft.; N33 57 29.6 W86 13 1
PMB 107, 3331 Rainbow Drive, Suite E, Rainbow City, AL 35906 US
(888) 239-2936; *Fax:* (719) 278-4339
supportservices@wayfm.com
License: Steele, St. Clair County, AL held by WAY-FM Media Group Inc.
Group Owner: WAY-FM Media Group Inc.
Arbitron Metro Market: Steele, AL; *Format:* Christian
Robert Augsburg, President

Stevenson

WMXN-FM
06-13-1977; 101.7 MHz FM; 2.3 kw; 541 ft.; N34 41 2 W85 48 4
19784 John T. Reid Pkway, P.O. Box 966, Scottsboro, AL 35768 USA
(256) 259-2341
www.1017thestorm.com
ron@1017thestorm.com
License: Stevenson, Jackson County, AL held by KEA Radio Inc.
Group Owner: KEA Radio Inc.; (acq 1996).
Wire Services: AP
Arbitron Metro Market: Stevenson, Al; *Format:* Contemporary Hits/Top 40
Charis Wise-Parker, Traffic Manager

Sylacauga

WFEB
03-01-1945; 1340 kHz AM; *Hrs Open:* 16; 1 kw-U, ND1; N33 10 16 W86 13 57
P. O. Box 2267, 1209 Miller Highway, Sylacauga, AL 35150 US
(256) 245-3281; *Fax:* (256) 245-3050
License: Sylacauga, AL held by Powers Broadcasting Co LLC
Regional Reps: Keystone (unwired net).
Arbitron Metro Market: Sylacauga, AL; *Format:* News, News/Talk, 84, Talk *Special Programming:* Gospel 6 hrs wkly; *Hrs. of News Programming:* news progmg 17 hrs wkly; *No. News Employees:* 3 *Target Audience:* 25-54.
Betty Heacock, General Manager
Dawn Stevens, Sales Manager

WYEA
05-16-1948; 1290 kHz AM; *Hrs Open:* 6 AM-8 PM
1 Motes Road, PO Box 629, Sylacauga, AL 35150 US
(256) 249-4263; *Fax:* (256) 245-4355
wyea@rocketmail.com
License: Sylacauga, AL held by Marble City Media LLC
Nat'l Network: USA; *Regional Network:* Alabama Radio Net; *Nat'l Reps:* Salem
Arbitron Metro Market: Sylacauga, AL; *Format:* Christian, Country; *Hrs. of News Programming:* News progmg 7 hrs wkly; *Target Audience:* General.; *Adv. Rates:* 6.25; 5.25; 6.25; na
John Vogel, President
Nelda Vogel, Operations Dir

Talladega

WTDR-FM
11-10-1972; 92.7 MHz FM; *Hrs Open:* 24; 2.6 kw; Ant 505 ft; N33 29 12 W85 59 15
1913 Barry Street, Suite B, Oxford, AL 35161
(256) 741-6000; *Fax:* (256) 741-6080
www.wtdrthunder.com
License: Talladega, Talladega County, AL held by Jeff Beck Broadcasting Group
Nat'l Network: AP Radio; *Wire Services:* AP
Population Served: 300,000; *No. News Employees:* 1; *Target Audience:* 25-54; adults; *Adv. Rates:* 30; 26; 27; 18
Jeff Beck, President
Shannon Wheeles, Director of Marketing & Sales

Tallassee

WQNR
10-29-1992; 99.9 MHz FM; 2.85 kw; 479 ft.; N32 26 32 W85 47 28
2514 S. College St., Suite 104, Auburn, AL 36832 US
(334) 887-9999; *Fax:* (334) 826-9599
www.katefm.com
License: Tallassee, Elmore County, AL held by Tiger Communications Inc.
Group Owner: Tiger Communications Inc.; (acq 1999)
Arbitron Metro Market: Auburn, AL; *Format:* Contemporary Hits/Top 40, Adult Contemp; *Target Audience:* 25-54; Adults; *Adv. Rates:* 28; 22; 25; 18
Brooke Myers, General Manager
Stacey Linn, Director of Sales

WTLS
06-01-1954; 1300 kHz AM
Mailing Address: PO Box 780146, Tallassee, AL 36078 US
Second Address: 2045 Hwy 229, Tallassee, AL 36078
(334) 283-8200; *Fax:* (334) 283-8622
www.1300wtls.com
mbutler@1300wtls.com
License: Tallassee, AL held by Michael Butler Broadcasting LLC
Arbitron Metro Market: Tallassee, AL; *Format:* Sports, Talk
Special Programming: Farm 6 hrs wkly,gospel 6 hrs wkly; *Adv. Rates:* 11; 8; 10; 7
Michael Butler, President
Leigh Anne Butler, General Sales Mgr
Steve Butler, Programming Director
Miles Hathcock, Promotions Manager
Terry Harper, Chief Engineer

Thomaston

WTID
01-01-2001; 103.9 MHz FM; 0.5 kw; 46 ft.; N32 16 49 W87 38 6
6930 Cahaba Valley Road, Suite 202, Birmingham, AL 35242-2673 US
(205) 949-4574
License: Thomaston, Marengo County, AL held by Great South Wireless LLC.
Arbitron Metro Market: Trinidad CO; *Format:* Christian
Joan Reynolds, CEO

Thomasville

WJDB
07-16-1956; 630 kHz AM; *Hrs Open:* Sunrise-sunset; 1 kw-D, ND2; 0.049 kw-N, ND2; N31 52 58 W87 44 42
P.O. 219, Thomasville, AL 36784 US
(334) 636-4438; *Fax:* (334) 636-4439
www.wjbdradio.com
wjdb@dixienet1.com
License: Thomasville, AL held by Griffin Broadcasting Corp.
Nat'l Network: CBS; *Regional Network:* Ark. Radio Net.
Format: Oldies; *Hrs. of News Programming:* news progmg 10 hrs wkly; *No. News Employees:* 1; *Target Audience:* General.
Ivy Griffin, President/General Manager

WJDB-FM
11-02-1972; 95.5 MHz FM; *Hrs Open:* 24; 9.6 kw; 525 ft.; N31 44 25 W87 45 43
Mailing Address: P.O. Box 219, Thomasville, AL 36784 US
Second Address: 2211 Hwy. 43 S., Thomasville, AL 36784
(334) 636-4438; *Fax:* (334) 636-4439
www.wjbdradio.com
wjdb@dixienet1.com
License: Thomasville, Clarke County, AL held by Griffin Broadcasting Corp.
Format: Contemporary Hits/Top 40, Country; *Hrs. of News Programming:* News progmg 10 hrs wkly; *Target Audience:* General.
Ivey Griffin, President/General Manager

***WDLG**
01-01-2007; 90.1 MHz FM; 0.5 kw; 249 ft.; N31 44 24 W87 45 43
P.O. Box 866, Pensacola, FL 32591 US
(850) 438-7667
www.catholicradio.us
mglin@aol.com
License: Thomasville, Clarke County, AL held by Divine Word Communications
Arbitron Metro Market: Thomasville, AL; *Format:* Christian, Religious
Gene Church, President

Trinity

WVNN-FM
10-04-1992; 92.5 MHz FM; *Hrs Open:* 24; 3.1 kw; 423 ft.; N34 42 36 W87 4 54 *Rebroadcasts:* Simulcasts WVNN-AM 100%
806 Governors Drive, Suite 101, Huntsville, AL 35801 US
(256) 830-8300; *Fax:* (256) 232-6842
www.wvnn.com
programdirector@wvnn.com
License: Trinity, Morgan County, AL held by Cumulus Licensing LLC.
Group Owner: Cumulus Media Inc.; (acq 4-4-2006; $3.3 million with WXQW(FM) Meridianville)
Nat'l Network: ABC; *Nat'l Reps:* Katz Radio
Arbitron Metro Market: Huntsville, AL; *Format:* News, News/Talk, 86; *Hrs. of News Programming:* 7 hrs news prgmg wkly; *No. News Employees:* 3
John Walker, General Manager
Matt Tobin, Sales Director
Dale Jackson, Programming Director
Stephanie Smith, Traffic Director

Troy

***WAXU**
01-01-2001; 91.1 MHz FM; *Hrs Open:* 24; 1.1 kw; 246 ft.; N31 47 22 W85 58 58
P.O. Box 3206, Tupelo, MS 38803 US
(662) 844-8888; *Fax:* (662) 842-6791
www.afr.net
faq@afa.net
License: Troy, Pike County, AL held by American Family Association.
Group Owner: American Family Radio
Format: Christian
Tim Wildmon, President
Donald Wildmon, Founder
Buddy Smith, Sr VP
Ed Vitagliano, Exec VP
Randy Sharp, Director Of Special Projects
Meeke Addison, Director Of Communications
Abraham Hamilton III, General Counsel

WTBF
02-25-1947; 970 kHz AM; *Hrs Open:* 24
67 Court Sq., Troy, AL 36081 US
(334) 566-0300; *Fax:* (334) 566-5689
www.wtbf.com
License: Troy, AL held by Troy Broadcasting Corp.
Format: Talk *Special Programming:* Farm 17 hrs wkly; *Hrs. of News Programming:* News progmg 20 hrs wkly; *Target Audience:* 35 plus; general; *Adv. Rates:* 25; 15; 25; 7:50
Joe Gilchrist, President
Jim Roling, General Manager
Dave Kirby, Programming Director
Dave Kirby, Operations Manager

WZHT
02-28-1973; 105.7 MHz FM; 100 kw; 1831 ft.; N31 58 28 W86 9 44
203 Gunn Road, Montgomery, AL 36117 US
(334) 274-6464; *Fax:* (334) 274-6467
www.myhot105.com
License: Troy, Pike County, AL held by Capstar TX LLC
Group Owner: iHeartMedia; (acq 8-30-00; grpsl)
Nat'l Network: ABC; Westwood One; *Nat'l Reps:* McGavren Guild
Arbitron Metro Market: Montgomery, AL; *Format:* Urban Contemporary; *Target Audience:* 18-49.
Becky Sweeney, Market President
Chris Coleman, Senior Vice President of Programming
Kimberly Brown, Promotions Director/Online Content Director
Kimberly Parker, Business Manager

Trussville

WQEN
10-07-1966; 103.7 MHz FM; 100 kw; 935 ft.; N33 26 38 W86 52 47
600 Beacon Parkway West, Suite 400, Birmingham, AL 35209 US
(205) 439-9600; *Fax:* (205) 439-8390
www.1037theq.com
License: Trussville, Jefferson County, AL held by Capstar TX LLC
Group Owner: iHeartMedia; (acq 8-30-2000; grpsl)
Arbitron Metro Market: Birmingham, AL; *Format:* Contemporary Hits/Top 40
Cyndi Collins, General Sales Mgr
Dino Conard, Programming Director
Kevin Klein, Senior Vice President of Sales

Tuscaloosa

WACT
09-01-1958; 1420 kHz AM; *Hrs Open:* 24; 5 kw-D, ND1; 0.108 kw-N, ND1; N33 10 30 W87 33 18
3900 11th Ave. S., Tuscaloosa, AL 35401 US
(205) 344-4589; *Fax:* (205) 366-9774
www.969myfm.com
License: Tuscaloosa, AL held by Capstar TX LLC
Group Owner: iHeartMedia; (acq 8-30-2000; grpsl)
Arbitron Metro Market: Tuscaloosa, AL; *Format:* Adult Contemp
Todd Robbins, Senior Vice President of Programming
Jackie Toye, Senior Vice President of Sales
Tom Canterbury, Promotions Director
Justin Barnett, Digital Manager

WJRD
10-10-1936; 1150 kHz AM; *Hrs Open:* 24; 20 kw-D, 1 kw-N, DA-N; N33 15 02 W87 36 35
Box 70937, Tuscaloosa, AL 23510
(205) 345-9573; *Fax:* (205) 366-9480
License: Tuscaloosa, Tuscaloosa County, AL held by JRD Inc.
Nat'l Network: ABC
Population Served: 100,000; *Arbitron Metro Market:* Tuscaloosa, AL; *Target Audience:* Adults 35 plus.
Jimmy Shaw, President

WTBC
12-23-1946; 1230 kHz AM; *Hrs Open:* 24
Mailing Address: P.O. Box 2000, Tuscaloosa, AL 35404 US
Second Address: 2110 McFarland Blvd. E., Suite C, Tuscaloosa, AL 35404
(205) 758-5523,(205) 732-9822; *Fax:* (205) 752-9696
www.wtbc1230.com
License: Tuscaloosa, AL held by John Sisty Enterprises Inc.
Nat'l Network: ABC; ESPN Radio *Regional Reps:* Alabama Net.
Arbitron Metro Market: Tuscaloosa, AL; *Format:* News, News/Talk, 84, Talk *Special Programming:* Relg 3 hrs wkly; *Hrs. of News Programming:* News progmg 3 hrs wkly; *Target Audience:* 25-54; upscale, affluent *Adv.Rates:* 28; 30; 28; 10
John Sisty, President/CEO
Brad Whittington, Operations Dir
Tara Hughes, General Sales Mgr

WTSK
02-01-1958; 790 kHz AM; 5 kw-D, 36 w-N; N33 11 17 W87 35 23
142 Skyland Blvd., Tuscaloosa, AL 35405
(205) 345-7200; *Fax:* (205) 349-1715
790wtsk.com
Todd.Livingston@townsquaremedia.com
License: Tuscaloosa, Tuscaloosa County, AL
Group Owner: Townsquare Media; (acq 7-31-2012; grpsl).
Population Served: 91,605; *Arbitron Metro Market:* Tuscaloosa, AL; *Target Audience:* 35 plus.
Todd Livingston, General Manager
Benjamin George, Programming Director
Tammy Boyd, Sales Director

*WUAL-FM
01-04-1982; 91.5 MHz FM; *Hrs Open:* 24; 100 kw; 518 ft.; N33 5 40 W87 24 47
P.O. Box 870370, Tuscaloosa, AL 35487 US
(205) 348-6644; *Fax:* (205) 348-6648
apr.org
aprnews@apr.org
License: Tuscaloosa, Tuscaloosa County, AL held by Board of Trustees of the University of Alabama.
Nat'l Network: PRI; NPR *Regional Reps:* Alabama Net.
Arbitron Metro Market: Tuscaloosa, AL; *Format:* Jazz, News, 62, Talk *Special Programming:* Folk 5 hrs, new age 20 hrs wkly; *Hrs. of News Programming:* news progmg 5 hrs wkly; *No. News Employees:* 3 *TargetAudience:* 35 plus.
Brian Poellnitz, Operations Manager & Fill-In Host
Elizabeth Brock, General Manager
Pat Duggins, News Director
Kathy Henslee, Development Director
David Duff, Music Director
Eva Lynch, Program Assistant

*WVUA-FM
90.7 MHz FM; 220 w; 56 meters; 33 12'34 N 87 32'56 W
P.O. Box 870170, Tuscaloosa, AL 35487-0170 US
(205) 348-6061; *Fax:* (205) 348-0375
wvuafm.ua.edu
stationmgr@wvuafm.ua.edu
License: Tuscaloosa, AL held by University of Alabama.
Arbitron Metro Market: Tuscaloosa, AL; *Format:* Alternative, Variety/Diverse; *Target Audience:* 18-25; high school & college students
Terry Siggers, General Manager
Ben Lankford, Station Manager
Gabrielle France, Music Director
Tina Turner, Digital Media Director
Cameron Johnson, Production Director

WMXB
12-10-1951; 1280 kHz AM; 5 kw-D, 500 w-N, DA-N; N33 13 07 W87 34 05
601 Greensboro Ave., Suite 507, Tuscaloosa, AL 35407
(205) 345-4787; *Fax:* (205) 345-4790
jwlawson@bellsouth.net
License: Tuscaloosa, Tuscaloosa County, AL held by Lawson of Tuscaloosa Inc.
Nat'l Network: Westwood One
Population Served: 75,000; *Arbitron Metro Market:* Tuscaloosa, AL *Special Programming:* Jazz 2 hrs wkly; *Target Audience:* 24-54; mature business audience
Jim Lawson, President
Mildred Porter, Operations Dir

*WMFT
06-06-2005; 88.9 MHz FM; *Hrs Open:* 24; 100 kW; 522 ft.; N33 20 19 W87 21 32 *Rebroadcasts:* Rebroadcasts WMBV(FM) Dixon Mills
5710 Watermelon Rd, Suite 316, Northport, AL 35473 USA
(205) 758-7900; *Fax:* (205) 758-0059
www.moodyradiosouth.fm
License: Tuscaloosa, Tuscaloosa County, AL held by The Moody Bible Institute of Chicago
Group Owner: Moody Radio
Nat'l Network: Moody; *Wire Services:* AP
Arbitron Metro Market: Tuscaloosa, AL; *Format:* Christian; *Hrs. of News Programming:* News progmg 6 hrs wkly; *Target Audience:* 35-54.

Tuscumbia

WVNA
04-05-1955; 1590 kHz AM; *Hrs Open:* 24; 5 kw-D, DAN; 1 kw-N, DAN; N34 45 24 W87 41 10
509 North Main Street, Tuscumbia, AL 35674 US
(256) 383-25275
License: Tuscumbia, AL held by Urban Radio Licenses LLC.
Group Owner: Urban Radio Licenses LLC; (acq 5-13-2005; grpsl).
Nat'l Network: CBS
Arbitron Metro Market: Tuscumbia, AL; *Format:* News, News/Talk, 84, Talk *Special Programming:* News; *Hrs. of News Programming:* news progmg 60 hrs wkly; *No. News Employees:* 3; *Target Audience:* 25-64.
Kevin Wagner, CEO
Derrick Robinson, Director of Sales
T.C. Kincaid, Programming Director
Donna Johnson, Business Manager

WZZA
04-17-1960; 1410 kHz AM; *Hrs Open:* 24; 0.5 kw-D, ND1; 0.051 kw-N, ND1; N34 42 29 W87 41 35
1570 Woodmont Drive, Tuscumbia, AL 35674 US
(256) 381-1862; *Fax:* (256) 381-6006
www.WZZARadio.com
ToriBailey@WZZARadio.com
License: Tuscumbia, AL held by Muscle Shoals Broadcasting
Nat'l Network: American Urban; *Wire Services:* Bloomberg Financial
Arbitron Metro Market: Tuscumbia, AL; *Format:* Black, Blues, 44, Jazz; *Hrs. of News Programming:* news-talk progmg 15 hrs wkly; *No. News Employees:* 3; *Target Audience:* Black; *Adv. Rates:* 20.00; 15.00; 15.00;12.50
Tori Bailey, CEO
Dorothy Owens, Operations Dir
Leonard Skipworth, Sales Manager
Darryl Luster, Programming Director
Tonyia Carter, News Director / Gospel Music Director
Odessa Bailey, CFO
LaFredia Thompson, Public ServiceDirector
Darryl Luster, Music Director
Dorothy Owens, Traffic Manager

Tuskegee

WACQ
07-01-1952; 580 kHz AM; 0.5 kw-D, ND1; 0.139 kw-N, ND1; N32 22 36 W85 39 28
320 Barnett Blvd., Tallassee, AL 36078 US
(334) 283-6888
www.wacqradio.com
wacqradio@elmore.rr.com
License: Tuskegee, Macon County, AL held by Tiger Communications Inc.
Group Owner: Tiger Communications Inc.; (acq 4-6-2006; $350,000 with WQSI(FM) Union Springs)
Population Served: 4,852; *Arbitron Metro Market:* Auburn, AL; *Format:* Contemporary Hits/Top 40; *Target Audience:* adults 25+.
Fred Randall Hughey, General Manager
Debra Hughey, Programming Director
Terry Harper, Chief Engineer

WQSI
07-12-1975; 95.9 MHz FM; 4.3 kw; 377 ft.; N32 28 17 W85 34 28
320 Barnett Blvd., Tallassee, AL 36078
(334) 887-9999; *Fax:* (334) 826-9599
License: Tuskegee, Macon County, AL held by New World Communications Inc.
Arbitron Metro Market: Montgomery, AL; *Format:* Talk; *Target Audience:* 18-34.; *Adv. Rates:* 27; 20; 25; 18
Brooke Myers, General Manager

Union Springs

WTGZ
10-15-1975; 93.9 MHz FM; *Hrs Open:* 24; 12.5 kw; 469 ft.; N32 19 04 W85 40 16
2514 S. College St., Suite 104, Auburn, AL 36832
(334) 887-9999
www.thetiger.fm
License: Union Springs, Bullock County, AL held by Tiger Communications Inc.
Group Owner: Tiger Communications Inc.; (acq 4-6-2006; $350,000 with WBIL(AM) Tuskegee)
Regional Network: Alabama Radio Net.
Population Served: 620,000; *Arbitron Metro Market:* Auburn, AL; *Format:* Rock/AOR; *Hrs. of News Programming:* News progmg 15 wkly; *Target Audience:* 25-54; 40+ boomers, active, affluent southerners *Adv. Rates:* 18; 18; 18; 12
Brooke Myers, General Manager
Stacey Linn, Director of Sales

Valley

WRLD
05-17-1993; 95.3 MHz FM; *Hrs Open:* 24; 25 kw; 253 ft.; N32 44 7 W85 8 55
1820 Wynnton Rd., Columbus, GA 31904 US
(706) 327-1217; *Fax:* (706) 596-4600
www.boomer953.com
License: Valley, Chambers County, AL held by PMB Broadcasting LLC.
Group Owner: PMB Broadcasting LLC; (acq 10-1-2008; grpsl)
Arbitron Metro Market: Columbus, GA; *Format:* Oldies; *Target Audience:* 35 plus.
Dave Arwood, Operations Manager
Helen Neal, Dir. of Sales

Valley Head

WQRX
02-10-1986; 870 kHz AM; *Hrs Open:* Sunrise-sunset
P.O. Box 510, Appling, GA 30802 US
(800) 926-4669
www.gnnradio.org
License: Valley Head, AL held by Barinowski Investment Company
Group Owner: Good News Network; (acq 10-13-99).
Target Audience: All Sp

Vernon

WJEC
04-01-1991; 106.5 MHz FM; *Hrs Open:* 24; 6 kw; 328 ft.; N33 51 15 W88 1 55
P.O. Box 630, Vernon, AL 35592 US
(205) 695-9191; *Fax:* (205) 695-9131
www.wjec1065.com
sales@wjec1065.com
License: Vernon, Lamar County, AL
Format: Gospel; *Adv. Rates:* 5; 5; 5; 5
R. William Davis, CEO/Program Director
Curt Smith, Station Manager
Glenn Crawford, Vice-President
Eric Otts, Disc Jockey
Randy Wright, Disc Jockey
Greg Fields, Disc Jockey
Wayne Barnes, Sales
Teresa Cantrell, Sales

WVSA
07-04-1966; 1380 kHz AM; 5 kw-D, ND1; 0.039 kw-N, ND1; N33 47 45 W88 7 3
P.O. Box 630, Vernon, AL 35592 US
(205) 695-9191; *Fax:* (205) 695-9131
www.wvsa1380.com
info@wjec1065.com

License: Vernon, AL held by Lamar County Broadcasting Co. Inc.
Arbitron Metro Market: Vernon, AL; *Format:* Sports; *Adv. Rates:* 3.50; 3.50; 3.50
R. William Davis, CEO/Programming Director
Curtis Smith, Station Manager
Kim Fowlkes, Sales
Glenn Crawford, Vice President
Teresa Cantrell, Sales

Warrior

WBHK
04-22-1992; 98.7 MHz FM; 39 kw; 1339 ft.; N33 29 4 W86 48 25
2700 Corporate Drive, Birmingham, AL 35242 US
(205) 322-2987; *Fax:* (205) 322-2390
www.987kiss.com
david.dubose@coxradio.com
License: Warrior, Jefferson County, AL held by SM-WBHK LLC
Group Owner: SummitMedia LLC
Nat'l Reps: Christal; *Wire Services:* Metro Weather Service Inc.
Arbitron Metro Market: Birmingham, AL; *Format:* Black, Blues; *Hrs. of News Programming:* news progmg 5 hrs wkly; *No. News Employees:* 2; *Target Audience:* 25-54; general; *Adv. Rates:* 400; 250; 250; 125
Kori White, Operations Dir
David DuBose, General Manager
Paul Bankston, General Sales Mgr
Darryl Johnson, Programming Director
Kori White, Promotions Manager
Reginald Green, News Director
Tom Scott, Chief Engineer
ChrisColeman, Music Director

Waverly

*WELL-FM
03-01-1990; 88.7 MHz FM; *Hrs Open:* 24; 60 kw vert; 423 ft.; N32 44 11 W85 29 54
P.O. Box 2208, Auburn, AL 36831 US
(334) 705-8004; *Fax:* (334) 705-8006
www.praise887.com/
cassiekeyes@hotmail.com
License: Waverly, Tallapoosa County, AL held by Alabama Christian Radio Inc.
Nat'l Network: USA
Arbitron Metro Market: Waverly, AL.; *Format:* Christian; *No. News Employees:* 1; *Target Audience:* 24 plus.
Jimmy Jarrell, President
Cassie Keyes, General Manager
Joe May, Programming Director

WGZZ
07-23-1989; 94.3 MHz FM; 4.2 kw; 394 ft.; N32 44 10.5 W85 29 54.2
Mailing Address: P.O. Box 950, Auburn, AL 36831 US
Second Address: 197 East University Drive, Auburn, AL 36830
(334) 826-2929; *Fax:* (334) 826-9151
www.wingsfm.com
hubbard@aunetwork.com
License: Waverly, Tallapoosa County, AL held by Auburn Network Inc.
Arbitron Metro Market: Waverly, AL; *Format:* Country *Special Programming:* Gospel 3 hrs wkly; *Target Audience:* 18-55.
Mike Hubbard, President/CEO
Al Mason, General Manager/VP Programming & Production
Chris Hines, Senior Vice-President
Tracy Ledbetter, Office Manager
Ann Bergman, Director of Marketing
Leah Sherriff, Account Executive
RichPerkins, Traffic Manager/Radio Host

Wetumpka

WRBZ
10-02-1954; 1250 kHz AM; *Hrs Open:* 24 hours; 5 kw-D, 80 w-N; N32 29 06 W86 12 25 *Rebroadcasts:* 95.7 FM
2821 U.S. Hwy. 231, Wetumpka, AL 36092
(334) 512-1250; *Fax:* (334) 567-7971
License: Wetumpka, Elmore County, AL held by J&W L.L.C.
Population Served: 450,000; *Arbitron Metro Market:* Montgomery, AL *Special Programming:* HIspanic; *Hrs. of News Programming:* 10; *Target Audience:* 12-100.; *Adv. Rates:* 22; 22; 22; 18
Johnny Roland, President
Pat Sullivan, General Manager

WJWZ
01-01-1998; 97.9 MHz FM; 3.7 kw; 303 ft.; N32 26 50 W86 12 37
4101-A Wall Street, Montgomery, AL 36121 US
(334) 244-0961; *Fax:* (334) 279-9563
License: Wetumpka, Elmore County, AL held by Bluewater Broadcasting Co. LLC
Arbitron Metro Market: Montgomery, AL; *Format:* Urban Contemporary
Rick Peters, President
Terry Barber, General Manager
Marvin Nugent, Programming Director
Susan Ashworth, Promotions Manager
Mary Brazell, Traffic Director
Jay Scott, Production Director/Vice President/Sales

Winfield

WKXM
08-23-1965; 1300 kHz AM; 5 kw-D, ND1; 0.03 kw-N, ND1; N33 55 52 W87 48 36
Mailing Address: PO Box 608, Winfield, AL 35594 US
Second Address: 655 Fairview Rd., Winfield, AL 35594
(205) 487-3261; *Fax:* (205) 487-6991
wkxm@dlis.net
License: Winfield, AL held by Ad-Media Management Corp.
Nat'l Network: Westwood One; ESPN Radio; NBC Radio;
Regional Network: Alabama Radio Net.
Format: Sports, Talk; *Target Audience:* General.; *Adv. Rates:* 9; 7; 9; 7
Maxine Harper, President/General Manager
Teresa Benton, Operations Dir
Doug Threadgill, News Director
Olen Booth, Engineering Dir

WKXM-FM
01-01-1991; 97.7 MHz FM; *Hrs Open:* 24; 3.9 kw; 404 ft.; N34 1 53 W87 48 6
Mailing Address: PO Box 608, Winfield, AL 35594 US
Second Address: 655 Fairview Rd., Winfield, AL 35594
(205) 487-3261; *Fax:* (205) 487-6991
License: Winfield, Marion County, AL
Nat'l Network: ABC
Format: Oldies; *Target Audience:* General.; *Adv. Rates:* 10; 8; 10; 8
Maxine Harper, President/General Manager
Teresa Benton, Operations Director/Traffic Manager

York

WSLY
09-01-1976; 104.9 MHz FM; *Hrs Open:* 24; 50 kw; 492 ft.; N32 16 54 W88 15 23
11474 Highway 11 North, York, AL 36925 US
(205) 392-5234; *Fax:* (203) 392-5536
www.espn1049.com
License: York, Sumter County, AL held by Sarah P. Grant.
Nat'l Network: Fox Sports
Format: Sports; *Target Audience:* 18-54; male & female
Sarah P. Grant, President

WYLS
11-01-1970; 670 kHz AM; *Hrs Open:* 7 AM-4:30 PM; 4.8 kw-D, NDD; N32 31 24 W88 15 28
11474 Us Hwy 11, York, AL 36925 US
(205) 392-5234; *Fax:* (205) 392-5536
License: York, AL held by Grantell Broadcasting Co.
Arbitron Metro Market: York, AL; *Format:* Gospel; *Target Audience:* 25-54+.
Sarah P. Grant, President

Alaska

Akiachak

*KHKY
01-01-2007; 92.7 MHz FM; 0.05 kw vert; 92 ft.; N60 54 35.6 W161 25 56.6
US
(907) 825-3600; *Fax:* (907) 825-3655
www.yupiit.org
License: Akiachak, Bethel County, AK held by Yupiit School District.
Arbitron Metro Market: Akiachak, AK; *Format:* Christian
Trevor Snyder, General Manager

Anchorage

KAFC
04-04-1999; 93.7 MHz FM; 27 kw; 663 ft.; N61 4 2 W149 44 36
Mailing Address: 2709 Boniface Pkway, Anchorage, AK 99504 US
Second Address: P.O. Box 210389, Anchorage, AK 99504
(907) 222-4826
www.kafc.org
License: Anchorage, Anchorage County, AK held by Christian Broadcasting Inc.
Group Owner: Christian Broadcasting
Arbitron Metro Market: Anchorage, AK; *Format:* Christian

KOAN
05-10-1975; 1080 kHz AM; 10 kw-U, ND1; N61 7 12 W149 53 43
3601 C Street, Suite 290, Anchorage, AK 99503 US
(907) 522-1018; *Fax:* (907) 522-1027
www.1080koan.com
License: Anchorage, AK held by Falcon Broadcasting LLC
Arbitron Metro Market: Anchorage, AK; *Format:* Talk; *Target Audience:* 25 plus.
Tetyana Savvina, Manager
Kathy Phillips, Programming Director

KASH-FM
12-01-1985; 107.5 MHz FM; *Hrs Open:* 24; 100 kw; 981 ft.; N61 20 11 W149 30 48
800 E. Dimond Blvd., Suite 3-370, Anchorage, AK 99515 US
(907) 522-1515; *Fax:* (907) 743-5184
www.kashcountry1075.com
anchorage@iheartmedia.com
License: Anchorage, Anchorage County, AK held by Capstar TX LLC
Group Owner: iHeartMedia; (acq 8-30-00; grpsl).
Arbitron Metro Market: Anchorage, AK; *Format:* Country; *Target Audience:* 25-54.
Andy Lohman, President/General Manager
Terri Bradley, Sales Manager
Matt Courtice, Digital Content Director

*KATB
06-01-1985; 89.3 MHz FM; *Hrs Open:* 24; 4.9 kw; 663 ft.; N61 4 2 W149 44 36
Mailing Address: 2709 Boniface Pkway, Anchorage, AK 99504 US
Second Address: P.O. Box 210389, Anchorage, AK 99504
(907) 222-4826
www.katb.org
License: Anchorage, Anchorage County, AK held by Christian Broadcasting Inc.
Group Owner: Christian Broadcasting Inc
Nat'l Network: Moody
Arbitron Metro Market: Anchorage, AK; *Format:* Religious; *Hrs. of News Programming:* News progmg 5 hrs wkly; *Target Audience:* 25-49; women

KBFX
10-01-1978; 100.5 MHz FM; 25 kw; 174 ft.; N61 11 52 W149 52 31
800 E. Dimond Blvd., Suite 3-370, Anchorage, AK 99515 US
(907) 522-1515; *Fax:* (907) 743-5184
www.1005thefox.com
anchorage@iheartmedia.com
License: Anchorage, Anchorage County, AK held by Capstar TX LLC
Group Owner: iHeartMedia; (acq 8-7-00; grpsl).
Arbitron Metro Market: Anchorage, AK; *Format:* Classic Rock
Andy Lohman, General Manager
Terri Bradley, Sales Manager
Joe Albrecht, Programming Director
Matt Courtice, Digital Content Director

KBRJ
11-01-1966; 104.1 MHz FM; *Hrs Open:* 24; 55 kw; 62 ft.; N61 7 12 W149 53 43
301 Arctic Slope Ave., Suite 200, Anchorage, AK 99518 US
(907) 344-9622; *Fax:* (907) 349-3299
www.kbrj.com
alaskawins@kbrj.com
License: Anchorage, Anchorage County, AK held by Alpha Media Licensee LLC
Group Owner: Alpha Media LLC; (acq 9-2-2015; grpsl).
Arbitron Metro Market: Anchorage, AK; *Format:* Country; *Target Audience:* 18-49.
Patrick Wright, Senior Marketing Manager
Carla Wyrick, General Sales Mgr

KBYR
01-01-1948; 700 kHz AM; *Hrs Open:* 24; 10 kw-U, ND1; N61 12 25 W149 55 20
833 Gambell Street, Anchorage, AK 99501 US
(907) 344-4045; *Fax:* (907) 522-6053
www.kbyr.com
License: Anchorage, AK held by Ohama Media Group LLC
Nat'l Network: ABC
Arbitron Metro Market: Anchorage, AK; *Format:* News, News/Talk, 86; *No. News Employees:* 1; *Target Audience:* 25-54.
Bill Sigma, General Manager/Vice President/COO
Debbie Rinckey, General Sales Mgr
Tom Oakes, Programming & Operations Manager/Vice President

Madisyn Vrem, Promotions Director
Gerritt Bode, Chief Engineer
Kristen Bolt, SalesDirector

KEAG
01-01-1987; 97.3 MHz FM; *Hrs Open:* 24; 55 kw; 62 ft.; N61 7 12 W149 53 43
301 Arctic Slope Ave., Suite 200, Anchorage, AK 99518 US
(907) 344-9622; *Fax:* (907) 349-3299
www.kool973.com
License: Anchorage, Anchorage County, AK held by Alpha Media Licensee LLC
Group Owner: Alpha Media LLC; (acq 9-2-2015; grpsl).
Arbitron Metro Market: Anchorage, AK; *Format:* Oldies; *Hrs. of News Programming:* news progmg 3 hrs wkly; *No. News Employees:* 1; *Target Audience:* 35-49.
Patrick Wright, Senior Marketing Manager
Carla Wyrick, General Sales Mgr
Dave Stroh, Programming Director

KENI
07-15-1967; 650 kHz AM; *Hrs Open:* 24; 50 kw-U, ND1; N61 9 58 W149 49 34
800 E. Dimond Blvd., Suite 3-370, Anchorage, AK 99515 US
(907) 522-1515; *Fax:* (907) 743-5186
www.650keni.com
License: Anchorage, AK held by Capstar TX LLC
Group Owner: iHeartMedia; (acq 8-30-2000; grpsl)
Nat'l Reps: Christal
Arbitron Metro Market: Anchorage, AK; *Format:* News, News/Talk, 86; *Hrs. of News Programming:* news progmg 5 hrs wkly; *No. News Employees:* 1; *Target Audience:* 25-64.
Andy Lohman, General Manager
Terri Bradley, Sales Manager
Mark Murphy, Programming Director
Matt Courtice, Digital Content Director

KFAT
04-01-1997; 92.9 MHz FM; *Hrs Open:* 24; 10 kw; 886 ft.; N61 20 11 W149 30 48
833 Gambell Avenue, Suite 200, Anchorage, AK 99518 US
(907) 344-4045
www.kfat929.com
License: Anchorage, Anchorage County, AK
Group Owner: Ohana Media Group LLC; (acq 7-30-99)
Nat'l Network: ABC
Arbitron Metro Market: Anchorage, AK *TV Affiliate:* KYES(TV) affil.; *Format:* Christian; *Target Audience:* 18-34; adults
Bill Sigmar, General Manager/Vice President/COO
Kirsten Bolt, Sales Director
Tom Oakes, Programming Director/Operations Manager/VP
Madisyn Vrem, Promotions Director
Gerrit Bode, Chief Engineer

KFQD
01-01-1924; 750 kHz AM; 50 kw-D, ND2; 50 kw-N, ND2; N61 20 18 W150 2 3
301 Arctic Slope Ave., Suite 200, Anchorage, AK 99518 US
(907) 344-9622; *Fax:* (907) 349-3299
www.kfqd.com
news@kfqd.com
License: Anchorage, AK held by Alpha Media Licensee LLC
Group Owner: Alpha Media LLC; (acq 9-2-2015; grpsl).
Nat'l Reps: Katz Radio
Arbitron Metro Market: Anchorage, AK *TV Affiliate:* KTUU; *Format:* News, News/Talk, 86 *Special Programming:* Red eye radio 24 hrs wkly; *Hrs. of News Programming:* News progmg 140 hrs wkly; *Target Audience:* 35plus; higher income, upper demo
Patrick Wright, Senior Marketing Manager
Kim Shuck, Sales Manager
Joe Campbell, Programming Director

KGOT
09-15-1975; 101.3 MHz FM; *Hrs Open:* 24; 26 kw; -66 ft.; N61 9 58 W149 49 34
800 E. Dimond Blvd., Suite 3-370, Anchorage, AK 99515 US
(907) 522-1515; *Fax:* (907) 743-5186
www.kgot.com
License: Anchorage, AK held by Capstar TX LLC
Group Owner: iHeartMedia
Arbitron Metro Market: Anchorage, AK; *Format:* Contemporary Hits/Top 40; *Hrs. of News Programming:* News progmg 2 hrs wkly; *Target Audience:* 12-44.
Andy Lohman, General Manager
Terri Bradley, Sales Manager
Casey Bieber, Programming Director
Matt Courtice, Digital Content Director

KHAR
01-07-1961; 590 kHz AM; *Hrs Open:* 24; 5 kw-U, ND1; N61 7 12 W149 53 43
301 Arctic Slope Ave., Suite 200, Anchorage, AK 99518 US
(907) 344-9622; *Fax:* (907) 349-3299
www.khar590.com
License: Anchorage, AK held by Alpha Media Licensee LLC
Group Owner: Alpha Media LLC; (acq 9-2-2015; grpsl).
Nat'l Network: CBS Sports Radio; *Nat'l Reps:* International Media
Arbitron Metro Market: Anchorage, AK; *Format:* Sports *Special Programming:* Religious 20 hrs wkly; *Hrs. of News Programming:* News progmg 3 hrs wkly; *Target Audience:* 35 plus; white collar, professional,upper-income demographics
Patrick Wright, Senior Marketing Manager
Carla Wyrick, General Sales Mgr
Joe Campbell, Programming Director

KDBZ
02-01-1973; 102.1 MHz FM; 23 kw; 82 ft.; N61 7 12 W149 53 43
83 Gambell Street, Anchorage, AK 99501 US
(907) 344-4045; *Fax:* (907) 522-6053
License: Anchorage, Anchorage County, AK
Group Owner: Ohana Media Group LLC; acq 8-12-99; $1.3 million).
Wire Services: AP
Arbitron Metro Market: Anchorage, AK; *Format:* Adult Contemp; *Target Audience:* 18-44; women
Tom Oakes, Operations Dir
Bill Sigmar, General Manager/Vice President/COO
Kirsten Bolt, Sales Director
Gerrit Bode, Chief Engineer

KLEF
09-16-1988; 98.1 MHz FM; *Hrs Open:* 24; 25 kw; Ant -85 ft; N61 11 17 W149 52 57
165 E. 56th Ave., Ste. 10, Anchorage, AK 99503
(907) 562-4434; *Fax:* (907) 562-4433
www.klef.com
klef@klef.com
License: Anchorage, Anchorage County, AK held by Chinook Concert Broadcasters Inc.
Regional Reps: None
Population Served: 300,000; *Arbitron Metro Market:* Anchorage, AK *Special Programming:* Children two hr wkly; *Target Audience:* 25-64; highly educated, affluent adults; *Adv. Rates:* Variable
Rick Goodfellow, President
Rick Goodfellow, Operations Dir
Rick Goodfellow, General Manager
Rick Goodfellow, Station Manager
Rick Goodfellow, General Sales Mgr
Rick Goodfellow, Programming Director
Rick Goodfellow, PromotionsManager
Ron Zastrow, Chief Engineer
Evelyn Burdick, Traffic Director

KMXS
09-01-1987; 103.1 MHz FM; *Hrs Open:* 24; 100 kw; 105 ft.; N61 11 33 W149 54 1
301 Arctic Slope Ave., Suite 200, Anchorage, AK 99518 US
(907) 344-9622; *Fax:* (907) 349-3299
www.kmxs.com
winner@kmxs.com
License: Anchorage, Anchorage County, AK held by Alpha Media Licensee LLC
Group Owner: Alpha Media LLC; (acq 9-2-2015; grpsl).
Nat'l Reps: McGavren Guild
Arbitron Metro Market: Anchorage, AK; *Format:* Adult Contemp; *Hrs. of News Programming:* news progmg 5 hrs wkly; *No. News Employees:* 1; *Target Audience:* 25-44; female listeners
Patrick Wright, Senior Marketing Manager
Kim Shuck, Sales Manager
Devan Mitchell, Programming Director

***KNBA**
09-01-1996; 90.3 MHz FM; *Hrs Open:* 24; 100 kw; 640 ft.; N61 25 22 W149 52 20
810 E. 9th Avenue, Anchorage, AK 99501 US
(907) 793-3500; *Fax:* (907) 793-3536
www.knba.org
feedback@knba.org
License: Anchorage, Anchorage County, AK held by Koahnic Broadcast Corp.
Arbitron Metro Market: Anchorage, AK; *Format:* Variety/Diverse; *Hrs. of News Programming:* news progmg 8 hrs wkly; *No. News Employees:* 3; *Target Audience:* 20-50; well off, public radio listeners *Adv. Rates:* 25; 25; 25; 25.
Jaclyn Sallee, President/Chief Executive Officer
Loren Dixon, Programming Director
Larry Cleland, Underwriting Director

KMVN
09-15-1960; 105.7 MHz FM; *Hrs Open:* 24; 51 kW; Ant 1,069 ft; N61 20 11 W149 30 48
4700 Business Park Blvd., Building E, Suite 44-A, Anchorage, AK 99503 USA
(907) 522-1018; *Fax:* (907) 522-1027
www.movin1057.com
License: Anchorage, Anchorage County, AK held by Alaska Integrated Media Inc.
Group Owner: Alaska Integrated Media
Nat'l Reps: Interep
Population Served: 15,893; *Arbitron Metro Market:* Anchorage, AK; *Format:* Urban Contemporary; *Hrs. of News Programming:* news progmg 9 hrs wkly; *No. News Employees:* 1; *Target Audience:* 25-54 plus. *Adv.Rates:* 30; 28; 32; 18

***KRUA**
02-14-1992; 88.1 MHz FM; *Hrs Open:* 24; 0.155 kw; 833 ft.; N61 20 11 W149 30 48
P. O. Box 755300, Fairbanks, AK 99775 US
(907) 786-6800; *Fax:* (907) 786-6806
aykrua1@uaa.alaska.edu
License: Anchorage, Anchorage County, AK held by University of Alaska-Anchorage.
Arbitron Metro Market: Anchorage, AK; *Format:* Alternative
Special Programming: Var/div music 20 hrs, sports one hr wklyVar/div music 20 hrs, American Indian 3 hrs, sports one hr wkly; *Hrs. of News Programming:* newsprogmg 10 hrs wkly; *No. News Employees:* 4; *Target Audience:* General; college community/div
Audri Pleas, Station Manager

***KSKA**
08-15-1978; 91.1 MHz FM; *Hrs Open:* 24; 100 kw; 617 ft.; N61 25 22 W149 52 20
3877 University Drive, Anchorage, AK 99508 US
(907) 550-8400; *Fax:* (907) 550-8401(907) 550-8403
www.kska.org
info@ksml.com
License: Anchorage, Anchorage County, AK held by Alaska Public Telecommunications Inc.
Nat'l Network: NPR; PRI; *Regional Network:* Alaska Pub.
Arbitron Metro Market: Anchorage, AK; *Format:* News; *Hrs. of News Programming:* news progmg 70 hrs wkly; *No. News Employees:* 2; *Target Audience:* 24 plus; professionals
Steve Lindbeck, CEO/GM
Torrie Allen, Chief Marketing & Development Officer
Slavik Boyechko, Digital Media Director
Bede Trantina, Programming Director
Lori Townsend, News Director
Bernie Washington, Chief Financial Officer

KTZN
05-02-1948; 550 kHz AM
800 Dimond Boulevard, Suite 3-370, Anchorage, AK 99515 US
(907) 522-1515; *Fax:* (907) 743-5184
www.550thezone.com
License: Anchorage, AK held by Capstar TX LLC
Group Owner: iHeartMedia; (acq 8-30-00; grpsl).
Nat'l Reps: D & R Radio
Arbitron Metro Market: Anchorage, AK; *Format:* Sports; *Target Audience:* 25-54.
Andy Lohman, General Manager
Terri Bradley, Sales Manager
Mark Murphy, Programming Director
Matt Courtice, Digital Content Director

KWHL
09-18-1982; 106.5 MHz FM; 100 kw; 52 ft.; N61 7 14 W149 53 42
301 Arctic Slope Ave., Suite 200, Anchorage, AK 99518 US
(907) 344-9622; *Fax:* (907) 344-3299
www.kwhl.com
studio@kwhl.com
License: Anchorage, Anchorage County, AK held by Alpha Media Licensee LLC
Group Owner: Alpha Media LLC; (acq 9-2-2015; grpsl).
Arbitron Metro Market: Anchorage, AK; *Format:* Rock/AOR; *Target Audience:* 18-44; medium income adults, mostly men
Patrick Wright, Senior Marketing Manager
Kim Shuck, Sales Manager
Brad Stennett, Programming Director
Matthew Grabowy, Promotions Manager

KYMG
01-01-1989; 98.9 MHz FM; *Hrs Open:* 24; 100 kw; -151 ft.; N61 9 58 W149 49 34
800 Dimond Boulevard, Suite 3-370, Anchorage, AK 99515 US
(907) 743-5239; *Fax:* (907) 743-5184
www.magic989fm.com
License: Anchorage, Anchorage County, AK held by Capstar TX LLC
Group Owner: iHeartMedia; (acq 8-30-00; grpsl).
Arbitron Metro Market: Anchorage, AK; *Format:* Adult Contemp
Special Programming: Relg one hr wkly; *Hrs. of News Programming:* news progmg 4 hrs wkly; *No. News Employees:* 1; *Target Audience:* 25-49; mostlywomen

Andy Lohman, General Manager
Terri Bradley, Sales Manager
Mark Murphy, Programming Director
Matt Courtice, Digital Content Director

***KAKL**
01-01-2004; 88.5 MHz FM; *Hrs Open:* 24; 11 kw; -82 ft.; N61 7 14 W149 53 42
5700 West Oaks Boulevard, Rocklin, CA 96765 US
(800) 525-5683; *Fax:* (916) 251-1650
www.klove.com
klove@klove.com
License: Anchorage, Anchorage County, AK held by Educational Media Foundation.
Group Owner: EMF Broadcasting
Nat'l Network: K-Love
Arbitron Metro Market: Anchorage, AK; *Format:* Christian; *No. News Employees:* 3; *Target Audience:* 25-44; Judeo Chrisitan, female
Mike Novak, President and CEO
David Pierce, Programming Director
Ed Lenane, News Director
Sam Wallington, Engineering Dir
Tracy Butler, Traffic Manager
Laura Daniels, News Reporter
Tim Luttrell, News Reporter
Kenny NobleCortes, News Reporter
Darren Vinson, News Reporter

***KAUG**
01-01-2007; 89.9 MHz FM; 0.004 kw horiz; 98 ft.; N61 24 33 W149 25 15
5530 East Northern Lights Boulevard, Anchorage, AK 99504-3135 US
(907) 742-4000; *Fax:* (907) 742-3545
License: Anchorage, Anchorage County, AK held by Anchorage School District.
Arbitron Metro Market: Anchorage, AK; *Format:* Variety/Diverse
Jim Browder, General Manager

KOAN
1080 kHz AM; 10 kW; N61 7 12 W149 53 43
4700 Business Park Blvd., Building E, Suite 44-A, Anchorage, AK 99503 USA
(907) 522-1018; *Fax:* (907) 522-1027
www.1080koan.com
License: Anchorage, Anchorage County, AK held by Alaska Integrated Media Inc.
Group Owner: Alaska Integrated Media
Arbitron Metro Market: Anchorage; *Format:* Talk

Barrow

***KBRW**
12-22-1975; 680 kHz AM; *Hrs Open:* 24; 10 kw-D, ND1; 10 kw-N, ND1; N71 15 24 W156 31 32
P.O. Box 109, Barrow, AK 99723 US
(907) 852-6811; *Fax:* (907) 852-2274
www.kbrw.org
info@kbrw.org
License: Barrow, AK held by Silakkuagvik Communications Inc.
Nat'l Network: PRI; NPR; *Regional Network:* Alaska Pub.
Format: Variety/Diverse *Special Programming:* Class 2 hrs, jazz 6 hrs, relg one hr, Filipino 2 h; *Hrs. of News Programming:* news progmg 24 hrs wkly; *No. News Employees:* 1; *Target Audience:* General.
Robert Sommer, Operations Dir
Jeff Seifert, General Manager
Jason Gilbert, Development Director
Isaac Tuckfield, Programming Director
Robert Thomas, News Director
Charles Laykatis, Chief Engineer
Kai Saxton, Operations Manager

***KBRW-FM**
09-01-1996; 91.9 MHz FM; *Hrs Open:* 7 AM-midnight; 0.89 kw; 72 ft.; N71 17 20 W156 45 31
P.O. Box 109, 1695 Okpik St, Barrow, AK 99723 US
(907) 852-6811; *Fax:* (907) 852-2274
License: Barrow, North Slope County, AK held by Silakkuagvik Communications Inc.
Nat'l Network: NPR; PRI; *Regional Network:* Alaska Pub.
Format: Adult Contemp, Big Band; *Hrs. of News Programming:* news progmg 80 hrs wkly; *No. News Employees:* 1; *Target Audience:* General.
Jeff Seifert, General Manager
Jason Gilbert, Development Director
Issac Tuckfield, Programming Director
Robert Thomas, News Director
Robert Sommer, Chief Engineer

Bethel

KYKD
11-01-1994; 100.1 MHz FM; *Hrs Open:* 24; 12 kw; 72 ft; N60 48 20 W161 47 14
P.O. Box 2428, Bethel, AK 99559
(907) 543-5953; *Fax:* (907) 543-5952
www.vfcm.org/kykd
kykd@vfcm.org
License: Bethel, Bethel County, AK held by Voice For Christ Ministries Inc.
Nat'l Network: Salem Radio Network; Moody
Special Programming: Christian Native; *Target Audience:* Native and Rural Alaskans; *Adv. Rates:* 20;20;20;20
Palmer Bailey, Station Manager
Derek Black, Webmaster

***KYUK**
05-13-1971; 640 kHz AM; 10 kw-U, ND1; N60 46 57 W161 53 0
Pouch 468- 640 Radio St., Bethel, AK 99559 US
(907) 543-3131; *Fax:* (907) 543-3130
www.kyuk.org
webmaster@kyuk.org
License: Bethel, AK held by Bethel Broadcasting Inc.
Nat'l Network: PRI; NPR; *Regional Network:* Alaska Pub.
Arbitron Metro Market: Bethel, AK *TV Affiliate:* *KYUK-TV affil; *Format:* Talk, Variety/Diverse *Special Programming:* Class 4 hrs, country 4 hrs wkly; *Target Audience:* General.
Shane Iverson, Operations/Programming Director
Mike Martz, General Manager
Angela Denning Barnes, News Director
Joseph Siebert, Chief Engineer

Big Lake

***KAGV**
11-01-2004; 1110 kHz AM; *Hrs Open:* 24/7
PO Box 940096, Houston, AK 99694 US
(907) 892-8820; *Fax:* (907) 892-8825
www.vfcm.org/kagv.htm
alaskaradio@vfcm.org
License: Big Lake, AK held by Voice for Christ Ministries Inc.
Nat'l Network: Salem Radio Network; Moody
Arbitron Metro Market: Big Lake, AK; *Format:* Christian, News, 62, Talk *Special Programming:* Native Alaskan 3 hrs wkly; *Hrs. of News Programming:* News progmg 20 hrs wkly; *Target Audience:* Native and Rural Alaska
Karl Thieme, Station Manager

Chevak

***KCUK**
01-01-1990; 88.1 MHz FM; 6 kw; 79 ft.; N61 31 46 W165 35 20
985 Ksd Way, Chevak, AK 99563 US
(907) 858-7015; *Fax:* (907) 858-7279
www.nv1.org/kcuk.htm
Nauliaran@yahoo.com
License: Chevak, Wade Hampton County, AK held by Kashunamiut School District.
Nat'l Network: NPR; *Regional Network:* Alaska Pub.
Arbitron Metro Market: Chevak, AK; *Format:* Variety/Diverse
Peter Tuluk, General Manager
Peter Tuluk, Station Manager

College

KTDZ
09-06-1984; 103.9 MHz FM; 2.95 kw; 823 ft.; N64 55 20 W147 42 55
819 First Avenue, Suite A, Fairbanks, AK 99701 US
(907) 451-5910; *Fax:* (907) 451-5999
www.mytedfm.com
1039koolfm@nnbradio.com
License: College, Fairbanks County, AK
Group Owner: Last Frontier Mediactive LLC; (acq 10-26-99; grpsl)
Nat'l Reps: Tacher
Arbitron Metro Market: College, AK; *Format:* Adult Contemp
Glenner Anderson, Operations Dir
Perry Walley, General Manager

Cordova

KCDV
100.9 MHz FM; 1.2 kw; -417 ft.; N60 32 20 W145 45 35
Haley Bader & Potts, 4350 N. Fairfax Dr, Arlington, VA 22203 US
(907) 424-3796; *Fax:* (907) 424-3737
License: Cordova, Valdez Cordova County, AK
Format: Adult Contemp
Raul Salvador, CFO
J.R. Lewis, President/General Manager

KLAM
05-01-1953; 1450 kHz AM; 0.25 kw-U, ND1; N60 32 20 W145 45 35
P.O. Box 60, #1 Forestry Way, Cordova, AK 99574 US
(907) 424-3796; *Fax:* (907) 424-3737
www.cordovaradio.com
License: Cordova, AK held by Bayview Communications Inc.
Nat'l Network: ABC
Arbitron Metro Market: Anchorage, AK; *Format:* Classic Rock, Country, 60; *Target Audience:* General.
J.R. Lewis, President/General Manager

Dillingham

***KDLG**
07-22-1975; 670 kHz AM; *Hrs Open:* 18; 10 kw-U, ND1; N59 2 43 W158 27 7
Box 670, Dillingham, AK 99576 US
(907) 842-5281; *Fax:* (907) 842-5645
www.kdlg.org
kdlgnews@kdlg.org
License: Dillingham, AK held by Dillingham City School District.
Nat'l Network: NPR; *Regional Network:* Alaska Pub.
Arbitron Metro Market: Dillingham, AK; *Format:* Adult Contemp, Country *Special Programming:* Yupik one hr wkly; *Hrs. of News Programming:* news progmg 20 hrs wkly; *No. News Employees:* 1
Rob Carpenter, General Manager
Jason Sear, Programming Director
Mike Mason, News Director
Larry Phares, Development Director

KRUP
08-01-1995; 99.1 MHz FM; *Hrs Open:* 24; 6 kw; 128 ft.; N59 2 31 W158 31 19
Mailing Address: P.O. Box 157, 301 Airport Road, Dillingham, AK 99576 US
Second Address: 301 Airport Rd., Dillingham, AK 99576
(907) 842-5364
License: Dillingham, Dillingham County, AK held by McCormick Broadcasting.
Format: Talk
Jackson McCormick, President

***KDLG-FM**
89.9 MHz FM; 0.25 kw; 82 ft.; N59 2 37 W158 27 47 US
(907) 842-5281; *Fax:* (907) 842-5645
www.kdlg.org
License: Dillingham, Dillingham County, AK held by Dillingham City School District.
Arbitron Metro Market: Dillingham, AK; *Format:* Religious
Rob Carpenter, General Manager
Jason Sear, Programming Director
Mike Mason, News Director
Larry Phares, Development Director

Eagle River

KVNT
1020 kHz AM; 10 kW; N61 29 7 W149 45 50
4700 Business Park Blvd., Building E, Suite 44-A, Anchorage, AK 99503 USA
(907) 522-1018; *Fax:* (907) 522-1027
www.1020kvnt.com
License: Eagle River, AK held by Alaska Integrated Media Inc.
Group Owner: Alaska Integrated Media
Format: News/Talk

Ester

KDJF
07-01-2007; 93.5 MHz FM; 20.5 kw; 1578 ft.; N64 52 45 W148 3 14
US
(907) 452-3697; *Fax:* (907) 456-3428
www.tvtv.com
chris@tvtv.com
License: Ester, Fairbanks North Star County, AK held by Tanana Valley Television Co.
Group Owner: Tanana Valley Television Co.; (acq 1-10-2008; $173,000 for CP)
Arbitron Metro Market: Ester, AK
William St. Pierre, President
Chris Fry, General Manager
Sam Oxman, News Director
Brian Virgin, Production

Fairbanks

KAKQ-FM
04-04-1981; 101.1 MHz FM; *Hrs Open:* 24; 46.2 kw; 571 ft.; N64 54 55 W147 38 52
546 9th Ave., Fairbanks, AK 99701 US
(907) 450-1000; *Fax:* (907) 450-1092
www.101magic.com
101magic@iheartmedia.com
License: Fairbanks, Fairbanks North Star County, AK held by Capstar TX LLC
Group Owner: iHeartMedia; (acq 8-30-00; grpsl).
Nat'l Network: Westwood One; *Nat'l Reps:* Christal
Arbitron Metro Market: Fairbanks, AK; *Format:* Contemporary Hits/Top 40; *Hrs. of News Programming:* news progmg one hr wkly; *No. News Employees:* 2; *Target Audience:* 25-44; working families & adults; *Adv. Rates:* 25; 18; 25; 14
Kim Williams, General Manager
Kathryn Harris, Programming Director

KCBF
01-01-1948; 820 kHz AM; *Hrs Open:* 24; 10 kw-U, ND1; N64 52 44 W147 40 6
630 West Fourth Avenue, Suite 300, Anchorage, AK 99501 US
(907) 451-5910; *Fax:* (907) 451-5999
License: Fairbanks, AK
Group Owner: Last Frontier Mediactive LLC; acq 8-12-99; grpsl).
Nat'l Network: CBS; Westwood One
Arbitron Metro Market: Fairbanks, AK; *Format:* Sports; *Hrs. of News Programming:* news progmg 4 hrs wkly; *No. News Employees:* 1; *Target Audience:* 35-54.; *Adv. Rates:* 10; 8; 10; 5
Glen Anderson, Operations Manager
Perry Walley, General Manager
Robert Smith, Programming Director

KFAR
01-01-1939; 660 kHz AM; 10 kw-U, ND1; N64 48 29 W147 29 34
1060 Aspen Street, Fairbanks, AK 99709 US
(907) 451-5910; *Fax:* (907) 451-5999
www.akradio.com
License: Fairbanks, AK
Arbitron Metro Market: Fairbanks, AK; *Format:* News, News/Talk, 86 *Special Programming:* Gospel 2 hrs wkly; *Target Audience:* 25 plus.
Glen Anderson, Operations Dir
Perry Walley, General Manager
Perry Walley, Sales Manager
Steve Floyd, Programming Director

KFBX
09-18-1972; 970 kHz AM; *Hrs Open:* 24; 10 kw-D, ND1; 10 kw-N, ND1; N64 52 48 W147 40 29
546 9th Ave., Fairbanks, AK 99701 US
(907) 450-1000; *Fax:* (907) 450-1092
www.970kfbx.com
kfbx@iheartmedia.com
License: Fairbanks, AK held by Capstar TX LLC
Group Owner: iHeartMedia; (acq 8-30-2000; grpsl)
Nat'l Reps: Christal
Arbitron Metro Market: Fairbanks, AK; *Format:* News, News/Talk, 86 *Special Programming:* The Wall Street Journal 7 hrs wkly; *Hrs. of News Programming:* news progmg 30 hrs wkly; *No. News Employees:* 1 *TargetAudience:* 35 plus; males
Kim Williams, General Manager

KIAK-FM
09-21-1983; 102.5 MHz FM; 92 kw; 571 ft.; N64 54 55 W147 38 52
546 9th Ave., Fairbanks, AK 99701 US
(907) 450-1000; *Fax:* (907) 450-1092
www.kiak.com
kiak@iheartmedia.com
License: Fairbanks, Fairbanks North Star County, AK held by Capstar TX LLC
Group Owner: iHeartMedia
Arbitron Metro Market: Fairbanks, AK; *Format:* Country; *Target Audience:* 18 plus; general; *Adv. Rates:* 35; 30; 35; 20
Kim Williams, General Manager

KKED
09-20-1962; 104.7 MHz FM; *Hrs Open:* 24; 46 kw; 571 ft.; N64 54 55 W147 38 52
546 Ninth Avenue, Fairbanks, AK 99701 US
(907) 450-1000; *Fax:* (907) 450-1092
www.1047theedge.com
License: Fairbanks, Fairbanks North Star County, AK held by Capstar TX LLC
Group Owner: iHeartMedia; (acq 8-30-00; grpsl).
Arbitron Metro Market: Anchorage, AK; *Format:* Rock/AOR
Kim Williams, Market Manager

***KSUA**
10-10-1985; 91.5 MHz FM; *Hrs Open:* 24; 3 kw; -16 ft.; N64 51 32 W147 49 41
202 Butrovich Building, Fairbanks, AK 99775 US
(907) 474-7054; *Fax:* (907) 474-6314
www.uaf.edu/ksua
fyksua@uaf.edu
License: Fairbanks, Fairbanks North Star County, AK held by The University of Alaska Board of Regents.
Arbitron Metro Market: Fairbanks, AK; *Format:* Alternative
Special Programming: Black 8 hrs, Sp 3 hrs, var/div music 19 hrs wkly; *Target Audience:* 14-35.
Brady Gross, General Manager
Matthew Harris, Programming Director

***KUAC**
01-01-1962; 89.9 MHz FM; *Hrs Open:* 24; 38 kw; 1660 ft.; N64 52 49 W148 3 8
P.O. Box 755620, Fairbanks, AK 99775 US
(907) 474-7491; *Fax:* (907) 474-5064
www.kuac.org
License: Fairbanks, Fairbanks North Star County, AK held by University of Alaska.
Nat'l Network: NPR; PRI; *Regional Network:* Alaska Pub.; *Wire Services:* AP
Arbitron Metro Market: Fairbanks, AK *TV Affiliate:* *KUAC-TV affil.; *Format:* News, News/Talk, 86, Variety/Diverse *Special Programming:* Jazz 15 hrs, folk 10 hrs, blues 4 hrs, new age 3 hrs wkly *Hrs. of NewsProgramming:* news progmg 32 hrs wkly; *No. News Employees:* 3; *Target Audience:* General.
Greg Petrowich, CEO
Matthew Schroder, Operations & Traffic Coordinator
Keith Martin, General Manager & Dir. of Engineering & Technology
Jerry Evans, Director of FM Programming & Operations
Chris Wadeson, Chief Engineer
GretchenGordon, Director of Development & Outreach

KWLF
10-31-1987; 98.1 MHz FM; 28 kw; 764 ft.; N64 55 20 W147 42 55
1060 Aspen Street, Fairbanks, AK 99709 US
(907) 451-5910; *Fax:* (907) 451-5999
www.kwolf981.com
License: Fairbanks, Fairbanks North Star County, AK
Group Owner: Last Frontier Mediactive LLC
Arbitron Metro Market: Fairbanks, AK; *Format:* Contemporary Hits/Top 40; *Target Audience:* 18 plus; general
Glen Anderson, Operations Dir
Perry Walley, General Manager
McConnell Adams, Programming Director

KXLR
07-01-1989; 95.9 MHz FM; *Hrs Open:* 24; 25 kw; -16 ft.; N64 52 38 W147 48 46
630 West Fourth Avenue, Suite 300, Anchorage, AK 99501 US
(907) 451-5910; *Fax:* (907) 451-5999
xrock959.com/
License: Fairbanks, Fairbanks North Star County, AK
Group Owner: Last Frontier Mediactive LLC
Arbitron Metro Market: Fairbanks, AK *TV Affiliate:* KTVF(TV) affil; *Format:* Classic Rock; *Target Audience:* 25-49.; *Adv. Rates:* 14; 13; 14; 10
Crys Castle, Programming Director

KYSC
01-01-2001; 96.9 MHz FM; *Hrs Open:* 24; 5.8 kw; 1608 ft.; N64 52 45 W148 3 14
P.O. Box 671003, Chugiak, AK 99567 US
(907) 452-3697; *Fax:* (907) 456-3428
www.tvtv.com
chris@tvtv.com
License: Fairbanks, Fairbanks North Star County, AK held by Tanana Valley Radio LLC
Group Owner: Tanana Valley Television Co.; (acq 9-28-2005; $700,000)
Nat'l Network: ABC
Arbitron Metro Market: Anchorage, AK *TV Affiliate:* KFXF(TV) affil; *Format:* Adult Contemp; *Adv. Rates:* 15; 11; 13; 9
Chris Fry, General Manager
Sam Oxman, News Director
Brian Virgin, Production Department Supervisor

KWDD(FM)
94.3 MHz FM; 28 kw; 233 meters; N64 55 21 W147 42 55
819 First Avenue, Suite A, Fairbanks, AK 99701-4449
(907) 451-5910; *Fax:* (907)451-5999
License: Fairbanks, North Star Borough County, AK held by Last Frontier Mediactive LLC
Group Owner: Last Frontier Mediactive LLC
Perry Walley, General Manager
Ken Vehmeier, Programming Director

Fort Yukon

***KZPA**
09-30-1993; 900 kHz AM; 5 kw-U, ND1; N66 33 24 W145 12 4
East Third Avenue, PO Box 50, Fort Yukon, AK 99740 US
(907 662-6356 OR (907) 662-8255; *Fax:* (907) 662-2915
kzparadio@hotmail.com
License: Fort Yukon, AK held by Gwandak Public Broadcasting Inc.
Arbitron Metro Market: Fort Yukon, AK; *Format:* Variety/Diverse; *Hrs. of News Programming:* News progmg 6 hrs wkly; *Target Audience:* All ages.
Loris A. Taylor, President/CEO
Vicki Thomas, Station Manager
Hans James, Programming Director

Galena

***KIYU**
07-04-1986; 910 kHz AM; *Hrs Open:* 24; 5 kw-U, ND1; N64 41 18 W156 43 29
Pob 165, Galena, AK 99741 US
(907) 656-1488; *Fax:* (907) 656-1734
www.kiyu.com
raven@kiyu.com
License: Galena, AK held by Big River Public Broadcasting Corp.
Nat'l Network: NPR; *Regional Network:* Alaska Pub.
Format: Variety/Diverse *Special Programming:* Jazz 4 hrs, Alaska native 2 hrs wkly; *Hrs. of News Programming:* news progmg 35 hrs wkly; *No. News Employees:* 1; *Target Audience:* General.
Russ Sweetsir, President
Jeremy Scott, Operations Dir

***KIYU-FM**
01-01-2008; 97.1 MHz FM; 0.1 kw; 49 ft.; N64 44 34 W156 50 30
US
(907) 656-1488; *Fax:* (907) 656-1734
www.kiyu.com
raven@kiyu.com
License: Galena, Yukon Koyukuk County, AK held by Big River Public Broadcasting Corp.
Arbitron Metro Market: Galena, AK; *Format:* Variety/Diverse
Russ Sweetsir, President
Jeremy Scott, Operations/ Program Director

Girdwood

***KEUL**
09-01-1998; 88.9 MHz FM; *Hrs Open:* 24; 1.4 kw horiz, 0 kw vert; 636 ft.; N60 57 44 W149 4 38
P O Box 29, Girdwood, AK 99587 US
(907) 754-2489
www.glaciercity.us
License: Girdwood, Anchorage County, AK held by Girdwood Community Club Inc.
Arbitron Metro Market: Anchorage, AK; *Format:* Variety/Diverse; *Target Audience:* Sole service provider.
Lewis Leonard, General Manager/COO
Denise Dargan, Underwriting Manager

Glennallen

KCAM
04-16-1964; 790 kHz AM; *Hrs Open:* 24; 5 kw-U; N62 06 52 W145 32 07
Box 249, Glennallen, AK 99833
(907) 822-5226; *Fax:* (907) 822-3761
www.kcam.org
kcam@kcam.org
License: Glennallen, Valdez-Cordova County, AK held by Northern Light Network.
Nat'l Network: Moody; USA
Population Served: 10,000; *Arbitron Metro Market:* Glennallen, AK *Special Programming:* American Indian one hr, class 10 hrs, contemp Chri; *Hrs. of News Programming:* News progmg 28 hrs wkly *Target Audience:* General.
Scott Yahr, President/Station Manager
Michael Eastty, Programming Director
Corey Emery, Engineering Dir
Scott Hill, Chief Engineer

***KXGA**
10-01-1994; 90.5 MHz FM; *Hrs Open:* 24; 3.2 kw; 751 ft.; N62 6 31 W146 10 25 *Rebroadcasts:* Rebroadcasts KCHU(AM) Valdez 100%

Mailing Address: P.O. Box 467, Valdez, AK 99686 US
Second Address: c/o KCHU(AM), 128 Pioneer Dr., Valdez, AK 99686
(907) 835-4665; *Fax:* (907) 835-2847
www.kchu.org
kchu@cvinternet.net
License: Glennallen, Valdez-Cordova County, AK held by Terminal Radio Inc.
Arbitron Metro Market: Valdez, AK; *Format:* Variety/Diverse
John Anderson, General Manager
Lanette Oliver, Development Director
Nancy Meador, Development Coordinator

Haines

*KHNS

10-04-1980; 102.3 MHz FM; *Hrs Open:* 24; 3 kw; -1220 ft.; N59 13 6 W135 25 29
P.O. Box 1109, Haines, AK 99827 US
(907) 766-2020; *Fax:* (907) 766-2022
www.khns.org
gm@khns.org
License: Haines, Haines County, AK held by Lynn Canal Broadcasting.
Nat'l Network: NPR; *Regional Network:* Alaska Pub.
Format: Talk *Special Programming:* Country 10 hrs wkly, Variety; *Hrs. of News Programming:* news progmg 100 hrs wkly; *No. News Employees:* 2; *Target Audience:* General.
Emily Seward, President
Kay Clements, General Manager
Leslie Ross, Development Director
Amelia Nash, Program Director
Macky Cassidy, Music Director
Margaret Friedenauer, News & Public Affairs Director

Homer

*KBBI

08-04-1979; 890 kHz AM; *Hrs Open:* 24; 10 kw-U, ND1; N59 40 14 W151 26 38
3913 Kachemak Way, Homer, AK 99603 US
(907) 235-7721; *Fax:* (907) 235-2357
www.kbbi.org
dorle@kbbi.org
License: Homer, AK held by Kachemak Bay Broadcasting Inc.
Nat'l Network: PRI; NPR; AP Radio; *Regional Network:* Alaska Pub.; *Wire Services:* AP
Arbitron Metro Market: Homer, AK; *Format:* News/Talk *Special Programming:* APM, AAA, jazz, rock; *Hrs. of News Programming:* news progmg 84 hrs wkly; *No. News Employees:* 15; *Target Audience:* General.
David Anderson, General Manager
Terry Rensel, Programming Director
Aaron Selbig, News Director
Paulette Wellington, Music Director
Josh Tobin, Development Director

KGTL

02-11-1981; 620 kHz AM; *Hrs Open:* 24; 5 kw-U, ND1; N59 41 3 W151 37 51
P.O. Box 109, Homer, AK 99603 US
(907) 235-6000; *Fax:* (907) 235-6683
kwavefm@xyz.net
License: Homer, AK held by Peninsula Communications Inc.
Group Owner: Peninsula Communications Inc.
Nat'l Network: USA
Format: Adult Contemp; *Hrs. of News Programming:* News progmg 20 hrs wkly; *Target Audience:* 35 plus; professionals
David Becker, President

KWVV-FM

09-22-1979; 103.5 MHz FM; *Hrs Open:* 24; 100 kw horiz; 1152 ft.; N59 41 3 W151 37 51
P.O. Box 109, Homer, AK 99603 US
(907) 235-6000; *Fax:* (907) 235-6683
kwavefm@xyz.net
License: Homer, Kenai Peninsula County, AK held by Peninsula Communications Inc.
Group Owner: Peninsula Communications Inc.
Format: Adult Contemp; *Hrs. of News Programming:* News progmg 14 hrs wkly; *Target Audience:* 18-49.; *Adv. Rates:* 240; 240; 240; 192
David Becker, President

KGTL(AM)

620 kHz AM; 5000 watts; non-directional; 59 41 03N 151 37 51W
PO Box 109, Homer, AK 99603 USA
(907) 235-6000; *Fax:* (907) 235-6683
License: Homer, AK
Group Owner: Penninsula Communications Inc
David Becker, President

Houston

KZND

04-01-1998; 94.7 MHz FM; *Hrs Open:* 24; 15 kW; 869 ft.; N61 20 12 W149 30 45
4700 Business Park Blvd., Building E, Suite 44-A, Anchorage, AK 99503 USA
(907) 522-1018; *Fax:* (907) 522-1027
www.947kznd.com
License: Houston, Matanuska-Susitna County, AK held by Alaska Integrated Media Inc.
Group Owner: Alaska Integrated Media
Arbitron Metro Market: Anchorage, AK; *Format:* Rock/AOR; *Target Audience:* 25-44; general

*KJHA

88.7 MHz FM; *Hrs Open:* 24; 1 kw; -131 ft.; N61 37 53 W149 48 46 *Rebroadcasts:* Rebroadcasts KJNP-FM North Pole midnight-7 AM and rebroadcasts KJNP(AM) North Pole 7 AM-midnight
P.O. Box 56359, North Pole, AK 99705 US
(907) 488-5246; *Fax:* (907) 488-5246
www.mosquitonet.com/~kjnp
kjnp@mosquitonet.com
License: Houston, Matanuska Susitna County, AK held by Evangelistic Alaska Missionary Fellowship Inc.
Format: Country, Gospel *Special Programming:* Athabaskan Indian 2 hrs, Eskimo 1/2 hr wkly
Yvonne Carriker, President
Richerd T. Olson, Operations Dir
Redgy Swedberg, Chief Engineer

KBBO-FM

01-01-1997; 92.1 MHz FM; *Hrs Open:* 24; 10 kw; 886 ft.; N61 20 11 W149 30 48
3700 Woodland Drive, Suite 700, Anchorage, AK 99217 US
(907) 344-4045; *Fax:* (907) 522-6053
License: Houston, Matanuska Susitna County, AK
Group Owner: Ohana Media Group LLC; (acq 8-12-99; $1.1 million).
Wire Services: AP
Arbitron Metro Market: Anchorage, AK; *Format:* Adult Contemp
Bill Sigmar, General Manager/Chief Operating Officer
Kirsten Bolt, Sales Director
Tom Oakes, Programming Director/Vice President of Operations
Trila Bumstead, CFO

KXLW

01-01-2000; 96.3 MHz FM; 10 kw; 886 ft.; N61 20 11 W149 30 48
5455 Highland Drive, Bellevue, WA 98006 US
(907) 344-4045; *Fax:* (907) 522-6053
www.963thewolf.com
bill.sigmar@ohanamediagroup.com
License: Houston, Matanuska Susitna County, AK
Group Owner: Ohana Media Group LLC; (acq 7-30-99)
Wire Services: AP
Arbitron Metro Market: Anchorage, AK; *Target Audience:* 20-49; men
Bill Sigmar, General Manager/Chief Operating Officer
Kirsten Bolt, Sales Director
Tom Oakes, Programming Director
Madisyn Vrem, Promotions Manager
Gerrit Bode, Chief Engineer

Juneau

*KRNN

01-01-1999; 102.7 MHz FM; 6 kw; -417 ft.; N58 17 9 W134 25 40
360 Egan Drive, Juneau, AK 99801 US
(907) 586-1670; *Fax:* (907) 586-3612
www.ktoo.org
License: Juneau, Juneau County, AK held by Capital Community Broadcasting Inc.
Group Owner: Capital Community Broadcasting Inc.; (acq 12-27-2006; $676,400 with KXLL(FM) Juneau)
Arbitron Metro Market: Juneau, AK; *Format:* Variety/Diverse
Bill Legere, President
Mike Sakarias, Operations Manager
Bill Legere, General Manager
Christy Ciambor, Development Director
Jeff Brown, Programming Director
Rosemarie Alexander, News Director
Richard Parker, Engineering Dir
Jeff Brown, Music Director

*KXLL

10-01-1999; 100.7 MHz FM; 6 kw; -417 ft.; N58 17 9 W134 25 40
360 Egan Drive, Juneau, AK 99801 US
(907) 586-1670; *Fax:* (907) 586-5692
www.kxll.org
License: Juneau, Juneau County, AK held by Capital Community Broadcasting Inc.
Group Owner: Capital Community Broadcasting Inc.; (acq 12-27-2006; $676,400 with KRNN(FM) Juneau)
Arbitron Metro Market: Juneau, AK; *Format:* Alternative, Triple A
Bill Legere, President/GM
Mike Sakarias, Operations Dir
Christy Ciambor, Development Director
Jeff Brown, Programming Director
Rosemarie Alexander, News Director
Richard Parker, Engineering Dir

KINY

05-28-1935; 800 kHz AM; *Hrs Open:* 24
3161 Channel Drive, Juneau, AK 99801 US
(907) 586-3630; *Fax:* (907) 586-3266
www.kinyradio.com
License: Juneau, AK held by Alaska-Juneau Communications Inc.
Format: Adult Contemp; *Hrs. of News Programming:* news progmg 4 hrs wkly; *No. News Employees:* 2; *Target Audience:* General.
Richard Burns, Group CEO
Kelly Peres, Operations/Programming Director
Terry Thomas, General Sales Mgr
Pete Carran, News Director
Chris Burns, Disc Jockey
Ron Davis, Disc Jockey

KJNO

10-19-1952; 630 kHz AM; *Hrs Open:* 24
3161 Channel Dr., Ste 202, Juneau, AK 99801 US
(907) 586-3630; *Fax:* (907) 463-3685
www.kjno.com
License: Juneau, AK held by Alaska Broadcast Communications Inc.
Group Owner: Alaska Broadcast Communications Inc.; (acq 1972; with co-located FM)
Nat'l Network: CBS Radio; *Nat'l Reps:* Tacher *Regional Reps:* Tacher
Format: Talk; *Target Audience:* 25-54.
Roy Paschal, President
Richard Burns, Operations Dir
Jeff McCoy, Programming Director

KSUP

12-01-1984; 106.3 MHz FM; *Hrs Open:* 24; 10 kw; -1007 ft.; N58 18 5 W134 26 26
1107 West 8th Street, Suite #2, Juneau, AK 99801 US
(907) 586-1063; *Fax:* (907) 586-3266
www.ksupradio.com
License: Juneau, Juneau County, AK held by Alaska-Juneau Communications Inc.
Arbitron Metro Market: Juneau, AK; *Format:* Classic Rock, Contemporary Hits/Top 40, 76
Kelly Peres, Programming Director/Operations Manager

KTKU

07-09-1984; 105.1 MHz FM; *Hrs Open:* 24; 3.8 kw; -1060 ft.; N58 19 47 W134 28 17
3161 Channel Dr. Suite 2, Juneau, AK 99801 US
(907) 586-3630; *Fax:* (907) 463-3685
License: Juneau, Juneau County, AK held by Alaska Broadcast Communications Inc.
Group Owner: Alaska Broadcast Communications Inc.
Arbitron Metro Market: Juneau, AK; *Format:* Country
Douglas Fisher, Chairman
Sheryl Lehman, General Sales Mgr
J.T. Gerlt, Programming Director

*KTOO

01-27-1974; 104.3 MHz FM; *Hrs Open:* 24; 1.4 kw; -1043 ft.; N58 18 4 W134 25 21
360 Egan Drive, Juneau, AK 99801 US
(907) 586-1670; *Fax:* (907) 586-3612(907) 586-2561 (news)
www.ktoo.org
info@ktoo.org
License: Juneau, Juneau County, AK held by Capital Community Broadcasting Inc.
Group Owner: Capital Community Broadcasting Inc.
Nat'l Network: NPR; PRI; *Regional Network:* Alaska Pub.
Arbitron Metro Market: Juneau, AK *TV Affiliate:* *KTOO-TV affil.; *Format:* News, Variety/Diverse *Special Programming:* Children one hrs, folk 8 hrs, Sp 2 hsr, French 2 hrs, jazz 14 hrs, Alaska native one hr wkly *Hrs.of News Programming:* news progmg 48 hrs wkly; *No. News Employees:* 14; *Target Audience:* General.
Bill Legere, President
Mike Sakarias, Operations Dir
Bill Legere, General Manager

Christy Ciambor, Development Director
Jeff Brown, Programming Director
Rosemarie Alexander, News Director
Richard Parker, Engineering Dir

KXXJ
01-01-2008; 1330 kHz AM; 10 kw-D, 3 kw-N; N58 18 05 W134 26 26
3161 Channel Drive, Juneau, AK 99801
(907) 586-3630
License: Juneau, Juneau County, AK held by Seattle Streaming Radio LLC.
Group Owner: Alaska Broadcast Communications
Nat'l Network: ESPN Radio

Richard Burns, Group CEO

***KAKI**
88.1 MHz FM; 10 kw vert; Ant -1,214 ft; N58 18 05 W134 26 26
Rebroadcasts: KLRD(FM) Yucaipa, California 100%
2351 Sunset Blvd., Suite 170-218, Rocklin, CA
(916) 251-1600; *Fax:* (916) 251-1650
License: Juneau, Juneau County, AK held by Educational Media Foundation
Group Owner: EMF Broadcasting

Mike Novak, President

***KNGW**
88.9 MHz FM; 0.125 kw; -420 ft.; N58 21 57 W134 37 58
P.O. Box 391, Twin Falls, ID 83303 US
(208) 733-3133
www.csnradio.com
License: Juneau, Juneau County, AK held by Calvary Chapel of Twin Falls, Inc.
Group Owner: CSN International; (acq 3-2-2009)
Arbitron Metro Market: Juneau, AK; *Format:* Christian, Religious

Kaltag

***KALG**
98.1 MHz FM; 0.1 kw; -253 ft.; N64 19 40 W158 43 36
165 Tiger Freeway, Galena, AK 99741 US
(907) 656-1488; *Fax:* (907) 656-1734
www.kiyu.com
raven@kiyu.com
License: Kaltag, Yukon Koyukuk County, AK held by Big River Public Broadcasting Corp.
Arbitron Metro Market: Galena, AK; *Format:* Variety/Diverse
Russ Sweetsir, President
Jeremy Scott, Operations/Program Director

Kasilof

***KABN-FM**
01-01-2003; 88.9 MHz FM; 3.2 kw vert; 335 ft.; N60 31 58 W151 4 52
3700 Woodland Drive, Suite 800, Anchorage, AK 99517 US
(907) 783-2256
License: Kasilof, Kenai Peninsula County, AK held by Alaska Educational Radio System Inc.
Arbitron Metro Market: Kasilof, AK

KFSE
11-22-2007; 106.9 MHz FM; *Hrs Open:* 24; 8 kw; 203 ft.; N60 25 55 W151 8 26
P.O. Box 769, Kasilof, AK 99610 US
(907) 283-8700; *Fax:* (907) 283-9177
info@radiokenai.com
License: Kasilof, Kenai Peninsula County, AK held by KSRM Inc.
Group Owner: KSRM Inc.; (acq 3-22-2007; $210,000 for CP)
Arbitron Metro Market: Medford-Ashland, OR
John Davis, President
Jake Thompson, Programming/Operations Manager
Matt Wilson, General Manager

Kenai

***KDLL**
01-01-1981; 91.9 MHz FM; *Hrs Open:* 24; 4.9 kw; 72 ft; N60 34 03 W151 07 25
Box 2111, Kenai, AK 99611
(907) 283-8433; *Fax:* (907) 283-6701
www.kdllradio.org
allen@kdllradio.org
License: Kenai, Kenai Peninsula County, AK held by Pickle Hill Public Broadcasting Inc.
Nat'l Network: NPR; PRI; *Regional Network:* Alaska Pub.
Population Served: 30,000 *Special Programming:* American Indian 10 hrs wkly; *Hrs. of News Programming:* news progmg 60 hrs wkly; *No. News Employees:* 1; *Target Audience:* Affluent.
Dave Anderson, General Manager
Allen Auxier, Station Manager
Terry Rensel, Programming Director
Aaron Selbig, News Director
Bobby Blue, Chief Engineer
Josh Tobin, Development Director

KWHQ-FM
11-18-1976; 100.1 MHz FM; *Hrs Open:* 24; 25 kw; 190 ft.; N60 30 49 W151 11 19
Route #2 Box 852, Soldotna, AK 99669 US
(907) 283-9430; *Fax:* (907) 283-9177
www.radiokenai.com
info@radiokenai.com
License: Kenai, Kenai Peninsula County, AK held by KSRM Inc.
Group Owner: KSRM Inc.
Wire Services: AP
Arbitron Metro Market: Kenai, AK; *Format:* Country; *Hrs. of News Programming:* news progmg 12 hrs wkly; *No. News Employees:* 2; *Target Audience:* 18-49.
John Davis, CEO/President
Jake Thompson, Programming/Operations Director
Matt Wilson, General Manager/ Marketing Manager
Andrew Rogers, News Director
Dan Gensel, Sports Director
Mark Gage, Marketing Consultant
Myra Arbelovsky,Office Manager/ Administrative Assistant/ Bookkeep
Nathan Jonhson, Marketing Consultant

***KOGJ**
88.1 MHz FM; 1.1 kw vert; 87 m; N60 31 58 W151 04 52
P.O. Box 391, Twin Falls, ID 83303 US
(208) 733-3133
www.csnradio.com
License: Kenai, Kenai Peninsula County, AK held by Calvary Chapel of Twin Falls, Inc.
Group Owner: CSN International
Format: Christian, Religious

Ketchikan

KFMJ
09-23-1996; 99.9 MHz FM; *Hrs Open:* 24; 0.115 kw; 2234 ft.; N55 21 40 W131 47 43
516 Stedman Street, Ketchikan, AK 58202 US
(907) 247-3699; *Fax:* (907) 247-5365
http://www.alaska.fm/kfmj/index.html
License: Ketchikan, Ketchikan County, AK held by TLP Communications Inc.
Nat'l Network: ABC; USA; *Wire Services:* AP
Arbitron Metro Market: Ketchikan, AK; *Format:* Oldies; *Hrs. of News Programming:* News progmg 18.5 hrs wkly; *Target Audience:* 30 plus, high disposable income adults; *Adv. Rates:* 15; 15; 15; 13.50
Robert Kern, Chairman
Julie Slanaker, General Sales Mgr
Stewart Whyte, Programming Director

KGTW
11-01-1987; 106.7 MHz FM; *Hrs Open:* 24; 0.44 kw; 2185 ft.; N55 21 39 W131 47 43
3161 Channel Drive, Suite 202, Juneau, AK 22203 US
(907) 225-2193; *Fax:* (907) 225-0444
License: Ketchikan, Ketchikan County, AK
Group Owner: Alaska Broadcast Communications Inc.
Format: Country; *Target Audience:* 18 plus.
Larry Snider, General Manager
Terry Thomas, Group Sales Manager
Jonathan Tulli, Programming Director

***KRBD**
05-01-1976; 105.3 MHz FM; *Hrs Open:* 24; 3.4 kw; 69 ft.; N55 20 23 W131 37 29
123 Stedman Street, Ketchikan, AK 99901 US
(907) 225-9655; *Fax:* (907) 247-0808
www.krbd.org
License: Ketchikan, Ketchikan County, AK held by Rainbird Community Broadcasting Corp.
Nat'l Network: NPR; PRI; *Regional Network:* Alaska Pub.; *Wire Services:* AP
Arbitron Metro Market: AK Panhandle *Special Programming:* Class 11 hrs, C&W 14 hrs, folk 10 hrs, jazz 10 hrs; *Hrs. of News Programming:* news progmg 2 hrs wkly; *No. News Employees:* 2; *Target Audience:* General.
Nathan Grambau, General Manager
Maria Dudzak, Programming Director
Leila Kheiry, News Director
Amanda Slevin

KTKN
01-01-1942; 930 kHz AM; *Hrs Open:* 24; 5 kw-D, ND1; 1 kw-N, ND1; N55 20 22 W131 38 12
3161 Channel Dr. Suite 2, Juneau, AK 99801 US
(907) 225-2193; *Fax:* (907) 225-0444
License: Ketchikan, AK held by Alaska Broadcast Communications Inc.
Group Owner: Alaska Broadcast Communications Inc.
Regional Reps: Tacher.
Arbitron Metro Market: Ketchikan, AK; *Format:* Adult Contemp, News, 62, Talk; *Hrs. of News Programming:* news progmg 20 hrs wkly; *No. News Employees:* 5; *Target Audience:* 25 plus.; *Adv. Rates:* 20; 20; 20; 18
Larry Snider, General Manager
Terry Thomas, Sales Manager
Jonathan Tulli, Programming Director

Kodiak

***KMXT**
06-01-1976; 100.1 MHz FM; *Hrs Open:* 24; 0.275 kw; 1020 ft.; N57 47 23 W152 25 56
620 Egan Way, Kodiak, AK 99615 US
(907) 486-3181; *Fax:* (907) 486-2733
www.kmxt.org
License: Kodiak, Kodiak Island County, AK held by Kodiak Public Broadcasting Corp.
Nat'l Network: NPR; PRI; *Regional Network:* Alaska Pub.
Format: News, Variety/Diverse; *Hrs. of News Programming:* news progmg 5 hrs wkly; *No. News Employees:* 2; *Target Audience:* General.
Willy Bethea, Operations/Program Director
Mike Wall, General Manager
Jay Barrett, News Director
Pam Foreman, Development Director

KRXX
01-01-1987; 101.1 MHz FM; 3.1 kw; 23 ft.; N57 47 3 W152 23 57
Mailing Address: 2435 Chilligan Drive, Anchorage, AK 99517 US
Second Address: 1315 Mill Bay Rd., Kodiak, AK 99615
(907) 486-5159; *Fax:* (907) 486-3044
kvok@ak.net
License: Kodiak, Kodiak Island County, AK
Arbitron Metro Market: Kodiak, AK; *Target Audience:* 18-56.
Chuck Wright, Operations Dir
Ellen Simeonoff, General Manager

KVOK
11-07-1974; 560 kHz AM; *Hrs Open:* 24; 1 kw-U, ND1; N57 46 33 W152 32 7
Mailing Address: 2435 Chilligan Drive, Anchorage, AK 99517 US
Second Address: 1315 Mill Bay Rd., Kodiak, AK 99615
(907) 486-5159; *Fax:* (907) 486-3044
www.kvok.com
kvok@ak.net
License: Kodiak, AK held by Kodiak Island Broadcasting Co. Inc.
Nat'l Network: ABC; *Wire Services:* AP
Arbitron Metro Market: Kodiak, AK; *Format:* Country, Talk; *Target Audience:* 25-56.; *Adv. Rates:* 180; 156; 132; 120
Chuck Wright, Operations Dir
Ellen Simeonoff, General Manager
Lesile Ann Heglin, Traffic/ Billing
Denise Simeonoff, Account Executive

***KBKO**
06-29-2012; 88.3 MHz FM; 0.1 kw; -26 ft.; N57 48 40 W152 21 40
US
(800) 949-1050; *Fax:* (425) 867-2340
sacredheartradio.org
info@sacredheartradio.org
License: Kodiak, AK held by Sacred Heart Radio, Inc.
Format: Religious *Special Programming:* Religious Forums
Dr Tom Curran, General Manager

Kotzebue

***KOTZ**
03-01-1973; 720 kHz AM; *Hrs Open:* 0600 - 0000; 10 kw-U, ND1; N66 50 22 W162 34 5
P.O Box 78, 396 Lagoon Street, Kotzebue, AK 99752 US
(907) 442-3434; *Fax:* (907) 442-2292
License: Kotzebue, AK held by Kotzebue Broadcasting Inc.
Nat'l Network: NPR; *Regional Network:* Alaska Pub.
Format: Variety/Diverse; *Target Audience:* General; 90% rural Eskimo, 10% white-collar caucasian
Rosie Hensley, General Manager
Johnson Greene, Programming Director
Pierre Lonewolf, Chief Engineer

***KINU**
06-04-2009; 89.9 MHz FM; *Hrs Open:* 24; 0.1 kw; 82 ft.; N66 53 46 W162 35 46
396 Lagoon Street, Kotzebue, AK 99752 US
(907) 442-3434; *Fax:* (907) 442-2292
www.kotz.org
message@kotz.org
License: Kotzebue, Northwest Arctic County, AK held by Kotzebue Broadcasting Inc.
Nat'l Network: NPR; *Regional Network:* Alaska Pub.
Arbitron Metro Market: Kotzebue, AK; *Format:* Variety/Diverse
Rosie Hensley, General Manager
Johnson Greene, Programming Director
Pierre Lonewolf, Chief Engineer

Koyukuk

***KOYU**
98.1 MHz FM; 0.1 kw; -23 ft.; N64 52 58 W157 42 10 US
(907) 656-1488; *Fax:* (907) 656-1734
www.kiyu.com
raven@kiyu.com
License: Koyukuk, Yukon Koyukuk County, AK held by Big River Public Broadcasting Corp.
Arbitron Metro Market: Galena, AK; *Format:* Variety/Diverse
Russ Sweetsir, President
Jeremy Scott, Operations/Program Director

McCarthy

***KXKM**
10-01-1994; 89.7 MHz FM; *Hrs Open:* 24; 102 w; -169 ft; N61 24 58 W143 01 19 *Rebroadcasts:* Rebroadcasts KCHU(AM) Valdez 100%
Mailing Address: c/o KCHU(AM), Box 467, Valdez, AK 99686
Second Address: c/o KCHU(AM), 128 Pioneer Dr., Valdez, AK 99686
(907) 835-4665; *Fax:* (907) 835-2847
www.kchu.org
kchu@cvinternet.net
License: McCarthy, Valdez-Cordova County, AK held by Terminal Radio Inc.
Nat'l Network: NPR; PRI; *Regional Network:* Alaska Pub.
Hrs. of News Programming: news progmg 10 hrs wkly; *No. News Employees:* 1; *Target Audience:* General.
John Anderson, Operations Dir
Danny Sparrell, General Manager
Tony Gorman, News Director
David Delahunt, Engineering Dir
Nancy Meador, Development Director

McGrath

***KMCG**
90.3 MHz FM; kw
US
(907) 524-3182
radiomcgrath@yahoo.com
License: McGrath, Yukon Koyukuk County, AK held by McGrath Community Radio.
Arbitron Metro Market: Carlsbad, CA
Jack Collins, General Manager

***KOGB**
91.3 MHz FM; kw
P.O. Box 89, Kasilof, AK 99610 US
(907) 262-0920
License: McGrath, Yukon Koyukuk County, AK held by Blessed Hope Baptist Mission.
Arbitron Metro Market: McGrath, AK
David McElwain, President

Meadow Lakes

KYKA
104.9 MHz FM; 20 kw; 266 meters; N61 20 12 W149 30 45
5700 West Oaks Boulevard, Rocklin, CA 95765 US
(916) 251-1600; *Fax:* (916) 251-1650
www.air1.com
License: Meadow Lakes, Matanuska-Susitna Borough County, AK
Group Owner: Educational Media Foundation

Mike Novak, President

Naknek

KAKN
05-01-1987; 100.9 MHz FM; *Hrs Open:* 24; 3 kw; 299 ft.; N58 44 40 W156 58 32
Mailing Address: P.O. Box 214, Naknek, AK 99633 US
Second Address: Mile 2 AK Peninsula Hwy., Naknek, AK 99633
(907) 246-7492; *Fax:* (907) 246-7462
www.kaknradio.org
studio@victoryradionetwork.com
License: Naknek, Bristol Bay County, AK held by Association of Free Lutheran Congregations Mission Corp.
Nat'l Network: USA
Arbitron Metro Market: Naknek, AK; *Format:* Adult Contemp, Christian; *Hrs. of News Programming:* News progmg 15 hrs wkly; *Target Audience:* General; mobile town/village population & coml fishermen *Adv. Rates:* 12.75; 12.75; 12.75; 29
Richard Long, President
Bob Lee, Station Manager

Nenana

KIAM
06-28-1985; 630 kHz AM; *Hrs Open:* 24; 10 kw-D, ND1; 3.1 kw-N, ND1; N64 28 43 W149 5 10
P.O. Box 474, Nenana, AK 99760 US
(907) 832-5426; *Fax:* (907) 832-5450
www.vfcm.org
Alaskaradio@vfcm.org
License: Nenana, AK held by Voice for Christ Ministries.
Nat'l Network: Salem Radio Network; Moody
Format: Christian, News, 62, Talk *Special Programming:* American Indian 3 hrs, class one hr wkly, family 3 hrs wkly; *Hrs. of News Programming:* News progm 10 hrs wkly; *Target Audience:* General.
Brian Blair, Station Manager

Nikiski

KXBA
03-04-2000; 93.3 MHz FM; 50 kw; 243 ft.; N60 30 39 W151 16 12
P O Box 109, Homer, AK 99603 US
(907) 262-6000(907) 283-7423; *Fax:* (907) 283-8461
License: Nikiski, Kenai Peninsula County, AK held by Peninsula Communications Inc.
Group Owner: Peninsula Communications Inc.
Format: Oldies; *Hrs. of News Programming:* News progmg 8 hrs wkly; *Target Audience:* 25-54.; *Adv. Rates:* 216; 216; 216; 180
David Becker, President/General Manager/Programming Director
Michael Becker, Sales Manager
Tim White, News Director

Nome

KICY
04-17-1960; 850 kHz AM; *Hrs Open:* 24
Mailing Address: P. O. Box 820, Nome, AK 99762 US
Second Address: 408 West D St., Nome, AK 99762
(907) 443-2213; *Fax:* (907) 443-2344
www.kicy.org
office@kicy.org; dennisw@kicy.org
License: Nome, AK held by Arctic Broadcasting Association
Nat'l Network: ABC; Moody; Salem Radio Network *Regional Reps:* Alaska Broadcast Media
Format: Gospel, Russian; *No. News Employees:* 1; *Target Audience:* 25-64.; *Adv. Rates:* 13; 10; 10; 7
Ted Haney, President
Dennis Weidler, General Manager

KICY-FM
09-11-1977; 100.3 MHz FM; *Hrs Open:* 24; 1 kw; -361 ft.; N64 30 9 W165 24 37
Mailing Address: P.O. Box 820, Nome, AK 99762 US
Second Address: 408 West D St., Nome, AK 99762
(907) 443-2213; *Fax:* (907) 443-2344
www.kicy.org
License: Nome, AK held by Arctic Broadcasting Association.
Nat'l Network: Salem Radio Network *Regional Reps:* Alaska Broadcast Media; *Wire Services:* AP
Format: Christian; *No. News Employees:* 1; *Target Audience:* 18-35.; *Adv. Rates:* 13; 10; 10; 7
Ted Haney, President
Dennis Weidler, General Manager

***KNOM**
07-14-1971; 780 kHz AM; *Hrs Open:* 24; 25 kw-D, ND1; 14 kw-N, ND1; N64 29 16 W165 17 58
1316 Peger Road, Fairbanks, AK 99709 US
(907) 443-5221; *Fax:* (907) 443-5757
www.knom.org
License: Nome, AK held by Catholic Bishop of Northern Alaska.
Wire Services: AP
Format: News, News/Talk, 86, Variety/Diverse, Religious *Special Programming:* Eskimo 6 hrs, CHR 12 hrs, relg 20 hrs, class 5 hrs; *Hrs. of News Programming:* news progmg 30 hrs wkly; *No. News Employees:* 2 *TargetAudience:* General.
Ric Schmidt, General Manager
Kelly Brabec, Programming Director
Laureli Kinneen, News Director

***KNOM-FM**
05-17-1993; 96.1 MHz FM; *Hrs Open:* 24; 1 kw; -138 ft.; N64 29 56 W165 23 56
1316 Peger Rd., Fairbanks, AK 99709 US
(907) 443-5221; *Fax:* (907) 443-5757
License: Nome, Nome County, AK
Nat'l Network: AP Radio; *Wire Services:* AP
Hrs. of News Programming: news progmg 30 hrs wkly; *No. News Employees:* 2
Ric Schmidt, General Manager
Kelly Brabec, Programming Director
Laureli Kinneen, News Director

North Nenana

***KIAM-FM**
04-10-2008; 91.9 MHz FM; *Hrs Open:* 24; 0.26 kw; -10 ft.; N64 33 50 W149 5 21
PO Box 474, 409 First Street, Nenana, AK 99760 US
(907) 832-5426; *Fax:* (907) 832-5450
www.vfcm.org
alaskaradio@vfcm.org
License: North Nenana, Yukon Koyukuk County, AK held by Voice for Christ Ministries Inc.
Nat'l Network: Salem Radio Network; Moody
Arbitron Metro Market: North Nenana, AK; *Format:* Christian
Brian Blair, Station Manager

North Pole

***KJNP**
10-11-1967; 1170 kHz AM; *Hrs Open:* 19 hrs; 50 kw-D, ND1; 21 kw-N, ND1; N64 45 34 W147 19 26
PO Box 56359, North Pole, AK 99705 US
(907) 488-2216; *Fax:* (907) 488-5246
www.mosquitonet.com
kjnp@mosquitonet.com
License: North Pole, AK held by Evangelistic Alaska Missionary Fellowship.
Format: Religious, Country *Special Programming:* Athabaskan Indian 2 hrs, Eskimo one hr wkly
Yvonne Carriker, President
Richard Olson, Operations Dir

***KJNP-FM**
10-11-1977; 100.3 MHz FM; 25 kw; 1572 ft.; N64 52 44 W148 3 10
P.O. Box 56359, North Pole, AK 99705 US
(907) 488-2216; *Fax:* (907) 488-5246
License: North Pole, Fairbanks North Star County, AK held by Evangelistic Alaska Missionary Fellowship.
TV Affiliate: *KJNP-TV affil..; *Format:* Religious
Yvonne Carriker, President
Richard Olson, Operations Dir

Nulato

***KNUL**
99.1 MHz FM; 0.1 kw; 16 ft.; N64 43 59 W158 6 25
US
License: Nulato, Yukon Koyukuk County, AK held by Big River Public Broadcasting Corp.
Arbitron Metro Market: Nulato, AK

Palmer

KMVN
08-07-1957; 95.5 MHz FM; *Hrs Open:* 24; kw
US
(818) 525-5000; *Fax:* (818) 525-5002
License: Palmer, Los Angeles County, AK held by KMVN License LLC.
Group Owner: Emmis Communications Corp.; (acq 9-26-2000; grpsl)
Arbitron Metro Market: Burbank, CA; *Format:* Adult Contemp
Janet Brainin, General Sales Mgr
Jimmy Steal, Programming Director
Dianna Jason, Promotions Manager
Dean Carter, General Sales Manager

***KJLP**
08-01-2005; 88.9 MHz FM; 0.25 kw; -210 ft.; N61 37 18 W149 1 16
Mailing Address: 6401 E Northern Lights B, Anchorage, AK 99504 US

Second Address: 6401 E. Northern Lights, Anchorage, AK 99521
(907) 333-5282; *Fax:* (907) 337-0003
www.katb.org
tom@katb.org
License: Palmer, Matanuska-Susitna County, AK held by Christian Broadcasting Inc.
Arbitron Metro Market: Palmer, AK; *Format:* Christian
Tom Steigleman, General Manager

Petersburg

***KFSK**
09-01-1977; 100.9 MHz FM; *Hrs Open:* 24; 2 kw; -482 ft.; N56 48 57 W132 57 6
Mailing Address: P. O. Box 149, Petersburg, AK 99833 US
Second Address: 404 N Second St, Petersburg, AK
(907) 772-3808; *Fax:* (907) 772-9296
www.kfsk.org
License: Petersburg, Wrangell Petersburg County, AK held by Narrows Broadcasting Corp.
Nat'l Network: PRI; NPR; AP Network News; *Regional Network:* Alaska Pub.; *Wire Services:* AP
Arbitron Metro Market: Petersburg, AK; *Format:* News, News/Talk, 86 *Special Programming:* Jazz 2 hrs wkly; *Hrs. of News Programming:* news prgmg 24 hrs wkly; *No. News Employees:* 2
Tom Abbott, General Manager
Matt Lichtenstein, News Director
Mindy Anderson, Development Director

Port Alsworth

***KGCU**
90.3 MHz FM; kw
, Port Alsworth, AK 99653 US
(907) 781-2243
License: Port Alsworth, Lake and Peninsula Boroug County, AK held by Lake Clark Bible Church.
Arbitron Metro Market: Port Alsworth, AK
James Walsh, General Manager

Ruby

***KRBY**
98.1 MHz FM; 0.1 kw; -69 ft.; N64 44 20 W155 28 48
PO Box 165, Galena, AK 99741-0165 US
(907) 656-1488; *Fax:* (907) 656-1734
www.kiyu.com
License: Ruby, Yukon Koyukuk County, AK held by Big River Public Broadcasting Corp.
Arbitron Metro Market: Ruby, AK
Russ Sweetsir, President
Brian Landrum, Operations/ Program Director

Sand Point

***KSDP**
03-02-1983; 830 kHz AM; *Hrs Open:* 24; 1 kw-U; N55 21 06 W160 28 02 *Rebroadcasts:* Rebroadcasts KDLG(AM) Dillingham
Box 328, City Bldg, Sand Point, AK 99661
(907) 383-5737; *Fax:* (907) 383-5737
www.ksdpradio.org
gm@ksdpradio.com
License: Sand Point, Aleutians East Borough County, AK held by Aleutian Peninsula Broadcasting Inc.
Nat'l Network: NPR; PRI
Population Served: 6,000 *Special Programming:* Gospel; *Target Audience:* General.
Austin Roof, General Manager
Virgil Porter, Programming Director

***KSPM**
90.3 MHz FM; kw
PO Box 329, Sand Point, AK 99661-0329 US
(907) 383-4551
radiosandpoint@yahoo.com
License: Sand Point, Aleutians East Borough County, AK held by Sand Point Baptist Church.
Arbitron Metro Market: Sand Point, AK
Craig Furlough, General Manager

Seward

KSEW
11-01-1948; 950 kHz AM; 1 kw-U, ND1; N60 5 27 W149 20 20
10914 E. 46th Avenue, Spokane, WA 99206 US
(907) 224-5793; *Fax:* (907) 224-4702
www.sewardradio.com
License: Seward, AK held by Seward Media Partners LLC
Arbitron Metro Market: Seaward, AK; *Format:* Country
James Spanos, Station Manager

Sitka

***KCAW**
02-19-1982; 104.7 MHz FM; *Hrs Open:* 24; 3.6 kw; -610 ft.; N57 3 13 W135 21 7
2b Lincoln Street, Sitka, AK 99835 US
(907) 747-5877; *Fax:* (907) 747-5977
www.kcaw.org
License: Sitka, Sitka County, AK held by Raven Radio Foundation.
Nat'l Network: NPR; PRI; *Regional Network:* Alaska Pub.
Arbitron Metro Market: Sitka, AK; *Format:* News, Variety/Diverse
Special Programming: Class 15 hrs, Indian 3 hrs wkly; *Target Audience:* General.
Ted Laufenberg, President
Ken Fate, General Manager
Robert Woolsey, News Director
Amy Kramer Johnson, Development Director

KIFW
09-01-1949; 1230 kHz AM; *Hrs Open:* 24; 1 kw-U, ND1; N57 3 27 W135 20 2
3161 Channel Dr. Suite 2, Juneau, AK 99801 US
(907) 747-6626; *Fax:* (907) 747-8455
License: Sitka, AK held by Alaska Broadcast Communications Inc.
Group Owner: Alaska Broadcast Communications Inc.; (acq 12-21-2000; grpsl)
Arbitron Metro Market: Sitka, AK; *Format:* Adult Contemp, News, 62, Oldies, Talk; *Hrs. of News Programming:* News progmg 60 hrs wkly; *Target Audience:* 18-49; all demographics
Larry Snider, General Manager
Terry Thomas, General Sales Mgr
Jonathan Tulli, Programming Director
Dominick Pannone, Chief Engineer

KSBZ
10-18-1990; 103.1 MHz FM; *Hrs Open:* 24; 3 kw; Ant 144 ft; N57 03 27 W135 20 02
611 Lake St., Sitka, AK 99801
(907) 747-6627; *Fax:* (907) 747-8455
www.ksbz.com
License: Sitka, Sitka County, AK held by Alaska Broadcast Communications Inc.
Group Owner: Alaska Broadcast Communications Inc.
Nat'l Reps: Tacher
Hrs. of News Programming: 2 hours; *No. News Employees:* 4; *Target Audience:* 25-54; *Adv. Rates:* 12 dollars per station/combo 1
Larry Snider, General Manager
Terry Thomas, General Sales Mgr
Dan Belair, Programming Director
Dominic Pannone, Engineering Dir

Soldotna

KKIS-FM
03-02-1994; 96.5 MHz FM; *Hrs Open:* 24; 10 kw; 259 ft.; N60 31 26 W151 3 23
44619 Sterling Highway, Soldotna, AK 99669 US
(907) 283-8700; *Fax:* (907) 283-9177
www.radiokenai.com
License: Soldotna, Kenai Peninsula County, AK held by KSRM Inc.
Group Owner: KSRM Inc.; (acq 12-7-2001; $350,000 with co-located AM)
Nat'l Network: ABC
Arbitron Metro Market: Anchorage, AK; *Format:* Adult Contemp; *Hrs. of News Programming:* news progmg 2 hrs wkly; *No. News Employees:* 1; *Target Audience:* 18-49.
John Davis, President/Chief Executive Officer

KPEN-FM
12-01-1984; 101.7 MHz FM; *Hrs Open:* 24; 25 kw; 240 ft.; N60 30 40 W151 16 12
P.O. Box 109, Homer, AK 99603 US
(907) 262-6000,(907) 283-7451; *Fax:* (907) 235-6683
kwavefm@xyz.net
License: Soldotna, Kenai Peninsula County, AK held by Peninsula Communications Inc.
Group Owner: Peninsula Communications Inc.
Nat'l Network: USA
Format: Country; *Target Audience:* 25-54.; *Adv. Rates:* 240; 240; 240; 180
David Becker, President/General Manager
Michael Becker, Sales Manager
Tim White, News Director

KSLD
04-06-1985; 1140 kHz AM; *Hrs Open:* 24; 10 kw-U, ND1; N60 31 26 W151 3 23
44619 Sterling Hwy, Soldotna, AK 99669 US
(907) 283-8700
www.radiokenai.com
info@radiokenai.com
License: Soldotna, AK held by KSRM Inc.
Group Owner: KSRM Inc.
Nat'l Network: Westwood One
Arbitron Metro Market: Kenai, AK; *Format:* Classic Rock; *Hrs. of News Programming:* News progmg one hr wkly; *Target Audience:* 25-59.
John C Davis, President/Chief Executive Officer
Matt Wilson, General Manager/Sales Manager
Jake Thompson, Programming Director
Andrew Rogers, News Director
Paul Jewusiak, Chief Engineer

KSRM
09-27-1967; 920 kHz AM; *Hrs Open:* 24; 5 kw-U, ND1; N60 30 49 W151 11 19
Hc-2 Box 852, Soldotna, AK 99669 US
(907) 283-5959; *Fax:* (907) 283-5811
www.radiokenai.com
info@radiokenai.com
License: Soldotna, AK held by KSRM Inc.
Group Owner: KSRM Inc.; (acq 4-72)
Arbitron Metro Market: Kenai, AK; *Format:* News, News/Talk, 86; *Hrs. of News Programming:* news progmg 105 hrs wkly; *No. News Employees:* 1; *Target Audience:* 25-54.
John Davis, President/Chief Executive Officer
Matt Wilson, General Manager/Sales Manager
Jake Thompson, Programming Director
Andrew Rogers, News Director
Paul Jewusiak, Chief Engineer

St. Paul

***KUHB-FM**
07-04-1984; 91.9 MHz FM; 15 kw horiz, 0.23 kw vert; 52 ft.; N57 7 14 W170 16 45
930 Tolstoi St, Box 905, St. Paul Island, AK 99660 US
(907) 546-2254; *Fax:* (907) 546-2367
www.kuhbradio.org
kuhbinfo@gmail.com
License: St. Paul, Pribilof Islands County, AK held by Pribilof School District.
Nat'l Network: NPR
Arbitron Metro Market: Saint Paul, AK; *Format:* Adult Contemp, Alternative, 22, Contemporary Hits/Top 40, Disco, News
Walt Gregg, General Manager
Walt Gregg, Station Manager
B.J. Kibbe, News Director

Sterling

KKNI
01-01-1998; 105.3 MHz FM; 7 kw; 284 ft.; N60 29 19.33 W150 44 42.83
10914 E. 46th Avenue, Spokane, WA 99206 US
Fax: (907) 224-4702
License: Sterling, Kenai Peninsula County, AK held by Seward Media Partners LLC

James Spanos, Station Manager

Talkeetna

***KTNA**
02-01-1993; 88.9 MHz FM; *Hrs Open:* 24; 7.2 kw; 72 ft.; N62 19 5 W150 17 52
P.O. Box 300, Talkeetna, AK 99676 US
(907) 733-1700; *Fax:* (907) 733-1781
www.ktna.org
info@ktna.org
License: Talkeetna, Matanuska Susitna County, AK held by Talkeetna Community Radio Inc.
Nat'l Network: NPR; PRI
Arbitron Metro Market: Talkeentna, AK; *Format:* News, News/Talk, 86 *Special Programming:* Blues 5 hrs, light rock 5 hrs wkly; *Hrs. of News Programming:* news progmg 15 hrs wkly; *No. News Employees:* 1 *TargetAudience:* General; rural Alaskans
Will Peterson, General Manager
Deborah Brock, Programming Director
Lorien Nettleton, News Director
Kristin Merkley-Business Manager
Deb Wessler, Development Director

Tok

***KUDU**
03-03-1998; 91.9 MHz FM; 0.2 kw; -121 ft.; N63 19 53 W143 7 2
402 E Yakima Avenue, Suite 1320, Yakima, WA 98901 US

(800) 775-4673; *Fax:* (907) 883-5245
www.lifetalk.net
office@lifetalk.net
License: Tok, Southeast Fairbanks County, AK held by Lifetalk Broadcasting Association.
Arbitron Metro Market: Tok, AK; *Format:* Religious, Talk
John Geli, Program/Operations Manager

Unalakleet

KNSA
01-01-1998; 930 kHz AM
P.O. Box 178, Unalakleet, AK 99684 US
(907) 624-3100; *Fax:* (907) 624-3130
License: Unalakleet, AK held by Unalakleet Broadcasting Inc.
Format: Variety/Diverse
Sam Towarak, Operations Dir
Henry Ivanoff, Station Manager

Unalaska

***KUCB**
10-01-2008; 89.7 MHz FM; 0.66 kw; -308 ft.; N53 52 35 W166 32 24
US
(907) 581-1888; *Fax:* (907) 581-1634
www.kucb.org
info@kucb.org
License: Unalaska, Aleutian Islands County, AK held by Unalaska Community Broadcasting Inc.
Nat'l Network: NPR; *Regional Network:* Alaska Pub.
Arbitron Metro Market: Unalaska, AK; *Format:* Public Affairs, News
Pipa Escalante, Operations Dir
Lauren Adams, General Manager
Stephanie Joyce, News Director
Daniel Weirich, Producer
Jane Bye, Development Director

Valdez

***KCHU**
08-03-1986; 770 kHz AM; *Hrs Open:* 24; 9.7 kw-U, ND1; N61 6 40 W146 15 39
Mailing Address: Box 467, Valdez, AK 99686 US
Second Address: 128 Poineer Dr., Valdez, AK
(907) 835-4665; *Fax:* (907) 835-2847
www.kchu.org
gm@kchu.org
License: Valdez, AK held by Terminal Radio Inc.
Nat'l Network: NPR; PRI; *Regional Network:* Alaska Pub.
Arbitron Metro Market: Valdez-Cordova Census Area, AK; *Format:* Variety/Diverse; *Hrs. of News Programming:* news progmg 40 hrs wkly; *No. News Employees:* 1; *Target Audience:* General.
John Anderson, Operations Dir
Danny Sparrell, General Manager
Tony Gorman, News Director
Nancy Meador, Development Coordinator

KVAK
01-01-1983; 1230 kHz AM; *Hrs Open:* 24; 1 kw-U, ND1; N61 7 16 W146 15 25
Mailing Address: 501 East Bremner, Valdez, AK 99686 US
Second Address: 501 E. Bremner St., Valdez, AK 99686
(907) 835-5825; *Fax:* (907) 835-5158
www.kvakradio.com
kvaksales@gci.net
License: Valdez, AK held by North Wave Communications Inc.
Arbitron Metro Market: Valdez, AK; *Format:* Country, Talk; *Hrs. of News Programming:* News progmg one hr wkly; *Target Audience:* General.
Laurie Prax, General Manager/Sales & Marketing Manager
Ashley Ney-Vollmer, News Director
Margaret Henry, Traffic & Billing

KVAK-FM
05-28-1999; 93.3 MHz FM; 1.2 kw; -1959 ft.; N61 7 16 W146 15 25
C/O Haley Bader & Potts, 4350 North Fairfax Dr, Arlington, VA 22203 US
(907) 835-5825; *Fax:* (907) 835-5158
www.kvakradio.com
kvaksales@gci.net
License: Valdez, Valdez Cordova County, AK
Arbitron Metro Market: Valdez, AK; *Format:* Adult Contemp; *Adv. Rates:* 10; 9; 10; 9
Laurie Prax, General Manager
Gary Pauly, Sales & Marketing
Mark Bone, Programming Director
Brooke Alexander, News Director
Margaret Henry, Traffic & Billing

Wasilla

KMBQ-FM
03-15-1985; 99.7 MHz FM; *Hrs Open:* 24; 51 kw; -187 ft; N61 38 03 W149 26 25
851 East West Point Drive, Suite 301, Wasilla, AK 99654
(907) 373-0222; *Fax:* (907) 376-1575
www.kmbq.com
License: Wasilla, Matanuska Susitna County, AK held by KMBQ Corp.
Nat'l Network: CNN Radio
Population Served: 91,000; *Arbitron Metro Market:* Anchorage, AK; *Hrs. of News Programming:* news progmg 13 wkly; *No. News Employees:* 2; *Target Audience:* 25-54; mid-upper class suburbanites & farm community *Adv.Rates:* 30; 25; 30; 20
Trila Bumstead, Chief Executive Officer
Bill Sigmar, General Manager/Vice President/COO
Kirsten Bolton, Sales Manager
Tom Oakes, Vice President/Operations Director
Gerrit Bode, Chief Engineer
Alena Carroll, Traffic Manager
ChuckGeiger, Programming Director

KAYO
01-23-2009; 100.9 MHz FM; 50 kw; -276 ft.; N61 38 21 W148 59 56
201 Arctic Slope Ave., Suite 200, Anchorage, AK 99518 US
(907) 344-1041; *Fax:* (907) 349-3299
www.countrylegends1009.com
License: Wasilla, Matanuska Susitna County, AK held by Alpha Media Licensee LLC
Group Owner: Alpha Media LLC; (acq 9-2-2015; grpsl).
Arbitron Metro Market: Wasilla, AK; *Format:* Country
Roxy Lennox, Operations Manager
Patrick Wright, Senior Marketing Manager
Scott Smith, Sales Manager
Paul Jewusiak, Chief Engineer
Margie Vanness, Account Executive
Sandy Weihs, Account Executive
Sandy Baker, Account Executive

KWAP
01-01-2008; 1430 kHz AM; 1 kw-U; N61 37 09 W149 17 17
2200 E. Parks Hwy., Wasilla, AK
(907) 373-0222; *Fax:* (907) 376-1575
www.kmbq.com
License: Wasilla, Matanuska Susitna County, AK held by Spirit of Alaska Broadcasting Inc.
Arbitron Metro Market: Anchorage, AK

Wrangell

***KSTK**
07-02-1977; 101.7 MHz FM; *Hrs Open:* 24; 3 kw; -184 ft.; N56 27 14 W132 22 54
Mailing Address: P.O. Box 1141, Wrangell, AK 99929 US
Second Address: 202 St. Michael's, Wrangell, AK 99929
(907) 874-2345; *Fax:* (907) 874-3293
www.kstk.org
info@kstk.com
License: Wrangell, Wrangell Petersburg County, AK held by Wrangell Radio Group Inc.
Nat'l Network: NPR; PRI; *Regional Network:* Alaska Pub.
Arbitron Metro Market: Wrangell, AK; *Format:* Variety/Diverse
Special Programming: Class 4 hrs, country 16 hrs, jazz 8 hrs wkly; *Hrs. of News Programming:* news progmg 20 hrs wkly; *No. News Employees:* 2 *TargetAudience:* General.; *Adv. Rates:* 11.80; 11.80; 11.80; na
Peter Helgeson, General Manager
Renee Claggett, Programming Director
Cindy Sweat, Development Director

American Samoa

Fagaitua

WVUV-FM
01-01-2008; 103.1 MHz FM; 1.3 kw; 1591 ft.; S14 19 21 W170 45 47
US
(684) 633-7793; *Fax:* (684) 633-4493
www.wvuv.com
License: Fagaitua, AS held by South Seas Broadcasting Inc.
Arbitron Metro Market: Faga'itua, AS
Shannon Cummings, General Manager

Leone

KNWJ
01-01-2001; 104.7 MHz FM; *Hrs Open:* 24; 0.28 kw; 1499 ft.; S14 19 21 W170 45 47
PO Box 997777, Leone, AS 96799 US
(684) 699 8127; *Fax:* (684) 699-8126
info@fm104.org
License: Leone, AS held by Showers of Blessings Radio
Format: Christian; *Target Audience:* Christian Adults
Dan Dalle, General Manager
Leatumauga F. Matai, Station Manager
Helen Fuiava, Marketing Manager

Nu'uuli

***KMOA**
89.7 MHz FM; 1.5 kw; 1463 ft.; S14 16 12 W170 41 10
US
(684) 699-2635
License: Nu'uuli, AS held by Society of Pure Truth Ministries Inc.
Arbitron Metro Market: Pago Pago, AS
Shannon Cummings, President

Pago Pago

KKHJ-FM
05-01-2000; 93.1 MHz FM; *Hrs Open:* 24; 1.1 kw; 1490 ft.; S14 16 12 W170 41 10
P.O. Box 6758, Pago Pago, AS 96799 US
(684) 633-7793; *Fax:* (684) 633-4493
License: Pago Pago, AS held by South Seas Broadcasting.
Group Owner: Contemporary Communications
Format: Adult Contemp; *Target Audience:* General.; *Adv. Rates:* 7; 6; 6.50; 5.50
Larry Fuss, President
Joey Cummings, General Manager/Vice President
Monica Miller, News Director
John Raynar, Sales Manager
Pam Berquist, Office Manager

KSBS-FM
04-14-1988; 92.1 MHz FM; *Hrs Open:* 6:00am-Midnight; 15 kw; -92 feet; S14 17 41 W170 39 44
Box 793, Pago Pago, AS 96799
(684) 633-7000; *Fax:* (684) 633-5727
www.ksbsfm.com
info@ksbsfm92.com
License: Pago Pago, AS held by Samoa Technologies Broadcasting and Media Group
Target Audience: Working adults.
Alex Sene, President
Esther Prescott, General Manager

Tafuna

KJAL
01-01-2005; 585 kHz AM
US
(417) 862-2781
www.apmedia.org/site
contact@apmedia.org
License: Tafuna, AS held by District Council of the Assemblies of God in AS.
Arbitron Metro Market: Tafuna, AS; *Format:* Christian
Viliamu Paaga, General Manager
Bill Snider, Director

Arizona

Apache Junction

KBSZ
01-27-1960; 1260 kHz AM; *Hrs Open:* 24; 3.5 kw-D, 50 w-N; N33 22 56 W111 32 09
340 W. Wickenburg Way, Suite. B, Wickenburg, AZ 20036
(928) 668-1250; *Fax:* (928) 668-1251
www.kbsz-am.com
amradio1tv@yahoo.com
License: Apache Junction, Maricopa County, AZ held by 1TV.Com Inc.
Group Owner: 1TV.Com Inc.; (acq 3-31-2008; $500,000)
Population Served: 25,000; *Arbitron Metro Market:* Phoenix, AZ; *Adv. Rates:* 5; 5; 5; na
Pete Peterson, General Manager

KVVA-FM
07-01-1973; 107.1 MHz FM; 23.5 kw; 335 ft.; N33 26 48 W111 37 32
501 N. 44th St., Suite 425, Phoenix, AZ 85008 US
(602) 776-1400
www.josephoenix.com
License: Apache Junction, Pinal County, AZ held by Entravision Holdings LLC.
Group Owner: Entravision Communications Corp.; (acq 7-28-00; grpsl).

Arbitron Metro Market: Apache Junction, AZ; *Format:* Spanish, Adult Contemp; *Target Audience:* 18-49; Hispanic
Dean Apostalides, Senior VP
Tom Duran, General Manager
Chris Moncayo, General Sales Mgr
Edgar Pineda, Programming Director

Arizona City

KKMR
04-13-1985; 106.5 MHz FM; *Hrs Open:* 24; 6 kw; 292 ft.; N32 50 4 W111 38 15
6006 S. 30th St., Phoenix, AZ 85042 US
(602) 243-3333; *Fax:* (602) 513-7409
www.univision.com
License: Arizona City, Pinal County, AZ held by Univision Radio License Corp.
Group Owner: Univision Radio; (acq 9-22-2003; grpsl).
Arbitron Metro Market: Phoenix, AZ; *Format:* Spanish; *Target Audience:* 25-54.; *Adv. Rates:* 50; 50; 50; 50
Roberto Yanez, Vice President and General Manager

Ash Fork

KAFZ
99.7 MHz FM; 10.5 kw; 325 meters
25 E. 86th St., New York, NY 10028 USA
(917) 535-0419
License: Ash Fork, AZ held by Alex Media Inc.
Group Owner: Alex Media Inc.
Format: Variety/Diverse
Alexander Berger, President

Bagdad

KFTT
01-01-2002; 107.7 MHz FM; 1 kw horiz; 1250 ft.; N34 33 25 W113 16 0
P.O. Box 1866, Lake Havasu City, AZ 86405 US
(928) 855-1051; *Fax:* (928) 855-7996
www.maddogwireless.net
info@maddog.net
License: Bagdad, Yava County, AZ held by Smoke and Mirrors LLC.
Group Owner: Smoke and Mirrors LLC; (acq 4-18-2001)
Arbitron Metro Market: Lake Havasu City, AZ; *Format:* Adult Contemp
Scott Gosselin, VP/GM
Kim Turner, Operations Manager

Benson

KAVV
04-01-1983; 97.7 MHz FM; *Hrs Open:* 24; 6 kw; 590 ft; N31 54 24 W110 27 08
Mailing Address: Box 18899, Tucson, AZ 85731
Second Address: 156 W. 5th St., Benson, AZ 85602
(520) 586-9797
www.cavefm.com
cave@gainbroadband.com
License: Benson, Cochise County, AZ held by Stereo 97 Inc.
Population Served: 60,000 *Special Programming:* Relg 3 hrs wkly; *Target Audience:* 25-49.
Paul Lotsof, Station Manager/Program Director/Chief Engineer

Bisbee

*KRMB
01-01-1997; 90.1 MHz FM; 0.115 kw; 2208 ft.; N31 28 55 W109 57 31 *Rebroadcasts:* Rebroadcasts KRMC(FM) Douglas 100%
Box 3765, McAllen, TX 78502 US
(956) 787-9788
www.moodyradio.org
License: Bisbee, Cochise County, AZ held by World Radio Network Inc.
Group Owner: World Radio Network Inc.
Format: Christian
Glen Lafitte, CEO
Kitty Stinson, COO
James Gablin, Director of Broadcast Operations
Jamie Sepulveda, Director of Finance and Administration

KWCD
10-12-1979; 92.3 MHz FM; *Hrs Open:* 24; 0.09 kw; 2129 ft.; N31 28 52 W109 57 30
P.O. Box 2770, Sierra Vista, AZ 85636 US
(520) 458-4313; *Fax:* (520) 458-4317
www.kwcdcountry.com
KWCD@cherrycreekradio.com
License: Bisbee, Cochise County, AZ held by CCR-Sierra Vista IV LLC.
Group Owner: Cherry Creek Radio LLC; (acq 12-19-2003; grpsl).
Nat'l Network: Westwood One; *Nat'l Reps:* Tacher
Arbitron Metro Market: Sierra Vista, AZ; *Format:* Country; *Hrs. of News Programming:* news progmg one hr wkly; *No. News Employees:* 1; *Target Audience:* 25-54; financially secure adults & military personnel
Grady Butler, Operations Dir
Randy Sueskind, General Manager

*KWRB
12-01-1996; 90.9 MHz FM; *Hrs Open:* 24; 0.99 kw vert; 2093 ft.; N31 28 58 W109 57 29
P.O. Box 3333, McAllen, TX 78502 US
(520) 452-8022; *Fax:* (520) 452-0927
www.kwrb.org
License: Bisbee, Cochise County, AZ held by World Radio Network Inc.
Arbitron Metro Market: Sierra Vista, AZ; *Format:* Christian, Religious; *Target Audience:* Women 35+.
Laia Daniels, Operations Dir

Black Canyon City

KBMB
03-30-1981; 710 kHz AM; *Hrs Open:* 24; 22 kw-D, 3.9 kw-N, DA-2; N34 04 50 W112 09 13
501 N. 44th St., Suite 425, Phoenix, AZ 85008 US
(602) 776-1400
www.espnradio710am.com
License: Black Canyon City, Yavapai County, AZ held by Entravision Holdings LLC.
Group Owner: Entravision Communications Corp.; (acq 7-28-00; grpsl).
Arbitron Metro Market: Phoenix, AZ; *Format:* Sports; *Target Audience:* 18-54.; *Adv. Rates:* 75; 75; 75; 50
Tom Duran, General Manager

Buckeye

KDVA
01-01-1992; 106.9 MHz FM; 6 kw; 305 ft.; N33 27 1 W112 35 58
501 N. 44th St., Suite 425, Phoenix, AZ 85008 US
(602) 776-1400; *Fax:* (602) 279-2921
www.josephoenix.com
License: Buckeye, Maricopa County, AZ held by Entravision Holdings LLC.
Group Owner: Entravision Communications Corp.; (acq 6-14-2001; $10 million)
Arbitron Metro Market: Phoenix, AZ; *Format:* Spanish
Dean Apostalides, Senior VP
Tom Duran, General Manager
Chris Moncayo, General Sales Mgr
Edgar Pineda, Programming Director

Bullhead City

KZZZ
11-15-1981; 1490 kHz AM
2350 Miracle Mile Rd., Suite 300, Bullhead City, AZ 86442 US
(928) 763-5586
www.talkatoz.com
License: Bullhead City, AZ held by Cameron Broadcasting Inc.
Group Owner: Cameron Broadcasting Inc.; acq 7-91; $1.28 million with KNKK(FM) Needles, CA;
Nat'l Network: Fox News Radio
Arbitron Metro Market: Bullhead City, AZ; *Format:* News/Talk; *No. News Employees:* 1; *Target Audience:* 35 plus.
Don Jaeger, Operations Dir

KFLG
10-01-1978; 1000 kHz AM; 1 kw-D, NDD; N35 10 10 W114 38 2
2350 Miracle Mile Rd., Suite 300, Bullhead City, AZ 86442 US
(928) 763-5586; *Fax:* (520) 763-3775
www.kflg947.com
License: Bullhead City, AZ held by Cameron Broadcasting Inc.
Group Owner: Cameron Broadcasting Inc.; acq 11-24-99).
Arbitron Metro Market: Bullhead City, AZ; *Format:* Country
Special Programming: Country Classic Sunday 10-2, American Country Countdown Sunday am; *Target Audience:* 18-64
Don Jaeger, Operations Dir

*KVIR
89.9 MHz FM; 18 kw vert; 2294 ft.; N35 14 54 W114 44 34
Rebroadcasts: Rebroadcasts KAWZ (FM), Twin Falls, ID 100%
Mailing Address: P.O. Box 391, Twin Falls, ID 83301 US
Second Address: 4002 North 3300 East, Twin Falls, ID 83301
(800) 357-4226; *Fax:* (208) 736-1958
www.csnradio.com
License: Bullhead City, Mohave County, AZ held by Calvary Chapel of Twin Falls, Inc.
Group Owner: CSN International
Arbitron Metro Market: Bullhead City, AZ; *Format:* Christian
Mike Kestler, President
Daniel Davidson, Operations Dir
Joe Jennings, Station Manager & Program Director
Mike Stocklin, Underwriting Director
Kelly Carlson, Engineering Dir

Camp Verde

KAJM
07-04-1984; 104.3 MHz FM; *Hrs Open:* 24; 40 kw; 2648 ft.; N34 13 47 W112 21 3
7434 E. Stetson Drive, Suite 255, Scottsdale, AZ 85251 US
(480) 994-9100; *Fax:* (480) 423-8770
www.mega1043.com
License: Camp Verde, Yavapai County, AZ held by Sierra H. Broadcasting Inc.
Nat'l Network: Westwood One; CNN Radio; *Nat'l Reps:* Roslin
Arbitron Metro Market: Scottsdale, AZ; *Format:* Blues; *Target Audience:* 25-54; general; *Adv. Rates:* 100; 80; 100; 60
Steven Szalay, Operations Dir
Michael Mallace, General Manager
Jack Preda, General Sales Mgr
Fred Rico, Programming Director
Matt Kirkpatrick, Promotions Manager
Michael Day, Chief Engineer
Alex Santa Maria, Music Director

Casas Adobes

KZLZ
08-31-1991; 105.3 MHz FM; *Hrs Open:* 24; 0.58 kw; 1906 ft.; N32 14 56 W111 6 58
1436 Auburn Boulevard, Sacramento, CA 95815 US
(530) 325-3054; *Fax:* (530) 325-3495
sonia@kzlzradio.com
License: Casas Adobes, Pinal County, AZ held by KZLZ LLC.
Group Owner: KZLZ LLC; (acq 12-1-2006; $4.75 million)
Arbitron Metro Market: Casas Adobes, AZ; *Target Audience:* General.
Sonya Tabanico, General Manager
Cesar Zalciora, Programming Director

Cave Creek

KFNX
06-27-1997; 1100 kHz AM; *Hrs Open:* 24; 50 kw-D, DA2; 1 kw-N, DA2; N33 47 52 W111 59 30
1185 N. Main Street, Providence, RI 02904 US
(602) 277-1100; *Fax:* (602) 248-1478
www.1100kfnx.com
License: Cave Creek, AZ held by Premier Radio Stations, LLC
Nat'l Network: CNN Radio; *Regional Network:* Arizona News Radio; *Wire Services:* CNN
Arbitron Metro Market: Phoenix, AZ; *Format:* Talk; *No. News Employees:* 1; *Target Audience:* 35 plus; Upscale; *Adv. Rates:* 75; 75; 75; 50
Francis Battaglia, President/Chief Executive Officer
Matthew Battaglia, Business Manager

Cedarville

KRMW
12-21-1992; 94.9 MHz FM; 21 kw; 761 feet; N35 51 00 W94 23 00
4209 Frontage Rd., Fayetteville, AR 72703 US
(479) 521-5566; *Fax:* (479) 521-0751
www.949nashicon.com
dan.hentschel@cumulus.com
License: Cedarville, AR held by Cumulus Licensing LLC
Group Owner: Cumulus Media Inc.
Format: Country
Dan Hentschel, Programming Director
Anita Cowan, Promotions Manager
Dale Daniels

Chandler

KMLE
06-18-1979; 107.9 MHz FM; *Hrs Open:* 24; 96 kW; 272 ft.; N33 20 3 W112 3 43
840 N Central Ave., Phoenix, AZ 85004 USA
(602) 452-1000; *Fax:* (602) 440-6530
www.kmle1079.com
License: Chandler, Maricopa County, AZ held by CBS Radio Stations Inc.
Group Owner: CBS Radio; (acq 8-7-00; grpsl).
Arbitron Metro Market: Phoenix, AZ; *Format:* Country *Special Programming:* Camel Views one hr wkly; *No. News Employees:* 2; *Target Audience:* 25-54
Tim Richards, Programming Director
Jackie Pulido, Promotions Manager

Chinle

KFXR-FM
08-01-1995; 107.3 MHz FM; *Hrs Open:* 24; 3.6 kw; 1,631 ft.; N36 21 7 W109 49 54 *Rebroadcasts:* Rebroadcasts KGLX(FM) Gallup
1632 S. 2nd St., Gallup, NM 87301 US
(505) 863-9391
License: Chinle, Apache County, AZ held by CC Licenses LLC.
Group Owner: iHeartMedia; (acq 8-18-2000).
Arbitron Metro Market: Gallup, NM; *Format:* Country
Chuck Hammond, Vice President/Market Manager

Chino Valley

KDDL
01-01-1999; 94.3 MHz FM; 4.1 kw; 810 ft.; N34 49 32 W112 34 9
530 Wilshire Blvd., Suite 301, Santa Monica, CA 90401 US
(928) 775-2530; *Fax:* (928) 775-2532
License: Chino Valley, Yavapai County, AZ held by Prescott Valley Broadcasting Co. Inc.
Group Owner: Prescott Valley Broadcasting Co. Inc.; (acq 10-15-2007; $1.2 million)
Format: Country
Patti Ezell, General Manager

Claypool

KIKO-FM
08-01-1991; 97.3 MHz FM; *Hrs Open:* 24; 0.67 kw; 3323 ft.; N33 17 20 W110 49 45
4501 Broadway, Miami, AZ 85539 US
(928) 425-4471; *Fax:* (928) 425-9393
radiokiko@cableone.net
License: Claypool, Gila County, AZ held by 1TV.com Inc.
Group Owner: 1TV.Com Inc.; (acq 4-30-2008; $1.025 million with KIKO(AM) Miami)
Nat'l Network: Jones Radio Networks
Format: Adult Contemp; *Hrs. of News Programming:* news progmg 6 hrs wkly; *No. News Employees:* 1; *Target Audience:* 21-55; blue collar, housewives, white collar; *Adv. Rates:* 12; 12; 12; 12
Shelly Harrison, General Manager
Bill Pettus, Director of Sales
Chelle Hodson, Office Manager

Clifton

KCUZ
07-31-1969; 1490 kHz AM; *Hrs Open:* 24; 1 kw-U, ND1; N33 2 30 W109 17 40 *Rebroadcasts:* Rebroadcasts KFMM(FM) Thatcher 100%
Mailing Address: C/O Frank H. Newell, P.O. Box 567, Green Valley, AZ 85622 US
Second Address: 301 B Hwy. 70 E., Safford, AZ 85546
(928) 428-0916; *Fax:* (928) 428-7797
www.saffordradio.com
License: Clifton, AZ held by Cochise Broadcasting LLC.
Group Owner: Cochise Broadcasting LLC; (acq 6-30-2007; $330,000 with KFMM(FM) Thatcher)
Format: Classic Rock *Special Programming:* Relg 2 hrs, loc talk 8 hrs wkly; *Hrs. of News Programming:* news progmg 7 hrs wkly; *No. News Employees:* 1; *Target Audience:* 25-54.; *Adv. Rates:* 12; 12; 12; 12.
Rick Schneider, General Manager
Darwin Morris, Programming Director

KWRQ
10-01-1986; 102.3 MHz FM; *Hrs Open:* 24; 4.3 kw; 2264 ft.; N32 53 23 W109 19 26
Mailing Address: 3335 W. 8th St., Thatcher, CA 95552 USA
Second Address: P.O. Drawer L., Safford, AZ 85546
(928) 428-1320; *Fax:* (928) 428-1311
www.mysouthernaz.com
traffic@mcmurrayradio.com
License: Clifton, Greenlee County, AZ held by McMurray Communications Inc.
Group Owner: McMurray Communications Inc.; acq 11-97; $350,000)
Nat'l Network: Jones Radio Networks
Arbitron Metro Market: Safford, AZ; *Format:* Adult Contemp; *Target Audience:* 20-35; working females

*K204CE
08-31-1996; 88.7 MHz FM; 0.25 kW; 2382 ft; N32 53 14 W109 18 48
820 N LaSalle Blvd, Chicago, IL 60610 USA
www.moodyradio.org/stations/satellators/graham-greenlee
License: Clifton, AZ held by The Moody Bible Institute of Chicago
Group Owner: Moody Radio
Nat'l Network: Moody
Arbitron Metro Market: Clifton, AZ; *Format:* Christian

Colorado City

KXFF
01-01-1993; 106.1 MHz FM; *Hrs Open:* 24; 35 kw; 1138 ft.; N37 5 41 W113 11 6
P.O. Box 711, Colorado City, AZ 86021 US
(435) 673-3579; *Fax:* (435) 673-8900
dhiatt@cherrycreekradio.com
License: Colorado City, Mohave County, AZ held by CCR-St. George IV LLC.
Group Owner: Cherry Creek Radio LLC; (acq 5-3-2006; grpsl)
Arbitron Metro Market: St. George, UT; *Format:* Oldies
Chris McCarthy, General Sales Mgr
Rick Parrish, Promotions Manager

Coolidge

KCKY
11-19-1964; 1150 kHz AM; *Hrs Open:* 18; 5 kw-D, DA2; 1 kw-N, DA2; N33 0 27 W111 32 54
13968 N Harmony Road, Coolidge, AZ 85228 US
(602) 426-1150; *Fax:* (602) 276-8119
License: Coolidge, AZ held by Cortaro Broadcasting Corp.
Arbitron Metro Market: Phoenix, AZ; *Format:* Christian; *No. News Employees:* 1; *Target Audience:* General.
Moses Herrera, President
Moses Herrera Jr., Station Manager

Cordes Lakes

KNRJ
01-01-2000; 101.1 MHz FM; *Hrs Open:* 24; 40 kw; 807 meters; N34 13 47 W112 21 03
7434 E. Stetson Dr., Suite 255, Scottsdale, AZ 85377
(480) 994-9100,(800) 254-7510; *Fax:* (480) 423-8770
www.azthebeat.com
License: Cordes Lakes, Gila County, AZ held by Sierra H. Broadcasting Inc.
Nat'l Network: Westwood One; CNN Radio
Arbitron Metro Market: Phoenix, AZ; *Adv. Rates:* 100; 80; 100; 60
Steve Szalay, Operations Dir
Michael Mallace, General Manager
Rod Carrillo, Programming Director

Cortaro

KVOI
09-23-1953; 1030 kHz AM; 10 kw-D, DA2; 1 kw-N, DA2; N32 20 51 W111 4 19
3222 South Richey Avenue, Tucson, AZ 85713 US
(520) 790-2440; *Fax:* (520) 790-2937
www.kvoi.com
info@kvoi.com
License: Cortaro, AZ held by Good News Broadcasting Inc.
Group Owner: Good News Communications Inc.; (acq 9-53).
Nat'l Reps: Salem
Arbitron Metro Market: Tucson, AZ; *Format:* News, Talk; *Hrs. of News Programming:* news progmg 10 hrs wkly; *No. News Employees:* 1; *Target Audience:* 35 plus.
Doug Martin, President
Ray Alan, Operations Director/Programming Director
Mary Martin, General Sales Mgr
Ed Alexander, Promotions Director
Larry Massey, Chief Engineer

Cottonwood

KVRD-FM
07-01-1991; 105.7 MHz FM; *Hrs Open:* 24; 0.3 kw; 2556 ft.; N34 41 12 W112 7 0
Mailing Address: P.O. Box 187, Cottonwood, AZ 86326 US
Second Address: 3405 E. Hwy. 89 A, Bldg. A, Cottonwood, AZ 86326
(928) 634-2286; *Fax:* (928) 634-2295
www.kvrdfm.com
License: Cottonwood, Yavapai County, AZ
Group Owner: Yavapai Broadcasting Corp.
Arbitron Metro Market: Cottonwood, AZ; *Format:* Country; *Hrs. of News Programming:* News progmg 2 hrs wkly; *Target Audience:* General.
David Kessel, General Manager
Mark Bachman, Programming Director
Paul David, News Director

KYBC
12-20-1964; 1600 kHz AM; *Hrs Open:* 24; 1 kw-D, ND1; 0.046 kw-N, ND1; N34 43 15 W111 59 55
Mailing Address: P.O. Box 187, Cottonwood, AZ 86326 US
Second Address: 3405 E. Hwy. 89 A, Bldg. A, Cottonwood, AZ 86326
(928) 634-2286; *Fax:* (928) 634-2295
www.myradioplace.com
kybc@myradioplace.com
License: Cottonwood, AZ held by Yavapai Broadcasting Corp.
Group Owner: Yavapai Broadcasting Corp.; acq 1-96; $750,000 with co-located FM).
Nat'l Network: Westwood One
Arbitron Metro Market: Cottowood, AZ; *Format:* Adult Contemp; *No. News Employees:* 2; *Target Audience:* 18-plus.
W. Grant Hafley, President
David Kessel, General Manager
Mike Puetz, General Sales Mgr
Bryan Saravo, Programming Director

KKLD
08-01-1983; 95.9 MHz FM; *Hrs Open:* 24; 21 kw; 2621 ft.; N34 41 12 W112 7 2
2690 E. Huntington Drive, Flagstaff, AZ 86004 US
(928) 634-2286; *Fax:* (928) 634-2295
www.kkld.com
License: Cottonwood, Yavapai County, AZ held by Yavapai Broadcasting Corp.
Group Owner: Yavapai Broadcasting Corp.; (acq 10-1-2000; grpsl).
Arbitron Metro Market: Cottonwood, AZ; *Format:* Oldies; *Hrs. of News Programming:* News progmg 7 hrs wkly; *Target Audience:* 18-49.
W. Grant Hafley, President
Rich Malone, Operations Dir
David Kessel, General Manager

Desert Hills

KRRK
09-09-1974; 100.7 MHz FM; *Hrs Open:* 24; 0.275 kw; 2697 ft.; N34 33 6 W114 11 37
2068 McCulloch Blvd, Lake Havasu City, AZ 86403 US
(928) 855-1051; *Fax:* (928) 855-7996
www.maddog.net
info@maddog.net
License: Desert Hills, Mohave County, AZ held by Smoke and Mirrors LLC.
Group Owner: Smoke and Mirrors LLC; (acq 11-29-99)
Arbitron Metro Market: Lake Havasu City, AZ; *Format:* Light Rock; *Hrs. of News Programming:* news progmg 5 hrs wkly; *No. News Employees:* 1; *Target Audience:* 18-34.
Kim Turner, Operations Dir
Scott Gosselin, General Manager

Dewey-Humboldt

KMVA
01-15-1988; 97.5 MHz FM; *Hrs Open:* 24; 42 kw; 2785 ft.; N34 14 5 W112 22 2
4745 North 7th Street, Suite 410, Phoenix, AZ 85014 US
(602) 222-9750; *Fax:* (602) 222-2297
License: Dewey-Humboldt, Yavapai County, AZ held by Riviera Broadcasting
Arbitron Metro Market: Phoenix, AZ; *Format:* Oldies
Michael Cutchall, CEO
Jose Rodiles, General Manager
Kristin Levy, General Sales Mgr

Dolan Springs

KOAS
01-07-1976; 105.7 MHz FM; *Hrs Open:* 24; 100 kw horiz; N35 50 11.9 W114 19 14.10
2920 S. Durango Dr., Las Vegas, NV 89117 US
(702) 730-0030; *Fax:* (702) 736-8447
www.oldschool1057.com
License: Dolan Springs, Mohave County, AZ held by Beasley Media Group LLC
Group Owner: Beasley Broadcast Group Inc.; (acq 10-3-2005; $38 million with KVGS(FM) Laughlin, NV)
Arbitron Metro Market: Las Vegas, NV; *Format:* Adult Contemp; *Target Audience:* 25-64; *Adv. Rates:* 55; 55; 55; 35
Tom Humm, General Manager
Lee Grau, General Sales Mgr
John Candelaria, Programming Director
Shayla Martinez, Promotions and Marketing Manager
Lamar Smith, Chief Engineer
Cory Cuddeback, Director of Sales/National Sales Manager
Sandy Ellis, Digital Director
Jesus Novo, Director of Business Affairs/Human Resources

*KLKI
91.9 MHz FM; 30 kw; Ant 2,270 ft.; N35 14 56 W114 44 34
P.O. Box 2098, Omaha, NE 68103-2098
(800) 525-5683
www.klove.com

License: Dolan Springs, Mohave County, AZ held by Educational Media Foundation
Group Owner: EMF Broadcasting
Format: Christian
Mike Novak, President

Doney Park

KZXK
01-01-2009; 98.9 MHz FM; 0.14 kw; 2001 ft.; N35 14 26 W111 35 51
PO Box 36717, Tucson, AZ 85740 US
(703) 812-0482
License: Doney Park, Coconino County, AZ held by Cochise Broadcasting LLC.
Group Owner: Cochise Broadcasting LLC
Arbitron Metro Market: Doney Park, AZ
Ted Tucker, General Manager

Douglas

KAPR
03-08-1958; 930 kHz AM; *Hrs Open:* 24; 2.5 kw-D, ND1; 0.071 kw-N, ND1; N31 22 8 W109 31 45 *Rebroadcasts:* KVOI
3222 South Richey Avenue, Tucson, AZ 85713 US
(520) 790-2440; *Fax:* (520) 790-2937
www.kvoi.com
info@kvoi.com
License: Douglas, AZ held by Good Music Inc.
Group Owner: Good News Communications Inc.; (acq 6-8-2001; $187,500)
Nat'l Network: Salem Radio Network; *Nat'l Reps:* Salem
Arbitron Metro Market: Tuscon, AZ; *Format:* News, News/Talk, 86; *Hrs. of News Programming:* News progmg 2 hrs wkly; *Target Audience:* General.; *Adv. Rates:* 5; 5; 5; 5
Doug Martin, CEO/President/GM
Ray Alan, Operations Dir
Ed Alexander, Promotions Manager
Ray Alan, Programming Director
Rhonda Curtis, CFO

KDAP
01-01-1946; 1450 kHz AM; 1 kw-U, ND1; N31 21 18 W109 33 6
2031 N. Sulphur Springs St., Douglas, AZ 85607 US
(520) 364-3486; (520) 364-3484; *Fax:* (520) 364-3483
License: Douglas, AZ held by Howard N. Henderson
Target Audience: General; loc Hispanic & Mexican residents
Howard Henderson, General Manager

KCDQ
03-15-1979; 95.3 MHz FM; *Hrs Open:* 24; 0.8 kw; 39 ft.; N31 22 8 W109 31 45
PO Box 36717, Tucson, AZ 85740 US
(520) 459-8201; *Fax:* (520) 458-7104
www.kcdq.com
License: Douglas, Cochise County, AZ held by Cochise Broadcasting LLC
Group Owner: Cochise Broadcasting LLC; (acq 6-8-2001; $137,500).
Nat'l Network: Westwood One
Arbitron Metro Market: Sierra Vista, AZ; *Format:* Contemporary Hits/Top 40; *Hrs. of News Programming:* News progmg 11 hrs wkly; *Target Audience:* 29-49.
Ted Tucker, General Manager

*KRMC
01-01-1996; 91.7 MHz FM; 3 kw; 236 ft.; N31 20 52 W109 28 42
Box 3333, McAllen, TX 78502 US
(520) 287-5206; *Fax:* (520) 364-5392
www.knog.org
License: Douglas, Cochise County, AZ held by World Radio Network Inc.
Arbitron Metro Market: Nogalas, AZ; *Format:* Spanish
David Johnson, President
Glen Lafitte, General Manager
James Heck, Engineering Dir

Drake

*KJZA
89.5 MHz FM; *Hrs Open:* 24; 0.25 kw; 2526 ft.; N35 12 0 W112 12 18
R.R. Box 308, Perkinsville, AZ 86334 US
(928) 541-1008
www.kjza.org
kjzafm@yahoo.com
License: Drake, Yavapai County, AZ held by St. Paul Bible College.
Nat'l Network: NPR; PRI
Arbitron Metro Market: Kingman, AZ; *Format:* Jazz

Nichole Erickson, Director & President
Tom Erickson, General Manager
Tom Erickson, Sales Manager

Duncan

KJIK
01-01-2003; 100.7 MHz FM; *Hrs Open:* 24; 9.73 kw; 2349 ft.; N32 53 21 W109 19 20
1850 West Thatcher Boulevard, Safford, AZ 85546 US
(928) 428-4100; *Fax:* (928) 348-9581
www.kjik.fm
traffic@kjk.fm
License: Duncan, Greenlee County, AZ held by Country Mountain Airwaves LLC.
Group Owner: Country Mountain Airwaves LLC
Arbitron Metro Market: Duncan, AZ; *Format:* Adult Contemp
Dan Curtis, General Manager
Roger Martin, Advertising
Roger Martin, Account Manager

Eagar

KTHQ
01-01-1996; 92.5 MHz FM; *Hrs Open:* 24; 62 kw; 1178 ft.; N34 15 6 W109 35 6
1491 Thatcher Blvd, Safford, AZ 85546 US
(928) 532-1010; *Fax:* (928) 532-0101
www.Qcountry92.com
mail@qcountry92.com
License: Eagar, Apache County, AZ held by Country Mountain Airwaves LLC.
Group Owner: Country Mountain Airwaves LLC
Arbitron Metro Market: Show Low, AZ; *Format:* Country
Camden Smith, General Manager
Laurie Pogson, News Director

Flagstaff

KAFF
10-15-1963; 930 kHz AM; *Hrs Open:* 5 AM-midnight; 5 kw-D, 50 w-N; N35 11 26 W111 40 37
Mailing Address: 1117 W. Rt. 66, Flagstaff, AZ 86001
Second Address: 1117 W. Hwy. 66, Flagstaff, AZ 86001
(928) 774-5231; *Fax:* (928) 779-2988
License: Flagstaff, Coconino County, AZ held by Guyann Inc.
Group Owner: Guyann Corp.; (acq 9-7-2005; grpsl).
Wire Services: AP
Population Served: 492,000; *Arbitron Metro Market:* Flagstaff, AZ; *No. News Employees:* 2; *Target Audience:* 25-54.
Steve Hoshor, General Manager
Jeff Basham, Programming Director
Ryan Oler, Chief Engineer

KAFF-FM
10-01-1968; 92.9 MHz FM; *Hrs Open:* 24; 98 kw; 1512 ft.; N34 58 7 W111 30 24
PO Box 1930, Flagstaff, AZ 86002 US
(928) 774-5231; *Fax:* (928) 779-2988
www.kaff.com
production@kaff.com
License: Flagstaff, Coconino County, AZ held by Guyann Inc.
Group Owner: Guyann Corp.
Nat'l Network: ABC; *Wire Services:* AP
Arbitron Metro Market: Flagstaff, AZ; *Hrs. of News Programming:* News progmg 4 hrs wkly; *No. News Employees:* 2
Jeff Basham, Programming & News Director
Ryan Older, Chief Engineer
Krista Kay, Disc Jockey

*KJTA
12-19-2001; 89.9 MHz FM; *Hrs Open:* 24; 1 kw; 1988 ft.; N35 14 25 W111 35 49
341 S. Washington, Lancaster, WI 53813 US
(928) 774-9514; *Fax:* (928) 774-9515
www.myflr.org
License: Flagstaff, Coconino County, AZ held by Family Life Broadcasting Inc.
Group Owner: Family Life Communications Inc.; (acq 5-23-2007; grpsl)
Format: Christian, Religious
Alonzo Williams, Vice President of Operations
Rod Robison, Vice President of Development

KVNA-FM
01-01-1999; 100.1 MHz FM; *Hrs Open:* 24; 5.2 kw; 1434 ft.; N34 58 5 W111 30 29
P. O. Box 1488, Sedona, AZ 86339 US
(928) 526-2700; *Fax:* (928) 634-2295
www.myradioplace.com
License: Flagstaff, Coconino County, AZ
Group Owner: Family Life Communications

Arbitron Metro Market: Flagstaff, AZ; *Format:* Adult Contemp

KMGN
01-01-1975; 93.9 MHz FM; *Hrs Open:* 24; 96 kw; 1509 ft.; N34 58 8 W111 30 28
Mailing Address: P.O. Box 1930, Flagstaff, AZ 86002 US
Second Address: 1117 W Rt. 66, Flagstaff, AZ 86001
(928) 774-5231; *Fax:* (928) 779-2988
www.kmgn.com
info@kmgn.com
License: Flagstaff, Coconino County, AZ held by Guyann Corp.
Group Owner: Guyann Corp.; (acq 9-7-2005; grpsl)
Nat'l Network: ABC; *Wire Services:* AP
Format: Classic Rock; *Hrs. of News Programming:* news progmg 4 hrs wkly; *No. News Employees:* 2; *Target Audience:* 25-54; upscale, educated, rgnl audience
Steve Hoshor, General Manager
Jeff Basham, Programming Director

*KPUB
10-01-1995; 91.7 MHz FM; *Hrs Open:* 24; 0.5 kw; 1837 ft.; N35 14 34 W111 36 40
Post Office Box 5764, Flagstaff, AZ 87011 US
(928) 523-5628; *Fax:* (928) 523-7647
www.knau.org
knau@nau.edu
License: Flagstaff, Coconino County, AZ held by Northern Arizona University.
Nat'l Network: NPR; PRI
Format: News; *Hrs. of News Programming:* News progmg 50 hrs wkly; *Target Audience:* 25-54; educated, socially conscious achievers
Brian Sanders, Operations Dir
Lisa Skinner, Traffic Manager
Shelly Watkins, Director of Underwriting
Stacy Murison, Development Director

*KNAU
11-24-1970; 88.7 MHz FM; *Hrs Open:* 24; 100 kw; 1460 ft.; N34 58 7 W111 30 24
P.O. Box 5764, Flagstaff, AZ 86001 US
(928) 523-5628; *Fax:* (928) 523-7647
www.knau.org
knau@nau.edu
License: Flagstaff, Coconino County, AZ held by Arizona Board of Regents for and on behalf of Northern Arizona University.
Nat'l Network: NPR; PRI
Format: News; *Hrs. of News Programming:* news progmg 50 hrs wkly; *No. News Employees:* 3; *Target Audience:* 25-54; educated, socially conscious achievers
Brian Sanders, Operations Dir
Jon Swett, Chief Engineer
Stacy Murison, Development Director

KVNA
08-08-1950; 600 kHz AM; *Hrs Open:* 24; 1 kw-D, ND1; 0.048 kw-N, ND1; N35 12 2 W111 36 49
2690 E. Huntington Drive, Flagstaff, AZ 86004 US
(928) 526-2700; *Fax:* (928) 774-5852
License: Flagstaff, AZ held by Yavapai Broadcasting Corp.
Group Owner: Yavapai Broadcasting Corp.; (acq 9-30-2000; grpsl).
Nat'l Network: Westwood One; AP Network News; Jones Radio Networks; *Regional Network:* Arizona News Radio
Arbitron Metro Market: Flagstaff-Prescott, AZ; *Format:* News, News/Talk, 84, Talk *Special Programming:* Sp 3 hrs wkly, folk music 4hrs wkly; *Hrs. of News Programming:* news progmg 25 hrs wkly; *No. News Employees:* 1 *Target Audience:* General.; *Adv. Rates:* 12; 12; 12; 12
W. Hafley, President
David Kessel, General Manager
Rich Malone, Programming Director

KZGL
01-01-2007; 103.7 MHz FM; 0.56 kw; 1959 ft.; N35 14 25 W111 35 53
US
(928) 779-1037
www.eagle1037.fm
studio@eagle1037.fm
License: Flagstaff, Coconino County, AZ held by Towers Investment Trust
Format: Triple A

Florence

KCDX
01-01-1999; 103.1 MHz FM; 2.7 kw; 3058 ft.; N33 17 55 W110 50 28
P.O. Box 36717, Tucson, AZ 85740 US
(520) 459-8201; *Fax:* (520) 458-7104
www.kcdx.com

License: Florence, Pinal County, AZ held by Desert West Air Ranchers Corp.
Format: Classic Rock
Ted Tucker, General Manager

Fountain Hills

***KLVK**
05-01-2000; 89.1 MHz FM; *Hrs Open:* 24; 30 kw; 2306 ft.; N33 35 33 W112 34 49
1425 N. Market Blvd., Suite 9, Sacramento, CA 95834 US
(800) 525-5683
www.klove.com
klove@klove.com
License: Fountain Hills, Maricopa County, AZ held by Educational Media Foundation.
Group Owner: EMF Broadcasting; (acq 3-11-03; grpsl).
Nat'l Network: K-Love
Arbitron Metro Market: Omaha, NB; *Format:* Christian; *No. News Employees:* 3; *Target Audience:* 25-33; Judeo Christian, female
Darrell Chambliss, Chairman
Mike Novak, President
Dan Beck, General Sales Mgr
David Pierce, Programming Director
Ed Lenane, News & Operations Director
Sam Wallington, Engineering Dir

Gilbert

KEXX(FM)
02-25-1981; 103.9 MHz FM; *Hrs Open:* 24; 99.59 kw; Ant 620 ft; N33 14 50 W111 31 49
7434 E. Stetson Dr., Suite 265, Scottsdale, AZ 85251
(480) 423-9255; *Fax:* (480) 423-9382
www.theedge1039.com
nat@theedge1039.com
License: Gilbert, Pinal County, AZ held by RBG Phoenix Licenses LLC
Group Owner: Riviera Broadcast Group LLC; (acq 11-21-2005; $30 million).
Nat'l Reps: Roslin
Population Served: 1,446,948; *Arbitron Metro Market:* Phoenix, AZ; *Hrs. of News Programming:* News progmg 2 hrs wkly; *Target Audience:* 18-34.; *Adv. Rates:* 200; 175; 175; 125
Tim Pohlman, CEO/General Manager
Nat Galvin, Operations Dir

Glendale

KPXQ
01-01-1946; 1360 kHz AM; *Hrs Open:* 24
4880 Santa Rosa Road, Suite 300, Camarillo, CA 93012 US
(602) 955-9600; *Fax:* (602) 955-7860
www.kpxq1360.com
License: Glendale, AZ held by Common Ground Broadcasting Inc.
Group Owner: Salem Communications Corp.; (acq 6-23-99; $5 million)
Nat'l Network: Salem Radio Network; *Nat'l Reps:* Salem
Arbitron Metro Market: Phoenix, AZ; *Format:* Talk, Religious; *Hrs. of News Programming:* news progmg 6 hrs wkly; *No. News Employees:* 1; *Target Audience:* 25-54; adults
Stuart Epperson, Chairman
Edward Atsinger, CEO
Heath Garlutzo, General Sales Mgr
Diane Zapponi-Paisley, Programming Director
Diane Johnson, News Director
John Bortowski, Chief Engineer
Laurie Larson, Operations Manager

KTAR-FM
12-19-1970; 92.3 MHz FM; 98 kw; 1,788 ft.; N33 19 58 W112 3 48
7740 N. 16th St., Suite 200, Phoenix, AZ 85020 US
(602) 274-6200
www.ktar.com
License: Glendale, Maricopa County, AZ held by Bonneville International Corporation
Group Owner: Bonneville International Corporation; (acq 7-11-2006; $77.5 million).
Arbitron Metro Market: Phoenix, AZ; *Format:* News, News/Talk, 86; *Target Audience:* 18-49.
Ryan Hatch, Vice President, Content and Operations
Scott Sutherland, Vice President and Market Manager
Jessica Webb, Vice President, Sales
Ben Hartman, Promotions and Events Manager
Paul Ihander, News Director
Jim Knapp, VicePresident, Business Development
Jeremy Hudson, Digital Services Manager
Connie Drushel, Human Resources Director
Rosemary Scarfo, Community Relations

KLNZ
01-01-1994; 103.5 MHz FM; *Hrs Open:* 24; 62 kw; 2428 ft.; N33 35 33 W112 34 49
501 N. 44th St., Suite 425, Phoenix, AZ 85008 US
(602) 776-1400
www.tricolor1035.com
License: Glendale, Maricopa County, AZ held by Entravision Holdings LLC.
Group Owner: Entravision Communications Corp.; (acq 7-28-00; grpsl).
Arbitron Metro Market: Phoenix, AZ; *Format:* Tejano; *Target Audience:* General.
Tom Duran, General Manager
Chris Moncayo, General Sales Mgr
Carrie Strait, Programming Director

Globe

KQMR
09-25-1980; 100.3 MHz FM; *Hrs Open:* 24; 90 kw; 2,047 ft.; N33 17 23 W110 51 53
6006 S. 30th St., Phoenix, AZ 85042 US
(602) 243-3333; *Fax:* (602) 513-7409
www.univision.com
License: Globe, Gila County, AZ held by Univision Radio License Corp.
Group Owner: Univision Radio; (acq 9-22-2003; grpsl).
Arbitron Metro Market: Phoenix, AZ; *Format:* Spanish; *Target Audience:* 18-49; upscale, well-educated, affluent adults
Roberto Yanez, Vice President and General Manager
Eric Bench, National Sales Manager

KJAA
01-01-1971; 1240 kHz AM; *Hrs Open:* 24; 1 kw-U, ND1; N33 22 51 W110 45 25 *Rebroadcasts:* KVOI
1240 South Saguaro Drive, Globe, AZ 85501 US
(520) 790-2440; *Fax:* (520) 790-2937
www.kvoi.com
info@kvoi.com
License: Globe, AZ held by 1TV.Com Inc.
Group Owner: 1TV.Com Inc.; (acq 11-7-2008; $300,000)
Format: News, News/Talk, 86; *Hrs. of News Programming:* 3 hrs wkly; *No. News Employees:* 3; *Target Audience:* 35 plus.; *Adv. Rates:* 5; 5; 5; 5
Ray Alan, Operations Manager
Doug Martin, General Manager
Mary Martin, Sales Manager

KRDE
10-13-1995; 94.1 MHz FM; *Hrs Open:* 24; 4.7 kw; 1039 Meters HAAT; N33 17 37 W110 50 09
Mailing Address: Box 1660, Globe, AZ 85203
Second Address: 800 N. Main St., Globe, AZ 85501
(928) 402-9222; *Fax:* (928) 425-5063
www.krde.com
krde@cableone.net
License: Globe, Gila County, AZ held by Linda C. Corso.
Nat'l Network: Fox News Radio; Westwood One; *Regional Network:* Arizona News Radio *Regional Reps:* Arizona News Network
Population Served: 2,000,000; *Arbitron Metro Market:* Phoenix, AZ *Special Programming:* Country Convoy; *Hrs. of News Programming:* news progmg 20 hrs wkly; *No. News Employees:* 1; *Target Audience:* 25-54;active, family building, western suburban; *Adv. Rates:* 45; 35; 15; 10
Linda Corso, Operations Dir
Linda Corso, General Manager
Mindy Ersey, Station Manager
Mindy Ersey, Programming Director
Mindy Ersey, Promotions Manager
Sean Cram, News/Web Director
Brad Hartman, Sport - Fishing

***KVJC**
01-01-2003; 91.9 MHz FM; *Hrs Open:* 24; 0.66 kw; 3396 ft.; N33 17 37 W110 50 9 *Rebroadcasts:* Rebroadcasts KAWZ (FM)
P.O. Box 391, Twin Falls, ID 83303 US
(800) 357-4226; *Fax:* (208) 736-1958
www.csnradio.com
csn@csnradio.com
License: Globe, Gila County, AZ held by Calvary Chapel of Twin Falls, Inc.
Group Owner: CSN International
Arbitron Metro Market: Phoenix, AZ; *Format:* Christian, Religious
Mike Kestler, President
Daniel Davidson, Operations Dir
Don Mills, Network Programming Director
Mike Stocklin, Underwriting Director
Kelly Carlson, Engineering Dir

***KLKA**
01-01-2008; 88.5 MHz FM; 1.5 kw vert; 2986 ft.; N33 17 55 W110 50 28 *Rebroadcasts:* Rebroadcasts KVLT(FM) Temple, TX 100%
1601 Belvedere Rd 204 E, West Palm Beach, FL 33406 US
(800) 525-5683; *Fax:* (916) 251-1650
www.klove.com
klove@klove.com
License: Globe, Gila County, AZ held by American Educational Broadcasting Inc.
Nat'l Network: K-Love
Arbitron Metro Market: Globe, AZ; *Format:* Christian; *No. News Employees:* 13
Mike Novak, President and CEO
James Auel, General Manager
David Pierce, Programming Director
Ed Lenane, News Director
Sam Wallington, Engineering Dir
Dan Antonelli, Chief Business Development Officer
Eric Moser, Chief FinancialOfficer
Tim Luttrell, News Reporter

Golden Valley

KYET
08-17-1992; 1170 kHz AM; *Hrs Open:* 24; 10 kw-D, ND1; 0.25 kw-N, ND1; N35 15 38 W112 10 55
138 West Bill Williams Avenue, Williams, AZ 86046 US
(928) 753-9100; *Fax:* (928) 753-1978
License: Golden Valley, AZ held by Grand Canyon Gateway Broadcasting L.L.C.

Rhonda Hart, President
Joe Hart, General Manager
Steve Levin, Programming Director
Dave Hawkins, News Director
Matt Krick, Engineering Dir
Deana Campbell, Traffic Manager

Grand Canyon

***KNAG**
90.3 MHz FM; 3 kw; 295 ft.; N35 56 44 W112 10 16
Rebroadcasts: KNAU-FM Flagstaff 100%
P . O. Box 5764, Flagstaff, AZ 86011 US
(928) 523-5628; *Fax:* (928) 523-7647
www.knau.org
knau@nau.edu
License: Grand Canyon, Coconino County, AZ held by Arizona Board of Regents/Northern Arizona University.
Arbitron Metro Market: Flagstaff, AZ; *Format:* News
Brian Sanders, Operations Director/Announcer
Cory Sheeley, Underwriting Sales Associate
Stacy Murison, Development Director
Shelly Watkins, Underwriting Manager
Laurel Morales, Fronteras Reporter
Mark Bevis, Content Manager

Green Valley

KFMA
02-20-1983; 92.1 MHz FM; *Hrs Open:* 24; 50 kw; 492 ft.; N32 0 11 W110 47 49
6290 Sunset Boulevard, Hollywood, CA 90028 US
(520) 407-4500
www.kfma.com
License: Green Valley, Pima County, AZ held by Arizona Lotus Corp.
Group Owner: Lotus Communications Corp.; (acq 5-10-93; $1.26 million;
Nat'l Reps: Christal
Arbitron Metro Market: Tucson, AZ; *Format:* Alternative *Special Programming:* Love night 20 hrs wkly; *Target Audience:* 18-34.
Ken Kwilosz, General Manager
Larry Mac, Operations Manager
Scott Romero, Local Sales Manager
Jessica Allen, Promotions Coordinator
Chris Firmage, Programming Director
Cindy Craig, Marketing Director

KYWD
10-21-1990; 97.1 MHz FM; *Hrs Open:* 24; 1.75 kw; 613 ft.; N31 58 37 W111 06 04
3202 N. Oracle Rd., Tucson, AZ 85705 US
(520) 618-2100
www.wildcountry971.com
License: Green Valley, Pima County, AZ held by Capstar TX LLC
Group Owner: iHeartMedia
Arbitron Metro Market: Tucson, AZ; *Format:* Country; *Hrs. of News Programming:* news progmg 2 hrs wkly; *No. News Employees:* 2; *Target Audience:* 18-35.

Richard J. Bressler, President

KGVY
09-23-1981; 1080 kHz AM; *Hrs Open:* 6 AM-sunset; 1 kw-D, NDD; N31 55 34 W110 59 45
Mailing Address: 1 Broadcast Center, Plano, IL 60545 US
Second Address: 1510 W. Camino Antigua, Sahuarita, AZ 85629
(520) 399-1000; *Fax:* (520) 399-9300
www.kgvy1080.com
DeAnnaS@kgvy1080.com
License: Green Valley, AZ held by KGVY LLC
Nat'l Network: ABC
Arbitron Metro Market: Tucson, AZ; *Format:* Oldies; *Hrs. of News Programming:* news progmg 13 hrs wkly; *No. News Employees:* 2; *Target Audience:* 35 plus; mature, well educated, higher income, retired; *Adv. Rates:* 31.75; 31.75; 31.75; na
James Walker, General Manager
Joey Lessa, Public Service Director

Holbrook

***KBMH**
01-01-2002; 90.3 MHz FM; 0.25 kw; 141 ft.; N34 55 5 W110 8 25
P.O. Box 3206, Tupelo, MS 38803 US
(662) 844-8888; *Fax:* (662) 842-6791
www.afr.net
faq@afa.net
License: Holbrook, Navajo County, AZ held by American Family Association.
Group Owner: American Family Radio
Format: Christian
Tim Wildmon, President
Donald Wildmon, Founder
Buddy Smith, Senior VP
Ed Vitagliano, Exec VP
Randy Sharp, Director Of Special Projects
Meeke Addison, Director Of Communications
Abraham Hamilton III, General Counsel & PublicPolicy Analyst

KDJI
10-01-1955; 1270 kHz AM; *Hrs Open:* 9 AM-4 PM
130 Hampton Point Dr., St. Simons Island, GA 31522-3031 US
(813) 948-2554
www.970kvwm.com
License: Holbrook, AZ held by Petracom of Holbrook L.L.C.
Group Owner: White Mountain Radio
Nat'l Network: ABC; Westwood One
Format: News, News/Talk, 86 *Special Programming:* Sports 10 hrs, farm 8 hrs wkly; *Target Audience:* 35-65; 46% female, 54% male
Bob Funk, General Manager/Sales Manager

KZUA
12-06-1993; 92.1 MHz FM; 100 kw; 256 ft.; N34 55 13 W110 7 53
1838 W. Commerce Dr., Suite A, Lakeside, AZ 85929 US
(928) 368-8100; *Fax:* (928) 368-8108
www.921kzua.com
License: Holbrook, Navajo County, AZ held by Petracom of Holbrook LLC.
Group Owner: White Mountain Radio; (acq 2-26-2002; $650,000 with co-located AM)
Nat'l Network: Westwood One; CNN Radio
Arbitron Metro Market: Holbrook, AZ.; *Format:* Country; *Target Audience:* 18-54; 57% female, 43% male; *Adv. Rates:* 15; 12; 12; 10
Steve Johnson, General Manager
Renee Beebe, General Sales Mgr

Hotevilla

***KUYI**
12-20-2000; 88.1 MHz FM; *Hrs Open:* 24; 69 kw; 407 ft.; N35 48 29 W110 16 23
P.O. Box 705, Hotevilla, AZ 86030 US
(928) 738-5505; *Fax:* (928) 738-5501
www.kuyi.net
info@kuyi.net
License: Hotevilla, Navajo County, AZ held by Hopi Foundation.
Arbitron Metro Market: Hotevilla, AZ; *Format:* News; *Hrs. of News Programming:* news progmg 6 hrs wkly; *No. News Employees:* 2; *Target Audience:* 30 plus.
Maria Garcia, Operations Dir
Richard Alun Davis, Station Manager
Davis Maho, Operations Manager
Macadio Namoki, Development and Marketing Coordinator

Kachina Village

KBTK(FM)
02-01-1995; 105.1 MHz FM; *Hrs Open:* 24; 1 kw; 1,968 ft; N35 14 26 W111 35 48
112 E. Rt. 66, Suite 105, Flagstaff, AZ 86001
(928) 779-1177; *Fax:* (928) 774-5179
www.1051thecanyon.com
ann@northlandradio.com
License: Kachina Village, Coconino County, AZ held by Grenax Broadcasting II LLC.
Group Owner: Grenax Broadcasting LLC; (acq 1-6-2006; grpsl)
Hrs. of News Programming: news progmg 4 hrs wkly; *No. News Employees:* 1; *Target Audience:* 28-54; males
Greg Dinetz, President/Chief Executive Officer
Jim Shipp, General Manager
Jay Arthur, Programming Director
Jon Sweat, Chief Engineer

Kaibito

***KECU**
88.5 MHz FM; kw
US
(580) 265-9475
License: Kaibito, Coconino County, AZ held by Union Valley Baptist Church Inc.
Arbitron Metro Market: Eureka, CA
Steve Vandegrift, General Manager

***KCHB**
90.1 MHz FM; kw
US
(918) 333-8700; *Fax:* (918) 333-3526
License: Kaibito, Coconino County, AZ held by South Central Oklahoma Christian Broadcasting Inc.
Arbitron Metro Market: Kaibito, AZ
Randall Christy, President

Kingman

KAAA
10-07-1949; 1230 kHz AM
2535 Hualapai Mountain Rd., Suite D, Kingman, AZ 86401
(928) 753-2537
www.talkatoz.com
License: Kingman, AZ held by Cameron Broadcasting Inc.
Group Owner: Cameron Broadcasting Inc.; (acq 11-24-99; grpsl)
Arbitron Metro Market: Kingman, AZ; *Format:* News/Talk *Special Programming:* Sports; *Target Audience:* 25 plus.
Don Jaeger, Operations Dir

KGMN
02-14-1984; 100.1 MHz FM; *Hrs Open:* 24; 0.91 kw; 2897 ft.; N35 6 37 W113 52 55
812 East Beale Street, Kingman, AZ 86401 US
(928) 753-9100; *Fax:* (928) 753-1978
www.kgmn.net
License: Kingman, Mohave County, AZ held by New West Broadcasting Systems Inc.
Nat'l Network: AP Radio; Jones Radio Networks
Format: Country; *Target Audience:* General
Joe Hart, CEO
Deana Campell, Operations Dir
Rhonda Hart, General Manager
Deana Campell, News Director

***KJZK**
90.7 MHz FM; 4.5 kw; 715 ft.; N35 10 37 W113 39 57
US
(928) 541-1008
kjzafm@yahoo.com
License: Kingman, Mohave County, AZ held by St. Paul Bible College.
Arbitron Metro Market: Kingman, AZ, Laughlin - Las Vegas, NV
Nichole Erickson, Director & President
Tom Erickson, General Manager

Lake Havasu City

KNTR
09-23-1970; 980 kHz AM; *Hrs Open:* 24
2068 McCulloch Blvd, Lake Havasu City, AZ 86403 US
(928) 855-9336; *Fax:* (928) 855-9333
www.kntram.com
office@myradiocentral.com
License: Lake Havasu City, AZ held by Steven M. Greeley.
Nat'l Network: PRI
Arbitron Metro Market: Lake Havasu City, AZ; *Format:* News, News/Talk, 86; *Hrs. of News Programming:* news progmg 12 hrs wkly; *No. News Employees:* 1; *Target Audience:* 35-64.
Steve Greeley, CEO
Traceye Jones, General Manager

KRCY-FM
01-01-1999; 96.7 MHz FM; 0.26 kw; 2707 ft.; N34 33 6 W114 11 37
1620 S. Palo Verde Ave, Lake Havasu City, AZ 86403 US
(928) 855-1051; *Fax:* (928) 855-7996
www.maddog.net
License: Lake Havasu City, Mohave County, AZ held by Rick L. Murphy.
Arbitron Metro Market: Lake Havasu City, AZ; *Format:* Oldies
Rick Murphy, President
Scott Gosselin, General Manager/Vice President
Alan Moir, Programming Director

***KNLB**
07-01-1983; 91.1 MHz FM; *Hrs Open:* 24; 8 kw; 453 ft.; N34 29 10 W114 13 6
Mailing Address: 510 North Acoma Blvd, Lake Havasu City, AZ 86403 US
Second Address: 510 N. Acoma Blvd., Lake Havasu City, AZ 86403
(928) 855-9110; *Fax:* (928) 453-2588
www.knlb.com
info@knlb.com
License: Lake Havasu City, Mohave County, AZ held by Advance Ministries.
Nat'l Network: USA
Format: Christian, Religious; *Hrs. of News Programming:* News progmg 8 hrs wkly; *Target Audience:* General.
Richard Tatham, President
Faron Eckelbarger, Station Manager

KZUL-FM
01-01-1986; 104.5 MHz FM; *Hrs Open:* 24; 0.23 kw; 2671 ft.; N34 33 6 W114 11 37
2068 McCulloch Blvd, Lake Havasu City, AZ 86403 US
(928) 855-4560; *Fax:* (928) 855-7996
www.hitsandfavorites.com
License: Lake Havasu City, Mohave County, AZ held by Mad Dog Wireless Inc.
Nat'l Network: ABC
Arbitron Metro Market: Lake Havasu City, AZ; *Format:* Adult Contemp, Classic Rock; *Target Audience:* 25-54.
Rick Murphy, President
Scott Gosselin, General Manager/Vice President
Ron Nickle, General Sales Mgr
Alan Moir, Programming Director

***KAIH**
01-01-2008; 89.3 MHz FM; 1.7 kw vert; -219 ft.; N34 27 52 W114 16 2 *Rebroadcasts:* Rebroadcasts KLRD(FM) Yucaipa, CA 100%
1425 N. Market Blvd, Suite 9, Sacramento, CA 95834 US
(888) 937-2471; *Fax:* (916) 251-1650
www.air1.com
info@air1.com
License: Lake Havasu City, Mohave County, AZ held by Educational Media Foundation.
Group Owner: EMF Broadcasting
Nat'l Network: Air 1
Arbitron Metro Market: Lake Havasu City, AZ; *Format:* Alternative, Christian
Darrell Chambliss, Chairman
Alan Mason, COO
Mike Novak, President and CEO
David Pierce, Programming Director
Ed Lenane, Promotions Director
Richard Hunt, News Director
Sam Wallington, Engineering Dir
Scott Smith, MusicDirector

Lake of the Woods

KZXQ
01-01-2005; 104.5 MHz FM; 0.5 kw; -751 ft.; N33 42 35 W108 45 56
P O Box 509, Ruidoso Downs, NM 88346 US
(623) 907-0267
License: Lake of the Woods, Catron County, AZ held by New Star Broadcasting LLC
Format: Talk
Karey Barbee, President
Vance Barbee, General Manager

Leupp

KQLP
101.5 MHz FM; kw
US

(512) 329-5843; *Fax:* (512) 329-5847
www.matineemedia.com
License: Leupp, McKinley County, AZ held by Ace Radio Corp.
Group Owner: Ace Radio Corp.
Arbitron Metro Market: Leupp, AZ
Stephen Hackerman, President

Mammoth

***KLTU**
88.1 MHz FM; 16 kw; 1939 ft.; N32 14 57 W111 6 57
P.O. Box 187, Humble, TX 77347 US
(800) 525-5683; *Fax:* (916) 251-1650
www.klove.com
klove@klove.com
License: Mammoth, Pinal County, AZ held by Good News Radio Broadcasting Inc.
Arbitron Metro Market: Mammoth, AZ; *Format:* Christian, Gospel; *No. News Employees:* 13
Darrell Chambliss, Chairman
Mike Novak, President and CEO
Doug Martin, General Manager
David Pierce, Programming Director
Ed Lenane, News Director
Sam Wallington, Engineering Dir
Dan Antonelli, Chief Business DevelopmentOfficer

Marana

KOHT
10-01-1984; 98.3 MHz FM; *Hrs Open:* 24; 6 kw; 184 ft.; N32 27 9 W111 5 11
3202 North Oracle Road, Tucson, AZ 85705 US
(520) 618-2100; *Fax:* (520) 618-2200
www.hot983.com
License: Marana, Pima County, AZ held by CC Licenses LLC.
Group Owner: iHeartMedia; (acq 6-22-2001; grpsl).
Arbitron Metro Market: Tucson, AZ; *Format:* Blues; *Hrs. of News Programming:* news progmg 4 hrs wkly; *No. News Employees:* 2; *Target Audience:* 18-49; Sp, contemp, white collar adults
Carl Anderson, Market President
Chris Abbott, Chief Engineer

KSAZ
01-01-1990; 580 kHz AM
1110 South Park Avenue, Tucson, AZ 85719 US
(520) 298-6880; *Fax:* (520) 298-6077
www.radioebenezer580am.com/
License: Marana, AZ held by Owl Broadcasting & Development Inc.
Nat'l Network: ABC
Arbitron Metro Market: Tucson, AZ; *Format:* Country *Special Programming:* International 2 hrs wkly; *Target Audience:* 35 plus.
Freddue Aragon, President
Jairo Aragon, Sales Manager

Maricopa

***KLVA**
04-08-1976; 105.5 MHz FM; *Hrs Open:* 24; 50 kw; 492 ft.; N33 0 14 W111 58 53
5700 West Oaks Boulevard, Rocklin, CA 95765 US
707-528-9236; *Fax:* 707-528-9246
www.klove.com
klove@klove.com
License: Maricopa, Pinal County, AZ held by Educational Media Foundation.
Group Owner: EMF Broadcasting; (acq 7-19-99).
Nat'l Network: K-Love
Format: Christian *Special Programming:* Sports 7 hrs wkly; *Target Audience:* 25-44; Judeo-Christian, female
Darell Chambliss, Chairman
Mike Novak, President
Chuck Pryor, Programming Director
Ed Lenane, Promotions Manager
Richard Hunt, News Director
Sam Wallington, Engineering Dir
Scott Smith, Music Director
Andrew Kelly, TrafficDirector
Tracy Butler, Traffic Manager

Mayer

KKFR
05-24-1996; 98.3 MHz FM; *Hrs Open:* 24; 41 kw; Ant 2,795 ft; N34 14 03 W112 22 01
4745 N. 7th St., Suite 410, Phoenix, AZ 86326
(602) 648-9800; *Fax:* (602) 283-0923
www.power983fm.com
License: Mayer, Yavapai County, AZ held by RBG Phoenix Licenses LLC.
Group Owner: Riviera Broadcast Group LLC; (acq 1-1-2007)
Nat'l Reps: Katz Eastman
Population Served: 75,000; *Arbitron Metro Market:* Phoenix, AZ
Jose Rodilles, General Manager/Chief Operations Officer
Todd Burden, General Sales Mgr
Mikey Fuentes, Programming Director
Deonne McBean, Promotions & Marketing Director

Meadview

KVGS
01-01-1991; 107.9 MHz FM; *Hrs Open:* 24; 100 kw horiz; Ant 1,781 ft; N35 50 11.9 W114 19 14.10
2920 S. Durango Dr., Las Vegas, NV 89117
(702) 730-0300; *Fax:* (702) 736-8447
www.starradiovegas.com
License: Meadview, Mohave County, AZ held by Beasley Media Group LLC
Group Owner: Beasley Broadcast Group Inc.; (acq 10-3-2005; $38 million with KOAS(FM) Dolan Springs, AZ)
Nat'l Network: ABC
Arbitron Metro Market: Las Vegas, NV; *Format:* Adult Contemp; *Target Audience:* 25-54; adults
Tom Humm, General Manager
Lee Grau, General Sales Mgr
Mike O'Brian, Programming Director
Shayla Martinez, Promotions and Marketing Manager
Lamar Smith, Chief Engineer
Cory Cuddeback, Director of Sales/National Sales Manager
SandyEllis, Digital Director
Jesus Novo, Director of Business Affairs/Human Resources

Mesa

KDKB
04-20-1968; 93.3 MHz FM; *Hrs Open:* 24; 100 kw; 1667 ft.; N33 20 0.8 W112 3 44.4
1167 West Javelina, Mesa, AZ 85210 US
(480) 897-9300
License: Mesa, Maricopa County, AZ held by Mesa Radio Inc.
Group Owner: Sandusky Radio; (acq 1977)
Nat'l Reps: Christal
Arbitron Metro Market: Phoenix, AZ; *Format:* Rock/AOR
Norman Rau, President
Chuck Artigue, General Manager/Vice President
Bob Weaver, General Sales Mgr
Buzz Casey, Programming Director
Kathy Perschke, News Director
Clayton Creekmore, Chief Engineer

KFNN
11-01-1962; 1510 kHz AM; *Hrs Open:* 24; 22 kw-D, DA2; 0.1 kw-N, DA2; N33 41 34 W112 0 9
4800 N. Centrl Avenue, Phoenix, AZ 85012 US
(602) 241-1510; *Fax:* (602) 241-1540
www.kfnn.com
License: Mesa, AZ held by CRC Broadcasting Co. Inc.
Nat'l Network: CNN Radio; *Wire Services:* Metro Weather Service Inc.
Arbitron Metro Market: Scottsdale, AZ; *Format:* News, News/Talk, 86 *Special Programming:* Real estate 10 hrs wkly; *Hrs. of News Programming:* news progmg 84 hrs wkly; *No. News Employees:* 3 *Target Audience:* 30 plus; upscale, investment-oriented professionals & entrepreneurs; decision makers; *Adv. Rates:* 70; 50; 60; 25
Ronald Cohen, President
Brian DuBose, Operations Director/Vice President
Brian Du Bose, Programming Director

KIHP
01-01-1946; 1310 kHz AM; *Hrs Open:* 24; 5 kw-D, 500 w-N, DA-N; N33 26 23 W111 50 09
4725 N. Scottsdale Rd., Suite 234, Scottsdale, AZ 85251
(480) 423-1310; *Fax:* (480) 423-3867
kxam@aol.com
License: Mesa, Maricopa County, AZ
Group Owner: IHR Educational Broadcasting; (acq 9-25-90)
Nat'l Network: Westwood One; ABC
Population Served: 2,500,000; *Arbitron Metro Market:* Phoenix, AZ; *Hrs. of News Programming:* News progmg 14 hrs wkly; *Target Audience:* 35-64.
Doug Sherman, President/Chief Executive Officer
Dick Jenkins, General Manager

KZZP
01-01-1967; 104.7 MHz FM; *Hrs Open:* 24; 100 kw; 1549 ft.; N33 20 4 W112 3 35
4686 East Van Buren Street, Phoenix, AZ 85282 US
(602) 374-6000; *Fax:* (602) 230-2781
www.1047kissfm.com
License: Mesa, Maricopa County, AZ held by Citicasters Licenses Inc.
Group Owner: iHeartMedia; (acq 6-99; grpsl).
Arbitron Metro Market: Phoenix, AZ; *Format:* Contemporary Hits/Top 40; *Hrs. of News Programming:* news progmg 7 hrs wkly; *No. News Employees:* 1; *Target Audience:* 18-34; women
Linda Little, Market President
Matt Mitchell, Programming Director

Miami

KIKO
06-13-1958; 97.3 MHz FM; *Hrs Open:* 24; 56 w; N33 24 41 W110 50 17
4501 Broadway, Miami, AZ 85539
(928) 425-7500 Business,(928) 425-4471 Contest; *Fax:* (928) 425-9393
www.kikonews.blogspot.com
radiokiko@cableone.net
License: Miami, Gila County, AZ held by 1TV.com Inc.
Group Owner: 1TV.Com Inc.; (acq 4-30-2008; $1.025 million with KIKO-FM Claypool)
Nat'l Network: Westwood One; ABC
Population Served: 35,000 *Hrs. of News Programming:* news progmg 8 hrs wkly; *No. News Employees:* 1; *Target Audience:* 21-70; industrial/blue collar workers in loc copper mines, highest hourly wage earners *Adv.Rates:* 15; 15; 15; 11
John Low, President
Shelly Harrison, General Manager
Roland Foster, News Director
Chelle Hodson, Office Manager
Randy Escobedo, Sports Commentator

KQSS
03-30-1987; 101.9 MHz FM; *Hrs Open:* 24; 6 kw; -79 ft.; N33 24 30 W110 48 14
Mailing Address: P.O. Box 292, Miami, AZ 85539 US
Second Address: 5734 McKinney, Globe, AZ 85501
(928) 425-7186; *Fax:* (928) 425-7982
www.gila1019.com
bill@gila1019.com
License: Miami, Gila County, AZ held by William D. Taylor.
Arbitron Metro Market: Globe, AZ; *Format:* Country; *Hrs. of News Programming:* news progmg 5 hrs wkly; *No. News Employees:* 1; *Target Audience:* 25-54.
Bill Taylor, General Manager

Mohave Valley

KVYL
93.7 MHz FM; 6 kw horiz; -89 ft.; N34 58 6 W114 31 58 US
(928) 855-9336
www.kvylfm.com
Office@MyRadioCentral.com
License: Mohave Valley, Mohave County, AZ held by Smoke and Mirrors LLC.
Group Owner: Smoke and Mirrors LLC
Arbitron Metro Market: Mohave Valley, AZ; *Format:* Oldies
Traceye Jones, General Manager
Carol Vasel, Account Executive

Morristown

KRPH
99.5 MHz FM; 50 kw; 492 ft.; N34 8 45.7 W112 41 56.1 US
(713) 528-2517
kdao@kdao.com
License: Morristown, Yavapai County, AZ held by Ace Radio Corp.
Group Owner: Grupo Multimedia LLC
Arbitron Metro Market: Morristown, AZ
Roberto de Jesus Medina, President

Munds Park

KFSZ
01-01-2009; 106.1 MHz FM; 4.3 kw; 1535 ft.; N34 58 6 W111 30 29 US
(928) 774-5231; *Fax:* (928) 779-2988
www.hits1061.com
info@lkcm.com
License: Munds Park, Coconino County, AZ held by LKCM Radio Group LP.
Group Owner: Guyann Corp.
Arbitron Metro Market: Munds Park, AZ; *Format:* Contemporary Hits/Top 40
Steve Hoshor, General Manager
Jeff Basham, Programming Director
Ryan Oler, Chief Engineer

Nogales

*KNOG
12-16-1995; 90.7 MHz FM; *Hrs Open:* 24; 100 w horiz, 50 kw vert; 52 meters; N31 21 33 W110 53 54
Mailing Address: Box 1614, Nogales, AZ 78502
Second Address: 150 W. First St., Nogales, AZ 85628
(520) 287-5206; *Fax:* (520) 287-3606
www.knog.org
License: Nogales, Santa Cruz County, AZ held by World Radio Network Inc.
Nat'l Network: Moody
Population Served: 60,000 *Special Programming:* Btfl music 5 hrs wkly; *Hrs. of News Programming:* News progmg 5 hrs wkly; *Target Audience:* 18-55; Hispanics
Marcos Romero, Station Manager
Mariana Romero, Programming Director
Concepcion Borrayo, News Director

KOFH
04-01-1999; 99.1 MHz FM; 6 kw; 167 ft.; N31 23 19 W110 56 35
934 N. Bejarano Street, Nogales, AZ 85621 US
(520) 287-6885; *Fax:* (520) 287-8290
www.maxima991.fm
noticieroalmaximo@hotmail.com
License: Nogales, Santa Cruz County, AZ held by Felix Corp.
Format: Contemporary Hits/Top 40
Oscar Felix Sr., General Manager
Rene Saylor, Programming Director

Oracle

KTGV
12-01-1984; 106.3 MHz FM; *Hrs Open:* 24; 430 w vert, 440 w horiz; 4,172 ft; N32 26 26 W110 47 12
7280 East Rosewood Street, Tucson, AZ 85710
(520) 722-5486; *Fax:* (520) 327-2260
License: Oracle, Pinal County, AZ held by Journal Broadcast Corp.
Group Owner: Journal Communications Inc.; (acq 4-15-98; $5.8 million)
Nat'l Reps: Christal
Population Served: 600,000; *Arbitron Metro Market:* Tucson, AZ; *Hrs. of News Programming:* News progmg 2 hrs wkly; *Target Audience:* 25-54; Hispanic and Anglo adults
Jim Arnold, General Manager/Vice President
Jennifer Nunn, Sales Manager

Oro Valley

KSZR
01-01-1992; 97.5 MHz FM; *Hrs Open:* 24; 6 kw; 93 meters; N32 19 45 W111 03 40
575 W. Roger Rd., Tucson, AZ 85705 US
(520) 887-1000
www.975thevibe.com
herb.crowe@cumulus.com
License: Oro Valley, AZ held by Radio License Holding CBC, LLC
Group Owner: Cumulus Media Inc.; (acq 4-26-01; grpsl).
Population Served: 800,000; *Arbitron Metro Market:* Tucson, AZ; *Format:* Urban Contemporary; *No. News Employees:* 2; *Target Audience:* 25-54.
Herb Crowe, Operations Dir
Keith Rosenblatt, General Sales Mgr
Chanel Carrasco, Promotions Manager

KCMT
01-01-2003; 102.1 MHz FM; 100 kw; 266 ft.; N32 17 23 W111 1 6
6290 Sunset Blvd, Suite 1600, Los Angeles, CA 90028 US
(520) 407-4500; *Fax:* (520) 407-4600
www.kcmt.com
steve@kcmt.com
License: Oro Valley, Pima County, AZ held by Arizona Lotus Corp.
Group Owner: Lotus Communications Corp.
Arbitron Metro Market: Tucson, AZ; *Format:* Tejano
Steve Groesbeck, General Manager
Tara Hungate, General Sales Mgr
Enrique Mayans, Programming Director
Carlos Gonzales, Promotions Manager
Tara Hungate, Director of Sales
Jorge Leyva, Promotions Coordinator

Page

*KNAD
01-01-1998; 91.7 MHz FM; 1 kw; 1634 ft.; N36 41 51 W111 37 57 *Rebroadcasts:* Rebroadcasts KNAU(FM) Flagstaff
P.O. Box 5764, Flagstaff, AZ 86011 US
(928) 523-5628; *Fax:* (928) 523-7647
www.knau.org
knau@nau.edu
License: Page, Coconino County, AZ held by Arizona Board of Regents on behalf of Northern Arizona University.
Format: News
Brian Sanders, Operations Dir
Lisa Skinner, Traffic Manager
Stacy Murison, Development Director

KPGE
05-15-1971; 1340 kHz AM; *Hrs Open:* 24; 1 kw-U, ND1; N36 54 23 W111 27 32
P.O. Box 1030, Page, AZ 86040 US
(928) 645-8181; *Fax:* (928) 645-3347
www.kpge.com
License: Page, AZ held by Lake Powell Communications Inc.
Nat'l Network: ABC
Arbitron Metro Market: Page-Lake Powell-Kanab-Fredonia; *Format:* Country; *Hrs. of News Programming:* news progmg 15 hrs wkly; *No. News Employees:* 4; *Target Audience:* 25-54.
Dan Brown, General Manager
Janet Brown, General Sales Mgr
Dave Weaver, Programming Director
Jim Wagoner, News Director
Dan the Man, DJ
Rachel Cates, Webmaster and DJ

KXAZ
09-22-1980; 93.3 MHz FM; *Hrs Open:* 24; 12.5 kw; 922 ft.; N37 0 42 W111 40 48
P O Box 1030, Page, AZ 86040 US
(928) 645-8181; *Fax:* (928) 645-3347
kxaz.com
sales@kxaz.com
License: Page, Coconino County, AZ
Arbitron Metro Market: Page, AZ; *Format:* Contemporary Hits/Top 40
Dudley Waller, General Manager
Janet Brown, Sales Manager
Dave Weaver, Programming Director

Paradise Valley

KHOT-FM
01-01-1996; 105.9 MHz FM; *Hrs Open:* 24; 36 kw; 577 ft.; N33 35 16 W111 45 38
6006 S. 30th St., Phoenix, AZ 85042 US
(602) 243-3333; *Fax:* (602) 513-7409
www.univision.com
License: Paradise Valley, Maricopa County, AZ held by Univision Radio License Corp.
Group Owner: Univision Radio; (acq 9-22-2003; grpsl).
Arbitron Metro Market: Phoenix, AZ; *Format:* Tejano; *Target Audience:* 18-49.
Roberto Yanez, Vice President and General Manager
Juan Villa, News Director

Parker

KLPZ
09-07-1974; 1380 kHz AM; *Hrs Open:* 24; 2.5 kw-D, ND1; 0.058 kw-N, ND1; N34 9 14 W114 17 15
P.O. Box 1247, Williston, ND 58802 US
(928) 669-9274; *Fax:* (928) 669-9300
www.klpz1380.com
info@klpz1380.com
License: Parker, AZ held by Keith Douglas Learn
Nat'l Network: Jones Radio Networks
Arbitron Metro Market: Phoenix, AZ; *Format:* Country, News, 62, Talk *Special Programming:* Farm one hr wkly; *Hrs. of News Programming:* news progmg 2 hrs wkly; *No. News Employees:* 2; *Target Audience:* 25-55. *Adv. Rates:* 14; 14; 14; na
Keith Learn, President

*KWFH
11-01-1984; 90.3 MHz FM; *Hrs Open:* 24; 800 w; 760 meters; N34 08 53 W114 16 44
Box 747, Parker, AZ 85344
(928) 669-5683,(928) 855-9110; *Fax:* (928) 669-5683
License: Parker, La Paz County, AZ held by Desert View Baptist Church.
Nat'l Network: Moody
Population Served: 12,000 *Target Audience:* General.
Gary Covert, Station Manager

KRIT
01-01-2003; 93.9 MHz FM; *Hrs Open:* 24; 7.6 kw; -154 ft.; N34 8 30 W114 17 50
P O Box 62, Keene, CA 93531 US
(602) 269-3121; *Fax:* (602) 269-3020
www.campesina.com
achavez@campesina.com
License: Parker, La Paz County, AZ held by Farmworker Educational Radio Network Inc.
Arbitron Metro Market: Parker, AZ; *Format:* Spanish
Bill Barquin, General Manager
Maria Barquin, Programming Director
Saul Madrid, News Director
Dave Whitehead, Chief Engineer
Michael Nowakowski, Executive Vice-President
Veronica Gonzalez, Executive Assistant
Gilbert Ochoa,National Sales

KPKR
12-23-2007; 97.3 MHz FM; *Hrs Open:* 24; 3.2 kw; 928 ft.; N34 7 29 W114 12 38
Mailing Address: US
Second Address: 1713 S. Kofa Ave., Suite E, Parker, AZ 85344
(928) 669-9999; *Fax:* (928) 669-8957
www.riverratradio.com
License: Parker, La Paz County, AZ held by Prescott Valley Broadcasting Co. Inc.
Group Owner: Prescott Valley Broadcasting Co. Inc.
Nat'l Network: Jones Radio Networks
Arbitron Metro Market: Parker, AZ; *Format:* Blues, Classic Rock; *Target Audience:* 25-54; fun loving recreationists
Sanford Cohen, President
Terry Cohen, Executive Vice President

Payson

KMOG
11-01-1983; 1420 kHz AM; *Hrs Open:* 24; 2.5 kw-D, DAN; 0.5 kw-N, DAN; N34 16 0 W111 18 54
500 E. Taylor Parkway, Payson, AZ 85541 US
(928) 474-5214; *Fax:* (928) 474-0236
http://and02.info/index.html
kmog@1420kmog.com
License: Payson, AZ held by Farrell Enterprises L.L.C.
Format: Country; *Hrs. of News Programming:* news progmg 2 hrs wkly; *No. News Employees:* 1; *Target Audience:* 25-54; working adults; *Adv. Rates:* 12; 16; 12; 10
Mike Farrell, President
Blaine Kimball, General Manager
Chris Higgins, Marketing Director

KMZQ-FM
01-01-2007; 99.3 MHz FM; 17 kw; 404 ft.; N34 11 4 W111 20 16 US
(702) 736-6161
License: Payson, Gila County, AZ held by Kemp Communications Inc.
Group Owner: Kemp Communications Inc.
Arbitron Metro Market: Payson, AZ
Will Kemp, President

Phoenix

KASA
01-06-1967; 1540 kHz AM; 10 kw-D, DA2; 0.019 kw-N, DA2; N33 22 36 W112 5 25
1445 West Baseline Road, Phoenix, AZ 85041 US
(602) 276-4241; *Fax:* (602) 276-8119
License: Phoenix, AZ held by KASA Radio Hogar Inc.
Arbitron Metro Market: Phoenix, AZ; *Format:* Religious; *Target Audience:* General.
Moses Herrera, President

*KBAQ
04-26-1993; 89.5 MHz FM; *Hrs Open:* 24; 29.7 kw; 1555 ft.; N33 19 58 W112 3 53
1435 S. Dobson Road, Mesa, AZ 85202 US
(480) 833-1122; *Fax:* (480) 774-8475
www.kbaq.org
License: Phoenix, Maricopa County, AZ held by College District.
Nat'l Network: NPR; PRI *Regional Reps:* Public Radio Partners;
Wire Services: AP
Arbitron Metro Market: Tempe, AZ; *Format:* News
Bill Shedd, Operations & Program Director
Lou Stanley, General Manager
Peter O'Dowd, News Director
Dave Atkins, Engineering Dir
Linda Pastori, Development Director

KESZ
07-01-1982; 99.9 MHz FM; *Hrs Open:* 24; 99 kw; 1,703 ft.; N33 20 1 W112 3 44
4686 E. Van Buren St., Suite 300, Phoenix, AZ 85008 US
(602) 374-6000
www.kez999.com

License: Phoenix, Maricopa County, AZ held by CC Licenses LLC.
Group Owner: iHeartMedia; (acq 5-14-99; $58 million)
Nat'l Network: AP Radio; *Nat'l Reps:* Katz Radio
Arbitron Metro Market: Phoenix, AZ; *Format:* Adult Contemp; *Target Audience:* General.
Richard J. Bressler, President

***KFLR-FM**
12-01-1985; 90.3 MHz FM; *Hrs Open:* 24; 100 kw; 1585 ft.; N33 20 2 W112 3 44
7355 North Oracle # 200, Tucson, AZ 85704 US
(602) 978-0903; *Fax:* (602) 548-8089
www.myflc.org
License: Phoenix, Maricopa County, AZ held by Family Life Broadcasting Inc.
Group Owner: Family Life Communications Inc.; (acq 7-30-78)
Nat'l Network: Salem Radio Network
Arbitron Metro Market: Albuquerque, NM; *Format:* Christian, Religious
Randy Carlson, President
Alonzo Williams, Vice President of Operations
Michael Bove, Engineering Dir

KGME
01-01-1940; 910 kHz AM; *Hrs Open:* 24; 5 kw-D, DAN; 5 kw-N, DAN; N33 32 0 W112 7 18
4686 E. Van Buren St., Suite 300, Phoenix, AZ 85008 US
(602) 374-6000
www.foxsports910.com
License: Phoenix, Maricopa County, AZ held by AMFM Radio Licenses L.L.C.
Group Owner: iHeartMedia; (acq 8-30-00; grpsl)
Nat'l Network: Fox Sports Radio
Arbitron Metro Market: Phoenix, AZ; *Format:* Sports, Talk *Special Programming:* Fantasy 2 hrs wkly; *No. News Employees:* 7; *Target Audience:* General.
Neil Larrimore, Programming Director

KFYI
10-01-1921; 550 kHz AM; *Hrs Open:* 24; 5 kw-D, ND1; 1 kw-N, ND1; N33 23 17 W112 0 22
4686 E. Van Buren St., Suite 300, Phoenix, AZ 85008 US
(602) 374-6000
www.kfyi.com
License: Phoenix, Maricopa County, AZ held by AMFM Radio Licenses LLC
Group Owner: iHeartMedia
Nat'l Network: Westwood One; *Nat'l Reps:* Christal
Arbitron Metro Market: Phoenix, AZ; *Format:* News, News/Talk, 86 *Special Programming:* Relg 2 hrs wkly; *Target Audience:* 50 plus.
Neil Larrimore, Programming Director

KIDR
02-01-1958; 740 kHz AM; *Hrs Open:* 24; 1 kw-D, DA2; 0.292 kw-N, DA2; N33 21 55 W112 6 30
8400 N.W. 52nd St., Ste-101, Miami, FL 33166 US
(702) 253-9800; *Fax:* (602) 234-8993
License: Phoenix, AZ held by Force Broadcasting LLC
TV Affiliate: CBS; *Format:* Children; *Hrs. of News Programming:* news progmg 10 hrs wkly; *No. News Employees:* 2; *Target Audience:* Under 18
Arthur Liu, CFO
Arturo Galvez, General Manager
Frank Feder, General Sales Mgr
Cat Thomas, Program Director
Juicy Balaoro, Promotions Director

***KJZZ**
01-01-1951; 91.5 MHz FM; *Hrs Open:* 24; 100 kw; 1608 ft.; N33 19 58 W112 3 53
1435 South Dobson Road, Mesa, AZ 85202 US
(480) 834-5627; *Fax:* (480) 774-8475
www.kjzz.org
License: Phoenix, Maricopa County, AZ held by Maricopa County Community College District.
Nat'l Network: NPR; PRI *Regional Reps:* Public radio partners; *Wire Services:* NOAA Weather; AP
Arbitron Metro Market: Phoenix, AZ; *Format:* Jazz, News; *Hrs. of News Programming:* news progmg 50 hrs wkly; *No. News Employees:* 6; *Target Audience:* 25-54.
Bill Shedd, Operations & Programming Director
Lou Stanley, General Manager
James Paluzzi, Station Manager
Peter O'Dowd, News Director
Dave Atkins, Engineering Dir
Linda Pastori, Development Director

KMVP-FM
07-01-1960; 98.7 MHz FM; *Hrs Open:* 24; 97 kw; 1,788 ft.; N33 19 58 W112 3 48
7740 N. 16th St., Suite 200, Phoenix, AZ 85020 US
(602) 274-6200
www.arizonasports.com
License: Phoenix, Maricopa County, AZ held by Bonneville International Corporation
Group Owner: Bonneville International Corporation
Nat'l Network: ESPN Radio
Arbitron Metro Market: Phoenix, AZ; *Format:* Sports, Talk; *Hrs. of News Programming:* news progmg 2 hrs wkly; *No. News Employees:* 1; *Target Audience:* Adults 25-54; *Adv. Rates:* 400; 300; 350; 150.
Ryan Hatch, Vice President, Content and Operations
Scott Sutherland, Vice President and Market Manager
Jessica Webb, Vice President, Sales
Ben Hartman, Promotions and Events Manager
Jim Knapp, Vice President, Business Development
Jeremy Hudson, Digital Services Manager
Tyler Bassett, Digital Content Manager
Connie Drushel, Human Resources Director
Rosemary Scarfo, Community Relations

KMVP
11-23-1949; 860 kHz AM; *Hrs Open:* 24; 0.94 kw-D, DAN; 1 kw-N, DAN; N33 25 14 W112 7 37
P.O. Box 322, Avondale, AZ 85323 US
(623) 533-3213
www.gospel860.com
License: Phoenix, Maricopa County, AZ held by Bonneville International Corporation
Group Owner: Bonneville International Corporation; (acq 1-14-2005; grpsl)
Arbitron Metro Market: Phoenix, AZ; *Format:* Gospel
Louis W. Bland, General Manager

KMXP
10-01-1964; 96.9 MHz FM; *Hrs Open:* 24; 98 kw; 1558 ft.; N33 20 3 W112 3 36
4686 E. Van Buren St., Suite 300, Phoenix, AZ 85008 US
(602) 374-6000; *Fax:* (602) 230-2781
www.mix969.com
License: Phoenix, Maricopa County, AZ held by Citicasters Licenses Inc.
Group Owner: iHeartMedia; (acq 5-4-99; grpsl).
Arbitron Metro Market: Phoenix, AZ; *Format:* Adult Contemp; *No. News Employees:* 1
Linda Little, Market President

***KNAI**
10-23-1991; 88.3 MHz FM; *Hrs Open:* 4 AM-7:30 PM; 22.5 kw; 997 ft.; N33 35 47 W112 5 29
PO Box 62, Keene, CA 93531 US
(928) 782-5995; *Fax:* (928) 782-3874
www.campesina.com
License: Phoenix, Maricopa County, AZ held by C,sar Ch vez Foundation
Group Owner: Farmworker Educational Radio Network, Inc.
Regional Reps: Vision Marketing
Arbitron Metro Market: Phoenix, AZ; *Format:* Tejano; *Target Audience:* 24-54; Hispanic market; *Adv. Rates:* 110; 100; 90; 0
Paul Chavez, President

KNIX-FM
09-01-1969; 102.5 MHz FM; *Hrs Open:* 24; 98 kw; 1621 ft.; N33 19 58 W112 3 53
4686 E. Van Buren St., Suite 300, Phoenix, AZ 85008 US
(602) 374-6000; *Fax:* (602) 374-6035
www.knixcountry.com
License: Phoenix, Maricopa County, AZ held by CC Licenses LLC.
Group Owner: iHeartMedia; (acq 6-1-99; $84 million)
Arbitron Metro Market: Phoenix, AZ; *Format:* Country; *Hrs. of News Programming:* news progmg one hr wkly; *No. News Employees:* 3; *Target Audience:* 25-54.
Linda Little, Market President
Steve Geofferies, Senior Vice President of Programming

KOOL
07-01-1980; 94.5 MHz FM; *Hrs Open:* 24; 95.6 kW; 217 ft.; N33 20 2 W112 3 42
840 N Central Ave., Phoenix, AZ 85004 USA
(602) 452-1000; *Fax:* (602) 440-6530
www.koolradio.com
License: Phoenix, Maricopa County, AZ held by CBS Radio Stations Inc.
Group Owner: CBS Radio; (acq 8-7-00; grpsl).
Nat'l Reps: Christal
Arbitron Metro Market: Phoenix, AZ; *Format:* Oldies; *Target Audience:* 25-54
Nat Galvin, Director of Sales
Tim Richards, Programming Director
Sandy Corcoran, Promotions Director

KOY
05-01-1949; 1230 kHz AM; *Hrs Open:* 24; 1 kw-U, ND1; N33 26 10 W112 6 34
4686 East Van Buren Street, Phoenix, AZ 85008 US
(602) 374-6000; *Fax:* (602) 374-6035
www.kfyi2.com
License: Phoenix, AZ held by AMFM Radio Licenses LLC.
Group Owner: iHeartMedia; (acq 8-30-00; grpsl).
Arbitron Metro Market: Phoenix, AZ; *Format:* Oldies
Linda Little, Market President
Steve Geofferies, Senior Vice President of Programming

***KPHF**
12-01-1991; 88.3 MHz FM; *Hrs Open:* 7:30 PM-4:30 AM; 22.5 kw; 974 ft.; N33 35 47 W112 5 31
Mailing Address: 4135 Northgate Blvd #1, Sacramento, CA 95834 US
Second Address: 290 Hegenberger Rd., Oakland, CA 94621
(800) 835-4810; *Fax:* (916) 641-8238
www.familyradio.com
info@familyradio.com
License: Phoenix, Maricopa County, AZ held by Family Stations Inc.
Group Owner: Family Stations Inc.; acq 12-91)
Arbitron Metro Market: Phoenix, AZ; *Format:* Christian, Religious
Harold Camping, President
David Manzi, Regional Manager

KPHX
06-10-1958; 1480 kHz AM; 5 kw-D, DA2; 0.5 kw-N, DA2; N33 24 2 W112 6 28
803 N. Rexford Dr., Beverly Hills, CA 90210 US
(602) 257-1351; *Fax:* (602) 256-0741
License: Phoenix, AZ held by Continental Broadcasting Corp. of Arizona Inc.
Nat'l Network: Music of Your Life
Arbitron Metro Market: Phoenix, AZ; *Format:* Talk
Kent Ennoms, CEO
Jonathan Molina, Operations Dir
Arthur Mobley, General Manager
Cam Maxwell, Station Manager

KKNT
06-01-1947; 960 kHz AM; *Hrs Open:* 24; 5 kw-D, DAN; 5 kw-N, DAN; N33 41 34 W112 0 9
4880 Santa Rosa Road, Suite 300, Camarillo, CA 93012 US
(602) 955-9600; *Fax:* (602) 955-7860
www.960thepatriot.com
License: Phoenix, AZ held by Common Ground Broadcasting Inc.
Group Owner: Salem Communications Corp.; (acq 1996; $6.5 million).
Nat'l Network: Salem Radio Network
Arbitron Metro Market: Phoenix, AZ; *Format:* News, News/Talk, 86 *Special Programming:* Insight bowl; *Hrs. of News Programming:* 6 hrs. news progmg wkly; *No. News Employees:* 2; *Target Audience:* 25-54; 35-64;upscale adults
Stuart Epperson, Chairman
Edward Atsinger, CEO
Joe Davis, President
Jon Horton, Operations Dir
James Ryan, General Manager
Heath Garlutzo, General Sales Mgr
Chris Llewellyn, Programming Director
Jean Laneri, PromotionsManager
Laurie Larson, Operations Director

KTAR
06-21-1922; 620 kHz AM; *Hrs Open:* 24; 5 kw-D, DAN; 5 kw-N, DAN; N33 28 44 W112 0 6
7740 N. 16th St., Suite 200, Phoenix, AZ 85020 US
(602) 274-6200
www.arizonasports.com
License: Phoenix, Maricopa County, AZ held by Bonneville International Corporation
Group Owner: Bonneville International Corporation; (acq 1-14-2005; grpsl)
Nat'l Network: ESPN Radio; *Nat'l Reps:* Interep; D & R Radio; *Wire Services:* UPI
Arbitron Metro Market: Phoenix, AZ; *Format:* Sports
Ryan Hatch, Vice President, Content and Operations
Scott Sutherland, Vice President and Market Manager
Jessica Webb, Vice President, Sales
Ben Hartman, Promotions and Events Manager
Jim Knapp, Vice President, Business Development
Jeremy Hudson, Digital Services Manager
Tyler Bassett, Digital Content Manager
Connie Drushel, Human Resources Director
Rosemary Scarfo, Community Relations

KXEG
01-01-1956; 1280 kHz AM; *Hrs Open:* 24; 2.5 kw-D, ND1; 0.049 kw-N, ND1; N33 29 32 W112 8 28
100 West Clarendon, #720, Phoenix, AZ 85013 US
(602) 296-3600; *Fax:* (602) 296-3624
www.kxeg1280.com
License: Phoenix, AZ held by Communicom Co. of Phoenix L.P.
Group Owner: Communicom Broadcasting LLC; (acq 12-14-2005; grpsl).
Nat'l Reps: Salem; Commercial Media Sales
Arbitron Metro Market: Phoenix, AZ; *Format:* Christian *Special Programming:* Sp 5 hrs wkly; *Target Audience:* 25 plus; educated adults with disposable income
Jess Spurgin, General Manager

KYOT-FM
10-31-1963; 95.5 MHz FM; *Hrs Open:* 24; 96 kw; 1572 ft.; N33 20 6 W112 3 39
840 North Central, Phoenix, AZ 85004 US
(602) 374-6000; *Fax:* (602) 374-6035
www.955themountain.com
License: Phoenix, Maricopa County, AZ held by AMFM Radio Licenses LLC
Group Owner: iHeartMedia; (acq 8-30-00; grpsl).
Arbitron Metro Market: Phoenix, AZ; *Format:* Adult Contemp; *No. News Employees:* 1; *Target Audience:* 25-54.
Linda Little, Market President
Matt Mitchell, Programming Director
John Baker, Chief Engineer

KZON
07-31-1992; 101.5 MHz FM; *Hrs Open:* 24; 100 kW; 226 ft.; N33 19 52 W112 3 46
840 N Central Ave., Phoenix, AZ 85004 USA
(602) 452-1000; *Fax:* (602) 440-6530
www.live1015phoenix.com
License: Phoenix, Maricopa County, AZ held by CBS Radio Stations Inc.
Group Owner: CBS Radio; (acq 12-20-99; grpsl)
Arbitron Metro Market: Phoenix, AZ; *Format:* Contemporary Hits/Top 40; *No. News Employees:* 1; *Adv. Rates:* 300; 250; 250; 150
Nat Galvin, Director of Sales
Tim Richards, Programming Director
Sandy Corcoran, Promotions Director

***KUFW**
10-23-1991; 90.5 MHz FM; *Hrs Open:* 4 AM-7:30 PM; 22.5 kw; 997 ft.; N33 35 47 W112 5 29
PO Box 62, Keene, CA 93531 US
(928) 782-5995; *Fax:* (928) 782-3874
www.campesina.com
License: Phoenix, Maricopa County, AZ held by C,sar Ch vez Foundation
Group Owner: Farmworker Educational Radio Network, Inc.
Regional Reps: Vision Marketing
Arbitron Metro Market: Phoenix, AZ; *Format:* Tejano; *Target Audience:* 24-54; Hispanic market; *Adv. Rates:* 110; 100; 90; 0
Paul Chavez, President

Pinetop

KNKI
106.7 MHz FM; 61.42 kw; 1171 ft.; N34 15 6 W109 35 6
1491 Thatcher Boulevard, Safford, AZ 85546 US
(928) 532-1010
www.italk1067.com
License: Pinetop, Navajo County, AZ held by William S. Konopnicki.
Arbitron Metro Market: Pinetop, AZ; *Format:* Talk, News/Talk
William Konopnicki, General Manager
Suzanne Barr, Chief of Staff

Pinetop-Lakeside

***KRCI**
01-01-2009; 89.5 MHz FM; 1 kw; 1125 ft.; N34 12 22 W109 58 34
US
(928) 368-6766
License: Pinetop-Lakeside, Navajo County, AZ held by Truth and Life Ministries.
Arbitron Metro Market: Lakeside, AZ; *Format:* Religious
Kevin Hansen, General Manager

Prescott

***KGCB**
12-05-1994; 90.9 MHz FM; *Hrs Open:* 24; 58 kw; 2,532 ft; N34 41 15 W112 07 02
3741 Karicio Ln., Prescott, AZ 86301
(928) 776-0909; *Fax:* (928) 776-1736
www.kgcb.org
info@radioshine.org
License: Prescott, Yavapai County, AZ held by Grand Canyon Broadcasters Inc.
Nat'l Network: Salem Radio Network
Target Audience: 25-54; adult, family audience
Sally Barton, Station Manager
Virginia Rayner, General Sales Mgr
Dan Young, Programming Director
Daniel White, Operations Director
Dave Schreiber, Production Director

KNOT
06-22-1957; 1450 kHz AM; *Hrs Open:* 24; 1 kw-U, ND1; N34 32 42 W112 26 46
P.O. Box 151, 116 S. Alto (86303), Prescott, AZ 86303 US
(928) 445-6880; *Fax:* (928) 445-6852
www.magic991.com
License: Prescott, AZ held by Guyann Corp.
Group Owner: Guyann Corp.; (acq 9-7-2005; grpsl).
Format: Country *Special Programming:* Jazz 2 hrs, sports 8 hrs wkly; *No. News Employees:* 1; *Target Audience:* 35 plus.
Steve Hoshor, General Manager
Jeff Basham, Programming Director
Jeff Basham, News Director
Ryan Oler, Chief Engineer

KTMG
11-11-1977; 99.1 MHz FM; *Hrs Open:* 24; 6 kw; 200 ft.; N34 34 29 W112 28 45
Mailing Address: P.O. Box 151, 116 S. Alto (86303), Prescott, AZ 86302 US
Second Address: 2225 E. Hwy. 69, Prescott, AZ 86301
(928) 445-6880; *Fax:* (928) 445-6852
License: Prescott, Yavapai County, AZ
Group Owner: Guyann Corp.
Nat'l Network: ABC
Format: Adult Contemp; *No. News Employees:* 1; *Target Audience:* 35 plus.
Lee Anderson, General Manager

***KNAQ**
09-01-1997; 89.3 MHz FM; 0.1 kw; 1585 ft.; N34 29 24 W112 31 59 *Rebroadcasts:* Rebroadcasts KNAU-FM Flagstaff 100%
P O Box 5764, Flagstaff, AZ 86011 US
(928) 523-5628; *Fax:* (928) 523-7647
www.knau.org
knau@nau.edu
License: Prescott, Yavapai County, AZ held by Northern Arizona University.
Format: News, Talk
Brian Sanders, Operations Dir
Lisa Skinner, Traffic Manager
Shelly Watkins, Director of Underwriting
Stacy Murison, Development Director

KYCA
08-01-1940; 1490 kHz AM; *Hrs Open:* 5 AM-1 AM; 1 kw-U, ND1; N34 33 3 W112 27 45
Mailing Address: P.O. Box 1631, Prescott, AZ 86302 US
Second Address: 500 Henry St., Prescott, AZ 86301
(928) 445-1700; *Fax:* (928) 445-5365
info@kyca.com
License: Prescott, AZ held by Southwest Broadcasting Co.
Nat'l Network: CBS; Westwood One
Arbitron Metro Market: Flagstaff-Prescott, AZ; *Format:* News, News/Talk, 86; *Hrs. of News Programming:* news progmg 20 hrs wkly; *No. News Employees:* 4; *Target Audience:* 35-64; mature adults; *Adv. Rates:* 20;16; 20; 16
Lou Silverstein, General Manager

***KJZP**
90.1 MHz FM; 0.027 kw; 1594 ft.; N34 29 24 W112 32 3
US
(928) 541-1008
www.kjza.org
kjzafm@yahoo.com
License: Prescott, Yavapai County, AZ held by St. Paul Bible College.
Nat'l Network: NPR
Arbitron Metro Market: Prescott, AZ; *Format:* Classical, Jazz, 80
Nichole Erickson, Director & President
Tom Erickson, General Manager

Prescott Valley

KPPV
09-01-1985; 106.7 MHz FM; *Hrs Open:* 24; 3.7 kw; 1617 ft.; N34 29 25 W112 32 0
Post Office Box 26523, Prescott Valley, AZ 86312 US
(928) 445-8289; *Fax:* (928) 442-0448
www.kppv.com
License: Prescott Valley, Yavapai County, AZ
Group Owner: Prescott Valley Broadcasting Co. Inc.
Nat'l Network: Jones Radio Networks; *Regional Network:* Arizona News Radio
Arbitron Metro Market: Flagstaff-Prescott, AZ; *Format:* Adult Contemp; *Hrs. of News Programming:* news progmg 6 hrs wkly; *No. News Employees:* 2; *Target Audience:* 25-54; middle to upper income professionals withfamilies and disposable income
Sanford Cohen, President
Ken Byers, Vice President of Broadcasting Operations
Allison Flannery, Vice President of Sales & Marketing
Terry Cohen, Executive Vice President

KQNA
06-28-1986; 1130 kHz AM; 1 kw-D, NDD; N34 37 46 W112 18 56
Mailing Address: P.O. Box 26523, Prescott Valley, AZ 86312 US
Second Address: 3755 Karicio Ln., Suite 2-C, Prescott, AZ 86303
(928) 445-8289; *Fax:* (928) 442-0448
www.kqna.com
License: Prescott Valley, AZ held by Prescott Valley Broadcasting Co.
Group Owner: Prescott Valley Broadcasting Co. Inc.; (acq 12-27-93; $75,000;
Nat'l Network: Fox News Radio; Salem Radio Network; CNN Radio; *Regional Network:* Arizona News Radio
Arbitron Metro Market: Prescott, AZ; *Format:* News, News/Talk, 84, Talk; *Hrs. of News Programming:* news progmg 84 hrs wkly; *No. News Employees:* 3; *Target Audience:* 35-64; middle - upper income, professionals & newconsumers
Sanford Cohen, President
Allison Flannery, Vice President of Sales & Marketing
Bill Monroe, News Director
Terry Cohen, Executive Vice President
Ken Byers, Vice President of Broadcast Operations

Quartzsite

KBUX
11-01-1988; 94.3 MHz FM; *Hrs Open:* 6 AM-10 PM; 0.205 kw; -161 ft.; N33 40 58 W114 13 59
P.O. Box 1, Quartzsite, AZ 85346 US
(928) 927-5111
kbuxradio@hotmail.com
License: Quartzsite, La Paz County, AZ held by Marvin D. Vosper
Arbitron Metro Market: Quartzite, AZ; *Format:* Country, Oldies, 94; *Target Audience:* General; retired motor home & trailer owners wintering in warmer climate
Marvin D. Vosper, Owner/General Manager
Marvin Vosper, Programming Director

Red Mesa

***KRMH**
01-01-1998; 89.7 MHz FM; 4.5 kw; 135 ft.; N36 57 48 W109 22 39
Hcr 6100 Box 40, Teec Nos Pos, AZ 86514 US
(928) 656-4100; *Fax:* (928) 656-4106
www.rmusd.net
License: Red Mesa, Apache County, AZ held by Red Mesa Unified School District No. 27.
Format: Variety/Diverse
Michele Scott, Business Manager

Safford

KATO
1230 kHz AM; *Hrs Open:* 24 Hours; 1 kw-U; N32 49 30 W109 45 30
Mailing Address: 3335 W. 8th St., Thatcher, AZ 85552
Second Address: P.O. Drawer L., Safford, AZ 85546
(928) 428-1230; *Fax:* (928) 428-1311
www.mysouthernaz.com
traffic@mcmurrayradio.com
License: Safford, Graham County, AZ held by McMurray Communications Inc.
Group Owner: McMurray Communications Inc.; acq 12-17-92; $10,000 with co-locat
Nat'l Network: ABC; TRN; Rush Limbaugh; Jerry Doyle; *Regional Network:* University of Arizona Sports; Arizona State University Sports; Phoenix Suns; *Nat'l Reps:* Regional Reps
Population Served: 36,000 *Hrs. of News Programming:* news progmg 25 hrs wkly; *No. News Employees:* 7; *Target Audience:* 25-54; upscale, intelligent; *Adv. Rates:* 15; 12; 14; 10

KXKQ
08-11-1979; 94.1 MHz FM; *Hrs Open:* 24; 1 kw; Ant 4,287 ft; N32 39 01 W109 50 53

Mailing Address: 3335 W. 8th St., Thatcher, AZ 95355
Second Address: P.O. Drawer L., Safford, AZ 95546
(928) 428-1230; *Fax:* (928) 428-1311
www.mysouthernaz.com
traffic@mcmurrayradio.com
License: Safford, Graham County, AZ held by McMurray Communications Inc.
Group Owner: McMurray Communications Inc.
Population Served: 40,000 *Hrs. of News Programming:* News progmg one hr wkly; *Target Audience:* 25-54.

Sahuarita

KEVT
10-12-1985; 1210 kHz AM
2919 East Broadway Boulevard, Suite 235, Tucson, AZ 85716 US
(520) 628-1200; *Fax:* (520) 326-4927
www.radiounica.com
License: Sahuarita, AZ held by One Mart Corp.
Arbitron Metro Market: Tucson, AZ; *Format:* Tejano
Francisco Zazueta, General Manager
Jim Parisi, Station Manager

Salome

KVGG
101.9 MHz FM; 5 kw; -164 ft.; N33 47 47.6 W113 33 27.9 US
(702) 385-6000; *Fax:* (702) 385-6001
License: Salome, La Paz County, AZ held by Kemp Communications Inc.
Group Owner: Kemp Communications Inc.
Arbitron Metro Market: Salome, AZ
Will Kemp, President

Scottsdale

KAZG
01-01-1956; 1440 kHz AM; *Hrs Open:* 8:30 AM - 5:30 PM; 5 kw-D, ND1; 0.052 kw-N, ND1; N33 28 43 W111 56 24
One Nationwide Plaza, 27th Floor, Columbus, OH 43216 US
(480) 941-1007; *Fax:* (602) 260-5759
kslx@kslx.com
License: Scottsdale, AZ held by Cactus Radio Inc.
Group Owner: Sandusky Radio; (acq 6-5-98; with co-located FM).
Arbitron Metro Market: Phoenix, AZ; *Format:* Oldies
Chuck Artigue, General Manager
Bob Weaver, General Sales Mgr
Jim Owen, Programming Director
Laura Johnson, Traffic Manager

KSLX-FM
08-01-1969; 100.7 MHz FM; 100 kw; 1841 ft.; N33 19 53 W112 3 47
4343 East Camelback Road, Suite 200, Phoenix, AZ 85018 US
(480) 941-1007; *Fax:* (602) 260-1007
www.kslx.com
License: Scottsdale, Maricopa County, AZ held by Cactus Radio Inc.
Group Owner: Sandusky Radio
Arbitron Metro Market: Phoenix, AZ; *Format:* Classic Rock
Chuck Artigue, General Manager
Bob Weaver, Sales Manager
Jim Owen, Programming Director
Laura Johnson, Traffic Manager

Sedona

KAZM
11-01-1974; 780 kHz AM; *Hrs Open:* 24; 5 kw-D, 250 w-N, DA-N; N34 51 38 W111 49 10
Box 1525, Sedona, AZ 86339
(928) 282-4154; *Fax:* (928) 282-2230
www.kazmradio.com
info@kazmradio.com
License: Sedona, Yavapai County, AZ held by Tabback Broadcasting Co.
Nat'l Network: Westwood One; ESPN Radio; Fox News Radio
Population Served: 280,000 *Hrs. of News Programming:* news progmg 16 hrs wkly; *No. News Employees:* 2; *Target Audience:* 25 plus; baby boomers, professions, tourists; *Adv. Rates:* 20; 20; 20; 14
Tom Tabback, General Manager

KQST
05-01-1984; 102.9 MHz FM; *Hrs Open:* 24; 90 kw; 1480 ft.; N34 58 5 W111 30 29
P.O. Box 187, Cottonwood, AZ 86326 US
(928) 634-2286; *Fax:* (928) 634-2295
www.myradioplace.com
License: Sedona, Coconino County, AZ held by Yavapai Broadcasting Corp.
Group Owner: Yavapai Broadcasting Corp.; (acq 12-1-2004; $3 million).
Arbitron Metro Market: Flagstaff-Prescott, AZ; *Format:* Contemporary Hits/Top 40; *Target Audience:* 24-59.
W. Grant Hafley, President
Dave Kessel, General Manager
Mike Puetz, General Sales Mgr
Bryan Saravo, Programming Director

KSED
08-01-1994; 107.5 MHz FM; *Hrs Open:* 24; 96 kw; 1463 ft.; N34 58 7 W111 30 24
2409 North 4th Street, Suite 101, Flagstaff, AZ 86004 US
(928) 779-1177; *Fax:* (928) 774-5179
www.koltcountry.com
License: Sedona, Coconino County, AZ held by Grenax Broadcasting II LLC.
Group Owner: Grenax Broadcasting LLC; (acq 1-6-2006; grpsl)
Nat'l Network: NBC
Arbitron Metro Market: Flagstaff, AZ; *Format:* Country; *No. News Employees:* 1
Greg Dinetz, President
Jay Arthur, Operations & Program Director
Stan Pierce, General Manager
Barb Richards, News Director
Jon Koger, Chief Engineer
Jan Hyslop, Traffic Manager

Seligman

KZKE
01-01-1995; 103.3 MHz FM; *Hrs Open:* 24; 7.7 kw; 453 ft.; N35 19 28 W112 45 52
422 West Highwy 66, Seligman, AZ 86337 US
(928) 753-9100; *Fax:* (928) 753-1978
License: Seligman, Yavapai County, AZ held by Route 66 Broadcasting L.L.C.
Arbitron Metro Market: Seligman, AZ; *Format:* Oldies
Joe Hart, President
Deana Campbell, Operations Dir
Rhonda Hart, General Manager
JoAnn Oxsen, General Sales Mgr
Tim Andrews, Programming Director
Dave Hawkins, News Director

Sells

***KOHN**
01-01-2004; 91.9 MHz FM; 10 kw; 1657 ft.; N32 7 59 W112 9 31 US
(520) 361-5011; *Fax:* (520) 361-3931
kohn@hotmail.com
License: Sells, Pima County, AZ held by Tohono O'Odham Nation.
Arbitron Metro Market: Sells, AZ; *Format:* Native American
Mary Lopez, Operations Dir
Sial Thonolig, General Manager

Show Low

***KNAA**
10-01-1997; 90.7 MHz FM; 3 kw; 817 ft.; N34 3 42 W109 54 22
Rebroadcasts: Rebroadcasts KNAU(FM) Flagstaff 100%
P.O. Box 5764, Flagstaff, AZ 86011 US
(928) 523-5628; *Fax:* (928) 523-7647
www.knau.org
knau@nau.edu
License: Show Low, Navajo County, AZ held by Arizona Board of Regents.
Nat'l Network: NPR
Format: News
Brian Sanders, Operations Dir
Stacy Murison, Development Director

KRFM
07-01-1983; 96.5 MHz FM; 100 kw; 994 ft.; N34 12 20 W109 56 26
1838 W. Commerce Dr., Suite A, Lakeside, AZ 85929 US
(928) 368-8100
www.965krfm.com
License: Show Low, Navajo County, AZ held by Petracom of Holbrook, LLC
Group Owner: White Mountain Radio
Nat'l Network: Jones Radio Networks
Arbitron Metro Market: White Mountains (AZ); *Format:* Adult Contemp; *Target Audience:* 18-34; 65% female & 35% male
Steve Johnson, General Manager
Renee Beebe, General Sales Mgr

KSNX
09-13-1964; 93.5 MHz FM; 25 kw; Ant 150 ft; N34 13 14 W110 01 49
130 Hampton Point Rd., St. Simons Island, GA 31522-1858 US
(813) 404-1858
www.1055ksnx.com
License: Show Low, Navajo County, AZ held by Petracom of Holbrook, LLC
Group Owner: White Mountain Radio
Arbitron Metro Market: Heber, AZ; *Format:* Oldies; *Target Audience:* 25-54; 50% female & 50% male
Renee Beebe, General Sales Mgr

KVSL
07-06-1968; 1450 kHz AM
3051 S. White Mountain Rd., Show Low, AZ 85901 US
(928) 368-8100; *Fax:* (928) 368-8108
www.whitemountainradio.com
License: Show Low, AZ
Nat'l Network: ABC; Fox News Radio
Arbitron Metro Market: Lakeside, AZ; *Format:* Oldies *Special Programming:* Farm 2 hrs wkly; *Target Audience:* 45-65; 46% female, 54% male
Steve Johnson, General Manager

KVWM
05-17-1957; 970 kHz AM
130 Hampton Point Dr., St. Simons Island, GA 31522-3031 US
(813) 948-2554
www.970kvwm.com
License: Show Low, AZ held by Petracom of Holbrook, LLC.
Group Owner: White Mountain Radio; (acq 11-17-2005; grpsl)
Nat'l Network: ABC; Westwood One
Arbitron Metro Market: Show low, AZ; *Format:* News/Talk; *Target Audience:* 35-65; 46% female & 54% male
Renee Beebe, General Sales Mgr

Sierra Vista

KKYZ
01-01-1995; 101.7 MHz FM; *Hrs Open:* 24; 3 kw; 328 ft.; N31 33 59 W110 13 57
P.O. Box 3037, Sierra Vista, AZ 85635 US
(520) 459-8201; *Fax:* (520) 458-7104
www.kkyz.com
info@kkyz.com
License: Sierra Vista, Cochise County, AZ held by Cochise Broadcasting L.L.C.
Group Owner: Cochise Broadcasting LLC; (acq 1-12-2001)
Arbitron Metro Market: Tucson, AZ; *Format:* Oldies; *Target Audience:* 25-54.
Ted Tucker, General Manager
Jeff Davenport, Station Manager

KNXN
06-20-1980; 1470 kHz AM; *Hrs Open:* 24
680 Avenida Del Sol, Sierra Vista, AZ 85635 US
(520) 790-2440; *Fax:* (520) 790-2937
www.kgms.com
doug@kvoi.com
License: Sierra Vista, AZ held by Good Music Inc.
Group Owner: Good News Communications Inc.; (acq 4-16-01; $300,000).
Format: Christian, Religious, 86; *Hrs. of News Programming:* news progmg 5 hrs wkly; *No. News Employees:* 1
Jeff Davenport, Operations Dir
Doug Martin, General Manager

KTAN
03-01-1957; 1420 kHz AM; *Hrs Open:* 24
Mailing Address: P.O. Box 2770, Sierra Vista, AZ 85636 US
Second Address: 2300 Busby Dr., Sierra Vista, AZ 85636
(520) 458-4313; *Fax:* (520) 458-4317
License: Sierra Vista, AZ held by CCR-Sierra Vista IV LLC.
Group Owner: Cherry Creek Radio LLC; (acq 12-19-2003; grpsl).
Nat'l Network: CBS; *Nat'l Reps:* Tacher
Arbitron Metro Market: Sierra Vista, AZ; *Format:* News, News/Talk, 84, Talk; *Hrs. of News Programming:* news progmg 20 hrs wkly; *No. News Employees:* 1; *Target Audience:* 25-54.
Grady Butler, Operations Dir
Tony Driskill, General Manager
Mary Nichols, News Director

KZMK
09-01-1973; 100.9 MHz FM; *Hrs Open:* 24; 3 kw; -46 ft.; N31 32 47 W110 16 29
Mailing Address: P.O. Box 2770, Sierra Vista, AZ 85636 US
Second Address: 2300 Busby Dr., Sierra Vista, AZ 85636
(520) 458-4313; *Fax:* (520) 458-4317
www.allhitskzmk.com/
License: Sierra Vista, Cochise County, AZ
Group Owner: Cherry Creek Radio LLC

Arbitron Metro Market: Sierra Vista, AZ; *Format:* Adult Contemp; *Hrs. of News Programming:* news progmg one hr wkly; *No. News Employees:* 1; *Target Audience:* 18-49.
Grady Butler III, Operations Dir
Tony Driskill, General Manager
Mary Nichols, News Director

South Tucson

KWFM(AM)
01-01-1957; 1330 kHz AM; 2 kw-D, 5 kw-N, DA-N; N32 18 51 W110 50 17
4433 E. Broadway, Suite 210, Tucson, AZ 85718
(520) 529-5865; *Fax:* (520) 529-9324
License: South Tucson, Pima County, AZ held by Hudson Communications Inc.
Population Served: 600,000; *Arbitron Metro Market:* Tucson, AZ
Kimberly Lopez, General Manager

KXEW
05-10-1963; 1600 kHz AM; *Hrs Open:* 24
889 W. El Puente Lane, Tucson, AZ 85713 US
(520) 618-2100; *Fax:* (520) 618-2165
www.tejano1600.com
License: South Tucson, AZ held by CC Licenses LLC.
Group Owner: iHeartMedia; (acq 9-25-2003).
Arbitron Metro Market: Tucson, AZ; *Format:* Tejano; *Target Audience:* 25-54; blue collar Hispanics
Carl Anderson, Market President
Melissa Santa Cruz, Promotions Director

Spring Valley

KAHM
09-09-1981; 102.1 MHz FM; *Hrs Open:* 24; 54 kw; 2526 ft.; N34 41 14 W112 7 1
Mailing Address: P.O. Box 2529, Prescott, AZ 86302 US
Second Address: 510 Henry St., Prescott, AZ 86301
(928) 445-7800
Kahm.info
License: Spring Valley, Yavapai County, AZ held by Southwest FM Broadcasting Co.
Arbitron Metro Market: Prescott, AZ; *Format:* Easy Listening; *Hrs. of News Programming:* news progmg 7 hrs wkly; *No. News Employees:* 3; *Target Audience:* 35-64; mature, affluent; *Adv. Rates:* 31; 24; 31; 20
Lou Silverstein, General Manager
Janice Derks, Sales Director
Nancy Bennett, Programming Director
Mark Parthe, Engineering Dir
Sue Mapp, Traffic Manager

Springerville

KQAZ
07-15-1984; 101.7 MHz FM; 55 kw; 1243 ft.; N34 15 6 W109 35 6
Mailing Address: P.O. Box 1069, Springerville, AZ 85938 US
Second Address: 691 E. Deuce of Clubs, Show Low, AZ 85901
(928) 532-1010; *Fax:* (928) 532-0101
www.majik101.com
mail@majik101.com
License: Springerville, Apache County, AZ held by Country Mountain Airwaves LLC.
Group Owner: Country Mountain Airwaves LLC; (acq 7-30-99; $175,000 with KRVZ(AM) Springerville)
Nat'l Network: AP Radio
Arbitron Metro Market: Show Low, AZ; *Format:* Adult Contemp
Camden Smith, General Manager
Laurie Pogson, News Director
Jack Jacobs, Disc Jockey

KRVZ
06-11-1982; 1400 kHz AM; *Hrs Open:* 24; 1 kw-U; N34 08 17 W109 16 10
Box 2020, Show Low, AZ 85938
(928) 532-1010; *Fax:* (928) 532-0101
krvz@frontiernet.net
License: Springerville, Apache County, AZ held by Country Mountain Airwaves LLC.
Group Owner: Country Mountain Airwaves LLC; (acq 7-30-99; $175,000 with KQAZ(FM) Springerville)
Nat'l Network: Jones Radio Networks

William Konopnicki, President
Dan Curtis, Operations Dir
Camden Smith, General Manager
Laurie Pogson, News Director

St. Johns

KWKM
01-01-2001; 95.7 MHz FM; *Hrs Open:* 24 hours; 100 kw; 1193 ft.; N34 14 58 W109 35 11
1520 B Commerce Dr., Show Low, AZ 85901 US
(928) 532-2949; *Fax:* (928) 532-3176
www.kwkm.com
jeanbarton@kwkm.com
License: St. Johns, Apache County, AZ held by KM Radio of St. Johns, LLC.
Group Owner: KM Communications Inc.
Nat'l Network: ABC
Arbitron Metro Market: Show Low, AZ; *Format:* Adult Contemp; *No. News Employees:* 1; *Target Audience:* 18-35 female
Myoung Hwa Bae, President

Sun City

KOMR
03-07-1975; 106.3 MHz FM; *Hrs Open:* 24; 23 kw; 725 ft.; N33 57 21 W112 28 34
6006 S. 30th St., Phoenix, AZ 85042 US
(602) 243-3333; *Fax:* (602) 513-7409
www.univision.com
License: Sun City, Maricopa County, AZ held by Univision Radio License Corp.
Group Owner: Univision Radio; (acq 9-22-2003; grpsl).
Arbitron Metro Market: Phoenix, AZ; *Format:* Spanish; *Target Audience:* 25-54.
Roberto Yanez, Vice President and General Manager
Juan Villa, News Director

Sun City West

KVIB
01-01-2005; 95.1 MHz FM; *Hrs Open:* 24; 41 kw; Ant 2,785 ft; N34 14 05 W112 22 02
4745 N. 7th Street, #410, Phoenix, AZ 85740
(602) 648-9800; *Fax:* (602) 648-4402
www.951latinovibefm.com
License: Sun City West, Maricopa County, AZ held by Riviera Broadcasting
Nat'l Reps: Katz Eastman
Target Audience: 18-34; Hispanic 2nd & 3rd generation
Marc Young, Operations & Programming Director
Jose Rodiles, General Manager
Jacqueline Bosque Diaz, General Sales Mgr
Meg Hall, Traffic Director

Superior

***KZAI**
01-01-2004; 89.9 MHz FM; 45 kw vert; 2031 ft.; N33 43 52 W111 20 39
5700 West Oaks Boulevard, Rocklin, CA 95765 US
(888) 937-2471; *Fax:* (916) 251-1650
www.air1.com
info@air1.com
License: Superior, Pinal County, AZ held by Educational Media Foundation.
Group Owner: EMF Broadcasting; (acq 2-10-2006; $2.5 million).
Nat'l Network: Air 1
Arbitron Metro Market: Superior, AZ; *Format:* Alternative, Christian
Alan Mason, COO
Mike Novak, President and CEO
Dan Beck, Operations Dir
David Pierce, Programming Director
Ed Lenane, News Director
Sam Wallington, Engineering Dir
Marya Morgan, News Reporter
Richard Hunt, News Reporter

Tanque Verde

KWCX-FM
07-08-1976; 104.9 MHz FM; *Hrs Open:* 24; 730 w; Ant 3,175 ft; N32 13 01 W109 36 26
900 West Patte Road, Willcox, AZ 85643
(520) 384-4626; *Fax:* (520) 384-4627
License: Tanque Verde, Pochise County, AZ held by KZLZ LLC.
Group Owner: KZLZ LLC; (acq 8-8-2007; $900,000 with KHIL(AM) Willcox)

Mark Lucke, General Manager
Cat Scalzo, Sales Manager

Teec Nos Pos

KNDN-FM
96.5 MHz FM; *Hrs Open:* 24 hours; 100 kw; 81 meters; N36 53 03 W109 03 53
1515 West Main Street, Farmington, NM
(505) 325-1996; *Fax:* (505) 327-2019
License: Teec Nos Pos, AZ held by KRJG Inc
Group Owner: Basin Broadcasting Company

Kerwin D Gober, President

Tempe

KDUS
04-16-1960; 1060 kHz AM; *Hrs Open:* 24; 5 kw-D, DAN; 0.5 kw-N, DAN; N33 21 43 W111 58 3
1167 W. Javelina Avenue, Mesa, AZ 85201 US
(480) 838-0400; *Fax:* (480) 820-8469
www.kdus.com
info@kdus.com
License: Tempe, AZ held by Tempe Radio Inc.
Group Owner: Sandusky Radio; (acq 1994; $20 million with co-located FM)
Arbitron Metro Market: Phoenix, AZ; *Format:* Sports; *No. News Employees:* 1; *Target Audience:* 18-34 males.
Chuck Artigue, General Manager
Dana Beaudin, General Sales Mgr
Angel Velasquez, Programming Director

KMIK
06-23-1960; 1580 kHz AM; *Hrs Open:* 24; 50 kw-D, DAN; 50 kw-N, DAN; N33 27 22 W111 50 1
4602 East University Drive, Phoenix, AZ 85034 US
(602) 381-1580; *Fax:* (602) 840-1488
www.radiodisney.com
License: Tempe, AZ held by Radio Disney Group LLC.
Group Owner: ABC Inc.; (acq 9-10-98; $5.85 million)
Nat'l Network: Radio Disney; *Nat'l Reps:* McGavren Guild
Arbitron Metro Market: Phoenix, AZ; *Format:* Children
Marni Gerber, Station Manager
Phil Guerini, VP/General Manager
Ivan Heredia, VP of Marketing

KUPD
04-01-1960; 97.9 MHz FM; 96 kw; 1621 ft.; N33 19 58 W112 3 53
1900 West Carmen, Tempe, AZ 85283 US
(480) 838-0400; *Fax:* (480) 820-8469
www.98kupd.com
mcfeelie@98kupd.com
License: Tempe, Maricopa County, AZ held by Tempe Radio Inc.
Group Owner: Sandusky Radio
Arbitron Metro Market: Phoenix, AZ; *Format:* Rock/AOR
Chuck Artigue, General Manager
Dana Beaudin, Sales Manager
Larry McFeelie, Programming Director
Debbie Marquez, Traffic Manager

Thatcher

KFMM
12-07-1981; 99.1 MHz FM; *Hrs Open:* 24; 50 kw; 2280 ft.; N32 53 22 W109 19 23 *Rebroadcasts:* Rebroadcasts KCUZ (AM) Safford 100%.
Mailing Address: 301 B Highway 70 East, Safford, AZ 85546 US
Second Address: 301 B Hwy. 70 E., Safford, AZ 85546
(928) 428-0916; *Fax:* (928) 428-7797
http://www.991theplanet.com/
License: Thatcher, Graham County, AZ held by Cochise Broadcasting LLC.
Group Owner: Cochise Broadcasting LLC
Arbitron Metro Market: Thatcher, AZ *Special Programming:* Children 2 hrs wkly; *Hrs. of News Programming:* news progmg 7 hrs wkly; *No. News Employees:* 1; *Adv. Rates:* Same as AM
Ted Tucker, General Manager
Jeff Davenport, Sales Manager

Tolleson

KNUV
01-23-1961; 1190 kHz AM; *Hrs Open:* 24; 5 kw-D, 250 w-N, DA-2; N33 26 42 W112 15 54
1601 N. 7th Street, #310, Phoenix, AZ 85006
(602) 759-1914; *Fax:* (602) 759-1776
www.onda1190am.com
License: Tolleson, Maricopa County, AZ held by New Radio Venture Inc.
Population Served: 2,000,000; *Arbitron Metro Market:* Phoenix, AZ
Laura Madrid, General Manager

KXXT
12-12-1962; 1010 kHz AM; *Hrs Open:* 24
PO Box 8085, Mitchell, IL 62040 US
(602) 296-3600; *Fax:* (602) 296-3624
jspurgin@communicom.com
License: Tolleson, AZ held by Communicom Co. of Arizona L.P.
Group Owner: Communicom Broadcasting LLC; (acq 12-14-2005; grpsl).
Arbitron Metro Market: Phoenix, AZ; *Format:* Religious; *No. News Employees:* 1
Ramon Bonilla, Operations Dir
Phillip French, Chief Engineer
Jess Spurgin, National Sales Director

Tuba City

KTBA
01-01-1980; 760 kHz AM
P.O. Box 9090, Window Rock, AZ 86515 US
(505) 371-5749; *Fax:* (505) 371-5588
License: Tuba City, AZ held by Western Indian Ministries Inc.
Arbitron Metro Market: Window Rock, AZ; *Format:* Adult Contemp; *Target Audience:* English & Navajo
Chuck Harper, General Manager

Tucson

KGMS
08-10-1963; 940 kHz AM; *Hrs Open:* 24
600 Congress Ave., Suite 1400, Austin, TX 78701 US
(520) 790-2440; *Fax:* (520) 790-2937
kgms.com
chrissy@kvoi.com
License: Tucson, AZ held by Good Music Inc.
Group Owner: Good News Communications Inc.; (acq 11-27-00; swap with KCEE(FM) Green Valley).
Nat'l Reps: Salem
Arbitron Metro Market: Tucson, AZ; *Format:* Christian, Talk; *Target Audience:* 25-54.; *Adv. Rates:* 25; 25; 25; 25
Doug Martin, President
Christina Willits, Operations Manager
Mary Martin, Sales Manager

KCUB
01-01-1929; 1290 kHz AM; *Hrs Open:* 24; 1 kw-U; N32 16 37 W110 58 50
575 W. Roger Rd., Tucson, AZ 85705 US
(520) 887-1000
www.sportsradio1290am.com
herb.crowe@cumulus.com
License: Tucson, AZ held by Radio License Holding CBC, LLC
Group Owner: Cumulus Media Inc.; (acq 4-26-2001; grpsl).
Population Served: 525,796; *Arbitron Metro Market:* Tucson, AZ; *Format:* Sports, Talk; *No. News Employees:* 1; *Target Audience:* 25-54.
Herb Crowe, Programming Director

KCEE
01-01-1994; 690 kHz AM; *Hrs Open:* 24
3222 S. Richey Avenue, Tucson, AZ 85713 US
(520) 889-8904; *Fax:* (520) 889-8573
www.1030kcee.com
License: Tucson, AZ held by Slone Broadcasting LLC
Arbitron Metro Market: Tucson, AZ; *Format:* Oldies; *Target Audience:* 24-54.; *Adv. Rates:* 30; 30; 25; 25
Araceli Espinoza, Operations Dir
Armando Zamora, General Manager
Steve Nunez, General Sales Mgr
Frank Luna, Engineering Dir

KFFN
01-01-1957; 1490 kHz AM; *Hrs Open:* 24; 1 kw-U, ND1; N32 14 56 W110 55 29
P.O. Box 693, Milwaukee, WI 53201 US
(520) 795-1490; *Fax:* (520) 327-2260
www.espntucson.com
License: Tucson, AZ held by Journal Broadcast Corp.
Group Owner: Journal Communications Inc.
Nat'l Network: ESPN Radio
Arbitron Metro Market: Tucson, AZ; *Format:* Sports; *Hrs. of News Programming:* News progmg 2 hrs wkly; *Target Audience:* 18-49.
Jim Arnold, General Manager/Vice President
Frank Arrotta, General Sales Mgr

***KFLT**
10-01-1977; 830 kHz AM; *Hrs Open:* 24; 50 kw-D, DAN; 1 kw-N, DAN; N32 26 39 W111 5 27
Mailing Address: P.O. Box 35300, Tuscan, AZ 85740 US
Second Address: 7355 N. Oracle Rd., Suite 102, Tucson, AZ 85704
(520) 797-3700; *Fax:* (520) 742-3375
www.myflr.org
abiddel@flr.org
License: Tucson, AZ held by Family Life Broadcasting System Inc.
Group Owner: Family Life Communications Inc.; (acq 10-86; $125,000;
Nat'l Network: Moody
Arbitron Metro Market: Tucson, AZ; *Format:* Christian, Religious; *Hrs. of News Programming:* news progmg 15 hrs wkly; *No. News Employees:* 1; *Target Audience:* 25-45; Christian families
Randy Carlson, President
Evan Carlson, Operations Dir
Adam Biddell, General Manager
Joe Rother, Chief Engineer
Rod Robison, Vice President of Development

KHYT
01-01-1993; 107.5 MHz FM; 92 kw; 620 meters; N32 24 54 W110 42 56
575 W. Roger Rd., Tucson, AZ 85705 US
(520) 887-1000
www.khit1075.com
License: Tucson, AZ held by Radio License Holding CBC, LLC
Group Owner: Cumulus Media Inc.; (acq 4-26-01; grpsl).
Arbitron Metro Market: Tucson, AZ; *Format:* Adult Contemp, Oldies; *Target Audience:* 25-54; adults
Herb Crowe, Operations Dir
Keith Rosenblatt, General Sales Mgr
Chanel Carrasco, Promotions Manager

KIIM
03-01-1954; 99.5 MHz FM; *Hrs Open:* 24; 93 kw; 2037 ft.; N32 14 56 W111 6 59
575 W. Roger Rd., Tucson, AZ 85705 US
(520) 887-1000; *Fax:* (520) 887-6397
www.kiimfm.com
License: Tucson, AZ held by Radio License Holding CBC, LLC
Group Owner: Cumulus Media Inc.
Nat'l Network: ABC; Premiere Radio Networks
Arbitron Metro Market: Tucson, AZ *TV Affiliate:* CMT; *Format:* Country *Special Programming:* CMT radio live 25 hrs wkly; *Target Audience:* Adult: 25-54.
Herb Crowe, Operations Dir
Keith Rosenblatt, General Sales Mgr
Chanel Carrasco, Promotions Manager

KLPX
06-01-1967; 96.1 MHz FM; 82 kw; 1952 ft.; N32 14 56 W111 6 59
3871 N. Commerce Drive, Tucson, AZ 85705 US
(520) 407-4500; *Fax:* (520) 407-4600
www.klpx.com
kkwilosz@azlotus.com
License: Tucson, Pima County, AZ
Group Owner: Lotus Communications Corp.; (Acq 6-79)
Nat'l Reps: D & R Radio
Arbitron Metro Market: Tucson, AZ; *Format:* Classic Rock; *Target Audience:* 25-54.
Steve Groesbeck, General Manager
Larry Mac, Programming Director
Jessica Allen, Promotions Coordinator
Cindy Craig, Marketing Director
John Covington, Local News Editor

KMXZ-FM
04-11-1973; 94.9 MHz FM; *Hrs Open:* 24; 97 kw; 1952 ft.; N32 14 56 W111 6 59
P.O. Box 693, Milwaukee, WI 53201 US
(520) 795-1490; *Fax:* (520) 327-2260
www.mixfm.com
mixfm@mixfm.com
License: Tucson, Pima County, AZ held by Journal Broadcast Corp.
Group Owner: Journal Communications Inc.; (acq 1996; grpsl)
Nat'l Network: AP Radio; *Wire Services:* AP
Arbitron Metro Market: Tucson, AZ; *Format:* Adult Contemp; *Hrs. of News Programming:* news progmg 3 hrs wkly; *No. News Employees:* 1; *Target Audience:* 25-54.
Darla Thomas, Operations Dir
Jennifer Nunn, General Sales Mgr
Bobby Rich, Programming Director
Larkin Gassman, Promotions Manager

KNST
10-01-1958; 790 kHz AM; *Hrs Open:* 24; 5 kw-D, DA1; 0.5 kw-N, DA1; N32 14 54 W111 0 30
600 Congress Ave., Suite 1400, Austin, TX 78701 US
(520) 618-2100; *Fax:* (520) 618-2135
www.knst.com
License: Tucson, AZ held by Capstar TX LLC
Group Owner: iHeartMedia; (acq 8-30-2000; grpsl)
Nat'l Network: Moody; *Nat'l Reps:* McGavren Guild
Arbitron Metro Market: Tucson, AZ; *Format:* News, News/Talk, 86; *No. News Employees:* 3; *Target Audience:* 25-54.
Carl Anderson, Senior Vice President of Programming
Garret Lewis, Programming Director
Paul Birmingham, News Director

KRQQ
02-01-1971; 93.7 MHz FM; 93 kw; 2011 ft.; N32 14 56 W111 6 59
3202 N. Oracle Rd., Tucson, AZ 85705 US
(520) 618-2100; *Fax:* (520) 618-2165
www.krq.com
License: Tucson, Pima County, AZ held by Capstar TX LLC
Group Owner: iHeartMedia
Arbitron Metro Market: Tucson, AZ; *Format:* Contemporary Hits/Top 40; *No. News Employees:* 1; *Target Audience:* 18-54.
Carl Anderson, Market President

KTKT
12-01-1949; 990 kHz AM; 10 kw-D, DA2; 1 kw-N, DA2; N32 15 19 W111 0 32
3871 North Commerce Drive, Tucson, AZ 85705 US
(520) 407-4500; *Fax:* (520) 407-4600
www.labuena943.com
License: Tucson, AZ held by Arizona Lotus Corp.
Group Owner: Lotus Communications Corp.; (acq 1973).
Nat'l Network: AP Radio; *Nat'l Reps:* Lotus Entravision Reps LLC
Arbitron Metro Market: Tucson, AZ; *Format:* Sports *Special Programming:* Black one hr, relg 2 hrs wkly; *Target Audience:* 25-54.
Steve Groesbeck, General Manager
Larry Mac, Programming Director
Cindy Craig, Marketing Director
Jessica Allen, Promotions Coordinator

KTUC
07-10-1926; 1400 kHz AM; 1 kw
575 W. Roger Rd., Tucson, AZ 85705 US
(520) 887-1000
www.ktucam.com
License: Tucson, AZ held by Radio License Holding CBC, LLC
Group Owner: Cumulus Media Inc.; (acq 4-26-01; grpsl).
Nat'l Network: CBS; *Nat'l Reps:* Katz Radio
Arbitron Metro Market: Tucson, AZ; *Format:* Adult Contemp, Oldies
Herb Crowe, Operations Dir
Keith Rosenblatt, Director of Sales
Chanel Carrasco, Dir of Marketing/Promotions

KTZR
02-27-1947; 1450 kHz AM; 1 kw-U; N32 12 04 W110 56 48
3202 N. Oracle Rd., Tucson, AZ 85713
(520) 618-2100; *Fax:* (520) 618-2200
www.lapreciosa1450.com
License: Tucson, Pima County, AZ held by CC Licenses LLC.
Group Owner: iHeartMedia; (acq 6-28-2001; grpsl).
Arbitron Metro Market: Tucson, AZ; *Format:* Spanish
Carl Anderson, Market President
Valerie Fanelli, Marketing Director

***KUAZ**
10-07-1968; 1550 kHz AM; *Hrs Open:* Sunrise-sunset; 50 kw-D, NDD; N32 22 21 W111 5 52
Mailing Address: Modern Lang Bldg, U of A, Tucson, AZ 85721 US
Second Address: Box 210067, Tucson, AZ
(520) 621-5828; *Fax:* (520) 621-3360
www.kuaz.org
License: Tucson, AZ held by Arizona Board of Regents for the Benefit of The University of Arizona.
Nat'l Network: NPR; PRI *Regional Reps:* Dana Homer; *Wire Services:* AP
Arbitron Metro Market: Tucson, AZ; *Format:* Jazz, News, 86; *Hrs. of News Programming:* 95+ hours per week; *No. News Employees:* 5
Jack Gibson, Director & General Manager
Achilles Calenti, Engineering Dir
Enrique Aldana, Director of Development
Julie Ben-Yeoshua, Underwriting Coordinator
Sue DeBenedette, Marketing Manager
Frank Fregoso, Chief Engineer
DanaHorner, General Sales Manager
Ed Kesterson, Programming Director

***KUAT-FM**
05-19-1975; 90.5 MHz FM; *Hrs Open:* 24; 12 kw; 3652 ft.; N32 24 55.1 W110 42 51.9
Mailing Address: University of Az, PO Box 210067, Tucson, AZ 85721 US
Second Address: Box 2100067, Tucson, AZ 85721-0067

(520) 621-5828; *Fax:* (520) 621-3360
www.kuatfm.org
License: Tucson, Pima County, AZ held by Arizona Board of Regents for the Benefit of The University of Arizona.
Nat'l Network: PRI *Regional Reps:* Dana Horner; *Wire Services:* AP
Arbitron Metro Market: Tucson, AZ; *Format:* Classical; *Target Audience:* 35 plus.
Jack Gibson, Director & General Manager
Achilles Calenti, Engineering Dir
Enrique Aldana, Director of Development
Julie Ben-Yeoshua, Underwriting Coordinator
Sue DeBenedette, Marketing Manager
Frank Fregoso, Chief Engineer
DanaHorner, General Sales Manager
Ed Kesterson, Programming Director

***KUAZ-FM**
04-27-1992; 89.1 MHz FM; *Hrs Open:* 24; 1.6 kw; 614 ft.; N32 12 53 W111 0 21
Mailing Address: Unv. of Az, P O Box 210067, Tucson, AZ 85721 US
Second Address: Box 210067, Tucson, AZ
(520) 621-5828; *Fax:* (520) 621-3360
www.kuaz.org
License: Tucson, Pima County, AZ held by Arizona Board of Regents for Benefit of the University of Arizona.
Nat'l Network: NPR; PRI; *Wire Services:* AP
Arbitron Metro Market: Tucson, AZ *TV Affiliate:* KUAT-TV affil; *Format:* Jazz, News, 62, Talk; *Hrs. of News Programming:* news progmg 95+ hrs wkly; *No. News Employees:* 5; *Target Audience:* General.
Jack Gibson, Director & General Manager
John Kelley, Station Manager
Ed Kesterson, Programming Director
Achilles Calenti, Engineering Dir
Enrique Aldana, Associate Director of Development
Pat Callahan, Director of Membership
MarkDuggan, Producer/Reporter

KMIY
05-18-1970; 92.9 MHz FM; *Hrs Open:* 24; 90 kw; 2,037 ft; N32 14 56 W111 06 59
3202 N. Oracle Rd., Tucson, AZ 78701
(520) 618-2100; *Fax:* (520) 618-2200
www.my929.com
License: Tucson, Pima County, AZ held by Capstar TX LLC
Group Owner: iHeartMedia
Population Served: 452,000; *Arbitron Metro Market:* Tucson, AZ; *Format:* Adult Contemp; *Hrs. of News Programming:* news progmg 21 hrs wkly; *No. News Employees:* 2
Carl Anderson, Market President

***KXCI**
12-17-1983; 91.3 MHz FM; *Hrs Open:* 24; 0.34 kw; 3642 ft.; N32 24 54 W110 42 56
220 South Fourth Avenue, Tucson, AZ 85701 US
(520) 623-1000 EXT. 11(520) 622-5924; *Fax:* (520) 623-0758
www.kxci.org
onfo@kxci.org
License: Tucson, Pima County, AZ held by Foundation for Creative Broadcasting Inc.
Arbitron Metro Market: Tucson, AZ; *Format:* Triple A *Special Programming:* American Indian 2 hrs, Black 4 hrs, folk 2 hrs, gospel 2 hrs, jazz 2 hrs, Sp 4 hrs wkly; *Hrs. of News Programming:* News progmg 4 hrs wkly *Target Audience:* 18-49.
Randy Peterson, General Manager/Development Director
Doug Groenhoff, Chief Engineer
Duncan Hudson, Music Director
Michelle Boulet-Stephenson, Membership Director
Amanda Shauger, Community Engagement Director

KQTH
05-04-1994; 104.1 MHz FM; *Hrs Open:* 24; 3 kw; 328 ft.; N32 17 23 W111 1 6
3438 N Country Club, Tucson, AZ 85716 US
(520) 722-5486; *Fax:* (520) 327-2260
www.1041thetruth.com
License: Tucson, Pima County, AZ held by Journal Broadcast Corp.
Group Owner: Journal Communications Inc.
Arbitron Metro Market: Tucson, AZ; *Format:* News; *Target Audience:* 25-54; males, persons
Darla Thomas, Operations Dir
Julie Brinks, General Manager
Jennifer Nunn, General Sales Mgr

***KFLT-FM**
01-01-2006; 88.5 MHz FM; 1.5 kw vert; 377 ft.; N32 0 11 W110 47 49
Mailing Address: 7355 N. Oracle, #200, Tucson, AZ 85740 US
Second Address: 7355 N. Oracle Rd., Suite 102, Tucson, AZ 85704
(800) 776-1070; *Fax:* (520) 742-6979
www.myflr.org
License: Tucson, Pima County, AZ held by Family Life Broadcasting Inc.
Group Owner: Family Life Communications Inc.
Arbitron Metro Market: Tucson, AZ; *Format:* Christian, Religious
Dr. Randy L. Carlson, President
Evan Carlson, Operations Dir
Adam Biddell, General Manager
Adam Biddell, Programming Director
Joe Rother, Chief Engineer
Bill Ronning, Music Director
Alonzo Williams, Vice President ofOperations
Rod Robison, Vice President of Development

***KAIC**
01-01-2006; 88.9 MHz FM; 1.8 kw vert; 26 ft.; N32 36 56 W110 38 38 *Rebroadcasts:* Rebroadcasts KLRD(FM) Yucaipa, CA 100%
1425 N Market Blvd., Suite 9, Sacramento, CA 95834 US
(888) 937-2471; *Fax:* (916) 251-1650
www.air1.com
info@air1.com
License: Tucson, Pima County, AZ held by Educational Media Foundation.
Group Owner: EMF Broadcasting
Nat'l Network: Air 1
Arbitron Metro Market: Tucson, AZ; *Format:* Alternative, Christian
Darrell Chambliss, Chairman
Mike Novak, President and CEO
Dan Beck, Operations Dir
Eric Allen, General Sales Mgr
David Pierce, Programming Director
Ed Lenane, News Director
Sam Wallington, Engineering Dir
Marya Morgan, NewsReporter
Eric Moser, Chief Financial Officer

Vail

KRDX
06-01-1978; 98.5 MHz FM; *Hrs Open:* 24; 3.9 kw; 410 ft.; N31 55 39 W110 37 57
Post Office Box 36717, Tucson, AZ 85740 US
(520) 459-8201; *Fax:* (520) 458-7104
www.fox985.com
License: Vail, Pima County, AZ held by Desert West Air Ranchers Corp.
Arbitron Metro Market: Tucson, AZ; *Format:* Variety/Diverse
Ted Tucker, General Manager

KXZK
01-01-2008; 103.7 MHz FM; 0.79 kw; 476 ft.; N31 55 39 W110 37 57
PO Box 36717, Tucson, AZ 85740 US
(520) 459-8201; *Fax:* (520) 458-7104
License: Vail, Pima County, AZ held by Cochise Broadcasting LLC.
Group Owner: Cochise Broadcasting LLC
Arbitron Metro Market: Vail, AZ
Ted Tucker, General Manager

Wellton

KCEC-FM
10-01-2000; 104.5 MHz FM; *Hrs Open:* 24; 1.75 kw; 1250 ft.; N32 40 22 W114 20 14
PO Box 62, Keene, CA 93531 US
(928) 782-5995; *Fax:* (928) 782-3874
www.campesina.com
License: Wellton, Yuma County, AZ held by Farmworker Educational Radio Network Inc.
Group Owner: Farmworker Educational Radio Network Inc.
Arbitron Metro Market: Yuma, AZ; *Format:* Tejano; *Target Audience:* 25-54; Hispanic market
Anthony Chavez, President
Mary Hudak, General Manager
Barbara Lane, General Sales Mgr
Pepe Escamilla, Programming Director
Isabel Eggert, News Director
Dave Whitehead, Chief Engineer

KUKY
95.9 MHz FM; 1.6 kw; 1263 ft.; N32 40 22 W114 20 11.2
2433 East Palo Verde Street, Yuma, AZ 85365 US
(928) 344-3727; *Fax:* (202) 293-7783
www.amigo959fm.com
radio.amigo@yahoo.com
License: Wellton, Yuma County, AZ held by Hispanic Target Media Inc.
Arbitron Metro Market: Wellton, AZ; *Format:* Tejano
Maria SanMillan, General Manager
Jose Vasquez, Marketing/Programming Director

Whiteriver

***KNNB**
09-11-1982; 88.1 MHz FM; *Hrs Open:* 18; 0.63 kw; 600 ft.; N33 45 47 W109 57 39
P. O. Box 310, Whiteriver, AZ 85941 US
(928) 338-5229; *Fax:* (928) 338-1744
License: Whiteriver, Navajo County, AZ held by Apache Radio Broadcasting Corp.
Format: Variety/Diverse *Special Programming:* Apache 8 hrs wkly; *Hrs. of News Programming:* news progmg 3 hrs wkly; *No. News Employees:* 1; *Target Audience:* 15-60.
Udell Opaha, Station Manager
Sylvia Browning, Programming Director

Wickenburg

KHOV-FM
12-02-1983; 105.3 MHz FM; *Hrs Open:* 24; 6 kw; 1,365 ft.; N34 11 32 W112 45 13
6006 S. 30th St., Phoenix, AZ 85042 US
(602) 243-3333; *Fax:* (602) 513-7409
www.univision.com
License: Wickenburg, Maricopa County, AZ held by Univision Radio License Corp.
Group Owner: Univision Radio; (acq 9-22-2003; grpsl).
Nat'l Network: Jones Radio Networks
Arbitron Metro Market: Phoenix, AZ; *Format:* Tejano; *Target Audience:* 18-49.
Roberto Yanez, Vice President and General Manager
Eric Bench, National Sales Manager

KSWG
01-01-1993; 96.3 MHz FM; *Hrs Open:* 24; 6.4 kw; 646 ft.; N33 55 34 W112 47 40
801 West Wickenburg Way, Wickenburg, AZ 85390 US
(928) 684-7804; *Fax:* (928) 684-7805
www.963realcountry.com
kswg@directpc.com
License: Wickenburg, Maricopa County, AZ held by Barna Broadcasting, LLC
Arbitron Metro Market: Wickenburg, AZ; *Format:* Country; *Adv. Rates:* 10; 10; 10; 10
Michael Barna, President
Kevin Mannion, Programming Director

Willcox

KHIL
12-02-1959; 1250 kHz AM; 5 kw-D, ND1; 0.196 kw-N, ND1; N32 16 0 W109 49 58
Mailing Address: 1491 Thatcher Blvd, Safford, AZ 85546 US
Second Address: 900 West Patte Rd., Willcox, AZ 85643
(520) 384-4626; *Fax:* (520) 384-4627
www.xwave1049.com
markelucke@qwestoffice.net
License: Willcox, AZ held by KZLZ LLC.
Group Owner: KZLZ LLC; (acq 8-8-2007; $900,000 with KWCX-FM Willcox)
Nat'l Network: USA
Format: Country
Mark Lucke, General Manager
Cat Scalzo, Account Manager

Williams

KWMX
01-01-1998; 96.7 MHz FM; 10.5 kw; 1066 ft.; N35 7 52 W112 8 3
2370 West Highway 89a, Suite 11-131, Sedona, AZ 86336 US
(928) 779-1177; *Fax:* (928) 774-5179
www.thewolf.com
License: Williams, Coconino County, AZ held by Grenax Broadcasting II LLC.
Group Owner: Grenax Broadcasting LLC; (acq 4-14-2005; grpsl)
Format: Classic Rock
Greg Dinetz, President
Jay Arthur, Operations & Programming Director
Stan Pierce, General Manager
Mike Mentor, Programming Director
Barb Richards, News Director
Jon Koger, Chief Engineer
Jan Hyslop

Window Rock

KTNN
02-26-1986; 660 kHz AM; *Hrs Open:* 12A - 12A; 50 kw-D, DAN; 50 kw-N, DAN; N35 53 42 W109 8 29
P.O.Box 2569, Window Rock, AZ 86515 US
(928) 871-3553; *Fax:* (928) 871-3479
www.ktnnonline.com
License: Window Rock, AZ held by The Navajo Nation
Wire Services: CNN
Arbitron Metro Market: Window Rock, AZ; *Format:* Country
Special Programming: Native American; *Hrs. of News Programming:* 1; *Target Audience:* Navajo Tribe of Native Americans
Troy Little, General Manager
Stan Bernally, Sales Manager
L.A. Williams, Programming Director
Marcia Peshlakai, Promotions Manager
Paul Jones, News Director

***KWIM**
09-21-1995; 104.9 MHz FM; 30 kw; 299 ft.; N35 39 19 W109 1 59
Post Office Box 9090, Window Rock, AZ 86515 US
(505) 371-5749; *Fax:* (505) 371-5588
www.westernindian.org
wim@westernindian.org
License: Window Rock, Apache County, AZ held by Western Indian Ministries Inc.
Arbitron Metro Market: Window Rock, AZ; *Format:* Adult Contemp, Christian, 74; *Adv. Rates:* 9; 9; 9; 9
Larry Harpor, General Manager
Chuck Harper, General Director
Greg Lewis, Programming Director
Marc Guiett, Chief Engineer

KWRK
10-01-1996; 96.1 MHz FM; *Hrs Open:* 24; 94 kw; 584 ft.; N35 33 36 W109 6 30
P. O. Box 2569, Window Rock, AZ 86515 US
(928) 871-3553; *Fax:* (928) 871-3479
License: Window Rock, Apache County, AZ held by The Navajo Nation.
Nat'l Network: Jones Radio Networks; *Wire Services:* AP
Arbitron Metro Market: Window Rock, AZ; *Format:* Country
Troy Little, General Manager
Stewart Begay, General Sales Mgr
L.A. Williams, Programming Director
Marcia Peshlakai, Promotions Manager
Leander Moffit, Program Coordinator

Winslow

KINO
12-18-1962; 1230 kHz AM; 1 kw-U, ND1; N35 2 15 W110 43 0
PO Box K, Winslow, AZ 86047 US
(928) 289-3364; *Fax:* (928) 289-3366
kinoradio@cableone.net
License: Winslow, AZ held by Sunflower Communications.
Nat'l Network: CBS; ESPN Radio; *Regional Network:* Arizona News Radio
Format: Country *Special Programming:* Sp 4 hrs wkly; *Target Audience:* General.; *Adv. Rates:* 7.75; na; na; na
Loy Engelhardt, General Manager

***KAWN**
91.3 MHz FM; 0.3 kw; 118 ft.; N35 1 36 W110 41 50
P.O. Box 3206, Tupelo, MS 38803 US
(662) 844-8888; *Fax:* (662) 842-6791
www.afr.net
faq@afa.net
License: Winslow, Navajo County, AZ held by American Family Association.
Group Owner: American Family Radio
Arbitron Metro Market: Winslow, AZ; *Format:* Christian
Tim Wildmon, President
Donald Wildmon, Founder
Buddy Smith, Sr VP
Ed Vitagliano, Exec VP
Randy Sharp, Director Of Special Projects
Meeke Addison, Director Of Communications
Abraham Hamilton III, General Counsel

Yuma

***KAWC**
07-11-1970; 1320 kHz AM; *Hrs Open:* 6 AM-6 PM
Mailing Address: PO Box 929, Yuma, AZ 85364 US
Second Address: 2020 S. Ave., # 8E, Yuma, AZ 85366
(928) 317-7690; *Fax:* (928) 317-7740
kawcradio.org
License: Yuma, AZ held by Arizona Western College.
Nat'l Network: NPR; PRI
Arbitron Metro Market: Yuma, AZ; *Format:* News, News/Talk, 86
Special Programming: Sp 15 hrs wkly; *No. News Employees:* 1; *Target Audience:* General.
Dave Riek, General Manager
Lou Gum, News/Operations Director

***KAWC-FM**
03-27-1992; 88.9 MHz FM; *Hrs Open:* 6 AM-9 PM; 2.4 kw; 108 ft.; N32 41 23 W114 30 1
9500 S. Avenue 8e, Yuma, AZ 85365 US
(928) 317-7690; *Fax:* (928) 317-7740
kawcradio.org
License: Yuma, Yuma County, AZ held by Arizona Western College
Arbitron Metro Market: Yuma, AZ; *Format:* Jazz, News; *No. News Employees:* 1
Dave Riek, General Manager

KBLU
03-01-1940; 560 kHz AM; *Hrs Open:* 24; 1 kw-D, DAN; 1 kw-N, DAN; N32 43 25 W114 38 39
600 Congress Avenue, Suite 1400, Austin, TX 78701 US
(928) 344-4980; *Fax:* (928) 344-4983
www.kbluam.com
License: Yuma, AZ held by EDB Yuma License LLC
Group Owner: Frontier Radio Management Inc.
Nat'l Network: ABC; Fox News Radio; Fox Sports; Premiere Radio Networks; *Regional Network:* Southwest Agri-Radio
Arbitron Metro Market: Yuma, AZ; *Format:* News, News/Talk, 86; *Target Audience:* Adults 25-54.
Dave Sturgeon, General Manager
Kelley Ray, Programming Director
Chris Reichman, News Director
Starr Favreau, Office Manager

***KCFY**
03-01-1992; 88.1 MHz FM; *Hrs Open:* 24; 3 kw; 240 ft.; N32 38 31 W114 33 34
Mailing Address: P.O. Box 1669, Yuma, AZ 85366 US
Second Address: 1921 S. Rail Ave., Yuma, AZ 85365
(928) 341-9730; *Fax:* (928) 341-9099
www.kcfyfm.com
kcfy@kcfyfm.com
License: Yuma, Yuma County, AZ held by Relevant Media Inc.
Format: Christian; *Hrs. of News Programming:* News progmg 4 hrs wkly; *Target Audience:* 25-45; young to middle aged families
Greg Myers, General Manager
Mike Bondora, Promotions Manager
Scott Garrett, News Director
Patty Larson, Traffic Manager

KCYK
12-11-1950; 1400 kHz AM; *Hrs Open:* 24; 1 kw; N32 39 06 W114 39 00
949 S. Avenue B, Yuma, AZ 85364
(928) 782-4321; *Fax:* (928) 343-1710
License: Yuma, Yuma County, AZ held by MonsterMedia L.L.C.
Nat'l Network: Jones Radio Networks; *Nat'l Reps:* McGavren Guild
Population Served: 160,000 *Hrs. of News Programming:* News progmg 6 hrs wkly; *Target Audience:* 35 plus.; *Adv. Rates:* 24; 24; 24; 15
Keith Lewis, CEO
Jennifer Blackwell, News Director

KLJZ
08-20-1972; 93.1 MHz FM; *Hrs Open:* 24; 100 kw; 82 ft.; N32 39 6 W114 39 4
Aztec Plaza, 949 S. Avenue B, Yuma, AZ 85364 US
(928) 782-4321; *Fax:* (928) 343-1710
todaysbestmusic@z93yuma.com
License: Yuma, Yuma County, AZ held by MonsterMedia L.L.C.
Nat'l Network: Jones Radio Networks; *Nat'l Reps:* McGavren Guild
Arbitron Metro Market: Phoenix, AZ; *Format:* Adult Contemp; *Hrs. of News Programming:* News progmg 2 hrs wkly; *Target Audience:* 18-49.; *Adv. Rates:* 42; 42; 42; 30

KTTI
11-06-1970; 95.1 MHz FM; *Hrs Open:* 24; 50 kw; 246 ft.; N32 38 31 W114 33 34
600 Congress Avenue, Suite 1400, Austin, TX 78701 US
(928) 344-4980; *Fax:* (928) 344-4983
www.kttifm.com
License: Yuma, Yuma County, AZ held by EDB Yuma License LLC
Group Owner: Frontier Radio Management Inc.; (acq 11-30-2007; grpsl)
Nat'l Network: Jones Radio Networks; *Regional Network:* Southwest Agri-Radio
Arbitron Metro Market: Yuma, AZ; *Format:* Country; *No. News Employees:* 3; *Target Audience:* 25-54; Adults
Jeff Edwards, Operations Dir
Jeff Harris, General Manager
Starr Favreau, Business Manager

KQSR
09-05-1986; 100.9 MHz FM; *Hrs Open:* 24; 3 kw; 262 ft.; N32 38 31 W114 33 34
600 Congress Avenue, Suite 1400, Austin, TX 78701 US
(928) 344-4980; *Fax:* (928) 344-4983
www.kqsrfm.com
License: Yuma, Yuma County, AZ held by EDB Yuma License LLC.
Group Owner: Frontier Radio Management Inc.; (acq 11-30-2007; grpsl)
Arbitron Metro Market: Yuma, AZ; *Format:* Adult Contemp; *Target Audience:* 25-54.
Jeff Harris, General Manager
Jay Wachs, General Sales Mgr
Jeff Edwards, Programming Director

***KYRM**
04-01-2000; 91.9 MHz FM; *Hrs Open:* 24; 6.3 kw; 1335 ft.; N33 3 18 W114 49 37
Mailing Address: Box 3765, McAllen, TX 78502 US
Second Address: 2690 3rd Ave., Yuma, AZ 85364
(928) 341-0919; *Fax:* (928) 314-4141
www.manantialyuma.org
kyrm@lwrn.org
License: Yuma, Yuma County, AZ held by World Radio Network.
Group Owner: World Radio Network Inc.
Arbitron Metro Market: Yuma, AZ.; *Format:* Christian, Religious
Special Programming: Children 6 hrs; *Hrs. of News Programming:* News progmg 6 hrs wkly; *Target Audience:* Hispanic population
Douglas Swanson, Station Manager
Rachel Swanson, Programming Director

Arkansas

Arkadelphia

KDEL-FM
06-12-1977; 100.9 MHz FM; *Hrs Open:* 24; 3 kw; 95 ft.; N34 6 39 W93 3 1
Mailing Address: P.O. Box 40, Arkadelphia, AR 71923 US
Second Address: 601 S. 7th St., Arkadelphia, AR 71923
(870) 246-9272; *Fax:* (870) 246-5878
www.arkadelphiaradio.com
License: Arkadelphia, Clark County, AR held by Southwest Arkansas Media LLC
Group Owner: Southwest Arkansas Media LLC
Arbitron Metro Market: Arkadelphia, AR; *Format:* Classic Rock
Pete Osteen, General Manager
Debbie Thompson, Station Manager
Gina Angel, Office/Traffic Manager
Kevin Hrabal, Production Manager

***KSWH-FM**
09-25-1969; 91.1 MHz FM; *Hrs Open:* 6 AM-midnight; 0.015 kw horiz; 49 ft.; N34 7 32 W93 3 48
Radio Station Kswh(Fm), P.O. Box 7872, Arkadelphia, AR 71923 US
(870) 230-5185; *Fax:* (870) 230-5144
kswh@hsu.edu
License: Arkadelphia, Clark County, AR held by Henderson State University.
Arbitron Metro Market: Arkadelphia, AR *Special Programming:* Alternative 15 hrs, contemp Christian 2 hrs, rap 15 hrs wkly; *Hrs. of News Programming:* news progmg 2 hrs wkly; *No. News Employees:* 2; *Target Audience:* 18-36; activity-orienated youthful females

KVRC
09-25-1947; 1240 kHz AM; *Hrs Open:* 24; 1 kw-U, ND1; N34 6 39 W93 3 1
Mailing Address: P. O. Box 40, Arkadelphia, AR 71923 US
Second Address: 601 S. 7th St., Arkadelphia, AR 71923
(870) 246-9272; *Fax:* (870) 246-5878
License: Arkadelphia, AR held by Southwest Arkansas Media LLC
Group Owner: Southwest Arkansas Media LLC; (acq 9-4-2013; grpsl)
Arbitron Metro Market: Arkadelphia, AR; *Format:* News, News/Talk, 86
Pete Osteen, General Manager
Debbie Thompson, Station Manager
Gina Angel, Office and Traffic Manager
Kevin Hrabal, DJ/ Production Manager

***KHED**
91.9 MHz FM; kw
1100 Henderson Street, Arkadelpjia, AR 71999 US
(870) 230-5091
License: Arkadelphia, Clark County, AR held by Henderson State University.

Ash Flat

KFCM
05-18-1981; 98.3 MHz FM; *Hrs Open:* 24; 25 kw; 318 ft.; N36 21 58 W91 28 35
PO Box 909, Cherokee Village, AR 72525 US
(870) 856-4408; *Fax:* (870) 895-4088
hometownradio@centurytel.net
License: Ash Flat, Sharp County, AR held by KFCM Inc.
Arbitron Metro Market: Cherokee Village, AR; *Format:* Oldies; *Hrs. of News Programming:* news progmg 25 hrs wkly; *No. News Employees:* 3; *Target Audience:* 25-54.; *Adv. Rates:* 18; 14; 16; 12
James Bragg, President

Ashdown

KMJI
05-25-1985; 93.3 MHz FM; *Hrs Open:* 24; 7.4 kw; 597 ft.; N33 30 24 W94 12 25
P O Box 311, Dequeen, AR 71832 US
(870) 772-3771; *Fax:* (870) 772-0364
www.mix933fm.com
wesspicher@gapbroadcasting.com
License: Ashdown, Little River County, AR held by Townsquare Media Texarkana License LLC
Group Owner: Townsquare Media; (acq 8-3-2007; grpsl)
Arbitron Metro Market: Texarkana, AR; *Format:* Adult Contemp *Special Programming:* Relg 4 hrs wkly; *Hrs. of News Programming:* news progmg 7 hrs wkly; *No. News Employees:* 1; *Target Audience:* General.
Ron Bird, General Manager
Jim Weaver, Brand Manager
Ron Bird, Director Of Sales
Jane Beckerdite, Digital Managing Editor

KPGG
05-19-1972; 103.9 MHz FM; *Hrs Open:* 24; 5.1 kw; 354 ft.; N33 36 6 W94 4 38
1578 Boston Road, New Boston, TX 75570 US
(903) 793-1109; *Fax:* (903) 794-4717
License: Ashdown, Little River County, AR held by American Media Investments Inc.
Group Owner: American Media Investments Inc.; (acq 2-17-2009; grpsl)
Nat'l Reps: Katz Radio
Arbitron Metro Market: Ashtown, AK; *Format:* Country; *No. News Employees:* 1; *Adv. Rates:* 35; 30; 30; 15
Kirk Keller, General Manager
Michael Brosius, Programming Director

Atkins

KCON
10-01-1999; 99.3 MHz FM; *Hrs Open:* 24; 4.1 kw; 394 ft.; N35 14 41 W92 52 51
P.O. Box 541, Morrilton, AR 72110 US
(501) 354-2484
www.993theeagle.com
rich@rivervalleyradio.com
License: Atkins, Pope County, AR held by EAB of Morrilton LLC
Group Owner: East Arkansas Broadcasters Inc.
Nat'l Reps: Christal; *Wire Services:* AP
Arbitron Metro Market: Morrilton, AK; *Format:* Classic Rock
Aaron Thomas, Operations Manager
Rich Moellers, Market Manager
Rhonda Dilbeck, Director of Sales

Augusta

***KJSM-FM**
08-27-1979; 97.7 MHz FM; 100 kw; 620 ft.; N35 10 36 W91 23 49
Mailing Address: 1206 No. Main, Beebe, AR 72012 US
Second Address: 8919 World Ministries Avenue, Baton Rouge, LA 70810
(225) 768-3688
www.jsm.org
kawikfish@yahoo.com
License: Augusta, Woodruff County, AR held by Family Worship Center Church Inc.
Group Owner: Family Worship Center Church Inc.; acq 3-4-2003; $2.75 million)
Arbitron Metro Market: Augusta, AR; *Format:* Christian
David Whitelaw, COO/General Manager
Jimmy Swaggart, President
John Santiago, Programming Director
Gene Snow, General Sales Manager

Barling

KFPW-FM
09-01-1987; 94.5 MHz FM; *Hrs Open:* 24; 18.5 kw; Ant 269 ft; N35 15 54 W94 21 52
323 N. Greenwood, Fort Smith, AR 72716
(479) 242-1047
www.thefort945fm.com
License: Barling, Sebastian County, AR held by Pharis Broadcasting Inc.
Group Owner: Pharis Broadcasting Inc.; (acq 3-14-2002;. $350,000 with KFPW
Nat'l Reps: Local Focus
Arbitron Metro Market: Fort Smith, AR; *Target Audience:* 25-54; general; *Adv. Rates:* 20; 20; 20; 20

Batesville

KAAB
08-01-1980; 1130 kHz AM; 1 kw-D, DA2; 0.02 kw-N, DA2; N35 44 40 W91 38 21
Mailing Address: Post Office Box 2077, Batesville, AR 72503
Second Address: Box 2077, Batesville, AR 72503
(870) 793-4196; *Fax:* (870) 793-5222
License: Batesville, AR held by WRD Entertainment Inc.
Group Owner: WRD Entertainment Inc.
Regional Network: Ark. Radio Net.
Arbitron Metro Market: Batesville, AR; *Format:* Tejano *Special Programming:* Farm 5 hrs wkly; *Target Audience:* 18-44.
Gary Bridgman, General Manager
Matt Johnson, Sales Manager
Ken Loggains, Programming Director
Gena Ries, Traffic Manager

KBTA
06-30-1950; 1340 kHz AM; *Hrs Open:* 24; 1 kw-U, ND1; N35 44 39 W91 38 21
P.O. Box 2077, Batesville, AR 72503 US
(870) 793-4196; *Fax:* (870) 793-5222
maxfm.com
License: Batesville, AR held by W.R.D. Entertainment Inc.
Group Owner: WRD Entertainment Inc.; acq 12-15-95).
Wire Services: AP
Format: Sports; *Hrs. of News Programming:* news progmg 22 hrs wkly; *No. News Employees:* 2; *Target Audience:* 18 plus.
Rob Grace, President
Gary Bridgman, General Manager
Matt Johnson, Sales Manager
Ken Loggains, Programming Director
Dale Johnson, Chief Engineer
Gina Ries, Traffic Manager

KBTA-FM
01-01-1999; 99.5 MHz FM; 3.4 kw; 427 ft.; N35 52 7 W91 35 14
P.O. Box 2077, Batesville, AR 72503 US
(870) 793-4196; *Fax:* (870) 793-5222
www.995hitsnow.com
License: Batesville, Independence County, AR held by W.R.D. Entertainment Inc.
Group Owner: WRD Entertainment Inc.
Arbitron Metro Market: Batesville, AR; *Format:* Adult Contemp
Rob Grace, President
Gary Bridgman, General Manager
Matt Johnson, General Sales Mgr
Ken Loggains, Programming Director
Dale Johnson, Chief Engineer

KZLE
03-03-1982; 93.1 MHz FM; 99 kw; 984 ft.; N35 53 29 W91 43 31
720 Ramsey Street, P.O. Box 2037, Batesville, AR 72503 US
(870) 793-4196; *Fax:* (870) 793-5222
maxfm.com
rob@maxfm.com
License: Batesville, Independence County, AR held by W.R.D. Entertainment Inc.
Group Owner: WRD Entertainment Inc.
Wire Services: AP
Arbitron Metro Market: Batesville, AR; *Target Audience:* 24 plus.
Rob Grace, President
Gary Bridgman, General Manager
Matt Johnson, Sales Manager
Dale Johnson, Engineering Dir

Beebe

***KOAR**
06-22-1991; 101.5 MHz FM; *Hrs Open:* 24; 6 kw; 328 ft.; N35 11 26 W91 54 45
1206 N. Main, Beebe, AR 72012 US
(916) 251-1600; *Fax:* (916) 251-1650
www.air1.com
info@air1.com
License: Beebe, White County, AR held by Educational Media Foundation.
Group Owner: EMF Broadcasting; (acq 6-9-2005; $525,000).
Nat'l Network: Air 1
Arbitron Metro Market: Searcy, AZ; *Format:* Christian
Darrell Chambliss, Chairman
Mike Novak, CEO
Mike Novak, President
Alan Mason, Operations Dir
Eric Moser, CFO

Bella Vista

KBVA
11-01-1991; 106.5 MHz FM; *Hrs Open:* 24; 37 kw; 567 ft; N36 18 21 W94 27 29
1512 Hwy. 72 S.E., Gravette, AR 72736
(479) 787-6411; *Fax:* (479) 787-6116
www.variety1065.com
gayla@variety1065.com
License: Bella Vista, Benton County, AR held by Gayla Joy McKenzie.
Arbitron Metro Market: Gravette, AR
Gayla Joy McKenzie, President

Bellefonte

KNWA
01-01-1986; 1600 kHz AM; 5 kw-D, ND1; 0.05 kw-N, ND1; N36 14 49 W93 5 6
Mailing Address: P.O. Box 2639, Gulfport, MS 39505 US
Second Address: 600 S. Pine, Harrison, AR 72601
(870) 741-1402; *Fax:* (870) 741-9702
kcwd@all.net
License: Bellefonte, AR held by Harrison Radio Stations Inc.
Format: Gospel
Roger Lowery, General Manager
Linda Peter, Sales Manager
Barbara Dean, Traffic Manager

Benton

KEWI
06-26-1953; 690 kHz AM; *Hrs Open:* 5 AM-10 PM; 0.25 kw-D, ND1; 0.073 kw-N, ND1; N34 31 57 W92 34 16
102 W. South Street, Benton, AR 72015 US
(501) 778-6677; *Fax:* (501) 778-7717
www.kewi690.com
kewi690@yahoo.com
License: Benton, AR held by Landers Broadcasting Co. Inc.
Nat'l Network: USA; *Regional Network:* Ark. Radio Net.
Arbitron Metro Market: Benton, AR; *Format:* Country, News, 64, Sports, Talk *Special Programming:* Farm 4 hrs, gospel 10 hrs, relg 5 hrs wkly; *Hrs. of News Programming:* news progmg 10 hrs wkly *No. News Employees:* 1; *Target Audience:* 25-65; all income levels; *Adv. Rates:* 13; 10; 12; 7
Jim Landers, CEO
Doris Landers, President

KHLR
01-01-1971; 106.7 MHz FM; *Hrs Open:* 24; kw
2400 Cottondale Lane, Little Rock, AR 72202 US
(501) 217-5000; *Fax:* (501) 228-9547
www.cool 95.com
cool95@cei.net
License: Benton, Pulaski County, AR held by CC Licenses LLC.
Group Owner: Signal Media of Arkansas
Nat'l Reps: D & R Radio
Arbitron Metro Market: Little Rock, AR; *Format:* Adult Contemp; *Hrs. of News Programming:* news progmg 5 hrs wkly; *No. News Employees:* 1; *Target Audience:* 25-54; baby boomers
Steve Jonsson, General Manager
Lesli Griffin, General Sales Mgr
Mike Kennedy, Programming Director
Chuck Gatlin, Promotions Director

Bentonville

KKEG
10-16-1964; 98.3 MHz FM; *Hrs Open:* 24; 100 kw; 617 ft.; N36 7 38 W93 59 23
4209 Frontage Road, Fayetteville, AR 72703 US
(479) 521-5566; *Fax:* (479) 521-0751

License: Bentonville, Washington County, AR held by Cumulus Licensing Corp.
Group Owner: Cumulus Media Inc.; (acq 2-1-99; grpsl)
Nat'l Reps: Roslin
Arbitron Metro Market: Fatetteville, AR; *Format:* Classic Rock, Rock/AOR; *No. News Employees:* 1; *Target Audience:* 18-49.
Dale Daniels, General Manager
Ray Daugherty, Sales Manager
Matt Miller, Programming Director
Anita Cowan, Promotions Director
Gregg Judd, Chief Engineer

KSEC
95.7 MHz FM; *Hrs Open:* 24; 6 kw; 328 ft.; N36 17 54 W94 10 21
Highway 72 East, Route 5, Gravette, AR 72736 US
(479) 756-8686; *Fax:* (479) 756-8687
www.ezspanishmedia.com
info@ezspanishmedia.com
License: Bentonville, Benton County, AR held by Lazeta 957 Co.
Arbitron Metro Market: Fayetteville, AR; *Format:* Tejano
Edward J. Vega, General Manager

Bentonville-Bella

KREB
02-05-1979; 1190 kHz AM; *Hrs Open:* Sunrise-sunset
10826 Hw 412, Alpena, AR 72611 US
(479) 582-3776; *Fax:* (479) 571-0995
www.newrock1049x.com
License: Bentonville-Bella, AR held by Butler Broadcasting Co. LLC
Nat'l Network: USA
Arbitron Metro Market: Fayetteville (Northwest Arkansas), AR; *Format:* Sports, Talk; *Target Audience:* 35 plus.
Steve Butler, General Manager
Dave Jackson, Programming Director

Berryville

KTHS-FM
12-19-1974; 107.1 MHz FM; *Hrs Open:* 24; 3.6 kw; 627 ft.; N36 20 45 W93 29 17
P.O. Bx 191, Berryville, AR 72616 US
(870) 423-2147; *Fax:* (870) 423-2146
www.kthsradio.com
frontdesk@kthsradio.com
License: Berryville, Carroll County, AR held by Carroll County Broadcasting Inc.
Group Owner: Carroll County Broadcasting Inc.
Nat'l Network: ABC
Arbitron Metro Market: Springfield, MO; *Format:* Country *Special Programming:* Tradio 8:30a - 10a; *Hrs. of News Programming:* news progmg 21.5 hrs wkly; *No. News Employees:* 1; *Target Audience:* General. *Adv. Rates:* :30 $10, :60 $13.50 net
Jay Bunyard, President
Jim Earls, General Manager
Jamie Hussey, General Sales Mgr
Linda Boyer, News Director
Sherri Linz, Traffic Director
Bree Adams, Sports

Blytheville

***KBCM**
01-01-2000; 88.3 MHz FM; *Hrs Open:* 24; 1.2 kw; 190 ft.; N35 54 45 W89 53 28
P.O. Box 3206, Tupelo, MS 38803 US
(662) 844-8888; *Fax:* (662) 842-6791
www.afr.net
faq@afa.net
License: Blytheville, Mississippi County, AR held by American Family Association.
Group Owner: American Family Radio
Arbitron Metro Market: Tupelo, MS; *Format:* Christian
Tim Wildmon, President
Donald Wildmon, Founder
Buddy Smith, Sr VP
Ed Vitagliano, Executive Vice President
Randy Sharp, Director Of Specialo Projects
Meeke Addison, Director Of Communications
Abraham Hamilton III, General Counsel& Public Policy Analyst

KHLS
01-01-1948; 96.3 MHz FM; 100 kw; 433 ft.; N35 53 56 W89 52 48
Mailing Address: P. O. Box 989, Blytheville, AR 72315 US
Second Address: 125 S. Second St., Blytheville, AR 72315
(870) 762-2093; *Fax:* (870) 763-8459
www.thundercountry963.com
License: Blytheville, Mississippi County, AR
Group Owner: Sudbury Services Inc.
Arbitron Metro Market: Memphis, TN; *Format:* Country
Keith Micheals, Operations Dir
Jean Anderson, General Manager
Dana Ham, General Sales Mgr
Tom Hill, Chief Engineer
Debbie Polk, Traffic Department

KLCN
01-01-1922; 910 kHz AM; 5 kw-D, ND2; 0.085 kw-N, ND2; N35 55 27 W89 52 18
Mailing Address: P. O. Box 989, Blytheville, AR 72316 US
Second Address: 125 S. Second St., Blytheville, AR 72315
(870) 762-2093; *Fax:* (870) 763-8459
License: Blytheville, AR held by Sudbury Services Inc.
Group Owner: Sudbury Services Inc.
Arbitron Metro Market: Memphis, TN; *Format:* News, News/Talk, 86
Dave Clark, General Manager
Tom Hill, Chief Engineer

Booneville

KQBK
11-01-1981; 104.7 MHz FM; *Hrs Open:* 24; 50 kw; 492 ft.; N35 11 1 W94 7 44
523 Garrison Ave., Suite 201, Ft. Smith, AR 72901 US
(479) 288-1047; *Fax:* (479) 785-2638
License: Booneville, Logan County, AR held by Pharis Broadcasting Inc.
Group Owner: Pharis Broadcasting Inc.; acq 11-20-97; $800,000)
Regional Network: Ark. Radio Net; *Nat'l Reps:* Commercial Media Sales *Regional Reps:* BRI
Arbitron Metro Market: Fort Smith, AR; *Format:* Oldies; *Hrs. of News Programming:* news progmg 10 hrs wkly; *No. News Employees:* 1; *Target Audience:* 18-54.; *Adv. Rates:* 20; 20; 20; 20

***KBHN**
01-01-2005; 89.7 MHz FM; 59 kw; 302 ft.; N35 8 25 W94 3 43
Box 6210, Fort Smith, AR 72906 US
(479) 646-6700; *Fax:* (479) 646-1373
www.kzkzfm.com
kzkzfm@kzkzfm.com
License: Booneville, Logan County, AR held by Vision Ministries Inc.
Arbitron Metro Market: Booneville, AR; *Format:* Christian
Marilyn Lynch, President
Jay Lynch, Owner/General Manager
Jay Lynch, Station Manager
Al Ross, Programming Director
Ashley Baker, Account Executives/Sales
Tiffany Snow, Account Executives/Sales

Brinkley

KBRI
10-25-1959; 1570 kHz AM; *Hrs Open:* 6 AM-10 PM; 0.25 kw-D, ND2; 0.023 kw-N, ND2; N34 52 2 W91 12 4
P.O. Box 789, Wynne, AR 72396 US
(870) 734-1570; *Fax:* (870) 734-1571
License: Brinkley, AR held by East Arkansas Broadcasters Inc.
Group Owner: East Arkansas Broadcasters Inc.
Regional Network: Ark. Radio Net.
Format: Gospel; *No. News Employees:* 1; *Target Audience:* General.
Bobby Caldwell, President
Scott Siler, General Manager
David Sills, General Sales Mgr
Lane Goodwin, Chief Engineer

Bryant

KKSP
04-01-1989; 93.3 MHz FM; *Hrs Open:* 24; 5.6 kw; 699 ft.; N34 47 31 W92 28 38
1402 Highway 270, Malvern, AR 72104 US
(501) 219-1919; *Fax:* (501) 225-4610
www.spirit933.com
License: Bryant, Saline County, AR held by Crain Media Group LLC.
Group Owner: Crain Media Group LLC; (acq 2-1-2008; grpsl)
Arbitron Metro Market: Little Rock, AR; *Format:* Christian
Don Burns, Programming Director

Cabot

KPZK
05-01-1993; 102.5 MHz FM; *Hrs Open:* 24; 3 kw; 328 ft.; N34 55 22 W92 0 32
700 Wellington Hills Rd., Little Rock, AR 72211 US
(501) 401-0200; *Fax:* (501) 401-0366
www.praise1025fm.com
License: Cabot, AR held by The Last Bastion Station Trust, LLC
Group Owner: The Last Bastion Station Trust, LLC
Arbitron Metro Market: Little Rock, AZ; *Format:* Gospel

KZTD
11-16-1980; 1350 kHz AM; 2.5 kw-D, ND1; 0.073 kw-N, ND1; N34 59 59 W92 1 41
#1 Shackleford Drive, Suite 400, Little Rock, AR 72211 US
(501) 378-0104; *Fax:* (501) 305-2977
kztd1350@hotmail.com
License: Cabot, AR held by New World LLC
Arbitron Metro Market: Cabot, AR; *Target Audience:* 18-49.
Arik Lev, President
Robert Tindle, Operations Dir
Phil Hall, General Manager
Christy Flynn, General Sales Mgr

Caddo Valley

KWPS-FM
99.7 MHz FM; 3 kw; 53 meters; N34 14 19.6 W93 00 19.1
805 Wood Duck Lane, Russellville, AR 72801 US
(479) 967-5921
michael.e.wilkins@gmail.com
License: Caddo Valley, AR held by Southwest Arkansas Media LLC
Group Owner: Southwest Arkansas Media LLC

Michael E. Wilkins, Manager

Cale

***KEJA**
91.7 MHz FM; 3 kw; 446 ft.; N33 28 34 W93 16 23
P.O. Box 3206, Tupelo, MS 38803 US
(662) 884-8888; *Fax:* (662) 842-6791
www.afr.net
faq@afa.net
License: Cale, Nevada County, AR held by American Family Association.
Group Owner: American Family Radio
Arbitron Metro Market: Cale, AR; *Format:* Christian, Gospel
Tim Wildmon, President
Donald Wildmon, Founder
Buddy Smith, Sr VP
Ed Vitagliano, Exec VP
Randy Sharp, Director Of Special Projects
Meeke Addison, Director Of Communications
Abraham Hamilton III, General Counsel

Calico Rock

KJMT
03-01-2007; 97.1 MHz FM; *Hrs Open:* 24; 5.2 kw; 715 ft.; N36 5 31 W92 15 46
US
(870) 425-4971; *Fax:* (870) 424-9717
www.mountaintalk97.com
License: Calico Rock, Izard County, AR held by Malvern Entertainment Corp.
Nat'l Network: Fox News Radio; Premiere Radio Networks; Talk Radio Network; Radio America
Arbitron Metro Market: Calico Rock, AR; *Format:* News, News/Talk, 86; *Hrs. of News Programming:* news progmg 29 hrs/week; *No. News Employees:* 1
Scott Gray, CEO, General Manager
Michael Wiseman, Operations/Engineering Director
Kim Szecksi, News Director
Dale Hoffman, Host, Producer
Roy Roane, Sales Representative

Camden

KAMD-FM
12-01-1968; 97.1 MHz FM; *Hrs Open:* 24; 50 kw; Ant 456 ft; N33 30 14 W92 48 38
612 Fairview Rd, Camden, AR 71701
(870) 836-9567; *Fax:* (870) 836-9500
www.k97online.com
radioworks@cablelynx.com
License: Camden, Ouachita County, AR held by Radio Works Inc.
Group Owner: Radio Works Inc.; (acq 12-13-2004; grpsl).
Population Served: 50,000; *Arbitron Metro Market:* Camden, AR
Greg Arnold, Operations Dir
Donna Stewart, Station Manager
Helen Aregood, News Director
Steve Halatyn, Chief Engineer

***KCAC**
06-11-1990; 89.5 MHz FM; *Hrs Open:* 8 AM-midnight; 10 kw horiz, 9.9 kw vert; 324 ft.; N33 39 16 W92 40 34
327 Stewart Street S.W., Camden, AR 71701 US

(501) 836-5289; *Fax:* (501) 836-4917
License: Camden, Ouachita County, AR held by Southern Arkansas University Tech
Nat'l Network: ABC
Arbitron Metro Market: Camden. AR; *Format:* Alternative; *Target Audience:* 18-35.
Quintin Green, Operations Dir
Rachelle Moore, General Manager

KMGC
11-18-1994; 104.5 MHz FM; *Hrs Open:* 24; 3 kw; 328 ft; N33 30 14 W92 48 38
133 Washington St., Camden, AR 71701
(870) 836-0104; *Fax:* (870) 836-9500
www.yesradioworks.com
cmbdenradioworks@hotmail.com
License: Camden, Ouachita County, AR held by Radio Works Inc.
Group Owner: Radio Works Inc.; (acq 12-13-2004; grpsl).
Helen Aregood, General Manager
Dan Murphy, General Sales Mgr

KNHD
08-08-1963; 1450 kHz AM; *Hrs Open:* 24; 1 kw-U, ND1; N33 33 49 W92 50 37
Mailing Address: 3109 Carlisle, Suite 212, Dallas, TX 75204 US
Second Address: 8917 World Ministry Ave., Baton Rouge, LA 70810
(225) 768-3688; *Fax:* (225) 768-3729
www.jsm.org
kawikfish@yahoo.com
License: Camden, AR held by Family Worship Center Church Inc.
Group Owner: Family Worship Center Church Inc.; (acq 3-7-2002; grpsl).
Format: Gospel; *No. News Employees:* 1; *Target Audience:* 35 plus.
David Whitelaw, COO
Jimmy Swaggart, President
John Santiago, Programming Director

Cash

KJBX
02-01-1991; 106.3 MHz FM; *Hrs Open:* 24; 25 kw; 312 ft.; N35 44 49 W90 37 50
314 Union Street, Jonesboro, AR 72401 US
(870) 933-8800; *Fax:* (870) 933-0403
www.themix1067.com
trey@triplefm.com
License: Cash, Poinsett County, AR held by Saga Communications of Arkansas LLC.
Group Owner: Saga Communications Inc.; (acq 11-8-02; grpsl).
Arbitron Metro Market: Jonesboro, AR; *Format:* Adult Contemp; *Hrs. of News Programming:* News progmg 2 hrs wkly; *Target Audience:* 25-54; women; *Adv. Rates:* 34; 43; 34; 59
Trey Stafford, President
Kevin Neathery, General Sales Mgr
Bill Pressly, Vice President of Programming
Al Simpson, Chief Engineer
Bill Blankenship, Production Director

Cave City

***KVMN**
01-01-1981; 89.9 MHz FM; 3.3 kw; 351 ft.; N35 57 7 W91 32 58
P.O. Box 190, Cave City, AR 72521 US
(870) 283-5331; *Fax:* (870) 283-3255
bsisk@cavecity.ncsc.k12.ar.us
License: Cave City, Sharp County, AR held by Cave City Schools.
Nat'l Network: USA
Arbitron Metro Market: Cave City, AR; *Format:* Variety/Diverse, Religious; *Target Audience:* General.
Becky Sisk, General Manager

Centerton

KLTK
03-02-1977; 1140 kHz AM
1912 South Walton Blvd, Suite A, Bentonville, AR 72712 US
(479) 899-6952; *Fax:* (479) 899-6953
License: Centerton, AR held by La Mas Mexicana LLC

Genaro Salas, General Manager

Cherry Valley

***KXRL**
01-01-2007; 90.1 MHz FM; 9 kw; 377 ft.; N35 22 31 W90 43 22
Rebroadcasts: Rebroadcasts WXHL-FM Christiana, DE 100%
3076 Glenfinnan Road, Memphis, TN 38128 US
(800) 220-8078; *Fax:* (302) 738-3090
www.thereachfm.com
License: Cherry Valley, Cross County, AR held by Priority Radio Inc.
Group Owner: Priority Radio Inc.; (acq 10-14-2005; $200,000 for CP)
Arbitron Metro Market: Cherry Valley, AR; *Format:* Christian
Steve Hare, President

Clarksville

KLYR
03-18-1957; 1360 kHz AM; *Hrs Open:* 16; 0.5 kw-D, ND2; 0.098 kw-N, ND2; N35 28 21 W93 29 28
P.O.188, Clarksville, AR 72830 US
(479) 754-3092
License: Clarksville, AR held by Randall P. Forrester.
Arbitron Metro Market: Fatetteville, AR; *Format:* Country *Special Programming:* Relg 8 hrs wkly; *Hrs. of News Programming:* News progmg 12 hrs wkly; *Target Audience:* General.
Randy Forrester, General Manager

KXIO
04-01-1991; 106.9 MHz FM; 5.9 kw; 112 ft.; N35 33 7 W93 24 33
205 Amy Lyn Place, Russellville, AR 72801 US
(479) 705-1069; *Fax:* (479) 754-5518
License: Clarksville, Johnson County, AR held by Jody Copeland
Format: Country
Gary Barnett, General Manager
Kelley Ray, Programming Director

Clinton

KGFL
10-01-1977; 1110 kHz AM; 5 kw-D; N35 33 30 W92 27 32
Mailing Address: Box 1349, Clinton, AR 72031
Second Address: Corner of Main & Griggs, Clinton, AR 72031
(501) 745-4474; *Fax:* (501) 745-4084
sid@khpq.com
License: Clinton, Van Buren County, AR held by King-Sullivan Radio
Population Served: 20,000 *Target Audience:* 35 plus.
Sid King, General Manager
Ali Sugg, General Sales Mgr
Sid King, Programming Director

KHPQ
12-23-1982; 92.1 MHz FM; 10 kw; 512 ft.; N35 38 37 W92 27 33
Mailing Address: Post Office Box 33, Clinton, AR 72031 US
Second Address: Corner of Main & Griggs, Clinton, AR 72031
(501) 745-4474; *Fax:* (501) 745-4084
www.infozark.net
sid@khpq.com
License: Clinton, Van Buren County, AR held by King-Sullivan Radio.
Nat'l Network: Jones Radio Networks
Format: Country; *Target Audience:* 25 plus.
Sid King, General Manager
Ali Sugg, General Sales Mgr
Sid King, Programming Director
Dave Britton, Chief Engineer

Coal Hill

KDYN-FM
01-01-1974; 92.7 MHz FM; *Hrs Open:* 16; 12.5 kw; 144 meters; N35 29 09.1 W93 53 29.5
P.O. 188, Clarksville, AR 72830 US
(479) 754-3092
License: Coal Hill, Johnson County, AR
Arbitron Metro Market: Fatetteville, AR; *Format:* Country
Randy Forrester, General Manager

Colt

KTRQ
10-01-1969; 102.3 MHz FM; 40 kw; 548 ft.; N35 3 16 W90 44 36
Mailing Address: P.O. Box 789, Highway 64 West, Wynne, AR 72396 US
Second Address: Hwy. 70 W., Brinkley, AR. 72021
(870) 734-1570; *Fax:* (870) 734-1571
www.ktrq.com
License: Colt, St. Francis County, AR held by East Arkansas Broadcasters Inc.
Group Owner: East Arkansas Broadcasters Inc.
Arbitron Metro Market: Brinkley, AR; *Format:* Oldies
Bobby Caldwell, General Manager

Conway

***KHDX**
05-01-1973; 93.1 MHz FM; 0.008 kw; 59 ft.; N35 6 1 W92 26 29
Washington & Indpendence, Conway, AR 72032 US
(501) 450-1339; *Fax:* (501) 450-1200
www.hendrix.edu
khdx@hendrix.edu
License: Conway, Faulkner County, AR held by Hendrix College.
Regional Network: Ark. Radio Net.
Format: Variety/Diverse
Julie Marvin, General Manager

KMJX
06-01-1967; 105.1 MHz FM; *Hrs Open:* 24; 79 kw; 1053 ft.; N34 47 53 W92 29 33
200 Concord Plaza, Suite 600, San Antonio, TX 78216 US
(501) 217-5000; *Fax:* (501) 228-9547
www.1051thewolf.com
License: Conway, Faulkner County, AR held by CC Licenses LLC.
Group Owner: iHeartMedia; (acq 5-5-96; grpsl)
Nat'l Reps: Clear Channel
Arbitron Metro Market: Little Rock, AR; *Format:* Country; *Hrs. of News Programming:* news progmg 3 hrs wkly; *No. News Employees:* 1; *Target Audience:* 18-34.
Ron Collar, Market Manager
Keli Williams, Senior Vice President of Sales
Chad Heritage, Senior Vice President of Programming
Matt Cruz, Promotions Director

KXXA(AM)
05-26-1961; 1330 kHz AM; 500 watts; N35 06 00 W92 26 41
Box 1266, 1117 Oak Street, Suite 300, Conway, AR 72033-1266
(501) 327-6611; *Fax:* (501) 327-7920
License: Conway, Faulkner County, AR held by Creative Media Inc.
Arbitron Metro Market: Little Rock, AR; *Format:* Sports *Special Programming:* Farm 6 hrs wkly
Michael Harrison, President
Elaine Harrison, Promotions Manager

***KUCA**
10-10-1966; 91.3 MHz FM; *Hrs Open:* 24; 5 kw; 154 ft; N35 02 55 W92 27 49
Mailing Address: Box U-5144, Univ of Central Arkansas, Conway, AR 72032
Second Address: 201 Donaghey Ave., Conway, AR
(501) 450-3326; *Fax:* (501) 450-5874
Montyr@uca.edu
License: Conway, Faulkner County, AR held by University of Central Arkansas.
Population Served: 80,000 *Hrs. of News Programming:* News progmg 10 hrs wkly; *Target Audience:* 18-54; educated adults
Monty Rowell, General Manager

Corning

KBKG
09-15-1983; 93.5 MHz FM; 3 kw; 138 ft.; N36 24 0 W90 35 5
P.O. Box 398, Corning, AR 72422 US
(870) 857-6646; *Fax:* (870) 857-6795
License: Corning, Clay County, AR held by Shields-Adkins Broadcasting Inc.
Nat'l Network: ABC
Arbitron Metro Market: Corning, AR; *Format:* Adult Contemp, Oldies
Jim Adkins, CEO

KCCB
02-19-1959; 1260 kHz AM; 1 kw-D, ND2; 0.031 kw-N, ND2; N36 24 0 W90 35 5
P.O. Box 398, Corning, AR 72422 US
(870) 857-6646; *Fax:* (870) 857-6795
License: Corning, AR held by Shields-Adkins Broadcasting Inc.
Nat'l Reps: Keystone (unwired net)
Arbitron Metro Market: Corning, AR; *Format:* Classic Rock; *Target Audience:* General.
Jim Adkins, President
Tina Privett, General Manager
Neil Raines, Programming Director
Palmer Johnson, Chief Engineer

Cotton Plant

KERL
01-01-2008; 99.3 MHz FM; 6 kw; Ant 328 ft; N34 58 07 W90 59 48
Box 711, Wynne, AR
(870) 238-8141; *Fax:* (870) 238-5997
bradfordcaldwell@yahoo.com

License: Cotton Plant, Woodruff County, AR held by Caldwell Media LLC.

Bradford Caldwell, CEO/COO
Bradford Caldwell, General Manager

Crossett

KAGH

01-01-1951; 800 kHz AM; *Hrs Open:* 24; 0.24 kw-D, NDD; N33 8 5 W91 56 49
P.O. Box 697, 117 Ashley 252, Crossett, AR 71635 US
(870) 364-2181; *Fax:* (501) 364-2183
kagh@alltell.net
License: Crossett, AR held by Ashley County Broadcasters Inc.
Nat'l Network: Westwood One; *Regional Network:* Ark. Radio Net.
Arbitron Metro Market: Crossett, AR; *Format:* Country
Kevin Medlin, President
Barry Medlin, General Manager
John Speeney, Sales Manager
Russ Miller, Programming Director
Bryan Bailey, News Director

KAGH-FM

03-16-1967; 104.9 MHz FM; 6 kw; 328 ft.; N33 8 5 W91 56 49
P.O. Box 697, 117 Ashley 252, Crossett, AR 71635 US
(870) 364-2181; *Fax:* (501) 364-2183
www.crossettradio.com/todayscountry1049
kagh@alltell.net
License: Crossett, Ashley County, AR held by Ashley County Broadcasters Inc.
Arbitron Metro Market: Crossett, AR; *Format:* Country
Barry Medlin, General Manager
John Speeney, General Sales Mgr
Russ Miller, Programming Director

Danville

KYEL

105.5 MHz FM; *Hrs Open:* 5am - 11pm; 4.4 kw; 381 ft.; N35 6 11 W93 13 58
3004 Kay Lane, Springdale, AR 72762 US
(479) 890-7207; *Fax:* (479) 967-5278
License: Danville, Yell County, AR held by Danville FM Inc.
Arbitron Metro Market: Russellville, AZ; *Format:* Country *Special Programming:* Cardinal Baseball
Diane Womack, General Manager
Chris Womack, Station Manager

Dardanelle

KCAB

03-24-1964; 980 kHz AM; 5 kw-D, ND2; 0.032 kw-N, ND2; N35 13 20 W93 10 8
2705 E. Pkwy., Russellville, AR 72802 US
(479) 968-6816; *Fax:* (479) 968-2946
www.rivertalk980.com
aaron@rivervalleyradio.com
License: Dardanelle, Yell County, AR held by EAB of Russellville LLC
Group Owner: East Arkansas Broadcasters Inc.; (acq 8-21-2013).
Nat'l Network: Premiere Radio Networks; *Regional Network:* Ark. Radio Net; *Nat'l Reps:* Christal; *Wire Services:* AP
Arbitron Metro Market: Russellville, AR; *Format:* News, News/Talk, 86; *Target Audience:* 25-54; adults
Aaron Thomas, Operations Manager
Rich Moellers, Market Manager
Rhonda Dilbeck, Director of Sales

KCJC

01-26-1966; 102.3 MHz FM; 1.45 kw; 1,322 ft.; N35 13 41 W93 15 20
2705 E. Pkwy., Russellville, AR 72802 US
(479) 968-6816; *Fax:* (479) 968-2946
www.rivercountrykcjc.com
License: Dardanelle, Yell County, AR held by EAB of Russellville LLC
Group Owner: East Arkansas Broadcasters Inc.
Nat'l Network: ABC; *Regional Network:* Ark. Radio Net; *Nat'l Reps:* Christal; *Wire Services:* AP
Arbitron Metro Market: Dardanelle, AR; *Format:* Country
Aaron Thomas, Operations Manager
Rich Moellers, Market Manager
Rhonda Dilbeck, Director of Sales

KWXT

10-01-1987; 1490 kHz AM; 1 kw-U, ND1; N35 13 8 W93 7 38
701 East Main Street, Russellville, AR 72801 US
(479) 754-3399; *Fax:* (479) 968-1337
www.kwxt1490am.com
kwxt1490am@ahoo.com
License: Dardanelle, AR held by George V. Domerese/Sherwood Broadcasting Co.
Arbitron Metro Market: Clarksville, AR; *Format:* Christian, Country, 44
Tim Domerese, General Manager
Jim Alexander, Chief Engineer

De Queen

*KBPU

01-01-2002; 88.7 MHz FM; 0.25 kw; 122 ft.; N34 2 38 W94 17 41
P. O. Box 1452, Washington, DC 20013 US
(208) 733-3551; *Fax:* (208) 734-0674
www.edgewaterbroadcasting.com
License: De Queen, Sevier County, AR held by Edgewater Broadcasting Inc.
Format: Christian
Clark Parrish, President

KDQN

08-01-1956; 1390 kHz AM; 0.5 kw-D, ND1; N34 1 57 W94 19 43
Mailing Address: P.O. Box 311, Dequeen, AR 71832 US
Second Address: 921 W Collin Raye Dr., De Queen, AR 71832
(870) 642-2446; *Fax:* (870) 642-2442
www.kdqn.net
numberonecountry@yahoo.com
License: De Queen, AR held by Jay W. Bunyard & Anne W. Bunyard.
Regional Network: Ark. Radio Net.
Arbitron Metro Market: De Queen, AR
Jay Bunyard, President
Jon Bunyard, General Manager
Victor Rojas, General Sales Mgr

KDQN-FM

10-06-1978; 92.1 MHz FM; 50 kw; 492 ft.; N34 13 35 W94 17 35
Mailing Address: P.O. Box 311, Dequeen, AR 71832 US
Second Address: 921 West Collin Raye Dr, DeQueen, AR 71832
(870) 642-2446; *Fax:* (870) 642-2442
www.kdqn.net
numberonecountry@yahoo.com
License: De Queen, Sevier County, AR held by Jay W. Bunyard & Anne W. Bunyard.
Arbitron Metro Market: De Queen, AR; *Format:* Country
Jon Bunyard, General Manager

De Witt

KDEW-FM

09-01-1970; 97.3 MHz FM; *Hrs Open:* 24; 50 kw; 272 ft.; N34 25 52 W91 26 8
P.O. Box 910, Stuttgart, AR 72160 US
(870) 673-1595; *Fax:* (870)673-8445
www.country973.com
kdew973@yahoo.com
License: De Witt, Arkansas County, AR held by Arkansas County Broadcasters Inc.
Group Owner: Arkansas County Broadcasters Inc.; acq 3-5-97; $150,000).
Format: Country; *No. News Employees:* 1; *Adv. Rates:* 16; 12; 12; 10
Scott Siler, General Manager
Scott Siler, Sales Manager
Mitch Mahan, Programming Director
Rob Shannon, News Director
Elizabeth Barnett

Dermott

KXSA-FM

08-24-1924; 103.1 MHz FM; *Hrs Open:* 24; 5.5 kw; 328 ft.; N33 31 56 W91 34 28
539 W. Gaines, Monticello, AR 71655 US
(870) 367-8528; *Fax:* (870) 367-9564
License: Dermott, Chicot County, AR held by Pines Broadcasting Inc.
Group Owner: Pines Broadcasting Inc.; (acq 3-14-2007; grpsl)
Arbitron Metro Market: Monticello, AR; *Format:* Country
Jimmy Sledge, President

Des Arc

KBDO

01-01-1999; 91.7 MHz FM; 56 kw vert; 682 ft.; N35 0 8 W91 44 41
P.O. Box 3206, Tupelo, MS 38803 US
(662) 844-8888; *Fax:* (662) 842-6791
www.afr.net
faq@afa.net
License: Des Arc, Prairie County, AR held by American Family Association.
Group Owner: American Family Radio
Arbitron Metro Market: Tupelo, MS; *Format:* Religious
Tim Wildmon, President
Donald Wildmon, Founder
Buddy Smith, Senior VP
Ed Vitagliano, Executive VP
Randy Sharp, Director Of Special Projects
Meeke Addison, Director Of Communications
Abraham Hamilton III, General Counsel & PublicPolicy Analyst

KFLI

01-01-2003; 104.7 MHz FM; 25 kw; 328 ft.; N35 0 23 W91 40 20
188 South Bellevue, Suite 222, Memphis, TN 38104 US
(800) 833-9211; *Fax:* (304) 455-1170
www.oldiesradioonline.com
License: Des Arc, Prairie County, AR held by George S. Flinn Jr.
Arbitron Metro Market: Little Rock, AR; *Format:* Oldies
Terry Murphy, General Manager

Dumas

KXFE

09-01-1980; 106.9 MHz FM; 25 kw; Ant 269 ft; N33 58 11 W91 32 58
Box 789, Wynne, AR 71601
(870) 238-8141; *Fax:* (870) 238-5997
License: Dumas, Desha County, AR held by Arkansas County Broadcasters Inc.
Group Owner: East Arkansas Broadcasters; (acq 8-31-2004; $130,000)
Population Served: 12,500
Bobby Caldwell, CEO
Scott Siler, General Manager
Chuck Cross, Sales Director

Earle

KCJF

01-01-2004; 103.9 MHz FM; 12.5 kw; 469 ft.; N35 27 1 W90 42 11
400 Tower Drive, Paragould, AR 72450 US
(870) 236-7627; *Fax:* (870) 336-3810
www.1039thegame.com
License: Earle, Crittenden County, AR held by Mor Media
Arbitron Metro Market: Jonesboro, AR; *Format:* Sports, Talk
Dina Mason, Presient/Chief Executive Officer

East Camden

KCXY

09-28-1987; 95.3 MHz FM; *Hrs Open:* 24; 100 kw; Ant 456 ft; N33 30 14 W92 48 38
Mailing Address: Box 957, 612 Fairvew Road, Camden, AR 71701
Second Address: 133 Washington St. S.W., Camden, AR 71701
(870) 836-9567; *Fax:* (870) 836-9500
radioworks@cablelynx.com
License: East Camden, Ouachita County, AR held by Radio Works Inc.
Group Owner: Radio Works Inc.; (acq 12-13-2004; grpsl).
Regional Network: Ark. Radio Net.
Population Served: 12,072; *Arbitron Metro Market:* Camden, AR; *Hrs. of News Programming:* news progmg 15 hrs wkly; *No. News Employees:* 1; *Target Audience:* 25-54.
Helen Aregood, General Manager
Dan Murphy, Programming Director
Terry Calahan, News Director
CC Schinz, Traffic Manager

El Dorado

KAGL

09-29-1993; 93.3 MHz FM; *Hrs Open:* 24; 18 kw; 354 ft.; N33 16 16 W92 39 17
2525 North West Avenue, El Dorado, AR 71730 US
(870) 863-6126; *Fax:* (870) 863-4555
www.eagle933.com
info@totalradio.com
License: El Dorado, Union County, AR held by Noalmark Broadcasting Corp.
Group Owner: Noalmark Broadcasting Corp.; acq 1-8-93; $10,000;
Nat'l Reps: Target Broadcast Sales
Arbitron Metro Market: El Dorado, AR; *Format:* Classic Rock; *Hrs. of News Programming:* news progmg 15 hrs wkly; *No. News Employees:* 1; *Target Audience:* 25-54; general

William Nolan, President
Jay Helm, General Manager
KC Wright, Programming Director
Edwin Alderson, Executive Vice President
Sharon Peterson, Traffic Manager

***KBSA**
12-01-1987; 90.9 MHz FM; *Hrs Open:* 24; 3 kw; 587 ft.; N33 16 19 W92 42 12 *Rebroadcasts:* Rebroadcasts KDAQ(FM) Shreveport, LA 100%
8515 Youree Drive, Shreveport, LA 71115 US
(800) 552-8502 (318) 798-0102; *Fax:* (318) 798-0107
www.redriverradio.org
listenermail@redriverradio.org
License: El Dorado, Union County, AR held by Board of Supervisors of Louisiana State University & A&M College.
Nat'l Network: NPR; PRI
Format: Classical, Jazz, 60; *Target Audience:* 25+.
Kermit Poling, General Manager
Bill Beckett, Programming Director
Ranae Moran, Director of Corporatie Support and Underwriting

KMRX
05-12-1984; 96.1 MHz FM; *Hrs Open:* 24; 100 kw; 446 ft.; N33 16 16 W92 39 17
2525 North West Avenue, El Dorado, AR 71730 US
(870) 863-6126; *Fax:* (870) 863-4555
www.totalradio.com
info@totalradio.com
License: El Dorado, Union County, AR held by Noalmark Broadcasting Corp.
Group Owner: Noalmark Broadcasting Corp.; acq 7-31-97).
Arbitron Metro Market: El Dorado, AR; *Format:* Adult Contemp; *Hrs. of News Programming:* news progmg 2 hrs wkly; *No. News Employees:* 1; *Target Audience:* 18-34.; *Adv. Rates:* 21; 11; 11; 11
Jay Helm, General Manager
KC Wright, Programming Director
Sharon Peterson, Traffic Manager

KDMS
05-08-1950; 1290 kHz AM
1904 W. Hillsboro, El Dorado, AR 71730 US
(870) 863-5121; *Fax:* (870) 863-6221
klbq@suddenlink.com
License: El Dorado, AR held by El Dorado Broadcasting Co.
Arbitron Metro Market: El Dorado, AR; *Format:* Adult Contemp
Rosh Partridge, President
Dan Murphy, Operations Dir
Don Travis, General Sales Mgr

KELD
10-17-1935; 1400 kHz AM; *Hrs Open:* 24; 1 kw-U, ND1; N33 14 14 W92 39 54
2525 North West Avenue, El Dorado, AR 71730 US
(870) 863-6126; *Fax:* (870) 863-4555
www.totalradio.com
info@totalradio.com
License: El Dorado, AR held by Noalmark Broadcasting Corp.
Group Owner: Noalmark Broadcasting Corp.; (acq 7-73)
Nat'l Network: Fox Sports; *Nat'l Reps:* Target Broadcast Sales
Arbitron Metro Market: El Dorado, AR; *Format:* Sports; *Target Audience:* General.
William Nolan Jr., President
Patrick Thomas, Operations Dir
Jay Helm, General Manager
KC Wright, Programming Director
Edwin Alderson, Executive Vice President
Sharon Peterson, Traffic Manager

KMLK
01-01-2000; 101.5 MHz FM; 6 kw; 328 ft.; N33 9 32 W92 37 47
4401 Fairgate Drive, Midland, TX 79707 US
(870) 875-1015; *Fax:* (870) 863-4555
www.randbandoldschool.com
License: El Dorado, Union County, AR held by Noalmark Broadcasting Corp.
Group Owner: Noalmark Broadcasting Corp.; acq 6-14-01).
Format: Adult Contemp *Special Programming:* Gospel 5 hrs wkly
Patrick Thomas, Operations Dir
Jay Helm, General Manager
KC Wright, Programming Director
Sharon Peterson, Traffic Manager

KIXB
12-09-1963; 103.3 MHz FM; *Hrs Open:* 24; 100 kw; 571 ft.; N33 13 20 W92 55 28
2525 North West Avenue, El Dorado, AR 71730 US
(873) 863-6126; *Fax:* (870) 863-4555
www.totalradio.com
License: El Dorado, Union County, AR held by Noalmark Broadcasting Corp.
Group Owner: Noalmark Broadcasting Corp.
Format: Country; *Hrs. of News Programming:* News progmg 15 hrs wkly; *Target Audience:* 18-54.
Jay Helm, General Manager
KC Wright, Programming Director
Sharon Peterson, Traffic Manager

KLBQ
12-23-1963; 98.7 MHz FM; 14 kw; 299 ft.; N33 12 30 W92 41 16
1904 W. Hillsboro, El Dorado, AR 71730 US
(870) 863-5121; *Fax:* (870) 863-6221
klbq@suddenlink.com
License: El Dorado, Union County, AR held by El Dorado Broadcasting Co.
Arbitron Metro Market: Monroe, LA; *Format:* Adult Contemp, Contemporary Hits/Top 40
Ross Partridge, President
Dan Murphy, Programming Director

***KAKV**
01-01-2003; 88.9 MHz FM; *Hrs Open:* 24; 26 kw; 377 ft.; N33 12 30 W92 42 30
188 S Bellevue, Suite 222, Memphis, TN 38104 US
(800) 525-5683; *Fax:* (916) 251-1650
www.klove.com
klove@klove.com
License: El Dorado, Union County, AR held by Educational Media Foundation.
Group Owner: EMF Broadcasting; (acq 1-23-2008; $320,000 with WLRK(FM) Greenville, MS)
Nat'l Network: K-Love
Arbitron Metro Market: El Dorado, AR; *Format:* Christian
Darrell Chambliss, Chairman
Mike Novak, President and CEO
David Pierce, Programming Director
Sam Wallington, Engineering Dir

England

KVDW
08-31-1979; 1530 kHz AM; *Hrs Open:* 24
#1 Shackleford Drive, Suite 400, Little Rock, AR 72211 US
(501) 864-7120; *Fax:* (501) 842-9308
victory1530@yahoo.com
License: England, AR held by Wells Broadcasting Inc.
Arbitron Metro Market: Little Rock, AR; *Format:* Gospel, Religious, 86 *Special Programming:* Farm 5 hrs, talk 10 hrs wkly; *Target Audience:* 18-54; professionals, farmers, college educated
Vernon Wells, General Manager

KHTE-FM
09-26-1988; 96.5 MHz FM; *Hrs Open:* 24; 10.5 kw; 495 ft.; N34 29 10 W92 9 27
111 North Spring Street, Searcy, AR 72143 US
(501) 219-1919; *Fax:* (501) 225-6140
donburns@crainmedia.com
License: England, Lonoke County, AR held by Crain Media Group LLC.
Group Owner: Crain Media Group LLC; (acq 2-1-2008; grpsl)
Arbitron Metro Market: Little Rock, AR; *Format:* Contemporary Hits/Top 40
Mike Horne, General Manager/Sales Manager

Eudora

KAVH
01-01-2001; 101.5 MHz FM; *Hrs Open:* 24; 6 kw; 328 ft.; N33 11 58 W91 15 39
1991 West Greenwood Road, Glendale, WI 53209 US
(414) 764-4953
License: Eudora, Chicot County, AR held by Joel J. Kinlow.
Arbitron Metro Market: Eudora, AR; *Format:* Variety/Diverse
Joel Kinlow, General Manager

Eureka Springs

KESA
05-13-1985; 100.9 MHz FM; *Hrs Open:* 6 AM-10 PM; 2 kw; 509 ft.; N36 22 48 W93 44 52
175 Sanctuary Road, Eureka Springs, AR 72632 US
(479) 253-9001; *Fax:* 4(79) 253-9002
License: Eureka Springs, Carroll County, AR held by Northeast Oklahoma Broadcast Network Inc.
Group Owner: Northeast Oklahoma Broadcast Network Inc.; (acq 5-7-2008; $302,000)
Regional Network: Ark. Radio Net.
Arbitron Metro Market: Grove, AR; *Format:* Adult Contemp
Special Programming: Class 10 hrs, hits of the 50s & 60s 2 hrs wkly; *Hrs. of News Programming:* news progmg 20 hrs wkly; *No. News Employees:* 1 *TargetAudience:* 35 plus; upper income & retired
Larry Hestand, Station Manager

Fairfield Bay

KFFB
12-31-1981; 106.1 MHz FM; *Hrs Open:* 24; 15.5 kw; 879 ft.; N35 44 0 W92 15 37
130 Liberty Lane, Batesville, AR 72501 US
(501) 884-6812; *Fax:* (501) 723-4861
www.kffb.com
kffb@kffb.com
License: Fairfield Bay, Van Buren County, AR held by Freedom Broadcasting Inc.
Group Owner: 2510 Licenses LLC
Nat'l Network: ABC; *Regional Network:* Ark. Radio Net.
Arbitron Metro Market: Fairfield Bay, AR; *Format:* Adult Contemp; *Hrs. of News Programming:* news progmg 8 hrs wkly; *No. News Employees:* 2; *Target Audience:* 35 plus; middle & upper income
Bob Connell, President
Bob Connell, General Manager
Carl Hampton, Music Director
Vic Schedler, Weather Director

Farmington

KFAY
12-15-1946; 1030 kHz AM; *Hrs Open:* 24; 10 kw-D, DA2; 1 kw-N, DA2; N36 6 34 W94 10 59
111 East Kilbourn Avenue, Suite 2700, Milwaukee, WI 53202 US
(479) 521-5566; *Fax:* (479) 521-0751
www.newstalk1030.com
info@kfayam.com
License: Farmington, AR held by Cumulus Licensing Corp.
Group Owner: Cumulus Media Inc.; (acq 2-1-99; grpsl)
Arbitron Metro Market: Fayetteville (Northwest Arkansas), AR; *Format:* News, News/Talk, 86; *Hrs. of News Programming:* news progmg 20 hrs wkly; *No. News Employees:* 6; *Target Audience:* 25-64; general
Ray Daugherty, Sales Manager
Dan Hentschel, Programming Director
Anita Cowan, Promotions Manager
Dale Daniels, Market Manager

Fayetteville

***KAYH**
06-26-2000; 89.3 MHz FM; *Hrs Open:* 24; 25 kw; 367 ft.; N36 10 48 W94 5 9
10550 Barkley St., Suite 100, Overland Park, KS 66212 US
(417) 336-1570
www.bottradionetwork.com
comments@bottradionetwork.com
License: Fayetteville, Washington County, AR held by Community Broadcasting Inc.
Group Owner: Bott Radio Network; (acq 1-14-2008; $450,000)
Arbitron Metro Market: Fayetteville (Northwest Arkansas), AR; *Format:* Christian, Talk
Eben Fowler, Operations Dir
Candy Green, Program Services Manager
Rachel Launius, Marketing Manager
Kenna Bennett, Area Account Manager

***KBNV**
01-01-2000; 90.1 MHz FM; *Hrs Open:* 24; 7.1 kw horiz, 16 kw vert; 466 ft.; N36 7 38 W93 59 23
P.O. Box 3206, Tupelo, MS 38803 US
(662) 844-8888; *Fax:* (662) 842-6791
www.afr.net
faq@afa.net
License: Fayetteville, Washington County, AR held by American Family Association.
Group Owner: American Family Radio
Arbitron Metro Market: Fayetteville (Northwest AR), AR; *Format:* Christian
Tim Wildmon, President
Donald Wildmon, Founder
Buddy Smith, Sr VP
Ed Vitagliano, Randy Sharp
Meeke Addison, Director Of Communication
Abraham Hamilton, General Counsel & Public Policy Analyst

KEZA
09-06-1983; 107.9 MHz FM; 99 kw; 1,260 ft.; N35 51 12 W94 1 33
2049 E. Joyce Blvd., Suite 101, Fayetteville, AR 72703 US
(479) 521-0104
www.magic1079.com

License: Fayetteville, Washington County, AR held by Capstar TX LLC
Group Owner: iHeartMedia; (acq 8-30-00; grpsl).
Arbitron Metro Market: Fayetteville (Northwest Arkansas), AR; *Format:* Adult Contemp *Special Programming:* Jazz, oldies; *Target Audience:* 25-54.
Clyde Bass, Regional Market President
Dave Ashcraft, Senior Vice President of Programming
Judy Hudson, Business Manager

KQSM-FM
11-07-1983; 92.1 MHz FM; *Hrs Open:* 24; 7.6 kw; 531 ft.; N36 7 38 W93 59 23
111 East Kilbourn Avenue, Suite 2700, Milwaukee, WI 53202 US
(479) 521-5566; *Fax:* (479) 521-0751
www.921theticket.com
License: Fayetteville, Benton County, AR held by Cumulus Licensing Corp.
Group Owner: Cumulus Media Inc.; (acq 2-1-99; grpsl).
Arbitron Metro Market: Fayetteville (Northwest Arkansas), AR; *Format:* Country *Special Programming:* Class 2 hrs wkly; *Target Audience:* 25-54.
Ray Daugherty, Sales Manager
Josh Bertaccini, Programming Director
Dale Daniels, Market Manager

KKIX
10-01-1966; 103.9 MHz FM; *Hrs Open:* 24; 100 kw; 482 ft.; N36 1 17 W94 13 4
600 Congress Ave., Suite 1400, Austin, TX 78701 US
(479) 521-0104; *Fax:* (479) 444-8600
www.kix104.com
License: Fayetteville, Washington County, AR held by Capstar TX LLC
Group Owner: iHeartMedia; (acq 8-30-00; grpsl).
Arbitron Metro Market: Fatetteville, AR; *Format:* Country; *Hrs. of News Programming:* news progmg 2 hrs wkly; *No. News Employees:* 1; *Target Audience:* 25-54.
Dave Ashcraft, Senior Vice President of Programming
Judy Hudson, Business Manager

KOFC
06-10-1957; 1250 kHz AM; *Hrs Open:* 16; 0.92 kw-D, ND2; 0.045 kw-N, ND2; N36 2 26 W94 16 32
10550 Barkley St., Suite 100, Overland Park, KS 66212 US
(417) 336-1570
www.bottradionetwork.com
comments@bottradionetwork.com
License: Fayetteville, Washington County, AR held by Community Broadcasting Inc.
Group Owner: Bott Radio Network; (acq 1-15-2008)
Arbitron Metro Market: Fayetteville (Northwest Arkansas), AR; *Format:* Christian, Talk; *Target Audience:* 35 plus; traditional Christian families
Eben Fowler, Operations Dir
Pat Rulon, Director of National Sales
Candy Green, Program Services Manager
Rachel Launius, Marketing Manager
Jason Potocnik, Director of Traffic Operations
Kenna Bennett, Area Account Manager

***KUAF**
01-15-1973; 91.3 MHz FM; *Hrs Open:* 24; 100 kw; 1089 ft.; N35 51 12 W94 1 32
406 Administration Bldg., Fayetteville, AR 72701 US
(479) 575-2556; *Fax:* (479) 575-8440
www.kuaf.com
kuaf.info@uark.edu
License: Fayetteville, Washington County, AR held by Board of Trustees University of Arkansas.
Nat'l Network: NPR
Arbitron Metro Market: Fayetteville, AR; *Format:* Jazz, News *Special Programming:* Folk 5 hrs, Black 5 hrs wkly; *Hrs. of News Programming:* news progmg 45 hrs wkly; *No. News Employees:* 3 *Target Audience:* 25-65.
Pete Hartman, Operations Dir
Rick Stockdell, Station Manager
P.J. Robowski, Music Director
Kyle Kellams, News Director
Doyle Garner, Chief Engineer
Molly Rawn, Major Giving/Membership
Rhonda Dillard, Underwriting Director
Christina Thomas, Development Coordinator/OAL Producer
Katy Henriksen, Classical Music/OAL & Arts Producer
Jacqueline Froelich, Ozarks at Large Producer/NPR Correspondent
Antoinette Grajeda, Ozarks At Large Producer

***KXUA**
04-04-2000; 88.3 MHz FM; *Hrs Open:* 24; 0 kw horiz, 0.47 kw vert; 262 ft.; N36 3 56 W94 10 30
406 Administration Bldg., Fayetteville, AR 72701 US
(479) 575-4273; *Fax:* (479) 575-2019
www.kxua.com
License: Fayetteville, Washington County, AR held by Board of Trustees of University of Arkansas.
Arbitron Metro Market: Fayetteville, AR; *Format:* Variety/Diverse; *Target Audience:* 12-24; high school and colege students
Tina Parker, Station Manager
Tyler Eck, Programming Director
Terry Johnson, Promotions Manager
David Zeek Martin, News Director
Paige Hermanson, Music Director
Harrison Grimwood, Production Manager

Fordyce

KBJT
08-01-1959; 1590 kHz AM; *Hrs Open:* 24
303 North Spring Street, Fordyce, AR 72742 US
(870) 352-7137; *Fax:* (870) 352-7139
kbjtkq.com
kbjt@windstream.net
License: Fordyce, AR held by KBJT Inc.
Arbitron Metro Market: Fordyce, AR; *Format:* News, News/Talk, 86 *Special Programming:* Gospel 11 hrs wkly; *Target Audience:* General.; *Adv. Rates:* 8; 8; 8; 8
Gary Coates, President
Gary Coates, General Manager
Carna Coates, Programming Director
Saxon Coates, News Director

KQEW
02-23-1982; 102.3 MHz FM; 25 kw; 328 ft.; N33 48 10 W92 26 10
303 Spring Street, Fordyce, AR 71742 US
(870) 352-7137; *Fax:* (870) 352-7139
www.kbjtkq.com
License: Fordyce, Dallas County, AR held by Dallas Properties Inc.
Format: News, Talk; *Target Audience:* General.; *Adv. Rates:* 12; 12; 12; 12

Forrest City

***KARH**
01-01-2000; 88.1 MHz FM; 4.2 kw; 508 ft.; N35 12 11 W90 33 57
P.O. Box 3206, Tupelo, MS 38803 US
(662) 844-8888; *Fax:* (662) 842-6791
www.afr.net
faq@afa.net
License: Forrest City, St. Francis County, AR held by American Family Association.
Group Owner: American Family Radio
Arbitron Metro Market: Tupelo, MO; *Format:* Religious
Tim Wildmon, President
Donald Wildmon, Founder
Buddy Smith, Senior VP
Ed Vitagliano, Executive VP
Randy Sharp, Director Of Special Projects
Meeke Addison, Director Of Communications
Abraham Hamilton III, General Counsel & PublicPolicy

KXJK
04-29-1949; 950 kHz AM; *Hrs Open:* 24; 5 kw-D, ND1; 0.087 kw-N, ND1; N34 58 53 W90 51 27
P. O. Box 707, Forrest City, AR 72336 US
(870) 633-1252; *Fax:* (870) 633-1259
www.kxjk.com
krystal@arkradio.com
License: Forrest City, AR held by Forrest City Broadcasting Co. Inc.
Regional Network: Ark. Radio Net. *Regional Reps:* Midsouth
Format: Classic Rock, News, 62, Talk *Special Programming:* Farm 16 hrs wkly; *Hrs. of News Programming:* news progmg 24 hrs wkly; *No. News Employees:* 2; *Target Audience:* General.
William Fogg, General Manager
Rob Johnson, Sales Manager
Rick Holt, News Director

Fort Smith

***KAOW**
01-01-1999; 88.9 MHz FM; *Hrs Open:* 24; 1.387 kw; 482 ft.; N35 26 50 W94 21 54
P.O. Box 3206, Tupelo, MS 38803 US
(662) 844-8888; *Fax:* (662) 842-6791
www.afr.net
faq@afa.net
License: Fort Smith, Sebastian County, AR held by American Family Association.
Group Owner: American Family Radio
Arbitron Metro Market: Fort Smith, AR; *Format:* Gospel
Tim Wildmon, President
Donald Wildmon, Founder
Buddy Smith, Sr. VP
Ed Vitagliano, Executive VP
Randy Sharp, Director Of Special Projects
Meeke Addison, Director Of Communications
Abraham Hamilton III, General Counsel & PublicPolisy

KLSZ-FM
07-27-1978; 100.7 MHz FM; *Hrs Open:* 24; 50 kw; 459 ft.; N35 13 32 W94 20 29
323 North Greenwood, Fort Smith, AR 72901 US
(479) 452-0681; *Fax:* (479) 452-0873
www.rock1007.com
License: Fort Smith, Sebastian County, AR held by Cumulus Licensing Corp.
Group Owner: Cumulus Media Inc.; (acq 5-1-99; $1 million)
Arbitron Metro Market: Fort Smith, AR; *Format:* Oldies; *Hrs. of News Programming:* News progmg 7 hrs wkly; *Target Audience:* 25-64.
Dale Daniels, General Manager
Ray Daugherty, Sales Manager
Josh Bertaccini, Programming Director
Anita Cowan, Promotions Manager

KENA
07-01-1950; 1450 kHz AM; *Hrs Open:* 24; 1 kw-U, ND1; N34 34 23 W94 14 55
Mailing Address: P.O. Box 1450, Mena, AR 71953 US
Second Address: 1600 S. Reine St., Mena, AR 71953
(501) 394-1450; *Fax:* (501) 394-1459
License: Fort Smith, AR held by Ouachita Broadcasting Inc.
Group Owner: Ouachita Broadcasting Inc.; (acq 1-14-99; $750,000 with co-located FM)
Format: Gospel; *Hrs. of News Programming:* news progmg 10 hrs wkly; *No. News Employees:* 1; *Target Audience:* 18 plus; industrial & agricultural workers, retirees, tourists & professionals
Dwight Douglas, General Manager

KFPW
07-27-1930; 1230 kHz AM; *Hrs Open:* 24
323 N. Greenwood, Fort Smith, AR 72916 US
(479) 242-1047
www.kfpwam.com
License: Fort Smith, AR held by Pharis Broadcasting Inc.
Group Owner: Pharis Broadcasting Inc.; (acq 3-14-2002; $850,000 with KFPW-FM Barling).
Nat'l Network: ABC; *Regional Network:* Ark. Radio Net; *Nat'l Reps:* Commercial Media Sales
Arbitron Metro Market: Fort Smith, AR; *Format:* News, Talk *Special Programming:* Sports 15 hrs wkly; *Hrs. of News Programming:* News progmg 13 hrs wkly; *Target Audience:* 35 plus; affluent; *Adv. Rates:* 12; 12;12; 12

KFSA
02-13-1947; 950 kHz AM; 1 kw-D, DA2; 0.5 kw-N, DA2; N35 25 58 W94 28 13
Four Glen Haven Dr., Fort Smith, AK 72901 US
(501) 646-6700; *Fax:* (501) 646-1373
License: Fort Smith, AR held by Fred H. Baker Jr.
Arbitron Metro Market: Fort Smith, AR; *Format:* Religious; *Target Audience:* General.
Fred Baker Jr., President

KFSW
01-01-2000; 1650 kHz AM; 10 kw-D, ND2; 1 kw-N, ND2; N35 16 29 W94 27 35
333 S. Kerr Blvd., Sallisaw, OK 74955 US
(479) 783-1650
License: Fort Smith, Sebastian County, AR held by G2 Media Group LLC
Group Owner: G2 Media Group LLC
Arbitron Metro Market: Fort Smith, AR; *Format:* News, News/Talk, 86
Delanna Nutter, Director of Sales
Marilyn Eckstein, Sales Consultant

KISR
08-13-1971; 93.7 MHz FM; *Hrs Open:* 24; 100 kw; 1250 ft.; N35 31 22 W94 23 32
Mailing Address: 4 Glen Haven Drive, Fort Smith, AR 72901 US
Second Address: 601 N. Greenwood, Fort Smith, AR 72901
(501) 785-2526; *Fax:* (479) 782-9127
www.kisr.net
info@kisr.net
License: Fort Smith, Sebastian County, AR held by Stereo 93 Inc.
Arbitron Metro Market: Fort Smith, AR; *Format:* Contemporary Hits/Top 40; *No. News Employees:* 1; *Target Audience:* 18-39.

Fred Baker Jr., General Manager
Gary Keifer, Station Manager
Carol Patterson, General Sales Mgr

KMAG
12-31-1964; 99.1 MHz FM; *Hrs Open:* 24; 94 kw; 1969 ft.; N35 4 26 W94 40 48
2049 East Joyce Boulevard, Suite 101, Fayetteville, AR 72703 US
(479) 782-8888; *Fax:* (479) 785-5946
www.kmag991.com
info@kmag991.com
License: Fort Smith, Sebastian County, AR held by Capstar TX LLC
Group Owner: iHeartMedia; (acq 8-30-00; grpsl).
Arbitron Metro Market: Fort Smith, AR; *Format:* Country; *No. News Employees:* 2; *Target Audience:* 25-54; females
Dave Ashcraft, Senior Vice President of Programming
Steve Knoll, Programming Director
Judy Hudson, Business Manager

KTCS
03-01-1956; 1410 kHz AM; 1 kw-D, ND2; 0.13 kw-N, ND2; N35 16 40 W94 22 35
Mailing Address: PO Box 180188, Fort Smith, AR 72918 US
Second Address: 5304 Hwy. 45 E, Fort Smith, AR 72916
(479) 646-6151; *Fax:* (479) 646-3509
www.ktcs.com
info@ktcs.com
License: Fort Smith, AR held by Big Chief Broadcasting Co.
Arbitron Metro Market: Fort Smith, AR; *Format:* Gospel
Lee Young, Station Manager
Lee Young, General Sales Mgr
Troy Eckelhoff, Programming Director
Melissa Eckelhoff, Promotions Manager
Sherry Bishop, Traffic Manager

KTCS-FM
08-15-1964; 99.9 MHz FM; 100 kw; 1919 ft.; N35 4 20 W94 40 50
Mailing Address: P. O. Box 6321, Fort Smith, AR 72906 US
Second Address: 5304 Hwy. 45 E., Fort Smith, AR 72916
(479) 646-6151; *Fax:* (479) 646-3509
www.ktcs.com
info@ktcs.com
License: Fort Smith, Sebastian County, AR held by Big Chief Broadcasting Co.
Arbitron Metro Market: Fort Smith, AR; *Format:* Country
Melissa Eckelhoff, Operations Dir
Lee Young, General Manager
Lee Young, Station Manager
Lee Young, General Sales Mgr
Troy Eckelhoff, Programming Director
Melissa Eckelhoff, Promotions Manager
Mary Livingston, News Director
Scott Reeves, Chief Engineer
Sherry Bishop, Traffic Manager

KWHN
11-22-1947; 1320 kHz AM; *Hrs Open:* 24; 5 kw-D, DAN; 5 kw-N, DAN; N35 24 36 W94 21 30
600 Congress Ave., Suite 1400, Austin, TX 78701 US
(479) 782-8888; *Fax:* (479) 785-5946
www.kwhn.com
License: Fort Smith, AR held by Capstar TX LLC
Group Owner: iHeartMedia
Arbitron Metro Market: Fort Smith, AR; *Format:* News, News/Talk, 86; *Hrs. of News Programming:* news progmg 40 hrs wkly; *No. News Employees:* 6; *Target Audience:* 25-54.
Clyde Bass, Regional Market President

***KEAF**
01-01-2009; 90.7 MHz FM; 26 kw vert; 2087 ft.; N35 9 56 W93 40 36 *Rebroadcasts:* Rebroadcasts WBFR(FM) Birmingham, AL 100%
4135 Northgate Blvd, Suite 1, Sacramento, CA 95834 US
(800) 543-1495; *Fax:* (510) 568-6190
www.familyradio.com
info@familyradio.com
License: Fort Smith, Sebastian County, AR held by Family Stations Inc.
Group Owner: Family Stations Inc.
Arbitron Metro Market: Fort Smith, AR; *Format:* Christian
Harold Camping, General Manager

Fouke

***KPOS**
01-01-2001; 104.3 MHz FM; *Hrs Open:* 24; 5 kw; 361 ft.; N33 21 5 W93 50 41
707 Green Cook Rd, Sunbury, OH 43074 US
(916) 251-1600; *Fax:* (916) 251-1650
www.air1.com
info@air1.com
License: Fouke, Miller County, AR held by Educational Media Foundation.
Group Owner: EMF Broadcasting; (acq 1-15-2004; $500,000)
Nat'l Network: Air 1
Format: Alternative, Christian; *No. News Employees:* 3; *Target Audience:* 25-44; Judeo Christian, female
Darrell Chambliss, Chairman
Mike Novak, CEO
Mike Novak, President
David Pierce, Programming Director
Richard Hunt, News Director

Glenwood

KHGZ
05-12-1980; 670 kHz AM; *Hrs Open:* 6 AM-midnight; 5 kw-D, NDD; N34 19 32 W93 33 27
Mailing Address: P.O. Box 740, Glenwood, AR 71943 US
Second Address: 180 Hwy. 70 E., Suite 11, Glenwood, AR 71943
(870) 356-2151(870) 356-2181; *Fax:* (870) 356-4684
License: Glenwood, AR held by MLS Broadcasting Inc.
Regional Reps: Rgnl Reps
Arbitron Metro Market: Glenwood, AR; *Format:* Gospel; *Hrs. of News Programming:* News progmg 8 hrs wkly; *Target Audience:* 34-54; affluent professionals; *Adv. Rates:* 10.59; 10.59; 10.59; 10.59
Bob DelGiorno, GM, News Director, Sports Director and Sales Mgr
Tony Evans, Chief Engineer
Ted Kelly, VP Programming, Webmaster
Jana Bradford, Attorney
Meghan DelGiorno, Owner, Human Resources, Chief Financial Officer

Goshen

KAKS
01-01-1955; 99.5 MHz FM; 14 kw; 443 ft.; N36 7 37 W93 51 57
70 North East St., Suite 100, Fayetteville, AR 72701 US
(479) 443-9960; *Fax:* (479) 444-9670
License: Goshen, Madison County, AR held by Carroll County Broadcasting Inc.
Group Owner: Carroll County Broadcasting Inc.; (acq 2-10-2005; $3.9 million with KCZZ(AM) Mission, KS).
Nat'l Network: ABC
Arbitron Metro Market: Fayetteville (Northwest Arkansas), AR; *Format:* Sports; *Target Audience:* 25-54; general
Steve Butler, General Manager

Gosnell

KAMJ
02-01-1999; 93.9 MHz FM; *Hrs Open:* 24; 1 kw; 489 ft.; N35 53 56 W89 52 48
P.O. Box 989, Blytheville, AR 72315 US
(870) 762-2093; *Fax:* (870) 763-8459
License: Gosnell, Mississippi County, AR held by Phoenix Broadcasting Group Inc.
Group Owner: Sudbury Services Inc.
Arbitron Metro Market: Gosnell, AR; *Format:* Urban Contemporary
Dave Clark, General Manager

Gould

KOTN(FM)
04-15-1999; 102.5 MHz FM; *Hrs Open:* 24; 6 kw; Ant 177 ft; N33 58 11 W91 32 58
Mailing Address: Box 910, Stuttgart, AR 92160
Second Address: 1818 S. Buerkle, Stuttgart, AR 92160
(870) 673-1595; *Fax:* (870) 673-8445
kdew973@yahoo.com
License: Gould, Lincoln County, AR held by Arkansas County Broadcasters Inc.
Group Owner: Arkansas County Broadcasters Inc.; acq 12-30-2003; $90,000)
Arbitron Metro Market: Gould, AR; *Format:* Country
Scott Siler, Station Manager
Rob Shannon, News Director

Gravette

KURM-FM
10-01-1989; 100.3 MHz FM; 1.75 kw; 610 ft.; N36 25 54 W94 30 46
113 E. New Hope, Rogers, AR 72758 US
(479) 633-0790; *Fax:* (479) 631-9711
www.kurm.net
License: Gravette, Benton County, AR held by KERM Inc.
Group Owner: KERM Inc.; (acq 4-4-2002; $350,000 with KLTK(AM) Centerton)
Arbitron Metro Market: Rogers, AK; *Format:* News, News/Talk, 86

Green Forest

KTHS
02-01-1958; 1480 kHz AM; *Hrs Open:* 24; 5 kw-D, ND1; 0.064 kw-N, ND1; N36 21 42 W93 33 40 *Rebroadcasts:* KUOA FM
Mailing Address: P.O. Bx 191, Berryville, AR 72616 US
Second Address: One Radio Dr., Berryville, AR 72616
(870) 423-2147; *Fax:* (870) 423-2146
www.kthsradio.com
studio@kthsradio.com
License: Green Forest, AR held by Carroll County Broadcasting Inc.
Group Owner: Carroll County Broadcasting Inc.; (acq 6-29-2006; $3.5 million with co-located FM)
Arbitron Metro Market: Springfield, MO; *Format:* Sports, Talk
Special Programming: Farm 15 hrs wkly; *No. News Employees:* 1; *Target Audience:* General.; *Adv. Rates:* $10 6a - 7p
Jay Bunyard, President
Tim Poynter, General Manager
William Autry, General Sales Mgr
Linda Boyer, Programming Director
Zeb Huffmaster, Chief Engineer
Sherri Linz, Traffic Manager

Greenbrier

KCNY
10-15-1984; 107.1 MHz FM; 12.5 kw; 466 ft.; N35 17 47 W92 19 11
1825 East Oak, Conway, AR 72032 US
(479) 832-0925; *Fax:* (501) 279-2900
www.y107fm.com
jrrunyon@crainmedia.com
License: Greenbrier, White County, AR held by Crain Media Group LLC
Group Owner: Crain Media Group LLC
Format: Adult Contemp
Mike Horne, General Manager
Lynn Dyer, General Sales Mgr
JR Runyon, Programming Director

Greenwood

KZKZ-FM
12-01-1981; 106.3 MHz FM; *Hrs Open:* 24; 15 kw; 397 ft.; N35 13 44 W94 15 45
6420 South Zero, Fort Smith, AR 72903 US
(479) 646-6700; *Fax:* (479) 646-1373
www.kzkzfm.com
kzkzfm@kzkzfm.com
License: Greenwood, Pike County, AR held by Family Communications Inc.
Arbitron Metro Market: Greenwood, AR; *Format:* Christian
Jay Lynch, General Manager
Jay Lynch, Station Manager
Dave Burdue, Programming Director

Gurdon

KYXK
12-01-1984; 106.9 MHz FM; *Hrs Open:* 24; 17.5 kw; 302 ft.; N33 56 42 W93 10 43
Mailing Address: P.O. Box 831, Arkadelphia, AR 71923 US
Second Address: 601 S. 7th St., Arkadelphia, AR 71923
(870) 246-9272; *Fax:* (870) 246-5878
License: Gurdon, Clark County, AR held by Southwest Arkansas Media LLC
Group Owner: Southwest Arkansas Media LLC; (acq 9-4-2013; grpsl)
Arbitron Metro Market: Gurdon, AR; *Format:* Country; *Target Audience:* 25-54; adults
Stephanie Collie, General Sales Mgr
Randy Seale, Programming Director
Ronna Pennington, News Director

Hamburg

KHMB
01-01-1996; 99.5 MHz FM; *Hrs Open:* 24; 3.2 kw; 312 ft.; N33 17 19 W91 52 45
203 Fairview Road, Crosset, AR 71635 US
(870) 364-4700; *Fax:* (870) 364-4770
www.QLiteradio.com
qlite@arkansas.net
License: Hamburg, Ash County, AR held by R&M Broadcasting

Format: Adult Contemp; *Target Audience:* 25-54
Dennis Maxwell, General Manager
Jane Austin, General Sales Mgr

Hampton

KELD-FM
11-26-1984; 107.1 MHz FM; *Hrs Open:* 24; 17.5 kw; 302 ft.; N33 32 23 W92 34 59
2525 North West Avenue, El Dorado, AR 71730 US
(870) 863-6126; *Fax:* (870) 863-4555
www.keldfm.com
License: Hampton, Calhoun County, AR held by Noalmark Broadcasting Corp.
Group Owner: Noalmark Broadcasting Corp.; acq 2-21-03; $250,000).
Nat'l Network: ABC; Fox News Radio
Arbitron Metro Market: Monroe, LA; *Format:* News, News/Talk, 86
Jay Helm, General Manager
KC Wright, Programming Director
Sharon Peterson, Traffic Manager

*KBPW
01-01-2001; 88.1 MHz FM; 60 kw vert; 338 ft.; N33 32 11 W92 28 7
221 S. Lee Hwy. 167 S., Hampton, AR 71744 US
(870) 798-3733
www.afr.net
License: Hampton, Calhoun County, AR held by American Family Association.
Group Owner: American Family Radio; (acq 4-19-01).
Arbitron Metro Market: Tupelo, MS; *Format:* Christian
Tim Wildmon, President
Donald Wildmon, Founder
Buddy Smith, Sr VP
Ed Vitagliano, Exec VP
Randy Sharp, Director Of Special Projects
Meeke Addison, Director Of Communications
Abraham Hamilton III, General Sales Mgr

Hardy

KOOU
10-04-1993; 104.7 MHz FM; *Hrs Open:* 24; 5.4 kw; 305 ft.; N36 16 29 W91 30 18
P.O. Box 909, Cherokee Village, AR 72525 US
(870) 856-3240; *Fax:* (870) 856-4408
License: Hardy, Sharp County, AR held by KOOU Inc.
Regional Network: Ark. Radio Net.
Format: Adult Contemp; *Hrs. of News Programming:* news progmg 10 hrs wkly; *No. News Employees:* 2; *Target Audience:* 25-60; female/professional; *Adv. Rates:* 12; 10; 11; 7
James Bragg, General Manager

Harrisburg

KWHF
05-15-1999; 95.9 MHz FM; *Hrs Open:* 24; 34 kw; 489 ft.; N35 47 42 W90 47 35
Mailing Address: P.O. Box 540, Jonesboro, AR 72403 US
Second Address: 407 W. Parker Rd., Jonesboro, AR 72404
(870) 932-8400; *Fax:* (870) 932-3814
License: Harrisburg, Poinsett County, AR held by CC Licenses LLC.
Group Owner: East Arkansas Broadcasters
Arbitron Metro Market: Jonesboro, AR; *Format:* Country; *Hrs. of News Programming:* news progmg 3 hrs wkly; *No. News Employees:* 2; *Target Audience:* 28-65; affluent baby boomers who have spendable income *Adv.Rates:* 16; 14; 16; 10
Scott Siler, General Manager
Chuck Crossno, General Sales Mgr
Mitch Mahan, Programming Director
Janice Reid, Traffic Manager

Harrison

*KBPB
01-01-2001; 91.9 MHz FM; *Hrs Open:* 24; 5.5 kw; 341 ft.; N36 22 12 W93 13 23
1411 Locust Street, St. Louis, MO 63103 US
(800) 228-5284; *Fax:* (573) 896-4376
License: Harrison, Boone County, AR held by New Life Evangelistic Center Inc.
Format: Christian, Gospel
Larry Rice, General Manager

KCWD
01-01-1982; 96.1 MHz FM; *Hrs Open:* 24; 8 kw; 1191 ft.; N36 6 41 W93 2 0
Mailing Address: P.O. Box 2639, Gulfport, MS 39505 US
Second Address: 600 S. Pine, Harrison, AR 72601
(870) 741-1402; *Fax:* (870) 741-9702
www.kcwdradio.com/index.php
kcwd@all.net
License: Harrison, Boone County, AR held by Harrison Radio Station Inc.
Arbitron Metro Market: Harrison, AR; *Format:* Classic Rock
Roger Lowery, General Manager
Linda Peter, General Sales Mgr
Barbara Dean, Traffic Manager

KHOZ
09-28-1946; 900 kHz AM; *Hrs Open:* 24; 1 kw-D, ND1; 0.062 kw-N, ND1; N36 14 35 W93 6 43
Pob 430 One Radio Aven., Harrison, AR 72601 US
(870) 741-2302; *Fax:* (870) 741-3299
www.khoz.com
scottieearls@krzk.com
License: Harrison, AR held by KHOZ LLC.
Group Owner: Earls Broadcasting Co.; (acq 6-16-2005; $3.7 million with co-located FM)
Nat'l Network: CBS; *Wire Services:* AP
Format: Country *Special Programming:* Sports 20 hrs wkly; *Hrs. of News Programming:* news progmg 15 hrs wkly; *No. News Employees:* 3; *Target Audience:* General.; *Adv. Rates:* 8.50; 8.50; 8.50; 8.50
Scottie Earls, General Manager
Marilyn Wallis, Station Manager
Rob McBee, Programming Director
Tammy Stevens, Office Manager
Kristin Clemmens, Traffic Manager

KHBZ
03-25-1963; 102.9 MHz FM; *Hrs Open:* 24; 100 kw; 981 ft.; N36 26 11 W93 14 43
P.O. Box 430, One Radio Avenue, Harrison, AR 72601 US
(870) 741-2301; *Fax:* (870) 741-3299
www.khoz.com
scottieearls@krzk.com
License: Harrison, Boone County, AR held by KHOZ LLC.
Group Owner: Earls Broadcasting Co.
Nat'l Network: CBS Radio; *Wire Services:* AP
Format: Country; *Hrs. of News Programming:* news progmg 15 hrs wkly; *No. News Employees:* 2; *Target Audience:* 25-54.; *Adv. Rates:* 37; 37; 37; 37
Scottie Earls, General Manager
Marilyn Wallis, Station Manager
Steve Kelly, Programming Director
Harold Smith, News Director
Tammy Stevens, Office Manager
Kristen Clemmens, Traffic Manager

Hatfield

KILX
01-01-2001; 104.1 MHz FM; *Hrs Open:* 24; 28.5 kw; 469 ft.; N34 32 42 W94 18 21
P.O. Box 1450, Mena, AR 71953 US
(479) 394-1450
License: Hatfield, Polk County, AR held by Ouachita Broadcasting Inc.
Group Owner: Ouachita Broadcasting Inc.; (acq 3-8-99).
Arbitron Metro Market: Hatfield, AR; *Format:* Adult Contemp
Dwight Douglas, General Manager

Heber Springs

KAWW
07-15-1967; 1370 kHz AM; *Hrs Open:* 6 AM-sunset (2 hrs past); 1 kw-D, NDD; N35 29 10 W92 2 5
#1 Shackleford Dr., Suite 400, Little Rock, AR 72211 US
(501) 268-7123; *Fax:* (501) 279-2900
jrrunyon@crainmedia.com
License: Heber Springs, AR held by Crain Media Group LLC
Group Owner: Crain Media Group LLC; acq 8-7-02; grpsl).
Regional Network: Ark. Radio Net.
Arbitron Metro Market: Heber Springs, AR; *Format:* News, News/Talk, 86; *Hrs. of News Programming:* news progmg one hr wkly; *No. News Employees:* 1; *Target Audience:* 25-65.; *Adv. Rates:* 8; 8; 8; 8
Larry Crain, CEO
Mike Horne, General Manager
Heath Shelby, Programming Director

*KBMJ
01-01-2002; 89.5 MHz FM; *Hrs Open:* 24; 70 kw vert; 735 ft.; N35 44 0 W92 15 37
P.O. Box 3206, Tupelo, MS 38803 US
(662) 844-8888; *Fax:* (662) 842-6791
www.afr.net
faq@afa.net
License: Heber Springs, Cleburne County, AR held by American Family Association.
Group Owner: American Family Radio
Format: Christian
Tim Wildmon, President
Donald Wildmon, Founder
Buddy Smith, Senior VP
Ed Vitagliano, Exec VP
Randy Sharp, Director Of Special Projects
Meeme Addison, Director Of Communications
Abraham Hamilton III, General Counsel & PublicPolicy Analyst

Helena

KFFA
11-19-1941; 1360 kHz AM; *Hrs Open:* 24; 1 kw-D, ND1; 0.09 kw-N, ND1; N34 31 39 W90 37 48
P.O. Box 430, Helena, AR 72342 US
(870) 338-8361(870) 338-8331; *Fax:* (870) 338-8332
www.kffa.com
kffa@arkansas.net
License: Helena, AR held by Delta Broadcasting Inc.
Arbitron Metro Market: Helena, AR; *Format:* Country *Special Programming:* Farm 16 hrs, blues 8 hrs, Black 10 hrs, sports 15 hrs, gospel 4 hrs wkly; *Hrs. of News Programming:* News progmg 25 hrs wkly; *Target Audience:* 18-54.
Jim Howe, President
Rose Seaton, Operations Dir
Louis Smith, Programming Director
Nancy Howie, News Director
Jerry Campbell, Engineering Dir

KFFA-FM
01-01-1972; 103.1 MHz FM; *Hrs Open:* 24; 13 kw; 318 ft.; N34 31 39 W90 37 46
Mailing Address: P.O. Box 430, Helena, AR 72342 US
Second Address: 1360 Radio Dr., Helena, AR 72342
(870) 338-8331; *Fax:* (870) 338-8332
www.kffa.com
kffa@arkansas.net
License: Helena, Phillips County, AR held by Delta Broadcasting Inc.
Arbitron Metro Market: Helana, AR; *Format:* Adult Contemp, Sports; *Hrs. of News Programming:* News progmg 4 hrs wkly
Jim Howe, CEO
Rose Seaton, Programming Director
Kacye Patton, News Director
Louis Smith, Music Critic

KJIW-FM
01-05-1989; 94.5 MHz FM; *Hrs Open:* 24; 14 kw; 413 ft.; N34 31 28 W90 35 47
204 Moore Street, Helena, AR 72342 US
(870) 338-2700
kjiwfm@ipa.net
License: Helena, Phillips County, AR held by Elijah Mondy Jr.
Format: Gospel
Elijah Mondy Jr., General Manager
April Mondy, Programming Director
Zipporah Mondy, Music Director

Hope

KHPA
04-21-1977; 104.9 MHz FM; 6 kw; 328 ft.; N33 43 12 W93 29 11
Mailing Address: P. O. Box 989, Blytheville, AR 72316 US
Second Address: 1600 S. Elm, Hope, AR 71801
(870) 777-8868; *Fax:* (870) 777-8888
www.supercountry105.com
SonyaOdom@supercountry105.com
License: Hope, Hempstead County, AR held by Newport Broadcasting Co.
Group Owner: Sudbury Services Inc.
Format: Country; *Target Audience:* General.
Alan Jeffries, Operations Dir
Kathy Davis, General Sales Mgr
Alan Jeffries, Programming Director
Tom Hill, Chief Engineer

KXAR
12-12-1947; 1490 kHz AM; 0.7 kw-U, ND1; N33 41 20 W93 35 55
Mailing Address: Box 320 Hwy 29 At I-30, Hope, AR 71801 US
Second Address: 1600 S. Elm, Hope, AR 71801
(870) 777-8868; *Fax:* (870) 777-8888
khpafm@supercountry105.com
License: Hope, AR held by Newport Broadcast Co.
Group Owner: Sudbury Services Inc.; (Acq 8-26-99; $51,000)
Regional Network: Ark. Radio Net.
Arbitron Metro Market: Hope, AR; *Format:* Talk; *Target Audience:* General; double income, stable, adult households
Alan Jeffries, Operations Manager/Programming Director
Kathy Davis, Sales Manager
Tom Hill, Chief Engineer

KBYB
12-31-1984; 101.7 MHz FM; *Hrs Open:* 24; 50 kw; 492 ft.; N33 40 46 W93 49 42
Highway 29 At I-30, Hope, AR 72801 US
(903) 793-4671; *Fax:* (903) 792-4261
www.1017bobfm.com
License: Hope, Hempstead County, AR held by Arklatex LLC.
Group Owner: Arklatex LLC; (acq 1-3-2007; grpsl)
Nat'l Reps: Interep
Arbitron Metro Market: Texarkana, TX; *Format:* Adult Contemp; *Target Audience:* 25-54.
Scott Gray, CFO

Horseshoe Bend

KKIK
01-01-2004; 106.5 MHz FM; 12 kw; 476 ft.; N36 15 22 W91 55 23
720 Ramsey Street, Batesville, AR 72503 US
(870) 793-4196; *Fax:* (870) 793-5222
License: Horseshoe Bend, Izard County, AR held by WRD Entertainment Inc.
Group Owner: WRD Entertainment Inc.
Arbitron Metro Market: Horseshoe Bend, AR; *Format:* Oldies
Gary Bridgman, General Manager
Matt Johnson, Sales Manager
Ken Loggains, Programming Director
Gena Ries, Traffic Manager

Hot Springs

***KALR**
05-01-1989; 91.5 MHz FM; *Hrs Open:* 24; 4.5 kw; 486 ft.; N34 37 31 W93 0 37
P.O. Box 8500, Hot Springs, AR 71910 US
(888) 937-2471
www.air1.com
info@air1.com
License: Hot Springs, Garland County, AR held by Educational Media Foundation.
Group Owner: EMF Broadcasting; (acq 6-28-2007; $275,000)
Nat'l Network: Air 1
Arbitron Metro Market: Omaha, NB; *Format:* Alternative, Christian
Mike Novak, CEO
Mike Novak, President

KZHS
03-10-1953; 590 kHz AM; 5 kw-D, ND2; 0.067 kw-N, ND2; N34 29 55 W92 58 45
P.O. Box 22265, Hot Springs, AR 79103 US
(501) 525-4600; *Fax:* (501) 525-4344
License: Hot Springs, AR held by Noalmark Broadcasting Corp.
Group Owner: Noalmark Broadcasting Corp.; (acq 12-13-2004; $140,000)
Nat'l Network: Fox Sports
Arbitron Metro Market: Hot Springs, AR; *Format:* News, News/Talk, 84, Talk
Paul Meacham, General Manager
Ron Chatman, Programming Director
Andrew Zupkoff, News Director

KLAZ
10-01-1971; 105.9 MHz FM; 95 kw; 994 ft.; N34 22 20 W93 2 51
P.O. Box 22265, Hot Springs, AR 79103 US
(510) 525-1301; *Fax:* (501) 525-4344
License: Hot Springs, Garland County, AR held by Noalmark Broadcasting Corp.
Group Owner: Noalmark Broadcasting Corp.
Arbitron Metro Market: Little Rock, AR; *Format:* Adult Contemp; *Target Audience:* 18-49.
Paul Meacham, General Manager
Paul Meacham, General Sales Mgr
Ron Chatman, Programming Director
Andrew Zupkoff, News Director
Gina Angel, Traffic Manager

KHTO(FM)
06-18-1965; 96.7 MHz FM; *Hrs Open:* 24; 940 w; Ant 807 ft; N34 24 13 W93 07 14
125 Corporate Terr., Hot Springs, AR 71913-7248
(501) 525-9700; *Fax:* (501) 525-9739
License: Hot Springs, Garland County, AR held by US Stations LLC.
Group Owner: US Stations LLC; (acq 2-1-2005; grpsl).
Population Served: 65,631 *Format:* Adult Contemp; *Target Audience:* 18 plus.
Craig Dale, Operations Dir
Gary Terrell, General Manager
Neal Gladner, General Sales Mgr
Melissa Waters, News Director

KQUS-FM
02-07-1969; 97.5 MHz FM; *Hrs Open:* 24; 100 kw; 860 ft; N34 24 11 W93 07 13
125 Corporate Terr., Hot Springs, AR 72702
(501) 525-9700; *Fax:* (501) 525-9739
www.us97country.com
info@usstations.com
License: Hot Springs, Garland County, AR
Group Owner: US Stations LLC; 10/1/2004
Nat'l Network: CBS; *Nat'l Reps:* Local Focus; *Wire Services:* AP
Population Served: 128,000; *Arbitron Metro Market:* Hot Springs, AR; *No. News Employees:* 1; *Target Audience:* 18-54.
Gary Terrell, General Manager
Paul Swint, General Sales Mgr
Craig Dale, Programming Director
Craig Dale, News Director
Gary Terrell, Chief Engineer
Tom Duke, Music Director

***KLRO**
03-20-1984; 90.1 MHz FM; *Hrs Open:* 24; 38 kw; 971 ft.; N34 30 18 W93 4 42
600 Garland Avenue, Hot Springs, AR 71913 US
(916) 251-1600; *Fax:* (916) 251-1650
www.klove.com
License: Hot Springs, Garland County, AR held by Educational Media Foundation.
Group Owner: EMF Broadcasting; (acq 9-24-2004; $1.2 million).
Nat'l Network: K-Love
Arbitron Metro Market: Rocklin, CA; *Format:* Christian
Darrell Chambliss, Chairman
Mike Novak, CEO/COO
Mike Novak, President
David Pierce, Programming Director
Ed Lenane, News Director
Sam Wallington, Engineering Dir

KBHS
10-06-1966; 1420 kHz AM; 5 kw-D, ND1; 0.087 kw-N, ND1; N34 27 19 W93 3 26
Mailing Address: P.O. Box 22265, Hot Springs, AR 79103 US
Second Address: 208 Buena Vista Rd., Hot Springs, AR 71902
(501) 525-4600; *Fax:* (501) 525-4344
www.klaz.com
License: Hot Springs, AR held by Noalmark Broadcasting Corp.
Group Owner: Noalmark Broadcasting Corp.
Nat'l Reps: Target Broadcast Sales
Format: Adult Contemp; *Target Audience:* 35 plus; upscale, high-income residents & business people
Paul Meacham, General Manager/Sales Manager
Ron Chatman, Programming Director
Andrew Zupkoff, News Director
Gina Angel, Traffic Manager

KZNG
01-01-1953; 1340 kHz AM; *Hrs Open:* 24; 1 kw-U, ND1; N34 29 43 W93 1 27
P.O. Box 22265, Hot Springs, AR 79103 US
(501) 525-9700; *Fax:* (501) 525-9739
www.myhotsprings.com
dck_antoine@yahoo.com
License: Hot Springs, AR held by US Stations LLC.
Group Owner: US Stations LLC; (acq 2-1-2005; grpsl).
Nat'l Network: ABC; Premiere Radio Networks; Westwood One; *Regional Network:* Ark. Radio Net.; *Wire Services:* AP
Arbitron Metro Market: Hot Springs, AR; *Format:* News, News/Talk, 86; *Hrs. of News Programming:* news progmg 10 hrs wkly; *No. News Employees:* 1; *Target Audience:* 18 plus.
Gary Terrell, General Manager
Paul Swint, Director Of Sales
Craig Dale, Programming Director

Hot Springs Village

KVRE
02-01-1994; 92.9 MHz FM; *Hrs Open:* 24; 25 kw; 328 ft.; N34 38 34 W93 4 8
P. O. Box 8439, Hot Springs Village, AR 71909 US
(501) 922-5678(501) 922-5880(501) 922-9444; *Fax:* (501) 922-6626
kvre@kvre.com
License: Hot Springs Village, Garland County, AR held by Caddo Broadcasting Co.
Nat'l Network: Music of Your Life
Arbitron Metro Market: Hot Springs, AR; *Format:* Adult Contemp; *Target Audience:* 35 plus; general
Tom Nichols, CEO
Alice Bates, Operations Dir
Polly Nichols, General Manager
Cyrie Wright, General Sales Mgr
John Chapman, News Director
Scotty Mack, Production Manager

Hoxie

***KJLV**
01-20-1988; 105.3 MHz FM; *Hrs Open:* 24; 25 kw; 328 ft.; N36 3 36 W91 2 44
Post Office Box 540, Jonesboro, AR 72403 US
(707) 528-9236; *Fax:* (707) 528-9246,(916) 251-1650
www.klove.com
License: Hoxie, Lawrence County, AR held by Educational Media Foundation.
Group Owner: EMF Broadcasting; (acq 11-1-01; $1.3 million with KJBR(FM) Marked Tree).
Arbitron Metro Market: Jonesboro, AR; *Format:* Christian; *Adv. Rates:* 10; 7; 10; na
Jon Taylor, CFO
Mike Novak, President
David Pierce, Promotions Manager
Ed Lenane, News Director
Sam Wallington, Engineering Dir

Humnoke

KVLO
01-01-1996; 101.7 MHz FM; 6 kw; 328 ft.; N34 32 58 W91 45 26
City Center West, 7201 W. Lake Mead Blvd, Las Vegas, NV 89128 US
(501) 401-0200; *Fax:* (501) 401-0366
License: Humnoke, Lonoke County, AR held by The Last Bastion Station Trust LLC, as Trustee
Arbitron Metro Market: Little Rock, AR; *Format:* Adult Contemp
Jim Beard, Operations Dir

Hunstville

***KGSF**
01-01-2008; 88.7 MHz FM; 5 kw vert; 595 ft.; N36 21 38 W93 44 54 *Rebroadcasts:* Rebroadcasts KAWZ(FM) Twin Falls, ID 100%
Mailing Address: P.O. Box 391, Twin Falls, ID 83303 US
Second Address: 4002 North 3300 East, Twin Falls, ID 83301
(208) 734-6633; *Fax:* (208) 736-1958
www.csnradio.com
License: Hunstville, Madison County, AR held by Calvary Chapel of Twin Falls Inc.
Group Owner: CSN International
Arbitron Metro Market: Green Forest, AR; *Format:* Christian, Religious
Mike Kestler, President
Daniel Davidson, Operations Dir
Joe Jennings, Station Manager & Program Director
Mike Stocklin, Underwriting Director
Kelly Carlson, Engineering Dir

Jacksonville

KDJE
09-29-1969; 100.3 MHz FM; *Hrs Open:* 24; 83 kw; 1053 ft.; N34 47 53 W92 29 33
10800 Colonel Glenn Rd., Little Rock, AR 72204 US
(501) 217-5000; *Fax:* (501) 374-0808
www.edgelittlerock.com
License: Jacksonville, Pulaski County, AR held by CC Licenses LLC.
Group Owner: iHeartMedia; (acq 5-15-96; grpsl).
Nat'l Reps: Clear Channel
Arbitron Metro Market: Little Rock, AR; *Format:* Rock/AOR; *Hrs. of News Programming:* news progmg 3 hrs wkly; *No. News Employees:* 1; *Target Audience:* 18-49.
Ron Collar, Market President
Keli Williams, Senior Vice President of Sales
Jeff Cage, Programming Director
Matt Cruz, Promotions Director

Jonesboro

***KAOG**
01-01-1999; 90.5 MHz FM; 40 kw; 397 ft.; N35 48 36 W90 48 45
P.O. Box 3206, Tupelo, MS 38803 US
(662) 844-8888; *Fax:* (662) 842-6791
www.afr.net
faq@afa.net
License: Jonesboro, Craighead County, AR held by American Family Association.
Group Owner: American Family Radio
Arbitron Metro Market: Tupelo, MO; *Format:* Religious
Time Wildmon, President
Donald Wildmon, Founder
Buddy Smith, Sr. VP
Ed Vitagliano, Executive VP
Randy Sharp, Director Of Special Projects

Meeke Addison, Director Of Communications
Abraham Mahilson III, General Counsel & PublicPolicy

***KASU**
05-17-1957; 91.9 MHz FM; *Hrs Open:* 24; 100 kw; 689 ft.; N35 53 27 W90 40 26
P.O. Box 2160, State University, AR 72467 US
(870) 972-2200; *Fax:* (870) 972-2997
www.kasu.org
kasu@astate.edu
License: Jonesboro, Craighead County, AR held by Arkansas State University.
Nat'l Network: PRI; NPR; *Wire Services:* AP
Arbitron Metro Market: State University, AZ; *Format:* Classical, Jazz, 60 *Special Programming:* New age, blues, folk 4 hrs, big band 2 hrs wkly; *Hrs. of News Programming:* news progmg 45 hrs wkly; *No. News Employees:* 1; *Target Audience:* General.
June Taylor, Operations Dir
Mike Doyle, Station Manager
Marty Scarbrough, Programming Director
Greg Chance, News Director
Eddy Arnold, Chief Engineer

KBTM
03-15-1930; 1230 kHz AM; *Hrs Open:* 24
Mailing Address: P.O. Drawer 1737, Jonesboro, AK 72403 US
Second Address: 407 W. Parker Rd., Jonesboro, AR 72404
(870) 935-5598; *Fax:* (870) 932-3814
License: Jonesboro, AR held by East Arkansas Broadcasters of Jonesboro LLC.
Group Owner: East Arkansas Broadcasters of Jonesboro LLC.
Regional Network: Ark. Radio Net.
Arbitron Metro Market: Jonesboro, AR; *Format:* News, News/Talk, 86; *Hrs. of News Programming:* news progmg 14 hrs wkly; *No. News Employees:* 2; *Target Audience:* 45 plus; upscale adults
Barbara Nelson, General Sales Mgr
Kevin Box, Promotions Manager
Janice Reid, News Director

KEGI
11-21-1986; 100.5 MHz FM; *Hrs Open:* 24; 38 kw; Ant 558 ft; N35 56 59 W90 39 58
314 Union Ave., Jonesboro, AR 72401
(870) 933-8800; *Fax:* (870) 933-0403
eagle1005.com
trey@triplefm.com
License: Jonesboro, Craighead County, AR held by Saga Communications of Arkansas LLC.
Group Owner: Saga Communications Inc.; (acq 11-8-2002; grpsl)
Arbitron Metro Market: Jonesboro, AR; *Hrs. of News Programming:* news progmg one hr wkly; *No. News Employees:* 1; *Target Audience:* 18-49.; *Adv. Rates:* 31; 36; 31; 11
Trey Stafford, President
Kevin Neathery, General Sales Mgr
Bill Pressly, Vice President of Programming
Rick Christian, Promotions Director
Al Simpson, Chief Engineer

KFIN
03-04-1974; 107.9 MHz FM; *Hrs Open:* 24; 98 kw; 600 ft.; N35 47 56 W90 44 31
407 West Parker Road, Jonesboro, AR 72404 US
(870) 932-1079; *Fax:* (870) 932-0892
www.kfin.com
License: Jonesboro, Craighead County, AR held by Capstar TX L.P.
Group Owner: East Arkansas Broadcasting
Arbitron Metro Market: Jonesboro, AR; *Format:* Country *Special Programming:* Farm 13 hrs wkly; *Hrs. of News Programming:* news progmg 9 hrs wkly; *No. News Employees:* 1; *Target Audience:* 25-54; broaddemographics
Scott Siler, General Manager
Chuck Crossno, Regional Sales Director
Mitch Mahan, Programming Director
Dennis Rogers, News Director
Janice Reid, Traffic Manager

KNEA
09-20-1950; 970 kHz AM; *Hrs Open:* 24
407 West Parker Road, Jonesboro, AR 72404 US
(870) 932-8400; *Fax:* (870) 932-3814
License: Jonesboro, AR held by CC Licenses LLC.
Group Owner: East Arkansas Broadcasting
Regional Network: Ark. Radio Net.
Arbitron Metro Market: Jonesboro, AR; *Format:* Gospel *Special Programming:* Farm 6 hrs wkly; *No. News Employees:* 5; *Target Audience:* General.
Scott Siler, General Manager
Chuck Crossno, Director of Sales (Regional)

***KJSB**
88.3 MHz FM; 1.9 kw vert; 299 ft.; N35 48 36 W90 48 45
P.O. Box 3206, Tupelo, MS 38803 US
(662) 844-8888; *Fax:* (662) 842-6791
www.afr.net
faq@afa.net
License: Jonesboro, Craighead County, AR held by American Family Association.
Group Owner: American Family Radio
Arbitron Metro Market: Jonesboro, AR; *Format:* Christian, Talk
Tim Wildmon, President
Donald Wildmon, Founder
Buddy Smith, Sr VP
Ed Vitagliano, Exec VP
Randy Sharp, Director Of Special Projects
Meeke Addison, Director Of Communications
Abraham Hamilton III, General Counsel

Judsonia

KVHU
01-01-2006; 95.3 MHz FM; *Hrs Open:* 24; 14 kw; Ant 440 ft; N35 13 41 W91 29 19
Box 10765, Searcy, AR
(501) 279-4886; *Fax:* (501) 279-4065
kvhu@harding.edu
License: Judsonia, White County, AR held by George S. Flinn Jr.
Target Audience: 35+.
Dutch Hoggatt, General Manager

Kensett

KEAZ
09-01-1972; 100.7 MHz FM; *Hrs Open:* 24; 50 kw; 328 ft.; N35 27 26 W92 2 11
111 North Spring Street, Searcy, AR 72143 US
(501) 268-7123; *Fax:* (501) 279-2900
jrrunyon@crainmedia.com
License: Kensett, Cleburne County, AR held by Crain Media Group LLC.
Group Owner: Crain Media Group LLC; (acq 8-7-2002; grpsl)
Arbitron Metro Market: Heber Springs, AR; *Format:* Adult Contemp; *Target Audience:* 25-54.
Larry Crain, CEO
Mike Horne, General Manager/Sales Manager

Lake City

KDXY
10-04-1971; 104.9 MHz FM; *Hrs Open:* 24; 25 kw; 480 ft; N35 49 29 W90 33 54
314 Union Ave., Jonesboro, AR 72401
(870) 933-8800; *Fax:* (870) 933-0403
www.thefox1049.com
trey@triplefm.com
License: Lake City, Craighead County, AR held by Saga Communications of Arkansas LLC.
Group Owner: Saga Communications Inc.; (acq 11-8-02; grpsl).
Population Served: 120,000 *Hrs. of News Programming:* news progmg 6 hrs wkly; *No. News Employees:* 1; *Target Audience:* 25-49.; *Adv. Rates:* 82; 76; 54; 10
Trey Stafford, President
Kevin Neathery, General Sales Mgr
Bill Pressly, Vice President of Programming
Bill Blankenship, Production Director

Lake Village

***KUUZ**
07-30-1977; 95.9 MHz FM; *Hrs Open:* 24; 20 kw; 302 ft.; N33 20 7 W91 7 33
Mailing Address: P. O. Box 1794, Greenville, MS 38702 US
Second Address: 8919 World Ministry Ave., Baton Rouge, LA 70810
(225) 768-3288; *Fax:* (225) 768-3729
www.jsm.org
onair@jsm.org
License: Lake Village, Chicot County, AR held by Family Worship Center Church Inc.
Group Owner: Family Worship Center Church Inc.; acq 6-12-02; $500,000).
Arbitron Metro Market: Lake Village, AR; *Format:* Religious
David Whitelaw, COO
John Santiago, Programming Director

Lakeview

KKTZ
05-01-1999; 93.5 MHz FM; 7.1 kw; 623 ft.; N36 29 13 W92 29 39
P.O. Box 2639, Gulfport, MS 39502 US
(870) 492-6022; *Fax:* (870) 492-2137
www.kktz.net
stewartbrunner@twinlakesradio.com
License: Lakeview, Baxter County, AR held by John M. Dowdy.
Arbitron Metro Market: Mountain Home, AR; *Format:* Adult Contemp; *Target Audience:* 24-25.
Morgan Dowdy, CEO
Stewart Brunner, Operations Dir
Stewart Brunner, General Manager
Bobby Van Haaren, Programming Director

Little Rock

KAAY
01-01-1924; 1090 kHz AM; 50 kw-D, DAN; 50 kw-N, DAN; N34 36 0 W92 13 30
700 Wellington Hills Rd., Little Rock, AR 72211 US
(501) 401-0386
www.1090kaay.com
License: Little Rock, AR held by Radio License Holding CBC, LLC
Group Owner: Cumulus Media Inc.; (acq 9-30-98; $5 million).
Nat'l Network: USA
Arbitron Metro Market: Little Rock, AR; *Format:* Christian; *Adv. Rates:* 14; 14; 14; 14
Richard Nickols, General Manager
Richard Nickols, Director of Sales

***KABF**
09-30-1984; 88.3 MHz FM; *Hrs Open:* 24; 91 kw; 778 ft.; N34 47 31 W92 28 38
2101 S Main Street, Suite 200, Little Rock, AR 72206 US
(501) 372-6119; *Fax:* (501) 376-3952
www.kabf.us
radiokabf@yahoo.com
License: Little Rock, Pulaski County, AR held by Arkansas Broadcasting Foundation.
Arbitron Metro Market: Little Rock, AR; *Format:* Black, Gospel, 52, Variety/Diverse *Special Programming:* Sp 10 hrs, folk 10 hrs, American Indian 3 hrs, blu; *Hrs. of News Programming:* news progmg 12 hrs wkly *No. NewsEmployees:* 1; *Target Audience:* General; low-moderate income & politically disenfranchised
Wade Rathke, General Manager
John Cain, Programming Director

KARN
01-01-1928; 920 kHz AM; *Hrs Open:* 24; 5 kw-D, DAN; 5 kw-N, DAN; N34 46 20 W92 14 45
700 Wellington Hills Rd., Little Rock, AR 72211 US
(501) 401-0200; *Fax:* (501) 401-0387
www.sportsanimal920.com
License: Little Rock, AR held by Radio License Holding CBC, LLC
Group Owner: Cumulus Media Inc.; (acq 8-27-97; grpsl).
Nat'l Network: CBS; *Regional Network:* Ark. Radio Net.; *Wire Services:* ESSA Weather Service
Arbitron Metro Market: Little Rock, AZ; *Format:* Sports; *Hrs. of News Programming:* news progmg 28 hrs wkly; *No. News Employees:* 10; *Target Audience:* 35-64.
Rich Nickols, General Manager

KTUV
10-01-1956; 1440 kHz AM; *Hrs Open:* 24; 5 kw-D, DAN; 0.24 kw-N, DAN; N34 42 46 W92 16 48
723 W. 14th St., Little Rock, AK 72202 US
(501) 562-2661; *Fax:* (501) 421-5255
www.birach.com
sima@birach.com
License: Little Rock, Pulaski County, AR held by Birach Broadcasting Corp.
Group Owner: Birach Broadcasting Corp.; (acq 1-31-2008; $1.5 million with KJMU(AM) Sand Springs, OK)
Arbitron Metro Market: Little Rock, AR; *Format:* Spanish; *Adv. Rates:* 35; 25; 35; 15
Sima Birach, President

KJBN
01-01-1946; 1050 kHz AM; 1 kw-D, ND1; 0.019 kw-N, ND1; N34 45 58 W92 17 38
1800 Maple Street, North Little Rock, AR 72114 US
(501) 791-1000; *Fax:* (501) 791-7121
License: Little Rock, AR held by Joshua Ministries and Community Development Corp.
Arbitron Metro Market: Little Rock, AR; *Format:* Gospel; *Target Audience:* Career-oriented people.
James Smith, General Manager
Chris Bryant, Station Manager

KKPT
10-26-1960; 94.1 MHz FM; *Hrs Open:* 24; 100 kw; 1601 ft.; N34 47 56 W92 29 44
P.O. Box 795365, Dallas, TX 75379 US

(501) 664-9410; *Fax:* (501) 664-5871
www.kkpt.com
License: Little Rock, Pulaski County, AR held by Signal Media of Arkansas.
Nat'l Reps: D & R Radio; *Wire Services:* AP
Arbitron Metro Market: Little Rock, AR; *Format:* Contemporary Hits/Top 40, Adult Contemp; *Hrs. of News Programming:* news progmg one hr wkly; *No. News Employees:* 1; *Target Audience:* 25-54; adults *Adv. Rates:* 90; 80; 85; 25
Philip Jonsson, President
Mike Kennedy, Programming Director
Chuck Gatlin, Promotions Manager

KPZK
01-01-1929; 1250 kHz AM; *Hrs Open:* 24; 2 kw-D, DA2; 1.2 kw-N, DA2; N34 42 5 W92 13 2
700 Wellington Hills Rd., Little Rock, AR 72211 US
(501) 401-0200; *Fax:* (501) 401-0374
www.power923.com
License: Little Rock, AR held by Radio License Holding CBC, LLC
Group Owner: Cumulus Media Inc.; (acq 9-19-97; grpsl).
Nat'l Reps: D & R Radio
Arbitron Metro Market: Little Rock, AR; *Format:* Urban Contemporary; *No. News Employees:* 1
Joe Booker, Programming Director

***KLRE-FM**
02-01-1973; 90.5 MHz FM; *Hrs Open:* 24; 40 kw; 246 ft.; N34 40 33.7 W92 19 7.5
2801 S University Avenue, Little Rock, AR 72204 US
(501) 569-8485; *Fax:* (501) 569-8488
License: Little Rock, Pulaski County, AR held by University of Arkansas.
Nat'l Network: PRI; NPR
Arbitron Metro Market: Little Rock, AR; *Format:* Talk; *Target Audience:* 35-54.
William Wagner, Operations Coordinator
Ben Fry, General Manager
Michael Hibblen, News Director
Mary Waldo, Development Director

KSSN
01-01-1966; 95.7 MHz FM; *Hrs Open:* 24; 92 kw; 1663 ft.; N34 47 57 W92 29 29
10800 Colonel Glenn Road, Little Rock, AR 72204 US
(501) 217-5000; *Fax:* (501) 228-9547
www.kssn.com
License: Little Rock, Pulaski County, AR held by CC Licenses LLC.
Group Owner: iHeartMedia; (acq 9-12-97; grpsl)
Nat'l Reps: Clear Channel
Arbitron Metro Market: Little Rock, AR; *Format:* Country; *Hrs. of News Programming:* news progmg 2 hrs wkly; *No. News Employees:* 1; *Target Audience:* 25-54.
Chad Heritage, Senior Vice President of Programming
Ron Collar, Market Manager
Keli Williams, Senior Vice President of Sales

KABZ
01-01-1967; 103.7 MHz FM; *Hrs Open:* 24; 100 kw; 1499 ft.; N34 47 56 W92 29 44
2400 Cottondale Lane, Little Rock, AR 72202 US
(501) 661-1037; *Fax:* (501) 664-5871
www.1037thebuzz.com; signalmedia.com
License: Little Rock, Pulaski County, AR held by Signal Media of Arkansas Inc.
Nat'l Network: ESPN Radio; Westwood One
Arbitron Metro Market: Little Rock, AR; *Format:* Talk; *Hrs. of News Programming:* news progmg 10 hrs wkly; *No. News Employees:* 1; *Target Audience:* 18-49.
Philip Jonsson, President
Steve Jonsson, General Manager/Vice President
Leslie Griffin, Sales Manager
Justin Acri, Programming Director
Matt Couch, Promotions Manager

***KUAR**
09-16-1986; 89.1 MHz FM; *Hrs Open:* 24; 63 kw; 1122 ft.; N34 47 49 W92 29 20
2801 S University Avenue, Little Rock, AR 72204 US
(501) 569-8485; *Fax:* (501) 569-8488
www.kuar.org
ben@kuar.org
License: Little Rock, Pulaski County, AR held by Board of Trustees of the University of Arkansas.
Nat'l Network: NPR; PRI
Arbitron Metro Market: Little Rock, AR; *Format:* Jazz, News, 62, Talk *Special Programming:* Folk 3 hrs wkly; *Hrs. of News Programming:* news progmg 86 hrs wkly; *No. News Employees:* 1; *Target Audience:* 35-54.
William Wagner, Operations Dir
Ben Fry, General Manager
Michael Hibblen, News Director
Mary Waldo, Development Director
Karen Tricot Steward, Web Communications Manager
Benita Norwood, Office Adminstrator

KURB
01-01-1993; 98.5 MHz FM; *Hrs Open:* 24; 100 kw; 1286 ft.; N34 47 56 W92 29 44
700 Wellington Hills Rd., Little Rock, AR 72211 US
(501) 401-0200; *Fax:* (501) 401-0349
www.b98.com
randy.cain@cumulus.com
License: Little Rock, AR held by Radio License Holding CBC, LLC
Group Owner: Cumulus Media Inc.
Arbitron Metro Market: Little Rock, AR; *Format:* Adult Contemp
Cindy Thompson, General Sales Mgr
Randy Cain, Programming Director

KDIS-FM
08-14-1992; 99.5 MHz FM; 3 kw; 312 ft.; N34 45 58 W92 17 38
13910 Cooper Orbit Cove, Little Rock, AR 72210 US
(501) 663-3300; *Fax:* (501) 663-3723
www.radiodisney.com
info@kdis.com
License: Little Rock, Pulaski County, AR held by Radio Disney Group LLC.
Group Owner: ABC Inc.; (acq 5-30-03; $2.56 million).
Arbitron Metro Market: Little Rock, AR; *Format:* Children
John Campbell, Station Manager
Lauren Eddins, Promotions Manager

Lonoke

KOLL
06-01-1982; 106.3 MHz FM; 50 kw; 492 ft.; N34 36 6 W91 51 40
1 Shackleford Drive, Suite 400, Little Rock, AR 72211 US
(501) 219-1919; *Fax:* (501) 225-4610
www.refreshingmix.com
License: Lonoke, Lonoke County, AR held by Crain Media Group LLC.
Group Owner: Crain Media Group LLC; (acq 2-1-2008; grpsl)
Arbitron Metro Market: Little Rock, AR; *Format:* Adult Contemp
Mike Horne, General Manager
Don Burns, Programming Director

Lowell

KMXF
06-30-1992; 101.9 MHz FM; *Hrs Open:* 24; 23 kw; 709 ft.; N36 26 28 W93 58 22
2049 East Joyce Boulevard, Suite 101, Fayetteville, AR 72703 US
(479) 442-0102; *Fax:* (479) 587-8255
www.hotmix1019.com
License: Lowell, Benton County, AR held by Capstar TX LLC
Group Owner: iHeartMedia; (acq 8-30-00; grpsl).
Wire Services: AP
Arbitron Metro Market: Fatetteville, AR; *Format:* Contemporary Hits/Top 40; *Hrs. of News Programming:* news progmg one hr wkly; *No. News Employees:* 1; *Target Audience:* 18-34; women; *Adv. Rates:* 45; 40; 40; 35
Dave Ashcraft, Senior Vice President of Programming
Judy Hudson, Business Manager

Magness

KBGB
01-01-2007; 105.7 MHz FM; 20 kw; Ant 426 ft; N35 17 20 W91 46 17
111 North Spring Street, Searcy, AR 72143
(501) 268-9700
License: Magness, White County, AR held by Crain Media Group LLC
Population Served: 1,284; *Arbitron Metro Market:* Deadwood, SD; *Format:* Adult Contemp
Mike Horne, General Manager

Magnolia

KVMA
04-01-1948; 630 kHz AM; *Hrs Open:* 24; 1 kw-D, NDD; 0.03 kw-N, ND1; N33 17 59 W93 13 57
Mailing Address: PO Box 430, Magnolia, AR 71753 US
Second Address: 131 S. Jackson, Magnolia, AR 71753
(880) 822-5862; *Fax:* (870) 234-5865
www.magnoliaradio.com
kvmakvmz@magnoliaradio.com
License: Magnolia, AR held by Noalmark Broadcasting Corp.
Group Owner: Noalmark Broadcasting Corp.; (acq 8-1-2005; $165,000)
Nat'l Network: ABC; *Regional Network:* Ark. Radio Net.
Arbitron Metro Market: Magnolia, AR; *Format:* Talk, Country
Special Programming: Farm 2 hrs wkly; *Hrs. of News Programming:* 20 hrs news progmg wkly; *Target Audience:* General.; *Adv. Rates:* 11; 8; 9; 5
William Nolan Jr., President
Paul Meacham, General Manager

Malvern

KBOK
08-01-1951; 1310 kHz AM; *Hrs Open:* Sunrise-sunset; 1 kw-D, NDD; N34 22 25 W92 49 52
1402 Hwy 270 West, Malvern, AR 72104 US
(501) 332-6981; *Fax:* (501) 332-6984
License: Malvern, AR held by Southwest Arkansas Media LLC
Group Owner: Southwest Arkansas Media LLC; (acq 9-4-2013; $35,000)
Regional Network: Ark. Radio Net.
Arbitron Metro Market: Little Rock, AR; *Format:* Country, News
Special Programming: Talk 6 hrs, gospel 8 hrs wkly; *Hrs. of News Programming:* News progmg 20 hrs wkly; *Target Audience:* General.
Malia Brown, General Manager

KIXV(FM)
04-01-1991; 101.5 MHz FM; *Hrs Open:* 24; 6 kw; Ant 322 ft; N34 28 24 W92 55 51
208 Buena Vista Rd., Hot Springs, AR 71913
(501) 525-4600; *Fax:* (501) 525-4344
License: Malvern, Hot Spring County, AR held by Noalmark Broadcasting Corp.
Group Owner: Noalmark Broadcasting Corp.; (acq 1-21-2003; $437,500).
Population Served: 120,000 *Format:* Easy Listening; *Hrs. of News Programming:* News progmg 3 hrs wkly; *Target Audience:* 35-60.
William Nolan Jr., President
Paul Meacham, General Manager
Paul Meacham, Sales Manager
Ron Chatman, Programming Director
Gina Angel, Traffic Manager

Mammoth Spring

KAMS
01-01-1956; 95.1 MHz FM; *Hrs Open:* 24; 100 kw; 650 ft.; N36 32 49 W91 25 47
Mailing Address: P. O. Box 193, Mammoth Spring, AR 72554 US
Second Address: N. Hwy. 63, Thayer, MO 65791
(417) 264-7211; *Fax:* (417) 264-7212
www.kkountry.com
License: Mammoth Spring, Fulton County, AR held by E-Communications LLC
Group Owner: E-Communications LLC; (acq 4-24-2008; $830,000 with KALM(AM) Thayer, MO)
Nat'l Network: ABC Daytime Direction; *Nat'l Reps:* Rgnl Reps
Regional Reps: Regional Reps
Arbitron Metro Market: Thayer, MT; *Format:* Country; *Hrs. of News Programming:* news progmg 11 hrs wkly; *No. News Employees:* 1; *Target Audience:* General.; *Adv. Rates:* :60-$30.50 :30-$20.50
Robert Eckman, President

Marianna

KAKJ
01-01-1994; 105.3 MHz FM; *Hrs Open:* 24; 6 kw; 328 ft.; N34 47 14 W90 46 3 *Rebroadcasts:* Rebroadcasts KCLT(FM) West Helena 90%
P.O. Box 2870, West Helena, AR 72390 US
(870) 572-9506; *Fax:* (870) 572-1845
www.force2radio.com
force2@sbcglobal.net
License: Marianna, Lee County, AR held by Raymond & L.T. Simes II.
Nat'l Network: ABC
Arbitron Metro Market: Helena-West Helena, AR; *Format:* Black; *No. News Employees:* 1; *Target Audience:* All ages.
Raymond Simes, President
L.T. Simes, Operations Dir
Raymond Simes, General Manager
Elaine Simes, Station Manager
Earnest Simes, Programming Director
Elaine Simes, Promotions Manager
Larry Evans, Operations Manager
Peter Turner,Promotions Director

Marion

KXHT
02-01-1986; 107.1 MHz FM; 2.75 kw; 479 ft.; N35 9 23 W90 5 46
188 South Bellevue, Suite 222, Memphis, TN 38104 US
(901) 375-9324; *Fax:* (901) 375-9331
www.flinn.com
License: Marion, Crittenden County, AR held by Flinn Broadcasting Corp.
Arbitron Metro Market: Memphis, TN; *Format:* Urban Contemporary
Lloyd Hetzer, General Manager
Duane Hargrove, Station Manager

Marked Tree

***KJBR**
01-01-1993; 93.7 MHz FM; *Hrs Open:* 24; 6 kw; 279 ft.; N35 34 34 W90 29 51
P.O. Box 540, Jonesboro, AR 72403 US
(916) 251-1600; *Fax:* (916) 251-1650
www.air1.com
info@air1.com
License: Marked Tree, Poinsett County, AR held by Educational Media Foundation.
Group Owner: EMF Broadcasting; (acq 11-1-01; $1.3 million with KJLV(FM) Hoxie).
Nat'l Network: Air 1
Format: Alternative, Christian
Mike Novak, President
David Pierce, Programming Director
Ed Lenane, News Director
Sam Wallington, Engineering Dir

Marshall

KBCN-FM
04-25-1983; 104.3 MHz FM; *Hrs Open:* 24; 100 kw; 820 ft; N35 52 17 W92 39 10
100 Blue Bird St., Harrison, AR 23225
(870) 743-1157; *Fax:* (870) 743-1168
ESPNArkansas.net
License: Marshall, Searcy County, AR held by Pearson Broadcasting of Marshall Inc.
Group Owner: Pearson Broadcasting; (acq 4-30-93; $450,000;
Special Programming: ESPN/Arkansas Razorbacks; *Adv. Rates:* Call for rates
Tommy Craft, Market Manager
Jamie Holt, General Manager
Dan Schauer, Sales Manager
Derek Ruscin, Programming Director

KCGS
05-24-1975; 960 kHz AM; *Hrs Open:* 24
Mailing Address: P.O. Box 178, Marshall, AR 72650 US
Second Address: 208 Battle St., Marshall, AR 72650
(870) 448-5567; *Fax:* (870) 448-5384
www.kcgs.com
License: Marshall, AR held by Southland Broadcasting Corp.
Nat'l Network: USA
Format: Gospel *Special Programming:* Bible answers live 7 hrs wkly; *Hrs. of News Programming:* news progmg 10 hrs wkly; *No. News Employees:* 2; *Target Audience:* General.; *Adv. Rates:* 84; 84; 84; na
Ronald Woolsey, President

***KCAV**
04-27-2009; 90.3 MHz FM; *Hrs Open:* 24/7; 0.057 kw; 676 ft.; N35 52 16 W92 39 10 *Rebroadcasts:* KCMH
US
(870) 425-2525; *Fax:* (870) 424-2626
www.kcmhradio.com
License: Marshall, Searcy County, AR held by Christian Broadcasting Group of Mountain Home Inc.
Nat'l Network: Moody; USA
Arbitron Metro Market: Marshall, AR; *Format:* Religious
Jim Holsted, President
Kyle Sexton, Station Manager
Michael Coolidge, Vice President
Lila Doyel, Secretary
Sondra McNelley, Receptionist

Marvell

***KLMK**
01-01-1999; 90.7 MHz FM; *Hrs Open:* 24; 50 kw; 486 ft.; N34 37 20 W90 58 44 *Rebroadcasts:* Rebroadcasts KLVR(FM) Middletown, CA 100%
113 Quapaw Trail, Helena, AR 72342 US
(916) 251-1600; *Fax:* (916) 251-1650
www.klove.com
License: Marvell, Phillips County, AR held by Educational Media Foundation.
Group Owner: EMF Broadcasting; (acq 8-28-2007; $300,000)
Nat'l Network: K-Love
Arbitron Metro Market: Marvell, AR; *Format:* Christian
Mike Novak, President

Maumelle

KHKN
01-01-1979; 94.9 MHz FM; *Hrs Open:* 24; 96 kw; 1,844 ft.; N34 26 31 W92 13 3
10800 Colonel Glenn Rd., Little Rock, AR 72204 US
(501) 217-5000; *Fax:* (501) 374-0808
www.949tomfm.com
tom@949tomfm.com
License: Maumelle, Pulaski County, AR held by CC Licenses LLC.
Group Owner: iHeartMedia; (acq 9-12-97; grpsl)
Arbitron Metro Market: Little Rock, AR; *Format:* Adult Contemp; *Target Audience:* 18-49.
Keli Williams, Senior Vice President of Sales

KWLR
01-01-1998; 96.9 MHz FM; 4.6 kw; 377 ft.; N34 53 33 W92 24 50
188 South Bellevue, Suite 222, Memphis, TN 38104 US
(501) 812 9700; *Fax:* (501) 812 9690
www.klove.com
kwlrword97@aol.com
License: Maumelle, Pulaski County, AR held by Flinn Broadcasting Corp.
Arbitron Metro Market: Memphis, TN; *Format:* Religious
Mike Novak, President
David Pierce, Promotions Manager
Ed Lenane, News Director

McGehee

KVSA
06-29-1953; 1220 kHz AM; *Hrs Open:* 6 AM-6:30 PM; 1 kw-D, ND1; 0.04 kw-N, ND1; N33 33 39 W91 23 6
P.O. Box 110, McGehee, AR 71654 US
(870) 222-4200(870) 538-5200; *Fax:* (870) 538-3389
kvsa1220@yahoo.com
License: McGehee, AR held by Southeast Arkansas Broadcasters Inc.
Regional Network: Ark. Radio Net; *Nat'l Reps:* Keystone (unwired net)
Arbitron Metro Market: McGehee, AR; *Format:* Variety/Diverse
Special Programming: Farm 5 hrs wkly; *Hrs. of News Programming:* 10 hrs wkly; *No. News Employees:* 2; *Adv. Rates:* 5.25; 5.25; 5.25; 5.25
Joyce Kinney, President
Dale Jones, Programming Director

Melbourne

***KLRM**
01-01-2008; 90.7 MHz FM; 7 kw vert; 617 ft.; N36 5 31 W92 15 46 *Rebroadcasts:* Rebroadcasts KLVR(FM) Middletown, CA 100%
88 Casey Jones Blvd., Jackson, TN 38305 US
(800) 877-5600; *Fax:* (916) 251-1650
www.klove.com
License: Melbourne, Izard County, AR held by Educational Media Foundation.
Group Owner: EMF Broadcasting; (acq 3-23-2007; grpsl)
Nat'l Network: K-Love
Arbitron Metro Market: Melbourne, AR; *Format:* Christian
Mike Novak, President
David Pierce, Programming Director

Mena

KQOR
01-01-2001; 105.3 MHz FM; 12.5 kw; 469 ft.; N34 32 42 W94 18 21
P.O. Box 311, Dequeen, AR 71832 US
www.classichitsradioonline.com
License: Mena, Polk County, AR held by Ouachita Broadcasting Inc.
Group Owner: Ouachita Broadcasting Inc.; (acq 3-8-99).
Arbitron Metro Market: Dallas, TX; *Format:* Oldies
Jay Bunyard, President
Dwight Douglas, General Manager
Dwight Douglas, Programming Director
Bevona Williams, Traffic Manager

KENA-FM
01-01-1969; 102.1 MHz FM; *Hrs Open:* 24; 12.5 kw; 469 ft.; N34 32 42 W94 18 21
Mailing Address: P.O. Box 311, Dequeen, AR 71832 US
Second Address: 1600 S. Reine St., Mena, AR 71953
(501) 394-1450; *Fax:* (501) 394-1459
License: Mena, Polk County, AR held by Ouachita Broadcasting Inc.
Group Owner: Ouachita Broadcasting Inc.
Nat'l Network: ABC
Format: Country; *Hrs. of News Programming:* news progmg 6 hrs wkly; *No. News Employees:* 1
Jay Bunyard, President
Dwight Douglas, General Manager
Dwight Douglas, Programming Director
Bevona Williams, Traffic Manager

KTTG
12-01-1994; 96.3 MHz FM; *Hrs Open:* 24; 47 kw; 1316 ft.; N34 41 24 W93 56 35
2937 Highway 71 North, Mean, AR 71593 US
(479) 394-6198; *Fax:* (479) 784-7290
www.espnradio.com
License: Mena, Polk County, AR held by Pearson Broadcasting of Mena Inc.
Group Owner: Pearson Broadcasting; (acq 1995; $175,000)
Nat'l Network: ESPN Radio; *Nat'l Reps:* ABC Radio Sales
Arbitron Metro Market: Mena, AR; *Format:* Sports, Talk; *No. News Employees:* 1; *Target Audience:* 18-49.; *Adv. Rates:* 14; 12; 14; 8
Max Pearson, CEO
Tommy Craft, General Manager
Dan Schauer, Sales Manager
Derek Ruscin, Programming Director
Betty LaClair, Traffic Manager

***K216FX**
91.1 MHz FM; 0.095 kW; N34 34 26 W94 14 3
820 N LaSalle Blvd, Chicago, IL 60610 USA
License: Mena, AR held by The Moody Bible Institute of Chicago
Group Owner: Moody Radio
Nat'l Network: Moody
Arbitron Metro Market: Mena, AR; *Format:* Christian

Monticello

KGPQ
05-01-1997; 99.9 MHz FM; 25 kw; 328 ft.; N33 43 49 W91 48 56
P.O. Box 308, Monticello, AR 71655 US
(870) 367-8525; *Fax:* (870) 367-9564
pinesradio@sbcglobal.net
License: Monticello, Drew County, AR held by Pines Broadcasting Inc.
Group Owner: Pines Broadcasting Inc.; (acq 3-14-2007; grpsl)
Format: Adult Contemp
Jimmy Sledge, President/General Manager

KHBM
04-01-1955; 1430 kHz AM; *Hrs Open:* 24; 1 kw-D, ND2; 0.03 kw-N, ND2; N33 36 18 W91 47 14
539 W. Gaines, Monticello, AR 71655 US
(870) 367-6854; *Fax:* (870) 367-9564
License: Monticello, AR held by Pines Broadcasting Inc.
Group Owner: Pines Broadcasting Inc.; (acq 3-14-2007; grpsl)
Regional Network: Ark. Radio Net.
Format: Contemporary Hits/Top 40; *Hrs. of News Programming:* news progmg 10 hrs wkly; *No. News Employees:* 1; *Target Audience:* General.
Jimmy Sledge, President

KHBM-FM
09-01-1967; 93.7 MHz FM; *Hrs Open:* 24; 23 kw; 417 ft.; N33 46 35 W91 43 2
539 W. Gaines, Monticello, AR 71655 US
(870) 367-6854; *Fax:* (870) 367-9564
License: Monticello, Drew County, AR held by Pines Broadcasting Inc.
Group Owner: Pines Broadcasting Inc.; (acq 3-14-2007; grpsl)
Regional Network: Ark. Radio Net.
Format: Contemporary Hits/Top 40, Adult Contemp; *Hrs. of News Programming:* news progmg 8 hrs wkly; *No. News Employees:* 1
Jimmy Sledge, President

Morrilton

KVOM
12-25-1952; 800 kHz AM; 0.25 kw-D, ND2; 0.04 kw-N, ND2; N35 9 28 W92 46 4
P.O. Box 541, Morrilton, AR 72110 US
(501) 354-2484; *Fax:* (501) 354-5629
www.kvom.com
newsroom@kvom.com
License: Morrilton, Conway County, AR held by EAB of Morrilton LLC

Group Owner: East Arkansas Broadcasters Inc.; (acq 8-21-2013).
Regional Network: Ark. Radio Net; *Nat'l Reps:* Christal; *Wire Services:* AP
Arbitron Metro Market: Morriton, AR; *Format:* Country; *Hrs. of News Programming:* news progmg 20 hrs wkly; *No. News Employees:* 2; *Target Audience:* General.; *Adv. Rates:* 14; 13; 14; 10
Aaron Thomas, Operations Manager
Rich Moellers, Market Manager
Rhonda Dilbeck, Director of Sales
Ashton Taylor, Programming Director
Eric Tyler, News and Sports Director

KVOM-FM
01-01-1981; 101.7 MHz FM; *Hrs Open:* 24; 6 kw; 205 ft.; N35 9 28 W92 46 4
P.O. Box 541, Morrilton, AR 72110 US
(501) 354-2484; *Fax:* (501) 354-5629
www.kvom.com
License: Morrilton, Conway County, AR held by EAB of Morrilton LLC
Group Owner: East Arkansas Broadcasters Inc.
Nat'l Reps: Christal
Arbitron Metro Market: Morrilton, AR; *Format:* Country; *Hrs. of News Programming:* news progmg 5 hrs wkly; *No. News Employees:* 2; *Target Audience:* General.
Aaron Thomas, Operations Manager
Rich Moellers, Market Manager
Rhonda Dilbeck, Director of Sales
Ashton Taylor, Programming Director
Eric Tyler, News and Sports Director

Mountain Home

***KCMH**
06-28-1988; 91.5 MHz FM; *Hrs Open:* 24; 26 kw vert; 472 ft.; N36 16 17 W92 25 20
P.O. Box 93, Mountain Home, AR 72653 US
(870) 425-2525; *Fax:* (870) 424-2626
www.kcmhradio.com
lorra@kcmhradio.com
License: Mountain Home, Baxter County, AR held by Christian Broadcasting Group of Mountain Home Inc.
Nat'l Network: Moody; USA
Arbitron Metro Market: Mountain Home, AR; *Format:* Religious; *Hrs. of News Programming:* News progmg 9 hrs wkly; *Target Audience:* General.
Jim Hewlett, President
Jesse Carraccio, General Manager
Eric Slusser, Programming Director
Sondra McNelley, Office & Traffic Manager

KOMT
10-25-1985; 107.5 MHz FM; *Hrs Open:* 24; 100 kw; 1017 ft.; N36 29 13 W92 29 39
2352 Highway 62 B, Mountain Home, AR 72653 US
(870) 492-6022; *Fax:* (870) 492-2137
www.twinlakesradio.com
radio@mountainhome.com
License: Mountain Home, Baxter County, AR held by MAC Partners.
Nat'l Network: ABC
Arbitron Metro Market: Fayetteville, AR; *Format:* Adult Contemp; *Target Audience:* 25-54; females
Morgan Dowdy, CEO
Stewart Brunner, General Manager
Bob Van Haaren, Programming Director
Kristen Speer, Marketing Specialist
Kim Garrett, Office Manager
Mary Vasiloff, PSA Director

KPFM
06-06-1984; 105.5 MHz FM; *Hrs Open:* 24; 19 kw; 797 ft.; N36 29 13 W92 29 39
US
(870) 492-6022; *Fax:* (870) 492-2137
www.twinlakesradio.com .
License: Mountain Home, Baxter County, AR held by Mountain Home Radio Station Inc.
Nat'l Network: ABC
Format: Country; *Hrs. of News Programming:* news progmg 15 hrs wkly; *No. News Employees:* 1; *Target Audience:* 24-54.
Morgan Dowdy, CEO
Stewart Brunner, Operations Dir
Bobby Van Haaren, Programming Director
Mary Vasiloff, PSA Director

KTLO
05-30-1953; 1240 kHz AM; *Hrs Open:* 24; 830 w
Mailing Address: P.O. Box 2010, Mountain Home, AR 72654 US
Second Address: 620 Hwy. 5 N., Mountain Home, AR 72653
(870) 425-3101; *Fax:* (870) 424-4314
www.ktlo.com
License: Mountain Home, Baxter County, AR held by KTLO LLC
Group Owner: KTLO LLC; (acq 5-1-91)
Arbitron Metro Market: Mountain Home, AR; *Format:* Country; *Hrs. of News Programming:* news progmg 11 hrs wkly; *No. News Employees:* 3; *Target Audience:* 18-55; general
Brad Haworth, Operations Manager
Bob Knight, General Manager
Danny Ward, Station Manager
Heather Loftis, Sales Manager
Sonny Elliot, News Director
Patty Sindlinger, Traffic Director
Tim Tibbs, Production Manager

KTLO-FM
01-11-1971; 97.9 MHz FM; 30 kw; 419 ft.; N36 20 55 W92 23 59
Mailing Address: P.O. Box 2010, Mountain Home, AR 72654 US
Second Address: 620 Hwy. 5 N., Mountain Home, AR 72653
(870) 425-3101; *Fax:* (870) 424-4314
www.ktlo.com
License: Mountain Home, Baxter County, AR held by KTLO LLC
Group Owner: KTLO LLC
Regional Network: Ark. Radio Net.
Arbitron Metro Market: Mountain Home, AR; *Format:* Adult Contemp, Easy Listening; *Target Audience:* 40 plus.
Brad Haworth, Operations Manager
Bob Knight, General Manager
Danny Ward, Station Manager
Heather Loftis, Sales Manager
Sonny Elliot, News Director
Patty Sindlinger, Traffic Director
Tim Tibbs, Production Manager

Mountain Pine

KLXQ
01-01-1996; 101.9 MHz FM; 3.1 kw; 407 ft.; N34 26 56 W93 15 59
125 Corporate Terrace, Hot Springs, AR 71913 US
(501) 525-9700; *Fax:* (501) 525-9739
www.myhotsprings.com
info@usstations.com
License: Mountain Pine, Garland County, AR held by US Stations LLC.
Group Owner: US Stations LLC; (acq 2-1-2005; grpsl)
Arbitron Metro Market: Mountain Pine, AR; *Format:* Classic Rock; *Target Audience:* 25-54.
Gary Terrell, General Manager
Paul Swint, Director Of Sales
Craig Dale, Programming Director
Tom Duke, Music Director

Mountain View

KWOZ
12-01-1981; 103.3 MHz FM; 100 kw; 988 ft.; N35 47 6 W91 57 44
Ridgeview Drive, N. County Road 269, Mountain View, AR 72560 US
(870) 793-4196; *Fax:* (870) 793-5222
www.arkansas103.com
arkansas103@hotmail.com
License: Mountain View, Stone County, AR held by WRD Entertainment Inc.
Group Owner: WRD Entertainment Inc.
Nat'l Network: ABC; *Wire Services:* AP
Arbitron Metro Market: Batesville, AR; *Format:* Country; *Hrs. of News Programming:* news progmg 3 hrs wkly; *No. News Employees:* 2; *Target Audience:* 18-54.
Matt Johnson, General Sales Mgr
Ken Loggains, Programming Director
Gena Ries

Murfreesboro

KMTB
05-18-1983; 99.5 MHz FM; *Hrs Open:* 24; 25 kw; 262 ft.; N34 0 41 W93 52 3
1513 S. Fourth St., Nashville, AR 71852 US
(870) 845-3601; *Fax:* (870) 845-3680
www.southwestarkansasradio.com
gm@southwestarkansasradio.com
License: Murfreesboro, Pike County, AR held by ARKLATEX Radio Inc.
Group Owner: ARKLATEX Radio Inc.; acq 8-28-2001; grpsl).
Format: Country
Brent Pinkerton, General Manager

Nashville

KBHC
05-01-1959; 1260 kHz AM; 0.5 kw-D, NDD; N33 55 45 W93 51 1
1513 S. Fourth St., Nashville, AR 71852 US
(870) 845-3601; *Fax:* (870) 845-3680
www.southwestarkansasradio.com
gm@southwestarkansasradio.com
License: Nashville, AR held by ARKLATEX Radio Inc.
Group Owner: ARKLATEX Radio Inc.; (acq 8-23-2001; grpsl).
Regional Network: Ark. Radio Net; *Nat'l Reps:* Keystone (unwired net)
Arbitron Metro Market: Nashville, AR; *Format:* Tejano
Brent Pinkerton, General Manager

KNAS
02-14-1977; 105.5 MHz FM; 6 kw; 203 ft.; N34 0 41 W93 52 3
1513 S. Fourth St., Nashville, AR 71852 US
(870) 845-3601; *Fax:* (870) 845-3680
www.southwestarkansasradio.com
gm@southwestarkansasradio.com
License: Nashville, Howard County, AR held by ARKLATEX Radio Inc.
Group Owner: ARKLATEX Radio Inc.
Format: Sports
Brent Pinkerton, General Manager

***KSSW**
01-01-2003; 96.9 MHz FM; 6 kw; 328 ft.; N34 0 41 W93 52 3
P O Box 989, Blytheville, AR 72316 US
(225)768-3224
www.jsm.org
onair@jsm.org
License: Nashville, Howard County, AR held by Family Worship Center Church Inc.
Group Owner: Family Worship Center Church Inc.; (acq 9-15-2005; $400,000)
Arbitron Metro Market: Texarkana, TX; *Format:* Religious
Van Michael, President
John Santiago, General Manager

***KNLL**
01-01-2008; 90.5 MHz FM; 100 kw vert; 481 ft.; N33 30 17 W93 34 47 *Rebroadcasts:* Rebroadcasts WAFR(FM) Tupelo, MS 100%
P.O. Box 3206, Tupelo, MS 38803 US
(662) 844-8888; *Fax:* (662) 842-6791
www.afr.net
faq@afa.net
License: Nashville, Howard County, AR held by American Family Association.
Group Owner: American Family Radio
Nat'l Network: American Family Radio
Arbitron Metro Market: Nashville, AR; *Format:* Christian
Tim Wildmon, President
Donald Wildmon, Founder
Buddy Smith, Sr VP
Ed Vitagliano, Exec VP
Randy Sharp, Director Of Special Projects
Meeke Addison, Director Of Communications
Abraham Hamilton III, General Counsel

Newark

***KLLN**
01-01-1985; 90.9 MHz FM; 4 kw; 456 ft.; N35 43 25 W91 26 40
1502 N. Hill Street, Newark, AR 72562 US
(870) 799-8969; *Fax:* (870) 799-8647
www.klln.fm
kllnfm@yahoo.com
License: Newark, Independence County, AR held by Newark Public School.
Arbitron Metro Market: Jonesboro, AR; *Format:* Gospel
Fred Ahlborn, General Manager

Newport

KNBY
10-12-1949; 1280 kHz AM; *Hrs Open:* 24; 1 kw-D, ND2; 0.088 kw-N, ND2; N35 36 38 W91 15 2
Mailing Address: P. O. Box 989, Blytheville, AR 72316 US
Second Address: 2025 McCarty Dr., Newport, AR 72112
(870) 523-5891; *Fax:* (870) 523-2967
License: Newport, AR held by Newport Broadcasting Co.
Group Owner: Sudbury Services Inc.
Format: News, News/Talk, 86; *Adv. Rates:* 9; 8; 9; 6
Harold Sudbury, President
Dale Turner, General Manager
Doug Holt, Programming Director

KOKR
09-01-1966; 96.7 MHz FM; 40 kw; 548 ft.; N35 29 16 W91 26 13
Mailing Address: P. O. Box 989, Blytheville, AR 72316 US
Second Address: 401 S. Spring Street, Searcy, AR 72143
(870) 523-5891; *Fax:* (870) 523_2967
License: Newport, Jackson County, AR
Group Owner: Sudbury Services Inc.
Format: Country; *Adv. Rates:* 10; 9; 10; 8
Dale Turner, General Manager

North Crossett

KWLT
05-01-1995; 102.7 MHz FM; *Hrs Open:* 24; 25 kw; 328 ft.; N33 8 5 W91 56 49
P.O. Box 697, Crossett, AR 71635 US
(870) 364-2181; *Fax:* (870) 364-2183
www.crossettradio.com
License: North Crossett, Ashley County, AR held by South Ark Broadcasting Inc.
Nat'l Network: ABC
Arbitron Metro Market: Crosset, AR; *Format:* Classic Rock; *Hrs. of News Programming:* News progmg 2 hrs wkly; *Target Audience:* General.; *Adv. Rates:* 14; 14; 14; 14
Kevin Medlin, President
Barry Medlin, General Sales Mgr

North Little Rock

KDXE
05-09-1957; 1380 kHz AM; *Hrs Open:* 24; 5 kw-D, DA2; 2.5 kw-N, DA2; N34 52 49 W92 14 1
10301 N. Rodney Parham Road, Suite C6, Little Rock, AR 72227 US
(501) 819-0625; *Fax:* (501) 835-4992
License: North Little Rock, AR held by Simmons Austin, LS LLC.
Group Owner: NC Communications Group
Nat'l Network: ESPN Radio
Arbitron Metro Market: Little Rock, AR; *Format:* Spanish *Special Programming:* 3 hrs wkly; *Hrs. of News Programming:* 2 hrs; *No. News Employees:* 1; *Target Audience:* 25-54; men; *Adv. Rates:* 12; 10; 12;10

Ola

KARV-FM
01-01-1998; 101.3 MHz FM; 0.74 kw; 909 ft.; N34 59 34 W93 11 35
201 West Second, Russellville, AR 72801 US
(479) 968-1184; *Fax:* (479) 967-5278
karv-kyel@yahoo.com
License: Ola, Yell County, AR held by KERM Inc.
Group Owner: KERM Inc.
Arbitron Metro Market: Ola, AR; *Format:* News, News/Talk, 86; *Hrs. of News Programming:* news progmg 20 hrs wkly; *No. News Employees:* 2; *Adv. Rates:* 120; 108; 108; 108
Kermit Womack, President
Chris Womack, General Manager

Osceola

KQMJ(FM)
09-01-1996; 107.3 MHz FM; 1.6 kw; Ant 335 ft; N35 45 59 W89 55 43
Box 989, Blytheville, AR 72316
(870) 762-2093; *Fax:* (870) 763-8459
License: Osceola, Mississippi County, AR held by Phoenix Broadcasting Group Inc.
Group Owner: Sudbury Services Inc.
Arbitron Metro Market: Memphis, TN; *Format:* Contemporary Hits/Top 40, Adult Contemp
Noel Showers, Programming Director

Ozark

KDYN
02-05-1969; 1540 kHz AM; *Hrs Open:* Sunrise-sunset; 0.5 kw-D, ND2; 0.001 kw-N, ND2; N35 29 16 W93 48 43
P. O. Box 1086, Ozark, AR 72949 US
(479) 667-4567; *Fax:* (479) 667-5214
www.kdyn.com
kdyn@centurytel.net
License: Ozark, AR held by Ozark Communications Inc.
Regional Network: Ark. Radio Net.
Arbitron Metro Market: Ozark, AR; *Format:* Country; *Hrs. of News Programming:* news progmg 20 hrs wkly; *No. News Employees:* 1; *Target Audience:* General.; *Adv. Rates:* 10; 10; 10; 7
Marc Dietz, President

KCYT
10-02-1980; 96.7 MHz FM; *Hrs Open:* 24; 10 kw; 486 ft.; N35 29 9.11 W93 53 29.49
Mailing Address: Highway 64, East Ozark, AR 72949 US
Second Address: 9331 Puddin Ridge Rd., Ozark, AR 72949
(479) 667-4567; *Fax:* (479) 667-5214
www.kdyn.com
kdyn@centurytel.net
License: Ozark, Franklin County, AR held by Hog Radio
Arbitron Metro Market: Ozark, AR
Jay Bunyard, President

Pangburn

KSMD
11-02-2003; 99.1 MHz FM; *Hrs Open:* 24; 25 kw; 328 ft.; N35 23 43 W91 44 17
P.O. Box 1488, Searcy, AR 72145 US
(501) 268-7123; *Fax:* (501) 279-2900
License: Pangburn, White County, AR held by Crain Media Group LLC
Group Owner: Crain Media Group LLC; acq 10-15-02; $180,000 for CP).
Arbitron Metro Market: Pangburn, AR; *Format:* News, News/Talk, 86
J.R. Runyon, Operations Dir

Paragould

KDRS
01-01-1947; 1490 kHz AM; *Hrs Open:* 24; 1 kw-U; N36 02 56 W90 27 44
400 Tower Dr., Paragould, AR 72401
(870) 236-7627; *Fax:* (870) 239-4583
dina@kdrs.com
License: Paragould, Greene County, AR held by MOR Media Inc.
Regional Network: Ark. Radio Net.
Population Served: 50,000 *Hrs. of News Programming:* News progmg 7 hrs wkly; *Adv. Rates:* 12; 12; 12; 12
Dina Mason, President
Brian Osborn, Operations & Programming Director
Leisa Rae, PSA & Traffic Manager

KDRS-FM
03-05-1983; 107.1 MHz FM; *Hrs Open:* 24; 3 kw; 410 ft; N36 01 48 W90 35 49
400 Tower Dr., Paragould, AR 72401
(870) 236-7627; *Fax:* (870) 239-4583
neajackfm.com
License: Paragould, Greene County, AR held by MOR Media Inc.
Target Audience: 18-44.; *Adv. Rates:* Same as AM
Dina Mason, General Manager
Dina Mason, General Sales Mgr
Brian Osborn, Programming Director
Leisa Rae, Public Service Director
Leisa Rae, Traffic Manager

Paris

KERX
05-01-1981; 95.3 MHz FM; 50 kw; 459 ft.; N35 17 13 W94 2 51
1912 Church Street, Barling, AK 72923 US
(479) 484-7285; *Fax:* (479) 784-7390
www.953maxfm.com/index2/
tommy@pearsonbroadcasting.com
License: Paris, Logan County, AR held by Pearson Broadcasting of Paris Inc.
Group Owner: Pearson Broadcasting; (acq 10-18-93; $42,000; *Wire Services:* AP
Arbitron Metro Market: Paris, AR; *Format:* Rock/AOR *Special Programming:* Blues 3 hrs wkly; *Target Audience:* 18-44; men & women; *Adv. Rates:* 16; 14; 16; 10
Tommy Craft, General Manager
Dan Schauer, Sales Manager
Jay James, Programming Director

Pearcy

KLBL
11-18-1991; 104.5 MHz FM; *Hrs Open:* 24; 3 kw; 407 ft.; N34 26 56 W93 15 59
P.O. Box 831, Arkadelphia, AR 71923 US
(501) 525-9700; *Fax:* (501) 525-9739
www.myhotsprings.com
pobriant@usstations.com
License: Pearcy, Garland County, AR held by US Stations LLC.
Group Owner: US Stations LLC
Nat'l Network: CBS Radio *Regional Reps:* Rgnl Reps
Arbitron Metro Market: Hot Springs, AR; *Format:* Country; *Hrs. of News Programming:* News progmg 7 hrs wkly; *Target Audience:* 25-50; general; *Adv. Rates:* 11.77; 11.77; 11.77; 11.77

Gary Terrel, General Manager
Paul Swint, General Sales Mgr
Craig Dale, Programming & News Director

Piggott

KBOA-FM
10-15-1983; 105.5 MHz FM; *Hrs Open:* 24; 6 kW; 299 ft.; N36 19 50 W90 7 24
5500 Poplar Ave, Suite 1, Memphis, TN 38119 USA
(901) 685-3993; *Fax:* (901) 685-3995
kboaradio.com/magic-105.html
License: Piggott, Clay County, AR held by Pollack Broadcasting Co.
Group Owner: Pollack Broadcasting Co.
Arbitron Metro Market: Piggott, AR; *Format:* Adult Contemp; *No. News Employees:* 1; *Target Audience:* 18-55; young adults, young professionals, farmers

Pine Bluff

***KCAT**
04-01-1963; 1340 kHz AM; 1 kw-U, ND1; N34 12 47 W92 1 53
P.O. Box 8808, Pine Bluff, AR 71601 US
(870) 534-5001; *Fax:* (870) 534-7985
www.kcatam.com
april@lordradio.com
License: Pine Bluff, AR held by Mondy Burke Smith Broadcasting Network
Arbitron Metro Market: Pine Bluff, AR; *Format:* Gospel; *Target Audience:* 18-55.; *Adv. Rates:* 20; 20; 20; 20
Elijah Mondy, General Manager
Darren Smith, General Sales Mgr
April Mondy, Programming Director
Belinda Mondy, News Director

KIPR
01-01-1963; 92.3 MHz FM; 100 kw; Ant 938 ft; N34 22 12 W92 10 07
700 Wellington Hills Rd., Little Rock, AR 72211 US
(501) 401-0200; *Fax:* (501) 401-0374
www.power923.com
License: Pine Bluff, AR held by Radio License Holding CBC, LLC
Group Owner: Cumulus Media Inc.; (acq 7-29-97; grpsl).
Population Served: 200,000; *Arbitron Metro Market:* Little Rock, AR; *Format:* Urban Contemporary; *Target Audience:* 18-44.
Joe Booker, Programming Director

***KUAP**
01-01-1995; 89.7 MHz FM; 50 kw; 268 ft.; N34 14 33 W92 1 2
P.O. Box 4145, Little Rock, AR 71601 US
(870) 575-8000; *Fax:* (870) 575-4666
www.uapb.edu
webadmin@uapb.edu
License: Pine Bluff, Jefferson County, AR held by Board of Trustees of Univ. of Arkansas.
Arbitron Metro Market: Pine Bluff, AR; *Format:* Jazz, Smooth Jazz
Finley Hill, Station Manager

Pocahontas

KPOC
11-15-1950; 1420 kHz AM; *Hrs Open:* 24
Mailing Address: P. O. Box 508, Pocahontas, AR 72455 US
Second Address: One Radio Dr., Pocahontas, AR 72455
(870) 892-5234; *Fax:* (870) 892-5235
info@kpoc.com
License: Pocahontas, AR held by Combined Media Group Inc.
Group Owner: Combined Media Group Inc.; (acq 12-20-2001; $410,000 with co-located FM).
Regional Network: Ark. Radio Net.
Format: Adult Contemp *Special Programming:* Farm 10 hrs wkly; *No. News Employees:* 1; *Target Audience:* 25-54; general
Timothy Scott, President
Larry Caldwell, Chief Engineer

KPOC-FM
04-25-1969; 104.1 MHz FM; *Hrs Open:* 24; 6 kw; 144 ft.; N36 16 38 W90 57 16
P. O. Box 508, Pocahontas, AR 72455 US
(870) 892-5234; *Fax:* (870) 892-5235
info@kpoc.com
License: Pocahontas, Randolph County, AR
Format: Adult Contemp

Prarie Grove

KMCK-FM
01-01-1947; 105.7 MHz FM; 100 kw; 476 ft; N36 11 07 W94 17 49
4209 N Frontage Road, Fayetteville, AR 53202

RADIO - U.S.

(479) 521-5566; *Fax:* (479) 521-0751
www.power1057.com
License: Prarie Grove, Benton County, AR held by Cumulus Licensing Corp.
Group Owner: Cumulus Media Inc.; (acq 12-10-98; grpsl)
Nat'l Reps: Christal
Population Served: 300,000; *Arbitron Metro Market:* Fayetteville (Northwest Arkansas), AR; *Target Audience:* 18-49; contemp adults
Dale Daniels, General Manager
Joe Kelley, Programming Director
Anita Cowan, Promotions Manager

Prescott

KTPA
12-01-1959; 1370 kHz AM; 1 kw-D, NDD; N33 47 36 W93 23 42
Mailing Address: P.O. Box 424, Hope, AR 71801 US
Second Address: 1600 So. Elm St., Hope, AZ 71802
(870) 777-8868(870) 777-8869; *Fax:* (870) 777-8888
khpafm@supercountry105.com
License: Prescott, AR held by Newport Broadcasting Co.
Group Owner: Sudbury Services Inc.; (acq 5-14-66)
Regional Network: Ark. Radio Net.
Arbitron Metro Market: Hope, AR; *Format:* Gospel
Robert Hill, General Manager
Sonya Odom, General Sales Mgr

Rogers

KAMO-FM
01-01-1971; 94.3 MHz FM; *Hrs Open:* 24; 25 kw; 692 ft.; N36 26 30 W93 58 26
111 East Kilbourn Avenue, Suite 2700, Milwaukee, WI 53202 US
(479) 521-5566; *Fax:* (479) 521-0751
www.us94.com
dale.daniels@cumulus.com
License: Rogers, Benton County, AR held by Cumulus Licensing Corp.
Group Owner: Cumulus Media Inc.; (acq 12-10-98; grpsl)
Arbitron Metro Market: Fayetteville, AZ; *Format:* Oldies
Joe Conway, General Manager
Dan Hinschell, Programming Director

KFFK
09-16-1954; 1390 kHz AM; *Hrs Open:* 24
70 North East Street, Suite 100, Fayetteville, AR 72701 US
(479) 582-3776; *Fax:* (479) 571-0995
License: Rogers, AR held by Butler Broadcasting Co. LLC
Nat'l Network: Fox Sports
Arbitron Metro Market: Fayetteville (Northwest Arkansas), AR; *Format:* News, News/Talk, 82, Talk; *Target Audience:* 25-54.
Steve Butler, President
Steve Bulter, General Manager
Dave Jackson, Programming Director

KURM
11-09-1979; 790 kHz AM; *Hrs Open:* 5 AM-11 PM; 5 kw-D, DAN; 0.5 kw-N, DAN; N36 18 10 W94 6 47
113 E. New Hope, Rogers, AR 72758 US
(479) 633-0790; *Fax:* (479) 631-9711
www.kurm.net
License: Rogers, AR held by KERM Inc.
Group Owner: KERM Inc.
Nat'l Network: CBS; *Regional Network:* Okla. News Net.
Arbitron Metro Market: Rogers, AR; *Format:* Variety/Diverse
Special Programming: Farm 10 hrs wkly; *Hrs. of News Programming:* news progmg 15 hrs wkly; *No. News Employees:* 2; *Target Audience:* 35

Russellville

KARV
02-25-1947; 610 kHz AM; *Hrs Open:* 24; 1 kw-D, DA2; 0.5 kw-N, DA2; N35 17 56 W93 9 9
201 West Second, Russellville, AR 72801 US
(479) 968-1184; *Fax:* (479) 967-5278
karv-kyet@yahoo.com
License: Russellville, AR held by KERM Inc.
Group Owner: KERM Inc.; acq 10-22-92; $250,000;
Nat'l Network: CBS; *Regional Network:* Ark. Radio Net.
Arbitron Metro Market: Ola, AR; *Format:* Sports, Talk *Special Programming:* Farm 5 hrs wkly; *Hrs. of News Programming:* news progmg 38 hrs wkly; *No. News Employees:* 4; *Target Audience:* 35 plus; affluentadults
Kermit Womack, President
Chris Womack, General Manager
Diane Womack, Sales Manager

*KMTC
06-01-1987; 91.1 MHz FM; *Hrs Open:* 24; 360 w; 62 ft; N35 18 11 W93 08 42
Mailing Address: Box 570, Russellville, AR 72811
Second Address: 305 Lake Front Dr., Russellville, AR 72802
(479) 967-7400; *Fax:* (479) 967-7894
License: Russellville, Pope County, AR held by Russellville Educational Broadcasting Foundation.
Nat'l Network: USA
Population Served: 30,000 *Hrs. of News Programming:* News progmg one hr wkly; *Target Audience:* 18-55; Christian
Tom Underhill, CEO
Debbie Bewley, General Manager
Melissa Krueger, Operations Manager
Jim Alexander, Chief Engineer

KWKK
09-29-1985; 100.9 MHz FM; *Hrs Open:* 24; 6 kw; 328 ft.; N35 17 37 W93 10 39
2705 E. Pkwy., Russellville, AR 72802 US
(479) 968-6816; *Fax:* (479) 968-2946
www.riverhitskwkk.com
License: Russellville, Pope County, AR held by EAB of Russellville LLC
Group Owner: East Arkansas Broadcasters Inc.; (acq 8-21-2013).
Nat'l Network: ABC; *Nat'l Reps:* Christal; *Wire Services:* AP
Arbitron Metro Market: Russellville, AR; *Format:* Adult Contemp
Special Programming: Arkansas Tech University Sports; *Hrs. of News Programming:* news progmg 5 hrs wkly; *No. News Employees:* 1; *Target Audience:* 18-49; young adults
Aaron Thomas, Operations Manager
Rich Moellers, Market Manager
Rhonda Dilbeck, Director of Sales

*KXRJ
04-03-1989; 91.9 MHz FM; *Hrs Open:* 24; 0.1 kw horiz; -92 ft.; N35 17 47 W93 8 18
Hwy 7 North, Russellville, AR 72801 US
(479) 964-0889 (479) 964-3282; *Fax:* (479) 498-6024
License: Russellville, Pope County, AR held by Arkansas Tech University.
Format: Jazz, Variety/Diverse *Special Programming:* Educ, jazz 15 hrs wkly; *Hrs. of News Programming:* News progmg 10 hrs wkly; *Target Audience:* General.
Anthony Caton, Director of Broadcasting

Salem

KHOM
09-01-1977; 100.9 MHz FM; 50 kw; 492 ft.; N36 35 38 W91 40 3
Post Office Box 107, West Plains, MO 65775 US
(417) 255-2548; *Fax:* (417) 255-2907
khom@centurytel.net
License: Salem, Fulton County, AR held by E-Communications LLC
Group Owner: E-Communications LLC; (acq 12-14-99).
Nat'l Network: ABC
Arbitron Metro Market: West Plains, MO; *Format:* Country; *No. News Employees:* 1; *Target Audience:* 35-54; adults

Searcy

KWCK
08-25-1951; 1300 kHz AM; 5 kw-D, NDD; N35 15 27 W91 43 49
100 East Arch, Searcy, AR 72143 US
(501) 268-7123; *Fax:* (501) 279-2900
www.kwck999.com
larrynokes@crainmedia.com
License: Searcy, AR held by Crain Media Group LLC.
Group Owner: Crain Media Group LLC; (acq 10-21-2002; grpsl).
Arbitron Metro Market: Searcy, AR; *Format:* Talk *Special Programming:* Farm 10 hrs wkly; *Target Audience:* 25-64.
Mike Horne, General Sales Manager/General Manager
Heath Shelby, Program Director/Music Director
Bill Bumpass, News Director
Tonya Moore, Traffic Manager

KWCK-FM
10-01-1973; 99.9 MHz FM; *Hrs Open:* 24; 50 kw; 492 ft.; N35 26 50 W91 56 52
Post Office Box 1300, Searcy, AR 72143 US
(501) 268-7123; *Fax:* (501) 279-2900
www.kwck999.com
License: Searcy, White County, AR
Group Owner: Crain Media Group LLC
Arbitron Metro Market: Searcy, AR; *Format:* Country; *Hrs. of News Programming:* news progmg 3 hrs wkly; *No. News Employees:* 1; *Target Audience:* 18-49.
Mike Horne, General Manager
Mike Horne, General Sales Mgr
Heath Shelby, Program Director/ Music Director
Bill Bumpass, News Director
Tonya Moore, Traffic Manager

Sheridan

*KANX
01-01-1999; 91.1 MHz FM; 40 kw; 522 ft.; N34 17 26 W92 29 36
P.O. Box 3206, Tupelo, MS 38803 US
(662) 844-8888; *Fax:* (662) 842-6791
www.afr.net
faq@afa.net
License: Sheridan, Grant County, AR held by American Family Association.
Group Owner: American Family Radio
Arbitron Metro Market: Tupelo, MO; *Format:* Religious
Tim Wildmon, President
Donald Wildmon, Founder
Buddy Smith, Sr. VP
Ed Vitagliano, Executive VP
Randy Sharp, Director Of Special Projects
Meeke Addison, Director Of Communications
Abraham Hamilton III, General Counsel & PublicPolicy

KARN-FM
11-01-1984; 102.9 MHz FM; *Hrs Open:* 24; 50 kw; 492 ft.; N34 32 6 W92 24 33
700 Willington Hills Road, Little Rock, AK 72211 US
(501) 401-0200; *Fax:* (501) 401-0387
www.sportsanimal920.com
License: Sheridan, Grant County, AR
Group Owner: Cumulus Media Inc.
Arbitron Metro Market: Little Rock, AR; *Format:* News, Talk; *Hrs. of News Programming:* news progmg 2 hrs wkly; *No. News Employees:* 1; *Target Audience:* 35-64.
Rich Nickols, General Sales Mgr
Dave Elswick, Programming Director
Jean Woods, Traffic Manager

Sherwood

KMTL
10-31-1983; 760 kHz AM; 10 kw-D, NDD; N34 49 34 W92 12 19
P.O. Box 6460, North Little Rock, AR 72124 US
(501) 835-1554
License: Sherwood, AR held by George V. Domerese.
Arbitron Metro Market: Little Rock, AR; *Format:* Religious
George Domerese, General Manager
Tom Rusk, Chief Engineer

KOKY
01-01-1956; 102.1 MHz FM; 4.1 kw; 387 ft; N34 44 38 W92 16 32
700 Wellington Hills Rd., Little Rock, AR 72211 US
(501) 401-0200; *Fax:* (501) 401-0374
License: Sherwood, AR held by The Last Bastion Station Trust, LLC
Group Owner: The Last Bastion Station Trust, LLC; (acq 10-23-97; grpsl).
Population Served: 525,000; *Arbitron Metro Market:* Little Rock, AR; *Format:* Urban Contemporary

Siloam Springs

*KLRC
10-01-1981; 9MHz FM; 3.1 kw; 453 ft.; N36 11 28 W94 33 58
2000 West Univ. Street, Siloam Springs, AR 72761 US
(479) 524-7101; *Fax:* (479) 524-7451
www.klrc.com
License: Siloam Springs, Benton County, AR held by John Brown University.
Nat'l Network: USA; *Wire Services:* UPI
Arbitron Metro Market: Fatetteville, AR; *Format:* Christian, Religious; *Hrs. of News Programming:* News progmg 2 hrs wkly; *Target Audience:* 25-49.
Charles Pollard, President
Sean Sawatzky, General Manager
Mark Michaels, Programming Director

KUOA
04-12-1923; 1290 kHz AM; *Hrs Open:* 24
2250 West Sunset Avenue, Suite 3, Springdale, AR 72762 US
(479) 303-2034; *Fax:* (479) 303-2037
www.hogsportsradio.com
dan@hogsportsradio.com
License: Siloam Springs, AR held by Hog Radio Inc.
Arbitron Metro Market: Siloam Springs, AR; *Format:* Sports
Jay Bunyard, President
Dan Storrs, General Manager
Lori Storrs, Local Sales Manager
Joe Morris, Production Director / Show Producer
Colleen Masters, Traffic Director

Springdale

KXNA
09-19-1968; 104.9 MHz FM; 2.75 kw; 486 ft.; N36 10 48 W94 5 7
70 North East Street, Suite 100, Fayetteville, AR 72701 US
(479) 582-3776; *Fax:* (479) 571-0995
License: Springdale, Washington County, AR held by Bulter Broadcasting LLC.
Nat'l Reps: Christal
Arbitron Metro Market: Fayetteville (Northwest AR), AR; *Format:* Alternative
Steve Butler, General Manager

KYNG
07-15-1966; 1590 kHz AM
4209 Frontage Road, Fayetteville, AR 72703 US
(479) 521-5566; *Fax:* (479) 521-0751
License: Springdale, AR held by Cumulus Licensing Corp.
Group Owner: Cumulus Media Inc.; (acq 12-10-98; grpsl)
Arbitron Metro Market: Springdale, AR; *Target Audience:* 18-54.
Dale Daniels, General Manager
Ray Daugherty, Sales Manager
Miguel Ramirez, Programming Director
Meghan Mathis, Traffic Manager

Stamps

KZHE
10-01-1980; 100.5 MHz FM; *Hrs Open:* 24; 50 kw; 492 ft.; N33 28 34 W93 16 23
406 West Union, Magnolia, AR 71753 US
(870) 234-7790; *Fax:* (870) 234-7791
www.kzhe.com
kzhe@kzhe.com
License: Stamps, Lafayette County, AR held by A-1 Communications Inc.
Arbitron Metro Market: Stamps, AR; *Format:* Country *Special Programming:* Gospel 8 hrs wkly; *Target Audience:* 25-54.
Troy Alphin, President
Sharon Alphin, Operations Dir
Dave Sehon, General Manager

Stuttgart

KWAK
05-15-1948; 1240 kHz AM; *Hrs Open:* 24
P.O. Box 910, Stuttgart, AR 72160 US
(870) 673-1595; *Fax:* (870) 673-8445
kdew973@yahoo.com
License: Stuttgart, AR held by Arkansas County Broadcasters Inc.
Group Owner: Arkansas County Broadcasters Inc.
Arbitron Metro Market: Stuttgart, AR; *Format:* News *Special Programming:* Farm 6 hrs wkly; *No. News Employees:* 1; *Target Audience:* General.
Bobby Caldwell, President
Scott Siler, General Manager
Mitch Mahan, Programming Director
Scott Shannon, News Director

KWAK-FM
12-15-1987; 105.5 MHz FM; *Hrs Open:* 24; 2.7 kw; 344 ft.; N34 25 52 W91 26 8
P.O. Box 910, Stuttgart, AR 72160 US
(870) 673-1595; *Fax:* (870) 673-8445
kdew973@yahoo.com
License: Stuttgart, Arkansas County, AR
Group Owner: Arkansas County Broadcasters Inc.
Nat'l Network: ABC
Arbitron Metro Market: Stuttgart, AR; *Format:* Oldies; *Hrs. of News Programming:* one.
Bobby Caldwell, President
Scott Siler, General Manager
Mitch Mahan, Programming Director
Scott Shannon, News Director

Texarkana

KOSY
11-15-1951; 790 kHz AM; *Hrs Open:* 24; 1 kw-D, DAN; 0.5 kw-N, DAN; N33 22 30 W94 1 0
2324 Arkansas Boulevard, Texarkana, AR 71854 US
(870) 772-3771; *Fax:* (870) 772-0364
www.kkyr.com
wesspicher@gapbroadcasting.com
License: Texarkana, AR held by Townsquare Media Texarkana License LLC
Group Owner: Townsquare Media
Arbitron Metro Market: Texarkana, TX; *Format:* Country; *No. News Employees:* 1; *Target Audience:* General.
Ron Bird, General Manager
Wes Spicher, Brand Manager
Ron Bird, Director Of Sales
Jane Beckerdite, Digital Managing Editor

KFYX(FM)
06-11-1968; 107.1 MHz FM; *Hrs Open:* 24; 2.9 kw; Ant 479 ft; N33 25 45 W94 07 11
615 Olive St., Texarkana, TX 75501
(903) 793-4671; *Fax:* (903) 792-4261
License: Texarkana, Miller County, AR held by ArkLaTex LLC.
Group Owner: Arklatex LLC; (acq 1-3-2007; grpsl)
Population Served: 36,501; *Arbitron Metro Market:* Texarkana TX; *Format:* Contemporary Hits/Top 40; *Target Audience:* 18-34.
Harold Sudbury, CEO
Scott Gray, CFO/Vice President

KYGL
01-01-1995; 106.3 MHz FM; 50 kw; 492 ft.; N33 18 30 W93 56 54
2324 Arkansas Boulevard, Texarkana, AR 71854 US
(870) 772-3771; *Fax:* (870) 770-0364
www.kygl.com
ron.bird@townsquaremedia.com
License: Texarkana, Miller County, AR held by Townsquare Media Texarkana License LLC
Group Owner: Townsquare Media
Arbitron Metro Market: Texarkana, AR; *Format:* Classic Rock
Ron Bird, General Manager
Ron Bird, Director Of Sales
Jane Meckerdite, Digital Managing Editor

*KKLT
01-01-2004; 89.3 MHz FM; 0.001 kw horiz, 23 kw vert; 505 ft.; N33 23 36 W93 51 34 *Rebroadcasts:* Rebroadcasts KLVR(FM) Santa Rosa, CA 100%
188 South Bellevue, Suite 222, Memphis, TN 38104 US
(800) 525-5683; *Fax:* (916) 251-1650
www.klove.com
klove@klove.com
License: Texarkana, Miller County, AR held by Educational Media Foundation.
Group Owner: EMF Broadcasting; (acq 1-11-2005; $125,000 for CP).
Nat'l Network: K-Love
Arbitron Metro Market: Texarkana, AR; *Format:* Christian; *No. News Employees:* 13
Darrell Chambliss, Chairman
Mike Novak, President and CEO
David Pierce, Chief Creative Officer and Programming Director
Ed Lenane, News Director
Sam Wallington, Engineering Dir

KTOY
01-01-1993; 104.7 MHz FM; *Hrs Open:* 24; 3.1 kw; 453 ft.; N33 25 45 W94 7 11
2409 College Drive, Texarkana, TX 75501 US
(903) 793-4671; *Fax:* (903) 792-4261
www.ktoy1047.com
scott@texarkanaradio.com
License: Texarkana, Miller County, AR held by Jo-Al Broadcasting Inc.
Group Owner: Arklatex LLC; (acq 1-3-2007; grpsl)
Nat'l Network: ABC; *Nat'l Reps:* Interep
Arbitron Metro Market: Texarkana, AR; *Format:* Adult Contemp; *Target Audience:* 25-54; blacks
John McCoy, Operations Dir
Scott Gray, General Sales Mgr
Soulman Billy Bland, Programming Director
Dee Dee Woods, Asst Program Director

Turrell

*WUMY
01-01-1989; 1180 kHz AM; *Hrs Open:* 24 hours; 5 kw-D, 26 w-N, 3.5 kw-CH; N35 08 31 W90 08 06
3710 Rawlins St., Suite 150, Dallas, TX 75219 US
(214) 273-6440
License: Turrell, Crittenden County, AR held by Memphis First Ventures, LP
Group Owner: Ronald and Terry Unkefer; (acq 10-20-2000; grpsl)
Population Served: 1,500,000; *Arbitron Metro Market:* Memphis, TN; *Format:* Country; *No. News Employees:* 3; *Target Audience:* 18-49 male
William H. Pollack, President

Van Buren

KHGG
11-24-1958; 1580 kHz AM; *Hrs Open:* 24
321 North Greenwood, Fort Smith, AR 72902 US
(479) 288-1047; *Fax:* (479) 785-2638
www.fortsmithradiogroup.com
License: Van Buren, AR held by Pharis Broadcasting Inc.
Group Owner: Pharis Broadcasting Inc.; acq 9-20-93; $110,000;
Nat'l Network: Fox Sports; *Regional Network:* Ark. Radio Net;
Nat'l Reps: Commercial Media Sales
Arbitron Metro Market: Fort Smith, AR; *Format:* Sports, Talk; *Target Audience:* General.; *Adv. Rates:* 15; 15; 15; 15
Ernie Witt, Programming Director

KBBQ-FM
05-22-1983; 102.7 MHz FM; 17 kw; 574 ft.; N35 26 51 W94 21 54
US
(479) 452-0681; *Fax:* (479) 452-0873
www.1027thevibe.com
License: Van Buren, Crawford County, AR held by Cumulus Licensing Corp.
Group Owner: Cumulus Media Inc.; (acq 8-99; $1.15 million)
Arbitron Metro Market: Fort Smith, AR; *Format:* Contemporary Hits/Top 40
Smitty O'Loughlin, General Manager
Dale Daniels, General Sales Mgr
JJ Ryan, Programming Director
Dina Godfrey, Promotions Manager
Michael Young, Business Manager
Anita Cowan, Events Manager

*KLFS
01-01-2004; 90.3 MHz FM; *Hrs Open:* 24; 2.4 kw vert; 256 ft.; N35 23 37 W94 33 7
1425 N Market Blvd., Suite 9, Sacramento, CA 95834 US
(800) 525-5683; *Fax:* (916) 251-1650
www.klove.com
klove@klove.com
License: Van Buren, Crawford County, AR held by Educational Media Foundation.
Group Owner: EMF Broadcasting
Nat'l Network: K-Love
Arbitron Metro Market: Van Buren, AR; *Format:* Christian; *No. News Employees:* 3; *Target Audience:* 25-44; Judeo Chrisitan, female
Darrell Chambliss, Chairman
Mike Novak, President and CEO
David Pierce, Programming Director
Ed Lenane, News Director
Sam Wallington, Engineering Dir

Vilonia

KASR
04-01-1984; 92.7 MHz FM; 25 kw; 328 ft.; N35 3 26 W92 4 16
1117 Oak Street, Suite 300, Conway, AR 72032 US
(501) 327-6611; *Fax:* (501) 327-6614
kasr@sbcglobal.net
License: Vilonia, Faulkner County, AR
Arbitron Metro Market: Conway, AR; *Format:* Sports
Mike Harrison, President
Josh Harrison, Operations Dir
Mike Harrison, General Manager
Michel Mace, Station Manager

Viola

KCMC-FM
05-01-2007; 94.3 MHz FM; *Hrs Open:* 24/7; 8.1 kw; Ant 571 ft; N36 19 30 W91 58 41
223 Russell St., Mountain Home, AR
(870) 425-4971; *Fax:* (870) 424-9717
License: Viola, Fulton County, AR held by MJFM LLC.
Population Served: 219,194 *Target Audience:* 25-54.
Mike Wiseman, COO
Scott Gray, General Manager

Waldo

KVMZ
01-01-2002; 99.1 MHz FM; 4.1 kw; 400 ft.; N33 17 59 W93 14 0
188 South Bellevue, Suite 222, Memphis, TN 38104 US
(870) 234-9901 (870) 234-5864; *Fax:* (870) 234-5865
www.magnoliaradio.com
kvmakvmz@magnoliaradio.com
License: Waldo, Columbia County, AR held by Noalmark Broadcasting Corp.
Group Owner: Noalmark Broadcasting Corp.; (acq 8-1-2005; $430,000)
Regional Network: Ark. Radio Net.
Arbitron Metro Market: Magnolia, AR; *Format:* Country; *Adv. Rates:* 10.59; 10.59; 10.59; 10.59
Ken Sibley, General Manager
Dan Gregory, Account Executive/Sports Director

Amanda Smith, Account Executive
Megan Black, Office Manager

Waldron

KHGG-FM

05-18-1982; 103.1 MHz FM; 6.1 kw; 1352 ft.; N34 58 44 W93 56 42 *Rebroadcasts:* Rebroadcasts KHGG(AM) 100%
321 N. Greenwood Ave., Fort Smith, AR 72901-3453 US
(479) 288-1047, (479) 783-5379; *Fax:* (479) 785-2638
sportshog1031.com
License: Waldron, Scott County, AR held by Pharis Broadcasting Inc.
Group Owner: Pharis Broadcasting Inc.; (acq 6-1-2003; $360,000).
Nat'l Network: Fox Sports; *Nat'l Reps:* Commercial Media Sales
Regional Reps: BRI
Format: Sports, Talk; *Hrs. of News Programming:* news progmg 10 hrs wkly; *No. News Employees:* 1; *Target Audience:* 25-54.; *Adv. Rates:* 12; 12; 12; 12

Walnut Ridge

KIYS

01-01-1947; 101.7 MHz FM; *Hrs Open:* 24; 10.5 kw; 1,073 ft.; N35 57 14 W90 41 41
407 E. Parker Rd., Jonesboro, AR 72404 US
(870) 934-5000; *Fax:* (870) 932-3814
www.kissjonesboro.com
License: Walnut Ridge, Lawrence County, AR held by East Arkansas Broadcasters Inc.
Group Owner: East Arkansas Broadcasters Inc.
Arbitron Metro Market: Jonesboro, AR; *Format:* Contemporary Hits/Top 40; *Target Audience:* 18-49; middle to upper middle income
Brandon Baxter, Programming Director

KRLW

06-29-1951; 1320 kHz AM; *Hrs Open:* 12; 1 kw-D, ND2; 0.152 kw-N, ND2; N36 3 58 W90 56 24
PO Box 30, Walnut Ridge, AR 72476 US
(870) 886-6666; *Fax:* (870) 886-5719
krlw@nex.net
License: Walnut Ridge, AR held by Combined Media Group Inc.
Group Owner: Combined Media Group Inc.; acq 7-25-01; with co-located FM).
Nat'l Network: CBS; *Regional Network:* Ark. Radio Net.
Arbitron Metro Market: Jonesboro, AR; *Format:* Oldies
Tim Scott, President

KJBX

03-27-1977; 106.3 MHz FM; *Hrs Open:* 24; 3 kw; 328 ft; N36 03 58 W90 56 24
314 Union Street, Jonesboro, AR 72401
(870) 933-8800; *Fax:* (870) 933-0403
BPresly@jonesbororadiogroup.com
License: Walnut Ridge, Lawrence County, AR held by Jonesboro Radio Group
Nat'l Network: CBS; *Regional Network:* Ark. Radio Net.
Population Served: 20,000; *Arbitron Metro Market:* Jonesboro, AR; *Format:* Contemporary Hits/Top 40
Tracy Stafford, General Manager
Chuck Crossno, General Sales Mgr
Bill Pressly, Vice President of Programming
Kevin Beathery, Advertising & Sales Manager
Ben Blankenship, Production Director

Warren

KWRF

08-01-1953; 860 kHz AM; *Hrs Open:* 24; 0.25 kw-D, ND1; 0.055 kw-N, ND1; N33 37 59 W92 3 51
1255 North Myrtle St, Warren, AR 71671 US
(870) 226-2653(870) 226-2654; *Fax:* (870) 226-3039
pines.broadcasting@sbcglobal.net
License: Warren, AR held by Pines Broadcasting Inc.
Regional Network: Ark. Radio Net.
Arbitron Metro Market: Warren, AR; *Format:* Classic Rock
Special Programming: Gospel 8 hrs wkly; *Hrs. of News Programming:* news progmg 10 hrs wkly; *No. News Employees:* 1; *Target Audience:* General.
Jimmy Sledge, President
Gwen Sledge, Operations Dir
Richard Garrison, Disc Jockey

KWRF-FM

06-21-1976; 105.5 MHz FM; *Hrs Open:* 24; 3 kw; 243 ft.; N33 38 8 W92 3 56
1255 N. Myrtle Street, Warren, AR 71671 US
(870) 226-2653; *Fax:* (870) 226-3039
License: Warren, Bradley County, AR
Arbitron Metro Market: Warren, AR
Jimmy Sledge, President
Gwen Sledge, Operations Director
Judy Moore, Programming Director
Richard Garrison, Disc Jockey
Allen Weise, Disc Jockey

West Helena

KCLT

12-17-1984; 104.9 MHz FM; *Hrs Open:* 24; 3 kw; 299 ft.; N34 30 56 W90 40 13
Mailing Address: P.O. Box 2870, West Helena, AR 72390 US
Second Address: 700 Dr. Martin Luther King Dr., Suite 1, West Helena, AR 72390
(870) 572-9506; *Fax:* (870) 572-1845
force2@sbcglobal.net
License: West Helena, Phillips County, AR held by West Helena Broadcasters Inc.
Arbitron Metro Market: West Helena, AR; *Format:* Urban Contemporary *Special Programming:* Gospel 15 hrs wkly; *Hrs. of News Programming:* news progmg one hr wkly; *No. News Employees:* 1; *Target Audience:* 25-54;general, mainly African-Americans
Raymond Simes, President
Larry Evans, Operations Dir
Elaine Sims, Station Manager

West Memphis

KQPN

12-01-1961; 730 kHz AM; *Hrs Open:* 24
342 River Oaks Blvd., Memphis, TN 38120 US
(901) 522-1919; *Fax:* (901) 522-1920
License: West Memphis, AR held by Simmons Austin, LS LLC.
Group Owner: Gow Broadcasting
Nat'l Network: ESPN Radio
Arbitron Metro Market: Memphis, TN; *Format:* Sports; *Target Audience:* 25-54; family types; *Adv. Rates:* 25; 25; 25; 20
David Gow, Chief Executive Officer
Craig Larson, Programming Director
Kent Abendroth, Chief Engineer

White Hall

KTRN

11-01-1997; 104.5 MHz FM; *Hrs Open:* 24; 3 kw; 289 ft.; N34 13 13 W92 4 37
6257 Brisa Del Mar, El Paso, TX 79925 US
(870) 536-5876 (on air)(870) 536 3282 (office); *Fax:* (870) 536-3475
License: White Hall, Jefferson County, AR held by Bayou Broadcasting Inc.
Arbitron Metro Market: Pine Bluff, AR; *Format:* Classic Rock; *Target Audience:* Women; 20 & up
Vickie Hooker, General Manager

Wilson

KOSE

10-11-1949; 860 kHz AM; 1 kw-D, ND1; 0.021 kw-N, ND1; N35 41 3 W89 58 57
125 S. Second St, Blytheville, AR 72315 US
(870) 762-2093; *Fax:* (870) 763-8459
License: Wilson, AR held by Newport Broadcasting Co.
Group Owner: Sudbury Services Inc.; (acq 1996)
Regional Network: Ark. Radio Net; *Nat'l Reps:* Roslin
Arbitron Metro Market: Memphis, TN; *Format:* Gospel *Special Programming:* Black 6 hrs, farm 5 hrs wkly; *Target Audience:* 24-55; middle-class, blue/white collar workers
Tom Hill, Chief Engineer

Wrightsville

KLAL

01-01-1998; 107.7 MHz FM; 100 kw; Ant 741 ft; N34 36 34 W92 14 14
700 Wellington Hills Rd., Little Rock, AR 72211 US
(501) 401-0200
www.alice1077.com
License: Wrightsville, AR held by Radio License Holding CBC, LLC
Group Owner: Cumulus Media Inc.; (acq 9-4-97).
Arbitron Metro Market: Little Rock, AR; *Format:* Contemporary Hits/Top 40
Sherry Lewis, General Sales Mgr
Randy Cain, Programming Director

Wynne

KWYN

09-28-1956; 1400 kHz AM; *Hrs Open:* 24; 1 kw-U, ND1; N35 15 21 W90 47 49
P.O. Box 789, Highway 64 West, Wynne, AR 72396 US
(870) 238-8141; *Fax:* (870) 238-5997
www.kwyn.com
eabwynne@cablelynx.com
License: Wynne, AR held by East Arkansas Broadcasters Inc.
Group Owner: East Arkansas Broadcasters Inc.
Nat'l Network: CBS; Westwood One; *Regional Network:* Ark. Radio Net.
Arbitron Metro Market: Wynne, AR; *Format:* Talk *Special Programming:* Farm 6 hrs wkly; *Target Audience:* General.
Bobby Caldwell, CEO/President
Scott Siler, General Manager
David Sills, General Sales Mgr
Bobby Caldwell, Programming Director
Jennifer Lynch, Traffic Manager
Renae Smith, Sales Representtive

KWYN-FM

05-15-1969; 92.5 MHz FM; *Hrs Open:* 24; 35 kw; 335 ft.; N35 11 59 W90 43 23
P.O. Box 789, Wynne, AR 72396 US
(870) 238-8141; *Fax:* (870) 238-5997
www.kwyn.com
License: Wynne, Cross County, AR held by East Arkansas Broadcasters Inc.
Group Owner: East Arkansas Broadcasters Inc.
Regional Network: Ark. Radio Net.
Arbitron Metro Market: Wynne, AR; *Format:* Country
Bobby Caldwell, CEO/President
Scott Siler, General Sales Mgr
Bobby Caldwell, Programming Director
Rob Shannon, News Director

Yellville

KCTT-FM

01-01-1986; 101.7 MHz FM; 6 kw; 285 ft.; N36 17 18 W92 30 37
Mailing Address: P.O. Box 2010, Mountain Home, AR 72654 US
Second Address: 620 Hwy. 5 N., Mountain Home, AR 72653
(870) 425-3101; *Fax:* (870) 424-4314
www.ktlo.com
License: Yellville, Marion County, AR held by KTLO LLC
Group Owner: KTLO LLC; (acq 5-29-98; $215,000)
Nat'l Network: ABC
Arbitron Metro Market: Mountain Home, AR; *Format:* Oldies
Special Programming: Folk 10 hrs wkly
Brad Haworth, Operations Manager
Bob Knight, General Manager
Danny Ward, Station Manager
Heather Loftis, Sales Manager
Sonny Elliot, News Director
Patty Sindlinger, Traffic Manager
Tim Tibbs, Production Manager

California

Adelanto

*KYZA

92.7 MHz FM; 0.28 kw; 1473 ft.; N34 36 44 W117 17 27
3101 North Federal Highway, Suite 601, Ft. Lauderdale, FL 33306 US
(949) 454-2475; *Fax:* (949) 454-1710
www.air1.com
License: Adelanto, Gallatin County, CA held by Educational Media Foundation
Group Owner: EMF Broadcasting
Arbitron Metro Market: Adelanto, CA; *Format:* Adult Contemp
Mike Novak, President/Chief Executive Officer

Alameda

KREV

08-01-1959; 92.7 MHz FM; 3.6 kw; 420 ft.; N37 47 54 W122 24 59
50 East Rivercenter Blvd., #1200, Covington, KY 41011 US
(415) 356-1600; *Fax:* (415) 356-1601
www.927rev.com
License: Alameda, Alameda County, CA held by Golden State Broadcasting LLC
Arbitron Metro Market: San Francisco, CA; *Format:* Contemporary Hits/Top 40
Ed Stolz, CEO
Autumn Larrick, Station Manager

Alturas

KALT-FM

07-01-2002; 106.5 MHz FM; 0.5 kw; 272 ft.; N41 29 57 W120 37 30
P.O. Box 106, Alturas, CA 96101 US

(530) 233-4842; *Fax:* (530) 233-4173
License: Alturas, Modoc County, CA held by Woodrow Michael Warren.
Group Owner: Woodrow Michael Warren Stns
Arbitron Metro Market: Alturas, CA; *Format:* Classic Rock
Mike Warren, General Manager

KCNO
12-04-1990; 94.5 MHz FM; *Hrs Open:* 14; 100 kw horiz; -194 ft.; N41 33 50 W120 24 55
P.O. Box 570, Alturas, CA 96101 US
(530) 233-3570; *Fax:* (530) 233-5470
englishradio@edimediainc.com
License: Alturas, Modoc County, CA held by EDI Media Inc.
Arbitron Metro Market: Alturas, CA; *Format:* Country; *Hrs. of News Programming:* News progmg 17 hrs wkly; *Target Audience:* General.
Bill Hansen, General Manager
Dodie McGoregh, News Director

KCFJ
06-04-1951; 570 kHz AM; *Hrs Open:* 6 AM-10 PM; 5 kw-D, 200 w-N; N41 30 07 W120 30 01
Box 580, Alturas, CA 96101
(530) 233-3570; *Fax:* (530) 233-5470
info@edimediainc.com
License: Alturas, Modoc County, CA held by EDI Media Inc.
Nat'l Network: USA
Population Served: 100,000 *Special Programming:* Farm one hr wkly; *Hrs. of News Programming:* news progmg 3 hrs wkly; *No. News Employees:* 1; *Target Audience:* General.
Bill Hansen, General Manager
Dodie McGough, News Director

Anderson

KEWB
03-20-1983; 94.7 MHz FM; 4.2 kw; 1565 ft.; N40 39 6 W122 31 32
1588 Charles Dr., Redding, CA 96003 US
(530) 244-9700; *Fax:* (530) 244-9707
power94radio.com
License: Anderson, Shasta County, CA held by Results Radio of Redding Licensee LLC.
Group Owner: Results Radio; (acq 6-28-2000; grpsl).
Arbitron Metro Market: Redding, CA; *Format:* Contemporary Hits/Top 40; *Target Audience:* 18-49.

Angwin

***KDFC**
09-01-1947; 89.9 MHz FM; *Hrs Open:* 24; 0.8 kw; 3035 ft.; N38 40 9 W122 37 53
PO Box 89, Angwin, CA 94508 US
(415) 764-1021; *Fax:* (415) 777-2291
www.kdfc.com
License: Angwin, San Francisco County, CA held by Entercom San Francisco License LLC.
Group Owner: Entercom Communications Corp.; (acq 3-14-2008; grpsl)
Arbitron Metro Market: San Francisco; *Format:* Talk; *Target Audience:* 25-54; educated, upscale
Bill Lueth, President
Rik Malone, Programming Director
Jude Heller, Promotions Manager
Rik Malone, Music Director
Len Mattson, Underwriting Director

***KNDL(FM)**
05-20-1961; 89.9 MHz FM; *Hrs Open:* 24; 794 w; Ant 3,010 ft; N38 40 09 W122 37 53
95 La Jota Dr., Angwin, CA 94508
(707) 965-4155; *Fax:* (707) 965-4161
www.thecandle.com
License: Angwin, Napa County, CA held by Howell Mountain Broadcasting Co. Inc.
Format: Christian; *Target Audience:* 35-49; general
Jim Aldred, General Manager

Apple Valley

KIXW
06-05-1954; 960 kHz AM; *Hrs Open:* 8:30 AM-5:30 PM; 5 kw-D, ND2; 0.02 kw-N, ND2; N34 31 0 W117 13 35
12370 Hesperia Road, Suite 16, Victorville, CA 92932 US
(760) 241-1313; *Fax:* (760) 241-0205
www.talk960.com
kimjennings@edbroadcasters.com
License: Apple Valley, CA held by EDB VV License LLC.
Group Owner: Frontier Radio Management Inc.; (acq 11-30-2007; grpsl)
Nat'l Reps: Christal
Format: Talk; *Target Audience:* 35+.
Tim Anderson, Vice President/General Manager
Kim Jennings, General Sales Mgr
Gregg Thomas, Programming Director

KWRN
01-26-1991; 1550 kHz AM; *Hrs Open:* 24; 5 kw-D, DAN; 0.5 kw-N, DA2; N34 32 12 W117 9 22 *Rebroadcasts:* Rebroadcasts KWRM(AM) Corona 100%
Mailing Address: 210 Radio Road, Corona, CA 91719 US
Second Address: 15165 7th St., Ste D, Victorville, CA 92392
(760) 955-8722; *Fax:* (760) 955-5751
License: Apple Valley, CA held by Major Market Stations Inc.
Nat'l Network: ABC
Arbitron Metro Market: Victorville, CA; *Format:* Contemporary Hits/Top 40; *Target Audience:* 34-54; adults with a stable job and disposable income; *Adv. Rates:* 20; 20; 20; 20
Marilynn Kramar, President
Esther Garzon, Vice President
Dick Vosper, Chief Engineer

KZXY-FM
05-17-1968; 102.3 MHz FM; 6 kw; 328 ft.; N34 24 40 W117 11 9
12370 Herperia Road, Suite 16, Victorville, CA 92395 US
(760) 241-1313; *Fax:* (760) 241-0205
www.y102fm.com
kimjennings@edbroadcasters.com
License: Apple Valley, San Bernardino County, CA held by EDB VV License LLC.
Group Owner: Frontier Radio Management Inc.
Nat'l Reps: Christal
Arbitron Metro Market: Apple Valley, CA; *Format:* Adult Contemp; *Target Audience:* 25-54; women; *Adv. Rates:* 25-75
Tim Anderson, Vice President/General Manager
Kim Jennings, General Sales Mgr
Colleen Quinn, Programming Director

Arcadia

KSSE
12-03-1960; 107.1 MHz FM; *Hrs Open:* 24; 6 kw; -43 ft.; N34 10 51 W118 1 38
5700 Wilshire Blvd., Suite 250, Los Angeles, CA 90036 US
(323) 900-6100; *Fax:* (323) 900-6119
www.superestrella.com
License: Arcadia, Los Angeles County, CA held by Entravision Holdings LLC.
Group Owner: Entravision Communications Corp.; (acq 4-1-03; grpsl).
Wire Services: SportsTicker
Arbitron Metro Market: Los Angeles, CA; *Format:* Spanish, Contemporary Hits/Top 40; *Target Audience:* 24-39; general
Juan Navarro, Interactive Sales Mgr
Nestor Rocha, Programming Vice President
Elias Autran, Promotions Manager

Arcata

***KHSU**
10-01-1960; 90.5 MHz FM; *Hrs Open:* 24; 8.5 kw; 1506 ft.; N40 43 37 W123 58 22
Radio Station Khsu-Fm, Arcata, CA 95521 US
(707) 826-4807; *Fax:* (707) 826-6082
www.khsu.org
khsu@humboldt.edu
License: Arcata, Humboldt County, CA held by Humboldt State University.
Nat'l Network: NPR; PRI
Format: News *Special Programming:* World 14 hrs, jazz 10 hrs wkly; *Hrs. of News Programming:* News progmg 28 hrs wkly
Kate Whiteside, Operations & Programming Director
Ed Subkis, General Manager
David Reed, Development Director
Kevin Sanders, Chief Engineer
Mark Shikuma, Music Director
Lorna Bryant, Administrative Assistant

KXGO
01-01-1970; 93.1 MHz FM; 50 kw; Ant 1,666 ft; N40 43 38 W123 58 22
1400 Main Street, Suite 104, Ferndale, CA 95501
(707) 786-5104; *Fax:* (707) 786-5100
www.theclassicrockstation.com
License: Arcata, Humboldt County, CA held by Lost Coast Communications
Group Owner: Lost Coast Communications; (acq 11-1-97).
Nat'l Reps: Christal
Population Served: 210,000 *Target Audience:* 25-54; upscale adults
Patrick Cleary, Managing Director
Brenda Boyd, Traffic & Office Manager
Patrick Cleary, General Sales Mgr
Charlie Fuentes, Programming Director
Cliff Berkowitz, Operations Manager

Arnold

KBYN
09-01-1995; 95.9 MHz FM; *Hrs Open:* 24; 0.86 kw; 863 ft.; N38 22 40 W120 11 33
4043 Geer Rd, P.O. Box 1039, Hughson, CA 95326 US
(209) 883-8760; *Fax:* (209) 883-8769
www.lafavorita.net
ngomez@lafavorita.net
License: Arnold, Calaveras County, CA held by KBYN Inc.
Nat'l Network: CBS
Arbitron Metro Market: Hughson, CA; *Format:* Spanish; *Target Audience:* 25-54; general
Nelson Gomez, General Manager
Marisol Valenzuela, Programming Director

KCFA
10-02-1995; 106.1 MHz FM; *Hrs Open:* 24; 3.8 kw; 843 ft.; N38 22 40 W120 11 33
4043 Geer Rd, Hughson, CA 95326 US
(209) 883-8760; *Fax:* (209) 883-8769
www.lafavorita.net
ngomez@lafavorita.net
License: Arnold, Calaveras County, CA held by La Favorita Radio Network, Inc.
Group Owner: La Favorita Radio Network; (acq 3-21-02).
Format: Spanish; *Hrs. of News Programming:* news progmg 5 hrs wkly; *No. News Employees:* 1; *Target Audience:* 30-50; Families
Nelson Gomez, General Manager
Marisol Valenzuela, Programming Director
Chuck Hughes, Chief Engineer

Arroyo Grande

KXTK
06-29-1962; 1280 kHz AM; *Hrs Open:* 24
10209 Southeast Division Street, Portland, OR 97266 US
(805) 547-1280; *Fax:* (805) 543-1508
espnradio1280.com
sports@espnradio1280.com
License: Arroyo Grande, CA held by Pacific Coast Media LLC
Nat'l Network: ESPN Radio; Westwood One
Arbitron Metro Market: San Luis Obispo, CA; *Format:* Sports; *Target Audience:* 25 plus.
Mike Chellsen, General Manager
Tom Barket, News Director
Bill Bordeaux, Engineering Dir
Max Woodcock, Production Manager

KIHC
09-01-2002; 890 kHz AM
1159 Fair Oaks Ave., Arroyo Grande, CA 93420 US
(805) 541-4343; *Fax:* (805) 541-9101
www.890online.com
License: Arroyo Grande, CA held by Jerry J. Collins.
Group Owner: Immaculate Heart Radio
Arbitron Metro Market: San Luis Obispo, CA; *Format:* Religious
Dick Jenkins, General Manager

Arvin

KMYX-FM
06-30-1999; 92.5 MHz FM; *Hrs Open:* 24; 0.62 kw; 1024 ft.; N35 11 41.1 W118 42 16
PO Box 62, Keene, CA 93531 US
(928) 782-5995; *Fax:* (928) 782-3874
www.campesina.com
License: Arvin, Kern County, CA held by Farmworker Educational Radio Network, Inc.
Group Owner: Farmworker Educational Radio Network, Inc.
Arbitron Metro Market: Bakersfield, CA; *Format:* Tejano; *Target Audience:* 25-54; Hispanic market
Paul Chavez, President

Atascadero

KSTT
05-19-1979; 104.5 MHz FM; *Hrs Open:* 24; 4.7 kw; 1444 ft.; N35 21 40 W120 39 21
3620 Sacramento Dr, Suite 204, San Luis Obispo, CA 93401 US
(805) 781-2750; *Fax:* (805) 781-2758
www.coast1045.com
License: Atascadero, San Luis Obispo County, CA held by AGM California, Inc.
Group Owner: American General Media; (acq 2-10-99; $1.5 million).
Nat'l Network: ABC

RADIO - U.S.

Arbitron Metro Market: San Luis Obispo, CA; *Format:* Adult Contemp; *Target Audience:* 25-55.
Kathy Signorelli, General Manager

Atherton

*KCEA
06-02-1979; 89.1 MHz FM; *Hrs Open:* 24; 0.1 kw; 128 ft.; N37 29 32 W122 16 28
555 Middlefield Road, Atherton, CA 94027 US
(650) 306-8823,(650) 306-8822; *Fax:* (650) 306-8834
www.kcea.org
info@kcea.org
License: Atherton, San Mateo County, CA held by Sequoia Union High School District.
Format: Big Band, Oldies; *Target Audience:* General.
Trish Millet, Operations Dir
Michael Isaacs, General Manager
John Mylod, News & Sports Director
Craig Roberts, Chief Engineer

Atwater

KBRE
10-01-1995; 92.5 MHz FM; *Hrs Open:* 24; 6 kw; 328 ft.; N37 16 41 W120 37 35
514 W. 19th St., Merced, CA 95340 US
(209) 723-2191; *Fax:* (209) 205-1013
www.1057thebear.com
License: Atwater, Merced County, CA held by Mapleton License of Merced LLC.
Group Owner: Mapleton Communications LLC; (acq 6-1-2002; grpsl)
Format: Rock/AOR; *Hrs. of News Programming:* news progmg 3 hrs wkly; *No. News Employees:* 1; *Target Audience:* Men 25-49
Diane Garcia, General Sales Mgr

Auberry

KKBZ
07-12-1992; 105.1 MHz FM; *Hrs Open:* 24; 0.6 kw; 1870 ft.; N37 4 25 W119 25 52
1110 E. Olive Ave., Fresno, CA 93728 US
(559) 497-1100; *Fax:* (559) 497-1125
mginsburg@lotusfresno.com
License: Auberry, Fresno County, CA held by Lotus Communications Corp.
Group Owner: Lotus Communications Corp.
Nat'l Reps: Lotus Entravision Reps LLC
Arbitron Metro Market: Fresno, CA; *Format:* Classic Rock; *Adv. Rates:* 40; 40; 40; 25
Howard Kalmenson, President/Chief Executive Officer
Kevin O'Rorke, General Manager
Mike Murray, Sales Manager
Andy Travis, Programming Director

Auburn

KAHI
11-13-1957; 950 kHz AM; *Hrs Open:* 24; 5 kw-D, DA2; 5 kw-N, DA2; N38 51 28 W121 1 39
605 West Lake Blvd., Suite 5, Tahoe City, CA 96145 US
(530) 885-5636; *Fax:* (530) 885-0166
www.kahi.com
info@KAHI.com
License: Auburn, CA held by IHR Educational Broadcasting.
Group Owner: IHR Educational Broadcasting; (acq 4-28-99; $475,000 with KSMH(AM) West Sacramento)
Nat'l Network: Radio America
Arbitron Metro Market: Auburm, CA; *Format:* Variety/Diverse *Special Programming:* community; *Hrs. of News Programming:* 6-9am, 12-1pm, 4-7pm; *Target Audience:* 25-54; Community focused; *Adv. Rates:* 25; 25; 25;18
Dave Rosenthal, Operations Dir
Jerry Henry, General Manager
Mike Remy, General Sales Mgr

KHYL
12-21-1961; 101.1 MHz FM; *Hrs Open:* 24; 36 kw; 577 ft.; N38 51 28 W121 1 39
1545 River Park Dr., Suite 500, Sacramento, CA 95815 US
(916) 929-5325
www.v101fm.com
License: Auburn, Placer County, CA held by AMFM Broadcasting Licenses LLC.
Group Owner: iHeartMedia; (acq 8-30-2000; grpsl).
Arbitron Metro Market: Sacramento, CA; *Format:* Urban Contemporary *Special Programming:* Soul 5 hrs wkly; *Hrs. of News Programming:* News progmg one hr wkly; *Target Audience:* 25-54.
John Geary, Market President
Sara McClure, Senior Vice President of Sales

Avalon

KBRT
06-01-1952; 740 kHz AM; 10 kw-D, DA2; 0.113 kw-N, DA2; N33 21 36 W118 22 18
3183 Airway Ave., Suite D, Costa Mesa, CA 92626 US
(714) 754-4450; *Fax:* (714) 754-0735
www.kbrt740.com
License: Avalon, CA held by Kierton Inc.
Group Owner: Crawford Broadcasting Co.; (acq 5-21-80)
Arbitron Metro Market: Los Angeles; *Format:* Talk, Religious; *Target Audience:* Christian adult.
Todd Stickler, Operations Dir
Sarah Davis, General Sales Mgr

*KISL
01-01-2000; 88.7 MHz FM; 0.2 kw; 20 ft.; N33 20 32 W118 19 11
P.O. Box 1980, Avalon, CA 90704 US
(310) 510-7469; *Fax:* (310) 510-1025
www.kisl.org
License: Avalon, Los Angeles County, CA held by Catalina Island Performing Arts Foundation
Format: Variety/Diverse
Aaron Pitts, Station Manager

Avenal

*KAAX
106.9 MHz FM; kw
12550 Brookhurst Street, Suite A, Garden Grove, CA 92840 US
License: Avenal, Kings County, CA held by Avenal Educational Services Inc.
Arbitron Metro Market: Garden Grove, CA
Alfredo Plascencia, President
Denny Jackson, Programming Director

Baker

KIXF
01-01-1994; 101.5 MHz FM; *Hrs Open:* 24; 4.3 kw; 1322 ft.; N35 26 10 W115 55 25 *Rebroadcasts:* Rebroadcasts KIXW-FM 100%
Mailing Address: 1611 East Main St, P.O.Box 1668, Barstow, CA 92312 US
Second Address: 101 Convention Center Dr, Suite 1001, Las Vegas, NV 89109
(760) 256-0326; *Fax:* (760) 256-9507
highwayradio.com
info@highwayradio.com
License: Baker, San Bernardino County, CA held by KHWY, Inc.
Group Owner: KHWY, Inc.; (acq 2-18-98; $1,741,444 with KIXW-FM Lenwood).
Nat'l Network: Westwood One; CNN Radio
Format: Country *Special Programming:* Hourly traf report to service interstate travelers; *No. News Employees:* 1; *Target Audience:* 25-54; interstate travelers to Las Vegas & Laughlin, NV
Kirk Anderson, President/COO
John Gregg, Operations Dir

KHRQ
01-01-2002; 94.9 MHz FM; 1.45 kw; 1325 ft.; N35 26 10 W115 55 25
Mailing Address: 1611 East Main St, P.O.Box 1668, Barstow, CA 92312 US
Second Address: 101 Convention Center Dr, Suite 1001, Las Vegas, NV 89109
(760) 256-0326; *Fax:* (760) 256-9507
highwayradio.com
info@highwayradio.com
License: Baker, San Bernardino County, CA held by The Drive LLC.
Group Owner: KHWY, Inc.; (acq 5-31-2003).
Nat'l Network: Jones Radio Networks
Arbitron Metro Market: Baker, CA; *Format:* Classic Rock
Kirk Anderson, President/COO
John Gregg, Operations Dir
Jeremy James, Programming Director

Bakersfield

KHTY
10-01-1946; 970 kHz AM; *Hrs Open:* 24; 1 kw-D, DA2; 5 kw-N, DA2; N35 27 0 W118 56 48
1100 Mohawk St., Suite 280, Bakersfield, CA 93309 US
(661) 322-9929; *Fax:* (661) 322-7239
www.foxsports970am.com
License: Bakersfield, Kern County, CA held by AMFM Radio Licenses LLC.
Group Owner: iHeartMedia; (acq 12-22-2000; $1.4 million)
Nat'l Network: Fox Sports
Arbitron Metro Market: Bakersfield, CA; *Format:* Sports
Jeremy Price, Market President
Kenn McCloud, Program Director and Promotions Director
Steve Mull, Chief Engineer

KLHC
02-01-1958; 1350 kHz AM; *Hrs Open:* 24; 1 kw-D, ND1; 0.033 kw-N, ND1; N35 21 0 W118 58 58
1400 Easton Road, Bakersfield, CA 93309 US
(661) 847-1450; *Fax:* (661) 847-1350
License: Bakersfield, CA held by Force Broadcasting LLC.
Group Owner: Centro Cristiano Vida Abundante
Arbitron Metro Market: Bakersfield, CA; *Format:* Religious
Maria Ochoa, General Manager

KCWR
03-21-1990; 107.1 MHz FM; *Hrs Open:* 24; 6 kw; 157 ft.; N35 22 11 W119 0 18
3223 Sillect Ave, Bakersfield, CA 93308 US
(661) 326-1011; *Fax:* (661) 328-7503(661) 328-7537(news)
License: Bakersfield, Kern County, CA held by Owens One Co. Inc.
Group Owner: Buck Owens Productions Inc.; (acq 5-24-2006; grpsl).
Arbitron Metro Market: Bakersfield, CA; *Format:* Country
Mel Owens Jr., CEO
Julie Randolph, General Sales Manager

KERI
01-03-1932; 1410 kHz AM; *Hrs Open:* 24; 1 kw-U, ND1; N35 21 7 W118 57 29
P.O. Box 444, Spartanburg, SC 29304 US
(888) 989-2299
www.wilkinsradio.com
denise@wilkinsradio.com
License: Bakersfield, CA held by Bob Wilkins Radio Network Broadcasting Inc.
Group Owner: Wilkins Communications Network Inc.; (acq 5-1-75)
Nat'l Reps: Christal; *Wire Services:* AP
Arbitron Metro Market: Bakersfield, CA; *Format:* Christian, Talk; *Target Audience:* 25-54.
Robert Wilkins, CEO/COO
Michael Benge, Local Sales Manager

*KFRB
08-01-1996; 91.3 MHz FM; *Hrs Open:* 24; 2.8 kw vert; 1368 ft.; N35 26 17 W118 44 22
Mailing Address: 4135 Northgate Blvd, Suite 1, Sacramento, CA 95834 US
Second Address: 290 Hegenberger Rd., Oakland, CA 94621
(805) 363-5576; *Fax:* (209) 389-0215
www.familyradio.com
info@familyradio.org
License: Bakersfield, Kern County, CA held by Family Stations Inc.
Group Owner: Family Stations Inc.
Arbitron Metro Market: Bakersfield, CA; *Format:* Christian, Religious *Special Programming:* Children's 10 hrs wkly
Harold Camping, President
David Manzi, Operations Dir

KGEO
01-01-1946; 1230 kHz AM; 1 kw-U, ND1; N35 20 53 W119 0 33
1400 Easton Dr, Suite 144-B, Bakersfield, CA 93309 US
(661) 631-1410; *Fax:* (661) 328-0873
www.bakersfieldespnsports.com
License: Bakersfield, CA held by AGM California, Inc.
Group Owner: American General Media; (acq 12-9-92; $1.75 million with co-located FM;
Nat'l Network: Westwood One; ESPN Radio; CBS; *Nat'l Reps:* McGavren Guild
Arbitron Metro Market: Bakersfield, CA; *Format:* News, News/Talk, 84, Talk *Special Programming:* Finance 13 hrs wkly; *Hrs. of News Programming:* news progmg 130 hrs wkly
Rogers Brandon, General Manager
Jeff Lemucchi, News Director

KGFM
10-01-1964; 101.5 MHz FM; 6.7 kw; 1299 ft.; N35 26 17 W118 44 22
1400 Easton Dr, Suite 144 B, Bakersfield, CA 93309 US
(661) 328-1410; *Fax:* (661) 328-0873
www.kgfm.com
rlewis@americangeneralmedia.com
License: Bakersfield, Kern County, CA held by AGM California, Inc.
Group Owner: American General Media
Arbitron Metro Market: Bakersfield, CA; *Format:* Adult Contemp; *Target Audience:* Adults 25-54

Robert Lewis, Director, Operations & Programming
Rogers Brandon, General Manager
Wayne Stephens, General Sales Mgr

KBFP
01-01-1959; 800 kHz AM; *Hrs Open:* 6 AM-12 AM; 1 kw-D, DA2; 0.44 kw-N, DA2; N35 20 44 W118 59 33
1100 Mohawk St., Suite 280, Bakersfield, CA 93309 US
(661) 322-9929; *Fax:* (661) 322-7239
www.comedy800.com
License: Bakersfield, Kern County, CA held by CC Licenses LLC.
Group Owner: iHeartMedia; (acq 10-11-2000; grpsl)
Arbitron Metro Market: Bakersfield, CA; *Format:* Comedy; *Target Audience:* 25-54, Spanish Adults
Jeremy Price, Market President
Kenn McCloud, Programming Director

KISV
01-01-1948; 94.1 MHz FM; *Hrs Open:* 24; 4.5 kw; 1332 ft.; N35 26 17 W118 44 22
1400 Easton Dr, Suite 144-B, Bakersfield, CA 93309 US
(661) 328-1410; *Fax:* (661) 328-0873
www.hot941.com
jreed@hot941.com
License: Bakersfield, Kern County, CA held by AGM California, Inc.
Group Owner: American General Media
Arbitron Metro Market: Bakersfield, CA; *Format:* Contemporary Hits/Top 40 *Special Programming:* Farm one hr, relg one hr wkly; *Target Audience:* Adults 18-49
Robert Lewis, Director, Operations & Programming
Rogers Brandon, General Manager
Wayne Stephens, Director, Sales
J. Reed, Program Director

KPSL-FM
12-15-1985; 96.5 MHz FM; *Hrs Open:* 24; 50 kw; 499 ft.; N35 29 8 W118 53 19
5100 Commerce Drive, Bakersfield, CA 93309 US
(661) 327-9711; *Fax:* (661) 327-0797
www.concierto965.com
info@thespanishradio.com
License: Bakersfield, Kern County, CA held by Illinois Lotus Corp.
Group Owner: Lotus Communications Corp.; (acq 8-24-99; grpsl).
Arbitron Metro Market: Bakersfield, CA; *Format:* Spanish
Greg Holcomb, General Manager
Sandy Ozuma, General Sales Mgr
Isidro Roman, Programming Director

KKBB
11-01-1991; 99.3 MHz FM; *Hrs Open:* 24; 10 kw; 390 ft.; N35 27 33 W119 1 13
3651 Pegasus Dr., Suite 107, Bakersfield, CA 93308 US
(661) 393-1900; *Fax:* (661) 393-1915
www.groove993.com
License: Bakersfield, Kern County, CA held by Alpha Media Licensee LLC
Group Owner: Alpha Media LLC; (acq 10-10-2014).
Nat'l Reps: D & R Radio
Arbitron Metro Market: Bakersfield, CA; *Format:* Oldies; *Target Audience:* 25-54; adults
Mary Lou Gunn, General Manager

KVMX
08-24-1963; 92.1 MHz FM; 4.2 kw; 397 ft.; N35 29 11 W118 53 21
5100 Commerce Drive, Bakersfield, CA 93309 US
(661) 327-9711; *Fax:* (661) 327-0797
www.965maxfm.com
License: Bakersfield, Kern County, CA held by Texas Lotus Corp.
Group Owner: Lotus Communications Corp.; (acq 7-29-2008; with KWID(FM) Las Vegas, NV in exchange for KZEP-FM San Antonio, TX)
Nat'l Reps: McGavren Guild
Arbitron Metro Market: Bakersfield, CA; *Format:* Classic Rock
Greg Holcomb, General Manager
Sandy Ozuna, General Sales Mgr
Kris Kingston, Programming Director

KNZR
01-01-1933; 1560 kHz AM; *Hrs Open:* 24; 25 kw-D, DAN; 10 kw-N, DAN; N35 18 30 W119 2 46
3651 Pegasus Dr., Suite 107, Bakersfield, CA 93308 US
(661) 393-1900; *Fax:* (661) 393-1915
www.knzr.com
License: Bakersfield, Kern County, CA held by Alpha Media Licensee LLC
Group Owner: Alpha Media LLC; (acq 10-10-2014).
Nat'l Network: CBS; *Nat'l Reps:* D & R Radio
Arbitron Metro Market: Bakersfield, CA; *Format:* News, News/Talk, 86 *Special Programming:* L.A. Dodgers; *Hrs. of News Programming:* news progmg 40 hrs wkly; *No. News Employees:* 4; *Target Audience:* 25-54.
Mary Lou Gunn, General Manager

***KPRX**
02-28-1987; 89.1 MHz FM; 11 kw; 499 ft.; N35 29 10 W118 53 20 *Rebroadcasts:* Rebroadcasts KVPR(FM) Fresno 100%
3437 W. Shaw #101, Fresno, CA 93711 US
(559) 275-0764; *Fax:* (559) 275-2202
www.kvpr.org
kvpr@kvpr.org
License: Bakersfield, Kern County, CA held by White Ash Broadcasting Inc.
Nat'l Network: NPR
Arbitron Metro Market: San Joaquin Valley, CA; *Format:* News
Mariam Stepanian, President
Mariam Stepanian, General Manager
Jim Meyers, Station Manager
Joe Moore, Programming Director
Steve Mull, Chief Engineer

***KTQX**
04-14-1989; 90.1 MHz FM; *Hrs Open:* 24; 0.57 kw; 3622 ft.; N35 27 11 W118 35 25
5005 E. Belmont Avenue, Fresno, CA 93727 US
(559) 455-5777; *Fax:* (559) 455-5778
www.radiobilingue.org
mail@radiobilingue.org
License: Bakersfield, Kern County, CA held by Radio Bilingue Inc.
Arbitron Metro Market: Bakersfield, CA; *Format:* Ethnic; *Hrs. of News Programming:* news progmg 11 hrs wkly; *No. News Employees:* 5; *Target Audience:* 16-60; Latino
Hugo Morales, CEO
Maria Erana, General Manager
Phil Traynor, General Sales Mgr
Samuel Orozco, News Director
Bill Bach, Chief Engineer

KUZZ
10-01-1946; 550 kHz AM; 5 kw-U, DA-N; N35 20 25 W118 56 14
3223 Sillect Ave., Bakersfield, CA 93308
(661) 326-1011; *Fax:* (661) 328-7503
www.kuzz.com
License: Bakersfield, Kern County, CA held by Buck Owens Productions Co., Inc.
Group Owner: Buck Owens Productions Inc.; (acq 5-24-2006; grpsl).
Population Served: 100,000; *Arbitron Metro Market:* Bakersfield, CA; *Target Audience:* 25-54.
Mel Owens Jr., CEO
Harvey Campbell, General Sales Mgr
Tom Jordan, Programming Director
Jerry Hufford, Promotions Manager
Suzanne Grant, News Director
Terry Gaiser, Chief Engineer
Toni Marie Faria, Music Director
HarveyCampbell, National Sales Manager

KUZZ-FM
01-01-1968; 107.9 MHz FM; kw
3223 Sillect Avenue, Bakersfield, CA 93308 US
(661) 326-1011; *Fax:* (661)328-7503
www.kuzz.com
hcampbell@buckowens.com
License: Bakersfield, Kern County, CA
Group Owner: Buck Owens Productions Inc.
Arbitron Metro Market: Bakersfield, CA; *Format:* Country
Harvey Campbell, General Sales Mgr
Tom Jordan, Programming Director
Jerry Hufford, Promotions Manager
Suzanne Grant, News Director

KWAC
01-01-1954; 1490 kHz AM; *Hrs Open:* 24
5200 Standard Street, Bakersfield, CA 93308 US
(661) 327-9711; *Fax:* (661) 327-0797
www.kwac.com
License: Bakersfield, CA held by Illinois Lotus Corp.
Group Owner: Lotus Communications Corp.; (acq 8-24-99; grpsl).
Nat'l Network: ESPN Radio; *Nat'l Reps:* Lotus Entravision Reps LLC
Arbitron Metro Market: Bakersfield, CA; *Format:* Tejano; *Hrs. of News Programming:* News progmg 5 hrs wkly; *Target Audience:* General.; *Adv. Rates:* 25; 25; 25; 15
Howard Kalmenson, President
Anna Gallegos, Operations Dir
Greg Holcomb, General Manager
Juan Martinez, Programming Director
Lloyd Moss, Chief Engineer

KAFY
01-01-2000; 1100 kHz AM; *Hrs Open:* 24
4043 Geer Rd, Hughson, CA 95326 US
(209) 883-8760; *Fax:* (209) 883-8769
www.lafavorita.net
ngomez@lafavorita.net
License: Bakersfield, Kern West County, CA held by La Favorita Radio Network, Inc.
Group Owner: La Favorita Radio Network; (acq 3-28-01).
Arbitron Metro Market: Bakersfield, CA; *Format:* Spanish, Oldies
Nelson Gomez, General Manager

Banning

KMET
01-01-1948; 1490 kHz AM; *Hrs Open:* 24; 1 kw-U; N33 55 49 W116 55 20
700 E. Redlands Blvd., Suite U, PMB 323, Redlands, CA 92026
(951) 849-4644,(909) 319-1177; *Fax:* NA
kmet1490talkradio@yahoo.com
License: Banning, Riverside County, CA held by Sunset Broadcasting Inc.
Nat'l Network: Talk Radio Network
Population Served: 375,000; *Arbitron Metro Market:* Riverside-San Bernardino, CA; *Hrs. of News Programming:* News progmg 3 hrs wkly; *Target Audience:* General; 25-54, 35-65
Mitch McClellan, General Manager
Sean Nickerson, Production Manager

***KRTM**
01-01-1989; 88.1 MHz FM; *Hrs Open:* 24; 0.114 kw; 2539 ft.; N34 2 16 W116 48 48
Mailing Address: 35200 Cathedral Canyon Dr, Suite G53, Cathedral City, CA 92234 US
Second Address: P.O. Box 913, Aledo, TX 76008
(855) 500-3759
www.krtmradio.org
steve@kdkr.org
License: Banning, Riverside West Inner County, CA held by Penfold Communications, Inc.
Group Owner: Penfold Communications, Inc.; (acq 6-11-98; $234,788)
Arbitron Metro Market: Temecula, CA; *Format:* Christian; *Target Audience:* 25-54.

Barstow

KDUC
06-04-1986; 94.3 MHz FM; 4.6 kw; 784 ft.; N34 58 15 W117 2 22
320 West College Avenue, Pleasant Gap, PA 16823 US
(760) 256-2121; *Fax:* (760) 256-5090
doscostascommunications@yahoo.com
License: Barstow, San Bernardino County, CA held by Dos Costas Communications Corp.
Group Owner: Dos Costas Communications Corp.; acq 6-18-03; grpsl).
Format: Contemporary Hits/Top 40; *Target Audience:* 12-44.;
Adv. Rates: Same as AM
Rolan Ulloa, General Manager/President
Manny Lopez, Vice President/Director of Sales
Mike Garcia, Programming Director

KIQQ
09-29-1960; 1310 kHz AM; *Hrs Open:* 24 *Rebroadcasts:* Simulcast with KAEH(FM) Beaumont 100%
16435 Wimbleton Drive, Victorville, CA 92392 US
(760) 255-2636; *Fax:* (760) 255-3236
License: Barstow, CA held by MBR Licensee LLC.
Group Owner: Moon Broadcasting; (acq 8-7-2000).
Nat'l Network: Westwood One
Format: Tejano; *Target Audience:* 45 plus.
Alicia Avila, General Manager

KSZL
06-25-1986; 1230 kHz AM; *Hrs Open:* 24; 1 kw-U, ND1; N34 54 44 W117 1 39
320 West College Avenue, Pleasant Gap, PA 16823 US
(760) 256-2121(760) 256-5382; *Fax:* (760) 256-5090
am1230kszl@yahoo.com
License: Barstow, CA held by Dos Costas Communications Corp.
Nat'l Network: Westwood One; *Nat'l Reps:* Western Regional Broadcast Sales
Arbitron Metro Market: Barstow, CA; *Format:* News, Talk; *Hrs. of News Programming:* news progmg 12 hrs wkly; *No. News Employees:* 2; *Target Audience:* 25 plus; Adults 35 years +; *Adv. Rates:* 15; 15; 15; 10

Rolan Ulloa, President/General Manager
Michael Garcia, Operations Dir
Manny Lopez, Vice President/Director of Sales

KXXZ
01-01-1989; 95.9 MHz FM; *Hrs Open:* 24; 8.9 kw; 486 ft.; N34 51 22 W117 3 0
320 West College Ave., Pleasant Gap, PA 16823 US
(760) 256-2121; *Fax:* (760) 256-5090
doscostas@yahoo.com
License: Barstow, San Bernardino County, CA held by Dos Costas Communications Corp.
Group Owner: Dos Costas Communications Corp.; acq 6-18-03; grpsl).
Arbitron Metro Market: Barstow; *Format:* Tejano
Rolan Ulloa, President/General Manager
Manny Lopez, Vice President/Director of Sales
Mike Garcia, Programming Director

*KWTH
01-01-2006; 91.3 MHz FM; 1.55 kw; 2296 ft.; N34 38 39 W116 37 38 *Rebroadcasts:* Rebroadcasts KWTW(FM) Bishop 100%
P O Box 637, Bishop, CA 93515 US
(866) 466-5989; *Fax:* (714) 979-8916
www.kwtw.org
recep@kwtw.org
License: Barstow, San Bernardino County, CA held by Living Proof Inc.
Arbitron Metro Market: Barstow, CA; *Format:* Christian, Religious
Daniel McClenaghan, President

*KODV
01-01-2005; 89.1 MHz FM; 5.8 kw; 768 ft.; N34 58 15.09 W117 2 21.51
Mailing Address: US
Second Address: 18280 Atlantic St., Hesperia, CA 92345
(760) 947-4300; *Fax:* (760) 245-6268
www.ondasdevida.com
License: Barstow, San Bernardino County, CA held by Ondas de Vida Network Inc.
Arbitron Metro Market: Barstow, CA
Hector Manzo, CEO

Bayside

*KNHM
04-15-1992; 91.5 MHz FM; *Hrs Open:* 24; 0.48 kw; 1722 ft.; N40 43 38 W123 58 22
2803 Greenwood Hgts Road, Kneeland, CA 95549 US
(541) 552-6301; *Fax:* (541) 552-8565
www.ijpr.org
License: Bayside, Humboldt County, CA held by JPR Foundation Inc.
Arbitron Metro Market: Bayside CA
Ronald Kramer, General Manager
Paul Westhelle, General Sales Mgr

Beaumont

KAEH
01-01-1996; 100.9 MHz FM; *Hrs Open:* 24; 1.5 kw; 479 ft.; N33 54 29 W116 59 45
PO Box 2235, Beaumont, CA 92223 US
(909) 381-0969; *Fax:* (909) 381-0943
www.lamaquinamusical.net
License: Beaumont, Riverside County, CA held by MBR Licensee LLC.
Group Owner: Moon Broadcasting; (acq 2-13-2002; $1.7 million).
Arbitron Metro Market: Beaumont, CA
Abel DeLuna, President
Alicia Avila, General Manager
Juan Ramirez, Programming Director
Manuel Garcia, News Director
Rick Hunt, Chief Engineer

Bella Vista

*KKRN
88.5 MHz FM; 0.6 kw; 2001 ft.; N40 54 23 W121 49 39 US
(530) 337-6736; *Fax:* (530) 337-6567
info@kkrn.org
License: Bella Vista, Shasta County, CA held by Acorn Community Enterprises.
Arbitron Metro Market: Bella Vista, CA
Staci Wadley, General Manager

Berkeley

*KALX
10-01-1967; 90.7 MHz FM; *Hrs Open:* 24; 0.5 kw; 781 ft.; N37 52 40 W122 14 44
300 Lakeside Dr. 8th Flr, Oakland, CA 94612 US
(510) 642-1111
kalx.berkeley.edu
mail@kalx.berkeley.edu
License: Berkeley, Alameda County, CA held by The Regents of the University of California.
Arbitron Metro Market: San Francisco, CA; *Format:* Variety/Diverse; *Hrs. of News Programming:* News progmg 4 hrs wkly
Sandra Wasson, General Manager
Lindsay Melnyk, Programming Director
Tristan Parker, News Director
Joe Tysl, Chief Engineer

KBLX-FM
04-29-1949; 102.9 MHz FM; *Hrs Open:* 24; 6.6 kw; 1289 ft.; N37 41 20 W122 26 7
55 Hawthorne St #900, San Francisco, CA 94105 US
((415) 284-1029; *Fax:* (415) 764-4959
www.kblx.com
info@kblx.com
License: Berkeley, Alameda County, CA
Group Owner: Entercom Communications Corp
Wire Services: Bay City News Service
Arbitron Metro Market: San Francisco; *Format:* Adult Contemp, Urban Contemporary; *Hrs. of News Programming:* Feature only; *No. News Employees:* 1; *Target Audience:* 25-54; adults
Renee Guillory, Operations Dir
Dwight Walker, Vice President/General Manager
Paul Marks, Chief Engineer
Kimmie Taylor, Music Director
Susie Lee, Public Service Director

KPFA
04-01-1949; 94.1 MHz FM; *Hrs Open:* 24; 59 kw horiz; 1329 ft.; N37 51 55 W122 13 12
1929 Mlk Jr Way, Berkeley, CA 94704 US
(510) 848-6767; *Fax:* (510) 848-3812
www.kpfa.org
info@kpfa.org
License: Berkeley, Alameda County, CA held by Pacifica Foundation.
Group Owner: Pacifica Foundation Inc.
Wire Services: Reuters; Pacifica Network News
Arbitron Metro Market: San Francisco; *Format:* Variety/Diverse
Special Programming: C&W 18 hrs, Black 18 hrs, jazz 15 hrs, folk 10 hrs, women 10 hrs, world 18 hrs wkly; *Hrs. of News Programming:* news progmg 11 hrs wkly; *No. News Employees:* 4; *Target Audience:* 25-50.
Richard Pirodsky, General Manager
Michael Yoshida, Chief Engineer
Maria Negret, Business Manager
Luis Medina, Music Director

*KPFB
02-01-1954; 89.3 MHz FM; 0.46 kw horiz; -98 ft.; N37 52 20 W122 16 18 *Rebroadcasts:* Simulcasts with *KPFA(FM) Berkeley except for pub affrs & special events progmg
1929 Martin L King Jr Wy, Berkley, CA 94704 US
License: Berkeley, Alameda County, CA held by Pacifica Foundation Inc.
Group Owner: Pacifica Foundation Inc.
Arbitron Metro Market: San Francisco
Richard Pirodsky, General Manager
Mark Mericle, News Director
Michael Yoshida, Chief Engineer
Luis Medina, Music Director
Maria Negret, Business Manager

KVTO
05-22-1922; 1400 kHz AM; *Hrs Open:* 24; 1 kw-U, ND1; N37 50 58 W122 17 44
55 Hawthorne Street, San Francisco, CA 94105 US
(415) 284-1029; *Fax:* (415) 764-4959
www.chineseradio.com
License: Berkeley, CA held by Urban Radio III L.L.C.
Group Owner: Pham Radio Communication, LLC; (acq 1979)
Nat'l Reps: D & R Radio
Arbitron Metro Market: San Francisco, CA; *Format:* Japanese, Korean, 18; *Target Audience:* 25-54.
Irene Fong, Operations Dir

Big Bear City

KBHR
12-17-1995; 93.3 MHz FM; *Hrs Open:* 24; 1.5 kw; 663 ft; N34 16 41 W116 47 31
Box 2979, ., Big Bear City, CA 92314
(909) 584-5247; *Fax:* (909) 584-5347
www.kbhr933.com
info@kbhr933.com
License: Big Bear City, San Bernardino County, CA held by Parallel Broadcasting Inc.
Nat'l Network: NBC News Radio
Population Served: 25,000; *Arbitron Metro Market:* Riverside-San B *Special Programming:* NBC News Radio 8 hrs, ski report, fish report; *Hrs. of News Programming:* news progmg 11 hrs wkly; *No. News Employees:* 1 *Target Audience:* 25-54; upscale second home owners, resort visitors; *Adv. Rates:* 30; 27; 30; 25
Rick Herrick, President
Cathy Herrick, Operations Dir
Jay Tunnell, General Sales Mgr
Mike Evans, Programming Director

Big Bear Lake

KXSB
05-01-1975; 101.7 MHz FM; *Hrs Open:* 24; 0.3 kw; 1414 ft.; N34 12 47 W116 51 59 *Rebroadcasts:* Rebroadcasts KXLM(FM) Oxnard 80%
200 S. A St., 4th Fl., Oxnard, CA 93030 US
(805) 240-2070
www.radiolazer.com
License: Big Bear Lake, San Bernardino County, CA held by Lazer Broadcasting Corp.
Group Owner: Lazer Broadcasting Corp.; acq 1995; $750,000)
Nat'l Reps: Lotus Entravision Reps LLC
Arbitron Metro Market: Riverside-San Bernardino, CA; *Format:* Contemporary Hits/Top 40, Spanish; *Hrs. of News Programming:* news progmg 2 hrs wkly; *No. News Employees:* 1; *Target Audience:* 25-54; adults, seriousminded; *Adv. Rates:* 75; 65; 65; 50

Big Pine

KRHV
01-01-1999; 93.3 MHz FM; 0.89 kw; 2904 ft.; N37 24 48 W118 11 8
Mailing Address: P.O. Box 1284, Mammoth Lakes, CA 93546 US
Second Address: 94 Laurel Mountain Rd., Mammouth Lakes, CA 93546
(760) 934-8888; *Fax:* (760) 934-2429
www.kmmtradio.com
kmmtradioworks@yahoo.com
License: Big Pine, Inyo County, CA held by David & Mary Digerness.
Format: Variety/Diverse, Classic Rock
Maryann Digerness, President
Shellie Woods, General Manager
Paul Payne, Station Manager
Paul Payne, General Sales Mgr
Spencer Myers, Programming Director
Ron Nelson, Engineering Dir

Big River

KFLG-FM
12-06-1974; 94.7 MHz FM; *Hrs Open:* 24; 19.5 kw; 2736 ft.; N34 33 6 W114 11 37
2350 Miracle Mile Rd., Suite 300, Bullhead City, AZ 86442 US
(928) 763-5586; *Fax:* (928) 763-3775
www.kflg947.com
License: Big River, San Bernardino County, CA held by Cameron Broadcasting Inc.
Group Owner: Cameron Broadcasting Inc.
Arbitron Metro Market: Big River, CA; *Format:* Country; *No. News Employees:* 1; *Target Audience:* 25-54
Don Jaeger, Operations Dir

Big Sur

KYZZ
95.9 MHz FM; 1 kw horiz; -111 meters; N36 13 24 W121 45 27
1500 Cotner Avenue, Los Angeles, CA
(310) 478-5540; *Fax:* (310) 445-1439
www.mountwilsoninc.com
License: Big Sur, Monterey County, CA held by Mount Wilson FM Broadcasters
Group Owner: Mount Wilson FM Broadcasters Inc.

Saul Levine, President

Bishop

KBOV
04-01-1953; 1230 kHz AM; 1 kw-U, ND1; N37 20 44 W118 23 43
P. O. Box 757, Bishop, CA 93515 US
(760) 873-6324; *Fax:* (760) 872-2639
www.kibskbov.com
kibskbov@qnet.com
License: Bishop, CA held by Great Country Broadcasting Inc.

Nat'l Reps: Western Regional Broadcast Sales
Format: Oldies; *Hrs. of News Programming:* news progmg 8 hrs wkly; *No. News Employees:* 1; *Target Audience:* General.; *Adv. Rates:* 8; 8; 8; 8
Steve Miller, Operations Dir
Lauren Brandt, General Manager

KIBS
11-01-1974; 100.7 MHz FM; *Hrs Open:* 24; 1 kw; 2959 ft.; N37 25 0 W118 11 0
PO Box 757, Bishop, CA 93515 US
(760) 873-6324; *Fax:* (760) 872-2639
www.kibskbov.com
kibskbov@kibskbov.com
License: Bishop, Inyo County, CA held by Great Country Broadcasting Inc.
Format: Country *Special Programming:* Sports 20 hrs wkly; *Hrs. of News Programming:* news progmg 8 hrs wkly; *No. News Employees:* 1; *Adv. Rates:* 12; 12; 13; 12
Steve Miller, Operations Dir
Steve Miller, General Manager
Ron Knox, Programming Director
Arnie Palu, News Director
Mike Cheuvront, Disc Jockey
John Young, Disc Jockey

***KWTW**
01-01-2002; 88.5 MHz FM; *Hrs Open:* 24; 0.9 kw; 2917 ft.; N37 24 48 W118 11 8
Mailing Address: P.O. Box 637, Bishop, CA 93515 US
Second Address: 125 S. Main St., Bishop, CA 93514
(760) 872-4225(866) 466-5989; *Fax:* (760) 872-4155
www.kwtw.org
recep@kwtw.org
License: Bishop, Inyo County, CA held by Living Proof Inc.
Arbitron Metro Market: Bishop, CA; *Format:* Christian, Religious; *Target Audience:* General; all who want to hear the gospel
Daniel McClenaghan, President

Blue Lake

KINS-FM
01-01-2007; 106.3 MHz FM; 3.3 kw; 1,693 ft.; N40 43 38.9 W123 58 17
1101 Marsh Rd., Eureka, CA 95501 US
(707) 442-5744
www.kins1063.com
License: Blue Lake, Humboldt County, CA held by Eureka Broadcasting Co. Inc.
Group Owner: Eureka Broadcasting Co. Inc.
Nat'l Network: Fox News Radio
Arbitron Metro Market: Eureka, CA; *Format:* News, News/Talk, 86
Brian Papstein, General Manager

Blythe

KJMB-FM
04-01-1975; 100.3 MHz FM; *Hrs Open:* 24; 36 kw horiz; 56 ft.; N33 37 16 W114 35 28
681 North 4th Street, Blythe, CA 92507 US
(760) 922-7143; *Fax:* (760) 922-2844
License: Blythe, Riverside County, CA held by Blythe Radio Inc.
Nat'l Network: USA
Format: Adult Contemp *Special Programming:* Farm 5 hrs wkly; *Hrs. of News Programming:* news progmg 10 hrs wkly; *No. News Employees:* 1; *Target Audience:* 18-40; adults; *Adv. Rates:* 16; 16; 16; 16
Jim Mayson, President
James Morris, General Manager

Borrego Springs

***KKJD**
91.3 MHz FM; 6 kw; -347 m; N33 14 39 W116 22 30
Box 2429, Borrego SpringsCA
(760)767-7447
www.kkjdradio.com
License: Borrego Springs, San Diego County, CA held by Borrego Springs Christian Center

Steve Mellor, President

Brawley

KROP
11-01-1946; 1300 kHz AM; *Hrs Open:* 24
2550 Fifth Ave., Suite 723, San Diego, CA 42102 US
(760) 344-1300; *Fax:* (760) 344-1763
q96radio@yahoo.com
License: Brawley, CA held by CCR-Brawley IV LLC.
Group Owner: Cherry Creek Radio LLC; acq 6-99; $2 million with co-located FM).
Arbitron Metro Market: Palm Springs, CA; *Format:* Country; *Target Audience:* 25-54; male
Tony Driskill, General Manager

KSEH
04-04-1988; 94.5 MHz FM; *Hrs Open:* 24; 50 kw; 302 ft.; N32 54 40 W115 31 40
1803 N. Imperial Ave., El Centro, CA 92243 US
(760) 482-7777
www.jose945.com
License: Brawley, Imperial County, CA held by Entravision Holdings LLC.
Group Owner: Entravision Communications Corp.
Nat'l Network: ABC
Arbitron Metro Market: El Centro, CA; *Format:* Spanish, Adult Contemp; *Target Audience:* 25-54.
Veronica Avila, Senior VP

Buena Park

***KBPK**
07-06-1970; 90.1 MHz FM; 0.019 kw; 10 ft.; N33 51 35 W118 0 53
6885 Orangethorpe Avenue, Buena Park, CA 90620 US
(714) 732-5459
kbpk-fm.com
License: Buena Park, Orange County, CA held by Buena Park School District.
Wire Services: AP
Arbitron Metro Market: Los Angeles; *Format:* Adult Contemp; *Target Audience:* 25-54.
Edward Ford, Operations Dir
Peg Berger, Programming Director
Tracy Thackrah, Music Director

Burbank

KIEV
01-01-1986; 1500 kHz AM
801 K Streeet 27th Fl, Sacramento, CA 95814 US
(916) 813-1065
License: Burbank, CA held by Royce International Broadcasting Co.
Nat'l Reps: McGavren Guild
Arbitron Metro Market: Los Angeles
Edward Stolz II, President

Burney

***KIBC**
11-15-1985; 90.5 MHz FM; *Hrs Open:* 24; 3 kw; 1457 ft.; N40 52 29 W121 46 13
P. O. Box 1717, Burney, CA 96013 US
(530) 335-5422; *Fax:* (530) 335-5422
www.kibcfm.org
License: Burney, Shasta County, CA held by Burney Educational Broadcasting Foundation.
Format: Gospel; *Target Audience:* General.
Wayne Hennessey, General Manager
Alvin Hennessey, Programming Director

***KNCA**
07-01-1992; 89.7 MHz FM; *Hrs Open:* 5 AM-2 AM; 29 kw; 2064 ft.; N40 54 21 W121 49 38
P.O. Box 3175, Eugene, OR 97403 US
(541) 552-6301
www.ijpr.org
info@ijpr.org
License: Burney, Shasta County, CA held by The State of Oregon, acting by and through the State Board of Higher Education.
Nat'l Network: NPR; PRI
Arbitron Metro Market: Redding, CA; *Format:* Jazz, News, 90
Special Programming: Blues 6 hrs, folk 3 hrs, pub affrs 7 hrs wkly; *Hrs. of News Programming:* news progmg 45 hrs wkly; *No. News Employees:* 1 *TargetAudience:* General.
Ronald Kramer, CEO
Bryon Lambert, Operations Dir
Paul Westhelle, General Sales Mgr
Mitchell Christian, CFO

KRRX
05-01-1985; 106.1 MHz FM; *Hrs Open:* 24; 100 kw; 1969 ft.; N40 54 21 W121 49 38
3360 Alta Mesa Dr., Redding, CA 96002 US
(530) 226-9500; *Fax:* (530) 221-4940
www.106x.com
duane@reddingradio.com
License: Burney, Shasta County, CA held by Mapleton License of Redding LLC.
Group Owner: Mapleton Communications LLC; (acq 11-30-2006; grpsl)
Arbitron Metro Market: Northern CA; *Format:* Rock/AOR; *No. News Employees:* 2; *Target Audience:* 25-54; upscale
Clark Schopflin, Programming Director

Calexico

***KQVO**
03-01-1984; 97.7 MHz FM; *Hrs Open:* 24; 6 kw; 305 ft.; N32 40 48 W115 25 36 *Rebroadcasts:* Rebroadcasts KPBS-FM San Diego 100%
2925 East Exposition Ave., Denver, CO 80209 US
(619) 594-6983; *Fax:* (619) 594-3812
www.kpbs.org
letters@kpbs.org
License: Calexico, Imperial County, CA held by State of California, San Diego State University
Nat'l Network: NPR; PRI
Arbitron Metro Market: San Diego, CA
Kathryn Nelson, Operations Dir
Tom Karlo, General Manager
Deanna Mackey, Station Manager
John Decker, Programming Director
Suzanne Marmion, News Director
Charlotte Albergertis, Director of Marketing and Corporate Support

***KUBO**
01-01-1989; 88.7 MHz FM; *Hrs Open:* 24; 3 kw; 272 ft.; N32 47 57 W115 30 12
5005 E. Belmont, Fresno, CA 93727 US
(559) 264-9191; *Fax:* (559) 455-5778
www.radiobilingue.org
ricardo@radiobilingue.org
License: Calexico, Imperial County, CA held by Radio Bilingue Inc.
Arbitron Metro Market: Calexico, CA; *Format:* Ethnic; *Hrs. of News Programming:* news progmg 3 hrs wkly; *No. News Employees:* 5; *Target Audience:* 16-60; Latino
Hugo Morales, Executive Director
Maria Erana, Operations Dir
Maria Esana, Programming Director
Samuel Orozco, News Director
Kenia Chavez, Marketing Director

California City

KMVE
05-22-1999; 106.9 MHz FM; *Hrs Open:* 24; 2.35 kw; 522 ft.; N35 12 44 W117 45 11
570 East Avenue Q-9, Palmdale, CA 93550 US
(661) 947-3107
License: California City, Kern County, CA held by High Desert Broadcasting
Group Owner: High Desert Broadcasting
Nat'l Network: ABC
Format: Tejano *Special Programming:* Gospel 3 hrs wkly; *No. News Employees:* 1; *Target Audience:* General.; *Adv. Rates:* 16; 16; 16; 14
John Hearne, CEO
Nelson Rasse, General Sales Mgr
Mark Benevento, Programming Director
Alizah Lipson, Promotions Director

Calipatria

KSSB
02-08-1997; 100.9 MHz FM; *Hrs Open:* 24; 3 kw horiz; 66 ft.; N33 7 12 W115 30 47
200 S. A St., 4th Fl., Oxnard, CA 93030 US
(805) 240-2070
www.radiolazer.com
License: Calipatria, Imperial County, CA held by Lazer Licenses LLC.
Group Owner: Lazer Broadcasting Corp.; (acq 9-22-2006; $925,000)
Arbitron Metro Market: Calipatria, CA *Special Programming:* Religious 6 hrs wkly; *Hrs. of News Programming:* news progmg 6 hrs wkly; *No. News Employees:* 1; *Target Audience:* 25 plus; female/male *Adv. Rates:* 12:50; 12:50; 12:50; 12:50

Calistoga

***KBBF**
05-30-1973; 89.1 MHz FM; 0.42 kw; 2767 ft.; N38 39 23 W122 36 54
P. O. Box 7189, Santa Rosa, CA 95401 US
(707) 545-8833; *Fax:* (707) 545-6244
www.kbbf-fm.org
License: Calistoga, Napa County, CA held by Bilingual Broadcasting Foundation Inc.

Arbitron Metro Market: Santa Rosa, CA; *Format:* Spanish
Alicia Sanchez, President
Josue Lopez, Director

Camarillo

KCAQ
09-27-1958; 95.9 MHz FM; 1.2 kw; 1457 ft.; N34 20 55 W119 20 13
2319 Alameda Ave, Suite 1D, Ventura, CA 93003 US
(805) 654-0414; (805) 289-1400
q959.fm
License: Camarillo, Ventura West County, CA held by Gold Coast Broadcasting LLC
Group Owner: Gold Coast Broadcasting LLC; (acq 1996; $3.65 million with KVTA(AM) Port Hueneme).
Nat'l Reps: Katz Radio
Arbitron Metro Market: Ventura, CA; *Format:* Contemporary Hits/Top 40; *Target Audience:* 18-44.
Chip Ehrhardt, National Sales Director
Steve Hess, General Sales Mgr
Brian Davis, Programming Director

*KMRO
01-19-1987; 90.3 MHz FM; *Hrs Open:* 24; 10.5 kw; 920 ft.; N34 24 40 W119 10 28
2310 Ponderosa Drive, Camarillo, CA 93010 US
(805) 482-4797; *Fax:* (805) 388-5202
www.nuevavida.com
info@nuevavida.com
License: Camarillo, Ventura County, CA held by The Association for Community Education Inc.
Arbitron Metro Market: Oxnard, CA; *Format:* Religious; *Target Audience:* General; Hispanics
Phil Guthrie, President
Mary Guthrie, General Manager

Camino

*KCPC
01-01-2005; 88.3 MHz FM; *Hrs Open:* 24; 0.055 kw vert; 446 ft.; N38 44 18 W120 42 8
US
(209) 477-3690; *Fax:* (209) 477-2762
www.kycc.org
kycc@kycc.org
License: Camino, El Dorado County, CA held by Nevada City Community Broadcast Group
Arbitron Metro Market: Kerville, TX; *Format:* Gospel, Religious; *Target Audience:* 35-55.
Shirley Garner, General Manager

Canyon Country

KHTS
06-01-1989; 1220 kHz AM; *Hrs Open:* 24; 1 kw-D, 500 w-N, DA-2; N34 27 55 W118 24 08
27225 Camp Plenty Rd., Suite 8, Santa Clarita, CA 41011
(661) 298-1220; *Fax:* (661) 298-2020
www.hometownstation.com
License: Canyon Country, Los Angeles County, CA held by Jeri Lyn Broadcasting Inc.
Arbitron Metro Market: Los Angeles
Carl Goldman, General Manager
Jen Serati, Station Manager
Kyle Jellings, Programming Director
Carol Rock, News Director
Bruce Smith, Chief Engineer

Carlsbad

KSSX
08-22-1965; 95.7 MHz FM; *Hrs Open:* 24; 29 kw; 639 ft; N32 50 24 W117 14 52
9660 Granite Ridge Rd., San Diego, CA 92123 US
(858) 292-2000; *Fax:* (858) 278-7957
www.957kissfm.com
License: Carlsbad, San Diego County, CA held by Citicasters Licenses Inc.
Group Owner: iHeartMedia; (acq 5-4-99; grpsl).
Nat'l Network: ABC
Population Served: 600,000; *Arbitron Metro Market:* San Diego, CA; *Format:* Oldies, Urban Contemporary; *Target Audience:* 25-54; general
Melissa Forrest, President/Market Manager
Sarah Dobbins, Sales Manager
Louie Cruz, Programming Director
Geoff Alan, Promotions Manager
Jean Arrollado, Marketing Director

Carmel

KKHK
12-04-1993; 95.5 MHz FM; *Hrs Open:* 24; 1.7 kw; 630 ft.; N36 33 9 W121 47 17
6 Garden Ct., Suite 300, Monterey, CA 93940 US
(831) 658-5200
www.955bobfm.com
kallen@radiomontereybay.com
License: Carmel, Monterey County, CA held by Mapleton License of Monterey LLC.
Group Owner: Mapleton Communications LLC; (acq 6-7-2005; $3.75 million)
Nat'l Reps: McGavren Guild
Arbitron Metro Market: Monterey-Salinas-Santa Cruz, CA; *Format:* Country
Jodi Morgan, General Sales Mgr
Kenny Allen, Programming Director

KCDU
04-29-1971; 101.7 MHz FM; *Hrs Open:* 24; 2.35 kw; 528 ft.; N36 33 9 W121 47 17
60 Garden Ct., Suite 300, Monterey, CA 93940 US
(831) 658-5200
www.1017thebeach.com
tdelrio@radiomontereybay.com
License: Carmel, Monterey County, CA held by Mapleton License of Monterey LLC.
Group Owner: Mapleton Communications LLC; (acq 1-17-2002; grpsl)
Nat'l Reps: McGavren Guild
Arbitron Metro Market: Monterey-Salinas-Santa Cruz, CA; *Format:* Adult Contemp; *Target Audience:* Women 25-54; upscale, educated, above average income
Jodi Morgan, General Sales Mgr
Tommy Del Rio, Programming Director

KRML
12-25-1957; 1410 kHz AM; *Hrs Open:* 24; 0.5 kw-D, ND1; 0.016 kw-N, ND1; N36 32 11 W121 54 13 *Rebroadcasts:* live streaming from www.krmlradio.com
Mailing Address: P.O. Drawer 22440, Carmel, CA 93922 US
Second Address: San Carlos near 5th, Carmel, CA 93921
(831) 624-6431; *Fax:* (831) 625-2417
www.krml.com
License: Carmel, CA held by Wisdom Broadcasting Co. Inc.
Regional Reps: McGavern Guild
Arbitron Metro Market: Monterey Bay; *Format:* Jazz *Special Programming:* Gospel 6 hrs wkly; *Hrs. of News Programming:* 10.5 hrs wkly; *Target Audience:* 35+.; *Adv. Rates:* 50; 40; 50; 25
David Kimball, General Manager

Carmel Valley

KRXA
07-10-1989; 540 kHz AM; *Hrs Open:* 18
2360 N.E. Coachman Road, Clearwater, FL 33765 US
(831) 394-5792
www.krxa540.com
hal@krxa540.com
License: Carmel Valley, CA held by KRFA-AM, LLC
Arbitron Metro Market: Monterey-Salinas-Santa Cruz, CA; *Format:* Talk *Special Programming:* Religious 5 hrs wkly, Health 2 hrs wkly; *Hrs. of News Programming:* News progmg 60 hrs wkly
Hal Ginsberg, General Manager
Larry Wrathall, General Sales Mgr
Fia Karim, Programming Director
Annabel Lund, News Director

Carmichael

KFIA
01-11-1979; 710 kHz AM; 25 kw-D, 1 kw-N, DA-2; N38 49 58 W121 19 03
1425 River Park Dr., Suite 520, Sacramento, CA 93012
(916) 924-0710; *Fax:* (916) 924-1587
www.kfia.com
info@kfia.com
License: Carmichael, Sacramento County, CA held by New Inspiration Broadcasting Co. Inc.
Group Owner: Salem Communications Corp.; (acq 2-15-95;
Population Served: 7,000,000; *Arbitron Metro Market:* Sacramento, CA; *Target Audience:* 35 plus; general
Edward Atsinger III, President
Steve Gasser, Operations Dir
Dale Hendry, General Manager
Max Miller, Programming Director

Carnelian Bay

KODS
01-01-1970; 103.7 MHz FM; 5.9 kw; 2986 ft.; N39 18 38 W119 53 1
961 Matley Lane, Suite 120, Reno, NV 89502 US
(775) 829-1964; *Fax:* (775) 825-3183
www.river1037.com
License: Carnelian Bay, Placer County, CA held by Reno Media Group L.P.
Group Owner: Americom Broadcasting; (acq 1996)
Nat'l Reps: CBS Radio
Arbitron Metro Market: Reno, NV; *Format:* Oldies
Tom Quinn, President
Lori Heeren, Vice President and General Manager
Heather Forcier, National Regional Sales Director
Carrie Carano, Local Sales Manager
Teresa Estabrook, Local Sales Manager

Carpinteria

KIST-FM
01-01-1998; 107.7 MHz FM; *Hrs Open:* 24; 930 w; Ant 1,627 ft; N34 30 10 W119 50 56
414 East Cota Street, Santa Barbara, CA 41011
(805) 879-8300; *Fax:* (805) 879-8430
License: Carpinteria, Santa Barbara County, CA held by Rincon License Subsidiary LLC.
Group Owner: Rincon Broadcasting LLC; (acq 7-11-2007; grpsl)
Nat'l Reps: Katz Radio
Arbitron Metro Market: Santa Barbara, CA
Keith Royer, Executive Vice President/General Manager
Tom Baker, General Manager
Jack Clarke, National Sales Manager
Jose Fierros, Programming Director
Lin Aubuchon, Promotions Manager
Steve Hess, Local Sales Manager

Cartago

KWTY
11-01-1989; 94.5 MHz FM; *Hrs Open:* 24; 2 kw horiz; -1788 ft.; N36 19 16 W118 1 22
P.O. Box 773, Big Pine, CA 93513 US
(760) 764-1111; *Fax:* (760) 764-1111
License: Cartago, Inyo County, CA held by Mark A. Miller
Wire Services: UPI
Format: Classic Rock; *Hrs. of News Programming:* News progmg 7 hrs wkly; *Target Audience:* General; 15-55 years (M-F), recreation/resort commuters; *Adv. Rates:* 5; 5; 5; 3
Mark Miller, General Manager
Dan Owen, General Sales Mgr

Cathedral City

KDES-FM
02-10-1963; 98.5 MHz FM; 43 kw; 528 ft.; N33 51 56 W116 26 4
2100 East Tahquitz Canyon Way, Palm Springs, CA 92262 US
(760) 325-2582; *Fax:* (760) 322-3562
License: Cathedral City, Riverside County, CA
Group Owner: RR Broadcasting
Arbitron Metro Market: Palm Springs, CA; *Format:* Oldies
Jack Broady, General Manager
Gregg Aratin, Vice President of Sales
Steve Kelly, Programming Director
Brian Garris, Promotions Manager
Gene Nichols, News Director
Mel Hill, Local Sales Manager

KWXY AM
01-19-1969; 1340 kHz AM; *Hrs Open:* 24; 50 kw; 499 ft; N33 51 55 W116 26 10
2100 East Tahquitz Canyon Way, Palm Springs, CA 92262
(760) 328-1104; *Fax:* (760) 328-7814
www.kwxy.com
License: Cathedral City, Riverside County, CA held by Glen Barnett Inc.
Wire Services: AP
Population Served: 45,573; *Arbitron Metro Market:* Palm Springs, CA; *Format:* Adult Contemp *Special Programming:* Canadian news 2 hrs wkly; *Hrs. of News Programming:* news progmg 16 hrs wkly; *No. News Employees:* 1; *Target Audience:* 35 plus; affluent adults; *Adv. Rates:* 37; 37; 37; 30
Jack Broady, General Manager
Gregg Aratin, Vice President of Sales
Ford Michaels, Programming Director
Gene Nichols, News Director
Mel Hill, Local Sales Manager
Kacy Consiglio, Traffic Director

Cayucos

KPYG
10-01-1984; 94.9 MHz FM; *Hrs Open:* 24; 25 kw; 328 ft.; N35 31 26 W121 3 40
396 Buckley Rd., San Luis Obispo, CA 93401 US
(805) 786-2580
www.kpig.com
License: Cayucos, San Luis Obispo County, CA held by Mapleton License of San Luis Obispo LLC
Group Owner: Mapleton Communications LLC; (acq 7-19-2002; grpsl)
Arbitron Metro Market: San Luis Obispo, CA; *Format:* Triple A; *Target Audience:* 25-54.

Cazadero

KTRY(FM)
106.3 MHz FM; 1620 watts; 194 meters; 38 29 20N 123 01 53W
3392 Mendocino Avenue, PO Box 100, Santa Rosa, CA 95402 USA
(707) 528-4434
License: Cazadero, Sonoma County, CA
Group Owner: Redwood Empire Stereocasters

Tom Skinner, Vice President/General Manager

Cedarville

KHAL
01-01-2008; 95.5 MHz FM; kw
US
(541) 298-4141
License: Cedarville, Gilliam County, CA held by Haystack Broadcasting Inc.
Arbitron Metro Market: Omaha-Council Bluffs, NE-IA
Danny Manciu, President

***KDUP**
01-01-2008; 88.1 MHz FM; 0.27 kw; -105 ft.; N41 38 13 W120 5 28
US
(775) 279-6677
openskyradio.org
klap@klap.fm
License: Cedarville, Modoc County, CA held by OpenSkyRadio Corp.
Arbitron Metro Market: Cedarville, CA; *Format:* Variety/Diverse
Jeffrey Cotton, General Manager

Ceres

***KBES**
09-01-1979; 89.5 MHz FM; 0.15 kw; 131 ft.; N37 35 21 W120 57 23
P.O. Box 4116, Modesto, CA 95352 US
(209) 538-4130; *Fax:* (209) 538-2795
www.betnahrain.org
License: Ceres, Stanislaus County, CA held by Bet Nahrain Inc.
Arbitron Metro Market: Modesto, CA; *Format:* Ethnic
Dr. Sargon Dadisho, General Manager
Janet Shamon, Programming Director
Seimon Mamio, Chief Engineer

KVIN
09-15-1963; 920 kHz AM; 0.5 kw-D, DA2; 2.5 kw-N, DA2; N37 35 49 W121 4 15; N37 37 55 W120 45 6
961 North Emerald Avenue, Suite A, Modesto, CA 95351 US
(209) 238-0920; *Fax:* (209) 544-1055
thevine@kvin.net
License: Ceres, CA held by Threshold Communications
Nat'l Reps: Interep
Arbitron Metro Market: Modesto, CA; *Format:* Adult Contemp; *Target Audience:* 35-64.
Doug Wulff, Operations Director/Music Director
Jim Bryan, General Manager/Programming Director
Sally Waterman, Office Manager

Chester

***KWLU**
04-06-1989; 98.9 MHz FM; *Hrs Open:* 24; 1 kw; 2474 ft.; N40 14 0 W121 1 11
395 Main St., Quincy, CA 95971 US
(916) 251-1600; *Fax:* (916) 251-1650
www.klove.com
License: Chester, Plumas County, CA held by Educational Media Foundation.
Group Owner: EMF Broadcasting; (acq 6-30-2005; $900,000 with KPCO(AM) Quincy)
Nat'l Network: K-Love
Format: Christian
Mike Novak, President
Ed Lenane, News Director
Sam Wallington, Engineering Dir

Chico

***KCHO**
04-22-1969; 91.7 MHz FM; *Hrs Open:* 24; 7.7 kw; 1220 ft.; N39 57 30 W121 42 48
First & Normal Sts., Chico, CA 95929 US
(530) 898-5896; *Fax:* (530) 898-4348
www.kcho.org
info@kcho.org
License: Chico, Butte County, CA held by California State University, Chico Research Foundation.
Nat'l Network: PRI; NPR
Arbitron Metro Market: Chico, CA; *Format:* Jazz, News; *Hrs. of News Programming:* news progmg 37 hrs wkly; *No. News Employees:* 1; *Target Audience:* General.
Brian Terhorst, General Manager
Lorraine Dechter, News Director
Jim Moore, Engineering Dir
Mike Birdsill, Chief Engineer
Beth Heberle, Underwriting Director

KFMF
02-01-1974; 93.9 MHz FM; *Hrs Open:* 24; 2 kw; 1129 ft.; N39 56 46 W121 43 17
1459 Humbolt Rd., Suite A, Chico, CA 95928 US
(530) 899-3600
www.939thehippo.com
dwilson@radiochicocomm.com
License: Chico, Butte County, CA held by Mapleton License of Chico LLC.
Group Owner: Mapleton Communications LLC; (acq 11-30-2006; grpsl)
Nat'l Reps: Christal
Arbitron Metro Market: Chico, CA; *Format:* Rock/AOR; *Hrs. of News Programming:* news progmg one hr wkly; *No. News Employees:* 1; *Target Audience:* 18-44.
Duane Davis, Operations Dir
Don Wilson, Programming Director
Christina Warner, Promotions Manager

***KHAP**
01-01-1999; 89.1 MHz FM; 12 kw; 285 ft.; N39 43 37 W121 40 45
Mailing Address: 4135 Northgate Blvd #1, Sacramento, CA 95834 US
Second Address: 290 Hegenberger Rd., Oakland, CA 94621
(916) 641-8191; *Fax:* (916) 641-8238
www.familyradio.com
info@familyradio.com
License: Chico, Butte County, CA held by Family Stations Inc.
Group Owner: Family Stations Inc.
Arbitron Metro Market: Chico, CA; *Format:* Christian, Religious
Special Programming: Family 25 hrs wkly; *Target Audience:* Christian Adults
Tom Evans, General Manager

KBQB
06-01-1993; 92.7 MHz FM; 1.5 kw; 643 ft.; N39 48 25 W121 37 35
856 Manzanita Ct., Chico, CA 95926 US
(530) 342-2200; *Fax:* (530) 342-2260
www.927bobfm.com
License: Chico, Butte County, CA held by Results Radio Licensee L.L.C.
Group Owner: Results Radio; (acq 6-11-99; grpsl)
Arbitron Metro Market: Chico, CA; *Format:* Adult Contemp

KMXI
11-16-1972; 95.1 MHz FM; 8.7 kw; 1171 ft.; N39 56 46 W121 43 17
4700 Sw Macadam Avenue, Portland, OR 97201 US
(530) 345-0021; *Fax:* (530) 893-2121
www.kmxi.com
License: Chico, Butte County, CA held by Deer Creek Broadcasting LLC
Group Owner: Deer Creek Broadcasting LLC
Arbitron Metro Market: Chico, CA; *Format:* Adult Contemp
Dino Corbin, General Manager
Jaime Perry, General Sales Mgr
Larry Scott, Programming Director
Heather Welch, News Director

KPAY
04-17-1935; 1290 kHz AM
4700 S.W. Macadam Ave., Portland, OR 97201 US
(530) 345-0021; *Fax:* (530) 893-2121
www.kpay.com
License: Chico, CA held by Deer Creek Broadcasting LLC.
Group Owner: Deer Creek Broadcasting LLC; (acq 9-8-2004; grpsl).
Nat'l Reps: Katz Radio
Arbitron Metro Market: Chico, CA; *Format:* News, News/Talk, 86; *Target Audience:* 25 plus.
Dino Corbin, General Manager
Larry Scott, Programming Director
Lisa Fitzgerald, Promotions Manager
Matt Ray, News Director
Karen Ulsh, Business Manager

***KZFR**
07-06-1990; 90.1 MHz FM; *Hrs Open:* 24; 6.3 kw; 587 ft.; N39 48 25 W121 37 35
Mailing Address: P.O. Box 3173, Chico, CA 95927 US
Second Address: 341 Broadway, Suite 411, Chico, CA 95928
(530) 895-0706/895-0788; *Fax:* (530) 895-0775
www.kzfr.org
info@kzfr.org
License: Chico, Butte County, CA held by Golden Valley Community Broadcasters.
Arbitron Metro Market: Chico, CA; *Format:* News, News/Talk, 86, Variety/Diverse *Special Programming:* American Indian 2 hrs, Sp 6 hrs wkly; *Hrs. of News Programming:* News progmg 8 hrs wkly
Jill Paydon, General Manager
Stacey Wear, Office Manager
Shelly Mariposa, Underwriting Director

China Lake

KSSI
01-01-1995; 102.7 MHz FM; *Hrs Open:* 24; 3 kw; -23 ft.; N35 39 6 W117 40 58
701 C. Inyokern Road, Ridgecrest, CA 93555 US
(760) 446-5774; *Fax:* (760) 446-5774
john@kssifm.com
License: China Lake, Kern County, CA held by Sound Enterprises.
Arbitron Metro Market: Ridgecrest, CA; *Format:* Rock/AOR; *Target Audience:* 25-54; general
John Perrige, General Manager
Don Fredette, Programming Director
Lisa Garcia, News Director

***KFRJ**
06-01-2005; 91.1 MHz FM; *Hrs Open:* 24; 5.5 kw; 1266 ft.; N35 28 38 W117 41 59
Mailing Address: 4135 Northgate Blve, Suite 1, Sacramenta, CA 95834 US
Second Address: 290 Hegenberger Rd., Oakland, CA 94621
(800) 543-1495; *Fax:* (916) 641-8238
www.familyradio.com
info@familyradio.com
License: China Lake, Kern County, CA held by Family Stations Inc.
Group Owner: Family Stations Inc.
Arbitron Metro Market: China Lake, CA; *Format:* Christian, Religious
Tom Evans, General Manager

Chowchilla

KNTO
08-01-1992; 93.3 MHz FM; *Hrs Open:* 24; 2.95 kw; 335 ft.; N37 13 2 W120 11 56
4043 Geer Road, Hughson, CA 95326 US
(209) 883-8760; *Fax:* (209) 883-8769
www.lafavorita.net
ngomez@lafavorita.net
License: Chowchilla, Madera County, CA held by La Favorita Radio Network, Inc.
Group Owner: La Favorita Radio Network; (acq 4-17-01; $450,000).
Arbitron Metro Market: Hughson, CA; *Format:* Spanish; *Target Audience:* 18-35; Hispanic
Nelson Gomez, General Manager
Marisol Valenzuela, Programming Director
Mawry Medina, Production Manager

Chualar

***KHDC**
06-28-1981; 90.9 MHz FM; .3 kw; 194 ft.; N36 34 54 W121 26 34
5005 E. Belmont, Fresno, CA 93727 US
(831) 757-8039; *Fax:* (831) 757-9854
www.radiobilingue.org
License: Chualar, Monterey County, CA held by Radio Bilingue Inc.
Format: Ethnic, Talk
Hugo Morales, Executive Director
Delia Saldivar, Station Manager
Maria Erana, Programming Director

Citrus Heights

*KLVB
11-01-1985; 99.5 MHz FM; *Hrs Open:* 24; 5.1 kw; 358 ft.; N38 38 32 W121 5 25 *Rebroadcasts:* Rebroadcasts KLVC(FM) Magalia 100%
1425 North Market Blvd., Suite 9, Sacramento, CA 95834 US
(916) 251-1600; *Fax:* (916) 251-1650
www.klove.com
klove@klove.com
License: Citrus Heights, Tehama County, CA held by Educational Media Foundation.
Group Owner: EMF Broadcasting; (acq 1-11-2001; $750,000).
Nat'l Network: K-Love; *Nat'l Reps:* D & R Radio
Arbitron Metro Market: Redding, CA; *Format:* Christian; *No. News Employees:* 3; *Target Audience:* 25-44; Judeo Christian, female
Darrell Chambliss, Chairman
Mike Novak, CEO/COO
Mike Novak, President
David Pierce, Programming Director
Ed Lenane, News Director
Sam Wallington, Engineering Dir

Claremont

*KSPC
02-01-1956; 88.7 MHz FM; 0.4 kw; 69 ft.; N34 8 33 W117 43 17
340 N. College Avenue, Claremont, CA 91711 US
(909) 621-8157
www.kspc.org
director@kspc.org
License: Claremont, Los Angeles County, CA held by Pomona College.
Arbitron Metro Market: Los Angeles; *Format:* Alternative, Jazz, 94 *Special Programming:* Pol 3 hrs, reggae 4 hrs, blues 4 hrs, pub affrs 3 hrs, hip hop/rap 6 hrs wkly; *Target Audience:* General.
Eric Tyron, Director of College Radio

Cloverdale

KSRT
01-01-2002; 107.1 MHz FM; *Hrs Open:* 24; 3.5 kw; 430 ft.; N38 48 34 W123 2 56
200 S. A St., 4th Fl., Oxnard, CA 93030 USA
(805) 240-2070
www.radiolazer.com
License: Cloverdale, Sonoma County, CA held by Lazer Licenses LLC.
Group Owner: Lazer Broadcasting Corp.; (acq 6-29-2006; $6.85 million with KJOR(FM) Windsor).
Format: Tejano

Clovis

KFPT
05-02-1977; 790 kHz AM; *Hrs Open:* 24
1071 West Shaw Avenue, Fresno, CA 93711 US
(559) 447-3570; *Fax:* (559) 447-3579
License: Clovis, CA held by Fat Dawgs 7 Broadcasting LLC
Group Owner: Fat Dawgs 7 LLC
Nat'l Network: ESPN Radio
Arbitron Metro Market: Fresno, CA; *Format:* Sports
Chris Pacheco, President
Paul Swearengin, Programming Director

KOND
09-30-1974; 92.1 MHz FM; 39 kw; 558 ft.; N37 7 40 W119 40 39
1436 Auburn Blvd., Sacramento, CA 95815 US
(559) 430-8510
www.univision.com
License: Clovis, Fresno County, CA held by Univision Radio License Corp.
Group Owner: Univision Radio; (acq 2-18-2004; $8 million).
Arbitron Metro Market: Fresno, CA; *Format:* Tejano
Angela Navarrete, Station Manager
Jose Luis Sanchez, Promotions Manager

Coachella

KNWZ
01-01-1954; 970 kHz AM; 5 kw-D, DA2; 1 kw-N, DA2; N33 41 12 W116 9 34
1321 N. Gene Autry Trail, Palm Springs, CA 92262 US
(760) 322-7890; *Fax:* (760) 322-5493
www.943knews.com
License: Coachella, Riverside County, CA held by Alpha Media Licensee LLC
Group Owner: Alpha Media LLC; (acq 9-2-2015; grpsl).
Arbitron Metro Market: Palm Springs, CA; *Format:* News, News/Talk, 86; *Target Audience:* 18-49.
Tricia Bastida, Senior Vice President and Market Manager
David Nola, General Sales Mgr
Paul Cashin, Programming Director
Cristine Constantinescu, Director of Promotions and Digital Media
Crystal White, National/Regional SalesManager

KCLB-FM
09-01-1960; 93.7 MHz FM; 26.5 kw; 646 ft.; N33 48 6 W116 13 28
1321 N. Gene Autry Trail, Palm Springs, CA 92262 US
(760) 322-7890; *Fax:* (760) 322-5493
www.937kclb.com
License: Coachella, Riverside County, CA held by Alpha Media Licensee LLC
Group Owner: Alpha Media LLC
Arbitron Metro Market: Palm Springs, CA; *Format:* Rock/AOR; *Target Audience:* 18-49
Tricia Bastida, Senior Vice President and Market Manager
David Nola, General Sales Mgr
Jennifer Shevlin, Program Director and Operations Manager
Cristine Constantinescu, Director of Promotions, Marketing & Digital Media
Bill Watson,Chief Engineer

*KPSH
90.9 MHz FM; 0.23 kw; 623 ft.; N33 52 3 W116 25 58
Mailing Address: 1905 Columbia Blvd, St Helens, OR 97051 US
Second Address: 8919 World Ministry Ave., Baton Rouge, LA 70826
(225) 768-3288; *Fax:* (225) 768-3729
www.jsm.org
onair@jsm.org
License: Coachella, Riverside County, CA held by Family Worship Center Church Inc.
Group Owner: Family Worship Center Church Inc.; acq 2-18-2004; $750,000 for CP).
Arbitron Metro Market: Coachella, CA; *Format:* Christian, Religious
Jimmy Swaggert, President/Chief Executive Officer
John Santiago, Operations Manager

KPST
01-01-2012; 103.5 MHz FM; 1.9 kw; 587 ft.; N33 39 23 W115 59 29
41601 Corporate Way, Palm Desert, CA 92260 US
(760) 341-5837; *Fax:* (760) 837-3711
www.jose947.com
vtocco@entravision.com
License: Coachella, Palm Springs County, CA held by Entravision Holdings LLC.
Group Owner: Entravision Communications Corp.; (acq 2-27-97).
Arbitron Metro Market: Palm Springs, CA; *Format:* Spanish, Adult Contemp
Victor Tocco, General Manager
Juliana Simmons, Promotions Manager
Sergio De La Torre, Chief Engineer

Coalinga

*KDKL
01-01-1999; 88.3 MHz FM; 1.4 kw vert; 2352 ft.; N36 22 11 W120 38 37
1601 Belvedere Rd, Suite 204e, West Palm Beach, FL 33406 US
(916) 251-1600; *Fax:* (916) 251-1650
www.klove.com
License: Coalinga, Fresno County, CA held by Educational Media Foundation
Group Owner: EMF Broadcasting; (acq 10-20-00; $80,000 for CP).
Nat'l Network: K-Love
Format: Christian
Mike Novak, President
David Pierce, Programming Director
Ed Lenane, News Director
Sam Wallington, Engineering Dir

KNGS
100.1 MHz FM; kw
12550 Brookhurst Street, Garden Grove, CA 92640 US
License: Coalinga, Fresno County, CA held by William L. Zawila.
Arbitron Metro Market: Fresno, CA
William Zawila, General Manager

*KFRP
11-01-2005; 90.7 MHz FM; 2.5 kw vert; 1253 ft.; N35 55 39 W120 22 46
Mailing Address: 4135 Northgate Blvd, Suite 1, Sacramento, CA 95834 US
Second Address: 290 Hegenberger Rd., Oakland, CA 94621
(800) 543-1495; *Fax:* (916) 641-8238
www.familyradio.com
info@familyradio.com
License: Coalinga, Fresno County, CA held by Family Stations Inc.
Group Owner: Family Stations Inc.
Arbitron Metro Market: Coalinga, CA; *Format:* Christian, Religious
Tom Evans, General Manager

Coarsegold

KRPW(FM)
94.5 MHz FM; 6 kw; Ant 103 ft; N37 15 56 W119 41 11
PO Box 2098, Omaha, NE NB 68103-2098
(312) 204-9900
License: Coarsegold, Madera County, CA held by Educational Media Foundation
Group Owner: Educational Media Foundation
Population Served: 1,840; *Arbitron Metro Market:* Coarsegold, CA
Mike Novak, President/CEO

Columbia

KCVR-FM
08-01-1995; 98.9 MHz FM; 6 kw; 328 ft.; N38 2 15 W120 22 5
6820 Pacific Ave., Floor 3A, Modesto, CA 95207 US
(209) 479-0154; *Fax:* (209) 474-0316
www.entravision.com
info@entravision.com
License: Columbia, Tuolumne County, CA held by Entravision Holdings LLC.
Group Owner: Entravision Communications Corp.; (acq 7-28-2000; grpsl).
Arbitron Metro Market: Stockton, CA; *Format:* Spanish, Contemporary Hits/Top 40
Lisa Vela, Senior VP

Colusa

KKCY
05-01-1990; 103.1 MHz FM; *Hrs Open:* 24; 0.135 kw; 1965 ft.; N39 12 21 W121 49 11
1479 Sanborn Dr., Yuba City, CA 95993 US
(530) 673-2200
gosunny.com
License: Colusa, Colusa County, CA held by Results Radio of Chico Licensee LLC.
Group Owner: Results Radio; (acq 6-11-99; grpsl)
Nat'l Reps: Katz Radio
Arbitron Metro Market: Chico, CA; *Format:* Country *Special Programming:* Sp one hr wkly; *Hrs. of News Programming:* news progmg 7 hrs wkly; *No. News Employees:* 1; *Target Audience:* 18-64.

KQPT
09-01-1986; 107.5 MHz FM; 28 kw; 633 ft.; N39 17 17 W122 20 2
1459 Humbolt Rd., Suite A, Chico, CA 95928 US
(530) 899-3600
www.1075nowfm.com
tdelrio@radiomontereybay.com
License: Colusa, Colusa County, CA held by Mapleton License of Chico LLC.
Group Owner: Mapleton Communications LLC; (acq 11-30-2006; grpsl)
Nat'l Reps: Christal
Arbitron Metro Market: Chico, CA; *Format:* Contemporary Hits/Top 40; *Target Audience:* 24-48.
Duane Davis, Operations Dir
Tommy Del Rio, Programming Director

Compton

KJLH
04-01-1965; 102.3 MHz FM; *Hrs Open:* 24; 5.6 kw; 338 ft.; N33 59 52 W118 21 32
161 North La Brea Ave, Inglewood, CA 90301 US
(310) 330-2200; *Fax:* (310) 330-5555,(310) 330-2244
www.kjlhradio.com
sales@kjlhradio.com
License: Compton, Los Angeles County, CA held by TAXI Productions Inc.
Nat'l Network: American Urban; ABC; *Nat'l Reps:* McGavren Guild
Arbitron Metro Market: Los Angeles; *Format:* Blues *Special Programming:* Relg 7 hrs, gospel 6 hrs, talk 8.5 hrs, Christian 6 hrs wkly; *Hrs. of News Programming:* news progmg 8.5 hrs wkly; *No. News Employees:* 2 *Target Audience:* 25-49; African-American audience

Stevland Morris, CEO
Karen Slade, General Manager
Al Ward, Vice President/National Sales Manager
Aundrae Russell, Programming Director
Jacquie Stephens, News Director
Barry Clark, Chief Engineer
Carrie Haynes, Traffic Manager

Concord

***KVHS**
05-16-1969; 90.5 MHz FM; *Hrs Open:* 25.?Â ?; 0.41 kw; 449 ft.; N38 1 49 W122 0 3
1101 Alberta Way, Concord, CA 94521 US
(925) 682-5847; *Fax:* (925) 609-5847
www.kvhs.com
License: Concord, Contra Costa County, CA held by Clayton Valley High School.
Wire Services: Bay City News Service
Arbitron Metro Market: Concord, CA; *Format:* Rock/AOR *Special Programming:* Flashback Show(Classic Rock); Punk & SKA Show; Metal Show(Hard Rock), Klub KVHS (Dance Mix); *Target Audience:* 18-34.(P-1) 18-49(P-2) 12+. *Adv. Rates:* 10.00 per CTBR
Melissa McConnell Wilson, General Manager

Concow

KBJK
01-01-1934; 100.3 MHz FM; 0.2 kw; -719 ft.; N39 56 25 W120 55 39
P.O. Box 77766, Stockton, CA 95267 US
(503) 223-1441; *Fax:* (503) 223-6909
www.espndeportesradio.com
License: Concow, Marion County, CA held by Sierra Radio Inc
Group Owner: Sierra Radio Inc.; (acq 10-22-98; $605,000)
Nat'l Network: ESPN Deportes *Regional Reps:* Allied Radio Partners.
Arbitron Metro Market: Portland, OR; *Format:* Sports
Tom F. Huth, President
Jack Hutchison, Executive Vice President

Copperopolis

KRVR
01-01-1995; 105.5 MHz FM; *Hrs Open:* 24; 1 kw; 781 ft; N37 56 55 W120 42 16
961 N. Emerald Ave., Suite A, Modesto, CA 95351
(209) 544-1055; *Fax:* (209) 544-8105
krvr.com
TheRiver@krvr.com
License: Copperopolis, Calaveras County, CA held by Threshold Communications.
Nat'l Reps: Interep
Population Served: 750,000; *Arbitron Metro Market:* Modesto, CA; *Target Audience:* 35-64.
Doug Wulff, Operations Dir
Jim Bryan, General Manager
Cheryl Miller, General Sales Mgr
Sally Waterman, News Director
R.J. Rose, Production Director

Corcoran

KBLO
01-01-1999; 102.3 MHz FM; *Hrs Open:* 24; 19.5 kw; 381 ft.; N36 11 4 W119 24 1
2171 Ralph Avenue, Stockton, CA 95206 US
(559) 740-4172; *Fax:* (559) 740-4177
www.radiolobo987.com
License: Corcoran, Kings County, CA held by Mapleton License of Visalia LLC
Group Owner: Mapleton Communications LLC; (acq 2-27-2009; $8 million)
Arbitron Metro Market: Corcoran, CA
Andrew Adams, Senior Vice President/General Manager
Diane Garcia, General Sales Mgr
Yolanda Navarro, Programming Director

Corning

KTHU
04-08-1988; 100.7 MHz FM; *Hrs Open:* 24; 50 kw; 272 ft.; N39 53 17 W122 37 38
856 Manzanita Ct., Chico, CA 95926 US
(530) 342-2200; *Fax:* (530) 342-2260
www.chicothunderheads.com
License: Corning, Tehama County, CA held by Results Radio Licensee L.L.C.
Group Owner: Results Radio; (acq 6-11-99; grpsl)
Arbitron Metro Market: Chico, CA; *Format:* Classic Rock *Special Programming:* Sp one hr wkly; *No. News Employees:* 1; *Target Audience:* 25-54.

Corona

KWRM
01-01-1948; 1370 kHz AM; *Hrs Open:* 24; 5 kw-D, DA2; 2.5 kw-N, DA2; N33 52 52 W117 32 33
Mailing Address: 210 Radio Road, Corona, CA 91719 US
Second Address: 210 Radio Rd., Corona, CA 92879
(951) 737-1370; *Fax:* (951) 735-9572
kwrm1370am.com
License: Corona, CA held by Major Market Stations Inc.
Arbitron Metro Market: Corona, CA; *Format:* Sports, Variety/Diverse; *Hrs. of News Programming:* news progmg 20 hrs wkly; *No. News Employees:* 2; *Target Audience:* 18-49; young Hispanic adults
Dr. William J. Roberts, President
Damian Vasquez, Operations Dir

Crescent City

KCRE-FM
03-21-1980; 94.3 MHz FM; 25 kw; Ant -305 ft; N41 45 35 W124 09 49
Mailing Address: Box 1089, Crescent City, CA 95531
Second Address: 1345 Northcrest Dr., Crescent City, CA 95531
(707) 464-9561; *Fax:* (707) 464-4303
www.kcrefm.com
License: Crescent City, Del Norte County, CA held by Bicoastal Media Licenses II, LLC
Nat'l Network: ABC
Population Served: 35,000
Mike Wilson, CEO/COO
Mike Wilson, President
Rene Shanle-Hutzell, General Manager
Dean Larson, Sr. Account Executive
John Pritchett, News Director
Kevin Sanders, Chief Engineer

KFVR
07-01-1950; 1310 kHz AM; *Hrs Open:* 24
PO Box 1089, Crescent City, CA 95531 US
(435) 623-4010; *Fax:* (435) 623-1451
www.lanueva1090.com
License: Crescent City, CA held by Del Rosario Talpa Inc.
Arbitron Metro Market: Beulah, CO; *Format:* Religious, Spanish
Mario Meza, General Manager

***KHSR**
07-01-1999; 91.9 MHz FM; *Hrs Open:* 24; 4.5 kw; -194 ft.; N41 45 35 W124 11 28 *Rebroadcasts:* Rebroadcasts KHSU-FM Arcata 100%
Khsu Humboldt State Univ, Arcata, CA 95521 US
(707) 826-4807; *Fax:* (707) 826-6082
www.khsu.org
khsu@humboldt.edu
License: Crescent City, Del Norte County, CA held by Humboldt State University.
Nat'l Network: NPR; PRI
Format: News *Special Programming:* World 14 hrs, jazz 10 hrs wkly
Katie Whiteside, Operations Dir
Ed Subkis, General Manager
David Reed, Development Director
Kevin Sanders, Chief Engineer
Mark Shikuma, Music Director
Lorna Bryant, Administrative Assistant

KPOD
12-05-1959; 1240 kHz AM; *Hrs Open:* 24; 778 w-U; N41 45 35 W124 11 28
1345 Northcrast Dr., Crescent City, CA 95531
(707) 464-9561; *Fax:* (707) 464-4303
www.kpod.com
License: Crescent City, Del Norte County, CA held by Bicoastal Media Licenses II, LLC
Group Owner: Bicoastal Media L.L.C.; (acq 3-31-00; $850,000 with co-loca
Nat'l Network: ABC
Population Served: 60,000 *Adv. Rates:* 12; 11; 11; 11
Mike Wilson, President & COO

KPOD-FM
01-01-1989; 97.9 MHz FM; *Hrs Open:* 24; 6 kw; Ant -128 ft; N41 45 35 W124 11 28
1345 Northcrest Dr., Crescent City, CA 95531
(707) 464-9561; *Fax:* (707) 464-4303
www.kpodfm.com
kpod@bicoastalmedia.com
License: Crescent City, Del Norte County, CA held by Bicoastal Media Licenses II, LLC
Group Owner: Bicoastal Media L.L.C.
Lane Carpenter, General Manager
Haley Wright, Office Manager
Carrie Okerlund, Assistant Office Manager

***KHEC**
91.1 MHz FM; 0.125 kw; 177 ft.; N41 48 11 W124 4 9
8823 Frey Road, Houston, TX 77034 US
(713) 944-8181
License: Crescent City, Del Norte County, CA held by Centro Cristiano Cosecha Final.
Arbitron Metro Market: Crescent City, CA
Francisco Diaz, President

Cupertino

***KKUP**
05-15-1972; 91.5 MHz FM; *Hrs Open:* 24; 0.2 kw; 2582 ft.; N37 6 40 W121 50 36
P. O. Box 820, Cupertino, CA 95015 US
(408) 260-2999
www.kkup.org
webmeister@kkup.org
License: Cupertino, Santa Clara County, CA held by Assurance Sciences Foundation Inc.
Arbitron Metro Market: San Jose, CA; *Format:* Alternative, Blues *Special Programming:* Brazilian 2 hrs, African 6 hrs, Indian 3 hrs, Sp 3; *Target Audience:* General.
Jim Thomas, Chairman
Jim Thomas, General Manager
Michael Berry, Programming Director
Peter Schwarz, Music Director
Dave Barnett, Chief Engineer
Record Rich, Webmaster
David Stafford, Studio Engineer

Cutten

KHUM
01-01-1996; 104.7 MHz FM; *Hrs Open:* 24; 50 kw; 2651 ft.; N40 7 15 W123 41 27
Mailing Address: PO Box 25, Ferndale, CA 95536 US
Second Address: 1400 Main St., Suite 104, Ferndale, CA 95536
(707) 786-5104; *Fax:* (707) 786-5100
www.khum.com
studio@khum.com
License: Cutten, Humboldt County, CA held by Lost Coast Communications Inc.
Group Owner: Lost Coast Communications Inc.; (acq 11-5-2001)
Nat'l Reps: McGavren Guild
Format: Triple A *Special Programming:* Jazz 20 hrs wkly; *Target Audience:* 25-54; general; *Adv. Rates:* 19; 19; 19; 9.
Cliff Berkowitz, Operations Dir
Tom Newhouse, General Manager
Jeffrey Smoeller, General Sales Mgr
Mike Dronkers, Programming Director
Kevin Sanders, Chief Engineer

Davis

***KDVS**
01-01-1968; 90.3 MHz FM; *Hrs Open:* 24; 9.2 kw; 105 ft.; N38 32 29 W121 45 3
1111 Franklin Street, 7th Floor, Oakland, CA 94607 US
(530) 752-0728; *Fax:* (530) 752-8548
www.kdvs.org
gm@kdvs.org
License: Davis, Yolo County, CA held by Regents of the University of California.
Arbitron Metro Market: Sacramento, CA; *Format:* Talk, Variety/Diverse; *Hrs. of News Programming:* News progmg 13 hrs wkly; *Target Audience:* General; loc community
Renner Burkle, General Manager
Mike Mastrangelo, General Sales Mgr
Michael Taber, Programming Director
Elizabeth Stitt, News Director
Rich Luscher, Chief Engineer
Sean Carson, Music Director
Natalie Roman, Music Director
GregCotta, Sports Director

KXSE
01-01-1978; 104.3 MHz FM; *Hrs Open:* 24; 3.4 kw; 436 ft.; N38 39 26 W121 43 12
1436 Auburn Blvd., Sacramento, CA 95815 US
(916) 646-4000; *Fax:* (916) 646-3237
www.jose1043.com
License: Davis, Sacramento County, CA held by Entravision Holdings LLC.

RADIO - U.S.

Group Owner: Entravision Communications Corp.; (acq 7-28-2000; grpsl).
Nat'l Network: ABC; Westwood One; CBS
Arbitron Metro Market: Sacramento, CA; *Format:* Adult Contemp, Spanish; *Target Audience:* 25-54.
Salvador Lopez, Promotions Manager

Delano

KCHJ
12-01-1951; 1010 kHz AM; *Hrs Open:* 24; 5 kw-D, DA2; 1 kw-N, DA2; N35 48 40 W119 19 18
5200 Standard Street, Bakersfield, CA 93308 US
(661) 327-9711; *Fax:* (661) 327-0797
www.elgallito.com
info@thespanishradio.com
License: Delano, CA held by Illinois Lotus Corp.
Group Owner: Lotus Communications Corp.; (acq 8-24-99; grpsl)
Wire Services: UPI
Arbitron Metro Market: Bakersfield, CA; *Format:* Oldies, Spanish
Special Programming: Sp 24 hrs, 7days a wk; *No. News Employees:* 2; *Target Audience:* 18 plus; Sp speaking adults
Howard Kalmenson, President
Greg Holcomb, General Manager
Vicente Arias, Programming Director
Lloyd Moss, Chief Engineer

KBFP-FM
10-02-1986; 105.3 MHz FM; 35 kw; 581 ft.; N35 30 53 W119 3 41
C/O Jodi M. Krame, 966 East Essex Drive, Fresno, CA 93720 US
(661) 322-9929; *Fax:* (661) 283-2963
www.lapreciosa1053.com
License: Delano, Kern County, CA held by CC Licenses LLC.
Group Owner: iHeartMedia; (acq 4-94)
Nat'l Reps: McGavren Guild
Arbitron Metro Market: Bakersfield, CA; *Format:* Spanish; *Target Audience:* 18-44.
Jeremy Price, Market President
Kenn McCloud, Program Director/Promotions
Lindsey Ponce, Public Affairs

KDFO
11-01-1968; 98.5 MHz FM; *Hrs Open:* 24; 8 kw; 581 ft.; N35 30 53 W119 3 41
1100 Mohawk St., Suite 280, Bakersfield, CA 93309 US
(661) 322-9929; *Fax:* (661) 322-7239
www.985thefox.com
License: Delano, Kern County, CA held by CC Licenses LLC.
Group Owner: iHeartMedia; (acq 10-16-2000; grpsl)
Arbitron Metro Market: Bakersfield, CA; *Format:* Classic Rock; *Target Audience:* 18-44.
Jeremy Price, Market President
Kenn McCloud, Programming Director
Adlai Wilson, Promotions Manager

Dinuba

KRDU
12-26-1946; 1130 kHz AM; *Hrs Open:* 24; 5 kw-D, DA2; 6.2 kw-N, DA2; N36 29 3 W119 15 57
83 E. Shaw Ave., Suite 150, Fresno, CA 93711 US
(559) 230-4300; *Fax:* (559) 243-4301
www.krdu1130.com
License: Dinuba, CA held by Capstar TX LLC
Group Owner: iHeartMedia; (acq 8-30-00; grpsl).
Arbitron Metro Market: Fresno-Visalia, CA; *Format:* Christian, Talk; *Hrs. of News Programming:* news progmg 7 hrs wkly; *No. News Employees:* 1; *Target Audience:* 18-65.
Steve Weed, Operations Manager/Program Director
Jeff Negrete, General Manager
Steve Darnell, Sales Director
David Abenojar, Promotions Director
Nik Ashjian, Digital Content Director

KSOF
06-05-1975; 98.9 MHz FM; *Hrs Open:* 24; 19 kw; 820 ft.; N36 38 15 W118 56 35
83 E. Shaw Ave., Suite 150, Fresno, CA 93711 US
(559) 243-4300; *Fax:* (559) 243-4301
www.softrock989.com
info@softrock989.com
License: Dinuba, Tulare County, CA held by Capstar TX LLC
Group Owner: iHeartMedia
Arbitron Metro Market: Fresno, CA; *Format:* Light Rock; *Hrs. of News Programming:* News progmg 2 hrs wkly; *Target Audience:* 25-54; women
Steve Weed, Operations Manager/Program Director
Jeff Negrete, General Manager
Steve Darnell, Sales Director
David Abenojar, Promotions Director
Nik Ashjian, Digital Content Director

Dunnigan

KSAC-FM
09-01-1983; 105.5 MHz FM; *Hrs Open:* 24; 2.55 kw; 1010 ft.; N38 47 17 W122 6 52
296 H Street, Third Floor, Chula Vista, CA 91910 US
(916) 924-0710; *Fax:* (916) 924-1587
License: Dunnigan, Yolo County, CA held by Caron Broadcasting Inc.
Group Owner: Salem Communications Corp.; (acq 1-11-2002; $8 million)
Format: Religious
Dale Hendry, General Manager
Max Miller, Programming Director
Veldon Leverich, Engineering Dir

Dunsmuir

KZRO
12-08-1992; 100.1 MHz FM; *Hrs Open:* 24; 12.5 kw; 233 ft.; N41 17 30 W122 14 21
Mailing Address: 111 E. Alma Street, Mt. Shasta, CA 96067 US
Second Address: 113 E. Alma St., Mt. Shasta, CA 96067
(530) 926-1332; *Fax:* (530) 926-0737
www.z100fm.net/
zmail@zchannelradio.com
License: Dunsmuir, Siskiyou County, CA held by Dennis Michael Crepps dba Big Tree Communications
Nat'l Network: Westwood One
Arbitron Metro Market: Dunsmuir, CA; *Format:* Classic Rock, Oldies *Special Programming:* Children 2 hrs wkly; *No. News Employees:* 1; *Target Audience:* 18-55; general
Dennis Michaels, General Manager
Rob Hanson, Chief Engineer

Earlimart

*KNAC
93.5 MHz FM; kw
12550 Brookhurst St. #A, Garden Grove, CA 92640 US
www.knac.com
License: Earlimart, Tulare County, CA held by Earlimart Educational Foundation Inc.

William Zawila, General Manager

East Los Angeles

KLAX-FM
04-22-1949; 97.9 MHz FM; 33 kw; 604 ft.; N34 9 49 W118 11 44
10281 West Pico Boulevard, Los Angeles, CA 90064 US
(310) 203-0900; *Fax:* (310) 843-4961
www.979laraza.com
info@979laraza.com
License: East Los Angeles, Los Angeles County, CA held by KLAX Licensing Inc.
Group Owner: Spanish Broadcasting System Inc.; (acq 2-87)
Arbitron Metro Market: Los Angeles, CA; *Format:* Spanish; *Target Audience:* 18-34.
Raul Alarcon Jr., CEO
Peter Remington, Vice President/General Manager
Eric Osuna, Vice President of Sales
Juan Carlos Hidalgo, Programming Director

East Porterville

KMQA
12-01-1989; 100.5 MHz FM; 2 kw; 2009 ft.; N35 45 36 W118 45 32
18319 Hart St., #19, Reseda, CA 91335 US
(559) 687-3170; *Fax:* (559) 687-3175
www.lamaquinamusical.net
License: East Porterville, Tulare County, CA held by MBP Licensee LLC.
Group Owner: Moon Broadcasting; (acq 12-29-98).
Nat'l Network: CNN Radio
Arbitron Metro Market: Visalia, CA; *Format:* Tejano; *Target Audience:* 25-40.
Mari Velazquez, General Manager
Victor Martinez, Programming Director
Rey Ponce, Promotions Manager

Edwards

KGBB
03-01-1990; 103.9 MHz FM; *Hrs Open:* 24; 6 kw; 328 ft.; N34 58 45 W118 10 2
42010 50th St. W., Quartz Hill, CA 93536 US
(661) 718-1552
www.bobfm1039.com
contact@adelmanbroadcasting.com
License: Edwards, Kern County, CA held by Adelman Broadcasting Inc.
Group Owner: Adelman Broadcasting Inc.
Arbitron Metro Market: Ridgecrest, CA; *Format:* Adult Contemp; *Target Audience:* 18-54.
Robert Adelman, President

El Cajon

*KECR
01-01-1955; 910 kHz AM; *Hrs Open:* 24
4135 Northgate Blvd, Suite 1, Sacramento, CA 95834 US
(619) 390-3481; *Fax:* (619) 443-7693
www.familyradio.com
kecr@nethere.com
License: El Cajon, CA held by Family Stations Inc.
Group Owner: Family Stations Inc.; acq 6-9-63)
Arbitron Metro Market: Lakeside, CA; *Format:* Religious; *Target Audience:* All ages; families
Harold Camping, President
Bill Babcock, Operations Dir
Jeff Zimmer, Chief Engineer
David Manzi, Regional Manager

KHTS-FM
01-01-1961; 93.3 MHz FM; *Hrs Open:* 24; 50 kw; 482 ft.; N32 43 48 W117 5 2
9660 Granite Ridge Dr., Suite 100, San Diego, CA 92123 US
(858) 292-2000
www.channel933.com
License: El Cajon, San Diego County, CA held by Citicasters Licenses Inc.
Group Owner: iHeartMedia; (acq 5-4-99; grpsl).
Arbitron Metro Market: San Diego, CA; *Format:* Contemporary Hits/Top 40; *Target Audience:* 18-34.
Melissa Forrest, President/Market Manager
Sarah Dobbins, Sales Manager
Jean Arrollado, Marketing Director

El Centro

KWST
06-21-1958; 1430 kHz AM; *Hrs Open:* 24; 1 kw-D, ND1; 0.036 kw-N, ND1; N32 48 27 W115 32 18
1803 N. Imperial Ave., El Centro, CA 92243 US
(760) 482-7777
www.jose945.com
License: El Centro, CA held by Entravision Holding L.L.C.
Group Owner: Entravision Communications Corp.; (acq 1998; $4.8 million)
Arbitron Metro Market: El Centro, CA; *Format:* Adult Contemp, Tejano; *Target Audience:* 25-49.
Albert Valdez, Operations & Programming Director
Veronica Avila, Senior VP

KXO
01-01-1927; 1230 kHz AM; *Hrs Open:* 24
420 Main Street, El Centro, CA 92243 US
(760) 352-1230
www.kxoradio.com
kxoamfm@kxoradio.com
License: El Centro, CA held by KXO Inc.
Nat'l Network: CBS; *Nat'l Reps:* McGavren Guild
Arbitron Metro Market: El Centro, CA; *Format:* Oldies *Special Programming:* Farm 7 hrs wkly; *Hrs. of News Programming:* news progmg 10 hrs wkly; *No. News Employees:* 1; *Target Audience:* 18-49.; *Adv. Rates:* 24; 23; 24; 23
Gene Brister, President
Caroll Buckley, Operations Director/Vice President
Doug Melanson, Chief Engineer

KXO-FM
08-02-1976; 107.5 MHz FM; *Hrs Open:* 24; 50 kw; 285 ft.; N32 48 24 W115 32 44
420 Main Street, El Centro, CA 92243 US
(760) 352-1230; *Fax:* (760) 352-0858
www.kxoradio.com
kxoamfm@kxoradio.com
License: El Centro, Imperial County, CA held by kxo.inc
Nat'l Reps: McGavren Guild
Arbitron Metro Market: El Centro, CA; *Format:* Adult Contemp; *Hrs. of News Programming:* News progmg 3 hrs wkly; *No. News Employees:* 1; *Target Audience:* 25-49.; *Adv. Rates:* 26; 24; 26; 24
Gene Brister, General Manager

El Cerrito

***KECG**
09-01-1978; 88.1 MHz FM; *Hrs Open:* 24; 0.017 kw; -95 ft.; N37 54 20 W122 17 34
Mailing Address: 540 Ashbury Avenue, El Cerrito, CA 94530 US
Second Address: 540 Ashbury Ave., El Cerrito, CA 94530
(510) 869-9910
prentisswoods@yahoo.com
License: El Cerrito, Contra Costa County, CA held by West Contra Costa Unified School District.
Arbitron Metro Market: San Francisco; *Format:* Jazz, Variety/Diverse *Special Programming:* Gospel 5 hrs, Sp 3 hrs, Filipino 2 hrs wkly; *Hrs. of News Programming:* News progmg 5 hrs wkly; *Target Audience:* General.
Prentiss Woods, Station Manager
Corey Mason, Programming Director

El Rio

KMLA
10-01-1996; 103.7 MHz FM; 1 kw; 804 ft.; N34 18 10 W119 13 41
555 South A Street, Suite 175, Oxnard, CA 93030 US
(805) 385-5656; *Fax:* (805) 385-5690
www.lam1037.com
willy@lam1037.com
License: El Rio, Ventura County, CA held by Gold Coast Radio L.L.C.
Arbitron Metro Market: Oxnard, CA
Gerardo Ceja, President
Guillermo Gonzalez, General Manager
Sonia Lopez, Station Manager
Veronica Gomez, Sales Manager
Gerardo Ceja, Programming Director
Rosa Rodriguez, Promotions Manager

Ellwood

KSPE-FM
02-06-1989; 94.5 MHz FM; *Hrs Open:* 24; 81 kw; Ant 2,949 ft; N34 31 32 W119 57 28
414 E. Cota St., Santa Barbara, CA 93101
(805) 879-8300; *Fax:* (805) 879-8430
License: Ellwood, Santa Barbara County, CA held by Rincon License Subsidiary LLC.
Group Owner: Point Broadcasting Company; (acq 7-11-2007; grpsl)
Population Served: 89,054; *Arbitron Metro Market:* Santa Barbara, CA; *Format:* Oldies
Keith Royer, Executive Vice President/General Manager
Steve Hess, Sales Manager
Lin Aubuchon, Director of Marketing & Promotions

Encinitas

KPRI
01-20-1962; 102.1 MHz FM; *Hrs Open:* 24; 30 kw; 632 ft.; N32 50 24 W117 14 52
5015 Shoreman Place, Suite 102, San Diego, CA 92122 US
(858) 678-0102; *Fax:* (858) 320-7024
www.kprifm.com
info@kprifm.com
License: Encinitas, San Diego County, CA held by Compass Radio of San Diego Inc.
Nat'l Reps: Katz Radio
Arbitron Metro Market: San Diego, CA; *Format:* Triple A; *Hrs. of News Programming:* news progmg 2 hrs wkly; *No. News Employees:* 1; *Target Audience:* 18-34; upscale, well educated, young adult contemp mus fans
Jonathan Schwartz, CFO
Bob Hughes, General Manager
Robert Burch, Station Manager
Clark Newton, Sales Manager
Haley Jones, Programming Director
Magi Aguilar, Promotions Manager

Escondido

KSOQ-FM
07-01-1966; 92.1 MHz FM; *Hrs Open:* 24; 0.58 kw; 1024 ft.; N33 6 39 W117 9 13 *Rebroadcasts:* Rebroadcasts KSON-FM San Diego 100%
Mailing Address: 4 Laguna Drive, Carlsbad, CA 92008 US
Second Address: 1615 Murray Canyon Rd., Suite 710, San Diego, CA 92108-4321
(619) 291-9797; *Fax:* (619) 543-1353
www.kson.com
ksonstudio@kson.com
License: Escondido, San Diego County, CA held by Entercom Radio
Group Owner: Entercom; (acq 2016)
Arbitron Metro Market: Escondido, CA; *Format:* Country *Special Programming:* Bluegrass Special 2 hrs wkly; *Target Audience:* 25-54
Rick Jackson, Senior Vice President/General Manager
Kevin Callahan, Programming Director
Bill Eisenhamer, Chief Engineer

KFSD
06-01-1958; 1450 kHz AM; *Hrs Open:* 24
550 Laguna Drive, Carlsbad, CA 92008 US
(760) 729-1000; *Fax:* (760) 476-9604
www.am1510kspa.com
License: Escondido, CA held by North County Broadcasting Corp.
Group Owner: Astor Broadcast Group; (acq 9-15-87; $3 million with co-located FM;
Arbitron Metro Market: Escondido, CA; *Format:* Adult Contemp; *Hrs. of News Programming:* News progmg 2 hrs wkly; *Target Audience:* 35-64.
Arthur Astor, CEO
Rick Roome, General Manager

Esparto

KLMG
01-01-1996; 97.9 MHz FM; 6 kw; 328 ft.; N38 45 33 W121 52 33
296 H Street, Suite 300, Chula Vista, CA 91910 US
(916) 368-6300; *Fax:* (916) 473-0146
www.latino979.com
acadenas@adelantemediagroup.com
License: Esparto, Yolo County, CA
Group Owner: Adelante Media Group LLC; (acq 12-15-2004; $21.7 million with KBBU(FM) Modesto)
Arbitron Metro Market: Esparto, CA; *Format:* Spanish, Christian
John Bustos, General Manager
Juan Gonzalez, Programming Director
Javier Gonzalez, Promotions Manager
Cynthia Sanchez, News Director
Mark Sedaka, Chief Engineer

Essex

KHWY
05-01-1991; 98.9 MHz FM; *Hrs Open:* 24; 9 kw; 1142 ft.; N34 52 50 W115 4 6 *Rebroadcasts:* Rebroadcasts KRXV(FM) Yermo 100%
Mailing Address: 1611 East Main Street, P.O.Box 1668, Barstow, CA 92312 US
Second Address: 101 Convention Center Dr, Suite 1001, Las Vegas, NV 89109
(760) 256-0326; *Fax:* (760) 256-9507
highwayradio.com
highwayradio@highwayradio.com
License: Essex, San Bernardino County, CA held by KHWY, Inc.
Group Owner: KHWY, Inc.
Nat'l Network: AP Radio
Format: Adult Contemp; *Hrs. of News Programming:* news progmg 28 hrs wkly; *No. News Employees:* 1; *Target Audience:* 35 plus; travelers on I-40 & I-15 & Mojave Desert residents
Kirk Anderson, President/COO
John Gregg, Operations Dir

Eureka

KATA
11-15-1957; 1340 kHz AM; 1 kw-U, ND1; N40 51 12 W124 5 0
5640 S. Broadway, Eureka, CA 95502 US
(707) 442-2000
www.kata1340.com
ddaniels@bicoastalmedia.com
License: Eureka, CA held by Bicoastal Media LLC.
Group Owner: Bicoastal Media L.L.C.; acq 7-28-99; grpsl)
Nat'l Network: ABC
Arbitron Metro Market: Eureka, CA; *Format:* Sports; *Target Audience:* 25-54; upscale adults
Mike Wilson, President & COO
Kevin Mostyn, VP & CTO

KEKA-FM
11-01-1983; 101.5 MHz FM; 89 kw; 2,051 ft.; N40 25 12 W124 5 0
1101 Marsh Rd., Eureka, CA 95501 US
(707) 442-5744
www.keka101.com
License: Eureka, Humboldt County, CA held by Eureka Broadcasting Co. Inc.
Group Owner: Eureka Broadcasting Co. Inc.; (acq 12-13-90; $430,189;
Nat'l Network: Fox News Radio; *Nat'l Reps:* Katz Radio
Arbitron Metro Market: Eureka, CA; *Format:* Country; *Target Audience:* 25-54.
Brian Papstein, General Manager

KFMI
01-01-1973; 96.3 MHz FM; 30 kw; 1581 ft.; N40 43 36 W123 58 18
5640 S. Broadway, Eureka, CA 95502 US
(707) 442-2000
www.power963.com
petemeyer@power963.com
License: Eureka, Humboldt County, CA held by Bicoastal Media LLC.
Group Owner: Bicoastal Media L.L.C.; acq 7-28-99; grpsl)
Nat'l Network: Jones Radio Networks
Arbitron Metro Market: Eureka, CA; *Format:* Adult Contemp *Special Programming:* Loveline 10 hrs wkly; *Target Audience:* 18-36; upscale adults
Mike Wilson, President/COO
Victoria Benning, Market Manager

KGOE
05-12-1933; 1480 kHz AM; *Hrs Open:* 24; 5 kw-D, ND2; 1 kw-N, ND2; N40 44 28 W124 12 5
5640 S. Broadway, Euroka, CA 95502 US
(707) 442-2000
www.kgoe.com
ltate@bicoastalmedia.com
License: Eureka, CA held by Bicoastal Media LLC.
Group Owner: Bicoastal Media L.L.C.; acq 7-28-99; grpsl)
Nat'l Network: Jones Radio Networks
Format: News, News/Talk, 86; *Hrs. of News Programming:* news progmg 100 hrs wkly; *No. News Employees:* 1; *Target Audience:* 25-54.
Laurie Tate, General Manager
Victoria Bennington, General Sales Mgr

KWSW
01-01-1946; 980 kHz AM; *Hrs Open:* 24; 5 kw-D, DAN; 0.5 kw-N, DAN; N40 48 02 W124 07 39
1101 Marsh Rd., Eureka, CA 95501 US
(707) 442-5744
www.eurekaradio.com
License: Eureka, Humboldt County, CA held by Eureka Broadcasting Co. Inc.
Group Owner: Eureka Broadcasting Co. Inc.; (acq 3-1-58).
Nat'l Network: CBS Radio; Wall Street
Population Served: 28,936; *Arbitron Metro Market:* Eureka, CA; *Format:* News, News/Talk, 86; *No. News Employees:* 2; *Target Audience:* 35 plus; upscale, educated
Brian Papstein, General Manager

KKHB
01-01-1994; 105.5 MHz FM; 28 kw; 1588 ft.; N40 43 50 W123 57 7 *Rebroadcasts:* Rebroadcasts KGO(AM) San Francisco
5640 S. Broadway, Eureka, CA 95502 US
(707) 442-2000
www.cool1055.com
ltate@bicoastalmedia.com
License: Eureka, Humboldt County, CA held by Bicoastal Media L.L.C.
Group Owner: Bicoastal Media L.L.C.; acq 11-9-98; grpsl)
Arbitron Metro Market: Redding, CA; *Format:* Oldies
Laurie Tate, General Manager
Victoria Bennington, General Sales Mgr

***KMUE**
08-09-1996; 88.1 MHz FM; 10 kw; 1621 ft.; N40 43 39 W123 58 17 *Rebroadcasts:* Rebroadcasts KMUD(FM) Garberville 100%
Mailing Address: P.O. Box 135, Redway, CA 95560 US
Second Address: 1144 Redway Dr., Redway, CA 95560
(707) 923-2513; *Fax:* (707) 923-2501
www.kmud.org
kmud@kmud.org
License: Eureka, Humboldt County, CA held by Redwood Community Radio Inc.
Format: Talk, Variety/Diverse
David Lippe, Operations Dir
Brenda Starr, General Manager
Marianne Knorzer, Programming Director

KRED
12-17-1979; 92.3 MHz FM; 25 kw; 1539 ft.; N40 43 37 W123 58 25
5640 S. Broadway, Eureka, CA 95502 US
(707) 442-2000
www.kred923.com
ltate@bicoastalmedia.com
License: Eureka, Humboldt County, CA held by Bicoastal Media LLC.
Group Owner: Bicoastal Media L.L.C.
Arbitron Metro Market: Eureka, CA; *Format:* Country; *Hrs. of News Programming:* news progmg 7 hrs wkly; *No. News Employees:* 1
Mike Wilson, President/COO

KEJY
01-01-2007; 790 kHz AM; 5 kw-D, ND1; 0.11 kw-N, ND1; 1,692 ft.; N40 48 9 W124 8 20
1101 Marsh Rd., Eureka, CA 95501 US
(707) 442-5744
www.eurekaradio.com
License: Eureka, Humboldt County, CA held by Eureka Broadcasting Co. Inc.
Group Owner: Eureka Broadcasting Co. Inc.
Arbitron Metro Market: Eureka, CA; *Format:* Spanish
Brian Papstein, General Manager

KIHH
07-26-2008; 1400 kHz AM
US
(916) 535-0500; *Fax:* (916) 535-0504
www.ihradio.org
info@ihradio.org
License: Eureka, CA held by IHR Educational Broadcasting.
Group Owner: IHR Educational Broadcasting
Nat'l Network: EWTN Radio
Arbitron Metro Market: Eureka, CA; *Format:* Christian
Douglas Sherman, President
Dick Jenkins, General Manager

Fair Oaks

KADO(FM)
11-25-1970; 94.7 MHz FM; 86.6 kw; 2,072 ft; N39 15 30 W119 42 36
5345 Madison Ave., Sacramento, CA 95841-3141
(916) 334-7777; *Fax:* (916) 339-4559
www.radio947.net
License: Fair Oaks, Sacramento County, CA held by Entercom Sacramento License L.L.C.
Group Owner: Entercom Communications Corp.; (acq 11-4-97; $15.9 million)
Population Served: 472,178; *Arbitron Metro Market:* Sacramento, CA; *Format:* Jazz, Smooth Jazz
Lee Hansen, Station Manager
Fred Hormel, General Sales Mgr
Lizann Hunt, Promotions Manager

Fairfield

***KASK**
91.5 MHz FM; 0.075 kw horiz; 650 ft.; N38 19 9 W121 59 31
160 Lighthouse Way, Vacaville, CA 95688 US
(707) 449-9300; *Fax:* (707) 447-0680
License: Fairfield, Solano County, CA held by Maranatha Broadcasting.
Arbitron Metro Market: Fairfield, CA; *Format:* Religious
Bob Michaels, Operations Dir
Michel Mace, Station Manager

Fairmead

***KLVY**
01-01-1998; 91.1 MHz FM; *Hrs Open:* 24; 39 kw; 558 ft.; N37 7 40 W119 40 39 *Rebroadcasts:* Rebroadcasts KLVN(FM) Livingston 100%
1425 N.Market Blvd,Ste.9, Sacramento, CA 95834 US
(707) 528-9236; *Fax:* (707) 528-9246
www.klove.com
klove@klove.com
License: Fairmead, Madera County, CA held by Educational Media Foundation Inc.
Group Owner: EMF Broadcasting
Nat'l Network: K-Love
Format: Christian; *No. News Employees:* 3; *Target Audience:* 25-44; Judeo-Christian, female
Darell Chambliss, Chairman
Mike Novak, President
David Pierce, Programming Director
Ed Lenane, News Director
Sam Wallington, Engineering Dir

Fall River Mills

***KKLC**
11-26-1977; 107.9 MHz FM; *Hrs Open:* 24; 13 kw; 2103 ft.; N40 54 23 W121 49 43 *Rebroadcasts:* Rebroadcasts KLVR(FM) Santa Rosa 100%
P. O. Box 448, Mount Shasta, CA 96067 US
(916) 251-1600; *Fax:* (916) 251-1650
www.klove.com
klove@klove.com
License: Fall River Mills, Siskiyou County, CA held by Educational Media Foundation
Group Owner: EMF Broadcasting; (acq 12-27-2002; $400,000).
Nat'l Network: K-Love
Format: Christian; *No. News Employees:* 3; *Target Audience:* 25-44; Judeo Christian, female
Mike Novak, President
David Pierce, Programming Director
Ed Lenane, News Director
Sam Wallington, Engineering Dir
Richard Hunt, News Director
Marya Morgan

Fallbrook

KSSD
11-22-1977; 107.1 MHz FM; *Hrs Open:* 24; 3 kw; 299 ft.; N33 23 1 W117 11 20
5700 Wilshire Blvd., Suite 250, Los Angeles, CA 90036 US
(323) 900-6100; *Fax:* (323) 900-6119
www.superestrella.com
License: Fallbrook, San Diego County, CA held by Entravision Holdings LLC.
Group Owner: Entravision Communications Corp.; (acq 4-1-03; grpsl).
Nat'l Reps: Lotus Entravision Reps LLC
Arbitron Metro Market: Los Angeles, CA; *Format:* Spanish, Contemporary Hits/Top 40; *Target Audience:* 18-34.; *Adv. Rates:* 100; 100; 150; 50
Juan Navarro, Interactive Sales Manager
Nestor Rocha, Programming Director
Elias Autran, Promotions Manager

Felton

KXZM
01-01-1999; 93.7 MHz FM; 0.41 kw; 2264 ft.; N37 9 35 W121 54 32
200 S. A St., 4th Fl., Oxnard, CA 93030 US
(805) 240-2070
www.radiolazer.com
License: Felton, Santa Cruz County, CA held by Lazer Broadcasting Corp.
Group Owner: Lazer Broadcasting Corp.; (acq 7-25-2005; $2.88 million with KXSM(FM) Hollister).

Firebaugh

***KYAF**
01-01-2006; 94.7 MHz FM; kw
C/O William Zawila, Esq., 12550 Brookhurst St. #A, Garden Grove, CA 92840 US
(559) 659-0100
kyafm.com
License: Firebaugh, Fresno County, CA held by Central Valley Educational Services Inc.
Arbitron Metro Market: Firebaugh, CA; *Format:* Oldies
Verne White, President

***KYCI**
01-01-2008; 90.5 MHz FM; 0.395 kw horiz; 1089 ft.; N36 43 32 W120 45 49 *Rebroadcasts:* Rebroadcasts KYCC(FM) Stockton 100%
9019 West Lane, Stockton, CA 95210 US
(209) 477-3690; *Fax:* (209) 477-2762
www.kycc.org
kycc@kycc.org
License: Firebaugh, Fresno County, CA held by Your Christian Companion Network Inc.
Arbitron Metro Market: Firebaugh, CA; *Format:* Gospel, Religious
Shirley Garner, President
Shirley Garner, General Manager
John Ramos, Promotions Manager
Vanessa Kudenov, Office Manager
Gary Harding, Production Manager

Ford City

KZPE
102.1 MHz FM; kw
12550 Brookhurst St. #A, Garden Grove, CA 92840 US
(714) 636-5040; *Fax:* (714) 636-5042
License: Ford City, Kern County, CA held by Estate of H.L. Charles, Robert Willing, executor
Arbitron Metro Market: Ford City, CA
William Zawila, Operations Dir

Forestville

KSXY
01-01-1996; 100.9 MHz FM; 2.5 kw; 513 ft.; N38 44 8 W122 50 55
3565 Standish Ave., Santa Rosa, CA 95407 US
(707) 588-0707; *Fax:* (707) 588-0777
www.allthehits.fm
License: Forestville, SONOMA County, CA held by Sinclair Telecable Inc.
Group Owner: Sinclair Communications Inc.; (acq 8-3-2001; $3.5 million)
Format: Adult Contemp; *Target Audience:* 18-45; *Adv. Rates:* 35; 30; 35; 20
Bob Sinclair, President
Debbie Morton, General Manager
Dray Lopez, Programming Director

Fort Bragg

KOZT
12-05-1981; 95.3 MHz FM; *Hrs Open:* 24; 35 kw; 515 ft.; N39 24 24 W123 44 4
110 South Franklin Stree, Fort Bragg, CA 95437 US
(707) 964-7277; *Fax:* (707) 964-9536
www.kozt.com
thecoast@kozt.com
License: Fort Bragg, Mendocino County, CA held by California Radio Partners Inc.
Format: Triple A; *Hrs. of News Programming:* news progmg one hr wkly; *No. News Employees:* 1; *Target Audience:* 25-49; affluent, educated consumers
Tom Yates, CEO
Vicky Watts, General Sales Mgr

***KJCU**
01-08-2010; 89.9 MHz FM; 0.13 kw; 348 ft.; N39 26 35 W123 43 58
C/O Living Proof, Inc., P.O. Box 637, Bishop, CA 93515 US
(866) 466-5989; *Fax:* (714) 979-8916
www.kwtw.org/kjcu.html
recep@kwtw.org
License: Fort Bragg, Mendocino County, CA held by Living Proof Inc.
Group Owner: Livinf Proof Inc.; (acq. 08-2010)
Arbitron Metro Market: Fort Bragg, CA; *Format:* Christian, Religious

Fortuna

KNCR
10-31-1966; 1090 kHz AM; *Hrs Open:* Sunrise-sunset; 10 kw-D; N40 33 30 W124 07 24
Box 109, Eureka, CA 95501
(707) 725-9363; *Fax:* (707) 726-9446
www.lanueva1090.com
mario@lanueva1090.com
License: Fortuna, Humboldt County, CA held by Del Rosario Talpa Inc.
Hrs. of News Programming: News progmg 2 hrs wkly; *Target Audience:* 25-54.
Mario Meza, General Manager
Sylvia Meza, General Sales Mgr

KWPT
05-15-1992; 100.3 MHz FM; *Hrs Open:* 24; 12 kw; 1894 ft.; N40 25 30.6 W124 6 18.9
1713 Main Street, Fortuna, CA 95540 US
(707) 786-5104; *Fax:* (707) 786-5100
www.kwpt.com
studio@kwpt.com
License: Fortuna, Humboldt County, CA held by KWPT Inc.
Group Owner: Lost Coast Communications Inc.; (acq 5-12-2005; $650,000)
Arbitron Metro Market: Eureka, CA; *Format:* Contemporary Hits/Top 40, Adult Contemp; *Target Audience:* 30-54; affluent, college educated
Cliff Berkowitz, Operations Dir
Tom Newhouse, General Manager
Jeffrey Smoeller, General Sales Mgr
Mike Dronkers, Programming Director

Fountain Valley

***KYLA(FM)**
01-01-1993; 92.7 MHz FM; *Hrs Open:* 24; 690 w; Ant 961 ft; N33 36 20 W117 48 35 *Rebroadcasts:* Rebroadcasts KLRD(FM) Yucaipa 100%
99 Long Ct., Suite 200, Thousand Oaks, CA 91360
(805) 497-8511; *Fax:* (805) 497-8514
www.air1.com
License: Fountain Valley, Orange County, CA held by Educational Media Foundation
Group Owner: EMF Broadcasting; (acq 1996; $5.5 million)
Nat'l Network: ABC
Population Served: 4,000,000 *Format:* Adult Contemp; *Target Audience:* 25-54.
Mike Novak, President/Chief Executive Officer

Fowler

KALZ
11-07-1980; 96.7 MHz FM; *Hrs Open:* 24; 25 kw; 328 ft.; N36 41 42 W119 43 56
83 E. Shaw Ave., Suite 150, Fresno, CA 93711 US
(559) 230-4300; *Fax:* (559) 243-4301
www.powertalk967.com
License: Fowler, Fresno County, CA held by Capstar TX LLC
Group Owner: iHeartMedia; (acq 8-30-2000; grpsl)
Arbitron Metro Market: Fresno, CA; *Format:* Talk; *Target Audience:* 25-54; women
Steve Weed, Operations Manager/Program Director
Jeff Negrete, Vice President/General Manager
Steve Darnell, Sales Director
David Abenojar, Promotions Director
Nik Ashjian, Digital Content Director

KQEQ
07-01-1962; 1210 kHz AM
2171 Ralph Avenue, Stockton, CA 95206 US
(559) 233-8803; *Fax:* (559) 233-8871
www.thehmongradio.com
rakradio@comcast.net
License: Fowler, CA held by RAK Communications Inc.
Arbitron Metro Market: Fresno, CA; *Hrs. of News Programming:* news progmg 10 hrs wkly; *No. News Employees:* 1; *Target Audience:* 13-Senior; Hmong and Lao; *Adv. Rates:* 12.10; 12.10; 12.10; 12.10
Dr. Daniel Moua, CEO
Pahoua Moua, General Manager

Frazier Park

KJPG
01-01-1994; 1050 kHz AM
P.O. Box 9775, Bakersfield, CA 93389 US
(916) 535-0500; *Fax:* (916) 535-0504
www.ihradio.org
info@ihradio.org
License: Frazier Park, CA held by IHR Educational Broadcasting.
Group Owner: IHR Educational Broadcasting; (acq 11-15-2003; $700,000).
Arbitron Metro Market: Bakersfield, CA; *Format:* Religious, Christian
Douglas Sherman, President
Dick Jenkins, General Manager

Freedom

KPIG-FM
12-01-1987; 107.5 MHz FM; *Hrs Open:* 24; 5.4 kw; 338 ft.; N36 50 6 W121 42 22
396 Buckley Rd., San Luis Obispo, CA 93401 US
(831) 722-9000
www.kpig.com
pd@kpig.com
License: Freedom, Santa Cruz County, CA held by Mapleton License of Monterey LLC.
Group Owner: Mapleton Communications LLC; (acq 11-16-2001; grpsl)
Nat'l Reps: McGavren Guild
Arbitron Metro Market: Monterey-Salinas-Santa Cruz, CA; *Format:* Blues, Country; *Target Audience:* 25-54.

Fremont

***KOHL**
09-23-1974; 89.3 MHz FM; *Hrs Open:* 24; 0.145 kw horiz, 0.115 kw vert; 407 ft.; N37 32 14 W121 54 14
43600 Mission Blvd., Fremont, CA 94539 US
(510) 659-6221; *Fax:* (510) 659-6001
www.kohlradio.com
kohl@kohlradio.com
License: Fremont, Alameda County, CA held by Fremont-Newark Community College Dist.
Format: Contemporary Hits/Top 40; *Hrs. of News Programming:* News progmg one hr wkly; *Target Audience:* 18-34.
Robert Dochterman, General Manager
Tom Gomez, Programming Director

Fresno

KHGE
01-06-1962; 102.7 MHz FM; *Hrs Open:* 24; 50 kw; 499 ft.; N36 49 7 W119 30 33
83 E. Shaw Ave., Suite 150, Fresno, CA 93711 US
(559) 230-4300; *Fax:* (559) 243-4301
www.1027thewolf.com
License: Fresno, Fresno County, CA held by Capstar TX LLC
Group Owner: iHeartMedia; (acq 8-30-2000; grpsl)
Nat'l Reps: Clear Channel
Arbitron Metro Market: Fresno, CA; *Format:* Country; *Hrs. of News Programming:* news progmg 20 hrs wkly; *No. News Employees:* 1; *Target Audience:* 25-54; women
Steve Weed, Operations Manager/Program Director
Jeff Negrete, General Manager
Steve Darnell, Sales Director
David Abenojar, Promotions Director
Nik Ashjian, Digital Content Director

KGED
01-01-2003; 1680 kHz AM
2171 Ralph Ave., Stockton, CA 95206 US
(559) 233-8803; *Fax:* (559) 233-8871
rakradio@comcast.net
License: Fresno, CA held by RAK Communications Inc.
Arbitron Metro Market: Fresno, CA; *Format:* Christian, Religious
Albert Perez, General Manager
Paul Kramer, Chief Engineer

KBIF
01-01-1947; 900 kHz AM; *Hrs Open:* 24; 1 kw-D, DAN; 0.5 kw-N, DAN; N36 41 30 W119 40 46
3401 W. Holland Ave., Fresno, CA 93722 US
(559) 222-0900; *Fax:* (559) 222-1573
www.900kbif.com
kbif@900kbif.com
License: Fresno, CA held by Overgaard Broadcasting Inc.
Group Owner: Cordell Overgaard
Nat'l Network: USA
Arbitron Metro Market: Fresno, CA; *Format:* Ethnic; *Hrs. of News Programming:* news progmg 10 hrs wkly; *No. News Employees:* 4; *Target Audience:* 25 plus;
Tony Donato, General Mgr/Operations Mgr
Moua Vang, Programming Director
Maya Xiong, News Director
Kong Her, Senior Advertising Mgr
Alice Jarnagin, Sales Rep/Audio Prod.

KCBL
06-26-1953; 1340 kHz AM; 1 kw-U, ND1; N36 45 51 W119 47 8
83 E. Shaw Ave., Suite 150, Fresno, CA 93711 US
(559) 230-4300; *Fax:* (559) 243-4301
www.foxsportsradio1340.com
License: Fresno, Fresno County, CA held by Capstar TX LLC
Group Owner: iHeartMedia; (acq 8-30-00; grpsl)
Nat'l Network: CNN Radio; Fox Sports; *Nat'l Reps:* Clear Channel
Arbitron Metro Market: Fresno, CA; *Format:* Sports; *Target Audience:* 18-49.
Steve Weed, Operations Manager/Program Director
Jeff Negrete, General Manager
Steve Darnell, Director of Sales
David Abenojar, Promotions Director
Nik Ashjian, Digital Content Director

***KEYQ**
10-14-1957; 980 kHz AM; *Hrs Open:* 24; 0.5 kw-D, ND1; 0.048 kw-N, ND1; N36 44 28 W119 51 12 *Rebroadcasts:* Rebroadcasts KMRO(FM) Camarillo 100%
2310 Ponderosa Drive, #28, Camarillo, CA 93010 US
(805) 482-4797; *Fax:* (805) 388-5202
www.nuevavida.com
info@nuevavida.com
License: Fresno, CA held by The Association for Community Education Inc.
Arbitron Metro Market: Camarillo, CA; *Format:* Religious; *Target Audience:* General; Sp-speaking
Phil Guthrie, President
Mary Guthrie, General Manager

***KFCF**
06-09-1975; 88.1 MHz FM; *Hrs Open:* 24; 2.4 kw; 1900 ft.; N37 4 23 W119 25 51 *Rebroadcasts:* Rebroadcasts KPFA(FM) Berkeley 85%
Mailing Address: PO Box 4364, Fresno, CA 93744 US
Second Address: 1449 N. Wishon Ave., Fresno, CA 93728
(559) 233-2221; *Fax:* (559) 233-5776
www.kfcf.org
License: Fresno, Fresno County, CA held by Fresno Free College Foundation.
Arbitron Metro Market: Fresno, CA; *Format:* Variety/Diverse
Special Programming: Southeast Asian languages one hr, American Indian 2 hrs, Sp 5 hrs wkly; *Hrs. of News Programming:* News progmg 12 hrs wkly *No. NewsEmployees:* 2; *Target Audience:* General; intelligent, discerning, questioning
Rebecca Caraveo, Operations Dir
Rychard Withers, General Manager
Frank Delgado, Promotions Manager
Rick Flores, Music Director

KFIG
01-01-1938; 1430 kHz AM; 5 kw-U, DA-1; N36 50 49 W119 40 46
351 W. Cromwell, Suite 108, Fresno, CA 93711
(559) 447-3570; *Fax:* (559) 447-3579
License: Fresno, Fresno County, CA held by Fat Dawgs 7 Broadcasting LLC
Nat'l Network: ESPN Radio
Population Served: 500,000; *Arbitron Metro Market:* Fresno, CA; *Target Audience:* 25 plus.
Joe Pacheco, President
Lane Ryan, General Manager
Nick Washington, Programming Director
Paul Kleinkramer, Chief Engineer

***KFNO**
02-12-1992; 90.3 MHz FM; 2.2 kw; 1949 ft.; N37 4 25 W119 25 52
4135 Northgate Blvd #1, Sacramento, CA 95834 US
1-(800) 543-1495; *Fax:* (916) 641-8238
http://www.familyradio.com
License: Fresno, Fresno County, CA held by Family Stations Inc.
Group Owner: Family Stations Inc.
Arbitron Metro Market: Fresno, CA; *Format:* Religious *Special Programming:* Children's 10 hrs wkly
Tom Evans, General Manager

KWRU
01-01-1937; 940 kHz AM; 50 kw-U, DA-2; N36 50 49 W119 39 46
27 William St., 11th Floor, New York, NY 10005 US
(212) 966-1059; *Fax:* (212) 625-2894
www.mrbi.net
License: Fresno, Fresno County, CA held by Multicultural Radio Broadcasting Licensee LLC.
Group Owner: Multicultural Radio Broadcasting Inc.; (acq 2-4-2004; grpsl).
Population Served: 180,500; *Arbitron Metro Market:* Fresno, CA; *Format:* Christian, Spanish; *Target Audience:* 25-54.
Arthur Liu, CEO/COO

***KFSR**
10-30-1982; 90.7 MHz FM; *Hrs Open:* 24; 2.55 kw; 66 ft.; N36 48 42 W119 44 43
5201 N. Maple Ave., Fresno, CA 93740 US
(559) 278-2598; *Fax:* (559) 278-6985
www.kfsr.org
kfsrfresno@hotmail.com
License: Fresno, Fresno County, CA held by California State University Fresno.
Arbitron Metro Market: Fresno, CA; *Format:* Jazz *Special Programming:* Evening eclectic 24 hrs wkly,; *Hrs. of News Programming:* News progmg 2 hrs wkly; *Target Audience:* General.
Don Priest, General Manager
Mike Stephens, Station Manager
Kyle Wheeler, Programming Director

KGST
01-01-1949; 1600 kHz AM; 5 kw-D, DAN; 5 kw-N, DAN; N36 42 36 W119 50 6
6290 Sunset Blvd, Ste 1600, Hollywood, CA 90028 US
(559) 497-1100; *Fax:* (559) 497-1125
www.espn1600am.com
mginsburg@lotusfresno.com
License: Fresno, CA held by Lotus Communications Inc.
Group Owner: Lotus Communications Corp.; (acq 8-1-85; $1.76 million;
Nat'l Reps: Lotus Entravision Reps LLC
Arbitron Metro Market: Fresno, CA *TV Affiliate:* ESPN; *Format:* Sports; *Hrs. of News Programming:* news progmg 2 hrs wkly; *No. News Employees:* 1; *Target Audience:* 18 plus; Hispanic adults
Adv. Rates: 30; 25; 25; 15
Kevin O'Rorke, General Manager
Melissa delCarlo, General Sales Manager
Howard Kalmenson, President
Francisco Villarreal, Regional Sales & Digital Assets Manager
Daniel Crotty, General Manager
Mr. Clean, Promotions Director

KIRV
10-01-1962; 1510 kHz AM; 10 kw-D, DAD; N36 42 42 W119 49 59
3401 W. Holland Ave., Fresno, CA 93722 US
(559) 222-0900; *Fax:* (559) 222-1573
www.1510kirv.com
kbifkirv@aol.com
License: Fresno, CA held by Centro Cristiano Viva Abundante, Inc.
Group Owner: Centro Cristiano Viva Abundante, Inc.

Arbitron Metro Market: Fresno, CA; *Format:* Christian; *Target Audience:* 25-54.
Tony Donato, General Mgr/Operations Mgr

KJFX
05-15-1970; 95.7 MHz FM; *Hrs Open:* 24; 17.5 kw; 850 ft.; N36 56 55 W119 29 9
966 East Essex Drive, Fresno, CA 93720 US
(559) 255-1041; *Fax:* (559) 230-0177
www.957thefox.com
License: Fresno, Fresno County, CA held by Wilks License Co.-Fresno LLC.
Group Owner: Wilks Broadcast Group LLC; (acq 6-1-2005; grpsl)
Nat'l Reps: McGavren Guild
Arbitron Metro Market: Fresno, CA; *Format:* Classic Rock
Kevin O'Rorke, General Manager
Rob Hasson, General Sales Mgr
Andrea Carter, Programming Director

KJWL
04-29-1994; 99.3 MHz FM; *Hrs Open:* 24; 14.5 kw; 344 ft.; N36 44 7 W119 47 9
670 P Street, Fresno, CA 93721 US
(559) 497-5118; *Fax:* (559) 497-9760
www.kjwl.com
License: Fresno, Fresno County, CA held by John E. Ostlund
Nat'l Network: CNN Radio
Arbitron Metro Market: Fresno, CA; *Format:* Classic Rock; *Target Audience:* 35 plus; upscale
John Ostlund, President
Bruce Campbell, Operations Dir
Mary Lou Gunn, General Manager
Dave Hull, General Sales Mgr
E. Curtis Johnson, Programming Director
Chris Gentile, Promotions Manager
Juanita Stevenson, News Director
LizRay, General Sales Manager
Jim Roberts, Production Manager
Joe Garcia, Traffic Manager
Kaarin Rosso, Business Administrator

KMGV
01-01-1949; 97.9 MHz FM; 2.1 kw; 2005 ft.; N37 4 29 W119 25 52
1071 W. Shaw Ave., Fresno, CA 93711 US
(559) 490-5800; *Fax:* (559) 490-4199
www.mega979.com
info@mega979.com
License: Fresno, CA held by Cumulus Licensing LLC
Group Owner: Cumulus Media Inc.; (acq 3-30-2007; grpsl).
Wire Services: UPI
Arbitron Metro Market: Fresno, CA; *Format:* Oldies; *Target Audience:* 25-54.; *Adv. Rates:* 100; 90; 90; 50
Patty Hixson, General Manager
Lori Garcia, National Sales Mgr
Jeff Davis, Programming Director
Timothy Wall, Promotions Assistant

KMJ
06-01-1925; 580 kHz AM; *Hrs Open:* 24; 50 kw; N36 39 33 W119 20 47
1071 W. Shaw Ave., Fresno, CA 93711 US
(559) 490-5800
www.kmjnow.com
License: Fresno, CA held by Cumulus Licensing LLC
Group Owner: Cumulus Media Inc.; (acq 3-30-2007; grpsl).
Nat'l Network: ABC
Arbitron Metro Market: Fresno, CA; *Format:* News/Talk; *No. News Employees:* 13; *Target Audience:* 25-64.
Patty Hixson, General Manager
Lori Garcia, National Sales Mgr
Blake Taylor, Programming Director
Joe Mauk, Chief Engineer

KLBN
03-15-1948; 101.9 MHz FM; *Hrs Open:* 24; 2.25 kw; 1959 ft.; N37 4 22 W119 25 53
Mailing Address: 600 New Hampshire Avenue, N.W., Suite 1200, Washington, DC 20037 US
Second Address: 1110 East Olive Avenue, Fresno, CA
(559) 497-1100; *Fax:* (559) 497-1125
www.1019labuena.com
kororke@lotusfresno.com
License: Fresno, Fresno County, CA held by Lotus Fresno Corp.
Group Owner: Lotus Communications Corp.; (acq 11-1-2007; $8.4 million)
Nat'l Reps: Lotus Entravision Reps LLC
Arbitron Metro Market: Fresno, CA; *Format:* Tejano; *Hrs. of News Programming:* news progmg one hr wkly; *No. News Employees:* 1; *Target Audience:* 25-54; adults
Kevin O'Rorke, General Manager
Melissa Del Carlo, General Sales Manager
Francisco Villerreal, Regional Sales & Digital Assets Manager
Armando Chaira, Public Service Director
Mr. Clean, Promotions Director

KMJ
12-08-1979; 105.9 MHz FM; *Hrs Open:* 24; 2.4 kw; 1959 ft.; N37 4 23 W119 25 51
1071 W. Shaw Ave., Fresno, CA 93711 US
(559) 490-5800; *Fax:* (559) 490-5878
www.kmjnow.com
License: Fresno, CA held by Cumulus Licensing LLC
Group Owner: Cumulus Media Inc.; (acq 3-30-2007; grpsl)
Arbitron Metro Market: Fresno, CA; *Format:* News/Talk
Patty Hixson, General Manager
Lori Garcia, General Sales Mgr
Blake Taylor, Programming Director
Chris Miller, Marketing Director

***KSJV**
07-04-1980; 91.5 MHz FM; *Hrs Open:* 24; 16 kw; 869 ft.; N36 38 15 W118 56 35
5005 E. Belmont, Fresno, CA 93727 US
(559) 455-5777; *Fax:* (559) 455-5778
www.radiobilingue.org
mail@radiobilingue.org
License: Fresno, Fresno County, CA held by Radio Bilingue Inc.
Arbitron Metro Market: Fresno, CA; *Format:* Ethnic; *Hrs. of News Programming:* news progmg 11 hrs wkly; *No. News Employees:* 5; *Target Audience:* 16-60; Latino
Hugo Morales, CEO
Maria Erana, General Manager
Phil Traynor, General Sales Mgr
Samuel Orozco, News Director
Bill Bach, Chief Engineer

KSKS
01-01-1946; 93.7 MHz FM; 68 kw; 1903 ft.; N37 4 39 W119 26 1
1071 W. Shaw Ave., Fresno, CA 93711 US
(559) 490-5800; *Fax:* (559) 490-5944
www.ksks.com
info@ksks.com
License: Fresno, CA held by Cumulus Licensing LLC
Group Owner: Cumulus Media Inc.
Arbitron Metro Market: Fresno, CA; *Format:* Country
Patty Hixson, General Manager
Karen Franz, General Sales Mgr
Darrin Arriens, Programming Director
Lori Garcia, National Sales Mgr

***KVPR**
10-15-1978; 89.3 MHz FM; *Hrs Open:* 24; 2.45 kw; 1890 ft.; N37 4 25 W119 25 52
3437 W. Shaw #101, Fresno, CA 93711 US
(559) 275-0764; *Fax:* (559) 275-2202
www.kvpr.org
kvpr@kvpr.org
License: Fresno, Fresno County, CA held by White Ash Broadcasting Inc.
Nat'l Network: NPR
Arbitron Metro Market: Fresno, CA; *Format:* News; *Hrs. of News Programming:* News progmg 52 hrs wkly
Ed Palacious, Chairman
Mariam Stepanian, President
Don Weaver, Production/ operations
Jim Meyers, Station Manager
David Parker, Secretary
Jim moore, Direct of Programme Content
Kristiana Richerdson, Assistant to President/General Manager
Shirin Sohraci, Business Manager
Shrin Sohrabi, Business Manager

KWYE
01-01-1963; 101.1 MHz FM; *Hrs Open:* 24; 10 kw; 1076 ft.; N36 55 48 W119 38 27
1071 W. Shaw Ave., Fresno, CA 93711 US
(559) 490-5800
www.y101hits.com
info@y101hits.com
License: Fresno, CA held by Cumulus Licensing LLC
Group Owner: Cumulus Media Inc.; (acq 3-30-2007; grpsl)
Nat'l Reps: Katz Radio
Arbitron Metro Market: Fresno, CA; *Format:* Adult Contemp; *Target Audience:* 18-49; emphasis on women
Patty Hixson, General Manager
Lori Garcia, National Sales Mgr
Jeff Davis, Programming Director

KXEX
09-01-1962; 1550 kHz AM; 5 kw-D, DA2; 2.5 kw-N, DA2; N36 46 14 W119 55 20
2171 Ralph Avenue, Stockton, CA 95206 US
(559) 233-8803; *Fax:* (559) 233-8871
rakradio@comcast.net
License: Fresno, CA held by RAK Communications Inc.
Arbitron Metro Market: Fresno, CA; *Format:* Religious
Ray Carrasco, General Manager
Paul Kramer, Chief Engineer

KYNO
10-01-1947; 1300 kHz AM; *Hrs Open:* 24; 5 kw-D, 1 kw-N, DA-N; N36 46 14 W119 45 00
1415 Fulton Street, Fresno, CA 93277
(559) 497-5118; *Fax:* (559) 452-0948
www.940espnfresno.com
info@940espnfresno.com
License: Fresno, Fresno County, CA held by John Ostlund and Katrina Ostlund
Population Served: 165,972; *Arbitron Metro Market:* Fresno, CA
Ray Carrasco, General Manager

Garberville

***KLVG**
01-01-1999; 103.7 MHz FM; *Hrs Open:* 24; 11 kw; 2349 ft.; N40 20 5 W124 6 32
1425 North Market Blvd, Suite 9, Sacramento, CA 95834 US
(727) 528-9236; *Fax:* (727) 528-9246
www.klove.com
klove@klove.com
License: Garberville, Humboldt County, CA held by Educational Media Foundation.
Group Owner: EMF Broadcasting
Nat'l Network: K-Love
Format: Christian; *No. News Employees:* 3; *Target Audience:* 25-44; female (Judeo-Christian)
Darell Chambliss, Chairman
Mike Novak, President
Eric Allen, General Sales Mgr
David Pierce, Programming Director
Ed Lenane, News Director
Sam Wallington, Engineering Dir
Scott Smith, Music Director
Marya Morgan, ScottSmith
Richard Hunt, News Reporter
Tracy Butler, Traffic Manager

***KMUD**
05-28-1987; 91.1 MHz FM; *Hrs Open:* 24; 0 kw horiz, 5.5 kw vert; 2602 ft.; N40 7 13 W123 41 31
Mailing Address: PO Box 135, 1144 Redway Drive, Redway, CA 95560 US
Second Address: 1144 Redway Dr., Redway, CA 95560
(707) 923-2513; *Fax:* (707) 923-2501
www.kmud.org
kmud@kmud.org
License: Garberville, Humboldt County, CA held by Redwood Community Radio Inc.
Format: Talk, Variety/Diverse *Special Programming:* Black 3 hrs, ethnic one hr, jazz 6 hrs, Sp 2 hrs,; *Hrs. of News Programming:* news progmg 6 hrs wkly; *No. News Employees:* 1; *Target Audience:* General.
David Lippe, Operations Dir
Brenda Starr, General Manager
Marianne Knorzer, Programming Director
Terri Klemetson, News Director
Simon Frech, Chief Engineer
Cynthia Elkins, News Coordinator

***KGKV**
01-01-2009; 89.1 MHz FM; 1.3 kw vert; 2510 ft.; N40 7 14 W123 41 31 *Rebroadcasts:* Rebroadcasts KLVR(FM) Middletown 100%
5700 West Oaks Boulevard, Rocklin, CA 95765 US
(916) 251-1600; *Fax:* (916) 251-1650
www.klove.com
klove@klove.com
License: Garberville, Humboldt County, CA held by Educational Media Foundation
Group Owner: Family Stations Inc.
Nat'l Network: K-Love
Arbitron Metro Market: Garberville, CA; *Format:* Christian, Religious
Mike Novak, President

Garden Grove

KEBN
06-21-1961; 94.3 MHz FM; *Hrs Open:* 24; 6 kw; 240 ft.; N33 46 51 W117 53 33
1845 Empire Ave, Burbank, CA 91504 US
(818) 729-5300; *Fax:* (818) 729-5683
www.kebnradio.com
lbiinfo@lbimedia.com

License: Garden Grove, Orange County, CA held by LBI Radio License LLC
Group Owner: Liberman Broadcasting Inc.; (acq 5-15-03; $35 million).
Arbitron Metro Market: Los Angeles, CA; *Format:* Spanish
Andrew Mars, General Manager
Daisy Ortiz, Director, Sales - TV & Radio, West Coast Region
Edward Leon, Programming Director
Gustave Aviles, News Director

George

KATJ-FM
06-29-1989; 100.7 MHz FM; 0.26 kw; 1549 ft.; N34 36 38 W117 17 18
15650 Seneca Road, Building A, Victorville, CA 92392 US
(760) 241-1313; *Fax:* (760) 241-0205
www.katcountry1007.com
kimjennings@edbroadcasters.com
License: George, San Bernardino County, CA held by EDB VV License LLC.
Group Owner: Frontier Radio Management Inc.; (acq 11-30-2007; grpsl)
Nat'l Network: CNN Radio; *Nat'l Reps:* Christal
Arbitron Metro Market: Victorville,CA; *Format:* Country; *Target Audience:* 25-54; adults; *Adv. Rates:* 25-60
Tom Hoyt, Operations Dir
Tim Anderson, General Manager
Kim Jennings, General Sales Mgr
Gregg Thomas, Programming Director

Gerber

KTOR
01-01-2003; 99.7 MHz FM; *Hrs Open:* 24; 0.09 kw; 2484 ft.; N40 14 21 W121 1 52
P O Box 1074, Chico, CA 95927 US
(530) 256-2400; *Fax:* (530) 256-3780
ktor@frontiernet.net
License: Gerber, Lassen County, CA held by Sierra Radio Inc.
Group Owner: Sierra Radio Inc.; (acq 9-4-2002; for 51% of CP).
Nat'l Network: ABC
Arbitron Metro Market: Chico, CA; *Format:* Classic Rock
Greg Heller, General Manager
Cari Catron, General Sales Mgr

Geyserville

KXTS
12-01-1993; 98.7 MHz FM; 2.65 kw; 503 ft.; N38 44 8 W122 50 55
2121 Diamond Mountain Ro, Calistoga, CA 94515 US
(707) 588-0707; *Fax:* (707) 588-0777
www.exitos98.7.fm
License: Geyserville, Sonoma County, CA held by Commonwealth Broadcasting LLC.
Group Owner: Sinclair Communications Inc.; (acq 8-3-2001; $5.5 million)
Arbitron Metro Market: San Francisco; *Format:* Tejano
Debbie Morton, General Manager
Alex Ballesteros, Programming Director

Gilroy

KAZA
09-01-1957; 1290 kHz AM; *Hrs Open:* 6 AM-midnight; 5 kw-D, DA2; 0.088 kw-N, DA2; N37 9 48 W121 38 28
355 Twn & Cntry Villiage, San Jose, CA 95128 US
(408) 776-3090; *Fax:* (408) 881-1292
License: Gilroy, CA held by Radio Fiesta Corp.
Arbitron Metro Market: San Jose, CA; *Format:* Oldies
Sonia Rodriquez, President
Juan Sidhu, Operations Dir

KBAY
01-01-1970; 94.5 MHz FM; *Hrs Open:* 24; 44 kw; 518 ft.; N37 12 32 W121 46 27
190 Park Center Plaza, Suite 200, San Jose, CA 95113 US
(408) 287-5775; *Fax:* (408) 293-3341
www.kbay.com
djang@nextmediagroup.net
License: Gilroy, Santa Clara County, CA held by Digity Digital LLC
Group Owner: Digity Digity LLC; (acq 12-6-2005; $80 million with KEZR(FM) San Jose).
Nat'l Reps: D & R Radio
Arbitron Metro Market: San Jose, CA; *Format:* Adult Contemp; *Hrs. of News Programming:* news progmg 4 hrs wkly; *No. News Employees:* 1; *Target Audience:* 35-54.; *Adv. Rates:* 300; 300; 300; 100
Dean Goodman, CEO
Sam Van Zandt, Public Affairs Director
Judy Dixon, General Sales Mgr
Dana Jang, Programming Director
Layna Thom, Promotions Coordinator

Glendale

KRLA
01-01-1928; 870 kHz AM; *Hrs Open:* 24
4880 Santa Rosa Road, Suite 300, Camarillo, CA 93012 US
(818) 956-5552; *Fax:* (818) 551-1110
www.krla870.com
License: Glendale, CA held by New Inspiration Broadcasting Co. Inc.
Group Owner: Salem Communications Corp.; (acq 6-23-98; $33.4 million).
Nat'l Network: Salem Radio Network; *Nat'l Reps:* Christal
Regional Reps: SRR; *Wire Services:* Metro Weather Service Inc.
Arbitron Metro Market: Los Angeles; *Format:* News, News/Talk, 86 *Special Programming:* Special Programming 20 hrs wkly, health 2 hrs wkly; *Hrs. of News Programming:* News progmg 100 hrs wkly; *Target Audience:* 35plus.
Jim Tinker, Operations Dir
Mark Pennington, General Sales Mgr
Craig Edwards, Programming Director
Kristi Charley, News Director
Bill Sheets, Chief Engineer

KSCA
03-01-1951; 101.9 MHz FM; *Hrs Open:* 24; 4.8 kw; 2,831 ft.; N34 13 26 W118 3 45
5999 Center Dr., Los Angeles, CA 90045 US
(310) 216-3434
www.univision.com
License: Glendale, Los Angeles County, CA held by Univision Radio License Corp.
Group Owner: Univision Radio; (acq 9-22-2003; grpsl).
Arbitron Metro Market: Los Angeles, CA; *Format:* Spanish, Tejano; *Target Audience:* 25-54.
Haz Montana, Operations Manager
Michelle Hohman, Regional Manager
Tom Koza, Chief Engineer

Goleta

KYGA
09-01-1957; 97.5 MHz FM; *Hrs Open:* 24; 17.5 kw; 890 meters; N34 31 31 W119 57 29 *Rebroadcasts:* Rebroadcasts KLRD(FM) Yucaipa 100%
5700 West Oaks Boulevard, Rocklin, CA 95765
(916) 251-1600; *Fax:* (916) 251-1650
www.air1.com
License: Goleta, Santa Barbara County, CA held by Educational Media Foundation
Group Owner: EMF Broadcasting; (acq 3-12-2001; grpsl).
Population Served: 650,000; *Arbitron Metro Market:* Santa Barbara, CA
Mike Novak, President

Gonzales

KKMC
09-22-1984; 880 kHz AM; *Hrs Open:* 24
30 E. San Joaquin St., #105, Salinas, CA 93901 US
(831) 424-5562; *Fax:* (831) 424-6437
www.kkmc.com
info@kkmc.com
License: Gonzales, CA held by Monterey County Broadcasters Inc.
Nat'l Network: USA; *Nat'l Reps:* Salem
Arbitron Metro Market: Monterey, CA; *Format:* Christian, Talk, 74 *Special Programming:* Sp 3 hrs wkly; *Hrs. of News Programming:* News progmg 7 hrs wkly; *Target Audience:* 25 plus; family oriented *Adv. Rates:* Call for4 rates and Packages
Carl Auel, President
John Dick, General Manager
Lorraine Dick, General Sales Mgr

KHIP
10-25-1990; 104.3 MHz FM; *Hrs Open:* 24; 2.6 kw; 509 ft.; N36 40 6 W121 31 9
60 Garden Ct., Suite 300, Monterey, CA 93940 US
(831) 658-5200
www.thehippo.com
kallen@radiomontereybay.com
License: Gonzales, Monterey County, CA held by Mapleton License of Monterey LLC.
Group Owner: Mapleton Communications LLC; (acq 11-16-2001; grpsl)
Nat'l Reps: McGavren Guild
Arbitron Metro Market: Monterey, CA; *Format:* Classic Rock; *Target Audience:* 18-49; upscale, active young professionals
Jodi Morgan, General Sales Mgr
Kenny Allen, Programming Director

Grass Valley

KNCO
10-01-1978; 830 kHz AM; *Hrs Open:* 24
1255 East Main St., A, Grass Valley, CA 95945 US
(530) 272-3424; *Fax:* (530) 272-2872
www.knco.com
info@knco.com
License: Grass Valley, CA held by Nevada County Broadcasters Inc.
Group Owner: Nevada County Broadcasters Inc.
Nat'l Network: CNN Radio; ABC; CBS Radio; *Wire Services:* AP
Arbitron Metro Market: Sacramento, CA; *Format:* News, News/Talk, 86 *Special Programming:* Christian 4 hrs wkly; *Hrs. of News Programming:* news progmg 30 hrs wkly; *No. News Employees:* 4; *Target Audience:* 35plus; adults of western Nevada County
Edward Sylvester, Chairman
Bob Breck, CEO
Scott Robertson, President
Tom Fitzsimmons, Operations Dir
Barbara Juneau, News Director
Tim Parish, Chief Engineer

KNCO-FM
09-07-1982; 94.1 MHz FM; *Hrs Open:* 24; 0.66 kw; 981 ft.; N39 14 44 W120 57 52
Mailing Address: 1255 E. Main Street, Grass Valley, CA 95945 US
Second Address: 1479 Sanborn Rd., Yuba City, CA 95993
(530) 272-3424; *Fax:* (530) 272-2872
www.mystarradio.com
info@mystarradio.com
License: Grass Valley, Nevada County, CA
Group Owner: Nevada County Broadcasters Inc.
Nat'l Network: Westwood One
Format: Adult Contemp; *Hrs. of News Programming:* news progmg 2 hrs wkly; *No. News Employees:* 1; *Target Audience:* 25-54; residents of western Nevada County
Tom Fitzsimmons, Programming Director
Hollie Grimaldi-Flores, Promotions Manager

KBAA
05-03-2004; 103.3 MHz FM; *Hrs Open:* 24; 0.53 kw; 1102 ft.; N39 14 45 W120 57 56
4880 Santa Rosa Rd, Camarillo, CA 93012 US
(916) 368-6300; *Fax:* (916) 473-0146
www.latino979.com
License: Grass Valley, Nevada County, CA
Group Owner: Adelante Media Group LLC; (acq 5-12-2006; $500,000)
Arbitron Metro Market: Grass Valley, CA; *Format:* Tejano
John Bustos, General Manager

Greenacres

*KAXL
05-04-1994; 88.3 MHz FM; *Hrs Open:* 24; 21 kw; 328 ft.; N35 24 55 W119 14 1
110 South Montclair, Suite 205, Bakersfield, CA 93309 US
(661) 832-2800; *Fax:* (661) 832-3164
www.kaxl.com
kaxl@kaxl.com
License: Greenacres, Kern County, CA held by Skyride Unlimted Inc.
Arbitron Metro Market: Bakersfield, CA; *Format:* Religious; *Hrs. of News Programming:* News progmg 4 hrs wkly; *Target Audience:* 35 plus; women; *Adv. Rates:* 25; 25; 25; 20
Dan Schaffer, Operations Dir
Terri Blankenship, Station Manager
Sheryl Giesbrecht, Promotions Manager
Matt Pelischek, Production Director

KRAB
10-01-1991; 106.1 MHz FM; *Hrs Open:* 24; 25 kw; 328 ft.; N35 21 33 W118 43 45
1100 Mohawk St., Suite 280, Bakersfield, CA 93309 US
(661) 322-9929; *Fax:* (661) 716-1616
www.krab.com
License: Greenacres, Kern County, CA held by CC Licenses LLC.
Group Owner: iHeartMedia
Nat'l Reps: McGavren Guild
Arbitron Metro Market: Bakersfield, CA; *Format:* Rock/AOR; *Target Audience:* 18-49; predominantely male
Jeremy Price, Market President
Danny Spanks, Programming Director
Kenn McCloud, Promotions Manager

Greenfield

KLOK-FM
01-01-1994; 99.5 MHz FM; 30 kw; 640 ft.; N36 27 51 W121 17 52
67 Garden Ct., Monterey, CA 93940 US
(831) 373-6767
www.tricolor995.com
tvalencia@entravision.com
License: Greenfield, Monterey County, CA held by Entravision Holdings LLC.
Group Owner: Entravision Communications Corp.; (acq 3-14-00; grpsl).
Nat'l Reps: Lotus Entravision Reps LLC
Arbitron Metro Market: Monterey, CA; *Format:* Tejano
Pedram Boloori, National Sales Mgr
Victor Ramos, Promotions Coordinator

KSEA
01-01-1998; 107.9 MHz FM; *Hrs Open:* 24; 0.87 kw; 1637 ft.; N36 23 0 W121 25 40
PO Box 62, Keene, CA 93531 US
(928) 782-5995; *Fax:* (928) 782-3874
www.campesina.com
License: Greenfield, Monterey County, CA held by Farmworker Educational Radio Network Inc.
Group Owner: Farmworker Educational Radio Network, Inc.; (acq 3-13-97; $600,000)
Arbitron Metro Market: Monterey-Salinas-Santa Cruz, CA; *Format:* Tejano; *Target Audience:* 18-54; Hispanic market
Paul Chavez, President

Greenville

***KPJP**
09-15-2004; 89.3 MHz FM; 4.5 kw vert; 2349 ft.; N40 13 59 W121 1 8
P. O. Box 180, Tahoma, CA 96142 US
(916) 535-0500; *Fax:* (916) 535-0504
www.ihradio.org
info@ihradio.org
License: Greenville, Plumas County, CA held by IHR Educational Broadcasting
Group Owner: IHR Educational Broadcasting
Arbitron Metro Market: Greenville, CA; *Format:* Religious
Douglas Sherman, President
Lori Erown, General Manager

Gridley

KHHZ
07-06-1979; 97.7 MHz FM; *Hrs Open:* 24; 1.5 kw; 1276 ft.; N39 30 18 W121 18 35
1436 Auburn Bloulevard, Sacramento, CA 95815 US
(530) 345-0021; *Fax:* (530) 893-2121
www.khhz.com
License: Gridley, Butte County, CA held by Deer Creek Broadcasting LLC.
Group Owner: Deer Creek Broadcasting LLC; (acq 9-8-2004; grpsl)
Nat'l Reps: Katz Radio
Arbitron Metro Market: Gridley, CA; *Format:* Spanish; *Target Audience:* 18-49.
Dino Corbin, General Manager
Bill Meyer, General Sales Mgr
Juan Villagrana, Programming Director
Matt Ray, News Director
Mark Miller, Chief Engineer
Heather Welch, Traffic Manager

Groveland

***KXSR**
05-08-1992; 91.7 MHz FM; *Hrs Open:* 24; 4 kw; 1591 ft.; N38 3 46 W120 14 45 *Rebroadcasts:* Rebroadcasts KXPR(FM) Sacramento 100%
3416 American River Dr., Suite B, Sacramento, CA 95864 US
(916) 278-8900 (877) 480-5900; *Fax:* (916) 278-8989
www.capradio.org
info@capradio.org
License: Groveland, Tuolumne County, CA held by California State University Sacramento.
Nat'l Network: NPR; PRI
Arbitron Metro Market: Sacramento, CA; *Format:* Talk; *Target Audience:* General; NPR listeners, eg. professionals, educators & administrators
Rick Eytcheson, President/General Manager
Constance Crawford, Director of Marketing/Public Relations
Arla Gibson, Director of Development
Carl Watanabe, Station Manager
Craig Murray, Managing Diretor
Jun Reina, CFO/COO
Al Gibes,Director, Digital Content
Joe Barr, Director of News and Information
Evan Matsler, Director of Operations
Paul Adams, Manager, Corporate Underwriting

Grover Beach

KURQ
07-04-1984; 107.3 MHz FM; *Hrs Open:* 24; 3.5 kw; 1650 ft.; N35 21 37 W120 39 18
966 East Essex Drive, Fresno, CA 93720 US
(805) 545-0101; *Fax:* (805) 541-5303
www.newrock1073.com
License: Grover Beach, San Luis Obispo County, CA held by EDB SLO License LLC.
Group Owner: Frontier Radio Management Inc.; (acq 11-30-2007; grpsl)
Arbitron Metro Market: San Luis Obispo; *Format:* Rock/AOR; *Hrs. of News Programming:* news progmg 8 hrs wkly; *No. News Employees:* 1; *Target Audience:* 18-44; emphasis on 25-34 year olds; *Adv. Rates:* 18; 18;18; 10
Ron Roy, VP
Rich Hawkins, General Manager
Pattie Wagner, General Sales Mgr
Tristan, Programming Director
Rebecca Crites, Promotions Manager

Guadalupe

KRTO
01-01-1992; 97.1 MHz FM; *Hrs Open:* 24; 0.36 kw; 1325 ft.; N34 53 52 W120 35 23
104 West Chapel Avenue, Santa Maria, CA 93454 US
(805) 928-4334; *Fax:* (805) 349-2765
www.mega971.com
mega971@gmail.com
License: Guadalupe, Santa Barbara County, CA held by Emerald Wave Media.
Group Owner: Emerald Wave Media; (acq 5-1-97; $475,000 with KTAP(AM) Santa Maria)
Arbitron Metro Market: Santa Maria-Lom; *Format:* Contemporary Hits/Top 40
August Ruiz, General Manager

Gualala

KTDE
08-01-1993; 100.5 MHz FM; *Hrs Open:* 24; 6 kw; 669 ft.; N38 49 33 W123 34 12
Mailing Address: P.O. Box 3463, Carefree, AZ 85377 US
Second Address: 38958 Cypress Way, Gualala, CA 95445
(707) 884-1000; *Fax:* (707) 884-1229
www.ktde.com
License: Gualala, Mendocino County, CA held by The Tide Community Broadcasting Inc.
Nat'l Network: CBS
Arbitron Metro Market: Gualala, CA; *Format:* Adult Contemp, Variety/Diverse *Special Programming:* Gospel one hr wkly; *Target Audience:* 30-55.
Joel E. Crockett, President
Diana Schmidt, Operations Dir
Paula Power, General Manager

***KGUA**
88.3 MHz FM; 2.8 kw; 787 ft.; N38 49 30 W123 34 19 US
(707) 884-4883; *Fax:* (707) 884-4883
www.kgua.org
License: Gualala, Mendocino County, CA held by Native Media Resource Center.
Arbitron Metro Market: Gualala, CA
Peggy Berryhill, President

Hamilton City

KCKS
09-01-1978; 101.7 MHz FM; *Hrs Open:* 24; 0.53 kw; 1099 ft.; N39 56 46 W121 43 17
Mailing Address: US
Second Address: Rt. 1 W. 11th St., Concordia, KS 66901
(530) 345-0021; *Fax:* (530) 894-4837
jperry@dcbchico.com
License: Hamilton City, Cloud County, CA held by KNCK, Inc.
Wire Services: National Weather Network
Arbitron Metro Market: Chico, CA; *Format:* Sports, Talk
Joe Jindra, President
Jaime Perry, General Sales Mgr

Hanford

KGEN-FM
01-01-1997; 94.5 MHz FM; *Hrs Open:* 24; 3.3 kw; 446 ft.; N36 12 16 W119 33 53
323 E. San Joaquin St., Tulare, CA 93274 US
(559) 686-1370; *Fax:* (559) 685-1394
License: Hanford, Kings County, CA held by Azteca Broadcasting Corp.
Group Owner: Azteca Broadcasting Corp.
Arbitron Metro Market: Visalia-Tulare, CA; *Format:* Tejano; *Target Audience:* 18 plus.

KIGS
02-01-1948; 620 kHz AM; *Hrs Open:* 24
6165 East Lacey Blvd., Hanford, CA 93230 US
(559) 582-0361; *Fax:* (559) 582-3981
info@kigs.com
License: Hanford, CA held by Perreira Broadcasting
Arbitron Metro Market: Hanford, CA; *Format:* Portugese; *Hrs. of News Programming:* News progmg 35 hrs wkly; *Target Audience:* 18-49, Portuguese
Tony Vieira, General Manager

KRDA
09-01-1976; 107.5 MHz FM; *Hrs Open:* 24; 24.6 kw; 705 ft.; N36 38 12 W118 56 34
500 S. Chinowth Rd., Visalia, CA 93277 US
(559) 430-8510
www.univision.com
License: Hanford, Kings County, CA held by Univision Radio License Corp.
Group Owner: Univision Radio; (acq 1-3-2006; $10 million).
Nat'l Reps: Lotus Entravision Reps LLC
Arbitron Metro Market: Fresno, CA; *Format:* Adult Contemp, Spanish; *Target Audience:* 35-54; high quality FM oriented news/talk listeners; *Adv. Rates:* 42; 38; 41; 20
Angela Navarrete, Station Manager

KFBT
01-01-1976; 103.7 MHz FM; 50 kw; 499 ft.; N36 33 12 W119 45 10
83 E. Shaw Ave., Suite 150, Fresno, CA 93711 US
(559) 230-4300; *Fax:* (559) 243-4301
www.thebeat1037.com
License: Hanford, Kings County, CA held by Capstar TX LLC
Group Owner: iHeartMedia
Arbitron Metro Market: Fresno, CA; *Format:* Adult Contemp
Steve Weed, Operations Manager/Program Director
Jeff Negrete, General Manager
Steve Darnell, Director of Sales
David Abenojar, Promotions Director
Nik Ashjian, Digital Content Director

Hayward

***KCRH**
04-10-1981; 89.9 MHz FM; 0.018 kw; -135 ft.; N37 38 23 W122 6 16
Po 25555 Hesperian Blvd, Hayward, CA 94545 US
(510) 723-6954
www.kcrhradio.com
kcrhradio@gmail.com
License: Hayward, Alameda County, CA held by South County Community College District.
Arbitron Metro Market: Hayward, CA; *Format:* Variety/Diverse, Adult Contemp *Special Programming:* Instructional one hr, pub affrs 5 hrs wkly; *Hrs. of News Programming:* News progmg 5 hrs wkly *Target Audience:* 17-35; general
Chad Mark Glen, Operations Dir
Chad Mark Glen, General Manager
Reid Alexander, Programming Director
Jesse Clark, Promotions Manager
Josh Hewitt, News Director

Healdsburg

KFGY
12-21-1979; 92.9 MHz FM; 2.3 kw; 1949 ft.; N38 45 45 W122 50 24
1410 Neotomas Avenue, Suite 200, Santa Rosa, CA 95405 US
(707) 543-0100; *Fax:* (707) 571-1097
www.froggy929.com
License: Healdsburg, Sonoma County, CA held by Amaturo Sonoma Media Group LLC
Group Owner: Sonoma Media Group
Arbitron Metro Market: San Francisco; *Format:* Country *Special Programming:* Jazz 5 hrs wkly; *Target Audience:* 18-44.
Kent Bjugstad, General Manager
Micheal Mitchell, General Sales Mgr
Jim Murphy, Programming Director

Dano, Promotions Manager
Stacy Hoblitzell, Music Director

KRSH
02-01-1996; 95.9 MHz FM; 2.65 kw; 502 ft.; N38 44 8 W122 50 55
126 Mill Street, Healdsburg, CA 95448 US
(707) 588-0707; *Fax:* (707) 588-0777
www.krsh.com
License: Healdsburg, Sonoma County, CA held by Deas Communications Inc.
Group Owner: Sinclair Communications Inc.; (acq 8-3-2001; $2.1 million).
Arbitron Metro Market: Santa Rosa, CA; *Format:* Triple A; *Target Audience:* 25-49.
Debbie Morton, General Manager
Dan Ethan, Chief Engineer

KNOB
01-01-2002; 96.7 MHz FM; 2.4 kw; 525 ft.; N38 44 8 W122 50 55
P O Box 968, Healdsburg, CA 95448 US
(707) 588-0707; *Fax:* (707) 588-0777
www.967bobfm.com
License: Healdsburg, Sonoma County, CA held by JYH Broadcasting.
Arbitron Metro Market: Santa Rosa, CA; *Format:* Adult Contemp
Judy Hughes, General Manager
Nate Campbell, Programming Director
Dan Ethan, Chief Engineer

Heber

KGBA
04-06-1946; 1490 kHz AM; *Hrs Open:* 24
2925 East Exposition Ave., Denver, CO 80209 US
(760) 357-5055; *Fax:* (760) 357-4168
www.kgba.com
License: Heber, CA held by The Voice of International Christian Evangelism Inc.
Arbitron Metro Market: Heber, CA; *Format:* Christian; *Target Audience:* 18-49; Hispanic
Douglas Hanson, General Manager
Paul Raine, General Sales Mgr
Noe Diaz, Programming Director

Hemet

KSDT
04-10-1959; 1320 kHz AM; *Hrs Open:* 24; 0.5 kw-D, DAD; 0.3 kw-N, DA2; N33 44 59 W116 59 53
200 S. a Street, Suite 400, Oxnard, CA 93030 US
(909) 925-1320; *Fax:* (909) 658-4843
www.radioimpacto.org
License: Hemet, CA held by Rudex Broadcasting Ltd.
Arbitron Metro Market: Riverside-San Bernardino, CA; *Format:* Christian
John Cooper, President

KXRS
11-09-1963; 105.7 MHz FM; *Hrs Open:* 24; 0.17 kw; 1024 ft.; N33 41 17 W116 55 32
200 S. A St., 4th Fl., Oxnard, CA 93030 US
(805) 240-2070
www.radiolazer.com
License: Hemet, Riverside County, CA held by Lazer Broadcasting Corp.
Group Owner: Lazer Broadcasting Corp.; acq 2-94).
Arbitron Metro Market: Riverside-San Bernardino, CA

Hesperia

KRAK
02-19-2001; 910 kHz AM; *Hrs Open:* 24; 0.7 kW; N34 23 19 W117 23 29
11920 Hesperia Rd., Hesperia, CA 92345 USA
(760) 244-2000
www.cbssportsradio910.com
License: Hesperia, San Bernardino County, CA held by CBS Radio Stations Inc.
Group Owner: CBS Radio; (acq 7-19-2000; $3,537,500 with KVFG(FM) Victorville).
Nat'l Network: ABC
Arbitron Metro Market: Hesperia, CA; *Format:* Sports; *Target Audience:* 40 plus
Jeff Salkin, General Sales Mgr
Lee Douglas, Programming Director
Leslie Bischoff, Promotions Manager

Hollister

KXSM
01-01-1979; 93.1 MHz FM; 0.48 kw; 2110 ft.; N36 54 13 W121 13 45
200 S. A St., 4th Fl., Oxnard, CA 93030 US
(805) 240-2070
www.radiolazer.com
License: Hollister, San Benito County, CA held by Lazer Broadcasting Corp.
Group Owner: Lazer Broadcasting Corp.; (acq 7-25-2005; $2.88 million with KXZM(FM) Felton).
Arbitron Metro Market: Monterey-Salinas-Santa Cruz, CA

KMPG
01-01-1966; 1520 kHz AM; *Hrs Open:* 14
P.O. Box 369, Hollister, CA 95024 US
(831) 722-4477; *Fax:* (831) 637-4031
License: Hollister, CA held by Promo Radio Corp.
Format: Spanish, Tejano; *Target Audience:* 18-49.
Adala Martinez, General Manager
Rafael Meza, Station Manager

***KHRI**
12-17-2000; 90.7 MHz FM; *Hrs Open:* 24; 0.17 kw; -364 ft.; N36 52 2 W121 23 58 *Rebroadcasts:* Rebroadcasts KLRD(FM) Yucaipa 100%
1601 Belvedere Rd., 204, West Palm Beach, FL 33406 US
(888) 937-2471; *Fax:* (916) 251-1650
www.air1.com
info@air1.com
License: Hollister, San Benito County, CA held by Educational Media Foundation.
Group Owner: EMF Broadcasting; (acq 11-7-00; $30,000 for CP).
Nat'l Network: Air 1
Arbitron Metro Market: Omaha, NE; *Format:* Alternative, Christian; *No. News Employees:* 3; *Target Audience:* 18-35; Judeo-Christian, female
Darrell Chambliss, Chairman
Mike Novak, President & CEO
Eric Allen, General Sales Mgr
David Pierce, Programming Director
Ed Lenane, News Director
Sam Wallington, Engineering Dir

Holtville

KGBA-FM
08-08-1983; 100.1 MHz FM; *Hrs Open:* 24; 6 kw; 328 ft.; N32 48 10 W115 29 54
605 State Street, El Centro, CA 92243 US
(406)243-6758; *Fax:* (760) 352-1883
www.kgba.org
kgba@kgba.org
License: Holtville, Imperial County, CA held by The Voice of International Christian Evangelism Inc.
Arbitron Metro Market: Missoula, MT; *Format:* Easy Listening
Special Programming: Politics 5 hrs wkly; *Hrs. of News Programming:* News progmg 3 hrs wkly; *Target Audience:* College Students
Chris Justice, General Manager
Mike Leonard, General Sales Mgr
Jon Van Dyke, Programming Director
Dean Imhof, Chief Engineer

Hoopa

***KIDE**
12-01-1980; 91.3 MHz FM; *Hrs Open:* 24; 0.195 kw; -1558 ft.; N41 3 51 W123 41 5
P.O.Box 1220, Hoopa, CA 95546 US
(530) 625-4245; *Fax:* (530) 625-4046
www.hoopa-nsn.gov
License: Hoopa, Humboldt County, CA held by Hoopa Valley Tribe.
Format: Easy Listening *Special Programming:* Native American 55 hrs wkly, youth 2 hrs wkly, Alternative 10 hrs wkly
Joseph Orozco, Station Manager
Floriene McCovey, Traffic Controller/Announcer
Jay Renzulli, Music Director/Announcer
Marian Mattz, Front Office/Traffic Assistant

Hopland

***KORB**
01-01-2009; 88.7 MHz FM; 0.1 kw vert; -1086 ft.; N38 58 15 W123 6 50
1425 North Market Blvd., Suite 9, Sacramento, CA 95834 US
(707) 526-2765
www.broken.fm
korb@broken.fm
License: Hopland, Mendocino County, CA held by One Ministries Inc.
Arbitron Metro Market: Hopland, CA; *Format:* Christian
Keith Leitch, President
Rynie Leitch, General Manager

Hornbrook

KRVC
01-01-2007; 98.9 MHz FM; 1.25 kw; 2484 ft.; N42 5 0 W122 42 0
US
(541) 772-0322; *Fax:* (541) 772-4233
www.hot989fm.com
License: Hornbrook, Siskiyou County, CA held by Opus Broadcasting Systems Inc.
Group Owner: Opus Broadcasting Systems Inc.
Nat'l Reps: Tacher
Arbitron Metro Market: Hornbrook, CA; *Format:* Contemporary Hits/Top 40
Dean Flock, General Manager
Brian Fraser, General Sales Mgr

Hydesville

KSLG-FM
04-13-2001; 94.1 MHz FM; 4.5 kw; 1731 ft.; N40 30 3.1 W124 17 8.1
Mailing Address: 1400 Main Street, #104, P.O. Box 25, Ferndale, CA 95536 US
Second Address: 1400 Main St., Suite 104, Ferndale, CA 95536
(707) 786-5104; *Fax:* (707) 786-5104
www.kslg.com
License: Hydesville, Humboldt County, CA held by Lost Coast Communications Inc.
Group Owner: Lost Coast Communications Inc.; (acq 11-5-2001)
Nat'l Reps: McGavren Guild
Arbitron Metro Market: Ferndale, CA; *Format:* Rock/AOR; *Target Audience:* 18-49.; *Adv. Rates:* 19; 19; 19; 9
Cliff Berkowitz, Operations Dir
Tom Newhouse, General Manager
Mike Dronkers, Programming Director
Kevin Sanders, Chief Engineer

Idyllwild

KATY-FM
12-01-1989; 101.3 MHz FM; *Hrs Open:* 24; 1.55 kw; 656 ft.; N33 43 31 W116 44 58
2519 Dundee Way, Vista, CA 92083 US
(951) 506-1222; *Fax:* (951) 506-1213
www.katyfm.com
katytraffic@linkline.com
License: Idyllwild, Riverside County, CA held by All Pro Broadcasting Inc.
Arbitron Metro Market: Riverside-San B; *Format:* Adult Contemp; *Hrs. of News Programming:* news progmg 2 hrs wkly; *No. News Employees:* 1; *Target Audience:* 25-49; affluent, upwardly mobile; *Adv. Rates:* 65; 65;65; 30
Willie Davis, CEO
Duane Davis, President
Bill McNulty, General Manager
Kevin Watson, Station Manager
Tom Lazar, Programming Director

Imperial

KMXX
09-17-1980; 99.3 MHz FM; *Hrs Open:* 24; 6 kw; 302 ft.; N32 54 40 W115 31 40
1803 N. Imperial Ave., El Centro, CA 92243 US
(760) 482-7777; *Fax:* (760) 482-0099
www.tricolor993.com
License: Imperial, Imperial County, CA held by Entravision Holdings LLC.
Group Owner: Entravision Communications Corp.; (acq 7-31-00; grpsl)
Format: Tejano; *Target Audience:* 18-49.
Veronica Avila, Senior VP
Albert Valdez, Programming Director

Independence

KSRW
04-12-1996; 92.5 MHz FM; *Hrs Open:* 24; 0.87 kw; 2949 ft.; N36 58 38 W118 7 13
P.O. Box 275, Independence, CA 93526 US
(760) 873-5329; *Fax:* (760) 873-5328
sierrawave.net
ksrw@sierrawave.net
License: Independence, Inyo County, CA held by Ms. Benett Kessler

Nat'l Network: CNN Radio
Arbitron Metro Market: Bishop, CA *TV Affiliate:* KSRW TV33; *Format:* Adult Contemp; *Hrs. of News Programming:* news progmg 10 hrs wkly; *No. News Employees:* 3; *Target Audience:* 30-65; professionals & retireeswith average to above average buying power
Benett Kessler, CEO/COO
Benett Kessler, News Director

Indian Wells

KAJR
08-25-2007; 95.9 MHz FM; 1.75 kw; 620 ft.; N33 48 4 W116 13 28
Mailing Address: US
Second Address: 441 S. Calle Encilia, Palm Springs, CA 92262
(760) 568-4550; *Fax:* (760) 541-7900
www.959theoasis.com
License: Indian Wells, Riverside County, CA held by A & J Media LLC.
Arbitron Metro Market: Indian Wells, CA; *Format:* Adult Contemp; *Target Audience:* Mostly Adults 45+, about 45% Women, 55% Men.
Arthur Rivkin, General Manager
Ken White, General Sales Mgr
Scott Herman, Digital Manager

Indio

*KCRI
01-01-1995; 89.3 MHz FM; 3.2 kw; 571 ft.; N33 48 5.7 W116 13 26.9 *Rebroadcasts:* Rebroadcasts KCRW(FM) Santa Monica 100%
1900 Pico Blvd., Santa Monica, CA 90405 US
(310) 450-5183(888) 600-kcrw; *Fax:* (310) 450-7172
www.kcrw.com
mail@kcrw.org
License: Indio, Riverside County, CA held by Santa Monica Community College.
Nat'l Network: NPR; *Wire Services:* AP
Arbitron Metro Market: Indio, CA; *Format:* News
Mike Newport, Operations Dir
Ruth Seymour, General Manager
Jennifer Ferro, Station Manager
David Kleinbart, General Sales Mgr

KESQ
01-01-1946; 1400 kHz AM; *Hrs Open:* 24; 1 kw-U, ND1; N33 43 37 W116 15 10 *Rebroadcasts:* Simulcasts KUNA(FM) 96.7
42-650 Melanie Place, Palm Desert, CA 92211 US
(760) 773-0342; *Fax:* (760) 568-3984
License: Indio, Riverside Central North County, CA held by Gulf-California Broadcast Co.
Group Owner: News-Press & Gazette Co.
Arbitron Metro Market: Palm Springs, CA *TV Affiliate:* KESQ-TV; *Format:* Tejano, Spanish; *Hrs. of News Programming:* news progmg 7 hrs wkly; *No. News Employees:* 1; *Target Audience:* Hispanic Adults *Adv.Rates:* 30; 25; 22; 12

KJJZ
03-01-1993; 102.3 MHz FM; *Hrs Open:* 24; 2.6 kw; 331 ft.; N33 52 14 W116 13 39
P.O. Box 1825, Palm Springs, CA 92263 US
(760) 320-4550; *Fax:* (760) 320-3037
www.102kjjz.com
License: Indio, Riverside County, CA held by R.M. Broadcasting L.L.C.
Nat'l Network: Westwood One; *Nat'l Reps:* McGavren Guild
Arbitron Metro Market: Palm Springs, CA; *Format:* Jazz, Smooth Jazz; *Hrs. of News Programming:* news progmg 3 hrs wkly; *No. News Employees:* 1; *Target Audience:* 25-49; Palm Springs baby boomers *Adv. Rates:* 50; 30; 30; 25
Todd Marker, Operations Dir
Hughes Hilles, General Sales Mgr
Jim Fitzgerald, Programming Director
Cary James, Promotions Manager
Jeff Michaels, News Director
Ben Manierre, Chief Engineer

KKUU
04-13-1984; 92.7 MHz FM; *Hrs Open:* 24; 4.2 kw; 394 ft.; N33 52 15 W116 13 37
1321 N. Gene Autry Trail, Palm Springs, CA 92262 US
(760) 322-7890; *Fax:* (760) 322-5493
www.927kkuu.com
License: Indio, Riverside County, CA held by Alpha Media Licensee LLC
Group Owner: Alpha Media LLC; (acq 9-2-2015; grpsl).
Nat'l Reps: Christal
Arbitron Metro Market: Palm Springs, CA; *Format:* Contemporary Hits/Top 40; *Target Audience:* 25-54.
Tricia Bastida, Senior Vice President and Market Manager
David Nola, General Sales Mgr
Scott Dwyer, Programming Director
Cristine Constantinescu, Director of Promotions and Digital Media
Bill Watson, Chief Engineer
Crystal White,National/Regional Sales Manager

Inglewood

KRCD
01-01-1959; 103.9 MHz FM; *Hrs Open:* 24; 4.1 kw; 387 ft.; N34 0 26 W118 21 54
610 S. Ardmore Ave., Los Angeles, CA 90005 US
(323) 468-5272; *Fax:* (323) 465-0230
www.univision.com
License: Inglewood, Los Angeles County, CA held by Univision Radio License Corp.
Group Owner: Univision Radio; (acq 9-22-2003; grpsl).
Arbitron Metro Market: Los Angeles, CA; *Format:* Adult Contemp, Spanish; *Target Audience:* 25-44; women, 60% African-American, 30% Hispanic
Haz Montana, Operations Manager
Michelle Hohman, Regional Manager
Jason Strongin, Director of Sales
Amalia Gonzalez, Programming Director
Olga Jaramillo, Promotions Manager
Tom Koza, Chief Engineer

KTYM
02-14-1958; 1460 kHz AM; *Hrs Open:* 24; 5 kw-D, DA2; 0.5 kw-N, DA2; N34 0 24 W118 21 52
6803 West Boulevard, Inglewood, CA 90302 US
(310) 672-3700; *Fax:* (310) 673-2259
www.ktym.com
License: Inglewood, CA held by Trans America Broadcasting Corp.
Arbitron Metro Market: Inglewood, CA *TV Affiliate:* KAIL(TV) affil; *Format:* Black, Variety/Diverse *Special Programming:* Japanese one hr, Pol 2 hrs, Russian 2 hrs wkly; *Hrs. of News Programming:* news progmg 2 hrswkly; *No. News Employees:* 2; *Target Audience:* 18-54.
Gerardo Borrego, President & General Manager
Gary Rehers, General Sales Mgr
Paul Wiren, Chief Engineer
Gary Rehers, Sales Director
Bobby Howe, Public Affairs
Jean Yamashita, Bookkeeper

Inyokern

*KZLU
01-01-2008; 88.5 MHz FM; 1 kw; 1299 ft.; N35 28 39 W117 41 58 *Rebroadcasts:* Rebroadcasts KLVR(FM) Middletown 100%
P.O. Box 637, Bishop, CA 93515 US
(800) 877-5600; *Fax:* (916) 251-1650
www.klove.com
License: Inyokern, Kern County, CA held by Educational Media Foundation.
Group Owner: EMF Broadcasting; (acq 9-14-2005)
Nat'l Network: K-Love
Arbitron Metro Market: Inyokern, CA; *Format:* Christian
Mike Novak, President
David Pierce, Programming Director
Ed Lenane, News Director
Sam Wallington, Engineering Dir
Marya Morgan, News Reporter
Richard Hunt, News Reporter

Irvine

*KUCI
10-01-1969; 88.9 MHz FM; *Hrs Open:* 24; 200 w; -10 ft; N33 38 41 W117 50 36
Box 4362, Irvine, CA 94612
(949) 824-6868
www.kuci.org
kuci@kuci.org
License: Irvine, Orange County, CA held by Regents of the University of California.
Population Served: 215,529; *Arbitron Metro Market:* Irvine, CA
Barbara DeMarco-Barrett, Operations Dir
Kevin Stockdale, General Manager
Heather McCoy, Programming Director
Lily Colovic, Promotions Manager
Adam O'Neal, News Director
Mike Boyle, Engineering Dir
Elaine Hawkes, ChiefEngineer
Matt Buga, Music Director
Angela Taslakian, Music Co-Director
Michelle Ma, Music Co-Director
Lauren Quijano, Public Affairs Director
Athena Matsudo, Marketing Director
Lily Colovic, Operations Manager

Isla Vista

KSBL
06-01-1981; 101.7 MHz FM; *Hrs Open:* 24; 6.9 kw; 389 meters; N34 00 09 W119 38 51.5
414 E. Cota St., Santa Barbara, CA 41011
(805) 879-8300; *Fax:* (805) 879-8430
License: Isla Vista, Santa Barbara County, CA held by Rincon License Subsidiary LLC.
Group Owner: Rincon Broadcasting LLC; (acq 7-11-2007; grpsl)
Population Served: 89,045; *Arbitron Metro Market:* Santa Barbara, CA; *Hrs. of News Programming:* news progmg 2 hrs wkly; *No. News Employees:* 1; *Target Audience:* 25-54; women
Keith Royer, Operations Dir
Keith Royer, General Manager
Jack Clarke, General Sales Mgr
Lin Aubuchon, Promotions Manager
Peter Bie, News Director
Andrea Shaparenko, Traffic Manager

Jackson

KTTA(FM)
08-16-1973; 94.3 MHz FM; 4.3 kw; Ant 790 ft; N38 24 10 W120 39 15
500 Media Place, Sacramento, CA 95815
(916) 368-6300; *Fax:* (916) 441-6480
License: Jackson, Amador County, CA held by Bustos Media of California License LLC.
Group Owner: Bustos Media LLC; (acq 5-12-2006; swap for KKFS(FM) Lincoln)
Population Served: 60,000
John Bustos, General Manager
Juan Gonzalez, Programming Director
Bobby Reynoso, Promotions Manager
Cynthia Sanchez, News Director
Mark Sedaka, Chief Engineer

KGRB(FM)
94.3 MHz FM; 4300 watts; 241 meters; non directional
PO Box 609, Jackson, CA 95642 USA
(916) 368-6300
www.radiogrande.com
License: Jackson, Amador County, CA
Group Owner: Adelante Media Of California License LLC

Johannesburg

KGIL
10-01-1947; 98.5 MHz FM; *Hrs Open:* 24; kw
US
(310) 478-5540; *Fax:* (310) 445-1439
www.kmozart.com
License: Johannesburg, Los Angeles County, CA held by Mount Wilson FM Broadcasters Inc.
Group Owner: Mount Wilson FM Broadcasters Inc.; (acq 11-20-92; $2.5 million;
Nat'l Network: AP Radio; *Nat'l Reps:* D & R Radio
Arbitron Metro Market: Los Angeles; *Format:* Classical *Special Programming:* Theater 2 hrs wkly
Saul Levine, President
Mike Johnson, Operations Dir
Kane Biscaya, General Sales Mgr

KRAJ
10-01-1998; 100.9 MHz FM; *Hrs Open:* 24; 1.5 kw; 1309 ft.; N35 28 38 W117 41 59
42010 50th St. W., Quartz Hill, CA 93536 US
(661) 718-1552; *Fax:* (661) 718-1553
www.theheat1009.com
contact@adelmanbroadcasting.com
License: Johannesburg, Kern County, CA held by Adelman Broadcasting Inc.
Group Owner: Adelman Broadcasting Inc.; (acq 12-28-99; $45,000).
Nat'l Network: Jones Radio Networks
Arbitron Metro Market: Antelope Valley; *Format:* Contemporary Hits/Top 40; *Target Audience:* 18-54.
Robert Adelman, President

Joshua Tree

KXCM
04-01-1965; 96.3 MHz FM; *Hrs Open:* 24; 6 kw; 243 ft.; N34 9 15 W116 11 50
P.O. Box 908, Twentynine Palms, CA 92277 US

(760) 362-4264
www.kxcmradio.com
coppermountainbroadcasting@yahoo.com
License: Joshua Tree, San Bernardino County, CA held by Copper Mountain Broadcasting Co.
Nat'l Network: Westwood One; Jones Radio Networks; *Nat'l Reps:* Interep
Arbitron Metro Market: Palm Springs, CA; *Format:* Country
Gary Demaroney, President
Carol Vaughn, Operations Dir
Gary Demaroney, General Manager
Scott Sear, Promotions Manager

Julian

***KLVJ**
10-23-1991; 100.1 MHz FM; *Hrs Open:* 24; 0.11 kw; 2228 ft.; N33 9 33 W116 36 53
1425 North Market Blvd, Ste 9, Sacramento, CA 95834 US
(727) 528-9236; *Fax:* (727) 528-9246
www.klove.com
klove@klove.com
License: Julian, San Diego County, CA held by Educational Media Foundation.
Group Owner: EMF Broadcasting; (acq 1-30-97; $34,168).
Nat'l Network: K-Love
Arbitron Metro Market: San Diego, CA; *Format:* Christian; *No. News Employees:* 3; *Target Audience:* 25-44; Judeo-Christian, female
Darell Chambliss, Chairman
Mike Novak, President
Fernando Chaidez, General Sales Mgr
David Pierce, Programming Director
Ed Lenane, News Director
Sam Wallington, Engineering Dir
Marya Morgan, News Reporter
Richard Hunt, MaryaMorgan

June Lake

***KWTM**
01-01-2002; 90.9 MHz FM; *Hrs Open:* 24; 0.91 kw; 344 ft.; N38 5 14 W119 10 31 *Rebroadcasts:* Rebroadcasts KWTW(FM) Bishop 100%
Mailing Address: 3000 W. Macarthur Blvd, Santa Ana, CA 92704 US
Second Address: 125 S. Main St., Bishop, CA 93514
(760) 872-4225; *Fax:* (760) 872-4155
www.kwtw.org
recep@kwtw.org
License: June Lake, Mono County, CA held by Living Proof Inc.
Format: Christian *Special Programming:* Talk 15 hrs wkly; *Target Audience:* Christian Families
Daniel McClenaghan, President
Brian Law, Operations Dir
Robert Branch, Chief Engineer

Kerman

KBHH
03-01-2001; 95.3 MHz FM; 6 kw; 328 ft.; N36 39 40 W120 9 59
Mailing Address: P O Box 62, Keene, CA 93531 US
Second Address: 2502 Merced St., Fresno, CA 93721
(661) 837-0745; *Fax:* (661) 837-1612
www.campesina.net
Achavez@campesina.com
License: Kerman, Fresno County, CA held by Farmworker Educational Radio Network Inc.
Arbitron Metro Market: Bakersfield, CA; *Format:* Spanish, Tejano; *Target Audience:* 25-54; Hispanic market
Cesar Chavez, General Manager
Cesar Chavez, Programming Director
Maria Urrutia, News Director
Dave Whitehead, Chief Engineer

KOKO-FM
04-16-1990; 94.3 MHz FM; *Hrs Open:* 24; 6 kw; 328 ft.; N36 44 29 W120 5 8
PO Box 398, Warrensburg, MO 64093 US
(559) 292-9494; *Fax:* (559) 294-7041
License: Kerman, Fresno County, CA held by Big Broadcasting Inc.
Arbitron Metro Market: Fresno, CA; *Format:* Oldies; *Hrs. of News Programming:* news progmg 14 hrs wkly; *No. News Employees:* 4; *Target Audience:* 18-54; Hispanic men & women
Art Laboe, General Manager
Anna Avila, General Sales Mgr
Paul Mendoza, Programming Director

Kernville

KCNQ
11-01-1985; 102.5 MHz FM; *Hrs Open:* 24; 0.13 kw; 1230 ft.; N35 37 21 W118 26 16
Mailing Address: 55 Valley View, Kernville, CA 93238 US
Second Address: 14 Sierra Dr., Kernville, CA 93238
(760) 379-4500; *Fax:* (760) 376-3119
todaysbestcountryonline.com
License: Kernville, Kern County, CA held by Robert J. Bohn & Katherine M. Bohn.
Nat'l Network: ABC
Arbitron Metro Market: Bakersfield, CA; *Format:* Country *Special Programming:* Relg one hr wkly; *Hrs. of News Programming:* news progmg 18 hrs wkly; *No. News Employees:* 1; *Target Audience:* General. *Adv.Rates:* 28; 28; 28; 24
Anthony Bohn, CEO
Robert Bohn, President
Gary Huff, General Sales Mgr
Bob Jamison, Programming Director
Scott Costa, News Director
Jullian King, Traffic Manager
Chris Potter, Webmaster

Kettleman City

***KWDS**
01-01-2006; 89.9 MHz FM; 50 kw vert; 251 ft.; N35 59 42 W119 58 6
P.O. Box 637, Bishop, CA 93515 US
(858) 277-4991; *Fax:* (858) 277-1365
www.horizonradio.org
License: Kettleman City, Kings County, CA held by Calvary Chapel of Costa Mesa Inc.
Arbitron Metro Market: Excelsior Springs, MO; *Format:* Christian
Mike MacIntosh, President

King City

***KDRH**
01-01-2001; 91.3 MHz FM; 0.3 kw vert; 75 ft.; N36 16 22 W121 5 2
1601 Belvedere Road, 204, West Palm Beach, FL 33406 US
www.air1.com
info@air1.com
License: King City, Monterey County, CA held by Educational Media Foundation.
Group Owner: EMF Broadcasting; (acq 11-7-00; $30,000 for CP).
Nat'l Network: Air 1
Arbitron Metro Market: Omaha, NB; *Format:* Alternative, Christian; *Hrs. of News Programming:* News progmg one hr wkly; *Target Audience:* 18-25; teen, young adult
Mike Novak, President
David Pierce, Programming Director
Ed Lenane, News Director
Sam Wallington, Engineering Dir
Marya Morgan, News Reporter
Richard Hunt, News Reporter
Tracy Butler, Traffic Manager

KRKC
09-21-1958; 1490 kHz AM; *Hrs Open:* 24; 1 kw-U, ND1; N36 13 34 W121 7 26
Mailing Address: P.O. Box B, King City, CA 93930 US
Second Address: 1134 San Antonio Dr., King City, CA 93930
(831) 385-5421; *Fax:* (831) 385-0635
www.krkc.com
bill@krkc.com
License: King City, CA held by Radio Del Rey.
Nat'l Network: CBS; *Nat'l Reps:* Farmakis; Katz Radio
Arbitron Metro Market: South Monterey County; *Format:* Country *Special Programming:* Farm 10 hrs, sports 9 hrs wkly; *No. News Employees:* 1; *Target Audience:* 25-54.
Bill Gittler, President
Bill Gittler, General Manager

KRKC-FM
01-30-1989; 102.1 MHz FM; *Hrs Open:* 24; 2.6 kw; 1821 ft.; N35 57 6 W121 0 3
P.O. Box B, King City, CA 93930 US
(831) 385-5421; *Fax:* (831) 385-0635
www.krkc.com
bill@krkc.com
License: King City, Monterey County, CA held by King City Communications Corp.
Nat'l Network: AP Radio
Arbitron Metro Market: Monterey-Salina; *Format:* Adult Contemp; *Hrs. of News Programming:* news progmg 1 hr wkly; *No. News Employees:* 1; *Target Audience:* 18-49; men and women
Bill Gittler, President
Jim Barker, Operations Dir
Bill Gittler, General Manager
David Magnum, News Director
Ron Warren, Chief Engineer

KEXA
01-01-1981; 93.9 MHz FM; *Hrs Open:* 24; 5.4 kw; 702 ft.; N36 22 48 W121 12 57
Mailing Address: 548 East Alisal Ste A, Salinas, CA 93905 US
Second Address: 548 E. Alisal St., Salinas, CA 93905
(831) 757-1910; *Fax:* (831) 757-8015
wolfhouseradio@yahoo.es
License: King City, Monterey County, CA held by Wolfhouse Radio Group Inc.
Group Owner: Wolfhouse Radio Group Inc.; (acq 8-31-2001; grpsl)
Arbitron Metro Market: King City, CA; *Format:* Tejano; *Target Audience:* General.
Ramon Castro, General Manager

Kings Beach

KSRN
01-01-1990; 107.7 MHz FM; 0.23 kw; 2867 ft.; N39 18 48 W119 52 59
200 S. A St., Oxnard, CA 93030 US
(805) 240-2070
www.radiolazer.com
License: Kings Beach, Placer County, CA held by Lazer Broadcasting Corp.
Group Owner: Lazer Broadcasting Corp.; (acq 12-12-2003; $2.5 million)
Nat'l Network: ABC; *Nat'l Reps:* Katz Radio
Arbitron Metro Market: Sacramento, CA; *Format:* Tejano *Special Programming:* Gospel one hr wkly; *Hrs. of News Programming:* News progmg 5 hrs wkly; *Target Audience:* 35-54; affluent, business professionals *Adv.Rates:* 12; 10; 10; 10

Kingsburg

***KVPW**
01-01-1992; 106.3 MHz FM; *Hrs Open:* 24; 16 kw; 420 ft.; N36 26 50 W119 37 10
1425 N Market Boulevard, Suite 9, Sacramento, CA 95834 US
707-528-9236; *Fax:* 707-528-9246
www.air1.com
License: Kingsburg, Fresno County, CA held by Pro-Active Communications-Fresno LLC
Arbitron Metro Market: Fresno, CA; *Format:* Christian
Darell Chambliss, Chairman
Gerald Clifton, CEO
Mike Novak, President
Brenda Brown, General Manager

La Mirada

KFSH-FM
04-16-1961; 95.9 MHz FM; 6 kw; 328 ft.; N33 49 53 W117 48 33
50 E. Rivercenter Blvd., Suite 1200, Covington, KY 41011 US
(714) 796-4458; *Fax:* (818) 551-1110
www.thefish959.com
License: La Mirada, Orange County, CA
Group Owner: Salem Communications Corp.
Arbitron Metro Market: Glendale, CA; *Format:* Christian; *Target Audience:* 18-49.
John Davis, President
Cherie Curry, General Manager

La Quinta

KUNA-FM
08-01-1987; 96.7 MHz FM; *Hrs Open:* 24; 0.97 kw; 581 ft.; N33 48 8 W116 13 30
42-650 Melanie Place, Palm Desert, CA 92211 US
(760) 568-6830; *Fax:* (760) 568-3984
www.kunamundo.com
License: La Quinta, Riverside County, CA held by Gulf California Broadcasting Co.
Group Owner: News-Press & Gazette Co.
Nat'l Reps: Univision Radio National Sales
Arbitron Metro Market: La Quinta, CA *TV Affiliate:* KUNA-TV; *Format:* Tejano; *Hrs. of News Programming:* news progmg 25 hrs wkly; *No. News Employees:* 1; *Target Audience:* 25-54.; *Adv. Rates:* 65; 60; 55;40
John Gilhuly, Operations Manager
Mike Stutz, General Manager and Corporate Director of News
Alex Silver, General Sales Mgr
Sonia Montano, Programming Director
Bob Smith, News Director
Susan Truesdale, Business Manager
CatherineFurguson, HR Coordinator
Kent Kay, Creative Services Director
Linda Gaston, Community Affairs Director
Tim Kiley, Assistant News Director

La Selva Beach

KOMY
01-01-1937; 1340 kHz AM; *Hrs Open:* 5 AM-midnight (M-S); 1 kw-D, ND2; 0.85 kw-N, ND2; N36 57 43 W121 58 51
2300 Portola Drive, Santa Cruz, CA 95062 US
(831) 475-1080; *Fax:* (831) 475-2967
www.1340komy.com
rosie@ksco.com
License: La Selva Beach, CA held by Zwerling Broadcasting System Ltd.
Format: Oldies, Sports; *Target Audience:* 25-64; people with an investment at risk in the community; *Adv. Rates:* 20; 20; 20; 15
Michael Zwerling, CEO
Ron Stevens, President
Michael Olson, General Manager
Rosemary Chalmers, Station Manager

Lake Arrowhead

KCXX
06-01-1978; 103.9 MHz FM; *Hrs Open:* 24; 400 w; Ant 1,797 ft; N34 14 03 W117 08 25
242 E. Airport Dr., Suite 106, San Bernardino, CA 90301
(909) 890-5904; *Fax:* (909) 890-9035
www.x1039.com
License: Lake Arrowhead, San Bernardino County, CA held by All-Pro Broadcasting Inc.
Nat'l Reps: Christal
Population Served: 1,300,000; *Arbitron Metro Market:* Riverside-San B; *Target Audience:* 18-49.; *Adv. Rates:* 120; 120; 120; 50
Willie Davis, CEO
Bill McNulty, General Manager
Coleen Bambrick, General Sales Mgr
John DeSantis, Programming Director
Monica Alonso, Promotions Manager

Lake Isabella

KQAB(AM)
07-15-1977; 1140 kHz AM; *Hrs Open:* Sunrise-sunset; 1 kw-D; N35 38 20 W118 28 22
14 Sierra Dr., PO Box 2008, Kernville, CA 93238
(760) 379-5636; *Fax:* (760) 376-3119
License: Lake Isabella, Kern County, CA held by Robert J. and Katherine M. Bohn.
Nat'l Network: ABC
Population Served: 29,000; *Arbitron Metro Market:* Bakersfield, CA; *Format:* News, Talk; *Hrs. of News Programming:* news progmg 14 hrs wkly; *No. News Employees:* 1; *Target Audience:* 40 plus; mature *Adv.Rates:* 11; 11; 11; 8.80
Robert Bohn, President
Anthony Bohn, General Manager
Gary Huff, General Sales Mgr
Bob Jamison, Programming Director
Scott Costa, News Director
Jillian King, Traffic Manager

KVLI(FM)
10-29-1992; 104.5 MHz FM; *Hrs Open:* 24; 200 w; 1,260 ft; N35 37 21 W118 26 16
14 Sierra Drive, Suite A, Kernville, CA 93238
(760) 376-4500; *Fax:* (760) 376-3119
www.classichitsradioonline.com
License: Lake Isabella, Kern County, CA held by Robert J. Bohn & Katerine M. Bohn
Nat'l Network: ABC
Population Served: 29,000; *Arbitron Metro Market:* Kernville, CA; *Format:* Oldies; *Hrs. of News Programming:* news progmg 12 hrs wkly; *No. News Employees:* 1; *Target Audience:* 25-54.; *Adv. Rates:* 28; 28;28; 24
Anthony Bohn, Station Manager
Gary Huff, General Sales Mgr
Scott Cosa, News Director
Bob Jamison, Engineering Dir
Jillian King, Traffic Manager

KRVQ-FM
05-01-2005; 104.5 MHz FM; 0.2 kw; 1260 ft.; N35 37 21 W118 26 16
55 Valley View, Kernville, CA 93238 US
(307) 732-0384
www.923theriver.com
bstphnsn@gmail.com
License: Lake Isabella, Teton County, CA held by Jackson Radio Group Inc.
Group Owner: Northeast Broadcasting Company Inc.; (acq 3-31-2006; $900,000 with KVRG(FM) Victor)
Arbitron Metro Market: Lake Isabella, CA; *Format:* Classic Rock
Steven Silberberg, President
Bruce Pollock, General Manager
Shay Richardson, Sales Manager
Bob Stephenson, Operations Mgr/Program Director
Mason Tibbs, Marketing Consultant/On Air

Lakeport

KNTI
10-21-1984; 99.5 MHz FM; *Hrs Open:* 24; 2.4 kw; 1919 ft.; N39 7 50 W123 4 32
140 N. Main St., Lakeport, CA 95453 US
(707) 263-6113; *Fax:* (707) 263-0939
www.knti.com
License: Lakeport, CA held by Bicoastal Media L.L.C.
Group Owner: Bicoastal Media L.L.C.; acq 7-28-99; grpsl)
Nat'l Network: CNN Radio
Format: Contemporary Hits/Top 40, Adult Contemp *Special Programming:* Sp 3 hrs, new adult contemp 3 hrs wkly; *Hrs. of News Programming:* news progmg 8 hrs wkly; *No. News Employees:* 1; *Target Audience:* 25-54;family oriented, upscale, professional adults
Mike Wilson, President & COO
Kevin Mostyn, VP & CTO

KXBX-FM
08-31-1984; 98.3 MHz FM; 4.8 kw; 367 ft.; N39 2 56 W122 46 3
775 East Blithedale Avenue, #143, Mill Valley, CA 94941 US
(707) 263-6113; *Fax:* (707) 263-0939
www.kxbxfm.com
License: Lakeport, Lake County, CA
Arbitron Metro Market: Lakeport, CA; *Format:* Adult Contemp
Jerry Del Core, General Manager

*KPFZ-FM
01-01-2008; 88.1 MHz FM; 0.1 kw vert; 2185 ft.; N38 59 23 W122 46 5
P O Box 1494, Lucerne, CA 95458 US
(707) 263-3640; *Fax:* (707) 263-3890
www.kpfz.org
kpfz@mchsi.com
License: Lakeport, Lake County, CA held by Lake County Community Radio Inc.
Arbitron Metro Market: Lakeport, CA; *Format:* Talk
Andy Weiss, Operations Dir
Andy Weiss, Station Manager
Tim Hoff, Programming Director
Bill Rett, Chief Engineer
Tee Watts, Music Director
Sandra Wade, Public/Cultural Affairs Director

Lancaster

KAVL
09-08-1950; 610 kHz AM; *Hrs Open:* 24; 4.9 kw-D, DA2; 4 kw-N, DA2; N34 42 22 W118 10 36
352 E. Ave. K-4, Lancaster, CA 93535 US
(661) 942-1121; *Fax:* (661) 723-5512
www.foxsports610.com
License: Lancaster, Los Angeles County, CA held by RZ Radio LLC
Group Owner: RZ Radio LLC; (acq 12-16-2011)
Nat'l Network: Fox Sports Radio
Arbitron Metro Market: Lancaster, CA; *Format:* Sports; *No. News Employees:* 2; *Target Audience:* 25-44; predominantly male, commuters, sports fans
Becky Smith, General Manager

KGMX
10-28-1970; 106.3 MHz FM; *Hrs Open:* 24; 3 kw; 135 ft.; N34 44 41 W118 7 30
100 Wilshire Blvd., Suite 1000, Santa Monica, CA 90401 US
(661) 947-3107; *Fax:* (661) 272-5688
www.kmix1063.com
psa@highdesertbroadcasting.com
License: Lancaster, Los Angeles County, CA held by High Desert Broadcasting LLC.
Group Owner: High Desert Broadcasting LLC
Arbitron Metro Market: Los Angeles; *Format:* Adult Contemp; *Hrs. of News Programming:* News 25 hrs wkly; *Target Audience:* 24-54.
John Hearne, CEO
Nelson Rasse, General Sales Mgr
Mark Benevento, Programming Director
Alizah Lipson, Promotions Director

KOSS
08-01-1956; 1380 kHz AM; *Hrs Open:* 24
100 Wilshire Blvd., Suite 1000, Santa Monica, CA 90401 US
(661) 947-3107; *Fax:* (661) 272-5688
www.newstalk1380.com
License: Lancaster, CA held by High Desert Broadcasting LLC.
Group Owner: High Desert Broadcasting LLC; (acq 1-21-97; with co-located FM)
Arbitron Metro Market: Los Angeles; *Format:* News, News/Talk, 86 *Special Programming:* Local 21 hrs wkly, finance 2 hrs wkly, good day Doug Stephan 4 hrs wkly; *Target Audience:* 18-49; homeowners, married couples withdiscretionary income
John Hearne, CEO
Nelson Rasse, General Sales Mgr
Mark Benevento, Programming Director
Alizah Lipson, Promotions Director

*KTLW
07-03-1997; 88.9 MHz FM; *Hrs Open:* 24; 5.8 kw; Ant 272 ft; N34 51 03 W118 09 22
14820 Sherman Way, Life On The Way Communications, Van Nuys, CA 91405
(818) 779-8444
www.ktlw.net
ktlwinfo@ktlw.net
License: Lancaster, Los Angeles County, CA held by Life On The Way Communications Inc.
Nat'l Network: AP Network News
Population Served: 4,500,000 *Hrs. of News Programming:* News progmg 6 hrs wkly; *Target Audience:* 25-54; 50% male, 50% female
Gary Curtis, Operations Dir
Rita Medall, Operations Manager

Laytonville

*KHKL
01-01-2002; 91.9 MHz FM; *Hrs Open:* 24; 0.1 kw; 2372 ft.; N39 41 38 W123 34 43
US
(800) 525-5683; *Fax:* (916) 251-1650
www.klove.com
klove@klove.com
License: Laytonville, Mendocino County, CA held by Educational Media Foundation.
Group Owner: EMF Broadcasting
Nat'l Network: K-Love
Arbitron Metro Market: Laytonville, CA; *Format:* Christian; *No. News Employees:* 3; *Target Audience:* 25-44; Judeo Christian, female
Darrell Chambliss, Chairman
Mike Novak, President and CEO
Eric Allen, General Sales Mgr
David Pierce, Programming Director
Ed Lenane, News Director
Sam Wallington, Engineering Dir

*KVUH
01-01-2005; 88.5 MHz FM; 1 kw vert; 2431 ft.; N39 41 38 W123 34 43 *Rebroadcasts:* Rebroadcasts KSJV(FM) Fresno 100%
4135 Northgate Blvd., Suite 1, Sacramento, CA 95834 US
(559) 264-9191; *Fax:* (559) 455-5778
www.radiobilingue.org
ricardo@radiobilingue.org
License: Laytonville, Mendocino County, CA held by Radio Bilingue Inc.
Arbitron Metro Market: Fresno, CA; *Format:* Ethnic
Hugo Morales, CEO
Maria Erana, General Manager
Phil Traynor, General Sales Mgr
Samuel Orozco, News Director
Bill Bach, Chief Engineer

*KLAI
01-01-2006; 90.3 MHz FM; 0.5 kw vert; 2431 ft.; N39 41 38 W123 34 43
Mailing Address: P O Box 135, Redway, CA 95560 US
Second Address: 1144 Redway Drive, Redway, CA 95560
(707) 923-2513; *Fax:* (707) 923-2501
www.kmud.org
License: Laytonville, Mendocino County, CA held by Redwood Community Radio Inc.
Arbitron Metro Market: Laytonville, CA; *Format:* Variety/Diverse
Michael Jacinto, Operations Dir
Brenda Starr, General Manager
Jeanette Todd, Interim Station Manager
Marianne Knorzer, Programming Director
Cynthia Elkins, News Coordinator
Simon Frech, Engineering Dir
Cynthia Click, MusicDirector and Volunteer Coordinator
Beth Comes-Westkamper, Traffic Cordinator
Terri Klemetson, News Coordinator
Dave Smith, Production Assistant
BR Graham, Underwriting Representative

Le Grand

*KEFR
01-11-1985; 89.9 MHz FM; 1.8 kw; 2142 ft.; N37 32 1 W120 1 50

Mailing Address: 4135 Northgate Blvd #1, Sacramento, CA 95834 US
Second Address: 290 Hegenberger Rd., Oakland, CA 94621
(916) 641-8191 (510) 568-6200; *Fax:* (916) 641-8238 (510) 633-7983
www.familyradio.com
kefr@k66.com
License: Le Grand, Merced County, CA held by Family Stations Inc.
Group Owner: Family Stations Inc.
Arbitron Metro Market: Oakland, CA; *Format:* Christian, Religious; *Target Audience:* General.
Harold Camping, President
Matt Pearce, Operations Dir
Larry Milliken, Station Manager
Craig Hulsebos, Programming Director

Lemoore

KJOP
12-23-1963; 1240 kHz AM
15279 Hanford Armona Road, Lemoore, CA 93245 US
(916) 535-0500; *Fax:* (916) 535-0504
www.ihradio.org
info@ihradio.org
License: Lemoore, CA held by IHR Educational Broadcasting.
Group Owner: IHR Educational Broadcasting; (acq 12-22-2000; $125,000)
Arbitron Metro Market: Visalia, CA; *Format:* Religious, Christian
Doug Sherman, President

Lenwood

KBTW
04-01-2001; 104.5 MHz FM; *Hrs Open:* 24; 1.1 kw; 768 ft.; N34 58 15 W117 2 22 *Rebroadcasts:* Rebroadcasts KXLM (FM) Oxnard 80%
200 S. A St., 4th Fl., Oxnard, CA 93030 USA
(805) 240-2070
www.radiolazer.com
License: Lenwood, San Bernardino County, CA held by Lazer Broadcasting Corp.
Group Owner: Lazer Broadcasting Corp.; (acq 10-27-99; 450,000).
Nat'l Reps: Lotus Entravision Reps LLC
Arbitron Metro Market: San Bernardino, CA; *Format:* Tejano; *Hrs. of News Programming:* News progmg 2 hrs wkly; *Target Audience:* 25-54; adult

KIXW-FM
01-01-1993; 107.3 MHz FM; 1 kw; 781 ft.; N34 58 15 W117 2 22
Mailing Address: 1611 East Main St, P.O.Box 1668, Barstow, CA 92312 US
Second Address: 101 Convention Center Dr, Suite 1001, Las Vegas, NV 89109
(760) 256-0326; *Fax:* (760) 256-9507
highwayradio.com
info@highwayradio.com
License: Lenwood, San Bernardino County, CA held by KHWY, Inc.
Group Owner: KHWY, Inc.; (acq 2-18-98; $1,741,444 with KIXF(FM) Baker).
Nat'l Network: CNN Radio; Westwood One
Format: Country
Kirk Anderson, President/COO
John Gregg, Operations Dir

KHDR
12-20-2002; 96.9 MHz FM; *Hrs Open:* 24; 1 kw; 801 ft.; N34 58 15 W117 2 23 *Rebroadcasts:* Rebroadcasts KHRQ(FM) Baker 100%
Mailing Address: 1611 East Main St, P.O.Box 1668, Barstow, CA 92312 US
Second Address: 101 Convention Center Dr, Suite 1001, Las Vegas, NV 89109
(760) 256-0326; *Fax:* (760) 256-9507
highwayradio.com
info@highwayradio.com
License: Lenwood, San Bernardino County, CA held by The Drive LLC.
Group Owner: KHWY, Inc.; (acq 2-25-2003).
Nat'l Network: AP Radio
Arbitron Metro Market: Lenwood, CA; *Format:* Classic Rock; *No. News Employees:* 1; *Target Audience:* General; travelers on I-15 and I-40
Kirk Anderson, President/COO
John Gregg, Operations Dir
Jeremy James, Programming Director
Kirk Anderson, Executive Vice President

Lincoln

KKFS
11-08-1974; 103.9 MHz FM; *Hrs Open:* 24; 6 kw; 328 ft.; N38 52 33 W121 7 30
P.O. Box 232, Yuba City, CA 95992 US
(916) 924-0710; *Fax:* (916) 924-1587
www.1039thefish.com
info@1039thefish.com
License: Lincoln, Placer County, CA held by Golden Gate Broadcasting Co. Inc.
Group Owner: Salem Communications Corp.; (acq 5-12-2006; swap for KTTA(FM) Jackson)
Arbitron Metro Market: Sacramento, CA; *Format:* Christian
Dale Hendry, General Manager
Max Miller, Programming Director
Veldon Leverich, Engineering Dir

Lindsay

KZPO
01-01-1999; 103.3 MHz FM; 0.28 kw; 2625 ft.; N36 17 14 W118 50 17
12550 Brookhurst St., #A, Garden Grove, CA 92840 US
members.aol.com/kingradio
License: Lindsay, Tulare County, CA held by Estate of Linda Ware, Cynthia Ramage, executor
Arbitron Metro Market: Lindsay, CA; *Format:* Oldies
Susan Crawford, General Manager

Livermore

KKIQ
05-01-1969; 101.7 MHz FM; *Hrs Open:* 24; 4.5 kw; 381 ft.; N37 35 42 W121 39 42
7901 Stoneridge Dr., Suite 525, Pleasanton, CA 94588 US
(925) 455-4500; *Fax:* (925) 416-1211
www.kkiq.com
gm@kkiq.com
License: Livermore, Alameda County, CA held by Alpha Media Licensee LLC
Group Owner: Alpha Media LLC; (acq 5-1-2015; grpsl).
Nat'l Network: AP Radio
Arbitron Metro Market: San Francisco, CA; *Format:* Adult Contemp; *Hrs. of News Programming:* news progmg 28 hrs wkly; *No. News Employees:* 1; *Target Audience:* 25-54; high income & highly educated adults *Adv.Rates:* 120; 110; 120; 60
Jim Hampton, Operations Manager
Kristi Willard, Local Sales Manager
Robin Mitchell, Director of Marketing and Promotions
Ken Hiemke, Sales Manager

*KLVS
09-01-1997; 107.3 MHz FM; *Hrs Open:* 24; 8.1 kw horiz; 1611 ft.; N37 49 17 W121 46 49 *Rebroadcasts:* Rebroadcasts KLVR(FM) Middletown, CA 100%
2171 Ralph Avenue, Stockton, CA 95206 US
(707) 528-9236; *Fax:* (707) 528-9246
www.klove.com
klove@klove.com
License: Livermore, Sacramento County, CA held by Educational Media Foundation.
Group Owner: EMF Broadcasting; (acq 9-12-96; $65,000).
Nat'l Network: K-Love
Arbitron Metro Market: Sacramento, CA; *Format:* Christian; *No. News Employees:* 3; *Target Audience:* 25-44; Judeo-Christian, female
Darell Chambliss, Chairman
Mike Novak, President
David Pierce, Programming Director
Ed Lenane, News Director
Sam Wallington, Engineering Dir
Marya Morgan, News Reporter
Richard Hunt, Marya Morgan

Livingston

*KLVN
01-01-1998; 88.3 MHz FM; *Hrs Open:* 24; 7.5 kw; 344 ft.; N37 36 31 W120 39 2 *Rebroadcasts:* Rebroadcasts KLVY(FM) Fairmead 100%
1425 N. Market Boulevard, Suite 9, Sacramento, CA 95834 US
(707) 528-9236; *Fax:* (707) 528-9246
www.klove.com
klove@klove.com
License: Livingston, Merced County, CA held by Educational Media Foundation.
Group Owner: EMF Broadcasting
Nat'l Network: K-Love
Arbitron Metro Market: Merced, CA; *Format:* Christian; *No. News Employees:* 3; *Target Audience:* 25-44; female (Judeo-Christian)
Darell Chambliss, Chairman
Mike Novak, President
David Pierce, Programming Director
Ed Lenane, News Director
Sam Wallington, Engineering Dir
Marya Morgan, News Reporter
Richard Hunt, Marya Morgan

KSKD
11-01-1984; 95.9 MHz FM; 3 kw; 305 ft.; N37 18 57 W120 43 20
2859 Greer Rd., Ste C, Turlock, CA 95382 US
(209) 883-8760; *Fax:* (209) 883-8769
www.lafavorita.net
ngomez@lafavorita.net
License: Livingston, Merced County, CA held by All American Broadcasting Co.
Nat'l Reps: Lotus Entravision Reps LLC
Arbitron Metro Market: Modesto, CA; *Format:* Adult Contemp
Nelson Gomez, President

*KCJH
01-01-1997; 89.1 MHz FM; *Hrs Open:* 24; 13.5 kw vert; 305 ft.; N37 18 57 W120 43 20 *Rebroadcasts:* Rebroadcasts KYCC(FM) Stockton 100%
9019 West Lane, Stockton, CA 95210 US
(209) 477-3690; *Fax:* (209) 477-2762
www.kycc.org
kycc@kycc.org
License: Livingston, Merced County, CA held by Your Christian Companion Network Inc.
Arbitron Metro Market: Stockton, CA; *Format:* Adult Contemp, Gospel, 74; *Target Audience:* 35-55.
Kenneth Haney, President
Shirley Garner, General Manager
Scott Mearns, Programming Director
John Ramos, Promotions Manager
Shirley Garner, Executive Vice President
Marina Tahod, Music Director
Vanessa Kudenov, Office Manager
Sharla Ogden, Accounting
Gary Harding, Production Manager

Lodi

KCVR
01-01-1946; 1570 kHz AM; 5 kw-D, DA2; 0.5 kw-N, DA2; N38 5 10 W121 12 57
6820 Pacific Ave., Floor 3A, Stockton, CA 95207 US
(209) 474-0154; *Fax:* (209) 474-0316
www.superestrella989.com
License: Lodi, CA held by Entravision Holdings LLC.
Group Owner: Entravision Communications Corp.; (acq 7-28-2000; grpsl).
Arbitron Metro Market: Stockton, CA; *Format:* Spanish, Contemporary Hits/Top 40
Lisa Vela, Senior VP

KWIN
12-24-1959; 97.7 MHz FM; *Hrs Open:* 24; 6 kw; 328 ft.; N38 4 17 W121 15 25
3127 Transworld Dr., Suite 270, Stockton, CA 95206 US
(209) 507-8500
www.kwin.com
info@kwin.com
License: Lodi, CA held by Radio License Holding CBC, LLC
Group Owner: Cumulus Media Inc.; (acq 5-9-03; grpsl).
Arbitron Metro Market: Stockton, CA; *Format:* Urban Contemporary
Bob Berger, General Manager
Joe Roberts, Programming Director
Jeff Bayani, Promotions Dir

KWNN
03-03-1978; 98.3 MHz FM; *Hrs Open:* 24; 6 kw; 390 ft.; N37 34 46 W120 50 48 *Rebroadcasts:* Simulcasts KWIN(FM) Lodi 95%
3127 Transworld Dr., Suite 270, Stockton, CA 95206 US
(209) 507-8500
www.kwin.com
License: Lodi, CA held by Radio License Holding CBC, LLC
Group Owner: Cumulus Media Inc.; (acq 12-12-03).
Nat'l Reps: Christal
Arbitron Metro Market: Stockton, CA; *Format:* Urban Contemporary
Bob Berger, General Manager
Joe Roberts, Programming Director
Jeff Bayani, Promotions Dir

*KCAI
89.7 MHz FM; 6.8 kw vert; Ant 396 ft; N38 23 01 W121 17 15
2351 Sunset Blvd., Suite 170-218, Rocklin, CA 95834

(916) 251-1600; *Fax:* (916) 251-1650
www.klove.com
License: Lodi, San Joaquin County, CA held by Educational Media Foundation.
Group Owner: EMF Broadcasting
Nat'l Network: K-Love
Arbitron Metro Market: Sacramento, CA
Mike Novak, President

Loma Linda

KCAA
11-01-1964; 1050 kHz AM; *Hrs Open:* 24
Mailing Address: 19939 Gatling Court, Katy, TX 77449 US
Second Address: 19939 Gatling Ct., Katy, TX 77449
(909) 885-8497; *Fax:* (909) 381-8935
www.KCAAradio.com
info@kcaaradio.com
License: Loma Linda, CA held by Broadcast Management Services Inc.
Nat'l Network: NBC Radio
Arbitron Metro Market: San Bernardino, CA; *Format:* News, Talk
Special Programming: Polka, swing era, sports; *Hrs. of News Programming:* news progmg 15 hrs wkly; *No. News Employees:* 3 *Target Audience:* General.; *Adv. Rates:* various
Fred Lundgren, CEO
Jim Hill, Operations Dir
Dennis Baxter, General Manager
Dick Vosper, Chief Engineer
Bill Bruns, Operations Manager
Paul Lane, Production Director

Lompoc

KSMY
01-01-1997; 106.7 MHz FM; 3.5 kw; 879 ft.; N34 44 31 W120 26 46
2100 West Northwest Highway, Suite 1150, Grapevine, TX 76051 US
(805) 925-2582; *Fax:* (805) 928-1544
License: Lompoc, Santa Barbara County, CA held by EDB SLO License LLC.
Group Owner: Frontier Radio Management Inc.; (acq 11-30-2007; grpsl)
Arbitron Metro Market: Santa Maria, CA; *Format:* Spanish, Tejano
Ron Roy, General Manager
Kathy Mansell, General Sales Mgr
Armando Lopez, Programming Director
Danny Fogle, Chief Engineer

KIDI-FM
01-01-1999; 105.1 MHz FM; *Hrs Open:* 24; 3.4 kw; 902 ft.; N34 44 31 W120 26 46
15275 Old Cazadero, Guerneville, CA 95446 US
(805) 928-4334; *Fax:* (805) 349-2765
www.labuena.fm
License: Lompoc, Santa Barbara County, CA held by Emerald Wave Media.
Group Owner: Emerald Wave Media; (acq 7-7-2006; $1.5 million)
Arbitron Metro Market: Santa Maria, CA; *Format:* Spanish; *Hrs. of News Programming:* news progmg 5 hrs wkly; *No. News Employees:* 1; *Target Audience:* 18-45; second generation bilingual Mexican Americans
August Ruiz, General Manager
Sofia Lariz, Regional Sales Manager

KBOX
12-24-1968; 104.1 MHz FM; *Hrs Open:* 24; 3.3 kw; 899 ft.; N34 44 30 W120 26 45
2325 Skyway Dr, Suite J, Santa Maria, CA 93455 US
(805) 922-1041; *Fax:* (805) 928-3069
listeners@1041pirateradio.com
License: Lompoc, Santa Barbara County, CA held by AGM California, Inc.
Group Owner: American General Media; (acq 2-1-2000)
Arbitron Metro Market: Santa Maria-Lompoc, CA; *Format:* Adult Contemp; *No. News Employees:* 1; *Target Audience:* Adults 18-49
Rich Watson, President
Emily Stich, General Sales Mgr
Luis Diaz, Programming Director
John Bartel, Chief Engineer

KRQK
12-18-1979; 100.3 MHz FM; *Hrs Open:* 24; 3.7 kw; 863 ft.; N34 44 30 W120 26 45
2325 Skyway Dr, Suite J, Santa Maria, CA 93455 US
(805) 922-1041; *Fax:* (805) 928-3069
listeners@1003laley.com
License: Lompoc, Santa Barbara County, CA held by AGM California, Inc.
Group Owner: American General Media; (acq 10-29-99; $1.3 million).
Arbitron Metro Market: Santa Maria-Lom; *Format:* Tejano; *Target Audience:* Hispanic Adults 18-49
Rich Watson, General Manager

*KRQZ
09-03-2000; 91.5 MHz FM; *Hrs Open:* 24; 4 kw; 781 ft.; N34 50 8 W120 24 6 *Rebroadcasts:* Rebroadcasts WUFM(FM) Columbus, OH 60%.
500 East North Avenue, Lompoc, CA 93436 US
(614) 839-7100; *Fax:* (805) 736-2642
www.radiou.com
License: Lompoc, Santa Barbara County, CA held by Trinity Church of the Nazarene.
Arbitron Metro Market: Westerville, OH; *Format:* Christian; *Target Audience:* 12-24 years.
Mark Hostand, Station Manager
Chris Hill, Chief Engineer

*KLWG
01-01-2006; 88.1 MHz FM; *Hrs Open:* 24; 2.5 kw; 1873 ft.; N34 54 36 W120 11 10
P O Box 1241, Lompoc, CA 93436 US
(805) 735-1511
License: Lompoc, Santa Barbara County, CA held by Calvary Chapel of Lompoc.
Arbitron Metro Market: Lompoc, CA; *Format:* Religious
Mark Galvan, General Manager
Landon Galvan, Programming Director

Long Beach

KBUE
08-01-1961; 105.5 MHz FM; *Hrs Open:* 24; 3 kw; 466 ft.; N33 51 29 W118 13 24
1845 Empire Ave, Burbank, CA 91504 US
(818) 729-5300; *Fax:* (818) 729-5678
aquisuena.estrellatv.com
lbiinfo@lbimedia.com
License: Long Beach, Los Angeles County, CA held by LBI Radio License LLC
Group Owner: Liberman Broadcasting Inc.; (acq 1995; $13 million)
Arbitron Metro Market: Los Angeles, CA; *Format:* Spanish;
Target Audience: 18-49; Spanish speaking adults
Andy Mars, General Manager
Daisy Ortiz, Director, Sales - TV & Radio West Coast Region
Pepe Garza Duron, Programming Director

*KFRN
09-19-1977; 1280 kHz AM; *Hrs Open:* 24
4135 Northgate Blvd, Suite1, Sacramento, CA 95834 US
(562) 427-7773; *Fax:* (562) 427-7723
www.familyradio.com
kfrn@familyradio.com
License: Long Beach, CA held by Family Stations Inc.
Group Owner: Family Stations Inc.; acq 9-19-77)
Nat'l Network: Family Radio *Regional Reps:* David Manzi
Arbitron Metro Market: Los Angeles, CA; *Format:* Christian, News; *Hrs. of News Programming:* News progmg 70 hrs wkly;
Target Audience: Family spectrum.
Harold Camping, President
Ward Cayot, Operations Dir
Suong Tran, Public Affairs Director

*KKJZ
01-03-1950; 88.1 MHz FM; *Hrs Open:* 24; 30 kw; 449 ft.; N33 47 58 W118 9 43
1250 Bellflower Blvd., Long Beach, CA 90840 US
(562) 985-2999; *Fax:* (562) 985-2982
www.jazzandblues.org
info@kkjz.org
License: Long Beach, Los Angeles County, CA held by California State University, Long Beach Foundation
Nat'l Network: NPR
Arbitron Metro Market: Los Angeles, CA; *Format:* Jazz *Special Programming:* Blues 15 hrs wkly; *Hrs. of News Programming:* news progmg 5 hrs wkly; *No. News Employees:* 1; *Target Audience:* 25-64; educated,opinion leaders, jazz & mus lovers
Mike Johnson, Operations Dir
Stephanie Levine-Fried, General Manager
Michael Levine, Programming Director
Denise Maynard, Promotions Manager

KLTX
01-01-1926; 1390 kHz AM; *Hrs Open:* 24; 5 kw-D, DA2; 3.6 kw-N, DA2; N33 53 30 W118 11 3
4880 Santa Rosa Rd, #300, Camarillo, CA 93012 US
(805) 482-4797; *Fax:* (805) 388-5202
www.nuevavida.com
License: Long Beach, CA held by Hi-Favor Broadcasting LLC
Group Owner: Hi-Favor Broadcasting LLC; acq 8-4-00; $30 million).
Arbitron Metro Market: Los Angeles, CA; *Format:* Religious;
Target Audience: 35 plus; mature audience
Mary Guthrie, Operations Dir

Los Altos

KFFG
10-01-1960; 97.7 MHz FM; 4 kw *Rebroadcasts:* Rebroadcasts KFOG-FM San Francisco 100%
750 Battery St., 3rd Floor, San Francisco, CA 94111 US
(415) 995-6800
www.kfog.com
License: Los Altos, CA held by Radio License Holding SRC, LLC
Group Owner: Cumulus Media Inc.; (acq 1995; $8.25 million).
Arbitron Metro Market: San Francisco; *Format:* Alternative, Oldies
Sheri Nelson, Promotions Manager

*KFJC
12-04-1959; 89.7 MHz FM; *Hrs Open:* 24; 0.11 kw; 1844 ft.; N37 19 14 W122 8 29
12345 - El Monte Road, Los Altos Hill, CA 94022 US
(650) 949-7260; *Fax:* (650) 948-1085
www.kfjc.org
info@kfjc.org
License: Los Altos, Santa Clara County, CA held by Foothill Community College Board of Trustees.
Arbitron Metro Market: Los Altos Hills, CA; *Format:* Variety/Diverse *Special Programming:* Country 8 hrs, bluegrass 8 hrs, jazz 7 hrs, progsv; *Hrs. of News Programming:* News progmg 9 hrs wkly *Target Audience:* 8-80; psychedelic speed freaks, radicals & other social outcasts
Eric Johnson, General Manager
Doc Penzel, Station Manager
Liz Clark, Promotions Manager
Mark Laubach, Chief Engineer
Dale Self
Brian Gilligan, Music Director

Los Angeles

KABC
07-01-1925; 790 kHz AM; 5 kw-D, DAN; 5 kw-N, DAN; N34 1 41 W118 22 22
3321 S La Cienega Blvd., Los Angeles, CA 90016 US
(310) 840-4900
www.kabc.com
License: Los Angeles, CA held by Radio License Holdings LLC
Group Owner: Cumulus Media Inc.; (acq 6-12-2007; grpsl).
Nat'l Network: ABC
Arbitron Metro Market: Los Angeles, CA; *Format:* News/Talk
Erik Braverman, Programming Director
Shelley Wagner, Promotions Manager

KBIG
02-15-1959; 104.3 MHz FM; 65 kw; 3,045 ft.; N34 13 36 W118 3 59
3400 W. Olive Ave., Suite 550, Burbank, CA 91505 US
(818) 559-2252; *Fax:* (818) 729-2818
www.1043myfm.com
License: Los Angeles, Los Angeles County, CA held by AMFM Broadcasting Licenses LLC
Group Owner: iHeartMedia
Arbitron Metro Market: Burbank, CA; *Format:* Adult Contemp;
Target Audience: 25-54.
Richard J. Bressler, President

KCBS-FM
07-12-1991; 93.1 MHz FM; *Hrs Open:* 24; 27.5 kW; 820 ft.; N34 13 55 W118 4 18
1800 K St. NW, Suite 920, Washington, DC 20006 USA
(202) 457-4518
www.kcbs.com
License: Los Angeles, Los Angeles County, CA held by CBS Radio East Inc.
Group Owner: CBS Radio
Nat'l Network: Westwood One; *Nat'l Reps:* Interep
Arbitron Metro Market: Los Angeles, CA *TV Affiliate:* KCBS-TV affil; *Format:* Adult Contemp; *Hrs. of News Programming:* news progmg 3 hrs wkly; *No. News Employees:* 1; *Target Audience:* 25-49
Kieran Geffert, General Sales Manager
Brad Bludau, Digital Sales Manager

KSWD
06-01-1957; 100.3 MHz FM; *Hrs Open:* 24; 5.4 kw; 2917 ft.; N34 13 35 W118 3 58
5900 Wilshire Blvd., 19th Fl., Los Angeles, CA 90036 US

(323) 634-1800; *Fax:* (323) 634-1888
www.thesoundla.com
heysound@thesoundla.com
License: Los Angeles, Los Angeles County, CA held by Bonneville International Corporation
Group Owner: Bonneville International Corporation; (acq 5-30-2008; $137.5 million)
Arbitron Metro Market: Los Angeles, CA; *Format:* Classic Rock; *Target Audience:* 25-54.
Peter Burton, General Manager
Mary Lea Wagner, General Sales Mgr
Dave Beasing, Programming Director

KMPC
09-22-1952; 1540 kHz AM
26 West 56th St, New York, NY 90064 US
(310) 452-7100; *Fax:* (310) 452-7880
www.radiokorea.com
rnadel@sportingnews.com
License: Los Angeles, CA held by P&Y Broadcasting Inc.
Arbitron Metro Market: Los Angeles; *Format:* Korean
Chris Canning, President

KSPN
02-18-1927; 710 kHz AM; *Hrs Open:* 24
77 West 66th St., 16th Fl., New York, NY 10023 USA
(310) 840-2800; *Fax:* (310) 840-2848
espn.go.com/losangeles/radio
License: Los Angeles, CA held by ABC Radio Los Angeles Assets LLC
Group Owner: ESPN Inc.
Nat'l Network: ESPN Radio
Arbitron Metro Market: Los Angeles; *Format:* Sports; *No. News Employees:* 2

KFI
04-16-1922; 640 kHz AM; 50 kw-D, ND2; 50 kw-N, ND2; N33 52 47 W118 0 47
3400 W. Olive Ave., Suite 550, Burbank, CA 91505 US
(818) 559-2252
www.kfiam640.com
License: Los Angeles, Los Angeles County, CA held by Capstar TX LLC
Group Owner: iHeartMedia; (acq 8-7-2000; grpsl)
Nat'l Reps: Christal
Arbitron Metro Market: Los Angeles, CA; *Format:* News, News/Talk, 86; *Target Audience:* 25-54.
Greg Ashlock, General Manager
Bill Denton, General Sales Mgr
Robin Bertolucci, Programming Director
Chris Little, News Director

KXOL-FM
01-01-1949; 96.3 MHz FM; *Hrs Open:* 24; 6.6 kw; 1306 ft.; N34 11 48 W118 15 30
10281 West Pico Boulevard, Los Angeles, CA 90064 US
(310) 229-3200
mega963fm.lamusica.com
max.ramirez@sbslosangeles.com
License: Los Angeles, Los Angeles County, CA held by KXOL Licensing Inc.
Group Owner: Spanish Broadcasting System Inc.; (acq 10-30-2003; $250 million).
Arbitron Metro Market: Los Angeles; *Target Audience:* 18-54.
Zev Levy, Advertising
Max Ramirez, Online Advertising

KIIS-FM
01-01-1948; 102.7 MHz FM; 8 kw; 2,959 ft.; N34 13 36 W118 3 57
3400 W. Olive Ave., Suite 500, Burbank, CA 91505 US
(818) 559-2252; *Fax:* (818) 729-2818
www.kiisfm.com
License: Los Angeles, Los Angeles County, CA held by Citicasters Licenses Inc.
Group Owner: iHeartMedia
Arbitron Metro Market: Los Angeles, CA; *Format:* Contemporary Hits/Top 40 *Special Programming:* Ryan Seacrest, Dr. Drew; *Target Audience:* 18-34.
Kevin LeGrett, Market President

KRRL
12-29-1948; 92.3 MHz FM; *Hrs Open:* 24; 42 kw; 2910 ft.; N34 13 36 W118 3 57
5900 Wilshire Blvd., Suite 1900, Los Angeles, CA 90036 US
(818) 559-2252; *Fax:* (818) 566-4517
www.real923la.com
info@hot92jamz.com
License: Los Angeles, Los Angeles County, CA held by AMFM Broadcasting Licenses LLC.
Group Owner: iHeartMedia; (acq 8-30-2000; grpsl).
Arbitron Metro Market: Los Angeles, CA; *Format:* Urban Contemporary; *Target Audience:* 18-49; females
Kevin LeGrett, Market President
David Howard, Vice President of Sales

KKGO
02-18-1959; 105.1 MHz FM; *Hrs Open:* 24; 18 kw; 2887 ft.; N34 13 45 W118 4 4
1500 Cotner Ave., Los Angeles, CA 90024 US
(310) 478-5540; *Fax:* (310) 445-1439
info@gocountry105.com
License: Los Angeles, Los Angeles County, CA held by Mt. Wilson FM Broadcasters Inc.
Group Owner: Mt. Wilson FM Broadcasters Inc.
Nat'l Network: AP Radio
Arbitron Metro Market: Los Angeles, CA; *Format:* Country
Saul Levine, President
Linda Vali, General Sales Mgr
Dave Wagner, Programming Director
Michael Levine, Promotions Manager
Susan Foreman, Promotions Director

***KHJ**
04-13-1922; 930 kHz AM; *Hrs Open:* 24; 5 kw-D, DAN 5 kw-N, DAN; N34 5 8 W118 15 24
3256 Penryn Rd, Suite 100, Loomis, CA 95650 US
(916) 535-0500; *Fax:* (916) 535-0504
www.ihradio.com
License: Los Angeles, CA held by IHR Educational Broadcasting
Group Owner: IHR Educational Broadcasting; (acq 11-06-2014 from LBI Media; $9.75 million)
Arbitron Metro Market: Los Angeles, CA; *Format:* Christian, Religious

KKLA-FM
01-01-1985; 99.5 MHz FM; *Hrs Open:* 24; 10 kw; 2959 ft.; N34 13 26 W118 3 44
Mailing Address: 4880 Santa Rosa Rd, #300, Camarillo, CA 93012 US
Second Address: 701 N. Brand Blvd., Suite 550, Glendale, CA 91203
(818) 956-5552; *Fax:* (818) 551-1110
www.kkla.com
info@kkla.com
License: Los Angeles, Los Angeles County, CA held by New Inspiration Broadcasting Inc.
Group Owner: Salem Communications Corp.
Nat'l Network: Salem Radio Network; *Nat'l Reps:* Salem; *Wire Services:* Metro Weather Service Inc.
Arbitron Metro Market: Los Angeles, CA; *Format:* Christian; *Target Audience:* 25-55.
Jim Tinker, Operations Dir
Terry Fahy, General Manager
Bill Price, General Sales Mgr
Chuck Tyler, Programming Director
Larry Marino, Operations Director

KLAC
01-01-1924; 570 kHz AM; *Hrs Open:* 24; 5 kw-D, DAN; 5 kw-N, DAN; N34 4 11 W118 11 36
3400 W. Olive Ave., Suite 550, Burbank, CA 91505 US
(818) 559-2252
www.am570lasports.com
License: Los Angeles, Los Angeles County, CA held by AMFM Broadcasting Licenses LLC.
Group Owner: iHeartMedia; (acq 8-30-2000; grpsl).
Arbitron Metro Market: Los Angeles, CA; *Format:* Sports; *Target Audience:* 35-54.
Kevin LeGrett, Market President
David Howard, Vice President of Sales

KLOS
12-30-1947; 95.5 MHz FM; 63 kw; 3130 ft.; N34 13 37 W118 3 58
3321 S. La Cienega Blvd., Los Angeles, CA 90016 USA
(310) 840-4900
www.955klos.com
License: Los Angeles, CA held by Radio License Holdings LLC
Group Owner: Cumulus Media Inc.
Arbitron Metro Market: Los Angeles, CA; *Format:* Rock/AOR
Leonard Madrid, General Sales Mgr
Norm Avery, Engineering Dir

KLVE
05-02-1959; 107.5 MHz FM; *Hrs Open:* 24; 29.5 kw; 2,999 ft.; N34 13 44 W118 4 2
5999 Center Dr., Los Angeles, CA 90045 US
(310) 846-2800
www.univision.com
License: Los Angeles, Los Angeles County, CA held by KLVE-FM License Corp.
Group Owner: Univision Radio
Wire Services: Reuters
Arbitron Metro Market: Los Angeles, CA; *Format:* Adult Contemp, Spanish; *Target Audience:* 18-49.
Luis Patino, General Manager
Jason Strongin, VP of Sales
Esmeralda Sosa, Promotions Director
Jim Coronado, Sales Manager
David Padilla, Sales Manager
Mariano Amador, Sales Manager

KNX
09-10-1920; 1070 kHz AM; *Hrs Open:* 24; 50 kW; N33 51 35 W118 20 56
5670 Wilshire Blvd., Suite 200, Los Angeles, CA 90036 USA
(323) 569-1070
www.knx1070.com
License: Los Angeles, Los Angeles County, CA held by CBS Radio East Inc.
Group Owner: CBS Radio; (acq 9-36).
Nat'l Network: CBS; *Nat'l Reps:* CBS Radio; *Wire Services:* Reuters
Arbitron Metro Market: Los Angeles; *Format:* News; *No. News Employees:* 40; *Target Audience:* General

KOST
10-09-1957; 103.5 MHz FM; 12.5 kw; 3114 ft.; N34 13 32 W118 3 52
3400 W. Olive Ave., Suite 550, Burbank, CA 91505 US
(818) 559-2252; *Fax:* (818) 729-2818
www.kost1035.com
License: Los Angeles, Los Angeles County, CA held by AMFM Broadcasting Licenses LLC.
Group Owner: iHeartMedia
Arbitron Metro Market: Los Angeles, CA; *Format:* Adult Contemp
Kevin LeGrett, Market President
David Howard, Vice President of Sales

***KPFK**
07-26-1959; 90.7 MHz FM; *Hrs Open:* 24; 110 kw; 2831 ft.; N34 13 45 W118 4 3
3729 Cahuenga Blvd West, North Hollywood, CA 91604 US
(818) 985-2711; *Fax:* (818) 763-7526
www.kpfk.org
gm@kpfk.org
License: Los Angeles, Los Angeles County, CA held by Pacifica Foundation.
Group Owner: Pacifica Foundation Inc.
Wire Services: AP; Catholic News Service; Reuters
Arbitron Metro Market: Los Angeles; *Format:* News, News/Talk, 86, Variety/Diverse *Special Programming:* Children one hr, jazz 5 hrs, gospel 2 hrs, Sp 15 hrs wkly; *Hrs. of News Programming:* news progmg 11 hrs wkly *No.News Employees:* 4; *Target Audience:* 25-55.
Zuberi Fields, Operations Dir
Eva Georgia, Station Manager
Sue Welsh, General Sales Mgr
Armando Gudino, Programming Director
Molly Paige, News Director
Fernando Velasquez, News Director

KPWR
12-20-1956; 105.9 MHz FM; *Hrs Open:* 24; 25 kw; 3035 ft.; N34 13 38 W118 4 0
2600 West Olive Ave., 8th Fl., Burbank, CA 91505 USA
(818) 953-4200; *Fax:* (818) 848-0961
www.power106.com
power106info@power106.com
License: Los Angeles, Los Angeles County, CA held by Emmis Radio License LLC
Group Owner: Emmis Communications Corp.
Nat'l Reps: D & R Radio
Arbitron Metro Market: Greater Los Angeles; *Format:* Urban Contemporary; *Target Audience:* 18-34; males
Janet Brainin, Director of Sales
Jimmy Steal, Programming Director
Dianna Jason, Sr. Director of Marketing & Promotions
Saul Perez, Chief Engineer

KRTH
04-13-1990; 101.1 MHz FM; 51 kW; 371 ft.; N34 13 38 W118 4 0
5670 Wilshire Blvd., Suite 200, Los Angeles, CA 90036 USA
(323) 936-5784; *Fax:* (323) 933-6072
www.kearth101.com
License: Los Angeles, Los Angeles County, CA held by CBS Radio East Inc.
Group Owner: CBS Radio; (acq 2-2-94; $116 million;
Nat'l Network: AP Network News; *Nat'l Reps:* CBS Radio
Arbitron Metro Market: Los Angeles, CA *TV Affiliate:* KCBS-TV affil; *Format:* Oldies; *Target Audience:* 25-64
Dan Kearney, General Manager
Ryan Lieberman, General Sales Mgr

Chris Ebbott, Programming Director
Mike Salas, Promotions Manager

KTNQ
01-01-1925; 1020 kHz AM; *Hrs Open:* 24; 50 kw-D, DA2; 50 kw-N, DA2; N34 2 0 W117 59 0
5999 Center Dr., Los Angeles, CA 90045 US
(310) 216-3434
www.univisionradio.com
License: Los Angeles, Los Angeles County, CA held by KTNQ-AM License Corp.
Group Owner: Univision Radio; (acq 9-22-2003; grpsl).
Wire Services: Reuters
Arbitron Metro Market: Los Angeles, CA; *Format:* News, News/Talk, 82, Talk; *Target Audience:* 25-54.
Haz Montana, Operations Manager
Michelle Hohman, Regional Manager

KTWV
11-20-1987; 94.7 MHz FM; *Hrs Open:* 24; 52 kW; 115 ft.; N34 13 29 W118 3 47
5670 Wilshire Blvd., Suite 200, Los Angeles, CA 90036 USA
(323) 937-9283; *Fax:* (323) 634-0947
www.947thewave.com
License: Los Angeles, Los Angeles County, CA held by CBA Radio East Inc.
Group Owner: CBS Radio; (acq 11-13-98; grpsl).
Arbitron Metro Market: Los Angeles, CA; *Format:* Adult Contemp; *Target Audience:* 25-54
Dan Kearney, General Manager
Ryan Lieberman, General Sales Mgr
Ralph Stewart, Programming Director
Mike Salas, Promotions Manager

***KUSC**
10-24-1946; 91.5 MHz FM; *Hrs Open:* 24; 39 kw; 2923 ft.; N34 12 48 W118 3 41
Mailing Address: P. O. Box 77913, Los Angeles, CA 90007 US
Second Address: 515 S. Figueroa St., Suite 2050, Los Angeles, CA 90071
(213) 225-7400; *Fax:* (213) 225-7410
www.kusc.org
kusc@kusc.org
License: Los Angeles, Los Angeles County, CA held by University of Southern California.
Nat'l Network: PRI; NPR
Arbitron Metro Market: Los Angeles, CA; *Format:* Talk; *Target Audience:* 35 plus.
Brenda Barnes, President
Steve Coghill, Operations Dir
Chris Mendez, Web Developer
Bill Leuth, VP/Programming Director
Minnie Priner, Development Director
Jamie Paisley, Music Director
Abe Shefa, Director of Underwriting
RinaRomero, Senior Business Manager
Ron Thompson, Director of Engineering

KWKW
04-14-1931; 1330 kHz AM; *Hrs Open:* 24
6290 Sunset Blvd, Ste 1600, Hollywood, CA 90028 US
(323) 851-5959; *Fax:* (323) 461-7347
www.radiodeportes.com
kwkw1330@aol.com
License: Los Angeles, CA held by Lotus Communications Corp.
Group Owner: Lotus Communications Corp.; (acq 1962)
Nat'l Reps: Lotus Entravision Reps LLC
Arbitron Metro Market: Los Angeles, CA; *Format:* Sports; *No. News Employees:* 30; *Target Audience:* 18-34 and 25 -54 males; *Adv. Rates:* upon request
Jim Kalmenson, President
Mike Addison, General Sales Mgr
Juan Rodriguez, Programming Director

***KXLU**
02-01-1957; 88.9 MHz FM; *Hrs Open:* 24; 2.9 kw horiz; 10 ft.; N33 58 16 W118 24 56
7900 Loyola Blvd, Los Angeles, CA 90045 US
(310) 338-2866(310) 338-5958; *Fax:* (310) 338-5959
www.kxlu.com
kxlu889fm@hotmail.com
License: Los Angeles, Los Angeles County, CA held by Loyola Marymount University Board of Trustees.
Arbitron Metro Market: Los Angeles, CA *Special Programming:* Black 10 hrs, Children one hr, folk one hr wkly; *Hrs. of News Programming:* News progmg 2 hrs wkly; *Target Audience:* 16-30.
Bennett Kongon, General Manager
Marcel Borbon, Programming Director
Mukta Mohan, Promotions Manager
Maki Tamura, Chief Engineer
Domenico DeCaro, Music Director
Robert Cifuentes, Production Director
Yolanda McClamb, Fine ArtsDirector
Lydia Ammossow, KXLU Advicer

KYPA
01-01-1926; 1230 kHz AM; *Hrs Open:* 24; 1 kw-U, ND1; N34 2 15 W118 16 35
27 William St., 11th Floor, New York, NY 10005 US
(212) 966-1059; *Fax:* (212) 625-2894
License: Los Angeles, CA held by Multicultural Radio Broadcasting Licensee LLC.
Group Owner: Multicultural Radio Broadcasting Inc.; (acq 2-20-98; grpsl).
Nat'l Network: ABC
Arbitron Metro Market: Los Angeles, CA; *Format:* Korean, News/Talk
Arthur Liu, CEO/COO

KYSR
06-30-1954; 98.7 MHz FM; *Hrs Open:* 24; 75 kw; 1181 ft.; N34 7 8 W118 23 30
3400 W. Olive Ave., Suite 550, Burbank, CA 91505 US
(818) 559-2252; *Fax:* (818) 566-4517
www.alt987fm.com
License: Los Angeles, Los Angeles County, CA held by AMFM Broadcasting Licenses LLC.
Group Owner: iHeartMedia; (acq 8-30-2000; grpsl).
Arbitron Metro Market: Los Angeles, CA; *Format:* Adult Contemp *Special Programming:* Pub affrs 2 hrs wkly; *Target Audience:* 25-54.
Mike Kaplan, Programming Director

KAMP
07-07-2009; 97.1 MHz FM; 21 kW; 141 ft.; N34 11 48.12 W118 15 29.58
CA USA
www.ampradio.com
License: Los Angeles, Los Angeles County, CA held by CBS Radio East Inc.
Group Owner: CBS Radio
Arbitron Metro Market: Los Angeles; *Format:* Contemporary Hits/Top 40

KEIB
01-01-1927; 1150 kHz AM; 50 kw-D, DA2; 44 kw-N, DA2; N34 2 0 W117 59 0
3400 W. Olive Ave., Suite 550, Burbank, CA 91505 US
(818) 559-2252
www.patriot.la
License: Los Angeles, Los Angeles County, CA held by Citicasters Licenses Inc.
Group Owner: iHeartMedia
Arbitron Metro Market: Los Angeles, CA; *Format:* Talk
Kevin LeGrett, Market President
David Howard, Vice President of Sales

Los Banos

KLBS
05-01-1961; 1330 kHz AM; *Hrs Open:* 24 hrs. a day; 0.42 kw-D, DAN; 5 kw-N, DAN; N37 5 51 W120 49 51
401 Pacheco Blvd., Los Banos, CA 93635 US
(209) 826-0578; *Fax:* (209) 826-1906
www.klbs.com
pr@klbs.com
License: Los Banos, CA held by Ethnic Radio Los Banos Inc.
Arbitron Metro Market: Merced, CA; *Format:* Portugese *Special Programming:* Relg 8 hrs wkly
Jose Encarnacao, General Manager

KQLB
11-01-1992; 106.9 MHz FM; *Hrs Open:* 24; 6 kw; 328 ft.; N36 55 35 W120 50 42
401-A Pacheco Boulevard, Los Banos, CA 93635 US
(209) 827-0123; *Fax:* (209) 826-1906
www.kqlb.com
pr@kqlb.com
License: Los Banos, Merced County, CA held by VLB Broadcasting Inc.
Arbitron Metro Market: Merced, CA; *Format:* Spanish
Batista Vieira, Chairman
Cidalia Sequeira, Operations Dir
J.J. Encarnacao, General Manager
Jose Berumen, Programming Director

Los Gatos

KRTY
07-09-1966; 95.3 MHz FM; *Hrs Open:* 24; 0.87 kw; 860 ft.; N37 12 17 W121 56 56
750 Story Rd, San Jose, CA 95122 US
(408) 293-8030; *Fax:* (408) 293-6124(408) 995-0823(studio)
www.krty.com
License: Los Gatos, Santa Clara County, CA held by KRTY Ltd.
Group Owner: Empire Broadcasting Corp.; (acq 2-93; $3.31 million;
Arbitron Metro Market: San Jose, CA; *Format:* Country; *No. News Employees:* 1; *Target Audience:* 25-54.
Bob Kieve, President
Mike Anthony, General Manager
Tina Ferguson, General Sales Mgr
George Sampson, Programming/News Director

Los Molinos

KCEZ
01-01-1999; 102.1 MHz FM; 25 kw; 220 ft.; N39 53 17 W122 37 38
856 Manzanita Ct., Chico, CA 95926 US
(530) 342-2200; *Fax:* (530) 342-2260
power102radio.com
License: Los Molinos, Tehama County, CA held by Results Radio Licensee L.L.C.
Group Owner: Results Radio; (acq 6-11-99; grpsl)
Arbitron Metro Market: Chico, CA; *Format:* Oldies

Los Osos-Baywood Par

KSTT-FM
01-01-1987; 101.3 MHz FM; *Hrs Open:* 24; 3.6 kw; 1647 ft.; N35 21 37 W120 39 18
966 East Essex Drive, Fresno, CA 93720 US
(805) 545-0101; *Fax:* (805) 541-5303
www.kstt.com
info@kstt.com
License: Los Osos-Baywood Par, San Luis Obispo County, CA held by EDB SLO License LLC.
Group Owner: Frontier Radio Management Inc.; (acq 11-30-2007; grpsl)
Arbitron Metro Market: San Luis Obispo, CA; *Format:* Adult Contemp; *Hrs. of News Programming:* news progmg 5 hrs wkly; *No. News Employees:* 1; *Target Audience:* 25-54.
Andrew Winford, Operations Dir
Rich Hawkins, General Manager
Josh Riley, General Sales Mgr
Andrew Cannon, Programming Director
Rebecca Crites, Promotions Manager

Lost Hills

KEBT
12-10-1995; 96.9 MHz FM; 15.5 kw; 413 ft.; N35 19 40 W119 42 58
1400 Easton Dr, Suite 144-B, Bakersfield, CA 93309 US
(661) 328-1410; *Fax:* (661) 328-0873
License: Lost Hills, Kern County, CA held by AGM California, LLC
Group Owner: American General Media; (acq 6-5-2006; $2.05 million)
Arbitron Metro Market: Bakersfield, CA; *Format:* Tejano *Special Programming:* Piolin Por La Manana; *Target Audience:* Adults 18-49
Rogers Brandon, General Manager
Wayne Stephens, General Sales Mgr
Erik Moreno, Programming Director

KQMX
105.7 MHz FM; 24.4 kw; 331 ft.; N35 30 54 W119 57 30 US
(512) 329-5843; *Fax:* (512) 329-5847
www.matineemedia.com
License: Lost Hills, Kern County, CA held by Ace Radio Corp.
Group Owner: Ace Radio Corp.
Arbitron Metro Market: Lost Hills, CA
Stephen Hackerman, President

Lucerne Valley

KIXA
11-01-1992; 106.5 MHz FM; *Hrs Open:* 24; 0.56 kw; 1066 ft.; N34 23 9 W117 3 24
50 E. Rivercenter Blvd, #180, Covington, KY 41011 US
(760) 241-1313; *Fax:* (760) 241-0205
www.thefox1065.com
kimjennings@edbroadcasters.com
License: Lucerne Valley, San Bernardino County, CA held by EDB VV License LLC.
Group Owner: Frontier Radio Management Inc.; (acq 11-30-2007; grpsl)
Nat'l Reps: Christal
Format: Classic Rock; *Hrs. of News Programming:* News progmg 18 hrs wkly; *Target Audience:* 16-45.; *Adv. Rates:* 25-60
Tom Hoyt, Operations Dir
Kim Jennings, General Sales Mgr
Joe Pagano, Programming Director

Ludlow

KDUQ
07-07-1995; 102.5 MHz FM; *Hrs Open:* 24; 6 kw; -164 ft.; N34 43 21 W116 10 4 *Rebroadcasts:* Rebroadcasts KDUC(FM) Barstow 100%
320 West College Avenue, Pleasant Gap, PA 16823 US
(760) 256-2121; *Fax:* (760) 256-5090
doscostas@yahoo.com
License: Ludlow, San Bernardino County, CA held by Dos Costas Communications Corp.
Group Owner: Dos Costas Communications Corp.; acq 6-18-03; grpsl).
Nat'l Network: ABC; CBS; *Nat'l Reps:* Western Regional Broadcast Sales
Format: Contemporary Hits/Top 40 *Special Programming:* Relg one hr wkly; *Hrs. of News Programming:* news progmg 7 hrs wkly; *No. News Employees:* 1; *Target Audience:* 25-54; adults
Roland Ulloa, Station Manager
Manny Lopez, General Sales Mgr
Mike Garcia, Programming Director
Brad Sobel, Chief Engineer

Madera

KHOT
12-31-1956; 1250 kHz AM; *Hrs Open:* 24
1436 Auburn Boulevard, Sacramento, CA 95815 US
(916) 535-0500; *Fax:* (916) 535-0504
www.ihradio.org
info@ihradio.org
License: Madera, CA held by Redwood Family Services Inc.
Arbitron Metro Market: Fresno, CA; *Format:* Religious *Special Programming:* Talk 70 hrs wkly; *Hrs. of News Programming:* news progmg 30 hrs wkly; *No. News Employees:* 1; *Target Audience:* 25-54.
Doug Sherman, President

KHIT-FM
10-01-1992; 107.1 MHz FM; 9.9 kw; 515 ft.; N37 7 40 W119 40 38
1110 E. Olive Avenue, Fresno, CA 93728 US
(559) 497-1100; *Fax:* (559) 497-1125
www.exitos1071.com
License: Madera, Madera County, CA held by Lotus Communications Corp.
Group Owner: Lotus Communications Corp.; (acq 3-10-99)
Nat'l Reps: Lotus Entravision Reps LLC
Arbitron Metro Market: Fresno, CA; *Format:* Spanish; *Target Audience:* 18-49.; *Adv. Rates:* 35; 35; 35; 30
Kevin O'Rorke, General Manager
Melissa Del Carlo, General Sales Manager
Francisco Villereal, Regional Sales Manager & Digital Assets
Armando Chaira, Public Service Director
Mr. Clean, Promotions Director

Magalia

***KLVC**
01-01-1993; 88.3 MHz FM; *Hrs Open:* 24; 5.7 kw; 1378 ft.; N39 57 45 W121 42 40 *Rebroadcasts:* Rebroadcasts KLVB-FM Red Bluff 100%
1425 N. Market Blvd. #9, Sacramento, CA 95834 US
(707) 528-9236; *Fax:* (707) 528-9246
www.klove.com
klove@klove.com
License: Magalia, Butte County, CA held by Educational Media Foundation Inc.
Group Owner: EMF Broadcasting
Nat'l Network: K-Love
Format: Christian; *No. News Employees:* 3; *Target Audience:* 33—40; Judeo-Christian, female
Darell Chambliss, Chairman
Mike Novak, President
Marya Morgan, News Director
Sam Wallington, Engineering Dir
Richard Hunt, News Reporter

Mammoth Lakes

KMMT
04-03-1973; 106.5 MHz FM; *Hrs Open:* 24; 0.36 kw; 2372 ft.; N37 37 42 W119 1 47
P. O. Box 1284, Mammoth Lakes, CA 93546 US
(760) 934-8888; *Fax:* (760) 934-2429
kmmtradioworks@yahoo.com
License: Mammoth Lakes, Mono County, CA held by Mammoth Mountain F.M. Associates Inc.
Format: Adult Contemp *Special Programming:* Jazz 2 hrs, classic rock 4 hrs wkly; *Hrs. of News Programming:* news progmg 2 hrs wkly; *No. News Employees:* 1; *Target Audience:* 18-54; active, athletic, affluent adults *Adv. Rates:* 15; 12; 15; 10

David Digerness, President
Shellie Woods, General Manager

Manteca

KCBC
04-05-1987; 770 kHz AM; *Hrs Open:* 24
P.O. Box 3003, Blue Bell, PA 19422 US
(209) 847-7700; *Fax:* (209) 847-1769
www.770kcbc.com
kcbcradio@surfside.net
License: Manteca, CA held by Kiertron Inc.
Group Owner: Crawford Broadcasting Co.; (acq 12-30-92; $1 million)
Arbitron Metro Market: Modesto, CA; *Format:* Religious, Christian; *Hrs. of News Programming:* news progmg 25 hrs wkly; *No. News Employees:* 1; *Target Audience:* 25-49.
Don Crawford Sr., President
John Yazel, Operations Dir
Laura Scotti, General Manager
Sarah Davis, Programming Director
Steve Minshall, Chief Engineer

Maricopa

KXTT
94.9 MHz FM; 6 kw; 312 ft.; N35 5 39 W119 27 40
200 S. A St., 4th Fl., Oxnard, CA 93030 US
(805) 240-2070
lamejornetwork.com
License: Maricopa, Kern County, CA held by Lazer Licenses LLC.
Group Owner: Lazer Broadcasting Corp.; (acq 6-11-2007; $3.85 million with KEAL(FM) Taft)
Arbitron Metro Market: Altus, OK

Marina

KTOM-FM
04-06-1982; 92.7 MHz FM; *Hrs Open:* 24; 6.9 kw; 620 ft.; N36 33 9 W121 47 17
903 N. Main St., Salinas, CA 93906 US
(831) 755-8181; *Fax:* (831) 755-8193
www.ktom.com
License: Marina, Monterey County, CA held by CC Licenses LLC.
Group Owner: iHeartMedia; (acq 9-22-97; grpsl).
Nat'l Reps: D & R Radio
Arbitron Metro Market: Monterey-Salinas, CA; *Format:* Country; *Hrs. of News Programming:* news progmg 5 hrs wkly; *No. News Employees:* 1; *Target Audience:* 25-54; men
Sean Beken, Market President
Sam Segovia, Program Director/Operations Manager
Maggie Fernandez, Promotions Director
Alyssa Oresco, Digital Content Director

Mariposa

KDJK
01-01-1992; 103.9 MHz FM; *Hrs Open:* 24; 0.071 kw; 2047 ft.; N37 32 0 W120 1 29 *Rebroadcasts:* Simulcasts KHKK-FM Modesto 95%
3127 Transworld Dr., Suite 270, Stocktons, CA 95206 US
(209) 507-8500
www.104thehawk.com
thehawk@104thehawk.com
License: Mariposa, CA held by Radio License Holding CBC, LLC
Group Owner: Cumulus Media Inc.; (acq 7-30-93; $6 million).
Nat'l Reps: Christal
Arbitron Metro Market: Merced, CA; *Format:* Classic Rock; *Target Audience:* 18-54.
Roy Williams, General Manager
Richard Perry, Programming Director

KUBB
07-04-1977; 96.3 MHz FM; *Hrs Open:* 24; 1.9 kw; 2,096 ft.; N37 32 1 W120 1 46
510 W. 19th St., Merced, CA 95340 US
(209) 383-7900; *Fax:* (209) 723-8461
www.kubb.com
License: Mariposa, Mariposa County, CA held by Alpha Media Licensee LLC
Group Owner: Alpha Media LLC; (acq 10-10-2014).
Nat'l Network: Westwood One; *Nat'l Reps:* D & R Radio
Arbitron Metro Market: Mariposa, CA; *Format:* Country *Special Programming:* Farm 2 hrs wkly; *Hrs. of News Programming:* news progmg 2 hrs wkly; *No. News Employees:* 1; *Target Audience:* 25-54.; *Adv. Rates:* 36; 32; 36; 22
Rene Roberts, Operations Manager
Mike McAdam, Vice President and Market Manager
Ed Monroe, General Sales Mgr

Marysville

KMYC
01-01-1940; 1410 kHz AM; *Hrs Open:* 6 AM-midnight; 5 kw-D, DA2; 1 kw-N, DA2; N39 8 18 W121 33 15
2905 South King Road, San Jose, CA 95122 US
(530) 742-5555; *Fax:* (530) 741-3758
www.kmyc.com
kmyc@xyix.com
License: Marysville, CA held by Thomas Huth.
Group Owner: Huth Broadcasting; .
Format: Talk *Special Programming:* Indian/Punjabi 2 hrs wkly; *No. News Employees:* 1; *Target Audience:* 18 plus; general
Thomas Huth, CEO
Jerry Snaper, Engineering Dir

KRCX-FM
10-12-1994; 99.9 MHz FM; *Hrs Open:* 24; 1.75 kw; 2182 ft.; N39 12 20 W121 49 10
1436 Auburn Blvd., Sacramento, CA 95815 US
(916) 646-4000; *Fax:* (916) 646-3237
www.tricolor999.com
License: Marysville, Yuba County, CA held by Entravision Holdings LLC.
Group Owner: Entravision Communications Corp.; (acq 3-14-2000; grpsl).
Arbitron Metro Market: Sacramento, CA; *Format:* Tejano; *No. News Employees:* 2; *Target Audience:* 18-49.
Salvador Lopez, Promotions Manager

McCloud

***KLDD**
01-01-2008; 91.9 MHz FM; 0.035 kw; 2375 ft.; N41 20 43 W122 11 42
P.O. Box 3175, Eugene, OR 97403 US
(541) 552-6301; *Fax:* (541) 552-8565
www.ijpr.org
jprinfo@sou.edu
License: McCloud, Siskiyou County, CA held by The State of Oregon Acting By and Through the Oregon State Board of Higher Education for Southern Oregon University.
Nat'l Network: NPR
Arbitron Metro Market: McCloud, CA; *Format:* Classical, News
Ron Kramer, General Manager
Valerie Ing-Miller, Programming Director
Darin Ransom, Engineering Dir
Betsy Byers, Administrative Assistant
Mitchell Christian, Director of Finance & Administration
Jill Hernandez, AccountantTechnician
Paul Westhelle, Executive Director

McFarland

KIWI
07-11-1989; 102.9 MHz FM; *Hrs Open:* 24; 25 kw; 322 ft.; N35 19 16 W119 42 26
Suite 102, 3701 Pegasus Dr., Bakersville, CA 93308 US
(661) 327-9711; *Fax:* (661) 327-0797
www.kiwifm.co.nz
License: McFarland, Kern County, CA
Group Owner: Lotus Communications Corp.; (Acq 12-18-00; $2.5 million including a $10,000 three-year noncompete agreement).
Nat'l Reps: Lotus Entravision Reps LLC
Arbitron Metro Market: Bakersfield, CA; *Format:* Tejano; *Target Audience:* General.
Bryan King, General Manager

KBQF
104.3 MHz FM; 6 kw; 327 ft.; N35 31 35 W119 18 43 US
(805) 486-4400
License: McFarland, Kern County, CA held by JAB Broadcasting LLC.
Arbitron Metro Market: McFarland, CA; *Format:* Spanish
Javier Orosco, General Manager

McKinleyville

***KNDZ**
01-01-2009; 89.3 MHz FM; 750 w vert; Ant 1,005 ft; N40 49 32 W124 00 05 *Rebroadcasts:* Rebroadcasts KVIP-FM Redding 100%
1139 Hartnell Ave., Redding, CA 94508
(530) 222-4455; *Fax:* (530) 222-4484
www.kvip.org
info@kvip.org
License: McKinleyville, Humboldt County, CA held by Pacific Cascade Communications Corp.
Group Owner: Pacific Cascade Communications Corp.; (acq 2-9-2009; $62,500 for CP)
Format: Christian

Phil Morrow, General Manager

KMDR
95.1 MHz FM; 2.3 kw; 1070 ft.; N40 49 32 W124 0 5
US
(707) 445-3699; *Fax:* (707) 445-3906
www.951mixfm.com
License: McKinleyville, Humboldt County, CA held by William W. McCutchen III.
Group Owner: William W. McCutchen III Stns
Arbitron Metro Market: McKinleyville, CA; *Format:* Adult Contemp
Randy Flavers, General Manager
Teresa Wold, Business Manager
Barbara Kennon, Account Manager

Mecca

KRCK-FM
01-01-2001; 97.7 MHz FM; 2 kw; 571 ft.; N33 48 4 W116 13 28
1425 River Park Drive, Sacramento, CA 95815 US
(760) 341-0123; *Fax:* (760) 341-7455
www.krck.com
License: Mecca, Riverside County, CA held by Playa Del Sol Broadcasters.
Arbitron Metro Market: Palm Springs, CA; *Format:* Contemporary Hits/Top 40; *Target Audience:* w18-49, A18-49
Edward Stolz, General Manager
Edward Morowski, Station Manager
Robert Scorpio, Programming Director
Debby McKay, National Sales Executive

Mendocino

***KAKX**
01-15-1997; 89.3 MHz FM; *Hrs Open:* 24; 0.25 kw vert; 233 ft.; N39 18 46 W123 46 57
Post Office Box 1154, Mendocino, CA 95460 US
(707) 937-1200
License: Mendocino, Mendocino County, CA held by Mendocino Unified School District.
Arbitron Metro Market: Mendocino, CA; *Format:* Rock/AOR, Variety/Diverse
Peter Davidson, President
Marshall Brown, General Manager

KMFB(FM)
11-01-1966; 92.7 MHz FM; *Hrs Open:* 24; 3 kw; 165 ft; N39 20 33 W123 46 51
101-E Boatyard Dr., Fort Bragg, CA 95437
(707) 964-5307; *Fax:* (707) 964-3299
www.kmfbfm.com
generalmail@kmfbfm.com
License: Mendocino, Mendocino County, CA held by Four Rivers Broadcasting Inc.
Group Owner: Four Rivers Broadcasting Inc.; (acq 7-21-2005; grpsl).
Wire Services: Agence France-Presse (AFP)
Population Served: 75,000 *Format:* Sports; *No. News Employees:* 4; *Target Audience:* 35-54.; *Adv. Rates:* 16; 14; 14; 12
Bob Woelfel, General Manager
Ed Kowas, News Director
Liz Helenchild, Music Director

***KPMO**
11-16-1966; 1300 kHz AM; *Hrs Open:* 24 hrs
1906 Coralino Drive, Henderson, NV 89014 US
(541) 552-6301; *Fax:* (541) 552-8565
www.ijpr.org
jprinfo@sou.edu
License: Mendocino, CA held by JPR Foundation Inc.
Nat'l Network: NPR; PRI; *Wire Services:* AP
Format: News, News/Talk, 86; *No. News Employees:* 1; *Target Audience:* General.
Ronald Kramer, CEO
Bryon Lambert, Operations Dir
Ronald Kramer, General Manager
Darin Ransom, Engineering Dir

Mendota

KMEN
01-01-2007; 100.5 MHz FM; 6 kw; 144 ft.; N36 38 50 W120 21 2
40 Bellan Blvd, No 10101, San Rafael, CA 94912 US
(213) 745-6224; *Fax:* (213) 745-7577
License: Mendota, Fresno County, CA held by MBP Licensee LLC.
Group Owner: Moon Broadcasting; (acq 3-30-2001; $350,000).
Arbitron Metro Market: Tulare, CA
Abel de Luna, President
Angelica Figueroa, General Sales Mgr
Yesenia de Luna, Programming Director

Menifee

KXFG
11-06-1996; 92.9 MHz FM; 6 kW; 115 ft.; N33 35 34.3 W117 8 50.8 *Rebroadcasts:* Rebroadcasts KFRG(FM) San Bernardino 100%
900 East Washington St., Suite 315, Colton, CA 92324 USA
(909) 433-3000
www.kfrog.com
License: Menifee, Riverside County, CA held by CBS Radio Stations Inc.
Group Owner: CBS Radio; (acq 11-13-98; grpsl).
Arbitron Metro Market: Colton, CA; *Format:* Country
Kimberly Martinez, General Sales Mgr
Lee Douglas, Programming Director
Leslie Bischoff, Promotions Director

Merced

KABX-FM
12-18-1975; 97.5 MHz FM; *Hrs Open:* 24; 8.8 kw; 1161 ft.; N37 26 44 W120 8 37
, Merced, CA US
(209) 384-3323
www.975kabx.com
License: Merced, Merced County, CA
Group Owner: Mapleton Communications LLC
Arbitron Metro Market: Merced, CA; *Format:* Oldies
Diane Garcia, Promotions Manager

***KAMB**
11-06-1967; 101.5 MHz FM; *Hrs Open:* 24; 1.85 kw; 2093 ft.; N37 32 1 W120 1 46
90 East 16th Street, Merced, CA 95340 US
(209) 723-1015; *Fax:* (209) 723-1945
www.celebrationradio.com
kamb@celebrationradio.com
License: Merced, Merced County, CA held by Central Valley Broadcasting Co. Inc.
Nat'l Network: AP Radio; Moody
Arbitron Metro Market: Merced, CA; *Format:* Christian; *Hrs. of News Programming:* news progmg 5 hrs wkly; *No. News Employees:* 1; *Target Audience:* 29-54; Christian adults in central California
Tim Land, CEO
Mike Boster, President
Dave Benton, Operations Dir
Tim Land, General Manager
Jinous Vartan, Promotions Manager

KBRE
11-01-1999; 1660 kHz AM; *Hrs Open:* 24
514 W. 19th St., Merced, CA 95340 US
(209) 723-2191; *Fax:* (209) 205-1013
www.1057thebear.com
License: Merced, CA held by Mapleton License of Merced LLC.
Group Owner: Mapleton Communications LLC; (acq 6-1-2002; grpsl)
Arbitron Metro Market: Modesto, CA; *Format:* Christian, Talk; *Target Audience:* 25-54.

KBKY
01-01-2002; 94.1 MHz FM; 6 kw; 328 ft.; N37 27 59 W120 14 9
1436 Auburn Blvd., Sacramento, CA 95815 US
(209) 385-9994; *Fax:* (209) 385-9982
License: Merced, Merced County, CA held by KM Radio of Merced L.L.C.
Arbitron Metro Market: Merced, CA; *Format:* Adult Contemp; *Target Audience:* Women Ages 24-54 Two Income Families; *Adv. Rates:* 20; 15; 20; 12.
Cynthia Masterson, General Manager
Roman Scanlon, General Sales Mgr
Matthew Stone, Programming Director

KGAM
01-01-1969; 106.3 MHz FM; *Hrs Open:* 24; 4 kw; 404 ft.; N37 25 35 W120 26 25
1020 W. Main Street, Merced, CA 95340 US
(760) 325-2582; *Fax:* (760) 322-3562
www.kgam.com
License: Merced, Riverside County, CA held by R & R Radio Corp.
Group Owner: RR Broadcasting; (acq 4-8-2002; with co-located FM)
Nat'l Reps: Christal
Arbitron Metro Market: Palm Springs, CA; *Format:* News, News/Talk, 86; *Hrs. of News Programming:* news progmg 5 hrs wkly; *No. News Employees:* 2; *Target Audience:* 25 plus; upscale, informed, involved adults
Jim Shea, CEO
Damien Galarza, General Manager
Diane Garcia, General Sales Manager
Yolanda Navarro, Programming Director
Rebecca Battis, Traffic Manager
Rick McMillion, Chief Engineer

KGAM(FM)
05-14-1992; 106.3 MHz FM; *Hrs Open:* 24; 4 kw; Ant 403 ft; N37 25 35 W120 26 25
200 S. A St., 4th Fl., Oxnard, CA 93030
(805) 240-2070
www.radiolazer.com
License: Merced, Merced County, CA held by Lazer Licenses LLC.
Group Owner: Lazer Broadcasting Corp.; (acq 6-1-2002; grpsl)
Arbitron Metro Market: Merced, CA; *Format:* Country; *Target Audience:* 25-54; upscale professionals

KYOS
10-01-1936; 1480 kHz AM; *Hrs Open:* 24
1020 W. Main St., Merced, CA 95340 US
(209) 723-2191
www.1480kyos.com
kyos@radiomerced.com
License: Merced, CA held by Mapleton License of Merced LLC.
Group Owner: Mapleton Communications LLC; acq 6-5-2002; grpsl)
Nat'l Network: CBS; *Nat'l Reps:* Christal
Arbitron Metro Market: Merced, CA; *Format:* News, News/Talk, 86 *Special Programming:* Farm 5 hrs, gospel one hr wkly; *Hrs. of News Programming:* news progmg 20 hrs wkly; *No. News Employees:* 2; *Target Audience:* 25-54.

Middletown

***KLVR**
10-15-1982; 91.9 MHz FM; *Hrs Open:* 24; 0.83 kw; 2989 ft.; N38 40 9 W122 37 53
1425 N. Market St, #9, Sacramento, CA 95834 US
(707) 528-9236; *Fax:* (707) 528-9236
www.klove.com
klove@klove.com
License: Middletown, Lake County, CA held by Educational Media Foundation.
Group Owner: EMF Broadcasting; (acq 1986).
Nat'l Network: K-Love
Arbitron Metro Market: San Francisco, CA; *Format:* Christian; *No. News Employees:* 3; *Target Audience:* 25-44; Judeo-Christian females
Darell Chambliss, Chairman
Mike Novak, President
David Pierce, Programming Director
Ed Lenane, News Director
Sam Wallington, Engineering Dir
Tracy Butler, Traffic Manager

Millers Ranch

KRBO(FM)
01-01-2012; 89.3 MHz FM; 100 w; -65.5 meters; N36 12 06 W121 27 48.9
975 West First Street, Azusa, CA 91702
(626) 969-7945
License: Millers Ranch, CA held by Christian Faith Center of the Valley

Samuel Martinez, President

Mission Viejo

***KSBR**
05-07-1979; 88.5 MHz FM; 620 w; 600 ft; N33 30 10 W117 36 06
28000 Marguerite Pkwy., Mission Viejo, CA 92675
(949) 582-5727; *Fax:* (949) 347-9693
www.ksbr.net
License: Mission Viejo, Orange County, CA held by South Orange County Community College District.
Nat'l Network: AP Network News; *Wire Services:* AP
Population Served: 500,000 *Special Programming:* Latin 3 hrs, blues 3 hrs, reggae 3 hrs, electronic 4 hrs, ragtime 2 hrs, folk 2 hrs wkly; *No. News Employees:* 1; *Target Audience:* 25-54.
Terry Wedel, Operations Dir
Dawn Kamber, News Director
Mark Schiffelbein, Engineering Dir

Modesto

***KADV**
11-01-1988; 90.5 MHz FM; *Hrs Open:* 24; 1.5 kw; 141 ft.; N37 36 26 W120 57 26
2031 Academy Place, Ceres, CA 95307 US
(559) 627-5276
www.mypromisefm.com

License: Modesto, Stanislaus County, CA held by Modesto Adventist Academy.
Nat'l Network: Moody; Salem Radio Network
Arbitron Metro Market: Visalia, CA; *Format:* Religious *Special Programming:* Sp one hr wkly; *Hrs. of News Programming:* News progmg 14 hrs wkly; *Target Audience:* 30 plus.
Steve White, General Manager
Jerry Moore, Chief Engineer

KESP
11-01-1951; 970 kHz AM; *Hrs Open:* 24; 1 kw-D, 1 kw-N; N37 41 23 W120 57 12
3127 Transworld Dr., Suite 270, Stockton, CA 95206 US
(209) 507-8500
www.sportsradio970.com
bob.berger@cumulus.com
License: Modesto, CA held by Radio License Holding CBC, LLC
Group Owner: Cumulus Media Inc.; (acq 5-18-92; $12.5 million grpsl, including co-located FM).
Nat'l Network: ESPN Radio; Cumulus Media Inc; *Nat'l Reps:* McGavren Guild
Arbitron Metro Market: Modesto, CA; *Format:* Sports; *Target Audience:* 35 plus.
Bob Berger, General Manager

KATM
01-01-1948; 103.3 MHz FM; 50 kw; 499 ft.; N37 34 30 W121 21 13
3127 Transworld Dr., Suite 270, Stockton, CA 95206 US
(209) 507-8500
www.katm.com
nikki@katm.com
License: Modesto, CA held by Radio License Holding CBC, LLC
Group Owner: Cumulus Media Inc.
Arbitron Metro Market: Stockton, CA; *Format:* Country; *Target Audience:* 25-64; mass appeal
Bob Berger, General Manager
Nikki Thomas, Programming Director

KBBU
01-01-1999; 93.9 MHz FM; *Hrs Open:* 24; 4 kw; 404 ft.; N37 39 0 W121 1 24 *Rebroadcasts:* Simulcast with KTTA(FM) Esparto 100%
P.O. Box 1022, Manteca, CA 95336 US
(916) 368-6300; *Fax:* (916) 441-6480
www.lakebuena.com
License: Modesto, Stanislaus County, CA
Group Owner: Adelante Media Group LLC; (acq 12-15-2004; $21.7 million with KLMG(FM) Esparto)
Arbitron Metro Market: Modesto, CA
John Bustos, General Manager
Juan Gonzalez, Programming Director
Javier Gonzalez, Promotions Manager
Adela Garcia, News Director
Mark Sedaka, Chief Engineer
Cynthia Sanchez, Traffic Manager

KFIV
01-01-1950; 1360 kHz AM; 4 kw-D, DA2; 0.95 kw-N, DA2; N37 41 23 W120 57 12
2121 Lancey Dr., Modesto, CA 95355 US
(209) 551-1306; *Fax:* (209) 551-3791
www.powertalk1360.com
License: Modesto, Stanislaus County, CA held by Capstar TX LLC
Group Owner: iHeartMedia; (acq 8-30-2000; grpsl)
Nat'l Network: Fox News Radio
Arbitron Metro Market: Modesto, CA; *Format:* News, News/Talk, 86 *Special Programming:* Afternoons live, 20 hrs wkly; *Hrs. of News Programming:* news progmg 148 hrs wkly; *Target Audience:* 25-54.
Greg Cobb, Sales Director
Kevin Fox, Promotions Director
Nik Ashjian, Digital Content Director

KHKK
01-01-1949; 104.1 MHz FM; *Hrs Open:* 24; 50 kw; 499 ft.; N37 39 10 W121 28 38
3127 Transworld Dr., Suite 270, Stocktons, CA 95206 US
(209) 507-8500
www.104thehawk.com
thehawk@104thehawk.com
License: Modesto, CA held by Radio License Holding CBC, LLC
Group Owner: Cumulus Media Inc.; (acq 10-1-93).
Nat'l Reps: McGavren Guild
Arbitron Metro Market: Modesto, CA; *Format:* Classic Rock; *Hrs. of News Programming:* news progmg 5 hrs wkly; *No. News Employees:* 1; *Target Audience:* 18-54
Roy Williams, General Manager
Richard Perry, Programming Director

KJSN
07-04-1977; 102.3 MHz FM; 6 kw; 289 ft.; N37 40 50 W120 55 26
600 Congress Avenue, Suite 1400, Auston, TX 78701 US
(209) 551-1306; *Fax:* (209) 551-1359
www.sunny102fm.com
License: Modesto, Stanislaus County, CA held by Capstar TX LLC
Group Owner: iHeartMedia
Arbitron Metro Market: Modesto, CA; *Format:* Adult Contemp; *Target Audience:* 25-49.
Greg Cobb, Sales Director
Kevin Fox, Promotions Director
Nik Ashjian, Digital Content Director

***KMPO**
01-01-1984; 88.7 MHz FM; *Hrs Open:* 24; 2.05 kw; 2041 ft.; N37 32 0 W120 1 29
5005 E. Belmont, Fresno, CA 93727 US
(559) 455-5777; *Fax:* (559) 455-5778
www.radiobilingue.org
mail@radiobilingue.org
License: Modesto, Stanislaus County, CA held by Radio Bilingue Inc.
Arbitron Metro Market: Modesto, CA; *Format:* Ethnic *Special Programming:* Black 3 hrs, folk 4 hrs, Filipino one hr wkly; *Hrs. of News Programming:* news progmg 11 hrs wkly; *No. News Employees:* 5; *Target Audience:* 16 plus; Latinos
Hugo Morales, CEO
Maria Erana, General Manager
Phil Traynor, General Sales Mgr
Samuel Orozco, News Director
Bill Bach, Chief Engineer

KMPH
07-10-2006; 840 kHz AM
US
(209) 527-8400; *Fax:* (209) 526-0820
License: Modesto, CA held by Pappas Radio of Modesto LLC.
Group Owner: Pappas Telecasting Companies; (acq 11-5-2003)
Nat'l Network: Salem Radio Network; Premiere Radio Networks; Talk Radio Network; *Nat'l Reps:* McGavren Guild
Arbitron Metro Market: Modesto, CA; *Format:* News, News/Talk, 86; *Hrs. of News Programming:* M-F 6am - 9am and Top of Each Hour; *No. News Employees:* 1; *Target Audience:* Adults: 35-64
Harry J. Pappas, CEO
Jim Pappas, Operations Dir
Jim P. Pappas, General Manager
Kevin Barrett, Programming Director

Mojave

KTPI
05-01-1958; 1340 kHz AM; *Hrs Open:* 24; 1 kw-U, ND1; N35 2 23 W118 8 57
352 E. Ave. K-4, Lancaster, CA 93535 US
(661) 942-1121; *Fax:* (661) 723-5512
www.magic1340.com
License: Mojave, Kern County, CA held by RZ Radio LLC
Group Owner: RZ Radio LLC; (acq 12-16-2011).
Nat'l Reps: Christal
Arbitron Metro Market: Lancaster, CA; *Format:* Adult Contemp; *Target Audience:* 35 plus; Adult Christian community
Becky Smith, General Manager

KTPI-FM
05-01-1966; 97.7 MHz FM; *Hrs Open:* 24; 3 kw; 299 ft.; N34 58 45 W118 10 2
352 E. Ave. K-4, Lancaster, CA 93535 US
(661) 942-1121; *Fax:* (661) 723-5512
www.ktpifm.com
License: Mojave, Kern County, CA held by RZ Radio LLC
Group Owner: RZ Radio LLC; (acq 12-16-2011).
Arbitron Metro Market: Lancaster, CA; *Format:* Country; *No. News Employees:* 1; *Target Audience:* 25-54.; *Adv. Rates:* 30; 22; 30; 24
Becky Smith, General Manager

***KCRY**
06-01-2000; 88.1 MHz FM; 10.5 kw; -95 ft.; N35 7 20 W118 12 25 *Rebroadcasts:* Rebroadcasts KCRW(FM) Santa Monica 100%
1900 Pico Blvd, Santa Monica, CA 90405 US
(310) 450-5183; *Fax:* (310) 450-7172
www.kcrw.com
mail@kcrw.org
License: Mojave, Kern County, CA held by Santa Monica Community College District.
Nat'l Network: NPR; *Wire Services:* AP
Arbitron Metro Market: Santa Monica, CA; *Format:* News
Michael Fleming, Chairman
Jennifer Ferro, President
Stu Bloomberg, Vice Chair
Tom Donner, Secretary/Treasurer

KCEL
01-01-2009; 96.1 MHz FM; 0.63 kw; 823 ft.; N35 5 38 W118 16 0
US
(661) 947-3107; *Fax:* (661) 256-8254
laquebuena961.com
psa@highdesertbroadcasting.com
License: Mojave, Kern County, CA held by Coloma Mojave LLC.
Arbitron Metro Market: Mojave, CA
John Hearne, CEO
Nelson Rasse, General Sales Manager
Mark Benevento, Programming Director
Alizah Lipson, Promotions Director

Monte Rio

KVRV
11-20-1977; 97.7 MHz FM; *Hrs Open:* 24; 2.05 kw; 1122 ft.; N38 32 25 W122 57 40
Mailing Address: 1410 Neotomas Avenue, Suite 200, Santa Rosa, CA 95405 US
Second Address: 1410 Neotomas Ave., Suite 200, Santa Rosa, CA 95405
(707) 543-0100; *Fax:* (707) 571-1097
www.977theriver.com
License: Monte Rio, Sonoma County, CA held by Amaturo Sonoma Media Group LLC
Group Owner: Sonoma Media Group; (acq 12-16-02; grpsl).
Arbitron Metro Market: San Francisco, CA; *Format:* Classic Rock; *Target Audience:* 25-54.
Jeff Clark, General Manager

Montecito

KJEE
03-01-1994; 92.9 MHz FM; 0.82 kw; 886 ft.; N34 27 57 W119 40 37
P. O. Box 22105, Santa Barbara, CA 93121 US
(805) 963-4676; *Fax:* (805) 963-8166
www.kjee.com
License: Montecito, Santa Barbara County, CA held by Montecito FM Inc.
Arbitron Metro Market: Santa Barbara, CA; *Format:* Rock/AOR; *Target Audience:* 18-34; general
Eddie Gutierrez, General Manager
Steve Meade, General Sales Mgr
Ryan Zoldas, Promotions Manager
John Palmmentari, News Director
Dean Burt, Chief Engineer

Monterey

KIDD
10-12-1995; 630 kHz AM; *Hrs Open:* 12a-12a; 1 kw-D, DA2; 1 kw-N, DA2; N36 41 28 W121 48 0
P.O. Box 250028, Los Angeles, CA 90025 US
(310) 478-5540; *Fax:* (310) 445-1439
www.mountwilsoninc.com
reception@mountwilsoninc.com
License: Monterey, Monterey County, CA held by Mount Wilson FM Broadcasters Inc.
Group Owner: Mount Wilson FM Broadcasters Inc.; (acq 4-2015).
Nat'l Reps: Eastman Radio; *Wire Services:* AP
Arbitron Metro Market: Monterey-Salina *TV Affiliate:* ESPN; *Format:* Sports, Talk
Saul Levine, President

KWAV
10-14-1961; 96.9 MHz FM; 18 kw; 2,451 ft.; N36 32 5 W121 37 14
60 Garden Crt., Suite 300, Monterey, CA 93940 US
(831) 658-5200
www.kwav.com
tdelrio@radiomontereybay.com
License: Monterey, Monterey County, CA held by Mapleton License of Monterey LLC
Group Owner: Mapleton Communications LLC; (acq 6-5-2014).
Nat'l Reps: Eastman Radio; *Wire Services:* AP
Arbitron Metro Market: Monterey-Salinas-Santa Cruz, CA; *Format:* Adult Contemp; *Target Audience:* 18-54; primarily women
Jodi Morgan, General Sales Mgr
Tommy Del Rio, Programming Director

Monterey Bay

KNRY
10-01-1935; 1240 kHz AM; *Hrs Open:* 24
2360 N.E. Coachman Road, Clearwater, FL 34625 US

(831) 372-1074; *Fax:* (831) 372-3585
www.knry.com
License: Monterey Bay, CA held by People's Radio Inc.
Nat'l Network: CBS
Arbitron Metro Market: Monterey, CA; *Format:* News, News/Talk, 86; *Target Audience:* 35 plus.
Jim Vossen, Operations Dir

Moraga

*KSMC
09-22-1977; 89.5 MHz FM; *Hrs Open:* 24; 0.8 kw horiz; 79 ft.; N37 50 25 W122 6 36
1928 St. Mary's Road, Moraga, CA 94575 US
(925) 631-4252(925) 631-4772; *Fax:* (925) 376-5766
www.ksmc895.com
ksmc@stmarys-ca.edu
License: Moraga, Contra Costa County, CA held by Associated Students of St. Mary's College of California.
Wire Services: Dow Jones News Service
Arbitron Metro Market: Moraga, CA; *Format:* Contemporary Hits/Top 40, News, 30 *Special Programming:* Relg 2 hrs, class 4 hrs, Sp 3 hrs, jazz 5 hrs wkly; *Target Audience:* 15-30; young, urban & willing to experiment
Noel Cilker, General Manager
Will McCoster, Programming Director
Jessica Fajardo, Promotions Manager
Ed Tywoniak, Chief Engineer
Nick McAlpine, Music Director

Moreno Valley

KHPY
01-16-2003; 1670 kHz AM
PO Box 87, Colton, CA 92324 US
(909) 247-5479; *Fax:* (909) 247-2790
License: Moreno Valley, CA held by Delbert L. Van Voorhis.
Format: Religious
Bill DeGeorge, General Manager

Morgan Hill

KSQQ
12-01-1990; 96.1 MHz FM; 4.7 kw; 161 ft.; N37 11 1 W121 48 9
1629-C Alum Rock Avenue, San Jose, CA 95116 US
(408) 258-9699; *Fax:* (408) 258-9770
www.ksqq.com
pr@ksqq.com
License: Morgan Hill, Santa Clara County, CA held by Coyote Communications Inc.
Arbitron Metro Market: San Jose, CA; *Format:* Ethnic
Batista Vieira, President
Peter Mieuli, Operations Dir
Alvaro Aguiar, General Sales Mgr
Elza Bettencourt-office manager

Morro Bay

*KESC
05-01-1991; 99.7 MHz FM; *Hrs Open:* 24; 0.285 kw; 1490 ft.; N35 21 40 W120 39 21 *Rebroadcasts:* Rebroadcasts KUSC(FM) Los Angeles 100%
P.O. Box 987, San Luis Obispo, CA 93406 US
(213) 225-7400; *Fax:* (213) 225-7410
www.kusc.org
kusc@kusc.org
License: Morro Bay, San Luis Obispo County, CA held by University of Southern California
Nat'l Reps: Michigan Spot Sales
Arbitron Metro Market: Los Angeles, CA; *Format:* Classical
Brenda Barnes, President
Steve Coghill, Operations Dir
Ron Thompson, Engineering Dir
Chris Mendez, Engineering Dir
Rina Romero, Senior Business Manager
Bill Lueth, VP/Program Director
Jamie Paisley, Music Director
Abe Shefa,Director of Underwriting
Minnie Priner, Development Director

Mount Bullion

KCIV
04-24-1989; 99.9 MHz FM; *Hrs Open:* 24; 1.9 kw; 2,094 ft.; N37 32 0 W120 1 29
1031 15th St., Suite 1, Modesto, CA 95354 US
(209) 524-8999; *Fax:* (209) 524-9088
www.bottradionetwork.com
comments@bottradionetwork.com
License: Mount Bullion, Mariposa County, CA held by Bott Communications Inc.
Group Owner: Bott Radio Network
Arbitron Metro Market: Fresno-Modesto, CA; *Format:* Christian, Talk; *Target Audience:* 25-54; Christian family audience; *Adv. Rates:* 29; 25; 26; 12
Richard Bott Sr., President & CEO
Eben Fowler, Operations Dir
Kathleen Reynolds, General Manager
Pat Rulon, Director of National Sales
Candy Green, Program Services Manager
Rachel Launius, Marketing Manager
Jason Potocnik,Director of Traffic Operations

Mount Shasta

KMJC
06-12-1947; 620 kHz AM; *Hrs Open:* 24
P. O. Box 448, Mt. Shasta, CA 96067 US
(541) 552-6301; *Fax:* (541) 552-8565
www.ijpr.org
info@ijpr.org
License: Mount Shasta, CA held by JPR Foundation Inc.
Nat'l Network: NPR; PRI; *Wire Services:* AP
Format: News, News/Talk, 86; *No. News Employees:* 1; *Target Audience:* General.
Bryon Lambert, Operations Dir
Ronald Kramer, General Manager
Paul Westhelle, General Sales Mgr

*KNSQ
01-01-1994; 88.1 MHz FM; *Hrs Open:* 5 AM-2 AM; 5 kw; 889 ft.; N41 13 22 W122 17 51
P.O. Box 3175, Eugene, OR 97403 US
(541) 552-6301; *Fax:* (541) 552-8565
www.ijpr.org
info@ijpr.org
License: Mount Shasta, Siskiyou County, CA held by The State of Oregon, acting by and through the State Board of Higher Education, for the benefit of Southern Oregon University.
Nat'l Network: NPR; PRI
Format: Jazz, News, 90 *Special Programming:* Blues 6 hrs, folk 3 hrs, pub affrs 7 hrs wkly; *Hrs. of News Programming:* news progmg 45 hrs wkly; *No. News Employees:* 1; *Target Audience:* General.
Ronald Kramer, CEO
Bryon Lambert, Operations Dir
Paul Westhelle, General Sales Mgr
Mitchell Christian, CFO

Mountain Pass

KHYZ
01-01-1980; 99.7 MHz FM; *Hrs Open:* 24; 8.4 kw; 1808 ft.; N35 29 27 W115 33 27
Mailing Address: 1611 East Main St, P.O.Box 1668, Barstow, CA 92312 US
Second Address: 101 Convention Center Dr, Suite 1001, Las Vegas, NV 89109
(760) 256-0326; *Fax:* (760) 256-9507
highwayradio.com
highwayradio@highwayradio.com
License: Mountain Pass, San Bernardino County, CA held by KHWY, Inc.
Group Owner: KHWY, Inc.
Nat'l Network: AP Radio
Format: Adult Contemp; *Hrs. of News Programming:* news progmg 16 hrs wkly; *No. News Employees:* 1; *Target Audience:* 35 plus; travelers & loc communities
Kirk Anderson, President/COO
John Gregg, Operations Dir

Mountain View

*KSFH
01-01-1974; 87.9 MHz FM; *Hrs Open:* 1 PM-9 PM (M-F); 0.01 kw; -246 ft.; N37 22 8 W122 5 2
1885 Miramonte Avenue, Mountain View, CA 94040 US
(650) 210-2435; *Fax:* (650) 968-1706
www.ksfh.com
License: Mountain View, Santa Clara County, CA held by St. Francis High School of Mountain View California Inc.
Arbitron Metro Market: Mountain, CA; *Format:* Rock/AOR; *Hrs. of News Programming:* News progmg 5 hrs wkly; *Target Audience:* General; young adult, high school, college
Bob Lautenslager, General Manager

Napa

KVON
12-17-1947; 1440 kHz AM; *Hrs Open:* 24; 5 kw-D, DA2; 1 kw-N, DA2; N38 15 45 W122 16 56
1124 Foster Road, Napa, CA 94558 US
(707) 258-1111; *Fax:* (707) 226-7544
www.kvon.com
License: Napa, CA held by Wine Country Broadcasting Co.
Nat'l Reps: Christal
Arbitron Metro Market: Napa, CA; *Format:* News, News/Talk, 86 *Special Programming:* Sp 2 hrs; *Hrs. of News Programming:* news progmg 30 hrs wkly; *No. News Employees:* 3; *Target Audience:* 35 plus. *Adv.Rates:* 60; 50; 60; 20
Jeff Schechtman, General Manager
Erica Pickett, Promotions Manager
Ben Webster, Chief Engineer
Dan Darnielle, Advertising & Sales Director

Needles

KLUK
05-01-1984; 97.9 MHz FM; 29.5 kw; 1552 ft.; N35 2 6 W114 22 9
2350 Miracle Mile Rd., Suite 300, Bullhead City, AZ 86442 US
(928) 763-5586; *Fax:* (928) 763-3775
www.lucky98fm.com
License: Needles, San Bernardino County, CA held by Cameron Broadcasting Inc.
Group Owner: Cameron Broadcasting Inc.; acq 1-18-02; grpsl).
Format: Classic Rock; *No. News Employees:* 1; *Target Audience:* 25-54
Don Jaeger, General Manager

KTOX
10-01-1952; 1340 kHz AM; *Hrs Open:* 24; 1 kw-U, ND1; N34 51 10 W114 37 19
Mailing Address: 2281 Mc Culloch Blvd., Suite 18, Lake Havasu City, AZ 86403 US
Second Address: P.O. Box 8766, Ft. Mahaur, AZ 86427
(760) 326-4500; *Fax:* (760) 326-6849
ktox1340@citlink.net
License: Needles, CA held by Creative Broadcasting Services Inc.
Nat'l Network: Jones Radio Networks; Premiere Radio Networks
Arbitron Metro Market: Needles, CA; *Format:* News, News/Talk, 86 *Special Programming:* Rt 66 program, 22 hrs of personalities and live local programming wkly; *Hrs. of News Programming:* news progmg 24 hrs wkly *No.News Employees:* 1; *Target Audience:* 18 plus.; *Adv. Rates:* 11;10; 11; 9
Robert Hayes, CEO
David Hayes, President
Paul Fix, Operations Dir
Kelly Hayes, General Sales Mgr

KNKK
107.1 MHz FM; *Hrs Open:* 24; 15.5 kw; 1909 ft.; N35 1 58 W114 21 57
2350 Miracle Mile Rd., Suite 300, Bullhead City, AZ 86442 US
(928) 763-5586; *Fax:* (928) 763-3775
www.theknack107.com
info@theknack107.com
License: Needles, San Bernardino County, CA held by Cameron Broadcasting Inc.).
Group Owner: Cameron Broadcasting Inc.; acq 3-13-01).
Arbitron Metro Market: Bullhead City, AZ; *Format:* Contemporary Hits/Top 40; *Target Audience:* 18-49
Don Jaeger, General Manager

*KJLC-FM
08-07-2012; 90.7 MHz FM; 1 kw; -259 ft.; N34 54 13 W114 38 38
US
(909)882-5330
License: Needles, San Bernadino County, CA held by Centro Cristiano Vida Abundante

Ramiro Lopez, President

Nevada City

*KVMR
07-17-1978; 89.5 MHz FM; *Hrs Open:* 24; 1.75 kw; 1132 ft.; N39 14 47 W120 57 48
401 Spring Street, Nevada City, CA 95959 US
(530) 265-9073; *Fax:* (530) 265-9077
www.kvmr.org
office@KVMR.org
License: Nevada City, Nevada County, CA held by Nevada City Community Broadcast Group.
Arbitron Metro Market: Nevada City, CA; *Format:* Variety/Diverse *Special Programming:* Country 7 hrs, Black 4 hrs, folk 13 hrs, blues 7 hrs, foreign/ethnic 20 hrs wkly; *Hrs. of News Programming:* news progmg 1 hr dailymon-fri; *No. News Employees:* 2; *Target Audience:* Full spectrum community radio; *Adv. Rates:* Upon Request
Erica Randall, Operations Dir
David Levin, General Manager

Brianna Caldwell, General Sales Mgr
Steve Baker, Programming Director
Felton Pruitt, News Director
Paul Patterson, Chief Engineer
Alice MacAllister, Music Director
Felton Pruitt, News Producer
John Button, Webmaster
Adrianna Kelly, Membership Coordinator
Briana Ezzell, Development Director
Julie Chiarelli, Business Manager

Newberry Springs

KIQQ-FM

01-01-2001; 103.7 MHz FM; *Hrs Open:* 24; 6 kw; 282 ft.; N34 53 7 W116 53 45 *Rebroadcasts:* Simulcast with KAEH(FM) Beaumont 100%
P.O. Box 191747, Atlanta, GA 31119 US
(760) 255-2636; *Fax:* (760) 255-3236
License: Newberry Springs, San Bernardino County, CA held by MBR Licensee LLC.
Group Owner: Moon Broadcasting; (acq 11-5-99).
Arbitron Metro Market: Barstow, CA
Alicia Avila, General Manager

Newman

KRUD

90.7 MHz FM; 1.9 kw horiz; 12.6 meters; N37 15 24 W120 59 59
Box 202, Newman, CA 95360-0202 US
(209) 862-4490
www.westsideradio.org
License: Newman, CA held by West Side Theatre Foundation

David Galatro, President

Newport Beach

KDLE

01-01-1962; 103.1 MHz FM; *Hrs Open:* 24; 0.3 kw; 965 ft.; N33 36 19 W117 48 38 *Rebroadcasts:* Simulcast with KDLD(FM) Santa Monica 100%
5700 Wilshire Blvd., Suite 250, Los Angeles, CA 90036 US
(323) 900-6100
www.joseradio.com
License: Newport Beach, Orange County, CA held by Entravision Holdings LLC.
Group Owner: Entravision Communications Corp.; (acq 2000; grpsl)
Arbitron Metro Market: Los Angeles, CA; *Format:* Spanish, Contemporary Hits/Top 40
Matt Cardenas, SVP Integrated Marketing Solution
Nestor Rocha, Programming Director
Elias Autran, Promotions Manager

North Fork

KLLE

01-01-1996; 107.9 MHz FM; 1.75 kw; 1,227 ft.; N37 17 42 W119 33 51
1360 W. 18th Street, Merced, CA 95341 US
(559) 430-8510
www.univision.com
License: North Fork, Madera County, CA held by Univision Radio License Corp.
Group Owner: Univision Radio; (acq 9-22-2003; grpsl).
Arbitron Metro Market: Fresno, CA; *Format:* Adult Contemp, Spanish
Angela Navarrete, Station Manager

North Highlands

*KQEI-FM

02-21-1992; 89.3 MHz FM; *Hrs Open:* 24; 3.3 kw; 354 ft.; N38 42 38 W121 28 54 *Rebroadcasts:* Rebroadcasts KQED-FM San Francisco 98%
4135 Northgate Blvd, Suite 1, Sacramento, CA 95834 US
(415) 864-2000; *Fax:* (415) 553-2241
www.kqed.org
fm@kqed.org
License: North Highlands, Sacramento County, CA held by KQED Inc.
Arbitron Metro Market: San Francisco, CA; *Format:* News
Jo Anne Wallace, General Manager
Traci Eckels, General Sales Mgr
Raul Ramirez, News Director
Sinclair Crockett, Director
Georgi Kelly, Senior Director
Jeff Rutledge, Project Manager

Northridge

*KCSN

11-01-1963; 88.5 MHz FM; *Hrs Open:* 24; 0.37 kw; 1644 ft.; N34 19 10 W118 33 15
18111 Nordhoff Street, Northridge, CA 91330 US
(818) 677-3090; *Fax:* (818) 677-3069
www.kcsn.org
info@kcsn.org
License: Northridge, Los Angeles County, CA held by California State University Northridge.
Nat'l Network: PRI; NPR
Arbitron Metro Market: Northridge, CA; *Format:* Variety/Diverse *Special Programming:* German 3 hrs, Jewish 3 hrs, bluegrass 5 hrs wkly; *Hrs. of News Programming:* news progmg 12 hrs wkly; *No. News Employees:* 1 *Target Audience:* 35 plus; middle/upper middle-class, well educated
Sky Daniels, General Manager
Laura Kelly, General Sales Mgr
Sky Daniels, Programming Director
Keith Goldstein, News Director
Conor S. Watson, Chief Engineer

Oak View

KRRF

01-30-1982; 106.3 MHz FM; *Hrs Open:* 24; 250 w; 827 ft; N34 27 55 W119 40 38
403 E. Montecito St., Suite A, Santa Barbara, CA 93101-1759
(805) 966-1755; *Fax:* (805) 650-6172
www.kmgq1063.com
License: Oak View, Santa Barbara County, CA held by Cumulus Licensing Corp.
Group Owner: Cumulus Media Inc.; (acq 3-12-2001; grpsl).
Nat'l Reps: McGavren Guild
Population Served: 350,000; *Arbitron Metro Market:* Santa Barbara, CA; *Format:* Adult Contemp, Jazz; *Target Audience:* 35-64; upscale, educated, professional, affluent; *Adv. Rates:* 30; 30; 30; 10
Nery Reyes, General Manager
Bruce Pollock, General Sales Mgr
Matt Stone, Programming Director
Tammy Myers, Promotions Manager
John Straker, Chief Engineer

Oakdale

KHOP

03-11-1985; 95.1 MHz FM; *Hrs Open:* 24; 29.5 kw; 633 ft.; N37 47 34 W120 31 8
3127 Transworld Dr., Suite 270, Stockton, CA 95206 US
(209) 507-8500
www.khop.com
programming@khop.com
License: Oakdale, CA held by Radio License Holding CBC, LLC
Group Owner: Cumulus Media Inc.; (acq 1996; $5 million).
Arbitron Metro Market: Modesto, CA; *Format:* Contemporary Hits/Top 40 *Special Programming:* Perez Hilton 20 hrs wkly; *Hrs. of News Programming:* news progmg 3 hrs wkly; *No. News Employees:* 1 *Target Audience:* 18-49.
Bob Berger, General Manager
Joe Roberts, Programming Director
Dustin Azevedo, Promotions Manager

Oakhurst

KAAT

11-01-1982; 103.1 MHz FM; *Hrs Open:* 24; 25 kw; -194 ft.; N37 27 10 W119 37 54
40356 Oak Park Way, Oakhurst, CA 93644 US
(559) 683-1031; *Fax:* (559) 683-5488
www.kaat.com
License: Oakhurst, Madera County, CA held by California Sierra Corp.
Group Owner: Moon Broadcasting; (acq 3-3-2005; $4.75 million with co-located AM).
Arbitron Metro Market: Fresno, CA; *Format:* Spanish *Special Programming:* Relg 2 hrs wkly; *Target Audience:* 25-54; general
Abel DeLuna, President
Denny Jackson, Programming Director

KTNS

11-20-1982; 1060 kHz AM; *Hrs Open:* 24
40356 Oak Pk Wy Box 2020, Oakhurst, CA 93644 US
(559) 683-1060(559) 683-1060; *Fax:* (559) 683-5488
www.ktnsradio.com
tammy@kaat.com
License: Oakhurst, CA held by California Sierra Corp.
Group Owner: Moon Broadcasting
Nat'l Network: CNN Radio; Westwood One
Arbitron Metro Market: Oakhurst, CA; *Format:* Adult Contemp; *No. News Employees:* 3; *Target Audience:* 25-49.
Becky Deaver, General Sales Mgr
Jesse Taylor, Programming Director

Oakland

KKSF

11-03-1947; 910 kHz AM; *Hrs Open:* 24; 1,470 ft
750 Battery Road, Suite 200, San Francisco, CA 94111 US
(415) 356-5500; *Fax:* (415) 975-5573
www.talk910.com
License: Oakland, CA held by AMFM Broadcasting Licenses LLC.
Group Owner: iHeartMedia; (acq 8-30-2000; grpsl).
Arbitron Metro Market: San Francisco, CA; *Format:* News, News/Talk, 86; *Hrs. of News Programming:* news progmg 5 hrs wkly; *No. News Employees:* 1; *Target Audience:* 25-49.
Kathryn Wilcox, Market President
Cheryle Hangartner, Market Sales Manager
Cory Callewaert, Programming Director
Mari Galaviz, Promotions Manager

KMKY

07-01-1922; 1310 kHz AM; *Hrs Open:* 24; 5 kw-U, DA1; N37 49 27 W122 19 10
77 West 66th Street, 16th Floor, New York, NY 10023 US
(650) 637-8800
www.radiodisney.com
License: Oakland, CA held by KGO-AM Radio Inc.
Group Owner: ABC Inc.; (acq 12-18-97; $6.25 million)
Nat'l Network: Radio Disney; *Nat'l Reps:* Interep
Arbitron Metro Market: San Francisco, CA; *Format:* Children; *Target Audience:* 2-14; kids, tweens & moms 25-54; *Adv. Rates:* 200; 150; 250; 100
Lynn Dooley, Station Manager
Shalon Rogers, Promotions Manager

KNEW

07-02-1921; 960 kHz AM; *Hrs Open:* 24; 5 kw-U, DA1; N37 49 40 W122 18 53
340 Townsend St., San Francisco, CA 94107 US
(415) 356-5500; *Fax:* (415) 975-5573
www.bloomberg.com
License: Oakland, Alameda County, CA held by AMFM Broadcasting Licenses LLC.
Group Owner: iHeartMedia; (acq 8-30-2000; grpsl).
Arbitron Metro Market: San Francisco, CA; *Format:* News, News/Talk, 86; *Hrs. of News Programming:* news progmg 65 hrs wkly; *No. News Employees:* 8; *Target Audience:* 25-54.
Kathryn Wilcox, Market President
Don Parker, Operations Dir

Oceano

KLMM

09-01-1997; 94.1 MHz FM; *Hrs Open:* 24; 0.34 kw; 1371 ft.; N34 53 52 W120 35 21
200 S. A St., 4th Fl., Oxnard, CA 93030 USA
(805) 240-2070
www.radiolazer.com
License: Oceano, San Luis Obispo County, CA held by Lazer Broadcasting Corp.
Group Owner: Lazer Broadcasting Corp.; (acq 8-7-2000; $1.115 million with KLUN(FM) Paso Robles)
Arbitron Metro Market: San Luis Obispo, CA; *Format:* Adult Contemp; *Hrs. of News Programming:* News progmg 6 hrs wkly; *Target Audience:* 25-54; general

Oceanside

*KKSM

07-04-1956; 1320 kHz AM; *Hrs Open:* 24; 0.5 kw-U, DA1; N33 12 8 W117 20 17
1140 West Mission Road, San Marcos, CA 92069 US
(760) 744-1150
License: Oceanside, CA held by Palomar Community College District.
Arbitron Metro Market: San Diego, CA; *Format:* Variety/Diverse; *Hrs. of News Programming:* news progmg 10 hrs wkly; *No. News Employees:* 1; *Target Audience:* 18-25; college age, mid-upper income, diverse ethnic *Adv. Rates:* 15; 10; 10; 8
Pat Hahn, Chairman, Media Studies

Oildale

KWVE(AM)

07-04-1988; 660 kHz AM; *Hrs Open:* 24; 10 kw-D, 1 kw-N, DA-2; N34 57 04 W120 22 38
1416 Hollister Ln., Los Osos, CA 93402
(805) 928-7707; *Fax:* (805) 922-8582
kgdp660@yahoo.com

License: Oildale, Santa Barbara County, CA held by Radio Representatives Inc.
Nat'l Network: USA
Population Served: 650,000; *Arbitron Metro Market:* Santa Maria, CA; *Format:* Christian, Talk; *Target Audience:* 35-65.; *Adv. Rates:* 22; 20; 19; 18
Crystal Stahl, Operations Dir
Steve Cox, General Manager
Bill Greenelsh, Promotions Manager
Gretchen England, News Director

KLLY
01-01-1985; 95.3 MHz FM; *Hrs Open:* 24; 12.5 kw; 463 ft.; N35 27 33 W119 1 13
3651 Pegasus Dr., Suite 107, Bakersfield, CA 93308 US
(661) 393-1900; *Fax:* (661) 393-1915
www.energy953.com
License: Oildale, Kern County, CA held by Alpha Media Licensee LLC
Group Owner: Alpha Media LLC; (acq 10-10-2014).
Nat'l Reps: D & R Radio
Arbitron Metro Market: Bakersfield, CA; *Format:* Contemporary Hits/Top 40; *Target Audience:* 25-44; adults
Mary Lou Gunn, General Manager
Liz Ray, Sales Manager
Miggy Santos, Programming Director

Ojai

KFYV
01-04-1972; 105.5 MHz FM; *Hrs Open:* 24; 0.31 kw; 1437 ft.; N34 20 55 W119 20 13
2319 Alameda Ave, Suite 1D, Ventura, CA 93003 US
(805) 289-1400; (805) 654-0414; *Fax:* (805) 644-7906
www.live1055.fm
License: Ojai, Ventura West County, CA held by Gold Coast Broadcasting LLC
Group Owner: Gold Coast Broadcasting LLC; (acq 5-15-97; $2 million with KUNX(AM) Ventura)
Nat'l Network: AP Radio; *Nat'l Reps:* Katz Radio
Arbitron Metro Market: Oxnard, CA; *Format:* Adult Contemp, Contemporary Hits/Top 40; *Hrs. of News Programming:* news progmg 3 hrs wkly; *No. News Employees:* 1; *Target Audience:* 25-49
Chip Ehrhardt, National Sales Director
Jack Clarke, National Advertising Sales
Mark Elliot, Programming Director

***KLFH**
01-01-2003; 89.5 MHz FM; 0.097 kw; 1322 ft.; N34 24 45 W119 11 16
35225 Avenue A, #204, Yucaipa, CA 92399 US
(805) 541-4343; *Fax:* (805) 541-9101
www.klife.org
info@klife.org
License: Ojai, Ventura County, CA held by Logos Broadcasting Corp.
Arbitron Metro Market: Ojai, CA; *Format:* Contemporary Hits/Top 40
Jim Fugler, General Manager
Noonie Fugler, Promotions Manager

Ontario

KSPA
01-26-1947; 1510 kHz AM; *Hrs Open:* 24; 10 kw-D, DA2; 1 kw-N, DA2; N34 5 41 W117 36 46
1045 South East, Anaheim, CA 97805 US
(909) 483-1500; *Fax:* (909) 483-1515
kspa1510@aol.com
License: Ontario, CA held by Ontario Broadcasting L.L.C.
Group Owner: Astor Broadcast Group; (acq 11-4-99)
Arbitron Metro Market: Riverside, CA; *Format:* Adult Contemp, Contemporary Hits/Top 40; *No. News Employees:* 1; *Target Audience:* 35+; *Adv. Rates:* 50; 50; 50; 30
Art Astor, President
Joe Lyons, Operations Dir
Peri Corso, General Manager
Susan Burke, Executive Vice President

KDEY-FM
01-26-1947; 93.5 MHz FM; *Hrs Open:* 24; 5 kw; Ant -131 ft; N34 10 32 W117 34 26
5055 Wilshire Blvd. #720, Los Angeles, CA 90036
(323) 337-1600; *Fax:* (323) 337-1633
www.935kday.com
sales@935kday.com
License: Ontario, San Bernardino County, CA held by KDAI Licensing LLC.
Population Served: 2,000,000; *Arbitron Metro Market:* Riverside-San Bernardino; *Format:* Urban Contemporary
Kimberly Fletcher, General Manager

Orange

KLAA
01-13-1992; 830 kHz AM; *Hrs Open:* 24
8910 University Center Lane, #130, San Diego, CA 92122 US
(818) 528-2050; *Fax:* (818) 784-8824
www.830am.com
License: Orange, CA held by LAA 1 LLC
Nat'l Network: NBC Radio
Arbitron Metro Market: Los Angeles; *Format:* News, Sports, 86
Special Programming: Sports; *Hrs. of News Programming:* News progmg 28 hrs wkly; *Target Audience:* 25-54; Male & female, high income, professionals *Adv. Rates:* 350; 350; 350; 75
Alan Fuller, General Manager

Orange Cove

KMAK
10-27-1990; 100.3 MHz FM; *Hrs Open:* 24; 0.072 kw; 2073 ft.; N36 44 45 W119 16 58
Mailing Address: 611 Willow Street, Visalia, CA 93291 US
Second Address: 640 Park Blvd., Orange Cove, CA 93646
(559) 626-7922; *Fax:* (559) 896-1631
kmakfm@sbcglobal.net
License: Orange Cove, Fresno County, CA held by Mr. Richard B. Smith.
Nat'l Network: CNN Radio
Arbitron Metro Market: Fresno, CA; *No. News Employees:* 1; *Target Audience:* 18-94.; *Adv. Rates:* 25; 25; 20; 15
Ms. Sue Jones, General Manager
Mr. Nelson Gomez, Promotions Manager
Mr. Richard Smith, Chief Engineer

Orcutt

KPAT
01-01-1993; 95.7 MHz FM; 3.3 kw; 899 ft.; N34 44 30 W120 26 45
2325 Skyway Dr, Suite J, Santa Maria, CA 93455 US
(805) 922-1041; *Fax:* (805) 928-3069
www.957thebeatfm.com
License: Orcutt, Santa Barbara County, CA held by AGM California, Inc.
Group Owner: American General Media; (acq 12-1-99; $900,000).
Nat'l Network: USA
Arbitron Metro Market: Santa Maria-Lompoc, CA; *Format:* Contemporary Hits/Top 40
Richard Watson, General Manager

Orland

KRQR
01-01-1994; 106.7 MHz FM; *Hrs Open:* 24; 50 kw; 308 ft.; N39 53 16 W122 37 38
856 Manzanita Ct., Chico, CA 95926 US
(530) 342-2200; *Fax:* (530) 342-2260
www.zrockfm.com
License: Orland, Glenn County, CA held by Results Radio Licensee L.L.C.
Group Owner: Results Radio; (acq 6-11-99; grpsl)
Arbitron Metro Market: Chico, CA; *Format:* Rock/AOR

Oroville

KNTF
08-04-1962; 1340 kHz AM; *Hrs Open:* 24 *Rebroadcasts:* Rebroadcasts KRER(FM) Hamilton City
1436 Auburn Boulevard, Sacramento, CA 95815 US
(530) 345-0021; *Fax:* (530) 893-2121
License: Oroville, CA held by Tom F. Huth
Group Owner: Huth Broadcasting
Arbitron Metro Market: Chico, CA; *Format:* Sports
Rosa Ramos, Programming Director

Oxnard

***KCRU**
01-01-1993; 89.1 MHz FM; 0.85 kw; 853 ft.; N34 6 47 W119 3 34 *Rebroadcasts:* Rebroadcasts KCRW(FM) Santa Monica 98%
1900 Pico Blvd, Santa Monica, CA 90405 US
(310) 450-5183(888) 660-kcrw; *Fax:* (310) 450-7172
www.kcrw.com
mail@kcrw.org
License: Oxnard, Ventura County, CA held by Santa Monica Community College District.
Arbitron Metro Market: Oxnard, CA; *Format:* News
Mike Newport, Operations Dir
Ruth Seymour, General Manager
Jennifer Ferro, Station Manager
David Kleinbart, General Sales Mgr
Ariana Morgenstern, Programming Director
Steve Herbert, Chief Engineer

KDAR
10-28-1974; 98.3 MHz FM; *Hrs Open:* 24; 1.5 kw; 1289 ft.; N34 20 55 W119 19 57
Mailing Address: 500 Esplanade Drive, Oxnard, CA 93030 US
Second Address: 500 Esplanade Dr., Suite 1500, Oxnard, CA 93036
(805) 485-8881; *Fax:* (805) 656-5330
www.kdar.com
radiomail@kdar.com
License: Oxnard, Ventura County, CA held by New Inspiration Broadcasting Co. Inc.
Group Owner: Salem Communications Corp.
Arbitron Metro Market: Oxnard-Ventura, CA; *Format:* Christian, Talk; *Hrs. of News Programming:* News progmg 2 hrs wkly; *Target Audience:* 25-54; upscale adults with large families
Ed Atsinger, President
Richard Trejo, General Manager
Terri Dawson, General Sales Mgr
Jeff Hunter, Programming Director

KOCP
08-15-1972; 104.7 MHz FM; *Hrs Open:* 24; 18 kw; 827 ft.; N34 25 20 W119 2 4
2319 Alameda Ave, Suite 1D, Ventura, CA 93003 US
(805) 289-1400; *Fax:* (805) 644-7906
oldschool1047.com
License: Oxnard, Ventura West County, CA held by Gold Coast Broadcasting LLC/Point Four LLC
Group Owner: Gold Coast Broadcasting LLC; (acq 1995; $1.2 million with KMXO(AM) Santa Paula).
Nat'l Reps: Katz Radio
Format: Oldies; *Target Audience:* 25-54.
Chip Ehrhardt, National Sales Director
Perry Van Houten, Programming Director

KOXR
06-11-1955; 910 kHz AM; *Hrs Open:* 24; 5 kw-D, DA2; 1 kw-N, DA2; N34 16 58 W119 7 36
200 S. A St., 4th Floor, Oxnard, CA 93030 US
(805) 240-2070
www.radiolazer.com
License: Oxnard, CA held by Lazer Broadcasting Corp.
Group Owner: Lazer Broadcasting Corp.; acq 1-11-99)
Nat'l Reps: Lotus Entravision Reps LLC
Arbitron Metro Market: Oxnard-Ventura, CA; *Target Audience:* 25-54.

KXLM
01-01-1991; 102.9 MHz FM; *Hrs Open:* 24; 5.5 kw; 112 ft.; N34 14 12 W119 12 11
Mailing Address: 200 S. a Street, Ste 400, Oxnard, CA 93030 US
Second Address: Box 6940, Oxnard, CA 93030
(805) 240-2070; *Fax:* (805) 240-5960
radiolazer.com
License: Oxnard, Ventura County, CA held by Kext Broadcasters Inc.
Arbitron Metro Market: Oxnard, CA; *Format:* Adult Contemp; *Hrs. of News Programming:* news progmg 2 hrs wkly; *No. News Employees:* 1; *Target Audience:* 25-59.; *Adv. Rates:* 65; 65; 65; 50
Alfredo Plascencia, President
Terry Janisch, General Sales Mgr

Pacific Grove

***KAZU**
10-01-1977; 90.3 MHz FM; *Hrs Open:* 24; 3.4 kw; 551 ft.; N36 33 9 W121 47 17
P.O. Box 210, Pacific Grove, CA 93950 US
(831) 582-5298; *Fax:* (831) 582-5299
www.kazu.org
programming@kazu.org
License: Pacific Grove, Monterey County, CA held by Foundation of California State University Monterey Bay
Nat'l Network: NPR
Arbitron Metro Market: Seaside, CA; *Format:* News *Special Programming:* Country 6 hrs, women's mus 6 hrs, gospel 4 hrs, fo; *Hrs. of News Programming:* News progmg 8 hrs wkly; *Target Audience:* 25-65; general
Mik Benedek, General Manager
Krista Almanzan, News Director

KOCN
04-10-1977; 105.1 MHz FM; *Hrs Open:* 24; 1.8 kw; 600 ft.; N36 33 9 W121 47 17
903 N. Main St., Salinas, CA 93906 US
(831) 755-8181; *Fax:* (831) 755-8193
www.1051kocean.com

License: Pacific Grove, Monterey County, CA held by CC Licenses LLC.
Group Owner: iHeartMedia; (acq 9-22-97; grpsl)
Nat'l Network: Westwood One; *Nat'l Reps:* Clear Channel
Arbitron Metro Market: Monterey-Salinas-Santa Cruz, CA; *Format:* Oldies; *No. News Employees:* 1; *Target Audience:* 25-54; at work, double income households
Sam Segovia, Operations Manager/Program Director
Sean Beken, Market President
Maggie Fernandez, Promotions Director
Alyssa Oresco, Digital Content Director

Pala

*KOPA(FM)

91.3 MHz FM; 100 w; Ant -1,066 ft; N33 22 00 W117 04 05
35008 Pala Temecula Road, Pala, CA 92059
(760) 891-3500
www.palatribe.com
hr@palatribe.com
License: Pala, San Diego County, CA held by Pala Band of Mission Indians.
Population Served: 1,326,179; *Arbitron Metro Market:* San Diego, California; *Format:* Variety/Diverse
Robert Smith, Chairman
Leroy Miranda, Vice Chairman
Theressa Villa, Secretary
Theresa J. Nieto, Treasurer
Dion Perez, Council Member
Sheila Lopez, Council Member

Palm Desert

KEZN

08-29-1983; 103.1 MHz FM; *Hrs Open:* 24; 1.9 kW; 56 ft.; N33 51 58.4 W116 25 58.6
915 Parkview Dr., Suite 72, Palm Desert, CA 92260 USA
(760) 340-9383; *Fax:* (760) 340-5756
www.sunny1031fm.com
License: Palm Desert, Riverside County, CA held by CBS Radio Stations Inc.
Group Owner: CBS Radio; (acq 11-13-98; grpsl).
Nat'l Network: Westwood One
Arbitron Metro Market: Palm Springs, CA; *Format:* Adult Contemp; *No. News Employees:* 1; *Target Audience:* 25-64
Kimberly Martinez, General Sales Mgr
Lee Douglas, Programming Director
Leslie Bischoff, Promotions Director

*KHCS

01-01-1993; 91.7 MHz FM; *Hrs Open:* 24; 0.96 kw; 574 ft.; N33 51 57 W116 25 56
5855 Naples Plaza, Long Beach, CA 90803 US
(760) 864-9620; *Fax:* (760) 864-9633
email@khcb.org
License: Palm Desert, Riverside County, CA held by Prairie Avenue Gospel Center.
Format: Christian, Religious; *Target Audience:* 20-85.
Dan Pike, President
R.F. Watts, Chief Engineer

Palm Springs

KNWQ

02-12-1946; 1140 kHz AM; 10 kw-D, DA2; 2.5 kw-N, DA2; N33 51 39 W116 28 20
1321 N. Gene Autry Trail, Palm Springs, CA 92262 US
(760) 322-7890; *Fax:* (760) 322-5493
www.943knews.com
License: Palm Springs, Riverside County, CA held by Alpha Media Licensee LLC
Group Owner: Alpha Media LLC; (acq 9-2-2015; grpsl).
Nat'l Network: CBS; *Nat'l Reps:* McGavren Guild
Arbitron Metro Market: Palm Springs, CA; *Format:* News, News/Talk, 86; *Target Audience:* 35-65.
Tricia Bastida, Senior Vice President and Market Manager
David Nola, General Sales Mgr
Paul Cashin, Programming Director
Cristine Constantinescu, Director of Promotions and Digital Media
Crystal White, National/Regional SalesManager

KPLM

01-24-1983; 106.1 MHz FM; *Hrs Open:* 24; 50 kw; 397 ft.; N33 52 14 W116 13 39
P.O. Box 1825, Palm Springs, CA 92263 US
(760) 568-4550; *Fax:* (760) 341-7600
thebig106.com
kplm@markerbroadcasting.com
License: Palm Springs, Riverside County, CA held by RM Broadcasting L.L.C.
Nat'l Reps: Katz Radio
Arbitron Metro Market: Palm Springs, CA; *Format:* Country; *Hrs. of News Programming:* news progmg 9 hrs wkly; *No. News Employees:* 1; *Target Audience:* 25-54.
Todd Marker, General Manager
Hughes Hilles, General Sales Mgr
Al Gordon, Programming Director
Kory James, Promotions Manager
Jeff Michaels, News Director
Nick Summers, Production Manager

*KPSC

04-01-1978; 88.5 MHz FM; *Hrs Open:* 24; 1.25 kw; 587 ft.; N33 51 56 W116 26 4 *Rebroadcasts:* Rebroadcasts KUSC 100%
Mailing Address: P. O. Box 77913, Los Angeles, CA 90007 US
Second Address: 515 S. Figueroa St., Suite 2050, Los Angeles, CA 90071
(213) 225-7400; *Fax:* (213) 225-7410
www.kusc.org
memberservices@kusc.org
License: Palm Springs, Riverside County, CA held by University of Southern California.
Nat'l Network: PRI; NPR
Arbitron Metro Market: Palm Springs, CA; *Format:* News/Talk, Classical; *Target Audience:* 35 plus; general
Brenda Barnes, President
Steve Coghill, Operations Dir
Bill Leuth, VP/Programming Director
Ron Thompson, Engineering Dir
Minnie Priner, Development Director
Jamie Paisley, Music Director
Abe Shefa, Director of Underwriting
RinaRomero, Senior Business Manager
Chris Mendez, Web Developer

KPSI

10-29-1956; 920 kHz AM; 5 kw-D, DA2; 1 kw-N, DA2; N33 51 29 W116 29 39
2100 E Tahquitz-Canyon W, Palm Springs, CA 92262 US
(760) 325-2582; *Fax:* (760) 322-3562
www.newstalk920.com
License: Palm Springs, CA held by R & R Radio Corp.
Group Owner: RR Broadcasting
Nat'l Reps: Christal
Arbitron Metro Market: Palm Springs, CA; *Format:* News, Talk
Special Programming: American Indian 2 hrs wkly; *Hrs. of News Programming:* news progmg 16 hrs wkly; *No. News Employees:* 4 *Target Audience:* 25-54.
Mike Keane, General Manager
Gregg Aratin, General Sales Mgr
Steve Kelly, Programming Director
Brian Garris, Promotions Manager
Gregg Nichols, News Director

KPSI-FM

06-01-1980; 100.5 MHz FM; *Hrs Open:* 24; 25 kw; Ant 121 ft; N33 56 44 W116 24 34
2100 E. Tahquitz Canyon Way, Palm Springs, CA 92262
(760) 325-2582; *Fax:* (760) 320-4632
www.mix1005.fm
License: Palm Springs, Riverside County, CA held by R & R Radio Corp.
Group Owner: RR Broadcasting
Population Served: 358,000; *Arbitron Metro Market:* Palm Springs, C
Scott Chrisman, CEO/COO
Ric Supple, President
Jack Brody, Operations Dir
Jack Brody, General Manager
Jack Brody, Station Manager
Gregg Aratin, General Sales Mgr
Bradley Ryan, Programming Director
Brian Garris, PromotionsManager
Gene Nichols, News Director
Barry O'Connor, Engineering Dir
Barry O'Connor, Chief Engineer

KPTR

10-04-1964; 1450 kHz AM; *Hrs Open:* 24
2100 E Tahquitz, Canyon Way, Palm Springs, CA 92262 US
(760) 325-2582; *Fax:* (760) 322-3562
www.kptr1450.com
License: Palm Springs, CA held by R & R Radio Corp.
Group Owner: RR Broadcasting; (acq 7-27-2006; $2.3 million).
Arbitron Metro Market: Palm Springs, CA; *Format:* Alternative, Talk; *No. News Employees:* 1
0, Chairman
Mike Keane, General Manager
Gregg Aratin, Gen. Sales Mgr.
Steve Kelly, Program Director
Lisa Childs, Program Director
Scott Cristman, Financial Officer
Mell Hill, Local Sales Mgr.
Ken Vincent, News Anchor/Reporter
Jazmin Anderson, Accounting
Jack Broady, Production Director
Kacy Broady, Traffic Director

Palmdale

KUTY

08-01-1957; 1470 kHz AM; *Hrs Open:* 24; 5 kw-D, DA2; 5 kw-N, DA2; N34 39 55 W118 0 40
100 Wilshire Boulevard, Suite 1000, Santa Monica, CA 90401 US
(661) 947-3107; *Fax:* (661) 272-5688
info@lameramera1470.com
License: Palmdale, CA held by High Desert Broadcasting LLC.
Group Owner: High Desert Broadcasting LLC; (acq 3-5-97)
Arbitron Metro Market: Palmdale, CA
John Hearne, CEO
Nelson Rasse, General Sales Mgr
Mark Benevento, Programming Director
Alizah Lipson, Promotions Director

Palo Alto

KDOW

01-01-1947; 1220 kHz AM; *Hrs Open:* 24; 5 kw-D, ND1; 0.145 kw-N, ND1; N37 29 4 W122 8 4
114 Sansome St, Sutie 1410, San Francisco, CA 94104 US
(510) 713-1100; *Fax:* (510) 505-1448
www.kdow.biz
comments@kdow.biz
License: Palo Alto, CA held by SCA-Palo Alto LLC.
Group Owner: Salem Communications Corp.; (acq 6-28-2001; $9 million)
Nat'l Network: Salem Radio Network; *Nat'l Reps:* Salem
Arbitron Metro Market: Fremont, CA; *Format:* Talk, News; *Hrs. of News Programming:* news progmg 70 hrs wkly; *No. News Employees:* 5; *Target Audience:* 25-54; general
Greg Edwards, Operations Dir
Mike Shields, General Manager
Mike Ginsburg, General Sales Mgr
Craig Roberts, Programming Director
Amy Nyquist, Promotions Manager
Craig Roberts, Chief Engineer

Palo Cedro

KWCA

101.1 MHz FM; 4.9 kw; 1476 ft.; N40 39 15 W122 31 12
188 South Bellevue, Suite 222, Memphis, TN 38104 US
(530) 727-8181; *Fax:* (530) 243-6642
www.mixredding.com
License: Palo Cedro, Trinity County, CA held by George S. Flinn Jr.
Arbitron Metro Market: Palo Cedro, CA
George S. Flinn Jr., President
Jose Pacheco, General Manager

Paradise

KHSL-FM

10-15-1983; 103.5 MHz FM; *Hrs Open:* 24; 1.5 kw; 1312 ft.; N39 57 29 W121 42 49
4700 S.W. Macadam Ave., Portland, OR 97201 US
(530) 345-0021; *Fax:* (530) 893-2121
www.khsl.com
License: Paradise, Butte County, CA held by Deer Creek Broadcasting LLC.
Group Owner: Deer Creek Broadcasting LLC; (acq 9-8-2004; grpsl).
Nat'l Reps: Katz Radio
Arbitron Metro Market: Chico, CA; *Format:* Country; *Hrs. of News Programming:* news progmg 6 hrs wkly; *No. News Employees:* 1; *Target Audience:* 25-54; active
Dino Corbin, General Manager
Bill Meyer, General Sales Mgr
Lisa Fitzgerald, Promotions Manager

KKXX

09-01-1960; 930 kHz AM
1601 Belvedere Road, West Palm Beach, FL 33406 US
(530) 894-7325; *Fax:* (530) 894-5372
www.kkxx.net
info@kkxx.net
License: Paradise, CA held by Butte Broadcasting Co.
Arbitron Metro Market: Chico, CA; *Format:* News, News/Talk, 86, Religious
Carl Auel, President
Andrew Palmquist, General Manager

KZAP
06-15-2007; 96.7 MHz FM; *Hrs Open:* 24; 1.5 kw; 1289 ft.; N39 57 45 W121 42 40 *Rebroadcasts:* Simulcast with KPIG-FM Freedom 100%
1459 Humboldt Rd., Suite A, Chico, CA 95928 US
(530) 899-3600
www.classichits967.com
duane@reddingradio.com
License: Paradise, Butte County, CA held by Mapleton License of Chico LLC.
Group Owner: Mapleton Communications LLC; (acq 11-30-2006; grpsl)
Nat'l Reps: Christal
Arbitron Metro Market: Paradise, CA; *Format:* Triple A; *Target Audience:* 25-49.
Duane Davis, Programming Director
Christina Warner, Promotions Manager

Pasadena

KAZN
09-12-1942; 1300 kHz AM; *Hrs Open:* 24
747 E. Green St., Suite 101, Pasadena, CA 91101 US
(626) 568-1300; *Fax:* (626) 568-3666
www.am1300.com
am1300LA@gmail.com
License: Pasadena, CA held by Multicultural Radio Broadcasting Licensee LLC.
Group Owner: Multicultural Radio Broadcasting Inc.; (acq 5-11-98; $12 million).
Arbitron Metro Market: Pasadena, CA; *Format:* Chinese; *Hrs. of News Programming:* News progmg 90 hrs wkly; *Target Audience:* Chinese.; *Adv. Rates:* 235; 205; 225; 195
Arthur Liu, CEO/COO

***KPCC**
09-01-1957; 89.3 MHz FM; *Hrs Open:* 24; 680 w; 2,922 ft; N34 13 35 W118 03 58
1570 E. Colorado Blvd., Pasadena, CA 91106
(626) 585-7000; *Fax:* (626) 585-7916
www.kpcc.org
License: Pasadena, Los Angeles County, CA held by Pasadena Area Community College District Board of Trustees.
Nat'l Network: NPR; PRI; CBC Radio One
Population Served: 342,000; *Arbitron Metro Market:* Los Angeles; *Hrs. of News Programming:* News progmg 6 hrs wkly; *Target Audience:* 25-55.
Bill Davis, CEO
Doug Johnson, Operations Dir
Julie Allen, General Sales Mgr
Craig Curtis, Programming Director
Paul Glickman, News Director

KDIS
02-07-1942; 1110 kHz AM; 50 kw-D, DA2; 20 kw-N, DA2; N34 6 50 W117 59 51
600 New Hampshire Ave. NW, Suite 1200, Washington, DC 20037 USA
(818) 569-5035
music.disney.com/radio-disney
License: Pasadena, CA held by ABC Radio Los Angeles Assets LLC
Group Owner: Disney Channels Worldwide
Nat'l Network: Radio Disney
Arbitron Metro Market: Los Angeles; *Format:* Contemporary Hits/Top 40
Gary Marsh, President & Chief Creative Officer

KROQ
08-03-1979; 106.7 MHz FM; *Hrs Open:* 24; 5.5 kW; 207 ft.; N34 11 49 W118 15 30
1800 K St. NW, Suite 200, Washington, DC 20006 USA
(202) 457-4518
www.kroq.com
License: Pasadena, Los Angeles County, CA held by CBS Radio Inc. of Los Angeles
Group Owner: CBS Radio; (acq 11-13-98; grpsl).
Arbitron Metro Market: Greater Los Angeles; *Format:* Alternative; *Target Audience:* 18-34

Paso Robles

KLUN
08-01-1995; 103.1 MHz FM; *Hrs Open:* 24; 1.1 kw; 761 ft.; N35 38 45 W120 44 16
200 S. A St., Oxnard, CA 93030 USA
(805) 240-2070
www.radiolazer.com
License: Paso Robles, San Luis Obispo County, CA held by Lazer Broadcasting Corp.
Group Owner: Lazer Broadcasting Corp.; acq 8-7-00; $1.115 million with KLMM(FM) Morro Bay)
Arbitron Metro Market: Santa Maria, CA; *Target Audience:* 18-49; general

KKAL
11-20-1972; 92.5 MHz FM; *Hrs Open:* 24; 4.8 kw; 1486 ft.; N35 21 40 W120 39 21
3620 Sacramento Dr, Suite 204, San Luis Obispo, CA 93401 US
(805) 781-2750; *Fax:* (805) 781-2758
www.krush925.com
License: Paso Robles, San Luis Obispo County, CA held by AGM California, Inc.
Group Owner: American General Media; (acq 1997; $675,000)
Arbitron Metro Market: San Luis Obispo, CA; *Format:* Adult Contemp; *Hrs. of News Programming:* news progmg 12 hrs wkly; *No. News Employees:* 1; *Target Audience:* Adults 18-65
Kathy Signorelli, General Manager
Mark Tobin, General Sales Mgr
Pepper Daniels, Programming Director

KPRL
10-01-1946; 1230 kHz AM; 1 kw-U, ND1; N35 39 15 W120 40 52
P.O. Box 5365, Santa Barbara, CA 93150 US
(805) 238-1230; *Fax:* (805) 238-5332
www.kprl.com
reception@kprl.com
License: Paso Robles, CA held by North County Communications LLC
Nat'l Reps: Western Regional Broadcast Sales
Arbitron Metro Market: San Luis Obispo; *Format:* News, News/Talk, 84, Talk; *Hrs. of News Programming:* news progmg one hr wkly; *No. News Employees:* 1; *Target Audience:* 25 plus.; *Adv. Rates:* 19; 17; 15; 12
Kevin Will, CEO

Patterson

KOSO
06-06-1966; 92.9 MHz FM; *Hrs Open:* 24; 6 kw; 328 ft.; N37 36 24.2 W121 2 37.2
2121 Lancey Dr., Modesto, CA 95355 US
(209) 551-1306; *Fax:* (209) 551-1359
www.b93fm.com
License: Patterson, Stanislaus County, CA held by Capstar TX LLC
Group Owner: iHeartMedia; (acq 8-30-00; grpsl).
Arbitron Metro Market: Modesto, CA; *Format:* Alternative; *Hrs. of News Programming:* news progmg 5 hrs wkly; *No. News Employees:* 1; *Target Audience:* 25-54.
Greg Cobb, Sales Director
Kevin Fox, Promotions Director
Nik Ashjian, Digital Content Director

KTSE-FM
01-01-1996; 97.1 MHz FM; *Hrs Open:* 24; 1.35 kw; 495 ft.; N37 29 34 W121 13 29
6820 Pacific Ave., Floor 3A, Modesto, CA 95207 US
(209) 474-0154; *Fax:* (209) 474-0316
www.superestrella989.com
License: Patterson, Stanislaus County, CA held by Entravision Holdings LLC.
Group Owner: Entravision Communications Corp.; (acq 7-28-00; grpsl).
Arbitron Metro Market: Patterson, CA; *Format:* Spanish, Adult Contemp
Lisa Vela, Senior VP
Esperanza Lopez, News Director

Pebble Beach

***KSPB**
09-22-1978; 91.9 MHz FM; 1 kw; 486 ft.; N36 35 11 W121 55 21
P.O. Box 657, Pebble Beach, CA 93953 US
(831) 626-5300(831) 625-5078; *Fax:* (831) 625-5208
www.kspb.org
webmaster@kspb.org
License: Pebble Beach, Monterey County, CA held by Robert Louis Stevenson School.
Arbitron Metro Market: Pebble Beach, CA; *Format:* Alternative *Special Programming:* Black 18 hrs, oldies 4 hrs, reggae 2 hrs, hard rock 2 hrs wkly
Matthew Arruda, Station Manager

Pescadero

***KPDO**
01-01-2006; 89.3 MHz FM; 0.1 kw; -118 ft.; N37 15 11.5 W122 24 37.2
Mailing Address: P O Box 25, Loma Mar, CA 94021 US
Second Address: 20748 Powder Horn Rd., Hidden Valley Lake, CA 95467
(831) 459-2811; *Fax:* (831) 459-4734
www.kpdo.org
License: Pescadero, San Mateo County, CA held by Pescadero Public Radio Service Inc.
Arbitron Metro Market: Pescadero, CA
Michael Bryant, General Manager

Petaluma

KTOB
01-10-1950; 1490 kHz AM; *Hrs Open:* 24; 1 kw-U; N35 39 15 W120 40 52
c/o Radio Station KRRS(AM), 1410 Neotomas Ave., Suite 104, Santa Rosa, CA 94953
(707) 545-1460; *Fax:* (707) 545-0112
License: Petaluma, Sonoma County, CA held by California Broadcasting Corp LLC
Nat'l Reps: Interep
Population Served: 812,826; *Arbitron Metro Market:* San Francisco; *Target Audience:* 25-54; contemporary Hispanic families; *Adv. Rates:* 45; 35; 45; 35
Ambrosio Vigil, CEO
Francisco Quirroz, Programming Director
Alberto Rosillo, Traffic Manager

Philo

***KZYX**
10-01-1989; 90.7 MHz FM; 3.4 kw; 1686 ft.; N39 1 22 W123 31 17
PO Box 1, 9300 Hwy 128, Philo, CA 95466 US
(707) 895-2324; *Fax:* (707) 895-2451
www.kzyx.org
uw@kzyx.org.
License: Philo, Mendocino County, CA held by Mendocino County Public Broadcasting.
Nat'l Network: NPR
Arbitron Metro Market: Philo, CA; *Format:* News, Talk, 94 *Special Programming:* Black 8 hrs, class 14 hrs, folk 8 hrs, gospel 2 hrs, jazz 11 hrs, blues 3 hrs; *Target Audience:* General.
Rich Culbertson, Operations Dir
John Coate, General Manager
David Steffen, General Sales Mgr
Mary Aigner, Programming Director
Paul Hanson, News Director

Piedmont

KSFN
05-01-1947; 1510 kHz AM; *Hrs Open:* 24; 8 kw-D, 230 w-N, DA-2; N37 49 02 W122 17 10 *Rebroadcasts:* Simulcast with KPIG-FM Freedom 100%
CA USA
License: Piedmont, Alameda County, CA held by Mapleton License of San Francisco LLC.
Group Owner: Mapleton Communications LLC; (acq 7-27-2005; $5.1 million)
Nat'l Reps: McGavren Guild
Population Served: 245,000; *Arbitron Metro Market:* San Francisco, CA; *Format:* Triple A

Pismo Beach

KXTZ
12-07-1974; 95.3 MHz FM; *Hrs Open:* 24; 4.2 kw; 390 ft.; N35 9 24 W120 38 11
795 Buckley Rd., Suite 2, San Luis Obispo, CA 93401 US
(805) 786-2570
www.953thebeach.com
eric.fahnoe@dimescentralcoast.com
License: Pismo Beach, San Luis Obispo County, CA held by Dimes Media Corporation
Group Owner: Dimes Media Corporation
Arbitron Metro Market: San Luis Obispo, CA; *Format:* Contemporary Hits/Top 40, Adult Contemp *Special Programming:* Talk one hr wkly; *Hrs. of News Programming:* news progmg one hr wkly; *No. News Employees:* 1 *Target Audience:* 18-49.
Eric Fahnoe, Promotions Manager

Pittsburg

KATD
09-01-1949; 990 kHz AM; *Hrs Open:* 24 *Rebroadcasts:* Rebroadcasts KIQI(AM) San Francisco 100%
44 Gough St., Suite 301, San Francisco, CA 94103 US
(415) 978-5378
www.kiqi1010am.com
License: Pittsburg, CA held by Way Broadcasting Licensee LLC.

Group Owner: Multicultural Radio Broadcasting Inc.; (acq 2-4-2004; grpsl).
Arbitron Metro Market: San Francisco, CA; *Format:* Spanish; *Hrs. of News Programming:* News progmg 50 hrs wkly; *Target Audience:* 25-54; middle upper income
Arthur Liu, CEO/COO

Placerville

KMJE
12-09-1982; 92.1 MHz FM; *Hrs Open:* 24; 6 kw; Ant 328 ft; 38Â° 38' 10"" N, 120Â° 38' 14"" W
298 Commerce Cir., Sacramento, CA 95815
(916) 576-7333; *Fax:* (916) 929-5330
www.921khits.com
rico@921khits.com
License: Placerville, El Dorado County, CA held by Results Radio of Sacramento LLC.
Group Owner: Fritz Communications Inc.; (acq 6-18-2008)
Nat'l Reps: McGavren Guild
Arbitron Metro Market: Sacramento, CA; *Target Audience:* Adults 35-64; *Adv. Rates:* 30; 40; 40; 20
Jack Fritz, CEO/General Manager
Kelly Andrews, General Sales Mgr
Rico Garcia, Programming/Promotions Manager
Ron Castro, Engineering Dir

Planada

KHTN
01-01-1966; 104.7 MHz FM; *Hrs Open:* 24; 1.95 kw; 2,080 ft.; N37 32 1 W120 1 46
510 W. 19th St., Merced, CA 95340 US
(209) 383-7900; *Fax:* (209) 723-8461
www.hot1047fm.com
License: Planada, Merced County, CA held by Alpha Media Licensee LLC
Group Owner: Alpha Media LLC; (acq 10-16-2014).
Nat'l Reps: D & R Radio
Arbitron Metro Market: Merced, CA; *Format:* Contemporary Hits/Top 40; *Target Audience:* 21-34; women; *Adv. Rates:* 36; 32; 36; 22
Rene Roberts, Operations Manager
Mike McAdam, Vice President and Market Manager
Ed Monroe, General Sales Mgr

Point Arena

KYOE
01-01-2003; 102.3 MHz FM; 1.2 kw; 1417 ft.; N38 53 44 W123 32 34
P. O. Box 1152, Fort Bragg, CA 95437 US
(707) 882-2323; *Fax:* (707) 882-3258
License: Point Arena, Mendocino County, CA held by Del Mar Trust.
Arbitron Metro Market: Point Arena, CA; *Format:* Country
Karen Hay, General Manager

Point Reyes Station

*KWMR
05-02-1999; 90.5 MHz FM; *Hrs Open:* 7 AM-12 AM; 0.235 kw; 1076 ft.; N38 4 48 W122 51 57
Mailing Address: P.O. Box 1262, Point Reyes Station, CA 94956 US
Second Address: 11431 State Rte. One #8, Point Reyes Station, CA 94956
(415) 663-8068; *Fax:* (415) 663-0746
www.kwmr.org
kwmr@kwmr.org
License: Point Reyes Station, Marin County, CA held by West Marin Community Radio Inc.
Arbitron Metro Market: Point Reyes Station, CA; *Format:* Talk
Kay Clements, General Manager
Amanda Eichstaedt, Executive Director/ Station Manager
Janet Galea, General Sales Mgr
Lyons Filmer, Programming Director
Alex Horvath, News Director
Richard Dillman, Chief Operator/ TransmitterWrangler
Marc Matheson, Office Administration/ Membership/ Volunteer Coord
Mia Jhonson, Underwriting
Ian Mcmurray, IT Desk
Janet Robbins, Classical Music Director

Pollock Pines

KFBK-FM
01-01-1946; 93.1 MHz FM; *Hrs Open:* 24; 50 kw; 364 ft.; N38 38 10.5 W120 38 14
1545 River Park Dr., Suite 500, Sacramento, CA 95815 US
(916) 929-5325
www.kfbk.com
news@kfbk.com
License: Pollock Pines, El Dorado County, CA held by CC Licenses LLC
Group Owner: iHeartMedia
Arbitron Metro Market: Sacramento, CA; *Format:* News, News/Talk, 86 *Special Programming:* West Texas Saturday Nights; *Hrs. of News Programming:* News progmg one hr wkly; *Target Audience:* 18-35
Sara McClure, Senior Vice President of Sales
Bill White, Programming Director
John Nelson, Director of Marketing

Pomona

KAHZ
05-12-1947; 1600 kHz AM; *Hrs Open:* 24; 5 kw-D, DAN; 5 kw-N, DAN; N34 1 48 W117 43 35
27 William St., 11th Floor, New York, NY 10005 US
(212) 966-1059; *Fax:* (212) 625-2894
www.mrbi.net
License: Pomona, CA held by Multicultural Radio Broadcasting Licensee LLC.
Group Owner: Multicultural Radio Broadcasting Inc.; (acq 11-17-98; $7.55 million).
Arbitron Metro Market: Los Angeles, CA; *Format:* Chinese; *Target Audience:* 30 plus; money oriented
Arthur Liu, CEO/COO

KWKU
12-23-1960; 1220 kHz AM; *Hrs Open:* 20; 0.25 kw-D, DA2; 0.25 kw-N, DA2; N34 1 11 W117 43 3 *Rebroadcasts:* Rebroadcasts KWKW(AM) Los Angeles 60%
449 Broadway, New York, NY 10013 US
(909) 865-3323; *Fax:* (909) 865-0342
License: Pomona, CA held by Lotus Communications Corp.
Group Owner: Lotus Communications Corp.; acq 2-00; $750,000).
Arbitron Metro Market: Pomona, CA; *Format:* News, News/Talk, 84, Talk *Special Programming:* Relg 15 hrs wkly; *Hrs. of News Programming:* news progmg 7 hrs wkly; *No. News Employees:* 1; *Target Audience:* 24-64.
Juan Rodriguez, General Manager
Mike Addison, General Sales Mgr
Maria Diaz, News Director

Port Hueneme

KKZZ
01-01-1948; 1520 kHz AM; 1 kw-U, ND1; N34 10 2 W119 8 2
2319 Alameda Ave, Suite 1D, Ventura, CA 93003 US
(805) 289-1400; *Fax:* (805) 644-7906
License: Port Hueneme, CA held by Gold Coast Broadcasting LLC
Group Owner: Gold Coast Broadcasting LLC; (acq 8-18-99; grpsl)
Arbitron Metro Market: Oxnard, CA; *Format:* News/Talk, Oldies, 94; *Target Audience:* 25-54.
Chip Ehrhardt, National Sales Director
Mark Elliott, Programming Director

Porterville

KIOO
08-01-1972; 99.7 MHz FM; *Hrs Open:* 24; 25 kw; 702 ft.; N36 6 26 W119 1 45
700 E. Mineral Ave., Visalia, CA 93277 US
(559) 553-1500; *Fax:* (559) 627-1496
www.997classicrock.com
License: Porterville, Tulare County, CA held by Momentum Broadcasting LP
Group Owner: Momentum Broadcasting LP
Nat'l Reps: Eastman Radio
Arbitron Metro Market: Visalia-Tulare-Hanford, CA; *Format:* Classic Rock; *Target Audience:* 25-44.
William Lynch, General Manager
Fawn Purdy, Sales Manager
Oriana Groppetti, National Sales

KTIP
01-01-1947; 1450 kHz AM; *Hrs Open:* 24; 1 kw-U, ND1; N36 5 44 W119 3 10
1660 North Newcomb St, Porterville, CA 93257 US
(559) 784-1450; *Fax:* (559) 784-2482
www.ktip.com
live@ktip.com
License: Porterville, CA held by Mayberry Broadcasting Co. Inc.
Nat'l Network: ABC; Westwood One *Regional Reps:* Rgnl Reps.
Arbitron Metro Market: Visalia-Tulare-Hanford, CA; *Format:* News, News/Talk, 86 *Special Programming:* Health show one hr, loc travel one hr wkly, national health 3hrs.,Trader's Market; *Hrs. of News Programming:* newsprogmg 23 hrs wkly; *No. News Employees:* 2; *Target Audience:* 25 plus.; *Adv. Rates:* 25; 23; 20; 10
Larry Stoneburner, President
Kent Hopper, Operations Dir
Larry & Mimi Stoneburner, General Manager
Michael Partipilo, General Sales Mgr
Mimi Stoneburner, Promotions Manager
P.K. Whitmire, News Director
Ron Neil, ChiefEngineer
Janice Dawson, Traffic Manager

Prunedale

*KLVM
02-28-1986; 89.7 MHz FM; *Hrs Open:* 24; 0.45 kw; 2346 ft.; N36 45 22 W121 30 6 *Rebroadcasts:* Rebroadcasts KLVR(FM) Santa Rosa 100%
Mailing Address: 8145 Prunedale North Rd., Prunedale, CA 93907 US
Second Address: 8145 Prunedale N. Rd., Salinas, CA 93907
(707) 528-9236; *Fax:* (707) 528-9246
www.klove.com
klove@klove.com
License: Prunedale, Monterey County, CA held by Prunedale Educational Association
Nat'l Network: K-Love
Format: Christian; *Target Audience:* 25-35; Judeo-Christian female
Darell Chambliss, Chairman
Mike Novak, President
David Pierce, Programming Director
Scott Smith, Music Director

Quincy

KNLF
06-10-1996; 95.9 MHz FM; *Hrs Open:* 24; 500 w; -499 ft; N39 58 03 W120 53 34
Box 117, 440 Lawrence St., Quincy, CA 95971
(530) 283-4144; *Fax:* (530) 283-5135
www.knlfradio.com
rtrumbo@excite.com
License: Quincy, Plumas County, CA held by New Life Broadcasting.
Nat'l Network: American Family Radio
Population Served: 20,000 *Hrs. of News Programming:* News progmg 10 hrs wkly; *Target Audience:* 18-54.; *Adv. Rates:* 8; 8; 8; 8
Ron Trumbo, President
Kip Sobel, Chief Engineer

KRAC
08-16-1963; 1370 kHz AM; *Hrs Open:* 24; 5 kw-D, DA2; 0.5 kw-N, DA2; N39 56 54 W120 53 54
395 Main St., Quincy, CA 95971 US
(530) 742-5555; *Fax:* (530) 741-3758
License: Quincy, CA held by Tom F. Huth
Group Owner: Huth Broadcasting; (acq 2-2-2006; $100,000)
Format: Talk
Cal Hunter, President
Tom Huth, General Manager

*KQNC
01-01-2005; 88.1 MHz FM; 0.5 kw; -1135 ft.; N39 56 14 W120 56 51 *Rebroadcasts:* Simulcast with KXJZ(FM) Sacramento 100%
US
(916) 278-8900; *Fax:* (916) 278-8989
www.csus.edu/npr
npr@csus.edu
License: Quincy, Plumas County, CA held by California State University, Sacramento.
Nat'l Network: NPR
Arbitron Metro Market: Quincy, CA; *Format:* Jazz, News
Rick Eytcheson, President & General Manager
Carl Watanabe, Station Manager
Joe Barr, Director of News and Information
Evan Matsler, Operations Director
Jun Reina, CFO/COO
Craig Murray, Managing Director
Constance Crawford,Director of Marketing & Public Relations
Arla Gibson, Director of Development
Al Gibes, Director of Digital Content

*KQNY
91.9 MHz FM; 2.7 kw; -1122 ft.; N39 56 15 W120 56 49
US
(530) 283-5494
License: Quincy, Plumas County, CA held by Plumas Community Radio
Arbitron Metro Market: Quincy, CA; *Format:* Blues, Rock/AOR

RADIO - U.S.

Mark Houston, President

Rancho Cordova

KSTE
04-19-1990; 650 kHz AM; *Hrs Open:* 24
1545 River Park Drive, Sacramento, CA 95815 US
(916) 929-5325; *Fax:* (916) 929-0118
www.kste.com
License: Rancho Cordova, CA held by AMFM Broadcasting Licenses LLC.
Group Owner: iHeartMedia; (acq 8-30-2000; grpsl).
Nat'l Network: ABC; Westwood One
Arbitron Metro Market: Sacramento, CA; *Format:* Talk; *Hrs. of News Programming:* news progmg 15 hrs wkly; *No. News Employees:* 4; *Target Audience:* 25-54.
Sara McClure, Senior Vice President of Sales
Bill White, Programming Director

Rancho Mirage

KMRJ
07-17-1998; 99.5 MHz FM; *Hrs Open:* 24; 3 kw; 328 ft.; N33 52 15 W116 13 37
25601 Paseo De La Paz, San Juan Capistrano, CA 92675 US
(760) 778-6995; *Fax:* (760) 778-1249
License: Rancho Mirage, Riverside County, CA held by Mitchell Media Inc.
Nat'l Network: Westwood One; *Nat'l Reps:* Katz Radio
Arbitron Metro Market: Palm Springs, CA; *Format:* Classic Rock; *Hrs. of News Programming:* News progmg 2 hrs wkly; *Target Audience:* 35-64; mid age families, working adults; *Adv. Rates:* 45; 30; 35; 20
Daniel Mitchell III, Chairman
Maurine Mitchell, CFO
Thomas Carr Mitchell, Station Manager
Adam Carolla, Programming Director
Veronica Ochoa, Promotions Manager
Carolina O'Connel, News Director
Mark Moceri, Engineering Dir
LordTim Hudson, Disc Jockey
Jeff Larsen

Randsburg

*KGBM
12-01-2001; 89.7 MHz FM; *Hrs Open:* 24; 6.8 kw; 1302 ft.; N35 28 39 W117 41 58
2009 South Sweet Gum Ave, Broken Arrow, OK 74012 US
(888) 937-2471; *Fax:* (916) 251-1650
www.air1.com
info@air1.com
License: Randsburg, Kern County, CA held by Educational Media Foundation.
Group Owner: EMF Broadcasting; (acq 4-19-02).
Nat'l Network: Air 1
Arbitron Metro Market: Bakersfield, CA; *Format:* Alternative, Christian; *No. News Employees:* 3; *Target Audience:* 18-35; Judeo-Christian female
Darrell Chambliss, Chairman
Mike Novak, President and CEO
David Pierce, Programming Director
Ed Lenane, News Director
Sam Wallington, Engineering Dir

Red Bluff

KALF
01-01-1978; 95.7 MHz FM; *Hrs Open:* 24; 7 kw; 1266 ft.; N39 55 2 W122 40 10
1459 Humbolt Rd., Suite A, Chico, CA 95928 US
(530) 899-3600
www.957thewolfonline.com
duane@reddingradio.com
License: Red Bluff, Tehama County, CA held by Mapleton License of Chico LLC.
Group Owner: Mapleton Communications LLC; (acq 11-30-2006; grpsl)
Arbitron Metro Market: Chico, CA; *Format:* Country; *Hrs. of News Programming:* news progmg 10 hrs wkly; *No. News Employees:* 1; *Target Audience:* 25-54.
Duane Davis, Operations Dir

KBLF
01-01-1946; 1490 kHz AM; 1 kw-U, ND1; N40 11 28 W122 12 54
113 East Alma, Mount Shasta, CA 95207 US
(530) 527-1490; *Fax:* (530) 527-3525
www.kblfam.com
kblfam@yahoo.com
License: Red Bluff, CA held by Tom Huth.
Group Owner: Huth Broadcasting; (acq 8-11-98; $5,000).
Nat'l Network: Westwood One; PRI
Arbitron Metro Market: Red Bluff, CA; *Format:* Oldies *Special Programming:* Farm 5 hrs, Sp 4 hrs wkly; *Target Audience:* 35-64.; *Adv. Rates:* 12; 8; 10; 5
Cal Hunter, General Manager

*KKRO
11-15-2002; 102.7 MHz FM; *Hrs Open:* 24; 5.5 kw; 1414 ft.; N40 20 41 W121 56 48 *Rebroadcasts:* Rebroadcasts KLRD(FM) Yucaipa 100%
1588 Charles Drive, Redding, CA 96003 US
(888) 937-2471; *Fax:* (916) 251-1650
www.air1.com
info@air1.com
License: Red Bluff, Shasta County, CA held by Educational Media Foundation Inc.
Group Owner: EMF Broadcasting
Nat'l Network: Air 1
Arbitron Metro Market: Redding, CA; *Format:* Alternative, Christian; *No. News Employees:* 3; *Target Audience:* 27-33; Judeo-Christian female
Darrell Chambliss, Chairman
Mike Novak, President and CEO
David Pierce, Programming Director
Ed Lenane, News Director
Sam Wallington, Engineering Dir

*KTHM
90.7 MHz FM; 0.1 kw vert; -135 ft.; N40 10 27 W122 13 55
P O Box 855, Los Molinos, CA 96055 US
(530) 347-0138
License: Red Bluff, Tehama County, CA held by Tehama County Community Broadcasters.
Arbitron Metro Market: Red Bluff, CA; *Format:* Variety/Diverse
Erik Mathisen, Station Manager

Redding

KNRO
01-01-2001; 1400 kHz AM
3360 Alta Mesa Dr., Redding, CA 96002 US
(530) 226-9500
www.foxsportsredding.com
duane@reddingradio.com
License: Redding, CA held by Mapleton License of Redding LLC.
Group Owner: Mapleton Communications LLC; (acq 11-30-2006; grpsl)
Nat'l Network: Fox Sports
Arbitron Metro Market: Redding, CA; *Format:* Sports

*KFPR
11-17-1994; 88.9 MHz FM; 0.75 kw; 3579 ft.; N40 36 10 W122 38 58 *Rebroadcasts:* Rebroadcasts KCHO(FM) Chico 100%
First and Normal, Chico, CA 95929 US
(530) 241-5246; *Fax:* (530) 241-5246
www.kcho.org
bterhorst@csuchico.edu
License: Redding, Shasta County, CA held by California State University, Chico Research Foundation.
Nat'l Network: NPR; PRI
Arbitron Metro Market: Redding, CA; *Format:* Jazz, News *Special Programming:* Sp 4 hrs wkly, BBC 40 hrs wkly; *Hrs. of News Programming:* news progmg 55 hrs wkly; *Target Audience:* General.
Brian Terhorst, General Manager
Mike Birdsill, Chief Engineer

KLXR
08-01-1956; 1230 kHz AM; *Hrs Open:* 24; 1 kw-U, ND1; N40 33 14 W122 22 53
P.O. Box 3463, Carefree, AZ 85377 US
(530) 244-5082; *Fax:* (530) 244-5698
KLXR1230@yahoo.com
License: Redding, CA held by Michael R. Quinn
Nat'l Network: Jones Radio Networks; *Wire Services:* AP
Arbitron Metro Market: Redding, CA; *Format:* Adult Contemp; *Target Audience:* 35 plus.
Mike Quinn, Programming Director
MIke Quinn, Promotions Manager

KNCQ
10-29-1985; 97.3 MHz FM; 28 kw; 3570 ft.; N40 36 10 W122 38 58
1588 Charles Dr., Redding, CA 96003 US
(530) 244-9700; *Fax:* (530) 244-9707
www.q97country.com
License: Redding, Shasta County, CA held by Results Radio of Redding Licensee LLC.
Group Owner: Results Radio
Nat'l Reps: D & R Radio
Arbitron Metro Market: Redding, CA; *Format:* Country; *Target Audience:* 25-54.

KQMS
09-14-1954; 1400 kHz AM; 1 kw-U, ND1; N40 33 31 W122 19 48
3360 Alta Mesa Dr., Redding, CA 96002 US
(530) 226-9500; *Fax:* (530) 221-6653
www.kqms.com
duane@reddingradio.com
License: Redding, CA held by Mapleton License of Redding LLC.
Group Owner: Mapleton Communications LLC; (acq 11-30-2006; grpsl)
Nat'l Reps: McGavren Guild
Arbitron Metro Market: Northern CA; *Format:* News, News/Talk, 86
Steve Gibson, News Director

KSHA
09-01-1981; 104.3 MHz FM; 100 kw; 1558 ft.; N40 39 14 W122 31 12
3360 Alta Mesa Dr., Redding, CA 96002 US
(530) 226-9500; *Fax:* (530) 221-4940
www.kshasta.com
License: Redding, Shasta County, CA held by Mapleton License of Redding, LLC
Group Owner: Mapleton Communications LLC
Arbitron Metro Market: Redding, CA; *Format:* Adult Contemp
Duane Davis, Operations Dir
Don Burton, Programming Director

*KSTN-FM
01-01-1962; 91.5 MHz FM; 0.42 kw vert; 1234 ft.; N40 54 27 W122 26 37
1425 N Market Blvd, Suite 9, Sacramento, CA 95834 US
(209) 948-5786
www.nuevavida.com
License: Redding, San Joaquin County, CA held by San Joaquin Broadcasting Co.
Arbitron Metro Market: Stockton, CA *Special Programming:* Sp, Por 4 hrs wkly; *Target Audience:* General.
Knox LaRue, President
Jose Rodriguez, Programming Director
Paul Shinn, Chief Engineer

*KVIP
01-04-1970; 540 kHz AM; *Hrs Open:* 24; 2.5 kw-D, 17 w-N; N40 37 25 W122 16 49
1139 Hartnell Ave., Redding, CA 96002 US
(530) 222-4455; *Fax:* (53) 222-4484
www.kvip.org
info@kvip.org
License: Redding, Shasta County, CA held by Pacific Cascade Communications Corp.
Group Owner: Pacific Cascade Communications Corp.; (acq 12-69)
Nat'l Network: Moody; Salem Radio Network
Population Served: 200,000; *Arbitron Metro Market:* Redding, CA; *Format:* Christian; *Hrs. of News Programming:* news progmg 14 hrs wkly; *No. News Employees:* 2; *Target Audience:* General.
Phil Morrow, General Manager

*KVIP-FM
10-19-1975; 98.1 MHz FM; *Hrs Open:* 24; 30 kw; Ant 1,710 ft; N40 36 10 W122 38 58
1139 Hartnell Ave., Redding, CA 96002 US
(530) 222-4455; *Fax:* (530) 222-4484
www.kvip.org
info@kvip.org
License: Redding, Shasta County, CA held by Pacific Cascade Communications Corp.
Group Owner: Pacific Cascade Communications Corp.
Nat'l Network: Moody; Salem Radio Network; *Wire Services:* AP
Population Served: 250,000; *Arbitron Metro Market:* Redding, CA; *Format:* Christian; *No. News Employees:* 2
Phil Morrow, General Manager

Redlands

KCAL(AM)
04-01-1959; 1410 kHz AM; *Hrs Open:* 24; 5 kw-D, 4 kw-N, DA-N; N34 04 08 W117 12 06
200 S. A St., 4th Fl., Oxnard, CA 93030
(805) 240-2070
www.radiolazer.com
License: Redlands, San Bernardino County, CA held by Lazer Broadcasting Corp.
Group Owner: Lazer Broadcasting Corp.; acq 8-7-01; $2.35 million).
Population Served: 680,000; *Arbitron Metro Market:* Riverside-San Bernardino, CA; *No. News Employees:* 2; *Target Audience:* 18-49, 25-64; Mexican origin, Latin American; *Adv. Rates:* 40; 40; 40; na.

KCAL-FM
01-01-1965; 96.7 MHz FM; 1.75 kw; 377 ft.; N34 11 51 W117 17 10
1940 Orange Tree Lane, Suite 200, Redlands, CA 92374 US
(909) 793-3554; *Fax:* (909) 798-6627
www.kcalfm.com
License: Redlands, San Bernardino County, CA held by SBR Broadcasting Corp.
Group Owner: Anaheim Broadcasting Corp.
Nat'l Reps: D & R Radio
Arbitron Metro Market: Redlands, CA; *Format:* Rock/AOR; *Target Audience:* 16-30.
Jeff Parke, General Manager
Dary Norsell, Programming Director
Brandon Kessel, Promotions Director
Curtis Parcell, Sales Manager
Doug Fleniken, Sales Manager
Dani Galante, Public Service Director

***KUOR-FM**
10-01-1966; 89.1 MHz FM; 0.035 kw; 2782 ft.; N34 11 47 W117 2 56 *Rebroadcasts:* Rebroadcasts KPCC(FM) Pasadena 100%
1200 East Colton Avenue, Redlands, CA 92374 US
www.scpr.org
License: Redlands, San Bernardino County, CA held by University of Redlands.
Nat'l Network: NPR
Arbitron Metro Market: Pasadena, CA; *Format:* Talk
Bill Davis, CEO
John Brenneise, Operations Dir
Mark Crowley, Vice President
Cheryl Dring, Programming Director
Joe Barr, News Director
Lance Harper, Chief Engineer
Russ Stanton, Vice President of Content
Melanie Sill, ExecutiveEditor
Bianca Ramirez, Associate Producer

Redondo Beach

KDAY
08-04-1961; 93.5 MHz FM; *Hrs Open:* 24; 4.2 kw; 384 ft.; N34 0 19 W118 21 44
222 North Sepulveda Blvd, Suite 1324, El Segundo, CA 90245 US
(760) 873-5329; *Fax:* (760) 873-5328
www.935kday.com
License: Redondo Beach, Los Angeles County, CA held by KDAY Licensing LLC.
Arbitron Metro Market: Los Angeles; *Format:* Urban Contemporary
Kimberly Fletcher, General Manager
Lisa Alta Moreno, General Sales Mgr
Anthony Acampora, Programming Director
Larry Slover, Chief Engineer

Ridgecrest

KLOA
12-11-1956; 1240 kHz AM
731 N. Balsam St., Ridgecrest, CA 93555 US
(760) 371-1700
www.cbssportsradio1240.com
contact@adelmanbroadcasting.com
License: Ridgecrest, CA held by Adelman Broadcasting Inc.
Group Owner: Adelman Broadcasting Inc.
Arbitron Metro Market: Bakersfield, CA; *Format:* Sports
Robert Adelman, President

KLOA
01-01-1979; 104.9 MHz FM; 1.5 kw; Ant 1,289 ft; N35 28 38 W117 41 59
42010 50th St. W., Quartz Hill, CA 93536 US
(661) 718-1552
contact@adelmanbroadcasting.com
License: Ridgecrest, CA held by Adelman Broadcasting Inc.
Group Owner: Adelman Broadcasting Inc.
Population Served: 70,000; *Arbitron Metro Market:* Bakersfield, CA; *Format:* Spanish
Robert Adelman, President

KWDJ
04-07-1974; 1360 kHz AM; *Hrs Open:* 24; 1 kw-D, ND1; 0.031 kw-N, ND1; N35 36 58 W117 38 35
121 W. Ridgecrest Blvd, Ridgecrest, CA 93555 US
(760) 384-4937; *Fax:* (760) 384-4978
foxtalk1360.com
eric@kziq.com
License: Ridgecrest, CA held by James & Donna Knudsen.
Nat'l Network: Fox News Radio; Jones Radio Networks; Premiere Radio Networks *Regional Reps:* Kim Kauffman
Arbitron Metro Market: Ridgecrest, CA; *Format:* News, Sports; *Hrs. of News Programming:* news progmg 168 hrs wkly; *No. News Employees:* 1; *Target Audience:* 25-54; educated adults with high disposable income
James Knudsen, President
Eric Kauffman, General Manager
Kim Kauffman, General Sales Mgr

KZIQ-FM
01-01-1978; 92.7 MHz FM; *Hrs Open:* 24; 3 kw; -131 ft.; N35 36 58 W117 38 35
121 West Ridgecrest Blvd, Ridgecrest, CA 93555 US
(760) 384-4937; *Fax:* (760) 384-4978
www.kziq.com
eric@kziq.com
License: Ridgecrest, Kern County, CA held by James & Donna Knudsen.
Arbitron Metro Market: Ridgecrest, CA; *Format:* Country; *Hrs. of News Programming:* News progmg 2 hrs wkly
Eric Kauffman, General Manager

***KWTD**
05-01-2005; 91.9 MHz FM; 7 kw; 1281 ft.; N35 28 38 W117 41 58 *Rebroadcasts:* Rebroadcasts KWTW(FM) Bishop 100%
P O Box 637, Bishop, CA 93515 US
(866) 466-5989; *Fax:* (760) 872-4155
www.kwtw.org
recep@kwtw.org
License: Ridgecrest, Kern County, CA held by Living Proof Inc.
Arbitron Metro Market: Ridgecrest, CA; *Format:* Christian
Daniel McClenaghan, President

***KRSF**
89.3 MHz FM; 4 kw horiz; 1480 ft.; N35 53 52.6 W117 17 18.3
Mailing Address: US
Second Address: 1209 W. Robert Ave., Ridgecrest, CA 93555-5936
(760) 375-2355
www.radio74.net
ejwitzel@mchsi.com
License: Ridgecrest, Kern County, CA held by Radio 74 Internationale.
Arbitron Metro Market: Ridgecrest, CA
Everet Witzel, President

Rio Dell

***KNHT**
01-01-1999; 107.3 MHz FM; *Hrs Open:* 5AM-2AM; 3.3 kw; 1703 ft.; N40 30 3 W124 17 10
67 Lakeview Terrace, Sandy Hook, CT 06482 US
(541) 552-6301; *Fax:* (541) 552-8565
www.ijpr.org
jprinfo@sou.edu
License: Rio Dell, Humboldt County, CA held by The State of Oregon, acting by and through the State Board of Higher Education, for the benefit of Southern Oregon University.
Nat'l Network: NPR; PRI; *Wire Services:* AP
Format: Classical, News; *Hrs. of News Programming:* news progmg 35 hrs wkly; *No. News Employees:* 1
Ronald Kramer, CEO
Bryon Lambert, Operations Dir
Paul Westhelle, General Sales Mgr
Darin Ransom, Engineering Dir
Mitchell Christian, CFO

Rio Vista

***KRVH**
11-07-1972; 91.5 MHz FM; 0.05 kw; 102 ft.; N38 9 17 W121 41 48
410 S. 4th Street, Rio Vista, CA 94571 US
(707) 374-6336; *Fax:* (707) 374-6810
www.radiorio.us
License: Rio Vista, Solano County, CA held by River Delta Unified School District.
Arbitron Metro Market: Rio Vista, CA; *Format:* Classic Rock; *Target Audience:* 13-19; young adult
Kevin MacGregor, General Manager

Riverbank

KMRQ
01-15-1979; 96.7 MHz FM; *Hrs Open:* 24; 6 kw; 299 ft.; N37 40 49.8 W120 55 25.5
600 Congress Avenue, Suite 1400, Auston, TX 78701 US
(209) 551-1306; *Fax:* (209) 551-1359
www.rock967.com
License: Riverbank, San Joaquin County, CA held by Capstar TX LLC
Group Owner: iHeartMedia; (acq 8-30-2000; grpsl)
Arbitron Metro Market: Modesto, CA; *Format:* Rock/AOR; *No. News Employees:* 1; *Target Audience:* 25-54.
Greg Cobb, Sales Director
Kevin Fox, Promotions Director
Nik Ashjian, Digital Content Director

Riverdale

KZLA
01-01-2003; 98.3 MHz FM; 0.1 kw; 43 ft.; N36 12 5 W120 5 53
Gammon & Grange Pc, 8280 Greensboro Dr, McLean, VA 22102 US
(559) 935-4191; *Fax:* (559) 935-4191
License: Riverdale, Fresno County, CA held by Huron Broadcasting LLC.
Arbitron Metro Market: Riverdale, CA; *Format:* Oldies
Rebecca Sexton, General Manager

Riverside

KGGI
01-23-1965; 99.1 MHz FM; *Hrs Open:* 24; 2.55 kw; 1,844 ft.; N34 14 4 W117 8 24
2030 Iowa Ave., Suite 100, Riverside, CA 92507 US
(951) 684-1991; *Fax:* (951) 274-4911
www.kggiradio.com
License: Riverside, Riverside County, CA held by AMFM Broadcasting Licenses LLC.
Group Owner: iHeartMedia; (acq 8-30-2000; grpsl).
Nat'l Reps: McGavren Guild
Arbitron Metro Market: Riverside-San Bernardino, CA; *Format:* Contemporary Hits/Top 40 *Special Programming:* Discussion 7 hrs wkly; *Target Audience:* 18-49.
Mark Thomas, Market President
Elston Butler, Senior Vice President of Sales
Rob Scorpio, Regional Senior Vice President of Programming
KC Morris, Promotions Director
Rich Mena, Engineering Dir
Jorge Lopez, Online ContentDirector

KPRO
06-22-1957; 1570 kHz AM; *Hrs Open:* 24; 5 kw-D, DA2; 0.194 kw-N, DA2; N33 55 54 W117 23 47
7351 Lincoln Avenue, Riverside, CA 92504 US
(951) 688-1570; *Fax:* (951) 688-7009
kproval@aol.com
License: Riverside, CA held by Impact Radio Inc.
Arbitron Metro Market: Riverside-San Bernardino, CA; *Format:* Christian, Religious; *Target Audience:* 18+; *Adv. Rates:* 20; 20; 20; 20
Ronnie Olenick, President
Valorie Stitely, General Manager

***KSGN**
01-01-1970; 89.7 MHz FM; *Hrs Open:* 24; 2.75 kw; 322 ft.; N34 11 50.9 W117 17 9.2
11498 Pierce Street, Riverside, CA 92505 US
(909) 583-2150; *Fax:* (909) 583-2170
www.ksgn.com
info@ksgn.com
License: Riverside, Riverside County, CA held by Good News Radio.
Arbitron Metro Market: Redlands, CA; *Format:* Christian, Religious; *Hrs. of News Programming:* News progmg 12 hrs wkly; *Target Audience:* General; Christians & church goers
Dennis Johnson, Chairman
Dawn Hibbard, General Manager
Bryan O'Neal, Programming Director
Brandi Lanai, News Director
Bruce Potterton, Chief Engineer
Heather Clough, Traffic Manager

KLYY
03-17-1959; 97.5 MHz FM; *Hrs Open:* 24; 72 kw; 1827 ft.; N34 14 4 W117 8 24
5700 Wilshire Blvd., Suite 250, Los Angeles, CA 90036 US
(323) 900-6100
www.joseradio.com
License: Riverside, Riverside County, CA held by Entravision Holdings LLC.
Group Owner: Entravision Communications Corp.; (acq 4-20-00; grpsl).
Nat'l Reps: Lotus Entravision Reps LLC
Arbitron Metro Market: Los Angeles; *Format:* Spanish, Adult Contemp; *Target Audience:* 18-49.
Matt Cardenas, SVP Integrated Marketing Solution
Nestor Rocha, Programming Director
Elias Autran, Promotions Manager

***KUCR**
10-01-1966; 88.3 MHz FM; 0.15 kw; 1621 ft.; N33 57 58 W117 17 14
300 Lakeside Dr. 8th Flr, Oakland, CA 94612 US
(951) 827-3737; *Fax:* (951) 827-3240
www.kucr.org
kucrinfo@kucr.org
License: Riverside, Riverside County, CA held by The Regents of the University of California.
Arbitron Metro Market: Riverside, CA; *Format:* Alternative, Variety/Diverse *Special Programming:* Black 18 hrs, class 14 hrs, jazz 6 hrs wkly
Jeff Armantrout, Operations Dir
Louis Vandenberg, General Manager
Walter Douglas, Promotions Manager
Bill Elledge, Chief Engineer

KFNY
01-01-1941; 1440 kHz AM; 1 kw-U, ND1; N34 1 36 W117 21 27
2030 Iowa Ave., Suite A, Riverside, CA 92507 US
(951) 684-1991; *Fax:* (951) 274-4949
www.newstalk1440.com
License: Riverside, Riverside County, CA held by Citicasters Licenses Inc.
Group Owner: iHeartMedia
Arbitron Metro Market: Riverside-San Bernardino, CA; *Format:* News, News/Talk, 86
Mark Thomas, Market President
Rob Scorpio, Regional Senior Vice President of Programming
Elston Butler, Senior Vice President of Sales
KC Morris, Promotions Director
Rich Mena, Chief Engineer
Jorge Lopez, Online Content Director

Rock Creek

***KRBP**
09-07-2012; 90.7 MHz FM; 1 kw; -2569 ft.; N39 54 20 W121 20 41
Mailing Address: US
Second Address: , (626) 969-7945,
License: Rock Creek, Plumas County, CA held by Christian Faith Center of the Valley
Format: Religious
Samuel Martinez, President

Rocklin

***KEBR**
07-27-1988; 1210 kHz AM; *Hrs Open:* 24
Mailing Address: 4135 Northgate Blvd #1, Sacramento, CA 95834 US
Second Address: 290 Hegenberger Rd., Oakland, CA 94621
(916) 641-8191; *Fax:* (916) 641-8238
www.familyradio.com
info@familyradio.com
License: Rocklin, CA held by Family Stations Inc.
Group Owner: Family Stations Inc.; 1988
Arbitron Metro Market: Sacramento, CA; *Format:* Religious; *Target Audience:* General.
Harold Camping, President
Peggy Renschler, Station Manager

Rohnert Park

KMHX
03-04-1986; 104.9 MHz FM; *Hrs Open:* 24; 6.6 kw; 548 ft.; N38 23 31 W122 40 40
6640 Redwood Drive, Suite 202, Rohnert Park, CA 94928 US
(707) 543-0100; *Fax:* (707) 543-1097
License: Rohnert Park, Sonoma County, CA held by Amaturo Sonoma Media Group LLC
Group Owner: Sonoma Media Group; (acq 6-5-2006; $7.7 million)
Arbitron Metro Market: Santa Rosa, CA; *Format:* Adult Contemp; *Target Audience:* 25-54.
Neysa Hinton, General Manager
Kent Bjugstad, General Sales Mgr
Danny White, Programming Director
Monika Weber, Promotions Manager

Rosamond

KQAV
09-01-1993; 93.5 MHz FM; *Hrs Open:* 24; 3 kw; Ant 207 ft; N34 51 03 W118 09 22
570 East Ave., Q-9, Palmdale, CA 93550
(661) 947-3107; *Fax:* (661) 272-5688
www.935thequake.com
info@thequake.com
License: Rosamond, Kern County, CA held by High Desert Broadcasting LLC
Group Owner: High Desert Broadcasting LLC; acq 3-7-2002; grpsl).
Nat'l Network: Westwood One
Population Served: 300,000; *Arbitron Metro Market:* Bakersfield, CA; *Format:* Classic Rock, News; *Target Audience:* 25-54.
Gary Wilson, Operations Dir
Nelson Rosse, General Manager
Greg Wood, General Sales Mgr
Jeff McElfresh, Promotions Manager
Amir Raheem, News Director

KVVS
03-01-1985; 105.5 MHz FM; *Hrs Open:* 24; 6 kw; 308 ft.; N34 51 3 W118 9 22 *Rebroadcasts:* Simulcast with KIIS-FM Los Angeles 100%
3400 W. Olive Ave., Suite 550, Burbank, CA 91505 US
(818) 559-2252; *Fax:* (818) 729-2818
www.kiisfm.com
License: Rosamond, Kern County, CA held by CC Licenses LLC.
Group Owner: iHeartMedia; (acq 11-21-2003; grpsl)
Arbitron Metro Market: Los Angeles, CA; *Format:* Contemporary Hits/Top 40
Kevin LeGrett, Market President
David Howard, Vice President of Sales

Roseville

KLIB
04-01-1968; 1110 kHz AM; *Hrs Open:* 24; 5 kw-D, DA2; 0.5 kw-N, DA2; N38 44 22 W121 12 50
27 William St., 11th Floor, New York, NY 10005 US
(212) 966-1059; *Fax:* (212) 625-2894
www.mrbi.net
License: Roseville, CA held by Way Broadcasting Licensee, LLC
Group Owner: Multicultural Radio Broadcasting, Inc.; (acq 4-20-2000; grpsl).
Arbitron Metro Market: Sacramento, CA; *Format:* Ethnic; *Target Audience:* 18 plus; Hispanic
Arthur Liu, CEO/COO

KFSG
01-01-2001; 1690 kHz AM
27 William St., 11th Floor, New York, NY 10005 US
(212) 966-1059; *Fax:* (212) 625-2894
www.mrbi.net
License: Roseville, CA held by Way Broadcasting Licensee, LLC
Group Owner: Multicultural Radio Broadcasting, Inc.; (acq 6-13-00; grpsl).
Arbitron Metro Market: Sacramento, CA; *Format:* Ethnic
Arthur Liu, CEO/COO

KQJK
06-01-1970; 93.7 MHz FM; *Hrs Open:* 24; 25 kw; 328 ft.; N38 44 22 W121 12 50
1545 River Park Dr., Suite 500, Sacramento, CA 95815 US
(916) 929-9370; *Fax:* (916) 925-0118
www.937jackfm.com
License: Roseville, Placer County, CA held by AMFM Texas Licenses LLC
Group Owner: iHeartMedia; (acq 4-1-2009; grpsl)
Arbitron Metro Market: Sacramento, CA; *Format:* Adult Contemp; *Hrs. of News Programming:* news progmg 2 hrs wkly; *No. News Employees:* 1; *Target Audience:* 25-54.
John Geary, Market President
Sara McClure, Senior Vice President of Sales

Sacramento

KHHM
10-01-1996; 103.5 MHz FM; *Hrs Open:* 24; 6 kw; 312 ft; N38 33 59 W121 28 47
1436 Auburn Blvd., Sacramento, CA 95815 US
(916) 646-4000; *Fax:* (916) 646-3237
www.hot1035.com
License: Sacramento, Sacramento County, CA held by Entravision Holdings LLC.
Group Owner: Entravision Communications Corp.; (acq 9-30-2004; $16.1 million).
Arbitron Metro Market: Sacramento, CA; *Format:* Urban Contemporary; *Target Audience:* 18-49.
Tosh Jackson, Programming Director

KDND
08-01-1945; 107.9 MHz FM; *Hrs Open:* 24; 50 kw; 404 ft.; N38 42 38 W121 28 54
401 City Avenue, Suite 409, Bala Cynwyd, PA 19004 US
(916) 334-7777; *Fax:* (916) 334-1092
www.endonline.com
License: Sacramento, Sacramento County, CA held by Entercom Sacramento License L.L.C.
Group Owner: Entercom Communications Corp.; (acq 6-3-97; $27.5 million).
Nat'l Reps: D & R Radio
Arbitron Metro Market: Sacramento, CA; *Format:* Contemporary Hits/Top 40; *No. News Employees:* 1; *Target Audience:* 25-44.
John Geary, Operations Dir
Dan Mason, Station Manager
Butch Mitchell, General Sales Mgr
Dayne Damme, Promotions Manager
Kat Maudru, News Director
Kristin Wong, General Sales Manager

***KEAR-FM**
05-01-1997; 88.1 MHz FM; *Hrs Open:* 24; 8.4 kw vert; 994 ft.; N38 14 50 W121 30 3
Mailing Address: 4135 Northgate Blvd., Suite 1, Sacramento, CA 95834 US
Second Address: 290 Hegenberger Rd., Oakland, CA 94621
(916) 641-8191; *Fax:* (916) 641-8238
www.familyradio.com
info@familyradio.com
License: Sacramento, Sacramento County, CA held by Family Stations Inc.
Group Owner: Family Stations Inc.; Built 1997
Arbitron Metro Market: Sacramento, CA; *Format:* Religious
Tom Evans, General Manager

KFBK
01-01-1922; 1530 kHz AM; *Hrs Open:* 24; 50 kw-D, DA2; 50 kw-N, DA2; N38 50 54 W121 28 58
1545 River Park Dr., Sutie 500, Sacramento, CA 95815 US
(916) 929-5325
www.kfbk.com
news@kfbk.com
License: Sacramento, Sacramento County, CA held by AMFM Broadcasting Licenses LLC.
Group Owner: iHeartMedia; (acq 8-30-2000; grpsl)
Wire Services: PR Newswire
Arbitron Metro Market: Sacramento, CA; *Format:* News, News/Talk, 86; *Hrs. of News Programming:* news progmg 45 hrs wkly; *No. News Employees:* 8
Sara McClure, Senior Vice President of Sales
Bill White, Programming Director
John Nelson, Director of Marketing

KHTK
03-02-1994; 1140 kHz AM; *Hrs Open:* 24; 50 kW; N38 23 34 W121 11 51
5244 Madison Ave., Sacramento, CA 95841 USA
(916) 338-9200; *Fax:* (916) 338-9208
www.khtk.com
License: Sacramento, Sacramento County, CA held by CBS Radio Stations Inc.
Group Owner: CBS Radio; (acq 11-13-98; grpsl)
Nat'l Network: FOX Sports; Westwood One
Arbitron Metro Market: Sacramento, CA *TV Affiliate:* CBS; *Format:* Sports; *Hrs. of News Programming:* News progmg 10 hrs wkly; *Target Audience:* 25-44
Kevin Sherrets, Programming Director

KJAY
05-23-1963; 1430 kHz AM; *Hrs Open:* 6 AM-8 PM; 0.5 kw-D, DAD; 0.02 kw-N, DA2; N38 30 17 W121 33 39
P.O. Box 1384, Carmichael, CA 95609 US
(916) 371-5101,(916) 371-5104; *Fax:* (916) 371-1459
kjay1430am@yahoo.com
License: Sacramento, CA held by KJAY L.L.C.
Arbitron Metro Market: Sacramento, CA; *Format:* Religious; *Target Audience:* 25-64.
Trudi Powell, President
Tiffany Powell, General Manager

KBEB
08-19-1976; 92.5 MHz FM; 50 kw; 449 ft.; N38 42 26 W121 28 33
1545 River Park Dr., Suite 500, Sacramento, CA 95815 US
(916) 929-5325
www.b92fm.com
License: Sacramento, Sacramento County, CA held by AMFM Broadcasting Licenses LLC
Group Owner: iHeartMedia; (acq 3-6-2008; $2.75 million)
Arbitron Metro Market: Sacramento, CA; *Format:* Country
Sara McClure, Senior Vice President of Sales
J.J. Ryan, Programming Director

KNCI
03-16-1994; 105.1 MHz FM; 50 kW; 299 ft.; N38 38 31 W121 5 25
5244 Madison Ave., Sacramento, CA 95841 USA
(916) 338-9200; *Fax:* (916) 338-9208
www.kncifm.com
License: Sacramento, Sacramento County, CA held by CBS Radio Stations Inc.
Group Owner: CBS Radio

Arbitron Metro Market: Sacramento, CA; *Format:* Country

KIID
08-01-1945; 1470 kHz AM
8265 Sierra College Boulevard, Roseville, CA 95661 US
(916) 780-1470
www.radiodisney.com
License: Sacramento, CA held by Radio Disney Group LLC.
Group Owner: ABC Inc.; (acq 12-19-00; $3.31 million).
Nat'l Network: Radio Disney
Arbitron Metro Market: Sacramento, CA; *Format:* Children
Phil Guerini, VP/General Manager
Judy Remy, Station Manager

KRXQ
11-01-1959; 98.5 MHz FM; *Hrs Open:* 24; 50 kw; 495 ft.; N38 38 53 W121 5 51
5345 Madison Avenue, Sacramento, CA 95841 US
(916) 334-7777; *Fax:* (916) 339-4274
www.krxq.net
License: Sacramento, Sacramento County, CA held by Entercom Sacramento License L.L.C.
Group Owner: Entercom Communications Corp.; (acq 7-28-98; grpsl)
Nat'l Reps: McGavren Guild
Arbitron Metro Market: Sacramento, CA; *Format:* Rock/AOR
Special Programming: Blues one hr wkly; *No. News Employees:* 1; *Target Audience:* 25-40; males
Sean Shannon, VP/Marketing Manager
Lance Richard, VP, Sales
Jim Fox, Operations Manager

KSEG
01-01-1959; 96.9 MHz FM; 50 kw; 499 ft.; N38 38 53 W121 28 38
5345 Madison Avenue, Sacramento, CA 95841 US
(916) 334-7777; *Fax:* (916) 339-4559
www.eagle969.com
License: Sacramento, Sacramento County, CA held by Entercom Sacramento License L.L.C.
Group Owner: Entercom Communications Corp.; (acq 1-7-97; $45 million with KRAK(FM) Roseville).
Nat'l Reps: D & R Radio
Arbitron Metro Market: Sacramento, CA; *Format:* Classic Rock; *Target Audience:* 18-49
Jim Fox, Operations Manager
Rich Ripley, General Sales Mgr
Sean Shannon, VP/Marketing Manager

KTKZ
01-01-1952; 1380 kHz AM; 5 kw-U, DA-2; N38 33 19 W121 10 51
1425 River Park Dr., Suite 520, Sacramento, CA 93012
(916) 924-0710; *Fax:* (916) 924-1587
www.ktkz.com
info@ktkz.com
License: Sacramento, Sacramento County, CA held by New Inspiration Broadcasting Co. Inc.
Group Owner: Salem Communications Corp.; (acq 3-11-97; $1.5 million).
Population Served: 1,110,000; *Arbitron Metro Market:* Sacramento, CA; *Target Audience:* 35 plus; general
Steve Gasser, Operations Dir
Dale Hendry, General Manager
Max Miller, Programming Director

KUDL
04-01-1957; 106.5 MHz FM; *Hrs Open:* 24; 50 kw; 410 ft.; N38 38 30 W121 5 25
5345 Masion Avenue, Sacramento, CA 95841 US
(916) 334-7777; *Fax:* (916) 339-4559
www.star1065.com
License: Sacramento, Sacramento County, CA held by Entercom Sacramento License LLC.
Group Owner: Entercom Communications Corp.; (acq 5-19-2003; $25 million).
Arbitron Metro Market: Sacramento, CA; *Format:* Adult Contemp; *Target Audience:* 18-49; new rock, mass appeal
Sean Shannon, VP/Marketing Manager
Butch Mitchell, General Sales Mgr
Lizann Hunt, Promotions Manager

***KXPR**
07-01-1991; 88.9 MHz FM; *Hrs Open:* 24; 50 kw; 492 ft.; N38 16 25 W121 30 11
3416 American River Dr., Suite B, Sacramento, CA 95864 US
(916) 278-8900; *Fax:* (916) 278-8989
www.capradio.org
npr@csus.edu
License: Sacramento, Sacramento County, CA held by California State University, Sacramento.
Nat'l Network: NPR; PRI
Arbitron Metro Market: Sacramento, CA; *Format:* Classical; *Target Audience:* General; NPR Listeners, eg. professionals, educators, administrators
Rick Eytcheson, President/General Manager
Constance Crawford, Director, Marketing/Public Relations
Arla Gibson, Director, Development
Craig Murray, Managing Director
Jun Reina, CFO/COO
Al Gibes, Director of Digital Content
CarlWatanabe, Station Manager
Evan Matsler, Director of Operations
Joe Barr, Director of News/Information
Paul Adams, Manager, Corporate Underwriting

***KXJZ**
10-01-1964; 90.9 MHz FM; *Hrs Open:* 24; 50 kw; 482 ft.; N38 42 38 W121 28 54
3416 American River Dr, Suite B, Sacramento, CA 95864 US
(916) 278-8900; *Fax:* (916) 278-8989
www.capradio.org
npr@csus.edu
License: Sacramento, Sacramento County, CA held by California State University, Sacramento.
Nat'l Network: NPR; PRI; AP Radio
Arbitron Metro Market: Sacramento, CA; *Format:* Jazz, News
Special Programming: World mus 2 hrs, blues 7 hrs wkly.; *Hrs. of News Programming:* news progmg 90 hrs wkly; *No. News Employees:* 5 *Target Audience:* General; NPR listeners,ex. professionals, educators & administrators
Rick Eytcheson, President/General Manager
Constance Crawford, Director, Marketing/Public Relations
Arla Gibson, Director of Development
Carl Watanabe, Station Manager
Craig Murray, Managing Director
Jun Reina, CFO/COO
Al Gibes,Director of Digital Content
Joe Barr, Director, News/Information
Evan Matsler, Director of Operations
Paul Adams, Manager, Corporate Underwriting

***KYDS**
01-24-1979; 91.5 MHz FM; *Hrs Open:* 7 AM-3:30 PM; 0.41 kw; 108 ft.; N38 36 33 W121 21 38
3738 Walnut Avenue, Carmichael, CA 95609 US
(916) 971-7430; *Fax:* (916) 971-7429
www.sanjuan.edu
kyds915station@live.com
License: Sacramento, Sacramento County, CA held by San Juan Unified School District.
Arbitron Metro Market: Sacramento, CA; *Format:* Variety/Diverse
Ed Santillanes, General Manager

KYMX
02-01-1990; 96.1 MHz FM; 50 kW; 486 ft.; N38 38 9 W121 33 11
280 Commerce Circle, Sacramento, CA 95815 USA
(916) 923-6800; *Fax:* (916) 922-2830
www.kymx.com
License: Sacramento, Sacramento County, CA held by CBS Radio Stations Inc.
Group Owner: CBS Radio; (acq 11-13-98; grpsl).
Arbitron Metro Market: Sacramento, CA; *Format:* Adult Contemp; *Hrs. of News Programming:* news progmg 3 hrs wkly; *No. News Employees:* 1; *Target Audience:* 25-54; Women ages 25-54

KZZO
04-28-1997; 100.5 MHz FM; 115 kW; 151 ft.; N38 38 30 W121 5 25
280 Commerce Circle, Sacramento, CA 95825 USA
(916) 923-6800
www.now100fm.com
License: Sacramento, Sacramento County, CA held by CBS Radio Stations Inc.
Group Owner: CBS Radio; (acq 11-13-98; grpsl).
Nat'l Reps: Christal
Arbitron Metro Market: Sacramento, CA; *Format:* Adult Contemp; *Hrs. of News Programming:* news progmg 3 hrs wkly; *No. News Employees:* 1; *Target Audience:* 25-44
Christian Salisbury, General Sales Mgr
Chad Rufer, Programming Director
Chad Skinner, Promotions Manager

Salinas

KDBV
07-17-1963; 980 kHz AM; *Hrs Open:* 24
1436 Auburn Boulevard, Sacramento, CA 95815 US
(805) 406-9157
License: Salinas, CA held by Centro Cristiano Vida Abundante Inc.
Wire Services: Accu-Weather
Arbitron Metro Market: Monterey-Salinas-Santa Cruz, CA; *Format:* Christian; *Target Audience:* 18-49; Hispanics
Ronald Stevens, General Manager

KDON-FM
12-01-1959; 102.5 MHz FM; 15 kw; 2,372 ft.; N36 45 23 W121 30 5
903 N. Main St., Salinas, CA 93906 US
(831) 755-8181; *Fax:* (831) 755-8193
www.kdon.com
License: Salinas, Monterey County, CA held by CC Licenses LLC.
Group Owner: iHeartMedia; (acq 9-22-97; grpsl)
Nat'l Reps: Christal
Arbitron Metro Market: Monterey-Salinas-Santa Cruz, CA; *Format:* Adult Contemp, Urban Contemporary; *No. News Employees:* 1; *Target Audience:* 18-54.
Sam Segovia, Operations Manager/Program Director
Sean Beken, Market President
Maggie Fernandez, Promotions Director
Alyssa Oresco, Digital Content Director

KMZT-FM
03-10-1997; 97.9 MHz FM; *Hrs Open:* 24; 2.9 kw; 479 ft.; N36 40 20 W121 31 28
1437 Auburn Boulevard, Sacramento, CA 95815 US
(831) 649-0969; *Fax:* (831) 649-3335
License: Salinas, Monterey County, CA held by Mount Wilson FM Broadcasters Inc.
Group Owner: Mount Wilson FM Broadcasters Inc.; (acq 12-21-2005; $3 million) .
Arbitron Metro Market: Monterey, CA; *Format:* Contemporary Hits/Top 40; *Target Audience:* 18-34; women
Kathy Baker, General Manager
Sean Stade, General Sales Mgr
Amy Challis, Programming Director
Ron Wharton, Chief Engineer

KRAY-FM
12-05-1977; 103.5 MHz FM; *Hrs Open:* 24; 2.5 kw; 512 ft.; N36 40 20 W121 31 28
Mailing Address: PO Box 1939, Salinas, CA 93902 US
Second Address: 548 E. Alisal St., Salinas, CA 93905
(831) 757-1910; *Fax:* (831) 757-8015
wolfhouseradio@yahoo.es
License: Salinas, Monterey County, CA held by Wolfhouse Radio Group Inc.
Group Owner: Wolfhouse Radio Group Inc.; (acq 7-13-2001; grpsl).
Arbitron Metro Market: Santa Cruz, CA; *Format:* Tejano
Ramon Castro, General Manager

KTGE
07-04-1963; 1570 kHz AM; *Hrs Open:* 24; 5 kw-D, DA2; 0.5 kw-N, DA2; N36 39 38 W121 32 29
Mailing Address: PO Box 1939, Salinas, CA 93902 US
Second Address: 548 E. Alisal St., Salinas, CA 93905
(831) 757-5911; *Fax:* (831) 757-8015
wolfhouseradio@yahoo.es
License: Salinas, CA held by Wolfhouse Radio Group Inc.
Group Owner: Wolfhouse Radio Group Inc.; (acq 7-13-2001; grpsl).
Arbitron Metro Market: Salinas, CA; *Format:* Tejano; *Target Audience:* Adults 24-54.
Ramon Castro, General Manager
Miguel Pelayo, Sales Manager
Vicente Romero, Programming Director
Ron Warren, Chief Engineer

KPRC-FM
09-16-1964; 100.7 MHz FM; 1.4 kw; 2385 ft.; N36 32 5 W121 37 14
903 North Main Street, Salinas, CA 93906 US
(831) 755-8181; *Fax:* (831) 755-8193
License: Salinas, Monterey County, CA held by CC Licenses LLC.
Group Owner: iHeartMedia; (acq 9-22-97; grpsl)
Arbitron Metro Market: Monterey-Salinas-Santa Cruz, CA; *Format:* Spanish
Sam Segovia, Operations Manager/Program Director
Sean Beken, Market President
Maggie Fernandez, Promotions Director
Alyssa Oresco, Digital Content Director

KION
01-01-1947; 1460 kHz AM; *Hrs Open:* 24; 10 kw-D, DA1; 10 kw-N, DA1; N36 43 59 W121 35 32
903 North Main Street, Salinas, CA 93906 US
(831) 755-8181; *Fax:* (831) 755-8193
www.powertalk1460.com
License: Salinas, CA held by CC Licenses LLC.
Group Owner: iHeartMedia

Arbitron Metro Market: Salinas, CA; *Format:* News, News/Talk, 86
Sam Segovia, Operations Manager/Program Director
Sean Beken, Market President
Maggie Fernandez, Promotions Director
Alyssa Oresco, Digital Content Director

San Andreas

*KARQ

01-01-2005; 89.3 MHz FM; *Hrs Open:* 24; 0.45 kw vert; 1926 ft.; N38 7 10 W120 43 27 *Rebroadcasts:* Rebroadcasts KLRD(FM) Yucaipa 100%
1425 N Market Blvd., Suite 9, Sacramento, CA 95834 US
(888) 937-2471; *Fax:* (916) 251-1650
www.air1.com
info@air1.com
License: San Andreas, Tuolumne County, CA held by Educational Media Foundation.
Group Owner: EMF Broadcasting
Nat'l Network: Air 1
Arbitron Metro Market: Ashdown, AR; *Format:* Alternative, Christian; *No. News Employees:* 3; *Target Audience:* 25-44; Judeo Christian, female
Darrell Chambliss, Chairman
Alan Mason, COO
Mike Novak, President and CEO
Ed Lenane, News Director
Sam Wallington, Engineering Dir
David Pierce, Chief Creative Officer

San Ardo

*KNBX

01-21-2001; 91.7 MHz FM; 2.7 kw; 1781 ft.; N35 57 6 W121 0 3 *Rebroadcasts:* Rebroadcasts KCBX(FM) San Luis Obispo 100%
P.O. 423, Santa Cruz, CA 95061 US
(805) 549-8855
www.kcbx.org
License: San Ardo, Monterey County, CA held by KCBX, Inc.
Nat'l Network: NPR; PRI
Arbitron Metro Market: San Ardo, CA; *Format:* Variety/Diverse; *Hrs. of News Programming:* News progmg 44 hrs wkly
Frank Lanzone, General Manager
Marisa Waddell, Programming Director
Ken Schreiner, Chief Engineer
Paul Severtson, Development Director
Neal Losey, Music Director

San Bernardino

KTDD

10-15-1947; 1350 kHz AM; *Hrs Open:* 24; 5 kw-D, DA2; 0.6 kw-N, DA2; N34 5 37 W117 17 57
2030 Iowa Ave., Suite A, Riverside, CA 92507 US
(951) 684-1991; *Fax:* (951) 274-4949
www.foxsportsradio1350.com
License: San Bernardino, San Bernardino County, CA held by Citicasters Licenses Inc.
Group Owner: iHeartMedia; (acq 5-4-99; grpsl).
Nat'l Network: Fox Sports Radio; *Nat'l Reps:* McGavren Guild
Arbitron Metro Market: Riverside-San Bernardino, CA; *Format:* Sports; *Hrs. of News Programming:* News progmg 15 hrs wkly; *Target Audience:* 25-64.
Mark Thomas, General Manager
Rob Scorpio, Regional Senior Vice President of Programming
Elston Butler, Senior Vice President of Sales

KFRG

12-03-1989; 95.1 MHz FM; *Hrs Open:* 24; 50 kW; 236 ft.; N34 11 51 W117 17 10
900 East Washington St., Suite 315, Colton, CA 92324 USA
(909) 433-3000
www.kfrog.com
License: San Bernardino, San Bernardino County, CA held by CBS Radio Stations Inc.
Group Owner: CBS Radio; (acq 11-13-98; grpsl).
Nat'l Reps: McGavren Guild
Arbitron Metro Market: Colton, CA; *Format:* Country; *Hrs. of News Programming:* news progmg 3 hrs wkly; *No. News Employees:* 1; *Target Audience:* 25-54; dual income families
Kimberly Martinez, General Sales Mgr
Lee Douglas, Programming Director
Leslie Bischoff, Promotions Manager

KKDD

01-01-1947; 1290 kHz AM; *Hrs Open:* 24; 5 kw-D, DA2; 5 kw-N, DA2; N34 7 27 W117 14 14
2001 Iowa Avenue, Suite 200, Riverside, CA 92507 US
(951) 684-1991; *Fax:* (951) 274-4911
www.lapreciosa1290.com
License: San Bernardino, CA held by AMFM Broadcasting Licenses LLC.
Group Owner: iHeartMedia; (acq 8-30-2000; grpsl).
Arbitron Metro Market: Riverside-San B; *Format:* Spanish; *Hrs. of News Programming:* news progmg 10 hrs wkly; *No. News Employees:* 1
Mark Thomas, Market President
Elston Butler, Senior Vice President of Sales
Rob Scorpio, Regional Senior Vice President of Programming
KC Morris, Promotions Manager
Rich Mena, Chief Engineer
Jorge Lopez, Online Content Director
Juan Marcos, Sales

KEZY

08-01-1947; 1240 kHz AM; *Hrs Open:* 24; 1 kw-U, ND1; N34 4 55 W117 18 17
4880 Santa Rosa Rd, #300, Camarillo, CA 93012 US
(626) 356-4230; *Fax:* (626) 795-9185
info@enuevavida.com
License: San Bernardino, CA held by Hi-Favor Broadcasting LLC
Group Owner: Hi-Favor Broadcasting LLC; acq 8-27-01; $4 million).
Nat'l Network: USA
Arbitron Metro Market: Riverside-San B; *Format:* Religious; *Hrs. of News Programming:* News progmg 2 hrs wkly; *Target Audience:* 30 plus.
Roland Hinz, President
Sergio Martinez, General Sales Mgr
Mary Guthrie, Programming Director

KOLA

06-15-1959; 99.9 MHz FM; *Hrs Open:* 24; 29.5 kw; 1663 ft.; N33 57 59 W117 17 16
1940 Orange Tree Lane, Suite 200, Redlands, CA 92374 US
(909) 793-3554; *Fax:* (909) 798-6627
www.kolafm.com
License: San Bernardino, San Bernardino County, CA held by Inland Empire Broadcasting Corp.
Group Owner: Anaheim Broadcasting Corp.; (acq 1995; $5 million)
Arbitron Metro Market: Riverside-San Bernardino, CA; *Format:* Oldies; *Hrs. of News Programming:* News progmg one hr wkly; *Target Audience:* 25-54.
Jeff Parke, General Manager
Gary Springfield, Programming Director
Alissa Ochoa, Promotions Director
Curtis Parcell, Sales Manager
Doug Fleniken, Sales Manager
Mylesha Davis, Promotions Coordinator
Irma Blanco, Public ServiceDirector

KTIE

01-01-1929; 590 kHz AM; *Hrs Open:* 24
992 Inland Center Drive, San Bernardino, CA 92408 US
(909) 885-6555 Ext. 101; *Fax:* (909) 383-8889
www.590ktie.com
License: San Bernardino, CA held by Caron Broadcasting Inc.
Group Owner: Salem Communications Corp.; (acq 8-29-2001; $7 million).
Arbitron Metro Market: San Bernardino, CA; *Format:* News, News/Talk, 86; *Target Audience:* 35-54; male /female upscale, educated, home owners, business decision makers
Jim Tinker, Operations Dir
Terry Fahy, General Manager
Brad Anderson, General Sales Mgr
Chuck Tyler, Programming Director
Pamela Tyus, Promotions Manager
Craig Edwards, Programming Director

*KVCR

12-01-1953; 91.9 MHz FM; *Hrs Open:* 24; 3.8 kw; 1621 ft.; N33 57 57 W117 17 5
701 S. Mt. Vernon Ave., San Bernardino, CA 92410 US
(909) 384-4444; *Fax:* (909) 885-2116
www.kvcr.org
License: San Bernardino, San Bernardino County, CA held by San Bernardino Community College Dist.
Nat'l Network: NPR
Arbitron Metro Market: Riverside-San Bernardino, CA *TV Affiliate:* KVCR-TV affil; *Format:* News, Talk; *Hrs. of News Programming:* news progmg 50 hrs wkly; *No. News Employees:* 3; *Target Audience:* General.
Kenn Couch, General Manager
Ken Vincent, Producer

San Clemente

KWVE-FM

11-16-1971; 107.9 MHz FM; *Hrs Open:* 24; 0.53 kw; 3793 ft.; N33 42 40 W117 31 55
3800 South Fairview, Santa Ana, CA 92704 US
(714) 918-6207; *Fax:* (714) 918-6256
www.kwve.com
License: San Clemente, Orange County, CA held by Calvary Chapel of Costa Mesa Inc.
Arbitron Metro Market: Santa Ana, CA; *Format:* Christian, Talk, 74 *Special Programming:* Children 3 hrs wkly; *Hrs. of News Programming:* news progmg 3-5 hrs wkly; *No. News Employees:* 2 *Target Audience:* General.; *Adv. Rates:* 120; 90; 90; 45
Charles Smith, President
Jeffrey Dorman, General Manager

San Diego

KBZT

03-06-1960; 94.9 MHz FM; 26.5 kw; 686 ft.; N32 50 17 W117 14 57
1615 Murray Canyon Road, San Diego, CA 92108 US
(619) 297-9595; *Fax:* (619) 543-1353
License: San Diego, San Diego County, CA held by Entercom Radio
Group Owner: Entercom; (acq 2016)
Arbitron Metro Market: San Diego, CA; *Format:* Alternative; *Target Audience:* 18-49.
Rick Jackson, Senior Vice President/General Manager
Kevin Callahan, Programming Director
Chris Turner, Promotions Manager
Eric Schecter, Chief Engineer
Copeland Isaac, Promotions Manager

KCBQ

01-01-1946; 1170 kHz AM; *Hrs Open:* 24
11521 Innfields Drive, Odessa, FL 33556 US
(858) 535-1210; *Fax:* (858) 535-1212
www.kcbq.com
info@kcbq.com
License: San Diego, CA held by New Inspiration Broadcasting Co. Inc.
Group Owner: Salem Communications Corp.; (acq 8-23-2000; $5 million).
Nat'l Network: AP Radio; ABC
Arbitron Metro Market: San Diego, CA; *Format:* News, News/Talk, 86; *Hrs. of News Programming:* News progmg 5 hrs wkly; *Target Audience:* 35-64; baby boomers that grew up in the 50s & early 60s
Heather Lloyd, Operations Dir
Dave Armstrong, Regional Vice President
Dawn Hockaday, Promotions Manager
Craig Caston, Chief Engineer

KFMB

05-19-1941; 760 kHz AM; *Hrs Open:* 24; 5 kw-D, DAN; 50 kw-N, DAN; N32 50 33 W117 1 30
Mailing Address: 7677 Engineer Road, San Diego, CA 92111 US
Second Address: 7677 Engineer Rd., San Diego, CA 92186
(619) 495-7548, *Fax:* (619) 279-7676
www.760kfmb.com
License: San Diego, CA held by Midwest Television Inc.
Nat'l Network: CBS; *Nat'l Reps:* McGavren Guild
Arbitron Metro Market: San Diego, CA; *Format:* News, News/Talk, 86 *Special Programming:* Financial 8 hrs wkly; *Hrs. of News Programming:* News 125 hrs wkly; *No. News Employees:* 10; *Target Audience:* 25-54.
August Meyer Jr., CEO
Ed Trimble, President
John Marquiss, General Sales Mgr
Dave Sniff, Programming Director
Mike Sommerville, Chief Engineer
Melanie Kartalija, Research Director

KFMB-FM

09-21-1959; 100.7 MHz FM; 30 kw; 620 ft.; N32 50 17 W117 14 57
Mailing Address: 7677 Engineer Road, San Diego, CA 92111 US
Second Address: 7677 Engineer Rd., San Diego, CA 92186
(619) 495-7548, *Fax:* (619) 279-7676
www.sandiegojack.com/
License: San Diego, San Diego County, CA held by Midwest Television Inc.
Arbitron Metro Market: San Diego, CA *TV Affiliate:* KFMB-TV affil.; *Format:* Adult Contemp; *Target Audience:* 18-35
Gina Landau, General Sales Mgr
Dave Sniff, Vice President/Programming Director
Kim Leeds, Promotions Manager

KGB-FM

01-01-1956; 101.5 MHz FM; *Hrs Open:* 24; 50 kw; 499 ft.; N32 43 48 W117 5 3
9660 Granite Ridge Dr., Suite 100, San Diego, CA 92123 US
(858) 292-2000
www.101kgb.com

License: San Diego, San Diego County, CA held by Citicasters Licenses Inc.
Group Owner: iHeartMedia
Arbitron Metro Market: San Diego, CA; *Format:* Classic Rock; *Target Audience:* 25-54.
Melissa Forrest, President/Marketing Manager
Terry King, Sales Manager
Shauna Moran, Programming Director
Bill Lennert, Promotion Director
Jean Arrollado, Marketing Director

KIFM
02-04-1960; 98.1 MHz FM; *Hrs Open:* 24; 26.5 kw; 686 ft.; N32 50 17 W117 14 57
1615 Murray Canyon Road, Suite 710, San Diego, CA 92108 US
(619) 297-3698; *Fax:* (619) 543-1353
www.sunny981sd.com/hd2/smooth-jazz-kifm
License: San Diego, San Diego County, CA held by Entercom Radio
Group Owner: Entercom; (acq 2016)
Nat'l Reps: CBS Radio
Arbitron Metro Market: San Diego, CA; *Format:* Jazz, Smooth Jazz *Special Programming:* Living Better San Diego 5 hrs wkly; *Hrs. of News Programming:* News progmg 2 hrs wkly; *Target Audience:* 25-54; upscale adults
Rick Jackson, General Manager
John D'Angelo, Promotions Manager
Bill Eisenhamer, Chief Engineer
Mike Vasquez, Program Director

KIOZ
01-01-1954; 105.3 MHz FM; *Hrs Open:* 24; 26 kw; 689 ft.; N32 50 20 W117 14 56
9660 Granite Ridge Dr., Suite 100, San Diego, CA 92123 US
(858) 292-2000
www.rock1053.com
License: San Diego, San Diego County, CA held by Citicasters Licenses Inc.
Group Owner: iHeartMedia; (acq 5-4-99; grpsl).
Arbitron Metro Market: San Diego, CA; *Format:* Rock/AOR; *Hrs. of News Programming:* news progmg one hr wkly; *No. News Employees:* 1; *Target Audience:* 18-49; upscale, well educated, young adult rock fans
Melissa Forrest, President/Market Manager
Terry King, Sales Manager
Shauna Moran, Programming Director
Bill Lennert, Promotions Director
Jean Arrollado, Marketing Director

KMYI
01-01-1949; 94.1 MHz FM; *Hrs Open:* 24; 77 kw; 689 ft.; N32 50 20 W117 14 56
9660 Granite Ridge Drive, Suite 100, San Diego, CA 92123 US
(858) 292-2000; *Fax:* (858) 715-3336
www.star941fm.com
License: San Diego, San Diego County, CA held by Citicasters Licenses Inc.
Group Owner: iHeartMedia; (acq 5-4-99; grpsl).
Arbitron Metro Market: San Diego, CA; *Format:* Adult Contemp; *Target Audience:* 35-54; general, women
Melissa Forrest, President/Marketing Manager
Sarah Dobbins, Sales Manager
John Peake, Programming Director
Geoff Alan, Promotion Director
Jean Arrollado, Marketing Director

KLNV
06-26-1960; 106.5 MHz FM; 50 kw; 440 ft.; N32 43 19 W117 4 7
600 W. Broadway, Suite 2150, San Diego, CA 92101 US
(619) 235-0600; *Fax:* (619) 744-4300
www.univision.com
License: San Diego, San Diego County, CA held by Univision Radio License Corp.
Group Owner: Univision Radio; (acq 9-22-2003; grpsl).
Wire Services: UPI
Arbitron Metro Market: San Diego, CA; *Format:* Tejano; *Target Audience:* 18-49; young adult, contemp mus fans, upscale, well-educated; *Adv. Rates:* 250; 250; 250; 125
Sabrina Widmann-Hernandez, Director of Sales
Nate Mendez, Promotions Director
Angel Ramos, Chief Engineer
Leslie Villem-Hamm, Local Sales Manager
Ivan Jurado, Marketing Director
Fernando Perez, Content Director
Mery Lopez-Gallo,Public Affairs Director

KLQV
05-20-1963; 102.9 MHz FM; *Hrs Open:* 24; 30 kw; 632 ft.; N32 50 24 W117 14 52
600 W. Broadway, Suite 2150, San Diego, CA 92101 US
(619) 235-0600; *Fax:* (619) 744-4300
www.univision.com
License: San Diego, San Diego County, CA held by Univision Radio License Corp.
Group Owner: Univision Radio; (acq 9-22-2003; grpsl).
Arbitron Metro Market: San Diego, CA; *Format:* Spanish; *Target Audience:* 25-44.; *Adv. Rates:* 350; 350; 350; 200
Sabrina Widmann-Hernandez, Director of Sales
Nate Mendez, Promotions Director
Angel Ramos, Chief Engineer
Leslie Villem-Hamm, Local Sales Manager
Ivan Jurado, Marketing Director
Fernando Perez, Content Director
Mery Lopez-Gallo,Public Affairs Director

KOGO
01-01-1926; 600 kHz AM; *Hrs Open:* 24
9660 Granite Ridge Dr., Suite 100, San Diego, CA 92123 US
(858) 292-2000; *Fax:* (858) 715-3364
www.kogo.com
License: San Diego, CA held by Citicasters Licenses Inc.
Group Owner: iHeartMedia; (acq 1999; grpsl).
Nat'l Network: Fox News Radio; *Wire Services:* AP
Arbitron Metro Market: San Diego, CA; *Format:* News, News/Talk, 86; *Hrs. of News Programming:* news progmg 22 hrs wkly; *No. News Employees:* 10; *Target Audience:* 25-54; issue oriented talk radio listeners
Melissa Forrest, President/Market Manager
Cassandra Jacob, Sales Manager
Brian Long, Programming Director
Bill Lennert, Promotions Director
Jean Arrollado, Marketing Director

*KPBS-FM
09-12-1960; 89.5 MHz FM; *Hrs Open:* 24; 2.7 kw; 1804 ft.; N32 41 53 W116 56 3
5200 Campanile Drive, Mc 5400, San Diego, CA 92182 US
(619) 594-1515, (619) 594-8100; *Fax:* (619) 594-3812
www.kpbs.org
letters@kpbs.org
License: San Diego, San Diego County, CA held by San Diego State University.
Nat'l Network: PRI; NPR; *Wire Services:* AP
Arbitron Metro Market: San Diego, CA; *Format:* News, News/Talk, 86; *Hrs. of News Programming:* news progmg 11 hrs wkly; *No. News Employees:* 15; *Target Audience:* 35 plus.
Tom Karlo, General Manager
John Decker, Programming Director

KEGY
04-28-1997; 103.7 MHz FM; *Hrs Open:* 24; 26.5 kW; 164 ft.; N32 50 20 W117 14 56
8033 Linda Vista Rd., San Diego, CA 92111 USA
(858) 571-7600; *Fax:* (858) 571-0326
www.energy1037.com
License: San Diego, San Diego County, CA held by CBS Radio Stations Inc.
Group Owner: CBS Radio; (acq 8-7-2000; grpsl)
Nat'l Reps: Christal
Population Served: 300,000; *Arbitron Metro Market:* San Diego, CA; *Format:* Contemporary Hits/Top 40

KLSD
07-14-1922; 1360 kHz AM; 5 kw-D, ND1; 1 kw-N, ND1; N32 43 49 W117 5 1
9660 Granite Ridge Drive, Suite 100, San Diego, CA 91213 US
(858) 292-2000; *Fax:* (858) 715-3372
www.1360sports.com
License: San Diego, CA held by Citicasters Licenses Inc.
Group Owner: iHeartMedia; (acq 1999; grpsl)
Nat'l Reps: CBS Radio
Arbitron Metro Market: San Diego, CA; *Format:* Sports
Melissa Forrest, President/Market Manager
Brian Wilson, Sales Manager
Brian Long, Programming Director
Bill Lennert, Promotions Director
Jean Arrollado, Marketing Director

KSDO
10-01-1947; 1130 kHz AM; *Hrs Open:* 24; 10 kw-D, DA2; 10 kw-N, DA2; N32 51 4 W116 57 51
136 Oak Knoll Avenue, Suite 200, Pasadena, CA 99101 US
(626) 356-4230; *Fax:* (626) 795-9185
www.ksdo.com
info@enuevavida.com
License: San Diego, CA held by Hi-Favor Broadcasting LLC
Group Owner: Hi-Favor Broadcasting LLC; acq 4-1-03; $10 million). .
Nat'l Network: ABC
Arbitron Metro Market: San Diego, CA; *Format:* Religious; *No. News Employees:* 10; *Target Audience:* 25-54.
Sean McCoy, General Manager
Sergio Martinez, General Sales Mgr
Mary Guthrie, Programming Director
Rudy Agus, Chief Engineer

*KSDS
12-01-1951; 88.3 MHz FM; *Hrs Open:* 24; 22 kw vert; Ant 246 ft; N32 48 19 W117 10 09
1313 Park Blvd., San Diego, CA 92108
(619) 388-3037; *Fax:* (619) 388-3928
License: San Diego, San Diego County, CA held by San Diego Community College District.
Nat'l Network: NPR
Population Served: 696,679; *Arbitron Metro Market:* San Diego, CA; *Hrs. of News Programming:* news progmg 7 hrs wkly; *No. News Employees:* 1; *Target Audience:* 25-65 plus; affluent, professional adults
Joseph Kocherhans, Operations Dir
Mark DeBoskey, Station Manager
Ann Bauer, Underwriting Account Manager
Claudia Russell, Programming Director
Natasha Collins, Promotions Manager
Bob Broms, News Director
Mike Rovatsos, WebProducer
Larry Quick, Chief Engineer
April Pendergraft, Membership Director
Joe Kocherhans, Music Director
Chad Fox, Assistant Music Director
Leslie Ebner, Office Manager

KNSN
01-01-1946; 1240 kHz AM; non directional
1615 Murray Canyon Road, Suite 710, San Diego, CA 92108 US
(619) 291-9797
License: San Diego, CA held by Multicultural Radio Broadcasting Licensee, LLC
Group Owner: Multicultural Radio Broadcasting Inc.; (acq 4-3-2006; grpsl)
Arbitron Metro Market: San Diego, CA; *Format:* Chinese
Marcel Gomez, General Manager

KSON
01-15-1964; 97.3 MHz FM; 50 kw; 440 ft.; N32 43 13 W117 4 14
1615 Murray Canyon Road, Suite 710, San Diego, CA 92108 US
(619) 291-9797; *Fax:* (619) 543-1353
www.kson.com
License: San Diego, San Diego County, CA held by Entercom Radio
Group Owner: Entercom; (acq 2016)
Arbitron Metro Market: San Diego, CA; *Format:* Country
Rick Jackson, General Manager
Colleen Davidson, Sales Manager
Kevin Callahan, Programming Director
John D'Angelo, Promotions Director
Eric Schecter, Chief Engineer
Chris Turner, Marketing Director

KURS
11-01-1992; 1040 kHz AM; *Hrs Open:* 24
296 H Street, Suite 300, Chula Vista, CA 91910 US
(619) 426-5645; *Fax:* (619) 425-1000
jc@psnradio.com
License: San Diego, CA held by Quetzal Bilingual Communications Inc.
Wire Services: UPI
Arbitron Metro Market: San Diego, CA; *Format:* Oldies
Jaime Bonilla, President

KYXY
01-01-1960; 96.5 MHz FM; *Hrs Open:* 24; 26.5 kW; 164 ft.; N32 50 20 W117 14 56
8033 Linda Vista Rd., San Diego, CA 92111 USA
(858) 571-7600; *Fax:* (858) 571-0326
www.kyxy.com
License: San Diego, San Diego County, CA held by CBS Radio Stations Inc.
Group Owner: CBS Radio; (acq 8-7-00; grpsl).
Nat'l Reps: Christal
Arbitron Metro Market: San Diego, CA; *Format:* Adult Contemp; *Target Audience:* 25-54; adults, women

San Fernando

KBUA
11-14-1958; 94.3 MHz FM; *Hrs Open:* 24; 6 kw; 85 ft.; N34 17 3 W118 28 17 *Rebroadcasts:* Rebroadcasts KBUE(FM) Long Beach 100%
1845 W. Empire Avenue, Burbank, CA 91504 US
(818) 729-5300; *Fax:* (818) 729-5678
aquisuena.estrellatv.com
License: San Fernando, Los Angeles County, CA held by LBI Radio License Corp.
Group Owner: Liberman Broadcasting Inc.; (acq 1997; $10.8 million)

Arbitron Metro Market: Los Angeles, CA; *Format:* Spanish
Lenard Liberman, President
Pepe Garza Duron, Programming Director

San Francisco

*KALW
03-20-1941; 91.7 MHz FM; *Hrs Open:* 24; 1.9 kw; 919 ft.; N37 45 17 W122 26 44
500 Mansell Street, San Francisco, CA 94134 US
(415) 841-4121; *Fax:* (415) 841-4125
www.kalw.org
kalw@kalw.org
License: San Francisco, San Francisco County, CA held by San Francisco Unified School District.
Nat'l Network: PRI; NPR
Arbitron Metro Market: San Francisco, CA; *Format:* Oldies, Variety/Diverse *Special Programming:* Diversified; *Hrs. of News Programming:* News progmg 68 hrs wkly; *Target Audience:* General; news & info-orientedlisteners
William Helgeson, Operations Dir
Matt Martin, General Manager
Annette Bistrup, Development Director
Holly Kernan, News Director

KCBS
04-01-1909; 740 kHz AM; 50 kW; N38 8 23 W122 31 45
865 Battery St., San Francisco, CA 94111 USA
(415) 765-4000
www.kcbs.com
License: San Francisco, San Francisco County, CA held by CBS Radio East Inc.
Group Owner: CBS Radio; (acq 1996)
Nat'l Network: CBS; *Wire Services:* Reuters; Bay City News Service; U.S. Weather Service
Arbitron Metro Market: San Francisco, CA; *Format:* News; *Target Audience:* 25-54
Brad Bludau, Digital Sales Manager
Kieran Geffert, Sales Manager

KFRC
05-22-2007; 106.9 MHz FM; *Hrs Open:* 24; 80 kW; 102 ft.; N37 51 4 W122 29 50 *Rebroadcasts:* Simulcast with KCBS(AM) San Francisco 100%
865 Battery St., San Francisco, CA 94111 USA
(415) 392-1069
www.kcbs.com
License: San Francisco, San Francisco County, CA held by CBS Radio Stations Inc.
Group Owner: CBS Radio; (acq 12-7-2005; $95 million)
Nat'l Network: CBS Radio; *Nat'l Reps:* CBS Radio
Arbitron Metro Market: San Francisco; *Format:* News; *No. News Employees:* 2
Kieran Geffert, Sales Manager
Brad Bludau, Digital Sales Manager

KEST
01-01-1926; 1450 kHz AM; *Hrs Open:* 24; 1 kw-U, ND1; N37 45 37 W122 22 56
44 Gough St., Suite 301, San Francisco, CA 94103 US
(415) 978-5378; *Fax:* (415) 865-0738
www.kestradio.com
kest1450@sbcglobal.net
License: San Francisco, CA held by Multicultural Radio Broadcasting Licensee LLC.
Group Owner: Multicultural Radio Broadcasting Inc.; (acq 3-31-98; grpsl).
Arbitron Metro Market: San Francisco; *Format:* Talk, Ethnic *Special Programming:* Chinese, Japanese, Indian, gospel, new age; *Hrs. of News Programming:* news progmg 6 hrs wkly; *No. News Employees:* 1 *TargetAudience:* 25 plus.
Arthur Liu, CEO/COO

KFAX
01-01-1925; 1100 kHz AM; *Hrs Open:* 24
4880 Santa Rosa Rd, #300, Camarillo, CA 93012 US
(510) 713-1100; *Fax:* (510) 505-1448
www.kfax.com
margow@salemsf.com
License: San Francisco, CA held by Golden Gate Broadcasting Co. Inc.
Group Owner: Salem Communications Corp.; (acq 9-1-84)
Nat'l Network: Salem Radio Network; *Nat'l Reps:* Salem
Arbitron Metro Market: San Francisco; *Format:* Talk, Religious *Special Programming:* Contemp Christian music 5 hrs weekly, children one hr wkly; *Hrs. of News Programming:* News progmg 4 hrs wkly *Target Audience:* 25-54; females, families, college educated
Greg Edwards, Operations Dir
Mike Shields, General Manager
Brian Rechten, General Sales Mgr
Wanda Cornelius, Promotions Manager
Craig Roberts, Chief Engineer
Margo Wiggins, Business Manager

KFOG
02-04-1960; 104.5 MHz FM; *Hrs Open:* 24; 7.1 kw; 1506 ft.; N37 45 19 W122 27 6
750 Battery St., 3rd Floor, San Francisco, CA 94111 US
(415) 995-6800
www.kfog.com
License: San Francisco, CA held by Radio License Holding SRC, LLC
Group Owner: Cumulus Media Inc.
Arbitron Metro Market: San Francisco, CA; *Format:* Alternative, Oldies
Sheri Nelson, Promotions Manager

KEAR
09-24-1924; 610 kHz AM
290 Hegenberger Road, Oakland, CA 94621-1436 US
(805) 363-5576; *Fax:* (209) 389-0215
www.familyradio.com
info@familyradio.com
License: San Francisco, CA held by Family Stations Inc.
Group Owner: Family Stations Inc.; (acq 4-28-2005; $35 million).
Nat'l Network: Family Radio
Arbitron Metro Market: Banning, CA; *Format:* Christian, Religious; *Target Audience:* General.
Matt Pearce, Operations Dir
Tom Evans, General Manager

KMVQ
05-22-2007; 99.7 MHz FM; 40 kW; 167 ft.; N37 41 15 W122 26 4
865 Battery St., San Francisco, CA 94111 USA
(416) 391-9970
www.997now.com
License: San Francisco, San Francisco County, CA held by CBS Radio KMVQ-FM Inc.
Group Owner: CBS Radio; (acq 1-96; grpsl)
Arbitron Metro Market: San Francisco; *Format:* Contemporary Hits/Top 40
Lindsay High, Sales Manager

KGO
01-01-1924; 810 kHz AM; 50 kw-U, DA1; N37 31 35 W122 6 2
750 Battery St., 2nd Floor, San Francisco, CA 94111 US
(415) 808-0810
www.kgoradio.com
producers@kgoradio.com
License: San Francisco, CA held by Radio License Holdings LLC
Group Owner: Cumulus Media Inc.; (acq 6-12-2007; grpsl).
Arbitron Metro Market: San Francisco, CA; *Format:* News/Talk; *Target Audience:* 25-54; general
Sheri Nelson, Promotions Manager

KIOI
10-27-1957; 101.3 MHz FM; *Hrs Open:* 24; 125 kw; 1161 ft.; N37 41 24 W122 26 13
340 Townsend St., Suite 5-101, San Francisco, CA 94107 US
(415) 975-5555; *Fax:* (415) 538-5953
www.1013.com
License: San Francisco, San Francisco County, CA held by AMFM Broadcasting Licenses LLC.
Group Owner: iHeartMedia; (acq 8-30-2000; grpsl).
Nat'l Reps: Christal
Arbitron Metro Market: San Francisco, CA; *Format:* Adult Contemp; *Hrs. of News Programming:* news progmg one hr wkly; *No. News Employees:* 1; *Target Audience:* 25-54.
Mark Adams, Programming Director
Val Klein, Promotions Manager

KIQI
01-01-1957; 1010 kHz AM; *Hrs Open:* 24; 10 kw-D, DA2; 0.5 kw-N, DA2; N37 49 33 W122 18 39
44 Gough St., Suite 301, San Francisco, CA 94103 US
(415) 978-5378
www.kiqi1010am.com
License: San Francisco, CA held by Multicultural Radio Broadcasting Licensee LLC.
Group Owner: Multicultural Radio Broadcasting Inc.; (acq 2-4-2004; grpsl).
Arbitron Metro Market: San Francisco; *Format:* Spanish; *No. News Employees:* 3; *Target Audience:* 24-54.
Arthur Liu, CEO/COO

KISQ
07-17-1958; 98.1 MHz FM; *Hrs Open:* 8 AM-5:30 PM; 75 kw; 1,016 ft.; N37 51 4 W122 29 50
340 Townsend St., Suite 5101, San Francisco, CA 94107 US
(415) 975-5555
www.981kissfm.com
License: San Francisco, San Francisco County, CA held by AMFM Broadcasting Licenses LLC.
Group Owner: iHeartMedia; (acq 8-30-2000; grpsl).
Nat'l Reps: McGavren Guild
Arbitron Metro Market: San Francisco, CA; *Format:* Oldies
Special Programming: Gospel 3 hrs wkly; *Target Audience:* 25-54; women
Kathryn Wilcox, Market President
Cheryle Hangartner, Sales Manager
Ricci Filiar, Programming Director
Ramona Gutierrez, Promotions Director

KITS
02-07-1983; 105.3 MHz FM; 15 kW; 187 ft.; N37 41 20 W122 26 7
865 Battery St., San Francisco, CA 94111 USA
(415) 478-5483
www.live105.com
License: San Francisco, San Francisco County, CA held by CBS Radio East Inc.
Group Owner: CBS Radio; (acq 5-7-97).
Arbitron Metro Market: San Francisco; *Format:* Alternative
Karl Isotalo, General Sales Mgr

KLLC
07-01-1996; 97.3 MHz FM; *Hrs Open:* 24; 82 kW; 92 ft.; N37 51 3 W122 29 51
865 Battery St., San Francisco, CA 94111 USA
www.radioalice.com
License: San Francisco, San Francisco County, CA held by CBS Radio East Inc.
Group Owner: CBS Radio
Nat'l Reps: CBS Radio
Arbitron Metro Market: San Francisco, CA; *Format:* Adult Contemp; *Target Audience:* 18-54
Lindsay High, Sales Manager

KMEL
11-30-1960; 106.1 MHz FM; *Hrs Open:* 24; 69 kw; 1289 ft.; N37 41 24 W122 26 13
433 E. Las Colinas Blvd, Suite 1130, Irving, TX 75039 US
(415) 356-5500; *Fax:* (415) 975-5573
www.kmel.com
License: San Francisco, San Francisco County, CA held by AMFM Broadcasting Licenses LLC.
Group Owner: iHeartMedia; (acq 8-30-2000; grpsl).
Nat'l Reps: Christal
Arbitron Metro Market: San Francisco, CA; *Format:* Urban Contemporary
Kathryn Wilcox, Market President
Don Parker, Vice President/Programming
Cheryle Hangartner, Director of Sales

KNBR
01-01-1922; 680 kHz AM; *Hrs Open:* 24; 50 kw-U, ND1; N37 32 50 W122 14 2
750 Battery St., 3rd Floor, San Francisco, CA 94111 US
(415) 995-6800; *Fax:* (415) 995-6867
www.knbr.com
License: San Francisco, CA held by Radio License Holding SRC, LLC
Group Owner: Cumulus Media Inc.; (acq 5-24-89; $17.5 million;)
Nat'l Network: ABC; Westwood One
Arbitron Metro Market: San Francisco, CA; *Format:* Sports, Talk; *Target Audience:* 18 plus; predominently men
Lee Hammer, Operations Dir
David Drutz, VP, Sales
Lee Hammer, Programming Director
Judi Ratto, General Sales Manager
Sheri Nelson, Judi Ratto
Daniel Erman, Sales Manager

KSFB
01-01-1926; 1260 kHz AM
P.O. Box 1160, Salt Lake City, UT 84110 US
(916) 535-0500; *Fax:* (916) 535-0504
www.ihradio.org
info@ihradio.org
License: San Francisco, CA held by IHR Educational Broadcasting.
Group Owner: IHR Educational Broadcasting; (acq 7-16-2007; $14 million)
Nat'l Network: EWTN Radio
Arbitron Metro Market: San Francisco; *Format:* Christian
Douglas Sherman, President
Lori Brown, General Manager

KOIT
01-01-1959; 96.5 MHz FM; 24 kw; 1575 ft.; N37 45 19 W122 27 6
201 3rd Street, Suite 1200, San Francisco, CA 94103 US

(415) 777-0965; *Fax:* (415) 896-0965
www.koit.com
License: San Francisco, San Francisco County, CA held by Entercom San Francisco License LLC.
Group Owner: Entercom Communications Corp.; (acq 3-14-2008; grpsl)
Arbitron Metro Market: San Francisco; *Format:* Adult Contemp; *Target Audience:* 25-54; upscale adults who earn an average of $30,000
Dwight Walker, General Manager
Steve DiNardo, General Sales Mgr
Andy Holt, Programming Director
Stacy Cunningham, Promotions Manager
Cheryl Hendrickson, Traffic Manager

***KPOO**
04-01-1971; 89.5 MHz FM; 0.27 kw horiz; 541 ft.; N37 47 33 W122 24 52
Mailing Address: P.O. Box 11008, San Francisco, CA 94101 US
Second Address: 1329 Divisadero St., San Francisco, CA 94142
(415) 346-5373; *Fax:* (415) 346-5173
www.kpoo.com
info@kpoo.com
License: San Francisco, San Francisco County, CA held by Poor Peoples' Radio Inc.
Arbitron Metro Market: San Francisco Bay Area; *Format:* Variety/Diverse
Terry Collins, President
Marilyn Fowler, Operations Dir
Jerome Parsons, General Manager
Harrison Chastang, News Director
Dave Billicci, Chief Engineer

***KQED-FM**
06-01-1969; 88.5 MHz FM; *Hrs Open:* 24; 110 kw; 1270 ft.; N37 41 23 W122 26 13
2601 Mariposa Street, San Francisco, CA 94110 US
(415) 553-2129; *Fax:* (415) 553-2241
www.kqed.org
fm@kqed.org
License: San Francisco, San Francisco County, CA held by KQED Inc.
Nat'l Network: NPR; PRI; *Wire Services:* Bay City News Service
Arbitron Metro Market: San Francisco-Oakland-San Jose-Sacramento *TV Affiliate:* KQED(TV) affil.; *Hrs. of News Programming:* news progmg 160 hrs wkly; *No. News Employees:* 9; *Target Audience:* General.
John Boland, President
Kevin E. Martin, SVP/COO
Traci Eckels, Chief Development Officer
David Shimada, Director of Corporate Support/General Sales Mngr.

KSFO
08-01-1925; 560 kHz AM; 5 kw; N37 44 44 W122 22 40
750 Battery St, 3rd Floor, San Francisco, CA 94105 US
(415) 808-5600
www.ksfo.com
License: San Francisco, CA held by Radio License Holdings LLC
Group Owner: Cumulus Media Inc.; (acq 6-12-2007; grpsl)
Arbitron Metro Market: San Francisco; *Format:* News/Talk; *Target Audience:* 25-54.
Melissa Galliani, General Sales Mgr
Jack Swanson, Programming Director

KSOL
12-10-1959; 98.9 MHz FM; *Hrs Open:* 24; 6.1 kw; 1,342 ft.; N37 45 19 W122 27 6
750 Battery St., Suite 200, San Francisco, CA 94111 US
(415) 989-5765
www.univision.com
License: San Francisco, San Francisco County, CA held by TMS License California Inc.
Group Owner: Univision Radio; (acq 9-22-2003; grpsl).
Arbitron Metro Market: San Francisco, CA; *Format:* Spanish, Tejano; *No. News Employees:* 1; *Target Audience:* 18-54.
Jose Luis Gonzalez, Operations Manager
Raul Rodriguez, Vice President and General Manager
Luz Maria Rodriguez, Marketing Director

KTCT
01-01-1948; 1050 kHz AM; *Hrs Open:* 24; 50 kw-D, 10 kw-N,; N37 39 2 W122 9 2
750 Battery St., 3rd Floor, San Francisco, CA 94111 US
(415) 995-6800; *Fax:* (415) 995-6867
www.knbr.com
License: San Francisco, CA held by Radio License Holding SRC, LLC
Group Owner: Cumulus Media Partners LLC; (acq 7-21-97; $15 million)
Nat'l Network: Westwood One
Arbitron Metro Market: San Francisco, CA; *Format:* Sports, Talk; *Target Audience:* 25-54.
Lee Hammer, Operations Dir
David Drutz, VP, Sales
Lee Hammer, Programming Director

KTRB
06-18-1933; 860 kHz AM
1192 Norwegian Avenue, Modesto, CA 95350 US
(415) 362-8686; *Fax:* (415) 391-6860
License: San Francisco, CA
Group Owner: Comerica Bank TRB Trust; (acq 3-30-2000)
Nat'l Network: Fox Sports; Sporting News Radio Network; *Nat'l Reps:* McGavren Guild
Arbitron Metro Market: San Francisco; *Format:* Sports *Special Programming:* Oakland A's, Stanford Football and Men's Basketball; *Target Audience:* Men: 25-54.
Michael Sher, Vice President/General Manager
Jack Chunn, General Sales Mgr
John Burger, Chief Engineer

KZDG
01-01-1947; 1550 kHz AM; *Hrs Open:* 24; 10 kw-U, DA-2
40931 Fremont Boulevard, Fremont, CA 94538
(510) 371-9999
www.radiozindagi.com
License: San Francisco, San Francisco County, CA held by CBS Radio East Inc. dba Radio Zindagi
Group Owner: CBS Radio; (acq 12-14-2000; grpsl)
Population Served: 715,674; *Arbitron Metro Market:* San Francisco; *Format:* Ethnic; *Target Audience:* 12 plus; affluent, home-owning, highly educated, business professionals
Sehba Shah, Director, Sales & Marketing

KRZZ
02-01-1959; 93.3 MHz FM; *Hrs Open:* 24; 6 kw; 1362 ft.; N37 41 13 W122 26 3
1420 Koll Circle, San Jose, CA 95112 US
(408) 546-4000; *Fax:* (408) 546-4041
www.yosoyraza.com
License: San Francisco, San Francisco County, CA held by KRZZ Licensing LLC.
Group Owner: Spanish Broadcasting System Inc.; (acq 12-7-2004).
Arbitron Metro Market: San Francisco; *Target Audience:* 18-49; Hispanics
Eric Osuna, VP/General Manager
Elena Jovel, Programming Director
George Anne Garcia Arana, Local Sales Manager
Sandra Gutierrez, Director, Promotions & Advertising
Jose Jimenez, Director, Production/Public Relations

KYLD
03-12-1958; 94.9 MHz FM; 30 kw; 1211 ft.; N37 41 22 W122 26 10
340 Townsend St., Suite 5101, San Francisco, CA 94107 US
(415) 541-5555; *Fax:* (415) 541-3087
www.wild949.com
License: San Francisco, San Francisco County, CA held by AMFM Broadcasting Licenses LLC.
Group Owner: iHeartMedia; (acq 8-30-2000; grpsl).
Arbitron Metro Market: San Francisco, CA; *Format:* Contemporary Hits/Top 40; *Target Audience:* 25-54.
Don Parker, Senior Vice President of Programming
Kathryn Wilcox, Market President
John Leathers, Sales Manager
Mark Adams, Programming Director

KGMZ(FM)
01-01-1959; 95.7 MHz FM; *Hrs Open:* 24; 6.9 kw; Ant 1,500 ft; N37 41 23 W122 26 12
201 Third St., Suite 1200, San Francisco, CA 94103-3143
(415) 957-0957; *Fax:* (415) 356-8394
www.957thegame.com/
thegame@957thegame.com
License: San Francisco, San Francisco County, CA held by Entercom San Francisco License LLC.
Group Owner: Entercom Communications Corp.; (acq 3-14-2008; grpsl)
Population Served: 812,846; *Arbitron Metro Market:* San Francisco,CA; *Format:* Sports; *Target Audience:* 25-54.
Stacy Cunningham, Operations Manager
Steve DiNardo, VP/Marketing Manager
Joe Cariffe, General Sales Mgr
Jason Barrett, Programming Director
Josh Pearlman, Promotions Manager
Shingo Kamada, Chief Engineer
Tony Cafarelli,Promotions Director

KOSF
11-03-1947; 103.7 MHz FM; 6.4 kw; 1,322 ft.; N37 41 17 W122 26 7
340 Townsend St., 4th Floor, San Francisco, CA 94107 US
(415) 975-5555; *Fax:* (415) 538-5953
www.big1037.com
License: San Francisco, San Francisco County, CA held by AMFM Broadcasting Licenses LLC.
Group Owner: iHeartMedia
Arbitron Metro Market: San Francisco, CA; *Format:* Oldies
Kathryn Wilcox, Market President
Val Klein, Promotions Manager

San Gabriel

KMRB
01-01-1942; 1430 kHz AM; *Hrs Open:* 24
747 E. Green St., Suite 208, Pasadena, CA 91101 US
(626) 773-1430; *Fax:* (626) 792-8890
www.am1430.net
am1430.net@gmail.com
License: San Gabriel, CA held by Multicultural Radio Broadcasting Licensee, LLC
Group Owner: Multicultural Broadcasting; (acq 1994).
Arbitron Metro Market: Los Angeles, CA; *Format:* Chinese *Special Programming:* Thai 2 hrs, Ethiopian 2 hrs wkly; *Target Audience:* General.
Arthur Liu, CEO/COO

San Jacinto

KRQB
08-01-2007; 96.1 MHz FM; *Hrs Open:* 24; 1.4 kw; 686 ft.; N34 2 13 W116 58 7
1845 Business Center Dr, Suite 106, San Bernardino, CA 92408 US
(909) 663-1961; *Fax:* (909) 663-1996
quebuena961.estrellatv.com
advertising@quebuena961.com
License: San Jacinto, Riverside West Inner County, CA held by LBI Radio License LLC.
Group Owner: Liberman Broadcasting Inc.; (acq 9-6-2007; $25 million)
Arbitron Metro Market: Riverside-San Bernardino, CA; *Format:* Spanish; *Adv. Rates:* 47; 47; 47; na
Jose Liberman, President
Winter Horton, Chief Operating Officer
Eduardo Leon, Vice President, Programming

San Joaquin

KJZN
01-01-1999; 105.5 MHz FM; *Hrs Open:* 24; 25 kw; 328 ft.; N36 36 28 W119 59 49
1066 East Shaw Avenue, Fresno, CA 93710 US
(559) 230-0104; *Fax:* (559) 230-0177
License: San Joaquin, Fresno County, CA held by Wilks License Co.-Fresno LLC.
Group Owner: Wilks Broadcast Group LLC; (acq 6-1-2005; grpsl)
Nat'l Reps: McGavren Guild
Arbitron Metro Market: Fresno, CA; *Format:* Talk; *Target Audience:* Adults 25-54.; *Adv. Rates:* 40; 40; 40; 10
Jeff Wilks, CEO
Mark Frank, VP, National Sales
Jeff Sanders, EVP, Programming
Jeff Bray, VP/Market Manager

San Jose

KBRG
03-04-1963; 100.3 MHz FM; *Hrs Open:* 24; 14.5 kw; 2,579 ft.; N37 6 40 W121 50 34
750 Battery St., Suite 200, San Francisco, CA 94111 US
(415) 989-5765
www.univision.com
License: San Jose, Santa Clara County, CA held by Univision Radio License Corp.
Group Owner: Univision Radio; (acq 1-1-2006; $90 million with KLOK(AM) San Jose).
Arbitron Metro Market: San Francisco, CA; *Format:* Adult Contemp, Spanish
Raul Rodriguez, Vice President and General Manager
Luz Maria Rodriguez, Marketing Director

KEZR
07-03-1967; 106.5 MHz FM; 42 kw; 535 ft.; N37 12 32 W121 46 27
190 Park Center Plaza, Suite 200, San Jose, CA 95113 US
(408) 287-5775; *Fax:* (408) 293-3341
www.mymix1065.com
License: San Jose, Santa Clara County, CA held by Digity Digity LLC
Group Owner: Digity Digity LLC; (acq 12-6-2005; $80 million with KBAY(FM) Gilroy)
Nat'l Reps: Christal

RADIO - U.S.

Arbitron Metro Market: San Jose, CA; *Format:* Adult Contemp; *Hrs. of News Programming:* news progmg 4 hrs wkly; *No. News Employees:* 1; *Target Audience:* 25-44.; *Adv. Rates:* 300; 300; 300; 100
Dean Goodman, CEO
Sam Van Zandt, Public Affairs Director
Judy Dixon, General Sales Mgr
Dana Jang, Programming Director
Layna Thom, Promotions Coordinator

*KMTG
05-17-1977; 89.3 MHz FM; 0.3 kw; -312 ft.; N37 12 6 W121 51 42
Mailing Address: 6677 Camden Avenue, San Jose, CA 95120 US
Second Address: 855 Linden Ave., San Jose, CA 95126
(408) 535-6310; *Fax:* (408) 535-2357
www.pioneerhigh.org
steve_dini@sjusd.org
License: San Jose, Santa Clara County, CA held by San Jose Unified School District.
Arbitron Metro Market: San Francisco, CA; *Format:* Variety/Diverse
Steve Dini, General Manager

KLIV
01-01-1946; 1590 kHz AM; *Hrs Open:* 24; 5 kw-D, DAN; 5 kw-N, DAN; N37 19 45 W121 51 23
750 Story Road, San Jose, CA 95122 US
(408) 293-8030; *Fax:* (408) 293-6124
www.kliv.com
License: San Jose, CA held by Empire Broadcasting Corp.
Group Owner: Empire Broadcasting Corp.; acq 7-1-67)
Nat'l Network: CNN Radio; *Nat'l Reps:* Christal; *Wire Services:* AP; Bay City News Service
Arbitron Metro Market: San Jose, CA; *Format:* News *Special Programming:* San Jose soccer earthquakes; *No. News Employees:* 8; *Target Audience:* General.; *Adv. Rates:* 75; 65; 65; 20
Robert Kieve, President
Mike Anthony, General Manager
Tina Ferguson, General Sales Mgr
George Sampson, Programming Director
George Sampson, News Director
Shawn Murphy, Sports Director

KLOK
10-19-1946; 1170 kHz AM; *Hrs Open:* 24
Mailing Address: 2905 South King Road, San Jose, CA 95122 US
Second Address: 2905 South King Rd., San Jose, CA 95122
(408) 440-0851; *Fax:* (408) 440-0853
www.klok1170am.com
klok1170am@aol.com
License: San Jose, CA held by Principle Bay Area Holding Co., LLC
Group Owner: Universal Media Access
Arbitron Metro Market: San Francisco, CA; *Format:* Ethnic; *Target Audience:* 18-49.
Brad Behnke, General Manager

KSJO
12-01-1946; 92.3 MHz FM; 32 kw; 446 ft.; N37 12 32 W121 46 27
55 Hawthorne Street, Suite 1000, San Francisco, CA 94105 US
(408) 453-5400; *Fax:* (408) 452-1330
License: San Jose, Santa Clara County, CA held by Clear Channel
Nat'l Reps: McGavren Guild
Arbitron Metro Market: San Jose, CA; *Format:* Alternative; *Target Audience:* 18-49; active adults
Jaysson Reno, General Sales Mgr

*KSJS
02-22-1963; 90.5 MHz FM; *Hrs Open:* 24; 1.5 kw; 472 ft.; N37 12 33 W121 46 30
1 Washington Square, Theatre Arts Dept, San Jose, CA 95192 US
(408) 924-5757(408) 924-4545; *Fax:* (408) 924-4558
www.ksjs.org
ksjs@ksjs.org
License: San Jose, Santa Clara County, CA held by San Jose State University.
Arbitron Metro Market: San Jose, CA; *Format:* Variety/Diverse; *Target Audience:* 18-34; students & community members
Nick Martinez, General Manager
Mike Adams, General Sales Mgr
Vincente Heredia, Programming Director

KSJX
06-24-1948; 1500 kHz AM; *Hrs Open:* 24; 10 kw-D, DA2; 5 kw-N, DA2; N37 21 28 W121 52 17
27 William St., 11th Floor, New York, NY 10005 US
(212) 966-1059; *Fax:* (212) 625-2894
www.mrbi.net
License: San Jose, CA held by Multicultural Radio Broadcasting Licensee LLC.
Group Owner: Multicultural Radio Broadcasting Inc.; (acq 2-20-98; grpsl).
Arbitron Metro Market: San Jose, CA; *Format:* Vietnamese *Special Programming:* Mandarin Chinese 10 hrs, Vietnamese; *No. News Employees:* 2; *Target Audience:* 25-54; managerial, professional, homeowners *Adv.Rates:* 80; 80; 80; 65
Arthur Liu, CEO/COO

KUFX
07-01-1959; 98.5 MHz FM; *Hrs Open:* 24; 10 kw; 879 ft.; N37 12 17 W121 56 56
201 Third Street, Suite 1200, San Francisco, CA 94103 US
(408) 200-9850; *Fax:* (408) 452-1330
www.kfox.com
License: San Jose, Santa Clara County, CA held by Entercom Communications
Nat'l Reps: CBS Radio
Arbitron Metro Market: San Jose, CA; *Format:* Classic Rock; *Target Audience:* 18-49; general
Steve DiNardo, VP/Market Manager
Chris Hoffman, Programming Director
Tony Cafarelli, National Sales Manager

KZSF
06-21-1947; 1370 kHz AM; *Hrs Open:* 24; 5 kw-U, DA1; N37 21 28 W121 52 17
2347 Bering Drive, San Jose, CA 95131 US
(408) 546-7201; *Fax:* (408) 247-4353
www.1370am.com
info@1370am.com
License: San Jose, CA held by Carlos A. Duharte
Regional Reps: Interep
Arbitron Metro Market: San Jose, CA; *Format:* Tejano; *Target Audience:* 18-49.; *Adv. Rates:* 150; 75; 75; 60
Carlos Duharte, CEO
Reyna Santillan, Promotions Manager

San Luis Obispo

*KCBX
07-25-1975; 90.1 MHz FM; *Hrs Open:* 24; 5.3 kw; 1421 ft.; N35 21 37 W120 39 17 *Rebroadcasts:* Rebroadcasts KSBX(FM) Santa Barbara 100%
4100 Vachell Lane, San Luis Obispo, CA 93401 US
(805) 549-8855; *Fax:* (805) 781-3025
www.kcbx.org
901kcbx@kcbx.org
License: San Luis Obispo, San Luis Obispo County, CA held by KCBX Inc.
Nat'l Network: NPR
Arbitron Metro Market: San Luis Obispo, CA; *Format:* Jazz, News *Special Programming:* Folk 15 hrs wkly; *Hrs. of News Programming:* News progmg 32 hrs wkly; *Target Audience:* General.
Frank Lanzone, President/General Manager
Hank Hadley, Operations Dir
Paul Severtson, General Sales Mgr
Guy Rathbun, Programming Director
Randal White, News Director
Paul Severtson, Development Director
Katherine Johnson, CFO
Greg Perry, Online Broadcast Manager

*KCPR
01-01-1968; 91.3 MHz FM; *Hrs Open:* 24; 0.31 kw; 1417 ft.; N35 21 38 W120 39 21
Building 26, Room 301, California Polytechnic State University, 1 Grand Avenue, San Luis Obispo, CA 93401 US
(805) 756-5998
www.kcpr.org
kcpr.internet@gmail.com
License: San Luis Obispo, San Luis Obispo County, CA held by California Polytechnic State University.
Arbitron Metro Market: San Luis Obispo, CA; *Format:* Variety/Diverse *Special Programming:* Sp 3 hrs, metal 3 hrs, blues 3 hrs; *Hrs. of News Programming:* News progmg 4 hrs wkly; *Target Audience:* General; Cal Polystudents, San Luis Obispo community
Tyler Deitz, General Manager
Kelly Stewart, Programming Director
Eric Buckthal, Music Director
Nick Cocores, Music Director
Bobak Beheshti, Music Director
Eli Becker, Webmaster

KYNS
12-13-1949; 1340 kHz AM; *Hrs Open:* 24
795 Buckley Rd., Suite 2, San Luis Obispo, CA 93401 US
(805) 786-2570
www.alt937.com
eric.fahnoe@dimescentralcoast.com
License: San Luis Obispo, CA held by Dimes Media Corporation
Group Owner: Dimes Media Corporation
Arbitron Metro Market: San Luis Obispo, CA; *Format:* Alternative, News, 62, Talk
Eric Fahnoe, Promotions Manager

KJDJ
02-08-1988; 1030 kHz AM; 2.5 kw-D, ND1; 0.7 kw-N, ND1; N35 17 58 W120 40 24
604 East Chapel Street, Santa Maria, CA 93454 US
(805) 928-1030
www.radiovidaabundante.com
oracion@radiovidaabundante.com
License: San Luis Obispo, CA held by Padre Serra Communications Inc.
Arbitron Metro Market: San Luis Obispo, CA; *Format:* Religious
Manuel Salvador, General Manager
Manny Aram, Programming Director

KKJG
01-01-1984; 98.1 MHz FM; 4.5 kw; 1519 ft.; N35 21 40 W120 39 21
3620 Sacramento Dr, Suite 204, San Luis Obispo, CA 93401 US
(805) 781-2750; *Fax:* (805) 781-2758
www.jugcountry.com
License: San Luis Obispo, San Luis Obispo County, CA held by AGM California, Inc.
Group Owner: American General Media; (acq 7-1-97; $1.5 million).
Arbitron Metro Market: San Luis Obispo, CA; *Format:* Country; *Target Audience:* Adults 25-54.
Kathy Signorelli, General Manager

KKJL
02-06-1960; 1400 kHz AM; *Hrs Open:* 24; 1 kw-U, ND1; N35 15 51 W120 39 56
Mailing Address: P.O. Box 1400, San Luis Obispo, CA 93406 US
Second Address: 51 Zaca Ln., Suite 90, San Luis Obispo, CA 93401
(805) 543-9400; *Fax:* (805) 543-0787
www.kkjl1400.com
info@kkjl1400.com
License: San Luis Obispo, CA held by Pacific Coast Media, LLC
Nat'l Network: CNN Radio
Arbitron Metro Market: San Luis Obispo, CA; *Format:* Sports, Adult Contemp *Special Programming:* SF Giants, SF 49ers, LA Lakers; *Target Audience:* 35 plus; adults males & females; *Adv. Rates:* 22; 22; 22; 16
Guy Hackman, President/General Manager
Kyle Ronemus, Operations Director/Vice President
Carol Mertes, Operations Manager
Greg Russo, Webmaster

*KLFF
09-26-1995; 89.3 MHz FM; *Hrs Open:* 24; 4.4 kw; 1529 ft.; N35 21 37 W120 39 17
P.O. Box 1561, San Luis Obispo, CA 93406 US
(805) 541-4343; *Fax:* (805) 541-9101
www.klife.org
info@klife.org
License: San Luis Obispo, San Luis Obispo County, CA held by Logos Broadcasting Corp.
Nat'l Network: Salem Radio Network
Arbitron Metro Market: San Luis Obispo, CA; *Format:* Christian; *Target Audience:* 18-34; Christians; *Adv. Rates:* 15; 15; 15; 15
Dr. Daniel Woods, CFO
Dan Lemburg, President
Jon Fugler, General Manager
Noonie Fugler, Promotions Manager

*KLVH
03-25-1999; 88.5 MHz FM; *Hrs Open:* 24; 2.8 kw; 1493 ft.; N35 21 37 W120 39 20
1425 N. Market Blvd., Suite 9, Sacramento, CA 95839 US
(707) 528-9236; *Fax:* (707) 528-9246
www.klove.com
klove@klove.com
License: San Luis Obispo, San Luis Obispo County, CA held by Educational Media Foundation.
Group Owner: EMF Broadcasting; (acq 5-12-99).
Nat'l Network: K-Love
Arbitron Metro Market: San Luis Obispo, CA; *Format:* Christian; *No. News Employees:* 3; *Target Audience:* 25-44; Judeo Christian, female
Darell Chambliss, Chairman
Mike Novak, President
Fernando Chaidez, General Sales Mgr

David Pierce, Programming Director
Ed Lenane, News Director
Sam Wallington, Engineering Dir

KSLY-FM
12-01-1959; 96.1 MHz FM; 3.6 kw; 1647 ft.; N35 21 37 W120 39 18
2215 Skyway Drive, Santa Maria, CA 93455 US
(805) 545-0101; *Fax:* (805) 541-5303
www.ksly.com
info@ksly.com
License: San Luis Obispo, San Luis Obispo County, CA held by EDB SLO License LLC.
Group Owner: Frontier Radio Management Inc.; (acq 11-30-2007; grpsl)
Arbitron Metro Market: San Luis Obispo, CA; *Format:* Country
Dave Daniels, Operations/Programming Director
Kathy Mansell, General Sales Mgr
Ron Roy, Regional Vice President

KVEC
05-01-1937; 920 kHz AM; *Hrs Open:* 24; 1 kw-D, ND2; 0.5 kw-N, ND2; N35 17 58 W120 40 24
3620 Sacramento Dr, Suite 204, San Luis Obispo, CA 93401 US
(805) 781-2750
www.920kvec.com
License: San Luis Obispo, San Luis Obispo County, CA held by AGM California, Inc.
Group Owner: American General Media
Nat'l Network: ABC; Fox News Radio; APNET; WWO
Arbitron Metro Market: San Luis Obispo, CA; *Format:* News, News/Talk, 86 *Special Programming:* Dodgers baseball, NFL/NCAA football, finance, senior focus, health, real estate; *Hrs. of News Programming:* news progmg 45hrs wkly; *No. News Employees:* 4; *Target Audience:* Adults 35+; *Adv. Rates:* 19; 17; 19; 17
Kathy Signorelli, General Manager

KZOZ
01-01-1962; 93.3 MHz FM; 23 kw; 1549 ft.; N35 21 40 W120 39 21
3620 Sacramento Dr, Suite 204, San Luis Obispo, CA 93401 US
(805) 781-2750; *Fax:* (805) 781-2758
www.kzoz.com
License: San Luis Obispo, San Luis Obispo County, CA held by AGM California, Inc.
Group Owner: American General Media; (acq 6-89; grpsl).
Arbitron Metro Market: San Luis Obispo, CA; *Format:* Classic Rock, Rock/AOR; *Target Audience:* Adults 18-49
Rogers Brandon, President
Kathy Signorelli, General Manager

San Marcos-Poway

KPRZ
01-01-1986; 1210 kHz AM; *Hrs Open:* 24
9255 Towne Center Drive, Suite 535, San Diego, CA 92121-3038 US
(858) 535-1210; *Fax:* (858) 535-1212
www.kprz.com
slopez@kprz.com
License: San Marcos-Poway, CA held by New Inspiration Broadcasting Co. Inc.
Group Owner: Salem Communications Corp.; (acq 1986)
Nat'l Network: Salem Radio Network
Arbitron Metro Market: San Diego, CA; *Format:* Christian, Talk, 74 *Special Programming:* Sp 22 hrs wkly; *Hrs. of News Programming:* News progmg 15 hrs wkly; *Target Audience:* 25-54; conservative, pro-family
Edward Astinger III, CEO
Heather Lloyd, Operations Dir
Dave Armstrong, VP/General Manager
Rob Babiarz, General Sales Mgr
Craig Caston, Chief Engineer
Evan Masyr, SVP/CFO

San Martin

KZSJ
11-01-1995; 1120 kHz AM; *Hrs Open:* 24; 5 kw-D, ND1; 0.15 kw-N, ND1; N36 57 49 W121 29 22
1436 Auburn Blvd., Sacramento, CA 95815 US
(408) 223-3130; *Fax:* (408) 223-3131
www.quehuongmedia.com
qhradio@aol.com
License: San Martin, CA held by Bustos Media Holdings L.L.C.
Group Owner: Bustos Media Holdings L.L.C.; (acq 2-26-99).
Arbitron Metro Market: San Martin, CA; *Format:* Vietnamese; *Target Audience:* Vietnamese; *Adv. Rates:* 50; 45; 50; 30
Amador Bustos, Chairman
Carlos A. Duharte, Operations Dir
Khoi Nguyen, General Manager

San Mateo

***KCSM**
10-01-1964; 91.1 MHz FM; 11 kw; 372 ft.; N37 32 8.1 W122 20 0
1700 West Hillsdale Boulevard, San Mateo, CA 94402 US
(650) 574-6586; *Fax:* (650) 524-6975
www.kcsm.org
License: San Mateo, San Mateo County, CA held by San Mateo County Community College District.
Nat'l Network: PRI; NPR
Arbitron Metro Market: San Mateo, CA *TV Affiliate:* *KCSM-TV affil.; *Format:* Jazz *Special Programming:* Blues 3 hrs wkly; *Target Audience:* 40 plus; males
Melanie Berzon, Operations Dir
Dante Betteo, Station Manager
Alisa Clancy, Programming Director
Michele Muller, Engineering Dir
Jesse Chuy Varela, Music Director
Barbara Lamb-Hall, Underwriting Representative

KSAN
09-01-1963; 107.7 MHz FM; 8.9 kw; 1161 ft.; N37 41 20 W122 26 7
750 Battery St., 3rd FloorCA 94105-3914 US
(888) 303-2663; *Fax:* (888) 709-2663
www.1077thebone.com
License: San Mateo, CA held by Radio License Holding SRC, LLC
Group Owner: Cumulus Media Inc.; (acq 5-29-97; $44 million)
Nat'l Reps: McGavren Guild
Arbitron Metro Market: San Francisco, CA; *Format:* Rock/AOR; *Target Audience:* 25-54.
Victor Nierva, Promotions Manager

San Rafael

KVVZ
06-01-1961; 100.7 MHz FM; 6 kw; 328 ft.; N37 58 49 W122 31 39 *Rebroadcasts:* Simulcasts KVVF-FM Santa Clara 100%
750 Battery St., Suite 200, San Francisco, CA 94111 US
(415) 989-5765
www.univision.com
License: San Rafael, Marin County, CA held by Univision Radio License Corp.
Group Owner: Univision Radio; (acq 3-1-2005; exchange for KOSL(FM) Jackson).
Arbitron Metro Market: San Francisco, CA; *Format:* Spanish
Raul Rodriguez, Vice President and General Manager
Leah Durflinger, National Sales Manager
Luz Maria Rodriguez, Marketing Director

***KSRH**
05-01-1980; 88.1 MHz FM; *Hrs Open:* 9 AM-3 PM; 0.007 kw; 66 ft.; N37 58 16 W122 30 47
185 Mission Street, San Rafael, CA 94901 US
(415) 485-2309 ext. 5213
info@ksrh.com
License: San Rafael, Marin County, CA held by San Rafael High School District.
Format: Black, Variety/Diverse *Special Programming:* Fr one hr wkly; *Hrs. of News Programming:* News progmg 5 hrs wkly; *Target Audience:* 12-29.
Marcos Cortez, Director

Santa Ana

KALI-FM
02-06-1980; 106.3 MHz FM; 6 kw; 302 ft.; N33 45 21 W117 51 18
449 Broadway, New York, NY 10013 US
(877) 595-3424; *Fax:* (626) 844-0156
License: Santa Ana, Orange County, CA held by KALI-FM Licensee LLC.
Arbitron Metro Market: Los Angeles, CA; *Format:* Japanese, Korean, 18; *Target Audience:* 18-44.
Arthur Liu, President
David Sweeney, General Manager
Alan Mok, Programming Director

KVNR
11-26-1926; 1480 kHz AM; 5 kw-D, DA2; 5 kw-N, DA2; N33 45 6 W117 54 38
14541 Brookhurst St, #C7-C8, Westminster, CA 92683 US
(714) 775-9042; *Fax:* (714) 531-6248
www.saigonradio.com
info@saigonradio.com
License: Santa Ana, Orange County, CA held by LBI Radio License Corp.
Group Owner: Liberman Broadcasting Inc.; (Acq 1-88; $6.25 million with co-located FM)
Arbitron Metro Market: Los Angeles, CA; *Format:* Vietnamese; *Target Audience:* 18-49.
Ninh Vu, President
Kathleen Bui, General Manager
Joe Dinh, Chief Engineer

KWIZ
01-01-1947; 96.7 MHz FM; *Hrs Open:* 24; 6 kw; 203 ft.; N33 48 8 W117 47 43
3101 Fifth St, Santa Ana, CA 92703 US
(714) 554-5000; *Fax:* (714) 554-9362
info@lbimedia.com
License: Santa Ana, Orange County, CA held by LBI Radio License LLC
Group Owner: Liberman Broadcasting Inc.; (acq 1997; $11.2 million).
Arbitron Metro Market: Los Angeles, CA; *Format:* Spanish
Winnie Coombs, Station Manager
Eduardo Leon, VP, Programming
Francisco Morales, Promotions Manager
Jesus Mar, Music Director

Santa Barbara

***KCSB-FM**
11-01-1964; 91.9 MHz FM; *Hrs Open:* 24; 0.62 kw; 2884 ft.; N34 31 31 W119 57 29
300 Lakeside Dr. 8th Flr, Oakland, CA 94612 US
(805) 893-3757; *Fax:* (805) 893-7832
www.kcsb.org
License: Santa Barbara, Santa Barbara County, CA held by Regents of the University of California.
Arbitron Metro Market: Santa Barbara, CA; *Format:* Variety/Diverse *Special Programming:* Sp 12 hrs, Japanese pop one hr, East Indian 2 hrs, reggae 6 hrs, American Indian 3 hrs wkly; *Hrs. of News Programming:* news progmg9 hrs wkly; *No. News Employees:* 2; *Target Audience:* Community radio/college radio
Ted Coe, Development Coordinator
Marta Ulvaeus, Assistant Director of Media Studies

KDB
02-14-1960; 93.7 MHz FM; *Hrs Open:* 24; 12.5 kw; 870 ft; N34 27 58 W119 40 37
Box 91660, Santa Barbara, CA 93101
(805) 966-4131; *Fax:* (805) 966-4788
www.kdb.com
License: Santa Barbara, Santa Barbara County, CA held by Pacific Broadcasting Co.
Population Served: 600,000; *Arbitron Metro Market:* Santa Barbara, CA; *Hrs. of News Programming:* News progmg one hr wkly; *Target Audience:* Adults; affluent, influential & educated; *Adv. Rates:* 30; 30; 30; 24
Richard Bickle, Operations Dir
Tim Owens, Executive VP/General Manager
Roby Scott, Station Manager
Roby Scott, General Sales Mgr
Steve Murphy, Programming Director
Roby Scott, Promotions Manager

KZER
10-31-1937; 1250 kHz AM; *Hrs Open:* 24; 2.5 kw-D, DA2; 1 kw-N, DA2; N34 25 6 W119 49 5
200 S. A St., 4th Fl., Oxnard, CA 93030 US
(805) 240-2070
www.radiolazer.com
License: Santa Barbara, CA held by Lazer Broadcasting Corp.
Group Owner: Lazer Broadcasting Corp.; acq 12-18-2003; $1.5 million).
Arbitron Metro Market: Oxnard, CA; *Hrs. of News Programming:* news progmg 140 hrs wkly; *No. News Employees:* 5; *Target Audience:* 25 plus; upscale, educated listeners

***KQSC**
07-01-1985; 1530 kHz AM; *Hrs Open:* 24; 12 kw; 866 ft.; N34 27 55 W119 40 37 *Rebroadcasts:* Rebroadcasts KUSC 100%
Mailing Address: PO Box 7913, Los Angeles, CA 90007 US
Second Address: 1149 S. Hill St., Suite H100, Los Angeles, CA 90015
(213) 225-7400; *Fax:* (213) 225-7410
License: Santa Barbara, Santa Barbara County, CA held by Kona Coast Radio, LLC.
Group Owner: Kona Coast Radio, LLC.
Nat'l Network: PRI; NPR
Arbitron Metro Market: Los Angeles, CA; *Format:* Oldies; *Hrs. of News Programming:* News progmg 3 hrs wkly; *Target Audience:* 35 plus.

KVYB
08-08-1961; 103.3 MHz FM; *Hrs Open:* 24; 105 kw; 2969 ft.; N34 31 29 W119 57 32
US

(805) 642-8595; *Fax:* (805) 656-5838
www.1033thevibe.com
License: Santa Barbara, Santa Barbara County, CA held by Cumulus Licensing Corp.
Group Owner: Cumulus Media Inc.; (acq 4-2000).
Nat'l Reps: McGavren Guild
Arbitron Metro Market: Ventura, CA; *Format:* Adult Contemp; *Target Audience:* 18-54; general; *Adv. Rates:* 75; 75;75; 20
Sommer Frisk, VP/Market Manager
Chris Cox, Operations Manager
Jennifer Demsey, Promotions Manager
Barbara Haser, Traffic Manager
Tim Koza, Chief Engineer

KTMS
08-11-1962; 990 kHz AM; *Hrs Open:* 24; 5 kw-D, DA2; 0.5 kw-N, DA2; N34 28 15 W119 40 33
414 E. Cota Street, Santa Barbara, CA 93101 US
(805) 879-8300
info@990am.com
License: Santa Barbara, CA held by Rincon Broadcasting LS LLC.
Group Owner: Rincon Broadcasting LLC; (acq 7-11-2007; grpsl)
Nat'l Network: ABC; CNN Radio
Arbitron Metro Market: Santa Barbara, CA; *Format:* Talk; *Hrs. of News Programming:* news progmg 4 hrs wkly; *No. News Employees:* 2; *Target Audience:* 25 plus; upscale adults
Keith Royer, Executive VP/General Manager
Lin Aubuchon, Promotions/Marketing Manager
Jack Clarke, National Sales Manager
Steve Hess, Local Sales Manager

KTYD
08-11-1972; 99.9 MHz FM; *Hrs Open:* 24; 34 kw; 1280 ft.; N34 28 15 W119 40 33
414 East Cota Street, Santa Barbara, CA 93101 US
(805) 879-8300; *Fax:* (805)879-8430
www.ktyd.com
keith.royer@rinconbroadcasting.com
License: Santa Barbara, Santa Barbara County, CA held by Rincon License Subsidiary LLC.
Group Owner: Rincon Broadcasting LLC; (acq 7-11-2007; grpsl)
Nat'l Reps: Katz Radio
Arbitron Metro Market: Santa Barbara, CA; *Format:* Rock/AOR
Special Programming: Pub affrs one hr wkly; *Hrs. of News Programming:* news progmg 3 hrs wkly; *No. News Employees:* 1; *Target Audience:* 18-49;upscale adults
Keith Royer, Operations & Programming Director
Keith Royer, Executive VP/General Manager
Steve Heff, General Sales Mgr
Lin Aubuchon, Promotions Manager
Ran Bullard, Chief Engineer
Jody McElfresh, Traffic Manager

KCLU
01-01-1946; 1340 kHz AM *Rebroadcasts:* Simulcast with KCLU-FM Thousand Oaks 100%
60 W. Olsen Road, #4400, Thousand Oaks, CA 91360 US
(805) 493-3900; *Fax:* (805) 493-3982
www.kclu.org
molson@callutheran.edu
License: Santa Barbara, CA held by California Lutheran University
Nat'l Network: NPR
Arbitron Metro Market: Thousand Oaks, CA; *Format:* News, News/Talk, 86
Jim Rondeau, Director of Operations and Programming
Mary Olson, General Manager
Lance Orozco, News Director
Mia Karnatz, Director of Member Services

KZSB
03-01-1961; 1290 kHz AM; *Hrs Open:* 24; 0.5 kw-D, ND1; 0.122 kw-N, ND1; N34 25 7 W119 41 10
1317 Santa Barbara Street, Santa Barbara, CA 93101 US
(805) 564-2000; *Fax:* (805) 966-6258
www.newspress.com
dkatich@newspress.com
License: Santa Barbara, CA held by Santa Barbara Broadcasting Inc.
Nat'l Network: Westwood One
Arbitron Metro Market: Santa Barbara, CA; *Format:* News, News/Talk, 86; *Target Audience:* 35-64.
Dennis Weibling, President
Richard Dugan, Operations Dir
Les Carroll, General Manager
Don Katich, News Director
Patrice Cardenas, Public Affairs Director

***KSBX**
04-01-2003; 89.5 MHz FM; *Hrs Open:* 24; 0.05 kw; 899 ft.; N34 27 57 W119 40 37 *Rebroadcasts:* Rebroadcassts KCBX(FM) San Luis Obispo 99%
4100 Vachell Lane, San Luis Obispo, CA 93401 US
(805) 549-8855
www.kcbx.org
License: Santa Barbara, Santa Barbara County, CA held by KCBX Inc.
Nat'l Network: NPR *Regional Reps:* Margaret Merisante
Arbitron Metro Market: Santa Barbara, CA; *Format:* Jazz; *Hrs. of News Programming:* News progmg 30 hrs wkly
Hank Hadley, Operations Dir
Frank Lanzone, General Manager
Marisa Waddell, Director of Programming & New Media
Claire Flaherty, Office Manager
Randol White, News Director
Katherine Johnson, CFO
Hank Hadley, Operations Manager
Katherine Johnson, Assistant General Manager
Neal Losey, Music Director
Rodger Mastako, Senior Account Executive
Greg Perry, KCBXnet Manager

Santa Clara

KVVF
09-25-1964; 105.7 MHz FM; *Hrs Open:* 24; 50 kw; 499 ft.; N37 21 32 W121 45 22
750 Battery St., Suite 200, San Francisco, CA 94111 US
(415) 989-5765
www.univision.com
License: Santa Clara, Santa Clara County, CA held by Univision Radio License Corp.
Group Owner: Univision Radio; (acq 9-22-2003; grpsl).
Arbitron Metro Market: San Francisco, CA; *Format:* Spanish
Raul Rodriguez, Vice President and General Manager
Luz Maria Rodriguez, Marketing Director

***KSCU**
07-01-1978; 103.3 MHz FM; *Hrs Open:* 24; 0.03 kw; -7 ft.; N37 20 50 W121 56 21
500 El Camino Real, Santa Clara, CA 95053 US
(408) 554-4413; *Fax:* (408) 554-5738
www.kscu.org
music@kscu.org
License: Santa Clara, Santa Clara County, CA held by President and Board of Trustees of Santa Clara University.
Arbitron Metro Market: San Francisco; *Format:* Alternative
Special Programming: Hip-hop 15 hrs, Blues 3 hrs, loud rock 6 hrs, world one hr wkly; *Hrs. of News Programming:* News progmg one hr wkly *Target Audience:* 14-34; Young adult who like modern music
Nick Leasure, General Manager
Morgan Johnson, Programming Director
Gordon Young, Media Advisor
Bill Orr, Engineering Dir

KVVN
12-18-1964; 1430 kHz AM; *Hrs Open:* 24
1125 East Santa Clara St., San Jose, CA 95116 US
(408) 998-0612; *Fax:* (408) 998-0583
kvvn@inlanguageradio.com
License: Santa Clara, CA held by Pham Radio Communication LLC
Regional Reps: In-Language Radio, SF
Arbitron Metro Market: Santa Clara, CA; *Format:* Vietnamese; *Hrs. of News Programming:* news progmg 14 hrs wkly; *No. News Employees:* 1; *Target Audience:* 23-34; Hispanic
Phung Dang, Operations Dir
Andrew Luu, Station Manager
Paul Marks, Chief Engineer

Santa Cruz

***KFER**
01-01-1992; 89.9 MHz FM; *Hrs Open:* 24; 0.2 kw; 26 ft.; N37 0 45 W121 58 25
PO Box 13, Santa Cruz, CA 95063 US
(831) 475-6651; *Fax:* (831) 464-8427
www.radioliberty.com
License: Santa Cruz, Santa Cruz County, CA held by Santa Cruz Educational Broadcasting Foundation.
Nat'l Network: Moody *Regional Reps:* Moody
Arbitron Metro Market: Monterey-Salinas-Santa Cruz, CA; *Format:* Variety/Diverse; *Hrs. of News Programming:* News progmg 15 hrs wkly; *Target Audience:* General.
Dr. Stan Monteith, General Manager

***KSRI**
02-28-2001; 90.7 MHz FM; *Hrs Open:* 24; 0.32 kw; 364 ft.; N37 0 10 W122 3 5 *Rebroadcasts:* Rebroadcasts KHRI(FM) Hollister 100%
500 Redwood Heights Road, Santa Cruz, CA 95003 US
(916) 251-1600; *Fax:* (916) 251-1650
www.air1.com
info@air1.com
License: Santa Cruz, Santa Cruz County, CA held by Educational Media Foundation.
Group Owner: EMF Broadcasting; (acq 8-17-00; $295,000).
Nat'l Network: Air 1
Format: Alternative, Christian; *No. News Employees:* 3; *Target Audience:* 18-35; Judeo-Christian, female
Mike Novak, President
David Pierce, Programming Director
Ed Lenane, News Director
Sam Wallington, Engineering Dir
Marya Morgan, News Reporter
Richard Hunt, Marya Morgan
Tracy Butler, Traffic Manager

KSCO
09-21-1947; 1080 kHz AM; *Hrs Open:* 24; 10 kw-D, DAN; 5 kw-N, DAN; N36 57 43 W121 58 51
2300 Portola Dr., Santa Cruz, CA 95062 US
(831) 475-1080; *Fax:* (831) 475-2967
www.ksco.com
License: Santa Cruz, CA held by Zwerling Broadcasting System Ltd.
Arbitron Metro Market: Monterey-Salinas-Santa Cruz, CA; *Format:* News, News/Talk, 86; *Hrs. of News Programming:* news progmg 35 hrs wkly; *No. News Employees:* 8; *Target Audience:* 25 plus; well educatedprofessionals, managers; *Adv. Rates:* 50; 50; 50; 35
Michael Zwerling, CEO
Michael Olson, General Manager
Michael Olson, General Sales Mgr
Rosemary Chalmers, Programming Director

***KUSP**
04-14-1972; 88.9 MHz FM; 1.25 kw; 2497 ft.; N36 32 5 W121 37 14
P. O. Box 423, Santa Cruz, CA 95061 US
(831) 476-2800; *Fax:* (831) 476-2802
www.kusp.org
License: Santa Cruz, Santa Cruz County, CA held by Pataphysical Broadcasting Foundation Inc.
Nat'l Network: NPR
Arbitron Metro Market: Santa Cruz, CA; *Format:* Variety/Diverse; *Hrs. of News Programming:* News progmg 44 hrs wkly
Duncan Lively, Operations Dir
Terry Green, General Manager
Johnny Simmons, Programming Director
J.D. Hillard, Director of News, Talk and Information Programs
J. D. Hillard, Producer
Steve Laufer, Director of New Media &kusp.org
Jen Switzer, Director of Individual Giving
Lola Brice, Director of Foundation and Business Support
Geo Warner, Volunteer Coordinator for Music Programming

KSQL
09-02-1961; 99.1 MHz FM; *Hrs Open:* 24; 1.1 kw; 2,612 ft.; N37 6 39 W121 50 37 *Rebroadcasts:* Simulcasts KSOL-FM San Francisco 100%
750 Battery St., Suite 200, San Francisco, CA 94111 US
(415) 989-5765
www.univision.com
License: Santa Cruz, Santa Cruz County, CA held by TMS License California Inc.
Group Owner: Univision Radio; (acq 9-22-2003; grpsl).
Arbitron Metro Market: Santa Cruz-San Francisco, CA; *Format:* Spanish, Tejano; *Hrs. of News Programming:* news progmg 4 hrs wkly; *No. News Employees:* 1; *Target Audience:* 25-54.
Raul Rodriguez, Vice President and General Manager
Luz Maria Rodriguez, Marketing Director

***KZSC**
08-01-1974; 88.1 MHz FM; *Hrs Open:* 24; 20 kw; 436 ft.; N37 0 10 W122 3 4
1111 Franklin Street, Oakland, CA 94607 US
(831) 459-5173; *Fax:* (831) 459-4734
www.kzsc.org
stationmanager@kzsc.org
License: Santa Cruz, Santa Cruz County, CA held by Regents of University of California.
Arbitron Metro Market: Santa Cruz, CA; *Format:* Variety/Diverse; *Hrs. of News Programming:* News progmg 40 hrs wkly; *Target Audience:* 18-plus; college students up till late 30's; *Adv. Rates:* 5; 15; 15; 15
Michael Bryant, General Manager

Santa Margarita

KWWV
07-21-1986; 106.1 MHz FM; *Hrs Open:* 24; 1.1 kw; 1447 ft.; N35 21 40 W120 39 21
795 Buckley Rd., Suite 2, San Luis Obispo, CA 93401 US
(877) 945-3106
www.wild1061.com
eric.fahnoe@dimescentralcoast.com
License: Santa Margarita, San Luis Obispo County, CA held by Dimes Media Corporation
Group Owner: Dimes Media Corporation
Arbitron Metro Market: San Luis Obispo, CA; *Format:* Contemporary Hits/Top 40; *Hrs. of News Programming:* news progmg 6 hrs wkly; *No. News Employees:* 2; *Target Audience:* 18-34; upscale homeowners
Eric Fahnoe, Promotions Manager

Santa Maria

KSBQ
09-01-1961; 1480 kHz AM; *Hrs Open:* 24; 1 kw-D, ND1; 0.061 kw-N, ND1; N34 57 2 W120 29 22
200 S. A St., 4th Fl., Oxnard, CA 93030 US
(805) 240-2070
www.radiolazer.com
License: Santa Maria, CA held by Lazer Broadcasting Corp.
Group Owner: Lazer Broadcasting Corp.; acq 12-29-99; $225,000)
Nat'l Reps: Lotus Entravision Reps LLC
Arbitron Metro Market: Santa Maria-Lompoc, CA; *Format:* Christian; *Target Audience:* 18-49; adults; *Adv. Rates:* 10; na; na; 5

KSMX
01-01-1946; 1240 kHz AM; 1 kw-U, ND1; N34 57 2 W120 29 27
2215 Skyway Drive, Santa Maria, CA 93455 US
(805) 925-2582; *Fax:* (805) 361-1366
www.1240ksmx.com
License: Santa Maria, CA held by EDB SLO License LLC.
Group Owner: Frontier Radio Management Inc.; (acq 11-30-2007; grpsl)
Nat'l Network: Premiere Radio Networks; Westwood One; Talk Radio Network
Arbitron Metro Market: Santa Maria-Lompoc, CA; *Format:* News, News/Talk, 86
Dave Daniels, Operations Dir
Ron Roy, Regional VP
Kathy Mansell, General Sales Mgr
Jennifer Grant, Programming Director
Niki Kozak, Webmaster/Promotions Director

KSNI-FM
01-01-1960; 102.5 MHz FM; 13.5 kw; 860 ft.; N34 50 8 W120 24 6
2325 Skyway Dr, Santa Maria, CA 93455 US
(805) 822-1041
www.sunnycountry.com
License: Santa Maria, Santa Barbara County, CA held by Agm California, Inc.
Group Owner: American General Media
Arbitron Metro Market: Santa Maria-Lompoc, CA; *Format:* Country; *Target Audience:* Adults 18-49
Richard Watson, General Manager

KTAP
06-10-1962; 1600 kHz AM; *Hrs Open:* 6 AM-midnight; 0.47 kw-D, ND2; 0.026 kw-N, ND2; N34 58 48 W120 27 12
104 West Chapel Ave., Santa Maria, CA 93454 US
(805) 928-4334; *Fax:* (805) 349-2765
License: Santa Maria, CA held by Emerald Wave Media.
Group Owner: Emerald Wave Media; (acq 3-6-97; $475,000 with KRTO(FM) Guadalupe)
Arbitron Metro Market: Santa Maria-Lompoc, CA; *Format:* Spanish; *Hrs. of News Programming:* news progmg 4 hrs wkly; *No. News Employees:* 1; *Target Audience:* General; first generation Mexicans
August Ruiz, General Manager

KSMA
05-25-1963; 1240 kHz AM; *Hrs Open:* 24
2325 Skyway Dr, Suite J, Santa Maria, CA 93455 US
(805) 922-1041
www.1240ksma.com
listeners@1240ksma.com
License: Santa Maria, Santa Barbara North County, CA held by AGM California, Inc.
Group Owner: American General Media
Arbitron Metro Market: Santa Maria-Lompoc, CA; *Format:* News, News/Talk, 86; *Target Audience:* Adults 35-64
Richard Watson, General Manager
Emily Reiswig, General Sales Mgr
Pepper Daniels, Programming Director

KUHL
04-01-1946; 1440 kHz AM; 5 kw-D, DAN; 1 kw-N, DAN; N34 59 2 W120 27 10
1101 S. Broadway, Suite C, Santa Maria, CA 93455 US
(805) 922-7727; *Fax:* (805) 349-0265
www.am1440.com
Shawn@knightbroadcasting.com
License: Santa Maria, CA held by Knight Broadcasting Inc.
Group Owner: Knight Broadcasting Inc.; (acq 7-31-2006; $1.2 million with KSMA(AM) Lompoc).
Arbitron Metro Market: Santa Maria, CA; *Format:* News, News/Talk, 86; *Target Audience:* 35-64; upscale news & sports listeners
Shawn Knight, General Manager
Lisa Hornick, General Sales Mgr
Jeff Williams, Programming Director
Beth Ward, Promotions Director/Traffic Manager
Ben Heighes, News Director

KXFM
01-01-1959; 99.1 MHz FM; 2.3 kw; 1906 ft.; N34 54 37 W120 11 8
2215 Skyway Drive, Santa Maria, CA 93455 US
(805) 925-2582; *Fax:* (805) 928-1544
www.991thefox.com
License: Santa Maria, Santa Barbara County, CA held by EDB SLO License LLC.
Group Owner: Frontier Radio Management Inc.; (acq 11-30-2007; grpsl)
Arbitron Metro Market: Santa Maria-Lompoc, CA; *Format:* Classic Rock; *Target Audience:* 18-49; contemp, active adults
Jennifer Grant, Operations Dir
Ron Roy, Regional VP
Jay Turner, Programming Director
Amy Fordyce, Promotions Director
Larissa Witts, Traffic Manager
Kathy Mansell, General Sales Manager
Rick Fulkerson, Chief Engineer

*KCLM
06-21-2005; 89.7 MHz FM; *Hrs Open:* 24; 2.45 kw vert; 1867 ft.; N34 54 37 W120 11 8
Mailing Address: 4135 Northgate Blvd, Suite 1, Sacramento, CA 95834 US
Second Address: 290 Hegenberger Rd., Oakland, CA 94621
(800) 543-1495; *Fax:* (916) 641-8238
www.familyradio.com
info@familyradio.com
License: Santa Maria, Santa Barbara County, CA held by California Lutheran University
Arbitron Metro Market: Santa Maria, CA; *Format:* Christian, Religious
Harol Camping, President
David Manzi, Operations Dir

*KGDP-FM
01-01-2003; 90.5 MHz FM; 17.5 kw; 827 ft.; N34 44 30 W120 26 45
PO Box 35300, Tuscon, CA 85740 US
(800) 776-1070; *Fax:* (805) 922-8582
www.myflr.org
License: Santa Maria, Santa Barbara County, CA held by People of Action.
Arbitron Metro Market: Santa Maria, CA; *Format:* Christian, Talk
Warren J. Bolthouse, Chairman
Dr. Randy L. Carlson, President
Steve Cox, General Manager
Adam Biddell, Programming Director
Alonzo Williams, Vice President of Operations
Rod Robison, Vice President of Development
Doug Goodall,Controller
Evan Carlson, Executive Dir. Marketing/Community Transformation

Santa Monica

KDLD
01-01-1960; 103.1 MHz FM; *Hrs Open:* 24; 3.7 kw; 269 ft.; N34 0 53 W118 22 50 *Rebroadcasts:* Simulcast with KDLE(FM) Newport Beach 100%
5700 Wilshire Blvd., Suite 250, Los Angeles, CA 90036 US
(323) 900-6100
www.joseradio.com
License: Santa Monica, Los Angeles County, CA held by Entravision Holdings LLC.
Group Owner: Entravision Communications Corp.; (acq 2000)
Arbitron Metro Market: Los Angeles; *Format:* Spanish, Contemporary Hits/Top 40; *Target Audience:* 25-54;; *Adv. Rates:* 150; 100; 125; 100
Matt Cardenas, SVP Integrated Marketing Solution
Nestor Rocha, Programming Director
Elias Autran, Promotions Manager

KBLA
01-01-1947; 1580 kHz AM; 50 kw-D, DA2; 50 kw-N, DA2; N34 5 8 W118 15 24
27 William St., 11th Floor, New York, NY 10005 US
(212) 966-1059; *Fax:* (212) 625-2894
www.mrbi.net
License: Santa Monica, CA held by Multicultural Radio Broadcasting Licensee LLC.
Group Owner: Multicultural Radio Broadcasting Inc.; (acq 2-4-2004; grpsl).
Arbitron Metro Market: Los Angeles, CA; *Format:* Christian, Spanish; *No. News Employees:* 1
Arthur Liu, CEO/COO

*KCRW
01-01-1946; 89.9 MHz FM; *Hrs Open:* 24; 6.9 kw; 1109 ft.; N34 7 8 W118 23 30
1900 Pico Blvd., Santa Monica, CA 90405 US
(310) 450-5183; *Fax:* (310) 450-7172
www.kcrw.org
mail@kcrw.org
License: Santa Monica, Los Angeles County, CA held by Santa Monica College District.
Nat'l Network: NPR; PRI; *Wire Services:* AP
Arbitron Metro Market: Santa Monica, CA; *Format:* News; *Hrs. of News Programming:* news progmg 14 hrs wkly; *No. News Employees:* 3; *Target Audience:* General; 18-55 year old consumers
Mike Newport, Operations Dir
Gary Scott, Programming Director
Steve Herbert, Chief Engineer
Jennifer Ferro, General Manager
Jill Smayo, Director of Development
Denise Anderman, Underwriting Director
Gregg Lewis, Marketing/ArtDirector
Nathan Lubeck, Director of Web Development

Santa Paula

KLJR-FM
10-04-1976; 96.7 MHz FM; *Hrs Open:* 24; 0.28 kw; 1499 ft.; N34 19 33 W119 2 18
200 South A St., 4th Floor, Oxnard, CA 93030 US
(805) 240-2070
lamejornetwork.com
License: Santa Paula, Ventura County, CA held by Lazer Broadcasting Corp.
Group Owner: Lazer Broadcasting Corp.; (acq 3-31-98; $925,000;
Nat'l Reps: Lotus Entravision Reps LLC
Arbitron Metro Market: Oxnard-Ventura, CA; *Format:* Adult Contemp; *Target Audience:* 25-54; general

KUNX
1400 kHz AM; 1 kw-U, ND1; N34 19 48 W119 5 31
2319 Alameda Ave, Suite 1D, Ventura, CA 93003 US
(805) 289-1400; *Fax:* (805) 644-7906
License: Santa Paula, Ventura West County, CA held by Gold Coast Broadcasting LLC
Group Owner: Gold Coast Broadcasting LLC; (acq 1996; $3.65 million with KCAQ(FM) Oxnard)
Arbitron Metro Market: Santa Paula, CA; *Format:* News, News/Talk, 86, Spanish; *Target Audience:* 25-54.
Chip Ehrhardt, National Sales Director
Steve Hess, General Sales Mgr
Tom Spence, Programming Director

Santa Rosa

KRRS
04-01-1962; 1460 kHz AM; *Hrs Open:* 24; 1 kw-D, 33 w-N, DA-2; N38 22 13 W122 43 39
1410 Neotomas Ave. #104, Santa Rosa, CA 90006
(707) 545-1460; *Fax:* (707) 545-0112
krrs@sonic.net
License: Santa Rosa, Sonoma County, CA held by California Broadcasting Corp LLC
Nat'l Reps: Interep
Population Served: 500,000; *Arbitron Metro Market:* Santa Rosa; *Target Audience:* 25-54; contemporary Hispanic families; *Adv. Rates:* 45; 35; 45; 35
Ambrosio Vigil, CEO
Francisco Quirroz, Programming Director
Alberto Rosillo, Traffic Manager

KSRO
05-01-1937; 1350 kHz AM; 5 kw-D, DAN; 5 kw-N, DAN; N38 26 22 W122 44 51
Mailing Address: 1410 Neotomas Avenue, Suite 200, Santa Rosa, CA 95405 US
Second Address: 1410 Neotomas Ave., Suite 200, Santa Rosa, CA 95405
(707) 543-0100; *Fax:* (707) 571-1097
www.ksro.com
License: Santa Rosa, CA held by Amaturo Sonoma Media Group LLC
Group Owner: Sonoma Media Group; (acq 12-16-02; grpsl).
Arbitron Metro Market: Santa Rosa, CA; *Format:* News, News/Talk, 86; *Target Audience:* 35-64.
Michael O'Shea, President
Kent Bjugstad, General Manager
Kent Bjusgastad, General Sales Mgr
Kent Bjugstad, Programming Director
Michelle Marques, Promotions Manager
Renee Bakos, News Director
Mick Rush, Chief Engineer

KZST
04-18-1971; 100.1 MHz FM; *Hrs Open:* 24; 6 kw; 246 ft.; N38 25 7 W122 40 33
Mailing Address: P.O Box 100, Santa Rosa, CA 95402 US
Second Address: 3392 Mendocino Ave., Santa Rosa, CA 95403
(707) 528-4434; *Fax:* (707) 527-8216
www.kzst.com
toms@kzst.com
License: Santa Rosa, Sonoma County, CA held by Redwood Empire Stereocasters.
Group Owner: Redwood Empire Stereocasters
Nat'l Reps: McGavren Guild; *Wire Services:* AP; Bay City News Service
Arbitron Metro Market: Santa Rosa, CA; *Format:* Adult Contemp; *No. News Employees:* 2; *Target Audience:* 25-54.
Tom Skinner, General Manager/Vice President
Brent Farris, Programming Director

KHTH
12-23-1974; 101.7 MHz FM; 2.2 kw; 1,056 ft; N38 30 31 W122 39 41
1410 Neotomas Avenue, Suite 200, Santa Rosa, CA 95405 US
(707) 543-0100; *Fax:* (707) 571-1097
www.hot1017online.com
License: Santa Rosa, CA held by Amaturo Sonoma Media Group LLC
Group Owner: Sonoma Media Group

Michael O'Shea, President

Santa Ynez

KRAZ
01-01-2001; 105.9 MHz FM; *Hrs Open:* 24; 0.065 kw; 2933 ft.; N34 31 32 W119 57 29
1101 S. Broadway, Suite C, Santa Maria, CA 93455 US
(805) 922-7727
www.krazfm.com
kathy@knightbroadcasting.com
License: Santa Ynez, Santa Barbara County, CA held by Knight Broadcasting Inc.
Group Owner: Knight Broadcasting Inc.; (acq 5-21-2001; $325,000 for CP).
Nat'l Network: ABC
Arbitron Metro Market: Santa Barbara, CA; *Format:* Country
Shawn Knight, General Manager
Lisa Hornick, General Sales Mgr
Jeff Williams, Programming Director
Beth Ward, Promotions Director/Traffic Manager
Ben Heighes, News Director

Seaside

KBOQ
10-01-1996; 103.9 MHz FM; *Hrs Open:* 24; 1.4 kw; Ant 604 ft; N36 30 17 W121 54 21
60 Garden Ct., Suite 300, Monterey, CA 93940
(831) 658-5200
kboq.radio.net
License: Seaside, Monterey County, CA held by Mapleton License of Monterey LLC.
Group Owner: Mapleton Communications LLC; (acq 1-24-2002; $1.85 million)
Nat'l Reps: McGavren Guild
Population Served: 500,000; *Arbitron Metro Market:* Monterey-Salinas-Santa Cruz, CA

KSES-FM
11-22-1972; 107.1 MHz FM; 1.85 kw; 587 ft.; N36 33 9 W121 47 17
67 Garden Crt., Monterey, CA 93940 US
(831) 373-6767
www.jose1071.com
License: Seaside, Monterey County, CA held by Entravision Holdings LLC.
Group Owner: Entravision Communications Corp.; (acq 3-14-00; grpsl).
Arbitron Metro Market: Monterey-Salinas-Santa Cruz, CA; *Format:* Spanish, Adult Contemp; *Target Audience:* 18-49.
Tony Valencia, General Sales Mgr
Victor Ramos, Promotions Manager

Sebastopol

KJZY
11-05-1995; 93.7 MHz FM; *Hrs Open:* 24; 6 kw; 217 ft.; N38 25 7 W122 40 33
P.O. Box 100, Santa Rosa, CA 95402 US
(707) 528-9393; *Fax:* (707) 527-8216
www.kjzy.com
info@kjzy.com
License: Sebastopol, Sonoma County, CA held by Redwood Empire Stereocasters.
Group Owner: Redwood Empire Stereocasters
Nat'l Reps: McGavren Guild; *Wire Services:* AP
Format: Jazz
Gordon Zlot, President
Tom Skinner, VP/General Manager
Patrick Stelzner, General Sales Mgr
Brent Farris, Programming Director
Steve Zabrskie, News Director
Eric Peter, Chief Engineer
Darlene Evart, Traffc Director

Selma

***KQKL**
08-06-2003; 88.5 MHz FM; *Hrs Open:* 24; 50 kw; 492 ft.; N36 26 50 W119 37 10
1425 N Market Blvd, Suite 9, Sacramento, CA 95834 US
(800) 525-5683; *Fax:* (916) 251-1650
www.klove.com
klove@klove.com
License: Selma, Fresno County, CA held by Educational Media Foundation.
Group Owner: EMF Broadcasting
Nat'l Network: K-Love
Arbitron Metro Market: Selma, CA; *Format:* Christian; *No. News Employees:* 3; *Target Audience:* 25-44; Judeo Christian, female
Darrell Chambliss, Chairman
Mike Novak, President and CEO
David Pierce, Programming Director
Ed Lenane, News Director
Sam Wallington, Engineering Dir
Marya Morgan, News Reporter
Richard Hunt, News Reporter
Laura Daniels, NewsReporter
Tim Luttrell, News Reporter
Kenny Noble Cortes, News Reporter
Darren Vinson, News Reporter

Shafter

KKXX-FM
01-01-1994; 93.1 MHz FM; *Hrs Open:* 24; 4 kw; 404 ft.; N35 28 21 W119 1 40
1400 Easton Drive, Suite 144, Bakersfield, CA 93309 US
(661) 328-1410; *Fax:* (661) 328-0873
www.hits931fm.com
License: Shafter, Kern County, CA held by AGM California.
Group Owner: American General Media; (acq 7-25-97; $1.5 million with KBID(AM) Bakersfield).
Arbitron Metro Market: Bakersfield, CA; *Format:* Adult Contemp, Contemporary Hits/Top 40; *Hrs. of News Programming:* news progmg 2 hrs wkly; *No. News Employees:* 4; *Target Audience:* Adults 18-34
Rogers Brandon, President
Bob Lewis, Operations Dir
Toni Snyder, General Manager
J. Reed, Programming Director

***KGZO**
06-06-1996; 90.9 MHz FM; *Hrs Open:* 24; 1.9 kw; 2070 ft.; N35 16 51 W119 44 52 *Rebroadcasts:* Rebroadcasts KMRO(FM) Camarillo 100%
2310 Ponderosa Drive, Suite 28, Camarillo, CA 93010 US
(805) 482-4797; *Fax:* (805) 388-5202
www.nuevavida.com
info@nuevavida.com
License: Shafter, Kern County, CA held by The Association for Community Education Inc.
Arbitron Metro Market: Bakersfield, CA; *Format:* Religious; *Target Audience:* General.
Phil Guthrie, President
Mary Guthrie, General Manager

KNZR-FM
03-03-1978; 97.7 MHz FM; *Hrs Open:* 24; 4.1 kw; 397 ft.; N35 27 33 W119 1 13
3651 Pegasus Dr., Suite 107, Bakersfield, CA 93308 US
(661) 393-1900; *Fax:* (661) 393-1915
www.knzr.com
License: Shafter, Kern County, CA held by Alpha Media Licensee LLC
Group Owner: Alpha Media LLC; (acq 10-10-2014).
Arbitron Metro Market: Bakersfield, CA; *Format:* News, News/Talk, 86; *Target Audience:* 18-49.
Mary Lou Gunn, General Manager
Steve Darnell, Programming Director
Kathy King, News Director

***KAIB**
01-01-2006; 89.5 MHz FM; 50 kw; 358 ft.; N35 36 53 W119 28 16 *Rebroadcasts:* Rebroadcasts KLRD(FM) Yucaipa 100%
US
(888) 937-2471; *Fax:* (916) 251-1650
www.air1.com
info@air1.com
License: Shafter, Kern County, CA held by Educational Media Foundation.
Group Owner: EMF Broadcasting; (acq 1-14-2005).
Nat'l Network: Air 1
Arbitron Metro Market: Shafter, CA; *Format:* Alternative, Christian
Darrell Chambliss, Chairman
Alan Mason, COO
Mike Novak, President and CEO
David Pierce, Programming Director
Ed Lenane, News Director
Sam Wallington, Engineering Dir
Tracy Butler, Traffic Manager
Eric Moser, Chief FinancialOfficer
Larry Moody, Director
Mitch Barnhart, Director

Shasta

KCNR
08-13-1967; 1460 kHz AM
4531 Shannon Place, Redding, CA 96001 US
(530) 244-5082; *Fax:* (530) 244-5698
License: Shasta, CA held by M C Allen Productions
Arbitron Metro Market: Redding, CA; *Format:* Sports, Talk; *Target Audience:* 24-55.
Mike Quinn, General Manager

Shasta Lake City

KESR
01-01-1998; 107.1 MHz FM; *Hrs Open:* 24; 1.4 kw; 1362 ft.; N40 39 6 W122 31 32
1588 Charles Dr., Redding, CA 96003 US
(530) 244-9700; *Fax:* (530) 244-9707
1071bobfm.com
License: Shasta Lake City, Shasta County, CA held by Results Radio of Redding Licensee LLC.
Group Owner: Results Radio; (acq 5-28-2000; grpsl).
Arbitron Metro Market: Redding, CA; *Format:* Adult Contemp

KNNN(FM)
10-26-1989; 99.3 MHz FM; 1.6 kw; Ant 1,525 ft; N40 39 15 W122 31 12
CA USA
tunein.com/radio/Hella-877-s104816
License: Shasta Lake City, Shasta County, CA held by Mapleton License of Redding LLC.
Group Owner: Mapleton Communications LLC; (acq 11-30-2006; grpsl)
Arbitron Metro Market: Redding, CA; *Format:* Country *Special Programming:* Jazz 3 hrs wkly; *Target Audience:* 25-54.

KJPR
01-01-2005; 1330 kHz AM; *Hrs Open:* 24 hrs
US
(541) 552-6301; *Fax:* (541) 552-8565
www.ijpr.org
jprinfo@sou.edu
License: Shasta Lake City, CA held by JPR Foundation Inc.
Arbitron Metro Market: Redding, CA; *Format:* News

Paul Westhelle, Executive Director
Eric Teel, Programming Director
Geoffrey Riley, News Director
Darin Ransom, Engineering Dir
Betsy Byers, Administrative Assistant
Mitchell Christian, Director of Finance & Administration
JillHernandez, Accountant Technician
Valerie Ing-Miller, Northern CA Program Coordinator
Abby Kraft, Development Associate
John Matthews, Classical Music Director

Shingle Springs

KNTY
05-01-1989; 101.9 MHz FM; *Hrs Open:* 24; 47 kw; 505 ft.; N38 51 12 W120 56 23
1436 Auburn Blvd., Sacramento, CA 95815 US
(916) 646-4000; *Fax:* (916) 646-3237
www.1019thewolf.com
License: Shingle Springs, El Dorado County, CA held by Entravision Holdings LLC.
Group Owner: Entravision Communications Corp.; (acq 3-14-2000; grpsl).
Arbitron Metro Market: Sacramento, CA; *Format:* Country; *Target Audience:* 25-54.
Tosh Jackson, Programming Director

Shingletown

KKXS
01-01-2001; 96.1 MHz FM; 1.9 kw; 1175 ft.; N40 29 18 W121 53 58
1588 Charles Dr., Redding, CA 96003 US
(530) 244-9700; *Fax:* (530) 244-9707
www.xs961.com
License: Shingletown, Shasta County, CA held by Results Radio of Redding Licensee LLC.
Group Owner: Results Radio; (acq 3-29-99; $125,000 for 50%).
Arbitron Metro Market: Redding, CA; *Format:* Jazz, Smooth Jazz

KRDG
08-01-1995; 105.3 MHz FM; *Hrs Open:* 24; 28 kw; 1243 ft.; N40 29 19 W121 54 23
3360 Alta Mesa Dr., Redding, CA 96002 US
(530) 226-9500; *Fax:* (530) 221-4940
www.1053classichits.com
License: Shingletown, Shasta County, CA held by Mapleton License of Redding LLC.
Group Owner: Mapleton Communications LLC; (acq 11-30-2006; grpsl)
Arbitron Metro Market: Northern CA; *Format:* Oldies; *Target Audience:* 25-54; active adults with families

Simi Valley

KIRN
09-21-1984; 670 kHz AM; *Hrs Open:* 24; 5 kw-D, DA1; 3 kw-N, DA1; N34 19 10 W118 42 56
6290 Sunset Boulevard, Suite #1600, Los Angeles, CA 90028 US
(323) 851-5476; *Fax:* (323) 512-7452
www.670amkirn.com
jimk@670amkirn.com
License: Simi Valley, CA held by Lotus Oxnard Corp.
Group Owner: Lotus Communications Corp.; (acq 12-11-96; $4.2 million)
Arbitron Metro Market: Simi Valley, CA; *Format:* Adult Contemp, Farsi, 60, News/Talk, Sports, Talk; *Hrs. of News Programming:* news progmg 14 hrs wkly; *No. News Employees:* 3; *Target Audience:* Persian, Iranian,Farsi Speaking Middle Eastern; *Adv. Rates:* $225 for 60""; $180 for 30""
Howard Kalmenson, President
John Paley, Operations Dir
Jim Kalmenson, General Manager
Poopak Mozaffari, Director of Administration & Sales
Afshin Gorgin, Programming Director
Poopak Mozaffari, Promotions Manager
Jason Houts,Chief Engineer

Soledad

***KFRS**
04-04-2002; 89.9 MHz FM; 0.25 kw vert; 305 ft.; N36 16 25 W121 16 12
Mailing Address: 4135 Northgate Blvd., Suite 1, Sacramento, CA 95834 US
Second Address: 290 Hegenberger Rd., Oakland, CA 94621
(916) 641-8191; *Fax:* (916) 641-8238
www.familyradio.com
info@familyradio.com
License: Soledad, Monterey County, CA held by Family Stations Inc.
Group Owner: Family Stations Inc.
Arbitron Metro Market: Soledad, CA; *Format:* Christian, Religious; *Target Audience:* Christian Adults
Matt Pearce, Operations Dir
Tom Evans, General Manager

KMJV
10-01-1991; 106.3 MHz FM; *Hrs Open:* 24; 4.7 kw; 371 ft.; N36 16 27 W121 16 15
548 East Alisal Street, Salinas, CA 93905 US
(831) 766-1200; *Fax:* (831) 757-8015
wolfhouseradio@yahoo.es
License: Soledad, Monterey County, CA held by Wolfhouse Radio Group Inc.
Group Owner: Wolfhouse Radio Group Inc.; (acq 7-13-2001; grpsl).
Arbitron Metro Market: Monterey, CA; *Format:* Tejano; *Target Audience:* 18-44.
Ramon Castro, General Manager
Nell Ahl, VP, Operations
Hector Villalobos, President
Vicente Romero, Programming Director

KMBX
01-01-1992; 700 kHz AM; 2.5 kw-D, ND1; 0.7 kw-N, ND1; N36 27 51 W121 17 52
67 Garden Crt., Monterey, CA 93940 US
(831) 373-6767
www.jose1071.com
License: Soledad, CA held by Entravision Holdings LLC.
Group Owner: Entravision Communications Corp.; (acq 3-14-00; grpsl).
Arbitron Metro Market: Monterey-Salinas-Santa Cruz, CA; *Format:* Religious; *Target Audience:* 18-49.
Tony Valencia, General Sales Mgr
Victor Ramos, Promotions Coordinator

Solvang

KSYV
09-22-1982; 96.7 MHz FM; *Hrs Open:* 24; 0.42 kw; 1217 ft.; N34 41 28 W120 15 58
1693 Mission Drive, Solvang, CA 93463 US
(805) 688-5798; *Fax:* (805) 688-2271
www.mix96.com
License: Solvang, Santa Barbara County, CA held by Knight Broadcasting Inc.
Group Owner: Knight Broadcasting Inc.; (acq 2-8-2002).
Nat'l Network: AP Network News
Arbitron Metro Market: Santa Maria-Lompoc, CA; *Format:* Adult Contemp; *Hrs. of News Programming:* News progmg 126 hrs wkly; *Target Audience:* 24-54; female 60%, male 40%
Shawn Knight, General Manager
Lisa Hornick, General Sales Mgr
Jeff Williams, Programming Director
Beth Ward, Promotions Director/Traffic Manager
Ben Heighes, News Director

Sonoma

***KSVY**
01-01-2005; 91.3 MHz FM; 0 kw horiz, 2.5 kw vert; -305 ft.; N38 16 47 W122 26 47
68 West Napa Street, Sonoma, CA 95476 US
(707) 933-0808; *Fax:* (707) 933-1573
www.ksvy.org
License: Sonoma, Sonoma County, CA held by Commonbond Foundation.
Arbitron Metro Market: Sonoma, CA; *Format:* Talk
Bill Hammett, President
Bob Taylor, General Manager
Stan Pappas, Programming Director

Sonora

KVML
01-01-1949; 1450 kHz AM; *Hrs Open:* 24; 0.94 kw-U, ND1; N38 00 30 W120 21 45
342 S. Washington St., Sonora, CA 95370 US
(209) 533-1450; *Fax:* (209) 533-9520
www.kvml.com
License: Sonora, Tuolumne County, CA held by Clarke Broadcasting Corp.
Group Owner: Clarke Broadcasting Corp.; acq 12-86; with co-located FM;
Nat'l Network: ABC; Fox News Radio
Population Served: 200,000; *Arbitron Metro Market:* Sonora, CA; *Format:* News, News/Talk, 86 *Special Programming:* Relg 3 hrs; *Hrs. of News Programming:* news progmg 50 hrs wkly; *No. News Employees:* 3 *TargetAudience:* 25 plus; general
H. Randolph Holder Jr., President
Larry England, General Manager/Director of Sales
Mark Truppner, Programming Director
MaryAnn Curmi, Promotions Director
B.J. Hansen, News Director
John Petter, Chief Engineer
D.J. Riendeau,Traffic Manager

KZSQ-FM
10-03-1973; 92.7 MHz FM; *Hrs Open:* 24; 0.38 kw; 1,289 ft.; N38 00 30 W120 21 44
342 S. Washington St., Sonora, CA 95370-5020 US
(209) 533-1450; *Fax:* (209) 533-9520
www.kzsq.com
License: Sonora, Tuolumne County, CA held by Clarke Broadcasting Corp.
Group Owner: Clarke Broadcasting Corp.; (acq 1986)
Nat'l Network: Fox News Radio
Population Served: 500,000; *Arbitron Metro Market:* Sonora, CA; *Format:* Adult Contemp; *Hrs. of News Programming:* news progmg 4 hrs wkly; *No. News Employees:* 3; *Target Audience:* 25-54.
H. Randolph Holder Jr., President
Larry England, General Manager/Director of Sales
Joe Marshall, Programming Director
MaryAnn Curmi, Promotions Director
B.J. Hansen, News Director
John Petter, Chief Engineer

Soquel

KYAA
01-01-2001; 1200 kHz AM
651 Cannery Road, Monterey, CA 93940 US
(831) 373-1234
www.knry.com
License: Soquel, CA held by IHR Educational Broadcasting
Arbitron Metro Market: Monterey-Salinas-Santa Cruz, CA; *Format:* Ethnic
Doug Sherman, CEO
Dick Jenkins, General Manager

South Lake Tahoe

KRLT
06-23-1976; 93.9 MHz FM; *Hrs Open:* 24; 3 kw; -105 ft.; N38 57 38 W119 56 32
Mailing Address: PO Box 1101, Zephyr Cove, NV 89448 US
Second Address: 276 Kingsbury Grade, Suite 203, Stateline, NV 89449
(775) 580-7130
www.krltfm.com
steve@krltfm.com
License: South Lake Tahoe, El Dorado County, CA held by CCR-Lake Tahoe IV LLC.
Group Owner: Cherry Creek Radio LLC; (acq 12-19-2003; grpsl).
Arbitron Metro Market: Lake Tahoe, CA/NE; *Format:* Contemporary Hits/Top 40; *Hrs. of News Programming:* News progmg 10 hrs wkly; *Target Audience:* 25-54.
Steve Harness, General Manager
George Alm, General Sales Mgr
Nick Reynolds, Programming Director

KTHO
03-17-1963; 590 kHz AM; *Hrs Open:* 24; 2.5 kw-D, DAN; 0.5 kw-N, DAN; N38 55 0 W119 57 46
P.O Box 1590, South Lake Tahoe, CA 96156 US
(530) 543-0590; *Fax:* (530) 543-1101
www.kthoradio.com
License: South Lake Tahoe, CA held by International Aerospace Solutions
Nat'l Network: ABC
Arbitron Metro Market: Reno, NV; *Format:* Oldies *Special Programming:* Jazz Trax Sundays 8pm; *Hrs. of News Programming:* news progmg 40 hrs wkly; *No. News Employees:* 1; *Target Audience:* 35-55; locals &visitors, working population and retired
Darrell Wampler, President
Ed Crook, Station Manager

KWYL
01-01-1966; 102.9 MHz FM; *Hrs Open:* 24; 39 kw; 2927 ft.; N39 18 38 W119 53 1
595 E. Plumb Ln., Reno, NV 89502 US
(775) 789-6700; *Fax:* (775) 789-6767
www.wild1029.com
r.boogie@cumulus.com
License: South Lake Tahoe, CA held by Radio License Holding CBC, LLC
Group Owner: Cumulus Media Inc.; (acq 5-9-03; grpsl).
Arbitron Metro Market: South Lake Tahoe, CA; *Format:* Contemporary Hits/Top 40; *Target Audience:* 25-54.

Jen Odom, General Sales Mgr
R. Boogie, Programming Director
Jay Schell, Digital Content/Promotions

KOWL
11-01-1956; 1490 kHz AM; 1 kw-U, ND1; N38 56 34 W119 57 25
Mailing Address: PO Box 1101, Zephyr Cove, NV 89448 US
Second Address: 276 Kingsbury Grade, Suite 203, Stateline, NV 89449
(775) 580-7130
www.krltfm.com
steve@krltfm.com
License: South Lake Tahoe, CA held by CCR-Lake Tahoe IV LLC.
Group Owner: Cherry Creek Radio LLC; (acq 12-19-2003; grpsl).
Arbitron Metro Market: South Lake Tahoe, CA; *Format:* News, News/Talk, 86
Steve Harness, General Manager
George Alm, Sales Manager
Nick Reynolds, Programming Director

South Oroville

KYIX
02-01-1994; 104.9 MHz FM; 0.26 kw; 1549 ft.; N39 39 4 W121 27 43
1601 Belvedere Rd, West Palm Beach, FL 33406 US
(530) 894-7325; *Fax:* (530) 894-5372
www.air1.com
License: South Oroville, Butte County, CA held by Butte Broadcasting Co.
Arbitron Metro Market: Chico, CA; *Format:* Alternative, Christian
Andrew Palmquist, General Manager

St. Helena

KVYN
11-01-1976; 99.3 MHz FM; 6 kw; 259 ft.; N38 25 34 W122 19 33
1124 Foster Road, Napa, CA 94558 US
(707) 252-1440(707) 258-1111; *Fax:* (707) 226-7544
www.kvyn.com
License: St. Helena, Napa County, CA held by Wine Country Broadcasting Co.
Nat'l Network: ABC; *Nat'l Reps:* Christal
Arbitron Metro Market: Saint Helena, CA; *Format:* Adult Contemp *Special Programming:* Folk 2 hrs wkly.; *Target Audience:* 25-45.; *Adv. Rates:* 60; 60; 55; 35
Roger Walther, President
Larry Sharp, General Manager
Carmen Shantz, Promotions Manager
Megan Goldsby, News Director
Ira Smith, Sports Director
Ben Webster, Chief Engineer
Tracy Webster, Business/Traffic Manager
Barry Rose,Sales Management Consultant

Stanford

***KZSU**
10-10-1964; 90.1 MHz FM; *Hrs Open:* 24; 500 w; -10 ft; N37 24 42 W122 10 41
Box 20190, Stanford, CA 94309
(650) 725-5865; *Fax:* (650) 725-5865
gm@kzsu.stanford.edu
License: Stanford, Santa Clara County, CA held by Trustees of Leland Stanford Jr. University.
Population Served: 13,000; *Arbitron Metro Market:* San Francisco; *Hrs. of News Programming:* news progmg 15 hrs wkly; *No. News Employees:* 40; *Target Audience:* 13-plus; independent-thinking individuals who valueunique programming
Francis Dickerson, Operations Dir
Emmerich Anklam, General Manager
Mark Mollineaux, Programming Director
Caleb Smith/Eliza Ridgeway, News Direcors
Mark Lawrence, Chief Engineer
Michael Peterson, Sports Director
Bill Cuevas, MusicDirector
Lois Kellerman, Promotions Director

Stockton

***KYCC**
02-24-1975; 90.1 MHz FM; 41 kw; 351 ft.; N37 57 30 W121 16 55
9019 West Lane, Stockton, CA 95210 US
(209) 477-3690; *Fax:* (209) 477-2762
www.kycc.org
kycc@kycc.org
License: Stockton, San Joaquin County, CA held by Your Christian Companion Network Inc.
Arbitron Metro Market: Stockton, CA; *Format:* Adult Contemp, Gospel, 74 *Special Programming:* Black 6 hrs, health one hr wkly; *Target Audience:* 35-55.
Shirley Garner, President
Shirley Garner, General Manager
Brent Randall, Programming Director
John Ramos, Promotions Manager
Vanessa Kudenov, Office Manager
Sharla Ogden, Accounting
Sandy Guerrero, Donor Relations
Gary Harding,Production Manager

KWSX
01-01-1947; 1280 kHz AM; *Hrs Open:* 24; 1 kw-D, DAN; 1 kw-N, DAN; N37 58 58 W121 13 46; N37 58 55 W121 13 44
2121 Lancey Dr., Modesto, CA 95355 US
(209) 551-1306; *Fax:* (209) 551-3791
www.powertalk1280.com
License: Stockton, San Joaquin County, CA held by Capstar TX LLC
Group Owner: iHeartMedia; (acq 8-30-2000; grpsl)
Arbitron Metro Market: Stockton, CA; *Format:* News, News/Talk, 86; *Target Audience:* 25-64.
Greg Cobb, Sales Director
Kevin Fox, Promotions Director
Nik Ashjian, Digital Content Director

KJOY
12-01-1946; 99.3 MHz FM; *Hrs Open:* 24; 4 kw; 322 ft.; N37 59 30 W121 17 17
3127 Transworld Dr., Suite 270, Stockton, CA 95206 US
(209) 507-8500; *Fax:* (209) 956-0907
www.993kjoy.com
License: Stockton, CA held by Radio License Holding CBC, LLC
Group Owner: Cumulus Media Inc.; (acq 5-9-03; grpsl).
Arbitron Metro Market: Stockton, CA; *Format:* Light Rock; *Target Audience:* 25-54.
Dirk Kooyman, Programming Director
Jeff Bayani, Promotions Manager

KQOD
01-24-1980; 100.1 MHz FM; 6 kw; 328 ft.; N37 59 47.8 W121 12 15.9
2121 Lancey Drive, Modesto, CA 95355 US
(209) 551-1306; *Fax:* (209) 551-53193791
www.mega100fm.com
License: Stockton, San Joaquin County, CA held by Capstar TX LLC
Group Owner: iHeartMedia; (acq 11-18-99).
Arbitron Metro Market: Stockton-Modesto, CA; *Format:* Oldies; *Target Audience:* 25-54.
Greg Cobb, Sales Director
Kevin Fox, Promotions Director
Nik Ashjian, Digital Content Director

KSTN
11-01-1949; 1420 kHz AM; *Hrs Open:* 24; 5 kw-D, DA2; 1 kw-N, DA2; N37 55 32 W121 14 44
2171 Ralph Avenue, Stockton, CA 95206 US
(209) 948-5786
www.valleyradio.org/kstn/
License: Stockton, CA held by San Joaquin Broadcasting Co.
Arbitron Metro Market: Stockton, CA; *Format:* Oldies *Special Programming:* Farm 3 hrs, relg 5 hrs wkly; *Hrs. of News Programming:* news progmg 20 hrs wkly; *No. News Employees:* 1; *Target Audience:* 18-40.
Knox LaRue, President
John Hampton, Music Director

***KUOP**
09-22-1947; 91.3 MHz FM; *Hrs Open:* 24; 7 kw; 1220 ft.; N37 28 48 W121 21 2
3601 Pacific Avenue, Stockton, CA 95211 US
(916) 278-8900; *Fax:* (916) 278-8989
www.capradio.org
npr@csus.edu
License: Stockton, San Joaquin County, CA held by University of the Pacific.
Nat'l Network: NPR; PRI
Arbitron Metro Market: Stockton, CA; *Format:* News; *Hrs. of News Programming:* news progmg 90 hrs wkly; *No. News Employees:* 1; *Target Audience:* General; NPR listeners, eg. professionals, educators, administrators
Rick Eytcheson, President/General Manager
Constance Crawford, Director, Marketing/Public Relations
Arla Gibson, Director of Development
Craig McMurray, Managing Director of Development
Jun Reina, CFO/COO
Al Gibes, Director, DigitalContent
Carl Watanabe, Station Manager
Joe Barr, Director, News/Information
Evan Matsler, Operations Director
Paul Adams, Manager, Corporate Underwriting

***KWG**
11-22-1921; 1230 kHz AM
1120 N. San Joaquin Street, Stockton, CA 95202 US
(209) 462-8307
www.ihradio.org
info@ihradio.org
License: Stockton, CA held by IHR Educational Broadcasting
Group Owner: IHR Educational Broadcasting; acq 10-18-99; $441,227).
Wire Services: Dow Jones News Service
Arbitron Metro Market: Loomis, CA; *Format:* Religious, Christian; *Target Audience:* 25-54.
Joseph Nesta, Station Manager
Dale Harry, Chief Engineer

Sunnyvale

KDFC
01-01-1961; 104.9 MHz FM; 6 kw; Ant -154 ft; N37 19 23 W121 45 15
201 Third Street, Suite 1200, San Francisco, CA 94103
(415) 546-8710
License: Sunnyvale, Santa Clara County, CA held by University of Southern California
Population Served: 967,487; *Arbitron Metro Market:* San Jose, CA; *Format:* Tejano; *Target Audience:* 18-49.
Bill Lueth, VP
Rik Malone, Programming Director
Len Mattson, Director of Underwriting

Susanville

KJDX
05-25-1983; 93.3 MHz FM; *Hrs Open:* 24; 100 kw; 1155 ft.; N40 27 13 W120 34 14
3015 Johnstonville Road, Susanville, CA 96130 US
(530) 257-2121; *Fax:* (530) 257-6955
www.theradionetwork.com
radiorod11@aol.com
License: Susanville, Lassen County, CA held by Sierra Broadcasting Corp.
Format: Country *Special Programming:* Class 5 hrs wkly
Rodney Chambers, President/General Manager
Wende Brewer, Account Executive
Ruth Dike, Office/Traffic Manager

KSUE
04-22-1948; 1240 kHz AM
3015 Johnstonville Rd, Susanville, CA 96130 US
(530) 257-2121; *Fax:* (530) 257-6955
radiorod11@aol.com
License: Susanville, CA held by Sierra Broadcasting Corp.
Arbitron Metro Market: Susanville, CA; *Format:* News, News/Talk, 86 *Special Programming:* Relg 3 hrs wkly; *Target Audience:* 35-54.
Rod Chambers, President
Ruth Dike, Operations Dir
Mike Smith, News Director
Mike Martindale, Chief Engineer
Kristin Volberg, Public Affairs Director

KLZN
01-01-2006; 1490 kHz AM; Ant -528 ft
US
(530) 257-6100; *Fax:* (530) 257-6107
License: Susanville, CA held by Sierra Radio Inc.
Group Owner: Sierra Radio Inc.
Arbitron Metro Market: Yakima, WA; *Format:* Adult Contemp
Gary Katz, President
Dennis Carlson, General Manager

Sutter

***KXJS**
01-01-2004; 88.7 MHz FM; 0.55 kw; 1978 ft.; N39 12 20 W121 49 10
3416 American River Dr, Suite B, Sacramento, CA 95864 US
(916) 278-8900; *Fax:* (916) 278-8989
www.csus.edu/npr
npr@csus.edu
License: Sutter, Sutter County, CA held by California State University, Sacramento.
Arbitron Metro Market: Sutter, CA; *Format:* Jazz, News
Rick Eytcheson, President & General Manager
Carl Watanabe, Station Manager
Joe Barr, Director of News and Information
Paul Adams, Manager, Corporate Underwriting
Constance Crawford, Director, Marketing/Public Relations
Arla Gibson,Director, Development

Craig Murray, Managing Director
Jun Reina, CFO/COO
Al Gibes, Director, Digital Content
Evan Matsler, Operations Director

Taft

KBDS

06-01-1986; 103.9 MHz FM; *Hrs Open:* 24; 6 kw; 328 ft.; N35 7 4 W119 27 33
6313 Schirra Court, Bakersfield, CA 93313 US
(661) 837-0745; *Fax:* (661) 837-1612
License: Taft, Kern County, CA held by Radio Campesina Bakersfield Inc.
Arbitron Metro Market: Bakersfield, CA
Bill Barquin, COO
Cesar Chavez, General Manager
Michelle Santillan, National Sales Director
Maria Barquin, Programming Director

KEAL

106.5 MHz FM; 6 kw; 285 ft.; N35 5 39 W119 27 40
200 S. A St., 4th Fl., Oxnard, CA 93030 US
(805) 240-2070
www.radiolazer.com
License: Taft, Kern County, CA held by Lazer Licenses LLC.
Group Owner: Lazer Broadcasting Corp.; (acq 6-11-2007; $3.85 million with KXTT(FM) Maricopa)
Arbitron Metro Market: Duluth-Superior, MN-WI

Tahoe City

*KKTO

10-03-1997; 90.5 MHz FM; *Hrs Open:* 24; 38 kw vert; 2940 ft.; N39 18 38 W119 53 1
Suite B, 3416 American River Dr., Sacramento, CA 95864 US
(916) 278-8900; *Fax:* (916) 278-8989
www.capradio.org
npr@csus.edu
License: Tahoe City, Placer County, CA held by California State University, Sacramento.
Nat'l Network: NPR; PRI
Arbitron Metro Market: Reno, NV; *Format:* News; *Hrs. of News Programming:* news progmg 90 hrs wkly; *No. News Employees:* 4; *Target Audience:* General; NPR listeners, eg. professionals, educators, administrators
Rick Eytcheson, President/General Manager
Constance Crafword, Director, Marketing/Public Relations
Evan Matsler, General Manager
Carl Watanabe, Station Manager
Arla Gibson, Director, Development
Craig Murray, Managing Director
AlGibes, Director, Digital Content
Joe Barr, Director of News/Information
Paul Adams, Manager, Corporate Underwriting
Jun Reina, CFO/COO

KLCA

04-05-1985; 96.5 MHz FM; *Hrs Open:* 24; 6.1 kw; 2963 ft.; N39 18 38 W119 53 1
961 Matley Lane, Suite 120, Reno, NV 89502 US
(775) 829-1964; *Fax:* (775) 825-3183
www.alice965.com
webmaster@alice965.com
License: Tahoe City, Placer County, CA held by Americom Limited Partnership
Group Owner: Americom Broadcasting; (acq 1996; $1.225 million)
Arbitron Metro Market: Reno, NV; *Format:* Adult Contemp, Contemporary Hits/Top 40 *Special Programming:* Metal shop 2 hrs wkly; *Hrs. of News Programming:* News progmg 3 hrs wkly; *Target Audience:* 18-34.
Tom Quinn, President
Lori Heeren, Vice President and General Manager
Heather Forcier, National Regional Sales Director
Carrie Carano, Local Sales Manager
Teresa Estabrook, Local Sales Manager

Tehachapi

KKZQ

01-01-2001; 100.1 MHz FM; 0.34 kw; 620 ft.; N35 4 30 W118 22 7
507 East Avenue, #29, Palmdale, CA 93350 US
(661) 947-3107; *Fax:* (661) 272-5688
www.edge100.com
info@edge100.com
License: Tehachapi, Kern County, CA held by High Desert Broadcasting LLC
Group Owner: High Desert Broadcasting LLC
Arbitron Metro Market: Bakersfield, CA; *Format:* Alternative; *Target Audience:* 18-49.
John Hearne, CEO
Nelson Rasse, General Sales Manager
Mark Benevento, Programming Director
Alizah Lipson, Promotions Director

KSRY

01-08-1982; 103.1 MHz FM; *Hrs Open:* 24; 1.9 kw; 577 ft.; N35 4 30 W118 22 8
3400 W. Olive Ave., Suite 550, Burbank, CA 91505 US
(818) 559-2252; *Fax:* (818) 729-2502
www.alt987fm.com
License: Tehachapi, Kern County, CA held by CC Licenses LLC.
Group Owner: iHeartMedia; (acq 11-21-2003; grpsl)
Nat'l Reps: Christal
Arbitron Metro Market: Los Angeles; *Format:* Alternative; *Hrs. of News Programming:* news progmg 2 hrs wkly; *No. News Employees:* 1
Mike Kaplan, Programming Director

*KBLV

01-01-2006; 88.7 MHz FM; 0.39 kw; 3694 ft.; N35 27 11 W118 35 25 *Rebroadcasts:* Rebroadcasts KLVR(FM) Middletown 100% US
(800) 877-5600; *Fax:* (916) 251-1650
www.klove.com
License: Tehachapi, Kern County, CA held by Educational Media Foundation.
Group Owner: EMF Broadcasting
Nat'l Network: K-Love
Arbitron Metro Market: Tehachapi, CA; *Format:* Christian
Mike Novak, President
David Pierce, Programming Director
Ed Lenane, News Director
Sam Wallington, Engineering Dir
Marya Morgan, News Reporter
Richard Hunt, News Reporter

Temecula

KMYT

01-01-2000; 94.5 MHz FM; *Hrs Open:* 24; 0.54 kw; 771 ft.; N33 28 51 W117 10 58 *Rebroadcasts:* Rebroadcasts KOGO(AM) San Diego
27349 Jefferson Avenue, Suite 116, Temecula, CA 92590 US
(951) 296-9050; *Fax:* (951) 296-9077
www.radio945fm.com
License: Temecula, Riverside County, CA held by CC Licenses LLC.
Group Owner: iHeartMedia; (acq 6-11-2001; $4.5 million including five-year noncompete agreement).
Arbitron Metro Market: Temecula, CA; *Format:* Triple A
Mark Thomas, Market President
Rob Scorpio, Regional Senior Vice President of Programming
Elston Butler, Sneior Vice President of Sales
Michael Dellinger, Programming Director
KC Morris, Promotions Director
Rich Mena, ChiefEngineer
Jorge Lopez, Online Content Director

KTMQ

01-01-2001; 103.3 MHz FM; 1.25 kw; 715 ft.; N33 28 51 W117 10 58
27349 Jefferson Avenue, Suite 116, Temecula, CA 92590 US
(951) 296-9050; *Fax:* (951) 296-9077
www.q1033.com
License: Temecula, Riverside County, CA held by CC Licenses LLC.
Group Owner: iHeartMedia; (acq 7-31-2001; $6.225 million).
Arbitron Metro Market: Temecula, CA; *Format:* Rock/AOR
Mark Thomas, Market President
Rob Scorpio, Regional Senior Vice President of Programming
Elston Butler, Senior Vice President of Sales
Michael Dellinger, Programming Director
KC Morris, Promotions Director
Rich Mena, ChiefEngineer
Jorge Lopez, Online Content Director

Templeton

KXDZ

01-01-2004; 100.5 MHz FM; 1.35 kw; 361 ft.; N35 30 19 W120 37 18
795 Buckley Rd., Suite 2, San Luis Obispo, CA 93401 US
(805) 786-2570
www.953thebeach.com
eric.fahnoe@dimescentralcoast.com
License: Templeton, San Luis Obispo County, CA held by Dimes Media Corporation
Group Owner: Dimes Media Corporation
Arbitron Metro Market: San Luis Obispo, CA; *Format:* Contemporary Hits/Top 40, Adult Contemp
Eric Fahnoe, Promotions Manager

Thermal

KKCM

03-12-1993; 92.1 MHz FM; *Hrs Open:* 24; 1.3 kw; 215 m; N33 39 18.00 W115 59 13.00
68474 29 Palms Highway Twenty-Nine, Palms, CA 92277
(760) 362-4264
www.kxcmradio.com
coppermountainbroadcasting@yahoo.com
License: Thermal, Riverside County, CA held by Copper Mountain Broadcasting Co.
Nat'l Network: Dial Global; Premiere; *Nat'l Reps:* Interep
Population Served: 350,000; *Arbitron Metro Market:* Palm Springs; *Target Audience:* 25-54.
Gary DeMaroney, President
Gary DeMaroney, General Manager
Carol Vaughn, Business Manager

Thousand Oaks

*KCLU-FM

10-20-1994; 88.3 MHz FM; *Hrs Open:* 24; 3.2 kw; 518 ft.; N34 13 5 W118 56 42
60 West Olsen Road, Thousand Oaks, CA 91360 US
(805) 493-3900; *Fax:* (805) 493-3982
www.kclu.org
kclu@callutheran.edu
License: Thousand Oaks, Ventura County, CA held by California Lutheran University.
Nat'l Network: NPR; PRI; *Wire Services:* AP
Arbitron Metro Market: Ventura County-Santa Barbara, CA; *Format:* News *Special Programming:* Jazz & blues 5 hrs wkly; *Hrs. of News Programming:* news progmg 125 hrs wkly; *No. News Employees:* 2; *Target Audience:* General.
Jim Rondeau, Director of Operations and Programming
Mary Olson, General Manager
Lance Orozco, News Director
Mia Karnatz-Shifflett, Director of Member Services

*KDSC

12-04-1979; 91.1 MHz FM; *Hrs Open:* 24; 4.8 kw; 1280 ft.; N34 24 47 W119 11 10 *Rebroadcasts:* Rebroadcasts KUSC(FM) Los Angeles 100%
Mailing Address: P. O. Box 77913, Los Angeles, CA 90007 US
Second Address: 515 S. Figueroa St., Suite 2050, Los Angeles, CA 90071
(213) 225-7400; *Fax:* (213) 225-7410
www.kusc.org
kusc@kusc.org
License: Thousand Oaks, Ventura County, CA held by University of Southern California
Nat'l Network: PRI; NPR
Arbitron Metro Market: Thousand Oaks, CA; *Format:* Talk; *Target Audience:* 35 plus.
Brenda Barnes, President
Steve Coghill, Operations Dir
Bill Lueth, VP/Programming Director
Ron Thompson, Engineering Dir
Jamie Paisley, Music Director
Rina Romero, Sr. Business Manager
Abe Shefa, Director of Underwriting
MinniePriner, Development Director
Chris Mendez, Web Developer

KYRA

04-01-1963; 92.7 MHz FM; *Hrs Open:* 24; 3.1 kw; Ant 462 ft; N34 12 21 W118 49 04
5700 W. Oaks Boulevard, Rocklin, CA 95765
(805) 497-8511; *Fax:* (805) 497-8514
www.927jillfm.com
License: Thousand Oaks, Ventura County, CA held by Educational Media Foundation
Population Served: 700,000 *Format:* Adult Contemp; *No. News Employees:* 1; *Target Audience:* 25-54; employed professional adults, especially women; *Adv. Rates:* 60; 65; 60; 50
Mike Novak, President
Joe Miller, Director of Broadcasting

*KYRA

05-01-2006; 92.7 MHz FM; *Hrs Open:* 24; 3.1 kw; 463 ft.; N34 12 21 W118 49 4 *Rebroadcasts:* Rebroadcasts KLRD(FM) Yucaipa 100%
3101 North Federal, Highway, Suite 601, Ft. Lauderdale, FL 33306 US
(877) 927-4927; *Fax:* (949) 454-1710
www.air1.com
License: Thousand Oaks, San Mateo County, CA held by Educational Media Foundation
Group Owner: EMF Broadcasting

Arbitron Metro Market: Malibu Vista, CA; *Format:* Adult Contemp; *Target Audience:* 18-54; adults
Mike Novak, President/Chief Executive Officer

Thousand Palms

KLOB
01-01-1993; 94.7 MHz FM; 1.65 kw; 640 ft.; N33 51 56 W116 25 58
41601 Corporate Way, Palm Desert, CA 92260 US
(760) 341-5837; *Fax:* (760) 837-3711
www.jose947.com
vtocco@entravision.com
License: Thousand Palms, Riverside County, CA held by Entravision Holdings LLC.
Group Owner: Entravision Communications Corp.; (acq 2-27-97).
Arbitron Metro Market: Palm Springs, CA; *Format:* Spanish, Adult Contemp
Victor Tocco, General Manager
Juliana Simmons, Promotions Manager
Sergio De La Torre, Chief Engineer

KXPS
11-14-1992; 1010 kHz AM; *Hrs Open:* 24; 3.6 kw-D, DA2; 0.4 kw-N, DA2; N33 50 35 W116 25 39
75-153 Merle Drive, Unit 9, Palm Desert, CA 92211 US
(760) 621-0100; *Fax:* (760) 322-5493
License: Thousand Palms, CA held by CRC Media West LLC
Arbitron Metro Market: Palm Springs, CA; *Format:* Sports, Talk
Special Programming: Relg 17 hrs wkly
Ron Cohen, President
Jeffrey O'Brien, General Manager

KFSQ
12-07-1963; 1270 kHz AM; *Hrs Open:* 24; 5 kw-D, DA2; 0.75 kw-N, DA2; N33 51 4 W116 23 36
1321 North Gene Autry Trail, Palm Desert, CA 92262 US
(760) 621-0100
License: Thousand Palms, CA held by Desert Radio Group
Arbitron Metro Market: Palm Springs, CA; *Format:* Talk; *Hrs. of News Programming:* news progmg 20 hrs wkly; *No. News Employees:* 3; *Target Audience:* 25 plus.
Angela Powers, Operations Dir
Jay White, General Manager
Don Nordin, General Sales Mgr
Mike Oakes, Programming Director
Charles Wolfe, Promotions Director
Christine Constantinescu, Director, Digital Media

Tipton

KCRZ
01-01-1997; 104.9 MHz FM; *Hrs Open:* 24; 2.3 kw; 528 ft.; N36 10 7 W119 15 4
1401 W. Caldwell Avenue, Visalia, CA 93277 US
(559) 553-1500; *Fax:* (559) 627-1496
License: Tipton, Tulare County, CA held by Momentum Broadcasting
Nat'l Network: ABC
Arbitron Metro Market: Visalia-Tulare-Hanford, CA; *Format:* Adult Contemp; *Target Audience:* 25-54.; *Adv. Rates:* 30; 25; 20; na
Don Groppetti, President
Bill Lynch, General Manager
Randy Hendrix, Programming Director
Genia Taylor, Business Manager

Torrance

KFOX
01-01-1998; 1650 kHz AM
4525 Wilshire Boulevard, Los Angeles, CA 90010 US
(323) 935-0606; *Fax:* (323) 935-8885
www.radioseoul1650.com
License: Torrance, CA held by HK Media Inc.
Format: Adult Contemp, Korean
Grant Chang, VP/Gereral Manager

Tracy

KMIX
12-14-1966; 100.9 MHz FM; 6 kw; 328 ft.; N37 37 32 W121 23 58
6820 Pacific Ave., Floor 3A, Stockton, CA 95207 US
(209) 474-0154; *Fax:* (209) 474-0316
www.entravision.com
License: Tracy, San Joaquin County, CA held by Entravision Holdings LLC.
Group Owner: Entravision Communications Corp.; (acq 7-28-00; grpsl).
Arbitron Metro Market: Stockton, CA; *Format:* Tejano
Lisa Vela, Senior Vice President

***KAIS(FM)**
01-01-2004; 90.7 MHz FM; *Hrs Open:* 24; 210 w; Ant 1,745 ft; N37 33 37 W121 36 19
PO Box 2098, Omaha, NE 68103-2098
(800) 525-5683; *Fax:* (916) 251-1650
www.klove.com
klove@klove.com
License: Tracy, San Joaquin County, CA held by Educational Media Foundation.
Group Owner: EMF Broadcasting
Nat'l Network: K-Love
Population Served: 967,487; *Arbitron Metro Market:* San Jose, CA; *Format:* Christian; *No. News Employees:* 3; *Target Audience:* 25-44; Judeo Christian, female
Darrell Chambliss, Chairman
Mike Novak, President and CEO
David Pierce, Programming Director
Ed Lenane, News Director
Sam Wallington, Engineering Dir
Marya Morgan, News Reporter
Richard Hunt, News Reporter
Laura Daniels, NewsReporter
Tim Luttrell, News Reporter
Kenny Noble Cortes, News Reporter
Darren Vinson, News Reporter

Truckee

KTKE
01-01-2003; 101.5 MHz FM; *Hrs Open:* 24; 0.14 kw; 1988 ft.; N39 14 29 W120 8 20
12030 Donner Pass Road, Truckee, CA 96161 US
(530) 587-9999; *Fax:* (530) 587-9119
www.truckeetahoeradio.com
info@truckeetahoeradio.com
License: Truckee, Nevada County, CA held by Todd Robinson, Inc
Arbitron Metro Market: Truckee, CA; *Format:* Triple A
Jon Robinson, President
Lindsay Romack, General Manager
Keith Thomas, Sales Manager
Lindsay Romack, Program Manager
Sue Waters, Music Director

Tulare

KBOS-FM
01-01-1965; 94.9 MHz FM; *Hrs Open:* 24; 16.5 kw; 863 ft.; N36 38 11.3 W118 56 33.1
83 E. Shaw Ave., Suite 150, Fresno, CA 93711 US
(559) 230-4300; *Fax:* (559) 243-4301
www.b95forlife.com
License: Tulare, Tulare County, CA held by Capstar TX LLC
Group Owner: iHeartMedia; (acq 8-30-00; grpsl).
Arbitron Metro Market: Fresno, CA; *Format:* Contemporary Hits/Top 40; *Target Audience:* 12-34.
Steve Weed, Operations Manager/Program Director
Jeff Negrete, General Manager
Steve Darnell, Director of Sales
David Abenojar, Promotions Director
Nik Ashjian, Digital Content Director

KGEN
01-01-1957; 1370 kHz AM; *Hrs Open:* 24
323 E. San Joaquin St., Tulare, CA 93274 US
(559) 686-1370; *Fax:* (559) 685-1394
License: Tulare, CA held by Azteca Broadcasting Corp.
Group Owner: Azteca Broadcasting Corp.
Arbitron Metro Market: Visalia-Tulare, CA; *Format:* Tejano; *Target Audience:* General.

KJUG
08-01-1946; 1270 kHz AM; *Hrs Open:* 24; 5 kw-D, DAN; 1 kw-N, DAN; N36 10 6 W119 15 12
1401 W. Caldwell Avenue, Visalia, CA 93277 US
(559) 553-1500; *Fax:* (559) 627-1496
www.kjugam.com
License: Tulare, CA held by Momentum Broadcasting
Nat'l Network: ABC; *Nat'l Reps:* Interep
Arbitron Metro Market: Visalia, CA; *Format:* Country *Special Programming:* Farm 5 hrs wkly; *Hrs. of News Programming:* news progmg 7 hrs wkly; *No. News Employees:* 1; *Target Audience:* 25-64.
Don Groppetti, President
Bill Lynch, General Manager
Genia Taylor, Business Manager
Randy Hendrix, Programming Director

KJUG-FM
05-06-1965; 106.7 MHz FM; *Hrs Open:* 24; 27.1 kw; 481 ft.; N36 14 31.9 W118 52 23.2
700 E. Mineral King Ave., Visalia, CA 93277 US
(559) 553-1500; *Fax:* (559) 627-1496
www.kjug.com
License: Tulare, Tulare County, CA held by Momentum Broadcasting LP
Group Owner: Momentum Broadcasting LP
Arbitron Metro Market: Visalia, CA; *Format:* Country; *Target Audience:* 18-54.
Don Groppetti, President
William Lynch, General Manager
Fawn Purdy, Sales Manager

Tulelake

KFLS-FM
07-23-1993; 96.5 MHz FM; *Hrs Open:* 24; 20 kw; 2156 ft.; N42 5 50 W121 37 59
Mailing Address: 1338 Oregon Avenue, Klamath Falls, OR 97601 US
Second Address: 1338 Oregon Ave., Klamath Falls, OR 97601
(541) 882-4656; *Fax:* (541) 884-2845
www.klamathradio.com
traffic@klamathradio.com
License: Tulelake, Siskiyou County, CA held by Wynne Enterprises LLC
Group Owner: Wynne Enterprises LLC
Regional Reps: Tacher.
Arbitron Metro Market: Klamath Falls, OR; *Format:* Country; *Target Audience:* 18-49.
Robert Wynne, CEO
Leslie Hougan, General Sales Mgr
Randy Adams, Programming Director
Lyle Ahrens, News Director
Russ Jump, Chief Engineer
Carol Fritch, Traffic Manager

Turlock

***KBDG**
01-01-1977; 90.9 MHz FM; *Hrs Open:* 24; 0.73 kw; 39 ft.; N37 31 1 W120 52 10
Mailing Address: P O Box 192, Turlock, CA 95381 US
Second Address: 1600 E. Canal Dr., Turlock, CA 95380
(209) 668-7176; *Fax:* (209) 668-2322
www.aaccot.org
License: Turlock, Stanislaus County, CA held by Assyrian American Civic Club.
Arbitron Metro Market: Turlock, CA; *Format:* Talk
Zaya Sargis, Station Manager

***KCSS**
08-13-1975; 91.9 MHz FM; *Hrs Open:* 20; 0.4 kw vert; 105 ft.; N37 31 35 W120 51 25
801 W. Monte Vista Ave., Turlock, CA 95382 US
(209) 667-3378 (office)(209) 667-3900 (stn); *Fax:* (209) 667-3901
www.kcss.net
License: Turlock, Stanislaus County, CA held by California State University, Stanislaus.
Arbitron Metro Market: Turlock, CA; *Format:* Variety/Diverse
Special Programming: Class 9 hrs, jazz 4 hrs, Americana 10 hrs, wkly; *Target Audience:* 18-54.
Greg Jacquay, General Manager
Garrett Neely, Station Manager
Clay Hobbs, Promotions Manager

KLOC
10-01-1949; 1390 kHz AM; 5 kw-D, DA2; 5 kw-N, DA2; N37 31 48 W120 41 37
4043 Geer Rd, Hughson, CA 95326 US
(209) 883-8760; *Fax:* (209) 883-8769
www.lafavorita.net
ngomez@lafavorita.net
License: Turlock, Stanislaus County, CA held by La Favorita Radio Network, Inc.
Group Owner: La Favorita Radio Network; (acq 5-16-03; $500,000).
Arbitron Metro Market: Hughson, CA; *Format:* Religious, Spanish
Nelson Gomez, General Manager

Twain Harte

KKBN
10-19-1985; 93.5 MHz FM; *Hrs Open:* 24; 0.4 kw; 1,262 ft.; N38 0 30 W120 21 44
342 S. Washington St., Sonora, CA 95370-5020 US
(209) 533-1450; *Fax:* (209) 533-9520
www.kkbn.com
License: Twain Harte, Tuolumne County, CA held by Clarke Broadcasting Corp.
Group Owner: Clarke Broadcasting Corp.; (acq 3-1-2000; $2.2 million)
Nat'l Network: Fox News Radio; *Wire Services:* AP

Arbitron Metro Market: Modesto, CA; *Format:* Country; *Hrs. of News Programming:* news progmg 4 hrs wkly; *No. News Employees:* 3; *Target Audience:* 25-54; general
H. Randolph Holder Jr., President
Larry England, General Manager/Director of Sales
Joe Marshall, Programming Director
MaryAnn Curmi, Promotions Director

Twentynine Palms

KCDZ
07-15-1989; 107.7 MHz FM; *Hrs Open:* 24; 6.7 kw; 305 ft.; N34 9 15 W116 11 50
6448 Hallee Road, #5, Joshua Tree, CA 92252 US
(760) 366-8471; *Fax:* (760) 366-2976
www.kcdzfm.com
License: Twentynine Palms, San Bernardino County, CA held by Morongo Basin Broadcasting Corp.
Nat'l Network: ABC; *Wire Services:* AP
Format: Adult Contemp; *Hrs. of News Programming:* news progmg 10 hrs wkly; *No. News Employees:* 6; *Target Audience:* 25-54; *Adv. Rates:* 18; 17; 18; 15
Cynthia Daigneault, President/General Sales Manager
Cody Joseph, Operations Manager
Eddie Hernandez, Chief Engineer
Gary Daigneault, Executive Vice President

KCLZ
12-01-1996; 95.5 MHz FM; *Hrs Open:* 24; 3.8 kw; 230 ft.; N34 9 16 W116 12 4
1321 N. Gene Autry Trail, Palm Springs, CA 92262 US
(760) 322-7890; *Fax:* (760) 322-5493
www.937kclb.com
License: Twentynine Palms, San Bernardino County, CA held by Alpha Media Licensee LLC
Group Owner: Alpha Media LLC
Nat'l Network: Fox News; Fox Sports; *Nat'l Reps:* Christal
Population Served: 64,000; *Arbitron Metro Market:* Twentynine Palms, CA; *Format:* Rock/AOR; *No. News Employees:* 1; *Target Audience:* 25-54
Tricia Bastida, Senior Vice President and Market Manager
David Nola, General Sales Mgr
Cristine Constantinescu, Director of Promotions, Marketing & Digital Media
Bill Watson, Chief Engineer

Ukiah

*KPRA
05-01-1987; 89.5 MHz FM; *Hrs Open:* 24; 1.6 kw; 1135 ft.; N39 7 1 W123 13 54
Mailing Address: 4135 Northgate Blvd #1, Sacramento, CA 95834 US
Second Address: 290 Hegenberger Rd., Oakland, CA 94621
(916) 641-8191; *Fax:* (916) 641-8238
www.familyradio.com
info@familyradio.com
License: Ukiah, Mendocino County, CA held by Family Stations Inc.
Group Owner: Family Stations Inc.; acq 2-3-86)
Format: Christian, Religious
Matt Pearce, Operations Dir
Tom Evans, General Manager

KQPM
02-01-1989; 105.9 MHz FM; *Hrs Open:* 24; 1.9 kw; 2018 ft.; N39 7 50 W123 4 32
140 N. Main St., Lakeport, CA 95453 US
(707) 263-6113; *Fax:* (707) 263-0939
www.kqpm.com
License: Ukiah, Mendocino County, CA held by Bicoastal Media L.L.C.
Group Owner: Bicoastal Media L.L.C.; acq 7-28-99; grpsl)
Format: Country; *Adv. Rates:* 20; 18; 20; 16
Mike Wilson, President & COO

KUKI
10-01-1950; 1400 kHz AM; *Hrs Open:* 24
1400 Kuki Lane, Ukiah, CA 95482 US
(707) 466-5868; *Fax:* (707) 468-5361
www.kukifm.com
ukiah@bicoastalspots.com
License: Ukiah, CA held by Bicoastal Media Licenses, LLC
Group Owner: Bicoastal Media L.L.C.; (acq 7-28-2006; grpsl)
Arbitron Metro Market: Ukiah, CA; *Format:* Spanish; *Hrs. of News Programming:* news progmg 25 hrs wkly; *No. News Employees:* 2; *Target Audience:* 25 plus; upwardly mobile adults
Mike Wilson, President & COO
Kristina Lebrett, Station Manager

KUKI-FM
10-16-1974; 103.3 MHz FM; 2.9 kw; 1778 ft.; N39 19 35 W123 16 11
1400 Kuki Lane, Ukiah, CA 95482 US
(707) 466-5868; *Fax:* (707) 468-5361
www.kukifm.com
ukiah@bicoastalspots.com
License: Ukiah, Mendocino County, CA held by Bicoastal Media Licenses, LLC
Group Owner: Bicoastal Media L.L.C.
Nat'l Network: ABC
Arbitron Metro Market: Ukiah, CA; *Format:* Country; *Hrs. of News Programming:* news progmg 7 hrs wkly; *No. News Employees:* 1; *Target Audience:* 25-54.
Mike Wilson, President & COO
Kristina Lebrett, Station Manager

KWNE
01-01-1968; 94.5 MHz FM; *Hrs Open:* 24; 2.2 kw; 1965 ft.; N39 7 50 W123 4 32
Mailing Address: P.O. Box 1056, Ukiah, CA 95482 US
Second Address: 1100 Hastings Rd., Suite B, Ukiah, CA 95482
(707) 462-1451(707) 462-0945; *Fax:* (707) 462-4670
www.kwine.com
kwine@kwine.com
License: Ukiah, Mendocino County, CA held by Broadcasting Corp of Mendocino County.
Arbitron Metro Market: Ukiah, CA; *Format:* Adult Contemp
Special Programming: Sp 4 hrs, farm one hr wkly; *Hrs. of News Programming:* news progmg 12 hrs wkly; *No. News Employees:* 1; *Target Audience:* 18-54;young adult; *Adv. Rates:* 30; 28; 30; 24
Guilford Dye, President
Gudrun Dye, Operations Dir
Mike Spencer, Station Manager

KXBX
06-17-1966; 1270 kHz AM; *Hrs Open:* 24; 0.5 kw-D, ND1; 0.097 kw-N, ND1; N39 0 50 W122 53 39
1400 Kuki Lane, Ukiah, CA 95482 US
(707) 466-5868; *Fax:* (707) 468-5361
www.kxbx.com
License: Ukiah, CA held by Bicoastal Media LLC.
Group Owner: Bicoastal Media L.L.C.; acq 7-28-99; grpsl)
Nat'l Network: Westwood One
Arbitron Metro Market: Lakeport, CA; *Format:* Adult Contemp, Oldies *Special Programming:* Sp 3 hrs, loc talk & info 5 hrs wkly; *Hrs. of News Programming:* news progmg 4 hrs wkly; *No. News Employees:* 1 *TargetAudience:* 40 plus; retirees; *Adv. Rates:* 16; 14; 16; 12
Mike Wilson, President & COO

*KULV
09-22-2003; 97.1 MHz FM; *Hrs Open:* 24; 0.13 kw; 1978 ft.; N39 7 50 W123 4 32
1425 North Market Blvd, Suite 9, Sacramento, CA 95834 US
(800) 525-5683; *Fax:* (916) 251-1650
www.klove.com
klove@klove.com
License: Ukiah, Mendocino County, CA held by Educational Media Foundation.
Group Owner: EMF Broadcasting
Nat'l Network: K-Love
Arbitron Metro Market: Ukiah, CA; *Format:* Christian; *No. News Employees:* 3; *Target Audience:* 25-44; Judeo Christian, female
Darrell Chambliss, Chairman
Mike Novak, President and CEO
David Pierce, Programming Director
Ed Lenane, News Director
Sam Wallington, Engineering Dir

Vacaville

KUIC
11-01-1968; 95.3 MHz FM; *Hrs Open:* 24; 0.49 kw; 2,024 ft.; N38 23 42 W122 5 57
555 Mason St., Suite 245, Vacaville, CA 95688 US
(707) 446-0200; *Fax:* (707) 446-0122
www.kuic.com
gm@kuic.com
License: Vacaville, Solano County, CA held by Alpha Media Licensee LLC
Group Owner: Alpha Media LLC; (acq 5-1-2015; grpsl).
Arbitron Metro Market: Vacaville, CA; *Format:* Adult Contemp; *Hrs. of News Programming:* news progmg one hr wkly; *No. News Employees:* 3; *Target Audience:* General; middle class, professionals; *Adv. Rates:* 120;110; 120; 90
Jim Hampton, Operations Manager
Kristi Willard, Local Sales Manager
Robin Mitchell, Director of Marketing and Promotions
Ken Hiemke, Sales Manager

Vallejo

KDIA
03-19-1996; 1640 kHz AM; *Hrs Open:* 24
3260 Blume Drive, Suite 520, San Pablo, CA 94806 US
(510) 222-4242; *Fax:* (510) 262-9054
www.kdia.com
andy.santamaria@kdia.com
License: Vallejo, CA held by Baybridge Communications L.L.C.
Arbitron Metro Market: San Francisco; *Format:* Religious *Special Programming:* Relg 5 hrs, Black 2 hrs, gospel 7 hrs wkly; *Hrs. of News Programming:* News progmg 5 hrs wkly; *Target Audience:* 25-54.
Clifford Brown, Operations Dir
Andy Santamaria, General Manager

KDYA
08-01-1947; 1190 kHz AM; *Hrs Open:* 24; 1 kw-D, NDD; N38 7 2 W122 15 20
600 East Main Street, Vacaville, CA 95688 US
(510) 222-4242; *Fax:* (510) 262-9054
www.gospel1190.net
andysantamaria@gospel1190.net
License: Vallejo, CA held by Baybridge Communications L.L.C.
Arbitron Metro Market: San Francisco; *Format:* Gospel *Special Programming:* Relg 5 hrs, Black 2 hrs, gospel 7 hrs wkly; *Hrs. of News Programming:* News progmg 5 hrs wkly; *Target Audience:* 25-54.
Andy Santamaria, President
Clifford Brown, Programming Director

Ventura

KBBY-FM
12-27-1962; 95.1 MHz FM; 12.5 kw; 876 ft.; N34 6 47 W119 3 34
1376 Walter Street, Ventura, CA 93003 US
(805) 642-8595; *Fax:* (805) 656-5838
www.b951.com
info@cumulus.com
License: Ventura, Ventura County, CA held by Cumulus Licensing Corp.
Group Owner: Cumulus Media Inc.; (acq 9-22-00; grpsl)
Nat'l Network: Westwood One
Arbitron Metro Market: Ventura, CA; *Format:* Adult Contemp; *Target Audience:* 18-54.
Chris Cox, Operations Dir
Sommer Frisk, VP/Marketing Manager

KHAY
01-01-1962; 100.7 MHz FM; 39 kw; 1211 ft.; N34 20 55 W119 19 57
1376 Walter Street, Ventura, CA 93003 US
(805) 642-8595; *Fax:* (805) 656-5838
www.khay.com
info@cumulus.com
License: Ventura, Ventura County, CA
Group Owner: Cumulus Media Inc.
Arbitron Metro Market: Oxnard-Ventura, CA; *Format:* Country; *Target Audience:* 18-54.
Tim Koza, Chief Engineer
Sommer Frisk, VP/Marketing Manager
Tom Watson, Programming Director
Chris Cox, Operations Manager
Dave Bradley, Production Director
Jennifer Dempsey, Promotions Director
Barbara Haser, Traffic Manager

KVTA
10-15-1994; 1590 kHz AM; 5 kw-D, DA2; 5 kw-N, DA2; N34 14 13 W119 12 9
2319 Alameda Ave, Suite 1D, Ventura, CA 93003 US
(805) 289-1400; *Fax:* (805) 644-7906
www.kvta.com
License: Ventura, Ventura West County, CA held by Gold Coast Broadcasting LLC.
Group Owner: Gold Coast Broadcasting LLC; (acq 2-10-97; $2 million with KFYV(FM) Ojai)
Nat'l Network: Premiere Networks; Westwood One; TheBlaze; Salem Radio Network
Arbitron Metro Market: Ventura, CA; *Format:* News, News/Talk, 86; *Target Audience:* 35 plus.
Chip Ehrhardt, National Sales Director
Mark Elliott, Programming Director

KVEN
03-01-1948; 1450 kHz AM; 1 kw-U, ND1; N34 15 39 W119 14 28
One Office Park Circle, Suite 300, Birmingham, AL 35223 US
(805) 642-8595; *Fax:* (805) 656-5838
www.kven.com
info@cumulus.com

RADIO - U.S.

License: Ventura, CA held by Cumulus Licensing Corp.
Group Owner: Cumulus Media Inc.; (acq 9-22-00; grpsl)
Arbitron Metro Market: Oxnard, CA; *Format:* Oldies; *Target Audience:* 25 plus; affluent, educated, professional with above average income
Gail Furillo, General Manager
Ernie Bingham, General Sales Mgr
Bo Jaxson, Programming Director
Jennifer Caldwell, Promotions Manager
Cyndy Abarre, News Director
J.D. Strahler, Chief Engineer
Sommer Frisk, Director of Sales
NeryReyes, Human Resources Manager

KSSC
11-01-1989; 107.1 MHz FM; *Hrs Open:* 24; 0.37 kw; 1296 ft.; N34 20 55 W119 19 57
5700 Wilshire Blvd., Los Angeles, CA 90036 US
(323) 900-6100; *Fax:* (323) 900-6119
www.superestrella.com
License: Ventura, Ventura County, CA held by Entravision Holdings LLC.
Group Owner: Entravision Communications Corp.; (acq 4-1-03; grpsl).
Arbitron Metro Market: Oxnard-Ventura, CA; *Format:* Spanish, Contemporary Hits/Top 40
Juan Navarr0, Interactive Sales Manager
Nestor Rocha, Programming Director
Elias Autran, Promotions Manager

Victorville

KVFG
09-11-2000; 103.1 MHz FM; *Hrs Open:* 24; 0.25 kW; N34 23 19 W117 23 29
11920 Hesperia Rd., Hesperia, CA 92345 USA
(760) 244-2000
www.cbsradio.com
License: Victorville, San Bernardino County, CA held by CBS Radio Stations Inc.
Group Owner: CBS Radio; (acq 7-19-00; $3,537,500 with KRAK(AM) Hesperia).
Nat'l Network: ABC
TV Affiliate: ESPN; *Format:* Oldies; *Target Audience:* 25-54
Jeff Salkin, General Sales Mgr
Lee Douglas, Programming Director
Leslie Bischoff, Promotions Manager

***KHMS**
01-03-1993; 88.5 MHz FM; *Hrs Open:* 24; 0.2 kw; 1512 ft.; N34 36 40 W117 17 20 *Rebroadcasts:* Rebroadcasts KSOS(FM) Las Vegas 100%
2201 South 6th Street, Las Vegas, NV 89104 US
(702) 731-5452; *Fax:* (702) 731-1992
www.sosradio.net
brad@sosradio.net
License: Victorville, San Bernardino County, CA held by Faith Communications Corp.
Group Owner: Faith Communications Corp.; (acq 4-5-91;
Format: Adult Contemp, Christian *Special Programming:* Family 2 hrs wkly; *Target Audience:* 25-44; young families
Brad Staley, General Manager
Scott Herrold, Programming Director
Chris Staley, VP of Programing/Administration
Dan Young, Music Director
Robert Forbes, Promotions Director
Tim Hunt, Director of Engineering

***KXRD**
10-18-1994; 89.5 MHz FM; *Hrs Open:* 24; 1.25 kw; 1411 ft.; N34 36 44 W117 17 27 *Rebroadcasts:* Rebroadcasts KLRD(FM) Yucaipa 100%
1425 North Market Blvd, Suite 9, Sacramento, CA 95834 US
(888) 937-2471; *Fax:* (916) 251-1650 (700) 528-9246
www.air1.com
info@air1.com
License: Victorville, San Bernardino County, CA held by Educational Media Foundation.
Group Owner: EMF Broadcasting; (acq 1-22-99).
Nat'l Network: Air 1
Arbitron Metro Market: Omaha, NE; *Format:* Alternative, Christian; *Hrs. of News Programming:* News progmg 7 hrs wkly; *Target Audience:* 18-34.
Mike Novak, President
Fernando Chaidez, Operations Dir
David Pierce, Programming Director
Ed Lenane, News Director
Sam Wallington, Engineering Dir
Marya Morgan, News Reporter
Richard Hunt, News Reporter

Visalia

***KARM**
01-01-1990; 89.7 MHz FM; 1 kw; 810 ft.; N36 38 10 W118 56 32
1300 South Woodland Dr., Visalia, CA 93291 US
(559) 627-5276; *Fax:* (559) 627-5288
www.mypromisefm.com
info@promisefm.com
License: Visalia, Tulare County, CA held by Harvest Broadcasting Co.
Nat'l Network: ABC
Arbitron Metro Market: Visalia, CA; *Format:* Christian, Religious
Dr. Richard Dunn, Chairman
Loren Olson, General Manager

***KDUV**
01-01-1992; 88.9 MHz FM; 1 kw; 2648 ft.; N36 17 14 W118 50 17
130 N. Kelsey, Ste H-123, Visalia, CA 93291 US
(559) 651-4111; *Fax:* (559) 651-4115
www.kduvfm.com
info@kduvfm.com
License: Visalia, Tulare County, CA held by Community Educational Broadcasting Inc.
Arbitron Metro Market: Visalia-Tulare-Hanford, CA; *Format:* Christian
Bob Croft, President
Bob Croft, General Manager
Michael Langley, Marketing Director
Jeremy Morris, News Director

KFSO-FM
09-01-1951; 92.9 MHz FM; 17.5 kw; 853 ft.; N36 38 8.7 W118 56 32.2
83 E. Shaw Ave., Suite 150, Fresno, CA 93710 US
(559) 230-4300; *Fax:* (559) 243-4301
www.lapreciosa929.com
License: Visalia, Tulare County, CA held by Capstar TX LLC
Group Owner: iHeartMedia; (acq 2-4-2009)
Arbitron Metro Market: Visalia, CA; *Format:* Spanish *Special Programming:* Religious 3 hrs wkly
Jeff Negrete, Market Manager
Steve Darnell, General Sales Mgr
Jose Robles, Promotions Director

KRZR
12-24-1976; 1400 kHz AM; *Hrs Open:* 24; 1 kw-U, ND1; 499 ft; N36 21 14 W119 17 2
83 East Shaw Avenue, Suite 150, Fresno, CA 93710 US
(559) 230-4300; *Fax:* (559) 243-4301
www.powertalk967.com
License: Visalia, CA held by Capstar TX LLC
Group Owner: iHeartMedia; (acq 8-30-00; grpsl).
Arbitron Metro Market: Fresno, CA; *Format:* News, News/Talk, 86; *Hrs. of News Programming:* News progmg one hr wkly; *Target Audience:* 18-34; male; *Adv. Rates:* 80; 80; 80; 50
Steve Weed, Operations Manager/Program Director
Jeff Negrete, General Manager
Steve Darnell, Sales Director
David Abenojar, Promotions Director
Nik Ashjian, Digital Content Director

KSEQ
10-01-1984; 97.1 MHz FM; 17 kw; 778 ft.; N36 38 8 W118 56 32
1110 E. Olive Ave., Fresno, CA 93728 US
(559) 497-1100
www.q97.com
kororke@lotusfresno.com
License: Visalia, Tulare County, CA held by Lotus Fresno Corp.
Group Owner: Lotus Communications Corp.; (acq 7-11-2014).
Nat'l Reps: Eastman Radio
Arbitron Metro Market: Visalia-Tulare-Hanford, CA; *Format:* Contemporary Hits/Top 40; *Target Audience:* 18-49.
Kevin O'Rorke, General Manager
Francisco Villarreal, Regional Sales Manager
Jon Ballard, Programming Director

Vista

KCEO
11-03-1967; 1000 kHz AM; *Hrs Open:* 24
2888 Loker Avenue, Carlsbad, CA 92010 US
(760) 729-1000; *Fax:* (760) 476-9604
reception@astorbroadcastgroup.com
License: Vista, CA held by North County Broadcasting Corp.
Group Owner: Astor Broadcast Group; (acq 4-30-97; $2.6 million).
Nat'l Network: Westwood One
Arbitron Metro Market: San Diego, CA; *Format:* Talk; *Hrs. of News Programming:* News progmg 20 hrs wkly; *Target Audience:* 35 plus.
Arthur Astor, President
Rick Roome, Operations Dir
Susan Burke, Executive Vice President/General Manager

Walnut

***KSAK**
01-10-1974; 90.1 MHz FM; *Hrs Open:* 24; 0.004 kw; 417 ft.; N34 2 46 W117 51 37
1100 N. Grand Avenue, Walnut, CA 91789 US
(909) 594-5611 EXT. 4678
www.ksak.com
ksak@mtsac.edu
License: Walnut, Los Angeles County, CA held by Mount San Antonio Community College District.
Wire Services: UPI
Arbitron Metro Market: Walnut, CA; *Format:* Christian; *Target Audience:* 18-25; students
Cason Smith, General Manager

Walnut Creek

KKDV
12-10-1959; 92.1 MHz FM; 3 kw; 79 ft.; N37 54 2 W122 5 7
7901 Stoneridge Dr., Suite 525, Pleasanton, CA 94588 US
(925) 944-6300; *Fax:* (925) 416-1211
www.kkdv.com
gm@kkdv.com
License: Walnut Creek, Contra Costa County, CA held by Alpha Media Licensee LLC
Group Owner: Alpha Media LLC; (acq 5-1-2015; grpsl).
Regional Reps: Lotus.
Arbitron Metro Market: San Francisco, CA; *Format:* Adult Contemp *Special Programming:* Hometown Mornings 24 hrs wkly; *Target Audience:* Adults; 25-54; *Adv. Rates:* 65; 65; 65;65
Jim Hampton, Operations Manager
Kristi Willard, Local Sales Manager
Robin Mitchell, Director of Marketing and Promotions
Ken Hiemke, Sales Manager

Wasco

***KFHL**
01-01-2005; 91.7 MHz FM; 6 kw; 240 ft.; N35 24 55 W119 14 1
PO Box 107, Keene, TX 76059 US
(661) 872-0030
www.kfhlradio.com
kfhlradio@yahoo.com
License: Wasco, Kern County, CA held by Mary V. Harris Foundation.
Arbitron Metro Market: Wasco, CA; *Format:* Christian, Talk
Robin Wade, Programming Director

Wasco-Greenacres

KERN
05-17-1950; 1180 kHz AM; *Hrs Open:* 24; 50 kw-D, DA2; 10 kw-N, DA2; N35 34 17 W119 19 26
1400 Easton Drive, Suite 144 B, Bakersfield, CA 93309
(661) 328-1410; *Fax:* (661) 283-7992
www.kernradio.com
License: Wasco-Greenacres, Kern West County, CA held by AGM California, Inc.
Group Owner: American General Media; (acq 9-27-2004; $1.83 million)
Nat'l Reps: Salem
Arbitron Metro Market: Bakersfield, CA; *Format:* News, News/Talk, 86; *Target Audience:* Adults 35+
Robert Lewis, Director, Operations & Operations
Wayne Stephens, Director, Sales

KERN
05-17-1950; 96.1 MHz FM; *Hrs Open:* 24; 50 kw-D, DA2; 10 kw-N, DA2; N35 34 17 W119 19 26
1400 Easton Drive, Suite 144 B, Bakersfield, CA 93309
(661) 328-1410; *Fax:* (661) 283-7992
www.kernradio.com
License: Wasco-Greenacres, Kern West County, CA held by AGM California, Inc.
Group Owner: American General Media; (acq 9-27-2004; $1.83 million)
Nat'l Reps: Salem
Arbitron Metro Market: Bakersfield, CA; *Format:* News, News/Talk, 86; *Target Audience:* Adults 35+
Robert Lewis, Director, Operations & Operations
Wayne Stephens, Director, Sales

Weaverville

KHRD
01-01-2000; 103.1 MHz FM; *Hrs Open:* 24; 0.6 kw; 3593 ft.; N40 36 10 W122 38 58

1588 Charles Dr., Reading, CA 96003 US
(530) 244-9700; *Fax:* (530) 244-9707
www.red1031.com
License: Weaverville, Trinity County, CA held by Results Radio of Redding Licensee LLC.
Group Owner: Results Radio; (acq 6-11-99; grpsl).
Arbitron Metro Market: Redding, CA; *Format:* Classic Rock

Weed

KSIZ
11-01-1983; 102.3 MHz FM; *Hrs Open:* 24; 15.5 kw; 1942 ft.; N41 21 30 W122 12 21
113 East Alma, Mt. Shasta, CA 96067 US
(530) 926-5946; *Fax:* (530) 926-0830
kcwhfm@yahoo.com
License: Weed, Siskiyou County, CA held by TRC Enterprises, LLC
Format: Contemporary Hits/Top 40, Adult Contemp *Special Programming:* Nostalgia 2 hrs wkly; *Hrs. of News Programming:* news progmg 6 hrs wkly; *No. News Employees:* 1; *Target Audience:* 25-54.; *Adv. Rates:* 13;12; 10; na
Rick Martin, General Manager
Al Blackmore, General Sales Mgr

West Covina

KALI
09-25-1963; 900 kHz AM; *Hrs Open:* 24; 0.5 kw-D, DA2; 0.079 kw-N, DA2; N34 1 54 W117 56 6
14541 Brookhurst St., Westminster, CA 92683 US
(562) 401-4030; *Fax:* (562) 401-4032
www.saigonradio.com
License: West Covina, CA held by Multicultural Radio Broadcasting Licensee LLC.
Group Owner: Multicultural Radio Broadcasting Inc.; (acq 10-5-98; $9 million).
Arbitron Metro Market: Downet, CA; *Format:* Vietnamese
Arthur Liu, CEO/COO

KRCV
11-18-1957; 98.3 MHz FM; *Hrs Open:* 24; 6 kw; 299 ft.; N34 4 18 W117 48 46
610 S. Ardmore Ave., Los Angeles, CA 90005 US
(323) 468-5272; *Fax:* (323) 465-0230
www.univision.com
License: West Covina, Los Angeles County, CA held by Univision Radio License Corp.
Group Owner: Univision Radio; (acq 9-22-2003; grpsl).
Arbitron Metro Market: Los Angeles, CA; *Format:* Oldies, Spanish; *Hrs. of News Programming:* News progmg 3 hrs wkly; *Target Audience:* 18-49; Sp speaking Hispanics, primarily of Mexican origin
Haz Montana, Operations Manager
Michelle Hohman, Regional Manager
Jason Strongin, Director of Sales
Amalia Gonzalez, Programming Director
Olga Jaramillo, Promotions Manager
Tom Koza, Chief Engineer

West Sacramento

KIFM
04-01-1945; 1320 kHz AM; *Hrs Open:* 24
5345 Madison Avenue, Sacramento, CA 95841 US
(916) 334-7777; *Fax:* (916) 339-4280
www.espn1320.net
License: West Sacramento, CA held by Entercom Sacramento License LLC.
Group Owner: Entercom Communications Corp.; (acq 10-17-97)
Nat'l Network: ESPN Radio
Arbitron Metro Market: Sacramento, CA; *Format:* Sports
Brian Lopez, Programming Director
Bryan Fox, Promotions Manager
Sean Shannon, VP/Market Manager
Lance Richard, VP Sales

KSMH
02-01-1999; 1620 kHz AM; *Hrs Open:* 24
7956 California Avenue, Fair Oaks, CA 95628 US
(916) 535-0500; *Fax:* (916) 535-0504
www.ihradio.org
info@ihradio.org
License: West Sacramento, CA held by IHR Educational Broadcasting.
Group Owner: IHR Educational Broadcasting; (acq 4-28-99; $475,000 with KAHI(AM) Auburn).
Arbitron Metro Market: Loomis, CA; *Format:* Religious
Doug Sherman, President
Frank Kavenik, Director
Dick Jenkins, General Manager

Westwood

*KWLK
88.5 MHz FM; 0.27 kw H 0.27 kw V; 2352 ft.; N40 20 14.50 W120 52 11.10
Mailing Address: P.O. Box 450, Susanville, CA 96130 US
Second Address: 450 Richmond Rd, Susanville, CA 96130
(530) 257-4833
www.kwlkradio.org
office@kwlkradio.org
License: Westwood, Lassen County, CA held by Calvary Chapel of Susanville
Group Owner: Calvary Chapel of Susanville
Arbitron Metro Market: Westwood, CA; *Format:* Religious

Williams

*KARA
10-28-2003; 99.1 MHz FM; *Hrs Open:* 24; 0.9 kw; 108 ft.; N39 8 7 W122 7 58
1425 N Market Blvd, Suite 9, Sacramento, CA 95834 US
(888) 937-2471; *Fax:* (916) 251-1650
www.air1.com
info@air1.com
License: Williams, Colusa County, CA held by Educational Media Foundation.
Group Owner: EMF Broadcasting
Nat'l Network: Air 1
Arbitron Metro Market: Sacramento, CA; *Format:* Alternative, Christian; *No. News Employees:* 3; *Target Audience:* 18-35; Judeo-Christian, female
Darrell Chambliss, Chairman
Alan Mason, COO
Mike Novak, President and CEO
Ed Lenane, News Director
Sam Wallington, Engineering Dir
Tracy Butler, Traffic Manager
Larry Moody, Director
Mitch Barnhart, Director
David R. Ferry,Director
Walter Golembeski, Director
David Pierce, Chief Creative Officer

Willits

KMKX
02-19-2000; 93.5 MHz FM; *Hrs Open:* 24; 0.89 kw; 2874 ft.; N39 30 59 W123 5 21
12 West Valley Street, 1799-2 Silverado Trail, Napa, CA 94558 US
(707) 462-1483; *Fax:* (707) 462-4670
www.maxrock.com
License: Willits, Mendocino County, CA held by Radio Millennium L L C
Nat'l Network: Westwood One
Arbitron Metro Market: Redding, CA; *Format:* Rock/AOR; *Hrs. of News Programming:* news progmg 1 hr wkly; *No. News Employees:* 1; *Target Audience:* 18-60; adults; *Adv. Rates:* 24; 22; 24; 18
Guilford Dye, President
Gudrun Dye, Operations Dir
Guilford Dye, General Manager
Mike Spencer, Station Manager

*KZYZ
01-01-1995; 91.5 MHz FM; *Hrs Open:* 18; 1.7 kw; 1788 ft.; N39 19 35 W123 16 10 *Rebroadcasts:* Rebroadcasts KZYX(FM) Philo 100%
P.O. Box 1, Philo, CA 95466 US
(707) 895-2324; *Fax:* (707) 895-2451
www.kzyx.org
License: Willits, Mendocino County, CA held by Mendocino County Public Broadcasting.
Arbitron Metro Market: Willits, CA; *Format:* News, Talk, 94
Rich Culbertson, Operations Dir
John Coate, Executive Director/General Manager
David Steffen, Business Support Coordinator
Mary Aigner, Programming Director

Willows

KIQS
12-29-1961; 1560 kHz AM; 0.25 kw-D, NDD; N39 31 44 W122 10 9
P. O. Box 7, Willows, CA 95988 US
(209) 277-8433; *Fax:* (209) 430-2733
avianhelpprogramcoordinator@yahoo.com
License: Willows, CA held by Radio Pan de Vida LLC
Format: Christian
Martin Godinez, General Manager

Windsor

KJOR
06-20-1997; 104.1 MHz FM; *Hrs Open:* 24; 0.9 kw; 305 ft.; N38 32 28 W122 54 5
200 S. A St., 4th Fl., Oxnard, CA 93030 US
(805) 240-2070
www.radiolazer.com
License: Windsor, Sonoma County, CA held by Lazer Licenses LLC.
Group Owner: Lazer Broadcasting Corp.; (acq 6-29-2006; $6.85 million with KSRT(FM) Cloverdale).
Nat'l Reps: Christal
Format: Oldies; *Target Audience:* 25-54.

*KRCB-FM
09-01-1993; 91.1 MHz FM; *Hrs Open:* 24; 0.12 kw; 732 ft.; N38 44 25 W122 50 46
5850 Labath Avenue, Rohnert Park, CA 94928 US
(707) 584-2000; *Fax:* (707) 585-1363
www.krcb.org
listener@krcb.org
License: Windsor, Sonoma County, CA held by Rural California Broadcasting Corp.
Nat'l Network: NPR; PRI; *Wire Services:* DAC
Arbitron Metro Market: Santa Rosa, CA *TV Affiliate:* *KRCB-TV affil.; *Format:* News, News/Talk, 86 *Special Programming:* Folk 6 hrs, jazz 6 hrs wkly; *Hrs. of News Programming:* news progmg 15 hrs wkly *No. NewsEmployees:* 1; *Target Audience:* General.
Nancy Dobbs, President/CEO
Robin Pressman, Programming Director
Bruce Robinson, News Director
Brian Griffith, Music Director
Larry Stratton, COO

*DKEZD
1580 kHz AM; Ant 43 ft
502 a Avenida Sevilla, Laguna Hills, CA 92653 US
(970) 669-9200
License: Windsor, CA held by Cedar Cove Broadcasting Inc.
Group Owner: Cedar Cove Broadcasting Inc.
Arbitron Metro Market: Estes Park, CO
Victor Michael Jr., President

Winton

KLOQ-FM
01-01-1994; 98.7 MHz FM; *Hrs Open:* 24; 6 kw; 299 ft.; N37 16 41 W120 37 35
1020 W. Main St., Merced, CA 95340 US
(209) 723-2191
www.radiolobo987.com
License: Winton, Merced County, CA held by Mapleton License of Merced LLC.
Group Owner: Mapleton Communications LLC; acq 6-1-2002; grpsl)
Arbitron Metro Market: Merced, CA; *Format:* Tejano; *Target Audience:* 25-49; Hispanic
Diane Garcia, General Sales Mgr
Yolanda Navarro, Programming Director

Woodlake

KFRR
09-01-1994; 104.1 MHz FM; *Hrs Open:* 24; 17 kw; 853 ft.; N36 38 12 W118 56 34
966 East Essex Drive, Fresno, CA 93720 US
(559) 230-0104; *Fax:* (559) 230-0177
License: Woodlake, Tulare County, CA held by Wilks License Co.-Fresno LLC.
Group Owner: Wilks Broadcast Group LLC; (acq 6-1-2005; grpsl)
Nat'l Reps: McGavren Guild
Arbitron Metro Market: Fresno, CA; *Format:* Alternative; *Target Audience:* 18-34; young affluent adults
Jeff Bray, VP/Marketing Manager
Jason Squires, Programming Director

Woodland

KCCL
10-01-1996; 101.5 MHz FM; 0.14 kw; 1975 ft.; N39 12 21 W121 49 11
500 Media Pl., Sacramento, CA 95815 US
(916) 576-7333; *Fax:* (916) 929-5330
1015khits.com
License: Woodland, Butte County, CA held by Results Radio Licensee L.L.C.
Group Owner: Results Radio; (acq 6-11-99; grpsl)
Arbitron Metro Market: Chico, CA; *Format:* Adult Contemp; *Hrs. of News Programming:* news progmg 7 hrs wkly; *No. News Employees:* 1

KSFM
02-04-1961; 102.5 MHz FM; 50 kW; 508 ft.; N38 35 20 W121 43 30
280 Commerce Circle, Sacramento, CA 95815 USA
(916) 923-6800; *Fax:* (916) 922-2830
www.ksfm.com
License: Woodland, Yolo County, CA held by CBS Radio of Sacramento Inc.
Group Owner: CBS Radio; (acq 11-13-98; grpsl).
Nat'l Network: Westwood One
Arbitron Metro Market: Sacramento, CA; *Format:* Contemporary Hits/Top 40; *Target Audience:* 12-44

Yermo

KRXV
02-05-1980; 98.1 MHz FM; *Hrs Open:* 24; 1.55 kw; 2280 ft.; N34 59 43 W116 50 15
Mailing Address: 1611 East Main St, P.O.Box 1668, Barstow, CA 92312 US
Second Address: 101 Convention Center Dr, Suite 1001, Las Vegas, NV 89109
(760) 256-0326; *Fax:* (760) 256-9507
highwayradio.com
info@highwayradio.com
License: Yermo, San Bernardino County, CA held by KHWY, Inc.
Group Owner: KHWY, Inc.
Nat'l Network: AP Radio
Arbitron Metro Market: Barstow, CA; *Format:* Adult Contemp; *Target Audience:* 25-54; travelers on I-15 & I-40 & loc communities
Kirk Anderson, President/COO
John Gregg, Operations Dir

Yreka

***KSYC**
07-27-1947; 1490 kHz AM; *Hrs Open:* 24 hrs
P.O. Box 3463, Carefree, AZ 85377 US
(541) 552-6301; *Fax:* (541) 552-8565
www.ijpr.org
info@ijpr.org
License: Yreka, CA held by JPR Foundation Inc.
Nat'l Network: NPR; PRI
Arbitron Metro Market: Ashland, OR; *Hrs. of News Programming:* news progmg 35 hrs wkly; *No. News Employees:* 1
Ronald Kramer, CEO
Bryon Lambert, Operations Dir
Paul Westhelle, General Sales Mgr
Eric Teel, Programming Director
Ransom,Darin, News Director
Darin Ransom, Engineering Dir
Mitchell Christian, CFO
Eric Alan, Music Director

KSYC-FM
06-01-1983; 103.9 MHz FM; 10 kw; 2359 ft.; N41 36 36 W122 37 26
Mailing Address: P.O. Box 3463, Carefree, AZ 85377 US
Second Address: 316 Lawrence Ln., Yreka, CA 96097
(530) 842-4158; *Fax:* (530) 842-7635
www.ksyc1039.com
ksyc@4fast.net
License: Yreka, Siskiyou County, CA held by Buffalo Broadcasting
Arbitron Metro Market: Yreka, CA; *Format:* Country; *Adv. Rates:* 21; 21; 21; 18
Kevin Sponsler, General Manager
Kevin Sponsler, Programming Director

***KNYR**
01-01-1995; 91.3 MHz FM; *Hrs Open:* 5AM-2am; 0.4 kw; 2365 ft.; N41 36 36 W122 37 26
P.O. Box 3175, Eugene, OR 97403 US
(541) 552-6301; *Fax:* (541) 552-8565
www.ijpr.org
jprinfo@sou.edu
License: Yreka, Siskiyou County, CA held by The State of Oregon, Acting By and Through the State Board of Higher Education for the Benefit of Southern Oregon University.
Nat'l Network: NPR; PRI
Arbitron Metro Market: Yreka, CA; *Format:* News; *Hrs. of News Programming:* news progmg 35 hrs wkly; *No. News Employees:* 1
Ronald Kramer, CEO
Bryon Lambert, Operations Dir
Paul Westhelle, General Sales Mgr
Eric Teel, Programming Director
Darin Ransom, Engineering Dir
Kurt Katzmar, Disc Jockey
Valerie Ing-Miller, Disc Jockey
Eric Alan, MusicDirector
Betsy Byers, Administrative Assistant
Mitchell Christian, Director of Finance & Administration
Jill Hernandez, Accountant Technician

Yuba City

KOBO
06-01-1953; 1450 kHz AM
449 Broadway, New York, NY 10013 US
(530) 742-5555; *Fax:* (530) 741-3758
License: Yuba City, CA held by Tom F. Huth.
Group Owner: Huth Broadcasting; (acq 12-17-2003; $200,000).
Format: Ethnic *Special Programming:* East Indian 3 hrs wkly
Thomas Huth, CEO

KUBA
01-01-1948; 1600 kHz AM; *Hrs Open:* 24
P.O. Box 309, Yuba City, CA 95992 US
(530) 673-1600; *Fax:* (530) 673-3010
www.kubaradio.com
info@lbimedia.com
License: Yuba City, CA held by Nevada County Broadcasters Inc.
Group Owner: Nevada County Broadcasters Inc.; (acq 8-9-2004; $500,000).
Nat'l Network: CBS Radio; *Regional Network:* Calif. Agri-Radio;
Wire Services: AP
Arbitron Metro Market: Yuba City, CA; *Format:* News, News/Talk, 86 *Special Programming:* Farm 4 hrs, gospel 2 hrs, relg 2 hrs wkly; *Hrs. of News Programming:* news progmg 15 hrs wkly; *No. News Employees:* 2 *Target Audience:* 35-64; community oriented; *Adv. Rates:* 29; 24; 24; 13
Dave Bear, Operations Dir
Robert Harlan, General Manager
Chris Gilbert, News Director
John Black, Promotions Director
Lucy Spears, Public Affairs Director

Yucaipa

***KLRD**
07-15-1986; 90.1 MHz FM; *Hrs Open:* 24; 0.55 kw; 3642 ft.; N34 3 18 W116 53 35
1425 North Market Blvd, Suite 9, Sacramento, CA 95834 US
(707) 528-9236; *Fax:* (916) 251-1650
www.air1.com
License: Yucaipa, San Bernardino County, CA held by Educational Media Foundation.
Group Owner: EMF Broadcasting; (acq 1-22-99).
Nat'l Network: Air 1
Format: Alternative, Christian; *Hrs. of News Programming:* News progmg 7 hrs wkly; *Target Audience:* 18-34; Christians
Mike Novak, President
Fernando Chaidez, Operations Dir
Eric Allen, General Sales Mgr
David Pierce, Programming Director
Ed Lenane, News Director
Sam Wallington, Engineering Dir
Paul Goldsmith, Music Director

Yucca Valley

KNWH
04-03-1961; 1250 kHz AM; 0.8 kw-D, ND2; 0.077 kw-N, ND2; N34 7 51 W116 22 12 *Rebroadcasts:* Rebroadcasts KNWQ(AM) Palm Springs 100%
1321 N. Gene Autry Trail, Palm Springs, CA 92262 US
(760) 322-7890; *Fax:* (760) 322-5493
www.943knews.com
License: Yucca Valley, San Bernardino County, CA held by Alpha Media Licensee LLC
Group Owner: Alpha Media LLC; (acq 9-2-2015; grpsl).
Arbitron Metro Market: Yucca Valley, CA; *Format:* News, News/Talk, 86; *Hrs. of News Programming:* 4.5 hrs. news progmg wkly; *No. News Employees:* 4; *Target Audience:* 25-54.
Tricia Bastida, Senior Vice President and Market Manager
David Nola, General Sales Mgr
Paul Cashin, Programming Director
Cristine Constantinescu, Director of Promotions and Digital Media
Bill Watson, Chief Engineer
Crystal White,National/Regional Sales Manager

KDGL
08-01-1988; 106.9 MHz FM; *Hrs Open:* 24; 4 kw horiz; 1,371 ft.; N34 4 55 W116 20 32
1321 N. Gene Autry Trail, Palm Springs, CA 92262 US
(760) 322-7890; *Fax:* (760) 322-5493
www.theeagle1069.com
License: Yucca Valley, San Bernardino County, CA held by Alpha Media Licensee LLC
Group Owner: Alpha Media LLC; (acq 9-2-2015; grpsl).
Nat'l Network: USA
Arbitron Metro Market: Yucca Valley, CA; *Format:* Contemporary Hits/Top 40, Adult Contemp; *Target Audience:* 25-54
Tricia Bastida, Senior Vice President and Market Manager
David Nola, General Sales Mgr
Cristine Constantinescu, Director of Promotions/Marketing and Digital Media
Bill Watson, Chief Engineer

Colorado

Alamosa

KALQ-FM
06-26-1969; 93.5 MHz FM; 2.8 kw; 131 ft.; N37 28 20 W105 51 13
Mailing Address: Box 179, Alamosa, CO 81101 US
Second Address: 292 Santa Fe, Alamosa, CO 81101
(719) 589-6644; *Fax:* (719) 589-0993
www.kalq935.com
info@kgiwkalq.com
License: Alamosa, Alamosa County, CO
Nat'l Network: ABC
Arbitron Metro Market: Alamosa, CO; *Format:* Country
Will Spears, President
Neil Hammer, General Manager
Helen Lozoya, General Sales Manager/Public Affairs Director
Evan Slack, Promotions Director
Mark Beatty, News Director
Will Williams, Chief Engineer

***KASF**
01-01-1967; 90.9 MHz FM; *Hrs Open:* 24; 1.1 kw; 89 ft.; N37 28 20 W105 52 39
110 Richardson Ave., Alamosa, CO 81101 US
(719) 587-7871; *Fax:* (719) 587-7522
www.adams.edu
License: Alamosa, Alamosa County, CO held by Adams State College.
Arbitron Metro Market: Alamosa, CO; *Format:* Contemporary Hits/Top 40 *Special Programming:* Gospel 4 hrs, talk 6 hrs, blues/jazz 6 hrs, reggae; *Hrs. of News Programming:* News progmg one hr wkly *Target Audience:* Community; college and local
Beth Dussault, General Manager

KGIW
02-27-1929; 1450 kHz AM; *Hrs Open:* 6 AM-11 PM; 1 kw-U, ND1; N37 28 20 W105 51 13
Box 179, Alamosa, CO 81101 US
(719) 589-6644; *Fax:* (719) 589-0993
License: Alamosa, CO held by Community Broadcasting Corp.
Nat'l Network: ABC
Format: Adult Contemp *Special Programming:* Sp 6 hrs, farm 6 hrs wkly; *Hrs. of News Programming:* news progmg 25 hrs wkly; *No. News Employees:* 1; *Target Audience:* 18-60.
Will Spears, President
Neil Hammer, General Manager
Helen Lozoya, General Sales Mgr
Mark Beatty, News Director
Will Williams, Chief Engineer
Christine Spears, Executive Vice President
Evan Slack, Promotions Manager

***KHUI**
03-01-1993; 89.1 MHz FM; *Hrs Open:* 24; 0.2 kw; 131 ft.; N37 30 33 W105 51 9
US
(808) 533-0065; *Fax:* (808) 524-2104
www.khuiradio.com
License: Alamosa, Honolulu County, CO held by Salem Media of Hawaii Inc.
Group Owner: Salem Communications Corp.; (acq 8-13-2004; $3.7 million with KHNR-FM Honolulu).
Nat'l Reps: McGavren Guild
Arbitron Metro Market: Honolulu, HI; *Format:* Ethnic
Steve Miller, General Manager

***KRZA**
10-26-1985; 88.7 MHz FM; *Hrs Open:* 5 AM-midnight; 9.8 kw; 2077 ft.; N36 51 32 W106 0 28
528 Ninth Street, Alamasa, CO 81101 US
(719) 589-8844; *Fax:* (719) 587-0032
www.krza.org
License: Alamosa, Alamosa County, CO held by Equal Representation of Media Advocacy Corp.
Nat'l Network: NPR
Arbitron Metro Market: Alamosa, CO; *Format:* Jazz, News
Special Programming: Sp 14 hrs, Latin American 3 hrs, news 4 hrs wkly; *Hrs. of News Programming:* news progmg 18 hrs wkly;

No. News Employees: 1 *TargetAudience:* General; adult progsv community oriented rural area
David Guerrero, President
Holly Felmlee, General Manager

Arvada

KDDZ

06-01-1998; 1690 kHz AM
12136 West Bayaud Avenue, Suite 125, Lakewood, CO 80228 USA
(303) 783-0880; *Fax:* (303) 761-1774
www.radiodisney.com
License: Arvada, CO held by Radio Disney Group LLC
Group Owner: Disney Channels Worldwide; Sale to Salem Media Group pending
Nat'l Network: Radio Disney
Arbitron Metro Market: Lakewood, CO; *Format:* Children
Gary Marsh, President & Chief Creative Officer

Aspen

*KAJX

07-07-1987; 91.5 MHz FM; *Hrs Open:* 24; 0.38 kw horiz, 0.37 kw vert; -988 ft.; N39 11 48 W106 48 14
110 E Hallam St #134, Aspen, CO 81611 US
(970) 920-9000; *Fax:* (970) 544-8002
www.kajx.org
License: Aspen, Pitkin County, CO held by Roaring Fork Public Radio Inc.
Nat'l Network: NPR; PRI; *Wire Services:* AP
Arbitron Metro Market: Aspen, CO; *Format:* Jazz, News *Special Programming:* Bluegrass 2 hrs wkly; *Hrs. of News Programming:* news progmg 50 hrs wkly; *No. News Employees:* 3; *Target Audience:* General; Aspenresidents & tourists
Roger Adams, News Director
Carolyne Heldman, Executive Director
Tom Egan, Operations Manager

KSPN-FM

02-14-1970; 103.1 MHz FM; *Hrs Open:* 24; 3 kw; -85 ft.; N39 13 33 W106 50 0
402 AABC, Suite D, Aspen, CO 81611 US
(970) 925-5776; *Fax:* (970) 925-1142
www.kspnradio.com
License: Aspen, Pitkin County, CO held by NRC Broadcasting Mountain Group LLC.
Group Owner: NRC Broadcasting Inc.; (acq 5-1-2007; grpsl)
Nat'l Reps: Christal
Arbitron Metro Market: Aspen, CO; *Format:* Triple A; *Hrs. of News Programming:* news progmg 6 hrs wkly; *No. News Employees:* 2; *Target Audience:* 25-49; affluent, well educated people who live in resort areas
Pete Benedetti, President/CEO
Kyle McCoy, VP Operations/Programming
Colleen Barill, General Manager
Krista Benedetti, VP, Sales

KPVW

01-01-2000; 107.1 MHz FM; *Hrs Open:* 24; 20.1 kw; 361 ft.; N39 18 56 W106 57 32
2425 Olympic Blvd., Suite 6000 W, Santa Monica, CA 90404-4030 US
(310) 447-3870
License: Aspen, Pitkin County, CO held by Entravision Holdings LLC.
Group Owner: Entravision Communications Corp.; (acq 12-13-01; $57,500).
Arbitron Metro Market: Grand Junction, CO; *Format:* Tejano; *Target Audience:* Latino; 18-34
Donald Daboub, SVP/Market Manager
Christopher Young, CFO
Jeffrey Liberman, COO

KTND

01-01-2006; 93.5 MHz FM; *Hrs Open:* 24; 21 kw; 295 ft.; N39 18 56 W106 57 32
PO Box 1099, Santa Monica, CA 90406-1099 US
(858) 456-7890
www.thunder935.com
License: Aspen, CO held by BS&T Wireless, Inc.
Group Owner: BS&T Wireless, Inc.
Arbitron Metro Market: Little Rock, AR; *Format:* Adult Contemp; *Target Audience:* WF 35-64.; *Adv. Rates:* 28; 28; 28; na
Lerman Senter, President

Aurora

KEZW

01-01-1954; 1430 kHz AM; *Hrs Open:* 24
4700 Syracuse Street, Suite 1050, Denver, CO 80237 US
(303) 967-2700; *Fax:* (303) 967-2747
www.kezw.com
info@kezw.com
License: Aurora, CO held by Entercom Denver License LLC.
Group Owner: Entercom Communications Corp.; (acq 7-24-02; with KOSI(FM) Denver).
Nat'l Reps: Katz Radio
Arbitron Metro Market: Denver-Boulder, CO; *Format:* Oldies, Big Band, 64; *Hrs. of News Programming:* News progmg 4 hrs wkly; *Target Audience:* 35 plus; general
Deborah Wallace, General Sales Mgr
Rick Crandall, Programming Director
Tina Lorraine, Promotions Manager
Stephanie Walrath, News Director
Jeff Garrett, Chief Engineer

KMXA

09-12-1972; 1090 kHz AM; 50 kw-D, 0.5 kw-N
1907 Mile High Stadium W. Cir., Denver, CO 80204 US
(303) 832-0050; *Fax:* (303) 832-3410
www.superestrella1090.com
License: Aurora, CO held by Entravision Holdings LLC.
Group Owner: Entravision Communications Corp.; (acq 3-14-2000; grpsl).
Arbitron Metro Market: Denver, CO; *Format:* Spanish, Adult Contemp; *Target Audience:* 18-54; Hispanics
Donald Daboub, Market Manager

Avon

KZYR

12-24-1984; 97.7 MHz FM; *Hrs Open:* 24; 15 kw; 440 ft.; N39 38 5 W106 26 47
275 N. Main Street, Garnet U201, Edwards, CO 81632 US
(970) 926-7625
www.kzyr.com
tony@kzyr.com
License: Avon, Eagle County, CO held by Cool Radio LLC
Arbitron Metro Market: Avon, CO.; *Format:* Triple A; *Target Audience:* 18-54.
Thomas Dobrez, President
Tony Mauro, General Manager

Basalt

KNFO

07-01-1995; 106.1 MHz FM; *Hrs Open:* 24; 1.6 kw; 364 ft.; N39 18 55 W106 57 36
402 AABC, Suite D, Aspen, CO 81611 US
(970) 925-5776; *Fax:* (970) 544-9101
License: Basalt, Eagle County, CO held by NRC Broadcasting Mountain Group LLC.
Group Owner: NRC Broadcasting Inc.; (acq 5-1-2007; grpsl)
Nat'l Network: CBS
Format: News, Sports, 86; *Hrs. of News Programming:* news progmg 13 hrs wkly; *No. News Employees:* 2; *Target Audience:* 35-64.
Pete Benedetti, President/CEO
Kyle McCoy, VP Operations/Programming
Colleen Barill, General Manager
Krista Benedetti, VP Sales
Dave Rogers, CFO

Bayfield

KLJH

07-01-2003; 107.1 MHz FM; 100 kw horiz; 1883 ft.; N37 21 46 W107 47 40
1105 West Apache, Farmington, NM 87401 US
(505) 327-7202; *Fax:* (505) 327-2163
www.kpcl.org
kpcl@kpcl.org
License: Bayfield, La Plata County, CO held by Voice Ministries of Farmington Inc.
Nat'l Reps: Salem
Arbitron Metro Market: Farmington, NM; *Format:* Christian
Fareed Ayoub, General Manager

Bennett

KFCO

01-01-1978; 107.1 MHz FM; *Hrs Open:* 24; 97 kw; 2,047 ft.; N39 55 22 W103 58 18
P.O. Box 2224, Greeley, CO 80632 US
(303) 872-1500; *Fax:* (303) 872-1501
www.flo1071.com
creighton@maxmediadenver.com
License: Bennett, Adams County, CO held by Max Radio of Denver LLC
Group Owner: MAX Media L.L.C.; (acq 10-24-2005; $14 million)
Population Served: 332,354; *Arbitron Metro Market:* Aurora, CO; *Format:* Urban Contemporary
Jeff Norman, President/General Manager
Sean Rhoads, General Sales Mgr
Brian DeGrasse, Director of Marketing and Promotions
Laurie Vigil, Business Manager
Cody Glasgo, Traffic Manager
Creighton Petro, Digital Director
JennaLeveille, Senior Account Executive
Rachel Makinen, Senior Account Executive
Joy B. Morrone, Senior Account Executive

Bethany

*KKWD(FM)

104.9 MHz FM; 25 kw; Ant 341 ft; N37 58 43 W103 34 48
3290 Peachtree Lane NW, Altanta, GA 67864-0991
(404) 949-0700
www.kjil.com
kjil@kjil.com
License: Bethany, OK held by Radio License Holding CBC LLC
Population Served: 74,523; *Arbitron Metro Market:* Dodge City - Garden City - Liberal, KS; *Format:* Christian, Religious
Robert Hughes, CEO
Glenn Hascall, Station Manager
Bill Lurwick, Program Director and Music Director
Delvin Kinser, News Director

Beulah

KFVR-FM

01-01-2001; 94.7 MHz FM; *Hrs Open:* 24; 18 kw; 387 ft.; N37 52 40 W104 57 19
1020 9th Street, Suite 201, Greeley, CO 80631 US
(719) 254-6300; *Fax:* (719) 254-6303
License: Beulah, Otero County, CO held by Greeley Broadcasting Corp.
Group Owner: Greeley Broadcasting Corp.; (acq 11-30-2006; $125,000)
Format: Tejano
Ricardo Salazar, President/General Manager

Black Forest

KLIM

05-08-1984; 1120 kHz AM; *Hrs Open:* 6 AM-sunset; 0.25 kw-D, NDD; N39 16 27 W103 42 49
Box 87, 165 E. Ave., Limon, CO 80828 US
(719) 775-8199
License: Black Forest, CO held by Kona Coast Radio II LLC
Group Owner: Kona Coast Radio LLC; (acq 3-7-96; $8,000).
Arbitron Metro Market: Colorado Sping, CO; *Format:* Oldies
Alan Olson, General Manager

Boulder

KBCO

10-01-1955; 97.3 MHz FM; 94 kw horiz, 80 kw vert; 1,539 ft.; N39 54 48 W105 17 32
Mailing Address: 4695 S. Monaco St., Denver, CO 80237 US
Second Address: 2500 Pearl St., Suite 315, Boulder, CO 80302
(303) 444-5600; *Fax:* (303) 930-6890
www.kbco.com
License: Boulder, Boulder County, CO held by Citicasters Licenses Inc.
Group Owner: iHeartMedia
Arbitron Metro Market: Denver, CO; *Format:* Triple A
Patrick Connor, Market President
Brigid Walje, Director of Sales
Scott Arbough, Programming Director

*KGNU-FM

05-22-1978; 88.5 MHz FM; *Hrs Open:* 24; 4 kw; 213 ft.; N39 59 33 W105 9 16
P.O. Box 885, Boulder, CO 80306 US
(303) 449-4885
www.kgnu.org
License: Boulder, Boulder County, CO held by Boulder Community Broadcast Association Inc.
Nat'l Network: PRI; NPR; *Regional Network:* Colo. Pub.
Arbitron Metro Market: Denver-Boulder, CO; *Format:* Variety/Diverse *Special Programming:* Black 7 hrs, folk 20 hrs, Sp 3 hrs, jazz 15 hrs, c; *Hrs. of News Programming:* news progmg 30 hrs wkly *No. News Employees:* 2; *Target Audience:* General.
Evan Perkins, Operations Dir
Sam Fuqua, Station Manager
Faye Lamb, General Sales Mgr
John Schaefer, Programming Director
Maeve Conran, News Director
Joel Edelstein, News Director

KVCU
11-14-1973; 1190 kHz AM; *Hrs Open:* 24
1305 University Avenue, Boulder, CO 80306 US
(303) 492-5031; *Fax:* (303) 492-1369
www.radio1190.org
dj@radio1190.org
License: Boulder, CO held by The University of Colorado Foundation.
Arbitron Metro Market: Denver-Boulder, CO; *Format:* Variety/Diverse *Special Programming:* Jazz 3 hrs wkly; *Hrs. of News Programming:* news progmg 3 hrs wkly; *No. News Employees:* 3; *Target Audience:* 25-44.
Mike Goldenberg, General Manager
Alex Sequin, Promotions Manager
Joe Oria, News Director
Henry Moffly, Production Director
Sam Goldner, Music Director
Michael Odbert, Student Operations Manager
Amy Moore-Shipley, Program Director& In-Studio/Interview Contact
Gracie Tomczak, Volunteer Coordinator
Allen Miller, Membership Coordinator

KCFC
02-15-1947; 1490 kHz AM
701 Montgomery St., Fourth Floor, San Francisco, CA 94111 US
(303) 871-9191; *Fax:* (303) 733-3319
www.cpr.org
License: Boulder, CO held by Public Broadcasting of Colorado Inc.
Nat'l Network: NPR
Arbitron Metro Market: Centennail, CO; *Format:* News; *Target Audience:* General.; *Adv. Rates:* 20; 20; 20; na
Max Wycisk, President
Sue Coughlin, General Sales Mgr

Breckenridge

KSMT
09-12-1975; 102.1 MHz FM; *Hrs Open:* 24; 6 kw; -210 ft.; N39 29 44 W106 1 44
Mailing Address: 1400 Easton Road, Bakersfield, CA 93303 US
Second Address: 130 Ski Hill Rd., Suite 240, Breckenridge, CO 80424
(970) 453-2234; *Fax:* (970) 453-5425
www.ksmtradio.com
License: Breckenridge, Summit County, CO held by NRC Broadcasting Mountain Group LLC.
Group Owner: NRC Broadcasting Inc.; (acq 5-1-2007; grpsl)
Arbitron Metro Market: Breckenridge, CO; *Format:* Triple A
Special Programming: Funk, hip hop, local & reggae; *Hrs. of News Programming:* news progmg 12 hrs wkly; *No. News Employees:* 1 *Target Audience:* 18-44; upscale adults, heavy ski & outdoor industry consumers; *Adv. Rates:* 35; 30; 35; 27
Lisa Korry-Cheek, General Manager

***KMPB**
06-01-2008; 90.7 MHz FM; *Hrs Open:* 24; 0.6 kw; -249 ft.; N39 29 44 W106 1 44
Mailing Address: US
Second Address: Ship 136 Lake Dillon Drive, Dillon, CO 80435
(970) 468-0905; *Fax:* (970) 468-0286
License: Breckenridge, Summit County, CO held by Community Radio for Northern Colorado
Nat'l Network: AP Network News; *Wire Services:* AP
Arbitron Metro Market: Breckenridge, CO; *Format:* Variety/Diverse; *Hrs. of News Programming:* news progmg 3 hrs wkly; *No. News Employees:* 2; *Target Audience:* 35+
M.R. Murray, President
Victor Michael Jr., Operations Dir

Breen

KLLV
09-19-1984; 550 kHz AM; *Hrs Open:* 24; 1.8 kw-D, NDD; N37 11 2 W108 4 54
Mailing Address: 14780 Hwy 140, Breen, CO 81326 US
Second Address: 14780 Hwy. 140, Breen, CO 81326
(970) 247-8955
License: Breen, CO held by Daystar Radio Ltd.
Arbitron Metro Market: Breen, CO; *Format:* Christian, Gospel, 74; *Hrs. of News Programming:* New progmg 2 hrs wkly; *Target Audience:* General.
Sharon Harper, General Manager
Debbie Baker, Programming Director
Jim Alexander, Chief Engineer

Brighton

KLVZ
04-26-1956; 810 kHz AM
2821 South Parker Road, Suite 1205, Aurora, CO 80014 US
(303) 433-5500; *Fax:* (303) 433-1555
www.810klvz.com
klvz@crawfordbroadcasting.com
License: Brighton, Adams County, CO held by KLZ Radio Inc.
Group Owner: Crawford Broadcasting Co.; (acq 12-10-93; $700,000;
Arbitron Metro Market: Denver, CO; *Format:* Oldies, Disco, 28; *Target Audience:* 18-49.
Mike Triem, General Manager
Jorge Carballo, Programming/Operations Director

Broomfield

KWOF
06-01-1967; 92.5 MHz FM; *Hrs Open:* 24; 57 kw horiz, 56 kw vert; 1237 ft.; N40 5 47 W104 54 4
433 E. Las Colina Blvd, #1130, Irving, TX 75039 US
(303) 832-5665; *Fax:* (303) 832-7000
www.925thewolf.com
License: Broomfield, Boulder County, CO held by Wilks License Co.-Denver LLC.
Group Owner: Wilks Broadcast Group LLC; (acq 3-5-2009; grpsl)
Arbitron Metro Market: Denver-Boulder, CO; *Format:* Country; *Hrs. of News Programming:* news progmg 2 hrs wkly; *No. News Employees:* 1; *Target Audience:* 35-64; educated, upscale, active professionals, ethnic
Barry Remington, General Manager
Brenda Egger, General Sales Mgr
Randy ""Shotgun"" Shannon, Programming Director
Barry Walters, Chief Engineer

Brush

KPRB
11-02-1998; 106.3 MHz FM; *Hrs Open:* 24; 7 kw; 249 ft.; N40 13 2 W103 41 46.1
Mailing Address: 231 Main Street, Fort Morgan, CO 80701 US
Second Address: 220 State St., Suite 106, Fort Morgan, CO 80701
(970) 867-7271; *Fax:* (970) 867-2676
www.b106.com
b106@b106.com
License: Brush, Morgan County, CO
Group Owner: Northeast Colorado Broadcasting LLC
Nat'l Network: ABC; *Wire Services:* AP
Format: Adult Contemp; *Hrs. of News Programming:* news progmg one hr wkly; *No. News Employees:* 1; *Target Audience:* 18-45; females
Alec Creighton, Programming Director

KSIR
08-01-1977; 1010 kHz AM; *Hrs Open:* 24; 25 kw-D, DA1; 0.28 kw-N, DA1; N40 18 50 W103 35 30
Mailing Address: 231 Main St, Ft Morgan, CO 80701 US
Second Address: 220 State St., Suite 106, Fort Morgan, CO 80701
(970) 867-7271; *Fax:* (970) 867-2676
www.ksir.com
ksir@necolorado.com
License: Brush, CO held by Northeast Colorado Broadcasting LLC
Group Owner: Northeast Colorado Broadcasting LLC; acq 7-1-2003; grpsl).
Nat'l Network: ABC; *Wire Services:* AP
Arbitron Metro Market: Fort Morgan, CO; *Format:* Agriculture, Sports, 86; *Hrs. of News Programming:* news progmg 5 hrs wkly; *No. News Employees:* 2; *Target Audience:* 25-65; farmers, ranchers, sports fans
Alec Creighton, General Manager
Theresa Leake, General Sales Mgr
Lorrie Boyer, Programming Director

***KLZV**
91.3 MHz FM; 6 kw; 423 ft.; N40 8 56 W103 17 4
16075 W Belleview Ave, Morrison, CO 80465 US
(800) 525-5683; *Fax:* (916) 251-1650
www.klove.com
klove@klove.com
License: Brush, Logan County, CO held by Educational Media Foundation.
Group Owner: EMF Broadcasting; (acq 10-2-2003; grpsl).
Nat'l Network: K-Love
Arbitron Metro Market: Brush, CO; *Format:* Christian; *No. News Employees:* 13; *Target Audience:* 25-44; Judeo Christian, female
Darrell Chambliss, Chairman
Mike Novak, President and CEO
Jennifer Lohman, Operations Dir
Eric Allen, General Sales Mgr
David Pierce, Chief Creative Officer and Programming Director
Ed Lenane, News Director
Sam Wallington,Engineering Dir
Scott Smith, Music Director
Richard Hunt, News Reporter
Marya Morgan, News Reporter
Tracy Butler, Traffic Manager
Alan Mason, Chief Operating Officer
Dan Antonelli, Chief Business Development Officer

***KBWA**
01-01-2006; 89.1 MHz FM; 6 kw vert; 145 ft.; N40 13 2.1 W103 41 46.2 *Rebroadcasts:* Rebroadcasts KXWA(FM) Loveland 100%
188 South Bellevue, Suite 222, Memphis, TN 38104 US
(877) 702-9293; *Fax:* (303) 702-9293
www.wayfm.com
supportservices@wayfm.com
License: Brush, Morgan County, CO held by WAY-FM Media Group Inc.
Group Owner: WAY-FM Media Group Inc.; (acq 2-23-2005; $25,000 for CP).
Arbitron Metro Market: Brush, CO; *Format:* Christian
Robert Augsburg, President

Buena Vista

KBVC
01-01-1975; 104.1 MHz FM; 0.6 kw; 1188 ft.; N38 44 45 W106 11 55
7600 County Rd. 120, Salida, CO 81201 US
(719) 539-2575; *Fax:* (719) 539-4851
www.eaglecountry104.com
License: Buena Vista, Chaffee County, CO held by Three Eagles Communications of Colorado LLC
Group Owner: Three Eagles Communications of Colorado LLC
Arbitron Metro Market: Salida, CO; *Format:* Country
Dead Johnson, Station Manager
Dan Ridenour, News Director
Doreen White, Business Manager

KSKE
08-22-1986; 1450 kHz AM; *Hrs Open:* 24
3402 C St. NE., Auburn, WA 98002 US
(253) 887-8464; *Fax:* (253) 887-8661
www.alwaysmountaintime.com
License: Buena Vista, CO held by Pilgrim Communications Inc.
Group Owner: Pilgrim Communications Inc.; (acq 12-11-97)
Nat'l Network: NBC Radio; *Nat'l Reps:* Interep
Arbitron Metro Market: Buena Vista, CO; *Format:* News/Talk; *Hrs. of News Programming:* news progmg 12 hrs wkly; *No. News Employees:* 3; *Target Audience:* Adults 25-54.; *Adv. Rates:* 40; 40; 40; 30
Holli Snyder, General Manager

Burlington

KNAB
07-11-1967; 1140 kHz AM; 1 kw-D, NDD; N39 17 41 W102 15 37
17534 County Road 49, Burlington, CO 80807 US
(719) 346-8600; *Fax:* (719) 346-8656
www.knabradio.com
knab@centurytel.net
License: Burlington, CO held by KNAB Inc.
Format: Adult Contemp; *Target Audience:* 18 plus.
Bette Bailly, CEO
Bette Bailly, General Manager
Paul O'Reilly, Programming Director
Beverly Schott, News Director
Chris Baylock, Disc Jockey

KNAB-FM
03-07-1980; 104.1 MHz FM; *Hrs Open:* 24; 51 kw; 361 ft.; N39 17 41 W102 15 37
P.O. Box 516, 17534 Colorado Road, Burlington, CO 80807 US
(719) 346-8600; *Fax:* (719) 346-8656
www.knabradio.com
knab@centurytel.net
License: Burlington, Kit Carson County, CO held by KNAB Inc.
Format: Country; *Adv. Rates:* 35; 30; 20; 12.50
Bette Bailly, General Manager

Burns

KIDN-FM
02-15-1985; 95.9 MHz FM; 6 kw; 650 ft.; N40 31 16 W107 17 46
1400 Easton Road, Bakersfield, CA 93303 US
(970) 879-5368; *Fax:* (970) 879-5843
www.alwaysmountaintime.com/kidn
License: Burns, Routt County, CO held by NRC Broadcasting Mountain Group LLC.
Group Owner: NRC Broadcasting Inc.; (acq 5-1-2007; grpsl)
Format: Contemporary Hits/Top 40; *Target Audience:* 21-54.

Steve Wodlinger, General Manager

Calhan

KKCS(FM)
104.7 MHz FM; 400 w horiz; Ant 476 ft; N38 59 57 W104 18 47
4843 South Ulster Street, Suite 700, Denver, CO 60611
(303) 446-5926
License: Calhan, El Paso County, CO held by Superior Broadcasting of Denver LLC.
Population Served: 2,707,120; *Arbitron Metro Market:* Chicago, IL
Christopher Devine, President

Canon City

KRLN
08-15-1947; 1400 kHz AM; *Hrs Open:* 24; 1 kw-U, ND1; N38 27 35 W105 13 26
PO Box 30181, Lincoln, NE 68503 US
(719) 275-7488; *Fax:* (719) 275-5132
starads@krln.cc
License: Canon City, CO held by Royal Gorge Broadcasting LLC.
Nat'l Network: CBS
Arbitron Metro Market: Fremont County; *Format:* News, News/Talk, 86; *Hrs. of News Programming:* news progmg 25 hrs wkly; *No. News Employees:* 1; *Target Audience:* 25-54; two income families & older discretionaryincome; *Adv. Rates:* 16; 12; 16; 12
Joan Wood, General Manager
Rosemary Lamberson, General Sales Mgr
Melissa Nunn, News Director

KSTY
06-01-1975; 104.5 MHz FM; 8.6 kw; 46 ft.; N38 18 54 W105 12 40
P. O. Box 30181, Lincoln, NE 68503 US
(719) 275-7488; *Fax:* (719) 275-5132
License: Canon City, Fremont County, CO held by Royal Gorge Broadcasting LLC.
Arbitron Metro Market: Canon City, CO; *Format:* Country; *Target Audience:* 25-60.; *Adv. Rates:* 30; 29; 30; 27
Missi Nunn, Operations Dir
Joan Wood, General Manager
Rosemary Lamberson, General Sales Mgr
Harry Russell, Engineering Dir
Ed Norden, Chief Engineer
Tanner Brandt, Music Director

***KTLC**
05-01-2001; 89.1 MHz FM; *Hrs Open:* 24; 1.15 kw; 1476 ft.; N38 45 21 W105 13 2 *Rebroadcasts:* Rebroadcasts KTLF(FM) Colorado Springs 100%
1665 Briargate Blvd, Colorado Springs, CO 80920 US
(719) 593-0600; *Fax:* (719) 593-2399
www.ktlf.org
lightpraise@ktlf.org
License: Canon City, Fremont County, CO held by Make a Difference Foundation Inc.
Arbitron Metro Market: Colorado Springs, CO; *Format:* Christian; *Target Audience:* 45-60; Christian
James Felix, Operations Dir
Tom Sullivan, General Manager
Sharick Wade, Programming Director
Robert Mumm, Chief Engineer

Carbondale

***KVOV**
04-15-1983; 90.5 MHz FM; 0.45 kw; 2543 ft.; N39 25 8 W107 22 10 *Rebroadcasts:* Rebroadcasts KVOD(FM) Denver 100%
P.O. Box 1388, Carbondale, CO 81623 US
(303) 871-9191; *Fax:* (303) 733-3319
www.cpr.org
License: Carbondale, Garfield County, CO held by Public Broadcasting of Colorado Inc.
Regional Network: Colo. Pub.
Arbitron Metro Market: Centennial, CO; *Format:* Classical
Max Wycisk, President
Mike Flanagan, Programming Director
Kelley Griffin, News Director

***KCJX**
09-06-2004; 88.9 MHz FM; 4 kw horiz, 3.5 kw vert; 2543 ft.; N39 25 8 W107 22 10
530 E. Main Street, Aspen, CO 81611 US
(970) 920-9000; *Fax:* (970) 544-8002
www.kajx.org
psa@aspenpublicradio.org
License: Carbondale, Garfield County, CO held by Roaring Fork Public Radio Inc.
Wire Services: AP
Arbitron Metro Market: West Glenwood Spring, CO; *Format:* Jazz, News; *No. News Employees:* 3
Tom Egan, Operations Dir
Carlyon Heldman, Executive Director
Roger Adams, News Director
Collins Kelly, Membership Director
Debbie Welden, Director of Development & Corporate Support
Rob St. Mary, Digital Content Manager

KUUR
01-01-2007; 96.7 MHz FM; 90 w; Ant 2,507 ft; N39 25 08 W107 22 10
Mailing Address: Box 11657, Aspen, CO
Second Address: 132 W. Main St., Aspen, CO 81611
(970) 920-9600; *Fax:* (970) 544-5239
www.aspenglenwood.com
sales@aspenglenwood.com
License: Carbondale, Garfield County, CO held by Colorado Radio Marketing LLC.

Marcos Rodriguez, General Manager

Castle Rock

KJMN
01-01-1979; 92.1 MHz FM; *Hrs Open:* 24; 42 kw; 535 ft.; N39 23 7 W105 2 52
1907 Mile High Stadium W. Cir., Denver, CO 80204 US
(303) 832-0050
www.jose921.com
License: Castle Rock, Douglas County, CO held by Entravision Holdings LLC.
Group Owner: Entravision Communications Corp.; (acq 3-14-00; grpsl).
Arbitron Metro Market: Denver-Boulder, CO; *Format:* Spanish, Adult Contemp; *Target Audience:* 25-54.
Daniel Daboub, Market Manager

Centennial

KXWA
03-11-2004; 101.9 MHz FM; *Hrs Open:* 24; 9.5 kw; 535 ft.; N39 23 7 W105 2 52
5145 Centennial Blvd, Ste 200, Colorado Springs, CO 80949 US
(303) 702-9293; *Fax:* (303) 485-1929
www.wayfm.com
supportservices@wayfm.com
License: Centennial, Larimer County, CO held by WAY-FM Media Group Inc.
Group Owner: WAY-FM Media Group Inc.; (acq 11-19-2002).
Arbitron Metro Market: Centennial, CO; *Format:* Christian; *Target Audience:* 18-34.
Lloyd Parker, COO
Bob Augsburg, President/Founder
Zach Cochran, General Manager
Jeff Connell, Programming Director

Center

KPAU
103.5 MHz FM; 0.46 kw horiz; 26 ft.; N37 47 20 W106 6 43
541 North Fairbanks Ct., Suite 1900A, Chicago, IL 60611 US
(312) 204-9900
License: Center, Saguache County, CO held by College Creek Media LLC.
Group Owner: College Creek Media LLC
Arbitron Metro Market: Center, CO
Christopher Devine, President/CEO

Central City

***KKKC**
88.9 MHz FM; 0.005 kw vert; 1604 ft.; N39 52 1 W105 32 37 US
(970) 669-9200
License: Central City, Gilpin County, CO held by Cedar Cove Broadcasting Inc.
Group Owner: Cedar Cove Broadcasting Inc.
Arbitron Metro Market: Central City, CO
Victor Michael Jr., President

Clifton

KMZK
09-08-1946; 106.9 MHz FM; *Hrs Open:* 24; 100 kw; 1444 ft.; N39 34 52 W108 57 36
US
(406) 245-3121; *Fax:* (406) 245-0822
License: Clifton, Yellowstone County, CO held by Unita Broadcasting LLC
Nat'l Network: Salem Radio Network; *Wire Services:* AP
Arbitron Metro Market: Billings, MT; *Format:* Christian; *Target Audience:* 18-44; young & energetic high school & college students & young adults
Doug Wylde, Operations Manager

Colona

KAVP
09-30-2000; 1450 kHz AM; *Hrs Open:* 24 *Rebroadcasts:* Rebroadcasts KWGL(FM) Ouray 100%
751 Horizon Ct., Suite 225, Grand Junction, CO 81506
(970) 241-6460
License: Colona, CO held by WS Communications LLC.
Group Owner: Western Slope Communications LLC
Format: Country
Louis Stark, Station Manager

Colorado City

KJQY
103.3 MHz FM; 100 kw; 541 ft.; N37 46 52 W104 32 3
2099 US 50, Pueblo, CO 81008 US
(719)-542-1033; *Fax:* (877) 842-6336
License: Colorado City, Huerfano County, CO held by Pueblo Broadcasting Group LLC
Arbitron Metro Market: Colorado City, CO; *Format:* Black
Steven Bartholomew, President/General Manager
Jack Kromer, Chief Engineer

Colorado Springs

***KEPC**
02-15-1957; 89.7 MHz FM; *Hrs Open:* 24; 10 kw; -256 ft.; N38 45 41 W104 47 4
5675 S. Academy Blvd., Colorado Springs, CO 80906 US
(719) 502-3131 (719) 502-3128
License: Colorado Springs, El Paso County, CO held by Pikes Peak Community College.
Arbitron Metro Market: Colorado Springs, CO; *Format:* Variety/Diverse; *Target Audience:* General.
Sharon Hogg, General Manager

KILO
01-21-1966; 94.3 MHz FM; 59.2 kw; 2198 ft.; N38 44 44 W104 51 42
1805 E. Cheyenne Rd., Colorado Springs, CO 80905 US
(719) 633-5456; *Fax:* (719) 634-5837
www.kilo943.com
License: Colorado Springs, El Paso County, CO held by Colorado Springs Radio Broadcasters Inc.
Group Owner: Bahakel Communications Ltd.; (acq 8-14-84)
Arbitron Metro Market: Colorado Springs; *Format:* Rock/AOR
Lou Mellini, General Manager
Ross Ford, Programming Director

KZNT
12-15-1956; 1460 kHz AM; *Hrs Open:* 24
5145 Centennial Blvd., Ste 200, Colorado Springs, CO 80949 US
(719) 531-5438; *Fax:* (719) 531-5588
www.newstalk1460.com
License: Colorado Springs, CO held by Bison Media Inc.
Group Owner: Salem Communications Corp.; (acq 10-6-03; $1.5 million).
Arbitron Metro Market: Colorado Spring, CO; *Format:* News, News/Talk, 86
Skip Snow, General Manager

KKFM
05-02-1959; 98.1 MHz FM; *Hrs Open:* 24; 71 kw; 2290 ft.; N38 44 36 W104 51 44
605 Corporate Drive, Suite 130, Colorado Springs, CO 80919 US
(719) 593-2700; *Fax:* (719) 593-2727
www.kkfm.com
License: Colorado Springs, CO held by Radio License Holding CBC, LLC
Group Owner: Cumulus Media Inc.; (acq 1-86; $2.5 million;).
Nat'l Reps: McGavren Guild
Arbitron Metro Market: Colorado Spring, CO; *Format:* Classic Rock; *Hrs. of News Programming:* News progmg one hr wkly; *Target Audience:* 25-54.
Scott Jones, General Sales Mgr
Bobby Irwin, Programming Director
Mark Stevens, Promotions Manager

***KRCC**
10-02-1951; 91.5 MHz FM; *Hrs Open:* 24; 2.1 kw; 2254 ft.; N38 44 43 W104 51 42
912 North Weber, Colorado Springs, CO 80903 US

RADIO - U.S.

(719) 473-4801; *Fax:* (719) 473-7863
www.krcc.org
info@krcc.org
License: Colorado Springs, El Paso County, CO held by The Colorado College.
Nat'l Network: NPR; PRI
Arbitron Metro Market: CO Springs, CO; *Format:* News/Talk
Special Programming: Celtic 5 hrs, reggae 6 hrs, jazz 15 hrs, blues 5 h; *Hrs. of News Programming:* News progmg 42 hrs wkly; *Target Audience:* 25-54;general
Mike Procell, Operations Dir
Delaney Utterback, General Manager
Jeff Bieri, Promotions Manager

KRDO
03-01-1947; 1240 kHz AM; *Hrs Open:* 24
399 S. 8th Street, Colorado Springs, CO 80905 US
(719) 632-1515; *Fax:* (719) 475-0815
www.krdo.com
m.lewis@krdo.com
License: Colorado Springs, CO held by News-Press & Gazette Co.
Group Owner: News-Press & Gazette Co.; (acq 6-26-2006; grpsl).
Nat'l Network: ABC; *Nat'l Reps:* D & R Radio
Arbitron Metro Market: Colorado Springs, CO *TV Affiliate:* KRDO-TV affil.; *Format:* News, News/Talk, 86
Jerry Killion, Operations Manager
JoAnne Rowley, Radio Sales Manager
Mike Lewis, Radio Program Director
Tim McSpadden, Promotions Manager
Mike Rausch, News Director
Joe Reed, Chief Engineer

KATC
10-01-1969; 95.1 MHz FM; *Hrs Open:* 24; 72 kw; 2280 ft.; N38 44 43 W104 51 39
6805 Corporate Dr., Suite 130, Colorado Springs, CO 80919 US
(719) 593-2700; *Fax:* (719) 593-2727
www.951nashfm.com
License: Colorado Springs, CO held by ERadio License Holding CBC, LLC
Group Owner: Cumulus Media Inc.; (acq 8-25-2006; $8.5 million).
Arbitron Metro Market: CO Spring, Pueblo CO; *Format:* Country
Bobby Irwin, Operations Dir
Scott Jones, General Sales Mgr
Mike Dylan, Programming Director
Alisha Scott, Promotions Manager

KKPK
10-05-2006; 92.9 MHz FM; 60 kw; 2198 ft.; N38 44 44 W104 51 42
6805 Corporate Dr., Suite 130, Colorado Springs, CO 80919 US
(719) 593-2700
www.929peakfm.com
License: Colorado Springs, CO held by Radio License Holding CBC, LLC
Group Owner: Cumulus Media Inc.
Wire Services: UPI
Arbitron Metro Market: Colorado Springs, CO; *Format:* Christian; *Target Audience:* 25-54.
Scott Jones, Sales/Advertising
Bobby Irwin, Programming Director
Jolana Miller, Promotions Manager

***KTLF**
02-27-1989; 90.5 MHz FM; *Hrs Open:* 24; 0 kw horiz, 20 kw vert; 2208 ft.; N38 44 43 W104 51 39
1665 Briargate Blvd., Colorado Springs, CO 80920 US
(719) 593-0600; *Fax:* (719) 593-2399
www.ktlf.org
lightpraise@ktlf.org
License: Colorado Springs, El Paso County, CO held by Educational Communications of Colorado Springs Inc.
Arbitron Metro Market: Colorado Springs, CO; *Format:* Christian; *Target Audience:* 45-60; Christian
Dr. Ron Johnson, Chairman
Sharick Wade, Operations Dir
Lynn Carmichael, Programming Director

KCSF
09-22-1922; 1300 kHz AM; *Hrs Open:* 24; 5 kw-D, ND1; 1 kw-N, ND1; N38 48 46 W104 48 51
6805 Corporate Dr., Suite 130, Colorado Springs, CO 80919 US
(719) 593-2700; *Fax:* (719) 593-2727
www.xtrasports1300.com
License: Colorado Springs, CO held by Radio License Holding CBC, LLC
Group Owner: Cumulus Media Inc.; (acq 1999; grpsl)
Nat'l Reps: McGavren Guild
Arbitron Metro Market: Colorado Springs, CO; *Format:* Sports
Bobby Irwin, Operations Mgr
Scott Jones, General Sales Mgr
Matt Pauley, Programming Director
Woody Powers, Community Officer

KREL
05-11-1951; 1580 kHz AM; *Hrs Open:* 6 AM-sunset
54 Monument Circle, Indianapolis, IN 46204 US
(940) 663-5711
License: Colorado Springs, CO held by First Broadcasters Investment Partners LLC.
Group Owner: First Broadcasting Operating Inc.; (acq 6-13-2005; grpsl)
Arbitron Metro Market: Dallas, TX; *Format:* Country; *Target Audience:* General.
Dean Goodman, President
Richard Womack, General Manager
Kimberly Long, Station Manager
Scott Kubala, Programming Director
Kevin Brooks, Chief Engineer

KVOR
09-22-1922; 740 kHz AM; 3.3 kw-D, DA2; 1.5 kw-N, DA2; N39 5 2 W104 42 41
9805 Corporate Dr., Suite 130, Colorado Springs, CO 80919 US
(719) 593-2700
www.kvor.com
bobby.irwin@cumulus.com
License: Colorado Springs, CO held by Radio License Holding CBC, LLC
Group Owner: Cumulus Media Inc.; (acq 1999; grpsl).
Nat'l Network: CBS; Wall Street
Arbitron Metro Market: Colorado Springs, CO; *Format:* News/Talk; *Target Audience:* General.
Scott Jones, General Sales Mgr
Bobby Irwin, Programming Director
Jim Arthur, News Director/Promotions

Commerce City

KLTT
04-01-1996; 670 kHz AM; N39 57 20 W104 43 50
2821 South Parker Road, Suite 1205, Aurora, CO 80014 US
(303) 481-1800; *Fax:* (303) 433-1555
www.670kltt.com
kltt@crawfordbroadcasting.com
License: Commerce City, CO held by KLZ Radio Inc.
Group Owner: Crawford Broadcasting Co.; (acq 1995; $750,000)
Arbitron Metro Market: Denver-Boulder,; *Format:* Religious, Talk; *Target Audience:* 30 plus; general
Mike Triem, General Manager

Cortez

KISZ-FM
09-28-1978; 97.9 MHz FM; *Hrs Open:* 20; 100 kw; 1309 ft.; N37 21 48 W108 9 0
Mailing Address: 427 Bedford Road, Pleasantville, CO 10570 US
Second Address: 2402 Hawkins, Cortez, CO 81321
(505) 325-3541; *Fax:* (505) 327-5796
License: Cortez, Montezuma County, CO held by Winton Road Broadcasting Co. LLC
Group Owner: Winton Road Broadcasting Co. LLC; (acq 5-3-01; grpsl).
Format: Country; *Hrs. of News Programming:* news progmg 4 hrs wkly; *No. News Employees:* 1; *Target Audience:* 18-49; young sophisticated adults; *Adv. Rates:* 350; 300; 350; 200
Dan Buchta, General Manager
Randy KLock, General Sales Mgr

KRTZ
12-01-1981; 98.7 MHz FM; *Hrs Open:* 24; 27 kw; 2900 ft.; N37 13 10 W108 48 26
1400 Easton Road, Bakersfield, CA 93303 US
(970) 565-6565; *Fax:* (970) 565-8567
krtzradio.com
License: Cortez, Montezuma County, CO
Arbitron Metro Market: Cortez, CO; *Format:* Adult Contemp
Special Programming: American Indian one hr, gospel one hr wkly; *Hrs. of News Programming:* news progmg 3 hrs wkly; *No. News Employees:* 1 *TargetAudience:* 20-55.; *Adv. Rates:* 228; 228; 228; 192
Kelly Turner, Programming Director
Desiree Bumham, Promotions Manager
Jim Burt, Engineering Dir

***KSJD**
07-01-1990; 91.5 MHz FM; *Hrs Open:* 24; 1.2 kw; 312 ft.; N37 28 57 W108 30 34
P.O. Box 970, Cortez, CO 81321 US
(970) 564-9727 (970) 564-0808
www.ksjd.org
License: Cortez, Montezuma County, CO held by Community Radio Project, Inc.
Arbitron Metro Market: Mancos, CO; *Format:* Variety/Diverse
Special Programming: Relg one hr wkly; *No. News Employees:* 1; *Target Audience:* 16-30; college level
Kristine Nunn, President
Jeff Pope, General Manager
Melissa Betrone, General Sales Mgr
Karen Mooneyhan, Programming Director

KVFC
02-27-1955; 740 kHz AM; *Hrs Open:* 24; 1 kw-D, DAN; 0.25 kw-N, DAN; N37 20 58 W108 32 29
1400 Easton Road, Bakersfield, CA 93303 US
(505) 325-3541; *Fax:* (505) 327-5796
www.kvfcradio.com
License: Cortez, CO held by Winton Road Broadcasting Co. LLC
Group Owner: Winton Road Broadcasting Co. LLC; acq 12-18-01; with co-located FM).
Nat'l Network: ABC; CNN Radio; Westwood One
Arbitron Metro Market: Farmington, NM; *Format:* News, News/Talk, 86; *Hrs. of News Programming:* news progmg 15 hrs wkly; *No. News Employees:* 2; *Target Audience:* 18-54; young adults
Anthony Brandon, CEO
Kelly Turner, Operations Dir
Bill Kruger, General Manager
Keri-Lyn Riley, General Sales Mgr
Jim Burt, Chief Engineer
L. Rogers Brandon, COO

***KZET**
09-03-2011; 90.5 MHz FM; 2 kw; 2865 ft.; N37 13 13 W108 48 24
US
(970) 749-9117
License: Cortez, Montezuma County, CO held by Community Radio Project.
Arbitron Metro Market: Cortez, CO; *Format:* Variety/Diverse
Jeffery Pope, General Manager

Craig

KRAI
01-01-1948; 550 kHz AM; *Hrs Open:* 19; 5 kw-D, DAN; 0.5 kw-N, DAN; N40 32 45 W107 31 52
Mailing Address: 1111 W. Victory Way, Craig, CO 81626 US
Second Address: 1111 W. Victory Way., Craig, CO 81626
(970) 824-6574; *Fax:* (970) 826-4581
www.krai.com
krai@krai.com
License: Craig, CO held by Wild West Radio Inc.
Nat'l Network: Westwood Edge; CNN Radio; *Wire Services:* AP
Format: Country, News, 84 *Special Programming:* Farm one hr wkly; *Hrs. of News Programming:* news progmg 12 hrs wkly; *No. News Employees:* 3; *Target Audience:* 25-54.
Frank Hanel, General Manager
Tammie Hanel, Station Manager

KRAI-FM
04-01-1976; 93.7 MHz FM; *Hrs Open:* 24; 100 kw; 980 ft; N40 34 35 W107 36 29
Mailing Address: 1111 West Victory Way, Craig, CO 81625
Second Address: 1111 W. Victory Way., Craig, CO 81626
(970) 824-6574; *Fax:* (970) 826-4581
www.krai.com
krai@krai.com
License: Craig, Moffat County, CO
Wire Services: AP
Population Served: 45,000 *Hrs. of News Programming:* news progmg 4 hrs wkly; *No. News Employees:* 3; *Target Audience:* 18-49.
Frank Hanel, General Manager
Tammie Hanel, Station Manager
Marci Marumoto, Account Executive

***KPYR**
01-01-2005; 88.3 MHz FM; 0.25 kw; 889 ft.; N40 33 50 W107 36 40 *Rebroadcasts:* Rebroadcasts KCFR(AM) Denver 100%
2249 S. Josephine St., Denver, CO 80210 US
(303) 871-9191; *Fax:* (303) 733-3319
www.cpr.org
License: Craig, Moffat County, CO held by Public Broadcasting of Colorado Inc.
Arbitron Metro Market: Craig, CO; *Format:* News
Max Wycisk, President

Crested Butte

***KBUT**
12-20-1986; 90.3 MHz FM; *Hrs Open:* 24; 0.225 kw; -636 ft.; N38 54 11 W106 58 23
Mailing Address: Box 308, Crested Butte, CO 81224 US
Second Address: 508 Maroon Ave., Crested Butte, CO 81224
(970) 349-5225; *Fax:* (970) 349-6440
www.kbut.org
kbut@kbut.org
License: Crested Butte, Gunnison County, CO held by Crested Butte Mountain Educational Radio Inc.
Nat'l Network: NPR; PRI
Arbitron Metro Market: Crested Butte, CO; *Format:* Variety/Diverse; *Hrs. of News Programming:* news progmg 72 hrs wkly; *No. News Employees:* 1; *Target Audience:* General.; *Adv. Rates:* 80; 80; 80; 70
Ryan Stringfellow, General Manager
Chad Reich, Programming Director

Del Norte

KSLV-FM
96.5 MHz FM; 930 w; Ant 1,589 ft; N37 43 47 W106 35 18
Box 631, Monte Vista, CO
(719) 852-3581; *Fax:* (719) 852-3583
www.kslvradio.com
kslv@amigo.net
License: Del Norte, Rio Grande County, CO held by San Luis Valley Broadcasting Inc.
Group Owner: San Luis Valley Broadcasting Inc.; 7-Jun
Nat'l Network: Dial Global Networks; *Wire Services:* AP
Special Programming: Local sports; *Hrs. of News Programming:* 2 hours weekly; *No. News Employees:* 1; *Target Audience:* 25 to 55 Adults
H. Robert Gourley III, President
Steven Howard, Operations Dir
Gerald Vigil, General Manager
Linda Pacheco, News Director

Delta

KDTA
01-14-1955; 1400 kHz AM; *Hrs Open:* 24; 1 kw-U; N38 45 38 W108 05 28 *Rebroadcasts:* Simulcast of KJOL(AM) Grand Junction 100%
1354 E. Sherwood Dr., Grand Junction, CO 81416
(970) 254-5565; *Fax:* (970) 254-5550
www.kjol.org
info@kjol.org
License: Delta, Delta County, CO held by United Ministries.
Group Owner: United Ministries; (acq 11-16-2004; $88,000).
Population Served: 30,000; *Arbitron Metro Market:* Grand Junction, CO
Ken Andrews, General Manager
Ken Andrews, Station Manager

KKNN
12-01-1985; 95.1 MHz FM; *Hrs Open:* 24; 100 kw; 969 ft; N38 52 40 W108 13 30
315 Kennedy Ave., Grand Junction, CO 81506
(970) 242-7788; *Fax:* (970) 243-0567
www.95rockfm.com
rick.carmean@townsquaremedia.com
License: Delta, Delta County, CO held by Townsquare Media Grand Junction License LLC
Group Owner: Townsquare Media; (acq 1-00).
Nat'l Reps: Katz Radio
Population Served: 225,000; *Arbitron Metro Market:* Grand Junction, CO; *Hrs. of News Programming:* news progmg 6 hrs wkly; *No. News Employees:* 1; *Target Audience:* 18-49; men
Rick Carmean, General Manager
Ray Michaels, Brand Manager
Clint Patterson, Digital Sales Manager
Tim Gray, Digital Managing Editor

***KPRU**
01-01-2001; 103.3 MHz FM; 12 kw; 988 ft.; N38 52 40 W108 13 32
2249 S Josephine St, Denver, CO 80210 US
(303) 871-9191; *Fax:* (303) 733-3319
www.cpr.org
License: Delta, Delta County, CO held by Public Broadcasting of Colorado Inc.
Format: Country
Max Wycisk, President
Sue Coughlin, General Sales Mgr
Sean Nethery, Programming Director
David Gomez, News Director
Bob Hensler, Chief Engineer

Denver

KALC
06-21-1965; 105.9 MHz FM; 96 kw; 1719 ft.; N39 43 58 W105 14 8
1200 17th Street, Suiye 2300, Denver, CO 80202 US
(303) 967-2700; *Fax:* (303) 967-2747
www.alice1059.com
info@alice1059.com
License: Denver, Denver County, CO held by Entercom Denver License LLC.
Group Owner: Entercom Communications Corp.; (acq 5-1-2002; $88 million).
Nat'l Reps: Christal
Arbitron Metro Market: Denver, CO; *Format:* Adult Contemp; *Target Audience:* 18-34; women
Jeff Silver, General Sales Mgr
Mike Peterson, Programming Director
Tina Lorraine, Promotions Manager
Stephanie Walrath, News Director
Jeff Garrett, Chief Engineer

KBJD
01-01-2001; 1650 kHz AM; *Hrs Open:* 24
4880 Santa Rosa Rd, Camarillo, CA 93012 US
(303) 283-0118
www.1650radioluz.com
production@salemdenver.com
License: Denver, CO held by Salem Media of Colorado Inc.
Group Owner: Salem Communications Corp.
Arbitron Metro Market: Aurora, CO; *Format:* Religious, Spanish, 86; *Hrs. of News Programming:* news progmg 15 hrs wkly; *No. News Employees:* 3
Brian Taylor, General Manager

KLDC
09-01-1954; 1220 kHz AM; 0.66 kw-D, ND1; 0.011 kw-N, ND1; N39 41 0 W105 0 24
2821 South Parker Road, Suite 1205, Aurora, CO 80014 US
(303) 433-5500; *Fax:* (303) 433-1555
www.1220kldc.com
License: Denver, CO held by KLZ Radio Inc.
Group Owner: Crawford Broadcasting Co.; (acq 8-11-99; $1.5 million)
Arbitron Metro Market: Denver-Boulder, CO; *Format:* Religious
Special Programming: Black 2 hrs wkly; *Target Audience:* 24-55; general
Mike Triem, General Manager

KBPI
06-19-1962; 106.7 MHz FM; *Hrs Open:* 24; 100 kw; 1,339 ft.; N39 43 58 W105 14 8
4695 S. Monaco St., Denver, CO 80237 US
(303) 713-8000; *Fax:* (303) 713-8744
www.kbpi.com
License: Denver, Denver County, CO held by Citicasters Licenses Inc.
Group Owner: iHeartMedia; (acq 5-4-99; grpsl).
Nat'l Network: ABC
Arbitron Metro Market: Denver-Boulder, CO; *Format:* Rock/AOR; *Target Audience:* 25-34; men
Patrick Connor, Market President
David Harwood, Sales

***KCFR-FM**
11-01-1970; 90.1 MHz FM; *Hrs Open:* 24; 44 kw; 909 ft.; N39 43 49 W105 14 59
2249 South Josephine St., Denver, CO 80210 US
(303) 871-9191; *Fax:* (303) 733-3319
www.cpr.org
info@cpr.org
License: Denver, Denver County, CO held by Public Broadcasting of Colorado Inc.
Nat'l Network: NPR
Arbitron Metro Market: Denver-Boulder, CO; *Format:* News, News/Talk, 86; *Hrs. of News Programming:* news progmg 50 hrs wkly; *No. News Employees:* 8; *Target Audience:* General.
Max Wycisk, President
Sue Coughlin, General Sales Mgr
Sean Nethery, Programming Director
Robert Hensler, Engineering Dir
Jenny Gentry, Executive Vice President

KPTT
03-31-1968; 95.7 MHz FM; 100 kw; 1,135 ft.; N39 43 59 W105 14 10
4695 S. Monaco St., Denver, CO 80237 US
(303) 713-8000
www.957theparty.com
License: Denver, Denver County, CO held by Citicasters Licenses Inc.
Group Owner: iHeartMedia
Arbitron Metro Market: Denver-Boulder, CO; *Format:* Contemporary Hits/Top 40; *Target Audience:* General.
Micah Goldberg, Vice President of Sales

KHOW
01-01-1925; 630 kHz AM; *Hrs Open:* 24; 5 kw-D, DA2; 5 kw-N, DA2; N39 54 36 W104 54 50
4695 S. Monaco St., Denver, CO 80237 US
(303) 713-8000
www.khow.com
License: Denver, Denver County, CO held by Citicasters Licenses Inc.
Group Owner: iHeartMedia; (acq 5-4-99; grpsl)
Arbitron Metro Market: Denver-Boulder, CO; *Format:* News, News/Talk, 86; *Target Audience:* 25-54.
Jessica Farias, General Sales Mgr
Crystalyn Portwood, Director of AM Sales

KIMN
08-01-1959; 100.3 MHz FM; *Hrs Open:* 24; 97 kw; 1132 ft.; N39 40 18 W105 13 12
1200 17th Street, Suite 2300, Denver, CO 80202 US
(303) 832-5665; *Fax:* (303) 832-7000
www.mix100.com
License: Denver, Denver County, CO held by Wilks License Co.-Denver LLC.
Group Owner: Wilks Broadcast Group LLC; (acq 3-5-2009; grpsl)
Nat'l Reps: Christal
Arbitron Metro Market: Denver-Boulder,; *Format:* Adult Contemp
Special Programming: Pub affrs 2 hrs wkly; *Target Audience:* 35-44; women
Barry Remington, General Manager
Geronimo, Programming Director

***KGNU**
01-01-1954; 1390 kHz AM; *Hrs Open:* 24 *Rebroadcasts:* Simulcast of KGNU-FM, Boulder 95%
828 Santa Fe Drive, Denver, CO 80204 US
(303) 449-4885
www.kgnu.org
sam@kgnu.org
License: Denver, CO held by Boulder Community Broadcast Association Inc.
Arbitron Metro Market: Denver-Boulder, CO; *Format:* Easy Listening
Sam Fuqua, General Manager

KQMT
10-02-1959; 99.5 MHz FM; *Hrs Open:* 24; 74 kw; 1624 ft.; N39 43 45 W105 14 6
10200 E. Girard Avenue, Suite B131, Denver, CO 80231 US
(303) 967-2700; *Fax:* (303) 967-2747
www.995themountain.com
info@995themountain.com
License: Denver, Denver County, CO held by Entercom Denver License LLC.
Group Owner: Entercom Communications Corp.; (acq 3-21-03).
Arbitron Metro Market: Denver, CO; *Format:* Classic Rock; *Hrs. of News Programming:* News progmg 4 hrs wkly; *Target Audience:* 25-54; upscale, educated
Amy Griesheimer, General Manager
Greg Carpenter, General Sales Mgr
Dylan Sprague, Programming Director

***KVOQ(AM)**
03-04-1956; 1340 kHz AM; *Hrs Open:* 24; 1 kw-U; N39 39 34 W105 00 44
7409 S. Alton Ct., Centennial, CO 80112
(303) 871-9191; *Fax:* (303) 733-3319
www.cpr.org
License: Denver, Denver County, CO held by Public Broadcasting of Colorado Inc.
Population Served: 1,250,000; *Arbitron Metro Market:* Denver, CO; *Format:* News
Max Wycisk, President
Sue Coughlin, General Sales Mgr

KLZ
03-10-1922; 560 kHz AM; *Hrs Open:* 24; N39 50 36 W104 57 14
2821 South Parker Road, Suite 1205, Aurora, CO 80014 US
(303) 481-1800; *Fax:* (303) 433-1555
www.560thesource.com
License: Denver, CO held by KLZ Radio Inc.
Group Owner: Crawford Broadcasting Co.; (acq 6-30-92; $1.5 million;
Arbitron Metro Market: Denver, CO; *Format:* Christian, Talk; *Target Audience:* 25-54; men
Mike Triem, General Manager

KNUS
01-01-1941; 710 kHz AM; *Hrs Open:* 24; 5 kw-U, DA1; N39 57 19 W104 51 1

4880 Santa Rosa Road, Suite 300, Camarillo, CA 93012 US
(303) 750-5687; *Fax:* (303) 696-8063
www.710knus.com
production@salemdenver.com
License: Denver, CO held by Salem Media of Colorado Inc.
Group Owner: Salem Communications Corp.; (acq 1996; $1.2 million)
Arbitron Metro Market: Denver-Boulder, CO; *Format:* News, News/Talk, 86; *Hrs. of News Programming:* news progmg 15 hrs wkly; *No. News Employees:* 3; *Target Audience:* 35-54; Adults
Brian Taylor, General Manager

KOA
12-15-1924; 850 kHz AM; *Hrs Open:* 24; 50 kw-U, ND1; N39 30 22 W104 45 57
4695 S. Monaco St., Denver, CO 80237 US
(303) 713-8000; *Fax:* (303) 713-8735
www.koanewsradio.com
License: Denver, CO held by Citicasters Licenses Inc.
Group Owner: iHeartMedia; (acq 5-4-99; grpsl).
Nat'l Network: CBS; *Wire Services:* CBS
Arbitron Metro Market: Denver-Boulder, CO; *Format:* News, News/Talk, 84, Talk; *Target Audience:* 25-54.
Garner Goin, Operations Manager
Patrick Connor, Market President
Crystalyn Portwood, Sales Director

KOSI
03-03-1968; 101.1 MHz FM; *Hrs Open:* 24; 74 kw; 1624 ft.; N39 43 45 W105 14 6
10200 E. Girard Avenue, Suite B-131, Denver, CO 80231 US
(303) 967-2700; *Fax:* (303) 967-2747
www.kosi101.com
info@kosi101.com
License: Denver, Denver County, CO held by Entercom Denver License LLC.
Group Owner: Entercom Communications Corp.; (acq 7-24-02; with KEZW(AM) Aurora).
Arbitron Metro Market: Denver-Boulder, CO; *Format:* Adult Contemp; *Hrs. of News Programming:* news progmg 5 hrs wkly; *No. News Employees:* 1; *Target Audience:* 25-54; women/families
Glynn Alan, General Sales Mgr
Dave Symonds, Programming Director

*KPOF
03-09-1928; 910 kHz AM; *Hrs Open:* 24; 5 kw-D, ND1; 1 kw-N, ND1; N39 50 47 W105 1 59
1302 Sherman St, Denver, CO 80203 US
(303) 428-0910; *Fax:* (303) 429-0910
www.am91.org
info@am91.org
License: Denver, CO held by Pillar of Fire Corp.
Group Owner: Pillar of Fire Inc.; acq 1928)
Nat'l Network: Moody
Arbitron Metro Market: Denver-Boulder, CO; *Format:* Christian, Religious; *Target Audience:* 18-plus; mature adult and families
Robert Dallenbach, President
Jerry Bauer, Operations Dir
Jack Pelon, General Manager

KRFX
06-01-1961; 103.5 MHz FM; 100 kw; 1135 ft.; N39 43 59 W105 14 10
50 East Rivercenter Blvd, Suite 1200, Covington, KY 41011 US
(303) 713-8000; *Fax:* (303) 713-8744
www.thefox.com
License: Denver, Denver County, CO held by Citicasters Licenses Inc.
Group Owner: iHeartMedia
Arbitron Metro Market: Denver, CO; *Format:* Classic Rock; *Target Audience:* 25-54.
Tim Hager, Market President

KRKS
08-01-1953; 990 kHz AM; *Hrs Open:* 24
4880 Santa Rosa Rd #300, Carmarillo, CA 93012 US
(303) 750-5687; *Fax:* (303) 696-8063
www.krks.com
krks@krks.com
License: Denver, CO held by Salem Media of Colorado Inc.
Group Owner: Salem Communications Corp.; (acq 10-93; $400,000)
Arbitron Metro Market: Denver-Boulder, CO; *Format:* Christian; *Target Audience:* 25 plus.
Brian Taylor, VP
Jules Dygert, General Sales Mgr
Cliff Mikkelson, Engineering Dir

*KUVO
08-29-1985; 89.3 MHz FM; *Hrs Open:* 24; 22.5 kw; 912 ft.; N39 43 49 W105 14 59
Mailing Address: P.O. Box 11111, Denver, CO 80211 US
Second Address: 2900 Welton St., Suite 200, Denver, CO 80205
(303) 480-9272; *Fax:* (303) 291-0757
www.kuvo.org
alfredo@kuvo.org
License: Denver, Denver County, CO held by Denver Educational Broadcasting.
Nat'l Network: NPR; PRI
Arbitron Metro Market: Denver, CO; *Format:* Jazz *Special Programming:* Sp 15 hrs wkly; *Target Audience:* 25-49.
Carlos Lando, COO/Program Director
Alfredo Cruz, CEO/President
Joey Kloss, Engineer/ISDN
Mike Pappas, Chief Engineer
Laura Jorstad, Business Manager
Tina Cartagena, Director of Development & Marketing
Victor Cooper, ProductionManager
Arturo G¢mez, Music Director
Martha Griego, Underwriting Account Executive
Denise Meny, Web Content Coordinator

KBNO
05-15-1948; 1280 kHz AM; *Hrs Open:* 24; 5 kw-D, DA2; 5 kw-N, DA2; N39 36 5 W104 58 48
1560 Broadway, Suite 1100, Denver, CO 80202 US
(303) 733-5266; *Fax:* (303) 733-5242
kbno@kbno.net
License: Denver, CO held by Latino Communications LLC
Group Owner: Latino Communications LLC; acq 11-21-00; $3.3 million).
Arbitron Metro Market: Denver-Boulder, CO; *Hrs. of News Programming:* news progmg 21 hrs wkly; *No. News Employees:* 27; *Target Audience:* 25-54; male
Zee Ferrufino, CEO
Michael Ferrufino, Operations Dir

KXKL-FM
12-01-1956; 105.1 MHz FM; *Hrs Open:* 24; 100 kw; 1168 ft.; N39 36 0 W105 12 35
433 E. Las Colina Blvd, #1130, Irving, TX 75039 US
(303) 228-2000; *Fax:* (303) 832-7000
www.kool105.com
License: Denver, Denver County, CO held by Wilks License Co.-Denver LLC.
Group Owner: Wilks Broadcast Group LLC; (acq 3-5-2009; grpsl)
Arbitron Metro Market: Denver, CO; *Format:* Oldies
Barry Remington, General Manager
Brenda Egger, General Sales Mgr
Cha Cha, Programming Director
Barry Walters, Chief Engineer

KYGO-FM
12-01-1953; 98.5 MHz FM; *Hrs Open:* 24; 96.6 kw; 1821 ft.; N39 40 35 W105 29 9
Mailing Address: 7800 E. Orchard Rd., Sutie 400, Greenwood Village, CO 80111 US
Second Address: 55 North 300 West, 2nd Floor, Salt Lake City, UT 84101
(303) 321-0950; *Fax:* (303) 333-2987
www.kygo.com
ageffre@bonneville.com
License: Denver, Denver County, CO
Group Owner: Bonneville Media; (acq. 2016)
Arbitron Metro Market: Greenwood Village, CO; *Format:* Country; *Target Audience:* 25-54.
Darlene Park, Sales Manager
Randy Weidner, National Sales
John E. Kage, Program Director
Garret Doll, Music Director
Randy Weidner, National Sales
Rita Gillespie-Stein, Webmaser
John ""JT"" Thomas, Program Director

Dolores

*KTCF
01-01-2004; 89.5 MHz FM; 0.5 kw; 174 ft.; N37 28 7 W108 32 48 *Rebroadcasts:* Rebroadcasts KTLF(FM) Colorado Springs 100%
1665 Briargate Blvd, Colorado Springs, CO 80920 US
(719) 593-0600; *Fax:* (719) 593-2399
www.ktlf.org
awagnon@ktlf.org
License: Dolores, Montezuma County, CO held by Educational Communications of Colorado Springs Inc.
Arbitron Metro Market: Crosby, MN; *Format:* Christian; *Target Audience:* 45-60; Christian
James Felix, Operations Dir
Tom Sullivan, General Manager
Lynn Carmichael, Programming Director
Marge Wallace, Office Manager
Alleen Wagnon, Office Assistant
Sharick Wade, KTPL Program Director

KKDC
10-21-2003; 93.3 MHz FM; 50 kw; 338 ft.; N37 27 59 W108 31 28
190 Turner Dr., Suite G, Durango, CO 81303 US
(970) 259-4444; *Fax:* (970) 247-1005
www.radiodolores.com
fcb@frontier.net
License: Dolores, Montezuma County, CO held by Four Corners Broadcasting LLC.
Group Owner: Four Corners Broadcasting LLC.
Arbitron Metro Market: Dolores, CO; *Format:* Rock/AOR; *No. News Employees:* 1; *Target Audience:* 35-54.
Kim Emanual, General Sales Mgr
Ed Lacy, Programming Director
Ryan Baker, Chief Engineer
Kristin Dills, Business Manager
Ward Holmes, Regional Manager

Durango

KDGO
04-18-1958; 1240 kHz AM; *Hrs Open:* 24; 1 kw-U, ND1; N37 18 18 W107 51 25
427 Bedford Rd, Pleasantville, NY 10570 US
(970) 247-1240; *Fax:* (970) 247-1771
License: Durango, CO held by Winton Road Broadcasting Co. LLC.
Group Owner: Winton Road Broadcasting Co. LLC; (acq 6-1-2001; grpsl)
Nat'l Network: ABC
Arbitron Metro Market: Durango, CO; *Format:* News, News/Talk, 86; *No. News Employees:* 1; *Target Audience:* 35-55.
Dan Buchta, General Manager
Ryan Nutter, Programming Director

*KDUR
01-01-1975; 91.9 MHz FM; 6 kw vert; -512 ft.; N37 16 41 W107 52 21
Fort Lewis College, 1000 Rim Drive, Durango, CO 81301 US
(970) 247-7634; *Fax:* (970) 247-7487
www.kdur.org
KDUR@fortlewis.edu
License: Durango, La Plata County, CO held by Board of Trustees for Fort Lewis College.
Nat'l Network: PRI
Arbitron Metro Market: Durango, CO; *Format:* Variety/Diverse
Special Programming: Bluegrass 6 hrs, blues 6 hrs, class 6 hrs, jazz 9 hrs, Native American folk 3 hrs wkly
Bryant Liggett, Station Manager
Jon Lynch, Programming Director
Rachel Perrault, Development Director
Jennifer Cossey, Office Manager
Chris Braun, Music Director

KIQX
10-15-1982; 101.3 MHz FM; *Hrs Open:* 24; 100 kw; 1995 ft.; N37 15 44 W107 54 08
190 Turner Dr., Suite G, Durango, CO 81303 US
(970) 259-4444; *Fax:* (970) 247-1005
fcb@frontier.net
License: Durango, La Plata County, CO held by Four Corners Broadcasting LLC.
Group Owner: Four Corners Broadcasting LLC.
Nat'l Network: CBS
Arbitron Metro Market: Albuquerque, NM; *Format:* Adult Contemp, Variety/Diverse; *No. News Employees:* 2; *Target Audience:* 25-54; mainstream business professionals & families; *Adv. Rates:* 15; 13; 15; 10
Kim Emanual, General Sales Mgr
Ed Lacy, Programming Director
Ryan Baker, Chief Engineer

KIUP
12-10-1935; 930 kHz AM; *Hrs Open:* 24; 5 kw-D, ND1; 0.1 kw-N, ND1; N37 18 18 W107 51 25
190 Turner Dr., Suite G, Durango, CO 81303 US
(970) 259-4444; *Fax:* (970) 247-1005
www.radiodurango.com
fcb@frontier.net
License: Durango, CO held by Four Corners Broadcasting LLC.
Group Owner: Four Corners Broadcasting LLC.
Nat'l Network: ESPN Radio; *Wire Services:* AP
Format: Sports; *Hrs. of News Programming:* news progmg 5 hrs wkly; *No. News Employees:* 2; *Target Audience:* 12 plus.; *Adv. Rates:* 15; 18; 15; 10
Kim Emanual, General Sales Mgr
Ed Lacy, Programming Director
Ryan Baker, Chief Engineer

KPTE
07-01-1995; 99.7 MHz FM; 9.2 kw; 1129 ft.; N37 20 21 W107 49 25
427 Bedford Rd, Pleasantville, NY 10570 US
(970) 247-1240; *Fax:* (970) 247-1771
99xdurango.com
kpte@997thepoint.com
License: Durango, La Plata County, CO held by Winton Road Broadcasting Co. LLC.
Group Owner: Winton Road Broadcasting Co. LLC
Arbitron Metro Market: Four Corners; *Format:* Adult Contemp, Contemporary Hits/Top 40; *Target Audience:* 18-44.
Dr. David Bryant, President
Russell Guthrie, General Manager

KRSJ
12-04-1972; 100.5 MHz FM; *Hrs Open:* 24; 100 kw; 1995 ft.; N37 15 47 W107 53 46
190 Turner Dr., Suite G, Durango, CO 81303 US
(970) 259-4444; *Fax:* (970) 247-1005
www.radiodurango.com
fcb@frontier.net
License: Durango, La Plata County, CO held by Four Corners Broadcasting LLC.
Group Owner: Four Corners Broadcasting LLC.
Nat'l Network: Fox News Radio; *Wire Services:* AP
Arbitron Metro Market: Durango,CO; *Format:* Country; *Hrs. of News Programming:* news progmg 6 hrs wkly; *No. News Employees:* 2; *Target Audience:* 25 plus.; *Adv. Rates:* 15; 12; 15; 10
Kim Emanual, General Sales Mgr
Ed Lacy, Programming Director
Ryan Baker, Chief Engineer

***KTDU**
05-02-2005; 88.5 MHz FM; 0 kw horiz, 4 kw vert; 371 ft.; N37 15 43 W107 54 24 *Rebroadcasts:* Rebroadcasts KTLF(FM) Colorado Springs 100%
1665 Briargate Blvd, Colorado Springs, CO 80920 US
(719) 593-0600; *Fax:* (719) 593-2399
www.ktlf.org
awagnon@ktlf.org
License: Durango, La Plata County, CO held by Educational Communications of Colorado Springs Inc.
Arbitron Metro Market: Durango, CO; *Format:* Christian; *Target Audience:* 45-60; Christian
James Felix, Operations Dir
Tom Sullivan, General Manager
Lynn Carmichael, Programming Director
Marge Wallace, Office Manager
Alleen Wagnon, Office Assistant
Sharick Wade, KTPL Program Director

***KDNG**
89.3 MHz FM; 0.2 kw; 322 ft.; N37 15 44 W107 53 58
P.O. Box 737, Ignacio, CO 81137 US
(970) 563-0255; *Fax:* (970) 563-0399
www.ksut.org
info@ksut.org
License: Durango, La Plata County, CO held by KUTE Inc.
Group Owner: KUTE Inc.
Arbitron Metro Market: Durango, CO
Eddie Box Jr., President

Eagle

KSKE-FM
01-01-1997; 101.7 MHz FM; *Hrs Open:* 24; 12 kw; 2188 ft.; N39 44 18 W106 47 58
Mailing Address: 225 N. Mill Street, Aspen, CO 81611 US
Second Address: 182 Avon Rd., Avon, CO 81620
(970) 949-0140; *Fax:* (970) 949-1464
www.kskeradio.com
info@kskeradio.com
License: Eagle, Eagle County, CO held by Superior Broadcasting of Denver LLC
Arbitron Metro Market: Avon, CO; *Format:* Country
Meredith Fox, Operations Dir
Steve Wodlinger, General Manager
Holli Snyder, General Sales Mgr
David Bach, News Director
Ken Laughlin, Chief Engineer

Eckley

KECK
95.3 MHz FM; 100 kw; 339 ft.; N40 0 33 W102 45 35
US
(719) 336-4227
License: Eckley, Yuma County, CO held by Arnold Broadcasting Inc.
Group Owner: Arnold Broadcasting Inc.; (acq 7-31-2008; grpsl)
Arbitron Metro Market: Eckley, CO
William Arnold, General Manager

El Jebel

KGHT
01-01-2006; 100.5 MHz FM; *Hrs Open:* 24; 6 kw; 295 ft.; N39 18 56 W106 57 32
PO Box 1099, Santa Monica, CA 90406-1099 US
(239) 263-7700
License: El Jebel, CO held by BS&T Wireless, Inc.
Group Owner: BS&T Wireless, Inc.; (acq 1-97)
Arbitron Metro Market: Little Rock, AR; *Format:* Contemporary Hits/Top 40; *Target Audience:* WF 35-64.; *Adv. Rates:* 28; 28; 28; na
Lerman Senter, President

Englewood

KNRV
01-01-1951; 1150 kHz AM; *Hrs Open:* 24; 10 kw-D, 1 kw-N, DA-2; N39 36 18 W104 50 25
1582 So. Parker Rd., Suite 204, Denver, CO 80203
(303) 696-5966; *Fax:* (303) 200-9190
www.onda1150am.com
hebertolv@amigomultimedia.com
License: Englewood, Arapahoe County, CO held by Amigo Multimedia Inc.
Population Served: 400,000; *Arbitron Metro Market:* Denver-Boulder,
Heberto Limas-Villers, President

Estes Park

KDEB(AM)
08-19-1967; 1470 kHz AM; *Hrs Open:* 24; 1 kw-D, 53 w-N; N40 20 15 W105 31 36
Mailing Address: Box 2810, Estes Park, CO 80517
Second Address: 184 E. Elkhorn Ave., Estes Park, CO 80517
(970) 586-9555; *Fax:* (970) 586-9561
keplradio@yahoo.com
License: Estes Park, Larimer County, CO held by WP Broadcasting of Colorado LLC.
Group Owner: Westburg Media Capital LP; (acq 6-30-2007)
Population Served: 5,976; *Arbitron Metro Market:* Estes Park, CO; *Format:* Talk; *Target Audience:* General.; *Adv. Rates:* 17; 16; 17; 10
Vince Lupo, General Manager

KRKY-FM
04-06-1998; 102.1 MHz FM; *Hrs Open:* 24; 6 kw horiz, 0 kw vert; 82 ft.; N40 21 38 W105 31 12
6807 Foxglove Drive, Cheyenne, WY 82009 US
(970) 453-2234; *Fax:* (970) 453-5425
www.alwaysmountaintime.com
jen@NRC365.com
License: Estes Park, Larimer County, CO held by NRC Broadcasting Inc.
Group Owner: United States CP LLC; (acq 8-31-2006; exchange for KSKE-FM Vail)
Nat'l Network: ABC
Arbitron Metro Market: Fort Collins, CO; *Format:* Spanish; *Target Audience:* Urban adults 19-34; Black, Hispanic, White; *Adv. Rates:* 120;120;120;80
Jen Radueg, General Manager
Tonya Everist, General Sales Mgr

***KHIH**
88.7 MHz FM; 0.1 kw vert; -161 ft.; N40 21 44 W105 31 4
US
(970) 669-9200
License: Estes Park, Lincoln County, CO held by Kona Coast Radio LLC.
Group Owner: Cedar Cove Broadcasting Inc.
Arbitron Metro Market: Estes Park, CO
Victor Michael Jr., General Manager

Evergreen

KXPK
06-08-1994; 96.5 MHz FM; *Hrs Open:* 24; 100 kw; 1739 ft.; N39 40 35 W105 29 9
1907 Mile High Stadium W. Cir., Denver, CO 80204 US
(303) 832-0050
www.965tricolor.com
License: Evergreen, Jefferson County, CO held by Entravision Holdings LLC.
Group Owner: Entravision Communications Corp.; (acq 5-1-02; $47.5 million).
Arbitron Metro Market: Denver-Boulder, CO; *Format:* Tejano; *No. News Employees:* 1
Don Daboub, General Manager

Fleming

KSIK
100.1 MHz FM; kw
US
(970) 669-9200
www.klove.com
License: Fleming, Lincoln County, CO held by Kona Coast Radio LLC.
Group Owner: Kona Coast Radio LLC
Arbitron Metro Market: Fleming, CO; *Format:* Christian
Victor Michael Jr., General Manager

Fort Collins

KIIX
03-01-1947; 1410 kHz AM; *Hrs Open:* 24; 1 kw-D, DAN; 1 kw-N, DAN; N40 35 34 W105 6 18
4270 Byrd Dr., Loveland, CO 80538 US
(970) 461-2560
www.kiixcountry.com
License: Fort Collins, Larimer County, CO held by Citicasters Licenses Inc.
Group Owner: iHeartMedia; (acq 5-4-99; grpsl)
Arbitron Metro Market: Fort Collins, CO; *Format:* Country; *Hrs. of News Programming:* news progmg 35 hrs wkly; *No. News Employees:* 2; *Target Audience:* 18-54; educated, affluent, professional
Garner Goin, Operations Manager
Stu Haskell, General Manager
Kathy Arias, General Sales Mgr
Mike Sanchez, Promotions Manager

***KCSU-FM**
09-20-1964; 90.5 MHz FM; *Hrs Open:* 24; 10 kw; -354 ft.; N40 36 0 W105 9 21
110 16th Street, Denver, CO 80202 US
(970) 491-7611; *Fax:* (970) 491-1690
www.kcsufm.com
License: Fort Collins, Larimer County, CO held by Colorado State Board of Agriculture.
Arbitron Metro Market: Fort Collins, CO; *Format:* Alternative
Special Programming: Hip-hop 3 hrs, jazz 3 hrs, Black 3 hrs wkly; *Hrs. of News Programming:* News progmg 3 hrs wkly;
Target Audience: 18-34; general
Nick Sbesta, Station Manager
Mario Caballero, General Sales Mgr

KPAW
07-27-1975; 107.9 MHz FM; *Hrs Open:* 24; 100 kw; 722 ft.; N40 53 42 W105 11 38
4270 Byrd Dr., Loveland, CO 80538 US
(970) 461-2560; *Fax:* (970) 461-0118
www.1079thebear.com
info@1079thebear.com
License: Fort Collins, Larimer County, CO held by Citicasters Licenses Inc.
Group Owner: iHeartMedia
Arbitron Metro Market: Fort Collins-Greeley, CO; *Format:* Classic Rock; *Target Audience:* 25-54; men
Garner Goin, Operations Manager
Stu Haskell, General Manager
Kathy Arias, General Sales Mgr
Doc Jarnagin, Programming Director
Mike Sanchez, Promotions Director

***KGCO**
01-01-2005; 88.3 MHz FM; *Hrs Open:* 24; 0.15 kw vert; 1194 ft.; N40 37 3 W105 19 40
P.O. Box 887, Brentwood, TN 37034 US
(800) 260-5676
www.nuevavida.com
info@nuevavida.com
License: Fort Collins, Larimer County, CO held by Educational Media Foundation.
Group Owner: EMF Broadcasting; (acq 10-2-2003; grpsl)
Arbitron Metro Market: Fort Collins, CO; *Format:* Christian; *No. News Employees:* 3; *Target Audience:* 25-44; Judeo Christian female
Mike Novak, President

***KRFC**
88.9 MHz FM; *Hrs Open:* 24; 0.01 kw horiz, 3 kw vert; 217 ft.; N40 34 53 W104 54 20
1840 Wallenberg Dr, Fort Collins, CO 80526 US
(970) 221-5075; *Fax:* (970) 221-5075
www.krfcfm.org
License: Fort Collins, Larimer County, CO held by Public Radio for the Front Range.
Arbitron Metro Market: Fort Collins, CO; *Format:* Variety/Diverse

Chris Kennison, Station Manager
Kristen Rasmussen, General Sales Mgr
Dennis Bigelow, Programming Director
Brian Hughes, Executive Director
Danielle Hastings, Development Director
Andrea Bradstreet, Volunteer Coordinator
AndrewSchneider, Web & Social Media

Fort Morgan

KFTM
05-22-1949; 1400 kHz AM; 1 kw-U, ND1; N40 15 31 W103 51 7
Mailing Address: 803 West Main, Sterling, CO 80751 US
Second Address: 16041 Hwy. 34, Fort Morgan, CO 80701
(970) 867-5674; *Fax:* (970) 542-1023
www.kftm.net
kftm@medialogic.com
License: Fort Morgan, CO held by Media Logic LLC
Group Owner: Media Logic LLC; acq 9-29-03; $415,000).
Nat'l Network: AP Radio; Jones Radio Networks; *Wire Services:* AP
Arbitron Metro Market: Fort Morgan, CO; *Format:* Adult Contemp, News, 62, Talk *Special Programming:* Farm news 6 hrs, talk 5 hrs, sports 10 hrs, local 3 hrs wkly; *Hrs. of News Programming:* news progmg 16 hrs wkly *No.News Employees:* 1; *Target Audience:* General; the people of (Morgan county) Colorado
Wayne Johnson, President
Wayne Johnson, General Manager
Dana Marini, General Sales Mgr
John Waters, Programming Director
Micheal Schaus, News Director

Fountain

KIBT
09-25-1992; 96.1 MHz FM; *Hrs Open:* 24; 0.46 kw; 2169 ft.; N38 44 44 W104 51 42
2864 S. Circle Dr., Suite 300, Colorado Springs, CO 80906 US
(719) 540-9200; *Fax:* (719) 579-0882
www.beatcolorado.com
info@beatcolorado.com
License: Fountain, El Paso County, CO held by AMFM Texas Licenses LLC.
Group Owner: iHeartMedia; (acq 7-1-2000; grpsl).
Nat'l Reps: Clear Channel
Arbitron Metro Market: CO Springs, CO Pueblo, CO; *Format:* Contemporary Hits/Top 40 *Special Programming:* Blues 3 hrs wkly; *Hrs. of News Programming:* News progmg 8-5 Monday - Friday; *No. News Employees:* 1 *Target Audience:* 25-44; men; *Adv. Rates:* 40; 35; 35; 15
Jason McCollim, Senior Vice President of Programming
Adam Burnes, Programming Director
Angela Cortez, Promotions Director

KJME
890 kHz AM; 5 kw-D, 580w-N, DA-2; 274 meters; N38 31 07 W104 36 03
965 South Irving Street, Denver, CO
(303) 937-1900
License: Fountain, CO held by Timothy C Cutforth

Tim Cutforth, General Manager

Fowler

KPCR
99.3 MHz FM; 0.1 kw horiz; -98 ft.; N38 7 49 W104 1 22 US
(314) 909-8569; *Fax:* (314) 835-9739
www.joyfmonline.org
License: Fowler, Kit Carson County, CO held by Youngers Colorado Broadcasting LLC.
Arbitron Metro Market: Fowler, CO
Sandi Brown, General Manager
Nick Spiniolas, Promotions Manager
Kelly Corday, News Director
Kim Underwood, Social Media Director
Jill Willis, Events Manager
Brenda Pacini, Office/Accounting Manager

Fraser

*KPOY(FM)
90.3 MHz FM; 150 w vert; Ant -1,007 ft; N39 56 49 W105 48 57
87 Jasper Lake Rd., Loveland, CO 80537
(970) 669-9200; *Fax:* (970) 669-0800
License: Fraser, Grand County, CO held by Cedar Cove Broadcasting Inc.
Group Owner: Cedar Cove Broadcasting Inc.
Population Served: 1,199; *Arbitron Metro Market:* Fraser, CO
Victor Michael Jr., President

Frisco

KYSL
05-27-1988; 93.9 MHz FM; *Hrs Open:* 24; 560 w; 1,050 ft; N39 33 22 W106 06 53
P.O. Box 27, Frisco, CO 80443
(970) 513-9393; *Fax:* (970) 262-3677
www.krystal93.com
feedback@krystal93.com
License: Frisco, Summit County, CO held by Krystal Broadcasting Inc.
Nat'l Network: AP Radio; *Nat'l Reps:* Interep
Hrs. of News Programming: news progmg 8 hrs wkly; *No. News Employees:* 1; *Target Audience:* 25-49; upscale adults; *Adv. Rates:* 27; 25; 27; 14
Ann Penny, President
John O'Connor, General Manager

Fruita

KEKB
05-24-1984; 99.9 MHz FM; *Hrs Open:* 24; 79 kw; 1,380 ft; N39 03 56 W108 44 52
315 Kennedy Ave., Grand Junction, CO 53202
(970) 242-7788; *Fax:* (970) 243-0567
www.kekbfm.com
pat.kelley@townsquaremedia.com
License: Fruita, Mesa County, CO held by Townsquare Media Grand Junction License LLC
Group Owner: Townsquare Media; (acq 7-9-98; grpsl).
Population Served: 100,000; *Arbitron Metro Market:* Grand Junction, CO; *Hrs. of News Programming:* news progmg 6 hrs wkly; *No. News Employees:* 2; *Target Audience:* 25-54.
Pat Kelley, General Manager
Justin Tyler, Brand Manager
Zandi Wilcox, Director Of Sales
Eric Davis, Digital Sales Manager
Madison Scruggs, Digital Managing Editor

KGJX
07-30-2012; 101.5 MHz FM; 3.15 kw; 418 m; N39 04 00 W108 44 45
3180 N. Mountain View Drive, San Diego, CA
(970)986-4900
License: Fruita, Mesa County, CO held by KBDX LLC

Glenwood Springs

*KLXV
08-01-1995; 91.9 MHz FM; *Hrs Open:* 24; 0.75 kw horiz, 0.185 kw vert; 2661 ft.; N39 25 30 W107 22 46
16075 W. Belleview Ave., Morrison, CO 80465 US
(916) 251-1600; *Fax:* (916) 251-1650
www.klove.com
klove@klove.com
License: Glenwood Springs, Garfield County, CO held by Educational Media Foundation.
Group Owner: EMF Broadcasting; (acq 12-28-00; grpsl).
Nat'l Network: K-Love
Arbitron Metro Market: Rocklin, CA; *Format:* Christian; *No. News Employees:* 3; *Target Audience:* 25-44; Judeo Christian, female
Darrell Chambliss, Chairman
Mike Novak, CEO/COO
Mike Novak, President
Jennifer Lohman, Operations Dir
David Pierce, Programming Director
Ed Lenane, News Director
Sam Wallington, Engineering Dir
Marya Morgan, News Reporter
Richard Hunt, News Reporter
Tracy Butler, Traffic Manager

KGLN
05-14-1950; 980 kHz AM; *Hrs Open:* 24
1360 E. Sherwood Dr., Grand Junction, CO 81501 US
(970) 254-2150
www.kgln.com
chrisb@gjradio.com
License: Glenwood Springs, CO held by MBC Grand Broadcasting Inc.
Group Owner: MBC Grand Broadcasting Inc.; (acq 1-16-2008; $250,000)
Nat'l Network: Fox News Radio
Format: Talk *Special Programming:* Finance 20 hrs wkly, religious 4 hrs wkly; *Hrs. of News Programming:* news 140 hrs wkly; *No. News Employees:* 1

KKCH
09-01-1997; 92.7 MHz FM; 55.2 kw; 2503 ft.; N39 25 7 W107 22 6
1400 Easton Road, Bakersfield, CA 93303 US
(970) 949-0140; *Fax:* (970) 949-1464
License: Glenwood Springs, Garfield County, CO held by NRC Broadcasting Mountain Group LLC.
Group Owner: NRC Broadcasting Inc.; (acq 5-1-2007; grpsl)

Steve Wodlinger, General Manager

KMTS
06-06-1977; 99.1 MHz FM; 10 kw; -226 ft.; N39 31 57 W107 20 30
P.O. Box 1028, Glenwood Springs, CO 81602 US
(970) 945-9124; *Fax:* (970) 945-5409
www.kmts.com
kmts@kmts.com
License: Glenwood Springs, Garfield County, CO held by Colorado West Broadcasting Inc.
Format: Country; *Target Audience:* 25-50.
Gabe Chenoweth, President
Kimberly Henrie, General Sales Mgr
Ron Milhorn, News Director

KRVG
10-01-2000; 95.5 MHz FM; *Hrs Open:* 24; 1 kw; 2416 ft.; N39 25 5 W107 22 1
751 Horizon Ct., Suite 225, Grand Junction, CO 81506 US
(970) 241-6460
www.wscradio.net
License: Glenwood Springs, Garfield County, CO held by Western Slope Communications LLC.
Group Owner: Western Slope Communications LLC
Arbitron Metro Market: Grand Junction, CO; *Format:* Classic Rock; *Hrs. of News Programming:* news progmg 20 hrs wkly; *No. News Employees:* 1
Cyrene Jagger, Station Manager

*KDNK
01-01-2004; 88.1 MHz FM; *Hrs Open:* 6 AM-1 AM (M-F); 7 AM-1 AM (S, Su); 1.2 kw horiz, 1.07 kw vert; 2543 ft.; N39 25 8 W107 22 10
2249 S Josephine Street, Denver, CO 80210 US
(970) 963-0139; *Fax:* (970) 963-0810
www.kdnk.org
License: Glenwood Springs, Garfield County, CO held by Carbondale Community Access Radio Inc.
Nat'l Network: NPR
Arbitron Metro Market: Grand Junction, CO; *Format:* News; *Hrs. of News Programming:* News progmg 21 hrs wkly
Nancy Emerson, President
Steve Skinner, Station Manager
Amy Kimberly, General Sales Mgr
Luke Nestler, Programming Director
Wick Moses, Advertising Director
Laura McCormick, Vice President
Nancy Smith, Treasurer
Susan Darrow,Secretary

Granby

KRKY
07-03-1986; 930 kHz AM; *Hrs Open:* 24; 4.5 kw-D, ND1; 0.121 kw-N, ND1; N40 2 26 W105 56 11
P.O.Drawer J, Dillon, CO 80435 US
(970) 453-2234; *Fax:* (970) 453-5425
www.alwaysmountaintime.com
License: Granby, CO held by New Field Broadcasting LLC
Format: Country *Special Programming:* Agriculture one hr, Sp one hr wkly; *Hrs. of News Programming:* news progmg 5 hrs wkly; *No. News Employees:* 2; *Target Audience:* 24-49; adults; *Adv. Rates:* 15; 12; 10; 8
Jen Radueg, General Manager
Tonya Everist, General Sales Mgr
Brandon Spence, Programming Director

Grand Junction

*KAFM
01-01-1999; 88.1 MHz FM; *Hrs Open:* 24; 0.3 kw; 1301 ft.; N39 4 0 W108 44 41
3684 G 4/10 Road, Palisade, CO 81526 US
(970) 241-8801
www.kafmradio.org
License: Grand Junction, Mesa County, CO held by Grand Valley Public Radio Co. Inc.
Arbitron Metro Market: Grand Junction, CO; *Format:* Talk; *Hrs. of News Programming:* News progmg 20 hrs wkly; *Target Audience:* 25-80.
Barry Barak, President
Tracy Baker, Operations Dir
Ryan Stringfellow, General Manager
Jon Rizzo, Programming Director
Marc Foster, Music Director

KBKL
01-01-1993; 107.9 MHz FM; *Hrs Open:* 24; 100 kw; 1,305 ft; N39 04 00 W108 44 41
315 Kennedy Ave., Grand Junction, CO 53202
(970) 242-7788; *Fax:* (970) 243-0567
www.kool1079.com
rick.carmean@townsquaremedia.com
License: Grand Junction, Mesa County, CO held by Townsquare Media Grand Junction License LLC
Group Owner: Townsquare Media; (acq 3-10-98; grpsl)
Arbitron Metro Market: Grand Junction, CO; *Target Audience:* 25-54.
Rick Carmean, General Manager
Ed Chandler, Brand Manager
Rick Carmean, Director Of Sales
Clint Patterson, Digital Sales Manager
Tim Gray, Digital Managing Editor
Marty Gausvik, CFO
Jonathan Pinch, COO

***KCIC**
03-04-1979; 88.5 MHz FM; *Hrs Open:* 24; 0.44 kw; -351 ft.; N39 4 41 W108 28 36
3102 E Road, Grand Junction, CO 81504 US
(970) 434-4113
License: Grand Junction, Mesa County, CO held by Pear Park Baptist Schools.
Arbitron Metro Market: Grand Junction, CO; *Format:* Religious *Special Programming:* Class 14 hrs wkly; *Hrs. of News Programming:* 2 hrs wkly
Randy David, President
Glenn Gardner, General Manager

KEXO
01-01-1942; 1230 kHz AM; *Hrs Open:* 24; 1 kw-U, ND1; N39 5 41 W108 34 41
715 Horizon Drive, Suite 430, Grand Junction, CO 81506 US
(970) 242-7788; *Fax:* (970) 243-0567
www.kexo1230.com
pat.kelley@townsquaremedia.com
License: Grand Junction, CO held by Townsquare Media Grand Junction License LLC
Group Owner: Townsquare Media; (acq 1-2000)
Arbitron Metro Market: Grand Junction, CO; *Format:* Talk; *No. News Employees:* 1; *Target Audience:* General.
Pat Kelley, General Manager
Justin Tyler, Brand Manager
Zandi Wilcox, Director Of Sales
Eric Davis, Digital Sales Manager
Madison Scruggs, Digital Managing Editor

***KLFV**
04-24-1982; 90.3 MHz FM; *Hrs Open:* 24; 3 kw; 1309 ft.; N39 3 57 W108 44 48
16075 W. Belleview Ave., Morrison, CO 80465 US
(916) 251-1600; *Fax:* (916) 251-1650
www.klove.com
klove@klove.com
License: Grand Junction, Mesa County, CO held by Educational Media Foundation.
Group Owner: EMF Broadcasting; (acq 12-28-00; grpsl).
Nat'l Network: K-Love
Arbitron Metro Market: Grand Junction, CO; *Format:* Christian *Special Programming:* Sp 2 hrs wkly; *No. News Employees:* 3; *Target Audience:* 25-44; Judeo Christian, female
Darrell Chambliss, Chairman
Mke Novak, CEO
Mike Novak, President
Jennifer Lohman, Operations Dir
Eric Moser, General Sales Mgr
David Pierce, Programming Director
Ed Lenane, News Director
Sam Wallington, Engineering Dir
AlanMason, Chief Operating Officer
D. Kevin Blair, Secretary and General Counsel
Amy Baumann, News Anchor
Jennifer James, News Anchor
Jennifer James, News Anchor
Mitch Barnhart, Director

KMOZ-FM
05-01-1960; 92.3 MHz FM; *Hrs Open:* 24; 100 kw; 1,378 ft; N39 04 00 W108 44 41
1360 E. Sherwood Dr., Grand Junction, CO 81501
(970) 254-2100
www.themoose923.com
License: Grand Junction, Mesa County, CO held by MBC Grand Broadcasting Inc
Group Owner: MBC Grand Broadcasting Inc.
Wire Services: AP
Population Served: 240,000; *Arbitron Metro Market:* Grand Junction, CO; *Hrs. of News Programming:* News progmg 8 hrs wkly; *Target Audience:* Adults; 25-54

***KMSA**
02-18-1975; 91.3 MHz FM; *Hrs Open:* 24; 3 kw; 1274 ft.; N39 3 58 W108 44 50
1175 Texas, Grand Junction, CO 81501 US
(970) 248-1442; *Fax:* (970) 248-1834
License: Grand Junction, Mesa County, CO held by Mesa State College.
Arbitron Metro Market: Grand Junction, CO; *Format:* Alternative, Reggae, 92 *Special Programming:* Black 6 hrs, folk 2 hrs, jazz 12 hrs wkly; *Hrs. of News Programming:* news progmg 10 hrs wkly; *No. News Employees:* 2 *Target Audience:* 18-60; college students and gen pub
Lucas Case, General Manager
Nickolas Patton, Operations Manager
Matt MacDonald, Promotions Manager

KMXY
01-01-1996; 104.3 MHz FM; 100 kw; 1,296 ft
315 Kennedy Ave., Grand Junction, CO 53202
(970) 242-7788; *Fax:* (970) 243-0567
www.mix1043fm.com
rick.carmean@townsquaremedia.com
License: Grand Junction, Mesa County, CO held by Townsquare Media Grand Junction License LLC
Group Owner: Townsquare Media; (acq 7-9-98; grpsl).
Arbitron Metro Market: Grand Junction, CO
Rick Carmean, General Manager
Ray Michaels, Brand Manager
Rick Carmean, Director Of Sales
Clint Patterson, Digital Sales Manager
Tim Gray, Digital Managing Editor

KNZZ
05-01-1926; 1100 kHz AM; *Hrs Open:* 24; 36 kw-C, DAN; 50 kw-D, DAN; DAN; 10 kw-N; N38 57 6 W108 25 10
1360 E. Sherwood Dr., Grand Junction, CO 81501 US
(970) 254-2100
www.1100knzz.com
License: Grand Junction, CO held by MBC Grand Broadcasting Inc.
Group Owner: MBC Grand Broadcasting Inc.; (acq 8-30-89).
Nat'l Network: Fox News Radio; *Wire Services:* AP
Arbitron Metro Market: Grand Junction, CO; *Format:* News, News/Talk, 86; *Hrs. of News Programming:* news progmg 44 hrs wkly; *No. News Employees:* 3; *Target Audience:* 25-64.

***KPRN**
04-01-1985; 89.5 MHz FM; *Hrs Open:* 24; 19.83 kw; 1319 ft.; N39 3 58 W108 44 43
2249 S Josephine Street, Denver, CO 80210 US
(303) 871-9191; *Fax:* (303) 733-3319
www.cpr.org
info@cpr.org
License: Grand Junction, Mesa County, CO held by Public Broadcasting of Colorado Inc.
Nat'l Network: NPR; *Regional Network:* Colo. Pub.
Arbitron Metro Market: Grand Junction, CO; *Format:* News; *Hrs. of News Programming:* news progmg 28 hrs wkly; *No. News Employees:* 1; *Target Audience:* 25 plus.
Max Wycisk, President
Sue Coughlin, General Sales Mgr
Sean Nethery, Programming Director
Robert Hensler, Engineering Dir
Jenny Gentry, Executive Vice President

KTMM
01-01-1959; 1340 kHz AM; *Hrs Open:* 24
1360 E. Sherwood Dr., Grand Junction, CO 81501 US
(970) 254-2100
www.theteam1340.com
License: Grand Junction, CO held by MBC Grand Broadcasting Inc.
Group Owner: MBC Grand Broadcasting Inc.
Nat'l Network: ESPN Radio
Arbitron Metro Market: Grand Junction, CO; *Format:* Sports; *Hrs. of News Programming:* news progmg 10 hrs wkly; *No. News Employees:* 1; *Target Audience:* 25-54; men

KMGJ
11-01-1973; 93.1 MHz FM; *Hrs Open:* 24; 100 kw; 1434 ft.; N39 3 59 W108 44 41
1360 E. Sherwood Dr., Grand Junction, CO 81501 US
(970) 254-2100
www.931magic.com
License: Grand Junction, Mesa County, CO held by MBC Grand Broadcasting, Inc.
Group Owner: MBC Grand Broadcasting Inc.; acq 5-94; with co-located AM).
Arbitron Metro Market: Grand Junction, CO; *Format:* Contemporary Hits/Top 40; *Hrs. of News Programming:* news progmg 6 hrs wkly; *No. News Employees:* 1; *Target Audience:* 18-49; women

KJOL
06-19-1957; 620 kHz AM; *Hrs Open:* 24; 5 kw-D, ND2; 0.079 kw-N, ND2; N39 7 35 W108 38 13
660 Rood Avenue, Grand Junction, CO 81501 US
(970) 254-5565; *Fax:* (970) 254-5550
www.kjol.org
info@kjol.org
License: Grand Junction, CO held by United Ministries.
Group Owner: United Ministries; (acq 5-1-2003).
Arbitron Metro Market: Grand Junction,; *Format:* Christian
Ken Andrews, General Manager
Ken Andrews, Station Manager
Rhonda Repshire, Promotions Manager
Kurt Neuswanger, Music Director

KKVT
03-27-1999; 100.7 MHz FM; *Hrs Open:* 24; 30 kw; 1558 ft.; N39 3 59.36 W108 44 40.94
1360 E. Sherwood Dr., Grand Junction, CO 81501 US
(970) 254-2100
www.thevault1007.com
License: Grand Junction, Mesa County, CO held by MBC Grand Broadcasting Inc.
Group Owner: MBC Grand Broadcasting Inc.
Arbitron Metro Market: Grand Junction, CO; *Format:* Country; *Hrs. of News Programming:* news progmg 2 hrs wkly; *No. News Employees:* 2; *Target Audience:* 25-54.

Greeley

KFKA
05-21-1921; 1310 kHz AM; *Hrs Open:* 24; 5 kw-D, DAN; 1 kw-N, DAN; N40 21 56 W104 43 56
P.O. Box K, Greely, CO 80632 US
(970) 356-1310; *Fax:* (970) 356-1314
www.1310kfka.com
info@1310kfka.com
License: Greeley, CO held by Music Ventures LLC dba Broadcast Media LLC
Nat'l Network: CBS Radio
Arbitron Metro Market: Greely, CO; *Format:* News, News/Talk, 86 *Special Programming:* Farm 15 hrs, Ger one hr, relg 4 hrs wkly; *Hrs. of News Programming:* news progmg 25 hrs wkly; *No. News Employees:* 2 *TargetAudience:* 25-54; community-minded, active people
Damon Sasso, Operations Dir
Justin Sasso, General Manager
Brady Hull, General Sales Mgr
Troy Coverdale, News Director
Joe Cross, Chief Engineer

KSME
12-25-1975; 96.1 MHz FM; *Hrs Open:* 24; 100 kw; 735 ft.; N40 40 50 W104 56 32
4270 Byrd Dr., Lovelandn, CO 80538 US
(970) 461-2560
www.kissfmcolorado.com
License: Greeley, Weld County, CO held by Citicasters Licenses Inc.
Group Owner: iHeartMedia; (acq 5-4-99; grpsl).
Nat'l Network: ABC
Arbitron Metro Market: Loveland, CO; *Format:* Contemporary Hits/Top 40; *No. News Employees:* 2; *Target Audience:* 10-44.
Garner Goin, Operations Manager
Stu Haskell, General Manager
Kathy Arias, General Sales Mgr
Mike Sanchez, Promotions Director

KGRE
08-24-1948; 1450 kHz AM; *Hrs Open:* 24; 1 kw-U, ND1; N40 26 15 W104 43 25
2132 N. Valley Street, Burbank, CA 91505 US
(970) 356-1450; *Fax:* (970) 356-8522
www.tigrecolorado.com
kgre@msn.com
License: Greeley, CO held by Greeley Broadcasting Corp.
Group Owner: Greeley Broadcasting Corp.; (acq 3-24-98)
Arbitron Metro Market: Fort Collins, CO *Special Programming:* Bienvenidos a America one hr wkly; *Target Audience:* 25-54; Hispanic; *Adv. Rates:* 25; 25; 25; 20
Ricardo Salazar, President

***KUNC**
01-01-1967; 91.5 MHz FM; *Hrs Open:* 24; 36 kw; 1260 ft.; N40 37 3 W105 19 39
University of N Colorado, Greeley, CO 80639 US

(970) 378-2579; *Fax:* (970) 378-2580
www.kunc.org
comment@kunc.org
License: Greeley, Weld County, CO held by Community Radio for Northern Colorado
Nat'l Network: NPR; PRI; *Wire Services:* AP
Arbitron Metro Market: Greeley, CO; *Format:* News, Variety/Diverse; *Hrs. of News Programming:* news progmg 65 hrs wkly; *No. News Employees:* 5; *Target Audience:* General.
Jamie Wood, CFO
Neil Best, President & CEO
Ryan Thompson, Operations Dir
Neil Best, General Manager
Michelle Kornich, General Sales Mgr
Kirk Mowens, Programming Director
Brian Larson, News Director
Ken Broeffle, ChiefEngineer
Robert Leja, Director of Corporate Support and Marketing
Netanya Hearne, Membership Associate
Kirk Mowers, Content Director
Nancy D'Albergaria, Development Director
Jim Hill, Digital Media Manager
Benjamin McPhail, MusicDirector

Greenwood Village

KDSP(FM)
07-19-1995; 102.3 MHz FM; *Hrs Open:* 24; 6 kw; Ant 210 ft; N39 39 55 W104 51 38 *Rebroadcasts:* Simulcast with KJAC(FM) Timnath 100%
1201 18th St., Suite 250, Denver, CO 80202
(303) 296-7025; *Fax:* (303) 296-7030
www.kcuvradio.com
info@kcuvradio.com
License: Greenwood Village, Arapahoe County, CO held by NRC Broadcasting Inc.
Group Owner: NRC Broadcasting Inc.; (acq 11-9-2005; $16 million)
Arbitron Metro Market: Denver, CO; *Format:* Adult Contemp
Timothy Brown, General Manager

Gunnison

KEJJ
01-01-1980; 98.3 MHz FM; *Hrs Open:* 24-7; 3 kw; 299 ft.; N38 31 22 W106 54 28 *Rebroadcasts:* at crested butte/lake city
P.O. Box 970, Montrose, CO 81401 US
(970) 641-4000; *Fax:* (970) 641-3300
kpkeharv@hotmail.com
License: Gunnison, Gunnison County, CO held by John Harvey Rees
Nat'l Network: Fox News Radio
Format: Oldies; *No. News Employees:* 2; *Target Audience:* 25-54.; *Adv. Rates:* 15; 12.50; 15; 6.50
John Rees, CEO
Matt Rees, Operations Dir

KPKE
08-23-1960; 1490 kHz AM; *Hrs Open:* 24; 1 kw-U, ND1; N38 33 57 W106 55 32
Box 1288, Gunnison, CO 81230 US
(970) 641-4000; *Fax:* (970) 641-3300
http://www.visitgunnison.com/businesspage.cfm?businessid=833
License: Gunnison, CO held by John Harvey Rees.
Nat'l Network: Fox News Radio
Format: Country *Special Programming:* Den Broncos; *Hrs. of News Programming:* news progmg 2 hrs wkly; *No. News Employees:* 1; *Target Audience:* 25-54.; *Adv. Rates:* 9.50; 4; 5; 2
John Rees, CEO
Matt Rees, Operations Dir

KVLE-FM
04-18-1980; 102.3 MHz FM; *Hrs Open:* 24; 3 kw; -459 ft.; N38 33 53 W106 55 38
1445 Hwy 135 N, Gunnison, CO 81230 US
(970) 648-4365
www.kvleradio.com
License: Gunnison, Gunnison County, CO held by Pilgrim Communications Inc.
Group Owner: Pilgrim Communications Inc.; (acq 4-30-98; $300,000)
Nat'l Network: ABC; *Wire Services:* CBS
Arbitron Metro Market: Longmont,CO; *Format:* Adult Contemp; *Hrs. of News Programming:* News progmg 12 hrs wkly; *Target Audience:* 25-54; males: 35-54.
Mick Whitecotton, President
Rick Johnson, Operations Dir

*KWSB-FM
01-26-1968; 91.1 MHz FM; *Hrs Open:* 18; 0.135 kw; 299 ft.; N38 31 22 W106 54 28
Kwsb Taylor Hall Rm. 111, Gunnison, CO 81231 US
(970) 943-3222; *Fax:* (970) 943-7069
www.kwsb.org
kwsb@western.edu
License: Gunnison, Gunnison County, CO held by Western State College of Colorado.
Nat'l Network: AP Radio
Arbitron Metro Market: Gunnison, CO; *Format:* Variety/Diverse
Special Programming: Jazz 3 hrs, reggae 6 hrs, blues 3 hrs, 60s hits 3 hrs, Sp one hr wkly; *Hrs. of News Programming:* News progmg 2 hrs wkly *TargetAudience:* 18-25.
Tory Maurer, General Manager
Brendan Kholer, Station Manager
Scott Stewart, Programming Director
Stephanie Bollini, Promotions Manager
Kelsey Hollenbaugh, Music Director
Trevor Bartez, Sports Director
Max Mulleneaux, DevelopmentPromotions Director
Patrick Ring, Production Director

Gypsum

*KLRY
01-01-2003; 91.3 MHz FM; *Hrs Open:* 24; 0.11 kw; 2818 ft.; N39 46 30 W106 50 45 *Rebroadcasts:* Rebroadcasts KLVR(FM) Santa Rosa, CA 100%
16075 W Belleview Ave., Morrison, CO 80465 US
(800) 525-5683; *Fax:* (916) 251-1650
www.klove.com
klove@klove.com
License: Gypsum, Eagle County, CO held by Educational Media Foundation.
Group Owner: EMF Broadcasting; (acq 10-2-2003; grpsl).
Nat'l Network: K-Love
Arbitron Metro Market: Gypsum, CO; *Format:* Christian; *No. News Employees:* 13; *Target Audience:* 25-44; Judeo Christian female
Darrell Chambliss, Chairman
Mike Novak, President and CEO
Alan Mason, COO
Eric Moser, CFO
David Pierce, Chief Creative Officer

KQSE
03-01-2005; 102.5 MHz FM; 1.35 kw; 2165 ft.; N39 44 18 W106 47 58
165 E Avenue, P O Box 87, Limon, CO 80828 US
(970) 949-0140; *Fax:* (970) 949-1464
www.alwaysmountaintime.com/kqse
License: Gypsum, Eagle County, CO held by Wildcat Communications L.L.C.
Arbitron Metro Market: Gypsum, CO
Holli Snyder, General Sales Mgr
Tonya Everist, Director of Sales

Hayden

KQZR
01-01-2000; 107.3 MHz FM; 29 kw; 650 ft.; N40 31 16 W107 17 46
300 East Lombard, Suite #620, Baltimore, MD 21202 US
(970) 879-5368; *Fax:* (970) 879-5843
www.alwaysmountaintime.com/zrock
ecampbell@nrcbroadcasting.com
License: Hayden, Routt County, CO held by NRC Broadcasting Mountain Group LLC.
Group Owner: NRC Broadcasting Inc.; (acq 5-1-2007; grpsl)
Arbitron Metro Market: Hayden, CO; *Format:* Classic Rock
Steve Wodlinger, General Manager
Eli Campbell, General Sales Mgr
John Johnston, Programming Director

*KHCO
01-01-2005; 90.1 MHz FM; 1.8 kw vert; 1713 ft.; N40 27 4 W106 45 6 *Rebroadcasts:* Rebroadcasts KLRD(FM) Yucaipa, CA 100%
188 South Bellevue, Suite 222, Memphis, TN 38104 US
(888) 937-2471; *Fax:* (916) 251-1650
www.air1.com
info@air1.com
License: Hayden, Routt County, CO held by Educational Media Foundation.
Group Owner: EMF Broadcasting; (acq 6-8-2005; $25,000 for CP).
Nat'l Network: Air 1
Arbitron Metro Market: Hayden, CO; *Format:* Alternative, Christian
Darrell Chambliss, Chairman
Alan Mason, COO
Mike Novak, President and CEO
Jennifer Lohman, Operations Dir
David Pierce, Programming Director

Ed Lenane, News Director
Sam Wallington, Engineering Dir
Marya Morgan, NewsReporter
Richard Hunt, News Reporter
Dan Antonelli, Chief Business Development Officer
Eric Moser, Chief Financial Officer
Brian Burger, Vice President of Human Resources
D. Kevin Blair, Secretary and General Counsel

Holyoke

KSTH
01-01-2002; 92.3 MHz FM; 1 kw; 210 ft.; N40 34 49 W102 19 11
P.O. Box 71, McCook, NE 69001 US
(308) 345-5400; *Fax:* (308) 345-4720
www.plansreporter.k2radio.net/ksth
License: Holyoke, Phillips County, CO held by Armada Media - McCook Inc.
Group Owner: Armada Media Corp.; (acq 1-17-2007; grpsl)
Format: Adult Contemp
Andrew Stossmeister, Operations Dir
Bryan Loker, General Manager

Idalia

KWDI
94.1 MHz FM; 0.1 kw; 190 ft.; N39 42 10 W102 17 32 US
(858) 277-4991; *Fax:* (858) 277-1365
License: Idalia, Yuma County, CO held by Conundrum Communications Investments Inc.
Arbitron Metro Market: Idalia, CO
Mike MacIntosh, President

Ignacio

*KSUT
06-09-1976; 91.3 MHz FM; *Hrs Open:* 24; 2 kw; 1631 ft.; N37 11 3 W107 29 6
Mailing Address: P.O. Box 737, Ignacio, CO 81137 US
Second Address: 123 Capote Dr., Ignacio, CO 81137
(970) 563-0255; *Fax:* (970) 563-0399
www.ksut.org
info@ksut.org
License: Ignacio, La Plata County, CO held by KUTE Inc.
Group Owner: KUTE Inc.
Nat'l Network: NPR; PRI
Arbitron Metro Market: Ignacio, CO; *Format:* Native American
Special Programming: American Indian 7 hrs, class 8 hrs, jazz 15 hrs wkly; *Hrs. of News Programming:* News progmg 30 hrs wkly; *Target Audience:* 24 plus;public radio audience
Ken Brott, Operations Dir
Stasia Lanier, Station Manager
Jim Belcher, Programming Director
Beth Warren, Promotions Manager

*KUTE
06-01-1998; 90.1 MHz FM; 3 kw vert; 1965 ft.; N37 21 51 W107 46 56
P O Box 737, Ignacio, CO 81137 US
(970) 563-0255; *Fax:* (970) 563-0399
www.ksut.org
bruce@ksut.org
License: Ignacio, La Plata County, CO held by KUTE Inc.
Group Owner: KUTE Inc.
Nat'l Network: NPR; PRI
Arbitron Metro Market: Ignacio, CO; *Format:* Triple A
Stasia Lanier, Station Manager
Beth Warren, Promotions Manager

Johnstown

KHNC
01-01-1993; 1360 kHz AM
26886 W.C.R. 17, Johnstown, CO 80534 US
(970) 587-5175; *Fax:* (970) 587-5450
www.americanewsnet.com
License: Johnstown, CO held by Donald A. and Sharon A. Wiedeman.
Format: News, News/Talk, 86; *Hrs. of News Programming:* news progmg 100 hrs wkly; *No. News Employees:* 5
Donald Wiedeman, President
Michael Golden, Operations Dir

Julesburg

KJBL
01-01-2002; 96.5 MHz FM; 0.265 kw; -106 ft.; N40 59 18 W102 15 44
P.O. Box 71, McCook, NE 69001 US
(308) 345-5400; *Fax:* (308) 345-4720
www.plainsreporter.k2radio.net

License: Julesburg, Sedgwick County, CO held by Armada Media - McCook Inc.
Group Owner: Armada Media Corp.; (acq 1-17-2007; grpsl)
Arbitron Metro Market: Julesburg, CO; *Format:* Country
Andrew Stossmeister, Operations Dir
Bryan Loker, General Manager

Kremmling

KIFT(FM)

11-01-1987; 106.3 MHz FM; *Hrs Open:* 24; 2.5 kw; 1,050 ft; N40 00 18 W106 26 57
130 Ski Hill Rd. #240, Breckenridge, CO 80424
(970) 453-2234; *Fax:* (970) 453-5425
www.alwaysmountaintime.com
jen@NRC365.com
License: Kremmling, Grand County, CO held by New Field Broadcasting LLC
Population Served: 25,000 *Format:* Contemporary Hits/Top 40; *Hrs. of News Programming:* news progmg 5 hrs wkly; *No. News Employees:* 2; *Target Audience:* 24-49.; *Adv. Rates:* 20; 15; 17; 12
Jen Radueg, General Manager
Tonya Everist, General Sales Mgr
Brandon Spence, Programming Director

La Jara

KZBR

97.1 MHz FM; 25 kw; 180 ft.; N37 22 5 W106 6 44 US
(719) 206-3013; *Fax:* (719) 480-6008
www.kzbr971.com
admin@kzbr971.com
License: La Jara, Conejos County, CO held by Lendsi Radio LLC.
Arbitron Metro Market: Alamosa, CO; *Format:* Variety/Diverse
Lina Jones, General Manager

La Junta

KTHN

08-28-1974; 92.1 MHz FM; 3 kw; 299 ft.; N37 59 15 W103 34 2
P. O. Box 485, La Junta, CO 81050 US
(719) 384-5456; *Fax:* (719) 384-5450
www.cherrycreekradio.com
kblj@secom.net
License: La Junta, Otero County, CO held by CCR-La Junta IV LLC
Group Owner: Cherry Creek Radio LLC
Arbitron Metro Market: La Junta, CO; *Format:* Country
Joe Schwartz, CEO
Pat Gittings, General Manager
Adrian Hart, General Sales Mgr
Pat McGee, Programming Director
Ken Eklund, Engineering Dir

KBLJ

07-23-1937; 1400 kHz AM; 1 kw-U, ND1; N37 59 14 W103 34 1
P. O. Box 485, La Junta, CO 81050 US
(719) 384-5456; *Fax:* (719) 384-5450
www.cherrycreekradio.com
pgittings@cherrycreekradio.com
License: La Junta, CO held by CCR-La Junta IV LLC.
Group Owner: Cherry Creek Radio LLC; (acq 12-19-2003; grpsl).
Nat'l Network: ABC
Arbitron Metro Market: La Junta, CO; *Format:* Contemporary Hits/Top 40, Adult Contemp; *Target Audience:* 30 plus; general; *Adv. Rates:* 21; 15; 15; 10
Pat Gittings, General Manager
Adrian Hart, General Sales Mgr
Pat McGee, Programming Director
Ken Eklund, Engineering Dir

*KECC

08-01-2002; 89.1 MHz FM; *Hrs Open:* 24; 0.74 kw; 299 ft.; N37 58 43 W103 34 48 *Rebroadcasts:* Rebroadcasts KRCC(FM) Colorado Springs 100%
14 East Cache La Poudre, Colorado Springs, CO 80903 US
(719) 473-4801; *Fax:* (719) 473-7863
www.krcc.org
info@krcc.org
License: La Junta, Otero County, CO held by The Colorado College.
Nat'l Network: NPR; PRI
Arbitron Metro Market: Colorado Springs, CO; *Format:* News, Variety/Diverse
Mike Procell, Operations Dir
Delaney Utterback, General Manager
Jeff Bieri, Promotions Manager
Joel Belik, Chief Engineer
Barbara Wilson, Human Resources

Lafayette

KRKS-FM

03-15-1971; 94.7 MHz FM; *Hrs Open:* 24; 100 kw; 984 ft.; N40 4 19 W105 21 14
4880 Santa Rosa Road, Suite 300, Camarillo, CA 93012 US
(303) 750-5687; *Fax:* (303) 696-8063
www.krks.com
krks@krks.com
License: Lafayette, Boulder County, CO held by Salem Media of Colorado Inc.
Group Owner: Salem Communications Corp.; (acq 12-15-93; $5 million;
Arbitron Metro Market: Denver-Boulder, CO; *Format:* Christian, Talk
Edward Atsinger, President
Joe Davis, Operations Dir
Brian Taylor, VP
Jules Dygert, General Sales Mgr
Cliff Mikkelson, Engineering Dir
Rob Adair, Regional Vice President

Lakewood

KEPN

01-08-1955; 1600 kHz AM; 5 kw-D, DAN; 5 kw-N, DAN; N39 39 20 W105 4 28
7800 East Orchard Road, Greenwood Village, CO 80111 US
(303) 321-0950; *Fax:* (303) 321-3383
www.1600thezone.com
License: Lakewood, CO held by Entercom Radio
Group Owner: Entercom; (acq 2016)
Nat'l Network: ESPN Radio; *Nat'l Reps:* CBS Radio
Arbitron Metro Market: Denver-Lakewood-Boulder, CO; *Format:* Sports
Don Benson, President/CEO
Robert Call, SVP/General Manager
Steve Price, General Sales Mgr
Nate Lundy, Programming Director
J.J. Pelini, Promotions Manager
Brad Hart, Engineering Dir
Randy Weidner, National Sales Manager
LisaPetrone, Director of Interactive Sales

KQKS

07-09-1966; 107.5 MHz FM; 91 kw; 1198 ft.; N39 41 45 W105 9 54
4700 South Syracuse Street, Suite 1050, Denver, CO 80237 US
(303) 967-2700; *Fax:* (303) 321-3383
www.ks1075.com
License: Lakewood, Jefferson County, CO held by Entercom
Group Owner: Entercom; (acq 2016)
Arbitron Metro Market: Denver-Boulder, CO; *Format:* Contemporary Hits/Top 40; *Target Audience:* 12-34.
Don Benson, President/CEO
Robert Call, SVP/General Manager
Steve Price, General Sales Mgr
John E. Kage, Programming Director
JJ Pellini, Promotions Manager

*KVOD

01-01-2005; 88.1 MHz FM; 1.2 kw vert; Ant 1,053 ft; N39 40 18 W105 13 05
Bridges Broadcast Center, 7409 S. Alton Ct., Centennial, CO 80226
(303) 871-9191; *Fax:* (303) 733-3319
www.cpr.org
info@cpr.org
License: Lakewood, Jefferson County, CO held by PRC Denver-I LLC
Regional Network: Colo. Pub.
Population Served: 2,548,279; *Arbitron Metro Market:* Denver-Boulder, CO *Special Programming:* 24 Hour Classsical; *No. News Employees:* 20; *Target Audience:* 18 Plus
Max Wycisk, President/General Manager
Mark Coulter, VP, Operations/Production
Sean Nethery, SVP, Programming
Sadie Babits, News Director
Jim East, VP, Development
Jennifer Flatt, VP, Marketing

Lamar

KLMR

12-01-1948; 920 kHz AM; *Hrs Open:* 24; 5 kw-D, DAN; 0.5 kw-N, DAN; N38 6 53 W102 37 16
Mailing Address: 7350 US Highway 50, Lamar, CO 81052 US
Second Address: 7350 US Hwy. 50, Lamar, CO 81052
(719) 336-2206; *Fax:* (719) 336-7973
klmraudio@yahoo.com
License: Lamar, CO held by CCR-Lamar IV LLC.
Group Owner: Cherry Creek Radio LLC; (acq 12-19-2003; grpsl).
Nat'l Network: ABC
Arbitron Metro Market: Pueblo; *Format:* Country; *Hrs. of News Programming:* News progmg 12 hrs wkly; *Target Audience:* 25-54.
Joe Schwartz, CEO
Pat Gittings, General Manager/Sales Manager
Ty Harmon, Programming Director
Ken Eklund, Engineering Dir
Robert Townsend, Business Manager
Ethan Denton, News Director

KLMR-FM

11-01-1978; 93.5 MHz FM; *Hrs Open:* 24; 100 kw; 479 ft.; N38 2 10 W102 35 58
7350 US Highway 50, Lamar, CO 81052 US
(719) 336-2206; *Fax:* (719) 336-7973
klmraudio@yahoo.com
License: Lamar, Prowers County, CO
Group Owner: Cherry Creek Radio LLC
Arbitron Metro Market: Lamar, CO; *Format:* Classic Rock; *Target Audience:* 25-54.
Joe Schwartz, CEO
Pat Gittings, General Manager/Sales Manager
Ty Harmon, Programming Director
Ethan Denton, News Director
Ken Eklund, Engineering Dir
Robert Townsend, Business Manager

KVAY

08-05-1991; 105.7 MHz FM; *Hrs Open:* 24; 100 kw; 479 ft.; N38 6 44 W102 57 39
P.O. Box 1176, 224 South Main, Lamar, CO 81052 US
(719) 336-8734; *Fax:* (719) 336-5977
www.kvay.com
deb@kvay.com
License: Lamar, Prowers County, CO held by Beacon Broadcasting LLC
Nat'l Network: AP Radio
Arbitron Metro Market: Lamar, CO; *Format:* Country *Special Programming:* Gospel 4 hrs, classic rock 4 hrs wkly; *No. News Employees:* 1; *Target Audience:* 25-55.; *Adv. Rates:* 15; 12; 12; 6
Cory Alan Forgue, Chief of Operations Engineer
Debbie Ellis, General Manager
Rich Lingle, Sales
Travis Williams, Operations/Programming Director
Thadeus Steele, Music Director
Cory Alan Forgue, News Contact
Frankie Carrillo,Office Manager/Traffic Directors
Anthony LaTour, Sports Team
Matthew Sizemore, Sports Team
Cory Alan Forgue, Sports Team

Las Animas

*KRKV

08-01-2008; 107.3 MHz FM; 80 kw; 354 ft.; N37 56 23 W103 26 8
Mailing Address: US
Second Address: 709 Coleman Ave., Athens, AL 35611
(256) 497-4502; *Fax:* NA
varietyrock@hotmail.com
License: Las Animas, Bent County, CO held by Alleycat Communications.
Arbitron Metro Market: Tulsa, OK; *Format:* Variety/Diverse, Rock/AOR; *Target Audience:* 18-54.
Richard Dabney, General Manager

Leadville

*KTOL

01-01-2006; 90.9 MHz FM; 0.45 kw; -679 ft.; N39 14 5 W106 17 59 *Rebroadcasts:* Rebroadcasts KTLF(FM) Colorado Springs 100%
1665 Briargate Blvd, Colorado Springs, CO 80920 US
(719) 593-0600; *Fax:* (719) 593-2399
www.ktlf.org
lightpraise@ktlf.org
License: Leadville, Lake County, CO held by Educational Communications of Colorado Springs Inc.
Arbitron Metro Market: Leadville, CO; *Format:* Christian; *Target Audience:* 45-60; Christian
James Felix, Operations Dir
Robyn Sedgwick, General Manager
Sharick Wade, Programming Director
Robert Mumm, Chief Engineer
Lauren Johnson, Operations Manager
Marge Wallace, Office Manager
Alleen Wagnon, Office Assistant

Limon

*KYCO
89.1 MHz FM; 1.8 kw; 328 ft.; N39 22 13 W103 42 50
US
(517) 999-3737
www.foundationradio.org
License: Limon, CO held by Saidnewsfoundation.
Arbitron Metro Market: Limon, CO
David Schaberg, General Manager

Littleton

KCKK
08-22-1957; 1510 kHz AM
1032 So. Union Boulevard, Suite 100, Lakewood, CO 80228 US
(303) 650-1795; *Fax:* (303) 524-3410
www.milehighsports.com
License: Littleton, CO held by Hunt Broadcasting
Group Owner: Hunt Broadcasting; (acq 4-26-2002; $2.7 million)
Arbitron Metro Market: Denver-Boulder, CO; *Format:* Sports
Janice Hunt, President

Loma

KDVC
01-01-2008; 102.5 MHz FM; 3.8 kw horiz; 1047 ft.; N37 56 29 W108 54 27
US
(312) 204-9900
License: Loma, Delores County, CO held by Cochise Media Licenses, LLC
Arbitron Metro Market: Loma, CO
Neal Robinson, President

Longmont

*KGUD
09-01-1975; 90.7 MHz FM; *Hrs Open:* 24; 100 w; Ant 270 ft; N40 14 24 W105 03 19
Mailing Address: Box 1534, Longmont, CO 80501
Second Address: Studio: 457 Fourth Ave., Longmont, CO 80501
(303) 485-9811
kgud907@gmail.com
License: Longmont, Boulder County, CO held by Longmont Community Radio
Population Served: 180,000; *Arbitron Metro Market:* Denver-Boulder,; *No. News Employees:* 2; *Target Audience:* 45 plus; retirees
George Baskos, General Manager
James Boynton Sr., Station Manager
N/A, Promotions Manager
N/A, News Director
N/A, Engineering Dir
N/A, Chief Engineer

KKFN
09-01-1964; 104.3 MHz FM; *Hrs Open:* 24; 91 kw; 676 ft.; N39 41 45 W105 9 54
7800 East Orchard Road, Greenwood Village, CO 80111 US
(303) 321-0950; *Fax:* (303) 321-3383
License: Longmont, Boulder County, CO held by Entercom Radio
Group Owner: Entercom Radio; (acq 2016)
Nat'l Network: Fox Sports
Arbitron Metro Market: Denver-Boulder, CO; *Format:* Sports; *Target Audience:* 18-34
Robert Call, SVP/General Manager
Nate Lundy, Programming Director
J.J. Pelini, Promotions Manager
Brad Hart, Chief Engineer

KRCN
12-01-1949; 1060 kHz AM; *Hrs Open:* 15; 18 (summer)
5151 US Hwy 40., Greenfield, IN 46140 US
(317) 894-2000
www.krcnradio.com
License: Longmont, CO held by Pilgrim Communications Inc.
Group Owner: Pilgrim Communications Inc.; (acq 5-27-98; $575,000)
Nat'l Network: ABC; *Nat'l Reps:* McGavren Guild
Arbitron Metro Market: Denver-Boulder,; *Format:* Christian; *Hrs. of News Programming:* news progmg 12 hrs wkly; *No. News Employees:* 3; *Target Audience:* 25-64; news & sports listeners; *Adv. Rates:* 150; 150;150; 120
Mick Whitecotton, President
Rick Johnson, Operations Dir

Loveland

KPIO
01-21-1955; 1570 kHz AM; *Hrs Open:* 24
1200 Rosewood Dr., Loveland, CO 80537 US
(816) 630-1090
www.thecatholicradionetwork.com
info@thecatholicradionetwork.com
License: Loveland, CO held by Catholic Radio Network Inc.
Group Owner: Catholic Radio Network Inc.; (acq 1-28-2009; $740,000)
Nat'l Network: EWTN Radio
Format: Christian; *Target Audience:* Christian Women
James O'Laughlin, General Manager

KTRR
02-05-1966; 102.5 MHz FM; 17 kw; 768 ft.; N40 38 31 W104 49 3
600 Main Street, Windsor, CO 80550 US
(970) 674-2700; *Fax:* (970) 686-7491
www.tri1025.com
maddison.scruggs@townsquaremedia.com
License: Loveland, Larimer County, CO
Group Owner: Townsquare Media; (acq 2-25-03).
Arbitron Metro Market: Windsor, CO; *Format:* Adult Contemp; *Target Audience:* 25-54.
Dave Jensen, General Manager

*KXGR
89.7 MHz FM; 0.1 kw horiz, 80 kw vert; 1220 ft.; N40 37 3 W105 19 40
16075 W Belleview Ave, Morrison, CO 80465 US
(303)628-7200
License: Loveland, CO held by Calvary Chapel Aurora
Format: Christian
Ed Taylor, President

Manitou Springs

KBIQ
05-01-1952; 102.7 MHz FM; *Hrs Open:* 24; 57 kw; 2280 ft.; N38 44 43 W104 51 39
7150 Campus Drive, Suite 150, Colorado Springs, CO 80920 US
(719) 531-5438; *Fax:* (719) 531-5588
www.kbiqradio.com
clakey@kbiqradio.com
License: Manitou Springs, El Paso County, CO held by Bison Media Inc.
Group Owner: Salem Communications Corp.; (acq 10-8-96; $2.825 million)
Arbitron Metro Market: CO Springs, CO; *Format:* Adult Contemp, Christian; *No. News Employees:* 1; *Target Audience:* 18-54.
Bret Stevens, Operations Dir
Skip Stow, General Manager
Jon Cobb, General Sales Mgr
Julie Smith, Promotions Manager
Kim Bratton, Business Manager
Jack Hamilton, Music Director
Lance Montgomery, Production Director
ElizabethMeredith, Traffic Manager

*KCME
09-01-1979; 88.7 MHz FM; *Hrs Open:* 24; 8.9 kw; 9,570 ft; N38 44 40 W104 51 41
1921 N. Weber St., Colorado Springs, CO 80907
(719) 578-5263; *Fax:* (719) 578-1033
www.kcme.org
kcme@kcme.org
License: Manitou Springs, El Paso County, CO held by Cheyenne Mt. Public Broadcast House Inc.
Population Served: 1,200,000; *Arbitron Metro Market:* Colorado Springs, CO; *Target Audience:* 45 plus; upper-middle class, mostly college graduates; *Adv. Rates:* 21; 21; 21; 21
George Preston, General Manager
Jeanna Wearing, Corporate Sponsorship Manager
Jana Lee, Programming Director
Melissa Anthony, Development Director
John Hassebrock, Chief Engineer
Brenda Bratton, Finance/Office Manager
KeithKauspedas, Traffic Director

KXRE
11-01-1956; 1490 kHz AM; *Hrs Open:* 24
600 Grant Street, Suite 600, Denver, CO 80203 US
(303) 733-5266; *Fax:* (303) 733-5242
kbno@kbno.net
License: Manitou Springs, CO held by Latino Communications LLC
Group Owner: Latino Communications LLC; acq 1-23-03; $350,000 with KAVA(AM) Pueblo).
Arbitron Metro Market: Denver, CO; *Hrs. of News Programming:* 21 hrs wkly; *No. News Employees:* 5; *Target Audience:* 25-54.; *Adv. Rates:* 35; 35; 35; 35
Zee Ferrufino, General Manager
Michael Ferrufino, Sales Manager

Merino

KRFD(FM)
01-01-2008; 94.5 MHz FM; 6.5 kw; Ant 226 ft; N40 28 33 W103 13 28
87 Jasper Lake Rd., Loveland, CO 80537
(970) 669-9200
License: Merino, Logan County, CO held by Northeast Colorado Broadcasting
Population Served: 37,395; *Arbitron Metro Market:* Roy, UT
Victor Michael Jr., General Manager

Minturn

*KVNC
06-01-2008; 90.9 MHz FM; 100 w; -211 meters; N39 36 58 W106 26 58 *Rebroadcasts:* Rebroadcasts KUNC(FM) Greeley 100%
1901 56th Avenue, Suite 200, Greeley, CO 80634-2950 US
(970) 378-2579; *Fax:* (970) 378-2580
www.kunc.org
License: Minturn, Eagle County County, CO held by Community Radio for Northern Colorado

Neil Best, President

Monte Vista

KSLV
02-01-1954; 1240 kHz AM; *Hrs Open:* 24; 1 kw-U, ND1; N37 36 10 W106 8 58
P.O. Box 631, Monte Vista, CO 81144 US
(719) 852-3581; *Fax:* (719) 852-3583
www.kslvradio.com
kslv@amigo.net
License: Monte Vista, CO held by San Luis Valley Broadcasting Inc.
Group Owner: San Luis Valley Broadcasting Inc.; (acq 4-1-79)
Nat'l Network: Jones Radio Networks; *Wire Services:* AP
Arbitron Metro Market: Monte Vista, CO; *Format:* Country *Special Programming:* Sp 10 hrs, farm one hr, gospel 4 hrs wkly; *Hrs. of News Programming:* news progmg 1 hour weekly; *No. News Employees:* 1 *TargetAudience:* 25-54.
Gerald Vigil, General Manager
Jerry Medina, Programming Director
Linda Pacheco, News Director

KYDN
01-01-1986; 95.3 MHz FM; *Hrs Open:* 24; 6 kw; 89 ft.; N37 36 10 W106 8 58
P. O. Box 631, Monte Vista, CO 81144 US
(719) 852-3581; *Fax:* (719) 852-3583
www.kslvradio.com
kslv@amigo.net
License: Monte Vista, Rio Grande County, CO held by San Luis Valley Broadcasting Inc.
Group Owner: San Luis Valley Broadcasting Inc.
Nat'l Network: Jones Radio Networks; *Wire Services:* AP
Arbitron Metro Market: Monte Vista, CO; *Format:* Country; *Hrs. of News Programming:* News progmg 6 hrs wkly
Gerald Vigil, General Manager
Jerry Medina, Programming Director
Linda Pacheco, News Director

Montrose

KKXK
12-01-1976; 94.1 MHz FM; *Hrs Open:* 24; 90 kw; 1883 ft.; N38 20 16 W107 38 23
Mailing Address: P.O. Box 970, Montrose, CO 81401 US
Second Address: 106 Rose Ln., Montrose, CO 81401
(970) 249-4546; *Fax:* (970) 249-2229
www.coloradoradio.com
porlando@cherrycreekradio.com
License: Montrose, Montrose County, CO held by Cherry Creek Radio IV, LLC
Group Owner: Cherry Creek Radio LLC
Nat'l Network: ABC
Arbitron Metro Market: Grand Junction, CO; *Format:* Country; *Hrs. of News Programming:* news progmg 4 hrs wkly; *No. News Employees:* 2; *Target Audience:* 25-54. Adults; *Adv. Rates:* 28; 28; 28; 17
Joe Schwartz, President
Bee Haddock, Operations Dir
Jay D. Austin, General Manager
Scott Staley, Programming Director
Jim Kerschner, Sports Director
Heather Glassman, Traffic Manager

*KPRH
10-01-1998; 88.3 MHz FM; 3.5 kw; 1677 ft.; N38 23 14 W107 40 28 *Rebroadcasts:* Rebroadcasts KCFR(FM) Denver 100%

2249 S Josephine St, Denver, CO 80210 US
(303) 871-9191; *Fax:* (303) 733-3319
www.cpr.org
License: Montrose, Montrose County, CO held by Public Broadcasting of Colorado Inc.
Nat'l Network: NPR
Format: News; *Target Audience:* General.
Max Wycisk, President
Sue Coughlin, VP, Development
Sean Nethery, Senior VP, Programming
Mark Coulter, VP, Production/Operations
Sadie Babits, News Director
Robert Hensler, Engineering Dir

KSTR-FM
04-10-1980; 96.1 MHz FM; 91 kw; 1099 ft.; N38 52 40 W108 13 33
1360 E. Sherwood Dr., Grand Junction, CO 81501 US
(970) 254-2100
www.961kstr.com
License: Montrose, Montrose County, CO held by MBC Grand Broadcasting Inc.
Group Owner: MBC Grand Broadcasting Inc.; (acq 5-25-2005; $600,000).
Arbitron Metro Market: Grand Junction, CO

KUBC
09-25-1947; 580 kHz AM; *Hrs Open:* 24; 5 kw-D, 1 kw-N, DA-N; N38 25 32 W107 52 57
Mailing Address: Box 970, Montrose, CO 81401
Second Address: 106 Rose Ln., Montrose, CO 81401
(970) 249-4546; *Fax:* (970) 249-2229
www.coloradoradio.com
License: Montrose, Montrose County, CO held by CCR-Montrose IV LLC.
Group Owner: Cherry Creek Radio LLC; (acq 8-19-2004; grpsl).
Nat'l Network: ABC; *Nat'l Reps:* TACHER
Population Served: 150,000; *Arbitron Metro Market:* Grand Junction, *Special Programming:* Sports 5 hrs, relg 3 hrs wkly; *Hrs. of News Programming:* News progmg 4 hrs wkly; *Target Audience:* 35+ *Adv. Rates:* 14; 14; 14; 10
Joseph Schwartz, President
Bee Haddock, Operations Dir
Scott Staley, Programming Director
James MacDonald, News Director
Jim Frank, Chief Engineer
James MacDonald, News Director
Heather Glassman, Traffic Manager

***KVMT**
01-01-1999; 89.1 MHz FM; *Hrs Open:* 24; 8 kw; 1581 ft.; N38 18 52 W108 12 2 *Rebroadcasts:* Rebroadcasts KVNF (FM) Paonia 100%
P.O. Box 1350, Paonia, CO 81428 US
(970) 527-4866; *Fax:* (970) 527-4865
www.kvnf.org
sally@kvnf.org; events@kvnf.org
License: Montrose, Montrose County, CO held by North Fork Valley Public Radio Inc.
Arbitron Metro Market: Paonia, CO; *Format:* News; *Hrs. of News Programming:* News progmg 35 hrs wkly
Jeff Reynolds, Operations Dir
Rick Watts, General Manager
Ali Lightfoot, Programming Director
Laura Palmisano, News Director

***KTMH**
01-01-2005; 89.9 MHz FM; 0 kw horiz, 4 kw vert; 1634 ft.; N38 23 15 W107 40 31 *Rebroadcasts:* Rebroadcasts KTLF(FM) Colorado Springs 100%
1665 Briargate Blvd, Colorado Springs, CO 80920 US
(719) 593-0600; *Fax:* (719) 593-2399
www.ktlf.org
awagnon@ktlf.org
License: Montrose, Ouray County, CO held by Educational Communications of Colorado Springs Inc.
Arbitron Metro Market: Montrose, CO; *Format:* Christian; *Target Audience:* 45-60; Christian
Lauren Johnson, Operations Dir
Robyn Sedgkwick, General Manager
Marge Wallace, Office Manager
Alleen Wagnon, Office Assistant
Sharick Wade, Program Director

***KJOL-FM**
91.9 MHz FM; 0.475 kw; -276 ft.; N38 28 8 W107 53 5
1354 East Sherwood Drive, Grand Junction, CO 81501 US
(970) 254-5565; *Fax:* (970) 254-5550
www.kjol.org
info@kjol.org
License: Montrose, Montrose County, CO held by United Ministries.
Arbitron Metro Market: Montrose, CO
Ken Andrews, General Manager
Ken Andrews, Station Manager
Rhonda Repshire, Promotions Manager
Kurt Neuswanger, Music Director
Dave Andrews, Public Affairs Director

Monument

KCBR
07-20-1986; 1040 kHz AM; *Hrs Open:* Sunrise-sunset
5050 Edison Avenue, Colorado Springs, CO 80915 US
(719) 570-1530; *Fax:* (719) 570-1007
License: Monument, CO held by DJR Broadcasting, LLC
Group Owner: United States CP LLC; (acq 1999; $750,000 with KCMN(AM) Colorado Springs)
Arbitron Metro Market: Colorado Springs, CO; *Format:* Christian, Talk; *Target Audience:* 25-54; 70% male, upper-middle income or higher
Don Crawford Jr., CEO
Don Crawford Sr, President
Tron Simpson, Operations Dir

Morrison

***KLDV**
03-27-1971; 91.1 MHz FM; *Hrs Open:* 24; 100 kw; 1168 ft.; N39 36 0 W105 12 35 *Rebroadcasts:* Rebroadcasts KLVR(FM) Middletown, CA 100%
16075 W. Belleview Ave., Morrison, CO 80465 US
(916) 251-1600; *Fax:* (916) 251-1650
www.klove.com
klove@klove.com
License: Morrison, Jefferson County, CO held by Educational Media Foundation.
Group Owner: EMF Broadcasting; (acq 12-28-2000; grpsl)
Nat'l Network: K-Love
Arbitron Metro Market: Morrison, CO; *Format:* Christian; *No. News Employees:* 3; *Target Audience:* 25-44; Judeo Christian, female
Mike Novak, President
Jennifer Lohman, Operations Director/Regional Manager

Mountain Village

KRKQ
95.5 MHz FM; 0.25 kw; 1470 ft.; N37 59 29 W107 58 21
US
(888) 948-1640
www.mountainchill.com
License: Mountain Village, San Miguel County, CO held by Lorenz E. Proietti.
Arbitron Metro Market: Mountain Village, CO; *Format:* Easy Listening
Lorenz Proietti, General Manager

New Castle

KTUN
04-16-1984; 94.5 MHz FM; *Hrs Open:* 24; 25 kw; -397 ft.; N39 33 56 W107 32 1
US
(970) 949-0140; *Fax:* (970) 949-1464
www.alwaysmountaintime.com
License: New Castle, Eagle County, CO held by NRC Broadcasting Mountain Group LLC.
Group Owner: NRC Broadcasting Inc.; (acq 5-1-2007; grpsl)
Arbitron Metro Market: New Castle, CO; *Format:* Classic Rock; *Hrs. of News Programming:* news progmg 4 hrs wkly; *No. News Employees:* 2; *Target Audience:* 25-63; affluent locals & tourists; *Adv. Rates:* 40; 38;40; 25
Meredith Fox, Operations Dir
Steve Wodlinger, General Manager

Norwood

KRYD
01-01-1998; 104.9 MHz FM; *Hrs Open:* 24; 23.62 kw; 1678 ft.; N38 18 59 W108 11 55
Mailing Address: 444 Seasons Drive, Grand Junction, CO 81507 US
Second Address: 475 Water St., Monrose, CO 81401
(970) 263-4100; *Fax:* (970) 263-9600
www.krydfm.com
billv@taousa.tv
License: Norwood, San Miguel County, CO held by Rocky III Investments Inc.
Arbitron Metro Market: Grand Junction, CO; *Format:* Country; *Hrs. of News Programming:* news progmg one hr wkly; *No. News Employees:* 3; *Target Audience:* 18 plus.; *Adv. Rates:* 45; 40; 45; 35
Bill Varecha, CEO
Jon Donofrio, Operations Dir
Paul Varecha, General Manager
Darnell Place-Wise, General Sales Mgr

Nunn

KIMX
01-01-2002; 96.9 MHz FM; 4.8 kw; 1027 ft.; N41 17 15 W105 26 38
302 S. 2nd Street, Laramie, WY 82070 US
(307) 745-5208; *Fax:* (307) 745-8570
mix967@fiberpipe.net
License: Nunn, Albany County, CO held by Appaloosa Broadcasting Co. Inc.
Group Owner: Northeast Broadcasting Company Inc.; (acq 11-12-2003; $775,000).
Format: Adult Contemp
Jim O'Reilly, General Manager

Oak Creek

KFMU-FM
09-22-1975; 104.1 MHz FM; *Hrs Open:* 24; 1.4 kw; 1073 ft.; N40 14 10 W106 52 30
Mailing Address: C/O Jerome S. Boros, 1290 Avenue of Americas, New York, NY 10104 US
Second Address: 2955 Village Dr., Steamboat Springs, CO 80487
(970) 879-5368; *Fax:* (970) 879-5843
http://alwaysmountaintime.com/kfmu/
ecampbell@nrcbroadcasting.com
License: Oak Creek, Routt County, CO held by NRC Broadcasting Mountain Group LLC.
Group Owner: NRC Broadcasting Inc.; (acq 5-1-2007; grpsl)
Arbitron Metro Market: Oak Creek, CO; *Format:* Triple A *Special Programming:* Jazz 4 hrs, modern mus 4 hrs wkly; *Hrs. of News Programming:* news progmg 10 hrs wkly; *No. News Employees:* 2 *Target Audience:* 21-54.; *Adv. Rates:* 18; 16; 16; 12
Pete Benedetti, President/CEO
Kyle McCoy, VP, Operations/Programming
John Johnston, General Manager
Krista Benedetti, VP, Sales

Olathe

***KUSZ**
01-01-2000; 106.5 MHz FM; kw
302 S. 2nd Street, Laramie, WY 82070 US
(307) 745-5208; *Fax:* (307) 745-8570
mix967@fiberpipe.net
License: Olathe, Albany County, CO held by Laramie Mountain Broadcasting LLC.
Format: Oldies
Jim O'Reilly, General Manager

Olney Springs

KRYE
01-01-2008; 104.9 MHz FM; 100 kw; 79 meters; N37 56 40 W104 59 56
2099 U.S. Hwy 50 W., #130A, Pueblo, CO
(970) 356-1452ÿ; *Fax:* (719) 562-0947
www.tigrecolorado.com
krye104.9@hotmail.com
License: Olney Springs, Pueblo County, CO held by United States CP LLC.
Group Owner: United States CP LLC
Population Served: 348; *Arbitron Metro Market:* Olney Springs, CO
Ricardo Salazar, General Manager

Ouray

KWGL
06-16-1986; 105.7 MHz FM; *Hrs Open:* 24; 60 kw horiz; 1752 ft.; N38 23 16 W107 40 28
751 Horizon Court, Suite 225, Grand Junction, CO 81506 US
(970) 241-6460; *Fax:* (970) 241-6452
www.range105.net
kelcie@wscradio.net
License: Ouray, Ouray County, CO held by WS Communications L.L.C.
Nat'l Network: Jones Radio Networks
Arbitron Metro Market: Grand Junction, CO; *Format:* Country; *Hrs. of News Programming:* news progmg 15 hrs wkly; *No. News Employees:* 1
Lou Stark, Station Manager
Michael Johnson, Programming Director
Katie Meyering, Business Manager

Bryan Fleming, Account Executive
Ward Holmes, Regional Manager

Pagosa Springs

KWUF

08-27-1975; 1400 kHz AM; *Hrs Open:* 24; 1 kw-U, ND1; N37 15 24 W107 1 6
702 S. 10th Street, Pagosa Springs, CO 81147 US
(970) 264-5983; *Fax:* (970) 264-5129
www.kwuf.com
admin@kwuf.com
License: Pagosa Springs, CO held by Wolf Creek Broadcasting L.L.C.
Nat'l Network: Westwood One
Arbitron Metro Market: Pagosa Springs, CO; *Format:* Country, News, 62, Sports, Talk; *Hrs. of News Programming:* News progmg 10 hrs wkly; *No. News Employees:* 1; *Target Audience:* General.; *Adv. Rates:* Same asFM
Will Spears, CEO
Christie Spears, General Sales Mgr
Chris Olivarez, Programming Director
Holly Heart, Production Manager

KWUF-FM

05-01-1986; 106.3 MHz FM; *Hrs Open:* 24; 0.255 kw; 1280 ft.; N37 11 32 W107 5 55
701 S. 10th Street, Pagosa Springs, CO 81147 US
(970) 264-5983; *Fax:* (970) 264-5129
www.kwuf.com
admin@kwuf.com
License: Pagosa Springs, Archuleta County, CO held by Wolf Creek Broadcasting L.L.C.
Nat'l Network: Westwood One
Arbitron Metro Market: Pagosa Springs, CO; *Format:* Adult Contemp *Special Programming:* Blues 10 hrs, jazz 10 hrs wkly; *Hrs. of News Programming:* News progmg 10 hrs wkly; *No. News Employees:* 1; *Target Audience:* 18 plus.; *Adv. Rates:* 9; 9; 9; na
Will Spears, CEO
Christie Spears, General Sales Mgr
Chirs Ulivarez, Programming Director
Chris Olivarez, Music/Sports/News

*KTPS

01-01-2003; 89.7 MHz FM; 0.2 kw; 1273 ft.; N37 11 35 W107 5 58 *Rebroadcasts:* Rebroadcasts KTLF(FM) Colorado Springs 100%
1665 Briargate Blvd., Colorado Springs, CO 80920 US
(719) 593-0600; *Fax:* (719) 593-2399
www.ktlf.org
awagnon@ktlf.org
License: Pagosa Springs, Archuleta County, CO held by Educational Communications of Colorado Springs Inc.
Arbitron Metro Market: Tacoma, WA; *Format:* Christian; *Target Audience:* 45-60; Christian
Lauren Johnson, Operations Dir
Robyn Sedgwick, General Manager
Marge Wallace, Office Manager
Alleen Wagnon, Office Assistant
Sharick Wade, Program Director

*KPGS

01-01-2008; 88.1 MHz FM; 1 kw vert; 1365 ft.; N37 11 48 W107 7 1 *Rebroadcasts:* Rebroadcasts KUTE(FM) Ignacio 100%
US
(970) 563-0255; *Fax:* (970) 563-0399
www.ksut.org
info@ksut.org
License: Pagosa Springs, Archuleta County, CO held by KUTE Inc.
Group Owner: KUTE Inc.
Nat'l Network: NPR
Arbitron Metro Market: Grand Junction, CO; *Format:* Triple A
Eddie Box Jr., President
Beth Warren, General Manager
Bruce Campbell, Development Director
Chris Aaland, Membership Manager
Rob Rawls, Administrative Director
Sheila Nanaeto, Tribal Radio Director
Ken Brott, Operations/ProgramDirector

Palisade

*KAAI

01-01-2007; 98.5 MHz FM; 0.26 kw; 2989 ft.; N39 3 14 W108 15 13
5700 West Oaks Boulevard, Rocklin, CA 95765 US
(888) 937-2471; *Fax:* (916) 251-1650
www.air1.com
info@air1.com
License: Palisade, Mesa County, CO held by Covenant Educational Media Inc.
Arbitron Metro Market: Palisade, CO; *Format:* Alternative, Christian
Darrell Chambliss, Chairman
Alan Mason, CEO/COO
Mike Novak, CEO
Doug Price, General Manager
David Pierce, Chief Creative Officer
Dan Antonelli, Chief Business Development Officer
Eric Moser, Chief Financial Officer
JenniferLohman, Regional Manager

Paonia

*KVNF

10-05-1979; 90.9 MHz FM; *Hrs Open:* 18; 2.6 kw; -72 ft.; N38 52 28 W107 39 40
Mailing Address: P. O. Box 1350, Paonia, CO 81428 US
Second Address: 233 Grand Ave., Paonia, CO 81428
(970) 527-4866; *Fax:* (970) 527-4865
www.kvnf.org
License: Paonia, Delta County, CO held by North Fork Valley Public Radio Inc.
Nat'l Network: NPR
Arbitron Metro Market: Paonia, CO; *Format:* News *Special Programming:* Class 15 hrs, jazz 17 hrs, blues 3 hrs, C&W 5 hrs, new age 6 hrs, Sp 2 hrs, gospel 3 hrs wkly
Jeff Reynolds, Operations Dir
Rick Watts, General Manager
Ali Lightfoot, Programming Director
Laura Palmisano, News Director
Candy Pennetta, Music Director

Parachute

KDBN

01-01-2008; 101.1 MHz FM; 425 w; -426 meters; N39 26 31 W108 01 15
398 Arroyo Drive, Parachute, CO 81635
License: Parachute, Garfield County, CO held by KSUN Community Radio Corp.

Mary Lee Mohrlang, President

Phippsburg

KEZZ

94.1 MHz FM; 1.75 kw; 1247 ft.; N40 22 3 W106 41 28
US
(970) 302-8444
License: Phippsburg, Jackson County, CO held by Youngers Colorado Broadcasting LLC.
Arbitron Metro Market: Phippsburg, CO
Kevin Youngers, General Manager

Pierce

KJMP

01-01-2004; 870 kHz AM
US
(307) 638-8921
License: Pierce, CO held by White Park Broadcasting Inc
Group Owner: Northeast Broadcasting Company Inc.; (acq 2-1-2006; $350,000)
Arbitron Metro Market: Fort Collins, CO; *Format:* Sports
Steven Silverburg., General Manager

Placerville

*KTEI

90.7 MHz FM; 0.25 kw horiz; 1474 ft.; N37 59 30 W107 58 21
Rebroadcasts: KTLF (FM) Colorado Springs 100%
1665 Briargate Blvd., Colorado Springs, CO 80920 US
(719) 593-0600; *Fax:* (719) 593-2399
www.ktlf.org
awagnon@ktlf.org
License: Placerville, San Miguel County, CO held by Educational Communications of Colorado Springs Inc.
Arbitron Metro Market: Placerville, CO; *Format:* Christian; *Target Audience:* 45-60; Christian
James Felix, Operations Dir
Tom Sullivan, General Manager
Lynn Carmichael, Programming Director
Marge Wallace, Office Manager
Alleen Wagnon, Office Assistant
Sharick Wade, KTPL Program Director

Poncha Springs

KWUZ

01-01-2008; 97.5 MHz FM; 0.029 kw; 2927 ft.; N38 27 11 W106 1 2
7600 CR 120, Salida, CO 81201 US
(719) 539-2575; *Fax:* (719) 539-4851
www.hippieradio975.com
License: Poncha Springs, CO held by Three Eagles Communications of Colorado, LLC
Group Owner: Three Eagles Communications of Colorado, LLC
Arbitron Metro Market: Poncha Springs, CO; *Format:* Contemporary Hits/Top 40, Adult Contemp
Dean Johnson, Station Manager
Dan Ridenour, News Director
Andrew Stossmeister, Sports Director
Doreen White, Office Manager

Pueblo

KAVA

06-01-1963; 1480 kHz AM; 1 kw-D, DA2; 0.107 kw-N, DA2; N38 18 56 W104 37 3
PO Box 1471, Evergreen, CO 80439 US
(303) 733-5266; *Fax:* (303) 733-5242
www.radioquebueno.com
kbno@kbno.net
License: Pueblo, CO held by Latino Communications LLC
Group Owner: Latino Communications LLC; acq 1-23-03; $350,000 with KXRE(AM) Manitou Springs).
Arbitron Metro Market: Pueblo, CO; *Hrs. of News Programming:* 21 hrs wkly; *No. News Employees:* 6; *Target Audience:* 25-54.; *Adv. Rates:* 25; 25; 25; 25
Zee Ferrufino, General Manager

KCCY-FM

08-23-1975; 96.9 MHz FM; 58 kw; 2,280 ft.; N38 44 43 W104 51 41
2864 S. Circle Dr., Suite 300, Colorado Springs, CO 80906 US
(719) 540-9200; *Fax:* (719) 579-0882
www.y969.com
License: Pueblo, Pueblo County, CO held by Capstar TX LLC
Group Owner: iHeartMedia; (acq 11-22-00; with KDZA-FM Pueblo).
Nat'l Reps: Christal
Arbitron Metro Market: Colorado Springs, CO; *Format:* Country; *Target Audience:* 25-54; general
Jason McCollim, Senior Vice President of Programming
Adam Burnes, Programming Director
Brian Taylor, Promotions Director

*KCFP

06-01-1986; 91.9 MHz FM; *Hrs Open:* 24; 0.6 kw horiz; 633 ft.; N38 22 23 W104 33 42 *Rebroadcasts:* Rebroadcasts KCFR(FM) Denver 100%
2249 South Josephine St, Denver, CO 80210 US
(303) 871-9191; *Fax:* (303) 733-3319
www.cpr.org
License: Pueblo, Pueblo County, CO held by Public Broadcasting of Colorado Inc.
Nat'l Network: NPR
Arbitron Metro Market: Pueblo, CO; *Format:* News; *Hrs. of News Programming:* news progmg 50 hrs wkly; *No. News Employees:* 8; *Target Audience:* General.
Max Wycisk, President
Sue Coughlin, General Sales Mgr

KCSJ

01-01-1947; 590 kHz AM; *Hrs Open:* 24; 1 kw-D, DA2; 1 kw-N, DA2; N38 21 30 W104 38 13
106 W. 24th St., Pueblo, CO 81003 US
(719) 545-2080
www.590kcsj.com
License: Pueblo, Pueblo County, CO held by CC Licenses LLC.
Group Owner: iHeartMedia; (acq 6-14-2001; with KDZA(AM) Pueblo)
Nat'l Network: ABC; *Nat'l Reps:* Christal
Arbitron Metro Market: Pueblo, CO; *Format:* News, News/Talk, 84, Talk; *Hrs. of News Programming:* news progmg 41 hrs wkly; *No. News Employees:* 2; *Target Audience:* 35-64; upscale; *Adv. Rates:* 20; 18; 18; 14
Jason McCollim, Senior Vice President of Programming
Darci Ewell, Market President

KDZA-FM

03-03-1987; 107.9 MHz FM; 32 kw; 2,211 ft.; N38 44 41 W104 51 46
2864 S. Circle Dr., Suite 300, Colorado Springs, CO 80906 US
(719) 540-9200
www.z1079rocks.com
License: Pueblo, Pueblo County, CO held by Capstar TX LLC
Group Owner: iHeartMedia; (acq 11-22-2000; with KCCY(FM) Pueblo)
Arbitron Metro Market: Pueblo, CO; *Format:* Classic Rock
Jason McCollim, Senior Vice President of Programming
Laura Trivett, Promotions Director

KFEL
08-01-1956; 970 kHz AM
P.O. Box 8055, Pueblo, CO 81008 US
(719) 543-7506 (970) 669-8000; *Fax:* (719) 543—0432 (970) 669-8000
www.thecatholicradionetwork.com
kfel970am@gmail.com
License: Pueblo, CO held by Catholic Radio Network Inc.
Group Owner: Catholic Radio Network Inc.; (acq 11-3-2006; $475,000)
Arbitron Metro Market: Pueblo, CO; *Format:* Religious; *Target Audience:* 25 plus.
John Koenig, Station Manager

KGFT
03-31-1988; 100.7 MHz FM; *Hrs Open:* 24; 77 kw; 2218 ft.; N38 44 43 W104 51 39
7150 Campus Drive, Suite 150, Colorado Springs, CO 80920 US
(719) 531-5438; *Fax:* (719) 531-5588
www.kgftradio.com
License: Pueblo, Pueblo County, CO held by Salem Communications Corp.
Group Owner: Salem Communications Corp.; (acq 1996; $3 million).
Nat'l Network: AP Radio
Arbitron Metro Market: Colorado Springs, CO; *Format:* Christian, News, 62, Talk, Religious *Special Programming:* Gospel 3 hrs, old time radio 11 hrs wkly; *Hrs. of News Programming:* news progmg 4 hrs wkly *No. NewsEmployees:* 1; *Target Audience:* 25 plus; Christian
Skip Stow, General Manager
Kim Bratton, Business Manager
Jon Cobb, General Sales Mgr
Bret Stevens, Programming Director
Julie Smith, Promotions Manager
Steve Altmaier, News Director

KCCY
02-01-1928; 1350 kHz AM; *Hrs Open:* 24; 1.3 kw-D, ND2; 0.15 kw-N, ND2; N38 21 28 W104 38 19
106 W. 24th St., Pueblo, CO 81003 US
(719) 545-2080
www.foxsportspueblo.com
License: Pueblo, Pueblo County, CO held by CC Licenses LLC.
Group Owner: iHeartMedia; (acq 6-14-2001; with KCSJ(AM) Pueblo)
Population Served: 130,000; *Arbitron Metro Market:* Pueblo, CO; *Format:* Sports; *Hrs. of News Programming:* news progmg one hr wkly; *No. News Employees:* 1; *Target Audience:* 35 plus.
Jason McCollim, Senior Vice President of Programming

KKMG
01-01-1983; 98.9 MHz FM; *Hrs Open:* 24; 57 kw; 2280 ft.; N38 44 43 W104 51 41
6805 Corporate Dr., Suite 130, Colorado Springs, CO 80919 US
(719) 593-2700; *Fax:* (719) 593-2727
www.989magicfm.com
License: Pueblo, CO held by Radio License Holding CBC, LLC
Group Owner: Cumulus Media Inc.; (acq 3-21-94; $912,500;).
Nat'l Reps: McGavren Guild
Arbitron Metro Market: Colorado Spring, CO; *Format:* Contemporary Hits/Top 40; *Target Audience:* 18-44.
Scott Jones, General Sales Mgr
Nikki Landry, Programming Director

KKPC
12-29-1947; 1230 kHz AM; *Hrs Open:* 24
900 West Orman, Pueblo, CO 81004 US
(303) 871-9191; *Fax:* (303) 733-3319
www.cpr.org
info@cpr.org
License: Pueblo, CO held by Public Broadcasting of Colorado Inc.
Arbitron Metro Market: Pueblo, CO; *Format:* News
Max Wycisk, President
Sean Nethery, Programming Director
Jenny Gentry, Executive Vice President

KNKN(FM)
11-01-1979; 106.9 MHz FM; 27.5 kw; Ant 666 ft; N38 06 22 W104 29 18
30 N. Electronic Dr., Pueblo West, CO 81007
(719) 547-0411; *Fax:* (719) 547-9301
knoffice@qwestoffice.net
License: Pueblo, Pueblo County, CO held by United States CP LLC.
Group Owner: United States CP LLC; (acq 3-10-2008; $1.75 million with KRMX(AM) Pueblo)
Population Served: 159,361; *Arbitron Metro Market:* Pueblo, CO; *Format:* Spanish; *Target Audience:* 18-54.
Lupe Brown, General Manager

***KTSC-FM**
10-01-1970; 89.5 MHz FM; 8 kw; 180 ft.; N38 18 38 W104 34 40
2200 Bonforte Blvd., Pueblo, CO 81001 US
(719) 549-2821 (719) 549-2822; *Fax:* (719) 549-2120
info@ktsc.com
License: Pueblo, Pueblo County, CO held by University of Southern Colorado.
Arbitron Metro Market: Pueblo, CO; *Format:* Blues
Mike Atencio, Station Manager

KVUU
01-01-1976; 99.9 MHz FM; *Hrs Open:* 24; 57 kw; 2198 ft.; N38 44 44 W104 51 42
2864 S. Circle Drive, Suite 300, Colorado Springs, CO 80906 US
(719) 540-9200; *Fax:* (719) 579-0882
www.my999radio.com
info@my999radio.com
License: Pueblo, Pueblo County, CO held by Capstar TX LLC
Group Owner: iHeartMedia; (acq 8-30-00; grpsl).
Nat'l Reps: Clear Channel
Arbitron Metro Market: Pueblo, CO; *Format:* Adult Contemp; *Hrs. of News Programming:* news progmg 3 hrs wkly; *No. News Employees:* 1; *Target Audience:* 25-54; upscale young adults; *Adv. Rates:* 80; 75; 75; 50
Jason McCollim, Senior Vice President of Programming
Adam Burnes, Programming Director
Deanna Regalado, Promotions Director

***KTPL**
01-01-2005; 88.3 MHz FM; 65 kw; 226 ft.; N37 56 40 W104 59 56
1665 Briargate Boulevard, Colorado Springs, CO 80920 US
(719) 593-0600; *Fax:* (719) 593-2399
www.ktpl.org
License: Pueblo, Pueblo County, CO held by Educational Communications of Colorado Springs Inc.
Arbitron Metro Market: Pueblo, CO; *Format:* Christian, Religious; *Target Audience:* 18-35; Christian
Lauren Johnson, Operations Dir
Robyn Sedgwick, General Manager
Sharick Wade, Programming Director
Robert Mumm, Chief Engineer
Marge Wallace, Office Manager
Alleen Wagnon, Office Assistant

***KFRY**
01-01-2006; 89.9 MHz FM; 0.87 kw; 2123 ft.; N38 2 29 W105 11 5 *Rebroadcasts:* Rebroadcasts KUFR(FM) Salt Lake City, UT 100%
4135 Northgate Blvd, Suite 1, Sacramento, CA 95834 US
(800) 543-1495; *Fax:* (916) 641-8238
www.familyradio.com
info@familyradio.com
License: Pueblo, Pueblo County, CO held by Family Stations Inc.
Group Owner: Family Stations Inc.
Arbitron Metro Market: Pueblo, CO; *Format:* Christian, Religious
Tom Evans, General Manager

KIQN-FM
106.9 MHz FM; 27,500 watts; 203 meters; 38 06 22N 104 29 18W
3715 Thatcher Avenue, Pueblo, CO 81005 USA
(719) 564-0899
License: Pueblo, Pueblo County, CO
Group Owner: Pueblo Radio Group LLC

M.R. Murray, General Manager
Hank Holloway, General Sales Mgr
Dave Moore, Programming Director
Ray Weston, News Director

Pueblo West

KRXP
01-01-1993; 103.9 MHz FM; *Hrs Open:* 24; 1.75 kw; 2156 ft.; N38 44 44 W104 51 42
1805 E. Cheyenne Rd., Colorado Springs, CO 80905 US
(719) 634-4896; *Fax:* (719) 634-5837
www.1039rxp.com
License: Pueblo West, Pueblo County, CO held by Colorado Springs Radio Broadcasters Inc.
Group Owner: Bahakel Communications Ltd.; (acq 2-22-99; grpsl)
Arbitron Metro Market: Pueblo, CO; *Format:* Alternative; *Hrs. of News Programming:* news progmg one hr wkly; *No. News Employees:* 1; *Target Audience:* 25-49; general
Lou Mellini, General Manager
Aaron Zytle, Programming Director
Coba Hunt, News Director

Red Feather Lakes

***KMKZ(FM)**
88.7 MHz FM; 26 w; Ant 853 ft; N40 52 04 W105 38 33
2134 Wedgewood Drive, Greeley, CO 80631
(970) 405-6405
License: Red Feather Lakes, Larimer County, CO held by 3G Learning Solutions
Population Served: 230,482; *Arbitron Metro Market:* Glendale, Az
Kaylynn Duvall, President

Redlands

KRZX
03-31-2010; 106.1 MHz FM; 0.87 kw; 1257 ft.; N39 4 1 W108 44 39
US
(520) 797-4434
License: Redlands, San Juan County, CO held by Cochise Media Licenses LLC
Group Owner: SkyWest Media L.L.C.
Arbitron Metro Market: Redlands, CO
Ted Tucker, General Manager

Rico

***KICO**
89.5 MHz FM; 125 kw horiz; -1319 ft.; N37 41 32 W108 1 55
PO Box 116, Cortez, CO 81321 US
(970) 564-9727; *Fax:* (970) 516-1927
www.ksjd.org
License: Rico, Dolores County, CO held by Community Radio Project.
Arbitron Metro Market: Rico, CO
Jeffrey Pope, Executive Director
Kim Welty, Membership Coordinator
Tom Yoder, Programming & Media Director
Amanda Puett, Director of Underwriting

Ridgway

KSNN-FM
01-01-2002; 103.7 MHz FM; *Hrs Open:* 24; 4.1 kw; Ant 1,574 ft; N38 23 15 W107 40 31
Mailing Address: Box 970, Montrose, CO 81402
Second Address: 106 Rose Lane, Montrose, CO 81401
(970) 249-4546; *Fax:* (970) 249-2229
www.coloradoradio.com
License: Ridgway, Ouray County, CO held by CCR-Montrose IV, LLC.
Group Owner: Cherry Creek Radio LLC; (acq 8-19-2004; grpsl).
Nat'l Reps: Tacher
No. News Employees: 1.5; *Target Audience:* 18-44 Adults; *Adv. Rates:* 15; 15; 15; 15
Joseph Schwartz, President
Bee Haddock, Operations Dir
John Craft, Regional Director
Dan Kerschner, Sales Manager
Scott Staley, Programming Director
Dan Lynch, News Director
Jim Frank, Chief Engineer
Heather Buchholtz, TrafficManager

Rifle

KRGS
06-09-1967; 690 kHz AM; *Hrs Open:* 24; 0.9 kw-D, ND1; 0.012 kw-N, ND1; N39 32 56 W107 46 11
751 Horizon Court, Suite 225, Grand Junction, CO 81506 US
(970) 241-6460
wscradio.net
License: Rifle, CO held by Western Slope Communications L.L.C.
Group Owner: Western Slope Communications LLC
Format: Sports; *Target Audience:* 18-54; males
Cyrene Jagger, Station Manager

KZKS
01-01-1994; 105.3 MHz FM; *Hrs Open:* 24; 60 kw; 2,437 ft; N39 25 57 W108 07 46
751 Horizon Ct., Suite 225, Grand Junction, CO 81506
(970) 241-6460
wscradio.net
License: Rifle, Garfield County, CO
Group Owner: Western Slope Communications LLC
Population Served: 320,000 *Hrs. of News Programming:* news progmg 20 hrs wkly; *No. News Employees:* 1
Cyrene Jagger, Station Manager

RADIO - U.S.

Rock Creek Park

KXCL
01-01-2008; 101.7 MHz FM; 2.1 kw; -9 meters; N38 43 11 W104 43 16
1200 W. Cornwallis, Greensboro, NC
(336) 286-2087
License: Rock Creek Park, Custer County, CO held by United States CP LLC.
Group Owner: United States CP LLC
Population Served: 58; *Arbitron Metro Market:* Rock Creek Park, CO
W. Philip Robinson, General Manager

Rocky Ford

KPHT
01-01-2002; 95.5 MHz FM; 100 kw; 735 ft.; N37 54 8 W104 16 0
1470 Ben Sawyer Blvd, Suite 16, Mount Pleasant, SC 29464 US
(719) 545-2080; *Fax:* (719) 543-9898
www.kpht955.com
License: Rocky Ford, Otero County, CO held by Capstar TX LLC
Group Owner: iHeartMedia; (acq 2-12-2001; $1 million).
Format: Oldies
Jason McCollim, Senior Vice President of Programming
Nick Donovan, Programming Director

Rye

*KRWA
08-24-2007; 90.9 MHz FM; 10 kw; 114 ft.; N37 56 40 W104 59 56
P.O. Box 704, Rye, CO 81069 US
(877) 702-9293; *Fax:* (719) 278-4339
supportservices@wayfm.com
License: Rye, Pueblo County, CO held by WAY-FM Media Group Inc.
Group Owner: WAY-FM Media Group Inc.; (acq 6-17-2005; $200,000 for CP)
Arbitron Metro Market: Rye, CO; *Format:* Christian
Robert Augsburg, President

Salida

KVRH
12-10-1948; 1340 kHz AM; *Hrs Open:* 24; 1 kw-U, ND1; N38 31 55 W106 0 54
7600 County Rd. 120, Salida, CO 81201 US
(719) 539-2575; *Fax:* (719) 539-4851
www.thepeak923.com
License: Salida, CO held by Three Eagles Communications of Colorado, LLC
Group Owner: Three Eagles Communications of Colorado, LLC
Arbitron Metro Market: Salida,CO; *Format:* Adult Contemp; *Hrs. of News Programming:* news progmg 10 hrs wkly; *No. News Employees:* 1; *Target Audience:* 25-54; general
Dean Johnson, Station Manager
Dan Ridenour, News Director
Doreen White, Business Manager

KVRH-FM
01-01-1971; 92.3 MHz FM; *Hrs Open:* 24; 0.22 kw; 2938 ft.; N38 27 11 W106 1 2
7600 County Rd. 120, Salida, CO 81201 US
(719) 539-2575; *Fax:* (719) 539-4851
www.thepeak923.com
License: Salida, Chaffee County, CO held by Three Eagles Communications of Colorado LLC
Group Owner: Three Eagles Communications of Colorado, LLC; (acq 4-12-2000; with co-located AM)
Arbitron Metro Market: Salida,CO; *Format:* Adult Contemp; *Hrs. of News Programming:* news progmg 10 hrs wkly; *No. News Employees:* 1
Dean Johnson, Station Manager
Dan Ridenour, News Director
Doreen White, Business Manager

KSBV
01-01-2002; 93.7 MHz FM; *Hrs Open:* 24; 1 kw; 2723 ft.; N38 26 47 W106 0 37
115 East 2nd Street, Salida, CO 81201 US
(719) 539-9377; *Fax:* (719) 539-7904
www.ksbv.net
License: Salida, Chaffee County, CO held by Arkansas Valley Broadcasting L.L.C.
Arbitron Metro Market: Salida, CO; *Format:* Classic Rock, Sports; *Target Audience:* 25-65.
Marc Scott, President
Melissa Scott, News Director

*KTPF
01-01-2007; 91.3 MHz FM; 0.39 kw; 2953 ft.; N38 26 48 W106 0 36 *Rebroadcasts:* Rebroadcasts KTLF(FM) Colorado Springs 100%
1665 Briargate Blvd., Colorado Springs, CO 80920 US
(719) 593-0600; *Fax:* (719) 593-2399
www.ktlf.org
lightpraise@ktlf.org
License: Salida, Chaffee County, CO held by Educational Communications of Colorado Springs Inc.
Arbitron Metro Market: Salida, CO; *Format:* Christian; *Target Audience:* 45-60; Christian
Lauren Johnson, Operations Dir
Ryan Sedgwick, General Manager
Sharick Wade, Programming Director
Robert Mumm, Chief Engineer
Marge Wallace, Office Manager
Alleen Wagnon, Office Assistant

*KMPZ
88.1 MHz FM; 0.2 kw; 2713 ft.; N38 26 48 W106 0 36
1921 North Weber Street, Colorado Springs, CO 80907 US
(719) 578-5263
www.kcme.org
genmanager@kcme.org
License: Salida, Chaffee County, CO held by Cheyenne Mountain Public Broadcast House Inc.
Arbitron Metro Market: Salida, CO; *Format:* Classical
George Preston, General Manager
Jeanna Wearing, Director of Underwriting
Melissa Anthony, Interim Development Director
Jana Lee, Music Director
Brenda Bratton, Finance/Office Manager
Jana Lee, Music Director
Bill Fodor, Directorof Broadcast Operations

Security

KRDO-FM
04-08-1973; 105.5 MHz FM; *Hrs Open:* 24; 1.6 kw horiz, 1.47 kw vert; 2238 ft.; N38 44 40 W104 51 41 *Rebroadcasts:* Simulcasts KRDO(AM) Colorado Springs 100%
825 Edmond St, St. Joseph, MO 64501 US
(719) 632-1515 (719) 473-1240; *Fax:* (719) 475-0815
www.krdo.com
m.lewis@krdo.com
License: Security, El Paso County, CO held by Pikes Peak Television, Inc.
Group Owner: News-Press & Gazette Co.; (acq 1989).
Arbitron Metro Market: Colorado Springs, CO; *Format:* News, News/Talk, 86
Jerry Killion, Operations Dir
Tim Larson, General Manager
JoAnne Rowley, Radio Sales Manager
Mike Lewis, Radio Program Director
Tim McSpadden, Promotions Manager
Baaron Pittenger, News Director
Joe Reed, Chief Engineer

Severance

KRKA
03-13-2008; 103.9 MHz FM; 16.5 kw; 1220 ft.; N40 37 3 W105 19 40
5700 West Oaks Boulevard, Rocklin, CA 95765 US
(916) 251-1600; *Fax:* (916) 251-1650
www.air1.com
License: Severance, Weld County, CO held by Educational Media Foundation
Group Owner: EMF Broadcasting
Arbitron Metro Market: Severance, CO; *Format:* Classic Rock
Mike Novak, President

Snowmass Village

KSNO-FM
04-01-1985; 103.9 MHz FM; *Hrs Open:* 24; 6 kw; 325 ft.; N39 14 51 W106 55 13
218 E. Valley Road, El Jebel, CO 81623 US
(970) 510-5361
www.ksno.us
les@thesoundfm.com
License: Snowmass Village, Pitkin County, CO held by Cool Radio LLC.
Nat'l Reps: Katz Radio; *Wire Services:* AP
Arbitron Metro Market: Aspen, CO; *Format:* Triple A; *Hrs. of News Programming:* news progmg 2 hrs wkly; *No. News Employees:* 1; *Target Audience:* 25-54.
Mark Michaud, General Manager/General Sales Manager
Les Helton, Programming Director

South Fork

*KTML
01-01-2009; 91.5 MHz FM; 0 kw horiz, 0.28 kw vert; 1614 ft.; N37 43 47 W106 35 18 *Rebroadcasts:* Rebroadcasts KTLF(FM) Colorado Springs 100%
1665 Briargate Bouelvard, Colorado Springs, CO 80920 US
(719) 593-0600; *Fax:* (719) 593-2399
www.ktlf.org
lightpraise@ktlf.org
License: South Fork, Rio Grande County, CO held by Educational Communications of Colorado Springs Inc.
Arbitron Metro Market: South Fork, CO; *Format:* Christian
Robyn Sedgwick, General Manager
Sharick Wade, Programming Director
Robert Mumm, Chief Engineer
Lauren Johnson, Operations Manager
Marge Wallace, Office Manager
Alleen Wagnon, Office Assistant

Springfield

*KTTE
91.9 MHz FM; 0.15 kw; 151 ft.; N37 24 36 W102 37 37 US
(405) 380-3516
www.klxfm.com
info@bpba.us
License: Springfield, Baca County, CO held by Better Public Broadcasting Association.
Arbitron Metro Market: Springfield, CO
Dennis Burton, General Manager

Starkville

*KCCS
01-01-2008; 91.7 MHz FM; 0.37 kw; 994 ft.; N36 59 33 W104 28 24 *Rebroadcasts:* Rebroadcasts KRCC(FM) Colorado Springs 100%
912 North Weber Street, Colorado Springs, CO 80903 US
(719) 473-4801; *Fax:* (719) 473-7863
www.krcc.org
info@krcc.org
License: Starkville, Las Animas County, CO held by The Colorado College.
Nat'l Network: NPR; PRI
Arbitron Metro Market: Starkville, CO
Delaney Utterback, General Manager

Steamboat Springs

KBCR
08-01-1976; 1230 kHz AM; *Hrs Open:* 24; 1 kw-U, ND1; N40 29 19 W106 50 57
Mailing Address: 815 Reed St, Lakewood, CO 80477 US
Second Address: 2110 Mt. Werner Rd., Steamboat Springs, CO 80487
(970) 879-2270; *Fax:* (970) 879-1404
kbcr.com
brian@kbcr.com
License: Steamboat Springs, CO held by Cool Radio LLC.
Nat'l Network: ESPN Radio
Arbitron Metro Market: Steamboat Springs, CO; *Format:* Sports; *No. News Employees:* 1; *Target Audience:* 24-55.
Brian Harvey, General Manager
Dave Lancaster, News Director
Tony Mauro, VP, Operations
Craig Koehn, Market Manager
Kri Hoy-Skubik, Digital Content Manager
Tom Dobrez, CEO

KBCR-FM
07-25-1974; 96.9 MHz FM; 10 kw; Ant 666 ft; N40 27 43 W106 50 57
Box 774050, Steamboat Springs, CO 80215
(970) 879-2270; *Fax:* (970) 879-1404
kbcr.com
License: Steamboat Springs, Routt County, CO held by Cool Radio LLC
Nat'l Network: ABC
Population Served: 25,000
Tom Dobrez, CEO
Tony Mauro, VP, Operations
Craig Koehn, Market Manager
Bri Hoy-Skubik, Digital Content Manager

*KLBV
01-01-2005; 89.3 MHz FM; *Hrs Open:* 24; 2.6 kw vert; 1732 ft.; N40 27 4 W106 45 6
16075 West Belleview Ave, Morrison, CO 80465 US

(800) 525-5683; *Fax:* (916) 251-1650
www.klove.com
klove@klove.com
License: Steamboat Springs, Routt County, CO held by Educational Media Foundation.
Group Owner: EMF Broadcasting; (acq 10-2-03; grpsl).
Nat'l Network: K-Love
Arbitron Metro Market: Steamboat Springs, CO; *Format:* Christian; *No. News Employees:* 13; *Target Audience:* 25-44; Judeo Christian, female
Darrell Chambliss, Chairman
Mike Novak, President and CEO
Jennifer Lohman, Operations Dir
David Pierce, Chief Creative Officer and Programming Director
Ed Lenane, News Director
Sam Wallington, Engineering Dir
Marya Morgan, NewsReporter
Richard Hunt, News Reporter
Alan Mason, Chief Operating Officer
Dan Antonelli, Chief Business Development Officer
Eric Moser, Chief Financial Officer
Brian Burger, Vice President of Human Resources

***KRNC**
01-23-2006; 88.5 MHz FM; 0.24 kw; 600 ft.; N40 27 43 W106 50 57 *Rebroadcasts:* Rebroadcasts KUNC(FM) Greeley 100%
US
(970) 378-2579; *Fax:* (970) 378-2580
www.kunc.org
comment@kunc.org
License: Steamboat Springs, Routt County, CO held by Community Radio of Northern Colorado
Nat'l Network: NPR; PRI; *Wire Services:* AP
Arbitron Metro Market: Steamboat Springs, CO; *Format:* News, Variety/Diverse
Jamie Wood, CFO
Neil Best, President and CEO
Ryan Thompson, Operations Dir
Kirk Mowers, Programming Director
Brian Larson, News Director
Ken Broeffle, Chief Engineer
Benjamin McPhail, Music Director
Dave Dennis, CorporateSupport Associate
Robert Leja, Director of Corporate Support and Marketing
Jim Hill, Digital Media Manager
Kirk Mowers, Content Director
Marc Applegate, Announcer/Producer

***KTSG**
01-01-2006; 91.7 MHz FM; 2.5 kw horiz, 0 kw vert; N40 27 43 W106 50 58 *Rebroadcasts:* Rebroadcasts KTLF(FM) Colorado Springs 100%
1665 Briargate Blvd., Colordo Springs, CO 80920 US
(719) 593-0600; *Fax:* (719) 593-2399
www.ktlf.org
lightpraise@ktlf.org
License: Steamboat Springs, Routt County, CO held by Educational Communications of Colorado Springs Inc.
Arbitron Metro Market: Steamboat Springs, CO; *Format:* Christian; *Target Audience:* 45-60; Christian
Lauren Johnson, Operations Dir
Ryan Sedgwick, General Manager
Sharick Wade, Programming Director
Robert Mumm, Chief Engineer
Skip Rice, Sonrise Host
Marge Wallace, Office Manager
Alleen Wagnon, Office Assistant

Sterling

KNNG
02-08-1974; 104.7 MHz FM; *Hrs Open:* 24; 100 kw; 650 ft.; N40 34 57 W103 1 56
P.O. Box 830, Sterling, CO 80751 US
(970) 522-1607; *Fax:* (970) 522-1322
knng@kci.net
License: Sterling, Logan County, CO held by Arnold Broadcasting Inc.
Group Owner: Arnold Broadcasting Inc.; (acq 7-31-2008; grpsl)
Nat'l Network: Jones Radio Networks; ABC
Format: Country; *Hrs. of News Programming:* news progmg 10 hrs wkly; *No. News Employees:* 1; *Target Audience:* General; country listeners
William Arnold, CEO

KPMX
08-19-1983; 105.7 MHz FM; *Hrs Open:* 24; 12 kw; 479 ft.; N40 31 57 W103 7 22
117 Main Street, Sterling, CO 80751 US
(970) 522-4800; *Fax:* (970) 522-3997
www.kpmx.com
andy@kpmx.com
License: Sterling, Logan County, CO held by Northeast Colorado Broadcasting LLC
Group Owner: Northeast Colorado Broadcasting LLC; acq 7-1-2003; grpsl).
Format: Adult Contemp; *Target Audience:* 18-54.; *Adv. Rates:* 12
Alec Creighton, General Manager
Theresa Leaks, General Sales Mgr
Andy Rice, Programming Director

KSTC
01-03-1925; 1230 kHz AM; *Hrs Open:* 24
P.O. Box 830, Sterling, CO 80751 US
(970) 522-1607; *Fax:* (970) 522-1322
knng@kci.net
License: Sterling, CO held by Arnold Broadcasting Inc.
Group Owner: Arnold Broadcasting Inc.; (acq 7-31-2008; grpsl)
Nat'l Network: ABC; Jones Radio Networks
Arbitron Metro Market: Sterling, CO; *Format:* Oldies *Special Programming:* Farm 15 hrs wkly; *Hrs. of News Programming:* news progmg 12 hrs wkly; *No. News Employees:* 1; *Target Audience:* General.
William Arnold, CEO
Betty Carlson, General Manager
Mike Walker, Programming Director
Montica Loft, Assistant Manager

***KDRE**
01-01-2005; 90.7 MHz FM; 1.6 kw vert; 506 ft.; N40 36 56 W103 2 2 *Rebroadcasts:* Rebroadcasts KLRD(FM) Yucaipa, CA 100%
5700 West Oaks Boulevard, Rocklin, CA 95765 US
(888) 937-2471; *Fax:* (916) 251-1650
www.air1.com
info@air1.com
License: Sterling, Logan County, CO held by Educational Media Foundation.
Group Owner: EMF Broadcasting; (acq 9-22-2005; $17,000 for CP)
Nat'l Network: Air 1
Arbitron Metro Market: Sterling, CO; *Format:* Alternative, Christian
Darrell Chambliss, Chairman
Alan Mason, COO
Mike Novak, President and CEO
Jennifer Lohman, Operations Dir
David Pierce, Programming Director
Ed Lenane, News Director
Sam Wallington, Engineering Dir
Marya Morgan, NewsReporter
Richard Hunt, News Reporter
Tracy Butler, Traffic Manager
Dan Antonelli, Chief Business Development Officer
Eric Moser, Chief Financial Officer
Brian Burger, Vice President of Human Resources

***KTAD**
01-01-2005; 89.9 MHz FM; 5 kw vert; 407 ft.; N40 31 57 W103 7 22 *Rebroadcasts:* Rebroadcasts KTPL(FM) Pueblo 100%
1665 Briargate Blvd., Colorado Springs, CO 80920 US
(719) 593-0600; *Fax:* (719) 593-2399
www.ktlf.org
License: Sterling, Logan County, CO held by Educational Communications of Colorado Springs Inc.
Arbitron Metro Market: Sterling, CO; *Format:* Christian, Religious; *Target Audience:* 18-35; Christian
Lauren Johnson, Operations Dir
Robyn Sedgwick, General Manager
Sharick Wade, Programming Director
Robert Mumm, Chief Engineer
Marge Wallace, Office Manager
Alleen Wagnon, Office Assistant

KSRX
01-01-2008; 97.5 MHz FM; 17 kw; Ant 561 ft; N40 27 15.1 W103 09 6.1
P.O. Box 430, Fort Morgan, CO
(970) 867-5674; *Fax:* (970) 542-1023
License: Sterling, Logan County, CO held by Media Logic LLC.
Group Owner: Media Logic LLC
Target Audience: 18-45; female, male
Wayne Johnson, President
Marc Romero, Station Manager

Strasburg

***KSJL**
97.7 MHz FM; 25 kw horiz; 52 ft.; N39 42 19 W104 12 17
P.O. Box 7346, Las Vegas, NV 89125 US
(210) 736-9700; *Fax:* (210) 735-8811
License: Strasburg, Adams County, CO held by Mary V. Harris Foundation.
Arbitron Metro Market: Strasburg, CO; *Format:* Oldies
Linda De Romanett, President

KJHM
01-01-1978; 101.5 MHz FM; *Hrs Open:* 24; 97 kw; 2,050 ft.; N39 55 22 W103 58 18
803 W. Main, Sterling, CO 80751 US
(303) 872-1500; *Fax:* (303) 872-1501
www.jammin1015.com
License: Strasburg, Adams County, CO held by Max Radio of Denver LLC
Group Owner: MAX Media L.L.C.
Arbitron Metro Market: Denver, CO; *Format:* Adult Contemp
Jeff Norman, President/General Manager
Sean Rhoads, General Sales Mgr
Brian DeGrasse, Director of Marketing and Promotions
Laurie Vigil, Business Manager
Cody Glasgo, Traffic Manager
Creighton Petro, Digital Director
JennaLeveille, Senior Account Executive
Rachel Makinen, Senior Account Executive
Joy B. Morrone, Senior Account Executive

Telluride

***KOTO**
10-01-1975; 91.7 MHz FM; 8.4 kw; -223 ft.; N37 55 59 W107 49 59
P.O. Box 1069, Telluride, CO 81435 US
(970) 728-4334; *Fax:* (970) 728-4326
www.koto.org
License: Telluride, San Miguel County, CO held by San Miguel Educational Fund.
Nat'l Network: NPR; PRI
Format: Variety/Diverse *Special Programming:* Class 9 hrs, country 12 hrs, jazz 9 hrs, blues 7 hrs, drama 3 hrs wkly; *Hrs. of News Programming:* news progmg 2 hrs wkly; *No. News Employees:* 2 *Target Audience:* General; community
Dina Coates Koebler, Executive Director
Ben Kerr, Station Manager
Cara Pallone, News Director
Corey Beaton, Music Director

Thornton

KKZN
05-30-1987; 760 kHz AM
4695 S. Monaco St., Denver, CO 80237 US
(303) 713-8000; *Fax:* (303) 713-8738
www.realtalk760.com
License: Thornton, CO held by Citicasters Licenses Inc.
Group Owner: iHeartMedia; (acq 5-4-99; grpsl).
Arbitron Metro Market: Denver-Boulder, CO; *Format:* Talk
Tim Hager, Market President

Timnath

KJAC
04-10-1989; 105.5 MHz FM; *Hrs Open:* 24; 50 kw; 1302 ft.; N40 37 3 W105 19 39
1806 Capitol Avenue, Cheyenne, WY 82001 US
(303) 296-7025; *Fax:* (303) 296-7030
www.1055jackfm.com
info@1055jackfm.com
License: Timnath, Larimer County, CO held by NRC Broadcasting Inc.
Group Owner: NRC Broadcasting Inc.; (acq 4-13-2004; $15 million)
Nat'l Network: Westwood One; *Nat'l Reps:* Target Broadcast Sales
Arbitron Metro Market: Fort Collins-Greeley, CO; *Hrs. of News Programming:* News progmg 10 hrs wkly; *Target Audience:* 18-54; general
Timothy Brown, General Manager
Roger Tighe, Chief Engineer

Trinidad

KCRT
05-21-1946; 1240 kHz AM; *Hrs Open:* 24; 0.25 kw-U, ND1; N37 8 45 W104 30 42
100 Fisher Drive, Trinidad, CO 81082 US
(719) 846-3355; *Fax:* (719) 846-4711
www.kcrtradio.com
kcrt@comcast.net
License: Trinidad, CO held by Phillips Broadcasting Inc.
Group Owner: Phillips Broadcasting Inc.; (acq 3-30-92; $235,000 with co-located FM;
Nat'l Network: ABC; Jones Radio Networks

Arbitron Metro Market: Trinidad, CO; *Format:* Country *Special Programming:* Farm one hr, relg 5 hrs wkly; *Hrs. of News Programming:* news progmg 15 hrs wkly; *No. News Employees:* 1; *Target Audience:* General. *Adv. Rates:* 8; 7; 6; 6
Anita Phillips, President
Lory Phillips, General Manager
David Phillips, Station Manager
Rick Neurauter, Advertising Director

KCRT-FM
08-01-1981; 92.5 MHz FM; *Hrs Open:* 24; 38.5 kw; 1020 ft.; N36 59 33 W104 28 24
100 Fisher Drive, Trinidad, CO 81082 US
(719) 846-3355; *Fax:* (719) 846-4711
www.kcrtradio.com
krct@comcast.net
License: Trinidad, Las Animas County, CO held by Phillips Broadcasting Inc.
Group Owner: Phillips Broadcasting Inc.
Arbitron Metro Market: Trinidad, CO; *Format:* Classic Rock; *Target Audience:* 25-54.; *Adv. Rates:* 12; 10; 8; 8
Anita Phillips, President
Lory Phillips, General Manager
David Phillips, Station Manager

***KJWA**
89.7 MHz FM; 0.9 kw; 791 ft.; N37 14 14 W104 30 52
Rebroadcasts: Rebroadcasts KXWA(FM) Loveland 100%
P.O. Box 704, Rye, CO 81069 US
(303) 702-9293; *Fax:* (303) 485-1929
www.wayfm.com
License: Trinidad, Pueblo County, CO held by WAY-FM Media Group Inc.
Group Owner: WAY-FM Media Group Inc.; (acq 6-19-2007)
Arbitron Metro Market: Trinidad, CO; *Format:* Christian
Zach Cochran, General Manager

***KTDL**
01-01-2007; 90.7 MHz FM; 0.45 kw; 971 ft.; N36 59 33 W104 28 24 *Rebroadcasts:* Rebroadcasts KTLF(FM) Colorado Springs 100%
1665 Briargate Blvd, Colorado Springs, CO 80920 US
(719) 593-0600; *Fax:* (719) 593-2399
www.ktlf.org
lightpraise@ktlf.org
License: Trinidad, Las Animas County, CO held by Educational Communications of Colorado Springs Inc.
Arbitron Metro Market: Trinidad, CO; *Format:* Christian; *Target Audience:* 45-60; Christian
Lauren Johnson, Operations Dir
Robyn Sedgwick, General Manager
Sharick Wade, Programming Director
Robert Mumm, Chief Engineer
Marge Wallace, Office Manager
Alleen Wagnon, Office Assistant

Vail

***KPRE**
09-01-1994; 89.9 MHz FM; *Hrs Open:* 24; 1.5 kw; 295 ft.; N39 38 5 W106 26 47 *Rebroadcasts:* Rebroadcasts KCFR(FM) Denver 100%
2249 S. Josephine Street, Denver, CO 80210 US
(303) 871-9191; *Fax:* (303) 733-3319
www.cpr.org
info@cpr.org
License: Vail, Eagle County, CO held by Public Broadcasting of Colorado Inc.
Nat'l Network: NPR
Format: News; *Hrs. of News Programming:* news progmg 50 hrs wkly; *No. News Employees:* 8; *Target Audience:* General.
Warren Olsen, Chairman
Max Wycisk, President
Sue Coughlin, General Sales Mgr
Bob Hensler, Engineering Dir

KVLE
07-25-1983; 610 kHz AM; 5 kw-D, ND1; 0.217 kw-N, ND1; N39 34 47 W106 24 54 *Rebroadcasts:* Simulcasts KSKE(AM) Buena Vista
1445 Hwy 135 N., Gunnison, CO 81230 US
(970) 648-4365; *Fax:* (970) 648-4367
www.kvleradio.com
License: Vail, CO held by Pilgrim Communications Inc.
Group Owner: Pilgrim Communications Inc.; (acq 3-2-2000; $150,000)
Nat'l Network: ABC
Arbitron Metro Market: Longmont, CO; *Format:* News/Talk; *Hrs. of News Programming:* news progmg 12 hrs wkly; *No. News Employees:* 3; *Target Audience:* 25-65.; *Adv. Rates:* 40; 40; 40; 30

Mick Whitecotton, President
Rick Johnson, Operations Dir

***KVJZ**
88.5 MHz FM; 5 kw; -791 ft.; N39 36 56 W106 26 57
P O Box 11111, Denver, CO 80211 US
(303) 480-9272; *Fax:* (303) 291-0757
www.kuvo.org
info@kuvo.org
License: Vail, Eagle County, CO held by Denver Educational Broadcasting Inc.
Arbitron Metro Market: Vail, CO
Carlos Lando, COO
Gene Craven, President

Walsenburg

KSPK-FM
03-01-1985; 102.3 MHz FM; *Hrs Open:* 24; 100 kw; 430 ft.; N37 37 39 W104 49 17
516 Main Street, Walsenburg, CO 81089 US
(719) 738-3636; *Fax:* (719) 738-2010
www.kspk.com
info@kspk.com
License: Walsenburg, Huerfano County, CO held by Mainstreet Broadcasting Co. Inc.
Nat'l Network: ABC; *Wire Services:* ABC
Arbitron Metro Market: Walsenburg, CO *TV Affiliate:* KSPK-TV; *Format:* Country, Sports *Special Programming:* Relg 2 hrs wkly; *Hrs. of News Programming:* news progmg 3 hrs wkly; *No. News Employees:* 2 *TargetAudience:* 24-59; upwardly mobile, two-income families; *Adv. Rates:* 20; 16; 18; 14
David Raye, Operations Dir
Paul Richards, General Manager
Paul Bossert, Chief Engineer
Michelle Lessar, Traffic Manager

***KTAW**
01-01-2008; 89.3 MHz FM; 0 kw horiz, 0.5 kw vert; 377 ft.; N37 37 39 W104 49 17 *Rebroadcasts:* Rebroadcasts KTLF(FM) Colorado Springs 100%
1665 Briargate Blvd, Colorado Sorings, CO 80920 US
(719) 593-0600; *Fax:* (719) 593-2399
www.ktlf.org
License: Walsenburg, Huerfano County, CO held by Educational Communications of Colorado Springs Inc.
Arbitron Metro Market: Walsenburg, CO; *Format:* Christian; *Target Audience:* 45-60; Christian
Lauren Johnson, Operations Dir
Robyn Sedgwick, General Manager
Sharick Wade, Programming Director
Robert Mumm, Chief Engineer
Skip Rice, Sonrise Host
Marge Wallace, Office Adminstrator
Alleen Wagnon, Office Assistant

KFEZ(FM)
01-01-2009; 101.3 MHz FM; 95.5 kw; Ant 1,000 ft; N37 47 20 W104 29 12
516 Main St., Walsenburg, CO 81089
(773) 592-9800
License: Walsenburg, Huerfano County, CO held by Edward Magnus.
Group Owner: DBA Soco Radio
Population Served: 2,980; *Arbitron Metro Market:* Walsenburg, CO
Mike Knar, General Manager
Jim Berry, Sales Manager
Jack Kromer, Chief Engineer

Weldona

****KFWA(FM)**
103.1 MHz FM; 25 kw; 135 meters; 39 28 12N 103 38 14W
1707 Ben Sawyer Blvd, Suite 16, Mount Pleasant, SC 29464 USA
kxwa.wayfm.com
License: Weldona, Morgan County, CO
Group Owner: Way-FM Media Inc

Wellington

KCOL
01-12-1959; 600 kHz AM; 5 kw-D, DA2; 0.5 kw-N, DA2; N40 39 0 W105 2 51
4270 Byrd Dr., Loveland, CO 80538 US
(970) 461-2560
www.600kcol.com
License: Wellington, Larimer County, CO held by Citicasters Licenses Inc.
Group Owner: iHeartMedia; (acq 5-8-98; $6.1 million with co-located FM)
Nat'l Reps: McGavren Guild
Arbitron Metro Market: Fort Collins, CO *TV Affiliate:* Fox; *Format:* News, News/Talk, 86 *Special Programming:* Farm 2 hrs, relg one hr, sports talk 7 hrs wkly; *Hrs. of News Programming:* News progmg 120 hrs wkly *Target Audience:* 35 plus.
Garner Goin, Operations Manager
Stu Haskell, General Manager
Kathy Arias, General Sales Mgr
Doc Jarnagin, Programming Director
Mike Sanchez, Promotions Director

KMAX-FM
01-01-2003; 94.3 MHz FM; *Hrs Open:* 24; 8.7 kw; 551 ft.; N40 55 41 W105 8 36
C/O Brill Media Co Lp, P O Box 3353, Evansville, IN 47732 US
(970) 674-2700; *Fax:* (970) 686-7491
www.943maxfm.com
pat.kelley@townsquaremedia.com
License: Wellington, Larimer County, CO
Group Owner: Townsquare Media; (acq 2-25-2003)
Arbitron Metro Market: Wellington, CO; *Format:* Classic Rock
Pat Kelley, General Manager
Justin Tyler, Brand Manager
Zandi Wilcox, Director Of Sales
Eric Davis, Digital Sales Manager
Madison Scruggs, Digital Managing Editor

Westcliffe

***KLZR**
91.9 MHz FM; kw
US
(785)843-1320; *Fax:* (785)841-1320
www.1059kissfm.com
License: Westcliffe, Custer County, CO
Group Owner: Cedar Cove Broadcasting Inc.

Jay Wachs, General Manager
Ammber Lee, Programming Director
Rebecca Supernaw, Advertising

Wheat Ridge

KTCL
09-01-1965; 93.3 MHz FM; 71 kw; 1135 ft.; N39 43 59 W105 14 10
4695 S. Monaco St., Denver, CO 80237 US
(303) 713-8000; *Fax:* (303) 713-8744
www.area93.com
License: Wheat Ridge, Jefferson County, CO held by Citicasters Licenses Inc.
Group Owner: iHeartMedia; (acq 5-8-98; $6.1 million with co-located AM)
Arbitron Metro Market: Denver-Boulder, CO; *Format:* Alternative *Special Programming:* Comedy one hr, loc bands one hr, reggae 2 hrs wkly; *Target Audience:* 18 plus.
Tim Hager, Market President

Widefield

KKLI
03-23-1987; 106.3 MHz FM; *Hrs Open:* 24; 1.6 kw; 2224 ft.; N38 44 41 W104 51 46
600 Congress Avenue, Suite 1400, Austin, TX 78701 US
(719) 540-9200; *Fax:* (719) 579-0882
www.sunny1063online.com
License: Widefield, El Paso County, CO held by Capstar TX LLC
Group Owner: iHeartMedia; (acq 8-30-00; grpsl).
Nat'l Reps: Clear Channel
Arbitron Metro Market: Colorado Springs, CO; *Format:* Adult Contemp; *Hrs. of News Programming:* news progmg 4 hrs wkly; *No. News Employees:* 1; *Target Audience:* 25-54; family-oriented, educated *Adv. Rates:* 100; 90; 90; 60
Jason McCollim, Senior Vice President of Programming
Laura Trivett, Promotions Director

Windsor

KUAD-FM
05-31-1975; 99.1 MHz FM; 100 kw; 837 ft.; N40 38 31 W104 49 3
P.O.Box 3353, Evansville, IN 47732 US
(970) 674-2700; *Fax:* (970) 686-7491
www.k99.com
pat.kelly@townsquaremedia.com
License: Windsor, Weld County, CO
Group Owner: Townsquare Media; (acq 2-25-03).
Arbitron Metro Market: Windsor, CO; *Format:* Country; *Target Audience:* 25-54; upscale country listeners, 60% women; *Adv. Rates:* 35; 35; 35; 25

Pat Kelley, General Manager
Justin Tyler, Brand Manager
Zandi Wilcox, Director Of Sales
Eric Davis, Digital Sales Manager
Madison Scruggs, Digital Managing Editor

KJJD
04-12-1969; 1170 kHz AM; *Hrs Open:* Sunrise-sunset; 1 kw-D, NDD; N40 27 46 W104 54 47
Mailing Address: P.O. Box 698, Windsor, CO 80550 US
Second Address: PO Box 698, Windsor, CO 80550
(970) 686-1170; *Fax:* (970) 686-5751
www.laley1170.com
secretaria1170@yahoo.com
License: Windsor, CO held by Rodriguez-Gallegos Broadcasting Corporation.
Format: Spanish *Special Programming:* Pub affrs; *Hrs. of News Programming:* News progmg 5 hrs wkly; *Target Audience:* 18-54; general
Jesse Rodriguez, General Manager
Danny Casas, Station Manager

Woodland Park

***KILE-FM**
89.5 MHz FM; 100 w vert; Ant -407 ft; N38 59 37 W105 02 21
4703 Orkney Dr., Missouri City, TX
(281) 923-7100; *Fax:* 713-559-8517
radioguy@airmail.net
License: Woodland Park, Teller County, CO held by Grace Public Radio.
Population Served: 10,200; *Arbitron Metro Market:* Colorado Springs, CO; *Target Audience:* Adults, 25-54
Fred Morton, Member
KT Morton, Member

Wray

KATR-FM
09-01-1983; 98.3 MHz FM; *Hrs Open:* 24; 100 kw; 554 ft.; N40 25 13 W102 58 10
519 W. Main Street, Sterling, CO 80751 US
(970) 521-2732; *Fax:* (970) 521-2733
www.katcountry983.com
medialogic@kci.net
License: Wray, Washington County, CO held by Media Logic LLC
Group Owner: Media Logic LLC; acq 10-28-2002; $700,000).
Arbitron Metro Market: Sterling, CO; *Format:* Country; *Hrs. of News Programming:* news progmg 15 hrs wkly; *No. News Employees:* 3; *Target Audience:* 16-70; males & females
Wayne Johnson, President/General Manager
Marc Romero, Station Manager
Dana Marini, General Sales Mgr
Michael Schaus, News Director
Henry Mowry, Marketing Director

KRDZ
01-11-1978; 1440 kHz AM; *Hrs Open:* 4:50 AM-midnight; 5 kw-D, ND1; 0.212 kw-N, ND1; N40 4 56 W102 11 25
P.O. Box 466, Wray, CO 80758 US
(970) 332-4171; *Fax:* (970) 332-4172
www.krdz.com
krdz@medialogicradio.com
License: Wray, CO held by Media Logic LLC
Group Owner: Media Logic LLC; acq 10-31-2002).
Nat'l Network: Jones Radio Networks; *Regional Network:* Brownfield
Format: Contemporary Hits/Top 40 *Special Programming:* Focus on family 2 hrs, farm 10 hrs wkly; *Hrs. of News Programming:* News progmg 10 hrs wkly; *Target Audience:* Farmers & ranchers.
Wayne Johnson/Owner, General Manager
Keith Lippoldt, Station Manager
Dana Marini, General Sales Mgr
Robert Lovell, Sports Director

***KGCD**
01-01-2006; 90.3 MHz FM; *Hrs Open:* 24; 0.43 kw vert; 253 ft.; N40 3 13 W102 13 32
US
(785) 694-2877; *Fax:* (785) 694-2875
kgcr@kgcr.org
License: Wray, Burleigh County, CO held by Educational Media Foundation.
Group Owner: EMF Broadcasting
Nat'l Network: K-Love
Arbitron Metro Market: Wray, CO; *Format:* Country, Gospel; *No. News Employees:* 3; *Target Audience:* 25-44; Judeo Christian, female
Mike Novak, President

Yuma

KNEC
01-01-1999; 100.9 MHz FM; 23 kw; 348 ft.; N40 0 33 W102 45 35
P O Box 830, 803 W Main St, Sterling, CO 80751 US
(970) 848-2302; *Fax:* (970) 848-2240
License: Yuma, Yuma County, CO held by Arnold Broadcasting Inc.
Group Owner: Arnold Broadcasting Inc.; (acq 7-31-2008; grpsl)
Format: Adult Contemp
Ashley Lynch, General Manager

Connecticut

Ansonia

WADS
05-08-1956; 690 kHz AM; 3.2 kw-D, DAD; N41 20 46 W73 6 51
P.O. Box 384, New Haven, CT 06513 US
(662) 844-8888; *Fax:* (662) 842-6791
www.afr.net
License: Ansonia, CT held by Radio Amor Inc.
Format: Christian, Religious
Tim Wildmon, President
Marvin Sanders, General Manager

Berlin

***WERB**
01-12-1979; 94.5 MHz FM; *Hrs Open:* 24; 27.5 w; 95 ft; N41 37 18 W72 45 13
Berlin High School Media Center, 139 Patterson Way, Berlin, CT 06037
(860) 828-0606,(860) 828-6577; *Fax:* (860) 829-0526
www.berlinwall.org
werb@berlinschools.org
License: Berlin, Hartford County, CT held by Berlin Board of Education.
Target Audience: Teenage listeners from Berlin High School
Chris Wolfe, General Manager

Bloomfield

WSDK
02-01-1964; 1550 kHz AM; *Hrs Open:* 24; 5 kw-D, DA2; 2.4 kw-N, DA2; N41 51 47 W72 44 1
160 Chapel Rd., Suite 103, Manchester, CT 06042 US
(860) 432-9735; *Fax:* (860) 432-8905
www.lifechangingradio.com
License: Bloomfield, Hartford County, CT held by Blount Masscom Inc.
Group Owner: Blount Communications Group
Arbitron Metro Market: Bloomfield, CT; *Format:* Religious; *Hrs. of News Programming:* news progmg 11 hrs wkly; *No. News Employees:* 1; *Target Audience:* 18-80; general; *Adv. Rates:* 32; 30; 32; 22
William Blount, President

Bridgeport

WCUM
09-01-1941; 1450 kHz AM; *Hrs Open:* 24; 1 kw-U, ND1; N41 13 10 W73 12 8
1862 Commerce Drive, Bridgeport, CT 06605 US
(203) 335-1450
www.radiocumbre.am
radiocumbre1450@aol.com
License: Bridgeport, CT held by Radio Cumbre Broadcasting Inc.
Arbitron Metro Market: Bridgeport, CT; *Hrs. of News Programming:* news progmg 14 hrs wkly; *No. News Employees:* 2; *Target Audience:* 25 plus.
Pablo De Jesus Colon Hijo, CEO
Migdalia Ramos Colon, Operations Director/Sales Manager
Allison Sheahan, General Manager

WDJZ
04-30-1977; 1530 kHz AM; 5 kw-D, DAD; N41 10 9 W73 13 14
175 Church Street, 3rd Floor, Naugatuck, CT 06770 US
(203) 368-4392; *Fax:* (203) 367-4551
www.wdjzradio.com
License: Bridgeport, CT held by People's Broadcast Network LLC
Arbitron Metro Market: Bridgeport, CT; *Format:* Ethnic, Gospel; *Target Audience:* 35 plus.
Milford Edwards Sr., General Manager

WEZN-FM
10-24-1960; 99.9 MHz FM; 27.5 kw; 669 ft.; N41 16 44 W73 11 8
3773 Howard Hughes Prwy, Suite 300n, Las Vegas, NV 89109 US
(203) 783-8200; *Fax:* (203) 783-8383
www.star999.com
kristin.okesson@coxinc.com
License: Bridgeport, Fairfield County, CT held by Connoisseur Media Licenses LLC
Group Owner: Connoisseur Media LLC; (acq 3-28-97; grpsl)
Arbitron Metro Market: Bridgeport, CT; *Format:* Adult Contemp; *Target Audience:* 25-54.; *Adv. Rates:* 275; 275; 275; 100
Kim Guthrie, President
Andy Alcosser, General Sales Mgr
Samantha Stevens, Programming Director
Stephen Donnarummo, Promotions Manager
Carol Roberts, News Director
Dom Bordonaro, Chief Engineer
Helaine Greenbaum, National SalesManager
Jennifer Chaves, Local Sales Manager
Kristin Okesson, VP/Market Manager

WICC
01-01-1926; 600 kHz AM; *Hrs Open:* 24; 1 kw-D, 500 w-N, DA-2; N41 09 36 W73 09 53
2 Lafayette Sq., Bridgeport, CT 06840
(203) 366-6000; *Fax:* (203) 384-0600,
www.wicc600.com
License: Bridgeport, Fairfield County, CT held by Cumulus Licensing Corp.
Group Owner: Cumulus Media Inc.; (acq 3-14-02; grpsl).
Nat'l Reps: Christal
Population Served: 450,000; *Arbitron Metro Market:* Bridgeport, CT *Special Programming:* It 5 hrs wkly; *Hrs. of News Programming:* news progmg 25 hrs wkly; *No. News Employees:* 3; *Target Audience:* 35-64.
Ann McManus, VP, Market Manager
Marrice Klebart, Sales Manager
Danny Lyons, Programming Director
Chris Mancini, Promotions Manager
Mike Bellamy, News Director
Curt Hansen, Operations Manager

***WPKN**
10-10-1963; 89.5 MHz FM; *Hrs Open:* 24; 10 kw; 554 ft.; N41 16 44 W73 11 8
244 University Ave., Bridgeport, CT 06601 US
(203) 331-9756
www.wpkn.org
wpkn@wpkn.org
License: Bridgeport, Fairfield County, CT held by WPKN Inc.
Arbitron Metro Market: Bridgeport, CT; *Format:* Variety/Diverse *Special Programming:* Class 2 hrs, Sp 4 hrs, Black 4 hrs, Fr 2 hrs, jazz 16 hrs wkly
Henry Minot, General Manager

Bristol

WPRX
11-22-1993; 1120 kHz AM; *Hrs Open:* 24; 1 kw-D, DAN; 0.5 kw-N, DAN; N41 39 29 W72 56 51
81 West Main Street, Suite G, New Britain, CT 06050 US
(860) 348-0667; *Fax:* (860) 348-0711
www.wprx1120.net
wprx1120@comcast.net
License: Bristol, CT held by Nievezquez Production Inc.
Arbitron Metro Market: Hartford-New Britain-Middletown, CT; *Format:* News, News/Talk, 86 *Special Programming:* Pol 2 hrs wkly; *Hrs. of News Programming:* news progmg 12 hrs wkly; *No. News Employees:* 2 *TargetAudience:* 23-54; Hispanic adults; *Adv. Rates:* 65; 60; 52; 30
Oscar Nieves, General Manager

Brookfield

WINE
05-09-1966; 940 kHz AM; 0.68 kw-D, ND1; 0.004 kw-N, ND1; N41 29 35 W73 25 45
600 14th Street, N.W., Suite 800, Washington, DC 20005 US
(203) 775-1212; *Fax:* (203) 775-6452
www.wineradio.com
License: Brookfield, CT held by Cumulus Licensing Corp.
Group Owner: Cumulus Media Inc.; (acq 1-23-2002; grpsl)
Nat'l Network: ESPN Radio
Arbitron Metro Market: Danbury, CT; *Format:* Sports; *Target Audience:* 25-54.
Tim Sheehan, Operations Dir
Brett Beshore, General Manager
Matt Carey, Programming Director
Lisa Harris, News Director
Peter Partenio, Chief Engineer

WRKI
12-24-1976; 95.1 MHz FM; 29.5 kw; 636 ft.; N41 29 36 W73 25 45
600 14th St., N.W., Suite800, Washington, DC 20005 US

(203) 775-1212; *Fax:* (203) 775-6452
www.i95rock.com
License: Brookfield, Fairfield County, CT held by Cumulus Licensing Corp.
Group Owner: Cumulus Media Inc.
Arbitron Metro Market: Danbury, CT; *Format:* Classic Rock
Tom Principi, General Sales Mgr
Taryn Polites, Promotions Manager

Danbury

WDAQ
01-01-1948; 98.3 MHz FM; *Hrs Open:* 24; 1.3 kw; 459 ft; N41 22 27 W73 26 47
98 Mill Plain Rd., Danbury, CT 06811 US
(203) 744-4800; *Fax:* (203) 778-4655
www.98q.com
License: Danbury, Fairfield County, CT held by Berkshire Broadcasting Corp.
Group Owner: Berkshire Broadcasting Corp.
Nat'l Reps: D & R Radio
Population Served: 250,000; *Arbitron Metro Market:* Danbury, CT; *Format:* Adult Contemp
Mike Delpha, General Sales Mgr
Rich Minor, Programming Director
Amanda Bale, Traffic Manager

*WFAR
07-19-1981; 93.3 MHz FM; 0.015 kw; 203 ft.; N41 23 44 W73 25 24
25 Chestnut Street, Danbury, CT 06810 US
(203) 748-0001; *Fax:* (203) 748-1101
www.radiofamilia.com
david@radiofamilia.com
License: Danbury, Fairfield County, CT held by Danbury Community Radio Inc.
Arbitron Metro Market: Danbury, CT; *Format:* Religious *Special Programming:* Sp 2 hrs wkly; *No. News Employees:* 1; *Target Audience:* Portuguese, Sp & It
David Abrantes, President
Helena Abrantes, Operations Dir
Jose Mingachos, News Director
David Abrantes, Director
Elio Ferreira, Director
Teresa Azevedo, Director
Octavio Rebelo, Director
Manuel Ramos, Director
AmericoVentura, Director

WLAD
10-01-1947; 800 kHz AM; *Hrs Open:* 24; 1 kw-D, 286 w-N; N41 22 27 W73 26 47
98 Mill Plain Rd., Danbury, CT 06811 US
(203) 744-4800; *Fax:* (203) 778-4655
www.wlad.com
License: Danbury, Fairfield County, CT held by Berkshire Broadcasting Corp.
Group Owner: Berkshire Broadcasting Corp.
Nat'l Network: NBC; Dial Global; *Nat'l Reps:* Katz
Population Served: 250,000; *Arbitron Metro Market:* Danbury, CT; *Format:* News/Talk
Mike Delpha, General Sales Mgr
Bart Busterna, Programming Director
Amanda Bale, Traffic Manager

*WXCI
02-10-1973; 91.7 MHz FM; *Hrs Open:* 6 AM-2 AM; 3 kw; 220 ft.; N41 23 42 W73 29 14
White Hall, 181 White Street, Danbury, CT 06810 US
(203) 837-9924
www.wxci.org
License: Danbury, Fairfield County, CT held by Western Connecticut State University Board of Trustees.
Arbitron Metro Market: Danbury, CT; *Format:* Alternative *Special Programming:* Club mus 3 hrs, jazz 3 hrs, reggae 2 hrs, new age; *Hrs. of News Programming:* News progmg 3 hrs wkly; *Target Audience:* 14-25.
Kristen King, General Manager
Darnell Carpenter, Chief Engineer

East Lyme

WNLC
04-01-1994; 98.7 MHz FM; *Hrs Open:* 24; 5.5 kw; 269 ft.; N41 23 6 W72 4 13
Mailing Address: P.O. Box 4368, Lancaster, PA 17604 US
Second Address: 89 Broad St., New London, CT 6320
(860) 442-5328; *Fax:* (860) 442-6532
www.wnlc.com
arussell@hallradio.com
License: East Lyme, New London County, CT held by Hall Communication Inc.
Group Owner: Hall Communications Inc.; acq 6-16-97; $2 million)
Nat'l Reps: Eastman Radio
Arbitron Metro Market: New London, CT; *Format:* Contemporary Hits/Top 40; *Target Audience:* Adults 25-49
Bonnie Rowbotham, Chairman
Arthur Rowbotham, President
Bill Baldwin, Operations Dir
Andy Russell, General Manager

Enfield

WMAS
12-01-1947; 94.7 MHz FM; 50 kw; 55 meters; N42 6 33 W72 36 40
1000 Hall of Fame Ave., Springfield, MA 01105 US
(413) 737-1414; *Fax:* (413) 737-1488
www.947wmas.com
info@947wmas.com
License: Enfield, CT held by Radio License Holding CBC, LLC
Group Owner: Cumulus Media Inc.
Arbitron Metro Market: Springfield, MA; *Format:* Adult Contemp
Craig Swimm, General Sales Mgr
Jim Raino, Programming Director
Erica Skubis, Promotions Manager

Fairfield

*WSHU-FM
02-01-1964; 91.1 MHz FM; *Hrs Open:* 24; 20 kw; 624 ft.; N41 16 45 W73 11 9
5151 Park Avenue, Fairfield, CT 06432 US
(203) 365-6604; *Fax:* (203) 371-7991
www.wshu.org
lombardi@wshu.org
License: Fairfield, Fairfield County, CT held by Sacred Heart University Inc.
Nat'l Network: NPR; PRI; *Wire Services:* AP
Format: News *Special Programming:* Folk 5 hrs, new age 6 hrs wkly; *Hrs. of News Programming:* news progmg 43 hrs wkly; *No. News Employees:* 4; *Target Audience:* General; all ages
Barbara Bashar, Operations Dir
George Lombardi, General Manager
Gillian Anderson, General Sales Mgr
Tom Kuser, Programming Director
Naomi Starobin, News Director
Paul Litwinovich, Chief Engineer

*WVOF
09-01-1970; 88.5 MHz FM; *Hrs Open:* 5 AM-2 AM; 0.1 kw; 33 ft.; N41 9 32 W73 15 35
North Benson Road, Barone Campus Center Box, Fairfield, CT 06430 US
(203) 254-4144; *Fax:* (203) 254-4224
www.wvof.org
License: Fairfield, Fairfield County, CT held by Fairfield University.
Arbitron Metro Market: Fairfield, CT; *Format:* Variety/Diverse; *Hrs. of News Programming:* news progmg 4 hrs wkly; *No. News Employees:* 5; *Target Audience:* 18-35.
Matt Dinnan, General Manager
Angelika Zbikowski, Station Manager
Robert Miller, Programming Director
Sarah Markham, Promotions Manager
Catherine Wolk, Music Director
Brian Alexander, Business Director
William Hollingsworth,Sports Director

Greenwich

WGCH
09-14-1964; 1490 kHz AM; *Hrs Open:* 24; 1 kw-U, ND1; N41 1 37 W73 37 59
1490 Dayton Ave., Greenwich, CT 06830 US
(203) 869-1490; *Fax:* (203) 869-3636
www.wgch.com
bob.small@wgch.com
License: Greenwich, CT held by BTR Greenwich Inc.
Group Owner: BusinessTalkRadio.Net Inc.; (acq 6-18-2003; $1.1 million)
Nat'l Network: Fox News Radio
Arbitron Metro Market: New York; *Format:* News, Talk *Special Programming:* High school sports 6 hrs, educ 2 hrs, Pol one hr,; *Hrs. of News Programming:* news progmg 35 hrs wkly; *No. News Employees:* 2 *TargetAudience:* 35 plus; very upscale, active, athletic, community-minded; *Adv. Rates:* 50; 50; 50; 50
Michael Metter, CEO
Michael Metter, President
Bob Small, Operations Dir
Elizabeth Kopyscinski, General Sales Mgr
Tony Savino, News Director
Jeff Weber, Executive Vice President
Rob Adams, Sports Commentator
Bob Small, TrafficManager

Groton

WQGN-FM
01-01-1971; 105.5 MHz FM; 3 kw; 276 ft.; N41 23 5 W72 4 13
1750 Rockville Pike, Suite 20, Rockville, MD 20852 US
(860) 443-1980; *Fax:* (860) 444-7970
www.q105.fm
License: Groton, New London County, CT
Arbitron Metro Market: New London, CT; *Format:* Contemporary Hits/Top 40; *Target Audience:* 18-49.; *Adv. Rates:* 100; 90; 100; 50
Shawn Murphy, Programming Director

WXLM
07-26-1958; 980 kHz AM; 1 kw-D, 72 w-N; N41 23 05 W72 04 13
7 Governor Winthrop Blvd., New London, CT 06320 US
(860) 443-1980; *Fax:* (860) 444-7970
www.wxlm.fm
jessica.vargas@cumulus.com
License: Groton, CT held by Radio License Holding CBC, LLC
Group Owner: Cumulus Media Inc.; (acq 4-26-2001; grpsl).
Nat'l Network: ABC
Population Served: 43,000; *Arbitron Metro Market:* New London, CT; *Format:* News/Talk, Sports; *Target Audience:* 25-49; middle income professionals
Julie Johnson, Programming Director
Jessica Vargas, Market Manager

Guilford

*WGRS
12-27-1993; 91.5 MHz FM; *Hrs Open:* 24; 3.1 kw; 82 ft.; N41 17 19 W72 39 32 *Rebroadcasts:* Rebroadcasts WMNR(FM) Monroe 100%
731 Main Street, Monroe, CT 06468 US
(203) 268-9667
www.wmnr.org
info@wmnr.org
License: Guilford, New Haven County, CT held by Monroe Board of Education.
Nat'l Network: PRI
Arbitron Metro Market: New Haven, CT; *Format:* Talk *Special Programming:* Big band 8 hrs, folk 2 hrs, new age one hr, Broadw
Jane Stadler, Operations Dir
Kurt Anderson, General Manager
Carol Babina, Development Director
Mark Morton, Engineering Dir
Rose Ryan, Membership Director

Hamden

WKCI-FM
02-10-1969; 101.3 MHz FM; 12 kw; 915 ft.; N41 26 1 W72 56 45
495 Benham St., Hamden, CT 06514 US
(203) 281-9600; *Fax:* (203) 407-4652
www.kc101.com
comments@kc101.com
License: Hamden, New Haven County, CT held by CC Licenses LLC
Group Owner: iHeartMedia; (Acq 7-24-92).
Arbitron Metro Market: New Haven, CT; *Format:* Contemporary Hits/Top 40
Zac Davis, Programming Director

*WQAQ
02-01-1973; 98.1 MHz FM; *Hrs Open:* Noon-2 AM (S-Su); 8 AM-2 AM (M-F); 0.018 kw; -79 ft.; N41 25 10.6 W72 54 22.6
275 Mount Carmel Avenue, Hamden, CT 06518 US
(203) 582-5278; *Fax:* (203) 582-8098
www.angelfire.com/ct2/wqaqradio/
License: Hamden, New Haven County, CT
Arbitron Metro Market: New Haven, CT; *Format:* Alternative, News, 62, Rock/AOR, Talk; *Hrs. of News Programming:* News progmg 10 hrs wkly; *Target Audience:* 18-30.
Bill Shoulders, Operations Dir
Chris Cooper, General Manager
Sally Densa, General Sales Mgr
Glenn Giangrande, Programming Director
Carlos Lanesee, Promotions Manager
Alison Keller, News Director
Jessie Elgarten, ProgrammingDirector

WQUN
07-17-1960; 1220 kHz AM; *Hrs Open:* 24
275 Mt. Carmel Avenue, Hamden, CT 06518 US

(203) 582-8984; *Fax:* (203) 582-5372
www.wqun.com
ray.andrewsen@quinnipiac.edu
License: Hamden, CT held by Quinnipiac University
Nat'l Network: CBS; Jones Radio Networks
Arbitron Metro Market: New Haven, CT; *Format:* News *Special Programming:* Irish 2 hrs, Broadway 2hrs, big bands 4 hrs wkly; *No. News Employees:* 2; *Target Audience:* General; community, business & cultural leaders
Ray Andrewsen, General Manager
Greg Little, News Director
Bob Radil, Chief Engineer

Hartford

WCCC-FM
06-07-1960; 106.9 MHz FM; *Hrs Open:* 24; 23 kw; 725 ft.; N41 47 48 W72 47 52
32 Fairfield Street, Boston, MA 02116 US
(860) 525-1069; *Fax:* (860) 246-9084
www.wccc.com
License: Hartford, Hartford County, CT
Nat'l Reps: Eastman Radio
Arbitron Metro Market: Hartford, CT; *Format:* Rock/AOR; *Target Audience:* 18-49; adult men
Howard (Woody) Tanger, CEO/COO
Howard ""Woody"" Tanger, President
Jon Skonieczny, Promotions Manager

WDRC
12-10-1922; 1360 kHz AM; *Hrs Open:* 24; 5 kw-D, DAN; 5 kw-N, DAN; N41 48 47 W72 41 48
869 Blue Hills Ave., Bloomfield, CT 06002 US
(860) 243-1115; *Fax:* (860) 286-8257
www.talkofconnecticut.com
License: Hartford, Hartford County, CT held by Connoisseur Media Licenses LLC
Group Owner: Connoisseur Media LLC; (acq 7-7-2014).
Nat'l Network: Westwood One; AP Radio; *Regional Network:* CRN; *Nat'l Reps:* Katz Radio; *Wire Services:* AP
Arbitron Metro Market: Hartford, CT; *Format:* News, News/Talk, 86; *No. News Employees:* 1; *Target Audience:* 40+.
Kristin Okesson, General Manager
Stu Gorlick, Director of Sales
Keith Dakin, Programming Director
Suzi Klonk, Marketing and Promotions Director
Rowena White, Local Sales Manager - Digital

WDRC-FM
01-01-1939; 102.9 MHz FM; *Hrs Open:* 24; 19.5 kw horiz, 19.54 kw vert; 810 ft.; N41 33 44 W72 50 40
869 Blue Hills Ave., Bloomfield, CT 06002 US
(860) 243-1115; *Fax:* (860) 286-8257
www.1029thewhale.com
License: Hartford, Hartford County, CT held by Connoisseur Media Licenses LLC
Group Owner: Connoisseur Media LLC
Wire Services: AP; Metro Weather Service Inc.
Population Served: 1,030,500; *Arbitron Metro Market:* Hartford-New Britain-Middletown, CT; *Format:* Classic Rock; *No. News Employees:* 1; *Target Audience:* 25-64.
Kristin Okesson, General Manager
Stu Gorlick, Director of Sales
Keith Dakin, Programming Director
Suzi Klonk, Marketing and Promotions Director
Rowena White, Local Sales Manager - Digital

WHCN
01-01-1939; 105.9 MHz FM; *Hrs Open:* 24; 16 kw; 866 ft.; N41 33 47 W72 50 42
10 Columbus Blvd., Hartford, CT 06106 US
(860) 723-6000; *Fax:* (860) 723-7090
www.theriver1059.com
License: Hartford, Hartford County, CT held by Capstar TX LLC
Group Owner: iHeartMedia; (acq 8-30-00; grpsl).
Nat'l Reps: Christal
Arbitron Metro Market: Hartford-New Britain-Middletown, CT; *Format:* Rock/AOR
Joe Madden, Sales
Dave Symonds, Programming Director
Sarah Hannon, Media Integration Director

*WJMJ
10-18-1976; 88.9 MHz FM; *Hrs Open:* 5 am-Midnight; 6.2 kw; 607 ft.; N41 45 9 W72 59 40
Archdioces of Hartford, 785 Asylum Avenue, Hartford, CT 06105 US
(860) 242-8800; *Fax:* (860) 242-4886
www.wjmj.org
License: Hartford, Hartford County, CT held by St. Thomas Seminary-Archdiocese of Hartford.
Nat'l Network: ABC; *Wire Services:* AP
Arbitron Metro Market: Hartford-New Britain-Middletown, CT; *Format:* Religious *Special Programming:* Educ, foreign one hr wkly; *Hrs. of News Programming:* news progmg 10 hrs wkly; *No. News Employees:* 1 *TargetAudience:* 40-65; working, middle-class, family group
Archbishop Henry Mansell, President
John Ellinger, General Manager
John Masternak, Programming Director
Ivor Hugh, Music Director

WPOP
07-01-1935; 1410 kHz AM; *Hrs Open:* 24; 5 kw-D, DA2; 5 kw-N, DA2; N41 41 35 W72 45 30
10 Columbus Blvd., Hartford, CT 06106 US
(860) 723-6000; *Fax:* (860) 723-7090
www.newsradio1410.com
License: Hartford, CT held by Capstar TX LLC
Group Owner: iHeartMedia
Nat'l Network: ESPN Radio
Arbitron Metro Market: Hartford-New Britain-Middletown, CT; *Format:* News, News/Talk, 86; *Hrs. of News Programming:* news progmg 25 hrs wkly; *No. News Employees:* 8; *Target Audience:* 35 plus.
Joe Madden, General Sales Mgr
Timothy Spence, Programming Director
Sarah Hannon, Media Integration Director

*WQTQ
11-01-1961; 89.9 MHz FM; *Hrs Open:* 24; 0.115 kw; 85 ft.; N41 47 47 W72 41 42
415 Granby Street, Hartford, CT 06112 US
(860) 695-1899,(860) 695-1900; *Fax:* (860) 722-6605
www.wqtq.com/wqtq
wqtqfm@yahoo.com
License: Hartford, Hartford County, CT held by Hartford Board of Education.
Arbitron Metro Market: Hartford-New Britain-Middletown, CT; *Format:* Gospel, Jazz, 72, Smooth Jazz *Special Programming:* Gospel 12 hrs, clean hip hop rap 19 hrs, reggae/calypso 6 hrs, jazz 12 hrs, Rhythm and blues 18 hrs wkly *Target Audience:* 15-45; literate, professional, quality mus listeners
Thomas Smith, COO
Connie Coles, President/General Manager
Shirley Minnifield, Business Manager

*WRTC-FM
02-01-1958; 89.3 MHz FM; *Hrs Open:* 24; 0.3 kw; 95 ft.; N41 45 6 W72 41 29
300 Summit Street, Hartford, CT 06106 US
(860) 297-2450; *Fax:* (860) 987-6214
www.wrtcfm.com
License: Hartford, Hartford County, CT held by Trustees of Trinity College.
Arbitron Metro Market: Hartford-New Br; *Format:* Variety/Diverse *Special Programming:* Class 4 hrs, gospel 6 hrs, West Indian 6 hrs, Pol; *Target Audience:* 15 plus.
Devon MacGillivary, General Manager
Matthew Mainuli, Station Manager
Benton Bair, Programming Director
Jonathan Costello, Promotions Manager

WTIC
02-10-1925; 1080 kHz AM; *Hrs Open:* 24; 50 kW; N41 46 39 W72 48 19
10 Executive Dr., Farmington, CT 06032 USA
(860) 677-6700
www.wtic.com
info@wtic.com
License: Hartford, CT held by CBS Radio Stations Inc.
Group Owner: CBS Radio; (acq 11-13-98; grpsl).
Nat'l Network: CBS
Arbitron Metro Market: Hartford, CT; *Format:* News/Talk, News, 86; *Hrs. of News Programming:* News progmg 30 hrs wkly; *Target Audience:* 35-59; intelligent, mature adults

WTIC-FM
12-01-1980; 96.5 MHz FM; *Hrs Open:* 24; 20 kW; 384 ft.; N41 46 27 W72 48 20
10 Executive Dr., Farmington, CT 06032 USA
(860) 677-6700
www.965tic.com
r.jones@entercom.com
License: Hartford, Hartford County, CT held by CBS Radio Stations Inc.
Group Owner: CBS Radio
Arbitron Metro Market: Hartford, CT; *Format:* Contemporary Hits/Top 40; *Hrs. of News Programming:* News progmg 8 hrs wkly; *Target Audience:* 18-34; intelligent, spirited, youthful adults
Stephanie Perl, General Sales Mgr
Ryan Jones, Programming Director
Katie Pallotta, Promotions Manager

WZMX
09-06-1990; 93.7 MHz FM; *Hrs Open:* 24; 17 kW; 174 ft.; N41 33 44 W72 50 42
10 Executive Dr., Farmington, CT 06032 USA
(860) 677-6700; *Fax:* (860) 674-8427
www.hot937.com
License: Hartford, Hartford County, CT held by CBS Radio Stations Inc.
Group Owner: CBS Radio; (acq 6-8-98; grpsl).
Arbitron Metro Market: Hartford, CT; *Format:* Urban Contemporary; *Target Audience:* 18-34; adults in Hartford & New Haven
Stephanie Perl, Sales Manager
DJ Buck, Programming Director
Jason Ricketts, Promotions Director

Hartford-Meriden

WKSS
06-01-1947; 95.7 MHz FM; 16.5 kw; 879 ft.; N41 33 41 W72 50 39
10 Columbus Blvd, Hartford, CT 06106 US
(860) 723-6000; *Fax:* (860) 493-7090
www.kiss957.com
License: Hartford-Meriden, Hartford County, CT held by Capstar TX LLC
Group Owner: iHeartMedia; (acq 8-30-00; grpsl).
Regional Network: Conn. Radio Net; *Nat'l Reps:* Christal
Arbitron Metro Market: Hartford-New Britain-Middletown, CT; *Format:* Contemporary Hits/Top 40; *Target Audience:* 18-34.
Steve Honeycomb, Regional Market Manager
Dave Symonds, Operations Manager
Joe Madden, General Sales Mgr
Zac Davis, Programming Director
Sarah Hannon, Media Integration Director

Ledyard

WWRX
11-30-1995; 107.7 MHz FM; *Hrs Open:* 24; 1.4 kw; 492 ft.; N41 27 35 W71 55 40
758 Colonel Ledyard Highway, Ledyard, CT 06339 US
(860) 464-1065; *Fax:* (860) 464-8143
www.jammin1077.com
License: Ledyard, New London County, CT held by Fuller Broadcasting International LLC
Arbitron Metro Market: New London, CT; *Format:* Contemporary Hits/Top 40; *Hrs. of News Programming:* News progmg one hr wkly; *Target Audience:* 25-54; mobile, upscale
John Fuller, President
Tim Burrows, General Sales Mgr
Brian Ram, Programming Director
Lori Robbins, Promotions Manager
Debbie Frenier, Traffic Manager

Litchfield

WZBG
07-08-1992; 97.3 MHz FM; *Hrs Open:* 24; 3 kw; 328 ft.; N41 48 8 W73 9 50
Mailing Address: 49 Commons Drive, Litchfield, CT 06759 US
Second Address: PO Box 1497, Litchfield, CT 06759
(860) 567-3697; *Fax:* (860) 567-3292
www.wzbg.com
info@wzbg.com
License: Litchfield, Litchfield County, CT held by Local Girls & Boys Broadcasting Corp.
Nat'l Network: CBS
Arbitron Metro Market: Litchfield, CT; *Format:* Adult Contemp, News *Special Programming:* Jazz 2 hrs wkly; *No. News Employees:* 3; *Target Audience:* 25-54.
Jennifer Parsons, General Manager

Manchester

WNEZ
05-18-1958; 1230 kHz AM; *Hrs Open:* 24
135 Burnside Ave., East Hartford, CT 06108 US
(860) 524-0001; *Fax:* (860) 548-1922
mtanderson2942@sbcglobal.net
License: Manchester, CT held by Gois Broadcasting
Arbitron Metro Market: Hartford-New Britain-Middletown, CT; *Format:* News, News/Talk, 86
Zzzzzzzzzzzzzzzzz, Chairman
Ivan Gois, President
Paul Gois, General Manager
Robbie Delgados, Programming Director

RADIO - U.S.

Meriden

WMMW
01-01-1946; 1470 kHz AM; *Hrs Open:* 24; 2.5 kw-D, DA2; 2.5 kw-N, DA2; N41 33 14 W72 48 7 *Rebroadcasts:* Rebroadcast WDRC (AM) Hartford 100%
869 Blue Hills Ave., Bloomfield, CT 06002 US
(860) 243-1115; *Fax:* (860) 286-8257
www.talkofconnecticut.com
License: Meriden, CT held by Connoisseur Media LLC
Nat'l Network: Westwood One; AP Radio; ABC; *Regional Network:* CRN; *Nat'l Reps:* McGavren Guild; *Wire Services:* ABC
Arbitron Metro Market: New Haven, CT; *Format:* News, Talk; *Target Audience:* 40 plus; middle income, grassroots America
Jeff Warshaw, CEO/COO
Keith Dakin, Operations Dir
Kristin Okesson, General Manager
Stu Gorlick, Director of Sales

***WNPR**
06-11-1978; 90.5 MHz FM; *Hrs Open:* 24; 18.5 kw horiz, 13.5 kw vert; Ant 1,148 ft; N41 33 42 W72 50 41
1049 Asylum Ave., Hartford, CT 06126
(860) 278-5310; *Fax:* (860) 275-7403
www.wnpr.org
info@wnpr.org
License: Meriden, New Haven County, CT held by Connecticut Public Television & Radio.
Nat'l Network: NPR; PRI
Population Served: 2,000,000 *Hrs. of News Programming:* news progmg 26 hrs wkly; *No. News Employees:* 5
Jerry Franklin, CEO/President
John Dankosky, News Director
Joseph Zareski, Chief Engineer

Middletown

***WESU**
09-01-1939; 88.1 MHz FM; *Hrs Open:* 24; 6 kw; 36 ft.; N41 33 12 W72 39 29
45 Bread Street, Middletown, CT 06457 US
(860) 685-7703/685-7700/685-7707; *Fax:* (860) 704-0608
www.wesufm.org
president@wesufm.org
License: Middletown, Middlesex County, CT held by Wesleyan University
Nat'l Network: NPR; *Wire Services:* UPI
Arbitron Metro Market: Middletown, CT; *Format:* Variety/Diverse *Special Programming:* NPR, Paacifica and Local Public affairs by day, Free form music at night and weekends Blues 10 hrs, gospel 6 hrs, reggae 10 hrs, metal 5hrs wkly; *Hrs. of News Programming:* 12hrs /day; *Target Audience:* discerning listeners; *Adv. Rates:* sliding scale underwriting opp
Mary Barrett, President
Ben Michael, General Manager
Hannah Ryan, Programming Director
Nate Brown, Tech Director
Virgil Taylor, Vice President
Rebecca Seidel, Personnel Director
Hannah Bahedry, Production Director
KatherineColien, Public Affairs Director
Danielle Pruitt, Public Relations Director
Reta Gasser & Ethan Hill, Music Directors

***WIHS**
10-11-1969; 104.9 MHz FM; *Hrs Open:* 24; 3 kw; 300 ft; N41 30 18 W72 39 32
1933 S. Main St., Hartford, CT 06457
(860) 346-1049; *Fax:* (860) 347-1049
www.wihsradio.org
wihs@snet.net
License: Middletown, Middlesex County, CT held by Connecticut Radio Fellowship Inc.
Nat'l Network: Moody
Population Served: 2,000,000 *Special Programming:* Children 9 hrs wkly; *Hrs. of News Programming:* News progmg 18 hrs wkly; *No. News Employees:* 2; *Target Audience:* General.; *Adv. Rates:* none
William Bacon, President
Paul Kretschmer, Operations Dir
G.J. Gerard, General Manager
Mark Channon, Station Manager
Ron Gangwer, Programming Manager
Paul Kretschmer, News Director
G.J. Gerard, Chief Engineer

WMRD
12-12-1948; 1150 kHz AM; *Hrs Open:* 24; 2.5 kw-D, ND1; 0.046 kw-N, ND1; N41 33 26 W72 37 13
167 North Seir Hill Rd, Norwalk, CT 06850 US
(860) 347-9673; *Fax:* (860) 347-7704
www.wliswmrd.net
radio@wliswmrd.net
License: Middletown, CT held by Crossroads Communications L.L.C.
Nat'l Network: Westwood One; CBS Radio; Jones Radio Networks; *Regional Network:* Conn. Radio Net.
Arbitron Metro Market: Hartford, CT; *Format:* Talk *Special Programming:* Pol 2 hrs, It 2 hrs, Celtic one hr, Caribbean one; *Hrs. of News Programming:* news progmg 8 hrs wkly; *No. News Employees:* 1 *TargetAudience:* 25-54; adults; *Adv. Rates:* 58; 47; 43; 38
Don DeCesare, President/General Manager

Milford

WFIF
09-04-1965; 1500 kHz AM; *Hrs Open:* Sunrise-sunset; 5 kw-D, DAD; N41 11 33 W73 6 5
90 Kay Ave., Milford, CT 06460 US
(203) 878-5915; *Fax:* (203) 882-8756
www.lifechangingradio.com
License: Milford, New Haven County, CT held by K.W. Dolmar Broadcasting Co. Inc.
Group Owner: Blount Communications Group; (acq 4-82; $425,000;
Nat'l Network: Salem Radio Network
Arbitron Metro Market: Milford, CT; *Format:* Religious *Special Programming:* Black 6 hrs wkly; *Target Audience:* General.
William Blount, President
Jon Vaught, Station Manager

Monroe

***WMNR**
01-31-1974; 88.1 MHz FM; *Hrs Open:* 24; 5 kw; 404 ft.; N41 19 8 W73 15 13
PO Box 920, Monroe, CT 06468 US
(203) 268-9667
www.wmnr.org
info@wmnr.org
License: Monroe, Fairfield County, CT held by Monroe Board of Education.
Nat'l Network: PRI
Arbitron Metro Market: Bridgeport, CT; *Format:* Talk *Special Programming:* Big band 8 hrs, folk 2 hrs, new age one hr, Broadw
Jane Stadler, Operations Dir
Kurt Anderson, General Manager
Carol Babina, Development Director
Mark Morton, Chief Engineer

Naugatuck

WFNW
02-26-1961; 1380 kHz AM; 5 kw-D, DA2; 0.5 kw-N, DA2; N41 30 35 W73 3 20
40 Mallane Lane, Naugatuck, CT 06770 US
(203) 723-0678
License: Naugatuck, CT held by Candido Broadcasting Inc.

Candido Carrelo, President

New Britain

***WFCS**
10-17-1972; 107.7 MHz FM; *Hrs Open:* 24; 0.036 kw; 108 ft.; N41 41 36 W72 45 49
1615 Stanley Street, New Britain, CT 06050 US
(860) 832-1883; *Fax:* (860) 832-3757
License: New Britain, Hartford County, CT held by Trustees of Central Connecticut State University.
Arbitron Metro Market: New Britain, CT *Special Programming:* Blues 12 hrs, Sp 2 hrs wkly; *Hrs. of News Programming:* news progmg 10 hrs wkly; *No. News Employees:* 4; *Target Audience:* 14-50.
Adam Morgan, General Manager
Mike McDonald, General Sales Mgr
Matt Rockwell, Programming Director

WLAT
05-20-1949; 910 kHz AM; *Hrs Open:* 24
135 Burnside Avenue, East Hartford, CT 06108 US
(860) 524-0001; *Fax:* (860) 548-1922
mtanderson2942@sbcglobal.net
License: New Britain, CT held by Freedom Communications of Connecticut Inc.
Group Owner: Freedom Communications of Connecticut Inc.; (acq 6-1-2004; $3 million with WNEZ(AM) Manchester)
Arbitron Metro Market: Hartford, CT; *Format:* Spanish
Ivon Gois, President
Paul Gois, General Manager
Robbie Delgado, Programming Director
Marion Thornton, Senior Marketing Manager

WRCH
09-28-1992; 100.5 MHz FM; *Hrs Open:* 24; 7.5 kW; 850 ft.; N41 42 13 W72 49 57
10 Executive Dr., Farmington, CT 06032 USA
(860) 677-6700
www.wrch.com
wrch@cbs.com
License: New Britain, Hartford County, CT held by CBS Radio Stations Inc.
Group Owner: CBS Radio; (acq 6-8-98; grpsl).
Arbitron Metro Market: Hartford-New Britain-Middletown, CT; *Format:* Adult Contemp; *Target Audience:* 25-54; women, adults
Geri DeRosa, General Sales Mgr
Allan Camp, Programming Director
Mike Stacy, Promotions Director
Mary Scanlon, News Director

WRYM
08-01-1946; 840 kHz AM; *Hrs Open:* 24; 1 kw-D, DAN; 0.125 kw-N, DAN; N41 41 10 W72 43 47
1056 Willard Ave., Newington, CT 06111 US
(860) 666-5646; *Fax:* (860) 666-5647
www.wrymradio.com
License: New Britain, CT held by Eight Forty Broadcasting Corp.
Nat'l Network: CNN Radio; *Nat'l Reps:* McGavren Guild
Arbitron Metro Market: Hartford-New Br *Special Programming:* Pol 5 hrs wkly, Italian 2 hrs wkly; *Hrs. of News Programming:* news progmg 8 hrs wkly; *No. News Employees:* 4; *Target Audience:* General; Hispanic
Dina Cassarino, Operations Dir
Walter Martinez, General Manager
Danny Delgado, News Director
John Ramsey, Chief Engineer
Silvina Martinez, Traffic Manager
Darvin Garcia, Music Director
Enzo Minniti, Webmaster

New Canaan

***WSLX**
01-01-1975; 91.9 MHz FM; 0.019 kw horiz; 174 ft.; N41 11 32 W73 29 46
377 North Wilton Road, New Canaan, CT 06840 US
(203) 966-5612; *Fax:* (203) 966-3409
www.wslx.org
info@stlukesct.org
License: New Canaan, Fairfield County, CT held by St. Luke's Foundation Inc.
Format: Variety/Diverse
Jeffrey Kress, General Manager
Troy Haynie, Broadcast Director

New Haven

WAVZ
09-01-1947; 1300 kHz AM; *Hrs Open:* 24; 1 kw-D, DAN; 1 kw-N, DAN; N41 17 16 W72 56 48
495 Benham Street, Hamden, CT 06514 US
(202) 281-9600
www.espnradio1300.com
License: New Haven, CT held by CC Licenses LLC.
Group Owner: iHeartMedia; (acq 12-18-92; $10 with WKCI-FM Hamden;
Nat'l Network: ESPN Radio; *Nat'l Reps:* Clear Channel
Arbitron Metro Market: New Haven, CT; *Format:* Sports, Talk
Steve Honeycomb, Regional Market Manager
Dave Symonds, Operations Manager
Thomas Principi, General Sales Mgr
Timothy Spence, Programming Director
Sarah Hannon, Media Integration Director

WELI
10-01-1935; 960 kHz AM; 5 kw-D, DAN; 5 kw-N, DAN; N41 22 14 W72 56 15
495 Benham Street, Hamden, CT 06514 US
(203) 281-9600
www.960weli.com
License: New Haven, CT held by CC Licenses LLC.
Group Owner: iHeartMedia; (acq 8-5-85).
Regional Network: Conn. Radio Net; *Nat'l Reps:* Katz Radio
Arbitron Metro Market: New Haven, CT; *Format:* News, News/Talk, 86; *Target Audience:* 18 plus.
Steve Honeycomb, Regional Market Manager
Dave Symonds, Operations Manager
Thomas Principi, General Sales Mgr
Timothy Spence, Programming Director
Sarah Hannon, Media Integration Director

WPLR
01-01-1944; 99.1 MHz FM; 15 kw; 906 ft.; N41 25 22 W72 57 6
600 Congress Ave., Suite 1400, Austin, TX 78701 US
(203) 783-8200; *Fax:* (203) 783-8373
www.wplr.com
License: New Haven, New Haven County, CT held by Connoisseur Media Licenses LLC
Group Owner: Connoisseur Media LLC; (acq 8-2000; grpsl)
Arbitron Metro Market: New Haven, CT; *Format:* Rock/AOR
Stu Gorlick, General Sales Mgr
Ed Sabatino, Programming Director
Samuel Tilery, Promotions Manager

WYBC
01-01-1944; 1340 kHz AM
5151 Park Avenue, Fairfield, CT 06825 US
(203) 365-0425; *Fax:* (203) 776-2446
www.wshu.org
info@wybc.com
License: New Haven, CT held by Yale Broadcasting Co. Inc.
Regional Network: Conn. Radio Net.
Arbitron Metro Market: New Haven, CT; *Format:* Easy Listening
Special Programming: Sp one hr wkly
George Lombardi, General Manager
Tom Kuser, Programming Director
Dan Katz, News Director
Paul Litwinovich, Chief Engineer
Gillian Anderson, Development Director
Lori Miller, Corporate Underwriting Director
Laurie Veillette,Business Manager

WYBC-FM
03-09-1959; 94.3 MHz FM; *Hrs Open:* 24; 3 kw horiz, 2.6 kw vert; 472 ft.; N41 20 59 W72 58 23
440 Wheelers Farms Road, Suite 302, Milford, CT 06461 US
(203) 783-8200; *Fax:* (203) 783-8383
www.943wybc.com
License: New Haven, New Haven County, CT held by Yale Broadcasting Co.
Group Owner: LMA Connoisseur Media, LLC
Nat'l Network: ABC
Arbitron Metro Market: Milford, CTÿ; *Format:* Urban Contemporary *Special Programming:* Gospel 8 hrs, jazz 8 hrs, folk 3 hrs wkly; *Hrs. of News Programming:* News progmg 10 hrs wkly; *Target Audience:* Urban & collegeage listeners.
Kristin Okesson, General Manager
Stu Gorlick, Director, Sales
Juan Castillo, Programming Director
Drew Carrano, Marketing/Promotions Director

New London

***WCNI**
01-01-1974; 90.9 MHz FM; *Hrs Open:* 1 PM-5 PM (M-F); 2 kw vert; 187 ft.; N41 22 53 W72 6 28
Box 4972, New London, CT 06320 US
(860) 439-2853 (860) 439-2850; *Fax:* (860) 439-2805
www.wcniradio.org
License: New London, New London County, CT held by Connecticut College Broadcasting Association Inc.
Arbitron Metro Market: New London, CT; *Format:* Variety/Diverse
Special Programming: Black 3 hrs, class 6 hrs, folk 9 hrs, gospel 3 hrs, jazz 9 hrs, Pol 3 hrs, Sp 3 hrs, women's 3 hrs wkly; *Target Audience:* General;all musical audiences except pop
John Tyler, General Manager/Chief Engineer

WKNL
01-01-1970; 100.9 MHz FM; *Hrs Open:* 24; 6 kw; 325 ft.; N41 26 27 W72 8 29
30 Cuprak Road, Norwich, CT 06360-0551 US
(860) 877-3511; *Fax:* (860) 442-6532
www.kool101fm.com
arussell@hallradio.com
License: New London, New London County, CT held by Hall Communications Inc.
Group Owner: Hall Communications Inc.; acq 1-19-95; $3.5 million with co-located AM;
Nat'l Reps: Eastman Radio
Arbitron Metro Market: New London, CT; *Format:* Oldies; *Hrs. of News Programming:* News progmg 2 hrs wkly; *Target Audience:* 25-54.
Bonnie Rowbotham, Chairman
Arthur Rowbotham, President
Bill Baldwin, Executive VP/Operations Director
Andy Russell, VP/General Manager
Bob Houde, Local Sales Manager
Jim Reed, Programming Director

Norfolk

***WSGG**
05-17-2001; 89.3 MHz FM; *Hrs Open:* 24; 0.14 kw vert; 92 ft.; N42 0 38 W73 12 8
P. O. Box 4594, Hartford, CT 06147 US
(860) 243-5630
www.revivalfm.com
License: Norfolk, Litchfield County, CT held by Revival Christian Ministries Inc.
Arbitron Metro Market: Hartford, CT; *Format:* Christian
Samuel Girona, General Manager

North Granby

***WWQA**
11-21-2011; 89.9 MHz FM; kw
US
(877) 700-8047
www.thelifefm.com
License: North Granby, CT held by The Power Foundation

Norwalk

WFOX
01-01-1966; 95.9 MHz FM; 3 kw; 299 ft.; N41 6 54 W73 26 6
600 Congress Ave., Suite 1400, Austin, TX 78701 US
(203) 783-8200; *Fax:* (203) 783-8383
www.959thefox.com/
steve.soyland@coxinc.com
License: Norwalk, Fairfield County, CT held by Connoisseur Media Licenses LLC
Group Owner: Connoisseur Media Licenses LLC
Arbitron Metro Market: Norwalk, CT; *Format:* Classic Rock
Christopher Gabrelcik, President
Michael Barone, Station Manager
Steve Soyland, Promotions Manager

WNLK
01-01-1948; 1350 kHz AM; *Hrs Open:* 24 *Rebroadcasts:* Rebroadcasts WSTC(AM) Stamford 100%
5151 Park Avenue, Fairfield, CT 06825 US
(203) 365-6604; *Fax:* (203) 371-7991
www.wshu.org
License: Norwalk, CT held by Sacred Heart University
Regional Network: Conn. Radio Net.
Arbitron Metro Market: Norwalk, CT; *Format:* News, News/Talk, 86; *Hrs. of News Programming:* news progmg 20 hrs wkly; *No. News Employees:* 4; *Target Audience:* 25-54.
Gillian Anderson, Devvelopment Director
Dan Katz, News Director
Laurie Veillette, Business Manager
Kate Remington, Music Director
Lori Miller, Director, Corporate Underwriting

Norwich

WCTY
05-01-1968; 97.7 MHz FM; *Hrs Open:* 24; 1.9 kw; 410 ft.; N41 28 28 W72 6 14
30 Cuprak Road, Norwich, CT 06360-0551 US
(860) 887-3511; *Fax:* (860) 886-7649
www.wcty.com
dave@wcty.com
License: Norwich, New London County, CT held by WICH Inc.
Group Owner: Hall Communications Inc.
Nat'l Reps: Eastman Radio; *Wire Services:* AP
Arbitron Metro Market: New London, CT; *Format:* Country; *Target Audience:* 25-54.
Andy Russell, VP/General Manager
Bob Houde, Sales Manager
Dave Elder, Programming Director

WICH
09-01-1946; 1310 kHz AM; *Hrs Open:* 24; 5 kw-U, DA-2; N41 33 10 W72 04 34
Box 551, 40 Cuprak Rd., Norwich, CT 17604
(860) 887-3511; *Fax:* (860) 886-7649
www.wich.com
License: Norwich, New London County, CT held by WICH Inc.
Group Owner: Hall Communications Inc.; (acq 7-1-65)
Nat'l Network: ABC; *Regional Network:* Conn. Radio Net; *Nat'l Reps:* Eastman Radio; *Wire Services:* AP
Population Served: 220,000; *Arbitron Metro Market:* New London, CT *Special Programming:* Pol 2 hrs wkly; *Hrs. of News Programming:* 5; *No. News Employees:* 2; *Target Audience:* 35 plus.
Bonnie Rowbotham, Chairman
Arthur Rowbotham, President
Bill Baldwin, Operations Dir
Andy Russell, General Manager
Bob Reed, Station Manager
Bob Houde, Local Sales Manager
Stu Bryer, Programming Director
Susan Harley, PromotionsManager
Roger Arnold, Chief Engineer

***WPKT**
10-17-1981; 89.1 MHz FM; *Hrs Open:* 24; 5.1 kw; Ant 590 ft; N41 31 11 W72 10 04 *Rebroadcasts:* Rebroadcasts WPKT(FM) Meriden 100%
1049 Asylum Ave., Hartford, CT 06106
(860) 278-5310; *Fax:* (860) 244-9624
www.wnpr.org
wherewelive@wnpr.org
License: Norwich, New London County, CT held by Connecticut Public Television & Radio.
Nat'l Network: NPR; PRI; AP Radio
Arbitron Metro Market: New London, CT; *Hrs. of News Programming:* news progmg 38 hrs wkly; *No. News Employees:* 13; *Target Audience:* General.
Jerry Franklin, President/CEO
Nancy Bauer, VP, Underwriting
John Dankosky, News Director
Joe Zareski, Chief Engineer
Eugene Amatruda, Production

Old Saybrook

WLIS
09-27-1956; 1420 kHz AM; *Hrs Open:* 24 hrs; 5 kw-D, DAN; 0.5 kw-N, DAN; N41 19 38 W72 23 21 *Rebroadcasts:* Rebroadcasts WMRD(AM) Middletown 90%
777 River Road, Middletown, CT 06457 US
(860) 347-9673; *Fax:* (860) 347-7704
www.wliswmrd.net
radio@wliswmrd.net
License: Old Saybrook, CT held by Crossroads Communications of Old Saybrook L.L.C.
Nat'l Network: CNN Radio; Westwood One; Talk Radio Network;
Regional Network: Conn. Radio Net.
Format: Talk *Special Programming:* Jazz 4 hrs wkly; *Hrs. of News Programming:* news progmg 8 hrs wkly; *No. News Employees:* 1; *Target Audience:* 25-64; Adults
Don DeCesare, President

Pawcatuck

WBMW
12-24-1992; 106.5 MHz FM; *Hrs Open:* 24; 3.1 kw; 459 ft.; N41 27 43 W72 1 27
756 Colonel Ledyard Hwy, Ledyard, CT 06339 US
(860) 464-1066; *Fax:* (860) 464-8143
www.wbmw.com
production@wbmw.com
License: Pawcatuck, New London County, CT held by Redwolf Broadcasting Corp.
Nat'l Network: USA
Arbitron Metro Market: New London, CT; *Format:* Adult Contemp; *No. News Employees:* 1; *Target Audience:* Adults 25-54 & women 25-54
John Fuller, President/General Manager
Tim Burrows, General Sales Mgr
Teresa Berry, Promotions Manager
Debbie Frenier, Traffic Manager

Pomfret

***WBVC**
01-01-2001; 91.1 MHz FM; 0.1 kw vert; 289 ft.; N41 53 27 W71 57 24
P O Box 128, Pomfret, CT 06258 US
(860) 963-5911; *Fax:* (860) 963-2086
www.web.pomfretschool.org/wbvc/
wbvc@pomfretschool.org
License: Pomfret, Windham County, CT held by Pomfret School.
Format: Variety/Diverse
Tim Peck, General Manager

Putnam

WINY
05-03-1953; 1350 kHz AM; *Hrs Open:* 24; 5 kw-D, ND1; 0.079 kw-N, ND1; N41 54 10 W71 53 43
P.O. Box 231, Putnam, CT 06260 US
(860) 928-1350; *Fax:* (860) 928-7878
www.winyradio.com
info@winyradio.com
License: Putnam, CT held by Osbrey Broadcasting Co.
Nat'l Network: AP Radio; Jones Radio Networks; *Wire Services:* AP
Format: Adult Contemp *Special Programming:* Talk 11 hrs wkly; *Hrs. of News Programming:* news progmg 18 hrs wkly; *No. News*

Employees: 3; *Target Audience:* 25-54 plus; adults; *Adv. Rates:* 31; 27; 31; 25
Gary Osbrey, President
Karen Osbrey, Operations Dir
Karen Osbrey, General Sales Mgr
Shaina Smith, News Director
John Wilbur, Sports Director
Kerri LeClerc, Traffic Manager
Adam Heath, Disc Jockey
Bill Alley, Disc Jockey
JasonBleau, Disc Jockey
Alyssa Moody, News Reporter

Ridgefield

WAXB
03-15-1985; 850 kHz AM; *Hrs Open:* 6 AM-10 PM; 2.5 kw; N41 17 27 W73 29 16
98 Mill Plain Rd., Danbury, CT 06811 US
(203) 744-4800; *Fax:* (203) 778-4655
www.b1073fm.com
License: Ridgefield, Fairfield County, CT held by Berkshire Broadcasting Corp.
Group Owner: Berkshire Broadcasting Corp.
Nat'l Network: ABC; *Nat'l Reps:* D & R Radio
Population Served: 500,000; *Arbitron Metro Market:* Danbury, CT; *Format:* Contemporary Hits/Top 40
Mike Delpha, General Sales Mgr
Amanda Bale, Traffic Manager

Salisbury

WKZE-FM
09-01-1992; 98.1 MHz FM; *Hrs Open:* 24; 1.8 kw; 604 ft.; N41 55 8 W73 34 22
7392 S. Broadway, Red Hook, NY 12571 US
(845) 758-9810; *Fax:* (845) 758-9819
www.wkze.com
info@wkze.com
License: Salisbury, Litchfield County, CT held by Willpower Radio L.L.C.
Nat'l Network: AP Radio
Arbitron Metro Market: Poughkeepsie, NY; *Format:* Triple A; *Hrs. of News Programming:* news progmg 2 hrs wkly; *No. News Employees:* 1; *Target Audience:* 25-54.; *Adv. Rates:* 35; 35; 35; na
Will Stanley, General Manager
Pete Nugent, Programming Director
Paul Higgins, Sales Manager

Sharon

WHDD
12-23-1986; 1020 kHz AM; *Hrs Open:* 6 AM-6 PM; 1.8 kw-C, NDD; 2.5 kw-D, NDD; N41 58 35 W73 31 27
67 Main Street, Sharon, CT 06069 US
(860) 364-4640; *Fax:* (860) 364-7035
www.am1020whdd.com
jg@robinhoodradio.com
License: Sharon, CT held by Willpower Radio L.L.C.
Arbitron Metro Market: Poughkeepsie, NY; *Format:* Talk
Marshall Miles, President/General Manager

WQQQ
10-07-1993; 103.3 MHz FM; *Hrs Open:* 24; 1.5 kw; 610 ft.; N41 55 8 W73 34 22
5151 Park Avenue, Fairfield, CT 06825 US
(860) 435-3333; *Fax:* (860) 435-3334
www.wqqq.com
WQQQfm@yahoo.com
License: Sharon, Litchfield County, CT held by The Ridgefield Broadcasting Corp.
Wire Services: AP
Format: Adult Contemp *Special Programming:* Oldies, Jazz, MOR; *Hrs. of News Programming:* news progmg 14 hrs wkly; *No. News Employees:* 1; *Target Audience:* Upscale adults; 25-54
George Lombardi, General Manager
Tom Kuser, Programming Director
Dan Katz, News Director
Paul Litwinovich, Chief Engineer
Gillian Anderson, Development Director
Lori Miller, Corporate Underwriting Director
Laurie Veillette,Business Manager

*WHDD-FM
05-05-2008; 91.9 MHz FM; *Hrs Open:* 24; 0.65 kw; -62 ft.; N41 53 32 W73 27 16
67 Main Street, Sharon, CT 06069 US
(860) 364-4640; *Fax:* (860) 364-7035
www.robinhoodradio.com
jg@robinhoodradio.com
License: Sharon, Litchfield County, CT held by Tri-State Public Communications Inc.
Nat'l Network: NPR; PRI
Arbitron Metro Market: Sharon, CT; *Format:* Public Affairs, News
Marshall Miles, President/General Manager

Shelton

*WRXC
01-01-1977; 90.1 MHz FM; *Hrs Open:* 24; 0.045 kw; 482 ft.; N41 21 43 W73 6 48 *Rebroadcasts:* Rebroadcasts WMNR(FM) Monroe 100%
PO Box 920, Monroe, CT 06468 US
(203) 268-9667
www.wmnr.org
info@wmnr.org
License: Shelton, Fairfield County, CT held by Monroe Board of Education.
Nat'l Network: PRI
Format: Talk *Special Programming:* Big band 8 hrs, folk 2 hrs, new age one hr, Broadw
Jane Stadler, Operations Dir
Kurt Anderson, General Manager
Carol Babina, Director, Development
Mark Morton, Chief Engineer

Somers

*WDJW
10-06-1986; 89.7 MHz FM; 0.009 kw horiz; -59 ft.; N41 57 43 W72 27 51 *Rebroadcasts:* Rebroadcasts WWUH(FM) West Hartford
Ninth District Road, Somers, CT 06071 US
(860) 749-2501(860) 749-0719; *Fax:* (860) 749-9264
License: Somers, Tolland County, CT held by Somers Board of Education.
Arbitron Metro Market: Somers, CT; *Format:* Alternative, Jazz
Peter Stone, President

South Kent

*WGSK
12-25-1987; 90.1 MHz FM; *Hrs Open:* 24; 0.077 kw; 128 ft.; N41 40 54 W73 29 13 *Rebroadcasts:* Rebroadcasts WMNR(FM) Monroe 100%
375 Monroe Turnpike, Monroe, CT 06468 US
(203) 268-9667
www.wmnr.org
info@wmnr.org
License: South Kent, Litchfield County, CT held by Monroe Board of Education.
Nat'l Network: PRI
Format: Talk *Special Programming:* Big band 8 hrs, folk 2 hrs, new age one hr, Broadw
Jane Stadler, Operations Dir
Kurt Anderson, General Manager
Carol Babina, General Sales Mgr

Southington

WXCT
09-02-1969; 990 kHz AM; *Hrs Open:* 24; 2.5 kw-D, DA2; 0.08 kw-N, DA2; N41 34 59 W72 53 1
440 Old Turnpike Road, Plantsville, CT 06479 US
(860) 621-1754; *Fax:* (860) 426-1172
www.canticonuevoradio.com
License: Southington, CT held by Davidson Media Station WXCT LLC.
Group Owner: Davidson Media Group LLC; (acq 4-30-2004; $1.4 million)
Arbitron Metro Market: Hartford, CT; *Format:* Christian
Chris McMurray, President
Joe Rizza, General Manager
Nelson Brudys, Programming Director

Stamford

*WEDW-FM
02-17-1992; 88.5 MHz FM; 2 kw horiz, 1.8 kw vert; 302 ft.; N41 2 49 W73 31 36 *Rebroadcasts:* Rebroadcasts WPKT (FM) Meriden100%
240 New Britain Avenue, Hartford, CT 06126 US
(860) 275-7550; *Fax:* (860) 244-9624
www.cpbn.org/
info@wnpr.org
License: Stamford, Fairfield County, CT held by Connecticut Public Broadcasting Inc.
Arbitron Metro Market: Stamford, CT; *Format:* News, News/Talk, 86
Kim Grehn, Station Manager
Nancy Bauer, Promotions Manager
John Dankosky, News Director
Joe Zareski, Chief Engineer

WSTC
09-18-1941; 1400 kHz AM; *Hrs Open:* 24
600 Congress Ave., Suite 1400, Austin, TX 78701 US
(203) 845-3030; *Fax:* (203) 229-1765
License: Stamford, CT held by Cox Radio Inc.
Group Owner: Cox Radio Inc.
Nat'l Network: CNN Radio; Westwood One; *Regional Network:* Conn. Radio Net; *Nat'l Reps:* Katz Radio
Arbitron Metro Market: New York; *Format:* News, News/Talk, 86; *Hrs. of News Programming:* news progmg 16 hrs wkly; *No. News Employees:* 4; *Target Audience:* 25-54.
Robin Faller, Operations Dir
Eric McDonald, Programming Director
Dawn Wachner, Promotions Manager

Stonington

WMOS
11-01-1981; 102.3 MHz FM; *Hrs Open:* 24; 3 kw; Ant 328 ft; N41 24 23 W71 50 15
Mailing Address: 7 Gov. Winthrop Blvd., New London, CT 06320 US
Second Address: 1 Mohegan Sun Blvd., Uncasville, CT
(860) 443-1980
www.1023thewolf.com
jessica.vargas@cumulus.com
License: Stonington, CT held by Radio License Holding CBC, LLC
Group Owner: Cumulus Media Inc.; (acq 4-26-2001; grpsl)
Population Served: 927; *Arbitron Metro Market:* Stonington, CT; *Format:* Classic Rock
Julie Johnson, Programming Director
Jessica Vargas, Market Manager

Storrs

*WHUS
01-01-1956; 91.7 MHz FM; *Hrs Open:* 24; 1.2 kw horiz, 4.4 kw vert; 492 ft.; N41 48 50 W72 15 36
Student U. Bldg Bx U-8r, Storrs, CT 06269 US
(860) 486-4007; *Fax:* (860) 486-2955
www.whus.org
info@whus.org
License: Storrs, Tolland County, CT held by Board of Trustees University of Connecticut.
Nat'l Network: AP Radio; NPR; *Wire Services:* AP
Arbitron Metro Market: Hartford-New Britain-Middletown, CT; *Format:* Variety/Diverse *Special Programming:* Sp 3 hrs wkly; *Hrs. of News Programming:* 18 hrs wkly; *No. News Employees:* 2; *Adv. Rates:* 25; 25; 25;25
Ryan King, General Manager
Sylvia Cunningham, News Director
Erin Walsh, Marketing Director
Barbara Becker, Business Manager
Trevor Morrison, Music Director
Santiago Pelaez, Promotions Director
John Zatowski, Chief Engineer

Torrington

*WAPJ
01-01-1997; 89.9 MHz FM; 0.04 kw; 276 ft.; N41 48 9 W73 9 54.3 *Rebroadcasts:* WWUH(FM) West Hartford
855 University Drive, Torrington, CT 06790 US
(860) 489-9033; *Fax:* (860) 482-7614
www.wapjfm.com
info@wapj.org
License: Torrington, Litchfield County, CT held by The I.B. and Zena H. Temkin Foundation Inc.
Arbitron Metro Market: Torrington, CT; *Format:* Variety/Diverse; *Hrs. of News Programming:* News progmg 10 hrs wkly; *Target Audience:* General; any and all
Mark Channon, Operations Manager
John Ramsey, General Manager

WSNG
610 kHz AM; *Hrs Open:* 24; 1 kw-D, DA2; 0.5 kw-N, DA2; N41 45 28 W73 3 6 *Rebroadcasts:* Rebroadcasts WDRC(AM) Hartford 100%
869 Blue Hills Ave., Bloomfield, CT 06002 US
(860) 243-1115; *Fax:* (860) 286-8257
www.talkofconnecticut.com
License: Torrington, Litchfield County, CT held by Connoisseur Media Licenses LLC
Group Owner: Connoisseur Media LLC
Nat'l Network: Westwood One; AP Radio; *Regional Network:* CRN; *Nat'l Reps:* Katz Radio; *Wire Services:* AP

Arbitron Metro Market: Hartford-New Britain-Middletown, CT; *Format:* News, News/Talk, 86; *Target Audience:* 40 plus; middle income, grassroots America
Kristin Okesson, General Manager
Stu Gorlick, Director of Sales
Keith Dakin, Programming Director
Suzi Klonk, Marketing and Promotions Director
Rowena White, Local Sales Manager - Digital

Vernon

***WCTF**
11-21-1982; 1170 kHz AM
4135 Northgate Blvd, Suite 1, Sacramento, CA 95834 US
(800) 543-1495; *Fax:* (916) 641-8238 (510) 633-7983
www.familyradio.com
familyradio@familyradio.org
License: Vernon, CT held by Family Stations Inc.
Group Owner: Family Stations Inc.; acq 1-86; $136,000;
Arbitron Metro Market: Hartford, CT; *Format:* Religious
Tom Evans, General Manager

Wallingford

***WWEB**
11-10-1976; 89.9 MHz FM; 0.015 kw horiz; -16 ft.; N41 27 34 W72 48 48 *Rebroadcasts:* Rebroadcasts WWUH (FM) West Hartford 80%
333 Christian Street, Wallingford, CT 06492 US
(203) 697-2506; *Fax:* (203) 697-2186
License: Wallingford, New Haven County, CT held by Choate Rosemary Hall Foundation.
Arbitron Metro Market: Wallingford, CT; *Format:* Variety/Diverse
Special Programming: Class 2 hrs, C&W 2 hrs wkly; *Target Audience:* High school students.
Chris Bielizna, General Manager

Waterbury

WATR
06-15-1934; 1320 kHz AM; *Hrs Open:* 24; 5 kw-D, DA2; 1 kw-N, DA2; N41 32 12 W73 1 52
1 Broadcast Lane, Waterbury, CT 06706 US
(203) 755-1121; *Fax:* (203) 574-3025
www.watr.com
talkback@watr.com
License: Waterbury, CT held by WATR Inc.
Nat'l Network: AP Radio
Arbitron Metro Market: Waterbury, CT; *Format:* News, News/Talk, 64, Talk *Special Programming:* Pol 2 hrs, It 3 hrs wkly; *Hrs. of News Programming:* news progmg 15 hrs wkly; *No. News Employees:* 2; *Target Audience:* 35-64.
Tom Chute, General Manager
Trish Torello, General Sales Mgr
Frank Marro, News/Sports Director

WMRQ-FM
12-25-1967; 104.1 MHz FM; *Hrs Open:* 24; 50 kw; Ant 859 ft; N41 33 41 W72 50 39
131 New London Turnpike, Suite 101, Glastonbury, CT 6033
(860) 657-1041; *Fax:* (860) 657-1042
www.radio1041.fm
sales@radio1041.fm
License: Waterbury, New Haven County, CT held by Red Wolf Broadcasting
Nat'l Network: ABC; *Nat'l Reps:* Christal
Population Served: 900,000; *Arbitron Metro Market:* Hartford, CT; *Format:* Adult Contemp; *Target Audience:* 18-49.
John Fuller, President
Brian Ram, VP, Programming

WWCO
01-01-1946; 1240 kHz AM; *Hrs Open:* 24; 1 kw-U, ND1; N41 33 59 W73 3 23 *Rebroadcasts:* Rebroadcasts WDRC(AM) Bloomfield 90%
869 Blue Hills Ave., Bloomfield, CT 06002 US
(860) 243-1115; *Fax:* (860) 286-8257
www.talkofconnecticut.com
License: Waterbury, New Haven County, CT held by Connoisseur Media Licenses LLC
Group Owner: Connoisseur Media LLC
Arbitron Metro Market: Hartford, CT; *Format:* News, News/Talk, 86; *No. News Employees:* 2; *Target Audience:* 35 plus.
Kristin Okesson, General Manager
Stu Gorlick, Director of Sales
Keith Dakin, Programming Director
Suzi Klonk, Marketing and Promotions Director
Rowena White, Local Sales Manager - Digital

WWYZ
08-01-1961; 92.5 MHz FM; *Hrs Open:* 24; 17 kw; 879 ft.; N41 33 47 W72 50 42
10 Columbus Boulevard, Hartford, CT 06106 US
(860) 723-6000; *Fax:* (860) 493-7090
www.country925.com
License: Waterbury, New Haven County, CT held by Capstar TX LLC
Group Owner: iHeartMedia; (acq 8-30-00; grpsl).
Nat'l Network: Westwood One; *Nat'l Reps:* Christal
Arbitron Metro Market: Waterbury, CT; *Format:* Country; *Hrs. of News Programming:* news progmg 5 hrs wkly; *No. News Employees:* 1; *Target Audience:* 25-54.
Dave Symonds, Senior Vice President of Programming
Bob Cleaver, Sales Manager
Sarah Hannon, Media Integration Director

West Hartford

WCCC
01-01-1947; 1290 kHz AM; *Hrs Open:* 24
1039 Asylum Avenue, Hartford, CT 06105 US
(860) 525-1069; *Fax:* (860) 246-9084
www.beethoven.com
License: West Hartford, CT held by Merlin Media
Nat'l Reps: Eastman Radio
Arbitron Metro Market: Hartford, CT; *Format:* Talk; *Target Audience:* 18-54.
Woody Tanger, CEO
Alan Tolz, COO
Mike Karolyi, Programming Director
John Ramsey, Chief Engineer
Michelle Bassos, Marketing Manager/Director of Sales

***WWUH**
07-15-1968; 91.3 MHz FM; *Hrs Open:* 24; 0.44 kw; 784 ft.; N41 46 27 W72 48 20
200 Bloomfield Avenue, West Hartford, CT 06117 US
(860) 768-4701; *Fax:* (860) 768-5701
www.wwuh.org
wwuh@hartford.edu
License: West Hartford, Hartford County, CT held by University of Hartford.
Wire Services: Pacifica Network News
Arbitron Metro Market: Hartford, CT; *Format:* Variety/Diverse
Special Programming: It 3 hrs, Por 3 hrs, Pol 3 hrs, It 3 hrs, foreign/; *Hrs. of News Programming:* News progmg 8 hrs wkly; *Target Audience:* General.
John Ramsey, President/General Manager

West Haven

***WNHU**
01-01-1973; 88.7 MHz FM; *Hrs Open:* 6 AM-2 AM; 1.7 kw; 161 ft.; N41 17 29 W72 57 40
300 Orange Avenue, West Haven, CT 06516 US
(203) 479-8800
www.wnhu.net
wnhu887@gmail.com
License: West Haven, New Haven County, CT held by University of New Haven Inc.
Arbitron Metro Market: New Haven, CT; *Format:* Variety/Diverse
Special Programming: Jazz 12 hrs, folk 6 hrs, Irish 5 hrs, metal 9 hrs,; *Hrs. of News Programming:* News progmg 12 hrs wkly; *Target Audience:* General.
Bryan Lane, General Manager

Westport

WEBE
09-01-1962; 107.9 MHz FM; *Hrs Open:* 24; 50 kw; 384 ft.; N41 10 14 W73 11 5
2 Lafayette Square, Bridgeport, CT 06604 US
(203) 333-9108; *Fax:* (203) 333-9108
www.webe108.com
danny@webe108.com
License: Westport, Fairfield County, CT held by Cumulus Licensing Corp.
Group Owner: Cumulus Media Inc.; (acq 3-14-02; grpsl).
Nat'l Reps: Christal
Arbitron Metro Market: Westport, CT; *Format:* Adult Contemp
Special Programming: Talk one hr wkly; *Hrs. of News Programming:* news progmg 3 hrs wkly; *No. News Employees:* 1; *Target Audience:* 25-54; upscalefemales; *Adv. Rates:* 330; 330; 330; 100
Danny Lyons, Operations Dir
Ann McManus, VP/Marketing Manager
Marnie Klebart, Sales Manager

***WSHU**
04-15-1959; 1260 kHz AM; *Hrs Open:* 6 AM-7 PM; 1 kw-D, DA2; 0.009 kw-N, DA2; N41 7 44 W73 23 20 *Rebroadcasts:* Rebroadcasts WSHU(FM) Fairfield 30%
5151 Park Avenue, Fairfield, CT 06432 US
(203) 365-0425; *Fax:* (203) 371-7991
www.wshu.org
lombardi@wshu.org
License: Westport, CT held by Sacred Heart University Inc.
Nat'l Network: NPR; PRI; *Wire Services:* AP
Arbitron Metro Market: New York, NY; *Format:* News, News/Talk, 86; *Hrs. of News Programming:* news progmg 45 hrs wkly; *No. News Employees:* 2; *Target Audience:* General.
George Lombardi, General Manager
Gillian Anderson, General Sales Mgr
Tom Kuser, Programming Director
Naomi Starobin, News Director
Paul Litwinovich, Chief Engineer

***WWPT**
01-01-1975; 90.3 MHz FM; 0.33 kw; 128 ft.; N41 10 19 W73 19 43
Mailing Address: 110 Myrtle Avenue, Westport, CT 06880 US
Second Address: 110 Myrtle Ave., Westport, CT 6880
(203) 341-1381; *Fax:* (203) 226-6875
License: Westport, Fairfield County, CT held by Board of Education, Town of Westport.
Arbitron Metro Market: Westport, CT; *Format:* Variety/Diverse
Special Programming: Slovak 3 hrs wkly; *Target Audience:* 14-24; youth
Mike Zito, Operations Dir
Jim Honeycutt, Faculty Advisor
Ian Goodman, Music Director
Steve Warshavsky, Sports Director

Willimantic

***WECS**
02-06-1982; 90.1 MHz FM; 0.43 kw; 381 ft.; N41 41 0 W72 13 1
83 Windham St., Willimantic, CT 06226 US
(860) 465-5354; *Fax:* (860) 465-5073
www.easternct.edu/wecs/
wecs@easternct.edu
License: Willimantic, Windham County, CT held by Eastern Connecticut State University.
Arbitron Metro Market: Willimantic, CT; *Format:* Rock/AOR
Special Programming: Jazz 16 hrs, relg 3 hrs, Sp 9 hrs wkly
John Zatowski, General Manager

WILI
10-05-1957; 1400 kHz AM; *Hrs Open:* 24; 1 kw-U, ND1; N41 42 54 W72 11 23
720 Main Street, Willimantic, CT 06226 US
(860) 456-1111; *Fax:* (860) 456-9501
www.wili.com
donna@wili.com
License: Willimantic, CT held by Nutmeg Broadcasting Co.
Group Owner: Hall Communications Inc.; (acq 8-30-2005; $1.8 million with co-located FM)
Nat'l Network: ABC; *Regional Network:* Conn. Radio Net; *Nat'l Reps:* Eastman Radio; *Wire Services:* AP
Format: Adult Contemp, News *Special Programming:* Ukrainian one hr, Sp one hr, relg 2 hrs,; *Hrs. of News Programming:* news progmg 10 hrs wkly; *No. News Employees:* 3; *Target Audience:* 25 plus; general *Adv.Rates:* 21; 18; 21; 15
Colin Rice, Executive VP
Andy Russell, General Manager
Donna Evan, General Sales Mgr
Mike Morrissette, News Director

WILI-FM
06-16-1975; 98.3 MHz FM; *Hrs Open:* 24; 1.05 kw; 525 ft.; N41 41 0 W72 12 59
720 Main Street, Williamantic, CT 06226 US
(860) 456-1111; *Fax:* (860) 456-9501
www.wili.com
donna@wili.com
License: Willimantic, Windham County, CT held by Nutmeg Broadcasting Co.
Group Owner: Hall Communications Inc.; 8/30/2005
Nat'l Reps: Eastman Radio; *Wire Services:* AP
Arbitron Metro Market: New London, CT; *Format:* Contemporary Hits/Top 40; *Hrs. of News Programming:* news progmg 6 hrs wkly; *No. News Employees:* 1; *Target Audience:* 22-44; college students, young married couples,young families; *Adv. Rates:* 38;34;38;32
Colin Rice, Executive VP
Andy Russell, General Manager
Donna Evan, General Sales Mgr
Mike Morrissette, News Director

Windsor

WKND
05-04-1961; 1480 kHz AM; 0.5 kw-D, DA2; 0.014 kw-N, DA2; N41 51 10 W72 40 43
544-J Windsor Ave, Windsor, CT 06095 US

(860) 524-0001; *Fax:* (860) 524-0336
www.wknd.fm
mtanderson2942@sbcglobal.net
License: Windsor, CT held by Gois Broadcasting LLC
Group Owner: Gois Broadcasting LLC; (acq 11-29-2004)
Nat'l Network: ABC
Arbitron Metro Market: Hartford-New Britain-Middletown, CT; *Format:* Blues, Talk *Special Programming:* Gospel 5 hrs, jazz 3 hrs wkly
Ivon Gois, President
Paul Gois, General Manager
Marion Anderson, General Sales Mgr

Windsor Locks

WUCS
07-01-1990; 97.9 MHz FM; 3.4 kw; 528 ft; N42 05 05 W72 42 14
10 Columbus Boulevard, Hartford, CT 06106
(860) 723-6000
www.979espn.com
License: Windsor Locks, Hartford County, CT held by Capstar TX LLC
Group Owner: iHeartMedia; (acq 8-30-00; grpsl).
Arbitron Metro Market: Hartford, CT; *Format:* Sports; *Target Audience:* 25-54.; *Adv. Rates:* 110; 100; 105; 55
Bob Cleaver, General Sales Mgr
Timothy Spence, Programming Director
Sarah Hannon, Media Integration Director

Delaware

Bethany Beach

WJKI
01-01-1996; 103.5 MHz FM; 1.45 kw; 479 ft.; N38 34 21 W75 6 58 *Rebroadcasts:* Simulcast w/ WGBG (FM) Seaford 100%
20200 Dupont Boulevard, Georgetown, DE 19947 US
(302) 856-2567; *Fax:* (302) 856-7633
www.bigclassicrock.com
wgbg@bigclassicrock.com
License: Bethany Beach, Sussex County, DE held by Adams Radio Group
Group Owner: Great Scott Broadcasting
Format: Classic Rock
Andrew Murr, Operations Manager
Jim McHugh, General Manager
Joanne Fitzhugh, Business Manager
Jeff Evans, Sales Manager

WKZP
01-01-1974; 95.9 MHz FM; 10.5 kw; Ant 469 ft; N38 25 20 W75 08 23
Gateway Crossing, 351 Tilghman Rd., Salisbury, MD 53202 US
(410) 742-1923; *Fax:* (410) 742-2329
www.kiss959fm.com
License: Bethany Beach, Sussex County, DE held by Capstar TX LLC
Group Owner: iHeartMedia; (acq 8-7-2000; grpsl).
Nat'l Reps: Clear Channel
Arbitron Metro Market: Salisbury-Ocean City, MD; *Format:* Contemporary Hits/Top 40; *Target Audience:* 18-34.
Chris Walus, Regional Market President
Jimmy Steele, Senior Vice President of Programming
Paul Burton, Senior Vice President of Sales
Victoria Kent, Promotions Director

Christiana

***WXHL-FM**
08-01-1994; 89.1 MHz FM; *Hrs Open:* 24; 0.001 kw horiz, 1.2 kw vert; 66 ft.; N39 40 38 W75 39 47
P.O. Box 372, Wilmington, DE 19899 US
(302) 731-0690; *Fax:* (302) 738-3090
www.thereachfm.com
listenercare@myreachradio.com
License: Christiana, New Castle County, DE held by Priority Radio Inc.
Group Owner: Priority Radio Inc.; (acq 12-10-99)
Arbitron Metro Market: Christiana, DE; *Format:* Christian, Religious
Dan Edwards, Operations Dir
Steve Hare, General Manager
Larry Humm, General Sales Mgr
Dave Kirby, Programming Director

Dover

WDOV
01-01-1948; 1410 kHz AM; *Hrs Open:* 24; 5 kw-D, DA2; 5 kw-N, DA2; N39 12 3 W75 33 55
1575 McKee Road, Dover, DE 19904 US
(302) 395-9800; *Fax:* (302) 674-5978
www.wdov.com
License: Dover, DE held by Capstar TX LLC
Group Owner: iHeartMedia; (acq 8-30-2000; grpsl)
Nat'l Network: Westwood One; *Nat'l Reps:* Clear Channel
Arbitron Metro Market: Dover, DE; *Format:* News, News/Talk, 84, Talk; *Hrs. of News Programming:* news progmg 162 hrs wkly; *No. News Employees:* 2; *Target Audience:* 25-54.
Chris Walus, Market Manager
Martha Masters, Sales Manager
Kyle Moran, Promotions Manager
Phil Feliceangeli, News Director

WDSD
01-01-1956; 94.7 MHz FM; 50 kw; 377 ft.; N39 12 3 W75 33 55
920 W. Basin Road, Suite 400, New Castle, DE 19720 US
(302) 395-9800; *Fax:* (302) 395-9808
www.wdsd.com
License: Dover, Kent County, DE held by Capstar TX LLC
Group Owner: iHeartMedia
Nat'l Network: Motor Racing Net; *Nat'l Reps:* Clear Channel
Arbitron Metro Market: Wilmington, DE; *Format:* Country; *Hrs. of News Programming:* news progmg 2 hrs wkly; *No. News Employees:* 1; *Target Audience:* 18-49.
Chris Walus, Market Manager
Martha Masters, Sales Manager
Sky Phillips, Programming Director
Kyle Moran, Promotions Manager

***WRTX**
04-05-1995; 91.7 MHz FM; *Hrs Open:* 24; 0 kw horiz, 0.58 kw vert; 315 ft.; N39 12 3 W75 33 55 *Rebroadcasts:* Rebroadcasts WRTI(FM) Philadelphia, PA 100%
1509 Cecil B. Moore Avenue, 3rd Floor, Philadelphia, PA 19121 US
(215) 204-8405; *Fax:* (215) 204-7027
www.wrti.org
comments@wrti.org
License: Dover, Kent County, DE held by Temple University of the Commonwealth System of Higher Education.
Nat'l Network: NPR; AP Radio
Format: Jazz; *No. News Employees:* 1; *Target Audience:* 30-65.
Tobias Poole, Operations Dir
David Conant, General Manager
William Johnson, Station Manager
Jane Kelly, Director of Development
Jack Moore, Programming Director
Jeffrey DePolo, Engineering Dir
Lorna Nixon, Traffic Manager
Jessica Schultz, Digital Content Manager

WRJE
09-28-2005; 1600 kHz AM; *Hrs Open:* 24; 5 kw-D, DA2; 1 kw-N, DA2; N39 10 11 W75 33 13
1076 South Chapel Street, Newark, DE 19702 US
License: Dover, DE held by K-5 Communications LLC

J. Roberto Ekonomo, General Manager
Vladimir Rosales, Programming Director
Aida Ekonomo, Marketing Director

Fenwick Island

***WLBW**
04-01-1994; 92.1 MHz FM; 3 kw; 469 ft.; N38 25 20 W75 8 23
5700 W. Oaks Boulevard, Rocklin, CA 95765 US
(410) 742-1923; *Fax:* (410) 742-2329
License: Fenwick Island, Sussex County, DE held by Educational Media Foundation
Arbitron Metro Market: Salisbury-Ocean City, MD; *Format:* Oldies; *Target Audience:* 25-54.; *Adv. Rates:* 50; 40; 50; 25
Mike Novak, President/CEO

Georgetown

WJWL
06-23-1951; 900 kHz AM; *Hrs Open:* 24; 10.5 kw-D, DA2; 1.08 kw-N, DA2; N38 42 29 W75 24 28
23 NE Front Street, Milford, DE 19963 US
(302) 422-2600; *Fax:* (302) 424-1630
digital900@aol.com
License: Georgetown, DE held by Adams Radio Group
Group Owner: Great Scott Broadcasting
Nat'l Network: CNN Radio; *Nat'l Reps:* ABC Radio Sales
Arbitron Metro Market: Salisbury-Ocean City, MD; *Format:* Spanish *Special Programming:* Relg 6 hrs wkly; *Hrs. of News Programming:* news progmg 10 hrs wkly; *No. News Employees:* 11; *Target Audience:* 25-54;mature adults
Jim McHugh, President
Danny Perez, General Manager
Lisette Perez, Programming Director
Kevin Andrade, Digital Media Director

WZBH
07-04-1969; 93.5 MHz FM; *Hrs Open:* 24; 11 kw; 486 ft.; N38 31 24 W75 17 55
119 Naylor Mill Road, Suite 10A, Salisbury, MD 21801 US
(410) 202-8102
www.wzbhrocks.com
License: Georgetown, Sussex County, DE held by Adams Radio Group
Group Owner: Great Scott Broadcasting
Arbitron Metro Market: Salisbury-Ocean City; *Format:* Contemporary Hits/Top 40; *Target Audience:* Adults; baby boomers
Johnnt Maze, Program Director
Garrett Mcauliffe, Promotions Director

WAKE-AM
07-04-1969; 1500 MHz AM; *Hrs Open:* 24; 11 kw; 486 ft.; N38 31 24 W75 17 55
2755 Sager Road, Valparaiso, IN 46383 US
(219)-462-6111; *Fax:* (219)-462-4880
www.wakeradio.com
License: Georgetown, Sussex County, DE held by Adams Radio Group
Group Owner: Adams Radio Group
Arbitron Metro Market: Salisbury-Ocean City; *Format:* Contemporary Hits/Top 40; *Target Audience:* Adults; baby boomers
Johnnt Maze, Program Director
Garrett Mcauliffe, Promotions Director

WLJE-FM
07-04-1969; 105.5 MHz FM; *Hrs Open:* 24; 11 kw; 486 ft.; N38 31 24 W75 17 55
2755 Sager Road, Valparaiso, IN 46383 US
(219)-462-6111; *Fax:* (219)-462-4880
www.wakeradio.com
License: Georgetown, Sussex County, DE held by Adams Radio Group
Group Owner: Adams Radio Group
Arbitron Metro Market: Salisbury-Ocean City; *Format:* Contemporary Hits/Top 40; *Target Audience:* Adults; baby boomers
Johnnt Maze, Program Director
Garrett Mcauliffe, Promotions Director

WZVN-FM
07-04-1969; 107.1 MHz FM; *Hrs Open:* 24; 11 kw; 486 ft.; N38 31 24 W75 17 55
2755 Sager Road, Valparaiso, IN 46383 US
(219)-462-6111; *Fax:* (219)-462-4880
www.1071thez.com
License: Georgetown, Sussex County, DE held by Adams Radio Group
Group Owner: Adams Radio Group
Arbitron Metro Market: Salisbury-Ocean City; *Format:* Adult Contemp; *Target Audience:* Adults; baby boomers
Johnnt Maze, Program Director
Garrett Mcauliffe, Promotions Director

WXRD-FM
07-04-1969; 103.9 MHz FM; *Hrs Open:* 24; 11 kw; 486 ft.; N38 31 24 W75 17 55
2755 Sager Road, Valparaiso, IN 46383 US
(219)-462-6111; *Fax:* (219)-462-4880
www.xrock1039.com
License: Georgetown, Sussex County, DE held by Adams Radio Group
Group Owner: Adams Radio Group
Arbitron Metro Market: Salisbury-Ocean City; *Format:* Adult Contemp; *Target Audience:* Adults; baby boomers
Johnnt Maze, Program Director
Garrett Mcauliffe, Promotions Director

KWML
07-04-1969; 104.5 MHz FM; *Hrs Open:* 24; 11 kw; 486 ft.; N38 31 24 W75 17 55
2755 Sager Road, Valparaiso, IN 46383 US
(219)-462-6111; *Fax:* (219)-462-4880
www.kool1045fm.com
License: Georgetown, Sussex County, DE held by Adams Radio Group
Group Owner: Adams Radio Group
Arbitron Metro Market: Salisbury-Ocean City; *Format:* Oldies; *Target Audience:* Adults; baby boomers
Aaron Criswell, General Manager
Ernesto Garcia, Operations Manager
Joey Hernandez, Program Director
Jim Halk, Program Director
Mike Jensen, General Sales Manager
Jaime Reddish, Promotions Director
Jorge Soto, Traffic Director

KWML-AM
07-04-1969; 570 MHz AM; *Hrs Open:* 24; 11 kw; 486 ft.; N38 31 24 W75 17 55
2755 Sager Road, Valparaiso, IN 46383 US
(219)-462-6111; *Fax:* (219)-462-4880
www.kool1045fm.com
License: Georgetown, Sussex County, DE held by Adams Radio Group
Group Owner: Adams Radio Group
Arbitron Metro Market: Las Cruces; *Format:* Oldies; *Target Audience:* Adults; baby boomers
Aaron Criswell, General Manager
Ernesto Garcia, Operations Manager
Joey Hernandez, Program Director
Jim Halk, Program Director
Mike Jensen, General Sales Manager
Jaime Reddish, Promotions Director
Jorge Soto, Traffic Director

KSNM-FM
07-04-1969; 570 MHz AM; *Hrs Open:* 24; 11 kw; 486 ft.; N38 31 24 W75 17 55
1355 California Ave., Las Cruces, MN 88001 US
575-525-9298; *Fax:* 575-525-9419
www.classichits987.com
License: Georgetown, Sussex County, DE held by Adams Radio Group
Group Owner: Adams Radio Group
Arbitron Metro Market: Las Cruces; *Format:* Classic Rock, Oldies; *Target Audience:* Adults; baby boomers
Aaron Criswell, General Manager
Ernesto Garcia, Operations Manager
Joey Hernandez, Program Director
Jim Halk, Program Director
Mike Jensen, General Sales Manager
Jaime Reddish, Promotions Director
Jorge Soto, Traffic Director

WLYV-AM
07-04-1969; 1450 MHz AM; *Hrs Open:* 24; 11 kw; 486 ft.; N38 31 24 W75 17 55
2000 Lower Huntington Road, Fort Wayne, IN 46819 US
(260) 747-1511; *Fax:* (260) 7474-1511
License: Georgetown, Sussex County, DE held by Adams Radio Group
Group Owner: Adams Radio Group
Arbitron Metro Market: Fort Wayne; *Format:* Oldies, Oldies; *Target Audience:* Adults; baby boomers
Aaron Criswell, General Manager
Ernesto Garcia, Operations Manager
Joey Hernandez, Program Director
Jim Halk, Program Director
Mike Jensen, General Sales Manager
Jaime Reddish, Promotions Director
Jorge Soto, Traffic Director

Harrington

***WKNZ**
88.7 MHz FM; 0 kw horiz, 25 kw vert; 322 ft.; N38 53 30 W75 34 48
PO Box 680, Milford, DE 19960 US
(302) 684-3149; *Fax:* (302) 684-2905
www.887thebridge.com
License: Harrington, Kent County, DE held by Eagle's Nest Fellowship Church.
Arbitron Metro Market: Harrington, DE
William Sammons, President

Laurel

WLYV-AM
11-19-1991; 103.3 MHz AM; *Hrs Open:* 24; 6 kw; 328 ft.; N38 30 12 W75 39 39
2000 Lower Huntington Road, Fort Wayne, IN 46819 US
(260) 747-1511; *Fax:* (260) 747-3999
taylor@argfw.com
License: Laurel, Sussex County, DE held by Adams Radio Group
Group Owner: Great Scott Broadcasting; acq 2-13-98; $1.5 million).
Arbitron Metro Market: Fort Wayne; *Format:* Adult Contemp; *Hrs. of News Programming:* News progmg 6 hrs wkly; *Target Audience:* 25-49.
Chris Monk, Vice President & Market Manager
Kevin Musselman, Director Of Sales
Eddie Didier, Chief Engineer
Susan Mullen, Business Manager

Lewes

WXDE
06-01-1991; 105.9 MHz FM; *Hrs Open:* 24; 6 kw; Ant 341 ft; N38 38 36 W75 13 00 *Rebroadcasts:* Rebroadcasts WKTT(FM) Salisbury, MD 100%
Box 909, Salisbury, MD 21803
(410) 219-3500,(410) 548-1543; *Fax:* (410) 548-1543
www.catcountryradio.com
License: Lewes, Sussex County, DE held by Delmarva Broadcasting Co.
Group Owner: Delmarva Broadcasting Co.; (acq 6-26-97; grpsl)
Nat'l Network: Motor Racing Net; *Nat'l Reps:* Katz Radio; *Wire Services:* AP
Population Served: 225,000; *Arbitron Metro Market:* Salisbury-Ocean City, MD *Special Programming:* NASCAR; *Hrs. of News Programming:* news progmg 3 hrs wkly; *No. News Employees:* 1; *Target Audience:* 25-54.
Mike Schollenberger, Sales Manager
Dan Gaffney, Programming Director
Mike Kazala, General Manager
Brian K. Hall, Promotions Manager
Amy Webb, Traffic Manager
Jeff Twilley, Chief Engineer

***WPBD**
06-20-2012; 91.5 MHz FM; kw
US
License: Lewes, DE held by Allied Communications Network Two

Middletown

***WXHM**
91.9 MHz FM; 0.28 kw vert; 319 ft.; N39 26 37 W75 43 24
US
(302) 731-0690; *Fax:* (302) 738-3090
License: Middletown, New Castle County, DE held by Priority Radio Inc.
Group Owner: Priority Radio Inc.
Arbitron Metro Market: Middletown, DE
Steve Hare, General Manager

Milford

WAFL
05-19-1973; 97.7 MHz FM; 3 kw; 328 ft.; N38 55 39 W75 29 20
Mailing Address: 2727 Shipley Rd., P.O. Box 7492, Wilmington, DE 19803 US
Second Address: 1666 Blairs Pond Rd., Milford, DE 19963
(302) 422-7575; *Fax:* (302) 422-3069
www.eagle977.com
mcobo@dbcmedia.com
License: Milford, Sussex County, DE held by Delmarva Broadcasting Co.
Group Owner: Delmarva Broadcasting Co.; (acq 6-26-97; grpsl).
Nat'l Network: Westwood One
Arbitron Metro Market: Salisbury-Ocean City, MD; *Format:* Adult Contemp *Special Programming:* Southern gospel 2 hrs wkly; *Target Audience:* 18-49; active, affluent adults in central & southern Delaware
Steve Monz, Operations Dir
Melody Booker, General Manager
Jody Trinsey, General Sales Mgr
Gary John, Programming Director
Jeff Twilly, Chief Engineer

WNCL
11-05-1990; 101.3 MHz FM; *Hrs Open:* 24; 3 kw; 328 ft.; N38 51 21 W75 29 2
Mailing Address: Wxpz County Road 626, Lincoln, DE 19960 US
Second Address: 1666 Blairs Pond Rd., Milford, DE 19963-5263
(302) 422-7575; *Fax:* (302) 422-3069
www.cool1013.com
cool@cool1013.com
License: Milford, Sussex County, DE held by Delmarva Broadcasting Co.
Group Owner: Delmarva Broadcasting Co.; acq 1-17-2003; $1.6 million).
Arbitron Metro Market: Salisbury-Ocean, MD; *Format:* Oldies; *Hrs. of News Programming:* News progmg 7 hrs wkly; *Target Audience:* 35-54; adults
Melody Booker, General Manager
Jody Trinsey, General Sales Mgr
Steve Monz, Programming Director
Jeff Twilly, Chief Engineer

WYUS
01-01-1953; 930 kHz AM; *Hrs Open:* 6 AM-midnight; 0.5 kw-D, DA2; 0.081 kw-N, DA2; N38 55 39 W75 29 20
1666 Blairs Pond Road, Milford, DE 19963 US
(302) 422-2428
www.laexitosa.com
rafael@wyusam.com
License: Milford, DE held by Delmarva Broadcasting Co.
Group Owner: Delmarva Broadcasting Co.
Arbitron Metro Market: Salisbury-Ocean *Special Programming:* Relg 10 hrs, Haitian 3 hrs wkly; *Target Audience:* 18 plus; Hispanic
Pete Booker, Michael Reath
VP, Operations Dir
Mike Kazala, General Manager
Mark Schollenberger, General Sales Mgr

Newark

***WVUD**
10-04-1976; 91.3 MHz FM; 0.79 kw horiz, 6.8 kw vert; 135 ft.; N39 41 26 W75 45 23
Perkins Student Center, Newark, DE 19716 US
(302) 831-2701; *Fax:* (302) 831-1399
www.wvud.org
ud.wvud@gmail.com
License: Newark, New Castle County, DE held by University of Delaware.
Nat'l Network: AP Radio
Arbitron Metro Market: Newark, DE; *Format:* Variety/Diverse *Special Programming:* Class 10 hrs, black 10 hrs, jazz 15 hrs, folk 15 h; *Target Audience:* General.
Steve Kramarck, Station Manager
Matt Wolfson, Programming Director
Phil Chinitz, Music Director
Dave Mackenzie, Chief Engineer

Ocean View

WZEB
01-12-1986; 101.7 MHz FM; 3.3 kw; 446 ft.; N38 31 24 W75 17 55 *Rebroadcasts:* Simulcast of WKDB (FM) Laurel 100%
20200 N. Dupont Highway, Georgetown, DE 19947 US
(302) 856-2567; *Fax:* (302) 856-7633
www.power1017.com
License: Ocean View, Sussex County, DE held by Adams Radio Group
Group Owner: Great Scott Broadcasting; acq 5-29-98; $1.5 million)
Arbitron Metro Market: Salisbury-Ocean City, MD; *Format:* Urban Contemporary
Jim McHugh, General Manager
Jeff Evans, Sales Manager
Karen Stevenson, Programming Director

Pike Creek

***WMHS**
04-01-2000; 88.1 MHz FM; *Hrs Open:* 24; 0.088 kw vert; 121 ft.; N39 45 27 W75 40 2
Mailing Address: 1400 Washington Street, P O Box 869, Wilmington, DE 19899 US
Second Address: 301 McKennans Church Rd., Wilmington, DE 19808
(302) 636-5652
wmhs881@gmail.com
License: Pike Creek, New Castle County, DE held by Red Clay Consolidated School District.
Wire Services: AP
Arbitron Metro Market: Pike Creek, DE; *Format:* Oldies; *Hrs. of News Programming:* news progmg 20 hrs wkly; *No. News Employees:* 11; *Target Audience:* 25-54; adults-baby boomers
Eric Stancell, Operations Dir
Sherry Gross, Principal

Rehoboth Beach

WGMD
09-21-1975; 92.7 MHz FM; *Hrs Open:* 24; 2.6 kw; 433 ft.; N38 42 14.4 W75 12 0.6
PO Box 530, Rehoboth Beach, DE 19971 US
(302) 945-2050; *Fax:* (302) 945-3781
www.wgmd.com
wgmd@wgmd.com
License: Rehoboth Beach, Sussex County, DE held by Resort Broadcasting Co. L.L.C.
Nat'l Reps: ABC Radio Sales
Arbitron Metro Market: Salisbury-Ocean City, MD; *Format:* News, News/Talk, 86 *Special Programming:* Farm 2 hrs, jazz 2 hrs, relg 2 hrs wkly; *Hrs. of News Programming:* news progmg 16 hrs wkly; *No. News Employees:* 3 *Target Audience:* 35 plus.; *Adv. Rates:* 50; 40; 50; 30
Walt Palmer, Operations/Programming Director
Mike Cobo, General Manager/Sales Manager
Donzene Sunkett, Traffic Manager

Seaford

WGBG
02-01-1972; 98.5 mhz FM; *Hrs Open:* 24; 6 kw; 322 ft.; N38 36 47 W75 35 12
119 Naylor Mill Road, Siute 10A, Salisbury, MD 21801 US
(410) 202-8102
www.bigclassicrock.com
wgbg@bigclassicrock.com
License: Seaford, Sussex County, DE held by Adams Radio Group
Group Owner: Adams Radio Group; (acq 4-27-98; $1.2 million with co-located AM)
Nat'l Network: CBS
Arbitron Metro Market: Salisbury-Ocean City, MD; *Format:* Classic Rock *Special Programming:* Farm one hr wkly; *Hrs. of News Programming:* News progmg 4 hrs wkly; *Target Audience:* 18-49; secondary 25-54, tertiary 35plus
Jim McHugh, General Manager
Jeff Evans, Sales Manager
Karen Stevenson, Programming Director
Terry Dalton, Chief Engineer

WJWK
01-01-1955; 1280 kHz AM; *Hrs Open:* 6 AM-midnight; 0.84 kw-D, ND1; 0.211 kw-N, ND1; N38 36 47 W75 35 12 *Rebroadcasts:* Simulcast with WKHI(FM) Fruitland 100%
20200 Dupont Boulevard, Georgetown, DE 19947 US
(302) 856-2567; *Fax:* (302) 856-7633
License: Seaford, DE held by Adams Radio Group
Group Owner: Great Scott Broadcasting
Arbitron Metro Market: Salisbury-Ocean City, MD; *Format:* News/Talk; *Hrs. of News Programming:* News progmg 4 hrs wkly; *Target Audience:* Black adults.
Jim McHugh, General Manager
Jeff Evans, Sales Manager
Karen Stevenson, Programming Director
Darius Godwin, Production Director

Selbyville

WOCM
03-01-1993; 98.1 MHz FM; *Hrs Open:* 24; 3 kw; 469 ft.; N38 25 20 W75 8 23
117 West 49th, Ocean City, MD 21842 US
(410) 723-3683; *Fax:* (410) 723-3698
www.irieradio.com
License: Selbyville, Sussex County, DE held by Irie Radio Inc.
Arbitron Metro Market: Salisbury-Ocean; *Format:* Triple A; *Target Audience:* 25-54; seasonal, beach residents & loc urban/farm; *Adv. Rates:* 20;20;20;20
Leighton Moore, President
David Rothner, General Manager
Brendan Kashuba, Programming Director
Lesley Bunting, Promotions Manager

Smyrna

WRDX
11-10-1993; 92.9 MHz FM; *Hrs Open:* 24; 1.7 kw; 377 ft.; N39 12 3 W75 33 55
600 Congress Avenue, Suite 1400, Austin, TX 78701 US
(302) 395-9800; *Fax:* (302) 395-9808
www.mix929fm.com
License: Smyrna, Kent County, DE held by Capstar TX LLC
Group Owner: iHeartMedia; (acq 8-30-2000; grpsl)
Nat'l Network: Westwood One; *Nat'l Reps:* Clear Channel
Arbitron Metro Market: Smyrna, DE; *Format:* Contemporary Hits/Top 40, Adult Contemp; *Target Audience:* 25-54.
Chris Walus, Market Manager
Martha Masters, Sales Manager
Kathryn Alt, Programming Director
Kyle Moran, Promotions Manager

Wilmington

WTMC
01-01-1947; 1380 kHz AM
115 South Justison St., Wilmington, DE 19801 US
(410) 964-5700; *Fax:* (410) 964-6478
www.deldot.net
License: Wilmington, DE held by State of Delaware Department of Transportation.
Arbitron Metro Market: Wilmington, DE; *Format:* Talk
Jonathan Weishaupt, President
William Brooks, General Manager

WDEL
01-01-1922; 1150 kHz AM; *Hrs Open:* 24
2727 Shipley Road, Wilmington, DE 19803 US
(302) 478-2700; *Fax:* (302) 478-0100
www.wdel.com
rgilbert@dbcmedia.com
License: Wilmington, DE held by Delmarva Broadcasting Co. Inc.
Group Owner: Delmarva Broadcasting Co.
Nat'l Network: Westwood One; *Nat'l Reps:* Katz Radio
Arbitron Metro Market: Wilmington, DE; *Format:* News, News/Talk, 86 *Special Programming:* Sp 2 hrs wkly; *Hrs. of News Programming:* news progmg 70 hrs wkly; *No. News Employees:* 10; *Target Audience:* 35-64.
Julian Booker, CEO
Michael Reath, General Manager
Ruth Gilbert, General Sales Mgr

WILM
10-01-1923; 1450 kHz AM; *Hrs Open:* 24; 1 kw-U, ND1; N39 43 46 W75 33 7
920 W. Basin Rd., New Castle, DE 19720 US
(302) 395-9800; *Fax:* (302) 395-9808
www.wilm.com
mail@wilm.com
License: Wilmington, DE held by Citicasters Licenses Inc.
Group Owner: iHeartMedia; (acq 10-29-2004; $3,986,000)
Nat'l Network: Wall Street; Fox News Radio; *Nat'l Reps:* Clear Channel; *Wire Services:* AP
Arbitron Metro Market: Wilmington, DE; *Format:* News, News/Talk, 86 *Special Programming:* Community Spotlight, Delaware Radio Magazine; *Hrs. of News Programming:* news progmg 168 hrs wkly; *No. News Employees:* 6 *Target Audience:* Adults 25-54.; *Adv. Rates:* na
Chris Walus, Market Manager
Martha Masters, Sales Manager
Kyle Moran, Promotions Director
Phil Feliceangeli, News Director

WWTX
04-21-1947; 1290 kHz AM; *Hrs Open:* 24; 2.5 kw-D, ND1; 0.032 kw-N, ND1; N39 44 3 W75 31 44
920 West Basin Rd., Suite 400, New Castle, DE 19720 US
(302) 395-9800; *Fax:* (302) 395-9808
www.foxsports1290am.com
License: Wilmington, DE held by Capstar TX LLC
Group Owner: iHeartMedia
Nat'l Reps: Clear Channel
Arbitron Metro Market: Wilmington, DE; *Format:* Sports, Talk; *Target Audience:* Males: 18-45.; *Adv. Rates:* na
Chris Walus, Market Manager
Martha Masters, Sales Manager
Kat Alt, Programming Director
Kyle Moran, Promotions Manager

WJBR-FM
01-01-1957; 99.5 MHz FM; *Hrs Open:* 24; 50 kw; 499 ft.; N39 50 2 W75 31 27
812 Philadelphia Pike, Suite C, Wilmington, DE 19809 US
(302) 765-1160
www.wjbr.com
License: Wilmington, New Castle County, DE held by Beasley Media Group LLC
Group Owner: Beasley Broadcast Group Inc.
Nat'l Reps: Christal
Arbitron Metro Market: Wilmington, DE; *Format:* Adult Contemp; *No. News Employees:* 1; *Target Audience:* 25-54.
Dan Sultzbach, Vice President/General Manager

***WMPH**
10-01-1969; 91.7 MHz FM; *Hrs Open:* 24; 0.1 kw vert; 144 ft.; N39 46 23 W75 30 25
5201 Washington St Ext, Wilmington, DE 19809 US
(302) 762-3671
www.brandywineschools.org/wmph
91.7wmph@gmail.com
License: Wilmington, New Castle County, DE held by Brandywine School District, Brd of Educ
Arbitron Metro Market: Wilmington, DE; *Format:* Variety/Diverse; *Hrs. of News Programming:* news progmg 2 hrs wkly; *No. News Employees:* 1; *Target Audience:* 13-27; high school & college students
Pat Bush, General Manager
Paul Wishengrad, Station Manager

WSTW
01-01-1950; 93.7 MHz FM; *Hrs Open:* 24; 47.1 kw; 502 ft.; N39 48 57 W75 31 47
2727 Shipley Road, P.O. Box 7492, Wilmington, DE 19803 US
(302) 478-2700; *Fax:* (302) 478-0100
License: Wilmington, New Castle County, DE
Group Owner: Delmarva Broadcasting Co.
Arbitron Metro Market: Wilmington, DE; *Format:* Adult Contemp *Special Programming:* Relg one hr, pub affrs one hr wkly; *Hrs. of News Programming:* News progmg 10 hrs wkly; *Target Audience:* 25-54.
Pete Booker, President
Ruth Gilbert, General Sales Mgr
Mike Rossi, Programming Director
Michael Reath, Vice President

District of Columbia

Annapolis

WLZL
12-12-2011; 107.9 MHz FM; *Hrs Open:* 24; 50 kW; 472 ft.; N38 59 46 W76 39 26
1015 Half St. SE, Suite 200, Washington, DC 20003
(202) 479-9227
www.elzolradio.com
License: Annapolis, Anne Arundel County, MD held by CBS Radio Annapolis LLC
Group Owner: CBS Radio; (acq 1-7-72)
Nat'l Network: Family Radio
Arbitron Metro Market: Washington, DC; *Format:* Spanish
Danny Bortnick, VP/Director of Sales
Rex Regner, Director of Digital Sales

Bethesda

WIAD
12-16-2009; 94.7 MHz FM; *Hrs Open:* 24; 20.5 kW; 784 ft.; N38 57 49 W77 6 18
1015 Half St. SE, Suite 200, Washington, DC 20003 USA
www.947freshfm.com
License: Bethesda, Montgomery County, MD held by CBS Radio East Inc.
Group Owner: CBS Radio; (acq 8-1-85; grpsl;
Nat'l Network: CNN Radio; *Nat'l Reps:* CBS Radio
Arbitron Metro Market: Washington, DC; *Format:* Adult Contemp; *Target Audience:* 25-49
Danny Bortnick, VP/Director of Sales

Bowie

WNEW
12-12-2011; 99.1 MHz FM; *Hrs Open:* 24; 45 kW; 463 ft.; N39 1 48 W76 44 25
1015 Half St. SE, Suite 200, Washington, DC 20003 USA
www.elzolradio.com
License: Bowie, Anne Arundel County, MD held by CBS Radio East Inc.
Group Owner: CBS Radio; (acq 11-13-98; grpsl)
Nat'l Reps: CBS Radio
Population Served: 5,000,000; *Arbitron Metro Market:* Washington, DC; *Format:* News; *Hrs. of News Programming:* news progmg 5 hrs wkly; *No. News Employees:* 1; *Target Audience:* Adults 18-49; upscaleprofessionals

Manassas

WJFK-FM
10-01-1991; 106.7 MHz FM; *Hrs Open:* 24; 22.5 kW; 663 ft.; N38 52 28 W77 13 24
1015 Half St. SE, Suite 200, Washington, DC 20003 USA
(800) 636-1067
www.1067thefandc.com
License: Manassas, Prince William County, VA held by CBS Radio Inc. of Washington, DC
Group Owner: CBS Radio; (acq 10-86; $13 million;
Arbitron Metro Market: Washington, DC; *Format:* Sports; *Hrs. of News Programming:* news progmg 3 hrs wkly; *No. News Employees:* 1; *Target Audience:* 25-54

Morningside

WJFK
01-29-2013; 1580 kHz AM; *Hrs Open:* 24; 50 kW; N38 52 9 W76 53 47
4200 Parliament Place, Lanham, MD 20706 USA
(301) 918-0955; *Fax:* (301) 459-9509
www.cbssportsradio1580.com
License: Morningside, Prince George's County, MD held by CBS Radio WPGC(AM) Inc.
Group Owner: CBS Radio; (acq 1994; with co-located FM)
Population Served: 756,510; *Arbitron Metro Market:* Washington, DC; *Format:* Sports; *Target Audience:* 18-54

WPGC
05-22-1987; 95.5 MHz FM; *Hrs Open:* 24; 50 kW; 351 ft.; N38 51 49 W76 54 40
1015 Half St. SE, Suite 200, Washington, DC 20003 USA
(301) 918-0955; *Fax:* (301) 459-9509
www.wpgc.com
License: Morningside, Prince George's County, MD held by CBS Radio Inc. of Maryland
Group Owner: CBS Radio

Arbitron Metro Market: Washington, DC; *Format:* Contemporary Hits/Top 40; *Target Audience:* 18-54
Danny Bortnick, VP/Director of Sales

Washington

*WAMU
10-23-1961; 88.5 MHz FM; *Hrs Open:* 24; 50 kw; 499 ft.; N38 56 10 W77 5 33
4400 Massachusetts Avenue N.W., Washington, DC 20016 US
(202) 885-1200; *Fax:* (202) 885-1269
www.wamu.org
feedback@wamu.org
License: Washington, DC held by American University.
Nat'l Network: NPR; PRI
Arbitron Metro Market: Washington, DC; *Format:* News, News/Talk, 86 *Special Programming:* Vintage radio 4 hrs, country 4 hrs, jazz 3 hrs wkly; *Hrs. of News Programming:* news progmg 120 hrs wkly; *No. News Employees:* 6; *Target Audience:* 25-54.
J.J. Yore, General Manager
Mark McDonald, Programming Director
Meymo Lyons, News Director
John Holt, Engineering Dir
Walt Gillette, Development Director
Anthony Hayes, Corporate Marketing Manager

WASH
01-01-1948; 97.1 MHz FM; 17.5 kw; 794 ft.; N38 57 1 W77 4 47
1801 Rockville Pike, 6th Floor, Rockville, MD 20852 US
(301) 984-9710; *Fax:* (301) 255-4314
www.washfm.com
License: Washington, DC held by AMFM Radio Licenses LLC.
Group Owner: iHeartMedia; (acq 8-30-00; grpsl).
Arbitron Metro Market: Washington, DC; *Format:* Adult Contemp
Aaron Hyland, Sales Manager
Kenny King, Programming Director
Sara Habibi, Promotions Coordinator
Matt Henry, Online Content Coordinator

WBIG-FM
06-03-1994; 100.3 MHz FM; *Hrs Open:* 24; 50 kw; 489 ft.; N38 53 13 W77 12 3
11300 Rockville Pike, Suite 905, Rockville, MD 20852 US
(240) 747-2700; *Fax:* (301) 770-0236
www.wbig.com
License: Washington, DC held by AMFM Radio Licenses LLC.
Group Owner: iHeartMedia; (acq 8-30-2000; grpsl)
Arbitron Metro Market: Rockville, MD; *Format:* Classic Rock; *Hrs. of News Programming:* news progmg one hr wkly; *No. News Employees:* 2; *Target Audience:* 35-54; professional, college, upscale
Aaron Hyland, Sales Manager
James Howard, Programming Director
Brianne Deerwester, Promotions Manager

*WCSP-FM
05-08-1982; 90.1 MHz FM; *Hrs Open:* 24; 36 kw; 568 ft.; N38 57 44 W77 1 36
400 North Capitol St, NW, Suite 650, Washington, DC 20001 US
(202) 737-3220; *Fax:* (202) 737-5554
www.c-span.org
radio@c-span.org
License: Washington, DC held by National Cable Satellite Corp.
Arbitron Metro Market: Washington, DC; *Format:* Public Affairs; *Target Audience:* General.
Brian Lamb, CEO
Kate Mills, General Manager

*WETA
04-19-1970; 90.9 MHz FM; *Hrs Open:* 24; 75 kw; 610 ft.; N38 53 30 W77 7 55
PO Box 2626, Washington, DC 20013 US
(703) 998-2600
www.weta.org/fm
radio@weta.com
License: Washington, DC held by Greater Washington Educational Telecommunications Association Inc.
Nat'l Network: NPR; PRI
Arbitron Metro Market: Washington, DC *TV Affiliate:* *WETA-TV affil; *Format:* Talk; *Target Audience:* General; educated adults
Timothy C. Coughlin, Chairman
Sharon Percy Rockefeller, President and Chief Executive Officer
Dan Devany, General Manager
Joseph B. Bruns, Executive Vice President and Chief Operating Offic
Dalton Delan, Executive Vice President andChief Programming Off
Polly Povejsil Heath, Senior Vice President and Chief Financial Officer

WWRC
01-01-1941; 1260 kHz AM; *Hrs Open:* 24
300 Crescent Court, Suite 600, Dallas, TX 75201 US
(301)231-7798; *Fax:* (301)881-8030
License: Washington, DC held by Red Zebra Broadcasting Licensee LLC.
Group Owner: Red Zebra Holdings LLC; (acq 7-29-2008; grpsl)
Nat'l Network: Westwood One; *Nat'l Reps:* Clear Channel
Arbitron Metro Market: Washington, DC; *Format:* Talk; *Target Audience:* 25-54; adults
Bill Hess, Operations Dir
Heather Steffan, General Sales Mgr
Dave Pugh, Promotions Manager
Jerry Phillips, News Director
Shaun Sandoval, Chief Engineer
Kathy Lennhoff, Promotions Director

WTOP-FM
09-01-1948; 103.5 MHz FM; *Hrs Open:* 24; 44 kw; 518 ft.; N38 56 10 W77 5 33
3400 Idaho Avenue NW, Washington, DC 20016 US
(202) 895-5000; *Fax:* (202) 895-5016
www.wtop.com
License: Washington, DC held by Hubbard Broadcasting
Group Owner: Hubbard Radio LLC; (acq 1-30-98; grpsl)
Nat'l Network: CBS Radio; *Nat'l Reps:* Katz Radio; *Wire Services:* Reuters
Arbitron Metro Market: Washington, DC; *Format:* News; *Target Audience:* General.
Ginny Morris, CEO/COO
Joel Oxley, General Manager
Skip Quast, General Sales Mgr
Laurie Cantillo, Programming Director
John D. Meyer, Director of Digital Media
Ralph Renzi, Director of Federal Sales

*WHUR-FM
12-10-1971; 96.3 MHz FM; *Hrs Open:* 24; 16.5 kw; 801 ft.; N38 57 1 W77 4 47
2400 Sixth Street N.W., Washington, DC 20059 US
(202) 806-3500; *Fax:* (202) 806-3522
www.whur.com
dickinson@whur.com
License: Washington, DC held by Howard University Board of Trustees.
Nat'l Network: CNN Radio; ABC; *Nat'l Reps:* D & R Radio; *Wire Services:* UPI
Arbitron Metro Market: Washington, DC; *Format:* Adult Contemp *Special Programming:* Gospel 14 hrs, Caribbean 6 hrs wkly; *Hrs. of News Programming:* news progmg 7 hrs wkly; *No. News Employees:* 3; *Target Audience:* 25-54.
Dr. H. Patrick Swygert, President
Millard Watkins III, General Manager
Jeanette Tyce, General Sales Mgr
David Dickinson, Programming Director

WIHT
01-01-1960; 99.5 MHz FM; *Hrs Open:* 24; 22 kw; 751 ft.; N38 57 49 W77 6 18
1801 Rockville Pike, Floor 5, Rockville, MD 20852 US
(240) 747-2700
www.hot995.com
info@hot995.com
License: Washington, DC held by AMFM Radio Licenses L.L.C.
Group Owner: iHeartMedia; (acq 9-00).
Arbitron Metro Market: Washington, DC; *Format:* Contemporary Hits/Top 40
Dennis Lamme, Market Manager
Aaron Hyland, Sales Manager
Tommy Chuck, Programming Director
Sydney Galkin, Promotions Manager

WKYS
08-01-1947; 93.9 MHz FM; *Hrs Open:* 24; 24.5 kw; 705 ft.; N38 56 24 W77 4 54
8515 Georgia Ave., 9th Floor, Silver Spring, MD 20910 US
(301) 306-1111; *Fax:* (301) 306-9540
www.kysdc.com
License: Washington, DC held by Radio One Licenses LLC
Group Owner: Radio One Inc.; (acq 6-95; $34 million;
Nat'l Reps: McGavren Guild
Arbitron Metro Market: Washington, DC; *Format:* Urban Contemporary; *Hrs. of News Programming:* news progmg 4 hrs wkly; *No. News Employees:* 3; *Target Audience:* 25-54; upscale Black adults
Jeff Wilson, General Manager
Neke Howse, Programming Director
Calvin Lewis, Promotions Manager
Ebony McMorris, News Director

WMAL
10-12-1925; 630 kHz AM; *Hrs Open:* 24; 10 kw-D, 5 kw-D; N39 00 55 W77 08 30
4400 Jenifer St. NW, Washington, DC 20015 US
(202) 686-3100
www.wmal.com
bill.hess@cumulus.com
License: Washington, DC held by Radio License Holdings LLC
Group Owner: Cumulus Media Inc.; (acq 6-12-2007; grpsl)
Nat'l Reps: ABC Radio Sales
Arbitron Metro Market: Washington, DC; *Format:* News/Talk
Jake McCann, General Sales Mgr
Bill Hess, Programming Director

WMZQ-FM
09-01-1968; 98.7 MHz FM; *Hrs Open:* 24; 50 kw; 489 ft.; N38 53 13 W77 12 3
1801 Rockville Pike, 5th Floor, Rockville, MD 20552 US
(240) 747-2700; *Fax:* (301) 984-4895
www.wmzq.com
License: Washington, DC held by AMFM Radio Licenses LLC
Group Owner: iHeartMedia; (acq 8-30-00; grpsl)
Nat'l Reps: Christal
Arbitron Metro Market: Washington, DC; *Format:* Country; *No. News Employees:* 1; *Target Audience:* 25-54.
Dennis Lamme, Market Manager
Aaron Hyland, Sales Manager
Meg Stevens, Programming Director
Sara Habibi, Promotions Coordinator
Heather O'Malley, Digital Content Coordinator

WOL
01-01-1924; 1450 kHz AM
8515 Georgia Ave., 9th Floor, Silver Spring, MD 20910 US
(301) 306-1111; *Fax:* (301) 306-9540
www.woldcnews.com
License: Washington, DC held by Radio One Licenses LLC
Group Owner: Radio One Inc.; (Acq 6-95)
Arbitron Metro Market: Washington, DC *TV Affiliate:* Talk; *Format:* Talk
Jeff Wilson, General Manager

*WPFW
02-28-1977; 89.3 MHz FM; *Hrs Open:* 24; 50 kw; 410 ft.; N38 56 9 W77 5 33
1929 Mlk, Jr Way, Berkeley, CA 94704 US
(202) 588-0999; *Fax:* (202) 588-0561
www.wpfw.org
bmwpfw@aol.com
License: Washington, DC held by Pacifica Foundation Inc.
Group Owner: Pacifica Foundation Inc.
Arbitron Metro Market: Washington, DC; *Format:* Jazz, News, 62, Talk *Special Programming:* Oldies 3 hrs, women 3 hrs, health one hr wkly; *Hrs. of News Programming:* News progmg 9 hrs wkly; *Target Audience:* 25-55.
Ron Pinchback, General Manager
Tiffany Jordan, General Sales Mgr

WRQX
05-15-1948; 107.3 MHz FM; 19.5 kw; 807 ft.; N38 57 1 W77 4 47
4400 Jenifer St. NW, Washington, DC 20015 US
(202) 686-3100
www.dcs1073.com
jake.mccann@cumulus.com
License: Washington, DC held by Radio License Holdings LLC
Group Owner: Cumulus Media Inc.
Nat'l Network: ABC
Arbitron Metro Market: Washington, DC; *Format:* Contemporary Hits/Top 40; *Target Audience:* 25-54.
Jeff Boden, President
Tom Grooms, Operations Dir
Carol Parker, Programming Director
Stella Pressley, News Director
David Sproul, Engineering Dir

WTEM
08-01-1923; 980 kHz AM; *Hrs Open:* 24; 50 kw-D, DA2; 5 kw-N, DA2; N38 57 43 W76 58 24
11300 Rockville Pike, Suite 707, Rockville, MD 20852 US
(301) 220-0980; *Fax:* (301) 255-4314
www.espn980.com
management@espn980.com
License: Washington, DC held by Red Zebra Broadcasting Licensee LLC.
Group Owner: Red Zebra Holdings LLC; (acq 7-29-2008; grpsl)
Nat'l Network: ESPN Radio; *Wire Services:* The Sports Network
Arbitron Metro Market: Washington, DC; *Format:* Sports, Talk; *Target Audience:* 25-54; men
Bruce Gilbert, President
Hartley Adkins, General Manager

WFED
09-25-1926; 1500 kHz AM; *Hrs Open:* 24; 50 kw-D, DA2; 50 kw-N, DA2; N39 2 31 W77 2 47
3400 Idaho Ave. N.W., Washington, DC 20016 US
(202) 895-5000; *Fax:* (202) 895-5144
www.federalnewsradio.com
License: Washington, DC held by Washington DC FCC License Sub LLC
Group Owner: Hubbard Broadcasting Inc.; (acq 1-19-2011)
Arbitron Metro Market: Washington, DC; *Format:* News, News/Talk, 86; *No. News Employees:* 4; *Target Audience:* General.
Lauren Larson, Broadcast Operations Manager
Joel Oxley, General Manager
Matt Mills, Director of Sales
Lisa Wolfe, Programming Director
Mary Kay LeMay, Marketing Director
Dave Garner, Chief Engineer
Jeffrey Wolinsky, Director ofFederal and National Sales
Jason Fornicola, Director of Custom Media

WUST
01-01-1949; 1120 kHz AM; 3 kw-C, NDD; 20 kw-D, NDD; N38 54 15 W77 9 54
2131crimmins Lane, Falls Church, VA 22043 US
(703) 532-0400
www.wust1120.com
contactwithwust@wust1120.com
License: Washington, DC held by New World Radio Inc.
Arbitron Metro Market: Falls Church, VA; *Format:* Ethnic *Special Programming:* Fr 15 hrs, Sp 15 hrs, Ger 7 hrs, Ethiopian 6 hrs,
Brian Edwards, Operations Dir
Alan Pendleton, General Manager

WWDC
01-01-1947; 101.1 MHz FM; *Hrs Open:* 24; 22.5 kw; 761 ft.; N38 59 59 W77 3 27
1801 Rockville Pike, 5th Floor, Rockville, MD 20852 US
(301) 587-7100; *Fax:* (301) 587-0225
www.dc101.com
License: Washington, DC held by AMFM Radio Licenses L.L.C.
Group Owner: iHeartMedia; (acq 8-30-00; grpsl).
Arbitron Metro Market: Washington, DC; *Format:* Rock/AOR
Aaron Hyland, Sales Manager
James Howard, Programming Director
Brianne Deerwester, Promotions Coordinator
Oswald Pinott, Chief Engineer
Matt Henry, Online Content Coordinator

WYCB
01-01-1978; 1340 kHz AM
8515 Georgia Ave., 9th Floor, Silver Spring, MD 20910 US
(301) 306-1111; *Fax:* (301) 306-9540
www.myspiritdc.com
jeffwilson@radio-one.com
License: Washington, DC held by Radio One Licenses LLC.
Group Owner: Radio One Inc.; (acq 11-8-01; grpsl).
Nat'l Network: American Urban
Arbitron Metro Market: Washington, DC; *Format:* Gospel
Jeff Wilson, General Manager
Karen Jackson, General Sales Mgr

Florida

Alachua

WNDT
01-01-1996; 92.5 MHz FM; *Hrs Open:* 24; 3.2 kw; 443 ft.; N29 44 22 W82 23 9 *Rebroadcasts:* Rebroadcasts WNDD(FM) Silver Springs 100%
3602 NE20th Place, Ocala, FL 32670 US
(352) 373-6644; *Fax:* (352) 375-1700
www.windfm.com
rkassi@windwogksales.com
License: Alachua, Alachua County, FL held by Ocala Broadcasting Corp. L.L.C.
Group Owner: Wooster Republican Printing Co.; (acq 10-22-97; $675,000 for stock)
Nat'l Reps: Katz Radio
Arbitron Metro Market: Gainesville, FL; *Format:* Light Rock; *Target Audience:* Adults; 25-54; *Adv. Rates:* 55; 70; 60; 25
Jim Robertson, Operations Dir
Robert Kassi, General Sales Mgr
Kevin Davis, Programming Director
Cheree Carr, News Director

Altamonte Springs

WORL
01-01-1986; 660 kHz AM
1188 Lake View Dr., Altamont Springs, FL 32714 US
(407) 682-9494; *Fax:* (407) 682-7005
www.worl660.com
License: Altamonte Springs, FL held by Salem Communications
Group Owner: Salem Communications Corp.; (acq 2-3-2006; swap in exchange for KNIT(AM) Dallas, TX)
Nat'l Reps: Salem
Arbitron Metro Market: Orlando, FL *TV Affiliate:* Talk; *No. News Employees:* 35-64; adult, male
CEO, CEO/COO
General Manager, General Manager
General Sales Manager, General Sales Mgr
Promotions Director, Promotions Manager

Apalachicola

WOYS
07-01-1988; 100.5 MHz FM; *Hrs Open:* 24; 12 kw; Ant 476 ft; N29 43 57 W84 53 24
Point Mall 35 Island Dr. #16, Eastpoint, FL 32328
(850) 670-8450; *Fax:* (850) 670-8492
www.oysterradio.com
manager@oysterradio.com
License: Apalachicola, Franklin County, FL held by East Bay Broadcasting Inc.
No. News Employees: 1; *Target Audience:* General.
Robert M. Allen, President
Michael Allen, Operations Director/GM/Station Manager
Bonnie Gomes, General Sales Mgr

WFCT
11-01-1997; 105.5 MHz FM; *Hrs Open:* 24; 50 kw; 315 ft.; N29 45 2 W84 52 18
4500 Illinois, Midland, TX 79703 US
(850) 227-9048; *Fax:* (850) 227-1101
wfct@gtcom.net
License: Apalachicola, Franklin County, FL held by Williams Communications Inc.
Group Owner: Williams Communications Inc.; acq 3-27-02; $650,000).
Arbitron Metro Market: Apalachicola, FL; *Format:* Adult Contemp
John Nichols, General Manager
Ken Carey, News Director

Arcadia

WFLN
09-03-1955; 1480 kHz AM; *Hrs Open:* 24; 1 kw-D, ND1; 0.131 kw-N, ND1; N27 13 43 W81 51 28
201 Asbury St., Arcadia, FL 34266 US
(863) 993-1480; *Fax:* (863) 499-1489
www.wflnradio.com
License: Arcadia, FL held by Integrity Radio of Florida LLC.
Nat'l Network: CBS Radio; CNN Radio; *Regional Network:* Florida's Radio Networks
Arbitron Metro Market: Arcadia, FL; *Format:* News, News/Talk, 86; *Target Audience:* 25-65; upscale adults
George S Kalman, President/General Manager
Rosemarie Carlucci, General Sales Mgr
Jack Welch, Programming Director
Phill Scott, Engineer
Kayo Keen, On Air Personality/Sales
Yerica Toscano, Office Manager

Atlantic Beach

WOKV-FM
03-10-1980; 104.5 MHz FM; *Hrs Open:* 24; 99 kw; 1014 ft.; N30 16 34 W81 33 53
8000 Belfort Parkway, Suite 100, Jacksonville, FL 32256 US
(904) 245-8500; *Fax:* (904) 245-8501
www.wokv.com
License: Atlantic Beach, Duval County, FL held by Cox Radio Inc.
Group Owner: Cox Radio Inc.; (acq 2000; grpsl)
Nat'l Network: Fox News Radio; *Nat'l Reps:* Katz Radio
Arbitron Metro Market: Jacksonville, FL; *Format:* News/Talk; *Target Audience:* 18-49; male oriented
Aaron Schachter, Aaron.Schachter@Coxinc.Com
Bob Deblois, Bob.Deblois@Coxinc.Com
Jodi Rainey, National Sales Manager
Ashley Testa, Digital Sales Manager
David Ratz, Promotions & Events Director
Rich Jones, News Director

WZNZ
08-01-1942; 1600 kHz AM
Post Office Box 51585, Jacksonville Beach, FL 32240 US
(904) 241-3311; *Fax:* (904) 241-1402
www.qopradio.com
License: Atlantic Beach, FL held by Queen of Peace Radio Inc.
Nat'l Network: EWTN Radio
Arbitron Metro Market: Jacksonville, FL; *Format:* Christian
Special Programming: 2 days - The 2012 Fall Sharethon; *Target Audience:* 25-54.
Tom Moran, General Manager

WZNZ
01-01-1984; 1600 kHz AM; *Hrs Open:* 24; 5 kw-D, 89 watts-N; N30 19 29 W81 25 48
(904) 470-4615
www.1023thebeach.com
feedback@1023thebeach.com
License: Atlantic Beach, FL held by Delmarva Educational Association
Group Owner: Delmarva Educational Association
Format: Oldies
Henry W. Hoot, Regional VP
Larry Stevens, Operations Mgr
Alexis Kimball, Sales & Marketing Director/Promotions
Courtney Banks, Producer

Auburndale

WTWB
10-10-1956; 1570 kHz AM; *Hrs Open:* 24; 5 kw-D, ND1; 0.013 kw-N, ND1; N28 4 32 W81 49 19
205 S. Hoover St., #400, Tampa, FL 33609 US
(863) 967-1570; *Fax:* (206) 350-6874
www.laraza1570.com
laraza1570@gmail.com
License: Auburndale, FL held by La Raza Media Group LLC
Arbitron Metro Market: Auburndale, FL; *Format:* Christian, News, 62, Talk; *Hrs. of News Programming:* news progmg 13 hrs wkly; *No. News Employees:* 1; *Target Audience:* 30 plus; middle income, 2-income family *Adv.Rates:* 15; 20; 20; 15
Lynne Breidenbach, General Manager
Justin Sargent, Programming Director

Avon Park

WFHT
10-01-1970; 1390 kHz AM; *Hrs Open:* 6 AM-10 PM
871 NW 167th St., Miami Gardens, FL 33168 US
(970) 356-1452ÿ; *Fax:* (719) 562-0947
www.tigrecolorado.com
krye104.9@hotmail.com
License: Avon Park, FL held by Azure Media
Nat'l Network: Jones Radio Networks
Arbitron Metro Market: Olney Springs, CO
Jhonson Napoleon, President

WWOJ
08-01-1982; 99.1 MHz FM; *Hrs Open:* 24; 10 kw; 515 ft.; N27 30 39 W81 31 54
3750 US 27 N., Sebring, FL 33870 US
(863) 382-9999
www.oj991.com
cohanradiogroup@htn.net
License: Avon Park, Highlands County, FL held by Cohan Radio Group Inc.
Group Owner: Cohan Radio Group Inc.; acq 11-1-98; $910,000 with WWTK(AM) Lake Placid)
Nat'l Network: ABC; *Regional Network:* Florida's Radio Networks; *Nat'l Reps:* Interep; *Wire Services:* AP
Arbitron Metro Market: Sebring, FL; *Format:* Country *Special Programming:* Bluegrass 2 hrs wkly; *Hrs. of News Programming:* news progmg 7 hrs wkly; *No. News Employees:* 1; *Target Audience:* 18 plus.
Peter Coughlin, President/General Manager

Baker

***WTJT**
05-01-1987; 90.1 MHz FM; *Hrs Open:* 24; 50 kw; 417 ft.; N30 49 19 W86 42 37
Rt 2, Box 204, Baker, FL 32531 US
(850) 537-2009; *Fax:* (850) 537-4663
wtjtradio@yahoo.com
License: Baker, Okaloosa County, FL held by Okaloosa Public Radio Inc.
Nat'l Network: USA
Arbitron Metro Market: Fort Walton Beach, FL; *Format:* Christian, Gospel, 86; *Target Audience:* 45 plus.
Earl Thompson, President
Jessica Walker, Station Manager
Ruth Thompson, Programming Director
Randy Henry, Chief Engineer

Baldwin

WJGM(FM)
07-30-1992; 105.7 MHz FM; 25 kw; Ant 328 ft; N30 22 28 W82 01 42

9090 Hogan Rd., Suite B, Jacksonville, FL 32216
(904) 425-3482
www.whjx.biz
License: Baldwin, Duval County, FL held by Tama Radio Licenses of Jacksonville, FL, Inc.
Group Owner: Tama Broadcasting Inc.; (acq 12-2-2001; $1.5 million)
Population Served: 827,908; *Arbitron Metro Market:* Jacksonville, FL; *Format:* Talk
Andy Johnson, General Manager

Bartow

WQXM
09-28-1953; 1460 kHz AM; *Hrs Open:* 24 hrs.; 1 kw-D, ND1; 0.155 kw-N, ND1; N27 54 34 W81 51 29
1355 North Maple Ave., Bartow, FL 33830 US
(863)533-1460
License: Bartow, FL held by Florida Broadcasting Media LLC
Arbitron Metro Market: Chehalis WA; *Format:* Country *Special Programming:* NFL Football; *Hrs. of News Programming:* 60 minutes weekly; *No. News Employees:* 1; *Adv. Rates:* 32
Osvaldo Vega, President

WWBF
09-16-1969; 1130 kHz AM; *Hrs Open:* 24; 2.5 kw-D, DAN; 0.5 kw-N, DAN; N27 54 31 W81 49 33
1130 Radio Road, Bartow, FL 33830 US
(863) 533-0744; *Fax:* (863) 533-8546
www.wwbf.com
tom@wwbf.com
License: Bartow, FL held by Thornburg Communications Inc.
Nat'l Network: CNN Radio; *Regional Network:* Florida's Radio Networks
Arbitron Metro Market: Bartow, FL; *Format:* Oldies *Special Programming:* Sports; *Hrs. of News Programming:* news progmg 10 hrs wkly; *No. News Employees:* 1; *Target Audience:* 35-54; affluent adults
Thomas Thornburg, President
Jeffrey Thornburg, Operations Dir
Susan Thornburg, Station Manager

Belle Glade

WBGF
10-10-1978; 93.5 MHz FM; 15.5 kw; 419 ft.; N26 41 0 W80 43 39
8895 N. Military Trail, Suite 206C, Palm Beach Gardens, FL 33410 US
(561) 627-9966; *Fax:* (561) 627-9993
www.935thebar.com
License: Belle Glade, Palm Beach County, FL held by JVC Media of South Fla LLC
Group Owner: JVC Broadcasting
Nat'l Network: ABC; *Regional Network:* Florida's Radio Networks
Regional Reps: Interep
Arbitron Metro Market: Belle Glade, FL; *Format:* Rock/AOR
Special Programming: Farm 5 hrs wkly; *Target Audience:* 25-54.
John Caracciolo, President

WSWN
10-07-1947; 900 kHz AM; 1 kw-D, ND1; 0.022 kw-N, ND1; N26 42 43 W80 40 59
8895 N. Military Trail, Suite 206C, Palm Beach Gardens, FL 33410 US
(561) 627-9966
www.900thetalk.com
License: Belle Glade, Palm Beach County, FL held by JVC Media of South Fla LLC
Group Owner: JVC Broadcasting; (acq 2014)
Nat'l Network: CBS Radio; *Regional Network:* Florida's Radio Networks; Southeast AgNet; *Nat'l Reps:* Interep
Arbitron Metro Market: West Palm Beach-Boca Raton, FL; *Format:* Talk *Special Programming:* Sports; *Target Audience:* 25-54.
Matthew Goldapper, General Manager

Belleview

*WYFZ
04-01-2001; 91.3 MHz FM; *Hrs Open:* 24; 0.9 kw; 318 ft.; N29 10 38 W82 8 42
6883 N.E. 79th Terrace, Wildwood, FL 34785 US
(800) 888-7077
www.bbnradio.org
bbn@bbnmedia.org
License: Belleview, Marion County, FL held by Bible Broadcasting Network Inc.
Group Owner: Bible Broadcasting Network; (acq 12-1-2005; $250,000)
Arbitron Metro Market: Belleview, FL; *Format:* Religious

Lowell Davey, President
Jason Padgett, Operations Manager

Beverly Beach

WBHQ
01-01-1978; 92.7 MHz FM; *Hrs Open:* 24; 5.5 kw; 341 ft.; N29 32 7 W81 15 50
50 East Rivercenter Blvd, Suite 1200, Covington, KY 41011 US
(386) 437-1992; *Fax:* (386) 437-8728
www.beach927.com
david@wnzf.com
License: Beverly Beach, Flagler County, FL held by Flagler County Broadcasting LLC
Format: Variety/Diverse
David Ayres, General Manager
Mary Hendley, General Sales Mgr
Marc Gilliland, Programming Director
Ron Charles, News Director
Dave Shy, Underwriting Manager
Mary Gergely, Office Manager
Dr. Dave West, Sports Director

Big Pine Key

WWUS
09-22-1980; 104.1 MHz FM; *Hrs Open:* 24; 100 kw horiz, 90.25 kw vert; 453 ft.; N24 39 39.8 W81 25 10.4
830 Crane Blvd., Sugarloaf Key, FL 33042 USA
(305) 745-2468
us1radio.com
License: Big Pine Key, Monroe County, FL held by Florida Keys Media LLC
Group Owner: Florida Keys Media LLC
Nat'l Network: Cumulus Media Networks
Arbitron Metro Market: Big Pine Key, FL; *Format:* Adult Contemp; *No. News Employees:* 1; *Target Audience:* 30-50.; *Adv. Rates:* 25; 25; 25; 25
Rick Lopez, General Manager
Amy Andrade, Sales Manager
Randy Perry, Chief Engineer

Bithlo

WNTF
07-31-1974; 1580 kHz AM
3765 N. John Young Pkwy., Orlando, FL 32804 US
(407) 291-1395
License: Bithlo, FL held by Unity Broadcasting LLC.
Group Owner: Unity Broadcasting LLC.; (acq 10-29-2002; $600,000 with WGAF(AM) Alachua)
Arbitron Metro Market: Orlando, FL; *Format:* Vietnamese
Shanti Persaud, President

Blountstown

WPHK
12-18-1968; 102.7 MHz FM; 13 kw; 318 ft.; N30 27 15 W85 2 32
269 Kelly Avenue, Blountstown, FL 32424 US
License: Blountstown, Calhoun County, FL held by Blountstown Communications
Format: Country *Special Programming:* Black 12 hrs wkly
Harry Hagen, General Manager

WYBT
09-08-1962; 1000 kHz AM
269 Kelly Avenue, Blountstown, FL 32424 US
(850) 674-5101; *Fax:* (850) 674-2965
License: Blountstown, FL held by Blountstown Communications
Arbitron Metro Market: Blountstown, FL; *Format:* Oldies *Special Programming:* Gospel & relg 15 hrs wkly
Shelley Shell

Boca Raton

WKIS
06-27-1988; 99.9 MHz FM; *Hrs Open:* 24; 98.4 kW; 984 ft.; N25 58 7 W80 13 20
194 NW 187th St., Miami, FL 33169 USA
(305) 654-1700; *Fax:* (305) 654-1715
www.wkis.com
License: Boca Raton, Palm Beach County, FL held by CBS Radio Stations Inc.
Group Owner: CBS Radio
Nat'l Network: Westwood One
Arbitron Metro Market: Miami-Fort Lauderdale-Hollywood, FL; *Format:* Country; *Hrs. of News Programming:* news progmg 2 hrs wkly; *No. News Employees:* 1; *Target Audience:* 25-54
Rob Morris, Programming Director
Sarah Lanieu, Promotions Manager

WSBR
04-01-1965; 740 kHz AM; 2.5 kw-D, DA2; 0.94 kw-N, DA2; N26 20 6 W80 15 55
1650 S. Dixie Hwy., 5th Fl., Boca Raton, FL 33432 US
(561) 995-8255; *Fax:* (561) 997-0476
www.wsbrradio.com
License: Boca Raton, Palm Beach County, FL held by Beasley Media Group LLC
Group Owner: Beasley Broadcast Group Inc.; (acq 3-14-2000; grpsl).
Arbitron Metro Market: West Palm Beach; *Format:* Talk
Duff Lindsey, Operations Manager/Program Director
Bob Morency, General Manager
Karen Ruggerie, Business Manager
Jodi Mibaum, Traffic Manager/Account Executive

Bonifay

WYYX
04-23-1983; 97.7 MHz FM; *Hrs Open:* 24; 100 kw; 830 ft.; N30 30 41 W85 29 24
3018 Thompson Lane, Murfreesboro, TN 37129 US
(850) 233-6606; *Fax:* (850) 233-1541
www.wyyx.com
info@wyyx.com
License: Bonifay, Holmes County, FL held by Magic Broadcasting II LLC
Group Owner: Magic Broadcasting II LLC; (acq 9-30-2002; grpsl)
Arbitron Metro Market: Panama City, FL; *Format:* Rock/AOR; *No. News Employees:* 1; *Target Audience:* 18-49.
Jim Storey, COO
J.P. Ferrell, General Sales Mgr
Karla Melvin, News Director

Bonita Springs

WRXK-FM
09-01-1974; 96.1 MHz FM; 100 kw; 1119 ft.; N26 25 22 W81 37 49
20125 S. Tamiami Trail, Estero, FL 33928 US
(239) 495-2100
www.96krock.com
License: Bonita Springs, Lee County, FL held by Beasley Media Group LLC
Group Owner: Beasley Broadcast Group Inc.; (acq 8-12-86).
Nat'l Network: ABC; *Nat'l Reps:* Katz Radio
Arbitron Metro Market: Fort Myers-Napl; *Format:* Rock/AOR; *Target Audience:* 18-49.
Brad Beasley, General Manager
Jon Parla, Sales Manager
Jeff Zito, Programming Director
AJ Lurie, Director of Sales
Diana Beasley, Digital Content Director

Boynton Beach

WLVJ
01-23-1973; 1040 kHz AM; *Hrs Open:* 24
2525 Ponce de Leon Blvd., #2, Miami, FL 33134 US
(954) 315-1515; *Fax:* (954) 315-1555
www.wlvj.com
License: Boynton Beach, FL held by Actualidad Radio
Arbitron Metro Market: West Palm Beach-Boca Raton, FL; *Format:* Religious
Adib Eden, President
Sergio Gomez, Operations Dir

*WRMB
04-15-1979; 89.3 MHz FM; *Hrs Open:* 24; 100 kW; 469 ft.; N26 31 4 W80 10 14
1511 W Boynton Beach Blvd, Boynton Beach, FL 33436 USA
(561) 737-9762; *Fax:* (561) 737-9899
www.moodyradio.org/stations/south-florida
License: Boynton Beach, Palm Beach County, FL held by The Moody Bible Institute of Chicago
Group Owner: Moody Radio
Nat'l Network: Moody; *Wire Services:* AP
Arbitron Metro Market: West Palm Beach-Ft. Lauderdale-Miami; *Format:* Christian; *No. News Employees:* 1; *Target Audience:* General.

Bradenton

*WJIS
01-01-1989; 88.1 MHz FM; 100 kw; 397 ft.; N27 7 54 W82 23 39
Post Office Box 7217, Lakeland, FL 33807 US
(941) 753-0401; *Fax:* (941) 753-2963
www.thejoyfm.com
thejoyfm@thejoyfm.com
License: Bradenton, Manatee County, FL held by WJIS FM Radio.

Arbitron Metro Market: Sarasota-Bradenton, FL; *Format:* Adult Contemp, Christian
Jeff McFarlane, General Manager
Steve Swanson, Programming Director
Carmen Brown, Promotions Manager
Steve Rieker, Chief Engineer

WWPR
01-01-1946; 1490 kHz AM; *Hrs Open:* 24
670 Ridge Pike, Lafayette Hill, PA 19444 US
(941) 761-8843; *Fax:* (941) 761-8683
www.1490wwpr.com
manager@1490wwpr.com
License: Bradenton, FL held by Greenrose Broadcasting Services Inc.
Nat'l Network: Talk Radio Network
Arbitron Metro Market: Tampa, FL; *Format:* Talk *Special Programming:* Community talk15 hrs, relg 6 hrs, gospel 6 hrs, sp; *Hrs. of News Programming:* news progmg 15 hrs wkly; *No. News Employees:* 1 *TargetAudience:* 35-64; general; *Adv. Rates:* 40; 30; 40; 20
Valerie Silver, General Manager

Brandon

WLCC
02-01-1988; 760 kHz AM
8121 Georgia Ave., 10th, Silver Spring, MD 20910 US
(813) 871-1819; *Fax:* (813) 871-1155
License: Brandon, FL held by Minority Media and Telecommunications Council Inc.
Arbitron Metro Market: Tampa-St. Petersburg-Clearwater, FL; *Target Audience:* 25-54.
Angela Cotto, CFO
Rafael Grullon, President

Brooksville

WWJB
10-11-1958; 1450 kHz AM; *Hrs Open:* 24
Mailing Address: P.O. Box 1507, Brooksville, FL 34605 US
Second Address: 55 W. Fort Dade Ave., Brooksville, FL 34605-1507
(352) 796-7469; *Fax:* (352) 796-5074
www.wwjb.com
info@wwjb.com
License: Brooksville, FL held by Hernando Broadcasting Co.
Nat'l Network: Westwood One; ABC; *Regional Network:* Florida's Radio Networks; *Nat'l Reps:* Dora-Clayton
Arbitron Metro Market: Tampa, FL; *Format:* News, News/Talk, 84, Talk; *No. News Employees:* 1; *Target Audience:* 25 plus.
Steve Manuel, President
Bill Willamson, General Sales Mgr
Peggy Hope, Promotions Manager
Bob Haa, News Director

Brunswick

WMUV
01-01-1984; 100.7 MHz FM; *Hrs Open:* 24; 5 kw-D, 89 watts-N; N30 19 29 W81 25 48
7235 Bonneval Rd., Jacksonville, FL 32256 US
(904) 641-9626
www.ilovethepromise.com
License: Brunswick, GA held by Delmarva Educational Association
Group Owner: Delmarva Educational Association
Format: Oldies
Henry W. Hoot, Regional VP
Larry Stevens, Operations Mgr
Alexis Kimball, Sales & Marketing Director/Promotions
Courtney Banks, Producer

Bunnell

WNZF
01-01-2008; 1550 kHz AM; *Hrs Open:* 24
US
(386) 437-1992
wnzf.com
newsradio@wnzf.com
License: Bunnell, FL held by Flagler County Broadcasting LLC
Nat'l Network: Fox Sports
Format: News, News/Talk, 86
David Ayers, General Manager
Ron Charles, News Director

Bushnell

WKFL
01-01-1987; 1170 kHz AM; *Hrs Open:* 6 AM-9 PM varies by season; 1 kw-D, NDD; N28 42 31 W82 7 36
P.O. Box 1000, Bushnell, FL 33513 US
(352) 568-3204; *Fax:* (407) 322-0431
License: Bushnell, FL held by TalknSports Inc.
Nat'l Network: Salem Radio Network
Format: News, News/Talk, 84, Talk; *Hrs. of News Programming:* news progmg 8 hrs wkly; *No. News Employees:* 1; *Target Audience:* 18-54; those who enjoy family progmg; *Adv. Rates:* 14; 13; 14; 13
Bruce Cox, President
Jan Hall, General Manager

Callahan

WEWC
01-01-1999; 1160 kHz AM; 5 kw-D, DAD; 0.25 kw-N, DAD; N30 22 28 W81 44 28
9373 West Sample Road, Coral Springs, FL 33065 US
(904) 549-2218; *Fax:* (904) 359-0070
License: Callahan, FL held by Norsan Consulting and Management Inc.
Group Owner: Norsan Consulting and Management Inc.; (acq 9-25-2007; $650,000)
Arbitron Metro Market: Callahan, FL
George Lopez, General Manager

WJBT
06-01-1983; 93.3 MHz FM; *Hrs Open:* 24; 98 kw
11700 Central Parkway, Jacksonville, FL 32224 US
(904) 636-0507; *Fax:* (904) 997-7713
www.wjbt.com
License: Callahan, Nassau County, FL held by Clear Channel Broadcasting Licenses Inc.
Group Owner: iHeartMedia; (acq 11-21-97; grpsl)
Arbitron Metro Market: Jacksonville, FL; *Format:* Urban Contemporary; *Target Audience:* 12-54; the young & young-at-heart
Aaron Wilborn, Senior Vice President of Sales
Nick Wize, Digital Content Director
Taylor Brown, Digital Content Coordinator
Carrie Thompson, Digital Sales Manager

Callaway

WAKT-FM
02-01-1990; 103.5 MHz FM; *Hrs Open:* 24; 100 kw; 423 ft.; N30 10 51 W85 29 45
Two Bala Plaza, Suite 801, Bala-Cynwyd, PA 19004 US
(850) 234-8858; *Fax:* (850) 234-6592
MelissaMiller@PanamaCityRadio.com
License: Callaway, Bay County, FL held by Double O Radio Corp.
Group Owner: Double O Radio L.L.C.; acq 3-10-2004; grpsl).
Nat'l Reps: Christal
Arbitron Metro Market: Panama City, FL; *Format:* Country; *Adv. Rates:* 50; 40; 40; 25
Harry Finch, General Manager
Melissa Miller, Programming Director

WKNK(FM)
103.5 MHz FM; 100,000 watts; 129 meters; 30 10 51N 85 29 45W
Two Bala Plaza, Suite 801, Bala Cynwyd, PA 19004 USA
(270) 432-0847; *Fax:* (270) 432-7601
License: Callaway, Bay County, FL
Group Owner: Powell Briadcasting Company LLC

Cantonment

WNVY
12-01-1955; 1070 kHz AM; 15 kw
2070 N. Palafox Rd., Pensacola, FL 32501 US
(850) 432-3658
www.wilkinsradio.com
denise@wilkinsradio.com
License: Cantonment, FL held by Pensacola Radio Corp.
Group Owner: Wilkins Communications Network Inc.; (acq 11-30-2006; $430,000)
Arbitron Metro Market: Pensacola, FL *TV Affiliate:* Relg; *Format:* Christian, Talk
Jessica Jordan, Station Manager

Cape Coral

WXKB
01-01-1975; 103.9 MHz FM; 100 kw; 1119 ft.; N26 25 22 W81 37 49
20125 S. Tamiami Trail, Estero, FL 33928 US
(239) 495-2100
www.b1039.com
License: Cape Coral, Lee County, FL held by Beasley Media Group LLC
Group Owner: Beasley Broadcast Group Inc.; (acq 11-18-94; $3.7 million;
Arbitron Metro Market: Fort Myers, FL; *Format:* Contemporary Hits/Top 40; *Target Audience:* General.
Brad Beasley, General Manager
Jon Parla, Sales Manager
Adam Star, Programming Director
AJ Lurie, Director of Sales
Diana Beasley, Digital Content Director

Carrabelle

WOCY
01-01-1999; 106.5 MHz FM; 100 kw; 482 ft.; N29 43 57 W84 53 24
Unit 16, 35 Island Drive, Eastpoint, FL 32328 US
(850) 670-8450; *Fax:* (850) 670-8492
http://www.hitz106fm.com/
manager@oysterradio.com
License: Carrabelle, Franklin County, FL held by Live Communications Inc.
Group Owner: 3G Broadcasting Inc.; (acq 8-30-2007; with WOYS(FM) Apalachicola)
Regional Network: Florida's Radio Networks
TV Affiliate: Top 40
Program Director, Jason Harrop
Promotions Director, Promotions Manager

Cedar Creek

***WKSG**
01-01-1999; 89.5 MHz FM; 22 kw; 375 ft.; N29 11 16 W81 52 55
1403 Indian River Ave., Titusville, FL 32780 US
(352) 369-8950; *Fax:* (352) 369-1109
License: Cedar Creek, Marion County, FL held by Daystar Public Radio Inc.
Format: Adult Contemp, Christian
Gary Linkus, General Manager

Cedar Key

WRGO
09-01-1996; 102.7 MHz FM; *Hrs Open:* 24; 12.5 kw; 459 ft.; N29 11 45 W82 59 46
3131 Bermuda Dunes Dr, Lecanto, FL 34461 US
(352) 795-1027; *Fax:* (352) 795-0002
License: Cedar Key, Levy County, FL held by WRGO Radio LLC.
Nat'l Network: Jones Radio Networks
Format: Oldies; *Target Audience:* 25-64.; *Adv. Rates:* 24; 20; 24; 18
Lou Cerra, General Manager

Century

WPFL
07-01-1989; 105.1 MHz FM; 8.6 kw; 558 ft.; N31 7 9 W87 16 5
Mailing Address: P.O. Box 1203, Century, FL 32535 US
Second Address: 2059 Old Fannie Rd., Flomaton, AL 36441
(251) 296-1051; *Fax:* (251) 296-1055
www.oldiesradioonline.com
wpflradio@bellsouth.net
License: Century, Escambia County, FL held by Tri-County Broadcasting Inc.
Arbitron Metro Market: Pensacola, FL; *Format:* Oldies
Ronnie Hammond, General Manager
Howard Macht, Chief Engineer

Charlotte Harbor

WIKX
09-01-1970; 92.9 MHz FM; *Hrs Open:* 24; 100 kw; 807 ft.; N26 53 47 W82 14 27
24100 Tiseo Blvd., Suite 10, Port Charlotte, FL 33980 US
(941) 206-1188; *Fax:* (941) 206-9296
www.kixcountry929.com
License: Charlotte Harbor, Charlotte County, FL held by Citicasters Licenses Inc.
Group Owner: iHeartMedia
Format: Country; *Hrs. of News Programming:* News progmg 10 hrs wkly; *Target Audience:* 25-54.
Robin Craig, Director of Sales

Chattahoochee

WTCL
11-01-1963; 1580 kHz AM; 10 kw-D, NDD; N30 40 14 W84 50 8
5004 - 27th Ave, Rockford, IL 61125 US
(850) 663-3857; *Fax:* (850) 663-8543
info@wtcl.com
License: Chattahoochee, FL held by Metz Inc.

Nat'l Network: USA; *Regional Network:* Florida's Radio Networks
Arbitron Metro Market: Chattahoochee, FL; *Format:* Gospel;
Target Audience: General.
Don Metz, President
David Garcia, General Manager

Chiefland

WLQH

06-06-1968; 940 kHz AM; *Hrs Open:* Sunrise-sunset
P.O. Box 99, Chiefland, FL 32626 US
(352) 498-0304; *Fax:* (352) 493-9909
www.suncoastradio.com
john@suncoastradio.com
License: Chiefland, FL held by Ocala Broadcasting Corp.
Format: Contemporary Hits/Top 40 *Special Programming:* Relg 9 hrs wkly
Bob Moody, Station Manager

WNDN

01-01-1991; 107.9 MHz FM; *Hrs Open:* 6 AM-midnight; 6 kw; 328 ft.; N29 30 54.9 W82 53 5
P.O. Box 99, Chiefland, FL 32626 US
(352) 493-4940; *Fax:* (352) 493-9909
www.windfm.com
hunter@windfm.com
License: Chiefland, Levy County, FL held by Ocala Broadcasting Corp.
Nat'l Network: Jones Radio Networks
Format: Rock/AOR
Robert McLimans, Operations Dir
Bob Kassi, General Sales Mgr
Rick Small, Operations Director
Emily Carey, Business Manager
Cheree Carr, Traffic

Chipley

WBGC

04-10-1956; 1240 kHz AM; 1 kw-U, ND1; N30 46 19 W85 33 31
1513 South Blvd, Chipley, FL 32428 US
(850) 638-0234; *Fax:* (850) 638-4333
License: Chipley, FL held by Jacquelyn Collier Pembroke
Regional Network: Florida's Radio Networks; *Nat'l Reps:* Keystone (unwired net)
Arbitron Metro Market: Chipley,FL; *Format:* Variety/Diverse
Todd Burnett, General Manager

Clearwater

WBTP

08-19-1963; 95.7 MHz FM; *Hrs Open:* 24; 100 kw; 607 ft.; N27 52 0 W82 37 27
4002 West Gandy Blvd., Tampa, FL 33611 US
(813) 832-1000; *Fax:* (813) 832-1090
www.957thebeat.com
License: Clearwater, Pinellas County, FL held by Clear Channel Broadcasting Licenses Inc.
Group Owner: iHeartMedia; (acq 10-94).
Nat'l Reps: Katz Radio; *Wire Services:* AP
Arbitron Metro Market: Tampa-St. Petersburg-Clearwater, FL;
Format: Urban Contemporary; *Target Audience:* 18-49; upwardly mobile adults
Fernando Bauermeister, Sales Manager
Mychal Maguire, Programming Director
Greg Wolf, Promotions Director
Brian Fink, Production Director
David Bell, Public Service Director
Marc Cerniglio, Digital Content Director

WTAN

06-01-1948; 1340 kHz AM; *Hrs Open:* 24
2360 N.E. Coachman Road, Clearwater, FL 33765 US
(727) 441-3311; *Fax:* (727) 441-1300
www.tantalk1340.com
License: Clearwater, FL held by Wagenvoord Advertising Group Inc.
Group Owner: Wagenvoord Advertising Group Inc.; acq 12-29-99; $100,000).
Arbitron Metro Market: Tampa-St. Petersburg-Clearwater, FL;
Format: News, Talk *Special Programming:* Big band 40 hrs wkly; *Hrs. of News Programming:* news progmg 12 hrs wkly; *No. News Employees:* 2 *TargetAudience:* 35-64.
Dave Wagenvoord, CEO
Lola Wagenvoord, General Manager

WXTB

12-01-1967; 97.9 MHz FM; *Hrs Open:* 24; 100 kw; 1503 ft.; N28 10 56 W82 46 6
4002 West Gandy Blvd., Tampa, FL 33611 US
(813) 832-1000; *Fax:* (813) 832-1090
www.98rock.com
License: Clearwater, Pinellas County, FL held by Citicasters Licenses Inc.
Group Owner: iHeartMedia; (acq 5-6-99; grpsl).
Nat'l Network: Premiere Radio Networks; *Nat'l Reps:* Katz Radio; *Wire Services:* AP
Arbitron Metro Market: Tampa-St. Peter, FL; *Format:* Rock/AOR
Special Programming: Pub affrs 4 hrs wkly; *Hrs. of News Programming:* news progmg 2 hrs wkly; *No. News Employees:* 1; *Target Audience:* 18-49; men
Sam Nein, Market President
Fernando Bauermeister, Sales Manager
Chris Sciortino, Promotions Director
John McMartin, Engineering Dir
Norm, Production Director
Josh Jenson, Creative Services Director
David Bell, Public ServiceDirector

Clermont

*WMYZ

07-18-1997; 88.7 MHz FM; *Hrs Open:* 24; 1.2 kw; 350 ft.; N28 38 56 W81 44 9 *Rebroadcasts:* Rebroadcasts WPOZ(FM) Union Park 100%
P. O. Box 980, Quebradillas, PR 0678 US
(407) 869-8000; *Fax:* (407) 869-0380
www.zradio.org
zcrew@zradio.org
License: Clermont, Lake County, FL held by Central Florida Educational Foundation Inc.
Format: Christian
James Hoge, President

WWFL

01-01-1962; 1340 kHz AM; *Hrs Open:* 24; 1 kw-U, ND1; N28 34 59 W81 42 19
5601 Windover Drive, OrlandO, FL 32819 US
(407) 351-3350; *Fax:* (407) 370-3524
www.cflradio.net
License: Clermont, FL held by Central Florida Investments Inc.
Arbitron Metro Market: Clermont, FL; *Format:* Adult Contemp
David Siegal, President

Clewiston

WAFC

02-16-1988; 590 kHz AM; *Hrs Open:* 24; 0.93 kw-D, ND1; 0.47 kw-N, ND1; N26 43 46 W80 54 49
530 East Alverdez Ave., Clewiston, FL 33440 US
(863) 983-5900; *Fax:* (863) 983-6109
www.wafcfm.com
License: Clewiston, FL held by Glades Media Company LLP
Nat'l Reps: Interep
Arbitron Metro Market: West Palm Beach-Boca Raton, FL; *Hrs. of News Programming:* News progmg 10 hrs wkly; *Target Audience:* General.; *Adv. Rates:* 20; 20; 20; 18
Robert Castellanos, CEO
KC Kelly, General Manager
Larry Parrish, General Sales Mgr
Jesus Castro, Programming Director
Debbie Pattison, News Director
Jim Johnson, CFO

*WJCB

88.5 MHz FM; 3 kw; 292 ft.; N26 43 46 W80 54 49
1150 West King Street, Cocoa, FL 32922 US
(321) 632-1000; *Fax:* (321) 636-0000
www.wjfp.com/site/page.php?pid=home
info@wjfp.com
License: Clewiston, Hendry County, FL held by Black Media Works Inc.
Group Owner: Black Media Works Inc.
Arbitron Metro Market: West Palm Beach, FL; *Format:* Gospel
Ray Kassis, General Manager

*WPSF

01-01-2008; 91.5 MHz FM; 0.7 kw vert; 387 ft.; N26 41 27 W80 47 18
1601 Belvedere Rd, 204 E, W Palm Beach, FL 33406 US
(786) 429-3606; *Fax:* (305) 251-2293
www.callfm.com
rob@callfm.com
License: Clewiston, Hendry County, FL held by American Educational Broadcasting Inc.
Arbitron Metro Market: Clewiston, FL; *Format:* Christian
Tim Pappas, Chairman
Rob Robbins, Ph.D., President
Rob Robbins, General Manager
Rob Robbins, Ph.D., Programming Director

Cocoa

*WMIE-FM

12-01-1984; 91.5 MHz FM; *Hrs Open:* 24; 20 kw horiz, 19 kw vert; 98 ft.; N28 21 21 W80 44 47
1150 West King Street, Cocoa, FL 32922 US
(321) 632-1000; *Fax:* (321) 636-0000
www.wjfp.com
info@wjfp.com
License: Cocoa, Brevard County, FL held by National Christian Network.
Arbitron Metro Market: Melbourne, FL; *Format:* Urban Contemporary; *Target Audience:* 18-49.
Raymond Kassis, President
Paul Esposito, General Manager
Jim Conn, Programming Director
Jan Ferguson, Chief Engineer

WMMV

10-04-1957; 1350 kHz AM; 1 kw-D, DAN; 1 kw-N, DAN; N28 21 58 W80 45 8
1388 S. Babcock St., Melbourne, FL 32901 US
(321) 821-7100; *Fax:* (321) 733-0904
www.wmmbam.com
billmick@iheartmedia.com
License: Cocoa, FL held by Capstar TX LLC
Group Owner: iHeartMedia; (acq 8-30-00; grpsl).
Nat'l Network: ABC; Westwood One; *Regional Network:* Florida's Radio Networks
Arbitron Metro Market: Melbourne, FL; *Format:* News, News/Talk, 86; *Target Audience:* General
Tom Davis, Market President
Ken Holiday, Operations Manager
Bill Mick, Programming Director
Deano Chaple, Promotions Director
Laurie Reid, Business Manager
Adam Schanz, Online Content Director

WWBC

07-01-1965; 1510 kHz AM; *Hrs Open:* Sunrise-sunset
1150 West King Street, Cocoa, FL 32922 US
(321) 632-1000; *Fax:* (321) 636-0000
www.wmiefm.com
josh@ncnradio.com
License: Cocoa, FL held by Astro Enterprises.
Arbitron Metro Market: Cocoa, FL; *Format:* Gospel, Talk, 74; *Target Audience:* 25 plus.
Ray Kassis, President
Paul Esposito, General Manager

WLRQ-FM

06-23-1982; 99.3 MHz FM; 50 kw; 492 ft.; N28 16 42 W80 42 3
1388 S. Babcock St., Melbourne, FL 32901 US
(321) 821-7100; *Fax:* (321) 733-0904
www.literock993.com
License: Cocoa, Brevard County, FL held by Capstar TX LLC
Group Owner: iHeartMedia
Population Served: 76,095; *Arbitron Metro Market:* Melbourne, FL; *Format:* Light Rock
Tom Davis, Market President
Ken Holiday, Operations Manager
Michael Lowe, Programming Director
Deano Chaple, Promotions Director
Laurie Reid, Business Manager
Adam Schanz, Webmaster

Cocoa Beach

WJRR

07-19-1962; 101.1 MHz FM; 95 kw; 1598 ft.; N28 34 51 W81 4 32
2500 Maitland Center Pkwy., Suite 401, Maitland, FL 32751 US
(407) 916-1011; *Fax:* (407) 916-7407
www.wjrr.com
programdirector@realrock1011.com
License: Cocoa Beach, Brevard County, FL held by Clear Channel Broadcasting Licenses Inc.
Group Owner: iHeartMedia; (acq 1-27-2009; with KYRK(FM) Houma, LA)
Arbitron Metro Market: Orlando, FL; *Format:* Rock/AOR; *Target Audience:* 18-34; men; *Adv. Rates:* 200.;180.,225.,50.
Linda Byrd, Market President
Lisa Kitchener, General Sales Mgr
Rick Everett, Programming Director
Lea Reynolds, Promotions Manager

WTKS-FM

05-08-1962; 104.1 MHz FM; *Hrs Open:* 24; 94 kw; 1598 ft.; N28 34 51 W81 4 32
2500 Maitland Center Pkwy., Suite 401, Maitland, FL 32751 US
(407) 916-1041; *Fax:* (407) 916-7511
www.realradio.fm

License: Cocoa Beach, Brevard County, FL held by Clear Channel Broadcasting Licenses Inc.
Group Owner: iHeartMedia; (acq 11-21-97; grpsl).
Nat'l Network: Premiere Radio Networks; *Nat'l Reps:* Clear Channel
Arbitron Metro Market: Orlando, FL; *Format:* Talk; *Target Audience:* Adults; 25-54; *Adv. Rates:* 300; 250; 450; 100
Linda Byrd, Market President
Mark Kanak, General Sales Mgr
Chris Kampmeier, Programming Director
Amanda Fraser, Promotions Manager

WMEL
06-22-1959; 1060 kHz AM; *Hrs Open:* 24; 5 kw-D, DA2; 1 kw-N, DA2; N28 20 38 W80 46 6
2355 Pluckebaum Rd., Cocoa, FL 32926 US
(321) 241-1060; *Fax:* (321) 631-9113
www.1060wmel.com
License: Cocoa Beach, FL held by Rama Communications Inc.
Group Owner: Rama Communications Inc.
Nat'l Network: ABC; Talk Radio Network
Arbitron Metro Market: Cocoa Beach, FL; *Format:* Talk; *Hrs. of News Programming:* news progmg 144 hrs wky; *No. News Employees:* 2; *Target Audience:* 35-64; decision making men & women
Shanti Persaud, President

Columbia City

WJTK
01-01-2006; 96.5 MHz FM; 5 kw; 359 ft.; N30 9 20 W82 38 14 US
(386) 758-9696; *Fax:* (386) 269-4361
www.northfloridanow.com
License: Columbia City, Columbia County, FL held by ABC Media Inc.
Arbitron Metro Market: Columbia City, FL; *Format:* News, News/Talk, 86
Cesta Newman, President

Coral Cove

WSRZ-FM
03-25-1995; 107.9 MHz FM; *Hrs Open:* 24; 47 kw; 509 ft.; N27 9 3 W82 27 51
1779 Independence Blvd., Sarasota, FL 34234 US
(941) 552-4800; *Fax:* (941) 552-4900
www.wsrz.com
License: Coral Cove, Sarasota County, FL held by Citicasters Licenses Inc.
Group Owner: iHeartMedia; (acq 5-4-99; grpsl).
Arbitron Metro Market: Sarasota-Bradenton, FL; *Format:* Oldies; *Target Audience:* 25-54.
William Ames, Local Sales Manager
Drew Thomas, Programming Director
Nikki Clark, Promotions Director

Coral Gables

WHIM
05-04-1964; 1080 kHz AM; *Hrs Open:* 24
2828 W. Flagler St, Miami, FL 33135 US
(407) 682-9494; *Fax:* (407) 682-7005
www.1520whim.com
whim@salemorlando.com
License: Coral Gables, FL held by Pennsylvania Media Associates Inc.
Group Owner: Salem Communications Corp.; (acq 1-23-2006; $600,000)
Nat'l Network: Salem Radio Network; *Nat'l Reps:* Salem
Arbitron Metro Market: Orlando, FL; *Format:* Christian, Talk; *Target Audience:* 35-64.
Edward Atsinger III, President
Dale Forbis, Operations Dir
David Koon, General Manager
John Stolz, General Sales Mgr

WHQT
11-15-1958; 105.1 MHz FM; 98 kw; 1007 ft.; N25 58 2 W80 12 34
2741 N. 29th Ave., Hollywood, FL 33020 US
(305) 444-4404; *Fax:* (954) 847-3240
www.hot105fm.com
pmt@coxradio.com
License: Coral Gables, Dade County, FL held by Cox Radio Inc.
Group Owner: Cox Radio Inc.; (acq 12-28-92;
Nat'l Reps: Christal
Arbitron Metro Market: Miami-Fort Lauderdale-Hollywood, FL; *Format:* Adult Contemp, Urban Contemporary; *Target Audience:* 18-49.
Phil Michael-Trueba, Director Of Branding

WRHC
01-01-1963; 1550 kHz AM; *Hrs Open:* 24; 10 kw-D, 500 k-N, DA-2; N25 51 27 W80 28 52
330 S.W. 27th Ave., Suite 207, Miami, FL 33135
(305) 541-3300; *Fax:* (305) 541-7470
www.wrhc.com
anavidal@lapoderosa.com
License: Coral Gables, Dade County, FL held by WRHC Broadcasting Corp.
Nat'l Reps: Lotus Entravision Reps LLC
Population Served: 1,800,000; *Arbitron Metro Market:* Miami-Fort Lauderdale-Hollywood, FL; *Hrs. of News Programming:* news progmg 4 hrs wkly; *No. News Employees:* 4; *Target Audience:* Central & South Americans
Jorge Rodriguez, President
Ana Vidal Rodriguez, Vice President
Miguel Melanio, Programming Director
Eduardo Aleman, News Director
Eduardo Rodriguez, Chief Engineer

WHIM(AM)
02-18-1949; 1080 kHz AM; *Hrs Open:* 24; 50 kw-D, 20 kw-N, DA-2; N25 44 53 W80 32 47
2828 W. Flagler St., Miami, FL 33135
(305) 644-0800; *Fax:* (305) 677-7585
www.1080theanswer.com
info@1080theanswer.com
License: Coral Gables, Dade County, FL held by Caron Broadcasting Inc.
Group Owner: Salem Communications Corp.; (acq 4-11-2008; $12.25 million)
Population Served: 408,750; *Arbitron Metro Market:* Miami, FL; *Format:* Christian, Religious
Tony Calatayud, General Manager
Jorge Guevara, General Sales Mgr
Mike Hernandez, Promotions Manager
Steve James, Chief Engineer
John Davitt, Traffic Director
Dania Hernandez, Media Specialist

***WVUM**
05-01-1968; 90.5 MHz FM; *Hrs Open:* 24; 0.1 kw horiz, 1.3 kw vert; 174 ft.; N25 43 2 W80 16 48
P.O. Box 248127, Coral Gables, FL 33124 US
(305) 284-3131; *Fax:* (305) 284-3132
www.wvum.org
info@wvum.org
License: Coral Gables, Dade County, FL held by WVUM Inc.
Arbitron Metro Market: Coral Gables, FL; *Format:* Alternative, Variety/Diverse *Special Programming:* Sports 5 hrs, Black 7 hrs, relg 6 hrs, Sp 2 hrs, o; *Hrs. of News Programming:* news progmg 3 hrs wkly *No. NewsEmployees:* 1; *Target Audience:* 13-plus.
Paul Driscoll, Operations Dir
Savanna Stiffÿ, General Manager
Jackson Alexander Parodiÿ, Programming Director
Ashley Gonzalezÿ, Promotions Manager
Ben Hampton, News and Public Affairs Directorÿ
Alex Faron, Engineering Dir
ZoeBrown, Digital Music Director
Christopher Lloyd, Office Manager
Giovanna Stallings-Blancheÿ, Music Director
Demetris Antoniouÿ, Training Director

Coral Springs

WZBR
1120 kHz AM; 9.5 kw-d; n26 16 54 w80 17 39
94 St Rose Street, Boston, MA
(617) 522-4889
License: Coral Springs, FL held by Langer Bradcasting Group LLC
Group Owner: Langer Broadcasting Group LLC

Alexander Langer, General Manager

Crawfordville

WAKU
01-01-1996; 94.1 MHz FM; *Hrs Open:* 24; 3 kw; 459 ft.; N30 4 34 W84 18 5
Mailing Address: P.O. Box 4106, Tallahassee, FL 32315 US
Second Address: 3225 Harstfield Rd., Tallahassee, FL 32303
(850) 926-8000; *Fax:* (850) 562-2730
www.wave94.com
dougapple@wave94.com
License: Crawfordville, Wakulla County, FL held by Altrua Investments International Corp.
Nat'l Network: Salem Radio Network
Arbitron Metro Market: Tallahassee, FL; *Format:* Christian; *Hrs. of News Programming:* News progmg 10 hrs wkly; *Target Audience:* 35-54; Adults; *Adv. Rates:* 20; 18; 18; 15
Mike Floyd, CEO
Doug Apple, General Manager

Crestview

WAAZ-FM
07-15-1965; 104.7 MHz FM; *Hrs Open:* 5 AM - MIDNIGHT; 100 kw; 486 ft.; N30 46 1 W86 35 7 *Rebroadcasts:* Simulcast with WJSB(AM) Crestview 100%
Mailing Address: P. O. Box 267, Crestview, FL 32536 US
Second Address: 506 W. First Ave., Crestview, FL 32536
(519) 357-1310; *Fax:* (519) 357-1897
www.945thebull.ca
License: Crestview, Okaloosa County, FL held by Crestview Broadcasting Co.
Nat'l Network: CBS Radio
Format: Rock/AOR
John Weese, General Manager

WJSB
1050 kHz AM; *Hrs Open:* daytime sunrise to sunset; Ant 485 ft
Rebroadcasts: Simulcast with WAAZ - FM Crestview 100%
Mailing Address: P.O. Box 267, Crestview, FL 32536 US
Second Address: 506 W. FIRST AVE., Crestview, FL 32536
(850) 682-3040; *Fax:* (850) 682-5232
waazwjsb@embarqmail.com
License: Crestview, FL held by Crestview Broadcasting Co.
Nat'l Network: CBS Radio
Arbitron Metro Market: Fort Walton Beach, FL; *Format:* Country
Special Programming: ATLANTA BRAVES BASEBALL; *No. News Employees:* 1
James T. Whitaker, General Manager
Cal Zethmayer, General Sales Mgr
Claude T. Strickland, Programming Director
Joe Dunn, Announcer
Buddy Shuman, Announcer
Sallie Stapleton, Office Manager
Tim English, Sports Director

Cross City

WZCC
11-01-1985; 1240 kHz AM; *Hrs Open:* 24; 1 kw-U, ND1; N29 36 35 W83 8 3
P.O. Box 2220, Cross City, FL 32628 US
(352) 498-0304; *Fax:* (352) 795-0002
www.suncoastradio.com
john@suncoastradio.com
License: Cross City, FL held by WRGO Radio LLC
Arbitron Metro Market: Gainesville-Ocala, FL; *Format:* Country
Lou Cerra, General Manager

WPLL
11-16-1987; 106.9 MHz FM; 100 kw; 469 ft.; N29 36 29 W82 51 1
P.O. Box 2220, Cross City, FL 32628 US
(352) 313-3150; *Fax:* (352) 313-3166
kevin.mangan@marcradio.com
License: Cross City, Dixie County, FL held by Marc Radio Gainesville LLC
Group Owner: Marc Radio Group; (acq 7-18-2011; grpsl)
Arbitron Metro Market: Gainesville-Ocala, FL; *Format:* Adult Contemp
Shawn Portmann, General Manager
Jeanie Edwards, General Sales Mgr
Kevin McKay, Programming Director
Alan Ritchie, National Sales Manager

***WWLC**
01-01-2006; 88.5 MHz FM; *Hrs Open:* 24; 1,000 w; Ant 193 ft; N29 39 09 W83 10 08
Spirit Radio of North Florida Inc., 500 N.E. 16th Ave., Gainesville, FL
(352) 372-2191; *Fax:* (352) 376-0575
License: Cross City, Dixie County, FL held by Spirit Radio of North Florida Inc.

Fr. Roland Julien, General Manager

WURB
97.7 MHz FM; 25 kw; 79 meters; N29 44 17 W82 51 26
414 S.W. 140th Terrace, Newberry, FL 32669 US
(352) 328-6232
License: Cross City, Dixie County, FL held by Urban One Broadcasting Network LLC
Group Owner: Urban One Broadcasting Network LLC
Format: Adult Contemp, Urban Contemporary
William Johnson, President

Crystal River

***WAQV**
01-01-1999; 90.9 MHz FM; *Hrs Open:* 24; 3.7 kw; 331 ft.; N29 1 54 W82 27 8 *Rebroadcasts:* Rebroadcasts WHIJ(FM) Ocala 100%
4741 S.W. 20th Street, Ocala, FL 34474 US
(800)456-8910; *Fax:* (352) 351-8917
www.thejoyfm.com
License: Crystal River, Citrus County, FL held by Radio Training Network Inc.
Arbitron Metro Market: Crystal River, FL; *Format:* Adult Contemp, Christian
Jeff MacFarlane, General Manager

WKTK
02-13-1976; 98.5 MHz FM; *Hrs Open:* 24; 100 kw; 981 ft.; N29 15 34 W82 34 5
401 City Ave., Suite 409, Bala Cynwyd, PA 19004 US
(352) 377-0985; *Fax:* (352) 377-1884
www.ktk985.com
dickoneil@entercom.com
License: Crystal River, Citrus County, FL held by Entercom Gainesville License LLC.
Group Owner: Entercom Communications Corp.; (acq 11-13-86; $3.6 million;
Arbitron Metro Market: Gainesville-Ocala, FL; *Format:* Adult Contemp; *Hrs. of News Programming:* news progmg 6 hrs wkly; *No. News Employees:* 1; *Target Audience:* 25-54.
Joseph Field, Chairman
David Field, CEO
Dick O'Neil, Operations Dir
Chris Malone, Programming Director

***WHGN**
11-01-1992; 91.9 MHz FM; *Hrs Open:* 24; 41 kW horiz, 39.3 kW vert; 541 ft.; N28 50 29 W82 30 21
PO Box 8889, St. Petersburg, FL 33738 USA
(727) 391-9994; *Fax:* (727) 397-6425
www.moodyradio.org/stations/florida
License: Crystal River, Citrus County, FL held by The Moody Bible Institute of Chicago
Group Owner: The Moody Bible Institute of Chicago; acq 4-11-03; $500,000).
Arbitron Metro Market: Crystal River-Ocala, FL; *Format:* Christian

Cypress Gardens

WHNR
11-29-1958; 1360 kHz AM; *Hrs Open:* 6 AM-midnight; 5 kw-D, DA2; 2.5 kw-N, DA2; N28 1 16 W81 42 2
1505 Dundee Road, Winter Haven, FL 33884 US
(863) 299-1141; *Fax:* (863) 293-6397
www.whnr1360am.com
License: Cypress Gardens, FL held by GB Enterprises Communication Corp.
Regional Network: Florida's Radio Networks
Arbitron Metro Market: Lakeland-Winter Haven, FL; *Format:* Urban Contemporary *Special Programming:* Relg 10 hrs wkly; *Hrs. of News Programming:* news progmg 20 hrs wkly; *No. News Employees:* 1; *Target Audience:* 55 plus.
P.J. Allen, Station Manager

Cypress Quarters

***WREH**
01-01-2004; 90.5 MHz FM; 100 kw horiz, 91.7 kw vert; 249 ft.; N27 20 51 W80 57 4
P. O. Box 637, Bishop, CA 93515 US
(954) 315-4315; *Fax:* (954) 315-4231
www.reachfm.org
License: Cypress Quarters, Okeechobee County, FL held by Reach Communications Inc.
Format: Christian
Carl Mims, General Manager
John Boone, Programming Director

Dade City

WDCF
12-01-1954; 1350 kHz AM; 1 kw-D, DAN; 0.5 kw-N, DAN; N28 20 4 W82 11 23
38141 Fifth Avenue, Zephyrhills, FL 33540 US
(727) 441-3311; *Fax:* (727) 441-1300
lola@tantalk1340.com
License: Dade City, FL held by Wagenvoord Advertising Group Inc.
Group Owner: Wagenvoord Advertising Group Inc.; acq 2-13-02).
Nat'l Network: ABC; *Regional Network:* Florida's Radio Networks
Arbitron Metro Market: Pasco County, Fl; *Format:* Religious; *Target Audience:* 25 plus; basic country demographics
Dave Wagenvoord, President
Lola Wagenvoord, Operations Dir

WTMP-FM
09-03-1993; 96.1 MHz FM; *Hrs Open:* 24; 2.8 kw; 482 ft.; N28 28 22 W82 17 45
8121 Georgia Ave 10th Fl, Silver Spring, MD 20910 US
(813) 259-9867; *Fax:* (813) 254-9867
www.wtmp.com
info@tamabroadcasting.com
License: Dade City, Pasco County, FL held by Tama Radio Licenses of Tampa, FL, Inc.
Group Owner: Tama Broadcasting Inc.; (acq 12-21-2001; $4.1 million).
Arbitron Metro Market: Tampa, FL; *Format:* Spanish; *Target Audience:* 35 plus; general
Glenn Cherry, CEO
Chris McMurray, General Manager
Lynn Tolliver, Programming Director

Davie

WAVS
08-21-1970; 1170 kHz AM; *Hrs Open:* 24; 5 kw-D, DAN; 0.25 kw-N, DAN; N26 4 39 W80 13 3
6360 Southwest 41st Pl., Davie, FL 33314 US
(601) 883-0848
www.vicksburgv105.com
mark@vicksburgv105.com
License: Davie, FL held by Alliance Broadcasting Inc.
Arbitron Metro Market: Redwood MS; *Format:* Oldies
Darrell Chambliss, Chairman
Mark Jones, CEO/COO
Dailon Huskey, Operations Dir
Lina Jones, General Manager
Stephen Donnovan, Engineering Dir

Daytona Beach

WMFJ
04-16-1935; 1450 kHz AM; *Hrs Open:* 24; 1 kw-U, ND1; N29 13 30 W81 1 30
4295 Ridgewood Ave., Port Orange, FL 32127 US
(386) 756-9094; *Fax:* (386) 760-7107
www.cornerstoneministry.org
wjlu@wjlu.org
License: Daytona Beach, FL held by Cornerstone Broadcasting Corp.
Nat'l Network: Moody; USA
Arbitron Metro Market: Daytona Beach, FL; *Format:* Religious; *Target Audience:* General.
Bill Powellў, President
William Powell, General Manager
Chris Johnson, Programming Director

WNDB
04-01-1948; 1150 kHz AM; *Hrs Open:* 24; 1 kw-D, DAN; 1 kw-N, DAN; N29 14 6 W81 4 19
126 W. Intl. Speedway Blvd., Daytona Beach, FL 32214 US
www.newsdaytonabeach.com
License: Daytona Beach, FL held by Southern Stone Communications
Group Owner: Southern Stone Communications; (acq 9-21-2001; grpsl).
Nat'l Network: CBS; *Wire Services:* UPI
Arbitron Metro Market: Daytona Beach, FL; *Format:* News, News/Talk, 84, Talk; *No. News Employees:* 2; *Target Audience:* 25-64; general

WROD
01-01-1947; 1340 kHz AM; *Hrs Open:* 24; 1 kw-U, ND1; N29 11 19 W81 0 28
Mailing Address: 1000 Olde Doubloon Drive, Vero Beach, FL 32963 US
Second Address: 2400 S. Ridgewood Ave., Suite 51, South Daytona, FL 32119
(386) 253-0000; *Fax:* (386) 255-3178
www.wrod.net
License: Daytona Beach, FL held by Volusia Broadcasting Co., LLC
Group Owner: Wilderness Communications LLC; 2008
Nat'l Network: NBC
Arbitron Metro Market: Daytona Beach, FL; *Format:* Adult Contemp, Contemporary Hits/Top 40; *Hrs. of News Programming:* news progmg 15 hrs wkly; *No. News Employees:* 1; *Target Audience:* 50 plus; adult standards *Adv. Rates:* 30; 30; 30; 30
Joseph Hopkins, President
Lori Bailey, Station Manager

De Funiak Springs

WDSP
03-01-1956; 1280 kHz AM; *Hrs Open:* 24; 5 kw-D, NDD; 0.046 kw-N, ND1; N30 42 41 W86 6 25
633 S. Second St., P.O. Box 90, Defuniak Springs, FL 32435 US
(850) 951-1280; *Fax:* (850) 951-1282
License: De Funiak Springs, FL held by The Sportzmax Inc.
Nat'l Network: ABC
Format: Country *Special Programming:* High School Sports; *Target Audience:* 25-54.; *Adv. Rates:* 10; 7; 10; na
Stephen Riggs III, President
Max Howell, Operations Dir
Arty Goodman, General Manager
Carolyn Mora, General Sales Mgr
Joshua Smith, Sales

WZEP
10-17-1955; 1460 kHz AM; *Hrs Open:* 24; 10 kw-D, 186 w-N; Single tower unipole; N30 43 45 W86 07 04
Mailing Address: 449 N. 12th St., De Funiak Springs, FL 32435
Second Address: Box 627, De Funiak Springs, FL 32435-0627
(850) 892-3158; *Fax:* (850) 892-9675
www.wzep1460.com
wzep@wzep1460.com
License: De Funiak Springs, Walton County, FL held by Walton County Broadcasting Inc.
Nat'l Network: CBS; *Regional Network:* Florida News Network
Population Served: 75,000; *Arbitron Metro Market:* Panama City, FL *Special Programming:* Gospel 13 hrs wkly; *Hrs. of News Programming:* news progmg 60 hrs wkly; *No. News Employees:* 1 *Target Audience:* General; residents & visitors to Walton & Holmes counties
Arthur Dees, President
Wes Richardson, Operations Dir
Arthur Dees, General Manager
Marty Dees, Station Manager
Rebecca King, General Sales Mgr
Stephanie King, Programming Director
Marty Dees, Promotions Manager
Kevin Chilcutt,News Director
Kevin Chilcutt, Engineering Dir
Terry Reeves, Chief Engineer
Wes Richardson, Traffic Manager

Defuniak Springs

***WAKJ**
01-01-1996; 91.3 MHz FM; *Hrs Open:* 24; 1.2 kw; 226 ft.; N30 41 5 W86 8 28
Mailing Address: Post Office Box 1305, Defuniak Springs, FL 32433 US
Second Address: 295 Hwy. 90 W., De Funiak Springs, FL 32435
(850) 892-2107; *Fax:* (866) 309-6532
www.eridan.websrvcs.com
WAKJradio@gmail.com
License: Defuniak Springs, Walton County, FL held by First Baptist Church Inc.
Arbitron Metro Market: De Funiak Springs, FL; *Format:* Christian
Zane Welch, General Manager
Jesse Knapp, Station Manager
John Gradick, Promotions Manager

Deland

WOCL
03-14-1986; 105.9 MHz FM; 96 kW; 1562 ft.; N28 55 10 W81 19 8
1800 Pembrook Dr., Suite 400, Orlando, FL 32810 USA
(407) 919-1000; *Fax:* (407) 919-1190
www.1059sunnyfm.com
License: Deland, Volusia County, FL held by CBS Radio Stations Inc.
Group Owner: CBS Radio; (acq 8-7-2000; grpsl)
Nat'l Reps: Christal
Arbitron Metro Market: Orlando, FL; *Format:* Oldies *Special Programming:* news progmg 20 hrs wkly; *Hrs. of News Programming:* 1; *No. News Employees:* 25-54
Lydia Frost, General Sales Mgr
Rick Stacy, Programming Director
Angela Schlesman, Promotions Manager

WTJV
01-01-1948; 1490 kHz AM; *Hrs Open:* 24; 1 kw-D, ND2; 1 kw-N, ND2; N29 01 5 W81 17 59
222 Hazard St, Orlando, FL 32804 US
(407) 841-8282; *Fax:* (407) 841-8250
License: Deland, Volusia West County, FL held by J&V Communications Inc.
Group Owner: J&V Communications Inc.; (acq 12-7-2005; $370,000)
Regional Network: Florida's Radio Networks

Arbitron Metro Market: Daytona Beach, FL; *Format:* Adult Contemp; *Target Audience:* 25-54

WYND
12-07-1956; 1310 kHz AM; *Hrs Open:* 24
316 E. Taylor Road, Deland, FL 32724 US
(386) 734-1310; *Fax:* (386) 734-8885
License: Deland, FL held by Buddy Tucker Association Inc.
Group Owner: Buddy Tucker Association Inc.; (acq 12-30-86; $255,000;
Nat'l Network: USA
Arbitron Metro Market: De Land, FL; *Format:* Christian, News, 62, Talk; *Hrs. of News Programming:* news progmg 45 hrs wkly; *No. News Employees:* 1; *Target Audience:* 25-55.; *Adv. Rates:* 20; 15; 20; 10
Buddy Tucker, General Manager
Art Taylor, Chief Engineer

Delray Beach

WDJA
02-01-1952; 1420 kHz AM; *Hrs Open:* 24; 5 kw-D, DA2; 0.5 kw-N, DA2; N26 27 22 W80 5 58
%Fletcher,Heald & Hildre, 1300 N 17th St- 11th Flr, Arlington, VA 22209 US
(561) 278-1420; *Fax:* (561) 278-7515
www.universo1420.com
info@universo1420.com
License: Delray Beach, FL held by Professional Broadcasting LLC
Arbitron Metro Market: West Palm Beach-Boca Raton, FL; *Format:* Reggae
Stan Rain, Operations Dir
Roy Bresky, General Manager

Deltona

WNUE-FM
09-01-1968; 98.1 MHz FM; *Hrs Open:* 24; 50 kw; N28 51 09 W81 04 03
523 Douglas Ave., Orlando, FL 32714 US
(407) 774-2626; *Fax:* (407) 774-3384
www.salsa981.com
License: Deltona, Brevard County, FL held by Entravision Holdings LLC.
Group Owner: Entravision Communications Corp.; (acq 3-24-2008; $24 million)
Nat'l Reps: SBS/Interep
Arbitron Metro Market: Daytona Beach, FL; *Format:* Variety/Diverse; *Hrs. of News Programming:* news progmg 2 hrs wkly; *No. News Employees:* 1; *Target Audience:* 25-54; Hispanic adults 25-54
Lilly Gonzalez, Senior VP

Destin

WNWF
01-01-2000; 1120 kHz AM; *Hrs Open:* 6 AM-6 PM; 1 kw-D, NDD; N30 30 34 W86 28 34
Mailing Address: Box 5780, Gainesville, FL 32602 US
Second Address: 415 Mountain Dr., Suite 7, Destin, FL 32541
(850) 654-1718; *Fax:* (850) 650-1619
www.destin1120am.com/
License: Destin, FL held by Flagship Communications Inc.
Arbitron Metro Market: Pensacola, FL; *Format:* News, News/Talk, 86; *No. News Employees:* 1; *Target Audience:* 35-64.; *Adv. Rates:* 12; 12; 12; 12
Dale Riddick, General Manager

WECQ
09-24-1981; 92.1 MHz FM; 25 kw; 279 ft; N30 31 06 W86 28 01
111 Ferry Rd., Fort Walton Beach, FL 32548 US
(850) 654-1000
www.q92online.com
dcollins@apexbroadcasting.com
License: Destin, Okaloosa County, FL held by Apex Broadcasting
Group Owner: Apex Broadcasting
Nat'l Reps: Katz Radio
Arbitron Metro Market: Fort Walton Beach, FL; *Format:* Contemporary Hits/Top 40; *Target Audience:* 18-49; general; *Adv. Rates:* 60; 60; 60; 30
Dan Collins, Operations Dir
Ron Raybourne, General Manager
Sean Mack, Programming Director

Dogwood Lakes Estate

***WAGE**
01-15-1992; 91.1 MHz FM; 0.7 kw; 180 ft.; N30 51 34 W85 47 45
Mailing Address: P.O. Box 1944, Dothan, AL 36301 US
Second Address: 2573 Hodgesville Rd, Dothan, AL 36302
(334) 793-3189; *Fax:* (334) 793-4344
www.bethanybc.edu
wjed911fm@bethanybc.edu
License: Dogwood Lakes Estate, Holmes County, FL held by Washington-Holmes Technical Center
Nat'l Network: USA
Format: Gospel, Religious; *Target Audience:* General; college students & relg community
Dr. H.D. Shuemake, CEO
Sylvia Green, Operations Dir
Dr. Samuel Shuemake, Station Manager

Dunedin

WGUL
11-21-1959; 860 kHz AM; *Hrs Open:* 24; 5 kw-D, 1.5 kw-N, DA-2; N27 59 55 W82 42 01
5211 W. Laurel St., Tampa, FL 34684
(813) 639-1903; *Fax:* (813) 639-1272
www.860wgul.com
barb@salemtampa.com
License: Dunedin, Pinellas County, FL held by Caron Broadcasting Inc.
Group Owner: Salem Communications Corp.; (acq 8-12-2005; $9.5 million with W
Nat'l Network: Salem Radio Network; *Nat'l Reps:* Salem
Population Served: 4,000,000; *Arbitron Metro Market:* Tampa-St. Peter
Joe Weaver, Operations Dir
Barbara Yoder, General Manager

Dunnellon

WTRS
03-11-1969; 102.3 MHz FM; *Hrs Open:* 24; 50 kw; 489 ft.; N29 11 15 W82 23 40
3357 S.W. 7th St., Ocala, FL 34474 US
(352) 732-9877; *Fax:* (352) 622-6675
www.mycountryfla.com
License: Dunnellon, Marion County, FL held by JVC Media of Florida, LLC.
Group Owner: JVC Broadcasting
Arbitron Metro Market: Ocala, FL; *Format:* Country
Sam Gerace, General Manager
Bo Hamilton, Programming Director

Eatonville

WRLZ
01-01-1957; 1270 kHz AM; *Hrs Open:* 24
Mailing Address: 4151 West Oakridge Road, Orlando, FL 32839 US
Second Address: 6106 B Hoffner Ave., Orlando, FL 32822
(407) 345-0700; *Fax:* (407) 345-1492
www.radioluz1270.com
License: Eatonville, FL held by Radio Luz Inc.
Arbitron Metro Market: Orlando, FL; *Format:* Spanish; *Target Audience:* General; Family; *Adv. Rates:* 35; 35; 35; 30.
Saturnino Gonzalez, President
John Maldonado, General Manager

Ebro

WBPC
07-15-2005; 95.1 MHz FM; *Hrs Open:* 24; 21 kw; Ant 285 ft; N30 34 06 W85 48 28
700 W. 23rd St., Suite E-40, Panama City, FL 32405 US
(850) 235-2195; *Fax:* (850) 235-2795
www.beach951.com
License: Ebro, FL held by Beach Radio Inc.
Group Owner: Randy Sheffield-Wayne Bishop; Startup
Nat'l Network: ABC News
Arbitron Metro Market: Panama City, FL; *Format:* Oldies; *Target Audience:* 35-64; adults; *Adv. Rates:* 40; 25; 30; 15
David Nolin, Operations Dir
Randy Sheffield, General Manager
David Nolin, Programming Director

Edgewater

***WKTO**
11-01-1997; 88.9 MHz FM; *Hrs Open:* 24; 25 kw; 395 ft.; N29 1 30 W81 8 52
P O Box 677, Mims, FL 32754 US
(386) 427-1095; *Fax:* (386) 427-8970
www.wkto.net
info@wkto.net
License: Edgewater, Volusia County, FL held by Mims Community Radio Inc.
Format: Religious *Special Programming:* Jazz 4 hrs, Pol 1.5 hrs, Ger 1.5 hrs, Sp 2 hr wkly; *Target Audience:* 18-50.
Carol Henry, CEO

Egypt Lake

WMGG
01-01-1955; 1470 kHz AM
Haley, Bader & Potts, 4350 N Fairfax Dr, Suite 9, Arlington, VA 22203 US
(813) 281-1040; *Fax:* (813) 281-1948
www.newstalkflorida.com
contactus@radiogenesis.com
License: Egypt Lake, FL held by Genesis Communications of Tampa Bay Inc.
Group Owner: Genesis Communications Inc.; (acq 3-5-2001; $2 million)
Regional Network: Florida's Radio Networks; *Nat'l Reps:* Interep; McGavren Guild; *Wire Services:* AP
Arbitron Metro Market: Tampa, FL; *Format:* Oldies *Special Programming:* Relg 2 hrs wkly; *Target Audience:* 40 plus.; *Adv. Rates:* 75; 55; 80; 40
Adam Lindemann, Chairman
Bruce Maduri, CEO
Steven Baltimore, General Manager
Dro Silva, Programming Director
Cindy Scheffer, News Director
Jerry Smith, Chief Engineer
Kimo Gray, Information Technology Director

WTMP
01-01-1954; 1150 kHz AM; *Hrs Open:* 24
5207 Washington Blvd, Tampa, FL 33619 US
(813) 259-9867; *Fax:* (813) 254-9867
www.wtmp.com
License: Egypt Lake, FL held by Tama Radio Licenses of Tampa, FL, Inc.
Group Owner: Tama Broadcasting Inc.; (acq 12-18-2001).
Nat'l Network: American Urban
Arbitron Metro Market: Tampa, FL; *Format:* Adult Contemp; *Target Audience:* 18-49; urban contemporary music listeners & adults; *Adv. Rates:* 80; 75; 80; 65
Dr. Glenn Cherry, CEO
Louis Muhammad, Operations Dir
Glenn Cherry, General Manager
Lynn Tolliver, Programming Director

Emeralda

***WGTT**
91.5 MHz FM; 1.1 kw; 135 ft.; N28 57 8 W81 47 29
P. O. Box 4291, Enterprise, FL 32725 US
License: Emeralda, Lake County, FL held by Sunbelt Educational Broadcasting Inc.

Raul Ortiz, President

Englewood

WENG
11-15-1964; 1530 kHz AM; *Hrs Open:* 24; 1 kW Day, 1 W Night; N26 58 15 W82 19 24
Mailing Address: PO Box 2908, Englewood, FL 34295 US
Second Address: 1355 S River Rd, Englewood, FL 34223
(941) 474-3231; *Fax:* (941) 475-2205
www.wengradio.com
info@wengradio.com
License: Englewood, FL held by Viper Communications Inc.
Group Owner: Viper Communications Inc.; (acq 10-21-02)
Nat'l Network: CBS; ABC; Dial Global; *Regional Network:* Florida's Radio Networks
Population Served: 150,000; *Arbitron Metro Market:* Englewood, FL; *Format:* News, News/Talk, 86; *No. News Employees:* 1

***WSEB**
05-01-1989; 91.3 MHz FM; *Hrs Open:* 24; 62 kw horiz, 60 kw vert; 282 ft.; N26 51 48 W82 17 54
517 Paul Morris Drive, Suite 4-2, Englewood, FL 34223 US
(941) 475-9732; *Fax:* (941) 473-7308
www.wsebfm.com
comments@wsebfm.com
License: Englewood, Sarasota County, FL held by Suncoast Educational Broadcasting Corp.
Arbitron Metro Market: Sarasota-Braden; *Format:* Religious; *Target Audience:* 35 plus; Christian families

WTZB
04-05-1999; 105.9 MHz FM; 25 kw; 295 ft.; N27 6 19 W82 23 59
1779 Independence Blvd., Sarasota, FL 34234 US
(941) 552-4800; *Fax:* (941) 552-4900
www.1059thebuzz.com
info@1059thebuzz.com

License: Englewood, Sarasota County, FL held by Citicasters Licenses Inc.
Group Owner: iHeartMedia; (acq 5-4-99; grpsl).
Arbitron Metro Market: Sarasota-Braden; *Format:* Alternative
William Ames, Local Sales Manager
Eddie Rupp, Programming Director
Nikki Clark, Promotions Director

Estero

WFSX-FM
12-16-1978; 92.5 MHz FM; *Hrs Open:* 24; 25 kw; Ant 620 ft; N26 19 00 W81 47 13
2824 Palm Beach Blvd., Fort Myers, FL 33916 US
(239) 479-5500
www.sbroadcast.com
License: Estero, Lee County, FL held by Sun Broadcasting Inc.
Group Owner: Sun Broadcasting Inc.; (acq 9-14-2012; grpsl
Nat'l Reps: McGavren Guild; *Wire Services:* AP
Population Served: 63,512; *Arbitron Metro Market:* Fort Myers, FL; *Format:* News/Talk; *Target Audience:* 25-44.
Mike Moody, General Sales Mgr
Ian Hickin, Programming Director

Eustis

WKIQ
06-01-1955; 1240 kHz AM; 0.79 kw-U, ND1; N28 50 19 W81 41 46
3765 N. John Young Pkwy., Orlando, FL 32804 US
(407) 291-1395
License: Eustis, FL held by Unity Broadcasting LLC.
Group Owner: Unity Broadcasting LLC.; (acq 10-15-2004; $180,000 with WQBQ(AM) Leesburg).
Format: Tejano
Shanti Persaud, President

***WIGW**
90.3 MHz FM; 9.4 kw; 233 ft.; N28 58 18 W81 45 15
35200 Cathedral Canyon Dr, Suite G53, Cathedral City, CA 92234 US
(714) 545-7868; *Fax:* (208) 736-1958
wigw.krtmradio.org
License: Eustis, Lake County, FL held by Penfold Communications, Inc.
Group Owner: Penfold Communications, Inc.
Arbitron Metro Market: Whitehouse, OH; *Format:* Christian

Everglades City

***WBGY**
08-01-2004; 88.1 MHz FM; 0 kw horiz, 0.11 kw vert; 59 ft.; N25 51 56 W81 23 9
1601 Belvedere Rd, 204 E, West Palm Beach, FL 33406 US
(239) 404-9849
wbby@earthlink.net
License: Everglades City, Collier County, FL held by Everglades City Broadcasting Co. Inc.
Arbitron Metro Market: West Palm Beach, FL; *Format:* Country
Robert Ladd, President

Fernandina Beach

WVOJ
01-01-1955; 1570 kHz AM; *Hrs Open:* 24
1218 S. Park Street, Kalamazoo, MI 49001 US
(904) 739-3660; *Fax:* (904) 739-9409
License: Fernandina Beach, FL held by Norsan Consulting and Management Inc.
Group Owner: Norsan Consulting and Management Inc.; (acq 9-14-2005; $2.1 million with WNNR(AM) Jacksonville).
Arbitron Metro Market: Jacksonville, FL; *Format:* Spanish, Christian
Norberto Sanchez, President
Bernie Daigle, General Manager

WJSJ
01-01-2000; 105.3 MHz FM; 3.9 kw; 410 ft.; N30 30 4 W81 35 14 *Rebroadcasts:* Simulcast with WJXL(AM) Jacksonville Beach 100%
1801 K St NW, Suite 400k, Washington, DC 20006 US
(904) 641-1011; *Fax:* (904) 641-1022
www.1010xl.com
SteveG@1010XL.com
License: Fernandina Beach, Nassau County, FL held by Tama Radio Licenses of Jacksonville, FL, Inc.
Group Owner: Tama Broadcasting Inc.; (acq 2-28-2003; $8.5 million with WSJF(FM) Saint Augustine Beach)
Nat'l Network: ESPN Radio
Arbitron Metro Market: Jacksonville, FL; *Format:* Sports
Steve Griffin, General Manager
Ken Brady, General Sales Mgr

Jason Dixon, Programming Director
Tom Champion, Promotions Manager
Michelle Thomas, Business Manager
Chadd Scott, Assistant Program Director
Terri Hill, AdministrativeAssistant
Steve Bute, Producer
Donna Murphy, Producer
Jessica Blaylock, Producer/Jaguars Reporter

Five Points

WCJX
01-01-1996; 106.5 MHz FM; *Hrs Open:* 24; 3.8 kw; 341 ft.; N30 15 14 W82 40 56
5348 N.W. US Highway 41, Lake City, FL 32055 US
(386) 755-9259
www.wcjx.com
License: Five Points, Columbia County, FL held by RTG Radio LLC.
Group Owner: Black Crow Media Group LLC; (acq 11-9-2001; grpsl).
Nat'l Network: ABC; Premiere Radio Networks
Arbitron Metro Market: Lake City, Florida; *Format:* Classic Rock

Flagler Beach

***WJLH**
08-23-1996; 90.3 MHz FM; 15 kw; 177 ft.; N29 22 26 W81 10 49
Rebroadcasts: Rebroadcasts WJLU(FM) New Smyrna Beach 100%
4295 Ridgewood Avenue, Port Orange, FL 32127 US
(386) 756-9094; *Fax:* (386) 760-7107
www.cornerstoneministry.org
thecornerstone@cornerstoneministry.org
License: Flagler Beach, Flagler County, FL held by Cornerstone Broadcasting Corp.
Format: Christian
Sandra Leisner, Operations Dir
William Powell, General Manager

Florida City

***WMFL**
10-01-1998; 88.5 MHz FM; *Hrs Open:* 24; 7.7 kw; 171 ft.; N25 19 31 W80 24 16
Mailing Address: 1601 Belvedere Road, West Palm Beach, FL 33406 US
Second Address: 290 Hegenberger Rd., OaklandCA 94621
(916) 641-8191; *Fax:* (916) 641-8238
www.familyradio.com
info@familyradio.com
License: Florida City, Dade County, FL held by Family Stations Inc.
Group Owner: Family Stations Inc.; acq 11-15-00; $75,000).
Nat'l Network: Family Radio
Arbitron Metro Market: Sacramento, CA; *Format:* Christian, Religious
Harold Camping, President
Stanley Jackson, Operations Dir
Rob Robbins, Operations Manager

Fort Lauderdale

***WYBP**
01-01-1974; 90.3 MHz FM; *Hrs Open:* 24; 8 kw; 280 ft; N26 9 12 W80 10 12
P.O. Box 7300, Charlotte, NC 28241
(800) 888-7077
www.bbnradio.org
bbn@bbnmedia.org
License: Fort Lauderdale, Broward County, FL held by Bible Broadcasting Network Inc.
Group Owner: Bible Broadcasting Network
Population Served: 1,700,000; *Arbitron Metro Market:* Miami-Fort Lauderdale-Hollywood, FL; *Format:* Christian; *Target Audience:* 30 plus; general
Lowell Davey, President
Jason Padgett, Operations Manager

WBGG-FM
07-01-1960; 105.9 MHz FM; 100 kw; 1030 ft.; N25 59 34 W80 10 27
7601 Riviera Blvd., Miramar, FL 33023 US
(954) 862-2000; *Fax:* (954) 862-4013
www.big1059.com
License: Fort Lauderdale, Broward County, FL held by Clear Channel Radio Licenses Inc.
Group Owner: iHeartMedia; (acq 2-24-94; $14 million;
Arbitron Metro Market: Miramar, FL; *Format:* Classic Rock
Todd Winick, Sales Manager
Adam Kirschner, Digital Program Director
Henry Herrera, Promotions Director

Anne Urist, Promotions Coordinator
Nicole Covar, PSA Director
Russell Wein, Digital and Integrated Media Sales Director

WFLL
09-16-1946; 1400 kHz AM; *Hrs Open:* 24; 1 kw-U, ND1; N26 9 13 W80 10 11
426 S. River Rd., Tryon, NC 28782 US
(844) 556-7872
www.nossaradiousa.com
License: Fort Lauderdale, FL held by ACM JCE IV B LLC.
Group Owner: ACM JCE IV B LLC.
Arbitron Metro Market: Miami-Fort Lauderdale-Hollywood, FL; *Target Audience:* 25 plus.
Mark Jorgenson, President

WHYI-FM
07-31-1960; 100.7 MHz FM; 98 kw; 1007 ft.; N25 58 2 W80 12 34
7601 Riviera Blvd., Miramar, FL 33023 US
(954) 862-2000; *Fax:* (954) 862-4012
www.y100.com
License: Fort Lauderdale, Broward County, FL held by Clear Channel Broadcasting Licenses Inc.
Group Owner: iHeartMedia; (acq 11-94; grpsl)
Nat'l Reps: McGavren Guild
Arbitron Metro Market: Miami-Fort Lauderdale-Hollywood, FL; *Format:* Contemporary Hits/Top 40
Tony Yip, General Sales Mgr
Alex Tear, Programming Director
Nicole Covar, Promotions Director
Russell Wein, Digital and Integrated Media Sales Director

WMIB
10-17-1959; 103.5 MHz FM; 100 kw; 1,007 ft; N25 57 59 W80 12 33
7601 Riviera Blvd., Miramar, FL 33023 US
(954) 862-2000; *Fax:* (954) 862-4013
www.1035thebeat.com
License: Fort Lauderdale, Broward County, FL held by Clear Channel Broadcasting Licenses Inc.
Group Owner: iHeartMedia; (acq 11-21-97; grpsl).
Population Served: 3,000,000; *Arbitron Metro Market:* Miami-Fort Lauderdale-Hollywood, FL; *Format:* Blues, Urban Contemporary
Damien Sweet, General Sales Mgr
Henry Herrera, Promotions Director
Russell Wein, Digital and Integrated Media Sales Director
Adam Kirschner, Digital Program Director

WRMA
08-15-1962; 106.7 MHz FM; *Hrs Open:* 24; 100 kw; 984 ft.; N25 59 34 W80 10 27
3191 Coral Way, Suite 805, Miami, FL 33145 US
(305) 444-9292; *Fax:* (305) 461-4466
License: Fort Lauderdale, Broward County, FL held by WRMA Licensing Inc.
Group Owner: Spanish Broadcasting System Inc.; (acq 7-11-97; $110 million with WXDJ(FM) North Miami Beach)
Nat'l Reps: D & R Radio
Arbitron Metro Market: Miami-Fort Lauderdale-Hollywood, FL; *Format:* Ethnic; *No. News Employees:* 1; *Target Audience:* 18-54; Hispanic adults
Raoul Alarcon, President
Jackie Nosti-Cambo, General Manager
Albert Rodriguez, General Sales Mgr
Tony Campos, Programming Director
John Caride, Promotions Manager
Tomas Regalado, News Director
Ralph Chambers, Chief Engineer
Yoli Machado, Traffic Manager

WSRF
01-01-1955; 1580 kHz AM; *Hrs Open:* 24; 10 kw-D, 5 kw-N, DA-2; N26 04 54 W80 13 34
1510 N.E. 162 St., Miami, FL 33314
(305) 940-1580; *Fax:* (305) 947-8050
info@wsrf.com
License: Fort Lauderdale, Broward County, FL held by Niche Radio Inc.
Population Served: 2,000,000; *Arbitron Metro Market:* Miami-Fort Lauderdale; *No. News Employees:* 8; *Target Audience:* Haitian-Creole
Jean Cherubin, CEO/COO
Emmanuel Cherubin, President
Rose P Coriolan, Operations Dir
Jean Cherubin, General Manager
Rose P Coriolan, General Sales Mgr
Ed Lozama, Programming Director
Rose P Coriolan, Promotions Manager
EdLozama, News Director
Ralph Chambers, Engineering Dir
Ralph Chambers, Chief Engineer

Fort Meade

WWRZ
03-07-1977; 98.3 MHz FM; *Hrs Open:* 24; 27 kw; 666 ft.; N27 51 10 W81 52 2
Mailing Address: One Cuprak Road, Norwich, CT 06360 US
Second Address: 404 West Lime Street, Lakeland, FL 33815-4651
(863) 682-8184; *Fax:* (863) 683-2409
www.max983fm.com
License: Fort Meade, Polk County, FL held by Hall Communications Inc.
Group Owner: Hall Communications Inc.; acq 10-1-96; $1,750,000).
Nat'l Reps: Eastman Radio; *Wire Services:* AP
Arbitron Metro Market: Lakeland, FL; *Format:* Adult Contemp; *Hrs. of News Programming:* news progmg 2 hrs wkly; *No. News Employees:* 3; *Target Audience:* 25-54; women
Bonnie Rowbotham, Chairman
Art Rowbotham, Operations Dir
Nancy Cattarius, General Manager
Mike James, Programming Director
Jessica Brown, Promotions Manager
Andrea Oliver, News & Public Affairs Director
Mike James, OperationsManager

Fort Myers

WCRM
08-22-1964; 1350 kHz AM; *Hrs Open:* 19; 2 kw-D, ND1; 0.15 kw-N, ND1; N26 37 31 W81 50 29
3448 Canal Street, Fort Meyers, FL 33916 US
(239) 334-1350 / (941) 332-1350; *Fax:* (305)969-8755
License: Fort Myers, FL held by Manna Christian Missions Inc.
Nat'l Network: USA
Arbitron Metro Market: Fort Myers, FL; *Format:* Christian; *Hrs. of News Programming:* news progmg 5 hrs wkly; *No. News Employees:* 1; *Target Audience:* General.
Salvador Santana, General Manager

***WGCU-FM**
09-12-1983; 90.1 MHz FM; *Hrs Open:* 24; 100 kw; 813 ft; N26 48 54 W81 45 44
10501 FGCU Blvd., Fort Myers, FL 33965
(239) 590-2500; *Fax:* (239) 590-2520
www.wgcu.org
License: Fort Myers, Lee County, FL held by Board of Trustees, Florida Gulf Coast University
Nat'l Network: NPR; PRI; BBC; APM; *Regional Network:* Fla. Pub. Radio; Fla. News Exchange
Population Served: 830,000; *Arbitron Metro Market:* Fort Myers-Napl *TV Affiliate:* WGCU; *No. News Employees:* 4; *Target Audience:* 24 plus.
Luc Martin, Operations Dir
Rick Johnson, General Manager
Amy Tardif, Station Manager
Terry Brennen, General Sales Mgr
Amy Tardif, Programming Director
Amy Tardif, News Director
Rick Carroll, Engineering Dir
Rick Carroll, ChiefEngineer

WINK-FM
10-10-1964; 96.9 MHz FM; *Hrs Open:* 24; 98 kw; 1499 ft.; N26 48 1 W81 45 48
2824 Palm Beach Blvd., Fort Myers, FL 33916 US
(239) 337-2346; *Fax:* (239) 332-0767
www.winkfm.com
License: Fort Myers, Lee County, FL held by Fort Myers Broadcasting Co.
Group Owner: Fort Myers Broadcasting Co.
Nat'l Reps: McGavren Guild
Arbitron Metro Market: Fort Myers-Naples-Marco Island, FL *TV Affiliate:* WINK-TV affil.; *Format:* Adult Contemp; *Target Audience:* 25-54; females
Wayne Simons, General Manager
Brad Foster, General Sales Mgr
Michael Hayes, Programming Director

WJPT
07-31-1991; 106.3 MHz FM; 50 kw; Ant 472 ft; N26 29 16 W81 55 49
20125 S. Tamiami Trail, Estero, FL 33928
(239) 495-2100
www.sunny1063.com
License: Fort Myers, Lee County, FL held by Beasley Media Group LLC
Group Owner: Beasley Broadcast Group Inc.; (acq 12-11-97; $5 million)
Arbitron Metro Market: Fort Myers-Naples-Marco Island, FL; *Format:* Adult Contemp; *Target Audience:* 45 plus.
Brad Beasley, General Manager
Jon Parla, Sales Manager
Randy Sherwyn, Programming Director
AJ Lurie, Director of Sales
Diana Beasley, Digital Content Director

***WJYO**
01-01-1988; 91.5 MHz FM; *Hrs Open:* 24; 3 kw; 285 ft.; N26 30 18 W81 51 14 *Rebroadcasts:* Rebroadcasts WBIY(FM) LaBelle 100%
Falls Road, Toccoa Falls, GA 30598 US
(239) 274-9150; *Fax:* (239) 274-0191
airwavesforJesus.com
wjyo@aol.com
License: Fort Myers, Lee County, FL held by Airwaves for Jesus Inc.
Arbitron Metro Market: Fort Myers-Naples-Marco Island, FL; *Format:* Christian *Special Programming:* Children 5 hrs wkly; *Hrs. of News Programming:* News progmg 10 hrs wkly; *Target Audience:* 44 plus; traditionalminded persons
Art Ramos, CEO
Jasmin Ramos, Operations Dir

WMYR
11-11-1952; 1410 kHz AM; *Hrs Open:* 24; 5 kw-D, DAN; 5 kw-N, DAN; N26 37 23 W81 51 18
P.O. Box 216, Fort Myers, FL 33902 US
(239) 732-9369; *Fax:* (239) 732-7267
wmyr@mail.com
License: Fort Myers, FL held by J&B WMYR LLC
Nat'l Network: USA; *Regional Network:* Florida's Radio Networks
Arbitron Metro Market: Fort Myers, FL; *Format:* News, Oldies; *No. News Employees:* 1; *Adv. Rates:* 35; 35; 35; 35
Bob Ladd, Operations Dir

WOLZ
01-01-1970; 95.3 MHz FM; 79 kw; 476 ft.; N26 30 18 W81 51 14
13320 Metro Parkway, Suite 1, Fort Myers, FL 33966 US
(239) 225-4300; *Fax:* (239) 225-4329
www.953theriver.com
info@wolz.com
License: Fort Myers, Lee County, FL held by Clear Channel Broadcasting Licenses Inc.
Group Owner: iHeartMedia; (acq 2-18-97; grpsl)
Nat'l Reps: Clear Channel
Arbitron Metro Market: Fort Myers-Napl *TV Affiliate:* Oldies; *Format:* Oldies *Special Programming:* news progmg 2 hrs wkly; *Hrs. of News Programming:* 1; *No. News Employees:* 35-54; upbeat, fun oldies
Kevin Miskimins, Senior Vice President of Sales

WWGR
12-02-1969; 101.9 MHz FM; *Hrs Open:* 24; 100 kw; 1119 ft.; N26 25 22 W81 37 49
Broadcast Plaza, Crane Ave., Pittsburgh, PA 15220 US
(239) 495-8383; *Fax:* (239) 495-0883
www.gatorcountry1019.com
wwgr@rendabroadcasting.com
License: Fort Myers, Lee County, FL held by Renda Broadcast Corp.
Group Owner: Renda Broadcasting Corp.; (acq 7-13-94; $4 million;
Arbitron Metro Market: Fort Myers, FL; *Format:* Country
Roger Harris, General Manager
Camellia Pflum, General Sales Mgr
Randy Savage, Programming Director
Buzzy Ford, Promotions Manager

***WMYE**
01-01-2008; 91.9 MHz FM; 1.2 kw; 328 ft.; N26 47 7.5 W81 47 46.6
US
(786) 429-3606; *Fax:* (305) 251-2293
www.callfm.com
rob@callfm.com
License: Fort Myers, Lee County, FL held by Call Communications Group Inc.
Arbitron Metro Market: Fort Myers, FL; *Format:* Christian; *Target Audience:* 13-25.
Tim Pappas, Chairman
Rob Robbins, Ph.D., Programming Director and General Manager

WFWN
10-14-1954; 1240 kHz AM; *Hrs Open:* 24; 1 kw; N26 37 28 W81 49 52
2824 Palm Beach Blvd., Fort Myers, FL 33916 US
(239) 479-5500
License: Fort Myers, FL held by Sun Broadcasting Inc.
Group Owner: Sun Broadcasting Inc.
Nat'l Network: CBS; *Nat'l Reps:* McGavren Guild
Arbitron Metro Market: Fort Myers, FL; *Format:* Sports; *Target Audience:* 35 plus.
Joseph Schwantzel, President
Keith Stulhmann, Engineering Dir

Fort Myers Beach

WWCN
01-01-1983; 99.3 MHz FM; 50 kw; 466 ft.; N26 29 16 W81 55 46
20125 S. Tamiami Trail, Estero, FL 33928 US
(239) 495-2100
www.993espn.com
License: Fort Myers Beach, Lee County, FL held by Beasley Media Group LLC
Group Owner: Beasley Broadcast Group Inc.; (acq 10-16-97; $6 million).
Arbitron Metro Market: Fort Myers-Naples-Marco Island, FL; *Format:* Sports, Talk; *Target Audience:* 18-49; adults
Brad Beasley, General Manager
Jon Parla, Sales Manager
John Cassio, Programming Director
AJ Lurie, Director of Sales
Diana Beasley, Digital Content Director

Fort Pierce

WIRA
05-18-1946; 1400 kHz AM; *Hrs Open:* 24; 1 kw-U, ND1; N27 26 7 W80 21 41
200 Concord Plaza, Suite 600, San Antonio, TX 78216 US
(772) 460-9356; *Fax:* (772) 460-2700
License: Fort Pierce, FL held by Team One Media LLC
Nat'l Network: ABC
Arbitron Metro Market: Fort Pierce-Stuart-Vero Beach, FL; *Format:* Gospel *Special Programming:* Relg one hr, pub affrs one hr wkly; *Target Audience:* 45 plus; male & female
Al Richards, General Manager

***WJFP**
01-15-1995; 91.1 MHz FM; *Hrs Open:* 6 AM-midnight; 6 kw; 157 ft.; N27 27 7 W80 21 34
1150 W. King Street, Cocoa, FL 32922 US
(772) 467-2400; *Fax:* (772) 467-9400
www.wjfp.com
info@wjfp.com
License: Fort Pierce, St. Lucie County, FL held by Black Media Works Inc.
Group Owner: Black Media Works Inc.; acq 1-21-98).
Arbitron Metro Market: Fort Pierce-Stuart-Vero Beach, FL; *Format:* Religious *Special Programming:* Sp 2 hrs, Haitian 8 hrs wkly; *Target Audience:* 12-49.
Kimberly Kassis, President

WJNX
12-24-1952; 1330 kHz AM; *Hrs Open:* 24; 5 kw-D, DA2; 1 kw-N, DA2; N27 27 20 W80 22 2
200 Concord Plaza, Suite 600, San Antonio, TX 78216 US
(772) 340-1590; *Fax:* (772) 340-3245
www.lagigante1330.com
wpsl@wpsl.com
License: Fort Pierce, FL held by Port St. Lucie Broadcasters Inc.
Nat'l Network: ESPN Deportes
Arbitron Metro Market: Fort Pierce-Stuart-Vero Beach, FL; *Format:* News, News/Talk, 86; *No. News Employees:* 1; *Target Audience:* 25-54.; *Adv. Rates:* 50; 30; 50; 40
Carol Wyatt, CEO
Greg Wyatt, General Manager

***WQCS**
04-01-1982; 88.9 MHz FM; 100 kw; 436 ft.; N27 25 17 W80 21 23
3209 Virginia Aveue, Fort Pierce, FL 33454 US
(772) 462-4744; *Fax:* (772) 462-4743
www.wqcs.org
info@wqcs.org
License: Fort Pierce, St. Lucie County, FL held by Indian River State College.
Nat'l Network: NPR; PRI; AP Radio
Arbitron Metro Market: Fort Pierce-Stuart-Vero Beach, FL; *Format:* News
Michelle Rhinesmith, Operations Dir
Madison Hodges, General Manager

Fort Walton Beach

WEDM(AM)
01-01-1956; 1400 kHz AM; 1 kw-U; N30 24 38 W86 37 23
21 Miracle Strip Pkwy. S.E., Fort Walton Beach, FL 32548
(850) 244-1400; *Fax:* (850) 243-1471
License: Fort Walton Beach, Okaloosa County, FL held by Star Broadcasting Inc.
Group Owner: Star Broadcasting Inc.; (acq 7-11-2005)

Population Served: 19,793; *Arbitron Metro Market:* Fort Walton Beach, FL; *Format:* Oldies *Special Programming:* Church program one hr wkly; *Target Audience:* 50 plus.
Ron Hale Sr., General Manager
David Kuntz, General Sales Mgr
Frank Hale, Programming Director

WFTW
11-20-1953; 1260 kHz AM; *Hrs Open:* 24; 2.5 kw-D, ND1; 0.131 kw-N, ND1; N30 24 49 W86 37 40
P.O. Box 2347, Fort Walton Beach, FL 32549 US
(850) 243-7676; *Fax:* (850) 664-0203
www.wftw.com
ken@wftw.com
License: Fort Walton Beach, FL held by Cumulus Licensing Corp.
Group Owner: Cumulus Media Inc.; (acq 1-10-03; grpsl).
Regional Network: Florida's Radio Networks
Arbitron Metro Market: Fort Walton Beach, FL; *Format:* News, News/Talk, 86 *Special Programming:* Rush Limbaugh affiliate
Lou Dickey, President
Ron Raybourne, General Manager
Georgia Edmiston, General Sales Mgr
Steve Williams, Programming Director
Lisa Captain, Promotions Manager
Gerald Lee, News Director
Bruce Campbell, Chief Engineer

WKSM
05-28-1965; 99.5 MHz FM; 50 kw; 438 ft.; N30 24 50 W86 37 40
P.O. Box 1699, Meridian, FL 39302 US
(850) 243-7676; *Fax:* (850) 243-6806
www.wksm.com
info@wksm.com
License: Fort Walton Beach, Okaloosa County, FL
Arbitron Metro Market: Fort Walton Beach, FL
Lee Leonard, General Sales Mgr
Nicci Garmon, Programming Director
Steve O'Day, Promotions Manager
Aimee Shaffer, News Director
Anthony Proffitt, Music Director
Steve Williams, Special Events Coordinator
Gerald Lee, TrafficManager

***WPSM**
07-01-1985; 91.1 MHz FM; *Hrs Open:* 24; 11 kw horiz, 10.78 kw vert; 344 ft.; N30 24 38 W86 37 22
Mailing Address: P.O. Box 1474, Ft. Walton Beach, FL 32549 US
Second Address: 233 N. Hill Ave., Fort Walton Beach, FL 32548
(850) 244-7667; *Fax:* (850) 244-3254
www.wpsm.com
contact@wpsm.com
License: Fort Walton Beach, Okaloosa County, FL held by Fort Walton Beach Educ. Broadcasting Corp.
Nat'l Network: USA
Arbitron Metro Market: Fort Walton Beach, FL; *Format:* Christian; *Hrs. of News Programming:* news progmg 14 hrs wkly; *No. News Employees:* 1; *Target Audience:* 25-55; young to middle-age adult Christians
Terry Thorne, General Manager

WZNS
01-01-1997; 96.5 MHz FM; *Hrs Open:* 24; 100 kw; 438 ft.; N30 24 50 W86 37 40
P.O. Box 1699, Meridian, MS 39302 US
(850) 664-0965; *Fax:* (850) 243-6806
www.z96.com
License: Fort Walton Beach, Okaloosa County, FL held by Cumulus Licensing Corp.
Group Owner: Cumulus Media Inc.; (acq 1-10-03; grpsl).
Arbitron Metro Market: Fort Walton Beach, FL; *Format:* Contemporary Hits/Top 40
Hayden Green, Programming Director

Fruit Cove

WSOS-FM
07-17-1982; 94.1 MHz FM; *Hrs Open:* 24; 5.5 kw; 505 ft.; N30 4 8 W81 38 50
2715 Stratton Blvd, St. Augustine, FL 32095 US
(904) 824-0833,(904) 722-9606; *Fax:* (904) 721-9322
tbryan@rendabroadcasting.com
License: Fruit Cove, St. Johns County, FL held by Renda Broadcasting Corp. of Nevada.
Group Owner: Renda Broadcasting Corp.; (acq 4-27-2005; $7.75 million).
Nat'l Reps: McGavren Guild
Arbitron Metro Market: Jacksonville, FL; *Format:* Adult Contemp; *Target Audience:* 25-54; upscale audience
Tony Renda, CEO
Tim Bryan, General Manager
Don Runk, General Sales Mgr
Briggs Bickley, Programming Director
Stacey Steiner, Promotions Manager
Brenda McArthur, News Director
Bob Dillehay, Chief Engineer
Jim Byard, PublicService Director

Gainesville

WAJD
05-31-1961; 1390 kHz AM; 5 kw-D, ND1; 0.051 kw-N, ND1; N29 39 56 W82 17 26
7120 Sw 24th Avenue, Gainesville, FL 32607 US
(352) 331-2200; *Fax:* (352) 331-0401
www.kiss1053.com
info@kiss1053.com
License: Gainesville, FL held by Gillen Broadcasting Corp.
Arbitron Metro Market: Gainesville, FL; *Format:* Children; *Target Audience:* 12-49.
Douglas Gillen, President
Doug Gillen, General Sales Manager

WGGG
02-01-1948; 1230 kHz AM; 1 kw-U, ND1; N29 40 56 W82 24 48
Mailing Address: P.O. Box 3930, Ocala, FL 34478 US
Second Address: 101 S.E. 2nd Pl., Grainesville, FL 32601
(352) 378-7378; *Fax:* (352) 629-1614
www.cflradio.net
License: Gainesville, FL held by Florida Sportstalk Inc.
Arbitron Metro Market: Gainesville-Ocala, FL; *Format:* Sports
Doug Gillen, General Manager

***WJLF**
08-26-1990; 91.7 MHz FM; *Hrs Open:* 24; 2 kw; 400 ft.; N29 38 34 W82 25 13 *Rebroadcasts:* Rebroadcasts WJIS(FM) Brandenton
2925 N.W. 39th Avenue, Gainesville, FL 32605 US
(352) 373-9553; *Fax:* (352) 373-9888
thejoyfm.com
thejoyfm@thejoyfm.com
License: Gainesville, Alachua County, FL held by Radio Training Network Inc.
Arbitron Metro Market: Gainesville-Ocala, FL; *Format:* Christian *Special Programming:* Youth 5 hrs, jazz 2 hrs, children 1 hr wkly; *Hrs. of News Programming:* news progmg 2 hrs wkly; *No. News Employees:* 1 *TargetAudience:* 18-49; young adults & young families
James Campbell, President
Andy Haynes, Station Manager

WDVH
10-01-1954; 980 kHz AM; *Hrs Open:* 6 AM-10 PM; 5 kw-D, ND1; 0.166 kw-N, ND1; N29 37 26 W82 17 19
9421 Holiday Drive, Indianapolis, IN 46260 US
(352) 313-3150; *Fax:* (352) 313-3199
www.flafnr.com
License: Gainesville, FL held by Marc Radio Gainesville LLC
Group Owner: Marc Radio Group LLC; (acq 7-18-2011; grpsl)
Nat'l Reps: Roslin
Arbitron Metro Market: Gainesville, FL; *Format:* News, News/Talk, 86; *Target Audience:* 35 plus.
Shawn Portmann, General Manager

WRUF
01-01-1928; 850 kHz AM; *Hrs Open:* 24; 5 kw-D, DAN; 5 kw-N, DAN; N29 38 34 W82 25 13
Mailing Address: P. O. Box 14444, Gainesville, FL 32604 US
Second Address: Univ. Of Florida, 3200 Wiemer Hall, Gainesville, FL 32611
(352) 392-0771; *Fax:* (352) 392-0519
info@am850.com
License: Gainesville, FL held by University of Florida, Board of Trustees
Nat'l Network: CBS; Westwood One; *Regional Network:* Florida's Radio Networks; *Wire Services:* CBS
Arbitron Metro Market: Gainesville-Oca *TV Affiliate:* WUFT-TV, WLUF-TV affils.; *Format:* News, News/Talk, 84, Talk *Special Programming:* Black 4 hrs wkly; *Hrs. of News Programming:* news progmg 54 hrs wkly *No.News Employees:* 3; *Target Audience:* 35-54; middle-to-upper income, decision makers
Robert Lawrence, Operations Dir
Larry Dankner, General Sales Mgr
Tom Ksynski, News Director
Don Rice, Chief Engineer
Steve Russell, Sports Commentator

WRUF-FM
01-01-1948; 103.7 MHz FM; *Hrs Open:* 24; 100 kw; 768 ft.; N29 42 34 W82 23 40
Mailing Address: 3200 Wimer Hall, P.O. Box 14444, Gainesville, FL 32604 US
Second Address: Univ. of Florida, 3200 Wiemer Hall, Gainesville, FL 32611
(352) 392-0771; *Fax:* (352) 392-0519
www.rock104.com
info@rock104.com
License: Gainesville, Alachua County, FL held by University of Florida, Board of Trustees
Arbitron Metro Market: Gainesville-Oca; *Format:* Contemporary Hits/Top 40 *Special Programming:* Alternative 6 hrs wkly; *Hrs. of News Programming:* news progmg 5 hrs wkly; *No. News Employees:* 3; *Target Audience:* 25-34; urban rockers
Harry Guscott, Operations Dir
Larry Dankner, General Manager
Tom Kyrnski, News Director
Don Rice, Chief Engineer
Monica Richs, Disc Jockey
Matt Lehtola, Disc Jockey
Cathy Ferguson, Traffic Manager

***WUFT-FM**
09-27-1981; 89.1 MHz FM; *Hrs Open:* 24; 100 kw; 771 ft.; N29 42 34 W82 23 40
2208 Weimer Hall, Gainesville, FL 32611 US
(352) 392-5551; *Fax:* (352) 392-5731
www.wuft.org
info@wuft.org
License: Gainesville, Alachua County, FL held by Board of Trustees, University of Florida.
Nat'l Network: NPR; PRI; *Regional Network:* Fla. Pub.
Arbitron Metro Market: Gainesville, FL *TV Affiliate:* *WUFT-TV affil.; *Format:* Jazz *Special Programming:* Black 4 hrs, folk one hr, wkly; *Hrs. of News Programming:* news progmg 15 hrs wkly; *No. News Employees:* 3; *Target Audience:* 35-65; general, educated (some college or degree)
Steve Seipp, Operations Dir
Larry Dankner, General Manager
Henri Pensis, Station Manager
Bill Beckett, Programming Director
Kevin Allen, News Director
Manis Samons, Chief Engineer
Richard Drake, Music Director

WTMN
01-01-1990; 1430 kHz AM
249 W. University Ave., Suite B, Gainesville, FL 32601 US
(352) 313-3150; *Fax:* (352) 338-0566
rejoice@musicalsoulfood.com
License: Gainesville, FL held by Marc Radio Gainesville LLC
Group Owner: Marc Radio Group; (acq 7-18-2011; grpsl)
Arbitron Metro Market: Gainesville, FL; *Format:* Gospel
Benjamin Hill, General Manager

***WYFB**
08-04-1985; 90.5 MHz FM; *Hrs Open:* 24; 97 kw; 679 ft.; N29 52 8 W82 12 4
P.O. Box 7300, Charlotte, NC 28241 US
(800) 888-7077
www.bbnradio.org
bbn@bbnmedia.org
License: Gainesville, Alachua County, FL held by Bible Broadcasting Network Inc.
Group Owner: Bible Broadcasting Network
Nat'l Network: Bible Bcstg Net; USA
Arbitron Metro Market: Gainesville, FL; *Format:* Religious; *Hrs. of News Programming:* News progmg 12 hrs wkly; *Target Audience:* General.
Lowell Davey, President
Jason Padgett, Operations Manager

WXJZ
05-01-1982; 100.9 MHz FM; *Hrs Open:* 24; 6 kw; 299 ft.; N29 38 3 W82 18 50
491 West University Ave., Suite 110, Gainesville, FL 32601 US
(352) 375-1317; *Fax:* (352) 375-6961
License: Gainesville, Alachua County, FL held by JVC Media of Florida, LLC.
Group Owner: JVC Broadcasting
Nat'l Network: Jones Radio Networks; *Nat'l Reps:* McGavren Guild
Arbitron Metro Market: Gainesville, FL; *Format:* Adult Contemp; *Target Audience:* 25-54; upscale, affluent, sophisticated; *Adv. Rates:* 30; 35; 30; 20
Sam Gerace, General Manager
Joey Cuffari, Business Manager

WYKS
05-04-1970; 105.3 MHz FM; 3 kw; 466 ft.; N29 37 53 W82 25 8
7120 Sw 24th Avenue, Gainesville, FL 32607 US

RADIO - U.S.

(352)331- 2200; *Fax:* (352) 331-0401
www.kiss1053.com
info@kiss1053.com
License: Gainesville, Alachua County, FL
Arbitron Metro Market: Gainesville, FL; *Format:* Contemporary Hits/Top 40
Stephen Puffer, President
Teresa Puffer, Operations Dir
Don Smith, Chief Engineer

Gifford

WPHR-FM
06-01-1994; 94.7 MHz FM; 25 kw; 295 ft; N27 33 21 W80 22 08
290 Hegenberger Rd, Oakland, CA 94621
1-800-543-1495; *Fax:* (801) 359-8112
www.familyradio.com
info@familyradio.com
License: Gifford, Indian River County, FL held by Aloha Station Trust LLC
Population Served: 33,704; *Arbitron Metro Market:* Butte MT; *Format:* Christian, Religious
Harold Camping, General Manager

Golden Gate

WNPL
09-01-2008; 1460 kHz AM; 7 kw-D, DA2 2 kw-N, DA2; N26 15 26 W81 40 33 *Rebroadcasts:* Simulcasts WJUA(AM) 1200
2824 Palm Beach Blvd, Fort Myers, FL 33916 US
(239) 334-1111; *Fax:* (239) 332-0767
juan1200.com
License: Golden Gate, Collier County, FL held by Fort Myers Broadcasting Co.
Group Owner: Fort Myers Broadcasting Co.; (acq 6-18-2007; $975,000 for CP)
Nat'l Network: Fox Sports; *Nat'l Reps:* McGavren Guild
Arbitron Metro Market: Ft.Myers-Naples, FL; *Format:* Adult Contemp
Wayne Simons, Operations Dir
Brad Foster, General Sales Mgr

Goulds

WRTO-FM
02-01-1976; 98.3 MHz FM; *Hrs Open:* 24; 100 kw; 1,407 ft.; N25 32 24 W80 28 7
800 Douglas Rd., Suite 111, Coral Gables, FL 33134 US
(305) 447-1140
www.univision.com
License: Goulds, Dade County, FL held by License Corporation #2
Group Owner: Univision Radio; (acq 9-22-2003; grpsl).
Arbitron Metro Market: Miami-Fort Lauderdale-Hollywood, FL; *Format:* Spanish
Claudia Puig, Senior Vice President and General Manager
Monica Rabassa, Vice President of Marketing and Public Affairs

Graceville

WTOT-FM
01-01-1996; 101.7 MHz FM; *Hrs Open:* 24; 6 kw; 328 ft.; N30 57 21 W85 29 53
9102 North Meridian St, Suite 500, Indianapolis, IN 46260 US
(850) 482-3046; *Fax:* (850) 482-3049
License: Graceville, Jackson County, FL held by GFR Inc.
Nat'l Network: ABC
Arbitron Metro Market: Graceville, FL; *Format:* Adult Contemp; *Target Audience:* 25+; female; *Adv. Rates:* 10; 8; 9; 6
Ed Cearley, General Manager

Green Cove Springs

WWJK
05-09-1977; 107.3 MHz FM; 98 kw
11700 Central Parkway, Jacksonville, FL 32224 US
(904) 636-0507; *Fax:* (904) 997-7713
License: Green Cove Springs, Clay County, FL held by Clear Channel Broadcasting Licenses Inc.
Group Owner: iHeartMedia
Arbitron Metro Market: Jacksonville, FL; *Format:* Adult Contemp
Rollin Isbell, Sales Manager
Skip Kelly, Programming Director
Jean Podbielski, Promotions Director
Nick Wize, Digital Content Director
Taylor Brown, Digital Content Coordinator

Gretna

WVFT
10-02-1989; 93.3 MHz FM; *Hrs Open:* 24; 8.7 kw; 499 ft.; N30 29 48 W84 27 33
Mailing Address: P.O.Box 919, 8 West Washington Street, Quincy, FL 32351 US
Second Address: 8 W. Washington, Quincy, FL 32351
(850) 627-7086; *Fax:* (850) 627-3422
License: Gretna, Gadsden County, FL held by Magic Broadcasting II LLC
Group Owner: Magic Broadcasting II LLC; (acq 9-18-91; $75,000;
Nat'l Network: USA
Format: Country *Special Programming:* Black 20 hrs wkly; *Hrs. of News Programming:* News progmg 21 hrs wkly; *Target Audience:* 25-54.
Pat Bitner, Operations Dir
Monte Bitner, General Manager
Jan Rogers, News Director
Jeff Fallaway, Chief Engineer

Gulf Breeze

WNRP
02-01-1998; 1620 kHz AM
P.O. Box 10, 805 N. Main St., Atmore, AL 36502 US
(850) 494-2800; *Fax:* (850) 494-0778
www.newsradio1620.com
License: Gulf Breeze, FL held by ADX Communications of Escambia
Arbitron Metro Market: Pensacola, FL; *Format:* News, News/Talk, 86; *Target Audience:* 35-64; 60% male, 40% female
Mary Hoxeng, General Manager
Bob Nieman, Station Manager
Jeff Wayne, General Sales Mgr
Tracey Castillo, Promotions Manager
Tim McEvoy, Engineering Dir

WRNE
11-01-1957; 980 kHz AM; *Hrs Open:* 24
312 E. Nine Mile Road, Suite 29-D, Pensacola, FL 32514 US
(850) 478-6000; *Fax:* (850) 484-8080
www.wrne980.com
hill@wrne980.com
License: Gulf Breeze, FL held by Media One Communications, Inc.
Nat'l Network: Cumulus; AURN; *Nat'l Reps:* Dora-Clayton
Arbitron Metro Market: Pensacola, FL; *Format:* Gospel *Special Programming:* 20 hrs/week Black Gospel; 5 hours/week Hispanic; *Hrs. of News Programming:* news progmg 5 hrs wkly; *No. News Employees:* 1 *TargetAudience:* 25-54; minorities
Robert Hill, President

WRRX
106.1 MHz FM; 3.9 kw; 407 ft.; N30 26 36 W87 14 4
300 East Rock Rd., (Wfmz-Tv), Allentown, PA 18103 US
(404) 949-0700; *Fax:* (404) 949-0740
www.cumulus.com
webmaster@cumulus.com
License: Gulf Breeze, Santa Rosa County, FL held by Cumulus Licensing Corp.
Arbitron Metro Market: Atlanta, GA; *Format:* Urban Contemporary
Lewis W. Dickey, Jr., Chairman, President & CEO
Debbie Dingwall, Operations Dir
Liz Hanlon, General Manager
Jonathan G. Pinch, Executive Vice President & Co-Chief Operating Offi
John W. Dickey, Executive Vice President & Co-ChiefOperating Offi
Richard S. Denning, Senior Vice President, Secretary & General Counsel
Joseph P. Hannan, Senior Vice President, Treasurer & Chief Financial
Linda A. Hill, Vice President, Corporate Controller & Chief Accou

Gulfport

WFUS
10-01-1963; 103.5 MHz FM; 66 kw; 1549 ft.; N27 49 9.7 W82 15 38.7
402 West Gandy Blvd., Tampa, FL 33611 US
(813) 832-1000; *Fax:* (813) 832-1090
www.us1035.com
webmaster@us1035.com
License: Gulfport, Pinellas County, FL held by Citicasters Licenses Inc.
Group Owner: iHeartMedia; (acq 6-99; grpsl)
Wire Services: AP
Arbitron Metro Market: Tampa, FL; *Format:* Country; *Target Audience:* 25-54; men
Heather Wallace, Sales Manager
Travis Daily, Programming Director
Rachel Pitts, Promotions Director
John McMartin, Engineering Dir
Josh Jensen, Creative Services Director
David Bell, Public Service Director
Marc Cemiglio,Digital Content Director

Haines City

***WLVF-FM**
04-11-1986; 90.3 MHz FM; *Hrs Open:* 24; 0.75 kw; 315 ft.; N28 6 49 W81 37 23
110 W. Scenic Highway, Haines City, FL 33844 US
(863) 422-5175; *Fax:* (863) 422-0110
www.gospel903.com
info@gospel903.com
License: Haines City, Polk County, FL held by Landmark Baptist Church
Nat'l Network: USA
Arbitron Metro Market: Haines City, FL; *Format:* Gospel
Lewis Cruz, Operations Dir
Steven Carter, General Manager
Lewis Cruz, Station Manager
Bobby Ogden, General Sales Mgr
Jeff Crews, Chief Engineer

Hammocks

***WMKL**
10-01-1998; 91.9 MHz FM; *Hrs Open:* 24; 25 kw vert; 318 ft.; N25 45 41.63 W80 49 10.77
1601 Belvedere Rd., 204e, West Palm Beach, FL 33406 US
(786) 429-3606; *Fax:* (305) 251-2293
www.callfm.com
callfm@callfm.com
License: Hammocks, Monroe County, FL held by Call Communications Group Inc.
Arbitron Metro Market: Hammocks, FL; *Format:* Christian; *Target Audience:* 13-25.
Robert Robbins, President
Kelly Downing, Programming Director
Jim Sorensen, Chief Engineer

Havana

WHTF
01-01-1986; 104.9 MHz FM; *Hrs Open:* 24; 47 kw; 505 ft.; N30 35 11 W84 14 11
25 Reliance Drive, Bristol, RI 02809 US
(850) 386-8004; *Fax:* (850) 442-1897
www.hot1049.com
License: Havana, Gadsden County, FL held by Opus Broadcasting Tallahassee LLC.
Group Owner: Opus Media Holdings LLC; (acq 9-2-2005; grpsl)
Nat'l Reps: McGavren Guild
Arbitron Metro Market: Tallahassee, FL; *Format:* Contemporary Hits/Top 40; *Target Audience:* 18-49.
Doug Purtee, Operations Dir
Hank Kestenbaum, General Manager

Hernando

WRZN
06-01-1989; 720 kHz AM; 10 kw-D, DAN; 0.25 kw-N, DAN; N28 55 21 W82 22 21
Mailing Address: 3974 Patch Drive, Tallahassee, FL 32308 US
Second Address: 3938 N. Roscoe Rd., Hernando, FL 34442
(352) 726-7221; *Fax:* (352) 726-3172
License: Hernando, FL held by Marc Radio Gainesville LLC
Group Owner: Marc Radio Group; (acq 7-18-2011; grpsl)
Format: Adult Contemp *Special Programming:* Loc news 4 hrs wkly; *Target Audience:* 45 plus.
Ben Hill, General Manager
Reggie Thomas, General Sales Mgr
Jim Brand, Programming Director

Hialeah

WACC
12-01-1987; 830 kHz AM; *Hrs Open:* 24; 1 kw-D, DA2; 1 kw-N, DA2; N25 46 22 W80 25 16
3785 N.W. 82nd Ave., Suite 312, Miami, FL 33166 US
(956) 487-8015
License: Hialeah, FL held by Radio Peace Catholic Broadcasting Inc.
Arbitron Metro Market: Reno NV; *Adv. Rates:* 100; 100; 100; 50
Eloy Vera, General Manager

WCMQ-FM
12-22-1969; 92.3 MHz FM; 31 kw; 617 ft.; N25 46 24 W80 11 18
3191 Coral Way, Suite 805, Miami, FL 33145 US
(305) 444-9292; *Fax:* (305) 883-7701
www.z92miami.com
saludos@clasica92fm.com
License: Hialeah, Dade County, FL held by WCMQ Licensing Inc.
Group Owner: Spanish Broadcasting System Inc.; (acq 12-22-86; grpsl;
Arbitron Metro Market: Miami-Fort Lauderdale-Hollywood, FL; *Format:* Adult Contemp
Tony Campos, Operations Dir
Jackie Nosti-Combo, General Manager
Albert Rodriguez, General Sales Mgr
John Caride, Promotions Manager

High Springs

***WUBA**
01-01-1923; 88.1 MHz FM; *Hrs Open:* 24; kw
US
(610) 617-8500; *Fax:* (610) 617-8501
License: High Springs, Philadelphia County, FL held by Neighborhoods United For a Better Alachua Inc.
Arbitron Metro Market: Philadelphia, PA
Joseph Tamburro, General Manager

WYGC
01-31-1984; 104.9 MHz FM; *Hrs Open:* 24; 3.2 kw; 449 ft.; N29 49 16 W82 34 25
491 West University Ave., Suite 110, Gainesville, FL 32601 US
(352) 375-6961; *Fax:* (352) 505-0318
License: High Springs, Alachua County, FL held by JVC Media of Florida, LLC.
Group Owner: JVC Broadcasting
Nat'l Network: CNN Radio; Westwood One
Arbitron Metro Market: Gainesville, FL; *Format:* Oldies; *Hrs. of News Programming:* News progmg 4 hrs wkly; *Target Audience:* 25-54.; *Adv. Rates:* 60; 60; 60; 20
Sam Gerace, General Manager
Wolf Bowers, Programming Director
Joey Cuffari, Business Manager

Hobe Sound

WOLL
01-01-2002; 105.5 MHz FM; 50 kw; 456 ft.; N26 45 42 W80 4 42
3071 Continental Drive, West Palm Beach, FL 33407 US
(561) 616-6600; *Fax:* (561) 616-6677
www.1055online.com
info@1055online.com
License: Hobe Sound, Martin County, FL held by Clear Channel Broadcasting Licenses Inc.
Group Owner: iHeartMedia; (acq 7-30-2008)
Arbitron Metro Market: West Palm Beach *TV Affiliate:* Classic Hits; *Format:* Adult Contemp; *No. News Employees:* 25-54.
Bryan Kelly, Director of Sales
Promotions Director, Promotions Manager
T.A. Walker, Brand Manager
Chad Tyson, Digital Program Director

Holiday

WSUN-FM
09-01-1978; 97.1 MHz FM; *Hrs Open:* 24; 11.5 kw; 731 ft.; N28 10 56 W82 46 6
11300 4th Street North, Suite 300, Saint Petersburg, FL 33716 US
(727) 579-2000; *Fax:* (727) 579-2662
www.97xonline.com
97xcomments@97xonline.com
License: Holiday, Pasco County, FL held by Cox Radio Inc.
Group Owner: Cox Radio Inc.; (acq 11-20-98)
Arbitron Metro Market: Tampa-St. Petersburg-Clearwater, FL; *Format:* Alternative, Rock/AOR; *Target Audience:* 35 plus.; *Adv. Rates:* 60; 50; 60; 40
Keith Lawless, Vice President & Marketing Manager
Stephanie Sabota, General Sales Manager
Jodi Rainey, National Sales Manager
Dan Connelly, Director Of Branding & Programming
Jenna Kesneck, Director Of Promotional Operations

Holly Hill

***WAPN**
10-01-1985; 91.5 MHz FM; *Hrs Open:* 24; 1.8 kw; 285 ft.; N29 15 6 W81 2 53
Mailing Address: 1508 State Avenue, Holly Hill, FL 32117 US
Second Address: 1508 State Ave., Daytona Beach, FL 32125
(386) 677-4272(386) 672-3333; *Fax:* (386) 677-7095
www.wapn.net
wapn@wapn.net
License: Holly Hill, Volusia County, FL held by Public Radio Capital Florida
Arbitron Metro Market: Holly Hill, FL; *Format:* Religious *Special Programming:* Sp 4 hrs wkly; *Target Audience:* General.
Shellye Lund-Vallance, General Manager
Earlyne Lund, Owner

WVYB
01-01-1997; 103.3 MHz FM; *Hrs Open:* 24; 6 kw; 295 ft.; N29 14 11 W81 4 22
126 W. Intl. Speedway Blvd., Daytona Beach, FL 32214 US
(386) 255-9300
1033wvyb.com
License: Holly Hill, Volusia County, FL held by Southern Stone Communications, LLC
Group Owner: Southern Stone Communications
Arbitron Metro Market: Daytona Beach, FL; *Format:* Adult Contemp; *Hrs. of News Programming:* News progmg 2 hrs wkly; *Target Audience:* 18-49.

Hollywood

WLQY
04-01-1953; 1320 kHz AM; 5 kw full time
1055 NE 125 St., Miami, FL 33161 US
(305) 891-1729; *Fax:* (305) 891-1583
www.entravision.com
License: Hollywood, FL held by Entravision Holdings LLC.
Group Owner: Entravision Communications Corp.; (acq 7-28-00; grpsl).
Arbitron Metro Market: Miami-Fort Lauderdale-Hollywood, FL; *Format:* Ethnic; *Target Audience:* 35 plus; female
Jeff Liberman, President
Rick Santos, General Manager

Holmes Beach

WBRN
12-07-1989; 98.7 MHz FM; 50 kw; N27 50 32 W82 48 52
P.O. Box 21061, Tampa, FL 33622
(727) 579-1925
License: Holmes Beach, Manatee County, FL held by WPOW License Limited Partnership
Group Owner: Beasley Broadcast Group Inc.
Nat'l Reps: CBS Radio
Arbitron Metro Market: Tampa-St. Petersburg-Clearwater, FL; *Format:* Rock/AOR
Jay Mulligan, General Sales Mgr
Hillary Hatch, Promotions Manager
Kelly Sedivy, Digital Sales Manager

Holt

WHWY
09-24-1981; 98.1 MHz FM; 100 kw; N30 24 38 W86 37 22
111 Ferry Rd., Fort Walton Beach, FL 32548 US
(850) 654-1000
www.highway98country.com
dcollins@apexbroadcasting.com
License: Holt, FL held by Apex Broadcasting
Group Owner: Apex Broadcasting
Nat'l Reps: Katz Radio
Arbitron Metro Market: Fort Walton Beach, FL; *Format:* Country; *Target Audience:* 18-49; general; *Adv. Rates:* 60; 60; 60; 30
Dan Collins, Operations Dir
Ron Raybourne, General Manager

Homestead

WOIR
11-04-1957; 1430 kHz AM
206 Washington Ave, Homestead, FL 33030 US
(305) 270-1430
http://www.zoe1430.com/
License: Homestead, FL held by Amanecer Christian Network Inc.
Arbitron Metro Market: Miami-Fort Laud *TV Affiliate:* Sp

***WRGP**
01-01-1999; 88.1 MHz FM; *Hrs Open:* 24; 0.165 kw; 423 ft.; N25 32 24 W80 28 7
University Park Campus, 11200 S.W. 8th Street, Miami, FL 33199 US
(305) 348-3071; *Fax:* (305) 348-6665
wrgp.org
wrgp@fiu.edu
License: Homestead, Dade County, FL held by Florida International University.
Arbitron Metro Market: Miami-Fort Lauderdale-Hollywood, FL; *Format:* Variety/Diverse *Special Programming:* Hip hop 12 hrs, news 3 hrs, raggae 3 hrs wkly; *Hrs. of News Programming:* News progmg 4 hrs wkly *TargetAudience:* General; young adults, mainly university students
Brennan Forsyth, General Manager
Jennifer Mojena, Programming Director

Homosassa Springs

WXCV
03-01-1983; 95.3 MHz FM; *Hrs Open:* 24; 6 kw; 328 ft.; N28 50 3 W82 39 34
P.O. Box 1408, Crystal River, FL 34423 US
(352) 628-4444; *Fax:* (352) 628-4450
www.citrus953.com
staff@citrus.com
License: Homosassa Springs, Citrus County, FL held by Westwind Broadcasting Inc.
Arbitron Metro Market: Homosassa Springs, FL; *Format:* Classic Rock *Special Programming:* Jazz 7 hrs, oldies 6 hrs wkly; *Hrs. of News Programming:* news progmg 7 hrs wkly; *No. News Employees:* 1; *Target Audience:* 25-54.
Laura Grady, General Manager
Ryan Downs, Programming Director
Jody Boles, Traffic Director
Annette Kimball, Senior Account Executive
Brittany Jones, Account Executive
Mary Castro, Account Executive

Immokalee

WAFZ
10-14-1964; 1490 kHz AM; *Hrs Open:* 24
2105 W. Immokalee Dr., Immokalee, FL 33934 US
(239) 657-9210; *Fax:* (239) 658-6109
www.wafz.com
iza@gladesmedia.com
License: Immokalee, FL held by Glades Media Company LLP.
Nat'l Network: CNN Radio; *Nat'l Reps:* Univision Radio National Sales
Arbitron Metro Market: Fort Myers-Naples-Marco Island, FL; *Target Audience:* Sp
Ricardo Chairez, Operations Dir
KC Kelly, General Manager
Jesus Castro, Programming Director
Robbie Castellanos, Partner

WAFZ-FM
01-01-1995; 92.1 MHz FM; *Hrs Open:* 24; 5.6 kw; 328 ft.; N26 26 54 W81 16 17
3061 Terrace Ave., Naples, FL 34104 US
(239) 657-9210; *Fax:* (239) 658-6109
www.radiofiesta.com
robbie@gladesmedia.com
License: Immokalee, Collier County, FL held by Glades Media Co. LLC
Nat'l Network: CNN Radio; *Nat'l Reps:* Univision Radio National Sales
Arbitron Metro Market: Fort Myers-Naples-Marco Island, FL; *Format:* Tejano; *Target Audience:* 18 plus; general; *Adv. Rates:* 20; 15; 20; 15
Robbie Castellanos, President
Ricardlo Chairez, Operations Dir
Alfredo Hernandez, General Manager

Indian Lakes Estates

***WLOQ**
01-01-1966; 88.7 MHz FM; *Hrs Open:* 24; kw
US
(407) 647-5557; *Fax:* (407) 647-4495
www.wloq.com
frontdesk@wloq.com
License: Indian Lakes Estates, Orange County, FL held by Gross Communications Corp.
Nat'l Reps: Interep
Arbitron Metro Market: Orlando, FL; *Format:* Jazz; *Target Audience:* 25-54; white collar/professionals
John Gross, CFO
Herbert Gross, President
Rick Weinkauf, Operations Dir
Ken Marks, General Sales Mgr

Indian River Shores

WOSN
01-01-1996; 97.1 MHz FM; 23 kw; 348 ft.; N27 44 6 W80 27 27
1235 16th St., Vero Beach, FL 32960 US
(772) 567-0937; *Fax:* (772) 562-4747
www.wosnfm.com

License: Indian River Shores, Indian River County, FL held by Vero Beach Broadcasters LLC
Group Owner: Vero Beach Broadcasters LLC; acq 2-15-01; $4.1 million).
Arbitron Metro Market: Fort Pierce-Stuart-Vero Beach, FL; *Format:* Adult Contemp
Jim Davis, General Manager
Karen Franke, Station Manager
Hamp Elliott, Programming Director
Miguel Santiesteban, Promotions Manager

Indian Rocks Beach

WXYB
05-11-1963; 1520 kHz AM; *Hrs Open:* Sunrise-sunset; 0.6 kw-D, NDD; N27 50 45 W82 46 21
27873 U.S. 19 North, Clearwater, FL 34621 US
(727) 725-5555; *Fax:* (813) 814-7500
www.wpso.com
wpso@wpso.com
License: Indian Rocks Beach, FL held by ASA Broadcasting Inc.
Arbitron Metro Market: Indian Rocks Beach, FL; *Format:* Ethnic, Greek, 60, News/Talk, Talk *Special Programming:* Indian 3 hrs, It 2 hrs, Pol 2 hrs, East Indian one; *Hrs. of News Programming:* News progmg 7 hrs wkly *Target Audience:* General; international, ethnic
Sam Agelatos, President
Angelo Agelatos, Station Manager

Indiantown

WIRK
08-01-1965; 103.1 MHz FM; 90 kw; 974 ft.; N27 1 31 W80 10 43
701 Northpoint Pkwy., Suite 500, West Palm Beach, FL 33407 USA
(561) 686-9505; *Fax:* (561) 686-0157
www.wirk.com
License: Indiantown, Martin County, FL held by Palm Beach Broadcasting LLC
Group Owner: Palm Beach Broadcasting LLC
Arbitron Metro Market: West Palm Beach-Stuart; *Format:* Country
Lee Strasser, Operations Dir
Tony Bonvini, General Sales Mgr

Inglis

WYKE(FM)
10-01-1994; 104.3 MHz FM; *Hrs Open:* 24; 4.4 kw; Ant 380 ft; N29 01 18 W82 41 20
11928 N. William St., Dunnellon, FL 34432
(352) 522-0172; *Fax:* (352) 564-8750
www.wow104.com
License: Inglis, Levy County, FL held by Nature Coast Broadcasting Inc.
Regional Network: Florida's Radio Networks
Population Served: 350,000; *Arbitron Metro Market:* Gainesville-Ocala, FL; *Format:* Adult Contemp; *Hrs. of News Programming:* News progmg one hr wkly; *Target Audience:* 25-54.; *Adv. Rates:* 20; 10; 15; 10
Lisa Cuppelli, CEO
Sab Cupelli, President
Marc Tyll, Operations Dir
Jeremy Howard, General Sales Mgr
Jon Kay, Operations Manager

WXRA
01-01-2008; 99.3 MHz FM; 3.7 kw; 420 ft.; N29 9 19 W82 27 1 US
(901) 375-9324; *Fax:* (901) 375-5889
www.flinn.com
mail@flinn.com
License: Inglis, Levy County, FL held by George S. Flinn Jr.
Arbitron Metro Market: Inglis, FL; *Format:* Christian
George Flinn Jr., President

Inverness

*WJUF
10-01-1995; 90.1 MHz FM; *Hrs Open:* 24; 21 kw; 397 ft.; N28 46 39 W82 28 5 *Rebroadcasts:* Rebroadcasts WUFT-FM Gainesville 100%
2208 Weimer Hall, University of Florida, Gainesville, FL 32611 US
(352) 392-5200; *Fax:* (352) 392-5741
www.wuft.org
info@wuft.org
License: Inverness, Citrus County, FL held by Board of Trustees, University of Florida.
Nat'l Network: NPR; PRI; *Regional Network:* Fla. Pub.
TV Affiliate: *WUFT-TV affil.; *Format:* Classical, Jazz, 60; *Hrs. of News Programming:* news progmg 15 hrs wkly; *No. News Employees:* 3; *Target Audience:* General.
Larry Dankner, General Manager
Henri Pensis, Station Manager

Islamorada

WWWK
10-15-1984; 105.5 MHz FM; 50 kw; 430 ft.; N25 5 29 W80 26 37
200 Concord Plaza, Suite 600, San Antonio, TX 78216 US
(270) 389-1550; *Fax:* (270) 389-1553
wmsk@bellsouth.net
License: Islamorada, Monroe County, FL held by LSM Radio Partners LLC
Arbitron Metro Market: Morganfield KY; *Format:* Country, Religious; *Hrs. of News Programming:* News progmg 20 hrs wkly; *Target Audience:* General; adults 25-64
Edward Henson, President
Bob Hite, Operations Dir
John Robinson, General Manager
Don Sheridan, General Sales Mgr
Rhonda Gibson, Traffic Manager

*WAZQ
89.3 MHz FM; kw
US
(561) 912-9002
License: Islamorada, Monroe County, FL held by Educational Public Radio Inc.
Arbitron Metro Market: Islamorada, FL; *Format:* Adult Contemp; *No. News Employees:* 12; *Target Audience:* 18-54; adults
Bill Lacy, President

WZFL
93.5 MHz FM; 50 kw; 113 meters; N 80 22 29.2 W
25 E. 86th St., New York, NY 10028 USA
(917) 535-0419
License: Islamorada, FL held by Alex Media Inc.
Group Owner: Alex Media Inc.
Format: Variety/Diverse
Alexander Berger, President

Jacksonville

WAPE-FM
01-01-1978; 95.1 MHz FM; 100 kw; 984 ft.; N30 19 22 W81 38 34
8000 Belfort Parkway, Suite 100, Jacksonville, FL 32256 US
(904) 245-8500; *Fax:* (904) 245-8501
www.wape.com
License: Jacksonville, Duval County, FL held by Cox Radio Inc.
Group Owner: Cox Radio Inc.; (acq 8-00; grpsl).
Nat'l Reps: Christal; *Wire Services:* AP
Arbitron Metro Market: Jacksonville, FL; *Format:* Contemporary Hits/Top 40
Todd Shannon, Program Director
Nichole Hartman, General Sales Manager
Jodi Rainey, National Sales Manager
Ashley Testa, Digital Sales Manager
David Ratz, Promotions & Events Director

WCGL
01-01-1948; 1360 kHz AM; *Hrs Open:* 24; 5 kw-D, ND2; 0.089 kw-N, ND2; N30 16 33 W81 38 12
6050-6 Moncrief Road, Jacksonville, FL 32209 US
(904) 766-9955; *Fax:* (904) 765-9214
www.wcgl1360.com
wcgl@aol.com
License: Jacksonville, FL held by JBD Communications Inc.
Arbitron Metro Market: Jacksonville, FL; *Format:* Religious; *Target Audience:* 25 plus.
Deborah Maiden, President
Kelvin Postell, Operations Dir

WEJZ
01-01-1949; 96.1 MHz FM; 100 kw; 984 ft.; N30 19 22 W81 38 34
Broadcast Plaza, Crane Ave., Pittsburgh, PA 15220 US
(904) 727-9696; *Fax:* (904) 721-9322
www.wejz.com
breese@rendabroadcasting.com
License: Jacksonville, Duval County, FL held by Renda Broadcasting Corp.
Group Owner: Renda Broadcasting Corp.; acq 6-90; grpsl;
Nat'l Reps: McGavren Guild; *Wire Services:* Metro Weather Service Inc.
Arbitron Metro Market: Jacksonville, FL; *Format:* Adult Contemp; *Target Audience:* 25-54; office, home & in-the-car audience
Tony Renda Sr., CEO
Bill Scull, General Manager
Bill Reese, General Sales Mgr
Chuck Beck, Programming Director
Woody Carlson, Promotions Manager
Jim Byard, News Director
Bob Dillehay, Chief Engineer
Jim Byard, Public ServiceDirector

WJAX
01-01-1958; 1220 kHz AM; *Hrs Open:* 24; 1 kw-D, ND2; 0.036 kw-N, ND2; N30 19 30 W81 34 15
5353 Arlington Expreway, Jacksonville, FL 32211 US
(904) 680-1220
kjones@jones.edu
License: Jacksonville, FL held by Jones College
Nat'l Network: CNN Radio
Arbitron Metro Market: Jacksonville, FL; *Format:* Adult Contemp; *Target Audience:* 40 plus.
Jamey Styer, Operations Dir
John Wharff III, General Manager
Andy Rex, Programming Director
Ralph Matheny, Chief Engineer

*WJCT-FM
04-17-1972; 89.9 MHz FM; 98 kw; 823 ft.; N30 16 51 W81 34 12
100 Festival Park Avenue, Jacksonville, FL 32206 US
(904) 353-7770; *Fax:* (904) 358-6352
www.wjct.org
wjct@wjct.org
License: Jacksonville, Duval County, FL held by WJCT Inc.
Nat'l Network: NPR; PRI; *Regional Network:* Fla. Pub.
Arbitron Metro Market: Jacksonville, FL *TV Affiliate:* *WJCT-TV affil.; *Format:* News, News/Talk, 86
Michael Boylan, CEO
Tom Patton, News Director

*WJFR
09-15-1987; 88.7 MHz FM; 8 kw; 351 ft.; N30 19 43 W81 41 42
4135 Northgate Blvd, Suite1, Sacramento, CA 95834 US
(904) 389-9088
www.familyradio.com
License: Jacksonville, Duval County, FL held by Family Stations Inc.
Arbitron Metro Market: Jacksonville, FL; *Format:* Religious; *Target Audience:* Conservative Christians.
Harold Camping, President
Harold Camping, General Manager
Marcy Morrison-Pearce, Programming Director
Phyllis Johnston, Music Director

WBOB(AM)
01-01-1945; 600 kHz AM
600 Congress Ave., Suite 1400, Austin, TX 78701 US
(904) 470-4615; *Fax:* (904) 296-1683
License: Jacksonville, FL held by Chesapeake-Portsmouth Broadcasting Corp.
Group Owner: Chesapeake-Portsmouth Broadcasting Corp.; (acq 12-5-2006; $1.8 million with WZNZ(AM) Jacksonville)
Arbitron Metro Market: Jacksonville, FL; *Format:* News, News/Talk, 86; *Target Audience:* 25-54.
Calvin Grabau, Operations Dir
Henry Hoot, General Manager

WJGL
07-01-1969; 106.1 MHz FM; *Hrs Open:* 24; 98 kw; 1014 ft.; N30 16 34 W81 33 53
8000 Belfort Parkway, Suite 100, Jacksonville, FL 32256 US
(904) 245-8500; *Fax:* (904) 245-8501
www.power1061.com
clarence.natto@coxinc.com
License: Jacksonville, Duval County, FL held by Cox Radio Inc.
Group Owner: Cox Radio Inc.
Nat'l Reps: Christal
Arbitron Metro Market: Jacksonville, FL; *Format:* Contemporary Hits/Top 40, Adult Contemp; *No. News Employees:* 1; *Target Audience:* Adults 25-54
Clarence Natto, Program Director
Eric Lauer, General Sales Manager
Jodi Rainey, National Sales Manager
Ashley Testa, Digital Sales Manager
David Ratz, Promotions & Events Director

*WKTZ-FM
02-08-1973; 90.9 MHz FM; *Hrs Open:* 24; 50 kw; 463 ft.; N30 16 36 W81 33 47
5353 Arlington Expresway, Jacksonville, FL 32211 US
(904) 731-1184
License: Jacksonville, Duval County, FL held by Jones College
Nat'l Network: AP Network News
Arbitron Metro Market: Jacksonville, FL; *Format:* Easy Listening; *Target Audience:* 40+.
Kenneth Jones, General Manager
Dick Jones, Chief Engineer
Tom Buetow, Music Director

WXXJ
11-01-1965; 102.9 MHz FM; *Hrs Open:* 24; 98 kw; 1014 ft.; N30 16 34 W81 33 53
8000 Belfort Parkway, Suite 100, Jacksonville, FL 32256 US
(904) 245-8500; *Fax:* (904) 245-8501
www.x1029.com
cody.black@coxinc.com
License: Jacksonville, Duval County, FL held by Cox Radio Inc.
Group Owner: Cox Radio Inc.; (acq 2-23-2000; grpsl)
Nat'l Reps: Christal
Arbitron Metro Market: Jacksonville, FL; *Format:* Rock/AOR; *Target Audience:* Men 18-34
Cody Black, Program Director
AJ Vaughan, General Sales Manager
Jodi Rainey, National Sales Manager
Ashley Testa, David Ratz
Promotions & Events Director, General Manager

***WCRJ**
03-16-1984; 88.1 MHz FM; *Hrs Open:* 24; 8 kw; 495 ft.; N30 16 34 W81 33 53
2361 Cortez Rd., Jacksonville, FL 32246 US
(904) 641-9626; *Fax:* (904) 645-9626
www.klove.com
calvin@fm88.org
License: Jacksonville, Duval County, FL held by The River Educational Media Inc.
Arbitron Metro Market: Jacksonville, FL; *Format:* Christian; *Target Audience:* 25-55; women
Roger Henderson, Operations Dir
Calvin Grabau, General Manager

WFXJ
11-01-1925; 930 kHz AM; 5 kw-D, DAN; 5 kw-N, DAN; N30 17 9 W81 44 52
11700 Central Parkway, Jacksonville, FL 32224 US
(904) 636-0507; *Fax:* (904) 997-7713
www.sportsradiojax.com
License: Jacksonville, FL held by Clear Channel Broadcasting Licenses Inc.
Group Owner: iHeartMedia
Arbitron Metro Market: Jacksonville, FL *TV Affiliate:* Sports; *Format:* Sports; *No. News Employees:* 25-49; men
Tommy BoDean, Senior Vice President of Programming
Aaron Wilborn, Senior Vice President of Sales
Nick Wize, Digital Content Director
Taylor Brown, Digital Content Coordinator
John Hakim, Digital Sales Manager

WYMM
11-18-1976; 1530 kHz AM; 50 kw-D, DAD; N30 21 50 W81 44 54
3801 Skillern Blvd, Flower Mound, TX 75028 US
(904) 786-2820; *Fax:* (904) 786-2661
am1530jax@yahoo.com
License: Jacksonville, FL held by Word Broadcasting Network Inc.
Group Owner: Word Broadcasting Network Inc.; (acq 7-29-2003; $1.25 million with WYRM(AM) Norfolk, VA).
Arbitron Metro Market: Jacksonville, F *TV Affiliate:* Sp; *Adv. Rates:* varies

WQIK-FM
09-01-1964; 99.1 MHz FM; *Hrs Open:* 24; 100 kw; 991 ft.; N30 16 51 W81 34 13
11700 Central Parkway, Jacksonville, FL 32224 US
(904) 636-0507; *Fax:* (904) 997-7707
www.991wqik.com
License: Jacksonville, Duval County, FL held by Citicasters Licenses Inc.
Group Owner: iHeartMedia; (acq 5-4-99; grpsl).
Nat'l Network: ABC
Arbitron Metro Market: Jacksonville, FL; *Format:* Country; *Hrs. of News Programming:* news progmg 4 hrs wkly; *No. News Employees:* 1; *Target Audience:* 18-54.
Aaron Wilborn, Senior Vice President of Sales
Cindy Spicer, Programming Director
Jean Podbielski, Promotions Director
John Hakim, Digital Sales Manager
Nick Wize, Digital Content Director
Taylor Brown, Digital ContentCoordinator

WQOP
01-30-1958; 1460 kHz AM
Mailing Address: 11521 Innfields Drive, Odessa, FL 33556 US
Second Address: 391 S. 14th Ave., Jacksonville Beach, FL 32250
(904) 241-3311; *Fax:* (904) 241-1402
www.qopradio.com
radioqop@aol.com
License: Jacksonville, FL held by Queen of Peace Radio, Inc.
Nat'l Network: USA
Arbitron Metro Market: Jacksonville, FL; *Format:* Talk, Religious
C. Williams, President
Tom Moran, General Manager

WROS
07-01-1955; 1050 kHz AM; *Hrs Open:* 6 AM-sunset; 5 kw-D, DA2; 0.013 kw-N, DA2; N30 21 14 W81 44 21
5590 Rio Grande, Jacksonville, FL 32205 US
(904) 353-1050; *Fax:* (904) 353-7076
www.wros.net
wros@wros.net
License: Jacksonville, FL held by The Rose of Jacksonville
Nat'l Network: USA *Regional Reps:* NRB
Arbitron Metro Market: Jacksonville, FL; *Format:* Christian; *Hrs. of News Programming:* news progmg 7 hrs wkly; *No. News Employees:* 1; *Target Audience:* 25-65; Christians & secular; *Adv. Rates:* 45; 45; 45; 45
Elwyn Hall, CEO
Robyne Hall, Station Manager
Yisrael Freedman, Programming Director
Jerry Smith, Chief Engineer

WNNR
01-01-1969; 970 kHz AM; 1 kw-D, DA2; 0.164 kw-N, DA2; N30 23 8 W81 40 4
2427 University Blvd. N., Jacksonville, FL 32211 US
(904) 739-3660; *Fax:* (904) 739-9409
www.larazalaraza.com
License: Jacksonville, FL held by Norsan Consulting and Management Inc.
Group Owner: Norsan Consulting and Management Inc.; (acq 9-15-2005; $2.1 million with WVOJ(AM) Fernandina Beach)
Arbitron Metro Market: Jacksonville, FL; *Format:* Sports; *Target Audience:* General.
Norberto Sanchez, President
Bernie Daigle, General Manager
Marci Koziolek, News Director

WZAZ
07-04-1950; 1400 kHz AM; *Hrs Open:* 24; 1 kw-U, ND1; N30 19 43 W81 41 42
8889 Pelican Bay Blvd., Suite 5100, Naples, FL 34108 US
(904) 470-4615; *Fax:* (904) 296-1683
www.1400wzaz.com
License: Jacksonville, FL held by Caron Broadcasting Inc.
Group Owner: Salem Communications Corp.; (acq 5-30-03; grpsl).
Nat'l Reps: Roslin
Arbitron Metro Market: Jacksonville, F; *Format:* Gospel; *Hrs. of News Programming:* news progmg 5 hrs wkly; *No. News Employees:* 2; *Target Audience:* 25-54; adult Black listeners
Henry Hoot, General Manager
Calvin Grabau, Programming Director

Jacksonville Beach

WJXL
01-01-1946; 1010 kHz AM; *Hrs Open:* 24
P.O. Box 16907, Jacksonville, FL 32245 US
(904) 641-1011; *Fax:* (904) 641-1022
www.1010xl.com
JasonD@1010XL.com
License: Jacksonville Beach, FL held by Seven Bridges Radio LLC
Nat'l Network: ESPN Radio; Motor Racing Net; *Wire Services:* AP
Arbitron Metro Market: Jacksonville, FL; *Format:* Sports *Special Programming:* NASCAR (MRN, PRN) Jacksonville University; *Target Audience:* M 25-54.; *Adv. Rates:* 30; 30; 30; 30
Steven Griffin, President
Jack O'Brien, General Sales Mgr
Jason Dixon, Programming Director

WFJO
11-01-1989; 92.5 MHz FM; 1.7 kw; 627 ft.; N30 16 34 W81 33 51
P.O. Box 1448, Kingsland, GA 31548 US
(904) 425-3482
License: Jacksonville Beach, Charlton County, FL held by Tama Radio Licenses of Jacksonville, FL Inc.
Group Owner: Tama Broadcasting Inc.; (acq 6-4-2003)
TV Affiliate: Talk; *No. News Employees:* General.

Jensen Beach

WMBX
12-10-1980; 102.3 MHz FM; *Hrs Open:* 24; 100 kw; 974 ft.; N27 1 31 W80 10 43
701 North Point Pkwy., West Palm Beach, FL 33407 USA
(561) 686-9505; *Fax:* (561) 684-6311
thex1023.com
License: Jensen Beach, Martin County, FL held by Palm Beach Broadcasting LLC
Group Owner: Palm Beach Broadcasting LLC
Arbitron Metro Market: West Palm Beach, FL; *Format:* Contemporary Hits/Top 40; *Hrs. of News Programming:* news progmg 17 hrs wkly; *No. News Employees:* 1; *Target Audience:* 25-54; women
Patricia Larschan, Operations Dir
Mark Krieger, General Sales Mgr
Danelle Sarvas, Promotions Manager
Pam Crosby, News Director
Jeff Clarke, Music Director
John O'Connell, Operations Manager

Juno Beach

WLDI
10-30-1969; 95.5 MHz FM; 100 kw; 925 ft.; N27 7 19 W80 23 20
3071 Continental Dr., West Palm Beach, FL 33407 US
(561) 616-6600; *Fax:* (561) 616-6677
www.wild955.com
info@wild955.com
License: Juno Beach, St. Lucie County, FL held by Clear Channel Broadcasting Licenses Inc.
Group Owner: iHeartMedia; (acq 6-17-98; grpsl).
Arbitron Metro Market: West Palm Beach-Boca Raton, FL; *Format:* Contemporary Hits/Top 40; *Target Audience:* 18-49; active, contemp
Bryan Kelly, Director of Sales
Chad Tyson, Digital Program Director
Ethan Briner, Promotions Director

Jupiter

WJBW
01-01-1997; 1000 kHz AM; *Hrs Open:* 24
2255 Glades Road, Suite 237w, Boca Raton, FL 33431 US
(772) 567-0937; *Fax:* (772) 562-4747
License: Jupiter, FL held by AM of Palm Beach Inc.
Arbitron Metro Market: West Palm Beach-Boca Raton, FL; *Format:* News, News/Talk, 86
Laurie Silvers, President
Jim Davis, General Manager
Karen Franke, Director of Sales
Brittany Hinger, Promotions Manager
Brittany Hinger, Webmaster

WUUB
08-02-2012; 106.3 MHz FM; 19 kW; 358 ft.; N26 47 59 W80 04 33
777 S. Flagler Dr., Suite 106, West Palm Beach, FL 33401
(561) 697-8353; *Fax:* (561) 697-8525
espnwestpalm.com
spolitziner@espnwestpalm.com
License: Jupiter, Palm Beach County, FL held by Good Karma Broadcasting LLC
Group Owner: Good Karma Broadcasting LLC
Arbitron Metro Market: Jupiter, FL; *Format:* Sports
Steve Politziner, General Manager
Evan Cohen, Programming Director
Stephanie Prince, Director of Marketing

Kendall

WURN
08-01-1999; 1020 kHz AM
1662 Willowmont Ave., San Jose, CA 95124 US
(305) 446-5444; *Fax:* (305) 493-1111
www.radiomega.net
License: Kendall, FL held by New World Broadcasting Inc.
Format: Ethnic; *Target Audience:* 25-55; adult
Alex Saintsuin, General Manager

Key Colony Beach

WKYZ
04-15-1999; 101.7 MHz FM; *Hrs Open:* 24; 100 kw horiz, 90.25 kw vert; 453 ft.; N24 39 39.8 W81 25 10.4
10144 Seagrape Way, Palm Beach Gardens, FL 33480 US
(305) 289-1013; *Fax:* (305) 743-9441
www.pirateradiokeywest.com
License: Key Colony Beach, Monroe County, FL held by Keys Media Co. Inc.
Format: Classic Rock; *Target Audience:* 25-54.
Joe Nascone, General Manager

***WYBW**
03-20-2013; 88.3 MHz FM; 0.25 kw; 92 ft.; N24 43 2 W81 4 18
P.O. Box 7300, Charlotte, NC 28241
(800) 888-7077
www.bbnradio.org
bbn@bbnmedia.org

License: Key Colony Beach, Monroe County, FL held by Bible Broadcasting Network Inc.
Group Owner: Bible Broadcasting Network
Population Served: 168,528; *Arbitron Metro Market:* Marathon, FL; *Format:* Christian, Religious
Lowell Davey, President
Jason Padgett, Operations Manager

Key Largo

***WLFE-FM**
01-01-2004; 90.9 MHz FM; 33 kw; Ant 308 ft; N25 14 07 W80 19 35
The New 88.3 19620 Pines Blvd, # 114, Pembroke Pines, FL 33029
(305) 406-2883; *Fax:* (305) 551-2737
www.lanuevafm.net
info@lanuevafm.net
License: Key Largo, Monroe County, FL held by Genesis License Subsidiary LLC.
Population Served: 408,750; *Arbitron Metro Market:* Miami, FL; *Format:* Christian
Kenny Reyes, General Manager

Key West

WAIL
12-01-1978; 99.5 MHz FM; *Hrs Open:* 24; 100 kw; 240 ft.; N24 39 32 W81 32 18
830 Crane Blvd., Sugarloaf Key, FL 33042 USA
(305) 745-2468
sun103.com
License: Key West, Monroe County, FL held by Florida Keys Media LLC
Group Owner: Florida Keys Media LLC
Regional Network: Florida's Radio Networks
Arbitron Metro Market: Key West, FL; *Format:* Classic Rock; *Target Audience:* 25-54; men
Rick Lopez, General Manager
Amy Andrade, Sales Manager
Randy Perry, Chief Engineer

WCNK
01-01-1986; 98.7 MHz FM; *Hrs Open:* 24; 100 kw horiz, 81 kw vert; 453 ft.; N24 39 39.8 W81 25 10.4
830 Crane Blvd., Sugarloaf, FL 33042 USA
(305) 745-2468
conchcountry.com
License: Key West, Monroe County, FL held by Florida Keys Media LLC
Group Owner: Florida Keys Media LLC
Nat'l Network: AP Radio
Arbitron Metro Market: Key West, Fl; *Format:* Country *Special Programming:* Armed Forces news one hr wkly; *Hrs. of News Programming:* News progmg one hr wkly; *Target Audience:* 24-55; military, baby boomers &largest income holders
Rick Lopez, General Manager
Amy Andrade, Sales Manager
Randy Perry, Chief Engineer

WEOW
02-01-1967; 92.7 MHz FM; *Hrs Open:* 24; 100 kw; 551 ft.; N24 40 36 W81 30 39
830 Crane Blvd., Sugarloaf Key, FL 33042 USA
(305) 745-2468
www.weow927.com
License: Key West, Monroe County, FL held by Florida Keys Media LLC
Group Owner: Florida Keys Media LLC
Regional Network: Florida's Radio Networks
Arbitron Metro Market: Key West, FL; *Format:* Contemporary Hits/Top 40
Rick Lopez, General Manager
Amy Andrade, Sales Manager
Randy Perry, Chief Engineer

WIIS
06-01-1978; 107.1 MHz FM; *Hrs Open:* 24; 2.5 kw; 203 ft.; N24 33 18 W81 48 7
517 Eaton Street, Key West, FL 33040 US
(305) 292-1133; *Fax:* (305) 292-6936
www.radiokeywest.com
johnrussin@hotmail.com
License: Key West, Monroe County, FL held by The Keyed Up Communications Co.
Format: Alternative *Special Programming:* Reggae 4 hrs, Metropolitan opera 4 hrs wkly; *Hrs. of News Programming:* news progmg 5 hrs wkly; *No. News Employees:* 1; *Target Audience:* 18-44; young, educated, activespenders for goods & svcs; *Adv. Rates:* 28; 24; 28; 17
John Russin, CEO
Linda Russin, COO

***WJIR**
12-01-1986; 90.9 MHz FM; *Hrs Open:* 24; 0.39 kw; 121 ft.; N24 33 7 W81 47 53
1209 United Street, Key West, FL 33040 US
(305) 296-4306; *Fax:* (305) 294-9547
www.wjir.org
License: Key West, Monroe County, FL held by Key West Educational Broadcasting.
Format: Christian, Religious; *Hrs. of News Programming:* News progmg 12 hrs wkly; *Target Audience:* General.
Ernie DeLoach, Station Manager

WKIZ
02-02-1959; 1500 kHz AM; *Hrs Open:* 24
P.O. Box 1471, Evergreen, CO 80439 US
(305) 296-1630; *Fax:* (305) 768-0282
www.konknet.com
wkizradio@aol.com
License: Key West, FL held by Seattle Streaming Radio L.L.C.
Group Owner: Seattle Streaming Radio LLC
Nat'l Network: CBS
Format: Religious, Spanish
Guy DeBoer, General Manager
Jim Spreitzer, General Sales Mgr

WKEY-FM
11-17-1985; 93.7 MHz FM; *Hrs Open:* 24; 26 kw; 138 ft.; N24 34 17 W81 44 25
Box 500940, Marathon, FL 33050 US
(305) 296-7511; *Fax:* (305) 296-0358
www.key93.com
License: Key West, Monroe County, FL held by The Great Marathon Radio Co.
Group Owner: The Great Marathon Radio Co.; (acq 7-30-2008)
Regional Network: Florida's Radio Networks
Format: Adult Contemp *Special Programming:* Classical 4 hrs, Sp 3 hrs wkly; *Hrs. of News Programming:* news progmg 8 hrs wkly; *No. News Employees:* 1; *Target Audience:* 25-54; affluent, upscale, culturallysupportive
Dewey Engstrom, Operations Dir
Rick Lopez, General Sales Mgr

WKWF
10-01-1945; 1600 kHz AM; *Hrs Open:* 24
5450 McDonald Ave., Suite 10, Key West, FL 33040 USA
(305) 294-2523; *Fax:* (305) 296-0358
sportsradio1600.com
License: Key West, FL held by Spottswood Partners II Ltd.
Format: Sports
Rick Lopez, General Manager
Amy Andrade, Sales Manager
Randy Perry, Chief Engineer

WMFM
01-01-1995; 107.9 MHz FM; 100 kw; 548 ft.; N24 40 35 W81 30 41 *Rebroadcasts:* Rebroadcasts WXDJ (FM) North Miami Beach 100%
26 West 56th Street, New York, NY 10019 US
(305) 447-9292; *Fax:* (305) 461-4466
www.lamusica.com
License: Key West, Monroe County, FL held by South Broadcasting System Inc.
Arbitron Metro Market: Coral Gables, FL
Jackie Nosti-Combo, General Manager
Albert Rodriguez, General Sales Mgr
Andrew Polsky, Advertising Contact

***WYBX**
06-01-2005; 88.3 MHz FM; *Hrs Open:* 24; 2 kw; 102 ft.; N24 34 20 W81 44 25 *Rebroadcasts:* Rebroadcasts WAFG(FM) Fort Lauderdale 100%
P.O. Box 7300, Charlotte, NC 28241
(800) 888-7077
www.bbnradio.org
bbn@bbnmedia.org
License: Key West, Monroe County, FL held by Bible Broadcasting Network Inc.
Group Owner: Bible Broadcasting Network; (acq 3-19-2009; $135,233)
Nat'l Network: Salem Radio Network
Population Served: 168,528; *Arbitron Metro Market:* Fort Lauderdale, FL; *Format:* Christian, News, 62, Talk, Religious; *Target Audience:* 25+
Lowell Davey, President
Jason Padgett, Operations Manager

***WKWR**
01-01-2005; 90.1 MHz FM; 0.25 kw; 69 ft.; N24 34 5 W81 44 53
188 South Bellevue, Suite 222, Memphis, TN 38104 US
(800) 525-5683; *Fax:* (916) 251-1650
www.klove.com
klove@klove.com
License: Key West, Monroe County, FL held by Broadcasting for the Challenged Inc.
Nat'l Network: K-Love
Arbitron Metro Market: Key West, FL; *Format:* Christian; *No. News Employees:* 13
Darrell Chambliss, Chairman
Mike Novak, President and CEO
George Flinn Jr., General Manager
David Pierce, Chief Creative Officer and Programming Director
Ed Lenane, News Director
Sam Wallington, Engineering Dir

Kissimmee

WHOO
04-01-1965; 1080 kHz AM; *Hrs Open:* 18
1040 West Cypress Street, Tampa, FL 33606 US
(813) 281-1040
www.sportstalkflorida.com
mytake@espnflorida.com
License: Kissimmee, FL held by Genesis Communications I Inc.
Group Owner: Genesis Communications Inc.; (acq 10-19-99)
Nat'l Network: ESPN Radio; *Regional Network:* Florida's Radio Networks; *Nat'l Reps:* Interep
Arbitron Metro Market: Orlando, FL; *Format:* Sports, Talk; *Target Audience:* 25-54; men; *Adv. Rates:* 75; 50; 100; 35
Bruce Maduri, President/General Manager
Len Weiner, Programming Director

WOTS
10-23-1978; 1220 kHz AM; *Hrs Open:* 24; 1 kw-D, NDD; 0.11 kw-N, ND1; N28 19 27 W81 23 44 *Rebroadcasts:* Rebroadcasts WPRD 1440 AM
222 Hazard St., Orlando, FL 32804
(407) 841-8282; *Fax:* (407) 841-8250
License: Kissimmee, Osceola County, FL held by J&V Communications Inc.
Group Owner: J&V Communications Inc.; (acq 1-12-99 for $450,000)
Arbitron Metro Market: Orlando, FL; *Format:* Spanish, Variety/Diverse *Special Programming:* Imus in the Morning; *No. News Employees:* 1
John Torrado, CEO & President
Jocelyn Torrado, Operations Dir
Lucas Soto, CO & GM
Jocelyn Torrado, Vice President & CFO
Jocelyn Torrado, Programming Director
Lou Mueller, Chief Engineer
Virgen Torrado, CEO
Janice Torrado, PSADirector

***WLAZ**
01-01-2000; 89.1 MHz FM; *Hrs Open:* 24; 5.2 kw vert; 522 ft.; N28 10 27 W81 17 1
Box 980, Quebradillas, PR 0678 US
(407) 518-7150; *Fax:* (407) 518-0062
www.laestaciondelafamilia.com
License: Kissimmee, Osceola County, FL held by Caguas Educational TV Inc.
Arbitron Metro Market: Kissimmee, FL; *Format:* Christian; *Hrs. of News Programming:* news progmg 10 hrs wkly; *No. News Employees:* 2
William Gutierrez, General Manager

La Belle

***WBIY**
01-01-1999; 88.3 MHz FM; *Hrs Open:* 24; 9 kw; 230 ft.; N26 43 22 W81 30 4
Falls Road, Toccoa Falls, GA 30598 US
1(888)400-9904; *Fax:* (863) 675-7584
www.oscaragueroministry.com
apostol@oscaraguero.com
License: La Belle, Hendry County, FL held by Oscar Aguero Ministry Inc.
Arbitron Metro Market: LaBelle, Fl; *Format:* Christian
Oscar Aguero, President
Roger Martinez, Station Manager

La Crosse

WBXY
10-01-1993; 99.5 MHz FM; *Hrs Open:* 24; 2.2 kw; 472 ft.; N29 44 22 W82 23 9
2848 East Oakland Park Blvd., Fort Lauderdale, FL 33306 US
(352) 375-1317; *Fax:* (352) 375-6961
www.thestar.fm
sales@thestar.fm

License: La Crosse, Alachua County, FL held by Asterisk Communications Inc.
Nat'l Network: Westwood One; Talk Radio Network; ABC; Fox Sports; *Nat'l Reps:* McGavren Guild
Arbitron Metro Market: Gainesville-Ocala, FL; *Format:* News, Sports, 86; *Target Audience:* 25-54; primarily baby boomers-upscale; *Adv. Rates:* 35; 30; 30; 20
John Starr, General Manager
Steve Cox, Programming Director

Lake City

WTUB
05-13-1956; 700 kHz AM; *Hrs Open:* Sunrise-sunset
Mailing Address: US
Second Address: 660 E. Main St., Orange, MA 1364
(978) 630-8700; *Fax:* (978) 630-3011
www.wjoeam.com/
License: Lake City, FL held by County Broadcasting Co. LLC.
Group Owner: Northeast Broadcasting Company Inc.; (acq 10-6-2003; $650,000 with WXRG(FM) Athol)
Arbitron Metro Market: Worcester, MA; *Format:* Oldies; *Target Audience:* 45 plus.
Spencer Marshall, General Manager

WDSR
05-06-1946; 1340 kHz AM; *Hrs Open:* 24; 1 kw-U, ND1; N30 9 20 W82 38 14
2485 South Marion Avenue, Lake City, FL 32025 US
(386) 961-9494; *Fax:* (386) 755-9369
www.northfloridanow.com/
John@Mix943.com
License: Lake City, FL held by Newman Media Inc.
Nat'l Network: CBS; *Regional Network:* Florida's Radio Networks
Regional Reps: Florida's Radio Net.
Arbitron Metro Market: Lake City, FL; *Format:* Oldies *Special Programming:* Black 1 hr wkly; *Target Audience:* 40-65.; *Adv. Rates:* 20; 20; 20; 15
John Newman, President
Barry Cole, Programming Director
Steve Rockford, Music Director

WGRO
11-14-1958; 960 kHz AM; *Hrs Open:* 6 AM-midnight (M-S); 7 AM-11 PM (Su; 0.5 kw-D, DAN; 1 kw-N, DAN; N30 11 47 W82 40 48
Rt 13, Box 318, Lake City, FL 32055 US
(386) 755-4102; *Fax:* (386) 752-9861
bandk@ISgroup.net
License: Lake City, FL held by Power Country Inc.
Regional Network: Florida's Radio Networks
Format: Country, Gospel
Louis Bolton II, President
Bob Hendrickson, General Manager

WNFB
05-28-1969; 94.3 MHz FM; *Hrs Open:* 24; 50 kw; 492 ft.; N30 7 44 W82 52 49
2485 South Marion Avenue, Lake City, FL 32025 US
(386) 961-9494; *Fax:* (386) 754-6915
www.northfloridanow.com
License: Lake City, Columbia County, FL held by Newman Media Inc.
Arbitron Metro Market: Lake City, FL; *Format:* Adult Contemp; *Target Audience:* 25-54.; *Adv. Rates:* 38; 35; 38; 25
John Newman, President
Barry Cole, Programming Director
Steve Rockford, Music Director

*WOLR
09-11-1986; 91.3 MHz FM; 0 kw horiz, 18 kw vert; 285 ft.; N30 2 56 W82 48 44
P O Box 1448, Live Oak, FL 32064 US
904-935-3300; *Fax:* (386) 935-2684
www.christianhitradio.net
License: Lake City, Columbia County, FL held by WOLR 91.3 FM Inc.
TV Affiliate: Relg

Lake Placid

WWTK
01-01-1989; 730 kHz AM; *Hrs Open:* 24; 0.5 kw-D, DA2; 0.34 kw-N, DA2; N27 24 25 W81 25 56
3750 US Hwy. 27, Suite 1, Sebring, FL 33870 US
(863) 382-9999; *Fax:* (863) 382-1982
www.tk730am.com
cohanradiogroup@htn.net
License: Lake Placid, FL held by Cohan Radio Group Inc.
Group Owner: Cohan Radio Group Inc.; (acq 11-1-98; $910,000 with WWOJ(FM) Avon Park).
Nat'l Network: USA; CBS Radio; ABC; Premiere Radio Networks; Talk Radio Network; *Regional Network:* Florida's Radio Networks; *Nat'l Reps:* Interep; *Wire Services:* AP
Arbitron Metro Market: Sebring, FL; *Format:* Talk; *Hrs. of News Programming:* news progmg 120 hrs wkly; *No. News Employees:* 1; *Target Audience:* 35 plus.
Peter Coughlin, President/GM

Lake Wales

WIPC
07-01-1951; 1280 kHz AM; *Hrs Open:* 24; 1 kw-D, DAN; 0.5 kw-N, DAN; N27 55 34 W81 36 4; N27 55 30 W81 36 16
630 Mountain Lake Cutoff Road, Lake Wales, FL 33859 US
(863) 679-7178; *Fax:* (863) 679-9395
wipc1280@yahoo.com
License: Lake Wales, FL held by Super W Media Group Inc.
Arbitron Metro Market: Lakeland-Winter Haven, FL; *Hrs. of News Programming:* news progmg 10 hrs wkly; *No. News Employees:* 1; *Target Audience:* 18+ Hispanics.; *Adv. Rates:* 29; 22; 29; 20
Robert Cubero, President/General Manager
Lupita Gonzalez, Programming Director
Frankie Cintron, Music Director

Lake Worth

WWRF
05-01-1959; 1380 kHz AM; *Hrs Open:* 24; 1 kw-D, ND1; 0.103 kw-N, ND1; N26 37 22 W80 4 20
2326 South Congress Avenue, Suite 2A, West Palm Beach, FL 33406 US
(561) 721-9950; *Fax:* (561) 721-9973
www.la1380.com/
info@gladesmedia.com
License: Lake Worth, FL held by Radio Fiesta Inc.
Arbitron Metro Market: West Palm Beach, FL; *Format:* Tejano
Special Programming: Sp relg 4 hrs wkly; *No. News Employees:* 1; *Target Audience:* 25-54; Hispanic
Robbie Castellanos, President/General Manager
Nelson Oseida, Operations Dir
Liza Flores, General Manager
Paul Danitz, General Sales Mgr
Nelson Oseida, Programming Director
Lisbeth Campos, Traffic Manager

Lakeland

*WKES
05-20-1975; 91.1 MHz FM; *Hrs Open:* 24; 100 kW; 325 ft.; N28 4 46 W82 2 27
PO Box 8889, St. Petersburg, FL 33738 USA
(727) 391-9994; *Fax:* (727) 397-6425
www.moodyradio.org/stations/florida
License: Lakeland, Polk County, FL held by The Moody Bible Institute of Chicago.
Group Owner: The Moody Bible Institute of Chicago; acq 10-10-96; $5 million)
Arbitron Metro Market: Lakeland-Tampa Bay, FL; *Format:* Christian

WLKF
01-01-1936; 1430 kHz AM; *Hrs Open:* 24; 5 kw-D, ND1; 1 kw-N, ND1; N28 2 27 W81 56 8
Mailing Address: P.O. Box 4368, Lancaster, PA 17604 US
Second Address: 404 W. Lime St., Lakeland, FL 33815-4651
(863) 682-8184; *Fax:* (863) 683-2409
www.wlkf.com
talk1430@wlkf.com
License: Lakeland, FL held by Hall Communications Ltd.
Group Owner: Hall Communications Inc.; (acq 10-1-96; $550,000)
Nat'l Network: ABC; *Regional Network:* Florida's Radio Networks;
Nat'l Reps: Eastman Radio; *Wire Services:* AP
Arbitron Metro Market: Lakeland-Winter Haven, FL; *Format:* News, News/Talk, 86; *Hrs. of News Programming:* News progmg 15 hrs wkly; *No. News Employees:* 3; *Target Audience:* 35 plus; middle to upper income adults
Bonnie Rowbotham, Chairman
Arthur Rowbotham, President
Nancy Cattarius, Station Manager
Bill Baldwin, Executive Vice President

WLLD
01-27-1992; 94.1 MHz FM; *Hrs Open:* 24; 100 kw; 1493 ft.; N27 40 23 W82 6 35
9721 Executive Center Dr., Suite 200, St. Petersburg, FL 33702 US
(727) 579-1925
www.wild941.com
License: Lakeland, Polk County, FL held by WDAS License Limited Partnership
Group Owner: Beasley Broadcast Group Inc.; (acq 11-13-98; grpsl).
Nat'l Network: CNN Radio
Arbitron Metro Market: Sarasota-Bradenton, FL; *Format:* Contemporary Hits/Top 40; *Target Audience:* 25 plus; professional, educated, upscale audience
Kent Denton, General Sales Mgr
J.J. Paone, Promotions Director
Kelly Sedivy, Digital Sales Manager

WONN
09-15-1949; 1230 kHz AM; 1 kw-U, ND1; N28 2 23 W81 57 39
Mailing Address: P.O. Box 4368, Lancaster, PA 17604 US
Second Address: 404 W. Lime St., Lakeland, FL 33815-4651
(863) 682-8184; *Fax:* (863) 683-2409
www.wonn.com
wonn@wonn.com
License: Lakeland, FL held by Hall Communications Inc.
Group Owner: Hall Communications Inc.; acq 10-1-81; $2 million with co-located FM;
Nat'l Network: CNN Radio; *Nat'l Reps:* Eastman Radio
Arbitron Metro Market: Lakeland-Winter *TV Affiliate:* MOR;
Format: Religious *Special Programming:* News progmg 20 hrs wkly; *Hrs. of News Programming:* 3; *Target Audience:* 35 Plus
Bonnie Rowbotham, Chairman
Nancy Cattarius, Station Manager

WWAB
09-01-1957; 1330 kHz AM; 1 kw-D, ND2; 0.118 kw-N, ND2; N28 2 40 W81 58 28
Mailing Address: P.O. Box 65, Lakeland, FL 33802 US
Second Address: 1203 Chase St., Lakeland, FL 33802
(863) 682-2998; *Fax:* (863) 683-9922
wwab@verizon.net
License: Lakeland, FL held by WWAB Inc.
Arbitron Metro Market: Lakeland, FL; *Format:* Blues, Talk *Special Programming:* Gospel 12 hrs wkly; *Target Audience:* 18-49.
Frank Clark, Operations Dir
Jerry Hughes, General Manager
Hugh Hughes, General Sales Mgr

*WYFO
03-01-1988; 91.9 MHz FM; 25 kw horiz, 23 kw vert; 328 ft.; N27 56 35 W81 54 45
P.O. Box 7300, Charlotte, NC 28241 US
(800) 888-7077
www.bbnradio.org
bbn@bbnmedia.org
License: Lakeland, Polk County, FL held by Bible Broadcasting Network Inc.
Group Owner: Bible Broadcasting Network; acq 9-21-89; $200,000;
Arbitron Metro Market: Lakeland, FL; *Format:* Christian, Religious
Jason Padgett, Operations Manager

Lantana

WPBR
01-01-1941; 1340 kHz AM; *Hrs Open:* 25.?Â ?; 0.81 kw-U, ND1; N26 37 12 W80 4 51
130 North Dixie Highway, Lake North, FL 33460 US
(561) 641-8882; *Fax:* (561) 641-8629
www.talk1340wpbram.com
adminandsales@1340wpbr.com
License: Lantana, FL held by Omni-Lingual Broadcasting Corp.
Nat'l Network: USA
Arbitron Metro Market: West Palm Beach-Boca Raton, FL;
Format: News, News/Talk, 86 *Special Programming:* Financial 9 hrs, medical 8 hrs, Jewish 3 hrs, Creole 30 hrs wkly; *Target Audience:* 35-64.
Emil Antonoff, President
Markes Pierre Louis, General Manager

Largo

WWBA
05-29-1972; 820 kHz AM; *Hrs Open:* 24; 50 kw-D, DA2; 1 kw-N, DA2; N27 54 30 W82 46 51
800 8th Avenue Southeast, Largo, FL 33771 US
(813) 281-1040; *Fax:* (813) 281-1948
www.newstalk820.com
License: Largo, FL held by Genesis Communications of Tampa Bay Inc.
Group Owner: Genesis Communications Inc.; (acq 1-13-2009; $3 million)
Nat'l Network: ABC
Arbitron Metro Market: Largo, FL; *Format:* News, News/Talk, 86; *No. News Employees:* 3; *Target Audience:* 25-54.
Laura Maduri, General Manager
Len Weiner, Programming Director
Roger Schulman, News Director
Gwen Schuler, Traffic Manager

Leesburg

WQBQ
09-12-1962; 1410 kHz AM; 5 kw-D, ND1; 0.09 kw-N, ND1; N28 47 13 W81 53 26
1920 Florida County Rd., 25A, Leesburg, FL 34748 US
(352) 315-1420
www.1410wqbq.com
License: Leesburg, FL held by Rama Communications Inc.
Group Owner: Rama Communications Inc.; (acq 10-15-2004; $180,000 with WKIQ(AM) Eustis).
Format: Adult Contemp
Shanti Persaud, President

Leesburg-Eustis

WLBE
08-01-1949; 790 kHz AM; *Hrs Open:* 24; 5 kw-D, DAN; 1 kw-N, DAN; N28 49 42 W81 47 10
32900 Radio Road, Leesburg, FL 34788 US
(352) 787-7900; *Fax:* (352) 787-1402
www.my790am.com
License: Leesburg-Eustis, FL held by WLBE 790 Inc.
Nat'l Network: CBS; *Regional Network:* Florida's Radio Networks; *Nat'l Reps:* Dora-Clayton
Format: Talk *Special Programming:* Black 3 hrs, farm 3 hrs, gospel 4 hrs, Pol 2 hrs w; *Hrs. of News Programming:* News progmg 25 hrs wkly; *Target Audience:* 45 plus.
MJ McNair, General Manager

Lehigh Acres

WCKT
01-01-1976; 107.1 MHz FM; *Hrs Open:* 24; 23.5 kw; 722 ft.; N26 19 0 W81 47 13
13320 Metro Parkway, Suite 1, Fort Myers, FL 33966 US
(239) 225-4300; *Fax:* (239) 275-4669
www.catcountry1071.com
License: Lehigh Acres, Lee County, FL held by Clear Channel Broadcasting Licenses Inc.
Group Owner: iHeartMedia; (acq 1996; grpsl)
Nat'l Reps: Clear Channel
Arbitron Metro Market: Fort Myers, FL; *Format:* Country; *Hrs. of News Programming:* news progmg 20 hrs wkly; *No. News Employees:* 1; *Target Audience:* 25-54.
Bob Pittman, Chairman
Louis Kaplan, Operations Manager
Kevin Miskimins, Senior Vice President of Sales
Todd Nixon, Programming Director

WWCL
04-29-1970; 1440 kHz AM; 5 kw-D, DA2; 1 kw-N, DA2; N26 36 5 W81 33 30
P.O. Box 61239, Fort Myers, FL 33906 US
(239) 337-1440; *Fax:* (239) 369-3386
energi1440@aol.com
License: Lehigh Acres, FL held by Latino Media Corp.
Arbitron Metro Market: Fort Myers, FL; *Format:* Christian
Angel Ramos, General Manager

Leisure City

WRAZ-FM
01-20-1990; 106.3 MHz FM; 50 kw; 308 ft.; N25 14 7 W80 19 35
3191 Coral Way, Suite 805, Miami, FL 33145 US
(305) 445-1063; *Fax:* (305) 446-9339
info@cima1063.com
License: Leisure City, Miami-Dade County, FL held by South Broadcasting System Inc.
Arbitron Metro Market: Leisure City, FL
Raoul Alarcon, President
Juan Fina, General Sales Mgr
Andy Vera, Programming Director
John Caride, Promotions Manager
Ralph Chambers, Chief Engineer
Berry Jasin, National Sales Manager
Barbara Guerra, Local Sales Manager
FelixLopez, Vice President of Sales
Yanin Mesa, Business Manager

Live Oak

WQHL
06-16-1949; 1250 kHz AM; *Hrs Open:* 24; 1 kw-D, ND2; 0.083 kw-N, ND2; N30 17 14 W82 57 56
1305 Helvenston St. S.E., Live Oak, FL 32064 US
(386) 362-1250,(386) 362-0981
www.wqhl981.com
dblackwell@blackcrow.fm
License: Live Oak, FL held by RTG Radio LLC.
Group Owner: Black Crow Media Group LLC; (acq 11-9-2001; grpsl).
Nat'l Network: ABC; *Regional Network:* Florida's Radio Networks
Format: Contemporary Hits/Top 40, Adult Contemp *Special Programming:* Gospel 7 hrs, relg 6 hrs wkly; *Hrs. of News Programming:* News progmg 12 hrs wkly; *Target Audience:* General.
Dean Blackwell, General Manager

WQHL-FM
10-01-1973; 98.1 MHz FM; *Hrs Open:* 24; 50 kw; 444 ft.; N30 17 14 W82 57 56
1305 Helvenston St. S.E., Live Oak, FL 32064 US
(386) 362-1250,(386) 362-0981
wqhl981.com
dblackwell@blackcrow.fm
License: Live Oak, Suwannee County, FL held by RTG Radio, LLC
Group Owner: Black Crow Media Group LLC
Nat'l Network: ABC; *Regional Network:* Southeast AgNet
Format: Country *Special Programming:* Nascar Racing, High School Football; *Target Audience:* General.
Dean Blackwell, General Manager

WILA
100.1 MHz FM; 6 kw; 328 feet; N30 13 43 W82 58 05
15722 96th Street, Live Oak, FL
(386) 364-6005
License: Live Oak, Suwannee County, FL held by Learning Avenue Inc

Sergio Martins, President

WJZS
106.1 MHz FM; 2.6 kw; 152 meters; N30 13 07 W82 59 26
295 Northwest Commons Loop 115, Box167, Lake City, FL 32055
(443) 507-5611
License: Live Oak, Suwannee County, FL held by The Estate of Leon F. Pettersen

Lynn Haven

WBYW(FM)
104.3 MHz FM; 6 kw; Ant 249 ft; N30 10 47 W85 38 11
1670 N.W. Federal Hwy., Stuart, FL 34994
(772) 692-9454; *Fax:* (772) 692-0258
License: Lynn Haven, Bay County, FL held by Horizon Broadcasting Co. Inc.
Population Served: 18,607; *Arbitron Metro Market:* Lynn Haven, FL
George Metcalf, President

Macclenny

WJXR
09-01-1978; 92.1 MHz FM; *Hrs Open:* 24; 25 kw; 328 ft; N30 17 54 W82 00 55
Box One, Jacksonville, FL 32063
(904) 259-2292; *Fax:* (904) 259-4488
License: Macclenny, Baker County, FL held by WJXR Inc.
Nat'l Network: ABC; *Regional Network:* Florida's Radio Networks *Arbitron Metro Market:* Jacksonville, F; *Hrs. of News Programming:* news progmg 7 hrs wkly; *No. News Employees:* 1; *Target Audience:* 25-54; middle class & upscale families; *Adv. Rates:* 30; 30; 30; 25
Gregory Perich, CEO
Sarah Perich, Vice President/Operations Director
Doug Rudowich, Station Manager
Avery Perich, Programming Director
Jerry Smith, Chief Engineer

Madison

WMAF
12-06-1956; 1230 kHz AM; 1 kw-U, ND1; N30 28 23 W83 26 9
Mailing Address: P. O. Box 776, Perry, FL 32347 US
Second Address: 2 Captain Brown Rd., Madison, FL 32341
(850) 973-3233; *Fax:* (850) 973-3097
License: Madison, FL held by Geneva Walker.
Regional Network: Florida's Radio Networks
Arbitron Metro Market: Madison, FL; *Format:* Country *Special Programming:* Oldies, gospel
Betty Evertt, General Manager

WXHT
11-01-2000; 102.7 MHz FM; 19 kw; 377 ft.; N30 38 23 W83 26 52
1711 Ellis Dr., Valdosta, GA 31601 US
(229) 244-8642
myhot1027.com
hot1027@gmail.com
License: Madison, Madison County, FL held by RTG Radio LLC
Group Owner: Black Crow Media Group LLC; (acq 6-4-2004; $3.4 million with WSTI-FM Quitman, GA).
Arbitron Metro Market: Valdosta, GA; *Format:* Contemporary Hits/Top 40; *Target Audience:* Adults 18-49.
Robert Ganzak, President
Jay Mathews, Programming Director
Kim Pelkowski, Director of Sales

***WAPB**
01-01-2005; 91.7 MHz FM; 0.2 kw; 224 ft.; N30 27 13 W83 24 17
Mailing Address: 1508 State Street, Holly Hill, FL 32117 US
Second Address: 1508 State Ave., Dayton Beach, FL 32125
(386) 677-4272; *Fax:* (386) 677-7095
wapn@wapn.net
License: Madison, Madison County, FL held by Public Radio Inc.
Arbitron Metro Market: Madison, FL; *Format:* Religious
Shellye Lund-Vallance, President

Maitland

WPYO
09-01-1968; 95.3 MHz FM; *Hrs Open:* 24; 12 kw; 450 ft.; N28 34 27 W81 27 46
4192 North John Young Parkway, Orlando, FL 32804 US
(321) 281-2000; *Fax:* (407) 290-1302
www.power953.com
info@power953.com
License: Maitland, Orange County, FL held by Cox Radio Inc.
Group Owner: Cox Radio Inc.; (acq 1999; $14.5 million)
Arbitron Metro Market: Orlando, FL; *Format:* Urban Contemporary; *Target Audience:* General.
Heather Reagan-Sticker, General Sales Manager
Stevie DeMann, Program Director
Keith Memoly, Director Of Marketing And Promotions
Mike McConnell, Promotions Manager

Marathon

WFFG
04-07-1962; 1300 kHz AM; *Hrs Open:* 24; 2.5 kw-U, DA1; N24 41 28 W81 6 30
One Boot Key, P.O. Box 500940, Marathon, FL 33050 US
(305) 743-5563(305) 743-5564; *Fax:* (305) 743-9441
keysradiogroup@aol.com
License: Marathon, FL held by The Great Marathon Radio Co.
Group Owner: The Great Marathon Radio Co.; (acq 11-5-90; grpsl;
Nat'l Network: Westwood One
Arbitron Metro Market: Marathon, FL; *Format:* News, News/Talk, 84, Talk; *Hrs. of News Programming:* News progmg 10 hrs wkly; *Target Audience:* 25-54; general
Joe Nascone, President/General Manager

WGMX
12-01-1976; 94.3 MHz FM; *Hrs Open:* 24; 50 kw; 276 ft.; N24 41 30 W81 6 31
P. O. Box 500940, Marathon, FL 33050 US
(305) 743-5563; *Fax:* (305) 743-9441
www.wgmxfm.com
keysradiogroup@aol.com
License: Marathon, Monroe County, FL held by The Great Marathon Radio Co.
Group Owner: The Great Marathon Radio Co.; (Acq 11-5-90; grpsl;
Nat'l Network: Westwood One
Format: Adult Contemp; *Adv. Rates:* Same as AM
Joe Nascone, President/General Manager
John Bartus, Operations Dir

WAVK
01-01-2002; 97.7 MHz FM; *Hrs Open:* 24; 50 kw horiz, 49 kw vert; 213 ft.; N24 46 2 W80 56 42
830 Crane Blvd., Sugarloaf Key, FL 33042 USA
(305) 745-2468
977thewave.com
License: Marathon, Monroe County, FL held by Florida Keys Media LLC
Group Owner: Florida Keys Media LLC
Nat'l Network: Cumulus Media Networks
Format: Adult Contemp
Rick Lopez, General Manager
Amy Andrade, Sales Manager
Randy Perry, Chief Engineer

***WKWM**
01-01-2008; 91.5 MHz FM; *Hrs Open:* 24; 12 kw; 462 ft.; N24 39 40 W81 25 10 *Rebroadcasts:* Rebroadcasts WLRN-FM Miami 100%
US

(305) 995-1717; *Fax:* (305) 995-2299
www.wlrn.org
info@wlrn.org
License: Marathon, Monroe County, FL held by The School Board of Miami-Dade County, FL.
Nat'l Network: NPR; PRI; *Regional Network:* Fla. Pub.; *Wire Services:* AP
Arbitron Metro Market: Bakersfield, CA; *Format:* News, News/Talk, 86 *Special Programming:* Haitian 3 hrs wkly; *Hrs. of News Programming:* news progmg 111 hrs wkly; *No. News Employees:* 7 *Target Audience:* General; well educated, moderate to high income bracket
John LaBonia, General Manager
Peter J. Moerz, Programming Director
Dan Grech, News Director

Marco

WGUF
01-01-1990; 98.9 MHz FM; *Hrs Open:* 24; 6 kw; 328 ft.; N26 1 50 W81 38 33
10915 K-Nine Drive, Bonita Springs, FL 34135 US
(239) 495-8383; *Fax:* (239) 495-0883
wguf@rendabroadcasting.com
License: Marco, Collier County, FL held by Renda Broadcasting Corp. of Nevada.
Group Owner: Renda Broadcasting Corp.; (acq 4-17-97; $2 million).
Arbitron Metro Market: Fort Myers-Naples-Marco Island, FL; *Format:* News, News/Talk, 86; *Hrs. of News Programming:* News progmg 7 hrs wkly; *Target Audience:* 35 plus; affluent southwest FL residents; *Adv. Rates:* 38;38; 38; 25
Tony Renda Jr., General Manager
Camellia Pflum, General Sales Mgr
Randy Savage, Programming Director
Buzzy Ford, Promotions Manager

*WMKO
02-08-1999; 91.7 MHz FM; *Hrs Open:* 24; 6.9 kw; 369 ft.; N26 3 10 W81 42 11 *Rebroadcasts:* Rebroadcasts WGCU-FM Fort Myers100%
10501 Fgcu Blvd S., Ft Myers, FL 33965 US
(239) 590-2500; *Fax:* (239) 590-2520
www.wgcu.org
License: Marco, Collier County, FL held by Board of Trustees, Florida Gulf Coast University
Nat'l Network: NPR
Arbitron Metro Market: Fort Myers, FL
Luc Martin, Operations Manager
Rick Johnson, General Manager
Amy Tardif, Station Manager/News Director

Marco Island

*WCNZ
05-01-1999; 1660 kHz AM; *Hrs Open:* 24
462 Merrimack Street, Methuen, MA 01844 US
(239) 732-9369; *Fax:* (239) 732-7267
www.avenuefla.com
bladd@mail.com
License: Marco Island, FL held by J & B WCNZ LLC
Nat'l Network: USA; *Regional Network:* Florida's Radio Networks
Arbitron Metro Market: Fort Myers, FL; *Format:* Jazz; *Hrs. of News Programming:* news progmg 10 hrs wkly; *No. News Employees:* 1
Robert Ladd, Station Manager

WVOI
01-01-1975; 1480 kHz AM; 1 kw-D, DA2; 1 kw-N, DA2; N25 59 30 W81 37 30
462 Merrimack Street, Methuen, MA 01844 US
(239) 732-9369; *Fax:* (239) 732-7267
http://www.avenue1410and1660.com/
bladd@mail.com
License: Marco Island, FL held by J&J WCNZ LLC
Nat'l Network: USA; *Regional Network:* Florida's Radio Networks
Arbitron Metro Market: Fort Myers-Napl *TV Affiliate:* AAA *Special Programming:* news progmg 5.5 hrs wkly; *Hrs. of News Programming:* 1; *No. News Employees:* 45 plus; upscale & profes; *Adv. Rates:* 10; 10; 10;10

Marianna

WTYS-FM
08-04-1995; 94.1 MHz FM; *Hrs Open:* 24; 4.4 kw; 384 ft.; N30 45 47 W85 13 52
Mailing Address: 2483 Jefferson, Marianna, FL 32448 US
Second Address: 2725 Jefferson St., Marianna, FL 32448
(850) 482-2131; *Fax:* (850) 526-3687
www.wtys.cc
wtysradio@embarqmail.com
License: Marianna, Jackson County, FL held by James L. Adams Jr.
Nat'l Network: CBS; *Regional Network:* Florida's Radio Networks
Arbitron Metro Market: Marianna, Fl; *Format:* Gospel; *Hrs. of News Programming:* news progmg 5 hrs wkly; *No. News Employees:* 1; *Target Audience:* 25-64; adults in Jackson county, FL & surrounding area
Jerry Jackson, Operations Dir
James Adams, General Manager
Tom O'Brien, News Director

WJAQ
09-01-1964; 100.9 MHz FM; *Hrs Open:* 24; 5.9 kw horiz; 331 ft.; N30 47 1 W85 15 18
P.O. Box 569, Marianna, FL 32447 US
(850) 482-3046; *Fax:* (850) 482-3049
wjaq@phon1.com
License: Marianna, Jackson County, FL
Nat'l Network: ABC; *Wire Services:* UPI
Format: Country; *Hrs. of News Programming:* news progmg 3 hrs wkly; *No. News Employees:* 1; *Target Audience:* General.; *Adv. Rates:* 25; 20; 22; 12
Bill Jones, Operations Dir
Gregory Kamishlian, Promotions Manager

*WAYP
05-01-1985; 88.3 MHz FM; *Hrs Open:* 24; 0.75 kw horiz, 70 kw vert; 344 ft.; N30 26 18.1 W85 25 27
P. O. Box 450, Marianna, FL 32446 US
(850) 422-1929; *Fax:* (850) 297-1888
wayp.wayfm.com
License: Marianna, Jackson County, FL held by WAY-FM Media Group Inc.
Group Owner: WAY-FM Media Group Inc.; (acq 11-13-2007; $210,000)
Arbitron Metro Market: Panama City, FL; *Format:* Christian
Bob Augsburg, President

WTOT
09-24-1958; 980 kHz AM; *Hrs Open:* 24; 1 kw-D, ND1; 0.34 kw-N, ND1; N30 47 1 W85 15 18
Mailing Address: 9102 N. Meridian Street, Ste 500, Indianapolis, IN 46260 US
Second Address: 4376 Lafayette St., Suite A, Marianna, FL 32446-3300
(850) 482-3046; *Fax:* (850) 482-3049
License: Marianna, FL held by MFR Inc.
Nat'l Network: ABC
Arbitron Metro Market: Marianna, FL; *Format:* Christian; *Target Audience:* 25 plus.; *Adv. Rates:* 10; 8; 9; 6
John Biddinger, CEO
Curtis Blount, Chief Engineer

WTYS
04-03-1947; 1340 kHz AM; *Hrs Open:* 24
Mailing Address: P.O. Box 777, Marianna, FL 32447 US
Second Address: 2725 Jefferson St., Marianna, FL 32448
(850) 482-2131; *Fax:* (850) 526-3687
www.wtys.cc
wtysradio@embarqmail.com
License: Marianna, FL held by James L. Adams Jr.
Regional Network: Florida's Radio Networks
Arbitron Metro Market: Dotham, AL; *Format:* Country *Special Programming:* Farm one hr, gospel 11 hrs wkly; *Hrs. of News Programming:* news progmg 7 hrs wkly; *No. News Employees:* 1; *Target Audience:* 25-64;adults in Jackson County & the surrounding area
Jerry Jackson, Operations Dir
James Adams, General Manager

*WHMF
91.1 MHz FM; kw
US
(850) 763-6489
License: Marianna, Jackson County, FL held by Health and Happiness Radio Inc.
Arbitron Metro Market: Panama City, FL
Leonard Moore, President

Mary Esther

WYZB
05-01-1986; 105.5 MHz FM; 25 kw; 305 ft.; N30 24 42 W86 37 14
P.O. Box 2347, Fort Walton Beach, FL 32549 US
(850) 243-2323
www.wyzb.com
License: Mary Esther, Okaloosa County, FL held by Cumulus Licensing Corp.
Group Owner: Cumulus Media Inc.; (acq 1-10-2003; grpsl)
Arbitron Metro Market: Fort Walton Bea; *Format:* Country; *Target Audience:* 25-54.
Kathy Kaufman, General Manager
Skip Davis, Programming Director
Lisa Captain, Promotions Manager

Mayo

*WGSG
01-01-1991; 89.5 MHz FM; 2.5 kw horiz, 20 kw vert; 249 ft.; N30 2 30 W83 7 45
P.O. Box 644, Mayo, FL 32066 US
(386) 294-2525; *Fax:* (386) 294-2525
License: Mayo, Lafayette County, FL held by True Concepts of Levy County Inc.
Format: Religious
Terri Simmons, General Manager

Melbourne

WAOA-FM
11-09-1972; 107.1 MHz FM; 100 kw; 486 ft.; N28 8 11 W80 42 12
1800 West Hibiscus Boulevard, Suite 138, Melbourne, FL 32901 US
(321) 984-1000; *Fax:* (321) 724-1565
www.wa1a.com
License: Melbourne, Brevard County, FL held by Cumulus Licensing Corp.
Group Owner: Cumulus Media Inc.
Arbitron Metro Market: Melbourne, FL; *Format:* Contemporary Hits/Top 40; *Target Audience:* 25-54.
Pete DeSimone, General Manager
Terry Simmons, Programming Director
Jennifer Armstrong, Promotions Manager
Jon Roberts, Chief Engineer
Christina Volonnino, Traffic Director

WFKS
12-25-1965; 95.1 MHz FM; *Hrs Open:* 24; 1.2 kw; Ant 210 ft; N28 04 41 W80 35 57
1388 S. Babcock St., Melbourne, FL 32901 US
(321) 821-7100; *Fax:* (321) 725-6821
www.mykiss951.com
kevincampbell@iheartmedia.com
License: Melbourne, Brevard County, FL held by Capstar TX LLC
Group Owner: iHeartMedia
Population Served: 76,095; *Arbitron Metro Market:* Melbourne, FL; *Format:* Contemporary Hits/Top 40; *Hrs. of News Programming:* News progmg one hr wkly
Tom Davis, Market President
Ken Holiday, Operations Manager
Kevin Campbell, Programming Director
Deano Chaple, Promotions Director
Laurie Reid, Business Manager
Adam Schanz, Webmaster
Mindy Levy, PSA Director

WCIF
01-01-1980; 106.3 MHz FM; 13.5 kw; 446 ft.; N28 8 15 W80 42 11
Mailing Address: 702 East New Haven Ave, Melbourne, FL 32901 US
Second Address: 3301 Dairy Rd., Melbourne, FL 32904
(321) 725-9243
www.wcif.com
info@wcif.com
License: Melbourne, Brevard County, FL held by First Baptist Church Inc.
Arbitron Metro Market: Melbourne-Palm bay, FL; *Format:* Religious
Martha Root, Operations Dir
Lee Martinez, General Manager

*WFIT
04-01-1975; 89.5 MHz FM; *Hrs Open:* 24; 900 w horiz, 4.6 kw vert; 112 ft; N28 03 51 W80 37 25
150 W. University Blvd., Melbourne, FL 32901
(321) 674-8950; *Fax:* (321) 674-8139
www.wfit.org
wfit@fit.edu
License: Melbourne, Brevard County, FL held by Florida Institute of Technology.
Population Served: 76,095; *Arbitron Metro Market:* Melbourne, FL; *Hrs. of News Programming:* News progmg 40 hrs wkly; *Target Audience:* 25-54; pub radio listeners
Terri Wright, General Manager
Todd Kennedy, Programming Director
Barbara Bingnear, Director of Gifts and Outreach
George Wilson, Sr. Underwriting Executive
Rose Mantle, Public Service Announcement Director, Membership S

WDMC
01-04-1956; 920 kHz AM; *Hrs Open:* 24; 5 kw-D, DA2; 1 kw-N, DA2; N28 8 11 W80 41 20
1800 Turtle Mound Road, Melbourne, FL 32934 US
(321) 757-7717; *Fax:* (321) 757-7705
License: Melbourne, FL held by Divine Mercy Communications Inc.
Arbitron Metro Market: Melbourne, FL; *Format:* Christian
Robert Groppe, President

WMMB
01-01-1947; 1240 kHz AM; *Hrs Open:* 24; 1 kw-U, ND1; N28 4 40 W80 35 55
1388 South Babcock Street, Melbourne, FL 32901 US
(321) 733-7100; *Fax:* (321) 733-0904
www.wmmbam.com
billmick@iheartmedia.com
License: Melbourne, FL held by Capstar TX LLC
Group Owner: iHeartMedia; (acq 8-30-00; grpsl)
Nat'l Network: Westwood One; *Regional Network:* Florida's Radio Networks
Arbitron Metro Market: Melbourne, FL; *Format:* News, News/Talk, 86; *Hrs. of News Programming:* news progmg 4 hrs wkly; *No. News Employees:* 3; *Target Audience:* 35 plus.
Tom Davis, Market President
Ken Holiday, Operations Manager
Bill Mick, Programming Director
Deano Chaple, Promotions Director
Laurie Reid, Business Manager
Adam Schanz, Online Content Director

WLZR(AM)
03-08-1968; 1560 kHz AM; *Hrs Open:* 6 AM-7 PM; 5 kw-D; N28 07 40 W80 42 29
1800 W. Hibiscus Blvd., Suite 138, Melbourne, FL 32901
(321) 984-1000; *Fax:* (321) 724-1565
www.espn1560.com
License: Melbourne, Brevard County, FL held by Cumulus Licensing Corp.
Group Owner: Cumulus Media Inc.; (acq 5-23-2001; with co-located FM)
Nat'l Network: ESPN Radio
Population Served: 76,095; *Arbitron Metro Market:* Melbourne, FL; *Format:* Sports; *Target Audience:* 35-64.
Sue Garrett, General Manager

Mexico Beach

WEBZ
11-28-1990; 99.3 MHz FM; *Hrs Open:* 24; 50 kw; 492 ft.; N30 0 21 W85 20 36
1834 Lisenby Avenue, Panama City, FL 32405 US
(850) 769-1408; *Fax:* (850) 769-0659
www.993thebeat.com
License: Mexico Beach, Bay County, FL held by Clear Channel Broadcasting Licenses Inc.
Group Owner: iHeartMedia; (acq 11-21-97; grpsl)
Format: Urban Contemporary; *Target Audience:* 30 plus; professional adults
Jackie Rinker, Vice President/Market Manager
Darrell Johnson, Senior Vice President of Sales

Miami

WAMR-FM
06-07-1974; 107.5 MHz FM; 93 kw; 1,007 ft.; N25 58 2 W80 12 34
800 Douglas Rd., Suite 111, Coral Gables, FL 33134 US
(305) 529-9272
www.univision.com
License: Miami, Dade County, FL held by WQBA-FM License Corp.
Group Owner: Univision Radio; (acq 9-22-2003; grpsl).
Arbitron Metro Market: Miami, FL; *Format:* Adult Contemp, Spanish
Claudia Puig, Senior Vice President and General Manager
Monica Rabassa, Vice President of Marketing and Public Affairs

WAQI
01-01-1939; 710 kHz AM; 50 kw-D, DA2; 50 kw-N, DA2; N25 58 7 W80 22 44
800 Douglas Rd., Suite 111, Coral Gables, FL 33134 US
(305) 447-1140; *Fax:* (305) 442-7676
www.univision.com
License: Miami, Dade County, FL held by License Corporation #1.
Group Owner: Univision Radio; (acq 9-22-2003; grpsl).
Arbitron Metro Market: Miami, FL; *Format:* News, News/Talk, 82, Talk
Claudia Puig, Senior Vice President and General Manager
Monica Rabassa, Vice President of Marketing and Public Affairs

***WDNA**
06-10-1980; 88.9 MHz FM; *Hrs Open:* 24; 7.4 kw horiz, 6.3 kw vert; 1145 ft.; N25 32 24 W80 28 7
P.O. Box 558636, Miami, FL 33255 US
(305) 662-8889; *Fax:* (305) 662-1975
www.wdna.org
License: Miami, Dade County, FL held by Bascomb Memorial Broadcasting Foundation Inc.
Arbitron Metro Market: Miami-Dade, FL; *Format:* Jazz *Special Programming:* World music 10 hrs wkly; *Hrs. of News Programming:* News progmg 10 hrs wkly; *Target Audience:* General; minorities; *Adv. Rates:* 30;25; 30; 20
Margarita Pelleya, General Manager
Ron Streeter, Chief Engineer
Sarah Cruz, Development Director
Howard Duperly, Marketing Manager
Michael Valentine, Music Director

WEDR
05-18-1963; 99 MHz FM; 100 kw; 919 ft.; N25 58 3 W80 12 34
2741 N 29th Avenue, Hollywood, FL 33020 US
(305) 444-4404; *Fax:* (305) 624-2736
www.wedr.com
info@wedr.com
License: Miami, Dade County, FL held by Cox Radio Inc.
Group Owner: Cox Radio Inc.; (acq 8-00; grpsl).
Arbitron Metro Market: Miami, FL; *Format:* Urban Contemporary
Jill Strada, Director Of Branding & Programming
Erik Velez, Director Of Integrated Marketing
Ralph Renzi, Director Of Sales
Angelina Rosario, General Sales Manager
Aj Punjabi, General Sales Manager
Crystal Gans, Digital SalesManager
Joanne Griswald, National Sales Manager
Antoine Edwards, Digital Content Producer

WMYM
08-15-1997; 990 kHz AM; *Hrs Open:* 24; 5 kw-D, DA2; 5 kw-N, DA2; N25 50 34 W80 25 12
2150 West 68th Street, Hialeah, FL 33016 US
(305) 823-0990; *Fax:* (305) 823-9322
www.radio.disney.com
gilbert.salguero@disney.com
License: Miami, FL held by Radio Disney Group LLC.
Group Owner: ABC Inc.; (acq 7-30-99; $7.4 million).
Arbitron Metro Market: Miami, FL; *Format:* Contemporary Hits/Top 40; *Target Audience:* Kids and families
Gilbert Salguero, General Manager

WFLC
07-20-1951; 97.3 MHz FM; 98 kw; 1007 ft.; N25 58 2 W80 12 34
2741 N. 29th Ave., Hollywood, FL 33020 US
(305) 444-4404; *Fax:* (954) 847-3223
www.hits973.com
License: Miami, Dade County, FL held by Cox Radio Inc.
Group Owner: Cox Radio Inc.
Nat'l Reps: Christal
Arbitron Metro Market: Miami-Fort Lauderdale-Hollywood, FL; *Format:* Oldies, Jazz; *Target Audience:* 25-54.
Jill Strada, Director Of Branding & Programming
Erik Velez, Director Of Integrated Marketing
Ralph Renzl, Director Of Sales
Angelina Rosario, General Sales Manager
AJ Punjabi, General Sales Manager
Crystal Gans, Digital SalesManager
Joanne Griswold, National Sales Manager
Antoine Edwards, Digital Content Manager

WINZ
01-01-1946; 940 kHz AM; *Hrs Open:* 24; 50 kw-D, DAN; 10 kw-N, DAN; N25 57 36 W80 16 13
7601 Riviera Boulevard, Miramar, FL 33023 US
(954) 862-2000; *Fax:* (954) 862-4012
www.940winz.com
License: Miami, FL held by Clear Channel Broadcasting Licenses Inc.
Group Owner: iHeartMedia; (acq 11-21-97; grpsl).
Nat'l Network: ABC; *Regional Network:* Florida's Radio Networks;
Nat'l Reps: Clear Channel
Arbitron Metro Market: Miami-Fort Lauderdale-Hollywood, FL; *Format:* Sports; *No. News Employees:* 20; *Target Audience:* 35-64; upscale, professional, managerial adults
Lonny Anger, Market President
Todd Winick, General Sales Mgr
Grace Blazer, Programming Director
Jessie Trujillo, Promotions Director
Adam Kirschner, Digital Program Director

WIOD
01-19-1926; 610 kHz AM; 5 kw-D, DA2; 5 kw-N, DA2; N25 50 58 W80 9 18
7601 Riviera Boulevard, Miramar, FL 33023 US
(954) 862-2000; *Fax:* (954) 862-4012
www.wiod.com
License: Miami, FL held by Clear Channel Broadcasting Licenses Inc.
Group Owner: iHeartMedia; (acq 11-21-97; grpsl)
Wire Services: UPI
Arbitron Metro Market: Miami-Fort Lauderdale-Hollywood, FL; *Format:* News, News/Talk, 86; *Target Audience:* 25-64.
Lonny Anger, Market President
Todd Winick, General Sales Mgr
Grace Blazer, Programming Director
Jessie Trujillo, Promotions Director
Adam Kirschner, Digital Program Director

***WLRN-FM**
02-01-1948; 91.3 MHz FM; *Hrs Open:* 24; 47 kw; 935 ft.; N25 58 46 W80 11 46
172 Northeast 15 Th Str., Miami, FL 33132 US
(305) 995-1717; *Fax:* (305) 995-2299
www.wlrn.org
info@wlrn.org
License: Miami, Dade County, FL held by School Board of Miami Dade County Florida.
Nat'l Network: NPR; PRI; *Regional Network:* Fla. Pub.; *Wire Services:* AP
Arbitron Metro Market: Miami-Fort Lauderdale-Hollywood, FL *TV Affiliate:* *WLRN-TV affil.; *Format:* News, News/Talk, 86 *Special Programming:* Haitian 3 hrs wkly; *Hrs. of News Programming:* news progmg 111 hrs wkly; *No. News Employees:* 7; *Target Audience:* General; well educated, moderate to high income bracket
Karen Echols, CFO
Antonio Zayas, Operations Dir
John Labonia, General Manager
Peter J. Maerz, Programming Director
Dan Grech, News Director
Jack Yaghdjian, Chief Engineer

WLYF
01-01-1948; 101.5 MHz FM; *Hrs Open:* 24; 100 kw; 814 ft.; N25 58 0 W80 12 42.8
20450 NW Second Aveune, Miami, FL 33169 US
(305) 521-5100; *Fax:* (305) 652-0098
www.litemiami.com
litefm@litemiami.com
License: Miami, Miami-Dade County, FL held by Entercom Radio
Group Owner: Entercom; (acq 2016)
Nat'l Reps: Interep; *Wire Services:* AP
Arbitron Metro Market: Miami, FL; *Format:* Adult Contemp; *Hrs. of News Programming:* News progmg 2 hrs wkly; *Target Audience:* 25-54; women
Doug Abernethy, Vice President & General Manager
Gina Sordo, Business Operations Manager
Rob Sidney, Director Of Programming
Kimba, Assistant Program Director
Gayle Garton, Music Director
Gary Blau, Director Of Engineering
AmandaWarrerman, Digital Producer & Webmaster
Amy Freeman, General Advertising Sales Manager
Cathy Kaufman, National Advertising Sales Manager
Dave Corey, Commercial Production Manager

***WKCP**
08-24-1970; 89.7 MHz FM; *Hrs Open:* 24; 100 kw; 1014 ft.; N25 32 24 W80 28 7
330 Southwest Second Street, Suite 207, Fort Lauderdale, FL 33312 US
(954)522-8755
classicalsouthflorida.publicradio.org
License: Miami, Miami-Dade County, FL held by American Public Media Group
Arbitron Metro Market: Miami, FL; *Format:* Talk
Nestor Rodriguez, President
Harold Chambers III, Operations Dir
Jason Hughes, General Manager
Claudia Polzin, Development Director

WOCN
12-22-1956; 1450 kHz AM
350 N.E. 71 Street, Miami, FL 33138 US
(305) 759-7280; *Fax:* (305) 759-2276
License: Miami, FL held by IM FL Licenses LLC.
Group Owner: Independence Media Holdings LLC; (acq 7-12-2006; $6 million)
Nat'l Network: ESPN Deportes; *Wire Services:* AP
Arbitron Metro Market: Miami-Fort Laud *TV Affiliate:* Sp; *No. News Employees:* General.; *Adv. Rates:* 50; 50; 50; 40

WPOW
06-23-1986; 96.5 MHz FM; 98 kW; 1004 ft.; N25 58 2 W80 12 34
194 NW 187th St., Miami, FL 33169 USA
(305) 654-1700; *Fax:* (305) 654-1715
www.power96.com
License: Miami, Dade County, FL held by CBS Radio Stations Inc.
Group Owner: CBS Radio; (acq 8-94).
Arbitron Metro Market: Miami-Fort Lauderdale-Hollywood, FL; *Format:* Contemporary Hits/Top 40
Rob Morris, Programming Director
Sarah Lanieu, Promotions Manager

WQAM
05-01-1921; 560 kHz AM; *Hrs Open:* 24; 5 kW-D, 1 kW-N; N25 44 36 W80 9 14
194 NW 187th St., Miami, FL 33169 USA
(305) 654-1700
www.wqam.com
info@wqam.com
License: Miami, FL held by CBS Radio Stations Inc.
Group Owner: CBS Radio
Nat'l Network: Sporting News Radio Network; *Nat'l Reps:* Eastman Radio
Arbitron Metro Market: Miami-Fort Lauderdale-Hollywood, FL; *Format:* Sports; *Target Audience:* 25-54; males
Rob Morris, Programming Director
Sarah Lanieu, Promotions Manager

WQBA
01-01-1947; 1140 kHz AM; 50 kw-D, DA2; 10 kw-N, DA2; N25 46 3 W80 29 10
800 S. Douglas Rd., Suite 111, Coral Gables, FL 33134 US
(305) 529-9272
www.univision.com
License: Miami, Dade County, FL held by WQBA-AM License Corp.
Group Owner: Univision Radio; (acq 9-22-2003; grpsl).
Arbitron Metro Market: Miami-Fort Lauderdale-Hollywood, FL; *Format:* News, News/Talk, 82, Talk
Claudia Puig, Senior Vice President and General Manager
Monica Rabassa, Vice President of Marketing and Public Affairs

WSUA
06-20-1969; 1260 kHz AM; *Hrs Open:* 24
2100 Coral Way, Miami, FL 33145 US
(305) 285-1260; *Fax:* (305) 858-5907
www.caracolusa.com
info@wsua.com
License: Miami, FL held by WSUA Broadcasting Corp.
Arbitron Metro Market: Miami-Fort Lauderdale-Hollywood, FL; *Format:* News, News/Talk, 86; *Hrs. of News Programming:* news progmg 31 hrs wkly; *No. News Employees:* 7; *Target Audience:* 18-54; Latin American audience
Tomas Martinez, General Manager

WFEZ(FM)
12-29-1947; 93.1 MHz FM; *Hrs Open:* 24; 100 kw; Ant 1,003 ft; N25 58 03 W80 12 34
2741 N. 29th Ave., Hollywood, FL 33020
(305) 444-4404; *Fax:* (954) 847-3223
rry.rushin@coxinc.com
License: Miami, Dade County, FL held by Cox Radio Inc.
Group Owner: Cox Radio Inc.; (acq 5-18-2000; grpsl)
Nat'l Reps: Christal
Population Served: 143,357; *Arbitron Metro Market:* Hollywood, FL; *Format:* Rock/AOR; *Target Audience:* 18-49; upscale, educ adults with hip active lifestyles; *Adv. Rates:* 210; 215; 265; 150
Gary Williams, Director Of Branding & Programming
Erik Velez, Director Of Integrated Marketing
Ralph Renzi, Director Of Sales
Angelina Rosario, General Sales Manager
AJ Punjabi, General Sales Manager
Crystal Gans, Digital SalesManager
Joanne Griswold, National Sales Manager
Antoine Edwards, Digital Content Manager
Lindsey Powell, Community Relations Manager

WWFE
07-01-1989; 670 kHz AM; *Hrs Open:* 24; 50 kw-D, 2.5 kw-N, DA-2; N25 51 27 W80 28 52
330 S.W. 27th Ave., Suite 207, Miami, FL 33135
(305) 541-3300; *Fax:* (305) 541-7470
www.lapoderosa.com
anavidal@lapoderosa.com
License: Miami, Dade County, FL held by Fenix Broadcasting Corp.
Nat'l Reps: Lotus Entravision Reps LLC
Population Served: 1,800,000; *Arbitron Metro Market:* Miami-Fort Lauderdale-Hollywood, FL; *Hrs. of News Programming:* news progmg 27 hrs wkly; *No. News Employees:* 4; *Target Audience:* 25-54.
Jorge Rodriguez, President
Ana Vidal Rodriguez, Vice President
Miguel Melanio, Programming Director
Eduardo Aleman, News Director
Eduardo Rodriguez, Chief Engineer

Miami Beach

WMIA-FM
07-01-1968; 93.9 MHz FM; 98 kw; 1007 ft.; N25 58 2 W80 12 34
7601 Riviera Boulevard, Miramar, FL 33023 US
(954) 862-2000; *Fax:* (954) 862-4013
www.my939miami.com
License: Miami Beach, Dade County, FL held by Clear Channel Broadcasting Licenses Inc.
Group Owner: iHeartMedia; (acq 11-21-97; grpsl)
Arbitron Metro Market: Miami Beach, FL; *Format:* Adult Contemp; *Target Audience:* 25-54.
Lonny Anger, Market President
Russell Wein, General Sales Mgr
Joey Brooks, Programming Director
Nicole Covar, Promotions Director

WMBM
01-01-1949; 1490 kHz AM; *Hrs Open:* 24; 1 kw-U; N25 46 10 W80 08 11
13242 NW 7 Ave., North Miami, FL 33139
(305) 769-1100; *Fax:* (305) 769-9975
www.wmbm.com
wmbm@wmbm.com
License: Miami Beach, Dade County, FL held by New Birth Broadcasting Corp.
Nat'l Network: American Urban; Westwood One
Population Served: 50,000; *Arbitron Metro Market:* Miami, FL; *Hrs. of News Programming:* news progmg 3 hrs wkly; *No. News Employees:* 1; *Target Audience:* 25 plus; mature Black, self-motivated, Christian,professionals; *Adv. Rates:* 140; 95; 140; 65
Victor Curry, President
Caroline Kelly, Operations Dir
Gregory Cooper, Programming Director

WMGE
01-01-1961; 94.9 MHz FM; 98 kw; 1007 ft.; N25 58 2 W80 12 34
7601 Riviera Boulevard, Miramar, FL 33023 US
(954) 862-2000; *Fax:* (954) 862-4147
www.mega949.com
License: Miami Beach, Dade County, FL held by Clear Channel Broadcasting Licenses Inc.
Group Owner: iHeartMedia; (acq 11-21-97; grpsl).
Nat'l Network: Westwood One
Arbitron Metro Market: Miramar, FL; *Format:* Ethnic; *Target Audience:* 18-34.
Lonny Anger, Market President
Armando Lapido, Sales Manager
Ray Hernandez, Programming Director
Jessie Trujillo, Promotions Director
Russell Wein, Digital & Integrated Media Sales Director

Miami Springs

WNMA
05-18-1958; 1210 kHz AM; *Hrs Open:* 24
27 William St., 11th Floor, New York, NY 10005 US
(212) 966-1059; *Fax:* (212) 625-2894
www.espndeportesmiami.com
License: Miami Springs, FL held by Multicultural Radio Broadcasting Licensee LLC.
Group Owner: Multicultural Radio Broadcasting Inc.; (acq 2-4-2004; grpsl).
Arbitron Metro Market: Miami, FL; *Format:* Sports, Spanish
Arthur Liu, CEO/COO

Micanopy

WSKY-FM
09-07-1985; 97.3 MHz FM; *Hrs Open:* 24; 50 kw; 492 ft.; N29 32 9 W82 19 18
3600 Northwest 43rd Street, Building B, Gainesville, FL 32606 US
(352) 377-0985; *Fax:* (352) 337-2968
www.thesky973.com
License: Micanopy, Alachua County, FL held by Entercom Gainesville License L.L.C.
Group Owner: Entercom Communications Corp.; (acq 3-18-98; $2.8 million).
Nat'l Reps: Christal
Arbitron Metro Market: Gainesville-Oca; *Format:* News, News/Talk, 86; *Target Audience:* 18-54.; *Adv. Rates:* 26; 22; 24; 19
Dick O'Neill, Vice President/General Manager
Eric Jewell, General Sales Mgr
Nick Allen, Programming Director
Beth Bouley, Traffic Manager

Middleburg

WGNE-FM
12-13-1973; 99.9 MHz FM; 48 kw; 984 ft.; N30 19 22 W81 38 34
6440 Atlantic Boulevard, Jacksonville, FL 32211 US
(904) 727-9696; *Fax:* (904) 721-9322
www.cflradio.net
License: Middleburg, Putnam County, FL held by Renda Broadcasting Corp.
Group Owner: Renda Broadcasting Corp.; (acq 1996; $6.5 million with WMUV(FM) Brunswick, GA)
Arbitron Metro Market: Daytona Beach, FL; *Format:* Country; *Target Audience:* 18-49.; *Adv. Rates:* 95; 65; 85; 55
Toney Renda, President
Bill Reese, General Manager
Charlie Jennings, General Sales Mgr
Chuck Beck, Programming Director
April Hartwich, Promotions Director
Rob Crouch, Digital Sales Manager

Midway

WFLA-FM
01-01-1996; 100.7 MHz FM; 11.5 kw; 489 ft.; N30 29 32 W84 17 13
325-G John Knox Road, Tallahassee, FL 32303 US
(850) 422-3107; *Fax:* (850) 383-0747
www.wflafm.com
License: Midway, Gadsden County, FL held by Clear Channel Broadcasting Licenses Inc.
Group Owner: iHeartMedia; (acq 11-21-97; grpsl).
Arbitron Metro Market: Tallahassee, FL; *Format:* Talk
Chuck Redden, Market Manager

Milton

WEBY
01-01-1978; 1330 kHz AM; *Hrs Open:* 24
7179 Printers Alley, Milton, FL 32583 US
(850) 983-2242; *Fax:* (850) 983-3231
www.1330weby.com
weby@1330weby.com
License: Milton, FL held by Spinnaker License Corp.
Nat'l Network: Jones Radio Networks
Arbitron Metro Market: Milton, FL; *Format:* News, Talk *Special Programming:* Christian 7 hrs wkly / Florida State football; *Hrs. of News Programming:* News progmg 15 hrs wkly; *No. News Employees:* 1 *TargetAudience:* 35 plus; affuent, educated adults; *Adv. Rates:* 25; 25; 25; 25
Mike Bates, President
Anthony Daughtery, Operations Dir
Dave Daughtry, News Director

***WEGS**
10-15-1985; 91.7 MHz FM; 20 kw; 367 ft.; N30 37 20 W87 5 12
Mailing Address: 505 Josephine St, Titusville, FL 32796 US
Second Address: 505 Josephine St., Titusville, FL 32796
(904) 474-1223; *Fax:* (850) 447-9650
www.olivebaptist.org
wegs917@aol.com
License: Milton, Santa Rosa County, FL held by Florida Public Radio Inc.
Arbitron Metro Market: Milton, FL; *Format:* Christian, Talk
Dave Talley, General Manager

WXBM-FM
04-28-1964; 102.7 MHz FM; 100 kw; 1601 ft.; N30 36 40 W87 36 26
6565 North W Street, Pensacola, FL 32505 US
(850) 994-5357; *Fax:* (850) 994-7191
www.wxbm.com
License: Milton, Santa Rosa County, FL held by Cumulus Licensing LLC
Group Owner: Cumulus Media Inc.
Arbitron Metro Market: Milton, FL; *Format:* Country
Kevin Peterson, Operations Manager
Mike Carr, Sales Manager
Lynn West, Programming Director
Terry Michaels, Promotions Manager
Yancty McNair, Chief Engineer
Hugh McPherson, Marketing Manager

Mims

WPGS
05-05-1986; 840 kHz AM; *Hrs Open:* Sunrise-sunset
805 North Dixie Ave, Titusville, FL 32796 US
(321) 383-1000
www.talkstar840.com
wpgs840@aol.com
License: Mims, FL held by WPGS Inc.
Nat'l Network: USA
Arbitron Metro Market: Melbourne-Titusville-Cocoa, FL; *Format:* Talk
Ed Shiflett, President
Jay Rowan, Chief Engineer

Miramar

WAXY-FM
104.3 MHz FM; 100 kw; 1273 ft.; N26 34 37 W80 14 32
600 New Hampshire Ave., N.W., Suite 1200, Washington, DC 20037 US
(305)521-5100; *Fax:* (305)521-1416
www.theticketmiami.com
License: Miramar, Palm Beach County, FL held by Entercom Radio
Group Owner: Entercom; (Acq 2016)

Tod Castleberry, Programming Director
Rick Malette, Market Controller
Von Freeman, Director of Marketing

Miramar Beach

WSBZ
10-18-1994; 106.3 MHz FM; 6 kw; 328 ft.; N30 23 7 W86 18 3
690 Little Canal Drive, Santa Rosa Beach, FL 32459 US
(850) 267-3279; *Fax:* (850) 231-1775
www.seabreeze.fm
office@wsbz.com
License: Miramar Beach, Walton County, FL held by Carter Broadcasting Inc.
Arbitron Metro Market: Fort Walton Bea; *Format:* Adult Contemp
Renee Carter, CFO
Mark Carter, General Manager

Monticello

*WFRF-FM
12-01-1996; 105.7 MHz FM; *Hrs Open:* 24; 16 kw; 410 ft.; N30 23 8 W83 50 5
2906 Clardy Road, Dothan, AL 36303 US
(850) 201-1070; *Fax:* (850) 201-1071
www.faithradio.us
mailbox@faithradio.us
License: Monticello, Jefferson County, FL held by Faith Radio Network Inc.
Nat'l Network: CBS
Arbitron Metro Market: Tallahassee, FL; *Format:* Religious; *Target Audience:* 12+.; *Adv. Rates:* 15; 25; 20; 13
Scott Beigle, President
Steve Huffman, Operations Dir
Brenda Beigle, Vice President
Suzanne Farrar, Administrative Assistant
Anna Moore, Administrative Assistant

*WKVH
03-01-2003; 91.9 MHz FM; *Hrs Open:* 24; 1.5 kw; 1322 ft.; N30 40 13 W83 56 26
1425 N. Market Blvd, Suite 9, Sacramento, CA 95834 US
(800) 525-5683; *Fax:* (916) 251-1650
www.klove.com
klove@klove.com
License: Monticello, Jefferson County, FL held by Educational Media Foundation.
Group Owner: EMF Broadcasting
Nat'l Network: K-Love
Arbitron Metro Market: Tallahassee, FL; *Format:* Christian; *No. News Employees:* 3; *Target Audience:* 25-44; Judeo Christian, female
Darrell Chambliss, Chairman
Mike Novak, President and CEO
Chip Bailey, Operations Dir
Eric Allen, General Sales Mgr
David Pierce, Programming Director
Ed Lenane, News Director
Sam Wallington, Engineering Dir
Marya Morgan, NewsReporter
Richard Hunt, News Reporter
Laura Daniels, News Reporter
Tim Luttrell, News Reporter
Kenny Noble Cortes, News Reporter
Darren Vinson, News Reporter

Mount Dora

WMGF
01-01-1966; 107.7 MHz FM; *Hrs Open:* 24; 98 kw; 1588 ft.; N28 55 10.1 W81 19 7.4
2500 Maitland Center Parkway, Suite 401, Maitland, FL 32751 US
(407) 916-7800; *Fax:* (407) 916-0329
www.magic107.com
info@magic107.com
License: Mount Dora, Lake County, FL held by Clear Channel Broadcasting Licenses Inc.
Group Owner: iHeartMedia; (acq 11-21-97; grpsl)
Regional Reps: Paul Rogers
Arbitron Metro Market: Orlando, FL; *Format:* Adult Contemp
Special Programming: Contemp Christian mus 20 hrs wkly; *Hrs. of News Programming:* news progmg 2 hrs wkly; *No. News Employees:* 1 *Target Audience:* 25-54; working women; *Adv. Rates:* 350.;350.;350.;170.
Linda Byrd, Market President
Chris Kampmeier, Senior Vice President of Programming
Barbara Latham, Senior Vice President of Sales
Laura Kam Downey, Promotions Manager

Murdock

WBCG
10-22-2001; 98.9 MHz FM; *Hrs Open:* 24; 5.5 kw; 341 ft.; N27 0 9 W82 10 54
24100 Tiseo Boulevard, Port Charlotte, FL 33980 US
(941) 639-1112; *Fax:* (941) 206-9296
www.989thebeach.com
wbcgbeachradio@cs.com
License: Murdock, Charlotte County, FL held by Concord Media Group Inc.
Regional Network: Florida's Radio Networks
Format: Adult Contemp; *Hrs. of News Programming:* News progmg 2 hrs wkly; *Target Audience:* Adults 25+; core 35-54 female; *Adv. Rates:* 20; 10; 10; 10
Robin Craig, General Sales Mgr
Todd Matthews, Programming Director
Ron Bigley, Traffic Manager

Naples

WARO
05-08-1962; 94.5 MHz FM; *Hrs Open:* 24; 99 kw; 1014 ft.; N26 20 26 W81 42 48
2824 Palm Beach Blvd., Fort Myers, FL 33916 US
(239) 479-5500
www.classicrock945.com
License: Naples, Collier County, FL held by Sun Broadcasting Inc.
Group Owner: Sun Broadcasting Inc.; (acq 9-24-2012; grpsl)
Arbitron Metro Market: Fort Myers, FL; *Format:* Classic Rock
Joe Corbett, General Sales Mgr

*WAYJ
10-01-1987; 89.5 MHz FM; *Hrs Open:* 24; 100 kw; 309 ft.; N26 7 12 W81 40 58
Mailing Address: 2132 Shadowlawn Drive, Naples, FL 33962 US
Second Address: 1860 Boy Scout Dr., Suite 202, Fort Myers, FL 33906
(800) 877-5600; *Fax:* (916) 251-1650
www.air1.com
info@air1.com
License: Naples, Lee County, FL held by WAY-FM Media Group Inc.
Group Owner: WAY-FM Media Group Inc.
Nat'l Network: USA
Arbitron Metro Market: Laramie WY; *Format:* Alternative, Christian
Darrell Chambliss, Chairman
Mike Novak, President
Alan Mason, Operations Dir
David Pierce, Programming Director
Ed Lenane, News Director
Sam Wallington, Engineering Dir
Marya Morgan, News Reporter
Richard Hunt, News Reporter

WNOG
10-14-1954; 1270 kHz AM; *Hrs Open:* 24; 5 kw; N26 37 28 W81 49 52 *Rebroadcasts:* Rebroadcasts WFWN Fort Myers 100%
2824 Palm Beach Blvd., Fort Myers, FL 33916 US
(239) 479-5500
www.thefan.am
License: Naples, FL held by Sun Broadcasting Inc.
Group Owner: Sun Broadcasting Inc.
Nat'l Network: CBS; *Nat'l Reps:* McGavren Guild
Arbitron Metro Market: Fort Myers, FL; *Format:* Sports; *Target Audience:* 35 plus.
Joseph Schwantzel, President
Keith Stulhmann, Engineering Dir

WSGL
05-10-1980; 104.7 MHz FM; *Hrs Open:* 24; 20 kw; 433 ft.; N26 7 35 W81 43 17
10915 K-Nine Drive, Bonita Springs, FL 34135 US
(239) 495-8383; *Fax:* (239) 495-0883
License: Naples, Collier County, FL held by Renda Broadcasting Corp. of Nevada.
Group Owner: Renda Broadcasting Corp.; (acq 11-10-98; $3.65 million).
Arbitron Metro Market: Fort Myers-Napl; *Format:* Adult Contemp
Special Programming: Classic rock 70s & 80s music 5 hrs wkly; *Hrs. of News Programming:* News progmg one hr wkly; *Target Audience:* 25-54; women
Tony Renda, General Manager
Camellia Pflum, General Sales Mgr
Randy Savage, Programming Director
Buzzy Ford, Promotions Manager
Melanie Hainkel, Music Director

*WSOR
01-01-1989; 90.9 MHz FM; *Hrs Open:* 24; 36 kW; 902 ft.; N26 20 29 W81 42 38
PO Box 8889, St. Petersburg, FL 33738 USA
(727) 391-9994; *Fax:* (727) 397-6425
www.moodyradio.org/stations/florida
License: Naples, Collier County, FL held by The Moody Bible Institute of Chicago
Group Owner: Moody Radio; (acq 1996)
Nat'l Network: Salem Radio Network; *Wire Services:* AP
Arbitron Metro Market: Naples-Fort Myers, FL; *Format:* Christian, Talk; *No. News Employees:* 1; *Target Audience:* 40 plus.

*WAYJ(FM)
08-01-1988; 89.5 MHz FM; *Hrs Open:* 24; 100 kw; Ant 309 ft; N26 07 12 W81 40 58
3805 The Lords Way, Naples, FL 34114
(239) 775-8950; *Fax:* (239) 774-5889
www.praisefm.com
praisefm895@msn.com
License: Naples, Collier County, FL held by Shadowlawn Association Inc.
Arbitron Metro Market: Fort Myers-Naples-Marco Island, FL; *Format:* Christian; *Target Audience:* 18-40.
Arnie Coones, General Manager

Naples Park

WAVV
05-30-1987; 101.1 MHz FM; *Hrs Open:* 24; 100 kw; Ant 980 ft; N26 10 58 W81 34 30
11800 Tamiami Tr. E., Naples, FL 33962
(239) 793-1011; *Fax:* (239) 793-7000
wavv101.com
w.tiburski@wavv101.com
License: Naples Park, Collier County, FL held by Alpine Broadcasting Corp.
Nat'l Network: AP Radio; *Nat'l Reps:* Christal
Arbitron Metro Market: Fort Myers-Napl *Special Programming:* Jazz 3 hrs wkly; *Hrs. of News Programming:* News progmg 8 hrs wkly; *Target Audience:* 35 plus; an economically qualified audience that is somewhat moreaffluent; *Adv. Rates:* 80; 80; 80; 50
Donna Alpert, CFO
Norman Alpert, President
Kenny Lamb, Operations Dir
Walt Tiburski, General Manager

WBTT
10-22-1987; 105.5 MHz FM; 23.5 kw; 722 ft.; N26 19 0 W81 47 13
13320 Metro Parkway, Suite 1, Fort Myers, FL 33966 US
(239) 225-4300; *Fax:* (239) 225-4329
www.1055thebeat.com
License: Naples Park, Collier County, FL held by Clear Channel Broadcasting Licenses Inc.
Group Owner: iHeartMedia; (acq 1996; grpsl)
Arbitron Metro Market: Fort Myers-Naples-Marco Island, FL; *Format:* Contemporary Hits/Top 40; *Target Audience:* 18-34.
Louis Kaplan, Operations Manager
Kevin Miskimins, Senior Vice President of Sales

Navarre

WKFP(FM)
01-01-1999; 95.7 MHz FM; 25 kw; Ant 282 ft; N30 27 02 W86 51 59
2070 N. Palafax St., Pensacola, FL 32501
(850) 434-1230; *Fax:* (850) 469-9698
praise957@hotmail.com

License: Navarre, Santa Rosa County, FL held by 550 AM Inc.
Arbitron Metro Market: Pensacola, FL; *Format:* Christian
Michael Glinter, President
Dara Glinter, Executive Vice President

Neptune Beach

WKSL
08-01-1965; 97.9 MHz FM; 12.5 kw
11700 Central Parkway, Jacksonville, FL 32224 US
(904) 636-0507; *Fax:* (904) 997-7713
www.979kissfm.com
License: Neptune Beach, Duval County, FL held by Clear Channel Broadcasting Licenses Inc.
Group Owner: iHeartMedia
Arbitron Metro Market: Jacksonville, FL; *Format:* Contemporary Hits/Top 40
Tommy BoDean, Senior Vice President of Programming
Aaron Wilborn, Senior Vice President of Sales
Jean Podbielski, Promotions Director
Nick Wize, Digital Content Director
Taylor Brown, Digital Content Coordinator
Rollin Isbell,Digital Sales Manager

New Port Richey

WDUV
09-19-1969; 105.5 MHz FM; *Hrs Open:* 24; 33 kw; 1503 ft.; N28 10 56 W82 46 6
11300 4th Street North, Suite 300, St. Petersburg, FL 33716 US
(727) 579-2000; *Fax:* (727) 579-2662
www.wduv.com
info@coxradio.com
License: New Port Richey, Pasco County, FL held by Cox Radio Inc.
Group Owner: Cox Radio Inc.; (acq 5-99)
Arbitron Metro Market: New Port Richey, FL; *Format:* Adult Contemp; *Target Audience:* 25-54.
Keith Lawless, Vice President & Market Manager
Bryan Kelly, General Sales Manager
Jodi Rainey, National Sales Manager
John Larson, Julia Freeman
Director Of Promotional Operations, General Manager

*WCIE
04-10-1985; 91.5 MHz FM; *Hrs Open:* 24; 16.5 kw; 305 ft.; N28 16 58 W82 42 43
5015 South Florida Ave, Suite 104, Lakeland, FL 33813 US
(727) 848-9150; *Fax:* (727) 848-1233
www.thejoyfm.com
jeff@thejoyfm.com
License: New Port Richey, Pasco County, FL held by Radio Training Network Inc.
Arbitron Metro Market: Tampa-St. Petersburg-Clearwater, FL; *Format:* Adult Contemp, Christian
James Campbell, President
Jeff MacFarlane, General Manager
Carmen Brown, Promotions Manager
Steve Rieker, Chief Engineer

WPSO
10-31-1963; 1500 kHz AM; *Hrs Open:* Sunrise-sunset
27873 U.S. 19 North, Clearwater, FL 34621 US
(727) 725-3500,(727) 725-5555; *Fax:* (813) 814-7500
www.wpso.com
wzra48@yahoo.com
License: New Port Richey, FL held by AKMA Broadcast Network Inc.
Arbitron Metro Market: Tampa-St. Petersburg-Clearwater, FL; *Format:* Greek, News, 62, Talk *Special Programming:* Pol two hrs, quiz/trivia program, relg 8 hrs, East Indian one hr, It 3 hrs wkly, Ethnic *Hrs. of NewsProgramming:* news progmg 35 hrs wkly; *No. News Employees:* 1; *Target Audience:* General; international, ethnic
Sam Agelatos, President
Angelo Agelatos, Operations Dir

New Smyrna Beach

*WJLU
09-07-1989; 89.7 MHz FM; *Hrs Open:* 24; 10 kw; 328 ft.; N29 0 32 W80 58 27
4295 Ridgewood Avenue, Port Orange, FL 32127 US
(386) 756-9094; *Fax:* (386) 760-7107
www.cornerstoneministry.org
License: New Smyrna Beach, Volusia County, FL held by Cornerstone Broadcasting Corp.
Nat'l Network: USA; Moody
Arbitron Metro Market: Daytona Beach, FL; *Format:* Religious; *Hrs. of News Programming:* News progmg 18 hrs wkly; *Target Audience:* General; families
William Powell, General Manager
Chris Johnson, Programming Director
Donna Crowley, Office Manager
Josh Jones, Webmaster
Edie Schmidt, Production & Traffic Manager

WSBB
01-01-1950; 1230 kHz AM; *Hrs Open:* 24; 1 kw-U; N29 01 57 W80 55 03
229 Canal St., New Smyrna Beach, FL 32170
(386) 428-9091; *Fax:* (386) 428-1924
License: New Smyrna Beach, Volusia County, FL held by Diegel Communications LLC
Nat'l Network: CNN Radio; *Regional Network:* Florida's Radio Networks
Population Served: 240,000; *Arbitron Metro Market:* Daytona Beach, FL *Special Programming:* Sundays: Boston Pops show, Jazz Journey show, Back To Live show, When Radio Was, Florida Roundtable, Best of Broadway *Hrs. of NewsProgramming:* News progmg 120 hrs wkly; *No. News Employees:* 1; *Target Audience:* 45 plus.; *Adv. Rates:* available on request
Skip Diegel, President
Skip Diegel, President/Owner/General Manager

Newberry

WHHZ
02-01-1999; 100.5 MHz FM; 44 kw; 469 ft.; N29 36 29 W82 51 1
100 Northwest 76th Drive, Suite 2, Gainesville, FL 32607 US
(352) 313-3130 / 3135; *Fax:* (352) 313-3166
www.1005thebuzz.com
themorningbuzz2004@yahoo.com
License: Newberry, Alachua County, FL held by Marc Radio Gainesville LLC
Group Owner: Marc Radio Group LLC; (acq 7-18-2011; grpsl)
Arbitron Metro Market: Gainesville-Ocala, FL; *Format:* Rock/AOR
Michael Ewing, General Manager
Diana Markowitz, Sales Manager
Kevin McKay, Programming Director
Max Sitero, Chief Engineer

Niceville

WTKE-FM
07-01-1950; 100.3 MHz FM; 3 kw; 469 ft.; N30 24 38 W86 37 22
P O Box 1699, Meridian, MS 39302 US
(850) 244-1400; *Fax:* (850) 243-1471
License: Niceville, Okaloosa County, FL held by Star Broadcasting Inc.
Group Owner: Star Broadcasting Inc.; (acq 2-14-2003)
Nat'l Reps: Roslin
Arbitron Metro Market: Fort Walton Beach, FL; *Format:* Sports, Talk; *Target Audience:* 25-54.
Ron Hale,Sr., General Manager
David Kuntz, General Sales Mgr
Frank Hale, Programming Director

Nocatee

WZSP
08-27-1998; 105.3 MHz FM; *Hrs Open:* 24; 4.1 kw; 400 ft.; N27 11 1 W81 56 57
300 Klispie Drive, Punta Gorda, FL 33950 US
(863) 494-4111; *Fax:* (863) 494-4443
www.lazeta.fm
info@lazeta.fm
License: Nocatee, De Soto County, FL held by Heartland Broadcasting Corp.
Regional Network: Florida's Radio Networks; *Nat'l Reps:* Lotus Entravision Reps LLC *Regional Reps:* Lotus-Entravision
Arbitron Metro Market: Zolfo Springs, FL; *Target Audience:* General; Sp speaking audience, Charlotte, Desto, Hardee, Sarasota, Polk & Highlands counties; *Adv. Rates:* 35; 30; 30; 24
Harold (Hal) Kneller Jr., President
Casey Williams, Sales & Station Manager
Sherry Good, Office Manager

North Fort Myers

WJBX
12-17-1983; 770 kHz AM; 10 kw-D, 0.63 kw-N; N26 46 30 W81 50 51
20125 S. Tamiami Trail, Estero, FL 33928 US
(239) 495-2100; *Fax:* (239) 992-8165
License: North Fort Myers, Lee County, FL held by Beasley Media Group LLC
Group Owner: Beasley Broadcast Group Inc.; (acq 12-16-87).
Arbitron Metro Market: Fort Myers, FL; *Format:* Sports, Talk
Brad Beasley, General Manager
AJ Lurie, Director of Sales
John Cassio, Programming Director
Jon Parla, Sales Manager
Diana Beasley, Digital Content Director

North Miami

WKAT
11-01-1937; 1360 kHz AM; 5 kw-D, ND1; 1 kw-N, ND1; N25 44 36 W80 9 14
13499 Biscayne Blvd., #1, North Miami, FL 33181 US
(305) 503-1340; *Fax:* (305) 677-7585
www.1360wkat.com
License: North Miami, FL held by Caron Broadcasting Inc.
Group Owner: Salem Communications Corp.; (acq 1-31-2005; $10 million)
Arbitron Metro Market: Miami-Fort Lauderdale-Hollywood, FL; *Format:* Classical, News, 62, Talk
Stephen James, Operations Dir
Tony Calatayud, General Manager

North Miami Beach

WXDJ
01-01-1986; 95.7 MHz FM; *Hrs Open:* 24; 40 kw; 548 ft.; N25 46 24 W80 11 18
3191 Coral Way, Suite 805, Miami, FL 33145 US
(305) 444-9292; *Fax:* (305) 461-4466
www.lamusica.com
License: North Miami Beach, Dade County, FL held by WXDJ Licensing Inc.
Group Owner: Spanish Broadcasting System Inc.; (acq 7-11-97; $110 million with WRMA(FM) Fort Lauderdale)
Arbitron Metro Market: North Miami Beach, FL; *Hrs. of News Programming:* News progmg 4 hrs wkly; *Target Audience:* 18-54; Hispanic Adults
Jackie Nosti Cambo, Vice President/General Manager
John Fina, General Sales Mgr
John Caride, Programming Director
Felix Lopez, Vice President of Sales

North Palm Beach

WSVU
10-13-2003; 960 kHz AM; 2.4 kw-D, 1.4 kw-N; N26 49 1 W80 15 7
8895 N. Military Trail, Suite 206C, Palm Beach Gardens, FL 33410 US
(561) 627-9966
www.959thepalm.com
License: North Palm Beach, Palm Beach County, FL held by JVC Media of South Fla LLC
Group Owner: JVC Broadcasting
Nat'l Network: CBS Radio
Arbitron Metro Market: North Palm Beach, FL; *Format:* Adult Contemp
Mike Balsamo, Operations Dir
Matthew Goldapper, General Manager

Ocala

*WHIJ
03-30-1990; 88.1 MHz FM; *Hrs Open:* 24; 1.25 kw vert; 394 ft.; N29 14 17 W82 7 17
814 N.E. 2nd Street, Ocala, FL 32670 US
(352) 351-8810; *Fax:* (352) 351-8917
www.thejoyfm.com
thejoyfm@thejoyfm.com
License: Ocala, Marion County, FL held by Radio Training Network Inc.
Arbitron Metro Market: Gainesville-Ocala, FL; *Format:* Adult Contemp, Christian; *Target Audience:* 20-50.
Jeff MacFarlane, General Manager

WMFQ
07-11-1977; 92.9 MHz FM; *Hrs Open:* 24; 50 kw; 476 ft.; N29 4 45 W82 5 31
3357 S.W. 7th St., Ocala, FL 34474 US
(352) 732-9877; *Fax:* (352) 622-6675
www.myq92.com
License: Ocala, Marion County, FL held by JVC Media of Florida, LLC.
Group Owner: JVC Broadcasting
Nat'l Reps: McGavren Guild
Arbitron Metro Market: Ocala, FL; *Format:* Adult Contemp, Contemporary Hits/Top 40; *Hrs. of News Programming:* news progmg 5 hrs wkly; *No. News Employees:* 1; *Target Audience:* 35 plus; upscale, female
Sam Gerace, General Manager
Bill Barr, Programming Director

WMOP
12-18-1953; 900 kHz AM; *Hrs Open:* 24; 2.7 kw-D, ND1; 0.023 kw-N, ND1; N29 14 16 W82 7 16
P.O. Box 3930, Ocala, FL 34478 US
(352) 732-2010; *Fax:* (352) 629-1614
http://www.espngo1.com
License: Ocala, FL held by Florida Sportstalk Inc.
Nat'l Network: ABC; *Nat'l Reps:* Dora-Clayton
Arbitron Metro Market: Gainesville, FL; *Format:* Sports, Talk; *Hrs. of News Programming:* news progmg 3 hrs wkly; *No. News Employees:* 1; *Target Audience:* 35 plus.
Don DePew, Operations Dir
Tom Catalano, General Manager
Carey David, General Sales Mgr
Chris Doering, Programming Director
Bill Boyer, Chief Engineer

WOCA
05-01-1957; 1370 kHz AM
Mailing Address: P.O. Box 1056, Ocala, FL 34478 US
Second Address: 1515 E. Silver Springs Blvd., Suite 134, Ocala, FL 34470
(352) 351-8000; *Fax:* 352-240-3858
www.woca.com
woca@woca.com
License: Ocala, FL held by Westshore Broadcasting Inc.
Nat'l Network: ABC; *Regional Network:* Florida's Radio Networks
Arbitron Metro Market: Gainesville-Oca *TV Affiliate:* News/talk; *Format:* Black *Special Programming:* news progmg 16 hrs wkly; *Hrs. of News Programming:* 2; *No. News Employees:* 35 plus.
Joe Martone, Chief Executive Officer/General Manager
Dan Martone, Programming Director

WOGK
11-07-1960; 93.7 MHz FM; 100 kw; 1348 ft.; N29 16 5 W82 4 51
3602 N.E. 20th Place, Ocala, FL 34470 US
(352) 622-5600; *Fax:* (352) 622-7822
www.937kcountry.com
ncfmrbob@earthlink.net
License: Ocala, Marion County, FL held by Ocala Broadcasting L.L.C.
Group Owner: Wooster Republican Printing Co.; (acq 9-27-86)
Nat'l Reps: Katz Radio
Arbitron Metro Market: Gainesville-Oca *TV Affiliate:* Country; *Format:* Country *Special Programming:* news progmg 3 hrs wkly; *Hrs. of News Programming:* 1; *No. News Employees:* 25-54; general *Adv. Rates:* 70; 75; 70; 25
Jim Robertson, Vice President/General Manager
Shanna McCoy, Sales Manager
Mr. Bob, Programming Director
Cheree Carr, Traffic Manager

Ocoee

WUNA
10-25-1962; 1480 kHz AM; 1 kw-D, ND1; 0.071 kw-N, ND1; N28 33 28 W81 32 28
127 Mamanasco Road, Ridgefield, CT 06877 US
(407) 656-9823; *Fax:* (407) 656-2092
www.lajefa1480.com
License: Ocoee, FL held by Way Broadcasting Licensee LLC
Regional Network: Florida's Radio Networks
Arbitron Metro Market: Ocoee, FL; *Format:* Spanish
Juan Nieves, General Manager
Sheila Rodriguez, General Sales Mgr
Lou Muller, Chief Engineer

Okeechobee

WAFC-FM
07-02-1979; 106.1 MHz FM; *Hrs Open:* 24; 12.5 kw; 279 ft.; N27 13 16.8 W80 52 5.8
US
(863) 902-0995; *Fax:* (863) 983-6109
License: Okeechobee, Hendry County, FL held by Glades Media Co. LLP.
Arbitron Metro Market: West Palm Beach-Boca Raton, FL; *Target Audience:* 18-49.
KC Kelly, General Manager
Jesus Castro, Programming Director

WOKC
02-06-1962; 1570 kHz AM
PO Box 1247, Okeechobee, FL 34973 US
(863) 467-1570; *Fax:* (863) 763-3171
www.gladesmedia.com
wokc@gladesmedia.com
License: Okeechobee, FL held by Glades Media Co. LLC
Regional Network: Florida's Radio Networks; Southeast AgNet
TV Affiliate: Country *Special Programming:* news progmg 10 hrs wkly; *Hrs. of News Programming:* 1; *No. News Employees:* General.; *Adv. Rates:* 12; 12; 12; 12
CEO, CEO/COO

Orange Park

*WAYR
05-28-1960; 550 kHz AM; *Hrs Open:* 24; 5 kw-D, DA2; 0.065 kw-N, DA2; N30 4 21 W81 47 24
2500 Russell Rd, Green Cove Springs, FL 32043 US
(800) 877-5600; *Fax:* (916) 251-1650
www.air1.com
info@air1.com
License: Orange Park, FL held by Good Tidings Trust Inc.
Arbitron Metro Market: McQueeney TX; *Format:* Alternative, Christian
Mike Novak, President
David Pierce, Programming Director
Ed Lenane, News Director
Sam Wallington, Engineering Dir
Marya Morgan, News Reporter
Richard Hunt, News Reporter

Orlando

WCFB
03-01-1947; 94.5 MHz FM; *Hrs Open:* 24; 97.5 kw horiz, 100 kw vert; 1480 ft.; N28 58 47 W81 27 20
4192 North John Young Parkway, Orlando, FL 32804 US
(321) 281-2000; *Fax:* (407) 290-6631
jimmy.farrell@coxinc.com
License: Orlando, Orange County County, FL held by Cox Radio Inc.
Group Owner: Cox Radio Inc.; (acq 3-28-97; grpsl)
Arbitron Metro Market: Orlando, FL; *Format:* Contemporary Hits/Top 40
Jimmy Farrell, General Sales Manager
Michael Saunders, Program Director
Keith Memoly, Marketing & Promotions Director
Dawn Campbell, Promotions Manager
Lynda Parker, Credit & Collections Manager

WDBO
05-24-1924; 580 kHz AM
4192 N John Young Parkway, Orlando, FL 32804 US
(407) 295-5858 (321) 281-2000; *Fax:* (407) 297-0156
www.wdbo.com
news@wdbo.com
License: Orlando, FL held by Cox Radio Inc.
Group Owner: Cox Radio Inc.; (acq 3-28-97; grpsl)
Arbitron Metro Market: Orlando, FL; *Format:* News, News/Talk, 86
Jimmy Farrell, General Sales Mgr
Drew Anderssen, Programming & Promotions Director
Joe Kelley, News Director
Steve Fluker, Chief Engineer
Susan Larkin, Vice President/Marketing Manager

WDYZ
12-05-1947; 990 kHz AM
1400 Lake Hearn Dr, Ne, Atlanta, GA 30319 US
(407) 566-2033; *Fax:* (407) 566-2034
www.radiodisney.com
License: Orlando, FL held by Radio Disney Group LLC.
Group Owner: ABC Inc.; (acq 1-23-01; $5 million cash).
Nat'l Network: Radio Disney; *Nat'l Reps:* Interep
Arbitron Metro Market: Orlando, FL; *Format:* Children; *Target Audience:* 4-16;25-49; children; mothers
Sean Cocchia, Senior Vice President/General Manager
Michael Bastone, Station Manager

WDBO(FM)
01-01-1952; 96.5 MHz FM; *Hrs Open:* 24; 100 kw; 1,600 ft; N28 34 51 W81 04 32 *Rebroadcasts:* Simulcast of WDBO
4192 John Young Pkwy, Orlando, FL 32804
(844) 932-6965
www.news965.com
License: Orlando, Orange County, FL held by Cox Radio Inc.
Group Owner: Cox Radio Inc.; (acq 1997)
Nat'l Network: Fox News Radio; *Nat'l Reps:* Christal
Population Served: 90,000; *Arbitron Metro Market:* Orlando, FL; *Format:* News/Talk; *No. News Employees:* 1; *Target Audience:* 25-54; Male

*WMFE-FM
07-14-1980; 90.7 MHz FM; *Hrs Open:* 24; 100 kw; 732 ft.; N28 36 8 W81 5 37
11510 East Colonial Drive, Orlando, FL 32817 US
(407) 273-2300; *Fax:* (407) 273-8462
www.wmfe.org
info@wmfe.org
License: Orlando, Orange County, FL held by Community Communications Inc.
Nat'l Network: PRI; NPR
Arbitron Metro Market: Orlando, FL; *Format:* News *Special Programming:* New instrumental 4 hrs wkly; *Hrs. of News Programming:* news progmg 48 hrs wkly; *No. News Employees:* 4; *Target Audience:* 35 plus;well-educated, executive, professional, upper-income
Sherry Alexander, Vice President/Chief Financial Officer
LaFontaine Oliver, President/General Manager

WMMO
08-19-1990; 98.9 MHz FM; *Hrs Open:* 24; 44 kw; 522 ft.; N28 34 27 W81 27 46
4192 North John Young Parkway, Orlando, FL 32804 US
(844) 862-9890; *Fax:* (407) 297-0156
www.wmmo.com
info@wmmo.com
License: Orlando, Orange County, FL held by Cox Radio Inc.
Group Owner: Cox Radio Inc.
Nat'l Reps: Christal
Arbitron Metro Market: Orlando, FL; *Format:* Classic Rock; *Hrs. of News Programming:* News progmg one hr wkly; *Target Audience:* 25-49
Hildi@Wmmo.Com, Program Director

WOMX
09-27-1989; 105.1 MHz FM; 94 kW; 1575 ft.; N28 34 51 W81 4 32
1800 Pembrook Dr., Suite 400, Orlando, FL 32810 USA
(407) 919-1000; *Fax:* (407) 919-1190
www.mix1051.com
License: Orlando, Orange County, FL held by CBS Radio Stations Inc.
Group Owner: CBS Radio; (acq 12-14-00; grpsl).
Arbitron Metro Market: Orlando, FL; *Format:* Adult Contemp; *Hrs. of News Programming:* 1
Michele Holland, Director of Sales
Dan Connors, Assistant Program Director
Angela Schlesman, Promotions Director

WRMQ
10-21-1985; 1140 kHz AM
1033 East Semoran Blvd, #253, Casselberry, FL 32707 US
(407) 830-0800; *Fax:* (407) 260-6100
mannyarroyo@qbcflorida.com
License: Orlando, FL held by Florida Broadcasters.
Arbitron Metro Market: Orlando, FL; *Format:* Gospel; *Target Audience:* 25-54.
George Arroyo, President

WRUM
07-01-1971; 100.3 MHz FM; *Hrs Open:* 24; 95 kw; 1588 ft.; N28 34 51 W81 4 32
2500 Maitland Center Parkway, Suite 401, Maitland, FL 32751 US
(407) 916-1003; *Fax:* (407) 916-0329
www.rumba1003.com
raymondtorres@rumba100.com
License: Orlando, Orange County, FL held by Clear Channel Broadcasting Licenses Inc.
Group Owner: iHeartMedia; (acq 1997; grpsl).
Arbitron Metro Market: Orlando, FL; *Format:* Spanish; *Target Audience:* 18-49.; *Adv. Rates:* 225; 200; 225; 125
Linda Byrd, Market President
Hector Marcano, General Sales Mgr
Raymond Torres, Programming Director
Lucy Torres, Promotions Director

WTLN
04-01-1940; 950 kHz AM; *Hrs Open:* 24
901 Douglas Ave, Ste 100, Altamonte Springs, FL 32714 US
(407) 618-1761; *Fax:* (407) 682-7005
www.wtln.com
office@salemorlando.comÿ
License: Orlando, FL held by Pennsylvania Media Associates Inc.
Group Owner: Salem Communications Corp.; (acq 12-7-2005; $9.4 million)
Nat'l Reps: Salem
Arbitron Metro Market: Orlando, FL; *Format:* Christian, Talk; *Target Audience:* 35-64.
Edward Atsinger III, President
Dale Forbis, Operations Dir
Bill Files, General Manager
John Stolz, General Sales Mgr
Pete Paquette, Programming Director
Joe Ferraro, Promotions Manager
Pete Paquette, Operations Manager
JeffSenas, ÿProducer/Production Assistant
Jim Turner, Weekend Board Operator/Producer
John Stolz, Director of Ministry Development

Christy Siron, Executive Assistant
Tatianna Irizarry, Traffic Manager

***WUCF-FM**
01-30-1978; 89.9 MHz FM; *Hrs Open:* 24; 0.36 kw horiz, 5.6 kw vert; 486 ft.; N28 35 27 W81 12 17
Mailing Address: P.O. Box 162199, Orlando, FL 32816 US
Second Address: 4000 Central Florida Blvd., Bldg. 75, Rm. 130, Orlando, FL 32816
(407) 823-0899; *Fax:* (407) 823-6364
wucf.org
wucfhost@mail.ucf.edu
License: Orlando, Orange County, FL held by University of Central Florida.
Nat'l Network: NPR; PRI
Arbitron Metro Market: Orlando, FL; *Format:* Jazz *Special Programming:* blues 4 hrs; seasonal opera; *Hrs. of News Programming:* news progmg 16 hrs wkly; *No. News Employees:* 10; *Adv. Rates:* $25/25-sec spot
John Hitt, President
Kayonne Riley, General Manager
Bruce Doerle, Engineering Dir
Patricia Stucky, Office Manager
Jan Whitehouse, Marketing Specialist
John Segers, Music Director

WWKA
04-24-1952; 92.3 MHz FM; *Hrs Open:* 24; 99 kw; 1457 ft.; N28 34 7 W81 3 16
4192 North John Young Parkway, Orlando, FL 32804 US
(844) 254-9232; *Fax:* (407) 299-4947
www.k923orlando.com
info@wwka.com
License: Orlando, Orange County, FL
Group Owner: Cox Radio Inc.
Arbitron Metro Market: Orlando, FL; *Format:* Country
J.R. Schumann, Programming Director
Amy Lynch, Promotions Director
Steve Fluker, Engineering Dir
Susan Larking, Vice President/Marketing Manager
Dennis Hopkins, Production Director

WYGM
01-01-1947; 740 kHz AM; 50 kw-D, DA2; 50 kw-N, DA2; N28 28 53 W81 39 43
2500 Maitland Center Parkway, Maitland, FL 32751 US
(407) 916-7800; *Fax:* (407) 916-0329
www.969thegame.com
License: Orlando, FL held by Clear Channel Broadcasting Licenses Inc.
Group Owner: iHeartMedia; (acq 11-21-97; grpsl)
Wire Services: AP
Arbitron Metro Market: Orlando, FL; *Format:* Sports; *Adv. Rates:* 65.; 65.; 65.; 35.
Linda Byrd, Market President
Lisa Kitchener, General Sales Mgr
Rick Everett, Programming Director
Lea Reynolds, Promotions Manager
Scott Harris, Program Coordinator

Orlovista

WRSO(AM)
01-01-2006; 810 kHz AM; *Hrs Open:* 24 hrs; 10 kw-D, 400 w-N, DA-2; N28 34 18 W81 26 02
999 Douglas Ave., Attamonte, FL 32714
(407) 774-8810; *Fax:* (407) 774-8895
License: Orlovista, Orange County, FL held by Star Over Orlando Inc.
Population Served: 243,195; *Arbitron Metro Market:* Orlando, FL; *Format:* Religious
Carl Tutera, President

Ormond Beach

WELE
08-01-1957; 1380 kHz AM; 5 kw-D, DA2; 2.5 kw-N, DA2; N29 16 9 W81 4 54
432 South Nova Road, Ormond Beach, FL 32174 US
(386) 523-1870; *Fax:* (386) 677-4123
www.goliathradio.com/
doug@wele1380.com
License: Ormond Beach, FL held by Wings Communications Inc.
Nat'l Network: CNN Radio; Westwood One
Arbitron Metro Market: Ormond Beach, FL; *Format:* News, News/Talk, 86; *Target Audience:* General; mature, adults interested in sports & local current events; *Adv. Rates:* 45; 45; 45; na
F. Douglas Wilhite, President
Kristin Cobb, Operations Dir
Mike Matsin, General Sales Mgr
Mike Johnson, Programming Director
Mike Johnson, News Director
Doug Wilhite, Engineering Dir
Greg Lake, Production Director

Ormond-By-The-Sea

WHOG-FM
01-01-1995; 95.7 MHz FM; 25 kw; 328 ft.; N29 14 11 W81 4 22
126 W. Intl. Speedway Blvd., Daytona Beach, FL 32214 US
(386) 255-9300
whog957.com
License: Ormond-By-The-Sea, Volusia County, FL held by Southern Stone Communitcations of Florida, LLC
Group Owner: Southern Stone Communication
Arbitron Metro Market: Daytona Beach, FL; *Format:* Classic Rock, Rock/AOR
Jonathan Wiley, Operations Dir
Greg Pretko, General Manager
Chris Chaos, Programming Director
Drita Travis, Promotions Manager

Oviedo

WONQ
11-21-1992; 1030 kHz AM
1355 East Altamonte Drive, Altamonte Springs, FL 32701 US
(407) 830-0800; *Fax:* (407) 260-6100
www.1030lagrande.com/
License: Oviedo, FL held by Florida Broadcasters.
Arbitron Metro Market: Orlando, FL *TV Affiliate:* Sp; *No. News Employees:* 25-54.

Palatka

***WHIF**
03-29-1996; 91.3 MHz FM; 1.7 kw; 318 ft.; N29 39 7 W81 35 32
3111 St. Johns Avenue, Palatka, FL 32177 US
(386) 325-3334; *Fax:* (386) 325-0934
www.whif.org
whif@gbso.net
License: Palatka, Putnam County, FL held by Putnam Radio Ministries Inc.
Format: Adult Contemp, Christian *Special Programming:* Relg educ 10 hrs wkly; *Target Audience:* 25-54; family-oriented, middle-class
Robin Toole, General Manager

WIYD
02-14-1947; 1260 kHz AM; *Hrs Open:* 24
P.O. Box 918, Palatka, FL 32078 US
(386) 325-4556; *Fax:* (386) 328-5161
www.wiydradio.com
wiyd@atlantic.net
License: Palatka, FL held by Hall Broadcasting Co.
Nat'l Network: ABC; *Regional Network:* Florida's Radio Networks
Format: Country *Special Programming:* Relg 5 hrs wkly; *Hrs. of News Programming:* news progmg 6 hrs wkly; *No. News Employees:* 1; *Target Audience:* 18-49; rich & powerful; *Adv. Rates:* 15; 15; 15; 10
Charles Alford Jr., President
Susan Player, Station Manager

WPLK
01-01-1957; 800 kHz AM; *Hrs Open:* 24; 1 kw-D, ND1; 0.334 kw-N, ND1; N29 39 7 W81 35 32
Mailing Address: P. O. Box 335, Palatka, FL 32178 US
Second Address: 1428 St. John's Ave., Palatka, FL 32177
(386) 325-5800; *Fax:* (386) 328-8725
wplk.com
wplk@wplk.com
License: Palatka, FL held by Radio Palatka Inc.
Nat'l Network: ABC
Format: Oldies; *Hrs. of News Programming:* news progmg 2 hrs wkly; *No. News Employees:* 1; *Target Audience:* General.
Charles Alford Jr., President
Susan Player, Station Manager

Palm Bay

***WEJF**
01-01-1993; 90.3 MHz FM; 0.1 kw horiz, 10 kw vert; 404 ft.; N28 2 49 W80 40 34
505 Josephine Street, Titusville, FL 32796 US
(321) 722-9998; *Fax:* (321) 724-0845
www.ggm.info/
License: Palm Bay, Brevard County, FL held by Florida Public Radio Inc.
Arbitron Metro Market: Palm Bay, FL; *Format:* Adult Contemp, Christian
Eric Sabo, Operations Dir

***WHYZ(FM)**
07-01-1997; 88.5 MHz FM; *Hrs Open:* 24; 600 w vert; Ant 108 ft; N28 02 54 W80 40 34
1065 Rainer Dr., Altamonte Springs, FL 32714-3847
(407) 869-8000; *Fax:* (407) 869-0380
www.zradio.org
License: Palm Bay, Brevard County, FL held by Central Florida Educational Foundation Inc.
Population Served: 41,727; *Arbitron Metro Market:* Altamonte Springs, FL; *Format:* Christian; *Target Audience:* Christian.
Jim Hoge, Founder, President andÿCEO
James Hoge, President
Dean O'Neal, Vice President, General Manager, Program Director
Carol Baker Ellingson, Promotions Manager
Mark Chambers, Chief Engineer
Judy Wise, HRÿ/ Office Manager
TateLuck, Assistant Program Director
Tim Wolf, Music Director
Jen Rose, Production
Jessica Bonano, Promotions Assistant
Randy Woods, Technical Director

Palm Beach

WRMF
01-01-1957; 97.9 MHz FM; *Hrs Open:* 24; 100 kw; 1348 ft.; N26 34 37 W80 14 32
2406 South Congress Aven, West Palm Beach, FL 33406 US
(561) 868-1100; *Fax:* (561) 868-1111
www.wrmf.com
License: Palm Beach, West Palm Beach County, FL held by Cobalt LLC
Nat'l Reps: McGavren Guild
Arbitron Metro Market: West Palm Beach-Boca Raton, FL; *Format:* Adult Contemp; *Target Audience:* 25-54; general
Mike Catchall, CEO
Elizabeth Hamma, Operations Dir
Mark Krieger, General Sales Mgr
Bob Neumann, Programming Director
Erika Ewald, Promotions Manager
Doris Dupee, CFO

Palm City

***WCNO**
04-01-1990; 89.9 MHz FM; 100 kw; 614 ft.; N27 7 20 W80 23 21
1150 West King Street, Cocoa, FL 32922 US
(772) 221-1100; *Fax:* (772) 221-8716
www.wcno.com
wcno@wcno.com
License: Palm City, Martin County, FL held by National Christian Network Inc.
Arbitron Metro Market: West Palm Beach,FL; *Format:* Adult Contemp, Christian
Ray Kassis, President
Tom Craton, General Manager

Palm Coast

***WHYZ**
91.1 MHz FM; 9.2 kw horiz, 9.16 kw vert; 175 ft.; N29 26 8 W81 9 21
P. O. Box 607883, Orlando, FL 32860 US
(407) 869-8000; *Fax:* (407) 869-0380
www.zradio.org
License: Palm Coast, Flagler County, FL held by Central Florida Educational Foundation Inc.
Arbitron Metro Market: Palm Coast, FL; *Format:* Christian
James Hoge, President
Dean O'Neal, Vice President

Palmetto

WBRD
10-01-1957; 1420 kHz AM; 2.5 kw-D, DA2; 1 kw-N, DA2; N27 32 42 W82 34 28
2101 Hammock Pl., Sarasota, FL 34235 US
(248) 557-3500; *Fax:* (248) 557-2950
www.birach.com
sima@birach.com
License: Palmetto, Manatee County, FL held by Birach Broadcasting Corp.
Group Owner: Birach Broadcasting Corp.
Arbitron Metro Market: Bradenton, FL; *Format:* Tejano; *Target Audience:* 35 plus.; *Adv. Rates:* 20; 25; 15; na
Sima Birach, Operations Manager

RADIO - U.S.

Panama City

WDIZ
04-01-1940; 590 kHz AM; 1.7 kw-D, DAN; 2.5 kw-N, DAN; N30 10 20 W85 36 49
1834 Lisenby Avenue, Panama City, FL 32405 US
(850) 769-1408; *Fax:* (850) 769-0659
www.963realfunbeachradio.com
License: Panama City, FL held by Clear Channel Broadcasting Licenses Inc.
Group Owner: iHeartMedia; (acq 11-21-97; grpsl)
Arbitron Metro Market: Panama City, FL; *Format:* Oldies
Jackie Rinker, Market President
Darrell Johnson, Senior Vice President of Sales

*WFSW
01-01-1995; 89.1 MHz FM; 100 kw; 404 ft.; N30 22 2 W85 55 29
1600 Red Barber Plaza, Tallahassee, FL 32310 US
(850) 487-3086; *Fax:* (850) 487-3293
www.wfsu.org
License: Panama City, Bay County, FL held by Florida State University.
Nat'l Network: NPR
Arbitron Metro Market: Panama City, FL; *Format:* News, Talk
Tim McGuire, Operations Dir
Pat Keating, General Manager
Caroline Austin, Station Manager
Stan Jastrebski, News Director
Doug Crall, Engineering Dir
Crystal Cumbo, Underwriting Manager
John Kwak, Development Director

WFSY
10-01-1971; 98.5 MHz FM; 100 kw; 1089 ft.; N30 30 41 W85 29 24
1834 Lisenby Avenue, Panama City, FL 32405 US
(850) 769-1408; *Fax:* (850) 769-0659
www.sunny985.com
help@sunny985.com
License: Panama City, Bay County, FL held by Clear Channel Broadcasting Licenses Inc.
Group Owner: iHeartMedia
Arbitron Metro Market: Panama City, FL; *Format:* Adult Contemp; *Target Audience:* 25-54.
Jackie Rinker, Vice President/Market Manager
Darrell Johnson, Senior Vice President of Sales

WILN
04-11-1985; 105.9 MHz FM; *Hrs Open:* 24; 50 kw; 384 ft.; N30 10 44 W85 46 55
7106 Laird Street, Suite 102, Panama City, FL 32408 US
(850) 230-5855; *Fax:* (850) 230-6988
www.island106.com
License: Panama City, Bay County, FL held by Magic Broadcasting II LLC
Group Owner: Magic Broadcasting II LLC; (acq 1-31-2003; grpsl)
Arbitron Metro Market: Panama City, FL; *Format:* Contemporary Hits/Top 40; *Hrs. of News Programming:* news progmg 2 hrs wkly; *No. News Employees:* 1; *Target Audience:* 18-49.
Melissa Allegretto, General Manager
Marc Summers, Programming Director

*WJTF
10-15-1998; 89.9 MHz FM; 100 kw; 105 ft.; N30 10 5 W85 40 30
341 S. Washington, Lancaster, WI 53813 US
(850) 874-9900; *Fax:* (850) 874-9930
License: Panama City, Bay County, FL held by Family Life Broadcasting Inc
Group Owner: Family Life Communications Inc.; (acq 5-23-2007; grpsl)
Nat'l Network: Moody
Arbitron Metro Market: Panama City, FL; *Format:* Religious, Christian; *Target Audience:* 35-90; general
Kelly Dickson, Operations Dir
Tom Bush, General Manager
Mickey Jacobs, Programming Director

*WKGC-FM
10-01-1982; 90.7 MHz FM; 100 kw; 356 ft.; N30 17 45 W85 39 42
5230 West US Highway 98, Panama City, FL 32401 US
(850) 873-3500; *Fax:* (850) 913-3299
www.wkgc.org
License: Panama City, Bay County, FL held by Gulf Coast Community College.
Nat'l Network: NPR; PRI; *Regional Network:* Fla. Pub.
Arbitron Metro Market: Panama City, FL; *Format:* News *Special Programming:* Black 6 hrs wkly; *Target Audience:* General.
Chris Thomes, Station Manager
Curtis Carter, Programming Director
Emily Balazs, News Director
Chris Thomes, Executive Director of Marketing & Communications

WPFM-FM
09-01-1963; 107.9 MHz FM; *Hrs Open:* 24; 98.5 kw; 781 ft.; N30 25 59 W85 24 51
118 Gwyn Drive, Panama City Beach, FL 32408 US
(850) 234-8858; *Fax:* (850) 234-6592
www.hot1079pc.com
neilknight@panamacityradio.com
License: Panama City, Bay County, FL
Group Owner: Powell Broadcasting Co. L.L.C.; acq 3-10-2004; grpsl).
Nat'l Reps: Christal
Arbitron Metro Market: Panama City, FL; *Format:* Contemporary Hits/Top 40; *Target Audience:* 18-49; active lifestyle, young adult audience; *Adv. Rates:* 50; 40; 40; 25
Neil Knight, Operations Dir
Neil Knight, Programming Director
Ira Rosenblatt, Market Manager

WLTG
12-11-1949; 1430 kHz AM; 5 kw-D, DA2; 5 kw-N, DA2; N30 9 55 W85 35 19
Mailing Address: P.O. Box 15635, Panama City, FL 32406 US
Second Address: 3100 E. 15th St., Springfield, FL 32405
(850) 784-9873; *Fax:* (850) 784-6908
www.1430newstalk.com
wltg@bellsouth.net
License: Panama City, FL held by Williams Communications Inc.
Group Owner: Williams Communications Inc.; acq 8-12-03; $500,000).
Nat'l Network: Premiere Radio Networks; Salem Radio Network;
Nat'l Reps: Commercial Media Sales
Arbitron Metro Market: Panama City, FL; *Format:* News, News/Talk, 84, Talk *Special Programming:* Black gospel 7 hrs wkly; *Target Audience:* General.
John Gay, General Manager

WPAP
03-30-1967; 92.5 MHz FM; *Hrs Open:* 24; 100 kw; 922 ft.; N30 30 41 W85 29 24
1834 Lisenby Avenue, Panama City, FL 32405 US
(850) 769-1408; *Fax:* (850) 769-0659
www.925wpap.com
help@925wpap.com
License: Panama City, Bay County, FL held by Clear Channel Broadcasting Licenses Inc.
Group Owner: iHeartMedia; (acq 11-21-97; grpsl)
Nat'l Reps: McGavren Guild
Arbitron Metro Market: Panama City, FL; *Format:* Country; *Target Audience:* 25-54.
Jackie Rinker, Market President
Darrell Johnson, Senior Vice President of Sales
Carolyn Mosley, Market Controller

*WFFL
01-01-2007; 91.7 MHz FM; 0.31 kw horiz, 0.304 kw vert; 207 ft.; N30 10 48 W85 38 10 *Rebroadcasts:* Rebroadcasts WJFM(FM) Baton Rouge, LA 100%
Mailing Address: 8030 Arrowridge Blvd, Charlotte, VA 28273 US
Second Address: 8919 World Ministry Ave., Baton Rouge, FL 70810
(225) 768-3224
www.jsm.org
License: Panama City, Bay County, FL held by Family Worship Center Church Inc.
Group Owner: Family Worship Center Church Inc.; (acq 10-12-2006; grpsl)
Arbitron Metro Market: Tucson, AZ; *Format:* Christian
David Whitelaw, COO

Panama City Beach

WASJ
01-01-1993; 105.1 MHz FM; *Hrs Open:* 24; 50 kw; 335 ft.; N30 10 44 W85 46 55
118 Gwyn Drive, Panama City Beach, FL 32408 US
(850) 234-8858; *Fax:* (850) 234-6592
www.bobatthebeach.com
ira.rosenblatt@panamacityradio.com
License: Panama City Beach, Bay County, FL
Group Owner: Powell Broadcasting Co. L.L.C.; acq 3-10-2004; grpsl)
Nat'l Network: ESPN Radio; *Nat'l Reps:* Christal
Arbitron Metro Market: Panama City, FL; *Format:* Sports; *Adv. Rates:* 50; 40; 40; 25
Neil Knight, Operations Manager/Programming Director
Ira Rosenblatt, General Manager

WPCF
09-23-1958; 1290 kHz AM; 0.27 kw-D, ND2; 0.055 kw-N, ND2; N30 10 44 W85 46 55
7106 Laird Street, Suite 102, Panama City, FL 32408 US
(850) 230-5855; *Fax:* (850) 230-6988
www.troprock1290.com
syoungblood@magicfl.com
License: Panama City Beach, FL held by Magic Broadcasting II LLC
Group Owner: Magic Broadcasting II LLC; (acq 9-30-2002; grpsl)
Arbitron Metro Market: Panama City, FL; *Format:* Country
Melissa Allegretto, General Manager
Steve Youngblood, Programming Director

WVVE
06-01-1988; 100.1 MHz FM; *Hrs Open:* 24; 12 kw; 404 ft.; N30 10 44 W85 46 55
P.O. Box 16626, Panama City, FL 32406 US
(850) 230-5855; *Fax:* (850) 230-6988
License: Panama City Beach, Bay County, FL held by Magic Broadcasting II LLC
Group Owner: Magic Broadcasting II LLC; (acq 9-30-2002; grpsl)
Arbitron Metro Market: Panama City, FL; *Format:* Adult Contemp; *Adv. Rates:* 20; 20; 20; na
Melissa Allegretto, General Manager
Marc Summers, Programming Director

Parker

WFLF-FM
08-01-1977; 94.5 MHz FM; *Hrs Open:* 24; 100 kw; 994 ft.; N29 49 9 W85 15 34
1834 Lisenby Avenue, Panama City, FL 32405 US
(850) 769-1408; *Fax:* (850) 769-0659
www.945wfla.com
help@945wfla.com
License: Parker, Bay County, FL held by Clear Channel Broadcasting Licenses Inc.
Group Owner: iHeartMedia; (acq 11-21-97; grpsl)
Nat'l Network: Fox News Radio
Arbitron Metro Market: Panama City, FL; *Format:* News, News/Talk, 86 *Special Programming:* Relg 5 hrs wkly
Jackie Rinker, Market President
Darrell Johnson, Senior Vice President of Sales

Pennsuco

*WGNK
01-01-1999; 88.3 MHz FM; *Hrs Open:* 24; 6 kw; 282 ft.; N25 52 24 W80 28 59
7205 S.W. 125 Avenue, Miami, FL 33183 US
(305) 406-2883; *Fax:* (305) 406-3030
www.lanueva883fm.com
License: Pennsuco, Dade County, FL held by Genesis License Subsidiary LLC
Format: Christian *Special Programming:* Children 6 hrs; *Hrs. of News Programming:* news progmg 3 hrs wkly; *No. News Employees:* 1; *Target Audience:* 18-35; Hispanic Christians
Edwin Ortiz, President
Mauricio Quintana, General Manager

Pensacola

WYCT
11-28-2003; 98.7 MHz FM; 100 kw; 981 ft.; N30 37 30 W87 26 39
72 Plantation Road, Pensacola, FL 32504 US
(850) 430-1987; *Fax:* (850) 494-0778
www.catcountry987.com
comments@CatCountry987.com
License: Pensacola, Escambia County, FL held by ADX Communications of Pensacola.
Arbitron Metro Market: Pensacola, FL; *Format:* Country
David Hoxeng, CEO
Kevin King, Operations Dir
Mary Hoxeng, General Manager
Mary Hoxeng, General Sales Mgr
Paul Stadden, Promotions Manager
Brit Smith, Chief Engineer

WBSR
09-01-1946; 1450 kHz AM; *Hrs Open:* 24; 1 kw-D, ND1; 1 kw-N, ND1; N30 25 44 W87 14 27
Mailing Address: P. O. Box 8057, Pensacola, FL 32505 US
Second Address: 1601 N. Pace Blvd., Pensacola, FL 32505
(850) 438-4982; *Fax:* (850) 433-7932
www.espnpensacola.com
License: Pensacola, FL held by Easy Media Inc.
Arbitron Metro Market: Pensacola, FL; *Format:* Adult Contemp; *Target Audience:* 35-54.
Frederic Brewer, President
Gene Pfalzer, Station Manager

WCOA
02-03-1926; 1370 kHz AM; *Hrs Open:* 24; 5 kw-D, DAN; 5 kw-N, DAN; N30 26 57 W87 15 46
6565 North W. Street, Pensacola, FL 32505 US
(850) 478-6011; *Fax:* (850) 478-3971
www.wcoapensacola.com
kevin.peterson@cumulus.com
License: Pensacola, FL held by Cumulus Licensing Corp.
Group Owner: Cumulus Media Inc.; (acq 10-25-99; with co-located FM)
Nat'l Network: ABC; *Nat'l Reps:* Katz Radio
Arbitron Metro Market: Vicinity-Pensacola, FL; *Format:* News, News/Talk, 86 *Special Programming:* Relg 3 hrs wkly; *Target Audience:* 25-54.
Kevin Peterson, Operations & Programming Director
Yancy McNair, Chief Engineer
Hugh McPherson, Marketing Manager

WMEZ
11-11-1960; 94.1 MHz FM; 77 kw; 1601 ft.; N30 36 40 W87 36 26
6565 North W Street, Pensacola, FL 32505 US
(850) 994-5357; *Fax:* (850) 994-7191
www.softrock941.com
License: Pensacola, Escambia County, FL held by Cumulus Licensing LLC
Group Owner: Cumulus Media Inc.
Arbitron Metro Market: Pensacola, FL; *Format:* Adult Contemp; *Target Audience:* 25-54. females
Kevin Peterson, Operations & Programming Director
Mike Carr, Sales Manager
Gerald Wilson, Chief Engineer
Hugh McPherson, Marketing Manager

***WPCS**
06-22-1971; 89.5 MHz FM; *Hrs Open:* 24; 95 kw; Ant 1,358 ft; N30 35 16 W87 33 13
Box 18000, Pensacola, FL 32503
(850) 479-6570; *Fax:* (850) 969-1638
www.rejoice.org
rbn@rejoice.org
License: Pensacola, Escambia County, FL held by Pensacola Christian College Inc.
Population Served: 1,025,018; *Arbitron Metro Market:* Pensacola, FL
Troy Shoemaker, President
Caleb Keener, Station Manager
Tonita Ohman, Programming Director
Ryan See, Chief Engineer

WPNN
10-01-1956; 790 kHz AM; 1 kw-D; N30 27 18 W87 14 22
3801 N. Pace Blvd., Pensacola, FL 32505
(850) 433-1141; *Fax:* (850) 433-1142
www.cnnpensacola.com
License: Pensacola, Escambia County, FL held by Miracle Radio Inc.
Population Served: 62,507; *Arbitron Metro Market:* Pensacola, FL
Gerald Schroeder, President
Gerald Schroeder, Operations Dir
Scott Schroeder, General Manager
Scott Schroeder, Station Manager

WTKX-FM
01-01-1971; 101.5 MHz FM; *Hrs Open:* 24; 100 kw; 1601 ft.; N30 36 40 W87 36 26.4
555 Broadcast Drive, Mobile, AL 36606 US
(850) 450-0100; *Fax:* (850) 473-0907
www.tk101.com
radio@tk101.com
License: Pensacola, Escambia County, FL held by Clear Channel Broadcasting Licenses Inc.
Group Owner: iHeartMedia; (acq 11-21-97; grpsl).
Arbitron Metro Market: Pensacola, FL; *Format:* Rock/AOR; *Target Audience:* 18-49; general
Ronnie Bloodworth, General Sales Mgr
Brett Mouron, Digital Content Director

***WUWF**
01-01-1981; 88.1 MHz FM; *Hrs Open:* 24; 100 kw; 614 ft.; N30 24 13 W86 59 34
11000 University Parkway, Pensacola, FL 32514 US
(850) 474-2787
www.wuwf.org
wuwf@wuwf.org
License: Pensacola, Escambia County, FL held by Board of Trustees, University of West Florida
Nat'l Network: PRI; NPR; *Regional Network:* Fla. Pub.
Arbitron Metro Market: Pensacola, GA; *Format:* Alternative, News; *Hrs. of News Programming:* news progmg 34 hrs wkly; *No. News Employees:* 2; *Target Audience:* General.
Joe Vincenza, Station Manager/Programming Director
Lynne Marshall, Promotions Director
Sandra Averhart, News Director
Dale Riegle, Technical Director
Pat Crawford, Executive Director
John Macdonell, IT Services Director
TheresaClark, Business Manager
Trish Allison, Development Director

WVTJ
11-01-1959; 610 kHz AM; *Hrs Open:* 24; 500 w-D, 157 w-N; N30 27 18 W87 14 22
2070 N. Palafox Rd., Pensacola, FL 32501
(850) 432-3658
www.wilkinsradio.com
denise@wilkinsradio.com
License: Pensacola, Escambia County, FL held by Pensacola Radio Corp.
Group Owner: Wilkins Communications Network Inc.; (acq 4-23-2007; $545,000)
Population Served: 480,000; *Arbitron Metro Market:* Pensacola, FL; *Format:* Gospel, Talk; *Target Audience:* 18-64.
Jessica Jordan, Station Manager

WCOA-FM
09-01-1965; 100.7 MHz FM; 100 kw; 1,555 ft; N30 37 35 W87 38 50
6565 N. W St., Pensacola, FL 32505
(850) 478-6011; *Fax:* (850) 478-3971
www.wcoapensacola.com
License: Pensacola, Escambia County, FL
Population Served: 52,197; *Arbitron Metro Market:* Pensacola, FL; *Format:* News, News/Talk, 86; *Target Audience:* 25-44.
Yancy McNair, Chief Engineer
Brian Newkirk, Assistant Program Director
Monte Saunders, Business Manager
Monica Ard, Traffic Manager

WDWR
01-01-1947; 1230 kHz AM; *Hrs Open:* 24
2070 North Palafox St., Pensacola, FL 32501 US
(850) 438-7667; *Fax:* (850) 437-3733
www.divinewordradio.com
info@divinewordradio.com
License: Pensacola, FL held by Divine Word Communications
Nat'l Network: EWTN Radio
Arbitron Metro Market: Pensacola, FL; *Format:* Christian
Gene Church, President

WRGV
01-01-1976; 107.3 MHz FM; 50 kw; 1601 ft.; N30 36 40 W87 36 27
555 Broadcast Drive, Mobile, AL 36606 US
(850) 450-0100; *Fax:* (850) 473-0907
www.1073kissfm.com
License: Pensacola, Escambia County, FL held by Clear Channel Broadcasting Licenses Inc.
Group Owner: iHeartMedia
Arbitron Metro Market: Pensacola, FL; *Format:* Contemporary Hits/Top 40; *Target Audience:* 18-49; general
Ronnie Bloodworth, General Sales Mgr
Matt McCoy, Programming Director
Brett Mouron, Digital Content Director

Perry

WNFK
12-01-1989; 92.1 MHz FM; 6 kw; 328 ft.; N30 5 17 W83 29 46
P.O. Box 779, Perry, FL 32347 US
(850) 584-9210; *Fax:* (850) 223-3492
www.powercountry102.com
License: Perry, Taylor County, FL held by Taylor County Broadcasting Inc.
Arbitron Metro Market: Perry, FL; *Format:* Country
Bob Hendrickson, General Manager
Keith Conway, Programming Director

WPRY
01-01-1953; 1400 kHz AM; *Hrs Open:* 24; 1 kw-U, ND1; N30 6 27 W83 34 0
P.O. Box 779, Perry, FL 32347 US
(850) 223-1400; *Fax:* (850) 223-3501
www.wpry.com
License: Perry, FL held by HF Broadcasting Perry LC
Format: Contemporary Hits/Top 40, Adult Contemp *Special Programming:* Black 2 hrs wkly; *Hrs. of News Programming:* 15 hrs news progmg wkly; *Target Audience:* 18 plus.
Gary Williams, General Manager

WFDZ
93.5 MHz FM; 6 kw; 252 ft.; N30 8 0 W83 35 45 US
(573) 701-4708
License: Perry, Taylor County, FL held by Dockins Telecommunications Inc.
Arbitron Metro Market: Perry, FL
Fred Dockins, General Manager

Pine Castle Sky Lake

WAMT
01-28-1977; 1190 kHz AM; *Hrs Open:* 24
1160 South Semoran Blvd, Suite A, Orlando, FL 32807 US
(813) 281-1040; *Fax:* (407) 382-7565
www.newstalkflorida.com
contactus@radiogenesis.com
License: Pine Castle Sky Lake, FL held by Genesis Communications I Inc.
Group Owner: Genesis Communications Inc.; (acq 3-20-2000; $2.1 million)
Nat'l Network: ABC; Westwood One; *Regional Network:* Florida's Radio Networks; *Nat'l Reps:* Interep; *Wire Services:* AP; Metro Weather Service Inc.
Arbitron Metro Market: Orlando, FL; *Format:* News, News/Talk, 86; *Target Audience:* 25-65; general; *Adv. Rates:* 50; 40; 50; 30
Bruce Maduri, President/General Sales Manager
Len Weiner, Programming Director
Amanda Berger, Promotions Director
Gwen Schuler, Traffic Manager

Pine Hills

WFLF
09-09-1955; 540 kHz AM; *Hrs Open:* 24
2500 Maitland Center Parkway, Maitland, FL 32751 US
(407) 916-7800; *Fax:* (407) 661-1940
www.1025wfla.com
License: Pine Hills, FL held by Clear Channel Broadcasting Licenses Inc.
Group Owner: iHeartMedia; (acq 11-21-97; grpsl)
Nat'l Network: Fox News Radio; *Regional Network:* Florida's Radio Networks; *Wire Services:* AP
Arbitron Metro Market: Orlando, FL; *Format:* News, News/Talk, 86 *Special Programming:* Florida Gaton football & basketball, Florida Marlins, Miami Dolphins; *Hrs. of News Programming:* news progmg 168 hrs wkly *No. NewsEmployees:* 5; *Target Audience:* 35-64.; *Adv. Rates:* 125; 150; 135; 25
Linda Byrd, Market President
Mark Kanak, Sales Manager
Jim Poling, Programming Director
Erika Plak, Promotions Director

Pine Island Center

WJUA
03-01-1940; 1200 kHz AM; 50 kw-D, DA2 1 kw-N, DA2; N26 42 52 W82 02 46
2824 Palm Beach Blvd., Fort Myers, FL 33916 US
(239) 334-1111; *Fax:* (239) 332-0767
www.juan1200.com
License: Pine Island Center, Lee Inner County, FL held by Fort Myers Broadcasting Co.
Group Owner: Fort Myers Broadcasting Co.
Nat'l Network: Jones Radio Networks; *Nat'l Reps:* McGavren Guild
Arbitron Metro Market: Fort Myers-Naples-Marco Island, FL; *Format:* Adult Contemp
Wayne Simons, General Manager
Brad Foster, General Sales Mgr
Michael Hayes, Programming Director

Pinellas Park

WHBO
11-01-1948; 1040 kHz AM
800 8th Avenue Southeast, Largo, FL 33771 US
(813) 281-1040; *Fax:* (813) 281-1948
www.sportstalkflorida.com
License: Pinellas Park, FL held by Genesis Communications of Tampa Bay Inc.
Group Owner: Genesis Communications Inc.; (acq 12-17-97; $1.5 million)
Nat'l Network: ESPN Radio; *Regional Network:* Florida's Radio Networks; *Nat'l Reps:* Interep; McGavren Guild; *Wire Services:* AP
Arbitron Metro Market: Tampa, FL; *Format:* Sports; *Target Audience:* 25-54.; *Adv. Rates:* 85; 50; 80; 45
Bruce Maduri, CEO/General Sales Manager
Len Weiner, Programming Director

RADIO - U.S.

Amanda Berger, Promotions Director
Gwen Schuler, Traffic Manager

Pinellas Park,

WTBN

11-12-1966; 570 kHz AM; *Hrs Open:* 24
5211 West Laurel Street, Tampa, FL 33607 US
(813) 639-1903; *Fax:* (813) 639-1272
www.bayword.com
info@bayword.com
License: Pinellas Park, FL held by Common Ground Broadcasting Inc.
Group Owner: Salem Communications Corp.; (acq 8-7-2001; $6.75 million).
Nat'l Network: Salem Radio Network; *Nat'l Reps:* Salem
Arbitron Metro Market: Tampa-St. Petersburg-Clearwater, FL; *Format:* Christian, Talk *Special Programming:* College (USF) sports football & basketball; *Hrs. of News Programming:* news progmg 30 hrs wkly *No. NewsEmployees:* 2; *Target Audience:* 25-64.
Joe Weaver, Operations Manager
Barb Yoder, General Manager
Denise Shreaves, Promotions & Marketing Director
Rey Noriega, News Director
Robert Hailey, Engineering Dir

Plant City

WTWD

07-01-1949; 910 kHz AM; *Hrs Open:* 24; 5 kw-U, DA1; N27 59 26 W82 12 31 *Rebroadcasts:* Rebroadcasts WTBN Pinnellas Park 100%
877 Executive Center Drive, #300, St. Petersburg, FL 33702 US
(813) 639-1903; *Fax:* (813) 639-1272
www.baywood.com
License: Plant City, FL held by South Texas Broadcasting Inc.
Group Owner: Salem Communications Corp.; (acq 7-27-00; grpsl).
Nat'l Network: Salem Radio Network; *Nat'l Reps:* Salem
Arbitron Metro Market: Tampa-St. Petersburg-Clearwater, FL; *Format:* Christian, Talk; *Target Audience:* 25-54.
Joe Weaver, Operations Manager
Barb Yoder, General Manager
Denise Shreaves, Promotions & Marketing Director
Robert Hailey, Chief Engineer

Plantation Key

WCTH

07-01-1969; 100.3 MHz FM; *Hrs Open:* 24; 100 kw; 463 ft.; N24 57 34 W80 34 30
93351 Overseas Hwy., Tavernier, FL 33070 USA
(305) 852-9085; *Fax:* (305) 852-2304
thundercountry.com
License: Plantation Key, Monroe County, FL held by Florida Keys Media LLC
Group Owner: Florida Keys Media LLC; (acq 2-99; $1.8 million)
Nat'l Network: Westwood One; *Regional Network:* Florida's Radio Networks; *Nat'l Reps:* Clear Channel
Arbitron Metro Market: Tavernier,FL; *Format:* Country *Special Programming:* NASCAR 3 hrs wkly; *Hrs. of News Programming:* news progmg 4 hrs wkly; *No. News Employees:* 1; *Target Audience:* 25-54; residents &tourists; *Adv. Rates:* 35; 30; 35; 20
Rick Lopez, General Manager
Amy Andrade, Sales Manager
Randy Perry, Chief Engineer

WFKZ

01-02-1984; 103.1 MHz FM; *Hrs Open:* 24; 50 kw; 449 ft.; N24 57 33 W80 34 30
93351 Overseas Hwy., Tavernier, FL 33070 USA
(305) 852-9085; *Fax:* (305) 852-2304
sun103.com
License: Plantation Key, Monroe County, FL held by Florida Keys Media LLC
Group Owner: Florida Keys Media LLC
Nat'l Network: AP Radio
Format: Classic Rock; *Hrs. of News Programming:* news progmg 8 hrs wkly; *No. News Employees:* 2; *Target Audience:* 25-54; adults; *Adv. Rates:* 28; 24; 28; 10
Rick Lopez, General Manager
Amy Andrade, Sales Manager
Randy Perry, Chief Engineer

Pompano Beach

WHSR

01-01-1959; 980 kHz AM; 5 kw-D, 2.2 kw-N; N26 20 6 W80 15 55
1650 S. Dixie Hwy., 5th Fl., Boca Raton, FL 33432 US
(561) 997-0074; *Fax:* (561) 997-0476
www.whsrradio.com
License: Pompano Beach, Broward County, FL held by Beasley Media Group LLC
Group Owner: Beasley Broadcast Group Inc.; (acq 3-17-2000; grpsl).
Arbitron Metro Market: Miami-Fort Lauderdale-Hollywood, FL; *Format:* Ethnic, Talk; *Target Audience:* 25-54; baby boomers weaned on electronic media as an info source
Duff Lindsey, Operations Manager/Program Director
Bob Morency, General Manager
Karen Ruggiere, Business Manager
Jodi Milbaum, Traffic Manager/Account Executive

WMXJ

01-01-1960; 102.7 MHz FM; 98 kw; 1007 ft.; N25 58 2 W80 12 34
20450 NW 2nd Avenue, Miami, FL 33169 US
(305) 521-5100; *Fax:* (305) 652-1888
www.thebeachmiami.com
webmasterWMXJ@wmxj.com
License: Pompano Beach, Broward County, FL held by Lincoln Financial Media Co. of Florida.
Group Owner: Entercom; (acq 2016).
Nat'l Reps: CBS Radio; *Wire Services:* AP
Arbitron Metro Market: Miami, FL; *Format:* Contemporary Hits/Top 40; *Target Audience:* 35-64.
Maureen Lesound, Senior Vice President/General Manager
Marc Telsey, General Sales Mgr
Sam Zniber, Programming Director
Eric Stenger, Promotions Director
Gary Blau, Engineering Dir
Marc Budine, Interactive & Online Sales Manager

WWNN

01-01-1959; 1470 kHz AM; *Hrs Open:* 24; 50 kw-D, DA2; 2.5 kw-N, DA2; N26 10 46 W80 13 15
1650 S. Dixie Hwy., 5th Fl., Boca Raton, FL 33432 US
(561) 988-5470; *Fax:* (561) 997-0476
www.wwnnradio.com
License: Pompano Beach, Broward County, FL held by Beasley Media Group LLC
Group Owner: Beasley Broadcast Group Inc.; (acq 3-14-2000; grpsl).
Arbitron Metro Market: Pompano Beach, FL; *Format:* Talk
Duff Lindsey, Operations Manager/Program Director
Bob Morency, General Manager
Karen Ruggerie, Business Manager
Jodi Mibaum, Traffic Manager/Account Executive

Ponte Vedra Beach

WEZI

07-01-1994; 106.5 MHz FM; *Hrs Open:* 24; 6 kw; 328 ft.; N30 16 35 W81 33 58
8000 Belfort Parkway, Suite 100, Jacksonville, FL 32256 US
(904) 245-8500; *Fax:* (904) 245-8501
www.easy1065.com
todd.shannon@coxinc.com
License: Ponte Vedra Beach, St. Johns County, FL held by Cox Radio Inc.
Group Owner: Cox Radio Inc.; (acq 9-18-2006; $7.65 million)
Arbitron Metro Market: Jacksonville, FL; *Format:* Christian; *Target Audience:* 35-64
Todd Shannon, Program Director
Bob Deblois, Director Of Sales
Jodi Ralney, National Sales Manager
Ashley Testa, Digital Sales Manager
David Ratz, Promotions & Events Director

Port Charlotte

WZJZ

10-01-1976; 100.1 MHz FM; *Hrs Open:* 24; 84 kw; 1060 ft.; N26 47 7 W81 47 47
13320 Metro Parkway, Suite #1, Fort Myers, FL 33966 US
(239) 225-4300
www.y100florida.com
License: Port Charlotte, Charlotte County, FL held by Clear Channel Broadcasting Licenses Inc.
Group Owner: iHeartMedia; (acq 2-18-97; grpsl)
Arbitron Metro Market: Fort Myers-Naples-Marco Island, FL; *Format:* Contemporary Hits/Top 40; *Target Audience:* 25-54.
Louis Kaplan, Operations Manager
Kevin Miskimins, Senior Vice President of Sales

*WVIJ

07-26-1987; 91.7 MHz FM; 1.9 kw; 207 ft.; N26 58 49 W82 4 3
3279 Sherwood Road, Port Charlotte, FL 33980 US
(941) 624-5000; *Fax:* (775) 243-0586
www.wvij.com
wvij@wvij.com
License: Port Charlotte, Charlotte County, FL held by Port Charlotte Educational Broadcasting Foundation Inc.
Arbitron Metro Market: Port Charlotte, FL; *Format:* Religious; *Target Audience:* 35 plus.
Daniel Kolenda Jr., President/General Manager

Port Orange

WKRO-FM

01-01-1993; 93.1 MHz FM; *Hrs Open:* 24; 15 kw; 427 ft.; N28 53 40 W80 53 8
126 W. Intl. Speedway Blvd., Daytona Beach, FL 32114 US
(386) 255-9300
931coast.com
License: Port Orange, Volusia County, FL held by Southern Stone Communications of Florida, LLC
Group Owner: Southern Stone Communications
Arbitron Metro Market: Daytona Beach, FL; *Format:* Country
Jonathan Wiley, Operations Dir
Greg Pretko, General Manager
Dallas Reese, Programming Director
Drita Travis, Promotions Manager

Port St. Lucie

WHLG

11-16-1998; 101.3 MHz FM; *Hrs Open:* 24; 6 kw; 299 ft.; N27 12 53 W80 15 24
1000 NW Alice Avenue, Stuart, FL 34994 US
(772) 692-9454; *Fax:* (772) 692-0258
www.coast1013.com
info@coast1013.com
License: Port St. Lucie, St. Lucie County, FL held by Horton Broadcasting Co. Inc.
Nat'l Network: Jones Radio Networks; *Nat'l Reps:* Interep
Format: Adult Contemp; *No. News Employees:* 10; *Target Audience:* 25-54; female/male 60/40%, 35 years old; *Adv. Rates:* 365; 40; 30; 20
George Metcalf, CEO
Lorna Potter, General Manager

WPSL

10-26-1985; 1590 kHz AM; *Hrs Open:* 24; 5 kw-D, ND1; 0.063 kw-N, ND1; N27 18 28 W80 18 26
8245 Business Park Drive, Port St Lucie, FL 34952 US
(772) 340-1590; *Fax:* (772) 340-3245
www.wpsl.com
wpsl@wpsl.com
License: Port St. Lucie, FL held by Port St. Lucie Broadcasters Inc.
Nat'l Network: CBS; ESPN Radio; *Regional Network:* Florida's Radio Networks
Arbitron Metro Market: Fort Pierce-Stuart-Vero Beach, FL; *Format:* News, News/Talk, 84, Talk *Special Programming:* Relg 6 hrs wkly; *Hrs. of News Programming:* news progmg 4 hrs wkly; *No. News Employees:* 1 *TargetAudience:* 45 plus; established families; *Adv. Rates:* 50 for:60—-40 for :30
Carol Wyatt, CEO
Greg Wyatt, Operations Dir

Punta Gorda

WCCF

09-15-1961; 1580 kHz AM; 1.25 kw-D, ND1; 0.11 kw-N, ND1; N26 53 37 W82 3 3
24100 Tiseo Boulevard, #10, Port Charlotte, FL 33981 US
(941) 206-1188; *Fax:* (941) 206-9296
www.wccfam.com
info@wccfam.com
License: Punta Gorda, FL held by Citicasters Licenses Inc.
Group Owner: iHeartMedia; (acq 2-1-99; grpsl).
Format: News, News/Talk, 86; *Target Audience:* 45 plus.; *Adv. Rates:* 35; 35; 35; 25
Sherri Griswold, Regional Market Manager
Robin Craig, Director of Sales

Punta Rassa

WTLQ-FM

05-03-1999; 97.7 MHz FM; *Hrs Open:* 24; 14.5 kw; 430 ft.; N26 29 16 W81 55 46
2824 Palm Beach Boulevard, Fort Myers, FL 33916 US
(239) 337-2346 / (239) 338-4325; *Fax:* (239) 334-0744
977latino.com
License: Punta Rassa, Lee Inner County, FL held by Fort Myers Broadcasting Co.
Group Owner: Fort Myers Broadcasting Co.; (acq 9-13-00; $7 million).
Nat'l Reps: McGavren Guild
Arbitron Metro Market: Fort Myers, FL; *Format:* Urban Contemporary; *Target Audience:* Hipanic Adults 18-49

Wayne Simons, General Manager
Brad Foster, General Sales Mgr

Quincy

WXSR
12-01-1966; 101.5 MHz FM; 37 kw; 489 ft.; N30 29 32 W84 17 13
325 John Knox Road, Building G, Tallahassee, FL 32303 US
(850) 422-3107; *Fax:* (850) 383-0747
www.x1015.com
License: Quincy, Gadsden County, FL held by Clear Channel Broadcasting Licenses Inc.
Group Owner: iHeartMedia; (acq 11-21-97; grpsl)
Arbitron Metro Market: Tallahassee, FL; *Format:* Rock/AOR; *Target Audience:* 18-34.; *Adv. Rates:* 50; 60; 60; 30
Chuck Redden, Market Manager
AJ Malone, Programming Director
Jason Taylor, Webmaster

***WFRU**
06-25-2008; 90.1 MHz FM; 32 kw vert; 328 ft.; N30 42 22 W84 37 39
954 Hwy C4-A, Baker, FL 32531 US
(850) 201-1070; *Fax:* (850) 201-1071
www.faithradio.us
License: Quincy, Gadsden County, FL held by Okaloosa Public Radio Inc.
Arbitron Metro Market: Quincy, FL; *Format:* Religious
Scott Beigle, General Manager
Steve Huffman, Operations Dir
Brenda Beigle, Vice President
Suzanne Farrar, Administrative Assistant
Anna Moore, Administrative Assistant

Riviera Beach

WHTY(AM)
08-17-1959; 1600 kHz AM; *Hrs Open:* 24; 5 kw-D, 4.7 kw-N, DA-2; N26 44 55 W80 08 02
2475 Mercer Avenue, Suite 104, West Palm Beach, FL 33401 US
(561) 459-5038; *Fax:* (561) 623-7668
www.radiovisionmedia.com
License: Riviera Beach, Palm Beach County, FL held by Travis License Partners LLC
Arbitron Metro Market: West Palm Beach-Boca Raton, FL; *Format:* Children
Robert Travis, Manager

WZZR
01-01-1971; 94.3 MHz FM; 50 kw; 456 ft.; N26 45 42 W80 4 42
3071 Continental Drive, West Palm Beach, FL 33407 US
(561) 616-6600; *Fax:* (561) 616-6677
www.wzzr.com
License: Riviera Beach, West Palm Beach County, FL held by Clear Channel Broadcasting Licenses Inc.
Group Owner: iHeartMedia; (acq 11-21-97; grpsl).
Arbitron Metro Market: West Palm Beach, FL; *Format:* Talk; *Target Audience:* 25-54.; *Adv. Rates:* 90; 75; 90; 60
Bryan Kelly, Director of Sales
Andrew Bednar, Promotions Director
Chad Tyson, Digital Program Director

Rock Harbor

WKLG
11-01-1984; 102.1 MHz FM; *Hrs Open:* 24; 100 kw; 430 ft.; N25 5 29 W80 26 37
Mailing Address: 513 Southard Street, Key West, FL 33040 US
Second Address: 1452 N. Krome Ave., Suite 103 E., Florida City, FL 33034
(305) 451-2202; *Fax:* (305) 453-2265
www.wklginc.com/radio
cs@wklginc.com
License: Rock Harbor, Monroe County, FL held by WKLG Inc.
Format: Adult Contemp; *Target Audience:* 25-54; majority are female 18 plus
Douglas LaRue, President

Rockledge

WHKR
11-25-1989; 102.7 MHz FM; *Hrs Open:* 24; 50 kw; 433 ft.; N28 20 59 W80 46 29
1800 Hibiscus Road, Suite 138, Melbourne, FL 32901 US
(321) 984-1000; *Fax:* (321) 724-1565
www.thehitkicker.com
Pete.DeSimone@cumulus.com
License: Rockledge, Brevard County, FL held by Cumulus Licensing Corp.
Group Owner: Cumulus Media Inc.; (acq 8-7-2000; grpsl).
Arbitron Metro Market: Melbourne-Titusville-Cocoa, FL; *Format:* Country *Special Programming:* Pub service one hr wkly; *Hrs. of News Programming:* news progmg 6 hrs wkly; *No. News Employees:* 2; *Target Audience:* 25-54.
Pete DeSimone, General Manager
Jim Callahan, Programming Director
Jennifer Armstrong, Promotions Manager
Jon Roberts, Chief Engineer
Christina Volonnino, Traffic Director

Royal Palm Beach

WMEN
04-01-1987; 640 kHz AM; *Hrs Open:* 24; 7.5 kw-D, DA2; 0.46 kw-N, DA2; N26 45 18 W80 22 0
701 Northpoint Pkwy., Suite 500, West Palm Beach, FL 33407 US
(561) 616-4777
www.640sports.com
License: Royal Palm Beach, FL held by ACM JCE IV B LLC.
Group Owner: ACM JCE IV B LLC.
Arbitron Metro Market: Royal Palm Beach, FL; *Format:* Sports
Mark Jorgenson, President

WPSP
02-01-1991; 1190 kHz AM; *Hrs Open:* 18
1033 East Semoran Blvd., #253, Casselberry, FL 32707 US
(561) 681-9777; *Fax:* (561) 687-3398
diaz1190am@aol.com
License: Royal Palm Beach, FL held by George M. Arroyo.
Arbitron Metro Market: West Palm Beach-Boca Raton, FL; *Format:* Spanish; *Hrs. of News Programming:* news progmg 20 hrs wkly; *No. News Employees:* 2; *Target Audience:* 25-54.; *Adv. Rates:* 30; 25; 30; 20
George Arroyo, President
Lissette Diaz, General Manager

Safety Harbor

WYUU
10-01-1983; 92.5 MHz FM; 50 kw; 489 ft.; N27 50 32 W82 48 52
9721 Executive Center Dr., Suite 200, St. Petersburg, FL 33702 US
(727) 579-1925
www.925maxima.com
License: Safety Harbor, Pinellas County, FL held by WQAM License Limited Partnership
Group Owner: Beasley Broadcast Group Inc.; (acq 10-15-98; $75 million with WLLD(FM) Holmes Beach).
Arbitron Metro Market: Tampa-St. Peter; *Format:* Spanish; *Target Audience:* 18-49.
Gretchen Pujals, Sales
Nio Encendio, Programming Director
Luzed Cruz, Promotions Manager
Luis Gonzalez, Production Director
Gerardo Cierra, Production Director

Saint Augustine

WAOC
12-01-1953; 1420 kHz AM; *Hrs Open:* 24; 2.18 kw-D, 250 w-N; N29 51 00 W81 19 50
Mailing Address: Box 3847, Saint Augustine, FL 93720
Second Address: 567 Lewis Point Rd. Ext., Saint Augustine, FL 32086
(904) 797-4444; *Fax:* (904) 797-3446
www.1420sports.com
kris@1420sports.com
License: Saint Augustine, St. Johns County, FL held by Philliips Broadcasting LLC
Nat'l Network: ESPN Radio; *Nat'l Reps:* Rgnl Reps *Regional Reps:* Rgnl Reps
Population Served: 150,000; *Arbitron Metro Market:* Jacksonville, FL *Special Programming:* University of Florida sports, NFL Jaguar affiliate, NASCAR; *Hrs. of News Programming:* news progmg 8 hrs wkly *No. NewsEmployees:* 1; *Target Audience:* 26 plus; affluent adults; *Adv. Rates:* 24; 18; 24; 12
Kristine Phillips, President
Matt Kraycinovich, Operations Dir

Saint Augustine Beach

WYRE-FM
09-01-1995; 105.5 MHz FM; *Hrs Open:* 24; 16 kw; Ant 410 ft; N29 51 00 W81 19 50
253 Zygmont Court, St. Augustin, FL 32084
(904) 824-5500; *Fax:* (904) 680-1051
www.tamabroadcasting.com
License: Saint Augustine Beach, St. Johns County, FL held by Tama Radio Licenses of Jacksonville, FL, Inc.
Group Owner: Cortona Media
Population Served: 175,000; *Arbitron Metro Market:* Jacksonville, FL; *Format:* Oldies; *Target Audience:* 20-45; general
Stephen Paul Garsh, General Manager

San Carlos Park

WDEO-FM
01-01-1995; 98.5 MHz FM; *Hrs Open:* 24; 18.5 kw; 371 ft.; N26 30 18 W81 51 14
7290 College Parkway, Suite 100, Fort Myers, FL 33907 US
(734) 930-5200; *Fax:* (734) 930-3179
www.avemariaradio.net
License: San Carlos Park, Lee County, FL held by Ave Maria University Inc.
Arbitron Metro Market: San Carlos Park, FL; *Format:* News, News/Talk, 86, Christian; *Target Audience:* 21 plus; adult Christian
Steve Clark, Operations Manager
Michael Jones, Vice President/General Manager
Gene Leger, General Sales Manager
Tom Loewe, Development Director

Sanford

WSDO
05-20-1947; 1400 kHz AM; *Hrs Open:* 24; 1 kw-U, ND1; N28 48 4 W81 15 6
222 Hazard St, Orlando, FL 32804 US
(407) 841-8282; *Fax:* (407) 841-8250
www.wprd.com
wprd1440@hotmail.com
License: Sanford, Seminole County, FL held by J&V Communications Co.
Group Owner: J&V Communications Inc.; (acq 6-5-92; $300,000)
Nat'l Network: Westwood One; *Regional Network:* Florida's Radio Networks
Arbitron Metro Market: Orlando, FL; *Format:* Spanish, Variety/Diverse *Special Programming:* Relg 3 hrs wkly; *Target Audience:* 21+
John Torrado, CEO
Jocelyn Torrado, Operations Dir

Sanibel

WXNX
12-01-1971; 93.7 MHz FM; *Hrs Open:* 24; 43 kw; 476 ft.; N26 30 18 W81 51 14
2824 Palm Beach Blvd., Fort Myers, FL 33916 US
(239) 479-5593
www.93x.fm
License: Sanibel, Collier County, FL held by Sun Broadcasting Inc.
Group Owner: Sun Broadcasting Inc.; (acq 9-24-2012; grpsl)
Nat'l Reps: McGavren Guild; *Wire Services:* AP
Arbitron Metro Market: Fort Myers, FL; *Format:* Rock/AOR; *No. News Employees:* 3; *Target Audience:* 25-54; women
Joseph Schwartzel, CEO

Santa Rosa Beach

WWAV
04-03-1985; 102.1 MHz FM; *Hrs Open:* 24; 50 kw; 374 ft.; N30 23 10 W86 17 48
111 Ferry Rd., Fort Walton Beach, FL 32548 US
(850) 654-1000
www.1021thewave.com
rraybourne@apexbroadcasting.com
License: Santa Rosa Beach, FL held by Qantum of Fort Walton Beach License Co. LLC.
Group Owner: Qantum Communications Corp.; (acq 7-2-2003; grpsl).
Nat'l Reps: Katz Radio
Arbitron Metro Market: Santa Rosa Beach, FL; *Format:* Adult Contemp; *Hrs. of News Programming:* News progmg one hr wkly; *Target Audience:* 25-54; general; *Adv. Rates:* 50; 50; 50; 25
Dan Collins, Operations Dir
Ron Raybourne, General Manager

WZLB
01-01-1974; 103.1 MHz FM; *Hrs Open:* 24; 50 kw; 374 ft.; N30 30 53 W86 13 12
111 Ferry Rd., Fort Walton Beach, FL 32548 US
(850) 654-1000
www.1031thewave.com
rraybourne@apexbroadcasting.com
License: Santa Rosa Beach, FL held by Apex Broadcasting
Group Owner: Apex Broadcasting
Nat'l Reps: Katz Radio
Arbitron Metro Market: Santa Rosa Beach, FL; *Format:* Rock/AOR; *Hrs. of News Programming:* News progmg one hr

wkly; *Target Audience:* 25-54; general; *Adv. Rates:* 50; 50; 50; 25
Dan Collins, Operations Dir
Ron Raybourne, General Manager

Sarasota

WCTQ
06-30-1965; 106.5 MHz FM; *Hrs Open:* 24; 13 kw; 584 ft.; N27 32 42 W82 34 27
1779 Independence Boulevard, Sarasota, FL 34234 US
(941) 552-4800; *Fax:* (941) 55-4900
www.1065ctq.com
eddierupp@clearchannel.com
License: Sarasota, Sarasota County, FL held by Citicasters Licenses Inc.
Group Owner: iHeartMedia
Arbitron Metro Market: Sarasota-Bradenton, FL; *Format:* Country; *Hrs. of News Programming:* News progmg one hr wkly; *Target Audience:* 25-54.
Eddie Rupp, Operations Manager
William Ames, Local Sales Manager
Todd Nixon, Programming Director
Nikki Clark, Promotions Director
Ty DeMeza, Promotions Coordinator

WHPT
01-01-1973; 102.5 MHz FM; *Hrs Open:* 24; 100 kw; 1650 ft.; N27 24 30 W82 15 0
11300 4th Street North, Suite 300, Saint Petersburg, FL 33716 US
(727) 579-2000; *Fax:* (727) 579-2271
theboneonline.com
info@coxradio.com
License: Sarasota, Sarasota County, FL held by Cox Radio Inc.
Group Owner: Cox Radio Inc.; (acq 5-99; grpsl)
Nat'l Reps: Clear Channel
Arbitron Metro Market: Sarasota-Bradenton, FL; *Format:* Alternative, Rock/AOR; *Target Audience:* 25-54.
Keith Lawless, Vice President & Market Manager
Aaron Miller, General Sales Manager
Jodi Rainey, National Sales Manager
John Brennan, Director Of Branding And Programming
Mike Oliviero, Director Of Promotional Operations

WLSS
05-23-1949; 930 kHz AM; *Hrs Open:* 24
5211 West Laurel Street, Suite A, Tampa, FL 33607 US
(941) 363-0930; *Fax:* (813) 639-1272
www.wlssradio.com
License: Sarasota, FL held by Caron Broadcasting Inc.
Group Owner: Salem Communications Corp.; (acq 8-12-2005; $9.5 million with WGUL(AM) Dunedin).
Nat'l Network: Salem Radio Network; *Nat'l Reps:* Salem
Arbitron Metro Market: Sarasota-Bradenton, FL; *Format:* News, News/Talk, 86
Joe Weaver, Operations Dir
Barb Yoder, General Manager

***WKZM**
10-21-1974; 104.3 MHz FM; *Hrs Open:* 24; 25 kW; 266 ft.; N27 16 30 W82 28 54 *Rebroadcasts:* Rebroadcasts WKES(FM) Lakeland 100%
PO Box 8889, St. Petersburg, FL 33738 USA
(727) 391-9994; *Fax:* (727) 397-6425
www.moodyradio.org/stations/florida
License: Sarasota, Sarasota County, FL held by The Moody Bible Institute of Chicago
Group Owner: The Moody Bible Institute of Chicago; acq 10-15-99)
Arbitron Metro Market: Sarasota-Bradenton, FL; *Format:* Religious; *Hrs. of News Programming:* News progmg 14 hrs wkly; *Target Audience:* General.

WSRQ
01-01-1961; 1220 kHz AM; 1 kw-D, DAD; 0.159 kw-N, DA2; N27 19 27 W82 29 47
3135 S.E. 27th Street, Gainesville, FL 32641 US
(941) 952-1220; *Fax:* (941) 365-2900
License: Sarasota, FL held by SRQ Radio LLC
Regional Network: Florida's Radio Networks
Arbitron Metro Market: Sarasota-Bradenton, FL; *Format:* News, News/Talk, 84, Talk; *Target Audience:* 25-64; men
Susan Nilon, General Manager
Howard Katz, Sales Director
Norm Vogele, Producer
Ian Dooley, Sports Director
Andrew Sanchez, Webmaster

***WSMR**
01-01-1993; 89.1 MHz FM; *Hrs Open:* 24; 54 kw; 443 ft.; N27 9 3 W82 27 51
4202 East Fowler Avenue, TVP 100, Tampa, FL 33620 US
(941) 906-9767; *Fax:* (941) 362-0377
www.wsmr.org
License: Sarasota, Sarasota County, FL held by Northwestern College.
Group Owner: University of South Florida
Arbitron Metro Market: Sarasota-Bradenton, FL; *Format:* Christian; *Hrs. of News Programming:* News progmg 6 hrs wkly; *Target Audience:* 30-55; with kids still at home
Dustin Hapli, Operations Manager
JoAnn Urofsky, General Manager
Douglas Poll, Station Manager
Sheila Rue, Programming Director
Cathy Coccia, Development Director

WSDV
12-07-1939; 1450 kHz AM; *Hrs Open:* 24; 1 kw-U, ND1; N27 20 11 W82 34 25
1779 Independence Boulevard, Sarasota, FL 34234 US
(941) 552-4800; *Fax:* (941) 552-4900
www.sunnyradioam.com
License: Sarasota, FL held by Citicasters Licenses Inc.
Group Owner: iHeartMedia; (acq 5-4-99; grpsl).
Arbitron Metro Market: Sarasota-Bradenton, FL; *Format:* Adult Contemp; *Hrs. of News Programming:* news progmg 40 hrs wkly; *No. News Employees:* 3; *Target Audience:* 25-54; general
Peter Norden, Market President
Nikki Clark, Promotions Director

WTMY
12-02-1960; 1280 kHz AM; *Hrs Open:* 24; 0.3 kw-D, 0.1 kw-N; N27 21 11 W82 29 13
1956 Main St., Sarasota, FL 34236 US
(941) 955-9387
www.wtmyradio.com
License: Sarasota, FL held by Southwest Florida Radio Broadcasting, LLC
Group Owner: Southwest Florida Radio Broadcasting, LLC
Arbitron Metro Market: Sarasota, FL; *Format:* Big Band, Adult Contemp *Special Programming:* Pol one hr, gospel 6 hrs, full service 2 hrs wkly; *Target Audience:* 40 plus; wealth & health oriented; *Adv. Rates:* 15;15; 15; na
Dave Dybas, Engineering Dir

Satellite Beach

WSBH
98.5 MHz FM; 6 kw; 328 ft.; N28 8 11 W80 42 12 US
(321) 752-9850; *Fax:* (321) 752-8717
www.beach985.com
License: Satellite Beach, Brevard County, FL held by Horton Broadcasting Co. Inc.
Arbitron Metro Market: Satellite Beach, FL
George Metcalf, President

Sebastian

WSJZ-FM
01-01-2001; 95.9 MHz FM; 25 kw; 289 ft.; N27 49 5 W80 37 18
1800 West Hibiscus Boulevard, Suite 138, Melbourne, FL 32901 US
(321) 984-1000; *Fax:* (321) 724-1565
www.espn959.com/
jennifer.armstrong@cumulus.com
License: Sebastian, Indian River County, FL held by Cumulus Licensing LLC.
Group Owner: Cumulus Media Inc.; (acq 11-8-2004; $5 million).
Arbitron Metro Market: Melbourne-Titusville-Cocoa, FL; *Format:* Sports
Peter DeSimone, General Manager
Jon Roberts, Programming Director
Jennifer Armstrong, Promotions Director
Christina Volonnino, Traffic Director

Sebring

WITS
11-24-1959; 1340 kHz AM; *Hrs Open:* 24
3750 US Hwy. 27N., Suite 1, Sebring, FL 33870 US
(863) 382-9999; *Fax:* (863) 382-1982
www.cohanradiogroup.com
cohanradiogroup@htn.net
License: Sebring, FL held by Cohan Radio Group Inc.
Group Owner: Cohan Radio Group Inc.; (acq 11-1-98; $735,000 with co-located FM plus WJCM(AM) Sebring)
Nat'l Network: ABC; *Nat'l Reps:* Interep; *Wire Services:* AP
Arbitron Metro Market: Sebring, FL; *Format:* Adult Contemp; *Hrs. of News Programming:* news progmg 5 hrs wkly; *No. News Employees:* 1; *Target Audience:* 40 plus; mature adults
Peter Coughlin, President/GM

WJCM
05-22-1950; 1050 kHz AM; *Hrs Open:* 24; 1 kw-D, ND1; 0.011 kw-N, ND1; N27 30 30 W81 25 20
3750 US Hwy 27N, Suite 1, Sebring, FL 33870 US
(863) 382-9999; *Fax:* (863) 382-1982
cohanradiogroup@htn.net
License: Sebring, FL held by Cohan Radio Group Inc.
Group Owner: Cohan Radio Group Inc.; (acq 11-1-98; $150,000).
Regional Network: Florida's Radio Networks; *Nat'l Reps:* Interep
Regional Reps: Interep; *Wire Services:* AP
Arbitron Metro Market: Sebring, FL; *Format:* Oldies; *Hrs. of News Programming:* news progmg 8 hrs wkly; *No. News Employees:* 1; *Target Audience:* 45+.
Peter Coughlin, President/GM

WWLL
07-01-1967; 105.7 MHz FM; *Hrs Open:* 24; 19 kw; Ant 351 ft; N27 21 29 W81 28 22
3750 US 27 N, Suite 1, Sebring, FL 33870 US
(863) 382-9999
www.lite1057fm.com
cohanradiogroup@htn.net
License: Sebring, Highlands County, FL held by Cohan Radio Group Inc.
Group Owner: Cohan Radio Group Inc.; (acq 11-1-98)
Nat'l Network: NBC Radio; *Nat'l Reps:* Interep; *Wire Services:* AP
Population Served: 90,000; *Arbitron Metro Market:* Sebring, FL; *Format:* Adult Contemp; *Hrs. of News Programming:* news progmg 2 hrs wkly; *No. News Employees:* 1; *Target Audience:* 25-54; adults
Peter Coughlin, President/GM

***WJFH**
01-01-2007; 91.7 MHz FM; 2 kw; 454 ft.; N27 22 52 W81 29 28
P.O. Box 7217, 5015 South Florida Ave., Lakeland, FL 33813 US
(800)456-8910; *Fax:* (863) 646-5326
www.thejoyfm.com
License: Sebring, Highlands County, FL held by Radio Training Network Inc.
Arbitron Metro Market: Sebring, FL; *Format:* Christian
James Campbell, President

Seffner

WHFS
11-07-1960; 1010 kHz AM; *Hrs Open:* 24; 50 kw-D, 5 kw-N, DA-2; N27 59 25 W82 15 06
9721 Executive Center Dr., Suite 200, St. Petersburg, FL 33702
(239) 263-5000; *Fax:* (239) 263-8191
www.moneytalk1010.com
License: Seffner, Hillsborough County, FL held by WDAS License Limited Partnership
Group Owner: Beasley Broadcast Group Inc.; (acq 11-21-87).
Nat'l Network: Sporting News Radio Network; Westwood One;
Nat'l Reps: CBS Radio
Arbitron Metro Market: Tampa-St. Petersburg-Clearwater, FL; *Format:* Talk
Charlie Ochs, Stations Manager/General Sales Manager
Kelly Sedivy, Digital Sales Manager

Shalimar

WNCV
10-25-1982; 93.3 MHz FM; *Hrs Open:* 24; 50 kw; 469 ft.; N30 24 38 W86 37 22
225 Northwest Hollywood Boulevard, Fort Walton Beach, FL 32548 US
(850) 243-7676; *Fax:* (850) 243-6806
www.wncv.com
License: Shalimar, Okaloosa County, FL held by Cumulus Licensing LLC.
Group Owner: Cumulus Media Inc.; (acq 8-2-2006; swap for WRKN(FM) Niceville)
Arbitron Metro Market: Fort Walton Beach, FL; *Format:* Adult Contemp
Mike DeMarco, General Manager
Hayden Green, Programming Director

Silver Springs

WNDD
02-01-1991; 95.5 MHz FM; *Hrs Open:* 24; 6 kw; 328 ft.; N29 16 55 W82 2 50
3602 NE20th Place, Ocala, FL 32670 US
(352) 622-9500; *Fax:* (352) 622-1900
www.windfm.com
rkassi@windwogksales.com
License: Silver Springs, Marion County, FL held by Ocala Broadcasting Corp. L.L.C.
Group Owner: Wooster Republican Printing Co.; (acq 9-1-97).

Nat'l Reps: Katz Radio
Arbitron Metro Market: Gainesville, FL; *Format:* Classic Rock, Rock/AOR; *Target Audience:* 25-54; adults; *Adv. Rates:* 70; 80; 70; 30
Jim Robertson, General Manager
Bob Kassi, General Sales Mgr
Hunter, Programming Director

Solana

WCVU
01-01-1994; 104.9 MHz FM; 6 kw; 318 ft.; N26 53 37.5 W82 3 2.7
24100 Tiseo Boulevard, #10, Port Charlotte, FL 33980 US
(941) 206-1188; *Fax:* (941) 206-9296
www.wcvu.com
License: Solana, Charlotte County, FL held by Citicasters Licenses Inc.
Group Owner: iHeartMedia; (acq 2-1-99; grpsl).
Nat'l Network: CNN Radio
Arbitron Metro Market: Fort Myers, FL; *Format:* Adult Contemp; *Adv. Rates:* 35; 30; 35; 25
Robin Craig, Director of Sales
Todd Matthews, Programming Director

WKII
11-19-1986; 1070 kHz AM; *Hrs Open:* 24
24100 Tiseo Boulevard, #10, Port Charlotte, FL 33980 US
(941) 206-1188; *Fax:* (941) 206-9296
www.1070nbcsports.com
License: Solana, FL held by Clear Channel Broadcasting Licenses Inc.
Group Owner: iHeartMedia
Regional Network: Florida's Radio Networks
Format: Sports; *Hrs. of News Programming:* news progmg 2 hrs wkly; *No. News Employees:* 1; *Target Audience:* 35 plus.
Robin Craig, Director of Sales

South Daytona

WPUL
06-13-1957; 1590 kHz AM; *Hrs Open:* 6 am-12 pm; 1 kw-D, ND1; 0.032 kw-N, ND1; N29 9 16 W81 1 20
Box 4010, South Daytona, FL 32121 US
(386) 239-7080 (Studio),(386) 226-2398; *Fax:* (386) 254-7510
ccherry2@aol.com
License: South Daytona, FL held by PSI Communications Inc.
Nat'l Network: American Urban
Arbitron Metro Market: Daytona Beach, FL; *Format:* Gospel, Talk; *Target Audience:* General.; *Adv. Rates:* 50; 40; 50; 35
Charles Cherry, CEO
Charles Cherry II, General Manager
Phinesse Demps, Programming Director

South Miami

WAXY
09-15-1947; 790 kHz AM; *Hrs Open:* 24; 25 kw-U, DA-2; N25 46 25 W80 38 13
20450 N.W. 2nd Ave., Miami, FL 33169
(305) 521-5100 / (887) 790-1015; *Fax:* (305) 521-1416
www.theticketmiami.com
vaguirre@790theticket.com
License: South Miami, Dade County, FL held by Entercom Radio
Group Owner: Entercom; (acq 2016).
Nat'l Reps: CBS Radio
Population Served: 2,800,000; *Arbitron Metro Market:* Miami-Fort Lauderdale-Hollywood, FL; *Target Audience:* 35 plus.
Gary Aybar, Operations Dir
Maureen Lesourd, Senior Vice President/General Manager
Larry Most, General Sales Mgr
Todd Castleberry, Programming Director
Eric Stenger, Promotions Director
Victoria Aguirre, Traffic Director

Southport

*WKGC
06-25-1965; 1480 kHz AM; *Hrs Open:* 6 AM-9 PM
5230 W. Highway 98, Panama City, FL 32401 US
(850) 873-3500; *Fax:* (850) 913-3299
www.wkgc.org
License: Southport, FL held by Gulf Coast Community College.
Nat'l Network: NPR
Arbitron Metro Market: Panama City, FL; *Format:* Easy Listening
Special Programming: Folk 2 hrs, educ 8 hrs wkly; *Hrs. of News Programming:* News progmg 25 hrs wkly; *Target Audience:* General; college students &older high school students
Jim Kerley, President
Harley Pummill, Operations Dir
Chris Thomes, General Manager

Sparr

*WTYG
91.5 MHz FM; 0.1 kw; 95 ft.; N29 20 21 W82 6 10
401 Groveland Road, Mt. Dora, FL 32757 US
(913) 669-8101
wtygfm@yahoo.com
License: Sparr, Marion County, FL held by Arts for the Community Inc.
Arbitron Metro Market: Mount Dora, FL; *Format:* Talk
De Miller, President

Spring Hill

WJQB
10-01-1992; 106.3 MHz FM; *Hrs Open:* 24 hours; 25 kw; 315 ft.; N28 31 41 W82 32 45
13825 U.S. Highway 19 N, Suite 400, Palm Harbor, FL 34667 US
(727) 697-1063; *Fax:* (727) 817-1063
www.trueoldies1063.com
License: Spring Hill, Hernando County, FL held by WGUL-FM Inc.
Nat'l Network: ABC Music Radio
Arbitron Metro Market: Tampa-St. Petersburg-Clearwater, FL; *Format:* Oldies; *Target Audience:* adults 35-64 adults 35+; *Adv. Rates:* 55; 45; 55; 15
Betty Marcocci, Chairman
Steve Schurdell, General Manager
Cem Maier, Sales Manager
Gordon A. Lienau, Traffic Manager

Springfield

WRBA
06-01-1986; 95.9 MHz FM; *Hrs Open:* 24; 50 kw; 282 ft.; N30 12 12 W85 36 57
118 Gwyn Drive, Panama City Beach, FL 32408 US
(850) 234-8858; *Fax:* (850) 234-6592
billyoung@panamacityradio.com
License: Springfield, Bay County, FL
Group Owner: Powell Broadcasting Co. L.L.C.; acq 3-10-2004; grpsl).
Arbitron Metro Market: Panama City, FL; *Format:* Classic Rock; *Target Audience:* 30-54; general; *Adv. Rates:* 50; 40; 40; 25
Steve Burns, Programming Director
Ira Rosenblatt, Marketing Manager

WYOO
03-02-1993; 101.1 MHz FM; *Hrs Open:* 24; 12 kw; 404 ft.; N30 10 44 W85 46 55
P.O. Box 16626, Panama City, FL 32406 US
(850) 230-5855; *Fax:* (850) 230-6988
www.talkradio101.com
License: Springfield, Bay County, FL held by Magic Broadcasting II LLC
Group Owner: Magic Broadcasting II LLC; (acq 9-30-2002; grpsl)
Regional Network: Florida's Radio Networks; *Nat'l Reps:* Christal
Arbitron Metro Market: Panama City, FL; *Format:* Talk; *Hrs. of News Programming:* news progmg 28 hrs wkly; *No. News Employees:* 1; *Target Audience:* 25-54; educated, upscale
Jeff Storey, COO
Mike Preble, Operations Dir

St. Augustine

*WAYL
05-22-1994; 91.9 MHz FM; *Hrs Open:* 24; 5 kw; 207 ft.; N29 51 0 W81 19 50
Mailing Address: 2701 Hodges Blvd., Jacksonville, FL 32225 US
Second Address: 1485 US Rt. 1 S., Saint Augustine, FL 32086
(906) 774-5731; *Fax:* (906) 774-4542
www.1067themountain.com
peterson.trisha@gmail.com
License: St. Augustine, St. Johns County, FL held by New Covenant Educational Ministries Inc.
Nat'l Network: Salem Radio Network
Arbitron Metro Market: Iron Mountain MI; *Format:* Oldies
Nancy Epperson, President

*WFCF
11-01-1993; 88.5 MHz FM; *Hrs Open:* 7 AM-midnight; 10 kw horiz, 9.8 kw vert; 201 ft.; N29 51 17 W81 20 9
P. O. Box 1027, St. Augustine, FL 32085 US
(904) 829-6481; *Fax:* (904) 826-3471
www.flagler.edu
wfcf@flagler.edu
License: St. Augustine, St. Johns County, FL held by Flagler College.
Arbitron Metro Market: St. Augustine, FL; *Format:* Variety/Diverse *Special Programming:* Sp 4 hrs, new age 4 hrs, folk 3 hrs, reggae 4 hrs, world 4 hrs, blues 4 hrs wkly; *Hrs. of News Programming:* News progmg one hrwkly; *Target Audience:* General.
Donna DeLorenzo Webb, General Manager
Daniel McCook, Station Manager
Don Runk, Underwriting Director

WFOY
07-07-1936; 1240 kHz AM; *Hrs Open:* 24
Mailing Address: One Radio Road, St. Augustine, FL 32085 US
Second Address: 567 Lewis Point Rd. Ext., Saint Augustine, FL 32086
(904) 797-1955; *Fax:* (904) 797-3446
www.1240news.com
kris@1240news.com
License: St. Augustine, FL held by Phillips Broadcasting LLC
Nat'l Network: Fox News Radio; Westwood One; Talk Radio Network; *Regional Network:* Florida's Radio Networks; *Nat'l Reps:* Rgnl Reps *Regional Reps:* Rgnl Reps
Arbitron Metro Market: Jacksonville, FL; *Format:* News, News/Talk, 84, Talk *Special Programming:* Rush Limbaugh affiliate; *Hrs. of News Programming:* news progmg 8 hrs wkly; *No. News Employees:* 1 *TargetAudience:* 26 plus; affluent adults; *Adv. Rates:* 29; 18; 29; 12
Kristine Phillips, President
Sheldon Petit, Production Manager
Mary-Jane Bunch, Traffic Manager

St. Augustine Beach

WSOS
10-15-1986; 1170 kHz AM; *Hrs Open:* 6 AM-9 PM
2820 Lewis Speedway, St. Augustine, FL 32084 US
(904) 739-3660; *Fax:* (904) 739-9409
www.classicrock941.com
License: St. Augustine Beach, FL held by Norsan Consulting and Management Inc.
Group Owner: Norsan Consulting and Management Inc.; (acq 1-13-2006; $300,000)
Arbitron Metro Market: Jacksonville, FL
Jorge Lopez, General Manager

St. Catherine

*WKFA
01-01-2005; 89.3 MHz FM; 0 kw horiz, 3.9 kw vert; 322 ft.; N28 32 22 W82 4 48
P O Box 1089, Silver Springs, FL 34489 US
(321) 267-3000; *Fax:* (321) 264-9370
www.noncomradio.com
wpio@gate.net
License: St. Catherine, Sumter County, FL held by Florida Public Radio Inc.
Arbitron Metro Market: Saint Catherine, FL; *Format:* Public Affairs, Religious
Randy Henry, President

St. Cloud

WIWA
01-01-2005; 1160 kHz AM
US
(407) 770-2500; *Fax:* (407) 770-2503
License: St. Cloud, FL held by Centro de la Familia Cristiana Inc.
Arbitron Metro Market: Saint Cloud, FL; *Format:* News, News/Talk, 82, Talk
Roberto Candelario, President

St. Marks

*WUJC
01-01-2005; 91.1 MHz FM; 74 kw; 312 ft.; N30 30 55 W83 52 17
Rebroadcasts: Rebroadcasts KAWZ (FM)
P.O. Box 391, Twin Falls, ID 83303 US
(800) 357-4226; *Fax:* (208) 736-1958
www.csnradio.com
csn@csnradio.com
License: St. Marks, Wakulla County, FL held by CSN International
Group Owner: CSN International
Arbitron Metro Market: Saint Marks-South Tallahassee, FL; *Format:* Christian, Religious
Mike Kestler, President
Daniel Davidson, Operations Dir
Don Mills, Network Programming Director
Mike Stocklin, Underwriting Director
Kelly Carlson, Engineering Dir

St. Petersburg

WXGL
09-01-1965; 107.3 MHz FM; *Hrs Open:* 24; 100 kw; 597 ft.; N28 2 22 W82 39 12
11300 4th Street North, Suite 300, Saint Petersburg, FL 33716 US
(727) 579-2000; *Fax:* (727) 579-2662
www.1073theeagle.com
1073comments@coxtampa.com
License: St. Petersburg, Pinellas County, FL held by Cox Radio Inc.
Group Owner: Cox Radio Inc.; (acq 7-1-88).
Nat'l Reps: Commercial Media Sales
Arbitron Metro Market: Tampa-St. Petersburg-Clearwater, FL; *Format:* Contemporary Hits/Top 40, Adult Contemp
Keith Lawless, Vice President / Marketing Manager
Aaron Mills, General Sales Manager
Jodi Rainey, National Sales Manager
John Larson, Program Director
Julia Freeman, Director Of Promotional Operations

WPOI
07-01-1961; 101.5 MHz FM; *Hrs Open:* 24; 97.1 kw; 1542 ft.; N27 49 10 W82 15 39
11300 4th Street North, Suite 300, St. Petersburg, FL 33716 US
(727) 579-2000; *Fax:* (727) 579-2662
www.hot1015tampabay.com
1015.lawless@coxinc.com
License: St. Petersburg, Pinellas County, FL held by Cox Radio Inc.
Group Owner: Cox Radio Inc.; (acq 1999; grpsl)
Nat'l Reps: Clear Channel
Arbitron Metro Market: Tampa-St. Petersburg-Clearwater, FL; *Format:* Contemporary Hits/Top 40; *Target Audience:* 25-54.
Keith Lawless, Vice President & Market Manager
Jodi Rainey, National Sales Manager
Jenna Kesneck, Director Of Promotional Operations

*WFTI-FM
06-01-1988; 91.7 MHz FM; *Hrs Open:* 24; 3 kw; 282 ft.; N27 46 15 W82 38 19
4135 Northgate Blvd., Suite 1, Sacramento, CA 95834 US
(727) 823-1140; *Fax:* (727) 823-5753
License: St. Petersburg, Pinellas County, FL
Group Owner: Radio Training Network
Arbitron Metro Market: Tampa-St. Petersburg-Clearwater, FLsburg-Clearwate; *Format:* Religious; *Hrs. of News Programming:* News progmg 9 hrs wkly; *Target Audience:* General.
Jim Campbell, President/Chief Executive Officer

WQYK-FM
05-01-1958; 99.5 MHz FM; *Hrs Open:* 24; 99 kw; 571 ft.; N27 55 53.8 W82 24 4.6
9721 Executive Center Dr., Suite 200, St. Petersburg, FL 33702 US
(727) 579-9999; *Fax:* (727) 563-8202
www.995qyk.com
License: St. Petersburg, Pinellas County, FL held by WDAS License Limited Partnership
Group Owner: Beasley Broadcast Group Inc.; (acq 12-1-86;
Nat'l Network: CBS; *Nat'l Reps:* Interep
Arbitron Metro Market: Tampa-St. Petersburg-Clearwater, FL *TV Affiliate:* WTOG(TV) affil; *Format:* Country; *Hrs. of News Programming:* news progmg 6 hrs wkly; *No. News Employees:* 1; *Target Audience:* 25-54.
Tee Gentry, Operations Manager/Program Director
Erika Beasley, General Sales Mgr
Hillary Hatch, Promotions Director
Kelly Sedivy, Digital Sales Manager
Kevin Ebel, Music Director

WGES
05-05-1950; 680 kHz AM; 0.69 kw-D, ND1; 0.125 kw-N, ND1; N27 51 24 W82 37 26
2700 W Martin Luther, King Blvd, Tampa, FL 34607 US
(813) 319-5757,(813) 637-8000; *Fax:* (813) 319-0029,(813) 637-8001
www.genesis680.com
License: St. Petersburg, FL held by ZGS Broadcasting of Tampa Inc.
Group Owner: ZG Communications; (acq 1-18-91; $200,000;
Regional Reps: Katz Hispanic Media
Arbitron Metro Market: Tampa-St. Petersburg-Clearwater, FL; *Format:* Spanish; *Target Audience:* General; adults 18-49
Evelyn Chaparro, General Manager

WDAE
11-01-1927; 620 kHz AM; *Hrs Open:* 24
4002 West Gandy Boulevard, Tampa, FL 33611 US
(813) 832-1000; *Fax:* (813) 832-1090
www.620wdae.com
License: St. Petersburg, FL held by Clear Channel Broadcasting Licenses Inc.
Group Owner: iHeartMedia; (acq 11-20-98; $9.75 million)
Nat'l Network: Fox Sports; *Nat'l Reps:* Katz Radio; *Wire Services:* AP
Arbitron Metro Market: Tampa-St. Peter; *Format:* Sports
Mark McCauley, Sales Manager
Doug Hamand, Programming Director
Greg Wolf, Promotions Director
John Mamola, Sports Director
Phil Azoon, Creative Services Director
David Bell, Public Service Director

WWMI
01-01-1939; 1380 kHz AM; *Hrs Open:* 24
77 W 66th St., 16th Fl., New York, NY 10023-6201 USA
(727) 577-4500; *Fax:* (727) 579-1340
www.radiodisney.com
License: St. Petersburg, FL held by Radio Disney Group LLC
Group Owner: Disney Channels Worldwide; Sale to Salem Media Group pending
Nat'l Network: Radio Disney; *Nat'l Reps:* Clear Channel; *Wire Services:* NOAA Weather
Arbitron Metro Market: Tampa-St. Peter, FL; *Format:* Children; *No. News Employees:* 2
Gary Marsh, President & Chief Creative Officer

St. Petersburg Beach

WRXB
01-01-1957; 1590 kHz AM; 5 kw-D, DA2; 1 kw-N, DA2; N27 44 3 W82 41 8
3551 42nd Ave. S., St. Petersburg, FL 33711 US
(727) 865-1591; *Fax:* (727) 866-1728
mediaguy@kentdgustafson.com
License: St. Petersburg Beach, FL held by Polnet Communications, Ltd.
Group Owner: Polnet Communications, Ltd.
Arbitron Metro Market: Tampa-St. Peter; *Format:* Gospel *Special Programming:* Jazz 15 hrs wkly; *Target Audience:* 23-54; urban contemp
Ed Edwards, General Manager

Starke

*WTLG
01-01-1982; 88.3 MHz FM; *Hrs Open:* 24; 7 kw; 285 ft.; N29 54 34 W82 6 2
P.O. Box 2098, Omaha, NE 68103-2098 US
(800) 525-5683
www.klove.com
License: Starke, Bradford County, FL held by Educational Media Foundation
Group Owner: EMF Broadcasting
Format: Christian
Mike Novak, President

Stuart

WSTU
12-09-1954; 1450 kHz AM; *Hrs Open:* 24; 1 kw-U, ND1; N27 12 53 W80 15 24
2435 S.E. Dixie Hgwy, Stuart, FL 34996 US
(772) 220-9788; *Fax:* (772) 340-3245
www.wstu1450.com
wpsl@wpsl.com
License: Stuart, FL held by Treasure Coast Broadcasters Inc.
Nat'l Network: ESPN Radio; ABC; *Regional Network:* Florida's Radio Networks
Arbitron Metro Market: Fort Pierce-Stuart-Vero Beach, FL; *Format:* News, News/Talk, 84, Talk; *No. News Employees:* 2; *Target Audience:* 35 plus.; *Adv. Rates:* 50 for :60— 40 for :30
Carol Wyatt, President

*WWFR
01-01-1988; 91.7 MHz FM; *Hrs Open:* 24; 2.65 kw; 499 ft.; N27 7 14 W80 23 59
Mailing Address: 4135 Northgate Blvd, Suite1, Sacramento, CA 95834 US
Second Address: 10400 NW 240th st, Okeechobee, FL 34973
(800) 543-1495
www.familyradio.com
info@familyradio.orgÿ
License: Stuart, Martin County, FL held by Family Stations Inc.
Group Owner: Family Stations Inc.
Nat'l Network: Family Radio
Arbitron Metro Market: Stuart, FL; *Format:* Christian *Special Programming:* Pub affrs 2 hrs wkly; *Hrs. of News Programming:* News progmg 11 hrs wkly; *Target Audience:* General.
Ed Dearborn, Operations Dir

WAVW
12-24-1964; 92.7 MHz FM; 50 kw; 482 ft.; N27 16 29 W80 17 11
3771 Jennings Road, Port St. Lucie, FL 34952 US
(772) 335-9300; *Fax:* (772) 335-3291
www.wave927.com
License: Stuart, Martin County, FL held by Capstar TX LLC
Group Owner: iHeartMedia; (acq 8-30-00; grpsl).
Arbitron Metro Market: Port St. Lucie, FL; *Format:* Country
Bryan Kelly, Director of Sales
Heath West, Programming Director
Chad Tyson, Digital Program Director

Summerland Key

WPIK
12-01-1991; 102.5 MHz FM; *Hrs Open:* 24; 50 kw; 413 ft.; N24 40 36 W81 30 39
Mailing Address: P.O. Box 420249, Summerland Key, FL 33042 US
Second Address: 22500 Pieces of Eight Rd., Cudjoe Key, FL 33042
(305) 745-9988; *Fax:* (305) 745-4165
www.myradioritmo.com
License: Summerland Key, Monroe County, FL held by Summerland Media LLC
Format: Ethnic
Lilliam Sierra, General Manager
Pepin Navarro, Programming Director

Sunrise

*WKPX
02-14-1983; 88.5 MHz FM; *Hrs Open:* 12; 3 kw; 98 ft.; N26 10 38 W80 15 23
8000 N.W. 44th Street, Sunrise, FL 33351 US
(754) 321-1000; *Fax:* (754) 321-1180
www.becon.tv
info@becon.tv
License: Sunrise, Broward County, FL held by School Board of Broward County.
Format: Alternative *Special Programming:* Black 3 hrs, blues 3 hrs wkly; *Target Audience:* 15-35; people interested in alternative progmg
Pat Swank, Station Manager
Jim Sorensen, Chief Engineer

Sweetwater

WZAB
01-01-2008; 880 kHz AM
2828 West Flagler Street, Miami, FL 33135 US
(305) 503-1340; *Fax:* (305) 677-7585
www.880thebiz.com
License: Sweetwater, FL held by Florida City Radio.
Arbitron Metro Market: Sweetwater, FL; *Format:* News/Talk, News
Tony Calatayud, General Manager
Jorge Guevara, Sales Manager

Tallahassee

WWOF(FM)
06-17-1976; 103.1 MHz FM; *Hrs Open:* 24; 50 kw; 295 ft; N30 29 43 W84 13 51
Opus Broadcasting, 3000 Olson Rd., Tallahassee, FL 32308
(850) 386-8004; *Fax:* (850) 422-1897
www.1031thewolf.com
hkestenbaum@opusbroadcasting.com
License: Tallahassee, Leon County, FL held by Opus Broadcasting Tallahassee LLC.
Group Owner: Opus Media Holdings LLC; (acq 9-2-2005; grpsl)
Nat'l Reps: McGavren Guild
Population Served: 182,965; *Arbitron Metro Market:* Tallahassee, FL; *Format:* Country; *Target Audience:* 25-54.
Doug Purtee, Operations Dir
Hank Kestenbaum, General Manager

*WANM
11-01-1976; 90.5 MHz FM; *Hrs Open:* 24; 1.6 kw vert; 167 ft.; N30 25 49 W84 17 27
P. O. Box 6202, Tallahassee, FL 32314 US
(850) 599-3000; *Fax:* (850) 561-2829
www.famu.edu/famcast
License: Tallahassee, Leon County, FL held by The Board of Trustees of Florida A&M University.
Nat'l Network: AP Radio; *Wire Services:* AP
Arbitron Metro Market: Tallahassee, FL; *Format:* News, Sports *Special Programming:* Reggae 3 hrs wkly, Gospel 18 hrs wkly, Jazz 15 hrs wkly.; *Hrs. of News Programming:* News progmg 5 hrs wkly *Target Audience:* General; urban African-American in area
Keith Miles, General Manager

WBZE
07-15-1962; 98.9 MHz FM; *Hrs Open:* 24; 99.2 kw; 604 ft.; N30 29 32 W84 17 2
3411 West Tharpe Street, Tallahassee, FL 32303 US
(850) 201-3000; *Fax:* (850) 561-8903
www.mystar98.com
john.dawson@cumulus.com
License: Tallahassee, Leon County, FL held by Cumulus Licensing Corp.
Group Owner: Cumulus Media Inc.
Nat'l Reps: Katz Radio
Arbitron Metro Market: Tallahassee, FL; *Format:* Adult Contemp; *Target Audience:* 25-54.; *Adv. Rates:* 90; 75; 75; 50
John Baker, Operations Manager
John Dawson, Programming Director
Estteffania Najera, Promotions Director
Dot Ealy, Vice President/Marketing Manager

WCVC
11-05-1953; 1330 kHz AM; *Hrs Open:* 6:30 AM-7 PM; 5 kw-D, NDD; N30 29 3 W84 17 13
117 1/2 Henderson Road, Tallahassee, FL 32312 US
(850) 386-1330
alanmccal@hotmail.com
License: Tallahassee, FL held by WCVC Inc.
Arbitron Metro Market: Tallahassee, FL
Wendell Borrink, President
Erwin O'Conner, General Manager

***WFRF**
08-01-1974; 1070 kHz AM; *Hrs Open:* Sunrise-senset
Mailing Address: P.O. Box 7617, Tallahassee, FL 32314 US
Second Address: 4015 N. Monroe St., Tallahassee, FL 32303
(850) 201-1070; *Fax:* (850) 201-1071
www.faithradio.us
mailbox@faithradio.us
License: Tallahassee, FL held by Faith Radio Network Inc.
Arbitron Metro Market: Tallahassee, FL; *Format:* Christian; *Target Audience:* 12 plus.
Scott Beigle, General Manager

***WFSQ**
05-01-1954; 91.5 MHz FM; *Hrs Open:* 24; 86 kw; 735 ft.; N30 21 31 W84 36 38
The Public Broadcast Cen, 1600 Red Barber Plaza, Tallahasse, FL 32310 US
(850) 487-3170; *Fax:* (850) 487-3093
www.wfsu.org
mail@wfsu.org
License: Tallahassee, Leon County, FL held by The Board of Regents of Florida acting for and on behalf of Florida State University.
Nat'l Network: NPR; PRI
Arbitron Metro Market: Tallahassee, FL *TV Affiliate:* WFSU TV; *Format:* Talk; *Hrs. of News Programming:* News progmg one hr wkly; *Target Audience:* 35 plus; highly educated
Tim McGuire, Operations Dir
Patrick Keating, General Manager
Caroline Austin, Station Manager
Doug Crall, Engineering Dir
John Kwak, Development Director
Crystal Cumbo, Underwriting Manager

***WFSU-FM**
10-14-1990; 88.9 MHz FM; *Hrs Open:* 24; 90 kw; 1243 ft.; N30 40 13 W83 56 26
The Public B/Cast Center, 1600 Red Barber Plaza, Tallahassee, FL 32310 US
(850) 487-3086; *Fax:* (850) 487-2611
www.wfsu.org
License: Tallahassee, Leon County, FL held by The Board of Regents of Florida acting for and on behalf of Florida State University.
Nat'l Network: NPR; PRI; *Regional Network:* Fla. Pub.
Arbitron Metro Market: Tallahassee, FL; *Format:* News, News/Talk, 86 *Special Programming:* Jazz 8 hrs wkly; *No. News Employees:* 9; *Target Audience:* 35-54; highly educated
Tim McGuire, Operations Dir
Pat Keating, General Manager
Caroline Austin, Station Manager
Doug Krall, Engineering Dir
John Kwak, Development Director

WGLF
12-01-1967; 104.1 MHz FM; *Hrs Open:* 24; 100 kw; 1411 ft.; N30 27 4 W84 0 42
3411 West Tharpe Street, Tallahassee, FL 32303 US
(850) 201-3000; *Fax:* (850) 561-8903
www.gulf104.com
john.baker@cumulus.com
License: Tallahassee, Leon County, FL held by Cumulus Licensing Corp.
Group Owner: Cumulus Media Inc.; (acq 6-22-99; $4 million)
Nat'l Reps: Katz Radio
Arbitron Metro Market: Tallahassee, FL; *Format:* Classic Rock, Rock/AOR; *Target Audience:* 25-54.; *Adv. Rates:* 75; 65; 60; 50
John Baker, Operations Manager
John Baker, Programming Director
Estteffania Najera, Marketing & Promotions Director
Dot Ealy, Vice President/Marketing Manager

WHBT
08-06-1959; 1410 kHz AM; *Hrs Open:* 24; 5 kw-D, ND1; 0.018 kw-N, ND1; N30 29 3 W84 17 13
3411 West Tharpe Street, Tallahassee, FL 32303 US
(850) 201-3000; *Fax:* (850) 561-8903
www.heaven1410.com
License: Tallahassee, FL held by Cumulus Licensing Corp.
Group Owner: Cumulus Media Inc.; (acq 10-28-97; grpsl)
Nat'l Reps: Katz Radio
Arbitron Metro Market: Tallahassee, FL; *Format:* Gospel; *Target Audience:* 18-54.; *Adv. Rates:* 15; 15; 15; 15
John Baker, Operations Manager
Doc D., Programming Director
Estteffania Najera, Promotions Director
Peter Walkowiak, Chief Engineer
Dot Ealy, Vice President/Marketing Manager

WHBX
06-28-1982; 96.1 MHz FM; *Hrs Open:* 24; 37 kw; 479 ft.; N30 16 8 W84 16 32
3411 West Tharpe Street, Tallahassee, FL 32303 US
(850) 201-3000; *Fax:* (850) 561-8903
961jamz.com
License: Tallahassee, Leon County, FL held by Cumulus Licensing Corp.
Group Owner: Cumulus Media Inc.; (acq 10-28-97; grpsl)
Nat'l Reps: Katz Radio
Arbitron Metro Market: Tallahassee, FL; *Format:* Urban Contemporary; *Target Audience:* 25-54.; *Adv. Rates:* 95; 90; 90; 50
Joe Bullard, Programming Director
Dot Ealy, Vice President/Marketing Manager

WTLY
10-15-1946; 1270 kHz AM; *Hrs Open:* 24
325 John Knox Road, Building G, Tallahassee, FL 32303 US
(850) 422-3107; *Fax:* (850) 383-0747
www.1053myfm.com
License: Tallahassee, FL held by Clear Channel Broadcasting Licenses Inc.
Group Owner: iHeartMedia
Arbitron Metro Market: Tallahassee, FL; *Format:* Adult Contemp; *Hrs. of News Programming:* news progmg 25 hrs wkly; *No. News Employees:* 1
Chuck Redden, Market Manager
Jason Taylor, Webmaster

WTAL
01-01-1935; 1450 kHz AM; *Hrs Open:* 24
1820 E. Park Ave, Tallahassee, FL 32301 US
(850) 671-1450,(850) 877-0105; *Fax:* (850) 877-5110
www.wtal1450.com
wtaal@nettally.com
License: Tallahassee, FL held by Live Communications Inc.
Nat'l Network: CBS; *Nat'l Reps:* Roslin
Arbitron Metro Market: Tallahassee, FL; *Format:* Christian, News, 62, Talk; *Hrs. of News Programming:* news progmg 21 hrs wkly; *No. News Employees:* 4; *Target Audience:* 25-54; educated, intelligent, affluent,involved, conservative; *Adv. Rates:* 15; 25; 20; 15
Dr. R.B. Holmes Jr., CEO
Richard Henderson, General Manager

WTNT-FM
07-24-1967; 94.9 MHz FM; 98 kw; 840 ft.; N30 34 42 W84 15 48
325 John Knox Road, Building G, Tallahassee, FL 32303 US
(850) 422-3107; *Fax:* (850) 383-0747
www.949tnt.com
License: Tallahassee, Leon County, FL held by Clear Channel Broadcasting Licenses Inc.
Group Owner: iHeartMedia; (acq 11-21-97; grpsl)
Nat'l Reps: Christal
Arbitron Metro Market: Tallahassee, FL; *Format:* Country; *Hrs. of News Programming:* News progmg one hr wkly; *Target Audience:* 25-54.
Chuck Redden, Market Manager
Jason Taylor, Promotions and Digital Content Director

***WVFS**
09-01-1987; 89.7 MHz FM; *Hrs Open:* 24; 7 kw vert; 180 ft.; N30 26 22 W84 17 29
420 Diffenbaugh Hall, Tallahassee, FL 32306 US
(850) 644-9692; *Fax:* (850) 644-8753
www.wvfs.fsu.edu
wvfs@wvfs.fsu.edu
License: Tallahassee, Leon County, FL held by Florida State University.
Arbitron Metro Market: Tallahassee, FL; *Format:* Alternative
Special Programming: Black 8 hrs, folk 3 hrs, Sp 2 hrs wkly; *Hrs. of News Programming:* News progmg 2 hrs wkly; *Target Audience:* General.
Misha Laurents, Ph.D., General Manager

WQTL
05-01-1992; 106.1 MHz FM; *Hrs Open:* 24; 2.25 kw; 543 ft.; N30 29 39 W84 14 0
300 Olson Road, Tallahassee, FL 32308 US
(850) 386-8004; *Fax:* (850) 422-1897
www.1061thepath.com
hkestenbaum@opusbroadcasting.com
License: Tallahassee, Leon County, FL held by Opus Broadcasting Tallahassee LLC.
Group Owner: Opus Media Holdings LLC; (acq 9-2-2005;. grpsl)
Arbitron Metro Market: Tallahassee, FL; *Format:* Rock/AOR; *Target Audience:* 18-49.
Hank Kestenbaum, Vice President/General Manager

Tampa

WMTX
11-01-1947; 100.7 MHz FM; *Hrs Open:* 24; 96 kw; 1549 ft.; N27 49 9.7 W82 15 38.7
4002 West Gandy Boulevard, Tampa, FL 33611 US
(813) 832-1000; *Fax:* (813) 832-1090
www.tampabaysmix.com
License: Tampa, Hillsborough County, FL held by Citicasters Licenses Inc.
Group Owner: iHeartMedia
Nat'l Network: Premiere Radio Networks; *Nat'l Reps:* Katz Radio; *Wire Services:* AP
Arbitron Metro Market: Tampa, FL; *Format:* Adult Contemp
Sam Nein, Market President
Doug Hamand, Senior Vice President of Programming
Fernando Bauermeister, Sales Manager
Randi West, Programming Director
Kim Cusmano, Promotions Director
Kristy Knight, Production Director
David Bell,Public Service Director

WAMA
01-01-1961; 1550 kHz AM; *Hrs Open:* 24; 10 kw-D, ND1; 0.133 kw-N, ND1; N27 55 16 W82 23 41
2000 North 14th Street, Suite 400, Arlington, VA 22201 US
(813) 319-1550; *Fax:* (813) 289-1554
www.holaciudad.com/tampa/home.html
traficlainvasora@gmail.com
License: Tampa, FL held by WAMA Inc.
Group Owner: ZG Communications; (acq 10-15-97; $2 million)
Nat'l Reps: Univision Radio National Sales; *Wire Services:* UPI
Arbitron Metro Market: Tampa, FL; *Format:* Tejano; *No. News Employees:* 1; *Target Audience:* 25-54; Hispanic Adults; *Adv. Rates:* 70; 60; 65; 45
Ron Gordon, Chairman
Norberto Vallejo, President

***WBVM**
05-27-1986; 90.5 MHz FM; *Hrs Open:* 24; 77 kw horiz, 74.7 kw vert; 965 ft.; N27 50 50.4 W82 15 50.1
Mailing Address: P.O. Box 18081, Tampa, FL 33679 US
Second Address: 3816 Morrison Ave., Tampa, FL 33629
(813) 289-8040; *Fax:* (813) 282-3580
www.spiritfm905.com
contact@spiritfm905.com
License: Tampa, Hillsborough County, FL held by The Bishop of the Diocese of St. Petersburg.
Arbitron Metro Market: Tampa, FL; *Format:* Christian *Special Programming:* Black 4 hrs, children 4 hrs, Sp 4 hrs wkly; *Target Audience:* 35 plus; families
John Morris, Operations Dir
Abby, Promotions Manager
Chris Sampson, Operations Manager

WHNZ
05-15-1922; 1250 kHz AM
4002 Gandy Blvd., Tampa, FL 33611 US
(813) 832-1000; *Fax:* (813) 832-1090
www.whnz.com
License: Tampa, FL held by Citicasters Licenses Inc.
Group Owner: iHeartMedia; (acq 5-4-99; grpsl)
Nat'l Reps: Katz Radio
Arbitron Metro Market: Tampa, FL; *Format:* News, News/Talk, 86; *Target Audience:* 25-54.

Sam Nein, Market President
Joe Kaim, Sales Manager
Doug Hamand, Programming Director
Greg Wolf, Promotions Director
Brian Fink, Production Director
Phil Azoon, Creative Services Director
David Bell, Public Service Director

WFLA
01-01-1924; 970 kHz AM; 25 kw-D, DA2; 11 kw-N, DA2; N28 1 14 W82 36 34
4002 West Gandy Boulevard, Tampa, FL 33611 US
(813) 832-1000; *Fax:* (813) 832-1090
www.970wfla.com
License: Tampa, FL held by Citicasters Licenses Inc.
Group Owner: iHeartMedia; (acq 5-4-99; grpsl).
Nat'l Network: Fox News Radio; *Nat'l Reps:* Katz Radio; *Wire Services:* AP
Arbitron Metro Market: Tampa-St. Petersburg-Clearwater, FLsburg-Clearwate; *Format:* News, News/Talk, 86 *Special Programming:* home imporvement, gardening 4 hrs wkly; *Hrs. of News Programming:* news progrmg 28 hrs wkly; *No. News Employees:* 5; *Target Audience:* 25-54.
Sam Nein, Market President
Mark McCauley, Sales Manager
Doug Hamand, Programming Director
Greg Wolf, Promotions Director
Steve Hall, News Director
Norm Kniess, Production Director
Phil Azoon, Creative Services Director
KimCusmano, Public Service Director

WFLZ-FM
01-01-1948; 93.3 MHz FM; 97 kw; 1549 ft.; N27 49 9.7 W82 15 38.7
4002 West Gandy Boulevard, Tampa, FL 33611 US
(813) 832-1000; *Fax:* (813) 831-4475
www.933flz.com
License: Tampa, Hillsborough County, FL held by Citicasters Licenses Inc.
Group Owner: iHeartMedia
Nat'l Reps: Katz Radio; *Wire Services:* AP
Arbitron Metro Market: Tampa-St. Petersburg-Clearwater, FL; *Format:* Contemporary Hits/Top 40; *Target Audience:* 18-34.
Fernando Bauermeister, General Sales Mgr
John Mayer, Programming Director
Kim Cusmano, Promotions Director
Brian Fink, Production Director
Drew Hall, Creative Services Director
David Bell, Public Service Director

***WMNF**
09-14-1979; 88.5 MHz FM; *Hrs Open:* 24; 70 kw; 1550 feet; N27 49 04 W82 14 31
1210 E. Martin Luther King Jr. Blvd., Tampa, FL 33603
(813) 238-8001
www.wmnf.org
wmnf@wmnf.org
License: Tampa, Hillsborough County, FL held by The Nathan B. Stubblefield Foundation.
Nat'l Network: NPR
Population Served: 2,800,000; *Arbitron Metro Market:* Tampa-St. Petersburg; *Hrs. of News Programming:* news progmg 24 hrs wkly; *No. News Employees:* 3; *Target Audience:* General.
Sheila Cowley, Operations Dir
Dr. Sydney White, Station Manager
Randy Wynne, Programming Director
Bill Brown, Chief Engineer
Laura Taylor, Development Director

WRBQ-FM
01-01-1954; 104.7 MHz FM; 99 kw; 571 ft.; N27 55 53.8 W82 24 4.6
9721 Executive Center Dr., Suite 200, St. Petersburg, FL 33702 US
(727) 579-1925
www.myq105.com
License: Tampa, Hillsborough County, FL held by WXTU License Limited Partnership
Group Owner: Beasley Broadcast Group Inc.; (acq 5-99).
Arbitron Metro Market: Tampa-St. Petersburg-Clearwater, FL; *Format:* Oldies; *Target Audience:* 18-49.
Ken Denton, General Sales Mgr
Tee Gentry, Programming Director
Kelly Sedivy, Digital Sales Manager

WTIS
01-01-1946; 1110 kHz AM; 10 kw-D, DAD; N27 52 26 W82 37 53
311 112th Ave., N.E., St Petersburg, FL 33716 US
(727) 576-1110; *Fax:* (727) 578-1110
wtis1110.com
License: Tampa, FL held by WTIS-AM Inc.
Arbitron Metro Market: St. Petersburg, FL; *Format:* Ethnic, Religious *Special Programming:* Sp one hr wkly; *Target Audience:* 25-54.
Ron Roseman, President
Tom Connolly, Operations/Program Director
Pete O'Shea, Promotions Manager
Ed Roseman, Executive Vice President
Joe Sparra, Sales Executive
Jodi Long, Sales Executive
Deborah Ray Roseman, Business Manager

***WUSF**
09-01-1963; 89.7 MHz FM; *Hrs Open:* 24; 71 kw; 942 ft.; N27 50 53 W82 15 48
4202 East Fowler Ave, Tampa, FL 33620 US
(813) 974-8700; *Fax:* (813) 974-5016
www.wusf.org
info@wusf.org
License: Tampa, Hillsborough County, FL held by Board of Trustees, University of South Florida.
Nat'l Network: NPR; PRI; *Regional Network:* Fla. Pub.; *Wire Services:* AP
Arbitron Metro Market: Tampa, FL *TV Affiliate:* *WUSF-TV affil; *Format:* Jazz, News; *Hrs. of News Programming:* news progmg 38 hrs wkly; *No. News Employees:* 8; *Target Audience:* General.
Dustin Hapli, Operations Manager
Jo Ann Urofsky, General Manager
Scot Kaufman, General Sales Mgr
Sheila Rue, Programming Director
Cathy Cocciaÿ, Development Directorÿ
Patricia J. Hickok, Member Services Directorÿ

WWRM
01-01-1958; 94.9 MHz FM; *Hrs Open:* 24; 97.3 kw; 1532 ft.; N27 49 10 W82 15 39
11300 North 4th Street, Suite 300, St. Petersburg, FL 33716 US
(727) 579-2000; *Fax:* (727) 579-2271
info@coxradio.com
License: Tampa, Hillsborough County, FL held by Cox Radio Inc.
Group Owner: Cox Radio Inc.; (acq 7-1-88).
Nat'l Reps: Christal
Arbitron Metro Market: Tampa, FL; *Format:* Adult Contemp; *Target Audience:* 25-54.
Keith Lawless, Vice President & Matketing Manager
Bryan Kelly, General Sales Manager
Jodi Rainey, National Sales Manager
Julia Freeman, Promotions Manager

Tarpon Springs

***WYFE**
06-14-1988; 88.9 MHz FM; 60 kw; 449 ft.; N28 22 40 W82 40 26
P.O. Box 7300, Charlotte, NC 28241 US
(800) 888-7077
www.bbnradio.org
bbn@bbnmedia.org
License: Tarpon Springs, Pinellas County, FL held by Bible Broadcasting Network Inc.
Group Owner: Bible Broadcasting Network; (acq 8-11-89)
Arbitron Metro Market: Tarpon Springs, FL; *Format:* Religious; *Target Audience:* General; Christians
Lowell Davey, President
Jason Padgett, Operations Manager

Tavares

WXXL
02-12-1969; 106.7 MHz FM; *Hrs Open:* 24; 100 kw; 823 ft.; N28 33 31 W81 35 38
2500 Maitland Center Parkway, Maitland, FL 32751 US
(407) 916-7800; *Fax:* (407) 916-7510
www.xl1067.com
License: Tavares, Lake County, FL held by AMFM Radio Licenses L.L.C.
Group Owner: iHeartMedia; (acq 8-30-00; grpsl)
Arbitron Metro Market: Orlando, FL; *Format:* Contemporary Hits/Top 40 *Special Programming:* Alternative 6 hrs wkly; *No. News Employees:* 1; *Target Audience:* 18-49; general; *Adv. Rates:* 350.;200.;260.;125.
Linda Byrd, Market President
Shannon Fraser, General Sales Mgr
Brian Mack, Programming Director
Glory Adona-Langstonÿ, Promotions Manager
Jana, Assistant Program/Music Director

Tavernier

WKEZ-FM
01-01-1999; 96.9 MHz FM; 25 kw; 223 ft.; N25 1 35 W80 30 30
Box 500940, Marathon, FL 33050 US
(305) 852-9085; *Fax:* (305) 852-5586
www.easy969.com
License: Tavernier, Monroe County, FL held by The Great Marathon Radio Co.
Group Owner: The Great Marathon Radio Co.; (acq 7-30-2008)
Format: Easy Listening
Mark Humenik, General Sales Mgr

Temple Terrace

WQBN
01-01-1956; 1300 kHz AM; *Hrs Open:* 6 AM-midnight
Mailing Address: 4023 North Armenia Bird Street, Tampa, FL 33607 US
Second Address: 5203 N. Armenia Ave., Tampa, FL 33603
(813) 871-1333; *Fax:* (813) 876-1333
superq1300@hotmail.com
License: Temple Terrace, FL held by Radio Tropical Inc.
Arbitron Metro Market: Tampa-St. Petersburg-Clearwater, FL; *Format:* Tejano, Variety/Diverse; *Hrs. of News Programming:* news progmg 20 hrs wkly; *No. News Employees:* 3; *Target Audience:* 25 plus; Hispanics
Efrain Archilla, President
Alvaro Lopez-Echevarry, Sales Manager
Joyce Cordero, Office Manager

Tice

WJGO
03-01-2000; 102.9 MHz FM; 96 kw; 466 ft.; N26 29 16 W81 55 46
10915 K-Nine Drive, Bonita Springs, FL 34135 US
(239) 495-8383; *Fax:* (239) 495-0883
www.1029bobfm.com
webguy@1029bobfm.com
License: Tice, Lee County, FL held by Renda Broadcasting Corp. of Nevada.
Group Owner: Renda Broadcasting Corp.; (acq 10-5-2000; $7 million)
Arbitron Metro Market: Fort Myers, FL; *Format:* Adult Contemp
Tony Renda Jr., General Manager
Randy Savage, Programming Director
Buzzy Ford, Promotions Manager

Titusville

WIXC
11-20-1957; 1060 kHz AM; *Hrs Open:* 24
3909 Champion Road, Titusville, FL 32796 US
(813) 281-1040; *Fax:* (321) 264-4246
www.newstalkflorida.com
contactus@radiogenesis.com
License: Titusville, FL held by Genesis Communications I Inc.
Group Owner: Genesis Communications Inc.; (acq 4-19-2000; $650,000)
Arbitron Metro Market: Titusville, FL; *Format:* News, News/Talk, 86; *Target Audience:* 35 plus.
Bruce Maduri, CEO/General Sales Manager
Len Weiner, Programming Director
Amanda Berger, Promotions Director
Jerry Smith, Chief Engineer
Gwen Schuler, Traffic Manager

***WPIO**
10-19-1975; 89.3 MHz FM; 7.1 kw; 335 ft.; N28 34 49 W80 51 0
505 Josephine Street, Titusville, FL 32796 US
(321) 267-3000; *Fax:* (321) 264-9370
www.noncomradio.net
License: Titusville, Brevard County, FL held by Florida Public Radio Inc.
Format: Religious
Randy Henry, President

Trenton

WDVH-FM
02-01-1988; 101.7 MHz FM; *Hrs Open:* 24; 3 kw; 143 meters; N29 36 29 W82 51 01
100 NW 76th Dr., Suite 2, Gainesville, FL 32607
(352) 313-3150; *Fax:* (352) 313-3166
www.pulse1017fm.com
kevin.mangan@marcradio.com
License: Trenton, Gilchrist County, FL held by Marc Radio Gainesville LLC
Group Owner: Marc Radio Group LLC; (acq 7-18-2011; grpsl)
Population Served: 181,843; *Arbitron Metro Market:* Gainesville-Ocala, FL; *Format:* Country *Special Programming:* Farm 2 hrs wkly; *Hrs. of News Programming:* News progmg 7 hrs wkly; *Target Audience:* 25 plus;working class & professionals
Shawn Portmann, Sales Manager
Kevin Mangan, Programming Director

Union Park

*WPOZ
08-09-1995; 88.3 MHz FM; *Hrs Open:* 24; 13 kw; 1333 ft.; N28 36 7 W81 5 37
1065 Rainer Drive, Altamonte Springs, FL 32714 US
(407) 869-8000; *Fax:* (407) 869-0380
www.zradio.org
zcrew@zradio.org
License: Union Park, Orange County, FL held by Central Florida Educational Foundation Inc.
Arbitron Metro Market: Orlando, FL; *Format:* Christian; *Target Audience:* 25-44.
James Hoge, President
Dean O'Neal, Vice President/GM/Programming Director

Venice

WDDV
02-01-1960; 1320 kHz AM
1779 Independence Boulevard, Sarasota, FL 34234 US
(941) 552-4800; *Fax:* (941) 552-4900
www.sunnyradioam.com
License: Venice, FL held by Citicasters Licenses Inc.
Group Owner: iHeartMedia; (acq 5-4-99; grpsl).
Arbitron Metro Market: Venice, FL; *Format:* Adult Contemp; *Target Audience:* 25-54; active, upscale, affluent
Eddie Rupp, Operations Manager/Programming Director
William Ames, Local Sales Manager
Nikki Clark, Promotions Director

WLTQ-FM
03-01-1974; 92.1 MHz FM; *Hrs Open:* 24; 11.5 kw; 476 ft.; N27 9 3 W82 27 51
1779 Independence Boulevard, Sarasota, FL 34234 US
(941) 552-4800
www.921thecoast.com
eddierupp@iheartmedia.com
License: Venice, Sarasota County, FL held by Citicasters Licenses Inc.
Group Owner: iHeartMedia
Arbitron Metro Market: Sarasota, FL; *Format:* Adult Contemp; *Target Audience:* 25-54; female
Eddie Rupp, Operations Manager
William Ames, Local Sales Manager
Nikki Clark, Promotions Director

Vero Beach

WAXE
05-01-1954; 1370 kHz AM; 1 kw-D, ND1; 0.074 kw-N, ND1; N27 36 1 W80 23 33
P.O. Box 0093, Port St. Lucie, FL 34985 US
(772) 335-9300
www.waxe1370.com
License: Vero Beach, FL held by Capstar TX LLC
Group Owner: iHeartMedia; (acq 8-30-2000; grpsl).
Arbitron Metro Market: Vero Beach, FL; *Format:* News, News/Talk, 86
Bryan Kelly, Director of Sales
Heath West, Programming Director
Chad Tyson, Webmaster

WCZR
05-29-1986; 101.7 MHz FM; 4.2 kw; 394 ft.; N27 44 7 W80 27 27
3071 Continental Drive, West Palm Beach, FL 33407 US
(561) 616-6600; *Fax:* (561) 616-6677
www.wzzr.com
License: Vero Beach, Indian River County, FL held by Capstar TX LLC
Group Owner: iHeartMedia; (acq 7-30-2008; grpsl)
Arbitron Metro Market: Fort Pierece-Stuart-Vero Beach, FL; *Format:* Talk; *Hrs. of News Programming:* news progmg 21 hrs wkly; *No. News Employees:* 3; *Target Audience:* 18-60.
Bryan Kelly, Director of Sales
Andrew Bednar, Promotions Director
Chad Tyson, Digital Program Director

WGYL
11-01-1970; 93.7 MHz FM; 50 kw; 479 ft.; N27 36 4 W80 23 33
1235 16th St., Vero Beach, FL 32960 US
(772) 794-7748; *Fax:* (772) 562-4747
www.937wgyl.com
License: Vero Beach, Indian River County, FL held by Vero Beach Broadcasters, LLC
Group Owner: Vero Beach Broadcasters, LLC
Arbitron Metro Market: Fort Pierce-Stuart-Vero Beach, FL; *Format:* Adult Contemp; *Target Audience:* 35-64; upscale adult
Jim Davis, General Manager
Karen Franke, Station Manager
John Anthony, Programming Director
Miguel Santiestaban, Promotions Manager

WJKD
01-01-1995; 99.7 MHz FM; 50 kw; 440 ft.; N27 44 7 W80 27 27
1235 16th St., Vero Beach, FL 32960 US
(772) 567-0937; *Fax:* (772) 562-4747
www.997jackfm.com
License: Vero Beach, Indian River County, FL held by Vero Beach Broadcasters, LLC.
Group Owner: Vero Beach Broadcasters, LLC.; (acq 2-11-2002).
Arbitron Metro Market: Fort Pierce-Stuart-Vero Beach, FL; *Format:* Adult Contemp
Jim Davis, General Manager
Karen Franke, Station Manager
Jesse Kriske, Programming Director
Miguel Santiestaban, Promotions Manager

WQOL
09-01-1979; 103.7 MHz FM; 50 kw; 476 ft.; N27 44 7 W80 27 27
1235 16th Street, Vero Beach, FL 32960 US
(772) 335-9300; *Fax:* (772) 335-3291
www.oldies1037fm.com
License: Vero Beach, Indian River County, FL held by Capstar TX LLC
Group Owner: iHeartMedia; (acq 8-30-00; grpsl).
Nat'l Network: Westwood One
Arbitron Metro Market: Fort Pierce-Stu; *Format:* Oldies; *Target Audience:* 35-64; baby boomers
Bryan Kelly, Director of Sales
Heath West, Programming Director

*WSCF-FM
02-01-1990; 91.9 MHz FM; *Hrs Open:* 24; 15.5 kw; 305 ft.; N27 38 10 W80 27 59
6767 20th Street, Vero Beach, FL 32966 US
(772) 569-0919; *Fax:* (772) 562-4892
www.wscf.com
License: Vero Beach, Indian River County, FL held by Central Educational Broadcasting Inc.
Nat'l Network: USA
Arbitron Metro Market: Fort Pierce-Stu; *Format:* Religious
Jon Hamilton, General Manager
Brad Bacon, General Sales Mgr
Paul Tipton, Programming Director
Bruce Douglas, News Director

WTTB
06-07-1954; 1490 kHz AM; 1 kw-U, ND1; N27 37 12 W80 25 1
1235 16th St., Vero Beach, FL 32960 US
(772) 567-0937; *Fax:* (772) 562-4747
www.wttbam.com
License: Vero Beach, FL held by Vero Beach Broadcasters LLC
Group Owner: Vero Beach Broadcasters LLC; acq 6-19-00; $5.15 million with co-located FM).
Nat'l Network: ABC; *Regional Network:* Florida's Radio Networks
Arbitron Metro Market: Vero Beach, FL; *Format:* News/Talk; *Target Audience:* General.
Jim Davis, General Manager
Karen Franke, Station Manager
Hamp Elliott, Programming Director
Miguel Santiestaban, Promotions Manager

WZTA
1370 kHz AM; 1 kw-D, ND1; 0.074 kw-N, ND1; N27 36 1 W80 23 33
P.O. Box 0093, Port St. Lucie, FL 34985 US
(772) 335-9300
www.waxe1370.com
License: Vero Beach, Indian River County, FL held by Capstar TX LLC
Group Owner: iHeartMedia
Arbitron Metro Market: Vero Beach, FL; *Format:* News, News/Talk, 86
Bryan Kelly, Director of Sales
Heath West, Programming Director
Chad Tyson, Digital Program Director

Watertown

WQLC
10-06-1990; 102.1 MHz FM; 9 kw; 531 ft.; N30 13 58 W82 48 18
3821 Cove Drive, Birmingham, AL 35213 US
(386) 755-4102; *Fax:* (386) 752-9861
www.powercountry102.com
License: Watertown, Columbia County, FL held by Power Country Inc.
Format: Country *Special Programming:* Gospel 4 hrs wkly; *Target Audience:* 18-54.
Louis Bolton II, President
Ron Peacock, General Manager

Wauchula

WAUC
01-07-1958; 1310 kHz AM; *Hrs Open:* 6 AM-midnight; 5 kw-D, DA2; 0.5 kw-N, DA2; N27 31 48 W81 49 8
Mailing Address: 1310 South Florida Avenue, Wauchula, FL 33873 US
Second Address: 1310 S. Florida Ave., Wauchula, FL 33873
(863) 773-9282(863) 773-5008(813) 773-5088; *Fax:* (863) 773-2032
wauc.radiostation@earthlink.net
License: Wauchula, FL held by Dora A. Cruz.
Regional Network: Florida's Radio Networks
Arbitron Metro Market: Grand Junction, CO; *Format:* Tejano; *Target Audience:* 35-54.
Robert Ayala, General Manager

Wellington

WKGR
05-01-1961; 98.7 MHz FM; 100 kw; 981 ft.; N27 1 31 W80 10 43
3071 Continental Drive, West Palm Beach, FL 33407 US
(561) 616-6600; *Fax:* (561) 616-6677
www.gaterrocks.com
License: Wellington, St. Lucie County, FL held by Clear Channel Broadcasting Licenses Inc.
Group Owner: iHeartMedia; (acq 9-16-97; grpsl)
Arbitron Metro Market: West Palm Beach-Boca Raton, FL; *Format:* Classic Rock; *Target Audience:* 25-54.
Bryan Kelly, Director of Sales
Chad Tyson, Digital Program Director
Andrew Bednar, Promotions Director

West Palm Beach

*WAYF
11-11-1993; 88.1 MHz FM; *Hrs Open:* 24; 0.05 kw horiz, 50 kw vert; 1053 ft.; N26 35 20 W80 12 44
P.O. Box 61275, Fort Myers, FL 33906 US
(307) 745-5208; *Fax:* (307) 745-8570
mix967@fiberpipe.net
License: West Palm Beach, Palm Beach County, FL held by WAY-FM Media Group Inc.
Group Owner: WAY-FM Media Group Inc.
Arbitron Metro Market: Medicine Bow WY; *Format:* Classic Rock
Steven Silberberg, President
Jim O'Reilly, General Manager

WJNO
07-15-1947; 1290 kHz AM
3071 Continental Drive, West Palm Beach, FL 33407 US
(561) 616-6600; *Fax:* (561) 616-6677
www.wjno.com
License: West Palm Beach, FL held by Clear Channel Radio Licenses Inc.
Group Owner: iHeartMedia; (acq 9-16-97; grpsl)
Nat'l Reps: Clear Channel
Arbitron Metro Market: West Palm Beach, FL; *Format:* News, News/Talk, 84, Talk; *Target Audience:* Adults; 25-64
Bryan Kelly, Director of Sales
Brian Mudd, Programming Director
Ethan Briner, Promotions Director
Joel Malkin, News Director
Chad Tyson, Digital Program Director

WFTL
01-01-1948; 850 kHz AM; *Hrs Open:* 24; 50 kw-D, 24 kw-N, DA-2; N26 32 30 W80 44 30
701 Northpoint Pkwy., Suite 500, Fort Lauderdale, FL 33407 US
(561) 616-4777
www.850wftl.com
License: West Palm Beach, Palm Beach County, FL held by ACM JCE IV B LLC.
Group Owner: ACM JCE IV B LLC.
Nat'l Network: ABC; NBC
Arbitron Metro Market: West Palm Beach-Boca Raton, FL; *Format:* News/Talk; *Target Audience:* 35 plus.
Mark Jorgenson, President

WEAT
06-01-2012; 107.9 MHz FM; 100 kW; 420 ft.; N26 45 47 W80 12 19
701 Northpoint Pkwy., Suite 500, West Palm Beach, FL 33407 USA
(561) 616-4777; *Fax:* (561) 868-1111
sunny1079.com
License: West Palm Beach, Palm Beach County, FL held by Palm Beach Broadcasting LLC
Group Owner: Palm Beach Broadcasting LLC
Nat'l Reps: Katz Radio
Arbitron Metro Market: West Palm Beach, FL; *Format:* Adult Contemp; *Target Audience:* 25-54

RADIO - U.S.

Christie Banks, Programming Director
Beth Stibal, Promotions Director

WBZT
07-31-1936; 1230 kHz AM; *Hrs Open:* 24; 1 kw-U, ND1; 0.8 kw-U, ND1; N26 45 33 W80 8 40; N26 15 18 W80 8 49
3071 Continental Drive, West Palm Beach, FL 33407 US
(561) 616-6600; *Fax:* (561) 616-6677
www.wbzt.com
info@wbzt.com
License: West Palm Beach, FL held by Capstar TX LLC
Group Owner: iHeartMedia; (acq 9-27-00; grpsl).
Arbitron Metro Market: West Palm Beach-Boca Raton, FL; *Format:* News, News/Talk, 86
Bryan Kelly, Director of Sales
Brian Mudd, Programming Director
Ethan Briner, Promotions Director
Joel Malkin, News Director

WRLX
12-13-1975; 92.1 MHz FM; 7.2 kw; 499 ft.; N26 47 58 W80 4 33
3071 Continental Drive, West Palm Beach, FL 33407 US
(561) 616-6600; *Fax:* (561) 616-6677
www.mia921.com
info@mia921.com
License: West Palm Beach, Palm Beach County, FL held by Capstar TX LLC
Group Owner: iHeartMedia; (acq 9-27-2000; grpsl)
Nat'l Reps: Clear Channel
Arbitron Metro Market: West Palm Beach-Boca Raton, FL; *Format:* Spanish
Bryan Kelly, Director of Sales
Jose Martinez, Programming Director
Ethan Briner, Promotions Director
Chad Tyson, Digital Program Director

***WPBI(FM)**
11-24-1969; 90.7 MHz FM; *Hrs Open:* 24; 38 kw; Ant 1,115 ft; N26 35 20 W80 12 44
Mailing Address: Box 6607, West Palm Beach, FL 33405
Second Address: 3401 S. Congress Ave., Boynton Beach, FL 33426
(561) 737-8000; *Fax:* (561) 369-3067
www.wxel.org
info@wxel.org
License: West Palm Beach, Palm Beach County, FL held by Barry Telecommunications Inc.
Nat'l Network: NPR; *Regional Network:* Fla. Pub.; *Wire Services:* AP
Population Served: 101,043; *Arbitron Metro Market:* West Palm Beach, FL; *Format:* News; *No. News Employees:* 7; *Target Audience:* 35 plus; career oriented (news & info)
Nestor Rodriguez, President
Jason Hughes, General Manager
Laura Galbrath, Sales Manager
Claudia Polzin, Development Director
Pam Szolscek, Traffic Manager

White City

WFLM
12-01-1993; 104.7 MHz FM; *Hrs Open:* 24; 17.5 kw; 390 ft.; N27 26 8 W80 22 40
6803 South Federal Hwy., Port St. Lucie, FL 34952 US
(772) 460-9356; *Fax:* (772) 460-2700
www.wflm.cc
License: White City, St. Lucie County, FL held by Midway Broadcasting Co.
Arbitron Metro Market: Fort Pierce-Stuart-Vero Beach, FLart-Vero Beach, F; *Format:* Blues *Special Programming:* Gospel 20 hrs, jazz 4 hrs, reggae 4 hrs wkly; *Target Audience:* 18-54.
Alice Lee, President

Wildwood

WVLG
09-01-1987; 640 kHz AM; *Hrs Open:* 6 AM-midnight; 930 w-D, 860 w-N; N28 54 16 W81 57 36
1161 Main St., The Villages, FL 34785
(352) 753-1119; *Fax:* (352) 259-4819
thevillagesdailysun.com/wvlg/WVLG.html
License: Wildwood, Sumter County, FL held by Senior Broadcasting Corp.
Regional Network: Southeast AgNet
Arbitron Metro Market: Gainesville-Ocala, FL; *Target Audience:* 18 plus; general
Frank Messing, Operations Dir
Rob Newton, General Manager
Ed Newlands, Station Manager
Laurie Shaw, General Sales Mgr
Ed Newlands, Programming Director
Rob Newton, Promotions Manager

Williston

WTMG
07-01-1983; 101.3 MHz FM; *Hrs Open:* 24; 3.5 kw; 433 ft.; N29 25 4 W82 32 58
249 University Avenue, Suite B, Gainesville, FL 32601 US
(352) 313-3150; *Fax:* (352) 313-3166
www.magic1013.com
rallen@marcradio.com
License: Williston, Levy County, FL held by Marc Radio Gainesville LLC
Group Owner: Marc Radio Group LLC; (acq 7-18-2011; grpsl)
Arbitron Metro Market: Gainesville, FL; *Format:* Adult Contemp; *Hrs. of News Programming:* news progmg 2 hrs wkly; *No. News Employees:* 1
Shawn Portmann, President
Russ Allen, Programming,Music & Promotion Director
Max Sitero, Chief Engineer
Keith Feeney, Business/ Finance
DJ Terrah, Mix Show Director

Wilton Manors

WEXY
06-01-1963; 1520 kHz AM
27 William St., 11th Floor, New York, NY 10005 US
(212) 966-1059; *Fax:* (212) 625-2894
www.mrbi.net
License: Wilton Manors, FL held by Multicultural Radio Broadcasting Licensee LLC.
Group Owner: Multicultural Radio Broadcasting Inc.; (acq 4-4-03; $2.75 million).
Nat'l Network: American Urban
Arbitron Metro Market: Wilton Manors, FL; *Format:* Gospel
Arthur Liu, CEO/COO

Windermere

WOTW
01-01-1966; 103.1 MHz FM; 22 kw; 745 ft.; N28 33 32 W81 35 39
3201 Lucien Way, Suite 180, Maitland, FL 32751 US
(407) 647-5557; *Fax:* (407) 647-4495
www.thewolf1031.com
License: Windermere, Orange County, FL held by JVC Media of Florida, LLC.
Group Owner: JVC Broadcasting
Arbitron Metro Market: Orlando, FL; *Format:* Country
Chris Ganoudis, General Manager
Elise Rossi, Music Director

Winter Garden

WLAA
01-01-1958; 1600 kHz AM
3765 N. John Young Pkwy., Orlando, FL 32804 US
(407) 293-9652
License: Winter Garden, FL held by Unity Broadcasting LLC.
Group Owner: Unity Broadcasting LLC.
Arbitron Metro Market: Orlando, FL *TV Affiliate:* Sp; *Format:* Tejano
Shanti Persaud, President

WOKB
02-22-2000; 1680 kHz AM
3765 N. John Young Pkwy., Orlando, FL 32868 US
(407) 894-1680
www.wokbradio.com
info@wokbradio.com
License: Winter Garden, FL held by Unity Broadcasting LLC.
Group Owner: Unity Broadcasting LIC.
Arbitron Metro Market: Orlando, FL; *Format:* Religious; *Target Audience:* 25-64; adults
Shanti Persaud, President

Winter Haven

WPCV
01-01-1962; 97.5 MHz FM; *Hrs Open:* 24; 100 kw; 1017 ft.; N28 7 35 W81 33 3
Mailing Address: P.O. Bo.X 4368, Lancaster, PA 17604 US
Second Address: 404 W. Lime St., Lakeland, FL 33815-4651
(863) 682-8184; *Fax:* (863) 683-2409
www.wpcv.com
wpcv@wpcv.com
License: Winter Haven, Polk County, FL held by Hall Communications Inc.
Group Owner: Hall Communications Inc.
Nat'l Reps: Eastman Radio; *Wire Services:* AP
Arbitron Metro Market: Lakeland-Winter Haven, FL; *Format:* Country; *Hrs. of News Programming:* news progmg 4 hrs wkly; *No. News Employees:* 3; *Target Audience:* 25-54.
Bonnie Rowbotham, Chairman
Art Rowbotham, President
Nancy Cattarius, Station Manager
Jeff Crews, Chief Engineer

WSIR
02-14-1947; 1490 kHz AM; *Hrs Open:* 24; 1 kw-U; N28 00 50 W81 45 02
665 Southwest Lake Howard Dr., Winter Haven, FL 33860
(863) 295-9411; *Fax:* (863) 401-9365
www.familyradio1490.com
joe.fisher@familyradio1490.com
License: Winter Haven, Polk County, FL held by Anscombe Broadcasting Group Ltd.
Nat'l Network: AURN; Sheridan Gospel Network; *Regional Network:* Florida's Radio Networks
Population Served: 683,000; *Arbitron Metro Market:* Lakeland-Winter *Special Programming:* Relg 8090; *Hrs. of News Programming:* News progmg 5 hrs wkly; *Target Audience:* 25-54; *Adv. Rates:* 40-60s / 35-30s
Steve Reszka, CEO
Tony Charles, Operations Dir
Joe Fisher, General Manager
Joe Fisher, General Sales Mgr
Joe Fisher, Programming Director
Pat Hughes, Promotions Manager
Steve Zagony, Engineering Dir
Steve Zagony, ChiefEngineer

Winter Park

WPRD
09-01-1954; 1440 kHz AM; *Hrs Open:* 24; 5 kw-D, DAN; 1 kw-N, DAN; N28 35 18 W81 22 53
222 Hazard St, Orlando, FL 32804 US
(407) 841-8282; *Fax:* (407) 841-8250
www.wprd.com
wprd1440@hotmail.com
License: Winter Park, Orange County, FL held by J&V Communications Inc.
Group Owner: J&V Communications Inc.; acq 11-94; $300,000)
Arbitron Metro Market: Orlando, FL; *Format:* Spanish, Variety/Diverse; *Target Audience:* 25-64
John Torrado, CEO
Jocelyn Torrado, Operations Dir
Hector Reyes, General Manager

***WPRK**
12-10-1952; 91.5 MHz FM; *Hrs Open:* 24; 1.3 kw; 105 ft.; N28 35 28 W81 20 55.7
1000 Holt Ave - 2745, Winter Park, FL 32789 US
(407) 646-2915,(407) 646-2241
www.rollins.edu/wprk
License: Winter Park, Orange County, FL held by Rollins College.
Arbitron Metro Market: Orlando, FL; *Format:* Urban Contemporary *Special Programming:* Jazz 3 hrs wkly; *Hrs. of News Programming:* News progmg 2 hrs wkly; *Target Audience:* General; non-traditional class and/or rocklisteners
Dan Seeger, General Manager

Woodville

WTSM(FM)
09-01-2003; 97.9 MHz FM; *Hrs Open:* 8:30 AM-5:30 PM; 6 kw; Ant 328 ft; N30 16 30 W84 07 39
435 St. Francis St., Tallahassee, FL 32301
(850) 561-8400; *Fax:* (850) 224-1553
License: Woodville, Leon County, FL held by 97.9 WJZTFM Inc.
Population Served: 182,965; *Arbitron Metro Market:* Tallahassee, FL; *Format:* Jazz, Smooth Jazz; *Target Audience:* 25-55.; *Adv. Rates:* 20; 15; 10; 8
Larry Wright, General Manager/Sales Manager
Tom Lang, Programming Director
Lauren Jones, Promotions Director
Jeff Cameron, Sports Director

Yankeetown

WXOF
01-01-1998; 96.7 MHz FM; 3.5 kw; 433 ft.; N29 1 18 W82 41 20
4554 Fouth Suncoast Boulevard, Homosassa, FL 34465 US
(352) 628-4444; *Fax:* (352) 628-4450
www.citrus953.com
License: Yankeetown, Levy County, FL held by WGUL-FM Inc.
Arbitron Metro Market: Yankeetown, FL; *Format:* Classic Rock
Laura Grady, General Manager
Ryan Downs, Programming Director
Annette Kimbally, Senior Account Executive

Jody Boles, Office & Traffic Manager
Jim Hathaway, Account Executive

Zephyrhills

WZHR
05-09-1962; 1400 kHz AM; *Hrs Open:* 24; 1 kw-U, ND1; N28 16 54 W82 12 30
706 North Myrtle Avenue, Clearwater, FL 33755 US
(727) 441-3311; *Fax:* (727) 441-1300
www.tantalk1340.com
lola@tantalk1340.com
License: Zephyrhills, FL held by Wagenvoord Advertising Group Inc.
Group Owner: Wagenvoord Advertising Group Inc.; acq 2-13-02).
Nat'l Network: CNN Radio; CBS Radio
Arbitron Metro Market: Tampa-St. Peter; *Format:* Gospel, Talk
Special Programming: CHR 10 hrs wkly; *Target Audience:* 35-64; men & women; *Adv. Rates:* 65; 65; 65; 65;
Dave Wagenvoord, CEO
Lola Wagenvoord, Operations Dir

Zolfo Springs

WZZS
11-01-1992; 106.9 MHz FM; *Hrs Open:* 24; 5 kw; 358 ft.; N27 21 59 W81 47 52
7891 US Highway 17 South, Zolfo Springs, FL 33890 US
(863) 494-4111; *Fax:* (863) 494-4443
License: Zolfo Springs, Hardee County, FL held by Heartland Broadcasting Corp.
Regional Network: Florida's Radio Networks
Arbitron Metro Market: Zolfo Springs, FL; *Format:* Country
Special Programming: Gospel 2 hrs, farm one hr daily; *Hrs. of News Programming:* news progmg one hr wkly; *No. News Employees:* 1 *Target Audience:* General; DeSoto, Hardee and Highlands counties
Harold Kneller Jr., President
Janet Kneller, Operations Dir
Casey Williams, Sales & Station Manager
Billy Brown, Programming Director
Michael Williams, Sales Representative
Sherry Good, Office Manager

Georgia

Adel

WDDQ
10-01-1979; 92.1 MHz FM; *Hrs Open:* 24; 2.6 kw; 506 ft.; N31 8 15 W83 23 41
1203 West 4th Street, Ste 11, Adel, GA 31620 US
(229) 259-9301; *Fax:* (229) 559-1332
www.talk921.com
lauren@talk921.com
License: Adel, Cook County, GA held by Adventure Radio Group LLC
Arbitron Metro Market: Valdosta, GA; *Format:* Talk; *Target Audience:* 18-50.
Ron Hester, General Manager
Scott James, Owner/Manager

Albany

WALG
01-01-1940; 1590 kHz AM; *Hrs Open:* 24; 5 kw-D, DA2; 1 kw-N, DA2; N31 37 19 W84 9 9
1104 West Broad Avenue, Albany, GA 31707 US
(229) 888-5000; *Fax:* (229) 888-6018
www.1590walg.com
matt.patrick@cumulus.com
License: Albany, GA held by Cumulus Licensing Corp.
Group Owner: Cumulus Media Inc.; (acq 11-3-98; grpsl).
Nat'l Network: ABC; *Regional Network:* Southern Farm; *Nat'l Reps:* Katz Radio
Arbitron Metro Market: Albany, GA; *Format:* News, News/Talk, 86; *Target Audience:* General.
Roger Russell, Programming Director
Katy Edwards, Promotions Director
Reid Reker, Marketing Manager

WSRA
07-10-1962; 1250 kHz AM; 1 kw-D, ND1; 0.053 kw-N, ND1; N31 37 0 W84 9 32
P. O. Box 90, Thomasville, GA 31799 US
(229) 432-1250; *Fax:* (229) 432-1927
www.wsraradio.com
info@wsra.com
License: Albany, GA held by Livingston Fulton
Arbitron Metro Market: Albany, GA; *Format:* Sports; *Target Audience:* 25-54.
Livingston Fulton, President

***WWVO**
07-12-1990; 90.7 MHz FM; *Hrs Open:* 16; 5.5 kw; 305 ft.; N31 38 42 W84 21 15
2724 Ledo Road, Albany, GA 31707 US
(229) 698-3473; *Fax:* (229) 874-5015
wwvothevoice@gmail.com
License: Albany, Dougherty County, GA held by Lamad Ministries Inc.
Arbitron Metro Market: Albany, GA; *Format:* Religious; *Hrs. of News Programming:* News progmg 4 hrs wkly; *Target Audience:* 35 plus.
C. William Eidenire, President
Eric Eidenire, General Manager

WGPC
01-01-1933; 1450 kHz AM; *Hrs Open:* 24; 1 kw-U, ND1; N31 34 55 W84 11 58
1104 West Broad Avenue, Albany, GA 31707 US
(229) 888-5000; *Fax:* (229) 888-5960
License: Albany, GA held by Cumulus Licensing Corp.
Group Owner: Cumulus Media Inc.; (acq 11-3-98; $2.25 million with co-locatd FM).
Nat'l Network: CBS; Fox Sports; *Regional Network:* Ga. News Net.
Arbitron Metro Market: Albany, GA; *Format:* Sports, Easy Listening; *Hrs. of News Programming:* News progmg 20 hrs wkly; *Target Audience:* 25 plus; middle to upper income
Becca Monroe, Local Sales Manager
John Blake, Programming Director
Katy Edwards, Promotions Director
Reid Reker, Marketing Manager

WJIZ-FM
01-01-1965; 96.3 MHz FM; 100 kw; 466 ft.; N31 39 16 W84 10 36
809 South Westover Blvd., Albany, GA 31707 US
(229) 439-9704; *Fax:* (229) 439-1509
www.wjiz.com
License: Albany, Dougherty County, GA held by CC Licenses LLC
Group Owner: iHeartMedia
Nat'l Network: American Urban
Arbitron Metro Market: Albany, GA; *Format:* Urban Contemporary; *Target Audience:* 18-54.; *Adv. Rates:* 60; 40; 60; 40
Jennifer Newman, Market President
Chuck Thompson, General Sales Mgr
Miss Monique, Programming Director
Wes Carroll, Digital Content Director

WJYZ
11-01-1952; 960 kHz AM; *Hrs Open:* 24; 5 kw-D, DA2; 0.39 kw-N, DA2; N31 37 5 W84 10 31
809 South Westover Road, Albany, GA 31707 US
(229) 439-9704; *Fax:* (229) 439-1509
www.wjyz.com
License: Albany, GA held by CC Licenses LLC.
Group Owner: iHeartMedia; (acq 7-12-2000; grpsl).
Nat'l Network: American Urban; *Nat'l Reps:* D & R Radio
Arbitron Metro Market: Albany, GA; *Format:* Gospel; *Hrs. of News Programming:* News progmg 3.5 hrs wkly; *Target Audience:* 25-54.; *Adv. Rates:* 12; 15; 12; 10
Jennifer Newman, Market President
Chuck Thompson, Director of Sales

WKAK
02-22-1963; 104.5 MHz FM; *Hrs Open:* 24; 98 kw; 981 ft.; N31 32 57 W84 0 19
1104 West Broad Avenue, Albany, GA 31707 US
(229) 888-5000; *Fax:* (229) 888-5960
www.kcountry104.com
License: Albany, Dougherty County, GA
Group Owner: Cumulus Broadcasting
Arbitron Metro Market: Albany, GA; *Format:* Country; *Hrs. of News Programming:* News progmg 25 hrs wkly
Becca Monroe, Sales Manager
John Blake, Programming Director
Katy Edwards, Promotions Director
Reid Reker, Marketing Manager

WQVE
12-17-1972; 101.7 MHz FM; 6 kw; 299 ft.; N31 37 15 W84 9 11 US
(229) 888-5000; *Fax:* (912) 888-5960
www.wqvealbany.com
matt.patrick@cumulus.com
License: Albany, Dougherty County, GA
Group Owner: Cumulus Media Inc.
Arbitron Metro Market: Albany, GA; *Format:* Contemporary Hits/Top 40
Becca Monroe, Local Sales Manager
Roger Russell, Programming Director
Katy Edwards, Promotions Director
Reid Reker, Market Manager

***WUNV**
01-01-1990; 91.7 MHz FM; *Hrs Open:* 24; 3 kw; 328 ft.; N31 40 20 W84 3 27 *Rebroadcasts:* Rebroadcasts WJSP-FM Warm Springs 100%
260 - 14th Street, N.W., Atlanta, GA 30318 US
(404) 685-2690; *Fax:* (404) 685-2684
www.gpb.org
ask@gpb.org
License: Albany, Dougherty County, GA held by Georgia Public Telecommunications Commission.
Nat'l Network: PRI; NPR; *Wire Services:* AP
Arbitron Metro Market: Atlanta, GA *TV Affiliate:* GBP-TV; *Format:* News; *Hrs. of News Programming:* news progmg 40 hrs wkly; *No. News Employees:* 10; *Target Audience:* Adults: 35 plus.
Milton Clipper, Chief Executive Officer
Teya Ryan, President
Tom Barclay, Operations Dir
Rob Maynard, Programming Director
Nancy Zintak, Promotions Manager
Bonnie Bean, CFO

WMRG
93.5 MHz FM; 25 kw; 328 ft; N31 44 05 W84 30 06
1570 Northside Dr., Bldg. 200, Suite B, Atlanta, GA 30318 USA
(240) 605-7820
www.streetz935.com
License: Albany, GA held by Core Communicators North LLC
Group Owner: Core Communicators Broadcasting LLC
Format: Urban Contemporary
Steve Hegwood, President

Alma

WAWO
10-01-1957; 1400 kHz AM; *Hrs Open:* 24; 1 kw-U; N31 31 50 W82 27 45
Drawer F, 208 Douglas St., Alma, GA 31510
(912) 632-1000; *Fax:* (912) 632-9696
License: Alma, Bacon County, GA held by Blueberry Broadcasting Co. Inc.
Nat'l Network: CNN Radio; *Regional Network:* Ga. News Net.
Population Served: 35,000 *Special Programming:* Farm 2 hrs wkly; *Hrs. of News Programming:* news progmg 6 hrs wkly; *No. News Employees:* 1; *Target Audience:* General.
Debra Deen, General Manager

WAJQ-FM
05-14-1987; 104.3 MHz FM; 4.5 kw; 371 ft.; N31 36 26 W82 32 46
208 Douglas Street, PO Box F, Alma, GA 31510 US
(912) 632-1000; *Fax:* (912) 632-9696
License: Alma, Bacon County, GA
Arbitron Metro Market: Brunswick GA; *Format:* Country; *Target Audience:* General.
Bob Sass, Promotions Manager

Alpharetta

WLTA
08-25-1986; 1400 kHz AM; 1 kw-U, ND1; N34 3 49 W84 16 34 *Rebroadcasts:* Rebroadcasts WNIV(AM) Atlanta 80%
2970 Peachtree Rd., N.W., Suite 970, Atlanta, GA 30305 US
(404) 995-7300; *Fax:* (404) 816-0748
www.faithtalk970.com
adam.asher@salematlanta.com
License: Alpharetta, GA held by South Texas Broadcasting Inc.
Group Owner: Salem Communications Corp.; (acq 11-17-99; $8 million with WNIV(AM) Atlanta)
Arbitron Metro Market: Atlanta, GA; *Format:* News, Talk, 74; *Target Audience:* 25-49; upper middle to upper income
Mike Moran, General Manager
Adam Asher, Station Manager
Mitch Ambler, General Sales Mgr
John Stirzaker, Programming Director

Ambrose

WDMG-FM
12-01-1983; 97.9 MHz FM; *Hrs Open:* 24; 3.5 kw; 316 ft.; N31 31 51 W82 54 34
603 West 2nd Street, PO Box 7, Tifton, GA 31754 US
(912) 389-0995; *Fax:* (912) 383-8552
www.979thebigdog.com
traffic@charter.net
License: Ambrose, Coffee County, GA held by Broadcast South LLC.
Group Owner: Broadcast South LLC; (acq 11-15-2006; grpsl)

Format: Classic Rock
John Higgs, General Manager

Americus

*WBJY
01-01-2002; 89.3 MHz FM; 65 kw vert; 614 ft.; N31 38 22 W83 44 58
P.O. Box 3206, Tupelo, MS 38803 US
(662) 844-8888; *Fax:* (662) 842-6791
www.afr.net
faq@afa.net
License: Americus, Sumter County, GA held by American Family Association.
Group Owner: American Family Radio
Arbitron Metro Market: Americus, GA; *Format:* Christian
Tim Wildmon, President
Donald Wildmon, Founder
Buddy Smith, Sr VP
Ed Vitagliano, Exec VP
Randy Sharp, Director Of Special Projects
Meeke Addison, Director Of Communications
Abraham Hamilton III, General Counsel

WDEC-FM
09-12-1964; 94.7 MHz FM; 25 kw; 328 ft.; N31 53 52 W84 18 53
239 Ezzard St., Lawrenceville, GA 30046 USA
(229) 924-1390, (229) 924-6500
www.americusradio.com
License: Americus, Sumter County, GA held by Sumter Broadcasting Co.
Group Owner: Sumter Broadcasting Co. Inc.; (acq 1994; with co-located AM)
Nat'l Reps: Rgnl Reps
Arbitron Metro Market: Albany, GA; *Format:* Adult Contemp
Special Programming: Black 5 hrs, farm one hr wkly; *Hrs. of News Programming:* news progmg 2 hrs wkly; *No. News Employees:* 2

WISK-FM
09-01-1973; 98.7 MHz FM; *Hrs Open:* 24; 25 kw; 302 ft.; N32 4 51 W84 15 20
239 Ezzard St., Lawrenceville, GA 30046 USA
(229) 924-1390, (229) 924-6500
www.americusradio.com
License: Americus, Sumter County, GA held by Sumter Broadcasting Co. Inc.
Group Owner: Sumter Broadcasting Co. Inc.
Nat'l Reps: Rgnl Reps
Format: Country

*WFRP
01-01-2005; 88.7 MHz FM; 4.2 kw; 230 ft.; N32 5 34 W84 16 56
Rebroadcasts: Rebroadcasts WBFR(FM) Birmingham, AL 100%
Mailing Address: 4135 Nothgate, Suite 1, Sacramento, CA 95834 US
Second Address: 290 Hegenberger Rd., Oakland, CA 94621
(800) 543-1495; *Fax:* (916) 641-8238
www.familyradio.com
info@familyradio.com
License: Americus, Sumter County, GA held by Family Stations Inc.
Group Owner: Family Stations Inc.
Arbitron Metro Market: Americus, GA; *Format:* Christian, Religious
Harold Camping, President
Stanley Jackson, Operations Dir

Aragon

WTSH-FM
08-01-1989; 107.1 MHz FM; 45 kw; Ant 518 ft; N34 15 03 W84 59 05
20 John Davenport Dr., Rome, GA 30160
(706) 291-9496; *Fax:* (706) 235-7107
www.south107.com
License: Aragon, Polk County, GA held by Woman's World Broadcasting Inc.
Population Served: 496,000 *Target Audience:* 25-54.; *Adv. Rates:* 32; 29; 32; 28
Kevin Daniels, Operations Manager/Programming Director
Randy Quick, General Manager
Howard Toole, Sales Manager
Dustin Sledge, Engineering/Information Technology Director

Arcade

WNGC
11-01-1947; 106.1 MHz FM; *Hrs Open:* 24; 100 kw; 1,132 ft; N34 43 46 W83 29 29
1010 Tower Place, Watkinsville, GA 30677
(706) 549-1340,(706) 549-6222; *Fax:* (706) 546-0441
License: Arcade, Stephens County, GA held by Cox Radio Inc.
Group Owner: Cox Radio Inc.; (acq 8-1-2008; grpsl)
Population Served: 850,000 *Format:* Country; *Hrs. of News Programming:* news progmg 10 hrs wkly; *No. News Employees:* 1; *Target Audience:* 25-54; adults with disposable income
Pete de Graaff, Program Director
Russell Lawson, General Sales Manager
Josh Hill, Promotions Director
Timy Bryant, News Director
Heather Taylor, Digital Brand Manager

Ashburn

WFFM
01-01-1990; 105.7 MHz FM; 6 kw; 328 ft.; N31 41 17 W83 38 38
114 Kent Rd., Tifton, GA 31794 US
(229) 382-1340; *Fax:* (229) 386-8658
www.burnincountryradio.com
License: Ashburn, GA held by Plant Broadcasting LLC
Group Owner: Plant Broadcasting
Arbitron Metro Market: Ashburn, GA; *Format:* Country
Nettie Hatcher, General Manager

Athens

WFSH-FM
01-01-1964; 104.7 MHz FM; *Hrs Open:* 24; 24 kw; 1657 ft.; N33 52 2 W83 49 44
2970 Peachtree Road, NW, Suite 700, Atlanta, GA 30305 US
(404) 995-7300; *Fax:* (404) 816-0748
www.thefishatlanta.com
License: Athens, Clarke County, GA held by South Texas Broadcasting Inc.
Group Owner: Salem Communications Corp.; (acq 7-27-2000; grpsl).
Arbitron Metro Market: Atlanta, GA; *Format:* Christian *Special Programming:* Gospel 2 hrs wkly
Mike Moran, General Manager/Vice President of Operations
Kevin Isaacs, Sales Director
Mike Blakemore, Programming Director
Chad Davis:, Promotions Manager
C. J. Jackson, Chief Engineer
Mike Stoudt, Music Director

WGAU
05-01-1938; 1340 kHz AM; *Hrs Open:* 24; 1 kw-U; N33 56 28 W83 24 13
850 Bobbin Mill Rd., Athens, GA 30606 USA
(706) 549-6222; *Fax:* (706) 353-1220
www.wgauradio.com
matt.caesar@coxinc.com
License: Athens, Clarke County, GA held by Cox Radio Inc.
Group Owner: Cox Radio Inc.; (acq 8-1-2008; grpsl)
Nat'l Network: ABC
Population Served: 175,000 *Format:* News/Talk; *No. News Employees:* 3; *Target Audience:* 25-65 Male
Matt Caesar, Program Director
Tim Bryant, News Director
Russell Lawson, General Sales Manager
Josh Hill, Promotions Director
Heather Taylor, Digital Brand Media

*WMSL
10-01-1987; 88.9 MHz FM; *Hrs Open:* 24; 20 kw; 299 ft.; N33 54 25 W83 29 35
585 Prince Avenue, Athens, GA 30601 US
(770) 725-8890; *Fax:* (678) 753-0088
www.wmsl.fm
gm@wmsl.fm
License: Athens, Clarke County, GA held by Prince Avenue Baptist Christian School.
Nat'l Network: USA
Arbitron Metro Market: Athens, GA; *Format:* Christian; *Hrs. of News Programming:* news progmg 11 hrs wkly; *No. News Employees:* 1; *Target Audience:* 25-54; women
Cliff Langston, Operations Dir
Jim Hutto, General Manager
Nathan Collins, Programming Director
Dianne Hutto, Promotions Manager
Mitch Kimbrell, News Director
James Hutto, Music Director

WRFC
05-01-1948; 960 kHz AM; *Hrs Open:* 24; 5 kw-D, DAN; 2.5 kw-N, DAN; N33 59 58 W83 26 0
1010 Tower Place, Watkinsville, GA 30677 US
(706) 549-6222
www.960theref.com
david.johnston@coxinc.com
License: Athens, GA held by Cox Radio Inc.
Group Owner: Cox Radio Inc.; (acq 8-1-2008; grpsl)
Nat'l Network: ESPN Radio
Format: Sports, Talk *Special Programming:* Black 15 hrs wkly; *Hrs. of News Programming:* news progmg 10 hrs wkly; *No. News Employees:* 3; *Target Audience:* 25-54
David Johnston, Program Director
Russell Lawson, General Sales Manager
Josh Hill, Promotions Director
Heather Taylor, Digital Brand Managerl Manager

*WUGA
08-28-1987; 91.7 MHz FM; *Hrs Open:* 24; 6 kw; 325 ft.; N33 55 13 W83 14 46
Mailing Address: 260 - 14th Street, N.W., Atlanta, GA 30318 US
Second Address: Georgia Public Radio (HQ), 260 14th St. N.W., Atlanta, GA 30318
(706) 542-9842; *Fax:* (706) 542-6718
www.wuga.org
wuga@uga.edu
License: Athens, Clarke County, GA held by Georgia Public Telecommunications Commission.
Nat'l Network: PRI; NPR; *Regional Network:* Georgia Public Radio; *Wire Services:* AP
Arbitron Metro Market: Athens, GA; *Format:* News *Special Programming:* Folk 4 hrs, jazz 4 hrs wkly; *Hrs. of News Programming:* news progmg 5 hrs wkly; *No. News Employees:* 3; *Target Audience:* Adults: 35 plus.
Michael Cardin, Operations Dir
Jimmy Sanders, Station Manager
Jeff Dantre, News Director
Walt Howard, Chief Engineer
Abbie Thaxton, Traffic Manager
Michael Cardin, Production and Operations Manager

*WUOG
10-16-1972; 90.5 MHz FM; *Hrs Open:* 24; 26 kw; 180 ft.; N33 56 59 W83 22 58
P.O. Box 2065, Athens, GA 30612 US
(706) 542-7100; *Fax:* (706) 542-0070
www.wuog.org
info@wuog.org
License: Athens, Clarke County, GA held by University of Georgia.
Regional Network: Ga. News Net.
Arbitron Metro Market: Athens, GA; *Format:* Alternative; *Hrs. of News Programming:* news progmg 4 hrs wkly; *No. News Employees:* 3; *Target Audience:* 18-25; students & faculty of Univ
Akeeme Martin, Operations Dir
Sarah Lawrence, General Manager
Eli Gaultney, Programming Director
Ella Grace Downs, Promotions Manager
Jason Flynn, News Director
David Sanders, Sports Director
Ryan Rudder, Music Director
Caroline Marchildon, Public Affairs Director

WXAG
06-10-1957; 1470 kHz AM
3166 Robinwood Trail, Decatur, GA 30034 US
(706) 552-1470; *Fax:* (706) 425-0847
www.1470wxag.com
License: Athens, GA held by Mecca Communications Inc.
Arbitron Metro Market: Athens, GA; *Format:* Gospel, Religious
Michael Thurmond, General Manager
James Ford, Station Manager
Yvonne Robert, Advertising Manager

Atlanta

*WABE
09-13-1948; 90.1 MHz FM; *Hrs Open:* 24; 100 kw; 1096 ft.; N33 45 33 W84 20 5
740 Bismark Road, N. E., Atlanta, GA 30324 US
(760) 954-6655; *Fax:* (760) 872-4155
License: Atlanta, Fulton County, GA held by Board of Education of the City of Atlanta.
Nat'l Network: NPR; PRI; *Wire Services:* AP
Arbitron Metro Market: Tucson AZ
Daniel McClenaghan, President

WAEC
01-01-1947; 860 kHz AM; 2.5 kw-C, DAN; 5 kw-D, DAN; 0.5 kw-N, DA; N33 43 45 W84 19 19
3033 Riviera Dr., Suite 200, Naples, FL 34103 US
(239) 263-5000; *Fax:* (239) 263-8191
www.love860.com
License: Atlanta, Fulton County, GA held by Beasley Media Group LLC
Group Owner: Beasley Broadcast Group Inc.; (acq 10-29-99)
Arbitron Metro Market: Atlanta, GA; *Format:* Christian, Religious; *Adv. Rates:* 40; 35; 35; 20
LeAnder Cooper, General Manager

WGKA
03-17-1922; 920 kHz AM
Suite 200, Bldg. 15, 1820 Powers Ferry Rd., Atlanta, GA 30339 US
(404) 995-7300; *Fax:* (404) 816-0748
www.talk920.com
adam.asher@salematlanta.com
License: Atlanta, GA held by Pennsylvania Media Associates Inc.
Group Owner: Salem Communications Corp.; (acq 6-28-2004; $16.4 million).
Arbitron Metro Market: Atlanta, GA; *Format:* News, News/Talk, 86; *Target Audience:* General.
Jeff Carter, Operations Dir
Mitch Amber, General Manager
David Koon, General Sales Mgr

WIFN
11-20-1965; 1340 kHz AM; *Hrs Open:* 24; 1 kw-U; N33 44 56 W84 24 26
3535 Piedmont Rd., Bldg. 14, Suite 1200, Atlanta, GA 30305
(404) 688-0068; *Fax:* (404) 995-4045
scottmcfarlane@680thefan.com
License: Atlanta, Fulton County, GA held by Dickey Broadcasting Co.
Group Owner: Dickey Broadcasting Co.; (acq 8-31-2000; grpsl)
Nat'l Network: Fox Sports; *Nat'l Reps:* McGavren Guild; *Wire Services:* AP
Population Served: 496,973; *Arbitron Metro Market:* Atlanta, GA; *Adv. Rates:* 100; 100; 100; 50
Scott McFarlane, Operations Dir
David Dickey, General Manager
Rob Hasson, General Sales Mgr

WAOK
03-15-1954; 1380 kHz AM; 25 kW-D, 4.2 kW-N; 364 ft.; N33 45 36 W84 28 45
1201 Peachtree St., Suite 800, Atlanta, GA 30361 USA
(404) 898-8900; *Fax:* (404) 898-8915
www.waok.com
License: Atlanta, Fulton County, GA held by CBS Radio East Inc.
Group Owner: CBS Radio; (acq 1996; grpsl).
Nat'l Network: CBS
Arbitron Metro Market: Atlanta, GA; *Format:* News/Talk, News, 86; *Hrs. of News Programming:* news progmg 50 hrs wkly; *No. News Employees:* 5; *Target Audience:* 25-54
Jean Ross, Operations Manager
Reggie Rouse, Programming Director
Jean Ross, News Director
Ashley Roberson, Digital Sales Director

***WCLK**
04-10-1974; 91.9 MHz FM; 6 kw; 308 ft.; N33 44 56 W84 24 26
111 James P Brawley Dr, S.W., Atlanta, GA 30314 US
(404) 880-8284(404) 880-8278; *Fax:* (404) 880-8869
www.wclk.com
wclkfm@cau.edu
License: Atlanta, Fulton County, GA held by Clark Atlanta University.
Nat'l Network: NPR; PRI
Arbitron Metro Market: Atlanta, GA; *Format:* Jazz *Special Programming:* Gospel 17 hrs, reggae 3 hrs, blues 3 hrs, info/talk 12 hrs wkly; *No. News Employees:* 16; *Target Audience:* 25-49; upscale, college educated,primarily African American
Wendy Williams, General Manager
Tammy Nobles, Station Manager
Aaron Cohen, Programming Director
Reginald Hicks, Development Director
Ray Cobb, Underwriting Manager

WDWD
07-01-1938; 590 kHz AM
77 West 66th Street, 16th Fl, New York, NY 10023 US
(770) 541-0590; *Fax:* (770) 952-7461
www.radiodisney.com/atlanta
License: Atlanta, GA held by Radio Disney Atlanta LLC.
Group Owner: ABC Inc.; (acq 5-17-85; $6.85 million;
Nat'l Network: ABC; *Nat'l Reps:* Interep
Arbitron Metro Market: Atlanta, GA; *Format:* Children; *Target Audience:* Children 6-14 Adults 25-54.; *Adv. Rates:* 125; 125; 125; 125
Melissa Munro, Operations Dir
Shawn Serra, Station Manager

WAFS
09-01-1955; 1190 kHz AM; *Hrs Open:* Sunrise-sunset
2970 Peachtree Road, Suite 700, Atlanta, GA 30305 US
(404) 995-7300; *Fax:* (404) 816-0748
www.biz1190.com
License: Atlanta, GA held by South Texas Broadcasting Inc.
Group Owner: Salem Communications Corp.; (acq 4-4-2000; $8 million).
Arbitron Metro Market: Atlanta, GA; *Format:* Gospel; *Target Audience:* 35-64.
Mike Moran, General Manager/Vice President of Operations

WGST
04-07-1988; 640 kHz AM; *Hrs Open:* 24; 50 kw-D, DA2; 1 kw-N, DA2; N33 45 43 W84 27 29 *Rebroadcasts:* Rebroadcasts WHEL(FM) Helen 100%
1819 Peachtree Road Northeast, Suite 700, Atlanta, GA 30309 US
(404) 367-0640; *Fax:* (404) 367-1100
www.640wgst.com
License: Atlanta, GA held by Citicasters Licenses Inc.
Group Owner: iHeartMedia
Wire Services: AP
Arbitron Metro Market: Atlanta, GA; *Format:* News, News/Talk, 86; *Target Audience:* 25-54.
Art Volpe, General Sales Mgr
Dan Hunt, Programming Director
Melissa Krinsky, Marketing Director
Steve Garza, Digital Program Director

WTZA
07-01-1947; 1010 kHz AM; *Hrs Open:* 24
2901 Mt. Industrial Blvd, Tucker, GA 30084 US
(770) 491-1010; *Fax:* (770) 491-3019
License: Atlanta, GA held by Dee Rivers Group.
Arbitron Metro Market: Atlanta, GA; *Format:* Talk, Religious; *Hrs. of News Programming:* News progmg one hr wkly; *Target Audience:* 25-54; working class
Georgia Salva, CEO
Erwin Hill, Operations Dir
Darrell Vick, General Manager

WWPW
12-02-1960; 96.1 MHz FM; *Hrs Open:* 24; 99 kw; Ant 984 ft; N33 48 27 W84 20 26
1819 Peachtree Rd. N.E., Suite 700, Atlanta, GA 30309 US
(404) 875-8080; *Fax:* (404) 367-1155
www.power961.com
License: Atlanta, Fulton County, GA held by Citicasters Licenses Inc.
Group Owner: iHeartMedia; (acq 5-4-99; grpsl)
Population Served: 3,500,000; *Arbitron Metro Market:* Atlanta, GA; *Format:* Contemporary Hits/Top 40; *Hrs. of News Programming:* News progmg 7 hrs wkly; *Target Audience:* 25-49; primarily male
Justin Schaflander, Market President
Art Volpe, General Sales Mgr
Dan Hunt, Programming Director
Matt Sheffield, Promotions Manager
Steven Garza, Digital Program Director

WNIV
01-01-1948; 970 kHz AM; *Hrs Open:* 24; 5 kw-D, ND2; 0.039 kw-N, ND2; N33 48 35 W84 21 14
2970 Peachtree Road, 8th Floor, Atlanta, GA 30305 US
(404) 995-7300; *Fax:* (404) 816-0748
www.faithtalk970.com
adam.asher@salematlanta.comÿ
License: Atlanta, GA held by South Texas Broadcasting Inc.
Group Owner: Salem Communications Corp.; (acq 11-17-99; $8 million with WLTA(AM) Alpharetta)
Arbitron Metro Market: Atlanta, GA; *Format:* Christian, Talk; *Hrs. of News Programming:* news progmg 7 hrs wkly; *No. News Employees:* 1; *Target Audience:* 25-49; educated adults, upper middle to upper income
Stuart Epperson, Chairman
Edward Atsinger III, President
Mike Moran, General Manager
Adam Asher, Station Manager
Mitch Ambler, General Sales Mgr
John Stirzaker, Programming Director
C. J. Jackson, Chief Engineer

WWWQ
01-01-1955; 99.7 MHz FM; 100 kw; 1115 ft.; N33 48 26 W84 20 22
780 Johnson Ferry Rd. NE, 5th Floor, Atlanta, GA 30342 US
(404) 497-4700
www.q100atlanta.com
License: Atlanta, GA held by Radio License Holding SRC, LLC
Group Owner: Cumulus Media Inc.; (acq 2-28-74)
Nat'l Reps: Cumulus Radio Sales
Arbitron Metro Market: Atlanta, GA; *Format:* Contemporary Hits/Top 40
Joyce Harms, Operations Dir

WUBL
02-18-1962; 94.9 MHz FM; *Hrs Open:* 24; 99 kw; 978 ft.; N33 48 27 W84 20 27
1819 Peachtree Road Northeast, Suite 700, Atlanta, GA 30309 US
(404) 875-8080; *Fax:* (404) 367-9490
www.949thebull.com
License: Atlanta, Fulton County, GA held by Citicasters Licenses Inc.
Group Owner: iHeartMedia
Nat'l Network: ABC
Arbitron Metro Market: Atlanta, GA; *Format:* Country
Jason Mosher, Vice President of Sales
Brian Michel, Programming Director
Melissa Krinsky, Promotions Manager
Steve Garza, Digital Program Director
Quenest Harrington, Online Content Manager

WQXI
10-01-1947; 790 kHz AM
210 Interstate North Circle, Suite 100, Atlanta, GA 30339 US
(404) 237-0079; *Fax:* (404) 231-5923
www.star941atlanta.com
License: Atlanta, GA held by Jefferson Pilot Communications Co.
Group Owner: Entercom; (acq 2016)
Arbitron Metro Market: Atlanta, GA; *Format:* Contemporary Hits/Top 40, Adult Contemp; *Target Audience:* 18-54; men
Neal Maziar, Operations Director/General Manager
Bob Richards, Programming Director
Leslie Smith, Promotions Manager
Leslie Hoar, Promotions Manager

***WRAS**
01-18-1971; 88.5 MHz FM; *Hrs Open:* 24; 100 kw; 436 ft.; N33 41 4 W84 17 23
University Plaza, Atlanta, GA 30303 US
(404) 413-1630; *Fax:* (404) 463-9535
www.wras.org
License: Atlanta, Fulton County, GA held by Georgia State University.
Arbitron Metro Market: Atlanta, GA; *Format:* Talk *Special Programming:* Classical 3 hrs, world 3 hrs, reggae 4 hrs, new age 3 hrs, rap/hip-hop 6 hrs wkly; *Hrs. of News Programming:* News progmg 6 hrs wkly *TargetAudience:* 18-34; college students
Dr. Kurt Keppler, CEO
Brady Rainey, General Manager
Andy Hawley, Programming Director
Michael Valania, Promotions Manager
Tom Taylor, Chief Engineer
Todd Wiese, Music Director

***WREK**
04-01-1968; 91.1 MHz FM; *Hrs Open:* 24; 100 kw; 335 ft.; N33 46 41 W84 24 22
165 Eighth Street, Atlanta, GA 30332 US
(404) 894-2468; *Fax:* (404) 894-6872
www.wrek.org
wrek@gatech.edu
License: Atlanta, Fulton County, GA held by Radio Communications Board, Georgia Institute of Technology.
Regional Network: Ga. News Net.
Arbitron Metro Market: Atlanta, GA; *Format:* Ethnic, Variety/Diverse *Special Programming:* Experimental 18 hrs, jazz 15 hrs, class 15 hrs wkly; *Target Audience:* General.
Andrea Kuklenyik, Operations Dir
Cody Turner, General Manager
Maria Sotnikova, Programming Director

***WRFG**
07-15-1973; 89.3 MHz FM; *Hrs Open:* 24; 65 kw; 486 ft.; N33 48 26 W84 20 22
1083 Austin Avenue Ne, Atlanta, GA 30307 US
(404) 523-3471; *Fax:* (404) 523-8990
www.wrfg.org
info@wrfg.org
License: Atlanta, Fulton County, GA held by Radio Free Georgia Broadcasting Foundation Inc.
Arbitron Metro Market: Atlanta, GA; *Format:* Easy Listening *Special Programming:* , Indian 3 hrs, Sp 5 hrs wkly; *Hrs. of News Programming:* News progmg 3 hrs wkly; *Target Audience:* 18-45; socially consciousAfrican-Americans
Wanique Shabazz, Operations Dir
Joan Baptist, Station Manager

WSB
03-15-1922; 750 kHz AM; *Hrs Open:* 24; 50 kw-U, ND1; N33 50 38 W84 15 12
1601 West Peachtree Street NE, Atlanta, GA 30309 US
(404) 897-7000; *Fax:* (404) 897-7363
www.wsbradio.com

License: Atlanta, GA held by Cox Radio Inc.
Group Owner: Cox Radio Inc.
Nat'l Network: Fox News; *Nat'l Reps:* Christal
Arbitron Metro Market: Atlanta, GA; *Format:* News, News/Talk, 86; *Hrs. of News Programming:* news progmg 168 hrs wkly; *No. News Employees:* 9; *Target Audience:* 25-54.
Pete Spriggs, Program Director
Ben Reed, VP, Market Manager

WSB-FM
11-10-1944; 98.5 MHz FM; 100 kw; 1027 ft.; N33 45 33 W84 20 5
3773 Howard Hughes Pwy, Suite 300n, Las Vegas, NV 89109 US
(404) 897-7500; *Fax:* (404) 897-7363
www.b985.com
License: Atlanta, Fulton County, GA
Group Owner: Cox Radio Inc.
Arbitron Metro Market: Atlanta, GA *TV Affiliate:* WSB-TV affil; *Format:* Adult Contemp; *Hrs. of News Programming:* news progmg 3.5 hrs wkly; *No. News Employees:* 1; *Target Audience:* 25-54.
Francisco Luciano, General Sales Mgr
Chris Eagan, Programming Director
Dave Clapper, Promotions Manager
Dan Kearney, VP, Market Manager

WVEE
07-01-1948; 103.3 MHz FM; 100 kW; 958 ft.; N33 45 33 W84 20 5
1201 Peachtree St., Suite 800, Atlanta, GA 30361 USA
(404) 898-8900; *Fax:* (404) 898-8915
www.v-103.com
License: Atlanta, Fulton County, GA held by CBS Radio East Inc.
Group Owner: CBS Radio
Arbitron Metro Market: Atlanta, GA; *Format:* Urban Contemporary; *No. News Employees:* 2; *Target Audience:* 18-49
Jean Ross, Operations Manager
Reggie Rouse, Programming Director
Jean Ross, News Director
Ashley Roberson, Digital Sales Manager

WYZE
06-01-1957; 1480 kHz AM
1776 Briarcliff Rd, Atlanta, GA 30306 US
(404) 622-7802; *Fax:* (404) 622-6767
am1480wyze@aol.com
License: Atlanta, GA held by GHB Broadcasting Inc.
Group Owner: GHB Radio Group
Regional Network: Ga. News Net.
Arbitron Metro Market: Atlanta, GA; *Format:* Black, Gospel
George Buck Jr., President
Jacob Bogan, Station Manager

WZGC
09-01-1965; 92.9 MHz FM; *Hrs Open:* 24; 64 kW; 1141 ft.; N33 48 26 W84 20 21.8
1201 Peachtree St., Suite 800, Atlanta, GA 30361 USA
(404) 898-8900; *Fax:* (404) 898-8916
www.929thegame.com
License: Atlanta, Fulton County, GA held by CBS Radio Inc. of Atlanta
Group Owner: CBS Radio; (acq 11-13-98; grpsl).
Nat'l Network: Westwood One; *Nat'l Reps:* Katz Radio
Arbitron Metro Market: Atlanta, GA; *Format:* Sports; *Hrs. of News Programming:* news progmg 2 hrs wkly; *No. News Employees:* 1; *Target Audience:* 25-54; upscale baby boomers
Ashley Roberson, Digital Sales Manager

Augusta

***WACG-FM**
06-02-1970; 90.7 MHz FM; *Hrs Open:* 24; 3.7 kw horiz; 1381 ft.; N33 24 18 W81 50 15 *Rebroadcasts:* Rebroadcasts WJSP-FM Warm Springs 75%
Mailing Address: 260 - 14th Street, N.W., Atlanta, GA 30318 US
Second Address: 2500 Walton Way, Augusta, GA 30904
(956) 487-8015
License: Augusta, Richmond County, GA held by Georgia Public Telecommunications Commission.
Nat'l Network: PRI; NPR; *Wire Services:* AP
Arbitron Metro Market: De Queen AR
Eloy Vera, General Manager

WRDW
01-01-2001; 1630 kHz AM; 10 kw-D, ND1; 1 kw-N, ND1; N33 31 0 W82 0 36
4051 Jimmie Dyess Pkwy., Augusta, GA 30909 US
(706) 396-7000
License: Augusta, Richmond County, GA held by Beasley Media Group LLC
Group Owner: Beasley Broadcast Group Inc.; (acq 2-23-2000).
Arbitron Metro Market: Augusta, GA; *Format:* Sports, Talk
Chris O'Kelley, Operations Manager
Kent Murphy, General Sales Mgr
Harley Drew, Programming Director
Mark Haddon, Vice President/Market Manager
Georgia Beasley, Digital Sales Manager

WYNF
01-12-1947; 1340 kHz AM; *Hrs Open:* 24; 1 kw-U; N33 27 46 W82 00 29
2743 Perimeter Pkwy., Bldg. 100, Suite 300, Augusta, GA 53202
(706) 396-6000; *Fax:* (706) 396-6010
www.foxsportsaugusta.com
License: Augusta, Richmond County, GA held by Capstar TX LLC
Group Owner: iHeartMedia
Population Served: 425,000; *Arbitron Metro Market:* Augusta, GA; *Format:* Sports; *Target Audience:* Children.
Ivy Elam, Market President
Sabrena Martin, General Sales Mgr
Cliff Bennett, Program Director/Digital Content Director
Andrew Harman, Promotions Coordinator
Cynthia Robinson, Business Manager

WBBQ-FM
03-01-1955; 104.3 MHz FM; *Hrs Open:* 24; 78 kw; 1430 ft.; N33 25 16.6 W81 50 18.6
2743 Perimeter Parkway, Bldg. 100, Suite 300, Augusta, GA 53202 US
(706) 396-6000
www.wbbq.com
License: Augusta, Richmond County, GA held by Capstar TX LLC
Group Owner: iHeartMedia; (acq 12-19-2000; grpsl).
Arbitron Metro Market: Augusta, GA; *Format:* Adult Contemp
Ivy Elam, Market President
Sabrena Martin, General Sales Mgr
Cliff Bennett, Program Director/Digital Content Director
Andrew Harman, Promotions Coordinator
Cynthia Robinson, Business Manager

WEKL
11-11-1967; 102.3 MHz FM; *Hrs Open:* 24; 1.5 kw; Ant 666 ft; N33 26 15 W82 05 27
2743 Perimeter Pkwy., Bldg. 100, Suite 200, Augusta, GA 53202
License: Augusta, Richmond County, GA held by Aloha Station Trust LLC
Arbitron Metro Market: Augusta, GA; *Hrs. of News Programming:* news progmg 3 hrs wkly; *No. News Employees:* 1; *Target Audience:* 18-34.
Tim Lawandus, General Sales Mgr
Bill West, Programming Director
Robb Tomas, Promotions Manager

WFAM
03-10-1952; 1050 kHz AM; *Hrs Open:* 24; 5 kw-D, ND2; 0.082 kw-N, ND2; N33 27 21 W81 56 20
552 Laney-Walker Blvd. Ext., Augusta, GA 30901 US
(706) 722-6077
www.wilkinsradio.com
denise@wilkinsradio.com
License: Augusta, GA held by J.J. & B. Broadcasting Inc.
Group Owner: Wilkins Communications Network Inc.; (acq 11-22-96; $330,000).
Nat'l Network: Salem Radio Network; *Nat'l Reps:* Salem
Arbitron Metro Market: Augusta, GA; *Format:* Christian, Talk; *Hrs. of News Programming:* News progmg 2 hrs wkly; *Target Audience:* 35 plus.; *Adv. Rates:* 30; 30; 30; 30
Michelle Mitchell, Station Manager

WFXA-FM
07-11-1968; 103.1 MHz FM; *Hrs Open:* 24; 6 kw; 302 ft.; N33 30 0 W81 56 3
6025 Broadcast Dr., North Augusta, SC US
(803) 279-2330
www.103jamzthefox.com
License: Augusta, Richmond County, GA held by Perry Broadcasting of Augusta Inc.
Group Owner: Perry Publishing & Broadcasting Co.; (acq 12-12-2007; grpsl)
Arbitron Metro Market: Augusta, GA; *Format:* Black; *Target Audience:* 25-34; females; *Adv. Rates:* 85; 80; 85; 75
Velvet Perry, General Sales Mgr

WGAC
01-01-1940; 580 kHz AM; 5 kw-D, 0.84 kw-N; N33 30 44 W82 4 48 *Rebroadcasts:* Simulcast with WGAC-FM Warrenton
4051 Jimmie Dyess Pkwy., Augusta, GA 30909 US
(706) 396-7000; *Fax:* (706) 396-7100
www.wgac.com
License: Augusta, Richmond County, GA held by Beasley Media Group LLC
Group Owner: Beasley Broadcast Group Inc.; (acq 5-19-92; assumption of debt;
Nat'l Network: CBS Radio; *Nat'l Reps:* D & R Radio
Arbitron Metro Market: Augusta, GA; *Format:* News, News/Talk, 84, Talk *Special Programming:* Farm 4 hrs, military 3 hrs wkly, Rush Limbaugh Affil.; *No. News Employees:* 5; *Target Audience:* 35-65.
Chris O'Kelley, Operations Manager
Kent Murphy, General Sales Mgr
Mark Haddon, Vice President/Market Manager
Georgia Beasley, Digital Sales Manager

WEZO
11-01-1993; 1230 kHz AM; *Hrs Open:* 24; 1 kw-U; N33 27 14 W82 01 47
1286 Broad St., Augusta, GA 30906
(706) 922-3834; *Fax:* (706) 922-3831
License: Augusta, Richmond County, GA held by Will Nunley Broadcasting LLC
Nat'l Network: CNN Radio; Premiere Radio Networks; Westwood One; *Regional Network:* Ga. News Net.
Population Served: 350,000; *Arbitron Metro Market:* Augusta, GA; *Hrs. of News Programming:* 24 hrs wkly; *No. News Employees:* 3; *Target Audience:* 25- women; 25+ men.; *Adv. Rates:* 7; 7; 7; 7
Will Nunley, General Manager
Teri Exrleben, General Sales Mgr

***WLPE**
11-17-1984; 91.7 MHz FM; *Hrs Open:* 24; 1.15 kw; 589 ft.; N33 34 21 W81 55 23
3213 Huxley Dr, Augusta, GA 30909 US
(706) 309-9610; *Fax:* (706) 309-9669
www.gnnradio.org
ctbarinowski@comcast.net
License: Augusta, Richmond County, GA held by Augusta Radio Fellowship Institute Inc.
Arbitron Metro Market: Augusta, GA; *Format:* Christian; *Hrs. of News Programming:* News progmg 12 hrs wkly; *Target Audience:* General.
Clarence Barinowski, General Manager

WTHB
05-01-1960; 1550 kHz AM; 5 kw-D, ND2; 0.011 kw-N, ND2; N33 30 0 W81 56 3
6025 Broadcast Dr., North Augusta, SC 29841 US
(803) 279-2330; *Fax:* (803) 279-8149
praise969.com
License: Augusta, GA held by Perry Broadcasting of Augusta Inc.
Group Owner: Perry Publishing & Broadcasting Co.
Nat'l Network: American Urban
Arbitron Metro Market: Augusta, GA; *Format:* Gospel; *Adv. Rates:* 40; 35; 40; 35
Velvet Perry, VP Director of Sales

WSCG
03-10-1952; 105.7 MHz FM; *Hrs Open:* 24; 100 kw; 1217 ft.; N33 25 17 W81 50 19
2743 Perimeter Parkway, Building 100, Suite 300, Augusta, GA 30909 US
(706) 396-6000; *Fax:* (706) 396-6010
www.g1057.com
License: Augusta, Richmond County, GA held by Capstar TX LLC
Group Owner: iHeartMedia; (acq 12-19-2000; grpsl)
Arbitron Metro Market: Augusta, GA; *Format:* Country; *Target Audience:* 18-44.
Ivy Elam, Market President
Sabrena Martin, General Sales Mgr
Jay Cruze, Programming Director
Andrew Harman, Promotions Coordinator
Cliff Bennett, Digital Content Director
Cynthia Robinson, Business Manager

Austell

WAOS
04-16-1968; 1600 kHz AM; *Hrs Open:* 24; 20 kw-D, ND2; 0.067 kw-N, ND2; N33 48 34 W84 39 25
5815 Westside Road, Austell, GA 30001 US
(770) 944-0900; *Fax:* (770) 944-9794
www.lamejorestacion.com
sammy@lamejorestacion.com
License: Austell, Cobb County, GA held by La Favorita Inc.
Group Owner: La Favorita Radio Network; (acq 1-24-90)
Arbitron Metro Market: Atlanta, GA; *Format:* Spanish; *Target Audience:* 18 plus; Hispanics in metro Atlanta & northeast GA
Samuel Zamarron, President
Nelson Gomez, General Manager

Avondale Estates

WMLB
11-01-2003; 1690 kHz AM; *Hrs Open:* 24
1200 West 4th Street, Adel, GA 31620 US
(307) 733-4030
www.jhcr.org
info@jhcr.org
License: Avondale Estates, GA held by JW Broadcasting Inc.
Format: Variety/Diverse
Jim Tallichet, General Manager

Bainbridge

WMGR
08-17-1947; 930 kHz AM; *Hrs Open:* 18; 5 kw-D, DAN; 0.5 kw-N, DAN; N30 54 25 W84 33 2
809 S. Westover Blvd., Albany, GA 31707 US
(229) 246-1650; *Fax:* (229) 246-1403
www.wmgr.net
wmgr@wmgr.net
License: Bainbridge, GA held by Decatur Broadcasting Inc.
Regional Network: Ga. News Net.
Arbitron Metro Market: Bainbridge, GA; *Format:* Oldies; *Hrs. of News Programming:* News progmg 10 hrs wkly; *Target Audience:* 30 plus.
Coley Voyles, President

WGEX
12-20-1967; 97.3 MHz FM; *Hrs Open:* 24; 100 kw; 1,200 ft; N31 09 12 W84 32 42
809 S. Westover Blvd., Albany, GA 31707 US
(229) 439-9704; *Fax:* (229) 439-1509
www.973hitmusicnow.com
License: Bainbridge, Decatur County, GA held by CC Licenses LLC.
Group Owner: iHeartMedia; (acq 7-11-2000; grpsl).
Nat'l Reps: Christal
Population Served: 900,000; *Arbitron Metro Market:* Albany, GA; *Format:* Contemporary Hits/Top 40; *Hrs. of News Programming:* News progmg 2 hrs wkly; *Target Audience:* 18-49.; *Adv. Rates:* 45; 40; 45; 35
Chuck Thompson, General Sales Mgr
Brian Thomas, Programming Director
Wes Carroll, Digital Content Director

WBGE
05-01-2001; 101.9 MHz FM; 6 kw; 328 ft.; N31 0 33 W84 25 16
4143 East River Road, Camilla, GA 31730 US
(229) 246-7776; *Fax:* (229) 246-9995
www.live1019.com
License: Bainbridge, Decatur County, GA held by Flint Media Inc.
Group Owner: Flint Media Inc.; (acq 7-15-2005; $485,000)
Format: Adult Contemp
Kevin Dowdy, General Manager

Barnesville

WBAF
07-23-1966; 1090 kHz AM; 1 kw-D, NDD; N33 3 13 W84 8 7
645 Forsyth Street, Barnesville, GA 30204 US
(309) 834-1100; *Fax:* (309) 834-4390
www.magic1007.fm
License: Barnesville, GA held by Barnesville Broadcasting Inc.
Regional Network: Ga. News Net.
Format: Adult Contemp; *Target Audience:* 25-54; adult
Jack Swart, General Manager
Grant Thompson, General Sales Mgr
Chad Fasig, Programming Director
Mark Hill, Chief Engineer

Baxley

WBYZ
07-01-1983; 94.5 MHz FM; *Hrs Open:* 24; 100 kw; Ant 1,014 ft; N31 47 10 W82 27 03
Mailing Address: Box 390, Baxley, GA 31513
Second Address: 4005 Golden Isles W., Baxley, GA 31515
(912) 367-3000; *Fax:* (912) 367-9779
www.wbyz.com
peggy@wbyz94.com
License: Baxley, Appling County, GA
Nat'l Network: ABC; *Regional Network:* Ga. News Net.
Target Audience: 20-55; those with buying power
Al Graham, President
Peggy Miles, Operations Dir
Peggy Miles, General Manager
Peggy Miles, Station Manager
Peggy Miles, General Sales Mgr
Al Graham, Programming Director
Peggy Miles, Promotions Manager
Cole Younger, NewsDirector
Dick Boekloo, Chief Engineer
Alan DuPriest, Music Director

WUFE
12-01-1954; 1260 kHz AM; *Hrs Open:* 6 AM-sunset; 5 kw-D; N31 48 00 W82 24 40
Mailing Address: Box 390, Baxley, GA 31513
Second Address: Hwy. 341 W., Baxley, GA 31515
(912) 367-3000; *Fax:* (912) 367-9779
License: Baxley, Appling County, GA held by South Georgia Broadcasters Inc.
Regional Network: Ga. News Net.
Population Served: 75,000 *Hrs. of News Programming:* News progmg 6 hrs wkly; *Target Audience:* General.
Al Graham, President
Peggy Miles, General Manager
Peggy Miles, Station Manager
Peggy Miles, General Sales Mgr
Dick Boeklod, Chief Engineer

Blackshear

WFNS
03-10-1961; 1350 kHz AM; 2.5 kw-D, ND1; 0.117 kw-N, ND1; N31 18 44 W82 14 0
245 Main Street, Blackshear, GA 31516 US
(912) 285-5002; *Fax:* (912) 285-3877
wgaradio@yahoo.com
License: Blackshear, GA held by MarMac Communications LLC.
Group Owner: MarMac Communications LLC; (acq 7-19-2001; $60,000)
Nat'l Network: CNN Radio; *Regional Network:* Ga. News Net.
Format: Sports *Special Programming:* Atlanta Braves, Hawks, Falcons, Ga Tech; *Target Audience:* General; families; *Adv. Rates:* 6; 5; 6; 5
Gary Marmitt, President
Sharon McKeand, Operations Dir
Charlie Kanons, General Sales Mgr
Kevin Thomas, News Director

WKUB
12-01-1979; 105.1 MHz FM; *Hrs Open:* 24; 50 kw; 348 ft.; N31 10 54 W82 22 51
Mailing Address: P.O. Box 112, Blackshear, GA 31516 US
Second Address: Box 1472, Waycross, GA 31502
(912) 449-3391; *Fax:* (912) 449-6284
www.waycrossradio.com
wkub@almatel.net
License: Blackshear, Pierce County, GA held by Mattox Broadcasting Inc.
Nat'l Network: ABC; *Regional Network:* Ga. News Net; *Nat'l Reps:* Dora-Clayton
Format: Country; *Hrs. of News Programming:* News progmg 4 hrs wkly; *Target Audience:* 25 plus.
G. Troy Mattox, President
Jim MIller, General Sales Mgr

Blakely

WBBK-FM
11-01-1984; 93.1 MHz FM; 45 kw; 328 ft.; N31 17 55 W85 3 18
P.O. Box 87, Donalsonville, GA 31745 US
(910) 253-6593
www.kjbbfm.com
info@kjbbfm.com
License: Blakely, Early County, GA held by Alabama Media LLC
Group Owner: Alabama Media LLC; (acq 5-13-2004; grpsl)
Arbitron Metro Market: Modesto CA; *Format:* Christian
Danny Hawkins, President

Blue Ridge

WPPL
01-01-1971; 103.9 MHz FM; *Hrs Open:* 24; 5.5 kw; 341 ft.; N34 52 3 W84 20 2
Mailing Address: 3350 Comberland Circl, Suite 1700 Riverwood, Atlanta, GA 30339 US
Second Address: 333 W. Highland St., Blue Ridge, GA 35013
(706) 632-9775; *Fax:* (706) 632-5922
www.mountaincountryradio.com
License: Blue Ridge, Fannin County, GA held by Fannin County Broadcasting Co. Inc.
Nat'l Network: AP Radio; *Regional Network:* Ga. News Net.
Arbitron Metro Market: Chattanooga, TN; *Format:* Country; *No. News Employees:* 9; *Target Audience:* 25-54; adults; *Adv. Rates:* 14; 14; 14; 12
Tim White, President
Jim Quinton, Operations Dir
Vicky Pulliam, General Manager

Bolingbroke

WWWD
01-01-2005; 102.1 MHz FM; 4.5 kw; 377 ft.; N32 54 30 W83 46 37
188 South Bellevue, Suite 222, Memphis, TN 38104 US
(901) 375-9324; *Fax:* (901) 375-0041
www.flinn.com
mail@flinn.com
License: Bolingbroke, Monroe County, GA held by George S. Flinn Jr.
Arbitron Metro Market: Memphis, TN
George Flinn Jr., General Manager

Boston

WTUF
07-18-1988; 106.3 MHz FM; *Hrs Open:* 24; 6 kw; 328 ft.; N30 47 40 W83 46 54
Mailing Address: P. O. Box 129, Thomasville, GA 31799 US
Second Address: 117 Remington Ave., Thomasville, GA 31792
(229) 225-1063; *Fax:* (229) 226-1361
www.wtufradio.com
lenrob@rose.net
License: Boston, Thomas County, GA held by Boston Radio Co.
Nat'l Network: AP Network News; *Regional Network:* Agrinet; Ga. News Net; *Nat'l Reps:* Rgnl Reps
Arbitron Metro Market: Boston, GA; *Format:* Country *Special Programming:* Bluegrass 5 hrs, gospel 7 hrs wkly; *Target Audience:* 18-65; adults
Len Robinson, President

Bostwick

WMOQ
01-01-1994; 92.3 MHz FM; 3 kw; 328 ft.; N33 44 49 W83 33 23
Mailing Address: 1081 N. Cherokee Road, Social Circle, GA 30275 US
Second Address: 1610 Launius Rd., Good Hope, GA
(770) 267-0923; *Fax:* (770) 342-8135
www.wmoqfm.com
julio@wmoqfm.com
License: Bostwick, Morgan County, GA held by Bostwick Broadcasting Group Inc.
Arbitron Metro Market: Bostwick, GA; *Format:* Country
B.R. Anderson, Sr, President
Julio, Operations Dir
David Malcolm, General Manager

Bowdon

WBZY
12-09-1996; 105.3 MHz FM; 61 kw; 1204 ft.; N33 24 41 W84 49 48
1819 Peachtree Road Northeast, Suite 700, Atlanta, GA 30309 US
(404) 875-8080; *Fax:* (404) 367-1111
www.elpatron1053.com
License: Bowdon, Carroll County, GA held by CC Licenses LLC.
Group Owner: iHeartMedia; (acq 11-24-2000; at least $7 million)
Arbitron Metro Market: Atlanta, GA; *Format:* Tejano
Cheryl Ervin, General Sales Mgr
Arnulfo Ramirez, Programming Director
Gabriel Diaz, Promotions Director
Steven Garza, Director of Digital Programming

Bremen

WGMI
10-01-1957; 1440 kHz AM; *Hrs Open:* 24; 2.5 kw-D, NDD; 0.062 kw-N, ND1; N33 42 56 W85 9 34
613 Tallapoosa Street, Bremen, GA 30110 US
(770) 537-0840; *Fax:* (770) 406-2324
wgmi1440@yahoo.com
License: Bremen, GA held by Garner Ministries Inc.
Format: Christian, Gospel, 74 *Special Programming:* High School Sports; *Hrs. of News Programming:* news progmg 3 hrs wkly; *No. News Employees:* 1; *Target Audience:* 25-54; majority married women with children *Adv. Rates:* Contact us for rates
Horace Garner, CEO
Peggy Garner, Operations Dir

Broxton

WULS
11-01-1993; 103.7 MHz FM; 6 kw; 328 ft.; N31 35 12 W82 52 25
P.O. Box 2450, Douglas, GA 31533 US
(912) 384-9857; *Fax:* (912) 384-0016
wuls@windstream.net
License: Broxton, Coffee County, GA held by WULS Inc.
Arbitron Metro Market: Broxton, GA; *Format:* Christian, Gospel

Wyndel Burnsed, Owner
Leona.M.Burnsed, Owner

Brunswick

*WAYR-FM

01-01-1996; 90.7 MHz FM; 14 kw; 328 ft.; N31 11 39 W81 29 30
2500 Russell Road, Green Cove Springs, FL 32043 US
(406) 721-6800; *Fax:* (406) 329-1850
www.trail1033.com
rharsell@simmonsmedia.com
License: Brunswick, Glynn County, GA held by Good Tidings Trust Inc.
Arbitron Metro Market: Florence MT; *Format:* Triple A; *No. News Employees:* 1; *Target Audience:* 25-54; adults
Rod Harsell, General Manager
Robert Chase, Programming Director

WGIG

03-05-1949; 1440 kHz AM; 5 kw-D, DAN; 1 kw-N, DAN; N31 10 7 W81 32 14
3833 US Highway 82, Brunswick, GA 31523 US
(912) 267-1025; *Fax:* (912) 264-5462
www.1440wgig.net
License: Brunswick, GA held by AMFM Radio Licenses LLC.
Group Owner: iHeartMedia; (acq 2014)
Nat'l Network: CBS; *Regional Network:* Ga. News Net.
Arbitron Metro Market: Brunswick, GA; *Format:* News, News/Talk, 86
Richard J. Bressler, President
Michelle Harrison, Business Manager

WBGA

06-01-1940; 1490 kHz AM; *Hrs Open:* 24; 0.6 kw-U, ND1; N31 9 42 W81 28 28
3833 US Highway 82, Brunswick, GA 31523 US
(912) 267-1025; *Fax:* (912) 264-5462
www.b963jams.com
License: Brunswick, GA held by AMFM Radio Licenses LLC.
Group Owner: iHeartMedia; (acq 2014)
Nat'l Reps: McGavren Guild
Arbitron Metro Market: Brunswick, GA; *Format:* Urban Contemporary *Special Programming:* Black 8 hrs, class one hr wkly; *Hrs. of News Programming:* news progmg 20 hrs wkly; *No. News Employees:* 1; *Target Audience:* 35 plus.
Richard J. Bressler, President
Michelle Harrison, Business Manager

WRJY

06-30-1994; 104.1 MHz FM; *Hrs Open:* 24; 4.2 kw; 390 ft.; N31 11 39 W81 29 30
108 Benedict Road, Brunswick, GA 31525 US
(912) 261-1000; *Fax:* (912) 265-8391
www.thewave1041.com
License: Brunswick, Glynn County, GA held by Golden Isles Broadcasting LLC
Nat'l Reps: Rgnl Reps
Arbitron Metro Market: Brunswick, GA; *Format:* Country; *Hrs. of News Programming:* News progmg 168 hrs wkly; *Target Audience:* 25-54; urban female; *Adv. Rates:* 15; 15; 15; 10
Ed Strang Steel, Operations Dir
Joe Willie Sousa, General Manager
Mark Stevens, Programming Director
Dick Boekeloo, Chief Engineer

WSFN

09-01-1966; 790 kHz AM; 0.5 kw-D, DA2; 0.115 kw-N, DA2; N31 8 40 W81 34 56
7515 Blythe Island Hwy, Brunswick, GA 31523 US
(912) 264-6251; *Fax:* (912) 264-9991
thefanradio@aol.com
License: Brunswick, GA held by MarMac Communications L.L.C.
Group Owner: MarMac Communications LLC; (acq 4-98; $350,000)
Nat'l Network: ABC; *Regional Network:* Ga. News Net.
Arbitron Metro Market: Brunswick, GA; *Format:* Sports
Gary Marmitt, President

WSOL-FM

09-01-1966; 101.5 MHz FM; *Hrs Open:* 24; 100 kw; 1463 ft.; N30 49 16 W81 44 14
1700 Central Parkway, Jacksonville, FL 32224 US
(904) 636-0507; *Fax:* (904) 997-7713
www.v1015.com
License: Brunswick, Glynn County, GA held by Citicasters Licenses Inc.
Group Owner: iHeartMedia; (acq 5-4-99; grpsl).
Arbitron Metro Market: Jacksonville, FL; *Format:* Urban Contemporary
Aaron Wilborn, Senior Vice President of Sales
Carrie Thompson, Digital Sales Manager
Nick Wize, Digital Content Director
Taylor Brown, Digital Content Coordinator

*WWIO-FM

02-28-1993; 88.9 MHz FM; *Hrs Open:* 24; 11.5 kw; 151 ft.; N31 11 20 W81 29 5 *Rebroadcasts:* Rebroadcasts WSVH(FM) Savannah 100%
260 - 14th Street, N.W., Atlanta, GA 30318 US
(404) 685-2690; *Fax:* (404) 685-2684
www.gpb.org
ask@gpb.org
License: Brunswick, Glynn County, GA held by Georgia Public Telecommunications Commission.
Nat'l Network: NPR; PRI; *Wire Services:* AP
Arbitron Metro Market: Brunswick, GA; *Format:* Classical, News; *Hrs. of News Programming:* news progmg 51 hrs wkly; *No. News Employees:* 10; *Target Audience:* Adults: 35 plus.
Michael H. McDougald, Chairman
Nancy Hall, CEO
Teya Ryan, President
Russell Wells, Operations Dir
Bob Houghton, General Manager
Eric Nauert, Station Manager
Rob Maynard, Programming Director
Susanna Capelouto, News Director
Bonnie Bean, CFO
Tom Barclay, Operations Manager
Janice Paul, Vice Chair

WMUV

11-08-1965; 100.7 MHz FM; *Hrs Open:* 24; 62 kw; 1473 ft.; N30 49 16 W81 44 14
Broadcast Plaza, Crane Ave., Pittsburgh, PA 15220 US
(904) 727-9696; *Fax:* (904) 721-9322
License: Brunswick, Glynn County, GA held by Renda Broadcasting Corp.
Group Owner: Renda Broadcasting Corp.; (acq 1996; $6.5 million with WGNE-FM Palatka, FL)
Nat'l Reps: McGavren Guild
Arbitron Metro Market: Jacksonville, FL; *Format:* Country; *Adv. Rates:* 50; 45; 60; 35
Tony Renda Sr., CEO
Bill Reese, General Manager
Charlie Jennings, General Sales Mgr
Chuck Beck, Programming Director
Stacey Steiner, Promotions Manager
Judy Riley, News Director
Bob Dillehay, Chief Engineer
Jim Byard, PublicService Director
Buffy Daum, Interactive Sales Manager
Leslie Rimer, Web Content Manager/ Web Designer

Buena Vista

WEAM-FM

06-21-2001; 105 MHz FM; *Hrs Open:* 24; 2.6 kw; 502 ft.; N32 20 33 W84 39 18
Mailing Address: P.O. Box 180, Hawkinsville, GA 31036 US
Second Address: 2203 Wynnton Rd., Columbus, GA 31906
(706) 576-3565; *Fax:* (706) 576-3683
foxie1049@aol.com
License: Buena Vista, Marion County, GA held by Davis Broadcasting Inc. of Columbus.
Group Owner: Davis Broadcasting Inc.; (acq 7-30-2003).
Arbitron Metro Market: Columbus, GA; *Format:* Gospel
Gregory Davis, Owner
Carl Conner, Operations Dir
Angela Verdejo, General Sales Mgr
Pam Dixon, Programming Director
Nicole Buffong, Promotions Manager
Anitra Strickland, Traffic Manager

Buford

WLKQ-FM

01-01-1970; 102.3 MHz FM; *Hrs Open:* 24; 4.2 kw; 390 ft.; N34 7 16 W83 58 35
6259 Woodlake Drive, Buford, GA 30518 US
(770) 623-8772; *Fax:* (770) 623-4722
www.laraza1023.com
info@laraza1023.com
License: Buford, Gwinnett County, GA held by Davis Broadcasting of Atlanta L.L.C.
Group Owner: Davis Broadcasting Inc.; (acq 9-30-2003; $5.25 million)
Regional Network: Ga. News Net.
Arbitron Metro Market: Atlanta, GA; *Format:* Spanish, Adult Contemp; *Hrs. of News Programming:* news progmg 6 hrs wkly; *No. News Employees:* 2; *Target Audience:* 35-54; upper-middle class professionals
Gregory Davis, President
Brian Barber, General Manager

WXEM

12-12-1957; 1460 kHz AM; 5 kw-D, ND1; 0.193 kw-N, ND1; N34 7 15 W83 58 35
5815 Westside Road, PO Box 746, Austell, GA 30001 US
(770) 944-0900; *Fax:* (770) 944-9794
www.lamejorestacion.com
sammy@lamejorestacion.com
License: Buford, Gwinnett County, GA held by La Favorita Inc.
Group Owner: La Favorita Radio Network; acq 6-12-91;
Arbitron Metro Market: Buford, GA; *Format:* Spanish; *Target Audience:* 18-49; Hispanic.
Samuel Zamarron, CEO
Gracie Zamarron, Station Manager

Byron

*WPWB

01-01-1988; 90.5 MHz FM; *Hrs Open:* 24; 16.5 kw; 453 ft.; N32 40 55 W83 22 10
P.O. Box 510, Appling, GA 30802 US
(800) 926-4669
www.gnnradio.org
License: Byron, Peach County, GA held by Augusta Radio Fellowship Institute Inc.
Group Owner: Good News Network
Format: Christian; *Hrs. of News Programming:* News progmg 12 hrs wkly; *Target Audience:* General.

Cairo

WGRA

10-01-1949; 790 kHz AM; 1 kw-D, ND2; 0.11 kw-N, ND2; N30 54 8 W84 14 3
Mailing Address: PO Box 120, Cairo, GA 31728 US
Second Address: 1809 U.S. 84 W., Cairo, GA 39828
(229) 377-4392; *Fax:* (229) 377-4564
www.wgra.net
jeff@wgra.net
License: Cairo, GA held by Lovett Broadcasting Enterprises Inc.
Regional Network: Ga. News Net; *Nat'l Reps:* Rgnl Reps
Format: News, News/Talk, 86 *Special Programming:* Black 6 hrs wkly; *Target Audience:* 30 plus; mainly women
Jeffrey Lovett, President

WWLD

06-01-1983; 102.3 MHz FM; 27 kw; 604 ft.; N30 29 32 W84 17 2
PO Box 120, Cairo, GA 31728 US
(850) 201-3000; *Fax:* (850) 205-3711
blazin1023.com
License: Cairo, Grady County, GA held by Cumulus Licensing LLC.
Group Owner: Cumulus Media Inc.; (acq 10-10-01; $1.5 million including noncompete agreement).
Nat'l Reps: Katz Radio
Arbitron Metro Market: Tallahassee, FL; *Format:* Urban Contemporary; *Target Audience:* 18-34.; *Adv. Rates:* 45; 40; 45; 50
Barry Kaye, General Manager
Jay Blaze, Programming Director

Calhoun

WEBS

11-01-1966; 1030 kHz AM
Mailing Address: Post Office Box 1299, Calhoun, GA 30701 US
Second Address: 427 S. Wall St., Calhoun, GA 30703
(706) 629-1110; *Fax:* (706) 629-7092
www.webscalhoun.com/
webs@webscalhoun.com
License: Calhoun, GA held by Radio WEBS Inc.
Nat'l Network: Jones Radio Networks
Arbitron Metro Market: Calhoun GA; *Format:* Oldies *Special Programming:* Black 2 hrs wkly; *Target Audience:* 18-52.; *Adv. Rates:* 18; 20; 20; 15
Ken Payne, President

WJTH

06-16-1977; 900 kHz AM; *Hrs Open:* 24; 1 kw-D, 266 w-N; 256 feet; N34 27 40 W84 53 44
Mailing Address: Box 1119, 329 RICHARDSON RD SE, Calhoun, GA 30701
Second Address: 329 Richardson Rd. S.E., Calhoun, GA 30701
(706) 629-6397; *Fax:* (706) 629-8463
www.wjth.com
am900@wjth.com
License: Calhoun, Gordon County, GA held by Cherokee Broadcasting Co.
Nat'l Network: ABC; Dial Global; *Regional Network:* Ga. News Net.; Southeast Agnet; *Nat'l Reps:* Rgnl Reps

Population Served: 50,000; *Arbitron Metro Market:* Atlanta, GA
Special Programming: Farm one hr, gospel 2 hrs, relg 16 hrs wkly; *Hrs. of News Programming:* news progmg 20 hrs wkly; *No. News Employees:* 1 *TargetAudience:* 18-64; general; *Adv. Rates:* 15; 14; 15; 14
Sam Thomas, General Manager
Keith Thomas, Station Manager
Gloria Cooley, General Sales Mgr
Sam Thomas, Programming Director
Phil Baker, Chief Engineer

WIPK-FM
11-01-2011; 94.5 MHz FM; 6 kw
1570 Northside Dr., Bldg. 200, Suite B, Atlanta, GA 30318 USA
(240) 605-7820
License: Calhoun, held by Core Communicators North LLC
Group Owner: Core Communicators Broadcasting LLC
Format: Contemporary Hits/Top 40
Steve Hegwood, President

Camilla

WZBN
04-01-1977; 105.5 MHz FM; *Hrs Open:* 24; 6 kw; 276 ft.; N31 18 51 W84 12 18
970 Martin Luther King Jr., Dr, Sw, Suite 202, Atlanta, GA 30314 US
(229) 888-5000; *Fax:* (912) 888-5960
License: Camilla, Mitchell County, GA held by Extreme Media Group LLC
Regional Network: Ga. News Net; *Nat'l Reps:* Katz Radio
Arbitron Metro Market: Albany, GA; *Format:* Urban Contemporary
Special Programming: Blues 5 hrs, gospel 16 hrs wkly; *Hrs. of News Programming:* news progmg 3 hrs wkly; *No. News Employees:* 1 *Target Audience:* 25-54; female
Paul Bucurel, General Manager

Canton

WCHK
04-11-1957; 1290 kHz AM
1176 Satellite Blvd, Suite 200, Suwanee, GA 30024 US
(770) 623-8772; *Fax:* (770) 623-4722
www.lamegatl.com
License: Canton, GA held by Davis Broadcasting of Atlanta L.L.C.
Group Owner: Davis Broadcasting Inc.; (acq 1-17-2007; $3.8 million with WNSY(FM) Talking Rock)
Arbitron Metro Market: Suwanee,GA; *Format:* Adult Contemp, Spanish, 28
Brian Barber, General Manager

WRDA-FM
08-01-1964; 105.7 MHz FM; *Hrs Open:* 24; 20 kw; 781 ft.; N34 3 58 W84 27 15
1819 Peachtree Rd. N.E., Suite 700, Atlanta, GA 30309 US
(404) 875-8080
www.radio1057.com
License: Canton, Cherokee County, GA held by CC Licenses LLC.
Group Owner: iHeartMedia; (acq 3-29-2004; $31 million).
Arbitron Metro Market: Atlanta, GA; *Format:* Alternative
Cameron Brown, General Sales Mgr
Aly Young, Programming Director
Matt Sheffield, Promotions Director
Steve Garza, Digital Program Director

Carrollton

WLBB
11-19-1975; 1330 kHz AM; *Hrs Open:* 24
100 Wexford Place, Athens, GA 30606 US
(678) 601-1330; *Fax:* (678) 601-8256
www.gradickcommunications.com
cworthington@newstalk1330.com
License: Carrollton, GA held by WYAI Inc.
Nat'l Network: CBS
Arbitron Metro Market: Carrollton, GA,; *Format:* News, News/Talk, 86; *No. News Employees:* 2
Steve Gradick, President
Colin Worthington, News Director
Michael Vincent, Production Director
Mitch Grey, Sports Director

WBTR-FM
01-01-1964; 92.1 MHz FM; *Hrs Open:* 24; 0.58 kw; 636 ft.; N33 33 54 W85 1 2
305 Courtyard Square, Carrollton, GA 30117 US
(770) 832-9685; *Fax:* (770) 830-1027
www.gradickcommunications.com
cworthington@newstalk1330.com
License: Carrollton, Carroll County, GA held by WYAI Inc.
Regional Network: Ga. News Net.
Arbitron Metro Market: Carrollton, GA,; *Format:* Country *Special Programming:* Black 5 hrs wkly; *Hrs. of News Programming:* news progmg 3 hrs wkly; *No. News Employees:* 1; *Target Audience:* 25-49.
Steven Gradick, President
Colin Worthington, News Director
Michael Vincent, Production Director
Mitch Grey, Sports Director

***WUWG**
02-19-1973; 90.7 MHz FM; *Hrs Open:* 24; 0.43 kw; 495 ft.; N33 33 50 W85 1 4 *Rebroadcasts:* WJSP, Warm Springs/Columbus, GA, 75%
Learning Resources Cntr, Carrollton, GA 30118 US
(404) 685-2690; *Fax:* (404) 685-2684
www.gpb.org
ask@gpb.org
License: Carrollton, Carroll County, GA held by Georgia Public Telecommunications Commission
Nat'l Network: NPR; PRI; *Wire Services:* AP
Arbitron Metro Market: Carrollton, GA; *Format:* Classical, News
Special Programming: Folk 2 hrs, bluegrass 2 hrs, new age 3 hrs; *Hrs. of News Programming:* news progmg 25-30 hrs wkly; *No. News Employees:* 10 *Target Audience:* General; students & area residents
Milton Clipper, Chief Executive Officer
Teya Ryan, President
Tom Barclay, Operations Dir
Rob Maynard, Programming Director
Nancy Zintak, Promotions Manager
Bonnie Bean, CFO
Steve Carey, Vice President of Production

Cartersville

WBHF
07-17-1946; 1450 kHz AM; *Hrs Open:* 24
406 Old Mill Road, Cartersville, GA 30120 US
(770) 386-1450; *Fax:* (770) 382-5390
www.wbhfradio.org/
news@wbhfradio.org
License: Cartersville, GA held by Anverse Inc.
Nat'l Network: ABC; AP Radio; *Wire Services:* AP
Arbitron Metro Market: Atlanta, GA; *Format:* News, Oldies, 84; *Hrs. of News Programming:* news progmg 10 hrs wkly; *No. News Employees:* 3
Ernestine Jones, Operations Dir
Matt Santini, General Manager

***WCCV**
01-24-1983; 91.7 MHz FM; *Hrs Open:* 6am-8pm; 7.3 kw; 935 ft.; N34 9 34 W85 2 13
779 South Erwin Street, Cartersville, GA 30120 US
(770) 387-0917; *Fax:* (770) 387-2856
www.ibn.org
License: Cartersville, Bartow County, GA held by Immanuel Broadcasting.
Arbitron Metro Market: Cartersville, GA; *Format:* Religious
Patrick Miller, CFO
Ed Tuten, President
Neil Hopper, General Manager
Howard Tuten, Station Manager
Billy Williams, Programming Director

WYXC
09-21-1961; 1270 kHz AM; *Hrs Open:* 24
1410 Highway 411, N.E., Cartersville, GA 30120 US
(770) 382-1306
www.newstalk1270.com
info@newstalk1270.com
License: Cartersville, GA held by Clarion Communications Inc.
Arbitron Metro Market: Atlanta, GA; *Format:* News, Sports, 86; *Hrs. of News Programming:* news progmg 15 hrs. wkly; *No. News Employees:* 1; *Target Audience:* 25-55.
Charles Shiflett, President
Jim Adams, Station Manager
Connie Dixon, General Sales Mgr
Charles Brachel, Programming Director
Allen Schmelz, Chief Engineer
Manny Garrett, Chief of Engineering

Chatsworth

***WNGH-FM**
11-13-1976; 98.9 MHz FM; *Hrs Open:* 24; 0.42 kw; 1729 ft.; N34 45 6 W84 42 54
613 Silver Circle, Dalton, GA 30721 US
(404) 685-2415
www.gpb.org
License: Chatsworth, Murray County, GA held by The Foundation for Public Broadcasting in Georgia Inc.
Nat'l Network: NPR; PRI; *Wire Services:* AP
TV Affiliate: WNGH-TV affil; *Format:* Classical, News *Special Programming:* Jazz 16 hrs wkly; *Hrs. of News Programming:* news progmg 41 hrs wkly; *No. News Employees:* 10; *Target Audience:* 35 plus; adults
Milton Clipper, Chief Executive Officer
Tom Barclay, Operations Dir
Rob Maynard, Programming Director
Bonnie Bean, CFO

Chauncey

WQIL
10-20-1995; 101.3 MHz FM; *Hrs Open:* 24; 50 kw; 492 ft.; N32 22 59 W83 7 8
P. O. Box 98, Milan, GA 31060 US
(478) 272-4422; *Fax:* (478) 275-4657
www.1013wqil.com
webmaster@1013wqil.com
License: Chauncey, Dodge County, GA held by GSW Inc.
Regional Reps: Regional Reps
Arbitron Metro Market: Macon, GA; *Format:* Gospel; *Hrs. of News Programming:* News progmg one hr wkly; *Target Audience:* 30 plus; Christians
G.S. Walker, Operations Dir
Rick Humphrey, General Manager
J. Morgan Dowdy, Partner

Clarkesville

WCHM
12-01-1989; 1490 kHz AM; *Hrs Open:* 24
Mailing Address: W Waters St, Clarkesville, GA 30523 US
Second Address: 1331 Washington St., Clarkesville, GA 30523
(706) 839-1490; *Fax:* (706) 754-8621
www.wchmradio.com/
License: Clarkesville, GA held by WCHM Radio LLC
Group Owner: Batten Communications Inc.; (acq 11-21-95; $70,000)
Nat'l Network: USA
Arbitron Metro Market: Clarkesville, GA; *Format:* Christian; *Hrs. of News Programming:* news progmg 5 hrs wkly; *No. News Employees:* 1; *Target Audience:* 25-62.
Brian Rothell, General Manager

WDUN-FM
01-01-1990; 102.9 MHz FM; *Hrs Open:* 24; 16 kw; 413 ft.; N34 29 05 W83 38 24
Mailing Address: PO Box 10, Gainesville, GA 30503
Second Address: 1102 Thompson Bridge Rd. N.E., Gainesville, GA 30501
(770) 532-9921; *Fax:* (770) 532-0459
MAJIC1029.com and AccessNorthGa.com
jay.jacobs@jacobsmedia.net
License: Clarkesville, Habersham County, GA held by JWJ Properties Inc.
Group Owner: Jacobs Media Corp.; (acq 3-19-92).
Nat'l Network: Westwood One; *Wire Services:* AP
Population Served: 500,000 *Target Audience:* 25-54; females with a median age of 41
John W. Jacobs Jr., Chairman
John W. Jacobs III, CEO
Joel Williams, General Manager
Bill Maine, Programming Director

Claxton

WCLA
07-20-1958; 1470 kHz AM; *Hrs Open:* 24; 1 kw-D, ND1; 0.26 kw-N, ND1; N32 10 12 W81 53 56
316 N. River St, Claxton, GA 30714 US
(912) 739-9252; *Fax:* (912) 739-0050
www.wclaradio.net
radioevans@bellsouth.net
License: Claxton, GA held by W. Danny Swain
Nat'l Network: ABC; *Regional Network:* Ga. News Net.
Arbitron Metro Market: Claxton, GA; *Format:* Oldies *Special Programming:* Farm 1.5 hrs, Hispanic 6 hrs, relg 4 hrs wkly; *No. News Employees:* 1; *Target Audience:* 35-64; adults; *Adv. Rates:* 10; 10; 10; 7
W. Swain, President
Herman Moody, Operations Dir
W. Smith, General Manager
Martin Foglia, Chief Engineer

WMCD
09-15-1972; 107.3 MHz FM; *Hrs Open:* 24; 25 kw; 328 ft.; N32 10 1 W81 54 7
Mailing Address: 607 Cricklewood Circle, Heathrow, FL 32746 US
Second Address: 561 E. Olliff St., Statesboro, GA 30458

RADIO - U.S.

(912) 764-6000; *Fax:* (912) 764-8827
spots@georgiaeagleradio.com
License: Claxton, Evans County, GA held by Georgia Eagle Media Inc.
Group Owner: Georgia Eagle Media Inc.; (acq 5-21-2007; grpsl)
Nat'l Network: Westwood One *Regional Reps:* Rgnl Reps
Arbitron Metro Market: Heathrow, FL; *Format:* Adult Contemp; *Hrs. of News Programming:* news progmg 7 hrs wkly; *No. News Employees:* 1; *Target Audience:* 25-50; general; *Adv. Rates:* 12; 12; 12; 12
Jeff Anderson, General Manager
Buddy Horne, Programming Director
Cornell Burgess, News Director

Clayton

WRBN

06-11-1990; 96.3 MHz FM; *Hrs Open:* 24; 0.37 kw; 1296 ft.; N34 54 24 W83 24 56
Mailing Address: P.O. Box 1149, Clayton, GA 30525 US
Second Address: 745 North Main St, Clayton, GA 30525
(706) 782-1041; *Fax:* (706) 243-6173
sky963.com
sky104wrbn@gmail.com
License: Clayton, Rabun County, GA held by Sutton Radiocasting Corp.
Group Owner: Georgia-Carolina Radiocasting Companies
Nat'l Network: ABC
Format: Adult Contemp, News *Special Programming:* NASCAR/Local Sports; *Hrs. of News Programming:* news progmg 2 hrs wkly; *No. News Employees:* 1; *Target Audience:* 25 plus
Scott Mazarky, Operations Manager
Adam Wright, VP/General Manager
Gene Gihl, News Director

Clemson

WSB(FM)

05-01-1948; 98.5 MHz FM; *Hrs Open:* 24; 40 kw; Ant 1,417 ft; N34 07 32 W83 51 32
1601 W. Peachtree St. N.E., Atlanta, GA 30309 US
(404) 897-7500; *Fax:* (404) 897-7363
License: Clemson, Pickens County, GA held by Cox Radio Inc.
Group Owner: Cox Radio Inc.; (acq 7-19-99; $78 million)
Population Served: 2,500,000; *Arbitron Metro Market:* Atlanta, GA; *Format:* Contemporary Hits/Top 40; *Target Audience:* 25-54
Chris Eagan, Program Director
Justin Tysinger, Promotions
Donna Hall, Vice President & Market Manager

Clermont

WNGA

105.1 MHz FM; 3.1 kw; 925 ft.; N34 33 58 W83 46 40
P.O. Box 2098, Omaha, NE 68103 US
(800) 525-5683
www.klove.com
License: Clermont, Hall County, GA held by Educational Media Foundation
Group Owner: EMF Broadcasting
Format: Adult Contemp, Christian
Darrell Chambliss, Chairman
Mike Novak, President & CEO

Cleveland

WAZX-FM

01-01-1989; 101.9 MHz FM; 0.35 kw; 1344 ft.; N34 30 32 W83 48 27
5113 Powers Ferry Road, Atlanta, GA 30327 US
(406) 657-2941; *Fax:* (406) 657-2977
www.yellowstonepublicradio.org
License: Cleveland, White County, GA held by WAZX-FM Inc.
Format: Classical, Jazz, 60
Lois Bent, General Manager

WRWH

09-27-1958; 1350 kHz AM; *Hrs Open:* 6 AM-sunset; 1 kw-D, ND2; 0.093 kw-N, ND2; N34 35 11 W83 46 1
Mailing Address: Box 181, Cleveland, GA 30528 US
Second Address: 681 Hood St., Cleveland, GA 30528
(706) 865-3181; *Fax:* (706) 865-0421
wrwh.com
wrwh@windstream.net
License: Cleveland, GA held by White County Media LLC
Regional Network: Ga. News Net.
Format: Religious; *Target Audience:* 35 plus.
Dean Dyer, President
Dean Dyer, General Manager

Cochran

*WMUM-FM

02-04-1985; 89.7 MHz FM; *Hrs Open:* 24; 43 kw horiz, 100 kw vert; 998 ft.; N32 28 11 W83 15 17 *Rebroadcasts:* Rebroadcasts WJSP-FM Warm Springs 80%
260 - 14th Street, N.W., Atlanta, GA 30318 US
(478) 301-5760; *Fax:* (404) 685-2684
www.gpb.org
ask@gpb.org
License: Cochran, Bleckley County, GA held by Georgia Public Telecommunications Commission.
Nat'l Network: NPR; PRI; *Wire Services:* AP
Arbitron Metro Market: Macon, GA *TV Affiliate:* WMUM-TV affil; *Format:* Classical, News *Special Programming:* Jazz 18 hrs wkly; *Hrs. of News Programming:* news progmg 40 hrs wkly; *No. News Employees:* 10 *Target Audience:* Adults 35+
Milton Clipper, Chief Executive Officer
Teya Ryan, President
Tom Barclay, Operations Dir
Rob Maynard, Programming Director
Nancy Zintak, Promotions Manager
Bonnie Bean, CFO

WDXQ

07-04-1965; 1440 kHz AM; *Hrs Open:* 24; 1 kw-D; N32 24 43 W83 21 42
157 Jac Arts Rd., Cochran, GA 31014
(478) 934-6337; *Fax:* (478) 934-0929
License: Cochran, Bleckley County, GA held by Georgia Eagle Media Inc.
Group Owner: Georgia Eagle Media Inc.; (acq 5-21-2007; grpsl)
Population Served: 30,000 *Special Programming:* Black 6 hrs, farm 3 hrs, gospel 6 hrs wkly; *Target Audience:* 18-54; adults
Tommy Palmer, General Manager
James Gay, Chief Engineer

WYPZ

07-04-1968; 107.5 MHz FM; 4 kw; 122.3 meters; N32 32 36 W83 27 55
6174 Highway 57, Macon, GA 31217 US
(404) 307-8079; *Fax:* (478) 742-2293
License: Cochran, Bleckley County, GA held by Praise 107.5 FM Radio LLC
Wire Services: UPI
Population Served: 10,291 *Target Audience:* Adults 18-54.

College Park

WNNX

01-12-2001; 100.5 MHz FM; *Hrs Open:* 24; 13.5 kw; 978 ft.; N33 45 34 W84 23 19
780 Johnson Ferry Rd. NE., 5th Floor, Atlanta, GA 30342 US
(404) 497-4700
www.atlantasclassicrock.com
hope.angelone@cumulus.com
License: College Park, Fulton County, GA held by Radio License Holding SRC, LLC
Group Owner: Cumulus Media Inc.
Nat'l Reps: Cumulus Radio Sales
Arbitron Metro Market: Atlanta, GA; *Format:* Classic Rock
Rob Roberts, Programming Director
Chris Murray, Vice President/Marketing Manager

Colquitt

*WCOQ

01-01-2008; 90.5 MHz FM; 4.5 kw vert; 154 ft.; N31 10 24 W84 43 33
10142 East County Rd 22, Columbia, AL 36319 US
(334) 798-6664
wcoqfm@yahoo.com
License: Colquitt, Miller County, GA held by D & K Communications Inc.
Arbitron Metro Market: Colquitt, GA; *Format:* Oldies
Robert Rogers, President

Columbus

WCGQ

07-15-1966; 107.3 MHz FM; *Hrs Open:* 24; 100 kw; 1010 ft.; N32 28 0 W85 3 20
1820 Wynnton Rd., Columbus, GA 31904 US
(706) 327-1217; *Fax:* (706) 596-4600
www.q1073.com
License: Columbus, Muscogee County, GA held by PMB Broadcasting LLC.
Group Owner: PMB Broadcasting LLC; (acq 10-1-2008; grpsl)
Arbitron Metro Market: Columbus, GA; *Format:* Contemporary Hits/Top 40; *Target Audience:* 18-49.; *Adv. Rates:* 41; 41; 41; 41
Dave Arwood, Operations Dir
Helen Neal, Dir. of Sales

WDAK

08-01-1940; 540 kHz AM
Mailing Address: C/O Haley, Bader & Potts, 4350 N. Fairfax Dr, #900, Arlington, VA 22203 US
Second Address: 1501 13th Ave., Columbus, GA 31901
(706) 576-3000; *Fax:* (706) 576-3010
www.newsradio540.com
scottmiller@newsradio540.com
License: Columbus, GA held by CC Licenses LLC.
Group Owner: iHeartMedia; (acq 5-9-2003; $2.73 million with WSTH-FM Alexander City, AL).
Nat'l Network: USA; Westwood One
Arbitron Metro Market: Columbus, GA; *Format:* News; *Target Audience:* 18-49; men
Derrick Greene, Operations Manager
Jennifer Newman, Market President
Chuck Thompson, Director of Sales
Scott Miller, Programming Director

WIOL

12-01-1954; 1580 kHz AM; *Hrs Open:* 20; 2.3 kw-D, 1 kw-N, DA-N; N32 27 55 W85 01 22
Box 1998, Columbus, GA 36107
(706) 576-3565; *Fax:* (706) 576-3683
www.957espn.com
info@dbicolumbus.com
License: Columbus, Muscogee County, GA held by Davis Broadcasting Inc. of Columbus.
Group Owner: Davis Broadcasting Inc.; (acq 4-20-01; $400,000).
Nat'l Network: USA
Population Served: 250,000; *Arbitron Metro Market:* Columbus, GA; *Format:* Sports, Talk; *Hrs. of News Programming:* News progmg 15 hrs wkly; *Target Audience:* General.
Gregory Davis, CFO

*WFRC

06-14-1985; 90.5 MHz FM; 25 kw; 240 ft.; N32 25 58 W84 57 2
4135 Northgate Blvd, Suite 1, Sacramento, CA 95834 US
(334) 291-0399; *Fax:* (510) 633-7983
www.familyradio.com
familyradio@familyradio.com
License: Columbus, Muscogee County, GA held by Family Stations Inc.
Group Owner: Family Stations Inc.
Arbitron Metro Market: Columbus, GA; *Format:* Religious *Special Programming:* Call-in 8 hrs wkly
Harold Camping, President
Sandra Salewski, Operations Dir

WFXE

09-22-1969; 104.9 MHz FM; 2.3 kw; 538 ft.; N32 27 59 W85 3 22
P.O. Box 1998, Columbus, GA 31994 US
(706) 576-3565; *Fax:* (706) 576-3683
info@dbicolumbus.com
License: Columbus, Muscogee County, GA held by Davis Broadcasting Inc.
Arbitron Metro Market: Columbus, GA; *Format:* Urban Contemporary
Gregory Davis, CEO
Bernie Corcoran, CFO

WBOJ

01-01-1947; 1270 kHz AM; *Hrs Open:* 19; 5 kw-D, ND1; 0.188 kw-N, ND1; N32 26 16 W85 1 10
Mailing Address: 1501 13th Avenue, Columbus, GA 31901 US
Second Address: 1501 13th Ave., Columbus, GA 31901
(706) 576-3000; *Fax:* (706) 576-3010
www.foxsportscolumbus.com
License: Columbus, GA held by 88.5 The Truth Inc.
Nat'l Reps: McGavren Guild
Arbitron Metro Market: Columbus, GA; *Format:* Sports; *Hrs. of News Programming:* News progmg 20 hrs wkly; *Target Audience:* 35-60.
Derrick Greene, Operations Dir
Chuck Thompson, General Sales Mgr
Jim Foster, Programming Director
Jennifer Newman, Marketing Manager

WOKS

03-02-1959; 1340 kHz AM; 1 kw-U, ND1; N32 27 7 W84 58 25
Mailing Address: P.O. Box 1998, Columbus, GA 31902 US
Second Address: 2203 Wynnton Rd., Columbus, GA 31906
(706) 576-3565; *Fax:* (706) 576-3683
info@dbicolumbus.com
License: Columbus, GA held by Davis Broadcasting Inc.
Group Owner: Davis Broadcasting Inc.; acq 7-24-92).
Nat'l Network: American Urban; *Nat'l Reps:* Katz Radio
Arbitron Metro Market: Columbus, GA *TV Affiliate:* Urban contemp; *Format:* Urban Contemporary; *No. News Employees:* 35-64.

WRCG
05-10-1928; 1420 kHz AM; *Hrs Open:* 24
1820 Wynnton Rd., Columbus, GA 31906 US
(706) 327-1217
jfoster@pmbradio.com
License: Columbus, GA held by PMB Broadcasting LLC.
Group Owner: PMB Broadcasting LLC; (acq 10-1-2008; grpsl)
Nat'l Network: CBS; *Regional Network:* Ga. News Net; *Nat'l Reps:* Christal
Arbitron Metro Market: Columbus, GA; *Format:* Country, News/Talk *Special Programming:* Farm 3 hrs wkly; *Hrs. of News Programming:* news progmg 24 hrs wkly; *No. News Employees:* 1; *Target Audience:* 35 plus;adults with discretionary income; *Adv. Rates:* 21; 21; 21; 21
Dave Arwood, Operations Dir
Helen Neal, Dir. of Sales

***WTJB**
12-15-1984; 91.7 MHz FM; *Hrs Open:* 6 AM-midnight; 5 kw horiz, 3.33 kw vert; 299 ft.; N32 25 20 W85 1 50 *Rebroadcasts:* Rebroadcasts WTSU(FM) Troy 100%
University Avenue, Department of Radio & Tv, Troy, AL 36082 US
(334) 670-3268; *Fax:* (334) 670-3934
www.troy.edu
License: Columbus, Muscogee County, GA held by Troy State University.
Nat'l Network: NPR; PRI
Arbitron Metro Market: Phoenix City, AL; *Format:* News *Special Programming:* Children one hr wkly; *Hrs. of News Programming:* News progmg 25 hrs wkly; *Target Audience:* General.
Judy Davis, Operations Dir
James Clower, General Manager
Fred Azbell, Programming Director
John Brunson, Chief Engineer
Donna Schubert, Associate Vice Chancellor for Marketing and Commun
Wade Giddens, Broadcast Engineer
DavidGriffin, Radio Engineer
Robert Barner, Production Coordinator

WVRK
11-16-1946; 102.9 MHz FM; 98 kw; 1568 ft.; N32 19 25.5 W84 46 46
1501 13th Avenue, Columbus, GA 31901 US
(706) 576-3000; *Fax:* (706) 576-3010
www.rock103columbus.com
License: Columbus, Muscogee County, GA held by CC Licenses LLC
Group Owner: iHeartMedia
Arbitron Metro Market: Columbus, GA; *Format:* Classic Rock, Rock/AOR
Jennifer Newman, General Manager
Chuck Thompson, Sales Manager
Rob Carter, Programming Director
Wes Carroll, Director of Digital Content

***WYFK**
07-01-1987; 89.5 MHz FM; 50 kw; 440 ft.; N32 40 13 W84 57 14
200 Hamilton Mulberry Grove Rd., Cataula, GA 31804 US
(800) 888-7077
www.bbnradio.org
bbn@bnnmedia.org
License: Columbus, Muscogee County, GA held by Bible Broadcasting Network Inc.
Group Owner: Bible Broadcasting Network
Arbitron Metro Market: Columbus, GA; *Format:* Religious; *Target Audience:* General.
Lowell Davey, President
Jason Padgett, Operations Manager

Commerce

WJJC
06-27-1957; 1270 kHz AM; *Hrs Open:* 24; 5 kw-D, ND1; 0.173 kw-N, ND1; N34 12 57 W83 26 9
Mailing Address: Company, Inc., PO Box 379, Commerce, GA 30529 US
Second Address: 1801 N. Elm St., Commerce, GA 30529
(706) 335-1270; *Fax:* (706) 335-1905
www.wjjc.net
wjjc@windstream.net
License: Commerce, GA held by Side Communications Inc.
Regional Network: Ga. News Net; *Nat'l Reps:* Rgnl Reps
Arbitron Metro Market: Atlanta, GA; *Format:* Talk *Special Programming:* Glenn Beck, Jim Rome, Dr. Laura; *Target Audience:* 25-55.
Rob Jordan, General Manager
Craig Fischer, Assistant General Manager

Conyers

WPBS
11-01-1979; 1040 kHz AM; *Hrs Open:* 12
1151 Flat Shoals Road, Conyers, GA 30208 US
(404) 932-5006
License: Conyers, GA held by PacificStar Media Corp.
Arbitron Metro Market: Atlanta, GA; *Format:* Christian, Spanish
Charles Kim, General Manager

Coosa

WSRM
01-01-2005; 93.5 MHz FM; 1.2 kw; 741 ft.; N34 14 2 W85 13 50
Rebroadcasts: Simulcast with WRGA(AM) Rome 100%
32 Saddle Mountain Rd, Rome, GA 30161 US
(706) 291-9496; *Fax:* (706) 235-7107
www.wrgarome.com
License: Coosa, Floyd County, GA held by Coosa Broadcasting Corp.
Group Owner: Southern Broadcasting Companies Inc.; (acq 5-31-2005; $1.1 million)
Arbitron Metro Market: Coosa, GA; *Format:* News, News/Talk, 86
Paul Stone, President
Randy Quick, General Manager

Cordele

***WAEF**
01-01-2001; 90.3 MHz FM; 11 kw vert; 505 ft.; N31 38 22 W83 44 58
P.O. Box 3206, Tupelo, MS 38803 US
(662) 844-8888; *Fax:* (662) 842-6791
www.afr.net
faq@afa.net
License: Cordele, Crisp County, GA held by American Family Association.
Group Owner: American Family Radio
Arbitron Metro Market: Hutchinson MN; *Format:* Religious, Talk *Special Programming:* Farm 15 hrs wkly; *Target Audience:* 25-54.
Tim Wildmon, President
Donald Wildmon, Founder
Buddy Smith, Senior VP
Ed Vitagliano, Executive VP
Randy Sharp, Director Of Special Projects
Meeme Addison, Director Of Communications
Abraham Hamilton III, General Sounsel & PublicPolicy Analyst

Cornelia

WCON
03-28-1953; 1450 kHz AM; *Hrs Open:* 24; 1 kw-U, ND1; N34 30 57 W83 32 20
Mailing Address: P. O. Box 100, Cornelia, GA 30531 US
Second Address: 540 N. Main St., Cornelia, GA 30531
(706) 778-2241; *Fax:* (706) 778-0576
www.wconfm.com
wcon@windstream.net
License: Cornelia, GA held by Habersham Broadcasting Co.
Nat'l Network: ABC; *Regional Network:* Ga. News Net.
Arbitron Metro Market: Cornelia,GA; *Format:* Country, Gospel; *No. News Employees:* 1; *Target Audience:* Adults.; *Adv. Rates:* 7; 6; 7; 5
Bobbie C. Foster, GM
John Foster, Operations Dir
Michael Harvey, News Director
Jimmy Dillard, Chief Engineer

WCON-FM
03-27-1965; 99.3 MHz FM; *Hrs Open:* 24; 19 kw; 807 ft.; N34 31 24 W83 40 46
Mailing Address: P.O. Box 100, Cornelia, GA 30531 US
Second Address: 540 N. Main St., Cornelia, GA 30531
(706) 778-2241; *Fax:* (706) 778-0576
www.wconfm.com
wcon@windstream.net
License: Cornelia, Habersham County, GA held by Habersham Broadcasting Co.
Arbitron Metro Market: Cornelia,GA; *Format:* Country; *No. News Employees:* 1; *Target Audience:* 18 plus.; *Adv. Rates:* 13; 11; 13; na.
Bobbie C. Foster, GM
Tom Thon, General Manager

Covington

WGFS
10-09-1946; 1430 kHz AM; *Hrs Open:* 6 AM-7 PM
Box 82141, Conyers, GA 30013 US
(404) 462-2633
www.irieatl.com
License: Covington, GA held by Multicultural Radio Broadcasting Licensee LLC.
Group Owner: Multicultural Radio Broadcasting Inc.; (acq 11-21-03; $700,000).
Nat'l Network: CBS; *Regional Network:* Ga. News Net.; *Wire Services:* CBS
Arbitron Metro Market: Atlanta, GA; *Format:* Christian, Ethnic; *Hrs. of News Programming:* news progmg 20 hrs wkly; *No. News Employees:* 1; *Target Audience:* General.
Arthur Liu, CEO/COO

Crawford

WGMG
04-01-1990; 102.1 MHz FM; 10 kw; 328 ft.; N33 55 18 W83 14 14
1010 Tower Place, Watkinsville, GA 30677 US
(706) 549-6222; *Fax:* (706) 546-0411
License: Crawford, Oglethorpe County, GA held by Cox Radio Inc.
Group Owner: Cox Radio Inc.; (acq 8-1-2008; grpsl)
Format: Adult Contemp; *Target Audience:* 18-49; general
Pete de Graaff, Program Director
Russell Lawson, General Sales Manager
Tim Bryant, News Director
Josh Hill, Promotions Director
Heather Taylor, Digital Brand Manager

Cumming

***WWEV-FM**
12-04-1981; 91.5 MHz FM; *Hrs Open:* 24; 8.9 kw; 961 ft.; N34 14 13 W84 9 36
Mailing Address: P.O. Box 248, Cumming, GA 30130 US
Second Address: 1705 Sawnee Dr., Cumming, GA 30040
(770) 781-9150; *Fax:* (770) 781-5003
info@wwev.org
License: Cumming, Forsyth County, GA held by Curriculum Development Foundation Inc.
Arbitron Metro Market: Cumming, GA; *Format:* Religious; *Target Audience:* 18-49; the family unit
Ray Haynes, General Manager
Ray Haynes, Promotions Manager
Marty Passmore, Chief Engineer
Denise Bell, Office Manager
Judy McDearis, Office Manager
Rhonda Haynes, Sales Rep
Suzan Cook, Sales Rep
Holly Bader, Sales Rep

Cusseta

WLTC
103.7 MHz FM; 6 kw; Ant 328 ft; N32 18 39 W84 45 45
1820 Wynnton Rd Suite B, Columbus, GA 31906
(706) 324-5850; *Fax:* (706) 256-2984
License: Cusseta, Chattahoochee County, GA held by Signature Broadcasting Ltd.
Arbitron Metro Market: Columbus, GA
Shirley Thrasher, General Manager

Dahlonega

WDGR
03-01-1982; 1210 kHz AM; 2.5 kw-C, NDD; 10 kw-D, NDD; N34 31 45 W84 0 23
9110 Four Mile Creek Rd, Dahlonega, GA 30506 US
(706) 864-4477; *Fax:* (404) 446-5981
License: Dahlonega, GA held by USK Broadcasting Inc.

Hye Kim, General Manager

WZTR
12-16-1996; 104.3 MHz FM; *Hrs Open:* 24; 3.7 kw; 417 ft.; N34 29 56 W84 8 32
1376 Ben Higgins Road, Dahlonega, GA 30533 US
(706) 867-9542; *Fax:* (706) 864-4364
www.thunder1043fm.com
License: Dahlonega, Lumpkin County, GA held by Grady W. Turner
Nat'l Network: ABC; *Regional Network:* Ga. News Net.
Format: Classic Rock, Country; *Hrs. of News Programming:* news progmg 4 hrs wkly; *No. News Employees:* 1; *Target Audience:* 25-54; general; *Adv. Rates:* 30; 22; 30; 15
Bo Wilson, Station Manager

***WNGU**
01-01-1998; 89.5 MHz FM; *Hrs Open:* 24; 0.75 kw; 459 ft.; N34 31 29 W83 59 50 *Rebroadcasts:* Rebroadcast WJSP, Warm Springs, Colombus, 100%
260 - 14th Street, N.W., Altanta, GA 30318 US

RADIO - U.S.

(404) 685-2690; *Fax:* (404) 685-2684
www.gpb.org
ask@gpb.org
License: Dahlonega, Lumpkin County, GA held by Georgia Public Telecommunications Commission.
Nat'l Network: NPR; PRI; *Wire Services:* AP
Arbitron Metro Market: Atlanta, GA; *Format:* Classical, News
Special Programming: Jazz; *Hrs. of News Programming:* news progmg 40 hrs wkly; *No. News Employees:* 10
Milton Clipper, Chief Executive Officer
Teya Ryan, President
Tom Barclay, Operations Dir
Rob Maynard, Programming Director
Nancy Zintak, Promotions Manager
Bonnie Bean, CFO

WCDG
10-17-1974; 88.7 MHz FM; 600 w; N34 33 10 W83 58 05
50 Millies Pl., Unit A, Dahlonega, GA 30533
(706) 482-0525
License: Dahlonega, GA held by Silver Dove Broadcasting, Inc.
Group Owner: Silver Dove Broadcasting, Inc.
Format: Christian
Laurel Hughes, General Manager
Ken Alcorn, Marketing Director

Dallas

WDPC
09-21-1979; 1500 kHz AM
8451 S. Cherokee Blvd, Suite B, Dougladcille, CA 30134 US
(770) 920-1520; *Fax:* (770) 920-4600
www.wordchristianbroadcasting.com
License: Dallas, GA held by Word Christian Broadcasting Inc.
Arbitron Metro Market: Dallas, GA; *Format:* Gospel, Religious; *Target Audience:* General.
Ken Johns, President

Dalton

WBLJ
04-08-1940; 1230 kHz AM; *Hrs Open:* 24; 1 kw-U, ND1; N34 45 23 W84 57 2
P.O. Box 809, Dalton, GA 30720 US
(706) 278-5511; *Fax:* (706) 226-8766
wblj1230.com
pscoggins@ngaradio.com
License: Dalton, GA held by North Georgia Radio Group L.P.
Group Owner: North Georgia Radio Group L.P.; (acq 3-20-2006; grpsl)
Nat'l Network: CBS Radio; *Regional Network:* Ga. News Net.
Arbitron Metro Market: Dalton, GA; *Format:* News, News/Talk, 86
Special Programming: Relg mus; *Hrs. of News Programming:* news progmg 28 hrs wkly; *No. News Employees:* 2; *Target Audience:* 18-54. *Adv.Rates:* 20; 30; 25; 10
Larry Gibson, Programming Director/Station Manager

WDAL
10-01-1954; 1430 kHz AM; *Hrs Open:* 24
Mailing Address: 1899 Cleveland Hwy, Dalton, GA 30720 US
Second Address: 613 Silver Cir., Dalton, GA 30721
(706) 278-5511(706) 278-3300; *Fax:* (706) 278-7966
License: Dalton, GA held by North Georgia Radio Group L.P.
Group Owner: North Georgia Radio Group L.P.; (acq 3-20-2006; grpsl)
Nat'l Network: CBS; *Nat'l Reps:* Rgnl Reps
Arbitron Metro Market: Chattanooga, TN; *Format:* Tejano; *Hrs. of News Programming:* news progmg 30 hrs wkly; *No. News Employees:* 3; *Target Audience:* 25-45.
Larry Gibson, Station Manager

WYYU
08-01-1995; 104.5 MHz FM; *Hrs Open:* 24; 6 kw; 328 ft.; N34 49 42 W84 53 41
Mailing Address: 104 South Pentz Street, Dalton, GA 30721 US
Second Address: 613 Silver Cir, Dalton, GA 30721
(706) 278-5511; *Fax:* (706) 278-7966
License: Dalton, Whitfield County, GA
Group Owner: North Georgia Radio Group L.P.
Arbitron Metro Market: Dalton, GA; *Format:* Adult Contemp; *No. News Employees:* 3
Lamar Studstill, Chairman
Cole Studstill, CFO
Lee Studstill, President

WTTI
06-17-1965; 1530 kHz AM; 10 kw-C, DAD; 10 kw-D, DAD; N34 47 9 W85 2 40
Mailing Address: P.O. Box 216, Dalton, GA 30720 US
Second Address: 111 W. Crawford St., Dalton, GA 30720
(706) 673-2222; *Fax:* (706) 673-7141
www.wttiradio.com
License: Dalton, GA held by Troy L. Hall.
Arbitron Metro Market: Dalton, GA; *Format:* Christian; *Target Audience:* 25-54; family, relg
Troy Hall, CEO
C.W. Queen, Station Manager

Darien

WHFX
05-13-1993; 107.7 MHz FM; *Hrs Open:* 24; 50 kw; 482 ft.; N31 10 9 W81 32 14
3833 US Highway 82, Brunswick, GA 31523 US
(912) 267-1025; *Fax:* (912) 264-5462
License: Darien, McIntosh County, GA held by AMFM Radio Licenses LLC.
Group Owner: iHeartMedia; (acq 2014)
Nat'l Reps: McGavren Guild
Arbitron Metro Market: Brunswick, GA; *Format:* Rock/AOR; *Hrs. of News Programming:* news progmg 4 hrs wkly; *No. News Employees:* 1; *Target Audience:* 25 plus; general; *Adv. Rates:* 25; 18; 20; 12
Richard J. Bressler, President
Michelle Harrison, Business Manager

Dawson

WMRZ
06-01-2005; 98.1 MHz FM; 25 kw; 262 ft.; N31 37 29 W84 19 20
809 South Westover Blvd., Albany, GA 31707 US
(229) 439-9704; *Fax:* (229) 439-1509
www.kissalbany.com
License: Dawson, Terrell County, GA held by CC Licenses LLC.
Group Owner: iHeartMedia; (acq 11-16-2005; $875,000)
Arbitron Metro Market: Dawson, GA; *Format:* Blues, Oldies, 92
Chuck Thompson, General Sales Mgr
Miss Monique, Programming Director
Wes Carroll, Digital Content Director

Decatur

WATB
07-19-1958; 1420 kHz AM; 1 kw-D, DA2; 0.051 kw-N, DA2; N33 47 13 W84 14 53
3589 N. Decatur Rd., Scottdale, GA 30079 US
(404) 508-1420; *Fax:* (404) 508-8930
www.watb1420.com
benv@mrbi.net
License: Decatur, GA held by Way Broadcasting Licensee LLC
Group Owner: Multicultural Broadcasting Radio Inc.; (acq 6-13-00; grpsl).
Arbitron Metro Market: Atlanta, GA; *Format:* Ethnic; *Target Audience:* General; ethnic groups from around the world
Benjamin Vannoy Jr., General Manager

WPBC
08-11-1964; 1310 kHz AM; *Hrs Open:* 24
3300 Buckeye Road, Suite 800, Atlanta, GA 30341 US
(678) 200-8540
License: Decatur, GA held by Hanmi Broadcasting Inc.
Arbitron Metro Market: Atlanta, GA
Chang Kim, General Manager

Demorest

***WPPR**
01-01-1997; 88.3 MHz FM; *Hrs Open:* 24; 7.3 kw; 636 ft.; N34 31 24 W83 40 46 *Rebroadcasts:* Rebroadcasts WJSP-FM Warm Springs 85%
260 - 14th Street, N.W., Atlanta, GA 30318 US
(404) 685-2690; *Fax:* (404) 685-2684
www.gpb.org
ask@spb.org
License: Demorest, Habersham County, GA held by Georgia Public Telecommunications Commission.
Nat'l Network: NPR; PRI; *Wire Services:* AP
Format: News *Special Programming:* Jazz; *Hrs. of News Programming:* news progmg 40 hrs wkly; *No. News Employees:* 10; *Target Audience:* Adults 35+
Milton Clipper, Chief Executive Officer
Teya Ryan, President
Tom Barclay, Operations Dir
Rob Maynard, Programming Director
Nancy Zintak, Promotions Manager
Bonnie Bean, CFO

Dock Junction

WXMK
05-01-1991; 105.9 MHz FM; *Hrs Open:* 24; 15 kw; 420 ft.; N31 11 39 W81 29 30
522 Old Mission Rd, Brunswick, GA 31520 US
(912) 261-1000; *Fax:* (912) 265-8391
www.magic1059.com
info@magic1059.com
License: Dock Junction, Glynn County, GA held by Golden Isles Broadcasting L.L C.
Arbitron Metro Market: Brunswick, GA; *Format:* Adult Contemp, Contemporary Hits/Top 40; *Target Audience:* 25-54; women; *Adv. Rates:* 25; 25; 25; 20
Mark Douglas, Operations Dir
Joe Willie Sousa, General Manager
Cathy Trimble, General Sales Mgr
Dick Boekeloo, Chief Engineer
Everett Armstrong, Business Manager
Laura Wisham, Senior Account Executive
Joey Miller, AccountExecutive
Mike Cornell, Production Director

Donalsonville

WGMK
09-01-1980; 106.3 MHz FM; 5.9 kw; 331 ft.; N31 4 26 W84 52 47
Mailing Address: P. O. Box 236, Donalsonville, GA 31745 US
Second Address: 91 North Way, Donalsonville, GA 31743
(229) 524-5123; *Fax:* (229) 524-2265
License: Donalsonville, Seminole County, GA
Group Owner: Flint Media Inc.
Format: Adult Contemp
Gilbert Kelley, General Manager

WSEM
02-12-1963; 1500 kHz AM; 1 kw-D, NDD; N31 4 26 W84 52 47
Mailing Address: P. O. Box 87, Donalsonville, GA 31745 US
Second Address: 91 North Way, Donalsonville, GA 31743
(229) 524-5123; *Fax:* (229) 524-2265
License: Donalsonville, GA held by Flint Media Inc.
Group Owner: Flint Media Inc.; (acq 6-22-2006; grpsl).
Regional Network: Ga. News Net.
Format: News, Talk; *Target Audience:* 25-49.; *Adv. Rates:* 20; 20; 20; na
Kevin Dowdy, President
Gilbert Kelley Jr., General Manager
Grace Kelley, General Sales Mgr

***WWGF**
08-01-1998; 107.5 MHz FM; *Hrs Open:* 24; 6 kw; 315 ft.; N30 58 45 W84 57 27
P.O. Box 510, Appling, GA 30802 US
(800) 926-4669
www.gnnradio.org
License: Donalsonville, Seminole County, GA held by Barinowski Investment Co.
Group Owner: Good News Network; (acq 1-21-99)
Arbitron Metro Market: Grovetown, GA; *Format:* Christian; *Target Audience:* All.

Douglas

WDMG
03-01-1947; 860 kHz AM; 5 kw-D, DAN; 5 kw-N, DAN; N31 30 23 W82 49 10
620 East Ward Street, Douglas, GA 31533 US
(912) 389-0995; *Fax:* (912) 383-8552
traffic@charter.net
License: Douglas, GA held by Broadcast South LLC.
Group Owner: Broadcast South LLC; (acq 11-15-2006; grpsl)
Nat'l Network: USA
Arbitron Metro Market: Albany, GA; *Format:* Sports *Special Programming:* Farm 4 hrs, relg 6 hrs wkly; *Hrs. of News Programming:* news progmg 20 hrs wkly; *No. News Employees:* 1; *Target Audience:* 25-54. *Adv.Rates:* 10; 9; 9; 6.
John Higgs, Station Manager

WOKA
12-10-1962; 1310 kHz AM; 3.9 kw-D, ND1; 0.039 kw-N, ND1; N31 31 24 W82 52 22
1310 W. Walker St., Douglas, GA 31533 US
(912) 384-1310; *Fax:* (912) 383-6328
License: Douglas, GA held by Coffee County Broadcasters Inc.
TV Affiliate: Sp; *No. News Employees:* General.; *Adv. Rates:* 12; 10; 12; 4.
CEO, Dwayne Gillis

WOKA-FM
07-01-1971; 106.7 MHz FM; 100 kw; 981 ft.; N31 40 21 W82 51 28
1310 West Walker Street, Douglas, GA 31533 US
(912) 384-8153; *Fax:* (912) 383-6328
www.dixiecountry.com
production@atc.cc
License: Douglas, Coffee County, GA held by Coffee County Broadcasters Inc.

TV Affiliate: Country; *Format:* Gospel; *No. News Employees:* Adults 25-54.; *Adv. Rates:* 25; 18; 20; 10
Jim Squires, Chief Executive Officer

Douglasville

WXJO
09-01-1969; 1120 kHz AM
6070 Rock Springs Road, Lithonia, GA 30038 US
(706) 276-2016; *Fax:* (706) 635-1018
wxjo1120.blogspot.ca
License: Douglasville, GA held by Exponent Broadcasting Inc.
Arbitron Metro Market: Atlanta, GA; *Format:* Oldies
Randy Gravley, President

WDCY
05-05-1993; 1520 kHz AM; *Hrs Open:* Sunrise-sunset
8451 Cherokee Blvd., Suite B, Douglasville, GA 30134 US
(770) 920-1520; *Fax:* (770) 920-4600
www.wordchristianbroadcasting.com
License: Douglasville, GA held by Word Christian Broadcasting Inc.
Arbitron Metro Market: Atlanta, GA; *Format:* Religious; *Hrs. of News Programming:* News progmg 10 hrs wkly; *Target Audience:* General.
Ken Johns, President

Dry Branch

WPLA
04-15-1998; 1670 kHz AM; *Hrs Open:* 24; 10 kw-D, 1 kw-N; N32 48 16 W83 36 16
7080 Industrial Hwy., Macon, GA 31216 US
(478) 781-1063; *Fax:* (478) 781-6711
www.foxsports1670.com
License: Dry Branch, Twiggs County, GA held by AMFM Radio Licenses LLC.
Group Owner: iHeartMedia; (acq. 2-15-2001; grpsl)
Nat'l Reps: Clear Channel
Population Served: 250,000; *Arbitron Metro Market:* Macon, GA; *Format:* Sports; *Target Audience:* General; adults
Thomas Bacote, Market President

Dublin

***WAWH**
01-01-2000; 88.3 MHz FM; 0.4 kw; 82 ft.; N32 32 27 W82 57 27
P.O. Box 3206, Tupelo, MS 38803 US
(662) 844-8888; *Fax:* (662) 842-6791
www.afr.net
faq@afa.net
License: Dublin, Laurens County, GA held by American Family Association.
Group Owner: American Family Radio
Format: Christian
Tim Wildmon, President
Donald Wildmon, Founder
Buddy Smith, Sr VP
Ed Vitagliano, Exec VP
Randy Sharp, Director Of Special Projects
Meeke Addison, Director Of Communications
Abraham Hamilton III, General Counsel

WKKZ
04-04-1967; 92.7 MHz FM; *Hrs Open:* 24; 50 kw; 417 ft.; N32 31 21 W82 54 0
Mailing Address: Post Office Box 967, Dublin, GA 31040 US
Second Address: 1006 Martin Luther King Blvd., Dublin, GA 31021
(478) 272-9270; *Fax:* (478) 275-3592
www.wkkz927.com
License: Dublin, Laurens County, GA held by Kirby Broadcasting Co.
Nat'l Network: ABC; *Nat'l Reps:* Dora-Clayton
Arbitron Metro Market: Macon, GA; *Format:* Contemporary Hits/Top 40
Ray Beck, General Manager

WMLT
01-12-1945; 1330 kHz AM; *Hrs Open:* 24; 5 kw-D, DAN; 0.5 kw-N, DAN; N32 33 50 W82 52 0
Mailing Address: PO Box 2639, Gulfport, MS 39505 US
Second Address: 807 Bellevue Ave., Dublin, GA 31021
(478) 272-4422; *Fax:* (478) 275-4657
richhumphrey@wqzy.com
License: Dublin, GA held by State Broadcasting Corporation.
Regional Network: Ga. News Net; *Nat'l Reps:* Rgnl Reps
Regional Reps: Regional Reps
Arbitron Metro Market: Dublin, GA; *Format:* Gospel; *No. News Employees:* 2; *Target Audience:* 25-54.
J. Morgan Dowdy, President
Rick Humphrey, General Manager

WQZY
01-01-1978; 95.9 MHz FM; *Hrs Open:* 24; 100 kw; 1024 ft.; N32 40 42 W82 33 26
P.O Box 2639, Gulfport, MS 39505 US
(478) 272-4422; *Fax:* (478) 275-4657
www.wqzy.com
webmaster@wqzy.com
License: Dublin, Laurens County, GA held by State Broadcasting Corporation
Regional Network: Ga. News Net. *Regional Reps:* Regional Reps
Format: Country; *Target Audience:* 18-54.; *Adv. Rates:* 28; 28; 26; 10
J. Morgan Dowdy, President
Rick Humphrey, General Manager
Robert Whitt, Programming Director

WXLI
03-16-1958; 1230 kHz AM; 0.7 kw-U, ND1; N32 31 21 W82 54 0
Mailing Address: P.O. Box 967, Dublin, GA 31040 US
Second Address: 1006 Martin Luther King Blvd., Dublin, GA 31021
(478) 272-4282; *Fax:* (478) 275-3592
License: Dublin, GA held by Laurens County Broadcasting Co.
Nat'l Network: CBS; *Nat'l Reps:* Dora-Clayton
Arbitron Metro Market: Dublin, GA; *Format:* Country, Gospel
Ray Beck, General Manager

East Dublin

WEDB
12-18-1966; 98.1 MHz FM; 9.6 kw; 525 ft.; N32 32 55 W82 38 49
P.O. Box 1590 2 Radio Loop, Swainsboro, GA 30401 US
(478) 237-1590; *Fax:* (478) 237-3559
www.magic98wedb.com/
License: East Dublin, Laurens County, GA held by RadioJones LLC.
Group Owner: RadioJones LLC
Arbitron Metro Market: East Dublin, GA; *Format:* Contemporary Hits/Top 40; *Hrs. of News Programming:* news progmg 10 hrs wkly; *No. News Employees:* 1; *Target Audience:* 18-50.; *Adv. Rates:* 16; 14; 14; 8
Dennis Jones, President
John Wagner, Operations Dir
Jolly Martin, General Sales Mgr
Bobby Duncan, Programming Director

East Point

WCFO
10-09-1994; 1160 kHz AM; *Hrs Open:* 24
1935 Sixth Street, Chamblee, GA 30341 US
(404) 681-9307; *Fax:* (404) 870-8859
www.newstalk1160.com
listeners@jwbroadcasting.com
License: East Point, GA held by JW Broadcasting Inc.
Arbitron Metro Market: Atlanta, GA; *Format:* News, News/Talk, 86
Jeff Davis, Operations Dir

WTJH
12-01-1949; 1260 kHz AM; 5 kw-D, ND2; 0.039 kw-N, ND2; N33 41 47 W84 28 29
645 Church St., Ste. 400, Norfolk, VA 23510 US
(404) 344-2233; *Fax:* (404) 346-0647
License: East Point, GA held by Christian Broadcasting of East Point Inc.
Group Owner: Willis Broadcasting Corp.
Arbitron Metro Market: Atlanta, GA; *Format:* Gospel, Religious
Christine Willis-Wiggs, General Manager

Eastman

WUFF
09-01-1961; 710 kHz AM
Mailing Address: 731 College Street, Eastman, GA 31023 US
Second Address: 855 College St., Eastman, GA
(478) 374-3437; *Fax:* (478) 374-3585
License: Eastman, GA held by Dodge Broadcasting Inc.
Arbitron Metro Market: Eastman,GA; *Format:* Country *Special Programming:* Black 5 hrs wkly

WUFF-FM
01-01-1976; 97.5 MHz FM; 4.62 kw; 371 ft.; N32 13 18 W83 13 4
Mailing Address: 731 College Street, Eastman, GA 31023 US
Second Address: 855 College St., Eastman, GA 31023
(478) 374-3437; *Fax:* (478) 374-3585
wolfcountry975.com
Greg@wolfcountry975.com
License: Eastman, Dodge County, GA
Arbitron Metro Market: Eastman, GA; *Format:* Gospel, News
Greg Grantham, General Manager/Program Director
Scott Morrison, Station Manager
Wanda Lancaster, General Sales Mgr
Quint Bush, News Director
Mike Cowan, Traffic/Billing

Eatonton

WKVQ
12-15-1966; 1540 kHz AM *Rebroadcasts:* Simulcast with WKRR(FM) Milledgeville
P.O. Box 3965, Eatonton, GA 31024 US
(706) 485-8792; *Fax:* (706) 485-3555
starstation@bellsouth.net
License: Eatonton, GA held by Craig Baker.
Format: Adult Contemp; *Target Audience:* General.
Craig Baker, President

WMGZ
02-08-1988; 97.7 MHz FM; *Hrs Open:* 24; 8.5 kw; 554 ft.; N33 20 41 W83 13 41
Mailing Address: P. O. Box 832, Milledgeville, GA 31061 US
Second Address: 156 Lake Laurel Rd., Milledgeville, GA 31061
(478) 453-9406; *Fax:* (478) 453-3298
www.z97.fm/
z97mail@yahoo.com
License: Eatonton, Putnam County, GA held by Southern Stone Broadcasting Inc.
Group Owner: Southern Broadcasting Companies Inc.; (acq 7-6-2005; $1.1 million with WKGQ(AM) Milledgeville)
Nat'l Network: ABC
Arbitron Metro Market: Eatonton, GA; *Format:* Adult Contemp; *Hrs. of News Programming:* news progmg 4 hrs wkly; *No. News Employees:* 1; *Target Audience:* 18-49.; *Adv. Rates:* 12; 10; 12; 8
Tony Taylor, Operations Dir
Tom Ptak, General Manager
Walter Reynolds, Promotions Manager

Elberton

WSGC
01-01-1947; 1400 kHz AM; *Hrs Open:* 24; 1 kw, ND1; N34 6 50 W82 52 52 *Rebroadcasts:* FM translator W243CI 96.5
P.O. Box 638, Elberton, GA 30458 US
(706) 213-1051; *Fax:* (706) 283-8710
www.wsgcradio.com
License: Elberton, GA held by Georgia-Carolina Radiocasting Co. LLC.
Group Owner: Georgia-Carolina Radiocasting Companies; (acq 7-25-2002; grpsl)
Nat'l Network: CBS Radio; *Regional Network:* Ga. News Net.
Arbitron Metro Market: Elberton, GA; *Format:* Adult Contemp; *Hrs. of News Programming:* news progmg 12 hrs wkly; *No. News Employees:* 1; *Target Audience:* 35+.
David Thompson, Operations Manager
Gary Bryant, Vice President/General Manager
David Stephens, News Director

Ellaville

WLEL
01-01-2009; 94.3 MHz FM; 4.8 kw; 328 ft.; N32 15 10 W84 13 50
US
(229) 937-9967; *Fax:* (229) 591-5743
www.wlelclassichits.com
License: Ellaville, Schley County, GA held by Gary S. Hess
Arbitron Metro Market: Ellaville, GA; *Format:* Contemporary Hits/Top 40, Adult Contemp
Roy Janes, General Manager
Cary Moore, Account Executive

Ellijay

WPGY
05-10-1978; 1580 kHz AM
P.O. Box 545, Ellijay, GA 30540 US
(706) 276-2016; *Fax:* (706) 635-1018
wlja@ellijay.com
License: Ellijay, GA held by Exponent Broadcasting Inc.
Format: Country; *Target Audience:* 18-75.; *Adv. Rates:* 15; 12; 15; 12
Randy Gravley, Operations Dir
Byron Dobbs, General Manager

WLJA-FM
11-01-1985; 101.1 MHz FM; *Hrs Open:* 6 AM-10 PM; 19 kw; 276 ft.; N34 42 59 W84 30 50
P.O. Box 545, Ellijay, GA 30540 US
(678) 454-9350; *Fax:* (678) 454-3950
www.wljaradio.com

RADIO - U.S.

License: Ellijay, Gilmer County, GA held by Tri-State Communications Inc.
Format: Country, Gospel; *Target Audience:* 18-75.; *Adv. Rates:* $15; 12; 15; 12
Millard Oakley, President
Craig Cantrell, Operations Dir
Joel Upton, General Manager
Carolyn Peterman, Station Manager
Mark Young, General Sales Mgr
Shirley Burnette, News Director
Austin Stinnett, Chief Engineer
Roger Ealey,News & Sports Director

Evans

WAEG
11-01-1991; 92.3 MHz FM; 6 kw; 328 ft.; N33 35 24.5 W82 13 52.5
6025 Broadcast Dr., North Augusta, SC 29841 US
(803) 279-2330; *Fax:* (803) 279-2330
www.923smoothjazz.com
License: Evans, Columbia County, GA held by Perry Broadcasting of Augusta Inc.
Group Owner: Perry Publishing & Broadcasting Co.; (acq 12-12-2007; grpsl)
Nat'l Reps: Christal
Arbitron Metro Market: Tyler-Longview TX; *Format:* Talk *Special Programming:* Relg 10 hrs wkly; *Hrs. of News Programming:* News progmg 3 hrs wkly; *Target Audience:* 35 plus; listeners with interest in classicalmusic; *Adv. Rates:* 35; 30; 30; 25

Fayetteville

WUMJ
03-08-1966; 97.5 MHz FM; 7.9 kw; 574 ft.; N33 29 29 W84 35 0
101 Marietta St., 12th Floor, Atlanta, GA 30303 US
(404) 765-9750; *Fax:* (404) 688-7686
www.majicatl.com
License: Fayetteville, Fayette County, GA held by Radio One Licenses, LLC
Group Owner: Radio One Inc.; (acq 11-8-2001; grpsl)
Arbitron Metro Market: Atlanta, GA; *Format:* Urban Contemporary
Tim Davies, General Manager

Fitzgerald

WBHB
10-08-1946; 1240 kHz AM; 1 kw-U, ND1; N31 42 23 W83 15 40
Box 100, Fitzgerald, GA 31750 US
(229) 423-2077; *Fax:* (229) 423-8313
License: Fitzgerald, GA held by Broadcast South LLC.
Group Owner: Broadcast South LLC; (acq 11-15-2006; grpsl)
Nat'l Network: Westwood One
Format: Black, Gospel; *Target Audience:* General.
John Higgs, General Manager

WRDO
01-01-1991; 96.9 MHz FM; *Hrs Open:* 24; 6 kw; 328 ft.; N31 44 33 W83 14 39
603 West 2nd Street, Pobox 7, Tifton, GA 31754 US
(912) 389-0995; *Fax:* (912) 383-8552
License: Fitzgerald, Ben Hill County, GA held by Broadcast South LLC.
Group Owner: Broadcast South LLC; (acq 11-15-2006; grpsl)
Nat'l Network: USA
Format: Adult Contemp *Special Programming:* Gospel 6 hrs wkly; *No. News Employees:* 1; *Target Audience:* 25-55; baby boomers
John Higgs, General Manager

Folkston

***WATY**
01-01-2000; 91.3 MHz FM; *Hrs Open:* 24; 0.6 kw; 322 ft.; N30 52 29 W82 1 10
Box 1448, Kingsland, GA 31548 US
(912)496-4484; *Fax:* (912)496-4086
www.gpb.org
ask@gpb.org
License: Folkston, Charlton County, GA held by The Foundation for Public Broadcasting in Georgia Inc.
Nat'l Network: NPR; *Regional Network:* Georgia Public Radio
Arbitron Metro Market: Jacksonville, FL
Milton Clipper, Chief Executive Officer
Teya Ryan, President
Rob Maynard, Programming Director
Nancy Zintak, Vice President of Marketing & Communications

***WECC-FM**
03-17-2002; 89.3 MHz FM; 30 kw; 489 ft.; N30 55 54 W81 42 30
P O Box 1190, St. Marys, GA 31558 US
(912) 882-8930; *Fax:* (912) 882-9322
www.thelighthousefm.org
mail@thelighthousefm.org
License: Folkston, Charlton County, GA held by Lighthouse Christian Broadcasting Corp.
Nat'l Network: Salem Radio Network
Arbitron Metro Market: Folkston, GA; *Format:* Christian
Paul Hafer, General Manager

Forsyth

WQMJ
11-22-1973; 100.1 MHz FM; 3 kw; 299 ft.; N32 58 27 W83 52 2
6070 Rock Springs Road, Lithonia, GA 30038 US
(478) 745-3301; *Fax:* (478) 742-2293
productionrci@aol.com
License: Forsyth, Monroe County, GA held by Roberts Communications Inc.
Arbitron Metro Market: Macon, GA; *Format:* Urban Contemporary
Mike Roberts, General Manager

***WBIB-FM**
89.1 MHz FM; 0.1 kw; 174 ft.; N33 3 1 W83 57 10 US
(478) 932-0036
www.wbibfm.com
wbibfm@yahoo.com
License: Forsyth, Monroe County, GA held by Believers in Broadcasting Inc.
Arbitron Metro Market: Forsyth, GA; *Format:* Christian
Travis Nunn, President
Jennifer Nunn, General Manager
Travis Nunn, Programming Director

Fort Benning South

WKCN
11-06-1992; 99.3 MHz FM; *Hrs Open:* 24; 29 kw; 548 ft.; N32 27 59 W85 3 22
1820 Wynnton Rd., Columbus, GA 31904 US
(706) 327-1217; *Fax:* (706) 596-4600
www.kissin993.com
License: Fort Benning South, Stewart County, GA held by PMB Broadcasting LLC.
Group Owner: PMB Broadcasting LLC; (acq 10-1-2008; grpsl)
Nat'l Reps: Christal
Arbitron Metro Market: Columbus, GA; *Format:* Country; *Target Audience:* 25-54; general
Dave Arwood, Operations Dir
Helen Neal, Dir. of Sales
Robert Grantham, Local Sales & Marketing Manager

Fort Gaines

***WJWV**
02-28-1993; 90.9 MHz FM; *Hrs Open:* 24; 20.5 kw horiz, 81 kw vert; 254 ft.; N31 36 16 W85 2 2 *Rebroadcasts:* Rebroadcasts WJSP-FM Warm Springs 100%
260 - 14th Street, N.W., Atlanta, GA 30318 US
(404) 685-2690; *Fax:* (404) 685-2684
www.gpb.org
ask@gpb.org
License: Fort Gaines, Clay County, GA held by Georgia Public Telecommunications Commission.
Arbitron Metro Market: Dothan, AL; *Format:* News *Special Programming:* Jazz 16 hrs wkly; *No. News Employees:* 10
Milton Clipper, Chief Executive Officer
Teya Ryan, President
Tom Barclay, Operations Dir
Rob Maynard, Programming Director
Nancy Zintak, Vice President of Marketing & Communications
Bonnie Bean, CFO

Fort Valley

WIBB-FM
03-03-1993; 97.9 MHz FM; *Hrs Open:* 24; 10.5 kw; 499 ft.; N32 34 12 W83 45 26
7080 Industrial Hwy., Macon, GA 31216 US
(478) 781-1063; *Fax:* (478) 781-6711
www.wibb.com
info@wibb.com
License: Fort Valley, Peach County, GA held by AMFM Radio Licenses LLC.
Group Owner: iHeartMedia; (acq 2-15-2001; grpsl).
Arbitron Metro Market: Macon, GA; *Format:* Blues, Urban Contemporary; *Hrs. of News Programming:* news progmg 14 hrs wkly; *No. News Employees:* 1; *Target Audience:* 18-44.
Brent Henslee, Operations Manager
Terrence Bibb, Programming Director
James Gay, Chief Engineer
Melissa Stinebaugh, Business Manager

***WJTG**
03-01-1989; 91.3 MHz FM; *Hrs Open:* 24; 100 kw; 459 ft.; N32 41 27 W83 51 45
341 S Washington, Lancaster, WI 53813 US
(478) 956-0085; *Fax:* (478) 956-0913
wjtg913@aol.com
License: Fort Valley, Peach County, GA held by Family Life Broadcasting Inc.
Group Owner: Family Life Communications Inc.; (acq 5-23-2007; grpsl)
Nat'l Network: USA
Arbitron Metro Market: Macon, GA; *Format:* Religious, Christian; *Target Audience:* General.
Tracy O. Wells, Operations Dir

WQBZ
04-06-1981; 106.3 MHz FM; *Hrs Open:* 24; 48 kw; 492 ft.; N32 45 31 W83 44 49
7080 Industrial Hwy., Macon, GA 31216 US
(478) 781-1063; *Fax:* (478) 781-6711
www.q106.fm
info@q106.fm
License: Fort Valley, Peach County, GA held by AMFM Radio Licenses LLC.
Group Owner: iHeartMedia; (acq 2-15-2001; grpsl).
Arbitron Metro Market: Macon, GA; *Format:* Classic Rock; *Target Audience:* 18-49.
Thomas Bacote, Market President
Brent Henslee, Operations Manager/Program Director
James Gay, Chief Engineer
Melissa Stinebaugh, Business Manager

WXKO
06-01-1951; 1150 kHz AM; *Hrs Open:* 24; 1 kw-D, ND1; 0.062 kw-N, ND1; N32 34 34 W83 54 17
6070 Rock Springs Road, Lithonia, GA 30038 US
(912) 825-5547; *Fax:* (912) 827-1273
clmurray11@aol.com
License: Fort Valley, GA held by WVKX-FM Radio LLC
Regional Network: Ga. News Net.
Arbitron Metro Market: Macon, GA; *Format:* Country; *Hrs. of News Programming:* news progmg 10 hrs wkly; *No. News Employees:* 1; *Target Audience:* 25 plus; Black
Christopher Murray, President

Gainesville

***WBCX**
01-01-1977; 89.1 MHz FM; *Hrs Open:* 24; 0.84 kw; 545 ft.; N34 19 1 W83 49 45
One Centinnial Circle, Gainesville, GA 30501 US
(307) 638-8921; *Fax:* (307) 638-8922
License: Gainesville, Hall County, GA held by Brenau University.
Nat'l Network: PRI; Jones Radio Networks
Arbitron Metro Market: Auburn WA; *Format:* Rock/AOR; *Adv. Rates:* 22; 15; 22; 15
Jay Andrews, Director of Broadcasting

WDUN
04-02-1949; 550 kHz AM; *Hrs Open:* 24; 10 kw-D, DAN; 2.5 kw-N, DAN; N34 20 8 W83 47 32
Mailing Address: P. O. Box 10, Gainesville, GA 30503 US
Second Address: 1102 Thompson Bridge Rd. N.E., Gainesville, GA 30501
(770) 532-9921; *Fax:* (770) 532-0459
WDUN.com or AccessNorthGA.com
jay.jacobs@jacobsmedia.net
License: Gainesville, GA held by JWJ Properties Inc.
Group Owner: Jacobs Media Corp.; (acq 9-83;
Nat'l Network: Fox News Radio; *Regional Network:* Ga. News Net.; *Wire Services:* AP
Arbitron Metro Market: Atlanta, GA; *Format:* News, News/Talk, 86; *Hrs. of News Programming:* Hourly; *No. News Employees:* 10; *Target Audience:* 25-65.; *Adv. Rates:* Varies
John W. Jacobs Jr., Chairman
Jay Jacobs, CEO
Bill Maine, Operations Dir
Joel Williams, General Manager
Jean Pethel, General Sales Mgr
Bill Maine, Programming Director

WSRV
11-01-1965; 97.1 MHz FM; 98 kw; 1585 ft.; N34 7 32 W83 51 32
1601 West Peachtree Street NE, Atlanta, GA 30303 US
(404) 897-7500; *Fax:* (404) 741-9797
www.971theriver.com
License: Gainesville, Hall County, GA held by Cox Radio Inc.
Group Owner: Cox Radio Inc.; (acq 8-16-2000; grpsl)
Arbitron Metro Market: Atlanta, GA; *Format:* Classical, Adult Contemp; *Hrs. of News Programming:* News progmg 3 hrs wkly; *Target Audience:* 35-54; baby boomers

Chris Eagan, Program Director
Justin Tysinger, Promotions Supervisor
Donna Hall, Vice President & Market Manager

WGGA
10-10-1941; 1240 kHz AM; *Hrs Open:* 24
Mailing Address: P.O. Box 10, Gainesville, GA 30503 US
Second Address: 1102 Thompson Bridge Rd. N.E., Gainesville, GA 30501
(770) 532-9921; *Fax:* (770) 532-0459
accesswdun.com
jay.jacobs@jacobsmedia.net
License: Gainesville, GA held by JWJ Properties Inc.
Group Owner: Jacobs Media Corp.; (acq 4-20-93; $360,000;
Nat'l Network: NBC; *Regional Network:* Ga. News Net.
Arbitron Metro Market: Atlanta, GA; *Format:* Sports, Talk; *Hrs. of News Programming:* Hourly; *No. News Employees:* 1; *Target Audience:* 18-49 men; *Adv. Rates:* Varies
John W. Jacobs Jr., Chairman
John W. Jacobs III, CEO
Joel Williams, General Manager

WLBA
01-26-1957; 1130 kHz AM; *Hrs Open:* Sunrise-sunset; 1 kw-C, NDD; 10 kw-D, NDD; N34 16 45 W83 46 33
PO Box 746, Austell, GA 30001 US
(770) 944-0900; *Fax:* (770) 944-9794
www.lafavorita.net
License: Gainesville, GA held by La Favorita Inc.
Group Owner: La Favorita Radio Network; acq 2-18-97; $275,000)
Format: Spanish
Samuel Zamarron, President
Ariel Zamarron, Station Manager

WYAY
04-03-1949; 106.7 MHz FM; 77 kw; 1657 ft.; N33 52 2 W83 49 44
780 Johnson Ferry Rd. NE, Atlanta, GA 30342 US
(404) 497-4700
www.newsradio1067.com
newsroom@newsradio1067.com
License: Gainesville, GA held by Radio License Holdings LLC
Group Owner: Cumulus Media Inc.
Arbitron Metro Market: Atlanta, GA; *Format:* News/Talk
Don Boyd, General Sales Mgr

Gibson

***WTHP**
01-01-2006; 94.3 MHz FM; 6.3 kw; 571 ft.; N33 17 5 W82 35 45
P.O. Box 510, Appling, GA 30802 US
(800) 926-4669
www.gnnradio.org
License: Gibson, Glascock County, GA held by Barinowski Investment Co. L.P.
Group Owner: Good News Network; (acq 2-15-2006)
Arbitron Metro Market: Grovetown, GA; *Format:* Christian

Glennville

WOAH
11-18-1977; 106.3 MHz FM; *Hrs Open:* 24; 6 kw; Ant 394 ft; N32 00 27 W81 54 51
25 Bristlecone Dr., Savannah, GA 30427
(912) 408-1063; *Fax:* (912) 876-6920
www.hotkiss1063.com
License: Glennville, Tattnall County, GA held by Broadcast Executives Corp.

James Lewis, General Manager

Gordon

WFXM
03-30-1976; 107.1 MHz FM; *Hrs Open:* 24; 3 kw; 466 ft.; N32 50 55 W83 28 29
6070 Rock Springs Road, Lithonia, GA 30038 US
(478) 745-3301(478) 745-1077; *Fax:* (478) 742-2293
productionrci@aol.com
License: Gordon, Wilkinson County, GA held by WFXM-FM Radio LLC
Arbitron Metro Market: Macon, GA; *Format:* Urban Contemporary
Special Programming: Jazz 3 hrs wkly; *Target Audience:* Middle & upper class Georgians
Mike Roberts, General Manager

Gray

WIHB-FM
01-01-1994; 96.5 MHz FM; *Hrs Open:* 24; 8 kw; 571 ft.; N32 58 31 W83 47 59
7080 Industrial Highway, Macon, GA 31216 US
(478) 781-1063; *Fax:* (478) 781-6711
www.965thebull.com
License: Gray, Jones County, GA held by AMFM Radio Licenses LLC.
Group Owner: iHeartMedia; (acq 2-1-2001; grpsl).
Arbitron Metro Market: Macon, GA; *Format:* Country; *Target Audience:* 18-54; adults
Thomas Bacote, Market President
Brent Henslee, Operations Manager
Blaine Jackson, Programming Director
James Gay, Chief Engineer
Melissa Stinebaugh, Business Manager

Grayson

WPLO
01-07-1959; 610 kHz AM; *Hrs Open:* 24; 1.5 kw-D, ND1; 0.225 kw-N, ND1; N33 57 11 W83 58 15
3055 Sugarloaf Club Dr, Duluth, GA 30097 US
(770) 237-9897; *Fax:* (770) 246-0054
License: Grayson, GA held by Teresa Prieto
Arbitron Metro Market: Atlanta, GA; *Format:* Spanish, Christian
Franca Vera, General Manager

Greensboro

WDDK
07-12-1980; 103.9 MHz FM; *Hrs Open:* 24; 5.3 kw; 328 ft.; N33 28 29 W83 14 46
1271-B East Broad Street, Greensboro, GA 30642 US
(706) 453-4140; *Fax:* (706) 453-7179
www.dock1039.com/wddk/
chip@dock1039.com
License: Greensboro, Greene County, GA held by Wyche Services Corp.
Nat'l Network: ABC; *Regional Network:* Ga. News Net.
Arbitron Metro Market: Greensboro, GA; *Format:* Oldies, Talk; *Hrs. of News Programming:* news progmg 4 hrs wkly; *No. News Employees:* 1; *Target Audience:* 24-60.; *Adv. Rates:* 12; 12; 12; 12
K.B. Travis, Operations Dir
Chip Lyness, General Manager
K.B. Travis, Operations Director

***WPMA**
12-01-2002; 102.7 MHz FM; *Hrs Open:* 24; 7.5 kw; 594 ft.; N33 30 10 W83 15 37
P.O. Box 510, Appling, GA 30802 US
(800) 926-4669
www.gnnradio.org
License: Greensboro, GA held by Barinowski Investment Co. L.P.
Group Owner: Good News Network
Format: Christian

Griffin

WHIE
12-15-1952; 1320 kHz AM; 5 kw-D, ND1; 0.083 kw-N, ND1; N33 14 30 W84 18 17
3707 Randall Mill Road, NW, Atlanta, GA 30327 US
(770) 227-9451; *Fax:* (770) 229-2291
License: Griffin, GA held by Chappell Communications L.L.C.
Arbitron Metro Market: Atlanta, GA; *Format:* Country, News, 62, Sports, Talk
Robert Chappell Jr., President

WKEU
01-01-1933; 1450 kHz AM; 1 kw-U, ND1; N33 14 24 W84 14 55
Mailing Address: P.O. Box 997, Griffin, GA 30224 US
Second Address: 1000 Memorial Dr., Griffin, GA 30224
(770) 227-5507; *Fax:* (770) 229-2291
www.wkeuradio.com
wkeu@aol.com
License: Griffin, GA held by WLT & Associates L.P.
Regional Network: Ga. News Net; *Nat'l Reps:* Rgnl Reps
Arbitron Metro Market: Atlanta, GA; *Format:* News, Oldies; *Target Audience:* 25 plus.
William Taylor, President

***WMVV**
04-16-1995; 90.7 MHz FM; *Hrs Open:* 24; 18 kw; 472 ft.; N33 22 12 W84 8 0
Mailing Address: 1984 Old Peachtree Rd, Lawrenceville, GA 30043 US
Second Address: 100 S. Hill St., Suite 100, Griffin, GA 30223
(770) 229-2020
www.newlife.fm
contactus@newlife.fm
License: Griffin, Spalding County, GA held by Life Radio Ministries Inc.
Nat'l Network: American Family Radio; *Wire Services:* AP
Arbitron Metro Market: Atlanta, GA; *Format:* Christian, Religious
Joseph Emert, President
James Stewart, Operations Dir

Hahira

WTHV
01-01-1990; 810 kHz AM; *Hrs Open:* 15; 2.5 kw-D; N30 52 33.7N 83 16 22.5W
4198 Rebecca Circle, Valdosta, GA 31602
(229) 245-9848; *Fax:* (229) 262-0809
wthv810am@yahoo.com
License: Hahira, Lowndes County, GA held by Eternal Life Ministries Inc.
Nat'l Network: Salem Radio Network
Population Served: 90,000; *Arbitron Metro Market:* Valdosta, GA
Special Programming: Spanish 5 hrs wkly; *Target Audience:* 24-55.; *Adv. Rates:* 84; 84; 84; na
Cody Fender, President
Phyllis Fender, Operations Dir
Cory Fender, General Manager
Cory Fender, Station Manager
Cory Fender, General Sales Mgr
Cory Fender, Programming Director
Cory Fender, Promotions Manager
Cory Fender, ChiefEngineer

Hampton

WHTA
10-19-1973; 107.9 MHz FM; kw
101 Marietta St., 12th Floor, Atlanta, GA 30303 US
(404) 765-9750; *Fax:* (404) 688-7686
www.hotspotatl.com
License: Hampton, Henry County, GA held by Radio One Licenses LLC.
Group Owner: Radio One Inc.; (acq 8-20-01; $60 million).
Arbitron Metro Market: Atlanta, GA; *Format:* Urban Contemporary
Tim Davies, General Manager

Hapeville

WWWE
01-07-1947; 1100 kHz AM; *Hrs Open:* Sunrise-sunset; 3.8 kw-C, NDD; 5 kw-D, NDD; N33 43 43 W84 19 20
3033 Riviera Dr., Suite 200, Naples, FL 34103 US
(239) 263-5000; *Fax:* (239) 263-8191
www.bbgi.com
License: Hapeville, Fulton County, GA held by Beasley Media Group LLC
Group Owner: Beasley Broadcast Group Inc.; (acq 10-29-99; $10 million with WAEC(AM) Atlanta)
Arbitron Metro Market: Atlanta, GA; *Format:* Talk *Special Programming:* Relg 12 hrs, news/talk 14 hrs, Ethiopian 2 hrs wk; *Hrs. of News Programming:* news progmg 8 hrs wkly; *No. News Employees:* 1 *TargetAudience:* 35 plus; mature audience
LeAnder Cooper, General Manager

Harlem

WGAC-FM
11-23-1992; 95.1 MHz FM; 5.7 kw; 538 ft; N33 29 7 W82 12 7
4051 Jimmie Dyess Pkwy., Augusta, GA 30909
(706) 396-7000; *Fax:* (706) 396-7100
www.wgac.com
License: Harlem, Columbia County, GA held by Beasley Media Group LLC
Group Owner: Beasley Broadcast Group Inc.; (acq 1-13-97; $1.2 million).
Arbitron Metro Market: Augusta, GA; *Format:* News, News/Talk, 86; *Target Audience:* 18-34; well-educated adults, upper demographics
Chris O'Kelley, Operations Manager
Kent Murphy, General Sales Mgr
Mark Haddon, Vice President/Market Manager
Georgia Beasley, Digital Sales Manager

Hartwell

WKLY
09-05-1947; 980 kHz AM; *Hrs Open:* 18; 1 kw-D, ND1; 0.149 kw-N, ND1; N34 21 28 W82 58 35
Mailing Address: PO Box 636, Hartwell, GA 30643 US
Second Address: 2235 Bowersville Hwy., Hartwell, GA 30643
(706) 376-2233; *Fax:* (706) 376-3100
www.wklyradio.com
wklyradio@hartcom.net
License: Hartwell, GA held by WKLY Broadcasting Co.
Nat'l Network: ABC Radio; CNN Radio; Westwood One; *Regional Network:* Ga. News Net.

Format: Country, Gospel; *Hrs. of News Programming:* news progmg 18 hrs wkly; *No. News Employees:* 2; *Target Audience:* 30 plus; middle class, working adults; *Adv. Rates:* 15; 15; 15; 10
Bruce Hicks, CFO
Bryan Hicks, General Manager

Hawkinsville

WCEH
12-11-1952; 610 kHz AM; *Hrs Open:* 24; 0.5 kw-D, ND1; 0.126 kw-N, ND1; N32 16 50 W83 26 37
500 Commerce Street, P.O. Box 180, Hawkinsville, GA 31036 US
(478) 892-9061; *Fax:* (478) 892-9063
www.houstoncountyradio.com/WCEH.html
License: Hawkinsville, GA held by Georgia Eagle Media Inc.
Group Owner: Georgia Eagle Media Inc.; (acq 1-12-2007; grpsl)
Arbitron Metro Market: Warner Robins, GA; *Format:* News, Sports; *Hrs. of News Programming:* 7; *Target Audience:* men 24-65; *Adv. Rates:* 8; 6; 8; 6
Cecil Staton, President
Jay Braswell, General Manager

WQXZ
09-26-1968; 103.9 MHz FM; 10.5 kw; 495 ft.; N32 10 3 W83 37 51
P. O. Box 489, Hawkinsville, GA 31036 US
(478) 892-9061; *Fax:* (478) 892-8663
License: Hawkinsville, Pulaski County, GA held by Georgia Eagle Media Inc.
Group Owner: Georgia Eagle Media Inc.; 2007
Nat'l Network: CNN Radio; *Regional Network:* Ga. News Net.
Arbitron Metro Market: Macon, GA; *Format:* Oldies; *Hrs. of News Programming:* 7; *No. News Employees:* 1; *Target Audience:* male and female, 25-65; *Adv. Rates:* 14; 12; 14; 12
Cecil Station, President
Jay Braswell, General Manager

Hazlehurst

WHJD
09-06-1962; 920 kHz AM; *Hrs Open:* 24; 500 w-D, 39 w-N; N31 51 02 W82 33 19
546 Baxley Hwy., Hazlehurst, GA 31539
(912) 375-4511; *Fax:* (912) 375-4512
License: Hazlehurst, Jeff Davis County, GA held by Broadcast South, LLC
Group Owner: Broadcast South LLC
Nat'l Network: Fox News Radio; *Regional Network:* Ga. News Net.
Population Served: 10,000 *TV Affiliate:* WVOH-LP affil *Special Programming:* Farm 2 hrs wkly; *No. News Employees:* 1; *Adv. Rates:* 11.00/60sec—9.00/30 sec 24/7
Tony Deloach, Station Manager

Helen

*WTFH
02-01-2001; 89.9 MHz FM; *Hrs Open:* 24; 0.015 kw; 561 ft.; N34 44 55 W83 43 43
Mailing Address: Falls Road, Toccoa Falls, GA 30598 US
Second Address: 292 Old Clarksville Hwy., Toccoa Falls, GA 30577
(800) 251-8326; *Fax:* (706) 282-6090
www.toccoafallsradio.org
radio@tfc.edu
License: Helen, White County, GA held by Toccoa Falls College.
Arbitron Metro Market: Helen, GA; *Format:* Christian
Marty Lee, Operations Dir
David Cornelius, General Manager
Bryan Race, Station Manager
Bryan Race, Programming Director
Mike Shelley, Assistant Manager
Mike Shelley, Music Director

Hephzibah

WAKB
01-01-1975; 100.9 MHz FM; *Hrs Open:* 24; 16 kw; 302 ft.; N33 22 40 W82 4 37
6025 Broadcast Dr., North Augusta, SC 29841 US
(803) 279-2330; *Fax:* (803) 279-8149
www.1009magic.com
vperry@perrybroadcasting.net
License: Hephzibah, Burke County, GA held by Perry Broadcasting of Augusta Inc.
Group Owner: Perry Publishing & Broadcasting Co.; (acq 12-12-2007; grpsl)
Arbitron Metro Market: Devil's Lake ND; *Format:* Religious
Velvet Perry, General Manager

Hiawassee

WJUL
1230 kHz AM; 1 kw-U; N34 56 34 W83 46 27
Mailing Address: 101 S. Main St., Ste 6, Hiawassee, GA
Second Address: 38 Kenmare Hall, N.E., Atlanta, GA 30324
(706 896-1230,(404) 266-2257
License: Hiawassee, Towns County, GA held by WJUL Radio LLC
Group Owner: Batten Communications Inc.; (acq 7-28-2006).

Rick Morris, General Manager
John Allen, Programming Director
Jackie Grizzle, Chief Engineer

Hinesville

WGML
12-09-1958; 990 kHz AM; *Hrs Open:* Sunrise-sunset; 0.25 kw-D, ND1; 0.076 kw-N, ND1; N31 51 1 W81 36 4
Mailing Address: P.O. Box 93, Hinesville, GA 31310 US
Second Address: 308 Rolland St., Hinesville, GA 31313
(912) 368-3399; *Fax:* (912) 368-4191
wgml@coastalnow.net
License: Hinesville, GA held by Powerhouse of Deliverance Church Inc.
Format: Gospel, Religious *Special Programming:* Sp one hr wkly; *Hrs. of News Programming:* News progmg 10 hrs wkly; *Target Audience:* General.; *Adv. Rates:* 7.50; 7; 7.50
Bishop Raymond Napper, CEO
Elder Mary Napper, President
Emanuel White, General Manager

WTHG
01-01-1994; 104.7 MHz FM; *Hrs Open:* 24; 12 kw; 469 ft.; N31 51 18 W81 44 28
Mailing Address: 120 Liberty St./#Cd-104, Hinesville, GA 31313 US
Second Address: 120 D Liberty St., Hinesville, GA 31313
(912) 368-9258; *Fax:* (912) 368-5526
rjp106@aol.com
License: Hinesville, Liberty County, GA held by Tama Radio Licenses of Savannah, GA Inc.
Group Owner: Tama Broadcasting Inc.; (acq 4-8-2004).
Arbitron Metro Market: Savannah, GA; *Format:* Classic Rock
Yvonne Clark, General Manager

WSGA
08-02-1982; 92.3 MHz FM; *Hrs Open:* 24; 50 kw; 482 ft.; N31 41 37 W81 23 27
Mailing Address: P.O. Box 1280, Hinesville, GA 31313 US
Second Address: 120 D Liberty St., Hinesville, GA 31313
(912) 368-9258; *Fax:* (912) 368-5526
office@923classiccountry.com
License: Hinesville, Liberty County, GA held by Tama Radio Licenses of Savannah, GA, Inc.
Group Owner: Tama Broadcasting Inc.; (acq 4-8-2004; $2.79 million).
Nat'l Reps: Rgnl Reps
Format: Adult Contemp; *Hrs. of News Programming:* News progmg 2 hrs wkly; *Target Audience:* 25-54; Savannah, Hinesville, Brunswick, 15 county area
Yvonne Clark, General Manager

Hogansville

WVCC
08-12-1985; 720 kHz AM; *Hrs Open:* Sunrise-sunset; 7.97 kw-D, NDD; N33 3 54 W84 57 23
154 Boone Dr., Newnan, GA 30263 US
(770) 683-7234; *Fax:* (770) 683-9846
www.720thevoice.com
License: Hogansville, GA held by Citicasters Licenses Inc.
Group Owner: iHeartMedia
Nat'l Network: Fox News Radio; Premiere Radio Networks; Salem Radio Network; *Regional Network:* Ga. News Net.
Arbitron Metro Market: Newnan, GA; *Format:* News, News/Talk, 86
Blaine Jackson, Programming Director

WMGP
09-03-1992; 98.1 MHz FM; *Hrs Open:* 24; 25 kw; 328 ft.; N33 3 54 W84 57 23
154 Boone Drive, Newnan, GA 30263 US
(770) 683-7234; *Fax:* (770) 683-9846
www.magic981.com
License: Hogansville, Troup County, GA held by Citicasters Licenses Inc.
Group Owner: iHeartMedia; (acq 1999; grpsl).
Arbitron Metro Market: Hogansville, GA; *Format:* Contemporary Hits/Top 40, Adult Contemp; *Target Audience:* 17-64; non-country listeners
Blaine Jackson, Programming Director

Homerville

WBTY
12-01-1980; 98.7 MHz FM; 6 kw; 299 ft.; N31 2 4 W82 51 50
Mailing Address: PO Bix 577, Homerville, GA 31634 US
Second Address: Intersection of Hwy's 168 & 37, Homerville, GA 31634
(781) 891-2808; *Fax:* (912) 487-3414
RadioBentley@gmail.com
License: Homerville, Clinch County, GA held by Southern Broadcasting & Investments.
Arbitron Metro Market: Waltham, MA; *Format:* Contemporary Hits/Top 40, Adult Contemp; *Target Audience:* General.
Nicholas Smits, President
Jim Strickland, Operations Dir
Michael Primes, General Manager
Vincent Menechino, Station Manager
Brian Irvine, Programming Director
Robbie LaBrie, Sports Director

Irwinton

WVKX
09-01-1995; 103.7 MHz FM; 6 kw; 328 ft.; N32 52 48 W83 11 7
P.O. Box 569, 104 High Hill Street, Irwinton, GA 31042 US
(478) 946-3445; *Fax:* (478) 946-2406
blackmaconweb.com
biggeorgeradio@cox.net
License: Irwinton, Wilkinson County, GA held by Wilkinson Broadcasting Inc.
Arbitron Metro Market: Irwinton, GA; *Format:* Blues, Gospel
Stan Carter, General Manager

Jackson

WJGA-FM
04-24-1967; 92.1 MHz FM; *Hrs Open:* 24; 2.15 kw; 374 ft.; N33 16 37 W83 57 59
P.O. Box 878, Jackson, GA 30233 US
(770) 775-3151; *Fax:* (770) 775-3153
License: Jackson, Butts County, GA held by Earnhart Broadcasting Co. Inc.
Nat'l Reps: Keystone (unwired net) *Regional Reps:* Rgnl Reps.; *Wire Services:* AP
Format: Adult Contemp, Black *Special Programming:* Gospel 15 hrs wkly; *Hrs. of News Programming:* news progmg 20 hrs wkly; *No. News Employees:* 1; *Target Audience:* General.; *Adv. Rates:* 15; 15; 15; 15
Don Earnhart, President

Jacksonville

WSIZ-FM
102.3 MHz FM; 5.5 kw; 335 ft.; N31 46 42 W83 5 7
US
(208) 733-3551
www.wayx.net
License: Jacksonville, Telfair County, GA held by World Radio Link Inc.
Group Owner: World Radio Link Inc.
Arbitron Metro Market: Jacksonville, GA; *Format:* Classic Rock, News, 86
Earl Williamson, President

Jasper

*WIVL
01-01-1999; 88.3 MHz FM; *Hrs Open:* 24; 0.2 kw; 3 ft.; N34 28 1 W84 25 49
321 Freeman Circle, Norcross, GA 30071 US
(770) 596-0739; *Fax:* (706) 425-1840
License: Jasper, Pickens County, GA held by Community Public Radio Inc.
Arbitron Metro Market: Jasper, GA; *Format:* Adult Contemp; *Target Audience:* 35-55; upper middle class, educated, Christian
Penny Jackson, President

WYYZ
05-25-1973; 1490 kHz AM; 1 kw-U, ND1; N34 28 32 W84 26 13
P.O. Box 280, Jasper, GA 30143 US
(706) 692-4100; *Fax:* (706) 692-4012
License: Jasper, GA held by Enlightment LLC
Nat'l Network: CBS
Arbitron Metro Market: Atlanta, GA; *Format:* Classic Rock
Mark Hellinger, General Manager

Jeffersonville

WPEZ
09-27-1993; 93.7 MHz FM; *Hrs Open:* 24; 100 kw; 679 ft.; N32 45 12 W83 33 46
173 First Street, Macon, GA 31202 US
(478) 746-6286; *Fax:* (478) 745-4383
www.z937.com
info@z937.com
License: Jeffersonville, Twiggs County, GA held by Cumulus Licensing Corp.
Group Owner: Cumulus Media Inc.; (acq 12-20-02; grpsl).
Arbitron Metro Market: Macon, GA; *Format:* Classic Rock; *Hrs. of News Programming:* News progmg one hr wkly; *Target Audience:* 25-54.; *Adv. Rates:* 120; 110; 110; 30
John Sheftic, General Manager

Jesup

***WTLD**
01-01-2004; 90.5 MHz FM; *Hrs Open:* 24; 6 kw; 171 ft.; N31 35 49 W81 56 14
207 Greenview Street, Jesup, GA 31545 US
(912) 695-7169; *Fax:* (912) 588-1822
WTLDFM@AOL.COM
License: Jesup, Wayne County, GA held by Resurrection House Ministries Inc.
Arbitron Metro Market: JESUP, GA; *Format:* Gospel; *Hrs. of News Programming:* News progmg 12 hrs wkly; *Target Audience:* 18 plus.
Dr. Leonard Small, CEO
Evangelist Marie Butler, General Manager

WIFO-FM
07-01-1968; 105.5 MHz FM; *Hrs Open:* 24; 25 kw; 308 ft.; N31 36 6 W81 56 0
P. O. Box 647, Jesup, GA 31545 US
(912) 427-3711; *Fax:* (912) 530-7717
www.bigdogcountry.com
bigdogstaff@bellsouth.net
License: Jesup, Wayne County, GA held by Jesup Broadcasting Corp.
Nat'l Network: ABC Information & Entertainment; *Regional Network:* Ga. News Net; *Nat'l Reps:* Rgnl Reps
Format: Country; *No. News Employees:* 1; *Target Audience:* General.
Charles Hubbard, CEO
Matt Hubbard, General Manager

WLOP
07-12-1949; 1370 kHz AM; 5 kw-D, ND1; 0.035 kw-N, ND1; N31 36 6 W81 56 0
Mailing Address: P. O. Box 647, Jesup, GA 31545 US
Second Address: 2420 Waycross Hwy, Jesup, GA 31545
(912) 427-3711; *Fax:* (912) 530-7717
bigdogstaff@bellsouth.net
License: Jesup, GA held by Jesup Broadcasting Corp.
Regional Network: Ga. News Net; *Nat'l Reps:* Rgnl Reps
Format: Sports; *Target Audience:* General.
Charles Hubbard Jr., President
Matt Hubbard, General Manager

***WLPT**
01-01-1988; 88.3 MHz FM; *Hrs Open:* 24; 20 kw; 801 ft.; N31 40 27 W81 53 12
P.O. Box 510, Augusta, GA 30802 US
(800) 926-4669
www.gnnradio.org
License: Jesup, Wayne County, GA held by Augusta Radio Fellowship Institute Inc.
Format: Christian; *Hrs. of News Programming:* News progmg 12 hrs wkly; *Target Audience:* General.

Kingsland

WKBX
02-23-1987; 106.3 MHz FM; *Hrs Open:* 24; 6 kw; 328 ft.; N30 48 4 W81 40 43
P.O. Box 2525, 111 N. Grove Boulevard, Kingsland, GA 31548 US
(912) 729-6106; *Fax:* (912) 729-4106
wkbx@k-bay106.com
License: Kingsland, Camden County, GA held by Radio Kings Bay Inc.
Nat'l Network: ABC
Format: Country; *Hrs. of News Programming:* news progmg one hr wkly; *No. News Employees:* 1; *Target Audience:* 18-54; contemp country audience; *Adv. Rates:* 20; 15.29; 20; 15.29
James Steele, President
John Fluery, Programming Director
Susan Pope, News Director
Wendy Steele, Executive Vice President
Jason Bishop, News Director

La Fayette

WQCH
11-01-1954; 1590 kHz AM; *Hrs Open:* 12; 5 kw-D; N34 42 57 W85 16 06
Box 746, La Fayette, GA 30728
(706) 638-3276; *Fax:* (706) 638-3896
www.wqch.net
WQCHRadio@aol.com
License: La Fayette, Walker County, GA held by Radix Broadcasting Inc.
Nat'l Network: AP Network News; *Regional Network:* Ga. News Net; *Nat'l Reps:* Rgnl Reps
Arbitron Metro Market: Chattanooga, TN *Special Programming:* Farm 2 hrs wkly; *Hrs. of News Programming:* news progmg 10 hrs wkly; *No. News Employees:* 1; *Target Audience:* 25 plus.; *Adv. Rates:* 11.50; 11.50;11.50; 11.50
C Rich Gwyn, General Manager

La Grange

WLAG
05-01-1941; 1240 kHz AM; *Hrs Open:* 24; 1 kw-U, ND1; N33 2 24 W85 1 27
Mailing Address: P.O. Box 1429, Lagrange, GA 30241 US
Second Address: 304 Broome St., La Grange, GA 30240
(706) 845-1023; *Fax:* (706) 845-8642
www.eagle1023.com
wlag@eagle1023.com
License: La Grange, GA held by Eagle's Nest Inc.
Group Owner: Eagle's Nest Inc.; acq 4-3-92; $10;
Format: Sports; *Hrs. of News Programming:* news progmg 4 hrs wkly; *No. News Employees:* 1; *Target Audience:* 25-54; general
Jim Vice, General Manager

***WOAK**
06-11-1984; 90.9 MHz FM; 3.4 kw; 299 ft.; N32 57 57 W84 59 8
1921 Hamilton Rd., Lagrange, GA 30240 US
(706) 884-2950; *Fax:* (706) 884-2930
woak.com
woak@woak.org
License: La Grange, Troup County, GA held by Oakside Christian School.
Nat'l Network: USA
TV Affiliate: Relg

***WBRQ**
91.9 MHz FM; 1 kw; 43 ft.; N33 0 48 W85 2 58
321 Freeman Circle, Norcross, GA 30071 US
(787) 529-8917
License: La Grange, Troup County, GA held by Family Educational Association Inc.
Arbitron Metro Market: La Grange, GA
Juan Carlos Matos, President

LaGrange

WTRP
01-09-1953; 620 kHz AM; 2.5 kw-D, ND2; 0.127 kw-N, ND2; N33 3 33 W85 1 40
Mailing Address: P.O. Box 561, LaGrange, GA 30240 US
Second Address: 806 New Franklin Rd., LaGrange, GA 30240
(706) 884-7022
www.wtrp620.com
License: LaGrange, Troup County, GA held by Tiger Communications Inc.
Group Owner: Tiger Communications Inc.; (acq 10-19-2006; $279,000 with WRLA(AM) West Point)
Arbitron Metro Market: LaGrange, GA; *Format:* Oldies
Thomas Hayley, President

Lakeland

WVGA
01-01-1994; 105.9 MHz FM; 10 kw; 328 ft.; N31 3 21 W83 13 54
1711 Ellis Dr., Valdosta, GA 31601 US
(229) 244-8642; *Fax:* (229) 242-7620
valdostatoday.com
kpelkowski@blackcrow.fm
License: Lakeland, Lanier County, GA held by RTG Radio LLC.
Group Owner: Black Crow Media Group LLC; (acq 11-9-2001; grpsl).
Arbitron Metro Market: Valdosta, GA; *Format:* News, News/Talk, 86
Jay Matthews, Operations Dir
Kim Pelkowski, General Manager

Lavonia

WLHR-FM
05-15-2008; 92.1 MHz FM; 4.2 kw; 338 ft; N34 22 2.7 W83 05 22
Mailing Address: P.O. Box 228, Lavonia, GA 30635
Second Address: 12715 Augusta Road, Lavonia, GA 30553
(706) 356-0921; *Fax:* (706) 356-5921
www.921wlhr.com
wlhr@gacaradio.com
License: Lavonia, Franklin County, GA held by Lake Hartwell Radio Inc.
Group Owner: Georgia-Carolina Radiocasting Companies; (acq 12-31-2008; $158,185 assumption of debt)
Nat'l Network: AP Network News
Format: Adult Contemp, Country, 60 *Special Programming:* Local News; *Hrs. of News Programming:* local news progmg 11 hrs wkly; *No. News Employees:* 1; *Target Audience:* 25+
Art Sutton, President
Michael Branch, Operations Dir
Daniel Brown, Vice President/General Manager
Daniel Brown, Programming Director
MJ Kneiser, News Director

Lawrenceville

WISK
08-28-1962; 990 kHz AM; *Hrs Open:* Sunrise-sunset
239 Ezzard St., Lawrenceville, GA 30046 USA
(229) 924-1390, (229) 924-6500
www.americusradio.com
License: Lawrenceville, GA held by Sumter Broadcasting Co. Inc.
Group Owner: Sumter Broadcasting Co. Inc.
Regional Network: Ga. News Net.
Format: Oldies; *No. News Employees:* 1; *Target Audience:* 19-65.

Leesburg

WJAD
10-01-1989; 103.5 MHz FM; 12.5 kw; 463 ft.; N31 40 18 W84 3 32
1104 West Broad Avenue, Albany, GA 31707 US
(229) 888-5000; *Fax:* (229) 888-5960
www.wjad.com
License: Leesburg, Lee County, GA held by Cumulus Licensing Corp.
Group Owner: Cumulus Media Inc.; (acq 7-7-98)
Nat'l Reps: Katz Radio
Arbitron Metro Market: Albany, GA; *Target Audience:* 25-40; Generation X, tail end of baby boomers
Becca Monroe, Sales Manager
John Blake, Programming Director
Katy Edwards, Promotions Manager
Reid Reker, Marketing Manager

Lithia Springs

WJTP
04-15-1959; 890 kHz AM; *Hrs Open:* Sunrise-sunset
P.O. Box 10, Walhalla, SC 29691 US
(239) 485-2100; *Fax:* (239) 992-8165
www.sunny1063.com
randy@sunny1063.com
License: Lithia Springs, GA held by New Life Broadcasting Inc.
Nat'l Network: ABC
Format: Oldies, Talk; *Hrs. of News Programming:* news progmg 6 hrs wkly; *No. News Employees:* 1; *Target Audience:* 25-54; emphasis on women
Juan Carlos Matos, President
Gary Butts, Operations Dir
Brad Beasley, General Manager
Randy Sherwyn, Programming Director
Jeff Hickcox, Promotions Manager
Dick Mangrum, News Director
Tim Stephens, Chief Engineer
Robert Hallman,Director of Sales
Dawn Krause, New Business Manager
AJ Lurie, National Sales Manager
Diana Beasley, Webmaster

Louisville

WPEH
09-10-1960; 1420 kHz AM; *Hrs Open:* 6 AM-midnight; 1 kw-D, ND1; 0.159 kw-N, ND1; N33 0 48 W82 23 33
PO Box 425, Louisville, GA 30434 US
(912) 625-7248; *Fax:* (912) 625-7249
www.wpeh.com
License: Louisville, GA held by Peach Broadcasting Co. Inc.
Regional Network: Ga. News Net.

Format: Country, Oldies; *Hrs. of News Programming:* News progmg 11 hrs wkly; *Target Audience:* General.
Ottis Stephens, President
Wendell Stephens, Programming Director

WPEH-FM
05-06-1971; 92.1 MHz FM; 6 kw; 299 ft.; N33 0 48 W82 23 33
PO Box 425, Louisville, GA 30434 US
(912) 625-7248; *Fax:* (912) 625-7249
wpeh@classicsouth.net
License: Louisville, Jefferson County, GA held by Peach Broadcasting Co. Inc.
Target Audience: 25 plus.
Otis Stephens, General Manager

Lumber City

***WMOC**
04-01-1997; 88.7 MHz FM; 50 kw; 210 ft.; N31 55 48 W82 41 6
Mailing Address: P.O. Box 176, Lumber City, GA 31549 US
Second Address: 412 Renwick St., Lumber City, GA 31549
(912) 363-2203; *Fax:* (912) 363-2106
http://www.mocradio.com
wmoc887@yahoo.com
License: Lumber City, Telfair County, GA held by Full Gospel Church of God Written in Heaven.
Arbitron Metro Market: Lumber City, GA; *Format:* Gospel; *Target Audience:* General , urban
Eddie Conaway, General Manager

Lumpkin

***WBOJ**
01-01-2008; 88.5 MHz FM; 23 kw; Ant 538 ft; N31 59 19 W84 55 59
Box 9382, Columbus, GA 31908
(706) 413-0342
License: Lumpkin, Stewart County, GA held by Spanish Cultural Education Inc.

Victor Molina, President

***WXIV**
90.1 MHz FM; kw
US
(205) 951-3700
License: Lumpkin, Stewart County, GA held by TBTA Ministries.
Arbitron Metro Market: Lumpkin, GA
Kenneth Layton, President

Lyons

WBBT
03-12-1959; 1340 kHz AM; *Hrs Open:* 24; 1 kw-U; N32 12 50 W82 19 51
300 Arboretum Place, Suite 590, Richmond, VA 23236 US
(912) 526-8122,(912) 526-6333; *Fax:* (912) 526-9155
www.bigoldies1073.com
rockinrobin_y101@yahoo.com
License: Lyons, Toombs County, GA held by T.C.B. Broadcasting Inc.
Nat'l Network: ABC
Population Served: 85,000 *Hrs. of News Programming:* news progmg 20 hrs wkly; *No. News Employees:* 2; *Target Audience:* General.; *Adv. Rates:* 5; 5; 5; 5
Ray Bilbrey, CEO
Robin Watson, Programming Director

WLYU
01-01-1989; 100.9 MHz FM; *Hrs Open:* 24; 6 kw; 328 ft.; N32 6 48 W82 23 52
P.O. Box 111, Lyons, GA 30436 US
(912) 526-8122; *Fax:* (912) 526-9155
www.toombsnow.com/y-101radio.html
barney@toombsnow.com
License: Lyons, Toombs County, GA
Nat'l Network: Fox News Radio
Arbitron Metro Market: Lyons, GA; *Format:* Country; *Hrs. of News Programming:* news progmg 8 hrs wkly; *No. News Employees:* 3; *Target Audience:* General.; *Adv. Rates:* 8; 8; 8; 7
Ray Bilbrey, President
Robin Watson, News Director

Mableton

WPZE
01-01-2001; 102.5 MHz FM; 3 kw; 469 ft.; N33 41 20 W84 30 38
101 Marietta St., 12th Floor, Atlanta, GA 30303 US
(404) 765-9750; *Fax:* (404) 688-7686
www.mypraiseatl.com
License: Mableton, Cobb County, GA held by Radio One Licenses, LLC
Group Owner: Radio One Inc.; (acq 7-8-2004; $31.5 million)
Arbitron Metro Market: Ebro FL; *Format:* Gospel; *Target Audience:* 35-64; adults
Tim Davies, General Manager

Macon

WDEN-FM
02-17-1947; 99.1 MHz FM; *Hrs Open:* 24; 100 kw; 581 ft.; N32 45 51 W83 33 32
544 Mulberry Street, 5th Floor, Macon, GA 31201 US
(478) 746-6286; *Fax:* (916) 251-1650
License: Macon, Bibb County, GA held by Cumulus Licensing Corp.
Group Owner: Cumulus Media Inc.
Nat'l Reps: Christal
Arbitron Metro Market: Whitehall MT; *Format:* Christian; *Adv. Rates:* 45; 45; 45; 15
Renee Coley, General Sales Mgr
Bobby Reed, Programming Director
Art Giles, Marketing Manager

***WBKG**
01-01-2002; 88.9 MHz FM; 5.5 kw; 502 ft.; N32 45 51 W83 33 32
P.O. Box 3206, Tupelo, MS 38803 US
(662) 844-8888; *Fax:* (662) 842-6791
www.afr.net
faq@afa.net
License: Macon, Bibb County, GA held by American Family Association.
Group Owner: American Family Radio
Arbitron Metro Market: Macon, GA; *Format:* Religious
Tim Wildmon, President
Donald Wildmon, Founder
Buddy Smith, Sr VP
Ed Vitagliano, Exec VP
Randy Sharp, Director Of Special Projects
Meeke Addison, Director Of Communications
Abraham Hamilton III, General Counsel

WBML
10-15-1940; 900 kHz AM; 2 kw-D, ND1; 0.145 kw-N, ND1; N32 50 58 W83 36 8; N32 50 58 W83 36 6
Mailing Address: 2301 West Main Street, Richmond, IN 47374 US
Second Address: 735 Reese St., Macon, GA 31217
(478) 743-5453; *Fax:* (912) 743-5453
License: Macon, GA held by WBML Inc.
Group Owner: Rodgers Broadcasting Corp.
Arbitron Metro Market: Richmond, IN; *Format:* Religious; *Target Audience:* 35 plus.
David Rogers, President

WDDO
11-25-1957; 1240 kHz AM; *Hrs Open:* 24; 1 kw-U, ND1; N32 50 18 W83 39 2
173 First Street, Macon, GA 31202 US
(478) 746-6286; *Fax:* (478) 745-4383
www.wddoam.com/info/contact.php
License: Macon, GA held by Cumulus Licensing Corp.
Group Owner: Cumulus Media Inc.; (acq 12-20-02; grpsl).
Nat'l Network: American Urban; *Nat'l Reps:* Christal
Arbitron Metro Market: Macon, GA; *Format:* Black, Gospel
John Sheftic, General Manager

WAYS
08-01-1967; 1500 kHz AM; 1 kw-D, NDD; N32 48 47 W83 37 36
P. O. Box 46, Macon, GA 31297 US
(478) 746-6286; *Fax:* (478) 742-8061
www.waysam.com
License: Macon, GA held by Cumulus Licensing Corp.
Group Owner: Cumulus Media Inc.; (acq 12-20-2002; grpsl).
Nat'l Network: Westwood One; *Nat'l Reps:* Christal
Arbitron Metro Market: Macon, GA; *Format:* Oldies; *Target Audience:* 25-54.
Steve Hazen, President
John Sheftic, General Manager

WROK-FM
06-10-1968; 105.5 MHz FM; *Hrs Open:* 24; 6.1 kw; Ant 659 ft; N32 53 48 W83 32 05
544 Mulberry St., Suite 500, Macon, GA 31297
(478) 746-6286
License: Macon, Bibb County, GA held by Volt Radio LLC
Group Owner: Cumulus Media Inc.
Nat'l Network: ESPN Radio
Population Served: 300,000; *Arbitron Metro Market:* Macon, GA
Renee Coley, General Sales Mgr
Bobby Reed, Programming Director
Art Giles, Marketing Manager

WIHB
11-01-1948; 1280 kHz AM; *Hrs Open:* 24; 5 kw-D, ND1; 0.099 kw-N, ND1; N32 48 16 W83 36 16
7080 Industrial Highway, Macon, GA 31216 US
(478) 781-1063; *Fax:* (478) 781-6711
www.973thebullicons.com
License: Macon, GA held by AMFM Radio Licenses LLC.
Group Owner: iHeartMedia; (acq 2-15-2001; grpsl)
Nat'l Reps: Clear Channel
Arbitron Metro Market: Macon, GA; *Format:* Country; *Target Audience:* General.
Thomas Bacote, Market President
Brent Henslee, Operations Manager/Program Director
James Gay, Chief Engineer
Melissa Stinebaugh, Business Manager

WMAC
10-30-1922; 940 kHz AM; *Hrs Open:* 24; 50 kw-D, DAN; 10 kw-N, DAN; N32 53 6 W83 43 50
544 Mulberry Street, 5th Floor, Macon, GA 31201 US
(478) 746-6286; *Fax:* (478) 742-8061
www.wmac-am.com
info@middlegeorgia.com
License: Macon, GA held by Cumulus Licensing Corp.
Group Owner: Cumulus Media Inc.; (acq 12-20-02; grpsl).
Nat'l Network: ABC; Westwood One; *Nat'l Reps:* McGavren Guild
Arbitron Metro Market: Macon, GA; *Format:* News, News/Talk, 86 *Special Programming:* Relg 4 hrs wkly; *Hrs. of News Programming:* news progmg 40 hrs wkly; *No. News Employees:* 2; *Target Audience:* 40 plus;upscale, college educated, household income $50K plus; *Adv. Rates:* 40; 40; 40; 10
Bill Hazen, General Manager
Renee Coley, General Sales Mgr
Bobby Reed, Programming Director
Art Giles, Marketing Manager

WNEX
04-01-1945; 1400 kHz AM
5962 Zebulon Road, Suite 306, Macon, GA 31210 US
(478) 745-5858; *Fax:* (478) 745-0500
License: Macon, GA held by Radio Peach Inc.
Nat'l Network: Radio Disney
Arbitron Metro Market: Macon, GA; *Format:* Gospel
Lowell Register, CEO
Debbie Hart, General Manager

WLZN
08-01-1992; 92.3 MHz FM; *Hrs Open:* 24; 3 kw; 328 ft.; N32 46 26 W83 38 15
544 Mulberry Street, 5th Floor, Macon, GA 31201 US
(478) 746-6286; *Fax:* (478) 742-8061
info@middlegeorgia.com
License: Macon, Bibb County, GA held by Cumulus Licensing Corp.
Group Owner: Cumulus Media Inc.; (acq 12-20-2002; grpsl).
Arbitron Metro Market: Macon, GA; *Format:* Urban Contemporary; *Hrs. of News Programming:* News progmg one hr wkly; *Adv. Rates:* 55; 60; 60; 20
Renee Coley, General Sales Mgr
Bobby Reed, Programming Director
Art Giles, Marketing Manager

Madison

WYTH
06-01-1955; 1250 kHz AM; *Hrs Open:* 6 AM-sunset; 1 kw-D, ND2; 0.079 kw-N, ND2; N33 34 45 W83 28 40
Mailing Address: P. O. Box 635, Madison, GA 30650 US
Second Address: 869 Church St., Eaton, GA 31024
(706) 485-8792; *Fax:* (706) 485-3555
starstation@bellsouth.net
License: Madison, GA held by Craig Baker and Debra Baker
Regional Network: Ga. News Net.
Arbitron Metro Market: Madison, GA; *Format:* Adult Contemp; *Hrs. of News Programming:* news progmg 15 hrs wkly; *No. News Employees:* 1; *Target Audience:* General.
Craig Baker, President

Manchester

WFDR
06-01-1957; 1370 kHz AM; *Hrs Open:* 6 AM-6 PM
PO Box 510, Manchester, GA 31816 US
(770) 487-4500; *Fax:* (706) 866-3494
www.georgia.thejoyfm.com
License: Manchester, GA held by Ploener Radio Group LLC
Arbitron Metro Market: Manchester, GA; *Format:* Gospel
Paul Ploener, President
Rick Davison, General Manager
Johanna Antes, Director of Support

Ken Hammock, Underwriting Specialist
Roxanne Davison, Office Manager

WVFJ-FM
01-01-1967; 93.3 MHz FM; *Hrs Open:* 24; 27 kw; 1611 ft.; N33 5 10 W84 46 10
P.O. Box 7217, 5015 South Florida Ave, Lakeland, FL 33813 US
(770) 487-4500; *Fax:* (770) 486-6400
www.j933.com
License: Manchester, Meriwether County, GA held by Provident Broadcasting Co.
Nat'l Reps: Rgnl Reps
Arbitron Metro Market: Atlanta, GA; *Format:* Christian; *No. News Employees:* 1; *Target Audience:* 25-45; women
Rick Davison, General Manager
John Zeiler, General Sales Mgr
Don Schaeffer, Programming Director
Steve Williams, Promotions Manager
Susan Ricards, News Director
Brian Chin, Chief Engineer
Dian Pena, Traffic Manager
RoxanneDavison, Office Manager

Marietta

WFOM
10-13-1946; 1230 kHz AM; *Hrs Open:* 24; 1 kw-D, ND2; 1 kw-N, ND2; N33 55 38 W84 30 8
2970 Peachtree Road, NW, Suite 700, Atlanta, GA 30305 US
(404) 688-0068; *Fax:* (404) 995-4045
www.1230thefan2.com
License: Marietta, GA held by Dickey Broadcasting Co.
Group Owner: Dickey Broadcasting Co.; (acq 8-31-2000; grpsl)
Nat'l Network: ESPN Radio; *Nat'l Reps:* McGavren Guild; *Wire Services:* AP
Arbitron Metro Market: Atlanta, GA; *Format:* Sports *Special Programming:* Notre Dame football (fall); *Target Audience:* 25-64.; *Adv. Rates:* 100; 100; 100; 50
David Dickey, President
Jim Mahanay, Operations Dir
David Dickey, General Manager
Colan Wheat, General Sales Mgr
Scott McFarlane, Programming Director
Laura Cowart, Controller
Rob Jenners, Creative Production Director
LindaPorter, Director of Traffic and Business Affairs
Josh Kluchka, Creative Production Assistant
Katie Kochman, Sales Coordinator

WFTD
11-14-1955; 1080 kHz AM; *Hrs Open:* Sunrise-sunset
3939 Gently Road, New Orleans, LA 70126 US
(770) 825-0095; *Fax:* (770) 246-0054
License: Marietta, GA held by Prieto Enterprises Inc.
Group Owner: Prieto Broadcasting Inc.; (acq 12-20-2001)
Arbitron Metro Market: Atlanta, GA; *Target Audience:* 21-45.
Filiberto Prieto, President

WKHX
01-01-1968; 101.5 MHz FM; *Hrs Open:* 24; 100 kw; 1079 ft.; N33 48 26 W84 20 22
780 Johnson Ferry Rd. NE, 5th Floor, Atlanta, GA 30342 US
(404) 741-1015
www.wkhx.com
jenn.fallin@cumulus.com
License: Marietta, GA held by Radio License Holdings LLC
Group Owner: Cumulus Media Inc.; (acq 6-12-2007; grpsl)
Nat'l Reps: ABC Radio Sales
Arbitron Metro Market: Atlanta, GA; *Format:* Country; *No. News Employees:* 1; *Target Audience:* 25-54.
Kevin Malone, General Sales Mgr

Martinez

WDRR
05-31-1984; 93.9 MHz FM; *Hrs Open:* 24; 14.5 kw; 433 ft.; N33 26 17 W82 5 19
4051 Jimmie Dyess Pkwy., Augusta, GA 30909 US
(706) 396-7000
www.ilovebobfm.com
License: Martinez, Columbia County, GA held by Beasley Media Group LLC
Group Owner: Beasley Broadcast Group Inc.; (acq 11-10-92; $810,000;
Arbitron Metro Market: Augusta, GA; *Format:* Variety/Diverse, Adult Contemp; *Target Audience:* 25 plus.
Chris O'Kelley, Operations Manager
Georgia Beasley, General Sales Mgr
Chuck Williams, Programming Director
Mark Haddon, Vice President/Market Manager

WPRW-FM
01-01-1994; 107.7 MHz FM; 24.5 kw; 577 ft.; N33 36 47 W82 17 51
2743 Perimeter Parkway, Building 100, Suite 300, Augusta, GA 30909 US
(706) 396-6000; *Fax:* (706) 396-6010
www.power107.net
License: Martinez, Columbia County, GA held by Capstar TX LLC
Group Owner: iHeartMedia; (acq 6-30-97; grpsl)
Arbitron Metro Market: Augusta, GA; *Format:* Urban Contemporary; *Target Audience:* General.
Ivy Elam, Market President
Sabrena Martin, General Sales Mgr
Minnesota Fattz, Programming Director
Cher Best, Promotions/Marketing Director
Cliff Bennett, Digital Content Director
Cynthia Robinson, Business Manager

Maysville

WXKT
12-01-1988; 103.7 MHz FM; *Hrs Open:* 24; 25 kw; Ant 546 ft; N34 14 13 W83 16 03
1010 Tower Place, Bogart, GA 30677 US
(706) 549-6222; *Fax:* (706) 353-1967
www.1037chuckfm.com
russell.lawson@coxinc.com
License: Maysville, Franklin County, GA held by Cox Radio Inc.
Group Owner: Cox Radio Inc.; (acq 8-1-2008; grpsl)
Population Served: 190,000 *Format:* Adult Contemp; *Target Audience:* 35-60; Male
Russell Lawson, General Sales Manager
Pete de Graaff, Program Director
Heather Taylor, Digital Brand Manager
Josh Hill, Promotions Director

McDonough

WKKP
04-02-1979; 1410 kHz AM; *Hrs Open:* 24; 2.5 kw-D, ND1; 0.058 kw-N, ND1; N33 25 47 W84 7 52 *Rebroadcasts:* Solid Gospel Network
Mailing Address: P.O. Box 878, Jackson, GA 30233 US
Second Address: 940 Brownlee Rd., Jackson, GA 30233
(770) 504-8410; *Fax:* (770) 775-3153
License: McDonough, GA held by Henry County Radio Co. Inc.
Nat'l Network: Jones Radio Networks; *Nat'l Reps:* Rgnl Reps
Arbitron Metro Market: Atlanta, GA; *Format:* Country; *Hrs. of News Programming:* News progmg 20 hrs wkly; *Target Audience:* General.; *Adv. Rates:* 8; 8; 8; 8
Susanne Earnhart, President
Tom Lynde, Operations Dir
Don Earnhardt, General Manager

McRae

WYIS
07-27-1957; 1410 kHz AM; 1 kw-D, NDD; N32 3 25 W82 51 56
Highway 341 South, McRae, GA 31055 US
(229) 868-5611; *Fax:* (229) 868-7552
License: McRae, GA held by Cinecom Broadcasting Systems Inc.
Nat'l Reps: Rgnl Reps
Arbitron Metro Market: McRae, GA; *Format:* Oldies *Special Programming:* Black 4 hrs wkly; *Target Audience:* 25-50; mature, wage earners
Jimmy Hussey, General Manager

Meigs

WQLI
09-08-2000; 92.3 MHz FM; 6 kw; 328 ft.; N31 5 12 W84 12 10
Rt 3 Box 514, Pelham, GA 31779 US
(229) 294-1909
License: Meigs, Mitchell County, GA held by Mitchell County Television.
Arbitron Metro Market: Pelham, GA; *Format:* Adult Contemp
Greg Jessen, Operations Dir
Buck Hein, General Sales Mgr
Brian Stenzel, Promotions Manager
Mark Heller, Chief Engineer
Jimmy Clark, Operations Manager

Metter

WBMZ
08-01-1971; 104.9 MHz FM; *Hrs Open:* 24; 3 kw; 299 ft.; N32 23 56 W82 2 36
Mailing Address: P. O. Box 238, Metter, GA 30439 US
Second Address: 1075 East Lillian Street, Metter, GA 30439
(912) 685-2136; *Fax:* (912) 685-2137
www.wbmzfm.com
License: Metter, Candler County, GA held by Radio Metter Inc.
Regional Network: Ga. News Net.
Format: Contemporary Hits/Top 40, Adult Contemp; *Target Audience:* General.; *Adv. Rates:* 8; 8; 8; 6
Jimmy Page, CEO

WHCG
12-22-1961; 1360 kHz AM; 1 kw-D, ND2; 0.059 kw-N, ND2; N32 23 56 W82 2 36
Mailing Address: P.O.Box 238, Metter, GA 30439 US
Second Address: 1075 E. Lillian St., Metter, GA 30439
(912) 685-2136; *Fax:* (912) 685-2137
License: Metter, GA held by Radio Metter Inc.
Format: Gospel; *Target Audience:* General.
Jimmy Page, President

Midway

WGCO
01-01-1974; 98.3 MHz FM; *Hrs Open:* 24; 100 kw; 981 ft.; N31 36 45 W81 21 37
401 Mall Blvd., Suite 101-D, Savannah, GA 31406 US
(912) 351-9830; *Fax:* (912) 352-4821
www.983hank.com
License: Midway, Liberty County, GA held by Alpha Media Licensee LLC
Group Owner: Alpha Media LLC; (acq 12-3-2012; grpsl).
Nat'l Reps: Christal
Arbitron Metro Market: Savannah, GA; *Format:* Country; *Hrs. of News Programming:* news progmg 2 hrs wkly; *No. News Employees:* 3; *Target Audience:* 25-54; yuppies; *Adv. Rates:* 50; 50; 50; 50
Rob Walker, Operations Manager
Gigi South, Vice President and Market Manager
Kathryn Wake, Director of Sales
John Marshall, Promotions Manager
Claire Beverly, News and Public Affairs Director
Carissa Lozinski-Doig, DigitalMarketing Director

Milan

WMCG
01-01-1982; 104.9 MHz FM; *Hrs Open:* 24; 36 kw; 564 ft.; N32 7 16 W83 16 5
P.O. Box 2639, Gulfport, GA 39505 US
(478) 272-4422; *Fax:* (478) 275-4657
www.1049wmcg.com
webmaster@1049wmcg.com
License: Milan, Telfair County, GA held by Tel-Dodge Broadcasting Inc.
Regional Reps: Dora-Clayton
Arbitron Metro Market: Macon, GA; *Format:* Country *Special Programming:* Farm one hr wkly; *Hrs. of News Programming:* News progmg 1 hr wkly; *Target Audience:* 35+.
J. Morgan Dowdy, Operations Dir
Rick Humphrey, General Manager

Milledgeville

***WGUR**
08-01-1975; 95.3 MHz FM; 85 w; Ant 3 ft; N33 04 44 W83 13 55
Box 3124, Georgia College & State University, Milledgeville, GA 31061
(478) 445-8256
License: Milledgeville, Baldwin County, GA held by Georgia College & State University
Population Served: 4,500 *Target Audience:* 18-24; college students
Sonya Barnes, General Manager

WKZR
06-30-1966; 102.3 MHz FM; 3.3 kw; 299 ft.; N33 4 58 W83 15 1
Box 519, Milledgeville, GA 31061 US
(478) 452-0586; *Fax:* (478) 452-5886
www.country102fm.com
License: Milledgeville, Baldwin County, GA held by WMVG Inc.
Format: Country
Carl Hirsch, Chairman
Steven Dinetz, CEO
Skip Weller, President
Barry Brown, General Manager
Art Greene, General Sales Mgr
Mark McKinney, Programming Director
Liza Van Horne, Promotions Manager
Trimeshia Jeffery, NewsDirector
Paul Matthews, Chief Engineer
Jeff Dinetz, COO

WLRR
07-24-1990; 100.7 MHz FM; 3 kw; 328 ft.; N33 6 50 W83 13 8
Rebroadcasts: Rebroadcasts WKVQ(AM) Eatonton 100%
P. O. Box 793, Milledgeville, GA 31061 US
(706) 485-8792; *Fax:* (706) 485-3555
License: Milledgeville, Baldwin County, GA held by Preston W. Small.
Format: Adult Contemp; *Target Audience:* 18-35.
Craig Baker, President

WMVG
03-29-1946; 1450 kHz AM; *Hrs Open:* 24; 1 kw-U, ND1; N33 4 58 W83 15 1
P. O. Box 519, Milledgeville, GA 31061 US
(478) 452-0586; *Fax:* (478) 452-5886
www.country102fm.com
License: Milledgeville, GA held by WMVG Inc.
Nat'l Reps: Rgnl Reps
Arbitron Metro Market: Milledgeville, GA; *Format:* News, Sports
Special Programming: Black 4 hrs wkly; *Hrs. of News Programming:* news progmg 25 hrs wkly; *No. News Employees:* 1; *Target Audience:* 18-49.
Randy Beasley, President

***WRGC-FM**
88.3 MHz FM; 4.8 kw; Ant 384 ft; N33 04 05 W83 16 30
Campus Box 97, Milledgeville, GA 31061-3375
(478) 445-6804; *Fax:* (478) 445-2364
License: Milledgeville, Baldwin County, GA held by Georgia College & State University.
Population Served: 17,499; *Arbitron Metro Market:* Milledgeville, GA
Dorothy Leland, President
Angela Criscoe, General Manager

Millen

WHKN
12-04-1989; 94.9 MHz FM; *Hrs Open:* 24; 14.5 kw; 400 ft.; N32 43 57 W81 51 43
P.O. Box 180, Hawkinsville, GA 32069 US
(912) 764-5496; *Fax:* (912) 764-8827
radiocenter@frontiernet.net
License: Millen, Jenkins County, GA held by Georgia Eagle Media Inc.
Group Owner: Georgia Eagle Media Inc.; acq 1-12-2007; grpsl)
Nat'l Network: ABC
Format: Country *Special Programming:* Farm 10 hrs, relg 2 hrs wkly; *Hrs. of News Programming:* news progmg 8 hrs wkly; *No. News Employees:* 1; *Target Audience:* 25-54; adults
Jeff Anderson, General Manager
Buddy Horne, Programming Director
Cornell Burgess, Traffic Director

Monroe

WKUN
02-04-1971; 1490 kHz AM; *Hrs Open:* 6 AM-6 PM
Mailing Address: 1081 Cherokee Road, Social Circle, GA 30279 US
Second Address: 1610 Launius Rd., Good Hope, GA 30641
(770) 267-0923; *Fax:* (706) 342-8135
www.wmoqfm.com
info@wmoqfm.com
License: Monroe, GA held by B.R. Anderson Sr. dba Radio Station WKUN
Regional Network: Ga. News Net.
Arbitron Metro Market: Atlanta, GA; *Format:* Gospel; *Hrs. of News Programming:* News progmg 3 hrs wkly; *Target Audience:* 25-65.; *Adv. Rates:* 8; 8; 8; na
B. R. Anderson Sr., President
Melanie Jackson, General Manager

Montezuma

WMNZ
11-29-1961; 1050 kHz AM; 0.25 kw-D, ND1; 0.041 kw-N, ND1; N32 17 53 W84 2 2
Mailing Address: P. O. Box 610, Montezuma, GA 31063 US
Second Address: 115 1/2 Cherry St., Montezuma, GA 31063
(478) 472-8386; *Fax:* (478) 472-8296
License: Montezuma, GA held by Macon County Broadcasting Co.
Arbitron Metro Market: Montezuma, GA; *Format:* Country, Gospel, 64
Danny Blizzard, President

WMGB
08-10-2001; 95.1 MHz FM; *Hrs Open:* 24; 46 kw; 390 ft.; N32 33 20 W83 44 14
P. O. Box 180, Hawkinsville, GA 31036 US
(478) 646-9510; *Fax:* (478) 745-4383
www.allthehitsb951.com
License: Montezuma, Macon County, GA held by Cumulus Licensing Corp.
Group Owner: Cumulus Media Inc.; (acq 12-20-02; grpsl).
Nat'l Network: Westwood One
Arbitron Metro Market: Macon, GA; *Format:* Contemporary Hits/Top 40
John Sheftic, General Manager

Morrow

WIGO
11-01-1956; 1570 kHz AM; 5 kw-D, ND1; 0.05 kw-N, ND1; N33 36 5 W84 18 40
2424 Old Rex Morrow Road, Morrow, GA 30260 US
(404) 361-1570; *Fax:* (404) 366-9772
www.wigoam.com
License: Morrow, GA held by MCL/MCM Georgia LLC.
Group Owner: Sheridan Broadcasting Corp.; (acq 12-29-2006; $1.75 million)
Arbitron Metro Market: Atlanta, GA; *Format:* Black, Gospel; *Target Audience:* 24-55.; *Adv. Rates:* 12;30 12;20 12;25
Larry Young, Operations Dir
Paul Ploener, General Manager

Moultrie

WMTM
11-10-1953; 1300 kHz AM; *Hrs Open:* 6 AM-sunset; 5 kw-D, ND2; 0.06 kw-N, ND2; N31 10 12 W83 44 50
Mailing Address: P.O. Box 788, Moultrie, GA 31776 US
Second Address: 100 WMTM Rd., Moultrie, GA 31768
(229) 985-1300; *Fax:* (229) 890-0905
www.cruisin94.com
License: Moultrie, GA held by Colquitt Broadcasting Co. L.L.C.
Nat'l Reps: Rgnl Reps
Arbitron Metro Market: Moultrie, GA; *Format:* Gospel, News
Special Programming: Farm 16 hrs wkly; *No. News Employees:* 1; *Target Audience:* General.
Jim Turner, President

WMTM-FM
11-17-1964; 93.9 MHz FM; *Hrs Open:* 6 AM-midnight; 100 kw; 554 ft.; N31 12 54 W83 47 13
P.O. Box 788, Moultrie, GA 31776 US
(229) 985-1300; *Fax:* (229) 890-0905
www.cruisin94.com
License: Moultrie, Colquitt County, GA held by Colquitt Broadcasting Co. LLC
Arbitron Metro Market: Albany, GA; *Format:* Contemporary Hits/Top 40
Jim Turner, Operations Dir

WHLJ(AM)
01-01-2002; 1400 kHz AM; *Hrs Open:* 24; 1 kw-U; N31 09 56 W83 46 01
Mailing Address: 1643 South Blvd., Moultrie, GA 31768
Second Address: Box 1305, Valdosta, GA 31603
(229) 890-2900; *Fax:* (229) 890-1497
License: Moultrie, Colquitt County, GA held by Lataurus Productions Two LLC
Population Served: 77,683; *Arbitron Metro Market:* Albany, GA
Ronnie Barnes, General Manager

***WBGP**
01-02-2012; 91.3 mhz
PO Box 181000, Tallahassee, FL
(877)801-1070; *Fax:* (850)201-1071
www.faithradio.us
scott@faithradio.us
License: Moultrie, GA
Group Owner: Faith Radio

Scott Beigle, President
Steve Huffman, Operations Dir
Brenda Beigle, Vice President

Mount Vernon

WYUM
08-03-1998; 101.7 MHz FM; 3.6 kw; 427 ft.; N32 13 12 W82 26 7
Box 900, Hwy 280 W., Vidalia, GA 30474 US
(912) 538-1017; *Fax:* (912) 537-4477
zfowler@vidaliacommunications.com
License: Mount Vernon, Montgomery County, GA held by Vidalia Communications Corp.
Group Owner: Vidalia Communications Corp.
Regional Network: Ga. News Net. *Regional Reps:* Rgnl Reps.
Arbitron Metro Market: Mount Vernon, GA; *Format:* Country; *Target Audience:* 25-49.
Zack Fowler, Station Manager
John Koon, General Sales Mgr
Jim Perry, Program Manager

Murrayville

WGTJ
11-01-1986; 1330 kHz AM; *Hrs Open:* 24 Hours; 1 kW-D, NDD, 500 W pre-sunrise, 34 W-N; N34 22 16 W83 56 47
PO Box 907038, 1716 Cleveland Hwy, Gainesville, GA 30501 USA
(770) 297-7485; *Fax:* (770) 297-8030
www.glory1330.com
mail@glory1330.com
License: Murrayville, GA held by Vision Communications of Georgia Inc.
Nat'l Network: SRN; *Regional Network:* GNN
Population Served: 500,000; *Arbitron Metro Market:* Gainesville, GA; *Format:* Christian; *No. News Employees:* 1; *Target Audience:* General; *Adv. Rates:* $12 net 30 sec, $18 net 60 sec
Mike Wofford, President
Mike Wofford, General Manager
Mike Wofford, General Sales Mgr
Mike Wofford, Programming Director
Mike Wofford, Promotions Manager

Nashville

***WVKV**
11-26-1986; 95.3 MHz FM; *Hrs Open:* 24; 29 kw; 522 ft.; N31 10 18 W83 21 57
104 E 7th Street, Tifton, GA 31794 US
(916) 251-1600; *Fax:* (916) 251-1650
www.klove.com
License: Nashville, Berrien County, GA held by Educational Media Foundation.
Group Owner: EMF Broadcasting; (acq 5-10-2007; $1.3 million)
Nat'l Network: K-Love
Arbitron Metro Market: Valdosta, GA; *Format:* Christian
Mike Novak, President

***WGCN**
01-01-2005; 90.5 MHz FM; 0.001 kw horiz, 50 kw vert; 292 ft.; N31 9 26 W83 22 28
US
(916) 251-1600; *Fax:* (916) 251-1650
www.nuevavida.com
info@nuevavida.com
License: Nashville, Berrien County, GA held by Educational Media Foundation.
Group Owner: EMF Broadcasting; (acq 1-7-2004)
Arbitron Metro Market: Nashville, GA; *Format:* Country, Gospel
Mike Novak, President

Newnan

WCOH
12-01-1947; 1400 kHz AM; 1 kw-U, ND1; N33 21 53 W84 48 42
154 Boone Drive, Newnan, GA 30263 US
(770) 683-7234; *Fax:* (770) 683-9846
www.foxsports1400.com
License: Newnan, GA held by Citicasters Licenses Inc.
Group Owner: iHeartMedia; (acq 5-4-99; grpsl)
Nat'l Network: Fox Sports; *Regional Network:* Ga. News Net.
Arbitron Metro Market: Atlanta, GA; *Format:* Sports; *Target Audience:* 25-54.
Janice Horne, General Sales Mgr

WNEA
04-18-1962; 1300 kHz AM; 1 kw-D, ND1; 0.05 kw-N, ND1; N33 22 31 W84 47 8
8 Madison Street, Newnan, GA 30264 US
(770) 920-1520; *Fax:* (770) 253-4711
www.wordchristianbroadcasting.com
License: Newnan, GA held by Word Christian Broadcasting Inc.
Regional Network: Ga. News Net.
Arbitron Metro Market: Atlanta, GA; *Format:* Religious *Special Programming:* Black, relg, gospel 15 hrs wkly; *Target Audience:* 18-64.
Ken Johns, CEO

Nicholls

WVOH-FM
12-09-1975; 93.5 MHz FM; 25 kw; 315 ft; N31 51 15 W82 34 00
546 Baxley Hwy., Hazlehurst, GA 31539
(912) 375-4511; *Fax:* (912) 375-4512
License: Nicholls, Coffee County, GA
Group Owner: Broadcast South LLC
Nat'l Network: Jones Radio Networks; *Regional Network:* Ga. News Net.

Tony DeLoach, Station Manager

North Atlanta

WCNN
12-04-1967; 680 kHz AM; *Hrs Open:* 24; 50 kw-D, DA2; 10 kw-N, DA2; N33 57 42 W84 15 48
2970 Peachtree Rd, Atlanta, GA 30305 US
(404) 688-0068; *Fax:* (404) 995-4045
www.680thefan.com
cwheat@680thefan.com
License: North Atlanta, GA held by Dickey Broadcasting Co.
Group Owner: Dickey Broadcasting Co.; acq 8-31-00; grpsl).
Regional Network: Nebraska Public Radio
Arbitron Metro Market: Atlanta, GA; *Format:* News, Sports
David Dickey, General Manager
Colan Wheat, Director of Sales
Scott McFarlane, Programming Director

Norwood

***WJGS**
91.5 MHz FM; 3 kw; 230 ft.; N33 30 13 W82 46 12
1405 Cecil Dye Rd., Norwood, GA 30821 US
(706) 465-3659
www.afr.net
License: Norwood, Warren County, GA held by American Family Association.
Group Owner: American Family Radio
Arbitron Metro Market: Norwood, GA; *Format:* Christian, Talk
Tim Wildmon, President
Donald Wildmon, Founder
Buddy Smith, Sr VP
Ed Vitagliano, Exec VP
Randy Sharp, Director Of Special Projects
Meeke Addison, Director Of Communications
Abraham Hamilton III, General Counsel

Ocilla

***WLPF**
12-01-1993; 98.5 MHz FM; *Hrs Open:* 24; 2.3 kw; 522 ft.; N31 28 11 W83 14 11
P.O. Box 510, Appling, GA 30802 US
(800) 926-4669
www.gnnradio.org
License: Ocilla, Irwin County, GA held by Barinowski Investment Co.
Group Owner: Good News Network; (acq 11-17-92; for CP;
Format: Christian; *Hrs. of News Programming:* News progmg 12 hrs wkly; *Target Audience:* General.

Omega

WTIF-FM
04-01-1993; 107.5 MHz FM; *Hrs Open:* 24; 6 kw; 328 ft.; N31 30 34 W83 31 13
114 Kent Rd., Tifton, GA 31794 US
(229) 382-1075; *Fax:* (229) 386-8658
www.wtif1075.com
mornings@wtif1075.com
License: Omega, GA held by Plant Broadcasting LLC
Group Owner: Plant Broadcasting
Regional Network: Ga. News Net.
Arbitron Metro Market: Tifton,GA; *Format:* Country; *No. News Employees:* 6; *Target Audience:* 18 plus.
Nettie Hatcher, General Manager

Palmetto

WALR-FM
09-01-1947; 104.1 MHz FM; 100 kw; 1217 ft.; N33 24 43 W84 50 3
1601 West Peachtree Street, Atlanta, GA 30309 US
(404) 897-7500; *Fax:* (404) 897-6495
www.kiss1041fm.com
License: Palmetto, Troup County, GA held by Cox Radio Inc.
Group Owner: Cox Radio Inc.; (acq 8-2000; $280 million)
Nat'l Reps: McGavren Guild
Arbitron Metro Market: Atlanta, GA; *Format:* Adult Contemp, Urban Contemporary; *Target Audience:* 25-54.
Tony Kidd, Program Director
Joe Tarver, Promotions
Donna Hall, Vice President & Market Manager

Patterson

***WNEE**
88.1 MHz FM; 6 kw; 161 ft.; N34 0 43 W83 17 38 US
(770) 596-0739
License: Patterson, Pierce County, GA held by Community Public Radio Inc.
Arbitron Metro Market: Patterson, GA
Penny Jackson, President

Peachtree City

WRDG
01-01-1948; 96.7 MHz FM; 2.15 kw; 551 ft.; N33 29 22 W84 34 7
1819 Peachtree Road Northeast, Atlanta, GA 30309 US
(404) 875-8080; *Fax:* (404) 367-9490
www.radio1057.com
License: Peachtree City, Fayette County, GA held by Citicasters Licenses Inc.
Group Owner: iHeartMedia; (acq 5-4-99; grpsl)
Arbitron Metro Market: Atlanta, GA; *Format:* Alternative
Cameron Brown, General Sales Mgr
Aly Young, Programming Director
Matt Shefield, Promotions Director
Steve Garza, Digital Program Director

***WMVW**
91.7 MHz FM; 13 kw; 246 ft.; N33 14 39 W84 25 49
P O Box 100, Lovejoy, GA 30250 US
(770) 229-2020
www.newlife.fm
License: Peachtree City, Fayette County, GA held by Life Radio Ministries Inc.
Arbitron Metro Market: Peachtree City, GA; *Format:* Christian
Joseph Emert, President
Jim Stewart, Operations Dir
Doug Doran, Vice President
Pete Chagnon, Production Director
Jenny Emert, Business Manager
Glenna Stewart, Administrative Assistant

Pembroke

WBAW-FM
08-31-1966; 99.3 MHz FM; 25 kw; 328 ft.; N33 13 25 W81 21 35
120 Liberty St., Ste. C&D, Hinesville, GA 31313 US
(605) 352-1933; *Fax:* (605) 352-1934
www.bigjimrocks.com
mlyon@kokk.com
License: Pembroke, Bryan County, GA held by Bullie Broadcasting Corp.
Format: Classic Rock
Linda Marcus, General Manager
Mike Lyon, General Sales Mgr

Perry

WPGA
01-01-1955; 980 kHz AM; *Hrs Open:* 24
P. O. Box 980, Perry, GA 31069 US
(478) 745-5858; *Fax:* (478) 745-5800
www.58abc.com
info@58abc.com
License: Perry, GA held by Register Communications Inc.
Arbitron Metro Market: Macon, GA; *Format:* Children; *No. News Employees:* 1; *Target Audience:* Children up to 12.
Loel Register, President
Debbie Hart, General Manager
Janice Register, Programming Director

WPGA-FM
05-03-1966; 100.9 MHz FM; 3.3 kw; 446 ft.; N32 33 20 W83 44 14
P.O. Box 5858, Macon, GA 31208 US
(478) 745-5500; *Fax:* (478) 745-5800
www.58abc.com
info@58abc.com
License: Perry, Houston County, GA held by Register Communications Inc.
Arbitron Metro Market: Macon, GA *TV Affiliate:* WPGA-TV affil; *Format:* Adult Contemp; *No. News Employees:* 1
Kristy Turner, General Sales Mgr
Janice Register, Programming Director

Pinehurst

WCEH-FM
02-22-1969; 98.3 MHz FM; *Hrs Open:* 24; 3.1 kw; 459 ft.; N32 10 3 W83 37 51
500 Commerce Street, P O Box 180, Hawkinsville, GA 31036 US
(478) 892-9061; *Fax:* (478) 892-9063
braswell@broadcast.net
License: Pinehurst, Dooly County, GA held by Georgia Eagle Media Inc.
Group Owner: Georgia Eagle Media Inc.; (acq 1-12-2007; grpsl)
Nat'l Network: CNN Radio; Jones Radio Networks; *Regional Network:* Ga. News Net.
Arbitron Metro Market: Macon, GA; *Format:* Adult Contemp; *Hrs. of News Programming:* news progmg 15 hrs wkly; *No. News Employees:* 1; *Target Audience:* 35-64; *Adv. Rates:* 18; 12; 15; 10
Dr. Joe S. Robinson, Chairman
Cecil P. Staton, Jr., CEO

Plainville

WRBF
104.9 MHz FM; 0.95 kw; 606 ft.; N34 20 35 W85 2 20 US
(817) 846-9535
www.1049therebel.com
License: Plainville, Gordon County, GA held by Howard C. Toole.
Arbitron Metro Market: Plainville, GA; *Format:* Classic Rock
Howard Toole, CEO/COO
Kevin Daniels, Operations Dir
Randy Quick, General Manager
Howard Toole, General Sales Mgr
Dustin Sledge, Programming Director
Cheryl Scott, Business Manager & Human Resource Director
Samantha Bell, BrandsManager
Rick Bradley, Production & Imaging Director
Nelle Reagan, Public Service Director

Port Wentworth

***WLFS**
01-01-2001; 91.9 MHz FM; 23.5 kw horiz, 23 kw vert; 338 ft.; N32 9 28 W80 59 31
P.O. Box 7217, 5015 South Florida Ave, Lakeland, FL 33813 US
(707) 526-2765
www.broken.fm
korb@broken.fm
License: Port Wentworth, Chatham County, GA held by Radio Training Network Inc.
Arbitron Metro Market: Hopland CA; *Format:* Christian
Keith Leitch, President
Rynie Leitch, General Manager

Portal

WXRS-FM
08-02-1982; 100.5 MHz FM; *Hrs Open:* 24; 3 kw; 299 ft.; N32 34 52 W82 23 14
P. O. Box 1590, Swainsboro, GA 30401 US
(478) 237-1590; *Fax:* (478) 237-3559
www.radiojones.com
License: Portal, Emanuel County, GA
Group Owner: RadioJones LLC
Arbitron Metro Market: Portal, GA; *Format:* Country; *Hrs. of News Programming:* news progmg 10 hrs wkly; *No. News Employees:* 1; *Target Audience:* 25 plus.; *Adv. Rates:* 16; 14; 14; 8
John Wagner, Operations Dir
Dennis Jones, General Manager
Jolly Martin, General Sales Mgr
Marty Foglia, Engineering Dir

Quitman

WSFB
11-19-1955; 1490 kHz AM; 1 kw-U, ND1; N30 46 51 W83 34 30
Rte 2 Bx 533, Tallahassee, FL 32311 US
(912) 263-4373
License: Quitman, GA held by Scott Matheson
Format: Contemporary Hits/Top 40, Adult Contemp; *Target Audience:* 30+.
Scott Matheson, General Manager

WSTI-FM
09-12-1986; 105.3 MHz FM; 25 kw; 318 ft.; N30 38 23 W83 26 52
1711 Ellis Dr., Valdosta, GA 31601 US
(229) 244-8642
mystar1053.com
star1053@gmail.com
License: Quitman, Brooks County, GA held by RTG Radio L.L.C.
Group Owner: Black Crow Media Group LLC; (acq 6-4-2004; $3.4 million with WXHT(FM) Madison, FL).
Arbitron Metro Market: Valdosta, GA; *Format:* Urban Contemporary *Special Programming:* Farm 5 hrs wkly; *Target Audience:* 25-54; white collar

Reidsville

WRBX
07-01-1993; 104.1 MHz FM; *Hrs Open:* 24; 4.9 kw; 361 ft.; N32 5 14 W82 7 48

P. O. Box 69, Reidsville, GA 30453 US
(912) 557-4140
License: Reidsville, Tattnall County, GA
Nat'l Network: USA
Format: Gospel; *Target Audience:* 8 plus; religious
William Keith Register, General Manager

WTNL
06-25-1976; 1390 kHz AM; *Hrs Open:* 6 AM-sunset; 0.5 kw-D, NDD; N32 5 14 W82 7 47
P.O. Box 69, 125 Friar Tuck Circle, Reidsville, GA 30453 US
(912) 557-3777; *Fax:* (912) 557-6956
License: Reidsville, GA held by WRBX/WTNL L.L.C.
Nat'l Network: USA
Arbitron Metro Market: Reidsville, GA; *Format:* Gospel; *Target Audience:* General.
Gary Frank, CEO
Jerry Richmond, News Director
Lisa Frank, COO

Richmond Hill

WRHQ
05-13-1991; 105.3 MHz FM; *Hrs Open:* 24; 11 kw; 485 ft; N32 02 52 W81 07 26
1102 E. 52nd St., Savannah, GA 31324
(912) 234-1053; *Fax:* (912) 354-6600
www.wrhq.com
qualityrock@wrhq.com
License: Richmond Hill, Bryan County, GA held by Thoroughbred Communications Inc.
Nat'l Network: AP Radio; *Nat'l Reps:* Christal
Arbitron Metro Market: Savannah, GA; *Hrs. of News Programming:* News progmg 2 hrs wkly; *Target Audience:* 25-54; 35-64; affluent
Jerry Rogers, President
Lyndy Brannan, Operations Dir
Mike Roberts, Programming Director
Phyllis Bright, News Director
Marty Foglia, Chief Engineer
Ray Williams, Regional Sales Manager

Rincon

WSSJ
05-01-1967; 100.1 MHz FM; *Hrs Open:* 24; 50 kw; 492 ft.; N32 16 49 W81 11 40
Mailing Address: 561 East Oliff Street, Statesboro, GA 30458 US
Second Address: 120 D. Liberty, Hinesville, GA 31313
(912) 691-1934; *Fax:* (912) 691-1936
www.myjoy100.com
rjp106@aol.com
License: Rincon, Effingham County, GA held by Tama Radio Licenses of Savannah, GA Inc.
Group Owner: Tama Broadcasting Inc.; (acq 4-28-2004)
Arbitron Metro Market: Savannah, GA; *Format:* Gospel; *No. News Employees:* 1; *Target Audience:* 18-45.; *Adv. Rates:* 14; 12; 14; na
Yvonne Clark, General Manager

Ringgold

WOCE
03-01-1989; 101.9 MHz FM; 1.3 kw; 702 ft.; N34 58 11 W85 5 10
P.O. 814, Ringgold, GA 30736 US
(423) 485-8987; *Fax:* (423) 553-9490
http://www.quebuena1019.com/
License: Ringgold, Catoosa County, GA held by North Georgia Radio Group L.P.
Group Owner: North Georgia Radio Group L.P.; (acq 7-28-2006; $2.15 milion)
Arbitron Metro Market: Chattanooga, TN; *Format:* Religious
Paul Fink, General Manager

Rochelle

WWKM
93.1 MHz FM; kw
US
(478)757-0983; *Fax:* (478)757-1305
License: Rochelle, Wilcox County, GA held by Georgia Eagle Media Inc.
Group Owner: Georgia Eagle Media Inc.

Cecil P. Staton, President

Rockmart

WZOT
08-28-1959; 1220 kHz AM; 0.5 kw-D, ND2; 0.103 kw-N, ND2; N34 0 14 W85 3 22
20 John Daveport Drive, Rome, GA 30161 US
(770) 684-7848; *Fax:* (770) 684-7848
www.hometown1220.com
License: Rockmart, GA held by Triple J's Broadcasting LLC
Regional Network: Ga. News Net.
Arbitron Metro Market: Rockmart, GA; *Format:* Gospel; *Target Audience:* 18-45.
Paul Stone, President
Kevin Daniels, Operations Dir
Randy Quick, General Manager
Dustin Sledge, Programming Director
Luke Brannon, Director of Engineering & IT
Cheryl Scott, Business Manager
Howard Tole, Sales Manager
SamanthaBell, Brands Manager
Rick Bradley, Production / Imaging Director
Nelle Reagan, Public Service Director

Rocky Ford

WZBX
09-06-1991; 106.5 MHz FM; 25 kw; 311 ft.; N32 43 57 W81 51 43
910 West Ogeechee Street, Sylvania, GA 30467 US
(912) 564-7461; *Fax:* (912) 564-7462
License: Rocky Ford, Screven County, GA held by Georgia Eagle Media Inc.
Group Owner: Georgia Eagle Media Inc.
Arbitron Metro Market: Rocky Ford, GA; *Format:* Classic Rock
Nate Hirsch, Station Manager
Scott Kidd, General Sales Mgr

Rome

***WGPB**
05-22-1965; 97.7 MHz FM; *Hrs Open:* 24; 4.2 kw; 791 ft.; N34 14 5 W85 13 48
Mailing Address: 710 Turner McCall Blvd., Rome, GA 30165 US
Second Address: Heritage Hall, 415 E. Third Ave., Rome, GA 30162
(706) 204-2276
www.gpb.org
ask@gpb.org
License: Rome, Floyd County, GA held by Georgia Public Telecommunications Commission
Nat'l Network: NPR; PRI; *Wire Services:* AP
Format: Classical, News *Special Programming:* Jazz 16 hrs wkly.; *Hrs. of News Programming:* news progmg 40 hrs wkly; *No. News Employees:* 10; *Target Audience:* Adults: 35 plus.
Milton Clipper, Chief Executive Officer
Teya Ryan, President
Tom Barclay, Operations Dir
Bob Houghton, General Manager
Rob Maynard, Programming Director
Nancy Zintak, Vice President of Marketing & Communications
Bonnie Bean,CFO

WLAQ
01-01-1947; 1410 kHz AM
2 Mt. Alto Road, Rome, GA 30165 US
(706) 232-7767; *Fax:* (706) 295-9225
www.wlaq1410.com
wlaq@comcast.net
License: Rome, GA held by Cripple Creek Broadcasting Co.
Nat'l Network: CBS
Format: News, News/Talk, 84, Talk
Randy Davis, President

WQTU
05-02-1966; 102.3 MHz FM; *Hrs Open:* 24; 1.1 kw; 745 ft.; N34 14 2 W85 13 50
P.O. Box 1187, Rome, GA 30162 US
(706) 295-1023; *Fax:* (706) 235-7107
q102rome@q102rome.com
License: Rome, Floyd County, GA held by McDougald Broadcasting Corp.
Group Owner: Southern Broadcasting Companies Inc.
Wire Services: National Weather Network
Format: Adult Contemp; *Hrs. of News Programming:* news progmg 6 hrs wkly; *No. News Employees:* 1; *Target Audience:* 25-54; upscale; *Adv. Rates:* 22; 18; 20; 12
Randy Quick, General Manager
Dustin Sledge, Programming Director

WRGA
11-01-1929; 1470 kHz AM; *Hrs Open:* 24; 5 kw-D, DAN; 5 kw-N, DAN; N34 18 5 W85 9 19
P. O. Box 1187, Rome, GA 30161 US
(706) 291-9496; *Fax:* (706) 235-7107
www.wrgarome.com
south107@aol.com
License: Rome, GA held by McDougald Broadcasting Corp.
Group Owner: Southern Broadcasting Companies Inc.; (acq 1-28-2002; $1.6 million with co-located FM).
Nat'l Network: ABC; CNN Radio; *Regional Network:* Ga. News Net.; *Wire Services:* National Weather Network
Format: News, News/Talk, 86; *Hrs. of News Programming:* news progmg 168 hrs wkly; *No. News Employees:* 2; *Target Audience:* General; upscale, involved, upwardly mobile
Paul Stone, President
Gregory Kamishlian, General Manager

WROM
12-26-1946; 710 kHz AM; *Hrs Open:* Sunrise-sunset
725 Calloway Dr., Rockmart, GA 30153 US
(706) 234-7171; *Fax:* (706) 234-8043
www.wromradio.com
wromradio@comcast.net
License: Rome, GA held by LGV Broadcasting Inc.
Nat'l Network: USA
Format: Gospel *Special Programming:* Christian teaching, contemp Christian mus; *Hrs. of News Programming:* news progmg 14 hrs wkly; *No. News Employees:* 1; *Target Audience:* 35 plus; middle class families, women,homeowners
Mark Lumpkin, General Manager

WGJK
08-01-1962; 1360 kHz AM; *Hrs Open:* 6 AM-12 PM; 0.5 kw-D, ND1; 0.047 kw-N, ND1; N34 16 15 W85 11 0
20 John Davenport Drive, Rome, GA 30161 US
(706) 291-9496; *Fax:* (706) 235-7107
sales@q102rome.com
License: Rome, GA held by Woman's World Broadcasting Inc.
Arbitron Metro Market: Rome, GA; *Format:* Urban Contemporary
Howard Toole, CEO
Randy Quick, General Manager
Kevin Daniels, Operation Manager & Programming Director
Luke Brannon, Engineering Director & IT
Dana Clark, Traffic Manager
Samantha Bell, Brands Manager
Nelle Reagan, Public ServiceDirector
Rick Bradley, Production & Imaging Director
Cheryl Scott, Business Manager & Human Resources Director

Rossville

WDYN
11-11-1958; 980 kHz AM; *Hrs Open:* Sunrise-sunset; 500 w-D; N34 58 03 W85 18 00
7413 Old Lee Hwy., Chattanooga, TN 53202
(423) 892-3333; *Fax:* (423) 899-7224
License: Rossville, Walker County, GA held by 3 Daughters Media Inc.
Group Owner: 3 Daughters Media Inc.; (acq 6-22-2007; grpsl)
Nat'l Reps: Clear Channel
Arbitron Metro Market: Chattanooga, TN; *Hrs. of News Programming:* news progmg 4 hrs wkly; *No. News Employees:* 1; *Target Audience:* 35-64; adults
Sammy George, General Manager

WRXR-FM
06-08-1966; 105.5 MHz FM; *Hrs Open:* 24; 1.8 kw; 604 ft.; N34 57 23 W85 17 32
7413 Old Lee Highway, Chatanooga, TN 37421 US
(423) 892-3333; *Fax:* (423) 899-7224
www.rock105.com
License: Rossville, Walker County, GA held by Capstar TX LLC
Group Owner: iHeartMedia; (acq 8-7-2000; grpsl)
Nat'l Reps: Clear Channel
Arbitron Metro Market: Chattanooga, TN; *Format:* Rock/AOR; *Hrs. of News Programming:* News progmg one hr wkly; *Adv. Rates:* 75; 45; 65; 20
Gator Harrison, Operations Manager
Jared Stehney, Market Manager/Sales Manager
Daniel Wyatt, Web Director

Roswell

WAMJ
01-01-1997; 107.5 MHz FM; 18 kw horiz, 33 kw vert; 607 ft.; N33 55 1 W84 12 6
101 Marietta St., 12th Floor, Atlanta, GA 30303 US
(404) 765-9750; *Fax:* (404) 688-7686
www.majicatl.com
License: Roswell, Fulton County, GA held by Radio One Licenses, LLC
Group Owner: Radio One Inc.; (acq 11-8-2001; grpsl)
Arbitron Metro Market: Atlanta, GA; *Format:* Adult Contemp, Urban Contemporary

Tim Davies, General Manager

Royston

WXFO

01-01-1971; 810 kHz AM; *Hrs Open:* Sunrise-sunset; 0.23 kw-D, NDD; N34 16 50 W83 7 9
1010 Tower Place, Bogart, GA 30622 US
(706) 246-0059; *Fax:* (706) 245-0890
www.newstalk810.com
License: Royston, GA held by Oconee River Broadcasting LLC
Nat'l Network: Fox News Radio; *Regional Network:* Ga. News Net.
Arbitron Metro Market: Royston, GA; *Format:* Talk; *Hrs. of News Programming:* news progmg 7 hrs wkly; *No. News Employees:* 3; *Target Audience:* General.; *Adv. Rates:* 7.50; 5.75; 7.50; 5.75
KJ Allen, General Manager

Sandersville

WSNT

05-11-1956; 1490 kHz AM; 1 kw-U; N32 58 23 W82 48 34
Mailing Address: Box 150, Sandersville, GA 30401
Second Address: 312 Morningside Dr., Sandersville, GA 31082
(478) 552-5182; *Fax:* (478) 553-0800
sales@waco100fm.com
License: Sandersville, Washington County, GA held by Radio Station WSNT Inc.
Nat'l Network: Salem Gospel; *Regional Network:* Ga. News Net; *Nat'l Reps:* Rgnl Reps *Regional Reps:* SE AgNet

Capers Brazzell, General Manager
Nancy Craig, General Sales Mgr
Jerry Knight, Programming Director
Taylor Everett, Promotions Manager

WSNT-FM

01-01-1975; 99.9 MHz FM; *Hrs Open:* 24; 6 kw; Ant 184 ft; N32 58 23 W82 48 34
Mailing Address: Box 150, Sandersville, GA 31082
Second Address: 312 Morningside Dr., Sandersville, GA 31082
(478) 552-5182; *Fax:* (478) 553-0800
www.waco100fm.com
sales@waco100fm.com
License: Sandersville, Washington County, GA held by Radio Station WSNT, Inc.
Nat'l Network: ABC Music Radio; *Regional Network:* Ga. News Net; *Nat'l Reps:* Rgnl Reps *Regional Reps:* SE AgNet
Hrs. of News Programming: 2; *No. News Employees:* 1
Mary Foster, Operations Dir
Capers Brazzell, General Manager
Nancy Craig, General Sales Mgr
Jerry Knight, Programming Director
Taylor Everett, Promotions Manager
Buddy Wommack, Chief Engineer

Sasser

WEGC

01-01-1995; 107.7 MHz FM; 11.5 kw; 312 ft.; N31 38 42 W84 21 15
1104 West Broad Avenue, Albany, GA 31707 US
(229) 888-5000(229) 878-1077; *Fax:* (229) 888-5960
www.mix107albany.com
april.bailey@cumulus.com
License: Sasser, Terrell County, GA held by Cumulus Licensing Corp.
Group Owner: Cumulus Media Inc.; (acq 7-7-98)
Nat'l Reps: Katz Radio
Arbitron Metro Market: Sasser, GA.; *Format:* Adult Contemp
Roger Russell, Programming Director
Katy Edwards, Promotions Manager
Reid Reker, Marketing Manager

Savannah

WAEV

02-04-1969; 97.3 MHz FM; 100 kw; 1299 ft.; N32 2 45 W81 20 27
245 Alfred Street, Savannah, GA 31408 US
(912) 964-7794; *Fax:* (912) 964-9414
www.973kissfm.com
info@973kissfm.com
License: Savannah, Chatham County, GA held by Capstar TX LLC
Group Owner: iHeartMedia
Nat'l Network: Westwood One
Arbitron Metro Market: Savannah, GA; *Format:* Contemporary Hits/Top 40; *Target Audience:* 25-54; affluent
Wesley Peper, Vice President of Sales

WBMQ

12-29-1939; 630 kHz AM
214 Television Circle, Savannah, GA 31406 US
(912) 961-9000; *Fax:* (912) 961-7070
License: Savannah, GA held by Cumulus Licensing Corp.
Group Owner: Cumulus Media Inc.; (acq 3-26-98; grpsl)
Nat'l Network: CBS
Arbitron Metro Market: Savannah, GA; *Format:* News, News/Talk, 86; *Target Audience:* 35 plus.
Eric Mastel, General Manager/Marketing Manager
Mike Miller, Programming Director
Gil Jones, Promotions Manager

WTKS

10-15-1929; 1290 kHz AM; 5 kw-D, DAN; 5 kw-N, DAN; N32 5 26 W81 8 55
245 Alfred St., Savannah, GA 31408 US
(912) 964-7794; *Fax:* (912) 964-9414
www.newsradio1290wtks.com
info@newsradio1290wtks.com
License: Savannah, GA held by Capstar TX LLC
Group Owner: iHeartMedia; (acq 8-30-00; grpsl).
Arbitron Metro Market: Savannah, GA; *Format:* News, News/Talk, 86; *Target Audience:* 25-64.
Sheryl Collison, Market President
Wesley Peper, Vice President of Sales

*WHCJ

08-18-1975; 90.3 MHz FM; *Hrs Open:* 16; 6 kw; 223 ft.; N32 1 28 W81 3 23
P. O. Box 20484, Savannah, GA 31404 US
(912) 356-2399; *Fax:* (912) 356-2041
License: Savannah, Chatham County, GA held by Savannah State University.
Arbitron Metro Market: Savannah, GA; *Format:* Variety/Diverse; *Target Audience:* 17-65; interested in jazz, reggae, blues & gospel
Theron Ike Carter, General Manager

WIXV

04-24-1972; 95.5 MHz FM; 98 kw; 988 ft.; N32 3 29 W81 20 19
330 East Kilbourn Avenue, Suite 250, Milwaukee, WI 53202 US
(912) 961-9000; *Fax:* (912) 961-7070
www.rockofsavannah.com
info@diane.hubelcumulus.com
License: Savannah, Chatham County, GA
Group Owner: Cumulus Media Inc.
Arbitron Metro Market: Savannah, GA; *Format:* Classic Rock; *Target Audience:* 18-49.
Greg Park, Station Manager
Steve Entrekin, Programming Director
Paul Galvin, Promotions Manager

WJCL-FM

06-18-1972; 96.5 MHz FM; *Hrs Open:* 24; 100 kw; 1161 ft.; N32 3 29 W81 20 19
214 Television Circle, Savannah, GA 31406 US
(912) 961-9000; *Fax:* (912) 961-7070
www.kix96.com
License: Savannah, Chatham County, GA held by Cumulus Licensing Corp.
Group Owner: Cumulus Media Inc.; (acq 3-12-98; $7.25 million)
Arbitron Metro Market: Savannah, GA; *Format:* Country; *No. News Employees:* 1; *Target Audience:* 25-54.
Eric Mastel, General Manager
Chris Miller, General Sales Mgr
Boomer Lee, Programming Director
Gil Jones, Promotions Director
Martin Gausvik, CFO

WJLG

10-06-1950; 900 kHz AM; 4.35 kw-D, ND1; 0.152 kw-N, ND1; N32 4 29 W81 4 17
214 Television Circle, Savannah, GA 31406 US
(912) 961-9000; *Fax:* (912) 961-7070
www.cumulus.com
License: Savannah, GA held by Cumulus Licensing Corp.
Group Owner: Cumulus Media Inc.; (acq 7-29-98; $5.25 million with co-located FM)
Nat'l Network: Fox Sports
Arbitron Metro Market: Savannah, GA; *Format:* Sports
Eric Mastel, General Manager
Chris Miller, General Sales Mgr
Boomer Lee, Programming Director
Gil Jones, Promotions Director

*WLXP

01-01-2002; 88.1 MHz FM; *Hrs Open:* 24; 5.5 kw; 341 ft.; N32 3 48 W81 2 56
P.O. Box 246, Savannah, GA 31402 US
(888) 937-2471; *Fax:* (916) 251-1650
www.air1.com
info@air1.com
License: Savannah, Chatham County, GA held by Christian Multimedia Network Inc.
Nat'l Network: Air 1
Arbitron Metro Market: Savannah, GA; *Format:* Christian; *No. News Employees:* 3; *Target Audience:* 18-35; Judeo-Christian, female; *Adv. Rates:* 12; 9; 12; 7.50
Mike Novak, CEO/COO
Mike Novak, President
Chip Bailey, Operations Dir

WQBT

11-29-1946; 94.1 MHz FM; 100 kw; 1299 ft.; N32 2 45 W81 20 27
245 Alfred St., Savannah, GA 31408 US
(912) 964-7794; *Fax:* (912) 964-9414
www.941thebeat.com
info@941thebeat.com
License: Savannah, Chatham County, GA held by Capstar TX LLC
Group Owner: iHeartMedia
Arbitron Metro Market: Savannah, GA; *Format:* Urban Contemporary
Wesley Peper, Vice President of Sales

WSEG

05-01-1956; 1400 kHz AM; *Hrs Open:* 24; 0.65 kw-D, ND1; 0.65 kw-N, ND1; N32 4 29 W81 4 17
2970 Peachtree Road, NW, Suite 970, Eighth Floor, Atlanta, GA 30305 US
(912) 264-6251
License: Savannah, GA held by MarMac Communications LLC.
Group Owner: MarMac Communications LLC; (acq 6-26-2007; $300,000)
Arbitron Metro Market: Savannah, GA; *Format:* Contemporary Hits/Top 40, Adult Contemp
Gary Marmitt, General Manager

WSOK

10-01-1946; 1230 kHz AM; 1 kw-U, ND1; N32 4 20 W81 4 35
245 Alfred St., Savannah, GA 31408 US
(912) 964-7794; *Fax:* (912) 964-9414
www.1230wsok.com
License: Savannah, GA held by Capstar TX LLC
Group Owner: iHeartMedia; (acq 8-30-00; grpsl).
Nat'l Network: American Urban
Arbitron Metro Market: Savannah, GA; *Format:* Gospel
Wesley Peper, Senior Vice President of Sales

*WSVH

04-20-1981; 91.1 MHz FM; *Hrs Open:* 24; 96 kw vert; 1414 ft.; N32 8 48 W81 37 5 *Rebroadcasts:* WJSP, Warm Springs, GA, 50-60%
Mailing Address: 260 - 14th Street, N.W., Atlanta, GA 30318 US
Second Address: 12 Ocean Science Cir., Savannah, GA 30602
(404) 685-2690 HQ; *Fax:* (404) 685-2684 HQ
www.gpb.org
ask@gpb.org
License: Savannah, Chatham County, GA held by Georgia Public Telecommunications Commission.
Nat'l Network: PRI; NPR; *Wire Services:* AP
Arbitron Metro Market: Savannah, GA; *Format:* Jazz, News; *Hrs. of News Programming:* news progmg 51 hrs wkly; *No. News Employees:* 10; *Target Audience:* Adults: 35 plus.
Milton Clipper, Chief Executive Officer
Teya Ryan, President
Tom Barclay, Operations Dir
Rob Maynard, Programming Director
Bonnie Bean, CFO

*WYFS

11-01-1986; 89.5 MHz FM; *Hrs Open:* 24; 100 kw horiz, 91 kw vert; 600 ft.; N32 4 4 W81 21 17
Mailing Address: P.O. Box 7300, Charlotte, NC 28241 US
Second Address: 11530 Carmel Commons Blvd., Charlotte, GA 28226
(800) 888-7077
www.bbnradio.org
bbn@bbnmedia.org
License: Savannah, Chatham County, GA held by Bible Broadcasting Network Inc.
Group Owner: Bible Broadcasting Network
Arbitron Metro Market: Savannah, GA; *Format:* Christian, Religious; *Target Audience:* General; christian progmg for the entire family
Lowell Davey, President
Jason Padgett, Operations Manager

Smithboro

*WAKP
89.1 MHz FM; 2.9 kw vert; 220 ft.; N33 19 0 W83 31 40
US
(864) 297-0216
License: Smithboro, Jasper County, GA held by Network of Glory Inc.
Arbitron Metro Market: Smithboro, GA
Lola Richey, General Manager

Smithville

WZIQ
01-01-1996; 106.5 MHz FM; *Hrs Open:* 24; 2.45 kw; 515 ft; N31 47 59 W84 14 54
P.O. Box 510, Appling, GA 30802
(800) 926-4669
www.gnnradio.org
License: Smithville, Lee County, GA held by Barinowski Investment Co.
Group Owner: Good News Network; (acq 1-21-98)
Population Served: 110,000; *Arbitron Metro Market:* Albany, GA

Smyrna

WAZX
03-01-1962; 1550 kHz AM; *Hrs Open:* 24
2460 Atlanta Road, Smyrna, GA 30080 US
(559) 935-4191; *Fax:* (559) 935-4191
License: Smyrna, GA held by GA-MEX Broadcasting Inc.
Arbitron Metro Market: Riverdale CA; *Format:* Oldies
Rebecca Sexton, General Manager

WSTR
05-01-1966; 94.1 MHz FM; 100 kw; 1018 ft.; N33 45 33 W84 20 5
210 Interstate North Circle, Suite 100, Atlanta, GA 30339 US
(404) 261-2970; *Fax:* (404) 365-9026
star94frontdesk@star94.com
License: Smyrna, Cobb County, GA held by Entercom Radio
Group Owner: Entercom; (acq 2016)
Arbitron Metro Market: Atlanta, GA; *Format:* Contemporary Hits/Top 40; *Target Audience:* 18-49; general
Don Benson, President
Mark Kanov, General Manager
Dan Bowen, Programming Director

Soperton

*WKTM
11-23-1982; 106.1 MHz FM; *Hrs Open:* 24; 6 kw; 299 ft.; N32 25 31 W82 33 26
3213 Huxley Drive, Augusta, GA 30909 US
(706) 309-9610
www.gnnradio.org
ctbarinowski@comcast.net
License: Soperton, Treutlen County, GA held by Barinowski Investment Co.

Clarence Barinowski, General Manager

Sparta

*WJDS
88.7 MHz FM; 0 kw horiz, 2 kw vert; 135 ft.; N33 18 48 W83 0 5
3213 Huxley Drive, Augusta, GA 30909 US
(800) 926-4669
www.gnnradio.org
brian@gnnradio.org
License: Sparta, Hancock County, GA held by Augusta Radio Fellowship Institute Inc.
Arbitron Metro Market: Appling, GA
Clarence Barinowski, General Manager

Springfield

WEAS-FM
08-01-1967; 93.1 MHz FM; 96.64 kw; 981 ft.; N32 2 45 W81 20 27
330 East Kilbourn Ave., Suite 250, Milwaukee, WI 53202 US
(912) 961-9000; *Fax:* (912) 961-7070
www.e93fm.com/
License: Springfield, Effingham County, GA held by Cumulus Licensing Corp.
Group Owner: Cumulus Media Inc.
Arbitron Metro Market: Springfield, GA; *Format:* Urban Contemporary
Barbara Haynes, General Manager
Lil G, Programming Director
Gil Jones, Promotions Manager
Duffy Egan, Chief Engineer

St. Marys

WWIO
10-15-1985; 1190 kHz AM; *Hrs Open:* Daytime
2101 Hwy 40 E., St. Marys, GA 31558 US
(912) 344-3565; *Fax:* (912) 344-3411
www.wsvh.org
publicradio@wsvh.org
License: St. Marys, GA held by Lighthouse Christian Broadcasting Corp.
Nat'l Network: USA; NPR; *Regional Network:* Georgia Public Radio; *Nat'l Reps:* Rgnl Reps; *Wire Services:* AP
Arbitron Metro Market: Savannah, GA; *Format:* Classical, News; *Hrs. of News Programming:* news progmg 40 hrs wkly; *No. News Employees:* 6; *Target Audience:* General; 35 yrs +
Russell Wells, Operations Dir
Eric Nauert, Station Manager
St. John Flynn, Programming Director
Mark Sehlig, Chief Engineer

St. Simons Island

WBGA
01-01-1990; 92.7 MHz FM; *Hrs Open:* 24; 6 kw; 328 ft.; N31 9 42 W81 28 28
3833 US Highway 82, Brunswick, GA 31523 US
(912) 265-9300; *Fax:* (912) 264-5462
License: St. Simons Island, Glynn County, GA held by Quantum of Brunswick License Co. LLC
Group Owner: Qantum Communications Corp.
Nat'l Network: ABC
Arbitron Metro Market: Brunswick, GA; *Format:* Urban Contemporary; *Target Audience:* 24-45.
Jonthan Havens, General Manager

Statenville

WHLJ-FM
01-01-1999; 97.5 MHz FM; 6 kw; Ant 328 ft; N30 46 47 W82 52 43
LaTaurus Productions Inc., Box 1305, Valdosta, GA 31601
(229) 242-9997; *Fax:* (229) 249-9765
WHLJ@BELLSOUTH.NET
License: Statenville, Echols County, GA held by LaTaurus Productions Inc.
Arbitron Metro Market: Valdosta, GA
Warren Lee, General Manager

Statesboro

WPMX
01-01-1995; 102.9 MHz FM; *Hrs Open:* 24; 25 kw; 328 ft.; N32 26 43 W81 58 7
P.O. Box 180, Hawkinsville, GA 31036 US
(912) 764-6000; *Fax:* (912) 764-8827
radiocenter@frontiernet.net
License: Statesboro, Bulloch County, GA held by Georgia Eagle Media Inc.
Group Owner: Georgia Eagle Media Inc.; acq 5-21-2007; grpsl)
Nat'l Network: ABC; *Regional Network:* Ga. News Net.
Format: Adult Contemp; *Target Audience:* General.
Jeff Anderson, General Manager
Buddy Horne, Programming Director

WPTB
04-04-1976; 850 kHz AM; *Hrs Open:* 24
1201 Third Avenue, Suite 3600, Seattle, WA 98101 US
(912) 764-6621; *Fax:* (912) 764-6622
espn850@frontiernet.net
License: Statesboro, GA held by Georgia Eagle Media Inc.
Group Owner: Georgia Eagle Media Inc.; (acq 5-21-2007; grpsl)
Nat'l Network: ESPN Radio; *Nat'l Reps:* Dora-Clayton *Regional Reps:* Regional Reps
Format: Sports *Special Programming:* Gospel 6 hrs wkly; *Hrs. of News Programming:* news progmg 7 hrs wkly; *No. News Employees:* 1; *Target Audience:* General.
Sandi Kirkland, Operations Dir
Nate Hirsch, General Manager
Bill Kent, Programming Director

*WVGS
01-01-1975; 91.9 MHz FM; *Hrs Open:* 24; 1 kw; 161 ft.; N32 25 32 W81 46 58
Lb 8128, Statesboro, GA 30460 US
(912) 681-0877; *Fax:* (912) 486-7113
class.georgiasouthern.edu
License: Statesboro, Bulloch County, GA held by Georgia Southern University
Arbitron Metro Market: Statesboro, GA; *Format:* Alternative; *Target Audience:* 18-25; college kids
Melonie Stone, General Manager

WWNS
12-01-1946; 1240 kHz AM; *Hrs Open:* 24; 0.71 kw-U, ND1; N32 27 19 W81 46 28
Mailing Address: 561 East Olliff St Bx958, Statesboro, GA 30458 US
Second Address: 561 E. Olliff St., Statesboro, GA 30458
(912) 764-5446; *Fax:* (912) 764-8827
License: Statesboro, GA held by Georgia Eagle Media Inc.
Group Owner: Georgia Eagle Media Inc.; (acq 5-21-2007; grpsl)
Nat'l Network: USA *Regional Reps:* Rgnl Reps
Arbitron Metro Market: Statesboro, GA; *Format:* News, News/Talk, 84, Talk; *Hrs. of News Programming:* news progmg 20 hrs wkly; *No. News Employees:* 1; *Target Audience:* 25-death.
Cornell Burgess, Operations Dir
Jeff Anderson, General Manager
Buddy Horne, Programming Director

*WSLT
88.5 MHz FM; 6 kw; 197 ft.; N32 38 9 W81 41 36
US
(912) 826-3833
License: Statesboro, Bulloch County, GA held by Salt and Light Communications Inc.
Arbitron Metro Market: Statesboro, GA
Linda Hand, CEO

Summerville

WGTA
08-27-1950; 950 kHz AM; *Hrs Open:* 6 AM-7 PM; 5 kw-D, ND2; 0.11 kw-N, ND2; N34 27 53 W85 21 12
2 Mount Alto Road, Rome, GA 30165 US
(770) 436-6171; *Fax:* (770) 436-0100
License: Summerville, GA held by Azteca Communications Inc.

Javier Macias, President
Patty Perez, General Manager

Swainsboro

WJAT
01-01-1950; 800 kHz AM; *Hrs Open:* 24
P.O. Box 1590 2 Radio Loop, Swainsboro, GA 30401 US
(478) 237-1590; *Fax:* (478) 237-3559
License: Swainsboro, GA held by RadioJones LLC.
Group Owner: RadioJones LLC; (acq 4-2-2004; grpsl)
Format: News, Sports, 86 *Special Programming:* Farm 5 hrs wkly; high school sports; *Hrs. of News Programming:* news progmg 10 hrs wkly; *No. News Employees:* 1; *Target Audience:* 25-64.; *Adv. Rates:* 10; 8; 8;5
Dennis Jones, President
Jolly Martin, General Sales Mgr
John Wagner, Programming Director
Marty Foglia, Engineering Dir

WXRS
03-10-1978; 1590 kHz AM; *Hrs Open:* 24; 2.5 kw-D, ND1; 0.023 kw-N, ND1; N32 33 25 W82 20 29
2 Radio Loop, PO Box 1590, Swainsboro, GA 30401 US
(478) 237-1590; *Fax:* (478) 237-3559
www.radiojones.com
License: Swainsboro, GA held by RadioJones LLC.
Group Owner: RadioJones LLC; (acq 4-2-2004; grpsl).
Arbitron Metro Market: Portal, GA; *Format:* Oldies; *Hrs. of News Programming:* news progmg 10 per day; *No. News Employees:* 1; *Target Audience:* 25-64.; *Adv. Rates:* 8; 6; 6; 3
Dennis Jones, President
John Wagner, Operations Dir
Jolly Martin, General Sales Mgr
Marty Foglia, Engineering Dir

Sylvania

WSYL
12-01-1955; 1490 kHz AM; *Hrs Open:* 24; 1 kw-U, ND1; N32 43 51 W81 37 4
910 W. Ogeechee Street, Sylvania, GA 30467 US
(912) 564-7461; *Fax:* (912) 564-7462
License: Sylvania, GA held by Georgia Eagle Media Inc.
Group Owner: Georgia Eagle Media Inc.; (acq 5-21-2007; grpsl)
Regional Network: Ga. News Net; *Nat'l Reps:* Rgnl Reps
Special Programming: Farm 5 hrs wkly
Nathan Hirsch, General Manager
Mary Lou Clontz, Programming Director
David Hartley, News Director

Sylvester

*WHKV
01-27-1993; 106.1 MHz FM; 6 kw; 328 ft.; N31 30 15 W83 55 46
1121 East Franklin St., Sylvester, GA 31791 US

(800) 525-5683
www.klove.com
klove@klove.com
License: Sylvester, Worth County, GA held by Educational Media Foundation.
Group Owner: EMF Broadcasting; (acq 4-30-2007; $615,000 with WFFM(FM) Ashburn)
Nat'l Network: K-Love
Arbitron Metro Market: Albany, GA; *Format:* Religious
Darrell Chambliss, Chairman
Alan Mason, COO
Mike Novak, President

WNUQ
08-01-1999; 102.1 MHz FM; 6 kw; 259 ft.; N31 31 40 W83 50 22
P.O. Box 364, Sylvester, GA 31791 US
(229) 888-5000; *Fax:* (229) 888-5960
www.q102albany.com
info18@cumulus.com
License: Sylvester, Worth County, GA held by Cumulus Licensing Corp.
Group Owner: Cumulus Media Inc.; (acq 3-12-2001; $550,000).
Nat'l Reps: Katz Radio
Arbitron Metro Market: Sylvester, GA; *Format:* Blues
Gregory Kamishlian, General Manager
Roshon Vance, Programming Director
Katy Edwards, Promotions Manager
April Bailey, Business Manager
Kelly Carpenter, Asst. Business Mgr. & Trafficÿ
Angel Taylor, Vice President of Salesÿ
MicheleHicks, Account Executive
Tiffany Cox, Account Executive
Susan Vancel, Account Executive

Talking Rock

WNSY
01-01-1999; 100.1 MHz FM; 7 kw; 617 ft.; N34 37 50 W84 29 29
Rebroadcasts: Rebroadcasts WLKQ-FM Buford 100%
1353 13th Avenue, Columbus, GA 31901 US
(770) 623-8772; *Fax:* (770) 623-4722
www.laraza1023.com
License: Talking Rock, Pickens County, GA held by Davis Broadcasting of Atlanta L.L.C.
Group Owner: Davis Broadcasting Inc.; (acq 1-17-2007; $3.8 million with WCHK(AM) Canton)
Arbitron Metro Market: Pickens, GA; *Format:* Spanish
Brian Barber, General Manager

Tallapoosa

WKNG
09-01-1977; 1060 kHz AM
Mailing Address: P.O. Box 606, Tallapoosa, GA 30176 US
Second Address: Hwy. 78, Golf Course Rd., Tallapoosa, GA 30176
(770) 574-1060; *Fax:* (770) 574-1062
www.wkng.com
License: Tallapoosa, GA held by WKNG LLC.
Nat'l Network: ABC; *Regional Network:* Ga. News Net.
Format: Country; *Target Audience:* 25-54.
Steven Gradick, President

***WEYY**
88.7 MHz FM; 0.25 kw; 98 ft.; N33 44 42.6 W85 17 16.2 US
(706) 965-2355
License: Tallapoosa, Haralson County, GA held by Old Time Gospel Ministries.
Arbitron Metro Market: Tallapoosa, GA
Robert Jarrell, President

WWGA
98.9 mhz; 1850 w; 597 ft; N33 39 03 W85 17 41
1 Golf Course Road, Tallapoosa, GA
(770)574-1060; *Fax:* (770)574-1062
www.gradickcommunications.com
License: Tallapoosa, GA held by Wkng LLC

Kim Fitzgerald Buhl, Traffic/Promotions
Colin Worthington, News Director
Michael Vincent, Production Director
Mitch Grey, Production Director

Tallulah Falls

***WNGM(FM)**
91.7 MHz FM; 130 w; Ant 1,030 ft; N34 43 46 W83 29 42
179 Cross Creek Dr., Toccoa, GA 30577
(706) 491-4457
License: Tallulah Falls, Habersham and Rabun County, GA held by Toccoa Foundation Inc.
Population Served: 2,986; *Arbitron Metro Market:* Pendleton, SC
Douglas Sutton, President

***WNGM(FM)**
90.3 MHz FM; 2.25 kw; Ant 325 ft; N33 49 50.4 W82 45 19.2
179 Cross Creek Drive, Toccoa, GA 30577
(706) 491-4457
License: Tallulah Falls, Wilkes County, GA held by Toccoa Foundation Inc.
Population Served: 168; *Arbitron Metro Market:* Tallulah Falls, GA
Douglas Sutton Jr., Operations Dir

WHTD
91.7 MHz FM; 25 watts; 1264 ft; N34 45 39.50 W83 24 44.50
179 Cross Creek Dr., Toccoa, GA 30577
(706) 491-4457
License: Tallulah Falls, GA held by Toccoa Foundation Inc.
Group Owner: Toccoa Foundation

Tennille

WJFL
10-14-1993; 101.9 MHz FM; 6 kw; 328 ft.; N32 54 49 W82 53 6
P.O. Box 1097, Sandersville, GA 31082 US
(478) 553-1019; *Fax:* (478) 553-1123
www.wjfl.com
wjfl@wjfl.com
License: Tennille, Washington County, GA held by Middle Georgia Broadcasting, Inc.
Format: Contemporary Hits/Top 40, Oldies
Michael Cowan, General Manager
Andrea Turner, Programming Director
Reba Barlow, Production Assistant
Tina Walker, Production Assistant

The Rock

***WKEU-FM**
01-01-2000; 88.9 MHz FM; 5 kw; 764 ft.; N32 59 11 W84 21 56
Mailing Address: 1000 Memorial Drive, Griffin, GA 30223 US
Second Address: 1000 Memorial Dr., Griffin, GA 30224
(770) 227-5507; *Fax:* (770) 229-2291
www.wkeuradio.com
wkeu@aol.com
License: The Rock, Upson County, GA held by Georgia Public Radio Inc.
Format: Classic Rock
William Taylor, Jr., President
William Taylor Jr., General Manager

Thomaston

WTGA
11-01-1962; 1590 kHz AM; 0.5 kw-D, ND1; 0.025 kw-N, ND1; N32 53 45 W84 18 10
Mailing Address: 208 South Center St, Thomaston, GA 30286 US
Second Address: Box 550, Thomaston, GA
(706) 647-7121; *Fax:* (706) 647-7122
License: Thomaston, GA held by Radio Georgia Inc.
Arbitron Metro Market: Thomaston, GA; *Format:* Adult Contemp
Special Programming: Black 4 hrs wkly
David Piper, President
Bill Bailey, General Sales Mgr
Robert Lyons, Chief Engineer

WTGA-FM
11-15-1982; 101.1 MHz FM; 6 kw; 308 ft; N32 51 49 W84 25 10
Mailing Address: 208 S. Center St., Thomaston, GA 30286
Second Address: Box 550, Thomaston, GA 30286
(706) 647-7121; *Fax:* (706) 647-7122
www.wtga.com
License: Thomaston, Upson County, GA
Population Served: 15,000
Dave Piper, President
Dave Piper, General Manager
Carl Pruett, General Sales Mgr
Charlie Steele, Programming Director
Bill Gentry, Promotions Manager
Mickey Thresher, News Director
Al Rhymeburg, Chief Engineer

Thomasville

WPAX
12-27-1922; 1240 kHz AM; *Hrs Open:* 24; 1 kw-U, ND1; N30 50 10 W83 59 19
Mailing Address: 117 Remington Ave, Thomasville, GA 31799 US
Second Address: 117 Remington Ave., Thomasville, GA 31799
(229) 226-1240; *Fax:* (229) 226-1361
www.wpaxradio.com
lenrob@rose.net
License: Thomasville, GA held by LenRob Inc.
Nat'l Network: CBS; *Regional Network:* Ga. News Net; *Nat'l Reps:* Rgnl Reps
Format: Contemporary Hits/Top 40; *Hrs. of News Programming:* news progmg 20 hrs wkly; *No. News Employees:* 1; *Target Audience:* 25 plus; mature with disposable income
Len Robinson, President

WSTT
01-01-1947; 730 kHz AM; *Hrs Open:* 5:30 AM-9 PM; 5 kw-D, NDD; 0.027 kw-N, ND1; N30 42 47 W84 8 20
210 S. Philip Rd., P.O. Box 213, Niles, MI 49120 US
(269) 683-4343
License: Thomasville, GA held by Marion R. Williams.
Group Owner: Marion R. Williams Stns; (acq 7-26-99; $300,000)
Nat'l Network: CBS
Arbitron Metro Market: Tallahassee, FL; *Format:* Gospel; *Target Audience:* 25-54; general

***WAYT**
01-01-2003; 88.1 MHz FM; 35 kw; 1286 ft.; N30 40 6 W83 58 10
P.O. Box 14884, Tallahassee, FL 32317 US
(850) 422-9293; *Fax:* (850) 297-1888
wayt.wayfm.com
supportservices@wayfm.com
License: Thomasville, Thomas County, GA held by WAY-FM Media Group Inc.
Group Owner: WAY-FM Media Group Inc.; acq 10-24-02).
Arbitron Metro Market: Tallahassee, FL; *Format:* Christian
Bob Augsburg, President/Founder
Steve Young, Station Manager

***WFSL**
03-01-2005; 90.7 MHz FM; 0.25 kw; 154 ft.; N30 50 12 W83 58 57
Florida St University, 1600 Red Baber Plaza, Talleahassee, FL 32310 US
(850) 487-3170; *Fax:* (850) 487-3093
www.wfsu.org
fprn@wfsu.org
License: Thomasville, Thomas County, GA held by Florida State University Board of Trustees.
Arbitron Metro Market: Tallahassee, FL; *Format:* Talk
Patrick Keating, General Manager
Caroline Austin, Station Manager
Krysta Brown, News Director
Doug Crall, Engineering Dir
Leo Barfield, Chief Engineer
Denison Graham, Finance Director
Sherri Leggett, Accounting Supervisor
Amanda DiLullo, Accounting Associate
Jacqueline Roark, Financial Specialist
Zhonta Stapleton, Accounting Associate
Melissa Roy, Administrative Specialist/HR

WGMY
107.1 MHz FM; 100 kw; 823 ft.; N30 35 12 W84 14 11
325 John Knox Road, Building G, Tallahassee, FL 32303 US
(850) 422-3107
www.kissfm1071.com
License: Thomasville, Orange County, GA held by CC Licenses LLC.
Group Owner: iHeartMedia
Arbitron Metro Market: Tallahassee, FL; *Format:* Contemporary Hits/Top 40
Richard J. Bressler, President
Jason Taylor, Digital Content Director

Thomson

WTHO-FM
02-22-1971; 101.7 MHz FM; 5.1 kw; 354 ft.; N33 28 20 W82 31 2
P.O. Box 900, 788 Cedar Rock Road NW, Thomson, GA 30824 US
(706) 595-5122; *Fax:* (706) 595-3021
wtho.com
traffic@wtho.com
License: Thomson, McDuffie County, GA held by Camellia City Communications Inc.
Regional Network: Ga. News Net; *Nat'l Reps:* Rgnl Reps
Arbitron Metro Market: Augusta, GA; *Format:* Country *Special Programming:* Farm 3 hrs, gospel one hr, relg 6 hrs wkly; *Hrs. of News Programming:* News progmg 2 hrs wkly; *No. News Employees:* 1; *Target Audience:* 25-54.
Mike Wall, General Manager
Mike Wall, General Sales Mgr
Steve Ferguson, Programming Director
Donna Branch, News Director

Mary Thomaston, Traffic Manager
Mike Wall, Station Owner

WTWA
01-10-1948; 1240 kHz AM; *Hrs Open:* 19; 1 kw-U, ND1; N33 28 20 W82 31 2
P.O. Box 900, Thomson, GA 30824 US
(706) 595-5122; *Fax:* (706) 595-3021
www.wtho.com
traffic@wtho.com
License: Thomson, GA held by Camellia City Communications Inc.
Arbitron Metro Market: Augusta, GA; *Format:* Adult Contemp; *No. News Employees:* 1; *Target Audience:* 35 plus.
Tom Thon, Operations Dir
Mike Wall, Station Manager
Steve Ferguson, Programming Director
Donna Branch, News Director

***WQAI**
89.5 MHz FM; 0.05 kw horiz, 49 kw vert; 476 ft.; N33 44 32 W82 31 17 *Rebroadcasts:* Rebroadcasts KLRD(FM) Yucaipa, CA 100%
P O Box 2440, Tupelo, MS 38803 US
(916) 251-1600; *Fax:* (916) 251-1650
www.air1.com
info@air1.com
License: Thomson, McDuffie County, GA held by Educational Media Foundation.
Group Owner: EMF Broadcasting; (acq 3-23-2007; grpsl)
Nat'l Network: Air 1
Arbitron Metro Market: Denison, IA; *Format:* Alternative, Christian
Mike Novak, President

Tifton

***WABR**
12-01-1973; 91.1 MHz FM; 30 kw; 249 ft.; N31 29 30 W83 31 49 *Rebroadcasts:* Rebroadcasts WJSP-FM Warm Springs 100%
260 - 14th Street, N.W., Atlanta, GA 30318 US
(308) 632-5667; *Fax:* (308) 635-1905
License: Tifton, Tift County, GA held by Georgia Public Telecommunications Commission.
Nat'l Network: NPR; *Regional Network:* Georgia Public Radio; *Wire Services:* AP
Arbitron Metro Market: Centennial CO; *Format:* Country
Julie Marshall, General Manager

WKZZ
01-01-2000; 92.5 MHz FM; 20.5 kw; 361 ft.; N31 31 40 W83 20 1
Box 100, Fitzgerald, GA 31750 US
(912) 389-0995; *Fax:* (912) 383-8552
traffic@charter.net
License: Tifton, Tift County, GA held by Broadcast South LLC.
Group Owner: Broadcast South LLC; (acq 11-15-2006; grpsl)
Format: Adult Contemp
John Higgs, General Manager

WOBB
01-01-1975; 100.3 MHz FM; 100 kw; 997 ft.; N31 25 51 W83 45 10
809 South Westover Blvd., Albany, GA 31707 US
(229) 439-9704; *Fax:* (229) 439-1509
www.b100wobb.com
License: Tifton, Tift County, GA held by CC Licenses LLC.
Group Owner: iHeartMedia; (acq 7-12-2000; grpsl).
Nat'l Reps: Christal
Arbitron Metro Market: Albany, GA *TV Affiliate:* Country; *Format:* Country *Special Programming:* News progmg 2 hrs wkly; *No. News Employees:* 25-49.; *Adv. Rates:* 45; 40; 45; 35
Chuck Thompson, General Sales Mgr
Paul Laseter, Programming Director
Wes Carroll, Digital Content Director

***WPLH**
01-01-1988; 103.1 MHz FM; 0.029 kw horiz; 177 ft.; N31 28 51 W83 31 38
Mailing Address: P.O. Box 20 Abac Station, Tifton, GA 31794 US
Second Address: 2802 Moore Hwy, Tifton, GA 31793
(229) 391-4977,(229) 391-4957; *Fax:* (229) 386-7158
License: Tifton, Tift County, GA held by Abraham Baldwin Agriculture College.
Regional Network: Georgia Public Radio
Format: Alternative
Eric Cash, General Manager

WTIF
01-01-1957; 1340 kHz AM; *Hrs Open:* 24; 1 kw-U, ND1; N31 28 16 W83 29 12
114 Kent Rd., Tifton, GA 31794 US
(229) 382-1340; *Fax:* (229) 386-8658
www.99rockfm.com
License: Tifton, GA held by Plant Broadcasting LLC
Group Owner: Plant Broadcasting
Nat'l Network: FOX; *Regional Network:* Ga. News Net.
Arbitron Metro Market: Tifton,GA; *Format:* Classic Rock; *No. News Employees:* 1; *Target Audience:* 18 plus.
Nettie Hatcher, General Manager

Tignall

WSGC-FM
05-15-1998; 105.3 MHz FM; *Hrs Open:* 24; 6 kw; 328 ft; N33 59 22 W82 46 23
562 Jones St, Elberton, GA 30635 US
(706) 283-1400; *Fax:* (706) 283-8710
www.wsgcradio.com
License: Tignall, Wilkes County, GA held by Georgia-Carolina Radiocasting Co. LLC.
Group Owner: Georgia-Carolina Radiocasting Companies; (acq 7-25-2002; grpsl)
Nat'l Network: ABC; CMLS; WWO
Population Served: 27,724 *Format:* Country, News/Talk, 84; *Hrs. of News Programming:* news progmg 5 hrs wkly; *No. News Employees:* 1; *Target Audience:* 25-54; general
David Thompson, Operations & Programming Director
Gary Bryant, Vice President/General Manager
David Stephens, News Director
Susie Larson, Office Manager

Toccoa

WNEG
04-21-1956; 630 kHz AM; *Hrs Open:* 24; 5.0 kw-D, 0.044 kw-N, ND2; N34 34 4 W83 19 26
Mailing Address: P.O. Box 1159, Toccoa, GA 30577 US
Second Address: 145 North Alexander St, Toccoa, GA 30577
(706) 886-2191; *Fax:* (706) 828-0819
www.wnegradio.com
wneg@windstream.net
License: Toccoa, Stephens County, GA held by Georgia-Carolina Radiocasting Co. LLC.
Group Owner: Georgia-Carolina Radiocasting Companies; (acq 7-25-2002; grpsl)
Nat'l Network: CBS Radio; *Regional Network:* Ga. News Net.
Arbitron Metro Market: Toccoa, GA; *Format:* News, Oldies; *Hrs. of News Programming:* news progmg 18 hrs wkly; *No. News Employees:* 1
Connie Gaines, Operations Manager
Phil Hobbs, General Manager
Ken Brady, General Sales Mgr
Charlie Bauder, News Director

Toccoa Falls

***WRAF**
09-04-1980; 90.9 MHz FM; *Hrs Open:* 24; 100 kw; 564 ft.; N34 35 57 W83 21 55
Mailing Address: Toccoa Falls College, Toccoa, GA 30598 US
Second Address: 292 Old Clarksville Hwy., Toccoa, GA 30577
(800) 251-8326,(706) 282-6030; *Fax:* (706) 282-6090
www.myfavoritestation.net
radio@tfc.edu
License: Toccoa Falls, Stephens County, GA held by Toccoa Falls College.
Nat'l Network: USA
Format: Adult Contemp, Religious; *Target Audience:* General; families
David Cornelius, General Manager

***WTXR**
09-01-1996; 89.7 MHz FM; *Hrs Open:* 24; 0.4 kw; 138 ft.; N34 35 57 W83 21 55
Mailing Address: Falls Road, Toccoa Falls, GA 30598 US
Second Address: 292 Old Clarkesville Hwy., Toccoa, GA 30577
(706) 282-6030; *Fax:* (706) 282-6090
radio@tfc.edu
License: Toccoa Falls, Stephens County, GA held by Toccoa Falls College.
Arbitron Metro Market: Toccoa Falls, GA; *Format:* Christian; *Target Audience:* 18-35; college students, young adults
David Cornelius, General Manager
Craig Salmon, Station Manager
Jennifer Doll, Programming Director
Kyle Atkins, Administrative Assistant
Allyn Griffith, Social Media Director

Toomsboro

***WZZG**
01-01-2009; 91.9 MHz FM; 2.3 kw; 479 ft.; N33 4 37.78 W83 8 48.25
US
(800) 926-4669; *Fax:* (706) 309-9669
www.gnnradio.org
License: Toomsboro, Wilkinson County, GA held by Augusta Radio Fellowship Institute Inc.
Arbitron Metro Market: Toomsboro, GA
C.T. Barinowski, President

Trenton

WBDX
01-01-1989; 102.7 MHz FM; *Hrs Open:* 24; 0.32 kw; 1375 ft.; N34 51 48 W85 23 35
2288 Gumbarrel Road, Ste. 111, Chattanooga, TN 37421 US
(254) 772-1900
License: Trenton, Dade County, GA held by Partners for Christian Media Inc.
Arbitron Metro Market: Eagle Pass TX; *Format:* Christian
Marvin Sanders, General Manager

WKWN
04-04-1982; 1420 kHz AM; *Hrs Open:* 24; 2.5 kw-D, ND2; 0.112 kw-N, ND2; N34 51 43 W85 29 59
Mailing Address: 11980 South Maine, Trenton, GA 30752 US
Second Address: 12544 N. Main St., Trenton, GA 30752
(706) 657-7594; *Fax:* (706) 657-6767
www.discoverdade.com
License: Trenton, GA held by Dade County Broadcasting Inc.
Regional Network: Ga. News Net.
Arbitron Metro Market: Chattanooga, TN; *Format:* News, News/Talk, 86; *Target Audience:* 25-54; locals
Evan Stone, CEO

Trion

WATG
01-01-1997; 95.7 MHz FM; *Hrs Open:* 24; 1.3 kw; 699 ft.; N34 28 10 W85 17 48
Mailing Address: 2 Mount Alto Road, Rome, GA 30165 US
Second Address: 10143 Commerce St., Summerville, GA 30747
(706) 857-2000; *Fax:* (706) 857-3652
www.theridge957.com/
License: Trion, Chattooga County, GA held by TTA Broadcasting Inc.
Nat'l Network: ABC; *Nat'l Reps:* Rgnl Reps
Arbitron Metro Market: Summerville,MA; *Format:* Oldies; *Hrs. of News Programming:* News progmg one hr wkly; *Target Audience:* 25-54; general
Jim Bojo, CFO
Randy Davis, President

WZQZ
04-01-1985; 1180 kHz AM; *Hrs Open:* 6am-10pm; 5 kw-D, NDD; N34 28 22 W85 19 31
Mailing Address: 3213 Huxley Dr., Augusta, GA 30909 US
Second Address: 4689 US Hwy. 27, Summerville, GA 30747
(706) 857-5555; *Fax:* (706) 857-2006
License: Trion, GA held by HS Productions Inc.
Nat'l Network: USA; CNN Radio; *Regional Network:* Ga. News Net.
Format: Talk; *Target Audience:* All ages; Northwest Georgia
Lebron Jimmy Charles Holbrook Jr., President
Terry Adams, General Manager

Tybee Island

WZAT
10-19-1971; 102.1 MHz FM; *Hrs Open:* 24; 98 kw; 1328 ft.; N32 3 29 W81 20 19
330 East Kilbourn Avenue, Suite 250, Milwaukee, WI 53202 US
(912) 961-9000; *Fax:* (912) 961-7070
www.z102.net
License: Tybee Island, Chatham County, GA held by Cumulus Licensing Corp.
Group Owner: Cumulus Media Inc.; (acq 7-29-98; $3.5 million)
Arbitron Metro Market: Savannah, GA; *Format:* Contemporary Hits/Top 40, Variety/Diverse
Lewis Dickey Jr., CEO
Sam Nelson, Operations Dir
Dale Powers, General Manager
Robert Combs, Engineering Dir
Martin Gausvik, CFO

Unadilla

WNNG-FM
06-01-1995; 99.9 MHz FM; *Hrs Open:* 24; 6 kw; 328 ft.; N32 18 29 W83 46 30
P.O. Box 510, Appling, GA 30802 US
(800) 926-4669
www.gnnradio.org

License: Unadilla, Dooly County, GA held by Augusta Radio Fellowship Institute Inc.
Group Owner: Good News Network; (acq 10-8-2007; $350,000)
Arbitron Metro Market: Unadilla, GA; *Format:* Adult Contemp

Valdosta

WAAC
01-01-1968; 92.9 MHz FM; 100 kw; 502 ft.; N30 48 13 W83 21 20
Mailing Address: Highway 84 West, Valdosta, GA 31601 US
Second Address: 2973 Hwy. 84 W., Valdosta, GA 31601
(229) 242-4513; *Fax:* (229) 247-7676
www.waacradio.com
mail@waacradio.com
License: Valdosta, Lowndes County, GA
Group Owner: Dee Rivers Radio Group
Nat'l Network: ABC
Arbitron Metro Market: Valdosta, GA; *Format:* Country; *Target Audience:* 25-54.; *Adv. Rates:* 53; 45; 53; 37
Robert Whitt, Operations Dir

*WAFT
11-25-1971; 101.1 MHz FM; *Hrs Open:* 24; 100 kw; 558 ft; N30 51 50 W83 23 39
215 Waft Hill Ln., Valdosta, GA 31603
(229) 244-5180; *Fax:* (229) 242-8808
www.waft.org
mail@waft.org
License: Valdosta, Lowndes County, GA held by Christian Radio Fellowship Inc.
Population Served: 56,019; *Arbitron Metro Market:* Valdosta, GA; *Hrs. of News Programming:* News progmg 3 hrs wkly; *Target Audience:* 40+ empty nesters
Bill Tidwell, GM

WRFV
11-03-1951; 910 kHz AM; 5 kw-D, DAN; 5 kw-N, DAN; N30 52 21 W83 20 36
3765 N. John Young Pkwy., Orlando, FL 32804 US
(407) 291-1395
License: Valdosta, GA held by Rama Communications Inc.
Group Owner: Rama Communications Inc.; (acq 2-28-2002; $255,000)
Arbitron Metro Market: Valdosta, GA
Shanti Persaud, President

WGUN
01-01-1939; 950 kHz AM; *Hrs Open:* 24; 3.5 kw-D, ND2; 0.063 kw-N, ND2; N30 48 13 W83 21 20
Mailing Address: Highway 84 West, Valdosta, GA 31601 US
Second Address: 2973 Hwy. 84 W., Valdosta, GA 31601
(229) 244-9590; *Fax:* (229) 247-7676
www.wgovradio.com
License: Valdosta, GA held by WGOV Inc.
Group Owner: Dee Rivers Radio Group
Nat'l Reps: Rgnl Reps
Arbitron Metro Market: Valdosta, GA; *Format:* Blues, Religious
Special Programming: Gospel 14 hrs, oldies 10 hrs wkly; *Hrs. of News Programming:* news progmg 3 hrs wkly; *No. News Employees:* 1; *Target Audience:* 18-45; Black; *Adv. Rates:* 28; 24; 28; 17
Lamar Freeman, Operations Dir
Loretta Grecco, General Sales Mgr
Jammie Brooks, Music Director

WQPW
09-01-1977; 95.7 MHz FM; *Hrs Open:* 24; 32 kw; 607 ft.; N30 42 7 W83 6 54
1711 Ellis Dr., Valdosta, GA 31601 US
(229) 244-8642
www.957themix.com
License: Valdosta, Lowndes County, GA held by RTG Radio LLC.
Group Owner: Black Crow Media Group LLC; (acq 11-9-2001; grpsl).
Arbitron Metro Market: Valdosta, GA; *Format:* Adult Contemp; *No. News Employees:* 14; *Target Audience:* 18-44.

WVLD
09-03-1959; 1450 kHz AM; *Hrs Open:* 24
1711 Ellis Dr., Valdosta, GA 31601 US
(229) 244-8642
rock1069.com
jmathews@blackcrow.fm
License: Valdosta, GA held by RTG Radio LLC
Group Owner: Black Crow Media Group LLC; (acq 11-9-2001; grpsl).
Nat'l Network: CBS
Arbitron Metro Market: Valdosta, GA; *Format:* Sports, Talk
Special Programming: Gospel 2 hrs wkly; *Hrs. of News Programming:* News progmg 10 hrs wkly; *Target Audience:* 35 plus.

*WVVS-FM
07-26-1971; 90.9 MHz FM; 5.3 kw horiz; 69 ft.; N30 50 50 W83 17 26
Vsu Box 142, Valdosta, GA 31698 US
(229) 259-2015
www.valdosta.edu/wvvs/
License: Valdosta, Lowndes County, GA held by Valdosta State University.
Arbitron Metro Market: Valdosta, GA; *Format:* Alternative; *Target Audience:* 18-25; students of VSU, population at large
Michael Taylor, General Manager
Daniel Oakes, Station Manager
Brian Auten, Promotions Manager

*WWET
12-01-1989; 91.7 MHz FM; *Hrs Open:* 24; 0 kw horiz, 0.43 kw vert; 85 ft.; N30 49 35 W83 16 40 *Rebroadcasts:* Rebroadcasts WJSP-FM Warm Springs 100%
260 - 14th Street, N.W., Atlanta, GA 30318 US
(404) 685-2690; *Fax:* (404) 685-2684
www.gpb.org
ask@gpb.org
License: Valdosta, Lowndes County, GA held by Georgia Public Telecommunications Commission.
Nat'l Network: NPR; PRI; *Wire Services:* AP
Arbitron Metro Market: Valdosta, GA; *Format:* News *Special Programming:* Jazz 16 hrs; *Hrs. of News Programming:* news progmg 40 hrs wkly; *No. News Employees:* 10; *Target Audience:* Adults: 35 plus.
Milton Clipper, Chief Executive Officer
Tom Barclay, Operations Dir
Rob Maynard, Programming Director
Nancy Zintak, Vice President of Marketing & Communications
Susanna Capelouto, News Director
Bonnie Bean, CFO

WWRQ-FM
02-01-1992; 107.9 MHz FM; 50 kw; 269 ft.; N31 3 21 W83 13 54
1711 Ellis Dr., Valdosta, GA 31601 US
(229) 244-8642
thebeat1079.com
jmathews@blackcrow.fm
License: Valdosta, Lowndes County, GA held by RTG Radio LLC.
Group Owner: Black Crow Media Group LLC; (acq 11-9-2001; grpsl).
Arbitron Metro Market: Valdosta, GA; *Format:* Classic Rock, Rock/AOR; *Target Audience:* 25-49; upscale suburban couples

WGOV-FM
06-01-1985; 96.7 MHz FM; *Hrs Open:* 24; 50 kw; Ant 328 ft; N30 48 13 W83 21 20
Mailing Address: Box 1207, Valdosta, GA 31601
Second Address: 2973 Hwy. 84 W., Valdosta, GA 31601
(229) 242-4513; *Fax:* (229) 247-7676
License: Valdosta, Lowndes County, GA held by W.G.O.V. Inc.
Group Owner: Dee Rivers Radio Group; (acq 4-19-2006; $2 million).
Arbitron Metro Market: Valdosta, GA; *Target Audience:* 18-49.
Joseph Jones, Operations Dir
Lamar Freeman, General Manager
Loretta Grecco, General Sales Mgr

*WVDA
01-01-2006; 88.5 MHz FM; 18.5 kw vert; 217 ft.; N30 47 50 W83 1 1 *Rebroadcasts:* Rebroadcasts KLRD(FM) Yucaipa, CA 100%
P.O. Box 3206, Tupelo, MS 38803 US
(662) 844-8888; *Fax:* (662) 842-6791
www.afr.net
faq@afa.net
License: Valdosta, Lowndes County, GA held by American Family Association.
Group Owner: American Family Radio
Arbitron Metro Market: Valdosta, GA; *Format:* Christian
Tim Wildmon, President
Donald Wildmon, Founder
Buddy Smith, Sr VP
Ed Vitagliano, Exec VP
Randy Sharp, Director Of Special Projects
Meeke Addison, Director Of Communications
Abraham Hamilton III, General Counsel

WJEM
08-01-1955; 1150 kHz AM; 5 kw-D, DA2; 0.101 kw-N, DA2; N30 50 49 W83 14 14
PO Box 5883, Valdosta, GA 31635 US
(229) 241-9797
www.thejock1150.com
License: Valdosta, GA held by WJEM Inc.
Arbitron Metro Market: Valdosta, GA; *Format:* Sports, Talk
John Staub, President
Joanna Staub, Operations Dir
Louis Scally, Programming Director
Tom Bradley, News Director
Jackie Hall, Traffic Manager

Vidalia

*WGPH
01-01-1988; 91.5 MHz FM; *Hrs Open:* 24; 31 kw; 604 ft.; N32 13 58 W82 28 51
P.O. Box 510, Appling, GA 30802 US
(800) 926-4669
www.gnnradio.org
brian@gnnradio.org
License: Vidalia, Toombs County, GA held by Augusta Radio Fellowship Institute Inc.
Group Owner: Good News Network
Format: Christian; *Hrs. of News Programming:* News progmg 12 hrs wkly; *Target Audience:* General.

WTCQ
03-05-1969; 97.7 MHz FM; 4.3 kw; 387 ft.; N32 13 12 W82 26 7
Mailing Address: Box 900, Hwy 280 W., Vidalia, GA 30474 US
Second Address: GA 30474
(912) 538-9898; *Fax:* (912) 537-4477
www.southeastgeorgiatoday.com
zfowler@vidaliacommunications.com
License: Vidalia, Toombs County, GA held by Vidalia Communications Corp.
Group Owner: Vidalia Communications Corp.
Nat'l Reps: Rgnl Reps
Arbitron Metro Market: Vidalia, GA; *Format:* Adult Contemp; *Target Audience:* 18-34.
Zack Fowler, Station Manager
John Koon, General Sales Mgr
Bob Roberts, Program Manager
Joyce Foskey, Account Executive and Office Manager

WVOP
12-02-1946; 970 kHz AM; *Hrs Open:* 24
Box 900, Hwy 280 W., Vidalia, GA 30474 US
(912) 537-9202; *Fax:* (912) 537-4477
www.southeastgeorgiatoday.com
License: Vidalia, GA held by Vidalia Communications Corp.
Group Owner: Vidalia Communications Corp.
Regional Network: Ga. News Net; *Nat'l Reps:* Rgnl Reps
Arbitron Metro Market: Vidalia, GA; *Format:* News/Talk; *Hrs. of News Programming:* news progmg 18 hrs wkly; *No. News Employees:* 1; *Target Audience:* 25-54.
Zack Fowler, Program Manager/Station Manager
John Koon, General Sales Mgr

Vienna

WKTF
11-17-1979; 1550 kHz AM; *Hrs Open:* 24
404 N. 6th Street, Vienna, GA 31092 US
(229) 268-1550
License: Vienna, GA held by LEN Radio Broadcasting of Vienna, Georgia LLC.
Arbitron Metro Market: Vienna, GA; *Format:* Christian, Contemporary Hits/Top 40
Thomas McCoy, General Manager

*WHHR
92.1 MHz FM; 5.1 kw; 348 ft.; N32 9 16 W83 47 55 US
(208) 733-3551; *Fax:* (208) 734-0674
www.edgewaterbroadcasting.com
License: Vienna, Dooly County, GA held by Radio Assist Ministry Inc.
Arbitron Metro Market: Vienna, GA
Clark Parrish, President
Jim Long, General Manager
Robert L. Jackson, Programming Director
Steve Atkin, Executive Director
Clark Parrish, Technical Director
Ben Mccarron, Chief Operating Engineer
Diana Atkin, Vice President
Earl Williamson, Secretary / Treasurer

Wadley

*WZAE
93.3 MHz FM; 4 kw; 144 ft.; N32 50 55 W82 24 10 US
(863) 644-3464; *Fax:* (863) 646-5326
License: Wadley, Jefferson County, GA held by Radio Training Network Inc.

Arbitron Metro Market: Wadley, GA
James Campbell, President

Warm Springs

*WJSP-FM

02-03-1985; 88.1 MHz FM; *Hrs Open:* 24; 42 kw; 1368 ft.; N32 51 8 W84 42 4
260 - 14th Street, N.W., Atlanta, GA 30318 US
(404) 685-2690; *Fax:* (404) 685-2684
www.gpb.org
ask@gpb.org
License: Warm Springs, Meriwether County, GA held by Georgia Public Telecommunications Commission.
Nat'l Network: NPR; PRI; *Wire Services:* AP
Arbitron Metro Market: Columbus, GA; *Format:* News, Talk
Special Programming: Jazz 18 hrs wkly; *Hrs. of News Programming:* news progmg 40 hrs wkly; *No. News Employees:* 10; *Target Audience:* 35-54; NPR-demo
Milton Clipper, Chief Executive Officer
Teya Ryan, President
Tom Barclay, Operations Dir
Rob Maynard, Programming Director
Nancy Zintak, Vice President of Marketing & Communications
Bonnie Bean, CFO

Warner Robins

WRWR

10-13-1954; 1350 kHz AM; *Hrs Open:* 24; 15 kw-D, 500 w-N, DA-N; N32 37 00 W83 39 00
1350 Radio Loop, Warner Robins, GA 31099
(478) 923-3416; *Fax:* (478) 923-3236
www.wnngthepatriot.com
License: Warner Robins, Houston County, GA held by Georgia Eagle Media Inc.
Group Owner: Georgia Eagle Media Inc.; (acq 1-3-2007; $650,000)
Nat'l Network: Fox News Radio; Westwood One; Talk Radio Network; Salem Radio Network; *Regional Network:* Ga. News Net.
Population Served: 200,000; *Arbitron Metro Market:* Macon, GA; *Hrs. of News Programming:* 12; *No. News Employees:* 2; *Target Audience:* 35-74; middle to upper class, working class, miltary, retired, business owners *Adv. Rates:* 18; 12; 18; 12
Cecil Staton, President
Jeff Scott, Programming Director

*WZCH

09-01-1994; 102.5 MHz FM; *Hrs Open:* 24; 4 kw; 328 ft.; N32 34 20 W83 40 13
750 West Sandtown Road, S.W., Marietta, GA 30064 US
(478) 781-1063; *Fax:* (478) 781-6711
www.peach965.com
ccw@clearchannel.com
License: Warner Robins, Houston County, GA held by Aloha Station Trust LLC, as Trustee
Arbitron Metro Market: Macon, GA; *Format:* Contemporary Hits/Top 40, Adult Contemp; *Target Audience:* 25-64.
John Lund, Operations Dir
Bill Clark, General Manager

WRBV

08-01-1969; 101.7 MHz FM; *Hrs Open:* 24; 4.9 kw; 354 ft.; N32 38 19 W83 38 33
7080 Industrial Hwy., Macon, GA 31216 US
(478) 781-1063; *Fax:* (478) 781-6711
www.v1017.com
License: Warner Robins, Houston County, GA held by AMFM Radio Licenses LLC.
Group Owner: iHeartMedia; (acq 2-1-2001; grpsl).
Nat'l Network: ABC
Arbitron Metro Market: Macon, GA; *Format:* Blues, Urban Contemporary; *Hrs. of News Programming:* News progmg one hr wkly; *Target Audience:* 21-54.
Thomas Bacote, Market President
Brent Henslee, Operations Manager
Terrence Bibb, Programming Director
James Gay, Chief Engineer
Melissa Stinebaugh, Business Manager

Warrenton

WCHZ-FM

01-01-1998; 93.1 MHz FM; 4.1 kw; Ant 400 ft; N33 29 59 W82 37 09 *Rebroadcasts:* Simulcast with WGAC(AM) Augusta
4051 Jimmie Dyess Pkwy., Augusta, GA 30909
(706) 396-7000
www.hotaugusta.com
License: Warrenton, Warren County, GA held by Beasley Media Group LLC
Group Owner: Beasley Broadcast Group Inc.; (acq 5-3-2000; $800,000 with WGUS(AM) Augusta).
Arbitron Metro Market: Augusta, GA; *Format:* Urban Contemporary; *No. News Employees:* 5
Chris O'Kelley, Operations Manager
Kent Murphy, General Sales Mgr
Jay Jones, Programming Director
Mark Haddon, Vice President/Market Manager
Georgia Beasley, Digital Sales Manager

Washington

WLOV

09-01-1955; 1370 kHz AM
Mailing Address: 330 Kilbourn Ave., Suite 250, Milwaukee, WI 53202 US
Second Address: 312 Old First National Bank Bldg., Elberton, GA 30635
(706) 678-0100; *Fax:* (706) 678-3394
www.wlovradio.com
License: Washington, GA held by Southern Stone Broadcasting Inc.
Group Owner: Southern Broadcasting Companies Inc.
Regional Network: Ga. News Net.
Format: Classic Rock
Leisa McCurley, News Director

Watkinsville

WPUP

06-01-1970; 100.1 MHz FM; *Hrs Open:* 24; 4.3 kw; 289 ft.; N33 56 28 W83 23 55
1010 Tower Place, Watkinsville, GA 30677 US
(706) 549-6222; *Fax:* (706) 546-0441
www.powerathens.com
License: Watkinsville, Oconee County, GA held by Cox Radio Inc.
Group Owner: Cox Radio Inc.; (acq 8-1-2008; grpsl)
Arbitron Metro Market: Watkinsville, GA; *Format:* Contemporary Hits/Top 40
Pete de Graaff, Program Director
Russell Lawson, General Sales Manager
Josh Hill, Promotions Director
Heather Taylor, Digital Brand Manager

Waverly Hall

WIOL-FM

07-04-1994; 95.7 MHz FM; *Hrs Open:* 24; 6 kw; Ant 876 ft; N32 50 48 W84 41 27
Mailing Address: Box 1998, Columbus, GA 31902
Second Address: 2203 Wynnton Rd., Columbus, GA 31906
(706) 576-3565; *Fax:* (706) 576-3683
info@dbicolumbus.com
License: Waverly Hall, Meriwether County, GA held by Davis Broadcasting of Columbus Inc.
Group Owner: Davis Broadcasting Inc.; (acq 11-4-97; $450,000).
Nat'l Network: CBS
Population Served: 250,000; *Arbitron Metro Market:* Columbus, GA; *Hrs. of News Programming:* news progmg 6 hrs wkly; *No. News Employees:* 2; *Target Audience:* 18-49; females 18-35 specifically
Gregory Davis, CEO

Waycross

*WASW

06-01-1998; 91.9 MHz FM; 18 kw; 289 ft.; N31 16 13 W82 39 19
P.O. Box 3206, Tupelo, MS 38803 US
(662) 844-8888; *Fax:* (662) 842-6791
www.afr.net
faq@afa.net
License: Waycross, Ware County, GA held by American Family Association.
Group Owner: American Family Radio
Arbitron Metro Market: Waycross, GA; *Format:* Christian, Religious
Tim Wildmon, President
Donald Wildmon, Founder
Buddy Smith, Sr VP
Ed Vitagliano, Exec VP
Randy Sharp, Director Of Special Projects
Meeke Addison, Director Of Communications
Abraham Hamilton III, General Counsel

WYNR

10-10-1971; 102.5 MHz FM; *Hrs Open:* 24; 97 kw; 994 ft.; N31 9 22 W81 58 19
3833 US Highway 82, Brunswick, GA 31523 US
(912) 267-1025; *Fax:* (912) 264-5462
www.1025wynr.com
License: Waycross, Ware County, GA held by AMFM Radio Licenses LLC.
Group Owner: iHeartMedia; (acq 2014)
Nat'l Reps: McGavren Guild
Arbitron Metro Market: Brunswick, GA; *Format:* Country; *Hrs. of News Programming:* news progmg one hr wkly; *No. News Employees:* 1; *Target Audience:* 25-54.
Richard J. Bressler, President
Michelle Harrison, Business Manager

WQGA

06-03-1972; 103.3 MHz FM; 100 kw; 1,100 ft; N31 15 42 W82 19 26
3833 US Highway 82, Brunswick, GA 31523 US
(912) 267-1025; *Fax:* (912) 264-5462
www.my103q.com
License: Waycross, Ware County, GA held by AMFM Radio Licenses LLC.
Group Owner: iHeartMedia; (acq 2014)
Nat'l Reps: McGavren Guild
Population Served: 250,000; *Arbitron Metro Market:* Brunswick, GA; *Format:* Adult Contemp *Special Programming:* Jazz 5 hrs wkly; *Target Audience:* 25-54.; *Adv. Rates:* 24; 20; 22; 12
Richard J. Bressler, President
Michelle Harrison, Business Manager

WWUF

01-25-1986; 97.7 MHz FM; *Hrs Open:* 24; 6 kw; 325 ft.; N31 11 5 W82 15 24
Mailing Address: 1350 Paces Forest Dr. NW, Atlanta, GA 30327 US
Second Address: 2132 Hwy. 84, Blackshear, GA 31516
(912) 449-3391; *Fax:* (912) 449-6284
www.waycrossradio.com/977/
wkub@almatel.net
License: Waycross, Ware County, GA held by Mattox Broadcasting Inc.
Nat'l Network: ABC; *Regional Network:* Ga. News Net; *Nat'l Reps:* Dora-Clayton
Arbitron Metro Market: Waycross, GA; *Format:* Contemporary Hits/Top 40, Adult Contemp; *Target Audience:* 25-54; general
Troy Mattox, President
Ray Williamson, Operations Dir
Jim Miller, General Sales Mgr

*WXVS

12-01-1985; 90.1 MHz FM; *Hrs Open:* 24; 79 kw horiz, 77.6 kw vert; 919 ft.; N31 13 17 W82 34 24 *Rebroadcasts:* WJSP, Warm Springs/Columbus, GA, 100%
260 - 14th Street, N.W., Atlanta, GA 30318 US
(404) 685-2690; *Fax:* (404) 685-2684
www.gpb.org
ask@gpb.org
License: Waycross, Ware County, GA held by Georgia Public Telecommunications Commission.
Nat'l Network: NPR; PRI; *Wire Services:* AP
Arbitron Metro Market: Waycross, GA; *Format:* Classical, News
Special Programming: Jazz 16 hrs; *Hrs. of News Programming:* news progmg 40 hrs wkly; *No. News Employees:* 10
Nancy Hall, CEO
Teya Ryan, President
Tom Barclay, Operations Dir
Bob Houghton, General Manager
Rob Maynard, Programming Director
Nancy Zintak, Promotions Manager
Susanna Capelouto, News Director
Bonnie Bean, CFO

WWGA(AM)

01-01-2004; 1230 kHz AM; *Hrs Open:* 24; 1 kw-U; N31 12 45 W82 22 20
1766 Memorial Dr., Suite 1, Waycross, GA 31501
(912) 285-5002; *Fax:* (912) 264-1991
www.gradickcommunications.com
License: Waycross, Ware County, GA held by MarMac Communications L.L.C.
Group Owner: MarMac Communications LLC
Format: News, News/Talk, 86
Gary Marmitt, General Manager
Dick Eoekeloo, Chief Engineer

Waynesboro

*WYFA

08-01-1991; 107.1 MHz FM; *Hrs Open:* 24; 25 kw; 295 ft.; N33 10 42 W81 59 24
Mailing Address: P.O. Box 7300, Charlotte, NC 28241 US
Second Address: 11530 Carmel Commons Blvd., Charlotte, NC 28226
(800) 888-7077
www.bbnradio.org
bbn@bbnmedia.org

License: Waynesboro, Burke County, GA held by Bible Broadcasting Network Inc.
Group Owner: Bible Broadcasting Network; acq 8-26-92; $225,000;
Arbitron Metro Market: Waynesboro, GA; *Format:* Religious
Jason Padgett, Operations Manager

West Point

WCJM-FM
07-18-1966; 100.9 MHz FM; 5.8 kw; 328 ft.; N32 51 7 W85 8 14
705 4th Avenue, West Point, GA 31833 US
(706) 645-2991; *Fax:* (706) 645-3364
www.wcjmthebull.com
License: West Point, Troup County, GA held by AMFM Radio Licenses LLC.
Group Owner: iHeartMedia; (acq 7-2-03; grpsl).
Regional Network: Ga. News Net.
Arbitron Metro Market: West Point, GA; *Format:* Country
Van Riggs, Senior Vice President of Programming

WRLA
05-01-1944; 1490 kHz AM; *Hrs Open:* 24; 1 kw-U, ND1; N32 52 26 W85 11 32
602 N. Cherry Dr., Lanett, AL 36863 US
(334) 644-1490
License: West Point, Troup County, GA held by Tiger Communications Inc.
Group Owner: Tiger Communications Inc.; (acq 10-19-2006; $279,000 with WTRP(AM) La Grange)
Regional Network: Ga. News Net.
Arbitron Metro Market: West Point, GA; *Format:* Oldies; *Hrs. of News Programming:* news progmg 9 hrs wkly; *No. News Employees:* 1; *Target Audience:* 18-55.
Brooke Myers, General Manager
Stacey Linn, Director of Sales

WPLV
08-01-1958; 1310 kHz AM; *Hrs Open:* 24
7050 Greenbower Lane, College Park, GA 30349 US
(706) 645-1310; *Fax:* (706) 645-3364
License: West Point, GA held by Qantum of Auburn License Co. LLC.
Group Owner: Qantum Communications Corp.; (acq 7-2-03; grpsl).
Format: Talk
Steve Wheeler, General Manager
Terry Harper, Chief Engineer

WPCH
1310 kHz AM; 1 kw-D, ND2; 0.025 kw-N, ND2; N32 53 48 W85 9 24
705 4th Avenue, West Point, GA 31833 US
(706) 645-2991; *Fax:* (706) 645-3364
License: West Point, Troup County, GA held by AMFM Radio Licenses LLC.
Group Owner: iHeartMedia
Arbitron Metro Market: West Point, GA; *Format:* Urban Contemporary
Van Riggs, Senior Vice President of Programming

Willacoochee

WKAA
04-07-1978; 99.5 MHz FM; *Hrs Open:* 24; 73 kw; 754 ft.; N31 10 18 W83 21 57
1711 Ellis Dr., Valdosta, GA 31601 US
(229) 244-8642
mykixcountry.com
jmathews@blackcrow.fm
License: Willacoochee, Atkinson County, GA held by RTG Radio LLC.
Group Owner: Black Crow Media Group LLC; (acq 11-9-2001; grpsl).
Arbitron Metro Market: Valdosta, GA; *Format:* Country; *Hrs. of News Programming:* news progmg 10 hrs wkly; *No. News Employees:* 1; *Target Audience:* 25-54.

Winder

WIMO
11-04-1952; 1300 kHz AM
P.O. Box 1540, Winder, GA 30680 US
(770) 867-1300; *Fax:* (770) 868-1962
License: Winder, GA held by Mark Myers
Nat'l Network: Salem Radio Network; Radio America; Fox News Radio; *Regional Network:* Ga. News Net.
Arbitron Metro Market: Atlanta, GA; *Format:* Gospel, Talk; *Target Audience:* General.
Jon Graham, Operations Dir
John Boyd, General Manager
Kurt Andrews, Programming Director

*WYFW
12-01-1987; 89.5 MHz FM; *Hrs Open:* 24; 6 kw; 200 ft.; N33 59 29 W83 45 46
P.O. Box 7300, Charlotte, NC 28241 US
(800) 888-7077
www.bbnradio.org
bbn@bbnmedia.org
License: Winder, Barrow County, GA held by Bible Broadcasting Network Inc.
Group Owner: Bible Broadcasting Network; acq 6-24-93; $104,000;
Arbitron Metro Market: Winder, GA; *Format:* Christian, Religious; *Hrs. of News Programming:* News progmg 7 hrs wkly; *Target Audience:* 35-44.
Lowell Davey, President
Jason Padgett, Operations Manager

Woodbine

WCGA
06-15-1987; 1100 kHz AM
Route 9, Box 280e, St. Simons Island, GA 31522 US
(912) 634-1100
License: Woodbine, GA held by Cox Broadcast Group Inc.
Arbitron Metro Market: St. Simons Island,GA; *Format:* News, News/Talk, 86; *Hrs. of News Programming:* news progmg 2 hrs wkly; *No. News Employees:* 2; *Target Audience:* Adults; 35-64; *Adv. Rates:* 25; 22; 23; 15.
Wesley Cox, General Manager

Woodbury

WFDR-FM
01-01-2007; 94.5 MHz FM; 2.75 kw; 492 ft.; N32 50 40 W84 37 25
US
(770) 487-4500; *Fax:* (706) 846-3494
License: Woodbury, Meriwether County, GA held by Ploener Radio Group LLC.
Arbitron Metro Market: Manchester, GA; *Format:* Christian
Rick Davison, General Manager
Roxanne Davison, Office Manager

Wrens

WTHB-FM
06-10-1979; 96.9 MHz FM; 6.2 kw; 397 ft.; N33 15 32.2 W82 19 10.1
6025 Broadcast Dr., North Augusta, SC 29841 US
(803) 279-2330; *Fax:* (803) 279-8149
csrapraise.com
vperry@perrybroadcasting.net
License: Wrens, Jefferson County, GA held by Perry Broadcasting of Augusta Inc.
Group Owner: Perry Publishing & Broadcasting Co.; (acq 12-12-2007; grpsl)
Arbitron Metro Market: Augusta, GA; *Format:* Gospel; *Target Audience:* Teen-49.
Velvet Perry, VP Director of Sales

Wrightsville

WDBN
05-27-1986; 107.9 MHz FM; *Hrs Open:* 24; 25 kw; 328 ft.; N32 37 5 W82 46 5
P.O. Box 2639, Gulfport, MS 39505 US
(478) 272-4422; *Fax:* (478) 275-4657
kris.bjorkman@statebroadcasting.com
License: Wrightsville, Johnson County, GA held by State Broadcasting Corp.
Regional Reps: Regional Reps
Arbitron Metro Market: Macon, GA; *Target Audience:* 12 plus.
J. Morgan Dowdy, President
Kris Bjorkman, General Manager

York

WSJA
91.3 MHz FM; *Hrs Open:* 24; N32 27 54 W88 16 54
P.O. Box 510, Appling, GA 30802 USA
(800) 926-4669
www.gnnradio.org
License: York, AL held by Augusta Radio Fellowship Institure Inc.
Group Owner: Good News Network
Arbitron Metro Market: York, AL; *No. News Employees:* 20

Young Harris

WJRB
01-01-2007; 95.1 MHz FM; 0.2 kw; 1585 ft.; N34 56 26 W83 55 8
US
(706) 379-9770; *Fax:* (706) 379-4104
License: Young Harris, Towns County, GA held by WJRB Radio LLC
Group Owner: Batten Communications Inc.
Arbitron Metro Market: Young Harris, GA
A.D. Frazier, President
Rebecca St. John, General Manager

Zebulon

WEKS
02-01-1994; 92.5 MHz FM; *Hrs Open:* 24; 12 kw; 476 ft.; N33 8 20 W84 31 31
4 Plum Lane, Newnan, GA 30263 US
(770) 412-8700; *Fax:* (770) 412-8080
www.925fmthebear.com
License: Zebulon, Pike County, GA held by Spalding Broadcasting Inc.
Arbitron Metro Market: Griffin, GA; *Format:* Country; *No. News Employees:* 1; *Target Audience:* 25-54.
Stephen Tarkenton, CEO
Les Reed, General Manager

Guam

Agana

*KPRG
01-27-1994; 89.3 MHz FM; *Hrs Open:* 24; 9.2 kw; 531 ft.; N13 29 17 E144 49 53
303 University Drive, Uog Station, Mangilao, GU 96923 US
(671) 734-8930; *Fax:* (671) 734-2958
www.kprgfm.org
License: Agana, GU held by Guam Educational Radio Foundation.
Nat'l Network: NPR
Arbitron Metro Market: Guam; *Format:* Jazz, Talk
Denise Mendiola, General Manager
Olympia Terral, General Sales Mgr
Lydia Taleu, Programming Director

KSTO
09-01-1973; 95.5 MHz FM; *Hrs Open:* 24; 25 kw; 583 ft.; N13 29 16.8 E144 49 53
P.O. Box 20249, Guam Main Facility, GU 96921 US
(671) 477-7108(671) 477-5786; *Fax:* (671) 477-6411
ksto@ite.net
License: Agana, GU held by Inter-Island Communications Inc.
Group Owner: Inter-Island Communications Inc.; acq 11-77).
Arbitron Metro Market: Hagatna, GU; *Format:* Adult Contemp
Special Programming: Country 12 hrs, gospel 6 hrs wkly; *Hrs. of News Programming:* news progmg 14 hrs wkly; *No. News Employees:* 1 *Target Audience:* 25-54.
Frances Poppe, CFO
Edward Poppe Jr., President
Joe Tighe, Operations Dir
Rosalin Koss, Programming Director
Edward Poppe III, Executive Vice President

KTWG
08-01-1975; 801 kHz AM; *Hrs Open:* 24; 10 kw-U, ND1; N13 27 7 E144 42 32 *Rebroadcasts:* Simulcasts KCNM(AM) Saipan, Northern Mariana Islands
PO Box 8700, Cary, NC 27512 US
(671) 477-5894; *Fax:* (671) 477-6411
www.ktwg.com
am800guam@gmail.com
License: Agana, GU held by Edward H. Poppe Jr. and Frances W. Poppe.
Group Owner: Inter-Island Communications Inc.; (acq 2-20-2002).
Arbitron Metro Market: Hag†t¤a, GU; *Format:* Religious; *Hrs. of News Programming:* news progmg 5 hrs wkly; *No. News Employees:* 1; *Target Audience:* 25-49; Christian
K. Leilani Dahilig, Station Manager
Richard Dahilig

KUAM
03-14-1954; 630 kHz AM
600 Harmon Loop Road, #102, Dededo, GU 96912 US
(671) 637-5826; *Fax:* (671) 637-9865
www.kuam.com
License: Agana, GU held by Pacific Telestations LLC
Nat'l Network: CBS
Arbitron Metro Market: Hag†t¤a, GU; *Format:* Adult Contemp
Joey Calvo, General Manager

KISH
01-01-2003; 102.9 MHz FM; *Hrs Open:* 24; 25 kw; 583 ft.; N13 29 16.8 E144 49 53

P O Box 20249, Guam Main Facility, Agana, Guam, GU 96921 US
(671) 477-9448; *Fax:* (671) 477-6411
License: Agana, GU held by Inter-Island Communications Inc.
Group Owner: Inter-Island Communications Inc.
Arbitron Metro Market: Hag†t¤a, GU; *Format:* Ethnic; *Hrs. of News Programming:* news progmg 15 hrs wkly; *No. News Employees:* 1; *Target Audience:* General; indiginous residents of Marianas Islands
Frances Poppe, CFO
Edward Poppe Jr., President
Joe Tighe, Operations Dir
Rosalin Koss, Programming Director
Edward Poppe III, Executive Vice President

KVOG
1530 kHz AM
US
(808) 521-4711; *Fax:* (808) 538-3269
License: Agana, GU held by Guam Power II Inc.
Arbitron Metro Market: Phoenix, AZ
Wagdy Guirguis, President

Agat

***KSDA-FM**
11-22-1990; 91.9 MHz FM; *Hrs Open:* 24; 3.8 kw; 1001 ft.; N13 25 53 E144 42 36
12501 Old Columbia Pike, Silver Spring, MD 20904 US
(671) 472-5732; *Fax:* (671) 477-4678
mail@joy92.net
License: Agat, GU held by Good News Broadcasting Corp.
Arbitron Metro Market: Agana Heights, GU; *Format:* Christian, Religious; *Hrs. of News Programming:* News progmg 7 hrs wkly; *Target Audience:* 25-54.
Robert Gibbons, Chairman
Brook Powers, President
Matthew Dodd, General Manager

Barrigada

***KHMG**
03-26-1996; 88.1 MHz FM; *Hrs Open:* 24; 8 kw; 472 ft; N13 29 17 W144 49 53
Box 23189, 170C Machaute St., Barrigada, GU 96921
(671) 477-6341; *Fax:* (671) 477-7136
www.hbcguam.net
khmg@hbcguam.net
License: Barrigada, GU held by Harvest Christian Academy.
Population Served: 140,000 *Special Programming:* Children 2 hrs wkly; *Hrs. of News Programming:* News progmg 5 hrs wkly; *Target Audience:* General; Christian, church and school families
John Collier, Station Manager

Chalan Kanoa-Saipan

***KRNM**
02-28-1998; 88.1 MHz FM; *Hrs Open:* 24; 1.8 kw; 125 ft.; N15 9 5 E145 43 11
P.O. Box 1250, Saipan, MP 96950 US
(670) 234-5766; *Fax:* (670) 235-0915
www.krnm.org
License: Chalan Kanoa-Saipan, MP held by Northern Marianas College.
Nat'l Network: NPR; PRI
Special Programming: Chamorro 2 hrs, Korean one hrs, Chinese one hr wkl; *Hrs. of News Programming:* News progmg 65 hrs wkly
Carl Pogue, General Manager
Joe Servino, Engineering Dir

Dededo

KGUM-FM
02-28-1999; 105.1 MHz FM; 12 kw; 502 ft.; N13 29 17 E144 49 30
P.O. Box Gm, Agana, GU 96932 US
(671) 477-5700; *Fax:* (671) 477-3982
License: Dededo, GU held by Sorensen Pacific Broadcasting Inc.
Group Owner: Sorensen Pacific Broadcasting Inc.; acq 6-23-03; grpsl).

Rex Sorensen, CEO
Jon Anderson, President
Albert Juan, Station Manager

KTKB
06-01-2003; 101.9 MHz FM; *Hrs Open:* 24; 46 kw; 479 ft.; N13 29 16 W144 49 36
3654 W. Jarvis Ave., Skokie, IL 60076 US
(847) 672-0864
www.ktkb.com
License: Dededo, Atkinson County, GU held by KM Broadcasting of Guam, LLC.
Group Owner: KM Communications Inc.
Format: Contemporary Hits/Top 40, Adult Contemp; *Target Audience:* 25-49; women ages 25-49; *Adv. Rates:* 17; 14; 16; 13
Myoung Hwa Bae, President

Garapan-Saipan

KPXP
11-05-1992; 99.5 MHz FM; *Hrs Open:* 24; 6.5 kw; 1493 ft.; N15 11 6 E145 44 30
P.O. Box Gm, Agana, GU 96932 US
(610) 784-3333; *Fax:* (610) 784-2075
www.power99.com
rex@spbguam.com
License: Garapan-Saipan, MP held by Sorensen Pacific Broadcasting Inc.
Group Owner: Sorensen Pacific Broadcasting Inc.; (acq 6-23-03; grpsl).
Arbitron Metro Market: Northern Mariana Islands; *Format:* Contemporary Hits/Top 40; *Hrs. of News Programming:* news progmg 14 hrs wkly; *No. News Employees:* 1; *Target Audience:* 14-39; affluent adults
Rex Sorensen, CEO
Jon Anderson, President
Curtis Dancoe, Station Manager
Wes Franks, General Sales Mgr
Ken Johnson, Programming Director
Joe McCollum, Promotions Manager
Marvin Palmer, Chief Engineer

KRSI
07-01-1992; 97.9 MHz FM; *Hrs Open:* 24; 6.5 kw; 1493 ft.; N15 11 6 E145 44 30
Caller Bx 10,000-Ppp-413, Garapan (Saipan), MP 96950 US
(670) 235-7996; *Fax:* (670) 235-7998
rex@spbguam.com
License: Garapan-Saipan, MP held by Sorensen Pacific Broadcasting Inc.
Group Owner: Sorensen Pacific Broadcasting Inc.; acq 6-23-03; grpsl).
Format: Classic Rock, Variety/Diverse *Special Programming:* Blues 6 hrs, reggae 19 hrs, Hawaiian 2 hrs, Chamdru 4 hrs, jazz one hr wkly; *Hrs. of News Programming:* News progmg one hr wkly; *Target Audience:* 25-49. *Adv. Rates:* 18; 16; 18; 12
Rex Sorensen, CEO
Curtis Dancoe, General Manager
Raymond Gibson, Programming Director
Laurence Bejerana, Promotions Manager
Marvin Palmer, Chief Engineer

KWAW
01-01-1999; 100.3 MHz FM; *Hrs Open:* 24; 1.1 kw; 1512 ft.; N15 11 5 E145 44 26
Mailing Address: Boon Bldg., 1270 N. Marine Dr., Tamuning, GU 96911 US
Second Address: Box 504651, Saipan, MP 96950
(670) 234-5929; *Fax:* (670) 234-2262
License: Garapan-Saipan, MP held by Leon Padilla Ganacias
Arbitron Metro Market: Garapan-Saipan, MI; *Hrs. of News Programming:* News progmg 150 minutes wkly
Victoria Borja, General Manager
Leo Ganacias, Programming Director

KZMI
01-01-1997; 103.9 MHz FM; *Hrs Open:* 24; 3.2 kw; 827 ft.; N15 11 0 E145 44 6
P.O. Box 20249, Guam Main Facility, GU 96921 US
(670) 234-7239; *Fax:* (670) 234-0447
License: Garapan-Saipan, MP held by Inter-Island Communications Inc.
Group Owner: Inter-Island Communications Inc.
Arbitron Metro Market: Garapan, MP; *Format:* Adult Contemp; *Hrs. of News Programming:* news progmg 16 hrs wkly; *No. News Employees:* 1
Frances Poppe, CFO
Edward Poppe Jr., President
Harry Blalock, General Manager
Edward Poppe III, Executive Vice President

***KORU**
89.9 MHz FM; 1.8 kw; 1493 ft.; N15 11 6 E145 44 30
US
(800) 775-4673; *Fax:* (671) 477-4678
www.lifetalk.net
License: Garapan-Saipan, MP held by Good News Broadcasting Corp.
Arbitron Metro Market: Garapan, MP
Robert Gibbons, President
John Geli, Program Manager
Matt Dodd, General Manager
Marcelo Vallado, Chief Engineer
Paul Willis, IT Director
Deloris Trujillo, HR Director

Hagatna

KGUM
02-01-1975; 567 kHz AM; *Hrs Open:* 24; 10 kw-U, ND1; N13 23 21 E144 45 34
P.O. Box Gm, Agana, GU 96932 US
(671) 477-5700; *Fax:* (671) 477-3982
License: Hagatna, GU held by Sorensen Pacific Broadcasting Inc.
Group Owner: Sorensen Pacific Broadcasting Inc.; (acq 6-23-2003; grpsl)
Nat'l Network: CBS; Westwood One
Format: News, News/Talk, 86 *Special Programming:* Educ one hr, computer 3 hrs, police one hr, health; *Hrs. of News Programming:* news progmg 20 hrs wkly; *No. News Employees:* 5; *Target Audience:* 35 plus; adultswith high income & education; *Adv. Rates:* 79; 45; 69; 45
Ray Gibson, Operations Dir
Rex Sorensen, General Manager

KOKU
04-28-1984; 100.3 MHz FM; *Hrs Open:* 24; 50 kw horiz, 49.7 kw vert; 541 ft.; N13 29 17 E144 49 35
530 West O'Brien Drive, Agana, GU 96910 US
Fax: (671) 477-5658
www.hitradio100.com
marketing@hitradio.com
License: Hagatna, GU held by Moy Communications Inc.
Format: Contemporary Hits/Top 40; *Target Audience:* 18-34; females; *Adv. Rates:* 96; 72; 83; 64
Kurt Moylan, President
Vince R. Limuaco, General Sales Mgr
Rick Nauta, Programming Director

KUAM-FM
09-01-1966; 93.9 MHz FM; 2 kw; 950 ft; N13 25 53 E144 42 36
600 Harmon Loop Rd., Suite 102, Dededo, GU 96912
(671) 637-0094; *Fax:* (671) 637-9865
License: Hagatna, GU

Joey Calvo, General Manager
Eli Monge, General Sales Mgr
Chris Barnett, Programming Director

KZGZ
12-01-1986; 97.5 MHz FM; *Hrs Open:* 24; 40 kw; 538 ft.; N13 29 17 E144 49 30
P. O. Box Gm, Agana, GU 96910 US
(671) 477-5700; *Fax:* (671) 477-3982
www.power98.com/
License: Hagatna, GU held by Sorensen Pacific Broadcasting Inc.
Group Owner: Sorensen Pacific Broadcasting Inc.
Arbitron Metro Market: Agana, GU; *Format:* Urban Contemporary; *Hrs. of News Programming:* News progmg 15 hrs wkly; *Target Audience:* 18-34; young affluent adults; *Adv. Rates:* 79; 59; 69; 45
Kazie Perkins, Operations Dir
Gene Colliflower, News Director

Saipan

KCNM
10-01-1984; 1080 kHz AM; *Hrs Open:* 24
P.O. Box 20249, Guam Main Facility, GU 96921 US
(670) 234-7239; *Fax:* (670) 234-0447
License: Saipan, MP held by Inter-Island Communications Inc.
Group Owner: Inter-Island Communications Inc.; (acq 8-6-84).
Nat'l Network: AP Network News
Arbitron Metro Market: Saipan, CNMI; *Format:* Religious; *Hrs. of News Programming:* news progmg 168 hrs wkly; *No. News Employees:* 1; *Target Audience:* General.; *Adv. Rates:* 10; 10; 10; 10
Harry Blalock, General Manager

Tamuning

KNUT
01-01-1999; 101.1 MHz FM; 8 kw; 193 meters; N13 29 15 E144 49 42
1868 Halsey Dr., Piti, GU 96921
(670) 234-7239; *Fax:* (671) 477-6411
License: Tamuning, GU held by Inter-Island Communications Inc.
Group Owner: Inter-Island Communications Inc.
Population Served: 65,000 *Hrs. of News Programming:* news progmg 16 hrs wkly; *No. News Employees:* 1
Frances Poppe, CFO
Edward Poppe Jr., President

Edward Poppe, General Manager
Harry Blalock, Station Manager
Lewis Tenorio, Programming Director

Tumon

KIJI
01-01-2006; 104.3 MHz FM; 12.5 kw; 292 ft.; N13 30 7 E144 47 21
US
(671) 478-0104; *Fax:* (671) 647-7840
www.kijifm104.com
License: Tumon, GU held by Guam Broadcast Services Inc.
Arbitron Metro Market: Tumon, GU; *Format:* Oldies
Yasunori Kawauchi, President
Kevin Yamazaki, Operations Dir

Hawaii

Aiea

KKOL-FM
09-01-1992; 107.9 MHz FM; *Hrs Open:* 24; 100 kw horiz, 80 kw vert; 1965 ft.; N21 23 51 W158 6 1
970 North Kalaheo Ave., Suite C-107, Kailua, HI 96734 US
(808) 533-0065; *Fax:* (808) 524-2104
www.1079koolgold.com
edkanoi@hawaii-radio.net
License: Aiea, Honolulu County, HI held by Salem Media of Hawaii Inc.
Group Owner: Salem Communications Corp.; (acq 1-3-2005 in exchange for KRTR(AM) Honolulu and KKNE(AM) Waipahu).
Arbitron Metro Market: Honolulu, HI; *Format:* Oldies; *No. News Employees:* 1; *Target Audience:* 35-54; adults
Steve Miller, General Manager
Rudi Camello, General Sales Mgr
Jenny Clipse, News Director
Bill Davis, Chief Engineer
Ed Kanoi, Program Director

Bellaire

KGOW(AM)
1560 kHz AM; 10 kw-U, DA-2; N19 47 02 W155 05 25
4703 Orkney Dr., Missouri City, TX 77459
(281) 923-7100
radioguy@neosoft.com
License: Bellaire, TX held by GOW Communications LLC

Fred Morton, General Manager

Captain Cook

KMWB
01-01-2007; 93.1 MHz FM; 10 kw; 3235 ft.; N19 43 14.9 W155 55 16
US
(808) 935-5461; *Fax:* (808) 935-7761
www.b97hawaii.com
sales@kwxx.com
License: Captain Cook, Hawaii County, HI held by Captain Cook Broadcasting Inc.
Arbitron Metro Market: Captain Cook, HI; *Format:* Contemporary Hits/Top 40, Adult Contemp
Joel Sellers, President

Eleele

KQNG
01-01-1939; 570 kHz AM; 1 kw-U, ND1; N21 59 33 W159 24 24
P.O. Box 15261, Santa Rosa, CA 95402 US
(808) 245-9527; *Fax:* (808) 245-3563
www.kongradio.com
kong@kongradio.com
License: Eleele, HI held by Ohana Broadcast Co. LLC
Group Owner: Ohana Broadcast Co. LLC
Arbitron Metro Market: Kauai; *Format:* News, News/Talk, 86; *Target Audience:* 25-54.
John Detz, CEO
Ron Middac, Chief Engineer

Fairfield

KINX
01-01-2008; 102.7 MHz FM; kw
738 Kaheka Street, Honolulu, HI 96814 US
(406) 761-8816; *Fax:* (406) 454-3484
License: Fairfield, Teton County, MT held by College Creek Media LLC.
Group Owner: College Creek Media LLC
Arbitron Metro Market: Great Falls, MT

Neal Robinson, President
Darnell Washington, General Manager

Haiku

KUAU
01-01-1995; 1570 kHz AM; *Hrs Open:* 24
707 Puunene Avenue, Kahului Maui, HI 96732 US
888) 404-7729; *Fax:* (808) 871-9708
www.kingscathedral.com
info@kingscathedral.com
License: Haiku, HI held by First Assembly of God-Kahului, Maui Inc.
Arbitron Metro Market: Haiku, HI
Ron Moody, General Manager
Dr James Marocco

KRYL(FM)
106.5 MHz FM; 72 kw; Ant 2,283 ft; N20 39 36 W156 21 50
Hochman Hawaii Five, 8215 Birch St., New Orleans, LA 70118
(504) 458-5976
License: Haiku, Maui County, HI held by Hochman Hawaii Five Inc
Population Served: 8,118; *Arbitron Metro Market:* Haiku, HI
Joel Sellers, President

Haliimaile

KPMW
01-01-1994; 105.5 MHz FM; 9 kw; 541 ft.; N20 44 40 W156 18 39
230 Hana Highway, Kahului, HI 96732 US
(808) 871-6251; *Fax:* (808) 871-5670
License: Haliimaile, Maui County, HI held by Rey-Cel Broadcasting Inc.
Arbitron Metro Market: Maui, HI; *Format:* Contemporary Hits/Top 40
Cecille Piros, General Manager
Cecille Pirose, General Sales Mgr
Bryan Pirose, Programming Director
Ray Piros, News Director

Hanalei

***KKCR**
08-02-1997; 90.9 MHz FM; *Hrs Open:* 24; 0.9 kw; -308 ft.; N22 13 2 W159 28 53
P.O. Box 825, Hanalei, HI 96714 US
(808) 826-7774; *Fax:* (808) 826-7977
www.kkcr.org
kkcr@kkcr.org
License: Hanalei, Kauai County, HI held by Kekahu Foundation Inc.
Arbitron Metro Market: Honolulu, HI; *Format:* Ethnic; *Hrs. of News Programming:* News progmg 5 hrs wkly; *Target Audience:* General; Kauai County residents
Harvey Cohen, President
Gwen Squyres, General Manager
Dean Rogers, Station Manager
Jessica Dofflemyer, General Sales Mgr
Donna Giarman, Engineering Dir
Erik Coopersmith, Development Director

Hanamaulu

KSHK
08-10-1999; 103.1 MHz FM; 51 kw; 919 ft.; N21 56 11 W159 26 43
P.O. Box 15261, Santa Rosa, CA 95402 US
(808) 245-9527
www.kongradio.com
License: Hanamaulu, Kauai County, HI held by Ohana Broadcast Co. LLC
Group Owner: Ohana Broadcast Co. LLC
Arbitron Metro Market: Lihue, HI; *Format:* Contemporary Hits/Top 40
Jim McKeon, Operations Dir
Denise Roberts, Promotions Manager
Ron Middag, Chief Engineer

Hilo

KHBC
10-01-1986; 92.7 MHz FM; 7.5 kw; -256 ft.; N19 50 19 W155 6 43
2447 Makiki Heights Dr, Honolulu, HI 96822 US
(808) 959-5700; *Fax:* (808) 959-5800
License: Hilo, Hawaii County, HI held by Hilo Broadcasting L.L.C.
Arbitron Metro Market: Hilo, HI; *Format:* Ethnic
Buddy Gordon, General Manager
Robert Turner, Chief Engineer

***KANO**
01-01-2001; 91.1 MHz FM; *Hrs Open:* 24; 30 kw; N19 35 31.4 W155 7 36
738 Kaheka Street, Honolulu, HI 96814 US
(808) 955-8821; *Fax:* (808) 946-3963
www.hawaiipublicradio.org
License: Hilo, Hawaii County, HI held by Hawaii Public Radio.
Nat'l Network: NPR; PRI
Arbitron Metro Market: Honolulu, HI; *Format:* Talk; *Hrs. of News Programming:* news progmg 35 hrs wkly; *No. News Employees:* 3
Valerie Yee, Operations Dir
Michael Titterton, General Manager
Kayla Rosenfeld, News Director
Gene Schiller, Music Director
Charles Husson, Operations Director

***KCIF**
07-01-1998; 90.3 MHz FM; 5 kw vert; -132 ft.; N19 38 14 W155 3 19
Mailing Address: 180 Kinoole St., Suite 310, Hilo, HI 96720 US
Second Address: Hilo Christian Broadcasting, P.O. Box 1066, Hilo, HI 96721
(808) 935-7434; *Fax:* (808) 961-6022
www.kcifhawaii.org
License: Hilo, Hawaii County, HI held by Hilo Christian Broadcasting.
Arbitron Metro Market: Hilo, HI; *Format:* Christian, Religious
Pastor David Shotwell, Chairman

KHLO
04-01-1950; 850 kHz AM; *Hrs Open:* 24; 5 kw-U, ND1; N19 41 48 W155 3 5
913 Kanoelehua Ave., Hilo, HI 96720 US
(808) 961-0651
www.espnhawaii.com
License: Hilo, HI held by Pacific Radio Group Inc.
Group Owner: Pacific Radio Group Inc.; acq 9-17-03; grpsl).
TV Affiliate: ESPN; *Format:* Sports; *Hrs. of News Programming:* news progmg 7 hrs wkly; *No. News Employees:* 2; *Target Audience:* 25-54.
Marc Miranda, General Sales Mgr
Josh Pacheco, Programming Director

KAPA
12-01-1988; 100.3 MHz FM; *Hrs Open:* 24; 35 kw; -256 ft.; N19 50 19 W155 6 43
75-5852 Alii Dr., Suite B1 & B2, Kailua-Kona, HI 96740 US
(808) 329-6633; *Fax:* (808) 327-5272
www.kaparadio.com
studio@kaparadio.com
License: Hilo, Hawaii County, HI held by Pacific Radio Group Inc.
Group Owner: Pacific Radio Group Inc.; (acq 8-11-2005; grpsl).
Format: Ethnic; *Target Audience:* 18-49.

KHNU
09-10-1947; 620 kHz AM; *Hrs Open:* 24; 5 kw-U, ND1; 10 kw-U, DA1; ND1; 5 kw-U; N19 51 2 W155 5 7; N19 44 12 W156 1 56; N19 018 W155 4037
2447 Makiki Heights Dr., Honolulu, HI 96822 US
(808) 329-8090; *Fax:* (808) 443-0888
www.lava105.com
info@lava105.com
License: Hilo, HI held by Mahalo Broadcasting L.L.C.
Group Owner: Mahalo Broadcasting L.L.C.; (acq 8-31-2007; grpsl)
Nat'l Network: ABC
Format: News, Talk; *No. News Employees:* 9; *Target Audience:* 35 plus.; *Adv. Rates:* 5; 5; 5; 5
Chip Begay, Operations Dir

KKBG
08-05-1980; 97.9 MHz FM; *Hrs Open:* 24; 51 kw; -65 ft.; N19 50 19 W155 6 43
913 Kanoelahua Ave., Hilo, HI 96720 US
(808) 961-0651
www.kbigfm.com
keith@kbigfm.com
License: Hilo, Hawaii County, HI held by Pacific Radio Group Inc.
Group Owner: Pacific Radio Group Inc.; (acq 9-17-2003; grpsl).
Arbitron Metro Market: Honolulu, HI; *Format:* Adult Contemp; *Hrs. of News Programming:* news progmg 10 hrs wkly; *No. News Employees:* 1

KNWB
08-03-1985; 97.1 MHz FM; *Hrs Open:* 5 AM-10:30 PM; 38 kw; -823 ft.; N19 47 2 W155 5 25
1145 Kilauea Avenue, Hilo, HI 96720 US
(808) 935-5461; *Fax:* (808) 935-7761
www.B97Hawaii.com
sales@kwxx.com

License: Hilo, Hawaii County, HI held by New West Broadcasting Corp.
Group Owner: New West Broadcasting Corp.; acq 1995; $270,000).
Format: Contemporary Hits/Top 40, Adult Contemp; *Hrs. of News Programming:* news progmg 8 hrs wkly; *No. News Employees:* 1; *Target Audience:* 25-45.
Chris Leonard, President
Gavin Tanouye, Station Manager

KPUA
01-01-1936; 670 kHz AM; *Hrs Open:* 24
1145 Kilauea Avenue, Hilo, HI 96720 US
(808) 935-5461; *Fax:* (808) 935-7761
License: Hilo, HI held by New West Broadcasting Corp.
Group Owner: New West Broadcasting Corp.; acq 5-18-92; $370,000 with co-located FM;
Nat'l Network: CBS; Westwood One
Format: News, Sports, 86 *Special Programming:* Japanese 6 hrs wkly; *Hrs. of News Programming:* news progmg 22 hrs wkly; *No. News Employees:* 3; *Target Audience:* 25 plus; upscale adults with interest in news
Christopher Leonard, General Manager
Ken Hupp, Programming Director
Triska LaRochell, Regional Sales Manager
John Orozco, Regional Sales Manager

KPVS
01-01-1995; 95.9 MHz FM; *Hrs Open:* 24; 39 kw; -256 ft.; N19 50 19 W155 6 43 *Rebroadcasts:* Rebroadcasts KLUA(FM) Kailua-Kona 100%
913 Kanoelehua Ave., Hilo, HI 96720 US
(808) 329-6633 ext. 225
thebeathawaii.com
jaz@pmghawaii.com
License: Hilo, Hawaii County, HI held by Pacific Radio Group Inc.
Group Owner: Pacific Radio Group Inc.; (acq 8-11-2005; grpsl).
Arbitron Metro Market: Hilo, HI; *Format:* Reggae; *Target Audience:* 25-54; women

KWXX-FM
12-16-1984; 94.7 MHz FM; *Hrs Open:* 24; 51 kw; -758 ft.; N19 47 2 W155 5 25
1145 Kilauea Avenue, Hilo, HI 96720 US
(808) 935-5461; *Fax:* (808) 935-7761
www.kwxx.com
sales@kwxx.com
License: Hilo, Hawaii County, HI
Nat'l Network: Westwood One
Arbitron Metro Market: Hilo, HI; *Format:* Adult Contemp *Special Programming:* Contemp Hawaiian 20 hrs, reggae 20 hrs wkly; *Hrs. of News Programming:* news progmg 3 hrs wkly; *No. News Employees:* 1 *TargetAudience:* 25 plus; upscale adults
Gavin Tawouye, Programming Director
Keoni Johnson, Disc Jockey
G. Kruz, Disc Jockey

KIPA
01-01-2008; 1060 kHz AM; Ant 3,113 ft
P.O. Box 4727, Hilo, HI 96720 US
(217) 607-0017; *Fax:* (808) 959-5800
www.konafm.com
License: Hilo, HI held by Parrott Broadcasting L.P.
Arbitron Metro Market: Hilo, HI; *Format:* Classic Rock
Buddy Gordon, General Manager

KHNU(AM)
09-10-1947; 620 kHz AM; *Hrs Open:* 24; 5 kw-U; N19 51 03 W155 05 09
74-5605 Luhia St., B-7, Kailua-Kona, HI 96740
(808) 329-8090; *Fax:* (808) 443-0888
www.lava105.com
info@lava105.com
License: Hilo, Hawaii County, HI held by Mahalo Broadcasting L.L.C.
Group Owner: Mahalo Broadcasting L.L.C.; (acq 8-31-2007; grpsl)
Nat'l Network: ABC
Population Served: 135,000; *No. News Employees:* 9; *Target Audience:* 35 plus.; *Adv. Rates:* 5; 5; 5; 5
Chip Begay, Operations Dir

*K220EO
02-03-1997; 91.9 MHz FM; 0.25 kW; N19 43 0 W155 8 13
820 N LaSalle Blvd, Chicago, IL 60610 USA
www.moodyradio.org/stations/satellators/hilo
License: Hilo, HI held by The Moody Bible Institute of Chicago
Group Owner: Moody Radio
Nat'l Network: Moody
Arbitron Metro Market: Hilo, HI; *Format:* Christian

Holualoa

KHWI
09-20-1992; 92.1 MHz FM; *Hrs Open:* 24; 4.5 kw; 3114 ft.; N19 43 15 W155 55 16
US
(208) 837-4104
License: Holualoa, Hawaii County, HI held by Parrott Broadcasting L.P.
Arbitron Metro Market: Sun Valley, ID; *Format:* Adult Contemp
Scott Parker, General Manager

Honolulu

KHCM
08-31-1956; 880 kHz AM; *Hrs Open:* 24
3555 Harding Avenue, Honolulu, HI 96816 US
(626) 912-3388; *Fax:* (626) 912-5604
License: Honolulu, HI held by Salem Media of Hawaii Inc.
Group Owner: Salem Communications Corp.; (Acq 11-10-99; with co-located FM)
Arbitron Metro Market: Honolulu, HI; *Format:* Chinese
Bruce Munsterman, General Manager
Dolly Martin, Programming Director
Bonnie BeMent, Assistant General Manager

KAIM-FM
11-01-1953; 95.5 MHz FM; *Hrs Open:* 24; 100 kw; 1854 ft.; N21 23 45 W158 5 58
3555 Harding Avenue, Honolulu, HI 96816 US
(808) 533-0065; *Fax:* (808) 524-2104
www.thefishhawaii.com
jwaters@salemhawaii.com
License: Honolulu, Honolulu County, HI held by Salem Media of Hawaii Inc.
Group Owner: Salem Communications Corp.; (acq 11-10-99; with co-located AM)
Nat'l Network: Salem Radio Network
Arbitron Metro Market: Honolulu, HI; *Format:* Christian; *Target Audience:* 25-49; female
Steve Miller, General Manager
Jack Waters, Programming Director

KKEA
11-01-1966; 1420 kHz AM; 5 kw-U, ND1; N21 19 26 W157 52 47
12381 Wilshire Blvd., Suite 105, PO Box 25606, Los Angeles, CA 90025 US
(808) 275-1047; *Fax:* (808) 548-0608
www.espn1420am.com
License: Honolulu, HI held by Blow Up LLC
Nat'l Network: CNN Radio; ESPN Radio; *Nat'l Reps:* Katz Radio
Arbitron Metro Market: Honolulu, HI; *Format:* Sports, Talk; *Target Audience:* 25-54; Male; *Adv. Rates:* 372; 372; 372; 372.
Randall Ikeda, General Manager
Chris Hart, Programming Director

KCCN-FM
05-21-1990; 100.3 MHz FM; 100 kw horiz, 81 kw vert; 1965 ft.; N21 23 51 W158 6 1
12381 Wilshire Blvd., Suite 105, PO Box 25606, Los Angeles, CA 90025 US
(808) 275-1000; *Fax:* (808) 536-2528
www.kccnfm100.com
info@kccnfm100.com
License: Honolulu, Honolulu County, HI held by SM-KCCN LLC
Group Owner: SummitMedia LLC
Arbitron Metro Market: Honolulu, HI; *Format:* Ethnic
Wayne Maria, Operations Dir
Michol Klabo, General Manager
Stuart Chang, General Sales Mgr
Shannon Scott, Promotions Manager

KHRA
03-01-1992; 1460 kHz AM; 5 kw-U, ND1; N21 19 26 W157 52 32
970 North Kalaheo Avenue, No. C-107, Kailua, HI 96734 US
(808) 593-1460; *Fax:* (808) 591-1986
License: Honolulu, HI held by KMC Broadcasting L.L.C.
Arbitron Metro Market: Honolulu, HI; *Format:* Korean
Tony Young Ho Kim, President
Chung Sangkit, General Manager

KGU
05-11-1922; 760 kHz AM; *Hrs Open:* 24; 10 kw-U, ND1; N21 17 41 W157 51 49
222 N. Sepulveda Blvd, Suite 1324, El Segundo, CA 90245 US
(808) 533-0065; *Fax:* (808) 524-2104
www.kguradio.com
License: Honolulu, HI held by Salem Media of Hawaii Inc.
Group Owner: Salem Communications Corp.; (acq 2-16-00)
Nat'l Network: Salem Radio Network; *Nat'l Reps:* Salem
Arbitron Metro Market: Honolulu, HI; *Format:* Christian, Talk; *Hrs. of News Programming:* News progmg 5 hrs wkly; *Target Audience:* 35-54; general
Jack Waters, Operations Dir
Steve Miller, General Manager
David Serrone, Programming Director
Jack Waters, Program Director

KPRP
01-01-1946; 650 kHz AM; *Hrs Open:* 24; 10 kw-U, ND1; N21 26 43 W158 3 49
222 N Sepulveda Blvd, Suite 1324, El Segundo, CA 90245 US
(808) 533-0065; *Fax:* (808) 524-2104
www.khnr.com
License: Honolulu, HI held by SM-KRTR-AM LLC
Group Owner: SummitMedia LLC
Nat'l Network: CNN Radio; CBS Radio; *Nat'l Reps:* Salem; *Wire Services:* AP
Arbitron Metro Market: Honolulu, HI; *Format:* News, Talk; *Hrs. of News Programming:* News progmg 55 hrs wkly; *Target Audience:* 25-54.
Jack Walters, Operations Dir
T.J. Malievsky, General Manager
Wayne Marla, Programming Director

*KHPR
11-13-1981; 88.1 MHz FM; *Hrs Open:* 24; 39 kw; 1686 ft.; N21 20 12 W157 49 3
738 Kaheka Street, Honolulu, HI 96814 US
(808) 955-8821; *Fax:* (808) 946-3863
www.hawaiipublicradio.org
mail@hawaiipublicradio.org
License: Honolulu, Honolulu County, HI held by Hawaii Public Radio.
Nat'l Network: NPR; PRI
Arbitron Metro Market: Honolulu, HI; *Format:* News; *Hrs. of News Programming:* news progmg 35 hrs wkly; *No. News Employees:* 1; *Target Audience:* General.
Charles Husson, Operations Dir
Michael Titterton, General Manager
Kayla Rosenfeld, News Director
Gene schiller, Music Director
Judy Neale, Director of Promotion
Bill Dorman, News Director

KHVH
04-01-1951; 830 kHz AM; *Hrs Open:* 24; 10 kw-U, ND1; N21 19 26 W157 52 32
650 Iwilei Rd., Suite 400, Honolulu, HI 96817 US
(808) 550-9200; *Fax:* (808) 550-9288
www.khvhradio.com
License: Honolulu, HI held by Capstar TX LLC
Group Owner: iHeartMedia; (acq 8-30-2000; grpsl)
Nat'l Reps: Clear Channel; *Wire Services:* AP
Arbitron Metro Market: Honolulu, HI; *Format:* News, News/Talk, 86; *Hrs. of News Programming:* news progmg 21 hrs wkly; *No. News Employees:* 5; *Target Audience:* 25-54.
Rob Welsh, General Sales Mgr
John Matthews, Programming Director
Ricardo Rosas, Promotions Director
Gregg Mueller, Account Executive

KIKI
03-18-1957; 990 kHz AM; *Hrs Open:* 24; 5 kw-U, ND1; N21 19 26 W157 52 32
650 Iwilei Rd., Suite 400, Honolulu, HI 96817 US
(808) 550-9200; *Fax:* (808) 550-9288
www.kikiradio.com
License: Honolulu, HI held by Capstar TX LLC
Group Owner: iHeartMedia
Nat'l Network: ABC; *Nat'l Reps:* Clear Channel
Population Served: 900,000; *Arbitron Metro Market:* Honolulu, HI; *Format:* News, News/Talk, 86; *Hrs. of News Programming:* News progmg 20 hrs wkly; *Target Audience:* 25-54.
Rob Welsh, General Sales Mgr
John Matthews, Programming Director
Ricardo Rosas, Promotions Director
Gregg Mueller, Account Executive

KINE-FM
11-01-1988; 105.1 MHz FM; 100 kw horiz, 81 kw vert; 1965 ft.; N21 23 51 W158 6 1
12381 Wilshire Blvd., Suite 105, PO Box 25606, Los Angeles, CA 90025 US
(808) 275-1000; *Fax:* (808) 536-2528
www.hawaiian105.com
info@hawaiian105.com
License: Honolulu, Honolulu County, HI held by SM-KINE LLC
Group Owner: SummitMedia LLC
Arbitron Metro Market: Honolulu, HI; *Format:* Contemporary Hits/Top 40, Ethnic; *Target Audience:* 25-44.

Michael Kelly, Operations Dir
John Aeto, General Sales Mgr
David Daniels, Programming Director
Scott MacKenzie, Promotions Manager
Jane Pascual, News Director
Wade Faildo, Promotions Manager
Ann Boots, Regional Sales Manager

***KIPO**
01-01-1989; 89.3 MHz FM; *Hrs Open:* 24; 38.5 kw; 1686 ft.; N21 20 12 W157 49 3
738 Kaheka Street, Honolulu, HI 96814 US
(808) 955-8821; *Fax:* (808) 946-3863
www.hawaiipublicradio.org
License: Honolulu, Honolulu County, HI held by Hawaii Public Radio.
Nat'l Network: PRI; NPR
Arbitron Metro Market: Honolulu, HI; *Format:* Jazz, News; *Hrs. of News Programming:* news progmg 50 hrs wkly; *No. News Employees:* 3; *Target Audience:* General.
Michael Titterton, General Manager
Kayla Rosenfeld, News Director
Gene Schiller, Music Director
Charles Husson, Operations Director

KREA
04-24-1973; 1540 kHz AM; *Hrs Open:* 24; 5 kw-U, ND1; N21 19 27 W157 52 47
1921 Sacramento Street, San Francisco, CA 94109 US
(808) 955-1234; *Fax:* (808) 946-9637
License: Honolulu, HI held by JMK Communications Inc.
Arbitron Metro Market: Honolulu, HI; *Format:* Korean
Young Lee, General Manager

KDNN
07-04-1988; 98.5 MHz FM; *Hrs Open:* 24; 51 kw; 59 ft.; N21 18 49 W157 51 43
600 Congress Ave., Suite 1400, Austin, TX 78701 US
(808) 550-9200; *Fax:* (808) 550-9510
www.island985.com
info@island985.com
License: Honolulu, Honolulu County, HI held by Capstar TX LLC
Group Owner: iHeartMedia; (acq 8-30-00; grpsl).
Nat'l Reps: Clear Channel
Arbitron Metro Market: Honolulu, HI; *Format:* Ethnic; *Target Audience:* 25-54; upscale, white collar, college educated
Jovi Santiago, Sales Manager
Jamie Hyatt, Programming Director
Ricardo Rosas, Promotions Director

KLHT
01-01-1946; 1040 kHz AM; *Hrs Open:* 24; 10 kw-U; N21 20 10 W157 53 33
98-1016 Komo Mai Dr., Aiea, HI 96817
(808) 524-1040; *Fax:* (808) 487-1040
www.klight.org
klht@hawaii.rr.com
License: Honolulu, Honolulu County, HI held by Calvary Chapel of Honolulu Inc.
Arbitron Metro Market: Honolulu, HI; *Target Audience:* General.
Jake O'Neil, General Manager
Clif Burchfield, General Sales Mgr
Josh Villoria, Programming Director

KPOI-FM
08-03-2000; 105.9 MHz FM; *Hrs Open:* 24; 100 kw horiz, 92 kw vert; 1965 ft.; N21 23 51 W158 6 1
45-602 Haamaile St, Kaneohe, HI 96744 US
(808) 947-1500; *Fax:* (808) 947-1506
kumu@kumu.com
License: Honolulu, Honolulu County, HI held by Ohana Broadcast Co. LLC
Group Owner: Ohana Broadcast Co. LLC
Arbitron Metro Market: Honolulu, HI; *Format:* Classic Rock; *Hrs. of News Programming:* news progmg 23 hrs wkly; *No. News Employees:* 1; *Target Audience:* 24-54; families, including single-parent families *Adv.Rates:* 36; 36; 36; 15
John Detz, General Manager
Greg Everett, General Sales Mgr
Dale Parsons, Programming Director
Gary Forsberg, News Director

KNDI
07-11-1960; 1270 kHz AM; *Hrs Open:* 24; 5 kw-U, ND1; N21 19 26 W157 52 47
Dba. Kndi Radio, 1734 S. King Street, Honolulu, HI 96826 US
(808) 946-2844; *Fax:* (808) 947-3531
www.kndi.com
kndiradio@hawaii.rr.com
License: Honolulu, HI held by Leona Jona dba KNDI Radio.
Arbitron Metro Market: Honolulu, HI; *Format:* Ethnic, Filipino; *Target Audience:* Limited english proficiency.; *Adv. Rates:* 45; 40; 35; 30
Leona Jona, President
Harvey Weinstein, Operations Dir
Ellen Kaiuwailani, Secretary/Office Mgr

KORL
12-01-1959; 1180 kHz AM; *Hrs Open:* 24
210 North 1000 East, St. George, UT 84770 US
(808) 875-8868; *Fax:* (808) 875-8870
License: Honolulu, HI held by Hochman-McCann Hawaii Inc.
Arbitron Metro Market: Honolulu, HI; *Format:* Ethnic; *Target Audience:* 25 plus.
George Hochman, CEO

KHCM-FM
03-06-1962; 97.5 MHz FM; *Hrs Open:* 24; 80 kw; Ant 46 ft; N21 17 37 W157 50 32
1160 N. King St., 2nd Fl., Honolulu, HI 79902
(808) 533-0065; *Fax:* (808) 524-2104
www.hawaiiscountrymusic.com
mtshawaii@yahoo.com
License: Honolulu, Honolulu County, HI held by Salem Media of Hawaii Inc.
Group Owner: Salem Communications Corp.; (acq 8-13-2004; $3.7 million with K
Population Served: 622,900; *Arbitron Metro Market:* Honolulu, HI
Leilani Williams, General Manager
Ed Kanol, Programming Director

KHNR
05-14-1947; 690 kHz AM; *Hrs Open:* 24; 10 kw-U; N21 17 41 W157 51 49
1160 N. King St., 2nd Fl., Honolulu, HI 79902
(808) 533-0065; *Fax:* (808) 524-2104
www.khnr.com
info@khnr.com
License: Honolulu, Honolulu County, HI held by Salem Media of Hawaii Inc.
Group Owner: Salem Communications; (acq 10-1-2006; exchange for KORL(AM) Honolulu)
Fox News Radio; Salem Radio Network
Population Served: 1,000,000; *Arbitron Metro Market:* Honolulu, HI
Stuart Epperson, Chairman
Edward G Atsinger, CEO/COO
Dave Santrella, President
Linnae Young, Operations Dir
Leilani Williams, General Manager
Jack Waters, Station Manager
Dita Holifield, General Sales Mgr
Jack Waters,Programming Director
Dave Kateley, Promotions Manager
Ernie Nearman, Chief Engineer

KQMQ-FM
10-01-1967; 93.1 MHz FM; 100 kw; 1854 ft.; N21 23 45 W158 5 58
4150 Pinnacle, El Paso, TX 79902 US
(808) 947-1500; *Fax:* (808) 947-1506
www.931dapaina.com
lauriemizuno@ohanabroadcast.com
License: Honolulu, Honolulu County, HI held by Ohana Broadcast Co. LLC
Group Owner: Ohana Broadcast Co. LLC
Arbitron Metro Market: Honolulu, HI; *Format:* Reggae
John Detz, General Manager
Laurie Mizuno, General Sales Mgr
Sean Lynch, Programming Director
Ryan Sean, Music Director

KSSK
01-01-1929; 590 kHz AM; *Hrs Open:* 24; 7.5 kw-U, ND1; N21 19 26 W157 52 32
650 Iwilei Rd., Suite 400, Honolulu, HI 96817 US
(808) 550-9200; *Fax:* (808) 550-9288
www.ksskradio.com
info@ksskradio.com
License: Honolulu, HI held by Capstar TX LLC
Group Owner: iHeartMedia; (acq 3-12-99; grpsl)
Nat'l Reps: Clear Channel; *Wire Services:* AP
Arbitron Metro Market: Honolulu, HI; *Format:* Adult Contemp; *Hrs. of News Programming:* news progmg 15 hrs wkly; *No. News Employees:* 5; *Target Audience:* 25-54.
Chuck Cotton, Vice President and General Manager
Rob Welsh, General Sales Mgr
Jamie Hyatt, Programming Director
Tiffany Garrett, Promotions Director

***KTUH**
01-01-1969; 90.3 MHz FM; *Hrs Open:* 24; 3 kw; -82 ft.; N21 18 14 W157 49 22
2444 Dole Street, Bachman Hall 209, Honolulu, HI 96822 US
(808) 956-7431; *Fax:* (808) 956-5271
www.ktuh.org
gm@ktuh.org
License: Honolulu, Honolulu County, HI held by University of Hawaii.
Arbitron Metro Market: Honolulu, HI; *Format:* Variety/Diverse; *Target Audience:* 18-59; no target, all kinds of people listen
Monty Anderson, General Manager
Travis Tokuyama, Programming Director
Loriel Macalma, Promotions Manager
Katie McClellen, News Director
Dale Machado, Chief Engineer

KHKA(AM)
03-01-1963; 1500 kHz AM; *Hrs Open:* 24; 10 kw-U; N21 17 08 W157 48 08
1088 Bishop Street, Suite LL2, Honolulu, HI 96813
(808) 536-3624
License: Honolulu, Honolulu County, HI held by Blow Up LLC
Nat'l Network: NBC Sports
Population Served: 374,658; *Arbitron Metro Market:* Honolulu, HI; *Format:* Talk; *Target Audience:* 35-64.
Mike Kelly, President
Randy McKone, Operations Dir
Laurie Mizuno, Director of Sales
Butch Thurman, News Director
J.J. Ford, Operations Manager

KUMU-FM
09-01-1967; 94.7 MHz FM; 100 kw; 79 ft.; N21 17 9 W157 50 19
765 Amana Street, Suite 206, Honolulu, HI 96814 US
(808) 947-1500; *Fax:* (808) 947-1506
www.kumu.com
lauriemizuno@ohanabroadcast.com
License: Honolulu, Honolulu County, HI held by Ohana Broadcast Co. LLC
Group Owner: Ohana Broadcast Co. LLC
Arbitron Metro Market: Honolulu, HI; *Format:* Adult Contemp; *Target Audience:* 25-54.
Jeff Coelho, General Manager
Laurie Mizuno, Director of Sales
Ed Kanoi, Programming Director
Sumee Mikkelson, Promotions Manager
Lilly Yamachika, News Director
Ernie Nearman, Chief Engineer

KWAI
01-21-1972; 1080 kHz AM; *Hrs Open:* 24; 5 kw-U, ND1; N21 17 41 W157 51 49
100 North Beretania St, Suite 401, Honolulu, HI 96817 US
(808) 523-3868; *Fax:* (808) 531-6532
www.kwai1080am.com
License: Honolulu, HI held by Radio Hawaii Inc.
Nat'l Network: USA
Arbitron Metro Market: Honolulu, HI; *Format:* News, News/Talk, 86 *Special Programming:* Filipino 7 hrs, Hawaiian 3hrs wkly, Samoan 14 hrs wkly; *Hrs. of News Programming:* News progmg 72 hrs wkly *Target Audience:* 25-64; general
Sam Wagenvoord, Operations Dir
Barry Wagenvoord, General Manager
Renee Rosehill, Operations Director
Ritchie Koseki, Account Executive
Jose Maldonado, Account Executive
Francis Andaya, Moderator/ Board Operator

KZOO
10-18-1963; 1210 kHz AM; 1 kw-U, ND1; N21 17 41 W157 51 49
250 Ward Avenue, Honolulu, HI 96814 US
(808) 593-2880; *Fax:* (808) 596-0083
www.kzoohawaii.com
License: Honolulu, HI held by Polynesian Broadcasting Inc.
Arbitron Metro Market: Honolulu, HI; *Format:* Japanese
David Furuya, President

KPHI
01-01-2008; 1130 kHz AM
188 South Bellevue, Ste 222, Memphis, TN 38104 US
(808) 538-1180; *Fax:* (808) 538-9548
www.hhawaiimedia.com
gh5512@aol.com
License: Honolulu, HI held by Hochman-McCann Hawaii Inc.
Arbitron Metro Market: Honolulu, HI; *Format:* Ethnic; *Target Audience:* 25 plus.; *Adv. Rates:* 30; 25; 25; 20
George Hochman, President

KHJZ
01-14-1979; 93.9 MHz FM; *Hrs Open:* 24; 100 kw; N21 19 26 W157 52 32
650 Iwilei Road, Suite 400, Honolulu, HI 96817 US
(808) 550-9200; *Fax:* (808) 550-9288
www.939jamz.com
License: Honolulu, Honolulu County, HI held by Capstar TX LLC
Group Owner: iHeartMedia
Nat'l Reps: Clear Channel
Arbitron Metro Market: Honolulu, HI; *Format:* Adult Contemp; *Target Audience:* 25-54; upscale, white collar, college educated
Jovi Santiago, Sales Manager
Jamie Hyatt, Programming Director
Ricardo Rosas, Promotions Director

Kahaluu

KLEO
01-01-1992; 106.1 MHz FM; 7.3 kw; 2995 ft.; N19 43 16 W155 55 15
75-5852 Alii Dr., Suite B1 & B2, Kailua-Kona, HI 96740 US
(808) 961-0651
www.kbigfm.com
keith@kbigfm.com
License: Kahaluu, Hawaii West County, HI held by Pacific Radio Group Inc.
Group Owner: Pacific Radio Group Inc.; acq 9-17-03; grpsl).
Arbitron Metro Market: Honolulu, HI; *Format:* Adult Contemp

Kahului

KMVI
03-17-1947; 550 kHz AM; *Hrs Open:* 24; 5 kw-U, ND1; N20 53 29 W156 29 23
311 Ano St., Kahului, HI 96732-1304 US
(808) 877-5566
www.espn550.com
License: Kahului, HI held by Pacific Radio Group Inc.
Group Owner: Pacific Radio Group Inc.; acq 12-10-99; grpsl)
Nat'l Network: ESPN Radio; ABC
Format: Sports; *No. News Employees:* 1; *Target Audience:* 18 plus; men, residents/tourists, educated professionals; *Adv. Rates:* 18; 18; 18; 11.
Pamela Tsutsui, General Manager

KJKS
06-22-1984; 99.9 MHz FM; 69 kw; 2283 ft.; N20 39 36 W156 21 50
311 Ano St., Kahului, HI 96732-1304 US
(808) 877-5566
www.kissfmmaui.com
License: Kahului, Maui County, HI
Group Owner: Pacific Radio Group Inc.
Nat'l Network: Westwood One
Format: Adult Contemp; *No. News Employees:* 1; *Target Audience:* 25-49.; *Adv. Rates:* 24; 24; 24; 15
Trance, Programming Director

KLHI-FM
10-01-1994; 92.5 MHz FM; *Hrs Open:* 24; 1.7 kw; 2211 ft.; N20 39 36 W156 21 50
311 Ano St., Kahului, HI 96732-1304 US
(808) 877-5566
native925.com
studio@native925.com
License: Kahului, Maui County, HI held by Pacific Radio Group Inc.
Group Owner: Pacific Radio Group Inc.; (acq 6-29-2007; swap for KORL-FM Waianae)
Arbitron Metro Market: Kahului, HI; *Format:* Contemporary Hits/Top 40; *No. News Employees:* 1; *Target Audience:* Adults 18-49; *Adv. Rates:* 33, 28, 30, 20

Kailua

KRTR-FM
10-09-1978; 96.3 MHz FM; *Hrs Open:* 24; 74 kw; 2116 ft.; N21 19 49 W157 45 24
970 N. Kalaheo Ave., Suite C-107, Kailua, HI 96734 US
(808) 275-1000; *Fax:* (808) 536-2528
License: Kailua, Honolulu County, HI held by SM-KRTR-FM LLC
Group Owner: SummitMedia LLC
Arbitron Metro Market: Honolulu, HI; *Format:* Adult Contemp; *Target Audience:* 25-54.
Carl Farmer, CEO
Wayne Maria, Operations Dir
Patti Milburn, General Manager
Wayne Maria, Station Manager
Michol Klabo, General Sales Mgr
Shannon Scott, Promotions Manager
Neil Johnston, CFO
Richard Ferguson, Executive VicePresident
Mimi Beams, General Sales Manager
Corinne Webb, National Sales Manager

Kailua Kona

KLUA
01-01-1991; 93.9 MHz FM; *Hrs Open:* 24; 7.3 kw; 3022 ft.; N19 43 16 W155 55 15 *Rebroadcasts:* Rebroadcasts KPVS(FM) Hilo 100%
75-5852 Alii Dr., Suite B1 & B2, Kona, HI 96740 US
(808) 329-6633; *Fax:* (808) 326-7886
License: Kailua Kona, Hawaii County, HI held by Pacific Radio Group Inc.
Group Owner: Pacific Radio Group Inc.; (acq 8-11-2005; grpsl).
Arbitron Metro Market: Kailuna Koa; *Format:* Adult Contemp; *Target Audience:* 25-54; women

Kalaheo

KTOH
06-01-2002; 99.9 MHz FM; 51 kw; 892 ft.; N21 56 10 W159 26 43
P.O. Box 1588, Clayton, GA 30525 US
(808) 246-4444; *Fax:* (808) 246-4405
www.hhawaiimedia.com
info@roostercountry.com
License: Kalaheo, Kauai County, HI held by Hochman Hawaii-One Inc.
Wire Services: AP
Arbitron Metro Market: Lihue, HI; *Format:* Contemporary Hits/Top 40, Adult Contemp; *Target Audience:* 25-54; adults; *Adv. Rates:* 25; 20; 20; 15
Dianna Hochman, General Manager
Mark James, Programming Director
George Hochman, Promotions Manager

Kaneohe

KPHW
10-17-1997; 104.3 MHz FM; *Hrs Open:* 24; 74 kw; 2116 ft.; N21 19 49 W157 45 24
970 North Kalaheo Avenue, Suite C-107, Kailua, HI 96734 US
(808) 275-1000; *Fax:* (808) 536-2528
www.power1043.com
patti@power1043.com
License: Kaneohe, Honolulu County, HI held by SM-KPHW LLC
Group Owner: SummitMedia LLC
Arbitron Metro Market: Honolulu, HI; *Format:* Contemporary Hits/Top 40; *Target Audience:* 18-34.
Carl Farmer, CEO
Wayne Maria, Operations Dir
Patti Milburn, VP and General Manager
KC Bejerana, Programming Director
Scott McKenzie, Digital Promotions Manager
Corinne Webb, National Sales Manager
Rhoda Kihikhi, HumanResources
Alan Yamamoto, National Sales Manager

Kapaa

KITH
01-01-1999; 98.9 MHz FM; 51 kw; 919 ft.; N21 56 10 W159 26 43
P.O. Box 80657, Baton Rouge, LA 70898 US
(808) 246-4444; *Fax:* (808) 246-4405
www.hhawaiimedia.com
License: Kapaa, Kauai County, HI held by Hochman Hawaii-Two Inc.
Wire Services: AP
Arbitron Metro Market: Lihue, HI; *Format:* Ethnic; *Hrs. of News Programming:* News progmg 10 hrs wkly; *Target Audience:* 18-44; adults; *Adv. Rates:* 25; 20; 20; 12
Dianna Hochman, General Manager

Kaunakakai

KMKK-FM
03-19-2007; 102.3 MHz FM; 1.9 kw; 1181 ft.; N21 7 55 W157 11 31
US
(808) 947-1500; *Fax:* (808) 244-8247
License: Kaunakakai, Maui County, HI held by Ohana Broadcast Co. LLC
Group Owner: Ohana Broadcast Co. LLC
Arbitron Metro Market: Kaunakakai, HI; *Format:* Adult Contemp
Jim McKeon, Operations Dir
John Detz, General Manager

Kawaihae

KWYI
11-01-1993; 106.9 MHz FM; *Hrs Open:* 6 AM-10 PM; 5.5 kw; 341 ft.; N19 53 9 W155 39 28
P.O.Box 58, Ookala, HI 96774 US
(808) 885-9866; *Fax:* (808) 885-6480
www.kwyi.com
info@kwyi.com
License: Kawaihae, Hawaii County, HI held by Colin H. Naito.
Format: Adult Contemp; *Target Audience:* 25-54.
Colin Naito, General Manager

Keaau

KBGX
04-16-2004; 105.3 MHz FM; *Hrs Open:* 24; 25.5 kw horiz, 0 kw vert; 92 ft.; N19 43 18 W155 27 23
133 North Superior St, De Pere, WI 54115 US
(808) 329-8090; *Fax:* (808) 443-0888
www.lava105.com
info@lava105.com
License: Keaau, Hawaii County, HI held by Mahalo Broadcasting L.L.C.
Group Owner: Mahalo Broadcasting L.L.C.; (acq 8-31-2007; grpsl)
Nat'l Network: ABC
Arbitron Metro Market: Kea'au, HI; *Format:* Oldies; *Target Audience:* Adults; 25-54; *Adv. Rates:* 30; 30; 30; 30
Chip Begay, Operations Dir

Kealakekua

KAOY
11-11-1982; 101.5 MHz FM; 6.5 kw; 2982 ft.; N19 43 15 W155 55 16
688 Kinoole St., Hilo, HI 96720 US
(808) 935-5461; *Fax:* (808) 935-7761
www.kwxx.com
sales@kwxx.com
License: Kealakekua, Hawaii County, HI held by New West Broadcasting Corp.
Group Owner: New West Broadcasting Corp.; acq 4-16-2004; $500,000).
Arbitron Metro Market: Hilo, HI; *Format:* Adult Contemp; *Target Audience:* 18-49.
Christopher Leonard, General Manager
Trisha LaRochelle, General Sales Mgr
Gavin Panouye, Programming Director
Ken Hupp, News Director
Yisa Var, Traffic Manager

KKON
10-01-1963; 790 kHz AM; *Hrs Open:* 24; 5 kw-U, ND1; N19 31 10 W155 55 8 *Rebroadcasts:* Rebroadcasts Khlo(AM) Hilo 100%
913 Kanoelehua Ave., Hilo, HI 96720 US
(808) 961-0651
www.espnhawaii.com
License: Kealakekua, HI held by Pacific Radio Group Inc.
Group Owner: Pacific Radio Group Inc.; (acq 8-11-2005; grpsl).
Arbitron Metro Market: Honolulu, HI; *Format:* Sports *Special Programming:* Hawaiian mus; *Target Audience:* 35 plus; general
Marc Miranda, General Manager

Kekaha

KUAI
06-30-1965; 720 kHz AM; *Hrs Open:* 5 AM-midnight; 5 kw-U, ND1; N21 53 37 W159 33 27
P. O. Box 720, Eleele, HI 96705 US
(808) 245-9527; *Fax:* (808) 245-3563
License: Kekaha, HI held by Ohana Broadcast Co. LLC
Group Owner: Ohana Broadcast Co. LLC
Arbitron Metro Market: Eleele, HI; *Format:* Adult Contemp, Country *Special Programming:* Hawaiian 5 hrs, jazz 4 hrs wkly; *Hrs. of News Programming:* News progmg 21 hrs wkly; *Target Audience:* 25-65; loc long-timeresidents, blue & white collar
John Detz, President

Kihei

KAOI
10-11-1979; 1110 kHz AM
Mailing Address: P.O. Box 15261, Santa Rosa, CA 95402 US
Second Address: Box 1437, Wailuku, HI 96793
(808) 244-9145; *Fax:* (808) 244-8247
www.vremaui.com
kaoi@kaoi.net
License: Kihei, HI held by Visionary Related Entertainment L.L.C.
Group Owner: Visionary Related Entertainment L.L.C.
Nat'l Network: CBS; Westwood One

Arbitron Metro Market: Wailuku, HI; *Format:* News, Sports, 86; *Target Audience:* 25-54.
J. Detz, News Director
Alex Kowalski, Chief Engineer

KKHI
01-28-1967; 107.7 MHz FM; kw
US
(303) 889-1019; *Fax:* (303) 962-5289
License: Kihei, Arapahoe County, HI held by Kona Coast Radio LLC.
Group Owner: Kona Coast Radio LLC.; (acq 9-29-2006; $17.5 million)
Arbitron Metro Market: Denver, CO; *Format:* Adult Contemp

KHEI-FM
01-01-2009; 107.5 MHz FM; *Hrs Open:* 24; 0.75 kw horiz; 3133 ft.; N20 46 31 W156 14 49
Mailing Address: US
Second Address: 1900 Main St., Suite 6, Wailuku, HI 96793
(808) 244-9145; *Fax:* (808) 244-8247
www.island1075.com
kaoi@kaoi.net
License: Kihei, Maui County, HI held by Visionary Related Entertainment LLC.
Group Owner: Visionary Related Entertainment L.L.C.
Arbitron Metro Market: Kihei, HI; *Format:* Ethnic
Alex Kowalaski, CEO
John Detz, General Manager
jim McKeon, Station Manager

Kilauea

***KAQA**
07-03-1997; 91.9 MHz FM; 6 kw horiz; 1690 ft.; N21 58 41 W159 29 55
P.O. Box 825, Hanalei, HI 96714 US
(808) 826-7774; *Fax:* (808) 826-7977
www.kkcr.org
kkcr@kkcr.org
License: Kilauea, Kauai County, HI held by Kekahu Foundation Inc.
Arbitron Metro Market: Hanalei, HI; *Format:* Ethnic; *Target Audience:* General; Kauai County residents
Harvey Cohen, President
Larry Lasota, General Manager
Dean Rogers, Station Manager
Douvn Jewell, General Sales Mgr
Ken Jannelli, Programming Director
Donna Lewis, News Director
Dean Rogers, Chief Engineer

Kurtistown

KTBH-FM
01-01-2008; 102.1 MHz FM; 50 kw horiz; N19 41 48 W155 3 5
US
(808) 935-2924; *Fax:* (808) 244-8247
License: Kurtistown, Hawaii County, HI held by Resonate Hawaii LLC
Arbitron Metro Market: Kurtistown, HI; *Format:* Adult Contemp

Lahaina

KPOA
10-24-1984; 93.5 MHz FM; *Hrs Open:* 24; 69 kw; 2283 ft.; N20 39 36 W156 21 50
311 Ano St., Kahului, HI 96732-1304 US
(808) 877-5566
www.kpoa.com
studio@kpoa.com
License: Lahaina, Maui County, HI held by Pacific Radio Group Inc.
Group Owner: Pacific Radio Group Inc.; acq 12-10-99; grpsl)
Format: Adult Contemp; *Hrs. of News Programming:* top of the hour; *No. News Employees:* 1; *Target Audience:* Adults; 25-54; *Adv. Rates:* 50; 40; 45; 30.
Alakai Paleka, Programming Director
Valerie Toro, Music Director

Lanai City

KONI
11-01-1993; 104.7 MHz FM; *Hrs Open:* 24; 69 kw; 2283 ft.; N20 39 36 W156 21 50
300 Ohukai Rd ,Ste C-318, Kihei, HI 96753 US
(808) 875-8866; *Fax:* (808) 875-8870
koni@hawaii.rr.com
License: Lanai City, Maui County, HI held by Hochman Hawaii Publishing Inc.
Wire Services: AP
Format: Oldies; *Hrs. of News Programming:* News progmg one hr wkly; *Target Audience:* 25-54; Maui county residents; *Adv. Rates:* 25; 20; 20; 12
George Hochman, COO
Jim Carroll, General Manager
Adrienne Owens, General Sales Mgr
Joe Hawkins, Programming Director
Byron McCann, Chief Engineer

Lihue

KJMQ
01-01-2001; 98.1 MHz FM; 51 kw; 13 ft.; N21 59 41 W159 24 36
3460 Torrance Blvd, Suite 303, Torrance, CA 90503 US
(808) 246-4444; *Fax:* (808) 246-4405
License: Lihue, Kauai County, HI held by Hochman Hawaii Four Inc.
Arbitron Metro Market: Lihue, HI; *Format:* Contemporary Hits/Top 40
George Hochman, President
Dianna Hochman, General Manager

KFMN
03-07-1988; 96.9 MHz FM; *Hrs Open:* 24; 100 kw; 400 ft; N21 59 54 W159 25 35
Box 1566, 1860 Leleiona St., Lihue, HI 96766
(808) 246-1197; *Fax:* (808) 246-9697
john.wada@fm97radio.com
License: Lihue, Kauai County, HI held by FM 97 Associates.
Population Served: 75,000 *Hrs. of News Programming:* news progmg 4 hrs wkly; *No. News Employees:* 1; *Target Audience:* 25-54; island residents & visitors
John Wada, General Manager
Valarie Rynda, General Sales Mgr
Jason Fujinaka, Programming Director
Jason Fujinaka, News Director
Russell Wada, Chief Engineer

KQNG-FM
10-17-1983; 93.5 MHz FM; 51 kw; 226 ft.; N21 59 33 W159 24 24
P.O. Box 15261, Santa Rosa, CA 95402 US
(808) 245-9527; *Fax:* (808) 245-3563
www.kongradio.com
kong@kongradio.com
License: Lihue, Kauai County, HI held by Ohana Broadcast Co. LLC
Group Owner: Ohana Broadcast Co. LLC
Arbitron Metro Market: Kauai; *Format:* Contemporary Hits/Top 40; *Target Audience:* 18-49.
John Detz, President
Ron Wiley, Operations Dir

***KHJC**
88.9 MHz FM; 2 kw; N22 00 17 W159 21 38 *Rebroadcasts:* Rebroadcasts KAWZ FM
Mailing Address: P.O. Box 391, Twqin Falls, ID 83303 US
Second Address: 4002 North 3300 East, Twin Falls, ID 83301
(800) 357-4226; *Fax:* (208) 736-1958
www.csnradio.com
License: Lihue, Kauai County, HI held by Calvary Chapel of Twin Falls
Group Owner: CSN International
Format: Christian
Mike Kestler, President
Daniel Davidson, Operations Dir
Don Mills, Network Programming Director
Mike Stocklin, Underwriting Director
Kelly Carlson, Engineering Dir

Makawao

KDLX
12-31-1980; 94.3 MHz FM; *Hrs Open:* 24; 0.76 kw horiz; 3061 ft.; N20 46 31 W156 14 49
P.O. Box 15261, Santa Rosa, CA 95402 US
(808) 244-9145; *Fax:* (808) 244-8247
License: Makawao, Maui County, HI held by Visionary Related Entertainment L.L.C.
Group Owner: Visionary Related Entertainment L.L.C.; acq 2-10-2004; grpsl).
Format: Country
John Detz, President
Jack Gist, Programming Director
Gary Forsberg, News Director
Alex Kowalski, Chief Engineer

Nanakuli

KNAN
106.7 MHz FM; 25 kw; -23 ft.; N21 18 46 W158 5 51
US
(702) 385-6000; *Fax:* (702) 385-6001
License: Nanakuli, Honolulu County, HI held by Big D Consulting Inc.
Arbitron Metro Market: Nanakuli, HI
Donald Hildre, President

Paauilo

KNUQ
01-01-1995; 103.7 MHz FM; *Hrs Open:* 24; 100 kw horiz; 1509 ft.; N20 38 13 W156 23 21
5501 Excelsior Blvd, Minneapolis, MN 55416 US
(808) 244-9145; *Fax:* (808) 244-8247
www.q103maui.com
License: Paauilo, Hawaii County, HI held by Visionary Related Entertainment LLC
Group Owner: Visionary Related Entertainment L.L.C.; acq 2-10-2004; grpsl).
Format: Ethnic; *No. News Employees:* 1; *Target Audience:* 18-49; young active adults
John Detz, CEO
Jim McKeon, Operations Dir
Shaggy Jenkins, Programming Director
Gary Forsberg, News Director
Alex Kowalski, Chief Engineer

Pahala

***KAHU**
91.7 MHz FM; 1.8 kw; -128 ft.; N19 6 2 W155 34 9
US
(808) 959-2726
www.kahufm.com
License: Pahala, Hawaii County, HI held by Haola Inc.
Arbitron Metro Market: Pahala, HI; *Format:* Ethnic
Wendell Kaehuaea, Operations Dir

Paia

***KMKV**
102.9 MHz FM; 1.5 kw; 2283 ft.; N20 39 36 W156 21 50
US
www.klov.com
License: Paia, Hawaii County, HI held by Educational Media Foundation
Group Owner: EMF Broadcasting
Arbitron Metro Market: Paia, HI; *Format:* Triple A
Mike Novak, President/Chief Executive Officer

Pearl City

KUPA
05-02-1990; 1370 kHz AM; *Hrs Open:* 24
738 Kaheka St., Honolulu, HI 96814 US
(801) 273-9200
License: Pearl City, HI held by Broadcasting Corp. of America.
Nat'l Network: Fox Sports
Arbitron Metro Market: Pearl City, HI; *Format:* Sports
Nathan Drage, President

KUCD
02-14-1995; 101.9 MHz FM; *Hrs Open:* 24; 100 kw horiz, 81 kw vert; 1965 ft.; N21 23 51 W158 6 1
650 Iwilei Rd., Suite 400, Honolulu, HI 96817 US
(808) 550-9200; *Fax:* (808) 550-9288
www.star1019fm.com
License: Pearl City, Honolulu County, HI held by Capstar TX LLC
Group Owner: iHeartMedia; (acq 8-30-00; grpsl).
Nat'l Reps: Clear Channel
Arbitron Metro Market: Honolulu, HI; *Format:* Alternative; *Target Audience:* 25-54; boomers & yuppies
Chuck Cotton, Vice President/General Manager
Jovi Santiago, Sales Manager
Jamie Hyatt, Programming Director
Ricardo Rosas, Promotions Director

Poipu

KSRF
08-14-1999; 95.9 MHz FM; 51 kw; 919 ft.; N21 56 11 W159 26 43
P.O. Box 15261, Santa Rosa, CA 95402 US
(808) 245-9527
www.kongradio.com
License: Poipu, Kauai County, HI held by Ohana Broadcast Co. LLC
Group Owner: Ohana Broadcast Co. LLC
Arbitron Metro Market: Lihue, HI; *Format:* Ethnic
John Detz, President
Shelly Cobb, Programming Director
Denise Roberts, News Director
Ron Middag, Chief Engineer

Pukalani

KJMD
06-15-1984; 98.3 MHz FM; *Hrs Open:* 24; 9.4 kw; 2306 ft.; N20 39 36 W156 21 50
311 Ano St., Kahului, HI 96732-1304 US
(808) 877-5566
www.dajam983.com
License: Pukalani, Maui County, HI held by Pacific Radio Group Inc.
Group Owner: Pacific Radio Group Inc.; acq 12-10-99; grpsl).
Format: Contemporary Hits/Top 40; *No. News Employees:* 1; *Target Audience:* 18-34; young active adults; *Adv. Rates:* 33; 28; 30; 20
Trance, Programming Director
Sherri Grimes, Promotions Manager

Volcano

KKOA
01-01-1996; 107.7 MHz FM; *Hrs Open:* 24; 25.5 kw horiz; 92 ft.; N19 43 18 W155 27 23
1090 Vermont Avenue, N.W., Suite 800, Washington, DC 20005 US
(808) 329-8090; *Fax:* (808) 443-0888
www.KOACountry.com
License: Volcano, Hawaii County, HI held by Mahalo Broadcasting L.L.C.
Group Owner: Mahalo Broadcasting L.L.C.; (acq 9-1-2007; grpsl)
Nat'l Network: ABC
Arbitron Metro Market: Honolulu, HI; *Format:* Country; *Target Audience:* Adults 18-64.; *Adv. Rates:* 30; 30; 30; 30
Chip Begay, Operations Dir

Wahiawa

***KHAI**
01-01-2007; 103.5 MHz FM; 2.2 kw horiz, 1.9 kw vert; 1959 ft.; N21 23 51 W158 6 1 *Rebroadcasts:* Rebroadcasts KLRD(FM) Yucaipa, CA 100%
US
(800) 877-5600; *Fax:* (916) 251-1650
www.air1.com
info@air1.com
License: Wahiawa, Oahu County, HI held by Educational Media Foundation.
Group Owner: EMF Broadcasting; (acq 12-19-2005; $2 million for CP)
Nat'l Network: Air 1
Arbitron Metro Market: McAllen-Brownsville-Harlingen, TX; *Format:* Alternative, Christian
Mike Novak, President

Wailea-Makena

KRKH
06-04-2008; 97.3 MHz FM; 1.446 kw; 2283 ft.; N20 39 36 W156 21 50
US
(808) 875-8866; *Fax:* (808) 875-8870
www.hhawaiimedia.com
License: Wailea-Makena, Maui County, HI held by Hochman Hawaii Publishing Inc.
Arbitron Metro Market: Wailea, HI; *Format:* Classic Rock
George Hochman, President
Jim Carroll, General Manager

Wailuku

KAOI-FM
06-01-1974; 95.1 MHz FM; *Hrs Open:* 24; 3.5 kw horiz; 3061 ft.; N20 46 31 W156 14 49
P.O. Box 15261, Santa Rosa, CA 95402 US
(808) 244-9145
License: Wailuku, Maui County, HI held by Visionary Related Entertainment L.L.C.
Group Owner: Visionary Related Entertainment L.L.C.; (acq 2-10-2004; grpsl).
Arbitron Metro Market: Wailuku, Hi; *Format:* Adult Contemp; *Hrs. of News Programming:* news progmg 5 hrs wkly; *No. News Employees:* 1; *Target Audience:* General.
Jim McKeon, Operations Dir
John Detz, General Manager
Dale Parsons, Programming Director
Gary Forsberg, News Director
Alex Kowalski, Chief Engineer

***KKUA**
04-15-1988; 90.7 MHz FM; *Hrs Open:* 24; 56 kw; 2556 ft.; N20 39 36 W156 21 50 *Rebroadcasts:* Rebroadcasts KHPR(FM) Honolulu 100%
738 Kaheka Street, Honolulu, HI 96814 US
(808) 955-8821; *Fax:* (808) 942-5477
www.hawaiipublicradio.org
mail@hawaiipublicradio.org
License: Wailuku, Maui County, HI held by Hawaii Public Radio Inc.
Nat'l Network: PRI; NPR
Arbitron Metro Market: Honolulu, HI; *Format:* News *Special Programming:* Hawaiian one hr, Pacific Island 2 hrs wkly; *Hrs. of News Programming:* news progmg 35 hrs wkly; *No. News Employees:* 3 *Target Audience:* General.
Charles Husson, Operations Dir
Michael Titterton, General Manager
Judy Neale, Programming Director
Bill Dorman, News Director
Gene Schiller, Music Director

***KMNO**
91.7 MHz FM; 140 w; 161.1 m; N20 42 19 W156 21 54
Box 1145, Wailuku, HI
(808)244-2032; *Fax:* (808)243-9626
www.manaoradio.com
License: Wailuku, Maui County, HI

Scott Sherley, President

Waimea

KAGB
01-01-2000; 99.1 MHz FM; 7.3 kw; 2991 ft.; N19 43 16 W155 55 15
75-5852 Alii Dr., Suite B1 & B2, Kailua-Kona, HI 96740 US
(808) 329-6633
www.kaparadio.com
studio@kaparadio.com
License: Waimea, Kauai County, HI held by Pacific Radio Group Inc.
Group Owner: Pacific Radio Group Inc.; (acq 8-11-2005; grpsl).
Arbitron Metro Market: Kailua-Kona, HI; *Format:* Ethnic

Waipahu

KKNE
09-20-1950; 940 kHz AM; *Hrs Open:* 24; 10 kw-U, ND1; N21 26 43 W158 3 49
711 Kapiolani Blvd., Suite 750, Honolulu, HI 96813 US
(808) 275-1000; *Fax:* (808) 536-2528
License: Waipahu, HI held by SM-KKNE LLC
Group Owner: SummitMedia LLC
Regional Network: Waitt Farm Net.
Arbitron Metro Market: Honolulu, HI; *Format:* Country; *Target Audience:* 25-44.
Michol Klabo, General Sales Mgr
Kimo Akane, Programming Director
Wade Faildo, Promotions Manager
Rhoda Kihikihi, Human Resources Manager
Patti Milburn, Marketing Manager

KDDB
11-23-1988; 102.7 MHz FM; 61 kw horiz, 60 kw vert; 1893 ft.; N21 23 49 W158 5 58
4150 Pinnacle, El Paso, TX 79902 US
(808) 947-1500; *Fax:* (808) 947-1506
License: Waipahu, Honolulu County, HI held by Ohana Broadcast Co. LLC
Group Owner: Ohana Broadcast Co. LLC
Nat'l Reps: McGavren Guild
Arbitron Metro Market: Honolulu, HI; *Format:* Contemporary Hits/Top 40; *Target Audience:* 18-34; young adults who enjoy many different types of music
John Detz, General Manager

KSSK-FM
12-30-1976; 92.3 MHz FM; *Hrs Open:* 24; 100 kw; 1949 ft.; N21 23 49 W158 5 58
650 Iwilei Rd., Suite 400, Honolulu, HI 96817 US
(808) 550-9200; *Fax:* (808) 550-9288
www.ksskradio.com
info@ksskradio.com
License: Waipahu, Honolulu County, HI held by Capstar TX LLC
Group Owner: iHeartMedia; (acq 9-1-00; grpsl)
Nat'l Reps: Clear Channel; *Wire Services:* AP; Metro Weather Service Inc.
Arbitron Metro Market: Honolulu, HI; *Format:* Adult Contemp; *Hrs. of News Programming:* news progmg 6 hrs wkly; *No. News Employees:* 3; *Target Audience:* 25-54.
Chuck Cotton, Vice President and General Manager
Rob Welsh, General Sales Mgr
Jamie Hyatt, Programming Director
Tiffany Garrett, Promotions Director

Idaho

Aberdeen

KQPI
01-01-2008; 99.5 MHz FM; 2.2 kw; 1959 ft.; N42 48 31 W112 29 10
US
(312) 204-9900
License: Aberdeen, Bingham County, ID held by College Creek Media LLC.
Group Owner: College Creek Media LLC
Arbitron Metro Market: Aberdeen, ID; *Format:* Country
Neal Robinson, President

American Falls

KORR
01-01-1995; 104.1 MHz FM; *Hrs Open:* 24; 56 kw; 1109 ft.; N42 51 46 W112 31 3
Mailing Address: P O Box 97, Pocatello, ID 83204 US
Second Address: 436 N. Main St., Pocatello, ID 83204
(208) 234-1290; *Fax:* (208) 234-9451
spots@kzbq.com
License: American Falls, Power County, ID held by Idaho Wireless Corp.
Group Owner: Idaho Wireless Corp.; acq 1996).
Format: Adult Contemp
Paul Anderson, General Manager
Harry Neuhardt, General Sales Mgr

Ammon

KSPZ
11-09-1957; 980 kHz AM; 5 kw-D, DA2; 1 kw-N, DA2; N43 31 23 W112 0 36
854 Lindsay Boulevard, Idaho Falls, ID 83401 US
(208) 522-1101; *Fax:* (208) 522-6110
www.lasupercaliente.com
License: Ammon, ID held by Sandhill Media Group LLC.
Group Owner: Sand Hill Media Corp.; (acq 2-27-2004; $2.65 million with co-located FM)
Nat'l Reps: McGavren Guild
Arbitron Metro Market: Ammon, ID
James Garshow, President
Ken Walker, General Sales Mgr
Domingo Munoz, Programming Director

Blackfoot

KCVI
09-22-1994; 101.5 MHz FM; *Hrs Open:* 24; 95 kw; 1512 ft.; N43 30 3 W112 39 43
810 West 200 North, Logan, UT 84321 US
(208) 785-1400; *Fax:* (208) 785-0184
www.kbear.fm
scott@kbear.fm
License: Blackfoot, Bingham County, ID held by Riverbend Communications LLC.
Group Owner: Riverbend Communications LLC; (acq 4-17-2006; grpsl).
Nat'l Reps: McGavren Guild
Arbitron Metro Market: Blackfoot, ID; *Format:* Rock/AOR; *Hrs. of News Programming:* news progmg 3 hrs wkly; *No. News Employees:* 1; *Target Audience:* 25-44; male
Jim Burgoyne, President
Delyn Hendricks, General Manager
Matt Burgoyne, General Sales Mgr
Scott Taylor, Programming Director
Tisa Cudmore, News Director

KBLI
11-01-1951; 690 kHz AM
980 North Michigan Ave, Ste-1880, Chicago, IL 60611 US
(208) 785-1400; *Fax:* (208) 785-0184
www.eastidahonews.com
License: Blackfoot, ID held by Riverbend Communications LLC.
Group Owner: Riverbend Communications LLC; (acq 4-17-2006; grpsl).
Arbitron Metro Market: Blackfoot, ID; *Format:* Talk
Mike Nelson, Operations Dir
Delyn Hendricks, General Manager
Tim Lewis, News Director

KLCE
10-15-1975; 97.3 MHz FM; 95 kw; 1512 ft.; N43 30 3 W112 39 43
810 West 200 North, Logan, UT 84321 US
(208) 785-1400; *Fax:* (208) 785-0184
www.klce.com
info@klce.com

License: Blackfoot, Bingham County, ID held by Riverbend Communications LLC
Group Owner: Riverbend Communications LLC
Nat'l Reps: McGavren Guild
Arbitron Metro Market: Boise, ID; *Format:* Adult Contemp; *Target Audience:* 18-49.
Chris Cross, General Manager
Mary Stapek, General Sales Mgr
Sea Stachura, News Director

Boise

KBOI
05-01-1947; 670 kHz AM; *Hrs Open:* 24; 50 kw; N43 25 44 W116 19 43
1419 W. Bannock St., Boise, ID 83702 US
(208) 336-3670; *Fax:* (208) 336-3734
www.kboi.com
License: Boise, ID held by Radio License Holding CBC, LLC
Group Owner: Cumulus Media Inc.; (acq 12-10-97; grpsl).
Nat'l Reps: Katz Radio *Regional Reps:* Allied Radio Partners
Arbitron Metro Market: Boise, ID; *Format:* News/Talk; *No. News Employees:* 3
Nick Coe, Sales
David Allen, Programming Director
Matt Nielsen, Promotions Manager

*KBSU-FM
12-04-1955; 730 kHz AM; 15 kw-D, 500 w-N, DA-2; N43 34 13 W116 20 45
213 SMITC, 1910 University Dr., Boise, ID 83725
(208) 426-3663; *Fax:* (208) 344-6631
License: Boise, Ada County, ID held by Idaho State Board of Education (Boise State University)
Population Served: 250,000; *Arbitron Metro Market:* Boise, ID; *Format:* Jazz, News, 62, Talk *Special Programming:* Folk
Brad Campbell, Operations Dir
John Hess, General Manager
Hy Kloc, General Sales Mgr
Ele Ellis, Programming Director
Sadie Babits, News Director
Tom Taylor, Chief Engineer
Betsy Micone, Business Director
Erik Jones, OperationsManager

*KBSU-FM
01-16-1977; 90.3 MHz FM; *Hrs Open:* 24; 17.5 kw; 2713 ft.; N43 45 21 W116 5 54
1910 University Drive, Boise, ID 83725 US
(208) 426-3663; *Fax:* (208) 344-6631
radio.boisestate.edu
License: Boise, Ada County, ID held by Boise State Board of Education.
Nat'l Network: PRI; NPR
Arbitron Metro Market: Boise, ID; *Format:* Talk; *Hrs. of News Programming:* News progmg 15 hrs wkly; *Target Audience:* General.
Erik Jones, Operations Dir
John Hess, General Manager
Ele Ellis, Programming Director
Sadie Babits, News Director

*KBSX
01-01-1994; 91.5 MHz FM; 3.7 kw; 2713 ft.; N43 45 21 W116 5 54
1910 University Drive, Boise, ID 83725 US
(208) 426-3663; *Fax:* (208) 344-6631
License: Boise, Ada County, ID held by Idaho State Board of Education.
Nat'l Network: NPR; *Wire Services:* AP
Arbitron Metro Market: Boise, ID; *Format:* News; *No. News Employees:* 4
Erik Jones, Operations Dir
John Hess, General Manager
Paul Stribling, Programming Director
Tom Taylor, Chief Engineer
Kelly Palmer, Development Director

KGEM
01-01-1945; 1140 kHz AM; *Hrs Open:* 24
P.O. Box 693, Milwaukee, WI 53201 US
(208) 344-4744; *Fax:* (208) 947-6765
www.saltandlightradio.com
License: Boise, ID held by Journal Broadcast Corp.
Group Owner: Journal Communications Inc.; (acq 5-13-98; grpsl)
Nat'l Reps: Katz Radio
Arbitron Metro Market: Boise, ID; *Format:* Christian, Religious, 86 *Special Programming:* Scripture 7 hrs wkly; *Target Audience:* 25-54.
Bob Rosenthal, Operations Dir
Cathy Prazenica, General Manager
Brook Bender, General Sales Mgr
Rick Kemp, Programming Director
Kristine Simoni, Promotions Manager
Dan McColly, Operations Manager
Paula Jensen, Traffic Manager

KFXD
11-09-1928; 630 kHz AM; 5 kw-D, DA2; 5 kw-N, DA2; N43 30 56 W116 19 43
50 East Rivercenter Blvd., Suite 1200, Covington, KY 41011 US
(208) 344-6363; *Fax:* (208) 344-1134
www.kfxd.com
License: Boise, ID held by Peak Broadcasting of Boise Licenses LLC.
Group Owner: Townsquare Media; (acq 6-28-2007; grpsl)
Arbitron Metro Market: Boise, ID; *Format:* Talk *Special Programming:* Religious 2.5 hrs wkly, finance 6 hrs wkly, gardening 1 hr wkly, gun 3 hr wkly, health 1 hr wkly; *Hrs. of News Programming:* news progmg 120 hrs wkly
Kevin Miller, Brand Manager
Mike Owens, Director Of Sales
Melissa Rogers, Digital Managing Editor

KIZN
08-01-1968; 92.3 MHz FM; *Hrs Open:* 24; 48 kw; 2717 ft.; N43 45 21 W116 5 54
1419 W. Bannock St., Boise, ID 83702 US
(208) 336-3670; *Fax:* (208) 336-3734
www.kizn.com
kissin92@kizn.com
License: Boise, ID held by Radio License Holding CBC, LLC
Group Owner: Cumulus Media Inc.; (acq 12-24-97; grpsl).
Arbitron Metro Market: Boise, ID; *Format:* Country; *No. News Employees:* 1; *Target Audience:* 25-54.
Bob Rosenthal, General Sales Mgr
Hank Aaron, Programming Director

KJOT
01-01-1979; 105.1 MHz FM; *Hrs Open:* 24; 53 kw; 2589 ft.; N43 45 18 W116 5 52
P.O. Box 693, Milwaukee, WI 53201 US
(208) 344-3511; *Fax:* (208) 947-6765
www.varietyrocks.com
License: Boise, Ada County, ID held by Journal Broadcast Corp.
Group Owner: Journal Communications Inc.
Nat'l Reps: Katz Radio
Arbitron Metro Market: Boise, ID; *Format:* Classic Rock; *Target Audience:* 25-49.
Marie McGlynn, General Manager
Brook Bender, General Sales Mgr
Rick Kemp, Programming Director
Kristine Simoni, Promotions Manager
Dan McColly, Operations Manager
Paula Jensen, Traffic Manager
Dan McColly

KMHR(AM)
04-08-1961; 950 kHz AM; 5 kw-D, 35 w-N; N43 37 14 W116 17 57
Box 1600, Nampa, ID 83653
(208) 463-1900
License: Boise, Ada County, ID held by First Western Inc.
Arbitron Metro Market: Boise, ID; *Format:* Religious *Special Programming:* Farm 5 hrs wkly
Steve Sumner, General Manager

KAWO
11-02-1979; 104.3 MHz FM; *Hrs Open:* Monday - Friday 8-5pm; 52 kw; 2579 ft.; N43 45 18 W116 5 52
50 East Rivercenter Blvd., Suite 1200, Covington, KY 41011 US
(208) 344-6363; *Fax:* (208) 342-0444
www.wow1043.com
rich.summers@townsquaremedia.com
License: Boise, Ada County, ID held by Peak Broadcasting of Boise Licenses LLC.
Group Owner: Townsquare Media
Arbitron Metro Market: Boise, ID; *Format:* Country; *Target Audience:* General.
Rich Summers, Brand Summers
Mike Owens, Director Of Sales
Ann Jacobs, Digital Sales Manager
Melissa Rogers, Digital Managing Editor

KQFC
11-01-1960; 97.9 MHz FM; *Hrs Open:* 24; 48 kw; 2717 ft.; N43 45 21 W116 5 54
3280 Peachtree Rd. NW, Suite 2300, Atlanta, GA 30305 US
(404) 949-0700
www.nashfm979.com
nick.coe@cumulus.com
License: Boise, ID held by Radio License Holding CBC, LLC
Group Owner: Cumulus Media Inc.
Arbitron Metro Market: Boise metropolitan area; *Format:* Country; *Target Audience:* 25-54; country lifestyle
Nick Coe, General Sales Mgr

KSPD
04-29-1959; 790 kHz AM; *Hrs Open:* 24; 1 kw-D, ND2; 0.061 kw-N, ND2; N43 33 57 W116 20 13
1477 South Five Mile Rd., Boise, ID 83709 US
(208) 377-3790; *Fax:* (208) 377-3792
www.myfamilyradio.com
info@myfamilyradio.com
License: Boise, ID held by KSPD Inc.
Group Owner: KSPD Inc.; acq 3-24-83;
Nat'l Network: Salem Radio Network
Arbitron Metro Market: Boise, ID; *Format:* Christian, Talk; *Target Audience:* 18-54.; *Adv. Rates:* 20; 20; 20; 15
Lee Schafer, President
David Schafer, Assistant Manager
Beth Schafer, Executive Vice President

Bonners Ferry

KBFI
09-01-1977; 1450 kHz AM; 1 kw-U, ND1; N48 41 20 W116 20 4
327 Marion Avenue, Sandpoint, ID 83864 US
(208) 263-2179; *Fax:* (208) 265-5440
prod@953kpnd.com
License: Bonners Ferry, ID held by Blue Sky Broadcasting.
Arbitron Metro Market: Bonners Ferry, ID; *Format:* News, News/Talk, 84, Talk; *No. News Employees:* 1; *Target Audience:* General.
Dylan Benefield, General Manager
Jim Tomchek, Programming Director

*KIBX
01-01-2000; 92.1 MHz FM; 0.074 kw; 2749 ft.; N48 36 37 W116 15 24
Mailing Address: 2319 North Monroe Street, Spokane, WA 99205 US
Second Address: , Bonners Ferry, ID
(509) 328-5729; *Fax:* (509) 328-5764
kpbx.org
kpbx@kpbx.org
License: Bonners Ferry, Boundary County, ID held by Spokane Public Radio Inc.
Nat'l Network: NPR; PRI
Arbitron Metro Market: Spokane, WA; *Format:* Classical, Jazz, 60; *Target Audience:* General, educated
Tom Parker, Chairman
Cary Boyce, President & General Manager
Kevin Brown, Programming Director
Paige Browning, News Correspondent, Announcer
Mary Cravens, Membership Coordinator
Brian Flick, Operations Manager, Jazz Host
MaryHarvill, Front Desk Receptionist

Buhl

*KTFY
08-01-2005; 88.1 MHz FM; *Hrs Open:* 24; 60 kw vert; 653 ft.; N42 43 48 W114 25 6
16115 South Montana Ave, Caldwell, ID 83605 US
(208) 735-0881; *Fax:* (208) 459-3144
License: Buhl, Twin Falls County, ID held by Southern Idaho Corp. of Seventh-Day Adventists dba Gem State Academy.
Arbitron Metro Market: Buhl, ID; *Format:* Christian; *Target Audience:* 25-54; women
Donald Klinger, Chairman
Stephen McPherson, President
Michael Agee, General Manager
Jerry Woods, Programming Director

Burley

KBAR
01-01-1968; 1230 kHz AM; 1 kw-U; N42 32 5 W113 48 54
3219 Laurelwood Dr., Twin Falls, ID 83301 US
(208) 733-2974
broc@hot100now.com
License: Burley, ID held by Eagle Rock Broadcasting Co Inc.
Group Owner: Lee Family Broadcasting Inc.
Format: News/Talk
Kim Lee, President
Benjamin Reed, Programming Director

*KBSY
10-01-1998; 88.5 MHz FM; 0.44 kw vert; 2083 ft.; N42 21 42 W113 27 17 *Rebroadcasts:* Rebroadcasts KBSX(FM) Boise 100%
1910 University Drive, Boise, ID 83725 US
(208) 426-3663; *Fax:* (208) 344-6631
radio.boisestate.edu

License: Burley, Cassia County, ID held by Idaho State Board of Education.
Nat'l Network: NPR
Format: News, News/Talk, 86
Erik Jones, Operations Dir
John Hess, General Manager
Ele Ellis, Programming Director
Tom Taylor, Engineering Dir

KZDX
02-15-1975; 99.9 MHz FM; 27 kw; 2450 ft.; N42 20 6 W113 36 15
Mailing Address: 3219 Laurelwood Dr., Twin Falls, ID 83301 US
Second Address: 47 N. 100 W., Jerome, ID 83301
(208) 324-8181
www.hot100now.com
kimlee@leeradio.net
License: Burley, ID held by Lee Family Broadcasting Inc.
Group Owner: Lee Family Broadcasting Inc.
Arbitron Metro Market: Burley, ID; *Format:* Adult Contemp
Kim Lee, General Sales Mgr
Broc Johnson, Programming Director

Caldwell

KSAS-FM
09-28-1982; 103.3 MHz FM; *Hrs Open:* 24; 54 kw; 2579 ft.; N43 45 18 W116 5 52
50 East Rivercenter Blvd., Suite 1200, Covington, KY 41011 US
(208) 344-6363; *Fax:* (208) 385-9064
kekeluv@gmail.com
License: Caldwell, Canyon County, ID held by Peak Broadcasting of Boise Licenses LLC.
Group Owner: Townsquare Media; (acq 6-28-2007; grpsl)
Arbitron Metro Market: Boise, ID; *Format:* Contemporary Hits/Top 40 *Special Programming:* Class 2 hrs, jazz 4 hrs wkly; *Hrs. of News Programming:* news progmg one hr wkly; *No. News Employees:* 1; *Target Audience:* 25-54; upscale, white collar
Kevin Godwin, Senior Vice President/General Manager
Mike Sutton, General Sales Mgr
Steve Kicklighter, Programming Director
Crystal Struthers, Promotions Manager
Dave Burnett, News Director
Susan Green, Traffic Manager

KBGN
10-05-1960; 1060 kHz AM; 10 kw-D, NDD; N43 43 13 W116 31 58
3303 E. Chicago, Caldwell, ID 83605 US
(208) 459-3635
www.kbgnradio.com
kbgn@kbgnradio.com
License: Caldwell, ID held by Nelson M. Wilson & Karen E. Wilson.
Nat'l Network: USA
Arbitron Metro Market: Caldwell, ID; *Format:* Christian, Religious, 86 *Special Programming:* Sp 5 hrs wkly; *Target Audience:* General.
Marnie Fillmore, Operations Dir
Nelson Wilson, General Manager

KBXL
02-22-1961; 94.1 MHz FM; *Hrs Open:* 24; 39 kw; 2635 ft.; N43 45 18 W116 5 52
1477 South Five Mile Rd, Boise, ID 83709 US
(208) 377-3790; *Fax:* (208) 377-3792
www.myfamilyradio.com
info@myfamilyradio.com
License: Caldwell, Canyon County, ID held by KSPD Inc.
Group Owner: KSPD Inc.; acq 4-26-89;
Nat'l Network: AP Network News; *Nat'l Reps:* Salem *Regional Reps:* Tacher
Arbitron Metro Market: Boise, ID; *Format:* Christian, Talk, 74; *Target Audience:* 25-54.; *Adv. Rates:* 35; 25; 35; 15.
Lee Schafer, President
David Schafer, Operations Dir
Beth Schafer, General Manager
Leigh Ann Schafer, Programming Director

KCID
01-01-1947; 1490 kHz AM; *Hrs Open:* 24; 1 kw-U, ND1; N43 39 51 W116 38 10
P.O. Box 693, Milwaukee, WI 53201 US
(208) 344-3511; *Fax:* (208) 947-6765
License: Caldwell, ID held by Journal Broadcast Corp.
Group Owner: Journal Communications Inc.; (acq 5-13-98; grpsl)
Nat'l Reps: Katz Radio
Arbitron Metro Market: Boise, ID; *Format:* Oldies; *Target Audience:* 35 plus.
Cathy Prazenica, General Manager
Brook Bender, General Sales Mgr
Rick Kemp, Programming Director
Dan McColly, Operations Manager
Paula Jensen, Traffic Manager

KTHI
12-01-1983; 107.1 MHz FM; *Hrs Open:* 24; 52 kw; 2579 ft.; N43 45 18 W116 5 52
P.O. Box 693, Milwaukee, WI 53201 US
(208) 344-3511; *Fax:* (208) 947-6765
www.khits.fm
License: Caldwell, Canyon County, ID held by Journal Broadcast Corp.
Group Owner: Journal Communications Inc.
Nat'l Reps: Katz Radio
Arbitron Metro Market: Boise, ID; *Format:* Oldies; *Target Audience:* General.; *Adv. Rates:* 35; 30; 30; 20
Cathy Prazenica, General Manager
Brook Bender, General Sales Mgr
Rick Kemp, Programming Director
Dan McColly, Operations Manager
KJ Mac, Program Director
Paula Jensen, Traffic Manager

***KTSY**
10-14-1990; 89.5 MHz FM; *Hrs Open:* 24; 8.3 kw; 2595 ft.; N43 45 18 W116 5 52
16115 S. Montana Avenue, Caldwell, ID 83605 US
(208) 459-5879; *Fax:* (208) 459-3144
www.ktsy.org
family@ktsy.org
License: Caldwell, Canyon County, ID held by Gem State Adventist Academy.
Arbitron Metro Market: Boise, ID; *Format:* Christian; *Hrs. of News Programming:* News progmg 4 hrs wkly; *Target Audience:* 25-45.
Donald Klinger, Chairman
Stephen McPherson, President
Michael Agee, General Manager
Jerry Woods, Programming Director

Chubbuck

KLLP
11-10-1984; 98.5 MHz FM; *Hrs Open:* 24; kw *Rebroadcasts:* Rebroadcasts KAWZ(FM) Twin Falls 65%
50 East Rivercenter Blvd., #1200, Covington, KY 41011 US
(208) 233-1133; *Fax:* (208) 232-1240
www.star985.com
kellymartinez@gapbroadcasting.com
License: Chubbuck, Bannock County, ID
Group Owner: Rich Broadcasting LLC; (acq 2-13-2008; grpsl)
Arbitron Metro Market: Boise, ID; *Format:* Adult Contemp *Special Programming:* Sp 4 hrs wkly; *Target Audience:* General.; *Adv. Rates:* 6; 4; 6; 4
Jeff Evans, Operations Dir
Ryan Doremus, General Sales Mgr
Kelly Martinez, Programming Director
Cami Chopski, News Director
Rhett Downing, Chief Engineer
Neica Kinney, Sales Manager

KRTK
01-01-1981; 1490 kHz AM; *Hrs Open:* 24; 1 kw-U, ND1; N42 55 38 W112 30 3
P.O. Box Zee, Pocatello, ID 83206 US
(208) 237-9500; *Fax:* (208) 237-4600
krtk@ltlink.com
License: Chubbuck, ID held by Broken Chains Inc.
Nat'l Network: ABC
Arbitron Metro Market: Pocatello, ID; *Format:* Christian; *Target Audience:* 35-55.; *Adv. Rates:* 12; 10; 12; 5
Stacy Dare, Station Manager

Coeur D'Alene

KICR
10-12-2001; 102.3 MHz FM; *Hrs Open:* 24; 0.172 kw; 1844 ft.; N47 39 35 W116 57 12 *Rebroadcasts:* Rebroadcasts KIBR-FM Sandpoint 100%
23547 Schoen Born, West Hills, CA 91304 US
(208) 663-2179; *Fax:* (208) 265-5440
www.themorningstampede.com
License: Coeur D'Alene, Kootenai County, ID held by Great Northern Broadcasting Inc.
Arbitron Metro Market: Spokane, ID; *Format:* Country
Dylan Benefield, General Manager
Jimmy Silver, Programming Director
Mike Brown, News Director

KVNI
11-01-1946; 1080 kHz AM; *Hrs Open:* 24; 10 kW-D, 1 kW-N; N47 36 59 W116 43 11
500 W Broome Ave, Spokane, WA 99201 USA
(509) 324-4000
kootenaifm.com
License: Coeur D'Alene, ID held by QueenB Radio Inc.
Group Owner: Morgan Murphy Media
Nat'l Reps: Katz Radio
Arbitron Metro Market: Spokane, WA; *Format:* Adult Contemp *Special Programming:* Christmas (Nov/Dec); *No. News Employees:* 2; *Target Audience:* 25 plus.
Tery Garras, General Sales Mgr
Denise Hombel, National/Regional Sales

Cottonwood

***KNWO**
01-01-1994; 90.1 MHz FM; *Hrs Open:* 24; 0.25 kw; 2008 ft.; N46 4 9 W116 27 54 *Rebroadcasts:* Rebroadcasts KRFA-FM Moscow, ID
Edu. Telecommns. & Tech., PO Box 642530, Pullman, WA 99164 US
(509) 335-6500; *Fax:* (509) 335-3772
www.nwpr.org
nwpr@wsu.edu
License: Cottonwood, Idaho County, ID held by Washington State University.
Format: News; *Hrs. of News Programming:* news progmg 37 hrs wkly; *No. News Employees:* 1; *Target Audience:* 25 plus.
Karen Olstad, COO
Scott Weatherly, Operations Dir
Dennis Haarsager, General Manager
Roger Johnson, Station Manager
Sarah McDaniel, General Sales Mgr
Mary Hawkins, Programming Director
Rachael McDonald, News Director
RalphHogan, Engineering Dir
Robin Rilette, Music Director

Culdesac

KZID
01-01-2003; 98.5 MHz FM; 6.3 kw; 420 ft.; N46 27 47 W116 54 25
Gammon & Grange Pc, 8280 Greensboro Dr 7th F, McLean, VA 22102 US
(336) 286-2087
License: Culdesac, Clearwater County, ID held by Torro Broadcasting.
Arbitron Metro Market: Culdesac, ID; *Format:* Rock/AOR
Eliot Keller, President
Julie Hein, General Sales Mgr
Greg Runyon, Programming Director
Jamie Burgin, Promotions Manager
Scott Schulte, News Director
Robert Norton Jr., Executive Vice President
Kellie Lala, General SalesManager
Ric Swann, Music Director

Donnelly

KMCL(AM)
10-15-1965; 1240 kHz AM; 1 kw-U; N44 46 52 W116 02 51
Mailing Address: Box 813, McCall, ID 83638
Second Address: 204 N. 3rd St., McCall, ID 83638
License: Donnelly, Valley County, ID held by Brundage Mountain Air Inc.
Population Served: 25,000
David Eaton, General Manager

Driggs

KCHQ
02-12-2004; 102.1 MHz FM; *Hrs Open:* 24; 4 kw; Ant 1899 ft; N43 42 42 W111 20 56
Mailing Address: 1406 Commerce Way, Idaho Falls, ID 83445
Second Address: P.O. Box 54, Driggs, ID 83422
(208) 524-5900; *Fax:* (208) 522-9696
www.rivercountryfm.com
delyn@richbroadcasting.com
License: Driggs, Teton County, ID held by Rich Broadcasting of Idaho LS
Group Owner: Rich Broadcasting LLC; 06/02/2011
Nat'l Reps: Eastman
Population Served: 95,000 *Hrs. of News Programming:* news progmg 8 hrs wkly; *No. News Employees:* 1; *Target Audience:* 25-54; adults; *Adv. Rates:* 20; 15; 18; 12.
Richard Mecham, President
DeLyn Hendricks, General Manager
Sandie Fulks, General Sales Mgr
Denis Miller, Programming Director

Eagle

KXLT-FM
09-01-1994; 107.9 MHz FM; 45 kw; 2684 ft.; N43 45 18 W116 5 52
50 East Rivercenter Boulevard, Suite 1200, Covington, KY 41011 US
(208) 344-6363; *Fax:* (208) 327-8800
www.lite108.com
License: Eagle, Ada County, ID held by Peak Broadcasting of Boise Licenses LLC.
Group Owner: Townsquare Media; (acq 6-28-2007; grpsl)
Nat'l Reps: McGavren Guild
Arbitron Metro Market: Boise, ID; *Format:* Adult Contemp; *Target Audience:* 25-54.
Jeff Connell, Brand Manager
Mike Owens, Director Of Sales
Ann Jacobs, Digital Sales Manager
Melissa Rogers, Digital Managing Editor

Emmett

KDBI
03-12-1973; 101.9 MHz FM; 57 kw; 2533 ft.; N43 45 18 W116 5 52
3982 Glendale, Boise, ID 83703 US
(208) 463-2900
www.bustosmedia.com
License: Emmett, Gem County, ID held by First Western Inc.
Group Owner: Adelante Media Group LLC; (acq 11-1-2003; $1.05 million).

Ed Distel, General Manager

KQBL
02-11-2015; 101.9 MHz FM; 52 kW; 144 ft.; N43 45 18 W116 5 52
5660 Franklin Rd., Suite 200, Nampa, ID 83687 USA
(208) 465-9966; *Fax:* (208) 465-2922
License: Emmett, Gem County, ID held by FM Idaho Co., LLC
Group Owner: FM Idaho Co., LLC; March 2, 2015
Arbitron Metro Market: Boise, ID; *Format:* Country
Chuck Reeves, Programming Director

Fairfield

KXML
99.9 MHz FM; 0.2 kw; -1312 ft.; N45 10 2 W113 52 14 US
(520) 797-4434
License: Fairfield, Lemhi County, ID held by SkyWest Media L.L.C.
Group Owner: SkyWest Media L.L.C.
Arbitron Metro Market: Fairfield, ID
Ted Tucker, General Manager

Garden City

KCIX
01-01-1985; 105.9 MHz FM; 49 kw; 2700 ft.; N43 45 18 W116 5 52
50 East Rivercenter Boulevard, Suite 1200, Covington, KY 41011 US
(208) 344-6363; *Fax:* (208) 385-9064
www.espnevansville.com
ladonne.craig@townsquaremedia.com
License: Garden City, Ada County, ID held by Peak Broadcasting of Boise Licenses LLC.
Group Owner: Townsquare Media; (acq 6-28-2007; grpsl)
Nat'l Reps: McGavren Guild
Arbitron Metro Market: Boise, ID; *Format:* Sports; *Target Audience:* 25-54.
LaDonne Craig, General Manager
Bobby Gates, Brand Manager
LaDonne Craig, Director Of Sales
Ashley Sollars, Digital Managing Editor

Gooding

KINF
12-02-1996; 100.7 MHz FM; *Hrs Open:* 24; 73 kw; 2192 ft.; N43 14 43 W115 26 12
616 Blue Lakes Blvd, North, #1270, Twin Falls, ID 83301 US
(208) 465-9966; *Fax:* (208) 465-2922
License: Gooding, Gooding County, ID held by FM Idaho Co. LLC.
Group Owner: FM Idaho Co. LLC dba Impact Radio Group; (acq 12-31-2006; grpsl)
Arbitron Metro Market: Boise, ID; *Format:* Tejano; *No. News Employees:* 35
Elliott Klein, President
Mikey Fuentes, Operations Dir
Darrell Calton, General Manager
Mark Broz, General Sales Mgr
Sarah McBride, Traffic Manager

KRXR
01-01-1992; 1480 kHz AM
910 5th St., Rupert, ID 83350 US
Fax: (208) 934-8630
License: Gooding, ID held by Maria Elena Juarez.

Efrain Ortega, General Manager

KXTA-2
01-01-1996; 97.5 MHz FM; 35 kw; 760 ft; N42 36 10 W113 43 21
3219 Laurelwood Dr., Twin Falls, ID 83301 US
(208) 324-8181
www.club975.com
radiobroc@gmail.com
License: Gooding, ID held by Lee Family Broadcasting Inc.
Group Owner: Lee Family Broadcasting Inc.; (acq 5-1-2012)
Nat'l Reps: McGavren Guild
Format: Contemporary Hits/Top 40
Kim Lee, President
Broc Johnson, Programming Director

Grangeville

KORT
10-08-1954; 1230 kHz AM; 1 kw-U; N45 55 52 W116 07 50
Box 510, Grangeville, ID 83530
(208) 983-1230; *Fax:* (208) 983-2744
License: Grangeville, Idaho County, ID held by 4-K Radio Inc.
Group Owner: 4-K Radio Inc.; (acq 6-1-71)
Population Served: 12,500 *Special Programming:* Farm 2 hrs wkly; *Hrs. of News Programming:* news progmg 8 hrs wkly; *No. News Employees:* 1; *Target Audience:* General.; *Adv. Rates:* 15; 15; 15; 15
Mike Ripley, President
Melinda Hall, General Manager
David Forsman, Chief Engineer
Ben Rivers, Disc Jockey
William, Disc Jockey
Tammy Lyson, Disc Jockey

KORT-FM
12-01-1979; 92.7 MHz FM; 360 w; 2,352 ft; N45 51 48 W116 07 24
Box 510, Grangeville, ID 83501
(208) 983-1230; *Fax:* (208) 983-2744
www.kortradio.com
License: Grangeville, Idaho County, ID
Group Owner: 4-K Radio Inc.
Nat'l Network: ABC
Population Served: 8,500
Mike Ripley, President
Mike Ripley, General Manager
Melinda Hall, Station Manager
Melinda Hall, General Sales Mgr
Melinda Hall, Programming Director
Jason Ford, News Director
David Forsman, Chief Engineer

***KKRH**
90.9 MHz FM; 1.9 kw; 2324 ft.; N45 51 42 W116 7 25 US
(208) 983-5433
www.calvarychapelgrangeville.com
License: Grangeville, Idaho County, ID held by Calvary Chapel of Grangeville Inc.
Arbitron Metro Market: Grangeville, ID; *Format:* Christian
Dean Huibregtse, President

Hailey

KYUN
01-01-2006; 106.7 MHz FM; 97 kw; 1578 ft.; N43 16 45 W114 9 14
US
(208) 735-8300; *Fax:* (208) 733-4196
License: Hailey, Blaine County, ID held by Locally Owned Radio LLC.
Group Owner: Locally Owned Radio LLC
Arbitron Metro Market: Hailey, ID; *Format:* Country
Larry Johnson, President
Jerre Fender, Operations Dir
Deb Uvieu, General Sales Mgr
Denis Jeffs, News Director

Hayden

KHTQ
11-01-1991; 94.5 MHz FM; *Hrs Open:* 24; 83 kW; 2182 ft.; N47 39 34 W116 57 48
500 W Boone Ave, Spokane, WA 99201 USA
(509) 324-4200
rock945.com
License: Hayden, Kootenai County, ID held by QueenB Radio Inc.
Group Owner: Morgan Murphy Media
Arbitron Metro Market: Spokane, WA; *Format:* Rock/AOR; *Target Audience:* 18-35
Tery Garras, General Sales Mgr
Denise Hombel, National/Regional Sales

Hazelton

KTPZ
01-01-2007; 92.7 MHz FM; 4.9 kw; 741 ft.; N42 43 54 W114 25 4
US
(208) 735-8300; *Fax:* (208) 733-4196
lorproduction@gmail.com
License: Hazelton, Jerome County, ID held by Locally Owned Radio LLC.
Group Owner: Locally Owned Radio LLC; (acq 9-8-2006; $2,911,000 with KIRQ(FM) Twin Falls)
Arbitron Metro Market: Hazelton, ID; *Format:* Christian
Larry Johnson, President
Jerre Fender, Operations Dir
Deb Uvieu, General Sales Mgr
Denis Jeffs, News Director

Homedale

KQTA
12-01-2004; 106.3 MHz FM; 100 kW; 1028 ft.; N43 37 15 W117 12 35
5660 E. Franklin Rd., Suite 305, Nampa, ID 83687 USA
(208) 713-7269
License: Homedale, Owyhee County, ID held by Radio Rancho, LLC
Group Owner: Radio Rancho, LLC
Arbitron Metro Market: Boise, ID; *Format:* Spanish
Kevin Terry, Owner

Idaho Falls

KSNA
08-18-1975; 100.7 MHz FM; *Hrs Open:* 24; 100 kw; 633 ft.; N43 21 6 W112 0 29
854 Lindsay Boulevard, Idaho Falls, ID 83402 US
(208) 522-1101; *Fax:* (208) 522-6110
www.sunny943.com
License: Idaho Falls, Madison County, ID held by Sand Hill Media Corp.
Group Owner: Sand Hill Media Corp.; acq 9-7-2001; $1.2 million with KQEO(FM) Idaho Falls plus 36-month employment agreement).
Nat'l Network: Jones Radio Networks; USA; *Nat'l Reps:* Tacher
Arbitron Metro Market: Idaho Falls, IN; *Format:* Contemporary Hits/Top 40
Mike Steele, Operations Dir
Keith Walker, General Manager
Chris Sheetz, General Sales Mgr
John Balginy, News Director

KFTZ
05-24-1986; 103.3 MHz FM; *Hrs Open:* 24; 100 kw; 659 ft.; N43 21 6 W112 0 22
Mailing Address: 980 North Michigan Ave., Suite 1880, Chicago, IL 60611 US
Second Address: 1190 Lincoln Rd., Idaho Falls, ID 83401
(208) 785-1400; *Fax:* (208) 785-0184
www.z103.fm
info@z103.fm
License: Idaho Falls, Bonneville County, ID held by Riverbend Communications LLC.
Group Owner: Riverbend Communications LLC; (acq 4-17-2006; grpsl).
Regional Reps: Christal Radio
Arbitron Metro Market: ID Falls, ID; *Format:* Contemporary Hits/Top 40; *Target Audience:* 18-34.
Jim Burgoyne, President
Delyn Hendricks, General Manager
Matt Burgoyne, General Sales Mgr
Jeremy Dresen, Programming Director
Tisa Cudmore, News Director

KBLY
09-10-1960; 1260 kHz AM; 5 kw-D, ND1; 0.064 kw-N, ND1; N43 31 15 W111 59 33
810 West 200 North, Logan, UT 84321 US
(208) 785-1400; *Fax:* (208) 785-0184
www.eastidahonews.com
tim@eiradio.com
License: Idaho Falls, ID held by Riverbend Communications LLC.
Group Owner: Riverbend Communications LLC; (acq 4-17-2006; grpsl).
Format: Talk *Special Programming:* Nutrition 1 hr wkly; *Hrs. of News Programming:* news 120 hrs wkly; *Target Audience:* 35 plus; upscale, mature adults
Jim Burgoyne, President
Mike Nelson, Operations Dir
Delyn Hendricks, General Manager
Matt Burgoyne, General Sales Mgr
Neal Larson, Programming Director
Tim Lewis, News Director

KID
01-01-1928; 590 kHz AM; 5 kw-D, DAN; 1 kw-N, DAN; N43 33 35 W111 55 15
50 East Rivercenter Blvd., Suite 1200, Covington, KY 41011 US
(208) 524-5900; *Fax:* (208) 522-9696
www,590kid.com
neal@590kid.com; DeLyn@radiopandemic.com; Sandie@radiopandemic.com
License: Idaho Falls, ID
Group Owner: Rich Broadcasting LLC; (acq 2-13-2008; grpsl)
Nat'l Network: CBS; *Nat'l Reps:* Target Broadcast Sales
Format: News, News/Talk, 86 *Special Programming:* Wall Street Journal 20 hrs wkly, sports 1 hr wkly; *Hrs. of News Programming:* News progmg 100 hrs wkly; *Target Audience:* 25-54; upscale decision-making professionals
Neica Kinney, General Manager
Sandie Fulks, General Sales Mgr
Bill Hatch, News Director
Neal Larson, Program/News Director
DeLyn Hendricks, Market Manager

KID-FM
05-01-1965; 96.1 MHz FM; 100 kw; 1503 ft.; N43 29 51 W112 39 50
50 East Rivercenter Blvd., Suite 1200, Covington, KY 41011 US
(208) 524-5900; *Fax:* (208) 522-9696
License: Idaho Falls, Bonneville County, ID
Group Owner: Rich Broadcasting LLC; (acq 2-13-2008; grpsl)
Format: Country *Special Programming:* Wall Street Journal 20 hrs wkly, sports 1 hr wkly
Joseph Orozco, General Manager
Sandie Fulks, General Sales Mgr
Neal Larson, Program/News Director
DeLyn Hendricks, Market Manager

KTHK
10-01-1993; 105.5 MHz FM; *Hrs Open:* 24; 100 kw; 659 ft.; N43 21 6 W112 0 22
980 North Michigan Ave., Suite 1880, Chicago, IL 60611 US
(208) 523-3722; *Fax:* (208) 525-2575
www.1055thehawk.com
License: Idaho Falls, Booneville County, ID held by Riverbend Communications LLC.
Group Owner: Riverbend Communications LLC; (acq 4-17-2006; grpsl).
Format: Country
Delyn Hendricks, General Manager
Sandie Fulks, General Sales Mgr

KQEO
04-01-2003; 107.1 MHz FM; 100 kw; 633 ft.; N43 21 6 W112 0 29
Mailing Address: P O Box 17, St Anthony, ID 83445 US
Second Address: 854 Lindsay Blvd., Idaho Falls, ID 83402
(208) 522-1101; *Fax:* (208) 522-6110
www.arrow107.com
contactus@arrow107.com
License: Idaho Falls, Bonneville County, ID held by Sand Hill Media Corp.
Group Owner: Sand Hill Media Corp.; acq 9-7-2001; $1.2 million with KSNA(FM) Rexburg plus 36-month employment agreement).
Arbitron Metro Market: Idaho Falls, ID; *Format:* Contemporary Hits/Top 40, Adult Contemp
Jim Garshow, General Manager

***KAIO**
01-01-2006; 90.5 MHz FM; 0.5 kw vert; 528 ft.; N43 32 37 W111 53 7 *Rebroadcasts:* Rebroadcasts KLRD(FM) Yucaipa, CA 100%
1425 North Market Blvd, Suite 9, Sacramento, CA 95834 US
(800) 877-5600; *Fax:* (916) 251-1650
www.air1.com
info@air1.com
License: Idaho Falls, Bonneville County, ID held by Educational Media Foundation.
Group Owner: EMF Broadcasting
Nat'l Network: Air 1
Format: Alternative, Christian
Mike Novak, President
Mike Lee, Operations Dir
David Pierce, Programming Director
Ed Lenane, News Director
Sam Wallington, Engineering Dir
Marya Morgan, News Reporter
Richard Hunt, News Reporter

Island Park

KOUW(FM)
11-01-1998; 102.9 MHz FM; *Hrs Open:* 24; 37 kw; 842 meters; N44 33 41 W111 26 32
1401 East Stillwood Drive, Salt Lake City, UT 84117
(801) 277-6139; *Fax:* (801) 294-5145
License: Island Park, Fremont County, ID held by RP Broadcasting Idaho LS LLC
Group Owner: Rich Broadcasting LLC; (acq 9-18-2007; with KEZQ(FM) West Yellowstone, MT)
Population Served: 100,000 *Format:* Classic Rock; *Hrs. of News Programming:* news progmg 10 hrs wkly; *No. News Employees:* 2; *Target Audience:* 18-45; Adults
Richard O. Mecham, Manager

Jerome

KART
08-01-1956; 1400 kHz AM; 1 kw-U, ND1; N42 43 51 W114 32 17
3219 Laurelwood Dr., Twin Falls, ID 83301 US
(208) 733-2974
kimlee@leeradio.net
License: Jerome, ID held by Lee Family Broadcasting Inc.
Group Owner: Lee Family Broadcasting Inc.; (acq 9-1-64).
Nat'l Network: CBS
Arbitron Metro Market: Jerome, ID; *Format:* Sports; *Target Audience:* 25 plus.
Kim Lee, President

KDIL
940 kHz AM
US
(208) 324-9268
License: Jerome, ID held by Scott Powell.
Arbitron Metro Market: Jerome, ID
Amy Meredith, President
Scott Powell, General Manager

KEDJ
08-01-1970; 103.1 MHz FM; 100 kw; N42 43 51 W114 32 17
3219 Laurelwood Dr., Twin Falls, ID 83301 US
(208) 733-2974
kimlee@leeradio.net
License: Jerome, ID held by Lee Family Broadcasting Inc.
Group Owner: Lee Family Broadcasting Inc.; (acq 9-1-64)
Nat'l Network: CBS
Arbitron Metro Market: Jerome, ID; *Format:* Rock/AOR; *Target Audience:* 25 plus.
Kim Lee, General Manager

Ketchum

KIKX
12-02-1996; 104.7 MHz FM; 97 kw; 1578 ft.; N43 16 45 W114 9 14
2660 Peachtree Road, N.W, #17f, Atlanta, GA 30305 US
(208) 733-5459; *Fax:* (208) 733-4196
kikx.com
lorproduction@gmail.com
License: Ketchum, Blaine County, ID held by Locally Owned Radio LLC.
Group Owner: Locally Owned Radio LLC; (acq 10-31-2003; grpsl)
Format: News
Larry Johnson, President
Jerre Fender, Operations Dir
Deb Uvieu, General Sales Mgr
Denis Jeffs, News Director

Kootenai

KTPO
01-01-2007; 106.7 MHz FM; 1.3 kw; 1158 ft.; N48 13 45 W116 30 30
US
(208) 263-2179; *Fax:* (208) 265-5440
www.1067thepoint.com
carolynp@953kpnd.com
License: Kootenai, Bonner County, ID held by Hellroaring Communications L.L.C.
Arbitron Metro Market: Kootenai, ID; *Format:* Classic Rock
Dylan Benefield, General Manager
Mike Brown, News Director
John Goes, Chief Engineer

Kuna

***KARJ**
01-01-2005; 88.3 MHz FM; *Hrs Open:* 24; 23 kw vert; 2161 ft.; N43 0 26 W116 42 23 *Rebroadcasts:* Rebroadcasts KLRD(FM) Yucaipa, CA 100%
1425 North Market Blvd., Suite 9, Sacramento, CA 95834 US
(888) 937-2471; *Fax:* (916) 251-1650
www.air1.com
info@air1.com
License: Kuna, Ada County, ID held by Educational Media Foundation.
Group Owner: EMF Broadcasting
Nat'l Network: Air 1
Arbitron Metro Market: Kuna, ID; *Format:* Alternative, Christian; *No. News Employees:* 3; *Target Audience:* 18-35; Judeo-Christian, female
Darrell Chambliss, Chairman
Alan Mason, COO
Mike Novak, President and CEO
Mike Lee, Operations Dir
Eric Allen, General Sales Mgr
David Pierce, Programming Director
Ed Lenane, News Director
Sam Wallington, Engineering Dir
Tracy Butler, Traffic Manager
Dan Antonelli, Chief Business Development Officer
Eric Moser, Chief Financial Officer

Lapwai

KZBG
01-01-2005; 97.7 MHz FM; 0.57 kw; 1060 ft.; N46 27 22 W117 2 56
721 South Hillcrest Dr, Colfax, WA 99111 US
(509) 751-0976; *Fax:* (509) 751-0975
bigcountryradio@clearwire.net
License: Lapwai, Nez Perce County, ID held by Xana Duke Radio Partners LLC
Arbitron Metro Market: Lapwai, ID; *Format:* Country
Thomas D. Hodgins, General Manager

Lewiston

KATW
10-02-1986; 101.5 MHz FM; *Hrs Open:* 24; 100 kw; 846 ft.; N46 27 38 W117 1 0
403 Capitol St., Lewiston, ID 83501 US
(208) 743-6564; *Fax:* (208) 798-0110
www.catfm.com
wecare@catfm.com
License: Lewiston, Nez Perce County, ID held by Pacific Empire Radio Corp.
Group Owner: Pacific Empire Radio Corp.; (acq 9-12-2008; grpsl)
Arbitron Metro Market: Lewiston, ID; *Format:* Adult Contemp; *Target Audience:* 18-49.
Evan Yeoman, Operations Manager
Ben Bonfield, General Manager
Leslie Gatherer, Traffic Manager

***KLCZ**
10-01-1967; 88.9 MHz FM; 0.23 kw; -840 ft.; N46 24 45 W117 1 31
3317 12th St., Lewiston, ID 83501 US
(208) 792-2418; *Fax:* (208) 792-2568
www.klcz.com
License: Lewiston, Nez Perce County, ID held by Lewis-Clark State College
Format: Variety/Diverse
Tate Smith, General Manager
Sandra Kelly, Station Manager
Jason Snyder, Music Manager

KMOK
03-01-1983; 106.9 MHz FM; *Hrs Open:* 24; 99 kw; 1230 ft.; N46 27 33 W117 2 18
805 Stewart Ave., Lewiston, ID 83501 US
(208) 743-1551
kelly@idavend.com

License: Lewiston, Nez Perce County, ID held by Inland Northwest Broadcasting
Group Owner: Inland Northwest Broadcasting
Nat'l Network: AP Radio
Format: Country; *Hrs. of News Programming:* news progmg 3 hrs wkly; *No. News Employees:* 1; *Target Audience:* 25-49; female; *Adv. Rates:* 20; 20; 20; 20
Kelly Wayne, Operations Dir

KOZE
10-06-1955; 950 kHz AM; *Hrs Open:* 24; 5 kw-D, DA2; 1 kw-N, DA2; N46 23 32 W117 2 3
P. O. Box 936, Lewiston, ID 83501 US
(208) 743-2502; *Fax:* (208) 743-1995
www.koze-sports.com
License: Lewiston, ID held by 4-K Radio Inc.
Group Owner: 4-K Radio Inc.; acq 6-1-71)
Regional Reps: Tacher Company.
Format: Talk *Special Programming:* Farm 2 hrs wkly; *No. News Employees:* 2; *Target Audience:* 25-54.; *Adv. Rates:* 15; 15; 15; 13
Michael Ripley, President
Chris Ripley, Station Manager
Lisa Jensen, General Sales Mgr
Jason Ford, News Director
David Forsman, Chief Engineer

KOZE-FM
01-17-1961; 96.5 MHz FM; *Hrs Open:* 24; 25 kw; 741 ft.; N46 27 48 W117 0 1
P.O. Box 936, Lewiston, ID 83501 US
(208) 743-2502; *Fax:* (208) 743-1995
www.koze.com
License: Lewiston, Nez Perce County, ID
Group Owner: 4-K Radio Inc.
Format: Rock/AOR; *Target Audience:* 18-49.
Lee McVey, Programming Director

KVTY
07-20-1998; 105.1 MHz FM; *Hrs Open:* 24; 0.5 kw; 1099 ft.; N46 27 33 W117 2 18
805 Stewart Ave., Lewiston, ID 83501 US
(208) 743-1551
kelly@idavend.com
License: Lewiston, Nez Perce County, ID held by Inland Northwest Broadcasting
Group Owner: Inland Northwest Broadcasting
Nat'l Network: AP Radio
Arbitron Metro Market: Lewiston, ID; *Format:* Contemporary Hits/Top 40; *Hrs. of News Programming:* news progmg 1 hr wkly; *No. News Employees:* 1; *Target Audience:* 18-44.; *Adv. Rates:* 20; 20; 20; 20
Kelly Wayne, Operations Dir

Lewiston-Clarkston

KRLC
03-01-1935; 1350 kHz AM; *Hrs Open:* 24; 5 kw-D, DAN; 1 kw-N, DAN; N46 23 39 W116 59 40
805 Stewart Ave., Lewiston, ID 83501 US
(208) 743-1551
kelly@idavend.com
License: Lewiston-Clarkston, ID held by Inland Northwest Broadcasting
Group Owner: Inland Northwest Broadcasting; (acq 11-1-81).
Arbitron Metro Market: Lewiston; *Format:* Country *Special Programming:* Farm 5 hrs, radio auction one hr wkly; *Hrs. of News Programming:* news progmg 10 hrs wkly; *No. News Employees:* 1; *Target Audience:* 25plus; adults; *Adv. Rates:* 20; 20; 20; 20.
Kelly Wayne, Operations Dir

Marsing

***KAWS**
01-01-2007; 89.1 MHz FM; 8.75 kw vert; 2192 ft.; N43 0 25 W116 42 13 *Rebroadcasts:* Rebroadcasts KAWZ(FM) Twin Falls 100%
P.O. Box 271, Twin Falls, ID 83303 US
(800) 357-4226; *Fax:* (208) 736-1958
www.csnradio.com
csn@csnradio.com
License: Marsing, Owyhee County, ID held by Calvary Chapel of Twin Falls Inc.
Arbitron Metro Market: Marsing, ID; *Format:* Christian
Mike Kestler, President
Daniel Davidson, Operations Dir
Mike Stocklin, General Manager
Don Mills, Network Programming Director / Music Director
Kelly Carlson, Engineering Dir
Jerry Johnson, Engineering Dir
Ray Gorney, AssistantDirector of Engineering
Dustin Pamplona, Engineer
Nolan Mather, Graphics / Website Maintenance
Mike Stocklin, National Underwriting
Austin Morris, Accounting
Lois Mills, FCC Applications / Translator Site Manager

***KAWS**
89.1 MHz FM; 6 kw; N32 31 7 W93 17 59 *Rebroadcasts:* Rebroadcasts KAWZ(FM)
P.O. Box 391, Twin Falls, ID 83303
(208) 734-6633; *Fax:* (208) 736-1958
www.csnradio.com
License: Marsing, Owyhee County, ID held by Calvary Chapel of Twin Falls Inc
Group Owner: CSN International
Format: Christian, Religious

McCall

***KBSK**
01-01-2002; 89.9 MHz FM; 0.22 kw; 1919 ft.; N45 0 38 W116 7 53
1910 University Drive, Boise, ID 83725 US
(208) 426-3663; *Fax:* (208) 344-6631
radio.boisestate.edu
License: McCall, Valley County, ID held by Idaho State Board of Education.
Format: Jazz
Erik Jones, Operations Dir
John Hess, General Manager
Hy Kloc, General Sales Mgr
Ele Ellis, Programming Director
Sadie Babits, News Director
Tom Taylor, Engineering Dir
Betsy Micone, Business Director
Brad Campell, OperationsManager

***KBSM**
01-20-1991; 91.7 MHz FM; *Hrs Open:* 24; 0.22 kw; 1913 ft.; N45 0 38 W116 7 53
1910 University Drive, Boise, ID 83725 US
(208) 426-3663; *Fax:* (208) 344-6631
radio.boisestate.edu
License: McCall, Valley County, ID held by Idaho State Board of Education.
Nat'l Network: PRI; NPR
Format: News *Special Programming:* Jazz; *Hrs. of News Programming:* News progmg 15 hrs wkly; *Target Audience:* General.
Erik Jones, Operations Dir
John Hess, General Manager
Hy Kloc, General Sales Mgr
Ele Ellis, Programming Director
Sadie Babits, News Director
Tom Taylor, Engineering Dir
Betsy Micone, Business Director
Brad Campbell, OperationsManager

KDZY
01-01-2001; 98.3 MHz FM; *Hrs Open:* 24; 0.5 kw horiz, 0 kw vert; N45 0 18 W116 8 1
2121 Diamond Mountain Road, Calistoga, CA 94515 US
(208) 377-3790(208) 634-3781; *Fax:* (208) 377-3792
www.kdzy98.com
daveh@myfamilyradio.com
License: McCall, Valley County, ID held by KSPD Inc.
Group Owner: KSPD Inc.; acq 4-15-02; $75,000).
Nat'l Network: AP Network News
Arbitron Metro Market: McCall, ID; *Format:* Country; *Target Audience:* 25 plus.; *Adv. Rates:* 13; 13; 13; 13
Lee Schafer, President

***KBSQ**
90.7 MHz FM; 0.22 kw; 1919 ft.; N45 0 38 W116 7 53
1910 University Drive, Boise, ID 83725 US
(208) 426-3663; *Fax:* (208) 344-6631
radio.boisestate.edu
boisestatepublicradio@boisestate.edu
License: McCall, Valley County, ID held by Idaho State Board of Education.
Arbitron Metro Market: Boise, ID; *Format:* News, Variety/Diverse
Erik Jones, Operations Dir
John Hess, General Manager
Hy Kloc, General Sales Mgr
Ele Ellis, Programming Director
Sadie Babits, News Director
Tom Taylor, Engineering Dir
Betsy Micone, Business Director
Brad Campbell, OperationsManager
Adrienne Zachary, Marketing & Special Events Coordinator
Arthur Balinger, Producer/ Program Host
Carol Wilke, Membership Assistant
Craig Morgan, Web & Graphic Designer

Middleton

***KOAY(FM)**
88.7 MHz FM; 5 kw; Ant 2,594 ft; N43 45 18 W116 05 52
16115 S. Montana Ave., Caldwell, ID 83605
(209) 459-5879; *Fax:* (208) 459-3144
fun@ktfy.org
License: Middleton, Canyon County, ID held by Southern Idaho Corp.
Population Served: 5,607; *Arbitron Metro Market:* Middleton, ID
Michael Agee, General Manager

Montpelier

KVSI
07-20-1965; 1450 kHz AM
24681 U.S. 89 Box 349, Montpelier, ID 83254 US
(208) 847-1450; *Fax:* (208) 847-1451
kvsi.com
kvsi@dcdi.net
License: Montpelier, ID held by Tri-States Broadcasting LLC
Arbitron Metro Market: Montpelier, ID; *Format:* Country *Special Programming:* Farm 4 hrs, relg 2 hrs wkly
Keith Martindale, Owner and General Manager
Ada Hillier, Programming Director
Ada Jane Hillier, Program and Traffic Director

Moscow

***KRFA-FM**
09-01-1963; 91.7 MHz FM; *Hrs Open:* 24; 28 kw vert; 925 ft.; N46 40 54 W116 58 13
PO Box 642530, Pullman, WA 99164 US
(509) 335-6500; *Fax:* (509) 335-6557
www.nwpr.org
nwpr@wsu.edu
License: Moscow, Latah County, ID held by Washington State University.
Nat'l Network: NPR; PRI
Format: News, News/Talk, 86 *Special Programming:* Folk, jazz; *Hrs. of News Programming:* news progmg 37 hrs wkly; *No. News Employees:* 1; *Target Audience:* General.
Gillian Coldsnow, Operations Dir
Kerry Swanson, Station Manager
Dave Deeney, General Sales Mgr
Robin Rilette, Programming Director
John Paxson, News Director
Sarah McDaniel, Membership Director

KRPL
05-20-1947; 1400 kHz AM; *Hrs Open:* 24; 1 kw-U; N46 44 47 W117 01 06
805 Stewart Ave., Lewiston, ID 83501 USA
(208) 743-1551
shad@inlandradio.com
License: Moscow, Latah County, ID held by Inland Northwest Broadcasting
Group Owner: Inland Northwest Broadcasting
Population Served: 60,000; *Arbitron Metro Market:* Pullman-Moscow area *Special Programming:* Farm 4 hrs, relg 2 hrs wkly; *Hrs. of News Programming:* news progmg 12 hrs wkly; *No. News Employees:* 4 *TargetAudience:* 25-54.
Shad Spreiter, Operations Dir

***KUOI-FM**
11-01-1945; 89.3 MHz FM; *Hrs Open:* 24; 0.4 kw vert; -115 ft.; N46 43 43 W117 0 22
S.U.B / 3rd Floor, Moscow, ID 83844 US
(208) 885-2218; *Fax:* (208) 885-2222
www.kuoi.org
nae@kuoi.org
License: Moscow, Latah County, ID held by University of Idaho.
Arbitron Metro Market: Moscow, ID; *Format:* Variety/Diverse *Special Programming:* Black 3 hrs, folk 3 hrs, jazz 4 hrs wkly; *Hrs. of News Programming:* news progmg 2 hrs wkly; *No. News Employees:* 3 *TargetAudience:* General; alternative mus listeners
Nae Hakala, Station Manager
Tim Goldy, Programming Director
Joseph Engle, News Director
Jeff Kimberling, Chief Engineer
Lindsay Stribling, Music Director
Nick McGarvey, Production Director and Chief Announcer
Shawn O'Neal,Advisor/Chief Operator

KZFN
02-24-1973; 106.1 MHz FM; *Hrs Open:* 24; 62 kw; 922 ft.; N46 40 51 W116 58 26
805 805 Stewart Ave., Lewiston, ID 83501 US

RADIO - U.S.

(208) 743-1551
shad@inlandradio.com
License: Moscow, Latah County, ID held by Inland Northwest Broadcasting
Group Owner: Inland Northwest Broadcasting
Arbitron Metro Market: Moscow, ID; *Format:* Contemporary Hits/Top 40; *Hrs. of News Programming:* news progmg 5 hrs wkly; *No. News Employees:* 4; *Target Audience:* 25-54.
Shad Spreiter, Operations Dir

Mountain Home

KMHI
03-20-1962; 1240 kHz AM; *Hrs Open:* 24; 1 kw-U, ND1; N43 9 3 W115 42 26
2660 Peachtree Road, N.W, #17f, Atlanta, GA 30305 US
(208) 465-9966; *Fax:* (208) 465-2922
www.impactradiogroup.com
barbara@impactradiogroup.com
License: Mountain Home, ID held by Calvary Chapel of Twin Falls, Inc.
Group Owner: CSN International
Nat'l Network: Westwood One
Format: Christian, Religious

KPDA
02-11-2015; 100.7 MHz FM; *Hrs Open:* 24 hours; 64 kW; 95 ft.; N43 14 49 W115 26 8
5660 E. Franklin Rd., Suite 305, Nampa, ID 83687 USA
(208) 713-7269
License: Mountain Home, Gooding County, ID held by Radio Rancho, LLC
Group Owner: Radio Rancho, LLC
Population Served: 82,755; *Arbitron Metro Market:* Nampa, ID; *Format:* Spanish

Nampa

KIDO
05-17-1920; 580 kHz AM; *Hrs Open:* 24; 5 kw-D, DAN; 5 kw-N, DAN; N43 33 35 W116 24 2
50 East Rivercenter Boulevard, Suite 1200, Covington, KY 41011 US
(208) 344-6363; *Fax:* (208) 344-1134
www.kidoam.com
kevin.miller@townsquaremedia.com
License: Nampa, ID held by Peak Broadcasting of Boise Licenses LLC.
Group Owner: Townsquare Media; (acq 6-28-2007; grpsl)
Arbitron Metro Market: Boise, ID; *Format:* News, Talk *Special Programming:* Religious 1 hr wkly, Gun talk 3 hrs wkly; *Target Audience:* 25-54.
Kevin Miller, Brand Manager
Mike Owens, Director Of Sales
Melissa Rogers, Digital Managing Editor

KRVB
01-10-1975; 94.9 MHz FM; 49 kw; 2694 ft.; N43 45 18 W116 5 52
455 Amity Road, Meridian, ID 83642 US
(208) 344-3511; *Fax:* (208) 947-6765
www.riverinteractive.com
License: Nampa, Canyon County, ID held by Journal Broadcast Corp.
Group Owner: Journal Communications Inc.; (acq 4-11-00).
Nat'l Reps: Katz Radio
Arbitron Metro Market: Boise, ID; *Format:* Classic Rock *Special Programming:* Talk 20 hrs wkly; *Target Audience:* 18-64.
Bob Rosenthal, Operations Dir
Cathy Prazenica, General Manager
Brook Bender, General Sales Mgr
Rich Kemp, Programming Director
Kristine Simoni, Promotions Manager
Tim Johnstone, Music Director
Dan McColly, Operations Manager
Paula Jensen, Traffic Manager

KKGL
02-01-1977; 96.9 MHz FM; *Hrs Open:* 24; 48 kw; 2717 ft.; N43 45 21 W116 5 54
3280 Peachtree Rd NW, Suite 2300, Atlanta, GA 30305 US
(404) 949-0700
www.kkgl.com
License: Nampa, ID held by Radio License Holding CBC, LLC
Group Owner: Cumulus Media Inc.; (acq 12-10-97; grpsl).
Nat'l Reps: Katz Radio
Arbitron Metro Market: Boise, ID; *Format:* Classic Rock
Bob Rosenthal, General Sales Mgr
Forrest Smithkors, Programming Director
Matt Nielsen, Promotions Manager

KTIK
01-01-1983; 1350 kHz AM; *Hrs Open:* 24; 5 kw-D, 500 w-N
1419 W. Bannock St., Boise, ID 83702 US
(208) 336-3670
www.ktik.com
License: Nampa, ID held by Radio License Holding CBC, LLC
Group Owner: Cumulus Media Inc.; (acq 4-1-03; $750,000).
Nat'l Network: ESPN Radio; Westwood One
Arbitron Metro Market: Boise, ID; *Format:* Sports; *Hrs. of News Programming:* News progmg one hr wkly; *Target Audience:* 25-54; sports oriented men; *Adv. Rates:* 25; 20; 25; 15
Tom Newman, General Sales Mgr

New Plymouth

KTIK
01-01-1982; 93.1 MHz FM; 48 kw; 828 meters; N43 45 21 W116 05 54
1419 W. Bannock St., Boise, ID 83702 US
(208) 336-3670
www.ktik.com
License: New Plymouth, ID held by Radio License Holding CBC, LLC
Group Owner: Cumulus Media Inc.

Tom Newman, General Sales Mgr

Notus

KWEI
12-01-1947; 1450 kHz AM; *Hrs Open:* Sunrise-sunset
6885 Highland Valley Rd., Boise, ID 83712 US
(208) 367-1859; *Fax:* (208) 383-9170
License: Notus, ID held by Treasure Valley Broadcasting Co.
Arbitron Metro Market: Boise, ID; *Format:* News, News/Talk, 86; *No. News Employees:* 1; *Target Audience:* 35-65; mass appeal
Hal Widsten, President
Cindy Aguirre, Operations Dir
Sennett Rockers, News Director
Richard Schuh, Chief Engineer
Sandra Valdez, Business/Traffic Manager
Darren Dunn, Operations Manager

Orofino

KLER
10-15-1958; 1300 kHz AM; 5 kw-D, DAN; 1 kw-N, DAN; N46 28 41 W116 14 34
P.O. Box 32, Orofino, ID 83544 US
(208) 476-5702; *Fax:* (208) 476-5703
kler@wildblue.net
License: Orofino, ID held by Central Idaho Broadcasting.
Nat'l Network: ABC; Jones Radio Networks
Arbitron Metro Market: Spokane, WA; *Format:* Country; *Hrs. of News Programming:* news progmg 8 hrs wkly; *No. News Employees:* 2; *Target Audience:* General; family or logging industry-federal employee workers *Adv.Rates:* 15; 15; 15; 15
Ben Dickson, Operations Dir
Jeff Jones, General Manager
Jason Ford, News Director
Jim Sheldon, Chief Engineer

KLER-FM
09-20-1979; 95.1 MHz FM; *Hrs Open:* 24; 2.3 kw; 676 ft.; N46 28 9 W116 16 40
P. O. Box 32, Orofino, ID 83544 US
(208) 476-5702; *Fax:* (208) 476-5703
License: Orofino, Clearwater County, ID
Nat'l Network: Jones Radio Networks
Arbitron Metro Market: Spokane, WA; *Format:* Adult Contemp; *Hrs. of News Programming:* news progmg 8 hrs wkly; *No. News Employees:* 2
Ben Dickson, Operations Dir
Jeff Jones, General Manager
Jason Ford, News Director
Jim Sheldon, Chief Engineer

Parma

KWYD
10-22-1990; 101.1 MHz FM; *Hrs Open:* 24; 96 kw; 1001 ft.; N43 24 9 W116 54 9
P.O. Box 813, McCall, ID 83638 US
(208) 465-9966; *Fax:* (208) 465-2922
www.wild101fm.com
License: Parma, Canyon County, ID held by FM Idaho Co. LLC.
Group Owner: FM Idaho Co. LLC dba Impact Radio Group; (acq 9-14-2007; $950,000)
Nat'l Network: ABC
Arbitron Metro Market: Boise, ID; *Format:* Contemporary Hits/Top 40; *No. News Employees:* 35; *Target Audience:* 18-34; women
Wendell M Stark, Operations Dir
Elliott Klein, General Manager

Payette

KWEI(AM)
12-20-1957; 1450 kHz AM; *Hrs Open:* 24; 1 kw-U; N44 03 47 W116 54 27
1406 N. Main St., Suite 107, Meridian, ID 83642-1798
(208) 267-5234; *Fax:* (208) 888-9647
www.kiov.com
sports@kiov.com
License: Payette, Payette County, ID held by Media Enterprises LLC.
Regional Reps: Tacher.
Population Served: 125,000 *Format:* Sports; *Target Audience:* 18-54; 65% male; *Adv. Rates:* 45; 25; 40; 10
Marshall Sage, Operations Dir
David Combes, General Manager

KQXR
12-01-1978; 100.3 MHz FM; *Hrs Open:* 24; 98 kw; 708 ft; N43 49 31 W116 30 29
5257 W. Fairview Ave., Suite 260, Boise, ID 53201
(208) 344-3511; *Fax:* (208) 947-6765
www.xrock.com
License: Payette, Payette County, ID held by Journal Broadcast Corp.
Group Owner: Journal Communications Inc.; (acq 5-13-98; grpsl)
Nat'l Reps: Katz Radio
Population Served: 293,600; *Arbitron Metro Market:* Boise, ID; *Target Audience:* 18-49.
Cathy Prazenica, General Manager
Brook Bender, General Sales Mgr
Rick Kemp, Programming Director
Kristine Simoni, Promotions Manager
Jeremi Smith, Music Director
Dan McColly, Operations Manager
Jeremy Nicolato, ProgramDirector
Paula Jensen, Traffic Manager

Plummer

*KWIS
88.3 MHz FM; 0 kw horiz, 2.4 kw vert; 945 ft.; N47 19 37 W116 42 55
US
(208) 686-5059; *Fax:* (208) 686-1182
www.cdatribe.com
hkeen@cdatribe-nsn.gov
License: Plummer, Benewah County, ID held by Coeur d'Alene Tribe.
Arbitron Metro Market: Plummer, ID
Chief Allan, Chairman
Helo Hancock, Legislative Director
Heather Keen, Public Relations
Ernie Stensgar, Vice Chairman
John Abraham, Secretary

Pocatello

*KISU-FM
04-15-1998; 91.1 MHz FM; *Hrs Open:* 24; 4.5 kw vert; 1043 ft.; N42 51 46 W112 31 3
Box 8310, Pocatello, ID 83209 US
(208) 282-3691; *Fax:* (208) 282-4600
www.kisu.org
milljerr@isu.edu
License: Pocatello, Bannock County, ID held by Idaho State University.
Nat'l Network: NPR; PRI
Format: Jazz, News, 86, Triple A; *Hrs. of News Programming:* 60+; *Adv. Rates:* 20; 18; 20; 12.
Jerry Miller, General Manager

KMGI
04-01-1978; 102.5 MHz FM; *Hrs Open:* 24; 100 kw; 1,024 ft.; N42 51 57 W112 30 46
544 N. Arthur Ave., Pocatello, ID 83204 US
(208) 233-2121
License: Pocatello, Bannock County, ID held by Idaho Wireless Corp.
Group Owner: Idaho Wireless Corp.
Nat'l Network: Westwood One
Arbitron Metro Market: Pocatello-Idaho Falls, ID; *Format:* Classic Rock; *Adv. Rates:* 276; 276; 276; 180
Paul Anderson, CEO

KOUU
12-20-1956; 1290 kHz AM; *Hrs Open:* 24
P.O. Box 97, Pocatello, ID 83204 US

(208) 234-1290; *Fax:* (208) 234-9451
License: Pocatello, ID held by Idaho Wireless Corp.
Group Owner: Idaho Wireless Corp.; (acq 3-86; with co-located FM;
Nat'l Network: ABC
Format: Country; *Target Audience:* 35-64; adults
Paul Anderson, General Manager
Harry Newhardt, General Sales Mgr

KPKY
08-18-1975; 94.9 MHz FM; 100 kw; 1004 ft.; N42 52 26 W112 30 48
50 East Rivercenter Blvd., Suite 1200, Covington, KY 41011 US
(208) 233-1133; *Fax:* (208) 232-1240
kellymartinez@gapbroadcasting.com
License: Pocatello, Bannock County, ID
Group Owner: Rich Broadcasting LLC; (acq 2-13-2008; grpsl)
Arbitron Metro Market: Pocatello, ID; *Format:* Classic Rock
Mike Hudson, General Sales Mgr
Scott Conners, Programming Director
Delyn Hendricks, Marketing Manager
Sandie Fulks, Sales Manager

KSEI
09-23-1926; 930 kHz AM; *Hrs Open:* 24; 5 kw-D, DAN; 5 kw-N, DAN; N42 57 44 W112 29 50
544 N. Arthur St., Pocatello, ID 83204 US
(208) 233-2121
License: Pocatello, Bannock County, ID held by Idaho Wireless Corp.
Group Owner: Idaho Wireless Corp.; (acq 11-18-2014).
Nat'l Reps: Katz Radio
Arbitron Metro Market: Pocatello, ID; *Format:* Oldies; *Target Audience:* General.; *Adv. Rates:* 120; 144; 110; 110
Paul Anderson, CEO

KWIK
09-01-1946; 1240 kHz AM; *Hrs Open:* 24
50 East Rivercenter Blvd., Suite 1200, Covington, KY 41011 US
(208) 524-5900; *Fax:* (208) 522-9696
www.590kid.com
License: Pocatello, ID
Group Owner: Rich Broadcasting LLC; (acq 2-13-2008; grpsl)
Regional Reps: Art Moore.
Arbitron Metro Market: Idhao Falls, ID; *Format:* News, News/Talk, 84, Talk *Special Programming:* Farm 3 hrs, gospel 2 hrs, relg one hr, American Indian one hr wkly; *Hrs. of News Programming:* news progmg 15 hrs wkly; *No. News Employees:* 3; *Target Audience:* 45 plus.
Tim Murphy, General Manager
Jodie Bates, General Sales Mgr
Neal Larson, Program/ News Director
Rhett Downing, Chief Engineer
Delyn Hendricks, Marketing Manager
Sandie Fulks, Sales Manager

KZBQ
12-27-1969; 93.7 MHz FM; *Hrs Open:* 24; 98 kw; 984 ft.; N42 51 57 W112 30 46
P. O. Box 97, Pocatello, ID 83204 US
(208) 234-1290; *Fax:* (208) 234-9451
www.kzbq.com/
Sales@EastIdahoRadio.com
License: Pocatello, Bannock County, ID
Group Owner: Idaho Wireless Corp.
Nat'l Network: ABC
Arbitron Metro Market: Pocatello, ID; *Format:* Country; *Target Audience:* 25-54; adults
Paul Anderson, Station Manager

KPTO
12-01-2005; 1440 kHz AM; *Hrs Open:* 24; 2.5 kw-D, 350 w-N, DA-2; N42 56 30 W112 27 17
Mailing Address: 2975 Valmont Road, St. George, UT
Second Address: 210 North 1000 East, St. George, UT 84770-3155
(208) 234-7000; *Fax:* (208) 232-1440,
legacy1@infowest.com
License: Pocatello, Bannock County, ID held by AM Radio 1440 Inc.
Group Owner: Legacy Media Corporation; (acq 12-6-2004).
Nat'l Network: CNN Radio; Westwood One
Hrs. of News Programming: On-The-Hour; *Target Audience:* 25-64.
Lee Weinstein, ESQ, Operations Dir

***KZJB**
01-01-2006; 90.3 MHz FM; 0.91 kw; 1031 ft.; N42 51 46 W112 31 3
4250 South 25th East, Idaho Falls, ID 83404 US
(208) 524-4747; *Fax:* (208) 524-0697
www.revelationradio.fm
info@revelationradio.fm
License: Pocatello, Bannock County, ID held by Watersprings Ministries
Group Owner: Watersprings Ministries
Arbitron Metro Market: Pocatello, ID; *Format:* Christian, Religious
Kelly Golden, Station Manager
Corey Wadsworth, Studio Engineer
Rick Brown, Senior Pastor
Buster Brown, Production

KEGE
07-23-2007; 92.1 MHz FM; 12 kw; 988 ft.; N42 52 26 W112 30 48
9148 Bonita Beach Road, Suite 205, Bonita Springs, FL 34135 US
(208) 522-5900; *Fax:* (208) 522-9696
www.590kid.com
neal@590kid.com
License: Pocatello, Bannock County, ID
Group Owner: Rich Broadcasting LLC; (acq 9-3-2008; $1.09 million)
Arbitron Metro Market: Pocatello, ID; *Format:* News, Talk
Neica Kinney, General Manager
Sandie Fulks, Sales Manager
Neal Larson, Program / News Director
DeLyn Hendricks, Market Manager

Post Falls

KCDA
06-29-1979; 103.1 MHz FM; *Hrs Open:* 24; 18.5 kw; 1,742 ft.; N47 34 52 W117 17 47
808 E. Sprague Ave., Spokane, WA 99202 US
(509) 242-2400; *Fax:* (509) 242-1160
www.1031kcda.com
License: Post Falls, Kootenai County, ID held by Capstar TX LLC
Group Owner: iHeartMedia; (acq 10-18-00; $4.7 million)
Nat'l Reps: Roslin
Arbitron Metro Market: Spokane, WA; *Format:* Adult Contemp; *Hrs. of News Programming:* news progmg one hr wkly; *No. News Employees:* 2; *Target Audience:* 25-54; active & affluent
Cal Hall, Market President
Brad Miller, Senior Vice President of Programming
Brent Phillipy, Sales Manager
Matt Auclair, Promotions Director
Andrea Williams, Digital Director

Preston

KACH
09-04-1948; 1340 kHz AM; *Hrs Open:* 24; 1 kw-U; N42 07 45 W111 51 00
1133 E. Glendale Rd., Preston, ID 83263
(208) 852-1340; *Fax:* (208) 852-1342
kach@plmw.com
License: Preston, Franklin County, ID held by Alan J. White, Nelada G. White.
Nat'l Network: ABC; *Nat'l Reps:* Interep; *Wire Services:* AP
Population Served: 10,500 *Special Programming:* Farm; *Hrs. of News Programming:* News progmg 12 hrs wkly; *Target Audience:* 18-54; general; *Adv. Rates:* 13.50; 10.50; 8.50; 6
Alan White, General Manager

KKEX
12-09-1993; 96.7 MHz FM; *Hrs Open:* 24; 100 kw; 217 ft.; N41 52 18 W111 48 31
Mailing Address: P.O. Box 3369, Logan, UT 84323 US
Second Address: 810 W. 200 N., Logan, UT 84321
(435) 752-1390; *Fax:* (435) 752-1392
License: Preston, Franklin County, ID held by Sun Valley Radio Inc.
Group Owner: Sun Valley Radio Inc.; acq 1994).
Format: Country
M. Kent Frandsen, President
Jay Eubanks, General Manager
Lynn Simmons, Programming Director
Dan Baker, Chief Engineer

Rathdrum

***KYMS**
89.9 MHz FM; *Hrs Open:* 24; 2.8 kw H 2.8 kw V; 1952 ft.; N48 4 42 W116 42 42
P.O. Box 998, Post Falls, ID 83877 US
(280) 457-7140
www.kymsradio.com
karla@todayschristiancountry.com
License: Rathdrum, Kootenai County, ID held by Legacy Broadcasting, Inc.
Group Owner: Legacy Broadcasting, LLC; (acq. 2011)
Arbitron Metro Market: Rathdrum, ID; *Format:* Christian, Religious
Sherry Nelson, President
Lee Lancaster, General Manager
Karla Lancaster, Business Manager

Rexburg

KGTM
01-17-1986; 98.1 MHz FM; *Hrs Open:* 24/7; 100 kw; 636 ft.; N43 32 34 W111 53 7
P.O. Box 3451, 228 E. 1st Street, Idaho Fall, ID 83401 US
(208) 235-7625; *Fax:* (208) 233-1133
www.star98radio.com
kelly@star98radio.com
License: Rexburg, Madison County, ID
Group Owner: Rich Broadcasting LLC; acq 7-25-2000; $495,000 with KRXK(FM) Rexburg).
Format: Contemporary Hits/Top 40, Adult Contemp; *Target Audience:* 35 plus.; *Adv. Rates:* 15; 15; 15; 6
Phil Jimenez, General Manager
Sandie Fulks, Programming Director
Kelly Martinez, Program Director
DeLyn Hendricks, Market Manager

***KBYI**
11-13-1972; 94.3 MHz FM; *Hrs Open:* 24; 99 kw; 692 ft.; N43 45 44 W111 57 30
Spori Building, Room 243, Rexburg, ID 83460 US
(208) 496-2411; *Fax:* (208) 496-2912
www.byuidahoradio.org
newsdesk@byui.edu
License: Rexburg, Madison County, ID held by Brigham Young University-Idaho.
Nat'l Network: NPR; PRI
Arbitron Metro Market: Southeastern ID; *Format:* Talk; *Hrs. of News Programming:* news progmg 33 hrs wkly; *No. News Employees:* 1; *Target Audience:* General.
Jim Clark, General Manager
Michelle Snyder, Promotions Manager
Mark Bailey, News Director

KRXK
01-01-1951; 1230 kHz AM; 1 kw-U, ND1; N43 50 50 W111 47 3
Rebroadcasts: Simulcast with KSEI (AM) Pocotello
341 West 1500 North, Rexburg, ID 83440 US
(208) 356-3651; *Fax:* (208) 356-8885
philjimenez@pacempire.com
License: Rexburg, ID
Group Owner: Rich Broadcasting LLC; (acq 7-25-2000; $495,000 with KGTM(FM) Rexburg).
Nat'l Reps: Target Broadcast Sales
Format: Sports; *Target Audience:* 25-54; male; *Adv. Rates:* 12; 10; 12; 6
Phil Jimenez, General Manager
Sean Green, Programming Director

KUPI-FM
08-16-1975; 99.1 MHz FM; 100 kw; 577 ft.; N43 32 33 W111 53 4
2464 Radio Rd, St. Anthony, ID 83445 US
(208) 522-1101; *Fax:* (208) 522-6110
www.99kupi.com
contactus@99kupi.com
License: Rexburg, Bonneville County, ID
Group Owner: Sand Hill Media Corp.
Arbitron Metro Market: Rexburg, ID; *Format:* Country
Tom Marhefka, CEO
Bob Eckman, General Manager
Jonathon Bergman, General Sales Mgr
Gary Lee, Programming Director
Mike Robertson, News Director
Jim White, Chief Engineer

***KBYR-FM**
01-01-1993; 91.5 MHz FM; *Hrs Open:* 24; 1 kw; 46 ft.; N43 49 2 W111 46 42
Spori Building, Room 294, Rexburg, ID 83460 US
(208) 496-1411; *Fax:* (208) 496-2912
www.byui.edu/kbyr
newsdesk@byui.edu
License: Rexburg, Madison County, ID held by Ricks College Corp.
Arbitron Metro Market: Rexburg, ID; *Format:* Adult Contemp; *Target Audience:* General.
Jim Clark, General Manager

Rigby

***KLRI**
01-01-2005; 89.5 MHz FM; *Hrs Open:* 24; 78 kw vert; 1527 ft.; N43 30 4 W112 39 44 *Rebroadcasts:* Rebroadcasts KLVR(FM) Santa Rosa, CA 100%
1425 North Market Blvd., Suite 9, Sacramento, CA 95834 US
(800) 525-5683; *Fax:* (916) 251-1650
www.klove.com
klove@klove.com
License: Rigby, Jefferson County, ID held by Educational Media Foundation.
Group Owner: EMF Broadcasting
Nat'l Network: K-Love
Arbitron Metro Market: Rigby, ID; *Format:* Christian; *No. News Employees:* 3; *Target Audience:* 25-44; Judeo Christian, female
Darrell Chambliss, Chairman
Mike Novak, President and CEO
Mike Lee, Operations Dir
David Pierce, Programming Director
Ed Lenane, News Director
Sam Wallington, Engineering Dir
Marya Morgan, News Reporter
Richard Hunt, NewsReporter
Laura Daniels, News Reporter
Tim Luttrell, News Reporter
Kenny Noble Cortes, News Reporter
Darren Vinson, News Reporter

Ririe

***KSQS**
01-01-2006; 91.7 MHz FM; 0.25 kw; 532 ft.; N43 32 37 W111 53 7
2201 S 6th St, Las Vegas, NV 89104 US
(702) 731-5452; *Fax:* (702) 731-1992
www.sosradio.net
info@sosradio.net
License: Ririe, Jefferson County, ID held by Faith Communications Corp.
Group Owner: Faith Communications Corp.
Arbitron Metro Market: Ririe, ID; *Format:* Adult Contemp, Christian
Brad Staley, General Manager
Bob Alzugarat, Station Manager
Scott Herrold, Programming Director
Rick Hall, Assistant Program Director/Music Director
Tim Hunt, Director of Network Engineering
Chris Staley, VP of Programming andAdministration

Rupert

KFTA
10-12-1955; 970 kHz AM; *Hrs Open:* 24; 2.5 kw-D, DAN; 0.9 kw-N, DAN; N42 36 7 W113 43 21; N42 36 10 W113 43 21
144 Seminole Circle, Jerome, ID 83338 US
(208) 436-4757; *Fax:* (208) 436-3050
lafantastica970@yahoo.com
License: Rupert, ID held by Tri-Market Radio Broadcasters Inc.
Group Owner: Tri-Market Radio Broadcasters Inc. & Eagle Rock Broadcasting Inc.; (acq 9-24-93; $700,000 with co-located FM;
Arbitron Metro Market: Rupert, ID; *No. News Employees:* 1
Kim Lee, General Manager
Ben Reed, Programming Director
Jerry Thaxton, Chief Engineer

KKMV
12-05-1978; 106.1 MHz FM; 25 kw; 2497 ft.; N42 20 6 W113 36 15
3219 Laurelwood Dr., Twin Falls, ID 83301 US
(208) 539-5288
www.kat106.com
License: Rupert, ID held by Lee Family Broadcasting Inc.
Group Owner: Lee Family Broadcasting Inc.
Arbitron Metro Market: Boise, ID; *Format:* Country; *No. News Employees:* 1; *Target Audience:* Adults: 25-54.
Kim Lee, General Manager

KXTA
10-24-1955; 970 kHz AM; 2.5 kw-D, 900 watts-N; 760 ft; N42 36 10 W113 43 21
3219 Laurelwood Dr., Twin Falls, ID 83301 US
(208) 733-2974
kimlee@leeradio.net
License: Rupert, ID held by Lee Family Broadcasting Inc.
Group Owner: Lee Family Broadcasting Inc.; (acq 5-1-2012)
Nat'l Reps: McGavren Guild
Format: Tejano
Kim Lee, President
Benjamin Reed, Programming Director

Salmon

KSRA
03-01-1959; 960 kHz AM; 1 kw-D, ND1; 0.056 kw-N, ND1; N45 11 2 W113 52 12
315 Riverfront Drive, Salmon, ID 83467 US
(208) 756-2218; *Fax:* (208) 756-2098
www.ksrafm.com
ksraradio@ksrafm.com
License: Salmon, ID held by Salmon River Communications Inc.
Nat'l Network: ABC
Arbitron Metro Market: Salmon, ID; *Format:* Adult Contemp, Country *Special Programming:* Farm 4 hrs, class one hr wkly; *Hrs. of News Programming:* 4
Jim Hone, President
Rick Sessions, General Manager
Leo Marshall, General Sales Mgr
Todd Skeen, Programming Director
Rockwell Smith, Chief Engineer
Shirley Sullivan, Office Manager

KSRA-FM
09-01-1979; 92.7 MHz FM; *Hrs Open:* 6 AM-10 PM; 1.5 kw; -879 ft.; N45 11 2 W113 52 12
315 Riverfront Drive, Salmon, ID 83467 US
(208) 756-2218; *Fax:* (208) 756-2098
www.ksrafm.com
License: Salmon, Lemhi County, ID held by Salmon River Communications, Inc.
Nat'l Network: ABC
Arbitron Metro Market: Salmon, ID
Jim Hone, CEO
Rick Sessions, General Manager
Leo Marshall, General Sales Mgr
Todd Skeen, Programming Director
Todd Skeen, Promotions Manager
Shirley Sullivan, Office Manager

Sandpoint

KIBR
01-01-1994; 102.5 MHz FM; *Hrs Open:* 24; 6 kw; -344 ft.; N48 18 16 W116 32 32 *Rebroadcasts:* Rebroadcasts KICR(FM) Coeur d'Alene 100%
327 Marion Ave, Sandpoint, ID 83864 US
(208) 263-2179; *Fax:* (208) 265-5440
carolynp@953kpnd.com
License: Sandpoint, Bonner County, ID held by Benefield Broadcasting Inc.
Nat'l Network: ABC
Arbitron Metro Market: Sandpoint, ID; *Format:* Country; *No. News Employees:* 1; *Target Audience:* 25-54.
Dylan Benefield, General Manager
Jimmy Silver, Programming Director
Mike Brown, News Director

KPND
05-19-1980; 95.3 MHz FM; *Hrs Open:* 24; 56 kw; 2503 ft.; N48 4 44 W116 57 11
327 Marion Avenue, Sandpoint, ID 83864 US
(208) 263-2179; *Fax:* (208) 265-5440
carolynp@953kpnd.com
License: Sandpoint, Bonner County, ID
Arbitron Metro Market: Spokane, WA; *Format:* Triple A
Jim Tomchek, News Director

KSPT
03-23-1949; 1400 kHz AM; *Hrs Open:* 24; 1 kw-U, ND1; N48 18 16 W116 32 32 *Rebroadcasts:* Rebroadcasts KBFI(AM) Bonners Ferry 100%
327 Marion Avenue, Sandpoint, ID 83864 US
(208) 263-2179; *Fax:* (208) 265-5440
www.kspt.org.pl
carolynp@953kpnd.com
License: Sandpoint, ID held by Blue Sky Broadcasting Inc.
Nat'l Network: ABC; USA; *Nat'l Reps:* Tacher
Arbitron Metro Market: Sandpoint, ID; *Format:* News, News/Talk, 84, Talk *Special Programming:* Relg 2 hrs wkly; *Target Audience:* 25 plus.
Dylan Benefield, General Manager
Mike Davis, News Director
Conrad Agtee, Chief Engineer
Jim Tomchek, Traffic Manager

Shelley

KQEZ(FM)
10-01-1999; 106.3 MHz FM; *Hrs Open:* 24/7; 100 kw; 636 ft; N43 06 45 W112 29 34
1406 Commerce Way., Idaho Falls, ID 83401
(208) 524-5900; *Fax:* (208) 529-6927
www.ezrockradio.com
scott@richbroadcasting.com
License: Shelley, Bingham County, ID
Group Owner: Rich Broadcasting LLC; acq 10-6-98; $788,500 with KATW(FM) Lewiston).
Population Served: 80,000; *Arbitron Metro Market:* ID Falls, ID; *Format:* Classic Rock; *Target Audience:* 25-54; adults; *Adv. Rates:* 20; 20; 20; 12
Phil Jimenez, General Manager
Sandie Fulks, General Sales Mgr
JJ Jeffrey, Programming Director

Soda Springs

KBRV
09-22-1957; 800 kHz AM
81 S. Main, Soda Springs, ID 83276 US
(208) 547-2400; *Fax:* (208) 547-4593
License: Soda Springs, ID held by Caribou Broadcasting Inc.
Format: Country
Tom Mathis, General Manager

KITT
10-17-1983; 100.1 MHz FM; *Hrs Open:* 24; 3 kw horiz; -276 ft.; N42 38 30 W111 36 40
Mailing Address: 81 S. Main, Box 777, Soda Springs, ID 83276 US
Second Address: Box 1450, 210 North 1000 East, St. George, UT 84771
(208) 547-2500; *Fax:* (208) 547-4593
License: Soda Springs, Caribou County, ID held by Tri-State Media Corp.
Group Owner: Legacy Media Corporation; (acq 7-8-2004; $234,000)
Arbitron Metro Market: Soda Springs, ID; *Format:* Country *Special Programming:* CNN radio 10 hrs wkly; *No. News Employees:* 2; *Target Audience:* 18-35
E. Morgan Skinner, Jr, President
Lavon Randall, Operations Dir
Jeffrey Bate, General Sales Mgr

St. Anthony

KIGO
07-10-1966; 1420 kHz AM; *Hrs Open:* 24 *Rebroadcasts:* 96.7 FM
PO Box 17, St. Anthony, ID 83445 US
(208) 280-1962
License: St. Anthony, ID held by Albino Ortega & Maria Juarez
Arbitron Metro Market: Saint Anthony, ID; *Target Audience:* 17-44; adults
Albino Ortega, General Manager

St. Maries

KOFE
03-01-1970; 1240 kHz AM; *Hrs Open:* 24; 1 kw-D, ND1; 0.5 kw-N, ND1; N47 19 14 W116 32 50
12260 Nacogdoches Road, Suite 102, San Antonio, TX 78217 US
(208) 245-1240; *Fax:* (208) 245-6525
KOFE@sm-email.com
License: St. Maries, ID held by Campbell River Holding Co. L.L.C.
Nat'l Network: Fox News Radio
Format: Contemporary Hits/Top 40, Adult Contemp; *Hrs. of News Programming:* news progmg 9 hrs wkly; *No. News Employees:* 2; *Target Audience:* 25-55.
Theresa Plank, General Manager
Phil Plank, Engineering Dir

***KXJO**
92.1 MHz FM; 0.2 kw; 22 ft.; N47 20 8.4 W116 34 18.2 US
(509) 328-5729; *Fax:* (509) 328-5764
www.kpbx.org
kpbx@kpbx.org
License: St. Maries, Benewah County, ID held by College Creek Media LLC.
Group Owner: College Creek Media LLC
Arbitron Metro Market: Saint Maries, ID
Neal Robinson, President

Sun Valley

KECH-FM
11-21-1988; 95.3 MHz FM; *Hrs Open:* 24; 0.1 kw; 2169 ft.; N43 39 42 W114 24 7
Boy 2750, Halley, ID 83333 US
(208) 788-7118; *Fax:* (208) 788-7119
License: Sun Valley, Blaine County, ID held by RP Broadcasting Idaho LS LLC

Group Owner: Rich Broadcasting LLC; acq 7-30-2004; grpsl). *Arbitron Metro Market:* Hailey, ID; *Format:* Classic Rock *Special Programming:* Alternative 5 hrs, blues 8 hrs, jazz 6 hrs wkly; *Hrs. of News Programming:* news progmg 6 hrs wkly; *No. News Employees:* 1 *TargetAudience:* 25-54; upscale adults; *Adv. Rates:* 18; 15; 18; 6

Scott Anderson, General Manager
Cathy Nikolaisons, General Sales Mgr
Lenny Joseph, Programming Director
Dayle Ohlau, News Director

KSKI-FM
08-03-1977; 94.5 MHz FM; *Hrs Open:* 24; 2.5 kw; 582 meters; N43 38 37 W114 23 50
P.O. Box 2158, Ketchum, ID 83340 US
(208) 726-5324; *Fax:* (208) 726-5459
License: Sun Valley, Blaine County, ID held by RP Broadcasting Idaho LS LLC
Group Owner: Rich Broadcasting LLC; (acq 7-30-2004; grpsl). *Arbitron Metro Market:* Hailey, ID; *Format:* Alternative; *Hrs. of News Programming:* news progmg 2 hrs wkly; *No. News Employees:* 1; *Target Audience:* 18-49; affluent, upscale consumers; *Adv. Rates:* 18; 12; 18;6

Scott Anderson, General Manager
Cathy Nikolaisons, General Sales Mgr
Bob Thompson, Programming Director
Sue Bailey, News Director

***KWRV**
07-29-1993; 91.9 MHz FM; 0.1 kw; 2154 ft.; N43 39 41 W114 24 8
45 East 7th Street, Saint Paul, MN 55101 US
(218) 751-8864; *Fax:* (218) 751-8640
www.mpr.org
kbooth@mpr.org
License: Sun Valley, Blaine County, ID held by Minnesota Public Radio.
Nat'l Network: PRI; *Regional Network:* Minn. Pub. Radio
Arbitron Metro Market: Bemidji, MN; *Format:* Talk

William Kling, President

KYZK
107.5 MHz FM; *Hrs Open:* 24; 0.1 kw; 2169 ft.; N43 39 42 W114 24 7
4350 N. Fairfax Dr.#900, Arlington, VA 22203 US
(208) 726-5324; *Fax:* (208) 726-5459
License: Sun Valley, Blaine County, ID held by RP Broadcasting Idaho LS LLC
Group Owner: Rich Broadcasting LLC
Nat'l Network: ABC *Regional Reps:* Allied Radio
Arbitron Metro Market: Sun Valley, OD; *Format:* Jazz

Scott Anderson, General Manager
Cathy Nikolaisons, General Sales Mgr
Bob Thompson, Programming Director
Sue Bailey, News Director
Don Mussell, Engineering Dir

***KBSS**
08-01-2004; 91.1 MHz FM; 0.7 kw; 1870 ft.; N43 38 36 W114 23 49
1910 University Drive, Boise, ID 83725 US
(208) 426-3663; *Fax:* (208) 344-6631
boisestatepublicradio@boisestate.edu
License: Sun Valley, Blaine County, ID held by Idaho State Board of Education.
Nat'l Network: NPR
Arbitron Metro Market: Boise, ID; *Format:* News

Erik Jones, Operations Dir
John Hess, General Manager
Hy Kloc, General Sales Mgr
Ele Ellis, Programming Director
Sadie Babits, News Director
Tom Taylor, Engineering Dir
Betsy Micone, Business Director
Brad Campbell, OperationsManager
Aaron Kunz, EarthFix Environmental Reporter
Adam Cotterell, News Reporter
Adrienne Zachary, Marketing & Special Events Coordinator
Arthur Balinger, Producer/ Program Host

Troy

KQZB
01-01-2008; 100.5 MHz FM; 0.9 kw; 1,598 ft.; N46 48 42 W116 54 59
403 Capital St., Lewiston, ID 83501 US
(208) 743-6564
License: Troy, Latah County, ID held by Pacific Empire Radio Corp.
Group Owner: Pacific Empire Radio Corp.
Arbitron Metro Market: Lewiston, ID; *Format:* Country

Evan Yeoman, Operations Manager
Ben Bonfield, General Manager
Keith Warrick, Sales Manager
Leslie Gatherer, Traffic Manager

Twin Falls

***KAWZ**
04-13-1988; 89.9 MHz FM; *Hrs Open:* 24; 100 kw vert; 991 ft.; N42 43 47 W114 24 52
Mailing Address: 241 Main Ave., West, Twin Falls, ID 83303 US
Second Address: 4002 N. 3300 E., Twin Falls, ID 83301
(208) 734-6633; *Fax:* (208) 736-1958
www.csnradio.com
csn@csnradio.com
License: Twin Falls, Twin Falls County, ID held by Calvary Chapel of Twin Falls Inc.
Group Owner: CSN International
Arbitron Metro Market: Twin Falls, ID; *Format:* Christian; *Hrs. of News Programming:* News progmg 2 hrs wkly; *Target Audience:* General; 18-80

Mike Kestler, President
Don Mills, Operations Dir
Mike Stocklin, General Manager

***KBSW**
05-15-1989; 91.7 MHz FM; *Hrs Open:* 24; 4.5 kw; 492 ft.; N42 43 48 W114 25 6
1910 University Drive, Boise, ID 83725 US
(208) 426-3663; *Fax:* (208) 344-6631
radio.boisestate.edu
License: Twin Falls, Twin Falls County, ID held by Idaho State Board of Education.
Nat'l Network: PRI; NPR
Format: Talk; *Hrs. of News Programming:* news progmg 15 hrs wkly; *No. News Employees:* 2; *Target Audience:* General.

Erik Jones, Operations Dir
John Hess, General Manager
Hy Kloc, General Sales Mgr
Ele Ellis, Programming Director
Sadie Babits, News Director
Tom Taylor, Engineering Dir
Betsy Micone, Business Director
Brad Campbell, OperationsManager

***KCIR**
12-12-1982; 90.7 MHz FM; *Hrs Open:* 24; 44.1 kw; 2513 ft.; N42 20 7 W113 36 17 *Rebroadcasts:* Rebroadcasts KILA(FM) Las Vegas 97%
2201 S. Sixth St., Las Vegas, NV 89104 US
(208) 734-5777; *Fax:* (702) 731-1992
www.sosradio.net
scott@sosradio.net
License: Twin Falls, Twin Falls County, ID held by Faith Communications Corp.
Group Owner: Faith Communications Corp.; (acq 9-29-82)
Nat'l Network: USA
Arbitron Metro Market: Twin Falls, ID; *Format:* Christian *Special Programming:* Children 2 hrs wkly; *Hrs. of News Programming:* News progmg 5 hrs wkly; *Target Audience:* 25-49; adults with families

Brad Staley, President and General Manager
Duane Luchsinger, Station Manager
Scott Herrold, Programming Director
Tim Hunt, Network Director of Engineering
Gary Thompson, Creative Services Director
Mike Mead, Donor Relations
Marney Domeraski, Donor Relations
Dawn Vincent, Listener Services
Rick Hall, Music Director
Chris Staley, Vice-President of Programming & Administration

***KEFX**
01-01-1996; 88.9 MHz FM; 100 kw vert; 991 ft.; N42 43 47 W114 24 52
Mailing Address: P.O. Box 391, Twin Falls, ID 83303 US
Second Address: 4002 North 3300 East, Twin Falls, ID 83301
(208) 734-2049; *Fax:* (208) 736-1958
www.effectradio.com
License: Twin Falls, Twin Falls County, ID held by Calvary Chapel Of Twin Falls, Inc.
Group Owner: Effect Radio
Arbitron Metro Market: Twin Falls, ID; *Format:* Christian, Religious, 76

Mike Kestler, President
Daniel Davidson, Operations Dir
Jon Gibson, Program & Music Director
Kelly Carlson, Engineering Dir

***KEZJ**
01-01-1946; 1450 kHz AM; 1 kw-U, ND1; N42 32 36 W114 28 14 *Rebroadcasts:* Rebroadcasts KBSU(AM) Boise
315 Falls Avenue, P.O. Box 1238, Twin Falls, ID 83303 US
(208) 733-7512; *Fax:* (208) 736-2188
www.957kezj.com
bradweiser@townsquaremedia.com
License: Twin Falls, ID held by Townsquare Media Twin Falls License LLC
Group Owner: Townsquare Media
Arbitron Metro Market: Twin Falls, ID; *Format:* Jazz, News, 62, Talk

Janice Degner, General Manager
Amanda Miller, General Sales Mgr
Brad Weiser, Programming Director

KEZJ-FM
03-15-1977; 95.7 MHz FM; 100 kw; 650 ft.; N42 43 42 W114 24 48
Mailing Address: 50 East Rivercenter Blv, Covington, KY 41011 US
Second Address: 415 Park Ave., Twin Falls, ID 83301
(208) 733-7512; *Fax:* (208) 733-7525
www.957kezj.com
bradweiser@clearchannel.com
License: Twin Falls, Twin Falls County, ID held by GAP Broadcasting Twin Falls License LLC.
Group Owner: GAPWEST Broadcasting; (acq 2-13-2008; grpsl)
Nat'l Network: ABC; *Nat'l Reps:* Clear Channel; *Wire Services:* ABC; AP
Arbitron Metro Market: Twin Falls, ID; *Format:* Country; *Target Audience:* 25-54.

Janice Degner, Operations Dir
Janice Degner, General Manager
Amanda Miller, General Sales Mgr
Brad Weiser, Programming Director
James Tidmarsh, News Director
Kelly Klaas, Chief Engineer
Brad Weiser, Operations Director

KLIX
12-12-1946; 1310 kHz AM; *Hrs Open:* 24; 5 kw-D, DAN; 2.5 kw-N, DAN; N42 33 6 W114 22 3
50 East Rivercenter, Blvd., Suite 1200, Covington, KY 41011 US
(208) 733-1310; *Fax:* (208) 733-7525
www.newsradio1310.com
janicedegner@townsquaremedia.com
License: Twin Falls, ID held by Townsquare Media Twin Falls License LLC
Group Owner: Townsquare Media; (acq 2-13-2008; grpsl)
Nat'l Network: ABC
Arbitron Metro Market: Boise, ID; *Format:* News, News/Talk, 86 *Special Programming:* Farm 2 hrs wkly; *Hrs. of News Programming:* news progmg 12 hrs wkly; *No. News Employees:* 1; *Target Audience:* 35-54. *Adv.Rates:* 16; 22; 16; 10.

Janice Degner, General Manager
Brad Weiser, Brand Manager
Amanda Miller, Director Of Sales
Doc Holliday, Digital Managing Editor

KLIX-FM
06-15-1974; 96.5 MHz FM; 100 kw; 131 ft.; N42 33 5 W114 30 59
50 East Rivercenter Blvd, Covington, KY 41011 US
(208) 733-1310; *Fax:* (208) 733-7525
License: Twin Falls, Twin Falls County, ID held by Townsquare Media Twin Falls License LLC
Group Owner: Townsquare Media; (acq 2-13-2008; grpsl)
Arbitron Metro Market: Boise, ID; *Format:* Oldies; *Target Audience:* 18-49.

Janice Degner, General Manager
Nate Bird, Brand Manager
Amanda Miller, Director Of Sales
Doc Holliday, Digital Managing Editor

KSNQ
09-01-2004; 98.3 MHz FM; 100 kw; 650 ft.; N42 43 42 W114 24 48
9148 Bonita Beach Road, Suite 205, Bonita Springs, FL 34135 US
(208) 733-7512; *Fax:* (208) 733-7525
www.983thesnake.com
kendra@983thesnake.com
License: Twin Falls, Twin Falls County, ID held by Intermart Broadcasting Twin Falls Inc.
Arbitron Metro Market: Twin Falls, ID; *Format:* Classic Rock

Patricia Woods, Operations Dir
Janice Degner, General Manager
Kendra Wolfe, Brand Manager

KIRQ
01-01-2007; 102.1 MHz FM; 5.2 kw; 722 ft.; N42 43 54 W114 25 4
US

(208) 735-8300; *Fax:* (208) 733-4196
www.irock1021.com
License: Twin Falls, Twin Falls County, ID held by Locally Owned Radio LLC.
Group Owner: Locally Owned Radio LLC; (acq 9-8-2006; $2,911,000 with KTPZ(FM) Hazelton)
Arbitron Metro Market: Twin Falls, ID
Rocky Metts, President
Jerre Fender, Operations Dir
Deb Uvieu, General Sales Mgr
Tiffany Seeley, Programming Director
Denis Jeffs, News Director
Charlie Knapp, Vice President

Ucon

KZKY(FM)
104.5 MHz FM; 28 kw; Ant 656 ft; N44 10 35 W111 25 51
980 N. Michigan Ave., Suite 1880, Chicago, IL 60611
(312) 204-9900
License: Ucon, Fremont County, ID held by Rich Broadcasting Idaho LS, LLC
Group Owner: Rich Broadcasting LLC
Population Served: 1,117; *Arbitron Metro Market:* Ashton, ID
Bruce Buzil, General Manager

Victor

KVRG
05-01-2005; 103.7 MHz FM; 0.821 kw; 1086 ft.; N43 29 27 W110 57 16
7901 Stoneridge Drive, Cheyenne, WY 82009 US
(307) 732-0384
www.1037therange.com
info@1037therange.com
License: Victor, Teton County, ID held by Jackson Radio Group Inc.
Group Owner: Northeast Broadcasting Company Inc.; (acq 3-31-2006; $900,000 with KRVQ(FM) Victor)
Arbitron Metro Market: Victor, ID; *Format:* Country
Steven Silberberg, President
Bruce Pollock, General Manager

Wallace

***KTWD**
12-01-2000; 103.5 MHz FM; *Hrs Open:* 24; 1.6 kw; 2215 ft.; N47 33 49 W115 50 1
35200 Cathedral Canyon Dr, Suite G53, Cathedral City, CA 92234 US
(714) 545-7868; *Fax:* (509) 244-2232
ktwd.krtmradio.org
License: Wallace, Shoshone County, ID held by Penfold Communications, Inc.
Group Owner: Penfold Communications, Inc.; (acq 2-24-2000; $50,000 for CP)
Format: Christian, Religious

KWAL
05-01-1938; 620 kHz AM; *Hrs Open:* 24; 1 kw-D, DAN; 1 kw-N, DAN; N47 30 29 W116 0 17
P.O. Box U, Osburn, ID 83849 US
(208) 752-1141(208) 752-1142; *Fax:* (208) 753-5111
kwalradio@usamedia.tv
License: Wallace, ID held by Silver Valley Broadcasters Inc.
Nat'l Network: Jones Radio Networks
Arbitron Metro Market: Wallace, ID; *Format:* Country
Paul Robinson, President
Paul Robinson, General Manager
George White, General Sales Mgr
John Davis, Programming Director

Weiser

KTRP
1260 kHz AM
2001 Penn Ave. NW, Fisher, Wayland Et Al, Washington, DC 20006 US
(208) 367-1859
www.ktrpradio.com
License: Weiser, ID held by JNE Investments Inc.
Arbitron Metro Market: Weiser, ID; *Format:* Talk

Wendell

KTFI
10-01-1928; 1340 kHz AM
Mailing Address: US
Second Address: 21361 Hwy 30, Twin Falls, ID 83301
(208) 735-8300; *Fax:* (208) 733-4196
License: Wendell, ID held by Locally Owned Radio LLC.
Group Owner: Locally Owned Radio LLC; (acq 10-31-2003; grpsl)
Format: Oldies *Special Programming:* Farm 3 hrs, relg 5 hrs, sports 3 hrs wkly; *Target Audience:* 35 plus.
Larry Johnson, President
Jerre Fender, Operations Dir
Deb Uvieu, General Sales Mgr
Denis Jeffs, News Director

Weston

KLZX
01-01-2001; 95.9 MHz FM; 25 kw; 217 ft.; N41 52 18 W111 48 31
2001 Pennsylvania Ave NW, Suite 400, Washington, DC 22206 US
(435) 752-5141; *Fax:* (435) 752-1392
www.klzxfm.com
will@cvradio.com
License: Weston, Franklin County, ID held by Sun Valley Radio Inc.
Group Owner: Sun Valley Radio Inc.
Arbitron Metro Market: Logan, UT; *Format:* Classic Rock
Lynn Simmons, General Manager
James Murdock, Sales Manager
Will Wheelwright, Programming Director

Illinois

Albion

***WBJW**
12-01-1997; 91.7 MHz FM; 1.7 kw; 499 ft.; N38 19 14 W88 2 37
Rebroadcasts: Rebroadcasts WBGW(FM) Fort Branch,
P O Box 4164, Evansville, IN 47724 US
(800)264-5550; *Fax:* (812) 768-5552
www.thyword.org
mail@thyword.org
License: Albion, Edwards County, IL held by Music Ministries Inc.
Arbitron Metro Market: Evansville,IN; *Format:* Religious
Floyd Turner, General Manager

Aledo

WRMJ
06-12-1979; 102.3 MHz FM; *Hrs Open:* 24; 3 kw; 299 ft.; N41 12 29 W90 48 10
P.O. Box 187, Aledo, IL 61231 US
(309) 582-5666; *Fax:* (309) 582-5667
wrmj.com
contactus@wrmj.com
License: Aledo, Mercer County, IL held by Western Illinois Broadcasting Co.
Regional Network: Brownfield
Arbitron Metro Market: Quad Cities, IA-IL (Davenport-Rock Island-Moline); *Format:* Country, News *Special Programming:* Relg 3 hrs wkly; *Hrs. of News Programming:* news progmg 20 hrs wkly; *No. News Employees:* 1 *Target Audience:* 25-54.; *Adv. Rates:* 11; 7; 7; 7
John Hoscheidt, General Manager
Judy Bedford, General Sales Mgr
Terry Tracy, Programming Director
Jim Taylor, News Director

Alton

WBGZ
01-01-1948; 1570 kHz AM; *Hrs Open:* 24; 1 kw-D, ND1; 0.074 kw-N, ND1; N38 55 44 W90 13 3
P.O. Box 615, Alton, IL 62002 US
(618) 465-1570; *Fax:* (618) 465-3546
www.wbgzradio.com
wbgz@wbgzradio.com
License: Alton, IL held by Metroplex Communications Inc.
Nat'l Network: USA
Arbitron Metro Market: St. Louis, MO; *Format:* News, News/Talk, 86 *Special Programming:* Gospel 4 hrs, relg 3 hrs wkly; *Hrs. of News Programming:* news progmg 20 hrs wkly; *No. News Employees:* 2; *Target Audience:* General.
Sam Stemm, General Manager
Nancy Bivens, Director of Sales
Mark Ellebracht, News Director
Mark Hilgert, Office Manager
Brent Burklund, Sports Director

Anna

WIBH
01-10-1957; 1440 kHz AM; *Hrs Open:* 24; 0.5 kw-D, ND1; 0.109 kw-N, ND1; N37 26 45 W89 15 0
330 South Main, Anna, IL 62906 US
(618) 833-9424; *Fax:* (618) 833-9091
www.wibhradio.com
License: Anna, IL held by WIBH Inc.
Wire Services: UPI
Format: Country; *Hrs. of News Programming:* news progmg 3 hrs wkly; *No. News Employees:* 1; *Target Audience:* 25-69.; *Adv. Rates:* 12; 12; 12; 11
Ronald Ellis, President
Maury Bass, Operations Dir
Maurice Bass, Programming Director

WKIB
01-13-1958; 96.5 MHz FM; *Hrs Open:* 24; 22 kw; 748 ft.; N37 21 44 W89 31 19
6120 Waldo Church Rd., Metropolis, IL 62960 US
(573) 339-7000; *Fax:* (573) 651-4100
www.mix965.net
License: Anna, Union County, IL held by W. Russell Withers Jr.
Group Owner: Withers Broadcasting Co.; (acq 10-22-2001; $2 million)
Nat'l Reps: Katz Radio
Format: Contemporary Hits/Top 40; *Hrs. of News Programming:* news progmg 10 hrs wkly; *No. News Employees:* 1; *Target Audience:* 18-45.
Rick Lambert, General Manager
Steve Thomas, Programming Director

Arcola

WKIO
12-19-1974; 107.9 MHz FM; *Hrs Open:* 24; 3.6 kw horiz, 3 kw vert; 427 ft.; N39 52 43 W88 11 51
206 South Willow, P.O. Box 988, Effingham, IL 62401 US
(217) 258-6060; *Fax:* (217) 258-6077
www.urock1079.com
License: Arcola, Moultrie County, IL held by Champaign Partners LLC
Arbitron Metro Market: Champaign, IL; *Format:* Christian; *Hrs. of News Programming:* news progmg 10 hrs wkly; *No. News Employees:* 1; *Target Audience:* 25-54.
Shirley Browning, General Manager

Arlington Heights

WCPY
12-17-1961; 92.7 MHz FM; *Hrs Open:* 24; 1.8 kW; 381 ft.; N42 08 14 W87 58 57
6020 W Higgins Ave, Chicago, IL 60630 USA
(773) 888-5152
polski.fm
info@polski.fm
License: Arlington Heights, IL held by WKIE Inc.
Group Owner: Newsweb Corp.; (acq 11-15-2004; grpsl)
Nat'l Network: CNN Radio
Arbitron Metro Market: Chicago, IL; *Format:* Polish

***WCLR**
11-01-2003; 88.3 MHz FM; *Hrs Open:* 24; 0.001 kw horiz, 1 kw vert; 59 ft.; N42 6 45 W87 58 58
502 West Euclid Avenue, Arlington Hiehgts, IL 60004 US
(888) 937-2471; *Fax:* (916) 251-1650
www.air1.com
info@air1.com
License: Arlington Heights, Cook County, IL held by Educational Media Foundation.
Group Owner: EMF Broadcasting; (acq 8-13-03).
Nat'l Network: Air 1
Arbitron Metro Market: Omaha, NE; *Format:* Alternative, Christian; *No. News Employees:* 3; *Target Audience:* 18-35; Judeo Christian, female
Darrell Chambliss, Chairman
Mike Novak, President & CEO
Ed Lenane, News Director
Sam Wallington, Engineering Dir
Marya Morgan, News Reporter
Richard Hunt, News Reporter
David R. Ferry, Director
Walter Golembeski, Director
David Pierce, Chief Creative Officer
Alan Mason, Chief Operating Officer

Assumption

WTIM
08-01-2014; 870 kHz AM; 0.5 kw, DAD; 374 ft.; N39 29 14 W88 57 31
Mailing Address: 918 East Park St, P.O. Box 169, Taylorville, IL 62568 US
Second Address: , Taylorville, IL 62568
(217) 824-3395; *Fax:* (217) 824-3301
taylorvilledailynews.com/wtim

License: Assumption, Christian County, IL held by Miller Communications Inc.
Group Owner: Miller Media Group
Nat'l Network: CNN Radio; CBS News; CBS Sports
Arbitron Metro Market: Davenport-Rock Island-Moline; *Format:* News, News/Talk, 86 *Special Programming:* Farm 20 hrs, relg 4 hrs wkly; *Hrs. of News Programming:* news progmg 25 hrs wkly; *No. News Employees:* 1 *Target Audience:* 35+
Randal Miller, President

Atlanta

WLCN
04-13-2001; 96.3 MHz FM; *Hrs Open:* 24; 6 kw; 266 ft.; N40 14 39 W89 15 51
PO Box 505, Atlanta, IL 61723 US
(217) 648-5510; *Fax:* (217) 648-2499
www.lincolncountry.com
lincolncountry@yahoo.com
License: Atlanta, Logan County, IL held by KM Radio of Atlanta, LLC.
Group Owner: KM Communications Inc.
Nat'l Network: ABC; *Wire Services:* AP; Metro Weather Service Inc.
Arbitron Metro Market: Atlanta, IL; *Format:* Country; *Target Audience:* 25-54.; *Adv. Rates:* 180; 180; 180; 180
Myoung Hwa Bae, President

Aurora

WBIG
12-13-1938; 1280 kHz AM; *Hrs Open:* 24; 1 kW; N41 46 10 W88 14 44
5500 Poplar Ave, Suite 1, Memphis, TN 38119 USA
(901) 685-3993; *Fax:* (901) 685-3995
www.wbig1280.com
whpollack@gmail.com
License: Aurora, IL held by Auril Broadcasting Co.
Group Owner: Pollack Broadcasting; 2016
Nat'l Network: Fox Sports
Arbitron Metro Market: Aurora-Chicago, IL; *Format:* Sports, Religious, 86 *Special Programming:* The Big Radio Shopping Show; *Hrs. of News Programming:* news progmg 10 hrs wkly; *No. News Employees:* 1 *TargetAudience:* 25-54; professional, upscale, suburbanites with children

WERV-FM
02-12-1961; 95.9 MHz FM; 2.85 kw; 338 ft.; N41 46 9 W88 16 2
1884 Plains Avenue, Aurora, IL 60307 US
(630) 898-1580; *Fax:* (630) 898-2463
License: Aurora, Du Page County, IL held by NM Licensing LLC.
Group Owner: NextMedia Group Inc.; (acq 11-26-2001; grpsl).
Nat'l Reps: McGavren Guild
Arbitron Metro Market: Chicago, IL; *Format:* Contemporary Hits/Top 40, Adult Contemp; *Hrs. of News Programming:* news progmg 5 hrs wkly; *No. News Employees:* 1; *Target Audience:* 25-54; suburban Chicago adults *Adv. Rates:* 50; 45; 50; 30
Brian Foster, General Manager

WLEY-FM
01-01-1965; 107.9 MHz FM; *Hrs Open:* 24; 21 kw; 761 ft.; N41 56 1 W88 4 23
3191 Coral Way, Suite 805, Miami, FL 33145 US
(312) 920-9500; *Fax:* (312) 920-9516
www.laley1079.com
info@laley1079.com
License: Aurora, Du Page County, IL held by WLEY Licensing Inc.
Group Owner: Spanish Broadcasting System Inc.; (acq 12-26-96; $33 million)
Arbitron Metro Market: Chicago, IL; *No. News Employees:* 1; *Target Audience:* 25-54.
Jeff Delgado, General Sales Mgr
Elena Castro, Promotions & Marketing Director
Sam Palerno, Chief Engineer

Ava

WXAN
01-11-1982; 103.9 MHz FM; *Hrs Open:* 24; 2.9 kw; 469 ft.; N37 51 19 W89 28 6
9077 Ava Road, Ava, IL 62907 US
(618) 426-3308; *Fax:* (618) 426-3310
www.mysoutherngospel.net
billmac@egyptian.netÿ
License: Ava, Jackson County, IL held by Southern Gospetality LLC.
Nat'l Network: Salem Radio Network
Arbitron Metro Market: Ava, IL; *Format:* Gospel, Religious; *Hrs. of News Programming:* News progmg 10 hrs wkly; *Target Audience:* 30-55; Christians & family-oriented listeners; *Adv. Rates:* 12; 12; 12; 12.

Harold Lawder, President
Will Stephens, General Manager
Bill McCarty, Lead Account Representative
Tish Brooks, Radio Jockey

Bartonville

WWCT
02-01-1997; 99.9 MHz FM; *Hrs Open:* 24; 1.5 kw; 584 ft.; N40 36 23 W89 32 20
P.O. Box 150846, Nashville, TN 37215 US
(309) 686-0101; *Fax:* (309) 686-0111
License: Bartonville, Peoria County, IL held by IM IL Licenses LLC.
Group Owner: Independence Media Holdings LLC; (acq 9-19-2006; grpsl)
Arbitron Metro Market: Peoria, IL; *Adv. Rates:* 30; 25; 30; 10
David Manning, General Manager
Jason Stuckwisch, General Sales Mgr
Gabe Reynolds, Programming Director

Beardstown

WRMS
11-01-1959; 790 kHz AM
108 East Main Street, Beardstown, IL 62618 US
(314) 752-7000
covenantnetwork@juno.com
License: Beardstown, IL held by Covenant Network.
Group Owner: Covenant Network; (acq 7-28-2004)
Format: Christian, Religious
Tony Holman, President
Jim Schaper, Programming Director

WRMS-FM
01-01-1976; 94.3 MHz FM; 6 kw; 299 ft.; N40 4 45 W90 25 58
108 East Main Street, Beardstown, IL 62618 US
(217) 323-1790; *Fax:* (217) 323-1705
wrmsfm@casscomm.com
License: Beardstown, Cass County, IL held by Conner Family Broadcasting Inc.
Format: Country
John Conner, General Manager
Glen Hopkins, Chief Engineer

Belleville

WSDZ
07-13-1947; 1260 kHz AM; *Hrs Open:* 24
77 W 66th St., 16th Fl., New York, NY 10023-6201 USA
(314) 428-4023; *Fax:* (314) 428-9119
www.radiodisney.com
License: Belleville, IL held by Radio Disney Group LLC
Group Owner: Disney Channels Worldwide; Sale to Salem Media Group pending
Nat'l Network: Radio Disney
Arbitron Metro Market: St. Louis, MO; *Format:* Contemporary Hits/Top 40 *Special Programming:* Caring is Cool 30 min wkly; *Target Audience:* 25-54 plus; 6-14; affluent, well-educated, business & professional Kids
Gary Marsh, President & Chief Creative Officer

Belvidere

WXRX
02-27-1971; 104.9 MHz FM; 4 kW; 400 ft.; N42 19 21 W88 57 14
2830 Sandy Hollow Rd, Rockford, IL 61108 USA
(815) 874-7861; *Fax:* (815) 874-2202
www.wxrx.com
License: Belvidere, Boone County, IL held by Mid-Way Radio, Inc.
Group Owner: Mid-West Family Broadcasting
Arbitron Metro Market: Rockford, IL; *Format:* Rock/AOR; *Target Audience:* 18-49.

Benton

WQRL
10-01-1973; 106.3 MHz FM; *Hrs Open:* 24; 12.5 kw; 459 ft.; N37 55 51 W88 40 52
Mailing Address: P.O. 818, Benton, IL 62812 US
Second Address: 303 N. Main St., Benton, IL 62812
(618) 435-8100; *Fax:* (618) 435-8102
wwqrlfm@shawneelink.net
License: Benton, Franklin County, IL held by Dana Communications Corp.
Arbitron Metro Market: Marion-Carbondale (Southern Illinois); *Format:* Oldies *Special Programming:* Farm 3 hrs wkly; *Hrs. of News Programming:* news progmg 15 hrs wkly; *No. News Employees:* 2 *Target Audience:* 25-49; adults & young adults preferring new country

Dana Withers, CEO
Gloria Holland, Station Manager
Jeff Oestreich, Chief Engineer
Bleu Withers, Executive Vice President

Berwyn

WVON
10-07-2003; 1690 kHz AM
111 East Kibourn Avenue, Suite 2700, Milwaukee, WI 53202 US
(773) 247-6200; *Fax:* (773) 247-5336
www.wvon.com
info@wvon.com
License: Berwyn, IL held by CC Licenses LLC.
Group Owner: iHeartMedia; (acq 1-18-2001)
Nat'l Network: ABC
Arbitron Metro Market: Chicago, IL; *Format:* Talk; *Target Audience:* 25-54; urban talk listeners
Melody Spann-Cooper, General Manager

Bethalto

WFUN-FM
04-01-1991; 95.5 MHz FM; *Hrs Open:* 24; 24.5 kw; 335 ft.; N38 48 38 W90 17 38
9666 Olive Blvd., Suite 610, St. Louis, MO 63132 US
(314) 989-9550; *Fax:* (314) 989-9551
www.oldschool955.com
License: Bethalto, Madison County, IL held by Radio One Licenses LLC.
Group Owner: Radio One Inc.; (acq 11-8-01; grpsl).
Arbitron Metro Market: St. Louis, MO; *Format:* Oldies; *Hrs. of News Programming:* News progmg 2 hrs wkly; *Target Audience:* General; families
Boogie D, Operations Mgr/Program Dir.
Gary Gunter, General Manager
Nate Dixon, General Sales Mgr
Gary Benett, Chief Engineer

Bloomington

WBNQ
01-01-1947; 101.5 MHz FM; 50 kw; 466 ft.; N40 27 1 W89 0 42
236 Greenwood Ave., Bloomington, IL 61704 US
(309) 829-1221
www.wbnq.com
License: Bloomington, IL held by Cumulus Licensing LLC
Group Owner: Cumulus Media Inc.
Arbitron Metro Market: Bloomington, IL; *Format:* Contemporary Hits/Top 40
Paula Williams, Sales Director
Brian Davis, Programming Director
Brandi McCarrey, Promotions Manager
Cody West, Music Director

*WESN
01-01-1972; 88.1 MHz FM; 0.12 kw; 98 ft.; N40 29 28 W88 59 37
P. O. Box 2900, Bloomington, IL 61701 US
(309) 556-2638; *Fax:* (309) 556-2949
www.wesn.org
wesn@iwu.edu
License: Bloomington, McLean County, IL held by Illinois Wesleyan University.
Nat'l Network: PRI
Arbitron Metro Market: Bloomington, IL; *Format:* Variety/Diverse
Special Programming: Black 18 hrs, class 6 hrs, jazz 6 hrs wkly
Patrick Nevels, Station Manager
Darek Jakubowski, Programming Director
Michael Kocourek, Promotions Manager
Al Maiocco, Technical Director
Patrick Cavanaugh, Music Director
Matt Siegert, Sports Director
Matt Siegert, SportsDirector
Sen "Jules" Wang, Assistant music director
Mike Kistner, Local show director
Rick Lindquist, Advisor

WJBC
05-01-1925; 1230 kHz AM; 1 kw-U, ND1; N40 27 1 W89 0 42
236 Greenwood Ave., Bloomington, IL 61704 US
(309) 829-1221
www.wjbc.com
talk@wjbc.com
License: Bloomington, IL held by Cumuls Licensing LLC
Group Owner: Cumulus Media Inc.; (acq 5-12-2004; grpsl)
Nat'l Reps: McGavren Guild
Arbitron Metro Market: Bloomington, IL; *Format:* News/Talk
Paula Williams, Director of Sales
Tim Lewis, Programming Director
Laura Ewan, Promotions Manager

***WJWR**
90.3 MHz FM; 18 kw; 327 ft.; N40 40 59.3 W88 45 43
Rr4, Box 184, Bloomington, IL 61704 US
(309) 963-4932
License: Bloomington, McLean County, IL held by Bloomington Normal Broadcasting Corp.
Arbitron Metro Market: Bloomington, IL
Jacqueline Dearing, President

Bluford

***WVYN**
90.9 MHz FM; 11 kw; 210 ft.; N38 13 10 W88 37 47 US
(618) 895-3030
www.wvyn.org
License: Bluford, Jefferson County, IL held by Real Life Radio Foundation Inc.
Arbitron Metro Market: Bluford, IL
Randall Lee Olson, President

Breese

WDLJ
01-01-2003; 97.5 MHz FM; 2.5 kw; 512 ft.; N38 36 33 W89 23 35
16808 Old Hwy 50, Carlyle, IL 62231 US
(618) 594-2620; *Fax:* (618) 594-2659
www.wdlj.com
License: Breese, Clinton County, IL held by KM Radio of Breese, LLC.
Group Owner: KM Communications Inc.
Arbitron Metro Market: Carlyle, IL; *Format:* Classic Rock
Bruce Loyd, General Manager
Roxanne Gillespie, Promotions Manager

Brookport

WRIK
10-01-1987; 750 kHz AM; 0.5 kw-D, NDD; N37 8 31 W88 38 58
6120 Waldo Church Road, Metropolis, IL 62960 US
Fax: (618) 564-3202
License: Brookport, IL held by Daniel S. Stratemeyer
Format: Talk
Samuel Stratemeyer, General Manager

Bushnell

WLMD
08-01-1992; 104.7 MHz FM; *Hrs Open:* 24; 3.3 kw; 377 ft.; N40 32 45 W90 29 15
P.O. Box 250, Macomb, IL 61455 US
(309) 833-5561; *Fax:* (309) 833-3460
www.radiomacomb.com
wlmd@macomb.com
License: Bushnell, McDonough County, IL held by Virden Broadcasting Corp.
Group Owner: Regional Media, A Virden Broadcasting Company; (acq 12-27-99; grpsl)
Nat'l Network: ABC; Jones Radio Networks; *Regional Network:* Brownfield; Ill. Radio Net.
Format: Country *Special Programming:* Farm 3 hrs wkly; *Hrs. of News Programming:* news progmg 2 hrs wkly; *No. News Employees:* 1; *Target Audience:* 25-54; general; *Adv. Rates:* 10; 10; 10; na
Vanessa Wetterling, Station Manager
Mike Weaver, Programming Director

Cairo

***WBEL**
01-01-2002; 88.5 MHz FM; 64 kw vert; 558 ft.; N36 59 32 W88 59 19
P.O. Box 3206, Tupelo, MS 38803 US
(662) 844-8888; *Fax:* (662) 842-6791
www.afr.net
faq@afa.net
License: Cairo, Alexander County, IL held by American Family Association.
Group Owner: American Family Radio
Arbitron Metro Market: Barling AR; *Format:* Religious
Tim Wildmon, President
Donald Wildmon, Founder
Buddy Smith, Sr VP
Ed Vitagliano, Exec VP
Randy Sharp, Director Of Special Projects
Meeke Addison, Director Of Communications
Abraham Hamilton III, General Counsel

WKRO
01-08-1942; 1490 kHz AM; *Hrs Open:* 24; 1 kw-U, ND1; N37 2 36 W89 11 2
Rural Route #1 Box 124, Thebes, IL 62990 US
(618) 734-1490; *Fax:* (618) 734-0884
djman75@hotmail.com
License: Cairo, IL held by Alexander Broadcasting Corp.
Nat'l Network: ABC
Format: Adult Contemp *Special Programming:* Gospel 12 hrs, farm 12 hrs wkly; *Hrs. of News Programming:* news progmg 12 hrs wkly; *No. News Employees:* 1; *Target Audience:* 25-54; general; *Adv. Rates:* 8.50;8.50; 8.50; 8.50
Danny McDonald, General Manager
Marti Nicholson, General Sales Mgr

Cambridge

KQCJ
08-30-2016; 93.9 MHz FM; *Hrs Open:* 24; 4.2 kw; 394 ft.; N41 22 56 W90 10 47
3815 N. Brady St, Davenport, IA 52806 US
(309) 798-4148
www.regionalmedia.info/page/rewind-93-9-wyec/
License: Cambridge, Henry County, IL held by Virden Broadcasting Corp.
Group Owner: Regional Media, A Virden Broadcasting Corporation; (acq. 11-30-2015 for $725,000)
Nat'l Network: CNN Radio; Fox News; *Regional Network:* RFD Illinois; Tom Kent Radio Network
Arbitron Metro Market: Davenport-Rock Island-Moline; *Format:* Adult Contemp; *Target Audience:* 25-64.
Fletcher M. Ford, President
Will Stevenson, News Director

Canton

WBYS
10-05-1947; 1560 kHz AM; *Hrs Open:* 6 AM-sunset
1000 East Linn St., Canton, IL 61520 US
(309) 647-1560; *Fax:* (309) 647-1563
www.1560wbys.com
wbysradio@yahoo.com
License: Canton, IL held by WPW Broadcasting Inc.
Group Owner: Prairie Radio Communications; (acq 1999; $210,000 for stock with co-located FM)
Nat'l Network: ABC
Arbitron Metro Market: Canton, IL; *Format:* News/Talk *Special Programming:* Farm 10 hrs wkly; *Hrs. of News Programming:* news progmg 25 hrs wkly; *No. News Employees:* 1; *Target Audience:* 30 plus;community-oriented with above average income; *Adv. Rates:* 13; 9; 11; 5
Don Tharp, General Manager
Vicki Kuzniar, General Sales Mgr

WCDD
10-07-1968; 107.9 MHz FM; *Hrs Open:* 24; 25 kw; 269 ft.; N40 32 40.5 W90 1 15.5
1000 East Linn St., Canton, IL 61520 US
(309) 647-1560; *Fax:* (309) 647-1563
www.1560wbys.com
wbysradio@yahoo.com
License: Canton, Fulton County, IL held by WPW Broadcasting, Inc.
Group Owner: Prairie Radio Communications
Nat'l Network: ABC
Arbitron Metro Market: Canton, IL; *Format:* Country *Special Programming:* High School Sports; *Hrs. of News Programming:* news progmg 10 hrs wkly; *No. News Employees:* 1; *Target Audience:* 35-54; males *Adv.Rates:* 15; 11; 13; 9
Don Tharp, General Manager

Carbondale

WCIL
11-14-1946; 1020 kHz AM; *Hrs Open:* Sunrise-sunset; 1 kw-D, NDD; N37 43 31 W89 15 25 *Rebroadcasts:* Rebroadcasts WJPF(AM) Herrin 100%
900 Laskin Rd., Virginia Beach, VA 23451 US
(618) 985-4843; *Fax:* (618) 985-6529
www.wjpf.com
License: Carbondale, Jackson County, IL held by MRR License LLC.
Group Owner: MAX Media L.L.C.; (acq 3-29-2004; grpsl).
Nat'l Reps: Christal
Arbitron Metro Market: Marion-Carbondale, IL; *Format:* News, News/Talk, 84, Talk *Special Programming:* Farm one hr wkly; *Hrs. of News Programming:* news progmg 10 hrs wkly; *No. News Employees:* 2; *Target Audience:* 35 plus.
Steve Falat, General Manager/Market Manager
Kim Debose, Sales Manager
Tom Miller, Programming Director
Michael Roberts, News Director
Bob Romonosky, Chief Engineer
Mike Murphy, Sports Director

WCIL-FM
07-01-1968; 101.5 MHz FM; *Hrs Open:* 24; 28.5 kw; 653 ft.; N37 42 4 W89 22 18
1431 Country Aire Dr., Carterville, IL 62918 US
(618) 985-4843; *Fax:* (618) 985-6529
www.cilfm.com
License: Carbondale, Jackson County, IL held by MRR License LLC
Group Owner: MAX Media L.L.C.
Nat'l Reps: Christal
Arbitron Metro Market: Marion-Carbondale, IL; *Format:* Contemporary Hits/Top 40; *Target Audience:* 18-34; adult females
Tom Miller, Operations Manager
Steve Falat, General Manager/Market Manager
Kim Debose, Sales Manager
Bob Romonosky, Chief Engineer

***WDBX**
02-01-1996; 91.1 MHz FM; *Hrs Open:* 7 AM-4 AM; 3 kw; 131 ft.; N37 43 43 W89 12 57
100 East Jackson Street, Carbondale, IL 62901 US
(618) 457-3691(618) 529-5900
www.wdbx.org
wdbx911@yahoo.com
License: Carbondale, Jackson County, IL held by Heterodyne Broadcasting Co.
Arbitron Metro Market: Marion-Carbondale, IL; *Format:* Variety/Diverse; *Hrs. of News Programming:* News progmg 2.5 hrs wkly; *Adv. Rates:* 5; 5; 5; 5
John Hochheimer, Chairman
Francis Murphy, President
Brian Powell, Station Manager

***WSIU**
09-15-1958; 91.9 MHz FM; *Hrs Open:* 24; 50 kw; 299 ft.; N37 42 29 W89 14 5 *Rebroadcasts:* Rebroadcasts WUSI(FM) Olney 100%, WVSI(FM) Mt. Venon 100%
Radio Station Wsiu, Carbondale, IL 62901 US
(618) 453-4343; *Fax:* (618) 453-6186
wsiu.org
jeff.williams@wsiu.org
License: Carbondale, Jackson County, IL held by Board of Trustees Southern Illinois University.
Nat'l Network: NPR; PRI; *Regional Network:* Ill. Radio Net.; *Wire Services:* AP
Arbitron Metro Market: Marion-Carbonda *TV Affiliate:* *WSIU-TV affil *Special Programming:* New age 4 hrs, big band 4 hrs, folk 3 hrs wkly; *Hrs. of News Programming:* news progmg 36 hrs wkly; *No. News Employees:* 3 *Target Audience:* 35-64; highly educated, upper income, socially conscious
Greg Petrowich, CEO
Jeff Williams, General Manager
Renee Dillard, General Sales Mgr
Mike Zelten, Programming Director
Terry Harvey, Chief Engineer
Delores Kerstein, CFO

Carlinville

***WIBI**
09-30-1975; 91.1 MHz FM; *Hrs Open:* 24; 50 kw; 476 ft.; N39 20 58 W89 48 16
P.O. Box 140, Carlinville, IL 62626 US
(217) 854-4800; *Fax:* (217) 854-4810
www.wibi.org
wibi@wibi.org
License: Carlinville, Macoupin County, IL held by Illinois Bible Institute Inc.
Group Owner: Illinois Bible Institute Inc.
Format: Adult Contemp, Christian; *Target Audience:* 25-49.
Barry Copeland, General Manager
Jeremiah Beck, Station Manager
Rob Regal, Programming Director
Jessica Barton, Promotions Manager
Sally Braundmeier, News Director
Joe Buchanan, Music Director
Liz Eilers, Underwriting Director

***WOLG**
12-08-1990; 95.9 MHz FM; 6 kw; 325 ft.; N39 14 25 W89 54 27
9 Cougar Road, Glen Carbon, IL 62034 US
(314) 752-7000
http://www.covenantnet.net/
covenantnetwork@juno.com
License: Carlinville, Macoupin County, IL held by Covenant Network.
Group Owner: Covenant Network; (acq 8-10-98; $300,000)
TV Affiliate: Relg

***WTSG**
08-11-1997; 90.1 MHz FM; *Hrs Open:* 24; 5 kw; 295 ft.; N39 20 58 W89 48 16
Box 140, Carlinville, IL 62626 US
(217) 854-4651; *Fax:* (217) 854-4610
www.wtsg.org
wibi@wibi.org
License: Carlinville, Macoupin County, IL held by Illinois Bible Institute Inc.
Group Owner: Illinois Bible Institute Inc.
Arbitron Metro Market: Carlinville, IL; *Format:* Gospel, Religious; *Target Audience:* 25-44.; *Adv. Rates:* 5; 5; 5; 5
Barry Copeland, General Manager
Jeremiah Beck, Station Manager
Rob Regal, Programming Director
Jessica Barton, Promotions Manager
Sally Braundmeier, News Director
Joe Buchanan, Music Director
Liz Eilers, Underwriting Director

Carmi

WROY
12-13-1948; 1460 kHz AM; *Hrs Open:* 24; 1 kw-D, ND1; 0.085 kw-N, ND1; N38 4 54 W88 12 4
101 North Church Street, Carmi, IL 62821 US
(618) 382-4161; *Fax:* (618) 382-4162
www.wrul.com
wroy1460@verizon.net
License: Carmi, IL held by W. Russell Withers Jr.
Group Owner: Withers Broadcasting Co.
Format: Oldies *Special Programming:* Farm 6 hrs wkly; *Hrs. of News Programming:* news progmg 25 hrs wkly; *No. News Employees:* 2; *Target Audience:* 35 plus; general; *Adv. Rates:* 16; 15; 16; 12
George Hinds, General Manager
Bill Perry Sr., Station Manager

WRUL
01-01-1951; 97.3 MHz FM; *Hrs Open:* 24; 50 kw; 489 ft.; N38 4 54 W88 12 4
101 North Church Street, Carmi, IL 62821 US
(618) 382-4161; *Fax:* (618) 382-4162
www.wrul.com
wrul973@verizon.net
License: Carmi, White County, IL held by W. Russell Withers Jr.
Group Owner: Withers Broadcasting Co.; (acq 5-1-2006; $1.1 million with co-located AM)
Nat'l Network: ABC
Format: Country; *Hrs. of News Programming:* news progmg 8 hrs wkly; *No. News Employees:* 1; *Target Audience:* 25-55.; *Adv. Rates:* 19; 17; 19; 13
Russell Withers, President
J.C. Tinsley, General Sales Mgr
Irma O'Dell, Programming Director
Bob Miller, News Director

***WYER**
90.5 MHz FM; 2.5 kw vert; 94 ft.; N38 4 28.6 W88 12 31.9 US
(765) 821-2180
License: Carmi, White County, IL held by Connersville Apostolic Lighthouse Inc.
Arbitron Metro Market: Carmi, IL
Blaine Lucas, Chairman
Sean Sebastian, President
Lee Ferraro, General Manager
Tony Pirollo, General Sales Mgr
Rosemary Welsch, Programming Director
Joe Resch, Disc Jockey

Carpentersville

***WWTG**
88.1 MHz FM; 2 kw vert; Ant 108 ft; N42 06 21 W88 22 38
238 Oak Avenue, Carpentersville, IL 98901
(847) 975-6000; *Fax:* (615) 216-7266
www.lifetalk.net
terryyounce@comcast.net
License: Carpentersville, Kane County, IL held by LifeTalk Radio Inc.
Nat'l Network: Life Talk Radio Network
Arbitron Metro Market: Chicago
Gabriel Bardan, Chairman
Terry Younce, Station Manager
John Geli, Programming Director

Carrier Mills

WBVN
01-08-1990; 104.5 MHz FM; *Hrs Open:* 24; 6 kw; 328 ft.; N37 46 25 W88 44 20
Route 7, Box 385b, Marion, IL 62959 US
(618) 252-2999; *Fax:* (618) 997-3194
www.wbvn.org
wbvn@wbvn.org
License: Carrier Mills, Saline County, IL held by Kenneth W. and Jane A. Anderson
Arbitron Metro Market: Marion,IL; *Format:* Christian; *No. News Employees:* 3; *Target Audience:* 18-45; general
Ken Anderson, President

Carterville

WUEZ
04-02-1992; 95.1 MHz FM; *Hrs Open:* 24; 17.6 kw; 390 ft.; N37 43 31 W89 15 25
1431 Country Aire Dr., Carterville, IL 62918 US
(618) 985-4843; *Fax:* (618) 985-6529
www.magic951.com
License: Carterville, Williamson County, IL held by MRR License LLC.
Group Owner: MAX Media L.L.C.; (acq 6-2-2004; grpsl)
Nat'l Reps: Christal
Arbitron Metro Market: Carterville, IL; *Format:* Adult Contemp; *Hrs. of News Programming:* news progmg 18 hrs wkly; *No. News Employees:* 2; *Target Audience:* 25-49; 60% women, 40% men, good spendable income; mgrs,supvrs, professionals
Tom Miller, Operations Manager
Steve Falat, General Manager/Market Manager
Kim DeBose, General Sales Mgr

Carthage

WCAZ
01-01-1922; 990 kHz AM; 1 kw-D, ND1; 0.009 kw-N, ND1; N40 24 30 W91 10 15
Mailing Address: 84 South Madison Street, Carthage, IL 62321 US
Second Address: 86 S. Madison, Carthage, IL 62321
(217) 357-3128; *Fax:* (217) 357-2014
www.wcazam990.com
License: Carthage, IL held by Ralla Broadcasting Co. Inc.
Arbitron Metro Market: Carthage, IL; *Format:* Talk
Rob Dunham, General Manager
Keith Yex, General Sales Mgr
Chuck Porter, Programming Director

WQKQ
11-01-1978; 92.1 MHz FM; *Hrs Open:* 24; 25 kw; 328 ft.; N40 35 37 W91 6 48
610 N. 4th St., Suite 300, Burlington, IA 52601 US
(319) 752-5402; *Fax:* (319) 752-4715
www.KQ92rocks.com
johnp@burlingtonradio.com
License: Carthage, Hancock County, IL held by Pritchard Broadcasting Corp.
Group Owner: Pritchard Broadcasting Corp.; (acq 12-1-99)
Nat'l Reps: Katz Radio
Arbitron Metro Market: Burlington, IA; *Format:* Rock/AOR; *Hrs. of News Programming:* news progmg 2 hrs wkly; *No. News Employees:* 2; *Target Audience:* 25-54.; *Adv. Rates:* 22; 22; 22; 11
Joe Bates, Operations Dir
John Pritchard, General Manager
Chet Young, General Sales Mgr
Jeff Holiday, Programming Director

WCEZ
01-01-2001; 93.9 MHz FM; *Hrs Open:* 24; 6 kw; 328 ft.; N40 24 54 W91 15 11
Mailing Address: P O Box 818, Benton, IL 62812 US
Second Address: 303 N. Main, Carthage, IL 62812
(319) 524-5410; *Fax:* (319) 524-7275
License: Carthage, Hancock County, IL held by Dana R. Withers.
Group Owner: Withers Broadcasting Co.; Gary M. Folluo, (319) 524-5410
Arbitron Metro Market: Keokuk, IA; *Format:* Adult Contemp; *Hrs. of News Programming:* news progmg 8 hrs wkly; *No. News Employees:* 1; *Target Audience:* 18-45; 60% female, 40% male; *Adv. Rates:* 13; 12; 11; 10
Dana Withers, President
Gary Folluo, General Manager
Judy Hall, Sales Manager
Preston Hampton, Program Director/Operations Manager
Matt Frisbee, News Director
Preston Hampton, News Director
Bill Reed, Sports Director
TaraWhitnah, Office Manager

Casey

WCBH
09-19-1988; 104.3 MHz FM; *Hrs Open:* 24; 11 kw; 495 ft.; N39 16 24 W87 55 39
209 Lake Land Boulevard, Mattoon, IL 61938 US
(217) 235-5624; *Fax:* (217) 937-4487
www.1043theparty.com
wcrc@wcrc975.com
License: Casey, Clark County, IL held by Two Petaz Inc.
Group Owner: The Cromwell Group Inc.; (acq 1-9-02; grpsl).
Arbitron Metro Market: Terre Haute, IN; *Format:* Contemporary Hits/Top 40
Chris Bullock, Market Manager
Tara Nickerson, Operations Manager
Cindy Hansen, Business Manager

WKZI
12-14-1963; 800 kHz AM; *Hrs Open:* 24; 250 w-U; N39 18 14 W87 58 15
18889 N. 23rd 50th St., Dennison, IL 62420
(217) 826-9673
wordpower.us
wkzi@rr1.net
License: Casey, Clark County, IL held by Word Power Inc.
Nat'l Network: Moody
Population Served: 358,500; *Arbitron Metro Market:* Terre Haute, IN; *Hrs. of News Programming:* News progmg 17 hrs wkly; *Target Audience:* General; 12 plus; *Adv. Rates:* 30; 30; 30; 30
Paul Dean Ford, President
Eleanor Jean Ford, Programming Director
Dan Watson, Engineering Dir

***WLHW**
01-01-2006; 91.5 MHz FM; *Hrs Open:* 24; 6 kw; 197 ft.; N39 18 14 W87 58 15
6 East Colorado Alley, P.O. Box 8, Casey, IL 62420 US
(217) 826-9673
www.wordpower.us
License: Casey, Clark County, IL
Arbitron Metro Market: Casey, IL; *Format:* Christian, Religious
Paul Ford, News Director
Eleanor Ford, Disc Jockey

WWGO-HD2
09-19-1988; 103.9 MHz FM; *Hrs Open:* 24; 11 kw; 495 ft.; N39 16 24 W87 55 39
209 Lake Land Boulevard, Mattoon, IL 61938 US
(217) 235-5624; *Fax:* (217) 937-4487
www.myradiolink.com/victory-103-9
License: Casey, Clark County, IL held by Two Petaz Inc.
Group Owner: The Cromwell Group Inc.; (acq 1-9-02; grpsl).
Arbitron Metro Market: Terre Haute, IN; *Format:* Sports, Talk
Chris Bullock, Market Manager
Tara Nickerson, Operations Manager
Cindy Hansen, Business Manager

Centralia

WILY
08-15-1946; 1210 kHz AM; *Hrs Open:* Sunrise-sunset
Mailing Address: 3501 Broadway, P.O. Box 1508, Mount Vernon, IL 62864 US
Second Address: 302 S. Poplar, Centralia, IL 62801
(618) 533-5700; *Fax:* (618) 533-5737
wrxx@mvn.net
License: Centralia, IL held by Withers Broadcasting Co. of West Virginia.
Group Owner: Withers Broadcasting Co.; (acq 11-4-97; $527,500 with co-located FM)
Regional Network: Brownfield; *Wire Services:* AP
Format: Oldies *Special Programming:* Business news; *Hrs. of News Programming:* news progmg 60 hrs wkly; *No. News Employees:* 2; *Target Audience:* 25-54.; *Adv. Rates:* 8.50; na; na; na
Russ Withers, President
Brenda Robinson, Operations Dir
Jared Kuhn, General Manager
Barrett Beach, Station Manager
Timmy Willmore, Chief Engineer
Nick Skok, Mobile Manager
Stephanie Domagalski, Public Relations Director
NhigelHinkson, Music Director

WRXX
12-24-1964; 95.3 MHz FM; *Hrs Open:* 24; 5.5 kw; 328 ft.; N38 33 46 W88 59 58
Mailing Address: 3501 Broadway, P.O. Box 1508, Mount Vernon, IL 62864 US
Second Address: 302 S. Poplar, Centralia, IL 62801

(618) 533-5700; *Fax:* (618) 533-5737
www.mywithersradio.com
centralia@mywithersradio.com
License: Centralia, Marion County, IL held by Withers Broadcasting Co. of West Virginia.
Group Owner: Withers Broadcasting Co.
Nat'l Network: ABC
Format: Rock/AOR; *Hrs. of News Programming:* news progmg 2 hrs wkly; *No. News Employees:* 2; *Target Audience:* 18-49.
Barry Drake, President
Curt Peterson, Operations Dir
Brad Stevens, Programming Director

Champaign

***WBGL**
10-31-1982; 91.7 MHz FM; *Hrs Open:* 24; 20 kw; Ant 459 ft; N40 09 12 W88 06 56
4101 Fieldstone Road, Champaign, IL 61821
(217) 359-8232; *Fax:* (217) 359-7374
www.wbgl.org
wbgl@wbgl.org
License: Champaign, Champaign County, IL held by Illinois Bible Institute Inc.
Group Owner: Illinois Bible Institute Inc.
Nat'l Network: USA
Arbitron Metro Market: Champaign, IL; *No. News Employees:* 1; *Target Audience:* 25-44.
Jeff Scott, Station Manager
Ryan Springer, Programming Director
Jennifer Briski, Promotions Manager
Joe Rother, Engineering Dir
Joe Buchanan, Music Director
Zoe Fuller, Underwriting Director

WDWS
01-24-1937; 1400 kHz AM; *Hrs Open:* 24; 1 kw-U, ND1; N40 5 4 W88 14 53
P.O. Box 3939, Champaign, IL 61826 US
(217) 351-5300; *Fax:* (217) 351-5385
www.wdws.com
talk@wdws.com
License: Champaign, IL held by D.W.S. Inc.
Nat'l Network: ABC; *Regional Network:* Ill. Radio Net; *Nat'l Reps:* Christal; *Wire Services:* AP
Arbitron Metro Market: Champaign, IL; *Format:* News, News/Talk, 84, Talk *Special Programming:* Farm 10 hrs, relg 4 hrs wkly; *Hrs. of News Programming:* news progmg 26 hrs wkly; *No. News Employees:* 6 *TargetAudience:* 35-64; adults
Mike Haile, Operations Dir
Mike Halle, General Manager
Dave Burns, General Sales Mgr
Carol Vorel, News Director
Jim Lewis, Operations Manager

***WEFT**
09-21-1981; 90.1 MHz FM; *Hrs Open:* 6 AM-2 AM; 10 kw horiz, 8.5 kw vert; 325 ft.; N40 10 51 W88 19 4
113 North Market, Champaign, IL 61820 US
(217) 359-9338
www.weft.org/
License: Champaign, Champaign County, IL held by Prairie Air Inc.
Nat'l Network: NPR; PRI
Arbitron Metro Market: Champaign, IL; *Format:* Variety/Diverse *Special Programming:* Black 8 hrs, blues 10 hrs, folk 10 hrs, pub affrs 5 hrs, Sp 3 hrs wkly; *Hrs. of News Programming:* News progmg 10 hrs wkly *TargetAudience:* General.
Mick Woolf, General Manager
George Uricoechea, Programming Director
Darren Martin, Chief Engineer

WHMS-FM
01-01-1948; 97.5 MHz FM; *Hrs Open:* 24; 50 kw; 358 ft.; N40 5 4 W88 14 53
Mailing Address: P.O. Box 3939, Champaign, IL 61826 US
Second Address: 2301 S. Neil, Champaign, IL 61820
(217) 351-5300; *Fax:* (217) 351-5385
www.whms.com
literock@whms.com
License: Champaign, Champaign County, IL
Wire Services: AP
Arbitron Metro Market: Champaign, IL; *Format:* Adult Contemp; *Hrs. of News Programming:* news progmg 10 hrs wkly; *No. News Employees:* 4; *Target Audience:* 25-54; adults
Mike Haile, General Manager
Ryan Aurthur, Programming Director

WIXY
06-01-1992; 100.3 MHz FM; 13 kw; 453 ft.; N40 0 45 W88 8 29
2603 W. Bradley Avenue, Champaign, IL 61821 US
(217) 355-4141; *Fax:* (217) 352-1256
www.wixy.com
info@wixy.com
License: Champaign, Champaign County, IL held by Saga Communications of Illinois LLC.
Group Owner: Saga Communications Inc.; (acq 11-4-92; $250,000;
Nat'l Reps: Katz Radio
Arbitron Metro Market: Champaign, IL; *Format:* Country; *Hrs. of News Programming:* News progmg 5 hrs wkly; *Target Audience:* 25 plus.
Ed Christian, CEO
Steve Goldstein, President
Alan Beck, General Manager

WLRW
01-01-1963; 94.5 MHz FM; *Hrs Open:* 24; 50 kw; 453 ft.; N40 7 35 W88 17 25
2603 W. Bradley Avenue, Champaign, IL 61821 US
(217) 352-4141; *Fax:* (217) 352-1256
www.mix945.com
info@mix945.com
License: Champaign, Champaign County, IL held by Saga Communications of Illinois LLC.
Group Owner: Saga Communications Inc.; (acq 10-86; grpsl;
Arbitron Metro Market: Champaign, IL; *Format:* Adult Contemp; *Target Audience:* 18-49.
Alan Beck, General Manager
Jonathan Drake, Programming Director

WPCD
01-01-1978; 88.7 MHz FM; 10.5 kw; N40 13 27 W88 17 56
2400 West Bradley Avenue, Champaign, IL 61820 US
(217) 351-2450; *Fax:* (217) 373-3899
wpcd.parkland.edu
wpcdradio@parkland.edu
License: Champaign, Champaign County, IL held by Parkland College Community College District No. 505.
Nat'l Network: USA News Network
Arbitron Metro Market: Champaign, IL; *Format:* Alternative, Urban Contemporary *Special Programming:* News 8 hrs, spanish 4 hrs wkly; *Hrs. of News Programming:* News progmg 8 hrs wkly; *Target Audience:* General
Eleni Kametas, General Manager

Charleston

***WEIU**
07-01-1985; 88.9 MHz FM; *Hrs Open:* 24; 4 kw; 167 ft.; N39 28 43 W88 10 21
Weiu Fm & Tv, Charleston, IL 61920 US
(217) 581-5956; *Fax:* (217) 581-6650
www.weiu.net
weiu@weiu.net
License: Charleston, Coles County, IL held by Eastern Illinois University.
Arbitron Metro Market: Charleston, IL *TV Affiliate:* *WEIU-TV affil; *Format:* Variety/Diverse *Special Programming:* Folks 4 hrs, jazz 4 hrs wkly; *Hrs. of News Programming:* news progmg 3 hrs wkly *No. NewsEmployees:* 1; *Target Audience:* 12 plus; 25-55 women; *Adv. Rates:* 10; 8; 9; 6
Denis Roche, General Manager
Jeff Owens, Station Manager
Linda Kingery, Programming Director
Kelly Runyon, News Director
John Wiley, Underwriting Director

WWGO
10-01-1965; 92.1 MHz FM; *Hrs Open:* 24; 6 kw; 328 ft.; N39 31 40 W88 21 23
P.O. Box 150846, Nashville, TN 37215 US
(217) 844-4487; *Fax:* (217) 235-6624
www.myradiolink.com
bub@radiomattoon.com
License: Charleston, Coles County, IL held by The Cromwell Group Inc. of Illinois.
Group Owner: The Cromwell Group Inc.; (acq 1993)
Nat'l Network: ABC
Arbitron Metro Market: Charleston, IL; *Format:* Classic Rock; *Hrs. of News Programming:* news progmg 20 hrs wkly; *No. News Employees:* 1; *Target Audience:* 25-54; upscale, educated adults
Bud Walters, President
Carol Floyd, General Manager
Bub McCullough, Programming Director
Kathie St. Clair, News Director
Josh Jamison, Chief Engineer

***WZGL**
01-01-2008; 88.1 MHz FM; 2.1 kw; 229 ft.; N39 28 38 W88 8 25
Rebroadcasts: Rebroadcasts WBGL(FM) Champaign 100%
P O Box 140, Carlinville, IL 62626 US
(217) 359-8232; *Fax:* (217) 359-7374
www.wbgl.org
License: Charleston, Coles County, IL held by Illinois Bible Institute Inc.
Group Owner: Illinois Bible Institute Inc.
Arbitron Metro Market: Charleston, IL; *Format:* Christian
Meridith Foster, Operations Dir
Jeff Scott, Station Manager
Ryan Springer, Programming Director
Jennifer Briski, Promotions Manager
Zoe Fuller, Office Manager/Underwriting Director
Jerilynn Jones, Volunteer Coordinator/Assistant toStation Manager
Sheryl Maxwell, Promotions Assistant
Jason Rackow, Production Director
Steve Thompson, Internet Media Director
Weez Stockton, Assistant Promotions Director

Chatham

WYMG
03-01-1948; 100.5 MHz FM; *Hrs Open:* 24; 50 kw; 489 ft.; N39 39 43 W89 55 22
1030 Durkin Drive, Springfield, IL 62704 US
(217) 753-5400; *Fax:* (217) 753-7902
www.wymg.com
wymg@wymg.com
License: Chatham, Sangamon County, IL held by Saga Communications of Illinois LLC.
Group Owner: Saga Communications Inc.; (acq 10-1-86).
Arbitron Metro Market: Chatham, IL; *Format:* Classic Rock; *Target Audience:* 25-54.
Mike Topoll, General Manager
Jane Cochran, Programming Director

Chester

KSGM
07-05-1947; 980 kHz AM; *Hrs Open:* 24; 1 kw-D, DAN; 0.47 kw-N, DAN; N37 47 16 W89 54 21 *Rebroadcasts:* Rebroadcasts KBDZ(FM) Perryville, MO
P.O. Box 428, Ste. Genevieve, MO 63670 US
(573) 883-2980 618-826-2980573-547-6780; *Fax:* (573) 883-2866
www.suntimesnews.com
suntimesnews@brick.net
License: Chester, IL held by Donze Communications Inc.
Arbitron Metro Market: Ste. Gene, MO; *Format:* Country, News, 62, Talk *Special Programming:* Farm 2 hrs, relg 6 hrs wkly; *Hrs. of News Programming:* news progmg 14 hrs wkly; *No. News Employees:* 2 *TargetAudience:* General; adults; *Adv. Rates:* 16; 14; 16; 14
Don Pritchard, News Director

Chicago

WBBM
11-14-1923; 780 kHz AM; *Hrs Open:* 24 hours; 50 kW; 696 ft.; N41 59 26 W88 1 39 *Rebroadcasts:* WCFS-FM HD2
180 North Stetson, Suite 1100, Chicago, IL 60601 USA
(312) 297-7800
www.wbbm780.com
License: Chicago, IL held by CBS Radio East Inc.
Group Owner: CBS Radio; (acq 1931)
Nat'l Network: CBS; CNN Radio; AP Network News; *Regional Network:* Ill. Radio Net.; *Wire Services:* AP; CBS; SportsTicker
Format: News; *Adv. Rates:* call sales dept

WBBM-FM
06-06-1979; 96.3 MHz FM; 3.3 kW; 1453 ft.; N41 52 44 W87 38 10
180 North Stetson, Suite 1100, Chicago, IL 60601 USA
(312) 861-9600
www.b96.com
License: Chicago, Cook County, IL held by CBS Radio East Inc.
Group Owner: CBS Radio
Nat'l Network: CBS; *Nat'l Reps:* CBS Radio
Format: Contemporary Hits/Top 40; *Target Audience:* 18-54

***WBEZ**
01-01-1942; 91.5 MHz FM; *Hrs Open:* 24; 5.7 kw; 1395 ft.; N41 53 56 W87 37 23
848 East Grand Avenue, Chicago, IL 60611 US
(312) 948-4600; *Fax:* (312) 832-3100
questions@wbez.org
License: Chicago, Cook County, IL held by The WBEZ Alliance Inc.
Nat'l Network: NPR; PRI
Arbitron Metro Market: Chicago,IL; *Format:* Jazz, News; *Hrs. of News Programming:* news progmg 45 hrs wkly; *No. News Employees:* 5; *Target Audience:* General; people who want to know about the world around them

Merrill Smith, Chairman
Donna Moore, CFO
Torey Malatia, President
Sally Eisele, Programming Director
Steve Edwards, Acting Program Manager

***WCRX**
07-29-1975; 88.1 MHz FM; *Hrs Open:* 24; 0.1 kw horiz, 0.09 kw vert; 128 ft.; N41 52 22 W87 38 52
600 South Michigan Ave., Chicago, IL 60605 US
(312) 663-3512; *Fax:* (312) 663-5204
www.colum.edu
License: Chicago, Cook County, IL held by Columbia College.
Nat'l Network: AP Radio; *Wire Services:* AP
Arbitron Metro Market: Chicago,IL; *Format:* News, Sports; *Hrs. of News Programming:* news progmg 20 hrs wkly; *No. News Employees:* 2; *Target Audience:* 18-24; Men
Cheryl Langston, General Manager
Tony Kwiecinski, Station Manager
Dave Dennis, Chief Engineer

WFMT
12-13-1951; 98.7 MHz FM; *Hrs Open:* 24; 6 kw; 1542 ft.; N41 52 44 W87 38 8
5400 N. St. Louis Ave., Chicago, IL 60625 US
(773) 279-2000; *Fax:* (773) 279-2199
www.networkchicago.com
finearts@wfmt.com
License: Chicago, Cook County, IL held by Window to the World Communications Inc.
Arbitron Metro Market: Chicago, IL *TV Affiliate:* WTTW(TV) affil; *Format:* Talk *Special Programming:* Folk 4 hrs, jazz 5 hrs wkly; *Hrs. of News Programming:* News progmg 7 hrs wkly; *Target Audience:* 25-54;upscale, professional, college educated, upper income adults
Dan Schmidt, CEO
Steve Robinson, Senior Vice President/General Manager
Paul Ansell, General Sales Mgr
Peter Van de Graaff, Programming Director
Gordon Carter, Chief Engineer
Don Mueller, Operations Manager

WGRB
01-01-1924; 1390 kHz AM; 5 kw-D, DA2; 5 kw-N, DA2; N41 44 13 W87 42 0
233 N. Michigan Ave., Suite 2800, Chicago, IL 60604 US
(312) 540-2000; *Fax:* (312) 938-4477
www.inspiration1390.com
License: Chicago, IL held by AMFM Broadcasting Licenses LLC.
Group Owner: iHeartMedia; (acq 8-30-2000; grpsl).
Nat'l Reps: Christal
Arbitron Metro Market: Chicago, IL; *Format:* Gospel
Matt Scarano, Market President
Adam Kurtz, General Sales Mgr
Sonya Blakey, Programming Director

WGCI-FM
12-11-1958; 107.5 MHz FM; 3.7 kw; 1549 ft.; N41 52 44 W87 38 8
233 N. Michigan Ave., Suite 2800, Chicago, IL 60601 US
(312) 540-2000; *Fax:* (312) 938-4477
www.wgci.com
License: Chicago, Cook County, IL held by AMFM Broadcasting Licenses LLC
Group Owner: iHeartMedia
Arbitron Metro Market: Chicago, IL; *Format:* Urban Contemporary
Matt Scarano, Market President
Adam Kurtz, General Sales Mgr

WGN(AM)
06-01-1924; 720 kHz AM; 50 kw-U; N42 00 42 W88 02 07
435 N. Michigan Ave., Chicago, IL 60611
(312) 222-4700; *Fax:* (312) 222-5165
www.wgnradio.com
info@wgnradio.com
License: Chicago, Cook County, IL held by WGN Continental Broadcasting Company
Group Owner: Tribune Broadcasting Co.; (acq 12-20-2007; grpsl)
Nat'l Network: ABC; *Nat'l Reps:* Christal; *Wire Services:* AP
Arbitron Metro Market: Chicago, IL *TV Affiliate:* WGN-TV affil; *Format:* News, News/Talk, 84, Talk *Special Programming:* Play-by-play: Chicago Cubs (MLB), Chicago Blackhaw; *No. News Employees:* 15 *TargetAudience:* 35-64.
Charlene Connaughton, CFO
Jimmy de Castro, President/General Manager
Jeff Hill, General Sales Mgr
Jim Carollo, Engineering Dir
Chenessa Roberson, HR Director
Jackie Paulus, Director of Marketing & Digital Innovation

***WHPK-FM**
03-15-1968; 88.5 MHz FM; *Hrs Open:* 24; 0.1 kw; 121 ft.; N41 47 40 W87 35 55
5706 S. University Ave, Chicago, IL 60637 US
(773) 702-8289; *Fax:* (773) 702-7718
whpk.uchicago.edu
whpk@uchicago.edu
License: Chicago, Cook County, IL held by The University of Chicago.
Arbitron Metro Market: Chicago, IL; *Format:* Jazz, Variety/Diverse *Special Programming:* Class 10 hrs, African one hr, Haitian 3 hrs, Isra; *Hrs. of News Programming:* News progmg 5 hrs wkly
Simon Wiener, Station Manager
Alec Mitrovich, Programming Director
Rachel Lazar, Promotions Manager
Theo Shure, Publicity Director
Mario Smith, Sponsorship Director
Rachel Schastock, Treasurer
Keegan Hankes, Music Director
RyanLavery, Training Director
Lillian Seonick, Traffic Director

WIND
01-01-1927; 560 kHz AM; 5 kw-D, DA2; 5 kw-N, DA2; N41 33 54 W87 25 11
3102 Oak Lawn Ave., Suite 215, Dallas, TX 75219 US
(847) 437-5200; *Fax:* (847) 956-5040
www.560wind.com
License: Chicago, IL held by Salem Media of Illinois LLC.
Group Owner: Salem Communications Corp.; (acq 1-7-2005; with KNIT(AM) Dallas and KKHT-FM Winnie, both TX, in exchange for WPPN(FM) Des Plaines, IL).
Arbitron Metro Market: Chicago, IL; *Format:* News, News/Talk, 86
Eric Thomas, Operations Dir
Jeff Reisman, General Manager
Marcus Brown, Programming Director

WJMK
07-27-1984; 104.3 MHz FM; 4.1 kW; 1568 ft.; N41 52 44 W87 38 8
180 North Stetson, Suite 900, Chicago, IL 60601 USA
(312) 729-3810
www.khitschicago.com
License: Chicago, Cook County, IL held by CBS Radio Inc. of Illinois
Group Owner: CBS Radio
Nat'l Network: Westwood One
Arbitron Metro Market: Chicago, IL; *Format:* Oldies; *Target Audience:* 25-54
Ben Ponzio, General Sales Mgr

***WKKC**
01-01-1975; 89.3 MHz FM; 280 w horiz, 250 w vert; Ant 111 ft; N41 46 48 W87 38 38
Kennedy-King College, 6800 S. Wentworth Ave., Chicago, IL 60621
(773) 602-5540; *Fax:* (773) 602-5532
www.ccc.edu
License: Chicago, Cook County, IL held by District 508 City College of Chicago.
Population Served: 250,000; *Arbitron Metro Market:* Chicago; *Target Audience:* 15-50.
Kevin Brown, General Manager

WKQX
01-01-1948; 95.9 MHz FM; *Hrs Open:* 24; 1 kw; 46 ft.; N40 46 17 W87 46 13
222 Merchandise Mart Plaza, Suite 230, Chicago, IL 60654 USA
(312) 527-8348; *Fax:* (312) 527-3620
www.101wkqx.com
License: Chicago, Cook County, IL held by Merlin Media License LLC
Group Owner: Cumulus Media
Nat'l Reps: D & R Radio
Arbitron Metro Market: Chicago, IL; *Format:* Alternative; *Target Audience:* 18-34.

WLIT-FM
04-07-1958; 93.9 MHz FM; *Hrs Open:* 24; 4 kw; 1581 ft.; N41 52 44 W87 38 8
233 N. Michigan Ave., Suite 2800, Chicago, IL 60601 US
(312) 540-2000; *Fax:* (312) 938-0111
www.939myfm.com
License: Chicago, Cook County, IL held by AMFM Broadcasting Licenses LLC.
Group Owner: iHeartMedia; (acq 8-30-2000; grpsl).
Nat'l Network: Premiere Radio Networks; *Nat'l Reps:* Clear Channel; *Wire Services:* AP
Arbitron Metro Market: Chicago, IL; *Format:* Adult Contemp; *Hrs. of News Programming:* news progmg one hr wkly; *No. News Employees:* 1; *Target Audience:* 25-54; affluent adults
Matt Scarano, Market President
Jerry Schnacke, Senior Vice President of Sales

WLS
04-12-1924; 890 kHz AM; 50 kw-U, ND1; N41 33 21 W87 50 54
190 North State St., 9th Floor, Chicago, IL 60601 US
(312) 984-0890; *Fax:* (312) 984-5305
www.wlsam.com
License: Chicago, IL held by Radio License Holdings LLC
Group Owner: Cumulus Media Inc.; (acq 6-12-2007; grpsl)
Arbitron Metro Market: Chicago, IL; *Format:* News/Talk
Lorraine Lynn, Promotions Director

WLUP-FM
01-01-1942; 97.9 MHz FM; *Hrs Open:* 24; 4 kw; 1394 ft.; N41 53 56 W87 37 23
222 Merchandise Mart Plaza, Suite 230, Chicago, IL 60654 US
(312) 245-1200; *Fax:* (312) 527-3620
www.wlup.com
License: Chicago, Cook County, IL held by Merlin Media License LLC
Nat'l Reps: D & R Radio
Arbitron Metro Market: Chicago, IL; *Target Audience:* 18-49.
Marv Nyren, General Manager

***WLUW**
09-19-1978; 88.7 MHz FM; *Hrs Open:* 24; 0.1 kw; 230 ft.; N42 0 4 W87 39 36
820 North Michigan Ave, Chicago, IL 60611 US
(773) 508-8080; *Fax:* (773) 508-8082
www.wluw.org
License: Chicago, Cook County, IL held by Loyola University, Chicago.
Wire Services: Pacifica Network News
Arbitron Metro Market: Chicago, IL; *Format:* Variety/Diverse; *Target Audience:* College students.
Danielle Basci, General Manager
Maxx McGathey, Programming Director
Katie Reese, Promotions Manager
Matt Malooly, News Director

WRTO
12-01-1988; 1200 kHz AM; *Hrs Open:* 24; 20 kw-D, DA2; 4.5 kw-N, DA2; N41 39 43 87 37 48
625 N. Michigan Ave., Suite 3, Chicago, IL 60611 US
(312) 981-1800; *Fax:* (312) 981-1806
www.univision.com
License: Chicago, Cook County, IL held by WLXX-AM License Corp.
Group Owner: Univision Radio; (acq 9-22-2003; grpsl).
Nat'l Reps: McGavren Guild
Arbitron Metro Market: Chicago, IL; *Format:* News, News/Talk, 82, Talk; *Hrs. of News Programming:* news progmg 10 hrs wkly; *No. News Employees:* 4; *Target Audience:* Urban Spanish.
Doug Levy, General Manager
Alicia Chavarria, Promotions Manager
Joshua Sigstad, Chief Engineer

WSCR
08-15-2000; 670 kHz AM; *Hrs Open:* 24; 50 kW; N41 56 3 W88 4 22
180 North Stetson, Suite 1250, Chicago, IL 60601 USA
(312) 729-3967
www.670thescore.com
License: Chicago, IL held by CBS Radio East Inc.
Group Owner: CBS Radio; (acq 11-13-98; grpsl).
Nat'l Network: Westwood One; *Regional Network:* Ill. Radio Net.
Arbitron Metro Market: Chicago,IL; *Format:* Sports; *Target Audience:* 25-54

***WMBI-AM**
07-28-1926; 1110 kHz AM; *Hrs Open:* Sunrise-sunset; 4.2 kW; N41 55 41 W88 0 25
820 N LaSalle Blvd, Chicago, IL 60610 USA
(312) 329-4300; *Fax:* (312) 329-4468
www.moodyradio.org/stations/wmbi-chicago
License: Chicago, IL held by The Moody Bible Institute of Chicago
Group Owner: The Moody Bible Institute of Chicago
Nat'l Network: Moody; *Wire Services:* AP
Arbitron Metro Market: Chicago, IL; *Format:* Spanish, Christian *Special Programming:* Sp 12 hrs wkly; *Target Audience:* 35-54; Hispanic Christians, children, English-speaking

***WMBI-FM**
07-25-1960; 90.1 MHz FM; *Hrs Open:* 24; 100 kW; 443 ft; N41 55 41 W88 00 25
820 N LaSalle Blvd, Chicago, IL 60610 USA

(312) 329-4300; *Fax:* (312) 329-4468
www.moodyradio.org/stations/wmbi-chicago
License: Chicago, Cook County, IL held by The Moody Bible Institute of Chicago
Group Owner: The Moody Bible Institute of Chicago
Nat'l Network: Moody; *Wire Services:* AP
Population Served: 7,400,000; *Arbitron Metro Market:* Chicago; *Format:* Christian; *No. News Employees:* 2; *Target Audience:* 35-54; Christian

WMVP
06-25-1926; 1000 kHz AM; *Hrs Open:* 24
77 W 66th St., 16th Fl., New York, NY 10023 USA
(312) 980-1000; *Fax:* (312) 980-1020
www.espnradio.com
License: Chicago, IL held by Sports Radio Chicago LLC
Group Owner: ESPN Inc.
Nat'l Network: ESPN Radio; *Nat'l Reps:* ABC Radio Sales
Arbitron Metro Market: Chicago, IL; *Format:* Comedy, Sports, 86; *Target Audience:* 25-54.

WDRV
07-09-1955; 97.1 MHz FM; *Hrs Open:* 24; 8.3 kw; 1,191 ft.; N41 53 6 W87 37 18
875 N. Michigan Ave., Suite 1510, Chicago, IL 60611 US
(312) 274-9710; *Fax:* (312) 274-1304
www.wdrv.com
License: Chicago, Cook County, IL held by Chicago FCC License Sub LLC
Group Owner: Hubbard Broadcasting Inc.; (acq 1-19-2011).
Nat'l Reps: Katz Radio
Arbitron Metro Market: Chicago, IL; *Format:* Classic Rock
John Gallagher, Vice President and Market Manager
David Kruse, General Sales Mgr
Curtiss Johnson, Programming Director
Matt Spaetzel, Sales Promotion Manager
Kathy Voltmer, News and Public Affairs Manager
Kent Lewin, ChiefEngineer
Tom Couch, Director of Creative Services
Paul Webber, Direct Marketing Manager
Jeff Buti, Digital Media Director

WSHE-FM
01-01-1947; 100.3 MHz FM; 5.7 kw; 1,394 ft.; N41 53 56 W87 37 23
130 E. Randolph St., Suite 2780, Chicago, IL 60601 US
(312) 297-5100; *Fax:* (312) 297-5155
www.wshechicago.com
License: Chicago, Cook County, IL held by Chicago FCC License Sub LLC
Group Owner: Hubbard Broadcasting Inc.; (acq 1-19-2011).
Arbitron Metro Market: Chicago, IL; *Format:* Adult Contemp; *Target Audience:* 25-49; women
John Gallagher, Vice President and Market Manager
Ryan Rusin, General Sales Mgr
Paul Webber, Programming Director
Dianne Sharp, Promotions Manager
Dave Karwowski, Marketing Director
Jeff Buti, Digital Media Director

WNTD
05-01-1922; 950 kHz AM; 1 kw-D, DAN; 5 kw-N, DAN; N41 51 39 W87 41 12; N41 38 12 W87 33 10
8400 NW 52nd Street, Suite 101, Miami, FL 33166 US
(312) 467-9755; *Fax:* (312) 467-9603
www.relevantradio.com
WNTD@relevantradio.com
License: Chicago, IL held by Sovereign City Radio Services LLC
Group Owner: Relevant Radio; (acq 10-18-2007; $15 million)
Arbitron Metro Market: Chicago, IL; *Format:* Religious; *Target Audience:* 25-54.
Scott Wert, General Manager

WEBG
03-09-1959; 95.5 MHz FM; 8.3 kw; 1175 ft.; N41 53 56 W87 37 23
233 N. Michigan Ave., Suite 2800, Chicago, IL 60601 US
(312) 540-2000; *Fax:* (312) 938-0712
www.big955chicago.com
License: Chicago, Cook County, IL held by AMFM Broadcasting Licenses LLC.
Group Owner: iHeartMedia; (acq 8-30-2000; grpsl).
Wire Services: UPI
Arbitron Metro Market: Chicago, IL; *Format:* Country; *Target Audience:* 25-54.
Matt Scarano, Market President

***WIIT**
06-01-1974; 88.9 MHz FM; *Hrs Open:* 24; 0.017 kw horiz; 89 ft.; N41 50 4 W87 37 43
3300 S. Federal St, Chicago, IL 60616 US
(312) 567-3087,(312) 567-3088; *Fax:* (312) 567-7042
wiit@iit.edu
License: Chicago, Cook County, IL held by Illinois Institute of Technology.
Arbitron Metro Market: Chicago; *Format:* Variety/Diverse *Special Programming:* Jazz 9 hrs, Ger 3 hrs, relg 2 hrs, Sp 5 hrs wkly; *Hrs. of News Programming:* News progmg 5 hrs wkly; *Target Audience:* 15-35; college &young urban community
Patrick Schneider, Station Manager

***WRTE**
12-01-1969; 90.5 MHz FM; *Hrs Open:* 24; 0.073 kw; 85 ft.; N41 50 26 W87 43 5
Mailing Address: 1401 West 18th Street, Chicago, IL 60608 US
Second Address: c/o Mexican Fine Arts Ctr. Museum, 1852 W. 19th St., Chicago, IL 60608-2706
(312) 455-9455; *Fax:* (312) 455-9755
valdivia@radioarte.org
License: Chicago, Cook County, IL held by Mexican Fine Arts Center Museum.
Arbitron Metro Market: Chicago; *Format:* Alternative; *Target Audience:* 15-35.
Jorge Valdivia, General Manager
Carlos Mendez, Programming Director
Shaaron Resendiz, Marketing/Underwriting Director
Adriana Diaz, Director of Youth Media Development & Research

WSBC
01-01-1925; 1240 kHz AM; *Hrs Open:* 24; 1 kW; N41 58 53 W87 46 20
5625 N Milwaukee Ave, Chicago, IL 60646 USA
(773) 792-1121; *Fax:* (773) 792-2904
accessradiochicago.com
mp@wsbcradio.com
License: Chicago, IL held by WSBC Inc.
Group Owner: Newsweb Corp.; (acq 2-23-98)
Arbitron Metro Market: Chicago; *Target Audience:* General.
Mark Pinski, General Manager

WYLL
10-13-1924; 1160 kHz AM; *Hrs Open:* 24; 50 kw-D, DA2; N42 2 30 W87 51 57
600 New Hampshire Ave, N.W., Suite 1200, Washington, DC 20037 US
(847) 956-5030; *Fax:* (847) 956-5040
www.wyll.com
License: Chicago, IL held by Salem Media Group LLC.
Group Owner: Salem Communications Corp.; (acq 12-20-2000; $29 million)
Arbitron Metro Market: Chicago; *Format:* Religious; *Target Audience:* 25-54; Upscale income adults
Eric Thomas, Operations Dir
Jeff Reisman, General Manager
James Herring, Station Manager
Marcus Brown, Programming Director
Frank McCoy, Chief Engineer

***WSSD**
09-15-1987; 88.1 MHz FM; 0.01 kw; 102 ft.; N41 43 44 W87 33 3
11026 South Wentworth, ', Chicago, IL 60628 US
(773) 928-8800; *Fax:* (773) 928-9009
License: Chicago, Cook County, IL held by Lakeside Communications Inc.
Arbitron Metro Market: Chicago; *Format:* Blues, Gospel, 86 *Special Programming:* Gospel, jazz, talk; *Target Audience:* 25 plus; Black
Huey Williams, President
Steven McKinney, Station Manager
Willie McPhatter, Programming Director

WKSC-FM
11-01-1957; 103.5 MHz FM; *Hrs Open:* 24; 4.3 kw; 1549 ft.; N41 52 44 W87 38 8
233 North Michigan Avenue, Suite 2800, Chicago, IL 60601 US
(312) 540-2000; *Fax:* (312) 938-0712
www.1035kissfm.com
License: Chicago, Cook County, IL held by AMFM Broadcasting Licenses LLC.
Group Owner: iHeartMedia; (acq 8-30-2000; grpsl).
Arbitron Metro Market: Chicago, IL; *Format:* Contemporary Hits/Top 40; *Hrs. of News Programming:* news progmg 15 hrs wkly; *No. News Employees:* 1; *Target Audience:* 18-34; upscale
Matt Scarano, Market President
Jerry Schnacke, Senior Vice President of Sales

WUSN
02-25-1982; 99.5 MHz FM; 5.7 kW; 1394 ft.; N41 56 3 W88 4 22
180 North Stetson, Suite 1000, Chicago, IL 60601 USA
(312) 649-0099; *Fax:* (312) 856-9586
www.us99.com
License: Chicago, Cook County, IL held by CBS Radio East Inc.
Group Owner: CBS Radio; (acq 1996; grpsl).
Arbitron Metro Market: Chicago, IL; *Format:* Country; *Target Audience:* 25-54
Paul Agase, General Sales Mgr

WLS
01-01-1948; 94.7 MHz FM; 4.4 kw; 1535 ft.; N41 52 44 W87 38 8
190 N. State St., 8th Floor, Chicago, IL 60601 US
(312) 984-9923
www.947wls.com
License: Chicago, IL held by Radio License Holdings LLC
Group Owner: Cumulus Media Inc.; (acq 6-12-2007; grpsl)
Arbitron Metro Market: Chicago, IL; *Format:* Classic Rock, Adult Contemp
Brian Thomas, Operations Dir
Jeff Smaluk, General Sales Mgr
Lorraine Lynn, Promotions Manager
Peter Bowen, VP/Market Manager
Scott Dirks, Production Director

WXRT
08-04-2011; 93.1 MHz FM; 6.7 kW; 1306 ft.; N41 53 56 W87 37 23
180 North Stetson, 10th Fl., Chicago, IL 60601 USA
(312) 649-0099; *Fax:* (312) 240-7973
www.wxrt.com
xrtcomments@wxrt.com
License: Chicago, Cook County, IL held by CBS Radio East Inc.
Group Owner: CBS Radio; (acq 11-13-98; grpsl)
Nat'l Reps: CBS Radio
Arbitron Metro Market: Chicago, IL; *Format:* Alternative; *No. News Employees:* 1; *Target Audience:* 25-54; upscale adults
Norm Winer, Vice President of Programming

***WZRD**
07-08-1974; 88.3 MHz FM; *Hrs Open:* 11 AM-midnight; 0.1 kw; 72 ft.; N41 58 56 W87 43 7
5500 N. St. Louis Avenue, Chicago, IL 60625 US
(773) 442-4578; *Fax:* (773) 442-4900
www.wzrdchicago.com
wzrdinexile@hotmail.com
License: Chicago, Cook County, IL held by Northeastern Illinois University.
Arbitron Metro Market: Chicago, IL; *Format:* Variety/Diverse; *Hrs. of News Programming:* news progmg 12 hrs wkly; *No. News Employees:* 29; *Target Audience:* General.
Dennis Sagel, Station Manager

WIQI
01-01-1948; 101.1 MHz FM; 5.7 kw; 425 meters; N41 53 56 W87 37 23
222 Merchandise Mart Plaza, Suite 230, Chicago, IL 60654 US
(312) 245-1200; *Fax:* (312) 527-3620
www.i101fm.com
License: Chicago, IL held by Merlin Media License LLC

Chillicothe

WPMJ
05-16-1977; 94.3 MHz FM; *Hrs Open:* 24; 6 kw; 299 ft.; N40 49 48 W89 29 54
5555 Gulf of Mexico Dr., Suite 201, Longboat Key, FL 34228 US
(309) 685-5975; *Fax:* (309) 685-9095
www.wpmjradio.com
info@wpmjradio.com
License: Chillicothe, Peoria County, IL held by Kelly Communications Inc.
Arbitron Metro Market: Peoria, IL
Bob Kelly, CEO

Christopher

WXLT
12-25-1990; 103.5 MHz FM; *Hrs Open:* 24; 6 kw; 328 ft.; N37 55 55 W88 57 31
1431 Country Aire Dr., Carterville, IL 62918 US
(618) 985-4843; *Fax:* (618) 985-6529
www.1035espn.com
License: Christopher, Franklin County, IL held by MRR License LLC.
Group Owner: MAX Media L.L.C.; (acq 6-2-2004; grpsl)
Nat'l Network: ESPN Radio; *Nat'l Reps:* Christal
Arbitron Metro Market: Christopher, IL; *Format:* Sports
Tom Miller, Operations Manager
Steve Falat, General Manager/Market Manager
Kim DeBose, General Sales Mgr
Dave McKenzie, Events Coordinator

Cicero

WCEV
10-01-1979; 1450 kHz AM; *Hrs Open:* 1-10PM(M-F);1-8:30PM(S);5AM-10PM(S); 1 kw; 305 ft.; N41 49 57 W87 42 40
5356 W. Belmont Ave., Chicago, IL 60641
(773) 282-6700; *Fax:* (773) 282-0123
www.wcev1450.com
wcev@wcev1450.com
License: Cicero, Cook County, IL held by Migala Communications Corp.
Wire Services: AP
Arbitron Metro Market: Chicago *Special Programming:* Ethnic Languages; *Hrs. of News Programming:* News progmg 7 hrs wkly; *Target Audience:* Adult ethnic Americans.; *Adv. Rates:* 65; 65; 65; 65
Estelle Migala, President
Barbara Holtzinger, Business Manager
George Migala, General Manager
Lucyna Migala, Programming Director
Dave Dybas, Chief Engineer

WRLL
01-01-1979; 1450 kHz AM; *Hrs Open:* Midnight-1 PM; 1 kw-U, ND1; N41 49 57 W87 42 20
3350 So. Kedzie Ave., Chicago, IL 60623 US
(773) 247-6200; *Fax:* (773) 247-5336
License: Cicero, IL held by Midway Broadcasting Corp.
Arbitron Metro Market: Chicago, IL
Melody Spann Cooper, Chairman
Pervis Spann, CEO/COO
Pervis Spann, President
Todd Ronczkowski, Operations Dir
Gustavo Rios, Station Manager
Juanita Maze, General Sales Mgr
Coz Carson, Programming Director
Denise King, NewsDirector
Bridget Goins, Executive Assistant

Clinton

WHOW
08-01-1947; 1520 kHz AM; *Hrs Open:* 24; 1 kw-C, NDD; 5 kw-D, NDD; N40 5 43 W88 57 51
918 East Park, P.O. Box 169, Taylorville, IL 62568 US
(217) 824-3395; *Fax:* (217) 824-3301
www.dewittdailynews.com
whow@randyradio.com
License: Clinton, De Witt County, IL held by Kaskaskia Broadcasting Inc.
Group Owner: Miller Media Group; (acq 1-4-2008; $400,000 with co-located FM)
Nat'l Network: CNN Radio; CBS News; CBS Sports
Format: Agriculture, News, 62, Talk; *Hrs. of News Programming:* news progmg 20 hrs wkly; *No. News Employees:* 1; *Target Audience:* 35+.; *Adv. Rates:* 12; 15; 7; na
Randall Miller, President
Jared White, Programming Director

WEZC
12-15-1975; 95.9 MHz FM; *Hrs Open:* 24; 6 kw; 308 ft.; N40 5 43 W88 57 51
918 East Park, P.O. Box 169, Clinton, IL 62568 US
(217) 824-3395; *Fax:* (217) 824-3301
dewittdailynews.com/community/wezc
whow@randyradio.com
License: Clinton, De Witt County, IL held by Kaskaskia Broadcasting Inc.
Group Owner: Miller Media Group; (acq 1-4-2008; $400,000 with co-located AM)
Nat'l Network: CNN Radio; SRN
Format: Adult Contemp; *Hrs. of News Programming:* 4 hrs news programing wkly; *No. News Employees:* 1; *Target Audience:* 35+.
Randal Miller, President
Jared White, Programming Director

Coal City

WRXQ
02-08-1991; 100.7 MHz FM; *Hrs Open:* 24; 2.45 kw; 482 ft.; N41 17 39 W88 10 15
8800 Route 14, Crystal Lake, IL 60012 US
(815) 556-0100; *Fax:* (815) 577-9231
mzander@nextmediachicago.com
License: Coal City, Grundy County, IL held by NM Licensing LLC.
Group Owner: NextMedia Group Inc.; (acq 11-26-01; grpsl).
Nat'l Reps: Christal
Arbitron Metro Market: Crest Hill IL; *Format:* Classic Rock; *Hrs. of News Programming:* News progmg 5 hrs wkly; *Target Audience:* 35-50; adults
Patrick Pendergast, General Manager
Doug Boyd, General Sales Mgr
Mark Zander, Programming Director
Dan Waddick, Promotions Manager

Colchester

WMQZ
01-01-1999; 104.1 MHz FM; 6 kw; 328 ft.; N40 32 1 W90 51 45
31 East Side Square, McComb, IL 61455 US
(309) 833-2121; *Fax:* (309) 836-3291
License: Colchester, McDonough County, IL held by Colchester Radio Inc.
Arbitron Metro Market: Colchester, IL; *Format:* Oldies
Bruce Foster, President
Nancy Foster, General Manager
Karen Kearne, General Sales Mgr
Mike Grillette, News Director
Shana Drake, Traffic Manager

WGNX
01-01-2007; 96.7 MHz FM; 1.8 kw; 328 ft.; N40 23 54 W90 43 55
US
(888) 357-5639; *Fax:* (217) 357-3001
www.wgnx.org
GoodNews@adams.net
License: Colchester, McDonough County, IL held by Patricia Van Zandt.
Arbitron Metro Market: Colchester, IL
Patricia Van Zandt, General Manager

Colfax

WRPW
01-01-1997; 92.9 MHz FM; 6 kw; 328 ft.; N40 29 28 W88 43 14
5555 Gulf of Mexico Drive, Suite 201, Longboat Key, FL 34228 US
(309) 888-4496; *Fax:* (309) 452-9677
License: Colfax, McLean County, IL held by Pilot Media LLC.
Group Owner: Great Plains Media Inc.; (acq 6-19-2007; grpsl)
Format: Contemporary Hits/Top 40
Kevin Trueblood, Operations Dir
Patti Donsbach, General Manager
Don Black, Programming Director
Amber Goodwin, Promotions Manager

Collinsville

KPNT
03-01-1967; 105.7 MHz FM; *Hrs Open:* 24; 54 kw; 254.4 meters; N38 34 27.7 W90 19 31.5
10706 Beaver Dam Road, Cockeysville, MD 21030 US
(314) 231-1057; *Fax:* (314) 621-3000
www.1057thepoint.com
stl.ms@emies.com
License: Collinsville, Ste. Genevieve County, IL held by Emmis Radio License LLC
Group Owner: Emmis Communications Corp.
Arbitron Metro Market: St. Louis, MO; *Format:* Rock/AOR; *Target Audience:* 18-34.
Jeff Smulyan, Chairman & CEO

Columbia

KBWX
02-15-1964; 104.9 MHz FM; *Hrs Open:* 24; 7.8 kw; 574 ft.; N38 34 24 W90 19 30
1001 E. Highlands Plaza Dr. W., St. Louis, MO 63110 US
(314) 333-8000
www.wild1049stl.com
License: Columbia, Monroe County, IL held by Citicasters Licenses Inc.
Group Owner: iHeartMedia; (acq 5-4-99; grpsl).
Arbitron Metro Market: St. Louis, MO; *Format:* Adult Contemp; *Target Audience:* 25-54; adults; *Adv. Rates:* 50; 30; 42; 15
Beth Davis, Regional Market President

Crest Hill

WCCQ
01-28-1976; 98.3 MHz FM; *Hrs Open:* 24; 3 kw; 469 ft.; N41 26 9 W88 11 4
2410-B Caton Farm Rd., Crest Hill, IL 60435 US
(815) 556-0100; *Fax:* (815) 577-9231
www.wccq.com
License: Crest Hill, Will County, IL held by NM License, LLC
Group Owner: Digity, LLC
Nat'l Network: ABC; *Nat'l Reps:* Christal; *Wire Services:* UPI
Arbitron Metro Market: Crest Hill IL; *Format:* Country; *Target Audience:* 25-54; general
Brian Foster, General Manager
Doug Boyd, General Sales Mgr
Roy Gregory, Programming Director
Dan Waddick, Promotions Director
Mike Dinger, Engineering Dir

Crete

***WBMF**
01-01-2002; 88.1 MHz FM; 0.09 kw; 374 ft.; N41 25 17 W87 38 39
851 W. New Monee Rd., Crete, IL 60417 US
(708) 367-0968
www.jsm.org
License: Crete, Will County, IL held by Family Worship Center Church Inc.
Group Owner: Family Worship Center Church Inc.
Arbitron Metro Market: Crete, IL; *Format:* Christian; *Hrs. of News Programming:* News progmg 2 hrs wkly
Jimmy Swaggart, President

WYCA
09-05-1965; 102.3 MHz FM; 1.05 kw; 499 ft.; N41 19 32 W87 37 15
6336 Calumet Ave., Hammond, IN 46324 US
(773) 288-9922; *Fax:* (219) 933-0323
www.wyca1023.com
License: Crete, Will County, IL held by Dontron Inc.
Group Owner: Crawford Broadcasting Co.; (acq 8-26-97; $1.8 million).
Arbitron Metro Market: Crete, IL; *Format:* Christian, Talk; *Target Audience:* 35 plus; adult, African-Americans
Donald Crawford, CEO
Taft Harris, General Manager

Crystal Lake

WAIT
10-01-1965; 850 kHz AM; *Hrs Open:* Sunrise-sunset; 2.5 kW; N42 15 30 W88 21 48
5625 N Milwaukee Ave, Chicago, IL 60646 USA
(773) 792-1121; *Fax:* (773) 792-2904
thepromise850.com
mp@wsbcradio.com
License: Crystal Lake, IL held by Chicago Newsweb Corp.
Group Owner: Newsweb Corp.; (acq 9-16-2003; $8.25 million)
Arbitron Metro Market: Chicago, IL; *Format:* Spanish, Christian

Danville

WDAN
10-01-1938; 1490 kHz AM; 1 kw-U, ND1; N40 8 58 W87 37 35
3001 Springmill Ste-B, Springfield, IL 62708 US
(217) 442-1700; *Fax:* (217) 431-1489
www.vermilioncountyfirst.com
BillPickett@neuhoffmedia.com
License: Danville, IL held by Neuhoff Family L.P.
Group Owner: Neuhoff Family L.P.; acq 11-5-03; grpsl).
Nat'l Reps: McGavren Guild
Arbitron Metro Market: Danville, Il; *Format:* News, News/Talk, 84, Talk *Special Programming:* Farm 20 hrs wkly; *Hrs. of News Programming:* news progmg 20 hrs wkly; *No. News Employees:* 1 *Target Audience:* 25-54.
Roger Neuhoff, President
Michael Hulvey, Operations Dir
Michelle Campbell, General Sales Mgr
Bill Pickett, News Director
Geoffery Neuhoff, Executive Vice President
Tom Barnes, Operations Manager

WDNL
05-01-1967; 102.1 MHz FM; *Hrs Open:* 24; 50 kw; 367 ft.; N40 8 58 W87 37 35
3001 Springmill, Ste-B, Springfield, IL 62708 US
(217) 442-1700; *Fax:* (217) 431-1489
www.wdnlfm.com
infowdnl@cooketech.net
License: Danville, Vermilion County, IL
Group Owner: Neuhoff Family L.P.
Arbitron Metro Market: Danville, Il; *Format:* Adult Contemp; *Hrs. of News Programming:* News progmg 2 hrs wkly; *Target Audience:* 18-49.
Michael Hulvey, Operations Dir
Tom Barnes, Programming Director
Carole Wade, Music Director

WYXY(FM)
03-02-1970; 99.1 MHz FM; 50 kw; Ant 500 ft; N40 08 52 W87 46 20
2603 W. Bradley Ave., Champaign, IL 61821
(217) 352-4141; *Fax:* (217) 352-1256

License: Danville, Vermilion County, IL held by Saga Communications of Illinois LLC.
Group Owner: Saga Communications Inc.; (acq 6-30-2004; $3.25 million).
Nat'l Reps: D & R Radio
Population Served: 469,000; *Arbitron Metro Market:* Champaign, IL; *Format:* Classic Rock
Alan Beck, General Manager
Bill Cain, Programming Director

WRHK
11-01-1992; 94.9 MHz FM; *Hrs Open:* 24; 6 kw; 328 ft.; N40 10 40 W87 28 55
1904 Oak Creek Road, Springfield, IL 62704 US
(217) 442-1700; *Fax:* (217) 431-1489
www.949krock.com
License: Danville, Vermilion County, IL held by Neuhoff Family L.P.
Group Owner: Neuhoff Family L.P.; acq 11-5-03; grpsl).
Nat'l Reps: McGavren Guild
Format: Classic Rock; *Hrs. of News Programming:* News progmg 5 hrs wkly; *Target Audience:* 18-49.
Roger Neuhoff, Chairman
Pat Odea, CFO
Geoffery Neuhoff, President
Michael Hulvey, General Manager
Michelle Campbell, General Sales Mgr
Tom Barnes, Programming Director
Don Russell, Chief Engineer

DeKalb

WCPT-FM
03-10-1960; 92.5 MHz FM; *Hrs Open:* 24; 20 kW; 489 ft.; N41 52 33 W88 45 16
5475 N Milwaukee Ave, Chicago, IL 60630 USA
(773) 792-0400
www.wcpt820.com
License: DeKalb, IL held by WDEK Inc.
Group Owner: Newsweb Corp.; (acq 11-15-2004; grpsl)
Nat'l Network: CNN Radio
Arbitron Metro Market: Chicago, IL; *Format:* Talk
Matt Comings, Operations Manager
Chris Schrage, Promotions Coordinator
Mike McCarthy, Chief Engineer

Decatur

WDZ
03-17-1921; 1050 kHz AM; 1 kw-D, ND1; 0.25 kw-N, ND1; N39 48 54 W89 0 8
1705 West Northwest Highway, Suite 275, Grapevine, TX 76051 US
(217) 423-9744; *Fax:* (217) 423-9764
www.espndecatur.com/
License: Decatur, IL held by Neuhoff Family L.P.
Group Owner: Neuhoff Family L.P.; (acq 2-23-2009; grpsl)
Nat'l Network: Fox Sports
Arbitron Metro Market: Decatur, IL; *Format:* Sports
Mark Hanson, General Manager
Tricia LeVeck, Programming Director

WDZQ
11-01-1976; 95.1 MHz FM; 50 kw; 492 ft.; N39 37 40 W89 4 51
1705 West Northwest Highway, Suite 275, Grapevine, TX 76051 US
(217) 423-9744; *Fax:* (217) 423-9764
www.95q.com
License: Decatur, Macon County, IL held by Neuhoff Family L.P.
Group Owner: Neuhoff Family L.P.; (acq 2-23-2009; grpsl)
Arbitron Metro Market: Decatur, IL; *Format:* Country
Mark Hanson, General Manager
Wendy Tohill, General Sales Mgr
Brad Wells, Programming Director
Tammy Moore, Promotions Manager

***WJMU**
03-10-1971; 89.5 MHz FM; *Hrs Open:* 7 AM-1 AM; 1.65 kw; 85 ft.; N39 50 30 W88 58 29
1184 West Main Street, Decatur, IL 62522 US
(217) 424-6377; *Fax:* (217) 424-3993
www.millikin.edu
License: Decatur, Macon County, IL held by Millikin University.
Arbitron Metro Market: Decatur, IL; *Format:* Alternative; *Hrs. of News Programming:* News progmg 8 hrs wkly; *Target Audience:* 20 plus; students, surrounding community
Dove Zemke, President
Matt Tucker, General Manager
Keith Chandler, Programming Director
Dan Bleyle, Promotions Manager

WSOY
01-01-1925; 1340 kHz AM; *Hrs Open:* 24
1705 West Northwest Hwy, Ste 275, Grapevine, TX 76051 US
(217) 877-5371; *Fax:* (217) 877-8777
www.wsoy.com
License: Decatur, IL held by Neuhoff Family L.P.
Group Owner: Neuhoff Family L.P.; (acq 2-23-2009; grpsl)
Arbitron Metro Market: Decatur, IL; *Format:* News, News/Talk, 84, Talk; *Hrs. of News Programming:* news progmg 13 hrs wkly; *No. News Employees:* 3; *Target Audience:* 25 plus.
Mark Hanson, General Manager
Ryan Forden, Programming Director

WSOY-FM
11-01-1946; 102.9 MHz FM; *Hrs Open:* 24; 54 kw; 443 ft.; N39 52 41 W88 56 32
1100 E. Pershing Road, Decatur, IL 62526 US
(217) 877-5371; *Fax:* (217) 877-8777
www.wsoy.com
License: Decatur, Macon County, IL held by Neuhoff Family L.P.
Group Owner: Neuhoff Family L.P.; (acq 2-23-2009; grpsl)
Nat'l Network: CBS; *Regional Network:* Ill. Radio Net.
Arbitron Metro Market: Decatur, IL; *Format:* Contemporary Hits/Top 40; *Hrs. of News Programming:* news progmg 3 hrs wkly; *No. News Employees:* 3; *Target Audience:* 25-54.
Mark Hanson, General Manager
Roy Jaynes, Programming Director

WYDS
01-01-1993; 93.1 MHz FM; *Hrs Open:* 24; 6 kw; 328 ft; N39 48 35 W88 59 31
410 N. Water St., Suite B, Decatur, IL 37215
(217) 428-4487; *Fax:* (217) 428-4501
www.decaturradio.com/93-1-fm-the-party/
cbullock@cromwellradio.com
License: Decatur, Macon County, IL held by WEJT Inc.
Group Owner: The Cromwell Group Inc.; (acq 4-9-93; $750,000;
Nat'l Reps: Eastman Radio
Population Served: 200,000; *Arbitron Metro Market:* Decatur, IL; *Hrs. of News Programming:* 24/7; *No. News Employees:* 1; *Target Audience:* 18-49; females average age of 26; *Adv. Rates:* 30; 28; 30; 20
Chris Bullock, General Manager
Tara Nickerson, Operations Manager
Cindy Hansen, Business Manager

WYDS-HD2
01-01-1993; 95.5 MHz FM; *Hrs Open:* 24; 6 kw; 328 ft; N39 48 35 W88 59 31
410 N. Water St., Suite B, Decatur, IL 37215
(217) 428-4487; *Fax:* (217) 428-4501
cbullock@cromwellradio.com
License: Decatur, Macon County, IL held by WEJT Inc.
Group Owner: The Cromwell Group Inc.; (acq 4-9-93; $750,000;
Nat'l Reps: Eastman Radio
Population Served: 200,000; *Arbitron Metro Market:* Decatur, IL; *Format:* Urban Contemporary, Gospel, 64; *Hrs. of News Programming:* 24/7; *No. News Employees:* 1; *Target Audience:* 18-49;; *Adv. Rates:* 30;28; 30; 20
Chris Bullock, General Manager
Tara Nickerson, Operations Manager
Cindy Hansen, Business Manager

Deerfield

WEEF
01-01-1963; 1430 kHz AM; 1.6 kw-D, DA2; 0.075 kw-N, DA2; N42 08 22 W87 53 7
4320 Dundee Rd., Northbrook, IL 60062 US
(847) 498-3350
License: Deerfield, IL held by Polnet Communications Ltd.
Group Owner: Polnet Communications Ltd.; (acq 5-20-2003; $1 million)
Arbitron Metro Market: Deerfield, IL; *Format:* Ethnic; *Target Audience:* General; Ethnic
Chris Bagat, Station Manager

Dekalb

WDKB
08-13-1990; 94.9 MHz FM; *Hrs Open:* 24; 3 kw; 328 ft.; N41 56 57 W88 53 44
2201 N. First St., #95, Dekalb, IL 60115 US
(815) 758-0950, (815) 758-4926; *Fax:* (815) 758-6226
www.b95fm.com
ontheair@b95fm.com
License: Dekalb, De Kalb County, IL held by De Kalb County Radio Ltd.
Wire Services: AP
Arbitron Metro Market: DeKalb, Il; *Format:* Adult Contemp
Special Programming: Relg one hr wkly; *Hrs. of News Programming:* news progmg 3hrs wkly; *No. News Employees:* 1; *Target Audience:* 25-54; adults withmoderate to upper incomes; *Adv. Rates:* 29; 29; 29; 20
Tana Knetsch, President
Dave Bavido, General Sales Mgr
Ken Misch, Programming Director

WLBK
12-07-1947; 1360 kHz AM; *Hrs Open:* 24 hours; 1 kw-D, ND1; 0.024 kw-N, ND1; N41 56 18 W88 45 3
Mailing Address: 11 Skyline Drive, Hawthorne, NY 10532 US
Second Address: 2410 Sycamore Rd. Suite C, De Kalb, IL 60115
(815) 758-8686; *Fax:* (815) 756-9723
www.wlbkradio.com
sales@1360wlbk.com
License: Dekalb, IL held by WPW Broadcasting Inc.
Group Owner: Prairie Radio Communications; (acq 4-12-2000).
Format: News, News/Talk, 86 *Special Programming:* Farm 12 hrs wkly; *Hrs. of News Programming:* news progmg 21 hrs wkly; *No. News Employees:* 1; *Target Audience:* General.; *Adv. Rates:* $35 6-10a.m., 3-7p.m.,$25 6a.
Larry Timpe, General Manager
Terry Ryan, Programming Director
Scott Zak, News Director

***WNIJ**
10-01-1954; 89.5 MHz FM; *Hrs Open:* 24; 50 kw; 420 ft.; N42 0 55 W89 0 7
801 North Frist Street, Dekalb, IL 60115 US
(815) 753-9000; *Fax:* (815) 753-9938
www.northernpublicradio.org
npr@niu.edu
License: Dekalb, De Kalb County, IL held by Northern Illinois University.
Nat'l Network: PRI; NPR
Arbitron Metro Market: Rockford, IL; *Format:* Jazz, News *Special Programming:* Folk 4 hrs wkly; *Hrs. of News Programming:* news progmg one hr wkly; *No. News Employees:* 2; *Target Audience:* General.
Staci Hoste, General Manager
Jan Kilgard, General Sales Mgr
Bill Drake, Programming Director
Guy Stephens, News Director
Jeff Glass, Chief Engineer

Des Plaines

WPPN
12-03-1971; 106.7 MHz FM; *Hrs Open:* 24; 50 kw; 423 ft.; N42 8 14 W87 58 57
625 N. Michigan Ave., Suite 3, Chicago, IL 60611 US
(312) 981-1800; *Fax:* (312) 981-1806
www.univision.com
License: Des Plaines, Cook County, IL held by Univision Radio License Corp.
Group Owner: Univision Radio; (acq 12-21-2004; asset exchange agreement).
Arbitron Metro Market: Chicago, IL; *Format:* Adult Contemp, Spanish
Doug Levy, Senior Vice President and General Manager
Hector Fabregas, Director of Local Sales
Victor Cerda, Programming Director
Alicia Chavarria, Promotions Manager
Joshua Sigstad, Chief Engineer
Adriene Drucker-Dibble, LocalSales Manager

Dixon

WIXN
07-01-1961; 1460 kHz AM; *Hrs Open:* 19; 1 kw-D, DA2; 0.023 kw-N, DA2; N41 49 38 W89 29 11
980 North Michigan Avenue, Suite 1880, Chicago, IL 60611 US
(815) 288-3341; *Fax:* (815) 284-1017
www.wixn.com
info@wixn.com
License: Dixon, IL held by NRG License Sub. LLC.
Group Owner: NRG Media LLC; (acq 10-31-2005; grpsl)
Format: News, Oldies *Special Programming:* Farm 11 hrs wkly; *Hrs. of News Programming:* news progmg 14 hrs wkly; *No. News Employees:* 2; *Target Audience:* 25-54.
Al Knickrehm, General Manager

WRCV
09-01-1965; 101.7 MHz FM; *Hrs Open:* 24; 6 kw; 328 ft.; N41 49 29 W89 29 51
980 North Michigan Avenue, Suite 1880, Chicago, IL 60611 US
(815) 288-3341; *Fax:* (815) 284-1017
www.wixn.com
License: Dixon, Lee County, IL held by NRG License Sub. LLC.
Group Owner: NRG Media LLC

Format: Country; *Hrs. of News Programming:* news progmg 10 hrs wkly; *No. News Employees:* 2
Steve Marco, Programming Director

Dorsey

*WARW
01-01-2006; 89.5 MHz FM; 1.5 kw; 318 ft.; N39 0 44 W89 57 13
Rebroadcasts: Rebroadcasts KLRD(FM) Yucaipa, CA 100%. US
(888) 937-2471; *Fax:* (916) 251-1650
www.air1.com
info@air1.com
License: Dorsey, Madison County, IL held by Educational Media Foundation.
Group Owner: EMF Broadcasting; (acq 9-22-2005; $30,000 for CP)
Nat'l Network: Air 1
Arbitron Metro Market: Dorsey, IL; *Format:* Alternative, Christian
Darrell Chambliss, Chairman
Alan Mason, COO
Mike Novak, President and CEO
Ed Lenane, News Director
Sam Wallington, Engineering Dir
Dan Antonelli, Chief Business Development Officer
Eric Moser, Chief Financial Officer
BrianBurger, Vice President of Human Resources
D. Kevin Blair, Secretary and General Counsel
Larry Moody, Director
Mitch Barnhart, Director

Downers Grove

*WDGC-FM
02-28-1969; 88.3 MHz FM; *Hrs Open:* 8 AM-10 PM (M-S); 0.25 kw horiz; 131 ft.; N41 48 16 W88 0 44
6301 Springside Avenue, Downers Grove, IL 60516 US
(630) 795-8490(630) 795-8400; *Fax:* (630) 795-8499
www.wdgc.csd99.org/
wdgcfm@hotmail.com
License: Downers Grove, Du Page County, IL held by High School District No. 99 Dupage County.
Arbitron Metro Market: Chicago, IL; *Format:* Variety/Diverse
Special Programming: Community affrs 6 hrs wkly; *Hrs. of News Programming:* News progmg 5 hrs wkly; *Target Audience:* General; all age groups
John Waite, General Manager

Dundee

WFXF
06-08-1967; 103.9 MHz FM; *Hrs Open:* 24; 2.55 kw; 322 ft.; N42 6 21 W88 22 37
1436 Auburn Boulevard, Sacramento, CA 95815 US
(815) 459-7000; *Fax:* (815) 459-7027
License: Dundee, Kane County, IL held by The Mile High Station Trust LLC, as Trustee
Arbitron Metro Market: Chicago; *Format:* Oldies
Doug Boyd, General Sales Mgr
Stew Cohen, News Director
Floyd Evans, VP, Regional Manager

Duquoin

WDQN
01-01-1951; 1580 kHz AM; *Hrs Open:* 5:30 AM-11 PM; 0.17 kw-D, ND1; 0.0066 kw-N, ND1; N38 1 56 W89 14 30
Mailing Address: P.O. Box 190, Duquoin, IL 62832 US
Second Address: 2337 US Rt. 51, Du Quoin, IL 62832
(618) 542-3894; *Fax:* (618) 542-4514
wdqnradio@onecliq.net
License: Duquoin, IL held by Du Quoin Broadcasting Co.
Nat'l Network: ABC; Motor Racing Net; *Regional Network:* Brownfield; *Wire Services:* AP
Arbitron Metro Market: Du Quoin, IL; *Format:* Adult Contemp, Country *Special Programming:* Farm 3 hrs, relg 5 hrs wkly; *Target Audience:* 25-64; male & female; *Adv. Rates:* 18; 18; 18
Marrianne Showalter, Operations Dir
Greg Showalter, General Manager
Michelle Klein, General Sales Mgr
Gordon Showalter, Programming Director
Ruth Showalter, Traffic & Accounts Rec

WDQN-FM
09-01-1969; 95.9 MHz FM; *Hrs Open:* 6 AM-11 PM; 6 kw; 328 ft.; N38 1 56 W89 14 30
Mailing Address: P.O. Box 190, Duquoin, IL 62832 US
Second Address: 3391 Charley Good Rd., West Frankfort, IL 62896
(618) 627-4651; *Fax:* (618) 627-2726
www.3abn.org
License: Duquoin, Perry County, IL held by Three Angels Broadcasting Network Inc.
Arbitron Metro Market: Du Quoin, IL; *Format:* Christian
Danny Shelton, President
Mollie Steenson, General Manager
Jim Morris, General Sales Mgr
Sandra Juarez, Programming Director
Moses Primo, Chief Engineer

Dwight

WJEZ
01-01-1998; 98.9 MHz FM; 1.3 kw; 489 ft.; N41 02 06 W88 26 10
315 N. Mill St., Pontiac, IL 61764 US
(815) 844-6101
www.wjez.com
cathi.coppinger@cumulus.com
License: Dwight, IL held by Cumulus Licensing LLC
Group Owner: Cumulus Media Inc.; (acq 5-12-2004; grpsl).
Format: Adult Contemp; *Target Audience:* 18-49; general
Paula Williams, General Sales Mgr
Cathi Coppinger, Programming Director
Brandi McCarrey, Promotions Manager
Mark Myre, Sports Director

Earlville

WMKB
02-03-2003; 102.9 MHz FM; *Hrs Open:* 24; 2.15 kw; 558 ft.; N41 37 16 W89 05 20
4756 E. 4th Rd., Mendota, IL 61342 US
(815) 538-7500; *Fax:* (866) 816-0064
www.wmkbradio.com
License: Earlville, La Salle County, IL held by KM Radio of Earlville, LLC.
Group Owner: KM Communications Inc.
Nat'l Network: ABC
Arbitron Metro Market: Brandon; *Format:* Tejano; *Target Audience:* 25-54.
Diana Cano, Sales Manager

East Moline

KUUL
02-23-1976; 101.3 MHz FM; 50 kw; 499 ft.; N41 37 10 W90 17 41
3535 East Kimberly Road, Davenport, IA 52807 US
(563) 344-7000; *Fax:* (563) 359-8524
www.1013kissfm.com
License: East Moline, Rock Island County, IL held by Citicasters Licenses Inc.
Group Owner: iHeartMedia; (acq 11-15-00; grpsl).
Nat'l Reps: Katz Radio
Arbitron Metro Market: East Moline, IL; *Format:* Classic Rock
Special Programming: Pub affrs 6 hrs, farm one hr wkly; *Target Audience:* 25-54; contemp, upscale adults
Jim O'Hara, Senior Vice President of Programming
Scott Bitting, Market President/Director of Sales
Kelly Meyer, Sales Manager
Todd Alan, Programming Director
Jessica Tillberg, Promotions Director
Mark Manuel, Web ContentDirector

*WDLM-AM
04-03-1960; 960 kHz AM; 1 kw-D; N41 24 57 W90 23 54
18239 E 200th St, Coal Valley, IL 61240 USA
(309) 234-5111; *Fax:* (309) 234-5114
www.moodyradio.org/stations/quad-cities
License: East Moline, IL held by The Moody Bible Institute of Chicago
Group Owner: The Moody Bible Institute of Chicago
Arbitron Metro Market: Quad Cities (NW Illinois and SE Iowa); *Format:* Christian

*WDLM-FM
01-20-1980; 89.3 MHz FM; 100 kW; 499 ft.; N41 32 52 W90 28 30
18239 E 200th St, Coal Valley, IL 61240 USA
(309) 234-5111; *Fax:* (309) 234-5114
www.moodyradio.org/stations/quad-cities
License: East Moline, Rock Island County, IL
Arbitron Metro Market: Quad Cities (NW Illinois and SE Iowa); *Format:* Christian

East St. Louis

*WCBW-FM
01-01-2001; 89.7 MHz FM; 0.25 kw; 187 ft.; N38 37 53 W90 12 9
1411 Locust Street, St. Louis, MO 63103 US
(314) 421-3020; *Fax:* (314) 421-1702
www.newlifeevangelisticcenter.org
larryr@hereshelpnet.org
License: East St. Louis, St. Clair County, IL held by New Life Evangelistic Center Inc.
Arbitron Metro Market: Saint Louis, MO; *Format:* Religious
Larry Rice, General Manager

WXOS
06-06-1965; 101.1 MHz FM; 100 kw; 986 ft.; N38 28 56 W90 23 53
11647 Olive Blvd., St. Louis, MO 63141 US
(314) 983-6000
www.101sports.com
webmaster@101sports.com
License: East St. Louis, St. Clair County, IL held by St. Louis FCC License Sub LLC
Group Owner: Hubbard Broadcasting Inc.; (acq 1-19-2011)
Nat'l Network: ESPN Radio; *Nat'l Reps:* McGavren Guild
Arbitron Metro Market: St. Louis, MO; *Format:* Sports, Talk; *Target Audience:* 25-49.
Mike Rowen, General Sales Mgr
Chris Neupert, Programming Director
Scott Wehner, Promotions Manager
Keith Kraus, Director of Sales
Kim Grant, Digital Media Director
Jerry England, Human Resources Director

Edwardsville

*WRYT
11-20-1987; 1080 kHz AM
664-A Coeur De Royale, Creve Coeur, MO 63141 US
(314) 752-7000
www.covenantnet.net
covenantnetwork@juno.com
License: Edwardsville, IL held by Covenant Network.
Group Owner: Covenant Network; (acq 10-2-97)
Arbitron Metro Market: St. Louis, MO; *Format:* Religious; *Target Audience:* General.
John Holman, President
Tony Holman, General Manager

*WSIE
09-04-1970; 88.7 MHz FM; *Hrs Open:* 24; 50 kw horiz, 41 kw vert; 499 ft.; N38 47 6 W89 59 10
Siue Box 1773, Edwardsville, IL 62026 US
(618) 650-2228; *Fax:* (618) 650-2233
www.wsieradio.com
License: Edwardsville, Madison County, IL held by Board of Trustees, Southern Illinois University.
Nat'l Network: NPR; PRI; *Regional Network:* Ill. Radio Net.
Arbitron Metro Market: St. Louis, MO; *Format:* Jazz *Special Programming:* New age 10 hrs wkly; *Hrs. of News Programming:* news progmg 20 hrs wkly; *No. News Employees:* 1; *Target Audience:* 25-49; adults seekinga sophisticated alternative
Gregory Conroy, General Manager
Jason Valentine, Programming Director
Justin Wingerter, News Director
John Masters, Chief Engineer

Effingham

WCRA
06-08-1947; 1090 kHz AM; 1 kw-D, NDD; N39 6 26 W88 33 44
405 South Banker Street, Suite 201, Effingham, IL 62401 US
(217) 342-4141; *Fax:* (217) 342-4143
www.effinghamradio.com
mphillips@cromwellradio.com
License: Effingham, IL held by Two Petaz Inc.
Group Owner: The Cromwell Group Inc.; (acq 1-9-02; grpsl).
Nat'l Network: CBS
Arbitron Metro Market: Effingham, Illinois; *Format:* News, News/Talk, 86; *Target Audience:* 25-54.
Sheila Myers, General Manager
Ethan Kruger, News Director
Eric Frye, Sports Director

WCRC
06-14-1963; 95.7 MHz FM; *Hrs Open:* 24; 50 kw; 479 ft.; N39 6 26 W88 33 44
405 South Banker Street, Suite 201, Effingham, IL 62401 US
(217) 342-4141; *Fax:* (217) 342- 4143
www.effinghamradio.com
wcrc@wcrc957.com
License: Effingham, Effingham County, IL held by Two Petaz Inc.
Group Owner: The Cromwell Group Inc.
Arbitron Metro Market: Effingham, Illinois; *Format:* Country
Sheila Myers, General Manager
Ethan Kruger, News Director
Eric Frye, Sports Director

WXEF
10-04-1982; 97.9 MHz FM; *Hrs Open:* 24; 6 kw; 312 ft.; N39 7 25 W88 38 28
P.O. Box 988, Effingham, IL 62401 US
(217) 347-5518; *Fax:* (217) 347-5519
www.thexradio.com
info@thexradio.com
License: Effingham, Effingham County, IL held by Premier Broadcasting Inc.
Nat'l Network: Fox News Radio
Arbitron Metro Market: Effingham, IL; *Format:* Adult Contemp
Special Programming: High school sports; *Hrs. of News Programming:* news progmg 15 hrs wkly; *No. News Employees:* 2; *Target Audience:* General.
Dave Ring, President
Tonya Siner, VP Operations, Sales Manager
Greg Sapp, Station Manager, News & Sports Directo
Kenna Endebrock, Promotions Manager
Angela James, Certified Radio & Digital Marketing Consultant
Teresa Klinger,Traffic, Office Manager
Mike Walker, Account Representative

***WEFI**
01-01-2006; 89.5 MHz FM; 0.4 kw; 164 ft.; N39 8 30 W88 33 36
Rebroadcasts: Rebroadcasts WAFR(FM) Tupelo, MS 100%
P.O. Box 3206, Tupelo, MS 38803 US
(662) 844-8888; *Fax:* (662) 842-6791
www.afr.net
faq@afa.net
License: Effingham, Effingham County, IL held by American Family Association.
Group Owner: American Family Radio
Arbitron Metro Market: Tyler-Longview, TX; *Format:* Christian
Tim Wildmon, President
Donald Wildmon, Founder
Buddy Smith, Sr VP
Ed Vitagliano, Exec VP
Randy Sharp, Director Of Special Projects
Meeke Addison, Director Of Communications
Abraham Hamilton, General Counsel

***WGMR**
91.3 MHz FM; 0.62 kw; 295 ft.; N39 7 2 W88 32 5
US
(314)752-7000
www.covenantnet.net
webmaster@covenantnet.net
License: Effingham, Effingham County, IL held by Brindisi Consortium.
Nat'l Network: EWTN Radio
Arbitron Metro Market: St. Louis, IL; *Format:* Christian
William Bence, President

WCRA
06-14-1963; 1090 MHz AM; *Hrs Open:* 24; 50 kw; 479 ft.; N39 6 26 W88 33 44
405 South Banker Street, Suite 201, Effingham, IL 62401 US
(217) 342-4141; *Fax:* (217) 342- 4143
www.effinghamradio.com
wcrc@wcrc957.com
License: Effingham, Effingham County, IL held by Two Petaz Inc.
Group Owner: The Cromwell Group Inc.
Arbitron Metro Market: Effingham, Illinois; *Format:* News, News/Talk, 86
Marv Philips, Market Manager
Beau Richards, Operations Manager
Cindy Hansen, Business Manager

WCRA-FM
06-14-1963; 1090 MHz FM; *Hrs Open:* 24; 50 kw; 479 ft.; N39 6 26 W88 33 44
405 South Banker Street, Suite 201, Effingham, IL 62401 US
(217) 342-4141; *Fax:* (217) 342- 4143
www.effinghamradio.com
wcrc@wcrc957.com
License: Effingham, Effingham County, IL held by Two Petaz Inc.
Group Owner: The Cromwell Group Inc.
Nat'l Network: WCRA AM 1090
Arbitron Metro Market: Effingham, Illinois; *Format:* News, News/Talk, 86
Marv Phillips, Market Manager
Beau Richards, Operations Manager
Cindy Hansen, Business Manager

Eldorado

WEBQ-FM
04-01-1972; 102.3 MHz FM; *Hrs Open:* 24; 3 kw; 299 ft.; N37 49 14 W88 27 11
701 South Commercial St, Harrisburg, IL 62946 US
(618) 253-7282; *Fax:* (618) 252-2366
www.webqradio.com
License: Eldorado, Saline County, IL held by W. Russell Withers Jr.
Group Owner: Withers Broadcasting Co.; (acq 7-28-2004; $450,000 with WEBQ(AM) Harrisburg).
Nat'l Network: ABC; *Regional Network:* Ill. Radio Net.
Arbitron Metro Market: Harrisburg, IL; *Format:* Adult Contemp; *Hrs. of News Programming:* news progmg 6 hrs wkly; *No. News Employees:* 1; *Target Audience:* 25-45; young middle class adults; *Adv. Rates:* 9.79;9.79; 7.79; 4.64
Cathy Horton, General Manager
Cathy Horton, Station Manager
Sonny Dotson, General Sales Mgr
Wyatt Drake, News Director
Bob Romonosky, Chief Engineer
Shelly Reeder, Traffic Manager

Elgin

***WEPS**
01-01-1950; 88.9 MHz FM; *Hrs Open:* 6; 0.74 kw; 43 ft.; N42 2 11 W88 16 34
355 E. Chicago Street, Elgin, IL 60120 US
(800) 747-7444; *Fax:* (847) 888-0272
www.wpr.org
Listener@wpr.org
License: Elgin, Kane County, IL held by Board of Education, Union School District 46.
Arbitron Metro Market: Elgin, IL; *Format:* Variety/Diverse *Special Programming:* Class 5 hrs, jazz 6 hrs, community affrs 3 hrs, educ 13 hrs wkly; *Target Audience:* Parents of students.
Steve Johnston, Director of Engineering & Operations
Jackie Olson Kold, Station Manager
Michael Leland, News Director
Mike Crane, Director of Radio
Michael Arnold, Associate Director
Sarah Jacobs, Audience Services Manager
Jeffrey Potter, Marketing Director
Rebecca Dopart, Membership and Corporate Support
Mary Kay Dadisman, Director of Development

WRMN
01-01-1949; 1410 kHz AM; 1 kW; N42 0 21 W88 17 55
5500 Poplar Ave, Suite 1, Memphis, TN 38119 USA
(901) 685-3993; *Fax:* (901) 685-3995
www.wrmn1410.com
License: Elgin, IL held by Elgin Community Broadcasting LLC
Group Owner: Pollack Broadcasting; 2016
Arbitron Metro Market: Elgin-Chicago, IL; *Format:* News/Talk
Special Programming: Sp 10 hrs wkly; *Hrs. of News Programming:* news progmg 5 hrs wkly; *No. News Employees:* 1; *Target Audience:* General.

Ellsworth

***WSPI**
89.5 MHz FM; 0.29 kw; 312 ft.; N40 24 16.9 W88 35 33.8
US
(309) 807-0100; *Fax:* (570) 644-2232
www.catholicspiritradio.com
License: Ellsworth, McLean County, IL held by 2820 Communications Inc.
Arbitron Metro Market: Ellsworth, IL; *Format:* Christian
Morgan Grammer, General Manager

Elmhurst

WJJG
10-10-1974; 1530 kHz AM; 760 w-D, DA; N41 52 03 W87 55 07
5629 St. Charles Rd., Suite 208, Berkeley, IL 60163
(708) 493-1530; *Fax:* (708) 493-1537
www.1530wjjg.com
License: Elmhurst, Du Page County, IL held by Joseph J. Gentile Inc.
Population Served: 5,000,000; *Arbitron Metro Market:* Chicago, IL; *Target Audience:* 45 plus; affluent adults
Joseph Gentile, President
Mike Baker, Operations Dir

***WRSE**
12-07-1962; 88.7 MHz FM; *Hrs Open:* 24; 0.32 kw; 95 ft.; N41 53 46 W87 56 45
190 Propect Avenue, Elmhurst, IL 60126 US
(630) 617-3729; *Fax:* (630) 617-3313
www.wrse.com
License: Elmhurst, Du Page County, IL held by Board of Trustees Elmhurst College.
Wire Services: AP
Arbitron Metro Market: Chicago; *Format:* Alternative, Oldies
Special Programming: Metal 3 hrs, hip hop 6 hrs wkly; *Hrs. of News Programming:* News progmg one hr wkly; *Target Audience:* 17-40; college & general
Jon Morgan, General Manager

Elmwood

WFYR
08-02-1993; 97.3 MHz FM; *Hrs Open:* 24; 25 kw; 338 ft.; N40 46 22 W89 44 50
120 Eaton St., Peoria, IL 61603 US
(309) 676-5000
www.973nashfm.com
License: Elmwood, Peoria County, IL held by Radio License Holding CBC, LLC
Group Owner: Cumulus Media Inc.; (acq 7-6-01; grpsl).
Nat'l Reps: Katz Radio
Arbitron Metro Market: Peoria, IL; *Format:* Country; *Target Audience:* 25-54; adults, family oriented & skewing female; *Adv. Rates:* 30; 30; 30; 10
Brad Creek, Director of Sales
Shelly Knight, Programming Director
Matt Harris, Promotions Manager

Elmwood Park

WCFS
11-21-2007; 105.9 MHz FM; *Hrs Open:* 24; 4.1 kW; 1575 ft.; N41 52 44 W87 38 8
180 North Stetson, Suite 1100, Chicago, IL 60601 USA
(312) 297-7800
www.wbbm780.com
License: Elmwood Park, Cook County, IL held by CBS Radio Holdings Corp. of Orlando
Group Owner: CBS Radio; (acq 1996)
Nat'l Network: Westwood One
Arbitron Metro Market: Chicago, IL; *Format:* News; *Hrs. of News Programming:* news progmg one hr wkly; *No. News Employees:* 1; *Target Audience:* 25-54

Eureka

WPIA
01-01-1989; 98.5 MHz FM; *Hrs Open:* 24; 6 kw; 328 ft.; N40 42 57 W89 27 50 *Rebroadcasts:* Simulcast with WWCT(FM) Farmington 100%
Post Office Box 150846, Nashville, TN 37215 US
(309) 686-0101; *Fax:* (309) 686-0111
www.kisspeoria.com/
mrea@ampillinois.com
License: Eureka, Woodford County, IL held by IM IL Licenses LLC.
Group Owner: Independence Media Holdings LLC; (acq 9-19-2006; grpsl).
Arbitron Metro Market: Eureka, IL; *Format:* Contemporary Hits/Top 40
Michael Rea, General Manager
Don Black, Programming Director

Evanston

WKTA
01-01-1953; 1330 kHz AM; *Hrs Open:* 24; 5 kw-D, DAD; 0.011 kw-N, DAD; N42 8 23 W87 53 9
3656 W. Belmont Ave., Chicago, IL 60618 US
(773) 588-6300; *Fax:* (773) 588-0834
www.pclradio.com
License: Evanston, IL held by Polnet Communications Ltd.
Group Owner: Polnet Communications Ltd.
Arbitron Metro Market: Chicago, IL; *Format:* Ethnic, News/Talk; *Hrs. of News Programming:* News progmg 5 hrs wkly; *Target Audience:* 18-54
Walter Kotaba, President

***WNUR-FM**
05-08-1950; 89.3 MHz FM; *Hrs Open:* 24; 7.2 kw; 98 ft.; N42 3 12 W87 40 33
1905 Sheridan Road, Evanston, IL 60201 US
(847) 491-7101; *Fax:* (847) 467-2058
www.wnur.org
gm@wnur.org
License: Evanston, Cook County, IL held by Northwestern University.
Arbitron Metro Market: Chicago, IL; *Format:* Jazz *Special Programming:* Folk 3 hrs, world mus 10 hrs, reggae 4 hrs wkly; *Hrs. of News Programming:* News progmg 3 hrs wkly; *Target Audience:* 18-34; general
Henry Bienen, President
Monica Yi, Operations Dir
Matt Ludwig, General Manager
Ethan Simonoff, Programming Director
Ashley Ayarza, Promotions Manager

WOJO
01-01-1946; 105.1 MHz FM; 5.7 kw; 1,394 ft.; N41 53 56 W87 37 23
625 N. Michigan Ave., Suite 3, Chicago, IL 60611 US
(312) 981-1800
www.univision.com
License: Evanston, Cook County, IL held by Tichenor License Corp.
Group Owner: Univision Radio; (acq 9-22-2003; grpsl).
Nat'l Reps: Katz Radio
Arbitron Metro Market: Chicago, IL *TV Affiliate:* Sp; *Format:* Tejano; *Hrs. of News Programming:* 1; *No. News Employees:* 18-35; regional/Mexican
Doug Levy, General Manager
Alicia Chavarria, Promotions Manager
Joshua Sigstad, Chief Engineer

WCGO
01-01-1947; 1590 kHz AM
2100 Lee Street, Evanston, IL 60202 US
(847) 475-1590; *Fax:* (847) 475-1590
www.1590wcgo.com
License: Evanston, IL held by Kovas Communications Inc.
Arbitron Metro Market: Chicago *TV Affiliate:* Sp; *Format:* Greek *Special Programming:* News progmg 8 hrs wkly; *No. News Employees:* General.

Fairbury

WIBL(FM)
08-08-2000; 107.7 MHz FM; *Hrs Open:* 24; 22.5 kw; Ant 351 ft; N40 37 45 W88 46 52
108 Boeykens Pl., Normal, IL 61761
(309) 888-4496; *Fax:* (309) 452-9677
License: Fairbury, Livingston County, IL held by Pilot Media LLC.
Group Owner: Great Plains Media Inc.; (acq 6-19-2007; grpsl)
Nat'l Network: AP Radio; *Wire Services:* AP
Population Served: 77,071; *Arbitron Metro Market:* Bloomington, IL; *Format:* Adult Contemp; *Hrs. of News Programming:* News progmg 2 hrs wkly; *Target Audience:* 25+; women
Kevin Trueblood, Operations Dir
Patti Donsbach, General Manager

Fairfield

WFIW
08-21-1953; 1390 kHz AM; *Hrs Open:* 24; 0.71 kw-D, ND1; 0.058 kw-N, ND1; N38 22 46 W88 19 33
Hwy. 15 E., PO Box 310, Fairfield, IL 62837 US
(618) 842-2159; *Fax:* (618) 847-5907
www.wfiwradio.com
License: Fairfield, IL held by The Original Company, Inc.
Group Owner: The Original Company, Inc.
Format: News/Talk, Sports; *Adv. Rates:* 23; 23; 23; 16
Mark Lange, President

WFIW
01-01-1965; 104.9 MHz FM; *Hrs Open:* 24; 4.9 kw; 364 ft; N38 22 46 W88 19 33
Hwy. 15 E., PO Box 310, Fairfield, IL 62837 US
(618) 842-2159; *Fax:* (618) 847-5907
www.wfiwradio.com
License: Fairfield, IL held by The Original Company, Inc.
Group Owner: The Original Company, Inc.
Population Served: 150,000 *Format:* Adult Contemp
Mark Lange, President

WOKZ
09-01-1996; 105.9 MHz FM; *Hrs Open:* 24; 4.9 kw; 328 ft; N38 22 46 W88 19 33
Hwy. 15 E., PO Box 310, Fairfield, IL 62837 US
(618) 842-2159; *Fax:* (618) 847-5907
www.wfiwradio.com
License: Fairfield, IL held by The Original Company, Inc.
Group Owner: The Original Company, Inc.
Population Served: 150,000 *Format:* Country; *Adv. Rates:* 23; 23; 23; 16
Mark Lange, President

Farmer City

WWHP
10-01-1983; 98.3 MHz FM; *Hrs Open:* 24; 5.2 kw; 351 ft.; N40 24 17 W88 35 34
401 North Main St, Farmer City, IL 61842 US
(309) 928-9876; *Fax:* (309) 928-3708
www.wwhp.com
wwhp@farmwagon.com
License: Farmer City, De Witt County, IL held by WMS1 Inc.
Arbitron Metro Market: Champaign, IL; *Format:* Triple A *Special Programming:* Gospel 3 hrs, comedy 1 hr; *Target Audience:* 18-65; reach city, suburbs & rural listeners in east central Illinois; *Adv. Rates:* 25; 25;25; 25
Larry Williams, Station Manager

Farmington

WZPN
01-01-1997; 96.5 MHz FM; 4.3 kw; 377 ft.; N40 40 10 W89 53 31
4530 N. Miller Ave., Peoria Heights, IL 61614 US
(309) 282-7625; *Fax:* (309) 686-0111
License: Farmington, Fulton County, IL held by IM IL Licenses LLC.
Group Owner: Independence Media Holdings LLC; (acq 3-30-2007; $600,000)
Nat'l Network: ESPN Radio
Format: Sports, Talk
Michael Rea, General Manager

Fisher

***WGNN**
04-07-1996; 102.5 MHz FM; *Hrs Open:* 24; 6 kw; 328 ft.; N40 20 21 W88 24 18
Mailing Address: P.O. Box 12345, Champaign, IL 61826 US
Second Address: 2421 N. 1450 E. Rd., White Heath, IL 61884
(217) 897-6333
www.greatnewsradio.org
staff@greatnewsradio.org
License: Fisher, Champaign County, IL held by Good News Radio Inc.
Nat'l Network: Moody; USA; Salem Radio Network
Format: News, News/Talk, 86, Religious; *Target Audience:* 35 plus; general
David Herriott, Chairman
Mark Burns, President
Carrie Burns, Operations Dir

Flora

WNOI
05-21-1971; 103.9 MHz FM; *Hrs Open:* 24; 3.3 kw; 299 ft.; N38 40 42 W88 29 14
P.O. Box 368, Flora, IL 62839 US
(618) 662-8331; *Fax:* (618) 662-2407
www.wnoi.com
info@wnoi.com
License: Flora, Clay County, IL held by H&R Communications Inc.
Nat'l Network: Jones Radio Networks
Arbitron Metro Market: Flora, IL; *Format:* Adult Contemp; *Hrs. of News Programming:* news progmg 12 hrs wkly; *No. News Employees:* 1; *Target Audience:* General.
Steven Lovellette, President
Patrick Garret, Operations Dir
Randy Poole, General Manager
Brenda Miller, General Sales Mgr
Patrick Garrett, Programming Director
Kirk Wallace, Chief Engineer

Flossmoor

***WHFH**
01-01-1965; 88.5 MHz FM; *Hrs Open:* 14; 1.5 kw horiz; 92 ft.; N41 32 43 W87 41 30
999 South Kedzie, Flossmoor, IL 60422 US
(708) 798-9434; *Fax:* (708) 799-3142
www.whfh.org
License: Flossmoor, Cook County, IL held by Community High School District No. 233.
Special Programming: News/talk one hr, sports talk one hr, live sports; *Hrs. of News Programming:* News progmg 4 hrs wkly; *Target Audience:* Teens-Adult.
Robert Comstock, General Manager
John Henry, Station Manager

Freeport

WFPS
11-01-1970; 92.1 MHz FM; *Hrs Open:* 24; 3.6 kw; 423 ft.; N42 19 41 W89 43 30
Mailing Address: 2830 Sandy Hollow Road, Rockford, IL 61109 US
Second Address: 834 N. Tower Rd., Freeport, IL 61032
(815) 235-7191; *Fax:* (815) 235-4318
www.wekz.com
License: Freeport, Stephenson County, IL held by Scott A. Thompson dba Big Radio
Format: Country; *Hrs. of News Programming:* news progmg 15 hrs wkly; *No. News Employees:* 4; *Target Audience:* 25-49.
Kent McConnell, Operations Dir
Wyatt Herrmann, Programming Director
Brad Hart, News Director
Todd Hausser, Chief Engineer
Becky Koester, Traffic Manager

WFRL
10-28-1947; 1570 kHz AM; *Hrs Open:* 24; 5 kw-D, 500 w-N, DA-2; N42 18 45 W89 35 38
Mailing Address: P.O. Box 807, Freeport, IL 61109
Second Address: 834 N. Tower Rd., Freeport, IL 61032
(815) 235-7191; *Fax:* (815) 235-4318
License: Freeport, Stephenson County, IL held by Scott A. Thompson dba Big Radio
Nat'l Network: ABC
Population Served: 50,000 *Hrs. of News Programming:* news progmg 24 hrs wkly; *No. News Employees:* 4; *Target Audience:* 25-34; *Adv. Rates:* 12; 10; 12; 8
Kent McConnell, Operations Dir
Wyatt Herrmann, Programming Director
Brad Hart, News Director
Todd Hausser, Chief Engineer
Becky Koester, Traffic Manager

***WNIE**
01-01-1999; 89.1 MHz FM; *Hrs Open:* 24; 6 kw; 361 ft.; N42 18 45 W89 35 38 *Rebroadcasts:* Rebroadcasts WNIJ(FM) De Kalb & WNIU(FM) Rockford 50%
801 North First Street, Dekalb, IL 60115 US
(815) 753-9000; *Fax:* (815) 753-9938
www.northernpublicradio.org
npr@niu.edu
License: Freeport, Stephenson County, IL held by Northern Illinois University.
Nat'l Network: PRI; NPR
Arbitron Metro Market: Freeport, IL; *Format:* News; *No. News Employees:* 2; *Target Audience:* General.
Staci Hoste, General Manager
Jan Kilgard, General Sales Mgr
Bill Drake, Programming Director
Guy Stephens, News Director
Jeff Glass, Chief Engineer

WXXQ
04-11-1965; 98.5 MHz FM; *Hrs Open:* 24; 11 kw; 492 ft.; N42 16 48 W89 19 59
C/O Putbrese Hunsaker, P. O. Box 217, Sterling, VA 20167 US
(815) 399-2233; *Fax:* (815) 484-2432
www.q985online.com
License: Freeport, Stephenson County, IL held by Cumulus Licensing Corp.
Group Owner: Cumulus Media Inc.; (acq 3-15-00; grpsl).
Arbitron Metro Market: Freeport, IL; *Format:* Country; *No. News Employees:* 1; *Target Audience:* 25-54.
Becky Riojas, General Manager/Marketing Manager
Scott Maenner, General Sales Mgr
Steve Summers, Programming Director
Priscilla Cantu, Promotions Manager

Galatia

WISH-FM
01-01-2001; 98.9 MHz FM; 4.1 kw; 400 ft.; N37 55 52 W88 40 50
P.O. Box 1508, Mount Vernon, IL 62864 US
(618) 643-2311; *Fax:* (618) 643-3299
License: Galatia, Saline County, IL held by W. Russell Withers Jr.
Group Owner: Withers Broadcasting Co.
Arbitron Metro Market: Mc Leansboro, IL; *Format:* Adult Contemp, Contemporary Hits/Top 40
Dana Withers, General Manager

Galena

WDBQ-FM
02-01-1989; 107.5 MHz FM; *Hrs Open:* 24; 6 kw; 328 ft.; N42 24 2 W90 23 55
111 East Kilbourn Avenue, Suite 2700, Milwaukee, WI 53202 US
(563) 690-2938; *Fax:* (563) 583-4535
www.myq1075.com
ken.peiffer@cumulus.com
License: Galena, Jo Daviess County, IL held by Peak Broadcasting of Fresno Licenses LLC
Group Owner: Townsquare Media; (acq 12-17-98; grpsl)
Arbitron Metro Market: Dubuque, IA; *Format:* Contemporary Hits/Top 40, Adult Contemp; *No. News Employees:* 1; *Target Audience:* 25-54.
Scott Lindahl, Promotions Manager

Galesburg

WAAG
12-15-1966; 94.9 MHz FM; *Hrs Open:* 24; 50 kw; 492 ft.; N40 56 34 W90 20 39
154 E. Simmons St., Galesburg, IL 61401 US
(309) 342-5131; *Fax:* (309) 342-0840
www.fm95online.com
fm95@fm95online.com
License: Galesburg, Knox County, IL held by Galesburg Broadcasting Co.
Group Owner: Galesburg Broadcasting Co.
Wire Services: AP
Arbitron Metro Market: Galesburg, IL; *Format:* Country; *Hrs. of News Programming:* news progmg 2 hrs wkly; *No. News Employees:* 4; *Target Audience:* 25-54.
Jim Lee, General Sales Mgr
Brian Prescott, Programming Director
Mike Perry, News Director

WAIK
01-01-1957; 1590 kHz AM; *Hrs Open:* 24; 5 kw-D, DA2; 0.055 kw-N, DA2; N40 57 43 W90 18 30
55 Public Sq., Monmouth, IL 61462 US
(309) 734-9452; *Fax:* (309) 342-3161
www.1330wram.com
loren.follmer@prairiecommunications.net
License: Galesburg, IL held by WPW Broadcasting Inc.
Group Owner: Prairie Radio Communications; acq 7-9-98; $439,500)
Nat'l Network: ABC
Arbitron Metro Market: Galesburg, IL; *Format:* News/Talk *Special Programming:* Talk 10 hrs, loc sports 10 hrs, relg 6 hrs wkly; *Hrs. of News Programming:* news progmg 24 hrs wkly; *No. News Employees:* 3 *TargetAudience:* 25 plus.
Mike Weaver, Operations Dir
Loren Follmer, General Manager
Amy Patterson, General Sales Mgr

WGIL
06-12-1938; 1400 kHz AM; *Hrs Open:* 24; 0.74 kw
154 E. Simmons St., Galesburg, IL 61401 US
(309) 342-9194; *Fax:* (309) 342-0840
www.wgil.com
wgil@wgil.com
License: Galesburg, IL held by Galesburg Broadcasting Co.
Group Owner: Galesburg Broadcasting Co.
Nat'l Network: Westwood One; *Regional Network:* Ill. Radio Net; *Nat'l Reps:* Interep; *Wire Services:* AP
Format: News/Talk; *Hrs. of News Programming:* news progmg 20 hrs wkly; *No. News Employees:* 4; *Target Audience:* 25-54.
Brian Prescott, Operations Dir
Roger Lundeen, General Manager
Chris McIntyre, Programming Director
Tyler Bachman, News Director

WLSR
01-01-1980; 92.7 MHz FM; *Hrs Open:* 24; 4.2 kw; 390 ft.; N40 56 34 W90 20 39
154 E. Simmons Street, Galesburg, IL 61401 US
(309) 342-5131; *Fax:* (309) 342-0840
www.thelaseronline.com
thelaser@thelaseronline.com
License: Galesburg, Knox County, IL held by Galesburg Broadcasting Co.
Group Owner: Galesburg Broadcasting Co.
Wire Services: AP
Arbitron Metro Market: Galesburg, IL; *Format:* Rock/AOR; *No. News Employees:* 4; *Target Audience:* 18-34.
John Pritchard, President
Brian Prescott, Operations Dir
Roger Lundeen, General Manager
Chris McIntyre, Programming Director

*WVKC
04-12-1961; 90.7 MHz FM; 1 kw horiz; 102 ft.; N40 56 46 W90 22 11
2 E. South Street, Galesburg, IL 61401 US
(309) 341-7000; *Fax:* (309) 341-7090
www.knox.edu/wvkc.xml
hengelma@knox.edu
License: Galesburg, Knox County, IL held by Knox College.
Arbitron Metro Market: Galesburg, IL; *Format:* Variety/Diverse
Special Programming: Black 6 hrs, jazz 15 hrs, class 18 hrs wkly
Roger Moore, President
Mark Iellski, General Manager

Galva

WJRE
05-01-2003; 102.5 MHz FM; *Hrs Open:* 24; 6 kw; 293 ft.; N41 13 36 W89 56 5
Mailing Address: 1020 Lincoln Rd, Bettendorf, IA 52722 US
Second Address: 3815 N. Brady St, Davenport, IA 52806
(309) 798-4148
License: Galva, Henry County, IL held by Virden Broadcasting Corp.
Group Owner: Regional Media, A Virden Broadcasting Corporation
Nat'l Network: NBC Radio News; NBC Sports
Arbitron Metro Market: Davenport-Rock Island-Moline; *Format:* Country *Special Programming:* Southern gospel one hr wkly; *No. News Employees:* 1
Fletcher M. Ford, President
Sean Patrick Kernan, Programming Director

Geneseo

*WAXR
01-01-2001; 88.1 MHz FM; 3 kw vert; 322 ft.; N41 28 47 W90 16 8
P.O. Box 3206, Tupelo, MS 38803 US
(662) 844-8888; *Fax:* (662) 842-6791
www.afr.net
faq@afa.net
License: Geneseo, Henry County, IL held by American Family Association.
Group Owner: American Family Radio
Format: Religious
Tim Wildmon, President
Donald Wildmon, Founder
Buddy Smith, Sr VP
Ed Vitagliano, Exec VP
Randy Sharp, Director Of Special Projects
Meeke Addison, Director Of Communications
Abraham Hamilton III, General Counsel

Geneva

WSPY
11-11-1961; 1480 kHz AM; *Hrs Open:* 24; 1 kw-D, DA2; 0.5 kw-N, DA2; N41 54 25 W88 17 43
1215 East Fern Avenue, Saint Charles, IL 60174 US
(630) 552-1000; *Fax:* (630) 552-9300
wspy@nelsonmultimedia.net
License: Geneva, IL held by Nelson Multi Media Inc.
Arbitron Metro Market: Chicago, IL; *Format:* Adult Contemp; *Hrs. of News Programming:* news progmg 2 hrs wkly; *No. News Employees:* 1; *Target Audience:* 35-65; baby boomers; *Adv. Rates:* 25; 20; 20; 10
Larry Nelson, President
Chris Schwemlein, Operations Dir
Vori Dhabolt, General Sales Mgr
Jenny Beckman, News Director
Lane Lindstrom, Chief Engineer
Beth Perrie, General Sales Manager

Genoa

WYRB
01-01-2001; 106.3 MHz FM; 3.8 kw; 413 ft.; N42 4 28 W88 49 24 *Rebroadcasts:* Rebroadcasts WSRB(FM) Lansing 100%
850 N. Church St., Suite 402, Rockford, IL 61103 US
(815) 209-2000; *Fax:* (815) 209-2490
www.mypower106.com
License: Genoa, De Kalb County, IL held by Dontron Inc.
Group Owner: Crawford Broadcasting Co.; (acq 9-28-01; $1.5 million).
Format: Black, Blues, 20, Blues, Urban Contemporary; *Target Audience:* 25-54; adult urban
Donald Crawford, CEO
Taft Harris, General Manager

Gibson City

WGCY
11-28-1983; 106.3 MHz FM; *Hrs Open:* 6 AM-midnight; 6 kw; 322 ft.; N40 33 57 W88 20 48
607 South Sangamon, Gibson City, IL 60936 US
(217) 784-8661; *Fax:* (217) 784-8677
www.wgcyradio.com
wgcyproduction@hotmail.com
License: Gibson City, Ford County, IL held by F & G Broadcasting Inc.
Nat'l Network: USA
Format: Easy Listening; *No. News Employees:* 1; *Target Audience:* 35 plus.
Gary McCollough, CEO/COO
Gary McCullough, General Manager
Frank McCullough, Sports Director
Tom Benefiel, Sports Commentator
Joni Cox, Sales Accounting
Rod Habermeyer, Sales Associate
Jim Cotter, News Reporter

Gilman

WYUR
01-01-2007; 103.7 MHz FM; 3.6 kw; 433 ft.; N40 53 53.3 W87 59 57.8
US
(815) 933-9287; *Fax:* (815) 933-8696
License: Gilman, Iroquois County, IL held by Milner Broadcasting Enterprises LLC
Group Owner: Milner Broadcasting Enterprises LLC
Arbitron Metro Market: Gilman, IL; *Format:* Contemporary Hits/Top 40
Jim Brandt, Operations Dir
Tim Milner, General Manager
Chris Swain, General Sales Mgr
Mickey Milner, Programming Director
Kathy Gagliano, Vice President, Sales
Gordy McCollum, Public Service Director
Chris Nickles, ProductionDirector

Glasford

WHPI
01-01-2000; 101.1 MHz FM; *Hrs Open:* 24; 3.3 kw; 449 ft.; N40 39 0 W89 46 46
P.O. Box 150846, Nashville, TN 37215 US
(256) 497-4502; *Fax:* NA
varietyrock@hotmail.com
License: Glasford, Peoria County, IL held by IM IL Licenses LLC.
Group Owner: Independence Media Holdings LLC; (acq 9-19-2006; grpsl)
Arbitron Metro Market: Tulsa OK; *Format:* Variety/Diverse, Rock/AOR; *Target Audience:* 18-54.
Richard Dabney, General Manager

Glen Ellyn

*WDCB
07-05-1977; 90.9 MHz FM; *Hrs Open:* 24; 5 kw; 300 ft; N41 50 36 W88 05 00
College of DuPage, 425 Fawell Blvd., Glen Ellyn, IL 60137
(630) 942-4200,(630) 942-3708; *Fax:* (630) 942-2788
www.wdcb.org
wdcbmktg@cdnet.cod.edu
License: Glen Ellyn, Du Page County, IL held by College of DuPage.
Special Programming: College classes 12 hrs, folk 12 hrs, gospel 2 hrs, var music 7 hrs wkly; *Hrs. of News Programming:* news progmg 13 hrs wkly; *No. News Employees:* 3; *Target Audience:* General.
Scott Wager, Station Manager
Ken Scott, General Sales Mgr
Mary Pat LaRue, Programming Director
Ken Scott, Promotions Manager
Brian O'Keefe, News Director
Paul Abella, Music Director

Glendale Heights

*WJKL
09-01-1960; 94.3 MHz FM; *Hrs Open:* 24; 3.5 kw; 440 ft.; N41 51 30 W87 57 16 *Rebroadcasts:* Rebroadcasts KLVR(FM) Santa Rosa, CA 100%
14 Douglas Avenue, Elgin, IL 60120 US
(916) 251-1600; *Fax:* (916) 251-1650
www.klove.com
License: Glendale Heights, Du Page County, IL held by Educational Media Foundation.
Group Owner: EMF Broadcasting; (acq 4-10-2007; $17 million)
Nat'l Network: K-Love
Arbitron Metro Market: Chicago, IL; *Format:* Christian
Mike Novak, President

Glenview

*WGBK
01-13-1979; 88.5 MHz FM; *Hrs Open:* 6:30 AM-8:00 AM; 3 PM-10 PM (M-F); 0.185 kw; 105 ft.; N42 6 39 W87 49 56
1835 Landwehr Rd, Glenview, IL 60025 US
(847) 486-4487; *Fax:* (847) 486-4439
www.wcbk.com
contest@wcbk.com
License: Glenview, Cook County, IL held by Glenbrook High School District 225.
Arbitron Metro Market: Chicago, IL; *Format:* Alternative, Sports
Special Programming: Sports talk 5 hrs, live sports 4 hrs; *Hrs. of News Programming:* News progmg 1 hr wkly; *Target Audience:* General; teens &adults
Dr. Daniel Oswald, General Manager

Godfrey

*WLCA
01-01-1974; 89.9 MHz FM; *Hrs Open:* 18; 1.5 kw; 394 ft.; N38 56 57 W90 11 47
5800 Godfrey Road, Godfrey, IL 62035 US
(618) 466-8936; *Fax:* (618) 466-7458
www.wlcafm.com
mlemons@lc.edu
License: Godfrey, Madison County, IL held by Lewis and Clark Community College.
Nat'l Network: USA
Format: Rock/AOR; *Adv. Rates:* 120; 120; 120; na
Mike Lemons, General Manager
Michael Lemons, Station Manager
Matthew Dorman, Programming Director
Dylan Brown, Promotions Manager
Dave Caires, Engineering Dir
Matt Maher, Music Director
Jon Mintert, Production Manager
JohnNeumann, Sports Director

Golconda

WKYX-FM
11-22-1990; 94.3 MHz FM; *Hrs Open:* 24; 3.1 kw; 449 ft.; N37 14 4 W88 29 48 *Rebroadcasts:* Simulcast with WKYX(AM) Paducah, KY 100%
P.O. Box 900, Bowling Green, KY 42102 US
(270) 554-8255; *Fax:* (270) 554-5468
www.wkyx.com
info@wkyx.com
License: Golconda, Pope County, IL held by Bristol Broadcasting Co. Inc.
Group Owner: Bristol Broadcasting Co. Inc.; (acq 2-20-2004; grpsl)
Arbitron Metro Market: Golconda, IL; *Format:* News, News/Talk, 86 *Special Programming:* Relg one hr wkly; *Target Audience:* 25-54.
Pete Ninninger, President
Gary Morse, General Manager

Granite City

WGNU
12-01-1961; 920 kHz AM; *Hrs Open:* 24; 0.45 kw-D, DA2; 0.5 kw-N, DA2; N38 45 33 W90 3 0
275 Union Blvd., St. Louis, MO 63108 US
(314) 454-0400; *Fax:* (314)448-4999
www.wgnu920am.com
info@wgnu920am.com
License: Granite City, IL held by 920 AM LLC
Arbitron Metro Market: St. Louis, MO; *Format:* Christian
Jay Madas, Operations Dir
Dirk Hallemeier, General Manager

WARH
11-24-1965; 106.5 MHz FM; 90 kw; 1,014 ft.; N38 34 27.7 W90 19 31.5
11647 Olive Blvd., St. Louis, MO 63141 US
(314) 983-6000
www.1065thearch.com
webmaster@1065thearch.com
License: Granite City, Madison County, IL held by St. Louis FCC License Sub LLC
Group Owner: Hubbard Broadcasting Inc.; (acq 1-19-2011)
Arbitron Metro Market: St. Louis, MO; *Format:* Contemporary Hits/Top 40
Mike Rowen, Local Sales Manager
Kevin Robinson, Programming Director
Sam Teferi, Promotions Director
Keith Kraus, Director of Sales
Kim Grant, Digital Media Director
Jerry England, Human Resources Director

Greenville

WGEL
12-20-1984; 101.7 MHz FM; *Hrs Open:* 24; 6 kw; 295 ft.; N38 48 11 W89 20 56
Box 177 309 W. Main Ave., Greenville, IL 62246 US
(618) 664-3300; *Fax:* (618) 664-3318
www.wgel.com
john@wgel.com
License: Greenville, Bond County, IL held by Bond Broadcasting.
Nat'l Network: USA
Format: Country *Special Programming:* Farm 19 hrs wkly; *No. News Employees:* 2; *Target Audience:* 25-64.
John Kennedy, President
Joe Doll, General Sales Mgr
Brad Rogers, Programming Director
Tom Kennedy, News Director

Harrisburg

WEBQ
09-01-1923; 1240 kHz AM; 1 kw-U, ND1; N37 43 3 W88 32 37
701 South Commercial, Harrisburg, IL 62946 US
(618) 253-7282; *Fax:* (618) 252-2366
www.webqradio.com
webq@yourclearwave.com
License: Harrisburg, IL held by W. Russell Withers Jr.
Group Owner: Withers Broadcasting Co.; (acq 7-28-2004; $450,000 with WEBQ-FM Eldorado).
Nat'l Network: ABC; *Regional Network:* Brownfield
Arbitron Metro Market: Harrisburg, IL; *Format:* Country *Special Programming:* Farm 6 hrs wkly; *Hrs. of News Programming:* news progmg 6 hrs wkly; *No. News Employees:* 1; *Target Audience:* Older area residents. *Adv. Rates:* 9.79; 9.79; 9.79; 4.64
Cathy Horton, General Manager
Sonny Dotson, General Sales Mgr
Shelly Reeder, News Director
Bob Romonosky, Chief Engineer

WOOZ-FM
09-01-1947; 99.9 MHz FM; 32 kw; 620 ft.; N37 36 45 W88 52 3
1431 Country Aire Dr., Carterville, IL 62918 US
(618) 985-3983; *Fax:* (618) 985-6529
www.z100fm.com
License: Harrisburg, Saline County, IL held by MRR License LLC.
Group Owner: MAX Media L.L.C.; (acq 3-29-2004; grpsl).
Nat'l Reps: Christal
Arbitron Metro Market: Marion-Carbondale, IL *TV Affiliate:* Country; *Format:* Country; *No. News Employees:* 18-49.
Tom Miller, Operations Manager
Steve Falat, General Manager/Market Manager
Kim DeBose, General Sales Mgr
Tracy McSherry-McKown, Programming Director

Harvey

WBGX
01-01-1955; 1570 kHz AM; *Hrs Open:* 24
15700 Campbell, Harvey, IL 60426 US
(800) 877-5600; *Fax:* (916) 251-1650
www.klove.com
License: Harvey, IL held by Great Lakes Radio-Chicago LLC
Arbitron Metro Market: Torrington WY; *Format:* Christian; *Adv. Rates:* 45; 25; 45; 25
Mike Novak, President

Hattiesburg

WFFX(AM)
08-01-1934; 1490 kHz AM; 1 kw-U, DA-2; N38 37 16 W90 09 36
6555 Highway 98 W., Suite 8, Hattiesburg, MS 39402
(601) 544-1037; *Fax:* (601) 296-9800
1037thefox.iheart.com
License: Hattiesburg, IL held by CC Licenses
Group Owner: IHeartMedia, Inc.
Nat'l Network: American Urban; *Nat'l Reps:* Katz Radio
Population Served: 46,626; *Arbitron Metro Market:* Hattiesburg, MS; *Format:* Blues, Gospel; *Target Audience:* 23-55.

Havana

WDUK
02-27-1970; 99.3 MHz FM; 3 kw horiz; 299 ft.; N40 18 43 W90 3 19
901 N. Promenade, Havana, IL 62644 US
(309) 543-3331
License: Havana, Mason County, IL held by Illinois Valley Radio.
Regional Network: Brownfield *Regional Reps:* Brownfield.
Arbitron Metro Market: Havana, IL; *Format:* Variety/Diverse, Country *Special Programming:* Farm 8 hrs wkly; *Target Audience:* General.; *Adv. Rates:* 3.70; 3.70; 3.70; 3.70
Edwin Stimpson, President

Henry

WRVY-FM
07-30-1990; 100.5 MHz FM; *Hrs Open:* 24; 3 kw; 328 ft.; N41 4 32 W89 21 10
PO Box 69, Princeton, IL 61356 US
(815) 875-8014
www.wzoe.com
License: Henry, Marshall County, IL held by WZOE, Inc.
Group Owner: WZOE, Inc.; (acq 5-8-98)
Nat'l Network: CBS; CNN Radio; *Regional Network:* Ill. Radio Net.
Format: Country *Special Programming:* Farm 4 hrs wkly; *Hrs. of News Programming:* news progmg 3 hrs wkly; *No. News Employees:* 3; *Target Audience:* 25-45.

Steve Samet, General Manager

Herrin

WJPF
08-28-1940; 1340 kHz AM; *Hrs Open:* 24; 0.77 kw-U, ND1; N37 50 4 W89 1 40
1431 Country Aire Dr., Carterville, IL 62918 US
(618) 985-5803; *Fax:* (618) 985-6529
www.wjpf.com
License: Herrin, Williamson County, IL held by MRR License LLC.
Group Owner: MAX Media L.L.C.; (acq 6-2-2004; grpsl)
Nat'l Network: Westwood One; *Regional Network:* Ill. Radio Net;
Nat'l Reps: Christal
Arbitron Metro Market: Marion-Carbondale, IL; *Format:* News, News/Talk, 84, Talk; *Hrs. of News Programming:* news progmg 10 hrs wkly; *No. News Employees:* 3; *Target Audience:* 35 plus; mature, middle-income wageearners
Tom Miller, Operations Manager
Steve Falat, General Manager/Market Manager
Kim DeBose, General Sales Mgr
Michael Roberts, News Director
Mike Murphy, Sports Director

WTAO-FM
08-01-1972; 92.7 MHz FM; *Hrs Open:* 24; 25 kw; 328 ft.; N37 46 28 W89 5 50
330 East Kilbourn Ave., Suite 250, Milwaukee, WI 53202 US
(618) 997-8123; *Fax:* (618) 993-2319
www.105tao.com
License: Herrin, Jackson County, IL held by Withers Broadcasting of Southern Illinois LLC.
Group Owner: Withers Broadcasting Co.; (acq 3-17-2008; grpsl)
Arbitron Metro Market: Marion-Carbondale (Southern Illinois); *Format:* Rock/AOR; *Target Audience:* M18-49.
Paxton Guy, Operations Dir
Jerry Crouse, General Manager
Mett Mellen, Programming Director
Tim Deterding, Chief Engineer

Heyworth

WBBE
06-06-2005; 97.9 MHz FM; 5.4 kw; Ant 344 ft; N40 27 08 W88 57 48
520 N. Center St., Bloomington, IL
(309) 834-1100; *Fax:* (309) 834-4390
www.bob979.com
License: Heyworth, McLean County, IL held by Connoisseur Media Licenses LLC.
Group Owner: Connoisseur Media LLC
Nat'l Reps: Christal
Target Audience: 18-54; Adults
Floyd Evans, General Manager
Michael Mendelssohn, General Sales Mgr
Adam Chandler, Programming Director
Mark Hill, Chief Engineer

Highland

WIJR
12-02-1963; 880 kHz AM; *Hrs Open:* 24; 1.7 kw-D, DA1; 0.16 kw-N, DA1; N38 45 23 W89 39 18
13063 Winu Dr., Highland, IL 62249 US
(618) 654-5615
www.birach.com
sima@birach.com
License: Highland, Madison County, IL held by Birach Broadcasting Corp.
Group Owner: Birach Broadcasting Corp.; (acq 8-15-2006; $1 million).
Regional Network: Brownfield
Arbitron Metro Market: St. Louis, MO; *Format:* Tejano *Special Programming:* Farm 3 hrs, Ger one hr wkly; *Hrs. of News Programming:* news progmg 18 hrs wkly; *No. News Employees:* 1; *Target Audience:* General;mature adults; *Adv. Rates:* 30; 30; 30; 20
Sima Birach, President

Highland Park

WVIV-FM
08-15-1963; 103.1 MHz FM; *Hrs Open:* 24; 6 kw; 328 ft.; N42 8 14 W87 58 57
625 N. Michigan Ave., Suite 3, Chicago, IL 60611 US
(312) 981-1800; *Fax:* (312) 981-1806
www.univision.com
License: Highland Park, Lake County, IL held by Univision Radio License Corp.
Group Owner: Univision Radio; (acq 9-22-2003; grpsl).

Arbitron Metro Market: Chicago, IL; *Format:* Spanish; *Target Audience:* 25-54.
Doug Levy, Senior Vice President and General Manager
Hector Fabregas, Director of Local Sales
Victor Cerda, Programming Director
Alicia Chavarria, Promotions Manager
Joshua Sigstad, Chief Engineer
Adriene Drucker-Dibble, LocalSales Manager

Hillsboro

WXAJ
09-01-2000; 99.7 MHz FM; *Hrs Open:* 24; 50 kw; 492 ft.; N39 21 12 W89 31 53
#2 Magnolia Drive, Centralia, IL 62801 US
(217) 528-3033; *Fax:* (217) 528-5348
www.997kissfm.com
kevinodea@neuhoffmedia.com
License: Hillsboro, Montgomery County, IL held by Neuhoff Family L.P.
Group Owner: Neuhoff Family L.P.; (acq 8-1-2007; grpsl)
Nat'l Reps: Christal
Arbitron Metro Market: Springfield, IL; *Format:* Contemporary Hits/Top 40; *Target Audience:* Adults; 18-49
Kevin O'Dea, General Manager
Kathy Byerly, Local Sales Manager
Frank Konwinski, Chief Engineer
Danielle Outlaw, Director of Sales
Morgan Jenkins, Receptionist
Jessica Ross, Traffic Manager
Dave Comstock, Production

Hinsdale

*WHSD
12-06-1970; 88.5 MHz FM; *Hrs Open:* 3 PM-10 PM; 0.125 kw horiz, 0.08 kw vert; 131 ft.; N41 47 18 W87 56 2
55th and Grant Streets, Hinsdale, IL 60521 US
(630) 570-8463; *Fax:* (630) 887-1362
License: Hinsdale, Du Page County, IL held by Hinsdale Twsp. High School District 86.
Format: Variety/Diverse; *Target Audience:* General.
Jerry Edwards, President
Darrel Kelly, Programming Director

Hoopeston

WHPO
05-29-1979; 100.9 MHz FM; *Hrs Open:* 24; 3 kw; 299 ft.; N40 28 36 W87 41 36
627 North Market, P.O.Box 55, Hoopeston, IL 60942 US
(217) 283-7744; *Fax:* (217) 283-6090
www.whporadio.com
License: Hoopeston, Vermilion County, IL held by Market Street Broadcasting LLC
Format: Country *Special Programming:* Southern gospel 7 hrs, big band 2 hrs wkly; *Hrs. of News Programming:* news progmg 6 hrs wkly; *No. News Employees:* 1; *Target Audience:* 25 plus; rural middle class
Blanche Voss, General Manager
Becky Voss, Programming Director

Jacksonville

WJIL
11-01-1961; 1550 kHz AM; *Hrs Open:* 24; 1 kw-D, DA2; 0.01 kw-N, DA2; N39 43 20 W90 11 43
P.O. Box 1065, Jacksonville, IL 62651 US
(217) 245-5119; *Fax:* (217) 245-1596
www.wjvofm.com
dianawjvo@mchsi.com
License: Jacksonville, IL held by Morgan County Broadcasting Co. Inc.
Nat'l Network: Westwood One; *Nat'l Reps:* Roslin
Format: News, News/Talk, 86 *Special Programming:* Farm 8 hrs wkly; *Hrs. of News Programming:* news progmg 9 hrs wkly; *No. News Employees:* 1; *Target Audience:* 35-64.
Ed Steele, Operations Dir
Sarah Hautala, General Manager
Diana McCutcheon, General Sales Mgr
Matt Lakis, Programming Director
Jeremy Ray, News Director
Glen Hopkiins, Chief Engineer
Julie Cambridge, Music Director
LouEstabrook, Office Manager

WLDS
12-09-1941; 1180 kHz AM; *Hrs Open:* Sunrise-sunset; 1 kw-D, NDD; N39 44 6 W90 11 50
P.O. Box 1180, Jacksonville, IL 62651 US
(217) 245-7171; *Fax:* (217) 245-6711
www.wlds.com
wlds@wlds.com
License: Jacksonville, IL held by Jacksonville Area Radio Broadcasters Inc.
Nat'l Network: CBS; *Regional Network:* Ill. Radio Net; *Nat'l Reps:* Katz Radio; *Wire Services:* AP
Format: Adult Contemp, News, 62, Talk *Special Programming:* Farm 20 hrs wkly; *Hrs. of News Programming:* news progmg 23 hrs wkly; *No. News Employees:* 3; *Target Audience:* 35 plus; business & professional people,farmers & housewives
Sue Shireman, Operations Dir
Gary Scott, General Manager
Mark Whalen, General Sales Mgr
Bob Thomas, Programming Director
Kevin Baxter, News Director
John Coe, Engineering Dir
Marty Megginson, Continuity Director
Gary Ballard,Music Director

Jerseyville

WJBM
10-11-1959; 1480 kHz AM; 0.5 kw-D, DA2; 0.032 kw-N, DA2; N39 6 46 W90 18 43
#1 Professional Plaza, P.O. Box 150, Pittsfield, IL 62363 US
(618) 498-8265; *Fax:* (618) 498-9830
www.wjbmradio.com
wjbm@wjbmradio.com
License: Jerseyville, IL held by DJ Two Rivers Radio Inc.
Regional Network: Brownfield
Arbitron Metro Market: St. Louis, MO; *Format:* Oldies *Special Programming:* Farm 18 hrs, sports 13 hrs, relg 3 hrs wkly; *Target Audience:* 25 plus; general market through retirement
J. Boyd Ingram, General Manager

Johnston City

WDDD-FM
11-22-1970; 107.3 MHz FM; *Hrs Open:* 24; 50 kw; 492 ft.; N37 45 15 W88 56 5
330 East Kilbourn Ave., Suite 250, Milwaukee, WI 53202 US
(618) 997-8123; *Fax:* (618) 993-2319
www.mywithersradio.com/w3d/
License: Johnston City, Williamson County, IL held by Withers Broadcasting of Southern Illinois LLC.
Group Owner: Withers Broadcasting Co.; (acq 3-17-2008; grpsl)
Arbitron Metro Market: Marion, IL; *Format:* Country; *Hrs. of News Programming:* news progmg 5 hrs wkly; *No. News Employees:* 2; *Target Audience:* P25-54.
Paxton Guy, Operations Dir
Janet Jensen, General Manager
Tim Deterding, Chief Engineer

Joliet

*WCSF
09-05-1988; 88.7 MHz FM; *Hrs Open:* 7 AM-2 AM (M-F); 0.1 kw; 128 ft.; N41 31 58 W88 5 54
500 North Wilcox Street, Joliet, IL 60435 US
(815) 740-3425(815) 740-3214; *Fax:* (815) 740-3697
www.stfrancis.edu
License: Joliet, Will County, IL held by University of St. Francis.
Arbitron Metro Market: Chicago,IL; *Format:* Rock/AOR *Special Programming:* Black 2 hrs, jazz 2 hrs, talk 4 hrs, requests 4 hrs, classic rock 4 hrs wkly; *Target Audience:* 18-45; males
Dr. Scott W. Marshall, General Manager

*WJCH
04-25-1986; 91.9 MHz FM; *Hrs Open:* 24; 50 kw; 495 ft.; N41 24 55 W88 16 19
4135 Northgate Blvd.Ste1, Sacramento, CA 95834 US
(815) 725-1331
www.familyradio.com
familyradio@familyradio.orgу
License: Joliet, Will County, IL held by Family Stations Inc.
Group Owner: Family Stations Inc.
Arbitron Metro Market: Chicago, IL; *Format:* Religious *Special Programming:* Class 2 hrs wkly
Harold Camping, President
Virginia Beehn, Operations Dir

WJOL
01-01-1924; 1340 kHz AM; *Hrs Open:* 24; 1 kw-U, ND1; N41 32 6 W88 3 15
2410 B Caton Carm Road, Crest Hill, IL 60403 US
(815) 556-0100; *Fax:* (815) 577-9231
www.wjol.com
License: Joliet, IL held by NM Licensing LLC.
Group Owner: NextMedia Group Inc.; (acq 11-26-2001; grpsl)
Nat'l Reps: Christal *Regional Reps:* Ill. Radio Net.
Arbitron Metro Market: Chicago, IL; *Format:* Talk *Special Programming:* Farm 3 hrs, gospel one hr, Pol one hr wkly; *Hrs. of News Programming:* news progmg 40 hrs wkly; *No. News Employees:* 2 *Target Audience:* 35 plus.
Patrick Pendergast, General Manager
Doug Boyd, General Sales Mgr
Scott Slocum, Programming Director
Dan Waddick, Promotions Director

WSSR
02-06-1960; 96.7 MHz FM; *Hrs Open:* 24; 3.1 kw; 466 ft.; N41 36 1 W87 58 44
2410 B Caton Farm Road, Crest Hill, IL 60403 US
(815) 556-0100; *Fax:* (815) 577-9231
www.star967.net
License: Joliet, Will County, IL held by NM Licensing LLC.
Group Owner: NextMedia Group Inc.
Nat'l Reps: Christal
Arbitron Metro Market: Chicago, IL; *Format:* Adult Contemp; *No. News Employees:* 1; *Target Audience:* 25-54; Adults
Scott Slocum, Operations Dir
Patrick Pendergast, General Manager
Doug Boyd, General Sales Mgr
Scott Childers, Programming Director

WWHN
04-10-1964; 1510 kHz AM; 0.6 kw-C, NDD; 1 kw-D, NDD; N41 30 50 W88 3 10
506 S. Dante Avenue, Glenwood, IL 60425 US
(773) 239-2300; *Fax:* (773) 239-9921
wwhn@aol.com
License: Joliet, IL held by Hawkins Broadcasting Co.
Arbitron Metro Market: Chicago, IL; *Format:* Gospel *Special Programming:* Sp one hr wkly; *Target Audience:* 18-54; affluent adults
Raymond Hawkins, President
Toni Hawkins, General Manager

Kankakee

*WAWF
01-01-2000; 88.3 MHz FM; 1.25 kw; 285 ft.; N41 4 39 W87 45 22
P.O. Box 262550, Baton Rouge, LA 70826 US
(225) 768-8300
www.jsm.org
License: Kankakee, Kankakee County, IL held by Family Worship Center Church Inc.
Group Owner: Family Worship Center Church Inc.
Arbitron Metro Market: Hewitt TX; *Format:* Religious
Jimmy Swaggart, President

WKAN
06-01-1947; 1320 kHz AM; *Hrs Open:* 24; 1 kw-D, DAN; 0.5 kw-N, DAN; N41 8 8 W87 49 10
2 Dearborn Square, Kankakee, IL 60901 US
(815) 935-9555; *Fax:* (815) 935-9593
www.wkan.com
wkan@starradio.com
License: Kankakee, IL held by STARadio Corp.
Group Owner: STARadio Corp.; (acq 2-7-94; $1.31 million with co-located FM;
Wire Services: UPI
Format: Talk *Special Programming:* Farm 10 hrs wkly; *Hrs. of News Programming:* news progmg 20 hrs wkly; *No. News Employees:* 1; *Target Audience:* 25-54.; *Adv. Rates:* 36; 36; 36; 20
Robert Kersmarki, President
Brendan Michaels, Operations Dir
Larry Regnier, General Sales Mgr

WVLI
09-21-1986; 92.7 MHz FM; *Hrs Open:* 24; 3 kw; 328 ft.; N41 7 22 W87 53 35
292 N. Convent, Bourbonnais, IK 60914 US
(773) 767-1000; *Fax:* (773) 767-1100
info@weplayanything.com
License: Kankakee, Kankakee County, IL held by Milner Broadcasting Enterprises LLC
Group Owner: Milner Broadcasting Enterprises LLC; (acq 7-27-2012; $1 million)
Nat'l Network: CNN Radio
Format: News
Jim Brandt, Operations Dir
Tim Milner, General Manager
Chris Swain, Local Sales Manager
Mickey Milner, Programming Director
Don Kerouac, Chief Engineer
Carl, Traffic Manager
Kathy Gagliano, VP, Sales
Gordy McCollum, PublicService Director

Chris Nickles, Production Director
Mike Ruble, Farm Director

***WONU**
01-01-1966; 89.7 MHz FM; 35 kw; 413 ft.; N41 9 24 W87 52 16
240 E. Marsile, Bourbonnais, IL 60914 US
(815) 939-5330; *Fax:* (815) 939-5087
www.shine.fm
shine@olivet.edu
License: Kankakee, Kankakee County, IL held by Olivet Nazarene University.
TV Affiliate: Relg; *No. News Employees:* 25-49; female, predominan
Justin Knight, General Manager/Director of Broadcast Operations

***WKCC**
06-01-1992; 91.1 MHz FM; *Hrs Open:* 24; 2.6 kw; 254 ft.; N41 9 38.9 W87 52 29.8
1711 Rt. 50 North, Ste 1, Bourbonnais, IL 60914 US
(815) 802-8230; *Fax:* (815) 935-5169
www.kcc.edu
wkcc@kcc.edu
License: Kankakee, Kankakee County, IL held by Kankakee Community College.
Arbitron Metro Market: Kankakee, IL; *Format:* Public Affairs; *Hrs. of News Programming:* News progmg 3 hrs wkly; *No. News Employees:* 1; *Target Audience:* General; travelers in northern IL
Mike Savage, General Manager

WFAV
10-22-1992; 95.1 MHz FM; *Hrs Open:* 24; 2.3 kw; 367 ft.; N41 4 39 W87 45 22
Mailing Address: 292 N Convent, Bourbonnais, IL 60914 US
Second Address: 292 N. Convent, Bourbonnais, IL 60914
(815) 933-9287; *Fax:* (815) 933-8696
www.wfav951.com
License: Kankakee, Kankakee County, IL held by Milner Broadcasting Enterprises LLC
Group Owner: Milner Broadcasting Enterprises LLC; (acq 3-17-95; $400,000).
Nat'l Network: AP Network News; *Wire Services:* AP
Arbitron Metro Market: Bourbonnais, IL; *Format:* Contemporary Hits/Top 40; *Hrs. of News Programming:* news progmg 20 hrs wkly; *No. News Employees:* 1; *Target Audience:* 25 plus.; *Adv. Rates:* 45; 45; 45; 35
Kathy Gagliano, VP/Sales
Jim Brandt, Operations Dir
Tim Milner, General Manager
Chris Swain, Local Sales Manager
Mickey Milner, Programming Director
Don Kerouac, Chief Engineer
Gordy McCollum, Public Service Director
MikeRuble, Farm Director
Carla, Traffic Manager
Chris Nickles, Production Director

***WEGN**
88.7 MHz FM; 5 kw; 213 ft.; N41 12 26.5 W87 58 21.6 US
(877) 700-8047; *Fax:* (217) 528-2400
www.thelifefm.com
License: Kankakee, Kankakee County, IL held by Cornerstone Community Radio Inc.
Arbitron Metro Market: Kankakee, IL
Richard Van Zandt, President

Kewanee

WKEI
09-11-1952; 1450 kHz AM; *Hrs Open:* 24
Mailing Address: 3815 N. Brady St, Davenport, IA 52806 US
Second Address: 1020 Lincoln Rd, Bettendorf, IA 52722
(563) 345-6454; *Fax:* (630) 225-5345
regionaldailynews.com/wkei
License: Kewanee, Henry County, IL held by Virden Broadcasting Corp.
Group Owner: Regional Media, A Virden Broadcasting Corporation
Nat'l Network: CBS Radio
Arbitron Metro Market: Davenport-Rock Island-Moline; *Format:* News, News/Talk, 86 *Special Programming:* Farm 20 hrs, relg 6 hrs wkly; *No. News Employees:* 1; *Target Audience:* 40+
Fletcher M. Ford, President
Jason Gilbraith, Station Manager

Knoxville

WKAY
12-13-2001; 105.3 MHz FM; *Hrs Open:* 24; 3.7 kw; 423 ft.; N40 56 34 W90 20 39
154 E. Simmons St., Galesburg, IL 61401 US
(309) 342-5131; *Fax:* (309) 342-0619
www.1053kfm.com
kfm@1053kfm.com
License: Knoxville, Knox County, IL held by Galesburg Broadcasting Co.
Group Owner: Galesburg Broadcasting Co.; (acq 4-1-99)
Wire Services: AP
Arbitron Metro Market: Eagle Pass TX; *Format:* Christian
Brian Prescott, Operations Dir
Roger Lundeen, General Manager
Chris McIntyre, Programming Director

La Grange

***WLTL**
01-05-1968; 88.1 MHz FM; *Hrs Open:* 24; 0.18 kw; 138 ft.; N41 48 45 W87 52 51
100 South Brainard Ave., La Grange, IL 60525 US
(708) 482-9585; *Fax:* (708) 482-7051
www.wltl.net
cthomas@wltl.net
License: La Grange, Cook County, IL held by Lyons Township High School.
Arbitron Metro Market: Chicago, IL; *Format:* Variety/Diverse, Rock/AOR *Special Programming:* Sports 5 hrs, news & views 10 hrs wkly; *Hrs. of News Programming:* News progmg 10 hrs wkly; *Target Audience:* 14-35; youngadults
Chris Thomas, General Manager
Jacob Alderman, Programming Director
Evan Boyd, Chief Engineer

WRDZ
10-01-1950; 1300 kHz AM; 4.5 kw-D, DA2; 4 kw-N, DA2; N41 40 29 W87 45 45
77 West 66th Street, 16th Floor, New York, NY 10023 US
(312) 683-1300; *Fax:* (312) 577-5994
License: La Grange, IL held by Radio Disney Chicago LLC.
Group Owner: ABC Inc.; (acq 5-12-99; with WPJX(AM) Zion).
Nat'l Network: ABC; *Wire Services:* City News Bureau
Arbitron Metro Market: Chicago; *Format:* Children; *Target Audience:* Children, mom's & dad's
Karyn Esken, Station Manager

La Salle

WAJK
12-04-1964; 99.3 MHz FM; 11 kw; 489 ft.; N41 24 47 W89 16 34
1 Broadcast Ln., Oglesby, IL 61348 USA
(815) 223-3100
www.lcbcradio.com/wakj
programdirector@classichits1039wlpo.com
License: La Salle, La Salle County, IL held by La Salle County Broadcasting Corp.
Group Owner: La Salle County Broadcasting Corp.
Arbitron Metro Market: LaSalle-Peru, IL; *Format:* Adult Contemp; *Target Audience:* 25-49.

***WNIW**
11-01-1998; 91.3 MHz FM; *Hrs Open:* 24; 36 kw vert; 331 ft.; N41 24 47 W89 16 34 *Rebroadcasts:* Rebroadcasts WNIJ(FM) De Kalb & WNIU(FM) Rockford 50%
801 North First Street, Dekalb, IL 60115 US
(815) 753-9000; *Fax:* (815) 753-9938
www.northernpublicradio.org
npr@niu.edu
License: La Salle, La Salle County, IL held by Northern Illinois University.
Nat'l Network: PRI; NPR
Arbitron Metro Market: Freeport, IL; *Format:* Classical, News; *No. News Employees:* 2; *Target Audience:* General.
Staci Hoste, General Manager
Jan Kilgard, General Sales Mgr
Bill Drake, Programming Director
Guy Stephens, News Director

Lake Forest

***WMXM**
09-10-1973; 88.9 MHz FM; *Hrs Open:* 18; 0.295 kw; 95 ft.; N42 14 59 W87 49 44
555 N. Sheridan Rd., Lake Forest, IL 60045 US
(847) 735-5220; *Fax:* (847) 735-6291
www.wmxm.org
wmxmgm@lakeforest.edu
License: Lake Forest, Lake County, IL held by Lake Forest College.
Arbitron Metro Market: Chicago, IL; *Format:* Classic Rock, Variety/Diverse *Special Programming:* Black 6 hrs, class 3 hrs, gospel 3 hrs, jazz 6 hrs; *Hrs. of News Programming:* news progmg 5 hrs wkly *No. NewsEmployees:* 2; *Target Audience:* 18-25; students
April Arellano, General Manager
Cleo Hehn, Programming Director

Lansing

WSRB
08-28-1961; 106.3 MHz FM; *Hrs Open:* 24; 4.1 kw; 397 ft.; N41 34 44 W87 32 47
6336 Calumet Avenue, Hammond, IN 46324 US
(773) 928-9230; *Fax:* (219) 933-4455ÿ
www.1063chicago.com
License: Lansing, Cook County, IL held by Dontron Inc.
Group Owner: Crawford Broadcasting Co.; (acq 4-10-97; $14.8 million).
Nat'l Network: ABC
Arbitron Metro Market: Chicago; *Format:* Black, Blues, 44, Religious; *Target Audience:* 25-54; urban, adult, African-American

Lasalle

WLPO
11-16-1947; 1220 kHz AM; *Hrs Open:* 24; 1 kw-D, DA2; 0.5 kw-N, DA2; N41 18 14 W89 5 44
1 Broadcast Ln., Oglesby, IL 61348 USA
(815) 223-3100
www.lcbcradio.com/wlpo
programdirector@classichits1039wlpo.com
License: Lasalle, IL held by La Salle County Broadcasting Corp.
Group Owner: La Salle County Broadcasting Corp.; (acq 8-1-49)
Format: News, News/Talk, 84, Talk; *Hrs. of News Programming:* news progmg 35 hrs wkly; *No. News Employees:* 3; *Target Audience:* 30 plus.

Lawrenceville

WAKO
06-09-1959; 910 kHz AM; *Hrs Open:* 5 AM-midnight; 0.5 kw-D, DA2; 0.05 kw-N, DA2; N38 43 23 W87 39 13
13799 US Hwy., Business 50, Lawrenceville, IL 62439-4921 US
(618) 943-3354
www.wakoradio.com
wakoradio@yahoo.com
License: Lawrenceville, IL held by DLC Media, Inc.
Group Owner: DLC Media, Inc.
Nat'l Network: Westwood One; *Wire Services:* AP
Arbitron Metro Market: Lawrenceville, IL; *Format:* Adult Contemp, Country; *Hrs. of News Programming:* news progmg 12 hrs wkly; *No. News Employees:* 1; *Target Audience:* 20-65+.
Gil T. Wilson, Operations Dir
David Foster, News Director

WAKO-FM
03-01-1965; 103.1 MHz FM; *Hrs Open:* 19; 6 kw; 328 ft.; N38 43 23 W87 39 13
13799 US Hwy., Business 50, Lawrenceville, IL 62439-4921 US
(618) 943-3354
www.wakoradio.com
wakoradio@yahoo.com
License: Lawrenceville, Lawrence County, IL held by DLC Media, Inc.
Group Owner: DLC Media, Inc.
AP
Arbitron Metro Market: Lawrenceville, IL; *Adv. Rates:* 15; 30; 20; 60
Gil T. Wilson, Operations Dir
David Foster, News Director

LeRoy

WBWN
10-15-1979; 104.1 MHz FM; *Hrs Open:* 24; 47 kw; 328 ft.; N40 25 26 W88 52 27
236 Greenwood Ave., Bloomington, IL 61704 US
(309) 829-1221
www.wbwn.com
dan@wbwn.com
License: LeRoy, IL held by Cumulus Licensing LLC
Group Owner: Cumulus Media Inc.; (acq 5-12-2004; grpsl).
Nat'l Reps: McGavren Guild
Arbitron Metro Market: Bloomington, IL; *Format:* Country; *Target Audience:* 25-45.; *Adv. Rates:* 70; 50; 50; 15
Paula Williams, Director of Sales
Dan Westhoff, Programming Director
Brandi McCarrey, Promotions Manager

RADIO - U.S.

Lemont

WVIX
04-17-1960; 93.5 MHz FM; *Hrs Open:* 24; 6 kw; 328 ft.; N41 36 39 W88 0 33 *Rebroadcasts:* Simulcast with WVIV-FM Highland Park
625 N. Michigan Ave., Suite 3, Chicago, IL 60611 US
(312) 981-1800; *Fax:* (312) 981-1806
www.univision.com
License: Lemont, Will County, IL held by Univision Radio License Corp.
Group Owner: Univision Radio; (acq 9-22-2003; grpsl).
Arbitron Metro Market: Chicago, IL; *Format:* Spanish; *Hrs. of News Programming:* one; *No. News Employees:* 1
Doug Levy, Senior Vice President and General Manager
Joshua Sigstad, Chief Engineer

Lena

WQLF
08-02-2002; 102.1 MHz FM; *Hrs Open:* 24; 5.2 kw; 351 ft.; N42 20 31 W89 48 21
Mailing Address: 530 Quail Drive, Lena, IL 61048 US
Second Address: 834 N. Tower Rd., Freeport, IL 61032
(815) 235-7191; *Fax:* (815) 235-4318
www.bigradio.fm
License: Lena, Stephenson County, IL held by Scott A. Thompson dba Big Radio
Arbitron Metro Market: Freeport, IL; *Format:* Contemporary Hits/Top 40, Adult Contemp *Special Programming:* Off the Record with Joe Benson 1 hr; Wolfman Jack Hits of the 70s & 80s 5 hrs; American Top 40 from the 80s *Hrs.of News Programming:* news progmg 3 hrs wkly; *No. News Employees:* 4; *Target Audience:* 20-49.; *Adv. Rates:* 12; 12; 12; 12
Kent McConnell, Operations Dir
Wyatt Herrmann, Programming Director
Becky Koester, News Director
Todd Hauser, Chief Engineer

Lexington

WZIM(FM)
01-01-2004; 99.5 MHz FM; *Hrs Open:* 24; 6 kw; Ant 328 ft; N40 34 30 W88 50 15
108 Boeykens Place, Normal, IL 61761
(309) 888-4496; *Fax:* (309) 452-9677
License: Lexington, McLean County, IL held by Pilot Media LLC.
Group Owner: Great Plains Media Inc.; (acq 6-19-2007; grpsl)
Wire Services: NBC
Population Served: 52,772; *Arbitron Metro Market:* Normal, IL; *Hrs. of News Programming:* News progmg 2 hrs wkly; *Target Audience:* 25-54.
Cody Welling, General Sales Manager
Robert Rees, Programming Director

Lincoln

WLLM
04-01-1951; 1370 kHz AM; *Hrs Open:* 24; 1 kw-D, ND1; 0.035 kw-N, ND1; N40 8 24 W89 23 10
3501 Sangamon Avenue, Springfield, IL 62707 US
(217) 735-9735; *Fax:* (217) 735-9736
www.wllmradio.com
License: Lincoln, IL held by Cornerstone Community Radio Inc.
Nat'l Network: USA
Format: Christian, Easy Listening
Beverly Tibbs, Operations Dir
Richard Van Zandt, General Manager
William Dolan, Station Manager
Pamela Pollard, Executive Assistant

***WLNX**
01-28-1974; 88.9 MHz FM; *Hrs Open:* 24; 0.225 kw; 69 ft.; N40 9 23 W89 21 40
300 Keokuk Street, Lincoln, IL 62656 US
(217) 732-3155; *Fax:* (217) 732-3715
www.wlnxradio.com
License: Lincoln, Logan County, IL held by Lincoln University.
Target Audience: 18-34; adults
John Malone, General Manager

Lincolnshire

***WAES**
01-01-2002; 88.1 MHz FM; 0.15 kw; 49 ft.; N42 11 59 W87 56 49
Two Stevenson Drive, Lincolnshire, IL 60069 US
(847) 634-4000 ext. 1710; *Fax:* (847) 634-0983
License: Lincolnshire, Lake County, IL held by Adlai E. Stevenson High School District No. 125.
Format: Variety/Diverse
Greg Sherwin, General Manager

Litchfield

WSMI
11-02-1950; 1540 kHz AM; 1 kw-D, NDD; N39 10 21 W89 34 14
Mailing Address: P. O. Box 10, Litchfield, IL 62056 US
Second Address: 6308 IL Rt. 16, Hillsboro, IL 62049
(217) 324-5921; *Fax:* (217) 532-2431
wsmiradio.com
wsmi@wsmiradio.com
License: Litchfield, IL held by Talley Broadcasting Corp.
Group Owner: Talley Radio Stations
Nat'l Network: CNN Radio; *Nat'l Reps:* Christal; *Wire Services:* AP
Format: Country, News, 62, Talk *Special Programming:* Farm 18 hrs wkly; *Hrs. of News Programming:* news progmg 15 hrs wkly; *No. News Employees:* 3; *Target Audience:* General.
Hayward Talley, President
Brian Talley, Operations Dir
Michael Niehaus, General Sales Mgr
Kevin Talley, Promotions Manager

WSMI-FM
03-05-1960; 106.1 MHz FM; *Hrs Open:* 4:30 AM-midnight; 50 kw; 500 ft; N39 15 21 W89 36 48
Mailing Address: Box 10, WSMI Bldg, Litchfield, IL 62056
Second Address: 6308 IL Rt. 16, Hillsboro, IL 62049
(217) 324-5921; *Fax:* (217) 532-2431
License: Litchfield, Montgomery County, IL
Group Owner: Talley Radio Stations
Nat'l Network: NBC; *Nat'l Reps:* Katz Radio; Christal; *Wire Services:* AP
Population Served: 600,000 *Special Programming:* Farm; *No. News Employees:* 3
Haywrd Talley, President
Brian Talley, Operations Dir
Mike Niehaus, General Sales Mgr
Terry Todt, Programming Director
Rick Davis, News Director
Tobin Ott, Local News Editor

Lockport

***WLRA**
11-01-1972; 88.1 MHz FM; *Hrs Open:* 24; 0.14 kw; 131 ft.; N41 36 10 W88 4 49
500 Independence Blvd, M/C 528, Romeoville, IL 60446 US
(815) 838-0500; *Fax:* (815) 838-9149
www.lewisu.edu/wlra
wlraradio@lewisu.edu
License: Lockport, Will County, IL held by Lewis University.
Nat'l Network: AP Network News; *Wire Services:* AP
Arbitron Metro Market: Chicago, IL; *Format:* Variety/Diverse
Special Programming: Black 15 hrs, class 6 hrs, jazz 15 hrs, sports 15; *Hrs. of News Programming:* News progmg 6 hrs wkly; *Target Audience:* 13-30;college bound or post-college
John Carey, General Manager

Loves Park

***WGSL**
03-28-1988; 91.1 MHz FM; 7 kw; 528 ft.; N42 19 20 W89 0 41
Mailing Address: 5375 Pebble Creek Trail, Rockford, IL 61111 US
Second Address: 5375 Pebble Creek Tr., Loves Park, IL 61111
(815) 654-1200; *Fax:* (815) 282-7779
License: Loves Park, Winnebago County, IL held by Quest for Life Inc.
Nat'l Network: USA
Arbitron Metro Market: Rockford, IL; *Format:* Religious; *Target Audience:* 35-50; older families
Ron Tietsort, Operations Dir
Ralph Trendadue, General Manager

WLUV
09-29-1962; 1520 kHz AM; 0.5 kw-D, ND2; 0.0125 kw-N, ND2; N42 19 48 W89 4 58
Mailing Address: 2272 Elmwood Rd, Loves Park, IL 61032 US
Second Address: 2272 Elmwood Rd., Rockford, IL 61103
(815) 877-9588; *Fax:* (815) 877-9649
License: Loves Park, IL held by Loves Park Broadcasting Co.
Arbitron Metro Market: Rockford, IL; *Format:* Country, Sports
Special Programming: Farm 6 hrs, polka 6 hrs wkly; *Target Audience:* 25-60; blue collar workers
Joe Salvi, General Manager

WKGL-FM
03-25-1964; 96.7 MHz FM; 2.2 kw; 551 ft.; N42 21 48 W89 8 6
2272 Elmwood Rd., Rockford, IL 61103 US
(815) 399-2233; *Fax:* (815) 484-2432
www.967theeagle.net
License: Loves Park, Winnebago County, IL held by Cumulus Licensing Corp.
Group Owner: Cumulus Media Inc.; (acq 3-12-2001).
Arbitron Metro Market: Rockford, IL; *Format:* Classic Rock
Becky Riojas, General Manager
Scott Maenner, General Sales Mgr
John Brizolla, Programming Director
Priscilla Cantu, Promotions Manager
John Huntley, Chief Engineer
Jan Thorp, Traffic Manager

W263BJ
100.5 MHz FM; 0.23 kW; N42 19 21 W88 57 14
2830 Sandy Hollow Rd, Rockford, IL 61109 USA
(815) 874-7861
License: Loves Park, IL held by Mid-Way Radio, Inc.
Group Owner: Mid-West Family Broadcasting
Arbitron Metro Market: Rockford, IL; *Format:* Easy Listening

Lynnville

WEAI
11-15-1989; 107.1 MHz FM; *Hrs Open:* 5 AM-midnight; 6 kw; 328 ft.; N39 37 16 W90 15 28
Mailing Address: P.O. Box 1180, Jacksonville, IL 62651 US
Second Address: 2161 Old State Rd., Jacksonville, IL 62651
(217) 245-7171; *Fax:* (217) 245-6711
www.wlds.com/
weai@weai.com
License: Lynnville, Morgan County, IL held by Jacksonville Area Radio Broadcasters Inc.
Nat'l Network: NBC Radio; *Regional Network:* Ill. Radio Net; *Nat'l Reps:* Katz Radio; *Wire Services:* AP
Arbitron Metro Market: Jacksonville, IL; *Format:* Oldies; *Hrs. of News Programming:* news progmg 6 hrs wkly; *No. News Employees:* 3; *Target Audience:* 20-40; active young adults
Gary Scott, General Manager
Mark Whalen, General Sales Mgr
Perry Brown, Programming Director
Kevin Baxter, News Director
John Coe, Chief Engineer
Troy Armstrong, Music Director
Marty Megginson, Traffic Manager

Macomb

***WIUM**
05-23-1956; 91.3 MHz FM; *Hrs Open:* 24; 50 kw; 486 ft.; N40 25 40 W90 40 58
1 University Circle, Macomb, IL 61455 US
(309) 298-2424; *Fax:* (309) 298-2133
www.tristatesradio.com
publicradio@wiu.edu
License: Macomb, McDonough County, IL held by Western Illinois University.
Nat'l Network: NPR; PRI
Format: News *Special Programming:* Folk/blues 7 hrs, jazz 5 hrs wkly; *Hrs. of News Programming:* news progmg 58 hrs wkly; *No. News Employees:* 2; *Target Audience:* General.
Ken Thermon, Operations Dir
Jonathan Ahl, General Manager
Rich Egger, News Director
Mark Garrett, Chief Engineer
Sharon Faust, Development Director
Ken Zahnle, Music Director

***WIUS**
02-01-1982; 88.3 MHz FM; 0.12 kw horiz; 82 ft.; N40 27 47 W90 41 0
1 University Circle, Macomb, IL 61455 US
(309) 298-3217; *Fax:* (309) 298-2133
www.wiu.edu/the dog/
License: Macomb, McDonough County, IL held by Western Illinois University.
Format: Alternative, Urban Contemporary *Special Programming:* Jazz 2 hrs, Sp 3 hrs, blues 4 hrs wkly; *Target Audience:* 18-30.
Patrick Stout, Station Manager
Tom Durso, Chief Engineer

WJEQ
02-01-1983; 102.7 MHz FM; *Hrs Open:* 24; 10 kw; 512 ft.; N40 25 3 W90 36 51
31 East Side Square, Macomb, IL 61455 US
(309) 833-2121; *Fax:* (309) 836-3291
www.wjeq.com
wjeq@macomb.com
License: Macomb, McDonough County, IL held by Prestige Communications
Format: Classic Rock *Special Programming:* Farm one hr wkly; *Hrs. of News Programming:* news progmg 10 hrs wkly; *No. News Employees:* 1; *Target Audience:* 18-49.

Bruce Foster, President
Nancy Foster, General Manager
Robin Johnson, General Sales Mgr
Kim Williams, Programming Director
Shana Drake, Traffic Manager
Kevin Dean, Music Director

WKAI
06-06-1966; 100.1 MHz FM; *Hrs Open:* 24; 25 kw; 282 ft.; N40 32 1 W90 51 45
P.O. Box 250, Macomb, IL 61455 US
(309) 833-5561; *Fax:* (309) 833-3460
www.radiomacomb.com
wkai@macomb.com
License: Macomb, McDonough County, IL held by Virden Broadcasting Company
Group Owner: Prestige Communications
Format: Adult Contemp; *Hrs. of News Programming:* news progmg 5 hrs wkly; *No. News Employees:* 1; *Target Audience:* 35 plus.; *Adv. Rates:* 10; 10; 10; na
Bruce Foster, President
Nancy Foster, General Manager
Robin Johnson, General Sales Mgr
Kim Williams, Programming Director
Kevin Dean, Music Director
Shana Drake, Traffic Manager

WLRB
07-04-1947; 1510 kHz AM; *Hrs Open:* Sunrise-sunset; 0.25 kw-C, NDD; 1 kw-D, NDD; N40 29 50 W90 40 30
P.O. Box 250, Macomb, IL 61455 US
(309) 833-5561; *Fax:* (309) 833-3460
wlrb@macomb.com
License: Macomb, IL held by WPW Broadcasting Inc.
Group Owner: Prestige Communications
Nat'l Network: Westwood One; Jones Radio Networks; *Regional Network:* Brownfield
Format: Contemporary Hits/Top 40 *Special Programming:* Farm 1.25 hrs wkly; *Hrs. of News Programming:* news progmg 6 hrs wkly; *No. News Employees:* 1; *Target Audience:* 45 plus.; *Adv. Rates:* 10; 10; 10; na
Bruce Foster, President
Nancy Foster, General Manager
Robin Johnson, General Sales Mgr
Kim Williams, Programming Director
Adam Stubinski, News Director
Kevin Dean, Music Director

WNLF
01-01-2003; 95.9 MHz FM; 6 kw; 328 ft.; N40 25 3 W90 36 51
C/O Wjeq Radio, 31 E Side Square, Macomb, IL 91455 US
(309) 833-2121; *Fax:* (309) 836-3291
License: Macomb, McDonough County, IL held by Nancy L. Foster.
Group Owner: Prestige Communications
Arbitron Metro Market: Macomb, IL; *Format:* Rock/AOR
Bruce Foster, President
Nancy Foster, General Manager
Adam Stubinski, News Director
Kendra Kessler, Traffic Manager

Macon

WZUS
05-05-1977; 100.9 MHz FM; *Hrs Open:* 24; 6 kw; Ant 328 ft; N39 47 11 W88 59 29
410 N. Water St., Suite B, Decatur, IL 62568
(217) 428-4487; *Fax:* (217) 428-4501
www.decaturradio.com
cbullock@cromwellradio.com
License: Macon, Macon County, IL held by The Cromwell Group Inc. of Illinois.
Group Owner: The Cromwell Group Inc.; (acq 4-16-02; $900,000).
Nat'l Network: Cumulus Radio Network; Premiere Radio Network; Talk Radio Network; *Regional Network:* Cromwell Ag Radio Network; *Nat'l Reps:* Eastman Radio
Population Served: 200,000; *Arbitron Metro Market:* Decatur, IL
Special Programming: Farm 8 hrs wkly; *Target Audience:* General.
Tara Nickerson, Business Manager
Tara Nickerson, Operations Manager
Chris Bullock, General Manager

Mahomet

WGKC
12-15-1990; 105.9 MHz FM; *Hrs Open:* 24; 2.5 kw; 512 ft.; N40 13 27 W88 17 56
400 North Broadway, Urbana, IL 61801 US
(217) 367-1195; *Fax:* (217) 367-3291
www.wgkc.net
ken.cunningham@sjbroadcasting.com
License: Mahomet, Champaign County, IL held by RadioStar Inc.
Group Owner: RadioStar Inc.; (acq 5-23-2006; grpsl).
Nat'l Reps: McGavren Guild
Arbitron Metro Market: Champaign, IL; *Format:* Classic Rock; *No. News Employees:* 1; *Target Audience:* 25-54; adult men
Jim Glassman, President
Roxanne Charles, General Manager
Steve Miller, General Sales Mgr
Ken Cunningham, Programming Director
Josh Laskowski, Promotions Manager
Jon Hall, Chief Engineer
Donna Keleher, Office Manager

Marion

***WAWJ**
01-01-2001; 90.1 MHz FM; 3 kw vert; 344 ft.; N37 51 23 W89 8 22
P.O. Box 3206, Tupelo, MS 38803 US
(662) 844-8888; *Fax:* (662) 842-6791
www.afr.net
faq@afa.net
License: Marion, Williamson County, IL held by American Family Association.
Group Owner: American Family Radio
Arbitron Metro Market: Great Falls MT; *Format:* Christian
Tim Wildmon, President
Donald Wildmon, Founder
Buddy Smith, Sr VP
Ed Vitagliano, Exec VP
Randy Sharp, Director Of Special Projects
Meeke Addison, Director Of Communications
Abraham Hamilton III, General Counsel

WGGH
09-24-1949; 1150 kHz AM; *Hrs Open:* 24 hrs; 5 kw-D, DA2; 0.044 kw-N, DA2; N37 43 47 W88 53 44
P.O. Box 340, Marion, IL 62959 US
(618) 993-8102; *Fax:* (618) 997-2305
www.wggh.net
License: Marion, IL held by Vine Broadcasting Inc.
Nat'l Network: Salem Radio Network; *Regional Network:* Ill. Radio Net.
Arbitron Metro Market: Marion-Carbondale (Southern Illinois); *Format:* Country, News, 62, Talk; *Hrs. of News Programming:* News progmg Hourly; *Target Audience:* 18 plus; general
Elaine Gomez, General Manager
Mat Canon, Programming Director
Brenda Bender, News Director
Johnny Gomez, Chief Engineer

Maroa

WDKR
05-01-1996; 107.3 MHz FM; *Hrs Open:* 24; 3 kw; 456 ft.; N39 57 56 W89 3 27
602 Woodland Court, Mt. Zion, IL 62549 US
(217) 864-4141; *Fax:* (217) 864-4727
License: Maroa, Macon County, IL held by WDKR Inc.
Arbitron Metro Market: Decatur, IL; *Format:* Oldies; *Target Audience:* 25-54; general; *Adv. Rates:* 23.55; 23.55; 23.55; 23.55
Mary Ellen Burns, General Manager

Marseilles

WLWF
03-01-1992; 96.5 MHz FM; *Hrs Open:* 24; 3 kw; 328 ft; N41 18 40 W88 49 07
1 Broadcast Ln., Oglesby, IL 61348 USA
(815) 233-3100
www.lcbcradio.com/wolf
programdirector@classichits1039wlpo.com
License: Marseilles, La Salle County, IL held by La Salle County Broadcasting Corp.
Group Owner: La Salle County Broadcasting Corp.; acq 6-99; $550,000
Nat'l Network: Jones Radio Networks
Format: Contemporary Hits/Top 40, Adult Contemp; *Hrs. of News Programming:* news progmg 8 hrs wkly; *No. News Employees:* 1; *Target Audience:* 35-54.

Marshall

WMMC
10-02-1989; 105.9 MHz FM; *Hrs Open:* 24; 2.3 kw; 528 ft.; N39 21 9 W87 49 19
Mailing Address: 1477 Radcliff Ln., Aurora, IL 60504 US
Second Address: 627 1/2 Archer Ave., Marshall, IL 62441
(217) 826-8017; *Fax:* (217) 826-8519
www.wmmcradio.com/
WMMC106@aol.com
License: Marshall, Clark County, IL held by JDL Broadcasting Inc.
Nat'l Network: ABC
Arbitron Metro Market: Terre Haute, IN; *Format:* Oldies; *Hrs. of News Programming:* News progmg 8 hrs wkly; *Target Audience:* 25-54; career-oriented men and women
J. Spangler, President
Lori Spangler, Operations Dir

Mattoon

WLBH
11-26-1946; 1170 kHz AM; *Hrs Open:* 6 AM-7 PM; 5 kw-D, DAD; N39 31 5 W88 22 15
PO Box 1848, North Route 45, Mattoon, IL 61938 US
(217) 234-6464; *Fax:* (217) 234-6019
License: Mattoon, IL held by Mattoon Broadcasting Co.
Group Owner: J.R. Livesay Group
Format: Adult Contemp, News, 62, Talk *Special Programming:* Relg 5 hrs wkly; *Hrs. of News Programming:* news progmg 20 hrs wkly; *No. News Employees:* 3; *Target Audience:* 25 plus.
J.R. Livesay, Chairman
J.R. Livesay II, CEO
Adam Kennedy, News Director
S.L. Herrington, CFO
Chase Arnold, Political Ed

WLBH-FM
08-01-1949; 96.9 MHz FM; *Hrs Open:* 24; 50 kw; 499 ft.; N39 31 2 W88 22 13
P. O. Box 1848, Mattoon, IL 61938 US
(217) 234-6464; *Fax:* (217) 234-6019
License: Mattoon, Coles County, IL held by Mattoon Broadcasting Co.
Group Owner: J.R. Livesay Group
Format: Adult Contemp; *Hrs. of News Programming:* news progmg 18 hrs wkly; *No. News Employees:* 3; *Target Audience:* 25 plus.
S.L. Herrington, CFO
J.R. Livesay II, General Manager
Adam Kennedy, News Director
J.R. Livesay, Chairman/CEO
Chase Arnold, Political Ed

***WLKL**
01-20-1975; 89.9 MHz FM; *Hrs Open:* 24; 1.3 kw; 203 ft.; N39 25 7 W88 22 55
Lake Land College, 5001 Lake Land Blvd, Mattoon, IL 61938 US
(217) 234-5373; *Fax:* (217) 234-5506
www.899themax.com
gpowers@lakeland.cc.il.us
License: Mattoon, Coles County, IL held by Community College District 517 Lake Land College.
Format: Rock/AOR; *Hrs. of News Programming:* news progmg 6 hrs wkly; *No. News Employees:* 1; *Target Audience:* 18-34; general; *Adv. Rates:* 5; 4; 4; 5
Greg Powers, General Manager

McLeansboro

WMCL
01-26-1968; 1060 kHz AM; *Hrs Open:* 24; 2.5 kw-D, DAD; 0.002 kw-N, DAD; N38 6 16 W88 33 48
303 North Main, P.O. Box 818, Benton, IL 62812 US
(618) 435-4392; *Fax:* (618) 643-3299
www.wqrlradio.com
wishfm989@gmail.com
License: McLeansboro, IL held by Dana Communications Corp.
Nat'l Network: CNN Radio
Arbitron Metro Market: McLeansboro, IL; *Format:* Country; *Target Audience:* 25-65; agricultural community
Dana Withers, President
Gloria Holland, Operations Dir

Mendota

WGLC
09-01-1965; 100.1 MHz FM; 6 kw; 328 ft.; N41 32 16 W89 06 25
3905 Progress Blvd., Peru, IL 61354 US
(815) 539-6741; *Fax:* (815) 225-2066
www.wglc.net
advertising@studstillmedia.com
License: Mendota, La Salle County, IL held by Mendota Broadcasting, Inc.
Group Owner: Studstill Broadcasting
Nat'l Network: ABC; *Nat'l Reps:* Rgnl Reps; *Wire Services:* AP
Arbitron Metro Market: La Salle-Peru, IL; *Format:* Country; *Target Audience:* 35 plus.
Cole Studstill, Managing of Programming

Metropolis

WMOK
02-04-1951; 920 kHz AM; *Hrs Open:* 24
3501 Broadway, P.O. Box 1508, Mount Vernon, IL 62864 US
(618) 524-4400; *Fax:* (618) 524-3133
http://www.920wmok.com
wmok920@frontier.com
License: Metropolis, IL held by Withers Broadcasting Co. of Paducah LLC.
Group Owner: Withers Broadcasting Co.; (acq 9-11-97; grpsl).
Arbitron Metro Market: Metropolis, IL; *Format:* Country *Special Programming:* Relg 5 hrs wkly; *No. News Employees:* 1; *Target Audience:* General.
Rick Lambert, General Manager
Melanie Shepherd, General Sales Mgr
Evan Spencer, Programming Director
Evan Spencer, News Director
Smokey King, Chief Engineer

WREZ
12-12-1988; 105.5 MHz FM; *Hrs Open:* 24; 6 kw; 328 ft.; N37 10 25 W88 42 29
3501 Broadway, P.O. Box 1508, Mount Vernon, IL 62864 US
(270) 538-5251; *Fax:* (270) 415-0599
License: Metropolis, Massac County, IL held by Withers Broadcasting Co. of Paducah LLC
Group Owner: Withers Broadcasting Co.
Format: Adult Contemp
Steve Thompson, Programming Director

WJLI
07-11-1984; 98.3 MHz FM; 100 kw; 699 ft.; N36 45 9 W88 29 58
6120 Waldo Church Rd, Metropolis, IL 62960 US
Fax: (618) 564-3202
License: Metropolis, Massac County, IL held by Sun Media Inc.
Format: Adult Contemp
Samuel Stratemeyer, President
Willie Kerns, Operations Dir

Milford

*WJCZ
01-01-2005; 91.3 MHz FM; 25 kw; 89 ft.; N40 35 7 W87 57 47
Rebroadcasts: Rebroadcasts WHLP (FM)
150 West Lincolnway, Suite 2001, Valpariso, IN 46383 US
(219) 548-5800
www.calvaryradionetwork.com
info@calvaryradionetwork.com
License: Milford, Iroquois County, IL held by Calvary Radio Network, Inc.
Group Owner: Calvary Radio Network
Arbitron Metro Market: Milford, IL; *Format:* Christian, Religious

Moline

WFXN
01-01-1946; 1230 kHz AM; *Hrs Open:* 24; 1 kw-U, ND1; N41 28 54 W90 31 49
3535 East Kimberly Road, Davenport, IA 52807 US
(563) 344-7000; *Fax:* (563) 359-8524
www.foxsportsradio1230.com
License: Moline, IL held by Citicasters Licenses Inc.
Group Owner: iHeartMedia; (acq 11-15-00; grpsl).
Arbitron Metro Market: Quad Cities, IA; *Format:* Sports *Special Programming:* Sports 8 hrs, pub affrs 4 hrs, farm one hr wkly; *Hrs. of News Programming:* news progmg 6 hrs wkly; *No. News Employees:* 1 *TargetAudience:* 25-54; upscale/contemp
Scott Bitting, Market President/Director of Sales
Jim O'Hara, Senior Vice President of Programming

WXLP
11-22-1970; 96.9 MHz FM; 50 kw; 499 ft.; N41 20 16 W90 22 46
1229 Brady Street, Davenport, IA 52803 US
(563) 326-2541; *Fax:* (563) 326-1819
www.97x.com
License: Moline, Rock Island County, IL held by Cumulus Licensing Corp.
Group Owner: Cumulus Media Inc.; (acq 3-15-2000; grpsl)
Nat'l Network: Westwood One
Arbitron Metro Market: Quad Cities, IA; *Format:* Classic Rock; *Target Audience:* 25-54.
Darren Pitra, Operations Dir
Joe Cook, General Sales Mgr
Richard Griesecke, Programming Director
Tracey Hall, News Director
Andy Andresen, Chief Engineer
Cheryl Riley-Hayles, Market Manager

Monee

*WGEN-FM
11-01-1995; 88.9 MHz FM; 0.1 kw vert; 177 ft.; N41 24 47.9 W87 46 2.8
820 N. Lasalle Blvd., Chicago, IL 60610 US
(312) 329-4300; *Fax:* (312) 329-4339
www.ktlw.org
License: Monee, Will County, IL held by Life on the Way Communications Inc.
Format: Christian, Religious; *Target Audience:* General.
Gary Curtis, Operations Dir
Doug Hastings, Station Manager
Pamela McCain, Operations Manager

Monmouth

WMOI
12-06-1967; 97.7 MHz FM; *Hrs Open:* 24; 3.4 kw; 440 ft.; N40 53 25 W90 36 31
55 Public Sq., Monmouth, IL 61462 US
(309) 734-9452; *Fax:* (309) 734-3276
www.1330wram.com
vanessa.wetterling@prairiecommunications.net
License: Monmouth, Warren County, IL held by WPW Broadcasting
Group Owner: Prairie Radio Communications
Regional Network: Tribune Radio Networks
Arbitron Metro Market: Monouth, IL; *Format:* Adult Contemp; *Hrs. of News Programming:* news progmg 40 hrs wkly; *No. News Employees:* 3; *Target Audience:* General.; *Adv. Rates:* 20; 20; 20; 14.50
Mike Weaver, Operations Dir
Loren Follmer, General Manager
Amy Patterson, General Sales Mgr

WRAM
05-01-1957; 1330 kHz AM; *Hrs Open:* 6 AM-6 PM; 1 kw-D, DA2; 0.05 kw-N, DA2; N40 56 59 W90 34 19
55 Public Sq., Monmouth, IL 61462 US
(309) 734-9452; *Fax:* (309) 734-3276
www.1330wram.com
loren.follmer@prairiecommunications.net
License: Monmouth, IL held by WPW Broadcasting Inc.
Group Owner: Prairie Radio Communications; (acq 12-24-97; $1.7 million with co-located FM)
Nat'l Network: ABC; *Regional Network:* Tribune Radio Networks
Format: Country *Special Programming:* Farm 18 hrs, relg 3 hrs wkly; *Hrs. of News Programming:* news progmg 20 hrs wkly; *No. News Employees:* 3; *Target Audience:* General; adult, mature
Mike Weaver, Operations Dir
Loren Follmer, General Manager
Amy Patterson, General Sales Mgr

Monticello

WCZQ
01-18-1972; 105.5 MHz FM; *Hrs Open:* 24; 6 kw; 328 ft.; N40 2 54 W88 34 25
1705 West Northwest Highway, Suite 275, Grapevine, TX 76051 US
(217) 762-2588; *Fax:* (217) 423-9764
License: Monticello, Piatt County, IL held by Neuhoff Family L.P.
Group Owner: Neuhoff Family L.P.; (acq 2-23-2009; grpsl)
Nat'l Network: ABC
Arbitron Metro Market: Champaign, IL; *Format:* Urban Contemporary *Special Programming:* Farm 11 hrs wkly; *Hrs. of News Programming:* News progmg 5 hrs wkly; *Target Audience:* 25-65; upscale suburban & prosperousfarm; *Adv. Rates:* 17; 17; 17; 17
Mark Hanson, General Manager
Wendy Tohill, General Sales Mgr
Jamie Pendleton, Programming Director
Cindy Hansen, News Director
Frank Konwinski, Chief Engineer

Morris

*WCFL
01-01-1962; 104.7 MHz FM; *Hrs Open:* 24; 50 kw; 496 ft; N41 21 17 W88 29 55 *Rebroadcasts:* Rebroadcasts WBGL(FM) Champaign 100%
4101 Fieldstone Road, Champaign, IL 61822
(217) 359-8232
www.wbgl.org
wbgl@wbgl.org
License: Morris, Grundy County, IL held by Illinois District Council of Assembly.
Nat'l Network: USA
Population Served: 1,500,000; *Arbitron Metro Market:* Chicago; *Target Audience:* 24-39.
Jeff Scott, Station Manager
Rick Smith, Director of Technology
Ryan Springer, Programming Director
Joe Roether, Chief Engineer
Jennifer Briski, Brand Manager
Joe Buchanan, Network Music Director
Zoe Fuller, UnderwritingDirector/Office Manager
Brian Miller, Donor Relations Director
Jason Rackow, Production Director
G. w. Van Alstine, Marketing Manager

WCSJ
01-15-1964; 1550 kHz AM; *Hrs Open:* 24; 0.25 kw-D, ND1; 0.006 kw-N, ND1; N41 20 29 W88 25 31
1 Broadcast Center, Plano, IL 60545 US
(815) 941-1000; *Fax:* (815) 941-9300
www.wcsjfm.com
news@NelsonMultimedia.net
License: Morris, IL held by Grundy County Broadcasters Inc.
Arbitron Metro Market: Chicago,IL; *Format:* Adult Contemp, News, 62, Talk; *Target Audience:* 35 plus.; *Adv. Rates:* 42; 31; 36; 25
Larry Nelson, President
Jack Daly, General Manager
Susan Pellegrini, General Sales Mgr

WCSJ-FM
01-01-1993; 103.1 MHz FM; *Hrs Open:* 24; 6 kw; 328 ft.; N41 17 35 W88 20 4
11 Skyline Drive, Hawthorne, NY 10532 US
(815) 941-1000; *Fax:* (815) 941-9300
License: Morris, Grundy County, IL held by Grundy County Broadcasters Inc.
Nat'l Network: ABC
Arbitron Metro Market: Chicago; *Format:* Adult Contemp, News, 62, Talk *Special Programming:* Farm 10 hrs wkly.; *Hrs. of News Programming:* news progmg 20 hrs wkly; *No. News Employees:* 1; *Target Audience:* 25plus; community oriented; *Adv. Rates:* 42; 31; 36; 25
Larry Nelson, President
Kevin Schramm, Operations Dir
Jack Daly, General Manager

*WBEQ
11-01-2003; 90.7 MHz FM; 1.45 kw; 468 ft.; N41 17 9 W88 25 49 *Rebroadcasts:* Rebroadcasts WBEZ(FM) Chicago 100%
848 East Grand Ave., Chicago, IL 60611 US
(312) 948-4600; *Fax:* (312) 832 3100
www.wbez.org
License: Morris, Grundy County, IL held by The WBEZ Alliance Inc.
Nat'l Network: NPR
Arbitron Metro Market: Morris, IL; *Format:* Jazz, News, 62, Talk
Merrill Smith, Chairman
Donna Moore, CFO
Torey Malatia, President and Chief Executive Officer
Greg Salustro, General Sales Mgr
Aurora Aguilar, Project Editor, Front & Center
Daniel O. Ash, Vice President, StrategicCommunications
Sally Eisele, Managing Editor, Public Affairs
Heidi Goldfein, Production Director
Matthew Green, Director of Digital Product Management
Vanessa Harris, Marketing Director

Morrison

WZZT
04-10-1991; 95.1 MHz FM; 6 kw; 328 ft.; N41 50 16 W89 55 29
3501 Broadway, P.O. Box 1508, Mount Vernon, IL 62864 US
(815) 625-3400; *Fax:* (815) 625-6940
wsdr1240@theramp.net
License: Morrison, Whiteside County, IL held by Withers Broadcasting Co. of Rock River LLC.
Group Owner: Withers Broadcasting Co.; (acq 1-21-98; grpsl).
Nat'l Network: ABC; *Regional Network:* Ill. Radio Net; *Nat'l Reps:* Christal
Arbitron Metro Market: Sterling, IL; *Format:* Classic Rock, Sports; *Target Audience:* 25-54; adults/men
Brian Zschiesche, General Manager
Kathy Wagner, Programming Director
Mary Carlson, News Director
Sherry Smith, Traffic Manager

Morton

WNGY
11-28-1976; 102.3 MHz FM; *Hrs Open:* 24; 4.1 kw; 400 ft.; N40 43 22 W89 30 40
331 Fulton St., Suite 1200, Peoria, IL 61602 US
(309) 637-3700; *Fax:* (309) 272-1476
www.energy1023.com

License: Morton, Tazewell County, IL held by Alpha Media Licensee LLC
Group Owner: Alpha Media LLC
Nat'l Network: Westwood One; CBS; *Regional Network:* Ill. Radio Net.
Population Served: 350,000; *Arbitron Metro Market:* Peoria, IL; *Format:* Contemporary Hits/Top 40 *Special Programming:* Relg one hr wkly; *Hrs. of News Programming:* news progmg 10 hrs wkly *No. News Employees:* 1; *Target Audience:* 25 plus; active, affluent males
Randy Rundle, Operations Manager
Mike Wild, General Manager
Matt Marchand, Sales Manager
Chris Stewart, Programming Director

Mount Carmel

WYNG
11-28-1960; 94.9 MHz FM; *Hrs Open:* 24; 50 kw; 420 ft.; N38 23 57 W87 47 18
P.O. Box 242, 1309 Old Orchard Road, Vincennes, IN 47591 US
(618) 263-3500; *Fax:* (618) 263-3520
www.wyng949.com
License: Mount Carmel, Wabash County, IL held by W. Russell Withers Jr.
Group Owner: Withers Broadcasting Co.; (acq 12-22-2006; $1.5 million)
Arbitron Metro Market: Mount Carmel, IL; *Format:* Adult Contemp
Scott Allen, General Manager
Terry Beckerman, General Sales Mgr
Josh Howard, Programming Director
Josh Baxter, News Director
Rodger Beard, Account Executive
Sally Voight, Account Executive
Denise Hodges, Traffic

*WVJC
07-23-1973; 89.1 MHz FM; *Hrs Open:* 24; 50 kw; 331 ft.; N38 26 29 W87 45 26
2200 College Drive, Mt. Carmel, IL 62863 US
(618) 262-8641; *Fax:* (618) 262-8989
www.bashradio.com
peachk@iecc.edu
License: Mount Carmel, Wabash County, IL held by Illinois Eastern Community Colleges.
Arbitron Metro Market: Evansville, IN; *Format:* Alternative; *Target Audience:* 12-24; general; *Adv. Rates:* N/A
Ryan Jenkins, Operations Dir
Kyle Peach, Programming Director

Mount Sterling

WPWQ
09-01-1995; 106.7 MHz FM; 25 kw; 328 ft.; N39 56 33 W90 57 44
P.O Box 196, 142 E. Washington Street, Rushville, IL 62681 US
(217) 224-4653; *Fax:* (217) 885-3233
wpwq106@adams.net
License: Mount Sterling, Brown County, IL held by WPW Broadcasting Inc.
Group Owner: Prairie Radio Communications; (acq 12-6-99; $550,000 with WKXQ(FM) Rushville)
Format: Oldies
Don Davis, President
Phil Alexander, General Manager
Brian Myles, Programming Director

Mount Vernon

WIBV
01-01-2001; 102.1 MHz FM; *Hrs Open:* 24; 10.5 kw; 509 ft.; N38 24 7 W89 8 9
6120 Waldo Church Road, Metropolis, IL 62960 US
(618) 249-6025; *Fax:* (618) 564-3202
jack@wibv102.com
License: Mount Vernon, Jefferson County, IL held by Benjamin Stratemeyer
Arbitron Metro Market: Mount Vernon-Centralia, IL; *Format:* Country; *Target Audience:* 18-54.
Samuel Stratemeyer, General Manager

*WAPO
01-01-1997; 90.5 MHz FM; 1.1 kw; 203 ft.; N38 18 39 W88 56 11
P.O. Box 3206, Tupelo, MS 38803 US
(662) 844-8888; *Fax:* (662) 842-6791
www.afr.net
faq@afa.net
License: Mount Vernon, Jefferson County, IL held by American Family Association.
Group Owner: American Family Radio
Arbitron Metro Market: Mount Vernon, IL; *Format:* Christian, Religious
Tim Wildmon, President
Donald Wildmon, Faounder
Buddy Smith, Sr VP
Ed Vitagliano, Randy Sharp
Director Of Special Projects, Meeke Addison
Director Of Communications, Abraham Hamilton III
General Counsel, General Sales Mgr

*WBMV
09-30-1997; 89.7 MHz FM; *Hrs Open:* 24; 10.5 kw vert; 492 ft.; N38 22 15 W88 55 20 *Rebroadcasts:* Rebroadcasts WIBI(FM) Carlinville 100%
P.O. Box 140, Carlinville, IL 62626 US
(217) 854-4800; *Fax:* (217) 854-4810
www.wibi.org/
wibi@wibi.org
License: Mount Vernon, Jefferson County, IL held by Illinois Bible Institute Inc.
Group Owner: Illinois Bible Institute Inc.
Arbitron Metro Market: Carlinville, IL; *Format:* Adult Contemp, Christian; *Target Audience:* 29-45.; *Adv. Rates:* 7; 7; 7; 7
Barry Copeland, General Manager
Tom Greene, Station Manager
Rob Regal, Programming Director
Jessica Barton, Promotions Manager
Sally Braundmeier, News Director
Joe Buchanan, Music Director
Liz Eilers, Underwriting Director
Angie Carpenter, Office Manager
Brian Miller, Donor Relations Director

WMIX
01-01-1947; 940 kHz AM; *Hrs Open:* 24; 5 kw-D, DA2; 1.5 kw-N, DA2; N38 22 14 W88 55 24; N38 21 15 W89 0 29
Mailing Address: 3501 Broadway, Mount Vernon, IL 62864 US
Second Address: 3501 Broadway, Mount Vernon, IL 62864
(618) 242-3500; *Fax:* (618) 242-2490
www.mywithersradio.com
wmix@mvn.net
License: Mount Vernon, IL held by Withers Broadcasting Co. of Illinois LLC.
Group Owner: Withers Broadcasting Co.; (acq 5-30-73).
Nat'l Network: Westwood One; *Wire Services:* AP
Arbitron Metro Market: Moutn Vernon, IL; *Format:* Adult Contemp
Special Programming: Farm 18 hrs wkly; *Hrs. of News Programming:* news progmg 15 hrs wkly; *No. News Employees:* 2; *Target Audience:* 25 plus.
W. Russell Withers Jr., President
Dana Withers, General Manager
Scott Smalls, General Sales Mgr
Nicholas Lemay, News Director

WMIX-FM
01-01-1946; 94.1 MHz FM; *Hrs Open:* 24; 50 kw horiz; 551 ft.; N38 22 15 W88 55 20
P. O. Box 1238, Mount Vernon, IL 62864 US
(618) 242-3500; *Fax:* (618) 242-2490
www.mywithersradio.com
wmix@mvn.net
License: Mount Vernon, Jefferson County, IL held by Withers Broadcasting Co. of Illinois LLC
Group Owner: Withers Broadcasting Co.
Arbitron Metro Market: Moutn Vernon, IL; *Format:* Country
Russell Withers, CEO
D.T. Brown, Programming Director
Craig Warner, News Director

Mount Zion

WXFM-FM
10-01-1984; 99.3 MHz FM; *Hrs Open:* 24; 1.15 kw; 495 ft; N39 48 35 W88 59 31
120 Wildwood Dr., Mount Zion, IL 62549
(217) 864-4141; *Fax:* (217) 864-4727
License: Mount Zion, Macon County, IL held by Technicom Inc.
Nat'l Network: CNN Radio; *Regional Network:* Brownfield
Population Served: 300,000 *Hrs. of News Programming:* News progmg 5 hrs wkly; *Target Audience:* Free spending, affluent adults.; *Adv. Rates:* 29; 29; 29; 29
Mary Ellen Burns, President

Mt. Vernon

*WVSI
01-01-2003; 88.9 MHz FM; *Hrs Open:* 24; 1.9 kw horiz, 4 kw vert; 338 ft.; N38 21 13 W88 56 32 *Rebroadcasts:* Rebroadcasts WSIU(FM) Carbondale
US
(618) 453-4343; *Fax:* (618) 453-6186
wsiu.org
jeff.williams@wsiu.org
License: Mt. Vernon, Jefferson County, IL held by The Board of Trustees of Southern Illinois University.
Nat'l Network: NPR; PRI; *Regional Network:* Ill. Radio Net.; *Wire Services:* AP
Arbitron Metro Market: Carbondale, IL; *Format:* News; *Hrs. of News Programming:* news progmg 36 hrs wkly; *No. News Employees:* 3
Greg Petrowich, CEO
Mike Zelten, Operations Dir
Jeff Williams, Station Manager
Renee Dillard, General Sales Mgr

Murphysboro

WINI
09-15-1954; 1420 kHz AM; *Hrs Open:* 24; 0.42 kw-D, DAN; 0.5 kw-N, DAN; N37 45 30 W89 14 2
1677 Business Highway 13, Murphysboro, IL 62966 US
(618) 684-2128; *Fax:* (618) 687-4318
www.winiradio.com
wini@intrnet.net
License: Murphysboro, IL held by Radio Station WINI.
Arbitron Metro Market: Marion-Carbondale (Southern Illinois); *Format:* News, News/Talk, 86 *Special Programming:* Relg 6 hrs wkly; *Hrs. of News Programming:* News progmg 22 hrs wkly; *Target Audience:* 25-59.
Nancy Engel, Operations Dir
Dale Adkins, General Manager

WVZA
03-01-1994; 105.1 MHz FM; *Hrs Open:* 24; 25 kw; 308 ft.; N37 45 15 W89 19 14
330 East Kilbourn Ave., Suite 250, Milwaukee, WI 53202 US
(618) 997-8123; *Fax:* (618) 993-2319
www.mywithersradio.com
License: Murphysboro, Williamson County, IL held by Withers Broadcasting of Southern Illinois LLC.
Group Owner: Withers Broadcasting Co.; (acq 3-17-2008; grpsl)
Arbitron Metro Market: Marion-Carbondale, IL; *Format:* Adult Contemp; *Target Audience:* W18-49, 25-54.
Paxton Guy, Operations Dir
Janet Jensen, General Manager
Gina Heern, General Sales Mgr
April Bennett, News Director
Tim Deterding, Chief Engineer

Naperville

*WONC
07-01-1968; 89.1 MHz FM; 1.5 kw; 164 ft.; N41 46 34 W88 11 41
30 N. Brainard St., Naperville, IL 60566 US
(630) 637-8989; *Fax:* (630) 637-5900
www.wonc.org
jvmadormo@noctrl.edu
License: Naperville, Du Page County, IL held by North Central College.
Wire Services: AP
Arbitron Metro Market: Chicago *TV Affiliate:* rock and roll; *Format:* Alternative, Religious *Special Programming:* 5; *No. News Employees:* 18-44.
General Manager, General Manager

Nashville

WNSV
07-10-1994; 104.7 MHz FM; *Hrs Open:* 24; 3.4 kw; 440 ft.; N38 26 2 W89 18 55
P. O. Box 818, Benton, IL 62812 US
(618) 327-4444; *Fax:* (618) 327-3716
www.v1047.com
angie@v1047.com
License: Nashville, Washington County, IL held by Dana K. Withers.
Arbitron Metro Market: Nashville, IL; *Format:* Adult Contemp; *Target Audience:* 30 plus.
Gloria Holland, Operations Dir
Dana Withers, General Manager

Neoga

WHQQ
09-01-1996; 98.9 MHz FM; *Hrs Open:* 24; 3.2 kw; 453 ft.; N39 14 59 W88 22 48
Mailing Address: 405 South Banker Street, Suite 201, Effingham, IL 62401 US
Second Address: 405 S. Banker St., #201, Effingham, IL 62401
(615) 361-7560; *Fax:* (615) 366-4313
www.effinghamradio.com

License: Neoga, Cumberland County, IL held by WSHY Inc.
Group Owner: The Cromwell Group Inc.
Nat'l Network: Jones Radio Networks
Format: Oldies *Special Programming:* Farm 7 hrs wkly; *Hrs. of News Programming:* News progmg 14 hrs wkly; *Target Audience:* 25-54; adults; *Adv. Rates:* 15; 12; 15; 10
Sheila Myers, General Manager
Ethan Kruger, News Director
Sports Director, Eric Frye

WMCI
08-24-1989; 101.3 MHz FM; *Hrs Open:* 24; 14.5 kw; 433 ft; N39 31 39 W88 21 23
209 Lakeland Blvd., Mattoon, IL 37215
(217) 235-5624,(217) 348-9292; *Fax:* (217) 235-6624
www.myradiolink.com
lenglum@cromwellradio.com
License: Neoga, Cumberland County, IL held by The Cromwell Group Inc. of Illinois.
Group Owner: The Cromwell Group Inc.
Regional Reps: Katz
Population Served: 100,000 *Special Programming:* Farm 5 hrs wkly; *Hrs. of News Programming:* news progmg 10 hrs wkly; *No. News Employees:* 1; *Target Audience:* 25-54.; *Adv. Rates:* 25; 18; 20; 15
Luci Englum, General Manager

Newton

WIKK
05-04-1992; 103.5 MHz FM; *Hrs Open:* 24; 25 kw; 328 ft.; N39 6 20 W88 10 21
P.O. Box 304, Newton, IL 62448 US
(618) 783-8000; *Fax:* (618) 783-4040
www.929thelegend.com
wikk1035@psbnewton.com
License: Newton, Jasper County, IL held by Forcht Broadcasting
Group Owner: Forcht Broadcasting
Nat'l Network: CNN Radio
Format: Classic Rock; *Hrs. of News Programming:* news progmg 8 hrs wkly; *No. News Employees:* 1; *Target Audience:* 25-49.
Mike Shipman, General Manager
Deb Ayers, Account Executive
Mark Weiler, News Director

Normal

***WGLT**
02-04-1966; 89.1 MHz FM; *Hrs Open:* 24; 25 kw; 377 ft.; N40 28 46 W89 3 12
310 Media Center, Normal, IL 61761 US
(309) 438-2255; *Fax:* (309) 438-7870
www.wglt.org
wglt@IllinoisState.edu
License: Normal, McLean County, IL held by Illinois State University.
Nat'l Network: NPR; PRI; AP Radio; *Regional Network:* Ill. Radio Net.; *Wire Services:* AP
Format: Blues, Jazz *Special Programming:* Folk 4 hrs, musical theater 2 hrs wkly; *Hrs. of News Programming:* news progmg 40 hrs wkly; *No. News Employees:* 3; *Target Audience:* 35-54.
Bruce Bergethon, General Manager
Aaron Wissmiller, General Sales Mgr
Mike McCurdy, Programming Director
Linda Healy, Promotions Manager
Willis Kern, News Director
Mark Hill, Chief Engineer
Jon Norton, Music Director
TravisMeadors, Broadcast Technologist
Jeff Paxton, Corporate Support Coordinator
Paat Peterson, Individual Giving Director
Chalrie Schlenker, Assistant News Director
Aaron Wissmiller, Development Director

WIHN
12-21-1973; 96.7 MHz FM; *Hrs Open:* 24; 3.9 kw; 410 ft.; N40 28 34 W89 2 2
555 Gulf of Mexico Dr, Suite 201, Longboat Key, FL 34228 US
(309) 834-1100; *Fax:* (309) 834-4390
www.967irock.com
License: Normal, McLean County, IL held by Connoisseur Media Licenses LLC
Group Owner: Connoisseur Media LLC; (acq 11-2-2006; $4 million)
Nat'l Network: ABC; *Nat'l Reps:* Christal
Arbitron Metro Market: Bloomington, IL; *Hrs. of News Programming:* news progmg 9 hrs wkly; *No. News Employees:* 1; *Target Audience:* 18-44.
Jack Swart, General Manager
Grant Thompson, General Sales Mgr

Adam Chandler, Programming Director
Mark Hill, Chief Engineer

Northbrook

WZRK
05-15-1964; 1550 kHz AM; 1 kw-D, DA2; 0.001 kw-N, DA2; N42 35 39 W88 23 24
Mailing Address: PO Box 700, Hwy 50 East, Lake Geneva, WI 53147 US
Second Address: 2300 Riverside Dr., Green Bay, WI 54301
(920) 271-1000; *Fax:* (920) 271-1010
www.sovcity.com
License: Northbrook, IL held by Sovereign City Radio Services LLC
Arbitron Metro Market: North Platte, NE
Scott Krusinski, Operations Dir

Oak Lawn

WNWI
12-31-1965; 1080 kHz AM; 3 kw-D, DAN; 2.6 kw-N, DAN; N41 38 36 W87 38 45
934 W. 138 St., Riverdale, MI 60827 US
(708) 201-9600; *Fax:* (248) 201-9674
www.birach.com
sima@birach.com
License: Oak Lawn, Cook County, IL held by Birach Broadcasting Corp.
Group Owner: Birach Broadcasting Corp.; (acq 6-30-95; $375,000).
Arbitron Metro Market: Chicago, IL *TV Affiliate:* Foreign language, Pol; *Format:* Ethnic
Sima Birach, Operations Manager

Oak Park

WPNA
10-07-1950; 1490 kHz AM; *Hrs Open:* 24; 1 kw-U, ND1; N41 52 52 W87 47 38
6100 N. Cicero Avenue, Chicago, IL 60646 US
(708) 848-8980; *Fax:* (708) 848-9220
email@wpna1490am.com
License: Oak Park, IL held by Alliance Communications Inc.
Wire Services: AP
Arbitron Metro Market: Chicago; *Format:* Ethnic, Polish *Special Programming:* Polka 15 hrs, gospel 2 hrs, blues 4 hrs, relg 4 hrs, Irish 3 hrs, Ukranian 2 hrs wkly; *Target Audience:* General.
Frank Spula, President
Alan Kearns, Operations Dir
Emily Leszczynski, General Manager
Jerry Obrecki, General Sales Mgr

WVAZ
10-17-1950; 102.7 MHz FM; *Hrs Open:* 24; 6 kw; 1171 ft.; N41 53 56 W87 37 23
233 North Michigan Avenue, Suite 2800, Chicago, IL 60601 US
(312) 540-2000; *Fax:* (312) 938-4404
www.v103.com
License: Oak Park, Cook County, IL held by AMFM Broadcasting Licenses LLC.
Group Owner: iHeartMedia; (acq 8-30-2000; grpsl).
Arbitron Metro Market: Chicago, IL; *Format:* Urban Contemporary *Special Programming:* Gospel 4 hrs, pub affrs 2 hrs wkly; *Hrs. of News Programming:* news progmg one hr wkly; *No. News Employees:* 2 *TargetAudience:* 25-54; Black adults
Matt Scarano, Market President
Jerry Schnacke, Senior Vice President of Sales
Derrick Brown, Programming Director
Paul Frede, Director of Marketing and Promotions

Oglesby

WALS
02-01-1993; 102.1 MHz FM; *Hrs Open:* 24; 2.25 kw; 545 ft.; N41 16 30 W88 57 56
3905 Progress Blvd., Peru, IL 61354 US
(815) 224-2480
www.walls102.com
advertising@studstillmedia.com
License: Oglesby, La Salle County, IL held by Laco Radio, Inc.
Group Owner: Studstill Broadcasting
Arbitron Metro Market: La Salle-Peru, IL; *Format:* Country; *Hrs. of News Programming:* news progmg 2 hrs wkly; *No. News Employees:* 2; *Target Audience:* 25-55.
Cole Studstill, Manager of Programming

Olney

***WPTH**
07-01-1992; 88.1 MHz FM; 2.9 kw; 200 ft.; N38 41 50 W88 2 13
817 Orchard Drive, Olney, IL 62450 US
(618) 863-2765; *Fax:* (618) 395-7064
License: Olney, Richland County, IL held by Olney Voice of Christian Faith Inc.
Format: Christian, Talk
Dr. Thomas Benson, President
Ron James, Operations Dir

WSEI
01-01-1953; 92.9 MHz FM; 50 kw; 289 ft.; N38 42 0 W88 4 49
Mailing Address: 304 South Museum Drive, Newton, IL 62448 US
Second Address: 4667 E. Radio Tower Ln., Olney, IL 62450
(618) 393-2156; *Fax:* (618) 392-4536
www.freedom929.com
License: Olney, Richland County, IL held by Forcht Broadcasting
Group Owner: Forcht Broadcasting
Format: Country
Mike Shipman, General Manager
Deb Ayers, Account Executive
Mark Weiler, News Director
Roger Johnson, Programming Director

***WUSI**
11-01-1992; 90.3 MHz FM; *Hrs Open:* 24; 25 kw; 472 ft.; N38 50 18 W88 7 46 *Rebroadcasts:* Rebroadcasts WSIU(FM) Carbondale 100%
1048 Commun. Bldg. Siuc, Carbondale, IL 62901 US
(618) 453-4343; *Fax:* (618) 453-6186
www.wsiu.org
wsiuradio@wsiu.org
License: Olney, Richland County, IL held by Southern Illinois University.
Nat'l Network: NPR; PRI; *Regional Network:* Ill. Radio Net.; *Wire Services:* AP
Arbitron Metro Market: Carbondale, IL *TV Affiliate:* WUSI-TV affil; *Format:* News; *Hrs. of News Programming:* news progmg 36 hrs wkly; *No. News Employees:* 3; *Target Audience:* 35-64; highly educated, upperincome, socially conscious
Greg Petrowich, CEO
Mike Zelten, Operations Dir
Jeff Williams, Station Manager

WVLN
11-11-1947; 740 kHz AM
Mailing Address: P.O. Box 1450, Corbin, KY 40702 US
Second Address: 4667 E. Radio Tower Ln., Olney, IL 62450
(618) 393-2156; *Fax:* (618) 392-4536
wvlnam.com
mishipman@forchtbroadcasting.com
License: Olney, IL held by Forcht Broadcasting
Group Owner: Forcht Broadcasting
Nat'l Network: ESPN Radio
Arbitron Metro Market: Olney, IL; *Format:* Sports
Mike Shipman, General Manager
Deb Ayers, Account Executive
Mark Weiler, News/Sports Director

Oreana

***WDCR**
03-04-1958; 88.9 MHz FM; *Hrs Open:* 24; 1.1 kw; 163 ft.; N39 55 49.9 W88 51 41
Mailing Address: US
Second Address: 3rd Fl., Robinson Hall, Dartmouth College, Hanover, NH 3826
(603) 646-3313(603) 646-3826; *Fax:* (603) 643-7655
www.webdcr.com
NEWSTIP@WebDCR.COM
License: Oreana, Grafton County, IL held by Trustees of Dartmouth College.
Arbitron Metro Market: Hanover, NH; *Format:* Rock/AOR; *Hrs. of News Programming:* news progmg 4 hrs wkly; *No. News Employees:* 2; *Target Audience:* General.
Heath Cole, Operations Dir
Ryan Zehner, General Manager
Julie Kaye, General Sales Mgr
Gregg Fox, Programming Director
Catherine Treyz, News Director

Oregon

WSEY
12-27-1999; 95.7 MHz FM; 3.2 kw; 358 ft.; N42 4 19 W89 25 8
P.O. Box 630, Marshfield, WI 54449 US
(815) 288-3341; *Fax:* (815) 284-1017
www.koolfm957.com
License: Oregon, Ogle County, IL held by NRG License Sub. LLC.
Group Owner: NRG Media LLC; (acq 10-31-2005; grpsl)
Format: Oldies
Allan Knickrehm, General Manager
Steve Marco, Programming Director

Danette Dallgas-Frey, News Director
Mark Baker, Chief Engineer

Ottawa

WCMY
03-05-1952; 1430 kHz AM; *Hrs Open:* 24; 0.5 kw-D, ND2; 0.038 kw-N, ND2; N41 20 53 W88 48 15
980 North Michigan Avenue, Suite 1880, Chicago, IL 60611 US
(815) 434-6050; *Fax:* (815) 434-5311
www.ottawaradio.net
License: Ottawa, IL held by NRG License Sub. LLC.
Group Owner: NRG Media LLC; (acq 10-31-2005; grpsl)
Nat'l Network: CBS Radio; Westwood One; *Regional Network:* Brownfield; *Nat'l Reps:* Interep; *Wire Services:* AP
Arbitron Metro Market: LaSalle, Ottawa, IL; *Format:* Adult Contemp, News, 62, Talk *Special Programming:* Farm 9 hrs wkly; *Hrs. of News Programming:* news progmg 35 hrs wkly; *No. News Employees:* 2 *TargetAudience:* 25 plus.
Jay Le Seuve, Operations Dir
Bill Jankowski, General Manager
Jill Williams, Promotions Manager
Rick Koshko, News Director
Kris Michaels, Creative Director

WRKX
09-01-1964; 95.3 MHz FM; 4.3 kw; 200 ft.; N41 23 0 W88 51 16
980 North Michigan Avenue, Suite 1880, Chicago, IL 60611 US
(815) 434-6050; *Fax:* (815) 434-5311
License: Ottawa, La Salle County, IL
Group Owner: NRG Media LLC
Wire Services: AP
Format: Adult Contemp
Jay LeSeure, Operations Dir
Bill Jankowski, General Manager
Kris Michaels, Promotions Manager
Rick Koshko, News Director
Jill Williams, Business Manager

*WWGN
09-24-1994; 88.9 MHz FM; *Hrs Open:* 24; 1.4 kw horiz, 4.1 kw vert; 487 ft.; N41 18 5 W88 57 11
807 La Salle St., Ottawa, IL 61350-2073 US
(815) 433-6000
License: Ottawa, LaSalle County, IL held by Family Worship Center Church Inc.
Group Owner: Family Worship Center Church Inc.; (acq 1-4-99; $250,000)
Format: Religious; *Hrs. of News Programming:* news progmg 14 hrs wkly; *No. News Employees:* 2; *Target Audience:* General.
Dan Hennenfent, General Manager

Palatine

*WHCM
01-01-2003; 88.3 MHz FM; 0.1 kw; 56 ft.; N42 4 54 W88 4 23
1200 W. Algonquin Rd, Palatine, IL 60067 US
(847) 925-6000
www.harpercollege.edu
servicedesk@harpercollege.edu
License: Palatine, Cook County, IL held by William Rainey Harper College.
Arbitron Metro Market: Palatine, IL; *Format:* Variety/Diverse
Diane Hill, Chairman
Dave Dluger, General Manager
Rita Canning, Vice-Chair
Walt Mundt, Secretary
Clara Moravec, Student Trustee

Pana

WMKR
07-12-1996; 94.3 MHz FM; *Hrs Open:* 24; 5.6 kw; 341 ft.; N39 27 8 W89 17 10
918 East Park St, P.O. Box 169, Taylorville, IL 62568 US
(217) 824-3395; *Fax:* (217) 824-3301
www.randyradio.com
License: Pana, Christian County, IL held by Miller Communications Inc.
Group Owner: Miller Media Group
Nat'l Network: CNN Radio; *Regional Network:* SRN
Arbitron Metro Market: Davenport-Rock Island-Moline; *Format:* Country; *Target Audience:* 25-54.
Randal Miller, President
Kami Payne, General Manager
Brandon Fellows, Programming Director
Steve Butera, News Director

Park Forest

WCPQ
01-05-1962; 99.9 MHz FM; *Hrs Open:* 24; 50 kW; 492 ft.; N41 18 4 W87 49 35
6020 W Higgins, Chicago, IL 60630 USA
(773) 888-5152; *Fax:* (773) 631-9858
www.polskifm.com
License: Park Forest, Cook County, IL held by WCLR Inc.
Group Owner: Newsweb Corp.; (acq 3-16-2004; $24 million with WNDZ(AM) Portage, IN)
Nat'l Network: CNN Radio
Arbitron Metro Market: Chicago; *Format:* Polish

Park Ridge

*WMTH
05-22-1960; 90.5 MHz FM; 0.008 kw; 102 ft.; N42 2 14 W87 51 30
1131 South Dee Road, Park Ridge, IL 60068 US
(847) 692-8495; *Fax:* (847) 692-8499
www.wmthalumni.org
dave@wmthalumni.com
License: Park Ridge, Cook County, IL held by Board of Education, Maine Twp. #207.
Arbitron Metro Market: Chicago, IL; *Format:* Variety/Diverse
Jim Wunderlich, General Manager

Paxton

*WRTK
11-01-1963; 90.5 MHz FM; kw
Mailing Address: US
Second Address: 124 N. Park Ave., Warren, OH 44482
(219) 228-2995; *Fax:* (330) 394-7701
www.thekeyfm.com
info@thekeyfm.com
License: Paxton, Trumbull County, IL held by Beacon Broadcasting Inc.
Group Owner: Beacon Broadcasting Inc.; (acq 9-14-2005; $400,000)
Arbitron Metro Market: Youngstown, IN; *Format:* Christian, Gospel *Special Programming:* It one hr, Pol one hr wkly
Harold Glunt, President
Dan Wolfe, General Manager
Jody McManus, Programming Director
Mike Azinger, Promotions Manager

WPXN
10-01-1984; 104.9 MHz FM; *Hrs Open:* 24; 3 kw; 299 ft.; N40 27 11 W88 6 11
361 N Railroad Avenue, Paxton, IL 60957 US
(217) 379-4333,(217) 892-9796; *Fax:* (217) 379-4334
wpxnradio.com
License: Paxton, Ford County, IL held by Paxton Broadcasting Corp.
Nat'l Network: CNN Radio; *Regional Network:* Brownfield; *Wire Services:* AP
Format: Oldies *Special Programming:* Farm 10 hrs wkly; *Hrs. of News Programming:* news progmg 8 hrs wkly; *No. News Employees:* 2; *Target Audience:* 25-54.
Dan Daugherity, President
Joel Cluver, Station Manager

Pekin

*WBNH
12-01-1988; 88.5 MHz FM; 48,000 kw; 495 ft; N40 38 34 W89 32 38
1915 Mayflower Drive, Pekin, IL 61555
(309) 636-8850; *Fax:* (877) 631-8850
www.wbnh.org
wbnh@wbnh.org
License: Pekin, Tazewell County, IL held by Central Illinois Radio Fellowship Inc.
Nat'l Network: Moody
Arbitron Metro Market: Peoria, IL; *Target Audience:* General.
Don Rice, President
Keith Lang, Operations Dir
Jim Huber, Station Manager
Wayne Miller, Chief Engineer

*WCIC
11-02-1983; 91.5 MHz FM; *Hrs Open:* 24; 47 kw; 505 ft.; N40 33 28 W89 34 4
3263 Court Street, Pekin, IL 61554 US
(309) 692-9242; *Fax:* (309) 692-9241
www.wcicfm.org
License: Pekin, Tazewell County, IL held by Illinois Bible Institute.
Group Owner: Illinois Bible Institute Inc.
Arbitron Metro Market: Peoria, IL; *Format:* Adult Contemp, Christian, 74; *Hrs. of News Programming:* News progmg 2 hrs wkly; *Target Audience:* 25-49.
Dave Brooks, General Manager
Dave Brooks, Station Manager
Jessie Browning, Promotions Manager
Joe Buchanan, Music Director
Katie Post, Office Manager
Trevor Moore, Audio/New Media Producer

WGLO
12-04-1964; 95.5 MHz FM; 7 kw; 620 ft.; N40 36 23 W89 32 20
120 Eaton St., Peoria, IL 61603 US
(309) 676-9595
www.955glo.com
matt.bahan@cumulus.com
License: Pekin, Tazewell County, IL held by Radio License Holding CBC, LLC
Group Owner: Cumulus Media Inc.
Nat'l Reps: D & R Radio
Arbitron Metro Market: Peoria, IL; *Format:* Classic Rock; *Target Audience:* 18-49.
Matt Bahan, Operations Dir
Matt Bahan, Programming Director
Brad Creek, Director of Sales

WVEL
04-21-1946; 1140 kHz AM; 5 kw-D
120 Eaton St., Peoria, IL 61603 US
(309) 676-5000
www.wvel.com
License: Pekin, IL held by Radio License Holding CBC, LLC
Group Owner: Cumulus Media Inc.; (acq 7-6-01; grpsl).
Arbitron Metro Market: Peoria, IL; *Format:* Gospel
Brad Creek, Director of Sales
Robert Butch Caruth, Programming Director
Matt Harris, Promotions Manager

WXCL
01-01-1973; 104.9 MHz FM; *Hrs Open:* 24; 6 kw; 328 ft.; N40 38 34 W89 32 38
331 Fulton St., Suite 1200, Peoria, IL 61602 US
(309) 637-3700; *Fax:* (309) 272-1476
www.1049thewolf.com
License: Pekin, Tazewell County, IL held by Alpha Media Licensee LLC
Group Owner: Alpha Media LLC; (acq 12-3-2012; grpsl).
Arbitron Metro Market: Peoria, IL; *Format:* Country; *No. News Employees:* 2; *Target Audience:* 25-54; affluent adults
Randy Rundle, Operations Manager
Mike Wild, General Manager
Matt Marchand, Sales Manager
Chris Michaels, Programming Director
Dirk Clemens, Promotions Manager
Ryan Madden, Production Director

Peoria

WZPW
11-01-1992; 92.3 MHz FM; 25 kw; 374 ft.; N40 47 10 W89 47 1
120 Eaton St., Peoria, IL 61603 US
(309) 676-5000
License: Peoria, IL held by Radio License Holding CBC LLC
Group Owner: Cumulus Media Inc.; (acq 9-19-2006; $11.75 million with WIXO(FM) Peoria).
Arbitron Metro Market: Peoria, IL; *Format:* Contemporary Hits/Top 40
Brad Creek, Director of Sales
Amanda King, Programming Director
Matt Harris, Promotions Manager

*WCBU
01-01-1970; 89.9 MHz FM; 26.5 kw; 647 ft.; N40 37 44 W89 34 12
1501 W. Bradley Ave., Peoria, IL 61625 US
(309) 677-3690; *Fax:* (309) 677-3462
www.wcbu.bradley.edu/
wcbu@bradley.edu
License: Peoria, Peoria County, IL held by Bradley University.
Nat'l Network: NPR; *Wire Services:* AP
Arbitron Metro Market: Peoria, IL; *Format:* Classical, News
Daryl Scott, Operations Dir
Thomas Hunt, General Manager
Cindy Dermody, General Sales Mgr
Nathan Irwin, Programming Director
Betty Beard, Promotions Manager
Jonathan Ahl, News Director
William Porter, Engineering Dir

WIRL
01-01-1947; 1290 kHz AM; 5 kw-D, DA2; 5 kw-N, DA2; N40 37 24 W89 35 27

331 Fulton St., Suite 1200, Peoria, IL 61602 US
(309) 637-3700; *Fax:* (309) 673-9562
www.1290wirl.com
License: Peoria, Peoria County, IL held by Alpha Media Licensee LLC
Group Owner: Alpha Media LLC; (acq 12-3-2012; grpsl).
Nat'l Reps: Christal
Arbitron Metro Market: Peoria, IL; *Format:* Oldies; *Target Audience:* 25-54; men
Randy Rundle, Operations Manager
Mike Wild, General Manager
Matt Marchand, Sales Manager
Ed Hammond, News Director
Wayne Miller, Chief Engineer
Kevin Cassulo, Executive Director of Business Development
Brenda Rundle, TrafficManager
Brian Rowell, Integrated Marketing Consultant
Ryan Madden, Production Manager

WMBD
01-01-1927; 1470 kHz AM; *Hrs Open:* 24; 5 kw-D, DA2; 5 kw-N, DA2; N40 34 22 W89 32 0
331 Fulton St., Suite 1200, Peoria, IL 61602 US
(309) 637-3700; *Fax:* (309) 673-9562
www.1470wmbd.com
License: Peoria, Peoria County, IL held by Alpha Media Licensee LLC
Group Owner: Alpha Media LLC; (acq 12-3-2012; grpsl).
Nat'l Network: Premiere Radio Networks; Westwood One; *Nat'l Reps:* Christal; *Wire Services:* U.S. Weather Service
Arbitron Metro Market: Peoria, IL; *Format:* News, News/Talk, 86
Special Programming: Farm 15 hrs wkly; *Hrs. of News Programming:* news progmg 40 hrs wkly; *No. News Employees:* 5; *Target Audience:* 35-64;upscale, well educated, professional, conservative
Mike Wild, General Manager
Matt Marchand, Sales Manager
David Van Camp, Programming Director

WOAM
02-08-1960; 1350 kHz AM; 1 kw-D, DA2; 1 kw-N, DA2; N40 35 41 W89 35 40
5555 Gulf of Mexico Dr, Suite 201, Longboat Key, FL 34228 US
(309) 685-0977; *Fax:* (309) 685-7150
License: Peoria, IL held by Kelly Communications Inc.
Arbitron Metro Market: Peoria, IL *TV Affiliate:* Hits of the 40s, 50s & 60s

WPBG
01-01-1947; 93.3 MHz FM; *Hrs Open:* 24; 40 kw; 551 ft.; N40 38 7 W89 32 19
331 Fulton St., Suite 1200, Peoria, IL 61602 US
(309) 637-3700; *Fax:* (309) 673-9562
www.933thedrive.com
License: Peoria, Peoria County, IL held by Alpha Media Licensee LLC
Group Owner: Alpha Media LLC
Arbitron Metro Market: Peoria, IL; *Format:* Contemporary Hits/Top 40, Adult Contemp; *Target Audience:* 25-54; baby boomers
Randy Rundle, Operations Manager
Mike Wild, General Manager
Matt Marchand, Sales Manager
Rick Hirschmann, Programming Director

WPEO
01-01-1946; 1020 kHz AM; 1 kw-D; N40 41 53 W89 31 31
Mailing Address: 1708 Highview Rd., East Peoria, IL 61611
Second Address: Box 1, Peoria, IL 61650
(309) 698-9736; *Fax:* (309) 698-9740
www.wpeo.com
wpeo@wpeo.com
License: Peoria, Peoria County, IL held by Pinebrook Foundation Inc.
Population Served: 500,000; *Arbitron Metro Market:* Peoria, IL; *Target Audience:* 35 plus.; *Adv. Rates:* 18; 18; 18; 18
John Wieland, President
Robert Ulrich, General Manager
Jeff Wineberry, General Sales Mgr
Nelson Hostetler, Programming Director
Jessica Wieland, News Director

WSWT
01-01-1964; 106.9 MHz FM; *Hrs Open:* 24; 50 kw; 479 ft.; N40 43 22 W89 30 40
331 Fulton St., Suite 1200, Peoria, IL 61602 US
(309) 637-3700; *Fax:* (309) 686-8659
www.mix1069.com
License: Peoria, Peoria County, IL held by Alpha Media Licensee LLC
Group Owner: Alpha Media LLC
Nat'l Reps: Christal; *Wire Services:* AP
Arbitron Metro Market: Peoria, IL; *Format:* Adult Contemp; *Hrs. of News Programming:* News progmg 2.5 hrs wkly; *Target Audience:* 25-54.; *Adv. Rates:* 85; 85; 85; 25
Randy Rundle, Operations Manager
Mike Wild, General Manager
Matt Marchand, Sales Manager
Wayne Miller, Chief Engineer

WIXO
05-14-1972; 105.7 MHz FM; 39 kw; 555 ft.; N40 43 25 W89 29 4
120 Eaton St., Peoria, IL 61603 US
(309) 676-5000
www.1057thexrocks.com
matt.bahan@cumulus.com
License: Peoria, IL held by Radio License Holding CBC, LLC
Group Owner: Cumulus Media Inc.
Arbitron Metro Market: Peoria, IL; *Format:* Rock/AOR
Brad Creek, Director of Sales
Matt Bahan, Programming Director
Matt Harris, Promotions Manager

***WAZU**
90.7 MHz FM; 0.5 kw; 266 ft.; N40 46 46 W89 39 18
138 Park Plaza Court, Canton, IL 61520 US
(309) 253-1951
License: Peoria, Peoria County, IL held by Sirius Syncope Inc.
Arbitron Metro Market: Peoria, IL; *Format:* Talk
Jeremy Styninger, President

Peru

WBZG
03-15-1970; 100.9 MHz FM; *Hrs Open:* 24; 3 kw; 328 ft.; N41 18 9 W89 14 11
3905 Progress Blvd., Peru, IL 61354 US
(815) 224-2100
www.wbzg.net
advertising@studstillmedia.com
License: Peru, La Salle County, IL held by Mendota Broadcasting Inc.
Group Owner: Studstill Broadcasting
Nat'l Reps: Rgnl Reps; *Wire Services:* AP
Arbitron Metro Market: La Salle-Peru, IL; *Format:* Rock/AOR; *No. News Employees:* 2; *Target Audience:* Men 18-54.
Cole Studstill, Manager of Programming

Petersburg

WLCE
03-01-1987; 97.7 MHz FM; *Hrs Open:* 24; 6 kw; 328 ft.; N39 54 35 W89 43 1
906 Gabbert Road, Springfield, IL 62707 US
(217) 629-7077; *Fax:* (217) 629-7952
www.alice.fm
alice@alice.fm
License: Petersburg, Menard County, IL held by Long-Nine Inc.
Group Owner: The Mid-West Family Broadcast Group; (acq 7-27-2001; $3 million)
Wire Services: AP
Arbitron Metro Market: Petersburg, IL; *Format:* Triple A *Special Programming:* Relg 5 hrs wkly; *Target Audience:* 18-34; female
Mark Birtch, General Manager
Dave Duetsch, General Sales Mgr
Josie O'Donnell, Programming Director
Jim Leach, News Director
Greg Stephens, Chief Engineer
Quinn Fagg, Traffic Manager

WQLZ
12-01-1967; 97.7 MHz FM; *Hrs Open:* 24; 6 kW; 328 ft.; N39 54 35 W89 43 1
1510 North 3rd St, Riverton, IL 62561 USA
(217) 629-7077; *Fax:* (217) 629-7952
www.wqlz.com
License: Petersburg, IL held by Long Nine, Inc.
Group Owner: Mid-West Family Broadcasting
Arbitron Metro Market: Petersburg, IL; *Format:* Rock/AOR; *Hrs. of News Programming:* news progmg 3 hrs wkly; *No. News Employees:* 4; *Target Audience:* Adults 18-49
Ken Carson, Operations Manager
Harvey Wells, General Manager
Mark Birtch, Director of Sales
Wes Styles, Programming Director

***WLWJ**
10-07-2001; 88.1 MHz FM; 6 kw; 328 ft.; N40 0 5 W89 41 49
600 West Mason Street, Springfield, IL 62702 US
(800) 932-9585; *Fax:* (217) 528-2400
www.wluj.org
comments@wluj.org
License: Petersburg, Menard County, IL held by Cornerstone Community Radio Inc.
Nat'l Network: USA
Arbitron Metro Market: Springfield, IL; *Format:* Christian, Religious, 86
Howard Fouks, Operations Dir
Richard Van Zandt, General Manager
David King, Station Manager
Richard Beaman, General Sales Mgr
Howard Fouks, Chief Engineer
Lonnie Lein, Production Manager
Richard Beaman, Senior Director ofUnderwriting
John McBride, Director of Special Ministries
Sherri McBride, Relational Phoning
Wayne Langhein, Finance
Claudia King, Office Assistant

Pittsfield

WBBA-FM
08-01-1966; 97.5 MHz FM; *Hrs Open:* 24; 10 kw; 305 ft.; N39 34 53 W90 47 52
#1 Professional Plaza, P.O. Box 150, Pittsfield, IL 62363 US
(304) 399-9603; *Fax:* (304) 399-9608
www.magic979.com
License: Pittsfield, Pike County, IL held by DJ Two Rivers Radio Inc.
Arbitron Metro Market: Oakland CA; *Format:* Adult Contemp
Newman Adkins, General Manager

***WIPA**
01-04-1993; 89.3 MHz FM; *Hrs Open:* 24; 50 kw; 492 ft.; N39 43 25 W90 41 9 *Rebroadcasts:* Rebroadcasts WUIS(FM) Springfield 100%
South Shepherd Road, Springfield, IL 62794 US
(217) 206-6516; *Fax:* (217) 206-6527
www.wuis.org
License: Pittsfield, Pike County, IL held by University of Illinois at Springfield.
Nat'l Network: NPR; PRI
Format: Jazz, News; *Hrs. of News Programming:* news progmg 45 hrs wkly; *No. News Employees:* 4; *Target Audience:* 25-54.
Sinta Seiber, Operations Dir
Bill Wheelhouse, General Manager
Lisa Clemmons-Stott, General Sales Mgr
Rick Bradley, News Director
Greg Manfroi, Chief Engineer

Plano

WSPY-FM
01-19-1974; 107.1 MHz FM; *Hrs Open:* 24; 1.5 kw; 466 ft.; N41 39 55 W88 34 34
1 Broadcast Center, Plano, IL 60545 US
(630) 552-1000; *Fax:* (630) 552-9300
wspy@nelsonmultimedia.net
License: Plano, Kendall County, IL held by Nelson Enterprises Inc.
Nat'l Network: ABC
Arbitron Metro Market: Chicago; *Format:* Variety/Diverse *Special Programming:* Farm 18 hrs wkly; *Hrs. of News Programming:* News progmg 12 hrs wkly; *Target Audience:* 25-54.
Liz Clark, CFO
Larry Nelson, President
Chris Schwemlein, Operations Dir
Vori Dhabolt, General Sales Mgr
Jeni Beckman, News Director
Lane Lindstrom, Chief Engineer
Beth Pierre, General Sales Manager

Polo

WLLT
12-12-1989; 107.7 MHz FM; *Hrs Open:* 24; 3 kw; 476 ft.; N41 53 51.9 W89 36 19.6
260 State Route 2, Dixon, IL 61021 US
(815) 284-1077
wllt@comcast.net
License: Polo, Ogle County, IL held by Sauk Valley Broadcasting Co.
Format: Adult Contemp
Bob Burns, President

Pontiac

WJBC
06-01-1969; 93.7 MHz FM; 12 kw; 472 ft.; N40 45 27 W88 37 40
236 Greenwood Ave., Bloomington, IL 61704 US
(309) 829-1221
www.937nashicon.com
License: Pontiac, IL held by Cumulus Licensing LLC
Group Owner: Cumulus Media Inc.; (acq 8-31-2006; $1 million).
Arbitron Metro Market: Jacksonville, FL; *Format:* Country

Paula Williams, Director of Sales
Dan Westhoff, Programming Director
Brandi McCarrey, Promotions Director

***WPJC**
01-01-2003; 88.3 MHz FM; 0.5 kw; 207 ft.; N40 52 51 W88 38 2
Rebroadcasts: Simulcasts WPRR (FM) 90.1
3777 44th St SE, Grand Rapids, MI 49512 US
(616) 656-1680; *Fax:* (616) 656-2158
www.publicrealityradio.org
info@publicrealityradio.org
License: Pontiac, Livingston County, IL held by Goodrich Radio L.L.C
Group Owner: Public Relaity Radio
Arbitron Metro Market: Warrenville, IL; *Format:* Talk
Robert Goodrich, President
Darren Gibson, Programming Director

Princeton

WZOE
10-25-1961; 1490 kHz AM; *Hrs Open:* 24; 1 kw-U, ND1; N41 21 8 W89 28 5
Mailing Address: PO Box 69, Princeton, IL 61356 US
Second Address: 2209 S. Main St., Princeton, IL 61356
(815) 875-8014
www.wzoe.com
License: Princeton, IL held by WZOE, Inc.
Group Owner: WZOE, Inc.
Nat'l Network: CBS; *Wire Services:* Metro Weather Service Inc.
Arbitron Metro Market: Princeton, IL; *Format:* News/Talk *Special Programming:* Farm 15 hrs wkly; *Hrs. of News Programming:* news progmg 84 hrs wkly; *No. News Employees:* 3
Steve Samet, General Manager

WZOE-FM
07-01-1980; 98.1 MHz FM; *Hrs Open:* 24; 6 kw; 299 ft.; N41 21 49 W89 23 36
Mailing Address: PO Box 69, Princeton, IL 61356 US
Second Address: 2209 S. Main St., Princeton, IL 61356
(815) 875-8014
www.wzoe.com
License: Princeton, Bureau County, IL held by WZOE, Inc.
Group Owner: WZOE, Inc.
Nat'l Network: CNN Radio; *Wire Services:* Metro Weather Service Inc.
Arbitron Metro Market: Princeton, IL; *Format:* Adult Contemp; *Hrs. of News Programming:* news progmg 8 hrs wkly; *No. News Employees:* 3
Steve Samet, General Manager

Quincy

WLIQ
12-13-1966; 1530 kHz AM; *Hrs Open:* Sunrise-sunset
15894 Highway 54 Pobox 1, Bowling Greeen, MO 63334 US
(573) 221-3450; *Fax:* (573) 221-5331
License: Quincy, IL held by Townsquare Media Quincy-Hannibal License LLC
Group Owner: Townsquare Media; (acq 2-29-2012).
Format: Adult Contemp
Ed Foxall, General Manager
Jeff Dorsey, Programming Director
John Hanvelt, News Director
Gary Glaenzer, Chief Engineer

***WGCA-FM**
09-20-1987; 88.5 MHz FM; 40 kw; 449 ft.; N39 58 18 W91 19 42
Post Office Box 467, Quincy, IL 62306 US
(217) 224-9422; *Fax:* (217) 228-0504
www.wgca.org
themix@wgca.org
License: Quincy, Adams County, IL held by Great Commission Broadcasting Corp.
Nat'l Network: USA
Format: Christian; *Target Audience:* 25-45.
Jim Tyler, Operations Dir
Bruce Rice, General Manager
Laura Cook, General Sales Mgr
Jim Taylor, Programming Director
Jim Wilson, Chief Engineer
Bruce Rice, Executive Director
Maxine Rice, Associate Director

WGEM
01-01-1948; 1440 kHz AM; 5 kw-D, DA2; 1 kw-N, DA2; N39 58 48 W91 19 24
Mailing Address: P.O. Box 80, 513 Hampshire, Quincy, IL 62306 US
Second Address: 513 Hampshire, Quincy, IL 62301
(217) 228-6600; *Fax:* (217) 228-6670
www.wgem.com
aelkins@wgem.com
License: Quincy, IL held by Quincy Broadcasting Co.
Group Owner: Quincy Newspapers Inc.
Nat'l Network: ESPN Radio; *Nat'l Reps:* Christal
Format: News, News/Talk, 84, Talk; *Hrs. of News Programming:* news progmg 25 hrs wkly; *Target Audience:* 25-54; general
Ralph Oakley, President
Carlos Fernandez, General Manager

WGEM-FM
01-01-1947; 105.1 MHz FM; *Hrs Open:* 24; 26.5 kw; 686 ft.; N39 57 4 W91 19 53
Mailing Address: 513 Hampshire, PO Box 80, Quincy, IL 62301 US
Second Address: 513 Hampshire, Quincy, IL 62301
(217) 228-6600; *Fax:* (217) 228-6670
www.wgem.com
License: Quincy, Adams County, IL
Group Owner: Quincy Newspapers Inc.
Regional Network: Miss. News Net; *Nat'l Reps:* Christal; *Wire Services:* AP
Format: News, News/Talk, 86; *Hrs. of News Programming:* News progmg 110 hrs wkly; *Target Audience:* 25-54.
Ralph Oakley, President
Carlos Fernandez, General Manager

WQCY
05-08-1989; 103.9 MHz FM; 1.8 kw; 436 ft.; N39 56 30 W91 35 3
2 Dearborn Square, Kankakee, IL 60901 US
(217) 224-4102; *Fax:* (217) 224-4133
www.1039thefox.com
wqcy@staradio.com
License: Quincy, Adams County, IL held by STARadio Corp.
Group Owner: STARadio Corp.; acq 8-13-98; grpsl)
Nat'l Network: CBS
Arbitron Metro Market: Quincy, IL; *Format:* Light Rock; *Target Audience:* 18-44; general
Michael Moyers, General Manager
Brenda Park, General Sales Mgr
Steve Boll, Programming Director
Mary Griffith, News Director
Phillip Reilly, Chief Engineer
Jerry Shoup, Traffic Manager

WCOY
01-01-1948; 99.5 MHz FM; *Hrs Open:* 24; 100 kw; 489 ft.; N39 56 30 W91 35 3
510 Maine Street, Quincy, IL 62306 US
(217) 224-4102; *Fax:* (217) 224-4133
License: Quincy, Adams County, IL
Group Owner: STARadio Corp.
Nat'l Network: CBS
Format: Country
Mike Moyers, Programming Director

***WQUB**
04-01-1974; 90.3 MHz FM; *Hrs Open:* 24; 28 kw; 417 ft.; N39 57 22 W91 23 22
1800 College Avenue, Quincy, IL 62301 US
(217) 228-5410; *Fax:* (217) 228-5616
www.wqub.org
info@wqub.org
License: Quincy, Adams County, IL held by Quincy University Corp.
Nat'l Network: NPR; AP Radio
Format: Jazz, News *Special Programming:* Folk 2 hrs, blues 2 hrs, alternative rock 12 hrs, hip hop 2 hrs, oldies 2 hrs wkly; *Hrs. of News Programming:* news progmg 31 hrs wkly; *No. News Employees:* 2; *Target Audience:* 25-64; male & female
Jim Lenz, Operations Dir
Patrick Mays, General Sales Mgr
Jim Cate, Chief Engineer

WTAD
07-25-1925; 930 kHz AM; *Hrs Open:* 24; 5 kw-D, DAN; 1 kw-N, DAN; N39 53 31 W91 25 25
2 Dearborn Square, Kankakee, IL 60901 US
(217) 224-4102; *Fax:* (217) 224-4133
www.wtad.com
License: Quincy, IL held by STARadio Corp.
Group Owner: STARadio Corp.; (acq 8-13-98; grpsl)
Nat'l Network: CBS; *Nat'l Reps:* McGavren Guild
Format: News, News/Talk, 86; *Hrs. of News Programming:* news progmg 22 hrs wkly; *No. News Employees:* 1; *Target Audience:* 35 plus; general
Brenda Parks, General Manager
Michael Moyers, General Manager

Ramsey

***WJLY**
01-01-1999; 88.3 MHz FM; *Hrs Open:* 24; 25 kw; 502 ft.; N39 8 6 W89 6 2
Mailing Address: P.O. Box 456, Ramsey, IL 62080 US
Second Address: R.R. 2 Box 51A, Ramsey, IL
(618) 423-2082; *Fax:* (618) 423-2394
www.wjly.org
wjly@frontiernet.net
License: Ramsey, Fayette County, IL held by Countryside Broadcasting.
Nat'l Network: Moody
Format: Christian; *Hrs. of News Programming:* News progmg 14 hrs wkly; *Target Audience:* 35 plus.
Richard Wheeler, General Manager
John Stanley, General Sales Mgr
Dave Carruthers, Programming Director
Henry Voss, Chief Engineer

WTRH
11-21-1990; 93.3 MHz FM; *Hrs Open:* 24; 3 kw; 466 ft.; N39 8 6 W89 6 2
P.O. Box 456, Ramsey, IL 62080 US
(618) 423-2082; *Fax:* (618) 423-2394
wtrh@frontiernet.net
wtrh@frontiernet.net
License: Ramsey, Fayette County, IL held by Countryside Broadcasting Inc.
Arbitron Metro Market: Ramsey, IL; *Format:* Oldies, Talk; *Hrs. of News Programming:* News progmg 14 hrs wkly; *Target Audience:* 35 plus; men & women who love old radio prgms & mus; *Adv. Rates:* 11; 11; 11; 11
Dick Wheeler, General Manager and Production Contact
Al Schumacher, Advertising Sales Contact

Rantoul

WKJR
02-01-1963; 1460 kHz AM; *Hrs Open:* 24; 0.5 kw-D, DA2; 0.065 kw-N, DA2; N40 18 37 W88 12 54
1012 W University, Urbana, IL 61801 US
(217) 893-1460; *Fax:* (217) 893-0884
www.1460sports.com
fanmail@1460sports.com
License: Rantoul, IL held by Ruben's Productions Inc.
Nat'l Network: ESPN Radio
Arbitron Metro Market: Champaign, IL; *Format:* Sports; *Target Audience:* General.; *Adv. Rates:* 20; 20; 20; 20
Rueben Acevero, General Manager
Armando Martinez, Programming Director
Scott Hudson, News Director

WQQB
01-01-1993; 96.1 MHz FM; *Hrs Open:* 24; 3.8 kw; 404 ft.; N40 13 27 W88 17 56
P.O. Box 3335, Peoria, IL 61612 US
(217) 367-1195; *Fax:* (217) 367-3291
www.wqqb.com
License: Rantoul, Champaign County, IL held by RadioStar Inc.
Group Owner: RadioStar Inc.; (acq 5-23-2006; grpsl).
Nat'l Reps: McGavren Guild
Arbitron Metro Market: Champaign, IL; *Format:* Contemporary Hits/Top 40; *Target Audience:* 18-34; female
Jim Glassman, President
Roxanne Charles, General Manager
Corey Berkemann, General Sales Mgr
Joe McIntyre, Programming Director
Donna Keleher, Office Manager

WJEK(FM)
03-15-1972; 95.3 MHz FM; *Hrs Open:* 24; 3 kw; Ant 425 ft; N40 13 05 W88 06 55
2702 Boulder Drive, Urbana, IL 61802
(217) 367-1195; *Fax:* (217) 367-3291
License: Rantoul, Champaign County, IL held by RadioStar Inc.
Group Owner: RadioStar Inc.; (acq 5-23-2006; grpsl)
Nat'l Reps: McGavren Guild
Population Served: 41,518; *Arbitron Metro Market:* Urbana, IL; *Format:* Country; *No. News Employees:* 1; *Target Audience:* 18-49.
Jim Glassman, President
Roxanne Charles, General Manager
Steve Miller, Sales Manager
Ken Cunningham, Programming Director
Josh Laskowski, Promotions Manager
Jon Hall, Engineering Dir
Donna Keleher, Office Manager
Diane Ducey,Promotions

River Grove

*WRRG
03-10-1975; 88.9 MHz FM; *Hrs Open:* 9 AM-midnight (M-F); 10 AM-midnight; 0.1 kw; 128 ft.; N41 54 56 W87 50 12
2000 N. 5th Avenue, River Grove, IL 60171 US
(708) 583-3110
www.wrrg.org
License: River Grove, Cook County, IL held by Triton College.
Arbitron Metro Market: Chicago; *Format:* Alternative, Contemporary Hits/Top 40 *Special Programming:* Jazz 5 hrs, loc 4 hrs, metal 4 hrs, world mus 3 hrs, oldies 11 hrs, classic rock 2 hrs wkly; *Target Audience:* 14-40.
Kelli Lynch, Station Manager

Robinson

WTAY
01-09-1956; 1570 kHz AM; *Hrs Open:* 24; 0.25 kw-D, ND2; 0.188 kw-N, ND2; N39 0 29 W87 46 41
Mailing Address: 522 Busseron St., Vincennes, IN 47591 USA
Second Address: PO Box 242, Vincennes, IN 47591
(812) 882-6060; *Fax:* (812) 882-7770
www.wtyefm.com
License: Robinson, IL held by The Original Company, Inc.
Group Owner: The Original Company, Inc
Format: Adult Contemp
Mark Lange, President
Jonathan Lange, Operations Mgr
Shanon O'Toole, General Sales Mgr

WTYE
01-04-1963; 101.7 MHz FM; 3.1 kw; 466 ft.; N39 0 29 W87 46 41
Mailing Address: 522 Busseron St., Vincennes, IN 47591 USA
Second Address: PO Box 242, Vincennes, IN 47591-0242
(618) 842-2159; *Fax:* (618) 847-5907
www.wtyefm.com
License: Robinson, IL held by The Original Company, Inc.
Group Owner: The Original Company, Inc
Arbitron Metro Market: Robinson, IL; *Format:* Adult Contemp
Mark Lange, President
Jonathan Lange, Operations Mgr
Shanon O'Toole, General Sales Mgr

Rochelle

WRHL
09-16-1966; 1060 kHz AM; *Hrs Open:* 24; 0.25 kw-D, DA2; 0.05 kw-N, DA2; N41 55 24 W89 3 30
Mailing Address: 400 May Mart Drive, Rochelle, IL 61068 US
Second Address: 400 May Mart Dr., Rochelle, IL 61068
(815) 562-7001; *Fax:* (815) 562-7002
www.wrhl.net
wrhlamfm@rochelle.net
License: Rochelle, IL held by Rochelle Broadcasting Co. Inc.
Nat'l Network: AP Network News; *Regional Network:* Ill. Radio Net.; Tribune Radio Networks; *Wire Services:* AP
Format: News, News/Talk, 86; *Hrs. of News Programming:* news progmg 140 hrs wkly; *No. News Employees:* 2; *Target Audience:* 25-75.; *Adv. Rates:* 13; 13; 13; 13
David Van Drew, General Manager
Penny Helm, General Sales Mgr
Greg Saunders, Programming Director
Jeffrey Leon, News Director
Doug White, Chief Engineer
Becky Leininger, Traffic Manager

WRHL-FM
10-05-1973; 102.3 MHz FM; *Hrs Open:* 24; 4.6 kw; 180 ft.; N41 55 24 W89 3 30
Mailing Address: Box 177, Rochelle, IL 61068 US
Second Address: 400 May Mart Dr., Rochelle, IL 61068
(815) 562-7001; *Fax:* (815) 562-7002
www.hitsandfavorites.com
License: Rochelle, Ogle County, IL
Nat'l Network: ABC
Format: Adult Contemp; *Hrs. of News Programming:* News progmg one hr wkly; *Target Audience:* 25-54; female
Becky Leininger, News Director

Rock Island

*WLKU
10-01-1947; 98.9 MHz FM; *Hrs Open:* 24; 39 kw; 922 ft.; N41 19 39 W90 22 46
P.O. Box 705, Mt. Pleasant, SC 29465 US
(916) 251-1600; *Fax:* (916) 251-1650
www.klove.com
License: Rock Island, Rock Island County, IL held by Educational Media Foundation.
Group Owner: EMF Broadcasting; (acq 2-3-2006; $3.5 million).
Nat'l Network: K-Love
Arbitron Metro Market: Quad Cities, IA; *Format:* Christian
Mike Novak, President
David Pierce, Programming Director
Ed Lenane, News Director
Sam Wallington, Engineering Dir
Marya Morgan, News Reporter
Richard Hunt, News Reporter

WKBF
02-16-1925; 1270 kHz AM; *Hrs Open:* 24; 5 kw-D, DAN; 5 kw-N, DAN; N41 29 40 W90 28 0
P.O. Box 705, Mt. Pleasant, SC 29465 US
(888) 321-1270
License: Rock Island, IL held by Quad Cities Media LLC
Arbitron Metro Market: Quad Cities, IA
Randall Melchert, President

*WVIK
02-25-1963; 90.3 MHz FM; *Hrs Open:* 24; 31 kw; 1096 ft.; N41 32 49 W90 28 35
639 38th Street, Rock Island, IL 61201 US
(309) 794-7500; *Fax:* (309) 794-1236
www.wvik.org
info@wvik.org
License: Rock Island, Rock Island County, IL held by Augustana College.
Nat'l Network: NPR; *Wire Services:* AP
Arbitron Metro Market: Rock Island, IL; *Format:* News *Special Programming:* Jazz 9 hrs wkly; *Hrs. of News Programming:* news progmg 35 hrs wkly; *No. News Employees:* 2; *Target Audience:* General.
David Garner, Operations Dir
Jay Pearce, General Manager
Sonita Oldfield-Carlson, General Sales Mgr
Mindy Heusel, Programming Director
Herb Trix, News Director
Colleen Sibthorp, Business Manager
Jim Peterson, Public AffairsDirector
Jennifer Blohm, Dvelopment Director
Mary McNeil, Underwriting Sales Associate

Rockford

*WFEN
08-25-1991; 88.3 MHz FM; 1 kw horiz, 8.5 kw vert; 574 ft.; N42 21 48 W89 8 6
4700 South Main Street, Rockford, IL 61102 US
(815) 964-9336; *Fax:* (815) 964-0550
www.wfen.org
License: Rockford, Winnebago County, IL held by Faith Center
Arbitron Metro Market: Rockford, IL; *Format:* Christian *Special Programming:* Sp one hr wkly; *Target Audience:* 35-54.
Fred Tscholl, General Manager
Fred Tscholl, Station Manager
Judy Gors, Manager of Underwriting
Kathy Tscholl, Station Secretary

*WNIU
04-28-1991; 90.5 MHz FM; *Hrs Open:* 24; 50 kw; 367 ft.; N42 0 55 W89 0 7
801 North First Street, Dekalb, IL 60115 US
(815) 753-9000; *Fax:* (815) 753-9938
www.northernpublicradio.org
npr@niu.edu
License: Rockford, Winnebago County, IL held by Northern Illinois University.
Nat'l Network: PRI; NPR
Arbitron Metro Market: Rockford, IL; *Format:* Classical *Special Programming:* New age 2 hrs, blues 4 hrs wkly; *Hrs. of News Programming:* news progmg 52 hrs wkly; *No. News Employees:* 2 *Target Audience:* General.
Staci Hoste, General Manager
Jan Kilgard, General Sales Mgr
Bill Drake, Programming Director
Guy Stephens, News Director
Jeff Glass, Chief Engineer

WNTA
12-24-1953; 1330 kHz AM; *Hrs Open:* 24; 1 kW; N42 13 32 W89 2 49
2830 Sandy Hollow Rd, Rockford, IL 61109 USA
(815) 874-7861; *Fax:* (815) 874-2202
www.sportsfanradio1330.com
License: Rockford, IL held by Mid-Way Radio, Inc.
Group Owner: Mid-West Family Broadcasting
Arbitron Metro Market: Rockford, IL; *Format:* Sports
Travis Winchester, Programming Director

*WQFL
05-02-1974; 100.9 MHz FM; *Hrs Open:* 24; 2.7 kw; 489 ft.; N42 19 20 W89 0 41
Mailing Address: 5375 Pebble Creek Trail, P. O. Box 2730, Rockford, IL 61111 US
Second Address: 5375 Pebble Creek Tr., Loves Park, IL 61111
(815) 654-1200; *Fax:* (815) 282-7779
www.101qfl.com
positive@101qfl.com
License: Rockford, Winnebago County, IL held by Quest for Life Inc.
Arbitron Metro Market: Rockford, IL; *Format:* Christian; *Hrs. of News Programming:* news progmg one hr wkly; *No. News Employees:* 1; *Target Audience:* 25-44; female dominant, educated, upscale & middle class
Ralph Trentadue, General Manager
Rick Hall, Programming Director

WROK
01-01-1923; 1440 kHz AM
3901 Brendenwood Road, Rockford, IL 61107 US
(815) 399-2233; *Fax:* (815) 399-8148
www.1440wrok.com
License: Rockford, IL held by Cumulus Licensing Corp.
Group Owner: Cumulus Media Inc.; (acq 10-2-00; grpsl).
Nat'l Network: CBS; Wall Street
Arbitron Metro Market: Rockford, IL; *Format:* News, News/Talk, 86; *Target Audience:* P35-64
Scott Maenner, General Sales Mgr
Scot Bertram, Programming Director
Priscilla Cantu, Promotions Manager
Jan Thorpe, News Director
John Huntley, Chief Engineer
Becky Riojas, Marketing Manager

WZOK
01-01-1949; 97.5 MHz FM; 50 kw; 452 ft.; N42 16 45 W89 2 15
3901 Brendenwood Road, Rockford, IL 61107 US
(815) 399-2233; *Fax:* (815) 484-2432
www.97zokonline.com
feedback@97zokonline.com
License: Rockford, Winnebago County, IL
Group Owner: Cumulus Media Inc.
Arbitron Metro Market: Rockford, IL; *Format:* Contemporary Hits/Top 40; *Target Audience:* 25-34.
Sweet Lenny, Programming Director
Priscilla Cantu, Promotions Manager
Becky Riojas, Marketing Manager
Scott Maenner, Sales Manager

Rockton

WGFB
03-01-1963; 103.1 MHz FM; *Hrs Open:* 24; 2.4 kW; 525 ft.; N42 22 2 W89 5 13
2830 Sandy Hollow Rd, Rockford, IL 61109 USA
(815) 874-7861; *Fax:* (815) 874-2202
www.b103fm.com
License: Rockton, Winnebago County, IL held by Mid-Way Radio, Inc.
Group Owner: Mid-West Family Broadcasting
Nat'l Reps: Katz Radio
Arbitron Metro Market: Rockford, IL; *Format:* Adult Contemp, Contemporary Hits/Top 40; *Target Audience:* Women

Rosemont

*WTZI
88.1 MHz FM; 0.3 kw; 72 ft.; N41 57 20 W87 52 2
150 West Lincolnway, Suite 2001, Valparaiso, IN 46383 US
(847) 895-3545; *Fax:* (847) 285-1462
License: Rosemont, Cook County, IL held by Calvary Radio Network, Inc.
Group Owner: Calvary Radio Network
Arbitron Metro Market: Rosemont, IL; *Format:* Religious

Rushville

WKXQ
05-01-1985; 92.5 MHz FM; *Hrs Open:* 5 AM-midnight; 6 kw; 328 ft.; N40 8 20 W90 39 26
108 East Main Street, Beardstown, IL 62618 US
(217) 323-1790
larry.bostwick@gmail.com
License: Rushville, Schuyler County, IL
Nat'l Network: CNN Radio
Format: Oldies *Special Programming:* Relg 6 hrs, farm 6 hrs wkly; *Hrs. of News Programming:* news progmg 12 hrs wkly; *No. News Employees:* 1; *Target Audience:* 18-54.
Larry Bostwick, President/General Manager
Jayneece Bostwick, Programming Director

Salem

WJBD
12-16-1956; 1350 kHz AM; *Hrs Open:* 24; 0.43 kw-D, ND1; 0.059 kw-N, ND1; N38 37 56 W88 55 2
Mailing Address: 980 North Michigan Ave, Suite 1880, Chicago, IL 60611 US
Second Address: 221 E. Broadway, Suite 107, Centralia, IL 62801
(618) 548-2000; *Fax:* (618) 548-2079
www.wjbdradio.com
wjbd@accessus.net
License: Salem, IL held by NRG License Sub. LLC.
Group Owner: NRG Media LLC; (acq 10-31-2005; grpsl)
Format: Country *Special Programming:* Farm 4 hrs, relg 6 hrs wkly; *Hrs. of News Programming:* news progmg 30 hrs wkly; *No. News Employees:* 3; *Target Audience:* General.
Bruce Kropp, General Manager

WJBD-FM
06-01-1972; 100.1 MHz FM; *Hrs Open:* 24; 1.15 kw; 449 ft.; N38 33 45 W88 59 57
Mailing Address: 980 North Michigan Ave, Suite 1880, Chicago, IL 60611 US
Second Address: 310 W. McMackin St., Salem, IL 62881
(618) 548-2000; *Fax:* (618) 548-2079
www.wjbdradio.com
wjbd@accessus.net
License: Salem, Marion County, IL held by NRG License Sub. LLC.
Group Owner: NRG Media LLC
Format: Adult Contemp, News
Matt Tackett, Operations Dir

***WSLE**
01-01-2005; 91.3 MHz FM; 0.77 kw; 154 ft.; N38 37 34 W88 56 41 *Rebroadcasts:* Rebroadcasts WAFR(FM) Tupelo, MS 100%
P.O. Box 3206, Tupelo, MS 38803 US
(662) 844-8888; *Fax:* (662) 842-6791
www.afr.net
faq@afa.net
License: Salem, Marion County, IL held by American Family Association.
Group Owner: American Family Radio
Arbitron Metro Market: Salem, IL; *Format:* Christian
Tim Wildmon, President
Donald Wildmon, Founder
Buddy Smith, Sr VP
Ed Vitagliano, Exec Vp
Randy Sharp, Director Of Special Projects
Meeke Addison, Director Of Communications
Abraham Hamilton III, General Sales Mgr

Sandwich

WAUR
05-01-1986; 930 kHz AM; *Hrs Open:* 24; 2.5 kw-D, DA2; 4.2 kw-N, DA2; N41 36 26 W88 27 11
8910 University Center Lane, #130, San Diego, CA 92122 US
(312) 461-8540 or (219) 309-9327; *Fax:* (312) 588-0168
aciabattari@relevantradio.com
License: Sandwich, IL held by Starboard Media Foundation Inc.
Group Owner: Relevant Radio; (acq 5-4-2004; $3.5 million).
Arbitron Metro Market: Hutchinson, MN; *Format:* Talk, Christian *Special Programming:* Farm 15 hrs wkly; *Target Audience:* 25-54.
Armand Ciabattari, General Manager

Savanna

WCCI
11-07-1971; 100.3 MHz FM; *Hrs Open:* 24; 9.6 kw; 515 ft.; N42 7 47 W90 8 24
P.O. Box 310, Savanna, IL 61074 US
(815) 273-7757; *Fax:* (815) 273-2760
www.wcciradio.com
License: Savanna, Carroll County, IL held by Carroll County Communications Inc.
Nat'l Network: Fox News Radio; *Regional Network:* Brownfield
Arbitron Metro Market: Savanna, IL; *Format:* Country, News; *Hrs. of News Programming:* news progmg 35 hrs wkly; *No. News Employees:* 1; *Target Audience:* 25-54.; *Adv. Rates:* 9; 9; 9; 9
John Miller, President
Edward Bock, Operations Dir
Brian Reusch, Station Manager
Leslie Smith, Programming Director
Mark Schoening, News Director

Seneca

WJDK-FM
01-01-1993; 95.7 MHz FM; 3 kw; 328 ft.; N41 13 12 W88 32 27
One Broadcast Center, Plano, IL 60545 US
(815) 941-1000; *Fax:* (815) 941-9300
www.wjdkfm.com
License: Seneca, La Salle County, IL held by Grundy County Broadcasters Inc.
Nat'l Network: ABC
Arbitron Metro Market: Chicago, IL; *Format:* Adult Contemp; *Hrs. of News Programming:* news progmg 14 hrs wkly; *No. News Employees:* 1; *Target Audience:* 25-49.; *Adv. Rates:* 42; 31; 36; 25
Larry Nelson, President
Mike Williams, Operations Dir
Jack Daly, General Manager

Sheffield

***WPRC**
88.7 MHz FM; 8.5 kw; 417 ft.; N41 36 33.3 W89 40 18.6 US
(309) 692-9242; *Fax:* (309) 692-9241
www.wcicfm.org
wcic@wcicfm.org
License: Sheffield, Bureau County, IL held by Illinois Bible Institute Inc.
Group Owner: Illinois Bible Institute Inc.
Arbitron Metro Market: Sheffield, IL; *Format:* Christian, Talk
Dave Brooks, General Manager
Dave Brooks, Station Manager
Jessie Browning, Promotions Manager
Joe Buchanan, Music Director
Katie Post, Office Manager
Trevor Moore, Audio/New Media Producer

Shelbyville

WINU
11-24-1972; 870 kHz AM; *Hrs Open:* 4:30 AM-7:30 PM
1411 Locust Street, St Louis, MO 63103 US
(314) 421-3020; *Fax:* (314) 421-1702
www.hereshelpnet.org
License: Shelbyville, IL held by New Life Evangelistic Center Inc.
Arbitron Metro Market: Decatur, IL; *Format:* Christian; *Target Audience:* 25-54.
Gary Scott, General Manager

WEJT
12-31-1969; 105.1 MHz FM; *Hrs Open:* 24/7; 13 kw; 466 ft.; N39 35 38 W88 50 45
P.O. Box 150846, Nashville, TN 37215 US
(217) 428-4487; *Fax:* (217) 428-4501
www.decaturradio.com
cbullock@cromwellradio.com
License: Shelbyville, Shelby County, IL held by Cromwell Group Inc. of Illinois.
Group Owner: The Cromwell Group Inc.; (acq 8-1-89; $320,000 with co-located AM;
Nat'l Reps: Eastman Radio
Arbitron Metro Market: Decatur, IL; *Format:* Contemporary Hits/Top 40, Adult Contemp, 22; *Target Audience:* 25-54; baby boomers; *Adv. Rates:* 30; 28; 30; 20
Tara Nickerson, Operations Dir
Chris Bullock, General Manager
Larry Timmons, Chief Engineer

Sherman

WQQL
05-10-1971; 93.9 MHz FM; 15 kw; 430 ft.; N39 59 25 W89 30 46
3501 Sangamon Avenue, Springfield, IL 62707 US
(217) 753-5400; *Fax:* (217) 753-7902
License: Sherman, Sangamon County, IL held by Saga Communications of Illinois LLC.
Group Owner: Saga Communications Inc.; (acq 7-96; grpsl).
Arbitron Metro Market: Sherman, IL; *Format:* Classic Rock, Adult Contemp; *Target Audience:* 25-54.
Leanne Arndt, General Manager
Kevin Anfield, General Sales Mgr
Bob Parrish, Programming Director
Brandy Moore, Promotions Manager
Michelle Eecles, News Director

Skokie

WTMX
08-18-1961; 101.9 MHz FM; *Hrs Open:* 24; 4.2 kw; 1,562 ft.; N41 52 44 W87 38 8
130 E. Randolph St., Suite 2700, Chicago, IL 60601 US
(312) 946-1019; *Fax:* (312) 946-4747
www.wtmx.com
License: Skokie, Cook County, IL held by Chicago FCC License Sub LLC
Group Owner: Hubbard Broadcasting Inc.; (acq 1-19-2011).
Nat'l Reps: Katz Radio
Arbitron Metro Market: Chicago, IL; *Format:* Contemporary Hits/Top 40; *No. News Employees:* 1
Sara McMurray, General Sales Mgr
Mary Ellen Kachinske, Programming Director
Dianne Sharp, Promotions Manager
Kent Lewin, Chief Engineer
Nikki Chuminatto, Music Director
Dave Karwowski, Marketing Director
Jeff Buti, Digital MediaDirector
Craig Volpe, Director of Sales
Erica Thornton, Vice President of Finance

Smithboro

***WSWS(FM)**
89.9 MHz FM; 10 kw; Ant 164 ft; N38 56 09 W89 13 56
5210 S.E. Washington Blvd., Bartlesville, OK 74006
(918) 333-8700; *Fax:* (918) 333-3526
License: Smithboro, Bond County, IL held by The Power Foundation
Population Served: 177; *Arbitron Metro Market:* Smithboro, IL
Danny Hester, President

South Jacksonville

WJVO
09-01-1986; 105.5 MHz FM; *Hrs Open:* 24; 6 kw; 328 ft.; N39 43 20 W90 11 43
P.O. Box 1055, Jacksonville, IL 62651 US
(217) 245-5119; *Fax:* (217) 245-1596
wjvofm.com
License: South Jacksonville, Morgan County, IL held by Morgan County Broadcasting Co. Inc.
Nat'l Network: Westwood One; ABC
Format: Country; *Hrs. of News Programming:* news progmg 4 hrs wkly; *No. News Employees:* 1; *Target Audience:* 25-54.
Sarah Hautala, General Manager

Sparta

WHCO
02-01-1955; 1230 kHz AM; *Hrs Open:* 24; 1 kw-U, ND1; N38 7 25 W89 43 20
Mailing Address: P.O. Box 255, Sparta, IL 62286 US
Second Address: 47 W. Maine, Mascoutah, IL 62258
(618) 443-2121; *Fax:* (618) 443-2800
www.whcoradio.com
Hoefft@Egyptian.Net
License: Sparta, IL held by Hirsch Communication Engineering Co.
Nat'l Network: CBS; Westwood One; *Regional Network:* Brownfield; Ill. Radio Net.
Arbitron Metro Market: St. Louis, MO; *Format:* News, News/Talk, 84, Talk *Special Programming:* Pol 2 hrs, farm 20 hrs, relg 10 hrs wkly; *Hrs. of News Programming:* news progmg 10 hrs wkly; *No. News Employees:* 2 *Target Audience:* 25-65.
Jack Scheper Sr., President
Mike Hoeft, News Director

Spring Valley

WIVQ
12-01-1993; 103.3 MHz FM; *Hrs Open:* 24; 4.9 kw; 361 ft.; N41 18 09 W89 14 11
3905 Progress Blvd., Peru, IL 61354 US
(815) 224-2103
www.qhitmusic.com
advertising@studstillmedia.com
License: Spring Valley, Bureau County, IL held by Mendota Broadcasting, Inc.
Group Owner: Studstill Broadcasting; (acq 7-17-97; $700,000 with WBZG(FM) Peru).
Nat'l Reps: Rgnl Reps; *Wire Services:* AP
Arbitron Metro Market: Spring Valley, IL; *Format:* Contemporary Hits/Top 40; *No. News Employees:* 2; *Target Audience:* 18-44.
Cole Studstill, Manager of Programming

***WSOG**
12-01-2002; 88.1 MHz FM; *Hrs Open:* 24; 4 kw vert; 262 ft.; N41 17 32 W89 7 59
515 West Minnesota, Spring Valley, IL 61362 US
(815) 220-1929; *Fax:* (815) 220-1929
www.wsogradio.com
wsog881@hotmail.com
License: Spring Valley, Bureau County, IL held by Spirit Education Association Inc.
Arbitron Metro Market: Spring Valley, IL; *Format:* Christian
Jim Perona, Sr., General Manager & Founder
Louis Perona, President
Jeremy Caldera, Voicing & Technical Support

Bob Gibson, Programming Planning, Voicing & Logging
Allen Drake, Project Coordinator

Springfield

WDBR

04-01-1948; 103.7 MHz FM; 50 kw; 299 ft.; N39 47 37 W89 36 18
3501 Sangamon Avenue, Springfield, IL 62707 US
(217) 753-5400; *Fax:* (217) 753-7902
www.wdbr.com
msmith@capitolradiogroup.com
License: Springfield, Sangamon County, IL
Group Owner: Saga Communications Inc.
Wire Services: UPI
Arbitron Metro Market: Springfield, IL; *Format:* Contemporary Hits/Top 40; *Target Audience:* 18-49; general
Mitch Smith, General Manager
Jason Addams, Programming Director
Scott Lindahl, Promotions Manager

WFMB

01-01-1922; 1450 kHz AM; *Hrs Open:* 24; 1 kw-U, ND1; N39 45 36 W89 39 5
600 Congress Ave., Suite 1400, Austin, TX 78701 US
(217) 528-3033; *Fax:* (217) 528-5348
www.sportsradio1450.com
sportsradio1450@sportsradio1450.com
License: Springfield, IL held by Neuhoff Family L.P.
Group Owner: Neuhoff Family L.P.; (acq 8-1-2007; grpsl)
Nat'l Network: ESPN Radio; ABC Information & Entertainment; *Regional Network:* Tribune Radio Networks; Brownfield; RFD Illinois; *Nat'l Reps:* Christal
Format: Sports; *Hrs. of News Programming:* news progmg 5 hrs wkly; *No. News Employees:* 2; *Target Audience:* 25-54; upscale professionals
Kevin O'Dea, General Manager
Kevin Anfield, General Sales Mgr
Danielle Outlaw, Programming Director
Frank Konwinski, Chief Engineer
Jeff Hofmann, News Director
John Price, Program Director

WFMB-FM

07-01-1965; 104.5 MHz FM; *Hrs Open:* 24; 43 kw; 430 ft.; N39 45 36 W89 39 5
600 Congress Ave., Suite 1400, Austin, TX 78701 US
(217) 528-3033; *Fax:* (217) 528-5348
www.wfmb.com
wfmb@wfmb.com
License: Springfield, Sangamon County, IL
Group Owner: Neuhoff Family L.P.
Nat'l Network: Motor Racing Net; *Nat'l Reps:* Christal
Format: Country; *No. News Employees:* 1; *Target Audience:* A 25-54.
Kevin O'Dea, General Manager
Kevin Anfield, General Sales Mgr
Danielle Outlaw, Programming Director
Dave Marsh, Promotions Manager
Kerri Cawley, Information Technology Director
John Spalding, Music Director
Jessica Ross, TrafficManager
Kathy Byerly, Local Sales Manager
Danielle Outlaw, Director of Sales

*WLUJ

05-24-1995; 89.7 MHz FM; 20 kw; 328 ft.; N39 48 30 W89 37 30
600 West Mason Street, Springfield, IL 62702 US
(217) 528-2300; *Fax:* (217) 528-2400
www.wluj.org
License: Springfield, Sangamon County, IL held by Cornerstone Community Radio Inc.
Nat'l Network: Moody
Format: Christian, Talk; *Target Audience:* General.
Arthur Gregg, Operations Dir
Richard Van Zandt, General Manager
John McBride, Station Manager
Richard Beaman, General Sales Mgr
Howard Fouks, Operations Manager
Dick Reed, Vice President

WMAY

10-15-1950; 970 kHz AM; 1 kW-D, 0.5 kW-N; N39 51 42 W89 32 32
1510 North 3rd St, Riverton, IL 62561 USA
(217) 629-7077; *Fax:* (217) 629-7952
www.wmay.com
License: Springfield, IL held by Long Nine, Inc.
Group Owner: The Mid-West Family Broadcast Group; (acq 12-7-76).
Nat'l Reps: D & R Radio
Arbitron Metro Market: Springfield, IL; *Format:* News/Talk; *Target Audience:* Men 35-54
Ken Carson, Operations Dir
Harvey Wells, General Manager
Mark Birtch, Director of Sales
Jim Leach, Programming Director
Jim Leach, News Director

WNNS

11-01-1980; 98.7 MHz FM; 50 kW; 469 ft.; N39 41 59 W89 46 55
1510 North 3rd St, Riverton, IL 62561 USA
(217) 629-7077; *Fax:* (217) 629-7952
www.wnns.com
License: Springfield, Sangamon County, IL held by Long Nine, Inc.
Group Owner: Mid-West Family Broadcasting
Arbitron Metro Market: Springfield, IL; *Format:* Adult Contemp
Special Programming: Jazz 6 hrs wkly
Ken Carson, Operations Manager
Harvey Wells, General Manager
Mark Birtch, Director of Sales
Chris Murphy, Programming Director
Deb West, Promotions Manager

*WQNA

08-31-1979; 88.3 MHz FM; *Hrs Open:* 24; 0.25 kw; 256 ft.; N39 44 3 W89 38 18
2201 Toronto Road, Springfield, IL 62707 US
(217) 529-5431; *Fax:* (217) 529-7861
www.wqna.org
info@wqna.org
License: Springfield, Sangamon County, IL held by Capital Area Career Center.
Regional Reps: Illinois Student News Network
Format: Variety/Diverse *Special Programming:* Varied; *Hrs. of News Programming:* news progmg 6 hrs wkly; *No. News Employees:* 1; *Target Audience:* 13-24; student, community, high school & college students
Jim Grimes, General Manager
Jim Pemberton, Programming Director
Kerri Donovan, Engineering Dir

WLFZ-FM

11-15-1993; 101.9 MHz FM; *Hrs Open:* 24; 50 kw; 272 ft.; N39 42 39 W89 38 42
1030 Durkin Drive, Springfield, IL 62704 US
(217) 753-5400; *Fax:* (217) 753-7902
www.cool1019.com
info@cool1019.com
License: Springfield, Sangamon County, IL held by Saga Communications of Illinois LLC.
Group Owner: Saga Communications Inc.; (acq 9-10-93; $1.44 million;
Nat'l Reps: Katz Radio
Format: Oldies; *Hrs. of News Programming:* News progmg 2 hrs wkly; *Target Audience:* 25 plus; upscale educated adults
Leanne Arndt, General Manager
Kevin Anfield, General Sales Mgr
Joey Mc Laughlin, Programming Director

*WSCT

11-01-1993; 90.5 MHz FM; *Hrs Open:* 24; 3.8 kw; 410 ft.; N39 38 38 W89 30 51 *Rebroadcasts:* Rebroadcasts WIBI(FM) Carlinville 100%
P.O. Box 140, Carlinville, IL 62626 US
(217) 854-4800; *Fax:* (217) 854-4810
www.wibi.org
wibi@wibi.org
License: Springfield, Sangamon County, IL held by Illinois Bible Institute.
Format: Religious; *Hrs. of News Programming:* News progmg 5 hrs wkly; *Target Audience:* 25-44; Christian & seeking non-Christians
Melody Miller, Operations Dir
Tom Greene, Station Manager
Rob Regal, Programming Director
G.W. Van Alstine, Promotions Manager
Joe Rother, Engineering Dir

WTAX

01-01-1930; 1240 kHz AM; 1 kw-U, ND1; N39 47 36 W89 36 18
PO Box 2759, Springfield, IL 62708 US
(217) 753-5400; *Fax:* (217) 753-7902
www.wtax.com
info@wtax.com
License: Springfield, IL held by Saga Communications of Illinois LLC.
Group Owner: Saga Communications Inc.; (acq 1996).
Nat'l Network: Moody; CBS; *Nat'l Reps:* Christal; *Wire Services:* UPI
Format: News, News/Talk, 84, Talk *Special Programming:* Farm 16 hrs wkly; *Hrs. of News Programming:* news progmg 20, hrs wkly; *No. News Employees:* 3; *Target Audience:* 30 plus.
Leanne Arndt, General Manager
Michelle Eccles, News Director

*WUIS

01-03-1975; 91.9 MHz FM; *Hrs Open:* 24; 50 kw; 499 ft.; N39 47 1.1 W89 26 45.9 *Rebroadcasts:* Rebroadcasts WIPA(FM) Pittsfield 100%
Mailing Address: South Sheperd Road, Springfield, IL 62794 US
Second Address: One University Plaza, MS CBM-130, Springfield, IL 62703
(217) 206-9847
www.wuis.org
License: Springfield, Sangamon County, IL held by University of Illinois at Springfield.
Nat'l Network: NPR; PRI
Arbitron Metro Market: Springfield, IL; *Format:* Jazz, News
Special Programming: NPR entertainment 15 hrs, bluegrass 2 hrs, Singer/; *Hrs. of News Programming:* news progmg 45 hrs wkly; *No. News Employees:* 5 *Target Audience:* 25-54.
Sinta Seiber, Operations Dir
Bill Wheelhouse, General Manager
Lisa Clemmons-Stott, General Sales Mgr
Sinta Seiber-Lane, Programming Director
Sean Crawford, News Director
Greg Manfroi, Chief Engineer
Sandra McGinnis, BusinessDirector
Randy Eccles, Development Director
Virginia Mitchelly, Development Assistant

St. Anne

WXNU

01-01-2006; 106.5 MHz FM; 1.95 kw; 463 ft.; N41 0 20 W87 41 42
US
(815) 935-9555; *Fax:* (815) 935-9593
wlan@starradio.com
License: St. Anne, Kankakee County, IL held by STARadio Corp.
Group Owner: STARadio Corp.
Arbitron Metro Market: Saint Anne, IL; *Format:* Country
Brendan Michaels, Operations Dir
Bob Kersmarki, General Manager
Larry Regnier, General Sales Mgr
Phil Reilly, Chief Engineer

St. Joseph

*WGNJ

01-01-1999; 89.3 MHz FM; *Hrs Open:* 24; 50 kw; 459 ft.; N40 5 16 W87 53 42
Mailing Address: P.O. Box 12345, Champaign, IL 61826 US
Second Address: 2421 N. 1450 E. Rd., White Heath, IL 61884
(217) 897-6333
www.greatnewsradio.org
staff@greatnewsradio.org
License: St. Joseph, Champaign County, IL held by Good News Radio Inc.
Nat'l Network: Salem Radio Network
Format: Christian, Religious, 86; *Target Audience:* 35 plus; general
David Herriott, Chairman
Mark Burns, President
Carrie Burns, Operations Dir

Staunton

WAOX

12-01-1999; 105.3 MHz FM; *Hrs Open:* 24; 6 kw; 285 ft.; N39 2 37 W89 44 56
P.O. Box 10, Litchfield, IL 62056 US
(618) 635-6000; *Fax:* (217) 532-2431
www.waox.com
waox@waoxradio.com
License: Staunton, Macoupin County, IL held by Talley Broadcasting Corp.
Group Owner: Talley Radio Stations
Nat'l Network: ABC; *Nat'l Reps:* Christal *Regional Reps:* Regional 'reps; *Wire Services:* AP
Arbitron Metro Market: Staunton, IL.; *Format:* Adult Contemp; *No. News Employees:* 2; *Target Audience:* 18-54.
Hayward Talley, President
Brian Talley, Operations Dir
Hayward Talley, General Manager
Beth Niehaus, News Director

Sterling

***WNIQ**
91.5 MHz FM; *Hrs Open:* 24; 2.4 kw; 328 ft.; N41 53 52 W89 36 20 *Rebroadcasts:* Rebroadcasts WNIJ(FM) De Kalb & WNIU(FM) Rockford 50%
801 North First Street, Dekalb, IL 60115 US
(815) 753-9000; *Fax:* (815) 753-9938
www.northernpublicradio.org
npr@niu.edu
License: Sterling, Whiteside County, IL held by Northern Illinois University.
Nat'l Network: PRI; NPR
Arbitron Metro Market: Freeport, IL; *Format:* News, News/Talk, 86; *Hrs. of News Programming:* News progmg 2 hrs wkly; *Target Audience:* General.
Staci Hoste, General Manager
Jan Kilgard, General Sales Mgr
Bill Drake, Programming Director
Guy Stephens, News Director

WSDR
08-21-1949; 1240 kHz AM; *Hrs Open:* 24; 0.5 kw-D, ND1; 1 kw-N, ND1; N41 48 59 W89 40 13
3501 Broadway, P.O. Box 1508, Mount Vernon, IL 62864 US
(815) 625-3400; *Fax:* (815) 625-6940
wsdr1240@theramp.net
License: Sterling, IL held by Withers Broadcasting Co. of Rock River LLC.
Group Owner: Withers Broadcasting Co.; (acq 1-21-98; grpsl).
Nat'l Network: CBS; ABC; *Regional Network:* Ill. Radio Net; *Nat'l Reps:* Christal
Format: News, Sports, 86 *Special Programming:* Farm 16 hrs, Sp 4 hrs wkly; *Hrs. of News Programming:* news progmg 10 hrs wkly; *No. News Employees:* 2; *Target Audience:* 25 plus.
Brian Zschiesche, General Manager
Sherry Smith, General Sales Mgr
Lisa Taylor, Programming Director

WSSQ
08-01-1966; 94.3 MHz FM; 6 kw; 299 ft.; N41 51 6 W89 42 38
3501 Broadway, P.O. Box 1508, Mount Vernon, IL 62864 US
(815) 625-3400; *Fax:* (815) 625-6940
wsdr1240@theramp.net
License: Sterling, Whiteside County, IL
Group Owner: Withers Broadcasting Co.
Nat'l Network: Westwood One; ABC; *Nat'l Reps:* Christal
Format: Adult Contemp; *Target Audience:* 25-54; women
T.J. Anzvino, General Manager

Streator

WSPL
09-26-1953; 1250 kHz AM; *Hrs Open:* 24; 0.5 kw-D, DA2; 0.064 kw-N, DA2; N41 09 30 W88 50 13
3905 Progress Blvd., Peru, IL 61354 US
(815) 673-8000
www.am1250wspl.com
advertise@studstillmedia.com
License: Streator, IL held by Mendota Broadcasting, Inc.
Group Owner: Studstill Broadcasting; (acq 5-30-2000; grpsl)
Arbitron Metro Market: La Salle-Peru, IL; *Format:* News/Talk; *Hrs. of News Programming:* news progmg 25 hrs wkly; *No. News Employees:* 3; *Target Audience:* 35 plus.
Cheryl Knirlberger, General Sales Mgr
Cole Studstill, Manager of Programming

WSTQ
09-15-1964; 97.7 MHz FM; *Hrs Open:* 24; 6 kw; 328 ft.; N41 10 49 W88 52 6
3905 Progress Blvd., Peru, IL 61354 US
(815) 224-2100
www.qhitmusic.com
advertising@studstillmedia.com
License: Streator, La Salle County, IL held by Mendota Broadcasting
Group Owner: Studstill Broadcasting
Arbitron Metro Market: La Salle-Peru, IL; *Format:* Contemporary Hits/Top 40; *Target Audience:* 18-44.
Cole Studstill, Managing of Programming

WYYS
01-01-1995; 106.1 MHz FM; *Hrs Open:* 24; 2.45 kw; 520 ft.; N41 16 30 W88 57 56
3905 Progress Blvd., Peru, IL 61354 US
(815) 224-2100
www.classichits106.com
advertising@studstillmedia.com
License: Streator, La Salle County, IL held by Mendota Broadcasting Inc.
Group Owner: Studstill Broadcasting; (acq 3-8-2000; grpsl)
Nat'l Network: ABC
Arbitron Metro Market: La Salle-Peru,; *Format:* Adult Contemp; *No. News Employees:* 2; *Target Audience:* 35 plus.
Cole Studstill, Manager of Programming

Sugar Grove

***WSRI**
01-01-2005; 88.7 MHz FM; *Hrs Open:* 24; 0.6 kw; 338 ft.; N41 42 16 W88 26 2 *Rebroadcasts:* Rebroadcasts KLRD(FM) Yucaipa, CA 100%
1425 N Market Blvd., Suite 9, Sacramento, CA 95834 US
(888) 937-2471; *Fax:* (916) 251-1650
www.air1.com
info@air1.com
License: Sugar Grove, Kane County, IL held by Educational Media Foundation.
Group Owner: EMF Broadcasting
Nat'l Network: Air 1
Arbitron Metro Market: Sugar Grove, IL; *Format:* Alternative, Christian; *Target Audience:* 25-44; female-Judeo/ Christian
Darrell Chambliss, Chairman
Alan Mason, COO
Mike Novak, President and CEO
David Pierce, Programming Director
Ed Lenane, News Director
Sam Wallington, Engineering Dir
Marya Morgan, News Reporter
Richard Hunt, News Reporter
Larry Moody, Director
Mitch Barnhart, Director
David R. Ferry, Director
Walter Golembeski, Director

Sullivan

WZNX
04-01-1992; 106.7 MHz FM; *Hrs Open:* 24; 9.5 kw; 550 ft; N39 36 38 W88 41 32
410 N. Water St., Suite B, Decatur, IL 37215
(217) 428-4487; *Fax:* (217) 428-4501
www.decaturradio.com
cbullock@cromwellradio.com
License: Sullivan, Moultrie County, IL held by WSHY Inc.
Group Owner: The Cromwell Group Inc.; (acq 2-14-97; $750,000)
Nat'l Network: Fox News Network; *Nat'l Reps:* Eastman Radio
Population Served: 300,000; *Arbitron Metro Market:* Decatur, IL; *Format:* Classic Rock; *Hrs. of News Programming:* 24/7; *No. News Employees:* 1; *Target Audience:* 25-54; strong men
Chris Bullock, General Manager
Tara Nickerson, Operations Manager
Cindy Hansen, Business Manager

Summit

***WARG**
01-01-1976; 88.9 MHz FM; *Hrs Open:* 8 AM-10 PM; 0.5 kw horiz, 0.46 kw vert; 82 ft.; N41 46 36 W87 48 17
7329 West 63rd Street, Summit, IL 60501 US
(708) 728-8368; *Fax:* (708) 728-3155
License: Summit, Cook County, IL held by Community High School District No. 217.
Arbitron Metro Market: Summit, IL; *Format:* Alternative; *Target Audience:* High School Students; alternative subculture
Jennifer Knapp, General Manager

Sycamore

WSQR
06-11-1981; 1180 kHz AM
1 Broadcast Center, Plano, IL 60545 US
(630) 552-1000; *Fax:* (630) 552-9300
wspy-news@nelsonmultimedia.net
License: Sycamore, IL held by De kalb County Broadcasters Inc.
Nat'l Network: ABC
Format: Adult Contemp *Special Programming:* Farm 6 hrs wkly; *Target Audience:* 35-55.
Pam Nelson, CFO
Larry Nelson, President
Beth Pierre, General Manager
Vori Dhabolt, General Sales Mgr

Taylorville

***WIHM**
01-01-1952; 1410 kHz AM
9 Cougar Road, Glen Carbon, IL 62034 US
(314) 752-7000
www.covenantnet.net
office@covenantnet.net
License: Taylorville, IL held by Covenant Network
Group Owner: Covenant Network; (acq 7-31-98; $60,000)
Format: Christian, Religious
Tony Holman, President

WRAN
11-25-1997; 97.3 MHz FM; *Hrs Open:* 24; 3.7 kw; 420 ft.; N39 16 48 W88 58 22
918 East Park St, P.O. Box 169, Taylorville, IL 62568 US
(217) 824-3395; *Fax:* (217) 824-3301
taylorvilledailynews.com/community/wran
License: Taylorville, Christian County, IL held by Miller Communications Inc.
Group Owner: Miller Media Group
Nat'l Network: CBS; *Regional Network:* SRN
Arbitron Metro Market: Davenport-Rock Island-Moline; *Format:* Oldies; *No. News Employees:* 1; *Target Audience:* 25-55
Randal Miller, President
Kami Payne, General Manager
Brandon Fellows, Programming Director
Steve Butera, News Director

WTIM
06-01-2016; 96.1 MHz FM *Rebroadcasts:* Repeater for 870 AM
Mailing Address: 918 East Park St, P.O. Box 169, Taylorville, IL 62568 US
Second Address: , Taylorville, IL 62568
(217) 824-3395; *Fax:* (217) 824-3301
taylorvilledailynews.com/wtim
License: Taylorville, Christian County, IL held by Miller Communications Inc.
Group Owner: Miller Media Group
Nat'l Network: CNN Radio; CBS News; CBS Sports
Arbitron Metro Market: Davenport-Rock Island-Moline; *Format:* News, News/Talk, 84, Talk; *Target Audience:* 35+
Randal Miller, President

WTIM
06-01-2016; 107.5 MHz FM *Rebroadcasts:* Repeater for 870 AM
Mailing Address: 918 East Park St, P.O. Box 169, Taylorville, IL 62568 US
Second Address: , Taylorville, IL 62568
(217) 824-3395; *Fax:* (217) 824-3301
taylorvilledailynews.com/wtim
License: Taylorville, Shelby County County, IL held by Miller Communications Inc.
Group Owner: Miller Media Group
Nat'l Network: CNN Radio; CBS News; CBS Sports
Arbitron Metro Market: Davenport-Rock Island-Moline; *Format:* News, News/Talk, 84, Talk; *Target Audience:* 35+
Randal Miller, President

WUSW
01-01-1971; 92.7 MHz FM; 11.5 kW; 482 ft.; N39 38 38 W89 30 51
1510 North 3rd St, Riverton, IL 62561 USA
(217) 629-7077; *Fax:* (217) 629-7952
www.us927.com
License: Taylorville, IL held by Long Nine, Inc.
Group Owner: Mid-West Family Broadcasting
Arbitron Metro Market: Springfield, IL; *Format:* Country; *Target Audience:* Adults 25-54
Ken Carson, Operations Manager
Harvey Wells, General Manager
Mark Birtch, Director of Sales
Chris Murphy, Programming Director

Terre Haute

WVGO
95.9 MHz FM
800 W. National Hwy., Washington, IN 475001 US
License: Terre Haute, IN held by DLC Media, Inc.
Group Owner: DLC Media, Inc.

Teutopolis

WKJT
01-01-1994; 102.3 MHz FM; *Hrs Open:* 24; 6 kw; 328 ft.; N39 8 30 W88 33 36
1100 Ave. of Mid-America, P.O. Box 566, Effingham, IL 62401 US
(217) 347-5518; *Fax:* (217) 347-5519
www.kjcountry.com
License: Teutopolis, Effingham County, IL held by Kirby Broadcasting Inc.
Nat'l Network: Fox News Radio
Format: Country
John Kirby, President
Tonya Siner, Operations Dir
Greg Sapp, Station Manager
George Flexter, Programming Director

Thomasboro

WKZS

06-01-1982; 103.3 MHz FM; *Hrs Open:* 24; 3 kw; 299 ft.; N40 8 46 W87 27 15
Mailing Address: 820 Railroad St. PO Bx67, Covington, IN 47932 US
Second Address: P.O. Box 67, Covington, IN 47932
(217) 443-4004; *Fax:* (765) 793-4644
www.kisscountryradio.com
info@kisscountryradio.com
License: Thomasboro, Fountain County, IL held by Benton-Weatherford Broadcasting Inc. of Indiana.
Nat'l Network: Jones Radio Networks; *Wire Services:* AP
Format: Country; *Hrs. of News Programming:* News progmg 10 hrs wkly; *No. News Employees:* 1; *Target Audience:* 18-49.
Larry Weatherford, President
Rhea Benton-Weatherford, General Manager
Greg Green, Station Manager
Tara Duncan, Promotions Manager

Tower Hill

WSVZ

06-01-2016; 98.3 MHz FM; 3.7 kw; 420 ft; N39 16 48 W88 58 22
Mailing Address: 918 East Park St, P.O. Box 169, Taylorville, IL 62568 US
Second Address: , Taylorville, IL 62568
(217) 824-3395; *Fax:* (217) 824-3301
taylorvilledailynews.com/community/wsvz
License: Tower Hill, Shelby County, IL held by Kaskaskia Broadcasting, Inc.
Group Owner: Miller Media Group
Regional Network: SRN
Arbitron Metro Market: Davenport-Rock Island-Moline; *Format:* Country; *Target Audience:* 25+
Randal Miller, President

Tuscola

WSJK(FM)

09-30-1970; 93.5 MHz FM; 6 kw; 308 ft; N39 54 24 W88 16 35
2702 Boulder Drive, Urbana, IL 61802
(217) 367-1195; *Fax:* (217) 367-3291
www.espncu.com
Steve.Miller@sjbroadcasting.com
License: Tuscola, Douglas County, IL held by RadioStar Inc.
Group Owner: RadioStar Inc.; (acq 5-23-2006; grpsl).
Nat'l Reps: McGavren Guild
Population Served: 81,291; *Arbitron Metro Market:* Champaign, IL; *Format:* Alternative; *Target Audience:* 18-49; adult professionals & college students
Jim Glassman, President
Roxanne Charles, General Manager
Steve Miller, General Sales Mgr
Ken Cunningham, Programming Director
Josh Laskowski, Promotions Manager
Jon Hail, Engineering Dir
Donna Keleher, Office Manager

Urbana

WBCP

01-01-1948; 1580 kHz AM
Unit D, 904 N. 4th St., Champaign, IL 61820 US
(563) 568-3477; *Fax:* (563) 568-3391
knei@kneiradio.com
License: Urbana, IL held by WBCP Inc.
Nat'l Network: American Urban; ABC
Arbitron Metro Market: Anchorage AK; *Format:* Oldies
Dr. D.L. Van Voorhis, President
Bill DeGeorge, General Manager

*WILL

03-28-1922; 580 kHz AM; *Hrs Open:* 24; 5 kw-D, DA2; 0.1 kw-N, DA2; N40 4 53 W88 14 18
300 North Goodwin Ave, Urbana, IL 61801 US
(217) 333-0850; *Fax:* (217) 244-9586
www.will.uiuc.edu
willamfm@uiuc.edu
License: Urbana, IL held by University of Illinois Board of Trustees.
Nat'l Network: NPR; PRI; *Wire Services:* AP
Arbitron Metro Market: Champaign, IL; *Format:* News, News/Talk, 86, Variety/Diverse *Special Programming:* Farm 7 hrs wkly; *Hrs. of News Programming:* news progmg 115 hrs wkly; *No. News Employees:* 3 *TargetAudience:* 25-60; educated, upper middle income, professionals
Mike Pritchard, Operations Dir
Mark Leonard, General Manager
Jay Pearce, Station Manager
Kate Dobrovolny, Promotions Manager
Tom Rogers, News Director
Rick Finnie, Chief Engineer
Denise Perry, Traffic Manager

*WILL-FM

09-01-1941; 90.9 MHz FM; *Hrs Open:* 24; 105 kw; 850 ft.; N40 2 18 W88 40 10
810 South Wright Street, 228 Gregory Hall, Urbana, IL 61801 US
(217) 333-0850; *Fax:* (217) 244-9586
willamfm@uiuc.edu
License: Urbana, Champaign County, IL held by University of Illinois Board of Trustees.
Wire Services: AP
Arbitron Metro Market: Champaign, IL *TV Affiliate:* *WILL-TV affil; *Format:* Variety/Diverse; *Hrs. of News Programming:* News progmg 2 hrs wkly; *Target Audience:* 35-70.
Jake Schumacher, Programming Director

WCFF

12-04-1967; 92.5 MHz FM; *Hrs Open:* 24; 16 kw; 410 ft.; N40 0 45 W88 8 29
504 South Neil Street, Champaign, IL 61820 US
(217) 352-4141; *Fax:* (217) 352-1256
www.925thechief.com
abeck@illiniradio.com
License: Urbana, Champaign County, IL held by Saga Communications of Illinois LLC.
Group Owner: Saga Communications Inc.; (acq 2000; $7 million).
Nat'l Reps: Katz Radio
Arbitron Metro Market: Champaign, IL; *Format:* Oldies; *Target Audience:* 35-64.
Ed Christian, CEO
Steve Goldstein, President
Jonathan Drake, Operations Dir
Alan Beck, General Manager
Karen Cochrane, General Sales Mgr
Gary Saladino, Promotions Manager
Mike Cation, News Director
Mark Spalding, ChiefEngineer
Ryan Leskis, Promotions Director
Sheila Wetherell, Business Manager

WPGU

04-17-1967; 107.1 MHz FM; *Hrs Open:* 24; 3 kw; 236 ft.; N40 6 34 W88 14 6
24 E. Green St., Ste 107, Champaign, IL 61820 US
(217) 337-3100; *Fax:* (217) 337-3162
www.wpgu.com
wpgu@wpgu.com
License: Urbana, Champaign County, IL held by Illini Media Co.
Arbitron Metro Market: Champaign, IL; *Format:* Alternative; *Hrs. of News Programming:* News progmg 7 hrs wkly; *Target Audience:* 18-34.
Mary Cory, General Manager
Scott Downs, General Sales Mgr
Becky Brothman, Programming Director
Beth Rehn, Promotions Manager
Jon Hansen, News Director
Melissa Pasco, Traffic Manager
Rachel Buenting, Traffic Manager

Vandalia

WKRV

05-28-1974; 107.1 MHz FM; *Hrs Open:* 24; 6 kw; 328 ft.; N38 59 48 W88 55 44
Mailing Address: 232 South Fourth Street, P.O. Box 100, Vandalia, IL 62471 US
Second Address: 232 S. 4th St., Vandalia, IL 62471
(618) 283-2325; *Fax:* (618) 283-1503
www.vandaliaradio.com
tstapleton@cromwellradio.com
License: Vandalia, Fayette County, IL held by Two Petaz Inc.
Group Owner: The Cromwell Group Inc.
Wire Services: Metro Weather Service Inc.
Format: Adult Contemp, Classic Rock; *Hrs. of News Programming:* news progmg 10 hrs wkly; *No. News Employees:* 1; *Target Audience:* 20-45.
Todd Stapleton, General Manager
Dan Michel, Program Director
Erica Foltz, Operations Director

WPMB

12-09-1963; 1500 kHz AM; *Hrs Open:* 6 AM-sunset
Mailing Address: 232 South Fourth Street, P.O. Box 100, Vandalia, IL 62471 US
Second Address: 232 S. 4th St., Vandalia, IL 62471
(618) 283-2325,(618) 283-2355; *Fax:* (618) 283-1503
www.vandaliaradio.com
wkrv@sbcglobal.net
License: Vandalia, IL held by Two Petaz Inc.
Group Owner: The Cromwell Group Inc.; (acq 2-3-2005; $350,000 with co-located FM).
Wire Services: Metro Weather Service Inc.
Format: Adult Contemp *Special Programming:* Farm 4 hrs, gospel 3 hrs wkly; *Hrs. of News Programming:* news progmg 8-10 hrs wkly; *No. News Employees:* 2; *Target Audience:* Women, 25-54
Todd Stapleton, General Manager
Dan Michel, Program Director
Erica Foltz, Operations Director
T, Programming Director

*WVNL

10-07-2002; 91.7 MHz FM; *Hrs Open:* 24 hrs; 0.1 kw; 164 ft.; N38 56 42 W89 6 10 *Rebroadcasts:* WIBI, Carlinville,IL, 100%
Box 140, Carlinville, IL 62626 US
(217) 854-4800; *Fax:* (217) 854-4810
www.wibi.org
wibi@wibi.org
License: Vandalia, Fayette County, IL held by Illinois Bible Institute Inc.
Arbitron Metro Market: Carlinville, IL; *Format:* Christian
Barry Copeland, General Manager
Tom Greene, Station Manager
Rob Regal, Programming Director
G. W. Van Alstine, Promotions Manager
Sally Braundmeier, News Director
Greg Kaurin, Chief Engineer
Joe Buchanan, Music Director
LizEilers, Underwriting Director
Angie Carpenter, Office Manager
Brian Miller, Donor Relations Director
Craig Norrenberns, Promotions Assistant & On-Air Weekends

Vernon Hills

WNVR

03-01-1988; 1030 kHz AM; 27 kw-D, 0.8 kw-N, 8 kw-CH
3656 W. Belmont Ave., Chicago, IL 60618 US
(773) 588-6300
www.polskieradio.com
License: Vernon Hills, IL held by Polnet Communications Ltd.
Group Owner: Polnet Communications Ltd.
Wire Services: AP
Arbitron Metro Market: Chicago *TV Affiliate:* Pol; *Format:* Ethnic *Special Programming:* news progmg 20 hrs wkly; *Hrs. of News Programming:* 7; *No. News Employees:* 18-54; Polish speaking au
Walter Kotaba, President

Virden

WCVS-FM

05-10-1982; 96.7 MHz FM; *Hrs Open:* 24; 6 kw; 328 ft.; N39 38 2 W89 48 50
600 Congress Ave., Suite 1400, Austin, TX 78701 US
(217) 528-3033; *Fax:* (217) 528-5348
www.wcvs.com
License: Virden, Macoupin County, IL held by Neuhoff Family L.P.
Group Owner: Neuhoff Family L.P.; (acq 8-1-2007; grpsl)
Nat'l Reps: Christal
Arbitron Metro Market: Springfield, IL; *Format:* Rock/AOR; *No. News Employees:* 1; *Target Audience:* 18-49; m/p
Kevin O'Dea, General Manager
Kevin Anfield, General Sales Mgr
Danielle Outlaw, Programming Director
Jeff Hofmann, News Director
Frank Konwinski, Chief Engineer
Jeremy Anderson, Program Director
Michelle Mitchell, PromotionsDirector

Virginia

WVIL

02-01-1998; 101.3 MHz FM; *Hrs Open:* 24; 4 kw; 390 ft; N40 00 52 W90 19 55
108 E. Main, Beardstown, IL 63105
(217) 323-1790; *Fax:* (217) 323-1705
www.wvilfm.com
License: Virginia, Cass County, IL held by LB Sports Productions LLC
Nat'l Network: Fox Sports; *Regional Network:* Ill. Radio Net.
Population Served: 65,000 *Hrs. of News Programming:* news progmg one hr wkly; *No. News Employees:* 1; *Target Audience:* 18-65; general
Larry Bostwick, General Manager
Missy DeGroot, Station Manager
Brenda Lawless, General Sales Mgr
Jayneece Bostwick, Programming Director
Gary Glaenzer, Chief Engineer

Warsaw

***WIUW**
05-17-1995; 89.5 MHz FM; *Hrs Open:* 24; 10.6 kw; 443 ft.; N40 20 44 W91 24 11 *Rebroadcasts:* Rebroadcasts WIUM(FM) Macomb 100%
1 University Circle, Macomb, IL 61455 US
(309) 298-2424; *Fax:* (309) 298-2133
www.tristatesradio.com
publicradio@wiu.edu
License: Warsaw, Hancock County, IL held by Western Illinois University.
Format: News; *Hrs. of News Programming:* news progmg 58 hrs wkly; *No. News Employees:* 2; *Target Audience:* General.
Ken Thermon, Operations Dir
Dorothy Vallillo, General Manager
Sharon Faust, General Sales Mgr
Rich Egger, News Director

Watseka

WGFA
09-01-1960; 1360 kHz AM; *Hrs Open:* 6 AM-6 PM; 1 kw-D, DAD; N40 47 37 W87 45 17
Rte 4, P.O. Box 100, Watseka, IL 60970 US
(815) 432-4955; *Fax:* (815) 432-4957
www.wgfaradio.com
info@wgfaradio.com
License: Watseka, IL held by Iroquois County Broadcasting Co.
Nat'l Network: Salem Radio Network; *Regional Network:* Ill. Radio Net.
Format: Talk; *Hrs. of News Programming:* news progmg 14 hrs wkly; *No. News Employees:* 2; *Target Audience:* 30-65; upscale
Justin Kaiser, Operations Dir
Margaret Martin, General Manager
Stacey Smith, Station Manager

WGFA-FM
03-02-1961; 94.1 MHz FM; *Hrs Open:* 24; 50 kw; Ant 364 ft; N40 47 37 W87 45 17
1973 E. 1950 North Rd., Watseka, IL 60970
(815) 432-4955; *Fax:* (815) 432-4957
www.wgfaradio.com
941fm@wgfaradio.com
License: Watseka, Iroquois County, IL held by Iroquois County Broadcasting Co.
Nat'l Network: ABC; *Nat'l Reps:* Farmakis; Katz Radio
Population Served: 150,000 *Special Programming:* Farm 18 hrs, business 2 hrs, sports 18 hrs wkly; *Hrs. of News Programming:* news progmg 12 hrs wkly; *No. News Employees:* 2; *Target Audience:* 25-54.
Don Elliot, Operations Dir
Margaret Martin, General Manager
Stacey Smith, Station Manager
Carl Gerdovich, News Director
Del Dayton, Chief Engineer
M'Lissa Long, Regional Sales Manager

Waukegan

WKRS
09-25-1949; 1220 kHz AM; *Hrs Open:* 24; 1 kw-D, DA2; 0.09 kw-N, DA2; N42 20 59 W87 52 53
980 N. Michigan Ave., Suite 1880, Chicago, IL 60611 US
(847) 336-7900; *Fax:* (847) 336-1523
www.wkrs.com
License: Waukegan, IL held by NM Licensing LLC.
Group Owner: NextMedia Group Inc.; (acq 11-26-01; grpsl).
Arbitron Metro Market: Chicago, IL; *Format:* News, News/Talk, 86; *Hrs. of News Programming:* news progmg 40 hrs wkly; *No. News Employees:* 4; *Target Audience:* 25 plus.
Kira La Fond, General Manager
Libby Collins, Programming Director

WXLC
05-01-1963; 102.3 MHz FM; 3 kw; 322 ft.; N42 20 59 W87 52 53
980 N. Michigan Ave., Suite 1880, Chicago, IL 60611 US
(847) 336-7900; *Fax:* (847) 336-1523
www.1023xlc.com
pwenzel@nextmediachicago.com
License: Waukegan, Lake County, IL
Group Owner: NextMedia Group Inc.
Arbitron Metro Market: Waukegan, IL; *Format:* Adult Contemp; *Target Audience:* 25-44.
Rory Fraley, General Manager
Mike Peof, General Sales Mgr
Haynes Johns, Programming Director
Paul Wenzel, Advertising

West Frankfort

WFRX
05-02-1951; 1300 kHz AM; 1 kw-D, ND1; 0.06 kw-N, ND1; N37 53 4 W88 55 44
330 East Kilbourn Ave., Suite 250, Milwaukee, WI 53202 US
(618) 997-8123; *Fax:* (618) 993-2319
License: West Frankfort, IL held by Withers Broadcasting of Southern Illinois LLC.
Group Owner: Withers Broadcasting Co.; (acq 3-17-2008; grpsl)
Nat'l Network: Jones Radio Networks
Arbitron Metro Market: Marion-Carbondale (Southern Illinois); *Format:* Big Band, News; *Hrs. of News Programming:* news progmg 20 hrs wkly; *No. News Employees:* 2; *Target Audience:* P45+.
Paxton Guy, Operations Dir
Janet Jensen, General Manager
Gina Heern, General Sales Mgr
Stavey Malick, Promotions Manager
Tim Deterding, Chief Engineer

West Terre Haute

WZJK
01-01-1967; 105.5 MHz FM; 295 ft.; N39 27 13 W87 28 15
2865 S. 325 W. Country Rd., Rockville, IN 47834 USA
(765) 569-3940; *Fax:* (765) 569-3945
www.1055wzjk.com
License: West Terre Haute, IN held by DLC Media, Inc.
Group Owner: DLC Media, Inc.

Jim Osborn, Operations Dir
Kandee Cook, General Sales Mgr
Denise Fields, Traffic Director

Wheaton

***WETN**
02-27-1962; 88.1 MHz FM; *Hrs Open:* 24; 0.25 kw; 141 ft.; N41 52 9 W88 5 56
501 E. College Avenue, Billy Graham Center, Wheaton, IL 60187 US
(630)752-5000; *Fax:* (630) 752-5286
www.wetn.org
wetn@wheaton.edu
License: Wheaton, Du Page County, IL held by Trustees of Wheaton College.
Arbitron Metro Market: Wheaton, IL; *Format:* Christian, Classical *Special Programming:* Live sports 5 hrs, live church svcs 3 hrs, live concerts 2 hrs wkly; *Hrs. of News Programming:* News progmg 2 hrs wkly *TargetAudience:* 18-49.
Dr. A. Duane Litfin, President
John Rorvik, General Manager
Mark Bartlebaugh, Station Manager

Willow Springs

WCPT-AM
01-01-1941; 820 kHz AM; *Hrs Open:* Daylight; 5.8 kW; N41 58 53 W87 46 20
5475 N Milwaukee Ave, Chicago, IL 60630 USA
(773) 792-0400
www.wcpt820.com
License: Willow Springs, IL held by WYPA Inc.
Group Owner: Newsweb Corp.; (acq 2-15-2001; $10.5 million)
Nat'l Network: CNN Radio
Arbitron Metro Market: Chicago; *Format:* Talk; *Target Audience:* 25-64; adults
Matt Comings, Operations Manager
Chris Schrage, Promotions Coordinator
Mike McCarthy, Chief Engineer

Wilmington

WYKT
09-29-1980; 105.5 MHz FM; 1.3 kw; 482 ft.; N41 17 11 W88 14 23
P.O. Box 92, Warrenville, IL 60555 US
(815) 935-9555; *Fax:* (815) 935-9593
wkan@starradio.com
License: Wilmington, Will County, IL held by STARadio Corp.
Group Owner: STARadio Corp.; acq 7-6-98)
Arbitron Metro Market: Wilmington, IL; *Format:* Oldies *Special Programming:* Gospel 4 hrs, pub svc 4 hrs, sports 12 hrs wkly; *Hrs. of News Programming:* news progmg 4 hrs wkly; *No. News Employees:* 1 *TargetAudience:* 25-54.
Robert Kersmarki, Operations Dir
Larry Regnier, General Sales Mgr
Brendan Michaels, Operations Manager

Winnebago

WRTB
01-01-1971; 95.3 MHz FM; *Hrs Open:* 24; 1.25 kW; 512 ft.; N42 17 26 W89 9 51
2830 Sandy Hollow Rd, Rockford, IL 61109 USA
(815) 874-7861
www.953thebull.com
License: Winnebago, Winnebago County, IL held by Mid-Way Radio, Inc.
Group Owner: Mid-West Family Broadcasting
Nat'l Reps: Katz Radio
Arbitron Metro Market: Rockford, IL; *Format:* Country, Adult Contemp; *Target Audience:* 25-54.
Mark Van Allen, Operations Dir
Mike Paterson, General Manager
Kim DiGiovanni, General Sales Mgr

Winnetka

***WNTH**
12-10-1960; 88.1 MHz FM; 0.1 kw; 82 ft.; N42 5 40 W87 43 7
385 Winnetka Avenue, Winnetka, IL 60093 US
(847) 784-2330; *Fax:* (847) 501-6400
License: Winnetka, Cook County, IL held by New Trier Township Board of Education.
Arbitron Metro Market: Cook, IL; *Format:* Variety/Diverse
Nina Lynn, Station Manager

Wonder Lake

***WTZY**
91.3 MHz FM; 4 kw; N42 27 53 W88 25 29
150 West Lincolnway, Suite 2001, Valparaiso, IN 46383 US
(219) 548-5800; *Fax:* (219) 548-5808
www.calvaryradionetwork.com
info@CalvaryRadioNetwork.com
License: Wonder Lake, IL held by Calvary Radio Network, Inc.
Group Owner: Calvary Radio Network
Format: Christian, Religious; *Target Audience:* 18-54

Wood River

KFNS
10-05-1961; 590 kHz AM; 1 kw-D, DA2; 1 kw-N, DA2; N38 55 43 W90 5 8 *Rebroadcasts:* Simulcast with KFNS-FM Troy, MO 100%
7000 Chippewa Avenue, Suite 200, St. Louis, MO 63119 US
(314) 962-0590; *Fax:* (314) 962-7576
www.kfns.com
License: Wood River, IL held by Big Stick One LLC.
Group Owner: Big League Broadcasting LLC; (acq 7-13-2004; grpsl)
Nat'l Reps: Interep
Arbitron Metro Market: Wood River, IL; *Format:* Sports; *Target Audience:* 25-54; men
Dave Greene, General Manager
James Oelklaus, General Sales Mgr

Woodlawn

WDML
11-05-1993; 106.9 MHz FM; *Hrs Open:* 24; 3 kw; 328 ft.; N38 21 29 W89 5 56
P.O. Box 1591, Mt. Vernon, IL 62864 US
(618) 242-3333; *Fax:* (618) 242-2490
www.wdml.com
wdml@mvn.net
License: Woodlawn, Jefferson County, IL held by Volunteer Broadcasting of Illinois Inc.
Nat'l Network: Westwood One
Arbitron Metro Market: Woodlawn, IL; *Format:* Rock/AOR *Special Programming:* Christian rock 3 hrs wkly, House of Blues Radio Hour; *Hrs. of News Programming:* everyday 5 3 minute segments; *No. News Employees:* 1 *Target Audience:* 30 plus; male; *Adv. Rates:* 15; 15; 15; 13
David Lister, CEO
Ryan Roddy, COO

Woodstock

WZSR
05-24-1974; 105.5 MHz FM; 1.6 kw; 568 ft.; N42 15 34 W88 21 45
8800 Route 14, Crystal Lake, IL 60012 US
(815) 459-7000; *Fax:* (815) 459-7027
www.star105.com
License: Woodstock, McHenry County, IL held by NM Licensing LLC.
Group Owner: NextMedia Group Inc.; (acq 11-26-01; grpsl).
Wire Services: UPI

Arbitron Metro Market: Crystal Lake, IL; *Format:* Adult Contemp
Special Programming: Relg one hr wkly; *Target Audience:* 25-54; female
Doug Boyd, General Sales Mgr
Steve Cherry, Programming Director
Erica Lorenz, Promotions Manager
Stew Cohen, News Director
Floyd Evans, VP, Regional Manager

***WZKL**
91.7 MHz FM; 6.5 kw vert; 354 ft.; N42 17 56 W88 35 34
600 W. Mason Street, Springfield, IL 62702 US
(916) 251-1600; *Fax:* (916) 251-1650
www.klove.com
License: Woodstock, McHenry County, IL held by Educational Media Foundation.
Group Owner: EMF Broadcasting; (acq 5-22-2008; $32,000 for CP)
Arbitron Metro Market: Woodstock, IL
Darrell Chambliss, Chairman
Alan Mason, CEO/COO
Mike Novak, President
David Pierce, Chief Creative Officer
Alan Mason, Chief Operating Officer
Eric Moser, Chief Financial Officer
Brian Burger, Vice President of Human Resources

Zion

WPJX
09-19-1967; 1500 kHz AM *Rebroadcasts:* Simulcast with WEEF(AM) Highland Park 100%
3656 W. Belmont Ave., Chicago, IL 60618 US
(773) 588-6300; *Fax:* (773) 588-0834
www.pclradio.com
License: Zion, IL held by Polnet Communications Ltd.
Group Owner: Polnet Communications Ltd.; (acq 5-15-2006; $230,000)
Arbitron Metro Market: Lake County, IL; *Format:* Spanish
Sara Vargas, General Manager

WWDV
01-01-1962; 96.9 MHz FM; 50 kw horiz, 38 kw vert; 486 ft.; N42 30 35 W87 53 11
875 N. Michigan Ave., Suite 1510, Chicago, IL 60611 US
(312) 274-9710; *Fax:* (312) 274-1304
www.wdrv.com
License: Zion, Lake County, IL held by Chicago FCC License Sub LLC
Group Owner: Hubbard Broadcasting Inc.; (acq 1-19-2011).
Population Served: 18,500; *Arbitron Metro Market:* Chicago, IL; *Format:* Classic Rock
John Gallagher, Vice President and Market Manager
David Kruse, General Sales Mgr
Curtiss Johnson, Programming Director
Matt Spaetzel, Sales Promotion Manager
Kathy Voltmer, News and Public Affairs Manager
Kent Lewin, ChiefEngineer
Tom Couch, Director of Creative Services
Paul Webber, Direct Marketing Manager
Jeff Buti, Digital Media Director

Indiana

Alexandria

WBKQ
96.7 MHz FM; 2.5 kw; 351 ft.; N40 10 38 W85 40 23
800 East 29th St, Muncie, IN 47302 US
(765) 288-4403; *Fax:* (765) 288-0429
www.967blakefm.com
blake@woofboom.com
License: Alexandria, Madison County, IN held by Woof Boom Radio Muncie License LLC
Group Owner: Woof Boom Radio, LLC; (acq. from Backyard Broadcasting)
Format: Country; *Adv. Rates:* 34; 34; 34; 18
J. Chapman, President
Steve Lindell, General Manager
Jay Garrison, Programming Director
Sean Mattingly, Director of Technical Operations
Blake, On-Air Personality

Anderson

***WBSB**
12-01-1996; 89.5 MHz FM; 0.4 kw vert; 364 ft.; N40 10 38 W85 40 23 *Rebroadcasts:* Rebroadcasts WBST(FM) Muncie 100%
Ad 103, Muncie, IN 47306 US
(765) 285-5888; *Fax:* (765) 285-8937
www.bsu.edu/ipr
info@bsu.edu/ipr
License: Anderson, Madison County, IN held by Ball State University.
Arbitron Metro Market: Muncie, IN; *Format:* News; *No. News Employees:* 1
Marcus Jackman, General Manager
Pam Coletti, General Sales Mgr
Steven Turpin, Programming Director
Carol Trimmer, Promotions Manager
Dorothy Marvell, News Director
Robert Mittendorf, Chief Engineer
Brian Beaver, News Reporter
Angie Rapp, Marketing Manager
Debbie Webb, Underwriting Adviser

***WGNR-AM**
01-01-1946; 1470 kHz AM; *Hrs Open:* 12 hrs; 1 kW-D, 0.036 kW-N; N40 3 43 W85 42 37
1920 W 53rd St, Anderson, IN 46013 USA
(888) 877-9467
www.radiomoody.org
License: Anderson, IN held by The Moody Bible Institute of Chicago
Group Owner: The Moody Bible Institute of Chicago
Nat'l Network: Radio Moody
Arbitron Metro Market: Anderson-Indianapolis; *Format:* Christian; *Target Audience:* 35-54.

***WGNR-FM**
09-11-1973; 97.9 MHz FM; *Hrs Open:* 24; 50 kW; 489 ft.; N40 3 43 W85 42 34
1920 W 53rd St, Anderson, IN 46013 USA
(888) 877-9467
www.moodyradio.org/stations/indiana
License: Anderson, Madison County, IN held by The Moody Bible Institute of Chicago
Group Owner: The Moody Bible Institute of Chicago; (acq 12-17-97; $5.5 million with co
Arbitron Metro Market: Indianapolis, IN; *Format:* Christian; *No. News Employees:* 1; *Target Audience:* 35-54.

WHBU
1240 kHz AM; *Hrs Open:* 24; 0.7 kw, ND2; N40 04 25 W85 41 58
Rebroadcasts: Translator: W279CL (FM) 103.7
800 East 29th Ste, Muncie, IN 47302 US
(765) 288-4403; *Fax:* (765) 288-0429
www.1240whbu.com
studio@1240whbu.com
License: Anderson, Madison County, IN held by Woof Boom Radio Muncie License, LLC
Group Owner: Woof Boom Radio
Format: News, News/Talk, 86; *Hrs. of News Programming:* news progmg 40 hrs wkly; *No. News Employees:* 1; *Target Audience:* 25-54.
Steve Lindell, Operations Dir
Brett Beshore, Promotions Manager

WQME
11-29-1990; 98.7 MHz FM; *Hrs Open:* 0000 - 2400, 24 hours per day, ever; 4.5 kw; 384 ft.; N39 58 59 W85 42 41
1100 East Fifth Street, Anderson, IN 46012 US
(765) 641-4349; *Fax:* (765) 641-3825
www.wqme.com
email@wqme.com
License: Anderson, Madison County, IN held by Anderson University Inc.
Nat'l Network: CNN Radio; *Wire Services:* AP
Format: Adult Contemp, Christian *Special Programming:* Relg 9 hrs wkly; *Hrs. of News Programming:* News progmg 8 hrs wkly; *Target Audience:* 25-54.; *Adv. Rates:* 20; 20; 20; 20
Donald Boggs, General Manager
Gerald Longenbaugh, General Sales Mgr
Matt Rust, Programming Director
Jill O'Malia, Promotions Manager
Norma Armogum, News Director
Jerry Morton, Engineering Dir

Angola

***WEAX**
09-01-1979; 88.3 MHz FM; *Hrs Open:* 24; 0.57 kw; 299 ft.; N41 41 12 W84 59 53
Stewart Hall W. Park St., Angola, IN 46703 US
(260) 665-4288
www.88xradio.com
License: Angola, Steuben County, IN held by Tri-State University.
Nat'l Network: CNN Radio
Arbitron Metro Market: Angola, IN.; *Format:* Alternative; *Hrs. of News Programming:* News progmg one hrs wkly; *Target Audience:* 18-44.
Josh Hornbacker, Operations Dir

WLKI
07-15-1974; 100.3 MHz FM; *Hrs Open:* 24; 4 kw; 394 ft.; N41 40 51 W85 0 5
Mailing Address: P.O. Box 999, Angola, IN 46703 US
Second Address: 2655 State Rd. 127N, Angola, IN 46703
(260) 665-9554; *Fax:* (260) 665-9064
www.wlki.com
wlki@wlki.com
License: Angola, Steuben County, IN held by Lake Cities Broadcasting Corp.
Group Owner: Lake Cities Broadcasting Corp.
Format: Adult Contemp; *Target Audience:* 25-49; adults with youthful outlook, skews female; *Adv. Rates:* 18.65; 18.65; 18.65; 18.65.
Thomas Andrews, President
Bill Kerner, Operations Dir
Andy St. John, Programming Director
Jim Measel, News Director
Greg Case, Chief Engineer

Attica

WSHP
04-01-1990; 95.7 MHz FM; 3.1 kw; 433 ft.; N40 23 2 W87 7 55
50 East Rivercenter Blvd, Suite 1200, Covington, KY 41011 US
(765) 474-1410; *Fax:* (765) 474-3442
License: Attica, Fountain County, IN held by Artistic Media Partners L.P.
Group Owner: Artistic Media Partners Inc.; (acq 10-3-94; $410,000;
Nat'l Reps: Christal
Arbitron Metro Market: Lafayette, IN; *Format:* Classic Rock; *Target Audience:* 25-54.; *Adv. Rates:* 32; 32; 32; 15
Arthur Angotti, General Manager
Steve Clark, Programming Director
Bob Henning, Chief Engineer

***WFWR**
01-01-2002; 91.5 MHz FM; 0.165 kw vert; 171 ft.; N40 16 47 W87 14 50
909 South McDonald St, Attica, IN 47918 US
(765) 764-1934
License: Attica, Fountain County, IN held by Fountain Warren Community Radio Corp.
Arbitron Metro Market: Attica, IN; *Format:* Variety/Diverse
Larry Grant, General Manager
Chris W. Gayler, Sales & Graphic Design
David W. Huckleberry, Web Design, Webmaster & Technical Support
A. Troy Sheridan, Sales & Web Design

Auburn

WGBJ
04-10-1967; 102.3 MHz FM; *Hrs Open:* 24; 6 kw; 315 ft.; N41 21 7 W85 9 55
2000 Lower Huntington Rd, Fort Wayne, IN 46819 US
(260) 482-4444; *Fax:* (260) 482-4410
www.radiounica1023.com
License: Auburn, De Kalb County, IN held by Three Amigo's Broadcasting Inc.
Nat'l Reps: McGavren Guild
Arbitron Metro Market: Fort Wayne, IN
Robert Britt, Operations Dir
Angie Phillips, General Manager

WGLL
09-03-1968; 1570 kHz AM; *Hrs Open:* 17; 0.5 kw-D, DA2; 0.151 kw-N, DA2; N41 20 1 W85 3 8 *Rebroadcasts:* Rebroadcasts WGL(AM) Fort Wayne 100
2000 Lower Huntington Rd, Fort Wayne, IN 46819 US
(260) 925-4300; *Fax:* (260) 432-0986
License: Auburn, IN held by Kovas Communications of Indiana Inc.
Nat'l Network: CBS; *Regional Network:* Network Indiana; *Nat'l Reps:* Rgnl Reps
Arbitron Metro Market: Fort Wayne, IN; *Format:* Religious; *Target Audience:* 25-54.
Raymond Alexander, President

Aurora

WSCH
10-29-1970; 99.3 MHz FM; *Hrs Open:* 24; 1.15 kw; 525 ft.; N38 57 55 W84 56 51
6857 Salem Ridge Road, Aurora, IN 47001 US

(812) 537-0944; *Fax:* (812) 537-5735
www.eaglecountryonline.com
info@eaglecountryonline.com
License: Aurora, Dearborn County, IN held by Wagon Wheel Broadcasting LLC.
Group Owner: Wagon Wheel Broadcasting LLC; (acq 2-1-2008; grpsl)
Nat'l Network: ABC; Motor Racing Net; *Regional Network:* Brownfield
Arbitron Metro Market: Cincinnati, OH; *Format:* Country *Special Programming:* Indiana University Basketball/Football, High Schoo; *Hrs. of News Programming:* 12 one-minute newscasts each weekday *No. News Employees:* 1; *Target Audience:* 25-plus.; *Adv. Rates:* 16; 16; 16; 16

Melissa Murphy, General Manager
Chelsie Shinkle, Programming Director
Mike Perleberg, News Director
Ted Ryan, Chief Engineer

Austin

WJAA

01-01-1991; 96.3 MHz FM; 3 kw; 328 ft.; N38 50 39 W85 49 26
1531 W. Tipton, Seymour, IN 47274 US
(812) 523-3343; *Fax:* (812) 523-5116
www.wjaa.net
coolbus@wjaa.net
License: Austin, Scott County, IN held by Midland Media Inc.
Nat'l Network: ABC; Westwood One
Arbitron Metro Market: Louisville, KY; *Format:* Classic Rock, Rock/AOR; *Hrs. of News Programming:* News progmg 5 hrs wkly; *Target Audience:* 25-54; men & women; *Adv. Rates:* 16; 14; 16; 12

Robert Becker, General Manager
Tony Starkey, General Sales Mgr
Shannon Pyle, Programming Director

WXKU-FM

12-01-1993; 92.7 MHz FM; *Hrs Open:* 24; 3.6 kw; 423 ft.; N38 49 20 W85 47 38
507 North State Street, North Vernon, IN 47265 US
(812) 346-1927; *Fax:* (812) 346-9722
www.wjcr.org
wjcrfm@yahoo.com
License: Austin, Scott County, IN held by BK Media LLC
Nat'l Network: USA
Arbitron Metro Market: Louisville, KY; *Format:* Country; *Hrs. of News Programming:* news progmg 21 hrs wkly; *No. News Employees:* 1; *Target Audience:* 25-65.

Marty Pieratt, General Manager

Batesville

WRBI

05-14-1977; 103.9 MHz FM; *Hrs Open:* 24; 1.95 kw; Ant 360 ft; N39 13 22 W85 15 28
133 S. Main St., Batesville, IN 45215
(812) 934-5111; *Fax:* (812) 934-2765
www.wrbiradio.com
wrbi@wrbiradio.com
License: Batesville, Ripley County, IN held by White River Broadcasting Co. Inc.
Group Owner: The Findlay Publishing Co.; (acq 7-31-97; grpsl).
Nat'l Reps: Rgnl Reps
Population Served: 102,000 *Special Programming:* Farm 5 hrs wkly; *Hrs. of News Programming:* news progmg 10 hrs wkly; *No. News Employees:* 1; *Target Audience:* General.; *Adv. Rates:* 22; 21; 20; 18

Maynard Meyer, CEO
Kris Kuechenmeister, Operations Dir
Ronald Green, General Manager
Caz Burdetter, Programming Director
Mary Mattingly, News Director

Battle Ground

WASK-FM

03-11-1993; 98.7 MHz FM; *Hrs Open:* 24; 4.4 kw; 384 ft.; N40 23 26 W86 51 53
Mailing Address: 3575 McCarty Lane, P O Box 7880, Lafayette, IN 47903 US
Second Address: 3575 McCarty Ln., Lafayette, IN 47905
(765) 447-2186; *Fax:* (765) 448-4452
www.wask.com
License: Battle Ground, Tippecanoe County, IN held by WASK Inc.
Group Owner: Schurz Communications Inc.; (acq 3-6-95; $860,000;
Nat'l Reps: Christal *Regional Reps:* Rgnl Reps.; *Wire Services:* AP
Arbitron Metro Market: Lafayette, IN; *Format:* Oldies; *Hrs. of News Programming:* news progmg 20 hrs wkly; *No. News Employees:* 4; *Target Audience:* 35 plus; general

John Trent, President
Mark Allen, Operations Dir
Brian Green, General Sales Mgr
Bryan McGarvey, Programming Director
Steve Truex, Chief Engineer

Bedford

WBIW

10-01-1948; 1340 kHz AM; *Hrs Open:* 24; 1 kw-U, ND1; N38 52 23 W86 28 34
P. O. Box 1307, Bedford, IN 47421 US
(812) 275-7555; *Fax:* (812) 279-8046
www.wbiw.com
comments@wbiw.com
License: Bedford, IN held by Ad-Venture Media Inc.
Nat'l Network: Westwood One; USA; *Regional Network:* Network Indiana; Brownfield; *Nat'l Reps:* Rgnl Reps
Arbitron Metro Market: Bedford, IN; *Format:* News, Sports, 86 *Special Programming:* Sports, weather, farm 3 hrs wkly; *Hrs. of News Programming:* news progmg 28 hrs wkly; *No. News Employees:* 1; *Target Audience:* 25 plus; general; *Adv. Rates:* 22; 17; 22; 16

Dean Spencer, President

WQRK

10-01-1975; 105.5 MHz FM; *Hrs Open:* 24; 2 kw; 400 ft.; N38 54 29 W86 28 28
P. O. Box 1307, Bedford, IN 47421 US
(812) 275-7555; *Fax:* (812) 279-8046
www.superoldies.net
oldies105@hpcisp.com
License: Bedford, Lawrence County, IN
Nat'l Network: ABC
Arbitron Metro Market: Indianapolis, I; *Format:* Oldies; *Hrs. of News Programming:* news progmg 8 hrs wkly; *No. News Employees:* 1; *Target Audience:* 35-55; upscale adults

Becky Riopel, General Manager

Beech Grove

WNTS

12-10-1956; 1590 kHz AM; *Hrs Open:* 24; 5 kw-D, DA2; 0.5 kw-N, DA2; N39 44 21 W86 5 29; N39 44 21 W86 5 26
4800 East Raymond St., Indianapolis, IN 46203 US
(317) 472-7137; *Fax:* (317) 472-7138
License: Beech Grove, IN held by Davidson Media Station WNTS Licensee LLC.
Group Owner: Davidson Media Group LLC; (acq 9-28-2005; $2 million)
Arbitron Metro Market: Indianapolis, IN

Steve Stiegelmeyer, General Manager
Mayra Arroyo, Programming Director

Berne

WZBD

08-27-1993; 92.7 MHz FM; *Hrs Open:* 5 AM-10 PM; 4.1 kw; 394 ft.; N40 46 15 W84 56 5
Mailing Address: 935 Sandy Hollow Lane, Portland, IN 47371 US
Second Address: 955 US 27 N., Berne, IN 46711
(260) 726-8729; *Fax:* (260) 726-4311
License: Berne, Adams County, IN held by Adams County Radio Inc.
Arbitron Metro Market: Fort Wayne, IN; *Format:* Adult Contemp, News; *Target Audience:* General.

Rob Weaver, President
Tony Giltner, Operations Dir

Bicknell

WUZR

06-04-1991; 105.7 MHz FM; *Hrs Open:* 24; 1.8 kw; 427 ft.; N38 43 47 W87 24 44
522 Busseron St., Vincennes, IN 47591 USA
(812) 882-6060; *Fax:* (812) 882-7770
www.wuzr.com
wuzr@originalcompany.com
License: Bicknell, IN held by The Original Company, Inc.
Group Owner: The Original Company Inc.
Arbitron Metro Market: Vincennes, IN; *Format:* Country

Mark Lange, President

Bloomfield

WMYJ-FM

101.1 MHz FM; 3.8 kw; 128 meters; N39 05 23 W86 44 25
Box 1970, Martinsville, IN 46151 US
(765) 349-1485; *Fax:* (765) 342-3569
www.spirit95fm.com
License: Bloomfield, IN held by Mid-America Radio Group Inc.
Group Owner: Mid-America Radio Group Inc.

David C. Keister, President

Bloomington

WBWB

07-17-1978; 96.7 MHz FM; *Hrs Open:* 24; 1.65 kw; 440 ft.; N39 9 46 W86 28 21
Mailing Address: 50 East Rivercenter Blvd, Suite 1200, Covington, KY 41011 US
Second Address: 304 State Rd. 446, Bloomington, IN 47401
(812) 336-8000; *Fax:* (812) 336-7000
www.wbwb.com
arthur@artisticradio.com
License: Bloomington, Monroe County, IN held by Artistic Media Partners L.P.
Group Owner: Artistic Media Partners Inc.; (acq 1-89; grpsl;
Nat'l Reps: McGavren Guild *Regional Reps:* Rgnl Reps.
Arbitron Metro Market: Bloomington, IN; *Format:* Contemporary Hits/Top 40; *No. News Employees:* 1; *Target Audience:* 18-49.

Arthur Angotti III, CEO/COO
Arthur Angotti III, President
Jim Wodock, General Manager
Jim Wodock, General Sales Mgr
Kevin Stockbridge, Programming Director
Bob Henning, Chief Engineer

*WFHB

12-01-1992; 91.3 MHz FM; *Hrs Open:* 24; 1.6 kw; 390 ft.; N39 1 18 W86 36 5
Mailing Address: P.O. Box 1973, Bloomington, IN 47402 US
Second Address: 108 W. 4th St., Bloomington, IN 47404
(812) 323-1200; *Fax:* (812) 323-0320
www.wfhb.org
volunteer@wfhb.org
License: Bloomington, Monroe County, IN held by Bloomington Community Radio Inc.
Arbitron Metro Market: Bloomington, IN; *Format:* News, Variety/Diverse *Special Programming:* Folk 10 hrs, Latin 3 hrs, Finnish 3 hrs wkly; *Hrs. of News Programming:* news progmg 5 hrs wkly; *No. News Employees:* 1 *Target Audience:* General.

Chad Carrothers, General Manager
Alycin Bektesh, News Director
Jeffrey Morris, Chief Engineer
Joe Crawford, Assistant News Director
Jim Manion, Music Director

*WFIU

09-30-1950; 103.7 MHz FM; *Hrs Open:* 24; 29 kw; 646 ft.; N39 8 31 W86 29 43
Indiana University, 1mu Messanine 005, Bloomington, IN 47405 US
(812) 855-1357; *Fax:* (812) 855-5600
www.indianapublicmedia.org
License: Bloomington, Monroe County, IN held by Trustees of Indiana University.
Nat'l Network: NPR
Arbitron Metro Market: Bloomington, IN *TV Affiliate:* *WTIU(TV) affil.; *Format:* Jazz, News; *Hrs. of News Programming:* news progmg 7 hrs wkly; *No. News Employees:* 1; *Target Audience:* General.

Donna Stroup, CFO
Brad Howard, Director of Engineering and Operations
Christina Kuzmych, Station Manager
Will Murphy, News Director
Bradley Howard, Chief Engineer
Eva Zogorski, Membership Director
John Wright, Computer Networkand Support
Marianne Woodruff, Corporate Development Manager
Scott Witzke, TV Marketing Director
Matt Stonecipher, Computer and Networking Support Analyst
Bill Shaw, News Coordinator

WGCL

03-11-1949; 1370 kHz AM; *Hrs Open:* 24
P.O. Box 2717, Bloomington, IN 47402 US
(812) 332-3366; *Fax:* (812) 331-4570
www.wgclradio.com
info@wgclradio.com
License: Bloomington, IN held by Sarkes Tarzian Inc.
Group Owner: Sarkes Tarzian Inc.
Nat'l Network: ABC; ESPN Radio; *Nat'l Reps:* Christal
Format: News, News/Talk, 86; *Hrs. of News Programming:* news progmg 5 hrs wkly; *No. News Employees:* 2; *Target Audience:* 30 plus.; *Adv. Rates:* 37; 37; 37; 25

Ron Tarsi, General Manager
Ducan Myers, General Sales Mgr

Don Pratt, Programming Director
Marc Antonetti, Chief Engineer

WTTS
01-07-1960; 92.3 MHz FM; *Hrs Open:* 24; 37 kw; 1089 ft.; N39 24 27 W86 8 52
P.O. Box 62, Bloomington, IN 47402 US
(317) 972-9887; *Fax:* (317) 972-9886
www.wttsfm.com
comments@wttsfm.com
License: Bloomington, Monroe County, IN
Group Owner: Sarkes Tarzian Inc.
Nat'l Reps: Christal
Arbitron Metro Market: Indianapolis, IN; *Format:* Triple A *Special Programming:* Blues 2 hrs, acoustic show 4 hrs wkly; *No. News Employees:* 1; *Target Audience:* 25-54.
Geoff Vargo, VP/General Manager
Daryl McIntire, General Sales Mgr
Brad Holtz, Programming Director
Josh Lantz, Promotions Manager
Laura Duncan, Music Director
Marcie Beasley, Controller
Jake Keebler, Production Director
ErinMasterson, Traffic Director

Bluffton

WFCV-FM
100.1 MHz FM; 6 kw; 299 ft.; N40 52 10 W85 10 20
3737 Lake Ave., Fort Wayne, IN 46805 US
(260) 423-2337
www.bottradionetwork.com
comments@bottradionetwork.com
License: Bluffton, Wells County, IN held by Bott Communications Inc.
Group Owner: Bott Radio Network
Arbitron Metro Market: Fort Wayne, IN; *Format:* Christian, Talk; *Target Audience:* 25-54; family oriented
Richard Bott Sr., President & CEO
Eben Fowler, Operations Dir
Dale Gerke, General Manager
Pat Rulon, Director of National Sales
Candy Green, Program Services Manager
Rachel Launius, Marketing Manager
Jason Potocnik, Director ofTraffic Operations

Boonville

WBNL
09-10-1950; 1540 kHz AM; *Hrs Open:* 24; 0.25 kw-D, ND2; 0.001 kw-N, ND2; N38 3 58 W87 16 27
Mailing Address: P.O. Box 270, Boonville, IN 47601 US
Second Address: 2177 N. Hwy. 61, Boonville, IN 47601
(812) 897-2080; *Fax:* (812) 897-2130
www.radio1540.net
rturpen@1540.net
License: Boonville, IN held by Turpen Communications LLC
Nat'l Network: USA; *Regional Network:* Network Indiana
Arbitron Metro Market: Boonville,IN; *Format:* Adult Contemp
Special Programming: Gospel 5 hrs wkly; *Hrs. of News Programming:* news progmg 14 hrs wkly; *No. News Employees:* 1; *Target Audience:* 25-54; Women25-54; *Adv. Rates:* 14; 14; 14; na
Ralph Turpen, President

WEJK
12-19-1967; 107.1 MHz FM; *Hrs Open:* 24; 1.6 kw; 640 ft.; N37 59 13 W87 16 11
Mailing Address: P. O. Box 270, Boonville, IN 47601 US
Second Address: 1162 Mt. Auburn Rd., Evansville, IN 47720
(812) 424-8284; *Fax:* (812) 421-3273
www.1071jackfm.com/
pbrayfield@southcentralmedia.com
License: Boonville, Warrick County, IN held by Boonville Broadcasting Co. Inc.
Group Owner: South Central Communications Corp.; (acq 8-14-2000; $400,000 for stock
Arbitron Metro Market: Evansville, IN
John Engelbrecht, CEO
Tim Huelsing, Operations Dir
Paul Brayfield, General Sales Mgr
Rsuty James, Programming Director
Chris Myers, Chief Engineer

WJPS
08-01-1992; 107.1 MHz FM; 1.6 kw; 295 ft.; N37 59 3 W87 16 11
522 Busseron St., Vincennes, IN 47591 US
(812) 882-6060
www.wjpsradio.com
marklange@originalcompany.com
License: Boonville, IN held by The Original Company, Inc.
Group Owner: The Original Company Inc.
Arbitron Metro Market: Vincennes, IN; *Format:* Adult Contemp
Mark Lange, President
Jonathan Lange, Operations Mgr.

Brazil

WAMB
01-01-1959; 1130 kHz AM; *Hrs Open:* 6 AM-2 hrs past sunset; 500 w-D, 20 w-N; N39 30 44 W87 08 18
111 W. National Ave., Brazil, IN 47834 USA
(812) 420-2518
wambradio.com
License: Brazil, Clay County, IN held by DLC Media, Inc.
Group Owner: DLC Media, Inc.
Regional Network: Network Indiana
Population Served: 25,000; *Arbitron Metro Market:* Brazil, IN; *No. News Employees:* 1; *Target Audience:* General; sports fans; *Adv. Rates:* 8; 8; 8; 4
Tyler Davis, News Director

WSDM-FM
11-13-1973; 92.7 MHz FM; *Hrs Open:* 24; 6 kw; Ant 298 ft; N39 30 44 W87 08 18
, Terre Haute, IN USA
License: Brazil, Clay County, IN held by Indiana Community Radio Corporation
Group Owner: Indiana Community Radio Coporation
Population Served: 100,000; *Arbitron Metro Market:* Terre Haute, IN; *Hrs. of News Programming:* news progmg 2 hrs wkly; *No. News Employees:* 1; *Adv. Rates:* 16; 16; 16; 16

WFNB
92.7 MHz FM; 6 kW
111 W. National Ave, Brazil, IN 47834 USA
(812) 420-2518
www.lite927wfnb.com
License: Brazil, IN held by DLC Media, Inc.
Group Owner: DLC Media, Inc.
Format: Adult Contemp
Tyler Davis, News Director

WFNF
1130 kHz AM; .5 kW
925 Wabash Ave., Suite 300, Terre Haute, IN 47807 USA
(812) 917-3901
License: Brazil, IN held by DLC Media, Inc.
Group Owner: DLC Media, Inc.
Format: Sports

Bremen

WHPZ
03-01-1993; 96.9 MHz FM; 2 kw; 463 ft.; N41 24 43 W86 1 51
P.O. Box 1538, Marion, IN 46952 US
(574) 291-8200; *Fax:* (574) 291-9043
www.pulsefm.com
License: Bremen, Marshall County, IN held by Le Sea Broadcasting Corp.
Group Owner: Le Sea Broadcasting; (acq 1-4-2000; $280,296).
Format: Christian
Tony Hale, CFO
Anna Riblet, Station Manager
Wes Hylton, Chief Engineer

Brookston

WBPE
04-16-1967; 95.3 MHz FM; *Hrs Open:* 24; 2.3 kw; 505 ft.; N40 32 48 W86 50 59
5520 East 75th Street, Indianapolis, IN 46250 US
(765) 474-1410; *Fax:* (765) 474-3442
www.wbpefm.com
License: Brookston, White County, IN held by Artistic Media Partners Inc.
Group Owner: Artistic Media Partners Inc.; (acq 9-1-98; $1.8 million)
Arbitron Metro Market: Lafayette, IN; *Format:* Adult Contemp; *Hrs. of News Programming:* news progmg 14 hrs wkly; *No. News Employees:* 1; *Target Audience:* 35 plus; affluent, educated & upscale
Ernie Caldemone, General Manager
Kit Osborne, General Sales Mgr
Jimmy Knight, Programming Director
Bob Henning, Chief Engineer

Brownsburg

***WKLU**
03-23-1992; 101.9 MHz FM; *Hrs Open:* 24; 4 kw; 361 ft.; N39 47 13 W86 17 57
733 Green Street, Brownsburg, IN 46112 US
(317) 841-1019; *Fax:* (317) 841-5167
www.wklu.net
bart@wklu.net
License: Brownsburg, Hendricks County, IN held by Indy Radio LLC
Arbitron Metro Market: Indianapolis, IN; *Format:* Oldies *Special Programming:* Beetles brunch; *No. News Employees:* 2; *Target Audience:* 25-54.
Bart Johnson, General Manager
Libby Zabriskie-Farr, Programming Director
Monica Lephart, Promotions Manager
Aimee McGrath, News Director

Cannelton

WCJZ
05-01-2001; 105.7 MHz FM; *Hrs Open:* 24; 2 kw; 584 ft.; N37 47 44 W86 50 58
Mailing Address: 71 Altdorf Lane, Cannelton, IN 47586 US
Second Address: 1115 Tamatack Rd., Suite 500, Owensboro, KY 42301
(812) 547-2345; *Fax:* (812) 547-2346
www.wtcjfm.com
jcatinna@cromwellradio.com
License: Cannelton, Perry County, IN
Group Owner: The Cromwell Group Inc.
Arbitron Metro Market: Tell CityM IN; *Format:* Classic Rock
Jan Catinna, General Manager
Mike Chaney, News Director

Carmel

***WHJE**
09-01-1963; 91.3 MHz FM; *Hrs Open:* 24; 0.4 kw; 98 ft.; N39 58 45 W86 7 10
5201 E. 131st Street, Carmel, IN 46032 US
(317) 571-4055; *Fax:* (317) 571-4066
www.whje.com
whje@whje.com
License: Carmel, Hamilton County, IN held by Carmel Clay Schools.
Regional Network: Network Indiana; *Wire Services:* UPI
Format: Alternative, Classic Rock; *Target Audience:* 12 plus.
Tom Schoeller, General Manager

Centerville

WHON
02-17-1964; 930 kHz AM; *Hrs Open:* 24; 0.5 kw-D, DA2; 0.144 kw-N, DA2; N39 53 32 W84 56 8
2626 Tingler Rd., Richmond, IN 47374 US
(765) 962-1595; *Fax:* (765) 966-4824
www.1017thepoint.com
License: Centerville, Wayne County, IN held by Brewer Broadcasting Corp.
Group Owner: Brewer Broadcasting Corp.; (acq 11-20-97)
Nat'l Reps: Rgnl Reps
Arbitron Metro Market: Richmond-Centerville, IN; *Format:* Adult Contemp; *No. News Employees:* 1; *Target Audience:* 35 plus.
Keith Landecker, Operations Manager
Jeff Lane, News Director
Lottie Jordan, Account Manager

Chandler

WLFW
04-02-1994; 93.5 MHz FM; *Hrs Open:* 24; 3.2 kW; 446 ft.; N38 01 27 W87 21 43
1162 Mt. Auburn Rd, Evansville, IN 47720 USA
(812) 424-8284; *Fax:* (812) 426-7928
935duke.com
License: Chandler, Warrick County, IN held by Midwest Communications Inc.
Group Owner: Midwest Communications Inc.
Nat'l Network: Westwood One
Arbitron Metro Market: Evansville, IN; *Format:* Country; *No. News Employees:* 3; *Target Audience:* 35-49.
Storm Avery, Brand Manager

Chesterton

***WBEW**
01-01-2001; 89.5 MHz FM; 4 kw; 597 ft.; N41 38 6 W87 2 59
P.O. Box 2011, Jersey City, NJ 07303 US
(312) 948-4632; *Fax:* (312) 948-4837
www.vocalo.org
info@vocalo.org
License: Chesterton, Porter County, IN held by The WBEZ Alliance Inc.
Arbitron Metro Market: Chicago, IL; *Format:* Jazz, News, 86
Torey Malatia, President
Greg Salustro, General Sales Mgr

***WDSO**
11-01-1976; 88.3 MHz FM; *Hrs Open:* 6 AM Monday through 5 PM Friday; 400 w; 135 ft; N41 36 29 W87 03 37
Chesterton High School, 2125 S. 11th St., Chesterton, IN 46304
(219) 983-3777; *Fax:* (219) 983-3775
License: Chesterton, Porter County, IN held by Duneland School Corp.
Regional Network: Network Indiana
Population Served: 149,200; *Arbitron Metro Market:* Chicago
Special Programming: Class one hr, specialty rock 8 hrs wkly; *Hrs. of News Programming:* News progmg 6 hrs wkly; *Target Audience:* General.
Michele Stipanovich, Operations Dir
Matthew Waters, Station Manager

Churubusco

WNHT
08-01-1994; 96.3 MHz FM; *Hrs Open:* 24; 6.7 kw; 554 ft.; N41 6 13 W85 10 44
2000 Lower Huntington Rd, Fort Wayne, IN 46819 US
(260) 747-1511; *Fax:* (260) 747-3999
wild963.com
jj@summitcityradio.com
License: Churubusco, Whitley County, IN held by Summit City License Sub, LLC.
Group Owner: Summit City Radio Group; (acq 11-6-2006; grpsl)
Nat'l Reps: Eastman Radio
Arbitron Metro Market: Churubusco, IN.; *Format:* Christian; *Target Audience:* 18-34; women
J.J. Fabini, Operations Dir
JJ Fabini, General Manager
Dave Reithmiller, General Sales Mgr
Shady Spencer, Programming Director
Katherine Whatley, Promotions Manager

Cicero

***WJCY**
01-01-2005; 91.5 MHz FM; 0.475 kw; 194 ft.; N40 11 53 W86 7 44 *Rebroadcasts:* Rebroadcasts WHLP (FM)
US
(219) 548-5800; *Fax:* (219) 548-5808
www.calvaryradionetwork.com
info@calvaryradionetwork.com
License: Cicero, Hamilton County, IN held by Calvary Radio Network, Inc.
Group Owner: Calvary Radio Network
Arbitron Metro Market: Cicero, IN; *Format:* Christian, Religious

Clarksville

WTFX-FM
01-01-1998; 93.1 MHz FM; *Hrs Open:* 24; 4.1 kw; 374 ft.; N38 17 2 W85 54 17
4000 #1 Radio Drive, Louisville, KY 40218 US
(502) 479-2222; *Fax:* (502) 479-2223
www.foxrocks.com
License: Clarksville, Clark County, IN held by CC Licenses LLC.
Group Owner: iHeartMedia
Arbitron Metro Market: Louisville, KY; *Format:* Rock/AOR
Kevin Hughes, Senior Vice President of Sales
Charlie Steele, Programming Director

Clinton

***WPFR-FM**
01-01-1998; 93.7 MHz FM; *Hrs Open:* 24; 2.3 kw; 531 ft; N39 33 18 W87 28 40
18889 N. 2350th St., Dennison, IL 62420
(217) 826-9673
wpfr@joink.com
License: Clinton, Vermillion County, IN held by Word Power Inc.
Nat'l Network: Moody
Population Served: 146,605; *Arbitron Metro Market:* Terre Haute, IN; *Hrs. of News Programming:* News progmg 17 hrs wkly; *Target Audience:* 12 plus.; *Adv. Rates:* 30; 30; 30; 30
Paul Ford, President
Eleanor Ford, Operations Dir
Jeff Tucker, Chief Engineer
Dan Watson, Chief of Operations

Cloverdale

***WSPM**
01-01-2003; 89.1 MHz FM; *Hrs Open:* 24; 0.0115 kw horiz, 22.5 kw vert; 423 ft.; N39 41 19 W86 42 3
6434 La Pas Trail, Indianapolis, IN 46268 US
(317) 870-8400; *Fax:* (317) 870-8404
www.catholicradioindy.org
info@catholicradioindy.org
License: Cloverdale, Putnam County, IN held by Hoosier Broadcasting Corp.
Group Owner: Hoosier Broadcasting Corp.
Arbitron Metro Market: Cloverdale, IN; *Format:* Religious
Chuck Cunningham, General Manager
Ed Roehling, General Sales Mgr
Bill Shirk, Programming Director
Jim Ganley, News Director
Marty Hensley, Chief Engineer

Cole

***WHUZ(FM)**
88.1 MHz FM; 100 w vert; Ant 121 ft; N40 27 37.5 W85 46 29.4
15 Wood St., Greenfield, IN 46140
(317) 467-1062
License: Cole, Grant County, IN held by Electronic Applications Radio Service Inc.
Group Owner: Electronic Applications Radio Service Inc.
Population Served: 16,042; *Arbitron Metro Market:* Crawfordsville, IN
Patrick Diemer, President

Columbia City

***WJHS**
08-12-1985; 91.5 MHz FM; *Hrs Open:* 24; 2.65 kw; 220 ft.; N41 10 4 W85 29 41
600 North Whitley Street, Columbia City, IN 46725 US
(260) 248-8915; *Fax:* (260) 244-5610
www.wjhs915.org
wallsll@wjhs915.org
License: Columbia City, Whitley County, IN held by Whitley County Consolidated Schools Board of Contr
Format: Alternative; *Target Audience:* Men 25-54; general
Krystal Walker Zoltek, Station Manager
Laurie Walls, Programming Director

Columbus

WCSI
01-01-1950; 1010 kHz AM; *Hrs Open:* 24; 0.33 kw-D, ND1; 0.018 kw-N, ND1; N39 11 12 W85 57 0
Mailing Address: Box 1789, 3212 Washington St., Columbus, IN 47203 US
Second Address: 3212 Washington St., Columbus, IN 47203
(812) 372-4448; *Fax:* (812) 372-1061
www.1010wcsi.com
License: Columbus, IN held by White River Broadcasting Co.
Group Owner: The Findlay Publishing Co.; (acq 11-1-57)
Regional Reps: Rgnl Reps.; *Wire Services:* CBS
Arbitron Metro Market: Columbus, IN; *Format:* News, News/Talk, 84, Talk; *No. News Employees:* 3; *Target Audience:* 35 plus.
Bob Morrison, Station Manager
Kevin Kelley, Brand Manager
John Foster, Morning Host
Christine Nelson, John Clark
News Director, Mike Sullivan
Manager Of Creative Services, Station Manager

WKKG
01-01-1958; 101.5 MHz FM; *Hrs Open:* 24; 50 kw; 492 ft.; N39 11 12 W85 57 0
Mailing Address: 3212 Washington Street, Columbus, IN 47202 US
Second Address: 3212 Washington St., Columbus, IN 47203
(812) 372-4448; *Fax:* (812) 372-1061
wkkg.com
wkkg@wkkg.com
License: Columbus, Bartholomew County, IN
Group Owner: The Findlay Publishing Co.
Format: Country; *Target Audience:* 25-54.
Scott Michaels, Programming Director
Judy Watkins, News Director
Sam Simmermaker, Sports Director

WINN
01-30-1975; 104.9 MHz FM; *Hrs Open:* 24; 6 kw; 299 ft.; N39 11 9 W85 57 37
Mailing Address: 507 North State Street, North Vernon, IN 47265 US
Second Address: 3212 Washington St., Columbus, IN 47203
(812) 372-4448
www.win1049.com
hits@win1049.com
License: Columbus, Bartholomew County, IN held by White River Broadcasting Co. Inc.
Group Owner: The Findlay Publishing Co.; (acq 1-8-2002)
Arbitron Metro Market: Columbus, IN; *Format:* Contemporary Hits/Top 40, Adult Contemp; *Target Audience:* 35-54.; *Adv. Rates:* 25; 25; 25; 25.
Kurt Kah, President
David Glass, Operations Dir
Tasha Mann, General Manager
Rich Anthony, Programming Director
Barry Wright, News Director
Chuck Weber, Engineering Dir
John Foster, Operations Manager
Sam Simmermaker, SportsDirector

WXCH
11-15-1984; 102.9 MHz FM; 5.1 kw; 318 ft.; N39 11 10 W85 57 29 *Rebroadcasts:* Rebroadcasts WSCH(FM) Aurora 98%
6857 Salem Ridge Road, Aurora, IL 47001 US
(812) 438-2777; *Fax:* (812) 537-5735
License: Columbus, Bartholomew County, IN held by Wagon Wheel Broadcasting LLC.
Group Owner: Wagon Wheel Broadcasting LLC; (acq 11-15-2007; grpsl)
Arbitron Metro Market: Columbus, IN; *Format:* Country
Dennis Drees, Operations Dir
Marty Pieratt, General Manager
Bob Shannon, News Director

***WKJD**
90.3 MHz FM; 3.4 kw vert; 269 ft.; N39 11 10 W85 57 29
1680 Hwy 62 Ne, Corydon, IN 47112 US
(812) 375-9947; *Fax:* (812) 375-2555
www.thebridgefm.org
License: Columbus, Bartholomew County, IN held by Good Samaritan Educational Radio Inc.
Arbitron Metro Market: Columbus, IN
Keith Reising, CEO
Matt Bond, Operations Dir
Melissa Burton, Office Manager

Connersville

WLPK
04-05-1948; 1580 kHz AM; *Hrs Open:* 24; 0.25 kw-D, ND1; 0.005 kw-N, ND1; N39 38 18 W85 8 54
Mailing Address: 2301 West Main Street, Richmond, IN 47374 US
Second Address: 406 Central Ave., Connersville, IN
(765) 825-6411; *Fax:* (765) 825-2411
www.wifefm.com
john@wifefm.com
License: Connersville, IN held by Rodgers Broadcasting Corp.
Group Owner: Rodgers Broadcasting Corp.; (acq 8-88; grpsl;
Regional Reps: Rgnl Reps.
Arbitron Metro Market: Indianapolis, IN; *Format:* Oldies *Special Programming:* Relg 12 hrs wkly; *Hrs. of News Programming:* news progmg 3 hrs wkly; *No. News Employees:* 2; *Target Audience:* 25-54; affluent,middle-aged country listeners; *Adv. Rates:* 19; 19; 19; 19
David Rodgers, President
John Trine, General Manager
John Westover, Station Manager
Ted Cramer, Programming Director
Brett Briscoe, News Director
Mike Peacock, Engineering Dir
Bob Hawkins, Chief Engineer
Barry Welsh, MusicDirector
Kristin Deiwert, News Director
Mike Reese, Programming Director

Corydon

WOCC
05-22-1964; 1550 kHz AM; 0.25 kw-D, ND1; 0.006 kw-N, ND1; N38 11 26 W86 8 0
Mailing Address: 211 N Capital Ave, Corydon, IN 47712 US
Second Address: 211 N. Capitol Ave, Corydon, IN 47112
(812) 738-9622; *Fax:* (812) 738-1676
License: Corydon, IN held by Richard Lee Brabandt.
Nat'l Network: USA; *Regional Network:* Network Indiana; *Nat'l Reps:* Rgnl Reps
Arbitron Metro Market: Louisville, KY *TV Affiliate:* Oldies *Special Programming:* news progmg 18 hrs wkly; *Hrs. of News Programming:* 1; *No. News Employees:* 34-55; baby boomers

WSFR
01-01-1994; 107.7 MHz FM; *Hrs Open:* 24; 8.2 kw; 568 ft.; N38 10 25 W85 54 50
3773 Howard Hughes Pwy, Suite 300n, Las Vegas, NV 89109 US
(502) 589-4800; *Fax:* (502) 583-4820
www.1077sfr.com
License: Corydon, Harrison County, IN held by SM-WRKA LLC
Group Owner: SummitMedia LLC
Arbitron Metro Market: Louisville, KY; *Format:* Rock/AOR; *Target Audience:* 25-54.

Shane Collins, Operations Dir
Todd Pitt, General Sales Mgr
Brian Eichenberger, Promotions Manager

Covington

*WFOF

06-17-1984; 90.3 MHz FM; *Hrs Open:* 24; 19 kW; 266 ft.; N40 9 8 W87 27 58
1920 W 53rd St, Anderson, IN 46013 USA
(888) 877-9467
www.moodyradio.org/stations/indiana
License: Covington, Fountain County, IN held by The Moody Bible Institute of Chicago
Group Owner: Moody Radio
Arbitron Metro Market: Covington, IN; *Format:* Christian

Crawfordsville

WCVL

12-12-1964; 1550 kHz AM
P.O. Box 603, Crawfordsville, IN 47933 US
(765) 362-8200; *Fax:* (765) 364-1550
www.wcvlam.com
dapeach@forchtbroadcasting.com
License: Crawfordsville, IN held by Forcht Brodcasting
Group Owner: Forcht Broadcasting; (acq 1986)
Nat'l Reps: Rgnl Reps
Arbitron Metro Market: West-Central Indiana; *Format:* Oldies; *Hrs. of News Programming:* Three Hours per Day; *No. News Employees:* 1; *Target Audience:* 45 plus.; *Adv. Rates:* $10
Dave Peach, General Manager
Steve Carter, COO
Brad Pendleton, Assistant Program Director
Phil Tompson, Account Executive
Dustin Zahn, Programming Director
Steven Halsema, News Director

WIMC

06-01-1974; 103.9 MHz FM; 1.35 kw; 495 ft.; N40 8 6 W86 54 14
P.O. Box 1450, Corbin, KY 40702 US
(765) 362-8200; *Fax:* (765) 364-1550
www.wimcfm.com
License: Crawfordsville, Montgomery County, IN held by Forcht Broadcasting
Group Owner: Forcht Broadcasting
Format: Contemporary Hits/Top 40, Adult Contemp; *Target Audience:* 25-49.
David Peach, General Manager
Brad Pendleton, Assistant Program Director
Phil Thompson, Account Executive
Scott Meier, Operations Dir
Stan Parman, Programming Director
Bob Friedle, Chief Engineer
Hal Maas, Music Director

*WNDY

01-01-1997; 91.3 MHz FM; *Hrs Open:* 24 hrs; 2.2 kw; 194 ft; N40 03 19 W86 55 57 *Rebroadcasts:* WFRI (PBS Indy) 3am - 5pm
Mailing Address: Box 352, Crawfordsville, IN 47933
Second Address: 301 W. Wabash, Crawfordsville, IN 47933
(765) 361-6240; *Fax:* (765) 361-7004
www.wabash.edu
License: Crawfordsville, Montgomery County, IN held by Wabash College Radio Inc.

Brent Harris, Faculty/Staff Advisor
Michael Brown, General Manager

WCDQ

08-13-1953; 106.3 MHz FM; *Hrs Open:* 24; 3.4 kw; 440 ft.; N40 3 19 W86 55 57
Mailing Address: 3800 Victory Parkway, Cincinnati, OH 45207 US
Second Address: 1800 N. 175 W., Crawfordsville, IN 47933
(765) 362-8200; *Fax:* (765) 364-1550
www.wcdqfm.com
dapeach@forchtbroadcasting.com
License: Crawfordsville, Montgomery County, IN held by Forcht Broadcasting
Group Owner: Forcht Broadcasting
Arbitron Metro Market: Crawfordsville, IN; *Format:* Country; *Hrs. of News Programming:* news progmg 48 hrs wkly; *No. News Employees:* 2; *Target Audience:* 25-49; middle & upper class, educated, socially aware
Dave Peach, General Manager
Dustin Zahn, Programming Director
Steven Halsema, News Director
Steve Carter, Chief Engineer

Crothersville

*WOJC

01-01-2005; 89.7 MHz FM; 0.3 kw vert; 244 ft.; N38 50 39 W85 49 26 *Rebroadcasts:* Rebroadcasts WJCY (FM)
150 West Lincolnway, Suite 2001, Valpariso, IN 46383 US
(219) 548-5800; *Fax:* (219) 548-5808
www.calvaryradionetwork.com
info@calvaryradionetwork.com
License: Crothersville, Jackson County, IN held by Calvary Radio Network, Inc.
Group Owner: Calvary Radio Network
Arbitron Metro Market: Crothersville, IN; *Format:* Christian, Religious

Crown Point

WXRD

11-10-1972; 103.9 MHz FM; *Hrs Open:* 24; 1.35 kw; 449 ft.; N41 19 24 W87 21 22
8105 Georgia St, Merrillville, IN 46360 US
(219) 462-6111; *Fax:* (219) 462-4880
www.xrock1039.com
License: Crown Point, Lake County, IN held by Porter County Broadcasting Holding Corporation, LL
Group Owner: Porter County Broadcasting Corp.; (acq 2-6-2004; $4.9 million with WZ
Nat'l Network: ABC; *Regional Network:* Network Indiana
Arbitron Metro Market: Crown Point, IN; *Format:* Classic Rock; *Hrs. of News Programming:* news progmg 12 hrs wkly; *No. News Employees:* 1; *Target Audience:* 25-54; women
Leigh Ellis, General Manager

*WRTW

90.5 MHz FM; 3.1 kw; 600 ft.; N41 20 56 W87 24 2
8400 Burr Street, Crown Point, IN 46307 US
(219) 228-2995; *Fax:* (219) 365-2029
www.thekeyfm.com
info@thekeyfm.com
License: Crown Point, Lake County, IN held by Hyles-Anderson College.
Arbitron Metro Market: Crown Point, IN; *Format:* Christian
Dan Wolfe, General Manager
Jody McManus, Programming Director
Mike Azinger, Promotions Manager
Bill Flowers, Production Director

Danville

WEDJ

01-10-1975; 107.1 MHz FM; *Hrs Open:* 24; 1.8 kw; 604 ft.; N39 48 6 W86 34 24
1800 N. Meridian St., Suite 605, Indianapolis, IN 46202 US
(317) 924-1071; *Fax:* (317) 924-7766
www.wedjfm.com
License: Danville, Hendricks County, IN held by Continental Broadcast Group Inc.
Nat'l Reps: Univision Radio National Sales
Arbitron Metro Market: Indianapolis, I; *Format:* Spanish; *Target Audience:* 18-54; hispanic adults; *Adv. Rates:* 60; 50; 60; 40.
Martha Miller, Operations Dir
Russ Dodge, General Manager
Manuel Sepulveda, Programming Director
Stephanie Tatay-Myers, Promotions Manager
Phil Alexander, Chief Engineer

Dayton

*WCNB

91.5 MHz FM; 0.7 kw; 10 ft.; N40 22 27.8 W86 44 25.8
6434 La Pas Trail, Indianapolis, IN 46268 US
(317) 870-8400; *Fax:* (317) 870-8404
License: Dayton, Boone County, IN held by Hoosier Broadcasting Corp.
Group Owner: Hoosier Broadcasting Corp.
Arbitron Metro Market: Dayton, IN
William Poorman, President

Decatur

WJZI(AM)

05-22-1964; 1540 kHz AM; *Hrs Open:* 6:00 am-8:45 pm; 250 w-D; N40 49 14 W84 55 12
Mailing Address: Box 471, Wauchula, FL 33873
Second Address: 133 West Main Street, Peru, IN 46970
(863) 773-9282(863) 773-5008(813) 773-5088; *Fax:* (863) 773-2032
wauc.radiostation@earthlink.net
License: Decatur, Adams County, IN held by Lewis Broadcasting LLC
Nat'l Network: USA; *Regional Network:* Network Indiana
Regional Reps: Indiana Broadcasters Assn

Population Served: 30,000; *Arbitron Metro Market:* Grand Junction CO; *Format:* Tejano; *Target Audience:* 35-54.; *Adv. Rates:* 7.00; 5.00; 6.00; 0.00
Robert Ayala, General Manager

Delphi

WXXB

05-24-1989; 102.9 MHz FM; *Hrs Open:* 24; kw
Mailing Address: 200 Monticello Dr, Dyer, IN 46311 US
Second Address: 3575 McCarty Ln., Lafayette, IN 47905
(765) 447-2186; *Fax:* (765) 448-4452
www.b1029.com
logan@b1029.com
License: Delphi, Carroll County, IN held by WASK, Inc.
Group Owner: Schurz Communications Inc.; (acq 10-00; $1 million)
Arbitron Metro Market: Lafayette, IN; *Format:* Contemporary Hits/Top 40; *No. News Employees:* 1; *Target Audience:* 18-49.
Robert Rhea, President
Ernie Caldemone, Operations Dir
John Trent, General Manager
John Schurz, General Sales Mgr
Anthony Bannon, Programming Director

Earl Park

WIBN

10-15-1983; 98.1 MHz FM; 25 kw; 328 ft.; N40 34 22 W87 27 12
Box D, 560 W. Amsler Rd., Rensselaer, IN 47978 USA
(765) 385-2373; *Fax:* (765) 385-2374
www.981wibn.com
License: Earl Park, IN held by Brothers Broadcasting Corp.
Group Owner: Brothers Broadcasting Corp.
Format: Oldies
John Balvich, General Manager
Kevin Ferrari, General Sales Mgr
Bob Kurtz, News Director
Bob Burt, Assistant General Mgr.

Edinburgh

WYGB

08-24-2000; 100.3 MHz FM; *Hrs Open:* 24; 4.9 kw; 361 ft.; N39 21 45 W85 54 23
PO Box 690, Columbus, IN 47202 US
(812) 348-1029; *Fax:* (812) 375-2555
www.korncountry.com
License: Edinburgh, Johnson County, IN held by Edinburgh Radio.
Arbitron Metro Market: Edinburgh, IN; *Format:* Country; *Target Audience:* 25-54; Bartholomew & Johnson county folks; *Adv. Rates:* 23; 20; 24; 9
Keith Reising, CEO

Elkhart

WBYT

04-01-1947; 100.7 MHz FM; 15 kw; 909 ft.; N41 36 58 W86 11 38
237 Edison Road, Suite 200, Mishawaka, IN 46545 US
(574) 258-5483; *Fax:* (574) 258-0930
www.b100.com
bwilliams@federatedmedia.com
License: Elkhart, Elkhart County, IN
Group Owner: Federated Media
Nat'l Reps: Christal
Arbitron Metro Market: Mishawaka, IN; *Format:* Country *Special Programming:* Relg 2 hrs wkly; *Target Audience:* 25-54.; *Adv. Rates:* 65; 65; 65; 45
Brad Williams, General Manager
Stephanie Michel, General Sales Mgr
Jesse Garcia, Programming Director
Greg Trobridge, Chief Engineer

WCMR

03-16-1956; 1270 kHz AM; *Hrs Open:* 24
P.O. Box 307, Elkhart, IN 46515 US
(574) 875-5166
solidgospel1270.com
License: Elkhart, IN held by Progressive Broadcasting System Inc.
Group Owner: Progressive Broadcasting System Inc.
Format: Christian, Talk, 74; *Target Audience:* 30 plus.; *Adv. Rates:* 15; 12; 13; 9.

WFRN-FM

06-10-1963; 104.7 MHz FM; *Hrs Open:* 24; 50 kw; 459 ft.; N41 37 18 W85 57 37
P.O. Box 307, Elkhart, IN 46515 US

(574) 875-5166
www.wfrn.com
comments@wfrn.com
License: Elkhart, Elkhart County, IN held by Progressive Broadcasting System Inc.
Group Owner: Progressive Broadcasting System Inc.
Nat'l Network: USA; *Regional Network:* Network Indiana
Arbitron Metro Market: South Bend, IN; *Format:* Christian; *No. News Employees:* 1; *Target Audience:* 25-54; families-primarily women; *Adv. Rates:* 35; 31; 33; 15.

WTRC
11-18-1931; 1340 kHz AM; *Hrs Open:* 24; 1 kw-U, ND1; N41 40 28 W85 56 51
P.O. Box 699, Elkhart, IN 46515 US
(574) 389-5100; *Fax:* (574) 389-5101
www.michiananewschannel.com
License: Elkhart, IN held by Pathfinder Communications Corp.
Group Owner: Federated Media
Nat'l Network: ABC; Jones Radio Networks; *Nat'l Reps:* Christal
Arbitron Metro Market: Elkhart, IN; *Format:* News, News/Talk, 86; *Hrs. of News Programming:* news progmg 21 hrs wkly; *No. News Employees:* 2; *Target Audience:* 35-64; Elkhart County residents; *Adv. Rates:* 55;34; 35; 17
Kathy Uebler, General Manager
Allan Strike, Programming Director
Gary Sieber, News Director

***WVPE**
05-01-1972; 88.1 MHz FM; *Hrs Open:* 24; 11.5 kw; 997 ft.; N41 36 49 W86 11 20
2720 California Road, Elkhart, IN 46514 US
(574) 262-5660; *Fax:* (574) 262-5520
www.wvpe.org
wvpe@wvpe.org
License: Elkhart, Elkhart County, IN held by Elkhart Community Schools Corp.
Nat'l Network: PRI; NPR; *Wire Services:* UPI
Arbitron Metro Market: South Bend, IN; *Format:* Jazz, News, 62, Talk *Special Programming:* Blues 15 hrs, folk 9 hrs wkly; *Hrs. of News Programming:* news progmg 13 hrs wkly; *No. News Employees:* 1 *TargetAudience:* 25-55.
Anthony Hunt, Station Manager
Lee Burdorf, Programming Director
Kim Macon, Development Director
Linda Picon, Office Manager

Ellettsville

WHCC
01-01-1992; 105.1 MHz FM; *Hrs Open:* 24; 1.7 kw; 620 ft.; N39 11 32 W86 41 46
Mailing Address: 5520 East 75th Street, Indianapolis, IN 46250 US
Second Address: 304 State Rd. 446, Bloomington, IN 47401
(812) 336-8000; *Fax:* (812) 336-7000
www.whcc105.com
jim@artisticradio.com
License: Ellettsville, Monroe County, IN held by Artistic Media Partners L.P.
Group Owner: Artistic Media Partners Inc.; (acq 7-96; $675,000).
Nat'l Network: Jones Radio Networks *Regional Reps:* Russ Dodge
Format: Country; *No. News Employees:* 2; *Target Audience:* 25-54.
Arthur Angotti III, CEO
Art Angotti, President
Rick Evans, Operations Dir
Jim Wodock, General Manager
Sandy Zehr, Station Manager
Junior Blondell, General Sales Mgr
Bob Henning, Chief Engineer
Shelly Hawkins, BusinessManager
Libby Hiple, Local Sales Manager
Jim Gray, Account Executive
Jane Rubeck, Account Executive
Torry Hamilton, Account Executive

Elwood

***WIKL(FM)**
07-01-1964; 101.7 MHz FM; *Hrs Open:* 24; 6 kw; Ant 328 ft; N40 16 33 W85 51 44 *Rebroadcasts:* Rebroadcasts KLVR(FM) Middletown, CA 100%
5700 West Oaks Boulevard, Rocklin, CA 95765
(916) 251-1600; *Fax:* (916) 251-1650
www.klove.com
License: Elwood, Madison County, IN held by Educational Media Foundation
Group Owner: EMF Broadcasting; (acq 12-1-02; grpsl).
Nat'l Network: K-Love

Population Served: 70,080; *Arbitron Metro Market:* Muncie, IN; *Format:* Oldies
Mike Novak, President

Evansville

WABX
01-01-1997; 107.5 MHz FM; *Hrs Open:* 24; 2 kW; 561 ft.; N37 59 21 W87 35 48
1162 Mt. Auburn Rd, Evansville, IN 47720 USA
(812) 424-8284; *Fax:* (812) 426-7928
wabx.net
License: Evansville, Vanderburgh County, IN held by Midwest Communications Inc.
Group Owner: Midwest Communications Inc.
Nat'l Reps: Katz Radio
Arbitron Metro Market: Evansville, IN; *Format:* Classic Rock
Rusty James, Brand Manager

WEOA
01-01-1935; 1400 kHz AM; *Hrs Open:* 24; 1 kw-U, ND1; N37 56 17 W87 31 51
P. O. Box 3848, Evansville, IN 47736 US
(812) 424-8864; *Fax:* (812) 424-9946
www.1400amweoa.com/
License: Evansville, IN held by South Central Communications Corp.
Group Owner: South Central Communications Corp.; acq 11-81)
Nat'l Network: ABC
Arbitron Metro Market: Evansville, IN; *Format:* Adult Contemp; *Hrs. of News Programming:* Hourly; *No. News Employees:* 2; *Target Audience:* 25-49; general
Ed Lander, President
Ed Lander, General Manager
Regina Lander, General Sales Mgr
Jerome Lander, Promotions Manager
Larry Switzer, News Director

WGBF
11-22-1923; 1280 kHz AM; *Hrs Open:* 24
136 Main Street, #202, Westport, CT 06880 US
(812) 425-4226; *Fax:* (812) 421-0005
License: Evansville, IN
Group Owner: Townsquare Media; (acq 12-3-2003; grpsl).
Nat'l Network: CNN Radio; Westwood One; *Nat'l Reps:* Katz Radio
Arbitron Metro Market: Evansville, IN; *Format:* News, News/Talk, 86; *Hrs. of News Programming:* news progmg 10 hrs wkly; *No. News Employees:* 1; *Target Audience:* 25-54; affluent, mature; *Adv. Rates:* 15; 30;25; 5
Syd Stewart, General Manager
Larry LeBlanc, Brand Manager
Bill Schmid, Director Of Sales
Lauren Bjork, Digital Managing Editor

WIKY
08-28-1948; 104.1 MHz FM; 39 kW; 571 ft.; N37 59 21 W87 35 48
1162 Mt. Auburn Rd, Evansville, IN 47720 USA
(812) 424-8284; *Fax:* (812) 426-7928
wiky.com
License: Evansville, Vanderburgh County, IN held by Midwest Communications Inc.
Group Owner: Midwest Communications Inc.
Arbitron Metro Market: Evansville, IN; *Format:* Adult Contemp *Special Programming:* Farm 17 hrs wkly; *Target Audience:* 25-54; females, workplace
Rusty James, Brand Manager

***WNIN-FM**
02-01-1982; 88.3 MHz FM; *Hrs Open:* 24; 17 kw; 840 ft.; N37 59 1 W87 16 13
405 Carpenter Street, Evansville, IN 47708 US
(812) 423-2973; *Fax:* (812) 428-7548
www.wnin.org
License: Evansville, Vanderburgh County, IN held by Tri-State Public Teleplex Inc.
Nat'l Network: PRI; NPR
Arbitron Metro Market: Evansville, IN; *Format:* News; *Hrs. of News Programming:* News progmg 20 hrs wkly; *Target Audience:* General.
David Dial, President
Jean Noyes, Station Manager
Daniel Moore, Programming Director

***WPSR**
09-01-1957; 90.7 MHz FM; *Hrs Open:* 6:45 AM-2:45 PM; 14 kw; 164 ft.; N38 1 44 W87 34 47
5400 First Avenue, Evansville, IN 47710 US
(812) 435-8241; *Fax:* (812) 435-8241

License: Evansville, Vanderburgh County, IN held by Evansville Vanderburg School Corp.
Regional Network: Network Indiana
Arbitron Metro Market: Evansville, IN; *Format:* Variety/Diverse; *Hrs. of News Programming:* News progmg 3 hrs wkly; *Target Audience:* General.
Michael Reininga, General Manager

***WSWI**
08-06-1947; 820 kHz AM; 0.25 kw-D, NDD; N37 57 53 W87 40 6
8600 University Blvd., Evansville, IN 47712 US
(812) 465-1665; *Fax:* (812) 461-5261
www.usi.edu/wswi
wswi@usi.edu
License: Evansville, IN held by University of Southern Indiana.
Arbitron Metro Market: Evansville, IN; *Format:* Alternative; *Hrs. of News Programming:* News progmg 3 hrs wkly; *Target Audience:* 18-54; students, faculty & community members
John Morris, General Manager

***WUEV**
04-01-1951; 91.5 MHz FM; *Hrs Open:* 24; 6.1 kw; 151 ft.; N37 58 24 W87 31 48
1800 Lincoln Ave, Evansville, IN 47722 US
(812) 479-2022; *Fax:* (812) 479-2320
wuev.evansville.edu
wuev@evansville.edu
License: Evansville, Vanderburgh County, IN held by University of Evansville.
Regional Network: Network Indiana; *Wire Services:* UPI
Arbitron Metro Market: Evansville, IN; *Format:* Jazz, Variety/Diverse *Special Programming:* Children 5 hrs, American Indian one hr wkly; *Hrs. of News Programming:* news progmg 10 hrs wkly; *No. News Employees:* 3
Mike Crowley, General Manager
Phil Bailey, Chief Engineer

WVHI
10-31-1948; 1330 kHz AM; 5 kw-D, DAN; 1 kw-N, DAN; N38 3 12 W87 35 40
3701 Fern Valley Road, Louisville, KY 40219 US
(812) 475-9930; *Fax:* (812) 425-2078
www.wvhi.com
License: Evansville, IN held by Word Broadcasting Network.
Group Owner: Word Broadcasting Network Inc.; (acq 3-17-99).
Arbitron Metro Market: Evansville, IN; *Format:* Adult Contemp, Religious; *Target Audience:* General.
Krista Denton, General Manager

WJLT
12-22-1964; 105.3 MHz FM; *Hrs Open:* 24; 50 kw; 492 ft.; N38 4 45 W87 36 36
136 Main Street, Suite 202, Westport, CT 06880 US
(812) 425-4226; *Fax:* (812) 421-0005
License: Evansville, Vanderburgh County, IN
Group Owner: Townsquare Media; (acq 12-3-2003; grpsl).
Nat'l Network: ABC
Arbitron Metro Market: Evansville, IN; *Format:* Oldies; *Target Audience:* 25-54.; *Adv. Rates:* 30; 30; 30; 20
Mike Sanders, Operations Dir
Mark Thomas, General Manager
Cindy Patrick, Programming Director
Kris Mattingly, Promotions Manager
Rick Crago, Chief Engineer

Ferdinand

WQKZ
11-01-1997; 98.5 MHz FM; 3.6 kw; 423 ft.; N38 10 2 W86 49 49
P.O. Box 167, Jasper, IN 47547 US
(812) 482-2131; *Fax:* (812) 482-9609
License: Ferdinand, DuBois County, IN held by Gem Communications L.L.P.
Nat'l Network: Jones Radio Networks
Format: Country; *Adv. Rates:* 16; 15; 16; 15
Gene Kuntz, General Manager/Sales & Operations Manager
Walt Ferber, Programming Director
Jim O'Neal, News Director
Jeri Weisheit, Business Manager

Fishers

WFMS
03-17-1957; 95.5 MHz FM; *Hrs Open:* 24; 13 kw; 991 ft.; N39 46 3 W86 0 12
6810 N. Shadeland Ave., Indianapolis, IN 46220 US
(317) 842-9550
www.wfms.com
info@wfms.com
License: Fishers, Marion County, IN held by Radio License Holding SRC, LLC
Group Owner: Cumulus Media Inc.; (acq 11-20-72)

Arbitron Metro Market: Indianapolis, IN; *Format:* Country
Lisa Juillerat, Programming Director
Christopher Wheat, Promotions Manager
Jake Robinson, Chief Engineer
Karyn Sullyvan, Public Service Announcements

Fort Branch

*WBGW
07-20-1990; 101.5 MHz FM; *Hrs Open:* 24; 2.1 kw; 561 ft.; N38 10 45 W87 29 13
Mailing Address: P.O. Box 4164, Evansville, IN 47724 US
Second Address: Box 4463 E. 1200 F, R.R. 2, Haubstadt, IN 47629
(800)264-5550; *Fax:* (812) 768-5552
www.thywordnetwork.org
mail@thyword.org
License: Fort Branch, Gibson County, IN held by Music Ministries Inc.
Nat'l Network: Moody; USA
Arbitron Metro Market: Evansville, IN; *Format:* Religious; *Hrs. of News Programming:* News progmg 12 hrs wkly; *Target Audience:* 35-54.
Floyd Turner, General Manager
Susan Turner, Promotions Manager
Floyd Turner, Chief Engineer
Susan Turner, Financial Secretary

Fort Wayne

WAJI
08-01-1959; 95.1 MHz FM; *Hrs Open:* 24; 39 kw; 679 ft.; N41 6 13 W85 11 28
PO Box 62, Bloomington, IN 47402 US
(260) 423-3676; *Fax:* (260) 422-5266
www.waji.com
barb@waji.com
License: Fort Wayne, Allen County, IN held by Sarkes Tarzian Inc.
Group Owner: Sarkes Tarzian Inc.
Nat'l Reps: Katz Radio; *Wire Services:* AP
Arbitron Metro Market: Fort Wayne, IN; *Format:* Adult Contemp; *No. News Employees:* 1; *Target Audience:* 25-54; women
Thomas Tarzian, CEO
Lee Tobin, General Manager
Dan Kennedy, Programming Director
Amy Collins, News Director
Geary Morrill, Chief Engineer
Robert Davis, CFO
Darlene Lee, Controller
Barb Richards, Programming Director

*WBCL
01-08-1976; 90.3 MHz FM; *Hrs Open:* 24; 26 kw; 692 ft.; N41 6 13 W85 11 46
1115 W. Rudisill Blvd., Fort Wayne, IN 46807 US
(260) 745-0576; *Fax:* (260) 456-2913
www.wbcl.org
License: Fort Wayne, Allen County, IN held by Taylor University Broadcasting Inc.
Group Owner: Taylor University Broadcasting

Ross McCampbell, Executive Director
Scott Tsuleff, Programming Director
Tiffany Schortgen, Promotions Director
Larry Bower, News Director

*WBOI
06-15-1978; 89.1 MHz FM; *Hrs Open:* 24; 34 kw; 604 ft.; N41 6 13 W85 10 44
Mailing Address: P.O. Box 8459, Fort Wayne, IN 46898 US
Second Address: 3204 Clairmont Ct., Fort Wayne, IN 46808
(260) 452-1189; *Fax:* (260) 452-1188
www.wbni.org/
jbrown@nipr.fm
License: Fort Wayne, Allen County, IN held by Northeast Indiana Public Radio Inc.
Nat'l Network: PRI; NPR; AP Radio; *Regional Network:* Network Indiana
Arbitron Metro Market: Fort Wayne, IN; *Format:* Jazz, News, 62, Talk; *Target Audience:* 25 plus.
Will Murphy, President
Katy Anderson, Operations Dir
Will Murphy, General Manager
Karen Fraser, General Sales Mgr
Sean Bueter, News Director
Ed Didier, Chief Engineer
Peggy Gaylord, Director of Underwriting

WFCV
06-17-1968; 1090 kHz AM; *Hrs Open:* Sunrise-sunset; 1 kw-C, DA2; 2.5 kw-D, DA2; N41 5 1 W85 4 32
3737 Lake Ave., Fort Wayne, IN 46805 US
(260) 423-2337
www.bottradionetwork.com
comments@bottradionetwork.com
License: Fort Wayne, Allen County, IN held by Bott Broadcasting Co.
Group Owner: Bott Radio Network; acq 5-1-80)
Nat'l Network: USA
Arbitron Metro Market: Fort Wayne, IN; *Format:* Christian, Talk; *Target Audience:* 25-54; family oriented
Richard Bott Sr., President & CEO
Eben Fowler, Operations Dir
Dale Gerke, General Manager
Pat Rulon, Director of National Sales
Candy Green, Program Services Manager
Rachel Launius, Marketing Manager
Jason Potocnik, Director ofTraffic Operations
John Beck, Network Development Manager

WOWO-FM
03-04-1993; 92.3 MHz FM; *Hrs Open:* 24; 2.2 kw; Ant 544 ft; N41 06 39 W85 11 44
2915 Maples Rd., Fort Wayne, IN 46816
(260) 447-5511; *Fax:* (260) 447-7546
www.wowo.com
License: Fort Wayne, Allen County, IN held by Pathfinder Communications Corp.
Group Owner: Federated Media; (acq 3-1-97)
Nat'l Network: ABC
Population Served: 380,000; *Arbitron Metro Market:* Fort Wayne, IN; *Format:* News, Talk; *Hrs. of News Programming:* news progmg 6 hrs wkly; *No. News Employees:* 1; *Target Audience:* 25-54; men and adults
John Dille, President
Jim Allgeier, General Manager
Ben Saurer, General Sales Mgr
Gregg Henson, Programming Director
Brian Sheikn, Promotions Manager
Dave Wheaton, News Director
Mogan David, Engineering Dir
Jack Didier, ChiefEngineer
Kayla Blakeslee, Traffic

WGL
01-24-1924; 1250 kHz AM; *Hrs Open:* 24
2000 Lower Huntington Rd, Fort Wayne, IN 46819 US
(260) 747-1511; *Fax:* (260) 747-3999
www.1250theriver.com
License: Fort Wayne, IN held by Summit City License Sub, LLC.
Group Owner: Summit City Radio Group; (acq 11-6-2006;. grpsl)
Nat'l Network: CBS
Arbitron Metro Market: Fort Wayne, IN; *Format:* Adult Contemp; *Hrs. of News Programming:* News progmg 2 hrs wkly
J.J. Fabini, Operations Dir
Dave Reithmiller, General Sales Mgr
Scott Howard, Local Sales Manager
Dave Riethmiller, Co-General Manager
J. Fabini, Co-General Manager

WKJG
11-01-1947; 1380 kHz AM
2915 Maples Rd., Ft. Wayne, IN 46816 US
(260) 447-5511; *Fax:* (260) 447-7546
www.espnfortwayne.com
License: Fort Wayne, IN held by Pathfinder Communications Corp.
Group Owner: Federated Media
Nat'l Network: ABC; *Nat'l Reps:* Christal
Arbitron Metro Market: Fort Wayne, IN; *Format:* Sports
Tony Richards, COO
Mark DePrez, General Manager
Jim Tighe, General Sales Mgr
Jon Zimney, Programming Director
Jack Didion, Engineering Dir
Mogan David, Chief Engineer
Eileen Strickland, Traffic Manager

*WLAB
08-23-1976; 88.3 MHz FM; *Hrs Open:* 24; 3.2 kw; 607 ft.; N41 6 13 W85 11 28
1145 South Barr Street, Fort Wayne, IN 46802 US
(260) 483-8236; *Fax:* (260) 482-7707
www.star883.com
don@star883.com
License: Fort Wayne, Allen County, IN held by STAR Educational Media Network (Pending)
Arbitron Metro Market: Fort Wayne, IN; *Format:* Adult Contemp, Christian; *Target Audience:* 25-54; Christian; *Adv. Rates:* 20; 17; 20; 15
Melissa Montana, General Manager
Don Buettner, Programming Director

WLDE
08-24-1970; 101.7 MHz FM; *Hrs Open:* 24; 3 kw; 328 ft.; N41 5 2 W85 4 39
PO Box 62, Bloomington, IN 47402 US
(260) 423-3676; *Fax:* (260) 422-5266
www.wlde.com
License: Fort Wayne, Allen County, IN held by Sarkes Tarzian Inc.
Group Owner: Sarkes Tarzian Inc.; acq 2-16-93;
Nat'l Network: CNN Radio; *Nat'l Reps:* Katz Radio; *Wire Services:* AP
Arbitron Metro Market: Fort Wayne, IN; *Format:* Contemporary Hits/Top 40, Adult Contemp; *No. News Employees:* 1; *Target Audience:* Adults 25-54.
Thomas Tarzian, CEO
R. Geoffrey Vargo, President
Lee Tobin, General Manager
Shelly Steckler, Programming Director
Aimee Collins, News Director
Geary Morrill, Chief Engineer
Robert Davis, CFO
Darlene Lee, Controller
ChrisDidier, Program Director

WLYV
03-28-1948; 1450 kHz AM; *Hrs Open:* 24; 1 kw-D, ND2; 1 kw-N, ND2; N41 4 14 W85 7 10
29200 Vassar Road, Suite 650, Livonia, MI 48152 US
(260) 436-1450; *Fax:* (260) 432-6179
www.redeemerradio.com
Info@redeemerradio.com
License: Fort Wayne, IN held by Fort Wayne Catholic Radio Group Inc.
Nat'l Network: USA
Arbitron Metro Market: Fort Wayne, IN; *Format:* Christian, Religious *Special Programming:* Spanish one hr wkly; *Target Audience:* 25-54; Christian adults
Chris Langford, President
Jason Garrett, General Manager
Patty Becker, Programming Director

WMEE
02-05-1965; 97.3 MHz FM; *Hrs Open:* 24; 26 kw; 689 ft.; N41 6 39 W85 11 44
2915 Maples Road, Fort Wayne, IN 46816 US
(260) 447-5511; *Fax:* (260) 447-7546
www.wmee.com
License: Fort Wayne, Allen County, IN held by Pathfinder Communications Corp.
Group Owner: Federated Media
Arbitron Metro Market: Fort Wayne, IN; *Format:* Adult Contemp; *Hrs. of News Programming:* News progmg one hr wkly; *Target Audience:* 25-54.
Bob Watson, CFO
John Dille, President
Mark Evans, Operations Dir
Allison Delagrange, General Sales Mgr
Rob Kiley, Programming Director
Brian Sheikh, Promotions Manager
Jack Didier, Engineering Dir
Chris Cage, Music Director

WOWO
03-31-1925; 1190 kHz AM; *Hrs Open:* 24
P.O. Box 487, Elkhart, IN 46515 US
(260) 447-5511; *Fax:* (260) 447-7546
www.wowo.com
License: Fort Wayne, IN held by Pathfinder Communications Corp.
Group Owner: Federated Media
Nat'l Network: CBS; *Nat'l Reps:* Christal
Arbitron Metro Market: Fort Wayne, IN; *Format:* News, News/Talk, 84, Talk; *No. News Employees:* 5; *Target Audience:* 25-54.
Tony Richards, COO
John Dille, President
Jon Zimney, Operations Dir
Mark DePrez, General Manager
Jim Tighe, General Sales Mgr
Andy Ober, News Director
Mogan David, Chief Engineer
Bob Watson, CFO

WXKE
05-06-1976; 103.9 MHz FM; *Hrs Open:* 24; 3 kw; 328 ft.; N41 6 32 W85 9 55
2541 Goshen Road, Fort Wayne, IN 46808 US
(260) 747-1511; *Fax:* (260) 747-3999
License: Fort Wayne, Allen County, IN held by Summit City License Sub, LLC.
Group Owner: Summit City Radio Group; (acq 11-6-2006; grpsl)

Nat'l Reps: Eastman Radio
Arbitron Metro Market: Fort Wayne, IN; *Format:* Classic Rock; *No. News Employees:* 1
J.J. Fabini, Operations Dir
Dave Reithmiller, General Sales Mgr
Doc West, Programming Director
Katherine Whatley, Promotions Manager

Frankfort

WILO
11-23-1953; 1570 kHz AM; *Hrs Open:* 5 AM-11 PM; 0.25 kw-D, ND1; 0.25 kw-N, ND1; N40 16 40 W86 29 7
Mailing Address: P.O. Box 545, Frankfort, IN 46041 US
Second Address: 1401 Barner St., Frankfort, IN 46041-1506
(765) 659-3338; *Fax:* (765) 659-3338
www.wilo.us
License: Frankfort, IN held by Kaspar Broadcasting Co. Inc.
Group Owner: Kaspar Broadcasting Group; (acq 10-1-59).
Nat'l Reps: Rgnl Reps
Format: Oldies *Special Programming:* Farm 12 hrs wkly
Vernon Kaspar, President
Russ Kaspar, Station Manager
Randy Lawson, Programming Director

WSHW
09-14-1962; 99.7 MHz FM; 50 kw; 459 ft.; N40 25 14 W86 24 47
Mailing Address: P. O. Box 545, Frankfort, IN 46041 US
Second Address: 1401 Barner St., Frankfort, IN 46041-1506
(765) 659-3338; *Fax:* (765) 654-3484
www.shine99.com
License: Frankfort, Clinton County, IN held by Kaspar Broadcasting Co. Inc.
Group Owner: Kaspar Broadcasting Group
Arbitron Metro Market: Lafayette, IN; *Format:* Adult Contemp
Special Programming: Farm 8 hrs wkly
Russ Kaspar, General Sales Mgr

Franklin

***WFCI**
10-15-1960; 89.5 MHz FM; *Hrs Open:* 8 AM-2 AM; 1.15 kw vert; 220 ft.; N39 24 29 W86 8 52
501 E. Monroe St., Franklin, IN 46131 US
(800)852-0232; *Fax:* (317) 738-8233
www.franklincollege.edu
info@franklincollege.edu
License: Franklin, Johnson County, IN held by Franklin College of Indiana.
Arbitron Metro Market: Indianapolis IN; *Format:* Contemporary Hits/Top 40; *Target Audience:* 12-24; college & high school students
Harold Camping, General Manager
Joe Papp, Chief Engineer

WFDM-FM
12-15-1961; 95.9 MHz FM; 3.4 kw; 299 ft.; N39 30 49 W86 4 7
645 Industrial Dr., Franklin, IN 46131 US
(317) 736-4040; *Fax:* (317) 736-4781
www.freedom95.us
info@freedom95.us
License: Franklin, Johnson County, IN held by Pilgrim Communications LLC.
Group Owner: Pilgrim Communications Inc.; (acq 7-2-99)
Nat'l Reps: Rgnl Reps
Arbitron Metro Market: Indianapolis, I; *Format:* Talk; *Adv. Rates:* 50; 35; 50; 25
Mick Whitecotton, President
Rick Johnson, Operations Dir

French Lick

WFLQ
04-12-1983; 100.1 MHz FM; *Hrs Open:* 24; 6 kw; 299 ft.; N38 35 41 W86 36 48
P. O. Box 100, French Lick, IN 47432 US
(812) 936-9100; *Fax:* (812) 936-9495
www.wflq.com
wflqfm@smithville.net
License: French Lick, Orange County, IN held by W.G. Willis dba Willtronics Broadcasting.
Nat'l Network: ABC
Format: Country *Special Programming:* Farm 3 hrs, relg 6 hrs, Gospel 4 hrs wkly; *Hrs. of News Programming:* news progmg 11 hrs wkly; *No. News Employees:* 1; *Target Audience:* 25 plus.; *Adv. Rates:* 10; 9; 10;9
Catherine Willis, Operations Dir
Col. W.G. Willis, General Manager
Randall Hamm, Programming Director
Joe Randolph, News Director
Bill Willis, Chief Engineer
Charlie Derek, Disc Jockey
Chaz Mixon, Disc Jockey
Kim Stewart, DiscJockey

Gary

***WGVE-FM**
01-01-1954; 88.7 MHz FM; 2.1 kw horiz; 92 ft.; N41 33 15 W87 19 5
620 East Tenth Place, Gary, IN 46402 US
(219) 962-9483; *Fax:* (219) 962-3726
License: Gary, Lake County, IN held by Gary Community School Corp.
Format: Talk; *Target Audience:* Northwest Indiana
Sarita Stevens, General Manager
Elizabeth Garcia, Programming Director

WLTH
11-05-1950; 1370 kHz AM; 1 kw-D, DAN; 0.5 kw-N, DAN; N41 34 17 W87 19 2; N41 32 22 W87 18 0
2019 Broadway, Gary, IN 46407 US
(219) 794-1370; *Fax:* (219) 794-1377
www.wlth1370.com
License: Gary, IN held by WLTH Radio Inc.
Nat'l Network: CNN Radio
Arbitron Metro Market: Chicago, IL; *Format:* News, News/Talk, 84, Talk; *Target Audience:* 30 plus Black
Pluria Marshall Jr., General Manager

WWCA
12-07-1949; 1270 kHz AM; 1 kw-U, DA1; N41 31 38 W87 22 36
645 Church St, Suite 400, Norfolk, VA 23510 US
(219) 309-9327
License: Gary, IN held by Starboard Media Foundation Inc.
Group Owner: Relevant Radio; (acq 7-1-2004; $1.5 million).
Arbitron Metro Market: Gary, IN; *Format:* Talk
Armand Ciabattari, Station Manager

Goshen

***WGCS**
10-02-1958; 91.1 MHz FM; *Hrs Open:* 24; 6 kw; 292 ft.; N41 33 29 W85 51 6
1700 South Main St., Goshen, IN 46526 US
(574) 535-7488; *Fax:* (574) 535-7293
www.globeradio.org
globe@goshen.edu
License: Goshen, Elkhart County, IN held by Goshen College Broadcasting Corp.
Nat'l Network: PRI
Arbitron Metro Market: South Bend, IN; *Format:* Variety/Diverse *Special Programming:* Sp 8 hrs, news 8 hrs, sports 10 hrs wkly; *Hrs. of News Programming:* News progmg 8 hrs wkly; *Target Audience:* Adults 25-49.
Jason Samuel, General Manager

WKAM
01-01-1954; 1460 kHz AM; *Hrs Open:* 24; 2.5 kw-D, DAN; 0.5 kw-N, DAN; N41 35 24 W85 48 56
26914 Marcellus Hwy, Dowagiac, MI 49047 US
(574) 533-1460; *Fax:* (574) 534-3698
License: Goshen, IN held by Fulmer Communications LLC
Nat'l Network: USA; *Regional Network:* Network Indiana; *Nat'l Reps:* Katz Radio; Rgnl Reps
Format: Adult Contemp *Special Programming:* Southern gospel 6 hrs wkly; *Hrs. of News Programming:* news progmg 20 hrs wkly; *No. News Employees:* 1; *Target Audience:* 30-65; mature, family oriented, goal oriented *Adv. Rates:* 12; 12; 12; 10
Kent Fulmer, General Manager

WSSM(FM)
01-17-1977; 97.7 MHz FM; *Hrs Open:* 24; 3 kw; Ant 482 ft; N41 36 04 W85 55 41
3371 Cleveland Rd., Suite 300, South Bend, IN 46628
(574) 273-9300; *Fax:* (574) 273-9090
Jobs@artisticradio.com
License: Goshen, Elkhart County, IN held by Artistic Media Partners Inc.
Group Owner: Artistic Media Partners Inc.; (acq 4-1-2002; $925,000)
Population Served: 101,081; *Arbitron Metro Market:* South Bend, IN; *Format:* Classic Rock; *Target Audience:* 25-54.; *Adv. Rates:* 52; 47; 52; 21
Jack Swart, General Manager
Carrie Jones, General Sales Mgr
Chili Walker, Programming Director
Teresa Holden, Promotions Manager
Rita Kinzie, News Director
Bob Henning, Chief Engineer
Carrie McCaffery, National Sales Manager
Jim Wodock, Bloomington General Manager

Greencastle

***WGRE**
04-25-1949; 91.5 MHz FM; *Hrs Open:* 24; 0.8 kw vert; 177 ft.; N39 38 19 W86 51 49
609 So. Locust Street, Greencastle, IN 46135 US
(765) 658-4642; *Fax:* (765) 658-4693
www.wgre.org
newton@depauw.edu
License: Greencastle, Putnam County, IN held by DePauw University.
Nat'l Network: AP Radio; *Wire Services:* AP
Format: Alternative *Special Programming:* Jazz 3 hrs, Intl 2 hrs, regl 2 hrs wkly; *Hrs. of News Programming:* News progmg 12 hrs wkly; *Target Audience:* 18-25; college campus & loc community
Jeff McCall, President
Chris Newton, Operations Dir
Greg Stephan, Chief Engineer

WREB
05-16-1966; 94.3 MHz FM; *Hrs Open:* 24; 3 kw horiz; 161 ft.; N39 39 38 W86 53 34
522 Busseron St., PO Box 242, Vincennes, IN 47591 USA
(812) 882-6060; *Fax:* (812) 882-7770
www.wrebfm.com
marklange@originalcompany.com
License: Greencastle, IN held by The Original Company, Inc
Group Owner: The Original Company Inc.
Format: Sports, News/Talk; *Adv. Rates:* 15; 15; 15; 15
Mark Lange, President

***WQRA**
01-01-2005; 90.5 MHz FM; 8.1 kw; 446 ft.; N39 35 22 W86 33 2
6434 La Pas Trail, Indianapolis, IN 46268 US
(888) 937-2471; *Fax:* (916) 251-1650
www.air1.com
info@air1.com
License: Greencastle, Putnam County, IN held by Educational Media Foundation.
Group Owner: EMF Broadcasting; (acq 11-1-2006; $2 million)
Nat'l Network: Air 1
Arbitron Metro Market: Greencastle, IN; *Format:* Alternative, Christian
Darrell Chambliss, Chairman
Alan Mason, COO
Mike Novak, President and CEO
Ed Lenane, News Director
Sam Wallington, Engineering Dir
Dan Antonelli, Chief Business Development Officer
Eric Moser, Chief Financial Officer
BrianBurger, Vice President of Human Resources
D. Kevin Blair, Secretary and General Counsel
Larry Moody, Director
Mitch Barnhart, Director

Greenfield

***WRGF**
01-01-2001; 89.7 MHz FM; 0.75 kw horiz, 2 kw vert; 164 ft.; N39 44 55 W85 40 50
Mailing Address: 110 West North St., Greenfield, IN 46140 US
Second Address: 810 N. Broadway, Greenfield, IN 46140
(317) 462-9211; *Fax:* (317) 467-6755
gcsc.k12.in.us
wrgf@insight66.com
License: Greenfield, Hancock County, IN held by Greenfield Central Community School Corp.
Format: Rock/AOR, Classic Rock
Tim Renshaw, General Manager

WZPL
06-01-1962; 99.5 MHz FM; 19 kw; 774 ft.; N39 45 36 W86 0 22
9245 N Meridian St #300, Indianapolis, IN 46260 US
(317) 816-4000; *Fax:* (317) 816-4080
www.wzpl.com
info@wzpl.com
License: Greenfield, Hancock County, IN held by Entercom Indianapolis License LLC.
Group Owner: Entercom Communications Corp.; (acq 8-26-2004; grpsl).
Nat'l Reps: McGavren Guild
Arbitron Metro Market: Indianapolis, IN; *Format:* Adult Contemp; *Target Audience:* 18-49; women; *Adv. Rates:* 200; 200; 200; 100
JR Ammons, Programming Director
Sheri Acquisto, Marketing Director
Jeff Kuhn, Promotions Director
Alex Keddie, Engineering Dir
Jenny Skjodt, VP/Marketing Manager
Ben Hoffman, Director, Sales
Nick Box, Webmaster

Greensburg

*WAUZ
09-01-1998; 89.1 MHz FM; *Hrs Open:* 24; 0.8 kw vert; 518 ft.; N39 14 13 W85 34 0
Mailing Address: 1680 Hwy 62 Ne, Corydon, IN 47112 US
Second Address: Box 487, Greensburg, IN 47201
(812) 738-3482; *Fax:* (812) 375-2555
www.wygs.org
ygs@wygs.org
License: Greensburg, Decatur County, IN held by Good Shepherd Radio Inc.
Arbitron Metro Market: Minneapolis-St. Paul, MN; *Format:* Christian, Gospel; *Target Audience:* 25-40.
Keith Reising, CEO

WRZQ-FM
12-01-1962; 107.3 MHz FM; *Hrs Open:* 24; 10.5 kw; 499 ft.; N39 13 35 W85 44 47
825 Washington Street, Columbus, IN 47201 US
(812) 379-1077; *Fax:* (812) 375-2555
www.qmix.com
qmix@qmix.com
License: Greensburg, Decatur County, IN
Format: Adult Contemp; *Hrs. of News Programming:* news progmg 4 hrs wkly; *No. News Employees:* 1; *Target Audience:* 18-49.; *Adv. Rates:* 34; 29; 34; 18
Keith Reising Jr., President
Dave Wineland, Operations Dir
Mike King, General Manager
Mike King, Station Manager
Michelle Hardcastle, General Sales Mgr
C.J. Miller, Programming Director
Sara Beth Clark, Promotions Manager
KeithMaddox, News Director
Jim Burgan, Engineering Dir
Mark Gravely, Disc Jockey
Matt Joyce, Promotions Director

WTRE
07-01-1968; 1330 kHz AM; *Hrs Open:* 18; 0.5 kw-D, DA2; 0.033 kw-N, DA2; N39 19 41 W85 30 6
825 Washington Street, Columbus, IN 47201 US
(812) 663-3000; *Fax:* (812) 663-8733
www.wtrecommunity.com
License: Greensburg, IN held by WTRE Inc.
Regional Network: Network Indiana
Arbitron Metro Market: Greensburg, IN; *Format:* Country, News, 62, Talk, Variety/Diverse *Special Programming:* Farm 10 hrs, relg 3 hrs wkly; *Hrs. of News Programming:* news progmg 24 hrs wkly; *No. News Employees:* 1 *Target Audience:* 25 plus.; *Adv. Rates:* 19; 15; 14; 12
Keith Reising Jr., President
Sandy Biddinger, Sales and News
Mark Gravely, Programming Director
Kathy Verseman, Promotions Manager
Robert Hawkins, Chief Engineer
Gene McCoy, Sales Executive

WTRE(FM)
89.9 MHz FM; 1 kw; 61.65 meters; N39 20 04 W85 35 55
15 Wood Street, Greenfield, IN 46140
(317) 467-1064
License: Greensburg, Decatur County, IN held by Hoosier Public Radio Corp

Martin Hensley, President

Greenville

WRZX
04-15-1962; 106.5 MHz FM; 50 kw; 479 ft.; N40 8 49 W84 36 36
101 Pine Street, Dayton, OH 45402 US
(937) 224-1137
www.big1065.com
License: Greenville, OH held by Aloha Station Trust LLC
Group Owner: iHeartMedia
Arbitron Metro Market: Dayton, OH; *Format:* Oldies
Dave Litteral, Senior Vice President of Sales

Greenwood

WTLC-FM
01-01-1994; 106.7 MHz FM; 6 kw; 325 ft.; N39 42 42 W86 8 45
21 E. St. Joseph St., Indianapolis, IN 46204 US
(317) 266-9600; *Fax:* (317) 328-3870
www.tlcnaptown.com
License: Greenwood, Johnson County, IN held by Radio One of Indiana LLC.
Group Owner: Radio One Inc.; (acq 2-15-01; grpsl).
Arbitron Metro Market: Indianapolis, IN; *Format:* Urban Contemporary
Chuck Williams, General Manager
Karen Vaughn, Programming Director

Hagerstown

*WBSH
12-01-1996; 91.1 MHz FM; 0.3 kw horiz, 8 kw vert; 200 ft.; N39 56 31 W85 11 41 *Rebroadcasts:* Rebroadcasts WBST(FM) Muncie 100%
Ad 103, Muncie, IN 47306 US
(765) 285-5888; *Fax:* (765) 285-8937
www.bsu.edu/ipr
info@bsu.edu/ipr
License: Hagerstown, Wayne County, IN held by Ball State University.
Arbitron Metro Market: Muncie, IN; *Format:* News; *Hrs. of News Programming:* news progmg 33 hrs wkly; *No. News Employees:* 1; *Target Audience:* General.
Marcus Jackman, General Manager
Pam Coletti, General Sales Mgr
Steven Turpin, Programming Director
Carol Trimmer, Promotions Manager
Dorothy Marvell, News Director
Robert Mittendorf, Chief Engineer
Brian Beaver, News Reporter

Hammond

WJOB
01-01-1928; 1230 kHz AM; *Hrs Open:* 24
6405 Olcutt Avenue, Hammond, IN 46320 US
(219) 989-8502; *Fax:* (219) 844-6190
www.heyregion.com
License: Hammond, IN held by Vazquez Development LLC
Arbitron Metro Market: Chicago, IL; *Format:* News, News/Talk, 86 *Special Programming:* Sports, Pol 2 hrs, relg 2 hrs, Greek one hr wkly; *Hrs. of News Programming:* news progmg 17 hrs wkly; *No. News Employees:* 10 *Target Audience:* 25-49; general
Michael Stewart, Operations Dir
Debbie Wargo, General Manager
Pat Renwick, General Sales Mgr
Michael Stewart, Programming Director
Ron Perzo, News Director
Tim Saldana, Production
Alexis Vazquez Dedelow, Owner

WPWX
09-14-1959; 92.3 MHz FM; *Hrs Open:* 24; 50 kw; 492 ft.; N41 37 50 W87 31 40
6336 Calumet Avenue, Hammond, IN 46324 US
(773) 734-4455; *Fax:* (219) 933-0323
www.power92chicago.com
License: Hammond, Lake County, IL held by Dontron Inc.
Group Owner: Crawford Broadcasting Co.; (acq 9-14-59).
Arbitron Metro Market: Chicago, IL; *Format:* Adult Contemp, Urban Contemporary, 12; *Target Audience:* 18-34; urban
Donald Crawford, President
Taft Harris, General Manager
Jay Allen, Programming Director

Hanna

*WHLP
01-01-2001; 89.9 MHz FM; 8 kw; 505 ft.; N41 26 9 W86 50 48
150 West Lincolnway, Suite 2001, Valparaiso, IN 46383 US
(219) 548-5800
calvaryradionetwork.com
info@calvaryradionetwork.com
License: Hanna, La Porte County, IN held by Calvary Radio Network, Inc.
Group Owner: Calvary Radio Network, Inc.
Arbitron Metro Market: South Bend, IN; *Format:* Religious

Hardinsburg

WKLO
01-01-2002; 96.9 MHz FM; 3.5 kw; 433 ft.; N38 28 21 W86 24 39
146 Shelly Court, Mt. Washington, KY 40047 US
(812) 295-9480; *Fax:* (812) 295-4455
www.1080wklo.com
john@1080WKLO.com
License: Hardinsburg, Washington County, IN held by Hembree Communications Inc.
Arbitron Metro Market: Loogootee, IN; *Format:* Adult Contemp
Larry Hembree, General Manager
Kim Lozano, General Sales Mgr

Hartford City

WMXQ
93.5 MHz FM; 3.4 kw; 442 ft.; N40 25 16 W85 25 40
800 East 29th St, Muncie, IN 47302 US
(765) 378-2080; *Fax:* (765) 378-2094
www.maxrocks.net
License: Hartford City, Blackford County, IN held by Woof Boom Radio Muncie License LLC
Group Owner: Woof Boom Radio, LLC; (acq. from Backyard Broadcasting)
Format: Classic Rock
J. Chapman, President
Steve Lindell, General Manager
Jay Garrison, Programming Director
Sean Mattingly, Director of Technical Operations

Hope

*WYGS
02-27-2003; 91.1 MHz FM; *Hrs Open:* 24; 0.38 kw vert; 328 ft.; N39 13 35 W85 44 47
Mailing Address: 1680 Hwy 62 Ne, Corydon, IN 47112 US
Second Address: 825 Washington St., Columbus, IN 47201
(812) 375-9947; *Fax:* (812) 375-2562
www.wygs.org
jhutson@wygs.org
License: Hope, Bartholomew County, IN held by Good Shepherd Radio Inc.
Arbitron Metro Market: Hope, IN; *Format:* Gospel
Keith Reising, Jr., Chairman
Matt Bond, Operations Dir
Mellissa Burton, Office Manager
Jim Hutson
Matt Bond
Keith Reising
Steve Fisher
Melissa Burton

Howe

*WQKO
01-01-1994; 91.9 MHz FM; 3 kw; 299 ft.; N41 38 01 W85 21 12
150 West Lincolnway, Suite 2001, Valparaiso, IN 46383 US
(219) 548-5800; *Fax:* (219) 548-5808
www.calvaryradionetwork.com
info@CalvaryRadioNetwork.com
License: Howe, Lagrange County, IN held by Calvary Radio Network, Inc.
Group Owner: Calvary Radio Network
Format: Christian, Religious; *Target Audience:* 18-54

Huntertown

WQHK-FM
11-08-1966; 105.1 MHz FM; 5.7 kw; 689 ft.; N41 6 39 W85 11 44
2915 Maples Road, Fort Wayne, IN 46816 US
(260) 447-5511; *Fax:* (260) 447-7546
www.k105fm.com
License: Huntertown, Adams County, IN held by Jam Communications Inc.
Group Owner: Federated Media
Arbitron Metro Market: Fort Wayne, IN; *Format:* Country
Rob Kelley, Operations Dir
Mark DePrez, General Manager
Mogan David, Chief Engineer

Huntingburg

WBDC
12-22-1975; 100.9 MHz FM; *Hrs Open:* 24; 11 kw; 492 ft.; N38 12 31 W86 54 0
Box 1009, Jasper, IN 47547 US
(812) 634-9232; *Fax:* (812) 482-3696
www.wbdc.us
License: Huntingburg, Dubois County, IN held by Dubois County Broadcasting Inc.
Group Owner: DCBroadcasting Inc.
Nat'l Network: CNN Radio; Jones Radio Networks; *Regional Network:* Brownfield; *Wire Services:* AP
Arbitron Metro Market: Salt Lake City-Ogden-Provo UT; *Format:* Country; *Adv. Rates:* 17; 15; 15; 13
Brian Schwenk, Programming Director
Kurt Gutgsell, Sports Director

Huntington

WBZQ
05-25-1957; 1300 kHz AM; *Hrs Open:* 24; 0.5 kw-D, DA2; 0.019 kw-N, DA2; N40 52 31 W85 28 27
2504 River Park Drive, Fort Wayne, IN 46825 US
(260) 482-8500
License: Huntington, IN held by Larko Communications Inc.
Arbitron Metro Market: Fort Wayne, IN; *Format:* Oldies; *Target Audience:* 25-65.

Chris Larko, General Manager

WGL-FM

09-01-1965; 102.9 MHz FM; *Hrs Open:* 24; 4.7 kw; 299 ft.; N40 55 33 W85 23 15
2541 Goshen Road, Fort Wayne, IN 46808 US
(260) 747-1511; *Fax:* (260) 747-3999
dave@summitcityradio.com
License: Huntington, Huntington County, IN held by Summit City License Sub, LLC.
Group Owner: Summit City Radio Group; (acq 11-6-2006; grpsl)
Nat'l Network: CBS; *Nat'l Reps:* Eastman Radio
Arbitron Metro Market: Huntington, IN; *Format:* Adult Contemp; *No. News Employees:* 1; *Target Audience:* 25-54.
JJ Fabini, Co-General Manager Operations
Dave Riethmiller, Co-General Manager (Sales)
J.J Fabini, Programming Director

***WVSH**

01-01-1950; 91.9 MHz FM; 0.92 kw horiz; 112 ft.; N40 53 32 W85 30 38
450 McGahn Street, Huntington, IN 46750 US
(260) 356-2019; *Fax:* (260) 358-2210
License: Huntington, Huntington County, IN held by Huntington County Community School Corp.
Regional Network: Network Indiana
Arbitron Metro Market: Huntington, IN; *Format:* Contemporary Hits/Top 40
Bill Walker, General Manager
George Castle, Engineering Dir

***WJCI**

102.9 MHz FM; 4.7 kw; N40 55 33 W85 23 15
150 West Lincolnway, Suite 2001, Valparaiso, IN 46383 US
(219) 548-5800; *Fax:* (219) 548-5808
www.calvaryradionetwork.com
info@CalvaryRadioNetwork.com
License: Huntington, Huntington County, IN held by Calvary Radio Network, Inc.
Group Owner: Calvary Radio Network; (acq. March 2014 from Adams Radio Group)
Format: Christian, Religious; *Target Audience:* 18-54

Indianapolis

***WBDG**

09-13-1965; 90.9 MHz FM; *Hrs Open:* 24; 0.4 kw; 79 ft.; N39 47 5 W86 17 27
1200 N. Girls School Rd., Indianapolis, IN 46224 US
(800) 877-5600; *Fax:* (916) 251-1650
www.klove.com
License: Indianapolis, Marion County, IN held by Metropolitan School District of Wayne Township.
Wire Services: Reuters
Arbitron Metro Market: Tulsa OK; *Format:* Christian
Mike Novak, President

WBRI

03-12-1964; 1500 kHz AM; *Hrs Open:* 6 AM-7 PM; 5 kw-D, DA; N39 52 14 W86 05 17
4802 East 62nd St., Indianapolis, IN 46220
(317) 255-5484
janet@wilkinsradio.com
License: Indianapolis, Marion County, IN held by Heritage Christian Radio Inc.
Group Owner: Wilkins Communications Network Inc.; (acq 7-1-2003; $1.5 million).
Nat'l Network: Salem Radio Network
Population Served: 1,800,000; *Arbitron Metro Market:* Indianapolis, I; *Format:* Christian, Talk; *Target Audience:* 35 plus.; *Adv. Rates:* 35; 35; 35; 35
Keith Smiley, Station Manager

***WEDM**

09-14-1970; 91.1 MHz FM; *Hrs Open:* 24; 0.18 kw vert; 217 ft.; N39 47 29 W85 59 53
9301 E. 18th Street, Indianapolis, IN 46229 US
(317) 532-6301; *Fax:* (317) 532-6199
License: Indianapolis, Marion County, IN held by Metropolitan School District of Warren Township.
Arbitron Metro Market: Indianapolis, IN; *Format:* Contemporary Hits/Top 40; *Hrs. of News Programming:* News progmg 3 hrs wkly; *Target Audience:* General; Warren Township residents
Daniel Henn, Station Manager

WFBQ

11-26-1959; 94.7 MHz FM; *Hrs Open:* 24; 58 kw; 804 ft.; N39 53 43 W86 12 4
6161 Fall Creek Rd., Indianapolis, IN 46220 US
(317) 257-7565; *Fax:* (317) 253-6501
www.q95.com
info@wfbq.com
License: Indianapolis, Marion County, IN held by Capstar TX LLC
Group Owner: iHeartMedia
Nat'l Network: AP Radio
Arbitron Metro Market: Indianapolis, IN; *Format:* Classic Rock
Rick Green, Market President
Michele Kiefer, Senior Vice President of Sales
Rob Cressman, Programming Director
Kristi Adams, Promotions Director
Melissa Laird, Digital Content Coordinator

***WFYI-FM**

10-01-1954; 90.1 MHz FM; *Hrs Open:* 24; 10 kw; 561 ft.; N39 53 59 W86 12 1
1401 North Meridian St., Indianapolis, IN 46202 US
(317) 636-2020; *Fax:* (317) 283-6645
www.wfyi.org
captions@wfyi.org
License: Indianapolis, Marion County, IN held by Metropolitan Indianapolis Public Broadcasting Inc.
Nat'l Network: PRI; NPR *Regional Reps:* Indiana Public Broadcasting Station; *Wire Services:* AP
Arbitron Metro Market: Indianapolis, IN *TV Affiliate:* *WFYI-TV affil.; *Format:* News, News/Talk, 86 *Special Programming:* Black 5 hrs, blues 4 hrs wkly; *Hrs. of News Programming:* News progmg 41 hrs wkly *TargetAudience:* 25-64; general
Anthony Lorenz, CFO
Lloyd Wright, President
Theresa Tetrault, General Sales Mgr
Michael Toulouse, Programming Director
Rena Barraclough, Promotions Manager
Steve Jensen, Engineering Dir
Jeanelle Adamak, Executive VicePresident
Alan Cloe, Executive Vice President
Lori Plummer, Promotions Manager

WHHH

10-28-1991; 96.3 MHz FM; *Hrs Open:* 24; 3.3 kw; 285 ft.; N39 46 32 W86 9 10
21 E. St. Joseph's St., Indianapolis, IN 46204 US
(317) 266-9600; *Fax:* (317) 328-3870
www.indyhiphop.com
License: Indianapolis, Marion County, IN held by Radio One of Indiana LLC.
Group Owner: Radio One Inc.; (acq 11-8-01; grpsl).
Nat'l Network: CNN Radio
Arbitron Metro Market: Indianapolis, IN; *Format:* Urban Contemporary; *Target Audience:* 18-49.
Chuck Williams, General Manager
Max Willams, Promotions Manager

WFNI

01-01-1938; 1070 kHz AM; *Hrs Open:* 24
One EMMIS Plaza, 40 Monument Circle, Suite 700, Indianapolis, IN 46204-3011 USA
(317) 266-9422; *Fax:* (317) 684-2021
www.emmis.com
IR@emmis.com
License: Indianapolis, IN held by Emmis Radio License LLC
Group Owner: Emmis Communications Corp.
Nat'l Network: ESPN Radio; *Nat'l Reps:* D & R Radio
Arbitron Metro Market: Indianapolis, IN; *Format:* Sports
Jeff Smulyan, Chairman & CEO

***WICR**

08-20-1962; 88.7 MHz FM; *Hrs Open:* 24; 8 kw; 685 ft.; N39 53 40 W86 12 21
1400 East Hanna Avenue, Indianapolis, IN 46227 US
(317) 788-3280; *Fax:* (317) 788-3490
wicr.uindy.edu
wicr@uindy.edu
License: Indianapolis, Marion County, IN held by University of Indianapolis.
Nat'l Network: PRI
Arbitron Metro Market: Indianapolis, IN; *Format:* Jazz; *Hrs. of News Programming:* News progmg 5 hrs wkly; *Target Audience:* 35 plus; Educated, Affluent, Older; *Adv. Rates:* 50; 40; 50; 40
Beverley Pitts, President
Scott Uecker, General Manager
Russell Maloney, Chief Engineer

***WJEL**

09-03-1975; 89.3 MHz FM; *Hrs Open:* 24; 1 kw vert; 115 ft.; N39 54 34 W86 7 39
1901 East 86th Street, Indianapolis, IN 46240 US
(317) 259-5278; *Fax:* (317) 259-5298
www.geocities.com/wjelpower
License: Indianapolis, Marion County, IN held by Metropolitan School District of Washington Townshi
Arbitron Metro Market: Indianapolis, IN; *Format:* Variety/Diverse
Tyler Hindman, Operations Dir
John King, General Manager
Robert Hendrix, Programming Director
Mike Rabey, Chief Engineer

WXNT

01-01-1923; 1430 kHz AM; *Hrs Open:* 24
9245 N Meridian Street, Ste 300, Indianapolis, IN 46260 US
(317) 816-4000; *Fax:* (317) 816-4035
www.newstalk1430.com
info@wxnt.com
License: Indianapolis, IN held by Entercom Indianapolis License LLC
Group Owner: Entercom Communications Corp.
Arbitron Metro Market: Indianapolis, IN; *Format:* Sports, News/Talk, 86 *Special Programming:* Big band 2 hrs wkly; *Hrs. of News Programming:* news progmg 18 hrs wkly; *No. News Employees:* 1 *Target Audience:* 35-64.
JR Ammons, Programming Director
Alex Keddie, Engineering Dir
Jenny Skjodt, VP/Marketing Manager
Ben Hoffman, Director, Sales
Sheri Acquisto, Marketing Director
Jeff Kuhn, Promotions Director
Nick Box, Webmaster

WIBC

12-05-1960; 93.1 MHz FM; 13.5 kw; 991 ft.; N39 46 3 W86 0 12
One EMMIS Plaza, 40 Monument Circle, Indianapolis, IN 46204-3011 USA
(317) 266-9422; *Fax:* (317) 684-2021
www.wibc.com
alan@wibc.com
License: Indianapolis, Marion County, IN held by Emmis Radio License LLC
Group Owner: Emmis Communications Corp.
Arbitron Metro Market: Indianapolis, IN; *Format:* News, Talk, 84; *No. News Employees:* 12; *Target Audience:* 25-54; white collar, above average income & education
Jeff Smulyan, Chairman & CEO

WNDE

10-23-1924; 1260 kHz AM; *Hrs Open:* 24; 5 kw-D, DAN; 5 kw-N, DAN; N39 51 54 W86 3 43
6161 Fall Creek Rd., Indianapolis, IN 46220 US
(317) 257-7565; *Fax:* (317) 254-9619
www.foxsports975.com
License: Indianapolis, IN held by Capstar TX LLC
Group Owner: iHeartMedia; (acq 8-30-00; grpsl).
Nat'l Network: AP Radio; ESPN Radio; *Nat'l Reps:* Clear Channel
Arbitron Metro Market: Indianapolis, IN; *Format:* Sports, Talk *Special Programming:* 0; *Target Audience:* 25-54.
Rick Green, Market President
Rob Cressman, Senior Vice President of Programming
Michele Kiefer, Senior Vice President of Sales
Kristi Adams, Promotions and Marketing Director
Melissa Laird, Digital Content Coordinator

***WRFT**

06-06-1978; 91.5 MHz FM; 0.13 kw; 180 ft.; N39 40 33 W86 0 56
6141 S. Franklin Road, Indianapolis, IN 46259 US
(317) 803-5552; *Fax:* (317) 862-7262
License: Indianapolis, Marion County, IN held by Franklin Township Community School Corp.
Arbitron Metro Market: Indianapolis, I; *Format:* Variety/Diverse; *Target Audience:* General.
Steve George, General Manager
Grace Phillippe, Programming Director
Reilly Schmalfeldt, Social Media Director
Noah Bousum, Operations Director
Britt Goodwin, Promotions Director

WSYW

05-15-1963; 810 kHz AM; *Hrs Open:* Sunrise-sunset; 0.25 kw-D, NDD; N39 43 32 W86 11 8
1800 N. Meridian St., Suite 603, Indianapolis, IN 46202 US
(317) 924-1071; *Fax:* (317) 924-7766
License: Indianapolis, IN held by Continental Broadcast Group Inc.
Nat'l Reps: Univision Radio National Sales
Arbitron Metro Market: Indianapolis, I; *Format:* Spanish; *Target Audience:* 18+; Hispanic Adults; *Adv. Rates:* 60; 50; 60; 40.
Martha Miller, Operations Dir
Bart Johnson, General Manager
Manuel Sepulveda, Programming Director
Ricard Guerrero, Promotions Manager
Phil Alexander, Chief Engineer
Amiee McGrath, Business Manager

WTLC

07-27-1941; 1310 kHz AM; *Hrs Open:* 24; 5 kw-D, DAN; 1 kw-N, DAN; N39 43 8 W86 10 33

21 E. Joseph St., Indianapolis, IN 46204 US
(317) 266-9600; *Fax:* (317) 328-3870
www.praiseindy.com
License: Indianapolis, IN held by Radio One of Indiana LLC.
Group Owner: Radio One Inc.; (acq 11-8-01; grpsl).
Nat'l Network: ABC; *Regional Network:* Network Indiana; *Nat'l Reps:* Katz Radio
Arbitron Metro Market: Indianapolis, IN; *Format:* Gospel; *Hrs. of News Programming:* News progmg one hr wkly; *Target Audience:* 35 plus; black females; *Adv. Rates:* 60; 50; 50; 30
Chuck Williams, VP/General Manager
Karen Vaughn, Programming Director

WYXB
01-22-1968; 105.7 MHz FM; *Hrs Open:* 24; 50 kw; 492 ft.; N39 46 3 W86 0 12
40 Monument Circle, Suite 600, Indianapolis, IN 46204 USA
(371) 681-1057
www.b1057.com
License: Indianapolis, Marion County, IN held by Emmis Radio License LLC
Group Owner: Emmis Communications Corp.
Nat'l Reps: D & R Radio
Arbitron Metro Market: Indianapolis, IN; *Format:* Light Rock
Special Programming: Gospel 10 hrs wkly; *Hrs. of News Programming:* news progmg 3 hrs wkly; *No. News Employees:* 1; *Target Audience:* 25-34; adults,(secondary is 25-54)
Bob Richards, Operations Dir
Taja Graham, Sales Manager
Bob Richards, Programming Director
Laura Bielenberg, Promotions Director

WNTR
10-15-1984; 107.9 MHz FM; *Hrs Open:* 24; 22 kw; 761 ft.; N39 53 43 W86 12 4
3135 North Meridian Stre, Indianapolis, IN 46204 US
(317) 816-4000; *Fax:* (317) 816-4035
License: Indianapolis, Marion County, IN held by Entercom Indianapolis License LLC
Group Owner: Entercom Communications Corp.; (acq 8-26-2004; grpsl).
Nat'l Reps: Christal
Arbitron Metro Market: Indianapolis, IN; *Format:* Adult Contemp
Special Programming: Jazz 6 hrs wkly; *No. News Employees:* 3; *Target Audience:* 25-54.
JR Ammons, Programming Director
Jeff Kuhn, Promotions Director
Alex Keddie, Engineering Dir
Jenny Skjodt, VP/Market Manager
Sheri Aquisto, Marketing Manager
Ben Hoffman, Director of Sales
Nick Box, Webmaster

WXLW
08-01-1948; 950 kHz AM; *Hrs Open:* 24; 5 kw-D, DA2; 0.117 kw-N, DA2; N39 51 5 W86 14 39
645 Industrial Drive, Franklin, IN 46131 US
(317) 736-4040; *Fax:* (317) 736-4781
www.xl950.com
dave@XL950.com
License: Indianapolis, IN held by Pilgrim Broadcasting, LLC
Nat'l Network: ABC; ESPN Radio
Arbitron Metro Market: Indianapolis, IN; *Format:* Sports, Talk
Special Programming: Gospel 5 hrs wkly; *Hrs. of News Programming:* News progmg 7 hrs wkly; *Target Audience:* 25-54; men, secondary women
Randy Tipmore, General Manager
Dan O'Brien, Marketing Director/Vice President
Jeremy Beutel, Programming Director

Jasper

WITZ
07-04-1948; 990 kHz AM; *Hrs Open:* Sunrise/Sunset; 1 kw-D, ND1; 0.006 kw-N, ND1; N38 21 2 W86 56 26
Mailing Address: P.O. Box 167, Jasper, IN 47546 US
Second Address: 1978 South WITZ Road, Jasper, IN 47546
(812) 482-2131; *Fax:* (812) 482-9609
www.witzamfm.com
witzamfm@psci.net
License: Jasper, IN held by Jasper On The Air Inc.

Gene Kuntz, General Manager/Sales & Operations Manager
Walt Ferber, Programming Director
Jim O'Neal, News Director
Jeri Weisheit, Business Manager

WITZ-FM
11-01-1954; 104.7 MHz FM; *Hrs Open:* 24; 50 kw; 390 ft.; N38 21 2 W86 56 26
Mailing Address: P. O. Box 167, Jasper, IN 47546 US
Second Address: 1978 South WITZ Road, Jasper, IN 47546
(812) 482-2131; *Fax:* (812) 482-9609
www.witzamfm.com
License: Jasper, Dubois County, IN held by Jasper On The Air Inc.
Nat'l Network: Fox News Radio; *Regional Network:* Network Indiana; *Nat'l Reps:* Rgnl Reps
Arbitron Metro Market: Evansville, IN; *Format:* Adult Contemp; *Target Audience:* 18-54.
Gene Kuntz, General Manager/General Sales Manager
Walt Ferber, Programming Director
Jim O'Neal, News Director
Jeri Weisheit, Traffic/Business Manager

***WJPR**
01-01-2006; 91.7 MHz FM; 2.6 kw; 276 ft.; N38 25 23 W86 49 47
1680 Hwy 62ne, Corydon, IN 47112 US
(812) 295-9480; *Fax:* (812) 295-3295
www.wjpr.org
License: Jasper, Dubois County, IN held by Jasper Public Radio Inc.
Arbitron Metro Market: Jasper, IN; *Format:* Oldies
Larry Hembree, General Manager

Jeffersonville

WXVW
06-26-1961; 1450 kHz AM; *Hrs Open:* 24; 1 kw-U; N38 17 41 W85 45 07
11027 Perwinkle Lane, Louisville, KY 40291
(502) 419-4744; *Fax:* (916) 251-1650
www.1450thesportsbuzz.com
License: Jeffersonville, Clark County, IN held by Ryan Media LLC
Nat'l Network: ESPN Radio *Regional Reps:* Rgnl Reps.
Population Served: 9,675; *Arbitron Metro Market:* Brownfield TX; *Adv. Rates:* 12; 15; 20; 8
Edward Dugan Ryan, Managing Member

WQMF
04-25-1974; 95.7 MHz FM; 28.5 kw; 643 ft.; N38 8 16 W85 56 5
4000 #1 Radio Drive, Louisville, KY 40218 US
(502) 479-2222; *Fax:* (502) 479-2227
www.wqmf.com
License: Jeffersonville, Clark County, IN held by CC Licenses LLC.
Group Owner: iHeartMedia; (acq 1-23-97; $13.5 million)
Arbitron Metro Market: Louisville, KY; *Format:* Classic Rock; *Target Audience:* 35-54; men
Kevin Hughes, Senior Vice President of Sales
Charlie Steele, Promotions Manager

Kendallville

WAWK
11-09-1955; 1140 kHz AM; 0.25 kw-D, NDD; N41 27 16 W85 15 48
931 N East Avenue, Kendallville, IN 46755 US
(913) 642-7770; *Fax:* (913) 642-1319
www.bottradionetwork.com
License: Kendallville, IN held by Northeast Indiana Broadcasting Inc.
Nat'l Network: USA; *Regional Network:* Network Indiana
Format: Christian, Talk; *Target Audience:* 25-55.; *Adv. Rates:* 16.00; 16.00; 16.00
Trace Thurlby, COO
Richard Bott, President
Richard Bott II, Operations Dir
Pat Rulon, General Sales Mgr
Candy Green, Programming Director
Rachel Moser, Promotions Manager
Jason Potocnik, News Director
Tom Holdeman, CFO
EbenFowler, Operations Director

WBTU
12-16-1964; 93.3 MHz FM; *Hrs Open:* 24; 18.5 kw; 384 ft.; N41 12 49 W85 12 4
9604 Coldwater Road, Fort Wayne, IN 46825 US
(260) 482-9288; *Fax:* (260) 482-8655
License: Kendallville, Noble County, IN held by Adams Radio Group
Arbitron Metro Market: Fort Wayne, IN; *Format:* Country; *Target Audience:* 18-54; upscale, young audience
Ron Stone, President/CEO
Kevin Musselman, Director of Sales
Mark Allen Carter, Programming Director
Shel Leshner, Market/General Manager

Kentland

WIVR
01-01-2000; 101.7 MHz FM; *Hrs Open:* 24; 3.2 kw; 453 ft.; N40 51 52 W87 35 14
292 N. Convent, Bourbonnais, IL 60914 US
(815) 933-9287; *Fax:* (815) 933-8696
www.rivervalleyradio.net
License: Kentland, Newton County, IN held by Milner Broadcasting Enterprises LLC
Group Owner: Milner Broadcasting; (acq 12-11-2000).
Nat'l Network: AP Network News; *Wire Services:* AP
Arbitron Metro Market: Watseka, IL; *Format:* Country; *Hrs. of News Programming:* news progmg 168 bcsts wkly; *No. News Employees:* 2; *Target Audience:* 12 plus; anthology country with current & recurrent hits *Adv.Rates:* 20; 20; 20; 15.
Tim Milner, General Manager
Chris Swain, Local Sales Manager
Mickey Milner, Programming Director
Jim Brandt, Operations Director
Don Kerouac, Chief Engineer
Carla, Traffic Manager
Kathy Gagliano, Vice President/Sales
GordyMcCollum, Public Service Director
Chris Nickles, Production Director
Mike Ruble, Farm Director

Knightstown

***WKPW**
09-07-1993; 90.7 MHz FM; 4.4 kw vert; 180 ft.; N39 46 1 W85 31 0
8149 W. US 40, Knightstown, IN 46148 US
(765) 345-9070; *Fax:* (765) 345-7039
License: Knightstown, Rush County, IN held by State of Indiana Eder Vocational Center
Wire Services: AP
Format: Country *Special Programming:* Gospel; *Target Audience:* General.
Paul Wilkinson, President
Mike York, General Manager/Radio Instructor
Bob Hawkins, Chief Engineer

Knox

WKVI
06-30-1969; 1520 kHz AM; 0.35 kw-C, NDD; 1.8 kw-D, NDD; N41 19 20 W86 36 17
P. O. Box 10, Knox, IN 46534 US
(574) 772-6241; *Fax:* (574) 772-5920
www.wkvi.com
info@spots.com
License: Knox, IN held by Kankakee Valley Broadcasting Co. Inc.
Format: Adult Contemp
Ted Hayes, General Manager
Lo Ann McDaniel, Programming Director
Anita Goodan, News Director
Jerry Curtis, General Manager
Lenny Dessauer, Programming Director
Nathan Welter, Sports Director
Tony Ross, Sales Manager
MarryPerren, News Director

WKVI-FM
07-21-1969; 99.3 MHz FM; 3.3 kw; 299 ft.; N41 19 20 W86 36 17
P. O. Box 10, 400 West Culver Road, Knox, IN 46534 US
(574) 772-6241; *Fax:* (574) 772-5920
www.wkvi.com
info@spots.com
License: Knox, Starke County, IN

Mike Novak, President/CEO
Keith Whipple, VP, Marketing
David Pierce, Programming Director
Ed Lenane, News Director
Sam Wallington, Engineering Dir
Marya Morgan, News Reporter
Richard Hunt, News Reporter
Karen Johnson, NewsReporter

Kokomo

WIOU
07-16-1948; 1350 kHz AM; *Hrs Open:* 24
Mailing Address: 60 North Wayne Street, Martinsville, IN 46151 US
Second Address: 671 E. 400 S., Kokomo, IN 46902
(765) 453-1212; *Fax:* (765) 455-3882
newsroom.wzwz.wiou@sbcglobal.net
License: Kokomo, IN held by Hoosier AM/FM LLC

Group Owner: Hoosier AM/FM LLC; (acq 3-24-93; $1.21 million with co
Nat'l Network: CBS
Format: News, News/Talk, 84, Talk; *Hrs. of News Programming:* news progmg 9 hrs wkly; *No. News Employees:* 2; *Target Audience:* 25-54.
Ernie Caldemore, VP/General Manager
Russ Dodge, General Sales Manager
Rop Rupe, Programming Director

***WIWC**
09-01-1993; 91.7 MHz FM; 2.1 kW; 299 ft.; N40 36 0 W86 18 8
1920 W 53rd St, Anderson, IN 46013 USA
(888) 877-9467
www.moodyradio.org/stations/indiana
License: Kokomo, Howard County, IN held by The Moody Bible Institute of Chicago
Group Owner: The Moody Bible Institute of Chicago
Arbitron Metro Market: Kokomo, IN; *Format:* Christian; *Target Audience:* 34-55; general

WWKI
10-21-1962; 100.5 MHz FM; *Hrs Open:* 24; 50 kw; 480 ft; N40 27 04 W86 02 12
519 N. Main St., Kokomo, IN 46901 US
(765) 459-4191; *Fax:* (765) 456-1111
www.wwki.com
License: Kokomo, IN held by Radio License Holding CBC, LLC
Group Owner: Cumulus Media Inc.; (acq 6-30-99; grpsl).
Population Served: 45,494; *Arbitron Metro Market:* Kokomo, IN; *Format:* Country
Allan James, Local Sales Manager

WZWZ
11-20-1964; 92.5 MHz FM; *Hrs Open:* 24; 6 kw; 325 ft.; N40 28 18 W86 9 52
Mailing Address: 60 North Wayne Street, Martinsville, IN 46151 US
Second Address: 671 E. 400 S., Kokomo, IN 46902
(765) 453-1212; *Fax:* (765) 455-3882
www.z925fm.com
Ernie@Z925fm.com
License: Kokomo, Howard County, IN held by Hoosier AM/FM LLC
Group Owner: Hoosier AM/FM LLC
Arbitron Metro Market: Kokomo, IN; *Format:* Adult Contemp; *Hrs. of News Programming:* News progmg 4 hrs wkly; *Target Audience:* 18-49.
Ernie Caldemone, VP/General Manager
Russ Dodge, Sales Manager
Chris Stevens, Programming Director
Jessica Green, Music Director

La Porte

WCOE
01-23-1964; 96.7 MHz FM; *Hrs Open:* 24; 3 kw horiz; 262 ft.; N41 38 0.55 W86 45 32.79
1700 Licolnway Place, Suite 8, Laporte, IN 46350 US
(219) 362-5290; *Fax:* (219) 324-7418
License: La Porte, La Porte County, IN held by La Porte County Broadcasting Company Inc.
Arbitron Metro Market: La Porte, IN; *Format:* Country; *Hrs. of News Programming:* news progmg 19 hrs wkly; *No. News Employees:* 2; *Target Audience:* 35-54; upper income, middle aged; *Adv. Rates:* 23; 21; 23; 21
Ken Coe, President
Dennis Siddall, General Manager
Cheryl Timm, General Sales Mgr
Stan Maddux, News Director
Charlie Gustafson, Chief Engineer
Jim O'Day, Production Director
DeEtta Coe, Business Manager
Chip Jones, SportsCommentator

WLOI
01-01-1948; 1540 kHz AM; *Hrs Open:* Sunrise-sunset
1700 Licolnway Place, Suite 8, Laporte, IN 46350 US
(219) 362-6144; *Fax:* (219) 324-7418
License: La Porte, IN held by La Porte County Broadcasting Company Inc.
Nat'l Network: ABC; Westwood One; *Regional Network:* Network Indiana; Va. News Net; *Nat'l Reps:* Rgnl Reps
Format: Adult Contemp *Special Programming:* Farm 8 hrs wkly; *Hrs. of News Programming:* news progmg 26 hrs wkly; *No. News Employees:* 2; *Target Audience:* 35 plus.; *Adv. Rates:* 21; 19; 21; 18
Ken Coe, President
Dennis Sidall, General Manager
Cheryl Timm, General Sales Mgr
Stan Maddux, News Director
Charlie Gustafson, Chief Engineer
Cathy Reese, Traffic Manager
Jim O'Day, Production Director
DeEtta Coe, BusinessManager

Lafayette

WASK
01-01-1942; 1450 kHz AM; *Hrs Open:* 24; 1 kw-U, ND1; N40 24 8 W86 50 59
Mailing Address: P. O. Box 7880, Lafayette, IN 47903 US
Second Address: 3575 McCarty Ln., Lafayette, IN 47903
(765) 447-2186; *Fax:* (765) 448-4452
www.wask.com
info@wask.com
License: Lafayette, IN held by WASK Inc.
Group Owner: Schurz Communications Inc.; (acq 1-28-91; $8.25 million with co
Nat'l Network: ESPN Radio; *Nat'l Reps:* Christal
Arbitron Metro Market: Lafayette, IN; *Format:* Sports *Special Programming:* Farm 2 hrs wkly; *Hrs. of News Programming:* news progmg 15 hrs wkly; *No. News Employees:* 6
John Trent, President
Brian Green, General Sales Mgr
Randy Jones, Programming Director
Steve Truex, Chief Engineer
Bryan McGarvey, Disc Jockey

WSHY
11-28-1959; 1410 kHz AM; *Hrs Open:* 24; 1 kw-D, DAD; 0.06 kw-N, DA2; N40 21 38 W86 52 38
5520 East 75th Street, Indianapolis, IN 45250 US
(800) 877-5600; *Fax:* (916) 251-1650
License: Lafayette, IN held by Artistic Media Partners Inc.
Group Owner: Artistic Media Partners Inc.; (acq 9-30-98; $275,000)
Nat'l Network: Fox News Radio; Fox Sports
Arbitron Metro Market: Melbourne AR; *Format:* Christian
Arthur Angotti, President/General Manager
Judy Perkins, Business Manager
Carrie Jones, National Sales Manager

WAZY-FM
03-01-1965; 96.5 MHz FM; *Hrs Open:* 24; 50 kw; 499 ft.; N40 23 2 W87 7 55
3824 S. 18th Street, Lafayette, IN 47909 US
(800) 877-5600; *Fax:* (916) 251-1650
License: Lafayette, Tippecanoe County, IN held by Artistic Media Partners L.P.
Group Owner: Artistic Media Partners Inc.; (acq 10-86; $2 million;
Nat'l Network: ABC; *Regional Network:* Network Indiana; *Nat'l Reps:* Christal
Format: Christian; *Adv. Rates:* 35; 27; 35; 27
Arthur Angotti, President/General Manager
Ski Anderson, Sales Manager
Chloe D., Programming Director
Judy Perkins, Business Manager

***WJEF**
02-07-1972; 91.9 MHz FM; *Hrs Open:* 24; 0.25 kw; 92 ft.; N40 23 52 W86 52 26
Mailing Address: 1801 South 18th Street, Lafayeytte, IN 47905 US
Second Address: 2300 Cason St., Lafayette, IN 47904
(765) 772-4700
www.jeff92.org
rbrist@lsc.k12.in.us
License: Lafayette, Tippecanoe County, IN held by Lafayette School Corp.
Arbitron Metro Market: Lafayette, IN; *Format:* Oldies; *Hrs. of News Programming:* News progmg 6 hrs wkly; *Target Audience:* General.
Randall Brist, General Manager

WKHY
01-01-1970; 93.5 MHz FM; *Hrs Open:* 24; 6 kw; 246 ft.; N40 23 13 W86 58 10
3575 McCarthy Lane, Lafayette, IN 47905 US
(765) 448-1566; *Fax:* (765) 448-1348
www.wkhy.com
License: Lafayette, Tippecanoe County, IN held by Stay Tuned Broadcasting Corp.
Group Owner: RadioWorks Inc.; (acq 5-12-99; grpsl)
Nat'l Network: AP Radio; *Nat'l Reps:* Katz Radio
Arbitron Metro Market: Lafayette, IN *TV Affiliate:* KHY TV;
Format: Classic Rock, Rock/AOR; *No. News Employees:* 1;
Target Audience: 25-54; adults that are active, mobile & moderately affluent
John Trent, General Manager
John Schurz, General Sales Mgr
Jeff Strange, Programming Director
Liz Hahn, Promotions Manager
Eric Burch, News Director
Steve Truex, Chief Engineer

WKOA
09-28-1964; 105.3 MHz FM; *Hrs Open:* 24; 50 kw; 308 ft.; N40 24 8 W86 50 59
Mailing Address: P. O. Box 7880, Lafayette, IN 47903 US
Second Address: 3575 McCarty Ln., Lafayette, IN 47903
(765) 447-2186; *Fax:* (765) 448-4452
www.wkoa.com
License: Lafayette, Tippecanoe County, IN
Group Owner: Schurz Communications Inc.
Arbitron Metro Market: Lafayette, IN; *Format:* Country *Special Programming:* Farm 3 hrs wkly; *Hrs. of News Programming:* news progmg 12 hrs wkly; *No. News Employees:* 3; *Target Audience:* 25-54.
Brian Green, President/General Manager
Mike Shamus, Programming Director
Joe Lacay, Director of Promotions/Digital Media
Steve Truex, Chief Engineer

***WQSG**
01-01-2005; 90.7 MHz FM; 17 kw vert; 328 ft.; N40 22 14 W86 30 32
P.O. Box 3206, Tupelo, MS 38803 US
(662) 844-8888; *Fax:* (662) 842-6791
www.afr.net
faq@afa.net
License: Lafayette, Tippecanoe County, IN held by American Family Association.
Group Owner: American Family Radio; (acq 7-29-2003).
Arbitron Metro Market: Lafayette, IN; *Format:* Christian
Tim Wildmon, President
Donald Wildmon, Founder
Buddy Smith, Sr VP
Ed Vitagliano, Exec VP
Randy Sharp, Director Of Special Projects
Meeke Addison, Director Of Communications
Abraham Hamilton III, General Counsel

Lafayette Township

***WCYT**
01-01-1995; 91.1 MHz FM; *Hrs Open:* 24; 0.125 kw horiz, 0.12 kw vert; 226 ft.; N40 58 51 W85 16 48
4310 Homestead Rd, Fort Wayne, IN 46804 US
(260) 431-2271; *Fax:* (260) 431-2330
www.wcyt.org
License: Lafayette Township, Allen County, IN held by Southwest Allen County Schools.
Arbitron Metro Market: Fort Wayne, IN; *Format:* Alternative *Special Programming:* Oldies 2 hrs, blues 2 hrs wkly; *Target Audience:* General.
Adam Schenkel, General Manager
Andy Dunn, Station Manager

Lagrange

WTHD
09-02-1994; 105.5 MHz FM; *Hrs Open:* 24; 2.4 kw; 522 ft.; N41 37 24 W85 20 49
206 S. High Street, Lagrange, IN 46761 US
(260) 463-8500; *Fax:* (260) 463-8580
www.wthd.net
wthd@wthd.net
License: Lagrange, Lagrange County, IN held by Swick Broadcasting Corp.
Group Owner: Lake Cities Broadcasting Corp.; (acq 7-14-93;
Nat'l Network: ABC
Arbitron Metro Market: Lagrange, IN; *Format:* Country; *Hrs. of News Programming:* news progmg 2 hrs wkly; *No. News Employees:* 1; *Target Audience:* 25-54.
Steve Swick, President/CEO
Mike Shamus, Operations Manager
Brian Green, General Manager
Scott Lindahl, Director of Sales
Bryan McGarvey, Programming Director
Joe Lacay, Promotions/Digital Director

Lanesville

WGZB-FM
06-20-1988; 96.5 MHz FM; 1.6 kw; 638 ft.; N38 10 25 W85 54 50
520 S. 4th St., Louisville, KY 40202 US
(502) 625-1220; *Fax:* (502) 625-1257
www.hiphopb965.com
b965jams@gmail.com
License: Lanesville, Harrison County, IN held by Alpha Media Licensee LLC
Group Owner: Alpha Media LLC

Arbitron Metro Market: Louisville, KY; *Format:* Urban Contemporary
Larry Wilson, Chairman
Bob Proffitt, President & CEO
Dale Schaefer, General Manager
George Demaree, General Sales Mgr
Phillip David March, Programming Director
Valerie Sickles, Director of Urban Promotions and Community Affairs

Lawrence

WRWM
02-01-1993; 93.9 MHz FM; *Hrs Open:* 24; 8.4 kw; Ant 480 ft; N39 49 39 W85 58 51
6810 N. Shadeland Ave., Indianapolis, IN 46220 US
(317) 842-9550; *Fax:* (317) 921-1996
www.939thebeat.com
jay.michaels@cumulus.com
License: Lawrence, Marion County, IN held by Radio License Holding SRC, LLC
Group Owner: Cumulus Media Inc.; (acq 5-5-2006; grpsl)
Population Served: 1,500,000; *Arbitron Metro Market:* Indianapolis, IN; *Format:* Urban Contemporary
Sherry Anno, General Sales Mgr
Jay Michaels, Programming Director
Jan Thoman, Marketing Director

***WRWM(FM)**
93.9 MHz FM; 1 w horiz, 100 w vert; Ant 82 ft; N39 18 27.1 W85 52 11.6
3280 Peachtree Road SW, Atlanta, GA 47203
(404) 949-0700
License: Lawrence, Bartholomew County, IN held by Susquehana Radio Corp
Population Served: 827,609; *Arbitron Metro Market:* Indianapolis, IN
Linda Jerome, President

Lebanon

***WIRE**
01-01-2001; 91.1 MHz FM; *Hrs Open:* 24; 3.2 kw vert; 210 ft.; N40 3 48 W86 26 29
107 S. Meridian Street, Suite 2022, Lebanon, IN 46052 US
(317) 870-8400; *Fax:* (317) 870-8404
www.radiomom.fm
License: Lebanon, Boone County, IN held by Hoosier Broadcasting Corp.
Group Owner: Hoosier Broadcasting Corp.
Format: Adult Contemp; *Target Audience:* 25-54; adults; *Adv. Rates:* 17; 17; 17; 17
Annie Martin, CFO
William Poorman, President
Chuck Cunningham, Operations Dir

Liberty

***WKWH**
89.7 MHz FM; 300 w vert; Ant 115 ft; N39 39 46.2 W84 55 38
134 Huston St., Connersville, IN
(765) 821-2180
License: Liberty, Union County, IN held by Hoosier Public Radio
Population Served: 2,133; *Arbitron Metro Market:* Liberty, IN
Martin Hensley, CEO

Ligonier

WLEG
06-10-1991; 102.7 MHz FM; *Hrs Open:* 24; 2 kw; 394 ft.; N41 27 52 W85 44 40
237 Edison Road, Mishawaka, IN 46545 US
(574) 389-5100; *Fax:* (574) 389-5101
www.espn1027.com
License: Ligonier, Noble County, IN held by Pathfinder Communications Corp.
Group Owner: Federated Media; (acq 9-26-2002; $550,000).
Format: Sports
John F. Dille, III, President
Roger Grossman, Programming Director
Jeff Snyder, Chief Engineer

Linton

WQTY
09-14-1970; 93.3 MHz FM; 12 kw; 476 ft.; N39 0 46 W87 22 23
522 Busseron St., Linton, IN 47591 USA
(812) 882-6060; *Fax:* (812) 882-7770
www.wqtyradio.com
marklange@originalcompany.com
License: Linton, IN held by The Original Company, Inc.
Group Owner: The Original Company Inc.
Arbitron Metro Market: Terre Haute, IN; *Format:* Oldies
Mark Lange, President

***WYTJ**
89.3 MHz FM; 1 kw; 292 ft.; N39 5 59 W87 10 59
Rr 3 Box 1034, Linton, IN 47441 US
(812) 847-7222
www.wytj893fm.com
wyjt@minerbroadband.com
License: Linton, Greene County, IN held by Bethel Baptist Church.
Arbitron Metro Market: Linton, IN; *Format:* Religious
Doug Cassel, General Manager
Harold Smith, Station Manager
Bro Smith

Logansport

WSAL
02-24-1949; 1230 kHz AM; *Hrs Open:* 24; 1 kw-U, ND1; N40 45 16 W86 18 40
P.O. Box 719, Logansport, IN 46947 US
(574) 722-4000; *Fax:* (574) 722-4010
www.indianasbestradio.com
License: Logansport, IN held by Logansport Radio Corp.
Nat'l Reps: Rgnl Reps
Format: Adult Contemp, News, 62, Talk *Special Programming:* Farm 10 hrs wkly; *Hrs. of News Programming:* news progmg 14 hrs wkly; *No. News Employees:* 2; *Target Audience:* General.
John Jenkins, CEO
Dan Keister, General Manager
Lisa Downham, General Sales Mgr
Bob Ehle, Jr., News Director
Jeff Smith, Chief Engineer

Loogootee

***WBHW**
09-01-1995; 88.7 MHz FM; 5.3 kw; 479 ft.; N38 34 4.66 W87 12 46.13 *Rebroadcasts:* Rebroadcasts WBGW(FM) Fort Branch 1
P.O. Box 4164, Evansville, IN 47724 US
(800)264-5550; *Fax:* (812) 768-5552
www.thyword.org
mail@thyword.org
License: Loogootee, Martin County, IN held by Music Ministries Inc.
Arbitron Metro Market: Evansville,IN; *Format:* Religious
Floyd Turner, President/General Manager/Chief Engineer
Susan Turner, Financial Secretary

WRZR
12-06-1984; 94.5 MHz FM; *Hrs Open:* 24; 1.8 kw; 427 ft.; N38 37 9 W86 58 27
Mailing Address: 514 Jfk Avenue, Loogootee, IN 47553 US
Second Address: 514 JFK Ave., Loogootee, IN 47553
(812) 634-9232; *Fax:* (812) 482-3696
www.wrzr.us/
mailbox@wrzr.us
License: Loogootee, Martin County, IN held by Hembree Communications Inc.
Regional Network: Brownfield; Network Indiana *Regional Reps:* Ron Spaulding; *Wire Services:* AP
Format: Classic Rock *Special Programming:* Farm 2 hrs wkly; *Hrs. of News Programming:* news progmg 2 hrs wkly; *No. News Employees:* 1; *Target Audience:* 24-45.; *Adv. Rates:* 17; 16; 17; 16
Paul Knies, President
Bill Potter, General Manager
Ron Spaulding, General Sales Mgr
Alan Williams, Programming Director
Mike Carie, News Director
David Ferguson, Chief Engineer

Lowell

WZVN
11-24-1972; 107.1 MHz FM; kw
6405 Olcott Avenue, Hammond, IN 46320 US
(219) 462-6111; *Fax:* (219) 462-4880
www.z1071.com
License: Lowell, Lake County, IN held by Adams Radio Group
Nat'l Network: ABC
Arbitron Metro Market: Valparaiso, IN; *Format:* Adult Contemp; *Target Audience:* 25-54.
Ron Stone, President/CEO

***WLPR-FM**
01-01-2006; 89.1 MHz FM; 2.4 kw; 253 ft.; N41 19 24 W87 21 22
P O Drawer 2440, Tupelo, MS 38803 US
(219) 756-5656; *Fax:* (219) 755-4312
www.afr.net
License: Lowell, Lake County, IN held by Northwest Indiana Public Broadcasting Inc.
Nat'l Network: NPR
Arbitron Metro Market: Cheney, WA; *Format:* News, News/Talk, 86
Thomas Carroll, CEO
Len Clark, Programming Director

Madison

WORX-FM
03-01-1950; 96.7 MHz FM; 1.05 kw; 551 ft.; N38 44 32 W85 21 43
Box 1009, Jasper, IN 47547 US
(812) 265-3322; *Fax:* (812) 273-5509
www.worxradio.com
thebestmusic@worxradio.com
License: Madison, Jefferson County, IN held by Dubois County Broadcasting Inc.
Group Owner: DCBroadcasting Inc.
Nat'l Network: Jones Radio Networks; *Regional Network:* Network Indiana; *Wire Services:* AP
Format: Adult Contemp *Special Programming:* news progmg 20 hrs wkly; *Hrs. of News Programming:* 1; *Adv. Rates:* 21; 21; 21; 19
Paul Knies, President

WXGO
03-01-1956; 1270 kHz AM; *Hrs Open:* 24; 1 kw-D, DA2; 0.058 kw-N, DA2; N38 44 28 W85 21 41
Box 1009, Jasper, IN 47547 US
(812) 634-9232; *Fax:* (812) 482-3696
www.worxradio.com
License: Madison, IN held by Dubois County Broadcasting Inc.
Group Owner: DCBroadcasting Inc.
Nat'l Network: USA; *Nat'l Reps:* Rgnl Reps
Arbitron Metro Market: Madison, IN; *Format:* Adult Contemp *Special Programming:* Farm 3 hrs, relg 6 hrs wkly; *Target Audience:* General.
Paul Knies, President

***WHMO**
91.1 MHz FM; kw
825 Washington Street, Suite 2C, Columbus, IN 47201 US
(812) 738-3482; *Fax:* (812) 375-2555
License: Madison, Jefferson County, IN held by Shepherd Radio Inc.
Arbitron Metro Market: Madison, IN
Keith Reising, General Manager

Marengo

***WBRO**
01-01-2000; 89.9 MHz FM; 1 kw; 279 ft.; N38 21 49 W86 25 13
1680 Hwy 62 Ne, Corydon, IN 47112 US
(812) 365-9276; *Fax:* (812) 365-2127
www.wbro.org
License: Marengo, Crawford County, IN held by Crawford County Community Radio Inc.
Format: Variety/Diverse
Shawn Scott, General Manager

Marion

WBAT
06-07-1947; 1400 kHz AM; *Hrs Open:* 24; 1 kw-U, ND1; N40 33 40 W85 41 30
820 Pennsylvania Street, Marion, IN 46953 US
(208) 734-6633; *Fax:* (208) 736-1958
www.csnradio.com
License: Marion, IN held by Hoosier AM/FM LLC
Group Owner: Hoosier AM/FM LLC
Nat'l Network: CBS; ESPN Radio *Regional Reps:* Regional Reps
Arbitron Metro Market: Green Forest AR; *Format:* Christian; *Adv. Rates:* 27; 24; 24; 20
Vanessa Miller, Operations Manager
Ernie Caldemone, VP/General Manager
John Clark, General Sales Mgr
Tim George, Programming Director
Ed Thurman, News Director
Jim Brunner, Sports Director
Sammy Edmonds, Webmaster

***WBSW**
01-01-1997; 90.9 MHz FM; 1 kw horiz, 2.4 kw vert; 308 ft.; N40 40 1 W85 37 50 *Rebroadcasts:* Rebroadcasts WBST(FM) Muncie 100%
Ad 103, Muncie, IN 47306 US
(765) 285-5888; *Fax:* (765) 285-8937
www.bsu.edu/ipr
License: Marion, Grant County, IN held by Ball State University.

Arbitron Metro Market: Muncie, IN; *Format:* News; *Hrs. of News Programming:* news progmg 33 hrs wkly; *No. News Employees:* 1; *Target Audience:* General.
John Strauss, General Manager
Angie Rapp, Marketing Director
Steven Turpin, Programming Director
Debbie Webb, Underwriting Coordinator
Genet Soule, Membership Development Coordinator
Terry Heifetz, News Director
RobertMittendorf, Chief Engineer

WMRI
05-11-1955; 860 kHz AM; *Hrs Open:* 24; 1 kw-D, DA2; 0.5 kw-N, DA2; N40 33 12 W85 38 45
820 S. Pennsylvania Street, Marion, IN 46953 US
(765) 664-7396; *Fax:* (765) 668-6767
www.wmri.com
race@wbat.com
License: Marion, IN held by Hoosier AM/FM LLC
Group Owner: Hoosier AM/FM LLC; (acq 5-12-2003; with co-located FM)
Nat'l Network: Music of Your Life; *Regional Network:* Network Indiana
Format: Oldies; *Target Audience:* 35-70.; *Adv. Rates:* 12; 10; 12; 8
Vanessa Miller, Operations Manager
Ernie Caldemone, VP/General Manager
John Clark, General Sales Mgr
Connor Owen, Programming Director
Ed Thurman, News Director
Jim Brunner, Sports Director
Sammy Edmonds, Webmaster

WXXC
12-19-1948; 106.9 MHz FM; *Hrs Open:* 24; 50 kw; 499 ft.; N40 35 52 W85 39 21
P O Box 1538, Marion, IN 46952 US
(765) 664-7396; *Fax:* (765) 668-6767
www.1069wxxc.com
studio@1069wxxc.com
License: Marion, Grant County, IN held by Hoosier AM/FM LLC
Group Owner: Hoosier AM/FM LLC
Nat'l Network: CNN Radio; *Regional Network:* Network Indiana
Arbitron Metro Market: Marion, IN; *Format:* Contemporary Hits/Top 40, Adult Contemp; *Target Audience:* 25-54.; *Adv. Rates:* 28; 28; 28; 18
Ernie Caldemone, VP/General Manager
John Clark, General Sales Mgr
Vanessa Miller, Programming/Operations Manager
Ed Thurman, News Director
Jim Brunner, Sports Director
Sammy Edmonds, Webmaster

Martinsville

WCBK-FM
10-15-1968; 102.3 MHz FM; 6 kw; 308 ft.; N39 26 18 W86 27 58
1639 Burton Lane, Martinsville, IN 46151 US
(765) 342-3394; *Fax:* (765) 342-5020
www.wcbk.com
License: Martinsville, Morgan County, IN held by Mid-America Radio Group Inc.
Group Owner: Mid-America Radio Group Inc.
Arbitron Metro Market: Martinsville, IN
Dave Keister, President
Ruth Arney, General Manager
John Taylor, Programming Director/Operations Manager

WMYJ
04-18-1967; 1540 kHz AM; 0.25 kw-C, NDD; 0.5 kw-D, NDD; N39 24 31 W86 25 10
Mailing Address: P.O. Box 1970, Martinsville, IN 46151 US
Second Address: 1639 Burton Ln., Martinsville, IN 46151-3004
(765) 342-3394; *Fax:* (765) 342-5020
License: Martinsville, IN held by Mid-America Radio Group Inc.
Group Owner: Mid-America Radio Group Inc.; (acq 8-4-97; with co-located FM)
Nat'l Network: USA
Arbitron Metro Market: Indianapolis, IN; *Format:* Gospel *Special Programming:* Farm one hr wkly; *Target Audience:* 25-54.
David Keister, General Manager

Michigan City

WEFM
09-15-1966; 95.9 MHz FM; *Hrs Open:* 24; 3 kw; 230 ft.; N41 42 58 W86 51 47
1903 Springland Avenue, Michigan City, IN 46360 US
(312) 649-0099; *Fax:* (219) 879-8202
us995.radio.com
jeff@cbsradio.com
License: Michigan City, La Porte County, IN held by Michigan City FM Broadcasters Inc.
Nat'l Network: Westwood One; NBC Radio; *Regional Network:* Network Indiana
Arbitron Metro Market: Chicago, IL; *Format:* Adult Contemp, Oldies *Special Programming:* Farm, relg 4 hrs wkly; *No. News Employees:* 1; *Target Audience:* General.; *Adv. Rates:* 21; 21; 21; 21
Thomas Burns, President
Ronald Miller, Station Manager
Ronald Miller, General Sales Mgr
Chuck van Cure, Programming Director

WIMS
08-10-1947; 1420 kHz AM; *Hrs Open:* 24; 5 kw-D, DA2; 5 kw-N, DA2; N41 40 26 W86 55 58
6405 Olcott Avenue, Hammond, IN 46320 US
(219) 879-9810; *Fax:* (219) 879-9813
www.wimsradio.com
ric@wimsradio.com
License: Michigan City, IN held by Gerard Media LLC
Format: Talk *Special Programming:* Pol 3 hrs wkly; *Target Audience:* 30 plus; general; *Adv. Rates:* 22; 18; 20; 12
Ric Federighi, General Manager
Mike Paine, Programming Director
Mary Gigliotti, Director of Marketing/Sales
Sherri Paine, Traffic Manager

Mitchell

***WMBL**
88.1 MHz FM; 1 kW; 400 ft.; N38 45 50 W86 31 15
1920 W 53rd St, Anderson, IN 46013 USA
(888) 877-9467
www.moodyradio.org/stations/indiana
License: Mitchell, Lawrence County, IN held by The Moody Bible Institute of Chicago
Group Owner: The Moody Bible Institute of Chicago
Arbitron Metro Market: Mitchell-Bloomington; *Format:* Christian

Monticello

WMRS
03-01-1989; 107.7 MHz FM; *Hrs Open:* 24; 2.45 kw; 515 ft.; N40 40 8 W86 41 44
132 N. Main Street, Monticello, IN 47960 US
(574) 583-8121; *Fax:* (574) 583-8933
www.wmrsradio.com
kevinp@wmrsradio.com
License: Monticello, White County, IN held by Monticello Community Radio Inc.
Nat'l Network: USA; Jones Radio Networks
Arbitron Metro Market: Lafayette, IN; *Format:* Adult Contemp, Talk, 94 *Special Programming:* Gospel 5 hrs, bluegrass 2 hrs wkly; *Hrs. of News Programming:* news progmg 20 hrs wkly; *No. News Employees:* 2 *TargetAudience:* 25-60; motivated, intelligent, diverse; *Adv. Rates:* 15; 15; 15; 15
Kevin Page, General Manager

Montpelier

***WJCO**
91.3 MHz FM; 0.35 kw; 196 ft.; N40 33 21 W85 17 39
Rebroadcasts: Rebroadcasts WQKO (FM)
150 West Lincolnway, Suite 2001, Valparaiso, IN 46383 US
(219) 548-5800; *Fax:* (219) 548-5808
www.calvaryradionetwork.com
info@calvaryradionetwork.com
License: Montpelier, Blackford County, IN held by Calvary Radio Network, Inc.
Group Owner: Calvary Radio Networks
Arbitron Metro Market: Montpelier, IN; *Format:* Christian, Religious

Morgantown

***WCJL**
12-31-2002; 90.9 MHz FM; 1 kw horiz, 13.5 kw vert; 213 ft.; N39 19 17 W86 31 8 *Rebroadcasts:* Rebroadcasts WHLP (FM)
150 West Lincolnway, Suite 2001, Valparaiso, IN 46383 US
(219) 548-5800
www.csnradio.com
csn@csnradio.com
License: Morgantown, Morgan County, IN held by Calvary Radio Network, Inc.
Group Owner: Calvary Radio Network; (acq. 05-2010)
Arbitron Metro Market: Morgantown, IN; *Format:* Christian, Religious, 86

Morristown

***WJCF-FM**
01-01-2000; 88.1 MHz FM; 2.7 kw vert; 151 ft.; N39 45 1 W85 33 19
Mailing Address: 7205 Mohawk Lane, Indianapolis, IN 46260 US
Second Address: 15 Wood St., Greenfield, IN 46140-2162
(317) 462-9523; *Fax:* (317) 467-1065
www.wjcfradio.com
wjcfradio@aol.com
License: Morristown, Shelby County, IN held by Indiana Community Radio Corp.
Arbitron Metro Market: Greenfield, IN; *Format:* Christian
Jennifer Cox-Hensley, General Manager
Marty Hensley, Programming Director

Mount Vernon

WYFX
08-01-1992; 106.7 MHz FM; 3 kw; 295 ft.; N37 56 3 W87 55 35
522 Busseron St., Vincennes, IN 47591 US
(812) 882-6060
www.wjpsradio.com
marklange@originalcompany.com
License: Mount Vernon, IN held by The Original Company, Inc.
Group Owner: The Original Company Inc.
Arbitron Metro Market: Vincennes, IN; *Format:* News/Talk
Mark Lange, President
Jonathan Lange, Operations Mgr.

Mt. Vernon

WRCY
08-21-1955; 1590 kHz AM; 0.5 kw-D, ND1; 0.035 kw-N, ND1; N37 56 3 W87 55 42
522 Busseron St., PO Box 242, Vincennes, IN 47591 USA
(812) 882-6060; *Fax:* (812) 882-7770
www.originalcompany.com
marklange@originalcompany.com
License: Mt. Vernon, IN held by The Original Company, Inc.
Group Owner: The Original Company, Inc
Arbitron Metro Market: Evansville, IN; *Format:* Country
Mark Lange, President

Muncie

***WBST**
09-12-1960; 92.1 MHz FM; *Hrs Open:* 24; 3 kw; 299 ft.; N40 12 48 W85 27 36
Ball State University, Ad 103, Muncie, IN 47306 US
(765) 285-5888; *Fax:* (765) 285-8937
www.bsu.edu/ipr
info@bsu.edu/ipr
License: Muncie, Delaware County, IN held by Ball State University.
Nat'l Network: PRI; NPR
Arbitron Metro Market: Muncie, IN; *Format:* Classical, News; *Hrs. of News Programming:* news progmg 33 hrs wkly; *No. News Employees:* 1; *Target Audience:* General.
John Strauss, General Manager
Angie Rapp, Marketing Director
Debbie Webb, Underwriting Coordinator
Steven Turpin, Programming Director
Genet Soule, Membership Development Coordinator
Terry Heiftez, News Director
Sean Ashcraft,Production Manager
Robert Mittendorf, Chief Engineer

WERK
104.9 MHz FM; *Hrs Open:* 24; 6 kw; 328 ft.; N40 9 19 W85 25 48
Rebroadcasts: Simulcasts WURK(FM) Elwood 80%
9821 South Co Rd 700 West, Daleville, IN 47334 US
(765) 288-4403; *Fax:* (765) 378-2090
www.werkradio.com
j.chapman@woofboom.com
License: Muncie, Delaware County, IN held by Woof Boom Radio Muncie License LLC
Group Owner: Woof Boom Radio, LLC; (acq. from Backyard Broadcasting)
Arbitron Metro Market: Muncie, IN; *Format:* Adult Contemp, Contemporary Hits/Top 40, 30, Classic Rock; *Adv. Rates:* 34; 34; 34; 18
J. Chapman, President
Steve Lindell, General Manager
Jay Garrison, Programming Director
Sean Mattingly, Director of Technical Operations

WLBC
06-01-2013; 104.1 MHz FM; 41 kw; 459 ft.; N40 9 40 W85 22 44
800 E. 29th Street, Munice, IN 47302 US

(765) 288-4403; *Fax:* (765) 288-0429
www.wlbc.com
steve@wlbc.com
License: Muncie, Delaware County, IN held by Woof Boom Radio Muncie License LLC
Group Owner: Woof Boom Radio, LLC; (acq. from Backyard Broadcasting - $4.45 M)
Nat'l Network: CMLS; *Wire Services:* AP
Format: Adult Contemp; *Hrs. of News Programming:* news progmg 19 hrs wkly; *No. News Employees:* 1; *Target Audience:* 18-49; female; *Adv. Rates:* 39; 37; 37; 29
J. Chapman, President/GM
Steve Lindell, VP/ Director, Operations
Sue Tschour, General Sales Mgr
Debbie Myers, Business Manager
Sean Mattingly, Director, Technical Operations
Dave Stout, News Reporter

WRFM
02-14-1965; 990 kHz AM; 0.25 kw-D, DA2; 0.001 kw-N, DA2; N40 6 54 W85 22 2
1506 S. Parker Dr., Evansville, IN 47714 USA
(765) 747-6970; *Fax:* (765) 747-5054
License: Muncie, Delaware County, IN held by Electronic Applications Radio Service Inc.
Group Owner: Electronic Applications Radio Service Inc.; (acq 3-16-99)
Nat'l Reps: Roslin; Rgnl Reps
Format: Gospel; *Target Audience:* 25-54; upscale adults & families, professional & blue collar; *Adv. Rates:* 18; 18; 18; 15
Steven Dugger, General Manager

***WWHI**
01-01-1950; 91.3 MHz FM; 0.001 kw horiz, 0.2 kw vert; 233 ft.; N40 11 56 W85 24 49
1601 E. 26th Street, Muncie, IN 47302 US
(765) 747-5339; *Fax:* (765) 747-5325
License: Muncie, Delaware County, IN held by Ball State University
Arbitron Metro Market: Muncie, IN; *Format:* Rock/AOR
Ken Wickliffe, General Manager

WXFN
11-01-1926; 1340 kHz AM; 1 kw-D 1 kw-N ND2; N40 9 42 W85 22 41 *Rebroadcasts:* Simulcast on WXFN 102.9 (FM)
800 E. 29th St, Muncie, IN 47302 US
(765) 288-4403; *Fax:* (765) 288-0429
www.wxfn.com
wxfn@woofboom.com
License: Muncie, IN held by Woof Boom Radio Muncie License LLC
Group Owner: Woof Boom Radio, LLC; (acq. from Backyard Broadcasting)
Nat'l Network: ABC; ESPN Radio; Sporting News Radio Network; FOX Sports Radio; *Regional Network:* Network Indiana; *Wire Services:* AP
Arbitron Metro Market: Muncie, IN; *Format:* Sports *Special Programming:* Black 3 hrs wkly; *Hrs. of News Programming:* news progmg 12 hrs wkly; *No. News Employees:* 2; *Target Audience:* 25-54. *Adv. Rates:* 22; 18; 18; 12
J.Chapman, President
Steve Lindell, VP/Operations Director
Sue Tschour, General Sales Mgr
Debbie Myers, Business Manager
Sean Mattingly, Chief Engineer

***WKMV**
88.3 MHz FM; 0.28 kw; 338 ft.; N40 9 22 W85 25 48
P. O. Box 106, Roaring Spring, PA 16673 US
(800) 877-5600; *Fax:* (916) 251-1650
www.klove.com
License: Muncie, Delaware County, IN held by Educational Media Foundation.
Group Owner: EMF Broadcasting; (acq 3-23-2007; grpsl)
Nat'l Network: K-Love
Format: Christian
Mike Novak, President

Nappanee

WRDI
12-16-1991; 95.7 MHz FM; *Hrs Open:* 24; 1.4 kw; 500 ft; N41 24 43 W86 01 51
3920 S. Old Highway 94, Suite 36, St. Charles, MO 63304
(636) 447-6000
License: Nappanee, Elkhart County, IN held by Redeemer Catholic Radio
Group Owner: Redeemer Catholic Radio; (acq 8-25-2000).
Nat'l Network: ABC; CBS
Population Served: 600,000 *Format:* Adult Contemp; *Hrs. of News Programming:* News progmg 10 hrs wkly; *Target Audience:* 35-70; secretaries, bankers
Lu Cortese, President
Dave Stevens, Executive Director
Greg Trobridge, Chief Engineer

Nashville

WVNI
08-01-1997; 95.1 MHz FM; *Hrs Open:* 24; 3.8 kw; 344 ft.; N39 13 52 W86 22 40
2723 N. Walnut Street, Bloomington, IN 47404 US
(812) 335-9500; *Fax:* (812) 335-8880
www.spirit95fm.com
spirit95@spirit95fm.com
License: Nashville, Brown County, IN held by Brown County Broadcasters Inc.
Group Owner: Mid-America Radio Group Inc.; (acq 10-29-97; $20,000 for 51% of s
Nat'l Network: Salem Radio Network
Arbitron Metro Market: Bloomington, IN; *Format:* Christian; *Target Audience:* 25-54.; *Adv. Rates:* 32;22;27;22
David Bruce, General Manager/Sales Manager
Jim Webster, Operations Director
Mike Peterson, Management Consultant
Shannon Reed, Sales Associate
Logan Roberson, Production Manager

New Albany

WFIA-FM
01-01-1996; 94.7 MHz FM; *Hrs Open:* 24; 3.3 kw; 394 ft.; N38 17 2 W85 54 17
9960 Campus Drive, Louisville, KY 40223 US
(502) 339-9470; *Fax:* (502) 423-3139
www.salemradiogroup.com
listeners@salemradiogroup.com
License: New Albany, Floyd County, IN held by Salem Media of Kentucky Inc.
Group Owner: Salem Communications Corp.; (acq 1999; $5 million with WRVI(FM) Valley Station, KY)
Nat'l Network: Salem Radio Network; *Nat'l Reps:* Salem
Arbitron Metro Market: Louisville, KY; *Format:* News, Talk, 74; *Target Audience:* 30 plus
Dave Reichel, Programming Director
Gregg Kramer, Traffic Manager
Charlie Strickland, Chief Engineer
Sherri Perciful, General Sales Manager
Stephanie Daniels, Marketing Director

***WNAS**
05-28-1949; 88.1 MHz FM; 2.85 kw; 3 ft.; N38 17 56 W85 48 45
618 E. Market St, PO Box 1087, New Albany, IN 47150 US
(812) 981-7625; *Fax:* (812) 949-6926
www.wnas.org
License: New Albany, Floyd County, IN held by New Albany-Floyd County Consolidated School Corp.
Arbitron Metro Market: Louisville, KY; *Format:* Contemporary Hits/Top 40
Jason Flener, General Manager

WNDA
06-15-1949; 1570 kHz AM; *Hrs Open:* 24; 1.5 kw-D, ND1; 0.233 kw-N, ND1; N38 19 40 W85 46 56
P.O. Box 655, New Albany, IN 47151 US
(812) 949-1570; *Fax:* (812) 949-9623
www.indiana1570.com
news@indiana9.comÿ
License: New Albany, IN held by New Albany Broadcasting Co. Inc.
Nat'l Network: CBS Radio; ESPN Radio
Arbitron Metro Market: Louisville, KY; *Format:* News, News/Talk, 86
David Smith, General Manager
Corissa Smith, General Sales Mgr
Ashley Robinson, News Director

New Carlisle

WSMM
07-02-1991; 102.3 MHz FM; *Hrs Open:* 24; 2 kw; 397 ft.; N41 43 38 W86 24 30
3371 Cleveland Rd., Suite 300, South Bend, IN 46628 US
(574) 273-9300; *Fax:* (574) 273-9090
www.wzow.com
License: New Carlisle, St. Joseph County, IN held by Artistic Media Partners Inc.
Group Owner: Artistic Media Partners Inc.; (acq 3-22-2002; $1.5 million)
Arbitron Metro Market: South Bend, IN; *Format:* Classic Rock; *Adv. Rates:* 52; 47; 52; 21
Arthur A. Angotti, III, President
Karen Right, Operations Manager
Paul Homan, General Manager
Carrie Jones, National Sales Manager
Rita Kinzie, Business Manager
Bob Henning, Chief Engineer

New Castle

WLTI
11-14-1960; 1550 kHz AM; 250 w-U, DA-2; N39 55 59 W85 24 26
1134 W. State Rd. 38, Box 690, New Castle, IN 47362 US
License: New Castle, IN held by Radio License Holding CBC, LLC
Group Owner: Cumulus Media Inc.; (acq 7-1-99; grpsl).
Regional Network: Network Indiana; *Nat'l Reps:* Katz Radio
Population Served: 24,000; *Arbitron Metro Market:* New Castle IN; *Format:* Country
Chris Carter, Programming Director

WMDH
01-01-1947; 102.5 MHz FM; *Hrs Open:* 24; 50 kw; 499 ft.; N40 3 18 W85 23 5
1134 W. State Rd. 38, New Castle, IN 47362 US
(765) 529-2600; *Fax:* (765) 529-1688
www.nashfm1025.com
License: New Castle, IN held by Radio License Holding CBC, LLC
Group Owner: Cumulus Media Inc.
Arbitron Metro Market: Muncie, IN; *Format:* Country
Chris Carter, Programming Director

New Haven

WJFX
04-01-1990; 107.9 MHz FM; *Hrs Open:* 24; 3.2 kw; 453 ft.; N41 1 26 W85 3 51
9604 Coldwater Road, Fort Wayne, IN 46825 US
(260) 493-9539; *Fax:* (260) 749-5151
www.hot1079online.com
License: New Haven, Allen County, IN held by Adams Radio Group
Nat'l Reps: Interep
Arbitron Metro Market: Fort Wayne, IN; *Format:* Contemporary Hits/Top 40; *Target Audience:* 18-49; adults; *Adv. Rates:* 65; 60; 70; 40
Ross Stone, President/CEO
Mark Allen Carter, Operations Dir
Kevin Musselman, Director of Sales
Phil Becker, Programming Director
Shel Leshner, Market Manager

New Washington

***WARA**
01-01-1994; 88.3 MHz FM; *Hrs Open:* 24; 0.95 kw; 300 ft.; N38 35 40 W85 28 6 *Rebroadcasts:* Rebroadcasts KLRD(FM) Yucaipa, CA 100%
402 E. Yakim, Suite 1320, Yakim, WA 98901 US
(916) 251-1600; *Fax:* (916) 251-1650
www.air1.com
info@air1.com
License: New Washington, Clark County, IN held by Educational Media Foundation.
Group Owner: EMF Broadcasting; (acq 10-2-2003; grpsl).
Nat'l Network: Air 1
Arbitron Metro Market: Louisville, KY; *Format:* Alternative, Christian; *No. News Employees:* 3; *Target Audience:* 18-35; Judeo Christian, female
Mike Novak, President
Chip Bailey, Operations Dir

New Whiteland

***WHZN**
88.3 MHz FM; 0.001 kw horiz, 7.8 kw vert; 725 ft.; N39 24 14 W86 8 41
7702 Indian Lake Rd, Indianapolis, IN 46236 US
(815) 939-5330; *Fax:* (815) 939-5087
www.shine.fm
License: New Whiteland, Johnson County, IN held by Olivet Nazarene University
Arbitron Metro Market: New Whiteland, IN; *Format:* Christian
Mike MacIntosh, President
Carl Fletcher, Operations Dir
Justin Knight, General Manager
Brian McIntre, Programming Director
Kurt Wallace, Promotions Manager
Seth Hurd, Digital Media Director

Shannon LaFrance, Impact Advocate
Jeff Enfield, Business Relations Director

Newburgh

WDKS
02-11-1991; 106.1 MHz FM; *Hrs Open:* 24; 6 kw; 328 ft.; N37 52 57 W87 32 28
117 SE 5th Street, Evansville, IN 47708 US
(812) 425-4226; *Fax:* (812) 428-5895
www.1061evansville.com
ryano@1061evansville.com
License: Newburgh, Warrick County, IN
Group Owner: Townsquare Media; (acq 12-3-2003; grpsl).
Nat'l Network: ABC; Westwood One
Arbitron Metro Market: Evansville, IN; *Format:* Contemporary Hits/Top 40; *No. News Employees:* 1; *Target Audience:* 18-34; women
LaDonne Craig, General Manager
Angie Ross, Director of Sales
Ryan O'Bryan, Programming Director

WGAB
03-05-1984; 1180 kHz AM; *Hrs Open:* 24 hrs
1180 Maple Lane, Newburgh, IN 47630 US
(812) 479-5342; *Fax:* (888) 708-8936
www.faith1180.com
info@faith1180.com
License: Newburgh, IN held by Faith Broadcasting LLC
Nat'l Network: ABC; Jones Radio Networks; Salem Radio Network; Westwood One
Arbitron Metro Market: Evansville, IN; *Format:* Christian; *Target Audience:* 18-54; men & women; *Adv. Rates:* 8;12;12;8
Gayle Russ, President
Daniel Wolfe, VP/Operations Manager
Jonathan Williams, Chief Engineer

Noblesville

WJJK
09-25-1950; 104.5 MHz FM; *Hrs Open:* 24; 50 kw; Ant 492 ft; N39 50 25 W86 10 34
6810 N. Shadeland Ave., Indianapolis, IN 46220 US
(317) 842-9550; *Fax:* (317) 921-1996
www.1045wjjk.com
jay.michaels@cumulus.com
License: Noblesville, Hamilton County, IN held by Radio License Holding SRC, LLC
Group Owner: Cumulus Media Inc.; (acq 5-5-2006; grpsl)
Population Served: 1,133,200; *Arbitron Metro Market:* Indianapolis, IN; *Format:* Adult Contemp; *No. News Employees:* 1; *Target Audience:* 25-54.
Sherry Anno, General Sales Mgr
Jay Michaels, Programming Director
Jan Thoman, Marketing Director

North Manchester

***WBKE-FM**
05-01-1967; 89.5 MHz FM; *Hrs Open:* 24; 3 kw horiz; 79 ft.; N41 0 40 W85 45 45 *Rebroadcasts:* Rebroadcasts WBNI-FM Ft. Wayne 50%
MU Box 19, Manchester University, Manchester, IN 46962 US
(260) 982-5272; *Fax:* (260) 982-5043
mefetters@manchester.edu
License: North Manchester, Wabash County, IN held by Manchester College.
Arbitron Metro Market: North Manchester, IN; *Format:* Variety/Diverse *Special Programming:* Class 10 hrs, Sp one hr, classic rock 6 hrs, AOR; *Hrs. of News Programming:* news progmg 10 hrs wkly *No. News Employees:* 1; *Target Audience:* General.
Judd Case, COO
Alicia Smith, Station Manager
Brandon Curry, Promotions Manager
Carley Staton, News Director
Mark Adkins, Faculty Advisor
Whittney Horn, Music Director
Mark Zinser, Sports Director

North Vernon

WWWY
03-19-1963; 106.1 MHz FM; *Hrs Open:* 24; 50 kw; 486 ft.; N39 4 2 W85 42 10
Mailing Address: P.O Box 1507, Findlay, OH 45839 US
Second Address: 3212 Washington St., Columbus, IN 47203
(419) 422-4545
www.1061theriver.com
License: North Vernon, Jennings County, IN held by White River Broadcasting Co. Inc.
Group Owner: The Findlay Publishing Co.; (acq 8-1-97; grpsl).
Target Audience: 25-44.; *Adv. Rates:* 35;35;35;35
Holly Lindsey, General Manager
Sarah Reinhard, General Sales Mgr

WJCP
01-08-1955; 1460 kHz AM; 1 kw-D, ND1; 0.092 kw-N, ND1; N38 59 46 W85 39 2
P.O. Box 15435, Cincinnati, OH 45215 US
(812) 346-1927; *Fax:* (812) 346-9722
License: North Vernon, IN held by Columbus Radio Inc.
TV Affiliate: Sports

Notre Dame

***WSND-FM**
09-17-1962; 88.9 MHz FM; *Hrs Open:* 7am to 2am M-F; 9am to 2am Sa/Su; 3.4 kw; 361 ft.; N41 36 19 W86 12 45
P O Box 532, Notre Dame, IN 46556 US
Studio (574) 63; *Fax:* (574) 631-3653
www.nd.edu/~wsnd
wsnd@nd.edu
License: Notre Dame, St. Joseph County, IN held by Voice of the Fighting Irish Inc.
Wire Services: UPI
Arbitron Metro Market: South Bend, IN; *Format:* Classical *Special Programming:* Jazz, Reggae, Celtic, Blues; *Hrs. of News Programming:* 10; *Target Audience:* General public radio.
Laurie McFadden, General Manager
Ed Jaroszewski, Programming Director
Patrick Brown, Student Manager

Oolitic

***WDCK**
01-01-2005; 88.9 MHz FM; 5.2 kw; 256 ft.; N38 59 14 W86 27 31
1680 Hwy 62 Ne, Corydon, IN 47112 US
(765) 349-1485; *Fax:* (765) 342-3569
License: Oolitic, Lawrence County, IN held by Spirit Educational Radio Inc.
Arbitron Metro Market: Oolitic, IN; *Format:* Gospel
David Keister, Chairman
Diana Nuchols, General Manager

Orland

***WCKZ**
02-02-2002; 91.3 MHz FM; *Hrs Open:* 24; 2 kw; 299 ft.; N41 44 36 W85 5 48
PO Box 8459, Fort Wayne, IN 46898 US
(260) 452-1189; *Fax:* (260) 452-1188
manager@nipr.fm
License: Orland, Steuben County, IN held by Northeast Indiana Public Radio Inc.
Nat'l Network: NPR
Arbitron Metro Market: Fort Wayne, IN; *Format:* Classical
Will Murphy, President / General Manager
Colleen Condron, Operations Dir
Karen Fraser, General Sales Mgr
Sean Bueter, News Director
Ed Didier, Chief Engineer
Janice Furtner, Music Director
Jackie Didier, Traffic Manager
KatyAnderson, Operations Manager
Sarah Delia, Reporter
Lea Denny, Office Manager/Special Events Coordinator
Jennifer DePoy, Finance Manager

Orleans

WPHZ
08-17-1991; 102.5 MHz FM; *Hrs Open:* 24; 6 kw; 282 ft.; N38 38 16 W86 27 11
PO Box 1307, Bedford, IN 47421 US
(812) 275-7555; *Fax:* (812) 279-8046
www.wphz.com
License: Orleans, Lawrence County, IN held by Mitchell Community Broadcast Co.
Nat'l Network: ABC; Jones Radio Networks; *Nat'l Reps:* Rgnl Reps
Arbitron Metro Market: Orleans, IN; *Format:* Adult Contemp; *Hrs. of News Programming:* news progmg 2 hrs wkly; *No. News Employees:* 1; *Target Audience:* General.
Holly Lindsey, General Manager
Sarah Reinhard, Sales Manager

Paoli

WSEZ
11-07-1963; 1560 kHz AM; *Hrs Open:* 6 AM-6 PM; 0.25 kw-D, NDD; N38 32 25 W86 28 42
192 South Court Street, Paoli, IN 47454 US
(812) 723-4484; *Fax:* (812) 723-4966
hitsandfavorites.com
wume@blueriver.net
License: Paoli, IN held by Diamond Shores Broadcasting
Regional Network: Network Indiana; *Nat'l Reps:* Rgnl Reps
Format: Oldies *Special Programming:* Farm 7 hrs wkly; *Hrs. of News Programming:* news progmg 7 hrs wkly; *No. News Employees:* 1; *Target Audience:* General.; *Adv. Rates:* 8; 8; 8; 6
Blair Trask, President/CEO
Jerry Wall, General Manager/General Sales Manager
Jason Archer, Programming Director
Dave Dedrick, News Director
Todd Edwards, Chief Engineer

WUME-FM
09-01-1972; 95.3 MHz FM; *Hrs Open:* 24; 3 kw; 299 ft.; N38 32 25 W86 28 42
192 South Court Street, Paoli, IN 47454 US
(812) 723-4484; *Fax:* (812) 723-4966
hitsandfavorites.com
License: Paoli, Orange County, IN held by Diamond Shores Broadcasting
Group Owner: Diamond Shores Broadcasting
Nat'l Network: ABC *Regional Reps:* Rgnl Reps
Arbitron Metro Market: Paoli, IN; *Format:* Contemporary Hits/Top 40; *Hrs. of News Programming:* news progmg 9 hrs wkly; *No. News Employees:* 1; *Target Audience:* General.; *Adv. Rates:* 15; 14; 14; 8
Blair Trask, President/CEO
Jerry Wall, General Manager
Jason Archer, Programming/Traffic Manager
Dave Dedrick, News Director
Todd Edwards, Chief Engineer

Paris

WWVR
01-20-1967; 98.5 MHz FM; 50 kW; 499 ft.; N39 36 20 W87 43 32
824 South 3rd St, Terre Haute, IN 47807 USA
985theriver.com
License: Paris, IL held by Midwest Communications Inc.
Group Owner: Midwest Communications Inc.
Arbitron Metro Market: Terre Haute, IN; *Format:* Classic Rock *Special Programming:* Gospel, news/talk, Black 6 hrs wkly; *Hrs. of News Programming:* News progmg 6 hrs wkly; *Target Audience:* 35-64.
Scott Steele, Brand Manager

Pendleton

***WEEM-FM**
11-01-1971; 91.7 MHz FM; *Hrs Open:* 24; 1.2 kw; 154 ft.; N39 59 52 W85 44 7
201 South East Street, Pendleton, IN 46064 US
(765) 778-2161; *Fax:* (765) 778-0605
www.917weem.org
jpetrey@smadison.k12.in.us
License: Pendleton, Madison County, IN held by South Madison Community School Corp.
Regional Network: Network Indiana
Arbitron Metro Market: Pendleton, IN; *Format:* Triple A *Special Programming:* High school sports 10 hrs, acoustic cafe 2 hrs, ed; *Target Audience:* Adults 18-45, students 13-18.
Jered Petrey, General Manager/Instructor
Morgan Landes, Programming Director
Kinsey Sturgeon, Production Director
Kerrigan McClain, Social Media Director

Peru

WARU
09-12-1954; 1600 kHz AM; *Hrs Open:* 24; 1 kw-D, ND2; 0.037 kw-N, ND2; N40 45 53 W86 2 26
Mailing Address: P. O. Box 1970, Martinsville, IN 46151 US
Second Address: 1711 E. Wabash Rd., Peru, IN 46970
(765) 473-4448; *Fax:* (765) 473-4449
waru@sbcglobal.net
License: Peru, IN held by Dram Weaver Marketing LLC
Group Owner: Dream Weaver Marketing LLC
Nat'l Network: AP Radio; *Nat'l Reps:* Rgnl Reps
Arbitron Metro Market: Peru, IN; *Format:* Country; *Hrs. of News Programming:* news progmg 20 hrs wkly; *No. News Employees:* 1; *Target Audience:* 25-54.; *Adv. Rates:* 14; 14; 14; 14
Wade Weaver, Owner/GM

WMYK
04-05-1965; 98.5 MHz FM; *Hrs Open:* 24; 6 kw; 328 ft.; N40 37 46 W86 2 30

Mailing Address: P. O. Box 1010, State Road 26, Peru, IN 46970 US
Second Address: 671 E. 400 S., Kokomo, IN 46902
(414)529-2122; *Fax:* (765) 455-3882
www.991themix.com
License: Peru, Miami County, IN held by Hoosier AM/FM, LLC
Group Owner: Hoosier AM/FM, LLC; (acq 1996; $360,000 with WARU(AM) P
Nat'l Network: ABC
Arbitron Metro Market: Peru, IN; *Format:* Classic Rock; *No. News Employees:* 2; *Target Audience:* 25-54.
Ernie Caldemone, President/General Manager
Russ Dodge, Sales Manager
Mike Turner, Programming Director
Lora Lacey, Senior Account Executive
Steve Ross, Chief Engineer

Petersburg

WBTO
10-08-1984; 102.3 MHz FM; *Hrs Open:* 24; 3 kw; 322 ft.; N38 30 33 W87 17 28
522 Busseron St., Vincennes, IN 47591 US
(812) 882-6060
www.wbtofm.com
License: Petersburg, IN held by The Original Company, Inc
Group Owner: The Original Company Inc.
Format: Classic Rock
Mark Lange, President

Plainfield

WRDZ-FM
07-01-2003; 98.3 MHz FM; *Hrs Open:* 24; 3 kw; 299 ft.; N39 45 33 W86 22 30
4802 East 62nd St, Indianapolis, IN 46220 US
(317) 574-2000; *Fax:* (317) 581-1985
www.radiodisney.com
License: Plainfield, Hendricks County, IN held by Radio Disney Group LLC.
Group Owner: ABC Inc.; (acq 7-1-03; $5.6 million).
Nat'l Network: Radio Disney; *Nat'l Reps:* McGavren Guild
Arbitron Metro Market: Indianapolis, IN; *Format:* Christian; *Target Audience:* W25-44. Kids 4-12; *Adv. Rates:* 75; 75; 75; 75
Jim McCondville, General Manager
Laura Sanchez, Promotions Manager

*WWDL
91.3 MHz FM; 0.2 kw; 141 ft.; N39 40 18 W86 21 30
Rebroadcasts: Rebroadcasts WRYP (FM)
7700 Indian Lake Rd, Indianapolis, IN 46236 US
(317) 823-2349; *Fax:* (858) 277-1365
License: Plainfield, Boone County, IN held by Horizon Christian Fellowship.
Group Owner: Horizon Christian Fellowship; (acq 3-6-2006).
Arbitron Metro Market: Plainfield, IN
Mike MacIntosh, President

Plymouth

WTCA
08-18-1964; 1050 kHz AM; *Hrs Open:* 24/7; 0.25 kw-D, DA2; 0.25 kw-N, DA2; N41 19 6 W86 18 41
112 West Washington, Plymouth, IN 46563 US
(574) 936-4096; *Fax:* (574) 936-6776
am1050.com
License: Plymouth, IN held by Community Service Broadcasters Inc.
Nat'l Network: Jones Radio Networks; *Regional Network:* Brownfield
Arbitron Metro Market: Plymouth, IN; *Format:* Contemporary Hits/Top 40, Adult Contemp *Special Programming:* Farm 3 hrs wkly religious 4hrs wkly; *Target Audience:* 25-65.
Ken Kunze, General Manager
Kathryn Bottorff, Station Manager
Jim Bottorff, General Sales Mgr
Tony Ross, Programming Director
Kathy Bottorff, News Director
James Kunze, Chief Engineer
Tony Ross, Sports Director

WZOC
07-20-1966; 94.3 MHz FM; 11.5 kW; 492 ft.; N41 31 42 W86 15 58
1301 East Douglas Rd, Mishawaka, IN 46545 USA
(574) 247-4343; *Fax:* (574) 273-4943
www.z943radio.com
License: Plymouth, Marshall County, IN held by WSJM, Inc.
Group Owner: Mid-West Family Broadcasting; (acq 9-12-96; $575,000)
Arbitron Metro Market: South Bend, IN; *Format:* Oldies
Bill Gamble, Operations Manager
Tony Gazzana, General Sales Mgr
Bill Gamble, Program Manager

*WIKV
01-01-2005; 89.3 MHz FM; 1.4 kw; 249 ft.; N41 20 51 W86 20 23
P O Drawer 2440, Tupelo, MS 38803 US
(800) 525-5683; *Fax:* (916) 251-1650
www.klove.com
klove@klove.com
License: Plymouth, Marshall County, IN held by Educational Media Foundation.
Group Owner: EMF Broadcasting; (acq 3-23-2007; grpsl)
Nat'l Network: K-Love
Arbitron Metro Market: Plymouth, IN; *Format:* Christian; *No. News Employees:* 13
Darrell Chambliss, Chairman
Mike Novak, President and CEO
David Pierce, Chief Creative Officer and Programming Director
Ed Lenane, News Director
Sam Wallington, Engineering Dir
Alan Mason, Chief Operating Officer
Dan Antonelli,Chief Business Development Officer
Eric Moser, Chief Financial Officer
Brian Burger, Vice President of Human Resources
D. Kevin Blair, Secretary and General Counsel
Tim Luttrell, News Reporter

Portage

WNDZ
05-13-1987; 750 kHz AM; *Hrs Open:* Daytime only; 15 kW; N41 33 49 W87 09 18
5625 N Milwaukee Ave, Chicago, IL 60646 USA
(773) 792-1121; *Fax:* (773) 792-2904
accessradiochicago.com
mp@wsbcradio.com
License: Portage, IN held by WNDZ Inc.
Group Owner: Newsweb Corp.; (acq 3-16-2004; $24 million with WCPQ(FM) Park Forest, IL)
Arbitron Metro Market: Chicago, IL; *Target Audience:* General.
Mark Pinski, General Manager

Portland

*WBSJ
12-01-1996; 91.7 MHz FM; 2 kw; 220 ft.; N40 24 26 W85 2 15
Rebroadcasts: Rebroadcasts WBST(FM) Muncie 100%
Ad 103, Muncie, IN 47306 US
(765) 285-5888; *Fax:* (765) 285-8937
www.bsu.edu/ipr
info@bsu.edu/ipr
License: Portland, Jay County, IN held by Ball State University.
Arbitron Metro Market: Muncie, IN; *Format:* News; *Hrs. of News Programming:* news progmg 33 hrs wkly; *No. News Employees:* 1; *Target Audience:* General.
John Strauss, General Manager
Angie Rapp, Marketing Director
Steven Turpin, Programming Director
Debbie Webb, Underwriting Coordinator
Genet Soule, Membership Development Coordinator
Terry Heifetz, News Director
RobertMittendorf, Chief Engineer

WPGW
01-14-1951; 1440 kHz AM; 0.5 kw-D, DAD; 0.045 kw-N, DAD; N40 26 10 W85 0 56
P. O. Box 1440, Portland, IN 47371 US
(260) 726-8729; *Fax:* (260) 726-4311
wpgw@jayco.net
License: Portland, IN held by WPGW Inc.
Nat'l Reps: Rgnl Reps
Format: Adult Contemp; *Target Audience:* General.
Robert Weaver, President

WPGW-FM
05-19-1975; 100.9 MHz FM; 4.6 kw; 180 ft.; N40 26 10 W85 0 54
P. O. Box 1440, Portland, IN 47371 US
(260) 726-8729; *Fax:* (260) 726-4311
wpgw@jayco.net
License: Portland, Jay County, IN held by WPGW Inc.
Format: Country; *Target Audience:* General.
Jeff Overholser, Programming Director
Laurette Horn, News Director

Princeton

WRAY
12-16-1950; 1250 kHz AM; *Hrs Open:* 24; 1 kw-D, ND1; 0.059 kw-N, ND1; N38 21 25 W87 35 25
P. O. Box 8, Princeton, IN 47670 US
(812) 386-1250; *Fax:* (812) 386-6249
www.wrayradio.com
wray@wrayradio.com
License: Princeton, IN held by Princeton Broadcasting Co. Inc.
Format: News, Talk; *No. News Employees:* 3; *Target Audience:* 25-54.
Stephen Lankford, General Manager
Lynn Roach, General Sales Mgr
Cliff Ingram, News Director
Dave Kunkel, Disc Jockey

WRAY-FM
05-15-1960; 98.1 MHz FM; *Hrs Open:* 24; 50 kw; 436 ft.; N38 21 25 W87 35 25
P. O. Box 8, Princeton, IN 47670 US
(812) 386-1250; *Fax:* (812) 386-6249
www.wrayradio.com
License: Princeton, Gibson County, IN
Format: Country
Stephen Lankford, General Manager
Cliff Ingram, News Director
Dave Kunkel, Disc Jockey

WSJD
10-01-1994; 100.5 MHz FM; *Hrs Open:* 24; 6 kw; 328 ft.; N38 23 24 W87 34 23
4314 Cherry Court, Evansville, IN 47714 US
(618) 262-4102; *Fax:* (618) 262-4103
wsjd@midwest.net
License: Princeton, Gibson County, IN held by WSJD Inc.
Group Owner: Southern Wabash Communications Corp.; (acq 8-3-01).
Regional Network: Ill. Radio Net.; Network Indiana; RFD Illinois
Arbitron Metro Market: Evansville, IN; *Format:* Oldies; *Hrs. of News Programming:* news progmg 20 hrs wkly; *No. News Employees:* 1; *Target Audience:* 25 plus.; *Adv. Rates:* 15; 12; 15; 5
Randolph Bell, President
Sally Dorgan Potts, Vice President
Scott Allen, General Manager/Programming Director

Rensselaer

WLQI
01-01-1973; 97.7 MHz FM; *Hrs Open:* 24; 3.3 kw; 299 ft.; N40 58 14 W87 9 10
Mailing Address: P.O. Box D, Rensselaer, IN 47978 US
Second Address: 560 W. Amster Rd., Rensselaer, IN 47978
(219) 866-5105; *Fax:* (219) 866-4104
www.1560wrin.com
License: Rensselaer, Jasper County, IN
Nat'l Network: Jones Radio Networks; *Regional Network:* Tribune Radio Networks
Format: Contemporary Hits/Top 40, Adult Contemp; *Hrs. of News Programming:* ndws progmg 10 hrs wkly; *No. News Employees:* 1; *Target Audience:* 25 plus.; *Adv. Rates:* 18; 13; 13; 7
Serap Jackson, Operations Dir
Michael Meeks, General Manager

*WPUM
09-06-1977; 93.3 MHz FM; *Hrs Open:* 24; 0.06 kw; 118 ft.; N40 55 12 W87 9 27
P.O. Box 651, U.S. Highway Route 231, Rensselaer, IN 47978 US
(219) 866-6000
License: Rensselaer, Jasper County, IN held by St. Joseph's College.
Nat'l Network: Superadio
Special Programming: Country 3 hrs, classical 3 hrs, blues 3 hrs, talk; *Hrs. of News Programming:* news progmg 10 hrs wkly; *No. News Employees:* 1; *Target Audience:* 18-34; general; *Adv. Rates:* 2; 2; 2; 2
Sally Nesselrode, Station Manager

WRIN
09-14-1963; 1560 kHz AM; 0.5 kw-C, NDD; 1 kw-D, NDD; N40 57 41 W87 9 7
Mailing Address: P.O. Box D, Rensselaer, IN 47978 US
Second Address: 560 W. Amster Rd., Rensselaer, IN
(219) 866-5105; *Fax:* (219) 866-5106
License: Rensselaer, IN held by Brothers Broadcasting Corp.
Nat'l Reps: Rgnl Reps
Format: Adult Contemp *Special Programming:* Farm 12 hrs, gospel 2 hrs, relg 10 hrs wkly; *Hrs. of News Programming:* news progmg 10 hrs wkly; *No. News Employees:* 1; *Target Audience:* 30+.

John Balvich, President
Connie Graham Luthi, General Sales Mgr
Bob Burt, Programming Director
Bob Kurtz, News Director

Richmond

*WECI

09-01-1964; 91.5 MHz FM; *Hrs Open:* 6 AM-3 AM; 0.4 kw; 125 ft.; N39 48 29 W84 54 47
Drawer 45, Richmond, IN 47374 US
(765) 983-1246; *Fax:* (765) 983-1641
www.weciradio.org/
Station.manager.weci@gmail.com
License: Richmond, Wayne County, IN held by Earlham College.
Arbitron Metro Market: Richmond, IN; *Format:* Country, Variety/Diverse *Special Programming:* Bluegrass/folk 19 hrs, classic rock 16 hrs, progsv
Katie Laushman & Rosa Ostrom, Station Managers
Ashley Girvin, Production Manager
David Walker, Business Manager
Krystnell Storr, News Director

WFMG

12-17-1960; 101.3 MHz FM; *Hrs Open:* 24; 20.5 kw; 272 ft.; N39 49 41 W84 55 57
2301 West Main Street, Richmond, IN 47374 US
(765) 962-6533; *Fax:* (765) 966-1499
www.g1013.com
info@g1013.com
License: Richmond, Wayne County, IN held by DBA Whitewater Broadcasting Corp.
Group Owner: DBA Whitewater Broadcasting Corp.
Format: Adult Contemp *Special Programming:* Miami University Sports 8 hrs wkly; *Hrs. of News Programming:* news progmg 2 hrs wkly; *No. News Employees:* 2; *Target Audience:* 18-44.; *Adv. Rates:* 22; 22; 22; 11
David Rodgers, President
Rick Duncan, Operations Dir
Michelle Bottomley, Station Manager
Rick Duncan, Programming Director
Dave Snow, Promotions Manager
Joel Brantingham, News Director
Steve Frey, Advertising
Andrew Hoover,Sales Manager/Public Service Announcements
John Rose, Production Manager

WKBV

09-27-1926; 1490 kHz AM; *Hrs Open:* 24; 1 kw-U; N39 49 30 W84 55 50
Box 1646, 2301 W. Main St., Richmond, IN 47374
(765) 962-6533; *Fax:* (765) 966-1499
License: Richmond, Wayne County, IN held by DBA Whitewater Broadcasting Corp.
Group Owner: DBA Whitewater Broadcasting Corp.
Nat'l Network: ABC; ESPN Radio; *Regional Network:* Network Indiana
Population Served: 500,000 *Special Programming:* Farm 4 hrs wkly; *Hrs. of News Programming:* news progmg 10 hrs wkly; *No. News Employees:* 2; *Target Audience:* 25-54.; *Adv. Rates:* 16; 16; 16; 8
David Rodgers, President
Rick Duncan, Operations/Programming Director
Michelle Bottomley, Station Manager
Dave Snow, Promotions Manager
Joel Brantingham, News Director
Andrew Hoover, Sales Manager/Public Service Announcements
John Rose, Production Manager

WQLK

10-15-1973; 96.1 MHz FM; *Hrs Open:* 24; 50 kw; 492 ft.; N39 53 28.5 W84 56 9.5
2626 Tingler Rd., Richmond, IN 47375 US
(765) 962-1595; *Fax:* (765) 966-4824
www.kicks96.com
License: Richmond, Wayne County, IN held by Brewer Broadcasting Corp.
Group Owner: Brewer Broadcasting Corp.
Arbitron Metro Market: Richmond, IN; *Format:* Country; *No. News Employees:* 1; *Target Audience:* 25-54.
Keith Landecker, Operations Manager
Dave Strycker, General Manager
Katie Alyea, Account Executive
Laura Bailey, Account Executive
Marty Hancock, Account Executive
John Westover, Account Executive

Roann

WARU-FM

01-01-2001; 101.9 MHz FM; *Hrs Open:* 24; 3.6 kw; 423 ft.; N40 48 30 W85 56 7
P.O. Box 1970, Martinsville, IN 46151 US
(765) 473-4448; *Fax:* (765) 473-4449
www.mitunes1019.com
License: Roann, Wabash County, IN held by Dream Weaver Marketing LLC
Group Owner: Dream Weaver Marketing LLC
Arbitron Metro Market: Peru, IN; *Format:* Adult Contemp; *Hrs. of News Programming:* news progmg 4 hrs wkly; *No. News Employees:* 1; *Adv. Rates:* 18; 18; 18; 18
Wade Weaver, Owner/GM
Julie Deniston, Sales Manager

Roanoke

*WBNI-FM

01-01-1991; 94.1 MHz FM; *Hrs Open:* 24; 3.4 kw; 328 ft.; N40 58 51 W85 16 48 *Rebroadcasts:* Simulcast with WCKZ(FM) Orland 100%
650 Madison Ave, New York, NY 10022 US
(260) 452-1189; *Fax:* (260) 452-1188
www.nipr.fm
jbrown@nipr.fm
License: Roanoke, Huntington County, IN held by Northeast Indiana Public Radio Inc.
Nat'l Network: NPR
Arbitron Metro Market: Fort Wayne, IN; *Format:* Classical
Bruce Haines, General Manager
Karen Fraser, General Sales Mgr
Colleen Condron, Programming Director
Jeanette Dillon, News Director

Rochester

WROI

08-29-1971; 92.1 MHz FM; *Hrs Open:* 24; 4.2 kw; 207 ft.; N41 3 14 W86 16 12
110 East 8th Street, Rochester, IN 46975 US
(574) 223-6059; *Fax:* (574) 223-2238
www.wroifm.com
wroi@rtcol.com
License: Rochester, Fulton County, IN held by Bair Communications Inc.
Nat'l Network: ABC Information & Entertainment; Westwood One; *Regional Network:* Brownfield; Network Indiana; *Nat'l Reps:* Rgnl Reps
Format: Oldies *Special Programming:* Farm 10 hrs, relg 6 hrs wkly; *Hrs. of News Programming:* news progmg 20 hrs wkly; *No. News Employees:* 1; *Target Audience:* General.
Tom Bair, President
Sue Bair, General Sales Mgr
Matt Bair, Programming Director
Baron Imhoof, News Director

Rockville

WAXI

08-01-1977; 104.9 MHz FM; *Hrs Open:* 24; 3000 kw; 440 ft.; N39 43 44 W87 17 56
2865 S. Co. Rd. 325 W., P.O. Box 104, Rockville, IN 47872 US
(765) 569-3940; *Fax:* (765) 569-3945
www.trueoldieswaxi.com
waxi1049@gmail.com
License: Rockville, Parke County, IN held by DLC Media INC.
Group Owner: DLC Media INC.; (acq 4-20-98; $485,000).
Nat'l Network: CBS; *Regional Network:* Brownfield Network; *Nat'l Reps:* Rgnl Reps
Arbitron Metro Market: Sulphur LA; *Format:* Christian *Special Programming:* Indiana Pacers, Brickyard 400, Indiana Sports Talk, Terre Haute Rex Baseball, Local high school sports; *Adv. Rates:* 13; 13; 13; 10
Barry Kent, Operations Dir
Tyler Davis, News Director

Royal Center

WHZR

10-16-1989; 103.7 MHz FM; *Hrs Open:* 24; 6 kw; 328 ft.; N40 48 43 W86 21 56
Logansport/Peru, Inc., 60 North Wayne Street, Martinsville, IN 46151 US
(574) 732-1037; *Fax:* (574) 739-1037
www.indianasbestradio.com
whzr@verizon.net
License: Royal Center, Cass County, IN held by Mid-America Radio Group of Logansport-Peru Inc.
Group Owner: Mid-America Radio Group Inc.; (acq 5-1-95; $450,000;
Format: Country; *Hrs. of News Programming:* news progmg 6 hrs wkly; *No. News Employees:* 1; *Target Audience:* 18-49; mass appeal; *Adv. Rates:* 15; 15; 15; 15
David Keister, President
Dan Keister, General Manager
Milt Hess, Sports Director
Laurie Novotny, Account Executive
Dale Lowe, Disc Jockey

Rushville

WIFE-FM

08-05-1971; 94.3 MHz FM; 1.05 kw; 561 ft.; N39 42 22 W85 29 41
102 North Perkins Street, Rushville, IN 46173 US
(765) 932-3983; *Fax:* (765) 938-1916
License: Rushville, Rush County, IN held by Rodgers Broadcasting Corp.
Group Owner: Rodgers Broadcasting Corp.; (acq 7-5-2007; $1.5 million)
Nat'l Reps: Christal; Rgnl Reps
Format: Country *Special Programming:* Farm 18 hrs wkly; *Target Audience:* 35 plus.
David Rodgers, President
Scott Huber, General Manager
Kevin Stone, General Sales Mgr
Doug Raab, Programming Director
Martha Swain, News Director

*WRLN

91.9 MHz FM; 225 w; Ant 263 ft; N39 37 10.8 W85 24 24
330 West 8th Street, Rushville, IN 45214
(765) 932-4186
www.wmub.org
License: Rushville, Rush County, IN held by Rush County Schools
Population Served: 6,303; *Arbitron Metro Market:* Rushville, IN
Edward Small, Broadcast Director

Salem

WNRW

01-01-1962; 98.9 MHz FM; *Hrs Open:* 24; 50 kw; 300 ft; N38 35 59 W86 05 17
4000 # 1 Radio Drive, Louisville, KY 40218-4568 US
(502) 479-2222; *Fax:* (502) 479-2308
www.989radionow.com
License: Salem, Washington County, IN held by CC Licenses LLC.
Group Owner: iHeartMedia; (acq 12-31-96)
Nat'l Reps: Clear Channel
Population Served: 942,300; *Arbitron Metro Market:* Louisville, KY; *Format:* Contemporary Hits/Top 40; *Target Audience:* 18-54; country music listeners
Earl Jones, Market President
Kevin Hughes, Senior Vice President of Sales
Kobi Kearney, Programming Director

WSLM

02-14-1953; 1220 kHz AM; *Hrs Open:* 18; 5 kw-D, DA2; 0.082 kw-N, DA2; N38 36 55 W86 5 10
Mailing Address: 1308 Hwy 56-E, PO Box 385, Salem, IN 47167 US
Second Address: 1308 Hwy 56 East, Salem, IN 47167
(812) 883-5750; *Fax:* (812) 883-2797
wslmradio.webs.com
wslm@blueriver.net
License: Salem, IN held by Don H. Martin.
Regional Network: Network Indiana; Tribune Radio Networks; *Nat'l Reps:* Rgnl Reps
Format: Religious; *Hrs. of News Programming:* news progmg 12 hrs wkly; *No. News Employees:* 5; *Target Audience:* 21-70.
Don Martin, President
J.R. Martin, Station Manager
Rebecca White, Programming Director
Becky White, Advertising Director

WSLM-FM

01-01-1992; 97.9 MHz FM; *Hrs Open:* 18; 3 kw; 328 ft.; N38 38 7 W86 10 37
Mailing Address: P.O. Box 385, 1308 Hwy 56-E, Salem, IN 47167 US
Second Address: 1308 Hwy 56 East, Salem, IN 47167
(812) 883-5750; *Fax:* (812) 883-2797
wslm@blueriver.net
License: Salem, Washington County, IN held by Rebecca L. White.
Format: Religious; *Hrs. of News Programming:* 3; *No. News Employees:* 2; *Target Audience:* 18-65.
Rebecca White, Programming Director
Don Martin, Programming Director

Santa Claus

WAXL
07-30-1996; 103.3 MHz FM; *Hrs Open:* 24; 3 kw; 463 ft.; N38 12 31 W86 54 0
Mailing Address: Box 1009, Jasper, IN 47546 US
Second Address: 458 3rd Ave., Jasper, IN 47546
(812) 482-2727; *Fax:* (812) 482-3696
www.waxl.us
mailbox@waxl.us
License: Santa Claus, Spencer County, IN held by Dubois County Broadcasting Inc.
Group Owner: DCBroadcasting Inc.; (acq 7-25-97)
Nat'l Network: ABC; *Regional Network:* Network Indiana; Brownfield; *Wire Services:* AP
Format: Adult Contemp; *Adv. Rates:* 18; 15; 15; 13
Paul Knies, President

Scottsburg

WMPI
12-16-1966; 105.3 MHz FM; *Hrs Open:* 24; 2.2 kw; 512 ft.; N38 42 44 W85 41 12
223 N. 820 West, Kokomo, IN 46901 US
(812) 752-5612; *Fax:* (812) 752-2345
www.i1053.com
rrice@i1053.com
License: Scottsburg, Scott County, IN held by D. R. Rice Broadcasting Inc.
Nat'l Reps: Rgnl Reps
Arbitron Metro Market: Louisville, KY; *Format:* Country; *Hrs. of News Programming:* news progmg 5 hrs wkly; *No. News Employees:* 1; *Target Audience:* 25-54.
Donald Rice, President
Raymond Rice, General Manager
Tom Cull, General Sales Mgr
John Ross, Programming Director
Steve Woodruff, Chief Engineer

Seelyville

*WVWG
88.9 MHz FM; 0.1 kw; N39 31 15 W87 13 34
150 West Lincolnway, Suite 2001, Valparaiso, IN 46383 US
(219) 548-5800; *Fax:* (219) 548-5808
www.calvaryradionetwork.com
info@CalvaryRadioNetwork.com
License: Seelyville, Vigo County, IN held by Calvary Radio Network, Inc.
Group Owner: Calvary Radio Network
Format: Christian, Religious; *Target Audience:* 18-54

Sellersburg

WLCL
01-01-1990; 93.9 MHz FM; *Hrs Open:* 24; 2.65 kw; Ant 328 ft; N38 15 21 W85 45 29
6721 W. 121st St., Overland Park, KS 66209 US
(913) 344-1500
License: Sellersburg, IN held by UB Louisville, LLC
Group Owner: UB Louisville, LLC
Population Served: 36,570; *Arbitron Metro Market:* New Albany, In; *Format:* Sports

Seymour

*WJLR
08-01-1995; 91.5 MHz FM; *Hrs Open:* 24; 30 kw; 381 ft.; N38 49 20 W85 47 38
1680 Highway 62 Ne, Corydon, IN 47112 US
(916) 251-1600; *Fax:* (916) 251-1650
www.klove.com
License: Seymour, Jackson County, IN held by Educational Media Foundation.
Group Owner: EMF Broadcasting; (acq 11-9-2004; $150,000).
Nat'l Network: K-Love
Format: Christian; *Target Audience:* 30-80; family oriented
Mike Novak, President
Eric Allen, General Sales Mgr
David Pierce, Programming Director
Ed Lenane, News Director
Sam Wallington, Engineering Dir
Marya Morgan, News Reporter
Richard Hunt, News Reporter
Chip Bailey, RegionalManager

WZZB
11-04-1949; 1390 kHz AM; *Hrs Open:* 24; 1 kw-D, ND1; 0.074 kw-N, ND1; N38 58 33 W85 53 21
Mailing Address: P.O Box 726, Jeffersonville, IN 47131 US
Second Address: 1534 Ewing St., Seymour, IN 47274
(812) 522-1390; *Fax:* (812) 522-9541
www.wzzb1390.com
info@wklo969.com
License: Seymour, IN held by Midnight Hour Broadcasting LLC.
Nat'l Network: USA; Jones Radio Networks; *Regional Network:* Network Indiana *Regional Reps:* Rgnl Reps.
Arbitron Metro Market: Seymour, IN; *Format:* News, Sports
Special Programming: Farm 2 hrs, relg 6 hrs wkly; *Hrs. of News Programming:* news progmg 17 hrs wkly; *No. News Employees:* 2; *Target Audience:* 25plus; community oriented
Blair Trask, President
Bud Shippee, Operations Dir
Bob Hawkins, Chief Engineer

Shelbyville

WLHK
11-06-1964; 97.1 MHz FM; *Hrs Open:* 24; 23 kw; 732 ft.; N39 40 6 W86 1 44
40 Monument Circle, Suite 600, Indianapolis, IN 46204 USA
(317) 266-9700; *Fax:* (317) 684-2021
www.hankfm.com
License: Shelbyville, Shelby County, IN held by Emmis Radio License LLC
Group Owner: Emmis Communications Corp.
Nat'l Reps: D & R Radio
Arbitron Metro Market: Shelbyville, IN; *Format:* Country; *No. News Employees:* 1; *Target Audience:* 25-54; female
Bob Richards, Operations Dir
Bill Davis, Sales Manager
Bob Richards, Programming Director
Lisa Wall, Promotions Manager

WSVX
01-14-1961; 1520 kHz AM
2356 North Morristown Road, Shelbyville, IN 46176 US
(317) 398-2200; *Fax:* (317) 392-3292
www.wsvx.com
info@wsvx.com
License: Shelbyville, IN held by 3 Towers Broadcasting Company, LLC
Regional Network: Brownfield
Arbitron Metro Market: Indianapolis, I *TV Affiliate:* adult contemp
Special Programming: news progmg 3 hrs wkly; *Hrs. of News Programming:* 1; *No. News Employees:* Shelby County.
Tyson Conrady, Programming/Operations Director
Scott Huber, General Manager
John Schoentrup, General Sales Mgr
Penny Lane, Promotions Director
Jessica McLean, Social Media Director
Johnny McRory, News/Sports Director

South Bend

*WETL
11-17-1958; 91.7 MHz FM; 3 kw; 299 ft.; N41 37 24 W86 14 15
635 South Main Street, South Bend, IN 46623 US
(574) 283-8432; *Fax:* (574) 283-8405
License: South Bend, St. Joseph County, IN held by South Bend Community School Corp.
Arbitron Metro Market: South Bend, IN; *Format:* Talk; *Target Audience:* General; student in the South Bend community school and community
Carl Brandt, General Manager
John Overmyer, Programming Director/Radio Instructor
Allen Wujcik, Chief Engineer

WHME
01-01-1968; 103.1 MHz FM; *Hrs Open:* 24; 3 kw; 299 ft.; N41 36 11 W86 12 51
61300 South Ironwood Rd, South Bend, IN 46614 US
(574) 291-8200; *Fax:* (574) 291-9043
www.whmefm.com
info@whme.com
License: South Bend, St. Joseph County, IN held by Le Sea Broadcasting Corp.
Group Owner: Le Sea Broadcasting
Arbitron Metro Market: South Bend, IN *TV Affiliate:* WHME-TV affil.; *Format:* 0, Christian; *Hrs. of News Programming:* News progmg 3 hrs wkly; *Target Audience:* 24-36; general
Pete Sumrall, President/CEO
Tony Agostino, CFO
Anna Riblet, Sales
Wes Hylton, Chief Engineer

WHLY
12-22-1947; 1580 kHz AM; *Hrs Open:* 24; 1 kw-D, DAN; 0.5 kw-N, DAN; N41 41 9 W86 9 53
930 East Lincoln Avenue, Goshen, IN 46528 US
(574) 533-3330
www.larazaindiana.com
lazrazaindiana@yahoo.com
License: South Bend, IN held by IB Communications Ltd.
Nat'l Network: EWTN Radio
Arbitron Metro Market: South Bend, IN; *Format:* Christian
Ignacio Zepeda, President/General Manager

WDND
01-01-1944; 1620 kHz AM; *Hrs Open:* 24
3371 Cleveland Road, Suite 300, South Bend, IN 46628 US
(574) 273-9300; *Fax:* (574) 273-9090
www.u93.com
License: South Bend, IN held by Artistic Media Partners Inc.
Group Owner: Artistic Media Partners Inc.; (acq 10-22-98; $6,123,180 with co-l
Nat'l Network: ESPN Radio; *Nat'l Reps:* McGavren Guild
Arbitron Metro Market: South Bend, IN; *Format:* Contemporary Hits/Top 40; *Target Audience:* 25-54.
Arthur Angotti, III, President
Karen Right, Operations Dir
Pam Homan, General Manager
Rita Kenzie, Business Manager
Jeff Smith, Local Sales Manager
Rob Sparks, Programming Director

WNDV-FM
01-01-1962; 92.9 MHz FM; *Hrs Open:* 24; 12 kw; 879 ft.; N41 36 20 W86 12 46
3371 Cleveland Road, Suite 300, South Bend, IN 46628 US
(574) 273-9300; *Fax:* (574) 273-9090
www.u93.com
License: South Bend, St. Joseph County, IN
Group Owner: Artistic Media Partners Inc.
Arbitron Metro Market: South Bend, IN; *Format:* Contemporary Hits/Top 40; *Target Audience:* 25-44; women
Athur Angotti, III, President
Karen Right, Operations Dir
Pam Homan, General Manager
Rita Kenzie, Business Manager
Jeff Smith, Local Sales Manager
Rob Sparks, Programming Director

WNSN
08-01-1962; 101.5 MHz FM; 13 kW; 971 ft.; N41 37 0 W86 13 1
1301 East Douglas Rd, Mishawaka, IN 46545 USA
(574) 247-4343; *Fax:* (574) 289-7382
www.sunny1015.com
License: South Bend, St. Joseph County, IN held by WSJM, Inc.
Group Owner: Mid-West Family Broadcasting
Arbitron Metro Market: South Bend, IN *TV Affiliate:* WSBT;
Format: Adult Contemp; *Hrs. of News Programming:* news progmg 2 hrs wkly; *No. News Employees:* 1; *Target Audience:* 25-54; adults
Bill Gamble, Operations Manager
Tony Gazzana, General Sales Mgr

WRBR-FM
01-01-1965; 103.9 MHz FM; 3 kw; 328 ft.; N41 41 53 W86 9 25
237 West Edison Road, Suite 200, Mishawaka, IN 46545 US
(574) 258-5483; *Fax:* (574) 258-0930
www.wrbr.com
License: South Bend, St. Joseph County, IN held by Talking Stick Communications L.L.C
Group Owner: Talking Stick Communications LLC; (acq 6-26-2002; $840,879)
Nat'l Reps: Christal
Arbitron Metro Market: South Bend, IN; *Format:* Rock/AOR; *Target Audience:* 25-54; affluent, older people
Clint Marsh, General Manager
Ann Earnhart, General Sales Mgr
Ron Stryker, Programming Director
Greg Trobridge, Chief Engineer

WSBT
04-01-1922; 960 kHz AM; *Hrs Open:* 24
1301 East Douglas Rd, Mishawaka, IN 46545 USA
(574) 233-3141; *Fax:* (574) 239-4231
www.wsbtradio.com
License: South Bend, IN
Group Owner: Mid-West Family Broadcasting
Nat'l Network: CBS Sports Radio
Arbitron Metro Market: South Bend, IN *TV Affiliate:* WSBT;
Format: News/Talk, Sports; *Hrs. of News Programming:* news progmg 10 hrs wkly; *No. News Employees:* 3; *Target Audience:* 25-54.

*WUBS
01-01-1993; 89.7 MHz FM; 1.5 kw; 79 ft.; N41 40 51 W86 15 34
P.O. Box 3931, South Bend, IN 46619 US
(574) 287-4700; *Fax:* (574) 287-2478
www.wubs.org
broshane@wubs.org
License: South Bend, St. Joseph County, IN held by Interfaith Christian Union Inc.

Arbitron Metro Market: South Bend, IN *TV Affiliate:* UBS-TV; *Format:* Religious
Rev. Sylvester Williams Jr., General Manager
Shane Williams, Programming Director
Brian Hoover, Chief Engineer

WUBU
10-01-1992; 106.3 MHz FM; *Hrs Open:* 24; 3 kw; 302 ft.; N41 40 35 W86 15 8
515 N. Ridgeland, Oak Park, IL 60302 US
(574) 233-3505; *Fax:* (574) 233-0580
www.wububfm.com
ghegland@wububfm.com
License: South Bend, St. Joseph County, IN held by Partnership Radio LLC
Nat'l Network: Jones Radio Networks; *Nat'l Reps:* Interep; McGavren Guild
Arbitron Metro Market: South Bend, IN; *Format:* Adult Contemp; *Target Audience:* 35-64; adults
Gene Walker, General Manager
Tonya Reed, General Sales Mgr
Greg Trobridge, Chief Engineer
Gary Hegland, Production Manger
Amy Mejer, Business Manager
April Miller, Production Assistant
Ron Moore, Sales Representative

South Whitley

WMYQ
12-02-1992; 101.1 MHz FM; *Hrs Open:* 24; 6 kw; 328 ft.; N41 5 58 W85 43 29
P.O.Box 5570, Ft. Wayne, IN 46895 US
(260) 213-4370; *Fax:* (260) 471-4447
License: South Whitley, Whitley County, IN held by Larko Communications Inc.
Nat'l Network: ABC
Arbitron Metro Market: Fort Wayne, IN; *Format:* Adult Contemp; *Target Audience:* 25-44.
Chris Larko, CEO
Dean Jackson, News Director

Speedway

WNOW
05-28-1967; 100.9 MHz FM; *Hrs Open:* 24; 6 kw; 328 ft.; N39 48 1 W86 4 39
21 E. St. Joseph St., Indianapolis, IN 46204 US
(317) 266-9600; *Fax:* (317) 261-4664
www.radionowindy.com
License: Speedway, Marion County, IN held by Radio One of Indiana LLC.
Group Owner: Radio One Inc.; (acq 11-8-2001; grpsl)
Nat'l Network: ABC; *Nat'l Reps:* Katz Radio
Arbitron Metro Market: Speedway, IN; *Format:* Contemporary Hits/Top 40; *Hrs. of News Programming:* news progmg 12 hrs wkly; *No. News Employees:* 2; *Target Audience:* 25-54.
Chuck Williams, General Manager
Andrea Geiger, General Sales Mgr
Max Williams, Promotions Manager

Spencer

WCLS
09-15-1983; 97.7 MHz FM; 6 kw; 328 ft.; N39 13 22 W86 38 40
PO Box 388, Spencer, IN 47460 US
(812) 935-7400; *Fax:* (812) 935-7404
www.wclsfm.com
classichits@wclsfm.com
License: Spencer, Owen County, IN held by Mid-America Radio of Indiana Inc.
Group Owner: Mid-America Radio Group Inc.; (acq 11-13-2002; $321,100).
Nat'l Network: Westwood One
Format: Contemporary Hits/Top 40, Adult Contemp *Special Programming:* Relg 6 hrs wkly
David Bruce, General Manager
David Bruce, General Sales Mgr
Michelle Pierce, Sales Associate
Johnnie Moore, Sales Associate
Denise Figg, Sales Associate

Sullivan

WNDI
10-07-1963; 1550 kHz AM; 0.25 kw-D, NDD; N39 4 32 W87 23 57
556 East State Road 94, Sullivan, IN 47882 US
(812) 268-6322; *Fax:* (812) 268-6652
License: Sullivan, IN held by JTM Broadcasting Corp.
Arbitron Metro Market: Terre Haute, IN; *Format:* Country *Special Programming:* Farm 6 hrs wkly; *Target Audience:* 24-54.
John Montgomery, General Manager

WNDI-FM
08-10-1982; 95.3 MHz FM; 6 kw; 328 ft.; N39 9 36 W87 32 32
556 East State Road 54, Sullivan, IN 47882 US
(812) 268-6322; *Fax:* (812) 268-6652
License: Sullivan, Sullivan County, IN held by JTM Broadcasting Corp.
Arbitron Metro Market: Terre Haute, IN
John Montgomery, General Manager

Syracuse

WAWC
05-31-1991; 103.5 MHz FM; *Hrs Open:* 24; 3 kw; 328 ft.; N41 22 57 W85 41 35
10129 North 800 East, Syracuse, IN 46567 US
(307) 232-2155
www.kted1005.com
License: Syracuse, Kosciusko County, IN held by Talking Stick Communications LLC.
Group Owner: Talking Stick Communications LLC; (acq 11-1-2006; $600,000)
Nat'l Network: CBS; *Regional Network:* Network Indiana
Arbitron Metro Market: Evansville, WY; *Adv. Rates:* 15; 15; 15; 5.30
Steven Silberberg, President
Rood Dogg, Programming Director
Courtney Williams, Sales Representative

Tell City

WTCJ
02-01-1948; 1230 kHz AM; *Hrs Open:* 24
Mailing Address: 409 Chestnut Street, A-154, Chattanooga, TN 18277 US
Second Address: 1115 Tamarack Rd., Suite 500, Owensboro, KY 42301
(270) 683-5200; *Fax:* (270) 688-0108
www.tellcityradio.com
jcatinna@cromwellradio.com
License: Tell City, IN held by Hancock Communications Inc.
Group Owner: The Cromwell Group Inc.; (acq 12-20-99; $25,000)
Nat'l Network: ABC; *Nat'l Reps:* Rgnl Reps
Arbitron Metro Market: Owensboro, KY; *Format:* Classic Rock
Special Programming: Gospel 6 hrs wkly; *No. News Employees:* 1; *Target Audience:* 25-54; community-oriented listeners; *Adv. Rates:* 7.50; 7.50; 7.50;7.50
Bayard Walters, President
Jan Catinna, General Manager
Jeff Morgan, Programming Director
Mike Chaney, News Director

Terre Haute

WIBQ
1230 kHz AM; 1 kW; N39 29 21 W87 25 10
824 South 3rd St, Terre Haute, IN 47807 USA
(812) 232-4161; *Fax:* (812) 234-9999
wibqam.com
License: Terre Haute, IN held by Midwest Communications Inc.
Group Owner: Midwest Communications Inc.
Arbitron Metro Market: Terre Haute, IN; *Format:* News/Talk
Scott Steele, Brand Manager

***WHOJ**
01-01-1997; 91.9 MHz FM; 1.5 kw; 46 ft.; N39 28 5 W87 23 59
P.O. Drawer 2440, Tupelo, MS 38803 US
(314) 752-7000
www.covenantnet.net
webmaster@covenantnet.net
License: Terre Haute, Vigo County, IN held by Covenant Network.
Group Owner: Covenant Network; (acq 3-30-2004; $112,500 with KBKC(FM) Moberly, MO)
Arbitron Metro Market: Terre Haute, IN; *Format:* Christian, Talk, 74
Tony Holman, General Manager

***WCRT-FM**
01-01-1992; 88.5 MHz FM; 550 w; 308 ft.; N39 30 14 W87 26 37
2108 W. Springfield, Champaign, IL 62626
(217) 359-8232; *Fax:* (217) 359-7374
www.wbgl.org
wbgl@wbgl.org
License: Terre Haute, Vigo County, IN held by Illinois Bible Institute.
Group Owner: Illinois Bible Institute Inc.
Nat'l Reps: 4101 Fieldstone
Arbitron Metro Market: Terre Haute, IN
Jeff Scott, Station Manager
Ryan Springer, Programming Director
Jennifer Briski, Promotions Manager
Joe Buchanan, Music Director
Zoe Fuller, Underwriting Director

***WISU**
09-13-1964; 89.7 MHz FM; *Hrs Open:* 11 AM-2 AM; 13.5 kw; 512 ft.; N39 30 26 W87 31 50
217 Dreiser Hall- Isu, Terre Haute, IN 47809 US
(812) 237-3248; *Fax:* (812) 237-8970
wisu.indstate.edu
License: Terre Haute, Vigo County, IN held by Indiana State University Board of Trustees.
Arbitron Metro Market: Terre Haute, IN; *Format:* Rock/AOR; *Hrs. of News Programming:* News progmg 4 hrs wkly; *Target Audience:* 18-25; young professionals, students
Joe Tenerelli, General Manager
David Sabaini, Programming Director
Dan Watson, Chief Engineer

WBOW
05-23-1958; 1300 kHz AM; *Hrs Open:* 24; 0.5 kw-D, ND1; 0.075 kw-N, ND1; N39 28 1 W87 25 34 *Rebroadcasts:* Rebroadcasts WSDX(AM) Brazil
925 Wabash Ave., Suite 300, Terre Haute, IN 47807 US
(812) 917-3901; *Fax:* (812) 234-0089
wibqam.com
License: Terre Haute, IN held by Midwest Communications Inc.
Group Owner: Midwest Communications Inc.
Arbitron Metro Market: Terre Haute, IN; *Format:* Sports; *Hrs. of News Programming:* News progmg 5 hrs wkly; *Target Audience:* 25-64; *Adv. Rates:* 8; 8; 8; 4

WMGI
06-13-1960; 100.7 MHz FM; 50 kW; 489 ft.; N39 27 28 W87 28 50
824 South 3rd St, Terre Haute, IN 47807 USA
(812) 232-4161; *Fax:* (812) 234-9999
mymixfm.com
License: Terre Haute, Vigo County, IN held by Midwest Communications Inc.
Group Owner: Midwest Communications Inc.; (acq 6-13-2005; $3.39 million with
Nat'l Network: Westwood One; *Nat'l Reps:* Christal
Arbitron Metro Market: Terre Haute, IN; *Format:* Contemporary Hits/Top 40; *Target Audience:* 18-34.; *Adv. Rates:* 43; 43; 43; 28
Steve Cannon, Brand Manager

***WZIS(FM)**
01-01-1981; 90.7 MHz FM; *Hrs Open:* 8 AM-2 AM; 1.4 kw; 230 ft.; N39 30 14 W87 26 37
5500 Wabash Avenue, Terre Haute, IN 47803 US
(812) 872-6923; *Fax:* (812) 872-6926
License: Terre Haute, Vigo County, IN held by Rose Hulman Institute of Technology.
Arbitron Metro Market: Terre Haute, IN; *Format:* Variety/Diverse
Special Programming: Classical 4 hrs, bluegrass one hr, Jazz 2 hrs, con; *Hrs. of News Programming:* News progmg 2 hrs wkly; *Target Audience:* Loc &college audience
Kevin Lanke, Faculty Advisor

WPFR
01-06-1948; 1480 kHz AM; *Hrs Open:* 24; 5 kw-D, 1 kw-N, DA-2; N39 30 02 W87 23 10
18889 N. 23 50th St., Dennison, IL 91505
(217) 826-9673
wpfr@joink.com
License: Terre Haute, Vigo County, IN held by Word Power Inc.
Nat'l Network: Moody
Population Served: 70,286; *Arbitron Metro Market:* Terre Haute, IN; *Target Audience:* 12 plus.; *Adv. Rates:* 30; 30; 30; 30
Paul Ford, President
Eleanor Ford, Operations Dir
Paul Ford, General Manager
Dan Watson, Chief of Operations

WTHI-FM
10-01-1948; 99.9 MHz FM; *Hrs Open:* 24; 50 kW; 489 ft.; N39 27 57 W87 24 12
824 South 3rd St, Terre Haute, IN 47807 USA
(812) 478-1499
hi99.com
License: Terre Haute, Vigo County, IN held by Midwest Communications Inc.
Group Owner: Midwest Communications Inc.
Arbitron Metro Market: Terre Haute, IN; *Format:* Country
Eric Michaels, Brand Manager

WDWQ
102.7 MHz FM; 28 kW; 659 ft.; N39 20 13 W87 28 0
824 South 3rd St, Terre Haute, IN 47807 USA

(812) 232-4161; *Fax:* (812) 234-9999
q1027.com
License: Terre Haute, Vigo County, IN held by Midwest Communications Inc.
Group Owner: Midwest Communications Inc.
Arbitron Metro Market: Terre Haute, IN; *Format:* Country
Steve Cannon, Brand Manager

Union City

*WJYW

06-01-1999; 88.9 MHz FM; *Hrs Open:* 24; 4.1 kw; 285 ft.; N40 11 32 W84 47 58 *Rebroadcasts:* 94.5-Richmond, IN, 97.7-News Paris
Mailing Address: P.O. Box 889, Blacksburg, VA 24063 US
Second Address: 505 S. Division St., Union City, OH 45390
(937) 968-5633; *Fax:* (937) 968-3320
www.889joyfm.com
License: Union City, Randolph County, IN held by Positive Alternative Radio Inc.
Nat'l Network: Salem Radio Network
Format: Christian; *Target Audience:* 25-54; Women
Vernon Baker, CEO
Dan Franks, General Manager

Upland

*WTUR

09-04-1995; 89.7 MHz FM; 0.15 kw; 112 ft.; N40 25 2 W85 29 31
500 West Reade Avenue, Upland, IN 46989 US
(800) 882-3456; *Fax:* (765) 998-4810
www.tayloru.edu/wtur
License: Upland, Grant County, IN held by Taylor University.
Arbitron Metro Market: Upland, IN; *Format:* Christian; *Target Audience:* College age.
Dr. Gene B. Habecker, Ph.D., J.D., President
Kathy Bruner, Faculty Advisor

Valparaiso

WAKE

11-04-1964; 1500 kHz AM; *Hrs Open:* 24
2755 Sager Road, Valparaiso, IN 46383 US
(219) 462-6111; *Fax:* (219) 462-4880
www.wakeradio.com
donclark@radiooneindiana.com
License: Valparaiso, IN held by Porter County Broadcasting Holding Corp. LLC.
Group Owner: Porter County Broadcasting Corp.
Nat'l Network: CNN Radio
Arbitron Metro Market: Northwest Indiana; *Format:* News; *Target Audience:* 30 plus; community oriented, middle to middle-upper class
Leigh Ellis, Chairman
O.J. Jackson, General Sales Mgr
Don Clark, Programming Director
Laura Waluszko, News Director
Carl Fletcher, Chief Engineer
Jennifer Malmquist, Traffic Manager

WLJE

10-06-1967; 105.5 MHz FM; 1.25 kw; 512 ft.; N41 31 28 W87 1 8
2755 Sager Road, Valparaiso, IN 46383 US
(219) 462-8125; *Fax:* (219) 462-4880
www.indiana105.com
License: Valparaiso, Porter County, IN
Group Owner: Adams Radio Group
Arbitron Metro Market: Chicago, IL; *Format:* Country; *Target Audience:* 25-55; family, middle income
Ron Stone, President/CEO
Linda Minar, CFO
Kim Mitchell, General Sales Mgr
OJ Jackson, Market General Manager
Alan Mulford, Chief Engineer

*WVUR-FM

09-25-1966; 95.1 MHz FM; *Hrs Open:* 24; 0.036 kw horiz; 125 ft.; N41 27 57 W87 2 29
Office of the Provost, Kretzmann Hall, Valparaiso, IN 46383 US
(219) 464-5383; *Fax:* (219) 464-6742
www.valpo.edu/wvur
License: Valparaiso, Porter County, IN held by The Lutheran University Association Inc.
Arbitron Metro Market: Valparaiso, IN; *Format:* Variety/Diverse *Special Programming:* Class 3 hrs, jazz 3 hrs, urban contemp 3 hrs, meta; *Hrs. of News Programming:* news progmg 8 hrs wkly; *No. News Employees:* 2 *Target Audience:* 18-34.
Olivia Adams, General Manager
Joey Basil, Programming Director
Andrew Whitmyer, News Director
Andrew Stem, Faculty Advisor

Van Buren

WCJC

08-28-1989; 99.3 MHz FM; *Hrs Open:* 24; 3 kw; 328 ft.; N40 40 1 W85 37 49
820 S. Pennsylvania Street, Marion, IN 46953 US
(765) 664-6239; *Fax:* (765) 662-0730
www.wcjc.com
bigjohn@wcjc.com
License: Van Buren, Grant County, IN held by Hoosier AM/FM LLC
Group Owner: Hoosier AM/FM LLC
Nat'l Network: ABC *Regional Reps:* Regional Reps
Arbitron Metro Market: Muncie, IN; *Format:* Country *Special Programming:* Relg 3 hrs wkly; *Hrs. of News Programming:* news progmg 25 hrs wkly; *No. News Employees:* 2; *Target Audience:* 25-54; consumer-orientedmodern country fans; *Adv. Rates:* 28; 28; 28; 25
David Keister, President
Ernie Caldemone, Vice President/General Manager
John Clark, Sales Manager
Ed Thurman, News Director
Tim George, Operations/Programming Manager

Veedersburg

WSKL

07-15-1999; 92.9 MHz FM; *Hrs Open:* 24; 4.5 kw; 269 ft.; N40 8 46 W87 27 15
PO Box 67, Danville, IL 61834 US
(217) 443-4004; *Fax:* (765) 793-4644
www.koololdies.net
fmkool929@aol.com
License: Veedersburg, Fountain County, IN held by Zona Communications Inc.
Nat'l Network: AP Radio; Jones Radio Networks; *Wire Services:* AP
Format: Oldies; *Hrs. of News Programming:* news progmg 5 hrs wkly; *No. News Employees:* 1; *Target Audience:* 35-65.
Rhea Benton-Weatherford, General Manager
Greg Green, News Director
Larry Weatherford, Sales/Operations Manager

Versailles

*WKRY

04-11-2003; 88.1 MHz FM; *Hrs Open:* 24; 0.5 kw vert; 302 ft.; N39 4 6 W85 15 58
825 Washington Street, Suite 2C, Columbus, IN 47201 US
(812) 375-9947; *Fax:* (812) 375-2562
www.wygs.org
jhutson@wygs.org
License: Versailles, Ripley County, IN held by Good Shepherd Radio Inc.
Arbitron Metro Market: Columbus, IN; *Format:* Religious
Keith Reising, Jr., Chairman
Keith Reising, CEO
Matt Bond, Operations Dir
Steve Fisher, Station Manager
Mellissa Burton, Office Manager

Vevay

WKID

09-06-1974; 95.9 MHz FM; *Hrs Open:* 24; 2.8 kw; 308 ft.; N38 50 12 W85 1 48
315 Ferry Street, Suite A, Vevay, IN 47043 US
(812) 427-9590; *Fax:* (812) 427-2492
www.k959froggy.com
License: Vevay, Switzerland County, IN held by Dial Broadcasting Inc.
Nat'l Network: Jones Radio Networks; *Regional Network:* Network Indiana *Regional Reps:* Regl Reps; *Wire Services:* AP
Format: Country; *Hrs. of News Programming:* News progmg 7 hrs wkly; *Target Audience:* 25-49; middle-income families; *Adv. Rates:* 18; 10; 16; 10
Greta Griffin, Operations Dir
Adam Griffin, General Manager
Susan Benning, Office Manager

Vincennes

WAOV

10-22-1940; 1450 kHz AM; *Hrs Open:* 24; 1 kw-D, ND1; 1 kw-N, ND1; N38 42 26 W87 29 42
Mailing Address: 522 Busseron St., Vincennes, IN 47591 US
Second Address: PO Box 242IN 47591-0242
(812) 882-6060
www.waovam.com
waov@originalcompany.com
License: Vincennes, IN held by The Original Company, Inc.
Group Owner: The Original Company Inc.; (acq 9-28-93; $250,000 with WWBL-FM)
Arbitron Metro Market: Vincennes, IN; *Format:* News/Talk
Mark Lange, President
Jonathan Lange, Operations Mgr
Aaron Lange, General Sales Mgr

*WATI

01-01-2002; 89.9 MHz FM; 0.5 kw; 157 ft.; N38 41 47 W87 26 27
P.O. Box 3206, Tupelo, MS 38803 US
(662) 844-8888; *Fax:* (662) 842-6791
www.afr.net
faq@afa.net
License: Vincennes, Knox County, IN held by American Family Association.
Group Owner: American Family Radio
Arbitron Metro Market: Vincennes, IN; *Format:* Christian, Religious
Tim Wildmon, President
Donald Wildmon, Founder
Buddy Smith, Sr VP
Ed Vitagliano, Exec VP
Randy Sharp, Director Of Special Projects
Meeke Addison, Director Of Communications
Abraham Hamilton III, General Counsel

WFML

05-16-1965; 96.7 MHz FM; *Hrs Open:* 24; 3000 kw; 386 ft.; N38 39 6 W87 28 37
P.O. Box 574, Vincennes, IN 47591 US
(812) 254-6761; *Fax:* (812) 254-3940
www.967jackfm.com
dlcmediainc@gmail.com
License: Vincennes, Knox County, IN held by DLC Media
Group Owner: DLC Media, INC; (acq 8-29-86).
Nat'l Network: CBS; *Regional Network:* Brownfield Network
Regional Reps: Rgnl Reps; *Wire Services:* AP
Format: Country *Special Programming:* Chicago Bears, Purdue Boilermakers; *Hrs. of News Programming:* news progmg 2 hrs wkly; *No. News Employees:* 2; *Target Audience:* 18-54.; *Adv. Rates:* 25; 25; 25; 25
Dave Crooks, President
Andy Morrison, Operations Dir
Dave Foster, News Director
Steve McClure, Chief Engineer
Bob Tester, Disc Jockey
Lisa Jackman, Traffic Director
Andy Morrison, Operations Manager

*WVUB

12-07-1970; 91.1 MHz FM; 50 kw; 499 ft.; N38 39 6 W87 28 37
1002 North First Street, Vincennes, IN 47591 US
(812) 888-4357; *Fax:* (812) 882-2237
www.blazer911wvub.com
blazerwvub@hotmail.com
License: Vincennes, Knox County, IN held by Board of Trustees for Vincennes University.
Nat'l Network: PRI
Arbitron Metro Market: Vincennes, IN *TV Affiliate:* WVUT(TV) affil; *Format:* Adult Contemp *Special Programming:* Class 6 hrs wkly
Phil Smith, Station Manager
Beth Davis, Sales Manager
Michael Woods, Programming Director
John Szink, News Director
Michael Murphy, Chief Engineer

WZDM

09-01-1988; 92.1 MHz FM; *Hrs Open:* 24; 4.1 kw; 400 ft.; N38 41 2 W87 26 8
Mailing Address: 522 Busseron St., Vincennes, IN 47591 US
Second Address: PO Box 242
(812) 882-6060
www.wzdm.com
wzdm@originalcompany.com
License: Vincennes, IN held by The Original Company, Inc
Group Owner: The Original Company Inc.
Arbitron Metro Market: Vincennes, IN; *Format:* Adult Contemp
Mark Lange, President
Jonathan Lange, Operations Mgr
Duncan Myers, General Sales Mgr

Wabash

WJOT

11-01-1971; 1510 kHz AM; 0.25 kw-D, NDD; N40 47 11 W85 49 19

1350 S. Wabash, Wabash, IN 46992 US
(260) 563-1161; *Fax:* (260) 563-0883
wjot@comtek.com
License: Wabash, IN held by Mid-America Radio of Wabash Inc.
Group Owner: Mid-America Radio Group Inc.
Nat'l Network: Westwood One

Wade Weaver, Promotions Manager

WJOT-FM
07-01-1993; 105.9 MHz FM; 6 kw; 318 ft.; N40 49 54 W85 48 36
1360 S. Wabash, Wabash, IN 46922 US
(260) 563-1161; *Fax:* (260) 563-0883
wjot@comtek.com
License: Wabash, Wabash County, IN held by Mid-America Radio of Wabash Inc.
Group Owner: Mid-America Radio Group Inc.; (acq 7-1-98; $190,000 with co-locat
Nat'l Network: Westwood One *Regional Reps:* Rgnl Reps.
Format: Oldies; *Target Audience:* 25-64.
Bill Barrows, Operations Dir
Wade Weaver, General Manager
Jack Elmore, Chief Engineer
Deb Dale, Traffic Manager

WKUZ
04-01-1965; 95.9 MHz FM; *Hrs Open:* 24; 4.2 kw; Ant 394 ft; N40 41 54 W85 45 03
Box 342, 1864 S. Wabash St., Wabash, IN 46992
(260) 563-4111; *Fax:* (260) 563-4425
www.wkuz.com
wkuz@kconline.com
License: Wabash, Wabash County, IN held by Upper Wabash Broadcasting Corp.
Nat'l Network: USA; *Regional Network:* Brownfield
Population Served: 500,000 *Special Programming:* Farm 5 hrs wkly; *Hrs. of News Programming:* news progmg 10 hrs wkly; *No. News Employees:* 1; *Target Audience:* General.; *Adv. Rates:* 10; 10; 10; 10
Toni Adams, President
Charles Adams, General Manager
Paul Adams, Chief Engineer

Wadesville

***WENS**
01-01-2005; 90.1 MHz FM; 6 kw vert; 285 ft.; N37 56 3 W87 55 35
Mailing Address: US
Second Address: 15 Wood St., Greenfield, IN 46140-2162
(317) 462-9523; *Fax:* (317) 467-1065
www.wjcfradio.com
wjcfradio@aol.com
License: Wadesville, Posey County, IN held by Indiana Community Radio Corp.
Arbitron Metro Market: Greenfield, IN; *Format:* Christian
Jennifer Cox-Hensley, President

Wakarusa

***WYBV**
01-01-2006; 89.9 MHz FM; 1.75 kw; 328 ft.; N41 27 50 W85 49 22
P.O. Box 7300, Charlotte, NC 28241 US
(800) 888-7077
www.bbnradio.org
bbn@bbnmedia.org
License: Wakarusa, Elkhart County, IN held by Bible Broadcasting Network Inc.
Group Owner: Bible Broadcasting Network
Arbitron Metro Market: Wakarusa, IN; *Format:* Christian
Lowell Davey, President
Jason Padgett, Operations Manager

Walton

WFRR
01-01-1995; 93.7 MHz FM; *Hrs Open:* 24; 6 kw; 328 ft.; N40 43 31 W86 10 33 *Rebroadcasts:* Rebroadcasts WFRN-FM Elkhart 85%
Mailing Address: P.O. Box 307, Elkhart, IN 46515 US
Second Address: 25802 CR 26, Elkhart, IN 46517
(574) 875-5166; *Fax:* (574) 875-6662
www.wfrn.com
moore@wfrn.com
License: Walton, Cass County, IN held by Progressive Broadcasting System
Nat'l Network: USA; *Regional Network:* Network Indiana; *Nat'l Reps:* Salem
Format: Christian; *No. News Employees:* 1; *Target Audience:* 25-54; general; *Adv. Rates:* 22; 16; 17; 9
Edwin Moore, President
James Carter, Programming Director
Don Wagner, News Director

Wanatah

***WTMK**
12-28-2010; 88.5 MHz FM; 3.4 kw; N41 18 15 W87 01 30
Mailing Address: One University Ave, Bourbonnais, IL 60914 US
Second Address: 9401 East 25th St, Indianapolis, IN 46229
(815) 939-5330
www.olivet.edu
License: Wanatah, La Porte County, IN held by Olivet Nazarene University
Group Owner: Olivet Nazarene University; (acq. 12-28-2010)
Regional Network: Regional Radio Sports Network
Arbitron Metro Market: Wanatah, IN; *Format:* Adult Contemp, Christian

Warsaw

WRSW
01-01-1951; 1480 kHz AM; *Hrs Open:* 24; 1 kw-D, DAN; 0.5 kw-N, DAN; N41 13 21 W85 50 17
1104 Kings Highway, Winona Lake, IN 46590 US
(574) 372-3064; *Fax:* (574) 267-2230
http://espnwarsaw.com/Home.aspx
License: Warsaw, IN held by Talking Stick Communications LLC.
Group Owner: Talking Stick Communications LLC; (acq 12-19-2003; $1.2 million with
Nat'l Network: Westwood One; *Regional Network:* Tribune Radio Networks; Network Indiana
Format: Sports; *Hrs. of News Programming:* news progmg 18 hrs wkly; *No. News Employees:* 1; *Target Audience:* General.; *Adv. Rates:* 21; 18; 21; 10.30
Clint Marsh, General Manager
Dan Daggett, General Sales Mgr
Roger Grossman, Programming Director
Jack Didier, Engineering Dir

WRSW-FM
01-01-1948; 107.3 MHz FM; 50 kw; 226 ft.; N41 13 21 W85 50 17
1104 Kings Highway, Winona Lake, IN 46590 US
(574) 372-3064; *Fax:* (574) 267-2230
www.wrsw.net
License: Warsaw, Kosciusko County, IN
Group Owner: Talking Stick Communications LLC
Nat'l Network: Westwood One; *Regional Network:* Network Indiana; *Nat'l Reps:* Rgnl Reps *Regional Reps:* Rgnl Reps
Format: Contemporary Hits/Top 40, Adult Contemp; *Target Audience:* General; affluent adults; *Adv. Rates:* 21; 18; 21; 10
Clint Marsh, General Manager
Dan Daggett, General Sales Mgr

***WQKV**
01-01-2006; 88.7 MHz FM; 14 kw; 86 meters; N41 08 19.8 W85 53 31
P O Drawer 240, Tupelo, MS 38801 US
(800) 525-5683; *Fax:* (916) 251-1650
www.klove.com
klove@klove.com
License: Warsaw, Fulton County, IN held by Educational Media Foundation.
Group Owner: EMF Broadcasting; (acq 3-23-2007; grpsl)
Nat'l Network: K-Love
Arbitron Metro Market: Rochester, IN; *Format:* Christian; *No. News Employees:* 13
Darrell Chambliss, Chairman
Mike Novak, President and CEO
David Pierce, Programming Director
Ed Lenane, News Director
Sam Wallington, Engineering Dir
Dan Antonelli, Chief Business Development Officer
Eric Moser, Chief FinancialOfficer
Brian Burger, Vice President of Human Resources
D. Kevin Blair, Secretary and General Counsel
Tim Luttrell, News Reporter

Washington

WAMW-AM
01-01-1955; 1580 kHz AM; *Hrs Open:* Daytime plus FM Translator is 24/7; 500 kw; N38 38 47 W87 16 48; N38 39 4 W87 9 55 *Rebroadcasts:* 95.9 W240CE 99 watts
800 W. National Hwy., Washington, IN 47501 US
www.wamwamfm.com
License: Washington, IN held by DLC Media, Inc.
Group Owner: DLC Media, Inc.
Regional Network: Brownfield Network
Format: Adult Contemp *Special Programming:* Brickyard 400, Cincinnati Reds, High School Sports; *Hrs. of News Programming:* 5; *No. News Employees:* 2; *Target Audience:* 25-64

WAMW-FM
11-20-1989; 107.9 MHz FM; *Hrs Open:* 24; 3000 kw; N38 38 47 W87 16 47
800 W. National Hwy., Washington, IN 47501 US
www.wamwamfm.com
License: Washington, Daviess County, IN held by DLC Media, Inc.
Group Owner: DLC Media, Inc.
Regional Network: Brownfield; Network Indiana; *Wire Services:* AP
Arbitron Metro Market: Washington, IN; *Format:* Contemporary Hits/Top 40, Adult Contemp *Special Programming:* Indy 500, IRL Racing, Cincinnati Bengals, Charlotte Hornets, Notre Dame Football, Local high school sports *Hrs.of News Programming:* 10; *No. News Employees:* 2; *Target Audience:* 25-64

WWBL
02-01-1948; 106.5 MHz FM; 50 kw; 341 ft.; N38 39 4 W87 9 55
Mailing Address: 522 Busseron St., Vincennes, IN 47591 USA
Second Address: Box 242, Vincennes, IN 47591-0242
(812) 882-6060
www.wwbl.com
marklange@originalcompany.com
License: Washington, IN held by Old Northwest Broadcasting Inc.
Group Owner: The Original Company Inc.
Arbitron Metro Market: Washington, IN; *Format:* Country
Mark Lange, President
Jonathan Lange, Operations Mgr
Duncan Myers, General Sales Mgr

Waynetown

***WSRC(FM)**
88.1 MHz FM; 10 kw vert; Ant 410 ft; N39 47 44 W86 48 04
5331 Mount Alifan Dr., Fredonia, NY 92111-2622
(858) 277-4991; *Fax:* (858) 277-1365
License: Waynetown, Hendricks County, IN held by Calvary Chapel of Crawfordsville Inc
Group Owner: Horizon Christian Fellowship
Population Served: 11,194; *Arbitron Metro Market:* Fredonia, NY
Michael MacIntosh, President

West Lafayette

***WKHL**
06-15-1992; 106.7 MHz FM; *Hrs Open:* 24; 6 kw; 328 ft.; N40 31 20 W86 58 57
2700 -A Kent Avenue, West Lafayette, IN 47906 US
(916) 251-1600; *Fax:* (916) 251-1650
www.klove.com
License: West Lafayette, Tippecanoe County, IN held by Educational Media Foundation.
Group Owner: EMF Broadcasting; (acq 4-17-2008; $1.2 million)
Nat'l Network: K-Love
Arbitron Metro Market: Lafayette, IN; *Format:* Christian
Mike Novak, President

***WHPL**
09-10-1993; 89.9 MHz FM; *Hrs Open:* 24; 2 kW; 328 ft.; N40 17 50 W86 54 5
1920 W 53rd St, Anderson, IN 46013 USA
(888) 877-9467
www.moodyradio.org/stations/indiana
License: West Lafayette, Tippecanoe County, IN held by The Moody Bible Institute of Chicago
Group Owner: The Moody Bible Institute of Chicago; acq 6-20-97)
Nat'l Network: Moody
Arbitron Metro Market: Lafayette, IN; *Format:* Christian, Adult Contemp; *Hrs. of News Programming:* News progmg 14 hrs wkly; *Target Audience:* 35 plus; relg

***WBAA**
04-04-1922; 920 kHz AM; 5 kw-D, DAN; 1 kw-N, DAN; N40 20 29 W86 53 1
1740 Elliott Hall, Rm 11, West Lafayette, IN 47907 US
(765) 494-5920; *Fax:* (765) 496-1542
www.wbaa.org
wbaa@wbaa.org
License: West Lafayette, IN held by Purdue University.
Nat'l Network: NPR; PRI
Arbitron Metro Market: West Lafayette, IN; *Format:* Jazz, News, 62, Talk; *Hrs. of News Programming:* news progmg 20 hrs wkly; *No. News Employees:* 3
Bette Carson Mogridge, Operations Dir
Mike Savage, General Manager
Greg Kostraba, Programming Director
Stan Jastrzebski, News Director

Chrissie Ankerberg, Chief Engineer
Brian Garrity, Corporate Support Manager
Christine Burr,Membership and Events Manager
Jenny Hood, Traffic Coordinator

***WBAA-FM**
02-01-1993; 101.3 MHz FM; 14 kw; 394 ft.; N40 17 50 W86 54 5
1740 Elliott Rm 11, West Lafayette, IN 47907 US
(765) 494-5920; *Fax:* (765) 496-1542
www.wbaa.org
wbaa@wbaa.org
License: West Lafayette, Tippecanoe County, IN held by Purdue University
Nat'l Network: NPR; PRI
Arbitron Metro Market: West Lafayette, IN; *Format:* Classical, News; *Hrs. of News Programming:* news progmg 20 rs wkly; *No. News Employees:* 3
Bette Carson Mogridge, Operations Dir
Mike Savage, General Manager
Greg Kostraba, Programming Director
Stan Jastrzebski, News Director
Chrissie Ankerberg, Chief Engineer
Brian Garrity, Corporate Support Manager
Christine Burr,Membership and Events Manager
Jenny Hood, Traffic Coordinator

Wilkinson

***WSMJ(FM)**
01-01-2008; 89.1 MHz FM; 150 w vert; Ant 102 ft; N39 52 46.4 W85 38 10.9
15 Wood St., Greenfield, IN 46140
(317) 467-1064
License: Wilkinson, Hancock County, IN held by Hoosier Public Radio Corp.
Population Served: 4,013; *Arbitron Metro Market:* North Wildwood, NJ
Martin Hensley, President

Winamac

WFRI
01-01-1998; 100.1 MHz FM; *Hrs Open:* 24; 6 kw; 328 ft.; N41 2 21 W86 30 55 *Rebroadcasts:* Rebroadcasts WFRN-FM Elkhart 80%
P. O. Box 307, Elkhart, IN 46515 US
(574) 875-5166
www.wfrn.com
comments@wfrn.com
License: Winamac, Pulaski County, IN held by Progressive Broadcasting System Inc.
Group Owner: Progressive Broadcasting System Inc.
Nat'l Network: USA; *Regional Network:* Network Indiana
Format: Christian; *Target Audience:* 25-54.; *Adv. Rates:* 13; 11; 12; 7

Winchester

WZZY
05-01-1967; 98.3 MHz FM; *Hrs Open:* 24; 3 kw; 299 ft.; N40 5 23 W84 56 13
P.O. Box 427, Winchester, IN 47394 US
(765) 962-6533; *Fax:* (765) 966-1499
www.todaysmusicmix.com
johnrose@g1013.com
License: Winchester, Randolph County, IN held by Rodgers Broadcasting Corp.
Group Owner: Rodgers Broadcasting Corp.; acq 1-1-00)
Regional Reps: Rgnl Reps.
Arbitron Metro Market: Richmond, IN; *Format:* Adult Contemp; *Hrs. of News Programming:* news progmg 10 hrs wkly; *No. News Employees:* 2; *Target Audience:* 25-54; general
David Rodgers, President
Rick Duncan, Operations Dir
Steve Frey, General Manager
Bob Phillips, News Director
Keith Wade, Disc Jockey

Woodburn

WBYR
10-01-1962; 98.9 MHz FM; 50 kw; 453 ft.; N40 57 14 W84 53 7
1005 Production Road, Fort Wayne, IN 46808 US
(260) 471-5100; *Fax:* (260) 471-5224
www.989thebear.com
License: Woodburn, Van Wert County, IN held by Pathfinder Communications Corp.
Group Owner: Federated Media; (acq 1996; $5.85 million)
Arbitron Metro Market: Fort Wayne, IN; *Format:* Rock/AOR; *Target Audience:* 18-49; men
Alec Dille, CEO
Jim Allgeier, Market General Manager

Stephanie Todich, General Sales Mgr
Marty Dehlhof, Programming Director

Zionsville

***WITT**
91.9 MHz FM; 6 kw; 297 ft.; N40 0 14 W86 28 14
PO Box 20563, Indianapolis, IN 46220 US
(317) 251-3851
www.919witt.org
radio@919witt.org
License: Zionsville, Boone County, IN held by Kids First Inc.
Arbitron Metro Market: Zionsville, IN; *Format:* Variety/Diverse
James Walsh, President
Matt Masters, Chief Engineer

Iowa

Adel

***KIHS**
01-01-2004; 88.5 MHz FM; 0.5 kw; 207 ft.; N41 36 9 W94 2 55
, Santa Ana, CA 92704 US
(800) 357-4226; *Fax:* (208) 736-1958
www.csnradio.com
csn@csnradio.com
License: Adel, Dallas County, IA held by St. Gabriel Communications
Group Owner: St. Gabriel Communications; acq. 09-24-2012; $600,000
Arbitron Metro Market: Des Moines, IA; *Format:* Christian, Religious

Albia

KIIC
06-15-1995; 96.7 MHz FM; 10 kw; 463 ft.; N41 0 38 W92 43 47
PO Box 654, Albia, IA 52531 US
(641) 932-2112; *Fax:* (641) 932-2113
License: Albia, Monroe County, IA held by Waveguide Communications Inc.
Nat'l Network: AP Network News; Jones Radio Networks;
Regional Network: Brownfield
Format: Country; *Hrs. of News Programming:* news prgmg 10 hrs wkly; *No. News Employees:* 1; *Target Audience:* 25-54.
Joe Milledge, President/General Manager
Tom Williamson, News Director
Gail Wirtjes, Account Executive

Algona

KLGA
01-01-1956; 1600 kHz AM; *Hrs Open:* 24
Mailing Address: P. O. Box 160, Algona, IA 50511 US
Second Address: 2102 80th Ave., Algona, IA 50511
(515) 295-2475; *Fax:* (515) 295-3851
www.waittmedia.com
License: Algona, IA held by NRG License Sub. LLC.
Group Owner: NRG Media LLC; (acq 10-31-2005; grpsl)
Nat'l Network: ABC; *Regional Network:* Radio Iowa
Arbitron Metro Market: Mason City, IA; *Format:* Adult Contemp
Special Programming: Farm, news, weather; *Hrs. of News Programming:* news progmg 44 hrs wkly; *No. News Employees:* 1; *Target Audience:* 25-54.
Bob Ketchum, General Manager
Dana Myee, Programming Director

KLGA-FM
08-17-1970; 92.7 MHz FM; *Hrs Open:* 6 AM-10:30 PM; 3.5 kw; 449 ft.; N43 4 5 W94 12 8
Mailing Address: P.O. Box 160, Algona, IA 50511 US
Second Address: 2102 80th Ave., Algona, IA 50511
(515) 295-2475; *Fax:* (515) 295-3851
License: Algona, Kossuth County, IA
Group Owner: NRG Media LLC
Arbitron Metro Market: Mason City, IA
Evan Armstrong, General Manager

Alta

KBVU-FM
01-01-1999; 97.5 MHz FM; 6 kw; 315 ft.; N42 38 5 W95 10 10
610 West 4th Street, Storm Lake, IA 50588 US
(712) 749-1234; *Fax:* (712) 749-1211
edge.bvu.edu
kbvu@bvu.edu
License: Alta, Buena Vista County, IA held by Buena Vista University.
Arbitron Metro Market: Storm Lake, IA; *Format:* Alternative;
Target Audience: 18-25; college students
Bruce Ellingson, General Manager/Faculty Advisor

Alton

***KRGO**
91.5 MHz FM; kw *Rebroadcasts:* WJRF/Duluth, MN
4604 Airpark Boulevard, Duluth, MN 55811 US
(218) 722-2727; *Fax:* (218) 722-1650
www.refugeradio.com
License: Alton, Sioux County, IA held by Refuge Media Group.
Arbitron Metro Market: Duluth, MN; *Format:* Christian
Daniel Hatfield, CFO/General Manager
Drew Jensen, Engineering Dir

Ames

KASI
01-01-1948; 1430 kHz AM; *Hrs Open:* 5 AM-midnight; 1 kw-D, ND1; 0.032 kw-N, ND1; N42 2 18 W93 40 53
415 Main St., Ames, IA 50010 US
(515) 232-1430; *Fax:* (515) 232-1439
www.1430kasi.com
License: Ames, Story County, IA held by Citicasters Licenses Inc.
Group Owner: iHeartMedia; (acq 8-24-99; with co-located FM).
Nat'l Network: CNN Radio; Fox Sports
Arbitron Metro Market: Ames, IA; *Format:* News, News/Talk, 84, Talk; *Hrs. of News Programming:* news progmg 25 hrs wkly; *No. News Employees:* 2; *Target Audience:* 25 plus.
Greg Chance, Senior Vice President of Programming
Joel McCrea, Regional Market Manager
Carol Kisling, Station Manager
Mel Crippen, Programming Director
Trent Rice, News Director
Dave Sprau, Sports Director

KCYZ
06-20-1968; 105.1 MHz FM; *Hrs Open:* 24; 25 kw; 328 ft.; N42 4 38 W93 38 54
415 Main St., Ames, IA 50010 US
(515) 232-1430; *Fax:* (515) 232-1439
www.now1051.com
License: Ames, Story County, IA held by Citicasters Licenses Inc.
Group Owner: iHeartMedia
Arbitron Metro Market: Ames, IA; *Format:* Adult Contemp; *Target Audience:* 18-40.
Greg Chance, Senior Vice President of Programming
Matt Gillon, Senior Vice President of Sales
Randy Sierra, Programming Director
Nick Bruns, Promotions Director

KLTI-FM
06-02-1967; 104.1 MHz FM; *Hrs Open:* 24; 100 kw; 1010 ft.; N41 54 9 W93 54 15
1416 Locust Street, Des Moines, IA 50309 US
(515) 280-1350; *Fax:* (515) 280-3011
www.lite1041.com
sallen@desmoinesradiogroup.com
License: Ames, Story County, IA held by Saga Communications of Iowa LLC.
Group Owner: Saga Communications Inc.; (acq 1-1-97; $3.2 million)
Nat'l Reps: Katz Radio; *Wire Services:* AP
Arbitron Metro Market: Des Moines, IA; *Format:* Adult Contemp; *Target Audience:* Women; 25-54
Ed Christian, CEO/President
Scott Allen, Operations Dir
Jeff Delvaux, General Manager
Pam Washington, Director of Sales
Scott Allen, Programming Director
Jay Wells, Promotions Manager
Luke Matthews, Digital Media Manager
TimWhite, Music Director
Geneva Walker, Business Manager

***KURE**
04-17-1970; 88.5 MHz FM; *Hrs Open:* 24; 0.63 kw; 72 ft.; N42 1 47 W93 38 51
1199 Friley Hall, Ames, IA 50012 US
(515) 294-4332; *Fax:* (515) 294-8093
www.kure885.org
generalmanager@kure885.org
License: Ames, Story County, IA held by Residence Associations Broadcasting Service Inc.
Arbitron Metro Market: Ames, IA; *Format:* Variety/Diverse; *Hrs. of News Programming:* News progmg 10 hrs wkly; *Target Audience:* 18-25; Iowa State Univ students & Ames community
John Harlow, General Manager
Dr. Dale Chimenti, Faculty Advisor

***WOI**
01-01-1922; 640 kHz AM; *Hrs Open:* 24; 5 kw-D, 1 kw-N, DA-N; N41 59 34 W93 41 27

3903 Westown Pkwy., West Des Moines, IA 50266 US
(515) 457-9645
www.weareiowa.com
License: Ames, Story County, IA held by Iowa State University.
Group Owner: Iowa State University
Nat'l Network: NPR; PRI; *Wire Services:* AP
Population Served: 3,000,000 *Hrs. of News Programming:* news progmg 40 hrs wkly; *No. News Employees:* 15; *Target Audience:* General.
Mary Grace Herrington, CEO/COO
Mary Grace Herrington, Programming Director
Steve Schoon, Chief Engineer

***WOI-FM**
07-01-1949; 90.1 MHz FM; 100 kw; 1490 ft.; N41 48 33 W93 36 53
204 Communications Bldg, Ames, IA 50011 US
(515) 294-2025; *Fax:* (515) 294-1544
www.iowapublicradio.org
License: Ames, Story County, IA held by Iowa State University.
Nat'l Network: NPR
TV Affiliate: class *Special Programming:* news progmg 12 hrs wkly; *Hrs. of News Programming:* 3; *No. News Employees:* General.
CEO, CEO/COO
Director of Operations, Operations Dir
Director, Fiscal Operations

Anamosa

KOSY-FM
02-14-2008; 95.7 MHz FM; 18 kw; N42 3 39 W91 32 35
600 Old Marion Road N.E., Cedar Rapids, IA 52402 US
(319) 395-0530
www.y957fm.com
License: Anamosa, Jones County, IA held by Citicasters Licenses Inc.
Group Owner: iHeartMedia
Arbitron Metro Market: Cedar Rapids, IA; *Format:* Contemporary Hits/Top 40
Joel McCrea, Regional Market President
J.J. Cook, Senior Vice President of Programming
Jeanne Kerr, Senior Vice President of Sales
Joni Sojka, Sales Manager
Brian Thomas, Production Director
Nicholas Bowers, Director of DigitalContent

Ankeny

KDXA
07-01-1991; 106.3 MHz FM; *Hrs Open:* 24/7; 25 kw; 328 ft.; N41 40 45 W93 35 46
2141 Grand Ave., Des Moines, IA 50312 US
(515) 245-8900
www.alt1063.com
License: Ankeny, Polk County, IA held by Citicasters Licenses Inc.
Group Owner: iHeartMedia; (acq 5-4-99; grpsl)
Nat'l Reps: Clear Channel; *Wire Services:* AP
Arbitron Metro Market: Des Moines, IA; *Format:* Triple A; *Target Audience:* 25-54.
Greg Chance, Senior Vice President of Programming
Matt Gillon, Senior Vice President of Sales
Mike Killabrew, Program Director/Music Director
Nick Bruns, Promotions Director

Asbury

WJOD
03-31-1994; 103.3 MHz FM; *Hrs Open:* 24; 6.6 kw; 643 ft.; N42 24 16 W90 34 12
111 East Kilbourn Ave., Suite 2700, Milwaukee, WI 53202 US
(563) 557-1040; *Fax:* (563) 583-4535
www.103wjod.com
License: Asbury, Dubuque County, IA held by Peak Broadcasting of Fresno Licenses LLC
Group Owner: Townsquare Media; (acq 2-6-98)
Nat'l Network: Jones Radio Networks
Arbitron Metro Market: Dubuque, IA; *Format:* Country; *Target Audience:* 18-49.
Ken Peiffer, Operations Dir
Scott Lindahl, General Manager

Atlantic

KJAN
09-01-1950; 1220 kHz AM; *Hrs Open:* 24; 0.178 kw-D, ND1; 0.062 kw-N, ND1; N41 25 2 W95 0 15
PO Box 389, Atlantic, IA 50022 US
(712) 243-3920; *Fax:* (712) 243-3937
www.kjan.com
License: Atlantic, IA held by Wireless Communications Corp.
Nat'l Network: Fox News Radio; *Regional Network:* Radio Iowa; Brownfield; *Nat'l Reps:* Commercial Media Sales; *Wire Services:* AP
Format: Adult Contemp, News *Special Programming:* Farm 12 hrs wkly; *Hrs. of News Programming:* news progmg 40 hrs wkly; *No. News Employees:* 1; *Target Audience:* 25 plus; general
James Field, General Manager
Chris Parks, Programming Director
Ric Hanson, News Director
Mark Saylor, Music Director
Stacie Linfor, Traffic Manager
Rod Christensen, Sales Manager

KSWI
07-01-2000; 95.7 MHz FM; *Hrs Open:* 24; 20 kw; 358 ft.; N41 26 7 W94 50 0
413 Chestnut Street, Atlantic, IA 50022 US
(712) 243-6885; *Fax:* (712) 243-1691
www.iowasuperstation.com
bill@iowasuperstation.com
License: Atlantic, Cass County, IA held by Meredith Communications L.C.
Nat'l Network: ABC
Arbitron Metro Market: Atlantic, IA; *Format:* Contemporary Hits/Top 40, Adult Contemp
Stephen Meredith, President
William Saluk, Vice President/General Manager
Frank Ulmstead, Programming Director
Tom Robinson, News/Sports Director
Tori Newell, Office Manager

Audubon

KSOM
08-01-1995; 96.5 MHz FM; *Hrs Open:* 24; 100 kw; 528 ft.; N41 26 7 W94 50 0
P O Box 88, Atlantic, IA 50022 US
(712) 243-6885; *Fax:* (712) 243-1691
www.iowasuperstation.com
ksom@mchsi.com
License: Audubon, Audubon County, IA held by Meredith Communications L.C.
Nat'l Network: ABC; Motor Racing Net; Premiere Radio Networks
Arbitron Metro Market: Atlantic, IA; *Format:* Country; *Hrs. of News Programming:* news progmg 6 hrs wkly; *No. News Employees:* 2; *Target Audience:* General; upscale & farmers
Bill Saluk, General Manager
Jill Christensen, Programming Director

Belle Plaine

KZAT-FM
05-30-1997; 95.5 MHz FM; *Hrs Open:* 24; 4.4 kw; 384 ft.; N41 56 35 W92 23 51
303 McClellan Street, Tama, IA 52339 US
(641) 484-5958; *Fax:* (641) 484-5962
www.radioz955.com
License: Belle Plaine, Benton County, IA held by Camrory Broadcasting Inc.
Nat'l Network: CBS; Westwood One; ABC; *Wire Services:* AP
Arbitron Metro Market: Belle Plaine, IA; *Format:* Contemporary Hits/Top 40, Adult Contemp *Special Programming:* Polka 2 hrs Sun am; *Hrs. of News Programming:* news progmg 6 hrs wkly; *No. News Employees:* 1 *TargetAudience:* 25-54; listeners who are professionals, laborers, commuters, tourists & truckers
Catherine Campbell Currier, President
Jeff Bayer, News Director

Bettendorf

KQCS
07-07-1984; 93.5 MHz FM; *Hrs Open:* 24; 6 kw; 318 ft.; N41 36 14 W90 24 43
1229 Brady Street, Davenport, IA 52803 US
(563) 326-2541; *Fax:* (563) 326-0844
quadcities.prod@cumulus.com
License: Bettendorf, Scott County, IA held by Cumulus Licensing Corp.
Group Owner: Cumulus Media Inc.; (acq 3-15-00; grpsl).
Arbitron Metro Market: Quad Cities, IA-IL (Davenport-Rock Island-Moline); *Format:* Rock/AOR; *Target Audience:* 18-34.
Cheryl Riley, General Manager/Marketing Manager
Joe Cook, General Sales Mgr
Darren Pitra, Programming Director
Andy Andresen, Chief Engineer

***KNSB(FM)**
91.1 MHz FM; 740 w; 116.8 meters; N41 32 43.8 W90 22 23.6
University of Northern Iowa, 324 Communications Arts Center, Cedar Falls, IA 50614-0359
(319) 273-6325
License: Bettendorf, Scott County, IA held by University of Northern Iowa.
Arbitron Metro Market: Quad Cities, IA-IL (Davenport-Rock Island-Moline)
Wayne Jarvis, General Manager

Boone

KFFF(AM)
01-01-1927; 1260 kHz AM; 5 kw-D, 33 w-N, DA-D; N42 02 55 W93 53 54
900 8th St., Boone, IA 50036
(515) 432-5014; *Fax:* (515) 432-2092
www.wolfradio933.com
mail@iowanewstalk.com
License: Boone, Boone County, IA held by Boone Biblical Ministries Inc.
Format: Talk
Robert Stumbo, President
Jamie Johnson, General Manager
Bob Pink, Chief Engineer

KFFF-FM
01-01-1950; 99.3 MHz FM; 5.2 kw; Ant 351 ft; N42 02 55 W93 53 54
900 8th St., Boone, IA 50036
(515) 432-5014; *Fax:* (515) 432-2092
License: Boone, Boone County, IA held by Boone Biblical Ministries Inc.
Format: Religious
Jamie Johnson, Programming Director

KWQW
05-15-1975; 98.3 MHz FM; *Hrs Open:* 24; 41 kw; 16.5 meters; N41 49 51 W93 43 54
4143 109th St., Urbandale, IA 50322 US
(515) 331-9200
www.983vibe.com
License: Boone, IA held by Radio License Holding CBC, LLC
Group Owner: Cumulus Media Inc.; (acq 8-29-2003; grpsl).
Nat'l Reps: Christal
Arbitron Metro Market: Des Moines, IA; *Format:* Urban Contemporary; *Target Audience:* 25-54.
Sean Elliott, Operations Mgr
Bob Jenkins, General Sales Mgr
Sean Elliott, Programming Director

KWBG
01-15-1950; 1590 kHz AM; *Hrs Open:* 6 AM-11 PM; 1 kw-D, DAN; 0.5 kw-N, DAN; N42 1 22 W93 52 36
P.O. Box 366, Boone, IA 50036 US
(515) 432-2046; *Fax:* (515) 432-1448
www.kwbg.com
License: Boone, IA held by NRG License Sub. LLC.
Group Owner: NRG Media LLC; (acq 10-31-2005; grpsl)
Nat'l Network: ABC; ESPN Radio; *Regional Network:* Brownfield
Arbitron Metro Market: Boone, IA; *Format:* News, News/Talk, 86 *Special Programming:* Farm 15 hrs wkly; *Hrs. of News Programming:* news progmg 36 hrs wkly; *No. News Employees:* 1; *Target Audience:* 35 plus;Boone County, Iowa residents; *Adv. Rates:* 24.90; 24.90; 15.90; 15.90
Brenda Miller, Operations Dir
Carol Kuster, General Manager
Ben Parsons, Webmaster and Sales
Jim Turbes, News Director
Ryan Wendt, Sports Director
Gena Treganza, Billing and Traffic

Britt

KHAM
01-01-2006; 103.1 MHz FM; 0.2 kw; 52 ft.; N43 5 47 W93 48 5
1296 Marian Lane, Green Bay, WI 54304 US
(641) 585-1073; *Fax:* (641) 585-2990
www.kiow.com
kiow@kiow.com
License: Britt, Hancock County, IA held by Coloff Media LLC
Arbitron Metro Market: Britt, IA
Tony Coloff, General Manager

Brooklyn

***KSKB**
03-01-1988; 99.1 MHz FM; 44 kw; 525 ft.; N41 41 23 W92 21 31
Mailing Address: 505 Josephine Street, Titusville, FL 32796 US
Second Address: 505 Josephine St., Titusville, FL 32796
(641) 522-7202; *Fax:* (641) 522-7239
noncomradio.net
wpio@gate.net
License: Brooklyn, Poweshiek County, IA held by Florida Public Radio Inc.

Arbitron Metro Market: Brooklyn, IA; *Format:* Adult Contemp, Christian *Special Programming:* Ger one hr, Pol one hr wkly; *Target Audience:* General.
Randy Henry, President
Archie Shetler, Vice President

Burlington

*KAYP
11-01-2000; 89.9 MHz FM; 9 kw vert; 440 ft.; N40 47 59 W91 32 35
P.O. Box 3206, Tupelo, MS 38803 US
(662) 844-8888; *Fax:* (662) 842-6791
www.afr.net
faq@afa.net
License: Burlington, Des Moines County, IA held by American Family Association.
Group Owner: American Family Radio
Format: Christian
Tim Wildmon, President
Donald Wildmon, Founder
Buddy Smith, Sr VP
Ed Vitagliano, Exec VP
Randy Sharp, Director Of Special Projects
Meeke Addison, Director Of Communications
Abraham Hamilton III, General Counsel & Public Policyanalyst

KBUR
07-01-1941; 1490 kHz AM; *Hrs Open:* 24; 0.76 kw-U, ND1; N40 49 26 W91 8 33
610 N. 4th St., Suite 300, Burlington, IA 52601 US
(319) 752-5402; *Fax:* (319) 752-4715
www.kbur.com
info@kbur.com
License: Burlington, IA held by Pritchard Broadcasting Corp.
Group Owner: Pritchard Broadcasting Corp.; (acq 6-6-2008; with KBKB(AM) Fort Madison)
Regional Network: Radio Iowa
Arbitron Metro Market: Burlington, IA; *Format:* Talk *Special Programming:* Farm 19 hrs wkly; *Hrs. of News Programming:* news progmg 28 hrs wkly; *No. News Employees:* 3; *Target Audience:* 25 plus; general
Joe Bates, Operations Dir
John Pritchard, General Manager
Chet Young, General Sales Mgr
Steve Hexom, Programming Director
Rob Sussman, News Director

KCPS
07-30-1965; 1150 kHz AM; *Hrs Open:* 24; 500 w-D, 67 w-N, DA-1; N40 51 11 W91 08 10
Mailing Address: Box 100, W.Burlington, IA 52601
Second Address: 205 S.Gear Av, W.Burlington, IA 52655
(319) 754-6698; *Fax:* (319) 754-8899
www.kcpsradio.com
kcps@aol.com
License: Burlington, Des Moines County, IA held by John Giannettino.
Nat'l Network: Premiere; Dial-Global; TRN; *Regional Network:* Chicago Cubs; Chicago Bears; Indy Racing; *Nat'l Reps:* Katz Radio
Population Served: 100,000 *Special Programming:* Agriculture-business 10 hrs, pro sports 10 hrs wkly; *Hrs. of News Programming:* news progmg 7 hrs wkly; *No. News Employees:* 1; *Target Audience:* 25-54; middle-aged,upscale & well-informed adults; *Adv. Rates:* 10; 10; 10; 8.50
John Giannettino, General Manager
Chip Giannettino, Station Manager
Chip Giannettino, General Sales Mgr
Chip Giannettino, Programming Director
Gary Saunders, News Director
Tracey Rogers, Chief Engineer

KDMG
07-19-1993; 103.1 MHz FM; 12 kw; 476 ft.; N40 44 4 W91 15 15
610 N. 4th St., Suite 300, Burlington, IA 52601 US
(319) 752-5402; *Fax:* (319) 752-4715
www.bigcountry1031.com
johnp@burlingtonradio.com
License: Burlington, Des Moines County, IA held by Pritchard Broadcasting Corp.
Group Owner: Pritchard Broadcasting Corp.
Nat'l Reps: Katz Radio
Arbitron Metro Market: Burlington, IA; *Format:* Country; *Hrs. of News Programming:* news progmg 2 hrs wkly; *No. News Employees:* 1; *Target Audience:* 25-54.; *Adv. Rates:* 24; 24; 24; 12
Joe Bates, Operations Dir
John Pritchard, General Manager
Chet Young, General Sales Mgr

KGRS
11-27-1968; 107.3 MHz FM; *Hrs Open:* 24; 100 kw; 430 ft.; N40 49 26 W91 8 33
Mailing Address: 50 East Rivercenter Blvd, #1200, Covington, KY 41011 US
Second Address: 1411 N. Roosevelt Ave., Burlington, IA 52601
(319) 752-2701; *Fax:* (319) 752-5287
www.thenewmix.com
License: Burlington, Des Moines County, IA held by GAP Broadcasting Burlington License LLC.
Group Owner: GAPWEST Broadcasting; (acq 2-13-2008; grpsl)
Format: Adult Contemp; *Hrs. of News Programming:* news progmg 15 hrs wkly; *No. News Employees:* 1; *Target Audience:* 18-45
Cosmo Leone, Programming Director
Mark Hempen, News Director
J.K. Martin, Local News Editor

KKMI
10-22-1981; 93.5 MHz FM; *Hrs Open:* 24; 6 kw; 305 ft.; N40 49 11 W91 7 2
610 N. 4th St., Suite 300, Burlington, IA 52601 US
(319) 752-5402; *Fax:* (319) 752-4715
www.935kkmi.com
johnp@burlingtonradio.com
License: Burlington, Des Moines County, IA held by Pritchard Broadcasting Corp.
Group Owner: Pritchard Broadcasting Corp.; (acq 8-5-91)
Nat'l Reps: Katz Radio
Arbitron Metro Market: Davenport, IA; *Format:* Adult Contemp; *Hrs. of News Programming:* news progmg 2 hrs wkly; *No. News Employees:* 2; *Target Audience:* 25-55; upscale; *Adv. Rates:* 15; 15; 15; 8
Joe Bates, Operations Dir
John Pritchard, General Manager
Chet Young, General Sales Mgr
Scott Michael, Programming Director

Carroll

KCIM
06-08-1950; 1380 kHz AM; 1 kw-D, DA2; 1 kw-N, DA2; N42 2 29 W94 53 6
1119 E. Plaza Drive, Carroll, IA 51401 US
(712) 792-4321
www.1380kcim.com
License: Carroll, IA held by Carroll Broadcasting Co.
Group Owner: Carroll Broadcasting Co.; acq 8-1-85; $1.5 million with co-located FM;
Nat'l Network: CBS; *Nat'l Reps:* Katz Radio
Arbitron Metro Market: Carroll, IA; *Format:* Oldies
John Ryan, Operations Dir
Deb Lupardus, General Sales Mgr

KKRL
01-18-1967; 93.7 MHz FM; *Hrs Open:* 24; 100 kw; 276 ft.; N42 2 57 W94 53 3
1119 E. Plaza Dr., Carroll, IA 51401 US
(712) 792-4321
www.1380kcim.com
License: Carroll, Carroll County, IA held by Carroll Broadcasting Co.
Group Owner: Carroll Broadcasting Co.
Nat'l Reps: Katz Radio
Arbitron Metro Market: Des Moines, IA; *Format:* Oldies; *No. News Employees:* 1; *Target Audience:* 18 plus.
John Ryan, Operations Dir
Deb Lupardus, General Sales Mgr

*KNSC(FM)
01-01-2004; 90.7 MHz FM; *Hrs Open:* 24; 10 kw; Ant 289 ft; N42 07 14 W94 48 49
2022 Communications Bldg. ISU, WOI Radio Group, Ames, IA 50011-3241
(515) 294-2025; *Fax:* (515) 294-1544
www.iowapublicradio.org
woi@iastate.edu
License: Carroll, Carroll County, IA held by Iowa State University of Science and Technology.
Nat'l Network: NPR; PRI
Hrs. of News Programming: News progmg 40 hrs wkly; *Target Audience:* General; educated
Mary Grace Herrington, Programming Director
Don Wirth, Director, Fiscal Operations

Castana

*KILV
01-01-2001; 107.5 MHz FM; *Hrs Open:* 24; 25 kw; 328 ft.; N42 12 26 W96 7 26
4232 Fowler Ave, Baltimore, MD 21236 US
(916) 251-1600; *Fax:* (916) 251-1650
www.klove.com
klove@klove.com
License: Castana, Monona County, IA held by Educational Media Foundation.
Group Owner: EMF Broadcasting; (acq 10-26-01).
Nat'l Network: K-Love
Format: Christian; *No. News Employees:* 3; *Target Audience:* 25-44; female-Judeo/Christian
Mike Novak, President
Glenn Goodwin, Operations Dir
David Pierce, Programming Director
Marya Morgan, News Director
Sam Wallington, Engineering Dir
Richard Hunt, News Reporter

Cedar Falls

KCFI(AM)
02-02-1958; 1250 kHz AM; *Hrs Open:* 24; 500 w-U, DA-2; N42 32 41 W92 29 16
Box 248, 721 Shirley St., Cedar Falls, IA 50613
(319) 277-1918; *Fax:* (319) 277-5202
www.1650thefan.com
Jesse@1650thefan.com
License: Cedar Falls, Black Hawk County, IA held by Fife Communications L.C.
Population Served: 68,653; *Arbitron Metro Market:* Waterloo, IA; *Adv. Rates:* 12; 12; 12; 12
Jim Coloff, President
Tony Coloff, Operations Dir
Jeff Ryant, Station Manager
Sue Coloff, Vice President, Operations

KCNZ
09-01-1998; 1650 kHz AM; *Hrs Open:* 24
721 Shirley St., Cedar Falls, IA 50613 US
(319) 277-1918; *Fax:* (319) 277-5202
www.1650thefan.com
radio@1650thefan.com
License: Cedar Falls, IA held by Fife Communications Co. LLC.
Nat'l Network: CBS
Arbitron Metro Market: Waterloo-Cedar Falls, IA; *Format:* Sports, Talk *Special Programming:* Farm 6 hrs; *Hrs. of News Programming:* news progmg 25 hrs wkly; *No. News Employees:* 2; *Target Audience:* 25-54;eastern Iowa adults; *Adv. Rates:* 22; 18; 14; 10
Jim Coloff, President/General Manager
Janelle Rench, Office Manager

*KHKE
04-01-1974; 89.5 MHz FM; *Hrs Open:* 24; 10 kw; 417 ft.; N42 23 55 W92 19 34
324 Comm Art Center, Cedar Falls, IA 50614 US
(515) 725-1700; *Fax:* (515) 725-1714
www.iowapublicradio.org
info@iowapublicradio.org
License: Cedar Falls, Black Hawk County, IA held by University of Northern Iowa.
Arbitron Metro Market: Waterloo-Cedar Falls, IA; *Format:* Talk; *Target Audience:* General.
Mary Grace Herrington, CEO
Kelly Edmister, Station Manager
Al Schares, Programming Director
Steve Schoon, Chief Engineer
Scott Rivers, Director of Network Operations
Al Shares, Music Director

KOEL-FM
01-07-1994; 98.5 MHz FM; *Hrs Open:* 24; 15 kw; 423 ft.; N42 26 32 W92 23 48
501 Sycamore Street, Suite 300, Waterloo, IA 50703 US
(319) 833-4800; *Fax:* (319) 833-4866
www.k985.com
License: Cedar Falls, Black Hawk County, IA held by Townsquare Media
Group Owner: Townsquare Media; (acq 3-15-00; grpsl).
Arbitron Metro Market: Waterloo, IA; *Format:* Country; *Hrs. of News Programming:* news progmg one hr wkly; *No. News Employees:* 1; *Target Audience:* 18-49; general
Josh Loeffler, General Manager
Lynette Fuller, Sales Manager
Bucky Doren, Programming Director

*KUNI
09-15-1960; 90.9 MHz FM; *Hrs Open:* 24; 94 kw; 1719 ft.; N42 18 59 W91 51 31
324 Communication Arts, Center, Cedar Falls, IA 50614 US
(515) 725-1700; *Fax:* (515) 725-1714
www.iowapublicradio.org
info@iowapublicradio.org

License: Cedar Falls, Black Hawk County, IA held by University of Northern Iowa.
Nat'l Network: NPR; PRI
Arbitron Metro Market: Cedar Falls, IA; *Format:* News, Triple A
Special Programming: Folk 4 hrs, rhythm and blues 2 hrs wkly; *Hrs. of News Programming:* news progmg 74 hrs wkly; *No. News Employees:* 3 *TargetAudience:* General.
Mary Grace Herrington, CEO
Al Schares, Programming Director
Steve Schoon, Chief Engineer
Kelly Edmister, Chief Administrative Officer
Scott Rivers, Director of Network Operations
Al Schares, Music Director

Cedar Rapids

*KCCK-FM

09-05-1972; 88.3 MHz FM; *Hrs Open:* 24; 10 kw; 420 ft.; N41 54 33 W91 39 17
6301 Kirkwood Blvd.,S.W., Cedar Rapids, IA 52406 US
(319) 398-5446; *Fax:* (319) 398-5492
www.kcck.org
studio@kcck.org
License: Cedar Rapids, Linn County, IA held by Kirkwood Community College.
Nat'l Network: NPR; *Wire Services:* AP
Arbitron Metro Market: Cedar Rapids, IA; *Format:* Jazz *Special Programming:* Blues 12 hrs, new age 7 hrs wkly; *Hrs. of News Programming:* news progmg 2 hrs wkly; *No. News Employees:* 1; *Target Audience:* 25-54;educated, affluent, active in community
Kathy Hall, President
George Dorman, Operations Dir
Dennis Green, General Manager
Lisa Baum, General Sales Mgr
Bob Stewart, Programming Director
George Dorman, News Director
Dave Maley, Engineering Dir
Dave Maley, ChiefEngineer

KGYM

12-20-1947; 1600 kHz AM; *Hrs Open:* 24; 5 kw-U, DA-N; N41 58 15 W91 32 01
1110 26th Ave. S.W., Cedar Rapids, IA 52401
(319) 363-2061; *Fax:* (319) 363-2948
www.kgymradio.com
info@kgymradio.com
License: Cedar Rapids, Linn County, IA held by KZIA Inc.
Nat'l Network: ESPN Radio; *Nat'l Reps:* Local Focus Radio; *Wire Services:* AP
Population Served: 315,000; *Arbitron Metro Market:* Cedar Rapids, I *Special Programming:* FM translator 106.3 in Iowa City; *Hrs. of News Programming:* News progmg one hr wkly; *Target Audience:* 18-49.
Rob Norton, President
Greg Runyon, Operations Dir
Julie Hein, General Manager
Joe Drahozal, General Sales Mgr
Scott Unash, Programming Director
Jamie Burks, Promotions Manager
Dorothy Roach, Traffic Manager
Robert Norton Jr.,Executive Vice President
Kellie Lala, General Sales Manager

KDAT

05-01-1971; 104.5 MHz FM; *Hrs Open:* 24; 100 kw; 551 ft.; N42 4 51 W91 41 45
600 Congress Ave., Suite 1400, Austin, TX 78701 US
(319) 365-9431; *Fax:* (319) 363-8062
www.kdat.com
License: Cedar Rapids, Linn County, IA held by Cumulus Media Inc.
Group Owner: Cumulus Media Inc.; (acq 8-7-00; grpsl).
Nat'l Reps: Christal
Arbitron Metro Market: Cedar Rapids, IA; *Format:* Adult Contemp; *Target Audience:* 25-54.; *Adv. Rates:* Contact Station
Tim Graves, Programming Director
Greg Sher, Promotions Manager

KHAK

07-01-1961; 98.1 MHz FM; *Hrs Open:* 24; 100 kw; 459 ft.; N41 55 28 W91 36 55
600 Congress Ave., Suite 1400, Austin, TX 78701 US
(319) 365-9431; *Fax:* (319) 363-8062
www.khak.com
khak@khak.com
License: Cedar Rapids, Linn County, IA held by Cumulus Licensing Corp.
Group Owner: Cumulus Media Inc.; (acq 8-7-00; grpsl).
Regional Network: Brownfield; *Nat'l Reps:* Christal
Arbitron Metro Market: Cedar Rapids, IA; *Format:* Country; *Target Audience:* 25-54; general; *Adv. Rates:* Contact Station
Bob James, Programming Director
Greg Sher, Promotions Manager

KMRY

08-01-1949; 1450 kHz AM; *Hrs Open:* 24; 1 kw-U, ND1; N42 0 25 W91 42 29
1957 Blairs Ferry Rd.,Ne, Cedar Rapids, IA 52402 US
(319) 393-1450; *Fax:* (319) 393-1407
www.kmryradio.com
kmry@kmryradio.com
License: Cedar Rapids, IA held by Sellers Broadcasting Inc.
Nat'l Network: CBS; *Wire Services:* AP
Arbitron Metro Market: Cedar Rapids, IA; *Format:* Adult Contemp
Special Programming: 50's oldies 3 hrs, polka 3 hrs, big band 2 hrs we; *Hrs. of News Programming:* news progmg 20 hrs wkly; *No. News Employees:* 1 *Target Audience:* 40 plus; affluent, upscale adults with large disposable income; *Adv. Rates:* 25; 20; 20; 10
Rick Sellers, President/General Manager
David Bolt, General Sales Mgr
Guy Dye, Programming Director
Bob Brooks, News/Sports Director
Jim Davies, Chief Engineer
Rick Sampson, Operations Manager

KMJM

07-01-1961; 1360 kHz AM; *Hrs Open:* 24; 1 kw-D, DA2; 0.124 kw-N, DA2; N41 55 28 W91 36 55
600 Old Marion Rd. N.E., Cedar Rapids, IA 52402 US
(319) 395-0530; *Fax:* (319) 393-9600
www.1360kmjm.com
License: Cedar Rapids, IA held by Capstar TX LLC
Group Owner: iHeartMedia; (acq 8-30-2000; grpsl).
Arbitron Metro Market: Cedar Rapids, IA; *Format:* Country
J.J. Cook, Senior Vice President of Programming
Joel McCrea, Regional Market President
Jeanne Kerr, Senior Vice President of Sales
Joni Sojka, Sales Manager
Brian Thomas, Production Director
Nicholas Bowers, Director of DigitalContent

KZIA

04-29-1975; 102.9 MHz FM; *Hrs Open:* 24; 100 kw; Ant 853 ft; N42 03 25 W91 41 42
1110 26th Ave. S.W., Cedar Rapids, IA 52404
(319) 363-2061; *Fax:* (319) 363-2948
www.kzia.com
kzia@kzia.com
License: Cedar Rapids, Linn County, IA held by KZIA Inc.
Nat'l Reps: Local Focus Radio; *Wire Services:* AP
Population Served: 315,000; *Arbitron Metro Market:* Cedar Rapids; *Hrs. of News Programming:* news progmg one hr wkly; *No. News Employees:* 1; *Target Audience:* 18-49.
Rob Norton, President
Greg Runyon, Operations Dir
Julie Hein, General Manager
Joe Drahozal, Station Manager
Greg Runyon, Programming Director
Jamie Burks, Promotions Manager
Scott Schulte, News Director
Rob Norton, ChiefEngineer
Rick Swann, Music Director

WMT

01-01-1922; 600 kHz AM; *Hrs Open:* 24
50 East Rivercenter Blvd., Suite 1200, Covington, KY 41011 US
(319) 395-0530; *Fax:* (319) 393-0918
License: Cedar Rapids, IA held by Citicasters Licenses Inc.
Group Owner: iHeartMedia; (acq 5-4-99; grpsl).
Nat'l Network: CBS
Arbitron Metro Market: Cedar Rapids, IA; *Format:* News, News/Talk, 84, Talk *Special Programming:* Farm 19 hrs wkly; *Target Audience:* 35 plus.
Joel McCrea, Regional Market President
JJ Cook, Senior Vice President of Programming
Jeanne Kerr, Senior Vice President of Sales
Randy Lee, Programming Director
Joni Sojka, Sales Manager

KKSY-FM

02-14-2008; 96.5 MHz FM; 100 kw; 518 ft.; N42 1 40 W91 38 25
600 Old Marion Road N.E., Cedar Rapids, IA 52402 US
(319) 395-0530; *Fax:* (319) 393-9600
www.965kisscountry.com
License: Cedar Rapids, Jones County, IA held by Citicasters Licenses Inc.
Group Owner: iHeartMedia
Arbitron Metro Market: Cedar Rapids, IA; *Format:* Country
Joel McCrea, Regional Market President
J.J. Cook, Senior Vice President of Programming
Jeanne Kerr, Senior Vice President of Sales
Joni Sojka, Sales Manager
Brian Thomas, Production Director
Nicholas Bowers, Director of DigitalContent

Centerville

KCOG

03-01-1949; 1400 kHz AM; *Hrs Open:* 5 AM-midnight; 0.5 kw-D, ND1; 1 kw-N, ND1; N40 44 40 W92 54 32
402 N. 12th Street, Centerville, IA 52544 US
(800) 373-4930
www.kmgo.com
carolyn@kmgo.com
License: Centerville, IA held by KCOG Inc.
Nat'l Network: USA; *Regional Network:* Brownfield
Arbitron Metro Market: Centerville, IA; *Format:* Adult Contemp
Fred Jenkins, President/General Manager
Larry Stout, Vice President
Carolyn Jenkins, Sales Manager
Edwin Brand, Programming Director
Russ Ocker, Music Director

KMGO

10-01-1974; 98.7 MHz FM; *Hrs Open:* 24; 100 kw; 449 ft.; N40 47 34 W92 52 47
402 N. 12th Street, Centerville, IA 52544 US
(641) 856-3996; *Fax:* (641) 856-3337
www.kmgo.com
License: Centerville, Appanoose County, IA held by KMGO Inc.
Nat'l Network: USA
Format: Country
Fred Jenkins, President/General Manager
Larry Stout, Vice President
Carloyn Jenkins, Sales Manager
Edwin Brand, Programming Director
Russ Ocker, Music Director

Chariton

KEDB

11-15-1979; 105.3 MHz FM; *Hrs Open:* 24; 34 kw; 597 ft.; N40 53 23 W93 1 29
C/O Fletcher Heald, 1300 N 17th St, 11th Fl, Arlington, VA 22209 US
(641) 895-7707; *Fax:* (641) 774-8495
www.kedb.fm
License: Chariton, Lucas County, IA held by Honey Creek Broadcasting LLC
Nat'l Network: Westwood One
Arbitron Metro Market: Chariton, IA; *Format:* Adult Contemp
Special Programming: Gosp 5 hrs wkly; *Hrs. of News Programming:* news progmg 30 hrs wkly; *No. News Employees:* 1; *Target Audience:* 28 plus. *Adv.Rates:* 10; 10; 10; 10
Cindy Spidle, General Sales Mgr
Nick Hoffman, Programming Director
John Johnston, News Director
Fred Jenkins, Engineering Dir
Jill Schull, Local News Editor

Charles City

KCHA

11-01-1949; 1580 kHz AM; *Hrs Open:* 24; 0.5 kw-D, ND1; 0.01 kw-N, ND1; N43 3 5 W92 40 0
207 North Main Street, Charles City, IA 50616 US
(641) 228-1000
www.kchaam.com
KCHA@KCHAAM.com
License: Charles City, IA held by Coloff Media, LLC.
Nat'l Network: ABC News/Talk; *Regional Network:* Radio Iowa
Arbitron Metro Market: Charles City - Floyd County, IA; *Format:* Adult Contemp; *Hrs. of News Programming:* news progmg 7 hrs wkly; *No. News Employees:* 1; *Target Audience:* 35 plus.
Jim Coloff, General Manager
Chris Berg, Programming Director
Angela Barton, News Director
Melissa Pitzenberger, Office Manager
Tad Barry, Account Executive
Kay Winkelman, Accoutn Executive
Jeanne Fullard, Special EventsCoordinator

KCHA-FM

10-01-1971; 95.9 MHz FM; *Hrs Open:* 24; 6 kw; 299 ft.; N43 3 5 W92 40 0
207 North Main Street, Charles City, IA 50616 US
(641) 228-1000
www.kchafm.com
License: Charles City, Floyd County, IA held by Coloff Media, LLC.
Nat'l Network: CNN Radio; *Regional Network:* Radio Iowa
Arbitron Metro Market: Charles City - Floyd County, IA; *Format:* Adult Contemp; *Hrs. of News Programming:* news progmg 7 hrs wkly; *No. News Employees:* 1; *Target Audience:* 25-54; adults

Jim Coloff, General Manager
Chris Berg, News Director and Program Director
Jeanne Fullard, Special Events Coordinator
Tad Barry, Account Executive
Kay Winkelman, Account Executive
Melissa Pitzenberger, Office Manager

Cherokee

KCHE

01-01-1953; 1440 kHz AM
201 S. 5th Street, Cherokee, IA 51012 US
(712) 225-2511; *Fax:* (712) 225-2513
www.kcheradio.com
kche1@ncn.net
License: Cherokee, IA held by J & J Radio Corp.
Group Owner: J&J Radio Corp.; (acq 11-14-03; $600,000 with co-located FM).
Nat'l Network: ABC; *Regional Network:* Radio Iowa
Arbitron Metro Market: Sioux City, IA; *Format:* Oldies *Special Programming:* Farm 12 hrs, Sp one hr wkly; *Hrs. of News Programming:* news progmg 14 hrs wkly; *No. News Employees:* 2; *Target Audience:* 45-80;general; *Adv. Rates:* 15; 15; 15; 15

Jeff Fuller, President
Curt Carlson, Sales Manager
Billy Bezoni, Programming Director
Nikki Thunder, News/Promotions Director
John O'Connor, Sports Director
Noel Deering, Computer Tech/Announcer
Keith Crane, Assistant News/SportsDirector
Kay O'Connor, Account Executive
Andrea McIrvin, Account Executive
Hallie Dessel, Office Manager
Jomi Anderson, Account Executive

KCHE-FM

12-09-1976; 92.1 MHz FM; *Hrs Open:* 24; 6 kw; 210 ft.; N42 47 21 W95 33 8
201 South 5th Street, Cherokee, IA 51012 US
(712) 225-2511
www.kcheradio.com
kche1@ncn.net
License: Cherokee, Cherokee County, IA held by J & J Radio Corp.
Nat'l Network: ABC; *Regional Network:* Radio Iowa; *Nat'l Reps:* Farmakis
Arbitron Metro Market: Cherokee, IA; *Format:* Adult Contemp; *Hrs. of News Programming:* news progmg 28 hrs wkly; *No. News Employees:* 2

Jeff Fuller, President and Owner
Curt Carlson, Operations Dir
Curt Carlson, General Sales Mgr
Bill Bezoni, Programming Director
Nikki Thunder, News and Promotions Director
Dick Keane, Chief of Operations
Hallie Dessell, TrafficManager
Noel Deering, Computer Tech and Announcer
Keith Crane, Assistant News/ Sports Director
John O'Connor, Sports Director
Andrea McIrvin, Account Executive

Clarinda

KMA-FM

09-25-1990; 99.1 MHz FM; *Hrs Open:* 24; 100 kw; 981 ft.; N40 48 4 W94 54 6
209 North Elm Street, Box 960, Shenandoah, IA 51601 US
(712) 246-5270; *Fax:* (712) 246-5275
www.kmaland.com
License: Clarinda, Page County, IA held by KMA Broadcasting L.P.
Nat'l Network: Westwood One; CNN Radio; *Wire Services:* AP
Format: Adult Contemp; *Hrs. of News Programming:* news progmg 5 hrs wkly; *No. News Employees:* 2; *Target Audience:* 25-44.

Edward May, President
Chuck Morris, Operations Dir
Mark Eno, General Manager
Don Hansen, Station Manager
Sandy Hansen, General Sales Mgr

Clarion

KIAQ

09-01-1992; 96.9 MHz FM; *Hrs Open:* 24; 100 kw; 578 ft; N42 40 18 W94 09 11
200 N. 10th St., Fort Dodge, IA 50501 US
(515) 955-5656; *Fax:* (515) 955-5844
www.yourfortdodge.com
sgossweiler@digity.me
License: Clarion, Wright County, IA held by Digity 3E License, LLC
Group Owner: Digity, LLC
Population Served: 304,000 *Format:* Country; *Target Audience:* 25-54.

Darren Helton, Operations Mgr
Steve Gossweiler, General Manager
Pat Kolar, Dir. of Sales
Darren Helton, Programming Director
Kelly Heinen, News Director

Clear Lake

KLKK

02-16-1978; 103.7 MHz FM; *Hrs Open:* 24; 25 kw; 328 ft.; N43 7 15 W93 11 36
330 East Kilbourn Avenue, Suite 250, Milwaukee, WI 53202 US
(641) 423-1300; *Fax:* (641) 423-2906
www.klkkfm.com
License: Clear Lake, Cerro Gordo County, IA
Nat'l Reps: Clear Channel
Arbitron Metro Market: Mason City, IA; *Format:* Classic Rock; *Hrs. of News Programming:* news progmg 42 hrs wkly; *No. News Employees:* 1; *Target Audience:* 25-54.; *Adv. Rates:* 50; 40; 35; 15

Hal Hofman, General Manager
Drew Kelly, Programming Director
Laurie Gansen, News Director

Clinton

KCLN

12-21-1956; 1390 kHz AM; *Hrs Open:* 24
1853 442nd Ave., Clinton, IA 52732 US
(563) 243-1390
www.947mac.com
chris.streets@prairiecommunications.net
License: Clinton, IA held by WPW Broadcasting, Inc.
Group Owner: Prairie Radio Communications; (acq 4-29-99; $800,000 with co-located FM)
Regional Network: Brownfield
Arbitron Metro Market: Davenport, IA; *Format:* Adult Contemp
Special Programming: Farm 10 hrs wkly; *Hrs. of News Programming:* news progmg 2 hrs wkly; *No. News Employees:* 1; *Target Audience:* 40 plus. *Adv.Rates:* 15; 12; 12; 10.

Chris Streets, General Manager
Chris Meyers, General Sales Mgr
Robert Bertam, News Dir/Sports Dir

KMXG

07-01-1974; 96.1 MHz FM; *Hrs Open:* 24; 100 kw; 981 ft.; N41 37 58 W90 24 38
1921 Gallows Rd., Suite 850, Vienna, VA 22182 US
(563) 344-7000; *Fax:* (563) 344-7006
www.mix96online.com
License: Clinton, Clinton County, IA held by Citicasters Licenses Inc.
Group Owner: iHeartMedia; (acq 11-15-00; grpsl).
Nat'l Reps: Christal
Arbitron Metro Market: Quad Cities, IA; *Format:* Adult Contemp
Special Programming: Jazz 3 hrs wkly; *Hrs. of News Programming:* news progmg 3 hrs wkly; *No. News Employees:* 1; *Target Audience:* 25-54; yuppies,baby boomers, upscale professional females; *Adv. Rates:* 75; 60; 40; 30

Jim O'Hara, Senior Vice President of Programming
Scott Bitting, Market President/Director of Sales
Kelly Meyer, Sales Manager
Ron Evans, Programming Director
Jessica Tillberg, Promotions Director
Mark Manuel, Web ContentDirector

KROS

09-28-1941; 1340 kHz AM; *Hrs Open:* 5:30 AM-midnight; 1 kw-U, ND1; N41 51 36 W90 12 18
870 13th Ave.N, P.O. Box0518, Clinton, IA 52733 US
(563) 242-1252; *Fax:* (563) 242-4825
www.krosradio.com
contactus@krosradio.com
License: Clinton, IA held by KROS Broadcasting Inc.
Nat'l Network: CNN Radio; *Regional Network:* Radio Iowa
Format: Variety/Diverse *Special Programming:* Folk 2 hrs, jazz one hr, blues one hr, gospel one; *Hrs. of News Programming:* news progmg 38 hrs wkly; *No. News Employees:* 1; *Target Audience:* General; loc audience *Adv. Rates:* 13; 13; 13; 6

Brad Parker, President
Dave Vickers, General Manager
Paul Clark, Programming Director
Dave Vickers, News Director
Tom Messerli, Engineering Dir
Gary Determan, Sports Director

KMCN

12-07-1970; 94.7 MHz FM; *Hrs Open:* 24; 3 kw; 328 ft.; N41 54 34 W90 13 28
1853 442nd Ave., Clinton, IA 52732 US
(563) 243-1390
www.947mac.com
chris.streets@prairiecommunications.net
License: Clinton, Clinton County, IA held by WPW Broadcasting Inc.
Group Owner: Prairie Radio Communications
Arbitron Metro Market: Clinton, IA; *Format:* Adult Contemp; *Hrs. of News Programming:* news progmg one hr wkly; *No. News Employees:* 1; *Target Audience:* 25-54.; *Adv. Rates:* 17; 15; 15; 10

Chris Streets, General Manager
Chris Meyers, General Sales Mgr
Robert Bertam, News Director

Council Bluffs

*KIWR

11-23-1981; 89.7 MHz FM; *Hrs Open:* 24; 100 kw; 1070 ft.; N41 18 40 W96 1 37
2700 College Road, Council Bluffs, IA 51503 US
(712) 325-3254; *Fax:* (712) 325-3391
www.897theriver.com
sjohn@iwcc.edu
License: Council Bluffs, Pottawattamie County, IA held by Iowa Western Community College.
Arbitron Metro Market: Omaha-Council Bluffs, NE-IA; *Format:* Alternative *Special Programming:* Var/div 16 hrs wkly; *Hrs. of News Programming:* News progmg 5 hrs wkly; *Target Audience:* 18-34; well-educated, upper &middle-upper income; *Adv. Rates:* 25; 25; 25; 15

Tom Johnson, CFO
Dan Kinney, President
Sophia John, General Manager/Programming Director

KLNG

01-01-1947; 1560 kHz AM; *Hrs Open:* 6 AM-sunset; 10 kw
120 S. 35th St., Suite 2, Council Bluffs, IA 51501 US
(712) 323-0100
www.wilkinsradio.com
denise@wilkinsradio.com
License: Council Bluffs, IA held by Wilkins Communications Network Inc.
Group Owner: Wilkins Communications Network Inc.; (acq 4-89; $250,000).
Nat'l Network: Salem Radio Network
Arbitron Metro Market: Omaha, IA; *Format:* Christian, Talk
Special Programming: Sp 10 hrs, Black 6 hrs wkly; *Target Audience:* 35 plus.; *Adv. Rates:* 35; 35; 35; 35

Chuck Yates, Station Manager

KQKQ-FM

01-01-1969; 98.5 MHz FM; 100 kw; 1102 ft.; N41 18 25 W96 1 37
1001 Farnam-On-The-Mall, Omaha, NE 68102 US
(402) 342-2000; *Fax:* (402) 346-5748
www.q985fm.com
License: Council Bluffs, Pottawattamie County, IA held by Waitt Omaha LLC.
Group Owner: Waitt Omaha LLC; (acq 1-7-2002; grpsl)
Arbitron Metro Market: Omaha-Council Bluffs, NE-IA; *Format:* Adult Contemp; *Target Audience:* 18-44.

Mary Quass, CEO
Jim McKernan, General Manager
Rhonda Gerrard, General Sales Mgr
Mark Todd, Programming Director
Brandon Pappas, Promotions Manager
Lori Storz, News Director
Chuck DuCoty, COO
Sam Coughlin, General SalesManager
Nevin Dane, Programming Director

Cresco

KCZQ

04-01-1991; 102.3 MHz FM; 3 kw; 328 ft.; N43 25 47 W92 9 49
116 1st Avenue West, Cresco, IA 52136 US
(563) 547-1000(563) 547-3366; *Fax:* (563) 547-2200
superc@iowatelecom.net
License: Cresco, Howard County, IA held by Mega Media Ltd.
Nat'l Reps: Farmakis; *Wire Services:* Agence France-Presse (AFP)
Format: Adult Contemp *Special Programming:* Farm 12 hrs wkly; *Target Audience:* General.

James Hebel, President
Debra Lowe, Operations Dir
Jim Bernard, Programming Director
Stan McHenry, Music Director

Creston

KSIB
12-07-1946; 1520 kHz AM; 1 kw-D, NDD; N41 2 16 W94 23 38
P.O. Box 426, Creston, IA 50801 US
(641) 782-2155; *Fax:* (641) 782-6963
www.ksibradio.com
License: Creston, IA held by G.O. Radio Ltd.
Nat'l Network: ABC; *Regional Network:* Brownfield
Arbitron Metro Market: Creston, IA; *Format:* Country; *Target Audience:* General.
Dave Rieck, President
Chad Rieck, General Manager
Chad Rieck, General Sales Mgr
Ben Walter, Programming Director
Terri Queck-Matzie, News Director
Charlie Maley, Chief Engineer

KSIB-FM
03-01-1966; 101.3 MHz FM; *Hrs Open:* 24; 19 kw; 364 ft.; N41 5 41 W94 22 30
P.O. Box 426, Creston, IA 50801 US
(641) 782-2155; *Fax:* (641) 782-6963
www.ksibradio.com
License: Creston, Union County, IA
Regional Network: Brownfield
Arbitron Metro Market: Creston, IA; *Format:* Country; *Target Audience:* General.
Adam Glenville, Operations Dir
Chad Rieck, General Manager
Kim Tate, Programming Director
Terri Queck-Matzie, News Director
Steve Sandlin, Chief Engineer
Joey Jeffery, Traffic Manager

*KLOX
01-01-2005; 90.9 MHz FM; 0 kw horiz, 4 kw vert; 335 ft.; N41 4 29 W94 22 35
505 Josephine St, Titusville, FL 32796 US
(321) 267-3000; *Fax:* (321) 264-9370
noncomradio.net
wpio@gate.net
License: Creston, Union County, IA held by Florida Public Radio Inc.
Arbitron Metro Market: Titusville, FL; *Format:* Adult Contemp, Christian
Randy Henry, President
Archie Shetler, Executive Vice President

Davenport

*KALA
11-04-1967; 88.5 MHz FM; *Hrs Open:* 24; 10 kw horiz, 9.33 kw vert; 323 ft.; N41 35 43.8 W90 40 43.7
518 W. Locust St., Davenport, IA 52803 US
(563) 333-6219; *Fax:* (563) 333-6218
kala@sau.edu
License: Davenport, Scott County, IA held by St. Ambrose University.
Arbitron Metro Market: Davenport, IA; *Format:* Jazz *Special Programming:* Sp 15 hrs, gospel 13 hrs wkly; *Hrs. of News Programming:* news progmg 34.5 hrs wkly; *No. News Employees:* 1; *Target Audience:* General.
David Baker, Operations Dir

KCQQ
09-01-1996; 106.5 MHz FM; *Hrs Open:* 24; 100 kw; 896 ft.; N41 37 58 W90 24 38
3535 E. Kimberly Rd., Davenport, IA 52807 US
(563) 344-7000
www.q106online.com
License: Davenport, Scott County, IA held by Citicasters Licenses Inc.
Group Owner: iHeartMedia; (acq 11-15-00; grpsl).
Arbitron Metro Market: Quad Cities, IA-IL (Davenport-Rock Island-Moline); *Format:* Classic Rock *Special Programming:* Relg one hr wkly; *Hrs. of News Programming:* news progmg 2 hrs wkly; *No. News Employees:* 1 *Target Audience:* 25-54.; *Adv. Rates:* 125; 90; 60; 30
Scott Bitting, Market President/Director of Sales
Jim O'Hara, Senior Vice President of Programming
Kelly Meyer, Sales Manager
Steve Gunner, Programming Director
Jessica Tillberg, Promotions Director
Mark Manuel, Web ContentDirector

KJOC
01-01-1947; 1170 kHz AM; *Hrs Open:* 24; 1 kw-D, DA2; 1 kw-N, DA2; N41 23 21 W90 31 0
1229 Brady Street, Davenport, IA 52803 US
(563) 326-2541; *Fax:* (563) 326-1819
www.kjoc.com
License: Davenport, IA held by Townsquare Media
Group Owner: Townsquare Media; (acq 3-15-2000; grpsl)
Nat'l Network: CBS
Arbitron Metro Market: Quad Cities, IA-IL (Davenport-Rock Island-Moline); *Format:* Oldies; *Target Audience:* 18-49.
Bruce Law, General Manager
Joe Cook, Director of Sales
Darren Pitra, Programming Director

WLLR-FM
10-01-1948; 103.7 MHz FM; *Hrs Open:* 24; 91 kw; 1191 ft.; N41 32 49 W90 28 35
3535 East Kimberly Road, Davenport, IA 52807 US
(563) 344-7000; *Fax:* (563) 344-7016
www.1037wllr.com
License: Davenport, Scott County, IA held by Citicasters Licenses Inc.
Group Owner: iHeartMedia
Arbitron Metro Market: Quad Cities, IA; *Format:* Country; *Hrs. of News Programming:* News progmg 2 hrs wkly; *Target Audience:* 25-54.
Scott Bitting, Market President/Director of Sales
Jim O'Hara, Senior Vice President of Programming
Kelly Meyer, Sales Manager
Jessica Tillberg, Promotions Director
Ron Evans, Music Director
Mark Manuel, Web Content Director

WOC
02-01-1922; 1420 kHz AM; 5 kw-D, DA2; 5 kw-N, DA2; N41 33 0 W90 28 37
3535 East Kimberly Road, Davenport, IA 52807 US
(563) 344-7000; *Fax:* (563) 344-7065
www.woc1420.com
License: Davenport, IA held by Citicasters Licenses Inc.
Group Owner: iHeartMedia; (acq 11-15-2000; grpsl).
Regional Network: Ill. Radio Net.; Radio Iowa; *Nat'l Reps:* Christal
Arbitron Metro Market: Quad Cities, IA *TV Affiliate:* Talk; *Format:* News, News/Talk, 86; *Hrs. of News Programming:* 5; *No. News Employees:* 35-64; info-oriented adul
Scott Bitting, Market President/Director of Sales
Jim O'Hara, Senior Vice President of Programming
Kelly Meyer, Sales Manager
Dan Kennedy, Programming Director
Jessica Tillberg, Promotions Director
Mark Manuel, Web ContentDirector

De Witt

KBOB-FM
01-12-1977; 104.9 MHz FM; *Hrs Open:* 24; 12.5 kw; 469 ft.; N41 43 11 W90 34 13
136 Main Street, Westport, CT 06880 US
(563) 326-2541; *Fax:* (563) 326-1819
www.rock1049.net
License: De Witt, Clinton County, IA held by Cumulus Licensing Corp.
Group Owner: Cumulus Media Inc.; (acq 10-2-2000; grpsl)
Arbitron Metro Market: Quad Cities, IA; *Format:* Rock/AOR
Cheryl Riley, General Manager
Joe Cook, General Sales Mgr
Dave Levora, Programming Director
Andy Andresen, Chief Engineer

Decorah

KDEC
05-01-1947; 1240 kHz AM; *Hrs Open:* 5 AM-10 PM (M-F); 1 kw-U; N43 19 26 W91 47 04
Mailing Address: Box 27, Decorah, IA 52101
Second Address: 110 Highland Dr., Decorah, IA 52101
(563) 382-4251; *Fax:* (563) 382-9540
www.kdecradio.com
kdec@kdecradio.com
License: Decorah, Winneshiek County, IA held by Decorah Broadcasting Inc.
Nat'l Network: Westwood One; *Nat'l Reps:* Farmakis
Population Served: 40,000 *Hrs. of News Programming:* news progmg 12 hrs wkly; *No. News Employees:* 2; *Target Audience:* 35 plus.; *Adv. Rates:* 7; 6; 6.50; 4.
Bob Holtan, President/General Manager
Jeni Grouws, Station/Promotions Manager
Darin Svenson, News/Sports Director

KDEC-FM
09-02-1986; 100.5 MHz FM; *Hrs Open:* 24; 30 kw; Ant 420 ft; N43 19 26 W91 47 04
Mailing Address: Box 27, Decorah, IA 52101
Second Address: 110 Highland Dr., Decorah, IA 52101
(563) 382-4251; *Fax:* (563) 382-9540
www.kdecradio.com
kdec@kdecradio.com
License: Decorah, Winneshiek County, IA held by Decorah Broadcasting Inc.
Population Served: 100,000 *Hrs. of News Programming:* news progmg 3 hrs wkly; *No. News Employees:* 2; *Target Audience:* 18-54.; *Adv. Rates:* 16; 12; 13; 5.50
Bob Holtan, President
Colleen Holtan, Operations Dir
Bob Holtan, General Manager
Jeni Grouws, Station Manager
Jeni Grouws, Programming Director
Darin Svenson, Promotions Manager
Eric Papenfuss, Chief Engineer

*KLCD
07-15-1977; 89.5 MHz FM; 0.1 kw; 180 ft.; N43 18 56 W91 47 18
45 East Seventh St., Saint Paul, MN 55101 US
(507) 282-0910; *Fax:* (507) 282-2107
www.mpr.org
mail@mpr.org
License: Decorah, Winneshiek County, IA held by Minnesota Public Radio Inc.
Nat'l Network: NPR; PRI
Format: Talk; *No. News Employees:* 1
John McTaggart, Chairman
Timothy Roesler, General Manager
Mary Stapek, General Sales Mgr
J.J. Yore, Vice President of Programming
Sea Stachura, News Director
Chris Worthington, Managing Director of News
Randy Yoder, Senior VicePresident/Chief Development Officer
Jim McGuinn, Programming Director

*KLNI
01-01-1993; 88.7 MHz FM; *Hrs Open:* 24; 0.1 kw; -36 ft.; N43 18 35 W91 48 30
480 Cedar Street, St. Paul, MN 55101 US
(651) 290-1500
www.mpr.org
mail@mpr.org
License: Decorah, Winneshiek County, IA held by Minnesota Public Radio
Nat'l Network: NPR
Format: News; *No. News Employees:* 1
Jon McTaggart, President/CEO
David Kansas, COO/Senior Vice President
Morris Goodwin, CFO/Senior Vice President
Chris Cross, Regional Network Manager
Mike Reszler, VP, Digital Media
Nick Kereakos, VP, Technology & Operations
MikeEdgerly, News Director
Chandra Kavati, Director of Development

*KWLC
12-01-1926; 1240 kHz AM
700 College Drive, Decorah, IA 52101 US
(563) 387-1240
kwlc.luther.edu
kwlcam@luther.edu
License: Decorah, IA held by Luther College.
Arbitron Metro Market: Decorah, IA; *Format:* Variety/Diverse; *Target Audience:* General.
Ashley Urspringer, Station Manager
Ryan Castelaz, Rock Music Director
Josh Bacon, Promotions Manager
Katherine Mohr, News Director
Peter Jarzyna, Rock Music Director
Leif Larson, Jazz Music Director
Chelsea Hall, World MusicDirector
Tyler Anderson, Loud Music Director/Production Manager
Dylan Hinton, Folk/Indigenous/Blues Music Director
Tony Chase, Hip-Hop Music Director

Denison

KDSN
04-11-1956; 1530 kHz AM; *Hrs Open:* 6am-10pm
Mailing Address: P.O. Box 670, Denison, IA 51442 US
Second Address: 1530 Ridge Rd., Denison, IA 51442
(712) 263-3141; *Fax:* (712) 263-2088
www.kdsnradio.com
info@kdsnradio.com
License: Denison, IA held by M & J Radio Corp.
Nat'l Network: ABC; *Regional Network:* Radio Iowa; *Nat'l Reps:* Farmakis
Arbitron Metro Market: Denison, IA; *Format:* Adult Contemp, Country *Special Programming:* Farm 12 hrs, polka 4 hrs, Sp 3

RADIO - U.S.

hrs wkly; *Hrs. of News Programming:* news progmg 8 rs wkly; *No. News Employees:* 1 *TargetAudience:* General.; *Adv. Rates:* 30; 30; 30; 30
Michael Dudding, President
Michael J. Dudding, General Sales Mgr
Deb Nelson, Promotions Manager
Mike Earl, News Director
Phyllis Rohlin, Executive Vice President

KDSN-FM
08-01-1968; 107.1 MHz FM; *Hrs Open:* 24; 6 kw; 302 ft.; N42 2 10 W95 19 44
Mailing Address: PO Box 670, Denison, IA 51442 US
Second Address: 1530 Ridge Rd., Denison, IA 51442
(712) 263-3141; *Fax:* (712) 263-2088
www.kdsnradio.com
info@kdsnradio.com
License: Denison, Crawford County, IA held by M & J Radio Corp.
Nat'l Network: ABC; *Nat'l Reps:* Farmakis
Arbitron Metro Market: Denison, IA; *Format:* Adult Contemp; *Hrs. of News Programming:* news progmg 8 hrs wkly; *No. News Employees:* 1; *Target Audience:* 21-65; *Adv. Rates:* Same as AM
Michael J. Dudding, President/General Sales Manager
Tom Hamilton, Programming Director
Deb Nelson, Promotions Manager
Mike Earl, News Director
Dick Keane, Engineering Dir
Kathy Dudding, Office Manager
Randy Grossman, SportsCommentator
Markita Mujica, Traffic Manager

Des Moines

KBGG
01-01-1998; 1700 kHz AM; *Hrs Open:* 24; 10 kw-D, ND2; 1 kw-N, ND2; N41 35 30 W93 31 43
3280 Peachtree Rd. NW, Suite 2300, Atlanta, GA 30305 US
(404) 949-0700
www.1700kbgg.com
License: Des Moines, IA held by Radio License Holding CBC, LLC
Group Owner: Cumulus Media Inc.; (acq 8-29-2003; grpsl).
Nat'l Network: ESPN Radio; *Nat'l Reps:* Christal; *Wire Services:* UPI
Arbitron Metro Market: Urbandale, IA; *Format:* Sports
Terry Peters, Operations Dir
Doug Wood, General Sales Mgr
Jack O'Brien, Operations Manager

***KDFR**
03-24-1989; 91.3 MHz FM; *Hrs Open:* 24; 32 kw; 446 ft.; N41 36 59 W93 31 36
Mailing Address: 4135 Northgate Blvd #1, Sacramento, CA 95834 US
Second Address: 2350 N.E. 44th Ct., Des Moines, IA 50317
(515) 262-0449
www.familyradio.com
kdfr@familyradio.org
License: Des Moines, Polk County, IA held by Family Stations Inc.
Group Owner: Family Stations Inc.
Arbitron Metro Market: Des Moines, IA; *Format:* Religious
Special Programming: Class 2 hrs wkly; *Hrs. of News Programming:* news progmg 6 hrs wkly; *No. News Employees:* 1; *Target Audience:* 25 plus; general
Tom Evans, President
Larry Vavroch, Operations Dir
Mike Destefano, Regional Manager

KXNO
07-21-1921; 1460 kHz AM; *Hrs Open:* 24; 5 kw-D, DAN; 5 kw-N, DAN; N41 38 45 W93 32 12
2141 Grand Ave., Des Moines, IA 50312 US
(515) 245-8900; *Fax:* (515) 245-8904
www.kxno.com
License: Des Moines, Polk County, IA held by Capstar TX LLC
Group Owner: iHeartMedia; (acq 8-30-2000; grpsl)
Nat'l Network: Fox Sports
Arbitron Metro Market: Des Moines, IA; *Format:* Sports; *Target Audience:* 35 plus; 25-54 Male
Greg Chance, Senior Vice President of Programming
Joel McCrea, General Manager
Mike Killabrew, Programming Director
Nick Bruns, Promotions Manager

KGGO
05-31-1964; 94.9 MHz FM; *Hrs Open:* 24; 100 kw; 325 meters; N41 37 55 W93 27 27
4143 109th St., Urbandale, IA 50322 US
(515) 331-9200; *Fax:* (515) 312-9292
www.kggo.com
License: Des Moines, IA held by Radio License Holding CBC, LLC
Group Owner: Cumulus Media Inc.; (acq 8-29-03; grpsl).
Nat'l Reps: Christal
Arbitron Metro Market: Des Moines, IA; *Format:* Classic Rock
Special Programming: Racing 2 hrs wkly
Sean Elliott, Operations Mgr
Bob Jenkins, General Sales Mgr

KHKI
01-01-1961; 97.3 MHz FM; *Hrs Open:* 24; 105 kw; Ant 469 ft; N41 39 46 W93 45 24
4143 109th St., Urbandale, IA 50322 US
(515) 331-9200
www.nashfm973.com
bob.jenkins@cumulus.com
License: Des Moines, IA held by Radio License Holding CBC, LLC
Group Owner: Cumulus Media Inc.; (acq 8-29-03; grpsl).
Nat'l Reps: Christal
Population Served: 400,000; *Arbitron Metro Market:* Des Moines, IA; *Format:* Country; *Target Audience:* 18-49.
Bob Jenkins, Promotions Manager

KIOA
09-18-1964; 93.3 MHz FM; *Hrs Open:* 24; 82 kw; 1066 ft.; N41 37 55 W93 27 26
73 Kercheval Avenue, Grosse Pointe Farms, MI 48236 US
(515) 280-1350; *Fax:* (515) 280-3011
www.kioa.com
License: Des Moines, Polk County, IA held by Saga Communications of Iowa LLC
Group Owner: Saga Communications Inc.; (acq 4-19-93; $2.7 million with co-located AM;
Arbitron Metro Market: Des Moines, IA; *Format:* Oldies; *Target Audience:* 25-54.
Jeff Delvaux, General Manager
Pam Washington, General Sales Mgr
Tim Fox, Programming Director
Lindsay Reinert, Promotions Manager
Jay Wells, News Director
Joe Farrington, Chief Engineer
Sarah Levere, Advertising Manager
Lee AnnRose, Traffic Manager

***KJMC**
05-01-1999; 89.3 MHz FM; *Hrs Open:* 24; 7.1 kw; 200 ft.; N41 39 21 W93 35 51
1169 25th Street, Des Moines, IA 50311 US
(515) 279-1811; *Fax:* (515) 279-1802
License: Des Moines, Polk County, IA held by Minority Communications Inc.
Nat'l Network: ABC
Arbitron Metro Market: Des Moines, IA; *Format:* Jazz, Oldies
Larry Neville, Operations Dir
Larry Rollins, General Manager
John Farington, Chief of Operations

KKDM
08-22-1995; 107.5 MHz FM; *Hrs Open:* 24; 100 kw; 722 ft.; N41 38 38 W93 17 20
2141 Grand Avenue, Des Moines, IA 50312 US
(515) 245-8900; *Fax:* (515) 245-8906
www.kiss1075.com
License: Des Moines, Polk County, IA held by Clear Channel Broadcasting Licenses Inc.
Group Owner: iHeartMedia; (acq 9-1-99; $7.35 million)
Nat'l Reps: Clear Channel
Arbitron Metro Market: Des Moines, IA; *Format:* Contemporary Hits/Top 40; *Target Audience:* 18-49.
Greg Chance, Senior Vice President of Programming
Nick Bruns, Promotions and Marketing Director

KDRB
02-01-1948; 100.3 MHz FM; *Hrs Open:* 24; 100 kw; 1795 ft.; N41 49 48 W93 36 54
2141 Grand Avenue, Des Moines, IA 50312 US
(515) 245-8900; *Fax:* (515) 245-8902
www.thebusfm.com
License: Des Moines, Polk County, IA held by Citicasters Licenses Inc.
Group Owner: iHeartMedia
Nat'l Reps: Clear Channel; *Wire Services:* AP
Arbitron Metro Market: Des Moines, IA; *Format:* Adult Contemp; *Target Audience:* 25-54.
Greg Chance, Senior Vice President of Programming
John McKeighan, Program Director and Music Director
Nick Bruns, Promotions Manager

KRNT
03-17-1935; 1350 kHz AM; *Hrs Open:* 24; 5 kw-D, DAN; 5 kw-N, DAN; N41 33 31 W93 34 45
1416 Locust Street, Des Moines, IA 50309 US
(515) 280-1350; *Fax:* (515) 280-3011
www.1350krnt.com
jbrown@desmoinesradiogroup.com
License: Des Moines, IA held by Saga Communications of Iowa LLC
Group Owner: Saga Communications Inc.
Nat'l Network: CBS; *Nat'l Reps:* Katz Radio; *Wire Services:* AP
Arbitron Metro Market: Des Moines, IA; *Format:* Adult Contemp; *Target Audience:* 50 plus.
Jeff Delvaux, General Manager
Pam Washington, General Sales Mgr
Mark McDowell, Programming Director
Luke Matthews, Digital Media Manager
Geneva Walker, Business Manager
Scott Allen, Operations Manager

KSTZ
01-01-1970; 102.5 MHz FM; *Hrs Open:* 24; 92 kw; 1260 ft.; N41 48 1 W93 36 27
1416 Locust Street, Des Moines, IA 50309 US
(515) 280-1350; *Fax:* (515) 280-3011
www.star1025.com
sallen@desmoinesradiogroup.com
License: Des Moines, Polk County, IA held by Saga Communications of Iowa LLC
Group Owner: Saga Communications Inc.; (acq 8-88; $3.2 million with co-located AM;
Nat'l Network: CNN Radio; *Nat'l Reps:* Katz Radio; *Wire Services:* AP
Arbitron Metro Market: Des Moines, IA; *Format:* Adult Contemp; *Target Audience:* 25-54; emphasis on upscale women
Scott Allen, Operations/Programming Director
Jeff Delvaux, General Manager
Pam Washington, General Sales Mgr
Geneva Walker, Business Manager
Michael Christiansen, Promotions Manager
Luke Matthews, Digital Media Manager

KWKY
02-02-1948; 1150 kHz AM; *Hrs Open:* 24
6626 Dubuqe Trail, Norwalk, IA 50211 US
(515) 223-1150; *Fax:* (515) 981-0840
www.kwky.com
info@kwky.com
License: Des Moines, IA held by St. Gabriel Communications
Nat'l Network: EWTN Radio
Arbitron Metro Market: Norwalk, IA; *Format:* Sports, Talk, 20
John Teeling, President
Martha Paz, Station Manager

KPSZ
04-01-1947; 940 kHz AM; *Hrs Open:* 24; 10 kw-D, DA2; 5 kw-N, DA2; N41 28 35 W93 22 26
1416 Locust Street, Des Moines, IA 50309 US
(515) 280-1350; *Fax:* (515) 280-3011
www.praise940.com
jbrown@desmoinesradiogroup.com
License: Des Moines, IA held by Saga Communications of Iowa LLC
Group Owner: Saga Communications Inc.
Nat'l Network: Salem Radio Network; *Nat'l Reps:* Katz Radio; *Wire Services:* AP
Arbitron Metro Market: Des Moines, IA; *Format:* Christian; *Target Audience:* Adult; adult christian, music and program format
Jeff Delvaux, General Manager
Pam Washington, General Sales Mgr
Jim Brown, Programming Director
Pam Washington, Sales Manager
Mark McDowell, Program Coordinator
Geneva Walker, Business Manager
Mary Sayre, Account Executive
LukeMatthews, Digital Media Manager

WHO
04-10-1924; 1040 kHz AM; *Hrs Open:* 24
2141 Grand Avenue, Des Moines, IA 50312 US
(515) 245-8900; *Fax:* (515) 245-8902
www.whoradio.com
License: Des Moines, IA held by Citicasters Licenses Inc.
Group Owner: iHeartMedia; (acq 5-4-99; grpsl)
Nat'l Network: Fox News Radio; *Nat'l Reps:* Clear Channel; *Wire Services:* AP
Arbitron Metro Market: Des Moines, IA; *Format:* News, News/Talk, 86 *Special Programming:* Farm 15 hrs wkly; *No. News Employees:* 7; *Target Audience:* Adults 25-54
Greg Chance, Senior Vice President of Programming
Joel McCrea, Market Manager

Mary Greig, Sales Manager
Van Harden, Programming Director
Nick Bruns, Promotions Director
Jim Boyd, News Director

Dubuque

KATF
06-25-1967; 92.9 MHz FM; *Hrs Open:* 24; 89.7 kw; 1014 ft.; N42 31 44 W90 36 58
Mailing Address: 7601 Ganser Wy, Madison, WI 53719 US
Second Address: 346 W. 8th St., Dubuque, IA 52001
(563) 690-0929
www.katfm.com
License: Dubuque, Dubuque County, IA held by Radio Dubuque Inc.
Group Owner: Radio Dubuque Inc.
Wire Services: NWS (National Weather Service)
Arbitron Metro Market: Dubuque, IA; *Format:* Adult Contemp; *Hrs. of News Programming:* News progmg 3 hrs wkly; *Target Audience:* 25-54; adults establishing families, careers & households
Thomas Parsley, General Manager

KDTH
05-04-1941; 1370 kHz AM; *Hrs Open:* 24; 5 kw-D, DAN; 5 kw-N, DAN; N42 29 6 W90 38 39
1055 University Avenue, Dubuque, IA 52001 US
(563) 690-0800; *Fax:* (563) 690-0858
www.kdth.com
kdth@kdth.com
License: Dubuque, IA held by Radio Dubuque Inc.
Group Owner: Radio Dubuque Inc.; (acq 7-1-2000; $3.68 million with co-located FM)
Nat'l Network: CBS; *Nat'l Reps:* Katz Radio; *Wire Services:* NWS (National Weather Service)
Arbitron Metro Market: Dubuque, IA; *Format:* Variety/Diverse *Special Programming:* Farm 17 hrs wkly; *Hrs. of News Programming:* news progmg 25 hrs wkly; *No. News Employees:* 3; *Target Audience:* 35 plus;responsible adults with established careers & households
Don Rabbitt, CEO
Thomas Parsley, President/General Manager
Perry Mason, General Sales Mgr
Michael Kaye, Programming Director
Ron Bock, News Director
Tim Lary, Sports Director

KLYV
09-01-1965; 105.3 MHz FM; 50 kw; 330 ft; N42 30 10 W90 42 11
5490 Saratoga Rd., Dubuque, IA 53202
(563) 557-1040; *Fax:* (319) 583-4535
www.y105online.com
License: Dubuque, Dubuque County, IA held by Peak Broadcasting of Fresno Licenses LLC
Group Owner: Townsquare Media
Population Served: 130,000; *Arbitron Metro Market:* Dubuque, IA; *Target Audience:* 18-49.
Scott Thomas, Programming Director

KXGE
03-08-1980; 102.3 MHz FM; *Hrs Open:* 24; 2 kw; 308 ft.; N42 35 7 W90 38 50
111 East Kilbourn Avenue, Suite 2700, Milwaukee, WI 53202 US
(563) 557-1040; *Fax:* (563) 583-4535
www.eagle102rocks.com
License: Dubuque, Dubuque County, IA held by Peak Broadcasting of Fresno Licenses LLC
Group Owner: Townsquare Media; (acq 12-17-98; grpsl)
Nat'l Network: ABC
Arbitron Metro Market: Dubuque, IA; *Format:* Classic Rock; *Hrs. of News Programming:* news progmg 2 hrs wkly; *No. News Employees:* 1; *Target Audience:* 18-49; in high school or college in the 60s & 70s
Dan Sullivan, General Manager
Doris Garius, General Sales Mgr
Scott Thomas, Programming Director
Tom Berryman, News Director

WDBQ
10-30-1933; 1490 kHz AM; 1 kw-U, ND1; N42 30 10 W90 42 24
111 East Kilbourn Avenue, Suite 2700, Milwaukee, WI 53202 US
(563) 557-1040; *Fax:* (563) 583-4535
www.wdbqam.com
heather.davis@cumulus.com
License: Dubuque, IA held by Peak Broadcasting of Fresno Licenses LLC
Group Owner: Townsquare Media; (acq 12-17-98; grpsl)
Nat'l Network: ABC; Westwood One
Arbitron Metro Market: Dubuque, IA; *Format:* News, Sports, 86
Jack Kilcoyne, Programming Director
Mike Field, Disc Jockey
Alan Williams, Traffic Manager

*KNSY(FM)
01-01-2005; 89.7 MHz FM; 530 w horiz, 2.6 kw vert; Ant 646 ft; N42 36 18 W90 47 57 *Rebroadcasts:* Rebroadcasts KUNI(FM) Cedar Falls 100%
324 Communications Arts Center, Univ. of Northern Iowa, Cedar Falls, IA 50614
(319) 273-6400; *Fax:* (319) 273-2682
www.kuniradio.org
License: Dubuque, Dubuque County, IA held by University of Northern Iowa.
Arbitron Metro Market: Dubuque, IA *Special Programming:* Blues 5 hrs, folk 4 hrs wkly; *Hrs. of News Programming:* news progmg 77 hours; *No. News Employees:* 3
Wayne Jarvis, General Manager
Scott Vezdos, Promotions Manager
Greg Shanley, News Director
Steve Schoon, Chief Engineer
Al Shares, Music Director

*KIAD
01-01-2006; 88.5 MHz FM; 0.75 kw vert; 518 ft.; N42 24 16 W90 34 12 *Rebroadcasts:* Rebroadcasts WAFR(FM) Tupelo, MS 100%
P.O. Box 3206, Tupelo, MS 38803 US
(662) 844-8888; *Fax:* (662) 842-6791
www.afr.net
faq@afa.net
License: Dubuque, Dubuque County, IA held by American Family Association.
Group Owner: American Family Radio
Arbitron Metro Market: Dubuque, IA; *Format:* Christian
Tim Wildmon, President
Donald Wildmon, Founder
Buddy Smith, Sr VP
Ed Vitagliano, Exec VP
Randy Sharp, Director Of Special Projects
Meeke Addison, Director Of Communications
Abraham Hamilton III, General Counsel

Dunkerton

KCOO
103.9 MHz FM; 6 kw; 312 ft.; N42 42 23.9 W92 13 3.7 US
(512) 329-5843; *Fax:* (512) 329-5847
www.matineemedia.com
License: Dunkerton, Black Hawk County, IA held by Matinee Media Corp.
Group Owner: Ace Radio Corp.
Arbitron Metro Market: Dunkerton, IA

Dyersville

KDST
08-25-1985; 99.3 MHz FM; *Hrs Open:* 24; 3 kw; 299 ft.; N42 25 43 W91 12 50
1931 20th Ave S.E., 600 N. Marquette Rd, Dyersville, IA 53821 US
(563) 875-8193; *Fax:* (563) 875-6001
www.realcountryonline.com
kdst993@iowatelecom.net
License: Dyersville, Dubuque County, IA held by Design Homes Inc.
Nat'l Network: ABC; *Regional Network:* Brownfield
Arbitron Metro Market: Dubuque, IA; *Format:* Country *Special Programming:* Farm; *No. News Employees:* 1; *Target Audience:* 45-60.; *Adv. Rates:* 19; 16.50; 16.50; 14.50
Randy Weeks, CEO
Franklin Weeks, President
Doug Langston, Operations Dir
Randy Weeks, General Manager
Doug Langston, Station Manager
Matt Monahan, News Director

Eagle Grove

*KJYL
02-20-1994; 100.7 MHz FM; *Hrs Open:* 24; 25 kw; 328 ft.; N42 39 18 W93 59 24
P.O. Box 72, County Rd 6, Blue Earth, MN 56013 US
(515) 448-4588; *Fax:* (515) 448-5267
www.kjyl.org
License: Eagle Grove, Wright County, IA held by Minn-Iowa Christian Broadcasting Inc.
Group Owner: Minn-Iowa Christian Broadcasting Inc.
Format: Christian; *No. News Employees:* 1; *Target Audience:* 30-55.
Jay Rudolph, Operations Dir
Matt Dorfner, General Manager
Mark Bohnett, Chief Engineer

Eddyville

KKSI
07-30-1990; 101.5 MHz FM; *Hrs Open:* 24; 49 kw; 499 ft.; N41 7 57 W92 42 12
416 E. Main St., Ottumwa, IA 52501 US
(641) 684-5563
www.ottumwaradio.com
License: Eddyville, Wapello County, IA held by O-Town Communications Inc.
Group Owner: Linder Broadcasting Group; (acq 12-10-99; $162,400)
Arbitron Metro Market: Des Moines, IA; *Format:* Classic Rock; *Hrs. of News Programming:* news progmg 4 hrs wkly; *No. News Employees:* 2; *Target Audience:* 25-54.; *Adv. Rates:* 29.68;29.68;29.68;27.68
Mike Buchanan, News Director

Eldon

KRKN
01-01-1996; 104.3 MHz FM; *Hrs Open:* 24; 23.5 kw; 341 ft.; N40 52 6 W92 18 20
416 E. Main St., Ottumwa, IA 52501 US
(641) 684-5563
www.ottumwaradio.com
License: Eldon, Wapello County, IA held by O-Town Communications Inc.
Group Owner: Linder Broadcasting Group.; (acq 12-10-99; $162,400).
Arbitron Metro Market: Ottumwa; *Format:* Country; *Hrs. of News Programming:* news progmg 4 hrs wkly; *No. News Employees:* 2; *Target Audience:* 18-54.; *Adv. Rates:* 29.68; 29.68; 29.68; 27.68
Mike Buchanan, News Director

Eldora

KDAO-FM
06-01-1992; 99.5 MHz FM; *Hrs Open:* 24; 3 kw; 328 ft.; N42 15 49 W93 3 57
Mailing Address: P.O. Box 538, Marshalltown, IA 50158 US
Second Address: 1930 N. Center St., Marshalltown, IA 50158
(641) 752-4122; *Fax:* (641) 752-5121
www.kdao.com
kdao@kdao.com
License: Eldora, Hardin County, IA held by Eldora Broadcasting Co. Inc.
Nat'l Network: Fox News Radio
Arbitron Metro Market: Marshaltown, IA; *Format:* Adult Contemp; *Target Audience:* 25-54.
Mark Osmundson, General Manager

Elkader

KADR
05-15-1983; 1400 kHz AM; 1 kw-U, ND1; N42 50 57 W91 24 43
600 N. Marquette Rd., P.O. Box 239, Prairie Du Chien, WI 53821 US
(563) 245-1400; *Fax:* (563) 245-1402
www.am1400online.com
License: Elkader, IA held by KADR-AM 14, div of Design Homes Inc.
Nat'l Reps: Farmakis
Arbitron Metro Market: Elkader, IA; *Format:* Adult Contemp
Troy Thein, Operations Dir
Dan Berns, General Manager

Emmetsburg

KUYY
01-10-1977; 100.1 MHz FM; *Hrs Open:* 24; 16 kw; 410 ft.; N43 7 24 W94 51 28
2215 Main Street, P.O. Box 390, Emmetsburg, IA 50536 US
(712) 264-1074; *Fax:* (712) 264-1077
www.y100-fm.com/info/
License: Emmetsburg, Palo Alto County, IA held by Jim Dandy Broadcasting Inc.
Arbitron Metro Market: Emmetsburg, IA; *Format:* Adult Contemp; *Target Audience:* 25-54.; *Adv. Rates:* 14; 12; 12; 10
Stan Calvert, Operations Dir
Marty Spies, General Manager
Stephanie Haviland, General Sales Mgr
Jeff Nixx, Programming Director
Abby Kohlhaas, Promotions Manager
Steve Schwaller, News Director
Steve Heaton, Chief Engineer

RADIO - U.S.

Epworth

KGRR
12-10-1994; 97.3 MHz FM; *Hrs Open:* 24; 25 kw; 328 ft.; N42 27 29 W90 46 40
Mailing Address: 2115 Jfk Road, Dubuque, IA 52002 US
Second Address: 346 W. 8th St., Dubuque, IA 52004
(563) 690-0800; *Fax:* (563) 588-5688
www.973therock.com
kgrr@kgrr.com
License: Epworth, Dubuque County, IA held by Radio Dubuque Inc.
Group Owner: Radio Dubuque Inc.; acq 7-1-00; $1.5 million).
Nat'l Reps: Katz Radio
Arbitron Metro Market: Dubuque, IA; *Format:* Classic Rock, Adult Contemp *Special Programming:* Chop Shop 5 hrs wkly, full metal jackie 2 hrs wkly; *Hrs. of News Programming:* news progmg 2 hrs wkly; *No. News Employees:* 1; *Target Audience:* 25-54; families
Don Rabbitt, CEO
Thomas Parsley, President
Paul Hemmer, Operations Dir
Perry Mason, Programming Director

Estherville

KILR
12-23-1967; 1070 kHz AM; *Hrs Open:* 6 AM-2 hrs past sunset
Mailing Address: P.O. Box 453, Estherville, IA 51334 US
Second Address: 3875 150th St., Estherville, IA 51334
(712) 362-2644; *Fax:* (712) 362-5951
kilrradio.com
KILRRADIO@HOTMAIL.COM
License: Estherville, IA held by Jacobson Broadcasting Co. Inc.
Nat'l Network: ABC; *Nat'l Reps:* Farmakis
Format: Country *Special Programming:* Farm 9 hrs, relg 11 hrs wkly; *Hrs. of News Programming:* news progmg 24 hrs wkly; *No. News Employees:* 1; *Target Audience:* 29-65; loc baby boomers; *Adv. Rates:* 20; 20.18; na
Barbara Jacobson, CFO
Roger Jacobson, President
Peggy Zahrt, Operations Dir
Ed Funston, News Director

KILR-FM
10-17-1969; 95.9 MHz FM; 25 kw; 325 ft.; N43 25 45 W94 49 23
P.O. Box 453, Estherville, IA 51334 US
(712) 362-2644; *Fax:* (712) 362-5951
kilrradio.com
KILRRADIO@HOTMAIL.COM
License: Estherville, Emmet County, IA held by Jacobson Broadcasting Co. Inc.
Nat'l Reps: Salem
Format: Country; *Target Audience:* 25-54.; *Adv. Rates:* 20; 19; 18; 18
Lou Mellini, General Manager

Fairfield

*KHOE
01-01-1994; 90.5 MHz FM; *Hrs Open:* 24; 0.1 kw; 98 ft.; N41 0 59 W91 58 9
1000 N. 4th Street, Fairfield, IA 52557 US
(641) 469-5463
www.khoe.org
khoe@mum.edu
License: Fairfield, Jefferson County, IA held by Fairfield Educational Radio Station.
Format: Classical, Variety/Diverse *Special Programming:* Children 3 hrs, folk 6 hrs, gospel 3 hrs, jazz 2 h; *Hrs. of News Programming:* News progmg 2 hrs wkly; *Target Audience:* 18-35; University & college audience
Stan Stansberry, General Manager

KKFD-FM
01-01-1977; 95.9 MHz FM; *Hrs Open:* 24; 4.1 kw; 400 ft.; N40 58 47 W92 5 45
57- 1/2 S. Court St, P.O. Box 648, Fairfield, IA 52556 US
(641) 472-4191; *Fax:* (641) 472-2071
www.exploreSEIowa.com
License: Fairfield, Jefferson County, IA held by Fairfield License Co. LLC.
Group Owner: GoodRadio.TV
Nat'l Network: ABC
Format: Classic Rock; *No. News Employees:* 1; *Target Audience:* Active, affluent adults 30-60
Marie Kiefer, Operations Dir
Tammy Jones, General Manager
Steve Smith, Programming Director
Andrew Zupkoff, News Director
Lee Muntz, Sports Director

KMCD
03-03-1958; 1570 kHz AM; *Hrs Open:* 24; 0.25 kw-D, ND2; 0.109 kw-N, ND2; N41 0 25 W92 0 50
57- 1/2 S. Court St., P.O. Box 648, Fairfield, IA 52556 US
(641) 472-4191; *Fax:* (641) 472-2071
www.fairfieldiowaradio.com
License: Fairfield, IA held by Fairfield License Co. LLC.
Group Owner: GoodRadio.TV; (acq 6-1-2007; $750,000 with co-located FM)
Nat'l Network: ABC; Jones Radio Networks; *Regional Network:* Radio Iowa
Format: Country; *No. News Employees:* 1; *Target Audience:* 30 plus; community leaders & Jefferson County
Tammy Jones, General Manager
Steve Smith, Programming Director
Andrew Zupkoff, News Director
Lee Muntz, Sports Director

Forest City

KIOW
11-08-1978; 107.3 MHz FM; *Hrs Open:* 24; 25 kw; 328 ft.; N43 17 2 W93 37 50
Mailing Address: P.O. Box 308, Forest City, IA 50436 US
Second Address: 18643 360th St., Forest City, IA 50436
(641) 585-1073; *Fax:* (641) 585-2990
www.kiow.com
kiow@kiow.com
License: Forest City, Winnebago County, IA held by Pilot Knob Broadcasting Inc.
Nat'l Network: CNN Radio; *Regional Network:* Radio Iowa; *Nat'l Reps:* Farmakis; *Wire Services:* AP
Format: Adult Contemp, Country, 60 *Special Programming:* Farm 15 hrs, contemp hits 19 hrs wkly; *Hrs. of News Programming:* news progmg 15 hrs wkly; *No. News Employees:* 1; *Target Audience:* General; Adults 25 + *Adv. Rates:* 15.35; 15.35; 15.35; 15.35
Susan Coloff, CFO
Tony Coloff, President

Fort Dodge

*KICB
09-01-1971; 88.1 MHz FM; 0.2 kw; 131 ft.; N42 29 27 W94 12 1
330 Avenue M, Fort Dodge, IA 50501 US
(515) 576-6049; *Fax:* (515) 576-5656
http://www.iccc.cc.ia.us/kicb
License: Fort Dodge, Webster County, IA held by Iowa Central Community College.
Format: Alternative *Special Programming:* Sports 2 hrs wkly, movies and games 2 hrs wkly, deans list 2 hrs wkly; *Target Audience:* 13-34; young men & women with progsv tastes
Robert Paxton, President
Brian Blessman, General Manager
Jeff Nelsen, Chief Engineer

KKEZ
01-01-1979; 94.5 MHz FM; *Hrs Open:* 24; 100 kw; 600 ft.; N42 29 43 W94 12 33
200 N. 10th St., Fort Dodge, IA 50501 US
(515) 955-5656; *Fax:* (515) 955-5844
www.yourfortdodge.com
sgossweiler@digity.me
License: Fort Dodge, Webster County, IA held by Digity 3E License, LLC
Group Owner: Digity, LLC
Arbitron Metro Market: Des Moines, IA; *Format:* Adult Contemp; *No. News Employees:* 3; *Target Audience:* 18-49.
Darren Helton, Operations Dir
Steve Gossweiler, General Manager
Pat Kolar, Dir. of Sales
Darren Helton, Programming Director
Kelly Heinen, News Director

*KNSH(FM)
09-15-1980; 91.1 MHz FM; *Hrs Open:* 24; 100 kw; Ant 1,052 ft; N42 49 03 W94 24 41
WOI Radio Group, 2022 Communications Bldg., Ames, IA 50011-3241
(515) 294-2025
www.iowapublicradio.org
woi@iastate.edu
License: Fort Dodge, Webster County, IA held by Iowa State University of Science and Technology.
Nat'l Network: NPR; PRI
Population Served: 17,000 *Hrs. of News Programming:* news progmg 41 hrs wkly; *No. News Employees:* 1; *Target Audience:* General; educated
Mary Grace Herrington, Programming Director
Don Wirth, Director, Fiscal Operations

KZLB
12-17-1990; 92.1 MHz FM; 6 kw; 321 ft; N42 28 44 W94 12 10
200 N. 10th Street, Fort Dodge, IA 50501 US
(515) 955-5656; *Fax:* (515) 955-5844
www.yourfortdodge.com
sgossweiler@digity.me
License: Fort Dodge, Webster County, IA held by Digity 3E License, LLC
Group Owner: Digity, LLC; (acq 7-1-2004; grpsl)
Population Served: 206,599; *Arbitron Metro Market:* Des Moines, IA; *Format:* Classic Rock
Steve Gossweiler, General Manager
Pat Kolar, Director of Sales
Darren Helton, Programming Director

KVFD
12-24-1939; 1400 kHz AM; *Hrs Open:* 24; 0.85 kw-U, ND1; N42 28 44 W94 12 10
200 N. 10th Street, Fort Dodge, IA 50501 US
(515) 955-1400; *Fax:* (515) 955-5844
www.yourfortdodge.com
sgossweiler@digity.me
License: Fort Dodge, IA held by Digity 3E License, LLC
Group Owner: Digity, LLC
Wire Services: AP
Arbitron Metro Market: Fort Dodge, IA; *Format:* Talk
Steve Gossweiler, General Manager
Pat Kolar, Director of Sales
Dan Jones, Programming Director

KWMT
04-01-1956; 540 kHz AM; 5 kw-D, DA2; 0.17 kw-N, DA2; N42 29 45 W94 12 33
200 N. 10th St., Fort Dodge, IA 50501 US
(515) 576-5656; *Fax:* (515) 955-5844
www.yourfortdodge.com
sgossweiler@digity.me
License: Fort Dodge, IA held by Digity 3E License, LLC
Group Owner: Digity, LLC; (acq 9-1-2007; grpsl)
Nat'l Reps: McGavren Guild
Arbitron Metro Market: Fort Dodge, IA; *Format:* Country; *Target Audience:* General.
Darren Helton, Operations Dir
Steve Gossweiler, General Manager
Pat Kolar, Dir. of Sales
Duane Murley, Programming Director
Kelly Heinen, News Director

*KAWV
01-01-2005; 89.5 MHz FM; 17 kw vert; 364 ft.; N42 40 18 W94 9 11
Mailing Address: 4136 Northgate Blvd., Suite 1, Sacramento, CA 95834 US
Second Address: 4136 Northgate Blvd., Suite 1, Sacramento, IA 95834
(800) 543-1495; *Fax:* (916) 641-8238
www.familyradio.com
info@familyradio.com
License: Fort Dodge, Webster County, IA held by Family Stations Inc.
Group Owner: Family Stations Inc.
Nat'l Network: Family Radio
Arbitron Metro Market: Fort Dodge, IA; *Format:* Religious
Harold Camping, President
Pat McMahon, Operations Dir
J.D. Freeman, General Manager

Fort Madison

KBKB
02-06-1948; 1360 kHz AM; *Hrs Open:* 18; 1 kw-D, ND1; 0.034 kw-N, ND1; N40 39 30 W91 16 20
610 N. 4th St., Suite 300, Burlington, IA 52601 US
(319) 752-5402; *Fax:* (319) 752-4715
www.bigcountry1031.com
johnp@burlingtonradio.com
License: Fort Madison, IA held by Pritchard Broadcasting Corp.
Group Owner: Pritchard Broadcasting Corp.; (acq 6-6-2008; with KBUR(AM) Burlington)
Arbitron Metro Market: Burlington, IA; *Format:* Country
Joe Bates, Operations Dir
John Pritchard, General Manager
Chet Young, General Sales Mgr

KBKB-FM
06-01-1973; 101.7 MHz FM; *Hrs Open:* 24; 50 kw; 466 ft.; N40 43 25 W91 13 49
Mailing Address: 50 East Rivercenter Blvd, #1200, Covington, KY 41011 US
Second Address: 1411 N. Roosevelt Ave., Burlington, IA 52601

(319) 752-2701; *Fax:* (319) 752-5287
www.1017thebull.com
License: Fort Madison, Lee County, IA held by GAP Broadcasting Burlington License LLC.
Group Owner: GAPWEST Broadcasting; (acq 2-13-2008; grpsl)
Nat'l Network: ABC
Arbitron Metro Market: Burlington, IA; *Format:* Country; *Hrs. of News Programming:* news progmg 7 hrs wkly; *No. News Employees:* 2
Kosmo Leone, Programming Director
J.K. Martin, News Director

Garnavillo

KCTN
12-06-1982; 100.1 MHz FM; *Hrs Open:* 24; 6 kw; 328 ft.; N42 53 6 W91 19 11
P.O. Box 239, 600 N. Marquette Rd, Prairie Du Chien, WI 53821 US
(563) 245-1400; *Fax:* (563) 245-1402
kctn.com
kctn@alpinecom.net
License: Garnavillo, Clayton County, IA held by KCTN-FM 100 div of Design Homes Inc.
Regional Network: Brownfield; *Nat'l Reps:* Farmakis
Arbitron Metro Market: Garnavillo, IA; *Format:* Country; *No. News Employees:* 1; *Target Audience:* 24-55; farmers & rural communities
Randy Weeks, CEO
Dan Berns, General Manager
Troy Thein, Chief of Operations

Glenwood

KXKT
04-08-1966; 103.7 MHz FM; *Hrs Open:* 24; 100 kw; 1086 ft.; N41 18 32 W96 1 33
600 Congress Avenue, Suite 1400, Austin, TX 78701 US
(402) 561-2000; *Fax:* (402) 551-4315
www.thekat.com
License: Glenwood, Mills County, IA held by Capstar TX LLC
Group Owner: iHeartMedia; (acq 8-30-2000; grpsl).
Arbitron Metro Market: Omaha, NE; *Format:* Country; *No. News Employees:* 1; *Target Audience:* 18-54; general
Richard J. Bressler, President

Grinnell

KGRN
11-15-1957; 1410 kHz AM
909 1/2 Main Street, Grinnell, IA 50112 US
(641) 236-1410; *Fax:* (641) 236-8896
www.http://myiowainfo.com
License: Grinnell, IA held by Grinnell License Co. LLC.
Group Owner: GoodRadio.TV; (acq 5-2-2007; $2.25 million)
Nat'l Reps: Farmakis
Format: News, News/Talk, 86; *Hrs. of News Programming:* News progmg 60 hrs wkly; *Target Audience:* 25-74
Dean Goodman, President
Ron McCarthy, General Manager

KRTI
05-01-1993; 106.7 MHz FM; *Hrs Open:* 24; 50 kw; 492 ft.; N41 48 16 W92 40 9
Mailing Address: P.O. Box 66, 1801 N. 13th Ave. East, Newton, IA 50208 US
Second Address: 1801 N. 13th Ave. E., Newton, IA 50208
(641) 792-5262; *Fax:* (641) 792-8403
www.energy1067.com
License: Grinnell, Poweshiek County, IA held by Newton License Co. LLC.
Group Owner: GoodRadio.TV; (acq 5-1-2007; grpsl)
Arbitron Metro Market: Grinnell, IA; *Format:* Contemporary Hits/Top 40
Tim Graves, Operations Dir
Ron McCarthy, General Manager

Grundy Center

KCRR
10-08-1983; 97.7 MHz FM; *Hrs Open:* 24; 16 kw; 407 ft.; N42 23 28 W92 31 57
2003 Elmcrest Drive, Marshalltown, IA 50158 US
(319) 833-4800; *Fax:* (319) 833-4866
www.kcrr.com
kcrr@kcrr.com
License: Grundy Center, Grundy County, IA held by Cumulus Licensing Corp.
Group Owner: Cumulus Media Inc.; (acq 3-15-00; grpsl).
Arbitron Metro Market: Waterloo-Cedar Falls, IA; *Format:* Classic Rock; *Hrs. of News Programming:* news progmg 3 hrs wkly; *No. News Employees:* 2; *Target Audience:* 25-54.

Lew Dickey, President/CEO
Keith Mitchell, Programming Director

Hampton

KLMJ
05-16-1983; 104.9 MHz FM; *Hrs Open:* 24; 6 kw; 305 ft.; N42 49 52 W93 11 20
Mailing Address: P.O. Box 495, Hampton, IA 50441 US
Second Address: 1509 4th St. N.E., Hampton, IA 50441
(641) 456-5656; *Fax:* (641) 456-5655
www.klmj.com
klmj@klmj.com
License: Hampton, Franklin County, IA held by C.D. Broadcasting Inc.
Nat'l Network: ABC; *Regional Network:* Radio Iowa; Brownfield;
Nat'l Reps: Farmakis
Arbitron Metro Market: Mason City, IA; *Format:* Adult Contemp, Country, 64 *Special Programming:* Iowa State & Univ. of Northern Iowa, farm 8 hrs wk; *Hrs. of News Programming:* news progmg 14 hrs wkly *No. NewsEmployees:* 2; *Target Audience:* 25 plus; general; *Adv. Rates:* 19; 19; 19; 19
Marlin Burrier, Operations Dir
Craig Donnelly, General Manager

Harlan

KNOD
11-12-1979; 105.3 MHz FM; *Hrs Open:* 24; 25 kw; 282 ft.; N41 37 0 W95 16 10
P.O. Box 723, 902 Chatburn Ave, Harlan, IA 51537 US
(712) 755-3883; *Fax:* (712) 755-7511
knodnews@harlannet.com
License: Harlan, Shelby County, IA held by Wireless Broadcasting L.L.C.
Regional Network: Brownfield
Format: Oldies *Special Programming:* Farm 3 hrs, relg 2 hrs wkly; *Hrs. of News Programming:* news progmg 5 hrs wkly; *No. News Employees:* 1; *Target Audience:* 25-50.; *Adv. Rates:* 12.25; 12.25; 12.25; 12.25.
Richard Keane, Operations Dir
Judy Storm, General Manager
Joel McCall, News Director
Paul Stessman, Traffic Manager

Hiawatha

*KXGM-FM
01-01-2002; 89.1 MHz FM; 0 kw horiz, 5.8 kw vert; 400 ft.; N42 3 13 W91 44 35
3232 Osage Rd, Waterloo, IA 50703 US
(319) 294-8910
www.891thespirit.com
License: Hiawatha, Linn County, IA held by Extreme Grace Media Inc.
Arbitron Metro Market: Cedar Rapids, IA; *Format:* Christian
Michael James, Station Manager

Hudson

KCVM
08-27-1997; 93.5 MHz FM; *Hrs Open:* 24; 6 kw; 325 ft.; N42 24 47 W92 26 15
506 North Clark Street, Forest City, IA 50436 US
(319) 277-1918(319) 266-6499; *Fax:* (319) 277-5202
www.mix96.net
themix@935themix.com
License: Hudson, Black Hawk County, IA held by Fife Communications Co. L.C.
Arbitron Metro Market: Waterloo-Cedar Falls, IA; *Format:* Adult Contemp; *Hrs. of News Programming:* news progmg 2 hrs wkly; *No. News Employees:* 1; *Target Audience:* 25-54; eastern Iowa adult females; *Adv. Rates:* 30; 30; 30; 30
Jim Coloff, President
Tony Coloff, Operations Dir
Jim Coloff, General Manager
Teri Lynn, Programming Director
Jay Rhymer, Promotions Manager
Jesse Gavin, News Director

Humboldt

KHBT
08-05-1970; 97.7 MHz FM; *Hrs Open:* 24; 5.8 kw; 276 ft.; N42 43 57 W94 12 23
Mailing Address: 3378 Raccoon Ridge, Adel, IA 50003 US
Second Address: 2196 Montana Ave., Humboldt, IA 50548
(515) 332-4100; *Fax:* (515) 332-2723
www.977thebolt.com
License: Humboldt, Humboldt County, IA held by NRG License Sub. LLC.

Group Owner: NRG Media LLC; (acq 10-31-2005; grpsl)
Wire Services: AP
Format: Adult Contemp *Special Programming:* Farm 10 hrs wkly; *Hrs. of News Programming:* news progmg 30 hrs wkly; *No. News Employees:* 1; *Target Audience:* 30-65; general
Bob Ketchum, General Manager

Ida Grove

KKIA
09-01-1981; 92.9 MHz FM; *Hrs Open:* 24; 25 kw; 328 ft.; N42 29 23 W95 17 40
Mailing Address: 2215 Main Street, P.O. Box 390, Emmetsburg, IA 50536 US
Second Address: P.O. Box 108, Storm Lake, IA 50588
(712) 732-3520; *Fax:* (712) 732-1746
www.stormlakeradio.com
info@stormlakeradio.com
License: Ida Grove, Ida County, IA held by Jim Dandy Broadcasting Inc.
Group Owner: NRG Media LLC; (acq 1-13-2003; $2.5 million with KUYY(FM) Emmetsburg)
Nat'l Network: Fox News Radio; *Nat'l Reps:* Farmakis
Format: Country *Special Programming:* Farm 10 hrs wkly; *Hrs. of News Programming:* news progmg 5 hrs wkly; *No. News Employees:* 1; *Target Audience:* 18-54.; *Adv. Rates:* 21; 21; 21; 21
Mary Quass, CEO
Buzz Paterson, General Manager
Chuck DuCoty, COO

Independence

KQMG
12-10-1959; 1220 kHz AM; 0.25 kw-D, ND1; 0.134 kw-N, ND1; N42 28 32 W91 52 26
3654 W. Jarvis Ave., Skokie, IL 60076 US
(847) 674-0864
License: Independence, IA held by KM Radio of Independence LLC.
Group Owner: KM Communications Inc.; (acq 10-9-03; $500,000 with co-located FM).
Nat'l Network: ABC
Arbitron Metro Market: Waterloo-Cedar Falls, IA
Myoung Hwa Bae, President

KQMG-FM
01-01-1972; 95.3 MHz FM; 2.9 kw; 410 ft.; N42 28 32 W91 52 26
231 1/2 First Street, East, Suite 953, Independence, IA 50644 US
(319) 334-3300; *Fax:* (319) 334-6158
kqmgfm@gmail.com
License: Independence, Buchanan County, IA
Group Owner: KM Communications Inc.
Arbitron Metro Market: Waterloo-Cedar Falls, IA; *Format:* Sports, Talk
Myoung Hwa Bae, President

Indianola

*KSTM
04-15-1994; 88.9 MHz FM; 0.15 kw; 125 ft.; N41 21 49 W93 33 37
701 North C Street, Indianola, IA 50125 US
(515) 961-1747(515) 961-1803; *Fax:* (515) 961-1674
www.889kstm.wordpress.com
License: Indianola, Warren County, IA held by Simpson College.
Arbitron Metro Market: Indianola, IA; *Format:* Alternative
Rich Ramos, General Manager

KXLQ
07-22-1963; 1490 kHz AM; 0.5 kw-D, ND1; 1 kw-N, ND1; N41 21 24 W93 35 16
810 Main St., P.O. Box 228, Pella, IA 50219 US
(248) 557-3500
www.birach.com
sima@birach.com
License: Indianola, Warren County, IA held by Birach Broadcasting Corp.
Group Owner: Birach Broadcasting Corp.; (acq 8-1-2007; $800,000 with WCXN(AM) Claremont, NC)
Arbitron Metro Market: Indianola, IA; *Format:* Sports
Sima Birach, President

Iowa City

KCJJ
10-14-1998; 1630 kHz AM; *Hrs Open:* 24
PO Box 2118, Iowa City, IA 52244 US

RADIO - U.S.

(319) 354-1242; *Fax:* (319) 354-1921
www.1630kcjj.com
kcjjam@gmail.com
License: Iowa City, IA held by River City Radio Inc.
Nat'l Network: ABC; CBS; *Wire Services:* AP
Arbitron Metro Market: Cedar Rapids, IA; *Format:* Talk; *No. News Employees:* 4; *Target Audience:* 25-54.; *Adv. Rates:* 32; 25; 28; 20
Steve Bridges, President
Tom Suter, General Manager
Kurt Means, Senior Account Executive
Deb Kelley-Melsha, Account Executive
Ginnie Collins, Board Operator

KKRQ
05-01-1966; 100.7 MHz FM; 100 kw; 531 ft.; N41 45 26 W91 31 31
1 Stephen Atkins Dr., Iowa City, IA 52245 US
(329) 354-9500; *Fax:* (319) 354-9504
www.kkrq.com
License: Iowa City, Johnson County, IA held by Citicasters Licenses Inc.
Group Owner: iHeartMedia
Arbitron Metro Market: Cedar Rapids, IA; *Format:* Classic Rock
Joel McCrea, Regional Market President
Jeanne Kerr, Senior Vice President of Sales
JJ Cook, Programming Director
Joni Sojka, Sales Manager

KRNA
10-04-1974; 94.1 MHz FM; *Hrs Open:* 24; 100 kw; 981 ft.; N41 45 0 W91 50 16
600 Congress Ave., Suite 1400, Austin, TX 78701 US
(319) 892-3573; *Fax:* (319) 363-8062
www.krna.com
License: Iowa City, Johnson County, IA held by Cumulus Licensing Corp.
Group Owner: Cumulus Media Inc.; (acq 2000; grpsl).
Nat'l Reps: Christal
Arbitron Metro Market: Cedar Rapids, IA; *Format:* Rock/AOR; *Target Audience:* 18-49.
Gregg Scharnau, Programming Director
Greg Sher, Promotions Manager

*KRUI-FM
03-28-1984; 89.7 MHz FM; *Hrs Open:* 24; 0.1 kw; 89 ft.; N41 39 29 W91 32 40
129 Grand Avenue Court, Iowa City, IA 52242 US
(319) 335-9525; *Fax:* (319) 335-9526
krui@uiowa.edu
License: Iowa City, Johnson County, IA held by Student Broadcasters Inc.
Arbitron Metro Market: Iowa City, IA; *Format:* Variety/Diverse; *Hrs. of News Programming:* News progmg 7 hrs wkly; *Target Audience:* 18-34; Univ
Aaron Roemig, Operations Dir
Nate George, Programming Director
Brian Anstey, Promotions Manager
Bill Penisten, News Director
Adam Erickson, Chief Engineer
Rick Oswavay, News Reporter
Ryal Brier, Sports Commentator

*KSUI
01-01-1948; 91.7 MHz FM; 100 kw; 1,292 ft; N41 43 15 W91 20 30
710 S. Clinton St. Bldg., Univ . of Iowa, Iowa City, IA 19103
(319) 335-5730; *Fax:* (319) 335-6116
License: Iowa City, Johnson County, IA held by University of Iowa
Nat'l Network: NPR; PRI; BBC

Joan Kjaer, Programming Director
Jim Davies, Engineering Dir

KXIC
06-07-1948; 800 kHz AM; 1 kw-D, DA2; 0.199 kw-N, DA2; N41 41 15 W91 32 39
1 Stephen Atkins Dr., Iowa City, IA 52245 US
(319) 354-9500; *Fax:* (319) 354-9504
www.kxic.com
License: Iowa City, IA held by Citicasters Licenses Inc.
Group Owner: iHeartMedia; (acq 5-4-99; grpsl).
Arbitron Metro Market: Cedar Rapids, IA; *Format:* News, News/Talk, 84, Talk
J.J. Cook, Senior Vice President of Programming
Joel McCrea, Regional Market President
Jeanne Kerr, Senior Vice President of Sales
Mark Pitz, Programming Director
Joni Sojka, Sales Manager

Brian Thomas, Production Director
Nicholas Bowers, Director of Digital Content

*WSUI
01-01-1919; 910 kHz AM
710 Clinton Street Bldg, Iowa City, IA 19103 US
(319) 335-5730; *Fax:* (319) 335-6116
wsui@uiowa.edu
License: Iowa City, IA held by The University of Iowa.
Nat'l Network: NPR
Format: News, News/Talk, 86
John Monick, General Manager
Dennis Reese, Programming Director
Jim Davis, Chief Engineer

Iowa Falls

KIFG
07-22-1962; 1510 kHz AM; 0.5 kw-C, NDD; 1 kw-D, NDD; N42 30 49 W93 12 57
410 Washington Avenue, Iowa Falls, IA 50126 US
(641) 648-4281; *Fax:* (641) 648-4606
www.kifgradio.com
kifg@iafalls.com
License: Iowa Falls, IA held by Times-Citizen Communications Inc.
Nat'l Network: CNN Radio; Westwood One; *Nat'l Reps:* Keystone (unwired net)
Format: Contemporary Hits/Top 40, Adult Contemp *Special Programming:* Farm 5 hrs wkly; *No. News Employees:* 1; *Target Audience:* 25 plus.
T.J. Norman, General Manager

KIFG-FM
10-01-1965; 95.3 MHz FM; *Hrs Open:* 24; 6 kw; 194 ft.; N42 30 49 W93 12 57
410 Washington Avenue, Iowa Falls, IA 50126 US
(641) 648-4281; *Fax:* (641) 648-4606
www.kifgradio.com
kifg@iafalls.com
License: Iowa Falls, Hardin County, IA held by Times-Citizen Communications Inc.
Format: News, Sports *Special Programming:* School news (during the school year); *No. News Employees:* 1
T.J. Norman, General Manager
Pat Dunn, Programming Director
Ann Denholm, Promotions Manager

Jefferson

KGRA
10-01-1981; 98.9 MHz FM; *Hrs Open:* 24; 11 kw; 499 ft.; N41 58 54 W94 31 12
Rr2 Box 106a, Lacrescent, MN 55947 US
(515) 386-2222; *Fax:* (515) 386-2215
kg98@netins.net
License: Jefferson, Greene County, IA held by Coon Valley Communications
Group Owner: M&M Broadcasting Inc.
Nat'l Network: ABC
Arbitron Metro Market: Jefferson, IA; *Format:* Classic Rock; *Hrs. of News Programming:* news progmg 9 hrs wkly; *No. News Employees:* 1; *Target Audience:* 25-49; Adults
Mel Suhr, President/CEO
Michael Suhr, VP/COO
John McGee, General Manager

Keokuk

*KMDY
01-01-2001; 90.9 MHz FM; 7.7 kw; 197 ft.; N40 30 41 W91 19 50
521 Main Street, Carthage, IL 62631 US
(217) 357-3000; *Fax:* (217) 357-3001
License: Keokuk, Lee County, IA held by Cornerstone Community Radio Inc.
Nat'l Network: Moody
Format: Christian
Richard Van Zandt, President

KOKX
10-19-1947; 1310 kHz AM; *Hrs Open:* 24; 1 kw-D, DAN; 0.5 kw-N, DAN; N40 22 50 W91 21 9
108 Washington Street, Keokuk, IA 52632 US
(319) 524-5410; *Fax:* (319) 524-7275
License: Keokuk, IA held by Withers Broadcasting of Iowa.
Group Owner: Withers Broadcasting Co.; (acq 7-15-81; $900,000 with co-located FM;
Format: News, News/Talk, 84, Talk, Adult Contemp *Special Programming:* Farm 6 hrs wkly; *Hrs. of News Programming:* news progmg 25 hrs wkly; *No. News Employees:* 2; *Target Audience:* 25-54.; *Adv. Rates:* 16;14; 14; 12

Dana Withers, President
Gary Folluo, General Manager
Dan Workman, Programming Director
Judy Hall, Sales Manager
Matt Frisbee, News Announcer/Reporter

KOKX-FM
10-15-2000; 95.3 MHz FM; *Hrs Open:* 24/7; 100 kw; 804 ft.; N40 24 1 W91 35 9
Mailing Address: 108 Washington Street, Keokuk, IA 52632 US
Second Address: 108 Washington St., Keokuk, IA 52632
(319) 524-5410; *Fax:* (319) 524-7275
License: Keokuk, Lee County, IA held by W. Russell Withers
Group Owner: Withers Broadcasting Co.
Nat'l Network: ABC
Arbitron Metro Market: Quad Cities, IA-IL (Davenport-Rock Island-Moline); *Format:* Oldies *Special Programming:* St. Louis Cardinals Baseball; *Hrs. of News Programming:* news progmg 4 hrs wkly; *No. News Employees:* 2 *Target Audience:* 25-54; women 50% men 50%; *Adv. Rates:* 24; 20; 18; 17
Gary M. Folluo, General Manager
Matt Frisbee, News Director
Dan Workman, Program Director

KRNQ
01-01-1999; 96.3 MHz FM; *Hrs Open:* 24/7; 19 kw; 804 ft.; N40 24 1 W91 35 9
108 Washington Street, Keokuk, IA 52632 US
(319) 524-5410; *Fax:* (319) 524-7275
gary@keokukradio.com
License: Keokuk, Lee County, IA held by David M. Lister.
Group Owner: Withers Broadcasting Co.; Gary M. Folluo, (319) 524-5410; gmkokx@mchsi.com
Arbitron Metro Market: Keokuk, IA/Burlington, IA/Quincy, IL; *Format:* Light Rock *Special Programming:* Local Sports; *Target Audience:* 18-45; 50/50 male, female; *Adv. Rates:* 17; 15; 16; 12.50
Gary Folluo, General Manager
Judy Hall, General Sales Mgr
Matt Frisbee, News Director
Tara Whitnah, Office Manager
Bill Reed, Sports Director

Knoxville

KNIA
08-30-1960; 1320 kHz AM; *Hrs Open:* 24; 0.5 kw-D, DA2; 0.222 kw-N, DA2; N41 19 50 W93 6 34
Mailing Address: PO Box 31, Knoxville, IA 50138 US
Second Address: 1610 N. Lincoln, Knoxville, IA 50138
(641) 842-3161; *Fax:* (641) 842-5606
www.kniakrls.com
kniaakrls@kniakrls.com
License: Knoxville, IA held by M & H Broadcasting Inc.
Regional Network: Radio Iowa
Format: Country *Special Programming:* Relg 18 hrs wkly; *Hrs. of News Programming:* news progmg 25 hrs wkly; *No. News Employees:* 3; *Target Audience:* 25-54; female; *Adv. Rates:* 14.60; 14.60; 14.60; 14.60
Jim Butler, General Manager
Trevor Castle, General Sales Mgr

KRLS
07-16-1973; 92.1 MHz FM; *Hrs Open:* 24; 15.5 kw; 308 ft.; N41 21 40 W93 0 15
Mailing Address: 1610 N. Lincoln Street, PO Box 31, Knoxville, IA 50138 US
Second Address: 1610 N. Lincoln, Knoxville, IA 50138
(641) 842-3161; *Fax:* (641) 842-5606
www.kniakrls.com
License: Knoxville, Marion County, IA
Group Owner: M&H Broadcasting Inc.
Wire Services: AP
Arbitron Metro Market: Knoxville/Pella, IA; *Format:* Adult Contemp; *Hrs. of News Programming:* news progmg 25 hrs wkly; *No. News Employees:* 3; *Target Audience:* 25-54; primarily female; *Adv. Rates:* 17:45;17:45; 17:45; 17:45.
Mel Suhr, President/CEO
Michael Suhr, VP/COO
Jim Butler, General Manager
Trevor Castle, General Sales Mgr

Lake City

KIKD
01-01-1997; 106.7 MHz FM; *Hrs Open:* 24; 25 kw; 328 ft.; N42 7 14 W94 48 49
1119 E. Plaza Dr., Carroll, IA 51401 US
(712) 792-4321
www.1380kcim.com
License: Lake City, Calhoun County, IA held by Carroll Broadcasting Co.

Group Owner: Carroll Broadcasting Co.; acq 1999; $975,000)
Nat'l Reps: Katz Radio
Format: Country; *Hrs. of News Programming:* 2; *Target Audience:* 18-49; contemp country with strong families
John Ryan, Operations Dir
Deb Lupardus, General Sales Mgr

Lamoni

*KNSL(FM)
01-01-2000; 97.9 MHz FM; *Hrs Open:* 24; 50 kw; Ant 492 ft; N40 48 52 W93 50 15 *Rebroadcasts:* WOI-AM
WOI Radio Group, 2022 Communications Bldg., Ames, IA 50011-3241
(515) 294-2025; *Fax:* (515) 294-1544
www.iowapublicradio.org
woi@iastate.edu
License: Lamoni, Decatur County, IA held by Iowa State University of Science and Technology
Nat'l Network: NPR; PRI
Hrs. of News Programming: 40 hrs wkly; *Target Audience:* General; Educated
Don Wirth, Programming Director
Mary Grace Herrington, Director, Iowa Public Radio

Le Mars

KKMA
01-01-1967; 99.5 MHz FM; 100 kw; 791 ft.; N42 28 56 W96 15 30
37 2nd Avenue NW, Box 1410, Le Mars, IA 51031 US
(712) 239-2100; *Fax:* (712) 239-3346
www.kool995.com
License: Le Mars, Plymouth County, IA
Group Owner: Powell Broadcasting Co. Inc.
Regional Reps: REGIONAL REPS
Arbitron Metro Market: Sioux City, IA; *Format:* Oldies; *Adv. Rates:* 20; 20; 20; 18
Kathy McCarty, Vice President
Julie Bockholt, Office Manager
Dennis Bullock, General Manager
Monica Stabile, General Sales Mgr
Scott McKenzie, Programming Director
Tim Guentz, Chief Engineer

KLEM
10-12-1954; 1410 kHz AM; *Hrs Open:* 24
37-2nd Avenue NW, Box 1410, Le Mars, IA 51031 US
(712) 546-4121; *Fax:* (712) 546-9672
www.klem1410.com
License: Le Mars, IA held by Powell Broadcasting Co Inc.
Group Owner: Powell Broadcasting Co. Inc.; (acq 7-6-99; with co-located FM)
Arbitron Metro Market: Sioux City, IA; *Format:* Adult Contemp, News, 84 *Special Programming:* Farm 18 hrs wkly; *No. News Employees:* 2
Tom Spies, President
Dennis Bullock, General Manager
Dave Grosenheider, Station Manager
Dave Ruden, Programming Director
Larry Schmitz, News Director
Stan Culley, Chief Engineer
Joanne Glamm, Reporter
Christi Rush

Madrid

*KNWM
08-21-1997; 96.1 MHz FM; *Hrs Open:* 24; 6 kw; 328 ft.; N41 51 5 W93 43 29
2825 East 13th Street, P.O. Box 1750, Ames, IA 50010 US
(515) 327-1071; *Fax:* (515) 327-1073
www.desmoines.fm
knwi@desmoines.fm
License: Madrid, Boone County, IA held by Northwestern College.
Group Owner: Northwestern College & Radio; (acq 12-30-2003; $1.8 million with KNWI(FM) Osceola).
Arbitron Metro Market: Des Moines, IA; *Format:* Christian
Richard Whitworth, General Manager
Dave St. John, Programming Director

Manchester

KMCH
12-05-1991; 94.7 MHz FM; *Hrs Open:* 24; 6 kw; 328 ft.; N42 31 42 W91 22 53
506 North Clark, Forest City, IA 50436 US
(563) 927-6249; *Fax:* (563) 927-4372
www.kmch.com
kmchradio@iowatelecom.net
License: Manchester, Delaware County, IA held by Coloff Media LLC.
Nat'l Network: CBS
Format: Adult Contemp, Country *Special Programming:* Farm 7 hrs, sports 7 hrs, relg 4 hrs wkly; *Hrs. of News Programming:* news progmg 20 hrs wkly; *No. News Employees:* 1; *Target Audience:* 25-64; northeast Iowaadults & farm population; *Adv. Rates:* 14.50; 14.50; 14.50; 14.50
Anthony Coloff, President
James Coloff, Operations Dir
Jackie Coates, Station Manager
Mike Johnson, Operations Manager

Manson

KXFT
09-01-1992; 99.7 MHz FM; 100 kw; 285 ft.; N42 40 18 W94 09 11
200 N. 10th St., Fort Dodge, IA 50501 US
(515) 955-5656; *Fax:* (515) 955-5844
www.yourfortdodge.com
sgossweiler@digity.me
License: Manson, Calhoun County, IA held by Digity 3E License, LLC
Group Owner: Digity, LLC; (acq 9-1-2007; grpsl)
Arbitron Metro Market: Manson, IA; *Format:* Country
Darren Helton, Operations Dir
Steve Gossweiler, General Manager
Pat Kolar, Dir. of Sales
Darren Helton, Programming Director
Kelly Heinen, News Director

Maquoketa

KMAQ
08-26-1958; 1320 kHz AM; *Hrs Open:* 6 AM-10 PM; 0.5 kw-D, ND1; 0.135 kw-N, ND1; N42 5 26 W90 37 43
129 North Main Street, Maquoketa, IA 52060 US
(563) 652-2426; *Fax:* (563) 652-6210
License: Maquoketa, IA held by Maquoketa Broadcasting Co.
Nat'l Network: USA; *Regional Network:* Brownfield; Radio Iowa; *Nat'l Reps:* Farmakis
Format: Country *Special Programming:* Farm 10 hrs, polka 3 hrs wkly; *Hrs. of News Programming:* news progmg 28 hrs wkly; *No. News Employees:* 1; *Target Audience:* General; adults, high percentage of farmers *Adv.Rates:* 15; 15; 15;15.
Dennis Voy, President
Leighton Hepker, Operations Dir
Tom Messerli, Chief Engineer

KMAQ-FM
09-01-1967; 95.1 MHz FM; 6 kw; 328 ft.; N42 5 26 W90 37 43
129 North Main Street, Maquoketa, IA 52060 US
(563) 652-2426; *Fax:* (563) 652-6210
License: Maquoketa, Jackson County, IA
Regional Network: Radio Iowa; *Wire Services:* AP
Hrs. of News Programming: news progmg 28 hrs wkly; *No. News Employees:* 1; *Adv. Rates:* 16; 16; 16; 13
Leighton Hepker, General Sales Mgr

Marshalltown

KDAO
12-16-1978; 1190 kHz AM; *Hrs Open:* 24
Box 538, Marshalltown, IA 50158 US
(641) 752-4122; *Fax:* (641) 752-5121
www.kdao.com
kdao@kdao.com
License: Marshalltown, IA held by MTN Broadcasting Inc.
Arbitron Metro Market: Marshaltown, IA *TV Affiliate:* KDAO-TV affil; *Format:* Adult Contemp; *Target Audience:* 25-54.
Mark Osmundson, General Manager

KFJB
06-01-1923; 1230 kHz AM; *Hrs Open:* 24; 1 kw-U, ND1; N42 4 1 W92 58 10
123 W. Main Street, Marshalltown, IA 50158 US
(641) 753-3361; *Fax:* (641) 752-7201
www.1230kfjb.com
office@marshalltownbroadcasting.com
License: Marshalltown, IA held by Marshalltown Broadcasting Inc.
Nat'l Network: ABC; *Regional Network:* Brownfield; *Nat'l Reps:* Katz Radio; *Wire Services:* AP
Arbitron Metro Market: Marshalltown, IW; *Format:* News, News/Talk, 86 *Special Programming:* Religious 3 hrs wkly, Sports 40 hrs wkly; *Hrs. of News Programming:* news progmg 20 hrs wkly; *No. News Employees:* 2 *Target Audience:* 35-64.; *Adv. Rates:* 35; 30; 33; 18
David Nelson, President
Kyle Martin, Operations Dir
Clark L. Wideman, General Manager
Mark Shaffer, Sales Manager
Kyle Martin, Programming Director
Chuck Shockley, News Director

KXIA
01-01-1968; 101.1 MHz FM; *Hrs Open:* 24; 100 kw; 656 ft.; N42 0 19 W92 55 45
Mailing Address: 123 West Main Street, Marshalltown, IA 50158 US
Second Address: 123 W. Main St., Marshalltown, IA 50158
(641) 753-3361; *Fax:* (641) 752-7201
www.kixweb.com
office@marshalltownbroadcasting.com
License: Marshalltown, Marshall County, IA held by Marshalltown Broadcasting Inc.
Nat'l Network: ABC; *Regional Network:* Brownfield; *Nat'l Reps:* Katz Radio; *Wire Services:* AP
Format: Country; *Hrs. of News Programming:* news progmg 6 hrs wkly; *No. News Employees:* 2; *Target Audience:* 25-54.; *Adv. Rates:* 45; 40; 42; 24
Todd Collins, Programming Director

*KRFH
88.7 MHz FM; 8.3 kw; 95 ft.; N42 4 17 W92 55 19
P O Box 538, Marshalltown, IA 50158 US
(641) 752-4122
License: Marshalltown, Marshall County, IA held by Marshalltown Education Plus Inc.
Arbitron Metro Market: Marshalltown, IA
Brett Gibson, General Manager
David Roble, Programming Director

Mason City

KCMR
05-03-1979; 97.9 MHz FM; *Hrs Open:* 24; 6 kw; 315 ft.; N43 7 18 W93 11 50
Mailing Address: P.O. Box 979, 600 First St, NW #101, Mason City, IA 50402 US
Second Address: 600 First St. N.W., Mason City, IA 50401
(641) 424-9300; *Fax:* (641) 423-2221
www.kcmrfm.com
License: Mason City, Cerro Gordo County, IA held by TLC Broadcasting Corp.
Arbitron Metro Market: Mason City, IA; *Format:* Religious *Special Programming:* Class 5 hrs, nostalgia 10 hrs wkly; *Target Audience:* Over 30.
Bill Schickel, General Manager
Bob Miller, General Sales Mgr

KGLO
01-17-1937; 1300 kHz AM; 5 kw-D, 5 kw-N
341 S. Yorktown Pike, Mason City, IA 50401 US
(641) 423-1300
www.discovernorthiowa.com
timothy.fleming@digity.me
License: Mason City, IA held by Digity 3E License, LLC
Group Owner: Digity, LLC
Nat'l Network: CBS
Arbitron Metro Market: Mason City, IA; *Format:* News/Talk; *No. News Employees:* 3; *Adv. Rates:* 20; 20; 20; 15.
Tim Fleming, Programming Director
Bob Fisher, News Director
Jesse Stewart, Farm Director
Joe Malone, Production Director

KIAI
11-01-1985; 93.9 MHz FM; 100 kw; 791 ft.; N43 10 04 W93 06 05
341 S. Yorktown Pike, Mason City, IA 50401 US
(641) 423-1300
www.discovernorthiowa.com
jstewart@digity.me
License: Mason City, IA held by Digity 3E License, LLC
Group Owner: Digity, LLC
Arbitron Metro Market: Mason City, IA; *Format:* Country; *Target Audience:* 24-54.; *Adv. Rates:* 30; 40; 35; 20.
Jesse Stewart, Programming Director
Bob Fisher, News Director

KLSS-FM
11-01-1967; 106.1 MHz FM; 100 kw; 315 ft.; N43 8 31 W93 6 40
341 S. Yorktown Pike, Mason City, IA 50401 US
(641) 423-1300
www.discovernorthiowa.com
jallen@digity.me
License: Mason City, Cerro Gordo County, IA held by Digity 3E License, LLC
Group Owner: Digity, LLC
Nat'l Network: ABC
Arbitron Metro Market: Mason City, IA; *Format:* Adult Contemp; *Target Audience:* 18-54.; *Adv. Rates:* 28; 28; 28; 25

RADIO - U.S.

John Swinton, Operations Dir
Jaren Allen, Programming Director
Bob Fisher, News Director

KRIB
04-01-1948; 1490 kHz AM; *Hrs Open:* 24; 1 kw-U, ND1; N43 8 6 W93 12 28
341 S. Yorktown Pike, Mason City, IA 50401 US
(641) 423-1300
www.discovernorthiowa.com
jallen@digity.me
License: Mason City, IA held by Digity 3E License, LLC
Group Owner: Digity, LLC
Nat'l Reps: McGavren Guild
Arbitron Metro Market: Mason City, IA; *Format:* Oldies; *No. News Employees:* 2; *Adv. Rates:* 23; 23; 23; 20.
Jaren Allen, Programming Director
Joe Malone, Production Director

***KRNI**
03-01-1948; 1010 kHz AM; *Hrs Open:* Sunrise-sunset; 0.76 kw-D, ND1; 0.016 kw-N, ND1; N43 8 31 W93 6 40 *Rebroadcasts:* Rebroadcasts KUNI(FM) Cedar Falls 100%
324 Communications Arts, Center, Cedar Falls, IA 50614 US
(515) 725-1700; *Fax:* (515) 725-1714
www.iowapublicradio.org
info@iowapublicradio.org
License: Mason City, IA held by University of Northern Iowa.
Nat'l Network: PRI; NPR
Arbitron Metro Market: Mason City, IA; *Format:* News *Special Programming:* Folk 4 hrs, blues 5 hrs wkly; *Hrs. of News Programming:* news progmg 77 hrs wkly; *No. News Employees:* 3; *Target Audience:* General.
Wayne Jarvis, General Manager
Scott Vezdan, Promotions Manager
Greg Shanley, News Director
Steve Schoon, Engineering Dir
Jeneane Beck, Local News Editor
Al Schares, Music Director
Pat Blank, Reporter
Tony Dehner, TrafficManager

***KNSM(FM)**
12-15-1987; 91.5 MHz FM; *Hrs Open:* 24; 8 kw vert; 371 ft; N43 09 27 W93 08 11 *Rebroadcasts:* Rebroadcast KUNI (FM) Cedar Falls 100%
c/o KUNI-FM, Univ. of Northern Iowa, Cedar Falls, IA 50614
(319) 273-6400; *Fax:* (319) 273-2682
www.kuniradio.org
kuni@uni.edu
License: Mason City, Cerro Gordo County, IA
Nat'l Network: PRI; NPR
Arbitron Metro Market: Mason City, IA; *Hrs. of News Programming:* news progmg 77 hrs wkly; *No. News Employees:* 3
Frank Muller, Operations Dir
David Reese, General Manager
Kim Lizny, Programming Director
Joe Sands, Chief Engineer

Milford

KUQQ
10-01-1996; 102.1 MHz FM; 50 kw horiz, 39 kw vert; 420 ft.; N43 24 20 W95 5 1
13906 Gold Circle, Suite 201, Omaha, NE 68144 US
(712) 336-5877; *Fax:* (712) 336-1634
www.kuqqfm.com
mspies@exploreokoboji.com
License: Milford, Dickinson County, IA held by Sorenson Broadcasting Corp.
Group Owner: Sorenson Broadcasting Corp.; (acq 7-1-2004; grpsl)
Arbitron Metro Market: Milford, IA; *Format:* Classic Rock; *Target Audience:* 18-44.
Neil Lipetzky, CEO
Dean Sorenson, President
Marty Spies, General Manager
Jeff Nixx, Programming Director
Abby Kohlhaas, Promotions Manager
Steve Schwaller, News Director
Steve Heaton, Chief Engineer
Chad Franzen, SportsDirector
Mary Treanor, Music Director
Terry Lowry, Office Manager
Matt Fallon, Production Director
Matt Fallon, Production Director

Mitchellville

***KICJ(FM)**
88.9 MHz FM; 1 kw; Ant 236 ft; N41 40 05 W93 19 43
Rebroadcasts: KUNI-FM,Cedar Falls, IA
2111 Grand Avenue, Suite 100, Des Moines, IA 50312
(800) 861-8000; *Fax:* (515) 725-1714
www.kuniradio.org
info@iowapublicradio.org
License: Mitchellville, Polk County, IA held by University of Northern Iowa.
Population Served: 206,599; *Arbitron Metro Market:* Des Moines, IA; *Format:* News, Triple A *Special Programming:* Folk 4hrs, Blues 5 hrs; *Hrs. of News Programming:* 77 hrs; *No. News Employees:* 3
Wayne Jarvis, General Manager
Scott Vezdos, Promotions Manager
Greg Shanley, News Director
Steve Schoon, Chief Engineer
Al Schares, Music Director

Montezuma

***KRNF**
89.7 MHz FM; 1.6 kw; 346 ft.; N41 43 55 W92 34 1
US
(641) 780-0017
License: Montezuma, Poweshiek County, IA held by American Radio Missions Foundation.
Arbitron Metro Market: Montezuma, IA; *Format:* Country
Doug Smiley, General Manager

Mount Pleasant

KILJ
12-01-1974; 1130 kHz AM; *Hrs Open:* 24
P.O. Box 311, Mt. Pleasant, IA 52641 US
(319) 385-8728; *Fax:* (319) 385-4517
www.kilj.com
License: Mount Pleasant, IA held by KILJ Inc.
Nat'l Network: ABC; *Regional Network:* Brownfield; Radio Iowa
Format: Country; *No. News Employees:* 1; *Adv. Rates:* 10; 10; 10; 10
Paul Dennison, President
John Kuhens, Station Manager
Anna Herreid, Production Manager
Theresa Rose, News Director
Paul Dennison, General Sales Manager
Lora Roth, Traffic Manager

KILJ-FM
10-01-1970; 105.5 MHz FM; *Hrs Open:* 24; 24 kw; 338 ft.; N40 56 55 W91 33 55
P.O. Box 281, Mt. Pleasant, IA 52641 US
(319) 385-8728; *Fax:* (319) 385-4517
www.kilj.com
kiljradio@kilj.com
License: Mount Pleasant, Henry County, IA held by KILJ Inc.
Regional Network: Brownfield; Radio Iowa
Format: Country; *No. News Employees:* 1; *Target Audience:* 25-54.; *Adv. Rates:* 10; 10; 10; 10
Paul Dennison, President
John Kuhens, General Manager
Paul Dennison, General Sales Mgr
Theresa Rose, News Director
Lora Roth, Traffic Manager

Mount Vernon

***KRNL-FM**
04-01-1948; 89.7 MHz FM; *Hrs Open:* Midnight-noon; 0.045 kw; 167 ft.; N41 55 34 W91 25 32
810 Commons Circle, Mt. Vernon, IA 52314 US
(319) 895-4431
www.cornellcollege.edu/kml/
kml@cornellcollege.edu
License: Mount Vernon, Linn County, IA held by Cornell College.
Nat'l Network: USA
Format: Talk *Special Programming:* Folk 2 hrs, Ger 2 hrs, jazz 2 hrs, Sp one hr wkly; *Target Audience:* 18-25; collegians & those seeking an alternative to coml radio
Jacob Gehl, General Manager
Ji 'Max' Zhang, Station Manager
Josh Boegner, Programming Director
Haley Severance, Promotions Manager

Moville

***KNSX(FM)**
97.1 MHz FM; 5.2 kw; 108.6 meters; N42 32 47.3 W96 01 08.2
Rebroadcasts: KUNI(FM) Cedar Falls 100%
Iowa Public Radio, 2111 Grand Avenue, Suite 100, Des Moines, IA 50312
(515) 725-1700; *Fax:* (515) 725-1714
iowapublicradio.org
License: Moville, Woodbury County, IA held by Iowa State University of Science & Technology

Mary Grace Herrington, CEO

Muscatine

KBEA-FM
02-01-1949; 99.7 MHz FM; *Hrs Open:* 24; 100 kw; 869 ft.; N41 36 22 W90 59 35
1229 Brady Street, Davenport, IA 52803 US
(563) 326-2541; *Fax:* (563) 326-1819
License: Muscatine, Muscatine County, IA held by Cumulus Licensing Corp.
Group Owner: Cumulus Media Inc.; (acq 3-15-00; grpsl).
Arbitron Metro Market: Quad Cities, IA-IL (Davenport-Rock Island-Moline); *Format:* Contemporary Hits/Top 40; *No. News Employees:* 1; *Target Audience:* 25-54.
Jack Swart, General Manager
Julie Derrer, General Sales Mgr
Steve Fuller, Programming Director
Tracy Hall, News Director
Andy Andresen, Chief Engineer

KMCS
06-16-1996; 93.1 MHz FM; *Hrs Open:* 24; 4.4 kw; 384 ft.; N41 26 34 W91 4 33
3128 Mulberry Ave., Muscatine, IA 52761 US
(563) 263-2442; *Fax:* (563) 263-9206
www.voiceofmuscatine.com
mail@voiceofmuscatine.com
License: Muscatine, Muscatine County, IA held by WPW Broadcasting, Inc.
Group Owner: Prairie Radio Communications
Nat'l Network: USA; AP Radio
Arbitron Metro Market: Muscatine, IA; *Format:* Rock/AOR; *Hrs. of News Programming:* News progmg 6 hrs wkly; *Target Audience:* 25-54.; *Adv. Rates:* Same as AM
Chris Streets, General Manager
Chris Meyers, General Sales Mgr
Robert Bertam, News Dir/Sports Dir

KWPC
01-05-1947; 860 kHz AM; *Hrs Open:* 24; 0.25 kw-D, ND1; 0.008 kw-N, ND1; N41 26 34 W91 4 33
3128 Mulberry Ave., Muscatine, IA 52761 US
(563) 263-2442; *Fax:* (563) 263-9206
www.voiceofmuscatine.com
mail@voiceofmuscatine.com
License: Muscatine, IA held by WPW Broadcasting Inc.
Group Owner: Prairie Radio Communications; (acq 11-5-99; $2.2 million with co-located FM)
Nat'l Network: USA
Arbitron Metro Market: Muscatine, IA; *Format:* Country *Special Programming:* Farm; *Hrs. of News Programming:* news progmg 20 hrs wkly; *No. News Employees:* 2; *Target Audience:* 25-54.; *Adv. Rates:* 17; 17;17; 17
Chris Streets, General Manager
Chris Meyers, General Sales Mgr
Robert Bertam, News Dir/Sports Dir

New Hampton

KCZE
12-01-1992; 95.1 MHz FM; 5.5 kw; 338 ft.; N43 2 46 W92 18 9
330 East Kilbourn Avenue, Suite 250, Milwaukee, WI 53202 US
(641) 228-1000; *Fax:* (641) 228-1200
www.951thebull.com
chrisberg@northiowabroadcasting.com
License: New Hampton, Chickasaw County, IA held by Coloff Media, LLC.
Nat'l Network: CNN Radio; *Regional Network:* Radio Iowa
Arbitron Metro Market: New Hampton, IA; *Format:* Country *Special Programming:* Farm 12 hrs wkly; *Target Audience:* General.
Jim Coloff, General Manager
Scott Lane, Station Manager
Chris Berg, Programming Director
Chris Berg, News Director
Chris Berg, News Director

New London

KHDK
10-05-2001; 97.3 MHz FM; *Hrs Open:* 24; 3.8 kw; 410 ft.; N40 47 53 W91 26 22
610 N. 4th St., Suite 300, Burlington, IA 52601 US

(319) 752-5402; *Fax:* (319) 752-4715
www.hot973online.com
johnp@burlingtonradio.com
License: New London, Henry County, IA held by Pritchard Broadcasting Corp.
Group Owner: Pritchard Broadcasting Corp.; (acq 12-27-99; $25,000 for CP)
Nat'l Reps: Katz Radio
Arbitron Metro Market: Burlington, IA; *Format:* Contemporary Hits/Top 40; *Hrs. of News Programming:* news progmg 1 hrs wkly; *No. News Employees:* 1; *Target Audience:* 25-54.; *Adv. Rates:* 17; 17; 17; 8
Joe Bates, Operations Dir
John Pritchard, General Manager
Chet Young, General Sales Mgr
Savanna Evans, Programming Director

New Sharon

KCWN
10-16-1995; 99.9 MHz FM; *Hrs Open:* 6 AM-11 PM; 25 kw; 282 ft.; N41 17 32 W92 40 24
Mailing Address: Box 999, Pella, IA 50219 US
Second Address: 304 Oskaloosa St., Pella, IA 50219
(641) 628-9999(888) 506-4562; *Fax:* (641) 628-9229
kcwn@kcwnfm.org
License: New Sharon, Mahaska County, IA held by Crown Broadcasting Co.
Arbitron Metro Market: Pella, IA; *Format:* Adult Contemp, Christian; *Adv. Rates:* 14; 14; 14; 14
Beverly DeVries, General Manager
Sharyl Fosenburg, General Sales Mgr
Nicole Fopma, Traffic Director

Newton

KCOB
09-15-1955; 1280 kHz AM; 0.73 kw-D, ND1; 0.019 kw-N, ND1; N41 44 11 W93 1 12
P.O. Box 66, 1801 N. 13th Ave. East, Newton, IA 50208 US
(641) 792-5262; *Fax:* (641) 792-8403
kcobradio.com
info@kcobradio.com
License: Newton, IA held by Newton License Co. LLC.
Group Owner: GoodRadio.TV; (acq 5-1-2007; grpsl)
Arbitron Metro Market: Newton, IA; *Format:* Country, News
Special Programming: Farm 2 hrs wkly; *Target Audience:* 25-50.
Dean Goodman, CEO
Ron McCarthy, General Manager
Terry Walter, Sports Director and Programming Director
Randy Van, News Director
Phil Benjamin, Chief Engineer

KCOB-FM
01-03-1969; 95.9 MHz FM; *Hrs Open:* 18; 5.1 kw; 354 ft.; N41 44 11 W93 1 12
P.O. Box 66, 1801 N. 13th Ave. East, Newton, IA 50208 US
(641) 792-5262; *Fax:* (641) 792-8403
kcobradio.com
info@kcobradio.com
License: Newton, Jasper County, IA held by Newton License Co. LLC.
Group Owner: GoodRadio.TV
Arbitron Metro Market: Newton, IA; *Format:* Country
Dean Goodman, CEO
Ron McCarthy, General Manager
Melanie Canon, General Sales Mgr
Terry Walter, Sports Director and Programming Director
Randy Van, News Director

***KKLG**
01-01-2005; 88.3 MHz FM; 0.4 kw; 218 ft.; N41 41 33 W93 0 37
Rebroadcasts: Rebroadcasts KLVR(FM) Santa Rosa, CA 100%
188 South Bellevue, Suite 222, Memphis, TN 38104 US
(800) 525-5683; *Fax:* (916) 251-1650
www.klove.com
klove@klove.com
License: Newton, Jasper County, IA held by Educational Media Foundation.
Group Owner: EMF Broadcasting; (acq 9-22-2005; $20,000 for CP)
Nat'l Network: K-Love
Arbitron Metro Market: Newton, IA; *Format:* Christian; *No. News Employees:* 13
Darrell Chambliss, Chairman
Mike Novak, President and CEO
Glenn Goodwin, General Sales Mgr
David Pierce, Chief Creative Officer and Programming Director
Ed Lenane, News Director
Sam Wallington, Engineering Dir

Marya Morgan, NewsReporter
Richard Hunt, News Reporter
Alan Mason, Chief Operating Officer
Dan Antonelli, Chief Business Development Officer
Eric Moser, Chief Financial Officer
Brian Burger, Vice President of Human Resources

Northwood

KYTC
01-01-1988; 102.7 MHz FM; *Hrs Open:* 24; 25 kw; 295 ft.; N43 29 18 W93 14 11
341 S. Yorktown Pike, Mason City, IA 50401 US
(641) 423-1300
www.discovernorthiowa.com
jallen@digity.me
License: Northwood, Worth County, IA held by Digity 3E License, LLC
Group Owner: Digital, LLC
Regional Network: Tribune Radio Networks
Arbitron Metro Market: Northwood, IA; *Format:* Adult Contemp; *No. News Employees:* 1; *Target Audience:* 25-64; primary audience men & women 35+; *Adv. Rates:* 23; 23; 23; 19
Jaren Allen, Programming Director
Bob Fisher, News Director

Oelwein

KOEL
07-23-1950; 950 kHz AM; *Hrs Open:* 24
136 Main Street, Westport, CT 06880 US
(319) 283-1234; *Fax:* (319) 283-3615
koelam@koel.com
License: Oelwein, IA held by Cumulus Licensing Corp.
Group Owner: Cumulus Media Inc.; (acq 3-15-00; grpsl).
Format: News, News/Talk, 84, Talk *Special Programming:* Farm 16 hrs wkly; *Hrs. of News Programming:* news progmg 30 hrs wkly; *No. News Employees:* 2; *Target Audience:* 35 plus.
Jeffrey Warshaw, President
Jeff Dientz, Operations Dir
Rob Murthum, General Manager
Craig Friedrich, General Sales Mgr
Rich Calvert, Programming Director
Matt Kelly, Music Director
Bob Fisher, National Sales Manager
DickStadlen, Operations Manager
April Walker, Promotions Manager

KKHQ-FM
12-29-1971; 92.3 MHz FM; *Hrs Open:* 24; 100 kw; 1,000 ft; N42 40 53 W91 52 52
Box 720, Blacks Bldg., Waterloo, IA 06880
(319) 833-4800,(800) 923-5635; *Fax:* (319) 833-4866
License: Oelwein, Fayette County, IA held by Cumulus Licensing LLC
Group Owner: Cumulus Media Inc.
Population Served: 150,000; *Arbitron Metro Market:* Waterloo-Cedar Falls, IA; *Hrs. of News Programming:* news progmg 2 hrs wkly; *No. News Employees:* 1; *Target Audience:* 35 plus.
Mark Anderson, General Sales Mgr
Bill Knight, Programming Director
April Walker, Promotions Manager
Elwin Huffman, News Director
Wes Davis, Chief Engineer

Okoboji

***KOJI**
01-01-2002; 90.7 MHz FM; *Hrs Open:* 24; 4.5 kw; 371 ft.; N43 9 53 W95 19 29 *Rebroadcasts:* Rebroadcasts KWIT(FM) Sioux City 100%
US
(712) 274-6406; *Fax:* (712) 274-6411
www.kwit-koji.org
gondekg@witcc.edu
License: Okoboji, Dickinson County, IA held by Western Iowa Tech Community College.
Nat'l Network: NPR; PRI; *Wire Services:* AP
Arbitron Metro Market: Sioux City, IA; *Format:* News, News/Talk, 86 *Special Programming:* Triple A 18 hrs, blues 4 hrs, jazz 17 hrs wkly; *Hrs. of News Programming:* news progmg 36 hrs wkly; *No. News Employees:* 1
Gretchen Gondek, General Manager
Dennis Semple, Chief Engineer
Duane Kraayenbrink, News Editor
Jake Moreland, Arts Producer
Margaret Holman, Account Executive
Mindy Thompson, Office Assistant
Steve Smith, Operations Manager

Onawa

KQNU(FM)
11-06-1995; 102.3 MHz FM; *Hrs Open:* 24; 100 kw; Ant 643 ft; N42 10 29 W96 23 13
2000 Indian Hills Dr., Sioux City, IA 51104
(712) 239-2100; *Fax:* (712) 239-3346
License: Onawa, Monona County, IA held by Powell Broadcasting Co. Inc.
Group Owner: Powell Broadcasting Co. Inc.; (acq 5-1-2007; $4.2 million with KKYY(FM) Whiting)
Population Served: 2,997; *Arbitron Metro Market:* Onawa, IA; *Format:* Variety/Diverse; *Hrs. of News Programming:* One; *Target Audience:* 25-54.; *Adv. Rates:* 18; 18; 18; 16
Dennis Bullock, General Manager

Osage

KSMA-FM
07-09-1980; 98.7 MHz FM; 25 kw; 328 ft.; N43 21 53 W93 2 53
111 East Kilbourn Ave, Suite 2700, Milwaukee, WI 53202 US
(641) 421-7744; *Fax:* (641) 423-2906
KISS@987KISSCountry.com
License: Osage, Mitchell County, IA
Nat'l Reps: Farmakis
Arbitron Metro Market: Mason City, IA; *Format:* Adult Contemp; *Target Audience:* General; 12-25; *Adv. Rates:* 40; 40; 35; 15
Tim Fleming, Operations Dir
Jim Coloff, General Manager
Dan Maynard, Programming Director
Tami Ramon, Promotions Manager
Laurie Gansen, News Director
J. Brooks, Operations Manager / Program Director
Michelle Horst, BusinessManager
Amber Nuehring, Office Assistant
Jamie Nelson, Marketing Consultants
Tami Ramon, Marketing Consultants
LuAnn Scholbrock, Marketing Consultants

Osceola

***KNWI**
10-04-1982; 107.1 MHz FM; *Hrs Open:* 24; 27 kw; 650 ft.; N41 1 34 W93 51 43
3737 Woodland Avenue, #111, West Des Moines, IA 50266 US
(515) 327-1071; *Fax:* (515) 327-1073
www.life1071.com
info@life1071.com
License: Osceola, Clarke County, IA held by Northwestern College.
Group Owner: Northwestern College & Radio; (acq 12-30-2003; $1.8 million with KNWM(FM) Madrid).
Arbitron Metro Market: Des Moines, IA; *Format:* Christian; *Target Audience:* 18-44; women
Dave St. John, General Manager
Dan Raymond, Programming Director
Erick David, Promotions Manager
Dave Dobes, Chief Engineer

Oskaloosa

KBOE
11-15-1950; 740 kHz AM; *Hrs Open:* 24; 0.229 kw-D, ND1; 0.01 kw-N, ND1; N41 19 15 W92 38 44
P.O. Box 380, Oskaloosa, IA 52527 US
(515) 673-3493; *Fax:* (515) 673-3495
www.kboeradio.com
kboe@kboeradio.com
License: Oskaloosa, IA held by Jomast Corp.
Regional Network: Brownfield; Radio Iowa
Format: Country *Special Programming:* Gospel 9 hrs wkly; *Hrs. of News Programming:* news progmg 15 hrs wkly; *No. News Employees:* 1; *Target Audience:* 25-50.
Brad Muhl, President
Glenda Lind-Booy, General Manager
Gary Wilson, Chief Engineer

KBOE-FM
02-07-1964; 104.9 MHz FM; *Hrs Open:* 24; 50 kw; 492 ft.; N41 19 15 W92 38 44
P.O. Box 380, Oskaloosa, IA 52577 US
(641) 673-3493; *Fax:* (641) 673-3495
www.kboeradio.com
License: Oskaloosa, Mahaska County, IA held by Jomast Corp.
Nat'l Network: ABC
Format: Country
Glenda Booy, General Manager

***KIGC**
01-01-1975; 88.7 MHz FM; *Hrs Open:* 24; 0.23 kw horiz; 121 ft.; N41 18 37 W92 38 49
201 Trueblood Avenue, Oskaloosa, IA 52577 US

(641) 673-1095; *Fax:* (641) 673-1396
License: Oskaloosa, Mahaska County, IA held by William Penn University
Format: Alternative, Black, 64 *Special Programming:* Jazz 12 hrs, gospel 12 hrs wkly; *Hrs. of News Programming:* News progmg one hr wkly; *Target Audience:* 13-25.
Larz Roberts, General Manager
James Roberts, Programming Director

Ottumwa

KBIZ
01-01-1941; 1240 kHz AM; 1 kw-U, ND1; N41 0 0 W92 23 23
416 E. Main St., Ottumwa, IA 52501 US
(641) 684-5563
www.ottumwaradio.com
License: Ottumwa, IA held by O-Town Communications, Inc.
Group Owner: Linder Broadcasting Group; (acq 10-20-2005; $890,000 with co-located FM).
Nat'l Network: CBS
Arbitron Metro Market: Ottumwa, IA; *Format:* News/Talk; *Target Audience:* 25-54.
Mike Buchanan, News Director

KLEE
08-01-1954; 1480 kHz AM; *Hrs Open:* 24
416 E. Main St., Ottumwa, IA 52501 US
(641) 684-5563
www.ottumwaradio.com
License: Ottumwa, IA held by O-Town Communications, Inc.
Group Owner: Linder Broadcasting Group; (acq 1-16-92; $400,000 with co-located FM;
Nat'l Network: Westwood One; *Regional Network:* Brownfield
Arbitron Metro Market: Des Moines, IA; *Format:* Oldies *Special Programming:* Gospel 6 hrs, polka one hr wkly; *Hrs. of News Programming:* news progmg 28 hrs wkly; *No. News Employees:* 1 *Target Audience:* General; people on the move
Mike Buchanan, News Director

KOTM-FM
03-22-1976; 97.7 MHz FM; 19 kw; 367 ft.; N41 1 28 W92 28 56
416 E. Main St., Ottumwa, IA 52501 US
(641) 684-5563
www.ottumwaradio.com
License: Ottumwa, Wapello County, IA held by O-Town Communications, Inc.
Group Owner: Linder Broadcasting Group
Nat'l Network: Westwood One
Format: Contemporary Hits/Top 40; *Target Audience:* Teens-50.
Mike Buchanan, News Director

KTWA
12-01-1984; 92.7 MHz FM; *Hrs Open:* 24; 50 kw; 318 ft.; N41 1 29 W92 28 9
416 E. Main St., Ottumwa, IA 52501 US
(641) 684-5563
www.ottumwaradio.com
License: Ottumwa, Wapello County, IA held by O-Town Communications Inc.
Group Owner: Linder Broadcasting Group.
Arbitron Metro Market: Ottumwa, IA; *Format:* Adult Contemp
Mike Buchanan, News Director

***KNSZ(FM)**
89.1 MHz FM; 13.5 kw; Ant 449 ft; N40 57 41 W92 22 13
2022 Communications Bldg., Iowa State University, Ames, IA 50011
(515) 294-2025; *Fax:* (515) 294-1544
www.iowapublicradio.org
License: Ottumwa, Wapello County, IA held by Iowa State University of Science and Technology.

Mary Grace Herrington, Programming Director
Don Wirth, Director, Fiscal Operations

Parkersburg

KQCR-FM
10-18-2000; 98.9 MHz FM; *Hrs Open:* 24; 6 kw; 328 ft.; N42 33 48 W92 57 22
Mailing Address: 1509 4th Street Ne, P O Box 495, Hampton, IA 50441 US
Second Address: 1509 4th St NE, Hampton, IA 50441-1106
(641) 456-5656; *Fax:* (641) 456-5655
www.kqcr.fm
kqcr@kqcr.fm
License: Parkersburg, Butler County, IA held by CD Broadcasting Inc.
Arbitron Metro Market: Hampton, IA; *Format:* Adult Contemp; *Hrs. of News Programming:* news progmg 12 hrs wkly; *No. News Employees:* 2; *Target Audience:* 25-45; Light, Soft AC 70's, 80's, 90's; *Adv. Rates:* 19;19; 19; 19
Marlin Burrier, Operations Dir
Craig Donnelly, General Manager
Duane Carstens, Sales Manager
Betsy Roberts, News Director
Steve Daniels, Chief Engineer
Kathy Donnelly, Bookkeeper/Office Managerager
Mike Betten, Music Director
Mandy Strother, Traffic
Sue Followwill, KLMJ/KQCR Sales Representative
Gladys Fanny, Receptionist
Jeff Moss, Sports Director

Pella

KAZR
08-01-1976; 103.3 MHz FM; *Hrs Open:* 24; 100 kw; 745 ft.; N41 32 18 W93 17 58
73 Kercheval Ave, Crosse Pointe, MI 48236 US
(515) 280-1350; *Fax:* (515) 280-3011
www.lazer1033.com
License: Pella, Marion County, IA held by Saga Communications of Iowa LLC.
Group Owner: Saga Communications Inc.; (acq 9-17-96; $2.7 million)
Nat'l Reps: Katz Radio; *Wire Services:* AP
Arbitron Metro Market: Des Moines, IA; *Format:* Rock/AOR; *Hrs. of News Programming:* news progmg 4 hrs wkly; *Target Audience:* 25-44.
Scott Allen, Operations Dir
Jeff Delvaux, General Manager
Pam Washington, General Sales Mgr
Ryan Patrick, Programming Director
Rob Lembke, Promotions Manager
Dan Abbuehl, Advertising Manager
Pam Washington, Sales Director

Perry

KDLS
05-10-1961; 1310 kHz AM; *Hrs Open:* 6 AM-10 PM; 0.5 kw-D, DA2; 0.3 kw-N, DA2; N41 49 58 W94 2 15
Mailing Address: 2260 141st Drive, P.O. Box 548, Perry, IA 50220 US
Second Address: 2260 141st Drive, Perry, IA 50220
(515) 465-5357; *Fax:* (515) 465-3952
License: Perry, IA held by Coon Valley Communications Inc.
Group Owner: Coon Valley Communications Inc.; (acq 2-15-2006; $300,000)
Nat'l Network: Westwood One; CNN Radio; *Nat'l Reps:* Farmakis; *Wire Services:* AP
Arbitron Metro Market: Des Moines, IA; *Format:* Variety/Diverse; *Hrs. of News Programming:* news progmg 25 hrs wkly; *No. News Employees:* 1; *Target Audience:* General.; *Adv. Rates:* 14; 11; 11; 6
Patrick Delaney, President
Tom Quinlan, Operations Dir
Patrick Graney, General Manager
Bob Pink, Chief Engineer
John Patrick, Operations Director
Marcia Murphy, Traffic Manager

KDLS-FM
02-26-1971; 105.5 MHz FM; *Hrs Open:* 6 AM-midnight; 10 kw; 515 ft.; N41 43 35 W93 51 38
P.O. Box 548, 2260 141st Drive, Perry, IA 50220 US
(515) 278-4117; *Fax:* (515) 254-1037
License: Perry, Dallas County, IA held by Perry Broadcasting Co.
Arbitron Metro Market: Des Moines, IA; *Adv. Rates:* 12; 12; 10; 6
Joel Garcia, General Manager

Pleasantville

KICL(FM)
03-12-2008; 96.3 MHz FM; 500 w; Ant 255 ft; N41 21 04 W93 13 58
1513 N. 1st St., Indianola, IA 50125
(515) 961-3338; *Fax:* (515) 961-3338
License: Pleasantville, Marion County, IA held by Iowas State University of Science and Technology
Population Served: 1,695; *Arbitron Metro Market:* Pleasantville, IA; *Format:* Country
Rebecca Orr, General Manager

Postville

***KPVL**
01-01-2003; 89.1 MHz FM; 3 kw; 246 ft.; N43 5 20 W91 33 54
116 E. Military Rd, Postville, IA 52162 US
(563) 864-7945; *Fax:* (563) 864-7940
www.kpvlradio.com
License: Postville, Allamakee County, IA held by Postville Chamber of Commerce.
Arbitron Metro Market: Postville, IA; *Format:* Talk, News
Randy Frank, General Manager

Red Oak

KOAK
08-16-1968; 1080 kHz AM; *Hrs Open:* Sunrise-sunset
P.O. Box 465, Red Oak, IA 51566 US
(712) 623-2584; *Fax:* (712) 623-2583
kcsifm.com
kcsi@kcsifm.com
License: Red Oak, IA held by Hawkeye Communications Inc.
Nat'l Network: ABC; *Regional Network:* Radio Iowa; *Wire Services:* AP
Format: Country
Jerry Dietz, President
Melanie West, General Sales Mgr
Marilyn Dietz, News Director

Rock Valley

KIHK
01-01-1998; 106.9 MHz FM; *Hrs Open:* 6 AM-6 AM; 25 kw; 328 ft.; N43 20 28 W96 19 3
1039 Radio Drive, Spirit Lake, IA 51360 US
(712) 722-1090; *Fax:* (712) 722-1102
www.ksoufm.com
License: Rock Valley, Sioux County, IA held by Sorenson Broadcasting Corp.
Group Owner: Sorenson Broadcasting Corp.; (acq 7-1-2004; grpsl)
Format: Country *Special Programming:* High School sports
Craig Aukes, General Manager
Dan Bonnema, General Sales Mgr
Doug Brock, News Director

Rockford

KYME
01-01-2008; 92.9 MHz FM; 0.375 kw; 33 ft.; N43 3 12 W92 57 15
US
(301) 759-1155
www.cumberlandsmagic.com
psullivan@alleganyradio.com
License: Rockford, Floyd County, IA held by Radioactive LLC.
Group Owner: Radioactive LLC
Arbitron Metro Market: Rockford, IA; *Format:* Adult Contemp
Benjamin Homel, President

Sac City

KEWS(FM)
104.7 MHz FM; 6 kw; Ant 159 ft; N42 24 40 W95 00 17
1717 Dixie Hwy., Suite 650, Fort Wright, KY 41011
(859) 331-9100
License: Sac City, Sac County, IA held by Radioactive LLC.
Group Owner: Radioactive LLC
Population Served: 2,197; *Arbitron Metro Market:* Sac City, IA
Benjamin Homel, President

Sageville

KIYX
01-01-1999; 106.1 MHz FM; *Hrs Open:* 24; 4.2 kW; 394 ft.; N42 41 27 W90 37 26
51 Means Dr, Platteville, WI 53818 USA
(608) 349-2000; *Fax:* (608) 349-2002
superhits106.com
superhits@queenbradio.com
License: Sageville, Dubuque County, IA held by QueenB Radio Wisconsin Inc.
Group Owner: Morgan Murphy Media; (acq 6-8-99)
Nat'l Network: Westwood One
Format: Oldies *Special Programming:* Christmas (Nov/Dec); *No. News Employees:* 1; *Adv. Rates:* 8; 6; 6; 6
Rick Sanson, Sales
Steve Hemmer, Programming Director

Sanborn

KXIM
98.3 MHz FM; 6 kw; 328 feet; N43 08 31 W95 37 13
6404 South Tomar Road, Sioux Falls, SD
(605) 929-0413
am770radioengineering@gmail.com
License: Sanborn, IA held by AM 770 Radio Engineering

Paul L Heeren, General Manager

Sheldon

KIWA
10-27-1961; 1550 kHz AM; *Hrs Open:* 24
411 Ninth Street, Sheldon, IA 51201 US
(712) 324-2597; *Fax:* (712) 324-2340
www.kiwaradio.com
newtips@kiwaradio.com
License: Sheldon, IA held by Sheldon Broadcasting Co. Inc.
Nat'l Network: ABC; *Regional Network:* Radio Iowa; *Nat'l Reps:* Farmakis
Format: News, News/Talk, 86; *Hrs. of News Programming:* news progmg 15 hrs wkly; *No. News Employees:* 2; *Target Audience:* General; adult
Walt Pruiksma, General Manager
Wayne Barahona, Programming Director
Tim Torkildson, News Director
Larry Ahrens, Sports Commentator
Jessica DeBoer, Traffic Manager

KIWA-FM
10-01-1971; 105.3 MHz FM; *Hrs Open:* 24; 50 kw; Ant 292 ft; N43 11 00 W95 52 05
411 9th St., Sheldon, IA 51201
(712) 324-2597; *Fax:* (712) 324-2340
www.kiwaradio.com
walt@kiwaradio.com
License: Sheldon, Obrien County, IA held by Sheldon Broadcasting Co. Inc.
Nat'l Reps: Farmakis
Population Served: 65,000 *Hrs. of News Programming:* news progmg 15 hrs wkly; *No. News Employees:* 2; *Target Audience:* General.
Walt Pruiksma, General Manager
Wayne Barahana, Chief Engineer

Shenandoah

KMA
08-12-1925; 960 kHz AM; *Hrs Open:* 24; 5 kw-D, DAN; 5 kw-N, DAN; N40 46 48 W95 21 23
209 North Elm Street, Shenandoah, IA 51601 US
(712) 246-5270; *Fax:* (712) 246-5275
www.kma960.com
License: Shenandoah, IA held by May Broadcasting Co.
Nat'l Network: ABC
Format: News, News/Talk, 86 *Special Programming:* Farm; *Hrs. of News Programming:* news progmg 15 hrs wkly; *No. News Employees:* 2; *Target Audience:* 35-54.; *Adv. Rates:* 135; 135; 85; 75
Edward May, President
Mark Eno, General Manager
Don Hansen, Station Manager

***KYFR**
01-01-1977; 920 kHz AM; *Hrs Open:* 24
Mailing Address: 4135 Northgate Blvd, Suite 1, Sacramento, CA 95834 US
Second Address: 700 W. Sheridan Ave., Shenandoah, IA 51601
(712) 246-5151
www.familyradio.com/english
info@familyradio.org
License: Shenandoah, IA held by Family Stations Inc.
Group Owner: Family Stations Inc.; (acq 1976)
Nat'l Network: Family Radio
Arbitron Metro Market: Oakland, CA; *Format:* Christian
Tom Evans, General Manager
Mike DeStefano, Station Manager

Sioux Center

***KDCR**
08-16-1968; 88.5 MHz FM; 100 kw; 495 ft.; N43 5 34 W96 9 23
Dordt College Campus, Sioux Center, IA 51250 US
(712) 722-0885; *Fax:* (712) 722-6244
kdcr@dordt.edu
License: Sioux Center, Sioux County, IA held by Dordt College Inc.
Nat'l Network: USA
Arbitron Metro Market: Sioux Center, IA; *Format:* Religious
Special Programming: Farm 2 hrs, Dutch one hr wkly
Dennis DeWaard, General Manager
Denny De Waard, Station Manager
Jim Bolkema, Programming Director
John Slegers, News Director
Ralph Goemaat, Chief Engineer
Jim Bolkema, Music Director
Mike Byker, Sports Director

KSOU
11-17-1969; 1090 kHz AM; *Hrs Open:* Sunrise-sunset; 0.5 kw-D, DAD; N43 3 22 W96 10 17
P.O. Box 528, Spirit Lake, IA 51360 US
(712) 722-1090(712) 722-1091; *Fax:* (712) 722-1102
www.ksoufm.com
License: Sioux Center, IA held by Sorenson Broadcasting Corp.
Group Owner: Sorenson Broadcasting Corp.; (acq 7-1-2004; grpsl)
Nat'l Reps: Farmakis
Arbitron Metro Market: Sioux Center, IA; *Format:* Christian; *Hrs. of News Programming:* news progmg 17 hrs wkly; *No. News Employees:* 1; *Target Audience:* General.
Shirley Wierda, Operations Dir
Craig Aukes, General Manager
Dan Bonnema, General Sales Mgr
James DeBoer, Programming Director
Doug Broek, News Director
Steve Heaton, Chief Engineer

KSOU-FM
10-17-1974; 93.9 MHz FM; *Hrs Open:* 24; 50 kw; 492 ft.; N43 5 1 W96 18 20
P.O. Box 298, Sioux Center, IA 51250 US
(712) 722-1090; *Fax:* (712) 722-1102
www.ksoufm.com
License: Sioux Center, Sioux County, IA
Group Owner: Sorenson Broadcasting Corp.
Nat'l Network: ABC
Arbitron Metro Market: Sioux Center, IA; *Format:* Adult Contemp
Steve Heaton, Operations Dir
Scott France, Programming Director
Shirley Wierda, Women's Int Ed

Sioux City

KGLI
03-11-1974; 95.5 MHz FM; *Hrs Open:* 24; 100 kw; 899 ft.; N42 30 53 W96 18 13
1113 Nebraska St., Sioux City, IA 51105 US
(712) 258-5595
www.kg95.com
License: Sioux City, Woodbury County, IA held by AMFM Radio Licenses LLC
Group Owner: iHeartMedia
Arbitron Metro Market: Sioux City, IA; *Format:* Adult Contemp; *Target Audience:* 18-49.
Rob Powers, Senior Vice President of Operations
Kelli Erickson, Market President

KMNS
05-01-1949; 620 kHz AM; *Hrs Open:* 24
Mailing Address: PO Box 3009, Sioux City, IA 51102 US
Second Address: 1113 Nebraska St., Sioux City, IA 51102
(712) 258-0628; *Fax:* (712) 252-2430
www.620kmns.com
License: Sioux City, IA held by AMFM Radio Licenses LLC.
Group Owner: iHeartMedia; (acq 10-1-2002; grpsl)
Nat'l Network: Fox Sports Radio; *Nat'l Reps:* Katz Radio
Arbitron Metro Market: Sioux City, IA; *Format:* Sports; *Target Audience:* 18-54.
Rob Powers, Senior Vice President of Operations
Kelli Erickson, Market President

***KMSC**
04-01-1978; 92.9 MHz FM; 0.012 kw; 184 ft.; N42 28 28 W96 21 34
1501 Morningside Ave, Sioux City, IA 51106 US
(712) 274-5665; *Fax:* (712) 274-5664
http://kmsc.morningside.edu/
kmsc@morningside.edu
License: Sioux City, Woodbury County, IA held by Morningside College Board of Directors.
Arbitron Metro Market: Sioux City, IA; *Format:* Alternative; *Target Audience:* General; high school, college students & young professionals
Ron Jorgensen, CFO
John Reinders, President
Dr. Mark Heistad, General Manager
Nick Brincks, Station Manager
Michael Lewis, Promotions Manager
Claire DeRoin, News Director
Bill Deeds, Executive Vice President

KSCJ
01-01-1927; 1360 kHz AM; *Hrs Open:* 24; 5 kw-D, DAN; 5 kw-N, DAN; N42 33 24 W96 20 12
P.O. Box 788, Baton Rouge, LA 70821 US
(712) 239-2100; *Fax:* (712) 239-3346
www.kscj.com
License: Sioux City, IA held by Powell Broadcasting Co.
Group Owner: Powell Broadcasting Co. Inc.; (acq 1996; $3.8 million with KSUX(FM) Winnebago, NE)
Nat'l Network: ABC *Regional Reps:* REGIONAL REPS
Arbitron Metro Market: Sioux City, IA; *Format:* News, News/Talk, 84, Talk; *Hrs. of News Programming:* news progmg 42 hrs wkly; *No. News Employees:* 2; *Target Audience:* 35-64; educated, higher income, issues-oriented *Adv. Rates:* 20; 20; 20; 15
Dennis Bullock, General Manager
Dave Grossenherder, General Sales Mgr
Steve Arthur, Programming Director
Randy Renshaw, News Director

KSEZ
02-06-1960; 97.9 MHz FM; *Hrs Open:* 24; 100 kw; 643 ft.; N42 28 56 W96 15 30
Mailing Address: P.O. Box 3009, Sioux City, IA 51102 US
Second Address: 1113 Nebraska St., Sioux City, IA 51105
(712) 258-5595; *Fax:* (712) 252-2430
www.z98rocks.com
License: Sioux City, Woodbury County, IA held by AMFM Radio Licenses LLC
Group Owner: iHeartMedia
Nat'l Network: ABC; *Nat'l Reps:* Katz Radio
Arbitron Metro Market: Sioux City, IA; *Format:* Classic Rock; *Target Audience:* 18-49.
Rob Powers, Senior Vice President of Operations
Kelli Erickson, Market President

***KTFC**
07-01-1965; 103.3 MHz FM; *Hrs Open:* 24; 100 kw; 633 ft.; N42 29 5.5 W96 18 18.9
1534 Buchanan Ave., Sioux City, IA 51106 US
(712) 252-4621
www.bottradionetwork.com
comments@bottradionetwork.com
License: Sioux City, Woodbury County, IA held by Community Broadcasting Inc.
Group Owner: Bott Radio Network; (acq 12-13-2007; $650,000 with KTFG(FM) Sioux Rapids)
Nat'l Network: USA
Arbitron Metro Market: Sioux City-Sioux Rapids, IA; *Format:* Christian, Talk *Special Programming:* Farm one hr, news 10 hrs, children 5 hrs wkly
Richard Bott Sr., President & CEO
Eben Fowler, Operations Dir
Pat Rulon, Director of National Sales
Candy Green, Program Services Manager
Rachel Launius, Marketing Manager
Kim Cotter, Office Manager

***KWIT**
01-31-1978; 90.3 MHz FM; *Hrs Open:* 24; 100 kw; 909 ft.; N42 28 56 W96 15 30
4647 Stone Avenue, Sioux City, IA 51102 US
(712) 274-6406; *Fax:* (712) 274-6411
www.kwit-koji.org
gondekg@witcc.edu
License: Sioux City, Woodbury County, IA held by Western Iowa Tech Community College.
Nat'l Network: PRI; NPR
Arbitron Metro Market: Sioux City, IA; *Format:* News, News/Talk, 86 *Special Programming:* Blues 2 hrs, Triple A 12 hrs, Sp 20 hrs wkly; *Hrs. of News Programming:* news progmg 36 hrs wkly; *No. News Employees:* 1 *Target Audience:* 25-54.
Steve Smith, Operations Dir
Gretchen Gondek, General Manager
Duane Kraayenbrink, News Director
Dennis Semple, Chief Engineer
Jake Moreland, Arts Producer
Mindy Thompson, Office Assistant

KWSL
04-01-1938; 1470 kHz AM; 5 kw-D, DA2; 5 kw-N, DA2; N42 24 42 W96 25 30
Mailing Address: 4700 S. Lewis Blvd, Sioux City, IA 51106 US
Second Address: 1113 Nebraska St., Sioux City, IA 51105
(712) 255-1470; *Fax:* (712) 252-2430
www.1470kwsl.com
License: Sioux City, IA held by AMFM Radio Licenses LLC.
Group Owner: iHeartMedia; (acq 10-1-2002; grpsl)
Nat'l Reps: Katz Radio
Arbitron Metro Market: Sioux City, IA; *Format:* Spanish; *Target Audience:* 25 plus.
Rob Powers, Senior Vice President of Operations
Kelli Erickson, Market President

Sioux Rapids

***KTFG**
01-01-1991; 102.9 MHz FM; 49 kw; 495 ft.; N42 54 34.6 W95 9 33.1 *Rebroadcasts:* Rebroadcasts KTFC(FM) Sioux City 100%
1534 Buchanan Ave., Sioux City, IA 51106 US
(712) 252-4621
www.bottradionetwork.com
comments@bottradionetwork.com

License: Sioux Rapids, Buena Vista County, IA held by Community Broadcasting Inc.
Group Owner: Bott Radio Network; (acq 12-13-2007; $650,000 with KTFC(FM) Sioux City)
Nat'l Network: USA
Arbitron Metro Market: Sioux City-Sioux Rapids, IA; *Format:* Christian, Talk *Special Programming:* Children 5 hrs wkly
Richard Bott Sr., President & CEO
Eben Fowler, Operations Dir
Pat Rulon, Director of National Sales
Candy Green, Program Services Manager
Rachel Launius, Marketing Manager
Kim Cotter, Office Manager

Spencer

KICD
12-01-1942; 1240 kHz AM; *Hrs Open:* 24
Mailing Address: P.O. Box 260, Spencer, IA 51301 US
Second Address: 2600 N. Hwy. Blvd., Spencer, IA 51301
(712) 262-1240; *Fax:* (712) 262-2076
www.kicdam.com
dputnam@spencerradiogroup.com
License: Spencer, IA held by Saga Communications of Iowa LLC.
Group Owner: Saga Communications Inc.; (acq 11-22-99; grpsl)
Nat'l Network: CBS
Format: Talk *Special Programming:* Farm 2 hrs wkly, religious 4 hrs wkly,; *Hrs. of News Programming:* news progmg 100 hrs wkly; *No. News Employees:* 1; *Target Audience:* 35 plus.
Kevin Tlam, Operations Dir
David Putnam, General Manager
Linda Maske, Station Manager
Brent Palm, News Director
Ryan Long, Engineering Dir
Dan Sketon, Chief Engineer
Troy Leninger, Farm Director
Mark Magnuson, FarmBroadcaster

KICD-FM
09-17-1965; 107.7 MHz FM; *Hrs Open:* 24; 100 kw; 285 ft.; N43 9 57 W95 8 46
Mailing Address: P.O. Box 260, Spencer, IA 51301 US
Second Address: 2600 N. Hwy. Blvd., Spencer, IA 51301
(712) 262-1240; *Fax:* (712) 262-2076
www.cd1077fm.com
License: Spencer, Clay County, IA held by Saga Communications of Iowa LLC.
Group Owner: Saga Communications Inc.
Nat'l Network: CBS
Format: Country; *No. News Employees:* 1; *Target Audience:* 25 plus.
David Putman, General Sales Mgr
Rhoda Wedeking, Programming Director

KLLT
02-01-1979; 104.9 MHz FM; *Hrs Open:* 24; 25 kw; 279 ft.; N43 17 13 W95 8 34
P.O. Box 260, Spencer, IA 51301 US
(712) 262-1240; *Fax:* (712) 262-2076
www.lite1049.com
License: Spencer, Clay County, IA held by Saga Communications of Iowa LLC.
Group Owner: Saga Communications Inc.; (acq 11-22-99; grpsl)
Nat'l Reps: Katz Radio
Format: Light Rock; *Hrs. of News Programming:* News progmg one hr wkly; *Target Audience:* 25-54.
Edward Christian, President/CEO
Kevin Tlam, Operations Dir
Dave Putnam, General Manager
Linda Maske, Office Manager
Ryan Long, News Director

Spirit Lake

KUOO
04-01-1985; 103.9 MHz FM; *Hrs Open:* 24; 50 kw; 492 ft.; N43 24 20 W95 5 1
13906 Gold Circle, Suite 201, Omaha, NE 68144 US
(712) 336-5800; *Fax:* (712) 336-1634
www.kuooradio.com
mspies@exploreokoboji.com
License: Spirit Lake, Dickinson County, IA held by Sorenson Broadcasting Corp.
Group Owner: Sorenson Broadcasting Corp.; (acq 7-1-2004; grpsl)
Nat'l Network: Fox News Radio
Arbitron Metro Market: Spirit Lake, IA; *Format:* Adult Contemp; *Hrs. of News Programming:* news progmg 16 hrs wkly; *No. News Employees:* 2; *Target Audience:* 25-54.
Neil Lipetzky, CEO
Dean Sorenson, President
Marty Spies, General Manager
Jeff Nixx, Programming Director
Abby Kohlhaas, Promotions Manager
Steve Schwaller, News Director
Steve Heaton, Chief Engineer
Chad Franzen, SportsDirector
Mary Treanor, Music Director
Terry Lowry, Office Manager
Matt Fallon, Production Director
Matt Fallon, Production Director

*KJIA
01-01-2002; 88.9 MHz FM; 50 kw; 272 ft.; N43 20 34 W95 12 24
PO Box 738, Okoboji, IA 51355 US
(712) 332-2428; *Fax:* (712) 332-2428
www.kjiaradio.com
kjia@kjiaradio.com
License: Spirit Lake, Dickinson County, IA held by Minn-Iowa Christian Broadcasting Inc.
Group Owner: Minn-Iowa Christian Broadcasting Inc.
Arbitron Metro Market: Okoboji, IA; *Format:* Christian
Matt Dorfner, Executive Director
Steve Ware, Programming Director
Mark Bohnett, Chief Engineer
Lynette Dorfner, Community Relations Representative
Bev Cother, Receptionist

St. Ansgar

*KJCY
09-01-2001; 95.5 MHz FM; *Hrs Open:* 24; 6 kw; 328 ft.; N43 21 52 W92 51 4
1296 Marian Lane, Green Bay, WI 54304 US
(641) 424-5529; *Fax:* (641) 424-5597
www.kjcy.com
kjcy@kjcy.com
License: St. Ansgar, Mitchell County, IA held by Minn-Iowa Christian Broadcasting Inc.
Group Owner: Minn-Iowa Christian Broadcasting Inc.; acq 3-20-01; $200,000).
Format: Christian
Matt Dorfner, President
Matt Donfner, General Manager

State Center

*KTDV
01-09-2009; 91.9 MHz FM; 22 kw; 307 ft.; N42 15 49 W93 3 57
P. O. Box 538, Marshalltown, IA 50158 US
(641) 752-4122; *Fax:* (641) 752-5121
ktdvradio.com
info@ktdvradio.com
License: State Center, Marshall County, IA held by Marshalltown Education Plus Inc.
Format: Adult Contemp, Christian
Mark Osmundson, General Manager

Storm Lake

KAYL
11-01-1948; 990 kHz AM; 0.25 kw-D, ND1; 0.006 kw-N, ND1; N42 38 5 W95 10 10
Mailing Address: 13906 Gold Circle, Suite 201, Omaha, NE 68144 US
Second Address: 606 1/2 Lake Ave., Storm Lake, IA 50588
(712) 732-3520; *Fax:* (712) 732-1746
www.stormlakeradio.com
info@stormlakeradio.com
License: Storm Lake, IA held by Sorenson Broadcasting Corp.
Group Owner: NRG Media LLC; (acq 7-1-2004; grpsl)
Nat'l Network: La Gran D
Arbitron Metro Market: Storm Lake, IA; *Adv. Rates:* 22; 22; 22; 22
Mary Quass, CEO
Buzz Paterson, General Manager
Chuck DuCoty, COO

KAYL-FM
02-01-1949; 101.7 MHz FM; 50 kw; 400 ft.; N42 38 5 W95 10 10
13906 Gold Circle, Suite 201, Omaha, NE 68144 US
(712) 732-3520; *Fax:* (712) 732-1746
www.stormlakeradio.com
info@stormlakeradio.com
License: Storm Lake, Buena Vista County, IA held by Sorenson Broadcasting Corp.
Group Owner: NRG Media LLC
Regional Network: Waitt Farm Net.
Arbitron Metro Market: Storm Lake, IA; *Format:* Adult Contemp; *Hrs. of News Programming:* news progmg 15 hrs wkly; *No. News Employees:* 1; *Target Audience:* 25-54; male & female; *Adv. Rates:* 28; 28; 28; 28
Mary Quass, CEO
Buzz Paterson, General Manager
Chuck DuCoty, COO

*KOIA
88.1 MHz FM; kw
US
License: Storm Lake, Buena Vista County, IA held by Ron Elmore Ministries Inc.
Arbitron Metro Market: Storm Lake, IA
Ron Elmore, President

Story City

*KHOI
89.1 MHz FM; kw
US
(515) 292-2878
www.khoifm.org
khoiradio@gmail.com
License: Story City, Story County, IA held by Unitarian Universalist Fellowship of Ames.
Arbitron Metro Market: Ames, IA; *Format:* Talk
Janet Klaas, President

Stuart

KKRF
08-11-1993; 107.9 MHz FM; 9.4 kw; 492 ft.; N41 27 40 W94 29 22
Mailing Address: Rr2 Box 106a, Lacrescent, MN 55947 US
Second Address: 204 S. Division St., Stuart, IA 50250-5021
(515) 465-5357; *Fax:* (515) 465-3952
License: Stuart, Guthrie County, IA held by Coon Valley Communications Inc.
Group Owner: Coon Valley Communications Inc.
Nat'l Network: ABC
Arbitron Metro Market: Des Moines, IA; *Format:* Country *Special Programming:* Farm 5 hrs wkly; *Hrs. of News Programming:* news progmg 10 hrs wkly; *No. News Employees:* 1; *Target Audience:* 25-64; general *Adv. Rates:* 13.50; 13.50; 13.50; 13.50
Pat Delaney, President
John France, Operations Dir
Sue Thomsen, General Manager

Twin Lakes

KTLB
10-05-1975; 105.9 MHz FM; *Hrs Open:* 18; 25 kw; 328 ft.; N42 32 9 W94 40 48
200 N. 10th St., Fort Dodge, IA 50501 US
(515) 955-5656; *Fax:* (515) 955-5844
www.yourfortdodge.com
sgossweiler@digity.me
License: Twin Lakes, Calhoun County, IA held by Digity 3E License, LLC
Group Owner: Digity, LLC
Arbitron Metro Market: Fort Dodge, IA; *Format:* Oldies; *No. News Employees:* 1; *Target Audience:* 35-54; baby boomers
Darren Helton, Operations Dir
Steve Gossweiler, General Manager
Pat Kolar, Dir. of Sales
Darren Helton, Programming Director
Kelly Heinen, News Director

Villisca

KCSI
09-01-1979; 95.3 MHz FM; *Hrs Open:* 24; 50 kw; 331 ft.; N41 1 35.2 W95 12 2
P.O. Box 465, Red Oak, IA 51566 US
(712) 623-2584; *Fax:* (712) 623-2583
www.kcsifm.com
kcsi@kcsifm.com
License: Villisca, Montgomery County, IA held by Hawkeye Communications Inc.
Nat'l Network: ABC; *Regional Network:* Radio Iowa; *Wire Services:* AP
Arbitron Metro Market: Villisca, CA; *Format:* Country
Jerry Dietz, CEO
Melanie West, General Sales Mgr
Marilyn Dietz, News Director

Vinton

KRQN
01-01-2005; 107.1 MHz FM; *Hrs Open:* 24; 4.7 kw; 371 ft.; N42 08 56 W91 52 50
425 Second St. E., 4th Floor, Cedar Rapids, IA 52401 US

(319) 365-9431
www.i1071.com
terry.peters@townsquaremedia.com
License: Vinton, IA held by George S. Flinn
Group Owner: Townsquare Media
Arbitron Metro Market: Cedar Rapids, IA; *Format:* Contemporary Hits/Top 40
Terry Peters, General Manager
Josh Loeffler, Director of Sales
Chris Hauger, Brand Manager
Bridget DeMeis, Digital Managing Editor

Wapello

*KAIP
01-01-2005; 88.9 MHz FM; 0.001 kw horiz, 13.5 kw vert; 494 ft.; N41 4 59 W91 10 18
US
(888) 937-2471; *Fax:* (916) 251-1650
www.air1.com
info@air1.com
License: Wapello, Louisa County, IA held by Educational Media Foundation.
Group Owner: EMF Broadcasting
Nat'l Network: Air 1
Arbitron Metro Market: Wapello, IA; *Format:* Alternative, Christian; *No. News Employees:* 3; *Target Audience:* 25-44; Judeo Christian, female
Darrell Chambliss, Chairman
Alan Mason, COO
Mike Novak, President and CEO
Glenn Goodwin, Operations Dir
David Pierce, Programming Director
Ed Lenane, News Director
Sam Wallington, Engineering Dir
Marya Morgan, News Reporter
Richard Hunt, News Reporter
Dan Antonelli, Chief Business Development Officer
Eric Moser, Chief Financial Officer
Brian Burger, Vice President of Human Resources
D. Kevin Blair, Secretary and General Counsel

Washington

KCII
11-12-1961; 1380 kHz AM; *Hrs Open:* 5 AM-11 PM; 0.5 kw-D, ND1; 0.025 kw-N, ND1; N41 18 18 W91 42 36
P.O. Box 31, 1610 N. Lincoln, Knoxville, IA 50138 US
(319) 653-2113; *Fax:* (319) 653-3500
kciiradio.com
kcii@kciiradio.com
License: Washington, IA held by Home Broadcasting Inc.
Nat'l Network: AP Radio
Arbitron Metro Market: Cedar Rapids, IA; *Format:* Adult Contemp, News; *Hrs. of News Programming:* news progmg 14 hrs wkly; *No. News Employees:* 1; *Target Audience:* 25-54; females; *Adv. Rates:* 17.47; 17.47;17.47; 17.47.
Joe Nichols, General Manager
Joe Nichols, General Sales Mgr
Nic Sabatke, Programming Director
Ben Stanton, News Director
Becky Helmick, Traffic Manager

KCII-FM
01-01-1975; 106.1 MHz FM; *Hrs Open:* 5 AM-11 PM; 3 kw; 299 ft.; N41 18 18 W91 42 36
P.O. Box 31, 1610 N. Lincoln, Knoxville, IA 50138 US
(319) 653-2113; *Fax:* (319) 653-3500
kciiradio.com
kcii@kciiradio.com
License: Washington, Washington County, IA held by Home Broadcasting Inc.
Arbitron Metro Market: Cedar Rapids, IA; *Format:* News, Oldies
Nic Sabatke, Operations Dir
Joe Nichols, General Manager
Ben Stanton, News Director
Dagan Miller, Sports Commentator

Waterloo

*KBBG
07-26-1978; 88.1 MHz FM; *Hrs Open:* 19; 9.5 kw; 154 ft.; N42 30 45 W92 19 24
918 Newell Street, Waterloo, IA 50703 US
(319) 234-1441; *Fax:* (319) 234-6182
www.kbbgfm.org
License: Waterloo, Black Hawk County, IA held by Afro-American Community Broadcasting Inc.
Nat'l Network: American Urban
Arbitron Metro Market: Waterloo, IA; *Format:* Blues, Gospel; *Target Audience:* General.
Lou Porter, CEO
Lou Porter, President
Beverly Douglas, Station Manager
Lou Porter, General Sales Mgr

KFMW
11-01-1968; 107.9 MHz FM; *Hrs Open:* 24; 77 kw; 1804 ft.; N42 24 2 W91 50 36
Mailing Address: Post Office Box 1540, Waterloo, IA 50704 US
Second Address: 514 Jefferson St., Waterloo, IA
(319) 234-2200; *Fax:* (319) 234-0149
www.rock108.com
cross@rock108.com
License: Waterloo, Black Hawk County, IA held by Woodward Communications Inc.
Group Owner: Woodward Communications Inc.
Nat'l Reps: Katz Radio
Arbitron Metro Market: Waterloo-Cedar Falls, IA; *Hrs. of News Programming:* news progmg 4 hrs wkly; *Target Audience:* 18-34; men
Michael Cross, Operations Dir
Tim Mathews, General Manager

*KNWS
01-01-1953; 1090 kHz AM; *Hrs Open:* Sunrise-sunset; 1 kw-D, NDD; N42 26 38 W92 17 58
3003 North Snelling Ave., Roseville, MN 55113 US
(319) 296-1975; *Fax:* (319) 296-1977
info@life1019.com
License: Waterloo, IA held by Northwestern College.
Group Owner: Northwestern College & Radio; (acq 4-2-53).
Nat'l Network: AP Radio
Arbitron Metro Market: Waterloo-Cedar Falls, IA; *Format:* Christian, Talk, 74; *Target Audience:* 35 plus.
Paul Virts, President
Doug Smith, Station Manager
Dan Raymond, Programming Director
David Dobes, Chief Engineer

*KNWS-FM
01-01-1965; 101.9 MHz FM; *Hrs Open:* 24; 100 kw; 1572 ft.; N42 24 2 W91 50 36
3003 North Snelling Ave., Roseville, MN 55113 US
(319) 296-1975; *Fax:* (319) 296-1977
www.life1019.com
License: Waterloo, Black Hawk County, IA
Arbitron Metro Market: Waterloo-Cedar Falls, IA; *Format:* Adult Contemp, Christian, 74; *Target Audience:* 30-50; women
Doug Smith, Station Manager
Mike Lanser, Programming Director
Dave Dobes, Engineering Dir
Richard Whitworth, Network Director
Brent Manion, Production Director
Dan Raymond, Program Director
Julia Taylor, Promotions Director

KOKZ
11-21-1962; 105.7 MHz FM; *Hrs Open:* 24; 100 kw; 1322 ft.; N42 24 35 W92 5 10
514 Jefferson Street, P.O. Box 1540, Waterloo, IA 50704 US
(319) 234-2200; *Fax:* (319) 234-0149
License: Waterloo, Black Hawk County, IA held by Woodward Communications Inc.
Group Owner: Woodward Communications Inc.
Nat'l Reps: Katz Radio
Arbitron Metro Market: Waterloo-Cedar Falls, IA; *Format:* Contemporary Hits/Top 40, Adult Contemp; *Target Audience:* 25-54.
Tim Mathews, General Manager

KWLO
11-01-1947; 1330 kHz AM; *Hrs Open:* 24; 5 kw-D, DA2; 5 kw-N, DA2; N42 28 1 W92 15 59
Mailing Address: Post Office Box 1540, Waterloo, IA 50704 US
Second Address: 514 Jefferson St., Waterloo, IA 50704
(319) 234-2200; *Fax:* (319) 234-0149
www.star1330.com
License: Waterloo, IA held by Woodward Communications Inc.
Group Owner: Woodward Communications Inc.; (acq 8-16-96; grpsl)
Nat'l Network: ABC; *Nat'l Reps:* Katz Radio
Arbitron Metro Market: Waterloo, IA; *Format:* Oldies; *Target Audience:* 35 plus.
Tom Woodward, President
Dennis Lowe, Operations Dir
Tim Mathews, General Manager
Amy Mollus, News Director
Mark Schumacher, Chief Engineer

KXEL
07-14-1942; 1540 kHz AM; *Hrs Open:* 24
514 Jefferson Street, P.O. Box 1540, Waterloo, IA 50704 US
(319) 234-2200; *Fax:* (319) 233-4946
www.kxel.com
License: Waterloo, IA held by Woodward Communications Inc.
Group Owner: Woodward Communications Inc.; (acq 1-11-58)
Nat'l Network: ABC; *Nat'l Reps:* Katz Radio
Arbitron Metro Market: Waterloo-Cedar Falls, IA; *Format:* News, News/Talk, 86 *Special Programming:* Relg 20 hrs wkly; *Hrs. of News Programming:* news progmg 28 hrs wkly; *No. News Employees:* 2; *Target Audience:* 45-65.
Tom Woodward, President
Dennis Lowe, Operations Dir
Bill Wells, General Manager
Cindy Hall, General Sales Mgr
Sarah Chase, Promotions Manager
Mark Schumacher, Chief Engineer
Ken Houser, Account Executive
Ken Hensley, AccountExecutive
Marica Downs, Account Executive

Waukon

KNEI-FM
09-01-1968; 103.5 MHz FM; 37 kw; 574 ft.; N43 18 28 W91 27 18
980 North Michigan Ave, Suite 1880, Chicago, IL 60610 US
(563) 568-3476; *Fax:* (563) 568-3391
knei@kneiradio.com
License: Waukon, Allamakee County, IA held by Wennes Communications Stations Inc.
Nat'l Network: CBS Radio; *Regional Network:* Radio Iowa; Brownfield
Format: Country; *Hrs. of News Programming:* News progmg one hr wkly; *Target Audience:* 25-45.
Greg Wennes, CEO
Chuck Bloxham, General Manager

KHPP(AM)
07-01-1967; 1160 kHz AM; 880 w-D, 26 w-N; N43 17 13 W91 28 06
14 W. Main St., Waukon, IA 52172
(563) 568-3477; *Fax:* (563) 568-3391
knei@kneiradio.com
License: Waukon, Allamakee County, IA held by Wennes Communications Stations Inc.
Population Served: 250,000; *Arbitron Metro Market:* Anchorage, AK; *Format:* Oldies
Dr. D.L. Van Voorhis, President
Bill DeGeorge, General Manager

Waverly

KWAY
05-06-1958; 1470 kHz AM; 1 kw-D, DA2; 0.061 kw-N, DA2; N42 42 13 W92 28 21
P.O. Box 307, 110 29th Ave Sw, Waverly, IA 50677 US
(319) 352-3550; *Fax:* (319) 352-3601
www.kwayradio.com
License: Waverly, IA held by Ael Suhr Enterprises Inc.
Arbitron Metro Market: Waverly, IA; *Format:* Country
Ael Suhr, President

KWAY-FM
12-21-1971; 99.3 MHz FM; 4.6 kw; 180 ft.; N42 42 13 W92 28 21
P.O. Box 307, Waverly, IA 50677 US
(319) 352-3550; *Fax:* (319) 352-3601
www.kwayradio.com
Kwayradio@kwayradio.com
License: Waverly, Bremer County, IA held by Ael Suhr Enterprises Inc.
Arbitron Metro Market: Waverly, IA; *Format:* Adult Contemp
Paul Bjornstad, General Manager

*KWVI
01-01-2006; 88.9 MHz FM; 20 kw vert; 274 ft.; N42 47 21 W92 14 22 *Rebroadcasts:* Rebroadcasts WAFR(FM) Tupelo, MS 100%
P.O. Box 3206, Tupelo, MS 38803 US
(662) 844-8888; *Fax:* (662) 842-6791
www.afr.net
faq@afa.net
License: Waverly, Bremer County, IA held by American Family Association.
Group Owner: American Family Radio
Format: Christian
Tim Wildmon, President
Donald Wildmon, Founder
Buddy Smith, Sr VP
Ed Vitagliano, Exec VP
Randy Sharp, Director Of Special Projects
Meeke Addison, Director Of Communications
Abraham Hamilton III, General Counsel

***KWAR**
01-01-2008; 89.9 MHz FM; *Hrs Open:* 24; 0.1 kw; 85 ft.; N42 43 37 W92 29 1
Eight St & First Ave NW, Waverly, IA 50677 US
(319) 352-8209; *Fax:* (319) 352-8610
yoursound.kwar@gmail.com
License: Waverly, Bremer County, IA held by Wartburg College.
Arbitron Metro Market: Waverly, IA; *Format:* Contemporary Hits/Top 40; *Target Audience:* General.
Matt Gruemmer, Station Manager
Holly Heljik, Programming Director

Webster City

KQWC
02-05-1950; 1570 kHz AM; 250 w-D, 132 w-N; 436 ft; N42 27 45 W93 48 05
Box 550, Webster City, IA 50595
(515) 832-1570; *Fax:* (515) 832-2079
kqradio.com
mharris@nrgmedia.com
License: Webster City, Hamilton County, IA held by NRG License Sub. LLC.
Group Owner: NRG Media LLC; (acq 10-31-2005; grpsl)
Population Served: 50,000 *Special Programming:* Farm 8 hrs wkly; *Hrs. of News Programming:* news progmg 45 hrs wkly; *No. News Employees:* 1; *Target Audience:* 50 plus; affluent with max spendable income *Adv.Rates:* 11; 9; 8; 6
Chuck DuCoty, COO
Mary Quass, CEO/Pressident
Mary Harris, General Manager
Rhonda Martin, Business Manager
Chris Lockwood, Programming Director
Pat Powers, News Director
George Nicholas, Chief Engineer
Chris Lockwood, DiscJockey
Doug Bremer, Sports Director

KQWC-FM
01-01-1969; 95.7 MHz FM; 25 kw; 436 ft; N42 28 04 W93 47 48
1020 East 2nd Street, Webster City, IA 50595
(515) 832-1570; *Fax:* (515) 832-2079
www.kqradio.com
License: Webster City, Hamilton County, IA
Group Owner: NRG Media LLC
Nat'l Network: ABC
Hrs. of News Programming: news progmg 35 hrs wkly; *No. News Employees:* 1; *Adv. Rates:* 24; 18; 16; 12
Chuck DuCoty, COO
Mary Quass, CEO/President
Mary Harris, General Manager
Rhonda Martin, Business Manager
Chris Lockwood, Programming Director
Pat Powers, News Director
George Nicholas, Chief Engineer
Chris Lockwood, DiscJockey
Doug Bremer, Sports Director

West Des Moines

KJJY
01-01-1978; 92.5 MHz FM; *Hrs Open:* 24; 41 kw; Ant 541 ft; N41 39 53 W93 45 25
4143 109th St., Urbandale, IA 50322 US
(515) 331-9200
www.925nashicon.com
License: West Des Moines, IA held by Radio License Holding CBC, LLC
Group Owner: Cumulus Media Inc.; (acq 8-29-03; grpsl).
Nat'l Reps: Christal
Population Served: 758,000; *Arbitron Metro Market:* Des Moines, IA; *Format:* Country; *Target Audience:* 25-54; general
Bob Jenkins, General Sales Mgr
Jonathan Monk, Programming Director

***KWDM**
03-01-1976; 88.7 MHz FM; *Hrs Open:* 14; 0.1 kw; 171 ft.; N41 35 25 W93 45 10
1140 35th Street, West Des Moines, IA 50265 US
(515) 226-2660; *Fax:* (515) 226-2609
kwdmfm@hotmail.com
License: West Des Moines, Polk County, IA held by West Des Moines Community School District.
Arbitron Metro Market: West Des Moines, IA; *Format:* Alternative
Special Programming: Sports 3 hrs wkly; *Hrs. of News Programming:* News progmg 3 hrs wkly; *Target Audience:* 12-25; educ facility-var progmg
Maren Tuttle/Ben Swanson, Station Managers
Jannell Mikels, Faculty Advisors

Whiting

KKYY
12-11-1979; 101.3 MHz FM; *Hrs Open:* 24; 50 kw; 492 ft.; N42 21 25 W96 8 2
P.O. Box 2307, Newburgh, NY 12550 US
(712) 258-5655
License: Whiting, Monona County, IA held by Powell Broadcasting Co. Inc.
Group Owner: Powell Broadcasting Co. Inc.; (acq 5-1-2007; $4.2 million with KZSR(FM) Onawa)
Nat'l Network: Motor Racing Net; Westwood One; ABC
Arbitron Metro Market: Sioux City, IA; *Format:* Country; *Hrs. of News Programming:* news progmg 20 hrs wkly; *No. News Employees:* 1; *Target Audience:* 18-54; adult men & women;
Adv. Rates: 15; 15; 15; 12
Jerry Haack, General Manager
Kelli Erickson, General Sales Mgr
Tim Guentz, Programming Director
Pam Guntz, Chief Engineer

Winterset

KPUL
03-01-1994; 99.5 MHz FM; *Hrs Open:* 24; 6 kw; 328 ft.; N41 24 2 W93 54 58
5911 Meredith Drive, Ste A, Des Moines, IA 50322 US
(515) 987-9995; *Fax:* (515) 987-9808
www.pulse995.com/
info@pulse995.com
License: Winterset, Madison County, IA held by Positive Impact Media Inc.
Arbitron Metro Market: Des Moines, IA; *Format:* Christian; *Target Audience:* Families.
David Nadler Jr., General Manager

Kansas

Abilene

KABI
04-08-1963; 1560 kHz AM; *Hrs Open:* 24; 0.25 kw-D, ND2; 0.058 kw-N, ND2; N38 55 46 W97 14 46
131 N. Sante Fe, P.O. Box 80, Salina, KS 67402 US
(785) 823-1111; *Fax:* (785) 823-2034
www.kabiabilene.com
License: Abilene, Dickinson County, KS held by Alpha Media Licensee LLC
Group Owner: Alpha Media LLC; (acq 9-2-2015; grpsl).
Nat'l Network: ABC; *Regional Network:* Kan. Agriculture
Arbitron Metro Market: Salina, KS; *Format:* Adult Contemp
Special Programming: Relg 4 hrs wkly; *Hrs. of News Programming:* news progmg 2 hrs wkly; *No. News Employees:* 1;
Target Audience: 35 plus; locresidents of Dickinson County; *Adv. Rates:* 12.22; 9.17; 11; 3.67
Bob Protzman, Station Manager
Mitch Drees, Sales Manager
John Anderson, Programming Director
Clarke Sanders, Promotions Manager
Todd Pittenger, News Director
Mark Beaver, Traffic Manager

KSAJ-FM
12-10-1968; 98.5 MHz FM; *Hrs Open:* 24; 100 kw; 440 ft.; N38 47 50 W97 13 1
131 N. Santa Fe, P.O. Box 80, Salina, KS 67402 US
(785) 823-1111; *Fax:* (785) 823-2034
www.trueoldies985.com
License: Abilene, Dickinson County, KS held by Alpha Media Licensee LLC
Group Owner: Alpha Media LLC
Nat'l Network: ABC; *Regional Network:* Kan. Info; *Nat'l Reps:* Katz Radio
Arbitron Metro Market: Salina, KS; *Format:* Oldies; *Hrs. of News Programming:* news progmg 3 hrs wkly; *No. News Employees:* 1;
Target Audience: 35-64; baby boomers; *Adv. Rates:* 16.53; 12.39; 14.87; 4.96
Bob Protzman, Station Manager
Mitch Drees, Sales Manager
John Anderson, Programming Director
Clarke Sanders, Promotions Manager
Todd Pittenger, News Director

Arkansas City

***KAXR**
01-01-2001; 91.3 MHz FM; 13.5 kw; 322 ft.; N36 55 32 W97 1 34
P.O. Box 3206, Tupelo, MS 38803 US
(662) 844-8888; *Fax:* (662) 842-6791
www.afr.net
faq@afa.net
License: Arkansas City, Cowley County, KS held by American Family Association.
Group Owner: American Family Radio
Arbitron Metro Market: Tupelo, MS; *Format:* Christian, Religious
Tim Wildmon, President
Donald Wildmon, Founder
Buddy Smith, Sr VP
Ed Vitagliano, Exec VP
Randy Sharp, Director Of Special Projects
Meeke Addison, Director Of Communications
Abraham Hamilton III, General Counsel & Public Policy

KACY
02-01-1999; 102.5 MHz FM; *Hrs Open:* 24; 6 kw; 328 ft.; N37 5 1 W96 55 46
P O Box 1704, Stafford, TX 77477 US
(620) 442-1102; *Fax:* (620) 442-8102
www.1025theriver.com
License: Arkansas City, Cowley County, KS held by Third Coast Broadcasting.
Arbitron Metro Market: Wichita, KS; *Format:* Rock/AOR, Triple A
Marshall Ice, General Manager

KSOK
01-01-1947; 1280 kHz AM; *Hrs Open:* 24; 1 kw-D, 100 w-N; N37 05 19 W97 01 56
334 E. Radio Ln., Arkansas City, KS 66762
(620) 442-5400; *Fax:* (620) 442-5401
www.ksokradio.com
ksok@ksokradio.com
License: Arkansas City, Cowley County, KS held by Cowley County Broadcasting Inc.
Nat'l Network: CBS; *Regional Network:* Kan. Agriculture
No. News Employees: 1; *Target Audience:* 22-55; blue collar, middle America, people who have children, are still working, & have mortgages; *Adv. Rates:* 26; 22; 24; 15
Brian Cunningham, Operations Dir
Marty Mutti, General Manager
Pam Miller, General Sales Mgr
Blake Carter, Promotions Manager
Shawn Wheat, News Director
Christy Bursack, Chief of Operations

KYQQ
11-01-1979; 106.5 MHz FM; 100 kw; 1280 ft.; N37 21 24 W96 57 55
3355 S. Valley View Boulevard, Las Vegas, NV 89102 US
(316) 436-1065; *Fax:* (316) 838-3607
www.radiolobo1065.com
License: Arkansas City, Cowley County, KS held by Journal Broadcast Corp.
Group Owner: Journal Communications Inc.; (acq 6-11-99; grpsl)
Arbitron Metro Market: Arkansas City, KS; *Format:* Tejano;
Target Audience: 18-49; Hispanic
Rob Burton, Operations Dir
Eric McCart, General Sales Mgr
Beverlee Brannigan, Programming Director
Manny Cowzinski, Promotions Manager

Arlington

KNZS
09-15-1989; 100.3 MHz FM; *Hrs Open:* 24 Hours; 14.5 kw; 443 ft.; N37 55 41 W98 17 58
10 E. 5th Ave., Hutchinson, KS 67501 US
(620) 665-5758; *Fax:* (620) 665-5758
www.adastraradio.com
ksku@adastra.kscoxmail.com
License: Arlington, Reno County, KS held by Ad Astra Per Aspera Broadcasting Inc.
Group Owner: Ad Astra Per Aspera Broadcasting Inc.; (acq 12-13-2007; exchange for KIBB(FM) Haven)
Nat'l Network: Jones Radio Networks
Arbitron Metro Market: Hutchinson, KS; *Format:* Classic Rock;
Hrs. of News Programming: 2 hours weekly; *No. News Employees:* 1; *Target Audience:* Adults 25-64

Atchison

KAIR
07-28-1939; 1470 kHz AM; 1 kw-U, DA1; N39 37 9 W94 59 27
P.O. Box G, 200 N. 5th St., Atchison, KS 66002 US
(913) 367-1470; *Fax:* (913) 367-7021
www.kairfm.com
kairradio@gmail.com
License: Atchison, KS held by KNZA Inc.
Group Owner: KNZA Inc.; (acq 8-13-2007 with KAIR-FM Horton)
Nat'l Network: EWTN Radio

Arbitron Metro Market: Atchison, KS; *Format:* Country; *Target Audience:* General; 25-65; *Adv. Rates:* 16; 14; 16; 10
J.C. Martin, Operations Dir
Neil Wieland, Programming Director

Augusta

KFXJ
04-01-1992; 104.5 MHz FM; *Hrs Open:* 24; 45 kw; 515 ft.; N37 48 15 W97 15 56
Mailing Address: 3355 S. Valley View Boulevard, Las Vegas, NV 89102 US
Second Address: 4200 N. Old Lawrence Rd., Wichita, KS 67219
(316) 838-9141; *Fax:* (316) 838-3607
www.1045thefox.com
License: Augusta, Butler County, KS held by Journal Broadcast Corp.
Group Owner: Journal Communications Inc.; (acq 6-11-99; grpsl)
Arbitron Metro Market: Wichita, KS; *Format:* Classic Rock; *Target Audience:* 25-54.
Rob Burton, Operations Dir
Eric McCart, General Sales Mgr
Manny Cowzinski, Promotions Manager
Ray Michaels, Operations Manager
Jason Wituk

KVWF
01-01-2006; 100.5 MHz FM; 25 kw; 276 ft.; N37 44 13 W97 9 25 US
(316) 558-8800; *Fax:* (316) 558-8802
kvwf@1005thewolf.com
License: Augusta, Butler County, KS held by Connoisseur Media Licenses LLC
Group Owner: Connoisseur Media Licenses LLC
Arbitron Metro Market: Augusta, KS; *Format:* Country
Trace Taul, Operations Dir
Doug Downs, General Manager
Ron Allen, Programming Director

Baldwin City

*KNBU
11-29-1965; 89.7 MHz FM; 0.1 kw; 118 ft.; N38 46 45 W95 11 15
PO Box 65, Baldwin City, KS 66006 US
(785) 594-6451; *Fax:* (785) 594-3570
License: Baldwin City, Douglas County, KS held by Baker University.
Special Programming: Jazz 15 hrs wkly
Tom Hedrick, General Manager

Baxter Springs

KCAR-FM
06-29-2000; 104.3 MHz FM; 6 kw; 299 ft.; N37 7 34 W94 42 12
C/O Putbrese, Hunsaker, P. O. Box 539, Sterling, VA 20167 US
(417) 781-1313; *Fax:* (417) 781-1316
www.lol1043.com
License: Baxter Springs, Cherokee County, KS held by American Media Investments Inc.
Group Owner: American Media Investments Inc.; (acq 2-17-2009; grpsl)
Arbitron Metro Market: Joplin, MO; *Format:* Classic Rock, Oldies
Dave Clemons, General Sales Mgr
Bubba Fontaine, Programming Director
Kathleen Pike, News Director

Belle Plaine

KHLT
03-04-1996; 99.7 MHz FM; *Hrs Open:* 24; 50 kw; 482 ft.; N37 20 8 W97 27 53
3436 Edgemont, Witchita, KS 67208 US
(316) 652-9275; *Fax:* (316) 683-0818
fiesta927@gmail.com
License: Belle Plaine, Sumner County, KS held by Air Capital Media Group
Arbitron Metro Market: Witchita, KS
Shane Krill, President

Belleville

KREP
06-26-1984; 92.1 MHz FM; *Hrs Open:* 24; 14.5 kw; 276 ft.; N39 45 0 W97 36 48
2307 West Frontage Road, Belleville, KS 66935 US
(785) 527-2266; *Fax:* (785) 527-5919
www.kr92country.com
kr-92@nckcn.com
License: Belleville, Republic County, KS held by First Republic Broadcasting Corp.
Nat'l Network: ABC
Format: Country; *Hrs. of News Programming:* news progmg 20 hrs wkly; *No. News Employees:* 1; *Target Audience:* 25-55.; *Adv. Rates:* 15.00;15.00;15.00;15.00
Deborah Sasser, President
Christine Strutt, General Sales Mgr
Eric Allgood, News Director
Marvin Hoffman, Chief Engineer
Eric Allgood, Sales/Sports Director

Beloit

KVSV
11-21-1979; 1190 kHz AM; *Hrs Open:* 6 AM-9 PM; 2.3 kw-D, DA1; 0.09 kw-N, DA1; N39 26 53 W98 4 45
PO Box 7, Beloit, KS 67420 US
(785) 738-2206; *Fax:* (785) 738-2208
www.kvsvradio.com
webmaster@kvsvradio.com
License: Beloit, KS held by McGrath Publishing Co.
Regional Network: Kan. Agriculture
Arbitron Metro Market: Beloit, KS; *Format:* Adult Contemp
Special Programming: Farm 9 hrs wkly; *Hrs. of News Programming:* news progmg 11 hrs wkly; *No. News Employees:* 1; *Target Audience:* General.
John Swanson, Station Manager
Sharon Keister, General Sales Mgr
Aaron Rut, Programming Director

KVSV-FM
11-11-1980; 105.5 MHz FM; *Hrs Open:* 24; 50 kw; 443 ft.; N39 28 9 W98 5 37
P.O. Box 7, Beloit, KS 67420 US
(785) 738-2206; *Fax:* (785) 738-2208
www.kvsvradio.com
webmaster@kvsvradio.com
License: Beloit, Mitchell County, KS
Arbitron Metro Market: Beloit, KS; *Format:* Easy Listening
John Swanson, Station Manager
Sharon Keister, General Sales Mgr

Bronson

*KBJQ
01-01-2002; 88.3 MHz FM; 36 kw; 381 ft.; N37 53 56 W95 0 9
P.O. Box 3206, Tupelo, MS 38803 US
(662) 844-8888; *Fax:* (662) 842-6791
www.afr.net
faq@afa.net
License: Bronson, Bourbon County, KS held by American Family Association.
Group Owner: American Family Radio
Arbitron Metro Market: Tupelo, MS; *Format:* Religious
Tim Wildmon, President
Donald Wildmon, Founder
Buddy Smith, Senior VP
Ed Vitagliano, Exec VP
Randy Sharp, Cirector Of Special Projects
Meeke Addison, Director Of Communications
Abraham Hamilton III, General Counsel & PublicPolicy Analyst

Burdett

KKDT
93.5 MHz FM; 95 kw; 1000 ft.; N38 36 32 W99 42 11 US
(785) 222-3400; *Fax:* (785) 222-3405
glen.hoyt@postrockradio.com
License: Burdett, Pawnee County, KS held by Post Rock Radio
Group Owner: Post Rock Radio
Arbitron Metro Market: Burdett, KS; *Format:* Adult Contemp
Glen Hoyt, General Manager

Burlington

KSNP
06-14-1990; 97.7 MHz FM; *Hrs Open:* 6 AM-11 PM; 17.2 kw; 584 ft.; N38 9 57 W95 32 19
PO Box 233, Burlington, KS 66839 US
(620) 364-8807
www.977thedawg.com
License: Burlington, Coffey County, KS held by My Town Media, Inc.
Group Owner: My Town Media, Inc.; (acq 1999; $230,000)
Regional Network: Mid-America Ag
Arbitron Metro Market: Burlington, KS; *Format:* Classic Rock
Special Programming: Farm 8 hrs, relg 3 hrs wkly; *Hrs. of News Programming:* news progmg 5 hrs wkly; *No. News Employees:* 1
Target Audience: 25-45; industrial employees; *Adv. Rates:* 9.25; na; 6; 3.50
Rob Gilligan, Station Manager

Caney

KEOJ
10-15-1992; 101.1 MHz FM; *Hrs Open:* 24; 6 kw; 328 ft.; N36 58 19 W95 53 47
P.O. Box 1250, Sapulpa, OK 74067 US
(918) 492-2660; *Fax:* (918) 492-8840
www.kxoj.com
kxoj@kxoj.com
License: Caney, Montgomery County, KS held by KXOJ Inc.
Group Owner: Adonai Radio Group; (acq 4-29-92; grpsl)
Arbitron Metro Market: Tulsa, OK; *Format:* Christian; *Target Audience:* 18-35; young married Christians
Mike Stephens, President
Joy Stephens, Operations Dir
David Stephens, General Manager
Bob Thornton, Programming Director
Darcy Kimble, News Director
Joe Hancock, Chief Engineer

Carbondale

KMAJ-FM
07-01-1971; 107.7 MHz FM; 53 kw; 772 ft.; N38 57 15 W95 54 43
330 East Kilbourn Ave., Suite 250, Milwaukee, WI 53202 US
(785) 272-2122; *Fax:* (785) 272-6219
www.kmaj.com
License: Carbondale, Shawnee County, KS held by Kansas City Trust LLC, Trustee
Nat'l Network: Westwood One
Arbitron Metro Market: Topeka, KS; *Format:* Adult Contemp
John Walker, General Manager
Keith Liefmann, General Sales Mgr
Rich Bowers, Programming Director
Carla Newman, Promotions Manager
Mike Manns, News Director

Cawker City

KZDY
01-01-1999; 96.3 MHz FM; *Hrs Open:* 24; 13 kw; 230 ft.; N39 30 29 W98 18 57
937 Jayhawk Rd., Marysville, KS 66508 US
(785) 562-2361
www.kdcountry94.com
License: Cawker City, Mitchell County, KS held by Dierking Communications Inc.
Group Owner: Dierking Communications Inc.; (acq 7-27-2006).
Nat'l Network: Jones Radio Networks; AP Radio
Arbitron Metro Market: Glen Elder, KS; *Format:* Adult Contemp; *Hrs. of News Programming:* news progmg 6 hrs wkly; *No. News Employees:* 1; *Target Audience:* 18-60.
Bruce Dierking, President/General Manager

Chanute

KKOY
11-17-1952; 1460 kHz AM; *Hrs Open:* 24
702 N. Plummer St., Chanute, KS 66801 US
(620) 431-3700
www.kkoy.com
License: Chanute, KS held by Southeast Kansas Broadcasting Co. Inc.
Group Owner: My Town Media, Inc.; (acq 5-21-97; $464,447 with co-located FM)
Nat'l Network: ESPN Radio
Arbitron Metro Market: Joplin, MO; *Format:* Country; *Target Audience:* 25-54.; *Adv. Rates:* 10.50; 7.50; 7.50; 5.00
Bill Wachter, President

KKOY-FM
01-01-1971; 105.5 MHz FM; *Hrs Open:* 24; 8 kw; 584 ft.; N37 35 59 W95 39 10
702 N. Plummer St., Chanute, KS 66801 US
(620) 431-3700
www.kkoy.com
License: Chanute, Neosho County, KS held by Southeast Kansas Broadcasting Co. Inc.
Group Owner: My Town Media, Inc.
Nat'l Network: ABC
Arbitron Metro Market: Joplin, MO; *Format:* Adult Contemp; *Adv. Rates:* Same as AM
Bill Wachter, President

*KANQ
90.3 MHz FM; 17 kw; Ant 528 ft; N37 35 59 W95 39 10
Box 14, Abilene, KS
(785) 263-7200; *Fax:* (785) 263-3876
www.kjil1057.com
radioforlife@kjil.com

License: Chanute, Neosho County, KS held by Great Plains Christian Radio Inc.

Robert Hughes, CEO

Cimarron

KMML
02-01-2008; 92.9 MHz FM; 32 kw; 610 ft.; N37 56 29.6 W100 18 44.3 *Rebroadcasts:* Rebroadcasts KSMM-FM Liberal 100% US
(620) 225-8080; *Fax:* (620) 624-4606
www.rockingmradio.com
License: Cimarron, Gray County, KS held by Radioactive LLC.
Group Owner: Radioactive LLC
Arbitron Metro Market: Cimarron, KS
Benjamin Homel, President
Enrique Franz, General Manager

Clay Center

KCLY
01-06-1978; 100.9 MHz FM; 35.5 kw; 581 ft.; N39 28 3 W97 3 45
Box 16, Clay Center, KS 67432 US
(785) 632-5661; *Fax:* (785) 632-5662
www.kclyradio.com
rhys@kclyradio.com
License: Clay Center, Clay County, KS held by Taylor Communications.
Nat'l Network: AP Network News; *Wire Services:* AP
Arbitron Metro Market: Topeka, KS; *Format:* Adult Contemp; *Target Audience:* 24-55; general
Kyle Bauer, General Manager
Rocky Downing, Station Manager
Joyce Beck, General Sales Mgr
Jamie Bloom, Programming Director
Michelle Tessaro, News Director
Rod Keen, Engineering Dir
Rhys Baker, Traffic/Billing
Duane Toews, FarmDirector
Susan Carlson, Advertising Consultant
Phil Casper, After Hours Director
Clay Dalquest, Sales Department
Angie Komar, Production Manager

Clearwater

KFH-FM
07-04-1995; 98.7 MHz FM; *Hrs Open:* 24; 50 kw; 492 ft.; N37 24 11 W97 35 22
331 Lookout Point, Hot Springs, AR 71913 US
(316) 685-2121; *Fax:* (316) 685-3408
www.kfhradio.com
letters@kfhradio.com
License: Clearwater, Sedgwick County, KS held by Entercom Witicha License LLC.
Group Owner: Entercom Communications Corp.; (acq 5-8-00; $2 million).
Arbitron Metro Market: Wichita, KS; *Format:* Sports, Talk; *Target Audience:* 18-49; general; *Adv. Rates:* 20; 20; 20; 20
Jackie Wise, General Manager
Mark Yearout, General Sales Mgr
Tony Duesing, Programming Director
Jessie Hosning, News Director
Craig Maudlin, Chief Engineer

Coffeyville

KGGF AM
01-01-1930; 690 kHz AM; 5 kW; N37 8 47 W95 28 42
306 West 8th St, Coffeyville, KS 67337 USA
(620) 251-3800
kggfradio.linkedupradio.com/kggf-am
License: Coffeyville, KS held by Sek Media
Group Owner: Sek Media
Nat'l Network: Fox News; *Regional Network:* Radio Oklahoma Network
Arbitron Metro Market: Coffeyville, KS; *Format:* News, News/Talk, 86; *No. News Employees:* 1; *Target Audience:* 35 plus.

KQQF
09-01-1983; 98.9 MHz FM; *Hrs Open:* 24; 3.2 kW; 361 ft.; N37 6 28 W95 43 22
306 West 8th St, Coffeyville, KS 67337 USA
(620) 251-3800; *Fax:* (620) 251-9210
kggfradio.linkedupradio.com/kqqf-fm
License: Coffeyville, Montgomery County, KS held by Sek Media
Group Owner: Sek Media
Arbitron Metro Market: Coffeyville, KS; *Format:* Contemporary Hits/Top 40; *No. News Employees:* 1; *Target Audience:* 35-54.

Colby

KRDQ
09-01-1971; 100.3 MHz FM; *Hrs Open:* 24; 100 kw; 610 ft.; N39 28 50 W100 54 34
1065 S. Range, Colby, KS 67701 US
(785) 462-3305; *Fax:* (785) 462-3307
www.nwksradio.com
sacha@rockingmradio.com
License: Colby, Thomas County, KS held by Melia Communications Inc.
Group Owner: Melia Communications Inc.
Nat'l Network: ABC; *Regional Network:* Mid-America Ag
Format: Adult Contemp; *Target Audience:* 18-49; general
Chelsea Kinnett, Operations Dir
Sacha Sanguinetti, General Manager
Will Sterrett, News Director

***KTCC**
05-01-1974; 91.9 MHz FM; *Hrs Open:* 24; 3 kw; 180 ft.; N39 22 34 W101 3 8
1255 South Range Ave, Colby, KS 67701 US
(785) 462-3984 EXT. 309; *Fax:* (785) 462-4600
www.colbycc.edu
License: Colby, Thomas County, KS held by Colby Community College.
Arbitron Metro Market: Colby, KS; *Format:* Contemporary Hits/Top 40 *Special Programming:* Sports 3 hrs, classic rock 3 hrs, hard rock 7 hrs, hip hop 4 hrs wkly; *Hrs. of News Programming:* news progmg 14 hrs wkly *No.News Employees:* 1; *Target Audience:* 18-25; young adults
Dr.Stephen M Vacik, President
Corey Sorenson, Station Manager

KWGB
09-01-1998; 97.9 MHz FM; *Hrs Open:* 24; 100 kw; 709 ft.; N39 23 24 W101 33 35
1065 S Range, Colby, KS 67701 US
(785) 462-3305; *Fax:* (785) 462-3307
www.nwksradio.com
sacha@rockingmradio.com
License: Colby, Thomas County, KS held by Melia Communications Inc.
Group Owner: Melia Communications Inc.
Format: Country
Chelsea Kinnett, Operations Dir
Sacha Sanguinetti, General Manager
Will Sterrett, News Director

KXXX
08-01-1947; 790 kHz AM; *Hrs Open:* 24; 5 kw-D, ND1; 0.024 kw-N, ND1; N39 23 35 W101 0 6
1660 N. Tyler, Wichita, KS 67212 US
(785) 462-3305; *Fax:* (785) 462-3307
www.nwksradio.com
sacha@rockingmradio.com
License: Colby, KS held by Rocking M Radio Inc.
Group Owner: Rocking M Radio Inc.; (acq 8-31-2007; grpsl)
Nat'l Network: Westwood One; *Regional Network:* Mid-America Ag
Arbitron Metro Market: Colby, KS; *Format:* Country; *Hrs. of News Programming:* news progmg 5 hrs wkly; *No. News Employees:* 1; *Target Audience:* 35-55; male, female, city & rural
Christopher Miller, Vice President
Sacha Sanguinetti, General Manager
Joe Vyzourek, Programming Director
Radonda Buford, Business Manager
Ross Volkmer, Farm Director

Coldwater

***KNJT**
90.3 MHz FM; 1 kw; 128 ft.; N37 16 6 W99 19 33
505 Josephine Street, Titusville, FL 32796 US
(321) 267-3000; *Fax:* (321) 264-9370
wpio@gate.net
License: Coldwater, Comanche County, KS held by Florida Public Radio Inc.
Arbitron Metro Market: Coldwater, KS
Randy Henry, President
Brian Larson, General Manager

Columbus

KMOQ
12-25-1982; 105.3 MHz FM; *Hrs Open:* 24; 13.6 kw; 305 ft.; N37 7 34 W94 42 12
2510 W. 20th Street, Joplin, MO 64804 US
(417) 781-1313; *Fax:* (417) 781-1316
License: Columbus, Cherokee County, KS held by American Media Investments Inc.
Group Owner: American Media Investments Inc.; (acq 2-17-2009; grpsl)
Nat'l Network: ABC
Arbitron Metro Market: Joplin, MO; *Format:* Contemporary Hits/Top 40; *Target Audience:* 25-54.
George DeMarco, General Manager
Dave Clemons, General Sales Mgr
Chris Stevens, Programming Director
Kathleen Pike, News Director

KJML(FM)
02-01-1980; 107.1 MHz FM; 11.7 kw; Ant 489 ft; N37 14 15 W94 44 15
2510 W. 20th St., Joplin, MO 64804
(417) 781-1313; *Fax:* (417) 781-1316
License: Columbus, Cherokee County, KS held by American Media Investments Inc.
Group Owner: American Media Investments Inc.; (acq 2-17-2009; grpsl)
Nat'l Network: ABC
Arbitron Metro Market: Joplin, MO; *Hrs. of News Programming:* news progmg 2 hrs wkly; *No. News Employees:* 1; *Target Audience:* 18-49; growing families with needs for a wide range of goods & svcs; *Adv. Rates:* 10;8; 8; 6
George DeMarco, General Manager
Dave Clemons, General Sales Mgr
Bubba Fontaine, Programming Director
Kathleen Pike, News Director

KJML
107.1 MHz FM; 11.5 kw; 489 ft.; N37 14 15 W94 44 15
2510 W. 20th St., Joplin, MO 64804 US
(213) 494-3377
License: Columbus, Riverside County, KS held by Ether Mining Corp.
Arbitron Metro Market: Columbus, KS
Mark Mueller, Operations Dir

Concordia

KNCK
02-06-1954; 1390 kHz AM; *Hrs Open:* 24; 0.5 kw-D, ND1; 0.054 kw-N, ND1; N39 33 58 W97 41 4
P.O. Box 629, Concordia, KS 66901 US
(785) 243-1414; *Fax:* (785) 243-1391
License: Concordia, KS held by KNCK Inc.
Format: Country *Special Programming:* Public affrs 2 hrs wkly; *Hrs. of News Programming:* news progmg 7 hrs wkly; *No. News Employees:* 1; *Target Audience:* 45 plus.
Joe Jindra, President
Marvin Hoffman, Chief Engineer

***KVCO**
05-01-1977; 88.3 MHz FM; 0.125 kw; 75 ft.; N39 33 17 W97 39 48
2221 Campus Drive, Concordia, KS 66901 US
(785) 243-1435(785) 243-4444; *Fax:* (785) 243-1043
kvco@cloud.edu
License: Concordia, Cloud County, KS held by Cloud County Community College.
Nat'l Network: CNN Radio
Arbitron Metro Market: Concordia, KS; *Format:* Variety/Diverse; *Target Audience:* 16-30 plus; students & young adults
John Chapin, General Manager

Copeland

***KHYM**
12-23-1997; 103.9 MHz FM; *Hrs Open:* 24; 100 kw; 751 ft.; N37 28 35 W100 35 59
P.O. Box 991, Meade, KS 67864 US
(620) 873-2991; *Fax:* (620) 873-2755
www.khymfm.org
mike@khym.org
License: Copeland, Gray County, KS held by Great Plains Christian Radio Inc.
Format: Christian, Religious; *Hrs. of News Programming:* Family 4 hrs wkly, talk 7 hrs wkly; *No. News Employees:* 1; *Target Audience:* 25-54, Christians
Michael Luskey, President/CEO
Jerry Mann, Operations Dir
Glenn Hascall, Station Manager
Darrin Kinser, Underwriting Director
Steve Larson, Chief Engineer

***KJIL**
09-05-1992; 99.1 MHz FM; *Hrs Open:* 24; 100 kw; 935 ft.; N37 28 35 W100 35 59
P.O. Box 991, Meade, KS 67864 US
(620) 873-2991; *Fax:* (620) 873-2755
www.kjil.com
kjil@kjil.com

License: Copeland, Gray County, KS held by Great Plains Christian Radio Inc.
Nat'l Network: Moody; USA
Format: Christian, Religious; *Target Audience:* 25-60; Evangelical Christians
Don Hughes, President
Michael Luskey, Operations Dir
Delvin Kinser, News Director
Steve Larson, Chief Engineer
Polly Hughes, Traffic Manager

KSKZ
05-01-1994; 98.1 MHz FM; *Hrs Open:* 24; 100 kw; 666 ft.; N37 46 48 W100 27 36
C/O Fisher Wayland: Cmc, 2001 Penn. Ave., NW, Washington, DC 20006 US
(620) 276-2366; *Fax:* (620) 276-3568
License: Copeland, Gray County, KS held by Ingstad Broadcasting Inc.
Group Owner: Robert Ingstad Broadcast Properties; (acq 1-27-95;
Arbitron Metro Market: Green City, KS; *Format:* Adult Contemp; *Target Audience:* 25-54.
Gil Wohler, General Manager
James Janda, Programming Director
Andrew Mahoney, News Director
Tom Dial, Chief Engineer
Rachel Wheet, Traffic Manager

Dearing

KUSN
10-01-1999; 98.1 MHz FM; *Hrs Open:* 24 hours daily; 9.7 kW; 403 ft.; N37 6 28 W95 43 22
306 West 8th St, Coffeyville, KS 67337 USA
(620) 251-3800
kggfradio.linkedupradio.com/kusn-fm
License: Dearing, Montgomery County, KS held by Sek Media
Group Owner: Sek Media
Format: Country; *Target Audience:* 18-49.

Derby

KZCH
01-01-1978; 96.3 MHz FM; *Hrs Open:* 24; 50 kw; 492 ft.; N37 43 6 W97 19 5
9323 E. 37th St. N., Wichita, KS 67226-2000 US
(316) 494-6600; *Fax:* (316) 494-6730
www.channel963.com
info@channel963.com
License: Derby, Sedgwick County, KS held by Capstar TX LLC
Group Owner: iHeartMedia; (acq 8-30-2000; grpsl).
Nat'l Reps: Clear Channel
Arbitron Metro Market: Wichita, KS; *Format:* Contemporary Hits/Top 40; *Target Audience:* 18-34; women
Tony Matteo, Senior Vice President of Programming
Jeff McCausland, Market President
Tom Libby, Senior Vice President of Sales
Tommy Castor, Programming Director
Morgan Huelsman, Digital Content Director

Dodge City

KDCC
01-01-1992; 1550 kHz AM; *Hrs Open:* 7 AM-10 PM; 1 kw-D, DA2; 0.09 kw-N, DA2; N37 47 14 W100 1 55
2500 North 14th Avenue, Dodge City, KS 67801 US
(620) 225-6783(620) 225-6720; *Fax:* (620) 225-0918
License: Dodge City, KS held by Dodge City Community College.
Format: News; *Hrs. of News Programming:* News progmg 35 hrs wkly; *Target Audience:* 18 plus.
John Ewy, General Manager

KGNO
06-30-1930; 1370 kHz AM; 5 kw-D, ND1; 0.23 kw-N, ND1; N37 45 36 W100 5 53
Mailing Address: 1660 North Tyler Road, Wichita, KS 67212 US
Second Address: 106 W Frontview, Dodge City, KS 67801
(620) 225-8080; *Fax:* (620) 225-6655
www.rockingmradio.com
rockswks@sbcgobal.net
License: Dodge City, KS held by Rocking M Radio Inc.
Group Owner: Rocking M Radio Inc.; (acq 8-31-2007; grpsl)
Nat'l Network: ESPN Radio; Fox News Radio; *Regional Network:* Mid-America Ag
Format: News, Sports, 86 *Special Programming:* Farm 15 hrs wkly; *Target Audience:* 25-54.
Brian Nugen, Operations Dir
Mark Hinca, General Manager
Peggy Burdick, General Sales Mgr
Candace Thomas, News Director

KAHE
05-01-1966; 95.5 MHz FM; *Hrs Open:* 24; 100 kw; 577 ft.; N37 38 28 W100 20 40
Mailing Address: 1660 N. Tyler Rd., Wichita, KS 67212 US
Second Address: 106 W Frontview, Dodge City, KS 67801
(620) 225-8080; *Fax:* (620) 225-6655
www.rockingmradio.com
License: Dodge City, Ford County, KS held by Rocking M Radio Inc.
Group Owner: Rocking M Radio Inc.
Nat'l Network: Fox Sports
Format: Oldies; *Hrs. of News Programming:* News progmg 5 hrs wkly; *Target Audience:* 25-49.
Sacha Sanguinetti, General Manager
Jim Groth, General Sales Mgr
Candice Thomas, Business Manager

***KONQ**
04-26-1978; 91.9 MHz FM; 2.6 kw horiz; 125 ft.; N37 46 33 W100 2 12
2501 North 14th Street, Dodge City, KS 67801 US
(620) 225-6783,(620) 225-6720; *Fax:* (620) 225-0918
License: Dodge City, Ford County, KS held by Dodge City Community College.
Format: Adult Contemp, Variety/Diverse *Special Programming:* Black 10 hrs, sports 5 hrs wkly; *Hrs. of News Programming:* News progmg 7 hrs wkly
John Ewy, General Manager

KZRD
12-01-1997; 93.9 MHz FM; 100 kw; 807 ft.; N37 55 56 W100 19 2
Mailing Address: 1660 N. Tyler, Wichita, KS 67212 US
Second Address: 106 W Frontview, Dodge City, KS 67801
(785) 565-0406; *Fax:* (785) 565-0437
www.rockingmradio.com
cmiller@rockingmradio.com
License: Dodge City, Ford County, KS held by Rocking M Radio Inc.
Group Owner: Rocking M Radio Inc.; (acq 8-31-2007; grpsl)
Arbitron Metro Market: South West KS
Brian Michaels, Operations Dir
Sacha Sanguinetti, General Manager
Jim Groth, General Sales Mgr
Candice Thomas, Business Manager

***KAIG**
01-01-2008; 89.9 MHz FM; 100 kw vert; 696 ft.; N37 55 56 W100 19 2 *Rebroadcasts:* Rebroadcasts KLRD(FM) Yucaipa, CA 100%
1425 N Market Blvd., Suite 9, Sacramento, CA 95834 US
(800) 877-5600; *Fax:* (916) 251-1650
www.air1.com
info@air1.com
License: Dodge City, Ford County, KS held by Educational Media Foundation.
Group Owner: EMF Broadcasting
Nat'l Network: Air 1
Arbitron Metro Market: Centralia, WA; *Format:* Alternative, Christian
Mike Novak, President
David Pierce, Programming Director
Ed Lenane, News Director
Sam Wallington, Engineering Dir
Marya Morgan, News Reporter
Richard Hunt, News Reporter

Downs

KDNS
04-11-1994; 94.1 MHz FM; *Hrs Open:* 5 AM-1 AM; 28 kw; 292 ft.; N39 30 29 W98 18 57
PO Box 88, Glen Elder, KS 67446 US
(785) 545-3220
www.kdcountry94.com
License: Downs, Osborne County, KS held by Dierking Communications Inc.
Group Owner: Dierking Communications Inc.; (acq 7-27-2006; $276,000).
Nat'l Network: Jones Radio Networks; *Regional Network:* Brownfield
Arbitron Metro Market: Glen Elder, KS; *Format:* Country *Special Programming:* Farm 6 hrs, gospel 5 hrs wkly; *Hrs. of News Programming:* news progmg 4 hrs wkly; *No. News Employees:* 1; *Target Audience:* 25-54.
Bruce Dierking, President/General Manager

Effingham

KDVB
03-12-2008; 96.9 MHz FM; 0.12 kw; 227 ft.; N39 33 7 W95 25 23
US
(785) 272-2122; *Fax:* (785) 272-6219
www.v100rocks.com
License: Effingham, Atchison County, KS held by Cumulus Licensing LLC.
Group Owner: Cumulus Media Inc.
Arbitron Metro Market: Effingham, KS
Spike Santee, General Manager
Ian, Promotions Manager

El Dorado

***KBTL**
03-01-1998; 88.1 MHz FM; 0.4 kw; 92 ft.; N37 48 16 W96 53 2
901 S. Haverhill Road, El Dorado, KS 67042 US
(316) 321-2222
License: El Dorado, Butler County, KS held by Butler County Community College.
Arbitron Metro Market: El Dorado, KS; *Format:* Variety/Diverse
Dr. Keith West, General Manager

KAHS
11-16-1953; 1360 kHz AM; *Hrs Open:* 24; 1 kw-D; N37 48 47 W96 48 44
201 N. Industrial Park Rd., Excelsior Springs, MO 74152
(316) 320-1360
www.1360kahs.com
1360kahs@gmail.com
License: El Dorado, Butler County, KS held by Catholic Radio Network Inc.
Group Owner: Catholic Radio Network Inc.; (acq 12-12-2005; $525,000)
Nat'l Network: CNN Radio; Westwood One
Population Served: 500,000; *Arbitron Metro Market:* Wichita, KS
Special Programming: Jazz 2 hrs wkly; *Target Audience:* 35-69.
James O'Laughlin, President

***KTLI**
02-15-1972; 99.1 MHz FM; 100 kw; 617 ft.; N37 56 22 W96 59 20
P.O. Box 1250, Sapulpa, OK 74067 US
(316) 303-9999; *Fax:* (316) 303-9900
k-love.com
License: El Dorado, Butler County, KS held by El Dorado Licenses Inc.
Group Owner: EMF Broadcasting; (acq 12-3-2004; $2.95 million).
Arbitron Metro Market: Wichita, KS; *Format:* Adult Contemp, Christian; *Hrs. of News Programming:* News progmg 25 hrs wkly; *Target Audience:* 25-54; women

Elk City

KIND-FM
94.9 MHz FM; 6 kw; 272 ft.; N37 15 42 W95 45 59
US
(620)331-6669; *Fax:* (620)331-8008
License: Elk City, KS
Group Owner: Tallgrass Broadcasting LLC
Format: Country

Emporia

KFFX
06-15-1966; 104.9 MHz FM; *Hrs Open:* 24; 3 kw; 279 ft.; N38 23 10 W96 10 36
P.O. Box 968, Emporia, KS 66801 US
(620) 342-1400; *Fax:* (620) 342-0804
www.todaysbesthits.com
License: Emporia, Lyon County, KS
Group Owner: Emporia's Radio Stations Inc.
Arbitron Metro Market: Emporia, KS; *Format:* Adult Contemp; *Hrs. of News Programming:* News progmg 4 hrs wkly; *Target Audience:* 20-40.
Steve Rocha, Programming Director
Esther Johnson, News Director

***KJLG**
01-11-1987; 91.9 MHz FM; *Hrs Open:* 24; 3 kw; Ant 263 ft; N38 24 35 W96 13 30
Box 506, 815 Graham St., Emporia, KS 66801
(620) 343-9292
kngm@osprey.net
License: Emporia, Lyon County, KS held by Great Plains Christian Radio Inc.
Population Served: 60,000; *No. News Employees:* 1; *Target Audience:* Young families and adults.
Robert Hughes, CEO

***KPOR**
06-19-2002; 90.7 MHz FM; *Hrs Open:* 24; 2 kw; 328 ft.; N38 26 50 W96 7 42
4135 Northgate Blvd, Suite 1, Sacramento, CA 95834 US
(316) 342-1474
www.familyradio.com
info@familyradio.com
License: Emporia, Lyon County, KS held by Family Stations Inc.
Group Owner: Family Stations Inc.
Arbitron Metro Market: Topeka, KS; *Format:* Religious
Tom Evans, General Manager

KANS
04-01-1998; 96.1 MHz FM; 6 kw; 318 ft.; N38 24 21 W96 14 13
1811 6th Avenue, Emporia, KS 66801 US
(620) 343-9393; *Fax:* (620) 342-7617
kans@ksradio.com
License: Emporia, Lyon County, KS held by C&C Consulting Inc.
Arbitron Metro Market: Emporia, KS; *Format:* Classic Rock
Marty Hill, General Manager
Lisa Vega, General Sales Mgr
Angie Boden, Programming Director
Brook Reed, News Director

KVOE
01-21-1939; 1400 kHz AM; 1 kw-U, ND1; N38 23 10 W96 10 36
P.O. Box 968, Emporia, KS 66801 US
(620) 342-1400; *Fax:* (620) 342-0804
www.kvoe.com
kvoe@kvoe.com
License: Emporia, KS held by Emporia Radio Stations Inc.
Group Owner: Emporia's Radio Stations Inc.; (acq 1-7-87)
Arbitron Metro Market: Emporia, KS; *Format:* Adult Contemp, News, 64 *Special Programming:* Sp 3 hrs wkly; *Target Audience:* 35-54.
Ron Thomas, General Manager
Erren Harter, Promotions Manager
Jeff O'Dell, News Director
Charlie Allen, Chief Engineer
Greg Rahe, Sports Commentator
Karri Kimberlin, Traffic
Gwen Longbine, Sales
Terry Bontrager,Receptionist/Traffic
Anne Orender, Sales

KVOE-FM
01-16-1985; 101.7 MHz FM; *Hrs Open:* 24; 3.2 kw; 299 ft.; N38 21 45 W96 7 0
P.O. Box 968, Emporia, KS 66801 US
(620) 342-1400; *Fax:* (620) 342-0804
www.kvoe.com
kvoe@kvoe.com
License: Emporia, Lyon County, KS held by Emporia Radio Stations Inc.
Group Owner: Emporia's Radio Stations Inc.; (acq 1994)
Arbitron Metro Market: Emporia, KS; *Format:* Country; *Hrs. of News Programming:* news progmg 7 hrs wkly; *No. News Employees:* 2; *Target Audience:* 25-54.
Steve Sauder, CEO
Ron Thomas, General Manager
Erren Harter, Promotions Manager
Charlie Allen, Chief Engineer
Greg Rahe, Sports Commentator
Karri Kimberlin, Traffic
Gwen Longbine, Sales
Terry Bontrager, Receptionist/Traffic
Anne Orender, Sales

***KANH**
01-01-2002; 89.7 MHz FM; 3 kw; 262 ft.; N38 21 45 W96 7 0
Broadcasting Hall, Lawrence, KS 66045 US
(785) 864-4530; *Fax:* (785) 864-5278
www.kpr.ku.edu
kpr@ku.edu
License: Emporia, Lyon County, KS held by University of Kansas.
Nat'l Network: NPR
Arbitron Metro Market: Lawrence, KS; *Format:* Jazz
Janet Campbell, General Manager
Darrell Brogdon, Programming Director
Mark Edwards, Promotions Manager
J. Schafer, News Director
Sheri Hamilton, Development Director
Kathleen Harrison, Membership Director
Nicci Banman, BusinessManager
Wendy Huggins, Administrative Associate

Enterprise

***KBMP**
03-06-2002; 90.5 MHz FM; *Hrs Open:* 24; 12.5 kw; 721 ft.; N39 6 16 W97 23 15 *Rebroadcasts:* Rebroadcasts KSIV-FM Saint Louis, MO 100%
10550 Barkley St., Suite 100, Overland Park, KS 66212 US
(913) 642-7770; *Fax:* (913) 642-1319
www.bottradionetwork.com
comments@bottradionetwork.com
License: Enterprise, Dickinson County, KS held by Community Broadcasting Inc.
Group Owner: Bott Radio Network; (acq 1-26-2006; $30,000 with KARF(FM) Independence)
Arbitron Metro Market: Abilene-Junction, KS; *Format:* Christian, Talk; *Target Audience:* 25-54; adults
Eben Fowler, Operations Dir
Pat Rulon, Director of National Sales
Candy Green, Program Services Manager
Rachel Launius, Marketing Manager
Tina Giffin, Area Account Manager

Eureka

KOTE
10-01-1988; 93.5 MHz FM; *Hrs Open:* 24; 3 kw; 322 ft.; N37 47 29 W96 17 25
Mailing Address: P.O. Box 331, Eureka, KS 67045 US
Second Address: 1275 P. Rd., Eureka, KS 67045
(620) 583-7414; *Fax:* (620) 583-7233
License: Eureka, Greenwood County, KS held by Niemeyer Communications LLC
Format: Classic Rock, Country; *No. News Employees:* 1; *Target Audience:* General.; *Adv. Rates:* 8; 8; 8; 8
Steve Niemeyer, General Manager

Fairway

KCNW
04-16-1953; 1380 kHz AM; *Hrs Open:* 24; 2.5 kw-D, ND1; 0.029 kw-N, ND1; N39 4 19 W94 40 58
4535 Metropolitan Ave, Kansas City, KS 66106 US
(913) 384-1380
www.wilkinsradio.com
denise@wilkinsradio.com
License: Fairway, KS held by Kansas City Radio Inc.
Group Owner: Wilkins Communications Network Inc.; (acq 1-17-2001; $725,000).
Nat'l Network: Westwood One
Arbitron Metro Market: Fairway, KS; *Format:* Christian, Talk; *No. News Employees:* 1; *Target Audience:* 35 plus; adults involved in community & family; *Adv. Rates:* 30; 30; 30; 30
Kevin Fears, Station Manager

Fort Scott

KMDO
10-08-1954; 1600 kHz AM
Mailing Address: PO Box 72, 2 North National Avenue, Fort Scott, KS 66701 US
Second Address: 2 North National Ave, Fort Scott, KS 66701
(620) 223-4500; *Fax:* (620) 223-5662
www.kombfm.com
amy@kombfm.com
License: Fort Scott, KS held by Fort Scott Broadcasting Co.
Nat'l Network: CNN Radio
Arbitron Metro Market: Joplin, MO; *Format:* Oldies; *Target Audience:* 17+
Tim McKenney, President

KOMB
01-23-1981; 103.9 MHz FM; *Hrs Open:* 24 hour; 25 kw; 328 ft.; N37 54 28 W94 46 2
P.O. Box 72, 2 N. National Ave, Fort Scott, KS 66701 US
(620) 223-4500,(620) 223-4501; *Fax:* (620) 223-5662
kombfm.com
tim@kombfm.com
License: Fort Scott, Bourbon County, KS
Nat'l Network: CNN Radio
Arbitron Metro Market: Joplin, MO; *Format:* Contemporary Hits/Top 40, Adult Contemp
Timothy McKenney, President
Deb McKenney, General Sales Mgr
Noel Connet, Programming Director
Amy Wood, Promotions Manager
Tom Knight, News Director

***KVCY**
11-01-1983; 104.7 MHz FM; *Hrs Open:* 24; 16 kw; 410 ft.; N37 52 43 W94 43 24
3434 West Kilbourn Ave., Milwaukee, WI 53208 US
(414) 935-3000; *Fax:* (414) 935-3015
www.vcyamerica.org
vcy@vcyamerica.org
License: Fort Scott, Bourbon County, KS held by VCY America Inc.
Group Owner: VCY America Inc.
Nat'l Network: USA; Moody
Arbitron Metro Market: Milwaukee, WI *TV Affiliate:* KVCX-TV;
Format: Christian, Religious
Vic Eliason, Operations Dir
Jim Schneider, Programming Director

Fredonia

KGGF FM
07-14-1997; 104.1 MHz FM; *Hrs Open:* 24/7; 7.3 kw; 380 ft.; N37 22 22 W95 43 37
306 West 8th St, Coffeyville, KS 67337 USA
(620) 251-3800
kggfradio.linkeduprradio.com/kggf-fm
License: Fredonia, Wilson County, KS held by Sek Media
Group Owner: Sek Media
Arbitron Metro Market: Fredonia, KS; *Format:* Oldies; *Target Audience:* 45-64

Galena

KQYX
01-01-1927; 1450 kHz AM; *Hrs Open:* 24
2702 Iowa Street, Joplin, MO 64804 US
(417) 781-1313; *Fax:* (417) 781-1316
License: Galena, KS held by American Media Investments Inc.
Group Owner: American Media Investments Inc.; (acq 2-17-2009; grpsl)
Arbitron Metro Market: Joplin, MO; *Format:* Oldies; *Target Audience:* 18-39.; *Adv. Rates:* 12; 12; 12; 10
Gene Bicknell, President
Dave Clemons, General Manager
Matt Kruger, Programming Director
Kathleen Pike, News Director

Garden City

***KANZ**
06-29-1980; 91.1 MHz FM; *Hrs Open:* 5 AM-midnight; 100 kw; 959 ft.; N37 46 43 W100 53 43.4 *Rebroadcasts:* Rebroadcasts KZNA(FM) Hill City 100%
201 N. 7th Street, Garden City, KS 67846 US
(620) 275-7444
www.hppr.org
License: Garden City, Finney County, KS held by KANZA Society Inc.
Nat'l Network: PRI; NPR
Arbitron Metro Market: Garden City, KS; *Format:* Variety/Diverse *Special Programming:* Jazz 15 hrs, folk 6 hrs, Sp 6 hrs wkly; *Hrs. of News Programming:* News progmg 39 hrs wkly; *Target Audience:* General.
Don Close, President
Dale Bolton, Operations Dir
Richard Hicks, General Manager
Robert Kirby, Programming Director

KIUL
05-20-1935; 1240 kHz AM; 1 kw-U, ND1; N37 59 52 W100 54 25
P.O. Box 364, Pierre, SD 57501 US
(620) 276-3251; *Fax:* (620) 276-3649
www.kiulradio.com
License: Garden City, KS held by Steckline Communications Inc.
Group Owner: Steckline Communications Inc.; (acq 11-28-2006; $550,000 with KYUL(AM) Scott City)
Nat'l Network: CBS; Westwood One
Format: News, News/Talk, 84, Talk *Special Programming:* Farm 5 hrs wkly; *Hrs. of News Programming:* news progmg 20 hrs wkly; *No. News Employees:* 2; *Target Audience:* 45 plus; upscale adults; *Adv. Rates:* 18;16; 18; 14
Theron Hayse, General Manager

KKJQ
11-20-1962; 97.3 MHz FM; *Hrs Open:* 24; 100 kw; 801 ft.; N37 46 48 W100 27 36
P.O. Box 907, Valley City, ND 58072 US
(620) 276-2366; *Fax:* (620) 276-3568
License: Garden City, Finney County, KS held by KBUF Partnership
Group Owner: Robert Ingstad Broadcast Properties
Nat'l Network: ABC
Arbitron Metro Market: Wichita, KS; *Format:* Adult Contemp, Country; *Target Audience:* 18-49.
Greg Lynn, Programming Director

Girard

KSEK-FM
09-01-1988; 99.1 MHz FM; 6 kw; 325 ft.; N37 29 2 W94 51 8
1612 Woodland Terrace, Pittsburg, KS 66762 US
(620) 232-9912; *Fax:* (620) 232-9915
License: Girard, Crawford County, KS held by Southeast Kansas Independent Living Resource Center Inc.
Group Owner: Southeast Kansas Independent Living Resource Center Inc.; (acq 11-30-2004; $700,000 with KSEK(AM) Pittsburg).
Nat'l Network: AP Network News
Arbitron Metro Market: Pittsburg, KS; *Format:* Classic Rock; *Hrs. of News Programming:* News progmg 10 hrs wkly; *Target Audience:* 25-54; resident adults & univ. students; *Adv. Rates:* 150; 120; 120; 120
Lynn Meredith, General Manager

Goodland

KGCR
03-01-1988; 107.7 MHz FM; *Hrs Open:* 24; 100 kw; 446 ft.; N39 22 2 W101 26 44
Mailing Address: P.O. Box 8, Aurora, NE 68818 US
Second Address: 3410 Rd. 66, Brewster, KS 67732
(785) 694-2877; *Fax:* (785) 694-2875
www.wordpress.kgcr.org
License: Goodland, Sherman County, KS held by The Praise Network Inc.
Nat'l Network: Moody; USA
Arbitron Metro Market: Goodland, KS; *Format:* Christian, Religious, 86 *Special Programming:* Farm 2 hrs wkly; *Hrs. of News Programming:* news progmg 30 hrs wkly; *No. News Employees:* 1; *Target Audience:* 25-54;Christian families
Lloyd Mintzmyer, CEO
James Claasson, General Manager

KKCI
09-15-1990; 102.5 MHz FM; *Hrs Open:* 24; 100 kw; 709 ft.; N39 23 24 W101 33 35
1065 S Range, Colby, KS 67701 US
(785) 462-3305; *Fax:* (785) 462-3307
www.nwksradio.com
sacha@rockingmradio.com
License: Goodland, Sherman County, KS held by Melia Communications, Inc.
Group Owner: Melia Communications, Inc.; (Acq 4-90; $40,000;
Nat'l Network: Jones Radio Networks
Arbitron Metro Market: Wichita, KS; *Format:* Classic Rock; *Target Audience:* 25-55.
Chelsea Kinnett, Operations Dir
Saha Sanguinetti, General Manager
Will Sterrett, News Director

KLOE
01-01-1947; 730 kHz AM; *Hrs Open:* 24; 1 kw-D, ND1; 0.02 kw-N, ND1; N39 20 4 W101 45 28
1065 S Range., Colby, KS 67701 US
(785) 462-3305; *Fax:* (785) 462-3307
www.kloe.com
License: Goodland, KS held by Melia Communications Inc.
Group Owner: Melia Communications Inc.; acq 1-26-96; $990,000 with co-located FM)
Nat'l Network: CBS; *Regional Network:* Kan. Agriculture
Arbitron Metro Market: Wichita, KS; *Format:* News/Talk; *Target Audience:* General.
Chelsea Kinnett, Operations Dir
Sacha Sanguinetti, General Manager
Will Sterrett, News Director

Great Bend

*KBDA
01-01-1999; 89.7 MHz FM; 1.4 kw; 112 ft.; N38 20 16 W98 45 48
P.O. Box 3206, Tupelo, MS 38803 US
(662) 844-8888; *Fax:* (662) 842-6791
www.afr.net
faq@afa.net
License: Great Bend, Barton County, KS held by American Family Association.
Group Owner: American Family Radio
Arbitron Metro Market: Tupelo, MS; *Format:* Christian, Religious
Tim Wildmon, President
Donald Wildmon, Founder
Buddy Smith, Sr VP
Ed Vitagliano, Executive VP
Randy Sharp, Director Of Special Projects
Meeke Addison, Director Of Communications
Abraham Hamilton III, General Counel & PublicPolicy Analyst

*KHCT
08-03-1992; 90.9 MHz FM; 50 kw; 781 ft.; N38 37 4 W98 56 32
815 N. Walnut, Suite 300, Hutchinson, KS 67501 US
(620) 662-6646
radiokansas.org
rfragoza@radiokansas.org
License: Great Bend, Barton County, KS held by Hutchinson Community College.
Nat'l Network: NPR
Format: News; *Target Audience:* General
Geralyn Smith, Operations Dir
Ken Baker, General Manager
Sharon Webb, General Sales Mgr
Ken Baker, Programming Director
Ric Jung, Chief Engineer

KVGB
03-10-1937; 1590 kHz AM; 5 kw-D, DAN; 5 kw-N, DAN; N38 18 50 W98 47 35
2703 Hall St., Suite 15, Hays, KS 67601 US
(785) 625-4000
www.greatbendpost.com
License: Great Bend, KS held by Eagle Communications Inc.
Group Owner: Eagle Communications Group; (acq 4-95).
Nat'l Network: ABC
Arbitron Metro Market: Great Bend, KS; *Format:* News, Talk
Special Programming: Farm 7 hrs, relg 2 hrs wkly; *Target Audience:* 28 plus.
Rick Nulton, General Manager

KVGB-FM
01-17-1977; 104.3 MHz FM; 96 kw; 810 ft.; N38 25 54 W98 46 18
2703 Hall St., Suite 15, Hays, KS 67601 US
(785) 625-4000
www.greatbendpost.com
License: Great Bend, Barton County, KS held by Eagle Communications, Inc.
Group Owner: Eagle Communications Group
Nat'l Network: ABC
Arbitron Metro Market: Great Bend, KS; *Format:* Classic Rock
Rick Nulton, General Manager

KZRS
02-03-1986; 107.9 MHz FM; *Hrs Open:* 24; 99 kw; 909 ft.; N38 46 16 W98 44 17
1660 N. Tyler, Wichita, KS 67212 US
(620) 792-7108; *Fax:* (620) 792-7051
www.rockingmradio.com/kzrs.htm
License: Great Bend, Barton County, KS held by Rocking M Radio Inc.
Group Owner: Rocking M Radio Inc.; (acq 8-31-2007; grpsl)
Regional Network: Mid-America Ag
Arbitron Metro Market: Great Bend, KS; *Format:* Adult Contemp; *Hrs. of News Programming:* news progmg 5 hrs wkly; *No. News Employees:* 1; *Target Audience:* 25-54.
Ken Schwamborn, General Manager
Chris Elson, Programming Director
Rod Rogers, Chief Engineer

*KWBI
10-10-2001; 91.9 MHz FM; *Hrs Open:* 24; 7.4 kw; 259 ft.; N38 20 16 W98 45 48
1425 North Market Blvd., Suite 9, Sacramento, CA 95834 US
(800) 525-5683; *Fax:* (916) 251-1650
www.klove.com
klove@klove.com
License: Great Bend, Barton County, KS held by Educational Media Foundation.
Group Owner: EMF Broadcasting
Nat'l Network: K-Love
Arbitron Metro Market: Omaha, NE; *Format:* Christian; *No. News Employees:* 13; *Target Audience:* 25-44; Judeo Christian, female
Darrell Chambliss, Chairman
Mike Novak, President/CEO
Eric Allen, General Sales Mgr
David Pierce, Programming Director
Ed Lenane, News Director
Sam Wallington, Engineering Dir
Marya Morgan, News Reporter
Richard Hunt, NewsReporter
Laura Daniels, News Reporter
Tim Luttrell, News Reporter
Kenny Noble Cortes, News Reporter
Darren Vinson, News Reporter

*KRTT
88.1 MHz FM; 0 kw horiz, 0.9 kw vert; 128 ft.; N38 21 46 W98 45 50
505 Josephine Street, Titusville, FL 32796 US
(321) 267-3000; *Fax:* (321) 264-9370
wpio@gate.net
License: Great Bend, Barton County, KS held by Florida Public Radio Inc.
Arbitron Metro Market: Great Bend, KS
Randy Henry, President
Archie Shetler, Vice President

Haven

KIBB
01-01-1998; 97.1 MHz FM; 18.5 kw; 823 ft.; N37 48 0.7 W97 31 29
106 North Main St., Hutchinson, KS 67501 US
(316) 558-8800; *Fax:* (316) 558-8802
www.971bobfm.com
License: Haven, Reno County, KS held by Connoisseur Media of Wichita LLC.
Group Owner: Connoisseur Media LLC; (acq 12-13-2007; exchange for KNZS(FM) Kingman)
Arbitron Metro Market: Wichita, KS; *Format:* Adult Contemp
Wichita,KS, General Manager
Kim Kretchmar, General Sales Mgr
Ron Allen, Programming Director

Hays

KAYS
10-15-1948; 1400 kHz AM; *Hrs Open:* 24; 1 kw-U, ND1; N38 53 29 W99 22 3
Mailing Address: 2300 Hall St., Box 6, Hays, KS 67601 US
Second Address: 2703 Hall St., Suite 15, Hays, KS 67601
(785) 625-2578; *Fax:* (785) 625-3632
www.hayspost.com
admin@hayspost.com
License: Hays, KS held by Eagle Communications Inc.
Group Owner: Eagle Communications Group; (Acq 3-20-91; grpsl;
Arbitron Metro Market: Hays, KS; *Format:* Oldies; *Hrs. of News Programming:* news progmg 6 hrs wkly; *No. News Employees:* 1; *Target Audience:* Adults.
Travis Kohlrus, General Manager

KHAZ
05-01-1985; 99.5 MHz FM; *Hrs Open:* 24; 100 kw; 515 ft; N38 56 29 W99 21 22
2300 Hall St., Box 6, Hays, KS 67601 US
(785) 625-2578; *Fax:* (785) 625-3632
www.hayspost.com
admin@hayspost.com
License: Hays, Ellis County, KS held by Eagle Communications Group
Group Owner: Eagle Communications Group
Nat'l Network: ABC
Format: Country *Special Programming:* Farm 10 hrs, gospel 3 hrs wkly; *Hrs. of News Programming:* news progmg 4 hrs wkly; *No. News Employees:* 2; *Target Audience:* 25-54.
Scott Boomer, Operations Dir
Travis Kohlrus, General Manager
Mark Goff, Chief Engineer

KJLS
06-27-1974; 103.3 MHz FM; *Hrs Open:* 24; 100 kw; 994 ft.; N39 1 15 W99 28 12
2300 Hall St., Box 6, Hays, KS 67601 US
(785) 625-2578; *Fax:* (785) 625-3632
www.hayspost.com
admin@hayspost.com
License: Hays, Ellis County, KS held by Eagle Communications Inc.
Group Owner: Eagle Communications Group; (acq 9-12-00; with KKQY(FM) Hill City).
Format: Adult Contemp; *Hrs. of News Programming:* news progmg 8 hrs wkly; *No. News Employees:* 1; *Target Audience:* 25-49; 60% female, 40% male
Travis Kohlrus, General Manager

*KPRD
01-01-1994; 88.9 MHz FM; 83 kw; 636 ft.; N38 46 16 W98 44 17
P.O. Box 8, Aurora, NE 68818 US
(785) 628-6300; *Fax:* (785) 628-6389
kprd@kprd.org
License: Hays, Ellis County, KS held by The Praise Network Inc.
Format: Religious; *Target Audience:* 20-48.
Lloyd Mintzmyer, CEO
David Breedon, Station Manager

*KZAN
91.7 MHz FM; *Hrs Open:* 24; 7.5 kw; 374 ft.; N38 57 29 W99 21 6.6 *Rebroadcasts:* Rebroadcast KANZ(FM) Garden City 100%
207 N. 7th St., Garden City, KS 67846 US

(620) 274-7444; *Fax:* (620) 275-7496
www.hppr.org
hppr@hppr.org
License: Hays, Ellis County, KS held by Kanza Society Inc.
Nat'l Network: NPR; PRI; AP Radio
Arbitron Metro Market: Hays, Kansas; *Format:* News, News/Talk, 86; *Target Audience:* 25-80; educated
Don Close, President
Richard Hicks, General Manager
Diana Gonzales, General Sales Mgr
Bob Kirby, Programming Director
Dale Bolton, Promotions Manager
Chuck Springer, Chief Engineer
Rod Buchele, Vice President
Quentin Hope,Treasurer
Gary Pitner, Secretary
Barb Blevins, Community Donor Relations Assistant
Dean Yates, Texas Underwriting Representative
Deb Oyler, Executive Director

***KHYS**
01-01-2009; 89.7 MHz FM; 0.45 kw; 285 ft.; N38 51 16 W99 22 53 *Rebroadcasts:* Rebroadcasts WAFR(FM) Tupelo, MS 100%
P.O. Box 3206, Tupelo, MS 38803 US
(662) 844-8888; *Fax:* (662) 842-6791
www.afr.net
faq@afa.net
License: Hays, Ellis County, KS held by American Family Association.
Group Owner: American Family Radio; (acq 6-9-2006)
Nat'l Network: American Family Radio
Arbitron Metro Market: Hays, KS; *Format:* Christian
Tim Wildmon, President
Donald Wildmon, Founder
Buddy Smith, Sr VP
Ed Vitagliano, Exec VP
Randy Sharp, Director Of Special Projects
Meeke Addison, Director Of Communications
Abraham Hamilton III, Generak Counsel

KRMR
06-16-2008; 105.7 MHz FM; 20.5 kw; 495 ft.; N38 55 59 W99 19 51
US
(785) 628-6108; *Fax:* (785) 628-1055
License: Hays, Ellis County, KS held by Radioactive LLC.
Group Owner: Radioactive LLC
Nat'l Network: Fox News Radio
Arbitron Metro Market: Hays, KS; *Format:* Contemporary Hits/Top 40
Benjamin Homel, President
Corey Sorenson, General Manager

Haysville

KFBZ
08-25-1985; 105.3 MHz FM; 98 kw; 1007 ft.; N37 48 1 W97 31 29
1850 K Street, NW, Suite 900, Washington, DC 20006 US
(316) 685-2121; *Fax:* (316) 685-3408
www.1053thebuzz.com
jwise@entercom.com
License: Haysville, Sedgwick County, KS held by Entercom Wichita License LLC.
Group Owner: Entercom Communications Corp.; (acq 2000; grpsl)
Arbitron Metro Market: Wichita, KS; *Format:* Adult Contemp
Special Programming: Relg 2 hrs wkly; *Hrs. of News Programming:* News progmg 2 hrs wkly; *Target Audience:* 25-54.
Jackie Wise, General Manager
Lisa Crider, General Sales Mgr
Dussty Hayes, Programming Director
Jennifer Lane, Webmaster

Herington

***KJRL**
09-06-1997; 105.7 MHz FM; *Hrs Open:* 24; 12.5 kw; 500 ft; N38 37 01 W96 59 09
Box 14, 805 S. Buckeye Avenue, Abilene, KS 67449
(785) 263-7200; *Fax:* (785) 263-3876
www.kjil1057.com
radioforlife@kjil.com
License: Herington, Dickinson County, KS held by Great Plains Christian Radio Inc.
Nat'l Network: Salem Radio Network; Moody; *Wire Services:* AP
Population Served: 320,000 *Hrs. of News Programming:* news progmg 16 hrs wkly; *No. News Employees:* 1; *Target Audience:* 18-54; military & professional including ag, railroad & transportation workers

Frank York, Chairman
Mike Luskey, CEO
Mike Luskey, President
Linda Emig, Operations Dir
Mark Hinca, Station Manager
Deb Hustis, Underwriting Director
Andrea Kunst, IT Director
Jennifer Pooler, Production Director
DelvinKinser, News Director
Steve Larson, Chief Engineer

Hiawatha

KNZA-FM
08-18-1977; 103.9 MHz FM; *Hrs Open:* 24; 50 kw; 492 ft.; N39 34 41 W95 33 46
1828 S. Hwy. 73, Hiawatha, KS 66434 US
(785) 547-3461; *Fax:* (785) 547-9900
www.knzafm.com
knza@rainbowtel.net
License: Hiawatha, Brown County, KS held by KNZA Inc.
Group Owner: KNZA Inc.; acq 6-83;
Nat'l Network: ABC; *Regional Network:* Brownfield; *Wire Services:* AP
Format: Country *Special Programming:* Farm 14 hrs wkly; *Hrs. of News Programming:* news progmg 10 hrs wkly; *No. News Employees:* 1; *Target Audience:* 18-54; general; *Adv. Rates:* 19; 15; 15; 13
Doug Weinberg, General Sales Mgr
L.J. Trant, Programming Director
Brian Hagen, News Director

Hill City

KKQY
08-29-1997; 101.9 MHz FM; *Hrs Open:* 24; 97 kw; 994 ft.; N39 1 15 W99 28 12
2300 Hall St., Box 6, Hays, KS 67601 US
(785) 625-2578; *Fax:* (785) 625-3632
www.hayspost.com
License: Hill City, Graham County, KS held by Eagle Communications Inc.
Group Owner: Eagle Communications Group; (acq 9-12-00; with KJLS(FM) Hays).
Arbitron Metro Market: Wichita, KS; *Format:* Country; *Hrs. of News Programming:* News progmg 5 hrs wkly; *Target Audience:* 25-54.
Scott Boomer, Operations Dir
Travis Kohlrus, General Manager
Mark Goff, Chief Engineer

***KZNA**
01-01-1986; 90.5 MHz FM; *Hrs Open:* 24; 100 kw; 659 ft.; N39 15 57 W99 50 0 *Rebroadcasts:* Rebroadcasts KANZ(FM) Garden City 100%
201 N. 7th Street, Garden City, KS 67846 US
(620) 275-7444; *Fax:* (620) 275-7496
www.hppr.org
hppr@hppr.org
License: Hill City, Graham County, KS held by Kanza Society Inc.
Nat'l Network: PRI; NPR; AP Radio
Arbitron Metro Market: Hill City, KS; *Format:* News, News/Talk, 86 *Special Programming:* Jazz 15 hrs, folk 6 hrs, Sp 6 hrs wkly; *Hrs. of News Programming:* News progmg 39 hrs wkly; *Target Audience:* 25-80; educated
Richard Hicks, General Manager
Bob Kirby, Programming Director
Chuck Springer, Chief Engineer

Hoisington

KHOK
01-01-1978; 100.7 MHz FM; *Hrs Open:* 24; 100 kw; 430 ft.; N38 32 49 W98 45 59
2703 Hall St., Suite 15, Hays, KS 67601 US
(785) 625-4000
www.greatbendpost.com
License: Hoisington, Barton County, KS held by Eagle Communications Inc.
Group Owner: Eagle Communications Group; (acq 9-1-86; grpsl;
Format: Country *Special Programming:* Relg 2 hrs wkly; *No. News Employees:* 1; *Target Audience:* 18-44.
Rick Nulton, General Manager

Holcomb

KBUF
01-01-1948; 1030 kHz AM; *Hrs Open:* 24
P.O. Box 907, Valley City, ND 58072 US
(620) 276-2366; *Fax:* (620) 276-3568
www.westernkansasnews.com
christaroy@wksradio.com
License: Holcomb, KS held by KBUF Partnership.
Group Owner: Robert Ingstad Broadcast Properties; (acq 11-1-79)
Regional Network: Mid-America Ag; *Wire Services:* NWS (National Weather Service); UPI
Arbitron Metro Market: Garden City, KS; *Format:* Talk, Country
Special Programming: Farm 15 hrs wkly; *No. News Employees:* 1; *Target Audience:* 25-54; people interested in class country & info progmg; *Adv. Rates:* 21.60; 21.60; 21.60; 14.40
Christa Roy, General Manager
James Janda, Programming Director

Horton

KAIR-FM
01-25-1995; 93.7 MHz FM; *Hrs Open:* 24; 25 kw; 328 ft.; N39 37 43 W95 18 53
P.O. Box G, 200 N. 5th St., Atchison, KS 66002 US
(913) 367-1470; *Fax:* (913) 367-7021
www.kairfm.com
kairradio@gmail.com
License: Horton, Brown County, KS held by KNZA Inc.
Group Owner: KNZA Inc.; (acq 8-13-2007; with KAIR(AM) Atchison)
Nat'l Network: AP Radio; *Wire Services:* AP
Arbitron Metro Market: Atchison, KS; *Format:* Country; *Hrs. of News Programming:* news progmg 133 hrs wkly; *No. News Employees:* 4; *Target Audience:* 25-54.; *Adv. Rates:* 16; 14; 16; 8
J.C. Martin, Operations Dir
Neil Wieland, Programming Director

Hugoton

KFXX-FM
09-16-1983; 106.7 MHz FM; *Hrs Open:* 24; 55 kw; 256 ft.; N37 18 57 W101 20 16
P.O. Box 907, Valley City, ND 58072 US
(503) 223-1441; *Fax:* (503) 223-6909
www.1080thefan.com
jaustin@entercom.com
License: Hugoton, Stevens County, KS held by KBUF Partnership.
Group Owner: Robert Ingstad Broadcast Properties
Arbitron Metro Market: Portland, OR *TV Affiliate:* ESPN; *Format:* Sports, Talk; *Target Audience:* 18-54, Men
Tim McNamara, General Manager
Jeff Austin, General Sales Mgr

Humboldt

KINZ
09-01-1998; 95.3 MHz FM; *Hrs Open:* 24; 24 kw; 335 ft.; N37 44 52 W95 33 39
117 South Grant St., Chanute, KS 66720 US
(620) 431-1333; *Fax:* (620) 431-1943
www.kinz.biz
mike@kinz.biz
License: Humboldt, Allen County, KS held by Sutcliffe Communications LLC.
Nat'l Network: CNN Radio
Format: Classic Rock *Special Programming:* Gospel 3 hrs wkly; *Target Audience:* 25-55.; *Adv. Rates:* 10; 10; 10; 7
Mike Sutcliffe, CEO
Sheri Sutcliffe, Operations Dir

Hutchinson

***KHCC-FM**
09-11-1972; 90.1 MHz FM; *Hrs Open:* 24; 100 kw; 1296 ft.; N38 3 22 W97 44 43
815 N. Walnut, Suite 300, Hutchinson, KS 67501 US
(620) 662-6646
www.radiokansas.org
rfragoza@radiokansas.org
License: Hutchinson, Reno County, KS held by Hutchinson Community College.
Nat'l Network: NPR
Format: News *Special Programming:* Car talk 2 hrs wkly; *Hrs. of News Programming:* News progmg 27 hrs wkly
Geralyn Smith, Operations Dir
Ken Baker, General Manager
Sharon Webb, Development Director
Ric Jung, Chief Engineer

KHUT
03-15-1972; 102.9 MHz FM; 98 kw; 430 ft.; N38 2 39 W98 0 56
PO Box 1036, Hutchinson, KS 67504 US
(620) 662-4486
www.hutchinsonscountrystation.com

License: Hutchinson, Reno County, KS held by Eagle Communications, Inc.
Group Owner: Eagle Communications Group
Format: Country; *Target Audience:* 25-54
Casey Osburn, Program Dir/Operations Dir
Travis Kohlrus, General Manager
Terry Drouhard, General Sales Mgr
Mark Goff, Chief Engineer

KWBW
05-28-1935; 1450 kHz AM; 1 kw-U, ND1; N38 4 22 W97 57 53
825 N. Main St., Hutchinson, KS 67501 US
(620) 662-4486; *Fax:* (620) 662-5357
www.bwradio.biz/
info@bwradio.biz
License: Hutchinson, KS held by Eagle Communications Inc.
Group Owner: Eagle Communications Group; (acq 11-4-91; with co-located FM).
Arbitron Metro Market: Hutchinson, KS; *Format:* Sports, News/Talk *Special Programming:* Black 2 hrs, gospel 11 hrs wkly
Casey Osburn, Operations Dir/Program Dir
Terry Drouhard, General Sales Mgr
Mark Goff, Chief Engineer

KZSN
10-07-1968; 102.1 MHz FM; *Hrs Open:* 24; 100 kw; 1027 ft.; N37 46 40 W97 30 37
9323 E. 37th St. N., Wichita, KS 67226 US
(316) 494-6600; *Fax:* (316) 494-6730
www.1021thebull.com
License: Hutchinson, Reno County, KS held by Capstar TX LLC
Group Owner: iHeartMedia; (acq 8-30-00; grpsl).
Nat'l Reps: Clear Channel
Arbitron Metro Market: Wichita, KS; *Format:* Country; *No. News Employees:* 1; *Target Audience:* 25-54; Adults
Tony Matteo, Senior Vice President of Programming
Jeff McCausland, Market President
Tom Libby, Senior Vice President of Sales
Brian Jennings, Programming Director
Morgan Huelsman, Digital Content Director

KWHK
01-01-2007; 95.9 MHz FM; *Hrs Open:* 24; 2.85 kw; 489 ft.; N38 2 57 W98 0 44
10 E. 5th Ave., Hutchinson, KS 67501 US
(620) 665-5758; *Fax:* (620) 665-5758
www.adastradradio.com
ksku@adastra.kscoxmail.com
License: Hutchinson, Reno County, KS held by Ad Astra Per Aspera Broadcasting Inc.
Group Owner: Ad Astra Per Aspera Broadcasting Inc.
Nat'l Network: ABC; *Regional Network:* Kan. Info.
Arbitron Metro Market: Dallas-Fort Worth; *Format:* Oldies; *Hrs. of News Programming:* news progmg 2 hrs wkly; *No. News Employees:* 1

Independence

***KARF**
01-01-1997; 91.5 MHz FM; 100 kw vert; 328 ft.; N37 3 55 W95 45 1
10550 Barkley St., Suite 100, Overland Park, KS 66212 US
(913) 642-7770; *Fax:* (913) 642-1319
www.bottradionetwork.com
comments@bottradionetwork.com
License: Independence, Montgomery County, KS held by Community Broadcasting Inc.
Group Owner: Bott Radio Network; (acq 1-26-2006; $30,000 with KBMP(FM) Enterprise)
Nat'l Network: USA
Arbitron Metro Market: Bartlesville, OK; *Format:* Christian, Talk
Eben Fowler, Operations Dir
Paul Sublett, General Manager
Pat Rulon, Director of National Sales
Candy Green, Program Services Manager
Rachel Launius, Marketing Manager
Jason Potocnik, Director of Traffic Operations

KIND
12-08-1947; 1010 kHz AM; *Hrs Open:* 24; 0.25 kw-D, ND1; 0.032 kw-N, ND1; N37 13 7 W95 43 30
Po Drawer A, Independence, KS 67301 US
(620) 331-3000; *Fax:* (620) 331-8008
a.bradshaw@tallgrassnation.com
License: Independence, KS held by Tallgrass Broadcasting Inc.
Group Owner: Tallgrass Broadcasting LLC; (acq 10-25-2006; $306,000 with co-located FM)
Nat'l Network: Westwood One; *Wire Services:* AP
Format: Adult Contemp *Special Programming:* Big band 2 hrs, class 3 hrs wkly; *Target Audience:* 35-65; baby boomers; *Adv. Rates:* 18; 18; 18; 18
Joseph Walker, President
Mark Wilson, General Manager

KBIK
05-10-1969; 102.9 MHz FM; *Hrs Open:* 24; 25 kw; Ant 272 ft; N37 15 42 W95 45 59
122 W. Myrtle, Independence, KS 67301
(620) 331-3000; *Fax:* (620) 331-8008
a.bradshaw@tallgrassnation.com
License: Independence, Montgomery County, KS held by Tallgrass Broadcasting Inc.
Group Owner: Tallgrass Broadcasting LLC
Nat'l Network: CNN Radio; *Wire Services:* AP
Population Served: 65,000 *Special Programming:* Alternative 4 hrs, Christian hot adult contemp 2 hrs wkly; *Target Audience:* 22-44.; *Adv. Rates:* 21; 21; 21; 21
Luis Medina, Operations Dir
Joe Jelddy, Station Manager

***KBQC**
01-01-2002; 88.5 MHz FM; 20 kw vert; 476 ft.; N37 3 11 W96 6 7
P.O. Box 3206, Tupelo, MS 38803 US
(662) 844-8888; *Fax:* (662) 842-6791
www.afr.net
faq@afa.net
License: Independence, Montgomery County, KS held by American Family Association.
Group Owner: American Family Radio; (acq 12-18-00; buyer paid construction & bcst costs of CP).
Arbitron Metro Market: Tupelo, MS; *Format:* Christian
Tim Wildmon, President
Donald Wildmon, Founder
Buddy Smith, Sr VP
Ed Vitagliano, Exec VP
Randy Sharp, Director Of Special Projects
Meeke Addison, Director Of Communications
Abraham Hamilton III, General Counsel

Ingalls

KERP
01-01-2001; 96.3 MHz FM; *Hrs Open:* 24; 100 kw; 699 ft.; N37 56 30 W100 18 44
Mailing Address: 1776 K Street NW, Washington, DC 20006 US
Second Address: 106 W Frontwiew, Dodge City, KS 67801
(620) 225-8080; *Fax:* (620) 225-6655
www.rockingmradio.com/kerp
rockswks@sbcglobal.net
License: Ingalls, Gray County, KS held by Rocking M Radio Inc.
Group Owner: Rocking M Radio Inc.; (acq 8-31-2007; grpsl)
Nat'l Network: Fox News Radio
Arbitron Metro Market: Dodge City, KS; *Format:* Country
Brian Nugen, Operations Dir
Mark Hinca, General Manager
Peggy Burdick, General Sales Mgr
Candace Thomas, News Director

KSSA
07-01-1999; 105.9 MHz FM; *Hrs Open:* 24; 100 kw; 666 ft.; N37 46 48 W100 27 36
Box 907, Valley City, ND 58072 US
(620) 276-3251; *Fax:* (620) 276-3568
License: Ingalls, Gray County, KS held by KBUF Partnership.
Group Owner: Robert Ingstad Broadcast Properties; (acq 1999; $250,000)
Arbitron Metro Market: Ingalls, KS
G.L. Wohler, General Manager
Rachel Wheet, News Director

Iola

KIOL
07-25-1961; 1370 kHz AM; *Hrs Open:* 24; 0.5 kw-D, DA2; 0.058 kw-N, DA2; N37 54 7 W95 24 26
P. O. Box 710, Iola, KS 66749 US
(620) 365-3151; *Fax:* (620) 365-5431
www.iolaradio.com
radistation@iolaradio.com
License: Iola, KS held by Iola Broadcasting Inc.
Arbitron Metro Market: Iola, KS; *Format:* Oldies
Tom Norris, General Manager

KIKS-FM
06-09-1977; 101.5 MHz FM; *Hrs Open:* 24; 11.5 kw; 289 ft.; N37 54 4 W95 24 4
P. O. Box 710, Iola, KS 66749 US
(620) 365-3151; *Fax:* (620) 365-5431
www.iolaradio.com
radiostation@iolaradio.com
License: Iola, Allen County, KS held by Iola Broadcasting Inc.
Format: Country *Special Programming:* Trading Post 20 hrs wkly
Tom Norris, General Manager

Junction City

KJCK
05-15-1949; 1420 kHz AM; *Hrs Open:* 24; 1 kw-D, DAN; 0.5 kw-N, DAN; N39 1 33 W96 48 36
2703 Hall St., Suite 15, Hays, KS 67601 US
(785) 625-4000
www.kjck.com
License: Junction City, KS held by Eagle Communications, Inc.
Group Owner: Eagle Communications, Inc.; (acq 9-4-86)
Nat'l Network: ABC; Fox News Radio; Sporting News Radio Network; *Wire Services:* AP
Format: News/Talk; *Hrs. of News Programming:* news progmg 75 hrs wkly; *No. News Employees:* 2; *Target Audience:* 35-54.; *Adv. Rates:* 14.25; 10.75; 14.25; 10.75
Travis Kohlrus, General Manager

KJCK-FM
07-22-1965; 97.5 MHz FM; *Hrs Open:* 24; 100 kw; 630 ft.; N39 0 53 W96 52 12
Box 789, Junction City, KS 66441 US
(785) 762-5525; *Fax:* (785) 762-5387
www.powerhits975.com
License: Junction City, Geary County, KS held by Eagle Communications, Inc.
Group Owner: Eagle Communications, Inc.
Wire Services: AP
Format: Contemporary Hits/Top 40; *Hrs. of News Programming:* news progmg one hr wkly; *No. News Employees:* 2; *Target Audience:* 18-34; young adults
Travis Kohlrus, General Manager

Kansas City

KDTD
01-01-1925; 1340 kHz AM; *Hrs Open:* 24; 0.2 kw-U, ND1; N38 16 1 W94 30 59
4121 Minnesota Ave., Kansas City, KS 66102 US
(913) 287-1480; *Fax:* (913) 287-5881
License: Kansas City, KS held by Davidson Media Station KCKN Licensee LLC.
Group Owner: Davidson Media Group LLC; (acq 10-11-2005; $1.9 million).
Arbitron Metro Market: Kansas City, MO-KS; *No. News Employees:* 2
Carlos Mercado, Operations Dir
Dan Perez, General Manager

KFKF-FM
05-28-1963; 94.1 MHz FM; 100 kw; 994 ft.; N39 0 57 W94 30 24
600 New Hampshire Avenue, N.W., Suite 1200, Washington, DC 20037 US
(816) 753-4000; *Fax:* (816) 753-4045
www.kfkf.com
info@kfkf.com
License: Kansas City, Wyandotte County, KS held by Wilks License Co.-Kansas City LLC.
Group Owner: Wilks Broadcast Group LLC; (acq 1-10-2007; grpsl)
Arbitron Metro Market: KS City, MO; *Format:* Country *Special Programming:* Country Classics 20 hrs wkly; *Target Audience:* 25-54
Mike Rowen, General Manager
Dale Carter, Programming Director
Jillian Gregg, News Director
Ben Weiss, Chief Engineer

KMBZ-FM
10-09-1959; 98.1 MHz FM; *Hrs Open:* 24; 100 kw; 994 ft; N39 04 23 W94 29 06
7000 Squibb Rd, Mission, KS 19004
(913) 744-3600; *Fax:* (913) 677-8061
www.kudl.com
info@kudl.com
License: Kansas City, Wyandotte County, KS held by Entercom Kansas City License L.L.C.
Group Owner: Entercom Communications Corp.; (acq 10-17-97; grpsl)
Population Served: 1,500,000; *Arbitron Metro Market:* Kansas City, MO-KS; *No. News Employees:* 1; *Target Audience:* 25-44; women
Tom McGinty, Operations Dir
Herndon Hasty, General Manager
Dan Prendiville, General Sales Mgr
Marcy Caldwell, Promotions Manager
Darcie Blake, News Director
Dave Alpert, General Manager

KYYS
01-01-1926; 1250 kHz AM; 25 kw-D, DA2; 3.7 kw-N, DA2; N39 11 6 W94 27 28
3270 Blazer Pkwy, Ste 101, Lexington, KY 40509 US
(913) 788-1255; *Fax:* (913) 788-1254
www.lasuperx1250.com
License: Kansas City, KS held by Entercom Kansas City License LLC.
Group Owner: Entercom Communications Corp.; (acq 3-3-99; $2.75 million)
Arbitron Metro Market: Kansas City, MO-KS; *Format:* Tejano
Juan C. Ramirez, General Manager

Kingman

***KCVW**
12-01-1997; 94.3 MHz FM; *Hrs Open:* 24; 100 kw; 830 ft.; N37 46 26 W97 30 52
10550 Barkley St., Suite 100, Overland Park, KS 66212 US
(316) 283-4592
www.bottradionetwork.com
comments@bottradionetwork.com
License: Kingman, Kingman County, KS held by Community Broadcasting Inc.
Group Owner: Bott Radio Network
Nat'l Network: USA
Arbitron Metro Market: Wichita, KS; *Format:* Christian, Talk; *Target Audience:* 25-55.
Richard Bott Sr., President & CEO
Eben Fowler, Operations Dir
Pat Rulon, Director of National Sales
Candy Green, Program Services Manager
Rachel Launius, Marketing Manager
Jason Potocnik, Director of Traffic Operations
TinaGiffin, Area Account Manager

Kiowa

KQZQ
01-01-2008; 98.3 MHz FM; 97 kw; 685 ft.; N37 24 9 W98 34 51 US
(620) 231-5620
www.coyotecountry983.com
License: Kiowa, Barber County, KS held by Troy Unruh.
Arbitron Metro Market: Kiowa, KS; *Format:* Country
Troy Unruh, General Manager

Larned

KBGL
01-01-2001; 106.9 MHz FM; 100 kw; 486 ft.; N38 27 6 W99 10 3
Box 6, Hays, KS 67601 US
(480) 657-9936
www.greatbendradio.com
License: Larned, Pawnee County, KS held by Hull Broadcasting Inc.
Group Owner: Eagle Communications Group; (acq 9-12-00; with KFIX(FM) Plainville).
Arbitron Metro Market: Larned, KS; *Format:* Contemporary Hits/Top 40
Rick Nulton, General Manager

KSOB
11-01-1965; 96.7 MHz FM; 3 kw; 266 ft.; N38 9 54 W99 6 5
1660 N. Tyler Road, Wichita, KS 67212 US
(620) 792-7108; *Fax:* (620) 792-7051
www.rockingmradio.com
cmiller@rockingmradio.com
License: Larned, Pawnee County, KS
Group Owner: Rocking M Radio Inc.
Format: Oldies; *Target Audience:* 30-60; baby boomers with disposable income
Dan Cormack, News Director
Chris Miller, Vice President

KNNS
11-04-1963; 1510 kHz AM; 0.5 kw-C, NDD; 1 kw-D, NDD; N38 9 54 W99 6 5
US
(620) 792-7108; *Fax:* (620) 792-7051
License: Larned, KS held by Rocking M Radio Inc.
Group Owner: Rocking M Radio Inc.; (acq 8-31-2007; grpsl)
Regional Network: Kan. Info.; Kan. Agriculture
Format: Sports *Special Programming:* Farm 10 hrs, gospel 6 hrs, relg 5 hrs wkly; *Target Audience:* General; people looking for loc info; *Adv. Rates:* 12; 10; 8; 5
Jen Schwamborn, General Manager
Chris Elsen, Programming Director

Lawrence

***KANU**
09-15-1952; 91.5 MHz FM; *Hrs Open:* 24; 100 kw; 699 ft.; N38 57 14 W95 16 11
226 Strong Hall, Lawrence, KS 66045 US
(785) 864-4530; *Fax:* (785) 864-5278
www.kansaspublicradio.org
kpr@ku.edu
License: Lawrence, Douglas County, KS held by University of Kansas.
Nat'l Network: PRI; NPR
Arbitron Metro Market: Lawrence, KS; *Format:* Jazz *Special Programming:* Bluegrass 4 hrs, Celtic 2 hrs, blues 4 hrs wkly; *Hrs. of News Programming:* news progmg 35 hrs wkly; *No. News Employees:* 3 *TargetAudience:* 25-49; upscale
Janet Campbell, General Manager
Darrell Brogdon, Programming Director
J. Schafer, News Director
Steve Kincaid, Engineering Dir

***KJHK**
01-01-1975; 90.7 MHz FM; *Hrs Open:* 24; 2.3 kw; 279 ft.; N38 57 14 W95 16 11
2051 Dole Center, Lawrence, KS 66045 US
(785) 864-4745; *Fax:* (785) 864-5173
www.kjhk.org
kjhk@mail.ku.edu
License: Lawrence, Douglas County, KS held by University of Kansas.
Format: Jazz *Special Programming:* Reggae 3 hrs, blues 2 hrs wkly; *Hrs. of News Programming:* News progmg 15 hrs wkly; *Target Audience:* 18-34; Univ & community population
Tom Johnson, General Manager
Danielle Basci, Station Manager
Tom Kimmel, Programming Director
Joe Noh, Promotions Manager

KLWN
02-22-1951; 1320 kHz AM; *Hrs Open:* 24; 0.5 kw-D, ND1; 0.25 kw-N, ND1; N38 56 5 W95 17 12
P.O. Box 1749, Cape Girardeau, MO 63702 US
(785) 843-1320; *Fax:* (785) 841-5941
www.klwn.com
License: Lawrence, KS held by Great Plains Media Inc.
Group Owner: Great Plains Media Inc.; (acq 6-30-2006; with co-located FM)
Format: News, News/Talk, 84, Talk *Special Programming:* Relg 4 hrs wkly; *Hrs. of News Programming:* news progmg 10 hrs wkly; *No. News Employees:* 2; *Target Audience:* 25-59; adults
John Flood, Programming Director

KKSW
08-20-1963; 105.9 MHz FM; *Hrs Open:* 24; 100 kw; 771 ft; N39 02 21 W95 26 59
3125 W. 6th St., Lawrence, KS 63702
(785) 843-1320; *Fax:* (785) 841-5924,(785) 843-4585
www.lazer.com
License: Lawrence, Douglas County, KS
Group Owner: Great Plains Media Inc.
Population Served: 100,000; *Arbitron Metro Market:* Topeka, KS; *Hrs. of News Programming:* news progmg one hr wkly; *No. News Employees:* 2; *Target Audience:* 18-34; young adults
Gary Katz, President
Dennis Carlson, General Manager

Leavenworth

KKLO
01-01-1946; 1410 kHz AM
481 Muncie Road, Leavenworth, KS 66048 US
(913) 351-1410; *Fax:* (913) 351-1410
www.hereshelpnet.org
License: Leavenworth, KS held by New Life Evangelistic Center Inc.
Arbitron Metro Market: Kansas City, MO; *Format:* Christian; *Target Audience:* 25-49; upscale, educated, loyal Christian listeners
Larry Rice, CEO
Saint Johns, General Manager

KQRC-FM
01-01-1962; 98.9 MHz FM; 98.5 kw; 1099 ft.; N39 1 20 W94 30 49
10706 Beaver Dam Road, Cockeysville, MD 21030 US
(913) 744-3600; *Fax:* (913) 677-8061
www.989therock.com
info@989therock.com
License: Leavenworth, Leavenworth County, KS held by Entercom Kansas City License LLC.
Group Owner: Entercom Communications Corp.; (acq 7-14-00; grpsl)
Arbitron Metro Market: Kansas City metro area; *Format:* Rock/AOR; *Target Audience:* 18-34; above average education & income; upscale professionals
Herndon Hasty, General Manager
John Karpinski, General Sales Mgr
Bob Edwards, Programming Director
Jennifer Morton, Promotions Manager
Dave Alpert, General Manager
Sammy Jo Behrens, Promotions

Leoti

KWKR
11-01-1983; 99.9 MHz FM; 97 kw; 397 ft.; N38 16 39 W101 17 50
Mailing Address: 1309 E. Fulton St., Garden City, KS 67846 US
Second Address: 1402 E. Kansas, Garden City, KS 67846
(620) 276-3251; *Fax:* (620) 276-3568
www.wksradio.com
info@wksradio.com
License: Leoti, Wichita County, KS held by KBUF Partnership.
Group Owner: Robert Ingstad Broadcast Properties; (acq 12-1-97; $841,170).
Nat'l Network: Westwood One
Arbitron Metro Market: Garden City, KS; *Format:* Classic Rock
Special Programming: Sp 3 hrs wkly; *Target Audience:* 25-44.
Scott Smith, General Manager
James Janda, Programming Director
Tim Boulware, News Director
Charlie Bay, Chief Engineer
Ivaree Previtt, Traffic Manager

Liberal

KLDG
10-01-1994; 102.7 MHz FM; *Hrs Open:* 24; 100 kw; 466 ft.; N37 2 45 W101 6 11
1410 North Western, Liberal, KS 67901 US
(620) 624-3891; *Fax:* (620) 624-7885
www.kscb.net
License: Liberal, Seward County, KS held by Seward County Broadcasting Co. Inc.
Group Owner: Seward County Broadcasting Co.
Nat'l Network: Jones Radio Networks; *Nat'l Reps:* Roslin
Arbitron Metro Market: Wichita, KS; *Format:* Country; *Hrs. of News Programming:* news progmg 2 hrs wkly; *No. News Employees:* 2; *Target Audience:* 18-49; young, mobile & impulsive consumers
John Landon, Chairman
Don Ford, President
Bob Larrabee, Operations Dir
Stuart Melchert, General Manager
Cheryl Collins, General Sales Mgr
Mikki Hofferber, News Director
John Mulhern, Chief Engineer
Mikki Hofferber, TrafficManager

KSCB
07-25-1948; 1270 kHz AM; *Hrs Open:* 24
1410 North Western, Liberal, KS 67901 US
(620) 624-3891; *Fax:* (620) 624-9472
www.kscb.net
kscb@kscb.net
License: Liberal, KS held by Seward County Broadcasting Co.
Group Owner: Seward County Broadcasting Co.
Nat'l Network: ABC; Westwood One; *Regional Network:* Kan. Info; *Nat'l Reps:* Roslin
Arbitron Metro Market: Liberal, KS; *Format:* News, News/Talk, 86
Special Programming: Farm 6 hrs wkly; *No. News Employees:* 3; *Target Audience:* 35 plus.
Terry Miller, Production Director
Stuart Melchart, General Manager
Tracy Utz, Business Manager
Cheryl Collins, General Sales Mgr
John Mulhern, Chief Engineer
Brock Kappelmann, News Director
Mikki Hofferber, Traffic Manager
Cameron Parsons, Webmaster

KSCB-FM
07-10-1978; 107.5 MHz FM; *Hrs Open:* 24; 100 kw; 466 ft.; N37 2 45 W101 6 11
1410 North Western, Liberal, KS 67901 US
(620) 624-3891; *Fax:* (620) 624-9472
www.kscb.net
License: Liberal, Seward County, KS held by Seward County Broadcasting Co.
Group Owner: Seward County Broadcasting Co.

Nat'l Network: Jones Radio Networks; *Regional Network:* Kan. Info; *Nat'l Reps:* Roslin
Arbitron Metro Market: Liberal, KS; *Format:* Adult Contemp; *Hrs. of News Programming:* news progmg 7 hrs wkly; *No. News Employees:* 2; *Target Audience:* 25-49; young adults
Mikki Hofferber, News Director

KSMM-FM
07-01-1978; 101.5 MHz FM; 100 kw; 541 ft.; N37 3 20 W100 48 40
US
(620) 624-8156; *Fax:* (620) 624-4606
www.rockingmradio.com
License: Liberal, Seward County, KS held by Rocking M Radio Inc.
Group Owner: Rocking M Radio Inc.; (acq 8-31-2007; grpsl)
Arbitron Metro Market: Liberal, KS
Enrique Frantz, General Manager
Christopher D. Miller-Vice President

KSMM
09-15-1960; 1470 kHz AM
1660 N. Tyler, Wichita, KS 67212 US
(620) 624-8156; *Fax:* (620) 624-4606
www.rockingmradio.com
License: Liberal, KS held by Rocking M Radio Inc.
Group Owner: Rocking M Radio Inc.; (acq 8-31-2007; grpsl)
Regional Network: Mid-America Ag; *Nat'l Reps:* McGavren Guild
Arbitron Metro Market: Liberal, KS; *Hrs. of News Programming:* News progmg one hr wkly; *Target Audience:* 25-54; Spanish speaking
Steve Schiffner, General Manager
Matt Younkin, Programming Director

KZQD
10-01-1997; 105.1 MHz FM; 50 kw; 387 ft.; N37 2 53 W100 54 34
P.O. Box 2636, Liberal, KS 67905 US
(620) 626-8282; *Fax:* (620) 626-8080
www.kzqdradiolibertad.com
License: Liberal, Seward County, KS held by Mario Loredo.
Arbitron Metro Market: Liberal, KS.; *Format:* Christian
Mario Loredo, General Manager

Lindsborg

KVOB
10-08-1985; 95.5 MHz FM; *Hrs Open:* 24; 15.5 kw; Ant 417 ft; N38 40 00 W97 41 30
641 W. Cloud, Salina, KS 67401
(785) 827-2100; *Fax:* (785) 827-3503
License: Lindsborg, Saline County, KS held by Rocking M Radio Inc.
Group Owner: Rocking M Radio Inc.; (acq 8-31-2007; grpsl)
Population Served: 325,000 *Hrs. of News Programming:* News progmg 2 hrs wkly; *Target Audience:* 25-49.; *Adv. Rates:* 21; 17; 14; 9
James Westling, Operations Dir
Christopher Miller, General Manager
Morgan Lillich, General Sales Mgr
James Westling, Programming Director
Rod Rogers, Chief Engineer

KDJM
01-01-2008; 101.7 MHz FM; 15.5 kw; 410 ft.; N38 40 0 W97 41 30
US
(785) 827-2100; *Fax:* (785) 827-3503
www.salina-radio.com
Mlillich@rockingmradio.com
License: Lindsborg, Saline County, KS held by Radioactive LLC.
Group Owner: Radioactive LLC
Arbitron Metro Market: Lindsborg, KS; *Format:* Country
Benjamin Homel, President
James Westling, Operations Dir
Pat Foster, General Manager
Morgan Lillich, Business Manager
Holliegh Henry, Business Development Executives
Russ Litteral, Business Development Executives

Lyons

KXKU
04-10-1970; 106.1 MHz FM; *Hrs Open:* 24; 100 kw; 656 ft.; N38 15 47 W97 54 8
10 E. 5th Ave., Hutchinson, KS 67501 US
(620) 665-5758; *Fax:* (620) 665-5758
www.adastraradio.com
ksku@adastra.kscoxmail.com
License: Lyons, Rice County, KS held by Ad Astra Per Aspera Broadcasting Inc.
Group Owner: Ad Astra Per Aspera Broadcasting Inc.; (acq 9-17-86; $366,816;
Nat'l Network: Jones Radio Networks; *Regional Network:* Kan. Info.
Arbitron Metro Market: Lyons, KS; *Format:* Country; *Hrs. of News Programming:* news progmg 2 hrs wkly; *No. News Employees:* 1; *Target Audience:* 25-64; listeners throughout central KS

Manhattan

KMAN
06-01-1950; 1350 kHz AM; *Hrs Open:* 24; 0.5 kw-D, ND1; 0.04 kw-N, ND1; N39 13 0 W96 33 30
2414 Casement Rd., Manhattan, KS 66502 USA
(785) 776-1350; *Fax:* (785) 539-1000
www.1350kman.com
dave@1350kman.com
License: Manhattan, KS held by Manhattan Broadcasting Co.
Group Owner: Seaton Stations
Nat'l Network: CBS; ESPN Radio; Westwood One; *Regional Network:* Kan. Info.
Format: News, News/Talk, 84, Talk; *Hrs. of News Programming:* news progmg 60 hrs wkly; *No. News Employees:* 1; *Target Audience:* 30 plus.; *Adv. Rates:* 18; 16; 18; 14
Dave Lewis, Programming Director
Cathy Dawes, News Director
John Kurtz, Sports Director

KMKF
09-01-1972; 101.5 MHz FM; *Hrs Open:* 24; 37 kw; 577 ft.; N39 15 55 W96 27 57
Mailing Address: P. O. Box 1350, Manhattan, KS 66502 US
Second Address: 2414 Casement Rd., Manhattan, KS 66502
(785) 776-1350; *Fax:* (785) 539-1000
www.purerock.com
License: Manhattan, Riley County, KS
Arbitron Metro Market: Topeka, KS; *Format:* Rock/AOR; *Hrs. of News Programming:* news progmg 2 hrs wkly; *No. News Employees:* 1; *Target Audience:* 18-35.
Richard Wartell, General Manager
Corey Dean, Programming Director
Kevin Block, Engineering Dir

***KSDB-FM**
01-01-1949; 91.9 MHz FM; *Hrs Open:* 24; 1.4 kw; 289 ft.; N39 9 49 W96 31 54
104 Kedzie Hall, Manhattan, KS 66502 US
(785) 532-2971; *Fax:* (785) 532-5484
www.wildcat919.com
radio@ksu.edu
License: Manhattan, Riley County, KS held by Kansas State University.
Arbitron Metro Market: Manhattan, KS; *Format:* Alternative, Urban Contemporary *Special Programming:* Black 4 hrs, gospel 3 hrs, jazz 3 hrs wkly; *Hrs. of News Programming:* news progmg 12 hrs wkly; *No. News Employees:* 1; *Target Audience:* 18-34; young adults; *Adv. Rates:* 10; 10; 10; 10
Steve Smethers, COO
Mary Shirk, Operations Dir
Kristin Russell, Station Manager
Jared Clark, Programming Director
Caitlin Whetstone, Promotions Manager
Dan Page, News Director

KXBZ
09-01-1994; 104.7 MHz FM; 50 kw; 488 ft.; N39 15 55 W96 27 59
2414 Casement Rd., Manhattan, KS 66502 US
(785) 776-1350
www.b1047.com
swick@z963.com
License: Manhattan, Riley County, KS held by Manhattan Broadcasting Co. Inc.
Group Owner: Seaton Stations; (acq 3-2-99).
Nat'l Network: Westwood One
Arbitron Metro Market: Manhattan, KS; *Format:* Country; *Target Audience:* 18-35; men & women
Chris Swick, Programming Director

***KGLV**
01-01-2008; 88.9 MHz FM; 11 kw; 1047 ft.; N39 0 22 W96 2 57
Rebroadcasts: Rebroadcasts KLVR(FM) Middletown, CA 100%
8030 Arrowridge Blvd, Charlotte, NC 28273 US
(916) 251-1600; *Fax:* (916) 251-1650
www.klove.com
klove@klove.com
License: Manhattan, Riley County, KS held by Educational Media Foundation.
Group Owner: EMF Broadcasting; (acq 10-27-2006; $325,000 for CP)
Nat'l Network: K-Love
Arbitron Metro Market: Manhattan, KS; *Format:* Christian
Darrell Chambliss, Chairman
Alan Mason, CEO/COO
Mike Novak, CEO
David Pierce, Chief Creative Officer
Dan Antonelli, Chief Business Development Officer
Eric Moser, Chief Financial Officer
Brian Burger, Vice President of HumanResources
D. Kevin Blair, Secretary and General Counsel

***KJIH**
89.9 MHz FM; 11 kw; Ant 230 ft; N39 24 04 W96 25 29
102 Red Branch Ln., Simpsonville, SC
(864) 297-0216; *Fax:* (864) 297-0344
networkofglory.com
info@networkofglory.org
License: Manhattan, Riley County, KS held by Network of Glory Inc.

Lola Richey, President

KMKF
101.5 MHz FM; *Hrs Open:* 24; 37 kw; 577 ft.; N54 15 39 W57 27 96
2414 Casement Rd., Manhattan, KS 66502 USA
(785) 776-1350
1015krock.com
crowley@purerock.com
License: Manhattan, KS held by Manhattan Broadcasting
Group Owner: Seaton Stations
Arbitron Metro Market: Manhattan, OK; *No. News Employees:* 5; *Target Audience:* 18+
Corey Reeves, General Manager
Andrea Besthorn, General Sales Mgr
Anderew Crowl, Programming Director

Marysville

KNDY
07-10-1956; 1570 kHz AM; *Hrs Open:* 24; 0.25 kw-D, ND2; 0.033 kw-N, ND2; N39 51 2 W96 38 52
937 Jayhawk Rd., Marysville, KS 66508 US
(785) 562-2361; *Fax:* (785) 562-2188
www.kndyradio.com
License: Marysville, KS held by Dierking Communications Inc.
Group Owner: Dierking Communications Inc.; (acq 9-6-88).
Nat'l Network: ABC; *Regional Network:* Mid-America Ag
Format: Country; *Hrs. of News Programming:* News progmg 24 hrs wkly; *Target Audience:* General.
Bruce Dierking, President/General Manager

KNDY-FM
07-23-1974; 95.5 MHz FM; *Hrs Open:* 24; 25 kw; 328 ft.; N39 57 36 W96 44 5
937 Jayhawk Rd., Marysville, KS 66508 US
(785) 562-2361; *Fax:* (785) 562-2188
www.kndyradio.com
License: Marysville, Marshall County, KS held by Dierking Communications, Inc.
Group Owner: Dierking Communications Inc.
Nat'l Network: ABC; *Regional Network:* Mid-America Ag
Format: Country
Bruce Dierking, President/General Manager
Myron Nolind, Chief Engineer

***KMLL**
91.7 MHz FM; 0.6 kw; 285 ft.; N39 52 12 W96 44 45
P.O. Box 3206, Tupelo, MS 38803 US
(662) 844-8888; *Fax:* (662) 842-6791
www.afr.net
faq@afa.net
License: Marysville, Marshall County, KS held by American Family Association.
Group Owner: American Family Radio
Arbitron Metro Market: Marysville, KS; *Format:* Christian
Tim Wildmon, President
Donald Wildmon, Founder
Buddy Smith, Sr VP
Ed Vitagliano, Exec VP
Randy Sharp, Director Of Special Projects
Meeke Addison, Director Of Communications
Abraham Hamilton III, General Counsel

McPherson

KBBE
01-12-1974; 96.7 MHz FM; *Hrs Open:* 24; 6 kw; 246 ft.; N38 20 30 W97 40 12
P.O. Box 1069, McPherson, KS 67460 US
(620) 241-1504; *Fax:* (620) 241-3196
midkansasradio.com
oldies96.7@midkansasradio.com
License: McPherson, McPherson County, KS

Nat'l Network: ABC
Arbitron Metro Market: McPherson, KS; *Format:* Oldies; *No. News Employees:* 1
Joe Johnston, General Manager

KNGL
01-04-1949; 1540 kHz AM; 0.25 kw-D, ND2; 0.002 kw-N, ND2; N38 20 30 W97 40 12
P.O. Box 1069, McPherson, KS 67460 US
(620) 241-1504; *Fax:* (620) 241-3196
midkansasradio.com
License: McPherson, KS held by Davies Communications Inc.
Nat'l Network: ABC; *Regional Network:* Kan. Info.; Kan. Agriculture
Format: Talk *Special Programming:* Relg 5 hrs wkly; *No. News Employees:* 1; *Target Audience:* 25-54.; *Adv. Rates:* 14; 11; 11; 8
Jerry Davies, President
Joe Johnston, General Manager/Sales Manager
Shawn White, Chief Engineer
Diane Davies, Executive Vice President
Nick Gosnell, Operations Manager

Medicine Lodge

***KREJ**
01-01-1990; 101.7 MHz FM; *Hrs Open:* 24; 50 kw; 476 ft.; N37 14 0 W98 39 44
505 Josephine Street, Titusville, FL 32796 US
(620) 886-3537; *Fax:* (321) 264-9370
www.krejksns.org
License: Medicine Lodge, Barber County, KS held by Florida Public Radio Inc.
Nat'l Network: Moody
Format: Religious; *Target Audience:* General.
Mike Henry, Operations Dir
Mike Henry, General Manager
Randy Henry, Chief Engineer

***KSNS**
04-01-1999; 91.5 MHz FM; 96 kw vert; 463 ft.; N37 14 2 W98 39 55
Mailing Address: 505 Josephine St, Titusville, FL 32796 US
Second Address: 505 Josephine St., Titusville, FL 32796
(620) 886-3537
License: Medicine Lodge, Barber County, KS held by Florida Public Radio Inc.
Format: Christian
Mike Henry, General Manager

Minneapolis

KZUH
02-24-1993; 92.7 MHz FM; *Hrs Open:* 24; 50 kw; 492 ft; N39 00 52 W97 37 42
641 W. Cloud, Salina, KS 67212
(785) 827-2100; *Fax:* (785) 827-3503
License: Minneapolis, Ottawa County, KS held by Rocking M Radio Inc.
Group Owner: Rocking M Radio Inc.; (acq 8-31-2007; grpsl)
Population Served: 150,000 *Target Audience:* 18-54.
Darren Irwin, General Manager
James Luelting, Operations Manager

Mission

KCZZ
10-01-1957; 1480 kHz AM; *Hrs Open:* 24; 1 kw-D, DA2; 0.5 kw-N, DA2; N39 4 5 W94 42 9
10706 Beaver Dam Road, Cockeysville, MD 21030 US
(913) 287-1480; *Fax:* (913) 287-5881
License: Mission, KS held by Davidson Media Station KCZZ Licensee LLC.
Group Owner: Davidson Media Group LLC; (acq 1-28-2005; $3.9 million with KAKS(FM) Huntsville, AR).
Nat'l Reps: Lotus Entravision Reps LLC
Arbitron Metro Market: Mission, KS; *Target Audience:* 18-49; adults; *Adv. Rates:* 40; 40; 40; 15
Carlos Mercado, Operations Dir
Dan Perez, General Manager

Ness City

KXNC
104.7 MHz FM; 16.5 kw; 896 ft.; N38 36 32 W99 42 11
108 West 8th Street, LaCrosse, KS 67548 US
(785) 222-3400; *Fax:* (785) 222-3405
kiss1047.net
glen.hoyt@postrockradio.com
License: Ness City, Ness County, KS held by Post Rock Radio, LLC
Group Owner: Post Rock Radio, LLC
Arbitron Metro Market: Ness City, KS; *Format:* Contemporary Hits/Top 40
Christopher Devine, General Manager
Glen Hoyt, General Sales Mgr
Chris Elsen, Programming Director

Newton

KJRG
05-24-1953; 950 kHz AM; 0.5 kw-D, ND2; 0.147 kw-N, ND2; N38 2 39 W97 22 21
209 Meridian Rd., Newton, KS 67114 US
(316) 283-4592; *Fax:* (316) 283-3177
www.bottradionetwork.com
comments@bottradionetwork.com
License: Newton, Harvey County, KS held by Community Broadcasting Inc.
Group Owner: Bott Radio Network; (acq 6-20-2006; $650,000)
Nat'l Network: USA
Arbitron Metro Market: Wichita, KS; *Format:* Christian, Talk; *Target Audience:* 25-54.
Richard Bott Sr., President & CEO
Eben Fowler, Operations Dir
Pat Rulon, Director of National Sales
Candy Green, Program Services Manager
Rachel Launius, Marketing Manager
Jason Potocnik, Director of Traffic Operations
TinaGiffin, Area Account Manager

KFTI-FM
01-01-1959; 92.3 MHz FM; *Hrs Open:* 24; 100 kw; 640 ft.; N38 1 12 W97 23 4
Mailing Address: P. O. Box 567, Newton, KS 67114 US
Second Address: 4200 N. Old Lawrence Rd., Wichita, KS 67219
(316) 838-9141; *Fax:* (316) 838-3607
info@classiccountry923.com
License: Newton, Harvey County, KS held by Journal Broadcast Corp.
Group Owner: Journal Communications Inc.; (acq 3-20-2000; $4.25 million)
Arbitron Metro Market: Wichita, KS; *Format:* Country
Rob Burton, Operations Dir
Eric McCart, General Sales Mgr
Ray Micheals, Programming Director
Manny Cowzinski, Promotions Manager

North Fort Riley

KBLS
01-01-1993; 102.5 MHz FM; 100 kw; 492 ft.; N38 57 5 W96 47 45
131 N. Santa Fe, P.O. Box 80, Salina, KS 67402 US
(785) 823-1111; *Fax:* (785) 823-2034
www.sunny1025.com
License: North Fort Riley, Geary County, KS held by Alpha Media Licensee LLC
Group Owner: Alpha Media LLC; (acq 9-2-2015; grpsl).
Arbitron Metro Market: Salina, KS; *Format:* Adult Contemp; *Hrs. of News Programming:* news progmg 2 hrs wkly; *No. News Employees:* 3; *Target Audience:* 25-54; women; *Adv. Rates:* 18.84; 14.13; 16.96; 5.65
Bob Protzman, Station Manager
Mitch Drees, General Sales Mgr
John Anderson, Programming Director
Clarke Sanders, Promotions Manager
Todd Pittenger, News Director

KBLS
07-12-1990; 102.5 MHz FM; 492 ft.; N38 57 05 W96 47 45
2414 Casement Rd., Manhattan, KS 66502 USA
(785) 776-1350
sunny1025.com
License: North Fort Riley, KS held by Manhattan Broadcasting Co.
Group Owner: Seaton Stations

Corey Reeves, General Manager
Andrea Besthorn, Station Manager
Andrew Crowl, Programming Director

North Newton

***KBCU**
04-06-1989; 88.1 MHz FM; *Hrs Open:* 24 (T-Su); 8 AM-midnight (M); 0.15 kw; 56 ft.; N38 4 26 W97 20 35
300 East 27th, North Newton, KS 67117 US
(316) 284-5228; *Fax:* (316) 284-5286
www.bethelks.edu/kbu
kbcu@bethelks.edu
License: North Newton, Harvey County, KS held by Bethel College.
Regional Network: Kan. Info.
Arbitron Metro Market: North Newton, KS; *Format:* Variety/Diverse *Special Programming:* Sp 2 hrs wkly; *Hrs. of News Programming:* News progmg 5 hrs wkly; *Target Audience:* General; college students & Harvey County
Christine Crouse-Dick, General Manager

Norton

KQNK
10-30-1963; 1530 kHz AM; 1 kw-D, NDD; N39 49 37 W99 52 8
17038 KQNK Rd., Norton, KS 67654 US
(785) 877-3378
www.kqnk.com
License: Norton, KS held by Dierking Communications Inc.
Group Owner: Dierking Communications Inc.; (acq 7-13-99; $165,000 with co-located FM).
Nat'l Reps: Keystone (unwired net)
Format: Contemporary Hits/Top 40
Bruce Dierking, President/General Manager

KQNK-FM
03-01-1993; 106.7 MHz FM; 21 kw; 358 ft.; N39 47 51 W99 53 29
1530 KQNK Rd., Norton, KS 67654 US
(785) 877-3378; *Fax:* (785) 877-3379
www.kqnk.com
License: Norton, Norton County, KS held by Dierking Communications Inc.
Group Owner: Dierking Communications Inc.
Format: Contemporary Hits/Top 40
Bruce Dierking, President/General Manager

***KSNB**
91.5 MHz FM; 0.25 kw; 171 ft.; N39 47 51 W99 53 29
P.O. Box 3206, Tupelo, MS 38803 US
(662) 844-8888; *Fax:* (662) 842-6791
www.afr.net
faq@afa.net
License: Norton, Norton County, KS held by American Family Association.
Group Owner: American Family Radio
Arbitron Metro Market: Norton, KS; *Format:* Christian
Tim Wildmon, President
Donald Wildmon, Founder
Buddy Smith, Sr VP
Ed Vitagliano, Exec VP
Randy Sharp, Director Of Special Projects
Meeke Addison, Director Of Communications
Abraham Hamilton III, General Counsel

Oberlin

KFNF
07-01-1977; 101.1 MHz FM; *Hrs Open:* 24; 100 kw; 443 ft.; N39 49 38 W100 38 48
1660 N. Tyler, Wichita, KS 67212 US
(785) 475-2225; *Fax:* (785) 475-2510
kfnf@highplainsradio.net
License: Oberlin, Decatur County, KS held by Armada Media - McCook Inc.
Group Owner: Armada Media Corp.; (acq 3-31-2007; grpsl)
Nat'l Network: ABC; *Regional Network:* Mid-America Ag
Arbitron Metro Market: Oberlin, KS; *Format:* Country *Special Programming:* Gospel 3 hrs wkly; *Target Audience:* 25-65; farmers; *Adv. Rates:* 13; 13; 13; na
Adam Kadavy, Operations Dir
Bryan Loker, General Manager

***KRLE**
01-01-2009; 89.7 MHz FM; 0.27 kw; 115 ft.; N39 48 11 W100 31 43 *Rebroadcasts:* Rebroadcasts KLVR(FM) Middletown, CA 100%
P O Box 1458, Washington, DC 20013 US
(916) 251-1600; *Fax:* (916) 251-1650
www.klove.com
klove@klove.com
License: Oberlin, Decatur County, KS held by Educational Media Foundation.
Group Owner: EMF Broadcasting; (acq 3-23-2007; grpsl)
Nat'l Network: K-Love
Arbitron Metro Market: Oberlin, KS; *Format:* Christian
Darrell Chambliss, Chairman
Alan Mason, CEO/COO
Mike Novak, CEO
David Pierce, Chief Creative Officer
Dan Antonelli, Chief Business Development Officer
Eric Moser, Chief Financial Officer
Brian Burger, Vice President of HumanResources
D. Kevin Blair, Secretary and General Counsel

Ogden

KQLA
02-14-1986; 103.5 MHz FM; *Hrs Open:* 24; 41 kw; 312 ft.; N39 9 21 W96 36 44
2703 Hall St., Suite 15, Hays, KS 67601 US
(785) 625-4000
www.qcountry1035.com
License: Ogden, Riley County, KS held by Eagle Communications, Inc.
Group Owner: Eagle Communications, Inc.; (acq 9-24-97; $650,000)
Nat'l Network: ABC *Regional Reps:* Regional Rep Corp
Format: Country; *Hrs. of News Programming:* news progmg 10 hrs wkly; *No. News Employees:* 1; *Target Audience:* 18-44; mobile, educated persons with quality income; *Adv. Rates:* 15; 12; 15; 12
Travis Kohlrus, General Manager

Oketo

*KOKN
88.7 MHz FM; kw
US
License: Oketo, Marshall County, KS held by Ron Elmore Ministries Inc.
Arbitron Metro Market: Hobs, MN
Ron Elmore, President

Olathe

KCCV-FM
12-01-1993; 92.3 MHz FM; *Hrs Open:* 24; 8.3 kw; 564 ft.; N38 56 10 W94 50 41
10550 Barkley St., Suite 100, Overland Park, KS 66212 US
(913) 642-7600; *Fax:* (913) 642-1319
www.bottradionetwork.com
comments@bottradionetwork.com
License: Olathe, Johnson County, KS held by Bott Broadcasting Co.
Group Owner: Bott Radio Network; acq 7-1-92; $537,500;
Nat'l Network: USA
Arbitron Metro Market: Kansas City, MO; *Format:* Christian, Talk; *Target Audience:* 25-54; family oriented
Richard Bott Sr., President & CEO
Eben Fowler, Operations Dir
Pat Rulon, Regional Manager
Candy Green, Program Services Manager
Rachel Launius, Marketing Manager
Jason Potocnik, Director of Traffic Operations

Olpe

KEKS
103.1 MHz FM; 2.45 kw; 315 ft.; N38 17 37 W96 13 3
US
(620) 343-6144; *Fax:* (620) 343-6844
kiss1031.net
License: Olpe, Lyon County, KS held by Andrew A. Wachter.
Arbitron Metro Market: Emporia, KS
Andrew Wachter, General Manager

Olsburg

*KANV
01-01-2003; 91.3 MHz FM; 6 kw; 328 ft.; N39 0 55 W96 53 55
Broadcasting Hall, Lawrence, KS 66045 US
(785) 864-4530; *Fax:* (785) 864-5278
www.kpr.ku.edu
kpr@ku.edu
License: Olsburg, Pottawatomie County, KS held by The University of Kansas.
Nat'l Network: NPR
Arbitron Metro Market: Topeka, KS; *Format:* Jazz; *No. News Employees:* 5
Janet Campbell, General Manager
Darrell Brogdon, Programming Director
J. Schafer, News Director
Steve Kincaid, Engineering Dir
Nicci Banman, Business Manager
Wendy Huggins, Administrative Associate
Mark Edwards, MusicDirector/Classical Announcer
Laura Lorson, All Things Considered Host/Producer
Bryan Thompson, Health Reporter
Stephen Koranda, Statehouse Reporter

Osage City

KMXN
07-26-1982; 92.9 MHz FM; *Hrs Open:* 24; 7.9 kw; Ant 538 ft; N38 48 21 W95 42 58
3125 W. 6th St., Lawrence, KS 66801
(785) 843-1320; *Fax:* (785) 841-5924
License: Osage City, Osage County, KS held by Great Plains Media Inc.
Group Owner: Great Plains Media Inc.; (acq 6-30-2006)
Arbitron Metro Market: Topeka, KS
Tim Robisch, General Manager
Tabatha LeVrault, Operations Manager
Morgan Grammer, Chief Engineer

Ottawa

KCHZ
03-01-1962; 95.7 MHz FM; 98 kw; Ant 981 ft; N39 00 45 W95 01 46
5800 Foxridge Dr., 6th Floor, Mission, KS 66202
(913) 514-3000; *Fax:* (913) 262-3946
www.957thevibe.com
License: Ottawa, KS held by CMP Houston-KC, LLC
Group Owner: Cumulus Media Inc.; (acq 5-3-2006; grpsl).
Population Served: 11,036; *Arbitron Metro Market:* Kansas City, MO-KS; *Format:* Contemporary Hits/Top 40
Jared Robb, General Sales Mgr
Maurive Devoe, Programming Director
Ashley Coppock, Promotions Manager

KOFO
09-24-1949; 1220 kHz AM; *Hrs Open:* 24; 250 w-D, 40 w-N; N38 35 04 W95 15 57
320 E. Radio Rd., Box 16, Ottawa, KS 66067
(785) 242-1220; *Fax:* (785) 242-1442
www.kofo.com
kofo@kofo.com
License: Ottawa, Franklin County, KS held by Brandy Communications Inc.
Nat'l Network: ABC; *Regional Network:* Kan. Agriculture
Population Served: 55,000; *Arbitron Metro Market:* Kansas City, MO *Special Programming:* Farm 2 hrs wkly; *Hrs. of News Programming:* news progmg 7 hrs wkly; *No. News Employees:* 1; *Target Audience:* 25-54; Male& Female
Brad Howard, President

*KRBW
01-01-1997; 90.5 MHz FM; 0.43 kw; 187 ft.; N38 35 4 W95 15 56
P.O. Box 3206, Tupelo, MS 38803 US
(662) 844-8888; *Fax:* (662) 842-6791
www.afr.net
faq@afa.net
License: Ottawa, Franklin County, KS held by American Family Association
Group Owner: American Family Radio; (acq 1-24-97)
Format: Christian
Tim Wildmon, President
Donald Wildmon, Founder
Buddy Smith, Sr VP
Ed Vitagliano, Exec VP
Randy Sharp, Director Of Special Projects
Meeke Addison, Director Of Communication
Abraham Hamilton III, General Counsel & Public PolicyAnalyst

*KTJO-FM
05-01-1951; 88.9 MHz FM; *Hrs Open:* 7 AM-midnight; 0.145 kw; 66 ft.; N38 36 16 W95 15 49
1001 South Cedar Street, Ottawa, KS 66067 US
(785) 242-5200; *Fax:* (785) 242-7429
License: Ottawa, Franklin County, KS held by Ottawa University.
Arbitron Metro Market: Ottawa, KS; *Format:* Christian, Variety/Diverse; *Hrs. of News Programming:* News progmg 5 hrs wkly; *Target Audience:* General; Ottawa Univ community & City of Ottawa, KS
Jesse Wemlinger, Station Manager

Overland Park

KCCV
01-01-1962; 760 kHz AM; *Hrs Open:* Sunrise-sunset; 6 kw-D, DA2; 0.2 kw-N, DA2; N39 2 26 W94 30 34
10550 Barkley St., Suite 100, Overland Park, KS 66212 US
(913) 642-7600; *Fax:* (913) 642-1319
www.bottradionetwork.com
comments@bottradionetwork.com
License: Overland Park, Johnson County, KS held by Bott Broadcasting Co.
Group Owner: Bott Radio Network; (acq 1962)
Nat'l Network: USA
Arbitron Metro Market: Kansas City, MO; *Format:* Christian, Religious, 86; *Target Audience:* 25-54; family-oriented
Richard Bott Sr., President & CEO
Eben Fowler, Operations Dir
Pat Rulon, Regional Manager
Candy Green, Program Services Manager
Rachel Launius, Marketing Manager
Jason Potocnik, Director of Traffic Operations

Parsons

KLKC
01-01-1948; 1540 kHz AM; 0.25 kw-D, ND2; 0.001 kw-N, ND2; N37 20 35 W95 13 55
PO Box 853, Parsons, KS 67357 US
(620) 421-6400; *Fax:* (620) 421-5570
klkc.com
lynnm@skilonline.com
License: Parsons, KS held by Southeast Kansas Independent Living Resource Center Inc.
Group Owner: Southeast Kansas Independent Living Resource Center Inc.; (acq 12-6-2005; $334,932 with co-located FM)
Arbitron Metro Market: Joplin, MO; *Format:* Sports, Talk *Special Programming:* Farm 2 hrs, relg 2 hrs, big band 3 hrs wkly; *Hrs. of News Programming:* News progmg 28 hrs wkly; *Target Audience:* 12-60; general *Adv. Rates:* 12.65; 9.90; 9.90; 9.90
Lynn Meredith, General Manager
Colt Smith, General Sales Mgr
Steve Lardy, Programming Director
Annette Tucker, News Director
Terry Blackburn, Music Director
Ed Hernandez

KLKC-FM
10-01-1978; 93.5 MHz FM; *Hrs Open:* 6 AM-11 PM; 3 kw; 266 ft.; N37 20 35 W95 13 55
PO Box 853, Parsons, KS 67357 US
(620) 421-6400; *Fax:* (620) 421-5570
lynnm@skilonline.com
License: Parsons, Labette County, KS
Arbitron Metro Market: Joplin, MO; *Format:* Oldies; *Adv. Rates:* Same as AM
James Auel, General Manager

Phillipsburg

KKAN
12-31-1959; 1490 kHz AM; *Hrs Open:* 24; 1 kw-U, ND1; N39 47 32 W99 19 55
205 F Street, P.O. Box 548, Phillipsburg, KS 67661 US
(785) 543-2151; *Fax:* (785) 543-2152
www.kkankqma.com
radio@kkankqma.com
License: Phillipsburg, KS held by RTY Broadcasting
Regional Network: Kan. Info.
Format: News, Variety/Diverse *Special Programming:* Farm 10 hrs, gospel 12 hrs wkly; *Target Audience:* General; rural population & small towns
Robert Yates, General Manager
Tad Felts, News/Sports Director
Robert Yates III, Systems Administrator

KQMA
07-14-1984; 92.5 MHz FM; 100 kw; 512 ft.; N39 37 2 W99 17 55
205 F Street, P.O. Box 548, Phillipsburg, KS 67661 US
(785) 543-2151; *Fax:* (785) 543-2152
www.kkankqma.com
License: Phillipsburg, Phillips County, KS held by RTY Broadcasting
Format: Variety/Diverse
Bob Yates, General Manager
Tad Felts, News Director
Tad Felts, Sports Director

Pittsburg

KKOW
10-11-1937; 860 kHz AM; *Hrs Open:* 24; 10 kw-D, DAN; 5 kw-N, DAN; N37 24 46 W94 38 16
1162 E Hwy 126, Pittsburg, KS 66762 US
(620) 231-7200; *Fax:* (620) 231-3321
www.kkowam.com
kkow@kkowradio.com
License: Pittsburg, KS held by American Media Investment Inc.
Nat'l Network: CBS; *Nat'l Reps:* McGavren Guild
Arbitron Metro Market: Joplin, MO; *Format:* Country; *Hrs. of News Programming:* news progmg 5 hrs wkly; *No. News Employees:* 2; *Target Audience:* General.
Chris Kelly, General Manager

KKOW-FM
04-20-1975; 96.9 MHz FM; 100 kw; 912 ft.; N37 18 44 W94 48 58
1162 E. Hwy 126, Pittsburg, KS 66762 US
(620) 231-7200; *Fax:* (620) 231-3321
www.kkowfm.com
kkow@kkowradio.com

License: Pittsburg, Crawford County, KS held by American Media Investments Inc.
Arbitron Metro Market: Joplin, MO; *Format:* Country
Chris Kelly, General Manager
Dave Fink, General Sales Mgr

***KRPS**
04-29-1988; 89.9 MHz FM; *Hrs Open:* 24; 100 kw; 1001 ft.; N37 18 44 W94 48 58
1701 South Broadway, Pittsburg, KS 66762 US
(620) 235-4288; *Fax:* 620(235-4290)
www.krps.org
krps@pittstate.edu
License: Pittsburg, Crawford County, KS held by Pittsburg State University.
Nat'l Network: NPR; PRI
Arbitron Metro Market: Four State area *Special Programming:* Folk 3 hrs; *Hrs. of News Programming:* News progmg 39 hrs wkly
Matt Larson, Operations Dir
Missi Kelly, General Manager
Vicki Pritchett, General Sales Mgr
Tim Metcalf, Programming Director

KSEK
01-01-1948; 1340 kHz AM; 1 kw-U, ND1; N37 23 44 W94 40 42
1604 E. Quincy, P.O. Box 383, Pittsburg, KS 66762 US
(620) 232-9912; *Fax:* (620) 232-9915
lynnm@skilonline.com
License: Pittsburg, KS held by Southeast Kansas Independent Living Resource Center Inc.
Group Owner: Southeast Kansas Independent Living Resource Center Inc.; (acq 11-30-2004; $700,000 with KSEK-FM Girard).
Nat'l Network: ESPN Radio; AP Network News
Arbitron Metro Market: Pittsburg, KS; *Format:* Sports *Special Programming:* High school basketball & football; *Hrs. of News Programming:* News progmg 10 hrs wkly; *Target Audience:* 25 plus.; *Adv. Rates:* 120;120; 120; 120
Lynn Meredith, General Manager

Plainville

KFIX
05-11-1998; 96.9 MHz FM; *Hrs Open:* 24; 10.5 kw; 876 ft.; N39 1 15 W99 28 12
Mailing Address: 2300 Hall St., Box 6, Hays, KS 67601 US
Second Address: 2703 Hall St., Suite 15, Hays, KS 67601
(785) 625-2578; *Fax:* (785) 625-3632
www.hayspost.com
admin@hayspost.com
License: Plainville, Rooks County, KS held by Hull Broadcasting Inc.
Group Owner: Eagle Communications Group; (acq 9-12-00; with KBGL(FM) Larned).
Arbitron Metro Market: Hays, KS; *Format:* Classic Rock; *Target Audience:* 25-64.
Travis Kohlrus, General Manager

Pleasanton

***KPIO-FM**
93.7 MHz FM; 25 kw; 328 ft.; N38 14 23 W94 56 36 US
(816) 630-1090
www.thecatholicradionetwork.com
info@thecatholicradionetwork.com
License: Pleasanton, Linn County, KS held by Kansas City Catholic Network Inc.
Arbitron Metro Market: Pleasanton, KS; *Format:* Christian
James O'Laughlin, President

Pratt

KHMY
07-01-1965; 93.1 MHz FM; *Hrs Open:* 24; 100 kw; 991 ft.; N37 55 43 W98 18 36
825 N. Main St., Hutchinson, KS 67501 US
(620) 662-4486
www.khmyfm.com
my931@cox.net
License: Pratt, Pratt County, KS held by Eagle Communications Inc.
Group Owner: Eagle Communications Group; (acq 3-17-03; swap for KSSH(FM) Ingalls).
Nat'l Reps: McGavren Guild
Arbitron Metro Market: Pratt, KS; *Format:* Adult Contemp, Contemporary Hits/Top 40
Casey Osburn, Operations Dir/Program Dir
Terry Drouhard, General Sales Mgr
Mark Goff, Chief Engineer

KMMM
09-19-1963; 1290 kHz AM; *Hrs Open:* 24; 5 kw-D, DA2; 0.5 kw-N, DA2; N37 38 34 W98 40 39
1660 N. Tyler, Wichita, KS 67212 US
(620) 672-5581; *Fax:* (620) 672-5583
License: Pratt, KS held by Rocking M Radio Inc.
Group Owner: Rocking M Radio Inc.; (acq 8-31-2007; grpsl)
Regional Network: Mid-America Ag; *Nat'l Reps:* McGavren Guild
Arbitron Metro Market: Pratt, KS; *Format:* Oldies; *Hrs. of News Programming:* news progmg 3 hrs wkly; *No. News Employees:* 1; *Target Audience:* 25 plus; rural
Eric Strobel, General Manager
Lisa Coss, Station Manager
Carl Raida, Programming Director

Riley

KACZ
09-16-2003; 96.3 MHz FM; 12.5 kw; 476 ft.; N39 13 34 W96 37 0
2414 Casement Rd., Manhattan, KS 66502 USA
(785) 776-1350
www.z963.com
dswick@z963.com
License: Riley, Riley County, KS held by Manhattan Broadcasting Co. Inc.
Group Owner: Seaton Stations
Wire Services: AP
Arbitron Metro Market: Topeka, KS; *Format:* Contemporary Hits/Top 40; *Hrs. of News Programming:* news progmg 4 hrs wkly; *No. News Employees:* 3; *Target Audience:* 18-59; woman; *Adv. Rates:* 18; 16; 18; 14
Chris Swick, Programming Director

Rozel

KKCV
01-01-2007; 102.5 MHz FM; *Hrs Open:* 24; 100 kw; 488 ft.; N37 57 28 W99 25 45.2
10550 Barkley St., Suite 100, Overland Park, KS 66212 US
(913) 642-7770
www.bottradionetwork.com
comments@bottradionetwork.com
License: Rozel, Pawnee County, KS held by Community Broadcasting Inc.
Group Owner: Bott Radio Network
Nat'l Network: USA
Arbitron Metro Market: Dodge City, KS; *Format:* Christian, Talk; *Target Audience:* 25-55.
Richard Bott Sr., President & CEO
Eben Fowler, Operations Dir
Pat Rulon, Director of National Sales
Candy Green, Program Services Manager
Rachel Launius, Marketing Manager
Jason Potocnik, Director of Traffic Operations
TinaGiffin, Area Account Manager

Russell

KRSL-FM
07-01-1965; 95.9 MHz FM; 1.35 kw; 486 ft.; N38 54 22 W98 51 39
P. O. Box 666, Russell, KS 67665 US
(785) 483-3121; *Fax:* (785) 483-6511
www.krsl.com
comments@krsl.com
License: Russell, Russell County, KS held by White Communications L.L.C.
Arbitron Metro Market: Russell, KS; *Format:* Contemporary Hits/Top 40, Adult Contemp; *Adv. Rates:* $13; 11; 11
Larry Calvery, General Manager
Mike McKenna, Station Manager
David Elliott, News Director

KRSL
01-11-1956; 990 kHz AM; 0.25 kw-D, ND1; 0.03 kw-N, ND1; N38 54 22 W98 51 39
P. O. Box 666, Russell, KS 67665 US
(785) 483-3121; *Fax:* (785) 483-6511
www.krsl.com
Comments@krsl.com
License: Russell, KS held by White Communications L.L.C.
Arbitron Metro Market: Russell ,KS; *Format:* Contemporary Hits/Top 40, Adult Contemp *Special Programming:* Polka 4 hrs, farm 2 hrs wkly; *Target Audience:* 24 plus; general; *Adv. Rates:* 13; 11; 11
Mike McKenna, General Manager
Brenda Calvery, General Sales Mgr
David Elliott, News Director

Sacramento

KUDL
01-01-2001; 102.9 Hz FM; *Hrs Open:* 24; 10 kw-D, 1 kw-N; N39 06 50 W94 40 45
5345 Madison Avenue, Sacramento, CA 95841
(916) 334-7777; *Fax:* (916) 339-4559
www.endonline.com
info@1065thewolf.com
License: Sacramento, CA held by Entercom Kansas City License LLC.
Group Owner: Entercom Communications Corp.
Arbitron Metro Market: Kansas City, MO-KS; *Format:* Contemporary Hits/Top 40
Herndon Hasty, General Manager
John Verlin, General Sales Mgr
Patrick Nease, Programming Director
Dave Alpert, General Manager

Saint Marys

KTOP-FM
12-04-1994; 102.9 MHz FM; 50 kw; 320 ft; N39 05 34 W95 47 05
825 S. Kansas Ave., Topeka, KS 12550
(785) 272-2122; *Fax:* (785) 272-6219
www.cumulus.com
oldieskqtp@aol.com
License: Saint Marys, Pottawatomie County, KS held by Cumulus Licensing Corp.
Group Owner: Cumulus Media Inc.; (acq 4-13-01; with KWIC(FM) Topeka).
Target Audience: 35-54.
John Walker, General Manager
Keith Liefmann, General Sales Mgr
Rich Bowers, Programming Director
Carla Newman, Promotions Manager
Mike Manns, News Director

Salina

***KAKA**
01-01-2002; 88.5 MHz FM; 46 kw; 394 ft.; N39 4 12 W97 51 14
P.O. Box 3206, Tupelo, MS 38803 US
(662) 844-8888; *Fax:* (662) 842-6791
www.afr.net
faq@afa.net
License: Salina, Saline County, KS held by American Family Association.
Group Owner: American Family Radio
Arbitron Metro Market: Tupelo, MS; *Format:* Religious
Tim Wildmon, President
Donald Wildmon, Founder
Buddy Smith, Sr. VP
Ed Vitagliano, Executive VP
Randy Sharp, Director Of Special Projects
Meeke Addison, Director Of Communications
Abraham Hamilton III, General Counsel & PublicPolicy

***KCVS**
01-01-1994; 91.7 MHz FM; *Hrs Open:* 24; 11.5 kw; 748 ft.; N38 39 58 W97 41 30
3434 West Kilbourn Avenue, Milwaukee, WI 53208 US
(414) 935-3000; *Fax:* (414) 935-3015
www.vcyamerica.org
vcy@vcyamerica.org
License: Salina, Saline County, KS held by VCY/America Inc.
Group Owner: VCY America Inc.; (acq 7-2-97).
Nat'l Network: Moody; USA
Arbitron Metro Market: Milwaukee, WI; *Format:* Christian
Vic Eliason, Operations Dir
Jim Schneider, Programming Director

KFRM
01-01-1947; 550 kHz AM; *Hrs Open:* sun up to sun down
P. O. Box 16, Clay Center, KS 67432 US
(785) 632-5661; *Fax:* (785) 632-5662
www.kfrm.com
webmaster@kfrm.com
License: Salina, KS held by Taylor Communications Inc.
Nat'l Network: AP Network News; *Wire Services:* AP
Arbitron Metro Market: Clay Center, KA; *Format:* Talk *Special Programming:* Gospel 5 hrs wkly; *Hrs. of News Programming:* news progmg 6 hrs wkly; *No. News Employees:* 2; *Target Audience:* 25-55; agricultural *Adv. Rates:* 120; 120;100; 25
Rod Keen, Operations Dir
Kyle Bauer, General Manager
Michelle Tessaro, News Director
Duane Toews, Farm Director
Rocky Downing, Sports Commentator
Joe Woodward, Traffic Manager
Phil Kasper, Weekend/Evening Manager

***KHCD**
01-28-1988; 89.5 MHz FM; *Hrs Open:* 24; 100 kw; 902 ft.; N39 6 16 W97 23 15 *Rebroadcasts:* Rebroadcasts KHCC-FM Hutchinson 100%
815 N. Walnut, Suite 300, Hutchinson, KS 67501 US
(620) 662-6646
www.radiokansas.org
rfragoza@radiokansas.org
License: Salina, Saline County, KS held by Hutchinson Community College.
Nat'l Network: NPR
Format: News *Special Programming:* Car talk 2 hrs wkly; *Hrs. of News Programming:* News progmg 27 hrs wkly
Geralyn Smith, Operations Dir
Ken Baker, General Manager
Sharon Webb, Development Director
Ric Jung, Chief Engineer

KINA
04-20-1964; 910 kHz AM; *Hrs Open:* 24 hrs; 0.5 kw-D, DA2; 0.029 kw-N, DA2; N38 45 52 W97 32 30
2703 Hall St., Suite 15, Hays, KS 67601 US
(785) 625-4000
License: Salina, KS held by Eagle Communications Inc.
Group Owner: Eagle Communications Group; (Acq 11-1-95; $235,000)
Nat'l Network: Fox News Radio; *Wire Services:* AP
Format: News/Talk; *Target Audience:* 45 plus; middle to upper income adults
Scott Boomer, Operations Dir
Travis Kohlrus, General Manager
Mark Goff, Chief Engineer

KSAL
05-18-1937; 1150 kHz AM; *Hrs Open:* 24; 5 kw-D, ND2; 5 kw-N, ND2; N38 53 3 W97 31 2
131 N. Santa Fe, P.O. Box 80, Salina, KS 67402 US
(785) 823-1111; *Fax:* (785) 823-2034
www.ksal.com
License: Salina, Saline County, KS held by Alpha Media Licensee LLC
Group Owner: Alpha Media LLC; (acq 9-2-2015; grpsl).
Nat'l Network: ABC; *Regional Network:* Kan. Agriculture; Kan. Info; *Nat'l Reps:* Katz Radio; *Wire Services:* AP
Arbitron Metro Market: Salina, KS; *Format:* News, News/Talk, 86 *Special Programming:* Farm 3 hrs wkly; *Hrs. of News Programming:* news progmg 20 hrs wkly; *No. News Employees:* 3; *Target Audience:* 35-64. *Adv. Rates:* 27.50; 20.63; 24.75; 8..25
Bob Protzman, Station Manager
Mitch Drees, Sales Manager
Rich Alexander, Programming Director
Clarke Sanders, Promotions Manager
Todd Pittenger, News Director
Aaron Coil, Chief Engineer
Nicole Novotny, Business and HumanResources

KSKG
01-01-1961; 99.9 MHz FM; *Hrs Open:* 24; 100 kw; 571 ft.; N38 47 36 W97 31 33
2703 Hall St., Suite 15, Hays, KS 67601 US
(785) 625-4000
License: Salina, Saline County, KS held by Eagle Communications Inc.
Group Owner: Eagle Communications Group
Arbitron Metro Market: Salina, KS; *Format:* Country *Special Programming:* Gospel 3 hrs wkly; *Target Audience:* 25-54; 51% female, 49% male (baby boomers)
Scott Boomer, Operations Dir
Travis Kohlrus, General Manager
Mark Goff, Chief Engineer

KYEZ
05-01-1975; 93.7 MHz FM; *Hrs Open:* 24; 100 kw; 509 ft.; N38 57 14 W97 36 29
131 N. Santa Fe, P.O. Box 80, Salina, KS 67402 US
(785) 823-1111; *Fax:* (785) 823-2034
www.y937.com
License: Salina, Saline County, KS held by Alpha Media Licensee LLC
Group Owner: Alpha Media LLC
Nat'l Reps: Katz Radio
Arbitron Metro Market: Salina, KS; *Format:* Country; *Hrs. of News Programming:* news progmg 2 hrs wkly; *No. News Employees:* 3; *Target Audience:* 25-54.; *Adv. Rates:* 25.40; 19.05; 22.86; 7.62
Clarke Sanders, Operations Manager
Bob Protzman, Station Manager
Mitch Drees, Sales Manager
Chad Allen, Programming Director
Todd Pittenger, News Director

KSAL-FM
10-01-1988; 104.9 MHz FM; 14 kw; 440 ft.; N38 52 36 W97 43 15
131 N. Santa Fe, P.O. Box 80, Salina, KS 67402 US
(785) 823-1111; *Fax:* (785) 823-2034
www.fm1049salina.com
License: Salina, Saline County, KS held by Alpha Media Licensee LLC
Group Owner: Alpha Media LLC; (acq 9-2-2015; grpsl).
Nat'l Reps: Katz Radio
Arbitron Metro Market: Salina, KS; *Format:* Contemporary Hits/Top 40; *Hrs. of News Programming:* news progmg 5 hrs wky; *No. News Employees:* 3; *Target Audience:* 18-44.; *Adv. Rates:* 21.20; 15.90; 19.08; 6.36
Bob Protzman, Station Manager
Mitch Drees, Sales Manager
Bill Ray, Programming Director
Clarke Sanders, Promotions Manager
Todd Pittenger, News Director

Scott City

KYUL
10-13-1962; 1310 kHz AM; 0.5 kw-D, ND1; 0.147 kw-N, ND1; N38 31 35 W100 54 42
P.O. Box 931, Huron, SD 57350 US
(620) 872-5345; *Fax:* (620) 872-5422
www.kiulradio.com
License: Scott City, KS held by Steckline Communications Inc.
Group Owner: Steckline Communications Inc.; (acq 11-28-2006; $550,000 with KIUL(AM) Garden City)
Regional Network: Kan. Info.; Kan. Agriculture
Arbitron Metro Market: Garden City, KS; *Format:* News, News/Talk, 86 *Special Programming:* Farm 5 hrs wkly, health 5 hrs wkly; *Hrs. of News Programming:* news prgomg 140 hrs wkly; *Target Audience:* 35-64
Rick Everett, General Manager
Alex Mayer, Programming Director

KSKL
11-09-1964; 94.5 MHz FM; 100 kw; 351 ft.; N38 31 35 W100 54 42
P.O. Box 907, Valley City, ND 58072 US
(620) 872-5345; *Fax:* (620) 872-5422
www.wksradio.com
info@wksradio.com
License: Scott City, Scott County, KS held by Western Kansas Wireless Inc.
Group Owner: Robert Ingstad Broadcast Properties; (acq 3-26-93; $175,000 with co-located AM;
Regional Network: Kan. Info.
Arbitron Metro Market: Scott City, KS; *Format:* Oldies
Christa Roy, General Manager
Bob Dale, Station Manager
James Janda, Programming Director
Jim Wagoner, News Director

***KJLJ**
88.5 MHz FM; 25 kw; 292 ft.; N38 32 55 W100 57 37
909 Carthage Street, Meade, KS 67864 US
(620) 873-2991; *Fax:* (620) 873-2755
www.kjil.com
kjil@kjil.com
License: Scott City, Scott County, KS held by Great Plains Christian Radio Inc.
Arbitron Metro Market: Scott City, KS; *Format:* Christian
Michael Luskey, President/CEO

Seneca

KMZA-FM
10-15-1992; 92.1 MHz FM; *Hrs Open:* 24; 6 kw; 404 ft.; N39 49 34 W96 1 45 *Rebroadcasts:* Rebroadcasts KNZA(FM) Hiawatha 90%
513 Main St., PO Box 92, Seneca, KS 66538 US
(785) 336-6166; *Fax:* (785) 336-3600
www.kmzafm.com
kmza@bbwi.net
License: Seneca, Nemaha County, KS held by KNZA Inc.
Group Owner: KNZA Inc.
Format: Country *Special Programming:* Farm 7 hrs wkly; *Hrs. of News Programming:* news progmg 10 hrs wkly; *No. News Employees:* 1; *Target Audience:* General.; *Adv. Rates:* 19; 15; 15; 13
Doug Weinberg, General Sales Mgr
L.J. Trant, Programming Director
Brian Hagen, News Director

Shawnee

KCMO-FM
05-04-1948; 94.9 MHz FM; *Hrs Open:* 24; 100 kw; 1119 ft.; N39 5 26 W94 28 18
401 City Avenue, Suite 409, Bala Cynwyd, PA 19004 US
(913) 514-3000; *Fax:* (913) 514-3004
www.710kcmo.com
bill.ryan@cumulus.com
License: Shawnee, Jackson County, KS held by CMP Houston-KC LLC
Group Owner: Cumulus Media Inc.
Nat'l Reps: Katz Radio
Arbitron Metro Market: Shawnee, KS; *Format:* Oldies; *Hrs. of News Programming:* news progmg 2 hrs wkly; *No. News Employees:* 1; *Target Audience:* 25-54.
Mark Sullivan, Senior Vice President, General Manager
Bill Ryan, General Sales Mgr
Don Daniels, Programming Director
Tom Bamford, Producer / PSA Director
Brian Goeke, Director of Marketing & Online
John Gallagher, Vice President ofSales

Silver Lake

KCVT
01-01-1996; 92.5 MHz FM; *Hrs Open:* 24; 6.7 kw; 387 ft.; N39 8 42 W95 55 37
534 S. Kansas Ave., Suite 930, Topeka, KS 66603 US
(785) 233-9250
www.bottradionetwork.com
comments@bottradionetwork.com
License: Silver Lake, Shawnee County, KS held by Richard P. Bott II.
Group Owner: Bott Radio Network
Nat'l Network: USA
Arbitron Metro Market: Topeka, KS; *Format:* Christian, Talk
Richard Bott Sr., President & CEO
Eben Fowler, Operations Dir
Pat Rulon, Regional Manager
Candy Green, Program Services Manager
Rachel Launius, Marketing Manager
Jason Potocnik, Director of Traffic Operations

Sterling

KSKU
06-12-1995; 94.7 MHz FM; *Hrs Open:* 24; 50 kw; 486 ft.; N38 13 50 W98 18 53
10 E. 5th Ave., Hutchinson, KS 67501 US
(620) 665-5758; *Fax:* (620) 665-5758
www.adastraradio.com
ksku@adastra.kscoxmail.com
License: Sterling, Rice County, KS held by Ad Astra Per Aspera Broadcasting Inc.
Group Owner: Ad Astra Per Aspera Broadcasting Inc.
Nat'l Network: Jones Radio Networks
Format: Contemporary Hits/Top 40; *Hrs. of News Programming:* news progmg 2 hrs wkly; *No. News Employees:* 1; *Target Audience:* 18-54; general

Topeka

***KBUZ**
01-01-1994; 90.3 MHz FM; 11 kw; 840 ft.; N39 0 19 W96 2 58
P.O. Box 3206, Tupelo, MS 38803 US
(662) 844-8888; *Fax:* (662) 842-6791
www.afr.net
faq@afa.net
License: Topeka, Shawnee County, KS held by American Family Association.
Group Owner: American Family Radio; (acq 12-30-94;
Arbitron Metro Market: Wichita, KS; *Format:* Religious
Tim Wildmon, President
Donald Wildmon, Founder
Buddy Smith, Senior VP
Ed Vitagliano, Exec VP
Randy Sharp, Director Of Special Projects
Meeke Addison, Director Of Communications
Abraham Hamiltong III, General Counsel & PublicPolicy Analyst

KDVV
05-29-1960; 100.3 MHz FM; 100 kw; 984 ft.; N38 57 15 W95 54 43
330 East Kilbourn Ave., Suite 250, Milwaukee, WI 53202 US
(785) 272-2122; *Fax:* (785) 272-6219
www.v100rocks.com
License: Topeka, Shawnee County, KS held by Cumulus Licensing LLC.
Group Owner: Cumulus Media Inc.
Nat'l Network: Westwood One

Arbitron Metro Market: Topeka, KS; *Format:* Rock/AOR; *Target Audience:* 18-54.
Benjamin Johnson, General Manager
David Nguyen, General Sales Mgr
Erik Magnuson, Programming Director
Lindsay Schrupp, News Director
Rich Lusch, Chief Engineer
A.J. Ramirez, Music Director
Sean Johannessen, Music Director
BryceFsch, Programming Director

***KJTY**
08-31-1985; 88.1 MHz FM; *Hrs Open:* 24; 35 kw; 584 ft.; N38 53 23 W95 17 17
341 S. Washington, Lancaster, WI 53813 US
(785) 357-8888; *Fax:* (785) 357-0100
www.myflr.org
License: Topeka, Shawnee County, KS held by Family Life Broadcasting Inc.
Group Owner: Family Life Communications Inc.; (acq 5-23-2007; grpsl)
Nat'l Network: USA
Arbitron Metro Market: Topeka, KS; *Format:* Religious, Religious *Special Programming:* Children 5 hrs wkly; *Hrs. of News Programming:* News progmg 15 hrs wkly; *Target Audience:* 25-49.
Randy Carlson, President
Adam Nash, Programming Director

KMAJ
07-01-1947; 1440 kHz AM
330 East Kilbourn Ave., Suite 250, Milwaukee, WI 53202 US
(785) 272-2122; *Fax:* (785) 272-6219
www.kmaj.com
info@kmaj.com
License: Topeka, KS held by Cumulus Licensing Corp.
Group Owner: Cumulus Media Inc.; (acq 7-31-98; grpsl)
Nat'l Network: ABC; ESPN Radio; Westwood One
Arbitron Metro Market: Topeka, KS; *Format:* News, News/Talk, 84, Talk; *Target Audience:* General.
John Walker, General Manager
Keith Liefmann, General Sales Mgr
Rose Diehl, Programming Director
Carla Newman, Promotions Manager
Mike Manns, News Director

KTOP
07-01-1947; 1490 kHz AM; 1 kw-U, ND1; N39 4 39 W95 40 46
330 East Kilbourn Ave., Suite 250, Milwaukee, WI 53202 US
(785) 272-2122; *Fax:* (785) 272-6219
www.ktop1490.com
License: Topeka, KS held by Cumulus Licensing Corp.
Group Owner: Cumulus Media Inc.; (acq 7-31-98; grpsl)
Nat'l Network: ESPN Radio
Arbitron Metro Market: Topeka, KS; *Format:* Sports
Kevin Klein, General Manager
Forrest Smithkors, Programming Director

KTPK
11-25-1974; 106.9 MHz FM; *Hrs Open:* 24; 100 kw; 1,211 ft.; N39 1 34 W95 55 1
1210 S.W. Executive Dr., Topeka, KS 66615 US
(785) 273-1069; *Fax:* (785) 273-0123
www.countrylegends1069.com
License: Topeka, Shawnee County, KS held by Alpha Media Licensee LLC
Group Owner: Alpha Media LLC; (acq 9-2-2015).
Nat'l Reps: Katz Radio
Arbitron Metro Market: Topeka, KS; *Format:* Country; *Hrs. of News Programming:* news progmg 6 hrs wkly; *No. News Employees:* 2; *Target Audience:* 25-64; mobile, family-oriented, high-income professional adults *Adv. Rates:* 29; 26; 26; 8
Larry Riggins, General Manager
Jeremy Lamb, Local Sales Manager
Roy Baum, Chief Engineer

KWIC
10-15-1993; 99.3 MHz FM; *Hrs Open:* 24; 6.8 kw; 538 ft.; N39 3 50 W95 45 49
P.O. Box 2307, Newburgh, NY 12550 US
(785) 272-2122; *Fax:* (785) 272-6219
www.eagle993.com
License: Topeka, Shawnee County, KS held by Cumulus Licensing Corp.
Group Owner: Cumulus Media Inc.; (acq 4-13-01; with KQTP(FM) Saint Marys).
Arbitron Metro Market: Topeka, KS; *Format:* Contemporary Hits/Top 40, Adult Contemp
John Walker, General Manager
Keith Liefmann, General Sales Mgr
Les Glenn, Programming Director
Carla Newman, Promotions Manager
Mike Manns, News Director

WIBW
05-08-1927; 580 kHz AM; *Hrs Open:* 24; 5 kw-D, DAN; 5 kw-N, DAN; N39 5 5 W95 46 58
1210 S.W. Executive Dr., Topeka, KS 66615 US
(785) 272-3456; *Fax:* (785) 228-7282
www.wibwnewsnow.com
License: Topeka, Shawnee County, KS held by Alpha Media Licensee LLC
Group Owner: Alpha Media LLC; (acq 9-2-2015; grpsl).
Nat'l Network: ABC; *Regional Network:* Kan. Agriculture; Kan. Info; *Nat'l Reps:* Katz Radio; *Wire Services:* AP
Arbitron Metro Market: Topeka, KS; *Format:* News, News/Talk, 84, Talk; *Hrs. of News Programming:* news progmg 15 hrs wkly; *No. News Employees:* 4; *Target Audience:* Adults 25+.
Larry Riggins, General Manager
Jeremy Lamb, Local Sales Manager
Keith Montgomery, Programming Director
Torey Berndt, Marketing and Promotions Director
Roy Baum, Chief Engineer
Jake Lebahn, Sports Director
Kelly Lenz, AgricultureDirector

WIBW-FM
09-01-1961; 94.5 MHz FM; *Hrs Open:* 24; 98.4 kw; 1,152 ft.; N39 0 22 W96 2 57
1210 S.W. Executive Dr., Topeka, KS 66615 US
(785) 272-3456; *Fax:* (785) 228-7282
www.94country.com
License: Topeka, Shawnee County, KS held by Alpha Media Licensee LLC
Group Owner: Alpha Media LLC
Regional Network: Kan. Info.; Kan. Agriculture; *Nat'l Reps:* Katz Radio
Arbitron Metro Market: Topeka, KS; *Format:* Country; *Hrs. of News Programming:* news progmg 4 hrs wkly; *No. News Employees:* 4; *Target Audience:* Adults 25-54.
Larry Riggins, General Manager
Jeremy Lamb, Local Sales Manager
Keith Montgomery, Programming Director
Torey Berndt, Marketing and Promotions Director
Roy Baum, Chief Engineer
Dave Navarro Jr., Digital Media Director

Ulysses

KULY
03-01-1965; 1420 kHz AM; *Hrs Open:* 24; 1 kw-D, DA2; 0.5 kw-N, DA2; N37 32 53 W101 21 49
P.O. Box 907, Valley City, ND 58072 US
(620) 276-2366; *Fax:* (620) 356-3635
www.wksradio.com
christaroy@wksradio.com
License: Ulysses, KS held by KBUF Partnership.
Group Owner: Robert Ingstad Broadcast Properties
Nat'l Network: Westwood One; *Regional Network:* Kan. Info.; Kan. Agriculture
Arbitron Metro Market: Ulysses, KS; *Format:* Country *Special Programming:* Farm 12 hrs, Sp 3 hrs wkly; *Hrs. of News Programming:* news progmg 24 hrs wkly; *No. News Employees:* 1; *Target Audience:* 21-65; middleto upper class workers, farmers & housewives
Christa Roy, General Manager
Bob Dale, Station Manager
James Janda, Programming Director
Jim Wagoner, News Director
Jerry Jones, Sports Director
Lory Williams, Farm Director

Wamego

KHCA
03-06-1986; 95.3 MHz FM; *Hrs Open:* 24; 6 kw; 325 ft.; N39 12 35 W96 21 5
Mailing Address: 103 North 3rd Street, Box 1471, Manhattan, KS 66502 US
Second Address: 103 N. 3rd, Manhattan, KS 66502
(785) 537-9595; *Fax:* (785) 537-2955
angel95@hotmail.com
License: Wamego, Pottawatomie County, KS held by KHCA Inc.
Nat'l Network: Salem Radio Network
Format: Adult Contemp, Christian *Special Programming:* Alternative 20 hrs wkly; *No. News Employees:* 1; *Target Audience:* Christian, 18-54
Jerry Hutchinson, President

Wellington

KLEY
11-19-1966; 1130 kHz AM; *Hrs Open:* 24; 0.25 kw-D, DA2; 0.001 kw-N, DA2; N37 14 28 W97 24 4
P.O. Box 707, Wellington, KS 67152 US
(620) 326-3341; *Fax:* (620) 326-8512
kley@sutv.com
License: Wellington, KS held by Johnson Enterprises Inc.
Group Owner: Johnson Enterprises Inc.; (acq 5-1-89; $575,000 with co-located FM;
Nat'l Network: USA; *Regional Network:* Kan. Info.; Kan. Agriculture
Arbitron Metro Market: Wichita, KS; *Format:* News, Talk *Special Programming:* Farm 10 hrs, relg 4 hrs wkly; *Hrs. of News Programming:* news progmg 20 hrs wkly; *No. News Employees:* 1; *Target Audience:* General. *Adv. Rates:* 7; 7; 7; 7
E. Gordon Johnson, President/General Manager
Larry Waggoner, Chief Engineer

KWME
08-27-1979; 92.7 MHz FM; *Hrs Open:* 24; 14 kw; 427 ft.; N37 20 8 W97 27 53
338 South Kley Drive, Wellington, KS 67152 US
(620) 326-3341; *Fax:* (620) 326-8512
www.kwme.com/
kley@sutv.com
License: Wellington, Sumner County, KS
Group Owner: Johnson Enterprises Inc.
Nat'l Network: USA
Arbitron Metro Market: Wellington. KS; *Format:* Oldies; *No. News Employees:* 1; *Target Audience:* 35-64.; *Adv. Rates:* 7; 7; 7; 7
E. Gordon Johnson, President/General Manager

Wichita

***KCFN**
04-23-1978; 91.1 MHz FM; *Hrs Open:* 24; 100 kw; 486 ft.; N38 1 9 W97 23 1
P.O. Box 3206, Tupelo, MS 38803 US
(662) 844-8888; *Fax:* (662) 842-6791
www.afr.net
faq@afa.net
License: Wichita, Sedgwick County, KS held by American Family Association
Group Owner: American Family Radio; (acq 5-94)
Arbitron Metro Market: Wichita, KS; *Format:* Christian *Special Programming:* Relg, news/talk; *Hrs. of News Programming:* News progmg 2 hrs wkly; *Target Audience:* 35-65; general
Tim Wildmon, President
Donald Wildman, Founder
Buddy Smith, Sr VP
Ed Vitagliano, Exec VP
Randy Sharp, Director Of Special Projects
Meeke Addison, Director Of Communiations
Abraham Hamilton III, General Counsel & Public PolicyAnalyst

KDGS
11-01-1993; 93.9 MHz FM; 25 kw; 328 ft.; N37 37 0 W97 20 11
9111 E. Douglas, Suite 130, Wichita, KS 67202 US
(316) 685-2121; *Fax:* (316) 685-3408
www.power939.com
info@power939.com
License: Wichita, KS held by Entercom Wichita License LLC.
Group Owner: Entercom Communications Corp.; (acq 4-21-00; $3.15 million).
Arbitron Metro Market: Wichita, KS; *Format:* Contemporary Hits/Top 40; *Target Audience:* 18-34.
Jackie Wise, General Manager
Mark Yearout, General Sales Mgr
Greg Williams, Programming Director

KEYN-FM
10-01-1968; 103.7 MHz FM; *Hrs Open:* 24; 98 kw; 1007 ft.; N37 48 1 W97 31 29
9111 E. Douglas, Suite 130, Wichita, KS 67207 US
(316) 685-2121; *Fax:* (316) 685-3408
www.keyn.com
info@keyn.com
License: Wichita, Sedgwick County, KS held by Entercom Wichita License LLC.
Group Owner: Entercom Communications Corp.; (acq 2000; grpsl)
Nat'l Network: ABC
Arbitron Metro Market: Wichita, KS; *Format:* Oldies *Special Programming:* Dr. Demento 2 hrs wkly; *Hrs. of News Programming:* News progmg 5 hrs wkly; *Target Audience:* 25-54; baby boomers
Jackie Wise, General Manager
Lisa Crider, General Sales Mgr

KLIO
09-01-1923; 1070 kHz AM; *Hrs Open:* 24; 10 kw-D, 1 kw-N, DA-N; N37 42 47 W97 19 59
Mailing Address: Box 1402, Wichita, KS 89102
Second Address: 4200 N. Old Lawrence Rd., Wichita, KS 67219
(316) 838-9141; *Fax:* (316) 838-3607
www.kfdi.com
info@kfdi.com
License: Wichita, Sedgwick County, KS held by Journal Broadcast Corp.
Group Owner: Journal Communications Inc.; (acq 6-11-99; grpsl)
Nat'l Network: ABC
Population Served: 411,000; *Arbitron Metro Market:* Wichita, KS; *No. News Employees:* 7; *Target Audience:* 25-54.
Beverlee Brannigan, Programming Director
Dan Dillon, News Director
Orin Friesen, Disc Jockey
Johnny Western, Disc Jockey
Dugg Collins, Disc Jockey
Krysti Bradford, Traffic Manager

KFDI-FM
06-06-1963; 101.3 MHz FM; 100 kw; 1138 ft.; N37 47 47 W97 31 59
Mailing Address: 3355 S. Valley View Boulevard, Las Vegas, NV 89102 US
Second Address: 4200 N. Old Lawrence Rd., Wichita, KS 67219
(316) 838-9141; *Fax:* (316) 838-3607
www.kfdi.com
License: Wichita, Sedgwick County, KS held by Journal Broadcast Corp.
Group Owner: Journal Communications Inc.
Arbitron Metro Market: Wichita, KS; *Format:* Country; *Target Audience:* 25-54; adults
Dugg Collins, Programming Director
Johnny Western, Disc Jockey
Orin Friesen, Disc Jockey

KNSS
05-26-1922; 1330 kHz AM; *Hrs Open:* 24; 5 kw-D, DAN; 5 kw-N, DAN; N37 42 47 W97 14 51
9111 E Douglas, Suite 130, Wichita, KS 67207 US
(316) 685-2121; *Fax:* (316) 685-3408
www.knssradio.com
info@knssradio.com
License: Wichita, KS held by Entercom Wichita License LLC.
Group Owner: Entercom Communications Corp.; (acq 2000; grpsl).
Nat'l Network: CBS; *Wire Services:* Weather Wire
Arbitron Metro Market: Wichita, KS; *Format:* News, News/Talk, 86; *Target Audience:* 25-54.
Jackie Wise, General Manager
Lisa Crider, General Sales Mgr
Tony Duesing, Programming Director
Steve McIntosh, News Director

KICT-FM
04-28-1972; 95.1 MHz FM; *Hrs Open:* 24; 100 kw; 899 ft.; N37 47 58 W97 31 58
3355 S. Valley View Boulevard, Las Vegas, NV 89102 US
(316) 838-9141; *Fax:* (316) 838-3607
www.t95.com
License: Wichita, Sedgwick County, KS held by Journal Broadcast Corp.
Group Owner: Journal Communications Inc.; (acq 6-14-99; grpsl)
Arbitron Metro Market: Wichita, KS; *Format:* Rock/AOR *Special Programming:* Dee Snider 2 hrs wkly; *Hrs. of News Programming:* news progmg 15 hrs wkly; *No. News Employees:* 2; *Target Audience:* 18-44.
Eric McCart, General Manager
Lisa Fetter, General Sales Mgr
Ray Michaels, Programming Director
Manny Cowzinski, Promotions Manager
Jason Wilson, Local Sales Manager

KTHR
04-17-1967; 107.3 MHz FM; *Hrs Open:* 24; 100 kw; 843 ft.; N37 46 40 W97 30 37
9323 E. 37th St. N., Wichita, KS 67226-2000 US
(316) 494-6600; *Fax:* (316) 494-6730
www.alt1073.com
License: Wichita, Sedgwick County, KS held by Capstar TX LLC
Group Owner: iHeartMedia; (acq 8-30-2000; grpsl).
Nat'l Reps: Clear Channel; *Wire Services:* UPI
Arbitron Metro Market: Wichita, KS; *Format:* Alternative; *Target Audience:* 25-54; Males
Jeff McCausland, Market President
Tom Libby, Senior Vice President of Sales
Tony Matteo, Senior Vice President of Programming
Morgan Huelsman, Digital Content Director

***KMUW**
04-26-1949; 89.1 MHz FM; *Hrs Open:* 24; 100 kw; 911 ft.; N37 46 26 W97 30 51.8
3317 E. 17th St. N., Wichita, KS 67208 US
(316) 978-6789; *Fax:* (316) 978-3946
www.kmuw.org
info@kmuw.org
License: Wichita, Sedgwick County, KS held by Wichita State University.
Nat'l Network: NPR; PRI; *Regional Network:* Kan. Info.; *Wire Services:* AP
Arbitron Metro Market: Wichita, KS; *Format:* Jazz, News, 90 *Special Programming:* Gospel 2 hrs, jazz 14 hrs, folk/world 5 hrs, AAA 1; *Hrs. of News Programming:* news progmg 121 hrs wkly; *No. News Employees:* 2 *Target Audience:* General.
Pat Hayes, Operations Dir
Mark McCain, General Manager
Larry Bennett, Programming Director
Lu Stephens, Promotions Manager
Jon Cyphers, Engineering Dir

KGSO
01-01-1950; 1410 kHz AM; *Hrs Open:* 24; 5 kw-D, DA2; 1 kw-N, DA2; N37 44 5 W97 21 6
3337 W. Central, Wichita, KS 67203 US
(316) 721-4407; *Fax:* (316) 721-8276
www.kgso.com
License: Wichita, KS held by Steckline Communications Inc.
Group Owner: Steckline Communications Inc.; (acq 7-1-2005; $1.3 million)
Nat'l Network: ESPN Radio; NBC Radio; USA; *Regional Network:* Mid-America Ag
Arbitron Metro Market: Wichita, KS; *Format:* Sports; *Target Audience:* Men 25-54.
Todd Johnson, General Manager

KFH
10-28-1947; 1240 kHz AM; 0.63 kw-U, ND1; N37 43 6 W97 19 5
600 Congress Ave., Suite 1400, Austin, TX 78701 US
(316) 685-2121; *Fax:* (316) 685-3408
www.kfhradio.com
letters@kfhradio.com
License: Wichita, KS held by Entercom Wichita License L.L.C.
Group Owner: Entercom Communications Corp.; (acq 2000; grpsl).
Nat'l Network: CBS; *Nat'l Reps:* D & R Radio
Arbitron Metro Market: Wichita, KS; *Format:* Sports, Talk; *Target Audience:* 35 plus; professionals
Jackie Wise, General Manager

KQAM
01-01-1936; 1480 kHz AM; 5 kw-D, DA2; 1 kw-N, DA2; N37 44 21 W97 16 14
1850 K Street, NW, Suite 900, Washington, DC 20006 US
(316) 685-2121; *Fax:* (316) 685-3408
www.kqamradio.com
License: Wichita, KS held by Radio Disney Group LLC.
Group Owner: ABC Inc.; (acq 7-29-02; $2 million).
Nat'l Network: Radio Disney
Arbitron Metro Market: Wichita, KS; *Format:* News, News/Talk, 86
Greg Steckline, President

KRBB
09-19-1948; 97.9 MHz FM; *Hrs Open:* 24; 100 kw; 1027 ft.; N37 46 40 W97 30 37
9323 E. 37th St. N., Wichita, KS 67226-2000 US
(316) 494-6600; *Fax:* (316) 494-6730
www.b98fm.com
info@b98fm.com
License: Wichita, Sedgwick County, KS held by Capstar TX LLC
Group Owner: iHeartMedia; (acq 8-30-00; grpsl)
Nat'l Reps: Clear Channel
Arbitron Metro Market: Wichita, KS; *Format:* Adult Contemp *Special Programming:* Jazz 2 hrs, Sp 3 hrs, love songs 18 hrs wkly; *No. News Employees:* 1; *Target Audience:* W 25-54; a 25-54; working & family oriented
Tony Matteo, Senior Vice President of Programming
Jeff McCausland, Market President
Tom Libby, Senior Vice President of Sales
Dave Wilson, Programming Director
Morgan Huelsman, Digital Content Director

KSGL
08-01-1957; 900 kHz AM; 0.25 kw-D, DA2; 0.028 kw-N, DA2; N37 41 33 W97 22 54
3337 West Central, Wichita, KS 67203 US
(316) 942-3231; *Fax:* (316) 942-9314
www.ksgl.com
License: Wichita, KS held by Agape Communications Inc.
Nat'l Network: USA
Arbitron Metro Market: Wichita, KS; *Format:* Religious
Don Clifford, President
Norbert Atherton, Operations Dir
Terry Atherton, General Manager

***KYFW**
09-24-1988; 88.3 MHz FM; *Hrs Open:* 24; 17 kw; 141 ft.; N37 40 22 W97 20 8
P.O. Box 7300, Charlotte, NC 28241 US
(800) 888-7077
www.bbnradio.org
bbn@bbnmedia.org
License: Wichita, Sedgwick County, KS held by Bible Broadcasting Network Inc.
Group Owner: Bible Broadcasting Network; acq 6-26-89)
Arbitron Metro Market: Charlotte, NC; *Format:* Christian; *Target Audience:* General.
Lowell Davey, President
Jason Padgett, Operations Manager

***KYWA**
06-17-2004; 90.7 MHz FM; *Hrs Open:* 24; 70 kw horiz, 67.5 kw vert; 472 ft.; N37 28 37 W97 4 28
110 S. Main Street, #1050, Wichita, KS 67202 US
(316) 831-0907; *Fax:* (316) 831-0910
supportservices@wayfm.com
License: Wichita, Sedgwick County, KS held by WAY-FM Media Group Inc.
Group Owner: WAY-FM Media Group Inc.; (acq 4-12-2004; $485,000)
Arbitron Metro Market: Wichita, KS; *Format:* Christian; *Target Audience:* 25-44; Females
Bob Augsburg, President
Lloyd Parker, COO
Dusty Rhodes, Senior Vice President
Paul Anthony, General Manager

Winfield

KSOK-FM
01-01-1996; 95.9 MHz FM; *Hrs Open:* 24; 15.2 kw; Ant 420 ft; N37 04 32 W96 56 13
334 E. Radio Ln., Arkansas City, KS 66762
(620) 442-5400; *Fax:* (620) 442-5401
www.ksokradio.com
ksok@ksokradio.com
License: Winfield, Cowley County, KS held by Cowley County Broadcasting Inc.
Nat'l Network: CBS; *Regional Network:* Kan. Agriculture
Population Served: 40,000; *No. News Employees:* 1; *Target Audience:* 22-55; blue collar, middle America, people who have children, are still working, & have mortgages; *Adv. Rates:* 26; 22; 24; 15
Brian Cunningham, Operations/Engineering Director
Marty Mutti, General Manager
Pam Miller, Station/General Sales Manager
Marty Mutti, Programming Director
Blake Carter, Promotions Manager
Shawn Wheat, News Director

***KBDD**
01-01-2000; 91.9 MHz FM; 48 kw; 492 ft.; N37 22 56 W96 57 20
Mailing Address: P O Drawer 2440, Tupelo, MS 38803 US
Second Address: 8919 World Ministry Ave., Baton Rouge, LA 70810
(225) 768-3688; *Fax:* (225) 768-3724
www.jsm.org
kawikfish@yahoo.com
License: Winfield, Cowley County, KS held by Family Worship Center Church Inc.
Group Owner: Family Worship Center Church Inc.; acq 6-10-2004; $1.15 million).
Format: Christian
David Whitelaw, COO
Jimmy Swaggart, President
John Santiago, Programming Director

KKLE
08-19-1963; 1550 kHz AM *Rebroadcasts:* Rebroadcasts KLEY(AM) Wellington 98%
P. O. Box 707,Kley Drive, Wellington, KS 67152 US
(620) 221-3341; *Fax:* (620) 326-8512
kley@sutv.com
License: Winfield, KS held by Johnson Enterprises Inc.
Group Owner: Johnson Enterprises Inc.; (acq 1990)
Nat'l Network: ESPN Radio; USA
Arbitron Metro Market: Wichita, KS; *Format:* Talk; *Target Audience:* General.; *Adv. Rates:* 7; 7; 7; 7
Gordon Johnson, President
Gordon Johnson, General Manager

KWLS
01-01-1980; 107.9 MHz FM; *Hrs Open:* 24; 50 kw; 492 ft.; N37 15 46 W96 53 42
1604 E. Quincy, Pittsburgh, KS 66762 US
(316) 776-9530; *Fax:* (316) 612-1077
www.kwlsradio.com
License: Winfield, Cowley County, KS held by Mid-America Ag Network Inc.
Nat'l Reps: McGavren Guild
Arbitron Metro Market: Wichita, KS; *Format:* Country; *Adv. Rates:* 16; 12; 12; 9.60
Larry Steckline, President
Chris Carter, Operations Dir
Denise Sherman, General Sales Mgr
Michael Carter, Promotions Manager

***KSWC**
11-01-1967; 100.3 MHz FM; 0.009 kw horiz; 43 ft.; N37 14 45 W96 58 15
100 College Street, Winfield, KS 67156 US
(620) 229-6263
www.scdigital.org/stream/
License: Winfield, Cowley County, KS held by Southwestern College.
Arbitron Metro Market: Winfield, KS; *Format:* Talk; *Target Audience:* 21 & younger.
Tom Jacobs, General Manager

Kentucky

Albany

WANY
10-25-1958; 1390 kHz AM; 1 kw-D, NDD; N36 41 54 W85 9 0
P. O. Box 400, Albany, KY 42602 US
(606) 387-5186; *Fax:* (606) 387-6595
mix1063@hotmail.com
License: Albany, KY held by Pamela Allred dba Albany Broadcasting Co.
Nat'l Reps: Keystone (unwired net)
Arbitron Metro Market: Albany, KY; *Format:* Country *Special Programming:* Farm 2 hrs, gospel 6 hrs wkly

WANY-FM
04-18-1966; 100.9 MHz FM; 2.7 kw horiz; 154 ft.; N36 41 54 W85 9 0
P. O. Box 400, Albany, KY 42602 US
(606) 387-5186; *Fax:* (606) 387-6595
License: Albany, Clinton County, KY
Arbitron Metro Market: Albany, KY; *Format:* Country
Pamela Allred, General Manager
Hank Thomas, Operations Manager
Paul Goodman, Sales Manager
Robert Huddleston, Chief Engineer

Allen

WMDJ-FM
09-01-1984; 100.1 MHz FM; 2.6 kw; 492 ft.; N37 35 12 W82 42 57
Mailing Address: P. O. Box 1530, Martin, KY 41649 US
Second Address: Old Hwy. Rt. 80, Martin, KY 41649
(606) 874-8005; *Fax:* (606) 874-0057
www.wmdjfm.com
fm100wmdj@mikrotec.com
License: Allen, Floyd County, KY held by Floyd County Broadcasting Co. Inc.
Nat'l Reps: Katz Radio
Arbitron Metro Market: Martin, KY; *Format:* Country, Oldies; *Target Audience:* 25-65.
Marty McKinney, Sales Manager
Sandra Howell, Traffic Manager
Robert Epps, Traffic Manager

Annville

WANV
01-01-2006; 96.7 MHz FM; 1.85 kw; 499 ft.; N37 13 24 W84 2 1 US
(606) 864-2148; *Fax:* (606) 528-9824
www.967wanv.com
License: Annville, Jackson County, KY held by Forcht Broadcasting
Group Owner: Forcht Broadcasting
Arbitron Metro Market: Annville, KY; *Format:* Contemporary Hits/Top 40, Adult Contemp
Bridgett Gambrel, General Manager
Terry Harris, Morning Hose
Matt Jones, Account Executive
Frances Wilhoit, Account Executive

Ashland

WCMI
01-01-1935; 1340 kHz AM; *Hrs Open:* 24; 1 kw-U; N38 28 02 W82 35 50
401 11th St., Suite 200, Huntington, WV 25701
(304) 523-8401; *Fax:* (304) 523-4848
License: Ashland, Boyd County, KY held by Fifth Avenue Broadcasting Co. Inc.
Group Owner: Kindred Communications Inc.; (acq 1-26-98; with WCMI-FM Catletts
Nat'l Network: NBC/ESPN
Population Served: 24,000; *Arbitron Metro Market:* Huntington-Ashl
Mike Kirtner, President
Reeves Kirtner, Operations Dir

WDGG
01-01-1948; 93.7 MHz FM; *Hrs Open:* 24; 100 kw; 741 ft.; N38 23 14 W82 39 45
401 11th T, Ste 200, Huntington, WV 25701 US
(304) 523-8401; *Fax:* (304) 523-4848
www.937thedawg.com
sales@937thedawg.com
License: Ashland, Boyd County, KY held by Fifth Avenue Broadcasting Co. Inc.
Group Owner: Kindred Communications Inc.; (acq 1988).
Nat'l Network: Jones Radio Networks; Motor Racing Net;
Regional Network: W. Va. MetroNews Network; *Nat'l Reps:* McGavren Guild; *Wire Services:* Accu-Weather; AP
Arbitron Metro Market: Huntington-Ashland, WV-KY; *Format:* Country; *Hrs. of News Programming:* news progmg 2 hrs wkly;
No. News Employees: 1; *Target Audience:* 25-49; male
Tom Wolf, CEO
Mike Kirtner, President
Rae Ann Parsons, General Sales Mgr
Cameron Smith, Engineering Dir

***WKAO**
91.1 MHz FM; 7 kw; 354 ft.; N38 25 11 W82 24 6
PO Box 889, Blacksburg, VA 24063 US
(540) 961-2377; *Fax:* (540) 951-5282
www.parfm.com
License: Ashland, Boyd County, KY held by Positive Alternative Radio Inc.
Group Owner: Positive Alternative Radio Inc.
Arbitron Metro Market: Ashland, KY
Edward Baker, President

Auburn

WBVR-FM
05-01-1965; 96.7 MHz FM; *Hrs Open:* 24; 45 kw; 423 ft.; N36 50 35 W86 15 30
PO Box 298, Russellville, KY 42276 US
(270) 843-3333; *Fax:* (270) 843-0454
www.beaverfm.com
travislee@beaverfm.com
License: Auburn, Logan County, KY held by Forever Communications Inc.
Group Owner: Forever Communications Inc.; (acq 1984)
Nat'l Reps: Christal
Arbitron Metro Market: Bowling Green, KY; *Format:* Country; *Target Audience:* 18-54.; *Adv. Rates:* 60; 60; 50; 25
Christine Hillard, President
Mark Mackey, General Manager
Myla Thomas, Programming Director

***WAYD**
01-01-2005; 88.1 MHz FM; 1 kw; 371 ft.; N36 57 37 W86 32 49
P.O. Box 887, Brentwood, TN 37024 US
(888) 339-2936; *Fax:* (615) 261-3967
supportservices@wayfm.com
License: Auburn, Logan County, KY held by WAY-FM Media Group Inc.
Group Owner: WAY-FM Media Group Inc.
Format: Christian
Matt Austin, General Manager
Bob Augsburg, Chief Engineer
Dusty Rhodes, CFO
Lloyd Parker, COO

Barbourville

WYWY
12-13-1955; 950 kHz AM; 1 kw-D, ND2; N36 50 26 W83 52 16
222 Daniel Boone Dr., Barbourville, KY 40906 US
(606) 546-4128; *Fax:* (606) 546-4138
wkkqproduction@yahoo.com
License: Barbourville, KY held by Choice Radio Group
Arbitron Metro Market: Barbourville, KY; *Format:* Gospel, Religious
Jonathan L. Smith, President
Karen Bowling, General Manager/General Sales Manager
Arvil Burnette, Chief Engineer

WKKQ
10-02-1974; 96.1 MHz FM; 25 kw; 328 ft.; N36 51 59 W83 54 0
222 Daniel Boone Drive, Barbourville, KY 40906 US
Fax: (606) 546-4138
wkkqproduction@yahoo.com
License: Barbourville, Knox County, KY held by Barbourville Commuity Broadcasting Co.
Arbitron Metro Market: Barbourville, KY; *Format:* Adult Contemp; *Target Audience:* 25-34.
Randy Brock, General Sales Mgr
Sean Terrell, Programming Director

Bardstown

WBRT
12-01-1954; 1320 kHz AM; 1 kw-D; N37 49 09 W85 29 10
106 S. 3rd St., Bardstown, KY 42141
(502) 348-3943; *Fax:* (502) 348-4043
www.wbrtcountry.com
info@wbrtcountry.com
License: Bardstown, Nelson County, KY held by Bardstown Radio Team, LLC
Nat'l Reps: Rgnl Reps
Population Served: 11,839; *Arbitron Metro Market:* Bardstown, Ky *Special Programming:* Farm 10 hrs wkly; *Target Audience:* 20 plus.
Kenny Fogle, General Manager

Beattyville

WLJC
05-12-1965; 102.1 MHz FM; 1.5 kw; 656 ft.; N37 36 47 W83 40 18
WLJC Drive, Beattyville, KY 41311 US
(606) 464-3600; *Fax:* (606) 464-5021
www.wljc.com
wljc@wljc.com
License: Beattyville, Lee County, KY held by Hour of Harvest Inc.
Nat'l Reps: Rgnl Reps
Format: Adult Contemp
Margaret Drake, President
Jonathan Drake, COO/General Manager
Kim Mitchell, General Sales Mgr
Alan Mulford, Chief Engineer

Benton

***WAAJ**
01-01-1996; 89.7 MHz FM; 6 kw vert; 299 ft.; N36 48 31 W88 13 26
Mailing Address: P O Box 281, Hardin, KY 42048 US
Second Address: 219 College St., Harding, KY 42048
(270) 437-4095; *Fax:* (270) 437-4098
www.hmiradio.com
info@hmiradio.com
License: Benton, Marshall County, KY held by Heartland Ministries.
Arbitron Metro Market: Benton, KY; *Format:* Gospel
Darrell Gibson, President
Adam Tarnowski, Operations Dir
Eddie Sheridan, General Manager

WCBL
12-13-1954; 1290 kHz AM; *Hrs Open:* 24; 5 kw-D, ND1; 0.053 kw-N, ND1; N36 51 31 W88 20 11
1039 Egner's Ferry Rd, P.O. Box 387, Benton, KY 42025 US
(270) 527-3102; *Fax:* (270) 527-5606
www.thelakecurrent.com
wcbl@freelandbroadcasting.com
License: Benton, KY held by Jim W. Freeland.
Group Owner: Freeland Broadcasting Stations; (acq 11-17-98; with co-located FM)
Format: Sports, Talk; *Hrs. of News Programming:* news progmg 7 hrs wkly; *No. News Employees:* 1; *Target Audience:* General.; *Adv. Rates:* 15; 15; 15; 15
Jim Freeland, President
Sherry Rickman, Operations Dir
Chris Freeland, General Manager
Gregg Leath, Programming Director
Sam Rickmon, News Director
Shane Freeland, Disc Jockey

***WTRT**
12-01-1998; 88.1 MHz FM; *Hrs Open:* 24; 0.6 kw vert; 253 ft.; N36 47 53 W88 20 50

Mailing Address: P.O. Box 281, Hardin, KY 42048 US
Second Address: 219 College St., Harding, KY 42048
(270) 437-4095; *Fax:* (270) 437-4098
www.hmiradio.com
info@hmiradio.com
License: Benton, Marshall County, KY held by Heartland Ministries
Arbitron Metro Market: Benton, KY; *Format:* Adult Contemp, Christian
Darrell Gibson, President
Eddie Sheridan, General Manager
Jeremy Johnson, Programming Director
Adam Tarnowski, Operations Coordinator

***WVHM**
06-01-1989; 90.5 MHz FM; 16.5 kw; 335 ft.; N36 48 31 W88 13 26
Mailing Address: P.O. Box 281, Hardin, KY 42048 US
Second Address: 219 College St., Hardin, KY 42048
(270) 437-4095; *Fax:* (270) 437-4098
www.hmiradio.com
info@hmiradio.com
License: Benton, Marshall County, KY held by Heartland Ministries.
Nat'l Network: USA
Arbitron Metro Market: Hardin, KY; *Format:* Gospel; *Target Audience:* 18-49.
Darrell Gibson, President
Eddie Sheridan, General Manager
Cecil Glass, Station Manager
Jeremy Johnson, Programming Director
Adam Tarnowski, Operations Coordinator

Berea

WKXO
07-18-1971; 1500 kHz AM; *Hrs Open:* 6 AM-7 PM; 0.25 kw-D, NDD; N37 35 12 W84 18 4
128 Big Hill Ave., Richmond, KY 40475 US
(859) 623-1389; *Fax:* (859) 623-1341
www.wkxoam.com
License: Berea, KY held by Wallingford Communications LLC.
Group Owner: Wallingford Broadcasting Co.; (acq 1999; grpsl)
Nat'l Network: Jones Radio Networks
Arbitron Metro Market: Lexington-Fayette, KY; *Format:* Gospel; *Hrs. of News Programming:* news progmg 3 hrs wkly; *No. News Employees:* 1; *Target Audience:* 21 plus.
Bill Clary, Operations Dir
Sean Hamilton, General Manager
Trizdon Reynolds, General Sales Mgr
Shelby Stlone, Promotions Manager
Ron Lykins, News Director

WLFX
09-27-1990; 106.7 MHz FM; *Hrs Open:* 24; 3.3 kw; 420 ft.; N37 39 40 W84 8 55
128 Big Hill Ave., Richmond, KY 40475 US
(859) 623-1386; *Fax:* (859) 623-1341
www.wlfxfm.com
License: Berea, Madison County, KY held by Wallingford Communications, LLC
Group Owner: Wallingford Broadcasting Co.
Arbitron Metro Market: Lexington-Fayette, KY; *Format:* Contemporary Hits/Top 40 *Special Programming:* Gospel 12 hrs wkly
Bill Clary, Operations Dir
Sean Hamilton, General Manager
Trizdon Reynolds, General Sales Mgr
Shelby Slone, Promotions Manager
Ron Lykins, News Director

Bowling Green

WBGN
11-24-1959; 1340 kHz AM; *Hrs Open:* 24; 1 kw-U, ND1; N37 0 34 W86 27 9
P.O. Box 900, Bowling Green, KY 42102 US
(270) 843-3333; *Fax:* (270) 783-0454
www.1340wbgn.com
joneal@forevercomm.com
License: Bowling Green, KY held by Forever Communications Inc.
Group Owner: Forever Communications Inc.; (acq 2001)
Nat'l Network: ABC; ESPN Radio; *Regional Network:* Ky. News Net; *Nat'l Reps:* Christal
Arbitron Metro Market: Bowling Green, KY; *Format:* Sports; *Target Audience:* 35-54.; *Adv. Rates:* 20; 20; 15; 10
Mark Mackey, General Manager
Joe O'Neal, General Sales Mgr
Chris Idle, Programming Director

***WCVK**
04-22-1986; 90.7 MHz FM; 14 kw; 449 ft.; N37 0 18 W86 31 19
1407 Scottsville Rd., Bowling Green, KY 42104 US
(270) 781-7326; *Fax:* (270) 781-8005
www.christianfamilyradio.com
mike@christianfamilyradio.com
License: Bowling Green, Warren County, KY held by Bowling Green Community Broadcasting Inc.
Nat'l Network: Salem Radio Network
Arbitron Metro Market: Bowling Green, KY; *Format:* Adult Contemp, Christian *Special Programming:* Christian Rock 10hrs weekly; *Target Audience:* 25-54; Christian men & women
Mike Wilson, General Manager
Susan ""West"" Woodard, Programming Director
Derek Gregory, Promotions Manager

WDNS
03-12-1973; 93.3 MHz FM; *Hrs Open:* 24; 12 kw; 472 ft.; N36 56 39 W86 15 11
P. O. Box 930, Bowling Green, KY 42102 US
(270) 781-2121; *Fax:* (270) 842-0232
www.wdnsfm.com
License: Bowling Green, Warren County, KY held by Daily News Broadcasting Co.
Arbitron Metro Market: Bowling Green, KY; *Format:* Classic Rock; *Hrs. of News Programming:* news progmg 7 hrs wkly; *No. News Employees:* 1; *Target Audience:* 18-54.
Sean Sheenan, Operations Dir
Art Kalemkarian, General Manager
Bryan Locke, Programming Director
John Blazek, Chief Engineer

WGGC
06-23-1961; 95.1 MHz FM; *Hrs Open:* 24; 100 kw; 988 ft.; N36 54 43 W86 11 21
245 West Dixie Ave., P.O. Box 517, Elizabethtown, KY 42701 US
(270) 783-8730; *Fax:* (270) 783-8665
www.wggc.com
darrin@wggc.com
License: Bowling Green, Warren County, KY held by Heritage Communications Inc.
Arbitron Metro Market: Bowling Green, KY; *Format:* Country
Bill Evans, General Manager
Darrin Evans, Station Manager
Dan Callahan, Disc Jockey
Maxwell P. Murphy, Disc Jockey

WKCT
11-01-1947; 930 kHz AM; *Hrs Open:* 24; 5 kw-D, DAN; 0.5 kw-N, DAN; N37 1 53 W86 26 18
Mailing Address: P. O. Box 930, Bowling Green, KY 42101 US
Second Address: 804 College St., Bowling Green, KY 42101
(270) 781-2121; *Fax:* (270) 842-0232
www.93wkct.com
alan@wdnsfm.com
License: Bowling Green, KY held by Daily News Broadcasting Co.
Nat'l Network: CBS
Arbitron Metro Market: Bowling Green, KY; *Format:* News, News/Talk, 86; *Hrs. of News Programming:* news progmg 25 hrs wkly; *No. News Employees:* 1; *Target Audience:* 25 plus.
Alan Cooper, General Manager
Chad Young, Programming Director
Al Arbogast, News Director
Claire Quinn, Sales Manager

***WKYU-FM**
11-01-1980; 88.9 MHz FM; *Hrs Open:* 24; 98 kw; 719 ft.; N37 5 23 W86 38 5
1 Big Red Way, Bowling Green, KY 42101 US
(270) 745-5489; *Fax:* (270) 745-6272
www.wkyu.org
wkyufm@wku.edu
License: Bowling Green, Warren County, KY held by Western Kentucky University.
Nat'l Network: NPR; PRI
Arbitron Metro Market: Bowling Green, KY *TV Affiliate:* *WKYU-TV affil; *Format:* News; *Hrs. of News Programming:* news progmg 35 hrs wkly; *No. News Employees:* 3; *Target Audience:* General.
Peter Bryant, General Manager

***WWHR**
08-18-1988; 91.7 MHz FM; *Hrs Open:* 24; 1.3 kw; 374 ft.; N37 0 19 W86 31 23
College Heights, 1 Big Red Way, Bowling Green, KY 42101 US
(270) 745-5439; *Fax:* (270) 745-5835
www.revolution.fm
License: Bowling Green, Warren County, KY held by Western Kentucky University.
Arbitron Metro Market: Bowling Green, KY; *Format:* Variety/Diverse *Special Programming:* Soul 2 hrs, punk 2 hrs, gothic 2 hrs, loc 2 hrs, e; *Hrs. of News Programming:* news progmg 5 hrs wkly; *No. News Employees:* 2 *Target Audience:* Adults 18-34.
Dr. Marjorie Yambor, General Manager
Nash Gumm, Station Manager
Savannah Burke, Programming Director
Nathan Smith, Production Director
Angela Conway, Public Relations Director
Salena Lisner, Human Resources Director
Sean Strain,Internet Director
Nick Lough, Underwriting Director

Brandenburg

WMMG
07-01-1984; 1140 kHz AM
Mailing Address: 1715 Bypass Road, P.O. Box 309, Bradenburg, KY 40108 US
Second Address: 1715 Bypass Rd., Brandenburg, KY 40108
(270) 422-4440; *Fax:* (270) 422-3464
www.wmmgradio.com
wmmg935@bbtel.com
License: Brandenburg, KY held by Meade County Communications Inc.
Nat'l Reps: Rgnl Reps
Arbitron Metro Market: Brandenburg, KY; *Format:* Country *Special Programming:* Relg 8 hrs wkly; *Adv. Rates:* 12; 12; 9; 12
Gwen Blevins, General Manager

WMMG-FM
08-23-1972; 93.5 MHz FM; 3.4 kw; 289 ft.; N37 59 5 W86 9 24
1715 Bypass Road, Brandenburg, KY 40108 US
(270) 422-4440; *Fax:* (270) 422-3464
www.wmmgradio.com
License: Brandenburg, Meade County, KY held by Meade County Communications Inc.
Nat'l Reps: Rgnl Reps
Arbitron Metro Market: Brandenburg, KY; *Target Audience:* 18-65.; *Adv. Rates:* Same as AM
J. Spangler, President
Lori Spangler, Operations Dir

Brownsville

WKLX
01-01-2000; 100.7 MHz FM; 8 kw; 584 ft.; N37 9 19 W86 19 33
1519 Euclid Avenue, Bowling Green, KY 42103 US
(270) 651-6050; *Fax:* (270) 651-7666
www.bowlinggreensam.com
License: Brownsville, Edmonson County, KY held by Charles M. Anderson.
Arbitron Metro Market: Bowling Green, OH; *Format:* Adult Contemp
Darron Steenbergen, General Manager

Buffalo

WXAM
11-26-1974; 1430 kHz AM; 1 kw-D, ND1; 0.042 kw-N, ND1; N37 31 49 W85 42 49
P.O. Box 177, Hodgenville, KY 42748 US
(270) 763-0800; *Fax:* (270) 769-6349
License: Buffalo, KY held by Mark Goodman Productions Inc.
Nat'l Network: ESPN Radio
Arbitron Metro Market: Buffalo, KY; *Format:* Sports, Talk
Roth Stratton, General Manager

Burkesville

WKYR-FM
10-01-1988; 107.9 MHz FM; *Hrs Open:* 24; 6 kw; 312 ft.; N36 47 26 W85 22 47
Mailing Address: P.O. Box 340, Burkesville, KY 42717 US
Second Address: Hwy. 90 E., Burkesville, KY 42717
(270) 433-7191; *Fax:* (270) 433-7195
wkyr@mchsi.com
License: Burkesville, Cumberland County, KY held by Cumberland Broadcasting LLC
Nat'l Network: ABC; Jones Radio Networks; *Regional Network:* Ky. News Net
Format: Country
Jessie Crabtree, General Manager

Burnside

WSFE
02-28-1984; 910 kHz AM; *Hrs Open:* 24
Mailing Address: P.O. Box 740, Somerset, KY 42501 US
Second Address: 101 First Radio Ln., Somerset, KY 42503

(606) 678-5151; *Fax:* (606) 678-2026
www.wsfeam.com
License: Burnside, KY held by Capstar TX LLC
Group Owner: iHeartMedia; (acq 12-8-2000; grpsl).
Format: News, News/Talk, 86; *Hrs. of News Programming:* news progmg 5 hrs wkly; *No. News Employees:* 1; *Target Audience:* 25-54.
Bruce Welker, Market President
Wynona Padgett, Promotion Director
Jim Mercer, Chief Engineer
Greg Wesley, Business Manager
Paula McKinney, Traffic Manager
Mike Murphy, Production Manager
Josh McKinney, Sports Director

WSEK
08-17-1985; 93.9 MHz FM; 50 kw; 492 ft.; N37 9 15 W84 27 35
Mailing Address: P.O. Box 740, Somerset, KY 42502 US
Second Address: 101 First Radio Ln., Burnside, KY 42503
(606) 678-5151; *Fax:* (606) 678-2026
www.k93country.com
License: Burnside, Pulaski County, KY held by Capstar TX LLC
Group Owner: iHeartMedia
Arbitron Metro Market: Burnside, KY; *Format:* Country
Bruce Welker, Market President
Rod Zimmerman, Senior Vice President of Programming
Wynona Padgett, Promotions Director
Jim Mercer, Chief Engineer
Greg Wesley, Business Manager
Paula McKinney, Traffic Manager
Mike Murphy,Production Manager

Cadiz

WKDZ
04-08-1966; 1110 kHz AM; *Hrs Open:* 24; 1 kw-D; N36 52 57 W87 50 44
Mailing Address: Box 1900, Cadiz, KY 42211
Second Address: 19 Wooldridge Ln., Cadiz, KY 42211-0316
(270) 522-3232; *Fax:* (270) 522-1110
www.oldies1480.com
bmann@wkdzradio.com
License: Cadiz, Trigg County, KY held by Ham Broadcasting Co. Inc.
Nat'l Network: Fox News
Population Served: 100,000 *Special Programming:* Farm 2 hrs wkly; *Hrs. of News Programming:* news progmg 18 hrs wkly; *No. News Employees:* 6; *Target Audience:* 25-54.
D.J. Everett III, President
Beth Mann, General Manager
Alan Watts, News Director

WKDZ-FM
05-18-1972; 106.5 MHz FM; *Hrs Open:* 24; 13.4 kw; 449 ft.; N36 48 29 W87 38 9
1487 Will Jackson Road, Cadiz, KY 42211 US
(270) 522-3232; *Fax:* (270) 522-1110
wkdzradio.com
wkdz@wkdzradio.com
License: Cadiz, Trigg County, KY held by Ham Broadcasting Co. Inc.
Format: Country; *Hrs. of News Programming:* news progmg 20 hrs wkly; *No. News Employees:* 2; *Target Audience:* 35-64.
Ryan McIntyre, Operations Dir
Evan Caposerri, General Manager
Casey Ross, Programming Director
Jim Cavanaugh, Chief Engineer

Calvert City

WCCK
01-01-1993; 95.7 MHz FM; *Hrs Open:* 24; 3.5 kw; 341 ft.; N37 6 47 W88 21 34
2 Aspen Street, Calvert City, KY 42029 US
(270) 395-5133; *Fax:* (270) 395-5231
www.thelakecurrent.com
wcck@freelandbroadcasting.com
License: Calvert City, Marshall County, KY held by Jim Freeland DBA Freeland Broadcasting.
Group Owner: Freeland Broadcasting Stations
Nat'l Network: AP Radio
Arbitron Metro Market: Calvert City,ky; *Format:* Country; *Hrs. of News Programming:* News progmg 10 hrs wkly; *Target Audience:* 30 plus; professionals and retired; *Adv. Rates:* 15; 13; 14; 10
Jim Freeland, President
Sherry Darnall, Operations Dir
Chris Freeland, General Manager
Gregg Leath, Programming Director
Sam Rickmon, News Director
Shane Freeland, Disc Jockey

Campbellsville

***WAPD**
01-01-1996; 91.7 MHz FM; 2.323 kw vert; 217 ft.; N37 19 59 W85 19 53
P.O. Box 3206, Tupelo, MS 38803 US
(662) 844-8888; *Fax:* (662) 842-6791
www.afr.net
faq@afa.net
License: Campbellsville, Taylor County, KY held by American Family Association.
Group Owner: American Family Radio
Arbitron Metro Market: Campbellsville, KY; *Format:* Christian
Tim Wildmon, President
Donald Wildmon, Founder
Buddy Smith, Sr VP
Ed Vitagliano, Exec VP
Randy Sharp, Director Of Special Projects
Meeke Addison, Director Of Communications
Abraham Hamilton III, General Counsel & Public PolicyAnalyst

WCKQ
12-01-1964; 104.1 MHz FM; *Hrs Open:* 24; 17 kw; 394 ft.; N37 20 7 W85 22 33
Mailing Address: P.O. Box 1505, Glasgow, KY 42141 US
Second Address: Box 1053, Campbellsville, KY 42719
(270) 789-2401; *Fax:* (270) 789-1450
www.myq104.com
License: Campbellsville, Taylor County, KY held by CBC of Marion and Taylor Counties Inc.
Group Owner: Commonwealth Broadcasting Corp.; (acq 6-30-97; $720,000 with co-located AM)
Nat'l Network: ABC; Jones Radio Networks; *Nat'l Reps:* Rgnl Reps
Arbitron Metro Market: Campbellsville, KY; *Format:* Adult Contemp; *Hrs. of News Programming:* news progmg 7 hrs wkly; *No. News Employees:* 1; *Target Audience:* 18-44.; *Adv. Rates:* 12; 12; 12; na
Steve Newberry, President
Marty Bagby, Operations Dir
Barb Smith, General Manager
Barb Smith, Station Manager
Greg Gribbins, General Sales Mgr
Rob Collins, Promotions Manager
Mike Graham, Chief Engineer

WTCO
03-01-1948; 1450 kHz AM; *Hrs Open:* 24; 1 kw-U, ND1; N37 20 7 W85 22 33
Mailing Address: P.O. Box 1505, Glasgow, KY 42142 US
Second Address: Box 1053, Campbellsville, KY 42718
(270) 469-9826
www.wtcosports.com
License: Campbellsville, KY held by CBC of Marion and Taylor Counties Inc.
Group Owner: Commonwealth Broadcasting Corp.
Nat'l Network: ESPN Radio
Arbitron Metro Market: Campbellsville, KY; *Format:* Sports; *No. News Employees:* 1; *Target Audience:* 25-64.; *Adv. Rates:* 6; 6; 6; na

***WLCU**
88.7 MHz FM; 0.8 kw; 207 ft.; N37 20 39 W85 21 34 US
(270) 789-5008
www.campbellsville.edu
License: Campbellsville, Taylor County, KY held by Campbellsville University.
Arbitron Metro Market: Campbellsville, KY
Jeannie Clark, General Manager
Benji Kelly, Vice President for Development
Kaleb Chowning, Research and Communications Coordinator

Campton

WCBJ
01-01-1999; 103.7 MHz FM; 4.1 kw; 397 ft.; N37 39 3 W83 26 21
129 College St., West Liberty, KY 41472 US
License: Campton, Wolfe County, KY held by Morgan County Industries Inc.
Group Owner: Morgan County Industries Inc.
Format: Adult Contemp
Merv Lawson, General Manager
Paul Lyons, Chief Engineer

Cannonsburg

WONS
12-01-1987; 1080 kHz AM; 1.8 kw-D; N38 23 10 W82 41 53
P.O. Box 7773, Huntington, WV 25701 US
(606) 923-4619
License: Cannonsburg, Boyd County, KY held by Expression Production Group LLC
Group Owner: Expression Production Group LLC
Arbitron Metro Market: Huntington, WV *TV Affiliate:* Relg; *Format:* Christian, Talk; *No. News Employees:* General.
Stephanie Skragg, President

Carlisle

WBVX
12-01-1994; 92.1 MHz FM; *Hrs Open:* 24; 32 kw; 610 ft.; N38 11 19 W84 22 13
401 West Main Street, Suite 301, Lexington, KY 40507 US
(859) 233-1515; *Fax:* (859) 233-1517
www.b92fm.com
License: Carlisle, Nicholas County, KY held by L.M. Communications of Kentucky LLC.
Group Owner: L M Communications Inc.; (acq 8-17-01; $4.8 million).
Nat'l Reps: Katz Radio
Arbitron Metro Market: Lexington-Fayette, KY; *Format:* Contemporary Hits/Top 40, Adult Contemp; *Hrs. of News Programming:* News progmg one hr wkly; *Target Audience:* General.
Lynn Martin, President
James MacFarlane, General Manager

Carrollton

WIKI
04-12-1968; 95.3 MHz FM; *Hrs Open:* 24; 1.8 kw; 423 ft.; N38 39 58 W85 16 51
507 North State Street, North Vernon, IN 47265 US
(812) 346-1927; *Fax:* (812) 346-9722
License: Carrollton, Carroll County, KY held by Wagon Wheel Broadcastiing LLC.
Group Owner: Wagon Wheel Broadcasting LLC; (acq 11-14-2007; grpsl)
Nat'l Network: Jones Radio Networks; CNN Radio; *Nat'l Reps:* Rgnl Reps
Format: Country; *Hrs. of News Programming:* News progmg 10 hrs wkly; *Target Audience:* 10-90; general
Marty Pieratt, General Manager

Catlettsburg

WCMI-FM
01-19-1972; 92.7 MHz FM; *Hrs Open:* 24; 2.35 kw; 531 ft.; N38 28 2 W82 35 50
401 11th Street, Suite 200, Huntington, WV 25701 US
(304) 523-8401; *Fax:* (304) 523-4848
www.planet927.com
reeves@kindredcom.net
License: Catlettsburg, Boyd County, KY held by Fifth Avenue Broadcasting Co. Inc.
Group Owner: Kindred Communications Inc.; (acq 7-7-98; with WCMI(AM) Ashland).
Regional Network: Ky. News Net; *Nat'l Reps:* McGavren Guild;
Wire Services: Accu-Weather; AP
Arbitron Metro Market: Huntington-Ashl; *Format:* Rock/AOR; *Hrs. of News Programming:* news progrmg 5 hrs wkly; *No. News Employees:* 1
Mke Kirtner, CEO
Mike Kirtner, President
Reeves Kirtner, Operations Dir
Rich Myhrwold, General Sales Mgr
Reeves Kirtner, Programming Director
Jim Kowalski, Engineering Dir
Rich Mhyrwold, Regional Sales Manager

Cave City

WHHT(FM)
09-02-1988; 103.7 MHz FM; *Hrs Open:* 24; 13.5 kw; 449 ft.; N36 57 34 W86 0 8
Mailing Address: P.O. Box 1505, Glasgow, KY 42142 US
Second Address: 113 W. Public Sq., Suite 400, Glasgow, KY 42141
(270) 651-6060; *Fax:* (270) 651-7666
www.1037thepoint.net
License: Cave City, Barren County, KY held by Commonwealth Broadcasting Corp.
Group Owner: Commonwealth Broadcasting Corp.; (acq 11-25-97)
Nat'l Network: Westwood One
Arbitron Metro Market: Bowling Green, KY; *Format:* Classic Rock; *Hrs. of News Programming:* news progmg 7 hrs wkly; *No. News Employees:* 1; *Target Audience:* 25-44.
Kellie Wood, Operations Dir
Darren Steenbergen, General Manager

Central City

WMTA
02-19-1955; 1380 kHz AM; *Hrs Open:* 24; 0.5 kw-D, ND1; 0.023 kw-N, ND1; N37 16 34 W87 8 39
One Wmta Drive, P.O. Box 973, Central City, KY 42330 US
(812) 479-5342; *Fax:* (812) 474-0483
License: Central City, KY held by Faith Broadcasting Company
Arbitron Metro Market: Central City, IN; *Format:* Religious; *Hrs. of News Programming:* News progmg 20 hrs wkly; *Target Audience:* General.
Gayle Russ, CEO
Jonathan Williams, Engineering Dir

WNES
01-01-1955; 1050 kHz AM; 1 kw-D, ND1; 0.172 kw-N, ND1; N37 16 9 W87 8 32
P. O. Box 471, Central City, KY 42330 US
(270) 754-3000; *Fax:* (270) 754-9484
License: Central City, KY held by Starlight Broadcasting.
Nat'l Network: CBS
Arbitron Metro Market: Central City, KY; *Format:* Sports, Talk
Special Programming: Farm 7 hrs wkly
Andy Anderson, CEO
Jowanna Bandy, General Manager
Stan Barnett, Programming Director

WQXQ
12-18-1956; 101.9 MHz FM; 100 kw; 669 ft.; N37 35 3 W86 59 29
P.O. Box 471, Central City, KY 42330 US
(270) 754-3000; *Fax:* (270) 754-9484
www.q1019.com
License: Central City, Muhlenberg County, KY held by Starlight Broadcasting
Format: Adult Contemp
Brian Schimmel, General Manager

Clinton

WQQR
11-02-1955; 94.7 MHz FM; *Hrs Open:* 24; 50 kw; 472 ft.; N36 45 19 W88 39 36.6
Mailing Address: 1715 Nashville Street, P.O. Box 298, Russellville, KY 42276 US
Second Address: 6000 Bristol Drive, Paducah, KY 42003
(270) 554-8255; *Fax:* (270) 554-5468
License: Clinton, Graves County, KY held by Bristol Broadcasting Co. Inc.
Group Owner: Bristol Broadcasting Co. Inc.
Regional Reps: Rgnl Reps.
Format: Classic Rock; *No. News Employees:* 1; *Target Audience:* 25 plus.; *Adv. Rates:* 26; 19; 26; 16
Nick Black, Programming Director

Coal Run

WPKE-FM
09-21-1974; 103.1 MHz FM; *Hrs Open:* 24; 1.2 kw; 741 ft.; N37 27 57 W82 33 4
1240 Radio Dr., PO Box 2200, Pikeville, KY 41501 US
(606) 437-4051; *Fax:* (606) 432-2809
www.wpke.com
License: Coal Run, Pike County, KY held by East Kentucky Broadcasting Corp.
Group Owner: East Kentucky Broadcasting Corp.; acq 6-94; $480,000 with WBPA(AM) Elkhorn City).
Nat'l Network: ABC *Regional Reps:* Rgnl Reps
Format: Classic Rock; *No. News Employees:* 1; *Target Audience:* General.
Cindy May Johnson, President/CEO

Columbia

WAIN
08-01-1951; 1270 kHz AM; *Hrs Open:* 24
Mailing Address: P.O. Box 69, Columbia, KY 42725 US
Second Address: 1521 Liberty Rd., Columbia, KY 42728
(270) 384-2135; *Fax:* (270) 384-6722
www.1270wain.com
wain@forchtbroadcasting.com
License: Columbia, KY held by Forcht Broadcasting
Group Owner: Forcht Broadcasting
Regional Network: Ky. News Net; *Nat'l Reps:* Rgnl Reps
Regional Reps: Rgnl Reps
Arbitron Metro Market: Columbia, KY; *Format:* Oldies *Special Programming:* Farm 2 hrs; *Hrs. of News Programming:* news progmg 8 hrs wkly; *No. News Employees:* 1; *Target Audience:* 16-65.; *Adv. Rates:* 14;13; 14; 10
Gary Phelps, General Manager
Louise Wooten, General Sales Mgr

WAIN-FM
03-01-1968; 93.5 MHz FM; *Hrs Open:* 24; 4.6 kw; 199 ft.; N37 6 26 W85 16 42
Mailing Address: P.O. Box 69, Columbia, KY 42728 US
Second Address: 1521 Liberty Rd., Columbia, KY 42728
(270) 384-2135; *Fax:* (270) 384-6722
www.935wain.com
wain@forchtbroadcasting.com
License: Columbia, Adair County, KY
Group Owner: Key Broadcasting Inc.
Nat'l Network: ABC
Arbitron Metro Market: Columbia, KY; *Format:* Country; *No. News Employees:* 1; *Target Audience:* 16-65.; *Adv. Rates:* Same as AM
Sherri Butler-McIver, General Manager
Delno Salmon, Sales Executive
Mary Kay Sullivan, Account Executive
Lisa Fisher, News Director
Delno Salmon, Disc Jockey

Corbin

WCTT
05-09-1947; 680 kHz AM; *Hrs Open:* 5 AM-midnight
Mailing Address: 701 South Main Street, Corbin, KY 40701 US
Second Address: 821 Adams Rd., Corbin, KY 40701
(606) 528-4717; *Fax:* (606) 528-4487
www.wctt.com
pdir@wkdp.com
License: Corbin, KY held by Encore Communications Inc.
Nat'l Network: ABC; *Nat'l Reps:* Rgnl Reps
Arbitron Metro Market: Corbin, KY; *Format:* Adult Contemp, News, 62, Oldies, Talk; *No. News Employees:* 1
Stephanie Mullins, General Manager
Lindsay Peterson, Programming Director
Leslie Fields, News Director

WCTT-FM
06-01-1967; 107.3 MHz FM; *Hrs Open:* 24; 50 kw; 492 ft.; N36 54 9 W84 4 55
Mailing Address: 701 South Main Street, Corbin, KY 40701 US
Second Address: 821 Adams Rd., Corbin, KY 40701
(606) 528-4717; *Fax:* (606) 528-4487
www.wctt.com
pdir@wkdp.com
License: Corbin, Whitley County, KY
Nat'l Reps: Rgnl Reps
Arbitron Metro Market: Corbin, KY; *Format:* Adult Contemp; *Hrs. of News Programming:* News progmg one hr wkly; *Target Audience:* 18-54.
Mark Wilson, Operations Dir
Lindsay Peterson, Programming Director
Leslie Fields, News Director
Matt Howell, Engineering Dir
Heidi Decker, Disc Jockey
Sammi Austin, Disc Jockey
Maverick Johnson, Disc Jockey
Tracy Black, PublicAffairs Director

WKDP
11-23-1961; 1330 kHz AM; 5 kw-D, DA2; 0.016 kw-N, DA2; N36 56 20 W84 4 44
Mailing Address: 701 South Main Street, Corbin, KY 40701 US
Second Address: 821 Adams Rd., Corbin, KY 40701
(606) 528-6617; *Fax:* (606) 528-4487
www.wkdp.com
swaggoner@wkdp.com
License: Corbin, KY held by Eubanks Broadcasting Inc.
Nat'l Reps: Rgnl Reps
Format: News, News/Talk, 86, Religious; *Target Audience:* 30-64.
Dallas Eubanks, President
Stephanie Mullins, General Manager
Derek Eubanks, Chief Engineer

WKDP-FM
01-01-1967; 99.5 MHz FM; 25 kw; 709 ft.; N36 57 14 W83 58 41
701 Main Street, Corbin, KY 40701 US
(606) 528-6617; *Fax:* (606) 528-4487
www.wkdp.com
swaggoner@wkdp.com
License: Corbin, Whitley County, KY held by Eubanks Broadcasting Inc.
Nat'l Network: ABC
Format: Country; *Target Audience:* General.
Rich Archut, Operations Dir

WRSL
11-01-1961; 1600 kHz AM; *Hrs Open:* Sunrise-sunset; 2 kw-D, 27 w-N; N37 01 06 W84 05 58
1100 S. Main St., London, KY 40484
(606) 878-1600; *Fax:* (606) 878-1116
License: Corbin, Whitley County, KY held by Lincoln-Garrard Broadcasting Co. Inc.
Population Served: 70,000
Johnathan Smith, President
Dave Colvin, General Manager

*WEKF
06-24-2003; 88.5 MHz FM; *Hrs Open:* 24; 21 kw vert; 499 ft.; N37 1 13 W84 23 41 *Rebroadcasts:* Rebroadcasts WEKU(FM) Richmond 100%
521 Lancaster Ave, Richmond, KY 40475 US
(800) 621-8890; *Fax:* (859) 622-6276
www.weku.fm
weku@eku.edu
License: Corbin, Whitley County, KY held by Eastern Kentucky University.
Nat'l Network: NPR; PRI; *Wire Services:* AP
Arbitron Metro Market: Corbin, KY; *Format:* Classical, News; *Hrs. of News Programming:* news progmg 35 hrs wkly; *No. News Employees:* 3; *Target Audience:* General.
Mary Ellyn Cain, Operations Dir
Tim Singleton, General Manager
Carol Siler, General Sales Mgr
Laura Allen, Programming Director
Charles Compton, News Director
Bill Browning, Chief Engineer

Covington

WCVG
10-29-1965; 1320 kHz AM; *Hrs Open:* 24; 0.5 kw-D, DA2; 0.43 kw-N, DA2; N39 2 44 W84 30 30
35 Island Drive, Eastpoint, FL 32328 US
(866) 305-1570; *Fax:* (859) 655-4345
www.gospel1320.com
License: Covington, KY held by Davidson Media Station WCVG Licensee LLC.
Group Owner: Davidson Media Group LLC; (acq 11-2-2006; $1.9 million)
Arbitron Metro Market: Cincinnati, OH; *Format:* Gospel; *Adv. Rates:* 40; 40; 40; 35
Jeff Eldred, Operations Dir
Simon Cipriano, General Manager
John Jones, Programming Director
Mayra Arroyo, Promotions Manager
Avery Corbin, Promotions Manager

Crab Orchard

WPBK
01-01-2008; 102.9 MHz FM; *Hrs Open:* 24; 2.75 kw; 361 ft.; N37 25 39 W84 39 21
US
(606) 365-2126
www.wpbkfm.com
renee@wpbkfm.com
License: Crab Orchard, Lincoln County, KY held by Radioactive LLC.
Group Owner: Radioactive LLC
Arbitron Metro Market: Crab Orchard, KY
Jonathan L. Smith, President
Renee Knies, Station Manager
David Smith, Chief Engineer

Cumberland

WCPM
10-01-1951; 1280 kHz AM; *Hrs Open:* 24 hrs a day; 1 kw-D, ND1; 0.115 kw-N, ND1; N36 58 25 W82 59 15
101 Keller Street, Cumberland, KY 40823 US
(606) 589-4623
wcpmradio@windstream.net
License: Cumberland, KY held by Cumberland City Broadcasting Inc.
Nat'l Network: Jones Radio Networks; AP Radio
Arbitron Metro Market: Cumberland,KY; *Format:* Country, News, 74 *Special Programming:* Black one hr, farm one hr wkly; *Hrs. of News Programming:* News progmg 9 hrs wkly; *Target Audience:* 18-49; general *Adv.Rates:* 6; 5; 6; 5
Susan Burton, General Manager
Susan Burton, Station Manager
Laura Hewitt, News Director

Cynthiana

WCYN
09-01-1956; 1400 kHz AM; 0.5 kw-D, ND1; 1 kw-N, ND1; N38 24 20 W84 17 32
10 Court Street, Cynthiana, KY 41031 US

(859) 234-1400; *Fax:* (859) 234-1425
www.wcyn.com
chris.winkle@wcyn.com
License: Cynthiana, KY held by WCYN Broadcasting Inc.
Nat'l Reps: Keystone (unwired net); Rgnl Reps
Arbitron Metro Market: Lexington, KY; *Format:* Oldies; *Target Audience:* General.
Chris Winkle, President
Chris Winkle, General Manager
Blake Bishop, News Director

WCYN-FM
06-01-1970; 102.3 MHz FM; 3.4 kw; 400 ft.; N38 24 39 W84 19 7 *Rebroadcasts:* Rebroadcasts WLXX(FM) Lexington 100%
10 Court Street, PO Box 398, Cynthiana, KY 41031 US
(859) 253-5900; *Fax:* (859) 253-5940
www.wvlkfm.net
License: Cynthiana, Harrison County, KY held by Cumulus Licensing LLC.
Group Owner: Cumulus Media Inc.; (acq 11-26-2002)
Arbitron Metro Market: Lexington, KY; *Format:* Country
Ken Fearnow, General Manager

Danville

***WDFB-FM**
09-01-1992; 88.1 MHz FM; *Hrs Open:* 24; 170 w; 328 ft; N37 35 46 W84 50 19
Mailing Address: Box 106, Danville, KY 40423
Second Address: 3596 Alum Springs Rd., Danville, KY 40422
(859) 236-9333; *Fax:* (859) 236-3348
www.wdfb.com
wdfb@wdfb.org
License: Danville, Boyle County, KY held by Alum Springs Educational Corp.
Nat'l Network: USA
Target Audience: General.; *Adv. Rates:* 6; 6; 5
Mildred Drake, President
Mildred Drake, General Sales Mgr
Cindy Pike, News Director

WHIR
10-27-1947; 1230 kHz AM; *Hrs Open:* 24; 1 kw-U, ND1; N37 40 28 W84 46 6
324 West Main Street, Danville, KY 40422 US
(859) 236-2711; *Fax:* (859) 236-1461
www.hometownlive.net
hometownradio@bellsouth.net
License: Danville, KY held by Hometown Broadcasting of Danville Inc.
Nat'l Network: Westwood One; Motor Racing Net; Sporting News Radio Network; Talk Radio Network; *Nat'l Reps:* Rgnl Reps
Arbitron Metro Market: Lexington-Fayette, KY; *Format:* News, News/Talk, 86; *Hrs. of News Programming:* news progmg 2 hrs wkly; *No. News Employees:* 1; *Target Audience:* 25-54; business owners, sports fans, housewives
Bruce Leslie, President
Jim Parman, Operations Dir
Robert Wagner, General Manager
Vicki Hyde, News Director

Drakesboro

WNTC
01-01-2001; 103.9 MHz FM; 1.95 kw; 407 ft.; N37 6 50 W87 3 52
810 Dominican Drive, Nashville, TN 37228 US
(615) 844-1039; *Fax:* (615) 777-2284
www.wnsr.com
info@wnsr.com
License: Drakesboro, Muhlenberg County, KY held by Nashville's SportsRadio Inc.
Group Owner: Southern Wabash Communications Corp.; (acq 10-17-01).
Arbitron Metro Market: Nashville, TN; *Format:* Sports
Randolph Bell, President
Tedd Johnson, Vice President/General Manager

Edmonton

WHSX
04-05-1990; 99.1 MHz FM; *Hrs Open:* 24; 6 kw; 328 ft.; N37 1 33 W85 33 14
P.O. Box 377, Edmonton, KY 42129 US
(270) 786-1000; *Fax:* (270) 786-4402
www.thehoss.com
License: Edmonton, Metcalfe County, KY held by Hart County Communications Inc.
Arbitron Metro Market: Bowling Green, KY; *Format:* Country
Special Programming: Farm 15 hrs wkly; *Hrs. of News Programming:* news progmg 10 hrs wkly; *No. News Employees:* 1; *Target Audience:* 25-54. *Adv.Rates:* 10; 10; 10; na

Dewayne Forbis, General Manager

Effingham

WJKG
11-18-1993; 105.5 MHz FM; *Hrs Open:* 24; 3 kw; 328 ft.; N37 41 50 W86 59 28
405 South Banker St., Suite 201, Effingham, IL 62401 US
(217) 342-4141; *Fax:* (217) 342-4143
www.wbio.com
jcatinna@cromwellradio.com
License: Effingham, Effingham County, IL held by Hancock Communications Inc.
Group Owner: The Cromwell Group Inc.; (acq 6-17-93; $90,565;
Nat'l Network: ABC; *Nat'l Reps:* Rgnl Reps
Arbitron Metro Market: Owensboro, Ky; *Format:* Contemporary Hits/Top 40, Classic Rock, 34; *Hrs. of News Programming:* news progmg 4 hrs wkly; *No. News Employees:* 1; *Target Audience:* 25-54.; *Adv. Rates:* 20;20; 20; 12
Brack Stacy, Market Manager
Brack Stacy, Operations Manager
Mel Iglenheart, Business Manager

Elizabethtown

WIEL
10-01-1950; 1400 kHz AM; *Hrs Open:* 24; 1 kw-U, ND1; N37 41 11 W85 52 19
406 South Mulberry St, Elizabethtown, KY 42701 US
(270) 763-0800; *Fax:* (270) 769-6349
License: Elizabethtown, KY held by Elizabethtown CBC Inc.
Group Owner: Commonwealth Broadcasting Corp.; (acq 5-12-00; grpsl)
Nat'l Network: ABC; *Nat'l Reps:* Rgnl Reps; *Wire Services:* AP
Format: Sports; *Hrs. of News Programming:* news progmg one hr wkly; *No. News Employees:* 1; *Target Audience:* 24-54; upscale adult; *Adv. Rates:* 10; 8; 10; 4.50
Dan Michaels, Operations Dir
Roth Stratton, General Manager
Holli Lee, News Director
Misty Monroe, News

***WKUE**
10-15-1990; 90.9 MHz FM; *Hrs Open:* 24; 5.2 kw; 633 ft.; N37 44 46 W85 53 18 *Rebroadcasts:* Rebroadcasts WKYU-FM Bowling Green 100%
College Heights, 1 Big Red Way, Bowling Green, KY 42101 US
(270) 745-5489; *Fax:* (270) 745-6272
wkyufm@wku.edu
License: Elizabethtown, Hardin County, KY held by Western Kentucky University.
Nat'l Network: NPR; PRI
Format: News *Special Programming:* Jazz 15 hrs, folk 5 hrs wkly; *Hrs. of News Programming:* news progmg 30 hrs wkly; *No. News Employees:* 3; *Target Audience:* General.
Peter Bryant, General Manager

WQXE
11-24-1969; 98.3 MHz FM; 8.5 kw; 531 ft.; N37 43 18 W86 2 10
P. O. Box 517, Elizabethtown, KY 42702 US
(270) 737-8000; *Fax:* (270) 737-7229
www.wqxe.com
bill@wqxe.com
License: Elizabethtown, Hardin County, KY held by Skytower Communications E'town Inc.
Nat'l Network: Westwood One
Format: Adult Contemp; *Target Audience:* 25-54; upscale, dual income families; *Adv. Rates:* 31; 29; 31; 25
Bill Evans, President

Elkhorn City

WEKB
11-24-1979; 1460 kHz AM; *Hrs Open:* 24; 5 kw-D, ND1; 0.114 kw-N, ND1; N37 18 25 W82 19 53 *Rebroadcasts:* Simulcast with WPKE(AM) Pikeville 100%
PO Box 2200, 1240 Radio Drive, Pikeville, KY 41502 US
(606) 437-4051; *Fax:* (606) 432-2809
www.myoldiesradio.com
License: Elkhorn City, KY held by East Kentucky Broadcasting Corp.
Group Owner: East Kentucky Broadcasting Corp.; (acq 6-94; $480,000 with co-located FM).
Nat'l Network: ABC *Regional Reps:* Rgnl Reps
Arbitron Metro Market: Pikeville,KY; *Format:* Oldies; *Target Audience:* 25-49.
Cindy May Johnson, General Manager

Elkton

WEKT
07-21-1977; 1070 kHz AM

P.O. Box 577, Elkton, KY 42220 US
(270) 265-5636; *Fax:* (270) 265-5637
www.wektgospelradio.com/
wektan1070@yahoo.com
License: Elkton, KY held by M&R Broadcasting Inc.
Nat'l Network: USA
Arbitron Metro Market: Elkton, KY; *Format:* Gospel
Marshall Sidebottom, General Manager
Nick Reed, Owner

Eminence

WLRS
06-01-1956; 1600 kHz AM; 500 w-D, 48 w-N; N38 21 02 W85 11 11
111 S. First St., La Grange, KY 40019
(502) 222-9171; *Fax:* (502) 222-9173
License: Eminence, Henry County, KY held by Metro East CBC Inc.
Group Owner: Commonwealth Broadcasting Corp.; (acq 4-13-00; $600,000 with WTSZ-FM Eminence).
Population Served: 16,000; *Arbitron Metro Market:* Louisville, KY; *Target Audience:* 25-54.
Dugan Ryan, General Manager

WTUV-FM
07-04-1988; 105.7 MHz FM; 3 kw; 328 ft.; N38 21 9 W85 11 9
P.O. Box 655, New Albany, IN 47151 US
(502) 671-8407; *Fax:* (502) 671-8743
License: Eminence, Henry County, KY held by Davidson Media Station WTSZ Licensee LLC.
Group Owner: Davidson Media Group LLC; (acq 5-3-2006; $500,000)
Arbitron Metro Market: Louisville, KY
Catalina Ibarraÿ, Station Manager
Paul Dendy, General Sales Mgr
Dennis Mendez, Programming Director
Jenny Sanchez, Traffic Manager

Erlanger

WIZF
09-22-1965; 101.1 MHz FM; 2.5 kw; 509 ft.; N39 6 18 W84 33 25
1 Centennial Plaza, 705 Central Ave., Cincinnati, OH 45202 US
(513) 679-6000; *Fax:* (513) 679-6014
www.wiznation.com
License: Erlanger, Kenton County, KY held by Blue Chip Broadcasting Licenses Ltd.
Group Owner: Radio One Inc.; (acq 4-30-2001; grpsl).
Arbitron Metro Market: Cincinnati, OH; *Format:* Urban Contemporary; *Target Audience:* 18-54.
Mitch Galvin, Station Manager

Falmouth

WIOK
06-01-1981; 107.5 MHz FM; *Hrs Open:* 24; 1.35 kw; 696 ft.; N38 35 13 W84 21 40
13297 Green Road, Walton, KY 41094 US
(859) 472-1075; *Fax:* (859) 472-2875
wiok@fuse.net
License: Falmouth, Pendleton County, KY held by Hammond Broadcasting Inc.
Nat'l Network: USA; *Nat'l Reps:* Rgnl Reps
Arbitron Metro Market: Cincinnati, OH; *Format:* Gospel; *Hrs. of News Programming:* News progmg 12 hrs wkly; *Target Audience:* 25-64; women; *Adv. Rates:* 144; 108; 144; 120
Jan Hammond, Operations Dir
Jamie Porter, General Sales Mgr

Fearsville

***WYJZ**
91.7 MHz FM; kw
US
(317) 467-1062
License: Fearsville, Christian County, KY held by Electronic Applications Radio Service Inc.
Group Owner: Electronic Applications Radio Service Inc.
Arbitron Metro Market: Lebanon, IN
Patrick Diemer, President

Flemingsburg

WFLE
11-01-1981; 1060 kHz AM; 0.5 kw-D, DAD; N38 27 1 W83 44 6
334 Recreation Park Rd., Flemingsburg, KY 41041 US
(606) 849-4433; *Fax:* (606) 845-9353
License: Flemingsburg, KY held by DreamCatcher Communications Inc.

Group Owner: DreamCatcher Communications Inc.; (acq 5-23-02; $607,491 with co-located FM).
Format: Country; *Target Audience:* 25-54.
Don Bowles, President
Kim Hester, Station Manager
Kim Hester, General Sales Mgr

WFLE-FM
02-01-1993; 95.1 MHz FM; 2.35 kw; 449 ft; N38 24 42 W83 34 41
334 Recreation Park Rd., Flemingsburg, KY 41041 US
(606) 849-4433; *Fax:* (606) 845-9353
License: Flemingsburg, KY held by DreamCatcher Communications Inc.
Group Owner: DreamCatcher Communications Inc.; 09/20/2004
Format: Country
Don Bowles, President
Kim Hester, Station Manager
Kim Hester, General Sales Mgr

Florence

WCVX
09-01-1984; 1160 kHz AM; *Hrs Open:* 24; 5 kw-D, 990 w-N, DA-2; N38 58 09 W84 40 56
635 W. 7th St., Suite 400, Cincinnati, OH 45203
(513) 533-2500; *Fax:* (513) 533-2528
www.christiantalk1160.com
License: Florence, Boone County, KY held by Christian Broadcasting System Ltd.
Group Owner: Christian Broadcasting System Ltd.; (acq 2-10-2006; swap of WDJO(AM) and WCVX(AM) Cincinnati, OH plus $6.75 million cash for WLQV(AM) Detroit, MI).
Population Served: 296,223; *Arbitron Metro Market:* Cincinnati, OH; *Format:* Oldies; *Hrs. of News Programming:* News progmg 6 hrs wkly; *Target Audience:* 25-54; 35-64; adults; *Adv. Rates:* 50; 45; 50; 15

Fort Campbell

WLFZ
07-27-1963; 1370 kHz AM; *Hrs Open:* 24; 1 kw-D, ND1; 0.053 kw-N, ND1; N36 38 28 W87 26 1
P.O. Box 2249, Clarksville, TN 37042 US
(320) 252-6200; *Fax:* (320) 252-9367
www.wmin1010.com
License: Fort Campbell, KY held by Saga Communications of Tuckessee L.L.C.
Group Owner: Saga Communications Inc.; (acq 2-1-2001; grpsl)
Arbitron Metro Market: Evanston WY; *Format:* Adult Contemp
Herb Hoppe, General Manager
Doug Kertz, General Sales Mgr
Gary Moore, Programming Director

WCVQ
08-01-1969; 107.9 MHz FM; *Hrs Open:* 24; 100 kw; 902 ft.; N36 32 23 W87 39 45
P.O. Box 2249, Clarksville, TN 37042 US
(931) 648-7720; *Fax:* (931) 648-7769
www.q108.com
Ryan@Q108.com
License: Fort Campbell, Christian County, KY held by Saga Communications of Tuckessee LLC.
Group Owner: Saga Communications Inc.; (acq 2-1-2001; grpsl)
Arbitron Metro Market: Clarksville-Hopkinsville, TN; *Format:* Adult Contemp; *Hrs. of News Programming:* news progmg 2 hrs wkly; *No. News Employees:* 1; *Target Audience:* 25-40.
Scott Chase, Operations Dir
Katie Gambill, General Manager

Fort Knox

WLVK
10-01-1967; 105.5 MHz FM; *Hrs Open:* 24; 3.2 kw; 456 ft.; N37 46 57 W85 54 38
Mailing Address: P.O. Box 2481, Elizabethtown, KY 42701 US
Second Address: 519 N. Miles St., Elizabethtown, KY 42702
(270) 766-1035; *Fax:* (270) 769-1052
www.bigcat1055.com
wlvk@bigcat1055.com
License: Fort Knox, Hardin County, KY held by W & B Broadcasting Co. Inc.
Arbitron Metro Market: Fort Knox, KY; *Format:* Country *Special Programming:* Lou Helton Country Countdown; *Hrs. of News Programming:* 4 hrs wkly; *No. News Employees:* 14; *Target Audience:* 25-49; young & middleage country fans; *Adv. Rates:* 32; 32; 32; 8
Bill Walters, President
Cale Tharp, Operations Dir
Rene Bell, General Manager

Fort Thomas

WYGY
01-01-1925; 97.3 MHz FM; *Hrs Open:* 24; 2.55 kw; 509 ft.; N39 12 1 W84 31 22
2060 Reading Rd., Cincinnati, OH 45202 US
(513) 699-5103; *Fax:* (513) 699-5000
www.theworldwidewolf.com
License: Fort Thomas, Campbell County, KY held by Cincinnati FCC License Sub LLC
Group Owner: Hubbard Broadcasting Inc.; (acq 1-19-2011)
Arbitron Metro Market: Cincinnati, OH; *Format:* Country; *Hrs. of News Programming:* News progmg 8 hrs wkly
Mike Fredrick, Vice President and Market Manager
Kehra Woolfolk, Account Executive

Frankfort

WKYW
02-01-1946; 1490 kHz AM; *Hrs Open:* 24
P.O. Box 1505, Glasgow, KY 42142 US
(502) 875-1130; *Fax:* (502) 875-1225
License: Frankfort, KY held by Forever South Licenses LLC.
Group Owner: Forever Communications Inc.; (acq 11-1-2007; grpsl)
Nat'l Network: Westwood One; *Nat'l Reps:* Rgnl Reps
Format: Oldies; *Hrs. of News Programming:* news progmg 12 hrs wkly; *No. News Employees:* 2; *Target Audience:* 25-55.; *Adv. Rates:* 28; 16; 18; 14
Brian Sands, General Manager

WSTV-FM
04-15-1991; 103.7 MHz FM; *Hrs Open:* 24; 2.5 kw; 358 ft.; N38 13 17 W84 54 52
P.O. Box 1505, Glasgow, KY 42142 US
(502) 875-1130; *Fax:* (502) 875-1225
www.star1037.com
License: Frankfort, Franklin County, KY held by Forever South Licenses LLC.
Group Owner: Forever Communications Inc.; (acq 11-1-2007; grpsl)
Nat'l Network: Westwood One
Format: Adult Contemp; *Hrs. of News Programming:* news progmg 4 hrs wkly; *No. News Employees:* 2; *Target Audience:* 25-54.
Brian Sands, General Manager

WFKY
01-01-1967; 104.9 MHz FM; *Hrs Open:* 24; 3.4 kw; 282 ft.; N38 13 18 W84 54 54
P.O. Box 1505, Glasgow, KY 42142 US
(502) 875-1130; *Fax:* (502) 875-1225
www.myfroggyville.com
License: Frankfort, Franklin County, KY
Group Owner: Forever Communications Inc.
Format: Country; *Hrs. of News Programming:* news progmg 168 hrs wkly; *No. News Employees:* 2; *Target Audience:* 25-54.; *Adv. Rates:* 18; 18; 18; 18
Brian Sands, General Manager
Jim Beam, Disc Jockey
Sally Mander, Disc Jockey
James Pond, Disc Jockey

Franklin

WFKN
04-25-1954; 1220 kHz AM; *Hrs Open:* 24; 0.25 kw-D, ND1; 0.09 kw-N, ND1; N36 44 20 W86 34 42
103 N. High Street, Franklin, KY 42134 US
(270) 586-4481; *Fax:* (270) 586-6031
www.franklinfavorite.com
wfkn@franklinfavorite.com
License: Franklin, KY held by WFKN LLC
Nat'l Reps: Rgnl Reps
Format: Country *Special Programming:* Relg, farm 6 hrs wkly; *Hrs. of News Programming:* news progmg 16 hrs wkly; *No. News Employees:* 2; *Target Audience:* General.
Kendra Holt, CEO/COO
Jamie Johnson, General Manager
Brownie Bennett, General Sales Mgr
James Mooneyhan, Sports Announcer

Fulton

WWKF
09-01-1954; 99.3 MHz FM; *Hrs Open:* 24; 3 kw; 299 ft.; N36 27 59 W88 56 47
1729 Nailing Drive, Union City, TN 38261 US
(731) 885-1240; *Fax:* (731) 885-3405
www.kf99kq105.com
acetj@acetj.com
License: Fulton, Fulton County, KY held by WENK of Union City Inc.
Group Owner: WENK of Union City Inc.; (acq 10-1-82; $473,131;
Nat'l Reps: Rgnl Reps
Arbitron Metro Market: Fulton, KY; *Format:* Contemporary Hits/Top 40; *No. News Employees:* 1; *Target Audience:* 18-34.
Terry Hailey, President & General Manager
Wilma Payne, Traffic Manager
Jerry McCain, Traffic Manager
JimAdcock, Sales Rep
Lorrie Matlock, Sales Rep
Brent Hinson, Website Enquiry

***WKMT**
89.5 MHz FM; 4.5 kw; 353 ft.; N36 34 10 W88 50 13 US
(270) 809-4745; *Fax:* (270) 809-4667
www.wkms.org
License: Fulton, Fulton County, KY held by Board of Regents, Murray State University.
Arbitron Metro Market: Fulton, KY; *Format:* Variety/Diverse
Randy Dunn, President
Kate Lochte, Station Manager

Garrison

WOKE
09-07-1998; 98.3 MHz FM; 5.2 kw; 351 ft.; N38 36 26 W83 2 33
Mailing Address: P.O. Box 926, South Shore, KY 41175 US
Second Address: 829 Main St., South Shore, KY 41175
(606) 932-2223; *Fax:* (606) 932-6132
License: Garrison, Lewis County, KY held by Expression Production Group LLC
Group Owner: Expression Production Group LLC
TV Affiliate: Relg; *Format:* Christian
Stephanie Skragg, President

Georgetown

***WKVO**
10-01-1963; 89.9 MHz FM; *Hrs Open:* 24; 50 kw; 410 ft.; N38 12 15 W84 32 51
400 E College St, Georgetown, KY 40324 US
(916) 251-1600
www.klove.com
klove@klove.com
License: Georgetown, Scott County, KY held by Educational Media Foundation.
Group Owner: EMF Broadcasting; (acq 3-12-2004; $1.7 million).
Nat'l Network: K-Love
Arbitron Metro Market: Lexington-Fayet; *Format:* Religious
Darrell Chambliss, Chairman
Alan Mason, COO
Mike Novak, President
Chip Bailey, Operations Dir
David Pierce, Programming Director
Ed Lenane, News Director
Sam Wallington, Engineering Dir
Marya Morgan, News Reporter
RichardHunt, News Reporter
Tracy Butler, Traffic Manager

WWTF
09-06-1957; 1580 kHz AM; 10 kw-D, DA2; 0.045 kw-N, DA2; N38 10 5 W84 35 37
2601 Nicholasville Road, Lexington, KY 40503 US
(859) 422-1000; *Fax:* (859) 422-1071
www.foxsports1580.com
License: Georgetown, KY held by Citicasters Licenses Inc.
Group Owner: iHeartMedia; (acq 6-30-97; grpsl)
Nat'l Reps: Christal
Arbitron Metro Market: Lexington, KY; *Format:* Sports; *Hrs. of News Programming:* News progmg 2 hrs wkly; *Adv. Rates:* 12; 12; 12; 4
Michael Jordan, Programming Director
Mandy Daugherty, Promotions Director
Marci Adams, Digital Program Director

WXZZ
09-10-1973; 103.3 MHz FM; 6 kw; 328 ft.; N38 3 56 W84 29 13
111 East Kilbourn Avenue, Suite 2700, Milwaukee, WI 53202 US
(859) 253-5900; *Fax:* (859) 253-5940
www.zrock103.com
john.lewis@cumulus.comy
License: Georgetown, Scott County, KY held by Cumulus Licensing Corp.
Group Owner: Cumulus Media Inc.; (acq 7-22-99; grpsl)
Arbitron Metro Market: Lexington, KY; *No. News Employees:* 3; *Target Audience:* 18-34.; *Adv. Rates:* 30; 30; 30; 15

John Lewis, General Manager
Scott Frazier, General Sales Mgr
Mario Anderson, Promotions Manager

Glasgow

WCLU
09-25-1946; 1490 kHz AM
PO Box 1628, Glasgow, KY 42142 US
(270) 651-9149; *Fax:* (270) 651-9222
www.wcluradio.com
emilyrose@wcluradio.com
License: Glasgow, KY held by Royse Radio Inc.
Nat'l Network: CBS
Arbitron Metro Market: Bowling Green, KY; *Format:* Variety/Diverse; *Target Audience:* 30 plus; listeners with disposable income
Henry Royse, President
Henry Royse, General Manager

WLYE-FM
01-01-1997; 94.1 MHz FM; *Hrs Open:* 24; 4.5 kw; 299 ft.; N36 59 2 W85 52 20
1919 Scottsville Road, Bowling Green, KY 42104 US
(270) 843-3333; *Fax:* (270) 843-0454
License: Glasgow, Barren County, KY held by Forever Communications Inc.
Group Owner: Forever Communications Inc.; acq 9-3-03).
Nat'l Reps: Christal
Arbitron Metro Market: Bowling Green, KY; *Format:* Country; *Hrs. of News Programming:* news progmg 6 hrs wkly; *No. News Employees:* 1; *Target Audience:* 25-54; adults, serving southern central Kentucky; *Adv. Rates:* 20; 20; 20; 10
Christine Hillard, President
Mark Mackey, General Manager
Jim O'Neal, General Sales Mgr

WPTQ
07-14-1972; 105.3 MHz FM; 15 kw; 433 ft.; N36 58 50 W86 6 10
Mailing Address: P.O. Box 1505, Glasgow, KY 42142 US
Second Address: 113 W. Public Sq., Suite 400, Glasgow, KY 42141
(270) 651-6050; *Fax:* (270) 651-7666
License: Glasgow, Barren County, KY held by Newberry Broadcasting Inc.
Group Owner: Commonwealth Broadcasting Corp.; (acq 11-25-97; grpsl)
Arbitron Metro Market: Bowling Green, KY; *Format:* Oldies
Derron Steenbergen, General Manager
Kelly McKay, Programming Director

*WSGP
01-01-2002; 88.3 MHz FM; 13 kw; 299 ft.; N36 49 5 W85 41 30
Mailing Address: PO Box 1423, Somerset, KY 42502 US
Second Address: 93 Rainbow Terr., Somerset, KY 45201
(606) 679-1342
www.kingofkingsradio.net
License: Glasgow, Barren County, KY held by Somerset Educational Broadcasting Foundation.
Arbitron Metro Market: Somerset, KY; *Format:* Religious
David Carr, General Manager
Carolyn Jones, Programming Director
Marvin Whitaker, Chief Engineer

WCDS
01-01-2007; 1230 kHz AM
Mailing Address: US
Second Address: 113 W Public Sq., Suite 400, Glasgow, KY 42141
(270) 651-6050; *Fax:* (270) 651-7666
License: Glasgow, KY held by Anderson Communications LLC.
Nat'l Network: ESPN Radio
Arbitron Metro Market: Glasgow, KY; *Format:* Sports
Charles Anderson, General Manager

Grand Rivers

WCBL-FM
03-03-1966; 99.1 MHz FM; 16 kw; 417 ft.; N37 6 47 W88 21 34
P.O. Box 387, 1039 Egner's Ferry Road, Benton, KY 42025 US
(270) 527-3102; *Fax:* (270) 527-5606
www.thelakecurrent.com
wcbl@freelandbroadcasting.com
License: Grand Rivers, Marshall County, KY
Group Owner: Freeland Broadcasting Stations
Format: Oldies; *Adv. Rates:* Same as AM
Jim Freeland, President/General Manager

Grayson

WGOH
06-01-1959; 1370 kHz AM; *Hrs Open:* 6 AM-2 hrs past sunset; 5 kw-D, ND1; 0.021 kw-N, ND1; N38 19 44 W82 58 33
PO Box 487, Grayson, KY 41143 US
(606) 474-5144; *Fax:* (606) 474-7777
www.wgohwugo.com
License: Grayson, KY held by Carter County Broadcasting Co.
Nat'l Network: CBS; *Regional Network:* Ky. News Net; *Nat'l Reps:* Rgnl Reps; *Wire Services:* AP
Arbitron Metro Market: Huntington-Ashland, WV-KY; *Format:* Country *Special Programming:* Bluegrass; *Hrs. of News Programming:* news progmg 30 hrs wkly; *No. News Employees:* 1; *Target Audience:* 35-65. *Adv.Rates:* 5; 4; 4; na
Jeff Roe, Operations Dir
Francis Nash, General Manager
Mike Phillips, Programming Director
Jim Phillips, News Director
William Craig, Engineering Dir
Melodie Carter, Traffic Manager

WUGO
02-01-1967; 9MHz FM; *Hrs Open:* 24; 4.8 kw; 360 ft; N38 19 44 W82 58 33
Box 487, 150 Radio Tower Dr., Grayson, KY 41143
(606) 474-5144; *Fax:* (606) 474-7777
www.wgohwugo.com
License: Grayson, Carter County, KY held by Carter County Broadcasting Co. Inc.
Nat'l Reps: Rgnl Reps; *Wire Services:* AP
Arbitron Metro Market: Huntington-Ashland, WV-KY; *Hrs. of News Programming:* News progmg 30 hrs wkly; *Target Audience:* 25-54.; *Adv. Rates:* 8; 6; 6; na
Francis Nash, General Manager

Greensburg

WGRK-FM
12-15-1977; 105.7 MHz FM; *Hrs Open:* 24; 5.1 kw; 358 ft.; N37 15 34 W85 30 57
Mailing Address: P.O. Box 457, Glasgow, KY 42141 US
Second Address: 50 Friendship Pike, Greensburg, KY 42719
(270) 932-7401; *Fax:* (270) 789-1450
www.kcountry1057.com
License: Greensburg, Green County, KY held by Green County CBC, Inc.
Group Owner: Commonwealth Broadcasting Corp.
Format: Country; *No. News Employees:* 1
Steve Newberry, President
Marty Bagby, Operations Dir
Barb Smith, General Manager
Greg Gribbins, General Sales Mgr
Trent Ford, Programming Director

Greenup

WLGC
04-01-1985; 1520 kHz AM; 5 kw-D; N38 35 44 W82 51 20
1401 Winchester Ave., Ashland, KY 41144
(606) 920-9565; *Fax:* (606) 920-9523
License: Greenup, Greenup County, KY held by Greenup County Broadcasting Inc.
Nat'l Network: Sporting News Radio Network
Arbitron Metro Market: Huntington-Ashl; *No. News Employees:* 1
Mark Justice, Operations Dir
Bobby Hall, General Manager
Scott Martin, Station Manager
Jim Forest, General Sales Mgr
Fred Francis, Chief Engineer

WLGC-FM
09-01-1982; 105.7 MHz FM; 12.5 kw; 466 ft.; N38 35 44 W82 51 22
P.O. Box 685, Greenup, KY 41144 US
(606) 920-9565; *Fax:* (606) 920-9523
wlgc@inet99.net
License: Greenup, Greenup County, KY held by Greenup County Broadcasting Inc.
Regional Network: Ky. News Net; *Wire Services:* AP
Arbitron Metro Market: Huntington-Ashland, WV-KY; *Format:* Country; *Hrs. of News Programming:* news progmg 3 hrs wkly; *No. News Employees:* 1; *Target Audience:* 25-54; middle income listeners; *Adv. Rates:* 15;13; 14; 10
Bob Hall, General Manager
Scott Martin, General Sales Mgr
Mark Justice, Programming Director

Greenville

WKYA
12-11-1981; 105.5 MHz FM; 3 kw horiz, 2.6 kw vert; 299 ft.; N37 11 45 W87 12 38
Highway 63 West, Box 471, Central City, KY 42330 US
(270) 338-6655; *Fax:* (270) 338-7388
License: Greenville, Muhlenberg County, KY held by Radio Active Media, Inc.
Group Owner: Starlight Broadcasting Co.; acq 1996; grpsl).
Format: Oldies; *Target Audience:* 18-40.
Andy Anderson, CEO
Richard Neathamer, Operations Dir
Stan Barnett, General Manager

Hardinsburg

WULF
07-09-1970; 94.3 MHz FM; 40 kw; 525 ft.; N37 52 18 W86 16 4
P.O. Box 1450, Corbin, KY 40702 US
(270) 765-0943; *Fax:* (270) 737-7229
943wulf.com
jodie@wqxe.com
License: Hardinsburg, Breckinridge County, KY held by Skytower Communications - 94.3 LLC
Arbitron Metro Market: Hardinsburg, KY; *Format:* Country
Bill Evans, President

WXBC
08-15-1992; 104.3 MHz FM; *Hrs Open:* 24; 2.3 kw; 377 ft.; N37 46 14 W86 26 7
Mailing Address: P.O. Box 104, Hardinsburg, KY 42301 US
Second Address: 110 S. Main St., Hardinsburg, KY 40143
(270) 756-1043; *Fax:* (270) 756-1086
wxbc1043.com
License: Hardinsburg, Breckinridge County, KY held by Breckinridge Broadcasting Co. Inc.
Nat'l Network: Fox News Radio
Arbitron Metro Market: Hardinsburg, KY; *Format:* Country; *Hrs. of News Programming:* news progmg 15 hrs wkly; *No. News Employees:* 1; *Target Audience:* 25-55.; *Adv. Rates:* 10;10;10;10
Lee Bramlett, CEO/General Manager
Dennis Day, Operations Dir
Ken Thornhill, News Director
Amanda Zimmer, Office Manager
Terry Henning Hopfer, Advertising Sales Manager

Harlan

WFSR
04-01-1976; 970 kHz AM; 5 kw-D, ND1; 0.024 kw-N, ND1; N36 52 2 W83 19 36
Mailing Address: PO Box 818, 125 S. Main St, Harlan, KY 40831 US
Second Address: 125 S. Main, Harlan, KY 40831
(606) 573-1470; *Fax:* (606) 573-1473
wtuk-wfsr@harlanonline.net
License: Harlan, KY held by Eastern Broadcasting Co.
Format: Gospel; *Target Audience:* 25-54; adult purchasers
Jeff Capps, General Manager

WHLN
05-30-1941; 1410 kHz AM; 5 kw-D, 94 w-N; N36 52 02 W83 19 36
Mailing Address: Box 898, Harlan, KY 40831
Second Address: 100 Eversole St., Suite 1, Harlan, KY 40831
(606) 573-2540; *Fax:* (606) 573-7557
whln@harlanonline.net
License: Harlan, Harlan County, KY held by Radio Harlan Inc.
Nat'l Network: ABC; *Nat'l Reps:* Rgnl Reps; *Wire Services:* AP
Population Served: 200,000 *Target Audience:* 25-54.; *Adv. Rates:* 14; 14; 14; 14
James O. Morgan, President
James O. Morgan, General Manager

WTUK
06-26-1991; 105.1 MHz FM; 0.53 kw; 1037 ft.; N36 54 9 W83 18 1
Mailing Address: P.O. Box 818, Harlan, KY 40831 US
Second Address: 125 S. Main, Harlan, KY 40831
(606) 573-1470; *Fax:* (606) 573-1473
www.wtuk1051.com
License: Harlan, Harlan County, KY held by Eastern Broadcasting Co.
Arbitron Metro Market: Harlan, KY; *Format:* Country *Special Programming:* Sports, news; *Hrs. of News Programming:* News prgmg every hour
Jeff Capps, Station Manager
Charles Anthony, Programming Director

Harold

WXLR
01-01-1994; 104.9 MHz FM; 0.37 kw; 922 ft.; N37 31 59 W82 29 40
Us Hwy 23 Main Street, Paulsboro Row, Harold, KY 41635 US
(606) 478-1200; *Fax:* (606) 478-4202
License: Harold, Floyd County, KY held by Adam D. Gearheart.
Arbitron Metro Market: Pikeville, KY; *Format:* Country
Adam Gearheart, President

Harrodsburg

WHBN
06-25-1955; 1420 kHz AM; *Hrs Open:* 24; 1 kw-D, ND1; 0.046 kw-N, ND1; N37 44 3 W84 48 50
2063 Shakertown Road, Danville, KY 40422 US
(859) 236-2711; *Fax:* (859) 236-1461
www.hometownlive.net
hometownradio@bellsouth.net
License: Harrodsburg, KY held by Hometown Broadcasting of Harrodsburg Inc.
Nat'l Network: Jones Radio Networks; AP Radio; *Regional Network:* Ky. News Net; *Nat'l Reps:* Rgnl Reps *Regional Reps:* Rgnl Reps.
Arbitron Metro Market: Lexington-Fayette, KY; *Format:* Country, Gospel; *Hrs. of News Programming:* news progmg 21 hrs wkly; *No. News Employees:* 1; *Target Audience:* General; residents of Mercer county; *Adv. Rates:* Call
Jim Parman, Operations Dir
Robert Wagner, General Manager
Vicki Hyde, News Director

Hartford

WXMZ
05-18-1972; 99.9 MHz FM; *Hrs Open:* 16; 6 kw; 328 ft; N37 26 36 W86 53 57 *Rebroadcasts:* Rebroadcasts WKYA(FM) Greenville 100%
Box 106, Hartford, KY 42330
(270) 298-3268; *Fax:* (270) 298-9326
License: Hartford, Ohio County, KY held by Starlight Broadcasting Co Inc
Population Served: 2,700; *Arbitron Metro Market:* Hartford, KY
Sherri Sawyer, General Manager
Dan Baron, General Sales Mgr
Michael Webb, Programming Director
Paula Davis, Promotions Manager
Gennora Reed, General Sales Manager

Hawesville

WKCM
11-07-1972; 1160 kHz AM; *Hrs Open:* 24; 2.5 kw-D, DAN; 1 kw-N, DAN; N37 54 20 W86 45 30
Mailing Address: PO Box 150846, Nashville, TN 37215 US
Second Address: 115 Tamarack Rd., Suite 500, Owensboro, KY 42301
(270) 683-5200; *Fax:* (270) 688-0108
www.owensbororadio.com
dpowers@cromwellradio.com
License: Hawesville, KY held by Hancock Communications Inc.
Group Owner: The Cromwell Group Inc.
Format: Country *Special Programming:* Farm 3 hrs, sports 6 hrs wkly; *Hrs. of News Programming:* news progmg 10 hrs wkly; *No. News Employees:* 1; *Target Audience:* 25-54; general; *Adv. Rates:* 5; 5; 5; 3.50
Brack Stacy, Market Manager
Brack Stacy, Operations Manager
Mel Ingleheart, Business Manager
Dale Powers, General Manager
Jeff Nalley, General Sales Mgr
Jeff Morgan, Programming Director
Amy Spalding, News Director

Hazard

*WEKH
02-01-1985; 90.9 MHz FM; *Hrs Open:* 24; 31 kw; 1063 ft.; N37 11 35 W83 11 17 *Rebroadcasts:* Rebroadcasts WEKU-FM Richmond 100%
102 Perkins Building, Richmond, KY 40475 US
(859) 622-1660; *Fax:* (859) 622-6276
www.weku.fm
wekunews@eku.edu
License: Hazard, Perry County, KY held by Board of Regents, Eastern Kentucky University.
Nat'l Network: NPR; PRI; *Wire Services:* AP
Arbitron Metro Market: Hazard, KY; *Format:* News; *Hrs. of News Programming:* news progmg 35 hrs wkly; *No. News Employees:* 3; *Target Audience:* General.
Mary Ellyn Cain, Operations Dir
Tim Singleton, General Manager
Carol Siler, General Sales Mgr
Laura Allen, Programming Director
Charles Compton, News Director
Bill Browning, Chief Engineer

WJMD
07-26-1989; 104.7 MHz FM; *Hrs Open:* 24; 0.48 kw; 1135 ft.; N37 11 36 W83 11 4
Mailing Address: P.O. Box 7001, Hazard, KY 41702 US
Second Address: 516 Main Street, Hazard, KY 41701
(606) 439-3358; *Fax:* (606) 439-3371
wjmd@windstream.net
License: Hazard, Perry County, KY held by Hazard Broadcasting Services
Nat'l Network: Salem Radio Network
Format: Religious; *Hrs. of News Programming:* news progmg 7 hrs wkly; *No. News Employees:* 2; *Target Audience:* General.
Michael Barnett, General Manager

WKIC(AM)
11-23-1947; 1390 kHz AM; 5 kw-D; N37 14 19 W83 12 41
Mailing Address: Box 7428, Hazard, KY 41702
Second Address: 516 Main St., Hazard, KY 41701
(606) 436-2121; *Fax:* (606) 436-4172
wsgsfm@alltel.net
License: Hazard, Perry County, KY held by Leslie County Broadcasting
Nat'l Network: Westwood One; *Nat'l Reps:* Rgnl Reps
Population Served: 5,459
Faron Sparkman, General Manager

WQXY
03-01-1988; 1560 kHz AM; 0.5 kw-C, NDD; 1 kw-D, NDD; N37 16 27 W83 11 29
PO Box 1981, Hazard, KY 41701 US
(606) 785-6129; *Fax:* (606) 785-0106
info@wqmg.com
License: Hazard, KY held by Black Gold Broadcasting.
Nat'l Network: Jones Radio Networks; AP Radio; CNN Radio
Format: Oldies; *Target Audience:* 25-54; educated, mobile, child-rearing couples in suburbs, blue collar workers
Randy Thompson, General Manager

WSGS
02-03-1959; 101.1 MHz FM; 100 kw horiz, 88 kw vert; 1463 ft.; N37 11 38 W83 10 52
P.O. Box 7898, Hazard, KY 41701 US
(606) 436-2121; *Fax:* (606) 436-4172
www.wsgs.com
License: Hazard, Perry County, KY held by Leslie County Broadcasting
Nat'l Network: ABC; *Regional Network:* Ky. News Net
Format: Country
Faron Sparkman, General Manager

Henderson

WGBF-FM
12-01-1971; 103.1 MHz FM; *Hrs Open:* 24; 3.2 kw; 453 ft.; N37 46 54 W87 37 24
136 Main St, Suite 202, Westport, CT 06880 US
(812) 425-4226; *Fax:* (812) 421-0005
www.103gbfrocks.com
info@103gbfrocks.com
License: Henderson, Henderson County, KY
Group Owner: Townsquare Media; (acq 12-3-2003; grpsl).
Nat'l Network: ABC
Arbitron Metro Market: Evansville, IN; *Format:* Rock/AOR; *No. News Employees:* 1; *Target Audience:* 18-49.; *Adv. Rates:* 60; 45; 50; 20
Mark Thomas, General Manager
Mike Sanders, Programming Director
Bobby Gates, Promotions Manager

WKDQ
01-01-1947; 99.5 MHz FM; *Hrs Open:* 24; 98 kw; 984 ft.; N37 52 57 W87 32 28
P.O. Box 3353, Evansville, IN 47732 US
(812) 425-4226
www.wkdq.com
License: Henderson, Henderson County, KY
Group Owner: Townsquare Media; (acq 2-25-03; grpsl).
Nat'l Reps: Christal
Arbitron Metro Market: Evansville, IN; *Format:* Country; *No. News Employees:* 2; *Target Audience:* 25-54.
Jon Prell, Programming Director
Lori Tevault, Promotions Manager

*WKPB
04-01-1990; 89.5 MHz FM; *Hrs Open:* 24; 43 kw; 377 ft.; N37 51 6 W87 19 43 *Rebroadcasts:* Rebroadcasts WKYU-FM Bowling Green 100%
1 Big Red Way, Bowling Green, KY 42101 US
(270) 745-5489; *Fax:* (270) 745-6272
www.wkyufm.org
wkyufm@wku.edu
License: Henderson, Henderson County, KY held by Western Kentucky University.
Nat'l Network: NPR; PRI
Arbitron Metro Market: Evansville, IN; *Format:* News; *Hrs. of News Programming:* news progmg 35 hrs wkly; *No. News Employees:* 3; *Target Audience:* General.
Peter Bryant, General Manager

WSON
12-17-1941; 860 kHz AM; *Hrs Open:* 24; 0.5 kw-D, DAN; 0.5 kw-N, DAN; N37 51 11 W87 32 12
Mailing Address: P. O. Box 418 ., 230 Second St., Henderson, KY 42420 US
Second Address: 230 2nd St., Henderson, KY 42420
(270) 826-3923; *Fax:* (270) 826-7572
www.wsonradio.com
License: Henderson, KY held by Henson Media of Henderson, CO
Nat'l Network: ABC; *Nat'l Reps:* Rgnl Reps; *Wire Services:* AP
Arbitron Metro Market: Evansville, IN; *Format:* Adult Contemp
Special Programming: Farm 2 hrs wkly; *Hrs. of News Programming:* news progmg 8 hrs wkly; *No. News Employees:* 1; *Target Audience:* 35+. *Adv.Rates:* 16; 14; 14; 12
Ed Henson, President
Darlene Hawkins, Operations Dir
Ed Henson, General Manager
Bill Stephens, News/PSA Director
Mary June Goodley, Sales Manager
Greg Busby, Sports Director

Highland Heights

*WNKU
04-29-1985; 89.7 MHz FM; *Hrs Open:* 21 (M-F); 20 (S); 19 (Su); 12 kw horiz, 9.9 kw vert; 318 ft.; N39 2 21 W84 27 57
P.O. Box 337, Highland Heights, KY 41076 US
(859) 572-6500; *Fax:* (859) 572-6604
www.wnku.org
radio@wnku.org
License: Highland Heights, Campbell County, KY held by Northern Kentucky University.
Nat'l Network: PRI; NPR
Arbitron Metro Market: Cincinnati, OH; *Format:* News, Triple A; *Hrs. of News Programming:* news progmg 40 hrs wkly; *No. News Employees:* 2; *Target Audience:* 35-49.
Grady Kirkpatrick, General Manager
Aaron Sharpe, General Sales Mgr

Hindman

WKCB
01-26-1971; 1340 kHz AM; 1 kw-U, ND1; N37 19 45 W83 0 17
Mailing Address: P.O. Box 864, Hindman, KY 41822 US
Second Address: 1517 Hwy. 550 W., Hindman, KY 41822
(606) 785-3129; *Fax:* (606) 785-0106
www.wkcb.com
request@wkcb.com
License: Hindman, KY held by Hindman Broadcasting Corp.
Nat'l Reps: Rgnl Reps
Format: Christian
Randy Thompson, General Manager
Paul Hoskins, Programming Director
Meralene Huff, Financial Manager

WKCB-FM
12-13-1974; 107.1 MHz FM; 1.55 kw; 650 ft.; N37 19 56 W82 56 52
Rt 550 West, Hindman, KY 41822 US
(606) 785-3129; *Fax:* (606) 785-0106
www.wkcb.com
request@wkcb.com
License: Hindman, Knott County, KY held by Hindman Broadcasting Corp.
Format: Rock/AOR
Hays McMakin, President
Tom McMakin, Operations Dir
Jeff Ray, General Manager
Robert Haydon, General Sales Mgr
Becky Black, Programming Director
Carol Lynn, Promotions Manager
Doug Walker, Chief Engineer
Chris Conkright,Information Technology
Ron Caudill, Sales Manager

Hodgenville

WRZI
03-01-1974; 107.3 MHz FM; 3.8 kw; Ant 420 ft; N37 40 21 W85 44 34
611 W. Poplar St., Suite C2, Elizabethtown, KY 42701
(270) 763-0800; *Fax:* (270) 769-6349
License: Hodgenville, Larue County, KY held by Elizabethtown CBC Inc.
Group Owner: Commonwealth Broadcasting Corp.; (acq 7-1-2000; grpsl)
Nat'l Reps: Keystone (unwired net); Rgnl Reps
Population Served: 98,000 *Special Programming:* Farm 2 hrs wkly; *Target Audience:* 18-44; females
Steve Newberry, President
Derron Steenberger, General Manager
Dale Thornhill, CFO/VP/Operations Director

Hopkinsville

WHOP
01-08-1940; 1230 kHz AM; *Hrs Open:* 24; 1 kw-U, ND1; N36 52 54 W87 30 44
Mailing Address: PO Box 709, Hopkinsville, KY 42240 US
Second Address: 220 Dink Embry's Buttermilk Rd., Hopkinsville, KY 42240-8802
(270) 885-5331; *Fax:* (270) 885-2688
www.whopam.com
michadwell@forchtbroadcasting.com
License: Hopkinsville, KY held by Forcht Broadcasting
Group Owner: Forcht Broadcasting
Nat'l Network: CBS; *Regional Network:* Ky. News Net; *Nat'l Reps:* Rgnl Reps
Arbitron Metro Market: Clarksville-Hopkinsville, TN-KY; *Format:* News, News/Talk, 86; *No. News Employees:* 2; *Target Audience:* 30 plus.; *Adv. Rates:* 16; 16; 16; 12
Mike Chadwell, General Manager
Traci Mason, General Sales Manager
Jeff Sisk, Program Director & Operations Manager
Dana Knight Hamilton, Account Executive
Adam May, News Director
Hannah Hegeman, News Reporter

WHOP-FM
05-01-1948; 95.3 MHz FM; *Hrs Open:* 24; 100 kw; Ant 620 ft; N36 55 41 W87 32 50
Box 709, Hopkinsville, KY 42241
(270) 885-5331; *Fax:* (270) 885-2688
www.whopam.com
License: Hopkinsville, Christian County, KY held by Forcht Broadcasting
Group Owner: Forcht Broadcasting
Nat'l Reps: Rgnl Reps
Population Served: 300,000; *Arbitron Metro Market:* Clarksville-Hopkinsville, TN-KY; *Hrs. of News Programming:* news progmg 15 hrs wkly; *No. News Employees:* 2; *Target Audience:* 18-54.; *Adv. Rates:* 30; 22; 22;15
Mike Chadwell, General Manager
Traci Mason, General Sales Manager
Jeff Sisk, Program Director
Dana Knight Hamilton, Account Executive
Todd Hamilton, Sports Director
Adam May, News Director
Hannah Hegeman, News Reporter

***WNKJ**
08-03-1981; 89.3 MHz FM; *Hrs Open:* 24; 12 kw; 330 ft; N36 48 34 W87 24 20
Mailing Address: Box 1029, Hopkinsville, KY 42240
Second Address: 1100 E. 18th St., Hopkinsville, KY 42240
(270) 886-9655; *Fax:* (270) 885-7210
www.wnkj.org
wnkj@wnkj.org
License: Hopkinsville, Christian County, KY held by Pennyrile Christian Community Inc.
Nat'l Network: Moody
Arbitron Metro Market: Clarksville-Hopkinsville, TN-KY *Special Programming:* Black 4.5 hrs, Korean 1/2 hr, Sp 3/4 hr wkly; *Hrs. of News Programming:* News progmg 12 hrs wkly; *Target Audience:* General.
Jim Dozier Adams, General Manager
Donald Griffey, Chief Engineer

WHVO
09-19-1954; 1480 kHz AM; *Hrs Open:* 24; 1 kw-D, ND1; 0.024 kw-N, ND1; N36 52 15 W87 30 43
PO Box 1900, Cadiz, KY 42211 US
(270) 886-1480; *Fax:* (270) 886-6286
License: Hopkinsville, KY held by Ham Broadcasting Inc.
Nat'l Network: AP Network News; Jones Radio Networks; Fox News Radio; *Regional Network:* Ky. News Net; *Nat'l Reps:* Rgnl Reps
Arbitron Metro Market: Clarksville-Hopkinsville, TN-KY; *Format:* Oldies *Special Programming:* Relg 6 hrs, gospel 3 hrs wkly; *Hrs. of News Programming:* news progmg 3 hrs wkly; *No. News Employees:* 2 *TargetAudience:* 35-54; Upscale Baby-boomers
D.J. Everett, President
Bill Booth, Operations Dir
Beth Mann, General Manager
Amy Berry, General Sales Mgr
Alan Watts, News/Farm Director

WVVR
07-01-1960; 100.3 MHz FM; *Hrs Open:* 24; 100 kw; 1001 ft.; N36 56 58 W87 40 18
1700 Dawson Springs Road, Hopkinsville, KY 42240 US
(931) 648-7720; *Fax:* (931) 648-7769
www.thebeaver.com
License: Hopkinsville, Christian County, KY held by Saga Communications of Tuckessee LLC.
Group Owner: Saga Communications Inc.; (acq 11-27-2000; $7 million)
Regional Reps: Rgnl Reps.
Arbitron Metro Market: Hopkinsville, KY; *Format:* Country; *Hrs. of News Programming:* news progmg 7 hrs wkly; *No. News Employees:* 1; *Target Audience:* 18-54; working class; *Adv. Rates:* 56; 48; 52; 32
Katie Gambill, General Manager

WZZP
02-28-2001; 97.5 MHz FM; 6 kw; 328 ft.; N36 45 47 W87 26 59
P O Box 2249, Clarksville, TN 37042 US
(931) 648-7720; *Fax:* (931) 648-7769
www.z975.com
courtney@z975.com
License: Hopkinsville, Christian County, KY held by Saga Communications of Tuckessee L.L.C.
Group Owner: Saga Communications Inc.; (acq 2-1-01; grpsl).
Arbitron Metro Market: Clarksville, TN
Scott Chase, Operations Dir
Katie Gambill, General Manager
Sande Cox, Sales Manager
Jared Mims, Programming Director

Horse Cave

WOVO
09-19-1994; 106.3 MHz FM; 3 kw; 476 ft.; N37 13 57 W85 52 6
Mailing Address: P.O. Box 1505, Glasgow, KY 42142 US
Second Address: 113 W. Public Sq., Suite 400, Glasgow, KY 42141
(270) 651-6050; *Fax:* (270) 651-7666
License: Horse Cave, Hart County, KY held by Commonwealth Broadcasting Corp.
Group Owner: Commonwealth Broadcasting Corp.; (acq 11-25-97; grpsl)
Nat'l Network: Westwood One
Arbitron Metro Market: Bowling Green, KY; *Format:* Adult Contemp
Kellie Wood, Operations Dir
Derron Steenbergen, General Manager

Hyden

WKIC
11-07-1988; 97.9 MHz FM; 1.75 kw; Ant 1,207 ft; N37 11 36 W83 11 04
Mailing Address: Box 7280, Hazard, KY 41749
Second Address: 516 Main St., Hazard, KY 41701
(606) 436-2121; *Fax:* (606) 436-4172
License: Hyden, Leslie County, KY held by Leslie County Broadcasting Inc.
Nat'l Network: ABC
Target Audience: General.
Stuart Sparkman, CEO
Faron Sparkman, General Manager
Bob Hale, Chief Engineer

Irvine

WCYO
08-01-1991; 100.7 MHz FM; *Hrs Open:* 24; 9.2 kw; 505 ft.; N37 39 40 W84 8 55
128 Big Hill Ave., Richmond, KY 40475 US
(859) 623-1386; *Fax:* (859) 623-1341
www.wcyofm.com
License: Irvine, Estill County, KY held by Kentucky River Broadcasting Co. Inc.
Group Owner: Wallingford Broadcasting Co.
Arbitron Metro Market: Richmond -Lexington, KY; *Format:* Country
Bill Clary, General Manager
Trizdon Reynolds, General Sales Mgr
Shelby Slone, Promotions Manager
Ron Lykins, News Director

WIRV
07-02-1960; 1550 kHz AM; 1 kw-D, ND1; 0.005 kw-N, ND1; N37 42 57 W83 58 29
128 Big Hill Ave., Richmond, KY 40475 US
(859) 623-1386; *Fax:* (859) 623-1241
www.wirvam.com
License: Irvine, KY held by Kentucky River Broadcasting Co Inc.
Group Owner: Wallingford Broadcasting Co.
Nat'l Reps: Rgnl Reps
Format: News/Talk
Bill Clary, Operations Dir
Sean Hamilton, General Manager
Trizdon Reynolds, General Sales Mgr
Shelby Slone, Promotions Manager
Ron Lykins, News Director

Jackson

WEKG
03-07-1969; 810 kHz AM; 5 kw-D, NDD; N37 34 41 W83 24 19
1024 College Avenuee, Jackson, KY 41339 US
(606) 666-7531; *Fax:* (606) 666-4946
kdavidson@wjsn.com
License: Jackson, KY held by Intermountain Broadcasting Co.
Arbitron Metro Market: Jackson, KY; *Format:* Gospel
Gloria Hay, CEO
Gloria Hay, General Manager
Doug Neace, General Sales Mgr

WJSN-FM
01-01-1979; 97.3 MHz FM; 19 kw; 814 ft.; N37 40 19 W83 24 21
1024 College Avenue, Jackson, KY 41339 US
(606) 666-7531; *Fax:* (606) 666-4946
wjsn.awardspace.com
License: Jackson, Breathitt County, KY
Format: Country
Hap Ritchey, Programming Director
Bill Reed, News Director
Larry Walters, Disc Jockey
Nicole Lewis, Disc Jockey
Deborah Walters, News Reporter
William Reed, Reporter
Cheryl Walters, Women's Int Ed

***WYLC**
89.7 MHz FM; 0.45 kw; 240 ft.; N37 35 8 W83 14 59
Mailing Address: US
Second Address: 3019 Hwy. 30 W., Jackson, KY 41339
(606) 295-3225
License: Jackson, Breathitt County, KY held by Breathitt Listeners Choice Radio Inc.
Arbitron Metro Market: Jackson, NY; *Format:* Children
Earl Lovely, Chairman

Jamestown

WJKY
09-03-1967; 1060 kHz AM; 1 kw-D, NDD; N37 1 31 W85 4 23
Mailing Address: P.O. Box 800, Jamestown, KY 42629 US
Second Address: 2804 South US Hwy 127, Russell Springs, KY 42642
(270) 866-3487; *Fax:* (270) 866-2060
www.lakercountry.com
License: Jamestown, KY held by Lake Cumberland Broadcasters
Format: Country
Mae Hoover, General Manager
Kem Bell, Advertising Manager
Greg Hammond, Sport Commentator
Audie Hammond, Sport Commentator

WJRS
09-03-1966; 104.9 MHz FM; 2 kw; 361 ft.; N37 1 31 W85 4 23
Mailing Address: P.O. Box 800, Jamestown, KY 42629 US
Second Address: 2804 South US Hwy 127, Russell Springs, KY 42642
(270) 866-3487; *Fax:* (270) 866-2060
www.lakercountry.com
License: Jamestown, Russell County, KY held by Lake Cumberland Broadcasters.
Wire Services: NWS (National Weather Service)
Format: Country
Jerry Hoover, General Manager

Jeffersontown

WGRK
03-15-1972; 1200 kHz AM; 0.5 kw-C, NDD; 1 kw-D, NDD; N37 15 34 W85 30 57
Mailing Address: 50 Friendship Pike, Campbellsville, KY 42718 US
Second Address: P.O. Box 1053, Campbellsville, KY 42719
(270) 932-7401
www.kcountry1057.com
wgrk@commonwealthbroadcasting.com
License: Jeffersontown, KY held by Green County CBC Inc.
Group Owner: Commonwealth Broadcasting Corp.; (acq 10-30-97; $600,000 with co-located FM)
Nat'l Network: ABC; Jones Radio Networks; *Nat'l Reps:* Rgnl Reps
Arbitron Metro Market: Jeffersontown, KY; *Format:* Country; *Hrs. of News Programming:* news progmg 7 hrs wkly; *No. News Employees:* 1; *Target Audience:* 25-54.
Denise Gilpin, Operations Dir
Barb Smith, General Manager
Teresa Bright, General Sales Mgr
Marty Bagby, News Director
Rob Collins, Production

WMJM
12-01-1978; 101.3 MHz FM; 2 kw; 194 ft.; N38 13 42 W85 38 22
520 S. 4th St., Louisville, KY 40202 US
(502) 625-1220; *Fax:* (502) 625-1259
www.1013online.com
1013online@gmail.com
License: Jeffersontown, Jefferson County, KY held by Alpha Media Licensee LLC
Group Owner: Alpha Media LLC; (acq 4-17-2014; grpsl).
Arbitron Metro Market: Louisville, KY; *Format:* Urban Contemporary
Larry Wilson, Chairman
Bob Proffitt, President & CEO
Dale Schaefer, General Manager
George Demaree, General Sales Mgr
Phillip David March, Programming Director
Valerie Sickles, Director of Urban Promotions and Community Affairs

Jenkins

WIFX-FM
05-10-1975; 94.3 MHz FM; *Hrs Open:* 24; 6.3 kw horiz, 6.24 kw vert; 1345 ft.; N37 9 59 W82 37 13
P.O. Box 1123, Jenkins, KY 41537 US
(606) 478-1200; *Fax:* (606) 478-4202
www.foxy943.com
wifx@foxy943.com
License: Jenkins, Letcher County, KY held by AJSPD LLC
Format: Rock/AOR; *Hrs. of News Programming:* News progmg 2 hrs wkly; *Target Audience:* 25-45.
Adam Gearheart, General Manager

WKVG
02-01-1970; 1000 kHz AM; *Hrs Open:* 7:30 AM- 6 PM; 1 kw-D, NDD; N37 9 59 W82 37 13
Mailing Address: P. O. Box 613, Pound, VA 24279 US
Second Address: Box 1474, Jenkins, KY 41537
(606) 832-4655; *Fax:* (606) 832-4656
License: Jenkins, KY held by Martins and Assoc. Inc.
Format: Gospel, Religious; *Hrs. of News Programming:* News progmg 9 hrs wkly; *Target Audience:* General.; *Adv. Rates:* 4.75; 4.75; 4.75; N/A
Jean Martin, Owner
Emma Martin, General Manager

Junction City

WDFB
05-20-1985; 1170 kHz AM; *Hrs Open:* Sunrise-sunset; 1 kw-D, DAD; N37 35 46 W84 50 19
Mailing Address: 3596 Alum Springs Road, Danvillle, KY 40422 US
Second Address: 3596 Alum Springs Rd., Danville, KY 40422
(859) 236-9333; *Fax:* (859) 236-3348
www.wdfb.com
wdfb@searnet.com
License: Junction City, KY held by Alum Springs Vision and Outreach Corp.
Nat'l Network: USA
Arbitron Metro Market: Junction City, KY; *Format:* Religious; *Target Audience:* General.; *Adv. Rates:* 6; 6; 6; 6
Cindy Pike, News Director
Mildred Drake, Executive Vice President

Keavy

***WVCT**
01-01-1984; 91.5 MHz FM; *Hrs Open:* 24; 0.1 kw horiz, 2.4 kw vert; 381 ft.; N36 59 1 W84 8 1
968 W. City Dam Road, Keavy, KY 40737 US
(606) 528-4671; *Fax:* (606) 526-0589
www.thegospeleagle.com
License: Keavy, Laurel County, KY held by Victory Training School Corp.
Arbitron Metro Market: Keavy, KY; *Format:* Gospel
Brenda Sivley, President
Charles Sivley, General Manager

Keene

WJMM-FM
12-09-1969; 99.1 MHz FM; *Hrs Open:* 24; 2.1 kw; 558 ft.; N38 3 56 W84 29 13
3950 Lexington Rd., Versailles, KY 40383 US
(859) 264-9700; *Fax:* (859) 264-9705
www.wjmm.com
benson.gregory@cbslradio.com
License: Keene, Jessamine County, KY held by Christian Broadcasting System Ltd.
Group Owner: Christian Broadcasting System Ltd.; (acq 7-1-2006; grpsl).
Format: Christian, Religious
Benson Gregory, Station Manager
Bruce Edwards, Programming Director
Morgan Fouts, Promotions Manager
Antoniette Parson, Business Manager
Kelly Rossi, Traffic Manager

La Center

WRJJ
01-01-2008; 104.3 MHz FM; 4 kw; 125 ft.; N37 4 30 W88 58 22
801 N. Garfield, Marion, IL 62959 US
(618) 967-3704
License: La Center, Ballard County, KY held by Janet Jensen.
Arbitron Metro Market: La Center, KY
Janet Jensen, General Manager

Lancaster

WRNZ
10-01-1988; 105.1 MHz FM; *Hrs Open:* 24; 3 kw; 325 ft; N37 36 06 W84 34 27
2063 Shakertown Rd., Danville, KY 41144
(859) 236-2711; *Fax:* (859) 236-1461
www.hometownLIVE.net
hometownradio@bellsouth.net
License: Lancaster, Garrard County, KY held by Hometown Broadcasting of Lancaster Inc.
Nat'l Reps: Rgnl Reps *Regional Reps:* Rgnl Reps
Population Served: 200,000; *Arbitron Metro Market:* Lexington-Fayet *Special Programming:* Relg 4 hrs wkly; *Hrs. of News Programming:* news progmg 2 hrs wkly; *No. News Employees:* 1; *Target Audience:* 25-54;upscale, white collar, baby boomers, business owners; *Adv. Rates:* Call
Jim Parman, Operations Dir
Robert Wagner, General Manager
Vicki Hyde, News Director

Lawrenceburg

WKYL
05-11-1993; 102.1 MHz FM; *Hrs Open:* 24; 6 kw; 328 ft.; N38 1 37 W84 52 59
1030 Burlington Lane, Frankfort, KY 40601 US
(502) 839-1021
www.weku.fm
License: Lawrenceburg, Anderson County, KY held by Davenport Broadcasting Inc.
Nat'l Network: Jones Radio Networks
Format: Jazz, Smooth Jazz *Special Programming:* Relg 2 hrs wkly; *Target Audience:* 30-50; higher income; especially at-work listeners
C. Michael Davenport, General Manager

Lebanon

WLBN
10-01-1954; 1590 kHz AM; *Hrs Open:* 24; 1 kw-D, ND1; 0.024 kw-N, ND1; N37 35 55 W85 14 47
P.O Box 457, Glasgow, KY 42141 US
(270) 692-3126; *Fax:* (270) 692-6003
License: Lebanon, KY held by CBC of Marion County Inc.
Group Owner: Commonwealth Broadcasting Corp.; (acq 7-3-97; $360,000 with co-located FM).
Nat'l Network: Jones Radio Networks; *Nat'l Reps:* Rgnl Reps
Format: Oldies *Special Programming:* Gospel 5 hrs, open mike 5 hrs wkly; *Hrs. of News Programming:* news progmg 13 hrs wkly; *No. News Employees:* 1; *Target Audience:* 35-64.; *Adv. Rates:* 8; 8; 8; 6
Andy Colley, Operations Dir
Lisa Kearnes, General Manager
Patty Brown, News Director
Mike Graham, Chief Engineer

WLSK
10-01-1979; 100.9 MHz FM; *Hrs Open:* 24; 6.6 kw; 413 ft.; N37 41 43 W85 19 6
P.O Box 457, Glasgow, KY 42141 US
(2700 692-3126; *Fax:* (270) 692-6003
License: Lebanon, Marion County, KY
Group Owner: Commonwealth Broadcasting Corp.
Format: Variety/Diverse; *Hrs. of News Programming:* news progmg 9 hrs wkly; *No. News Employees:* 1; *Target Audience:* 30-49.; *Adv. Rates:* 12; 12; 12; 12.
Andy Colley, Operations Dir
Patty Brown, News Director
Lisa Kearnes, Marketing & Sales Manager

Lebanon Junction

WKMO
10-01-1979; 99.3 MHz FM; 6 kw; 312 ft.; N37 44 26 W85 49 28
PO Box 457, Glasgow, KY 42141 US
502-769-0800; *Fax:* 502-769-6349
License: Lebanon Junction, Bullittt County, KY held by Elizabethtown CBC Inc.
Group Owner: Commonwealth Broadcasting Corp.; (acq 12-23-2002; $900,000)
Nat'l Reps: Rgnl Reps
TV Affiliate: Country *Special Programming:* news progmg one hr wkly; *Hrs. of News Programming:* 1; *Adv. Rates:* 22; 18; 22; 15
Dale Thornhill, Vice President/General Manager
Sarah Hart, Sales Manager

Ledbetter

***WKYP**
01-01-2004; 90.1 MHz FM; 1 kw vert; Ant 328 ft; N37 06 10 W88 24 15
Mailing Address: Box 281, Hardin, KY 42048
Second Address: 219 College St., Harding, KY 42048
(270) 437-4095; *Fax:* (270) 437-4098
www.hmiradio.com
info@hmiradio.com
License: Ledbetter, Livingston County, KY held by Heartland Ministries Inc.

Darrell Gibson, President
Jeremy Johnson, Programming Director

Leitchfield

WKHG
10-29-1967; 104.9 MHz FM; 3.5 kw; 272 ft.; N37 30 40 W86 17 15
2160 Brandenburg Road, Leitchfield, KY 42754 US
(270) 259-5692; *Fax:* (270) 259-5692
www.k105.com
news@k105.com
License: Leitchfield, Grayson County, KY held by Heritage Media of Kentucky Inc.
Format: Adult Contemp
Mark Buckles, President
Christy Buckles, General Manager

WMTL
01-17-1959; 870 kHz AM; 0.5 kw-D, NDD; N37 30 40 W86 17 15
2160 Branderburg Road, Leitchfield, KY 42754 US
(270) 259-3165; *Fax:* (270) 259-5693
news@k105.com
License: Leitchfield, KY held by Heritage Media of Kentucky Inc.
Arbitron Metro Market: Leitchfield, KY; *Format:* Country
Mark Buckles, President
Christy Buckles, General Manager
Ed Thomas, Chief Engineer

Lerose

***WEBF**
03-01-1999; 88.3 MHz FM; *Hrs Open:* 3 PM-9 PM (M-F); 1 kw; Ant 321 ft; N37 36 23 W83 41 16
Owsley County High School, Hwy. 28/ E. Shepherd Ln., Booneville, KY 41314
(606) 593-5185; *Fax:* (606) 593-6312
www.owsley.kyschools.us
License: Lerose, Owsley County, KY held by Board of Regents - Morehead State University

Population Served: 15,000 *Target Audience:* 12-35; poor & uneducated in need of information
Diana Gross, Chairman
Stephen Jackson, CEO
Dan Conti, General Manager
Bill Hodges, Programming Director
Jerry McIntosh, CFO

Lewisport

WLME
07-01-1990; 102.7 MHz FM; *Hrs Open:* 24; 2.25 kw; 545 ft.; N37 47 44 W86 50 58
Mailing Address: P.O. Box 150846, Nashville, TN 37215 US
Second Address: 1115 Tamarack Rd., Suite 500, Owensboro, KY 42301
(270) 683-5200; *Fax:* (270) 688-0108
spots@wrioradio.com
License: Lewisport, Perry County, KY held by WLME Inc.
Group Owner: The Cromwell Group Inc.
Nat'l Network: Jones Radio Networks; *Nat'l Reps:* Rgnl Reps
Format: Sports, Talk *Special Programming:* Sports 6 hrs wkly; *Hrs. of News Programming:* news progmg 3 hrs wkly; *No. News Employees:* 1; *Target Audience:* 25-54; general
Bayard Walters, President
Rich Chiaino, General Manager
Ross DiFranco, Sales Director
John Lassman, Programming Director

Lexington

WBUL-FM
07-15-1969; 98.1 MHz FM; 100 kw; 561 ft.; N38 2 7 W84 27 2
2601 Nicholasville Rd., Lexington, KY 40503 US
(859) 422-1000; *Fax:* (859) 422-1038
www.wbul.com
License: Lexington, Fayette County, KY held by Citicasters Licenses Inc.
Group Owner: iHeartMedia; (acq 5-4-99; grpsl).
Arbitron Metro Market: Lexington, KY; *Format:* Country; *Target Audience:* 25-49; baby boomers who grew up with Stones & Beatles
Michael Jordan, Programming Director
Mandy Daugherty, Promotions Director
Marci Adams, Digital Program Director

WLAP
09-01-1922; 630 kHz AM; *Hrs Open:* 24; 5 kw-D, DA2; 1 kw-N, DA2; N38 7 25 W84 26 45
2601 Nicholasville Road, Lexington, KY 40503 US
(859) 422-1000; *Fax:* (859) 422-1038
www.wlap.com
License: Lexington, KY held by Citicasters Licenses Inc.
Group Owner: iHeartMedia
Nat'l Network: CBS; *Nat'l Reps:* Christal
Arbitron Metro Market: Lexington-Fayette, KY; *Format:* News, News/Talk, 86; *No. News Employees:* 1; *Target Audience:* 18-49; men
Michael Jordan, Programming Director
Mandy Daugherty, Promotions Director
Marci Adams, Digital Program Director

WLXG
01-01-1946; 1300 kHz AM; 2.5 kw-D, 1 kw-N, DA-N; N38 05 50 W84 31 45
401 W. Main St., Suite 301, Lexington, KY 40578
(859) 233-1515; *Fax:* (859) 233-1517
www.wlxg.com
jmac@lmcomm.com
License: Lexington, Fayette County, KY held by L.M. Communications Inc.
Group Owner: L M Communications Inc.; (acq 7-1-84)
Nat'l Network: ESPN Radio; *Nat'l Reps:* Katz Radio
Population Served: 190,000; *Arbitron Metro Market:* Lexington-Fayet; *Format:* Sports; *Hrs. of News Programming:* News progmg 5 hrs wkly; *Target Audience:* 25-54; adults
Lynn Martin, Sports Director
Shawn Seay, Program Director
James MacFarlane, General Manager

WMXL
01-01-1940; 94.5 MHz FM; *Hrs Open:* 24; 85 kw; 636 ft.; N38 7 24 W84 26 37
2601 Nicholasville Rd., Lexington, KY 40503 US
(859) 422-1000; *Fax:* (859) 422-1038
www.mymix945.com
info@wmxl.com
License: Lexington, Fayette County, KY held by Citicasters Licenses Inc.
Group Owner: iHeartMedia; (acq 5-4-99; grpsl).
Arbitron Metro Market: Lexington, KY; *Format:* Adult Contemp; *Hrs. of News Programming:* News progmg 3 hrs wkly; *Target Audience:* 25-54; women
Michael Jordan, Programming Director
Mandy Daugherty, Promotions Director
Marci Adams, Digital Program Director

*WRFL
03-03-1988; 88.1 MHz FM; 7.9 kw; 285 ft.; N38 2 19 W84 30 16
026 Grehan Journalism Bl, Lexington, KY 40506 US
(859) 257-4636,(859) 257-9735; *Fax:* (859) 323-1039
License: Lexington, Fayette County, KY held by Radio Free Lexington Inc.
Arbitron Metro Market: Lexington-Fayette, KY; *Format:* Variety/Diverse
John Clark, General Manager

*WUKY
03-13-1941; 91.3 MHz FM; *Hrs Open:* 24; 100 kw; 779 ft.; N37 52 45 W84 19 33
340 McVey Hall, Lexington, KY 40506 US
(859) 257-3221; *Fax:* (859) 257-6291
wuky.org
npr.rocks@email.uky.edu
License: Lexington, Fayette County, KY held by University of Kentucky
Nat'l Network: NPR; PRI; *Wire Services:* AP
Arbitron Metro Market: Lexington, KY; *Format:* News, Triple A; *Hrs. of News Programming:* news progmg 62 hrs wkly; *No. News Employees:* 25; *Target Audience:* 25-54; *Adv. Rates:* non-commercial
John Lumagui, Operations Dir
Tom Godell, General Manager
Rusty Sharp, Programming Director
Gail Bennett, Promotions Manager
Alan Lytle, News Director
John Lumagui, Engineering Dir
Lori Horine, Business Manager
Mike Graves,Music Director

WVLK
10-01-1947; 590 kHz AM; *Hrs Open:* 24
111 East Kilbourn Avenue, Suite 2700, Milwaukee, WI 53202 US
(859) 253-5959; *Fax:* (859) 253-5940
www.wvlkam.com
License: Lexington, KY held by Cumulus Licensing Corp.
Group Owner: Cumulus Media Inc.; (acq 7-22-99; grpsl).
Nat'l Network: CBS
Arbitron Metro Market: Lexington, KY; *Format:* News, News/Talk, 84, Talk; *No. News Employees:* 5; *Target Audience:* 25-54.
Scott Frazier, General Manager
Andrea Ayers, Sales Manager
Scott Johnson, Programming Director
Mario Anderson, Marketing & Promotions Director

WLXX
02-01-1962; 92.9 MHz FM; *Hrs Open:* 24; 100 kw; 850 ft.; N38 2 22 W84 24 11
111 East Kilbourn Avenue, Suite 2700, Milwaukee, WI 53202 US
(859) 253-5900; *Fax:* (859) 253-5940
www.wlxxthebear.com
License: Lexington, Fayette County, KY
Arbitron Metro Market: Lexington, KY; *Format:* Country
John Lewis, General Manager
Scott Frazier, Sales Manager
Dale O'Brian, Programming Director
Mario Anderson, Promotions Manager

Lexington-Fayette

WLKT
07-30-1992; 104.5 MHz FM; 50 kw; 466 ft.; N38 4 9 W84 18 44
2601 Nicholasville Road, Lexington, KY 40503 US
(859) 422-1000; *Fax:* (859) 422-1038
www.1045thecat.com
License: Lexington-Fayette, Fayette County, KY held by Citicasters Licenses Inc.
Group Owner: iHeartMedia; (acq 5-4-99; grpsl).
Arbitron Metro Market: Lexington-Fayette, KY; *Format:* Contemporary Hits/Top 40
Michael Jordan, Programming Director
Mandy Daugherty, Promotions Director
Marci Adams, Digital Program Director

Liberty

WKDO
11-01-1963; 1560 kHz AM; 1 kw-D, NDD; N37 18 22 W84 55 2
Mailing Address: P. O. Box 990, Liberty, KY 42539 US
Second Address: 988 Dry Ridge Rd., Liberty, KY 42539
(606) 787-7331; *Fax:* (606) 787-2166
License: Liberty, KY held by Radio Station WKDO.
Nat'l Network: USA
Format: Country; *Target Audience:* 18-49.
Carlos Wesley, President
David Smith, Chief Engineer

WKDO-FM
01-01-1977; 98.7 MHz FM; *Hrs Open:* 16; 25 kw; 240 ft.; N37 18 22 W84 55 2
P.O. Box 990, Liberty, KY 42539 US
(606) 787-7331; *Fax:* (606) 787-2166
License: Liberty, Casey County, KY held by Radio Station WKDO.
Hrs. of News Programming: news progmg 21 hrs wkly; *No. News Employees:* 3; *Target Audience:* 15-35.
Rich Archut, Operations Dir

London

WFTG
09-01-1955; 1400 kHz AM; *Hrs Open:* 24
534 Tobacco Road, London, KY 40741 US
(606) 864-2148; *Fax:* (606) 864-0645
License: London, KY held by Forcht Broadcasting
Group Owner: Forcht Broadcasting; (acq 8-5-92; $410,000)
Regional Network: Ky. News Net
Format: Talk; *No. News Employees:* 1; *Target Audience:* 40 plus.
Mike Tarter, President
Brisgett Gambret, General Manager
Travis Stevens, Programming Director
Phillip Fraley, Chief Engineer

WGWM
08-08-1981; 980 kHz AM; *Hrs Open:* 24
948 Moriah Church Road, London, KY 40741 US
(606) 878-0980; *Fax:* (606) 878-0980
License: London, KY held by WGWM Broadcasting Inc.
Format: Gospel; *Hrs. of News Programming:* News progmg 5 hrs wkly; *Target Audience:* 25-54; male/female
Elmer Oakley, President/General Manager

WWEL
09-15-1970; 103.9 MHz FM; *Hrs Open:* 24; 5.4 kw; 348 ft.; N37 8 30 W84 4 45
Mailing Address: P. O. Box 1450, Corbin, KY 40702 US
Second Address: 534 Tobacco Rd., London, KY 40741
(606) 864-2148; *Fax:* (606) 864-0645
www.sam1039.com
License: London, Laurel County, KY held by Forcht Broadcasting
Group Owner: Key Broadcasting Inc.
Nat'l Network: NBC Radio; *Regional Network:* Ky. News Net
Arbitron Metro Market: London, KY; *Format:* Classic Rock; *Hrs. of News Programming:* news progmg 21 hrs wkly; *No. News Employees:* 1; *Target Audience:* 18-40.; *Adv. Rates:* 1; 10
Mike Tarter, President
Bridgett Gambrel, General Manager
Terry Harris, Programming Director
Dave Begley, News Director
Frances Wilhoit, Account Executive

WYGE
01-01-1994; 92.3 MHz FM; *Hrs Open:* 24; 23.5 kw; 732 ft.; N37 9 1 W83 59 32
201 East Second St, London, KY 40741 US
(606) 877-1326; *Fax:* (606) 883-6424
www.good-news-outreach.org
wygeradio@yahoo.com
License: London, Laurel County, KY held by Ethel Huff Broadcasting LLC.
Nat'l Network: Salem Radio Network; USA
Arbitron Metro Market: London, KY; *Format:* Religious; *Adv. Rates:* 10; 9; 10; 7
Ethel Huff, Chairman
Arlene Zawko, General Manager

Louisa

WZAQ
05-17-1991; 92.3 MHz FM; 4.5 kw; 377 ft.; N38 10 33 W82 37 39
P.O. Box 176, Louisa, KY 41230 US
(304) 529-2517
www.92jack.com
License: Louisa, Lawrence County, KY held by Expression Production Group LLC
Group Owner: Expression Production Group LLC
Arbitron Metro Market: Lawrence-Boyd, KY; *Format:* Adult Contemp
Stephanie Skragg, President

Louisville

WAMZ
09-01-1966; 97.5 MHz FM; *Hrs Open:* 24; 100 kw; 673 ft.; N38 3 50 W85 43 52
4000 #1 Radio Dr., Louisville, KY 40218 US
(502) 479-2222; *Fax:* (502) 479-2308
www.wamz.com
License: Louisville, Jefferson County, KY held by CC Licenses LLC.
Group Owner: iHeartMedia
Arbitron Metro Market: Louisville, KY; *Format:* Country
Kevin Hughes, Senior Vice President of Sales
Michael Jordan, Programming Director

WDJX
08-01-1963; 99.7 MHz FM; 24 kw; 715 ft.; N38 21 53 W85 50 18
520 S. 4th St., Suite 200, Louisville, KY 40202 US
(502) 625-1220; *Fax:* (502) 625-1256
www.wdjx.com
License: Louisville, Jefferson County, KY held by Alpha Media Licensee LLC
Group Owner: Alpha Media LLC; (acq 4-17-2014; grpsl).
Arbitron Metro Market: Louisville, KY; *Format:* Contemporary Hits/Top 40
Dale Schaefer, General Manager
Otis Maher, Programming Director
Billy S. Garland, Promotions Director
Jo Ellen Embry, Market Controller

WFIA
03-01-1947; 900 kHz AM; *Hrs Open:* 24
50 East Rivercenter Blvd, Suite 1200, Covington, KY 41011 US
(502) 339-9470; *Fax:* (502) 423-3139
www.salemradiogroup.com
pcopass@salemradiolouisville.com
License: Louisville, KY held by Salem Media Group LLC.
Group Owner: Salem Communications Corp.; (acq 1-24-2001; $1.75 million)
Nat'l Reps: Salem
Arbitron Metro Market: Louisville, KY; *Format:* Christian, Talk; *Hrs. of News Programming:* News progmg 2 hrs wkly; *Target Audience:* 30 plus; general
Tim Hartlage, General Manager
Sherry Perciful, Sales Manager
Dave Reichel, Programming Director
Carrie Baylor, Promotions Manager
Gregg Kramer, Accounting/Traffic
Patty Copass, Human Resources/Business Office
Todd Burns, AccountExecutive

*WFPK
10-04-1954; 91.9 MHz FM; *Hrs Open:* 24; 6.8 kw; 774 ft.; N38 21 55 W85 50 24
301 York St., Louisville, KY 40203 US
(502) 814-6500; *Fax:* (502) 814-6599
www.wfpk.org
License: Louisville, Jefferson County, KY held by Kentucky Public Radio Inc.
Nat'l Network: PRI; NPR
Arbitron Metro Market: Louisville, KY; *Format:* Alternative; *Target Audience:* 25 plus.
Donovan Reynolds, General Manager
Stacy Owen, Programming Director

*WFPL
02-20-1950; 89.3 MHz FM; *Hrs Open:* 24; 21 kw; 774 ft.; N38 21 55 W85 50 24
301 York St., Louisville, KY 40203 US
(502) 814-6500; *Fax:* (502) 814-6599
www.wfpl.org
tmundt@louisvillepublicmedia.org
License: Louisville, Jefferson County, KY held by Kentucky Public Radio Inc.
Nat'l Network: NPR; PRI
Arbitron Metro Market: Louisville, KY; *Format:* News, News/Talk, 86; *Hrs. of News Programming:* news progmg 124 hrs wkly; *No. News Employees:* 3; *Target Audience:* General.
Donovan Reynolds, General Manager
Daniel Gilliam, Programming Director
Gabe Bullard, News Director
Dennis Stovall, Business Manager
Kirsten Pfalzgraf, Marketing Director

WHAS
07-18-1922; 840 kHz AM; *Hrs Open:* 24; 50 kw-U, ND1; N38 15 40 W85 25 43
4000 #1 Radio Drive, Louisville, KY 40218 US
(502) 479-2222; *Fax:* (502) 479-2308
www.whas.com
info@whas.com
License: Louisville, KY held by CC Licenses LLC.
Group Owner: iHeartMedia; (acq 8-86; with co-located FM)
Nat'l Reps: Clear Channel
Arbitron Metro Market: Louisville, KY; *Format:* News, News/Talk, 86; *Hrs. of News Programming:* news progmg 14 hrs wkly; *No. News Employees:* 12; *Target Audience:* 25-54.
Earl Jones, Market President
Kevin Hughes, Senior Vice President of Sales
Kelly Carls, Programming Director

WKJK
11-01-1948; 1080 kHz AM; *Hrs Open:* 24; 10 kw-D, DA2; 1 kw-N, DA2; N38 18 29 W85 49 45; N38 18 28 W85 49 45
4000 Radio Drive #1, Louisville, KY 40218 US
(502) 479-2222; *Fax:* (502) 479-2308
www.talkradio1080.com
jimfenn@clearchannel.com
License: Louisville, KY held by CC Licenses LLC.
Group Owner: iHeartMedia; (acq 9-13-96; $1 million with intellectual property of WSFR(FM) Corydon, IN)
Nat'l Network: CBS Radio; *Nat'l Reps:* Clear Channel
Arbitron Metro Market: Louisville, KY; *Format:* News, News/Talk, 86; *Target Audience:* 35-64; men
Earl Jones, Market President
Kevin Hughes, Senior Vice President of Sales
Jim Fenn, Programming Director
Kellie Burton, Promotions Director

WGTK
12-30-1933; 970 kHz AM; *Hrs Open:* 24; 5 kw-D, DA2; 5 kw-N, DA2; N38 19 5 W85 44 39
888 - 7th Avenue, New York, NY 10106 US
(502) 339-9470; *Fax:* (502) 423-3139
www.970wgtk.com
License: Louisville, KY held by Salem Media of Kentucky Inc.
Group Owner: Salem Communications Corp.; (acq 10-4-2000)
Arbitron Metro Market: Louisville, KY; *Format:* News, News/Talk, 86; *Hrs. of News Programming:* news progmg 21 hrs wkly; *No. News Employees:* 1; *Target Audience:* 35 plus; people with most discretionary incomes
CC Matthews, Operations Dir
Tim Hartlage, General Manager

WLLV
06-01-1940; 1240 kHz AM; 1 kw-U, ND1; N38 14 49 W85 42 19
3270 Blazer Pkwy S101, Lexington, KY 40509 US
(502) 776-1240; *Fax:* (502) 776-1250
License: Louisville, KY held by Davidson Media Station WLLV Licensee LLC.
Group Owner: Davidson Media Group LLC; (acq 4-12-2006; $2.65 million with WLOU(AM) Louisville).
Arbitron Metro Market: Louisville, KY; *Format:* Black, Gospel
Vivien Ogburn, Station Manager

WLOU
01-01-1948; 1350 kHz AM; 2.2 kw-D, DAN; 0.5 kw-N, DAN; N38 13 52 W85 49 22
3270 Blazer Pkwy, Suite 101, Lexington, KY 40509 US
(502) 776-1240; *Fax:* (502) 776-1250
www.wlouonline.com
License: Louisville, KY held by Davidson Media Station WLOU Licensee LLC.
Group Owner: Davidson Media Group LLC; (acq 4-12-2006; $2.65 million with WLLV(AM) Louisville).
Nat'l Network: American Urban
Arbitron Metro Market: Louisville, KY; *Format:* Gospel; *Target Audience:* 25-54; mature adults
Vivien Ogburn, Station Manager

WXMA
10-01-1964; 102.3 MHz FM; *Hrs Open:* 24; 6 kw; 285 ft.; N38 14 37 W85 45 34
520 S. 4th St., Suite 200, Louisville, KY 40202 US
(502) 625-1220; *Fax:* (502) 625-1255
www.themaxfm.com
themaxfm@gmail.com
License: Louisville, Jefferson County, KY held by Alpha Media Licensee LLC
Group Owner: Alpha Media LLC; (acq 4-17-2014; grpsl).
Arbitron Metro Market: Louisville, KY; *Format:* Adult Contemp; *Target Audience:* 25-49; young adults who enjoy modern/alternative rock; *Adv. Rates:* 110; 100; 110; 80
Dale Schaefer, General Manager
Tom Ulmer, General Sales Mgr
Sarah Jordan, Programming Director
Billy S. Garland, Promotions Director

WRKA
01-01-1974; 103.9 MHz FM; *Hrs Open:* 24; 1.35 kw; 489 ft.; N38 15 22 W85 45 29
612 South 4th Street, Louisville, KY 40202 US
(502) 589-4800; *Fax:* 502-561-2988
www.countrylegends1039.com
Shane.Collins@summitmedia.com
License: Louisville, Jefferson County, KY held by SM-WRKA LLC
Group Owner: SummitMedia LLC
Nat'l Reps: Christal; *Wire Services:* AP
Arbitron Metro Market: Louisville, KY; *Format:* Country; *Hrs. of News Programming:* News progmg one hr wkly; *Target Audience:* 25-54; emphasis on 25-44
Shane Collins, Operations Dir
Todd Schumacher, Vice President/General Manager
Todd Pitt, General Sales Mgr
Matt Killion, Programming Director
Brian Eichenberger, Promotions Manager

WLGX
06-07-1993; 100.5 MHz FM; *Hrs Open:* 24; 37.4 kw; Ant 554 ft; N38 03 49 W85 43 52
4000 #1 Radio Dr., Louisville, KY 40218 US
(502) 479-2222; *Fax:* (502) 479-2308
www.myfmlouisville.com
License: Louisville, Jefferson County, KY held by Clear Channel Broadcasting Licenses Inc.
Group Owner: iHeartMedia; (acq 9-13-96; $6.9 million with co-located AM).
Nat'l Reps: Clear Channel
Arbitron Metro Market: Louisville, KY; *Format:* Adult Contemp; *Hrs. of News Programming:* News progmg 3 hrs wkly; *Target Audience:* 18-49; general
Earl Jones, Market President
Kevin Hughes, Senior Vice President of Sales
Kobi Kearney, Programming Director

WTUV
08-20-1958; 620 kHz AM; *Hrs Open:* 24; 0.5 kw-D, DA2; 0.5 kw-N, DA2; N38 18 59 W85 42 8
162 W. Broadway, Louisville, KY 40202 US
(502) 583-6200; *Fax:* (502) 473-7500
www.lapoderosaky.com
License: Louisville, KY held by Davidson Media Station WTMT Licensee LLC.
Group Owner: Davidson Media Group LLC; (acq 6-30-2006; $1 million).
Arbitron Metro Market: Louisville, KY
Paul Dendy, General Manager
Catalina Ibarra, Station Manager
Dennis Mendez, Programming Director
Jenny Sanchez, Traffic Manager

*WUOL-FM
12-20-1976; 90.5 MHz FM; *Hrs Open:* 24; 21 kw; 774 ft.; N38 21 55 W85 50 24
2301 South 3rd Street, Louisville, KY 40292 US
(502) 814-6500; *Fax:* (502) 814-6599
www.wuol.org
dgilliam@louisvillepublicmedia.org
License: Louisville, Jefferson County, KY held by Kentucky Public Radio Inc.
Arbitron Metro Market: Louisville, KY; *Format:* Talk; *Hrs. of News Programming:* News progmg 2 hrs wkly; *Target Audience:* General; those interested in quality music & info
Donovan Reynolds, General Manager
Daniel Gilliam, Programming Director
Gabe Bullard, News Director
Gray Smith, Development Director
Kristen Pfalzgraf, Marketing Manager

WKRD
01-01-1936; 790 kHz AM; *Hrs Open:* 24; 5 kw-D, DA2; 1 kw-N, DA2; N38 11 34 W85 31 14 *Rebroadcasts:* Simulcast with WKRD-FM Shelbyville 100%
4000 #1 Radio Drive, Louisville, KY 40218 US
(502) 479-2222; *Fax:* (502) 479-2308
www.790krd.com
License: Louisville, KY held by CC Licenses LLC
Group Owner: iHeartMedia; (acq 1996)
Nat'l Network: Fox Sports; Premiere Radio Networks; *Nat'l Reps:* Clear Channel
Arbitron Metro Market: Louisville, KY; *Format:* Sports; *Hrs. of News Programming:* News progmg 2 hrs wkly; *Target Audience:* 25-54.
Kevin Hughes, Senior Vice President of Sales
Jim Fenn, Programming Director
Kellie Burton, Promotions Director

Lyndon

WQNU
10-19-1964; 103.1 MHz FM; *Hrs Open:* 24; 23 kw; 554 ft.; N38 19 28 W85 33 0
612 South 4th Street, Louisville, KY 40202 US

(502) 589-4800
newcountryq1031.com
License: Lyndon, Jefferson County, KY held by SM-WQNU LLC
Group Owner: SummitMedia LLC
Nat'l Reps: Christal; *Wire Services:* AP
Arbitron Metro Market: Louisville, KY; *Format:* Country; *Target Audience:* 35-54
Matt Killion, Programming Director
Brian Eichenberger, Promotions Manager
Todd Pitt, General Sales Manager/Internet Sales
David Dubose, Marketing Manager

Madisonville

WFMW
01-01-1947; 730 kHz AM; *Hrs Open:* 24
Mailing Address: 2380 North Main Street, Madisonville, KY 42431 US
Second Address: 2380 N. Main St., Madisonville, KY 42431
(270) 821-4096; *Fax:* (270) 821-5954
www.wfmw.net
wfmw@wfmw.net
License: Madisonville, KY held by Sound Broadcasters Inc.
Nat'l Network: CNN Radio; *Nat'l Reps:* Rgnl Reps; *Wire Services:* AP
Format: Country; *Hrs. of News Programming:* news progmg 13 hrs wkly; *No. News Employees:* 1; *Target Audience:* 18 plus.; *Adv. Rates:* 15; 15; 15; 15
Robert Kelley, President
Danny Koeber, Programming Director
Chris Gardener, News Director
Chris Meyers, Chief Engineer

WKTG
04-19-1949; 93.9 MHz FM; *Hrs Open:* 24; 35 kw; 584 ft.; N37 31 26 W87 24 11
Mailing Address: P. O. Box 338, Madisonville, KY 42431 US
Second Address: 2380 N. Main St., Madisonville, KY 42431
(270) 821-1156
www.wktg.com
wktg@wktg.com
License: Madisonville, Hopkins County, KY
Nat'l Network: USA
Format: Rock/AOR; *Hrs. of News Programming:* news progmg 3 hrs wkly; *No. News Employees:* 1; *Target Audience:* 20-45.; *Adv. Rates:* 18; 18; 18; 18
Robert Kelley, Station Manager
Bill McClone, Programming Director
Kevin O'Connor, Disc Jockey
Erin Grant, Disc Jockey

*WSOF-FM
02-01-1977; 89.9 MHz FM; 39 kw; 282 ft.; N37 21 26 W87 28 41
1415 Island Ford Rd, Madisonville, KY 42431 US
(270) 825-3004
www.wsof.org
comments@wsof.org
License: Madisonville, Hopkins County, KY held by Temple Broadcasting Co.
Nat'l Network: USA
Format: Christian; *Target Audience:* General; Christian
Gary Hall, General Manager

WTTL
09-16-1956; 1310 kHz AM; *Hrs Open:* 24; 1.5 kw-D, DAN; 0.5 kw-N, DAN; N37 20 12 W87 32 41
Mailing Address: 265 South Main Street, Madisonville, KY 42431 US
Second Address: 265 S. Main St., Madisonville, KY 42431
(270) 821-1310; *Fax:* (270) 825-3260
License: Madisonville, KY held by Madisonville CBC Inc.
Group Owner: Commonwealth Broadcasting Corp.; (acq 2-8-2000; $1.31 million with co-located FM)
Arbitron Metro Market: Madisonville, KY; *Format:* News, Sports, 86; *Target Audience:* 25-54.
Tom Rogers, General Manager
Lee Ann Oliver, General Sales Mgr
Stephanie Vandygraiff, News Director

WTTL-FM
09-07-1992; 106.9 MHz FM; *Hrs Open:* 24; 2 kw; 528 ft; N37 22 51 W87 28 04
Mailing Address: Box 1310, Madisonville, KY 42431
Second Address: 265 S. Main St., Madisonville, KY 42431
(270) 825-1079; *Fax:* (270) 825-3260
License: Madisonville, Hopkins County, KY
Group Owner: Commonwealth Broadcasting Corp.
Nat'l Network: ABC; Jones Radio Networks
Target Audience: 25-34.
Dex Gage, General Manager
Ed Wilhelm, Chief Engineer

*WKMD
90.9 MHz FM; 20.5 kw; 400 ft.; N37 21 47 W87 30 56
2108 University Station, Murray, KY 42071 US
(270) 809-4359; *Fax:* (270) 809-4667
www.wkms.org
msu.wkms@murraystate.edu
License: Madisonville, Hopkins County, KY held by Board of Regents, Murray State University.
Arbitron Metro Market: Madisonville, KY
Kate Lochte, Station Manager
Tracy Ross, Programming Director

Manchester

WKLB
09-26-1981; 1290 kHz AM; *Hrs Open:* 24; 5 kw-D, ND1; 0.034 kw-N, ND1; N37 8 15 W83 46 50
Mailing Address: P. O. Box 448, Manchester, KY 40962 US
Second Address: 106 Richmond Rd., Manchester, KY 40962
(606) 598-2445; *Fax:* (606) 598-2653
www.wklb.com
wklb1stchoice@yahoo.com
License: Manchester, KY held by Barker Broadcasting Co.
Nat'l Reps: Rgnl Reps *Regional Reps:* Barker Broadcasting
Format: Country; *Hrs. of News Programming:* news progmg 8 hrs wkly; *No. News Employees:* 1; *Target Audience:* 24-65; working people
Larry Barker, President

WTBK
10-01-1989; 105.7 MHz FM; *Hrs Open:* 19; 5 kw; 715 ft.; N37 8 59 W83 45 8
Mailing Address: PO Box 453, Manchester, KY 40962 US
Second Address: 107 Dickerson St., Manchester, KY 40962
(606) 598-7588; *Fax:* (606) 598-7598
wtbkradio@yahoo.com
License: Manchester, Clay County, KY held by Manchester Communications Inc.
Nat'l Network: Westwood One; ABC
Format: Classic Rock *Special Programming:* Talk 8 hrs wkly; *Hrs. of News Programming:* news progmg 10 hrs wkly; *No. News Employees:* 1; *Target Audience:* General; 18 plus in the morning, 16-45 at night
Tim Finley, General Manager

WWLT
08-09-1967; 103.1 MHz FM; *Hrs Open:* 24; 2.1 kw; 564 ft.; N37 4 30 W83 49 14
100 Thompson-Poynter Rd., London, KY 40741 US
(707) 528-9236; *Fax:* (707) 528-9246
www.klove.com
License: Manchester, Clay County, KY held by Educational Media Foundation
Group Owner: EMF Broadcasting; (acq 1956)
Nat'l Network: K-Love
Arbitron Metro Market: Manchester, KY; *Format:* Christian
Mike Novak, President & CEO

WWXL
01-01-1956; 1450 kHz AM; *Hrs Open:* 24 Hours; 1 kw-U, ND1; N37 9 4 W83 45 45
4260 East Laurel Road, London, KY 40741 US
(606) 598-9995; *Fax:* (606) 598-9995
License: Manchester, KY held by Juanita H. Nolan
Arbitron Metro Market: Manchester, KY; *Format:* Sports, Talk; *Hrs. of News Programming:* news progmg 3 hrs wkly; *No. News Employees:* 1; *Target Audience:* 35-54; programmed for adults 35-54 *Adv. Rates:* 20,20,20,10
Jonathan Dobson, General Manager
Juanita Nolan, Owner

Mannsville

WVLC
12-31-1994; 99.9 MHz FM; *Hrs Open:* 24; 11 kw; 492 ft.; N37 10 4 W85 11 26
Mailing Address: P.O. Box 4190, Campbellsville, KY 42719 US
Second Address: 101 East Main St., Campbellsville, KY 42719
(270) 789-4998; *Fax:* (270) 789-4584
www.wvlc.com
bigdawg@wvlc.com
License: Mannsville, Taylor County, KY held by Patricia Rodgers.
Nat'l Network: Jones Radio Networks; CNN Radio
Arbitron Metro Market: Campbellsville, KY; *Format:* Country; *No. News Employees:* 2; *Target Audience:* General.
Lash Franklin, Operations Dir
Jan Royce, General Manager
Chase McBridge, News Director
Mike Wilson, News Reporter
Tammy Sexton, Office Manager

Brent Thompson, Sales Rep
Teresa Schwoebel, Sales Rep

Marion

WMJL
07-10-1968; 1500 kHz AM; *Hrs Open:* 6 AM-sunset; 0.175 kw-D, NDD; N37 20 16 W88 4 3
Mailing Address: P. O. Box 68, Marion, KY 42064 US
Second Address: 251 Club Dr., Marion, KY 42064
(270) 965-2271; *Fax:* (270) 965-4464
License: Marion, KY held by Joe Myers Production Inc.
Nat'l Reps: Rgnl Reps
Arbitron Metro Market: Marion, KY; *Hrs. of News Programming:* news progmg 12 hrs wkly; *No. News Employees:* 1; *Target Audience:* General.
Joe Myers, President

WMJL-FM
06-01-1993; 102.7 MHz FM; *Hrs Open:* 24; 6 kw; 328 ft.; N37 20 16 W88 4 3
P.O. Box 68, Marion, KY 42064 US
(270) 965-2271; *Fax:* (270) 965-4464
License: Marion, Crittenden County, KY held by Joe Myers Production Inc.
Arbitron Metro Market: Marion, KY; *Format:* Oldies
Randy Hugg, Operations Dir
Lisa Rich, General Manager
Todd Lewis, General Sales Mgr
Steve Shoffner, News Director
Gary Homza, Chief Engineer

Mayfield

WLLE
01-01-1997; 102.1 MHz FM; 50 kw; 472 ft.; N36 45 57.8 W88 38 49.8
Mailing Address: P O Box 900, Bowling Green, KY 42102 US
Second Address: 1176 State Rt. 45 N., Mayfield, KY 42066
(270) 554-0093; *Fax:* (270) 554-4613
www.willieradio.com
jamiefutrell@wkyq.com
License: Mayfield, Hickman County, KY held by Bristol Broadcasting Co. Inc.
Group Owner: Bristol Broadcasting Co. Inc.; (acq 3-15-2004; grpsl)
Arbitron Metro Market: Mayfield, Ky; *Format:* Country; *No. News Employees:* 1
Jamie Futrell, General Manager

WNGO
01-07-1947; 1320 kHz AM; *Hrs Open:* 5 AM-10 PM; 1 kw-D, ND1; 0.097 kw-N, ND1; N36 45 37 W88 38 20 *Rebroadcasts:* Rebroadcasts WKYX(AM) Paducah 90%
Mailing Address: 1715 Nashville Street, P.O. Box 298, Russellville, KY 42276 US
Second Address: 6000 Bristol Dr., Paducah, KY 42003
(270) 554-8255; *Fax:* (270) 554-5468
www.wkyx.com
License: Mayfield, KY held by Bristol Broadcasting Co. Inc.
Group Owner: Bristol Broadcasting Co. Inc.; acq 2-20-2004; grpsl).
Format: News, News/Talk, 86; *Hrs. of News Programming:* news progmg 12 hrs wkly; *No. News Employees:* 1; *Target Audience:* 24-54.
Jamie Futrell, General Manager
Greg Dunker, Programming Director
Donna Groves, News Director
Greg Walker, Chief Engineer

WYMC
10-18-1976; 1430 kHz AM; *Hrs Open:* 24; 1 kw-D, DAN; 1 kw-N, DAN; N36 47 12 W88 39 16
Mailing Address: P. O. Box V, 197 Wymc Road, Mayfield, KY 42066 US
Second Address: 197 WYMC Rd., Mayfield, KY 42066
(270) 247-1430; *Fax:* (270) 247-1825
radio@wymcradio.com
License: Mayfield, KY held by JDM Communications Inc.
Arbitron Metro Market: Mayfield, KY; *Format:* Adult Contemp; *No. News Employees:* 1; *Target Audience:* 35-64; affluent, business oriented; *Adv. Rates:* 20; 9; 12; 8.10
Jim Moore, General Manager
Shan Moore, Traffic Manager

Maysville

WFTM
01-01-1948; 1240 kHz AM; *Hrs Open:* 6 AM-11 PM; 1 kw-U, ND1; N38 38 10 W83 45 38
626 Forest Ave., Maysville, KY 41056 US

(606) 564-3361; *Fax:* (606) 564-4291
www.wftm.net
License: Maysville, KY held by Standard Tobacco Co.
Nat'l Reps: Keystone (unwired net); Rgnl Reps
Format: Contemporary Hits/Top 40 *Special Programming:* Farm 6 hrs, gospel 5 hrs, relg 5 hrs wkly; *Hrs. of News Programming:* news progmg 10 hrs wkly; *No. News Employees:* 1; *Target Audience:* 50-70.
J.A. Finch, President
Jeff Cracraft, Operations Dir
Doug McGill, General Manager
Dave Gray, News Director

WFTM-FM
10-26-1965; 95.9 MHz FM; *Hrs Open:* 24; 3 kw; 308 ft.; N38 38 35 W83 46 47
626 Forest Avenue, Maysville, KY 41056 US
(606) 564-3361; *Fax:* (606) 564-4291
www.wftm.net
License: Maysville, Mason County, KY
Nat'l Network: AP Radio
Format: Classic Rock; *No. News Employees:* 1; *Target Audience:* 18-55.
Robert Roe, General Manager
Danny Weddle, General Sales Mgr
Ben Smith, Sales & Promotions Manager
Travis Scaggs, News Director
Lisa Jarrell, Traffic Manager
Danny Weddle, Sports Director

McDaniels

***WBFI**
09-07-1987; 91.5 MHz FM; *Hrs Open:* 24; 5 kw; 328 ft.; N37 36 6 W86 22 13
P.O. Box 2, McDaniels, KY 40152 US
(270) 257-2689(888) 333-9234; *Fax:* (270) 257-8344
License: McDaniels, Breckenridge County, KY held by Bethel Fellowship Inc.
Nat'l Network: USA
Format: Adult Contemp, Christian; *Hrs. of News Programming:* News progmg 20 hrs wkly; *Target Audience:* General; Christians
Ronald Miller, President
Roger Goostree, General Manager
Daryl Cook, Programming Director

McKee

WWAG
11-01-1990; 107.9 MHz FM; *Hrs Open:* 24; 3.9 kw; 410 ft.; N37 23 39 W83 54 27
Star Route; Box 16, Sand Gap, KY 40481 US
(606) 287-9924
www.wwagfm.com
License: McKee, Jackson County, KY held by Dandy Broadcasting Inc.
Nat'l Network: ABC; *Nat'l Reps:* Rgnl Reps
Arbitron Metro Market: Jackson County, KY; *Format:* Country *Special Programming:* Bluegrass 9 hrs wkly, gospel 8 hrs on Sunday; *Hrs. of News Programming:* news progmg 10 hrs wkly; *No. News Employees:* 1 *TargetAudience:* General.; *Adv. Rates:* 10; 8; 10; 6.25
Dan Brockman, President
Sherry Brockman, General Manager

***KYAI**
01-01-2008; 89.3 MHz FM; 50 kw; 165 m; N37 04 30 W83 49 14
Rebroadcasts: Rebroadcasts KLVR(FM) Middletown, CA 100%
2351 Sunset Blvd., Suite 170-218, Rocklin, CA 38104
(916) 251-1600; *Fax:* (916) 251-1650
www.klove.com
License: McKee, Terry County, KY held by Educational Media Foundation.
Group Owner: EMF Broadcasting; (acq 11-1-2006; grpsl)
Nat'l Network: K-Love

Mike Novak, President

Middlesboro

WFXY
03-01-1969; 1490 kHz AM; *Hrs Open:* 24; 1 kw-U, ND1; N36 36 47 W83 42 34
Mailing Address: PO Box 999, Middlesboro, KY 40965 US
Second Address: 2118 Cumberland Ave., Middlesboro, KY 40965
(606) 248-9528; *Fax:* (606) 248-6397
www.1490wfxy.com
katcountry@gmail.com
License: Middlesboro, KY held by Penelope Inc.
Nat'l Network: Jones Radio Networks; *Regional Network:* Tenn. Radio Net; *Nat'l Reps:* Rgnl Reps
Format: Adult Contemp *Special Programming:* Black 2 hrs, gospel 3 hrs, relg 3 hrs wkly; *Hrs. of News Programming:* news progmg 20 hrs wkly; *No. News Employees:* 2; *Target Audience:* 25-54; community-oriented
Frank Smith, Operations Dir
Brian O'Brien, General Manager
Penny Smith, General Sales Mgr

WMIK
11-15-1948; 560 kHz AM; 2.5 kw-D, ND1; 0.088 kw-N, ND1; N36 37 38 W83 42 52
Mailing Address: P. O. Box 608, Middlesboro, KY 40965 US
Second Address: N. 19th St., Middlesboro, KY 40965
(606) 248-5842; *Fax:* (606) 248-7660
www.wmikradio.com/
wmikradio@bellsouth.net
License: Middlesboro, KY held by Gateway Broadcasting Inc.
Arbitron Metro Market: Middlesboro, KY; *Format:* Gospel *Special Programming:* Farm one hr, gospel 2 hrs wkly
Michael Barnett, Station Manager
Chuck Owens, Chief Engineer

WMIK-FM
06-04-1971; 92.7 MHz FM; 0.35 kw; 1345 ft.; N36 35 39 W83 47 42
P.O. Box 608, Middlesboro, KY 40965 US
(606) 248-5842; *Fax:* (606) 248-7660
www.wmikradio.com/
ÿwmikradio@bellsouth.netÿÿÿÿ
License: Middlesboro, Bell County, KY held by Gateway Broadcasting Inc.
Regional Network: Tenn. Radio Net.
Arbitron Metro Market: Middlesboro, KY; *Format:* Religious

Midway

WBTF
01-01-1998; 107.9 MHz FM; 6 kw; 328 ft.; N38 11 41 W84 38 25
401 West Main Street, Suite 301, Lexington, KY 40507 US
(859) 233-1515; *Fax:* (859) 233-1517
www.1079thebeat.com
jayalexander@lmcomm.com
License: Midway, Woodford County, KY held by L.M. Communications of Kentucky L.L.C.
Group Owner: L M Communications Inc.; (acq 4-10-01).
Nat'l Reps: Katz Radio
Arbitron Metro Market: Lexington-Fayette, KY; *Format:* Urban Contemporary, Christian; *Hrs. of News Programming:* News progmg 24 hrs wkly; *Target Audience:* 18-49; adults
Jay Alexander, Program Director
Craig Olive, Market Manager
Don Trail, General Sales Manager
Dawn Trail, Sales Manager
Christine Navarro, Traffic Manager

Monticello

WFLW
05-19-1955; 1360 kHz AM; *Hrs Open:* 6 AM-6 PM
P. O. Box 427, Monticello, KY 42633 US
(606) 348-8427; *Fax:* (606) 348-3867
License: Monticello, KY held by Stephen Staples Jr.
Nat'l Reps: Rgnl Reps
Format: Gospel *Special Programming:* Farm 5 hrs, news/talk 10 hrs wkly; *No. News Employees:* 1; *Target Audience:* General.
Stephen Staples Jr., General Manager/Programming Director
Debbie Brown, Traffic Manager
Bruce Correll, Chief Engineer

WKYM
12-19-1965; 101.7 MHz FM; *Hrs Open:* 24; 1.75 kw; 617 ft.; N36 48 36 W84 50 49
P.O. Box 427, Monticello, KY 42633 US
(606) 348-8427
www.wkym.com
License: Monticello, Wayne County, KY
Nat'l Reps: Rgnl Reps
Format: Classic Rock; *Target Audience:* 18-50; baby boomers
Stephen Staples Jr., Programming Director

WMKZ
06-01-1990; 93.1 MHz FM; *Hrs Open:* 24; 1.45 kw; 676 ft.; N36 48 29 W84 50 46
183 Old Hwy 90, Monticello, KY 42633 US
(606) 348-3393; *Fax:* (606) 348-3330
www.wmkz.com
License: Monticello, Wayne County, KY held by Monticello-Wayne County Media Inc.
Nat'l Network: USA
Arbitron Metro Market: Monticello, KY; *Format:* Country; *Hrs. of News Programming:* News progmg 9 hrs wkly; *Target Audience:* 24-55; general
Joel Catron, General Manager

Morehead

***WBMK**
01-01-2002; 88.5 MHz FM; 0.6 kw; 522 ft.; N38 10 38 W83 24 24
P.O. Box 3206, Tupelo, MS 38803 US
(662) 844-8888; *Fax:* (666) 842-6791
www.afr.net
faq@afa.net
License: Morehead, Rowan County, KY held by American Family Association.
Group Owner: American Family Radio; (acq 11-26-99)
Arbitron Metro Market: Morehead, KY; *Format:* Christian
Tim Wildmon, President
Donald Wildmon, Founder
Buddy Smith, Sr VP
Ed Vitagliano, Exec VP
Randy Sharp, Director Of Special Projects
Meeke Addison, Director Of Commmunications
Abraham Hamilton, General Counsel

WIVY
07-01-1994; 96.3 MHz FM; *Hrs Open:* 24; 2.15 kw; 518 ft.; N38 10 33 W83 24 28
123 E. 1st St., Morehead, KY 40351 US
(606) 784-9966; *Fax:* (606) 674-6700
www.wivyradio.com
info@wivyradio.com
License: Morehead, Rowan County, KY held by Gateway Radio Works Inc.
Group Owner: Gateway Radio Works Inc.
Nat'l Network: ABC
Arbitron Metro Market: Lexington-Fayette, KY; *Format:* Adult Contemp; *No. News Employees:* 2; *Target Audience:* 25 plus; affluent, well educ, mature adult, higher spendable income; *Adv. Rates:* 18; 14; 18; 10
Hays McMakin, CEO/President
Tom McMakin, Operations Dir
Jeff Ray, General Manager
Vernice Taylor, Station Manager
Robert Haydon, General Sales Mgr
Becky Black, Programming Director

***WMKY**
06-01-1965; 90.3 MHz FM; *Hrs Open:* 24; 37 kw; 904 ft.; N38 10 38 W83 24 17
Upo Box 903, Morehead, KY 40351 US
(606) 783-2001; *Fax:* (606) 783-2335
www.msuradio.com
wmky@moreheadstate.edu
License: Morehead, Rowan County, KY held by Morehead State University
Nat'l Network: PRI; NPR; *Regional Network:* Ky. News Net; *Wire Services:* AP
Arbitron Metro Market: Lexington, KY; *Format:* Variety/Diverse *Special Programming:* Bluegrass, Blues, Jazz, Storytelling; *No. News Employees:* 10; *Target Audience:* 25-54
Greg Jenkins, Operations Dir
Paul Hitchcock, General Manager
Chuck Mraz, News Director

WMOR
02-18-1955; 1330 kHz AM
129 College St., West Liberty, KY 41472 US
License: Morehead, KY held by Morgan County Industries Inc.
Group Owner: Morgan County Industries Inc.; acq 3-16-99; $300,000 with co-located FM)
Nat'l Network: Moody
Arbitron Metro Market: Morehead, KY; *Format:* Oldies
Merv Lawson, General Manager
Paul Lyons, Chief Engineer

WMOR-FM
06-15-1965; 106.1 MHz FM; 19.5 kw; 374 ft.; N38 10 56 W83 26 56
129 College St., West Liberty, KY 41472 US
www.mix106wmor.com
License: Morehead, Rowan County, KY held by Morgan County Industries Inc.
Group Owner: Morgan County Industries Inc.
Arbitron Metro Market: Morehead, KY; *Format:* Adult Contemp
Merv Lawson, General Manager
Paul Lyons, Chief Engineer

Morganfield

***WKVN**
08-08-1967; 95.3 MHz FM; 25 kw; 269 ft.; N37 46 38 W87 37 26
P. O. Box 369, Morganfield, KY 42437 US

RADIO - U.S.

(916) 251-1600; *Fax:* (916) 251-1650
www.klove.com
License: Morganfield, Union County, KY held by Educational Media Foundation.
Group Owner: EMF Broadcasting; (acq 1-21-2009)
Nat'l Network: K-Love
Arbitron Metro Market: Morganfield, CA; *Format:* Christian; *Target Audience:* 25-64; general
Mike Novak, President

WMSK
11-21-1960; 1550 kHz AM; *Hrs Open:* 24; 250 w-D; N37 40 00 W87 55 40
Mailing Address: Box 369, Morganfield, KY 42437
Second Address: 1339 US 60 W., Morganfield, KY 42437
(270) 389-1550; *Fax:* (270) 389-1553
wmsk@bellsouth.net
License: Morganfield, Union County, KY held by Henson Media Inc.
Nat'l Network: Jones Radio Networks; *Regional Network:* Ky. News Net; *Nat'l Reps:* Rgnl Reps; *Wire Services:* AP
Population Served: 50,000 *Hrs. of News Programming:* News progmg 20 hrs wkly; *Target Audience:* General; adults 25-64; *Adv. Rates:* 6.25; 6.25; 6.25; 6.25
Edward Henson, President
Bob Hite, Operations Dir
John Robinson, General Manager
Don Sheridan, General Sales Mgr
Rhonda Gibson, Traffic Manager

***WBOO**
90.3 MHz FM; 1 kw vert; 108 ft.; N37 36 41.8 W87 57 19.1 US
(317) 467-1062
License: Morganfield, Union County, KY held by Electronic Applications Radio Service Inc.
Group Owner: Electronic Applications Radio Service Inc.
Arbitron Metro Market: Morganfield, KY
Patrick Diemer, President

***WEUC**
12-29-2008; 88.7 MHz FM; 0 kw horiz, 3 kw vert; 259 ft.; N37 44 9 W87 59 45
US
(270) 389-4281; *Fax:* (270) 389-3581
www.weuc.org
License: Morganfield, Union County, KY held by Saint Ann Radio Group Inc.
Nat'l Network: EWTN Radio
Arbitron Metro Market: Morganfield, KY; *Format:* Christian
Richard A Nally, President
Ed Thomas, Chief Engineer
Dr Darrell R French, Vice President

Morgantown

WLBQ
01-01-1976; 1570 kHz AM; *Hrs Open:* 6 AM-10 PM
P. O. Box 130, Morgantown, KY 42261 US
(270) 526-3321; *Fax:* (270) 526-5393
License: Morgantown, KY held by Butler County Broadcasting Co.
Nat'l Network: ABC
Format: Country; *Hrs. of News Programming:* news progmg 8 hrs wkly; *No. News Employees:* 1; *Target Audience:* General; residents of Morgantown & Butler County, KY
Charles Black, President
Jan Embry, Operations Dir
Howard Phelps, Station Manager

WWKN
99.1 MHz FM; 0.65 kw; 226 ft.; N37 13 38 W86 41 54
US
(469) 619-1001
License: Morgantown, Butler County, KY held by Independence Media Holdings LLC.
Group Owner: Independence Media Holdings LLC
Arbitron Metro Market: Morgantown, KY
David Jacobs, CEO

Mount Sterling

***WAXG**
01-01-1998; 88.1 MHz FM; 0.3 kw; 174 ft.; N38 3 39 W83 57 20
2597 Grassy Lick Rd., Mount Sterling, KY 40353 US
(859) 499-3537
www.afr.net
License: Mount Sterling, Montgomery County, KY held by American Family Association.
Group Owner: American Family Radio
Arbitron Metro Market: Jackson WY; *Format:* Christian
Tim Wildmon, President
Donald Wildmon, Founder
Buddy Smith, Sr VP
Ed Vitagliano, Exec VP
Randy Sharp, Director Of Special Projects
Meeke Addison, Director Of Communications
Abraham Hamilton III, General Counsel

WKYN
12-01-1983; 107.7 MHz FM; *Hrs Open:* 24; 6 kw; 328 ft.; N38 6 8 W83 50 12
22 W. Main St., Mount Sterling, KY 40353 US
(859) 498-1077; *Fax:* (859) 498-7930
www.wkynradio.com
License: Mount Sterling, Bath County, KY held by Gateway Radio Works Inc.
Group Owner: Gateway Radio Works Inc.
Nat'l Network: NBC Radio
Arbitron Metro Market: Lexington-Fayette, KY; *Format:* Country; *Hrs. of News Programming:* 10 hrs wkly; *No. News Employees:* 2; *Adv. Rates:* 18; 14; 18; 10
Hays McMakin, President
Tom McMakin, Operations Dir
Jeff Ray, General Manager
Vernice Taylor, Station Manager

WMST
10-17-1957; 1150 kHz AM; *Hrs Open:* 24
22 W. Main St., Mount Sterling, KY 40353 US
(859) 498-1150; *Fax:* (859) 498-7930
www.wmstradio.com
License: Mount Sterling, KY held by Gateway Radio Works Inc.
Group Owner: Gateway Radio Works Inc.; Acq. Jan-1-00
Nat'l Network: CBS Radio *Regional Reps:* Rgnl. Reps.
Arbitron Metro Market: Lexington, KY; *Format:* Adult Contemp
Special Programming: Farm 2 hrs wkly; *Hrs. of News Programming:* 37 hrs wkly; *No. News Employees:* 2; *Target Audience:* 25 plus; affluent, matureadult, high spendalbe income, well educated; *Adv. Rates:* 18; 14; 18; 10
Hays McMakin, President
Tom McMakin, Operations Dir
Jeff Ray, General Manager
Vernice Taylor, Station Manager

Mount Vernon

WRVK
04-30-1957; 1460 kHz AM; *Hrs Open:* 6 AM-9 PM
P.O. Box 1288, Mt. Vernon, KY 40456 US
(606) 256-2146; *Fax:* (606) 256-9146
www.wrvk1460.com
manager@wrvk1460.com
License: Mount Vernon, KY held by Saylor Broadcasting Inc.
Format: Country, Gospel; *Target Audience:* General.; *Adv. Rates:* 9:50; 9:50; na; 9:50
Charles Saylor, President
Charles Saylor, Station Manager
Charles Napier, General Sales Mgr

Mt Washington

WLCR
10-29-1955; 1040 kHz AM
3600 Goldsmith Lane, Louisville, KY 40220 US
(502) 451-9527; *Fax:* (502) 451-9527
www.wlcr.net
License: Mt Washington, KY held by LCR Partners L.P.
Arbitron Metro Market: Louisville, KY; *Format:* Religious; *Target Audience:* General; Those interested in the existance of God
Vince Heuser, General Manager

Mt. Sterling

WWRW
05-28-1968; 105.5 MHz FM; 3 kw; 300 ft; N38 05 36 W83 56 39
2601 Nicholasville Rd., Lexington, KY 40502
(859) 422-1000; *Fax:* (859) 422-1038
www.wmkj.com
info@wmkj.com
License: Mt. Sterling, Montgomery County, KY held by Clear Channel Media and Entertainment
Population Served: 28,000
Gene Guinn, General Manager
Mike Boyle, Sales Manager
Michael Jordan, Programming Director
Mandy Daugherty, Marketing & Promotions Manager

Munfordville

WCLU-FM
08-01-1964; 102.3 MHz FM; 2.8 kw; 410 ft.; N37 10 41 W85 55 15
P.O. Box 1628, Glasgow, KY 42142 US
(270) 651-9149; *Fax:* (270) 651-9222
www.wcluradio.com
emilyrose@wcluradio.com
License: Munfordville, Hart County, KY held by Royse Radio Inc.
Arbitron Metro Market: Bowling Green, KY; *Format:* Adult Contemp
Henry Royse, President
Henry Royse, General Manager

WLOC
02-01-1993; 1150 kHz AM; *Hrs Open:* 24
P.O. Box 98, Glasgow, KY 42142 US
(270) 786-4400; *Fax:* (270) 786-4402
www.wloconline.com
License: Munfordville, KY held by Forbis Communications Inc.
Arbitron Metro Market: Bowling Green, KY; *Format:* Country, Gospel; *Target Audience:* 25 plus; serve entire area
DeWayne Forbis, President
Dewayne Forbis, General Manager
Chris Jessie, Programming Director
Joe Berry, News Director

Murray

WFGS
06-23-1967; 103.7 MHz FM; *Hrs Open:* 24; 100 kw; 659 ft.; N36 32 58 W88 19 52
1715 Nashville Street, Russellville, KY 42276 US
(270) 753-2400; *Fax:* (270) 753-9434
www.froggy103.com
License: Murray, Calloway County, KY held by Forever Communications Inc.
Group Owner: Forever Communications Inc.
Nat'l Network: Westwood One
Arbitron Metro Market: Murray, KY; *Format:* Country; *Hrs. of News Programming:* news progmg 4 hrs wkly; *No. News Employees:* 1; *Target Audience:* 18-45.; *Adv. Rates:* 23; 19; 16; 13
Scott Swalls, General Manager
Tony Doolin, Programming Director
Neal Bradley, Sports Director

***WKMS-FM**
05-11-1970; 91.3 MHz FM; *Hrs Open:* 24; 100 kw; 600 ft.; N36 55 17 W88 5 48
2018 University Station, Murray, KY 42071 US
(800) 599-4737; *Fax:* (270) 809-4667
www.wkms.org
License: Murray, Calloway County, KY held by Board of Regents, Murray State University.
Nat'l Network: NPR; PRI; *Wire Services:* AP
Format: News, Variety/Diverse *Special Programming:* Class 15 hrs, folk & bluegrass 3 hrs, AAA 3 hrs, u; *Hrs. of News Programming:* news progmg 82 hrs wkly; *No. News Employees:* 2; *Target Audience:* 35 plus; lifelong learners
Tracy Ross, Operations & Programming Director
Kate Lochte, Station Manager
Mark Welch, Programming Director
Chad Lampe, News Director
Allen Fowler, Chief Engineer
Asia Burnett, Development Director
Ronda Gibson, UnderwritingDirector

WNBS
07-01-1948; 1340 kHz AM; *Hrs Open:* 24; 1 kw-U, ND1; N36 37 42 W88 18 4
1715 Nashville Street, Russellville, KY 42276 US
(270) 753-2400; *Fax:* (270) 753-9434
www.1340wnbs.com
License: Murray, KY held by Forever Communications Inc.
Group Owner: Forever Communications Inc.; acq 12-31-02; grpsl).
Nat'l Network: ESPN Radio; CBS Radio; *Regional Network:* Ky. News Net *Regional Reps:* Rgnl Reps.
Arbitron Metro Market: Murray, KY; *Format:* News, Sports, 86; *Hrs. of News Programming:* news progmg 10 hrs wkly; *No. News Employees:* 1; *Target Audience:* 25-55.
Debbie Howard, General Manager
Neal Bradley, Programming Director
Candi Freeland, News Director

WOFC
09-12-1978; 1130 kHz AM; *Hrs Open:* 24
1715 Nashville Street, Russellville, KY 42276 US
(270) 753-2400; *Fax:* (270) 753-9434
License: Murray, KY held by Forever Communications Inc.

Group Owner: Forever Communications Inc.; (acq 12-31-2002; grpsl)
Nat'l Network: ESPN Radio *Regional Reps:* Rgnl reps.
Format: Sports; *Adv. Rates:* 12; 11; 10; 9
Scott Swalls, General Manager
Neal Bradley, Programming Director
Adam Bittel, Chief Engineer

Neon

WIZD
08-31-1956; 1480 kHz AM; *Hrs Open:* 12; 5 kw-D; N37 11 54 W82 42 42
486 Lakeside Dr., Jenkins, KY 41829
(606) 634-9430
License: Neon, Letcher County, KY held by Letcher County Broadcasting Inc.
Population Served: 150,000 *Target Audience:* 24-60; general
Ernestine Kincer, President
G.C. Kincer, General Manager

Newburg

WHBE
01-01-1992; 680 kHz AM; *Hrs Open:* 24; 1.3 kw-D, 450 w-N, DA-2; N38 05 31 W85 40 56
11700 Commonwealth Dr., Suite 800, Louisville, KY 40219
(502) 240-0602; *Fax:* (502) 240-0940
www.radiodisney.com
License: Newburg, Breckinridge County, KY held by Radio Disney Group LLC.
Group Owner: ABC Inc.; (acq 2-14-02; $1.92 million).
Arbitron Metro Market: Louisville, KY; *Target Audience:* Age 25-44 mothers of children; Mothers of children younger than 15
John Salzman, Station Manager

Newport

WNOP
08-21-1948; 740 kHz AM; *Hrs Open:* 24
5440 Moeller Avenue, Cincinnati, OH 45212 US
(513) 731-7740; *Fax:* (513) 731-6465
www.sacredheartradio.com
info@sacredheartradio.com
License: Newport, KY held by Sacred Heart Radio, Inc.
Arbitron Metro Market: Cincinnati, OH; *Format:* Talk, Christian
Bill Levitt, Station Manager

Nicholasville

WCGW
09-15-1986; 770 kHz AM; 1 kw-D, NDD; N37 53 7 W84 31 46
3950 Lexington Rd., Versailles, KY 40383 US
(859) 873-8844; *Fax:* (859) 873-1318
www.wcgwam.com
770AM@CKCRadio.com
License: Nicholasville, KY held by Christian Broadcasting System Ltd.
Group Owner: Christian Broadcasting System Ltd.; (acq 7-1-2006; grpsl).
Nat'l Network: USA
Arbitron Metro Market: Versailles, KY; *Format:* Gospel; *Target Audience:* 25-54; above average in educ, family size, income;
Adv. Rates: 20; 20; 20; na
Benson Gregory, Station Manager
Bruce Edwards, Programming Director
Morgan Fouts, Promotions Manager
Antoinette Parson, Business Manager
Kelly Rossi, Traffic Manager

WLTO
08-29-1988; 102.5 MHz FM; *Hrs Open:* 24; 4.6 kw; 373 ft.; N37 57 37 W84 32 42
300 West Vine Street, Lexington, KY 40507 US
(859) 253-5900; *Fax:* (859) 253-5940
www.hot102.net
steve.bearance@cumulus.com
License: Nicholasville, Jessamine County, KY held by Cumulus Licensing Corp.
Group Owner: Cumulus Media Inc.; (acq 7-22-99; grpsl)
Arbitron Metro Market: Lexington, KY; *Format:* Contemporary Hits/Top 40; *Target Audience:* 18-44
Scott Frazier, General Manager
Andrea Ayers, General Sales Mgr
Tabatha Levrault, Programming Director

WMJR
10-19-1954; 1380 kHz AM; *Hrs Open:* 24
2909 Richmond Road, Suite 5, Lexington, KY 40509 US
(859) 278-0894; *Fax:* (859) 278-0426
info@wmjr.net
License: Nicholasville, KY held by Thy Kingdom Come Network Inc.
Arbitron Metro Market: Lexington, KY; *Format:* Religious; *Target Audience:* 35-64.
Leo Brown, President

North Corbin

WKFC
01-01-2008; 101.9 MHz FM; 6 kw; 328 ft.; N37 2 9 W84 5 5 US
(606) 878-9532; *Fax:* (606) 878-1116
www.wkfcfm.com
License: North Corbin, Laurel County, KY held by Radioactive LLC.
Group Owner: Radioactive LLC
Arbitron Metro Market: North Corbin, KY; *Format:* Country
Jonathan Smith, President
Karen Moses Bowling, General Manager

Oak Grove

WEGI-FM
08-31-1964; 94.3 MHz FM; *Hrs Open:* 24; 6 kw; 256 ft.; N36 38 28 W87 26 1
401 Church St., Nashville, TN 37219 US
(931) 648-7720; *Fax:* (931) 648-7769
eagle943.com
License: Oak Grove, Christian County, KY held by Saga Communications of Tuckessee LLC.
Group Owner: Saga Communications Inc.; (acq 10-4-2002; $1.5 million with co-located AM)
Arbitron Metro Market: Clarksville-Hopkinsville, TN-KY; *Format:* Contemporary Hits/Top 40, Adult Contemp; *Hrs. of News Programming:* news progmg 5 hrs wkly; *No. News Employees:* 1; *Target Audience:* 25-54.
Scott Chase, Operations Dir
Katie Gambill, General Manager
Sande Cox, Sales Manager
J.T. Daniels, Programming Director
Lee Erwin, News Director

Okolona

*WJIE-FM
01-01-1988; 88.5 MHz FM; *Hrs Open:* 24; 24.5 kw horiz, 18.5 kw vert; 623 ft.; N38 1 59 W85 45 16
Mailing Address: 5400 Minors Lane, Louisville, KY 40219 US
Second Address: 5400 Minors Ln., Louisville, KY 40219
(502) 968-1220; *Fax:* (502) 962-3143
www.wjie.org
jimfraser@wjie.org
License: Okolona, Jefferson County, KY held by Evangel Schools Inc.
Nat'l Network: Moody
Format: Christian; *Hrs. of News Programming:* News progmg 7 hrs wkly; *Target Audience:* 25-49; Christian adults; *Adv. Rates:* 25; 20; 25; 10
James Fraser, General Manager
Jim Galipeau, Programming Director
Christin Ray, Disc Jockey
Chris Crain, Assistant Program Director
Ceci Labarge, Disc Jockey
Jason Brock, Disc Jockey
Jaclyn Olson, Traffic Manager
Randy Ollis,Staff Meterologist

Owensboro

WBKR
01-01-1948; 92.5 MHz FM; *Hrs Open:* 24; 91 kw; 1050 ft.; N37 36 29 W87 3 15
3301 Frederica Street, Owensboro, KY 42301 US
(800)-666-1031; *Fax:* (270) 683-2128
wbkr.com
License: Owensboro, Daviess County, KY
Group Owner: Townsquare Media
Arbitron Metro Market: Owensboro, KY; *Format:* Country *Special Programming:* Farm 2 hrs wkly; *No. News Employees:* 2; *Target Audience:* 25-54.
LaDonne Craig, General Manager
Traci Davis, Director of Sales
Moon Mullins, Programming Director
Chadwick Benefield, Promotions Director
Dave Spenser, Music Director
Michael Owns, Traffic Manager

*WKWC
01-21-1983; 90.3 MHz FM; *Hrs Open:* 24; 5 kw; 82 ft.; N37 44 32 W87 7 27
3000 Frederica St., Owensboro, KY 42301 US
(270) 852-3601; *Fax:* (270) 852-3599
patherradio@kwc.edu
License: Owensboro, Daviess County, KY held by Kentucky Wesleyan College.
Format: Triple A; *Hrs. of News Programming:* News progmg 2 hrs wkly; *Target Audience:* 12 plus.
Derik Hancock, Programming Director

WOMI
03-07-1938; 1490 kHz AM; 0.83 kw-U, ND1; N37 44 29 W87 6 58
C/O Brill Media Co, PO Box 3353, Evansville, IN 47708 US
(270) 683-1558; *Fax:* (270) 683-2128
www.1490womi.com
License: Owensboro, KY
Group Owner: Townsquare Media; (acq 2-25-03; with co-located FM).
Nat'l Reps: Christal
TV Affiliate: Talk; *Hrs. of News Programming:* 2; *No. News Employees:* 35-64.
LaDonne Craig, General Manager
Traci Davis, Sales Manager
Moon Mullins, Programming Director

WSTO
06-07-1948; 96.1 MHz FM; *Hrs Open:* 24; 100 kW; 1001 ft.; N37 46 20 W87 21 27
1162 Mt. Auburn Rd, Evansville, IN 47720 USA
(812) 424-8284; *Fax:* (812) 426-7928
hot96.com
License: Owensboro, Daviess County, KY held by Midwest Communications Inc.
Group Owner: Midwest Communications Inc.
Arbitron Metro Market: Evansville, IN; *Format:* Contemporary Hits/Top 40; *Hrs. of News Programming:* news progmg one hr wkly; *No. News Employees:* 4; *Target Audience:* 18-34.
Matthew Ozee, Brand Manager

WVJS
11-26-1947; 1420 kHz AM; *Hrs Open:* 24
Mailing Address: P.O. Box 3353, Evansville, IN 47732 US
Second Address: 1115 Tamarack Rd., Suite 500, Owensboro, TK 42301
(270) 683-5200; *Fax:* (270) 688-0108
www.oldiesowensboro.com
jcatinna@cromwellradio.com
License: Owensboro, KY held by Cromwell Group Inc. of Kentucky.
Group Owner: The Cromwell Group Inc.; (acq 11-20-02; $300,000).
Nat'l Network: ABC; *Nat'l Reps:* Rgnl Reps
Arbitron Metro Market: Owensboro, KY; *Format:* News, Sports
Special Programming: Farm one hr wkly; *Hrs. of News Programming:* One; *No. News Employees:* 1; *Target Audience:* 35-54.
Brack Stacy, Market Manager
Brack Stacy, Operations Manager
Business Manager, Mel Ingleheart
Janet Catinna, General Manager
Kelsey Turner, Sales Manager
Steve Horn, Programming Director
Mel Ford, News Director

*WJVK
01-01-2004; 91.7 MHz FM; 0.1 kw; 174 ft.; N37 44 48 W87 6 58
Rebroadcasts: WCVK(FM)
Mailing Address: 1407 Scottsville Rd, Bowling Green, KY 42104 US
Second Address: 1407 Scottsville Rd., Bowling Green, KY 42104
(270) 781-7326; *Fax:* (270) 781-8005
www.christianfamilyradio.com
License: Owensboro, Daviess County, KY held by Bowling Green Community Broadcasting Inc.
Arbitron Metro Market: Owensboro, KY; *Format:* Christian
Ken Burns, Operations Dir
Mike Wilson, General Manager
Susan ""West"" Woodard, Programming Director
Derek Gregory, Promotions Manager
Donna Brown, Office Manager/Bookkeeper
Mary Beth Warren, Administrative Assistant
DaleMcCubbins, Production Manager

Paducah

WDDJ
11-26-1946; 96.9 MHz FM; *Hrs Open:* 24; 100 kw; 778 ft.; N37 2 56 W88 36 52
Mailing Address: 901 East Valley Drive, Bristol, VA 24201 US
Second Address: 6000 Bristol Dr., Paducah, KY 42003

(270) 534-9690; *Fax:* (270) 554-5468
www.electric969.com
pd@electric969.com
License: Paducah, McCracken County, KY held by Bristol Broadcasting Co. Inc.
Group Owner: Bristol Broadcasting Co. Inc.; (acq 6-24-97; $2.7 million with co-located AM).
Arbitron Metro Market: Paducah, KY; *Format:* Contemporary Hits/Top 40; *Hrs. of News Programming:* news progmg 2 hrs wkly; *No. News Employees:* 2; *Target Audience:* 18-49; active, white & blue collar adults *Adv.Rates:* 75; 75; 75; 40
Gary Morse, General Manager
Jamie Futrell, General Sales Mgr
Mark Summer, Programming Director
Greg Walker, Chief Engineer

WDXR
12-24-1957; 1450 kHz AM; *Hrs Open:* 24; 1 kw-U, ND1; N37 5 55 W88 37 19
Mailing Address: P.O. Box 900, 948 Fairview Avenue, Bowling Green, KY 42102 US
Second Address: 1176 Stat Rt. 45 N., Paducah, KY
(270) 247-5122; *Fax:* (270) 554-5468
License: Paducah, KY held by Bristol Broadcasting Co. Inc.
Group Owner: Bristol Broadcasting Co. Inc.; (acq 3-15-2004; grpsl)
Nat'l Network: ABC
Arbitron Metro Market: Paducah, KY; *Format:* Urban Contemporary; *Hrs. of News Programming:* news progmg 5 hrs wkly; *No. News Employees:* 1; *Target Audience:* 30-65.
Gary Morse, General Manager

***WGCF**
12-01-1996; 89.3 MHz FM; *Hrs Open:* 24; 12 kw; 492 ft.; N37 11 31 W88 58 41
1112 Kentucky Ave., Kevil, KY 42053 US
(270) 462-3020; *Fax:* (270) 462-3024
www.afr.net
License: Paducah, McCracken County, KY held by American Family Association.
Group Owner: American Family Radio; (acq 11-25-2003; $200,000).
Format: Christian, Religious
Tim Wildmon, President
Donald Wildmon, Founder
Buddy Smith, Sr VP
Ed Vitagliano, Exec VP
Randy Sharp, Director Of Special Projects
Meeke Addison, Director Of Communications
Abraham Hamilton III, General Counsel

WKYQ
01-01-1947; 93.3 MHz FM; *Hrs Open:* 24; 100 kw; 915 ft.; N37 2 56 W88 36 52
Mailing Address: P.O. Box 1389, Bristol, VA 24203 US
Second Address: 6000 Bristol Drive, Paducah, KY 42003
(270) 554-8255; *Fax:* (270) 554-5468
www.wkyq.com
production@wkyq.com
License: Paducah, McCracken County, KY
Group Owner: Bristol Broadcasting Co. Inc.
Format: Country; *No. News Employees:* 3; *Target Audience:* 25-54.; *Adv. Rates:* 85; 85; 85; 45
Bobby Cook, Operations Dir
Jamie Futrell, General Manager
Jeff Lawrence, Programming Director
Donna Groves, News Director
Greg Walker, Engineering Dir

WKYX
01-01-1946; 570 kHz AM; *Hrs Open:* 24; 1 kw-D, DA2; 0.5 kw-N, DA2; N37 0 53 W88 36 46 *Rebroadcasts:* Simulcast with WKYX-FM Golconda, IL 100%
Mailing Address: P. O. Box 1389, Bristol, VA 24203 US
Second Address: 6000 Bristol Dr., Paducah, KY 42003
(270) 554-8255; *Fax:* (270) 554-5468
www.wkyx.com
License: Paducah, KY held by Bristol Broadcasting Co. Inc.
Group Owner: Bristol Broadcasting Co. Inc.; (acq 11-23-71)
Nat'l Reps: Christal
Format: News, News/Talk, 86; *Hrs. of News Programming:* news progmg 20 hrs wkly; *No. News Employees:* 3; *Target Audience:* 25-54; middle to upper income; *Adv. Rates:* 35; 35; 35; 15
Jamie Futrell, General Manager
Greg Dunker, Programming Director
Donna Groves, News Director

WPAD
08-23-1930; 1560 kHz AM; *Hrs Open:* 24; 10 kw-D, DA3; 1 kw-N, DA3; DA3; 5 kw-N; N37 3 8 W88 36 3
Mailing Address: 901 East Valley Drive, Bristol, VA 24201 US
Second Address: 6000 Bristol Dr., Paducah, KY 42003
(270) 534-9690; *Fax:* (270) 554-4613
www.electric969.com
info@electric969.com
License: Paducah, KY held by Bristol Broadcasting Co. Inc.
Group Owner: Bristol Broadcasting Co. Inc.
Nat'l Network: Westwood One
Format: Sports; *Hrs. of News Programming:* news progmg 22 hrs wkly; *No. News Employees:* 2; *Target Audience:* 35-64; upscale, white-collar; *Adv. Rates:* Same as FM
Alfonso Gimenez-Porrata, CEO
Alfonso Gimenez-Lucchetti, Operations Dir
Sayda Ortiz, General Sales Mgr
Maria Luisa Gimenez-Lucchetti, Vice President, Operations

***WNFC**
91.7 MHz FM; 15 kw; 297 ft.; N37 3 41.4 W88 50 25.7 US
(270) 369-8614; *Fax:* (270) 369-7402
www.wjcr.org
donjrwjcr@yahoo.com
License: Paducah, McCracken County, KY held by FM 90.1 Inc.
Arbitron Metro Market: Paducah, KY
Don Powell, General Manager

Paintsville

WKYH
03-18-1985; 600 kHz AM
P.O. Box 1407, Ste 6 Woodland Place, Paintsville, KY 41240 US
(606) 789-3333; *Fax:* (859) 402-0260
ckbelhasen@belsouth.net
License: Paintsville, KY held by Highlands Broadcasting Corp.
Nat'l Network: Westwood One
Format: News, News/Talk, 84, Talk; *Target Audience:* 25-49; middle to upper class adults
Charles K. Belhasen, President
Charles Belhasen, General Manager

WKLW-FM
06-18-1993; 94.7 MHz FM; *Hrs Open:* 24; 4.9 kw; 732 ft.; N37 47 42 W82 48 3
Mailing Address: P.O. Drawer 1407, Ste Six Woodland Pl, Paintsville, KY 41240 US
Second Address: 865 S. Mayo Tr., Paintsville, KY 41240
(606) 789-6664; *Fax:* (606) 789-6669
www.wklw.com
wklwfm@belsouth.net
License: Paintsville, Johnson County, KY held by B & G Broadcasting Inc.
Format: Adult Contemp
Alan Burton, General Manager

WSIP
04-24-1949; 1490 kHz AM; 1 kw-U, ND1; N37 48 21 W82 46 1
Mailing Address: P.O. Box 1450, Corbin, KY 40702 US
Second Address: 127 Main St., Paintsville, KY 41240
(606) 789-5311; *Fax:* (606) 789-7200
www.wsipam.com
wsipradio@bellsouth.net
License: Paintsville, KY held by S.I.P. Broadcasting Inc.
Group Owner: Forcht Broadcasting; (acq 2-84)
Nat'l Reps: Rgnl Reps
Format: Oldies; *Target Audience:* General.
Mike Tarter, President/Chief Executive Officer
Spike Berkhimer, General Manager
Tim Collins, Programming & Music Director
Dan Lyons, Sales & Promotions Director
Scott Ratliff, News & Sports Director
Deanna Meadows, MarketingDirector

WSIP-FM
01-12-1965; 98.9 MHz FM; *Hrs Open:* 24; 100 kw; 627 ft.; N37 51 30 W82 47 41
Mailing Address: P. O. Box 1450, Corbin, KY 40702 US
Second Address: 127 Main St., Paintsville, KY 41240
(606) 789-5311; *Fax:* (606) 789-7200
www.wsipfm.com
wsipradio@bellsouth.net
License: Paintsville, Johnson County, KY
Group Owner: Forcht Broadcasting
Format: Country
Mike Tarter, President/Chief Executive Officer
Spike Berkheimer, General Manager
Tim Collins, Programming & Music Director
Dan Lyons, Sales & Promotions Director
Scott Ratliff, News & Sports Director
Deanna Meadows, MarketingDirector

Paris

WGKS
06-05-1968; 96.9 MHz FM; 50 kw; 492 ft.; N38 7 32 W84 21 12
401 W Main St., Suite 301, Lexington, KY 40511 US
(859) 233-1515; *Fax:* (859) 233-1517
www.969kissfm.com
jmac@lmcomm.com
License: Paris, Bourbon County, KY held by L.M. Communications Inc.
Group Owner: L M Communications Inc.
Nat'l Network: ABC; *Nat'l Reps:* Katz Radio
Arbitron Metro Market: Lexington-Fayette, KY; *Format:* Adult Contemp; *Hrs. of News Programming:* news progmg 10 hrs wkly; *No. News Employees:* 1
Lynn Martin, President
Craig Olive, General Manager
Dawn Trail, General Sales Mgr
Skip Eliot, Programming Director
Christine Navarro, Traffic Manager

WYGH
01-01-1993; 1440 kHz AM; *Hrs Open:* 24
13297 Green Road, Walton, KY 41094 US
(859) 472-1075; *Fax:* (859) 472-2875
wiok@fuse.net
License: Paris, KY held by Hammond Broadcasting Inc.
Arbitron Metro Market: Lexington-Fayet; *Format:* Gospel
John Smith, General Manager
Cecil Bowling, Programming Director

***WPTJ**
08-01-2003; 90.7 MHz FM; *Hrs Open:* 24; 10 kw; 315 ft.; N38 19 40 W84 7 44
Mailing Address: 1811 Cynthiana, Millersburg Rd, Paris, KY 40361 US
Second Address: Lay Witness Broadcasting, Box 7, Paris, KY 40362-0007
(859) 484-9691
License: Paris, Bourbon County, KY held by Lay Witness Outreach Inc.
Arbitron Metro Market: Paris, KY; *Format:* Religious; *Adv. Rates:* 150; 120; 150; 100
John Smith, General Manager
John Brett, Programming Director

Philpot

WBIO
11-18-1993; 94.7 MHz FM; *Hrs Open:* 24; 3 kw; 328 ft.; N37 41 50 W86 59 28
Mailing Address: P. O. Box 150846, Nashville, TN 37215 US
Second Address: 115 Tamarack Rd., Suite 500, Owensboro, KY 42301
(270) 683-5200; *Fax:* (270) 688-0108
www.wbio.com
jcatinna@cromwellradio.com
License: Philpot, Daviess County, KY held by Hancock Communications Inc.
Group Owner: The Cromwell Group Inc.; (acq 6-17-93; $90,565;
Nat'l Network: ABC; *Nat'l Reps:* Rgnl Reps
Arbitron Metro Market: Owensboro, Ky; *Format:* Country; *Hrs. of News Programming:* news progmg 4 hrs wkly; *No. News Employees:* 1; *Target Audience:* 25-54.; *Adv. Rates:* 20; 20; 20; 12
Brack Stacy, Market Manager
Brack Stacy, Operations Manager
Mel Iglenheart, Business Manager

WPRT-HD2
11-18-1993; 102.1 MHz AM; *Hrs Open:* 24; 3 kw; 328 ft.; N37 41 50 W86 59 28
Mailing Address: P. O. Box 150846, Nashville, TN 37215 US
Second Address: 115 Tamarack Rd., Suite 500, Owensboro, KY 42301
(270) 683-5200; *Fax:* (270) 688-0108
www.wbio.com
jcatinna@cromwellradio.com
License: Philpot, Daviess County, TN held by Hancock Communications Inc.
Group Owner: The Cromwell Group Inc.; (acq 6-17-93; $90,565;
Nat'l Network: ABC; *Nat'l Reps:* Rgnl Reps
Arbitron Metro Market: Owensboro, Ky; *Format:* Christian, Religious, 44; *Hrs. of News Programming:* news progmg 4 hrs wkly; *No. News Employees:* 1; *Target Audience:* 25-54.; *Adv. Rates:* 20; 20; 20; 12
Brack Stacy, Market Manager
Brack Stacy, Operations Manager
Mel Iglenheart, Business Manager

Pikeville

WDHR
03-25-1966; 93.1 MHz FM; *Hrs Open:* 24; 22 kw; 758 ft.; N37 27 57 W82 33 4
PO Box 2200, 1240 Radio Dr., Pikeville, KY 41501 US
(606) 437-4051; *Fax:* (606) 432-2809
www.wdhr.com
wdhr@wdhr.com
License: Pikeville, Pike County, KY held by East Kentucky Broadcasting Corp.
Group Owner: East Kentucky Broadcasting Corp.
Nat'l Network: ABC
Arbitron Metro Market: Pikeville, KY; *Format:* Country; *No. News Employees:* 2
Walter E. May, Owner/Founder
Cindy May Johnson, President/CEO
Beverly Newman, General Sales Mgr
Dave Stanford, Programming Director

***WJSO**
04-01-1989; 90.1 MHz FM; *Hrs Open:* 24; 3.8 kW; 456 ft.; N37 27 52 W82 32 45
PO Box 3237, Pikeville, KY 41502 USA
www.moodyradiopikeville.fm
License: Pikeville, Pike County, KY held by The Moody Bible Institute of Chicago
Group Owner: The Moody Bible Institute of Chicago; acq 12-18-91; donation;
Nat'l Network: Moody
Arbitron Metro Market: Pikeville, KY; *Format:* Christian; *Hrs. of News Programming:* News progmg 15 hrs wkly; *Target Audience:* 35-55.

WLSI
01-20-1949; 900 kHz AM; *Hrs Open:* 24 *Rebroadcasts:* Simulcast with WPRT(AM) Prestonburg 100%
1240 Radio Dr., PO Box 2200, Pikeville, KY 41501 US
(606) 437-4051; *Fax:* (606) 432-2809
License: Pikeville, KY held by East Kentucky Broadcasting Corp.
Group Owner: East Kentucky Broadcasting Corp.; (acq 5-14-2003; $531,273 with WZLK(FM) Virgie)
Nat'l Network: CNN Radio; NBC Radio; Sporting News Radio Network
Format: Talk, Sports; *Hrs. of News Programming:* news progmg 21 hrs wkly; *No. News Employees:* 1; *Target Audience:* 25-49.
Cindy May, President/General Manager

WPKE
07-31-1949; 1240 kHz AM; *Hrs Open:* 24 *Rebroadcasts:* Rebroadcasts WBPA(AM) Elkhorn City 100%
1240 Radio Dr., PO Box 2200, Pikeville, KY 41502 US
(606) 437-4051; *Fax:* (606) 432-2809
www.myoldiesradio.com
License: Pikeville, KY held by East Kentucky Broadcasting Corp.
Group Owner: East Kentucky Broadcasting Corp.; acq 1962).
Nat'l Reps: Rgnl Reps *Regional Reps:* Rgnl Reps
Format: Oldies; *Hrs. of News Programming:* news progmg 5 hrs wkly; *No. News Employees:* 1; *Target Audience:* General.
Cindy May Johnson, President/General Manager

Pineville

WANO
03-16-1957; 1230 kHz AM; 1 kw-U, ND1; N36 46 7 W83 42 59
P.O. Box 999, Middlesboro, KY 40965 US
(606) 248-8993; *Fax:* (606) 248-6397
www.1230wano.com
katcountryky@gmail.com
License: Pineville, KY held by Cumberland Media Group Inc.
Arbitron Metro Market: Pineville, KY.; *Format:* Oldies
Brian O'Brien, Operations Dir

WRIL
02-24-1973; 106.3 MHz FM; 1.15 kw; 748 ft.; N36 45 16 W83 42 12
Mailing Address: P.O. Box 693, Pineville, KY 40977 US
Second Address: 25 E. Log Mountain, Pineville, KY 40977
(606) 337-5202; *Fax:* (606) 337-8020
wrilcountry@yahoo.com
License: Pineville, Bell County, KY held by Pine Hills Broadcasting Inc.
Format: Country
Gayle McPherson, General Manager

Pippa Passes

***WWJD**
11-01-1986; 91.7 MHz FM; *Hrs Open:* 24; 7.3 kw; 545 ft.; N37 19 45 W82 52 30
100 Purpose Road, Pippa Passes, KY 41844 US
(606) 368-6131; *Fax:* (606) 368-6017
wwjd@alc.edu
License: Pippa Passes, Knott County, KY held by Alice Lloyd College.
Arbitron Metro Market: Pippa Passes, KY; *Format:* Adult Contemp, Christian; *Target Audience:* 13-25.
Jason Stowers, General Manager

Plum Springs

WWKU
10-01-1962; 1450 kHz AM
Mailing Address: P.O. Box 457, Glasgow, KY 42141 US
Second Address: 113 W. Public Sq., Suite 400, Glasgow, KY 42141
(270-651-6050; *Fax:* (270-651-7666
www.espn1450.net/
License: Plum Springs, KY held by Newberry Broadcasting Inc.
Group Owner: Commonwealth Broadcasting Corp.
Arbitron Metro Market: Glasgow,KY; *Format:* Sports
Derron Steenbergen, Vice President/General Manager

Prestonsburg

WDOC
11-01-1957; 1310 kHz AM; *Hrs Open:* Sunrise-sunset
P.O. Box 307, Prestonsburg, KY 41653 US
(606) 886-2338(606) 886-8409; *Fax:* (606) 263-4923
www.q95fm.net
gorm.collins@wdocinc.com
License: Prestonsburg, KY held by WDOC Inc.
Nat'l Reps: Rgnl Reps
Arbitron Metro Market: Prestonsburg, KY; *Format:* Gospel; *Target Audience:* 25-64.; *Adv. Rates:* 7; 5; 6; na
Gormon Collins Jr., President
Gormon Collins, Jr., General Manager
Samantha Osborne, General Sales Mgr
Jamie Howell, News Director

WPRT
12-05-1952; 960 kHz AM *Rebroadcasts:* Simulcast with WLSI(AM) Pikeville 100%
1240 Radio Dr., PO Box 2200, Pikeville, KY 41502 US
(606) 437-4051; *Fax:* (606) 432-2809
www.900wlsi.com
cmjohnson@ekbradio.com
License: Prestonsburg, KY held by East Kentucky Broadcasting.
Group Owner: East Kentucky Broadcasting.; (acq 10-26-2001)
Nat'l Network: CNN Radio; NBC Radio; Sporting News Radio Network
Format: Talk, Sports
Cindy May Johnson, President/General Manager

WQHY
02-11-1968; 95.5 MHz FM; *Hrs Open:* 24; 100 kw; 1001 ft.; N37 41 45 W82 45 24
University Drive, P.O. Box 309, Prestonsburg, KY 41653 US
(606) 886-2338,(606) 886-8409; *Fax:* (606) 886-1026
www.q95fm.net
q95prod@bellsouth.net
License: Prestonsburg, Floyd County, KY held by WDOC, Inc.
Nat'l Network: ABC; *Nat'l Reps:* Rgnl Reps
Format: Contemporary Hits/Top 40; *Hrs. of News Programming:* news progmg 2 hrs wkly; *No. News Employees:* 1; *Target Audience:* 18-34.; *Adv. Rates:* 24; 20; 22; 14
Gormon Collins, Jr., General Manager
Samantha Osborne, General Sales Mgr
Jessica Sparks, Programming Director
Russ Lafforty, Chief Engineer
Carla Hughes, Traffic Manager

WXKZ-FM
02-10-1967; 105.3 MHz FM; 4.7 kw; 371 ft.; N37 39 24 W82 45 58
P.O. Box 1049, Harold, KY 41635 US
(606) 478-1200; *Fax:* (606) 478-4202
www.thedoublex.com
wifx@foxy943.com
License: Prestonsburg, Floyd County, KY held by Adam Gearheart dba WXLR-FM
Format: Oldies
Barry Boyd, General Manager
Mel Stevens, Programming Director

Princeton

WAVJ
04-01-1969; 104.9 MHz FM; *Hrs Open:* 24; 6 kw; 174 ft.; N37 7 14 W87 51 31
Mailing Address: P.O. Box 1505, Glasgow, KY 42142 US
Second Address: 108 W. Main St., Princeton, KY 42445
(877) 702-9293; *Fax:* (303) 702-9293
www.wayfm.com
supportservices@wayfm.com
License: Princeton, Caldwell County, KY held by Caldwell County CBC Inc.
Group Owner: Commonwealth Broadcasting Corp.
Arbitron Metro Market: Brush CO; *Format:* Christian
Robert Augsburg, President

WPKY
03-15-1950; 1580 kHz AM; *Hrs Open:* 24; 0.25 kw-D, ND1; 0.009 kw-N, ND1; N37 7 14 W87 51 31
Mailing Address: P.O. Box 1505, Glasgow, KY 42142 US
Second Address: 108 W. Main St., Princeton, KY 42445
(270) 365-2072; *Fax:* (270) 365-2073
License: Princeton, KY held by Caldwell County CBC Inc.
Group Owner: Commonwealth Broadcasting Corp.; (acq 6-25-98; $362,000 with co-located FM)
Nat'l Network: ESPN Radio
Format: Sports; *Hrs. of News Programming:* news progmg 11 hrs wkly; *No. News Employees:* 1; *Target Audience:* General.
Tom Rogers, General Manager
LeeAnn Oliver, General Sales Mgr
Ed Thomas, Chief Engineer

Providence

WWKY
04-09-1976; 97.7 MHz FM; *Hrs Open:* 24; 6 kw; 328 ft.; N37 24 52 W87 34 23
Mailing Address: P.O. Box 1505, Glasgow, KY 42142 US
Second Address: 265 S. Main St., Madisonville, KY 42431
(270) 825-9779; *Fax:* (270) 825-3260
License: Providence, Webster County, KY held by Hopkins-Webster CBC Inc.
Group Owner: Commonwealth Broadcasting Corp.; (acq 5-21-98; $425,000).
Nat'l Network: CNN Radio; *Regional Network:* Ky. News Net
Format: Oldies; *Hrs. of News Programming:* news progmg 21 hrs wkly; *No. News Employees:* 2; *Target Audience:* 25-54.
Tom Rogers, General Manager
Lee Oliver, General Sales Mgr
Stephanie Vandygraiff, News Director

Radcliff

WAKY
11-01-1991; 103.5 MHz FM; *Hrs Open:* 24; 3.5 kw; N37 52 45 W85 43 03
519 N. Miles St., Suite 3, Elizabethtown, KY 42701 US
(270) 766-1035
www.waky1035.com
rbell@waky1035.com
License: Radcliff, KY held by W & B Broadcasting Inc.
Group Owner: W & B Broadcasting Inc.
Nat'l Network: ABC
Population Served: 513,878 *Format:* Oldies; *Hrs. of News Programming:* news progmg 4 hrs wkly; *No. News Employees:* 14; *Target Audience:* 25-54; baby boomers; *Adv. Rates:* 32; 32; 32; 8
Ren, Bell, General Sales Mgr

WAKY
11-01-1991; 620 kHz AM; *Hrs Open:* 24; 3.5 kw; N37 52 45 W85 43 03
519 N. Miles St., Suite 3, Elizabethtown, KY 42701 US
(270) 766-1035
www.waky1035.com
License: Radcliff, KY held by W & B Broadcasting Inc.
Group Owner: W & B Broadcasting Inc.
Nat'l Network: ABC
Population Served: 513,878 *Format:* Oldies; *Hrs. of News Programming:* news progmg 4 hrs wkly; *No. News Employees:* 14; *Target Audience:* 25-54; baby boomers; *Adv. Rates:* 32; 32; 32; 8
Ren, Bell, General Sales Mgr

Reidland

WZZL
10-01-1992; 106.7 MHz FM; *Hrs Open:* 24; 4.7 kw; 371 ft.; N37 5 55 W88 37 19
3501 Broadway, P.O. Box 1508, Mount Vernon, IL 62864 US
(270) 538-5251; *Fax:* (270) 415-0599
www.wzzl.com
rlambert@withersradio.net
License: Reidland, McCracken County, KY held by Withers Broadcasting Co. of Paducah LLC.
Group Owner: Withers Broadcasting Co.; (acq 9-11-97; grpsl).
Arbitron Metro Market: Paducah, KY; *Format:* Rock/AOR; *Target Audience:* 18-49.

Rick Lambert, General Manager
Jolie Birchfield, Sales Manager
Melanie Shepherd, Account Executive
Jana Adams, Account Executive

Richmond

WCBR
03-01-1969; 1110 kHz AM; *Hrs Open:* Sunrise-sunset; 0.25 kw-D, NDD; N37 44 9 W84 16 5
Mailing Address: PO Box 570, Richmond, KY 40476 US
Second Address: 509 Leighway Dr., Richmond, KY 40475
(859) 623-1235; *Fax:* (859) 623-7094
wcbrradio@bellsouth.net
License: Richmond, KY held by WCBR Inc.
Nat'l Network: USA
Arbitron Metro Market: Richmond,KY; *Format:* Gospel *Special Programming:* Loc talk shows, news, sports & relg talk 35 hrs wkly; *Hrs. of News Programming:* News progmg 5 hrs wkly; *Target Audience:* 35 plus; olderadult listener; *Adv. Rates:* 8.50; 8.50; 8.50; 8.50
Malissa Blair, News Director
David Humes, Executive Vice President

*WEKU
09-01-1968; 88.9 MHz FM; *Hrs Open:* 24; 50 kw; 719 ft.; N37 52 45 W84 19 33
102 Perkins Building, Richmond, KY 40475 US
(859) 622-1660; *Fax:* (859) 622-6276
www.weku.fm
weku@eku.edu
License: Richmond, Madison County, KY held by Board of Regents, Eastern Kentucky University.
Nat'l Network: NPR; PRI; *Wire Services:* AP
Arbitron Metro Market: Richmond, KY; *Format:* News; *Hrs. of News Programming:* news progmg 35 hrs wkly; *No. News Employees:* 3; *Target Audience:* General.
Jonese Franklin, Operations Dir
Roger Duvall, General Manager
John Hingsgergen, Programming Director
Charles Compton, News Director
Bill Browning, Chief Engineer
Michael Carter, Music Director
Carol Siler, Development Director

WEKY
10-17-1953; 1340 kHz AM; *Hrs Open:* 24; 1 kw-U, ND1; N37 43 0 W84 18 25
128 Big Hill Ave., Irvine, KY 40475 US
(859) 623-1386; *Fax:* (859) 623-1341
www.wekyam.com
coyote@wcyofm.com
License: Richmond, KY held by Wallingford Communications Inc.
Group Owner: Wallingford Broadcasting Co.; (acq 1999; grpsl)
Regional Network: Ky. News Net; *Nat'l Reps:* Rgnl Reps
Arbitron Metro Market: Richmond, KY; *Format:* News/Talk
Special Programming: Black 12 hrs, relg 6 hrs wkly; *Hrs. of News Programming:* news progmg 3 hrs wkly; *No. News Employees:* 1; *Target Audience:* 25-54.
Kelly Wallingford, President

WVLK-FM
05-12-1972; 101.5 MHz FM; *Hrs Open:* 24; 9 kw; 541 ft.; N37 52 45 W84 19 33
111 East Kilbourn Avenue, Suite 2700, Milwaukee, WI 53202 US
(859) 253-5900; *Fax:* (859) 253-5940
www.wvlkam.com
License: Richmond, Madison County, KY held by Cumulus Licensing Corp.
Group Owner: Cumulus Media Inc.; (acq 10-5-99; grpsl)
Arbitron Metro Market: Lexington-Fayette, KY; *Format:* Sports, Talk; *Hrs. of News Programming:* news progmg 6 hrs wkly; *No. News Employees:* 1
Scott Frazier, General Manager
John Laing, Sales Manager
Scott Johnson, Programming Director
Mario Anderson, Promotions & Marketing Director

Russell Springs

WHVE
01-01-1993; 92.7 MHz FM; 6 kw; 328 ft.; N37 4 40 W85 10 28
Mailing Address: PO Box 927, Columbia, KY 42728 US
Second Address: 7955 Russell Springs Rd., Russell Springs, KY 42642
(270) 384-7979; *Fax:* (270) 384-6244
www.ridingthewave.com
thewave@ridingthewave.com
License: Russell Springs, Russell County, KY held by Shoreline Communications Inc.
Format: Adult Contemp
Don Salmon, Operations Dir
Jan Royse, General Manager
Ted Beckman, General Sales Mgr
Larry Smith, Programming Director

WIDS
10-14-1982; 570 kHz AM; *Hrs Open:* 24
13297 Green Road, Walton, KY 41094 US
(859) 472-1075; *Fax:* (859) 472-2875
wiok@fuse.net
License: Russell Springs, KY held by Hammond Broadcasting Inc.
Format: Gospel
Jan Hammond, General Manager

Russellville

WUBT
03-28-1965; 101.1 MHz FM; *Hrs Open:* 24; 47 kw; 1289 ft.; N36 31 36 W86 41 14
55 Music Square West, Nashville, TN 37203 US
(615) 664-2400; *Fax:* (615) 664-2457
www.1011thebeat.com
info@1011thebeat.com
License: Russellville, Logan County, KY held by Capstar TX LLC
Group Owner: iHeartMedia; (acq 8-30-00; grpsl).
Arbitron Metro Market: Nashville, TN; *Format:* Urban Contemporary
Melissa Kent, General Sales Mgr
Emma Applebome, Promotions Manager
Karlie Powell, Digital Program Director

WRUS
08-28-1953; 610 kHz AM; *Hrs Open:* 24; 1.8 kw-D, ND1; 0.059 kw-N, ND1; N36 50 40 W86 55 21
1715 Nashville Street, P.O. Box 298, Russellville, KY 42276 US
(270) 726-6100; *Fax:* (270) 726-3095
www.wrusam.com
wrus@bellsouth.net
License: Russellville, KY held by Logan Radio Inc.
Format: Variety/Diverse
Chris McGinnis, General Manager

Salt Lick

WKCA
04-19-1976; 97.7 MHz FM; *Hrs Open:* 24; 3 kw; 469 ft.; N38 10 33 W83 24 28
123 E. 1st St., Morehead, KY 40351 US
(606) 674-2266; *Fax:* (606) 674-6700
www.wkcaradio.com
License: Salt Lick, Bath County, KY held by Gateway Radio Works Inc.
Group Owner: Gateway Radio Works Inc.; (acq 9-7-2007)
Nat'l Network: CBS Radio
Arbitron Metro Market: Ravenna NE; *Format:* Country; *Adv. Rates:* 18;14;18;10
Tom McMakin, Operations Dir
Jeff Ray, General Manager
Becky Black, Programming Director

Salyersville

WRLV
09-01-1979; 1140 kHz AM; *Hrs Open:* 12; 1 kw-D, NDD; N37 44 58 W83 5 19
129 College St., West Liberty, KY 41472 US
(606) 349-6125; *Fax:* (606) 349-6129
License: Salyersville, KY held by Morgan County Industries Inc.
Group Owner: Morgan County Industries Inc.; (acq 7-5-2007; $460,000 with co-located FM)
Nat'l Reps: Rgnl Reps
Format: Country; *Hrs. of News Programming:* news progmg 5 hrs wkly; *No. News Employees:* 2; *Target Audience:* 35-65; middle age to elderly; *Adv. Rates:* 3.50; 3.50; 3.50; na
Merv Lawson, General Manager
Kathy Puckett, General Sales Mgr
Paul Lyons, Chief Engineer

WRLV-FM
08-25-1989; 106.5 MHz FM; *Hrs Open:* 24; 5.9 kw; 331 ft.; N37 45 27 W83 3 50
129 College St., West Liberty, KY 41472 US
(606) 349-6125; *Fax:* (606) 349-6129
License: Salyersville, Magoffin County, KY held by Morgan County Industries, Inc.
Group Owner: Morgan County Industries, Inc.
Nat'l Reps: Rgnl Reps
Format: Country; *Hrs. of News Programming:* news progmg 5 hrs wkly; *No. News Employees:* 2; *Target Audience:* 18-80; young to elderly; *Adv. Rates:* 8.75; 8.75; 8.75; 8.75
Merv Lawson, General Manager
Kathy Puckett, General Sales Mgr
Paul Lyons, Chief Engineer

Science Hill

WYKY
01-01-2008; 106.1 MHz FM; 1.95 kw; 584 ft.; N37 7 53 W84 32 21
290 WTLO Road, Somerset, KY 42502 US
(606) 678-8151; *Fax:* (606) 678-8152
www.somerset106.com
License: Science Hill, Pulaski County, KY held by Forcht Broadcasting
Group Owner: Forcht Broadcasting
Arbitron Metro Market: Science Hill, KY; *Format:* Adult Contemp
Terry Forcht, President
Mike Tarter, General Manager
Kevin Wilson, General Sales Mgr
Greg Moore, Programming Director

Scottsville

WLCK
02-27-1958; 1250 kHz AM; *Hrs Open:* 6 AM-9 PM; 0.86 kw-D, ND1; 0.076 kw-N, ND1; N36 44 25 W86 10 31
Mailing Address: P.O. Box 158, Scottsville, KY 42164 US
Second Address: 102 1/2 Public Sq., Scottsville, KY 42164
(270) 237-3149; *Fax:* (270) 237-3533
License: Scottsville, KY held by Skytower Communications Group LLC
Nat'l Network: USA
Arbitron Metro Market: Bowling Green, KY; *Format:* Religious; *Hrs. of News Programming:* news progmg 12 hrs wkly; *No. News Employees:* 1; *Target Audience:* General.
Darrin Evans, President
Chris Nelson, General Manager
Max Murphy, Chief Engineer

WVLE
02-26-1967; 99.3 MHz FM; 6 kw; 328 ft.; N36 44 25 W86 10 31
Mailing Address: P.O. Box 158, Scottsville, KY 42164 US
Second Address: 104 1/2 Public Sq., Scottsville, KY 42164
(270) 237-3148; *Fax:* (270) 237-3533
www.wvle.net
License: Scottsville, Allen County, KY
Arbitron Metro Market: Bowling Green, KY; *Format:* Country
Greg Gribbins, General Manager

Shelbyville

WCND
06-03-1964; 940 kHz AM; 0.25 kw-D, ND2; 0.01 kw-N, ND2; N38 12 48 W85 10 16
P.O. Box 1505, Glasgow, KY 42142 US
(248) 557-3500; *Fax:* (248) 557-2950
www.birach.com
sima@BIRACH.Com
License: Shelbyville, KY held by Birach Broadcasting Corporation
Arbitron Metro Market: Louisville, KY; *Format:* Oldies; *Hrs. of News Programming:* news progmg one hr wkly; *No. News Employees:* 1; *Target Audience:* 35-64; upscale, white collar
Rick Loesch, President
Cuervo Curtis, Operations Dir
Tom Charity, General Sales Mgr
Sam Walker, Programming Director

WVKY(FM)
09-30-1989; 101.7 MHz FM; *Hrs Open:* 24; 6 kw; Ant 328 ft; N38 12 48 W85 10 16 *Rebroadcasts:* Simulcasts WKRD(AM) Louisville 100%
4000 Radio Drive, Louisville, KY 40218
(502) 479-2222; *Fax:* (502) 479-2308
www.790wkrd.com
License: Shelbyville, Shelby County, KY held by Southern Belle LLC
Nat'l Network: Fox Sports
Population Served: 750,000; *Arbitron Metro Market:* Louisville, KY
Jim Fenn, Programming Director
Bill Gentry, Promotions Manager

WVKY
12-01-1962; 101.7 MHz FM; *Hrs Open:* 24; 6 kw; 328 ft.; N38 12 48 W85 10 16
115 W. Maine St., Frankfort, KY 40601 US
(502) 875-1130
froggykycountry.com
License: Shelbyville, Jessamine County, KY held by Christian Broadcasting System Ltd.
Group Owner: Christian Broadcasting System Ltd.; (acq 7-1-2006; grpsl).

Arbitron Metro Market: Lexington, KY; *Format:* News, News/Talk, 86

Shepherdsville

WGHL

01-01-1993; 105.1 MHz FM; 1.9 kw; 591 ft.; N38 4 55 W85 47 6
520 S. 4th St., 2nd Fl., Louisville, KY 40202 US
(502) 625-1220; *Fax:* (502) 584-1051
www.oldschool1051.com
easyrock1051@gmail.com
License: Shepherdsville, Bullitt County, KY held by Alpha Media Licensee LLC
Group Owner: Alpha Media LLC; (acq 4-17-2014; grpsl).
Arbitron Metro Market: Louisville, KY; *Format:* Urban Contemporary
Dale Schaefer, Vice President and Market Manager
Tom Ulmer, General Sales Mgr
Tommy Lee Gudding, Programming Director
Sarah Jordan, Promotions Director

Smiths Grove

WUHU

12-01-1986; 107.1 MHz FM; *Hrs Open:* 24; 50 kw; 492 ft.; N36 50 35 W86 15 30
P. O. Box 900, Bowling Green, KY 42102 US
(270) 843-3333; *Fax:* (270) 843-0454
www.allhitwuhu107.com
License: Smiths Grove, Warren County, KY held by Forever Communications Inc.
Group Owner: Forever Communications Inc.; (acq 2001)
Nat'l Reps: Christal
Arbitron Metro Market: Bowling Green, KY; *Format:* Adult Contemp; *Target Audience:* 18-49.; *Adv. Rates:* 40; 35; 35; 20
Christine Hillard, President
Joe O'Neal, General Sales Mgr
Brooke Summers, Programming Director
Executive VP of Sales

*WBFK

91.1 MHz FM; 750 watts; 190 meters; N37 06 39 W89 58 44
PO Box 7441, Amarillo, TX
(806) 353-1488; *Fax:* (806) 353-1542
www.calvaryamarillo.org
License: Smiths Grove, KY held by Grace Community Church of Amarillo

William Gehm, President

Somerset

*WDCL-FM

07-01-1985; 89.7 MHz FM; *Hrs Open:* 24; 100 kw; 571 ft.; N37 9 29 W85 9 50 *Rebroadcasts:* Rebroadcasts WKYU-FM Bowling Green 100%
1 Big Red Way, Bowling Green, KY 42101 US
(270) 745-5489(800) 599-9598; *Fax:* (270) 745-6272
www.wkyufm.org
wkyufm@wku.edu
License: Somerset, Pulaski County, KY held by Western Kentucky University.
Nat'l Network: PRI; NPR
Arbitron Metro Market: Somerset, KY; *Format:* News *Special Programming:* Folk 5 hrs, jazz 15 hrs wkly; *Hrs. of News Programming:* news progmg 35 hrs wkly; *No. News Employees:* 3; *Target Audience:* General.
John Campbell, Operations Dir
Peter Bryant, General Manager/Station Manager
Kevin Willis, News Director
Don Eastman, Chief Engineer
Lee Stott, Music Director

WLLK-FM

08-14-1989; 102.3 MHz FM; *Hrs Open:* 24; 6 kw; 328 ft.; N37 4 41 W84 40 39
Mailing Address: P.O. Box 740, Somerset, KY 42502 US
Second Address: 101 First Radio Ln., Somerset, KY 42503
(606) 678-5151; *Fax:* (606) 678-2026
www.lake1023.com
License: Somerset, Pulaski County, KY held by Capstar TX LLC
Group Owner: iHeartMedia; (acq 12-8-2000; grpsl).
Format: Adult Contemp; *Hrs. of News Programming:* news progmg 6 hrs wkly; *No. News Employees:* 1; *Target Audience:* 25-54.; *Adv. Rates:* 20; 15; 18; 10
Bruce Welker, Market President
Rod Zimmerman, Programming Director
Wynona Padgett, Promotions Director
Jim Mercer, Chief Engineer
Greg Wesley, Business Manager
Paula McKinney, Traffic Manager
Mike Murphy, Production Manager
Josh McKinney, Sports Director

WKEQ

09-01-1964; 97.1 MHz FM; 27.5 kw; 659 ft.; N36 57 40 W84 34 7
Mailing Address: P.O. Box 740, Somerset, KY 42501 US
Second Address: 101 First Radio Ln., Somerset, KY 42503
(606) 678-5151; *Fax:* (606) 678-2026
www.q97rock.com
License: Somerset, Pulaski County, KY held by Capstar TX LLC
Group Owner: iHeartMedia
Wire Services: NOAA Weather
Format: Classic Rock
Bruce Welker, Market President
Rod Zimmerman, Senior Vice President of Programming
Wynona Padgett, Promotions Director
Jim Mercer, Chief Engineer
Paula McKinney, Traffic Manager
Mike Murphy, Production Manager
Josh McKinney,Sports Director

WSFC

12-14-1947; 1240 kHz AM; *Hrs Open:* 24; 0.79 kw-U, ND1; N37 7 3 W84 36 42
Mailing Address: P.O.Box 740, Somerset, KY 42501 US
Second Address: 101 First Radio Ln., Somerset, KY 42503
(606) 678-5151; *Fax:* (606) 678-2026
www.wsfcam.com
License: Somerset, KY held by Capstar TX LLC
Group Owner: iHeartMedia; (acq 12-8-2000; grpsl).
Nat'l Reps: Rgnl Reps; *Wire Services:* NOAA Weather
Format: Sports; *Hrs. of News Programming:* news progmg 15 hrs wkly; *No. News Employees:* 1; *Target Audience:* General.
Rod Zimmerman, Senior Vice President of Programming
Wynona Padgett, Promotions Director
Mike Murphy, Production Manager

*WTHL

07-16-1987; 90.5 MHz FM; 50 kw; 591 ft.; N37 7 52 W84 33 15
93 Rainbow Terrace Road, Somerset, KY 42503 US
(606) 679-6300
www.kingofkingsradio.net
License: Somerset, Pulaski County, KY held by Somerset Educational Broadcasting Foundation.
Nat'l Network: Moody
Arbitron Metro Market: Somerset,KY; *Format:* Religious *Special Programming:* Gospel under 20 hrs wkly; *Target Audience:* 40 plus; people with conservative, traditional & relg values & interests
David Carr, General Manager
Carolyn Jones, Programming Director
Marvin Whitaker, Chief Engineer

WTLO

11-01-1958; 1480 kHz AM
Mailing Address: P.O. Box 1480, P.O. Drawer, Somerset, KY 42501 US
Second Address: 290 WTLO Rd., Somerset, KY 42503
(606) 678-8151; *Fax:* (606) 678-8152
www.wtloam.com
wtlo@usa.com
License: Somerset, KY held by Forcht Broadcasting
Group Owner: Forcht Broadcasting
Nat'l Network: ABC
Arbitron Metro Market: Somerset, KY; *Format:* Oldies *Special Programming:* Farm one hr, relg 4 hrs wkly; *Target Audience:* 45 plus; upscale & highly mobile
Greg Moore, Program Director
Amy Strouf, Digital Marketing Director
Kevin Wilson, General Advertising Manager
Misty Raines, Account Executive
Mike Tarter, General Manager
Dave Childders, General Sales Mgr
Josh Good, ProgrammingDirector
Kevin Wilson, Account Executive
Amy Stroud, Digital Media Coordinator
Greg Moore, Production

*WKVY

01-01-2004; 88.1 MHz FM; *Hrs Open:* 24; 4 kw vert; 526 ft.; N37 4 36 W84 48 39
1425 N Market Blvd., Suite 9, Sacramento, CA 95834 US
(800) 525-5683; *Fax:* (916) 251-1650
www.klove.com
klove@klove.com
License: Somerset, Pulaski County, KY held by Educational Media Foundation.
Group Owner: EMF Broadcasting
Nat'l Network: K-Love
Arbitron Metro Market: Somerset, KY; *Format:* Christian; *No. News Employees:* 13; *Target Audience:* 25-44; Judeo Christian, female
Darrell Chambliss, Chairman
Mike Novak, President and CEO
Chip Bailey, Operations Dir
David Pierce, Chief Creative Officer and Programming Director
Ed Lenane, News Director
Sam Wallington, Engineering Dir
Marya Morgan, NewsReporter
Richard Hunt, News Reporter
Alan Mason, Chief Operating Officer
Dan Antonelli, Chief Business Development Officer
Eric Moser, Chief Financial Officer
Brian Burger, Vice President of Human Resources

Springfield

WYSB

02-17-1989; 102.7 MHz FM; *Hrs Open:* 24; 4 kw; 354 ft.; N37 41 43 W85 19 6
253 West Main Street, Lebanon, KY 40033 US
(502) 348-1027; *Fax:* (888) 531-6397
www.1027wysb.com
info@1027wysb.com
License: Springfield, Washington County, KY held by Washington County CBC Inc.
Group Owner: Commonwealth Broadcasting Corp.; (acq 10-30-97; $350,000).
Nat'l Network: ABC; *Regional Network:* Ky. News Net
Arbitron Metro Market: Springfield, KY; *Format:* Adult Contemp *Special Programming:* Sports 12 hrs, farm 10 hrs wkly; *Hrs. of News Programming:* news progmg 20 hrs wkly; *No. News Employees:* 1; *Target Audience:* 25-55.
Dale Thornhill, General Manager
Greg Gribbins, General Sales Mgr
Andrew Colley, Programming Director
Tom Redmon, News Director

St. Matthews

WVEZ

04-01-1967; 106.9 MHz FM; 24.5 kw; 669 ft.; N38 22 19 W85 49 33
3773 Howard Hughes Pwy, Suite 300n, Las Vegas, NV 89109 US
(502) 589-4800; *Fax:* (502) 583-4820
www.lite1069.com
info@lite1069.com
License: St. Matthews, Jefferson County, KY held by SM-WVEZ LLC
Group Owner: SummitMedia LLC
Arbitron Metro Market: Louisville, KY; *Format:* Adult Contemp *Special Programming:* Delilah; *Target Audience:* 24-54; upper-scale, working women
Shane Collins, Operations Dir
Todd Pitt, General Sales Mgr
Don Nordin, Programming Director
Brian Eichenberger, Promotions Manager

Stamping Ground

WLXO

12-15-1994; 96.1 MHz FM; 6 kw; 328 ft.; N38 12 15 W84 32 51
401 W. Main Street, Suite 301, Lexington, KY 40507 US
(859) 294-0961; *Fax:* (859) 233-1517
www.hank961.com
License: Stamping Ground, Scott County, KY held by Clarity Communications Inc.
Nat'l Network: Talk Radio Network; *Nat'l Reps:* Katz Radio
Arbitron Metro Market: Lexington-Fayette, KY; *Format:* Talk; *Hrs. of News Programming:* News progmg 20 hrs wkly
Charlie Cohn, President
James MacFarlane, General Manager

Stanford

*WXKY-FM

05-22-1967; 96.3 MHz FM; 4.9 kw; 732 ft.; N37 31 27 W84 52 12
P. O. Box 300, Stanford, KY 40484 US
(916) 251-1600; *Fax:* (916) 251-1650
www.klove.com
License: Stanford, Lincoln County, KY held by Educational Media Foundation.
Group Owner: EMF Broadcasting; (acq 10-20-2004; $800,000).
Nat'l Network: K-Love
Format: Christian
Mike Novak, President
Chip Bailey, Operations Dir
David Pierce, Programming Director

Ed Lenane, News Director
Sam Wallington, Engineering Dir
Marya Morgan, News Reporter
Richard Hunt, News Reporter

Stanton

WBFC
06-21-1975; 1470 kHz AM
Mailing Address: P.O. Box 577, Stanton, KY 40380 US
Second Address: 2401 Paint Creek Rd., Stanton, KY 40380
(606) 663-6631; *Fax:* (606) 663-2267
www.wbfcam.com
License: Stanton, KY held by Combs Broadcasting Inc.
Arbitron Metro Market: Stanton,KY; *Format:* Gospel
James H. Combs, CEO/COO
James Harold Combs, President
Beverly Combs, General Manager
Daniel Morton, Vice President
Beverly Combs, Secretary and Treasurer

WSKV-FM
08-10-1974; 104.9 MHz FM; *Hrs Open:* 24; 720 w; 680 ft; N37 45 43 W83 50 36
Mailing Address: Box 610, Stanton, KY 40380
Second Address: 28 W. Hall's Rd., Stanton, KY 40380
(606) 663-2811; *Fax:* (606) 663-2895
www.wskvfm.com
License: Stanton, Powell County, KY held by Moore Country 104 LLC
Nat'l Network: KNN
Population Served: 120,000 *Hrs. of News Programming:* 6 hrs per week; *Target Audience:* General.
A.C. Moore, Owner
Ethan Moore, General Manager
Ethan Moore, General Sales Mgr
Mary Moore, Programming Director
Ethan Moore, Promotions Manager
Ethan Moore, Chief Engineer

Sturgis

WMSK-FM
11-21-1960; 101.3 MHz FM; *Hrs Open:* 24; 6 kw; N37 40 00 W87 55 40
Mailing Address: P.O. Box 369, Morganfield, KY
Second Address: 1339 US 60 W., Morganfield, KY 42437
(270) 389-1550; *Fax:* (270) 389-1553
wmsk@bellsouth.net
License: Sturgis, Union County, KY held by Henson Media Inc.
Nat'l Network: Jones Radio Networks; *Regional Network:* Ky. News Net; *Nat'l Reps:* Rgnl Reps; *Wire Services:* AP
Hrs. of News Programming: News progmg 20 hrs wkly; *Target Audience:* General; adults 25-64; *Adv. Rates:* 7.00; 7.00; 7.00; 7.00
Edward Henson, President
John Robinson, General Manager
Doug Collins, General Sales Mgr
Rhonda Gibson, Traffic Manager

Tompkinsville

WTKY
05-28-1960; 1370 kHz AM; *Hrs Open:* daytimer; 2.1 kw-D, NDD; N36 43 27 W85 40 53
341 Radio Station Road, Tompkinsville, KY 42167 US
(270) 487-6119; *Fax:* (270) 487-8462
kixcountry@scrtc.com
License: Tompkinsville, KY held by Whittimore Enterprises Inc.
Nat'l Network: USA; *Nat'l Reps:* Rgnl Reps
Arbitron Metro Market: Tompkinsville, KY; *Format:* Country
Special Programming: gospel/religious & bluegrass; *Hrs. of News Programming:* progmg 4 hrs wkly; *No. News Employees:* 2; *Target Audience:* 55+. *Adv. Rates:* 35; 28; 32; 28
Randy Kerr, General Manager

WTKY-FM
01-20-1972; 92.1 MHz FM; *Hrs Open:* 6AM-11PM; 5.3 kw; 351 ft.; N36 49 7 W85 39 32
341 Radio Station Road, Tompkinsville, KY 42167 US
(270) 487-6119; *Fax:* (270) 487-8462
kixcountry@scrtc.com
License: Tompkinsville, Monroe County, KY held by Whittimore Enterprises Inc.
Nat'l Network: USA; *Nat'l Reps:* Rgnl Reps
Arbitron Metro Market: Tompkinsville, KY; *Format:* Country; *Hrs. of News Programming:* news progmg 2 hrs wkly; *No. News Employees:* 2; *Target Audience:* Female 18-45.; *Adv. Rates:* 35; 28; 32; 28
Randy Kerr, General Manager

WKWY
01-01-2003; 102.7 MHz FM; *Hrs Open:* 6AM - 11PM; 6 kw; 315 ft.; N36 43 27 W85 40 53
341 Radio Station Road, Tompkinsville, KY 42167 US
(270) 487-6119; *Fax:* (270) 487-8462
License: Tompkinsville, Monroe County, KY held by Whittimore Enterprises
Nat'l Network: USA; *Nat'l Reps:* Rgnl Reps
Arbitron Metro Market: Tompkinsville, KY; *Format:* Country; *Hrs. of News Programming:* news progmg 2 wkly; *No. News Employees:* 2; *Adv. Rates:* 35; 28; 32; 28
Randy Kerr, General Manager

Upton

***WJCR-FM**
02-01-1990; 90.1 MHz FM; *Hrs Open:* 24; 100 kw; 384 ft.; N37 25 57 W86 1 50
Mailing Address: P.O. Box 91, Upton, KY 42784 US
Second Address: 13101 Raider Hollow Rd., Upton, KY 42784
(270) 369-8614; *Fax:* (270) 369-7402
www.wjcr.org
wjcrfm@yahoo.com
License: Upton, Hardin County, KY held by FM 90.1 Inc.
Format: Gospel *Special Programming:* 5 hrs live prayline wkly; *Target Audience:* General.
Lauree K. Powell, CFO
Don Powell, President
Gary Richardson, Station Manager/Programming Director
Larry Baysinger, Chief Engineer

Valley Station

WSYI
01-01-1982; 105.9 MHz FM; 1.9 kw; 413 ft; N38 08 16 W85 56 06
9960 Corporate Campus Dr., Suite 3600, Louisville, KY 93012
(502) 339-9470; *Fax:* (502) 423-3139
www.salemradiogroup.com
License: Valley Station, Jefferson County, KY held by WAY Media Group Inc.
Group Owner: WAY Media Group Inc.; (acq 10-2-2008; $3 million)
Nat'l Network: Salem Radio Network; *Nat'l Reps:* Salem
Arbitron Metro Market: Louisville, KY
CC Matthews, Operations Dir
Tim Hartlage, General Manager

Vanceburg

WKKS
06-01-1958; 1570 kHz AM; 1 kw-D, NDD; N38 35 50 W83 20 50
1106 Fairlane Drive, Vanceburg, KY 41179 US
(606) 796-3031; *Fax:* (606) 796-6186
License: Vanceburg, KY held by Brown Communications Inc.
Format: Country
Dennis Brown, President

WKKS-FM
01-01-1983; 104.9 MHz FM; 3 kw; 299 ft.; N38 36 19 W83 19 57
1106 Fairlane Drive, P.O. Box 10, Vanceburg, KY 41179 US
(606) 796-3031; *Fax:* (606) 796-6186
License: Vanceburg, Lewis County, KY held by Brown Communications Inc.
Format: Contemporary Hits/Top 40
Dennis Brown, President

Vancleve

WMTC-FM
01-01-1991; 99.9 MHz FM; *Hrs Open:* 24; 6 kw; 328 ft.; N37 36 23 W83 26 48
1036 Highway 541, Jackson, KY 41339 US
(606) 666-5006; *Fax:* (606) 666-7534
www.mountaingospel.org
studio@mountaingospel.org
License: Vancleve, Breathitt County, KY held by Kentucky Mountain Holiness Assn.
Arbitron Metro Market: Vancleve, KY; *Format:* Christian, Religious *Special Programming:* Farm one hr wkly; *Adv. Rates:* 3; 3; 3; 3
Seldon Short, Operations Dir
Dan Lorimer, General Manager
Jennifer Cox, Programming Director
Theresa Kerley, Disc Jockey
Gordon Sampsel, Music Director

Versailles

WCDA
07-16-1973; 106.3 MHz FM; *Hrs Open:* 24; 3.7 kw; 420 ft.; N38 2 51 W84 29 57
401 West Main Street, Suite 301, Lexington, KY 40507 US
(859) 280-1063; *Fax:* (859) 233-1517
www.your1063.com
License: Versailles, Woodford County, KY held by L.M. Communications Inc.
Group Owner: L M Communications Inc.; acq 9-3-98).
Nat'l Reps: Katz Radio
Arbitron Metro Market: Lexington, KY; *Format:* Adult Contemp; *Hrs. of News Programming:* news progmg 2 hrs wkly; *No. News Employees:* 1; *Target Audience:* 25-49; female
Lynn Martin, President
James MacFarlane, General Manager
James McFarlane, Promotions Manager

Vine Grove

WTHX
10-05-1993; 101.5 MHz FM; *Hrs Open:* 24; 6 kw; 328 ft; N37 35 07 W85 50 20
611 W. Poplar St., Suite C2, Elizabethtown, KY 42701
(270) 763-0800; *Fax:* (270) 769-6349
License: Vine Grove, Hardin County, KY held by Elizabethtown CBC Inc.
Group Owner: Commonwealth Broadcasting Corp.; (acq 7-1-00; grpsl).
Regional Reps: Rgnl Reps.
Population Served: 200,000 *Hrs. of News Programming:* news progmg 3 hrs wkly; *No. News Employees:* 1; *Target Audience:* 25-45; males; *Adv. Rates:* 18; 18; 18; 10
Steve Newberry, President
Dan Diaz, Operations Dir
Barb Smith, General Manager
Sarah Hart, Sales Manager
Mark Conover, Programming Director
Mike Graham, Engineering Dir

Virgie

WZLK
11-15-1992; 107.5 MHz FM; 1.45 kw; 679 ft.; N37 27 57 W82 33 4
1240 Radio Dr., PO Box 2200, Pikeville, KY 41501 US
(606) 437-4051; *Fax:* (606) 432-2809
www.1075z.com
License: Virgie, Pike County, KY held by East Kentucky Broadcasting Corp.
Group Owner: East Kentucky Broadcasting Corp.; (acq 5-14-2003; $531,273 with WLSI(AM) Pikeville).
Arbitron Metro Market: Virgie, KY; *Format:* Contemporary Hits/Top 40
Jill Fraley, General Sales Mgr

Warfield

***WNON**
91.3 MHz FM; kw
Highway 292 South, Warfield, KY 41267 US
(606) 395-6831
License: Warfield, Martin County, KY held by Calvary Temple Community Church.
Regional Network: ABN Radio
Arbitron Metro Market: Lebanon, IN
Arnold Damron, President

West Liberty

WLKS
07-25-1965; 1450 kHz AM; *Hrs Open:* 24; 1 kw-U, ND1; N37 55 36 W83 16 41
129 College St., West Liberty, KY 41472 US
License: West Liberty, KY held by Morgan County Industries Inc.
Group Owner: Morgan County Industries Inc.
Nat'l Reps: Rgnl Reps
Format: Oldies *Special Programming:* Farm 5 hrs wkly; *Hrs. of News Programming:* news progmg 35 hrs wkly; *No. News Employees:* 1; *Target Audience:* General.; *Adv. Rates:* 4; 4; 4; 4
Merv Lawson, General Manager
Paul Lyons, Chief Engineer

WLKS-FM
01-01-1994; 102.9 MHz FM; *Hrs Open:* 24; 6 kw; 328 ft.; N38 2 16 W83 20 18
129 College St., West Liberty, KY 41472 US
License: West Liberty, Morgan County, KY held by Morgan County Industries Inc.
Group Owner: Morgan County Industries Inc.
Format: Country
Merv Lawson, General Manager
Paul Lyons, Chief Engineer

Whitesburg

*WMMT
11-01-1985; 88.7 MHz FM; *Hrs Open:* 24; 1 kw horiz, 15 kw vert; 1470 ft.; N37 6 38 W82 44 15
306 Madison Street, Whitesburg, KY 41858 US
(606) 633-0108; *Fax:* (606) 633-1009
www.appalshop.org
wmmtfm@appalshop.org
License: Whitesburg, Letcher County, KY held by Appalshop Inc.
Regional Network: Kentucky Educational Television
Arbitron Metro Market: Whitesburg, KY; *Format:* Variety/Diverse; *Target Audience:* General.
Cheryl Marshall, General Manager

WTCW
02-19-1953; 920 kHz AM; 4.2 kw-D, ND1; 0.043 kw-N, ND1; N37 8 46 W82 46 1
P.O. Box 288, Mayking, KY 41837 US
(606) 633-2711; *Fax:* (606) 633-4445
www.wtcwam.com
wxkq@yahoo.com
License: Whitesburg, KY
Group Owner: Forcht Broadcasting; (acq 1-1-86; $765,000 with co-located FM;
Nat'l Network: CBS; *Nat'l Reps:* Rgnl Reps
Arbitron Metro Market: Whitesburg, KY; *Format:* Country; *Target Audience:* 30 plus.
Kevin Day, General Manager
Bob Scott, On-Air and Production Director
Lisa Elkins, Account Executive

WXKQ-FM
11-25-1964; 103.9 MHz FM; 0.28 kw; 1500 ft.; N37 6 38 W82 44 15
P.O. Box 288, Corbin, KY 40702 US
(606) 633-2711; *Fax:* (606) 633-4445
www.1039thebulldog.com
License: Whitesburg, Letcher County, KY held by Forcht Broadcasting
Group Owner: Forcht Broadcasting
Arbitron Metro Market: Whitesburg, KY; *Format:* Contemporary Hits/Top 40
Kevin Day, General Manager
Bob Scott, Production Director
Beth Wright, Business Marketing Specialist
Doc West, Programming Director
Lisa Elkins, Account Executive

Whitesville

WXCM
05-01-1993; 97.1 MHz FM; 4 kw; 404 ft.; N37 41 50 W86 59 28
Mailing Address: P.O. Box 150846, Nashville, TN 37215 US
Second Address: 1115 Tamarack Rd., Suite 500, Owensboro, KY 42301
(270) 683-5200; *Fax:* (270) 688-0108
www.owensbororadio.com
License: Whitesville, Daviess County, KY held by The Cromwell Group Inc. of Kentucky.
Group Owner: The Cromwell Group Inc.; (acq 1993; $170,000;
Arbitron Metro Market: Whitesville, KY; *Format:* Rock/AOR; *No. News Employees:* 1; *Target Audience:* Males in 30's.; *Adv. Rates:* 20; 20; 20; 15
Brack Stacy, Market Manager
Brack Stacy, Operations Manager
Mel Ingleheart, Business Manager
Kevin Riecke, Operations Dir
Jan Catinna, General Manager
Jeff Nalley, General Sales Mgr
Mike Chaney, News Director

Whitley City

WHAY
12-01-1990; 98.3 MHz FM; *Hrs Open:* 24; 5.1 kw; 354 ft.; N36 39 40 W84 26 53
Box 69, Whitley City, KY 42653 US
(606) 376-2218; *Fax:* (606) 376-5146
www.hay98.com
whayradio@highland.net
License: Whitley City, McCreary County, KY held by Tim Lavender.
Format: Triple A; *Hrs. of News Programming:* News progmg 5 hrs wkly; *Target Audience:* 30 plus.
Tim Lavender, General Manager

Wickliffe

WBCE
01-04-1981; 1200 kHz AM; 1 kw-D, NDD; N36 58 54 W89 4 39
Mailing Address: P. O. Box 128, Wickliffe, KY 42087 US
Second Address: 1136 Barlow Rd., Wickliffe, KY 42087
(740) 548-5919; *Fax:* (740) 548-5911
License: Wickliffe, KY held by WBCE Inc.
Format: Christian
Holly Casagrande, General Manager
Margaret Litton, Programming Director

WGKY
01-01-1987; 95.9 MHz FM; *Hrs Open:* 24; 2.45 kw; 361 ft.; N36 56 17 W88 58 1
930 Wickliffe Road, P.O. Box 500, Wickliffe, KY 42087 US
(270) 538-5251; *Fax:* (270) 415-0599
www.959wgky.com
License: Wickliffe, Ballard County, KY held by W. Russell Withers Jr.
Group Owner: Withers Broadcasting Co.; (acq 2-21-2006; $400,000)
Nat'l Network: Jones Radio Networks; *Regional Network:* Brownfield *Regional Reps:* Rgnl Reps.
Format: Oldies; *Hrs. of News Programming:* News progmg 5 hrs wkly; *Target Audience:* 24-54; rural homeowners, farmers
Clay Reed, Operations Dir
Rick Lambert, General Manager
Kathy Duncan, Station Manager

Williamsburg

WEKC
09-21-1981; 710 kHz AM; 4.2 kw-D, NDD; N36 46 28 W84 10 5
Mailing Address: Rt 550 West, Hindman, KY 41822 US
Second Address: 402 Main St., Williamsburg, KY 40769
(606) 549-3000; *Fax:* (606) 539-0916
License: Williamsburg, KY held by Gerald Parks
Nat'l Network: USA
Arbitron Metro Market: Williamsburg, KY; *Format:* Gospel, Religious; *Hrs. of News Programming:* News progmg 5 hrs wkly; *Target Audience:* General; young adults, All ages, race & creed; *Adv. Rates:* 10, 10, 10, 6
Kay Parks, Station Manager

*WCWC
03-07-1959; 1430 kHz AM; *Hrs Open:* Daylight
C/O Fletcher, Heald Esq, 1300 N 17th Sr, 11th Flr, Arlington, VA 22209 US
radiowcwc@bellsouth.net
License: Williamsburg, KY held by Whitley County Board of Education
Arbitron Metro Market: Williamsburg, KY
David Estes, General Manager

WEZJ-FM
11-01-1990; 104.3 MHz FM; 6.2 kw; 656 ft.; N36 44 43 W84 11 24
522 Main Street, Williamsburg, KY 40769 US
(606) 549-2285; *Fax:* (606) 549-5565
License: Williamsburg, Whitley County, KY held by Whitley Broadcasting Co. Inc.
Nat'l Reps: Rgnl Reps
Arbitron Metro Market: Williamsburg, KY; *Format:* Country
David Estes, General Manager

Williamstown

WNKR
04-01-1992; 106.7 MHz FM; *Hrs Open:* 24; 1.8 kw; 607 ft.; N38 41 19 W84 35 7
11 N Main Street, Dry Ridge, KY 41035 US
(859) 824-9106; *Fax:* (859) 824-9835
www.1067wnkr.com
wnkrproduction@fuse.net
License: Williamstown, Grant County, KY held by Grant County Broadcasters Inc.
Regional Network: Ky. News Net; *Nat'l Reps:* Rgnl Reps
Arbitron Metro Market: Cincinnati, OH; *Format:* Country; *Hrs. of News Programming:* news progmg 6 hrs wkly; *No. News Employees:* 1; *Target Audience:* 35-54; adults; *Adv. Rates:* 60;60; 60; 50
Robert Wallace, President
Jay Anthony, Operations Dir
Jeffrey Ziesmann, General Manager
Laura Eisenmenger, General Sales Mgr
Jim Stitt, Chief Engineer

Wilmore

*WLAI
10-27-1969; 107.1 MHz FM; *Hrs Open:* 24; 3.6 kw; 128 m; N37 40 28 W84 46 06 *Rebroadcasts:* Rebroadcasts KLRD(FM) Yucaipa, CA 100%
2351 Sunset Blvd., Suite 170-218, Rocklin, CA 41144
(916) 251-1600; *Fax:* (916) 251-1650
www.air1.com
info@air1.com
License: Wilmore, Boyle County, KY held by Educational Media Foundation.
Group Owner: EMF Broadcasting; (acq 5-20-2005; $1 million).
Nat'l Network: Air 1
Population Served: 200,000; *Arbitron Metro Market:* Lexington, KY
Mike Novak, President
Chip Bailey, Operations Dir
David Pierce, Programming Director
Ed Lenane, News Director
Sam Wallington, Engineering Dir
Marya Morgan, News Reporter
Richard Hunt, News Reporter

WVRB
09-18-1995; 95.3 MHz FM; *Hrs Open:* 24; 4.1 kw; 397 ft.; N37 57 37 W84 32 42
8686 Michael Lane, Fairfield, OH 45014 US
(707) 528-9236; *Fax:* (707) 528-9246
License: Wilmore, Jessamine County, KY held by Vernon R. Baldwin Inc.
Group Owner: Vernon R Baldwin Broadcasting Inc.; acq 7-26-94;
Arbitron Metro Market: Lexington, KY; *Format:* Christian; *Target Audience:* 20-45; Christians baby boomers
Marcella Baldwin, President

Winchester

WKQQ
01-01-1974; 100.1 MHz FM; *Hrs Open:* 24; 20 kw; 636 ft.; N38 7 24 W84 26 37
2601 Nicholasville Road, Lexington, KY 40503 US
(859) 422-1000; *Fax:* (859) 422-1038
www.wkqq.com
info@wkqq.com
License: Winchester, Clark County, KY held by Citicasters Licenses Inc.
Group Owner: iHeartMedia; (acq 5-4-99; grpsl).
Arbitron Metro Market: Lexington-Fayette, KY; *Format:* Classic Rock; *Hrs. of News Programming:* news progmg 3 hrs wkly; *No. News Employees:* 1; *Target Audience:* 18-49; women
Michael Jordan, Programming Director
Mandy Daugherty, Promotions Director
Marci Adams, Digital Program Director

Louisiana

Abbeville

KFTE
06-01-1974; 105.1 MHz FM; *Hrs Open:* 24; 25 kw; 300 ft; N30 00 40 W92 07 21
1749 Bertrand Dr., Lafayette, LA 70510
(337) 233-6000; *Fax:* (337) 234-7360
License: Abbeville, Vermilion County, LA
Group Owner: Townsquare Media
Arbitron Metro Market: Lafayette, LA; *Adv. Rates:* 25; 22; 25; 17
Mike Grimsley, General Manager
Frank Malambri, Sales Director
Tard, Programming Director

KROF
07-09-1948; 960 kHz AM; *Hrs Open:* 24; 1 kw-D, ND1; 0.095 kw-N, ND1; N30 0 40 W92 7 21
1749 Bertrand Drive, Lafayette, LA 70506 US
(337) 233-6000; *Fax:* (337) 234-7360
www.talkradio960.com
License: Abbeville, LA
Group Owner: Townsquare Media; (acq 12-7-2001; grpsl)
Arbitron Metro Market: Lafayette, LA; *Format:* Talk; *Adv. Rates:* 22; 15; 15; na
Mike Grimsley, General Manager
Frank Malambri, General Sales Mgr
Bernadette Lee, Programming Director
Kyle Vidrine, Chief Engineer

Alexandria

*KAPM
06-01-1998; 91.7 MHz FM; 1 kw; 128 ft.; N31 16 4 W92 26 24
P.O. Box 3206, Tupelo, MS 38803 US
(662) 844-8888; *Fax:* (662) 842-6791
www.afr.net
faq@afa.net
License: Alexandria, Rapides County, LA held by American Family Association.
Group Owner: American Family Radio
Arbitron Metro Market: Tupelo, MO; *Format:* Christian, Religious

Tim Wildmon, President
Donald Wildmon, Founder
Buddy Smith, Sr. VP
Ed Vitaglio, Executive VP
Randy Sharp, Director Of Special Requests
Meeke Addison, Director Of Communications
Abraham Hamilton III, General Counsel & PublicPolicy

KDBS
12-01-1953; 1410 kHz AM; *Hrs Open:* 24
600 Congress Avenue, Suite 1400, Austin, TX 78701 US
(318) 443-7454(318) 445-1234; *Fax:* (318) 445-7231
www.kdixie.com
daveg@kswl.com
License: Alexandria, LA held by Cenla Broadcasting Licensing Co. LLC.
Group Owner: Cenla Broadcasting Co. Inc.; (acq 11-13-2006; grpsl)
Nat'l Network: ESPN Radio
Arbitron Metro Market: Alexandria, LA; *Format:* Sports
Charlie Sopraz, Operations Dir
Taylor Thompson, General Manager
Tish Robertson, General Sales Mgr
Dave Grachien, Programming Director
Sybil Ford, News Director
Linnie Dupree, Chief Engineer

KEDG
01-01-2001; 106.9 MHz FM; 6 kw; 328 ft.; N31 18 26 W92 23 56
Mailing Address: 188 South Bellevue, Suite 222, Memphis, TN 38104 US
Second Address: 1115 Texas Ave, Alexandria, LA 71301
(318) 445-1234(318) 487-1035; *Fax:* (318) 473-1960
License: Alexandria, Rapides County, LA held by Flinn Broadcasting Corp.
Arbitron Metro Market: Alexandria, LA; *Format:* Urban Contemporary
Taylor Thompson, General Manager
Randy James, Programming Director

KMXH
02-01-1993; 93.9 MHz FM; 6 kw; 328 ft.; N31 16 4 W92 26 24
P O Box 5504, Alexandria, LA 71307 US
(318) 445-0800; *Fax:* (318) 445-1445
License: Alexandria, Rapides County, LA held by FM Broadcasting Corp.
Arbitron Metro Market: Alexandria, LA; *Format:* Urban Contemporary
Cathy Rogers, CFO
Kevin Wagner, President
Bruce Pattani, General Sales Mgr
Cheron Holland, News Director
Charles Washam, Local Sales Manager

KJMJ
09-21-1935; 580 kHz AM; *Hrs Open:* 24
601 Washington Street, Alexandria, LA 71301 US
(318) 561-6145; *Fax:* (318) 449-9954
www.radiomaria.us
info.usa@radiomaria.org
License: Alexandria, LA held by Radio Maria Inc.
Group Owner: Radio Maria Inc.; acq 9-20-99).
Arbitron Metro Market: Alexandria, LA; *Format:* Christian, Talk, 74; *Hrs. of News Programming:* News progmg 8 hrs wkly; *Target Audience:* Homebound, prisoners & sick
Fr. Robert Young, Director
Carla Rachal, General Manager
Frank Hare, Production Manager

***KLSA**
01-01-1987; 90.7 MHz FM; *Hrs Open:* 24; 100 kw; 1243 ft.; N31 33 56 W92 32 50 *Rebroadcasts:* Rebroadcasts KDAQ(FM) Shreveport 100%
99 Lakeshore Drive, Baton Rouge, LA 70805 US
(318) 797-5150; *Fax:* (318) 797-5265
www.redriverradio.org
License: Alexandria, Rapides County, LA held by Board of Supervisors Louisiana State University & Agricultural Mechanical College.
Nat'l Network: NPR; PRI
Arbitron Metro Market: Alexandria, LA; *Format:* Classical, Jazz, 60; *Hrs. of News Programming:* Nws progmg 40 hrs wkly
Kermit Poling, General Manager
Bill Beckett, Programming Director
Ranae Moran, Director of Corporate Support & Underwriting
Henry Edwards, Membership Director

***KLXA**
11-01-1998; 89.9 MHz FM; *Hrs Open:* 24; 3 kw; 328 ft.; N31 22 40 W92 28 27
6652 North Club Dr., Shreveport, LA 71107 US
(916) 251-1600; *Fax:* (916) 251-1650
www.klove.com
klov@klove.com
License: Alexandria, Rapides County, LA held by Educational Media Foundation.
Group Owner: EMF Broadcasting; (acq 12-1-03; $125,000).
Nat'l Network: K-Love
Arbitron Metro Market: Alexandria, LA; *Format:* Christian; *No. News Employees:* 3; *Target Audience:* 25-44; Judeo Christian, female
Mike Novak, President
Chip Bailey, Operations Dir
David Pierce, Programming Director
Ed Lenane, News Director
Sam Wallington, Engineering Dir
Marya Morgan, News Reporter
Richard Hunt, News Reporter
Tracy Butler, TrafficManager

KQID-FM
09-17-1978; 93.1 MHz FM; 97 kw; 1522 ft.; N31 38 20 W92 12 18
Mailing Address: 1115 Texas Avenue, Alexandria, LA 71301 US
Second Address: 1115 Texas Ave., Alexandria, LA 71306
(318) 445-1234; *Fax:* (318) 473-1960
www.q93fm.com
License: Alexandria, Rapides County, LA
Group Owner: Cenla Broadcasting Co. Inc.
Arbitron Metro Market: Alexandria, LA; *Format:* Contemporary Hits/Top 40
MaryElin Macht, Programming Director

KRRV-FM
05-11-1969; 100.3 MHz FM; *Hrs Open:* 24; 98 kw; 1053 ft.; N31 1 59 W92 30 8
600 Congress Avenue, Suite 1400, Austin, TX 78701 US
(318) 445-1234; *Fax:* (318) 473-1960
www.krrvonline.com
License: Alexandria, Rapides County, LA held by Cenla Broadcasting Licensing Co. LLC.
Group Owner: Cenla Broadcasting Co. Inc.
Arbitron Metro Market: Alexandria area; *Format:* Country
Hollywood Harrison, Programming Director

KSYL
04-01-1947; 970 kHz AM; 1 kw-D, DAN; 1 kw-N, DAN; N31 19 33 W92 29 17
Mailing Address: 1115 Texas Avenue, Alexandria, LA 71301 US
Second Address: 1115 Texas Ave., Alexandria, LA 71301
(318) 445-1234; *Fax:* (318) 442-8255
www.ksyl.com
License: Alexandria, LA held by Cenla Broadcasting Inc.
Group Owner: Cenla Broadcasting Co. Inc.; (acq 8-1-80)
Arbitron Metro Market: Alexandria, LA; *Format:* Talk
Taylor Thompson, President
Chad Soprano, Sales Manager
Dave Graichen, Programming Director

KZMZ
01-01-1947; 96.9 MHz FM; *Hrs Open:* 24; 98 kw; Ant 1,053 ft; N31 01 59 W92 30 08
1115 Texas Ave, Alexandria, LA 78701
(318) 445-1234; *Fax:* (318) 445-7231
chad@cenlabroadcasting.com
License: Alexandria, Rapides County, LA held by Cenla Broadcasting Licensing Co. LLC.
Group Owner: Cenla Broadcasting Co. Inc.; (acq 11-13-2006; grpsl)
Population Served: 475,000; *Arbitron Metro Market:* Alexandria, LA; *Hrs. of News Programming:* news progmg 2 hrs wkly; *No. News Employees:* 1; *Target Audience:* Adults 25-54
Taylor Thompson, General Manager
Chad Soprano, General Sales Mgr

Amite

WABL
01-01-1956; 1570 kHz AM; *Hrs Open:* 12; 0.5 kw-D, ND2; 0.015 kw-N, ND2; N30 42 31 W90 31 31
Mailing Address: 12515 Bankston Road, Amite, LA 70422 US
Second Address: 12515 Bankston Rd., Amite, LA 70422
(780) 672-9822; *Fax:* (780) 672-4678
www.981camfm.com
License: Amite, LA held by Spotlight Broadcasting LLC
Group Owner: Spotlight Broadcasting LLC; acq 6-8-01; $70,000).
Arbitron Metro Market: Norfolk NE; *Format:* Contemporary Hits/Top 40, Adult Contemp
Richard Dees, General Manager
David Gilmore, General Sales Mgr

WTGG
03-03-1997; 96.5 MHz FM; *Hrs Open:* 24; 6 kw; 328 ft.; N30 37 24 W90 24 19
200 E. Thomas St., Hammond, LA 70401 US
(985) 345-0060; *Fax:* (985) 542-9377
www.tangiradio.net
License: Amite, Tangipahoa County, LA held by Charles W. Dowdy, Debtor-In-Possession
Group Owner: Charles W. Dowdy; acq 4-8-98; $650,000)
Nat'l Network: Westwood One; *Regional Network:* La. Net.
Arbitron Metro Market: Baton Rouge, LA; *Format:* Oldies; *Hrs. of News Programming:* news progmg one hr wkly; *No. News Employees:* 1; *Target Audience:* 25-54; women
Charles W. Dowdy, Owner/General Manager
Richard Clark, Dir. of Operations

Angola

***KLSP**
08-12-1986; 91.7 MHz FM; 0.105 kw; 52 ft.; N30 57 17 W91 35 45
LA. State Penitentiary, Angola, LA 70712 US
(225) 655-2281; *Fax:* (225) 655-2273
License: Angola, West Feliciana County, LA held by Angola Educational Foundation Inc.
Arbitron Metro Market: Baton Rouge, LA; *Format:* Variety/Diverse
Special Programming: Black 10 hrs, C&W 6 hrs, jazz 7 hrs, poets corner; *Target Audience:* General.
Burl Cain, General Manager
Maurice Rabalais, Station Manager

Arcadia

***KHCL**
01-20-2001; 92.5 MHz FM; *Hrs Open:* 24; 6 kw; 328 ft.; N32 27 27 W92 59 38 *Rebroadcasts:* Rebroadcasts KHCB-FM Houston, TX 95%
2424 South Blvd., Houston, TX 77098 US
(713) 520-5200
www.khcb.org
email@khcb.org
License: Arcadia, Bienville County, LA held by Houston Christian Broadcasters Inc.
Group Owner: Houston Christian Broadcasters Inc.
Nat'l Network: Moody
Arbitron Metro Market: Houston, TX; *Format:* Christian
Bruce E. Munsterman, President

Atlanta

KCIJ
01-01-2002; 106.5 MHz FM; *Hrs Open:* 24; 25 kw; 328 ft.; N31 48 29 W92 48 22
213 Renee Street, Nachitoches, LA 71457 US
(318) 354-4000; *Fax:* (318) 352-9598
License: Atlanta, Winn County, LA held by North Face Broadcasting L.L.C.
Arbitron Metro Market: Alexandria, LA; *Format:* Contemporary Hits/Top 40, Adult Contemp; *Target Audience:* 25-54; general
John Brewer, Operations Dir
Bill Vance, Station Manager

Baker

WBRP
06-16-1994; 107.3 MHz FM; *Hrs Open:* 24; 4.6 kw; 328 ft; N30 37 24 W91 09 50
Mailing Address: Box 2231, Baton Rouge, LA 70802
Second Address: 929-B Government St., Baton Rouge, LA 70802
(225) 388-9898; *Fax:* (225) 383-3700
owen.weber@gbcradio.com
License: Baker, East Baton Rouge County, LA held by Guaranty Broadcasting Co. of Baton Rouge LLC.
Group Owner: Guaranty Broadcasting Co. of Baton Rouge, LLC; (acq 2-5-97).
Population Served: 750,000; *Arbitron Metro Market:* Baton Rouge, LA *Special Programming:* LSU WOMEN'S BASKETBALL; *Target Audience:* Adults 25-54;
Flynn Foster, President
Gordy Rush, General Manager/Marketing Manager
T.J. Solis, Sales Manager
Darren Gauthier, Programming Director
James Gilmore, Digital Marketing Manager

Ball

KBKK
09-01-1998; 105.5 MHz FM; *Hrs Open:* 24; 6 kw; 318 ft.; N31 25 39 W92 24 18
92 West Shamrock, Pineville, LA 71360 US

(318) 487-1035; *Fax:* (318) 487-4419
www.1055kbuck.com
License: Ball, Rapides County, LA held by Opus Broadcasting Alexandria LLC.
Group Owner: Opus Media Holdings LLC; (acq 9-30-2004; $3.38 million with KLAA-FM Tioga).
Nat'l Reps: Christal; *Wire Services:* AP
Arbitron Metro Market: Alexandria, LA; *Format:* Country *Special Programming:* Nascar; *Target Audience:* 50 plus.
Kim Jones, President

KWDF
01-01-1987; 840 kHz AM; 8 kw-D, NDD; N31 22 40 W92 28 27
3735 Rigolette Rd., Pineville, LA 71360 US
(318) 640-4373
www.wilkinsradio.com
denise@wilkinsradio.com
License: Ball, LA held by Capital City Radio Corp.
Group Owner: Wilkins Communications Network Inc.; (acq 4-5-2006).
Nat'l Network: USA
Arbitron Metro Market: Pineville, LA; *Format:* Christian, Talk; *Adv. Rates:* 6; 6; 6; na
John Ponthier, Station Manager

KWDF
01-01-1987; 99.7 kHz FM; 8 kw-D, NDD; N31 22 40 W92 28 27
3735 Rigolette Rd., Pineville, LA 71360 US
(318) 640-4373
www.wilkinsradio.com
denise@wilkinsradio.com
License: Ball, LA held by Capital City Radio Corp.
Group Owner: Wilkins Communications Network Inc.; (acq 4-5-2006).
Nat'l Network: USA
Arbitron Metro Market: Pineville, LA; *Format:* Christian, Talk; *Adv. Rates:* 6; 6; 6; na
John Ponthier, Station Manager

Basile

KYBG
05-04-1990; 102.1 MHz FM; *Hrs Open:* 24; 3 kw; Ant 328 ft; N30 28 52 W92 35 50
Box 60571, Lafayette, LA 70526
(337) 783-2521; *Fax:* (337) 783-5744
www.kqis.com
License: Basile, Evangeline County, LA held by Third Partner Broadcasting Inc.
Nat'l Network: ABC
Arbitron Metro Market: Lafayette, LA; *Hrs. of News Programming:* News progmg 3 hrs wkly; *Target Audience:* 25-55; middle-income
Phil Lizotte, General Manager
Hans Nelson, Programming Director
Christa Broussard, Account Executive

Bastrop

***KAXV**
01-01-2000; 91.9 MHz FM; 12 kw; 456 ft.; N32 49 22 W92 7 28
P.O. Box 3206, Tupelo, MS 38803 US
(662) 844-8888; *Fax:* (662) 842-6791
www.afr.net
faq@afa.net
License: Bastrop, Morehouse County, LA held by American Family Radio.
Group Owner: American Family Radio
Arbitron Metro Market: Tupelo, MS; *Format:* Christian, Religious
Tim Wildmon, President
Donald Wildmon, Founder
Buddy Smith, Sr VP
Ed Vitagliano, Exec VP
Randy Sharp, Director Of Special Projects
Meeke Addison, Director Of Communications
Abraham Hamilton III, General Counsel & Public PolicyAnalyst

KJMG
01-01-1996; 97.3 MHz FM; *Hrs Open:* 24; 5.9 kw; 328 ft.; N32 40 20 W91 55 6
Mailing Address: 5021 - 6th Place, Meridian, LA 39305 US
Second Address: Box 4808, Monroe, LA 71211
(318) 388-2323; *Fax:* (318) 388-0569
www.majic97.com
License: Bastrop, Morehouse County, LA held by Holladay Broadcasting of Louisiana LLC
Group Owner: Holladay Broadcasting of Louisiana LLC; acq 9-30-98; $700,000).
Nat'l Network: ABC; *Nat'l Reps:* McGavren Guild
Arbitron Metro Market: Monroe, LA; *Format:* Adult Contemp *Special Programming:* Blues 12 hrs wkly; *Target Audience:* 25-54.
Bob Holladay, President

KRVV
01-01-1977; 100.1 MHz FM; *Hrs Open:* 24; 50 kw; 492 ft.; N32 40 20 W91 55 6
Mailing Address: 1108 Hudson Lane, Monroe, LA 71211 US
Second Address: 1109 Hudson Ln., Monroe, LA 71201
(318) 388-2323; *Fax:* (318) 388-0569
www.thebeat.net
krvv@bayou.com
License: Bastrop, Morehouse County, LA held by Holladay Broadcasting of Louisiana LLC
Group Owner: Holladay Broadcasting of Louisiana LLC; acq 10-15-91; $1 million;
Nat'l Network: ABC; *Nat'l Reps:* McGavren Guild
Arbitron Metro Market: Monroe, LA; *Format:* Urban Contemporary *Special Programming:* Gospel 4 hrs wkly; *Target Audience:* 18-49.
Bob Holladay, President

Baton Rouge

KBRH
01-01-1953; 1260 kHz AM; *Hrs Open:* 24; 5 kw-D, ND1; 0.127 kw-N, ND1; N30 27 38 W91 14 37
1050 South Foster Drive, Baton Rouge, LA 70806 US
(225) 383-3243; *Fax:* (225) 379-7685
License: Baton Rouge, LA held by East Baton Rouge Parish School Board
Arbitron Metro Market: Baton Rouge, LA; *Format:* Blues; *Target Audience:* 35 plus.
Larry Davis Gryzbac, General Manager

***KLSU**
10-01-1981; 91.1 MHz FM; *Hrs Open:* 24; 5.7 kw; 161 ft.; N30 24 37 W91 10 37
B-39 Hodges, Lsu, Baton Rouge, LA 70803 US
(225) 578-8688; *Fax:* (225) 388-1698
License: Baton Rouge, East Baton Rouge County, LA held by Louisiana State University.
Nat'l Reps: Rgnl Reps
Arbitron Metro Market: Baton Rouge, LA; *Format:* Variety/Diverse; *Hrs. of News Programming:* News progmg one hr wkly; *Target Audience:* 18-25; university students & college age listeners
Angela Schifani, Station Manager

***WBRH**
09-01-1977; 90.3 MHz FM; *Hrs Open:* 24; 3.5 kw; 478 ft.; N30 26 36.31 W91 10 53.61
1050 South Foster Drive, Baton Rouge, LA 70806 US
(225) 388-9030; *Fax:* (225) 379-7685
www.baton-rouge.com/wbrh/
License: Baton Rouge, East Baton Rouge County, LA held by East Baton Rouge Parish School Board
Nat'l Network: NPR
Arbitron Metro Market: Baton Rouge, LA; *Format:* Jazz; *Target Audience:* 25-54; men
Larry Davis Gryzbac, General Manager

WDGL
10-01-1968; 98.1 MHz FM; *Hrs Open:* 24; 95 kw; 1499 ft.; N30 21 58 W91 12 47
Mailing Address: P.O. Box 2231, Baton Rouge, LA 70821 US
Second Address: 929-B Government St., Baton Rouge, LA 70802
(225) 388-9898; *Fax:* (225) 383-3700
www.eagle981.com
gordy.rush@gbcradio.com
License: Baton Rouge, East Baton Rouge County, LA held by Guaranty Broadcasting Co. of Baton Rouge LLC.
Group Owner: Guaranty Broadcasting Co. of Baton Rouge, LLC
Wire Services: AP
Arbitron Metro Market: Baton Rouge, LA; *Format:* Classic Rock *Special Programming:* LSU FOOTBALL AND BASEBALL PLAY BY PLAY BROADCASTS; Don Dubuc Fishing; *Target Audience:* Adults 25-54
Flynn Foster, President
Gordy Rush, General Manager
T.J. Solis, Sales Manager
Darren Gauthier, Programming Director
James Gilmore, Digital Marketing Manager

WPYR
01-01-1956; 1380 kHz AM
600 Congress Ave., Suite 1400, Austin, TX 78701 US
(225) 448-3754; *Fax:* (226) 231-1879
www.brcatholicradio.com
info@brcatholicradio.com
License: Baton Rouge, LA held by Davidson Media Station WPYR Licensee LLC.
Group Owner: Davidson Media Group LLC; (acq 9-16-2008; exchange for WBZK(AM) York, SC)
Arbitron Metro Market: Baton Rouge, LA; *Format:* Christian, Talk, 74; *Adv. Rates:* 25; 25; 25; na
David Dawson, Station Manager

WIBR
07-18-1948; 1300 kHz AM; 5 kw-D, 1 kw-N, DA-2; N30 28 25 W91 13 34
650 Wooddale Blvd., Baton Rouge, LA 85281
(225) 926-1106; *Fax:* (225) 928-1606
License: Baton Rouge, East Baton Rouge County, LA held by Radio License Holding CBC, LLC
Group Owner: Cumulus Media Inc.; (acq 1999; grpsl).
Nat'l Network: ABC; *Regional Network:* La. Net; *Nat'l Reps:* McGavren Guild; *Wire Services:* UPI
Population Served: 245,752; *Arbitron Metro Market:* Baton Rouge, LA; *Format:* Sports

WJBO
12-11-1934; 1150 kHz AM; 5 kw-U, DA1; N30 27 47 W91 16 10
5555 Hilton Ave., Suite 500, Baton Rouge, LA 70808 US
(225) 231-1860; *Fax:* (225) 231-1873
www.wjbo.com
info@wjbo.com
License: Baton Rouge, LA held by Capstar TX LLC
Group Owner: iHeartMedia; (acq 8-30-2000; grpsl)
Nat'l Network: CBS; Westwood One
Arbitron Metro Market: Baton Rouge, LA; *Format:* News, Sports, 86; *Target Audience:* 20 plus.
Michael Hudson, Market President
Bruce Collins, Programming Director
David Sorge, Online Content Director

***WJFM**
06-01-1995; 88.5 MHz FM; *Hrs Open:* 24; 25.5 kw; 279 ft.; N30 23 6 W91 5 23
Mailing Address: P. O. Box 262550, Baton Rouge, LA 70826 US
Second Address: 8919 World Ministry Ave., Baton Rouge, LA 70810
(225) 768-3688; *Fax:* (225) 768-3729
www.jsm.org
kawikfish@yahoo.com
License: Baton Rouge, East Baton Rouge County, LA held by Family Worship Center Church Inc.
Group Owner: Family Worship Center Church Inc.; (acq 12-15-99).
Arbitron Metro Market: Baton Rouge, LA; *Format:* Christian; *Hrs. of News Programming:* news progmg 2 hrs wkly; *No. News Employees:* 1; *Target Audience:* 25-54; full gospel Christians & anyone searching for hope
David Whitelaw, COO
Jimmy Swaggart, President
John Santiago, Programming Director

WFMF
01-01-1941; 102.5 MHz FM; 96 kw; 1499 ft.; N30 19 34 W91 16 36
5555 Hilton Ave., Suite 500, Baton Rouge, LA 70808 US
(225) 231-1860; *Fax:* (225) 231-1873
www.wfmf.com
License: Baton Rouge, East Baton Rouge County, LA held by Capstar TX LLC
Group Owner: iHeartMedia
Arbitron Metro Market: Baton Rouge, LA; *Format:* Contemporary Hits/Top 40; *Target Audience:* 18-34; female
Michael Hudson, Market President
Bob Murphy, Programming Director

WUBR
11-01-1946; 910 kHz AM
3000 Tecumseh Street, Baton Rouge, LA 70805 US
(517) 351-3333
License: Baton Rouge, LA held by Communications Capital Co. III LLC.
Group Owner: Communications Capital Managers LLC; (acq 2-17-2006; $75,000)
Arbitron Metro Market: Baton Rouge, LA; *Target Audience:* 18-59.
Michael Oesterle, CEO
Sandra Pate, General Manager

WPFC
01-01-1963; 1550 kHz AM; *Hrs Open:* Sunrise-sunset; 5 kw-D, ND2; 0.042 kw-N, ND2; N30 30 7 W91 12 39
6940 Harry Drive, Baton Rouge, LA 70806 US
(225) 926-1506; *Fax:* (225) 926-4974

License: Baton Rouge, LA held by Victory and Power Ministries Inc.
Nat'l Network: USA
Arbitron Metro Market: Baton Rouge, LA; *Format:* Gospel, Religious; *Hrs. of News Programming:* news progmg 3 hrs wkly; *No. News Employees:* 2; *Target Audience:* 35-59; middle-class female
Pastor Moore, CEO
Keith Richard, Station Manager

*WRKF
01-18-1980; 89.3 MHz FM; *Hrs Open:* 24; 28 kw; 935 ft.; N30 22 22 W91 12 16
3050 Valley Creek Drive, Baton Rouge, LA 70808 US
(225) 926-3050; *Fax:* (225) 926-3105
www.wrkf.org
License: Baton Rouge, East Baton Rouge County, LA held by Public Radio Inc.
Nat'l Network: NPR; PRI
Arbitron Metro Market: Baton Rouge, LA; *Format:* News, News/Talk, 86; *Hrs. of News Programming:* news progmg 35 hrs wkly; *No. News Employees:* 1; *Target Audience:* General.
Blythe Earl, General Manager
Malcolm Robinson, General Sales Mgr

WTGE
09-10-1966; 100.7 MHz FM; *Hrs Open:* 24; 97 kw; 1,499 ft; N30 19 35 W91 16 36
Mailing Address: Box 2231, Baton Rouge, LA 70802
Second Address: 929-B Government St., Baton Rouge, LA 70802
(225) 388-9898; *Fax:* (225) 383-3700
www.newcountry1007.com
owen.weber@gbcradio.com
License: Baton Rouge, East Baton Rouge County, LA held by Guaranty Broadcasting Co. of Baton Rouge LLC.
Group Owner: Guaranty Broadcasting Co. of Baton Rouge, LLC; (acq 1996; $5.5 million).
Population Served: 750,000; *Arbitron Metro Market:* Baton Rouge, LA *Special Programming:* NEW ORLEANS SAINTS FOOTBALL PLAY BY PLAY and LSU MEN'S BASKETBALL; *Target Audience:* Adults 25-54
Flynn Foster, President
Gordy Rush, General Manager
T.J. Solis, Sales Manager
Darren Gauthier, Programming Director
James Gilmore, Digital Marketing Manager

WYNK-FM
12-07-1968; 101.5 MHz FM; *Hrs Open:* 24; 97 kw; 1499 ft.; N30 19 34 W91 16 36
5555 Hilton Avenue, Suite 500, Baton Rouge, LA 70808 US
(225) 231-1860; *Fax:* (225) 231-1873
www.wynkcountry.com
License: Baton Rouge, East Baton Rouge County, LA held by Capstar TX LLC
Group Owner: iHeartMedia; (acq 8-30-2000; grpsl)
Arbitron Metro Market: Baton Rouge, LA; *Format:* Country; *No. News Employees:* 2; *Target Audience:* 18-54.
Michael Hudson, Market President
Kahilla Hakimzadeh, Senior Vice President of Sales

Bayou Vista

KQKI-FM
12-31-1976; 95.3 MHz FM; 16.5 kw; 400 ft.; N29 39 28 W91 17 41
107 Pluto Street, Morgan City, LA 70380 US
(985) 395-2853; *Fax:* (985) 395-5094
jaboyne@cox.net
License: Bayou Vista, St. Mary County, LA held by Teche Broadcasting Corp.
Nat'l Network: ABC; *Regional Network:* La. Net.
Format: Country; *Hrs. of News Programming:* news progmg 17 hrs wkly; *No. News Employees:* 1; *Target Audience:* 30 plus; general; *Adv. Rates:* 18; 17; 17.50; 15
Paul Cook/Owner, CEO/COO
Julie Boyne, General Manager
Julie Boyne, General Sales Mgr
J. J. Starbuck, Programming Director
Jennifer Protich, Traffic Manager

Belle Chasse

KKND
03-01-1990; 102.9 MHz FM; 4.7 kw; Ant 604 ft; N29 57 14 W89 56 58
201 St. Charles Ave., Suite 201, New Orleans, LA 70170 US
(504) 581-7002; *Fax:* (504) 566-4857
www.power1029.com
info@power1029.com
License: Belle Chasse, LA held by Radio License Holding CBC, LLC
Group Owner: Cumulus Media Inc.; (acq 8-29-2003; grpsl).
Population Served: 2,965,100; *Arbitron Metro Market:* New Orleans, LA; *Format:* Contemporary Hits/Top 40
Greg Capogna, General Manager

Benton

KSYR
01-01-1981; 92.1 MHz FM; *Hrs Open:* 24; 6 kw; 322 ft.; N32 39 19 W93 41 36
3712 Cornell Drive, Shreveport, LA 71107 US
(318) 222-3122; *Fax:* (318) 459-1493
License: Benton, Bossier County, LA held by Access. 1 Louisiana Holding Co. LLC.
Group Owner: Access.1 Communications Corp.; (acq 5-5-00; grpsl).
Nat'l Network: ABC
Arbitron Metro Market: Shreveport, LA; *No. News Employees:* 1; *Target Audience:* 35 plus; upper income, upwardly mobile
Cary Camp, President/General Manager
Don Zimmerman, General Sales Mgr

Berwick

KBZE
07-04-1990; 105.9 MHz FM; 4 kw; 404 ft.; N29 45 27 W91 10 25
Mailing Address: Po Drawer N, Morgan City, LA 70380 US
Second Address: 1320 Victor II Blvd., Morgan City, LA 70380
(985) 385-6266; *Fax:* (985) 385-6268
kbze@petronet.net
License: Berwick, St. Mary County, LA held by HubCast Broadcasting Inc.
Nat'l Network: ABC
Arbitron Metro Market: Morgan City, La; *Format:* Adult Contemp, Sports, 74; *Hrs. of News Programming:* news progmg 10 hrs wkly; *No. News Employees:* 1; *Target Audience:* 24-54; middle to upper income
Howard Castay Jr., President
Darlene Castay, Operations Dir

Blanchard

KDKS-FM
10-19-1998; 102.1 MHz FM; *Hrs Open:* 24; 20 kw; 367 ft.; N32 35 57 W93 54 1
208 N. Thomas Dr., Shreveport, LA 71137 US
(318) 222-3122
www.kdks.fm
License: Blanchard, Caddo County, LA held by Alpha Media Licensee LLC
Group Owner: Alpha Media LLC; (acq 4-14-2015; grpsl).
Arbitron Metro Market: Shreveport, LA; *Format:* Urban Contemporary; *No. News Employees:* 1; *Target Audience:* 25-54.
Cary Camp, General Manager
Melvin Jones, Urban Market Sales Manager
Quinn Echols, Programming Director
Johnette Robinson, General Sales Manager

*KFLO-FM
01-01-2006; 89.1 MHz FM; 38 kw; 406 ft.; N32 18 28 W93 58 34
Mailing Address: P.O. Box 7277, Shreveport, LA 71137 US
Second Address: 2097 N. Hearne Ave., Shreveport, LA 71107
(318) 550-2000; *Fax:* 318-550-2002
miracle891.org
info@miracle891.org
License: Blanchard, Caddo County, LA held by Family Life Educational Foundation
Arbitron Metro Market: Dallas-Fort Worth; *Format:* Religious
Dan Perkins, Operations Dir
Donna Cole, General Manager
Mike Duncan, Traffic Manager
Ray Cole, Programming Director

Bogalusa

WBOX
03-01-1954; 920 kHz AM; 1 kw-D, NDD; N30 50 29 W89 50 6
P. O. Box 351, Columbia, MS 39429 US
(504) 732-4288
License: Bogalusa, LA held by Best Country Broadcasting LLC
Arbitron Metro Market: Columbia, MS; *Format:* Country
Ben Strickland, President

Bossier City

KBCL
09-01-1957; 1070 kHz AM; 0.25 kw-D, NDD; N32 32 14 W93 43 28
316-B Gregg Street, Shreveport, LA 71104 US
(318) 861-1070
www.kbclthebridge.org
kbcl_radio@bellsouth.net
License: Bossier City, LA held by Barnabas Center Ministries
Arbitron Metro Market: Shreveport, LA; *Format:* Christian, Talk
Leon McKee, General Manager
Jean McKee, Programming Director

Boyce

KBCE
03-29-1982; 102.3 MHz FM; 21 kw; 289 ft.; N31 22 21 W92 38 9
2826 Lee Street, Suite 6, Alexandria, LA 71409 US
(318) 445-0800; *Fax:* (318) 445-1445
License: Boyce, Rapides County, LA held by Trinity Broadcasting Corp.
Nat'l Network: American Urban; *Nat'l Reps:* D & R Radio
Arbitron Metro Market: Alexandria, LA; *Format:* Urban Contemporary; *No. News Employees:* 2; *Target Audience:* General.
Kevin Wagner, President
Bruce Pattani, General Sales Mgr
Cheron Holland, News Director

Breaux Bridge

KPEL-FM
05-01-1993; 96.5 MHz FM; *Hrs Open:* 24; 22.5 kw; 328 ft; N30 06 09 W91 59 30
1749 Bertrand Dr., Lafayette, LA 70505
(337) 233-6000; *Fax:* (337) 234-7360
www.965kvki.com
amyfletcher@townsquaremedia.com
License: Breaux Bridge, St. Martin County, LA
Group Owner: Townsquare Media; (acq 12-7-2001; grpsl)
Arbitron Metro Market: Lafayette, LA *Special Programming:* Local 1 hr wkly; *Target Audience:* 18-35
Amy Fletcher, General Manager
Erin Bristol, Brand Manager
Lisa Janes, Director Of Sales
Chasity Spears, Digital Managing Editor

Broussard

*WHFG
01-01-2008; 91.3 MHz FM; 6 kw; 367 ft.; N29 58 4 W91 55 31
516 South 4th St, Las Vegas, NV 89101 US
(817) 641-3495
License: Broussard, Lafayette County, LA held by Mary V. Harris Foundation.
Arbitron Metro Market: Windom, MN
Linda De Romanett, President

Brusly

KRVE
09-09-1989; 96.1 MHz FM; *Hrs Open:* 24; 50 kw; 449 ft.; N30 29 37 W91 0 19
5555 Hilton Ave., Suite 500, Baton Rouge, LA 70808 US
(225) 231-1860; *Fax:* (225) 231-1869
www.961theriver.com
sam@961theriver.com
License: Brusly, West Baton Rouge County, LA held by Capstar TX LLC
Group Owner: iHeartMedia; (acq 8-30-00; grpsl).
Arbitron Metro Market: Baton Rouge, LA; *Format:* Adult Contemp; *No. News Employees:* 3; *Target Audience:* 25-54; women
Michael Hudson, Market President
Kahilla Hakimzadeh, Senior Vice President of Sales

Bunkie

KEZP
01-01-1993; 104.3 MHz FM; *Hrs Open:* 24; 19.2 kw; 374 ft.; N31 5 14 W92 21 34
1605 Murray Street, Suite 120, Alexandria, LA 71301 US
(318) 487-1035; *Fax:* (318) 487-1045
License: Bunkie, Avoyelles County, LA held by Opus Broadcasting Alexandria LLC.
Group Owner: Opus Media Holdings LLC; (acq 9-30-2004; $1.83 million)
Nat'l Network: Westwood One
Arbitron Metro Market: Alexandria, LA; *Format:* Rock/AOR; *No. News Employees:* 1; *Target Audience:* 35-64.
Mark Jones, General Manager

Buras

*KMRL
04-22-1995; 91.9 MHz FM; 11.5 kw; 787 ft.; N29 33 45 W89 49 46

P.O. Box 1307, Buras, LA 70041 US
(504) 362-3379
License: Buras, Plaquemines County, LA held by New Orleans Quality Radio Inc.
Target Audience: General.
W. Christopher Beary, President

Carencro

KLWB

06-08-2010; 103.7 MHz FM; 10 kw; 466 ft.; N30 20 32 W91 57 46
3501 NW Evangeline Thruway, Carencro, LA 70520 USA
(337) 896-1600
www.1037thegame.com
License: Carencro, LA held by Delta Media Corp.
Group Owner: Delta Media Corp.
Format: Sports, Talk
Charles Chatelain, CEO/COO

Church Point

*KCKR

01-01-2007; 91.9 MHz FM; 12.5 kw horiz, 12.4 kw vert; 466 ft.; N30 19 47 W92 5 6
Mailing Address: 17967 Brownsferry Road, Athens, AL 35611 US
Second Address: 8919 World Ministry Ave., Baton Rouge, LA 70810
(225) 768-3102
www.jsm.org
License: Church Point, Acadia County, LA held by Family Worship Center Church Inc.
Group Owner: Family Worship Center Church Inc.; (acq 10-22-2007; $3.6 million)
Arbitron Metro Market: Fayetteville (Northwest Arkansas), AR; *Format:* Religious
Jimmy Swaggart, President

Clinton

*WBKL

09-23-1981; 92.7 MHz FM; *Hrs Open:* 24; 32 kw; 604 ft.; N30 51 3 W91 4 31 *Rebroadcasts:* Rebroadcasts KLVR(FM) Santa Rosa, CA 100%.
13855 Plank Road, Baker, LA 70714 US
(916) 251-1600; *Fax:* (916) 251-1650
www.klove.com
License: Clinton, East Feliciana County, LA held by Educational Media Foundation.
Group Owner: EMF Broadcasting; (acq 7-1-2005; $3.2 million)
Nat'l Network: K-Love
Arbitron Metro Market: Baton Rouge, LA; *Format:* Christian
Mike Novak, President
Chip Bailey, Operations Dir
David Pierce, Programming Director
Ed Lenane, News Director
Sam Wallington, Engineering Dir
Marya Morgan, News Reporter
Richard Hunt, News Reporter

*WWRA

01-01-2008; 91.9 MHz FM; 5 kw; 269 ft.; N30 49 0 W90 48 42
3953 N. Flannery Road, Baton Rouge, LA 70814 US
(225) 791-1429
www.amorradio.org
License: Clinton, East Feliciana County, LA held by Victory Harvest Church.
Arbitron Metro Market: Clinton, LA; *Format:* Religious
Dulio Canossa, General Manager

Columbia

KNNW

01-21-1980; 103.1 MHz FM; *Hrs Open:* 24; 25 kw; 328 ft.; N32 11 44 W92 9 48
1200 N. 18th St., Suite D, Monroe, LA 71201 US
(318) 387-3922
www.1031nowfm.com
tcollins@lagniappebroadcasting.com
License: Columbia, Caldwell County, LA held by Mapleton License of Monroe, LLC.
Group Owner: Mapleton Communications
Arbitron Metro Market: Columbia, LA; *Format:* Urban Contemporary
Taurian Collins, Programming Director

Coushatta

KSBH

11-15-1992; 94.9 MHz FM; *Hrs Open:* 24; 25 kw; 328 ft.; N31 51 34 W93 13 0
505 Royal St., Suite B, Natchitoches, LA 71547 US
(318) 354-4000; *Fax:* (318) 352-9598
License: Coushatta, Red River County, LA held by KSBH L.L.C.
Arbitron Metro Market: Natchitoches, LA; *Format:* Country; *Target Audience:* 18-54.
John Brewer, Operations Dir
Bill Vance, Station Manager
Shane Evath, News Director

KRRP

05-01-1981; 950 kHz AM; *Hrs Open:* 24; 0.5 kw-D, DA2; 0.209 kw-N, DA2; N31 56 49 W93 20 13
P.O. Box 1362, 1519 Ringgold Avenue, Coushatta, LA 71019 US
(318) 932-6704; *Fax:* (318) 932-9700
krrp@cp-tel.net
License: Coushatta, LA held by Roberto Feliz
Nat'l Network: ESPN Radio
Arbitron Metro Market: Coushatta, LA; *Format:* Sports; *Hrs. of News Programming:* news progmg 20 hrs wkly; *No. News Employees:* 1; *Target Audience:* 35 plus; mature, educated, affluent listeners *Adv. Rates:* 15; 15; 15; 12
Chris Boyd, General Manager
George Moore, Programming Director
Robert Abrahams, Chief Engineer

Crowley

KAJN-FM

10-01-1977; 102.9 MHz FM; *Hrs Open:* 24; 95 kw; 1499 ft.; N30 2 19 W92 22 15
Mailing Address: P.O. Box 1469, Crowley, LA 70527 US
Second Address: 110 W. 3rd St., Crowley, LA 70526
(337) 783-1560; *Fax:* (337) 783-1674
www.kajn.com
License: Crowley, Acadia County, LA held by Agape Broadcasters Inc.
Nat'l Network: USA; *Wire Services:* AP
Arbitron Metro Market: Crowley, LA; *Format:* Religious *Special Programming:* Black 2 hrs wkly; *Hrs. of News Programming:* news progmg 3 hrs wkly; *No. News Employees:* 1; *Target Audience:* 25-44; female, familyoriented; *Adv. Rates:* 40.56; 36.30; 36.36; 30.65
Barry Thompson, CEO/General Manager
Janet Thompson, Operations Dir
Bryan Rivera, General Sales Mgr
Craig Thompson, Programming Director
Paula St. Cyr, Traffic Manager
Steve Cook, News Director
Tony Evans, Chief Engineer

KSIG

05-01-1947; 1450 kHz AM; 1 kw-U, ND1; N30 13 45 W92 20 59
Mailing Address: 320 North Parkerson Ave., Crowley, LA 70526 US
Second Address: 320 N. Parkerson Ave., Crowley, LA 70527
(337) 783-2520; *Fax:* (337) 783-5744
www.ksig.com
License: Crowley, LA held by Acadia Broadcast Partners Inc.
Arbitron Metro Market: Crowley, LA; *Format:* Oldies *Special Programming:* Fr 18 hrs, farm 5 hrs wkly
Phil Lizotte, President
Jimmy Cole, General Sales Mgr
Hans Nelson, Programming Director
Tony Evans, Chief Engineer

De Quincy

KTSR

11-01-1985; 92.1 MHz FM; *Hrs Open:* 24; 13.5 kw; 448 ft.; N30 13 16 W93 18 40
900 North Lakeshore Drive, Lake Charles, LA 70601 US
(337) 433-1641; *Fax:* (337) 433-2999
www.kissfm921.com
leslie.guidry@townsquaremedia.com
License: De Quincy, Calcasieu County, LA held by Townsquare Media Lake Charles License LLC
Group Owner: Townsquare Media; (acq 2-6-2008; grpsl)
Arbitron Metro Market: Lake Charles metro area; *Format:* Contemporary Hits/Top 40
Leslie Guidry, General Manager
Erik Tee, Brand Manager
Brad Burley, Director Of Sales
Kristian Bland, Digital Managing Editor

De Ridder

KDLA

11-11-1950; 1010 kHz AM; *Hrs Open:* Sunrise-sunset; 1 kw-D, ND1; 0.04 kw-N, ND1; N30 52 43 W93 17 25
1825 Pelican Road, DeRidder, LA 70634 US
(318) 462-1000; *Fax:* (318) 462-1000
License: De Ridder, LA held by Christian Broadcasting of De Ridder Inc.
Nat'l Network: Reach Satellite
Format: Gospel; *Target Audience:* 18-54.
Guy Giuliano, President
Dawson Austin, Operations Dir

KQLK

09-06-1991; 97.9 MHz FM; *Hrs Open:* 24; 50 kw; 492 ft.; N30 36 57 W93 13 31
P.O. Box 19090, Lake Charles, LA 70616 US
(337) 436-7277; *Fax:* (337) 433-7278
www.kqlk.com
info@kqlk.com
License: De Ridder, Beauregard County, LA held by Cumulus Licensing LLC.
Group Owner: Cumulus Media Inc.; (acq 12-6-2004; $3 million with KAOK(AM) Lake Charles).
Arbitron Metro Market: Lake Charles, LA; *Format:* Adult Contemp
Eric Nielson, Operations Dir
Jimmie Cole, General Manager/General Sales Manager
Adrian Scott, Programming Director
Kevin Goode, Promotions Manager
Richard Rhodes, Chief Engineer

DeRidder

*KBAN

01-01-2001; 91.5 MHz FM; 20.5 kw; 361 ft.; N30 38 10 W93 2 33
P.O. Box 3206, Tupelo, MS 38803 US
(662) 844-8888; *Fax:* (662) 842-6791
www.afr.net
faq@afa.net
License: DeRidder, Beauregard County, LA held by American Family Association.
Group Owner: American Family Radio
Arbitron Metro Market: Tupelo, MS; *Format:* Christian, Religious
Tim Wildmon, President
Donald Wildmon, Founder
Buddy Smith, Sr VP
Ed Vitagliano, Exec VP
Randy Sharp, Director Of Special Projects
Meeke Addison, Director Of Communications
Abraham Hamilton III, General Source & Public PolicyAnalyst

Delhi

KGGM

09-01-1991; 93.5 MHz FM; 6 kw; 328 ft.; N32 27 45 W91 33 13
Box 426, Delhi, LA 71232 US
(318) 878-8255; *Fax:* (318) 728-3571
License: Delhi, Richland County, LA held by Kenneth W. Diebel
Format: Gospel
Ken Diebel, President

Denham Springs

WLRO

04-15-1959; 1210 kHz AM; *Hrs Open:* 18; 10 kw-D, 1 kw-N, DA-N; N30 31 20 W90 58 15
5555 Hilton Ave., Suite 500, Baton Rouge, LA 78701
(225) 231-1860; *Fax:* (225) 231-1869
www.1210thescore.com
License: Denham Springs, Livingston County, LA held by Capstar TX LLC
Group Owner: iHeartMedia; (acq 8-30-00; grpsl)
Nat'l Network: Westwood One
Population Served: 750,000; *Arbitron Metro Market:* Baton Rouge, LA; *Format:* Sports; *No. News Employees:* 2; *Target Audience:* 25-54.
Michael Hudson, Market President

Donaldsonville

KNXX

01-01-1972; 104.9 MHz FM; *Hrs Open:* 24; 6 kw; Ant 299 ft; N30 05 57 W91 00 13 *Rebroadcasts:* Rebroadcasts WNXX(FM) Jackson 100%
Mailing Address: Box 2231, Baton Rouge, LA 70346
Second Address: 929 B Government St., Baton Rouge, LA 70802-6033
(225) 388-9898 ext 148; *Fax:* (225) 499-9800
License: Donaldsonville, Ascension County, LA held by Guaranty Broadcasting Co. of Baton Rouge LLC.

Group Owner: Guaranty Broadcasting Co. of Baton Rouge, LLC; (acq 2-18-2000; $1.2 million).
Nat'l Reps: McGavren Guild
Population Served: 150,000; *Arbitron Metro Market:* Baton Rouge, LA; *Hrs. of News Programming:* News progmg 2 hrs wkly; *Target Audience:* 18-34.; *Adv. Rates:* 18.40; 18.40; 18.40; 18.40
Flynn Foster, President
Owen Weber, Operations Dir
Gordy Rush, General Manager
Dave Dunaway, Operations Manager

Dry Prong

***KVDP**
08-13-1985; 89.1 MHz FM; 4.5 kw; 295 ft.; N31 35 20 W92 30 59
Mailing Address: P. O. Box 214, Dry Prong, LA 71423 US
Second Address: 160 Bud Walker Rd., Dry Prong, LA 71423
(318) 899-5837; *Fax:* (318) 899-7624
License: Dry Prong, Grant County, LA held by Dry Prong Educational Broadcasting Foundation Inc.
Nat'l Network: USA
Arbitron Metro Market: Dry Prong, LA; *Format:* Christian, Religious
Greg Capogna, General Manager
J. Michael, Programming Director
Darris Cline, Chief Engineer

Dubach

KNBB
06-04-1984; 97.7 MHz FM; *Hrs Open:* 5 AM-11 PM; 50 kw; 464 ft.; N32 40 9 W92 37 58
Mailing Address: P.O. Box 977, Ruston, LA 71273 US
Second Address: 500 N. Monroe St., Ruston, LA 71270
(318) 255-5000; *Fax:* (318) 255-5084
www.espn977.com
seanfox@espn977.com
License: Dubach, Lincoln County, LA held by Red Peach, LLC
Group Owner: Red Peach LLC
Nat'l Network: ESPN Radio
Arbitron Metro Market: Monroe, LA; *Format:* Sports, Talk; *Target Audience:* 25-44; men
Gary McKenney, General Manager

Dulac

KDLC
08-04-2011; 97.7 MHz FM; 100 kW; 438 ft.; N29 20 48 W90 49 49.4
PO Box 2639, Gulfport, MS 39505-2639 USA
228-896-5500
License: Dulac, LA held by Coast Radio Group, Inc.
Group Owner: Coast Radio Group, Inc.

Steve Spillman, General Sales Mgr
Pat McGowan, Programming Director

Empire

KWMZ-FM
06-01-2001; 104.5 MHz FM; 7.8 kw; Ant 850 ft; N29 33 45 W89 49 46
c/o Hartman Leito & Bolt LLP, 6100 Southwest Blvd., Suite 500, Fort Worth, TX 29564
(817) 738-2400
License: Empire, Plaquemines County, LA held by On Top Communications of Louisiana LLC, Debtor-in-Possession

Bryan Rice, General Manager

Erath

KHXT
04-01-1992; 107.9 MHz FM; *Hrs Open:* 24; 25 kw; 328 ft; N30 02 54 W91 59 49
1749 Bertrand Dr., Lafayette, LA 70505
(337) 233-6000; *Fax:* (337) 234-7360
www.1079ishot.com
info@1079ishot.com
License: Erath, Vermilion County, LA
Group Owner: Townsquare Media; (acq 12-7-2001; grpsl)
Regional Network: La. Net; *Nat'l Reps:* Katz Radio
Population Served: 300,000; *Arbitron Metro Market:* Lafayette, LA; *Hrs. of News Programming:* News progmg 25 hrs wkly; *Target Audience:* 12-34.
Mike Grimsley, General Manager
DJ Digital, Brand Manager
Frank Malambri, Director Of Sales
Dave Landry, Digital Managing Editor

Erwinville

***KPAE**
09-30-1985; 91.5 MHz FM; *Hrs Open:* 24; 10 kw; 164 ft.; N30 32 9 W91 24 52 *Rebroadcasts:* Rebroadcasts WPAE (FM) Centreville, MS 75%
Mailing Address: 13028 Us Hwy 190 West, Erwinville, LA 70767 US
Second Address: 122 E. Main St., Centreville, MS 39631
(601) 645-6515; *Fax:* (225) 627-4970,(601) 645-9122
www.soundradio.org
wpaefm@telepak.net
License: Erwinville, West Baton Rouge County, LA held by Port Allen Educational Broadcasting Foundation.
Nat'l Network: Moody
Format: Religious; *Target Audience:* General.
Willie Kennedy, President

Eunice

KEUN
10-01-1952; 1490 kHz AM; *Hrs Open:* 24; 1 kw-U, ND1; 150 ft.; N30 28 17 W92 24 51
P. O. Box 1049, Eunice, LA 70535 US
(337) 457-3041; *Fax:* (337) 457-3081
www.keunworldwide.com
spots@keunworldwide.com
License: Eunice, LA held by Tri-Parish Broadcasting Co. Inc.
Nat'l Network: Radio America; *Regional Network:* La. Net.
Arbitron Metro Market: Lafayette, LA; *Format:* News, News/Talk, 86 *Special Programming:* Cajun one hr wkly; *Hrs. of News Programming:* news progmg 6 min every hr; *No. News Employees:* 1; *Target Audience:* 25plus.; *Adv. Rates:* 8; 8; 8; 3
Rick Nesbitt, General Manager
Tony Evans, Chief Engineer

KEUN-FM
10-22-1981; 105.5 MHz FM; *Hrs Open:* 24; 1 kw; 486 ft.; N30 26 16 W92 26 49
PO Box 1049, 330 West Laurel Ave, Eunice, LA 70535 US
(337) 457-3041; *Fax:* (337) 457-3081
www.keunworldwide.com
spots@keunworldwide.com
License: Eunice, St. Landry County, LA held by Tri-Parish Broadcasting Co. Inc.
Nat'l Network: ABC
Arbitron Metro Market: Lafayette, LA; *Format:* Country *Special Programming:* Cajun music 12 hrs wkly; *Hrs. of News Programming:* Local news progmg one hr wkly; *No. News Employees:* 1; *Target Audience:* P 25-54. *Adv. Rates:* 18; 17; 18; 15
Rick Nesbitt, General Manager

Farmerville

KBYO-FM
04-19-1979; 92.7 MHz FM; *Hrs Open:* 24; 6 kw; 328 ft.; N32 40 31 W92 19 10
Po Drawer 399, 408 Cedar, Farmerville, LA 71241 US
(318) 516-3033; *Fax:* (318) 323-3719
www.fun927fm.com/
License: Farmerville, Union County, LA held by Union Broadcasting Co. Inc.
Arbitron Metro Market: Monroe, LA; *Format:* Adult Contemp; *Target Audience:* 24-65; adult audience with incomes to buy
Lee Fletcher, General Manager

Ferriday

KFNV-FM
10-01-1971; 107.1 MHz FM; *Hrs Open:* 24; 18.5 kw; 233 ft.; N31 36 8 W91 32 27
Mailing Address: P.O. Box 1319, Columbia, LA 71418 US
Second Address: 917 S. EE Wallace Blvd., Ferriday, LA 71334
(800) 784-1071; *Fax:* (318) 757-7689
License: Ferriday, Concordia County, LA held by Tom D. Gay
Group Owner: The Radio Group
Arbitron Metro Market: Ferriday LA; *Format:* Contemporary Hits/Top 40, Adult Contemp; *Hrs. of News Programming:* News progmg 2 hrs wkly; *Target Audience:* 25-55; baby boomers; *Adv. Rates:* 9; 8; 8; 5
Desiree Smith, General Manager

Folsom

WJSH
03-01-1996; 104.7 MHz FM; *Hrs Open:* 24; 6 kw; 328 ft.; N30 39 55 W90 4 49
PO Box 30, Magnolia, MS 39652 US
(601) 783-6600
License: Folsom, St. Tammany County, LA held by Charles W. Dowdy, Debtor-In-Possession
Group Owner: Charles W. Dowdy; (acq 11-17-2000).
Arbitron Metro Market: Folsom, LA; *Format:* Smooth Jazz
Charles W. Dowdy, Owner/General Manager

Franklin

KDDK
05-09-1975; 105.5 MHz FM; 3 kw; Ant 300 ft; N29 50 14 W91 32 22 *Rebroadcasts:* Rebroadcasts KJCB(AM) Lafayette 100%
5047 Hwy. 1148, Plaquemine, LA 23261
(225) 687-2882
www.kddkfm.com
kddk@bellsouth.net
License: Franklin, St. Mary County, LA held by Radio & Investments Inc.
Population Served: 100,000
Ken Noble, General Manager

KFRA
06-04-1961; 1390 kHz AM; 0.5 kw-D, ND1; 0.244 kw-N, ND1; N29 50 14 W91 32 22
P.O. Box 27224, Richmond, VA 23261 US
(337) 924-7100
http://www.1390kfra.com/
kbze.kfra@gmail.com
License: Franklin, LA held by Castay Media Inc.
Arbitron Metro Market: Franklin, LA
Howard Castay, President

Franklinton

WOMN
12-05-1966; 1110 kHz AM; *Hrs Open:* Sunrise-sunset; 1 kw-D, NDD; N30 51 34 W90 9 57
P.O.Box 604, Franklinton, LA 70438 US
(985) 624-9452; *Fax:* (985) 624-9559
mpittman@pittmanbroadcasting.com
License: Franklinton, LA held by Pittman Broadcasting Services LLC.
Group Owner: Pittman Broadcasting Services LLC; (acq 6-4-2002; with co-located FM)
Arbitron Metro Market: New Orleans, LA; *Format:* Country; *Target Audience:* General.
Mike Mitchell, General Sales Mgr
Tony Evans, Chief Engineer

WUUU
03-03-1997; 98.9 MHz FM; *Hrs Open:* 24; 6 kw; 108 ft.; N30 51 34 W90 9 57
P O Box 604, Franklinton, LA 70438 US
(985) 624-9452; *Fax:* (985) 624-9559
mpittman@pittmanbroadcasting.com
License: Franklinton, Washington County, LA held by Pittman Broadcasting Services LLC.
Group Owner: Pittman Broadcasting Services LLC
Arbitron Metro Market: New Orleans, LA
Joe Mule, General Manager
Dale Mitchell, Programming Director

Galliano

WTIX-FM
11-16-1975; 94.3 MHz FM; *Hrs Open:* 24; 100 kw; 981 ft.; N29 33 45 W89 49 46
1206 Decatur Street, New Orleans, LA 70116 US
(504) 454-9000; *Fax:* (504) 454-9002
wtixfm.com
info@wtixfm.com
License: Galliano, Lafourche County, LA held by Fleur de Lis Broadcasting Inc.
Nat'l Network: ABC
Arbitron Metro Market: New Orleans, LA; *Format:* Oldies; *Hrs. of News Programming:* News progmg 4 hrs wkly; *Target Audience:* 25-54.; *Adv. Rates:* 35; 35; 35; 20
Michael Costello, President/General Manager

Garyville

***WCKW**
12-22-1970; 1010 kHz AM; *Hrs Open:* 24
3501 North Causeway Blvd, Ste 700, Metairie, LA 70002 US
(314) 752-7000; *Fax:* (314) 752-7702
www.covenantnet.net
License: Garyville, LA held by Covenant Network
Group Owner: Covenant Network; (acq 10-17-2006)
Arbitron Metro Market: River Parishes; *Format:* Religious; *Target Audience:* 18-54.
John Anthony Holman, President

Gibsland

KBEF
05-23-2001; 104.5 MHz FM; 6 kw; 328 ft.; N32 31 59 W93 11 34
P.O. Box 218, Dubberly, LA 71024 US
(318) 377-1240; *Fax:* (318) 377-4619
www.kbef.com
kaso1240@yahoo.com
License: Gibsland, Bienville County, LA held by Amistad Communications Inc.
Group Owner: Amistad Communications Inc.; (acq 7-12-2000; $375,000 for CP with KASO(AM) Minden).
Arbitron Metro Market: Minden, LA; *Format:* Christian
Mike Griffith, General Manager

Golden Meadow

KLEB
05-13-1963; 1600 kHz AM; *Hrs Open:* 24; 5 kw-D, DA2; 0.25 kw-N, DA2; N29 23 43 W90 16 1
PO Box 1350, Larose, LA 70373 US
(985) 798-7792; *Fax:* (985) 798-7793
www.klrzfm.com
klrz@mobiletel.com
License: Golden Meadow, LA held by Coastal Broadcasting of Larose Inc.
Arbitron Metro Market: New Orleans, LA; *Format:* Oldies, Country; *Target Audience:* 25 plus; general; *Adv. Rates:* 20; 15; 20; 10
Andrea Galjour, Operations Dir
Jerry Gisclair, General Manager

***KUHN**
88.9 MHz FM; 1 kw; 75 ft.; N29 20 53 W90 14 55
US
(985) 475-6640; *Fax:* (985) 475-7109
www.unitedhoumanation.org
License: Golden Meadow, Lafourche County, LA held by United Houma Nation Inc.
Arbitron Metro Market: Golden Meadow, LA
Brenda Robichaux, General Manager

Grambling

***KGRM**
01-01-1974; 91.5 MHz FM; *Hrs Open:* 24; 50 kw; 492 ft.; N32 30 56 W92 43 27
Mailing Address: P.O. Box 417, Grambling, LA 71245 US
Second Address: Washington Johnson Complex 2nd Fl., 403 Main St., Grambling, LA 71245
(318) 274-6343; *Fax:* (318) 274-3245
evansjb@gram.edu
License: Grambling, Lincoln County, LA held by Grambling State University.
Format: Gospel *Special Programming:* Jazz 56 hrs wkly, blues 9 hrs wkly; *Target Audience:* Black community.
Joyce Evans, General Manager

Gray

KCIL
08-01-1967; 96.7 MHz FM; *Hrs Open:* 24; 12 kw; Ant 476 ft; N29 41 39 W90 59 58
Mailing Address: Box 2068, Houma, LA 70802
Second Address: 120 Prevost Dr., Houma, LA 70364
(985) 851-1020; *Fax:* (985) 872-4403
info@mix967.net
License: Gray, St. Mary County, LA held by Sunburst Media-Louisiana LLC.
Group Owner: Sunburst Media-Louisiana LLC; (acq 1-23-2007; grpsl)
Nat'l Network: Jones Radio Networks
Hrs. of News Programming: News progmg 2 hrs wkly; *Target Audience:* 18-34; majority women
Eric Gill, Operations Dir
Hilary Domangue, General Manager

Gretna

KGLA
01-06-1969; 1540 kHz AM; 1 kw-D, NDD; N29 53 15 W90 5 3
PO Box 428, Marrero, LA 70072 US
(504) 799-4242
info@kgla.tv
License: Gretna, LA held by Crocodile Broadcasting Corp.
Arbitron Metro Market: New Orleans, LA; *Format:* Spanish
Ernesto Schweikert, General Manager
Miriam Danilov, General Sales Mgr
Mario Raul Zavala, Programming Director

KKNO
09-10-1989; 750 kHz AM; *Hrs Open:* Sunrise-sunset; 0.25 kw-D, NDD; N29 53 15 W90 5 3
P.O. Box 641403, Kenner, LA 70064 US
(504) 347-7775; *Fax:* (504) 347-7440
kkno750am@aol.com
License: Gretna, LA held by Robert C. Blakes Enterprises Inc.
Arbitron Metro Market: New Orleans, LA; *Format:* Christian, Gospel, 74; *Hrs. of News Programming:* News progmg 10 hrs wkly; *Target Audience:* General.; *Adv. Rates:* 18.00; 18.00; 18.00; na
Robert Blakes Sr., President
Lois Blakes, General Manager
Stacey Blakes, General Sales Mgr

Hammond

***KSLU**
11-11-1974; 90.9 MHz FM; *Hrs Open:* 24; 3 kw; 141 ft.; N30 30 53 W90 27 59
D Vickers Hall, Room 112, SLU 10783, Hammond, LA 70402 US
(985) 549-2330; *Fax:* (985) 549-3960
www.kslu.org
kslu@selu.edu
License: Hammond, Tangipahoa County, LA held by Southeastern Louisiana University.
Nat'l Network: PRI
Arbitron Metro Market: Hammond, LA; *Format:* Alternative; *Hrs. of News Programming:* news progmg 30 hrs wkly; *No. News Employees:* 1; *Target Audience:* General.; *Adv. Rates:* 15; 10; 10; 8
Todd Delaney, General Manager
Don Ellzey, News Director
Steve Portier, Chief Engineer

WRQQ
04-03-1965; 103.3 MHz FM; *Hrs Open:* 24; 100 kw; Ant 1,004 ft; N30 24 06 W90 50 43
631 Main St., Baton Rouge, LA 70806-2930 US
(225) 926-1106
www.classichits1033.com
License: Hammond, LA held by Radio License Holding CBC, LLC
Group Owner: Cumulus Media Inc.; (acq 1999; grpsl).
Nat'l Network: ABC; *Regional Network:* La. Net; *Nat'l Reps:* McGavren Guild
Arbitron Metro Market: Baton Rouge, LA; *Format:* Adult Contemp; *Hrs. of News Programming:* news progmg 3 hrs wkly; *No. News Employees:* 1; *Target Audience:* 25-54.
J'Michael Francios, Operations Mgr
Pat Galloway, General Manager
Tiffany Faul, General Sales Mgr
Jeff Johnson, Programming Director
Deontray Alexander, Promotions Manager

WFPR
11-15-1947; 1400 kHz AM; *Hrs Open:* 24; 1 kw-U, ND1; N30 30 31 W90 30 18
PO Box 1829, Hammond, LA 70404 US
(985) 345-0060; *Fax:* (985) 542-9377
License: Hammond, LA held by North Shore Broadcasting Co. Inc.
Nat'l Network: CBS
Format: Country *Special Programming:* Farm one hr, gospel 12 hrs wkly; *Hrs. of News Programming:* news progmg 7 hrs wkly; *No. News Employees:* 1; *Target Audience:* 35-64.; *Adv. Rates:* 20; 15; 15; 10
Wayne Dowdy, President
Eloise Dowdy, General Manager
Ben Bickham, Programming Director

WHMD
08-26-1974; 107.1 MHz FM; 6 kw; 328 ft.; N30 25 32 W90 17 1
200 East Thomas Street, Hammond, LA 70401 US
(985) 345-0060; *Fax:* (985) 542-9377
License: Hammond, Tangipahoa County, LA
Group Owner: Northshore Broadcasting
Format: Country; *Adv. Rates:* 25; 20; 20; 15
Moss Bresnahan, President
Brian Shirey, General Manager/Sales Manager
Richard Clark, Programming Director
Ruth Joiner, Business Manager

Haughton

KBTT
01-01-1993; 103.7 MHz FM; *Hrs Open:* 24; 6 kw; 328 ft.; N32 33 11 W93 34 56
208 N. Thomas Dr., Shreveport, LA 71137 US
(318) 222-3122; *Fax:* (318) 320-0102
www.kbtt.fm
License: Haughton, Bossier County, LA held by Alpha Media Licensee LLC
Group Owner: Alpha Media LLC; (acq 4-14-2015; grpsl).
Arbitron Metro Market: Shreveport, LA; *Format:* Urban Contemporary; *No. News Employees:* 1; *Target Audience:* 18-34.
Cary Camp, General Manager
Melvin Jones, Urban Market Sales Manager
Quinn Echols, Program Manager

Heflin

***KIMW**
105.5 MHz FM; 6 kw; N32 31 7 W93 17 59 *Rebroadcasts:* Rebroadcasts KAWZ(FM)
P.O. Box 391, Twin Falls, ID 83303
(208)733-3133; *Fax:* (208) 736-1958
www.csnradio.com
License: Heflin, Webster County, LA held by Calvary Chapel of Twin Falls Inc
Group Owner: CSN International
Format: Christian, Religious

Hodge

KRLQ
08-15-2007; 94.1 MHz FM; 47 kw; 507 ft.; N32 24 35 W92 53 49
Mailing Address: US
Second Address: 1319 N. Vienna, Ruston, LA 71270
(318) 255-7941; *Fax:* (318) 255-8211
krlq941fm@bellsouth.net
License: Hodge, Jackson County, LA held by William W. Brown.
Nat'l Network: ABC; *Regional Network:* La. Net.
Arbitron Metro Market: Hodge, LA; *Format:* Country, Sports, 86
Bob Day, Programming Director
Cherie Freeman, Office Manager
Larry Allen, Music Director

Homer

***KYXA**
03-01-1998; 106.7 MHz FM; 50 kw; 459 ft.; N32 44 39 W93 22 52
3712 Cornell Drive, Shreveport, LA 71107 US
(916) 251-1600; *Fax:* (916) 251-1650
www.klove.com
License: Homer, Claiborne County, LA held by Educational Media Foundation.
Group Owner: EMF Broadcasting; (acq 5-30-2006).
Nat'l Network: K-Love
Format: Christian
Mike Novak, President
Chip Bailey, Operations Dir
David Pierce, Programming Director
Ed Lenane, News Director
Sam Wallington, Engineering Dir
Marya Morgan, News Reporter
Richard Hunt, News Reporter

Houma

KJIN
04-01-1946; 1490 kHz AM; *Hrs Open:* 24; 1 kw-U, ND1; N29 34 14 W90 43 42
Mailing Address: P.O Box 2068, Houma, LA 70360 US
Second Address: 120 Prevost Dr., Houma, LA 70364
(985) 851-1020; *Fax:* (985) 872-4403
License: Houma, LA held by Sunburst Media-Louisiana LLC.
Group Owner: Sunburst Media-Louisiana LLC; (acq 1-23-2007; grpsl)
Nat'l Network: ABC; *Nat'l Reps:* Roslin
Format: Sports; *Hrs. of News Programming:* news progmg 3 hrs wkly; *No. News Employees:* 1; *Target Audience:* 35 plus.; *Adv. Rates:* 15; 15; 15; 10
John Delise, Operations Dir
Danny Fletcher, General Manager
Cade Voison, Programming Director
Bo Hoover, Chief Engineer

KVDU
11-15-1968; 104.1 MHz FM; *Hrs Open:* 24; 100 kw; Ant 1,945 ft; N29 57 13 W90 43 25
929 Howard Ave., New Orleans, LA 70360
(504) 679-7300; *Fax:* (504) 679-7358
www.voodoo104.com
License: Houma, Terrebonne County, LA held by Clear Channel Broadcasting Licenses Inc.
Group Owner: iHeartMedia; (acq 1-27-2009; with WJRR(FM) Cocoa Beach, FL)
Nat'l Reps: Clear Channel
Population Served: 2,500,000; *Arbitron Metro Market:* New Orleans, LA; *Format:* Contemporary Hits/Top 40; *Hrs. of News*

Programming: news progmg 2 hrs wkly; *No. News Employees:* 1; *Target Audience:* 25-54.
Nicky Sparrow, Senior Vice President of Sales

Iota

*KITA
01-01-2008; 89.5 MHz FM; 19 kw vert; 433 ft.; N30 11 17 W92 37 55 *Rebroadcasts:* Rebroadcasts KLRD(FM) Yucaipa, CA 100%
188 South Bellevue, Suite 222, Memphis, TN 38104 US
(888) 937-2471; *Fax:* (916) 251-1650
www.air1.com
info@air1.com
License: Iota, Acadia County, LA held by Educational Media Foundation.
Group Owner: EMF Broadcasting; (acq 11-1-2006; grpsl)
Nat'l Network: Air 1
Arbitron Metro Market: Iota, LA; *Format:* Alternative, Christian
Darrell Chambliss, Chairman
Alan Mason, COO
Mike Novak, President and CEO
Chip Bailey, Operations Dir
Ed Lenane, News Director
Sam Wallington, Engineering Dir
Eric Moser, Chief Financial Officer
Brian Burger, Vice President ofHuman Resources
D. Kevin Blair, Secretary and General Counsel
Larry Moody, Director
Mitch Barnhart, Director

Jackson

WNXX
10-17-2001; 104.5 MHz FM; *Hrs Open:* 24; 3 kw; 472 ft.; N30 44 44 W91 7 32 *Rebroadcasts:* Rebroadcasts KNXX(FM) Donaldsonville 100%
Mailing Address: 729 Champagne Drive, Kenner, LA 70065 US
Second Address: 929-B Government St., Baton Rouge, LA 70802
(225) 388-9898; *Fax:* (225) 383-3700
www.1045espn.com
cindy.manzella@gbcradio.com
License: Jackson, East Feliciana County, LA held by Guaranty Broadcasting Co. of Baton Rouge LLC.
Group Owner: Guaranty Broadcasting Co. of Baton Rouge, LLC; (acq 10-5-2000; $1.044 million)
Arbitron Metro Market: Baton Rouge, LA; *Format:* Alternative; *Target Audience:* Adults 18-49.
George Foster Jr., Chairman
Bridger Eglin, President
Owen Weber, Operations Dir
Dave Dunaway, Operations Manager
Charles Hanagriff, Sports Director
James Gilmore, Online Marketing Manager
Gordy Rush, Market Manager

Jean Lafitte

KXMG
12-31-1965; 107.5 MHz FM; 69 kw; Ant 650 ft; N29 26 48 W90 44 34
Mailing Address: Box 2068, Houma, LA 70802
Second Address: 120 Prevost Dr., Houma, LA 70364
(985) 851-1020; *Fax:* (985) 872-4403
www.1075kcil.net
info@1075kcil.net
License: Jean Lafitte, Terrebonne County, LA held by Sunburst Media-Louisiana LLC.
Group Owner: Sunburst Media-Louisiana LLC
Population Served: 250,000; *Arbitron Metro Market:* New Orleans, LA; *Hrs. of News Programming:* news progmg 2 hrs wkly; *No. News Employees:* 1; *Target Audience:* Adults; 25-54; *Adv. Rates:* 55; 55; 45; 25
John Brewer, Operations Dir
Danny Fletcher, General Manager
Bill Vance, Station Manager
Shane Evath, News Director

Jena

*KAYT
01-01-2001; 88.1 MHz FM; 15.5 kw horiz, 70 kw vert; 1007 ft.; N31 33 55 W92 33 0
2721 East Erwin Street, Tyler, TX 75708 US
(318) 484-2500; *Fax:* (318) 487-0909
www.kaytfm.com
License: Jena, La Salle County, LA held by Black Media Works Inc.
Group Owner: Black Media Works Inc.
Arbitron Metro Market: Alexandria, LA; *Format:* Religious
Raymond Kassis, General Manager
Jocelyn Jacob, Station Manager

KJNA-FM
11-01-1976; 102.7 MHz FM; *Hrs Open:* 24; 6 kw; 299 ft.; N31 41 51 W92 5 43
Mailing Address: 2nd and Elm Street, Jena, LA 71342 US
Second Address: 1791 N. 2nd St., Jena, LA 71342
(318) 992-4155; *Fax:* (318) 992-4479
kjnafm@hotmail.com
License: Jena, La Salle County, LA held by Little River Radio Co.
Group Owner: The Radio Group
Format: Country; *Hrs. of News Programming:* news progmg 20 hrs wkly; *No. News Employees:* 1; *Target Audience:* 25-54.
Sean Riley, Operations Manager

Jennings

KJEF
11-01-1950; 1290 kHz AM; *Hrs Open:* 24; 1 kw-D, ND1; 0.28 kw-N, ND1; N30 12 38 W92 39 55
1215 S. Lake Arthur Ave., Jennings, LA 70546 US
(337) 433-1641; *Fax:* (337) 433-2999
www.cajunradio.net
leslie.guidry@townsquaremedia.com
License: Jennings, LA held by Townsquare Media Lake Charles License LLC
Group Owner: Townsquare Media; (acq 2-6-2008; grpsl)
Regional Network: La. Net.
Format: Ethnic; *Target Audience:* General.
Leslie Guidry, General Manager
Mike Soileau, Brand Manager
Brad Burley, Director Of Sales
Kristian Bland, Digital Managing Editor

KHLA
01-01-1963; 92.9 MHz FM; *Hrs Open:* 24; 30 kw; 640 ft.; N30 10 48 W93 1 52
1215 S. Lake Arthur Ave., Jennings, LA 70546 US
(337) 433-1641; *Fax:* (337) 433-2999
www.929thelake.com
leslie.guidry@townsquaremedia.com
License: Jennings, Jefferson Davis County, LA held by Townsquare Media Lake Charles License LLC
Group Owner: Townsquare Media; (acq 2-6-2008; grpsl)
Format: Contemporary Hits/Top 40, Adult Contemp
Leslie Guidry, General Manager
Gary Shannon, Brand Manager
Brad Burley, Director Of Sales
Kristian Bland, Digital Managing Editor

Jonesboro

*KTOC-FM
10-01-1967; 104.9 MHz FM; 25 kw; 236 ft.; N32 13 28 W92 43 27
Mailing Address: 3712 Cornell Dr., Shreveport, LA 71107 US
Second Address: 8919 World Ministry Ave., Baton Rouge, LA 70810
(225) 768-3688(225) 768-8300; *Fax:* (225) 768-3729
www.jsm.org
kawikfish@yahoo.com
License: Jonesboro, Jackson County, LA held by Family Worship Center Church Inc.
Group Owner: Family Worship Center Church Inc.; (acq 9-25-2002; $200,000 with co-located AM).
Arbitron Metro Market: Baton Rouge, LA; *Format:* Christian
David Whitelaw, COO
Jimmy Swaggart, President
John Santiago, Programming Director

Jonesville

KZKR
01-01-2001; 105.1 MHz FM; 6 kw; Ant 315 ft; N31 36 21 W91 50 06
2 O'Ferrall St., Natchez, MS 39120 USA
(601) 442-4895; *Fax:* (601) 446-8260
listenupyall.com
License: Jonesville, Catahoula County, LA held by First Natchez Radio Group
Group Owner: First Natchez Radio Group; (acq 8-30-99; $150,000).

Kaplan

KMDL
08-01-1981; 97.3 MHz FM; *Hrs Open:* 24; 38 kw; 561 ft.; N30 2 54 W91 59 49
1749 Bertrand Drive, Lafayette, LA 70506 US
(337) 233-6000; *Fax:* (337) 234-7360
www.973thedawg.com
mike.grimsley@townsquaremedia.com
License: Kaplan, Vermilion County, LA
Group Owner: Townsquare Media; (acq 12-7-2001; grpsl)
Nat'l Network: AP Radio
Arbitron Metro Market: Lafayette, LA; *Format:* Country; *Hrs. of News Programming:* News progmg 7 hrs wkly; *Target Audience:* 25-54.
Mike Grimsley, General Manager
Jude Walker, Brand Manager
Frank Malambri, Director Of Sales
Dave Landry, Digital Managing Editor

Kenner

WWL-FM
09-08-1970; 105.3 MHz FM; 96 kw; 1004 ft.; N29 58 57 W89 57 9
400 Poydras Street, Suite 800, New Orleans, LA 70130 US
(504) 593-6376; *Fax:* (504) 593-1850
www.wwl.com
info@wwl.com
License: Kenner, Jefferson County, LA held by Entercom New Orleans License LLC.
Group Owner: Entercom Communications Corp.; (acq 12-13-99; grpsl).
Arbitron Metro Market: New Orleans, LA; *Format:* News, Talk
Chris Claus, General Manager
Malcolm Pelham, General Sales Mgr
Diane Newman, Programming Director
Helen Centanni, Promotions Director
Dave Cohen, News Director
Joe Pollet, Chief Engineer

Kentwood

WEMX
12-14-1967; 94.1 MHz FM; *Hrs Open:* 24; 100 kw; 981 ft; N30 51 18 W90 39 59
631 Main St., Baton Rouge, LA 70806 US
(225) 926-1106
www.max94one.com
License: Kentwood, Tangipahoe County, LA held by Radio License Holding CBC, LLC
Group Owner: Cumulus Media Inc.; (acq 1-14-99; grpsl).
Population Served: 2,225; *Arbitron Metro Market:* Kentwood, LA; *Format:* Contemporary Hits/Top 40
F'Michael Francios, Operations Dir
Greg Benefield, General Manager
Tiffany Faul, General Sales Mgr
J'Michaels Francios, Programming Director
Deondray Alexander, Promotions Director

*WPEF
91.5 MHz FM; 6 kw; 292 ft.; N31 2 2 W90 25 27
US
(504) 816-8000; *Fax:* (504) 816-8580
License: Kentwood, Tangipahoe County, LA held by Providence Educational Foundation Inc.
Arbitron Metro Market: Kentwood, LA
Clay Corvin, General Manager
Lindsay Flood, Underwriting Manager

LaPlace

WRKN
01-10-1966; 92.3 MHz FM; *Hrs Open:* 24; 100 kw; Ant 1,945 ft; N29 57 10 W90 43 26
201 St. Charles Ave., Suite 201, New Orleans, LA 70170 US
(504) 581-7002
www.nashfm929.com
License: LaPlace, LA held by Radio License Holding CBC, LLC
Group Owner: Cumulus Media Inc.; (acq 1-30-2004; $14.25 million).
Nat'l Reps: Christal *Regional Reps:* Christal Radio
Population Served: 65,187; *Arbitron Metro Market:* Jackson, TN; *Format:* Country
Greg Benefeld, General Manager
Ray Mariner, Programming Director

Lacombe

WYLK
03-01-1996; 94.7 MHz FM; *Hrs Open:* 24; 2.9 kw; 479 ft.; N30 23 8 W89 55 33
69170 Hwy. 190, Covington, LA 70433 USA
(985) 867-5990; *Fax:* (985) 867-9550
lake947sports.wordpress.com
License: Lacombe, St. Tammany County, LA held by North Shore Broadcasting Co. Inc.

Group Owner: C. Wayne Dowdy
Arbitron Metro Market: Lacombe, LA; Format: Christian; Hrs. of News Programming: news progmg 2 hrs wkly; No. News Employees: 1; Target Audience: 25-54; general

Lafayette

KFXZ
08-26-2004; 1520 kHz AM; Hrs Open: 24; 10 kW-D, .5 kW-N; N30 16 51 W92 0 53
3501 NW Evangeline Thruway, Carencro, LA 70520 USA
(337) 896-1600; Fax: (337) 993-5510
License: Lafayette, LA held by Delta Media Corp.
Group Owner: Delta Media Corp.
Arbitron Metro Market: Lafayette, LA; Format: Spanish, Adult Contemp
Charles Chatelain, CEO/COO

KJCB
04-09-1982; 770 kHz AM; 1 kw-D, DAN; 0.5 kw-N, DAN; N30 17 55 W91 59 30
413 Jefferson Street, Lafayette, LA 70501 US
License: Lafayette, LA held by R & M Broadcasting Inc.
Arbitron Metro Market: Lafayette, LA; Format: Gospel; Target Audience: 25-54.

KPEL
01-02-1950; 1420 kHz AM; 1 kw-D, DAN; 0.75 kw-N, DAN; N30 16 38 W92 3 51
1749 Bertrand Drive, Lafayette, LA 70506 US
(337) 233-6000; Fax: (337) 234-7360
www.espn1420.com
mike.grimsley@townsquaremedia.com
License: Lafayette, LA
Group Owner: Townsquare Media; (acq 12-7-2001; grpsl)
Regional Network: La. Net; Nat'l Reps: Christal
Arbitron Metro Market: Lafayette, LA; Format: Sports; Target Audience: 35-54; male
Mike Grimsley, General Manager
Scott Prather, Brand Manager
Frank Malambri, Director Of Sales
Dave Landry, Digital Managing Editor

KRRQ
03-01-1996; 95.5 MHz FM; 50 kw; 443 ft; N30 21 08 W92 10 51
202 Galbert Rd., Lafayette, LA 70506 US
(337) 232-1311
www.krrq.com
License: Lafayette, LA held by Radio License Holding CBC, LLC
Group Owner: Cumulus Media Inc.; (acq 1-14-99; grpsl).
Arbitron Metro Market: Lafayette Metro area; Format: Urban Contemporary
Lance Knoll, General Sales Mgr
Jackson Brown, Programming Director
Lynette Batiste, Promotions Director

*KRVS
01-01-1962; 88.7 MHz FM; 27.5 kw horiz, 100 kw vert; 1243 ft.; N30 19 20 W92 22 40
Mailing Address: Usl Box 42171, Lafayette, LA 70504 US
Second Address: 231 Hebrard Blvd., Lafayette, LA 70503
(337) 482-5787; Fax: (337) 482-6101
www.krvs.org
krvs@louisiana.edu
License: Lafayette, Lafayette County, LA held by University of Southwestern Louisiana.
Nat'l Network: NPR
Arbitron Metro Market: Lafayette, LA; Format: Blues, Jazz; Target Audience: General.
James Hebert, Operations Dir
Karl Fontenot, Chief Engineer
Judith Meriwether, Development Director

*KIKL
02-07-1988; 90.9 MHz FM; Hrs Open: 24; 8.2 kw; 377 ft.; N30 17 5 W92 4 3
107 Parkgate Drive, Tupelo, MS 38803 US
(916) 251-1600; Fax: (916) 251-1650
www.klove.com
klove@klove.com
License: Lafayette, Lafayette County, LA held by Educational Media Foundation.
Group Owner: EMF Broadcasting; (acq 4-25-2005; $1.5 million).
Nat'l Network: K-Love
Arbitron Metro Market: Rocklin, CA; Format: Christian
Darrell Chambliss, Chairman
Mike Novak, CEO/COO

KSMB
01-01-1964; 94.5 MHz FM; 100 kw; Ant 1,079 ft; N30 21 44 W92 12 53
202 Galbert Rd., Lafayette, LA 70506 US
(337) 232-1311
www.ksmb.com
License: Lafayette, LA held by Radio License Holding CBC, LLC
Group Owner: Cumulus Media Inc.; (acq 4-26-01; grpsl).
Population Served: 122,130; Arbitron Metro Market: Lafayette, LA; Format: Contemporary Hits/Top 40; Target Audience: 18-49; active on-the-go adults
Bobby Novosad, Programming Director
Lynette Batiste, Promotions Director

KTDY
09-15-1966; 99.9 MHz FM; 100 kw; 984 ft.; N30 12 6 W91 46 37
1749 Bertrand Dr, Lafayette, LS 70506 US
(337) 237-5839
www.999ktdy.com
License: Lafayette, Lafayette County, LA
Group Owner: Townsquare Media
Arbitron Metro Market: Lafayette, LA; Format: Adult Contemp; Target Audience: 25-54; female
Mike Grimsley, General Manager
Pam Begnaud, General Sales Mgr
C.J. Clements, Programming Director

KVOL
05-18-1935; 1330 kHz AM; 5 kw-D, DAN; 1 kw-N, DAN; N30 14 29 W92 3 31
3225 Ambassador Caffery Parkwa, Lafayette, LA 70506 US
(337) 896-1600; Fax: (337) 896-2695
License: Lafayette, LA held by Delta Media Corp.
Group Owner: Delta Media Corp.; (acq 1-28-2004; grpsl).
Nat'l Network: Westwood One
Arbitron Metro Market: Lafayette, LA; Format: News, Talk; Target Audience: 25-54; middle & upper income
Charles Sagona, General Manager

Lake Charles

KAOK
05-10-1947; 1400 kHz AM; Hrs Open: 24; 1 kw-D, ND1; 1 kw-N, ND1; N30 14 10 W93 10 2
425 Broad Street, Lake Charles, LA 70601 US
(337) 439-3300; Fax: (337) 433-7278
www.kaok.com
License: Lake Charles, LA held by Cumulus Licensing LLC.
Group Owner: Cumulus Media Inc.; (acq 12-6-2004; $3 million with KQLK(FM) De Ridder).
Nat'l Network: CBS; Regional Network: La. Net.
Arbitron Metro Market: Lake Charles, LA; Format: News, News/Talk, 86; Hrs. of News Programming: news progmg 168 hrs wkly; No. News Employees: 1; Target Audience: 24 plus; baby boomers
Eric Nielson, Operations Dir
Jimmie Cole, General Sales Mgr
Eric Nielson, Programming Director
Kevin Goode, Promotions Manager
Richard Rhodes, Chief Engineer

KBIU
12-01-1976; 103.3 MHz FM; Hrs Open: 24; 35 kw; 479 ft.; N30 14 41 W93 20 37
111 East Kilbourn Avenue, Suite 2700, Milwaukee, WI 53202 US
(337) 439-3300; Fax: (337) 433-7701
www.kbiu.com
License: Lake Charles, Calcasieu County, LA held by Cumulus Licensing Corp.
Group Owner: Cumulus Media Inc.; (acq 12-17-98; grpsl)
Nat'l Reps: Katz Radio
Arbitron Metro Market: Lake Charles, LA; Format: Adult Contemp; Target Audience: 25-54; adult
Eric Nielson, Operations Dir
Jimmie Cole, General Sales Mgr
Kevin Goode, Promotions Manager
Holly Fontenot, News Director
Richard Rhodes, Chief Engineer

KNGT
11-08-1965; 99.5 MHz FM; 100 kw; 1171 ft.; N30 17 26 W93 34 35
P.O. Box 3067, Lake Charles, LA 70602 US
(337) 433-1641; Fax: (337) 433-2999
www.gator995.com
leslie.guidry@townsquaremedia.com
License: Lake Charles, Calcasieu County, LA held by Townsquare Media Lake Charles License LLC
Group Owner: Townsquare Media; (acq 2-6-2008; grpsl)
Nat'l Reps: Christal
Arbitron Metro Market: Lake Charles, LA; Format: Country
Special Programming: Local 20 hours wkly; Target Audience: 25-54.
Leslie Guidry, General Manager
Erik Tee, Brand Manager
Brad Burley, Director Of Sales
Kristian Bland, Digital Managing Editor

KLCL
05-12-1935; 1470 kHz AM; 5 kw-D, ND1; 0.5 kw-N, ND1; N30 15 31 W93 16 7
P.O. Box 3067, Lake Charles, LA 70502 US
(337) 433-1641; Fax: (337) 433-2999
www.cajunradio.net
leslie.guidry@townsquaremedia.com
License: Lake Charles, LA held by Townsquare Media Lake Charles License LLC
Group Owner: Townsquare Media; (acq 2-6-2008; grpsl)
Regional Network: La. Net.
Arbitron Metro Market: Lake Charles, L; Format: Ethnic; Target Audience: 18-64.
Leslie Guidry, General Manager
Mike Soileau, Brand Manager
Brad Burley, Director Of Sales
Kristian Bland, Digital Managing Editor

*KOJO
01-01-1990; 91.1 MHz FM; Hrs Open: 24; 4 kw horiz, 14 kw vert; 387 ft.; N30 12 7 W92 56 47 Rebroadcasts: Rebroadcasts KJMJ(AM) Alexandria
601 Washington St, Alexandria, LA 71301 US
(888)408-0201; Fax: (318) 449-9954
www.radiomaria.us
License: Lake Charles, Calcasieu County, LA held by Radio Maria Inc.
Group Owner: Radio Maria Inc.; acq 10-13-99).
Arbitron Metro Market: Lake Charles, LA; Format: Christian, Talk, 74; Target Audience: General; Christians seeking training & encouragement through Bible teaching programs

KJMH
08-01-1998; 107.5 MHz FM; Hrs Open: 24; 50 kw; 463 ft.; 39 26 29 N 91 02 W
900 North Lakeshore Drive, Lake Charles, LA 70601 US
(337) 433-1075
www.107jamz.com
leslie.guidry@townsquaremedia.com
License: Lake Charles, Jefferson Davis County, LA held by Townsquare Media Lake Charles License LLC
Group Owner: Townsquare Media; (acq 2-6-2008; grpsl)
Arbitron Metro Market: Lake Charles metro area; Format: Urban Contemporary; No. News Employees: 1; Target Audience: 25-54.
Leslie Guidry, General Manager
Erik Tee, Brand Manager
Brad Burley, Director Of Sales
Kristian Bland, Digital Managing Editor

KXZZ
01-01-1947; 1580 kHz AM; Hrs Open: 24; 1 kw-D, DAN; 1 kw-N, DAN; N30 15 28 W93 11 55
425 Broad Street, Lake Charles, LA 70601 US
(337) 439-3300; Fax: (337) 433-7701
www.kxzz1580am.com
License: Lake Charles, LA held by Cumulus Licensing Corp.
Group Owner: Cumulus Media Inc.
Nat'l Network: American Urban; Nat'l Reps: Katz Radio
Arbitron Metro Market: Lake Charles, LA; Format: Black; Target Audience: 25-54; adult
Eric Nielson, Operations Dir
Jimmie Cole, General Sales Mgr
Kevin Goode, Promotions Manager

KYKZ
01-01-1976; 96.1 MHz FM; Hrs Open: 24; 100 kw; 479 ft.; N30 14 41 W93 20 37
111 East Kilbourn Avenue, Suite 2700, Milwaukee, WI 53202 US
(337) 436-7277; Fax: (337) 436-7278
www.kykz.com
License: Lake Charles, Calcasieu County, LA held by Cumulus Licensing Corp.
Group Owner: Cumulus Media Inc.; (acq 12-17-98; grpsl)
Arbitron Metro Market: Lake Charles, LA; Format: Country; Hrs. of News Programming: news progmg 8 hrs wkly; No. News Employees: 3; Target Audience: General.
Jimmie Cole, General Sales Mgr
Eric Nielson, Programming Director
Kevin Goode, Promotions Manager
Richard Rhodes, Chief Engineer
Chuck Bortnick, Marketing Manager

*KYLC
01-01-2001; 90.3 MHz FM; 80 kw vert; 469 ft.; N30 38 10 W93 2 33
P.O. Box 3206, Tupelo, MS 38803 US

(662) 844-8888; *Fax:* (662) 842-6791
www.afr.net
faq@afa.net
License: Lake Charles, Calcasieu County, LA held by American Family Association.
Group Owner: American Family Radio; (acq 3-14-01).
Arbitron Metro Market: Tupelo, MS; *Format:* Christian, Religious
Tim Wildmon, President
Donald Wildmon, Founder
Buddy Smith, Sr VP
Ed Vitagliano, Exec VP
Randy Sharp, Director Of Special Projects
Meeke Addison, Director Of Communications
Abraham Hamilton III, General Counsel

Lake Providence

KLPL(AM)
06-27-1957; 1050 kHz AM; 250 w-D, 22 w-N; N32 48 59 W91 12 22
645 Church St., Willis Broadcasting Corp., Norfolk, VA 23510
(757) 622-4600; *Fax:* (757) 624-6515
License: Lake Providence, East Carroll County, LA held by Willis Broadcasting Corp.
Group Owner: Willis Broadcasting Corp.; acq 4-21-98; $120,000 with co-located FM).
Population Served: 10,300 *Target Audience:* General.
Robert Dominguez, General Manager
Toya Hall, Programming Director

KLPL(FM)
01-28-1975; 92.7 MHz FM; 3 kw; Ant 154 ft; N32 48 59 W91 12 22
645 Church St., Willis Broadcasting Corp., Norfolk, LA 23510
(757) 622-4600; *Fax:* (757) 624-6515
License: Lake Providence, East Carroll County, LA
Population Served: 10,300
Angela Carter, General Manager
Chris Hertlein, Programming Director

Larose

KLRZ
03-29-1993; 100.3 MHz FM; *Hrs Open:* 24; 89 kw; 586 ft.; N29 33 1 W90 21 4
P.O. Box 1350, Larose, LA 70373 US
(985) 798-7792; *Fax:* (985) 798-7793
www.klrzfm.com
License: Larose, Lafourche County, LA held by Coastal Broadcasting of Larose Inc.
Nat'l Network: Westwood One
Arbitron Metro Market: New Orleans, LA; *Format:* Ethnic; *Hrs. of News Programming:* news progmg 22 hrs wkly; *No. News Employees:* 1; *Target Audience:* 25-54; professionals
Andrea Galjour, Operations Dir
Jerry Gisclair, General Manager

Leesville

KJAE
10-01-1979; 93.5 MHz FM; 7.5 kw; 328 ft.; N31 8 28 W93 17 44
PO Box 1323 ., 101 Lees Lane, Leesville, LA 71466 US
337-238-5523
www.kjae935.com
License: Leesville, Vernon County, LA
Format: Country

KLLA
09-01-1956; 1570 kHz AM
Mailing Address: 101 Lees Lane, PO Box 1323, Leesville, LA 71446 US
Second Address: 101 Lees Ln., Leesville, LA 71446
(337) 239-3402; *Fax:* (337) 238-9283
License: Leesville, LA held by Pene Broadcasting Co.
Arbitron Metro Market: Alexandria, LA; *Format:* Country
Penny Scogin, General Manager
Peggy Merritt, General Sales Mgr
Tony Evans, Chief Engineer

KVVP
01-20-1977; 105.7 MHz FM; *Hrs Open:* 24; 13.5 kw; 449 ft.; N31 0 19 W93 16 42
P.O. Drawer K, Leesville, LA 71496 US
(337) 537-5887; *Fax:* (337) 537-4152
www.kvvp.com
License: Leesville, Vernon County, LA held by Stannard Broadcasting Co. Inc.
Arbitron Metro Market: Leesville, LA; *Format:* Country *Special Programming:* Relg 9 hrs wkly; *Hrs. of News Programming:* news progmg 15 hrs wkly; *No. News Employees:* 1; *Target Audience:* 18-54; adults withspending power

KBDV
01-01-2008; 92.7 MHz FM; *Hrs Open:* 24 hours; 6 kw; 328 ft.; N31 7 7 W93 11 12
605 San Antonio Avenue, Many, LA 71449 US
(318) 256-5924; *Fax:* (318) 256-0950
www.bdcradio.com
License: Leesville, Vernon County, LA held by Baldridge-Dumas Communications Inc.
Group Owner: Baldridge-Dumas Communications Inc.
Arbitron Metro Market: Leesville, LA; *Format:* Adult Contemp
Michael Parker, Operations Dir
Rhonda Leach, General Manager
Donna Johnson, Station Manager

Mamou

KBON
06-01-1997; 101.1 MHz FM; *Hrs Open:* 24; 25 kw; 328 ft.; N30 29 50 W92 15 59
109 South 2nd Street, Eunice, LA 70535 US
(337) 546-0007; *Fax:* (337) 546-0097
www.kbon.com
101.1@kbon.com
License: Mamou, Evangeline County, LA held by Rose Ann Marx.
Format: Country
Paul Marx, General Manager

Mansfield

KJVC
09-01-1976; 92.7 MHz FM; *Hrs Open:* 24; 3 kw; 299 ft.; N32 1 18 W93 44 18
805 Polk St., Mansfield, LA 71052 US
(318) 871-0093; *Fax:* (318) 871-2927
www.kjvcfm.com
kjvc@kjvcfm.com
License: Mansfield, De Soto County, LA held by Leon Hunt
Group Owner: Star Radio Network
Format: Country; *Adv. Rates:* 6; 6; 6; 6
Leon Hunt, President

*KHMD
05-01-1994; 104.7 MHz FM; *Hrs Open:* 24; 25 kw; 328 ft.; N31 57 49 W93 53 58
2424 South Blvd., Houston, TX 77098 US
(713) 520-5200
www.khcb.org
email@khcb.org
License: Mansfield, De Soto County, LA held by Houston Christian Broadcasters Inc.
Group Owner: Houston Christian Broadcasters Inc.; (acq 12-30-2008; $150,000)
Arbitron Metro Market: Shreveport, LA; *Format:* Christian
Bruce E. Munsterman, President

*KMSL
01-01-2006; 91.7 MHz FM; 12 kw vert; 339 ft.; N32 10 39 W93 55 2 *Rebroadcasts:* Rebroadcasts WAFR(FM) Tupelo, MS 100%
180 Fisher Lane, Mansfield, LA 71052 US
(318) 933-8218
www.afr.net
License: Mansfield, DeSoto County, LA held by American Family Association.
Group Owner: American Family Radio; (acq 5-13-2005; $10 for CP)
Nat'l Network: American Family Radio
Arbitron Metro Market: El Dorado, AR; *Format:* Christian
Tim Wildmon, President
Donald Wildmon, Founder
Buddy Smith, Sr VP
Ed Vitagliano, Exec VP
Randy Sharp, Director Of Special Projects
Meeke Addison, Director Of Communications
Abraham Hamilton III, General Counsel

Mansura

KZLG
07-01-2000; 95.9 MHz FM; *Hrs Open:* 24; 6 kw; 322 ft.; N35 14 25 w111 35 53
4659 N Us Hwy 89, Flagstaff, AZ 86004 US
(928) 522-8282
www.eaglerocksonline.com
License: Mansura, Avoyelles County, LA held by Towers Investment Trust
Nat'l Network: AP Radio; *Regional Network:* La. Net.
Arbitron Metro Market: Flagstaff, AZ; *Format:* Adult Contemp; *Hrs. of News Programming:* 3 hrs; *Target Audience:* 25 plus.; *Adv. Rates:* 8; 8; 8; 8

Many

*KAVK
06-01-1998; 89.3 MHz FM; 12 kw; 427 ft.; N31 32 5 W93 25 21
P.O. Box 3206, Tupelo, MS 38803 US
(662) 844-8888; *Fax:* (662) 842-6791
www.afr.net
faq@afa.net
License: Many, Sabine County, LA held by American Family Association.
Group Owner: American Family Radio
Arbitron Metro Market: Tupelo, MS; *Format:* Christian, Religious
Tim Wildmon, President
Donald Wildmon, Founder
Buddy Smith, Sr. VP
Ed Vitagliano, Executive VP
Randy Sharp, Director Of Special Projects
Meeke Addison, Director Of Communications
Abraham Hamilton III, General Counsel & PublicPolicy

KWLV
11-12-1977; 107.1 MHz FM; 25 kw; 253 ft.; N31 36 27 W93 24 5
595 San Antonio Avenue, Many, LA 71449 US
(318) 256-5177; *Fax:* (318) 256-0950
www.bdcradio.com
kwlv@bellsouth.net
License: Many, Sabine County, LA
Arbitron Metro Market: Many, LA; *Format:* Country; *Target Audience:* 20 plus.
Rhonda Benson Leach, General Manager
Donna Johnson, Station Manager
Kenny Carter, Chief Engineer

Marksville

KAPB-FM
08-14-1971; 97.7 MHz FM; 6 kw; 328 ft.; N31 7 27 W92 4 40
P. O. Box 1319, Columbia, LA 71418 US
(318) 253-5272; *Fax:* (318) 253-5262
License: Marksville, Avoyelles County, LA held by Three Rivers Radio Co.
Group Owner: The Radio Group
Arbitron Metro Market: Alexandria, LA; *Format:* Country

Maurice

KYMK-FM
06-13-1985; 106.3 MHz FM; 2.6 kw; 495 ft.; N30 4 16 W92 11 53
140 South Ash Ave., Tempe, AZ 85281 US
(337) 993-5500; *Fax:* (337) 993-5510
www.1063radiolafayette.com
License: Maurice, Vermilion County, LA held by Delta Media Corp.
Group Owner: Delta Media Corp.
Arbitron Metro Market: Maurice, LA; *Format:* Adult Contemp
Charles Chatelain, CEO/COO
Charles Sagona, General Manager

Minden

KASO
04-01-1952; 1240 kHz AM; *Hrs Open:* 24; 1 kw-U, ND1; N32 37 50 W93 16 56
Post Office Box 1240, Minden, LA 71058 US
www.kbef.com
License: Minden, LA held by Minden Broadcasting
Nat'l Network: Jones Radio Networks; *Regional Network:* La. Net.
Arbitron Metro Market: Minden, LA; *Format:* Adult Contemp; *Hrs. of News Programming:* News progmg 102 hrs wkly; *Target Audience:* 35-64; male & female; *Adv. Rates:* 33; 16; 16; 16
Fred Caldwell, President
Mike Griffith, General Manager
Mark Cheesne, Programming Director

KLKL
07-01-1978; 95.7 MHz FM; *Hrs Open:* 24; 50 kw; 469 ft.; N32 33 16 W93 31 47
208 N. Thomas Dr., Shreveport, LA 71137 US
(318) 222-3122
www.klkl.fm
License: Minden, Webster County, LA held by Alpha Media Licensee LLC
Group Owner: Alpha Media LLC; (acq 4-14-2015; grpsl).
Arbitron Metro Market: Shreveport, LA; *Format:* Oldies; *No. News Employees:* 1; *Target Audience:* 25-54.
Cary Camp, Market Manager
Johnette Robinson, General Market Sales Manager
J.J. O'Brien, Programming Director

Monroe

KRJO
05-01-2001; 1680 kHz AM; *Hrs Open:* 24
Mailing Address: 3436 Hwy 45 North, Meridan, MS 39302 US
Second Address: 1109 Hudson Ln., Monroe, LA 71201
License: Monroe, LA held by Holladay Broadcasting of Louisiana LLC
Group Owner: Holladay Broadcasting of Louisiana LLC; acq 11-21-2003; grpsl).
Nat'l Reps: McGavren Guild

*KBMQ
08-15-1999; 88.7 MHz FM; *Hrs Open:* 24; 25 kw horiz, 24.5 kw vert; 458 ft.; N32 24 15 W92 2 7
130 Art Alley, Suite C, Monroe, LA 71201 US
(318) 387-1230; *Fax:* (318) 387-8856
www.887fm.org
License: Monroe, Ouachita County, LA held by Media Ministries Inc.
Arbitron Metro Market: Monroe, LA; *Format:* Christian; *Hrs. of News Programming:* News progmg one hr wkly; *Target Audience:* 25-54; women; *Adv. Rates:* 25; 25; 25; 20

*KEDM
04-23-1991; 90.3 MHz FM; *Hrs Open:* 24; 100 kw; 856 ft.; N32 39 38 W91 59 28
150 Riverside Mall, Baton Rouge, LA 70801 US
(318) 342-5556; *Fax:* (318) 342-5570
www.kedm.org
License: Monroe, Ouachita County, LA held by University of Louisiana at Monroe
Nat'l Network: NPR; *Regional Network:* La. Net.; *Wire Services:* AP
Arbitron Metro Market: Monroe, LA; *Format:* Classical, Jazz, 60
Jay Curtis, Programming Director
Bob Lenox, News Director
Kenneth Sanders, Chief Engineer
Lila Strode, Development Director

KJLO-FM
07-01-1946; 104.1 MHz FM; *Hrs Open:* 24; 97 kw; 1017 ft.; N32 39 36 W92 5 15
Mailing Address: US
Second Address: 1109 Hudson Ln., Monroe, LA 71201
(318) 388-2323; *Fax:* (318) 388-0569
www.kjlo.com
License: Monroe, Ouachita County, LA held by Holladay Broadcasting of Louisiana LLC.
Group Owner: Holladay Broadcasting of Louisiana LLC; (acq 10-1-2006; $500,000)
Nat'l Reps: McGavren Guild
Format: Country *Special Programming:* Gospel 4 hrs wkly; *No. News Employees:* 1; *Target Audience:* 25-54.
Robert Holladay, President

KLIP
04-01-1993; 105.3 MHz FM; *Hrs Open:* 24; 50 kw; 433 ft.; N32 33 8 W92 8 33
1109 Hudson Lane, Monroe, LA 71201 US
(318) 388-2323
www.la105.com
la105@bayou.com
License: Monroe, Ouachita County, LA held by Holladay Broadcasting of Louisiana LLC
Group Owner: Holladay Broadcasting of Louisiana LLC; acq 11-21-2003; grpsl).
Nat'l Network: ABC; *Nat'l Reps:* McGavren Guild
Arbitron Metro Market: Monroe, LA; *Format:* Contemporary Hits/Top 40, Adult Contemp; *Hrs. of News Programming:* News progmg 2 hrs wkly; *Target Audience:* 25-54.
Bob Holladay, President

KXRR
11-15-1965; 106.1 MHz FM; 97 kw; 1017 ft.; N32 39 36 W92 5 15
1200 North 18th Street, Suite D, Monroe, LA 71201 US
(318) 387-3922; *Fax:* (318) 322-4585
rock106kxrr.com
License: Monroe, Ouachita County, LA held by Opus Broadcasting Monroe L.L.C.
Group Owner: Opus Media Holdings LLC; (acq 7-19-2004; grpsl).
Nat'l Reps: Christal
Arbitron Metro Market: Monroe, LA; *Target Audience:* 25-49.
Chris Zimmerman, General Manager
Don Kellogg, Programming Director

*KXUL
05-09-1973; 91.1 MHz FM; *Hrs Open:* 24; 8.5 kw; 715 ft.; N32 39 38 W91 59 28
128 Stubbs Hall, 40 Bayou Drive, Monroe, LA 71209 US
(318) 342-5985
www.kxul.com
License: Monroe, Ouachita County, LA held by University of Lousiana at Monroe.
Arbitron Metro Market: Monroe, LA; *Format:* Alternative; *Target Audience:* 12-34.
Mason Howard, Music Director

KMLB
07-01-1931; 540 kHz AM
1400 Oliver Road, Monroe, LA 71201 US
(318) 388-2323; *Fax:* (318) 388-0569
www.kmlb.com
talk540@bayou.com
License: Monroe, LA held by Holliday Broadcasting of Louisiana LLC.
Group Owner: Holladay Broadcasting of Louisiana LLC; (acq 3-4-2008; $150,000)
Nat'l Network: ABC; ABC Information & Entertainment; Fox News Radio; Premiere Radio Networks; Talk Radio Network; *Regional Network:* La. Net.; La. Agri-News; Yancey AG Network; Agri-Net;
Nat'l Reps: Eastman Radio
Arbitron Metro Market: Monroe, LA; *Format:* News, Talk *Special Programming:* New Orleans Saints/LSU; *Hrs. of News Programming:* 3hrs / day; *No. News Employees:* 1; *Target Audience:* 25 plus.
Bob Holladay, General Manager

KMVX
01-29-1967; 101.9 MHz FM; 97 kw horiz, 96 kw vert; 1516 ft.; N32 11 50 W92 4 14
PO Box 4067, Monroe, LA 71211 US
(318) 807-3285; *Fax:* (318) 325-9466
www.starradiomonroe.com
License: Monroe, Ouachita County, LA held by Holladay Broadcasting of Louisiana LLC
Arbitron Metro Market: Monroe, LA; *Format:* Contemporary Hits/Top 40
Bobby Richards, Programming Director

*KYFL
10-08-1992; 89.5 MHz FM; *Hrs Open:* 24; 25 kw; 377 ft.; N32 33 8 W92 8 33
115 Warren Dr., West Monroe, LA 71291 US
(318) 396-6284; *Fax:* (318) 396-6284
www.bbnradio.org
bbn@bbnmedia.org
License: Monroe, Ouachita County, LA held by Bible Broadcasting Network Inc.
Group Owner: Bible Broadcasting Network
Arbitron Metro Market: Charlotte, NC; *Format:* Christian; *Hrs. of News Programming:* News progmg 3 hrs wkly; *Target Audience:* General.
Jason Padgett, Operations Manager

Moreauville

KLIL
07-25-1980; 92.1 MHz FM; 6 kw; 299 ft.; N31 2 53 W91 59 47
Mailing Address: P.O. Box 365, Moreauville, LA 71355 US
Second Address: 10586 Hwy. 1, Moreauville, LA 71355
(318) 985-2929; *Fax:* (318) 985-2995
klil@kricket.net
License: Moreauville, Avoyelles County, LA held by Cajun Broadcasting Inc.
Nat'l Network: AP Radio; *Regional Network:* La. Net.
Arbitron Metro Market: Alexandria, LA; *Format:* Oldies; *Target Audience:* 20 plus; working adults; *Adv. Rates:* 7; 7; 7; 7
Louis Coco Jr., President

Morgan City

KMRC
04-01-1954; 1430 kHz AM; *Hrs Open:* 24; 0.5 kw-D, NDD; N29 45 3 W91 10 24
P.O. Box 83, Morgan City, LA 70380 US
(504) 450-4225
www.kmrcradio.com
kmrc@kmrc1430.com
License: Morgan City, LA held by Spotlight Broadcasting L.L.C.
Group Owner: Spotlight Broadcasting LLC; acq 2-1-00; $109,000).
Format: Adult Contemp; *Hrs. of News Programming:* news progmg 5 hrs wkly; *No. News Employees:* 1; *Target Audience:* 25-54; middle to upper income; *Adv. Rates:* 12; 10; 10; 6.
John Stork, General Manager

Moss Bluff

KZWA
08-12-1994; 104.9 MHz FM; 25 kw; 328 ft.; N30 27 15 W93 8 20
P. O. Box 699, Lake Charles, LA 70602 US
(337) 491-9955; *Fax:* (337) 433-8097
www.kzwafm.com/
info@kzwa.com
License: Moss Bluff, Calcasieu County, LA held by B & C Broadcasting Inc.
Arbitron Metro Market: Moss Bluff, LA.; *Format:* Urban Contemporary; *Target Audience:* 18-34.

Natchitoches

*KBIO
07-02-2002; 89.7 MHz FM; 0.1 kw; 295 ft.; N31 47 13 W93 7 52
Rebroadcasts: Rebroadcasts KJMJ(AM) Alexandria
P O Drawer 2440, Tupelo, MS 38803 US
(318) 561-6145; *Fax:* (318) 449-9954
www.radiomaria.us
info.usa@radiomaria.org
License: Natchitoches, Natchitoches County, LA held by Radio Maria Inc.
Group Owner: Radio Maria Inc.; (acq 9-6-2001)
Arbitron Metro Market: Alexandria, LA; *Format:* Christian, Talk, 74

KDBH-FM
07-01-1965; 97.5 MHz FM; 6 kw; 220 ft.; N31 48 17 W93 1 27
720 Front Street, PO Box 607, Natchitoches, LA 71457 US
(318) 352-9696; *Fax:* (318) 357-9595
License: Natchitoches, Natchitoches County, LA held by Baldridge-Dumas Communications Inc.
Group Owner: Baldridge-Dumas Communications Inc.; acq 5-14-01; $340,000 with co-located AM including two-year noncompete agreement).
Nat'l Network: Jones Radio Networks; *Regional Network:* La. Net.
Arbitron Metro Market: Many, LA; *Format:* Country
Rhonda Benson Leach, General Manager
Donna Johnson, Station Manager
Kenny Carter, Chief Engineer

KNOC
05-01-1947; 1450 kHz AM; *Hrs Open:* 24; 1 kw-U, ND1; N31 45 47 W93 3 47
PO Box 607, Natchitoches, LA 71457 US
(318) 354-4000; *Fax:* (318) 352-9598
License: Natchitoches, LA held by North Face Broadcasting L.L.C.
Nat'l Network: ABC
Format: News, News/Talk, 86; *Hrs. of News Programming:* news progmg 20 hrs wkly; *No. News Employees:* 1; *Target Audience:* 35 plus; upper-middle class; *Adv. Rates:* 20; 20; 20; 10
John Brewer, Operations Dir
Bill Vance, Station Manager
Shane Erath, News Director

*KNWD
09-01-1975; 91.7 MHz FM; *Hrs Open:* 24; 0.255 kw horiz; 164 ft.; N31 44 51 W93 5 47
P. O. Box 3038, Natchiloches, LA 71497 US
(318) 357-5693
www.nsula.edu/thedemon
knwd@nsula.edu
License: Natchitoches, Natchitoches County, LA held by Northwestern State University of Louisiana.
Format: Variety/Diverse; *Hrs. of News Programming:* news progmg 3 hrs wkly; *No. News Employees:* 1; *Target Audience:* 18-25.
Brady Renard, General Manager

KZBL
10-08-1985; 100.7 MHz FM; *Hrs Open:* 24; 25 kw; 276 ft.; N31 48 17 W93 1 27
1115 Washington Street, Natchitoches, LA 71457 US
(318) 357-1007; *Fax:* (318) 357-9595
www.kzblradio.com/
License: Natchitoches, Natchitoches County, LA held by Baldridge-Dumas Communications Inc.
Group Owner: Baldridge-Dumas Communications Inc.; acq 6-21-99; $400,000).
Nat'l Network: Jones Radio Networks
Arbitron Metro Market: Natchitoches, LA; *Format:* Oldies; *Hrs. of News Programming:* News progmg 10 hrs wkly; *Target Audience:* 25-50.; *Adv. Rates:* 16; 12; 12; 10
Rhonda Benson Leach, General Manager
Donna Johnson, Station Manager

New Iberia

KANE
08-01-1946; 1240 kHz AM; *Hrs Open:* 24; 1 kw-U, ND1; N30 1 3 W91 50 10
P.O. Box 1350, Larose, LA 70373 US

(337) 365-3434; *Fax:* (337) 365-9117
www.kane1240.com
kane@kane1240.com
License: New Iberia, LA held by Coastal Broadcasting of Lafourche L.L.C.
Group Owner: Coastal Broadcasting; (acq 12-31-01).
Regional Network: La. Net.
Arbitron Metro Market: New Iberia, LA; *Format:* Ethnic; *Hrs. of News Programming:* News progmg 30 hrs wkly; *Target Audience:* 25-54.; *Adv. Rates:* 21; 16; 19; 14
Andrea Galjour, Operations Dir
Jerry Gisclair, General Manager

KNIR
06-01-1951; 1360 kHz AM; *Hrs Open:* 24
601 Washington Street, Alexandria, LA 71301 US
(318) 561-6145; *Fax:* (318) 449-9954
www.radiomaria.us
info.usa@radiomaria.org
License: New Iberia, LA held by Radio Maria Inc.
Group Owner: Radio Maria Inc.; (acq 6-10-2003; $45,000).
Arbitron Metro Market: Lafayette, LA; *Format:* Christian
Father Stenzel, General Manager

KYFJ
06-01-1992; 93.7 MHz FM; *Hrs Open:* 24; 100 kw; Ant 971 ft; N30 20 19 W91 31 23
202 Galbert Rd., Lafayette, LA 70506 US
(337) 232-1311
www.bbnradio.org
License: New Iberia, LA held by Bible Broadcasting Network Incorporated
Group Owner: Bible Broadcasting Network; (acq 10-8-99; $9.5 million)
Population Served: 500,000; *Arbitron Metro Market:* Baton Rouge, LA; *Format:* Religious

KXKC
01-01-1969; 99.1 MHz FM; *Hrs Open:* 24; 100 kw; 1,039 ft; N30 12 06 W91 46 37
202 Galbert Rd., Lafayette, LA 70560 US
(337) 232-1311
www.nashfm991.com
License: New Iberia, LA held by Radio License Holding CBC, LLC
Group Owner: Cumulus Media Inc.; (acq 12-5-2003; $7.6 million).
Population Served: 122,130; *Arbitron Metro Market:* Lafayette, LA; *Format:* Country; *Target Audience:* 18-49.
Mary Galyean, General Manager
Kris Vandyke, Programming Director
Lynette Batiste, Promotions, Marketing & Events
Wayne Mulling, VP/Market Mgr

New Orleans

WBOK
02-01-1951; 1230 kHz AM; 1 kw-U, ND1; N29 59 18 W90 2 45
1639 Gentilly Boulevard, New Orleans, LA 70119 US
(504) 942-0106; *Fax:* (291) 291-6804
www.wbok1230am.com
License: New Orleans, LA
Arbitron Metro Market: New Orleans, LA; *Format:* Gospel; *Target Audience:* 25 plus.

***WBSN-FM**
02-05-1979; 89.1 MHz FM; *Hrs Open:* 24; 11 kw; 440 ft.; N29 55 11 W90 1 29
3939 Gentilly Blvd., New Orleans, LA 70126 US
(504) 816-8000
www.lifesongs.com
onair@lifesongs.com
License: New Orleans, Orleans County, LA held by Providence Educational Foundation.
Arbitron Metro Market: New Orleans, LA; *Format:* Christian; *Target Audience:* 25-49; active, Christian oriented families

WEZB
09-01-1945; 97.1 MHz FM; 99 kw; 984 ft.; N29 55 11 W90 1 29
400 Poydras Street, 8th Floor, New Orleans, LA 70130 US
(504) 260-9797
www.b97.com
ino@b97.com
License: New Orleans, Orleans County, LA held by Entercom New Orleans License LLC.
Group Owner: Entercom Communications Corp.; (acq 12-13-99; grpsl)
Arbitron Metro Market: New Orleans, LA; *Format:* Contemporary Hits/Top 40; *Target Audience:* 18-34; females
Ken Beck, General Manager
Patrick Galloway, General Sales Mgr
Mike Kaplan, Programming Director
Joe Pollet, Chief Engineer

WGSO
01-27-1946; 990 kHz AM; *Hrs Open:* 24; 1 kw-D, ND1; 0.4 kw-N, ND1; N29 57 24 W90 4 34
110 Veterans Blvd., Suite 300, Metairie, LA 70005 US
(985) 639-3820; *Fax:* (985) 639-3869
www.wgso.com
info@wgso.com
License: New Orleans, LA held by Northshore Radio LLC
Arbitron Metro Market: New Orleans, LA; *Format:* News, News/Talk, 86
Mike Starr, General Manager

WLMG
03-15-1970; 101.9 MHz FM; *Hrs Open:* 24; 99 kw; 984 ft.; N29 55 11 W90 1 29
400 Poydras Street, 8th Floor, New Orleans, MD 70130 US
(504) 593-6376
www.magic1019.com
License: New Orleans, Orleans County, LA
Group Owner: Entercom Communications Corp.
Arbitron Metro Market: New Orleans, LA; *Format:* Adult Contemp

WLNO
05-26-1995; 1060 kHz AM; *Hrs Open:* 24
401 Whitney Avenue, Suite 160, Gretna, LA 70056 US
(504) 362-9800; *Fax:* (504) 362-5541
www.wlno.com
License: New Orleans, LA held by Communicom Co. of Louisiana L.P.
Arbitron Metro Market: New Orleans, LA; *Format:* Christian, Religious; *Target Audience:* General.
Carl DiMaria, CEO
Richard Kylberg, President

WNOE-FM
09-15-1968; 101.1 MHz FM; *Hrs Open:* 24; 100 kw; 1004 ft.; N29 58 57 W89 57 9
929 Howard Ave., New Orleans, LA 70113 US
(504) 679-7300; *Fax:* (504) 679-7343
www.wnoe.com
ProgramDirector@WNOE.com
License: New Orleans, Orleans County, LA held by Clear Channel Broadcasting Licenses Inc.
Group Owner: iHeartMedia; acq 1996; grpsl)
Nat'l Network: ABC; Westwood One; *Nat'l Reps:* Clear Channel
Arbitron Metro Market: New Orleans, LA; *Format:* Country; *No. News Employees:* 1; *Target Audience:* 25-54.
Nicky Sparrow, Senior Vice President of Sales
Richard Atwood, Chief Engineer

WODT
07-23-1923; 1280 kHz AM; 5 kw-U, DA1; N29 53 43 W90 0 16
929 Howard Avenue, New Orleans, LA 70113 US
(504) 679-7300; *Fax:* (504) 679-7345
www.foxsportsam1280.com
License: New Orleans, LA held by Clear Channel Broadcasting Licenses Inc.
Group Owner: iHeartMedia; (acq 7-24-92)
Nat'l Reps: Clear Channel
Arbitron Metro Market: New Orleans, LA *TV Affiliate:* Urban Gospel; *Format:* Sports *Special Programming:* News progmg one hr wkly; *No. News Employees:* 35 plus; general
Nicky Sparrow, Senior Vice President of Sales

WQUE-FM
01-01-1949; 93.3 MHz FM; *Hrs Open:* 24; 98.8 kw; 984 ft.; N29 55 11 W90 1 29
929 Howard Avenue, New Orleans, LA 70113 US
(504) 679-7300; *Fax:* (504) 679-7345
www.Q93.com
webmaster@Q93.com
License: New Orleans, Orleans County, LA held by Clear Channel Broadcasting Licenses Inc.
Group Owner: iHeartMedia
Nat'l Network: Premiere Radio Networks; *Nat'l Reps:* Clear Channel
Arbitron Metro Market: New Orleans, LA; *Format:* Urban Contemporary; *Hrs. of News Programming:* 2; *No. News Employees:* 1
Nicky Sparrow, Senior Vice President of Sales
Richard Atwood, Chief Engineer

***WRBH**
01-01-1980; 88.3 MHz FM; *Hrs Open:* 24; 51 kw; 623 ft.; N29 56 59 W89 57 28
3606 Magazine Street, New Orleans, LA 70115 US
(504) 899-1144; *Fax:* (504) 899-1165
www.wrbh.org
License: New Orleans, Orleans County, LA held by Radio for the Blind and Print Handicapped Inc.
Arbitron Metro Market: New Orleans, LA; *Format:* News; *Hrs. of News Programming:* News progmg 28 hrs wkly; *Target Audience:* Blind & print handicapped.
Natalia Gonzalez, Executive Director
Jackie Bullock, Programming Director
Ernie Kain, Chief Engineer

WRNO-FM
10-17-1967; 99.5 MHz FM; 100 kw; 1004 ft.; N29 58 57 W89 57 9
929 Howard Avenue, New Orleans, LA 70113 US
(504) 679-7300; *Fax:* (504) 679-7345
www.wrno.com
License: New Orleans, Orleans County, LA held by Clear Channel Broadcasting Licenses Inc.
Group Owner: iHeartMedia; (acq 8-8-2002; swap for KKND(FM) Port Sulphur).
Nat'l Network: Premiere Radio Networks; ABC; Fox News Radio; Westwood One
Arbitron Metro Market: New Orleans, LA; *Format:* News, News/Talk, 86; *No. News Employees:* 3
Nicky Sparrow, Senior Vice President of Sales
Richard Atwood, Chief Engineer

WSHO
01-01-1926; 800 kHz AM; 1 kw-D, DA2; 0.233 kw-N, DA2; N29 50 42 W90 6 39
1001 Howard Avenue, Suite 4304, New Orleans, LA 70113 US
(504) 527-0800; *Fax:* (504) 527-0881
www.wsho.com
whso@wsho.com
License: New Orleans, LA held by Shadowlands Communications L.L.C.
Nat'l Network: Salem Radio Network
Arbitron Metro Market: New Orleans, LA; *Format:* Religious; *Target Audience:* 25-54.
William Ainsworth, President

WWWL
04-21-1925; 1350 kHz AM; *Hrs Open:* 24; 5 kw-D, DAN; 5 kw-N, DAN; N29 55 27 W90 2 4
2000 West 41st St., Baltimore, MD 21211 US
(504) 593-6376
www.3wl1350.com
License: New Orleans, LA held by Entercom New Orleans License LLC.
Group Owner: Entercom Communications Corp.; (acq 12-13-99; grpsl)
Nat'l Network: ESPN Radio
Arbitron Metro Market: New Orleans, LA; *Format:* Sports
Ken Beck, General Manager
Malcolm Pelham, General Sales Mgr
Diane Newman, Programming Director
Joe Pollet, Chief Engineer
Mark Broudreaux, General Sales Manager

WQNO
01-01-1948; 690 kHz AM; *Hrs Open:* 24; 10 kw-D, DA2; 5 kw-N, DA2; N29 57 53 W89 57 31
1206 Decatur Street, New Orleans, LA 70116 US
(504) 552-2412; *Fax:* (504) 552-2430
www.wistradio.com
License: New Orleans, LA held by WTIX Inc.
Group Owner: GHB Radio Group; (acq 2-12-92; $800,000;
Arbitron Metro Market: New Orleans, LA; *Format:* Oldies, Talk; *Hrs. of News Programming:* News progmg 30 hrs wkly; *Target Audience:* 25 plus; affluent, educated, professional; *Adv. Rates:* 50; 40; 40; 50
Daniel Frazier, General Manager
John Bradley, Sales Representative

WKBU
02-01-1953; 95.7 MHz FM; 99.5 kw; 984 ft.; N29 55 11 W90 1 29
400 Poydras Street, New Orleans, LA 70130 US
(504) 593-6376; *Fax:* (504) 593-1850
bayou957.com
mail@entercom.com
License: New Orleans, Orleans County, LA held by Entercom New Orleans License LLC.
Group Owner: Entercom Communications Corp.; (acq 12-13-99; grpsl)
Arbitron Metro Market: New Orleans, LA; *Format:* Classic Rock; *Target Audience:* 25-54.
Patrick Galloway, General Sales Mgr
Mike Kaplan, Programming Director
Dave Cohen, News Director
Joe Pollet, Chief Engineer

***WTUL**
11-14-1974; 91.5 MHz FM; *Hrs Open:* 24; 1.5 kw; 161 ft.; N29 56 18 W90 7 7
Tulane University Center, Box 5069, New Orlans, LA 70118 US
(504) 865-5887
www.wtul.fm
wtul@tulane.edu
License: New Orleans, Orleans County, LA held by Tulane Educational Fund.
Arbitron Metro Market: New Orleans, LA; *Format:* Alternative; *Hrs. of News Programming:* News progmg 3 hrs wkly; *Target Audience:* General.
Sarah Gersten, General Manager
Chelsea O'Lansen, Programming Director

WVOG
04-23-1964; 600 kHz AM; *Hrs Open:* 5:30 AM-8:30 PM; 1 kw-D, ND2; 0.031 kw-N, ND1; N29 57 25 W90 9 33
2730 Loumor Ave, Matairie, LA 70001 US
(504) 831-6941; *Fax:* (504) 831-2647
www.600wvog.com
License: New Orleans, LA held by F.W. Robbert Broadcasting Co. Inc.
Group Owner: F W Robbert Broadcasting Co. Inc.; acq 6-28-74).
Arbitron Metro Market: New Orleans, LA; *Format:* Christian, Talk; *Hrs. of News Programming:* News progmg 2 hrs wkly; *Target Audience:* 30 plus.; *Adv. Rates:* 9; 9; 9; na
Fred P. Westenberger, President
Eric Westenberger, Station Manager
Eric Martin, Sales Director
Earnie Harvey, Chief Engineer
Gina Marino, Secretary

WWL
03-31-1922; 870 kHz AM; *Hrs Open:* 24; 50 kw-U, DA1; N29 50 14 W90 7 55
400 Poydras Street, New Orleans, MD 70130 US
(504) 260-1870
www.wwl.com
info@wwl.com
License: New Orleans, LA held by Entercom New Orleans License LLC.
Group Owner: Entercom Communications Corp.; (acq 12-13-99; grpsl)
Nat'l Network: CBS; *Nat'l Reps:* D & R Radio
Arbitron Metro Market: New Orleans, LA; *Format:* News, News/Talk, 84, Talk
Diane Newman, Operations & Program Director
Chris Claus, Vice President/General Manager
Malcolm Pelham, General Sales Mgr
Helen Centanni, Producer

***WWNO**
02-20-1972; 89.9 MHz FM; *Hrs Open:* 24; 35 kw; 984 ft.; N29 55 11 W90 1 29
2000 Lakeshore Drive, New Orleans, LA 70148 US
(504) 280-7000
www.wwno.org
License: New Orleans, Orleans County, LA held by Louisiana State University.
Nat'l Network: PRI; NPR; *Wire Services:* AP
Arbitron Metro Market: New Orleans, LA; *Format:* Jazz, News; *Hrs. of News Programming:* News progmg 39 hrs wkly; *Target Audience:* 35 plus; well-educated professionals, mgrs, artists & art patrons
Ron Curtis, Operations Dir
Chuck Miller, General Manager
Karen Anklam, General Sales Mgr
Fred Kasten, Programming Director
Eileen Fleming, News Reporter
Ron Biava, Development and Marketing Manager
Jameeta Youngblood, BusinessManager
Jenni Lawson, Production Manager

***WWOZ**
12-06-1980; 90.7 MHz FM; *Hrs Open:* 24; 4 kw; 509 ft.; N29 57 24 W90 4 31
US
(504) 568-1239; *Fax:* (504) 558-9332
www.wwoz.org
wwoz@wwoz.org
License: New Orleans, Orleans County, LA held by Friends of WWOZ Inc.
Arbitron Metro Market: New Orleans, LA; *Format:* Blues, Jazz; *Hrs. of News Programming:* News progmg 5 hrs wkly; *Target Audience:* 35-55; upscale & educated males
Jorge Fuentes, Operations Dir
David Freedman, General Manager
Dwayne Breashears, Programming Director
Damond Jacob, Chief Engineer
Tony Guillory, IT Manager
Scott Borne, Music Director
Beau Royster, Chief Financial and BusinessDevelopment Officer
Crystal Gross, Development Director
Molly Cobb, Membership Director

WYLD
01-01-1949; 940 kHz AM; *Hrs Open:* 24
929 Howard Avenue, New Orleans, LA 70113 US
(504) 679-7300; *Fax:* (504) 679-7345
www.am940.com
info@am940.com
License: New Orleans, LA held by Clear Channel Broadcasting Licenses Inc.
Group Owner: iHeartMedia; (acq 3-25-93;
Nat'l Network: ABC; Westwood One; *Nat'l Reps:* Clear Channel
Arbitron Metro Market: New Orleans, LA; *Format:* Gospel; *Target Audience:* 25-54.
Nicky Sparrow, Senior Vice President of Sales

WYLD-FM
01-01-1971; 98.5 MHz FM; *Hrs Open:* 24; 97.8 kw; 984 ft.; N29 55 11 W90 1 29
929 Howard Avenue, New Orleans, LA 70113 US
(504) 679-7300; *Fax:* (504) 679-7345
www.wyldfm.com
License: New Orleans, Orleans County, LA held by Clear Channel Broadcasting Licenses Inc.
Group Owner: iHeartMedia
Arbitron Metro Market: New Orleans, LA; *Format:* Adult Contemp, Urban Contemporary; *Hrs. of News Programming:* news progmg 5 hrs wkly; *No. News Employees:* 2
Nicky Sparrow, Senior Vice President of Sales

New Roads

KQXL
01-01-1979; 106.5 MHz FM; *Hrs Open:* 24; 50 kw; Ant 485 ft; N30 37 24 W91 09 50
631 Main St., Baton Rouge, LA 85281 US
(225) 926-1106
www.q106dot5.com
License: New Roads, LA held by Radio License Holding CBC
Group Owner: Cumulus Media Inc.; (acq 1-14-99; grpsl).
Nat'l Network: CBS
Population Served: 600,000; *Arbitron Metro Market:* Baton Rouge, LA; *Format:* Urban Contemporary; *No. News Employees:* 1
J'Michael Francios, Operations Dir
Tiffany Faul, General Sales Mgr
J'Michael Francios, Programming Director
Deontray Alexander, Promotions Manager

***KPCP**
88.3 MHz FM; 6 kw horiz, 5.53 kw vert; 299 ft.; N30 43 20.4 W91 35 45.6
P.O. Box 450, New Roads, LA 70760 US
(225) 638-6822; *Fax:* (225) 638-6822
rgremillion@bellsouth.net
License: New Roads, Pointe Coupee County, LA held by Stop the Violence/Save the Children Inc.
Arbitron Metro Market: New Roads, LA; *Format:* Adult Contemp
Roosevelt Gremillion, President

KCLF
08-19-1964; 1500 kHz AM; 1 kw-D, ND1; N30 44 8 W91 24 58
P.O. Box 450, New Roads, LA 70760 US
(225) 638-6822; *Fax:* (225) 638-6882
www.kclf1500am.com
rgremillion@bellsouth.net
License: New Roads, LA held by New World Broadcasting Co. Inc.
Arbitron Metro Market: New Roads, LA; *Format:* Urban Contemporary
Roosevelt Gremillion, President

Norco

WFNO
01-01-1987; 830 kHz AM; 5 kw-D, DA2; 0.75 kw-N, DA2; N30 3 0 W90 22 41
3500 North Causeway Boulevard, Suite 830, Metairie, LA 70002 US
(504) 832-3555; *Fax:* (504) 838-7700
License: Norco, LA held by Davidson Media Station WFNO Licensee LLC.
Group Owner: Davidson Media Group LLC; (acq 1-11-2007; $2 million)
Wire Services: AP
Arbitron Metro Market: New Orleans, LA; *Format:* Spanish; *Hrs. of News Programming:* news progmg 12 hrs wkly; *No. News Employees:* 2; *Target Audience:* 18-44.

***WNKV**
01-01-2007; 91.1 MHz FM; 4.7 kw vert; 230 ft.; N29 48 34 W90 25 17 *Rebroadcasts:* Rebroadcasts KLVR(FM) Middletown, CA 100%
188 South Bellevue, Suite 222, Memphis, TN 38104 US
(800) 525-5683; *Fax:* (916) 251-1650
www.klove.com
klove@klove.com
License: Norco, St. Charles County, LA held by Educational Media Foundation.
Group Owner: EMF Broadcasting; (acq 11-1-2006; grpsl)
Nat'l Network: K-Love
Arbitron Metro Market: Norco, LA; *Format:* Christian; *No. News Employees:* 13
Darrell Chambliss, Chairman
Mike Novak, President and CEO
Chip Bailey, Operations Dir
David Pierce, Programming Director
Ed Lenane, News Director
Sam Wallington, Engineering Dir
Dan Antonelli, Chief Business DevelopmentOfficer
Eric Moser, Chief Financial Officer
Brian Burger, Vice President of Human Resources
D. Kevin Blair, Secretary and General Counsel
Tim Luttrell, News Reporter

North Fort Polk

KUMX
05-10-1995; 106.7 MHz FM; *Hrs Open:* 24; 6 kw; 315 ft.; N31 3 5 W93 16 41
168 K V V P Drive, Leesville, LA 71446 US
(337) 537-9000; *Fax:* (337) 537-4152
www.kumxfm.com
info@kumxfm.com
License: North Fort Polk, Vernon County, LA held by West Central Broadcasting Co. Inc.
Nat'l Network: ABC
Arbitron Metro Market: Leesville, LA; *Format:* Adult Contemp, Christian *Special Programming:* Tom Joiner; *Hrs. of News Programming:* 12pm, 5pm; *No. News Employees:* 12; *Target Audience:* 22-42.; *Adv. Rates:* 78; 78; 78; 78
Alan Taylor, CFO
Doug Stannard, General Manager

Oak Grove

KWCL-FM
01-30-1973; 96.7 MHz FM; *Hrs Open:* 24; 23 kw; 341 ft.; N32 51 32 W91 21 22
Mailing Address: 230 East Main, Oak Grove, LA 71263 US
Second Address: 230 E. Main St., Oak Grove, LA 71263
(318) 428-9670
www.kwclfm.com
License: Oak Grove, West Carroll County, LA held by KWCL-FM Broadcasting Co. Inc.
Nat'l Network: ABC; Jones Radio Networks
Arbitron Metro Market: Oak Grove, LA; *Format:* Oldies; *Hrs. of News Programming:* news progmg 17 hrs wkly; *No. News Employees:* 1; *Target Audience:* General.; *Adv. Rates:* 8; 8; 8; 6
Irene Robinson, President
Kelley Lovell, Programming Director

Oakdale

KKST
01-01-1972; 98.7 MHz FM; *Hrs Open:* 24; 48 kw; Ant 1,053 ft; N31 01 59 W92 30 08
1115 Texas Ave., Alexandria, LA 78701
(318) 445-1234; *Fax:* (318) 445-7231
www.cenlabroadcasting.com
chad@cenlabroadcasting.com
License: Oakdale, Allen County, LA held by Cenla Broadcasting Licensing Co. LLC.
Group Owner: Cenla Broadcasting Co. Inc.; (acq 11-13-2006; grpsl)
Population Served: 150,000; *Arbitron Metro Market:* Alexandria, LA; *Hrs. of News Programming:* news progmg 20 hrs wkly; *No. News Employees:* 1; *Target Audience:* 18-49; women
Taylor Thompson, General Manager
Chad Soprano, General Sales Mgr

Oil City

KRMD-FM
08-01-1948; 101.1 MHz FM; 97.7 kw; 345.7 meters; N32 41 08 W93 56 00
270 Plaza Loop, PO Box 5459, Bossier City, LA 78701
(318) 549-8500; *Fax:* (318) 549-8505
www.krmd.com
krmd@cumulus.com

License: Oil City, Caddo County, LA held by Cumulus Licensing Corp.
Group Owner: Cumulus Media Inc.; (acq 8-7-2000; grpsl)
Nat'l Reps: Christal
Population Served: 369,800; *Arbitron Metro Market:* Shreveport, LA; *No. News Employees:* 2; *Target Audience:* 25-54.; *Adv. Rates:* 100; 85; 95; 45
Steve Lucchesi, Vice President
Christy Reed, General Sales Mgr
James Anthony, Programming Director
Miranda Martin, Promotions Manager
Jordan Evans, Engineering Dir

Opelousas

KOGM
107.1 MHz FM; *Hrs Open:* 24; 0.75 kW; 935 ft.; N30 20 32 W91 57 46
3501 NW Evangeline Thruway, Carencro, LA 70520 USA
(337) 896-1600
www.mustang877.com
License: Opelousas, LA held by Delta Media Corp.
Group Owner: Delta Media Corp.
Regional Network: La. Net.
Arbitron Metro Market: Lafayette, LA; *Format:* Country; *Hrs. of News Programming:* 1 hour per week; *No. News Employees:* 1; *Target Audience:* 25 plus.
Charles Chatelain, CEO/COO

KSLO
09-21-1947; 1230 kHz AM; *Hrs Open:* 24; 1 kW; N30 31 30 W92 6 22
3501 NW Evangeline Thruway, Carencro, LA 70520 USA
(337) 896-1600
License: Opelousas, St. Landry County, LA held by Delta Media Corp.
Group Owner: Delta Media Corp.
Nat'l Network: Westwood One; *Regional Network:* La. Agri-News; La. Net.
Arbitron Metro Market: Opelousas, LA; *Format:* Spanish, News; *Hrs. of News Programming:* 10 hrs. per week; *No. News Employees:* 1; *Adv. Rates:* 15.55; 15.55; 15.55; 15.55
Charles Chatelain, CEO/COO

KFXZ-FM
08-03-1989; 105.9 MHz FM; 3.4 kw; 433 ft.; N30 27 59 W92 4 31
202 Galbert Rd., Lafayette, LA 70506 US
(337) 706-0112
www.z1059.com
License: Opelousas, St. Landry County, LA held by Delta Media Corp.
Group Owner: Delta Media Corp.; (acq 1-28-2004; grpsl)
Arbitron Metro Market: Lafayette, LA; *Format:* Urban Contemporary
Charles Chatelain, CEO/COO
Charles Sagona, General Manager

KDCG-CD
01-01-1991;; 15 kw; N30 20 32 W91 58 32
3501 NW Evangeline Thruway, Carencro, LA 70520 USA
(337) 896-1600
www.kdcg.com
License: Opelousas, LA held by Delta Media Corp.
Group Owner: Delta Media Corp.

Charles Chatelain, CEO/COO

Pineville

KTTP
09-13-1974; 1110 kHz AM; 2 kw-D, NDD; N31 21 52 W92 27 15
34-D Macarthur Drive, Alexandria, LA 71303 US
(318) 473-4388; *Fax:* (318) 449-1779
kttpam1110@aol.com
License: Pineville, LA held by Benjamin-Dane LLC
Arbitron Metro Market: Alexandria, LA; *Format:* Gospel; *Target Audience:* 25-70.; *Adv. Rates:* 120; 120; 120; na
Ronald Reeves, President
Carolyn Frazier, Station Manager

Plaquemine

*KPAQ
88.1 MHz FM; 2.9 kw vert; 308 ft.; N30 15 41 W91 18 40
P.O. Box 3206, Tupelo, MS 38803 US
(662) 844-8888; *Fax:* (662) 842-6791
www.afr.net
faq@afa.net
License: Plaquemine, Iberville County, LA held by American Family Association.
Group Owner: American Family Radio
Arbitron Metro Market: Plaquemine, LA; *Format:* Christian
Tim Wildmon, President
Donald Wildmon, Founder
Buddy Smith, Sr VP
Ed Vitagliano, Exec VP
Randy Sharp, Director Of Special Projects
Meeke Addison, Director Of Communications
Abraham Hamilton III, General Counsel

Port Allen

WXOK
02-01-1953; 1460 kHz AM; *Hrs Open:* 24; 4.7 kw-D, 290 w-N; N30 28 25 W91 13 34
631 Main St., Baton Rouge, LA 70801 US
(225) 926-1106
www.heaven1460.com
License: Port Allen, LA held by Radio License Holding CBC, LLC
Group Owner: Cumulus Media Inc.; (acq 1-14-99).
Population Served: 230,139; *Arbitron Metro Market:* Baton Rouge, LA; *Format:* Gospel
J'Michael Francios, Operations Mgr/Program Dir
Greg Benefield, General Manager
Tiffany Faul, General Sales Mgr
Deontray Alexander, Promotions Manager

Port Sulphur

KAGY
08-17-1966; 1510 kHz AM; *Hrs Open:* 6 AM-6 PM; 1 kw-D, NDD; N29 29 3 W89 42 15
P.O. Box 8888, Metairie, LA 70011 US
(504) 450-4225
www.kagyradio.com
License: Port Sulphur, LA held by Spotlight Broadcasting of New Orleans LLC
Group Owner: Spotlight Broadcasting LLC; (acq 12-30-2002; $250,000).
Arbitron Metro Market: Metairie, LA; *Format:* Adult Contemp; *Target Audience:* 24-54; general; *Adv. Rates:* 12; 12; 12; 12

KKND
07-04-1989; 102.9 MHz FM; *Hrs Open:* 24; 4.7 kw; Ant 981 ft; N29 48 30 W89 45 42
201 St. Charles Ave., Suite 201, New Orleans, LA 70170 US
(504) 581-7002; *Fax:* (504) 566-4857
www.power1029.com
info@power1029.com
License: Port Sulphur, LA held by Radio License Holding CBC, LLC
Group Owner: Cumulus Media Inc.; (acq 8-29-2003; grpsl).
Nat'l Reps: Clear Channel
Arbitron Metro Market: New Orleans, LA; *Format:* Contemporary Hits/Top 40; *No. News Employees:* 1; *Target Audience:* 25-54.
Benjamin Duncan, Promotions Director

Rayne

KLEJ
01-01-1993; 106.7 MHz FM; 3 kw; Ant 328 ft; N30 18 17 W92 20 47
Mailing Address: Box 228, Crowley, LA 70527
Second Address: 320 N. Parkerson Ave., Crowley, LA 70526
(337) 783-2520; *Fax:* (337) 783-5744
www.countrylegends1067.com
License: Rayne, Acadia County, LA held by Broadcast Partners Inc.
Arbitron Metro Market: Lafayette, LA
Phil Lizotte, President
Jimmy Cole, General Sales Mgr
Hans Nelson, Programming Director
Tony Evans, Chief Engineer

Rayville

KMYY
09-01-1984; 92.3 MHz FM; *Hrs Open:* 16; 11.5 kw; 486 ft.; N32 29 1 W91 54 10
1200 North 18th Street, Suite D, Monroe, LA 71201 US
(318) 387-3922; *Fax:* (318) 322-4585
923thewolf@gmail.com
License: Rayville, Richland County, LA held by Opus Broadcasting Monroe L.L.C.
Group Owner: Opus Media Holdings LLC; (acq 7-19-2004; grpsl).
Arbitron Metro Market: Monroe, LA; *Format:* Country
Mike Downhoar, General Manager

Reserve

WPRF
08-01-1991; 94.9 MHz FM; *Hrs Open:* 24; 50 kw; Ant 482 ft; N29 43 48 W90 43 37
770 N. Jefferson St., Milwaukee, WI 70068
(414) 273-3776; *Fax:* (414) 291-3776
License: Reserve, St. John the Baptist County, LA held by Southeastern Broadcasting Inc.
Population Served: 156,929; *Arbitron Metro Market:* Eugene-Springfield OR
Craig Karmazin, President
C.J. Knee, Operations Dir
Bill Johnson, Programming Director
Warren Jorgenson, News Director

Richwood

KHLL
03-01-1995; 100.9 MHz FM; 25 kw; 328 ft.; N32 24 25 W92 4 13
704-C Trenton Street, West Monroe, LA 71291 US
(318) 322-1009; *Fax:* (318) 323-6680
www.hillradio.com
mail@hillradio.com
License: Richwood, Ouachita County, LA held by Dan Gilliland.
Format: Christian
Rick Godley, General Manager

KLIC
01-01-1950; 1230 kHz AM; *Hrs Open:* 24; 1 kw-U; N32 25 43 W92 04 43
130 N 2nd St. Ste C, Monroe, LA 71211
(318) 387-1230; *Fax:* (318) 387-8856
License: Richwood, Ouachita County, LA held by Media Ministries Inc.
Nat'l Network: Salem Radio Network
Population Served: 150,000; *Arbitron Metro Market:* Monroe, LA; *Hrs. of News Programming:* News progmg 14 hrs wkly; *Target Audience:* 25-54; Adults 35 +; *Adv. Rates:* 14; 13; 14; 9
Tony Davis, President
Mike Downhour, General Manager
Diane Osborne, General Sales Mgr
Naomi Thompson, News Director
Ernie Sandidge, Engineering Dir
Mark Kemp, Traffic Manager

Ruston

*KAPI
02-01-1998; 88.3 MHz FM; 0.3 kw; 197 ft.; N32 33 8 W92 39 21
P.O. Box 3206, Tupelo, MS 38803 US
(662) 844-8888; *Fax:* (662) 842-6791
www.afr.net
faq@afa.net
License: Ruston, Lincoln County, LA held by American Family Association.
Group Owner: American Family Radio
Arbitron Metro Market: Tupelo, MO; *Format:* Religious
Tim Wildmon, President
Donad Wildmon, Founder
Buddy Smith, Sr. VP
Ed Vitagliano, Executive VP
Randy Sharp, Director Of Special Projects
Meeke Addison, Director Of Communications
Abraham Hamilton III, General Counsel & PublicPolicy

*KLPI
01-01-1973; 89.1 MHz FM; 4 kw; 285 ft.; N32 31 41 W92 38 50
100 Wysteria Street, Ruston, LA 71272 US
(318) 257-4851
www.klpi.latech.edu
License: Ruston, Lincoln County, LA held by Louisiana Tech University.
Arbitron Metro Market: Monroe, LA; *Format:* Alternative; *No. News Employees:* 2; *Target Audience:* 18-24; college students

KPCH
01-01-1999; 99.3 MHz FM; *Hrs Open:* 24; 24.5 kw; 331 ft.; N32 28 53 W92 40 34
Mailing Address: 109 Llanfair Drive, Ruston, LA 71270 US
Second Address: 500 N. Monroe St., Ruston, LA 71270
(866-414-4427)
www.thepeach993.com
License: Ruston, Lincoln County, LA held by Communications Capital Co. II of Louisiana LLC.
Group Owner: Communications Capital Managers LLC; (acq 3-4-2002; grpsl)
Regional Network: La. Net.
Arbitron Metro Market: Monroe, LA; *Format:* Oldies; *Adv. Rates:* 19; 19; 19; 19
Gary McKenney, General Manager
Tommy Gray, Chief Engineer

KRUS
11-07-1947; 1490 kHz AM; 1 kw-U, ND1; N32 30 48 W92 39 56
Mailing Address: P. O. Box 430, Ruston, LA 71270 US
Second Address: 500 N. Monroe St., Ruston, LA 71270

(318) 255-5000
z1075fm@bayou.com
License: Ruston, LA held by Communications Capital Co. II of Louisiana LLC.
Group Owner: Communications Capital Managers LLC; (acq 3-4-2002; grpsl)
Arbitron Metro Market: Ruston, LA; *Format:* Black, Gospel; *Target Audience:* 25-55; Black
Gary McKenney, General Manager
James Cooper, Programming Director
Tommy Gray, Chief Engineer

KXKZ
06-29-1966; 107.5 MHz FM; *Hrs Open:* 24; 100 kw; 1066 ft.; N32 26 37 W92 42 43
Mailing Address: 500 N. Monroe, P.O. Box 430, Ruston, LA 71270 US
Second Address: 500 N. Monroe St., Ruston, LA 71270
(318) 255-5000
www.z1075fm.com
License: Ruston, Lincoln County, LA held by Red Peach LLC
Group Owner: Communications Capital Managers LLC
Nat'l Network: ABC; *Wire Services:* ESSA Weather Service
Arbitron Metro Market: Ruston, LA; *Format:* Country; *Hrs. of News Programming:* news progmg 7 hrs wkly; *No. News Employees:* 1; *Target Audience:* 25-54.
Matt McKenney, Programming Director

Shreveport

KVMA-FM
01-01-2001; 102.9 MHz FM; *Hrs Open:* 24; 42 kw; 535 ft.; N32 29 36 W93 45 55
270 Plaza Loop, Bossier City, LA 71111 US
(318) 549-8500; *Fax:* (318) 549-8505
magic1029fm.com
cumulus.shreveport@cumulus.com
License: Shreveport, Caddo County, LA held by Cumulus Licensing Corp.
Group Owner: Cumulus Media Inc.; (acq 10-23-2000)
Wire Services: AP
Arbitron Metro Market: Bossier City, LA; *Format:* Urban Contemporary
Susan Lucchesi, President/Marketing Manager
Christy Reed, General Sales Mgr
Nina Montgomery, Programming Director
Jordan Evans, Chief Engineer

***KDAQ**
12-21-1984; 89.9 MHz FM; *Hrs Open:* 24; 100 kw; 932 ft.; N32 40 40 W93 55 30
P.O. Box 5250, Shreveport, LA 71135 US
(318) 798-0102
www.redriverradio.org
listenermail@redriverradio.com
License: Shreveport, Caddo County, LA held by Louisiana State University Board of Supervisors.
Nat'l Network: NPR; PRI
Arbitron Metro Market: Shreveport, LA; *Format:* Classical, Jazz, 60; *Hrs. of News Programming:* News progmg 40 hrs wkly; *Target Audience:* General.
Kermit Poling, General Manager
Bill Beckett, Programming Director

KEEL
01-01-1922; 710 kHz AM; *Hrs Open:* 24; 50 kw-D, DA2; 5 kw-N, DA2; N32 40 35 W93 51 35
50 East Rivercenter Boulevard, #1200, Covington, KY 41011 US
(318) 688-1130; *Fax:* (318) 687-8574
www.710keel.com
info@710keel.com
License: Shreveport, LA held by Townsquare Media Shreveport License LLC
Group Owner: Townsquare Media; (acq 8-3-2007; grpsl)
Regional Network: La. Net; *Nat'l Reps:* D & R Radio
Arbitron Metro Market: Shreveport, LA; *Format:* News, Talk; *Hrs. of News Programming:* news progmg 6 hrs wkly; *No. News Employees:* 5; *Target Audience:* 25-54; men
Lisa Janes, General Manager
Casey Ryan, General Sales Mgr
John Lee, Programming Director
Craig Westbrook, Chief Engineer

KSYB
07-10-1975; 1300 kHz AM; *Hrs Open:* 24; 5 kw-D, ND1; 0.03 kw-N, ND1; N32 31 48 W93 48 16
Mailing Address: 2807 Hilry Huckaby III Avenue, Shreveport, LA 71107 US
Second Address: 1526 Corporate Dr., Shreveport, LA 71107
(318) 222-2744
License: Shreveport, LA held by Amistad Communications Inc.
Group Owner: Amistad Communications Inc.; (acq 10-26-2000; $900,000).
Arbitron Metro Market: Shreveport, LA; *Format:* Christian, Gospel
Special Programming: Sports 10 hrs wkly; *Target Audience:* Christian families; *Adv. Rates:* 16; 16; 16; 16
Fred Caldwell, CEO
Rhonda Phillips-Sanders, General Manager
James W. Lane Jr., General Sales Mgr
Tawanna Gadson, Programming Director

KIOU
01-01-1950; 1480 kHz AM; *Hrs Open:* 6 AM-6 PM; 1 kw-D, ND2; 0.129 kw-N, ND2; N32 34 18 W93 44 39
2438 E. Texas St., Suite 7, Bossier City, LA 71111 US
(318) 752-2115
www.wilkinsradio.com
denise@wilkinsradio.com
License: Shreveport, LA held by Capital City Radio Corp.
Group Owner: Wilkins Communications Network Inc.; acq 10-97; $70,500)
Arbitron Metro Market: Shreveport, LA; *Format:* Christian, Talk; *Target Audience:* General.
Fred Flournoy, Station Manager

KXKS-FM
05-17-1968; 93.7 MHz FM; 95 kw; 1010 ft.; N32 40 39 W93 55 41
50 East Rivercenter Boulevard, #1200, Covington, KY 41011 US
(318) 688-1130; *Fax:* (318) 687-8574
License: Shreveport, Caddo County, LA held by Townsquare Media Shreveport License LLC
Group Owner: Townsquare Media
Arbitron Metro Market: Shreveport, LA; *Format:* Country; *Target Audience:* 25-54; 30 yr old female
Amy Fletcher, General Manager
Gary McCoy, Brand Manager
Lisa Janes, Director Of Sales
Chasity Spears, Digital Managing Editor

KMJJ-FM
12-05-1976; 99.7 MHz FM; 23.5 kw; 533 ft.; N32 29 36 W93 45 55
600 Congress Avenue, Suite 1400, Austin, TX 78701 US
(318) 549-8500; *Fax:* (318) 549-8505
www.997kmjj.com
cumulus.shreveport@cumulus.com
License: Shreveport, Caddo County, LA held by Cumulus Licensing Corp.
Group Owner: Cumulus Media Inc.; (acq 8-7-00; grpsl).
Arbitron Metro Market: Shreveport, LA; *Format:* Urban Contemporary; *Hrs. of News Programming:* News progmg one hr wkly; *Target Audience:* 18-49; African American & general; *Adv. Rates:* 75; 65; 75; 35
Susan Lucchesi, President/Marketing Manager
Christy Reed, General Sales Mgr
Doug Davis, Programming Director
Gary Robinson, Promotions Manager
Jasen Bragg, Chief Engineer

KOKA
08-01-1954; 980 kHz AM; *Hrs Open:* 24; 5 kw-D, ND2; 0.079 kw-N, ND2; N32 31 30 W93 48 30
208 N. Thomas Dr., Shreveport, LA 71137 US
(318) 222-3122
www.koka.am
License: Shreveport, Caddo County, LA held by Alpha Media Licensee LLC
Group Owner: Alpha Media LLC; (acq 4-14-2015; grpsl).
Nat'l Reps: D & R Radio
Arbitron Metro Market: Shreveport, LA; *Format:* Gospel, Urban Contemporary; *No. News Employees:* 1; *Target Audience:* 25-64; middle-aged, middle class, Black adults
Cary Camp, Market Manager
Melvin Jones, Urban Market Sales Manager
Eddie Giles, Programming Director

KRMD
06-01-1928; 1340 kHz AM; *Hrs Open:* 24; 1 kw-U, ND1; N32 29 36 W93 45 55
600 Congress Ave., Suite 1400, Austin, TX 78701 US
(318) 549-8500; *Fax:* (318) 549-8505
www.supertalk1340.com
krmd@cumulus.com
License: Shreveport, LA held by Cumulus Licensing Corp.
Group Owner: Cumulus Media Inc.
Arbitron Metro Market: Shreveport, LA; *Format:* Talk
Susan Lucchesi, Vice President
John Sherman, Programming Director
Benjamin Duncan, Promotions Director
Sandy Clark, Traffic Manager

KRUF
11-05-1948; 94.5 MHz FM; *Hrs Open:* 24; 99 kw; 1096 ft.; N32 40 13 W93 55 59
6341 Westport Avenue, Shreveport, LA 71129 US
(318) 688-1130; *Fax:* (318) 687-8574
www.k945.com
info@k945.com
License: Shreveport, Caddo County, LA
Group Owner: Townsquare Media
Arbitron Metro Market: Shreveport, LA; *Format:* Contemporary Hits/Top 40
Amy Fletcher, General Manager
Erin Bristol, Brand Manager
Lisa Janes, Director Of Sales
Chasity Spears, Digital Managing Editor

***KSCL**
03-11-1976; 91.3 MHz FM; *Hrs Open:* 24; 2.6 kw; 184 ft.; N32 28 51.4 W93 43 51.1
2911 Centenary Blvd, PO Box 41188, Shreveport, LA 71134 US
(318) 869-5296
www.centenary.edu
License: Shreveport, Caddo County, LA held by Centenary College of Louisiana.
Arbitron Metro Market: Shreveport, LA; *Format:* Alternative; *Hrs. of News Programming:* news progmg 4 hrs wkly; *No. News Employees:* 1; *Target Audience:* General; college students & adults interested in div music
David Rowe, CEO/COO
John Schleass, Station Manager
Alyson Escude, Programming Director
Tyler Davis, Music Director
Jon Schleuss, Station Manager

KVKI-FM
05-01-1959; 96.5 MHz FM; *Hrs Open:* 24; 95 kw; 797 ft.; N32 35 38 W93 51 39
US
(318) 688-1130; *Fax:* (318) 688-9839
www.kpel965.com
License: Shreveport, Caddo County, LA held by Townsquare Media Shreveport License LLC
Group Owner: Townsquare Media; (acq 8-3-2007; grpsl)
Nat'l Reps: D & R Radio
Arbitron Metro Market: Shreveport, LA; *Format:* Adult Contemp; *No. News Employees:* 1; *Target Audience:* 25-54; female
Lisa Janes, General Manager
Steve King, Programming Director
Casey Ryan, Director of Sales

KWKH
09-01-1925; 1130 kHz AM; *Hrs Open:* 24
50 East Rivercenter Boulevard, #1200, Covington, KY 41011 US
(318) 688-1130; *Fax:* (318) 687-8574
www.kwkhonline.com
amyfletcher@townsquaremedia.com
License: Shreveport, LA held by Townsquare Media Shreveport License LLC
Group Owner: Townsquare Media; (acq 8-3-2007; grpsl)
Nat'l Reps: D & R Radio
Arbitron Metro Market: Shreveport, LA; *Format:* Country; *Hrs. of News Programming:* news progmg 18 hrs wkly; *No. News Employees:* 4; *Target Audience:* Male 25-54.
Amy Fletcher, General Manager
Greg, Brand Manager
Lisa Janes, Director Of Sales
Chasity Spears, Digital Managins Editor

Simmesport

KSLO
01-12-2011; 105.3 MHz FM; 3 kW; 466 ft.; N30 54 7 W91 56 7
3501 NW Evangeline Thruway, Carencro, LA 70520 USA
(337) 896-1600
License: Simmesport, Avoyelles County, LA held by Delta Media Corp.
Group Owner: Delta Media Corp.
Nat'l Network: Westwood One
Format: Spanish
Charles Chatelain, CEO/COO

Slidell

WSLA
12-05-1963; 1560 kHz AM; *Hrs Open:* Daytime; 1 kw-D, NDD; N30 15 0 W89 45 46
Mailing Address: P.O. Box 1175, Slidell, LA 70459 US
Second Address: 38230 Coast Blvd., Slidell, LA 70458
(985) 643-1560; *Fax:* (985) 649-9822
License: Slidell, LA held by MAPA Broadcasting L.L.C.
Nat'l Network: USA; *Regional Network:* La. Net.

Arbitron Metro Market: New Orleans, LA; *Format:* Sports; *Target Audience:* 25 plus; news intensive audience & sports fans; *Adv. Rates:* 35; 15; 25
George Mayoral, General Manager
Jim Sommers, Programming Director

South Fort Polk

KROK
02-22-2003; 95.7 MHz FM; *Hrs Open:* 24hrs; 25 kw; 294 ft.; N31 3 5 W93 16 41
168 KVVP Drive, Leesville, LA 71446 US
(337) 537-9292; *Fax:* (337) 537-4152
www.krok.com
krok@krok.com
License: South Fort Polk, Vernon County, LA held by West Central Broadcasting Co. Inc.
Arbitron Metro Market: South Fort Polk, LA; *Format:* Alternative; *Target Audience:* 18-54.
Alan Taylor, CFO
Doug Stannard, President

Springhill

KTKC
06-30-1954; 1460 kHz AM; *Hrs Open:* Sunrise-sunset; 1 kw-D, 220 w-N; N33 00 28 W93 28 43
226 N. Main St., Springhill, LA 71075 US
(318) 539-6000; *Fax:* (318) 539-6002
www.ktkcfm.com
License: Springhill, Webster County, LA held by Leon Hunt
Group Owner: Star Radio Network
Population Served: 25,000; *Arbitron Metro Market:* Shreveport, LA; *Format:* Oldies
Leon Hunt, President

KTKC
09-05-1975; 92.9 MHz FM; *Hrs Open:* 24; 40 kw horiz, 13.3 kw vert; 548 ft.; N33 0 30 W93 28 38
226 N. Main St., Springhill, LA 71075 US
(318) 539-6000; *Fax:* (318) 539-6002
www.ktkcfm.com
License: Springhill, Webster County, LA held by Leon Hunt
Group Owner: Star Radio Network
Nat'l Network: ABC
Arbitron Metro Market: Shreveport, LA; *Format:* Country; *Target Audience:* 35-54.
Leon Hunt, President

St. Martinville

*KSJY
01-01-2005; 89.9 MHz FM; 30 kw; 466 ft.; N30 8 3 W91 51 46
P.O. Box 3206, Tupelo, MS 38803 US
(662) 844-8888; *Fax:* (662) 842-6791
www.afr.net
faq@afa.net
License: St. Martinville, St. Martin County, LA held by American Family Association.
Group Owner: American Family Radio
Arbitron Metro Market: Tupelo, MO; *Format:* Christian, Religious
Tim Wildmon, President
Donald Wildmon, Founder
Buddy Smith, Sr. VP
Ed Vitagliano, Executive VP
Randy Sharp, Director Of Special Projects
Meeke Addison, Director Of Communications
Abraham Hamilton III, Generalcounsel & PublicPolicy

Sulphur

KEZM
01-01-1955; 1310 kHz AM; *Hrs Open:* 24; 0.5 kw-D, DA2; 0.05 kw-N, DA2; N30 13 27 W93 22 44
101 West Napoleon Street, Sulphur, LA 70663 US
(337) 527-3611; *Fax:* (337) 527-0213
www.kezmonline.com
License: Sulphur, LA held by Merchant Broadcasting Inc.
Nat'l Network: Sporting News Radio Network
Arbitron Metro Market: Lake Charles, LA; *Format:* Sports; *Hrs. of News Programming:* news progmg 5 hrs wkly; *No. News Employees:* 1; *Target Audience:* 18-63; upscale baby-boomers; *Adv. Rates:* 4; 4; 4; 3
Bruce Merchant, President
Kathy Soileau, General Sales Mgr

KKGB
12-17-1977; 101.3 MHz FM; *Hrs Open:* 24; 12 kw; 479 ft.; N30 14 41 W93 20 37
111 East Kilbourn Avenue, Suite 2700, Milwaukee, WI 53202 US
(337) 439-3300; *Fax:* (337) 436-7278
www.kkgb.com
License: Sulphur, Calcasieu County, LA held by Cumulus Licensing Corp.
Group Owner: Cumulus Media Inc.; (acq 12-17-98; grpsl)
Nat'l Reps: Christal
Arbitron Metro Market: Lake Charles, L; *Format:* Classic Rock; *No. News Employees:* 1; *Target Audience:* General; baby boomers
Eric Nielson, Operations Dir
Jimmie Cole, General Sales Mgr
Kevin Goode, Promotions Manager

*KRLR
01-01-2007; 89.1 MHz FM; 0.001 kw horiz, 16 kw vert; 394 ft.; N30 21 6 W93 23 49 *Rebroadcasts:* Rebroadcasts KLVR(FM) Santa Rosa, CA 100%
188 S. Bellevue, Suite 222, Memphis, TN 38104 US
(800) 877-5600; *Fax:* (916) 251-1650
www.klove.com
License: Sulphur, Calcasieu County, LA held by Educational Media Foundation.
Group Owner: EMF Broadcasting; (acq 11-1-2006; grpsl)
Nat'l Network: K-Love
Arbitron Metro Market: Sulphur, LA; *Format:* Christian
Darrell Chambliss, Chairman
Mike Novak, President
Chip Bailey, Operations Dir

Tallulah

KBYO
09-04-1954; 1360 kHz AM; 0.5 kw-D, ND2; 0.131 kw-N, ND2; N32 25 37 W91 13 15
Mailing Address: 3046 Indiana Ave, Suite 231, Vicksburg, MS 39180 US
Second Address: 1109 Hudson Ln., Monroe, LA 71201
(318) 388-2323; *Fax:* (318) 388-0569
License: Tallulah, LA held by Retail Social Activities Center Inc, (R-Sac)
Group Owner: Holladay Broadcasting of Louisiana LLC; (acq 9-8-2011)
Arbitron Metro Market: Monroe, LA
Evan Doss III, President
Russell Kendrick, Chief Engineer

KLSM
04-29-1983; 104.5 MHz FM; 25 kw; 328 ft.; N32 22 13 W91 7 39
900 Belmont Street, Vicksburg, MS 39180 US
(601) 636-2340; *Fax:* (601) 638-0869
License: Tallulah, Madison County, LA held by Holladay Broadcasting of Louisiana LLC.
Group Owner: Holladay Broadcasting of Louisiana LLC
Arbitron Metro Market: Vicksburg, MS; *Format:* Adult Contemp; *Target Audience:* 25-54.
Bob Holladay, General Manager

KTJZ
01-01-2008; 97.5 MHz FM; 6 kw; 308 ft.; N32 25 42 W91 18 47 US
(225) 334-7490; *Fax:* (225) 334-7491
License: Tallulah, Madison County, LA held by Mid South Communications Co. Inc.
Arbitron Metro Market: Tallulah, LA; *Format:* Blues, Gospel
Ernest Johnson, Chairman

Thibodaux

*KNSU
02-15-1972; 91.5 MHz FM; *Hrs Open:* 10 AM-2 AM (M-F); noon-2 AM (S, Su); 0.25 kw vert; 148 ft.; N29 47 29 W90 48 7
P. O. Box 2664, Thibodaux, LA 70310 US
(985) 448-4446; *Fax:* (985) 449-7106
www.nicholls.edu/knsu
lance.arnold@nicholls.edu
License: Thibodaux, Lafourche County, LA held by Board of Trustees, Nicholls State University.
Format: Alternative; *Hrs. of News Programming:* News progmg 10 hrs wkly; *Target Audience:* 18 plus.
Katie Kingdon, Station Manager
Jonathan DeSilvie, Programming Director

KTIB
12-24-1953; 640 kHz AM; *Hrs Open:* 24; 5 kw-D, DA2; 1 kw-N, DA2; N29 51 5 W90 54 48
108 Green Street, P.O. Box 682, Thibodaux, LA 70301 US
(985) 447-6404; *Fax:* (985) 447-6464
www.ktib640.com
License: Thibodaux, LA held by Gap Broadcasting LLC
Nat'l Network: Jones Radio Networks; Premiere Radio Networks; Talk Radio Network; *Regional Network:* La. Net; *Nat'l Reps:* Commercial Media Sales
Arbitron Metro Market: Thibodaux, LA
George Laughlin, CEO
Linda Bellanger, General Manager

*KTLN
05-01-1995; 90.5 MHz FM; *Hrs Open:* 24; 0.2 kw vert; 358 ft.; N29 43 18 W90 46 33 *Rebroadcasts:* Rebroadcasts WWNO(FM) New Orleans 100%
Library Building Rm 450, 2000 Lakeshore Drive, New Orleans, LA 70148 US
(504) 280-7000; *Fax:* (504) 280-6061
www.wwno.org
info@wwno.org
License: Thibodaux, Lafourche County, LA held by Board of Supervisors of Louisiana State University and Agricultural and Mechanical College, University of New Orleans.
Nat'l Network: NPR; PRI
Arbitron Metro Market: New Orleans, LA; *Format:* Jazz, News; *Hrs. of News Programming:* News progmg 39 hrs wkly; *Target Audience:* 35-70; well educated professionals, managers, artists & arts patrons

KXOR-FM
05-01-1966; 106.3 MHz FM; *Hrs Open:* 24; 25 kw; 328 ft.; N29 38 52 W90 41 34
120 Prevost Drive, Houma, LA 70364 US
(985) 851-1020; *Fax:* (985) 872-4403
www.LA1063.com
info@rock1063.net
License: Thibodaux, Lafourche County, LA held by Sunburst Media-Louisiana LLC.
Group Owner: Sunburst Media-Louisiana LLC; (acq 1-23-2007; grpsl)
Regional Network: La. Agri-News
Hrs. of News Programming: News progmg 20 hrs wkly; *Target Audience:* 18-54.; *Adv. Rates:* 25; 20; 25; 15
John Delise, Operations Dir
Danny Fletcher, General Manager

Tioga

KLAA-FM
05-25-1984; 103.5 MHz FM; *Hrs Open:* 24; 50 kw; 476 ft.; N31 25 39 W92 24 18
92 West Shamrock Street, Pineville, LA 71360 US
(318) 487-1035; *Fax:* (318) 487-4419
www.la103.com
License: Tioga, Rapides County, LA held by Mapleton Communications
Group Owner: Opus Media Holdings LLC; (acq 9-30-2004; $3.38 million with KBKK(FM) Ball).
Nat'l Reps: Christal; *Wire Services:* AP
Arbitron Metro Market: Alexandria, LA; *Format:* Country; *Hrs. of News Programming:* news progmg 4 hrs wkly; *No. News Employees:* 1; *Target Audience:* 25-54; working people, upscale professionals
Kim Jones, President

Varnado

WBOX-FM
11-01-1985; 92.9 MHz FM; 3 kw; 322 ft.; N30 54 10 W89 57 36
P. O. Box 351, Columbia, MS 39429 US
(504) 732-4288; *Fax:* (985) 732-4288
License: Varnado, Washington County, LA held by Best Country Broadcasting LLC
Arbitron Metro Market: Columbia, MS; *Format:* Country
Ben Strickland, President

Vidalia

KWTG
01-01-1994; 104.7 MHz FM; 3 kw; 266 ft.; N31 35 5 W91 23 18
Mailing Address: 381 John R. Junkin Drive, Natchez, MS 39120 US
Second Address: 917 S.E.E. Wallace Blvd., Ferriday, LA 71334
(318) 757-4200; *Fax:* (318) 757-7689
License: Vidalia, Concordia County, LA held by Tom D. Gay.
Group Owner: The Radio Group
Arbitron Metro Market: Vidalia, LA; *Format:* Country
Desiree Smith, General Manager

Ville Platte

KVPI
11-01-1953; 1050 kHz AM; *Hrs Open:* 6 AM-midnight; 250 w-D, 10 w-N; N30 41 39 W92 18 46
Mailing Address: P.O. Box J, Ville Platte, LA 73586
Second Address: 809 W. LaSalle St., Ville Platte, LA 70586

(337) 363-2124; *Fax:* (337) 363-3574
Kvpionline.com
kvpiamfm@gmail.com
License: Ville Platte, Evangeline County, LA held by Ville Platte Broadcsting Co.
Nat'l Network: CBS Radio National Network
Population Served: 79,692; *Arbitron Metro Market:* Lafayette, LA *Special Programming:* Cajun 12 hrs wkly; *Hrs. of News Programming:* news progmg 12 hrs wkly; *Target Audience:* 32-65.
Mark Layne, General Manager
Dave Graichen, Chief Engineer

KVPI-FM
02-26-1967; 92.5 MHz FM; *Hrs Open:* 24; 3.9 kw horiz; Ant 220 ft; N30 41 39 W92 18 46
Mailing Address: Box J, Ville Platte, LA 70586
Second Address: 809 W. LaSalle St., Ville Platte, LA 70586
(337) 363-2124; *Fax:* (337) 363-3574
www.oldies925.com
kvpiamfm@gmail.com
License: Ville Platte, Evangeline County, LA held by Ville Platte Broadcsting Co.
Nat'l Network: NBC Radio; *Wire Services:* AP
Population Served: 72,940 *Special Programming:* Cajun French 6 hrs wkly.; *Hrs. of News Programming:* news progmg 12 hrs wkly; *No. News Employees:* 1; *Target Audience:* 32-65.

Vivian

KNCB
04-09-1966; 1320 kHz AM; *Hrs Open:* Sunrise-sunset; 5 kw-D, ND1; 0.057 kw-N, ND1; N32 54 7 W93 58 58
Mailing Address: P. O. Box 1072, Vivian, LA 71082 US
Second Address: 17525 Hwy. 1 N., Vivian, LA 71082
(318) 375-3278; *Fax:* (318) 375-3329
rjc1072@cs.com
License: Vivian, LA held by North Caddo Broadcasting Co.
Arbitron Metro Market: Shreveport, LA; *Format:* Country, Gospel, 60, News/Talk, Talk; *Target Audience:* General.; *Adv. Rates:* 16; 14; 10; 8.15

KNCB-FM
09-28-1996; 105.3 MHz FM; *Hrs Open:* 24; 3.2 kw; 449 ft.; N32 55 54 W93 54 22
Mailing Address: P.O. Box 1072, Vivian, LA 71082 US
Second Address: 17525 Hwy. 1 N., Vivian, LA 71082
(318) 375-3278; *Fax:* (318) 375-3329
rjc1072@cs.com
License: Vivian, Caddo County, LA
Nat'l Network: ABC
Arbitron Metro Market: Shreveport, LA; *Format:* Country; *Adv. Rates:* 16; 14; 10; 8.15

Washington

KNEK
08-18-1980; 1190 kHz AM; 250 w-D; N30 35 09 W92 04 00
202 Galbert Rd., Lafayette, LA 70506 US
(337) 232-1311
www.knek.com
License: Washington, LA held by Radio License Holding CBC, LLC
Group Owner: Cumulus Media Inc.; (acq 1-14-99; grpsl)
Regional Network: La. Net.
Arbitron Metro Market: Lafayette, LA; *Format:* Urban Contemporary; *Target Audience:* 25-54.
Jim Beard, General Manager
Deidre Williams, Programming Director
Lynette Batiste, Promotions Manager

KNEK
01-01-1989; 104.7 MHz FM; *Hrs Open:* 24; 25 kw; 328 ft.; N30 25 17 W92 6 50
202 Galbert Rd., Lafayette, LA 70506 LA
(337) 232-1311
www.knek.com
License: Washington, LA held by Radio License Holding CBC, LLC
Group Owner: Cumulus Media Inc.
Arbitron Metro Market: Lafayette, LA; *Format:* Urban Contemporary
Jim Beard, General Manager
Deidre Williams, Programming Director
Lynette Batiste, Promotions Manager
Jared Verrett, Chief Engineer

West Monroe

KMBS
08-01-1956; 1310 kHz AM; 5 kw-D, ND1; 0.049 kw-N, ND1; N32 29 2 W92 9 10
613 N 5th Street, P.O. Box 547, West Monroe, LA 71291 US
(318) 323-1310
License: West Monroe, LA held by Red Bear Broadcasting
Nat'l Network: ABC
Arbitron Metro Market: Monroe, LA; *Format:* Sports
Chuck Redden, General Manager

KZRZ
08-01-1967; 98.3 MHz FM; *Hrs Open:* 24; 50 kw; 492 ft.; N32 39 38 W91 59 28
350 Park Avenue, 20th Floor, New York, NY 10022 US
(318) 387-3922; *Fax:* (318) 322-4585
www.sunny983.com
License: West Monroe, Ouachita County, LA held by Opus Broadcasting Monroe L.L.C.
Group Owner: Opus Media Holdings LLC; (acq 7-19-2004; grpsl).
Arbitron Metro Market: Monroe, LA; *Format:* Adult Contemp; *Target Audience:* 18-54; mid to upper income

White Castle

KKAY
11-01-1976; 1590 kHz AM; *Hrs Open:* 24; 1 kw-D, ND1; 0.067 kw-N, ND1; N30 11 1 W91 6 27
3365 Hwy - 1 South, Donaldsonville, LA 70346 US
(225) 473-6397; *Fax:* (225) 473-5764
www.kkay1590.com
License: White Castle, LA held by Cactus Communications LLC.
Arbitron Metro Market: Baton Rouge, LA; *Format:* Variety/Diverse; *Adv. Rates:* 13.25; 13:25; 13.25; na
David Dawson, General Manager

Winnfield

KVCL-FM
11-03-1966; 92.1 MHz FM; *Hrs Open:* 24; 6 kw; 210 ft.; N31 56 54 W92 37 37
P. O. Box 548, Winnfield, LA 71483 US
(318) 628-5822; *Fax:* (318) 628-7355
License: Winnfield, Winn County, LA held by Baldridge-Dumas Communications Inc.
Group Owner: Baldridge-Dumas Communications Inc.; (acq 12-28-2006; $300,000 with co-located AM)
Arbitron Metro Market: Alexandria LA; *Format:* Country; *Hrs. of News Programming:* news progmg 22 hrs wkly; *No. News Employees:* 2
Ted Dumas, General Manager

Winnsboro

KMAR-FM
08-01-1969; 95.9 MHz FM; *Hrs Open:* 24; 6 kw; 178 ft.; N32 11 2 W91 44 51
P. O. Box 1319, Columbia, LA 71418 US
(318) 435-5141; *Fax:* (318) 435-5749
kmarfm@bellsouth.net
License: Winnsboro, Franklin County, LA held by Boeuf River Broadcasting Co.
Group Owner: The Radio Group; (acq 11-89; $200,000 with co-located AM;
Nat'l Network: ABC; *Wire Services:* UPI
Format: Country; *Hrs. of News Programming:* news progmg 20 hrs wkly; *No. News Employees:* 1; *Target Audience:* 30-60; adults; *Adv. Rates:* 12; 12; 12; 12
Rene Johnston, General Manager

Zwolle

KTEZ
07-04-2002; 99.9 MHz FM; *Hrs Open:* 24 hours; 6 kw; 328 ft.; N31 39 17 W93 29 4
P O Box 11196, College Station, TX 77842 US
(318) 256-5924; *Fax:* (318) 256-0950
www.bdcradio.com
kwlv@bellsouth.net
License: Zwolle, Sabine County, LA held by Baldridge-Dumas Communications Inc.
Group Owner: Baldridge-Dumas Communications Inc.; (acq 2-25-2002).
Format: Adult Contemp
Tedd Dumas, Operations Dir
Rhonda Leach, General Manager
Cindy Ezernack, Station Manager

Maine

Auburn

WTHT
02-01-1977; 99.9 MHz FM; *Hrs Open:* 24; 28.5 kw; 643 ft.; N43 57 7 W70 17 46
912 Washington Street, Auburn, ME 04210 US
(207) 797-0780; *Fax:* (207) 797-0368
www.999thewolf.com
info@999thewolf.com
License: Auburn, Androscoggin County, ME held by WBIN Media Co. Inc.
Group Owner: WBIN Media Co. Inc.
Arbitron Metro Market: Portland, ME; *Format:* Country; *Target Audience:* Women 18-34, women 25-54; Maine's kiss 99.9
Stan Manning, Operations Dir
Pat Collins, General Manager
Tim Gatz, General Sales Mgr
Stann Bennett, Programming Director
Corey Garrison, Promotions Manager
Bill Ryall, Chief Engineer

Augusta

WJZN
02-23-1932; 1400 kHz AM; *Hrs Open:* 24; 1 kw-U; N44 17 30 W69 46 27 *Rebroadcasts:* Rebroadcasts WTVL(AM) Waterville 100%
56 Western Avenue, Suite 13, Augusta, ME 13203
(207) 623-4735; *Fax:* (207) 626-5948
www.1400and1490.com
augusta@catomm.com
License: Augusta, Kennebec County, ME
Group Owner: Townsquare Media; (acq 4-26-2001; grpsl).
Nat'l Reps: D & R Radio
Population Served: 19,103; *Arbitron Metro Market:* Augusta, ME; *No. News Employees:* 1; *Target Audience:* 20-40; young adults
Al Perry, General Manager
Julie Beaulieu, General Sales Mgr
Renee Nelson, News Director
Bob Perry, Chief Engineer

WVQM
07-01-1961; 101.3 MHz FM; 41 kw; 371 ft.; N44 18 36 W69 49 51 *Rebroadcasts:* Simulcast with WVOM(FM) Howland 100%
Mailing Address: 330 East Kilbourn Avenue, Suite 250, Milwaukee, WI 53202 US
Second Address: 125 Community Drive, Suite 201, Augusta, ME 04330
(207) 623-9000; *Fax:* (207) 623-9007
www.wvomfm.com
kellyslater@clearchannel.com
License: Augusta, Kennebec County, ME held by Blueberry Broadcasting LLC.
Group Owner: Blueberry Broadcasting LLC; (acq 7-29-2008; grpsl)
Arbitron Metro Market: Augusta-Waterville, ME; *Format:* News, News/Talk, 86
Steve Smith, Operations Dir
Kelly Slater, General Manager
Rick Dugal, General Sales Mgr

***WMDR**
10-02-1946; 1340 kHz AM; *Hrs Open:* 24
160 Bangor Street, Augusta, ME 04330 US
(207) 622-1340; *Fax:* (207) 623-2874
www.worshipradionetwork.org
denise@worshipradionetwork.org
License: Augusta, ME held by Light of Life Ministries Inc.
Arbitron Metro Market: Augusta, ME; *Format:* Religious *Special Programming:* stories; *Hrs. of News Programming:* News progmg 5 hrs wkly; *Target Audience:* General.

WMME-FM
01-14-1981; 92.3 MHz FM; 50 kw; 499 ft.; N44 20 7 W69 41 1
1064 James Street, Syracuse, NY 13203 US
(207) 623-4735; *Fax:* (207) 626-5948
www.92moose.fm
License: Augusta, Kennebec County, ME
Group Owner: Townsquare Media
Arbitron Metro Market: Augusta, ME; *Format:* Contemporary Hits/Top 40; *Target Audience:* General
J. Spangler, President
Lori Spangler, Operations Dir

***WWTP**
01-01-2011; 89.5 MHz FM; 2 kw; 902 ft.; N45 3 26 W69 11 27
Mailing Address: PO Box 10660, Portland, ME 04104 US
Second Address: 4 Washington St., Auburn, ME 04104
(207) 689-9939
www.thepresence.fm
info@thepresence.fm
License: Augusta, ME held by The Presence Radio Network Inc.
Group Owner: The Presence Radio Network Inc.
Format: Religious
Craig Foster, President
Eric Marenghi, Operations Mgr
Richard A. Hyatt, Engineering Consultant
Cynthia Nickless, Executive Director

***WXBP**
01-01-2011; 90.3 MHz FM; 2 kw; 902 ft.; N45 3 26 W69 11 27
Mailing Address: PO Box 10660, Portland, ME 04104 US
Second Address: 4 Washington St., Auburn, ME 04104
(207) 689-9939
www.thepresence.fm
info@thepresence.fm
License: Augusta, ME held by The Presence Radio Network Inc.
Group Owner: The Presence Radio Network Inc.
Format: Religious
Craig Foster, President
Eric Marenghi, Operations Mgr
Richard A. Hyatt, Engineering Consultant
Cynthia Nickless, Executive Director

Bangor

WAEI
01-01-1924; 910 kHz AM; *Hrs Open:* 18
27 State Street, 6th Flr, Bangor, ME 04401 US
(858) 277-4991; *Fax:* (858) 277-1365
www.ksrdradio.com
License: Bangor, ME held by Blueberry Broadcasting LLC.
Group Owner: Blueberry Broadcasting LLC; (acq 7-29-2008; grpsl)
Arbitron Metro Market: Portland OR; *Adv. Rates:* 25; 20; 22; 10
Mike MacIntosh, President
Brian KC Jones, General Manager

WEZQ
06-09-1976; 92.9 MHz FM; *Hrs Open:* 24; 20 kw; 787 ft; N44 45 35 W68 33 55
49 Acme Road, Brewer, ME 53202
(207) 989-5631; *Fax:* (207) 989-5685
www.wezq-fm.com
info@wezq-fm.com
License: Bangor, Penobscot County, ME held by Townsquare Media Bangor License LLC
Group Owner: Townsquare Media; (acq 3-1-99; grpsl)
Nat'l Reps: D & R Radio
Population Served: 33,011; *Arbitron Metro Market:* Bangor, ME; *No. News Employees:* 1; *Target Audience:* 25-54.
Paul Dupuis, Operations Dir
Tom Preble, General Manager
Dorian Daniels, Programming Director

***WHCF**
08-10-1981; 88.5 MHz FM; *Hrs Open:* 24; 35 kw; 1621 ft.; N45 7 46 W68 21 28
Mailing Address: 1476 Broadway, Bangor, ME 04401 US
Second Address: 1476 Broadway, Bangor, ME 4401
(207) 947-2751; *Fax:* (207) 947-0010
whcffm.com
contact@whcffm.com
License: Bangor, Penobscot County, ME held by Bangor Baptist Church
Nat'l Network: Salem Radio Network
Arbitron Metro Market: Bangor, ME; *Format:* Christian, Gospel, 74 *Special Programming:* Children 2 hours wkly; *Hrs. of News Programming:* 2 Min. hourly; *Target Audience:* 35-55; Adults
Stacey Brann, Chief Engineer

***WHSN**
09-01-1974; 89.3 MHz FM; *Hrs Open:* 24; 3 kw; 85 ft.; N44 49 46 W68 47 39
1 College Circle, Bangor, ME 04401 US
(207) 941-7116; *Fax:* (207) 947-3987
www.whsn-fm.com
License: Bangor, Penobscot County, ME held by Husson University Board of Trustees.
Wire Services: AP
Arbitron Metro Market: Bangor, ME; *Format:* Alternative; *Hrs. of News Programming:* news progmg 7 hrs wkly; *No. News Employees:* 1; *Target Audience:* 12-35; high school & college students
Ben Haskell, General Manager
Mark Nason, Programming Director

***WMEH**
09-14-1970; 90.9 MHz FM; *Hrs Open:* 24; 13.5 kw; 807 ft.; N44 45 45 W68 33 58
Mailing Address: 1450 Lisbon Street, Lewiston, ME 04240 US
Second Address: 1450 Lisbon St., Lewiston, ME 4240
(207) 783-9101; *Fax:* (207) 942-2857
www.mpbn.net
cbeck@mpbn.net
License: Bangor, Penobscot County, ME held by Maine Public Broadcasting Corp.
Nat'l Network: NPR; PRI
Arbitron Metro Market: Bangor, ME; *Format:* Jazz, News
Mark Vogelzang, CEO
Alexander G. Maxwell, Operations Dir
Mary Mayo, General Sales Mgr
Charles Beck, Programming Director
Keith Shortall, News Director
Christopher Amann, CFO
Alexander G. Maxwell,Jr., COO

WBFB
03-15-1961; 97.1 MHz FM; *Hrs Open:* 24; 5 kw; Ant 1,230 ft; N44 42 13 W69 04 07
184 Target Industrial Cir., Bangor, ME 04401
(207) 947-9100; *Fax:* (207) 942-8039
www.weei.com
License: Bangor, Penobscot County, ME held by Blueberry Broadcasting LLC.
Group Owner: Blueberry Broadcasting LLC; (acq 7-29-2008; grpsl)
Population Served: 200,000; *Arbitron Metro Market:* Bangor, ME; *Target Audience:* General.; *Adv. Rates:* 22; 18; 20; 10
Holly Rae, Programming Director

WZON
12-01-1926; 620 kHz AM; *Hrs Open:* 24; 5 kw-D, DAN; 5 kw-N, DAN; N44 49 44 W68 47 8
Mailing Address: PO Box 1929, Bangor, ME 04401 US
Second Address: 861 Broadway, Bangor, ME 04401
(207) 990-2800; *Fax:* (207) 990-2444
www.wzonthepulse.com
License: Bangor, ME held by The Zone Corp.
Group Owner: The Zone Corp.; (acq 9-1-93; $236,200;)
Arbitron Metro Market: Bangor, ME; *Format:* Talk; *No. News Employees:* 1; *Target Audience:* General; info & entertainment seekers; *Adv. Rates:* 20; 15; 20; 14
Stephen King, CEO
Bobby Russell, Programming Director

Bar Harbor

WBFE
06-01-1992; 99.1 MHz FM; *Hrs Open:* 24; 45 kw; 397 ft.; N44 26 41 W68 1 22
P.O. Box 9494, Ellsworth, ME 04605 US
(207) 947-9100; *Fax:* (207) 942-8039
www.971thebear.com
License: Bar Harbor, Hancock County, ME held by Blueberry Broadcasting LLC.
Group Owner: Blueberry Broadcasting LLC; (acq 7-29-2008; grpsl)
Nat'l Network: ABC; *Nat'l Reps:* Christal
Format: Country; *No. News Employees:* 1; *Target Audience:* General.
Jack O'Brien, Operations Dir
Josh Scroggins, General Manager
Bruce Biette, General Sales Mgr
Paul Dupuis, Programming Director

WBKA
05-06-1995; 107.7 MHz FM; *Hrs Open:* 24; 11.5 kw; 489 ft.; N44 33 13 W68 5 40 *Rebroadcasts:* Rebroadcasts WBQQ (FM) Kennebunk 90%
P.O. Box 6111, Bar Harbor, ME 04609 US
(207) 667-9800; *Fax:* (207) 967-8671
www.wbachradio.com
License: Bar Harbor, Hancock County, ME held by Blueberry Broadcasting LLC
Group Owner: Blueberry Broadcasting LLC
Nat'l Network: CBS; Westwood One
Arbitron Metro Market: Bar Harbor, ME; *Format:* Talk *Special Programming:* Blues 15 hrs wkly; *Hrs. of News Programming:* news progmg 6 hrs wkly; *No. News Employees:* 1; *Target Audience:* 25-54; baby boomers
Pat Collins, General Manager

Bath

WBCI
06-01-1971; 105.9 MHz FM; 50 kw; 499 ft.; N44 4 9 W69 55 28
122 Main St., Suite 4B, Topsham, MA 04086 US
(207) 725-9224; *Fax:* (207) 725-2686
www.lifechangingradio.com
License: Bath, Sagadahoc County, ME held by Blount Communications Inc.
Group Owner: Blount Communications Group; (acq 4-20-95; $375,000)
Nat'l Network: Salem Radio Network; *Nat'l Reps:* Salem
Arbitron Metro Market: Lewiston-Auburn-Augusta-Waterville, ME; *Format:* Religious; *Adv. Rates:* 16; 16; 16; 16
William Blount, President
Lee Pelletier, Manager

WJTO
09-30-1957; 730 kHz AM; *Hrs Open:* 24; 1 kw-D, ND2; 0.006 kw-N, ND2; N43 52 39 W69 50 49
P.O. Box 474, Rowley, MA 01969 US
(207) 443-6671
License: Bath, ME held by Blue Jey Broadcasting Co.
Arbitron Metro Market: Portland, ME; *Format:* Adult Contemp; *Hrs. of News Programming:* News progmg 2 hrs wkly; *Target Audience:* 35 plus; adults along the Maine coastline
Bob Bittner, General Manager

***WTBP**
01-01-2011; 89.7 MHz FM; 2 kw; 902 ft.; N45 3 26 W69 11 27
Mailing Address: PO Box 10660, Portland, ME 04104 US
Second Address: 4 Washington St., Auburn, ME 04104
(207) 689-9939
www.thepresence.fm
info@thepresence.fm
License: Bath, ME held by The Presence Radio Network Inc.
Group Owner: The Presence Radio Network Inc.
Format: Religious
Craig Foster, President
Eric Marenghi, Operations Mgr
Richard A. Hyatt, Engineering Consultant
Cynthia Nickless, Executive Director

Belfast

WBAK
03-07-1986; 104.7 MHz FM; *Hrs Open:* 24; 10 kw; 1,099 ft; N44 34 51 W68 53 51
184 Target Industrial Circle, Bangor, ME 04605
(207) 947-9100; *Fax:* (207) 942-8039
www.1047the bear.com
License: Belfast, Waldo County, ME held by Blueberry Broadcasting LLC.
Group Owner: Blueberry Broadcasting LLC; (acq 7-29-2008; grpsl)
Population Served: 300,000; *Arbitron Metro Market:* Bangor, ME; *No. News Employees:* 2; *Target Audience:* 18-49.
Josh Scroggins, General Manager

Benedicta

***WRPB**
89.3 MHz FM; 0.145 kw; 207 ft.; N45 47 11 W68 24 44 US
(207) 622-1340; *Fax:* (207) 623-2874
www.worshipradionetwork.org
info@worshipradionetwork.org
License: Benedicta, Aroostook County, ME held by Light of Life Ministries Inc.
Arbitron Metro Market: Augusta, ME; *Format:* Christian
Denise La Fountain, General Manager

Biddeford

WCYY
08-01-1972; 94.3 MHz FM; *Hrs Open:* 24; 11.5 kw; 482 ft.; N43 32 39 W70 24 16
One City Ctr., Portland, ME 04101 US
(207) 774-6364
www.wcyy.com
brian.lang@townsquaremedia.com
License: Biddeford, ME held by Townsquare Media Portland License, LLC
Group Owner: Townsquare Media; (acq 7-7-99; grpsl).
Nat'l Reps: Christal
Arbitron Metro Market: Portland, ME; *Format:* Rock/AOR; *No. News Employees:* 1
Brian Lang, General Manager
Mike Marcello, General Sales Mgr
Herb Ivy, Brand Mgr
Digital Managing Editor, Stephen Lenz

WGIN
01-01-1948; 1400 kHz AM; *Hrs Open:* 24; 1 kw-U, ND1; N43 28 52 W70 29 8
110 Main St Ste 1102, Saco, ME 04072 US
(207) 774-4561; *Fax:* (207) 774-3788
www.ilovethebay.com
info@ilovethebay.com
License: Biddeford, ME held by Saga Communications of New England LLC.
Group Owner: Saga Communications Inc.; (acq 11-17-03; $350,000).
Nat'l Network: Jones Radio Networks
Format: Adult Contemp *Special Programming:* Relg 2 hrs wkly; *No. News Employees:* 1; *Target Audience:* 35 plus; upscale professional
Harry Nelson, Station Manager

Blue Hill

*WERU-FM
06-01-1988; 89.9 MHz FM; *Hrs Open:* 6 AM-1 AM; 11.5 kw; 856 ft.; N44 26 4 W68 35 25
Mailing Address: 1186 Acadia Hwy, East Orland, ME 04431 US
Second Address: 1186 Acadia Hwy., East Orland, ME 4431
(207) 469-6600; *Fax:* (207) 469-8961
www.weru.org
amy@weru.org
License: Blue Hill, Hancock County, ME held by Salt Pond Community Broadcasting Co.
Arbitron Metro Market: Blue Hill, ME; *Format:* Variety/Diverse; *Target Audience:* General.

Boothbay Harbor

WTQX
04-01-1984; 96.7 MHz FM; *Hrs Open:* 24; 15.5 kw; 417 ft.; N44 1 31 W69 34 17 *Rebroadcasts:* Simulcast with WTOS-FM Skowhegan 100%
Mailing Address: 330 East Kilbourn Avenue, Suite 250, Milwaukee, WI 53202 US
Second Address: 125 Community Drive, Suite 201, Augusta, ME 04330
(207) 623-9000; *Fax:* (207) 623-9007
www.wtosfm.com
jackobrien@blueberrybroadcasting.com
License: Boothbay Harbor, Lincoln County, ME held by Blueberry Broadcasting LLC.
Group Owner: Blueberry Broadcasting LLC; (acq 7-29-2008; grpsl)
Arbitron Metro Market: Lincoln County, Maine; *Target Audience:* 25-49.
Jeff O'Brien, Operations Dir
Mark White, General Sales Mgr

Brewer

WKIT
02-14-1979; 100.3 MHz FM; *Hrs Open:* 24; 16 kw; 883 ft.; N44 40 39 W68 45 15
Mailing Address: PO Box 1929, Bangor, ME 04402 USA
Second Address: 861 Broadway, Bangor, ME 04402
(207) 990-2800; *Fax:* (207) 990-2444
www.zoneradio.com
License: Brewer, Penobscot County, ME held by The Zone Corp.
Group Owner: The Zone Corp.; (acq 9-95; $800,000 with co-located AM)
Arbitron Metro Market: Bangor, ME; *Format:* Classic Rock; *No. News Employees:* 2; *Target Audience:* 18-49.
Stephen King, CEO
Bobby Russell, Programming Director

WQCB
01-20-1986; 106.5 MHz FM; *Hrs Open:* 24; 98 kw; 1079 ft.; N45 3 26 W69 11 27
Mailing Address: 330 East Kilbourn Ave, Suite 250, Milwaukee, WI 53202 US
Second Address: 49 Acme Rd., Brewer, ME 4412
(207) 989-5631; *Fax:* (207) 989-5685
www.wqcb-fm.com
q1065@midmaine.com
License: Brewer, Penobscot County, ME held by Townsquare Media Bangor License LLC
Group Owner: Townsquare Media; (acq 2-20-98; $6.4 million with WBZN(FM) Old Town)
Nat'l Reps: McGavren Guild
Arbitron Metro Market: Bangor, ME; *Format:* Country; *Hrs. of News Programming:* news progmg 4 hrs wkly; *No. News Employees:* 2; *Target Audience:* 25-54; general
Paul Dupuis, Operations Dir
Tom Preble, General Manager
Darin Ingersoll, Programming Director

Brunswick

*WBOR
04-01-1957; 91.1 MHz FM; *Hrs Open:* 7 AM-2 AM; 0.3 kw horiz; 154 ft.; N43 54 34 W69 57 43
Music Directors, Smith Union, Bowdoin College, Brunswick, ME 04011 US
(207) 725-3250
www.wbor.org
wbor@bowdoin.edu
License: Brunswick, Cumberland County, ME held by Trustees of Bowdoin College.
Format: Variety/Diverse; *Target Audience:* General.
Walter Kennedy, Station Manager
Steven McClelland, Programming Director
Noah Fardon, Music Director

WCME(AM)
12-01-1955; 900 kHz AM; *Hrs Open:* 24; 1 kw-D, 66 w-N; N43 55 40 W69 59 43 *Rebroadcasts:* Simulcasts WJAE(AM) Westbrook
Atlantic Coast Radio, 779 Warren Ave., Portland, ME 04103-1007
(207) 773-9695; *Fax:* (207) 761-4406
www.thebigjab.com
shoe@thebigjab.com
License: Brunswick, Cumberland County, ME held by Blue Jey Broadcasting Co. Inc.
Nat'l Reps: McGavren Guild
Population Served: 35,000; *Arbitron Metro Market:* Portland, ME; *Format:* Sports, Talk; *Hrs. of News Programming:* news progmg 4 hrs wkly; *No. News Employees:* 2; *Target Audience:* 25-54.; *Adv. Rates:* 30;25; 20; 15.
David Shumacher, Operations Manager

Calais

*WMED
11-01-1983; 89.7 MHz FM; 30 kw; 525 ft.; N45 1 45 W67 19 26 *Rebroadcasts:* Rebroadcasts WMEH(FM) Bangor 100%
Mailing Address: 1450 Lisbon Street, Lewiston, ME 04240 US
Second Address: 1450 Lisbon St., Lewiston, ME 4240
(207) 783-9101; *Fax:* (207) 942-2857
www.mpbn.net
cbeck@mpbn.net
License: Calais, Washington County, ME held by Maine Public Broadcasting Corp.
Nat'l Network: NPR; PRI
Arbitron Metro Market: Calais, ME; *Format:* Jazz, News
P. James Dowe, Jr, CEO
Mary Mayo, General Sales Mgr
Charles Beck, Programming Director
Christopher Amann, CFO
Alexander G. Maxwell, Jr, COO

WQDY-FM
01-14-1976; 92.7 MHz FM; *Hrs Open:* 24; 3 kw; 299 ft.; N45 10 2 W67 16 38
P.O. Box 403, Calais, ME 04619 US
(207) 454-7545; *Fax:* (207) 454-3062
www.wqdy.fm
wqdy@wqdy.fm
License: Calais, Washington County, ME held by WQDY Inc.
Nat'l Network: Jones Radio Networks; ABC; *Wire Services:* AP
Format: Classic Rock; *No. News Employees:* 1
Bill McVicar, President
Roger Holst, Chief Engineer

Camden

WQSS
05-01-1988; 102.5 MHz FM; *Hrs Open:* 24; 7.9 kw; 1201 ft.; N44 12 40 W69 9 6
184 Target Industrial Circle, Bangor, ME 04401 US
(207) 623-9000; *Fax:* (207) 623-9007
License: Camden, Knox County, ME held by Blueberry Broadcasting LLC.
Group Owner: Blueberry Broadcasting LLC; (acq 7-29-2008; grpsl)
Format: Adult Contemp
Bruce Biette, Operations Dir

*WMEP
10-01-2002; 90.5 MHz FM; 0 kw horiz, 2 kw vert; 1217 ft.; N44 12 40 W69 9 6 *Rebroadcasts:* Rebroadcasts WMEH(FM) Bangor 100%
Mailing Address: 65 Texas Avenue, Bangor, ME 04401 US
Second Address: 1450 Lisbon St., Lewiston, ME 4240
(800) 884-1717; *Fax:* (207) 942-2857
www.mpbn.net
csweet@mpbn.net
License: Camden, Knox County, ME held by Maine Public Broadcasting Corp.
Nat'l Network: NPR; PRI
Arbitron Metro Market: Bangor, ME; *Format:* Jazz, News
Mark Vogelzang, President & CEO
Mary Mayo, General Sales Mgr
Charles Beck, Programming Director
Keith Shortall, News & Public Affairs Director
Christopher Amann, CFO
Alexander G. Maxwell, Jr, COO
Charles Beck, V.P. , Director ofRadio & Television
Jennifer Foley, V.P. Development: Philanthropic Giving
Gil Maxwell, V.P. Technology & Chief Technology Officer
Pam Smart, Membership Director

Caribou

WCXU
11-15-1986; 97.7 MHz FM; *Hrs Open:* 24; 20 kw; 318 ft.; N46 47 26 W67 55 7
152 East Green Ridge Rd., Caribou, ME 04736 US
(800) 660-9298; *Fax:* (207) 472-3221
www.channelxradio.com
channelxradio@yahoo.com
License: Caribou, Aroostook County, ME held by The Canxus Broadcasting Corp.
Group Owner: Canxus Broadcasting Corp.
Regional Reps: Cyr Associates.
Arbitron Metro Market: Aroostook County, ME; *Format:* Adult Contemp, News, 64; *Hrs. of News Programming:* news progmg 21 hrs wkly; *No. News Employees:* 1; *Target Audience:* 25-54; educated, div occupations, affluent
Dennis Curley, President/CEO
Richard Chandler, General Manager/Station Manager

*WFST
07-15-1956; 600 kHz AM; *Hrs Open:* 24; 5 kw-D, ND1; 0.127 kw-N, ND1; N46 53 12 W68 2 44
P.O. Box 600, Cariboo, ME 04736 US
(207) 492-6000; *Fax:* (207) 493-3268
wfst@maine.rr.com
License: Caribou, ME held by Northern Broadcast Ministries Inc.
Nat'l Network: Moody; Salem Radio Network
Format: Christian, Gospel, 74; *Target Audience:* General.
Donald Flewelling, President

Dennysville

WCRQ
05-01-1998; 102.9 MHz FM; *Hrs Open:* 24; 100 kw; 456 ft.; N45 1 44 W67 19 25
637 Main Street, Calais, ME 04619 US
(207) 454-7545; *Fax:* (207) 454-3062
www.wcrqfm.com
onair@wcrqfm.com
License: Dennysville, Washington County, ME held by WQDY Inc.
Arbitron Metro Market: St. Stephen, Dennysville,ME; *Format:* Adult Contemp; *Hrs. of News Programming:* News progmg 6 hrs wkly; *Target Audience:* 18-49; mass appeal
Bill McVicar, President
Bill Conley, Programming Director

Dexter

*WKVZ
01-01-1993; 102.1 MHz FM; *Hrs Open:* 24; 23 kw; 673 ft.; N45 2 40 W69 15 1
378 Main Street, Dexter, ME 04930 US
(916) 251-1600; *Fax:* (916) 251-1650
www.klove.com
License: Dexter, Penobscot County, ME held by Educational Media Foundation.
Group Owner: EMF Broadcasting; (acq 4-6-2009; $550,000 with WFZX(FM) Searsport)
Nat'l Network: K-Love
Arbitron Metro Market: Bangor, ME; *Format:* Christian

Dover-Foxcroft

WZLO
11-01-1980; 103.1 MHz FM; *Hrs Open:* 24; 1.5 kw; N45 05 37 W69 05 0
Mailing Address: PO Box 1929, Bangor, ME 04401 USA
Second Address: 861 Broadway, Bangor, ME 04401
(207) 990-2800; *Fax:* (207) 990-2444
www.wzlofm.com
License: Dover-Foxcroft, ME held by The Zone Corp.
Group Owner: The Zone Corp.; (acq 9-1-93; $236,200;)
Arbitron Metro Market: Bangor, ME; *Format:* Adult Contemp, Alternative; *No. News Employees:* 1; *Target Audience:* General; info & entertainment seekers; *Adv. Rates:* 20; 15; 20; 14
Stephen King, CEO
Bobby Russell, Programming Director

Eastport

*WSHD
04-01-1984; 91.7 MHz FM; 0.012 kw; 115 ft.; N44 54 30 W66 59 24
89 High Street, Eastport, ME 04631 US
(207) 853-6254; *Fax:* (207) 853-2919
www.shead.org
License: Eastport, Washington County, ME held by Shead High School.
Format: Variety/Diverse; *Target Audience:* General.

Ellsworth

WDEA
12-13-1958; 1370 kHz AM; 5 kw-U, DA-2; N44 28 00 W68 28 11
Mailing Address: 49 Acme Road, Brewer, ME 53202
Second Address: 49 Acme Rd., Brewer, ME 4412
(207) 989-5631; *Fax:* (207) 989-5685
www.am1370wdea.com
q1065@midmaine.com
License: Ellsworth, Hancock County, ME held by Townsquare Media Bangor License LLC
Group Owner: Townsquare Media; (acq 1999; grpsl)
Nat'l Network: CBS; *Nat'l Reps:* D & R Radio
Population Served: 54,578; *Arbitron Metro Market:* Hancock County, ME; *Target Audience:* 35 plus.
Tom Preble, General Manager
Dan Groshon, Director of Sales
Fred Miller, Programming Director
Michael O'Hara, Promotions Manager
Jodi Hersey, News Director
Richard Hyatt, Chief Engineer
Fred Mille, Brand Manager:

WKSQ
05-27-1982; 94.5 MHz FM; *Hrs Open:* 24; 11.5 kw; 1027 ft.; N44 39 31 W68 36 17
184 Target Industrial Circle, Bangor, ME 04401 US
(207) 947-9100; *Fax:* (207) 942-8039
www.kissfm.net
License: Ellsworth, Hancock County, ME held by Blueberry Broadcasting LLC.
Group Owner: Blueberry Broadcasting LLC; (acq 7-29-2008; grpsl)
Nat'l Reps: Christal
Arbitron Metro Market: Bangor, ME; *Format:* Adult Contemp; *Hrs. of News Programming:* news progmg 7 hrs wkly; *No. News Employees:* 3; *Target Audience:* 25-54.
Jon Shields, Operations Dir
Josh Scroggins, General Sales Mgr

WWMJ
12-27-1965; 95.7 MHz FM; 11.5 kw; 1030 ft.; N44 39 31 W68 36 20
49 Acme Road, Ellsworth, ME 04412 US
(207) 989-5631
www.wwmj-fm.com
License: Ellsworth, Hancock County, ME
Arbitron Metro Market: Bangor, ME; *Format:* Contemporary Hits/Top 40, Adult Contemp; *Target Audience:* 25-54.
Tom Preble, General Manager
Sabrina Colson, Director of Sales
Fred Miller, Programming Director

Fairfield

WCTB
11-01-1993; 93.5 MHz FM; 10.5 kw; 499 ft.; N44 44 42 W69 41 32
295 Kennedy Memorial Dr., Waterville, ME 04901 US
(207) 660-4888; *Fax:* (207) 660-4889
www.935trueoldies.com
License: Fairfield, Somerset County, ME held by Mountain Wireless Inc.
Group Owner: Mountain Wireless Inc.; acq 4-20-94; $60,000
Arbitron Metro Market: Augusta-Waterville, ME; *Format:* Oldies
Alan W. Anderson, President

Farmington

WKTJ-FM
08-21-1973; 99.3 MHz FM; *Hrs Open:* 24; 1.5 kw; 400 ft.; N44 39 22 W70 11 48
Voter Hill Road, Farmington, ME 04938 US
(207) 778-3400; *Fax:* (207) 778-3000
www.wktj.com
License: Farmington, Franklin County, ME held by Franklin Broadcasting Corp.
Format: Oldies; *Hrs. of News Programming:* News progmg 12 hrs wkly; *Target Audience:* 25-54.; *Adv. Rates:* 20; 16; 20; 12
Rick Davis, General Manager
Steve Bull, General Sales Mgr
Kathy Shrewsbury, News Director

Fort Kent

*WMEF
03-01-1994; 106.5 MHz FM; 7.4 kw; 302 ft.; N47 15 30 W68 33 30 *Rebroadcasts:* Rebroadcasts WMEH(FM) Bangor 100%.
Mailing Address: 1450 Lisbon Street, Lewiston, ME 04240 US
Second Address: 1450 Lisbon St., Lewiston, ME 4240
(207) 783-9101; *Fax:* (207) 942-2857
www.mpbn.net
cbeck@mpbn.net
License: Fort Kent, Aroostook County, ME held by Maine Public Broadcasting Corp.
Nat'l Network: PRI; NPR
Arbitron Metro Market: Fort Kent, ME; *Format:* Jazz, News;
Target Audience: General
Mark Vogelzang, CEO

Freeport

*WMSJ
12-01-1997; 89.3 MHz FM; 7.5 kw vert; 505 ft.; N43 45 45 W70 19 30
P O Box 432, Freeport, ME 04032 US
(207) 865-3448; *Fax:* (207) 865-1763
www.positive.fm
info@positive.fm
License: Freeport, Cumberland County, ME held by The Positive Radio Network.
Arbitron Metro Market: Freeport, ME; *Format:* Christian; *Target Audience:* 25-48.
Suzanne Happs, General Manager
Kenny Robinson, Programming Director

Gardiner

WABK
04-01-1974; 104.3 MHz FM; 50 kw; 371 ft.; N44 18 36 W69 49 51
330 East Kilbourn Avenue, Suite 250, Milwaukee, WI 53202 US
(403) 362-3418; *Fax:* (403) 362-8168
License: Gardiner, Kennebec County, ME held by Blueberry Broadcasting LLC.
Group Owner: Blueberry Broadcasting LLC; (acq 7-29-2008; grpsl)
Arbitron Metro Market: Portland OR; *Format:* Adult Contemp
Douglas Kirk, Chairman
Thomas Pippy, CFO
Steve Kassay, Operations Dir
Simon Constam, General Sales Mgr
Cathy Philippo, News Director

WFAU
09-23-1968; 1280 kHz AM; *Hrs Open:* 24; 5 kw-D, DAN; 5 kw-N, DAN; N44 14 53 W69 48 51 *Rebroadcasts:* Simulcasts with WRKD(AM) Rockland 100%
330 East Kilbourn Avenue, Suite 250, Milwaukee, WI 53202 US
(207) 623-9000; *Fax:* (207) 623-9007
License: Gardiner, ME held by Blueberry Broadcasting LLC.
Group Owner: Blueberry Broadcasting LLC; (acq 7-29-2008; grpsl)
Arbitron Metro Market: Gardiner, ME; *Format:* Sports; *Hrs. of News Programming:* news progmg 34 hrs wkly; *No. News Employees:* 1; *Target Audience:* 25-54.
Kelly Slater, General Manager
Sharon Griffith, News Director

Gorham

WLVP
03-03-1980; 870 kHz AM; 10 kw-D, DA2; 1 kw-N, DA2; N43 39 46 W70 29 41 *Rebroadcasts:* Simulcasts WLAM(AM) Lewiston 100%
912 Washington St, Auburn, ME 04240 US
(207) 797-0780; *Fax:* (207) 797-0368
License: Gorham, ME held by Nassau Broadcasting III L.L.C.
Group Owner: WBIN Media Co. Inc.
Arbitron Metro Market: Portland, ME; *Format:* Oldies
Stan Manning, Operations Dir
Patrick Collins, General Manager
Tim Gatz, General Sales Mgr
Sean Baker, Programming Director
Bill Ryall, Chief Engineer

*WMPG
09-01-1973; 90.9 MHz FM; *Hrs Open:* 24; 4.5 kw; 640 ft.; N43 44 37.7 W70 20 0.8
96 Falmouth Street, Portland, ME 04104 US
(207) 780-4943
www.wmpg.org
stationmanager@wmpg.org
License: Gorham, Cumberland County, ME held by Trustees University of Maine.
Arbitron Metro Market: Gorham, ME; *Format:* Variety/Diverse
Special Programming: Sp 4 hrs, Balkan 2 hrs, Cambodian 2 hrs, African; *Hrs. of News Programming:* News progmg 10 hrs wkly;
Target Audience: General; anygroup currently underserved by other loc stns
Jim Rand, Station Manager
Lisa Bunker, Programming Director

Gray

WJJB-FM
11-15-1975; 96.3 MHz FM; 40 kw; Ant 1,410 ft; N44 15 03 W70 25 16
779 Warren Ave., Portland, ME 02116
(207) 773-9695
www.thebigjab.com
shoe@thebigjab.com
License: Gray, Cumberland County, ME held by Atlantic Coast Radio L.L.C.
Group Owner: Atlantic Coast Radio L.L.C.; (acq 9-8-2000; grpsl)
Nat'l Network: Sporting News Radio Network; *Nat'l Reps:* McGavren Guild
Population Served: 950,000; *Arbitron Metro Market:* Portland, ME
Morgan Grumbach, General Sales Mgr

Harpswell

*WYFP
07-08-1993; 91.9 MHz FM; *Hrs Open:* 24; 6 kw; 144 ft.; N43 44 14 W69 59 39
P.O. Box 7300, Charlotte, NC 28241 US
(800) 888-7077
www.bbnradio.org
bbn@bbnmedia.org
License: Harpswell, Cumberland County, ME held by Bible Broadcasting Network Inc.
Group Owner: Bible Broadcasting Network; acq 9-30-97; $150,000)
Nat'l Network: USA
Arbitron Metro Market: Harpswell, ME; *Format:* Religious *Special Programming:* Christian rock 4 hrs, praise & worship 3 hrs wkly;
Target Audience: 25-49.
Jason Padgett, Operations Manager

Houlton

WHOU-FM
01-13-1976; 100.1 MHz FM; *Hrs Open:* 24; 9.6 kw; 525 ft.; N46 8 35 W68 6 50
Mailing Address: 39 Court Street, Suite 215, Houlton, ME 04730 US
Second Address: 39 Court St., Suite 215, Houlton, ME 4730
(207) 532-3600; *Fax:* (207) 521-0056
www.whoufm.com
sales@whoufm.com
License: Houlton, Aroostook County, ME held by County Communications Inc.
Nat'l Network: ABC
Format: Adult Contemp *Special Programming:* Sacred one hr wkly; *Hrs. of News Programming:* News progmg 8 hrs wkly;
Target Audience: 25-54.
David Moore, President
Fred Grant, General Manager
JoLene Ledger, Station Manager

Howland

WVOM-FM
06-01-1993; 103.9 MHz FM; 90 kw; 1509 ft.; N45 7 46 W68 21 28 *Rebroadcasts:* Rebroadcasts WBYA(FM) Searsport 80%
263 State Street, Bangor, ME 04401 US
(207) 947-9100; *Fax:* (207) 942-8039
License: Howland, Penobscot County, ME held by Blueberry Broadcasting LLC.
Group Owner: Blueberry Broadcasting LLC; (acq 7-29-2008; grpsl)
Nat'l Network: CBS; Westwood One
Arbitron Metro Market: Bangor, ME; *Format:* News, News/Talk, 86; *Target Audience:* 25-64; upper income, professional, managerial
Jon Shields, Operations Dir
Josh Scroggins, General Manager
Katrina Walls, Programming Director

Islesboro

WBYA
01-01-1999; 105.5 MHz FM; 25 kw; 305 ft.; N44 18 58 W68 58 12
20 South Street, Bangor, ME 04401 US
(702) 736-6161
License: Islesboro, Waldo County, ME held by WBIN Media Co. Inc.
Group Owner: WBIN Media Co. Inc.
Arbitron Metro Market: Payson AZ
Will Kemp, President

Kennebunk

WBQQ
11-01-1991; 99.3 MHz FM; *Hrs Open:* 24; 3 kw; 328 ft.; N43 24 16 W70 26 15
169 Port Road, Kennebunk, ME 04043 US
(207) 797-0780; *Fax:* (207) 967-8671
www.999thewolf.com/
License: Kennebunk, York County, ME held by WBIn Media Co. Inc.
Group Owner: WBIN Media Co. Inc.
Nat'l Network: ABC
Format: Talk; *Target Audience:* 35-64; upscale
Pat Collins, Operations Dir
Patrick Collins, General Manager
Tim Gatz, General Sales Mgr
Stan Bennett, Programming Director
Corey Garrison, Promotions Manager
Stan Manning, Operations Director

Kennebunkport

WHTP
12-01-1994; 104.7 MHz FM; 6 kw; Ant 292 ft; N43 26 36 W70 26 38
89 Mussey Road, Suite 100, Scarborough, ME 04074
(207) 883-0615; *Fax:* (207) 883-1258
www.hot1047maine.com
License: Kennebunkport, York County, ME held by Mainstream Media LLC
Nat'l Network: AP Radio
Special Programming: Jazz 5 hrs wkly; *Target Audience:* 25-54; upscale, affluent, management, professionals
Pat Collins, Operations Dir
Scott Hooper, Programming Director
Stan Manning, Operations Director

***WMEK**
88.3 MHz FM; 250 w; Ant 138 ft; N43 24 16 W70 26 15
P.O. Box 398, New Durham, NH 03855 US
(603) 859-9170; *Fax:* (603) 859-8172
www.communityliferadio.org
License: Kennebunkport, York County, ME held by Word Radio Educational Foundation
Group Owner: Word Radio Educational Foundation
Format: Religious
Ronald R. Malone, President
Sharon Malone, Operations Manager

Kittery

WSHK
08-01-1992; 105.3 MHz FM; *Hrs Open:* 24; 2.2 kw; 371 ft; N43 10 28 W70 46 50 *Rebroadcasts:* Rebroadcasts WSAK-FM Hampton
292 Middle Rd., Dover, NH 03820 US
(603) 749-9750
www.shark1053.com
License: Kittery, ME held by Townsquare Media Portsmouth License, LLC
Group Owner: Townsquare Media; (acq 7-7-99; grpsl).
Population Served: 9,543; *Arbitron Metro Market:* Kittery, ME; *Format:* Adult Contemp
Brian Lang, General Manager
Paul Kelley, Director of Sales
Jonathan Smith, Brand Manager
Rob Michaelson, Digital Managing Editor

Lewiston

***WARX**
02-29-1948; 93.9 MHz FM; *Hrs Open:* 24; 27.5 kw; 633 ft.; N44 8 40 W70 1 22
P.O. Box 2118, Omaha, NE 68103 US
(888) 937-2471; *Fax:* (916) 251-1650
www.air1.com
License: Lewiston, Androscoggin County, ME held by Educational Media Foundation.
Group Owner: EMF Broadcasting; (acq 6-5-2008; $1 million)
Nat'l Network: Air 1
Arbitron Metro Market: Lewiston-Auburn, ME; *Format:* Christian
Alan Mason, COO
Mike Novak, President

***WRBC**
10-06-1958; 91.5 MHz FM; *Hrs Open:* 24; 0.12 kw; 16 ft.; N44 6 18 W70 12 32
141-145 Nichols Street, Lewiston, ME 04240 US
(207) 786-6330; *Fax:* (207) 795-8793
www.bates.edu/wrbc
License: Lewiston, Androscoggin County, ME held by President and Trustees of Bates College.
Format: Christian; *Target Audience:* General; anyone searching for something different
Ky Windborn, General Manager

WFNK
03-01-1973; 107.5 MHz FM; 100 kw; 928 ft.; N44 0 12 W70 25 24
P.O. Box 929, Lewiston, ME 04240 US
(207) 797-0780; *Fax:* (207) 797-0368
www.1075frank.com
info@1075frank.com
License: Lewiston, Androscoggin County, ME held by WBIN Media Co. Inc.
Group Owner: WBIN Media Co. Inc.
Nat'l Reps: D & R Radio
Arbitron Metro Market: Portland, ME; *Format:* Classic Rock
Pat Collins, General Manager
Tim Gatz, General Sales Mgr
Stan Bennett, Programming Director
Corey Garrison, Promotions Manager
Stan Manning, Operations Director
Amy Ryan, Production Director

WEZR
08-21-1938; 1240 kHz AM; *Hrs Open:* 24; 1 kw-U; N44 06 55 W70 14 56
555 Center St., Auburn, ME 04268
(207) 784-4700; *Fax:* (207) 784-4700
dickgleason@gmail.com
License: Lewiston, Androscoggin County, ME held by Mountain Valley Broadcasting Inc.
Group Owner: Gleason Radio Group; (acq 11-28-90)
Nat'l Network: USA; *Nat'l Reps:* CYR Associates *Regional Reps:* CYR Associates
Population Served: 100,000; *Arbitron Metro Market:* Lewiston-Auburn, ME; *Hrs. of News Programming:* Top & bottom of each hour; *No. News Employees:* 3; *Target Audience:* General.; *Adv. Rates:* 20; 20; 20; 20
Richard Gleason, President/General Manager

WLAM
09-04-1947; 1470 kHz AM; 5 kw-U, DA1; N44 3 47 W70 15 0
P.O. Box 929, Lewiston, ME 04240 US
(207) 797-0780; *Fax:* (207) 797-0368
License: Lewiston, ME held by WBIN Media Co. Inc.
Group Owner: WBIN Media Co. Inc.
Nat'l Reps: D & R Radio
Arbitron Metro Market: Portland, ME; *Format:* Oldies
Tim Gatz, General Sales Mgr
Stan Manning, Operations Director

Lincoln

***WHMX**
04-01-1975; 105.7 MHz FM; *Hrs Open:* 24; 48 kw; 466 ft.; N45 20 38 W68 30 24
1476 Broadway, Bangor, ME 04401 US
(207) 947-2751
www.solutionfm.com
contact@solutionfm.com
License: Lincoln, Penobscot County, ME held by Bangor Baptist Church.
Arbitron Metro Market: Bangor, ME; *Format:* Christian; *Target Audience:* 18-35.
Pencil Boone, General Manager
Tim Collins, Programming Director

***WWLN**
90.5 MHz FM; 0.065 kw; 492 ft.; N45 20 41 W68 30 30 US
(207) 622-1340; *Fax:* (207) 623-2874
License: Lincoln, Penobscot County, ME held by Light of Life Ministries Inc.
Arbitron Metro Market: Lincoln, ME
Ryan Gagne, Operations Dir
Raymond Bouchard, General Manager
Roger Jackson, Programming Director

Machias

WALZ-FM
11-25-1978; 95.3 MHz FM; *Hrs Open:* 24; 3 kw; 220 ft.; N44 44 8 W67 30 11 *Rebroadcasts:* Rebroadcasts WQDY-FM Calais 100%
P.O. Box 403, Calais, ME 04619 US
(207) 454-7545; *Fax:* (207) 454-3062
www.wqdy.fm
wqdy@wqdy.fm
License: Machias, Washington County, ME held by William McVicar & Roger Holst, general partnership
Nat'l Network: ABC; Jones Radio Networks; *Wire Services:* AP
Arbitron Metro Market: Calais, ME; *Format:* Contemporary Hits/Top 40, Adult Contemp *Special Programming:* Boston Red Sox; *No. News Employees:* 1
William McVicar, General Manager

***WUMM**
01-01-2008; 91.7 MHz FM; 0.1 kw; 72 ft.; N44 42 33 W67 27 29 US
(207) 255-1371
www.umm.maine.edu/wumm
wumm@maine.edu
License: Machias, Washington County, ME held by University of Maine System.
Arbitron Metro Market: Machias, ME; *Format:* Variety/Diverse
Brian Corliss, General Manager

Madawaska

WCXX
01-30-1988; 102.3 MHz FM; *Hrs Open:* 24; 1.2 kw; 423 ft.; N47 19 51 W68 20 26 *Rebroadcasts:* Rebroadcasts WCXU(FM) Caribou 50%
152 E. Green Ridge Rd, Caribou, ME 04736 US
(207) 473-7513; *Fax:* (207) 472-3221
www.channelxradio.com
channelxradio@yahoo.com
License: Madawaska, Aroostook County, ME held by Canxus Broadcasting Corp.
Group Owner: Canxus Broadcasting Corp.
Nat'l Network: CNN Radio *Regional Reps:* Cyr Associates.
Arbitron Metro Market: Aroostook County, ME; *Format:* Adult Contemp, News, 64; *Hrs. of News Programming:* news progmg 16 hrs wkly; *No. News Employees:* 1; *Target Audience:* 18-54.; *Adv. Rates:* 20; 15; 18; 12
Richard Chandler, Station Manager
Douglas Christensen, News Director

Madison

WQSK
01-01-1995; 97.5 MHz FM; *Hrs Open:* 24; 6 kw; 328 ft.; N44 47 32 W69 58 10
330 East Kilbourn Avenue, Suite 250, Milwaukee, WI 53202 US
(207) 623-9000; *Fax:* (207) 623-9007
www.foxsportsmaine.com
donaldshields@clearchannel.com
License: Madison, Somerset County, ME held by Blueberry Broadcasting LLC.
Group Owner: Blueberry Broadcasting LLC; (acq 7-29-2008; grpsl)
Regional Reps: Cyr Associates.
Format: Sports; *Target Audience:* 25-54.
Kelly Slater, General Manager
Rick Dugal, General Sales Mgr
Donald Shield, Programming Director

Mexico

WTBM
09-15-1988; 100.7 MHz FM; *Hrs Open:* 24; 0.85 kw; 1273 ft.; N44 34 56 W70 37 59 *Rebroadcasts:* Simulcast with WOXO-FM Norway 99%
5243 Main Street, Norway, ME 04268 US
(207) 743-5911; *Fax:* (207) 743-5913
www.woxo.com
info@oxocountry.com
License: Mexico, Oxford County, ME held by Mountain Valley Broadcasting Inc.
Group Owner: Gleason Radio Group; (acq 12-90;
Nat'l Network: USA; *Nat'l Reps:* CYR Associates
Arbitron Metro Market: Portland, ME; *Format:* Country, Sports
Special Programming: Financial Advise 3 hrs; *Hrs. of News Programming:* news progmg 12 hrs wkly; *No. News Employees:* 2; *Target Audience:* General. *Adv. Rates:* 20; 20; 20; 20
Dick Gleason, President/General Manager

Milbridge

WRMO
01-01-2005; 93.7 MHz FM; *Hrs Open:* 24 hours; 22.5 kw; 669 ft.; N44 38 33 W68 10 18
93 Cottage Street, Suite 101, Ben Harbor, ME 04609 US
(207) 812-3878
www.937thewave.com
License: Milbridge, Washington County, ME held by Steven A. Roy, Personal Representative, Estate of Lyle Evans
Nat'l Reps: Rgnl Reps
Arbitron Metro Market: Milbridge, ME; *Format:* Adult Contemp; *Hrs. of News Programming:* 5am, 6am, 7am, 8am, 9am, 12pm, 5pm; *Target Audience:* 35+; *Adv. Rates:* 15; 15; 10; 8

Millinocket

WSYY
12-07-1963; 1240 kHz AM; *Hrs Open:* 24; 1 kw-U, ND1; N45 40 24 W68 43 7
Lake Road, PO Box 1240, Millinocket, ME 04462 US
(207) 723-9657; *Fax:* (207) 723-5900
www.themountain949.com
calendar@themountain949.com
License: Millinocket, ME held by Katahdin Communications Inc.
Nat'l Network: ESPN Radio *Regional Reps:* Cyr Associates.
Arbitron Metro Market: Bangor, ME; *Format:* Sports; *Target Audience:* General.; *Adv. Rates:* 6; 6; 6; 6
James Talbot, President

WSYY-FM
04-12-1978; 94.9 MHz FM; *Hrs Open:* 24; 23.5 kw; 692 ft.; N45 42 58 W68 47 54
P.O. Box 1240, Lake Rd., Millinocket, ME 04462 US
(207) 723-9657; *Fax:* (207) 723-5900
www.themountain949.com
License: Millinocket, Penobscot County, ME
Nat'l Network: CBS Radio
Arbitron Metro Market: Bangor, ME; *Format:* Variety/Diverse; *Target Audience:* 20-45.

Monticello

WXME
09-02-1981; 780 kHz AM
297 Britton Road, Monticello, ME 04760 US
(207) 538-9180
License: Monticello, ME held by Allan H. Weiner
Format: Talk
Allan Weiner, President

WBCQ-FM
09-01-2008; 94.7 MHz FM; 6 kw; 312 ft.; N46 20 30 W67 49 4
297 Britton Road, Monticello, ME 04760 US
(207) 538-9180; *Fax:* (207) 521-0056
License: Monticello, Aroostook County, ME held by Allan H. Weiner & Barbara A. Weiner dba WBCQ Radio.
Arbitron Metro Market: Monticello, ME; *Format:* Country
David Moore, General Manager

North Windham

WXTP
01-01-1996; 106.7 MHz FM; *Hrs Open:* 24; 810 w; Ant 623 ft; N43 51 06 W70 19 40
Mailing Address: Box 10660, Portland, ME 04104 US
Second Address: 4 Washington St., Auburn, ME 04210
(207) 689-9939
www.thepresence.fm
info@thepresence.fm
License: North Windham, ME held by The Presence Radio Network Inc.
Group Owner: The Presence Radio Network Inc.
Arbitron Metro Market: Portland, ME; *Target Audience:* 35 plus; general
Craig Foster, Eric Marenghi
Operations Mgr, Operations Dir
Richards A. Hyatt, Engineering Consultant

North Yarmouth

WCLZ
04-11-1965; 98.9 MHz FM; 48 kw; 400 ft.; N43 55 40 W69 59 42
420 Western Avenue, South Portland, ME 04106 US
(207)774-4561
www.989wclz.com
License: North Yarmouth, Cumberland County, ME held by Saga Communications of New England LLC.
Group Owner: Saga Communications Inc.; (acq 10-15-2007; $3.5 million)
Nat'l Reps: Christal
Arbitron Metro Market: Portland, ME; *Format:* Triple A
Larry Julius, General Sales Mgr
Ethan Minton, Brand Manager

Norway

WOXO-FM
12-12-1970; 92.7 MHz FM; *Hrs Open:* 24; 5.2 kw; 735 ft.; N44 17 47 W70 37 5 *Rebroadcasts:* Rebroadcasts WTBM(FM) Mexico 99%
243 Main Street, Norway, ME 04268 US
(207) 743-7812
www.woxo.com
info@woxo.com
License: Norway, Oxford County, ME held by Mountain Valley Broadcasting Inc.
Group Owner: Gleason Radio Group; (acq 12-12-75).
Nat'l Network: USA; *Nat'l Reps:* CYR Associates
Arbitron Metro Market: Portland, ME; *Format:* Country, Sports; *Hrs. of News Programming:* news progmg 12 hrs wkly; *No. News Employees:* 2; *Target Audience:* General.; *Adv. Rates:* 20; 20; 20; 20

Oakland

***WMDR-FM**
01-01-2006; 88.9 MHz FM; *Hrs Open:* 24; 100 kw; 1283 ft.; N44 14 58 W70 25 25
160 Bangor Street, Augusta, ME 04330 US
(207) 622-1340; *Fax:* (207) 623-2874
www.worshipradionetwork.org
License: Oakland, Kennebec County, ME held by Light of Life Ministries Inc.
Arbitron Metro Market: Oakland, ME; *Format:* Christian, Country; *Hrs. of News Programming:* News progmg one hr wkly
Ray Bouchard, CEO/COO
Denise Lafountain, General Manager

Old Town

WBZN
01-01-1995; 107.3 MHz FM; 50 kw; 308 ft; N45 02 06 W68 40 57
Mailing Address: 49 Acme Road, Brewer, ME 53202
Second Address: 49 Acme Rd., Brewer, ME 4412
(207) 989-5631; *Fax:* (207) 989-5685
www.wbzn-fm.com
License: Old Town, Penobscot County, ME held by Townsquare Media Bangor License LLC
Group Owner: Townsquare Media; (acq 2-20-98; $6.4 million with WQCB(FM) Brewer)
Population Served: 9,474; *Arbitron Metro Market:* Brewer, ME
Paul Dupuis, Operations Dir
Tom Preble, General Manager
Dick Hyatt, Chief Engineer

Orono

***WMEB-FM**
04-01-1963; 91.9 MHz FM; *Hrs Open:* 24; 10 kw; 171 ft.; N44 55 8 W68 40 0
5748 Memorial Union, Orono, ME 04469 US
(207) 581-2333
www.wmeb.fm
wmeb919@hotmail.com
License: Orono, Penobscot County, ME held by Board of Trustees, University of Maine.
Arbitron Metro Market: Orono, ME; *Format:* Variety/Diverse; *Target Audience:* General.

Pittsfield

***WJCX**
12-01-1993; 99.5 MHz FM; 6 kw; 328 ft.; N44 48 11 W69 10 6
154 River Rd, Orrington, ME 04474 US
(207) 991-9555; *Fax:* (207) 991-9553
www.ccbangor.org/radio
wjcx99.5@ccbangor.org
License: Pittsfield, Somerset County, ME held by Calvary Chapel of Bangor
Format: Christian, News, 62, Talk, Religious; *Target Audience:* 18-54

Pittston Farm

***WHPF**
88.1 MHz FM; 0.25 kw; -240 ft.; N45 53 38 W69 57 54 US
(207) 622-1340; *Fax:* (207) 623-2874
www.worshipradionetwork.org
info@worshipradionetwork.org
License: Pittston Farm, Somerset County, ME held by Light of Life Ministries Inc.
Arbitron Metro Market: Augusta, ME; *Format:* Christian
Denise LaFountain, General Manager

Portland

WBAE
03-01-1946; 1490 kHz AM; *Hrs Open:* 24
290 Hegenberge Road, Oakland, CA 94621 US
(801) 359-3147; *Fax:* (801) 359-8112
www.familyradio.com
info@familyradio.com
License: Portland, ME held by Saga Communications of New England LLC.
Group Owner: Saga Communications Inc.; (acq 1996; $10 million with co-located FM).
Nat'l Network: CNN Radio
Arbitron Metro Market: Newport OR; *Format:* Christian, Religious
Harold Camping, General Manager

WBLM
02-01-1966; 102.9 MHz FM; 100 kw; 1,460 ft; N43 55 28 W70 29 28
One City Ctr., Portland, ME 04101 US
(207) 774-6364
www.wblm.com
brian.lang@townsquaremedia.com
License: Portland, ME held by Townsquare Media Portland License, LLC
Group Owner: Townsquare Media; (acq 7-7-99; grpsl).
Nat'l Reps: Christal
Population Served: 593,820; *Arbitron Metro Market:* Portland, ME; *Format:* Classic Rock; *Target Audience:* 25-54; active, involved, fun-loving
Brian Lang, General Manager
Mike Marcello, Director of Sales
Herb Ivy, Brand Mgr
Stephen Lenz, Digital Managing Editor

WGAN
08-03-1938; 560 kHz AM
420 Western Ave, South Portland, ME 04106 US
(207) 774-4561; *Fax:* (207) 774-3788
www.560wgan.com
wgan@560wgan.com
License: Portland, ME held by Saga Communications of New England LLC.
Group Owner: Saga Communications Inc.; (acq 6-2-92; grpsl, including co-located FM).
Nat'l Network: CNN Radio
Arbitron Metro Market: Portland, ME; *Format:* News, News/Talk, 86; *Hrs. of News Programming:* news progmg 20 hrs plus wkly
Cary Pahigian, President
Jeff Wade, Programming Director

WJBQ
06-01-1960; 97.9 MHz FM; 16 kw; 889 ft; N43 51 06 W70 19 40
One City Ctr., Portland, ME 04101 US
(207) 774-6364
www.wjbq.com
License: Portland, ME held by Townsquare Media Portland License, LLC
Group Owner: Cumulus Media Inc.; (acq 7-7-99; grpsl).
Population Served: 150,000; *Arbitron Metro Market:* Portland, ME; *Format:* Contemporary Hits/Top 40
Brian Lang, General Manager
Mike Marcello, Dir of Sales
AJ Dukette, Brand Manager
Stephen Lenz, Digital Managing Editor

WLOB
02-02-1957; 1310 kHz AM; *Hrs Open:* 24; 5 kw-U, DA-2; N43 41 22 W70 20 06 *Rebroadcasts:* Simulcast with WLOB-FM Topsham 100%
779 Warren Ave., Portland, ME 04103
(877) 393-8255
wlobradio.com
License: Portland, Cumberland County, ME held by Atlantic Coast Radio L.L.C.
Group Owner: Atlantic Coast Radio L.L.C.; (acq 9-8-00; grpsl).
Nat'l Network: Fox News Radio; *Nat'l Reps:* McGavren Guild
Population Served: 250,000; *Arbitron Metro Market:* Portland, ME; *Hrs. of News Programming:* News progmg 17 hrs wkly; *Target Audience:* General.

***WMEA**
04-01-1974; 90.1 MHz FM; *Hrs Open:* 24; 24.5 kw; 1896 ft.; N43 51 30 W70 42 41 *Rebroadcasts:* Rebroadcasts WMEH(FM) Bangor 100%
1450 Lisbon Street, Lewiston, ME 04240 US
(800) 884-1717; *Fax:* (207) 942-2857
www.mpbn.net
cbeck@mpbn.net
License: Portland, Cumberland County, ME held by Maine Public Broadcasting Corp.
Nat'l Network: NPR; PRI
Arbitron Metro Market: Portland, ME; *Format:* News, Triple A; *Hrs. of News Programming:* news progmg 20 hrs wkly; *No. News Employees:* 8; *Target Audience:* 25-64.
Mark Vogelzang, CEO/President

WMGX
06-10-1977; 93.1 MHz FM; 50 kw; 443 ft.; N43 41 17 W70 15 27
420 Western Ave, South Portland, ME 04106 US
(207) 774-4561; *Fax:* (207) 774-3788
www.coast931.com
info@coast931.com
License: Portland, Cumberland County, ME

Group Owner: Saga Communications Inc.
Arbitron Metro Market: Portland, ME; *Format:* Adult Contemp
Bruce Simel, General Manager

WPOR

10-31-1967; 101.9 MHz FM; *Hrs Open:* 24; 32 kw; 610 ft.; N43 45 33 W70 19 15
420 Western Ave, South Portland, ME 04106 US
(207) 774-4561; *Fax:* (207) 774-3788
www.wpor.com
wpor@wpor.com
License: Portland, Cumberland County, ME
Group Owner: Saga Communications Inc.
Arbitron Metro Market: Portland, ME; *Format:* Country
Matty Jeff, General Manager

WZAN

07-13-1925; 970 kHz AM; 5 kw-D, DAN; 5 kw-N, DAN; N43 36 19 W70 19 18
420 Western Ave, South Portland, ME 04106 US
(207) 774-4561; *Fax:* (207) 774-3788
www.970wzan.com
feedback@970wzan.com
License: Portland, ME held by Saga Communications of New England LLC.
Group Owner: Saga Communications Inc.; (acq 6-23-93; $350,000 with WYNZ-FM Westbrook;
Nat'l Network: CBS; CNN Radio; *Nat'l Reps:* Katz Radio
Arbitron Metro Market: Portland, ME; *Format:* Talk; *Target Audience:* 25-54 Males.
Chris May, Operations Manager

Presque Isle

WBPW

09-01-1973; 96.9 MHz FM; *Hrs Open:* 24; 100 kw; 440 ft; N46 45 52 W67 59 23
551 Main St., Presque Isle, ME 13203
(207) 769-6600; *Fax:* (207) 764-5274
www.bigcountry969.com
License: Presque Isle, Aroostook County, ME
Group Owner: Townsquare Media; (acq 4-26-00; grpsl).
Nat'l Network: ABC; *Nat'l Reps:* Katz Radio
Population Served: 9,641; *Arbitron Metro Market:* Presque Isle, ME *Special Programming:* NASCAR, American Country Countdown; *Hrs. of News Programming:* news progmg 2 hrs wkly; *No. News Employees:* 1 *TargetAudience:* 25-54.; *Adv. Rates:* 34; 30; 34; 18
Lisa Miles, General Manager
Lisa Miles, Director of Sales
Chris O'Brien, Programming Director
Mark Shaw, News Director

WEGP

06-24-1960; 1390 kHz AM; *Hrs Open:* 24
3 State Street Place, Presque Isle, ME 04769 US
(207) 762-6700; *Fax:* (207) 762-3319
www.wegp.net
sandy@wegp.net
License: Presque Isle, ME held by Decelles/Smith Media Inc.
Nat'l Network: Fox News Radio; Premiere Radio Networks; Talk Radio Network; Westwood One
Arbitron Metro Market: Presque Isle, ME.; *Format:* News, Talk; *Target Audience:* Adults; mature listeners over age 29
Brian Lawrence, Programming Director

*WMEM

01-01-1975; 106.1 MHz FM; 100 kw; 1073 ft.; N46 33 6 W67 48 38 *Rebroadcasts:* Rebroadcasts WMEH(FM) Bangor 100%
Mailing Address: 1450 Lisbon Street, Lewiston, ME 04240 US
Second Address: 1450 Lisbon St., Lewiston, ME 4240
(207) 783-9101; *Fax:* (207) 942-2857
www.mpbn.net
cbeck@mpbn.net
License: Presque Isle, Aroostook County, ME held by Maine Public Broadcasting Corp.
Nat'l Network: NPR; PRI
Arbitron Metro Market: Presque Isle, ME; *Format:* Jazz, News
Mark Vogelzang, CEO
Charles Beck, Vice President
Keith Shortall, News Director
Claire Hannan, CFO
Cory Morrissey, Director of Marketing & Corporate Support

WOZI

02-02-1981; 101.9 MHz FM; *Hrs Open:* 24; 7.9 kw; Ant 1,207 ft; N46 32 51 W67 48 35
551 Main St., Presque Isle, ME 13203
(207) 769-6600; *Fax:* (207) 764-5274
www.102therock.com
License: Presque Isle, Aroostook County, ME
Group Owner: Townsquare Media; (acq 4-26-01; grpsl).
Nat'l Network: Westwood One; *Nat'l Reps:* Katz Radio
Population Served: 150,000 *Hrs. of News Programming:* news progmg one hr wkly; *No. News Employees:* 1; *Target Audience:* 25-54.; *Adv. Rates:* 15; 12; 13; 6
Lisa Miles, General Manager
Chris O' Brien, Programming Director

WQHR

01-01-1981; 96.1 MHz FM; *Hrs Open:* 24; 95 kw; 1,309 ft; N46 32 55 W67 48 35
551 Main St., Presque Isle, ME 13203
(207) 769-6600; *Fax:* (207) 764-5274
www.HitMusicQ96.com
License: Presque Isle, Aroostook County, ME
Group Owner: Townsquare Media; (acq 4-26-01; grpsl).
Nat'l Network: ABC; *Nat'l Reps:* Katz Radio
Population Served: 250,000 *Hrs. of News Programming:* news progmg 2 hrs wkly; *No. News Employees:* 1; *Target Audience:* 18-49.; *Adv. Rates:* 34; 30; 34; 18
Lisa Miles, General Manager
Mark Shaw, Programming Director

*WUPI

07-26-1973; 92.1 MHz FM; *Hrs Open:* 24; 0.017 kw horiz; -39 ft.; N46 40 15 W68 1 0
107 Main Street, Bangor, ME 04401 US
(207) 768-9741; *Fax:* (207) 768-9742
www.umpi.maine.edu
License: Presque Isle, Aroostook County, ME held by University of Maine Trustees.
Arbitron Metro Market: Presque Isle, ME; *Format:* Variety/Diverse; *Hrs. of News Programming:* news progmg 5 hrs wkly; *No. News Employees:* 2; *Target Audience:* 16-35.
Dr. Don Zillman, President
Marjorie McNamara, General Manager
Larry French, Station Manager
Laura Mooney, General Sales Mgr
Meg Medlinskas, Programming Director
Jeffery Carmicheal, Engineering Dir

Rockland

WMCM

04-16-1968; 103.3 MHz FM; *Hrs Open:* 24; 16 kw; 771 ft.; N44 7 35 W69 8 18
184 Target Industrial Circle, Bangor, ME 04861 US
(207) 623-9000; *Fax:* (207) 623-9007
License: Rockland, Knox County, ME held by Blueberry Broadcasting LLC.
Arbitron Metro Market: Rockland, ME; *Format:* Country; *No. News Employees:* 1; *Target Audience:* General.; *Adv. Rates:* 30; 25; 25; 15

WVOM

10-01-1952; 1450 kHz AM; *Hrs Open:* 24; 1 kw-U, ND1; N44 7 34 W69 8 19
15 Payne Ave., Rt #1 South, Rockland, ME 04841 US
(207) 623-9000; *Fax:* (207) 623-9007
License: Rockland, ME held by Blueberry Broadcasting LLC.
Group Owner: Blueberry Broadcasting LLC; (acq 7-29-2008; grpsl)
Nat'l Network: Westwood One; *Nat'l Reps:* CYR Associates
Format: Sports; *Hrs. of News Programming:* news progmg 11 hrs wkly; *No. News Employees:* 1; *Target Audience:* 35 plus.; *Adv. Rates:* 30; 25; 25; 15
Kelly Slater, General Manager
Rick Dugal, General Sales Mgr
Don Shields, Programming Director

Rumford

WTME

08-21-1953; 780 kHz AM *Rebroadcasts:* Simulcast with WKTQ(AM) South Paris 100%
P.O. Box 72, Norway, ME 04268 US
(207) 743-5911; *Fax:* (207) 743-5913
www.wtme.com
info@woxo.com
License: Rumford, ME held by Mountain Valley Broadcasting Inc.
Group Owner: Gleason Radio Group; (acq 11-2-2000; $50,000)
Nat'l Network: USA; USA; *Nat'l Reps:* CYR Associates
Format: Talk; *Hrs. of News Programming:* Top of each hour; *No. News Employees:* 1; *Target Audience:* General.; *Adv. Rates:* 10; 10; 10; 10

Saco

WPEI

07-18-1982; 95.9 MHz FM; *Hrs Open:* 24; 4.1 kw; 397 ft.; N43 32 33 W70 24 17
20 Guest St., Third Floor, Brighton, MA 02135-2040 US
(617) 779-3500
www.weei.com
License: Saco, ME held by Atlantic Coast Radio L.L.C.
Group Owner: Atlantic Coast Radio L.L.C.; acq 7-12-99; $1.15 million)
Nat'l Network: Westwood One; *Nat'l Reps:* McGavren Guild; *Wire Services:* AP
Arbitron Metro Market: Portland, ME; *Format:* Sports; *Target Audience:* 18-34.; *Adv. Rates:* 50; 45; 45; 45

Sanford

WXEX-FM

10-10-1975; 92.1 MHz FM; *Hrs Open:* 24; 1.2 kw; 525 ft; N43 35 24 W70 22 20
P.O. Box 1540, Exeter, NH 03833
(603) 749-5900; *Fax:* (603) 749-0088
www.wxexradio.com
info@fnxradio.com
License: Sanford, York County, ME held by FNX Broadcasting LLC.
Group Owner: Phoenix Media Communications Group
Nat'l Reps: McGavren Guild
Arbitron Metro Market: Portsmouth-Dover-Rochester, NH *Special Programming:* Jazz 6 hrs, talk 2 hrs wkly; *No. News Employees:* 1; *Target Audience:* General.
Gary Kurtz, General Manager

*WSEW

03-02-1992; 88.7 MHz FM; 10 kw; 564 ft.; N43 25 5 W70 48 4
P.O. Box 398, New Durham, NH 03855 US
(603) 859-9170; *Fax:* (603) 859-8172
www.wsew.org
License: Sanford, York County, ME held by Word Radio Educational Foundation
Group Owner: Word Radio Educational Foundation
Nat'l Network: Moody
Format: Religious
Ronald R. Malone, President
Sharon Malone, Operations Manager

WWSF

11-09-1957; 1220 kHz AM; *Hrs Open:* 24; 1 kw-D, 234 w-N; N43 25 53 W70 45 44
One Washington St., Dover, NH 20036
(603) 749-5900; *Fax:* (603) 749-0088
fnxradio.com
License: Sanford, York County, ME held by FNX Broadcasting LLC.
Group Owner: Phoenix Media Communications Group; (acq 5-17-99; $1.025 million with co-located FM).
Population Served: 20,000
Sam Pseifle, General Manager

Scarborough

WHXR

01-01-1960; 106.3 MHz FM; 3 kw; Ant 299 ft; N43 35 24 W70 22 20
477 Congress St., Suite 3 A, 3rd Fl. Annex, Portland, ME 04043
(207) 797-0780; *Fax:* (207) 797-0368
www.boneradio.com
License: Scarborough, Cumberland County, ME held by WBIN Media Co. Inc.
Group Owner: WBIN Media Co. Inc.
Population Served: 200,000; *Arbitron Metro Market:* Portland, ME
Pat Collins, Operations Dir
Stan Manning, Operations Director

Searsport

*WKVV

10-10-1994; 101.7 MHz FM; *Hrs Open:* 6 AM-midnight; 2.65 kw; 1004 ft.; N44 34 51 W68 53 47
263 State St., Bangor, ME 04401 US
(916) 251-1600; *Fax:* (916) 251-1650
www.klove.com
License: Searsport, Waldo County, ME held by Educational Media Foundation.
Group Owner: EMF Broadcasting; (acq 4-6-2009; $550,000 with WGUY(FM) Dexter)
Nat'l Network: K-Love
Format: Christian
Mike Novak, President

Skowhegan

WFMX

09-01-1989; 107.9 MHz FM; 22 kw; 387 ft.; N44 37 1 W69 37 31
295 Kennedy Memorial Dr., Penny Hill Park, ME 04901 US
(207) 660-4888
www.mixmaine.com

License: Skowhegan, Somerset County, ME held by Mountain Wireless Inc.
Group Owner: Mountain Wireless Inc.; (acq 11-20-97; $222,355)
Arbitron Metro Market: Augusta-Waterville, ME; *Format:* Adult Contemp; *Target Audience:* 25-54; baby boomers who grew up with Top-40 radio
Alan W. Anderson, President

WSKW
01-01-1956; 1160 kHz AM; 10 kw-D, ND1; 0.73 kw-N, ND1; N44 44 43 W69 41 36; N44 44 42 W69 41 32
Mailing Address: PO Box 159, Skowhegan, ME 04976 US
Second Address: 208 Middle Rd., Skowhegan, ME 4976
(207) 474-5171; *Fax:* (207) 474-3299
License: Skowhegan, ME held by Mountain Wireless Inc.
Group Owner: Mountain Wireless Inc.; (acq 1999; $1.6 million with WCTB(FM) Fairfield)
Nat'l Network: ESPN Radio
Arbitron Metro Market: Augusta-Watervi; *Format:* Country; *Target Audience:* 12 plus; loc sports fans
Alan W. Anderson, President

WTOS-FM
11-13-1969; 105.1 MHz FM; *Hrs Open:* 24; 57 kw; 2451 ft.; N45 1 54 W70 18 50
125 Community Drive, Augusta, ME 04330 US
(207) 621-9867
www.wtosfm.com
reverend@clearchannel.com
License: Skowhegan, Somerset County, ME held by Blueberry Broadcasting LLC.
Group Owner: Blueberry Broadcasting LLC; (acq 7-29-2008; grpsl)
Arbitron Metro Market: Augusta, ME; *Format:* Rock/AOR; *Hrs. of News Programming:* news progmg 3 hrs wkly; *No. News Employees:* 1; *Target Audience:* 18-49.

South Paris

WKTQ
10-28-1955; 1450 kHz AM; *Hrs Open:* 24; 1 kw-U, ND1; N44 13 16 W70 31 43 *Rebroadcasts:* Simulcast with WTME(AM) Rumford 100%
P.O. Box 72, Norway, ME 04268 US
(207) 743-5911; *Fax:* (207) 743-5913
www.wtme.com
dick@gleasonmedia.com
License: South Paris, ME held by Mountain Valley Broadcasting Inc.
Group Owner: Gleason Radio Group; (acq 7-27-76).
Nat'l Network: USA; USA; *Nat'l Reps:* CYR Associates
Format: Talk; *Hrs. of News Programming:* Top of each hour; *No. News Employees:* 1; *Target Audience:* General.; *Adv. Rates:* 20; 20; 20; 20
Richard Gleason, President
Victor Hodgkins, Station Manager

South Portland

WYNZ
02-01-1976; 100.9 MHz FM; 25 kw; Ant 305 ft; N43 41 26 W70 19 05
420 Western Ave., South Portland, ME 04106
(207) 774-4561; *Fax:* (207) 774-3788
www.y1009.com
bighits@y1009.com
License: South Portland, Cumberland County, ME held by Saga Communications of New England LLC.
Group Owner: Saga Communications Inc.; (acq 6-23-93; $350,000 with WYNZ(AM) Portland;
Nat'l Network: CNN Radio; *Nat'l Reps:* Katz Radio
Arbitron Metro Market: Portland, ME; *Target Audience:* 25-54.
Matty Jeff, Brand Manager
Chris Mae, Promotions Manager
Tina Seuerstrom, General Sales Manager

Thomaston

WBQX
05-29-1992; 106.9 MHz FM; *Hrs Open:* 24; 29.5 kw; 633 ft.; N44 6 30 W69 9 28 *Rebroadcasts:* Rebroadcasts WBQQ(FM) Kennebunk 100%
477 Congress Street, Portland, ME 04210 US
(207) 594-9283; *Fax:* (207) 594-1620
www.wbachradio.com
License: Thomaston, Knox County, ME held by Nassau Broadcasting III L.L.C.
Group Owner: Nassau Broadcasting Partners L.P.; (acq 4-6-2004; grpsl).
Regional Reps: Kettell-Carter.
Arbitron Metro Market: Rockland, ME; *Format:* Talk *Special Programming:* Jazz 2 hrs, children one hr wkly; *Hrs. of News Programming:* News progmg 4 hrs wkly; *Target Audience:* 35 plus; affluent, upscale adults
Pat Collins, Operations Dir
Scott Hooper, Programming Director

Topsham

WPPI
01-01-1993; 95.5 MHz FM; *Hrs Open:* 24; 6 kw; Ant 456 ft; N43 54 12 W70 02 13 *Rebroadcasts:* Simulcasts with WEEI(AM) Boston, MA
20 Guest St., Brighton, MA 02135-2040
(617) 779-3500
www.weei.com
License: Topsham, Sagadahoc County, ME held by Atlantic Coast Radio L.L.C.
Group Owner: Atlantic Coast Radio L.L.C.; (acq 9-30-99)
Nat'l Network: ESPN; *Nat'l Reps:* McGavren Guild
Population Served: 700,000 *Target Audience:* 25-49; middle class, active lifestyle with discretionary income; *Adv. Rates:* 125; 70; 60; 20

Van Buren

WCXV
98.1 MHz FM; 6 kw; 3 ft.; N47 10 4 W67 57 43 *Rebroadcasts:* Rebroadcasts WCXU (FM) Caribou 100%
Rural Route 2, Box 2100, Caribou, ME 04736 US
(207) 473-7513; *Fax:* (207) 472-3221
www.channelxradio.com
channelxradio@yahoo.com
License: Van Buren, Aroostook County, ME held by Canxus Broadcasting Corp.
Group Owner: Canxus Broadcasting Corp.
Arbitron Metro Market: Van Buren, ME; *Format:* Adult Contemp, News, 64
Dennis Curley, President
Richard Chandler, Vice President
Douglas Christensen, News Director
Phillip Shaw Neal, Music Director / Production Directo
Pamela Curley, Traffic Director
Cheryl LaFrance, Continuity Director
StaceySkinner, Advertising Sales Representatives
Greg Beidelman, Advertising Sales Representatives

Veazie

WNZS
08-01-2002; 1340 kHz AM; *Hrs Open:* 24
P.O. Box 8526, Bangor, ME 04402 US
(207) 989-8863
License: Veazie, ME held by Waterfront Communications Inc.
Nat'l Network: Salem Radio Network; Talk Radio Network; ABC Information & Entertainment; *Nat'l Reps:* Commercial Media Sales *Regional Reps:* Cyr Association
Arbitron Metro Market: Bangor, ME; *Format:* News, News/Talk, 86; *Hrs. of News Programming:* news progmg 15 hrs wkly; *No. News Employees:* 2; *Target Audience:* 25-54; 35-64; adults in metro Banger area; *Adv. Rates:* 10; 7; 8; 5.

WWNZ
08-01-2004; 1400 kHz AM; *Hrs Open:* 24; 1 kw-D, 810 w-N; N44 50 50 W68 40 48
Mailing Address: Box 8526, Bangor, ME
Second Address: 379 Riverside Dr., Eddington, ME 4428
(207) 989-8863
wnzproduction@aol.com
License: Veazie, Penobscot County, ME held by Waterfront Communications Inc.
Nat'l Network: USA; Fox News Radio; Wall Street; *Nat'l Reps:* Commercial Media Sales *Regional Reps:* Cyr Associates
Population Served: 150,000; *Arbitron Metro Market:* Bangor, ME; *Target Audience:* 25-54; 35-64; Banger metro area adults 25 plus; *Adv. Rates:* 10; 7; 8; 5
Daniel Priestley, President
Jocelynn Priestley, Station Manager

Waterville

WEBB
03-26-1968; 98.5 MHz FM; *Hrs Open:* 24; 61 kw; 305 ft; N44 33 52 W69 36 39
Mailing Address: 56 Western Avenue, Suite 13, Augusta, ME 13203
Second Address: 56 Western Ave. Suite 13, Augusta, ME 4330
(207) 623-4735; *Fax:* (207) 626-5948
www.b985.fm
License: Waterville, Kennebec County, ME
Group Owner: Townsquare Media
Population Served: 15,697; *Arbitron Metro Market:* Waterville, ME; *No. News Employees:* 1
Dean O'Neal, Operations Dir
Al Perry, General Manager
Julie Beaulieu, Director of Sales

***WMEW**
11-01-1983; 91.3 MHz FM; *Hrs Open:* 24; 3 kw; 299 ft.; N44 29 23 W69 39 5 *Rebroadcasts:* Rebroadcasts WMEH(FM) Bangor 100%
Mailing Address: 1450 Lisbon Street, Lewiston, ME 04240 US
Second Address: 1450 Lisbon St., Lewiston, ME 4240
(207) 783-9101; *Fax:* (207) 942-2857
www.mpbn.net
cbeck@mpbn.net
License: Waterville, Kennebec County, ME held by Maine Public Broadcasting Corp.
Nat'l Network: NPR; PRI
Arbitron Metro Market: Waterville, ME; *Format:* Jazz, News; *Hrs. of News Programming:* news progmg 20 hrs wkly; *No. News Employees:* 8; *Target Audience:* 25-64.
Mark Vogelzang, CEO
Charles Beck, VP/Programming Director

***WMHB**
10-01-1974; 89.7 MHz FM; *Hrs Open:* 6 AM-12 AM; 0.11 kw vert; 105 ft.; N44 33 57 W69 39 49
Mayflower Hill Drive, Colby College, Waterville, ME 04901 US
(207) 859-5454
www.wmhb.org
info@wmhb.org
License: Waterville, Kennebec County, ME held by Mayflower Hill Broadcasting Corp.
Arbitron Metro Market: Augusta, ME; *Format:* Variety/Diverse
Special Programming: Indie, Folk, Hip-hop, Jazz, World, Rock, Loud Rock; *Hrs. of News Programming:* News progmg 2.5 hrs wkly; *Target Audience:* 5-100; wecater to everyone
Benjy Ogden, President
Dan Echt, Operations Dir
Kathleen Fallon, General Manager
Kelly Wharton, General Sales Mgr
Luke Bowe, Programming Director
Jeffrey Oakes, Programming Director

WTVL
06-19-1946; 1490 kHz AM; 1 kw-U, ND1; N44 33 52 W69 36 39
Mailing Address: 1064 James Street, Syracuse, NY 13203 US
Second Address: 52 Western Ave., Augusta, ME 4330
(207) 623-4735; *Fax:* (207) 626-5948
www.1400and1490.com
mac.dickson@townsquaremedia.com
License: Waterville, ME
Group Owner: Townsquare Media; (acq 4-26-2001; grpsl).
Arbitron Metro Market: Augusta, ME; *Format:* Oldies; *Target Audience:* 25-54.
Farid Suleman, CEO
Julie Beaulieu, General Manager
Al Perry, General Sales Mgr
Mac Dickson, Programming Director
Renee Nelson, News Director
Bob Perry, Chief Engineer
Al Perry, Regional Sales Manager

Westbrook

WRED
11-08-1959; 1440 kHz AM; 5 kw-D, DAN; 5 kw-N, DAN; N43 40 50 W70 22 47
779 Warren Ave., Portland, ME 04103 US
(207) 773-9695
www.thebigjab.com
shoe@thebigjab.com
License: Westbrook, ME held by Atlantic Coast Radio L.L.C.
Group Owner: Atlantic Coast Radio L.L.C.; (acq 9-99)
Nat'l Network: Sporting News Radio Network; *Nat'l Reps:* McGavren Guild
Arbitron Metro Market: Portland, ME; *Format:* Sports, Talk; *Target Audience:* General; male
Morgan Grumbach, General Sales Mgr

***WRKJ**
88.5 MHz FM; 2 kw; 354 ft.; N43 41 10 W70 30 30
P.O. Box 398, New Durham, NH 03855 US
(603) 859-9170; *Fax:* (603) 859-8172
www.communityliferadio.org
License: Westbrook, Cumberland County, ME held by Word Radio Educational Foundation
Group Owner: Word Radio Educational Foundation
Arbitron Metro Market: Westbrook, ME; *Format:* Christian
Ronald R. Malone, President
Sharon Malone, Operations Manager

Winslow

***WWWA**
04-23-1999; 95.3 MHz FM; *Hrs Open:* 24; 12 kw; 673 ft.; N44 42 48 W69 43 39
P.O. Box 332, Litchfield, ME 04330 US
(207) 622-1340; *Fax:* (207) 623-2874
www.worshipradionetwork.org
License: Winslow, Kennebec County, ME held by Light of Life Ministries Inc.
Arbitron Metro Market: Winslow, ME; *Format:* Christian
Denise LaFountain, Station Manager
Brad Taylor, Programming Director

Winter Harbor

WNSX
01-01-1999; 97.7 MHz FM; 50 kw; 489 ft.; N44 33 13 W68 5 40
53 Main St. Suite 202, Bar Harbor, ME 04609 US
(207) 667-0002; *Fax:* (207) 667-0627
www.wnsxradio.com
billd@wnsx.net
License: Winter Harbor, Hancock County, ME held by Stony Creek Broadcasting LLC
Wire Services: AP
Arbitron Metro Market: Hancock County, ME; *Format:* Classic Rock; *Hrs. of News Programming:* News progmg 4 hrs. wkly; *No. News Employees:* 1; *Target Audience:* Adults; 25+
Bill Da Butler, Operations Dir
Mark Osborne, General Manager
Irene Hafford, General Sales Mgr
Bill Ducharme, Chief Engineer
Natalie Knox, Sales

Yarmouth

***WYAR**
11-16-1998; 88.3 MHz FM; *Hrs Open:* 24; 1 kw horiz; 79 ft.; N43 45 56 W70 8 27
P.O. Box 414, Yarmouth, ME 04096 US
(207) 847-3169
www.wyar.org
wyar@maine.rr.com
License: Yarmouth, Cumberland County, ME held by Heritage Radio Society Inc.
Arbitron Metro Market: Yarmouth, ME; *Format:* Big Band, Oldies; *Target Audience:* General; senior citizens & young people
Gary King Sr., CEO

York Center

WTBU
06-01-1987; 95.3 MHz FM; *Hrs Open:* 24; 1.45 kw; 676 ft.; N43 13 25 W70 41 37
815 Lafayette Road, Portsmouth, NH 03801 US
(603) 436-7300; *Fax:* (603) 430-9415
www.953fmthebull.com
License: York Center, York County, ME held by Capstar TX LLC
Group Owner: iHeartMedia; (acq 8-30-2000; grpsl)
Nat'l Reps: Katz Radio
Arbitron Metro Market: Portsmouth, NH; *Format:* Country; *Hrs. of News Programming:* news progmg 7 hrs wkly; *No. News Employees:* 1; *Target Audience:* 18-34. 60% females
Tim Moore, Programming Director
Marc Provenzano, Promotions Manager
Matt Provost, Digital Content Director

Maryland

Aberdeen

WAMD
05-01-1957; 970 kHz AM; *Hrs Open:* 24
400 Hiob Lane, Aberdeen, MD 21001 US
(410) 306-6270
www.970wamd.com
studio@970wamd.com
License: Aberdeen, MD held by Radio Broadcast Communications Inc.
Group Owner: Radio Broadcast Communications Inc.
Arbitron Metro Market: Aberdeen, MD; *Format:* Contemporary Hits/Top 40; *Target Audience:* 25+
Rebecca Chappel, Operations Dir
Libby Parris, Station Manager
Libby Parris, General Sales Mgr
Mike Parris, Programming Director

Annapolis

WNAV
01-01-1949; 1430 kHz AM; 5 kw-D, DAN; 1 kw-N, DAN; N38 59 0 W76 31 21
236 Admiral Drive, Annapolis, MD 21401 US
(410) 263-1430; *Fax:* (410) 268-5360
www.1430wnav.com
stevehopp@wnav.com
License: Annapolis, MD held by Sajak Broadcasting Corp.
Nat'l Network: CBS Radio; Westwood One
Arbitron Metro Market: Baltimore, MD; *Format:* Adult Contemp
Special Programming: Baltimore Orioles baseball, Naval Academy sports; *No. News Employees:* 2; *Target Audience:* 35 plus.
Steve Hopp, General Manager
Dan O'Neil, General Sales Mgr
Bill Lusby, Programming Director
Barbara Cox, News Director

WYRE
01-01-1946; 810 kHz AM; *Hrs Open:* Sunrise-Sunset; 0.25 kw-D, NDD; N38 58 13 W76 30 28
13321 New Hampshire Avenue, Silver Spring, MD 20904 US
301-879-2422; *Fax:* 301-879-2562
License: Annapolis, MD held by Bay Broadcasting Corp.
Arbitron Metro Market: Baltimore, MD
Richard Dent, President

Baltimore

WBAL
11-02-1925; 1090 kHz AM; *Hrs Open:* 24; 50 kw-U, DA-N; N39 22 33 W76 46 21
3800 Hooper Ave., Baltimore, MD 21211
(410) 467-3000
www.wbal.com
news@wbal.com
License: Baltimore, Baltimore County, MD held by WBAL Div., The Hearst Corp.
Nat'l Network: CBS Radio; *Nat'l Reps:* Eastman
Population Served: 2,100,000; *Arbitron Metro Market:* Baltimore, MD; *Target Audience:* 25-54.
Cary Pahigian, General Manager
Lori Smyth, Promotions Manager
Michelle Butt, News Director

WFSI
07-27-1955; 860 kHz AM; 2.5 kw-D, 66 w-N, DA-2; N39 18 43 W76 29 26
600 Washington Ave., Towson, MD 20037
(410) 825-7700
www.familyradio.com
info@familyradio.com
License: Baltimore, Baltimore County, MD held by Family Stations Inc.
Group Owner: Family Stations Inc.; (acq 3-2-2005; $7.5 million with WBMD(AM) Baltimore)
Population Served: 905,759; *Arbitron Metro Market:* Baltimore, MD; *Format:* Christian, Religious; *Target Audience:* 18-49.

***WBJC**
04-06-1951; 91.5 MHz FM; 50 kw; 499 ft.; N39 23 11 W76 43 52 US
(410) 580-5800; *Fax:* (410) 580-5858
www.wbjc.com
License: Baltimore, Baltimore County, MD held by Baltimore City Community College
Nat'l Network: PRI
Arbitron Metro Market: Baltimore, MD; *Format:* Classical
Kati Harrison, Operations Dir
Joseph M. Hutchins, General Manager

WBMD
12-07-1947; 750 kHz AM; *Hrs Open:* Sunrise-sunset; 0.73 kw-D, NDD; N39 19 26 W76 32 56
US
(410) 821-9000; *Fax:* (410) 268-0931
www.familyradio.com
familyradio@familyradio.org
License: Baltimore, MD held by Family Stations Inc.
Group Owner: Family Stations Inc.; (acq 3-2-2005; $7.5 million with WBGR(AM) Baltimore)
Arbitron Metro Market: Oakland, CA; *Format:* Religious; *Target Audience:* 12 plus.

WCAO
05-08-1922; 600 kHz AM; 5 kw-U, DA1; N39 25 47 W76 45 42
711 W. 40th St., Baltimore, MD 21211 US
(410) 366-7600; *Fax:* (410) 467-0011
www.heaven600.com
License: Baltimore, MD held by Citicasters Licenses Inc.
Group Owner: iHeartMedia; (acq 5-99; grpsl).
Arbitron Metro Market: Baltimore, MD; *Format:* Gospel
Kevin Friedman, Sales Manager
Lee Michaels, Programming Director
Ali Jarvis, Promotions Manager

WCBM
01-01-1924; 680 kHz AM; *Hrs Open:* 24
1205 York Rd-Penthouse, Lutherville, MD 21093 US
(410) 580-6800; *Fax:* (410) 580-6810
www.wcbm.com
bpettit@wcbm.com
License: Baltimore, MD held by M-10 Broadcasting
Nat'l Network: CBS
Arbitron Metro Market: Baltimore, MD; *Format:* Talk; *Hrs. of News Programming:* news progmg 11 hrs wkly; *No. News Employees:* 3; *Target Audience:* 25-54; informed adults with major purchasing power
Nick Mangione Jr., Website Manager
Marc Beaving, General Manager

***WEAA**
01-10-1977; 88.9 MHz FM; *Hrs Open:* 24; 12.5 kw; 220 ft.; N39 20 31 W76 35 13
1700 East Cold Spring Lane, Baltimore, MD 21251 US
(443) 885-3564; *Fax:* (443) 885-8206
www.weaa.org
License: Baltimore, Baltimore County, MD held by Morgan State University.
Nat'l Network: NPR; *Wire Services:* AP
Arbitron Metro Market: Baltimore, MD; *Format:* Jazz, News, 62, Talk *Special Programming:* Urban oldies 5 hrs, Caribbean 7 hrs, African world 4 hrs, gospel 13 hrs, hip hop 5 hrs wkly; *Hrs. of News Programming:* newsprogmg 10 hrs wkly; *No. News Employees:* 1; *Target Audience:* 25-54; *Adv. Rates:* 65; 65; 65; 55

WERQ-FM
01-01-1960; 92.3 MHz FM; *Hrs Open:* 24; 37 kw; 571 ft.; N39 20 20 W76 40 2
1705 Whitehead Rd., Gwynn Oak, MD 21207 US
(410) 332-8200
www.92q.com
hmazer@radio-one.com
License: Baltimore, Baltimore County, MD held by Radio One Licenses LLC
Group Owner: Radio One Inc.; (acq 6-21-93; $9 million with co-located AM;
Arbitron Metro Market: Baltimore, MD; *Format:* Urban Contemporary; *Target Audience:* 18-34; young adults
Howard Mazer, General Manager

WRBS
03-01-1941; 1230 kHz AM; *Hrs Open:* 24; 1 kw-U; N39 18 58 W76 36 03
3500 Commerce Dr., Baltimore, MD 93012
(410) 247-4100; *Fax:* (410) 247-4533
www.wrbsam.com
info@wrbs.com
License: Baltimore, Baltimore County, MD held by WRBS-AM LLC
Population Served: 8,000,000; *Arbitron Metro Market:* Baltimore, MD

WIYY
12-07-1958; 97.9 MHz FM; 13.5 kw; 945 ft.; N39 20 5 W76 39 3
3800 Hooper Avenue, Baltimore, MD 21211 US
(410) 467-3000; *Fax:* (410) 338-6483
classic98rock@hearst.com
License: Baltimore, Baltimore County, MD
Arbitron Metro Market: Baltimore, MD; *Format:* Rock/AOR; *Target Audience:* 18-49.
Hugues Jean, General Sales Mgr
Dave Hill, Programming Director
Lori Smyth, Promotions Manager
Steve Hartman, Regional Sales Manager

WJZ
11-03-2008; 1300 kHz AM; *Hrs Open:* 24; 5 kW-D, 5 kW-N; N39 20 0 W76 46 13 *Rebroadcasts:* Rebroadcasts WJFK-FM Manassas, VA 77%
1423 Clarkview Rd., Suite 100, Baltimore, MD 21209 USA
(410) 825-1000
www.cbssportsradio1300.com
License: Baltimore, MD held by CBS Radio WLIF-AM Inc.
Group Owner: CBS Radio; (acq 5-29-89; $32 million with co-located FM;
Nat'l Network: ESPN Radio; *Nat'l Reps:* CBS Radio
Arbitron Metro Market: Baltimore, MD; *Format:* Sports, Talk; *Target Audience:* 18-49; men

Dave Labrozzi, Programming Director
Dave Burgess, Promotions Manager

***WYPR**
05-23-1979; 88.1 MHz FM; 15.5 kw; 425 ft.; N39 19 53 W76 39 28
2216 N. Charles Street, Baltimore, MD 21218 US
(410) 235-1660; *Fax:* (410) 235-1161
www.wypr.org
tbrandon@wypr.org
License: Baltimore, Baltimore County, MD held by WYPR License Holding LLC
Nat'l Network: NPR; PRI
Arbitron Metro Market: Baltimore, MD; *Format:* Jazz, News, 62, Talk
Anthony Brandon, President
Andy Bienstock, Programming Director

WLIF
02-11-1994; 101.9 MHz FM; 13.5 kW; 843 ft.; N39 25 7.6 W76 33 16.1
1423 Clarkview Rd., Suite 100, Baltimore, MD 21209 USA
(410) 825-1000; *Fax:* (410) 296-9543
www.todays1019.com
License: Baltimore, Baltimore County, MD held by CBS Radio WLIF Inc.
Group Owner: CBS Radio
Arbitron Metro Market: Baltimore, MD; *Format:* Adult Contemp
Special Programming: Jazz 8 hrs wkly
Jon Blum, Sales Manager
Greg Carpenter, Programming Director
Hal Martin, Promotions Manager

WZFT
01-01-1949; 104.3 MHz FM; 13 kw; Ant 964 ft; N39 20 10 W76 38 59
711 W. 40th St., Suite 350, Baltimore, MD 41011 US
(410) 366-7600; *Fax:* (410) 467-0011
www.z1043.com
License: Baltimore, Baltimore County, MD held by Citicasters Licenses Inc.
Group Owner: iHeartMedia; (acq 5-4-99; grpsl)
Nat'l Reps: Katz Radio
Population Served: 1,300,000; *Arbitron Metro Market:* Baltimore, MD; *Format:* Contemporary Hits/Top 40; *Target Audience:* 25-44.
Lynn Polovoy, Sales Manager
Ali Jarvis, Promotions Coordinator

WOLB
11-25-1947; 1010 kHz AM
1705 Whitehead Rd., Gwynn Oak, MD 21207 US
(410) 481-1010
www.wolbbaltimore.newsone.com
License: Baltimore, MD held by Radio One Licenses LLC
Group Owner: Radio One Inc.
Nat'l Reps: Katz Radio
Arbitron Metro Market: Baltimore, MD *TV Affiliate:* Talk; *Format:* Talk; *No. News Employees:* 35 plus; African American
Howard Mazer, General Manager
Dave Wilner, General Sales Mgr
Kellen Wynder, Promotions Manager

WPOC
01-01-1959; 93.1 MHz FM; 16 kw; 866 ft.; N39 17 13 W76 45 16
711 West 40th Street, Baltimore, MD 21211 US
(410) 366-7600
www.wpoc.com
License: Baltimore, Baltimore County, MD held by Citicasters Licenses Inc.
Group Owner: iHeartMedia; (acq 4-29-99; grpsl).
Arbitron Metro Market: Baltimore, MD; *Format:* Country
Kevin Friedman, Sales Manager
Tommy Chuck, Programming Director
Dustin Sugar-Moore, Promotions Coordinator
Heather O'Malley, Digital Content Coordinator

WRBS-FM
08-01-1964; 95.1 MHz FM; *Hrs Open:* 24; 50 kw; 499 ft; N39 15 21 W76 40 29
3500 Commerce Drive, Baltimore, MD 21227
(410) 247-4100; *Fax:* (410) 247-4533
www.951shinefm.com
info@wrbs.com
License: Baltimore, Baltimore County, MD held by Peter and John Radio Fellowship Inc.
Population Served: 200,000; *Arbitron Metro Market:* Baltimore, MD; *Hrs. of News Programming:* news progmg 6 hrs wkly; *No. News Employees:* 1
Steven Lawhon, General Manager

WWIN
01-01-1951; 1400 kHz AM; *Hrs Open:* 24
1705 Whitehead Rd., Baltimore, MD 20707 US
(410) 332-8200; *Fax:* (410) 944-1047
www.mybaltimorespirit.com
License: Baltimore, MD held by Radio One Licenses LLC.
Group Owner: Radio One Inc.; (acq 1-23-92; $7.5 million with WWIN-FM Glen Burnie)
Nat'l Reps: Katz Radio
Arbitron Metro Market: Baltimore, MD; *Format:* Gospel; *Hrs. of News Programming:* news progmg one hr wkly; *No. News Employees:* 1; *Target Audience:* 25-54; Black, relg
Howard Mazer, General Manager
Dave Willner, General Sales Mgr
Kelly Wynder, Programming Director

WWMX
10-17-1986; 106.5 MHz FM; *Hrs Open:* 24; 11 kW; 900 ft.; N39 20 4.6 W76 39 3.1
1423 Clarkview Rd., Suite 100, Baltimore, MD 21209 USA
(410) 825-1000; *Fax:* (410) 321-4548
www.mix1065.net
License: Baltimore, Baltimore County, MD held by CBS Radio Stations Inc.
Group Owner: CBS Radio
Arbitron Metro Market: Baltimore, MD *TV Affiliate:* WJZ-TV; *Format:* Adult Contemp; *Target Audience:* 25-54
Tracy Brandys, General Sales Mgr
Dave Labrozzi, Programming Director
Dave Burgess, Promotions Manager

WQSR
12-15-1947; 102.7 MHz FM; 50 kw; 436 ft.; N39 23 11 W76 43 52
711 West 40th Street, Baltimore, MD 21211 US
(410) 366-7600; *Fax:* (240) 747-3747
www.1027jackfm.com
License: Baltimore, Baltimore County, MD held by Citicasters Licenses Inc.
Group Owner: iHeartMedia; (acq 4-1-2009; grpsl)
Arbitron Metro Market: Baltimore, MD; *Format:* Adult Contemp
Lynn Polovoy, General Sales Mgr
Kenny King, Programming Director
Dustin Sugar-Moore, Promotions Manager
Matt Henry, Online Content Coordinator

Bel Air

***WHFC**
01-01-1972; 91.1 MHz FM; *Hrs Open:* 24; 1.1 kw; 226 ft.; N39 33 22 W76 16 48
401 Thomas Run Road, Bel Air, MD 21015 US
(443) 412-2305
www.whfc911.org
whfc@harford.edu
License: Bel Air, Harford County, MD held by Harford Community College.
Arbitron Metro Market: Baltimore, MD; *Format:* Variety/Diverse
Special Programming: AAA 15 hrs, class 18 hr, jazz 18 hrs, Christian 6; *Target Audience:* 24-42; upwardly mobile professionals
Gary Helton, General Manager

Berlin

WOCQ
06-25-1981; 103.9 MHz FM; 6 kw; 328 ft.; N38 22 58 W75 18 58
2000 Lower Huntington Road, Fort Wayne, IN 46819 US
www.softrock1039.com
License: Berlin, Worcester County, MD held by Adams Radio Group
Group Owner: Great Scott Broadcasting; acq 11-7-97; $2.775 million)
Arbitron Metro Market: Salisbury-Ocean *TV Affiliate:* Hip Hop
Special Programming: news progmg 4 hrs wkly; *Hrs. of News Programming:* 1; *No. News Employees:* 18-49.

Bethesda

WMMJ
11-12-1961; 102.3 MHz FM; 2.9 kw; 479 ft.; N38 56 10 W77 5 33
8515 Georgia Ave., 9th Floor, Silver Spring, MD 20910 US
(301) 306-1111
www.mymajicdc.com
mymajicdc@interactiveone.com
License: Bethesda, Montgomery County, MD held by Radio One Licenses LLC.
Group Owner: Radio One Inc.; (acq 11-8-01; grpsl).
Arbitron Metro Market: Washington, DC; *Format:* Urban Contemporary; *Target Audience:* 25-54
David Howard, General Sales Mgr
Kashon Powell, Programming Director
Cynthia Bullock, Traffic Mgr

Braddock Heights

WTLP
04-08-1972; 103.9 MHz FM; *Hrs Open:* 24; 0.35 kw; 958 ft.; N39 27 50 W77 29 44 *Rebroadcasts:* Rebroadcasts WTOP-FM Washington, DC 100%
3400 Idaho Ave. N.W., Washington, DC 20016 US
(202) 895-5000
www.wtop.com
License: Braddock Heights, Frederick County, MD held by Washington DC FCC License Sub LLC
Group Owner: Hubbard Broadcasting Inc.; (acq 1-19-2011)
Nat'l Network: CBS Radio; *Nat'l Reps:* Katz Radio
Arbitron Metro Market: Washington, DC; *Format:* News; *No. News Employees:* 4; *Target Audience:* General.
Joel Oxley, General Manager
Matt Mills, Director of Sales
Mike McMearty, Director of News and Programming
Mary Kay LeMay, Director of Marketing
John Meyer, Director of Digital Operations
Skip Quast, Sales Manager
Steve Goldstein,Digital Sales Manager
Jeffrey Wolinsky, Federal Sales

Brunswick

WTRI
10-02-1966; 1520 kHz AM
P.O. Box 123, Crownsville, MD 21032 US
www.radioearl.com
License: Brunswick, MD held by WTRI Holding LLC
Arbitron Metro Market: Brunswick, MD; *Format:* Country

California

WKIK-FM
12-01-1994; 102.9 MHz FM; *Hrs Open:* 24; 4 kw; 394 ft.; N38 22 3 W76 36 55 *Rebroadcasts:* Simulcast with WKIK(AM) La Plata 100%
2805 Three Notch Rd., Mechanicsville, MD 20659 US
(301) 884-5550; *Fax:* (301) 884-0280
www.country1029wkik.com
License: California, St. Marys County, MD held by Somar Communications Inc.
Group Owner: Somar Communications Inc.; acq 1993; $130,000; *Format:* Country; *Target Audience:* 25-54.

Cambridge

WCEM
01-01-1947; 1240 kHz AM; *Hrs Open:* 24
2 Bay St., Cambridge, MD 21613 US
(410) 228-4800
www.mtslive.com
news@mtslive.com
License: Cambridge, MD held by MTS Broadcasting LC.
Group Owner: MTS Broadcasting, LC; (acq 6-20-93; $1.8 million with co-located FM;)
Nat'l Network: Westwood One; ESPN Radio
Format: Adult Contemp *Special Programming:* Relg 5 hrs wkly; *No. News Employees:* 1; *Target Audience:* 25-54.
Shane Walker, Operations Mgr
Troy Hill, General Manager

WCEM-FM
01-29-1968; 106.3 MHz FM; 6 kw; 325 ft.; N38 35 3 W76 4 54
2 Bay St., Cambridge, MD 21613 US
(410) 228-4800
www.mtslive.com
news@mtslive.com
License: Cambridge, Dorchester County, MD held by MTS Broadcasting, LC
Group Owner: MTS Broadcasting, LC
Format: Contemporary Hits/Top 40; *Target Audience:* 18-49.
Shane Walker, Operations Mgr
Troy Hill, General Manager

Catonsville

WJZ-FM
11-03-2008; 105.7 MHz FM; *Hrs Open:* 24; 50 kW; 541 ft.; N39 19 26 W76 32 56
USA
www.1057thefan.com
License: Catonsville, Baltimore County, MD held by CBS Radio Stations Inc.
Group Owner: CBS Radio; (acq 11-13-98; grpsl)
Nat'l Reps: Christal
Arbitron Metro Market: Baltimore, MD; *Format:* Sports; *No. News Employees:* 1; *Target Audience:* 25-54

Chestertown

WCTR
06-16-1963; 1530 kHz AM; 0.27 kw-C, NDD; 1 kw-D, NDD; N39 13 35 W76 5 20
231 Flatland Road, Chestertown, MD 21620 US
(410) 778-1530; *Fax:* (410) 778-4800
www.wctr.com
info@wctr.com
License: Chestertown, MD held by WCTR Broadcasting LLC
Nat'l Network: ABC *Regional Reps:* Rgnl Reps
Arbitron Metro Market: Kent County, MD; *Format:* Oldies; *Hrs. of News Programming:* News progmg 10 hrs wkly; *Target Audience:* 35 plus.
Richard Gelfman, President

College Park

***WMUC-FM**
09-10-1979; 88.1 MHz FM; *Hrs Open:* 24; 0.01 kw; 3 ft.; N38 58 59 W76 56 37
3130 S Campus Dining Hal, College Park, MD 20742 US
(301) 314-7867; *Fax:* (301) 314-7879
www.wmucradio.com
License: College Park, Prince Georges County, MD held by University of Maryland.
Arbitron Metro Market: Washington, DC; *Format:* Variety/Diverse; *Target Audience:* College students.
Christina Gatte, Operations Dir
Scott Kornberg, General Manager
Lealin Queen, Programming Director
Adam Rosenfeld, Promotions Manager
Liz Lane, News Director

Crisfield

WBEY-FM
07-01-1995; 97.9 MHz FM; 4.3 kw; 379 ft.; N38 1 45 W75 45 5
1637 Dunn Swamp Road, Pocomoke City, MD 21851 US
(410) 957-1904
www.easternshoremedia.net
bay979@gmail.com
License: Crisfield, Somerset County, MD held by Bay Broadcasting.
Arbitron Metro Market: Crisfield, MD; *Format:* Country

Cumberland

WCBC
06-24-1953; 1270 kHz AM; 5 kw-D, DA2; 1 kw-N, DA2; N39 40 28 W78 46 48
P.O. Box 1290, Cumberland, MD 21501 US
(301) 724-5000; *Fax:* (301) 722-8336
www.wcbcradio.com
License: Cumberland, MD held by Cumberland Broadcasting Co. Inc.
Nat'l Network: ABC; Westwood One
Arbitron Metro Market: Cumberland, MD; *Format:* News, News/Talk, 86; *Hrs. of News Programming:* news progmg 3 hrs wkly; *No. News Employees:* 2; *Target Audience:* 25 plus.; *Adv. Rates:* 19.50; 19.50; 19.50; 19.50
David Aydelotte Sr., President

WKGO
04-01-1962; 106.1 MHz FM; *Hrs Open:* 24; 5.4 kw; 1411 ft.; N39 34 54 W78 53 58
Mailing Address: 350 Byrd Avenue, Cumberland, MD 21502 US
Second Address: 350 Byrd Ave., Cumberland, MD 21502
(301) 722-6666; *Fax:* (301) 722-0945
www.go106.com
go106@go106.com
License: Cumberland, Allegany County, MD held by WTBO-WKGO Corp. L.L.C.
Group Owner: Wooster Republican Printing Co.
Nat'l Network: Westwood One
Format: Classic Rock; *Hrs. of News Programming:* news progmg one hr wkly; *No. News Employees:* 1; *Target Audience:* 25-54.
Rich Cornwell, General Manager

WCMD
01-01-1948; 1230 kHz AM; *Hrs Open:* 24; 1.0 kw-D, ND2; 1.0 kw-N, ND2; N39 38 38 W78 44 32
15 E. Industrial Park, Cumberland, MD 21502 US
(301) 759-1005
www.1390espn.com
License: Cumberland, MD held by West Virginia Radio Corporation of the Alleghenies
Group Owner: West Virginia Radio Corp.; (acq. 04-2008 for $350, 000)
Nat'l Network: CMLS; ESPN
Arbitron Metro Market: Cumberland, MD; *Format:* Sports; *Hrs. of News Programming:* news progmg 20 hrs wkly; *No. News Employees:* 2; *Target Audience:* 25-55.
Dale Miller, President

WTBO
12-13-1928; 1450 kHz AM; *Hrs Open:* 24; 1 kw-U, ND1; N39 38 43 W78 45 5
Mailing Address: 350 Byrd Avenue, Cumberland, MD 21502 US
Second Address: 350 Byrd Ave., Cumberland, MD 21502
(301) 722-6666; *Fax:* (301) 722-0945
www.wtboam.com
License: Cumberland, MD held by WTBO-WKGO Corp. LLC.
Group Owner: Wooster Republican Printing Co.; (acq 11-1-77).
Nat'l Network: CSN
Arbitron Metro Market: Cumberland, MD; *Format:* Oldies; *Hrs. of News Programming:* news progmg 20 hrs wkly; *No. News Employees:* 1; *Target Audience:* 40 plus.; *Adv. Rates:* 18; 14; 18; 12
G. Dix II, President
Richard Cornwell, General Manager

Denton

WKDI
12-27-1988; 840 kHz AM; *Hrs Open:* Sunrise-sunset; 1 kw-D, DAD; N38 53 53 W75 51 10
Mailing Address: P.O. Obx 889, Blacksburg, VA 24063 US
Second Address: 24580 Station Rd., Denton, MD 21629
(410) 479-2288; *Fax:* (410) 479-5188
wkdi@broadcast.net
License: Denton, MD held by Bayshore Communications Inc.
Format: Christian, Talk; *Hrs. of News Programming:* News progmg 12 hrs wkly; *Target Audience:* 25-49; middle-income Christians
Edward Baker, CEO
Michael McCoy, General Manager

Easton

WKHZ
09-29-1960; 1460 kHz AM; 1 kw-D, 500 w-N, DA-2; N38 46 13 W76 04 55
101 Federal Street, Easton, MD 21061
(443) 385-0353; *Fax:* (410) 822-0576
stacie@wceiradio.com
License: Easton, Talbot County, MD
Nat'l Network: Jones Radio Networks
Population Served: 70,000 *Target Audience:* 45 plus; mature adults

WCEI-FM
05-14-1975; 96.7 MHz FM; *Hrs Open:* 24; 12.5 kw; 463 ft.; N38 57 21.8 W76 5 35.6
306 Port St., Easton, MD 21601 US
(410) 822-3301; *Fax:* (410) 822-0576
www.wceiradio.com
studio@wceiradio.com
License: Easton, Talbot County, MD held by First Media Radio, LLC
Group Owner: First Media Radio, LLC
Arbitron Metro Market: Easton,MD; *Format:* Adult Contemp; *No. News Employees:* 1; *Target Audience:* 25-54.
Matt Spence, Operations Dir
Julia Fickes, General Manager

Elkton

***WOEL-FM**
09-01-1978; 89.9 MHz FM; 3 kw; 259 ft.; N39 35 35 W75 51 49 US
410-392-3225; *Fax:* 410-392-3229
apd.saved@juno.com
License: Elkton, Cecil County, MD held by Maryland Baptist Bible College.
Nat'l Network: USA
TV Affiliate: Relg

WSRY
08-22-1963; 1550 kHz AM; 1 kw-D, DA2; 0.001 kw-N, DA2; N39 35 45 W75 47 50
179 Stanton Christiana Road, Christiana, DE 19702 US
(302) 731-7270; *Fax:* (302) 738-3090
www.myreachradio.com
listenercare@myreachradio.com
License: Elkton, MD held by Priority Radio Inc.
Group Owner: Priority Radio Inc.; (acq 12-10-99)
Nat'l Network: ESPN Radio
Arbitron Metro Market: Wilmington, DE; *Format:* Religious
Special Programming: Relg 3 hrs, farm one hr wkly; *Target Audience:* 25-64.; *Adv. Rates:* 21; 17; 19; 13
Dan Edwards, General Manager

Emmitsburg

***WMTB-FM**
10-01-1977; 89.9 MHz FM; *Hrs Open:* Noon-3 PM; 0.1 kw; 144 ft.; N39 41 2 W77 21 25
US
(301) 447-5240
www.msmary.edu/wmtb
License: Emmitsburg, Frederick County, MD held by Mount Saint Mary's College.
Arbitron Metro Market: Emmitsburg, MD; *Format:* Alternative
Special Programming: Folk one hr, gospel one hr, relg 4 hrs wkly; *Hrs. of News Programming:* News progmg 2 hrs wkly; *Target Audience:* General; college &community
Randy Gray, General Manager

Federalsburg

WTDK
12-02-1978; 107.1 MHz FM; *Hrs Open:* 24; 3.9 kw; 407 ft.; N38 46 2 W75 44 46
2 Bay St., Cambridge, MD 21613 US
(410) 228-4800
www.mtslive.com
news@mtslive.com
License: Federalsburg, Caroline County, MD held by MTS Broadcasting.
Group Owner: MTS Broadcasting; acq 1-30-97)
Nat'l Network: USA; Westwood One
Arbitron Metro Market: Federalsburg, MD; *Format:* Oldies; *Hrs. of News Programming:* News progmg 4 hrs wkly; *Target Audience:* 25-54; affluent listeners
Shane Walker, Operations Mgr
Troy Hill, General Manager

Frederick

WFMD
01-01-1936; 930 kHz AM; *Hrs Open:* 24; 5 kw-D, DA2; 2.5 kw-N, DA2; N39 24 55 W77 27 41
5966 Grove Hill Road, Frederick, MD 21703 US
(301) 663-4181; *Fax:* (301) 682-8018
www.wfmd.com
info@wfmd.com
License: Frederick, MD held by Aloha Station Trust LLC
Nat'l Network: ABC; *Wire Services:* AP
Arbitron Metro Market: Frederick, MD; *Format:* News, News/Talk, 84, Talk; *Hrs. of News Programming:* news pogmg 20 hrs wkly; *No. News Employees:* 3; *Target Audience:* 35-64.

WFRE
02-19-1961; 99.9 MHz FM; *Hrs Open:* 24; 7.6 kw; 1165 ft.; N39 30 0 W77 29 58
5966 Grove Hill Road, Frederick, MD 21703 US
(301) 663-4181; *Fax:* (301) 682-8018
www.wfre.com
JessicaMitko2@clearchannel.com
License: Frederick, Frederick County, MD held by Aloha Station Trust LLC
Nat'l Reps: Clear Channel; *Wire Services:* AP
Arbitron Metro Market: Frederick, MD; *Format:* Country; *Hrs. of News Programming:* news progmg one hr wkly; *No. News Employees:* 3; *Target Audience:* 25-54.
Jim Condron, General Manager
Linda Beaulieu, General Sales Mgr

***WYPF**
05-01-1991; 88.1 MHz FM; *Hrs Open:* 24; 1 kw; 1115 ft.; N39 29 31 W77 30 0
2216 North Charles Street, Baltimore, MD 21218 US
(410) 235-1660; *Fax:* (410) 235-1161
www.wypr.org
frontdesk@wypr.org
License: Frederick, Frederick County, MD held by Your Public Radio Corp.
Nat'l Network: NPR; PRI
Format: News, News/Talk, 86; *Target Audience:* General.
Anthony Brandon, President
Brian Crompwell, Business Manager
Paul Hollis, Public Information Assistant
Kristin Beno, Director of Membership
Alexandra Price, Director of Development
Kyle Leslie, Director of New Media
AmiDougherty, Traffic Assistant

WWFD
12-15-1960; 820 kHz AM; *Hrs Open:* 24; 4.3 kw-D, DAN; 0.43 kw-N, DAN; N39 24 42 W77 28 20
6633 Mount Phillip Rd., Frederick, MD 21703 US
(202) 895-5000; *Fax:* (202) 895-5149
License: Frederick, Frederick County, MD held by Washington DC FCC License Sub LLC

RADIO - U.S.

Group Owner: Hubbard Broadcasting Inc.; (acq 1-19-2011)
Nat'l Reps: Katz Radio
Arbitron Metro Market: Washington, DC; *Format:* Variety/Diverse; *Target Audience:* General.
David Kolesar, Engineering Dir

Frostburg

WFRB
12-20-1958; 560 kHz AM; *Hrs Open:* 24; 5 kw-D, ND1; 0.055 kw-N, ND1; N39 41 2 W78 57 57
242 Finzel Road, Frostburg, MD 21532 US
(301) 689-8871; *Fax:* (301) 689-8880
www.talkradio560.com
wfrb@wfrb.com
License: Frostburg, MD held by WTBO-WKGO Corp. L.L.C.
Group Owner: Wooster Republican Printing Co.; (acq 6-1-97; $3.5 million with co-located FM).
Format: Talk; *Hrs. of News Programming:* news progmg 10 hrs wkly; *No. News Employees:* 1; *Target Audience:* 40 plus; those gainfully employed in the market for goods & svcs; *Adv. Rates:* 18; 14; 18; 12
Rich Cornwell, General Manager

WFRB-FM
10-01-1965; 105.3 MHz FM; *Hrs Open:* 24; 13.5 kw; 958 ft.; N39 41 2 W78 57 57
242 Finzel Road, Frostburg, MD 21532 US
(301) 689-8871; *Fax:* (301) 689-8880
www.wfrb.com
License: Frostburg, Allegany County, MD
Group Owner: Wooster Republican Printing Co.
Format: Country; *Hrs. of News Programming:* news progmg 5 hrs wkly; *No. News Employees:* 2
Rich Cornwell, General Manager

***WFWM**
04-01-1986; 91.9 MHz FM; *Hrs Open:* 24; 0.255 kw horiz, 1.3 kw vert; 1424 ft.; N39 34 54 W78 53 53
101 Braddock Road, Frostburg, MD 21532 US
(301) 687-4143; *Fax:* (301) 687-7040
www.wfwm.org
wfwm@frostburg.edu
License: Frostburg, Allegany County, MD held by Frostburg State University.
Nat'l Network: NPR; *Wire Services:* AP
Format: Classical, Jazz *Special Programming:* Educ 11 hrs wkly; *Hrs. of News Programming:* news progmg 2 hrs wkly; *No. News Employees:* 1; *Target Audience:* General.
Chuck Dicken, General Manager
Jeff Rosedale, News Director

***WLIC**
10-01-1989; 97.1 MHz FM; *Hrs Open:* 24; 0.15 kw; 1355 ft.; N39 34 54 W78 53 58 *Rebroadcasts:* Rebroadcasts WAIJ(FM) Grantsville 100%
Mailing Address: 34 Springs Road, P.O. Box 540, Frostburg, MD 21532 US
Second Address: He's Alive Corp. Offices, 34 Springs Rd., Grantsville, MD 21536
(301) 895-3292; *Fax:* (301) 895-3293
www.hesalive.net
hesalive@hesalive.net
License: Frostburg, Alleghany County, MD held by He's Alive Inc.
Group Owner: He's Alive Inc.
Nat'l Network: USA
Format: Adult Contemp, Christian, 44; *Target Audience:* 18-35.
Melissa Flores, President

Fruitland

WKHI
01-01-1972; 107.7 MHz FM; *Hrs Open:* 24; 5.3 kw; 348 ft.; N38 23 0 W75 24 53
55 Hawthorne Street, San Francisco, CA 94105 US
(302) 856-2567; *Fax:* (302) 856-7633
www.1077thebone.com
sue@greatscottbroadcasting.com
License: Fruitland, Wicomico County, MD held by Adams Radio Group
Group Owner: Great Scott Broadcasting; (acq 7-16-99; $700,000 with WXSH(FM) Pocomoke City, MD)
Nat'l Network: NBC
Arbitron Metro Market: Salisbury-Ocean City, MD; *Format:* Country *Special Programming:* Black 5 hrs, gospel 5 hrs wkly; *Target Audience:* 25-54.

Gaithersburg

WMET
01-31-1983; 1160 kHz AM; *Hrs Open:* 24
8945 N. Westland Drive, Ste 302, Gaithersburg, MD 20877 US
(877) 636-1160; *Fax:* (301) 585-1682
www.wmetllgo.com
ylevin@wmet1160.com
License: Gaithersburg, MD held by Beltway Acquisition Corp.
Nat'l Network: NBC Radio
Arbitron Metro Market: Gaithersburg, MD; *Format:* Religious; *Target Audience:* 25 plus.
Irene Lagan, General Manager

Glen Burnie

WFBR
05-15-1963; 1590 kHz AM; 1 kw-U, DA-2; N39 10 36 W76 37 20
159 8th Ave. NW., Glen Burnie, MD 21061 US
(410) 761-1590
www.1590wfbr.com
License: Glen Burnie, Anne Arundel County, MD held by Way Broadcasting Licensee, LLC
Group Owner: Multicultural Radio Broadcasting, Inc.; (acq 8-1-2005; exchange for WKDV(AM))
Population Served: 1,300,000; *Arbitron Metro Market:* Baltimore, MD; *Format:* Talk
Jean Alston, Station Manager

WWIN-FM
09-15-1964; 95.9 MHz FM; *Hrs Open:* 24; 3 kw horiz, 3 kw vert; 299 ft; N39 12 16 W76 34 07
1705 Whitehead Rd., Baltimore, MD 20706
(410) 332-8200; *Fax:* (410) 944-1282
www.magicbaltimore.com
hmazer@radio-one.com
License: Glen Burnie, Anne Arundel County, MD held by Radio One Licenses LLC.
Group Owner: Radio One Inc.; (acq 1-23-92; $7.5 million with WWI
Nat'l Network: ABC; *Nat'l Reps:* Christal
Population Served: 915,800; *Arbitron Metro Market:* Baltimore, MD; *Format:* 0, Urban Contemporary; *Hrs. of News Programming:* news progmg one hr wkly; *No. News Employees:* 1; *Target Audience:* 25-54; Black adult
Howard Mazer, General Manager

Grantsville

***WAIJ**
10-01-1984; 90.3 MHz FM; *Hrs Open:* 19; 10 kw horiz, 8.8 kw vert; 561 ft.; N39 42 14 W79 5 31
Mailing Address: 34 Springs Road, P.O. Box 540, Grantsville, MD 21536 US
Second Address: He's Alive Corp. Offices, 34 Springs Rd., Grantsville, MD 21536
(301) 895-3292; *Fax:* (301) 895-3293
www.hesalive.net
info@hesalive.net
License: Grantsville, Garrett County, MD held by He's Alive Inc.
Group Owner: He's Alive Inc.
Nat'l Network: USA
Arbitron Metro Market: Oakland, MD; *Format:* Christian, Gospel; *Target Audience:* 18-35.
Melissa Flores, General Manager

Grasonville

WRNR-FM
04-01-1980; 103.1 MHz FM; 6 kw; 328 ft.; N38 56 37 W76 10 43
179 Admiral Cochrane Drive, Annapolis, MD 21401 US
(410) 626-0103; *Fax:* (410) 267-7634
www.wrnr.com
info@wrnr.com
License: Grasonville, Queen Annes County, MD held by Empire Broadcasting System Inc.
Nat'l Network: CBS Radio
Arbitron Metro Market: Baltimore, MD; *Format:* Alternative, Variety/Diverse; *Hrs. of News Programming:* news progmg 2 hrs wkly; *No. News Employees:* 1; *Target Audience:* 25-54; adults
Bob Waugh, Operations Dir

Hagerstown

WARK
07-20-1947; 1490 kHz AM; *Hrs Open:* 24; 1 kw-U, ND1; N39 37 35 W77 42 40 *Rebroadcasts:* Rebroadcasts WAFY(FM) Middletown 20-30%
880 Commonwealth Ave., Hagerstown, MD 21740 US
(301) 733-4500; *Fax:* (301) 733-0040
License: Hagerstown, MD held by Manning Broadcasting Inc.
Group Owner: Manning Broadcasting Inc.
Arbitron Metro Market: Hagerstown, MD; *Format:* Talk *Special Programming:* Jazz 2 hrs wkly; *Hrs. of News Programming:* news progmg 8 hrs wkly; *No. News Employees:* 2; *Target Audience:* 25-54.
Rick Mussleman, General Manager
Marcia Cason, General Sales Mgr
Caroline Henneberger, News Director
Bill McCarrey, Engineering Dir

***WGMS**
06-15-1993; 89.1 MHz FM; *Hrs Open:* 24; 0.9 kw; 1339 ft.; N39 41 47 W77 30 50 *Rebroadcasts:* Rebroadcasts WETA-FM Washington 100%
3939 Campbell Avenue, Arlington, VA 22206 US
(703) 998-2600
www.weta.org/fm
radio@weta.com
License: Hagerstown, Washington County, MD held by Greater Washington Education Telecommunication Association.
Nat'l Network: NPR; PRI
Arbitron Metro Market: Hagerstown, MD; *Format:* Talk; *Target Audience:* General; educated adults

WJEJ
10-01-1932; 1240 kHz AM; *Hrs Open:* 24; 1 kw-U, ND1; N39 40 0 W77 43 30
1135 Haven Road, Hagerstown, MD 21740 US
(301) 739-2323; *Fax:* (301) 797-7408
www.wjejradio.com
wjej@myactv.net
License: Hagerstown, MD held by Hagerstown Broadcasting Co. Inc.
Nat'l Network: CBS; *Wire Services:* Metro Weather Service Inc.
Arbitron Metro Market: Hagerstown-Chambersburg-Waynesboro, MD-PA; *Format:* Easy Listening; *Hrs. of News Programming:* news progmg 24 hrs wkly; *No. News Employees:* 1; *Target Audience:* 35 plus.

WAYZ
01-01-1946; 104.7 MHz FM; *Hrs Open:* 24; 8.3 kw; 1378 ft.; N39 41 47 W77 30 47
10960 John Wayne Drive, Greencastle, PA 17225 US
(717) 597-9200; *Fax:* (717) 597-9210
www.wayz.com
info@wayz.com
License: Hagerstown, Washington County, MD held by H.J.V. L.P.
Group Owner: VerStandig Broadcasting; (acq 8-28-2000; $2.5 million and WWMD(FM) Waynesboro, PA).
Wire Services: UPI
Arbitron Metro Market: Hagerstown, MD; *Format:* Country *Special Programming:* Relg 3 hrs wkly; *Target Audience:* 25-54.

***WZXH**
01-01-2009; 91.7 MHz FM; 900 w; Ant 423 ft; N39 27 39 W77 41 58 *Rebroadcasts:* Rebroadcasts WBYO(FM) Sellersville, PA 100%
Box 186, Sellersville, PA
(215) 721-2141; *Fax:* (215) 721-9811
www.wordfm.org
License: Hagerstown, Washington County, MD held by Four Rivers Community Broadcasting Corp.
Group Owner: Four Rivers Community Broadcasting Corp.
Arbitron Metro Market: Hagerstown-Chambersburg-Waynesboro, MD-PA
Charles Loughery, President
Meg Sabulsky, Operations Dir
David Baker, General Manager
Meg Sabulsky, Programming Director
William Dunn, Promotions Manager
Charles Doughery, Engineering Dir

Halfway

WHAG
06-09-1962; 1410 kHz AM; *Hrs Open:* 6 AM-7 PM; 1 kw-D, DA2; 0.099 kw-N, DA2; N39 37 3 W77 44 17
255 Penncraft Ave., Chambersburg, PA 17201 US
(301) 797-7300; *Fax:* (301) 797-2659
www.thenewfm963.com
License: Halfway, Washington County, MD held by Alpha Media Licensee LLC
Group Owner: Alpha Media LLC; (acq 4-17-2014; grpsl).
Arbitron Metro Market: Hagerstown-Chambersburg-Waynesboro, MD-PA; *Format:* Oldies; *Hrs. of News Programming:* news progmg 7 hrs wkly; *No. News Employees:* 2; *Target Audience:* 25-64.
Rich Bateman, General Manager
Ed Dorsey, Sales Manager

WDLD
01-01-1965; 96.7 MHz FM; 4.8 kw; 164 ft.; N39 37 3 W77 44 17
25 Penncraft Ave., Chambersburg, PA 17201 US
(717) 263-0813; *Fax:* (717) 263-9649
www.wild967.fm
wild@wild967.com

License: Halfway, Washington County, MD held by Alpha Media Licensee LLC
Group Owner: Alpha Media LLC
Nat'l Network: ABC
Arbitron Metro Market: Hagerstown-Chambersburg-Waynesboro, MD-PA; *Format:* Contemporary Hits/Top 40; *Target Audience:* 18-54; adults, young families
Rick Alexander, Operations Manager
Rich Bateman, General Manager
Artie Shultz, Programming Director
Tammy Heckman, Promotions Director

Havre De Grace

WJSS
05-15-1948; 1330 kHz AM; *Hrs Open:* 24; 5 kw-D, DAN; 0.5 kw-N, DAN; N39 33 55 W76 7 8
1205 York Road, Lutherville, MD 21093 US
(410) 939-0800; *Fax:* (410) 939-2156
www.wjss1330.com
info@wjss.com
License: Havre De Grace, MD held by Benjamin-Dane LLC
Arbitron Metro Market: Havre de Grace, MD; *Format:* News, News/Talk, 86; *Target Audience:* General.
Ronald Reeves, President

WXCY
06-19-1960; 103.7 MHz FM; *Hrs Open:* 24; 37 kw; 551 ft.; N39 33 52 W76 6 7
707 Revolution Street, Havre de Grace, MD 21078 US
(410) 939-1100; *Fax:* (410) 939-1104
www.wxcyfm.com
wxcy@wxcyfm.com
License: Havre De Grace, Harford County, MD held by Delmarva Broadcasting Co.
Group Owner: Delmarva Broadcasting Co.
Wire Services: Metro Weather Service Inc.
Arbitron Metro Market: Wilmington, DE; *Format:* Country *Special Programming:* Relg 2 hrs, NASCAR info updates on race day 6 hrs; *No. News Employees:* 2; *Target Audience:* 25-54.; *Adv. Rates:* 70; 60; 70; 50

Hurlock

WAAI
06-01-1989; 100.9 MHz FM; *Hrs Open:* 24; 1.3 kw; 502 ft.; N38 37 28 W75 53 20
2 Bay St., Cambridge, MD 21613 US
(410) 228-4800
www.mtslive.com
news@mtslive.com
License: Hurlock, Dorchester County, MD held by MTS Broadcasting.
Group Owner: MTS Broadcasting; acq 1-30-97)
Nat'l Network: ABC; *Nat'l Reps:* Rgnl Reps; *Wire Services:* ABC
Arbitron Metro Market: Hurlock, MD; *Format:* Country *Special Programming:* Gospel 4 hrs wkly; *Hrs. of News Programming:* news progmg 6 hrs wkly; *No. News Employees:* 4; *Target Audience:* 25-54; general
Shane Walker, Operations Mgr
Troy Hill, General Manager

Indian Head

WWGB
06-01-1986; 1030 kHz AM; *Hrs Open:* Sunrise-sunset; 50 kw-D, DAD; N38 33 53 W76 49 1
0710 Oxon Hill Road, Oxon Hill, MD 20745 US
(301) 899-1444; *Fax:* (301) 899-7244
www.wwgb.com
radio@wwgb.com
License: Indian Head, MD held by Good Body Media LLC.
Group Owner: Mountain Broadcasting Corp.; (acq 7-15-2002).
Arbitron Metro Market: Indian Head, MD; *Format:* Christian

La Plata

WKIK
10-01-1965; 1560 kHz AM; *Hrs Open:* 12; 0.25 kw-C, NDD; 1 kw-D, NDD; N38 32 36 W76 59 37
2805 Three Motch Rd., Mechanicsville, MD 20659 US
(301) 884-5550; *Fax:* (301) 884-0280
www.country1029wkik.com
License: La Plata, MD held by Somar Communications Inc.
Group Owner: Somar Communications Inc.; acq 4-12-91; $65,000;
Nat'l Network: ABC
Arbitron Metro Market: Washington, DC; *Format:* Country *Special Programming:* Local news, Baltimore Ravens football; *Hrs. of News Programming:* News progmg 5 hrs wkly; *Target Audience:* 25-54.

Laurel

WILC
12-23-1965; 900 kHz AM; *Hrs Open:* 5 AM-4 AM; 1.9 kw-D, DA2; 0.5 kw-N, DA2; N39 4 57 W76 50 19
1550 Hemlock Street, N.W, Washington, DC 20012 US
(301) 419-2122; *Fax:* (301) 419-2409
viva900@tvcontacto.net
License: Laurel, MD held by ZGS Radio Inc.
Group Owner: ZGS Communications; (acq 2-11-02; $5.5 million).
Nat'l Network: CNN Radio; *Nat'l Reps:* Univision Radio National Sales
Arbitron Metro Market: Washington, DC; *Format:* Adult Contemp; *Hrs. of News Programming:* News progmg 10 hrs wkly; *Target Audience:* General.; *Adv. Rates:* 100; 80; 80; 70
Patricia Omana, General Manager
Sergio Uriola, Programming Director
Mavi Raez, News Director

Lexington Park

WPTX
07-01-1998; 1690 kHz AM
2805 Three Notch Rd., Mechanicsville, MD 20659 US
(301) 884-5550; *Fax:* (301) 884-0280
wsmdfm@aol.com
License: Lexington Park, MD held by Somar Communications Inc.
Group Owner: Somar Communications Inc.; (acq 2-12-2001; $2.25 million with WMDM(FM) Lexington Park including three-year, $100,000 noncompete agreement)
Arbitron Metro Market: Lexington Park, MD; *Format:* News/Talk

WMDM
12-16-1976; 97.7 MHz FM; 6 kw; 328 ft.; N38 16 58 W76 33 39
28095 Three Notch Rd., Mechanicsville, MD 20659 US
(301) 884-5550; *Fax:* (301) 884-0280
www.977therocket.com
License: Lexington Park, St. Marys County, MD held by Somar Communications Inc.
Group Owner: Somar Communications Inc.; (acq 2-12-2001; $2.25 million with WPTX(AM) Lexington Park including three-year, $100,000 noncompete agreement)
Arbitron Metro Market: Lexington, MD; *Format:* Classic Rock; *Target Audience:* 25-54.

Maugansville

***WHGT**
12-05-2006; 1590 kHz AM; *Hrs Open:* 24
16621 National Pike, Hagerstown, MD 21740 US
(301) 582-0378; *Fax:* (301) 582-1620
License: Maugansville, MD held by Emmanuel Baptist Temple
Arbitron Metro Market: Maugansville, MD; *Format:* Christian *Special Programming:* Church worship svc one hr wkly; *Hrs. of News Programming:* News progmg 14 hrs wkly; *Target Audience:* Conservative Christian

Mechanicsville

WSMD-FM
09-01-1988; 98.3 MHz FM; *Hrs Open:* 24; 3 kw; 328 ft.; N38 24 49 W76 46 31
28095 Three Notch Rd., Mechanicsville, MD 20659 US
(301) 884-5550; *Fax:* (301) 884-0280
www.star983.com
License: Mechanicsville, St. Marys County, MD held by Somar Communications Inc.
Group Owner: Somar Communications Inc.
Nat'l Network: ABC
Format: Contemporary Hits/Top 40 *Special Programming:* Local news; *Hrs. of News Programming:* news progmg 6 hrs wkly; *No. News Employees:* 1; *Target Audience:* 25-54.

Middletown

WAFY
05-07-1990; 103.1 MHz FM; *Hrs Open:* 24; 1 kw; 571 ft.; N39 25 5 W77 30 3
5742 Industry Lane, Frederick, MD 21704 US
(301) 620-7700(301) 620-1031; *Fax:* (301) 696-0509
www.key103radio.com
License: Middletown, Frederick County, MD held by Manning Broadcasting Inc.
Group Owner: Manning Broadcasting Inc.
Nat'l Reps: Katz Radio
Arbitron Metro Market: Frederick, MD; *Format:* Adult Contemp; *No. News Employees:* 2; *Target Audience:* 25-54; upscale, well-educated, great radio commitment
Rick Musselman, COO
Larry Veihmeyer, Director of Sales
Tom Shinn, Programming Director
Brian Corson, Promotions Manager
Mick Rapeer, Chief Engineer
Rona Mensah, Disc Jockey
Marc Richards, Disc Jockey
Dan Stevens, DiscJockey
Larry Veihmeyer, DOS

Midland

WDZN
08-29-1988; 99.5 MHz FM; *Hrs Open:* 24; 1.05 kw; 787 ft.; N39 40 29.5 W78 57 43.3
15 E. Industrial Blvd., Cumberland, MD 21502 US
(301) 759-1005
License: Midland, MD held by West Virginia Radio Corporation of the Alleghenies
Group Owner: West Virginia Radio Corp.
Nat'l Network: Jones Radio Networks
Arbitron Metro Market: Midland, MD; *Format:* Adult Contemp; *Hrs. of News Programming:* news progmg 15 hrs wkly; *No. News Employees:* 1; *Target Audience:* 25-55.; *Adv. Rates:* 18; 18; 18; 13
Dale Miller, President

***WLVV**
88.3 MHz FM; 2 w vert; Ant 1,351 ft; N39 34 51 W78 54 01
4271 Muncy-Exchange Rd., Turbotville, PA
(570) 412-6295
License: Midland, Allegany County, MD held by Muncy Hills Broadcasting Inc.

Van Michael, President

Mountain Lake Park

WKHJ
07-09-1990; 104.5 MHz FM; *Hrs Open:* 24; 1.5 kw; 663 ft.; N39 24 37 W79 17 15
P.O. Box 2337, Mtn. Lake Park, MD 21550 US
(301) 334-4272; *Fax:* (301) 334-2152
www.wkhj.com
License: Mountain Lake Park, Garrett County, MD held by Broadcast Communications II Inc.
Group Owner: Broadcast Communications Inc.; (acq 11-14-2005)
Nat'l Network: CNN Radio
Format: Adult Contemp; *Hrs. of News Programming:* news progmg 12 hrs wkly; *No. News Employees:* 1; *Target Audience:* 18-49.; *Adv. Rates:* 24; 18; 24; 18
Terry King, General Manager
Pam Trickett, Promotions Manager
James Shaffer, News Director
Paul Mullan, Chief Engineer

Myersville

WWEG
03-01-1957; 106.9 MHz FM; *Hrs Open:* 24; 15.5 kw; 853 ft.; N39 29 57 W77 36 42
880 Commonwealth Ave., Hagerstown, MD 21740 US
(301) 733-4500; *Fax:* (301) 733-0040
www.1069theeagle.com
info@1069theeagle.com
License: Myersville, Washington County, MD held by Manning Broadcasting Inc.
Group Owner: Manning Broadcasting Inc.
Nat'l Network: Westwood One
Arbitron Metro Market: Hagerstown,MD; *Format:* Contemporary Hits/Top 40, Adult Contemp; *No. News Employees:* 2
Peter Stover, President
Kym McKay, Programming Director

Oakland

WMSG
05-19-1963; 1050 kHz AM; 1 kw-D, ND1; 0.075 kw-N, ND1; N39 23 32 W79 23 54
P.O. Box 449, Oakland, MD 21550 US
(301) 334-3800; *Fax:* (301) 334-2152
www.wmsg.com
office@wkhj.com
License: Oakland, MD held by Broadcast Communications II Inc.
Group Owner: Broadcast Communications Inc.; (acq 11-14-2005; with co-located FM)
Nat'l Network: CBS
Arbitron Metro Market: Oakland, MD; *Format:* Oldies; *Target Audience:* General.
Paul Mullan, General Manager

WWHQ
01-01-1966; 92.3 MHz FM; 1.4 kw; 689 ft.; N39 26 41 W79 31 42
P.O. Box 449, Oakland, MD 21550 US

(301) 334-3800; *Fax:* (301) 334-2152
office@wkhj.com
License: Oakland, Garrett County, MD held by Broadcast Communications II Inc.
Group Owner: Broadcast Communications Inc.
Nat'l Network: ABC
Arbitron Metro Market: Oakland, MD; *Format:* Country
Paul Mullen, Operations Dir
Paul Mullen, General Manager

Ocean City

WIJK(AM)
07-01-1960; 1590 kHz AM; *Hrs Open:* 24; 1 kw-D, 500 w-N, DA-2; N38 24 16 W75 07 37
Mailing Address: 11500 Coastal Hwy., Sea Watch Suite #1, Ocean City, MD 21842
Second Address: 12216 Parklawn Dr., Suite 203, Rockville, MD 20852
(410) 723-9100
khzradio.com
wkhz1590@aol.com
License: Ocean City, Worcester County, MD held by Radio Broadcast Communications Inc.
Population Served: 550,000; *Arbitron Metro Market:* Salisbury-Ocean City, MD; *Hrs. of News Programming:* News progmg 2 hrs wkly; *Target Audience:* 25-54; active, thinking, responsive, affluent adults, with high disposableincome
Bill Parris, President

***WYPO**
04-15-1994; 106.9 MHz FM; 4.5 kw; 384 ft.; N38 19 39 W75 11 50
US
www.wypr.org
tbrandon@wypr.org
License: Ocean City, Worcester County, MD held by WYPR License Holding LLC
Nat'l Network: NPR; PRI
Arbitron Metro Market: Salisbury-Ocean; *Format:* Jazz, News, 62, Talk
Anthony Brandon, President/General Manager

***WSDL**
02-13-1998; 90.7 MHz FM; *Hrs Open:* 24; 18.5 kw; 331 ft.; N38 30 6 W75 10 7
P O Box 2596, Salisbury, MD 21802 US
(410) 543-6895; *Fax:* (410) 548-6000
www.publicradiodelmarva.net
prd@salisbury.edu
License: Ocean City, Worcester County, MD held by Salisbury State University Foundation Inc.
Nat'l Network: NPR; PRI
Arbitron Metro Market: Salisbury-Ocean; *Format:* News; *Hrs. of News Programming:* news progmg 24 hrs wkly; *No. News Employees:* 1; *Target Audience:* General.

WWFG
06-30-1978; 99.9 MHz FM; 38 kw; 469 ft.; N38 25 20 W75 8 23
351 Tilghman Road, Salisbury, MD 21804 US
(410) 742-1923; *Fax:* (410) 742-2329
www.froggy999.com
License: Ocean City, Worcester County, MD held by Capstar TX LLC
Group Owner: iHeartMedia; (acq 8-7-00; grpsl).
Nat'l Reps: Clear Channel
Arbitron Metro Market: Ocean City, MD; *Format:* Country; *Target Audience:* 25-54; affluent, upwardly mobile
Chris Walus, Regional Market President
Jimmy Steele, Senior Vice President of Programming
Paul Burton, Senior Vice President of Sales
Victoria Kent, Promotions Director/Digital Content Director

***WRAU**
88.3 MHz FM; 50 kw; 492 ft.; N38 23 12 W75 17 27
4400 Massachusetts Ave., NW, Washington, DC 20016 US
(202) 885-1200; *Fax:* (202) 885-1269
www.wamu.org
License: Ocean City, Worcester County, MD held by Exec. Comm. of Bd. of Trustees of American University.
Arbitron Metro Market: Ocean City, MD

Ocean City-Salisbury

WQHQ
07-31-1965; 104.7 MHz FM; 33 kw; 610 ft.; N38 23 15 W75 17 30
351 Tilghman Road, Salisbury, MD 21804 US
(410) 742-1923; *Fax:* (410) 742-2329
www.q105fm.com
License: Ocean City-Salisbury, Worcester County, MD held by Capstar TX LLC
Group Owner: iHeartMedia
Arbitron Metro Market: Salisbury-Ocean City, MD; *Format:* Adult Contemp; *Target Audience:* 25-54.
Chris Walus, Regional Market President
Paul Burton, Senior Vice President of Sales
Jimmy Steele, Programming Director
Victoria Kent, Promotions Director

Ocean Pines

WAVD
03-01-1994; 97.1 MHz FM; *Hrs Open:* 24; 4.6 kw; 374 ft; N38 22 75 W75 10 32
Mailing Address: Box 909, Salisbury, MD 19803
Second Address: 919 Ellegood St., Salisbury, MD 21801
(410) 219-3500; *Fax:* (410) 548-1543
License: Ocean Pines, Worcester County, MD held by Delmarva Broadcasting Co.
Group Owner: Delmarva Broadcasting Co.; acq 6-26-97; grpsl)
Nat'l Reps: Katz Radio; *Wire Services:* AP
Arbitron Metro Market: Salisbury-Ocean City, MD; *No. News Employees:* 1; *Target Audience:* 30-60.
Joe Edwards, Operations Dir
Joe Beail, General Manager
Jeff Twilley, Chief Engineer

Pikesville

WQAL(AM)
04-05-1955; 1370 kHz AM; 50 kw-D, 7.7 kw-N, DA-2; N39 26 23 W76 21 20
Hilton Plaza, 1726 Reisterstown, Baltimore, MD 21208
(410) 580-6800; *Fax:* (410) 580-6810
www.v1370.com
License: Pikesville, Baltimore County, MD held by M-10 Broadcasting Inc.
Nat'l Network: Fox Sports
Population Served: 619,493; *Arbitron Metro Market:* Baltimore, MD; *Format:* Sports
Nick Mangione Jr., Operations Dir
Bob Pettit, General Manager
Marc Beavin, General Sales Mgr
Eddie Applefeld, Promotions Manager
Terry Trouyet, Operations Director

Pocomoke City

WGOP
08-01-1955; 540 kHz AM; 0.5 kw-D, ND1; 0.243 kw-N, ND1; N38 3 11 W75 34 11
1637 Dun Swamp Rd., Pocomoke City, MD 21851 US
(410) 957-0540
www.birach.com
sima@birach.com
License: Pocomoke City, Worcester County, MD held by Birach Broadcasting Corp.
Group Owner: Birach Broadcasting Corp.; acq 11-25-92; $127,500;
Arbitron Metro Market: Pocomoke City, MD; *Format:* Sports
Sima Birach, President
Mike Powell, Operations Manager

WXSH
05-01-1992; 106.1 MHz FM; 4 kw; 341 ft.; N38 4 36 W75 32 18
1508 Market Street, Pocomoke City, MD 21851 US
(410) 957-6081; *Fax:* (410) 957-6080
bay979@gmail.com
License: Pocomoke City, Worcester County, MD held by Adams Radio Group
Group Owner: Great Scott Broadcasting; (acq 7-16-99; $700,000 with WKHI(FM) Fruitland)
Arbitron Metro Market: Salisbury-Ocean City, MD; *Format:* Urban Contemporary
Michael Powell, General Manager

WICO-FM
10-01-2000; 92.5 MHz FM; 2.95 kw; 472 ft.; N38 8 35 W75 39 53
P.O. Box 909, Salisbury, MD 21803 US
(410) 219-3500; *Fax:* (410) 548-1543
www.wicotalk.com
License: Pocomoke City, Worcester County, MD held by Delmarva Broadcasting Co.
Group Owner: Delmarva Broadcasting Co.; acq 7-10-2000; $425,000)
Nat'l Network: CBS; *Nat'l Reps:* Katz Radio; *Wire Services:* AP
Arbitron Metro Market: Salisbury, MD; *Format:* Talk; *Hrs. of News Programming:* news progmg 2 hrs wkly; *No. News Employees:* 1; *Target Audience:* Adults 35-54; baby boomers

W245CA
05-01-1992; 96.9 MHz FM; 4 kw; 341 ft.; N38 4 36 W75 32 18
2000 Lower Huntington Road, Fort Wayne, IN 46819 US
(260) 747-1511; *Fax:* (260) 747-3999
www.b969fm.com
bigkess@argfw.com
License: Pocomoke City, Worcester County, MD held by Adams Radio Group
Group Owner: Great Scott Broadcasting; (acq 7-16-99; $700,000 with WKHI(FM) Fruitland)
Arbitron Metro Market: Salisbury-Ocean City, MD; *Format:* Urban Contemporary
Michael Powell, General Manager

WXKE-FM
05-01-1992; 96.3 MHz FM; 4 kw; 341 ft.; N38 4 36 W75 32 18
2000 Lower Huntington Road, Fort Wayne, IN 46819 US
(260) 747-1511; *Fax:* (260) 747-3999
www.963xke.com
jjfabini@argfw.com
License: Pocomoke City, Worcester County, MD held by Adams Radio Group
Group Owner: Great Scott Broadcasting; (acq 7-16-99; $700,000 with WKHI(FM) Fruitland)
Arbitron Metro Market: Ft. Wayne; *Format:* Urban Contemporary
Chris Monk, Vice President & Market Manager
Kevin Musselman, Director Of Sales
Eddie Didier, Chief Engineer
Susan Mullen, Business Manager

Potomac-Cabin John

WCTN
01-01-1965; 950 kHz AM; *Hrs Open:* 24
7825 Tuckerman Lane, Potomac, MD 20854 US
(301) 879-2422; *Fax:* (301) 879-2562
www.radiolajefa.com
hernan@radiolajefa.com
License: Potomac-Cabin John, MD held by Win Radio Broadcasting Corp.
Arbitron Metro Market: Washington, DC; *Format:* Oldies
Richard Yoon, President

Prince Frederick

WWXT
08-01-1971; 92.7 MHz FM; *Hrs Open:* 24; 2.85 kw; 476 ft.; N38 40 26 W76 35 41
P. O. Box 547, Prince Frederick, MD 20678 US
(301) 230-3500; *Fax:* (240) 430-2675
License: Prince Frederick, Calvert County, MD held by Red Zebra Broadcasting Licensee LLC.
Group Owner: Red Zebra Holdings LLC; (acq 5-9-2006; grpsl).
Nat'l Network: ESPN Radio
Arbitron Metro Market: Washington, DC; *Format:* Sports

Princess Anne

***WESM**
03-29-1987; 91.3 MHz FM; *Hrs Open:* 24; 45 kw; 299 ft.; N38 12 37 W75 40 56
Backbone Road, Princess Anne, MD 21853 US
(410) 651-8001; *Fax:* (410) 651-8005
www.wesm913.org
wesm913@umes.edu
License: Princess Anne, Somerset County, MD held by University of Maryland Eastern Shore.
Nat'l Network: NPR; PRI
Arbitron Metro Market: Princess Anne, MD; *Format:* Blues, Jazz
Special Programming: Blues 5 hrs, reggae 2 hrs, big band 10 hrs, gospel 20 hrs wkly; *Hrs. of News Programming:* news progmg 15 hrs wkly *No. NewsEmployees:* 1; *Target Audience:* General.
Dr. Thelma Thompson, President
Angel Resto Jr., Operations Dir
Stephen Williams, General Manager
Yancy Carrigan, Programming Director
Brian Daniels, Webmaster
Daphne Chatham, Administrative Assistant
Yancy Carrigan, MusicDirector

WOLC
12-24-1976; 102.5 MHz FM; 50 kw; 499 ft.; N38 6 43 W75 39 14
P. O. Box 130, Princess Anne, MD 21853 US
(410) 543-9652; *Fax:* (410) 651-9652
www.wolc.org
wolc@wolc.org
License: Princess Anne, Somerset County, MD held by Maranatha Inc.
Arbitron Metro Market: Salisbury-Ocean *TV Affiliate:* Relg; *No. News Employees:* 25-64.

Rockville

WLXE
11-01-1951; 1600 kHz AM; *Hrs Open:* 24; 1 kw-D, 500 w-N, DA-N; N39 05 51 W77 09 07
27 William St., 11th Floor, New York, NY 10005 US
(212) 966-1059; *Fax:* (212) 625-2894
www.mrbi.net
License: Rockville, Montgomery County, MD held by Multicultural Radio Broadcasting Licensee LLC.
Group Owner: Multicultural Radio Broadcasting Inc.; (acq 7-31-01; $800,000).
Population Served: 4,000,000; *Arbitron Metro Market:* Washington, DC; *Format:* Spanish
Arthur Liu, CEO/COO

Salisbury

*WDIH
06-01-1990; 90.3 MHz FM; 0.38 kw; 180 ft.; N38 24 28 W75 36 16
P.O. Box 186, Salisbury, MD 21801 US
(443) 736-4257
www.wdihradio90-3.org
wdihradio@comcast.net
License: Salisbury, Wicomico County, MD held by Salisbury Educational Broadcasting Foundation.
Arbitron Metro Market: Salisbury, MD; *Format:* Christian

WICO
09-01-1957; 1320 kHz AM; *Hrs Open:* 24; 1 kw-D, ND1; 0.028 kw-N, ND1; N38 21 39 W75 37 0
Mailing Address: 2727 Shipley Rd., P.O. Box 7492, Wilmington, DE 19803 US
Second Address: 919 Ellegood St., Salisbury, MD 21801
(410) 219-3500; *Fax:* (410) 548-1543
www.wicoam.com
License: Salisbury, MD held by Delmarva Broadcasting Co.
Group Owner: Delmarva Broadcasting Co.; (acq 6-26-97; grpsl)
Nat'l Network: CBS Radio; *Nat'l Reps:* Katz Radio; *Wire Services:* AP
Arbitron Metro Market: Salisbury-Ocean City, MD; *Format:* News, News/Talk, 84, Talk *Special Programming:* Farm one hr wkly; *Hrs. of News Programming:* news progmg 18 hrs wkly; *No. News Employees:* 2 *TargetAudience:* 35-64.
Joe Edwards, Operations Dir
Mike Kazala, General Manager
Bill Reddish, News Director
Jeff Twilley, Chief Engineer

WKTT
09-03-1969; 97.5 MHz FM; *Hrs Open:* 24; 4.5 kw; 299 ft.; N38 21 39 W75 37 0 *Rebroadcasts:* Rebroadcasts WZKT(FM) Lewes, DE 100%
Mailing Address: 2727 Shipley Rd., P.O. Box 7492, Wilmington, DE 19803 US
Second Address: 919 Ellegood St., Salisbury, MD 21801
(410) 219-3500; *Fax:* (410) 548-1543
www.catcountryradio.com
catcountry@radiocenter.com
License: Salisbury, Wicomico County, MD held by Delmarva Broadcasting Co.
Group Owner: Delmarva Broadcasting Co.; 1997
Nat'l Network: Motor Racing Net; *Nat'l Reps:* Katz Radio; *Wire Services:* AP
Arbitron Metro Market: Salisbury-Ocean City, MD; *Format:* Country; *Hrs. of News Programming:* news progmg 3 hrs wkly; *No. News Employees:* 1; *Target Audience:* 25-54.
Joe Edwards, Operations Dir
Mike Kazala, General Manager
E.J. Foxx, Programming Director
Dixie Kelly, Promotions Manager
Jeff Twiley, Chief Engineer

WJDY
03-14-1958; 1470 kHz AM; *Hrs Open:* 6 AM-midnight; 5 kw-D, DAD; 0.043 kw-N, DA2; N38 23 30 W75 38 48
351 Tilghman Rd., Salisbury, MD 21804 US
(410) 742-1923; *Fax:* (410) 742-2329
www.newsradio1470.com
License: Salisbury, MD held by Capstar TX LLC
Group Owner: iHeartMedia
Arbitron Metro Market: Salisbury-Ocean City, MD; *Format:* News, News/Talk, 86; *Target Audience:* 04-12.
Josh Wolff, Operations Manager
Chris Walus, Market Manager
Paul Burton, Sales Manager
Randy Scott, Programming Director
Victoria Kent, Promotions Director

*WLVW
07-25-1982; 105.5 MHz FM; 2.1 kw; Ant 384 ft; N38 24 26 W75 35 57
Gateway Crossing, 351 Tilghman Rd., Salisbury, MD 53202
(410) 742-1923; *Fax:* (410) 742-2329
www.kiss1055.com
kissfm@kiss1055.com
License: Salisbury, Wicomico County, MD held by Educational Media Foundation
Nat'l Reps: EMT
Arbitron Metro Market: Salisbury-Ocean City, MD; *No. News Employees:* 1; *Target Audience:* 18-44.
Mike Novak, President
Thompson Malone, General Manager
Don Roudebush, Development Director

WSBY-FM
12-13-1989; 98.9 MHz FM; *Hrs Open:* 24; 6 kw; 325 ft.; N38 18 0 W75 37 41
351 Tilghman Road, Salisbury, MD 21804 US
(410) 742-1923; *Fax:* (410) 742-2329
www.mymagic989.com
License: Salisbury, Wicomico County, MD held by Capstar TX LLC
Group Owner: iHeartMedia; (acq 8-7-00; grpsl).
Arbitron Metro Market: Salisbury-Ocean; *Format:* Urban Contemporary; *No. News Employees:* 1; *Target Audience:* 25-54.
Chris Walus, Regional Market President
Jimmy Steele, Senior Vice President of Programming
Paul Burton, Senior Vice President of Sales
Victoria Kent, Promotions Director/Digital Content Director

*WSCL
05-29-1987; 89.5 MHz FM; *Hrs Open:* 24; 33 kw; 584 ft.; N38 39 15 W75 36 42
Mailing Address: P.O. Box 2596, Salisbury, MD 21802 US
Second Address: S. Salisbury Blvd., Salisbury, MD 21802
(410) 543-6895; *Fax:* (410) 548-3000
www.delmarvapublicradio.net
dpr@salisbury.edu
License: Salisbury, Wicomico County, MD held by Salisbury State University Foundation Inc.
Nat'l Network: NPR; PRI; AP Radio
Arbitron Metro Market: Salisbury-Ocean; *Format:* Talk; *Hrs. of News Programming:* news progmg 29 hrs wkly; *No. News Employees:* 1; *Target Audience:* General.
Dana Whitehair, General Manager
Chris Ranck, Programming Director
Don Rush, News Director

WTGM
09-13-1940; 960 kHz AM; *Hrs Open:* 24; 5 kw-D, DA2; 5 kw-N, DA2; N38 25 44 W75 37 26
341 Tilghman Road, Salisbury, MD 21804 US
(410) 742-1923; *Fax:* (410) 742-2329
www.foxsports960.com
License: Salisbury, MD held by Capstar TX LLC
Group Owner: iHeartMedia; (acq 8-7-00; grpsl).
Arbitron Metro Market: Salisbury, MD; *Format:* Sports; *No. News Employees:* 1; *Target Audience:* 25-64.
Chris Walus, Regional Market President
Jimmy Steele, Senior Vice President of Programming
Paul Burton, Senior Vice President of Sales
Randy Scott, Programming Director
Victoria Kent, Promotions Director/Digital Content Director

Silver Spring

WBQH
12-07-1946; 1050 kHz AM; *Hrs Open:* 24; 10 kw-D, ND2; 0.044 kw-N, ND2; N39 00 51 W77 01 46
8121 Georgia Ave., 10th Fl., Silver Spring, MD 20910 US
(202) 244-6482
www.lameramera1050.com
License: Silver Spring, Montgomery County, MD held by Washington DC FCC License Sub LLC
Group Owner: Hubbard Broadcasting Inc.; (acq 1-19-2011)
Wire Services: AP
Population Served: 3,500,000; *Arbitron Metro Market:* Washington, DC; *Format:* Tejano
Carlos Navarro, General Manager

Snow Hill

WAMS-FM
02-01-2004; 101.1 MHz FM; *Hrs Open:* 24; 1.2 kw; Ant 489 ft; N38 12 57 W75 19 21
Snow Hill Broadcasting L.L.C., 7200 Coastal Hwy., Ocean City, MD 21817
(410) 524-6862; *Fax:* (410) 524-6808
www.wqmr.com
License: Snow Hill, Worcester County, MD held by Snow Hill Broadcasting L.L.C.
Population Served: 296,100; *Arbitron Metro Market:* Salisbury-Ocean City, MD *Special Programming:* Power Talk(local) Travel Show/Car Doc/Garison Show/ Tasting Room/ Satellite Sisters; *Target Audience:* 18-64 Persons. *Adv. Rates:* 20; 20; 20; 20
Jack Gillen, President
Kevin Brenahan, Operations Dir
R.J. Shingleton, General Sales Mgr
Corey Duices, Programming Director
Heather Shingleton, News Director

St. Mary's City

*WGWS
88.1 MHz FM; 1.1 kw; 174 ft.; N38 8 43 W76 22 22
P.O. Box 391, Twin Falls, ID 83303 US
(800) 357-4226
License: St. Mary's City, Saint Mary's County, MD held by Calvary Chapel of Twin Falls, Inc.
Group Owner: CSN International
Arbitron Metro Market: Saint Mary'S City, MD; *Format:* Christian, Religious

St. Michaels

WINX-FM
01-01-2000; 94.3 MHz FM; 4.6 kw; 361 ft.; N38 37 49 W76 3 25
306 Port Street, Easton, MD 21601 US
(410) 822-3301; *Fax:* (410) 822-0576
www.winxfm.com
License: St. Michaels, Talbot County, MD held by First Media Radio LLC
Arbitron Metro Market: Saint Michaels, MD; *Format:* Country
Matt Spence, Operations Dir
Stacie Monz, General Manager

Takoma Park

*WGTS
05-08-1957; 91.9 MHz FM; *Hrs Open:* 24; kw
7600 Flower Avenue, Takoma Park, MD 20912 US
(301) 891-4200; *Fax:* (301) 270-9191
www.wgts919.com
wgts@wgts919.com
License: Takoma Park, Montgomery County, MD held by Columbia Union College Broadcasting Inc.
Arbitron Metro Market: Washington, DC; *Format:* Religious; *Target Audience:* General.

Thurmont

WTHU
06-12-1967; 1450 kHz AM; *Hrs Open:* 24; 0.5 kw-D, ND1; 0.4 kw-N, ND1; N39 37 37 W77 24 11
10 Radio Lane, Thurmont, MD 21788 US
(301) 637-6736
www.wthu.org
License: Thurmont, MD held by Christian Radio Coalition Inc.
Arbitron Metro Market: Thurmont, MD; *Format:* Talk

Towson

WNST
10-27-1955; 1570 kHz AM; 5 kw-D, ND1; 0.237 kw-N, ND1; N39 25 4 W76 33 23
1550 Hart Road, Towson, MD 21286 US
(410) 821-9678
www.wnst.net
info@wnst.net
License: Towson, MD held by Nasty 1570 Sports LLC.
Arbitron Metro Market: Baltimore, MD; *Format:* Sports
Paul Kopelke, General Manager
Steve Hennessey, General Sales Mgr

*WTMD
02-12-1976; 89.7 MHz FM; *Hrs Open:* 24; 10 kw; 236 ft.; N39 23 45 W76 36 29
Towson University, 8000 York Road, Towson, MD 21252 US
(410) 704-8938; *Fax:* (410) 704-2609
www.wtmd.org
wtmd@towson.edu
License: Towson, Baltimore County, MD held by Towson University.
Arbitron Metro Market: Towson, MD; *Format:* Triple A; *Hrs. of News Programming:* News progmg 6 hrs wkly; *Target Audience:* 25-64.
Scott Mullins, Programming Director

RADIO - U.S.

Waldorf

WPRS-FM
02-01-1965; 104.1 MHz FM; *Hrs Open:* 24; 20 kw; 801 ft.; N38 37 7.4 W76 50 39
8515 Georgia Ave., 9th Floor, Silver Spring, MD 20910 US
(301) 306-1111
www.praisedc.com
License: Waldorf, Charles County, MD held by Radio One Licenses LLC.
Group Owner: Radio One Inc.; (acq 9-5-2007)
Arbitron Metro Market: Waldorf, MD; *Format:* Gospel
Jeffrey Wilson, General Manager

Walkersville

WDMV
12-01-1994; 700 kHz AM; 5 kw-D, DAD; N39 27 27 W77 19 27
702 Russell Ave., Suite 306, Gaithersburg, MD 20877 US
(301) 990-0700
www.radiolajefa.com
contacto@radiolajefa.com
License: Walkersville, Frederick County, MD held by Birach Broadcasting Corp.
Group Owner: Birach Broadcasting Corp.; (acq 9-95).
Arbitron Metro Market: Walkersville, MD; *Format:* Spanish
Sima Birach, President
Hernan Molina, General Manager
Ernesto Molina, Programming Director
Josefina Rodriguez, Administrative Manager
Vanesa Merino, Traffic Department

Westernport

WWPN
10-01-1993; 101.1 MHz FM; 0.32 kw; 1368 ft.; N39 22 58 W79 4 43
Box 3382, Lavale, MD 21502 US
(301) 463-5100
www.spirit101.com
License: Westernport, Allegany County, MD held by Ernest F. Santmyire.
Arbitron Metro Market: Westernport, MD; *Format:* Christian, Religious; *Target Audience:* 18-45; working class

Westminster

WZBA
11-01-1959; 100.7 MHz FM; *Hrs Open:* 24; 25 kw; 689 ft.; N39 26 50 W76 46 48
11350 McCormick Road, Hunt Valley, PA 21031 US
(410) 771-8484; *Fax:* (410) 771-1616
www.thebayonline.com
License: Westminster, Carroll County, MD held by Shamrock Communications Inc.
Group Owner: Shamrock Communications Inc.; (acq 4-7-81; $1.74 million with co-located AM;
Arbitron Metro Market: Baltimore, MD; *Format:* Classic Rock; *Hrs. of News Programming:* News progmg one hr wkly; *Target Audience:* 25-49; men & women active in the country life group
Jefferson Ward, General Manager
Dan Michaels, Programming Director

WTTR
07-01-1953; 1470 kHz AM; *Hrs Open:* 24; 1 kw-D, DAN; 1 kw-N, DAN; N39 34 37 W77 1 21
101 WTTR Lane, Westminster, MD 21158 US
(410) 876-1515; *Fax:* (410) 876-5095
www.wttr.com
info@wttr.com
License: Westminster, MD held by Sajak Broadcasting Corp.
Arbitron Metro Market: Baltimore, MD; *Format:* Contemporary Hits/Top 40, Adult Contemp *Special Programming:* Farm 4 hrs wkly; *Hrs. of News Programming:* news progmg 12 hrs wkly; *No. News Employees:* 1 *TargetAudience:* 35-64.
Pat Sajak, CEO

Wheaton

WACA
01-01-1954; 1540 kHz AM; 1 kw-C, NDD; 5 kw-D, NDD; N39 0 50 W77 1 46
2000 K St., N.W., Suite 600, Washington, DC 20006 US
(512) 467-0643
License: Wheaton, MD
Arbitron Metro Market: Monterey-Salinas-Santa Cruz CA

Williamsport

***WCRH**
07-24-1976; 90.5 MHz FM; *Hrs Open:* 24; 10 kw; 879 ft.; N39 39 34 W77 57 56
Mailing Address: P.O. Box 439, Williamsport, MD 21795 US
Second Address: 12146 Cedar Ridge Rd., Williamsport, MD 21795
(301) 582-0285; *Fax:* (301) 582-2707
www.wcrh.org
wcrh@wcrh.org
License: Williamsport, Washington County, MD held by Cedar Ridge Children's Home and School Inc.
Nat'l Network: Moody
Arbitron Metro Market: Hagerstown, MD; *Format:* Religious; *Hrs. of News Programming:* news progmg 9 hrs wkly; *No. News Employees:* 1; *Target Audience:* 25-45.
David Swacina, CEO
Jeff Ward, Operations Dir

WICL
11-15-1972; 95.9 MHz FM; *Hrs Open:* 24; 3.3 kw; 299 ft.; N39 36 18 W77 46 49
1606 W. King St., Martinsburg, WV 25401 US
(304) 263-8868; *Fax:* (304) 263-8906
www.bigdawgfm.com
License: Williamsport, Washington County, MD held by West Virginia Radio Corporation of the Alleghenies
Group Owner: West Virginia Radio Corp.; (acq 3-10-98; $1.05 million).
Nat'l Network: WWO; NBCNEW
Arbitron Metro Market: Williamsport, MD; *Format:* Country; *Hrs. of News Programming:* News progmg 15 hrs wkly; *Target Audience:* 25+
Mike McGough, General Manager

Worton

***WKHS**
03-28-1974; 90.5 MHz FM; 17.5 kw; 217 ft.; N39 16 55 W76 5 26
Mailing Address: 25301 Lambs Meadow Road, Worton, MD 21678 US
Second Address: Rts. 297 & 298, Worton, MD 21678
(410) 778-4249; *Fax:* (410) 778-3802
www.wkhsradio.org
wkhsradio@gmail.com
License: Worton, Kent County, MD held by Board of Education of Kent County.
Format: Variety/Diverse *Special Programming:* Oldies 6 hrs, children 5 hrs, country 2 hrs, big b; *Target Audience:* 12 plus.

Massachusetts

Acton

***WHAB**
08-01-1979; 89.1 MHz FM; *Hrs Open:* 10 AM-5:30 PM (M-F); 0.008 kw; 26 ft.; N42 28 48 W71 27 28
96 Hayward Road, Acton, MA 01720 US
(978) 264-4700
License: Acton, Middlesex County, MA held by Acton-Boxborough Regional School District.
Format: News, Variety/Diverse

Amherst

***WAMH**
01-01-1955; 89.3 MHz FM; *Hrs Open:* 24; 0.15 kw; 719 ft.; N42 21 51 W72 25 24
P.O. Box 2292, Amherst, MA 01002 US
(413) 542-2224(413) 542-2288
www.amherst.edu/~wamh
wamh@amherst.edu
License: Amherst, Hampshire County, MA held by Trustees of Amherst College.
Arbitron Metro Market: Amherst, MA; *Format:* Variety/Diverse; *Hrs. of News Programming:* News progmg 2 hrs wkly; *Target Audience:* 16-32; youth of today
Bob Neel, General Manager
Blaine Werner, Programming Director

***WFCR**
05-06-1961; 88.5 MHz FM; *Hrs Open:* 24; 13 kw; Ant 895 ft; N42 21 49 W72 25 24
131 County Circle, Hampshire House, Amherst, MA 01003
(413) 545-0788
www.nepr.net
radio@nepr.net
License: Amherst, Hampshire County, MA held by University of Massachusetts.
Nat'l Network: PRI; NPR; *Wire Services:* AP
Population Served: 1,183,119; *Arbitron Metro Market:* Springfield, MA *Special Programming:* Sp 2 hrs wkly; *Hrs. of News Programming:* news progmg 40 hrs wkly; *No. News Employees:* 6; *Target Audience:* General.
Martin Miller, General Manager

***WMUA**
01-01-1949; 91.1 MHz FM; *Hrs Open:* 24; 0.45 kw; 128 ft.; N42 23 37 W72 31 21
105 Campus Center, Amherst, MA 01003 US
(413) 545-2876; *Fax:* (413) 545-0682
www.wmua.org
manager@wmua.org
License: Amherst, Hampshire County, MA held by Board of Trustees of University of Massachusetts.
Arbitron Metro Market: Hampshire, MA; *Format:* Variety/Diverse; *Hrs. of News Programming:* News progmg 3 hrs wkly; *Target Audience:* General; Univ

WRNX
11-12-1990; 100.9 MHz FM; kw
1331 Main Street, 4th Floor, Springfield, MA 01103 US
(413) 781-1011; *Fax:* (413) 734-4434
www.mykix1009.com
License: Amherst, Hampshire County, MA held by CC Licenses LLC.
Group Owner: iHeartMedia; (acq 4-1-2007; grpsl)
Arbitron Metro Market: Springfield, MA; *Format:* Country
Sean Davey, Market Manager
Danielle Veronesi, Marketing and Promotions Director
Nora Drapalski, Digital Content Director

WPNI
04-02-1963; 1430 kHz AM; *Hrs Open:* 6 AM-midnight; 5 kw-D, DA2; 0.011 kw-N, DA2; N42 21 25 W72 29 13
98 Lower Westfield Rd, Holyoke, MA 01040 US
(413) 536-1105; *Fax:* (413) 536-1153
License: Amherst, MA held by 6 Johnson Road Licenses Inc.
Group Owner: Pamal Broadcasting Ltd.; (acq 5-29-2003; $8 million with co-located FM)
Arbitron Metro Market: Springfield, MA; *Format:* News, News/Talk, 86
Fred Caruso, Operations Dir
Jeff Fisher, General Manager
Jess Levitan, General Sales Mgr
Amy Bates, News Director
Cathy Keizer, Traffic Manager

Andover

WXRV
06-01-1959; 92.5 MHz FM; *Hrs Open:* 24; 25 kw; 712 ft.; N42 46 23 W71 6 1
30 How Street, Haverhill, MA 01830 US
(978) 374-4733; *Fax:* (978) 373-8023
www.wxrv.com
info@wxrv.com
License: Andover, Essex County, MA held by Beanpot License Corp.
Group Owner: Northeast Broadcasting Company Inc.; (acq 1981).
Arbitron Metro Market: Andover, MA; *Format:* Adult Contemp, Triple A; *Target Audience:* 25-54.
Terry Lieberman, General Manager
Steve Young, General Sales Mgr
Ron Bowen, Programming Director
John Mullett, Promotions Manager
AJ Crozby, Production Director
Rita Cary, Air Staff
Carolyn Morrell, Air Staff
Matt Phipps, AirStaff
Irene Collins, Air Staff

Ashland

WSRO
05-01-1967; 650 kHz AM
22942 Captain Kidd Lane, Cudjoe Key, FL 33042 US
(508) 424-2568; *Fax:* (508) 820-2473
www.wsro.com
wsroam650@yahoo.com
License: Ashland, MA held by Langer Broadcasting Group L.L.C.
Group Owner: Langer Broadcasting Group L.L.C.; acq 1996; $10,000).
Arbitron Metro Market: Boston; *Format:* Talk, Religious; *Target Audience:* 20-80; general
Carl Abrams, General Manager

Athol

WFNX
12-04-1989; 99.9 MHz FM; *Hrs Open:* 24; 1.85 kw; 407 ft.; N42 35 39 W72 12 2
P.O. Box 1230, Claremont, NH 03743 US

(978) 374-4733; *Fax:* 978-373-8023
www.wxrv.com
info@wxrv.com
License: Athol, Worcester County, MA held by County Broadcasting Co. LLC.
Group Owner: Northeast Broadcasting Company Inc.; (acq 10-6-2003; $650,000 with WJOE(AM) Orange-Athol).
Nat'l Network: ABC
Arbitron Metro Market: Haverhill, Ma; *Format:* Classic Rock
Glenn Cardinal, General Manager
Spencer Marshall, Programming Director
John Mullett, Promotions Manager
AJ Crozby, Production Director

Attleboro

WARL
10-08-1950; 1320 kHz AM; 5 kw-D, DA2; 5 kw-N, DA2; N41 57 33 W71 19 37
100 Bedford Street, New Bedford, MA 02719 US
(508) 989-5013; *Fax:* (401) 521-5878
License: Attleboro, MA held by The ADD Radio Group Inc.
Arbitron Metro Market: Providence-Warwick-Pawtucket, RI; *Format:* News, News/Talk, 84, Talk; *Target Audience:* 18 plus; middle to upper middle class
Scott MacPherson, General Manager

Baptist Village

***WWQZ**
89.5 MHz FM; 40 w horiz, 35 w vert; Ant 384 ft; N42 05 01 W72 24 51
52 New Hartford Rd., Barkhamsted, CT
(860) 379-3365; *Fax:* (860) 828-6109
License: Baptist Village, Hampden County, MA held by Morgan Brook Chirstian Radio Inc.

G. Thomas Palmer, President

Barnstable

WQRC
07-20-1970; 99.9 MHz FM; *Hrs Open:* 24; 50 kw; 381 ft.; N41 41 19 W70 20 49
737 W. Main St., Hyannis, MA 02601 US
(508) 771-1224
www.wqrc.com
wqrc@wqrc.com
License: Barnstable, Barnstable County, MA held by Sandab Communications Limited Partnership II
Group Owner: Sandab Communications L.P. II; acq 4-16-92; grpsl;
Nat'l Network: AP Radio; *Nat'l Reps:* Clear Channel; *Wire Services:* AP
Arbitron Metro Market: Cape Cod, MA; *Format:* Adult Contemp; *Hrs. of News Programming:* news progmg 32 hrs wkly; *No. News Employees:* 4; *Target Audience:* Adults/women; 25-54

Bayview

***WPMW**
88.5 MHz FM; 0.14 kw; 177 ft.; N41 38 22.6 W70 58 4.9
600 Pleasant Street, New Bedford, MA 02740 US
(508) 996-8274
www.radiocormariae.com
webmaster@radiocormariae.com
License: Bayview, Bristol County, MA held by Academy of the Immaculate Inc.
Nat'l Network: EWTN Radio
Arbitron Metro Market: New Bedford, MA; *Format:* Christian

Boston

WBMX
08-12-2009; 104.1 MHz FM; *Hrs Open:* 24; 21 kW; 837 ft.; N42 20 50 W71 4 59
83 Leo M. Birmingham Pkwy., Boston, MA 02135 USA
(617) 746-1300
www.mix1041.com
License: Boston, Suffolk County, MA held by CBS Radio Stations Inc.
Group Owner: CBS Radio; (acq 6-5-98; grpsl)
Nat'l Network: CBS; *Nat'l Reps:* Christal
Arbitron Metro Market: Boston, MA; *Format:* Adult Contemp
Barbara Jean Scannell, General Manager
Doreen Wong, General Sales Mgr
Steve Salhany, Programming Director
Dana Zabilski, Promotions Manager
Mike Mullaney, Music Director

***WBUR-FM**
03-01-1950; 90.9 MHz FM; *Hrs Open:* 24; 12 kw; 1001 ft.; N42 18 27 W71 13 27
890 Commonwealth Avenue, Boston, MA 02215 US
(617) 353-0909; *Fax:* (617) 353-4747
www.wbur.org
info@wbur.org
License: Boston, Suffolk County, MA held by The Executive Committee of Trustees of The Boston University.
Nat'l Network: NPR; PRI
Arbitron Metro Market: Boston, MA; *Format:* News, Talk; *Target Audience:* 25-54; intelligent adults interested in news natl, internatl & local
Jean Wong, CFO
Paul LaCamera, General Manager
Corey Lewis, Station Manager
Sam Fleming, Programming Director
John Davidow, News Director
Jeff Hutton, Engineering Dir

WBZ
09-19-1921; 1030 kHz AM; *Hrs Open:* 24; 50 kW; N42 16 44 W70 52 34
1170 Soldiers Field Rd., Boston, MA 02134 USA
(617) 787-7000; *Fax:* (617) 787-5969
www.wbz.com
License: Boston, MA held by CBS Radio East Inc.
Group Owner: CBS Radio
Nat'l Network: ABC; CBS; *Nat'l Reps:* CBS Radio
Arbitron Metro Market: Boston,MA; *Format:* News; *Target Audience:* 25-54

WEEI
12-01-1926; 850 kHz AM; *Hrs Open:* 24
401 City Ave., Suite 409, Bala Cynwyd, PA 19004 USA
(617) 779-3500; *Fax:* (617) 779-3557
www.weei.com/weei/shows-schedules/espn-weei-850-am
License: Boston, MA held by Entercom License LLC
Group Owner: Entercom Communications
Nat'l Network: ESPN Radio
Arbitron Metro Market: Boston, MA; *Format:* Sports; *No. News Employees:* 6; *Target Audience:* 25-54.

***WERS**
11-14-1949; 88.9 MHz FM; *Hrs Open:* 24; 4 kw; 610 ft.; N42 21 8 W71 3 25
120 Boylston Street, Boston, MA 02116 US
(617) 824-8890; *Fax:* (617) 824-8804
www.wers.org
info@wers.org
License: Boston, Suffolk County, MA held by Emerson College.
Wire Services: AP
Arbitron Metro Market: Boston, MA; *Format:* Variety/Diverse; *Hrs. of News Programming:* news progmg 3.5 hrs wkly; *No. News Employees:* 6
Howard D. Simpson, Operations Dir
Dr. Jack Casey, General Manager
Luca Pace, News Director

WEZE
590 kHz AM; *Hrs Open:* 24; 5 kw-U, DA1; N42 24 24 W71 5 14
500 Victory Road, Quincy, MA 02171 US
(617) 328-0880
www.wezeradio.com
contactus@salemradioboston.com
License: Boston, MA held by Pennsylvania Media Associates Inc.
Group Owner: Salem Communications Corp.; (acq 1-31-97; $6 million)
Arbitron Metro Market: Boston, MA; *Format:* Talk, Religious; *Hrs. of News Programming:* News progmg 5 hrs wkly; *Target Audience:* 25 plus.
Pat Ryan, General Manager

***WGBH(FM)**
10-06-1951; 89.7 MHz FM; *Hrs Open:* 24; 98 kw; 650 ft; N42 12 42 W71 06 51
1 Guest St., Brighton, MA 2135
(617) 300-5400
www.wgbh.org
License: Boston, Suffolk County, MA held by WGBH Educational Foundation.
Nat'l Network: PRI; NPR
Population Served: 330,000; *Arbitron Metro Market:* Boston TV *Affiliate:* *WGBH-TV, *WGBX-TV affils; *Format:* Jazz, News
Special Programming: Folk 10 hrs, blues 8 hrs, Irish 2 hrs, cultural 3 *Hrs. of NewsProgramming:* News progmg 22 hrs wkly; *Target Audience:* General.
John Abbott, President
Marita Rivero, General Manager

WILD
01-01-1946; 1090 kHz AM
US
License: Boston, MA held by Radio One of Boston Licenses LLC.
Group Owner: Radio One Inc.; (acq 12-20-2000; $5 million in cash & stock merger)
Nat'l Network: ABC; *Nat'l Reps:* Roslin
Arbitron Metro Market: Boston; *Format:* News, News/Talk, 86; *Target Audience:* General.

WJMN
03-31-1948; 94.5 MHz FM; 9.2 kw; 1158 ft.; N42 18 27 W71 13 27
10 Cabot Road, Suite 302, Medford, MA 02155 US
(781) 663-2500; *Fax:* (781) 290-0722
www.jamn945.com
feedback@jamn945.com
License: Boston, Suffolk County, MA held by AMFM Radio Licenses L.L.C.
Group Owner: iHeartMedia; (acq 8-30-00; grpsl)
Nat'l Reps: Katz Radio
Arbitron Metro Market: Boston; *Format:* Contemporary Hits/Top 40; *Target Audience:* 12-44.; *Adv. Rates:* 400; 400; 450; 300
Alan Chartrand, Market President

WMJX
01-06-1982; 106.7 MHz FM; 21.5 kw; 771 ft.; N42 20 50 W71 4 59
55 Morrissey Boulevard, Boston, MA 02125 US
(617) 822-9600; *Fax:* (617) 822-6571
License: Boston, Suffolk County, MA held by Greater Boston Radio Inc.
Group Owner: Beasley Broadcast Group; (acq 2-85)
Nat'l Reps: Katz Radio
Arbitron Metro Market: Boston, MA; *Format:* Adult Contemp
Rob Hogan, Programming Director

WWDJ
02-04-2008; 1150 kHz AM; *Hrs Open:* 24
US
www.radioluzboston.com
License: Boston, MA held by Pennsylvania Media Associates Inc.
Group Owner: Salem Communications Corp.; (acq 10-31-2003; $8.6 million)
Arbitron Metro Market: Boston, MA; *Format:* Christian

WWZN
01-01-1934; 1510 kHz AM; 50 kw-U, DA-2; N42 23 10 W71 12 01
308 Victory Road, Quincy, MA 02171
(617) 237-1234
License: Boston, Suffolk County, MA held by Blackstrap Broadcasting LLC
Group Owner: Rose City Radio Corp.
Nat'l Network: Sporting News Radio Network
Population Served: 535,000; *Arbitron Metro Market:* Boston; *Target Audience:* 25-54.

WODS
10-09-1987; 103.3 MHz FM; 8.7 kW; 1191 ft.; N42 18 27.4 W71 13 26.7
83 Leo M. Birmingham Pkwy., Boston, MA 02135 USA
(617) 787-7500
www.1033ampradio.com
License: Boston, Suffolk County, MA held by CBS Radio East Inc.
Group Owner: CBS Radio; (acq 11-13-98; grpsl)
Nat'l Reps: CBS Radio
Arbitron Metro Market: Boston; *Format:* Contemporary Hits/Top 40
Barbara Jean Scanell, General Manager
Steve Salhany, Programming Director
Rachel Kennedy, Promotions Manager

WMKI
01-01-1922; 1260 kHz AM
226 Lincoln Street, Allston, MA 02134 US
(617) 787-0146
License: Boston, MA held by Radio Disney Group LLC.
Group Owner: ABC Inc.; (acq 8-22-00; grpsl).
Nat'l Network: USA
Arbitron Metro Market: Boston; *Format:* Children; *Target Audience:* 6-14.; *Adv. Rates:* 100; 100; 100; 40

***WRBB**
10-01-1970; 104.9 MHz FM; *Hrs Open:* 24; 0.019 kw; 89 ft.; N42 20 19 W71 5 28
360 Huntington Avenue, Boston, MA 02115 US
(617) 373-4338
www.wrbbradio.org
License: Boston, Suffolk County, MA held by Northeastern University.

RADIO - U.S.

Arbitron Metro Market: Boston; *Format:* Variety/Diverse; *Hrs. of News Programming:* news progmg 2 hrs wkly; *No. News Employees:* 1; *Target Audience:* 12-35; college, urban
Stephanie Smith, General Manager
Rae Fagin, Programming Director

WRKO
01-01-1922; 680 kHz AM; 50 kw-D, DA2; 50 kw-N, DA2; N42 29 25 W71 13 5
20 Guest Street, Brighton, MA 02135 US
(617) 779-3400; *Fax:* (617) 779-3467
www.wrko.com
License: Boston, MA held by Entercom Boston License L.L.C.
Group Owner: Entercom Communications Corp.; (acq 10-15-98; $82 million with WEEI(AM) Boston)
Nat'l Network: ABC
Arbitron Metro Market: Boston; *Format:* Talk; *Target Audience:* 25-54.
Bill Cooksey, Programming Director

WROL
10-08-1950; 950 kHz AM; *Hrs Open:* 24; 5 kw-D, NDD; 0.09 kw-N, ND1; N42 26 15 W70 59 40
US
www.wrolboston.com
License: Boston, MA held by Salem Media Group LLC.
Group Owner: Salem Communications Corp.; (acq 3-2-2001; $11 million)
Arbitron Metro Market: Boston; *Format:* Christian *Special Programming:* Irish music programming; Car Doctor; *Target Audience:* Adults.
Patricia Ryan, General Sales Mgr

WBQT
01-01-1945; 96.9 MHz FM; 22.5 kw; 735 ft.; N42 20 50 W71 4 59
P.O. Box 1059, East Brunswick, NJ 08816 US
(617) 822-9600; *Fax:* (617) 822-6871
License: Boston, Suffolk County, MA held by Greater Boston Radio Inc.
Group Owner: Beasley Broadcast Group; (acq 3-31-93; $11.65 million;
Nat'l Reps: Katz Radio
Arbitron Metro Market: Boston; *Format:* Talk
Nika Desautels, General Sales Mgr
Grace Blazer, Programming Director
Hisham Fayed, Promotions Manager

***WUMB-FM**
09-19-1982; 91.9 MHz FM; *Hrs Open:* 24; 0.66 kw; 207 ft.; N42 15 27 W71 1 44
100 Morrissey Boulevard, Boston, MA 02125 US
(617) 287-6900
www.wumb.org
wumb@umb.edu
License: Boston, Suffolk County, MA held by The University of Massachusetts.
Nat'l Network: PRI; NPR
Arbitron Metro Market: Boston, MA; *Format:* Variety/Diverse; *Hrs. of News Programming:* News progmg 5 hrs wkly; *Target Audience:* 25-40.

WZLX
10-29-1985; 100.7 MHz FM; 21.5 kW; 837 ft.; N42 20 50 W71 4 59
83 Leo M Birmingham Pkwy., Boston, MA 02135 USA
(617) 746-5100; *Fax:* (617) 746-5105
www.wzlx.com
License: Boston, Suffolk County, MA held by CBS Radio Inc. of Boston
Group Owner: CBS Radio; (acq 11-13-98; grpsl)
Nat'l Network: CBS; *Nat'l Reps:* CBS Radio
Arbitron Metro Market: Boston, MA; *Format:* Classic Rock; *Target Audience:* 25-54; males
Barbara Jean Scanell, General Manager
David Place, General Sales Mgr
Mike Thomas, Programming Director
Adam Luciano, Promotions Coordinator

WBZ-FM
08-05-2009; 98.5 MHz FM; 9 kW; 1191 ft.; N42 18 27 W71 13 27
83 Leo Birmingham Pkwy., Boston, MA 02135 USA
(617) 779-0985
www.985thesportshub.com
License: Boston, MA held by CBS Radio Stations Inc.
Group Owner: CBS Radio
Format: Sports
Kelley Anderson, Promotions Manager

Boxford

***WBMT**
01-30-1978; 88.3 MHz FM; *Hrs Open:* 2:30 PM-9 PM(M-F); 10 AM-6 PM(S,Su); 0.66 kw; 33 ft.; N42 37 38 W70 58 32
20 Endicott Road, Topsfield/Boxford, MA 01983 US
(978) 887-8830
www.masconomet.org
wbmtradio@masconomet.org
License: Boxford, Essex County, MA held by Masconomet Regional High School System.
Arbitron Metro Market: Topsfieldboxford, MA; *Format:* Rock/AOR
Joseph Czarnecki, General Manager

Brewster

***WZAI**
01-01-2006; 94.3 MHz FM; 4.7 kw; Ant 372 ft; N41 46 36 W70 00 40 *Rebroadcasts:* Rebroadcasts WCAI-FM Woods Hole 100%
3 Water Street, Box 3, Woods Hole, MA 02543
(508) 548-9600
www.capeandislands.org
License: Brewster, Barnstable County, MA held by WGBH Educational Foundation.
Nat'l Network: NPR

John Voci, Station Manager

Bridgewater

***WBIM-FM**
11-01-1972; 91.5 MHz FM; *Hrs Open:* 24; 0.18 kw; 72 ft.; N41 59 15 W70 58 21
731 Summer Street, Bridgewater, MA 02325 US
(508) 531-2858; *Fax:* (508) 531-1786
www.bridgew.edu/wbim
wbim@bridgew.edu
License: Bridgewater, Plymouth County, MA held by Bridgewater State College.
Arbitron Metro Market: Bridgewater, MA; *Format:* Variety/Diverse; *Hrs. of News Programming:* news progmg 14 . hrs wkly; *No. News Employees:* 1; *Target Audience:* 18-35; college students & loc residents

Brockton

WXBR
11-27-1946; 1460 kHz AM; 5 kw-D, DAN; 1 kw-N, DAN; N42 2 54 W71 3 20
211 Jason Street, Pittsfield, MA 02101 US
(508) 587-2400; *Fax:* (508) 587-4786
www.1460wxbr.com
License: Brockton, MA held by BTR Boston Inc.
Group Owner: BusinessTalkRadio.Net Inc.; (acq 11-13-2006; $1 million)
Arbitron Metro Market: Brockton, MA; *Format:* News, News/Talk, 84, Talk; *Target Audience:* 35 plus; general; *Adv. Rates:* 16; 12; 9; 6
Richard Muserlian, General Manager
Richard Muserlian, Marketing Specialist

WAAF
07-21-1948; 97.7 MHz FM; 2.05 kw; 568 ft.; N42 12 42 W71 6 51 *Rebroadcasts:* simulcasts WAAF (FM) Westborough 100%
211 Jason Street, Pittsfield, MA 02101 US
(617) 779-5400
www.waaf.com
License: Brockton, Plymouth County, MA held by Entercom Boston License L.L.C.
Group Owner: Entercom Communications Corp.; (acq 12-27-2006; $30 million)
Arbitron Metro Market: Boston, Ma; *Format:* Rock/AOR; *Adv. Rates:* 16; 16; 13; 6
Julie Kahn, General Manager

WMSX
07-17-1961; 1410 kHz AM; 1 kw-D, DA2; 0.156 kw-N, DA2; N42 3 30 W71 2 40
288 Linwood Street, Brockton, MA 02401 US
(508) 587-5454; *Fax:* (508) 537-1903
License: Brockton, MA held by Kingdom Church
Arbitron Metro Market: Boston, MA; *Format:* Spanish

Brookline

WBOS
01-01-1955; 92.9 MHz FM; *Hrs Open:* 24; 18.5 kw; 735 ft.; N42 20 50 W71 4 59
55 Morrissey Boulevard, Boston, NJ 02125 US
(617) 822-9600; *Fax:* (617) 822-6771
www.alt929boston.com
kwest@myradio929.com
License: Brookline, Norfolk County, MA held by Greater Los Angeles Radio Inc.
Group Owner: Greater Media Inc.; (acq 7-23-97)
Nat'l Reps: Katz Radio
Arbitron Metro Market: Boston, MA; *Format:* Triple A; *Hrs. of News Programming:* news progmg 3 hrs wkly; *No. News Employees:* 1; *Target Audience:* 25-49; baby boomers seeking diverse quality music

WUNR
01-01-1947; 1600 kHz AM
60 Temple Place, Boston, MA 02111 US
(617) 367-9003; *Fax:* (617) 367-2265
wunr.com
info@wunr.com
License: Brookline, MA held by Champion Broadcasting System Inc.
Arbitron Metro Market: Boston, MA; *Format:* Ethnic

Cambridge

WHRB
05-01-1957; 95.3 MHz FM; *Hrs Open:* 24; 1.45 kw; 607 ft.; N42 21 8 W71 3 25
389 Harvard Street, Cambridge, MA 02138 US
(617) 495-9472
www.whrb.org
mail@whrb.org
License: Cambridge, Middlesex County, MA held by Harvard Radio Broadcasting Co. Inc.
Arbitron Metro Market: Boston; *Format:* Jazz, Rock/AOR; *Hrs. of News Programming:* News progmg 4 hrs wkly; *Adv. Rates:* 36; 32; 36; 32
Lilli Beard, President
Martin Kiik, General Manager
William Holub-Moorman, Programming Director

WJIB
01-01-1948; 740 kHz AM; *Hrs Open:* 24; 0.25 kw-D, ND1; 0.005 kw-N, ND1; N42 23 13 W71 8 21
443 Concord Avenue, Cambridge, MA 02138 US
(617) 868-7400
License: Cambridge, MA held by Bob Bittner Broadcasting Inc.
Arbitron Metro Market: Boston; *Format:* Adult Contemp *Special Programming:* French 10 hrs, gospel 4 hrs wkly; *Hrs. of News Programming:* News progmg 3 hrs wkly; *Target Audience:* 40-75; locally-programmed for thoseenjoying good adult mus

***WMBR**
04-10-1961; 88.1 MHz FM; *Hrs Open:* 6 AM-2 AM; 0.72 kw; 295 ft.; N42 21 42 W71 5 3
C/O Wmbr, 3 Ames Street, Cambridge, MA 02142 US
(617) 253-4000
License: Cambridge, Middlesex County, MA held by Technology Broadcasting Corp.
Arbitron Metro Market: Boston, MA; *Format:* Variety/Diverse; *Target Audience:* General.
Gloria Apolinario, General Manager
Christopher Bobko, Station Manager
Dugan Hayes, General Manager

Charlton

***WYQQ**
01-01-1976; 90.1 MHz FM; *Hrs Open:* 24; 0.1 kw; 390 ft.; N42 8 1 W71 57 26
57 Muggett Hill Rd, Charlton, MA 01507 US
(508) 248-0049; *Fax:* (508) 248-4518
www.wycm.com
License: Charlton, Worcester County, MA held by Christian Mix Radio Inc.
Arbitron Metro Market: Charlton, MA; *Format:* Christian
Stephen Binley, Station Manager
Judy Pelletier, Promotions Manager

Chatham

WFCC-FM
03-24-1987; 107.5 MHz FM; *Hrs Open:* 24; 50 kw; 341 ft.; N41 44 14 W70 0 40
737 W. Main St., Hyannis, MA 02601 US
(508) 771-1224; *Fax:* (508)775-2065
www.wfcc.com
info@capecodbroadcasting.com
License: Chatham, Barnstable County, MA held by Cape Cod Broadcasting License I LLC
Group Owner: Sandab Communications L.P. II; (acq 1-31-2008; $7.5 million with WOCN-FM Orleans)

Arbitron Metro Market: Chatham, MA; *Format:* Classical; *Hrs. of News Programming:* News progmg 2 hrs wkly; *No. News Employees:* 2; *Target Audience:* 25 plus; upscale, affluent, educated adults

Chicopee

WACE
12-01-1946; 730 kHz AM; *Hrs Open:* 24; 5 kw-D, ND1; 0.008 kw-N, ND1; N42 10 2 W72 37 31
P.O. Box 1, Springfield, MA 01101 US
(413) 594-6654
License: Chicopee, MA held by Carter Broadcasting Corp.
Arbitron Metro Market: Las Vegas NV
Eloy Vera, General Manager

Concord

WBNW
08-28-1989; 1120 kHz AM; *Hrs Open:* 5 AM-10 PM; 5 kw-D, DA2; 1 kw-N, DA2; N42 26 54 W71 25 39
144 Gould Street, Needham, MA 02494 US
(781) 474-5180
www.moneymattersboston.com
License: Concord, MA held by Money Matters Radio Inc.
Regional Reps: New England.
Arbitron Metro Market: Needham, MA; *Format:* News, Talk; *Hrs. of News Programming:* News progmg 17 hrs wkly; *Target Audience:* 35 plus; upscale, suburban families

*WIQH
12-01-1971; 88.3 MHz FM; *Hrs Open:* 1-9:30 PM (M-F); 10 AM-10 PM (S); 0.1 kw horiz; 23 ft.; N42 26 48 W71 20 49
500 Walden Street, Concord, MA 01742 US
(978) 369-2440
www.wiqh.org
License: Concord, Middlesex County, MA held by Concord-Carlisle Regional School District.
Arbitron Metro Market: Boston; *Format:* Rock/AOR; *Target Audience:* 12-21; teenagers
Joe Jacobs, General Manager
Margaret Gill, Co-Programming Director
Holly McGrory, Co-Programming Director

Dedham

WAMG
06-01-2005; 890 kHz AM; *Hrs Open:* 24
122 Green Street, Worcester, MA 01604 US
(508) 791-2111
www.megaboston.com/
igois@goisbroadcasting.com
License: Dedham, MA held by J Sports Licensee LLC
Nat'l Network: ESPN Radio; *Nat'l Reps:* McGavren Guild
Arbitron Metro Market: Worcester, MA; *Format:* Sports; *Target Audience:* 18 plus; males

Dennis

WEII
06-15-1981; 96.3 MHz FM; *Hrs Open:* 24; 25 kw; 297 ft.; N41 43 44 W70 10 2
154 Barnstable Rd., Hyannis, MA 02601 US
(508) 778-2888; *Fax:* (508) 778-9651
License: Dennis, Barnstable County, MA held by AMFM Radio Licenses LLC.
Group Owner: iHeartMedia
Nat'l Reps: Eastman Radio
Arbitron Metro Market: Cape Cod, MA; *Format:* Sports
Richard J. Bressler, President

Dudley

*WXRB
01-01-1975; 95.1 MHz FM; *Hrs Open:* 24; 0.014 kw horiz; 125 ft.; N42 2 40 W71 55 52
501 Washington Street, South Easton, MA 02375 US
(508) 213-2138
www.wxrbfm.com
wxrbfm@yahoo.com
License: Dudley, Worcester County, MA held by WXRB-FM Educational Broadcasting Inc.
Arbitron Metro Market: Whitman, MA; *Format:* Oldies *Special Programming:* Nichols College sports; *Target Audience:* 18 plus.
Peter Q. George, Station Manager

East Longmeadow

WHNP
01-01-1947; 1600 kHz AM; *Hrs Open:* daytime only; 2.5 kw-D, NDD; N42 4 25 W72 31 28 *Rebroadcasts:* simulcast of WHMP (AM) Northampton
15 Hampton Avenue, Northampton, MA 01060 US
(413) 586-7400; *Fax:* (413) 585-0927
www.whmp.com
License: East Longmeadow, MA held by Saga Communications of New England LLC.
Group Owner: Saga Communications Inc.; (acq 6-2-92; grpsl).
Nat'l Network: CBS Radio; *Wire Services:* AP
Arbitron Metro Market: Springfield, MA; *Format:* News, News/Talk, 86; *Target Audience:* 18-49; upscale young adults
Dave Musante, General Manager
Denise Vozella, News Director

Easthampton

WWEI
10-01-1967; 105.5 MHz FM; *Hrs Open:* 24; 720 w horiz, 706 w vert; Ant 918 ft; N42 14 29 W72 38 57 *Rebroadcasts:* Simulcast with WEEI (AM) Boston 100%
20 Guest Street, Brighton, MA 02135
(617) 779-3500
www.weei.com
License: Easthampton, Hampshire County, MA held by Entercom Springfield License LLC.
Group Owner: Entercom Communications Corp.; (acq 9-5-2007; $5.75 million)
Nat'l Network: Fox Sports; Westwood One; *Nat'l Reps:* D & R Radio; Interep
Population Served: 139,000; *Arbitron Metro Market:* Springfield, MA; *Format:* Sports; *Target Audience:* 25-54; men; adults

Easton

*WSHL-FM
01-01-1973; 91.3 MHz FM; *Hrs Open:* 24; 0.1 kw; 66 ft.; N42 3 27 W71 4 47
320 Washington Street, Easton, MA 02356 US
(508) 565-1919; *Fax:* (508) 565-1974
www.stonehill.edu
License: Easton, Bristol County, MA held by Stonehill College.
Wire Services: UPI
Format: Variety/Diverse; *Target Audience:* 19-30.

Everett

WKOX
01-20-1952; 1430 kHz AM; *Hrs Open:* 24; 5 kw-D, 1 kw-N, DA-N; N42 24 11 W71 04 29
10 Cabot Road, Suite 302, Medford, MA 02155 US
(781) 663-2500; *Fax:* (781) 290-0722
www.talk1430.com
License: Everett, Middlesex County, MA held by AMFM Radio Licenses L.L.C.
Group Owner: iHeartMedia; (acq 8-30-2000; grpsl)
Population Served: 743,900; *Arbitron Metro Market:* Boston; *Format:* Talk
Alan Chartrand, Market President

Fairhaven

WFHN
03-01-1989; 107.1 MHz FM; *Hrs Open:* 24; 5.4 kw; 344 ft.; N41 38 25 W70 55 3
1750 Rockville Pike, Suite 20, Rockville, MD 20852 US
(508) 999-6690; *Fax:* (508) 999-1420
www.fun107.com
jr.reitz@townsquaremedia.com
License: Fairhaven, Bristol County, MA
Group Owner: Townsquare Media; (acq 2-23-00; grpsl).
Nat'l Reps: McGavren Guild
Arbitron Metro Market: Fairhaven, MA; *Format:* Contemporary Hits/Top 40; *Target Audience:* 18-49.
Wayne Leland, President
Gail Leblanc, General Manager and Director of Sales
JR Reitz, Brand Manager

Fall River

WHTB
05-13-1948; 1400 kHz AM; *Hrs Open:* 5 AM-11 PM; 1 kw-U, ND1; N41 41 23 W71 8 43
456 Rock Street, Fall River, MA 02722 US
(508) 678-9727; *Fax:* (508) 673-0310
License: Fall River, MA held by SNE Broadcasting Ltd.
Nat'l Reps: McGavren Guild
Arbitron Metro Market: Providence-Warwick-Pawtucket, RI; *Format:* Ethnic, Talk *Special Programming:* English 10 hrs, Pol one hr, Cambodian one hr, Fr o; *Target Audience:* 25-64; Portuguese (ethnic); *Adv. Rates:* 24;22; 20; 18
Robert Karam, President

WSAR
01-01-1921; 1480 kHz AM; 5 kw-U, DA1; N41 43 26 W71 11 21
1 Home Street, Somerset, MA 02725 US
(508) 678-9727; *Fax:* (508) 673-0310
www.wsar.com
hector@wsar.com
License: Fall River, MA held by Bristol County Broadcasting Inc.
Arbitron Metro Market: Providence-Warw; *Format:* News, News/Talk, 84, Talk *Special Programming:* Por 3 hrs wkly; *Target Audience:* 25 plus.
Ric Oliveira, General Manager

Falmouth

WCIB
01-01-1970; 101.9 MHz FM; 50 kw; 479 ft.; N41 33 31 W70 35 46
154 Barnstable Road, Hyannis, MA 02601 US
(508) 778-2888; *Fax:* (508) 778-9651
www.cool102.com
License: Falmouth, Barnstable County, MA held by AMFM Radio Licenses LLC
Group Owner: iHeartMedia
Nat'l Reps: Eastman Radio
Arbitron Metro Market: Cape Cod, MA; *Format:* Contemporary Hits/Top 40, Adult Contemp; *Target Audience:* 25-54.
Richard J. Bressler, President

*WFPB-FM
01-01-1996; 91.9 MHz FM; 0.3 kw horiz, 6 kw vert; 250 ft.; N41 36 50 W70 35 56 *Rebroadcasts:* Rebroadcasts WUMB-FM Boston 100%
100 Morrissey Blvd., Boston, MA 02125 US
(617) 287-6900; *Fax:* (617) 287-6916
www.wumb.org
wumb@umb.edu
License: Falmouth, Barnstable County, MA held by University of Massachusetts.
Nat'l Network: NPR
Format: Variety/Diverse
Patricia Domeniconi, General Manager
Jay Moberg, Programming Director

Fitchburg

WPKZ
10-06-1941; 1280 kHz AM; *Hrs Open:* 24; 5 kw-D, DA2; 1 kw-N, DA2; N42 35 40 W71 50 12
762 Water Street, Fitchburg, MA 01420 US
(978) 343-3766; *Fax:* (978) 345-6397
www.wpkz.net/
License: Fitchburg, MA held by Central Broadcasting Co. LLC
Nat'l Network: ABC
Arbitron Metro Market: Fitchburg, MA; *Format:* Sports, Talk; *Hrs. of News Programming:* news progmg 10 hrs wkly; *No. News Employees:* 2; *Target Audience:* 28 plus; loc listeners in the heart of New England *Adv.Rates:* 30; 20; 30; 10

WFGL
02-01-1950; 960 kHz AM; *Hrs Open:* 24; 2.5 kw-D, DA2; 1 kw-N, DA2; N42 35 24 W71 49 43 *Rebroadcasts:* Rebroadcasts WRYP (FM)
356 Broad St, Fitchburg, MA 01420 US
(978) 665-9111; *Fax:* (978) 696-0610
info@renewfm.org
License: Fitchburg, MA held by Horizon Christian Fellowship
Group Owner: Horizon Christian Fellowship
Arbitron Metro Market: Fitchburg, MA; *Format:* Christian, Religious; *Target Audience:* 25-54

WXLO
08-01-1960; 104.5 MHz FM; *Hrs Open:* 24; 37 kw; 564 ft.; N42 30 27 W71 49 37
250 Commercial St., Suite 530, Worceser, MA 01608 US
(508) 752-1045; *Fax:* (508) 793-0824
www.wxlo.com
License: Fitchburg, MA held by Radio License Holding CBC, LLC
Group Owner: Cumulus Media Inc.
Arbitron Metro Market: Worcester, MA; *Format:* Adult Contemp
Lance Ballance, Operations Dir
Bob Goodell, VP/Market Manager

*WXPL
08-01-1985; 91.3 MHz FM; 0.1 kw; -135 ft.; N42 35 18 W71 47 26
160 Pearl Street, Fitchburg, MA 01420 US
(978) 665-3163; *Fax:* (978) 665-3693
License: Fitchburg, Worcester County, MA held by Fitchburg State College.
Arbitron Metro Market: Fitchburg, MA; *Format:* Triple A; *Target Audience:* 16-25.

Framingham

***WDJM-FM**
01-01-1973; 91.3 MHz FM; 0.1 kw; 89 ft.; N42 17 44 W71 26 18
100 State Street, Framingham, MA 01701 US
(508) 626-4622; *Fax:* (508) 626-4939
wdjmfm@gmail.com
License: Framingham, Middlesex County, MA held by Framingham State College.
Arbitron Metro Market: Boston, MA; *Format:* Alternative; *Target Audience:* 15-35; college, surrounding community & commuters

WROR-FM
01-01-1959; 105.7 MHz FM; 23 kw; 735 ft.; N42 20 50 W71 4 59
55 Morrissey Boulevard, Boston, MA 02125 US
(617) 822-9600; *Fax:* (617) 822-6471
www.wror.com
License: Framingham, Middlesex County, MA held by Greater Boston Radio Inc.
Group Owner: Beasley Broadcast Group; (acq 10-11-96)
Arbitron Metro Market: Boston; *Format:* Contemporary Hits/Top 40, Adult Contemp; *Target Audience:* 25-54.

Franklin

***WGAO**
01-01-1975; 88.3 MHz FM; 0.175 kw; 190 ft.; N42 5 8 W71 23 54
99 Main Street, Franklin, MA 02038 US
(508) 528-4210; *Fax:* (508) 528-7846
www.dean.edu
License: Franklin, Norfolk County, MA held by Dean College.
Nat'l Network: AP Radio
Arbitron Metro Market: Boston; *Format:* Classic Rock *Special Programming:* Relg 8 hrs wkly; *Target Audience:* 15-25.

Gardner

WGAW
01-01-1946; 1340 kHz AM; 1 kw-U, ND1; N42 35 33 W71 59 20
362 Green Street, Gardner, MA 01440 US
(978) 632-1340; *Fax:* (978) 632-1332
www.wgaw1340.com
License: Gardner, MA held by County Broadcasting Co. LLC.
Group Owner: Northeast Broadcasting Company Inc.; (acq 12-2-2003; $235,000).
Nat'l Network: ABC
Format: News, News/Talk, 86

***WJWT**
91.7 MHz FM; 0.85 kw H 0.85 kw V; 276 ft.; N42 33 29 W72 3 6
Rebroadcasts: Rebroadcasts WRYP (FM)
365 Broad St, Fitchburg, MA 01420 US
(714) 825-9663; *Fax:* (714) 825-9661
www.renewfm.org
info@renewfm.org
License: Gardner, Worcester County, MA held by Horizon Christian Fellowship
Group Owner: Horizon Christian Fellowship
Arbitron Metro Market: Gardner, MA; *Format:* Christian, Religious

Gloucester

WBOQ
09-14-1964; 104.9 MHz FM; *Hrs Open:* 24; 3.2 kw; 446 ft.; N42 35 36 W70 43 28
8 Enron Street, Beverly, MA 01915 US
(978) 927-1049; *Fax:* (978) 921-2635
www.northshore1049.com
promo@northshore1049.com
License: Gloucester, Essex County, MA held by Westport Communications L.P.
Arbitron Metro Market: Beverly, MA; *Format:* News, Sports; *Hrs. of News Programming:* News progmg 3 hrs wkly; *Target Audience:* 25-54; mass appeal classical favorites
Todd Tanger, President

Great Barrington

***WAMQ**
11-01-1988; 105.1 MHz FM; *Hrs Open:* 24; 0.73 kw; 919 ft.; N42 9 36 W73 28 48 *Rebroadcasts:* Rebroadcasts WAMC-FM Albany, N.Y. 100%
318 Central Avenue, Albany, NY 12206 US
(800) 323-9262
www.wamc.org
mail@wamc.org
License: Great Barrington, Berkshire County, MA held by WAMC.
Group Owner: WAMC/Northeast Public Radio; (acq 3-5-93; $325,000;
Nat'l Network: NPR; PRI; *Wire Services:* AP
Arbitron Metro Market: Great Barrington, MA; *Format:* News, News/Talk, 86 *Special Programming:* Folk 7 hrs, jazz 13 wkly; *Target Audience:* General.

WSBS
12-01-1956; 860 kHz AM; *Hrs Open:* 24; 2.7 kW; N42 12 53 W73 20 43
425 Stockbridge Rd., Great Barrington, MA 01230 USA
(413) 528-0860; *Fax:* (413) 528-2162
www.wsbs.com
License: Great Barrington, MA held by Berkshire Broadcasting Co. Inc.
Group Owner: amma Broadcasting LLC
Nat'l Network: AP Radio; *Nat'l Reps:* D & R Radio; *Wire Services:* AP
Format: Adult Contemp, Talk; *Hrs. of News Programming:* news progmg 10 hrs wkly; *No. News Employees:* 3; *Target Audience:* 25 plus; general
Peter Barry, Vice President
Dave Isby, General Sales Mgr
Jesse Stewart, Programming Director
Tom Conklin, News Director

Greenfield

WIZZ
08-26-1980; 1520 kHz AM; 10 kw-D, DAD; N42 36 12 W72 36 21
Mailing Address: P. O. Box 983, Claremont, NH 01302 US
Second Address: 369 S. Shelburne Rd., Greenfield, MA 1370
(413) 774-5757
www.wizzradio.com
phild@wizzradio.com
License: Greenfield, MA held by P. & M. Radio LLC
Nat'l Network: AP Network News
Format: Oldies
Phillip Drumheller, President/Owner/General Manager

WHMQ
05-15-1938; 1240 kHz AM; *Hrs Open:* 24; 1 kw-U; N42 35 21 W72 37 08 *Rebroadcasts:* Rebroadcasts WHMP(AM) Northampton 100%
15 Hampton Ave., Northampton, MA 01301
(413) 586-7400; *Fax:* (413) 585-0927
License: Greenfield, Franklin County, MA held by Saga Communications of New England LLC.
Group Owner: Saga Communications Inc.; (acq 4-1-2001; $2.2 million with co-located FM)
Nat'l Network: CBS Radio; *Wire Services:* AP
Population Served: 65,000 *Hrs. of News Programming:* news progmg 20 hrs wkly; *No. News Employees:* 2; *Target Audience:* 35 plus.; *Adv. Rates:* 40; 28; 34; 23
Barbara Kuschka, Operations Dir
David Musante, General Manager
David Musante, General Sales Mgr
Denise Uozella, News Director

WHAI
05-15-1948; 98.3 MHz FM; *Hrs Open:* 24; 2 kw; 404 ft.; N42 34 15 W72 38 42
81 Woodard Road, Greenfield, MA 01301 US
(413) 774-4301; *Fax:* (413) 773-5637
whai.com
info@whai.com
License: Greenfield, Franklin County, MA held by Saga Communications of New England LLC.
Group Owner: Saga Communications Inc.
Format: Adult Contemp; *No. News Employees:* 1; *Target Audience:* 25-54.; *Adv. Rates:* 40; 32; 32; 20
Dan Guin, General Manager
Nick Danjer, Brand Manager

WPVQ
07-26-1981; 95.3 MHz FM; *Hrs Open:* 24; 0.57 kw; 761 ft.; N42 41 50 W72 36 20
81 Woodard Road, Greenfield, MA 01301 US
(413) 774-4301; *Fax:* (413) 773-5637
www.bear953.com
info@whai.com
License: Greenfield, Franklin County, MA held by Saga Communications of New England LLC.
Group Owner: Saga Communications Inc.; (acq 2-13-2004; grpsl).
Format: Country; *Target Audience:* 18-45.
Dan Guin, General Manager
Nick Danjer, Brand Manager

Harwich Port

WFRQ
93.5 MHz FM
234 South Street, Hyannis, MA 02601 US
(508) 778-6000
License: Harwich Port, Barnstable County, MA
Group Owner: Codcomm Inc.

Haverhill

WCEC
01-01-1947; 1490 kHz AM; *Hrs Open:* 24; 1 kw-U, ND1; N42 46 22 W71 6 1
462 Merrimack St., Methuen, MA 01844 US
(978) 686-9966
www.impacto1490.com
WCEC impacto@costaeagleradio.com
License: Haverhill, MA held by Costa-Eagle Radio Ventures L.P.
Group Owner: Costa-Eagle Radio Ventures L.P.; (acq 1998)
Nat'l Reps: Roslin
Arbitron Metro Market: Boston; *Format:* Talk; *Target Audience:* Sp speaking.

Holliston

***WHHB**
04-17-1979; 99.9 MHz FM; 0.017 kw; 203 ft.; N42 12 42 W71 26 36
370 Hollis Street, Holliston, MA 01746 US
(508) 429-0677; *Fax:* (508) 429-8225
License: Holliston, Middlesex County, MA held by Holliston High School.
Format: Variety/Diverse
Christopher Murphy, General Manager

Holyoke

***WCCH**
01-01-1977; 103.5 MHz FM; *Hrs Open:* 6 AM-11 PM; 0.009 kw; 259 ft.; N42 11 55 W72 38 27
303 Homestead Avenue, Holyoke, MA 01040 US
(413) 538-7000
License: Holyoke, Hampden County, MA held by Holyoke Community College.
Arbitron Metro Market: Springfield, MA; *Format:* Variety/Diverse

Hyannis

WCOD-FM
06-02-1967; 106.1 MHz FM; *Hrs Open:* 24; 50 kw; 430 ft.; N41 43 44 W70 10 2
278 South Sea Ave., West Yarmouth, MA 02673 US
(508) 760-5252; *Fax:* (508) 760-5353
www.106wcod.com
License: Hyannis, Barnstable County, MA held by AMFM Radio Licenses LLC.
Group Owner: iHeartMedia
Nat'l Reps: Eastman Radio
Arbitron Metro Market: Cape Cod, MA; *Format:* Adult Contemp; *No. News Employees:* 2; *Target Audience:* 25-54.
Richard J. Bressler, President

WPXC
01-09-1987; 102.9 MHz FM; *Hrs Open:* 24; 3.1 kw; 463 ft.; N41 41 20 W70 20 49
154 Barnstable Road, Hyannis, MA 02601 US
(508) 775-5678; *Fax:* (508) 862-6329
www.pixy103.com
License: Hyannis, Barnstable County, MA
Group Owner: Codcomm Inc.; (acq 11-8-2005; grpsl)
Nat'l Reps: McGavren Guild
Arbitron Metro Market: Cape Cod, MA; *Hrs. of News Programming:* news progmg 4 hrs wkly; *No. News Employees:* 3; *Target Audience:* General.
Jake Demmin, General Manager
Suzanne Tonaire, Programming Director

Lawrence

WNNW
08-01-1947; 800 kHz AM; *Hrs Open:* 24
462 Merrimack St., Methuen, MA 01844 US
(978) 688-8000
www.power800am.com
License: Lawrence, MA held by Costa-Eagle Radio Ventures L.P.
Group Owner: Costa-Eagle Radio Ventures L.P.; acq 3-27-98; $405,000).
Nat'l Network: CNN Radio; *Nat'l Reps:* Lotus Entravision Reps LLC; *Wire Services:* AP
Arbitron Metro Market: Methuen, MA; *Hrs. of News Programming:* news progmg 10 hrs wkly; *No. News Employees:* 2; *Target Audience:* 35-64; general; *Adv. Rates:* 100; 75; 100; 35

WEEI(FM)
04-01-1960; 93.7 MHz FM; *Hrs Open:* 24; 50 kw; 430 ft; N42 40 26 W71 11 26
Entercom Boston, 20 Guest St., 3rd Fl., Brighton, MA 2135
(617) 779-5300; *Fax:* (617) 931-7827
www.937mikefm.com
info@937mikefm.com
License: Lawrence, Essex County, MA held by Entercom Boston II License L.L.C.
Group Owner: Entercom Communications Corp.; (acq 10-15-98; grpsl)
Population Served: 300,000; *Arbitron Metro Market:* Boston; *Format:* Sports; *Target Audience:* 25-54.
Julie Kahn, General Manager
Christina Anders, Promotions Manager

WEEI-FM
10-17-1967; 93.7 MHz FM; *Hrs Open:* 24; 34 kw; 584 ft.; N42 31 53 W70 59 12
401 City Avenue, Suite 409, Bala Cynwyd, PA 19004 US
(401) 751-9334; *Fax:* (401) 351-8109
www.weei.com/weei/
info@weei.com
License: Lawrence, Washington County, MA held by Entercom Providence License LLC.
Group Owner: Entercom Communications Corp.; (acq 6-15-2004; $14.5 million).
Nat'l Network: Westwood One
Arbitron Metro Market: Providence, RI; *Format:* Sports, Talk; *No. News Employees:* 1; *Target Audience:* 25-49.
Joseph Field, Chairman
David Field, CEO
Joseph Harrington, Station Manager
Rod Morrison, Promotions Manager

Leicester

WVNE
06-19-1991; 760 kHz AM; *Hrs Open:* Sunrise-sunset; 8.6 kw-C, NDD; 25 kw-D, NDD; N42 14 57 W72 4 41
70 James St., Suite 201, Worcester, MA 01603 US
(508) 831-9863; *Fax:* (508) 831-7964
www.lifechangingradio.com
License: Leicester, Worcester County, MA held by Blount Masscom Inc.
Group Owner: Blount Communications Group; (acq 5-15-90;
Nat'l Network: Salem Radio Network
Arbitron Metro Market: Leicester, MA; *Format:* Christian, Religious; *Target Audience:* 25-54.; *Adv. Rates:* 25.20; 15.30; 25.20; na
William Blount, President
Emanuel DaCunha, Programming Director

Leominster

WCMX
11-13-1967; 1000 kHz AM; *Hrs Open:* 6 AM-2 hrs past sundown; 1 kw-D, NDD; N42 31 25 W71 44 7
194 Electric Avenue, Lunenburg, MA 01462 US
(978) 582-8282; *Fax:* (978) 582-4978
License: Leominster, MA held by Twin City Baptist Temple Inc.
Nat'l Network: Salem Radio Network
Arbitron Metro Market: Lunenburg, MA; *Format:* Christian; *Hrs. of News Programming:* News progmg 7 hrs wkly; *Target Audience:* 35-54 women.; *Adv. Rates:* 12; 10; 12; 8

Lowell

WCAP
06-10-1951; 980 kHz AM; *Hrs Open:* 24; 5 kw-D, DA2; 5 kw-N, DA2; N42 39 16 W71 21 43
243 Central Street, Lowell, MA 01852 US
(978) 454-0404; *Fax:* (978) 458-9124
www.980wcap.com
sam@980wcap.com
License: Lowell, MA held by Merrimack Valley Radio LLC
Nat'l Network: ABC *Regional Reps:* LOCAL; *Wire Services:* AP
Arbitron Metro Market: Lowell, Ma; *Format:* News, Talk; *Hrs. of News Programming:* News progmg 20 hrs wkly; *Target Audience:* 25 plus; business people, professionals, factory workers, housewives; *Adv. Rates:* 60; 40;60; 40
Ryan Johnston, Operations Dir

***WUML**
11-06-1967; 91.5 MHz FM; *Hrs Open:* 18; 1.4 kw; 207 ft.; N42 39 7 W71 19 15
1 University Avenue, Lowell, MA 01854 US
(978) 934-4969
www.wuml.org
wuml@wuml.org
License: Lowell, Middlesex County, MA held by University of Massachusetts-Lowell Board of Trustees.
Arbitron Metro Market: Boston; *Format:* Variety/Diverse; *Target Audience:* 16-25.
Nate Osit, General Manager
Joe Keefe, Programming Director

WCRB
01-01-1947; 99.5 MHz FM; 27 kw; 653 ft.; N42 39 14 W71 13 2
P.O. 1059, East Brunswick, NJ 08816 US
(781) 893-7080; *Fax:* (781) 893-0038
www.wcrb.com
License: Lowell, Middlesex County, MA held by WGBH Educational Foundation
Arbitron Metro Market: Boston; *Format:* Classical; *Target Audience:* 30-64; adults
Nancy Dieterich, General Manager
Mark Edwards, Programming Director
Tim Neill, Promotions Manager

WLLH
06-01-2005; 1400 kHz AM; *Hrs Open:* 24; 1 kw-U, ND1; N42 42 27 W71 9 51
8121 Georgia Avenue, 10th Floor, Silver Spring, MD 20910 US
(617) 830-1000
License: Lowell, MA held by J Sports Licensee LLC
Nat'l Network: ESPN Radio; *Nat'l Reps:* McGavren Guild
Arbitron Metro Market: Boston; *Format:* Sports; *Target Audience:* Males 18+.
Jessamy Tang, General Manager
Neil Kelleher, General Sales Mgr
Kara Lachance, Programming Director
Len Weiner, Programming Director

Lynn

WBWL
08-05-1963; 101.7 MHz FM; *Hrs Open:* 24; 1.7 kw; 626 ft; N42 21 08 W71 03 25
10 Cabot Rd., Suite 302, Medford, MA 02155
(781) 663-2500; *Fax:* (781) 290-0722
www.thebull1017.com
feedback@thebull1017.com
License: Lynn, Essex County, MA held by AMFM Radio Licenses LLC
Group Owner: iHeartMedia
Nat'l Reps: McGavren Guild; *Wire Services:* AP
Population Served: 3,880,000; *Arbitron Metro Market:* Boston, MA; *Format:* Country *Special Programming:* Jazz 8 hrs, loc music 2 hrs wkly; *Hrs. of News Programming:* news progmg 2 hrs wkly *No. News Employees:* 1; *Target Audience:* 18-49; well-educated, affluent & socially active trend setters
Alan Chartrand, Market President
Dylan Sprague, Vice President of Programming

WLYN
11-01-1947; 1360 kHz AM; *Hrs Open:* 24; 700 w-D, 76 w-N; N42 27 17 W70 58 44
27 William St., 11th Floor, New York, NY 10005 US
(212) 966-1059; *Fax:* (212) 625-2894
www.mrbi.net
License: Lynn, Essex County, MA held by Multicultural Radio Broadcasting Licensee LLC.
Group Owner: Multicultural Radio Broadcasting Inc.; (acq 8-7-2002; $1.78 million)
Population Served: 3,000,000; *Arbitron Metro Market:* Boston; *Format:* Ethnic; *Target Audience:* Hispanic (Spanish & Portuguese); *Adv. Rates:* 50; 50; 50; 50
Arthur Liu, CEO/COO

Marion

***WWTA**
01-01-1996; 88.5 MHz FM; 0.1 kw; 52 ft.; N41 42 32 W70 45 57
Front Street, Marion, MA 02738 US
(508) 748-2000; *Fax:* (508) 291-6666
www.taboracademy.org
kkistler@taboracademy.org
License: Marion, Plymouth County, MA held by Tabor Academy.
Arbitron Metro Market: Marion, MA; *Format:* Variety/Diverse
Karl Kistler, General Manager

Marshfield

WATD-FM
12-05-1977; 95.9 MHz FM; *Hrs Open:* 24; 1.6 kw; 469 ft.; N42 6 39 W70 42 17
130 Enterprise Drive, Marshfield, MA 02050 US
(781) 837-1166; *Fax:* (781) 837-1978
www.959watd.com
news@959watd.com
License: Marshfield, Plymouth County, MA held by Marshfield Broadcasting Co.
Arbitron Metro Market: Boston.MA; *Format:* Adult Contemp, Blues, 64; *Hrs. of News Programming:* news progmg 10 hrs wkly; *No. News Employees:* 2; *Target Audience:* 25-64; South Shore residents
Edward Perry, Jr, President

Mashpee

WHYA(FM)
02-12-1987; 101.1 MHz FM; *Hrs Open:* 24; 3.7 kw; Ant 253 ft; N41 36 50 W70 35 56 *Rebroadcasts:* Rebroadcasts WFQR(FM) Harwich Port 100%
278 South Sea Ave., West Yarmouth, MA 2673
(508) 775-5678; *Fax:* (508) 862-6329
www.frankplaysitall.com
License: Mashpee, Barnstable County, MA held by Codcomm Inc
Group Owner: Codcomm Inc.; (acq 11-7-2005; grpsl)
Nat'l Reps: Katz Radio
Arbitron Metro Market: Cape Cod, MA; *No. News Employees:* 1; *Target Audience:* 35-64.
Terri Gamble, General Manager

Maynard

***WAVM**
04-01-1973; 91.7 MHz FM; *Hrs Open:* 24; 0.5 kw horiz; 77 ft.; N42 25 17 W71 27 10
Wavm - 1 Tiger Drive, Maynard, MA 01754 US
(978) 897-5213
www.wavm.org
License: Maynard, Middlesex County, MA held by Maynard Public Schools.
Format: Oldies
Steven Silberberg, President
Roger Ingram, General Manager

Medford

***WMFO**
03-01-1971; 91.5 MHz FM; 0.125 kw; 135 ft.; N42 24 27 W71 7 15
Mailing Address: 44 Professors Row, Room 110, Medford, MA 02155 US
Second Address: 474 Boston Ave., Medford, MA 2155
(617) 625-0800; *Fax:* (617) 625-6072
www.wmfo.org
wmfo@wmfo.org
License: Medford, Middlesex County, MA held by Tufts University.
Arbitron Metro Market: Boston, MA; *Format:* Variety/Diverse
Annie Ross, General Manager

WXKS-FM
09-01-1960; 107.9 MHz FM; *Hrs Open:* 24; 20.5 kw; 771 ft.; N42 20 50 W71 4 59
10 Cabot Road, Suite 302, Medford, MA 02155 US
(781) 396-1430; *Fax:* (781) 290-0722
www.kiss108.com
feedback@kiss108.com
License: Medford, Middlesex County, MA held by AMFM Radio Licenses L.L.C.
Group Owner: iHeartMedia
Arbitron Metro Market: Medford, MA; *Format:* Contemporary Hits/Top 40; *Target Audience:* 25-54.
Alan Chartrand, Market President

Middleborough Center

WVBF
01-01-1993; 1530 kHz AM; *Hrs Open:* 24
Mailing Address: 123 Broadway, Taunton, MA 02780 US
Second Address: 130 Enterprise Dr., Marshfield, MA 2050
(508) 822-1106
www.hometowntalkradio.com
WVBF1530@hotmail.com
License: Middleborough Center, MA held by Steven J. Callahan.
Nat'l Network: Westwood One; NBC Radio
Arbitron Metro Market: Taunton, MA; *Format:* Public Affairs, News
Tony Lopes, General Manager

Milford

WMRC
10-06-1956; 1490 kHz AM; *Hrs Open:* 24; 1 kw-U, ND1; N42 8 12 W71 30 50
258 Main Street, Milford, MA 01757 US
(508) 473-1490
www.wmrcdailynews.com
wmrc@wmrcdailnews.comÿ
License: Milford, MA held by First Class Radio Corp.

Arbitron Metro Market: Worcester, MA; *Format:* Adult Contemp; *Hrs. of News Programming:* news progmg 32 hrs wkly; *No. News Employees:* 2; *Target Audience:* 25-54.; *Adv. Rates:* 36; 24; 36; 24
Thomas McAuliffe Sr., President
Rick Michaels, Operations Dir
Thomas McAuliffe II, General Manager
Ray Auger, Promotions Manager
Ed Thompson, News Director

Milton

*WMLN-FM
04-01-1975; 91.5 MHz FM; *Hrs Open:* 24; 0.17 kw; 95 ft.; N42 14 28 W71 6 52
1071 Blue Hill Avenue, Milton, MA 02186 US
(617) 333-0500
License: Milton, Norfolk County, MA held by Curry College.
Nat'l Network: CNN Radio; *Wire Services:* AP
Arbitron Metro Market: Boston, MA; *Format:* Adult Contemp, News, 62, Talk, Variety/Diverse; *Hrs. of News Programming:* News progmg 15 hrs wkly; *Target Audience:* General.
Alan Frank, General Manager

Nahant

WESX
01-01-1939; 1230 kHz AM
90 Everett Avenue, Chelsea, MA 02150 US
(617) 884-4500; *Fax:* (617) 884-4515
www.wesx1230am.com
info@wesx1230am.com
License: Nahant, MA held by North Shore Broadcasting Corp.
Nat'l Network: ABC; Westwood One; *Wire Services:* AP
Arbitron Metro Market: Nahant, MA; *Format:* Ethnic *Special Programming:* Auto repair 2 hrs, gardening 2 hrs, home improvement 2 hrs, restaurant/dining 2 hrs, Pol 2 hrs wkly; *Hrs. of News Programming:* news progmg 25 hrswkly; *No. News Employees:* 2; *Target Audience:* 35 plus; general; *Adv. Rates:* 55; 31; 55; 17
Charles Banta, General Manager

Nantucket

*WNAN
03-15-2000; 91.1 MHz FM; 2.3 kw vert; 210 ft.; N41 17 6 W70 8 39 *Rebroadcasts:* Rebroadcasts WCAI-FM Woods Hole 100%
Mailing Address: 125 Western Avenue, Boston, MA 02134 US
Second Address: 3 Water St., Woods Hole, MA 2543
(508) 548-9600; *Fax:* (508) 548-5517
www.wgbh.org
cainan@wgbh.org
License: Nantucket, Nantucket County, MA held by WGBH Educational Foundation.
Nat'l Network: NPR
Arbitron Metro Market: Nantucket, MA; *Format:* News, News/Talk, 86
John Voci, Station Manager

*WNCK
06-28-2002; 89.5 MHz FM; *Hrs Open:* 24; 0.078 kw horiz, 0.5 kw vert; 118 ft.; N41 17 6 W70 8 39 *Rebroadcasts:* Rebroadcasts WGBH(FM) Boston 100%
19 Old South Road, Nantucket, MA 02554 US
(617) 300-2000; *Fax:* (617) 300-1025
License: Nantucket, Nantucket County, MA held by Nantucket Public Radio Inc.
Arbitron Metro Market: Boston, MA; *Format:* Variety/Diverse; *Target Audience:* 40 plus.
Benjamin Godley, COO
Jonathan C. Abbott, President and Chief Executive Officer
David Bernstein, Vice President and General Manager
Winifred Lenihan, Promotions Manager
Michael Foti, Engineering Dir
Margaret Drain, Vice Presidentfor National Programming
Jeanne M. Hopkins, Vice President, Communications and Government Rela
Joseph M. Igoe, Vice President and Chief Technology Officer
Susan L. Kantrowitz, Vice President and General Counsel
Vinay Mehra, Chief FinancialOfficer, Vice President for Financ

WAZK
06-13-2012; 97.7 mhz; 1750 w; 236 ft; N41 17 06 W70 08 25
19 Old South Road, Nantucket, MA
(508)228-9770
www.ackfm.com
info@ackfm.com
License: Nantucket, MA
Group Owner: Vertical Resources LLC
Justin Tyler, Operations Dir
Jennifer McAllister, Business Manager
Lauren Sleeth, General Sales Mgr

Natick

WQOM
11-01-1972; 1060 kHz AM; *Hrs Open:* 24; 40 kw-D, 2.5 kw-N, 22 kw-CH, DA-3; N42 17 17 W71 25 55
6325 Sheridan Drive, Williamsville, NY 14221
(508) 820-2430
www.wbix.com
alex@wbix.com
License: Natick, Middlesex County, MA held by WBIX Corp.
Group Owner: Langer Broadcasting Group L.L.C.; (acq 11-29-2005).
Population Served: 2,900,000; *Arbitron Metro Market:* Boston
Alex Langer, General Manager
Jim Harris, General Sales Mgr

New Bedford

WBSM
07-17-1949; 1420 kHz AM; 5 kw-D, DA2; 1 kw-N, DA2; N41 39 2 W70 54 58
1750 Rockville Pike, Suite 20, Rockville, MD 20852 US
(508) 999-6690; *Fax:* (508) 999-1420
www.wbsm.com
pete.braley@townsquaremedia.com
License: New Bedford, MA
Group Owner: Townsquare Media; (acq 4-26-2001; grpsl)
Nat'l Reps: Christal
Arbitron Metro Market: Fairhaven, MA; *Format:* News, News/Talk, 84, Talk
Gail Le Blanc, General Manager
Gail LeBlanc, Director of Sales
Pete Braley, Programming Director
Deborah Aguiar, Promotions Manager

WCTK
12-09-1946; 98.1 MHz FM; *Hrs Open:* 24; 47.3 kw; 508 ft; N41 37 21 W70 55 07
75 Oxford St., Providence, RI 17604
(401) 467-4366
www.wctk.com
twall@hallradio.com
License: New Bedford, Bristol County, MA held by Hall Communications Inc.
Group Owner: Hall Communications Inc.
Nat'l Reps: Eastman Radio
Population Served: 1,594,300; *Arbitron Metro Market:* Providence-Warwick-Pawtucket, RI; *Target Audience:* 25-54.; *Adv. Rates:* 140; 130; 130; 50
Tom Wall, Vice President
Bob Walker, Programming Director
Briget D'Antonio, Promotions Manager

WJFD-FM
02-22-1949; 97.3 MHz FM; *Hrs Open:* 24; 50 kw; 499 ft.; N41 38 20 W70 52 27
651 Orchard Street, New Bedford, MA 02744 US
(508) 997-2929; *Fax:* (508) 990-3893
www.wjfd.com
claudia@wjfd.com
License: New Bedford, Bristol County, MA held by Edmund Dinis, trustee
Arbitron Metro Market: Providence-Warwick-Pawtucket, RI; *Format:* Ethnic; *Target Audience:* General; Portuguese-speaking community
Jorge Morais, General Manager

WNBH
05-21-1921; 1340 kHz AM; *Hrs Open:* 24; 1 kw-U, ND1; N41 37 21 W70 55 7 *Rebroadcasts:* Simulcast with WLKW(AM) West Warwick, RI
75 Oxford Street, Providence, RI 02905 US
(401) 467-4366
www.wnbhradio.com
twall@hallradio.com
License: New Bedford, MA held by Hall Communications Inc.
Group Owner: Hall Communications Inc.; (acq 10-1-66)
Nat'l Network: ESPN Radio; *Nat'l Reps:* Eastman Radio
Arbitron Metro Market: Providence,RI; *Format:* Sports *Special Programming:* Pol 2 hrs wkly; *Hrs. of News Programming:* News progmg 3 hrs wkly; *Target Audience:* Men 25-54; *Adv. Rates:* 30; 20; 20; 10
Bonnie Rowbotham, Chairman
Arthur Rowbotham, President
Tom Wall, Operations Dir

*WFHL
01-01-2003; 88.1 MHz FM; 0.3 kw; 135 ft.; N41 38 15 W70 52 19
Mailing Address: P.O. Box 3025, New Bedford, MA 02741 US
Second Address: 71 William, New Bedford, MA 2740
(508) 991-7600
www.radiowfhl.com
License: New Bedford, Bristol County, MA held by New Bedford Christian Radio Inc.
Arbitron Metro Market: New Bedford, MA; *Format:* Portugese
Manuel Pereira, General Manager

Newburyport

WNBP
03-10-1957; 1450 kHz AM; *Hrs Open:* 24; 1 kw-U, ND1; N42 49 23 W70 51 42
44 Merrimac St., Second Floor East, Newburyport, MA 01950 US
(978) 462-1450; *Fax:* (978) 462-0333
www.wnbp.com
License: Newburyport, MA held by Port Broadcasting LLC
Nat'l Network: AP Radio; *Wire Services:* AP
Arbitron Metro Market: Boston, MA; *Format:* Adult Contemp *Special Programming:* Irish 4 hrs wkly; *Hrs. of News Programming:* news progmg 5 hrs wkly; *No. News Employees:* 1; *Target Audience:* 25-54.
Peter Falconi, Operations Dir
Carl Strube, General Manager
Ted Brouse, General Sales Mgr
Charlie Curtis, Programming Director

*WNEF
91.7 MHz FM; 0.001 kw horiz, 1 kw vert; 328 ft.; N42 51 56 W70 56 17 *Rebroadcasts:* Rebroadcasts WUMB-FM Boston 100%
100 Morrissey Blvd., Boston, MA 02125 US
(617) 287-6900; *Fax:* (617) 287-6916
www.wumb.org
wumb@umb.edu
License: Newburyport, Essex County, MA held by University of Massachusetts.
Arbitron Metro Market: Boston, MA; *Format:* Variety/Diverse
Patricia Monteith, General Manager
Danielle Knight, General Sales Mgr
Brian Quinn, Programming Director

Newton

WXKS
04-01-1947; 1200 kHz AM; *Hrs Open:* 24; 50 kw-U, DA-2; N42 17 20 W71 11 21
3071 Continental Drive, West Palm Beach, FL 33407
(781) 396-1430; *Fax:* (781) 391-3064
License: Newton, Middlesex County, MA held by Capstar TX LLC
Group Owner: iHeartMedia; (acq 2-15-2001; $10 million)
Population Served: 1,700,000; *Arbitron Metro Market:* Boston; *Format:* News, News/Talk, 86
Alan Chartrand, Market President

WNTN
04-01-1968; 1550 kHz AM; 10 kw-D, ND2; 0.003 kw-N, ND2; N42 21 27 W71 14 30
134 Rumford Ave, Newton, MA 02446 US
(617) 969-1550
www.wntn.com
info@wntn.com
License: Newton, MA held by Colt Communications LLC.
Arbitron Metro Market: Boston, MA; *Format:* Greek *Special Programming:* Irish 6 hrs, Indian 2 hrs wkly; *Target Audience:* 40 plus.
Paul Roberts, Operations Dir
Rob Rudnick, General Manager
John Frassica, General Sales Mgr
Leo Sullivan, Chief Engineer

*WZBC
04-01-1974; 90.3 MHz FM; *Hrs Open:* 24; 1 kw; 220 ft.; N42 20 5 W71 10 31
Boston College, Chestnut Hill, MA 02167 US
(617) 552-3511; *Fax:* (617) 552-1738
www.wzbc.org
License: Newton, Middlesex County, MA held by Trustees of Boston College.
Arbitron Metro Market: Boston; *Format:* Alternative; *Target Audience:* 18-34.
Alexis Murphy, General Manager

Norfolk

WDIS
03-20-1978; 1170 kHz AM; *Hrs Open:* Day Time

100 Pond Street, Norfolk, MA 02056 US
(508) 384-8255; *Fax:* (508) 384-1530
www.wdisam.com
info@wdisam.com
License: Norfolk, MA held by Discussion Radio Inc.
Nat'l Network: Salem Radio Network
Arbitron Metro Market: Boston, MA; *Format:* News, News/Talk, 86; *Hrs. of News Programming:* news progmg 6 hrs wkly; *No. News Employees:* 1; *Target Audience:* 35-64.; *Adv. Rates:* 24; 24; 24; 24.
Corine Slade, General Manager
Dan Collier, Programming Director

North Adams

*WJJW
09-05-1973; 91.1 MHz FM; 0.423 kw; -830 ft.; N42 41 27 W73 6 16
375 Church Street, North Adams, MA 01247 US
(413) 662-5405
www.mcla.edu
webmaster@mcla.edu
License: North Adams, Berkshire County, MA held by Massachusetts College of Liberal Arts.
Harris Elder, General Manager
Nick Strassel, Programming Director
Paul Wiley, Chief Engineer

WUPE-FM
07-12-1964; 100.1 MHz FM; 1.3 kw; 502 ft.; N42 41 51 W73 3 52
211 Jason St., Pittsfield, MA 01247 USA
(413) 499-3333; *Fax:* (413) 442-1590
www.wupe.com
fun@wupe.com
License: North Adams, Berkshire County, MA held by Berkshire Broadcasting Co. Inc.
Group Owner: Gamma Broadcasting LLC
Arbitron Metro Market: North Adams, MA; *Format:* Oldies; *Target Audience:* 35 plus.
Peter Barry, VP/Marketing Manager

WNAW
11-23-1947; 1230 kHz AM; 1 kw-U, ND1; N42 41 3 W73 6 23
PO Box 707, North Adams, MA 01247 USA
www.wnaw.com
License: North Adams, MA held by Berkshire Broadcasting Co. Inc.
Group Owner: Gamma Broadcasting LLC
Nat'l Network: AP Radio; *Nat'l Reps:* McGavren Guild
Arbitron Metro Market: Baltimore, MD; *Format:* Adult Contemp; *No. News Employees:* 2; *Target Audience:* Adults.
Bob Heck, Sales Manager

North Dartmouth

*WTKL
09-01-1973; 91.1 MHz FM; 1.2 kw; 299 ft.; N41 37 43 W71 0 24
285 Old Westport Road, North Dartmouth, MA 02747 US
(916) 251-1600; *Fax:* (916) 251-1650
www.klove.com
License: North Dartmouth, Bristol County, MA held by Educational Media Foundation.
Group Owner: EMF Broadcasting; (acq 6-30-2006; $725,000).
Nat'l Network: K-Love
Format: Christian
Mike Novak, President
Glenn Goodwin, Operations Dir

*WUMD
06-10-2006; 89.3 MHz FM; *Hrs Open:* 24; 0.096 kw horiz, 9.6 kw vert; 305 ft.; N41 37 43 W71 0 24
285 Old Westport Road, North Dartmouth, MA 02747 US
(508) 999-8149
www.893wumd.org
wumd@umassd.edu
License: North Dartmouth, Bristol County, MA held by University of Massachusetts.
Arbitron Metro Market: North Dartmouth, MA; *Format:* Variety/Diverse; *Target Audience:* 13-60; general, high school, college, community
Jennifer Mulcare-Sullivan, Station Manager

Northampton

WEIB
01-01-2001; 106.3 MHz FM; *Hrs Open:* 24; 3 kw; 289 ft.; N42 22 25 W72 40 26
8 North King Street, Northampton, MA 01060 US
(413) 585-1112; *Fax:* (413) 585-9138
www.weibfm.com
weibfm@aol.com
License: Northampton, Hampshire County, MA held by Cutting Edge Broadcasting Inc.
Arbitron Metro Market: Northampton, MA; *Format:* Jazz, Smooth Jazz
Carol Cutting, President
Drew Dawson, Programming Director

WHMP
12-01-1950; 1400 kHz AM; *Hrs Open:* 24; 1 kw-U; N42 19 36 W72 39 28
15 Hampton Ave., Northampton, MA 78701
(413) 586-7400; *Fax:* (413) 585-0927
www.whmp.com
License: Northampton, Hampshire County, MA held by Saga Communications of New England LLC.
Group Owner: Saga Communications Inc.; (acq 2000; $12 million with co-loca
Nat'l Network: CBS Radio; *Nat'l Reps:* Katz Radio; *Wire Services:* AP
Population Served: 100,000; *Arbitron Metro Market:* Springfield, MA *Special Programming:* Pol 3 hrs wkly; *Hrs. of News Programming:* news progmg 40 hrs wkly; *No. News Employees:* 2; *Target Audience:* 35 plus;upscale, well educated
David Musante, General Manager
Chris Belmonte, Brand Manager
Denise Vozella, News Director

WLZX
11-01-1956; 99.3 MHz FM; *Hrs Open:* 24; 5.8 kw; 331 ft.; N42 22 25 W72 40 26
45 Fisher Avenue, East Longmeadow, MA 01028 US
(413) 525-4141; *Fax:* (413) 525-4334
www.lazer993.com
info@lazer993.com
License: Northampton, Hampshire County, MA held by Saga Communications of New England LLC.
Group Owner: Saga Communications Inc.; (acq 2000; $12 million with co-located AM).
Arbitron Metro Market: Springfield, MA; *Format:* Rock/AOR; *No. News Employees:* 2; *Target Audience:* 18-34; male
Jay Schultz, General Manager

*WOZQ
01-01-1981; 91.9 MHz FM; *Hrs Open:* 6 AM-2 AM; 0.2 kw horiz, 0.175 kw vert; -115 ft.; N42 19 13 W72 38 14
College Hall, Northampton, MA 01063 US
(413) 585-4956,(413) 585-4977; *Fax:* (413) 585-4166
www.smith.edu/wozq
wozq@email.smith.edu
License: Northampton, Hampshire County, MA held by Trustees of Smith College.
Format: Variety/Diverse; *Target Audience:* 15 plus; college students & area businesses
Rachel McDonald, Station Manager

Orange

WJDF
01-01-1995; 97.3 MHz FM; 5.8 kw; 82 ft.; N42 36 3 W72 23 1
P.O. Box 973, Orange, MA 01364 US
(978) 544-0957; *Fax:* (978) 544-2131
www.wjdf.com
info@wjdf.com
License: Orange, Franklin County, MA held by Deane Brothers Broadcasting Corp.
Format: Adult Contemp
Donn Deane, General Manager
Chad Songer, General Sales Mgr
Jay Deane, Programming Director

Orleans

WFPB
04-10-1970; 1170 kHz AM; *Hrs Open:* 24; 1 kw-D, DAD; N41 46 48 W70 0 36 *Rebroadcasts:* Rebroadcasts WUMB-FM Boston 100%
100 Morrissey Boulevard, Boston, MA 02125 US
(617) 287-6900; *Fax:* (617) 287-6916
www.wumb.org
wumb@umb.edu
License: Orleans, MA held by University of Massachusetts.
Arbitron Metro Market: Cape Cod, MA; *Format:* Variety/Diverse
Patricia Domeniconi, General Manager
Jay Mobera, Programming Director

WOCN-FM
07-25-1974; 104.7 MHz FM; *Hrs Open:* 24; 50 kw horiz, 36 kw vert; 459 ft.; N41 46 48 W70 0 36
737 W. Main St., Hyannis, MA 02601 US
(508) 771-1224
www.ocean1047.com
License: Orleans, Barnstable County, MA held by Cape Cod Broadcasting License II LLC.
Group Owner: Sandab Communications L.P. II; (acq 7-10-2007; $7.5 million with WFCC-FM Chatham)
Nat'l Network: AP Radio; *Nat'l Reps:* Clear Channel; *Wire Services:* AP
Arbitron Metro Market: Cape Cod, MA; *Format:* Variety/Diverse, Classic Rock; *Hrs. of News Programming:* news progmg 32 hrs wkly; *No. News Employees:* 4; *Target Audience:* Adults 25-64.

*WFMR
91.3 MHz FM; 1.15 kw; 282 ft.; N41 46 36 W70 0 40
494 Commercial Street, Provicetown, MA 02657 US
(508) 487-2619; *Fax:* (508) 487-5524
www.womr.org
info@womr.org
License: Orleans, Barnstable County, MA held by Lower Cape Communications Inc.
Arbitron Metro Market: Orleans, MA; *Format:* Public Affairs
John Braden, Executive Director

Petersham

*WNGB
91.3 MHz FM; 0.6 kw; -174 ft.; N42 31 30 W72 16 42 US
(518) 686-0975; *Fax:* (518) 686-0975
www.wngn.org
wngn@wngn.org
License: Petersham, Worcester County, MA held by Northeast Gospel Broadcasting Inc.
Arbitron Metro Market: Petersham, MA; *Format:* Christian, Gospel
Brian Larson, General Manager
Bill Dagle, Vice President

Pittsfield

WBEC
03-01-1947; 1420 kHz AM; *Hrs Open:* 24; 1 kw-D, DAN; 1 kw-N, DAN; N42 26 40 W73 16 43
211 Jason St., Pittsfield, MA 01247 USA
(413) 399-3333; *Fax:* (413) 442-1590
www.live959.com
License: Pittsfield, MA held by Gamma Broadcasting LLC
Group Owner: Gamma Broadcasting LLC
Nat'l Network: ABC News Radio; FOX News Radio; FOX Sports Radio; Westwood One
Arbitron Metro Market: Odessa-Midland TX; *Format:* News/Talk
Larry Kratka, News Director

WBRK
02-20-1938; 1340 kHz AM; *Hrs Open:* 24; 1 kw-U, ND1; N42 27 0 W73 12 55
100 North Street, Pittsfield, MA 01201 US
(413) 442-1553; *Fax:* (413) 445-5294
www.wbrk.com
WBRK@WBRK.COM
License: Pittsfield, MA held by WBRK Inc.
Nat'l Network: CBS; Westwood One *Regional Reps:* interep loca focus
Arbitron Metro Market: PITTSFIELD MA; *Format:* Variety/Diverse
Special Programming: Pol 2 hrs, Irish one hr, relg 2 hrs wkly; *No. News Employees:* 2; *Target Audience:* 35 plus.
Robert Shade, VP Sales
Cheryl Tripp, VP Office
John Campoli, Sales

WBRK-FM
10-10-1970; 101.7 MHz FM; *Hrs Open:* 24; 3 kw; 144 ft.; N42 28 31 W73 16 7
100 North Street, Pittsfield, MA 01201 US
(413) 442-1553; *Fax:* (413) 445-5294
www.wbrk.com
WBRK@WBRK.COM
License: Pittsfield, Berkshire County, MA
Nat'l Network: ABC
Arbitron Metro Market: PITTSFIELD MA; *Format:* Adult Contemp; *Target Audience:* 25-54.
Robert Shade, VP Sales
Cheryl Tripp, VP Office
John Campoli, Sales

WUPE
09-09-1971; 1110 kHz AM; *Hrs Open:* 24; 5 kw-D, DAD; N42 26 22 W73 17 30
211 Jason St., Pittsfield, MA 01247 USA
(413) 499-3333; *Fax:* (413) 442-1590
www.wupe.com
fun@wupe.com

License: Pittsfield, MA held by Gamma Broadcasting LLC
Group Owner: Gamma Broadcasting LLC
Nat'l Reps: D & R Radio
Arbitron Metro Market: Pittsfield, MA; *Format:* Oldies; *Hrs. of News Programming:* news progmg 14 hrs wkly; *No. News Employees:* 1; *Target Audience:* 25-54; baby boomers; *Adv. Rates:* 17; 14; 17; na
Peter Barry, VP/Marketing Manager

WBEC-FM
01-01-1975; 95.9 MHz FM; *Hrs Open:* 24; 1 kw; 558 ft.; N42 24 44 W73 17 5
211 Jason Street, Pittsfield, MA 01247 USA
(413) 399-3333; *Fax:* (413) 442-1590
www.live959.com
License: Pittsfield, Berkshire County, MA held by Gamma Broadcasting LLC
Group Owner: Gamma Broadcasting LLC
Arbitron Metro Market: Pittsfield, MA; *Format:* Adult Contemp; *Hrs. of News Programming:* news progmg 28 hrs wkly; *No. News Employees:* 1; *Target Audience:* 25-54; young adults with families; *Adv. Rates:* 25;22; 25; 20
Peter Barry, VP/Marketing Manager
Larry Kratka, News Director

Plymouth

WPLM
08-08-1955; 1390 kHz AM; 5 kw-D, DA2; 5 kw-N, DA2; N41 58 5 W70 42 6
P.O. Box 1390, North Plymouth, MA 02362 US
(508) 746-1390; *Fax:* (508) 830-1128
alana@991.com
License: Plymouth, MA held by Plymouth Rock Broadcasting Co. Inc.
Nat'l Reps: Roslin
Arbitron Metro Market: Boston; *Format:* Adult Contemp, Talk
Dr. Laurie Campbell, President
Alan Anderson, General Manager
Sean Casey, Promotions Manager
Chip Morgan, Chief Engineer
Pat Carroll, Public Service Director

WPLM-FM
06-25-1961; 99.1 MHz FM; 50 kw; 430 ft.; N41 58 2 W70 42 4
17 Columbus Road, North Plymouth, MA 02362 US
(508) 746-1390; *Fax:* (508) 830-1128
License: Plymouth, Plymouth County, MA held by Plymouth Rock Broadcasting Co. Inc.
Arbitron Metro Market: Boston; *Format:* Adult Contemp
Joe Harrington, General Manager
Kevin Cronon, Programming Director

Provincetown

***WOMR**
03-21-1982; 92.1 MHz FM; 6 kw; 161 ft.; N42 3 54 W70 9 31
P.O. Box 975, Provincetown, MA 02657 US
508-487-2619; *Fax:* (508) 487-5524
www.womr.org
info@womr.org
License: Provincetown, Barnstable County, MA held by Lower Cape Communications Inc.
Arbitron Metro Market: Cape Cod, MA *TV Affiliate:* Variety; *Format:* Black *Special Programming:* News progmg 5.5 hrs wkly; *No. News Employees:* General; div; *Adv. Rates:* 12; 12; 12; 12
John Braden, Executive Director
Matthew Dunn, Operations Dir
Operations Manager

Quincy

WJDA
09-13-1947; 1300 kHz AM; *Hrs Open:* 24; 1 kw-D, ND1; 0.072 kw-N, ND1; N42 15 35 W70 58 36
90 Everett Avenue, Chelsea, MA 02150 US
(617) 884-4500; *Fax:* (617) 884-4515
www.wjda1300am.com
info@wjda1300am.com
License: Quincy, MA held by South Shore Broadcasting Co.
Nat'l Network: ABC
Arbitron Metro Market: Boston; *Format:* Ethnic *Special Programming:* Cantonese 3 hrs wkly; *Hrs. of News Programming:* news progmg 10 hrs wkly; *No. News Employees:* 2; *Target Audience:* 35 plus.; *Adv. Rates:* 40; 32
Charles Banta, President
Mike Logan, News Director

Rockland

***WRPS**
02-08-1974; 88.3 MHz FM; *Hrs Open:* 24; 0.105 kw; 138 ft.; N42 7 43 W70 55 1
34 Mackinlay Way, Rockland, MA 02370 US
(781) 871-0724
License: Rockland, Plymouth County, MA held by Rockland Public Schools.
Arbitron Metro Market: Boston; *Format:* Adult Contemp; *Target Audience:* General.
David Cable-Murphy, General Manager
Robert Mulligan, Chief Engineer

Salem

***WMWM**
01-01-1976; 91.7 MHz FM; *Hrs Open:* 7 AM-midnight; 0.13 kw; 79 ft.; N42 30 14 W70 53 26
352 Lafayette Street, Salem, MA 01970 US
(978) 219-9170
wmwmsalem@gmail.com
License: Salem, Essex County, MA held by Salem State College.
Arbitron Metro Market: Boston, MA; *Format:* Variety/Diverse; *Target Audience:* General.
Ben Schaefer, General Manager
Danny Carter, Programming Director

Sandwich

***WSDH**
01-01-1976; 91.5 MHz FM; *Hrs Open:* 10 AM-4 PM (M-F); 0.31 kw; 151 ft.; N41 44 6 W70 27 35
Quaker Meetinghouse Road, East Sandwich, MA 02537 US
(508) 888-0420; *Fax:* (508) 833-8392
License: Sandwich, Barnstable County, MA held by Sandwich Public Schools.
Format: Variety/Diverse; *Hrs. of News Programming:* News progmg 4 hrs wkly; *Target Audience:* 12-40.
Chip Hill, General Manager

Scituate

***WSMA**
05-01-2006; 90.5 MHz FM; 0.005 kw horiz, 7.7 kw vert; 492 ft.; N41 56 2 W70 35 10 *Rebroadcasts:* Rebroadcasts KAWZ (FM)
P.O. Box 391, Twin Falls, ID 83303 US
(800) 357-4226; *Fax:* (208) 736-1958
www.csnradio.com
csn@csnradio.com
License: Scituate, Plymouth County, MA held by Calvary Chapel of Twin Falls
Group Owner: CSN International
Arbitron Metro Market: Scituate, MA; *Format:* Christian, Gospel, 86
Mike Kestler, President
Daniel Davidson, Operations Dir
Don Mills, Network Programming Director
Mike Stocklin, Underwriting Director
Kelly Carlson, Engineering Dir

Sheffield

***WBSL-FM**
09-01-1973; 91.7 MHz FM; 0.23 kw horiz; -75 ft.; N42 6 57 W73 25 0
245 N. Undermountain Rd., Sheffield, MA 01257 US
(413) 229-8511
www.berkshireschool.org
bclough@berkshireschool.org
License: Sheffield, Berkshire County, MA held by Berkshire School Inc.
Format: Variety/Diverse *Special Programming:* Jazz 15 hrs, Black 2 hrs, folk 2 hrs, Sp 2 hrs, Pol one hr wkly; *Target Audience:* General.
John Weinner, Station Manager
Thomas Jaworski, Engineering Dir
Coleen Cox, Station Advisor
James Harris, Station Advisor
Vickie Sheppard, Station Manager

South Hadley

***WMHC**
05-14-1957; 91.5 MHz FM; 0.1 kw; -16 ft.; N42 15 12 W72 34 40
3 Carr Lab, South Hadley, MA 01075 US
(413) 538-2044; *Fax:* (413) 538-2431
www.mtholyoke.edu/org/wmhc
amlewis@mtholyoke.edu
License: South Hadley, Hampshire County, MA held by President & Trustees of Mount Holyoke College.
Nat'l Network: AP Radio
Arbitron Metro Market: South Hadley, MA; *Format:* Rock/AOR; *Target Audience:* General; Mount Holyoke College Community
Catherine Moldonado, Programming Director

South Yarmouth

WKPE-FM
08-01-1994; 103.9 MHz FM; 5.5 kw; 341 ft.; N41 41 26 W70 11 21
737 W. Main St., Hyannis, MA 02601 US
(508) 771-1224
www.capecountry104.com
License: South Yarmouth, Barnstable County, MA held by Sandab Communications L.P. II.
Group Owner: Sandab Communications L.P. II; acq 6-19-98; $1.2 million)
Nat'l Reps: Clear Channel
Arbitron Metro Market: Cape Cod, MA *TV Affiliate:* Country; *No. News Employees:* P 18 - 54

Southbridge

WESO
03-20-1955; 970 kHz AM; *Hrs Open:* 24; 1 kw-D, ND1; 0.021 kw-N, ND1; N42 3 59 W71 59 28
16 Walker Avenue, Westfield, MA 01085 US
(508) 909-0970; *Fax:* (508) 764-2682
thespirit970.com
License: Southbridge, MA held by Money Matters Inc.
Arbitron Metro Market: Southbridge, MA; *Format:* Country, News, 62, Sports, Talk *Special Programming:* Pol 3 hrs; *Hrs. of News Programming:* news progmg 30 hrs wkly; *No. News Employees:* 2 *Target Audience:* 34-59.; *Adv. Rates:* 24; 20; 24; 18
Dick Vaughan, COO
Lia Zaido, Operations Dir
Camie Luke, Promotions Manager
J.P. Ellery, News Director

WWFX
11-01-1968; 100.1 MHz FM; *Hrs Open:* 24; 2.85 kw; 479 ft.; N42 13 28 W71 52 51
250 Commercial St., Worcester, MA 01608 US
(508) 752-1045; *Fax:* (508) 793-0824
www.pikefm.com
License: Southbridge, MA held by Radio License Holding CBC, LLC
Group Owner: Cumulus Media Inc.; (acq 4-26-01; grpsl).
Nat'l Network: Jones Radio Networks
Arbitron Metro Market: Worcester, MA; *Format:* Adult Contemp
John Sutherland, Sales

Springfield

***WAIC**
02-01-1967; 91.9 MHz FM; 0.23 kw horiz; 66 ft.; N42 6 44 W72 33 29
170 Wilbraham Road, Springfield, MA 01109 US
(413) 205-3941
License: Springfield, Hampden County, MA held by American International College.
Arbitron Metro Market: Springfield, MA; *Format:* Variety/Diverse *Special Programming:* Gospel; *Target Audience:* 16-40.
Will Hughes, CEO
Jean Paul, Operations Dir
Doc Holiday, General Manager
Christopher Flynn, Director of Major Gifts & Planned Giving

WAQY
12-17-1966; 102.1 MHz FM; *Hrs Open:* 24; 17 kw; 781 ft.; N42 5 0 W72 42 16
45 Fisher Ave, East Longmeadow, MA 01028 US
(413) 525-4141; *Fax:* (413) 525-4334
www.rock102.com
rcressman@lazer993.com
License: Springfield, Hampden County, MA held by Saga Communications of New England LLC.
Group Owner: Saga Communications Inc.; (acq 6-2-92; grpsl).
Nat'l Reps: Katz Radio
Arbitron Metro Market: Springfield, MA; *Format:* Classic Rock; *Target Audience:* General; upscale young adults with high income
Jay Schultz, Sales Manager
Lenny Diana, Brand Manager

WHYN
01-01-1941; 560 kHz AM; *Hrs Open:* 24
1331 Main Street, 4th Floor, Springfield, MA 01103 US
(413) 781-1011
www.whyn.com
License: Springfield, MA held by CC Licenses LLC.
Group Owner: iHeartMedia; (acq 1996; grpsl)

Arbitron Metro Market: Springfield, MA; *Format:* News, News/Talk, 86; *No. News Employees:* 6; *Target Audience:* General.
Sean Davey, Market Manager

WHYN-FM
01-01-1946; 93.1 MHz FM; 8.6 kw; 1001 ft.; N42 14 28 W72 38 56
1331 Main Street, 4th Floor, Springfield, MA 01103 US
(413) 781-1011; *Fax:* (413) 734-4434
www.mix931.com
fm@mix931.com
License: Springfield, Hampden County, MA held by CC Licenses LLC.
Group Owner: iHeartMedia
Arbitron Metro Market: Springfield, MA; *Format:* Adult Contemp; *Target Audience:* 25-54.
Sean Davey, Market Manager
Danielle Veronesi, Marketing and Promotions Director

WHLL
09-01-1932; 1450 kHz AM; 1 kw-U, ND1; N42 6 32 W72 36 44
1000 Hall of Fame Ave., Springfield, MA 01105 US
(413) 737-1414; *Fax:* (413) 737-1488
www.1450thehall.com
info@947wmas.com
License: Springfield, MA held by Radio License Holding CBC, LLC
Group Owner: Cumulus Media Inc.
Nat'l Network: ABC
Arbitron Metro Market: Springfield, MA; *Format:* Sports
Craig Swimm, General Sales Mgr
Jim Raino, Programming Director
Erica Skubis, Promotions Manager

***WNEK-FM**
02-17-1976; 105.1 MHz FM; 0.013 kw; -23 ft.; N42 6 55 W72 31 5
US
(413) 782-1586; *Fax:* (413) 796-2008
www.wnek.wneclubs.org/
License: Springfield, Hampden County, MA held by Trustees of Western New England College.
Arbitron Metro Market: Springfield, MA; *Format:* Variety/Diverse; *Target Audience:* 15-35; college community, greater Springfield area
Specer Bracco, Operations Dir
Ian Martin, General Manager

***WSCB**
03-01-1958; 89.9 MHz FM; 0.1 kw; 36 ft.; N42 5 59 W72 33 30
263 Alden Street, Springfield, MA 01109 US
(413) 748-3000
License: Springfield, Hampden County, MA held by President & Trustees of Springfield College.
Arbitron Metro Market: Springfield, MA; *Format:* Variety/Diverse
Kyle Belanger, Faculty Advisor

WSPR
06-01-1936; 1270 kHz AM; 5 kw-D, DA2; 1 kw-N, DA2; N42 5 24 W72 36 11
270 Union Street, New Bedford, MA 02740 US
(413) 781-5200; *Fax:* (413) 734-2240
www.wspr1270.com
License: Springfield, MA held by Davidson Media Station WSPR Licensee LLC.
Group Owner: Davidson Media Group LLC; (acq 5-16-2005; $6.8 million with WACM(AM) West Springfield)
Arbitron Metro Market: Springfield, MA
Paul Gois, General Manager

***WTCC**
08-19-1971; 90.7 MHz FM; 4 kw; 92 ft.; N42 6 32 W72 34 45
Mailing Address: P.O. Box 9000, Springfield, MA 01105 US
Second Address: One Armory Sq., Springfield, MA 01105
(413) 736-2781; *Fax:* (413) 781-3747
www.wtccfm.org
fkrampits@stcc.edu
License: Springfield, Hampden County, MA held by Springfield Technical Community College.
Arbitron Metro Market: Springfield, MA; *Format:* Variety/Diverse; *Target Audience:* General.
Ernest Johnson, General Manager

Sudbury

***WYAJ**
09-01-1980; 97.7 MHz FM; 0.004 kw; 220 ft.; N42 22 30 W71 24 28
390 Lincoln Rd., Sudbury, MA 01776 US
(978) 443-9961; *Fax:* (978) 443-8824
www.lsrhs.net
contact.us@lsrhs.net
License: Sudbury, Middlesex County, MA held by Lincoln-Sudbury Regional School District.
Arbitron Metro Market: Sudbury, MA; *Format:* Variety/Diverse
Special Programming: Black 6 hrs, class 3 hrs, jazz 5 hrs, loc rock art; *Target Audience:* General.
Paul Sarapas, General Manager

Taunton

WSNE-FM
01-26-1966; 93.3 MHz FM; 31 kw; 591 ft.; N41 51 56 W71 17 22
75 Oxford Street, Suite 302, Providence, RI 02905 US
(401) 781-9979; *Fax:* (401) 781-9329
www.coast933.com
feedback@coast933.com
License: Taunton, Bristol County, MA held by Capstar TX LLC
Group Owner: iHeartMedia; (acq 8-30-00; grpsl).
Nat'l Network: AP Radio; Premiere Radio Networks; *Nat'l Reps:* Clear Channel
Arbitron Metro Market: Providence-Warwick-Pawtucket, RI; *Format:* Adult Contemp *Special Programming:* Pub affrs 4 hrs wkly; *Target Audience:* 25-54; mostly women
Rhonda Lapham, Market Manager

Tisbury

WBUA
06-01-1981; 92.7 MHz FM; *Hrs Open:* 21; 3 kw; 315 ft.; N41 26 16 W70 36 51
Mailing Address: P.O. Box 958, 211 Jason St., Pittsfield, MA 01202 US
Second Address: 57 Carrolls Way, Vineyard Haven, MA 2568
(508) 693-5000; *Fax:* (508) 693-8211
www.mvyradio.com
gorcutt@mvyradio.com
License: Tisbury, Dukes County, MA held by Executive Committee of the Trustees of Boston University
Nat'l Network: Moody; AP Radio; *Nat'l Reps:* McGavren Guild
Arbitron Metro Market: Cape Cod, MA; *Format:* Rock/AOR
Special Programming: Class 4 hrs, jazz 4 hrs wkly; *No. News Employees:* 1; *Target Audience:* 25-49; upper income, active consumer group
Joseph Gallagher, President
Greg Orcutt, General Manager
P.J. Finn, Programming Director
Nick Ward, Promotions Manager

Truro

WGTX
01-01-2000; 102.3 MHz FM; 2.15 kw; 266 ft.; N42 1 20 W70 4 28
P.O. Box 508, Provincetown, MA 02657 US
(508) 487-1002
License: Truro, Barnstable County, MA held by Dunes 102FM LLC
Arbitron Metro Market: Provincetown, MA; *Format:* News, News/Talk, 86
Rob Robin, Owner

Turners Falls

WRSI
07-01-1984; 93.9 MHz FM; *Hrs Open:* 24; 2.5 kw; 358 ft.; N42 32 1 W72 35 34
15 Hampton Road, Northampton, MA 01060 US
(413) 586-7400; *Fax:* (413) 585-0927
www.wrsi.com
License: Turners Falls, Franklin County, MA held by Saga Communications of New England LLC.
Group Owner: Saga Communications Inc.; (acq 2-13-2004; grpsl).
Nat'l Network: CBS Radio
Arbitron Metro Market: Springfield, MA; *Format:* Triple A; *Hrs. of News Programming:* News progmg 9 hrs wkly; *Target Audience:* 18-54; young, educated, spend money; *Adv. Rates:* 35; 25; 30; 15
Dave Musante, General Manager
Chris Belmonte, Programming Director

Waltham

***WBRS**
02-05-1968; 100.1 MHz FM; *Hrs Open:* 24; 0.025 kw; 151 ft.; N42 22 9 W71 15 28
415 South Street, Waltham, MA 02254 US
(781) 736-5277
www.wbrs.org
gm@wbrs.org
License: Waltham, Middlesex County, MA held by Brandeis University.
Wire Services: UPI
Arbitron Metro Market: Waltham, MA; *Format:* Variety/Diverse; *Hrs. of News Programming:* News progmg 5 hrs wkly; *Target Audience:* General.
Lee Nisson, General Manager

WKLB-FM
01-01-1948; 102.5 MHz FM; *Hrs Open:* 24; 14 kw; 906 ft.; N42 18 37 W71 14 14
55 Morrissey Boulevard, Boston, MA 02125 US
(617) 822-6880; *Fax:* (617) 822-6659
www.country1025.com
mbrophey@wklb.com
License: Waltham, Middlesex County, MA held by Charles River Broadcasting WCRB License Corp.
Group Owner: Beasley Broadcast Group; (acq 11-15-2006)
Nat'l Reps: Katz Radio
Arbitron Metro Market: Boston,MA; *Format:* Country; *Target Audience:* 25-54.
Phil Redo, General Manager
Mark Keaney, General Sales Mgr
Mike Brophey, Programming Director
Dawn Santolucito, Promotions Manager

Ware

WARE
07-11-1948; 1250 kHz AM
3 Converse Street, Palmer, MA 01069 US
(413) 289-2300; *Fax:* (413) 289-2323
www.realoldies1250.net
manager@realoldies1250.net
License: Ware, MA held by Success Signal Broadcasting Inc.
Nat'l Network: Fox News Radio; *Nat'l Reps:* Rgnl Reps
Arbitron Metro Market: Springfield, MA; *Format:* Oldies *Special Programming:* Pol 4 hrs wkly; *No. News Employees:* 3; *Target Audience:* 30 plus.
Marshall Sanft, President

Watertown

WRCA
01-01-1948; 1330 kHz AM; *Hrs Open:* 24; 25 kw-D, 17 kw-N; N42 17 20 W71 11 21
552 Massachusetts Ave., Suite 201, Cambridge, MA 02139 US
(617) 492-3300; *Fax:* (617) 492-2800
License: Watertown, Middlesex County, MA held by Beasley Media Group LLC
Group Owner: Beasley Broadcast Group Inc.; (acq 5-2000; $6 million)
Arbitron Metro Market: Boston, MA; *Format:* Ethnic; *Hrs. of News Programming:* News progmg 10 hrs wkly; *Target Audience:* General.; *Adv. Rates:* 35; 35; 35; 35
Stu Fink, General Manager

WAZN
01-01-1958; 1470 kHz AM; *Hrs Open:* 24; 1.4 kw-D, 3.4 kw-N, DA-2; N42 24 49 W71 12 40 *Rebroadcasts:* Rebroadcasts WLYN(AM) Lynn (partial
27 William St., 11th Floor, New York, NY 10005 US
(212) 966-1059; *Fax:* (212) 625-2894
www.mrbi.net
License: Watertown, Middlesex County, MA held by Multicultural Radio Broadcasting Licensee LLC.
Group Owner: Multicultural Radio Broadcasting Inc.; (acq 12-11-2002; $1.8 million)
Population Served: 2,000,000; *Arbitron Metro Market:* Boston; *Format:* Variety/Diverse; *Target Audience:* Russian, Hispanic (Sp & Portuguese); *Adv. Rates:* 50; 50; 50; 50
Arthur Liu, CEO/COO

Webster

WGFP
04-01-1980; 940 kHz AM; *Hrs Open:* 24; 1 kw-D, ND2; 0.004 kw-N, ND2; N42 3 17 W71 50 0
27 Douglas Road, Webster, MA 01570 US
(508) 943-9400; *Fax:* (508) 943-0405
www.coolcountry940.com
barry@coolcountry940.com
License: Webster, MA held by Just Because Inc.
Arbitron Metro Market: Worcester, MA; *Format:* Country *Special Programming:* live high school sports; *Hrs. of News Programming:* News progmg 25 hrs wkly; *Target Audience:* 25-54.
Barry Sims, CEO

WORC
04-08-1994; 98.9 MHz FM; 1.87 kw; 410 ft.; N42 2 11 W71 59 22

250 Commercial St., 5th Floor, Worcester, MA 01608 US
(508) 752-1045; *Fax:* (508) 973-0824
www.nashicon989.com
License: Webster, MA held by Radio License Holding CBC, LLC
Group Owner: Cumulus Media Inc.; (acq 6-8-99; $3.5 million).
Arbitron Metro Market: Worcester, MA; *Format:* Country
Bob Goodell, VP/Market Manager

Wellesley

***WZLY**
09-20-1976; 91.5 MHz FM; 0.007 kw; 154 ft.; N42 17 35 W71 18 21
106 Central Street, Wellesley, MA 02481 US
(781) 283-2690
www.wzly.net
gm@wzly.net
License: Wellesley, Norfolk County, MA held by Wellesley College.
Arbitron Metro Market: Wellesley, MA; *Format:* Variety/Diverse; *Target Audience:* General; Wellesley town and college community
Gabriella Lanze, General Manager
Jasmyne Keimig, Promotions Manager

Wellfleet

***WRYP**
90.1 MHz FM; 2.5 kw vert; 80 ft.; N42 1 53 W70 5 26
365 Broad St, Fitchburg, MA 01420 US
(888) 310-7729
renewfm.org
info@renewfm.org
License: Wellfleet, Barnstable County, MA held by Horizon Christian Fellowship
Group Owner: Horizon Christian Fellowship
Arbitron Metro Market: Wellfleet, MA; *Format:* Christian

West Barnstable

***WKKL**
09-19-1977; 90.7 MHz FM; *Hrs Open:* 24; 0.205 kw; 125 ft.; N41 41 31 W70 20 16
2240 Iyannough Road, West Barnstable, MA 02668 US
(508) 375-4027
www.geocities.com/wkkl247
wkkl247@yahoo.com
License: West Barnstable, Barnstable County, MA held by Board of Trustees Cape Cod Community Colleges.
Arbitron Metro Market: Cape Cod, MA; *Format:* Alternative
Lisa Zinsius, General Manager

West Springfield

WACM
08-28-1949; 1490 kHz AM; 0.47 kw-U, ND1; N42 5 55 W72 37 45
34 Sylvan Street, W. Springfield, MA 01089 US
License: West Springfield, MA held by Davidson Media Station WACM Licensee LLC.
Group Owner: Davidson Media Group LLC; (acq 5-16-2005; $6.8 million with WSPR(AM) Springfield)

Raul Ortiz, President

West Yarmouth

***WBUR**
10-01-1940; 1240 kHz AM; *Hrs Open:* 24; 1 kw-U, ND1; N41 38 7 W70 14 6 *Rebroadcasts:* Rebroadcasts WBUR-FM Boston 98%
890 Commonwealth Ave, Attn. Gm C/O Wbur, Boston, MA 02215 US
(617) 353-0909
www.wbur.org
info@wbur.org
License: West Yarmouth, MA held by The Executive Committee of Trustees of The Boston University
Arbitron Metro Market: Boston, MA; *Format:* News, News/Talk, 86 *Special Programming:* Sp 5 hrs wkly; *Hrs. of News Programming:* News progmg 78 hrs wkly; *Target Audience:* 25-54; intelligent adults interested in news& politics
Jean Wong, CFO
Paul LaCamera, General Manager
Corey Lewis, Station Manager
Sam Fleming, Programming Director
John Davidson, News Director
Jeffrey Hutton, Engineering Dir

WXTK
12-30-1948; 95.1 MHz FM; 50 kw; 262 ft.; N41 38 8 W70 14 6
154 Barnstable Road, Hyannis, MA 02601 US
(508) 778-2888; *Fax:* (508) 778-9651
www.95wxtk.com
info@95wxtk.com
License: West Yarmouth, Barnstable County, MA held by AMFM Radio Licenses LLC.
Group Owner: iHeartMedia
Nat'l Network: ABC; *Nat'l Reps:* Eastman Radio
Arbitron Metro Market: Cape Cod, MA; *Format:* News, News/Talk, 84, Talk; *No. News Employees:* 1; *Target Audience:* 25 plus.
Richard J. Bressler, President

Westborough

WAAF
06-15-1961; 107.3 MHz FM; 9.6 kw; 1099 ft.; N42 20 9 W71 42 57
20 Guest Street, Boston, MA 02135 US
(617) 779-5400; *Fax:* (617) 931-1073
www.waaf.com
rvaleri@entercom.com
License: Westborough, Worcester County, MA
Group Owner: Entercom Communications Corp.
Arbitron Metro Market: Westborough, MA; *Format:* Rock/AOR; *Target Audience:* 25-54.
Julie Kahn, General Manager

Westfield

***WNNZ-FM**
05-01-1982; 91.7 MHz FM; *Hrs Open:* 7 AM-8 PM (M-F); 4 AM-11 PM (S); 7; 100 w; 314 ft; N42 32 05 W72 35 32
131 Country Circle, Amherst, MA 01003
(413) 545-0788; *Fax:* (413) 772-1100
License: Westfield, Franklin County, MA held by Trustees of Deerfield Academy.
Population Served: 150,000 *Target Audience:* 10-20; teens, young adults, pre-teens
Christopher Stacy, General Manager

WNNZ
07-08-1987; 640 kHz AM; *Hrs Open:* 24
131 Country Circle, Amherst, MA 01003 US
(413) 545-0788
www.nepr.net
radio@nepr.net
License: Westfield, MA held by New England Public Radio Foundation Inc.
Nat'l Network: NPR
Arbitron Metro Market: Springfield, MA; *Format:* News; *Target Audience:* 25-54; upscale adults
Martin Miller, CEO/COO
Bart Rankin, Operations Dir
Sean Davey, General Manager
Helen Barrington, Programming Director
Fred Bever, News Director
Charles Dube, Chief Engineer

***WSKB**
10-01-1974; 89.5 MHz FM; 0.1 kw; -217 ft.; N42 7 55 W72 47 51
605 Loomis St, Westfield, MA 01085 US
(413) 572-5683
www.wsc.ma.edu/wskb
License: Westfield, Hampden County, MA held by Westfield State College.
Format: Variety/Diverse; *Target Audience:* General.
Jimmy Hewitt, General Manager
Ryan O'Rourke, Programming Director

Williamstown

***WCFM**
09-08-1958; 91.9 MHz FM; 0.44 kw; -837 ft.; N42 42 38 W73 12 6
Paresky Ctr., Williamstown, MA 01267 US
(413) 597-3265; *Fax:* (413) 597-2259
wcfm.williams.edu
wcfmbd@wso.williams.edu
License: Williamstown, Berkshire County, MA held by The President & Trustees of Williams College.
Arbitron Metro Market: Twin Falls, ID
Adam Ain, General Manager

Winchendon

***WKMY**
01-01-2006; 91.1 MHz FM; 0.06 kw; 450 ft.; N42 42 9 W72 2 18
Rebroadcasts: Rebroadcasts KLVR(FM) Middletown, CA 100%
Falls Road, Toccoa Falls, GA 30598 US
(800) 877-5600; *Fax:* (916) 251-1650
License: Winchendon, Worcester County, MA held by Educational Media Foundation.
Group Owner: EMF Broadcasting; (acq 6-30-2005; $15,000 for CP)
Nat'l Network: K-Love
Arbitron Metro Market: Winchendon, MA; *Format:* Christian
Darrell Chambliss, Chairman
Mike Novak, President
Glenn Goodwin, Operations Dir

Woods Hole

***WCAI**
09-25-2000; 90.1 MHz FM; 1.3 kw vert; 249 ft.; N41 26 16 W70 36 51
3 Water Street, Woods Hole, MA 02543 US
(508) 548-9600; *Fax:* (508) 548-5517
www.wgbh.org
cainan@wgbh.org
License: Woods Hole, Barnstable County, MA held by WGBH Educational Foundation
Nat'l Network: NPR
Arbitron Metro Market: Woods Hole, MA; *Format:* News, News/Talk, 86
John Voci, Station Manager
Susan Loucks, General Sales Mgr
Steve Young, Programming Director

Worcester

***WBPR**
01-01-1994; 91.9 MHz FM; 0.37 kw; 699 ft.; N42 18 11 W71 53 52 *Rebroadcasts:* Rebroadcasts WUMB-FM Boston 100%
100 Morrissey Boulevard, Boston, MA 02125 US
(617) 287-6900; *Fax:* (617) 287-6916
www.wumb.org
wumb@umb.edu
License: Worcester, Worcester County, MA held by University of Massachusetts.
Arbitron Metro Market: Boston, MA; *Format:* Variety/Diverse; *No. News Employees:* 25; *Target Audience:* 25-45.
Patricia Monteith, General Manager
Danielle Knight, General Sales Mgr
Brian Quinn, Programming Director

***WCHC**
09-12-1977; 88.1 MHz FM; *Hrs Open:* 7 AM-2 AM; 0.1 kw vert; -7 ft.; N42 14 15 W71 48 31
1 College Street, Worcester, MA 01610 US
(508) 793-2474
License: Worcester, Worcester County, MA held by Trustees of the College of the Holy Cross.
Arbitron Metro Market: Worcester, MA; *Format:* Alternative
Special Programming: Black 8 hrs, class 6 hrs, jazz 6 hrs, metal 6 hrs, funk 3 hrs wkly; *Hrs. of News Programming:* News progmg 5 hrs wkly; *Target Audience:* 12-35; adventurous
James Borders, General Manager

WCRN
12-05-1994; 830 kHz AM
50 Braintree Hill Park, Boston, MA 02184 US
(617) 423-0210
www.wcrnradio.com
chris@wcrnradio.com
License: Worcester, MA held by Carter Broadcasting Corp.
Arbitron Metro Market: Worcester, MA; *Format:* Talk; *Target Audience:* 25-54.
Tony Chavez, Operations Dir
Chris Thompson, General Sales Mgr

***WCUW**
12-04-1973; 91.3 MHz FM; *Hrs Open:* 24; 0.63 kw; 144 ft.; N42 15 46 W71 47 59
US
www.wcuw.org
wcuw@wcuw.org
License: Worcester, Worcester County, MA held by WCUW Inc.
Arbitron Metro Market: Worcester, MA; *Format:* Variety/Diverse
Special Programming: Fr 2 hrs, Sp 19 hrs, Ger 2 hrs, Pol 6 hrs, ethnic 10 hrs wkly; *Hrs. of News Programming:* News progmg one hr wkly; *Target Audience:* General.
Joe Cutroni, General Manager

***WICN**
11-21-1969; 90.5 MHz FM; *Hrs Open:* 24; 1.1 kw; 810 ft.; N42 18 11 W71 53 52
50 Portland Street, Worcester, MA 01608 US
(508) 752-0700; *Fax:* (508) 752-7518
www.wicn.org
webmaster@wicn.org
License: Worcester, Worcester County, MA held by WICN Public Radio Inc.
Nat'l Network: NPR

Arbitron Metro Market: Worcester, MA; *Format:* Big Band, Jazz; *Hrs. of News Programming:* News progmg 12 hrs wkly; *Target Audience:* 35 plus; high education, high income; *Adv. Rates:* 30-40 a spot
Mike Gorman, President
Thomas Kenney, Operations Dir
Brian Barlow, General Manager
Tyra Penn, General Sales Mgr
Kyle Warren, Operations Director

WNEB
12-18-1946; 1230 kHz AM; *Hrs Open:* 24; 1 kw-U, ND1; N42 16 23 W71 49 23
P.O. Box 20027, Worcester, MA 01602 US
(508) 767-1230
www.1230radio.com
info@1230radio.com
License: Worcester, Worcester County, MA held by Emmanuel Communications Inc.
Group Owner: Emmanuel Communications Inc.
Arbitron Metro Market: Worcester, MA; *Format:* Religious; *Target Audience:* 25-54.; *Adv. Rates:* 20; 20; 20; 10
Raymond Lauring, President
Cindy R. Dorsey, General Manager

WORC
02-01-1925; 1310 kHz AM; 5 kw-D, DA2; 1 kw-N, DA2; N42 13 19 W71 49 2
122 Green Street, Worcester, MA 01604 US
(508) 791-2111; *Fax:* (508) 752-6897
www.megaworcester.com/
License: Worcester, MA held by Antonio F. Gois.
Nat'l Network: Westwood One
Arbitron Metro Market: Worcester, MA *TV Affiliate:* Sp; *Format:* Sports; *Hrs. of News Programming:* 1; *No. News Employees:* 29-54; Latinos

WSRS
06-17-1940; 96.1 MHz FM; *Hrs Open:* 24; 16.5 kw; 863 ft.; N42 18 34 W71 54 13
96 Stereo Lane, Paxton, MA 01612 US
(508) 757-9696; *Fax:* (508) 757-1779
www.wsrs.com
info@wsrs.com
License: Worcester, Worcester County, MA held by Capstar TX LLC
Group Owner: iHeartMedia
Nat'l Network: ABC
Arbitron Metro Market: Worcester, MA; *Format:* Adult Contemp; *Hrs. of News Programming:* news progmg 5 hrs wkly; *No. News Employees:* 1; *Target Audience:* 25-54.
Sean Davey, Market Manager
Joe Flynn, Sales Manager
Tony Bristol, Programming Director
Danielle Veronesi, Promotions Director
Chris Tracy, Chief Engineer
Joel Palmer, Production Manager
Julianne Nideur, Market Controller

WTAG
05-01-1924; 580 kHz AM; *Hrs Open:* 24; 5 kw-D, DA2; 5 kw-N, DA2; N42 20 13 W71 49 15
58 Stereo Lane, Paxton, MA 01612 US
(508) 795-0580; *Fax:* (508) 757-1779
www.wtag.com
License: Worcester, MA held by Capstar TX LLC
Group Owner: iHeartMedia; (acq 8-30-2000; grpsl).
Nat'l Network: CBS
Arbitron Metro Market: Worcester, MA; *Format:* News, News/Talk, 86 *Special Programming:* Sports; *Hrs. of News Programming:* news progmg 40 hrs wkly; *No. News Employees:* 6; *Target Audience:* 25-54.
Sean Davey, Market Manager
Joe Flynn, Director of Sales
Kevin Johnson, Programming Director
Danielle Veronesi, Promotions Director
Dan Kelleher, Chief Engineer

WVEI
01-01-1926; 1440 kHz AM; *Hrs Open:* 24; 5 kw-D, DAN; 5 kw-N, DAN; N42 17 25 W71 50 47 *Rebroadcasts:* Simulcast with WEEI(AM) Boston 100%
401 City Avenue, Suite 409, Bala Cynwyd, PA 19004 US
(508) 752-5611; *Fax:* (508) 752-1006
www.weei.com
jsheridan@entercom.com
License: Worcester, MA held by Entercom Boston II License LLC.
Group Owner: Entercom Communications Corp.; (acq 10-15-98; grpsl)
Nat'l Reps: CBS Radio
Arbitron Metro Market: Worcester, MA; *Format:* Sports
Julie Kahn, Station Manager
Jack Sheridan, General Sales Mgr
Eric Fitch, Chief Engineer

Mexico

Tijuana

XETRA
01-01-1934; 690 kHz AM; *Hrs Open:* 24
MX
(818) 972-4200; *Fax:* (818) 972-4210
www.wradio690.com
License: Tijuana, BN held by Clear Channel Communications Inc.
Nat'l Network: ABC
Arbitron Metro Market: Burbank, CA; *Format:* Adult Contemp; *Target Audience:* 25-54; men
Dan Weiner, General Sales Mgr

XETRAFM
01-01-1978; 91.1 MHz FM; *Hrs Open:* 24; kw
6160 Cornerstone Court East, San Diego, CA 92121 MX
(858) 535-2500
www.91x.com
gwolfson@lmasandiego.com
License: Tijuana, BN held by Clear Channel Communications Inc.
Arbitron Metro Market: San Diego, CA; *Format:* Alternative; *No. News Employees:* 1; *Target Audience:* 18-49; very active, college educated, above market average income, single
Megan Kennedy, Sales Manager
Christy Taylor, Programming Director

XHRMFM
01-01-1981; 92.5 MHz FM; *Hrs Open:* 24; kw
6160 Cornerstone Court East, San Diego, CA 92121 MX
(619) 570-1925; *Fax:* 858) 522-5717
www.magic925.com
gwolfson@lmasandiego.com
License: Tijuana, BN held by The Rivas Kaloyan Family.
Arbitron Metro Market: San Diego, CA; *Format:* Adult Contemp, Oldies; *Target Audience:* 18-49.
Megan Kennedy, Sales Manager
Christy Taylor, Programming Director

Michigan

Ada

WPRR
01-01-1998; 1680 kHz AM; *Hrs Open:* 24; 10 kw, ND2; N42 56 9 W85 27 26
3777 44th Street, Grand Rapids, MI 49512 US
(616) 656-1680; *Fax:* (616) 656-2619
www.publicrealityradio.org
info@publicrealityradio.org
License: Ada, MI held by Goodrich Radio L.L.C.
Group Owner: Public Reality Radio
Arbitron Metro Market: Grand Rapids, MI; *Format:* Talk; *No. News Employees:* 1; *Adv. Rates:* 26; 21; 21; 15
Robert Goodrich, Chairman
Robert Goodrich, President
Darren Gibson, Programming Director

Adrian

WABJ
11-13-1946; 1490 kHz AM; *Hrs Open:* 24; 1 kw-U, ND1; N41 54 2 W84 0 51
121 W. Maumec, Adrian, MI 49221 US
(219) 756-5656; *Fax:* (219) 755-4312
www.afr.net
License: Adrian, MI held by Friends Communications of Michigan Inc.
Group Owner: Friends Communications Inc.; (acq 10-1-90; grpsl;
Regional Network: Mich. Farm *Regional Reps:* Michigan.
Arbitron Metro Market: Cheney WA; *Format:* News, News/Talk, 86
Thomas Carroll, CEO
Len Clark, Programming Director

WLEN
06-09-1965; 103.9 MHz FM; *Hrs Open:* 24; 3 kw; 299 ft; N41 54 11 W83 59 13
P.O. Box 687, Adrian, MI 49221
(517) 263-1039; *Fax:* (517) 265-5362
www.wlen.com
License: Adrian, Lenawee County, MI held by Lenawee Broadcasting Co.
Nat'l Network: CBC News Radio
Special Programming: Sp 4 hrs wkly; *No. News Employees:* 1; *Target Audience:* 25-54.
Julie Koehn, President
Julie Koehn, General Manager
Julie Koehn, Station Manager
Pat Hayes, General Sales Mgr
Dale Gaertner, Programming Director
Dominic Fracassa, News Director
Tom Peterson, Engineering Dir
Tom Peterson, ChiefEngineer

WQTE
09-01-1976; 95.3 MHz FM; *Hrs Open:* 24; 3 kw; 299 ft.; N41 48 15 W84 5 25
121 West Maunee Street, Adrian, MI 49221 US
(517) 265-1500; *Fax:* (517) 263-4525
License: Adrian, Lenawee County, MI held by Friends Communications of Michigan Inc.
Group Owner: Friends Communications Inc.; (acq 10-1-90; grpsl;
Format: Country; *Hrs. of News Programming:* News progmg 2 hrs wkly; *Target Audience:* 25-54.
Larry Augustine, General Manager
Patricia Wendt, News Director
Harry Bingaman, Chief Engineer

***WVAC-FM**
02-13-1967; 107.9 MHz FM; 0.087 kw; 84 ft.; N41 53 49 W84 3 40
110 S. Madison, Adrian, MI 49221 US
(517) 264-3913
www.adrian.edu
License: Adrian, Lenawee County, MI held by Adrian College Board of Trustees.
Arbitron Metro Market: Adrian, MI; *Format:* Variety/Diverse; *Target Audience:* 18-23; those affiliated to the college lifestyle
Janaye Powers, Programming Director

Albion

***WUFN**
04-01-1971; 96.7 MHz FM; *Hrs Open:* 24; 3.2 kw; 456 ft.; N42 15 56 W84 38 43
7335 N. Oracle, Tucson, AZ 85704 US
(800) 776-1070
www.myflr.org
License: Albion, Calhoun County, MI held by Family Life Broadcasting System.
Group Owner: Family Life Communications Inc.
Nat'l Network: USA; AP Radio
Arbitron Metro Market: Battle Creek, MI; *Format:* Christian, Religious; *Hrs. of News Programming:* News progmg 1.5 hrs wkly; *Target Audience:* 25-54; Christian families
Randy Carlson, President
Dawn Bumstead, General Manager

Allendale

***WGVU-FM**
07-15-1983; 88.5 MHz FM; *Hrs Open:* 24; 4 kw; 295 ft.; N43 3 24 W85 57 37
301 West Fulton Street, Grand Rapids, MI 49504 US
(616) 331-6666
www.wgvu.org
wgvu@gvsu.edu
License: Allendale, Ottawa County, MI held by Board of Control of Grand Valley State University.
Nat'l Network: NPR; AP Radio
Format: Jazz, News; *Hrs. of News Programming:* news progmg 26 hrs wkly; *No. News Employees:* 5; *Target Audience:* 25 plus; mid to upper educ & income levels
Ken Kolbe, Operations Dir
Michael Walenta, General Manager
Gary Hunt, Programming Director
Pamela Holtz, Promotions Manager
Fred Martino, News Director

Alma

WFYC
08-17-1948; 1280 kHz AM; *Hrs Open:* 24
PO Box 665, Alma, MI 48801 US
(989) 463-3175; *Fax:* (989) 463-6674
www.wqbxradio.com
wqbx@cmsinter.net
License: Alma, MI held by Jacom Inc.
Format: Sports *Special Programming:* Farm 4 hrs wkly; *Target Audience:* 25-50.; *Adv. Rates:* 10.50; 10.50; 10.50; 9
James Sommerville, President
Susan Sommerville, Promotions Manager

RADIO - U.S.

***WQAC**
03-27-1993; 90.9 MHz FM; *Hrs Open:* 7 AM-2 AM (M-F); noon-2 AM (S, Su); 0.1 kw; 66 ft.; N43 22 46 W84 40 25
614 West Superior Street, Alma, MI 48801 US
(989) 463-7095; *Fax:* (989) 463-7277
License: Alma, Gratiot County, MI held by Alma College.
Format: Alternative; *Target Audience:* 13-24; high school & college students
Steven Best, General Manager

Alpena

WZTK
06-01-2014; 105.7 MHz FM; *Hrs Open:* 20; 4.5 kw; 285 ft.; N45 3 58 W83 29 6
123 Prentiss St., Alpena, MI 49707 US
(989) 354-8400; *Fax:* (989) 354-3436
www.watz.com
watz@watz.com
License: Alpena, Alpena County, MI held by WATZ Radio Inc.
Group Owner: Midwestern Broadcasting Co.
Regional Network: Mich. Farm
Arbitron Metro Market: Alpena, MI; *Format:* News, News/Talk, 86
Special Programming: Farm 3 hrs, Ger 2 hrs, Pol 2 hrs, relg 2 hrs wkly; *Hrs. of News Programming:* news progmg 31 hrs wkly; *No. News Employees:* 2 *Target Audience:* 35-64.
Mike Centala, General Sales Mgr
Steve Wright, Programming Director
Bruce Johnson, News Director
Mary Thurston, Production Director

WATZ-FM
01-01-1967; 99.3 MHz FM; *Hrs Open:* 20; 17 kw; 843 ft.; N44 51 25 W83 32 34
Mailing Address: 123 Prentiss St., Alpena, MI 49707 US
Second Address: 300 E. Front St., Suite 450, Traverse City, MI 49684
(989) 354-8400; *Fax:* (989) 354-3436
www.watz.com
watz@watz.com
License: Alpena, Alpena County, MI held by WATZ Radio Inc.
Group Owner: Midwestern Broadcasting Co.
Arbitron Metro Market: Alpena, MI; *Format:* Country; *Target Audience:* 25-54.
Mike Centala, General Sales Mgr
Steve Wright, Programming Director
Bruce Johnson, News Director
Mary Thurston, Production Director

***WCML-FM**
04-24-1978; 91.7 MHz FM; *Hrs Open:* 24; 92 kw; 1194 ft.; N45 8 17.3 W84 9 43.6 *Rebroadcasts:* Rebroadcasts WCMU-FM Mount Pleasant 100%
3965 E Broomfield Road, Mt. Pleasant, MI 48859 US
(989) 774-3105; *Fax:* (989) 774-4427
www.wcmu.org
schud1ra@cmich.edu
License: Alpena, Alpena County, MI held by Central Michigan University.
Nat'l Network: NPR; PRI; *Wire Services:* AP
Arbitron Metro Market: Michigan, Upper Peninsula,MS *TV Affiliate:* *WCML(TV) affil; *Format:* Jazz, News; *Hrs. of News Programming:* news progmg 45 hrs wkly; *No. News Employees:* 2; *Target Audience:* General.
Edward Grant, General Manager
Ray Ford, Programming Director

WHSB
05-01-1965; 107.7 MHz FM; 100 kw; 610 ft.; N45 3 46 W83 42 56
1491 M-32 W., Alpena, MI 49707 US
(989) 354-4611; *Fax:* (989) 354-4014
www.truenorthradionetwork.com
thebay@truenorthradionetwork.com
License: Alpena, Alpena County, MI held by Edwards Communications LC.
Group Owner: Edwards Communications LC.; (acq 12-21-2004; grpsl).
Nat'l Reps: Michigan Spot Sales; *Wire Services:* UPI
Format: Adult Contemp; *Target Audience:* 25-54.
Darrel Kelly, General Manager
Phil Heimerl, News Director

Ann Arbor

WAAM
10-01-1947; 1600 kHz AM; *Hrs Open:* 24; 5 kw-D, DA2; 5 kw-N, DA2; N42 11 32 W83 41 9
US
(225) 768-8300
www.jsm.org
kawikfish@yahoo.com
License: Ann Arbor, MI held by Ann Arbor First Ventures L.P.
Nat'l Network: Westwood One
Arbitron Metro Market: El Dorado AR; *Format:* Christian, Religious; *Adv. Rates:* 38; 38; 34; 20
David Whitelaw, COO

***WCBN-FM**
01-23-1972; 88.3 MHz FM; *Hrs Open:* 24; 0.2 kw vert; 177 ft.; N42 16 37 W83 44 7
5000 Ls & a Bldg, 5th Flr, Ann Arbor, MI 48109 US
(734) 647-4122(734) 763-3535
www.wcbn.org
License: Ann Arbor, Washtenaw County, MI held by Regents of the University of Michigan.
Arbitron Metro Market: Ann Arbor, MI; *Format:* Variety/Diverse; *Target Audience:* 18-49.
Rob Goldey, General Manager
Kristin Sumrall, Programming Director
Alex Sergay, Chief Engineer

WWWW-FM
03-01-1962; 102.9 MHz FM; *Hrs Open:* 24; 50 kw; 440 ft.; N42 14 46 W83 50 58
1100 Victors Way, Suite 100, Ann Arbor, MI 48108 US
(734) 302-8100; *Fax:* (734) 213-7508
www.w4country.com
programming@w4country.com
License: Ann Arbor, Washtenaw County, MI held by Cumulus Licensing LLC
Group Owner: Cumulus Media Inc.; (acq 2007)
Nat'l Reps: Cumulus Radio Sales
Arbitron Metro Market: Ann Arbor, MI; *Format:* Country
Matt Spaulding, Market Manager
Brian Cowan, Programming Director
Sarah Thomas, Promotions Director
Brian Welch, Production Director

WQKL
02-14-1967; 107.1 MHz FM; 3 kw; 289 ft.; N42 16 41 W83 44 32
1100 Victors Way, Ann Arbor, MI 48108 US
(734) 302-8100; *Fax:* (734) 213-7508
www.annarbors107one.com
License: Ann Arbor, Washtenaw County, MI
Nat'l Reps: Cumulus Radio Sales
Arbitron Metro Market: Ann Arbor, MI; *Format:* Triple A; *Hrs. of News Programming:* news progmg 4 hrs wkly; *No. News Employees:* 1; *Target Audience:* 25-50; women
Brent Dingman, General Sales Mgr
Chris Ammel, Programming Director
Chris Wachner, Promotions Manager
Brian Larsen, News Director

WTKA
04-26-1945; 1050 kHz AM; 10 kw-D, DA2; 0.5 kw-N, DA2; N42 8 46 W83 39 36
1100 Victors Way, Suite 100, Ann Arbor, MI 48108 US
(734) 302-8100; *Fax:* (734) 213-7508
www.wtka.com
programming@wtka.com
License: Ann Arbor, MI held by Cumulus Licensing LLC
Group Owner: Cumulus Media Inc.
Nat'l Network: CBS Sports Radio; *Nat'l Reps:* Cumulus Radio Sales
Arbitron Metro Market: Ann Arbor, MI; *Format:* Sports; *No. News Employees:* 1; *Target Audience:* 18-34; male
Matt Spaulding, Market Manager

***WUOM**
01-01-1948; 91.7 MHz FM; *Hrs Open:* 24; 93 kw; 778 ft.; N42 24 27 W83 54 50
535 W. William Street, Ann Arbor, MI 48103 US
(734) 764-9210; *Fax:* (734) 647-3488
www.michiganradio.org
michigan.radio@umich.edu
License: Ann Arbor, Washtenaw County, MI held by The Regents of University of Michigan.
Nat'l Network: NPR; PRI; *Wire Services:* AP
Arbitron Metro Market: Ann Arbor, MI; *Format:* News, News/Talk, 86; *Hrs. of News Programming:* news progmg 140 hrs wkly; *No. News Employees:* 7
Peggy Watson, Operations Dir
Tamar Charney, Programming Director
Vincent Duffy, News Director
Larry Jonas, Director of Development
Steve Chrypinski, Marketing Director
Kathy Agosta, Director of Corporate Support

Ashley

WJSZ
03-14-1994; 92.5 MHz FM; *Hrs Open:* 24; 4 kw; 400 ft.; N43 10 56 W84 27 3
1907 W-M-21, Owosso, MI 48867 US
(989) 725-1925; *Fax:* (989) 725-7925
www.z925.com
rodk@voyager.net
License: Ashley, Gratiot County, MI held by Krol Communications Inc.
Regional Network: Mich. Farm
Format: Adult Contemp; *Hrs. of News Programming:* 90 mins wkly; *Target Audience:* 25-54; general; *Adv. Rates:* 30; 24; 24; 15
Rob Krol, President
Angie Bucsf, General Manager

Atlanta

WFDX
10-20-1988; 92.5 MHz FM; *Hrs Open:* 24; 100 kw; 869 ft.; N45 1 0 W84 21 10
1020 Hastings, Traverse City, MI 49686 US
(231) 947-5369
www.943thefoxfm.com
charlie@wklt.com
License: Atlanta, Montmorency County, MI held by Northern Michigan Radio Inc.
Nat'l Reps: Christal
Arbitron Metro Market: Traverse City, MI; *Format:* Contemporary Hits/Top 40, Adult Contemp; *No. News Employees:* 1; *Target Audience:* 25-54.
Rich Nadkau, Programming Director

Auburn Hills

***WAHS**
01-01-1975; 89.5 MHz FM; 0.1 kw; 141 ft.; N42 37 42 W83 13 56
2800 Waukegan, Auburn Hills, MI 48326 US
(248) 852-9247; *Fax:* (248) 852-0595
License: Auburn Hills, Oakland County, MI held by Avondale School District.
Arbitron Metro Market: Auburn Hills, MI; *Format:* Contemporary Hits/Top 40
Rick Kreinbring, General Manager

***WXOU**
08-01-1995; 88.3 MHz FM; *Hrs Open:* 24; 0.11 kw; 256 ft.; N42 42 35 W83 13 50
69 Oakland Center, Rochester, MI 48309 US
(248) 370-4273
www.wxou.org
wxou@wxou.org
License: Auburn Hills, Oakland County, MI held by Oakland University.
Arbitron Metro Market: Auburn Hills, MI; *Format:* Variety/Diverse; *Hrs. of News Programming:* 8 hrs wkly; *No. News Employees:* 5; *Target Audience:* General; univ & loc community not serviced by coml media
Sean Varicalli, General Manager
Christine Stover, General Sales Mgr
Christina Venditti, Programming Director
Josh Nagy, Promotions Manager
Ashley Allison, News Director
Patrick Cymbalski, Assistant Program Director
Matt Pocket,Sports Director
Joe Iaconis, IT Director

Bad Axe

WLEW
01-01-1950; 1340 kHz AM; *Hrs Open:* 24; 1 kw-D, DAD; 1 kw-N, DAD; N43 48 3 W83 1 23
935 South Van Dyke Rd, Bad Axe, MI 48413 US
(989) 269-9931; *Fax:* (989) 269-7702
www.thumbnet.net
info@thumbnet.net
License: Bad Axe, MI held by Thumb Broadcasting Inc.
Format: Country; *Hrs. of News Programming:* news progmg 19 hrs wkly; *No. News Employees:* 2; *Target Audience:* 18-50.
Richard Aymen, General Manager

WLEW-FM
01-01-1956; 102.1 MHz FM; *Hrs Open:* 24; 50 kw; Ant 492 ft; N43 53 28 W83 07 26
935 S. Van Dyke Rd., Bad Axe, MI 48413
(989) 269-9931; *Fax:* (989) 269-7702
License: Bad Axe, Huron County, MI held by Thumb Broadcasting Inc.
Population Served: 620,000 *Target Audience:* 25-50.

Richard Aymen, Operations Dir
Matthew Aymen, General Sales Mgr
Craig Routzhan, News Director
Jerry Stocker, Chief Engineer
Tina Hind, Traffic Manager

Baraga

***WVCN**
01-01-1998; 104.3 MHz FM; *Hrs Open:* 24; 100 kw; 860 ft.; N46 39 50 W88 23 6
3434 W Kilbourn Ave, Milwaukee, WI 53208 US
(800) 729-9829; *Fax:* (414) 935-3015
www.vcyamerica.org
wvcn@vcyamerica.org
License: Baraga, Baraga County, MI held by Keweenaw Bay Broadcasting Inc.
Group Owner: VCY America Inc.; (acq 7-8-99)
Format: Christian
Dr. Randall Melchert, President
Vic Eliason, Operations Dir
Jim Schneider, Programming Director
Gordon Morris, News Director
Andy Eliason, Chief Engineer
Tom Schlueter, Music Director

Battle Creek

WBCK
07-09-1948; 930 kHz AM; 5 kw-D, 1 kw-N, DA-2; N42 17 40 W85 11 00
390 Golden Ave., Battle Creek, MI 49015
(269) 963-5555
License: Battle Creek, Calhoun County, MI held by Stratus Radio LLC
Population Served: 170,000; *Arbitron Metro Market:* Battle Creek, M
Tim Collins, Programming Director

WBCK-FM
02-28-1975; 95.3 MHz FM; 3 kw; 269 ft.; N42 17 17 W85 9 54
390 Golden Ave., Battle Creek, MI 49015 US
(269) 963-5555; *Fax:* (269) 963-5185
www.wbckfm.com
License: Battle Creek, Calhoun County, MI held by Townsquare Media Battle Creek License LLC
Group Owner: Townsquare Media; (acq 11-14-2013).
Arbitron Metro Market: Battle Creek, MI; *Format:* News, News/Talk, 86; *Target Audience:* 25-54.
Kate Conley, General Manager
Kelly Troff, Director of Sales
Tim Collins, Brand Manager
Kayla Kiley, Digital Managing Editor

WKFR-FM
06-11-1963; 103.3 MHz FM; *Hrs Open:* 24; 50 kw; 482 ft.; N42 21 20 W85 20 28
4154 Jennings Drive, Kalamazoo, MI 49048 US
(269) 344-0111
www.wkfr.com
radio@wkfr.com
License: Battle Creek, Calhoun County, MI held by Cumulus Licensing Corp.
Group Owner: Cumulus Media Inc.; (acq 5-26-98; grpsl)
Arbitron Metro Market: Kalamazoo, MI; *Format:* Contemporary Hits/Top 40; *Hrs. of News Programming:* news progmg 3 hrs wkly; *No. News Employees:* 1; *Target Audience:* 25-54.
Dana Marshall, Programming Director

WBFN
07-01-1993; 1400 kHz AM
390 Golden Avenue, Battle Creek, MI 49015 US
(601) 776-2931
www.flc.org
License: Battle Creek, MI held by Aloha Station Trust LLC
Arbitron Metro Market: Battle Creek, MI; *Format:* Christian
Randy Carlson, President

Bay City

***WCHW-FM**
09-01-1973; 91.3 MHz FM; 0.11 kw horiz; 125 ft.; N43 35 19 W83 52 28
1624 Columbus Avenue, Bay City, MI 48708 US
(989) 892-1741
www.wchwonline.freewebspace.com
License: Bay City, Bay County, MI held by School District Bay City.
Arbitron Metro Market: Bay City, MI; *Format:* Rock/AOR
Jeremy Powers, General Manager

WHNN
01-01-1947; 96.1 MHz FM; *Hrs Open:* 24; 100 kw; 1020 ft.; N43 33 10 W83 41 24
1740 Champagne Dr. N., Saginaw, MI 48604 US
(989) 776-2100
www.whnn.com
License: Bay City, MI held by Radio License Holding CBC, LLC
Group Owner: Cumulus Media Inc.; (acq 4-26-01; grpsl).
Arbitron Metro Market: Saginaw-Bay City-Midland, MI; *Format:* Adult Contemp; *No. News Employees:* 1
Julia Richardson, Marketing

WIOG
11-12-1961; 102.5 MHz FM; *Hrs Open:* 24; 86 kw; 801 ft.; N43 28 24 W83 50 40
1740 Champagne Dr. N., Saginaw, MI 48604 US
(989) 776-2100
www.wiog.com
nate@wiog.com
License: Bay City, MI held by Radio License Holding CBC, LLC
Group Owner: Cumulus Media Inc.; (acq 2-8-99; grpsl).
Nat'l Network: ABC
Arbitron Metro Market: Saginaw-Bay City-Midland, MI; *Format:* Contemporary Hits/Top 40
Julia Richardson, General Sales Mgr

WMAX
06-05-1925; 1440 kHz AM; *Hrs Open:* 24; 5 kw-D, DA2; 2.5 kw-N, DA2; N43 31 27 W83 57 58 *Rebroadcasts:* WDEO(AM) Ypsilanti 97%
P.O. Box 504, Ann Arbor, MI 48106 US
(734) 930-5200; *Fax:* (989) 930-3101
www.avemariaradio.net
mjones@avemariaradio.net
License: Bay City, MI held by 990 Investors L.L.C.
Nat'l Network: EWTN Radio
Arbitron Metro Market: Saginaw, MI; *Format:* Talk, Christian; *Hrs. of News Programming:* news progmg 14 hrs wkly; *No. News Employees:* 2; *Target Audience:* 25-54; adult Christian; *Adv. Rates:* 25; 25; 45; 25
Al Kresta, CEO
Michael Jones, President

***WLKB**
07-25-1993; 89.1 MHz FM; *Hrs Open:* 24; 50 kw vert; 371 ft.; N43 33 42 W83 58 52 *Rebroadcasts:* Rebroadcasts KLVR(FM) Santa Rosa, CA 100%
919 29th St., Bay City, MI 48708 US
(800) 525-5683
www.klove.com
klove@klove.com
License: Bay City, Bay County, MI held by Educational Media Foundation.
Group Owner: EMF Broadcasting; (acq 8-8-2006; $800,000)
Nat'l Network: K-Love
Arbitron Metro Market: Rocklin, CA; *Format:* Christian; *No. News Employees:* 3; *Target Audience:* 25-44; female-Judeo Christian
Darrell Chambliss, Chairman
Mike Novak, CEO
Mike Novak, President
Pam Patrick-Thompson, Operations Dir
David Pierce, Programming Director
Ed Lenane, News Director
Sam Wallington, Engineering Dir
Marya Morgan, News Reporter
Richard Hunt, News Reporter
Mitch Barnhart, Director
Larry Moody, Director
Dr.David.R.Ferry, Director

***WUCX-FM**
09-01-1989; 90.1 MHz FM; 30 kw; 479 ft.; N43 33 10 W83 41 24
1961 Delta Road, University Center, MI 48710 US
(877) 472-7677
wucx@delta.edu
License: Bay City, Bay County, MI held by Central Michigan University.
Nat'l Network: NPR; PRI
Arbitron Metro Market: Bay City, MI; *Format:* Blues, Jazz, 60; *Target Audience:* General.
Barry Baker, General Manager
Joe Yezak, Program Manager

Bear Creek Township

***WTLI**
09-16-1998; 89.3 MHz FM; 17 kw vert; 1024 ft.; N45 10 12 W84 45 4 *Rebroadcasts:* rebroadcast of WLGH(FM) Leroy Township
148 East Grand River Road, Williamston, MI 48895 US
(888) 887-7139; *Fax:* (877) 850-0881
www.positivehits.com
411@smile.fm
License: Bear Creek Township, Emmet County, MI held by Superior Communications.
Group Owner: Superior Communications
Arbitron Metro Market: Petoskey, MI; *Format:* Christian
Jenn Czelada, General Manager
Ed Czelada, Programming Director

Bear Lake

WCUZ
11-02-1987; 100.1 MHz FM; 2.05 kw; 564 ft.; N44 30 54 W86 6 53 *Rebroadcasts:* Simulcasts WLDR-FM Traverse City 100%
Mailing Address: P.O. Box 262, Bear Lake, MI 49617 US
Second Address: 1532 Forrester Rd, Frankfort, MI 49635
(231) 947-3220; *Fax:* (231) 947-7201
License: Bear Lake, Manistee County, MI held by Roy E. Henderson.
Group Owner: Fort Bend Broadcasting Co.; (acq 9-27-2000; $590,000 with WOUF(FM) Beulah)
Format: Country
Roy Henderson, General Manager

Beaverton

WMRX-FM
09-15-1980; 97.7 MHz FM; 4.1 kw; 400 ft.; N43 53 16 W84 31 45 *Rebroadcasts:* Rebroadcasts WMPX(FM) Midland 100%
Mailing Address: 1510 Bayliss Street, Midland, MI 48640 US
Second Address: 1510 Bayliss St., Midland, MI 48640
989-631-1490; *Fax:* (989) 631-6357
www.wmpxwmrx.com
admin@wmpxwmrx.com
License: Beaverton, Gladwin County, MI held by Steel Broadcasting Inc.
Nat'l Network: ABC
Arbitron Metro Market: Saginaw, MI; *Format:* Oldies, Adult Contemp *Special Programming:* Sounds of Sinatra 2 hrs wkly; *Hrs. of News Programming:* News progmg 8 hrs wkly; *No. News Employees:* 1; *Target Audience:* General; 35+
Thomas Steel, President
Jon Walding, General Sales Mgr
Brad Morgan, Programming Director
Tom Steel, News Director

Belding

***WSLI**
01-01-2009; 90.9 MHz FM; 11.5 kw vert; 240 ft.; N43 5 12 W85 18 59 *Rebroadcasts:* Rebroadcasts WLGH(FM) Leroy Township 100%
148 East Grand River Road, Williamston, MI 48895 US
(888) 887-7139
www.smile.fm
411@smile.fm
License: Belding, Ionia County, MI held by Smile FM.
Group Owner: Superior Communications
Arbitron Metro Market: Belding, MI; *Format:* Christian
Edward Czelada, President
Jenn Czelada, General Manager
Dale Mazzoline, Feature Production
Ed Czelada, Administration, Programming & Engineering
Clayton Hewitt, Administration and Engineering
Aaron Burrell, Administration

Benton Harbor

WSJM-FM
06-15-1998; 94.9 MHz FM; *Hrs Open:* 24; 2.2 kW; 381 ft.; N42 4 19 W86 22 14
PO Box 107, St. Joseph, MI 49085 USA
(269) 925-1111; *Fax:* (269) 925-1011
www.wsjm.com
news@wsjm.com
License: Benton Harbor, Berrien County, MI held by WSJM, Inc.
Group Owner: Mid-West Family Broadcasting
Regional Reps: Michigan Spot Sales
Arbitron Metro Market: St. Joseph, MI; *Format:* News/Talk
Dave Doetsch, President & General Manager
Paul Layendecker, Operations Manager
Bob Bucholtz, General Sales Mgr
Ray Gustafson, Programming Director
Ray Gustafson, News Director

WHFB-FM
10-10-1947; 99.9 MHz FM; 50 kw; 407 ft.; N41 57 42 W86 21 2
1301 East Douglas Road, Mishawaka, MI 46545 US
(574) 233-3141
License: Benton Harbor, Berrien County, MI held by WHFB Broadcast Associates L.P.

Format: Country; *Target Audience:* 25-54.
Bill Gamble, Programming Director

WSJM-AM
11-18-1956; 1400 kHz AM; *Hrs Open:* 24; 0.88 kW; N42 5 12 W86 26 40
PO Box 107, St. Joseph, MI 49085 USA
(269) 925-1111; *Fax:* (269) 925-1011
www.wsjmsports.com
License: Benton Harbor, MI held by WSJM, Inc.
Group Owner: Mid-West Family Broadcasting; (acq 1-1-59)
Nat'l Network: ABC; *Regional Network:* Mich. Talk; *Wire Services:* AP
Format: Sports; *No. News Employees:* 4; *Target Audience:* 35 plus.
Gayle Olson, Chairman
Dave Doetsch, President & General Manager
Ray Gustafson, Operations Manager
Bob Bucholtz, General Sales Mgr
Lindsay Kay, Promotions Manager
Ray Gustafson, News Manager
Terry Green, Engineering Dir

***WCXB**
89.9 MHz FM; 0.25 kw; 335 ft.; N42 4 19 W86 22 14
Rebroadcasts: WCSG(FM) Grand Rapids 100%
1159 E. Beltline Ave. N.E., Grand Rapids, MI 49525 US
(616) 942-1500; *Fax:* (616) 942-7078
www.wcsg.org
License: Benton Harbor, Berrien County, MI held by Cornerstone University.
Arbitron Metro Market: Benton Harbor, MI; *Format:* Christian; *Target Audience:* Teens, young adults.

WQLQ
94.3 MHz FM; 50 kW; 407 ft.; N41 57 42 W86 21 2
1301 East Douglas Rd, Mishawaka, IN 46545 USA
(574) 247-4343
www.live999radio.com
License: Benton Harbor, MI held by WSJM, Inc.
Group Owner: Mid-West Family Broadcasting
Arbitron Metro Market: South Bend, IN; *Format:* Contemporary Hits/Top 40

Benton Harbor-St. Jo

WHFB
09-22-1947; 1060 kHz AM; 2.5 kw-C, ND1; 5 kw-D, ND1; ND1; 0.0013; N42 4 44 W86 28 1; N42 4 44 W86 28 0
2100 Fairplain Avenue, Benton Harbor, MI 49022 US
(269) 934-5137
License: Benton Harbor-St. Jo, MI held by WHFB Broadcast Associates L.P.
Regional Network: Mich. Farm
Format: News, News/Talk, 86; *No. News Employees:* 1; *Target Audience:* General.
Bill Stanley, General Manager
Jill Ferraro, General Sales Mgr

Berrien Springs

***WAUS**
01-01-1971; 90.7 MHz FM; *Hrs Open:* 24; 50 kw; 492 ft.; N41 57 42 W86 21 2
WAUS, Berrien Springs, MI 49104 US
(269) 471-3400; *Fax:* (269) 471-3804
www.waus.org
waus@andrews.edu
License: Berrien Springs, Berrien County, MI held by Andrews Broadcasting Corp.
Nat'l Network: PRI
Arbitron Metro Market: Tyler-Longview, TX; *Format:* Talk *Special Programming:* Relg 10 hrs wkly; *Hrs. of News Programming:* News progmg 3 hrs wkly; *Target Audience:* 35 plus; listeners with interest in classicalmusic
Niels-Erik Andreasen, Chairman
Sharon Dudgeon, General Manager
Bill Brent, Programming Director

Beulah

WOUF
01-01-1998; 99.3 MHz FM; 50 kw horiz; 430 ft.; N44 36 38 W86 9 38
1532 Forrester Road, Frankfort, MI 49635 US
(231) 947-3220; *Fax:* (231) 947-7201
License: Beulah, Benzie County, MI held by Roy E. Henderson.
Group Owner: Fort Bend Broadcasting Co.; acq 9-27-2000; $590,000 with WCUZ(FM) Bear Lake)
Arbitron Metro Market: Traverse City,MI; *Format:* Country; *Target Audience:* 18-54; male
Roy Henderson, General Manager

Big Rapids

WBRN
01-06-1953; 1460 kHz AM; *Hrs Open:* 24
1820 16 Mile Road, Big Rapids, MI 49307 US
(231) 796-7000; *Fax:* (231) 796-7951
www.wbrn.com
news@bigrapidsradionetwork.com
License: Big Rapids, MI held by Mentor Partners Inc.
Group Owner: Mentor Partners Inc.; (acq 6-21-2005; $850,000 with co-located FM).
Nat'l Network: ESPN Radio; *Regional Network:* Minn. News Net;
Nat'l Reps: Michigan Spot Sales
Arbitron Metro Market: Big Rapids, MI; *Format:* News, News/Talk, 84, Talk; *Hrs. of News Programming:* news progmg 12 hrs wkly; *No. News Employees:* 1; *Target Audience:* 35 plus; adults; *Adv. Rates:* 8.35; 8.35;8.35; 8.35
Jeffrey Scarpelli, President
Brian Goodenow, Operations Dir
Jeff Scarpelli, General Manager
Brian Goodenow, Programming Director
Steve Gove, News Director
Mark Wittkoski, Chief Engineer

WWBR
09-01-1964; 100.9 MHz FM; *Hrs Open:* 24; 6 kw; 318 ft.; N43 39 49 W85 28 54
17964 River's Edge Dr., Big Rapids, MI 49307 US
(231) 796-7000; *Fax:* (231) 796-7951
License: Big Rapids, Mecosta County, MI
Group Owner: Mentor Partners Inc.
Regional Network: Mich. Radio; *Wire Services:* AP
Arbitron Metro Market: Big Rapids, MI; *Format:* Country; *Hrs. of News Programming:* news progmg 10 hrs wkly; *No. News Employees:* 1; *Target Audience:* 25-54.; *Adv. Rates:* 24;20;22;18
Jeff Scarpelli, General Manager
Steve Gove, News Director
Mark Wittkoski, Chief Engineer

WODJ
10-21-1959; 1590 kHz AM; *Hrs Open:* 24
US
(231) 830-0176; *Fax:* (231) 830-0194
License: Big Rapids, MI
Group Owner: Cumulus Media Inc.; (acq 9-28-2005; grpsl).
Arbitron Metro Market: Muskegon, MI; *Format:* Talk
Jeff Morton, General Manager

WYBR
06-30-1982; 102.3 MHz FM; *Hrs Open:* 24; 10.5 kw; 436 ft.; N43 41 1 W85 34 56
18720 16 Mile Road, Big Rapids, MI 49307 US
(231) 796-7000; *Fax:* (231) 796-7951
www.wybr.com
License: Big Rapids, Mecosta County, MI held by Mentor Partners Inc.
Group Owner: Mentor Partners Inc.; (acq 8-10-98).
Arbitron Metro Market: Big Rapids, MIý; *Format:* Adult Contemp
Special Programming: Relg one hr wkly; *Hrs. of News Programming:* news progmg 8 hrs wkly; *No. News Employees:* 2; *Target Audience:* 25-49. *Adv.Rates:* 22; 19; 20; 16
Jeffrey Scarpelli, General Manager
Diane Scarpelli, General Sales Mgr
Mark Wittkoski, Chief Engineer

Birmingham

WCSX
03-14-1987; 94.7 MHz FM; *Hrs Open:* 24; 13.5 kw; 951 ft.; N42 27 13 W83 9 50
1 Radio Plaza Street, Feundale, NJ 48220 US
(248) 398-9470
www.wcsx.com
License: Birmingham, Oakland County, MI held by Greater Michigan Radio Inc.
Group Owner: Beasley Broadcast Group; (acq 7-3-73)
Nat'l Reps: McGavren Guild
Arbitron Metro Market: Detroit,MI; *Format:* Classic Rock; *Target Audience:* 25-54; males
Tom Bender, Operations Dir

Bloomfield Hills

***WBFH**
10-01-1976; 88.1 MHz FM; *Hrs Open:* 24; 0.36 kw; 180 ft.; N42 34 42 W83 17 10
7273 Wing Lake Road, Bloomfield Hills, MI 48301 US
(248)-341-5400; *Fax:* (248) 341-5449
www.wbfh.fm
thebiff@Radio.fm
License: Bloomfield Hills, Oakland County, MI held by Board of Education of Bloomfield Hills School District.
Arbitron Metro Market: Bloomfield Hills, MI; *Format:* Sports, Talk
Special Programming: Prep sports 6 hrs wkly; *Target Audience:* 12-34.
Justin Lopas, Operations Dir
Pete Bowers, General Manager
Paul Stewart, Station Manager
Paul Stewart, Programming Director
Grace McIlhon & Sean Shepard, Promotions Manager
Eric Bloom, News Director
Randy Carr, Engineering Dir
Danny Harwood, Production Director
Jeremy Fishman, Music Director
Bryan Furlong, Video Department Director
Michael Blumenthal, Sports Director
Joshua Lumsden, Public Affairs Director

Boyne City

WBCM
04-10-1978; 93.5 MHz FM; *Hrs Open:* 24; 14 kw; 928 ft.; N45 19 27 W84 52 44 *Rebroadcasts:* Simulcast of WTCM-FM Traverse City, MI
314 E. Front St., P.O. Box 472, Traverse City, MI 49684 US
(231) 947-7675; *Fax:* (231) 929-3988
www.wtcmi.com
wtcm@wtcmradio.com
License: Boyne City, Charlevoix County, MI held by WBCM Radio Inc.
Group Owner: Midwestern Broadcasting Co.; (acq 9-6-90; $250,000;
Nat'l Reps: Katz Radio
Arbitron Metro Market: Petoskey, MI; *Format:* Country
Paul Binsfield, General Sales Mgr
Jack O'Malley, Programming Director
Joel Franck, News Director
Steve Cook, Production Manager

Bridgeport

WHHQ
11-26-1956; 1250 kHz AM; *Hrs Open:* 24; 5 kw-D, 1.1 kw-N, DA-2; N43 20 31 W83 53 57
Box 504, Ann Arbor, MI 48607
(734) 930-5200
www.avemariaradio.net
License: Bridgeport, Saginaw County, MI held by Ave Maria Communications
Arbitron Metro Market: Saginaw-Bay City-Midland, MI
Al Kresta, President/Chief Executive Officer

Bridgman

WYTZ
03-01-1993; 97.5 MHz FM; *Hrs Open:* 24; 3.8 kW; 413 ft.; N41 59 24 W86 31 47
580 E Napier Ave, Benton Harbor, MI 49022 USA
(269) 925-1111; *Fax:* (269) 925-1011
www.975ycountry.com
License: Bridgman, Berrien County, MI held by WSJM, Inc.
Group Owner: Mid-West Family Broadcasting; (acq 1996; grpsl)
Nat'l Reps: Christal
Arbitron Metro Market: Bridgman, MI; *Format:* Country; *No. News Employees:* 5; *Target Audience:* 25-54.
Gayle Olson, Chairman
Dave Doetsch, President & General Manager
Paul Layendecker, Operations Manager
Bob Bucholtz, General Sales Mgr
Ray Gustafson, News Director

Bronson

***WCVM**
01-01-1998; 94.7 MHz FM; *Hrs Open:* 24; 4 kw; 404 ft.; N41 44 30 W85 14 32 *Rebroadcasts:* Repeater for WBCL 90.3 FM
1115 West Rudisill Blvd, Fort Wayne, IN 46807 US
(260) 745-0576; *Fax:* (260) 456-2913
www.wbcl.org
License: Bronson, Branch County, MI held by Taylor University Broadcasting, Inc.
Group Owner: Taylor University Broadcasting, Inc.
Arbitron Metro Market: Bronson, MI; *Format:* Christian, Religious; *Target Audience:* 25+

Brooklyn

WKHM-FM
01-01-1994; 105.3 MHz FM; *Hrs Open:* 24; 2.2 kw; 377 ft.; N42 9 14 W84 24 7
1700 Glenshire Dr., Jackson, MI 49201 US
(517) 787-9546; *Fax:* (517) 787-7517
www.k1053.com
steve@wkhm.com

License: Brooklyn, Jackson County, MI held by Jackson Radio Works Inc.
Group Owner: Jackson Radio Works Inc.; (acq 12-8-97; grpsl).
Regional Reps: Michigan Spot Sls
Format: Adult Contemp; *No. News Employees:* 2; *Target Audience:* 18-49.
Bruce Goldsen, President
Sue Goldsen, Operations Dir
Jamie McKibbin, Station Manager
Michael Bradford, Chief Engineer

Buchanan

WSMK
01-01-1991; 99.1 MHz FM; *Hrs Open:* 24; 3 kw; 328 ft.; N41 52 51 W86 18 13
210 Philip Rd., P.O. 213, Niles, MI 49120 US
(269) 683-4343
www.wsmkradio.com
License: Buchanan, Berrien County, MI held by Marion R. Williams.
Group Owner: Marion R. Williams Stns
Arbitron Metro Market: South Bend, IN; *Format:* Adult Contemp; *Target Audience:* 25 - 44; females

Burton

*WTAC
01-01-2002; 89.7 MHz FM; 15 kw vert; 361 ft.; N42 44 56 W83 42 59 *Rebroadcasts:* simulcasts WLGH (FM) Leroy Township 100%
3302 North Van Dyke, Imlay City, MI 48444 US
(888) 887-7139; *Fax:* (877) 850-0881
www.smile.fm
411@smile.fm
License: Burton, Genesee County, MI held by Superior Communications.
Group Owner: Superior Communications
Arbitron Metro Market: Burton, MI; *Format:* Christian
Edward Czelada, President
Dale Mazzoline, Feature Production
Ed Czelada, Administration, Programming & Engineering
Clayton Hewitt, Administration and Engineering
Aaron Burrell, Administration

Cadillac

WATT
09-01-1945; 1240 kHz AM; *Hrs Open:* 24; 1 kw-U; N44 13 27 W85 24 06
7825 S. Mackinaw Tr., Cadillac, MI 49601 US
(231) 775-1263; *Fax:* (231) 779-2844
License: Cadillac, Wexford County, MI held by MacDonald Garber Broadcasting Inc.
Group Owner: MacDonald Garber Broadcasting Co.; (acq 11-17-98; grpsl)
Nat'l Network: Fox News Radio; Radio America; *Nat'l Reps:* Eastman *Regional Reps:* Eastman
Population Served: 11,500 *Target Audience:* General.; *Adv. Rates:* 18; 18; 18; 18
Trish Garber, President

WCKC
09-15-1985; 107.1 MHz FM; 2.75 kw; 482 ft.; N44 10 16 W85 20 13 *Rebroadcasts:* WGFM-FM Cheboygan 100%
8082 E. M-115, Suite B, Cadillac, MI 49601 US
(231) 876-1079; *Fax:* (231) 876-1071
1071thedrive.com
1071thedrive@gmail.com
License: Cadillac, Wexford County, MI held by Up North Radio, LLC
Group Owner: Up North Radio, LLC; (acq 9-29-16; grpsl)
Arbitron Metro Market: Northern Michigan and Upper Peninsula; *Format:* Classic Rock; *Target Audience:* 25-54.

WLJW
03-15-2004; 1370 kHz AM; *Hrs Open:* 24; 5 kw-D, DA2; 1 kw-N, DA2; N44 13 54 W85 24 45 *Rebroadcasts:* Simulcast with WLJN(AM) Elmwood Township
P.O. Box 1408, Traverse City, MI 49685 US
(231) 946-1400; *Fax:* (231) 946-3959
www.wljn.com
info@wljn.com
License: Cadillac, MI held by Good News Media Inc.
Group Owner: Good News Media Inc.; acq 3-5-2004; $85,001).
Nat'l Network: Moody; Salem Radio Network; *Nat'l Reps:* Katz Radio; *Wire Services:* AP
Format: Christian, Talk, 74; *Target Audience:* General.
D.C. Cavender, Operations Dir
Brian Harcey, General Manager
Pete Lathrop, Programming Director
Don Parker, Chief Engineer
Jane Cavender, Disc Jockey
Carla Wanlass, Business Administrator
Lisa Lempke, Administrator to theExecutive Director
Dave Stockfish, Disc Jockey

WJZQ
10-15-1961; 92.9 MHz FM; *Hrs Open:* 24; 100 kw; 912 ft.; N44 35 41 W85 11 53
300 E. Front St., Suite 450, Traverse City, MI 49684 US
(231) 946-6211; *Fax:* (231) 946-1914
www.z93hits.com
License: Cadillac, Wexford County, MI held by WKJF Radio Inc.
Group Owner: Midwestern Broadcasting Co.; (acq 10-29-2001; with co-located AM).
Nat'l Reps: Katz Radio
Arbitron Metro Market: Traverse City-Petoskey, MI; *Format:* Contemporary Hits/Top 40; *Hrs. of News Programming:* news progmg 2 hrs wkly; *No. News Employees:* 1; *Target Audience:* 35-64; affluent adults; *Adv. Rates:* 20; 20; 20; 20
Ron Pritchard, Programming Director
Chris Davis, Marketing Director
Courtney Rehmer, News Director
Jordan Anderson, Production Manager
George Bliss, Account Manager
Linda Francomb, Account Manager
Judy Gill, Account Manager
Heather Barelmay, Account Manager

WLXV
07-07-1974; 96.7 MHz FM; 7.2 kw; 604 ft.; N44 22 51 W85 33 24
7825 S. Mackinaw Trail, Cadillac, MI 49601 US
(231) 775-1263; *Fax:* (231) 779-2844
www.mix96cadillac.com
rich@mix96cadillac.com
License: Cadillac, Wexford County, MI held by MacDonald Garber Broadcasting Co.
Group Owner: MacDonald Garber Broadcasting Co.
Arbitron Metro Market: Traverse City, MI; *Format:* Adult Contemp; *Hrs. of News Programming:* news progmg one hr wkly; *No. News Employees:* 1; *Adv. Rates:* 28; 28; 28; 28
Trish Garber, President
Kerry Davis, General Sales Mgr

*WOLW
05-26-1988; 91.1 MHz FM; 50 kw horiz, 28 kw vert; 699 ft.; N44 16 33 W85 42 49 *Rebroadcasts:* Rebroadcasts WPHN(FM) Gaylord 100%
P.O. Box 695, Gaylord, MI 49735 US
(800) 545-8857
promisefm.com
info@thepromisefm.com
License: Cadillac, Wexford County, MI held by Northern Christian Radio Inc.
Group Owner: Northern Christian Radio Inc.
Nat'l Network: Moody
TV Affiliate: Relg *Special Programming:* News progmg 10 hrs wkly; *No. News Employees:* 35-54.; *Target Audience:* Joe Sereno

*WGCP
91.9 MHz FM; 2.1 kw; 144 ft.; N44 17 8 W85 29 20
P.O. Box 567, Cadillac, MI 49601 US
(231) 468-2087
License: Cadillac, Wexford County, MI held by West Central Michigan Media Ministries.
Arbitron Metro Market: Cadillac, MI; *Format:* Religious
David Bolduc, President

Caro

WKYO
05-19-1962; 1360 kHz AM; 1 kw-D, DA2; 1 kw-N, DA2; N43 27 32 W83 23 39
125 Eagles Nest Dr., Seneca, SC 29678 US
(989) 673-3181; *Fax:* (989) 673-5662
www.tuscolatoday.com
License: Caro, MI held by Edwards Communications LC.
Group Owner: Edwards Communications LC.; (acq 2-25-98; with co-located FM).
Format: Oldies
Tim Murphy, General Manager
Stacey Linn, Programming Director

Carrollton

WSGW-FM
03-11-1991; 100.5 MHz FM; *Hrs Open:* 24; 6 kw; 328 ft.; N43 33 42 W83 58 52
1795 Tittabawassee Road, Saginaw, MI 48604 US
(989) 752-3456; *Fax:* (989) 754-5046
www.fmtalk1005.com
License: Carrollton, Saginaw County, MI held by NM Licensing LLC.
Group Owner: NextMedia Group Inc.; (acq 12-30-2002; grpsl)
Wire Services: Metro Weather Service Inc.
Arbitron Metro Market: Saginaw, MI; *Format:* Talk; *No. News Employees:* 1; *Target Audience:* 18-49; women & teens
David Mauer, Programming Director
Shannone Dunlap, VP

Cass City

WIDL
10-16-1974; 92.1 MHz FM; 6 kw; 318 ft.; N43 28 51 W83 20 31
1521 W. Caro Rd., PO Box 106, Caro, MI 48723 US
(989) 672-1360; *Fax:* (989) 673-0256
License: Cass City, Tuscola County, MI held by Edwards Communications LC.
Group Owner: Edwards Communications LC.
Format: Adult Contemp
Tim Murphy, General Manager
Stacey Linn, Programming Director

Cassopolis

WGTO
08-01-1988; 910 kHz AM; *Hrs Open:* 24; 1 kw-D, DA2; 0.035 kw-N, DA2; N41 57 14 W86 0 59
Mailing Address: 6036 S. Bishop St, Chicago, IL 60636 US
Second Address: 58176 O'Keefe Rd, Cassopolis, MI 49031
(269) 782-9010; *Fax:* (269) 782-5107
www.wgtoradio.com
License: Cassopolis, MI held by Larry Langford Jr.
Arbitron Metro Market: South Bend, IN; *Format:* Oldies *Special Programming:* Blues 4 hrs, gospel 10 hrs wkly; *Target Audience:* 25-49; middle class Black adults
Larry Langford, President
Chris Cole, Station Manager

Charlevoix

WKHQ-FM
05-16-1980; 105.9 MHz FM; *Hrs Open:* 24; 100 kw; 892 ft.; N45 10 49 W85 5 50
5148 US 31 N, Williamsburg, MI 49690 US
(231) 941-0963; *Fax:* (231) 941-9626
www.106khq.com
info@106khq.com
License: Charlevoix, Charlevoix County, MI held by MacDonald Garber Broadcasting Co.
Group Owner: MacDonald Garber Broadcasting Co.; acq 11-17-98; grpsl)
Nat'l Network: ABC; *Nat'l Reps:* McGavren Guild
Arbitron Metro Market: Traverse City-Petoskey, MI; *Format:* Contemporary Hits/Top 40; *No. News Employees:* 1; *Target Audience:* 18-34.
Trish Garber, President

WMKT
07-20-1974; 1270 kHz AM; *Hrs Open:* 24
209 US 131 S., Petoskey, MI 49770 US
(231) 347-8713
www.wmktthetalkstation.com
advertise@106khq.com
License: Charlevoix, MI held by MacDonald Garber Broadcasting Co.
Group Owner: MacDonald Garber Broadcasting Co.
Arbitron Metro Market: Traverse City, MI; *Format:* News, News/Talk, 86; *Target Audience:* 35 plus; listeners with spendable income
Bill Michaels, Operations Dir

WCZW
01-31-2003; 107.9 MHz FM; *Hrs Open:* 24; 5 kw; 164 ft.; N45 20 00 W85 14 47 *Rebroadcasts:* Rebroadcasts WCCW-FM Traverse City, MI
300 E. Front St., Suite 450, Traverse City, MI 49684 US
(231) 946-6211; *Fax:* (231) 946-1914
www.wccw.fm
License: Charlevoix, Charlevoix County, MI held by WCCW Radio Inc.
Group Owner: Midwestern Broadcasting Co.
Nat'l Network: ABC; *Nat'l Reps:* Katz Radio
Arbitron Metro Market: Traverse City, MI; *Format:* Contemporary Hits/Top 40; *Target Audience:* 35 plus; baby boomers; *Adv. Rates:* 12; 12; 12; 12
Ross Biederman, President
Dave Gauthier, Programming Director
Chris Davis, Marketing Director
Courtney Rehmer, News Director
Jordan Anderson, Production Manager
George Bliss, Account Manager
Linda Francomb, Account Manager

JudyGill, Account Manager
Heather Bartelmay, Account Manager

***WTCK**
01-01-2006; 90.9 MHz FM; *Hrs Open:* all; 5.5 kw; 996 ft.; N45 30 5.2 W85 1 48.7
P.O. Box 1109, Indian River, MI 49749 US
(231) 238-0811; *Fax:* (231) 238-0803
www.baragabroadcasting.com
License: Charlevoix, Charlevoix County, MI held by Baraga Broadcasting Inc.
Arbitron Metro Market: Charlevoix, MI; *Format:* Christian
Harry Speckman, Chaplain
Christine Schicker, Station Manager
Brian Brachel, Chief Engineer

Charlotte

WJXQ
05-30-1976; 106.1 MHz FM; *Hrs Open:* 24; 49 kW; 496 ft; N42 23 28 W84 37 22
2495 Cedar St, Holt, MI 48842 USA
(517) 699-0111; *Fax:* (517) 699-1880
q106fm.com
License: Charlotte, Jackson County, MI held by Midwest Communications Inc.
Group Owner: Midwest Communications Inc.
Wire Services: AP
Population Served: 500,000; *Arbitron Metro Market:* Lansing, MI; *Format:* Rock/AOR; *Hrs. of News Programming:* news progmg one hr wkly; *No. News Employees:* 1; *Target Audience:* 25-44; baby boomers with aninclination for rock and roll
Mojo, Brand Manager

Cheboygan

WCBY
10-28-1954; 1240 kHz AM; 1 kw-U, ND1; N45 39 38 W84 29 26
1356 Mackinaw Ave., Cheboygan, MI 49721 US
(231) 627-2341; *Fax:* (231) 627-7000
bigcountrygold.com
License: Cheboygan, MI held by Black Diamond Broacast Holdings, LLC
Group Owner: Black Diamond Broadcast Group; (acq 05-2016; grpsl)
Nat'l Reps: Michigan Spot Sales
Arbitron Metro Market: Cheboygan, MI; *Format:* Big Band, Oldies; *Target Audience:* 35-64.

WGFM
08-15-1968; 105.1 MHz FM; 43 kw; 968 ft.; N45 10 12 W84 45 4
514 Munson Ave., Traverse City, MI 49686 US
(231) 922-4981; *Fax:* (231) 922-3633
rock105.fm
License: Cheboygan, Cheboygan County, MI held by Black Diamond Broadcast Holdings, LLC.
Group Owner: Black Diamond Broadcast Group, LLC.
Arbitron Metro Market: Traverse City-Petoskey, MI; *Format:* Classic Rock

Chocolay Township

WUPZ
01-01-2008; 94.9 MHz FM; 100 kw; 512 ft.; N46 30 51.7 W87 28 40.2
715 W. Washington St., Marquette, MI 49855 US
(906) 255-0656
www.radioresultsnetwork.com
License: Chocolay Township, Iron County, MI held by Radioactive LLC.
Group Owner: Radioactive LLC
Arbitron Metro Market: Chocolay Township, MI; *Format:* Contemporary Hits/Top 40

Clare

WCFX
06-28-1967; 95.3 MHz FM; *Hrs Open:* 24; 6 kw; 328 ft.; N43 44 41 W84 48 9
5847 Venture Way, Mt. Pleasant, MI 48858 US
(989) 772-4173; *Fax:* (989) 773-1236
www.wcfx.com
kent@wcfx.com
License: Clare, Clare County, MI held by Grenax Broadcasting LLC
Group Owner: Grenax Broadcasting LLC; (acq 2-5-2004).
Arbitron Metro Market: Mount Pleasant,MI; *Format:* Christian; *Target Audience:* 18-49.; *Adv. Rates:* 28; 30; 28; 20
Greg Dinetz, President
Kent Bergstrom, Operations Dir
Jim Spangenberg, General Manager
Rob Ryan, Promotions Manager

Clyde Township

***WPRR-FM**
90.1 MHz FM; *Hrs Open:* 24; 5 kw; N42 33 29 W85 56 7
Rebroadcasts: Translator for WPRR AM
3777 - 44th St, Grand Rapids, MI 49512 US
(616) 656-1680; *Fax:* (616) 656-2619
www.publicrealityradio.org
info@publicrealityradio.org
License: Clyde Township, Allegan County, MI held by Goodrich Radio L.L.C.
Group Owner: Public Reality Radio; (acq 11-19-2012 from Larlen Commuications)
Nat'l Network: Pacifica Radio
Arbitron Metro Market: Grand Rapids, MI; *Format:* Talk
Robert Goodrich, Chairman
Robert Goodrich, President
Darren Gibson, Programming Director

Coldwater

WNWN-FM
11-11-1950; 98.5 MHz FM; 50 kW; 469 ft.; N42 03 27 W84 59 53
70 W Michigan Ave, Suite 700, Battle Creek, MI 49017 USA
(269) 968-1991; *Fax:* (269) 968-1881
wincountry.com
License: Coldwater, Branch County, MI held by Midwest Communications Inc.
Group Owner: Midwest Communications Inc.; acq 6-1-95; grpsl)
Nat'l Reps: Christal; *Wire Services:* Accu-Weather
Arbitron Metro Market: Battle Creek, MI; *Format:* Country *Special Programming:* news progmg 5 hrs wkly; *Hrs. of News Programming:* 3; *No. News Employees:* 25-54.
PJ Lacey, Brand Manager

WTVB-AM
08-07-1949; 1590 kHz AM; *Hrs Open:* 24; 5 kW; N41 54 34 W85 0 21
182 N Angola Rd, Coldwater, MI 49036 USA
(517) 279-1590; *Fax:* (517) 279-4695
wtvbam.com
License: Coldwater, MI held by Midwest Communications Inc.
Group Owner: Midwest Communications Inc.; acq 6-1-95; grpsl)
Nat'l Reps: Christal; *Wire Services:* NOAA Weather
Arbitron Metro Market: Coldwater, MI; *Format:* News/Talk *Special Programming:* Farm 6 hrs wkly; *Hrs. of News Programming:* news progmg 10 hrs wkly; *No. News Employees:* 2
Ken Delaney, Brand Manager

***WYBA**
07-15-2008; 90.1 MHz FM; 32 kw; Ant 62 ft; N42 8 39 W85 12 35
Mailing Address: P.O. Box 7300, Charlotte, NC 28241
Second Address: 11530 Carmel Commons Blvd., Charlotte, NC 28226
(800) 888-7077
www.bbnradio.org
bbn@bbnmedia.org
License: Coldwater, Branch County, MI held by Bible Broadcasting Network Inc.
Group Owner: Bible Broadcasting Network
Nat'l Network: Bible Bcstg Net
Arbitron Metro Market: Coldwater, MI; *Format:* Christian
Lowell Davey, President
Jason Padgett, Operations Manager

Coleman

***WPRJ**
12-07-1992; 101.7 MHz FM; *Hrs Open:* 24; 4.6 kw; 374 ft.; N43 48 39 W84 27 50
5444 N. Coleman Rd., P,O, Box 236, Coleman, MI 48618 US
(989) 465-9775; *Fax:* (989) 465-1060
License: Coleman, Midland County, MI held by Come Together Ministries Inc.
Arbitron Metro Market: Saginaw-Bay City-Midland, MI; *Format:* Adult Contemp, Christian; *Target Audience:* 18 plus; youth, young singles & married
Gary Bugh, President
Connie Wieber, Station Manager

Coopersville

WHTS
09-14-1983; 105.3 MHz FM; 20 kw; 794 ft.; N43 18 35 W85 54 45
60 Monroe Center, Grand Rapids, MI 49503 US
(616) 774-8461; *Fax:* (616) 451-3299
www.1053hotfm.com
beau.derek@cumulus.com
License: Coopersville, MI held by Radio License Holding CBC, LLC
Group Owner: Cumulus Media Inc.; (acq 11-29-2005; $4.1 million)
Arbitron Metro Market: Grand Rapids, MI; *Format:* Contemporary Hits/Top 40; *Target Audience:* 25-54; adult women
John Crenshaw, Operations Manager
Rich Berry, General Sales Mgr
Marcus Bradman, Dir of Marketing/Promotions
Jeff Cartwright, Regional VP/Market Mgr

Crystal Falls

WOBE
06-01-2000; 100.7 MHz FM; 100 kw; 653 ft.; N45 49 16 W88 2 34
212 West J. Street, Iron Mountain, WI 49801 US
(906) 774-5731; *Fax:* (906) 774-4542
peterson.trisha@gmail.com
License: Crystal Falls, Iron County, MI held by Results Broadcasting of Iron Mountain Inc.
Group Owner: Results Broadcasting; (acq 11-1-2001; $800,000).
Nat'l Network: ABC
TV Affiliate: Classic hits; *Hrs. of News Programming:* 1; *No. News Employees:* 25-65.
Trisha Peterson, General Manager

DeWitt

WQHH
01-01-1991; 96.5 MHz FM; 6 kW; 322 ft.; N42 50 58 W84 40 4
600 W Cavanaugh Rd, Lansing, MI 48910 USA
(517) 393-1320; *Fax:* (517) 393-0882
www.power965fm.com
License: DeWitt, Clinton County, MI held by The MacDonald Broadcasting Company
Group Owner: MacDonald Broadcasting; (acq 10-3-2006; $3.65 million with WXLA(AM) Dimondale)
Nat'l Reps: D & R Radio
Arbitron Metro Market: Lansing; *Format:* Urban Contemporary; *Target Audience:* 18-49; *Adv. Rates:* 25; 25; 25; 25
Duane Alverson, President
Cindy Tuck, Vice President

Dearborn

***WHFR**
12-20-1985; 89.3 MHz FM; *Hrs Open:* 24; 270 w; 98 ft; N42 19 26 W83 14 09
Henry Ford Community College, 5101 Evergreen Rd., Dearborn, MI 48128
(313) 845-9676,(313) 845-9842; *Fax:* (313) 317-4034
www.whfr.fm
whfr@hfcc.edu
License: Dearborn, Wayne County, MI held by Henry Ford Community College.
Nat'l Network: PRI
Population Served: 800,000; *Arbitron Metro Market:* Detroit
Special Programming: Jazz 10 hrs, world mus 2 hrs, big band 6 hrs, blues 12 hrs wkly; *Hrs. of News Programming:* News progmg one hr wkly; *Target Audience:* General.
Lara Hrycaj, Operations Dir
Susan McGraw, General Manager

WNIC
12-01-1946; 100.3 MHz FM; *Hrs Open:* 24; 32 kw; 600 ft.; N42 23 22 W83 8 53
27675 Halsted Rd., Farmington Hills, MI 48331 US
(248) 324-5800; *Fax:* (248) 848-0297
www.wnic.com
License: Dearborn, Wayne County, MI held by AMFM Radio Licenses L.L.C.
Group Owner: iHeartMedia; (acq 8-30-00; grpsl).
Arbitron Metro Market: Detroit, MI; *Format:* Adult Contemp; *Hrs. of News Programming:* news progmg 2 hrs wkly; *No. News Employees:* 1; *Target Audience:* 25-54; female
Nick Gnau, Market President
Liz Walterhouse, General Sales Mgr
Cody Trombley, Promotions Director

WDTW
12-29-1946; 1310 kHz AM; *Hrs Open:* 24; 5 kw-D, DA2; 5 kw-N, DA2; N42 15 50 W83 15 14
US
License: Dearborn, MI held by Pedro Zamora
Nat'l Network: Westwood One
Arbitron Metro Market: Detroit; *Format:* Alternative, Talk; *Hrs. of News Programming:* news progmg 27 hrs wkly; *No. News Employees:* 4; *Target Audience:* 25-54; men 25-54

Dearborn Heights

WNZK
10-12-1985; 690 kHz AM; 2.5 kw-D, DA2; 2.5 kw-N, DA2; N42 5 55 W83 19 48
21700 Northwestern Hwy., Suite 1190, Tower 14, Southfield, MI 48075 US
(248) 557-3500; *Fax:* (248) 557-2950
www.birach.com
sima@birach.com
License: Dearborn Heights, Wayne County, MI held by Birach Broadcasting Corp.
Group Owner: Birach Broadcasting Corp.; (acq 1984).
Arbitron Metro Market: Detroit *TV Affiliate:* Ethnic; *Format:* Ethnic, Talk; *No. News Employees:* General.
Sima Birach, Operations Manager

Detroit

*WDET-FM
02-13-1949; 101.9 MHz FM; *Hrs Open:* 24; 48 kw; 554 ft.; N42 21 6 W83 3 48
4600 Cass Avenue, Detroit, MI 48201 US
(313) 577-4146; *Fax:* (313) 577-1300
www.wdetfm.org
wdetfm@wdetfm.org
License: Detroit, Wayne County, MI held by Wayne State University.
Nat'l Network: NPR
Arbitron Metro Market: Detroit, MI; *Format:* News *Special Programming:* Jazz 15 hrs, folk 3 hrs, bluegrass 2 hrs, gospel 2 hrs, blues 3 hrs, reggae 2 hrs wkly; *Hrs. of News Programming:* news progmg 118 hrs wkly *No.News Employees:* 6; *Target Audience:* 35-64; public radio & news consumers
Yolanda Dunn, CFO
J.Mikel Ellcessor, General Manager
Tim Hygh, Station Manager
Ron Jones, Programming Director
Jerome Vaughn, News Director
Jerome Vaughn, News/Programming Director

WDFN
12-17-1939; 1130 kHz AM; 50 kw-D, DA2; 10 kw-N, DA2; N42 6 39 W83 11 52
27675 Halstead Road, Farmington Hills, MI 48331 US
(248) 324-5800; *Fax:* (248) 848-0396
www.wdfn.com
License: Detroit, MI held by AMFM Radio Licenses L.L.C.
Group Owner: iHeartMedia; (acq 8-30-2000; grpsl).
Nat'l Network: Westwood One
Arbitron Metro Market: Detroit, MI; *Format:* Sports, Talk; *Target Audience:* 25-54.
Liz Walterhouse, General Sales Mgr
Aaron Klauber, Promotions Director

WDRQ
07-09-1947; 93.1 MHz FM; *Hrs Open:* 24; 26.5 kw; 669 ft.; N42 28 16 W83 12 3
3011 W. Grand Blvd., Suite 800, Detroit, MI 48202 US
(313) 871-9300
www.nashfm931.com
lori.bennett@cumulus.com
License: Detroit, Wayne County, MI held by Radio License Holdings LLC
Group Owner: Cumulus Media Inc.; (acq 6-12-2007; grpsl)
Nat'l Reps: ABC Radio Sales; *Wire Services:* AP
Arbitron Metro Market: Detroit, MI; *Format:* Country; *No. News Employees:* 1
Steve Kosbau, President

WDMK
05-26-1960; 105.9 MHz FM; 20 kw; 725 ft.; N42 28 16 W83 12 3
3250 Franklin St., Detroit, MI 48207 US
(313) 259-2000; *Fax:* (313) 259-7011
www.kissdetroit.com
License: Detroit, Wayne County, MI held by Radio One of Detroit LLC.
Group Owner: Radio One Inc.; (acq 11-8-2001; grpsl).
Arbitron Metro Market: Detroit, MI; *Format:* Urban Contemporary; *Target Audience:* 25-49.
Nate Bell, Operations Dir
George Jones, General Sales Mgr
Toya Menzie, Promotions Manager

*WRCJ-FM
02-05-1948; 90.9 MHz FM; *Hrs Open:* Midnight-noon; 42 kw horiz, 38 kw vert; 541 ft.; N42 22 25 W83 6 50
123 Selden Street, Detroit, MI 48201 US
(313)494-6400; *Fax:* (313) 494-6087
www.wrcjfm.org/
90.9@dptv.org
License: Detroit, Wayne County, MI held by Board of Education, City of Detroit.
Arbitron Metro Market: Detroit, MI; *Format:* Jazz; *No. News Employees:* 15; *Target Audience:* General; intergenerational-urban/suburban
Donald Walker, Operations Dir
Robert Scott, General Manager
Dave Wagner, Programming Director
Ken Sands, Promotions Manager
Steve Johnson, Chief Engineer

WGPR
01-01-1961; 107.5 MHz FM; *Hrs Open:* 24; 50 kw; Ant 405 ft; N42 21 28 W83 03 55
3250 Franklin St., Detroit, MI 48207 US
(313) 259-2000; *Fax:* (313) 259-7011
www.hothiphopdetroit.com
License: Detroit, Wayne County, MI held by WGPR Inc.
Group Owner: Radio One.; (acq 7-64)
Population Served: 151,148; *Arbitron Metro Market:* Detroit *TV Affiliate:* WGPR-TV affil; *Format:* Urban Contemporary; *Target Audience:* 25-54
Armando Rivera, Operations Dir
George Jones, General Sales Mgr
Kelli Harrison, Promotions Manager

WJLB
01-01-1926; 97.9 MHz FM; 50 kw; 489 ft.; N42 24 22 W83 6 44
27675 Halstead Road, Farmington Hills, MI 48331 US
(248) 324-5800; *Fax:* (313) 965-3965
www.fm98wjlb.com
License: Detroit, Wayne County, MI held by AMFM Radio Licenses L.L.C.
Group Owner: iHeartMedia; (acq 8-30-00; grpsl)
Arbitron Metro Market: Detroit; *Format:* Urban Contemporary; *Target Audience:* 18-49; Black adults
Colleen Grant, General Sales Mgr

WJR
05-04-1922; 760 kHz AM; 50 kw-U, ND1; N42 10 5 W83 12 54
3011 West Grand Blvd., Detroit, MI 48202 US
(313) 875-4440
www.wjr.net
License: Detroit, MI held by Radio License Holdings LLC
Group Owner: Cumulus Media Inc.; (acq 6-12-2007; grpsl)
Nat'l Reps: ABC Radio Sales
Arbitron Metro Market: Detroit; *Format:* News/Talk, Sports; *Target Audience:* 12 plus.
Tom O'Brien, General Sales Mgr

WKQI
02-12-1949; 95.5 MHz FM; *Hrs Open:* 24; 100 kw; 427 ft.; N42 28 23 W83 11 59
27675 Halstead Road, Farmington Hills, MI 48331 US
(248) 324-5800; *Fax:* (248) 848-0272
www.channel955.com
programming@channel955.com
License: Detroit, Wayne County, MI held by AMFM Radio Licenses L.L.C.
Group Owner: iHeartMedia; (acq 8-30-00; grpsl).
Nat'l Network: Premiere Radio Networks
Arbitron Metro Market: Detroit; *Format:* Contemporary Hits/Top 40; *Target Audience:* 18-49; active, upscale women
Tony Travatto, Programming Director
Cody Trombley, Promotions Director

WXYT-FM
10-03-2007; 97.1 MHz FM; 15 kW; 909 ft.; N42 28 58 W83 12 19
26455 American Dr., Southfield, MI 48034 USA
(248) 327-2900
www.971theticket.com
License: Detroit, Wayne County, MI held by CBS Radio East Inc.
Group Owner: CBS Radio; (acq 3-9-89;
Nat'l Network: ESPN Radio; Westwood One
Arbitron Metro Market: Detroit; *Format:* Sports; *No. News Employees:* 3
Rich Renko, General Sales Mgr
Jimmy Powers, Programming Director

WLQV
01-01-1925; 1500 kHz AM; *Hrs Open:* 24; 50 kw-D, 10 kw-N, DA-2; N42 13 52 W83 11 58
Two Radio Plaza, Ferndale, MI 48152
(248) 581-1234; *Fax:* (248) 581-1231
www.faithtalk1500.com
License: Detroit, Wayne County, MI held by Caron Broadcasting Inc.
Group Owner: Salem Communications Corp.; (acq 2-10-2006; swap for WDJO(AM) Florence, KY and WCVX(AM) Cincinnati, OH plus $6.75 million cash)
Nat'l Network: Salem Radio Network
Arbitron Metro Market: Detroit; *Hrs. of News Programming:* news progmg 2 hrs wkly; *No. News Employees:* 1; *Target Audience:* 25-65 plus; middle class
Steve Dealy, Operations Dir
Chris MacCourtney, General Manager
Brad Smith, General Sales Mgr

WMUZ
11-11-1958; 103.5 MHz FM; 50 kw; 466 ft.; N42 22 40 W83 14 32
12300 Radio Place, Detroit, MI 48228 US
(313) 272-3434; *Fax:* (313) 272-5045
www.wmuz.com
station@wumz.com
License: Detroit, Wayne County, MI held by WMUZ Radio Inc.
Group Owner: Crawford Broadcasting Co.
Arbitron Metro Market: Detroit, MI; *Format:* Christian, Religious, 86
Donald Crawford, President
Rich Hanovich, Operations Dir
Frank Franciosi, General Manager

WMXD
12-08-1964; 92.3 MHz FM; 45 kw; 479 ft.; N42 19 55 W83 2 42
27675 Halsted Rd., Farmington Hills, MI 48331 US
(248) 324-5800; *Fax:* (313) 965-3965
www.mix923fm.com
contact@mix923fm.com
License: Detroit, Wayne County, MI held by AMFM Radio Licenses L.L.C.
Group Owner: iHeartMedia; (acq 8-30-00; grpsl).
Arbitron Metro Market: Detroit, MI; *Format:* Urban Contemporary
Nick Gnau, Market President
Colleen Grant, General Sales Mgr

WOMC
03-05-1948; 104.3 MHz FM; 190 kW; 367 ft.; N42 28 10 W83 6 54
26455 American Dr., Southfield, MI 48034 USA
(248) 327-2900; *Fax:* (248) 399-1043
www.womc.com
License: Detroit, Wayne County, MI held by CBS Radio Inc. of Michigan
Group Owner: CBS Radio; (acq 4-28-88)
Nat'l Network: Westwood One
Arbitron Metro Market: Detroit; *Format:* Oldies *Special Programming:* news progmg 4 hrs wkly; *Hrs. of News Programming:* 1; *No. News Employees:* 25-54; upscale
Kelly Turner, General Sales Mgr
Tim Roberts, Programming Director
Debbie Kenyon, Market Manager

WDVD
06-01-1948; 96.3 MHz FM; 20 kw; 787 ft.; N42 27 13 W83 09 50
3011 West Grand Blvd., Suite 800, Detroit, MI 48202 US
(313) 871-3030; *Fax:* (313) 871-8974
www.963wdvd.com
License: Detroit, MI held by Radio License Holdings LLC
Group Owner: Cumulus Media Inc.
Arbitron Metro Market: Detroit; *Format:* Adult Contemp
Ron Harrell, Programming Director
\, News Director

WDTK
01-01-1926; 1400 kHz AM; 1 kw-U, ND1; N42 24 22 W83 6 44
2 Radio Plaza, Ferndale, MI 48220 US
(248) 581-1234; *Fax:* (248) 581-1231
www.wdtkam.com
License: Detroit, MI held by Pennsylvania Media Associates Inc.
Group Owner: Salem Communications Corp.; (acq 9-30-2004; $4.75 million).
Nat'l Reps: Salem
Arbitron Metro Market: Detroit; *Format:* News, News/Talk, 86
Steve Dealy, Operations Dir
Christian MacCourtney, General Manager
Brad Smith, General Sales Mgr

WRIF
01-01-1948; 101.1 MHz FM; *Hrs Open:* 24; 27 kw; 879 ft.; N42 28 14 W83 15 1
1 Radio Plaza, Ferndale, MI 48220 US
(248) 547-0101; *Fax:* (248) 542-8800
wrif.com
License: Detroit, Wayne County, MI held by Greater Media Inc.
Group Owner: Beasley Broadcast Group; acq 12-15-87)
Nat'l Reps: Katz Radio
Arbitron Metro Market: Detroit; *Format:* Rock/AOR; *Target Audience:* 18-49; men
Tom Bender, General Manager

WDZH
05-03-2010; 98.7 MHz FM; 50 kW; 443 ft.; N42 23 42 W83 08 58
26455 American Dr., Southfield, MI 48034 USA
(248) 327-2900
www.987ampradio.com
License: Detroit, Wayne County, MI held by CBS Radio East Inc.
Group Owner: CBS Radio; (acq 12-89; grpsl;
Population Served: 3,500,000; *Arbitron Metro Market:* Detroit;
Format: Contemporary Hits/Top 40
Jay Jennings, General Sales Mgr
Rayne, Programming Director
Rebecca Falk, Marketing Director

WWJ
08-20-1920; 950 kHz AM; *Hrs Open:* 24; 50 kW; N42 1 90 W83 14 23
26455 American Dr., Southfield, MI 48034 USA
(248) 327-2900
www.wwj.com
wwjnewsroom@cbsradio.com
License: Detroit, Wayne County, MI held by CBS Radio East Inc.
Group Owner: CBS Radio; (acq 3-9-89;
Nat'l Network: CBS
Population Served: 7,065,585; *Arbitron Metro Market:* Detroit, MI *TV Affiliate:* WWJ-TV affil; *Format:* News; *No. News Employees:* 32; *Target Audience:* General

WMGC-FM
03-06-1960; 105.1 MHz FM; 50 kw; 492 ft.; N42 27 13 W83 9 50
1 Radio Plaza, Ferndale, MI 48220 US
(248) 414-5600; *Fax:* (248) 542-7700
www.detroitmagic.com
License: Detroit, Wayne County, MI held by Greater Boston Radio Inc.
Group Owner: Beasley Broadcast Group; (acq 12-5-96)
Arbitron Metro Market: Detroit, MI; *Format:* Adult Contemp;
Target Audience: General; professional, upscale, educated
Peter Smyth, President
Tom Bender, General Manager

WXYT
10-09-1984; 1270 kHz AM; *Hrs Open:* 24; 50 kW; N42 1 39 W83 20 42
26455 American Dr., Southfield, MI 48034 USA
(248) 327-2900
www.cbssportsradio1270.com
License: Detroit, MI held by CBS Radio Inc. of Detroit
Group Owner: CBS Radio; (acq 11-13-98; grpsl)
Arbitron Metro Market: Detroit, MI; *Format:* Sports; *Target Audience:* 25-54
Rich Renko, General Sales Mgr
Jimmy Powers, Programming Director

WYCD
07-01-1993; 99.5 MHz FM; 17.5 kW; 781 ft.; N42 27 13 W83 9 50
26455 American Dr., Southfield, MI 48034 USA
(248) 327-2900
www.wycd.com
License: Detroit, Wayne County, MI held by CBS Radio Inc. of Michigan
Group Owner: CBS Radio; (acq 1-96; grpsl)
Arbitron Metro Market: Southfield, MI; *Format:* Country; *Target Audience:* 12-34
Debbie Kenyon, General Manager
Jay Jennings, General Sales Mgr
Tim Roberts, Programming Director

WDTW-FM
10-16-1960; 106.7 MHz FM; 61 kw; 509 ft.; N42 19 55 W83 2 42
27675 Halsted Road, Farmington Hills, MI 48331 US
(248) 324-5800; *Fax:* (248) 848-0396
www.thedrocks.com
License: Detroit, Wayne County, MI held by AMFM Radio Licenses L.L.C.
Group Owner: iHeartMedia
Arbitron Metro Market: Farmington Hills, MI; *Format:* Classic Rock
Liz Walterhouse, General Sales Mgr
Aaron Klauber, Director of Marketing and Promotions

Dimondale

WXLA
09-20-1982; 1180 kHz AM; *Hrs Open:* 12; 10 kW; N42 39 01 W84 34 49
PO Box 1776, Saginaw, MI 48605 USA
(989) 752-8161
License: Dimondale, Eaton County, MI held by The MacDonald Broadcasting Company
Group Owner: MacDonald Broadcasting; (acq 10-3-2006; $3.65 million)
Nat'l Reps: D & R Radio
Population Served: 1,237; *Arbitron Metro Market:* Lansing;
Format: Adult Contemp
Kenneth MacDonald Jr., CEO
Cindy Tuck, General Manager
Sharon Crane, General Sales Mgr

Dowagiac

WHPD
01-01-1971; 92.1 MHz FM; *Hrs Open:* 24; 3.3 kw; 299 ft.; N41 59 52 W86 3 14 *Rebroadcasts:* Simulcast with WHPZ(FM) Bremen, IN
61300 Ironwood Road, South Bend, IN 46614 US
(574) 291-8200
www.pulsefm.com
info@whpd.com
License: Dowagiac, Cass County, MI held by LeSea Broadcasting Corp.
Group Owner: Le Sea Broadcasting; (acq 4-12-2005; $950,000 with co-lo
Nat'l Reps: Michigan Spot Sales
Arbitron Metro Market: South Bend, IN; *Format:* Christian; *Target Audience:* 25-64.; *Adv. Rates:* 15; 12; 12; 8
Pete Sumrall, General Manager
Tom Scott, Programming Director

Eagle

***WJOM**
01-01-2006; 88.5 MHz FM; 4.3 kw vert; 131 ft.; N42 48 25 W84 47 18
148 East Grand River, Williamston, MI 48895 US
(888) 887-7141
www.smile.fm
Jennc@smile.fm
License: Eagle, Clinton County, MI held by Michigan Community Radio.
Arbitron Metro Market: Eagle, MI; *Format:* Christian
Ed Czelada, President
Ed Czelada, Administration, Programming & Engineering
Clayton Hewitt, Administration and Engineering
Aaron Burrell, Administration
Dale Mazzoline, Production

East Jordan

***WICV**
06-25-1989; 100.9 MHz FM; *Hrs Open:* 24; 2.8 kw; 489 ft.; N45 10 40 W85 5 57 *Rebroadcasts:* Rebroadcasts WIAA(FM) Interlochen 100%
P.O. Box 199, Interlochen, MI 49643 US
(231) 276-4400; *Fax:* (231) 276-4417
www.interlochen.org/ipr
ipr@interlochen.org
License: East Jordan, Charlevoix County, MI held by Interlochen Center for the Arts
Nat'l Network: NPR; PRI; ABC; *Regional Network:* Mich. Radio
Format: Classical, News; *Target Audience:* 35-80; upper income, arts-oriented, civic-minded professionals
Thom Paulson, Operations Dir

East Lansing

***WDBM**
02-24-1989; 88.9 MHz FM; *Hrs Open:* 24; 2 kw; 279 ft.; N42 42 20 W84 28 30
G-4 Holden Hall, East Lansing, MI 48824 US
(517) 353-4414
www.impact89fm.org
manager@impact89fm.org
License: East Lansing, Ingham County, MI held by Board of Trustees of Michigan State University.
Arbitron Metro Market: East Lansing, MI; *Format:* Alternative
Special Programming: Blues 4 hrs, jazz 5 hrs, heavy metal 4 hrs, progsv country 4 hrs, Christian rock 4 hrs wkly; *Hrs. of News Programming:* News progmg 10hrs wkly; *Target Audience:* 18-34; students of MSU
Gary Reid, General Manager
Aaron Young, Station Manager
Aiman Farooq, Programming Director
Devin Culham & Sam Riddle, Promotions Manager
Emanuele Berry, News Director
Josh Rickert, Production Director

***WKAR**
08-18-1922; 870 kHz AM; 10 kw-D, DAD; N42 42 19 W84 28 30
404 Wilson Road, East Lansing, MI 48824 US
(517) 884-4700; *Fax:* (517) 432-3858
www.wkar.org
mail@wkar.org
License: East Lansing, MI held by Board of Trustees of Michigan State University.
Nat'l Network: NPR; PRI
Arbitron Metro Market: Lansing-East Lansing, MI; *Format:* News, News/Talk, 86 *Special Programming:* Sp 3 hrs wkly; *Hrs. of News Programming:* news progmg 25 hrs wkly; *No. News Employees:* 5
Gene Purdum, Operations Dir
DeAnne Hamilton, General Manager
Cindy Herfindahl, General Sales Mgr
Curt Gilleo, Programming Director
Diane Hutchens, Promotions Manager
Kevin Laveny, News Director
Gary Blievernicht, EngineeringDir

***WKAR-FM**
10-10-1948; 90.5 MHz FM; 85 kw; 884 ft.; N42 42 7 W84 24 48
84 Wilson Road, East Lansing, MI 48824 US
(517) 432-9527; *Fax:* (517) 353-7124
www.wkar.org
mail@wkar.org
License: East Lansing, Ingham County, MI held by Board of Trustees of Michigan State University.
Arbitron Metro Market: Lansing-East Lansing, MI *TV Affiliate:* *WKAR-TV affil; *Format:* News *Special Programming:* Jazz 7 hrs wkly
Huberto Biaggi, President
Raul Muxo, General Sales Mgr
Carlos Gonzalez, Programming Director

WVFN
01-20-1965; 730 kHz AM; *Hrs Open:* 24; 0.5 kw-D, DAD; 0.05 kw-N, DAD; N42 38 45 W84 33 39
3420 Pine Tree Rd., Lansing, MI 48911 US
(517) 394-7272
www.thegame730am.com
License: East Lansing, MI held by Townsquare Media Lansing License, LLC
Group Owner: Townsquare Media; (acq 2000; grpsl).
Arbitron Metro Market: Lansing, MI; *Format:* Sports; *Target Audience:* 25-54.
Zoe Burdine-Fly, General Manager
Darin White, Director of Sales
Nick Chase, Brand Manager
Brandon Howell, Digital Managing Editor

Elmwood Township

***WLJN**
12-23-1982; 1400 kHz AM; *Hrs Open:* 24; 0.64 kw-U, ND1; N44 46 36 W85 39 43 *Rebroadcasts:* Simulcast with WLJW(AM) Cadillac
Mailing Address: PO Box 1400, Traverse City, MI 49685 US
Second Address: 1101 Cass St., Traverse City, MI 49684
(231) 946-1400; *Fax:* (231) 946-3959
www.wljn.com
info@wljn.com
License: Elmwood Township, MI held by Good News Media Inc.
Group Owner: Good News Media Inc.
Format: Talk, Religious; *Hrs. of News Programming:* News progmg 4 hrs wkly; *Target Audience:* General.
Brian Harcey, General Manager
Pete Lathrop, Programming Director

Escanaba

WCHT
12-01-1958; 600 kHz AM; 0.57 kw-D, DA1; 0.134 kw-N, DA1; N45 48 19 W87 10 13
524 Ludington St., Suite 300, Escanaba, MI 49829 US
(906) 789-9700
www.rrnsports.com
jack@radioresultsnetwork.com
License: Escanaba, MI held by Lakes Radio Inc.
Group Owner: Lakes Radio Inc.
Nat'l Network: CBS Radio
Arbitron Metro Market: Escanaba, MI; *Format:* News, News/Talk, 86 *Special Programming:* Farm one hr, forestry one hr wkly; *Hrs. of News Programming:* 24; *No. News Employees:* 4; *Target Audience:* 25-54.

WDBC
09-04-1941; 680 kHz AM; *Hrs Open:* 24; 10 kw-D, DA2; 1 kw-N, DA2; N45 45 53 W87 5 48
604 Ludington St., Escanaba, MI 49829 US
(906) 786-3800; *Fax:* (906) 789-9959
www.kmbbroadcasting.com/wdbc
wykxinfo@yahoo.com
License: Escanaba, MI held by Sovereign Communications

Group Owner: Sovereign Communications
Nat'l Network: ABC; *Regional Network:* Mich. Radio; *Nat'l Reps:* Katz Radio; *Wire Services:* AP
Arbitron Metro Market: Escanaba, MI; *Format:* Oldies *Special Programming:* Relg 4 hrs, children one hr wkly; *Hrs. of News Programming:* news progmg 12 hrs wkly; *No. News Employees:* 1; *Target Audience:* 25-54.
Craig Woerpel, News Director
Jim Pinar, Sports Director

WGLQ
09-11-1976; 97.1 MHz FM; 100 kw; 1070 ft.; N46 8 4 W86 56 52
524 Ludinton St., Suite 300, Escanaba, MI 49829-3900 US
(906) 228-9700
radioresultsnetwork.com
License: Escanaba, Delta County, MI held by Lakes Radio, Inc.
Group Owner: Lakes Radio, Inc.; 4/1/1982
Nat'l Network: NBC
Format: Adult Contemp; *No. News Employees:* 4

WYKX
12-22-1977; 104.7 MHz FM; *Hrs Open:* 24; 100 kw; 351 ft.; N45 55 41 W87 16 0
604 Ludington St., Escanaba, MI 49829 US
(906) 786-3800; *Fax:* (906) 789-9959
www.kmbbroadcasting.com/wykx
wykxprod@yahoo.com
License: Escanaba, Delta County, MI held by Sovereign Communications, LLC
Group Owner: Sovereign Communications
Nat'l Network: ABC; Jones Radio Networks; *Wire Services:* AP
Arbitron Metro Market: Escanaba, MI; *Format:* Country; *Hrs. of News Programming:* news progmg 4 hrs wkly; *No. News Employees:* 1; *Target Audience:* General; 25-54
Craig Woerpel, News Director
Jim Pinar, Sports Director

***WUPJ**
90.9 MHz FM; 100 kw vert; 66 meters; N34 41 15 W82 59 13
409 Rainbow Circle, Kingsport, TN
(423) 963-9548
License: Escanaba, MI held by Clean Air Broadcasting Corp

David Purin, President

Essexville

WMJO
01-01-1992; 97.3 MHz FM; *Hrs Open:* 24; 3 kW; 324 ft.; N43 30 51 W83 45 51
PO Box 1776, Saginaw, MI 48605 USA
(989) 752-8161; *Fax:* (989) 752-8102
www.973joefm.com
admin@973joefm.com
License: Essexville, Bay County, MI held by The MacDonald Broadcasting Company
Group Owner: MacDonald Broadcasting; (acq 12-20-2001; grpsl).
Nat'l Reps: Eastman Radio *Regional Reps:* Eastman Radio; *Wire Services:* AP
Arbitron Metro Market: Flint-Saginaw-Bay City; *Format:* Adult Contemp, Variety/Diverse, 64; *No. News Employees:* 1; *Target Audience:* Adults 25-54; 50% Male, 50% Female
Kenneth MacDonald Jr., CEO
Duane Alverson, President
Jim Kramer, Operations Dir
Mary Yearham, General Sales Mgr
Cindy Tuck, Vice President

Farmington Hills

WFDF
05-25-1922; 910 kHz AM; *Hrs Open:* 24
2302 Lapeer Road, Flint, MI 48503 US
(810) 238-7300
www.radiodisney.com/detroit
kimberly.r.munoz@disney.com
License: Farmington Hills, MI held by Radio Disney Group LLC.
Group Owner: ABC Inc.; (acq 8-15-2002; $3 million).
Nat'l Network: Radio Disney; *Nat'l Reps:* McGavren Guild
Arbitron Metro Market: Farmington Hills, MI; *Format:* Children; *Target Audience:* M/F 6-16, F25-49
Rich Padgen, General Manager
Brian Christy, Promotions Manager
Elise Bennett, Promotions Manager

Fenton

WCXI
11-15-1985; 1160 kHz AM; 1 kw-U, DA1; N42 48 30 W83 43 50
15130 N. Rd., Fenton, MI 48430 US
(810) 750-1911
www.birach.com
sima@birach.com
License: Fenton, Genesee County, MI held by Birach Broadcasting Corp.
Group Owner: Birach Broadcasting Corp.; acq 9-13-99; $708,000)
Nat'l Network: American Urban
Arbitron Metro Market: Flint, MI; *Format:* Oldies, Talk; *Target Audience:* General; average age 35, primarily female, average income $35,000
Brenda Charette, Operations Manager

Flint

WCRZ
11-04-1961; 107.9 MHz FM; 50 kw; 331 ft.; N42 58 49 W83 34 40
Mr. John Risher, Gm, G-33387 E. Bristol Road, Flint, MI 48501 US
(810) 743-1080; *Fax:* (810) 742-5170
www.wcrz.com
License: Flint, Genesee County, MI held by Townsquare Media of Flint Inc.
Group Owner: Townsquare Media
Arbitron Metro Market: Flint, MI; *Format:* Adult Contemp
Kelly Quinn, General Manager
Kelly Quinn, General Sales Mgr

WDZZ-FM
09-29-1979; 92.7 MHz FM; 3 kw; 328 ft.; N43 2 29 W83 41 28
6317 Taylor Drive, Flint, MI 48501 US
(810) 238-7300; *Fax:* (810) 743-2500
www.wdzz.com
jeff.wade@cumulus.com
License: Flint, Genesee County, MI held by Cumulus Licensing Corp.
Group Owner: Cumulus Media Inc.; (acq 3-15-00; grpsl).
Arbitron Metro Market: Flint, MI; *Format:* Urban Contemporary *Special Programming:* Gospel 8 hrs, teen talk one hr, concerned pastors one hr wkly; *Target Audience:* Adults.
August Wallace, Programming Director

WFBE
10-05-1953; 95.1 MHz FM; *Hrs Open:* 5 AM-1 AM; 32 kw; 243 ft; N42 58 24 W83 39 02
6317 Taylor Dr., Flint, MI 48507 US
(810) 238-7300; *Fax:* (810) 725-2500
www.nashfm951.com
timothy.shickles@cumulus.com
License: Flint, Genesee County, MI held by Radio License Holding CBC, LLC
Group Owner: Cumulus Media Inc.; (acq 4-26-01; grpsl).
Nat'l Network: PRI
Population Served: 15,000; *Arbitron Metro Market:* Flint, MI; *Format:* Country; *Target Audience:* General; country music listeners
Bobby Nies, General Sales Mgr
April Rose, Programming Director
Donna Luce, Promotions Manager

WFLT
12-05-1955; 1420 kHz AM; *Hrs Open:* 24
718 Beach Street, Flint, MI 48502 US
(810) 239-5733; *Fax:* (810) 239-7134
wflt1420am@aol.com
License: Flint, MI held by C.E.B.A.
Arbitron Metro Market: Flint, MI; *Format:* Black, Gospel; *Hrs. of News Programming:* news progrmg 6 hrs wkly; *No. News Employees:* 2; *Target Audience:* Adults 35+; *Adv. Rates:* $20.00
Sammie L. Jordan Jr., General Manager

WFNT
04-10-1953; 1470 kHz AM; *Hrs Open:* 24; 5 kw-D, DA2; 1 kw-N, DA2; N42 58 22 W83 38 24
John Risher/Gen. Manager, G-33387 E. Bristol Road, Flint, MI 48501 US
(810) 743-1080; *Fax:* (810) 742-5170
www.wfnt.com
License: Flint, MI
Group Owner: Townsquare Media; (acq 8-13-98; grpsl).
Arbitron Metro Market: Flint, MI; *Format:* Oldies; *No. News Employees:* 3
John Risher, General Manager

***WFUM(FM)**
08-23-1985; 91.1 MHz FM; *Hrs Open:* 24; 18 kw; 489 ft; N42 53 57 W83 27 42 *Rebroadcasts:* Rebroadcasts WUOM(FM) Ann Arbor 100%
535 W. William St., Suite 110, Ann Arbor, MI 48103
(734) 764-9210; *Fax:* (734) 647-3488
michiganradio.org
michigan.radio@umich.edu
License: Flint, Genesee County, MI held by Regents of the University of Michigan.
Nat'l Network: NPR
Arbitron Metro Market: Flint, MI *TV Affiliate:* *WFUM-TV affil
Peggy Watson, Operations Dir
Michael Leland, News Director

***WAKL**
09-01-1997; 88.9 MHz FM; *Hrs Open:* 24; 0.38 kw vert; 263 ft.; N42 58 49 W83 34 40
503 Wood St., Fenton, MI 48430 US
(916) 251-1600; *Fax:* (916) 251-1650
www.klove.com
klove@klove.com
License: Flint, Genesee County, MI held by Educational Media Foundation.
Group Owner: EMF Broadcasting; (acq 11-19-01; $450,000).
Nat'l Network: K-Love
Arbitron Metro Market: Flint, MI; *Format:* Christian; *No. News Employees:* 3; *Target Audience:* 25-44; female-Judeo Christian
Mike Novak, President
David Pierce, Programming Director
Ed Lenane, News Director
Sam Wallington, Engineering Dir
Marya Morgan, News Reporter
Richard Hunt, News Reporter

WSNL
04-26-1946; 600 kHz AM; *Hrs Open:* 24
5210 S. Saginaw Rd., Flint, MI 48507 US
(810) 694-4146; *Fax:* (810) 694-0661
www.wsnlradio.com
License: Flint, MI held by Christian Broadcasting System Ltd.
Group Owner: Christian Broadcasting System Ltd.; (acq 1-22-93; $400,000;
Arbitron Metro Market: Flint, MI; *Format:* Christian, Talk; *Target Audience:* 25-54; 35+.
Graham Parker, Station Manager
Antoniette Parson, Business Manager
Mike Demasellis, Production Assistant

WTRX
10-01-1947; 1330 kHz AM; 5 kw-D, DA2; 1 kw-N, DA2; N42 58 24 W83 39 2
6317 Taylor Dr., Flint, MI 48507 US
(810) 238-7300; *Fax:* (810) 725-2500
www.wtrxsports.com
timothy.shickles@cumulus.com
License: Flint, MI held by Radio License Holding CBC, LLC
Group Owner: Cumulus Media Inc.; (acq 10-6-00; $180,000).
Arbitron Metro Market: Flint, MI; *Format:* Sports
Bobby Nies, General Sales Mgr
April Rose, Programming Director
Donna Luce, Promotions Manager
Dan Greer, Chief Engineer

WWCK
11-11-1946; 1570 kHz AM; 1 kw-D, ND1; 0.179 kw-N, ND1; N43 0 39 W83 39 3
6317 Taylor Drive, Flint, MI 48507 US
(810) 238-7300; *Fax:* (810) 238-7310
License: Flint, MI held by Cumulus Licensing Corp.
Group Owner: Cumulus Media Inc.; (acq 3-15-00; grpsl).
Nat'l Network: Westwood One
Arbitron Metro Market: Flint, MI; *Format:* News, News/Talk, 86; *Target Audience:* 18-34.
Bobby Nies, General Manager
Dan Greer, Chief Engineer
Pam Cantar, Traffic Director

WWCK-FM
09-01-1964; 105.5 MHz FM; 25 kw; 328 ft.; N43 0 39 W83 39 4
6317 Taylor Drive, Flint, MI 48507 US
(810) 238-7300; *Fax:* (810) 238-7310
www.wwck.com
info@wwck.com
License: Flint, Genesee County, MI
Arbitron Metro Market: Flint, MI; *Format:* Contemporary Hits/Top 40
Bobby Nies, General Manager

Fowler

WQBX
11-01-1964; 104.7 MHz FM; *Hrs Open:* 24; 6 kw; 328 ft.; N43 22 8 W84 36 19
PO Box 669, Alma, MI 48801 US
(989) 463-3175; *Fax:* (989) 463-6674
License: Fowler, Gratiot County, MI

Nat'l Network: ABC
Format: Adult Contemp; *Adv. Rates:* 15.25; 15.25; 15.25; 13
Randy Wanek, General Sales Mgr
Jeff Lynn, Programming Director

Frankenmuth

WRCL

01-01-2001; 93.7 MHz FM; *Hrs Open:* 24; 3.5 kw; 436 ft.; N43 18 19.4 W83 33 5.4
3338 East Bristol Road, Burton, MI 48529 TS
(810) 235-4937
www.club937.com
clay@club937.com
License: Frankenmuth, Saginaw County, MI
Group Owner: Townsquare Media; (acq 11-9-01; $7 million with WFGR(FM) Grand Rapids).
Nat'l Network: CNN Radio; Westwood One
Arbitron Metro Market: Burton, MI; *Format:* Christian; *Target Audience:* 12-34; children & adults
Clay Church, Programming Director

Frankfort

WBNZ

10-02-1978; 92.3 MHz FM; *Hrs Open:* 24; 50 kw; 446 ft.; N44 36 38 W86 9 38
1532 Forrester Road, Frankfort, MI 49635 US
(231) 352-6374; *Fax:* (231) 352-4335
License: Frankfort, Benzie County, MI held by The Kalil Holding Group LLC.
Nat'l Reps: Patt
Arbitron Metro Market: Traverse City-Petoskey, MI; *Format:* Classic Rock *Special Programming:* Folk 2 hrs, big band 2 hrs wkly; *Hrs. of News Programming:* news progmg 3 hrs wkly; *No. News Employees:* 1 *TargetAudience:* 25-54.; *Adv. Rates:* 14; 12; 14; 8
Roy Henderson, General Manager

Freeland

*WTRK

01-01-2005; 90.9 MHz FM; 0.43 kw; 324 ft.; N43 33 42 W83 58 52
P.O. Drawer 2440, Tupelo, MS 38803 US
(888) 937-2471; *Fax:* (916) 251-1650
www.air1.com
info@air1.com
License: Freeland, Saginaw County, MI held by Educational Media Foundation.
Group Owner: EMF Broadcasting; (acq 6-29-2005; $75,000)
Nat'l Network: Air 1
Arbitron Metro Market: Freeland, MI; *Format:* Alternative, Christian
Darrell Chambliss, Chairman
Alan Mason, COO
Mike Novak, President and CEO
David Pierce, Programming Director
Ed Lenane, News Director
Sam Wallington, Engineering Dir
Marya Morgan, News Reporter
Richard Hunt, News Reporter
Tracy Butler, Traffic Manager
Mitch Barnhart, Director
David R. Ferry, Director
Walter Golembeski, Director

Gagetown

*WCTP

01-01-2006; 88.5 MHz FM; *Hrs Open:* 24; 6 kw; 328 ft.; N43 45 36 W83 5 45
4330 Farver Road, Gagetown, MI 48735 US
(989) 315-8043; *Fax:* (989) 872-3700
www.wctpradiofm.com
info@wctpradiofm.com
License: Gagetown, Tuscola County, MI held by Plonta Broadcasting Inc.
Arbitron Metro Market: Gagetown, MI; *Format:* Gospel; *No. News Employees:* 3
Duane Plonta, President

Gaylord

*WBLW

01-01-2000; 88.1 MHz FM; *Hrs Open:* 24 hours; 5 kw vert; 853 ft.; N45 10 12 W84 45 4
PO Box 177, Gaylord, MI 49734 US
(989) 705-7464
www.wblwradio.com
info@wblwradio.com
License: Gaylord, Otsego County, MI held by Gaylord Baptist Christian School.
Nat'l Network: USA
Arbitron Metro Market: Gaylord, MI,; *Format:* Christian
Jay Towne, General Manager
Bro. Tim Ramsey, Station Manager
Tim Ramsey, Programming Director
Bro. Dominic Garrisi, Assistant Chief Engineer

WSRT

11-18-1972; 106.7 MHz FM; *Hrs Open:* 24; 100 kw; 581 ft.; N45 2 44 W84 50 46
2215 Oak Industrial Dr., Grand Rapids, MI 49505 US
(231) 947-0003; *Fax:* (231) 947-7002
License: Gaylord, Otsego County, MI held by Northern Radio of Gaylord Inc.
Nat'l Reps: Christal
Arbitron Metro Market: Traverse City-Petoskey, MI; *Format:* Adult Contemp; *Target Audience:* 18-49; rgnl orientation including Traverse City, Petoskey, Cheboygan-active life style
Charlie Ferguson, General Manager
Greg Marsh, General Sales Mgr
Dennis Winslow, Programming Director
Kristal Flateau, News Director
Dennis Murray, Chief Engineer

WMJZ-FM

01-01-1984; 101.5 MHz FM; 50 kw; 492 ft.; N45 1 10 W84 24 28
3687 Old US Hwy. 27 S., Gaylord, MI 49735 US
(989) 732-2341; *Fax:* (989) 732-6202
www.radioeaglegaylord.com
License: Gaylord, Ostego County, MI held by Darby Advertising Inc.
Group Owner: Darby Advertising Inc.; (acq 1-1-98; with co-located AM)
Nat'l Network: Motor Racing Net
Arbitron Metro Market: Gaylod, MI; *Format:* Variety/Diverse; *Target Audience:* 25-54.; *Adv. Rates:* 25; 25; 25; 25
Kent Smith, President
Chip Aledge, Programming Director

*WPHN

04-07-1985; 90.5 MHz FM; *Hrs Open:* 24; 100 kw; 1001 ft.; N45 8 17 W84 9 44
P.O. Box 695, Gaylord, MI 49734 US
(800) 545-8857
promisefm.com
info@thepromisefm.com
License: Gaylord, Otsego County, MI held by Northern Christian Radio Inc.
Group Owner: Northern Christian Radio Inc.
Nat'l Network: Moody; USA
Format: Christian, Religious; *Hrs. of News Programming:* News progmg 10 hrs wkly; *Target Audience:* 25-55.

Gladstone

WGKL

02-15-1999; 105.5 MHz FM; 10 kw; 377 ft.; N45 48 17 W87 10 15
524 Ludington St., Suite 300, Escanaba, MI 49829-3900 US
(906) 789-9700
www.radioresultsnetwork.com
License: Gladstone, Delta County, MI held by Lakes Radio Inc.
Group Owner: Lakes Radio Inc.
Nat'l Network: ABC
Format: Oldies; *No. News Employees:* 4; *Target Audience:* adults 25-64

Gladwin

WGDN

12-07-1974; 1350 kHz AM
3601 W. Woods Rd, Gladwin, MI 48624 US
(989) 426-1031; *Fax:* (989) 426-9436
www.103country.com
steve@103country.com
License: Gladwin, MI held by Apple Broadcasting Co. Inc.
Format: Religious; *Target Audience:* 35 plus.
Steve Coston, General Manager

WGDN-FM

02-07-1978; 103.1 MHz FM; 11.5 kw; 486 ft.; N43 57 17 W84 32 59
3601 West Woods Road, Gladwin, MI 48624 US
(989) 426-1031; *Fax:* (989) 426-9436
www.103country.com
steve@103country.com
License: Gladwin, Gladwin County, MI
Nat'l Network: Westwood One
Format: Country
George Jones, Chairman
Marlon Kiser, CEO
Steve Coston, General Manager
Winnette Jessup, General Sales Mgr
Corey Pratt, Production
Winnette Jessup, Traffic Manager

Glen Arbor

WGFN

02-01-1991; 98.1 MHz FM; *Hrs Open:* 24; 21 kw; 738 ft.; N44 49 16 W85 59 47 *Rebroadcasts:* WGFN-FM Cheboygan 100%
514 Munson Ave., Traverse City, MI 49686 US
(231) 922-4981; *Fax:* (231) 627-7000
classicrockthebear.com
License: Glen Arbor, Leelanau County, MI held by Black Diamond Broadcast Holdings, LLC.
Group Owner: Black Diamond Broacast Group, LLC.; (acq 05-2016; grpsl)
Arbitron Metro Market: Traverse City-Petoskey, MI; *Format:* Classic Rock; *No. News Employees:* 1

Good Hart

*WJOG

01-01-2006; 91.3 MHz FM; 6 kw vert; 623 ft.; N45 30 33 W85 2 11 *Rebroadcasts:* simulcasts WJOM (FM) Eagle 100% US
(888) 887-7139
www.smile.fm
Jennc@smile.fm
License: Good Hart, Emmet County, MI held by Michigan Community Radio.
Arbitron Metro Market: Jackson, TN; *Format:* Gospel
Ed Czelada, President
Ed Czelada, Administration, Programming & Engineering
Clayton Hewitt, Administration and Engineering
Aaron Burrell, Administration
Dale Mazzoline, Production

Goodland Township

*WHYT

01-01-2004; 88.1 MHz FM; 0.4 kw vert; 581 ft.; N43 10 30 W83 4 2
601 Savidge St, Reed City, MI 49677 US
(888) 887-7139; *Fax:* (877) 850-0881
www.smile.fm
Jennc@smile.fm
License: Goodland Township, Lapeer County, MI held by Smile FM.
Group Owner: Superior Communications
Arbitron Metro Market: Goodland Township, MI; *Format:* Christian
Ed Czelada, President
Jenn Czelada, General Manager
Ed Czelada, Administration, Programming & Engineering
Clayton Hewitt, Administration and Engineering
Aaron Burrell, Administration
Dale Mazzoline, Production

Grand Haven

WGHN

07-16-1956; 1370 kHz AM; *Hrs Open:* 24; 500 w-D, 22 w-N; N43 02 17 W86 13 46
Box 330, One S. Harbor, Grand Haven, MI 49417
(616) 842-8110; *Fax:* (616) 842-4350
www.sportsradio1370.com
License: Grand Haven, Ottawa County, MI held by WGHN Inc.
Nat'l Network: ESPN Radio; *Nat'l Reps:* Patt
Population Served: 120,000; *Arbitron Metro Market:* Grand Rapids, M; *Adv. Rates:* 18; 15; 17; 10
Will Tieman, President
Eric Kaelin, General Manager

WGHN-FM

01-28-1969; 92.1 MHz FM; *Hrs Open:* 24; 6 kw; 213 ft.; N43 3 25 W86 14 28
One South Harbor, Box 330, Grand Haven, MI 49417 US
(616) 842-8110; *Fax:* (616) 842-4350
www.wghn.com
License: Grand Haven, Ottawa County, MI
Nat'l Network: CBS Radio; *Regional Network:* Mich. Farm
Arbitron Metro Market: Grand Rapids, MI; *Format:* Adult Contemp *Special Programming:* Farm 5 hrs wkly; *Hrs. of News Programming:* news progmg 30 hrs wkly; *No. News Employees:* 2; *Target Audience:* 25-54.
Vicki Coulson, Station Manager
Jesse Bruce, Programming Director
Walt Zerlaut, News Director

Grand Ledge

WLMI
92.9 MHz FM; 5.4 kW; 344 ft; N42 43 58 W84 33 13
2495 Cedar St, Holt, MI 48842 USA
License: Grand Ledge, MI held by Midwest Communications Inc.
Group Owner: Midwest Communications Inc.
Arbitron Metro Market: Lansing, MI; *Format:* Contemporary Hits/Top 40
Artimis, Brand Manager

Grand Rapids

*WCXG
05-18-1978; 89.9 MHz FM; *Hrs Open:* 24; 4.9 kw; 207 ft.; N42 58 40 W85 35 44 *Rebroadcasts:* Rebroadcasts WCSG(FM) Grand Rapids 100%
1159 East Beltline, Grand Rapids, MI 49525 US
(616) 942-1500; *Fax:* (616) 942-7078
www.wcsg.org
License: Grand Rapids, Kent County, MI held by Cornerstone University
Arbitron Metro Market: Guernsey WY; *Format:* Oldies

WBCT
10-01-1951; 93.7 MHz FM; *Hrs Open:* 24; 320 kw; 781 ft.; N42 37 56 W85 32 16
77 Monroe Center Avenue, Grand Rapids, MI 49503 US
(616) 459-1919
www.b93.com
License: Grand Rapids, Kent County, MI held by CC Licenses LLC.
Group Owner: iHeartMedia; (acq 1996; grpsl)
Nat'l Reps: Clear Channel
Arbitron Metro Market: Grand Rapids, MI; *Format:* Country
Tim Feagan, Regional Market President

*WBLU-FM
08-18-1979; 88.9 MHz FM; 0.65 kw; 400 ft.; N42 59 15 W85 37 26 *Rebroadcasts:* Rebroadcasts WBLV(FM) Twin Lake 100%
300 East Crystal Lake Road, Twin Lake, MI 49457 US
(231) 894-2616(231) 458-9258; *Fax:* (231) 893-2457
radio@bluelake.org
License: Grand Rapids, Kent County, MI held by Blue Lake Fine Arts Camp.
Nat'l Network: PRI; NPR
Arbitron Metro Market: Twin Lake, MI; *Format:* Jazz, News
Special Programming: Folk 5 hrs wkly; *Target Audience:* Adults.
Heidi Stansell, Vice President
James Chick, Business Manager

*WCSG
06-09-1973; 91.3 MHz FM; 37 kw; 571 ft.; N42 47 46 W85 38 58
1159 E. Beltline Avenue, Northeast, Grand Rapids, MI 49505 US
(616) 942-1500
www.wcsg.org
wcsg@wcsg.org
License: Grand Rapids, Kent County, MI held by Cornerstone University.
Nat'l Network: AP Radio
Arbitron Metro Market: Grand Rapids, MI; *Format:* Christian; *Hrs. of News Programming:* news progmg 2 hrs wkly; *No. News Employees:* 2; *Target Audience:* 35-49.
Dr. Joseph Stowell, President
Lee Geysbeek, Operations Dir
Chris Lemke, General Manager
Patty Riva, Promotions Manager
Tom Bosscher, Chief Engineer

WBFX
01-01-1965; 101.3 MHz FM; *Hrs Open:* 24; 50 kw; 420 ft.; N43 2 28 W85 21 28
77 Monroe Center St. N.W., Suite 1000, Grand Rapids, MI 49503 US
(616) 459-1919; *Fax:* (616) 242-6599
www.1013thebrew.com
License: Grand Rapids, Kent County, MI held by CC Licenses LLC
Group Owner: iHeartMedia
Arbitron Metro Market: Grand Rapids, MI; *Format:* Classic Rock
Tim Feagan, Regional Market President

WFGR
08-09-1992; 98.7 MHz FM; 2.75 kw; 492 ft.; N43 1 57 W85 41 47
220 Lyon St, NW Ste 425, Grand Rapids, MI 49503 US
(616) 451-4800
www.wfgr.com
jerry.tarrants@townsquaremedia.com
License: Grand Rapids, Kent County, MI
Group Owner: Townsquare Media; (acq 9-25-01; $3.9 million for stock).
Arbitron Metro Market: Grand Rapids, MI; *Format:* Oldies; *Target Audience:* 25 plus; affluent, well-educated professionals
Tim Cook, Programming Director

WFUR
11-01-1947; 1570 kHz AM; *Hrs Open:* 24; 1 kw-D, ND1; 0.307 kw-N, ND1; N42 57 14 W85 41 52
399 Garfield Avenue S.W., Grand Rapids, MI 49504 US
(616) 451-9387
www.wfuramfm.com
wfuramfm@cbcglobal.net
License: Grand Rapids, MI held by Furniture City Broadcasting Corp.
Group Owner: Kuiper Stns; (acq 3-10-50)
Nat'l Network: USA
Arbitron Metro Market: Grand Rapids, MII; *Format:* Religious; *Hrs. of News Programming:* News progmg 5 hrs wkly; *Target Audience:* 35 plus; 60% female, 30% male
William Kuiper Sr., President
Steven Kuiper, Operations Dir
Dave Kuiper, News Director
Bill Kuiper Jr., Chief Engineer
Pat Deja, Public Affairs Director

WFUR-FM
09-01-1960; 102.9 MHz FM; *Hrs Open:* 24; 50 kw; 492 ft.; N42 57 13 W85 41 55
399 Garfield Avenue S.W., Grand Rapids, MI 49504 US
(616) 451-9387
www.wfuramfm.com
License: Grand Rapids, Kent County, MI
Nat'l Network: USA
Arbitron Metro Market: Grand Rapids, MII; *Format:* Religious; *Hrs. of News Programming:* News progmg 5 hrs wkly; *Target Audience:* 35-64; Christian family music listeners & homeowners
Pat Deja, Programming Director
Doug Wentworth, News Director
Dave Kuiper, Disc Jockey

WGRD-FM
08-01-1962; 97.9 MHz FM; *Hrs Open:* 24; 13 kw; 591 ft.; N42 47 46 W85 38 58
600 Congress Ave., Suite 1400, Austin, TX 78701 US
(616) 451-4800; *Fax:* (616) 451-0113
www.wgrd.com
License: Grand Rapids, Kent County, MI
Group Owner: Townsquare Media; (acq 8-7-00; grpsl).
Nat'l Reps: Katz Radio
Arbitron Metro Market: Grand Rapids, MII; *Format:* Alternative; *Hrs. of News Programming:* news progmg 3 hrs wkly; *No. News Employees:* 1; *Target Audience:* 18-49.
Russ Hines, General Manager
Dustin Wood, General Sales Mgr
Jerry Tarrants, Programming Director

WLAV
01-01-1947; 96.9 MHz FM; *Hrs Open:* 24; 50 kw; 489 ft.; N43 02 1 W85 31 15
60 Monroe Ctr., Grand Rapids, MI 49503 US
(616) 774-8461; *Fax:* (616) 451-3299
www.wlav.com
rob.brandt@cumulus.com
License: Grand Rapids, MI held by Radio License Holding CBC, LLC
Group Owner: Cumulus Media Inc.; (acq 5-30-00; grpsl).
Nat'l Network: ABC
Arbitron Metro Market: Grand Rapids, MI; *Format:* Classic Rock; *Target Audience:* 25-49.
John Crenshaw, Operations Dir
Rich Berry, General Sales Mgr
Rob Brandt, Programming Director
Marcus Bradman, Director of Marketing/Promotions

WLHT-FM
02-28-1962; 95.7 MHz FM; 40 kw; 551 ft.; N43 1 57 W85 41 47
600 Congress Ave., Suite 1400, Austin, TX 78701 US
(616) 451-4855; *Fax:* (616) 451-9595
www.wlht.com
License: Grand Rapids, Kent County, MI held by Townsquare Media of Grand Rapids Inc.
Group Owner: Townsquare Media
Arbitron Metro Market: Grand Rapids, MI; *Format:* Adult Contemp; *Target Audience:* 25-54.
Terry Jacobs, President
Bill Bailey, Programming Director

WNWZ
11-01-1947; 1410 kHz AM; 1 kw-D, ND1; 0.048 kw-N, ND1; N42 59 14 W85 37 26
600 Congress Ave., Suite 1400, Austin, TX 78701 US
616-451-4800; *Fax:* (616) 451-9595
http://funny1410am.com/help/
Russ.Hines@townsquaremedia.com
License: Grand Rapids, MI
Group Owner: Townsquare Media; (acq 8-7-00; grpsl).
Nat'l Network: Jones Radio Networks
Arbitron Metro Market: Grand Rapids, M *TV Affiliate:* Comedy; *No. News Employees:* 35 plus; professionals
Russ Hines, General Manager
Tim Huston, General Sales Mgr
Jerry Tarrants, Programming Director
Brand Manager

WOOD
01-01-1924; 1300 kHz AM
77 Monroe Center St. N.W., Suite 1000, Grand Rapids, MI 49503 US
(616) 459-1919; *Fax:* (616) 723-3303
www.woodradio.com
info@woodradio.com
License: Grand Rapids, MI held by CC Licenses LLC.
Group Owner: iHeartMedia; (acq 5-10-96; grpsl)
Nat'l Network: ABC; *Nat'l Reps:* Clear Channel
Arbitron Metro Market: Grand Rapids, MI *TV Affiliate:* Talk; *Format:* News, News/Talk, 86 *Special Programming:* news progmg 24 hrs wkly; *Hrs. of News Programming:* 6; *No. News Employees:* 35-54.
Doug Montgomery, Operations Manager
Tim Feagan, General Manager
Henry Capogna, Sales Manager
Phil Tower, Programming Director
Samantha Bennett, Promotions Director
Matt Benson, Digital Sales Manager
Laura Murdoch, BusinessManager
Kelly Norton, Director of Sales

WSRW-FM
01-01-1962; 105.7 MHz FM; *Hrs Open:* 24; 265 kw; Ant 810 ft; N42 41 13 W85 30 35
77 Monroe Center St. N.W., Suite 1000, Grand Rapids, MI 49503 US
(616) 459-1919; *Fax:* (616) 723-3303
www.westmichiganstar.com
License: Grand Rapids, Kent County, MI held by CC Licenses LLC.
Group Owner: iHeartMedia
Arbitron Metro Market: Grand Rapids, MI; *Format:* Adult Contemp; *Hrs. of News Programming:* News progmg 10 hrs wkly
Doug Montgomery, Operations Manager
Tim Feagan, General Manager
Amanda Alexander, General Sales Mgr
Dave Taft, Programming Director
Samantha Bennett, Promotions Manager
Matt Benson, Digital Sales Manager
Laura Murdoch, BusinessManager
Kelly Norton, Director of Sales

WTKG
02-01-1945; 1230 kHz AM; *Hrs Open:* 24; 1 kw-D, ND2; 1 kw-N, ND2; N42 59 42 W85 40 36
77 Monroe Center St. N.W., Grand Rapids, MI 49503 US
(616) 459-1919; *Fax:* (616) 723-3303
www.wtkg.com
info@wtkg.com
License: Grand Rapids, MI held by CC Licenses LLC.
Group Owner: iHeartMedia; (acq 1996; grpsl).
Nat'l Reps: Clear Channel
Arbitron Metro Market: Grand Rapids, MI; *Format:* Talk; *Hrs. of News Programming:* news progmg 7 hrs wkly; *No. News Employees:* 2; *Target Audience:* 25-54; conservative
Doug Montgomery, Operations Manager
Tim Feagan, General Manager
Henry Capogna, General Sales Mgr
Phil Tower, Programming Director
Samantha Bennett, Promotions Manager
Matt Benson, Digital Sales Manager
Laura Murdoch, BusinessManager

*WVGR
12-07-1961; 104.1 MHz FM; *Hrs Open:* 24; 96 kw; 725 ft.; N42 39 17 W85 31 38 *Rebroadcasts:* Rebroadcasts WUOM(FM) Ann Arbor 100%
535 West William Street, Ann Arbor, MI 48103 US
(734) 764-9210; *Fax:* (734) 647-3488
www.michiganradio.org
michigan.radio@umich.edu
License: Grand Rapids, Kent County, MI held by Regents of the University of Michigan.
Nat'l Network: NPR; PRI

RADIO - U.S.

Arbitron Metro Market: Grand Rapids, MI; *Format:* News, News/Talk, 86; *Hrs. of News Programming:* news progmg 140 hrs wkly; *No. News Employees:* 12
Peggy Watson, Operations Dir
Vincent Duffey, News Director
Bob Skon, Chief Engineer
Sarah Hulett, Assistant News Director
Jennifer Guerra, Reporter/Producer
Lester Graham, Investigative Reporter

WJRW
09-18-1040; 1340 kHz AM; 1 kw-U; N42 57 05 W85 41 55
60 Monroe Ctr., Grand Rapids, MI 49503 US
(616) 774-8461; *Fax:* (616) 451-3299
www.1340wjrw.com
dave.jaconette@cumulus.com
License: Grand Rapids, MI held by Radio License Holding CBC, LLC
Group Owner: Cumulus Media Inc.
Format: News/Talk
John Crenshaw, Operations Dir
Rich Berry, General Sales Mgr
Dave Jaconette, Programming Director
Marcus Bradman, Dir of Marketing/Promotions
Jeff Cartwright, Market Manager

Grayling

WGRY
08-01-1970; 1230 kHz AM; *Hrs Open:* 24; 0.75 kw-U, ND1; N44 39 5 W84 44 18
6514 Old Lake Road, Grayling, MI 49738 US
(989) 348-6171; *Fax:* (989) 348-6181
www.gannonbroadcasting.com
radio@i2k.net
License: Grayling, MI held by Blarney Stone Broadcasting Inc.
Group Owner: Blarney Stone Broadcasting Inc.
Nat'l Reps: Michigan Spot Sales
Format: Contemporary Hits/Top 40; *Hrs. of News Programming:* news progmg 16 hrs wkly; *No. News Employees:* 1; *Target Audience:* 25 plus.
William Gannon, President
Pete Michaels, Operations Dir

WQON
06-16-1977; 100.3 MHz FM; 60 kw; 430 ft.; N44 34 15 W84 41 33
6514 Old Lake Rd., Grayling, MI 49738 US
(989) 348-6171; *Fax:* (989) 348-6181
www.gannonbroadcasting.com
radio@i2k.net
License: Grayling, Crawford County, MI held by Blarney Stone Broadcasting Inc.
Group Owner: Blarney Stone Broadcasting Inc.
Nat'l Network: ABC; *Nat'l Reps:* Patt
Format: Country; *Target Audience:* 25-54.
William Gannon, President
Pete Michaels, Operations Dir

Greenville

WGLM
05-19-1960; 1380 kHz AM
Mailing Address: 9181 S. Greenville Road, Greenville, MI 48838 US
Second Address: 9181 S. Greenville Rd., Greenville, MI
(616) 754-1063
License: Greenville, MI held by Packer Radio Greenville Inc.
Format: News, Sports, 86
Chris Loiselle, CFO
Bruce Bentley, Operations Dir
John Clark, General Manager
Ralph Haines, Chief Engineer

***WDPW**
91.9 MHz FM; 4 kw vert; 207 ft.; N43 5 12 W85 18 59
P.O. Box 6465, Grand Rapids, MI 49516 US
(616) 698-1831
License: Greenville, Montcalm County, MI held by Larlen Communications Inc.
Arbitron Metro Market: Polson, MT
P.R. Frank, Operations Dir
Ken Kreitzer, General Manager
Christopher Hartley, Programming Director
Tom Nornhold, Chief Engineer
Jennifer Bryant, Assistant Music Director

WBBL
01-01-1979; MHz FM; 50 kw; 492 feet; N43 01 10 W85 20 58
60 Monroe Ctr., 3rd Floor, Grand Rapids, MI 49503 US
(616) 774-8461; *Fax:* (616) 451-3299
www.wbbl.com
dave.jaconette@cumulus.com
License: Greenville, MI held by Radio License Holding CBC, LLC
Group Owner: Cumulus Media Inc.
Format: Sports
John Crenshaw, Operations Dir
Dave Jaconette, Programming Director
Marcus Bradman, Dir of Marketing/Promotions
Jeff Cartwright, Regional VP/Market Manager

Gulliver

WCMM
01-01-1982; 102.5 MHz FM; 100 kw; 814 ft.; N45 58 1 W86 29 18
524 Ludington St., Suite 300, Escanaba, MI 49829-3900 US
(906) 789-4102
radioresultsnetwork.com
countrymoose@radioresultsnetwork.com
License: Gulliver, Schoolcraft County, MI held by Lakes Radio Inc.
Group Owner: Lakes Radio Inc.; acq 11-30-99; grpsl)
Nat'l Network: ABC
Arbitron Metro Market: Gulliver, MI; *Format:* Country; *No. News Employees:* 4; *Target Audience:* 18-54; younger, contemp, mobile adult workers

Gwinn

WUPT
01-01-2008; 100.3 MHz FM; 100 kw; 512 ft.; N46 30 51.7 W87 28 40.2
715 W. Washington St., Marquette, MI 49855 US
(906) 228-9700
www.radioresultsnetwork.com
License: Gwinn, Marquette County, MI held by Radioactive LLC.
Group Owner: Radioactive LLC
Arbitron Metro Market: Gwinn, MI; *Format:* Contemporary Hits/Top 40, Adult Contemp

Hancock

WMPL
03-02-1957; 920 kHz AM; 1 kw-D, ND1; 0.206 kw-N, ND1; N47 6 5 W88 35 26
326 Quincy Street, Hancock, MI 49930 US
(906) 482-3700; *Fax:* (906) 482-1540
www.wmpl920.com
rick@wmpl920.com
License: Hancock, MI held by J & J Broadcasting Inc.
Nat'l Network: USA; *Nat'l Reps:* Michigan Spot Sales
Arbitron Metro Market: Hancock, MI; *Format:* News, Sports, 86; *Hrs. of News Programming:* news progmg 15 hrs wkly; *No. News Employees:* 1; *Target Audience:* General.; *Adv. Rates:* 10; 8; 8; 5
Jerry Hackman, President
Jay Nix, Operations Dir
Ken Waldrop, General Manager
Mariann Schulze, General Sales Mgr
Mitchell Lake, News Director
Ted Franz, Chief Engineer
Josh Ylitalo, Traffic Manager

WKMJ-FM
01-01-1968; 93.5 MHz FM; 13.5 kw; 456 ft.; N47 6 6 W88 34 11
326 Quincy Street, Hancock, MI 49930 US
(906) 482-3700; *Fax:* (906) 482-1540
www.themix93.com
rick@wmpl920.com
License: Hancock, Houghton County, MI held by J & J Broadcasting Inc.
Nat'l Network: Jones Radio Networks
Arbitron Metro Market: Hancock, MI; *Format:* Adult Contemp, Sports; *No. News Employees:* 1; *Target Audience:* 18-45.; *Adv. Rates:* 14; 13; 13; 9
Kate Lochte, Station Manager

WGLI
02-11-2003; 98.7 MHz FM; *Hrs Open:* 24; 100 kw; 522 ft.; N47 6 13 W88 34 4
PO Box 550, Bavaga, MI 44908 US
(906) 353-9287; *Fax:* (906) 483-4910
www.keepitintheup.com
eagleadmin@up.net
License: Hancock, Houghton County, MI held by Keweenaw Bay Indian Community
Nat'l Network: Jones Radio Networks
Arbitron Metro Market: Traverse City, MI; *Format:* Classic Rock
Special Programming: Loc talk 5 hrs wkly
Ed Janisse, General Manager
John Preston, General Sales Mgr

Hanover

***WJKZ**
90.9 MHz FM; kw
PO Box 4872, East Lansing, MI 48826 US
(517) 999-3737
License: Hanover, Jackson County, MI held by Saidnewsfoundation.
Arbitron Metro Market: Hanover, MI
David Schaberg, General Manager

Harbor Beach

***WSMB**
03-01-1925; 89.3 MHz FM; kw
P.O. Box 88, Attica, MI 48412 US
(901) 767-0104; *Fax:* (901) 767-0582
www.smile.fm
License: Harbor Beach, Shelby County, MI held by Entercom Memphis License LLC.
Group Owner: Entercom Communications Corp.; (acq 12-13-99; grpsl)
Nat'l Network: Fox Sports
Arbitron Metro Market: Memphis, TN; *Format:* Sports
Dan Barron, Operations Dir
Kory Myers, General Sales Mgr
Dennis Fuller, Programming Director
Rondi Atkinson, Promotions Manager
Mike Schwartz, Chief Engineer

WCZE
01-01-2005; 103.7 MHz FM; 43 kw; 528 ft.; N43 41 10 W82 59 40
6940 Armstrong Rd #N, Imlay City, MI 48444 US
(888) 887-7139; *Fax:* (877) 850-0881
www..smile.fm
jennc@smile.FM
License: Harbor Beach, Huron County, MI held by Jennifer & Edward Czelada.
Format: Christian
Jenn Czelada, General Manager
Ed Czelada, Programming Director
Aaron Burrell, Administration
Clayton Hewitt, Administration and Engineering
Ed Czelada, Administration, Programming & Engineering
Dale Mazzoline, Production

Harbor Springs

***WCMW-FM**
08-15-1988; 103.9 MHz FM; *Hrs Open:* 24; 12 kw; 1001 ft.; N45 30 8 W85 1 44 *Rebroadcasts:* Rebroadcasts WCMU-FM Mount Pleasant 100%
3965 East Broomfield Rd., Mt Pleasant, MI 48859 US
(989) 774-3105; *Fax:* (989) 774-4427
www.wcmu.org
schud1ra@cmich.edu
License: Harbor Springs, Emmet County, MI held by Central Michigan University.
Nat'l Network: NPR; PRI; *Wire Services:* AP
Arbitron Metro Market: Michigan, Upper Peninsula, MS; *Format:* Jazz, News; *Hrs. of News Programming:* news progmg 45 hrs wkly; *No. News Employees:* 2
Ed Grant, General Manager

***WHBP**
90.1 MHz FM; 1.2 kw; 1004 ft.; N45 30 8 W85 1 44 US
(231) 276-4400; *Fax:* (231) 276-4417
www.interlochen.org/ipr
License: Harbor Springs, Emmet County, MI held by Interlochen Center for the Arts.
Arbitron Metro Market: Harbor Springs, MI
Thom Paulson, General Manager

Harrietta

WKAD
01-01-2003; 93.7 MHz FM; 4.3 kw; Ant 390 ft; N44 16 41 W85 35 28
Box 520, Cadillac, MI 49412
(231) 775-1263; *Fax:* (231) 779-2844
License: Harrietta, Wexford County, MI held by Cadillac Broadcasting LLC
Population Served: 14,894; *Arbitron Metro Market:* Traverse City, MI
Eric Sharp, Operations Manager

Harrison

***WBHL**
90.7 MHz FM; 100 w; Ant 98 ft; N44 01 02 W84 47 56

Box 567, Cadillac, MI 49601
(231) 468-2087
License: Harrison, Clare County, MI held by West Central Michigan Media Ministries

David Bodluc, President

Harrisville

*WSFP
01-01-2006; 88.1 MHz FM; 0.48 kw; 472 ft.; N45 3 50 W83 42 57 *Rebroadcasts:* Simulcasts WJOM(FM) Eagle 100% US
(888) 887-7139
411@smile.fm
License: Harrisville, Montmorency County, MI held by Michigan Community Radio.
Arbitron Metro Market: Harrisville, MI; *Format:* Christian
Edward Czelada, President
Dale Mazzoline, Feature Production
Ed Czelada, Administration, Programming & Engineering
Clayton Hewitt, Administration and Engineering
Aaron Burrell, Administration

Hart

WWKR
07-01-1995; 94.1 MHz FM; *Hrs Open:* 24; 5 kw; 682 ft.; N43 40 34 W86 14 20
5399 W. Wallace Ln., Ludington, MI 49431 US
(231) 843-0941; *Fax:* (231) 843-9411
www.94k-rock.com
License: Hart, Oceana County, MI held by Synergy Lakeshore Licenses, LLC
Group Owner: Synergy Broadcast Group; (acq 4-10-98; $250,000)
Nat'l Network: AP Network News; *Nat'l Reps:* Michigan Spot Sales *Regional Reps:* Michigan Spot Sales
Arbitron Metro Market: Mason, MI; *Format:* Classic Rock; *Hrs. of News Programming:* news progmg 2 hrs wkly; *Target Audience:* 25-54; baby boomers
Todd Mohr, President
Stacy Johnson, Operations Dir
Tom Green, Chief Engineer

Hartford

WCXT
10-31-1981; 98.3 MHz FM; 3.7 kW; 427 ft.; N42 15 14 W86 20 9
PO Box 107, St. Joseph, MI 49085 USA
(269) 925-1111; *Fax:* (269) 925-1011
www.983thecoast.com
License: Hartford, Van Buren County, MI held by WSJM, Inc.
Group Owner: Mid-West Family Broadcasting; (acq 10-95; with WCSY(AM) South Haven)
Arbitron Metro Market: Hartford, MI; *Format:* Adult Contemp
Gayle Olson, Chairman
Dave Doetsch, President & General Manager
Paul Layendecker, Operations Dir
Bob Bucholtz, General Sales Mgr
Zack East, Programming Director

Hastings

WBCH
11-01-1957; 1220 kHz AM; *Hrs Open:* 24
Mailing Address: P. O. Box 88, Hastings, MI 49058 US
Second Address: 119 W. State St., Hastings, MI 49058
(301) 759-1005; *Fax:* (301) 759-3124
www.cumberlandsmagic.com
License: Hastings, MI held by Barry Broadcasting Co.
Regional Network: Mich. Farm *Regional Reps:* Patt.; *Wire Services:* NOAA Weather
Arbitron Metro Market: Spencer IA; *Format:* Adult Contemp; *Adv. Rates:* 18; 14; 18; 10
Dale Miller, President
Jerry Hannahs, Promotions Manager

WBCH-FM
12-01-1967; 100.1 MHz FM; *Hrs Open:* 24; 3 kw; 295 ft.; N42 37 34 W85 16 41
119 West State Street, Hastings, MI 49058 US
(269) 945-3414
License: Hastings, Barry County, MI
Nat'l Network: ABC; *Wire Services:* NOAA Weather
Arbitron Metro Market: Billings MT; *Format:* Easy Listening
Marcos Rodriguez, General Manager

Hemlock

WCEN-FM
08-08-1963; 94.5 MHz FM; 100 kw; 981 ft.; N43 43 36 W84 36 16
2929 S. Isabella Rd., Mt. Pleasant, MI 48858 US
(989) 752-3456; *Fax:* (989) 754-5046
www.945themoose.com
License: Hemlock, Saginaw County, MI held by NM Licensing LLC.
Group Owner: NextMedia Group Inc.; (acq 12-30-02; grpsl).
Wire Services: Metro Weather Service Inc.
Arbitron Metro Market: Saginaw-Bay City-Midland, MI; *Format:* Country; *Target Audience:* 25-54; medium income, rural & urban
Shannone Dunlap, Operations Dir
Joby Phyllips, Programming Director

Highland Park

*WHPR-FM
05-21-1954; 88.1 MHz FM; *Hrs Open:* 24; 0.012 kw; 105 ft.; N42 24 29 W83 5 30
160 Victor Street, Detroit, MI 48203 US
(313) 868-6612; *Fax:* (313) 868-8725
www.whprradio.com
tv68whpr@aol.com
License: Highland Park, Wayne County, MI held by R.J.s Late Night Entertainment Corp.
Format: Oldies, Talk; *Target Audience:* 21 & over; African Americans 40 plus politically aware & motivated
R. J. Watkins, Operations Dir
Henry Tyler, Vice President

Hillman

WKJZ
12-14-1993; 94.9 MHz FM; 50 kw; 492 ft.; N45 1 15 W83 55 21
Rebroadcasts: Rebroadcasts WQLB(FM) Tawas City 85%
523 Meadow Rd., Tawas City, MI 48763 US
(989) 362-3417
www.hitsfm.net
License: Hillman, Montmorency County, MI held by Carroll Enterprises Inc.
Group Owner: Carroll Enterprises Inc.; acq 6-29-92;
Format: Variety/Diverse
John Carroll Jr., General Manager

Hillsdale

WCSR
05-21-1959; 1340 kHz AM; 0.5 kw-D, ND1; 0.25 kw-N, ND1; N41 55 41 W84 38 10 *Rebroadcasts:* Simulcast with WCSR-FM Hillsdale 98%
P.O. Box 273, Hillsdale, MI 49242 US
(517) 437-4444; *Fax:* (517) 437-7461
www.radiohillsdale.com
wcsrinc@comcast.net
License: Hillsdale, MI held by WCSR Inc.
Regional Network: Mich. Farm
Arbitron Metro Market: Hillsdale, MI; *Format:* Adult Contemp
Special Programming: Farm 3 hrs, relg 10 hrs wkly; *Target Audience:* 25 plus; county-wide
Anthony Flynn, President
Michael Flynn, General Manager

WCSR-FM
05-19-1973; 92.1 MHz FM; 6 kw; 243 ft.; N41 55 41 W84 38 10
Mailing Address: 170 N. West St, Box 273, Hillsdale, MI 49242 US
Second Address: 170 N. West St., Hillsdale, MI 49242
(517) 437-4444; *Fax:* 517) 437-7461
www.radiohillsdale.com
License: Hillsdale, Hillsdale County, MI
Arbitron Metro Market: Hillsdale, MI
Brian Lamb, CEO
Kate Mills, General Manager

Holland

WHTC
07-31-1948; 1450 kHz AM; *Hrs Open:* 24; 1 kW; N42 47 41 W86 6 22
87 Central Ave, Holland, MI 49423 USA
(616) 392-3121; *Fax:* (616) 392-8066
whtc.com
License: Holland, MI held by Midwest Communications Inc.
Group Owner: Midwest Communications Inc.; (acq 8-1-00; grpsl).
Nat'l Network: CBS; *Nat'l Reps:* Christal
Arbitron Metro Market: Holland, MI; *Format:* News/Talk *Special Programming:* Sp 3 hrs wkly; *Hrs. of News Programming:* news progmg 15 hrs wkly; *No. News Employees:* 1; *Target Audience:* 35 plus.; *Adv. Rates:* 25; 20; 20; 15
Brent Alan, Brand Manager

WTNR
03-21-1961; 94.5 MHz FM; *Hrs Open:* 24; 50 kw; 499 ft.; N42 51 20 W85 57 45
60 Monroe Ctr., 3rd Floor, Grand Rapids, MI 49503 US
(616) 774-8461; *Fax:* (616) 451-3299
www.nashfm945.com
john.crenshaw@cumulus.com
License: Holland, MI held by Radio License Holding CBC, LLC
Group Owner: Cumulus Media Inc.; (acq 4-26-2001; grpsl).
Nat'l Network: ABC; *Nat'l Reps:* Katz Radio
Arbitron Metro Market: Grand Rapids, MI; *Format:* Country
John Crenshaw, Program Dir/Operation Mgr
Rich Berry, General Sales Mgr
Marcus Bradman, Dir of Marketing/Promotions

*WTHS
10-15-1984; 89.9 MHz FM; *Hrs Open:* 24; 1 kw; 154 ft; N42 47 16 W86 06 02
Box 9000, Hope College, Holland, MI 49422
(616) 395-7878,(616) 395-7880
http://wths.hope.edu
wths@hope.edu
License: Holland, Ottawa County, MI held by Hope College Board of Trustees.
Hrs. of News Programming: News progmg 7 hrs wkly; *Target Audience:* 15-30; students & adults
Tom Zahari, General Manager
John Pattrick, Director
William DeBoar, Production Director

WMAX-FM
09-01-1962; 96.1 MHz FM; *Hrs Open:* 24; 50 kw horiz, 45 kw vert; 492 ft.; N42 49 10 W85 52 9
77 Monroe Center St. N.W., Suite 1000, Grand Rapids, MI 49503 US
(616) 459-1919; *Fax:* (616) 235-9600
www.espn961.com
License: Holland, Ottawa County, MI held by CC Licenses LLC.
Group Owner: iHeartMedia; (acq 1-27-2009)
Nat'l Reps: Clear Channel
Arbitron Metro Market: Grand Rapids, MI; *Format:* Sports; *Target Audience:* 25-34; women
Doug Montgomery, Operations Manager
Tim Feagan, Market Manager
Matt Benson, Digital Sales Manager

Holt

WLCM
08-25-1956; 1390 kHz AM; *Hrs Open:* 24 Hours; 5 kw-D, 4.5 kw-N, DA-D; N42 34 02 W84 51 58 (day), N42 33 07 W84 33 05 (night)
1613 Lawrence Hwy, P.O. Box 338, Charlotte, MI 48813 USA
(517) 543-8200; *Fax:* (517) 543-7779
www.wlcmradio.com
jeff.frank@cbslradio.com
License: Holt, Ingham County, MI held by Christian Broadcasting System Ltd.
Group Owner: Christian Broadcasting System Ltd.; (acq 1-5-93; assumption of land contract;
Population Served: 700,000; *Arbitron Metro Market:* Lansing-East Lansing, MI *Special Programming:* Gospel 3 hrs wkly; *Hrs. of News Programming:* News progmg 2 hrs wkly; *Target Audience:* 25-55; general
Kim Bailey, Operations Dir
Jeff Frank, Station Manager
Antoniette Parson, Business Manager

Holton

WVIB
01-01-2002; 100.1 MHz FM; 2.9 kw; 472 ft.; N43 18 50 W86 9 17
3375 Merriam, Suite 201, Muskegon Heights, MI 49444 US
(231) 830-0176; *Fax:* (231) 830-0104
www.v100fm.com
ronald.gates@cumulus.com
License: Holton, MI held by Radio License Holding CBC, LLC
Group Owner: Cumulus Media Inc.; (acq 9-28-2005)
Arbitron Metro Market: Muskegon, MI; *Format:* Urban Contemporary
Jon Russell, Operations Dir
Ron Gates, General Sales Mgr
Rich Berry, VP/Market Manager

Honor

WSRJ
01-01-2002; 105.5 MHz FM; 17 kw; 367 ft.; N44 39 41 W85 48 53 *Rebroadcasts:* Rebroadcasts WSRT(FM) Gaylord 75%
2215 Oak Indust. Dr. Ne, Grand Rapids, MI 49505 US
(231) 947-0003; *Fax:* (231) 947-7002
License: Honor, Benzie County, MI held by Northern Radio of Michigan Inc.
Arbitron Metro Market: Grand Rapids, MI; *Format:* Classic Rock
Charlie Ferguson, General Manager

Houghton

WCCY
01-01-1929; 1400 kHz AM; *Hrs Open:* 24; 1 kw-U, ND1; N47 8 6 W88 33 53
313 Montezuma Avenue, Houghton, MI 49931 US
(906) 482-7700; *Fax:* (906) 482-7751
www.wccy.com
jharju@up.net
License: Houghton, MI
Group Owner: Houston Community Broadcasting Corporation; (acq 1-6-2005; grpsl).
Nat'l Network: ABC; ESPN Radio; Jones Radio Networks; *Regional Network:* Mich. Radio; *Nat'l Reps:* Michigan Spot Sales
Arbitron Metro Market: Houghton, MI; *Format:* Sports, Adult Contemp *Special Programming:* Relg one hr, pub affrs one hr wkly; *Hrs. of News Programming:* news progmg 18 hrs wkly; *No. News Employees:* 1 *TargetAudience:* 35+.
Kevin Ericson, Operations Dir
Jeff Harju, General Manager

***WGGL-FM**
02-01-1982; 91.1 MHz FM; *Hrs Open:* 24; 100 kw; 860 ft.; N47 2 8 W88 41 43
45 East 7th Street, Saint Paul, MN 55101 US
(651) 290-1500; *Fax:* (651) 290-1224
www.mpr.org
License: Houghton, Houghton County, MI held by Minnesota Public Radio Inc.
Nat'l Network: PRI; NPR; *Regional Network:* Minn. Pub. Radio
Format: News; *No. News Employees:* 1; *Target Audience:* General.
William Kling, President
Erik Nycklemoe, Operations Dir
Larissa Anderson, Assistant Producer
Sasha Aslanian, Producer/Reporter
Elizabeth Baier, Reporter

WHKB
09-01-1989; 102.3 MHz FM; 6 kw; 548 ft.; N47 8 6 W88 33 53
313 East Montezuma Avenue, Houghton, MI 49931 US
(906) 482-7700; *Fax:* (906) 482-7751
www.kbear102.com
License: Houghton, Houghton County, MI
Group Owner: Houston Community Broadcasting Corporation; (acq 1-6-2005; grpsl).
Nat'l Network: ABC; Jones Radio Networks; *Regional Network:* Mich. Radio; *Nat'l Reps:* Michigan Spot Sales
Format: Country; *Hrs. of News Programming:* news prgmg 18 hrs/week; *No. News Employees:* 1; *Target Audience:* 25-54.
Kevin Ericson, Operations Dir
Jeff Harju, General Manager

***WMTU-FM**
01-26-1994; 91.9 MHz FM; 0 kw horiz, 4.4 kw vert; 479 ft.; N47 8 27 W88 32 26
West Wadsworth Hall Mtu, Houghton, MI 49931 US
(906) 487-2333; *Fax:* (906) 487-3016
www.wmtu.mtu.edu
wmtu@mtu.edu
License: Houghton, Houghton County, MI held by Michigan Technological University.
Arbitron Metro Market: Houghton, MI; *Format:* Variety/Diverse
George Olszewski, General Manager
Lindsay Worden, Station Manager
Matt Derucki, Programming Director
Dea Occhietti, Promotions Manager
Josh Martin, Chief Engineer

WOLV
03-07-1980; 97.7 MHz FM; 6.5 kw; 591 ft.; N47 8 6 W88 33 53
313 Montezuma Ave., Houghton, MI 49931 US
(906) 482-7700; *Fax:* (906) 482-7751
www.thewolf.com
License: Houghton, Houghton County, MI
Nat'l Network: ABC; Jones Radio Networks; *Regional Network:* Mich. Radio; *Nat'l Reps:* Michigan Spot Sales
TV Affiliate: Classic Hits *Special Programming:* news prgmg 18 hrs/week; *Hrs. of News Programming:* 1; *No. News Employees:* 25-54.
Kevin Ericson, Operations Dir
Jeff Harju, General Manager

Houghton Lake

WTWS
03-26-1975; 92.1 MHz FM; *Hrs Open:* 24; 0.92 kw; 748 ft.; N44 17 21 W84 44 32
P.O. Box 468, Prudenville, MI 48651 US
(989) 366-5364; *Fax:* (989) 366-6200
License: Houghton Lake, Clare County, MI held by Coltrace Communications Inc.
Format: Country
Michael Jay, Programming Director

WUPS
07-01-1961; 98.5 MHz FM; *Hrs Open:* 24; 100 kw; Ant 981 ft; N44 17 18 W84 44 30
Box 468, Prudenville, MI 48651
(989) 366-5364; *Fax:* (989) 366-6200
www.wups.com
wupsfm@yahoo.com
License: Houghton Lake, Roscommon County, MI held by Coltrace Communications Inc.
Nat'l Network: ABC; *Nat'l Reps:* Rgnl Reps
Population Served: 200,000 *Hrs. of News Programming:* news progmg 6 hrs wkly; *No. News Employees:* 1; *Target Audience:* 25-54; general
Michael Jay, Programming Director

Howell

WHMI-FM
09-01-1977; 93.5 MHz FM; *Hrs Open:* 24; 5.2 kw; 354 ft.; N42 39 47 W83 56 23
P.O. Box 935, Howell, MI 48844 US
(517) 546-0860; *Fax:* (517) 546-1758
www.whmi.com
whmi@whmi.com
License: Howell, Livingston County, MI held by The Livingston Radio Co.
Nat'l Network: CNN Radio; *Nat'l Reps:* Michigan Spot Sales
Arbitron Metro Market: Detroit; *Format:* Contemporary Hits/Top 40, Adult Contemp; *Hrs. of News Programming:* news progmg 10 hrs wkly; *No. News Employees:* 3; *Target Audience:* 25-64.
Marcia Jablonski, CEO
Reed Kittredge, Operations Dir
Greg Jablonski, General Manager
Debbie Platt, General Sales Mgr

Hudson

WBZV
03-01-1995; 102.5 MHz FM; *Hrs Open:* 24; 6 kw; 328 ft.; N41 53 3 W84 31 24
121 W. Maumee Street, Adrian, MI 49221 US
(517) 265-9500; *Fax:* (517) 263-4525
friends@tc3net.com
License: Hudson, Lenawee County, MI held by Friends Communications of Hudson Inc.
Group Owner: Friends Communications Inc.
Nat'l Network: ABC; *Nat'l Reps:* Michigan Spot Sales
Arbitron Metro Market: Hudson, MI; *Format:* Classic Rock; *Hrs. of News Programming:* news progmg 6 hrs wkly; *No. News Employees:* 1; *Target Audience:* 25-54.
Bob Elliot, Chairman

Imlay City

***WDTR**
12-01-2000; 89.1 MHz FM; 1.5 kw; Ant 171 ft; N43 03 42 W83 05 44
3302 N. Van Dyke, Imlay City, MI 48444
(810) 721-0891; *Fax:* (413) 410-9708
www.positivehits.com
info@joyfm.net
License: Imlay City, Lapeer County, MI held by Michigan Community Radio.

Jenn Czelada, General Manager
Ed Czelada, Programming Director

Indian River

WMKC
02-08-1982; 102.9 MHz FM; 100 kw; 1102 ft.; N45 30 8 W85 1 44
514 Munson Ave., Traverse City, MI 49686 US
(231) 627-2341; *Fax:* (231) 627-7000
www.1029bigcountry.com
License: Indian River, Mackinac County, MI held by Black Diamond Broadcast Holdings, LLC.
Group Owner: Black Diamond Broadcast Group, LLC.
Arbitron Metro Market: Traverse City, MI; *Format:* Country

Inkster

WDRJ
11-01-1956; 1440 kHz AM; *Hrs Open:* 24
2994 East Grand Boulevard, Detroit, MI 48202 US
(313) 871-1440
www.1440wdrj.com
1440@communicom.com
License: Inkster, MI held by Davidson Media Station WMKM Licensee LLC.
Group Owner: Davidson Media Group LLC; (acq 5-28-2004; $5.75 million)
Arbitron Metro Market: Detroit, MI; *Format:* Religious; *Target Audience:* 35 plus; adult Black church audience
Rich Kylberg, President
Raymond Burkhart, General Manager
Carl Dimaria, General Sales Mgr

Interlochen

***WIAA**
07-22-1963; 88.7 MHz FM; *Hrs Open:* 24; 100 kw; 1033 ft.; N44 16 33 W85 42 49
Mailing Address: PO Box 199, Interlochen, MI 49643 US
Second Address: One Lyon St., Interlochen, MI 49643
(231) 276-4400; *Fax:* (231) 276-4417
www.interlochen.org/ipr
ipr@interlochen.org
License: Interlochen, Grand Traverse County, MI held by Interlochen Center for the Arts.
Nat'l Network: NPR; PRI
Arbitron Metro Market: Traverse City-Petoskey, MI; *Format:* Classical, News; *Target Audience:* 35-80; professional, arts-oriented, upper-income
Thom Paulson, Operations Dir

Ionia

WION
02-01-1953; 1430 kHz AM; *Hrs Open:* 24
1150 Haynor Road, Iona, MI 48846 US
(616) 527-9466; *Fax:* (616) 775-5908
www.i1430.com
office@i1430.com
License: Ionia, MI held by Packer Radio WION LLC
Nat'l Network: CNN Radio; Sporting News Radio Network; *Regional Network:* Mich. Radio
Arbitron Metro Market: Grand Rapids, MI; *Format:* Variety/Diverse; *No. News Employees:* 1
Jim ""Carlyle"" Angus, CEO
Jim Carlyle, General Manager
Jim Aaron, Programming Director
Jim Aaron, Co-owner and Disc Jockey
Garry Osborn, Disc Jockey
Phil Cloud, Disc Jokcey and Account Representative
Dan Ferguson, SalesRepresentative
Scott Beetman, Engineer

Iron Mountain

WIMK
12-27-1981; 93.1 MHz FM; *Hrs Open:* 24; 100 kw; 591 ft.; N45 49 16 W88 2 28 *Rebroadcasts:* Rebroadcasts WUPK-FM Marquette 100%
1411 Ashmun St., Sault Ste. Marie, MI 49783 US
(855) 876-2536
www.rock101.net
Theresa@sovcomm.net
License: Iron Mountain, Dickinson County, MI held by Sovereign Communications
Group Owner: Sovereing Communications; acq 01-01-2010
Format: Classic Rock, Rock/AOR; *No. News Employees:* 1; *Target Audience:* 25-54.; *Adv. Rates:* 20; 17.50; 15; 10
Theresa Henderson, General Sales Mgr

WJNR-FM
08-17-1972; 101.5 MHz FM; 100 kw; 614 ft.; N45 49 16 W88 2 34
212 West J Street, Iron Mountain, MI 49801 US
(906) 774-5731
www.frogcountry.com
peterson.trisha@gmail.com
License: Iron Mountain, Dickinson County, MI held by Results Broadcasting of Michigan Inc.
Group Owner: Results Broadcasting; (acq 6-5-97).
Nat'l Network: ABC
Format: Country; *Target Audience:* 25-54.
Trisha Peterson, General Manager

WMIQ
01-01-1947; 1450 kHz AM; *Hrs Open:* 24; 1 kw-U, ND1; N45 49 16 W88 3 16
101 E. Kent St., Iron Mountain, MI 49801 US
(906) 774-4321
www.wmiq.net
talk1450wmiq@uplogon.com
License: Iron Mountain, MI held by Sovereign Communications
Group Owner: Sovereign Communications
Nat'l Network: USA
Arbitron Metro Market: Iron Mountain, MI; *Format:* News, News/Talk, 84, Talk; *Hrs. of News Programming:* news progmg 24 hrs wkly; *No. News Employees:* 1; *Target Audience:* 35-64; educated, middle to upper incomelisteners; *Adv. Rates:* Same as FM

***WVCM**
91.5 MHz FM; *Hrs Open:* 24; 0.5 kw vert; 600 ft.; N45 49 15 W88 2 25
3434 West Kilbourn Ave, Milwaukee, WI 53208 US
(414) 935-3000; *Fax:* (414) 935-3015
www.vcyamerica.org
vcy@vcyamerica.org
License: Iron Mountain, Dickinson County, MI held by VCY America Inc.
Group Owner: VCY America Inc.
Arbitron Metro Market: Milwaukee, WI; *Format:* Christian
Randall Melchert, President
Vic Eliason, Operations Dir
Jim Schneider, Programming Director

WHTO
01-01-2003; 106.7 MHz FM; 6.1 kw; 676 ft.; N45 49 16 W88 2 34
400 East Maple, Fremont, MI 49412 US
(906) 774-5731; *Fax:* (906) 774-4542
www.1067themountain.com
peterson.trisha@gmail.com
License: Iron Mountain, Dickinson County, MI held by Results Broadcasting of Iron Mountain Inc.
Group Owner: Results Broadcasting; (acq 6-29-2005; $650,000)
Nat'l Network: ABC
Arbitron Metro Market: Iron Mountain, MI; *Format:* Oldies
Trisha Peterson, General Manager

Iron River

WFER
11-18-1949; 1230 kHz AM; *Hrs Open:* 5 AM-11 PM; 1 kw-U; N46 03 55 W88 38 17
Box AC, 809 W. Genesee St., Iron River, MI 49935
(906) 265-5104; *Fax:* (906) 265-3486
wikb@sbcglobal.net
License: Iron River, Iron County, MI held by Iron River Community Broadcasting Corporation
Group Owner: Stephen Marks; (acq 5-10-2004; $1.25 million with co-located FM)
Nat'l Reps: Roslin
Population Served: 20,000 *Hrs. of News Programming:* news progmg 15 hrs wkly; *No. News Employees:* 1; *Target Audience:* General.
Jay Barry, General Manager
Margaret Henschel, General Sales Mgr
Jeff Bonno, Chief Engineer

WIKB-FM
09-25-1981; 99.1 MHz FM; *Hrs Open:* 5 AM-11 PM; 60 kw; 492 ft.; N46 6 3 W88 32 23
Mailing Address: P. O. Box Ac, Iron River, MI 49935 US
Second Address: 809 W. Genesee St., Iron River, MI 49935
(906) 265-5104; *Fax:* (906) 265-3486
www.wikb.com
wikb@sbcglobal.net
License: Iron River, Iron County, MI held by Iron River Community Broadcasting Corporation
Group Owner: Stephen Marks
Format: Adult Contemp
Kirk Tollett, General Manager
Scott Humphrey, News Director
Jennifer Tollett, Traffic Manager

Ironwood

WIMI
03-01-1976; 99.7 MHz FM; 100 kw; 561 ft.; N46 25 25 W90 14 53
222 S. Lawrence Street, Ironwood, MI 49938 US
(906) 932-2411; *Fax:* (906) 932-2485
www.wimifm.com
wimi@broadcast.net
License: Ironwood, Gogebic County, MI held by Magellan Broadcasting LLC.
Format: Adult Contemp
Anna Bolich, Sales Manager
Al Rice, Programming Director
Bob Friedle, Chief Engineer
Hal Maas, Music Director

WJMS
11-03-1931; 590 kHz AM; *Hrs Open:* 24; 5 kw-D, DAN; 1 kw-N, DAN; N46 25 25 W90 12 30
222 S. Lawrence Street, Ironwood, MI 49938 US
(906) 932-2411; *Fax:* (906) 932-2485
www.wjmsam.com
wimi@broadcast.net
License: Ironwood, MI held by Magellan Broadcasting LLC.
Nat'l Network: CBS; *Nat'l Reps:* D & R Radio
Format: Country, Talk; *No. News Employees:* 1; *Target Audience:* 25 plus.
Anna Bolich, Sales Manager
Al Rice, Programming Director

WUPM
10-17-1977; 106.9 MHz FM; 53 kw; 495 ft.; N46 28 18 W90 0 43
209 Harrison Street, Ironwood, MI 49938 US
(906) 932-5234
www.wupm-whry.com
License: Ironwood, Gogebic County, MI held by Big G Little O Inc.
Nat'l Network: ABC
Arbitron Metro Market: Ironwood, MI; *Format:* Adult Contemp
Charles Gervasio, President
Laura Keller, Programming Director

***WKIW**
01-01-2008; 88.3 MHz FM; 300 w vert; Ant 515 ft; N46 26 28 W90 11 26 *Rebroadcasts:* Rebroadcasts KLVR(FM) Middletown, CA 100%
PO Box 2098, Omaha, NE 68103
www.klove.com
License: Ironwood, Gogebic County, MI held by Educational Media Foundation.
Group Owner: EMF Broadcasting; (acq 7-23-2007; grpsl)
Nat'l Network: K-Love

Mike Novak, President

Ishpeming

WIAN
01-01-1947; 1240 kHz AM
1009 W. Ridge St., Suite A, Marquette, MI 49855 US
(906) 225-1313; *Fax:* (906) 225-1492
info@wjpd.com
License: Ishpeming, MI held by Sovereign Communications LLC
Group Owner: Sovereign Communications LLC
Format: News, News/Talk, 86
Keith Neve, Chief Operating Office
Coral Howe, Chief Engineer

WJPD
05-15-1975; 92.3 MHz FM; 100 kw; 509 ft.; N46 30 51 W87 28 58
1009 W. Ridge St., Suite A, Marquette, MI 49855 US
(906) 225-1313; *Fax:* (906) 225-1492
www.wjpd.com
news@wjpd.com
License: Ishpeming, Marquette County, MI held by Sovereign Communications LLC
Group Owner: Sovereign Communications LLC
Wire Services: UPI
Format: Country
Derek Miceli, Operations Dir
Keith Neve, Chief Operating Officer
Coral Howe, Chief Engineer
Heather DeGrave, Marketing Consultant
Gordon Mielke, Marketing Consultant
Betty Gunville, Marketing Consultant

WMQT-FM
01-26-1974; 107.7 MHz FM; *Hrs Open:* 24; 98 kw; 639 ft.; N46 30 8 W87 38 52
121 North Front Street, Marquette, MI 49855 US
(906) 225-9100; *Fax:* (906) 225-5577
www.wmqt.com
tom@wmqt.com
License: Ishpeming, Marquette County, MI held by Taconite Broadcasting Inc.
Arbitron Metro Market: Ishpeming, MI; *Format:* Adult Contemp; *No. News Employees:* 1; *Target Audience:* 18-49.
Tom Mogush, General Manager
Jim Koski, Programming Director

WZAM
06-26-1959; 970 kHz AM; *Hrs Open:* 24; 5 kw-D, ND2; 0.062 kw-N, ND2; N46 30 20 W87 32 24
PO Box467, Ishpeming, MI 49849 US
(906) 225-9100; *Fax:* (906) 225-5577
www.espn970.com
tom@wmqt.com
License: Ishpeming, MI held by Taconite Broadcasting Inc.
Nat'l Network: ESPN Radio
Arbitron Metro Market: Ishpeming, MI; *Format:* Sports, Talk; *No. News Employees:* 1; *Target Audience:* 25-54.
Tom Mogush, General Manager
Jim Koski, Programming Director
Casey Ford, News Director

Jackson

WIBM
01-01-1925; 1450 kHz AM; *Hrs Open:* 24
1700 Glenshire Dr., Jackson, MI 49201 US
(517) 787-9546; *Fax:* (517) 787-7517
www.espnradio1450.com
steve@wkhm.com
License: Jackson, MI held by Jackson Radio Works Inc.
Group Owner: Jackson Radio Works Inc.; acq 11-14-97; grpsl)
Nat'l Network: ESPN Radio *Regional Reps:* Michigan Spot Sales
Format: Sports *Special Programming:* Polish, Spanish; *Hrs. of News Programming:* news progmg one hr wkly; *No. News Employees:* 2; *Target Audience:* 18-49; sports enthusiasts
Bruce Goldsen, President
Susan Goldsen, VP of Sales/Marketing

***WJKN**
01-01-1962; 1510 kHz AM; 5 kw-D, DAD; N42 11 10 W84 22 39
P.O. Box 468, Prudenville, MI 48651 US
(517) 750-9723; *Fax:* (517) 750-6619
info@home.fm
License: Jackson, MI held by Spring Arbor University
Nat'l Network: CBS; Westwood One; *Nat'l Reps:* Patt
Arbitron Metro Market: Lansing-East Lansing, MI; *Format:* Religious
Carl Fletcher, General Manager
Dave Benson, Chief Engineer

WKHM
12-07-1951; 970 kHz AM; *Hrs Open:* 24; 1 kw-D, DA2; 1 kw-N, DA2; N42 11 39 W84 25 50
1700 Glenshire Dr., Jackson, MI 49201 US
(517) 787-9546; *Fax:* (517) 787-7517
www.wkhm.com
steve@wkhm.com
License: Jackson, MI held by Jackson Radio Works Inc.
Group Owner: Jackson Radio Works Inc.; acq 12-8-97; grpsl).
Nat'l Network: ABC; *Regional Network:* Mich. Radio *Regional Reps:* Mich. Spot Sales
Format: News/Talk; *Hrs. of News Programming:* news progmg 15 hrs wkly; *No. News Employees:* 1; *Target Audience:* 25-64.
Bruce Goldsen, President
Susan Goldsen, VP of Sales/Marketing

WWDK
01-01-1955; 94.1 MHz FM; 40 kW; 551 ft; N42 23 31 W84 40 00
2495 Cedar St, Holt, MI 48842
(517) 699-0111; *Fax:* (517) 699-1880
941theduke.com
License: Jackson, Jackson County, MI held by Midwest Communications Inc.
Group Owner: Midwest Communications Inc.
Population Served: 864,300; *Arbitron Metro Market:* Lansing, MI; *Format:* Country
Joe Cassady, Brand Manager

Kalamazoo

***WCXK**
02-03-1997; 88.3 MHz FM; *Hrs Open:* 24; 10 kw vert; 397 ft.; N42 18 23 W85 39 25 *Rebroadcasts:* Rebroadcasts WCSG(FM) Grand Rapids 100%
1159 E. Beltline Ave. N.E., Grand Rapids, MI 49525 US
(616) 942-1500; *Fax:* (616) 942-7078
www.wcsg.org
License: Kalamazoo, Kalamazoo County, MI held by Cornerstone University.
Arbitron Metro Market: Rye CO; *Format:* Christian

***WIDR**
07-07-1975; 89.1 MHz FM; *Hrs Open:* 24; 0.1 kw; 187 ft.; N42 16 55 W85 37 5
1501 Faunce Student Services, Kalamazoo, MI 49008 US
(269) 387-6301; *Fax:* (269) 387-2839
www.widrfm.org
info@widr.org

License: Kalamazoo, Kalamazoo County, MI held by Western Michigan University Board of Trustees.
Arbitron Metro Market: Kalamazoo, MI; *Format:* Variety/Diverse; *Hrs. of News Programming:* News progmg 7 hrs wkly; *Target Audience:* 18-25; college students
Jax Kappeler, General Manager
Taylor Larson, Programming Director

***WKDS**
10-01-1982; 89.9 MHz FM; *Hrs Open:* 24; 0.14 kw; 125 ft.; N42 14 36 W85 34 19
606 East Kilgore Road, Kalamazoo, MI 49001 US
(269) 343-2211; *Fax:* (269) 343-3710
License: Kalamazoo, Kalamazoo County, MI held by Kalamazoo Board of Education.
Arbitron Metro Market: Kalamazoo, MI; *Format:* Variety/Diverse; *Hrs. of News Programming:* News progmg 3 hrs wkly; *Target Audience:* High school & college students.
Mark Monk, Operations Dir

WKMI
08-01-1947; 1360 kHz AM; *Hrs Open:* 24
4154 Jennings Drive, Kalamazoo, MI 49048 US
(269) 344-0111; *Fax:* (269) 344-4223
www.wkmi.com
radio@wkmi.com
License: Kalamazoo, MI held by Cumulus Licensing Corp.
Group Owner: Cumulus Media Inc.; (acq 5-26-98; grpsl)
Arbitron Metro Market: Kalamazoo, MI; *Format:* News, News/Talk, 86 *Special Programming:* Sports; *Hrs. of News Programming:* news progmg 30 hrs wkly; *No. News Employees:* 1; *Target Audience:* 25 plus.
Dave Benson, Programming Director

WKPR
10-20-1960; 1440 kHz AM; *Hrs Open:* 6 AM-sunset
Box 50867, Kalamazoo, MI 49005 US
(269) 381-1420
License: Kalamazoo, MI held by Kalamazoo Broadcasting Co.
Group Owner: Kuiper Stns
Nat'l Network: USA
Arbitron Metro Market: Kalamazoo, MI; *Format:* Religious; *Target Audience:* 25 plus.
William Kuiper Sr., President
Stan Gebben, Station Manager
William Kuiper Jr., Chief Engineer

WKZO
09-10-1931; 590 kHz AM; *Hrs Open:* 24; 5 kW; N42 20 55 W85 33 48
4200 W Main St, Kalamazoo, MI 49006 USA
(269) 345-7121; *Fax:* (269) 345-1436
wkzo.com
License: Kalamazoo, MI held by Midwest Communications Inc.
Group Owner: Midwest Communications Inc.; (acq 5-1-2006; grpsl).
Nat'l Network: CBS; *Nat'l Reps:* Christal
Arbitron Metro Market: Kalamazoo, MI; *Format:* News/Talk *Special Programming:* Farm 10 hrs, relg 5 hrs wkly; *No. News Employees:* 5; *Target Audience:* 25 plus; upscale, 60% male, 40% female
Ken Lanphear, Brand Manager

***WMUK**
01-08-1951; 102.1 MHz FM; *Hrs Open:* 24; 50 kw; 489 ft.; N42 25 3 W85 31 55
1903 West Michigan Avenue, Western Michigan University, Kalamazoo, MI 49008 US
(269) 387-5715; *Fax:* (269) 387-4630
www.wmuk.org
License: Kalamazoo, Kalamazoo County, MI held by Western Michigan University Board of Trustees.
Nat'l Network: NPR; PRI; *Regional Network:* Minn. Pub. Radio
Arbitron Metro Market: Kalamazoo, MI; *Format:* Jazz, News *Special Programming:* Bluegrass 4 hrs wkly; *Hrs. of News Programming:* news progmg 38 hrs wkly; *No. News Employees:* 3; *Target Audience:* General;educated adults
Gordon Bolar, General Manager
Klayton Woodworth, Programming Director
Andrew Robins, News Director

WVFM
06-19-1964; 106.5 MHz FM; 33 kW; 600 ft.; N42 28 35 W85 29 5
4200 W Main St, Kalamazoo, MI 49006 USA
(269) 345-7121; *Fax:* (269) 345-1436
myfm1065.com
License: Kalamazoo, Kalamazoo County, MI held by Midwest Communications Inc.
Group Owner: Midwest Communications Inc.; (acq 5-1-2006; grpsl)
Nat'l Reps: Christal
Arbitron Metro Market: Kalamazoo, MI; *Format:* Oldies
Mark Hamlin, Brand Manager

WQLR
1660 kHz AM; *Hrs Open:* 24; 50 kW; N42 03 27 W84 59 53
4200 W Main St, Kalamazoo, MI 49006 USA
(269) 349-1660; *Fax:* (269) 345-1436
1660thefan.com
License: Kalamazoo, MI held by Midwest Communications Inc.
Group Owner: Midwest Communications Inc.
Arbitron Metro Market: Kalamazoo, MI; *Format:* Sports
James McKinney, Brand Manager

Kalkaska

WKLT
04-08-1979; 97.5 MHz FM; *Hrs Open:* 24; 32 kw; 617 ft.; N44 47 29 W85 14 20
1020 Hastings Street, Traverse City, MI 49686 US
(231) 947-0003
www.wklt.com
License: Kalkaska, Kalkaska County, MI held by Northern Radio of Michigan
Nat'l Reps: Christal
Arbitron Metro Market: Traverse City-Petoskey, MI; *Format:* Rock/AOR *Special Programming:* Sunday night classics, blues 2 hrs wkly; *Hrs. of News Programming:* News progmg 2 hrs wkly; *Target Audience:* 25-54; babyboomers & young adults
Charlie Ferguson, Sales Manager
Terri Ray, Programming Director

Kentwood

***WGVU**
12-25-1954; 1480 kHz AM; *Hrs Open:* 24
301 W. Fulton, Grand Rapids, MI 49504 US
(616) 331-6666
www.wgvu.org
wgvu@gvsu.edu
License: Kentwood, MI held by Grand Valley State Univ.
Nat'l Network: NPR; PRI
Arbitron Metro Market: Grand Rapids, MI; *Format:* News; *Hrs. of News Programming:* news progmg 89 hrs wkly; *No. News Employees:* 3; *Target Audience:* 35-44; college-educated men with average income
Ken Kolbe, Operations Dir
Michael Walenta, General Manager
Pamela Holtz, Promotions Manager
Fred Martino, News Director
Bob Lumbert, Chief Engineer
Jim Rademaker, Special Events Coordinator
Ed Spier, Traffic Manager

WVHF
09-18-1978; 1140 kHz AM; *Hrs Open:* 15 hrs; 5 kw-D, DA; N42 56 13 W85 27 20
2504 Ardmore Street, Grand Rapids, MI 49506
(616) 475-4299 Ext. 11; *Fax:* (616) 475-4335
License: Kentwood, Kent County, MI held by WJNZ Radio L.L.C.
Nat'l Network: ABC; Premiere Radio Networks
Population Served: 703,400; *Arbitron Metro Market:* Grand Rapids, MI *Special Programming:* Jazz 6 hrs, gospel 4 hrs; *Hrs. of News Programming:* Top of the hour 6a-7p; *Target Audience:* 25-54; Baby Boomers *Adv.Rates:* 25; 23; 26; 17
Mike St. Cyr, President
Selina James, Office Manager

Kingsford

***WEUL**
02-11-1990; 98.1 MHz FM; 1 kw; 466 ft.; N45 49 58 W88 4 57
Rebroadcasts: Simulcast with WHWL(FM) Marquette, WHWG(FM) Trout Lake
830 Carmen Drive, Marquette, MI 49855 US
(906) 249-1423
www.whwl.net
whwl@whwl.net
License: Kingsford, Dickinson County, MI held by Gospel Opportunities Inc.
Arbitron Metro Market: Kingsford, MI; *Format:* Religious; *No. News Employees:* 3
Andy Larsen, News Director
Curt Marker, Manager
Beth Marker, Part-time Bookkeeper
Kathy Kantola, Executive Assistant

Kingsley

WJNL
04-17-1947; 1210 kHz AM; 2.5 kw-C, NDD; 50 kw-D, NDD; N44 33 34 W85 35 37
Mailing Address: 2175 Click Road, Petoskey, MI 49770 US
Second Address: 310 West Front St., Traverse City, MI 49684
(231) 947-1210
www.wjml.com
License: Kingsley, MI held by Stone Communications Inc.
Nat'l Network: CBS Radio; *Regional Network:* Mich. Talk
Format: News, Sports, 86; *Hrs. of News Programming:* News progmg 72 hrs wkly; *Target Audience:* 25 plus.; *Adv. Rates:* 25; 25; 25; 18.
Richard Stone, President
Philip Clever, Station Manager

L'Anse

WCUP
01-01-1998; 105.7 MHz FM; *Hrs Open:* 24; 51 kw; 856 ft.; N46 39 50 W88 23 6
PO Box 550, Baraga, MI 49908 US
(906) 353-9287; *Fax:* (906) 353-9200
www.keepitintheup.com
eagleadmin@up.net
License: L'Anse, Baraga County, MI held by Keweenaw Bay Indian Community
Nat'l Network: ABC
Arbitron Metro Market: L'anse, MI; *Format:* Country *Special Programming:* American Indian 2 hrs; polka 2 hrs wkly; *Hrs. of News Programming:* News progrmg one hr wkly; *Target Audience:* 18 plus.
Ed Janisse, General Manager
John Preston, General Sales Mgr

Lake City

***WAIR**
104.9 MHz FM; 1.6 kw; 489 ft.; N44 14 56 W85 18 48
3302 N. Van Dyke, Imlay City, MI 48444 US
(888) 887-7139; *Fax:* (877) 850-0881
www.positivehits.com
jennc@smile.FM
License: Lake City, Missaukee County, MI held by Superior Communications.
Group Owner: Superior Communications
Arbitron Metro Market: Lake City, MI; *Format:* Christian
Jenn Czelada, General Manager
Ed Czelada, Programming Director
Aaron Burrell, Administration
Clayton Hewitt, Administration and Engineering
Ed Czelada, Administration, Programming & Engineering
Dale Mazzoline, Production

Lake Isabella

WRAX
98.9 MHz FM; 6 kw; Ant 328 ft; N43 52 51 W86 13 04
, Lake Isabella, MI
(859) 331-9100
License: Lake Isabella, Mason County, MI held by Radioactive LLC.
Group Owner: Radioactive LLC

Benjamin Homel, President

Lakeview

WGLM-FM
11-01-1989; 106.3 MHz FM; 3 kw; 328 ft.; N43 24 33 W85 15 53
9181 S. Greenville RoadMI 48838 US
(616) 754-1063
License: Lakeview, Montcalm County, MI held by Packer Radio Greenville Inc.
Format: Country
Bruce Bentley, Operations Dir
John Clark, General Manager

Lansing

WFMK
07-16-1959; 99.1 MHz FM; *Hrs Open:* 24; 28 kw; 600 ft.; N42 40 33 W84 30 0
3420 Pine Tree Rd., Lansing, MI 48911 US
(517) 394-7272
www.99wfmk.com
fly@townsquaremedia.com
License: Lansing, Ingham County, MI held by Townsquare Media Lansing License, LLC
Group Owner: Townsquare Media; (acq 2000; grpsl).
Nat'l Reps: Christal
Arbitron Metro Market: Lansing-East Lansing, MI; *Format:* Adult Contemp; *No. News Employees:* 1; *Target Audience:* 25-54.
Zoe Burdine-Fly, General Manager
Darin White, Director of Sales
Oe, Engineering Dir

WHZZ
01-01-1967; 101.7 MHz FM; *Hrs Open:* 24; 4.1 kW; 420 ft.; N42 41 29 W84 33 29
600 W Cavanaugh Rd, Lansing, MI 48910 USA
(517) 393-1320; *Fax:* (517) 393-0882
1017mikefm.com
License: Lansing, Ingham County, MI held by The MacDonald Broadcasting Company
Group Owner: MacDonald Broadcasting
Nat'l Reps: D & R Radio; *Wire Services:* AP
Arbitron Metro Market: Lansing; *Format:* Adult Contemp
Cindy Tuck, General Manager
Mark Prince, Production Director
Gary Harding, Chief Engineer

WILS
07-17-1947; 1320 kHz AM; 25 kW Day, 2 kW Night; N42 37 19 W84 38 38
600 W Cavanaugh Rd, Lansing, MI 48910-5254 USA
(517) 393-1320; *Fax:* (517) 393-0882
www.1320wils.com
License: Lansing, MI held by The MacDonald Broadcasting Company
Group Owner: MacDonald Broadcasting; (acq 12-20-2001; grpsl)
Nat'l Network: Fox News Radio; *Regional Network:* Michigan Radio Network; *Nat'l Reps:* D & R Radio
Arbitron Metro Market: Lansing; *Format:* News, News/Talk, 86; *Adv. Rates:* 45; 45; 45; 30
Cindy Tuck, General Manager
Mark Price, Production Director
Lee Cohen, Sales
Dave Horski, Traffic Director
Mark Pruchniewski, Production Director

WITL
01-01-1965; 100.7 MHz FM; 26.5 kw; 643 ft.; N42 40 33 W84 30 0
3420 Pine Tree Rd., Lansing, MI 48911 US
(517) 363-2233
www.witl.com
fly@townsquaremedia.com
License: Lansing, MI held by Townsquare Media Lansing License, LLC
Group Owner: Townsquare Media; (acq 2000; grpsl).
Arbitron Metro Market: Lansing-East Lansing, MI; *Format:* Country; *No. News Employees:* 1
Zoe Burdine-Fly, General Manager
Chris Tyler, Director of Sales
Chris Tyler, Brand Manager
Brandon Howell, Digital Managing Editor

WJIM
08-22-1934; 1240 kHz AM; *Hrs Open:* 24; 890 w-D, 890 w-N
3420 Pine Tree Rd., Lansing, MI 48911 US
(517) 394-7272; *Fax:* (517) 394-3391
www.wjimam.com
fly@townsquaremedia.com
License: Lansing, MI held by Townsquare Media Lansing License, LLC
Group Owner: Townsquare Media; (acq 2000; grpsl)
Nat'l Network: Westwood One; ABC
Arbitron Metro Market: Lansing-East Lansing, MI; *Format:* News/Talk
Zoe Burdine-Fly, General Manager
Darin White, Director of Sales
Nick Chase, Brand Manager
Brandon Howell, Digital Managing Editor

WJIM
06-01-1960; 97.5 MHz FM; *Hrs Open:* 24; 45 kw; 512 ft.; N42 40 33 W84 30 0
3420 Pine Tree Rd., Lansing, MI 48911 US
(517) 363-2975
www.975now.com
zoe.burdine-fly@townsquaremedia.com
License: Lansing, MI held by Townsquare Media Lansing License, LLC
Group Owner: Townsquare Media
Arbitron Metro Market: Lansing-East Lansing, MI; *Format:* Contemporary Hits/Top 40
Zoe Burdine-Fly, General Manager
Darin White, Director of Sales
Josh Strickland, Brand Manager
Brandon Howell, Digital Managing Editor

***WLNZ**
02-11-1994; 89.7 MHz FM; 0 kw horiz, 0.42 kw vert; 98 ft.; N42 44 15 W84 33 12
PO Box 40010, Lansing, MI 48933 US
(517) 483-1000
License: Lansing, Ingham County, MI held by Lansing Community College.
Nat'l Network: PRI; NPR
Arbitron Metro Market: Lansing-East Lansing, MI; *Format:* Blues, Jazz, 90 *Special Programming:* Reggae 4 hrs, big band 3 hrs, folk 3 hrs, Sp 4 hrs
Daedalian Lowry, Station Manager

WMMQ
11-16-1963; 94.9 MHz FM; 50 kw; 492 ft.; N42 38 45 W84 33 38
3420 Pine Tree Rd., Lansing, MI 48911 US
(517) 394-7272
www.wmmq.com
fly@townsquaremedia.com
License: Lansing, MI held by Townsquare Media Lansing License, LLC
Group Owner: Townsquare Media
Arbitron Metro Market: Lansing, MI; *Format:* Classic Rock; *No. News Employees:* 1
Zoe Burdine-Fly, General Manager
Darin White, Director of Sales
Chris Tyler, Brand Manager
Brandon Howell, Digital Managing Editor

Lapeer

WLCO
11-16-1962; 1530 kHz AM; 5 kw-D, DAD; N43 1 35 W83 17 12
63338 Bristol Road, Burton, MI 48529 US
(810) 743-1080; *Fax:* (810) 742-5170
info@wlco.com
License: Lapeer, MI
Group Owner: Townsquare Media; (acq 7-18-2002; $1.3 million with co-located FM)
Nat'l Network: ABC; *Nat'l Reps:* Patt
Arbitron Metro Market: Flint, MI; *Format:* Country; *Target Audience:* 35 plus.; *Adv. Rates:* 20; 25; 20; na
Zoe Burdine-Fly, General Manager

***WMPC**
12-06-1926; 1230 kHz AM; *Hrs Open:* 24; 1 kw-U, ND1; N43 4 46 W83 18 35
P. O. Box 104, Lapeer, MI 48446 US
(810) 664-6211; *Fax:* (810) 664-5361
License: Lapeer, MI held by The Calvary Bible Church of Lapeer Inc.
Nat'l Network: Moody; *Wire Services:* AP
Arbitron Metro Market: Detroit, MI; *Format:* Religious; *Hrs. of News Programming:* news progmg 24 hrs wkly; *No. News Employees:* 1; *Target Audience:* General.
Bob Baldwin, General Manager

WQUS
02-06-1968; 103.1 MHz FM; 2.6 kw; 341 ft.; N43 4 43 W83 11 24
3338 East Bristol Road, Burton, MI 48529 US
(810) 743-1080; *Fax:* (810) 742-5170
www.us103.com
License: Lapeer, Lapeer County, MI
Group Owner: Townsquare Media
Arbitron Metro Market: Flint, MI; *Format:* Rock/AOR *Special Programming:* AOR, gospel, blues; *Target Audience:* 25-40; college educated men & women; *Adv. Rates:* 50; 35; 45; 30
Pete Clinton, General Sales Mgr
J. Patrick, Programming Director

Leland

WFCX
08-09-1991; 94.3 MHz FM; *Hrs Open:* 24; 20.5 kw; 764 ft.; N44 46 19 W85 40 58 *Rebroadcasts:* Rebroadcasts WFDX(FM) Atlanta 100%
1020 Hastings, Traverse City, MI 49686 US
(231) 947-5396; *Fax:* (231) 947-7002
License: Leland, Leelanau County, MI held by Northern Michigan Radio Inc.
Nat'l Reps: Christal
Arbitron Metro Market: Traverse City, MI; *Format:* Contemporary Hits/Top 40, Adult Contemp *Special Programming:* Relg one hr wkly; *Hrs. of News Programming:* news progmg 7 hrs wkly; *No. News Employees:* 1 *TargetAudience:* 25-54.
Amanda Pashall, Programming Director

Leroy Township

***WLGH**
12-01-1996; 88.1 MHz FM; 0.001 kw horiz, 6.7 kw vert; 571 ft.; N42 42 20 W84 21 27
601 Savidge St, Reed City, MI 49677 US
(517) 381-0573; *Fax:* (877) 850-0881
www.positivehits.com
info@positivehits.com
License: Leroy Township, Osceola County, MI held by Superior Communications.
Group Owner: Superior Communications
Format: Christian
Jenn Czelada, General Manager
Ed Czelada, Programming Director

Lexington

WBTI
07-13-1991; 96.9 MHz FM; *Hrs Open:* 24; 3 kw; 328 ft.; N43 12 34 W82 32 10
808 Huron Ave., Port Huron, MI 48060 US
(810) 982-9000; *Fax:* (810) 987-9380
www.wbti.com
amilano@radiofirst.net
License: Lexington, Sanilac County, MI held by Liggett Communications LLC.
Group Owner: Liggett Communications LLC.
Arbitron Metro Market: Port Huron, Mi; *Format:* Contemporary Hits/Top 40; *Target Audience:* 18-34.
Alisa Milano, Director of Sales
Ben Coburn, Programming Director

Linwood

WSAG
11-01-2002; 104.1 MHz FM; 4.6 kW; 338 ft.; N43 43 30 W83 56 50
PO Box 1776, Saginaw, MI 48605 USA
(989) 752-8161
thebay104fm.com
License: Linwood, Bay County, MI held by The MacDonald Broadcasting Company
Group Owner: MacDonald Broadcasting; (acq 6-30-2005)
Nat'l Reps: Eastman Radio *Regional Reps:* Eastman Radio; *Wire Services:* AP
Arbitron Metro Market: Flint-Saginaw-Bay City; *Format:* Oldies
Special Programming: Polka (weekends), Christmas (Nov./Dec.); *No. News Employees:* 1
Ken MacDonald Jr., CEO
Duane Alverson, President
Jim Kramer, Operations Dir
Mary Yearham, General Sales Mgr
Cindy Tuck, Vice President

Livonia

WCAR
10-23-1963; 1090 kHz AM; 0.25 kw-D, DA2; 0.5 kw-N, DA2; N42 19 46 W83 21 43
32500 Park Lane Ave., Garden City, MI 48135 US
(734) 525-1111; *Fax:* (734) 525-3608
www.birach.com
sima@birach.com
License: Livonia, Wayne County, MI held by Birach Broadcasting Corp.
Group Owner: Birach Broadcasting Corp.; (acq 7-6-98; $2 million)
Arbitron Metro Market: Garden City, MI; *Format:* Sports, Talk
Special Programming: Ethnic; *Target Audience:* 25 plus.
Sima Birach, President

Ludington

WKLA
10-09-1944; 1450 kHz AM; *Hrs Open:* 24; 1 kw-U, ND1; N43 57 5 W86 25 28
5399 W. Wallace Ln., Ludington, MI 49431 US
(231) 843-0941; *Fax:* (231) 843-9411
License: Ludington, MI held by Synergy Media, Inc.
Group Owner: Synergy Broadcast Group
Format: Oldies; *No. News Employees:* 1; *Target Audience:* 40 plus; mature adults

WKLA-FM
05-01-1971; 106.3 MHz FM; 4.9 kw; 361 ft.; N44 3 27 W86 24 58
5399 W. Wallace Ln., Ludington, MI 49431 US
(231) 843-0941; *Fax:* (231) 843-9411
www.wkla.com
License: Ludington, Mason County, MI held by Synergy Media, Inc.
Group Owner: Synergy Broadcast Group
Nat'l Network: ABC *Regional Reps:* Patt Media
Format: Adult Contemp; *Hrs. of News Programming:* news progmg 3 hrs wkly; *No. News Employees:* 2; *Target Audience:* 25-50.; *Adv. Rates:* 24; 20; 22; 14

RADIO - U.S.

Luna Pier

WMIM
07-16-1967; 98.3 MHz FM; *Hrs Open:* 24; 3.4 kw; Ant 443 ft; N41 40 05 W83 27 11
14 S. Monroe Street, Monroe, MI 48161
(734) 242-6600; *Fax:* (734) 242-6599
License: Luna Pier, Monroe County, MI held by Cumulus Licensing Corp
Group Owner: Cumulus Media Inc.; (acq 7-98; $2.8 million)
Nat'l Reps: Michigan Spot Sales
Population Served: 300,000; *Arbitron Metro Market:* Toledo, OH
Special Programming: Relg 3 hrs wkly; *Hrs. of News Programming:* news progmg 3 hrs wkly; *No. News Employees:* 1; *Target Audience:* 25-54.
Sandy Frankhouse, General Manager

Mackinaw City

***WIAB**
10-01-2000; 88.5 MHz FM; 0.001 kw horiz, 20 kw vert; 430 ft.; N45 40 0 W84 38 5 *Rebroadcasts:* Simulcast with WIAA(FM) Interlochen 100%
P O Box 334, Stanwood, MI 49346 US
(616) 726-0193
License: Mackinaw City, Cheboygan County, MI held by Interlochen Center for the Arts
Arbitron Metro Market: Scottsdale AZ
Timothy Woodson, Chairman

WYPV
09-06-1989; 94.5 MHz FM; 50 kw; 361 ft.; N45 40 0 W84 38 5
P.O. Box 432, Elk Rapids, MI 49629 US
(231) 360-5140
patriotvoice.net
patriotvoice2012@gmail.com
License: Mackinaw City, Cheboygan County, MI held by Michigan Broadcasters, LLC
Group Owner: Michigan Broadcasters, LLC.
Arbitron Metro Market: Traverse City-Petoskey, MI; *Format:* Country

Manistee

WMTE
06-07-1951; 1340 kHz AM; *Hrs Open:* 24; 1 kw-U, ND1; N44 14 7 W86 19 5
13999 S. W. Bayshore Dr., Traverse City, MI 49684 US
(231) 947-3220
License: Manistee, MI held by Roy E. Henderson
Group Owner: Lake Michigan Broadcasting Inc.; (acq 9-20-96; grpsl).
Nat'l Network: ABC; *Nat'l Reps:* Michigan Spot Sales
Arbitron Metro Market: Manistee, MI; *Format:* News/Talk; *No. News Employees:* 1; *Target Audience:* General.; *Adv. Rates:* 12; 12; 12; 7.
Lynn Baerwolf, CEO/COO
Jason Wilder, Operations Dir
Ben Failor, General Sales Mgr

WMLQ
08-01-1970; 97.7 MHz FM; *Hrs Open:* 24; 2.5 kw; 515 ft.; N44 12 40 W86 17 53
5399 Wallace Ln., Ludington, MI 49431 US
(213) 843-0941
License: Manistee, Manistee County, MI held by Synergy Lakeshore Licenses, LLC
Group Owner: Synergy Broadcast Group; (acq 6-1-2006; $380,000).
Regional Network: Mich. Farm; *Nat'l Reps:* Michigan Spot Sales
Regional Reps: Michigan Spot Sales
Arbitron Metro Market: Manistee, MI; *Format:* Adult Contemp, Easy Listening; *Target Audience:* 35-64; Adults
Todd Mohr, President

WMTE-FM
06-22-1994; 101.5 MHz FM; 6 kw; 262 ft.; N44 12 41 W86 17 53
4225 E. Burt Lake Rd., Chemboygan, MI 49721 US
(231) 290-1107; *Fax:* (607) 749-2374
License: Manistee, Manistee County, MI held by Mitten Media, LLC
Group Owner: Mitten Media, LLC
Regional Reps: Patt Media
Arbitron Metro Market: Manistee, MI
Todd Mohr, President

***WLMN**
89.7 MHz FM; 15 kw; 282 ft.; N44 6 18 W86 15 1
P.O. Box 199, 9350 Lyon Street, Interlochen, MI 49643 US
(231) 276-4400; *Fax:* (231) 276-4417
www.interlochen.org/ipr
License: Manistee, Manistee County, MI held by Interlochen Center for the Arts.
Arbitron Metro Market: Manistee, MI; *Format:* News
Thom Paulson, General Manager

Manistique

WTIQ
02-11-1968; 1490 kHz AM; 1 kw-U, ND1; N45 57 51 W86 16 37
524 Ludington St., Suite 300, Escanaba, MI 49829-3900 US
(906) 789-9700
www.radioresultsnetwork.com
License: Manistique, MI held by Lakes Radio Inc.
Group Owner: Lakes Radio Inc.; acq 11-30-99; grpsl)
Regional Network: MNN
Arbitron Metro Market: Manistique, MI; *Format:* Oldies; *Target Audience:* 25-54

Marine City

WHLX
12-10-1951; 1590 kHz AM; *Hrs Open:* 24; 1 kw-D, DA2; 0.102 kw-N, DA2; N42 43 42 W82 31 15
808 Huron Ave., Port Huron, MI 48060 US
(810) 982-9000; *Fax:* (810) 987-9380
License: Marine City, MI held by Liggett Communications, LLC.
Group Owner: Liggett Communications, LLC.; (acq 5-1-2000).
Nat'l Network: ABC
Arbitron Metro Market: Detroit; *Format:* Rock/AOR; *Target Audience:* 25-54.
Robert Liggett, President

Marlette

WBGV
07-25-1999; 92.5 MHz FM; *Hrs Open:* 24; 3 kw; 328 ft.; N43 17 10 W82 58 17
19 S. Elk Street, Sandusky, MI 48422 US
(810) 648-2700; *Fax:* (810) 648-3242
www.sanilacbroadcasting.com
boba@sanilacbroadcasting.com
License: Marlette, Sanilac County, MI held by GB Broadcasting Co.
Nat'l Network: ABC
Arbitron Metro Market: Sandusky, MI; *Format:* Country; *Hrs. of News Programming:* news progmg 2 hrs wkly; *No. News Employees:* 1; *Target Audience:* General.; *Adv. Rates:* 13; 13; 13; 13
George Benko, President

Marquette

WDMJ
07-01-1931; 1320 kHz AM
1009 W. Ridge St., Suite A, Marquette, MI 49855 US
(906) 255-1313; *Fax:* (906) 225-1492
news@wjpd.com
License: Marquette, MI held by Sovereign Communications LLC
Group Owner: Sovereign Communications LLC
Nat'l Reps: Michigan Spot Sales
Arbitron Metro Market: Marquette, MI; *Format:* News, News/Talk, 86; *Target Audience:* 25-54.
Keith Neve, Chief Operating Officer
Coral Howe, Chief Engineer

WFXD
04-06-1974; 103.3 MHz FM; *Hrs Open:* 24; 100 kw; 938 ft.; N46 36 14 W87 37 15
3060 US 41 W., Marquette, MI 49855 US
(906) 227-8888, (906) 228-6800; *Fax:* (906) 228-8128
www.wfxd.com
contact@wfxd.com
License: Marquette, Marquette County, MI held by Great Lakes Radio Inc.
Group Owner: Great Lakes Radio Inc.; (acq 11-30-99; grpsl)
Format: Country; *Target Audience:* 25-54.

***WHWL**
12-16-1965; 95.7 MHz FM; 100 kw; 531 ft.; N46 29 52 W87 24 59
130 Carmen Drive, Marquette, MI 49855 US
(906) 249-1423
www.whwl.net
whwl@whwl.net
License: Marquette, Marquette County, MI held by Gospel Opportunities Inc.
Format: Religious
W. Curtis Marker, General Manager

***WNMU-FM**
08-01-1963; 90.1 MHz FM; *Hrs Open:* 24; 100 kw; 928 ft.; N46 21 9 W87 51 32
1401 Presque Isle Avenue, Marquette, MI 49855 US
(906) 227-2600
www.nmu.edu/wnmufm
esmith@nmu.edu
License: Marquette, Marquette County, MI held by Board of Trustees of Northern Michigan University.
Nat'l Network: NPR; PRI; *Wire Services:* AP
Arbitron Metro Market: Marquette, MI *TV Affiliate:* *WNMU-TV affil; *Format:* Jazz, News *Special Programming:* Educ; *Hrs. of News Programming:* News progmg 31 hrs wkly
Eric Smith, General Manager
Evelyn Massaro, Station Manager
Stan Wright, Programming Director
Nicole Walton, News Director
Mike Perucco, Chief Engineer

WUPK
05-01-1992; 94.1 MHz FM; *Hrs Open:* 24; 4.4 kw; 381 ft.; N46 30 51 W87 28 58 *Rebroadcasts:* Rebroadcasts WIMK(FM) Iron Mountain 100%
1411 Ashmun St., Sault Ste. Marie, MI 49783 US
(906) 225-1313
www.94rockradio.net
License: Marquette, Marquette County, MI held by Sovereign Communications LLC
Group Owner: Sovereign Communications LLC
Nat'l Reps: Patt
Arbitron Metro Market: Marquette, MI; *Format:* Classic Rock, Rock/AOR; *Hrs. of News Programming:* news progmg 3 hrs wkly; *No. News Employees:* 1; *Target Audience:* 25-54; baby boomers
Coral Howe, Chief Engineer

***WUPX**
01-01-1994; 91.5 MHz FM; *Hrs Open:* 24; 1.7 kw; 436 ft.; N46 30 52 W87 29 7
1204 University Center, Marquette, MI 49855 US
(906) 227-2348; *Fax:* (906) 227-2344
www.wupx.com
wupx@nmu.edu
License: Marquette, Marquette County, MI held by Board of Control of Northern Michigan University.
Arbitron Metro Market: Marquette, MI *TV Affiliate:* *WNMU-TV affil; *Format:* Alternative *Special Programming:* Black 6 hrs, jazz 2 hrs wkly; *Target Audience:* College.
Marcela Godoy, General Manager
Adam Holloway, Station Manager
Jeffrey Matthias, Programming Director
Jacob Stipe, Promotions Manager
Marcus Davenportÿ, Station Engineer
Will Getts, Production Director
Jack Meeks, MusicDirector
Vanesa Taylor, Public Affairs Coordinator

Marshall

WBXX
10-01-1968; 104.9 MHz FM; 6 kw; 328 ft.; N42 18 47 W84 55 46
390 Golden Avenue, Battle Creek, MI 49015 US
(269) 963-5555; *Fax:* (269) 963-5185
www.mix1049online.com
License: Marshall, Calhoun County, MI held by Townsquare Media Battle Creek License LLC
Group Owner: Townsquare Media
Arbitron Metro Market: Battle Creek, MI; *Format:* Adult Contemp; *Target Audience:* 18-49.
Kate Conley, General Manager
Kelly Troff, Director of Sales
Tim Collins, Brand Manager
Kayla Kiley, Digital Managing Editor

Mason

***WUNN**
05-11-1967; 1110 kHz AM; *Hrs Open:* Sunrise-sunset; 1 kw-D, DAD; N42 33 4 W84 24 15
PO Box 35300, Tucson, AZ 85704 US
(800) 776-1070
License: Mason, MI held by Family Life Broadcasting System.
Group Owner: Family Life Communications Inc.; (acq 1-1-69).
Arbitron Metro Market: Albion, MI; *Format:* Religious, Christian; *Hrs. of News Programming:* News progmg 1.5 hrs wkly; *Target Audience:* 25-54; Christian families
Randy Carlson, President
Dawn Bumstead, General Manager
Bob Wolfe, Chief Engineer

Mattawan

WZUU
04-01-1991; 92.5 MHz FM; *Hrs Open:* 24; 6000 w; 1000 ft; N42 34 52 W85 45 17
706 East Allegan Street, Otsego, MI 49078

(269) 343-1717
www.wzuu.com
License: Mattawan, Van Buren County, MI held by Forum Communications Inc.
Group Owner: Forum Communications Co.; (acq 6-1-97)
Regional Reps: Michigan Spot Sales
Population Served: 500,000; *Arbitron Metro Market:* Kalamazoo, MI *Special Programming:* Bob and Tom, NASCAR Sprint Cup; *Hrs. of News Programming:* news progmg 1 hr wkly; *No. News Employees:* 1; *Target Audience:* 25-54; *Adv. Rates:* On request
Scotty Melun, Programming Director
Bill Mitchell, News Director
Walker Sisson, Chief Engineer

McMillan

WMJT
01-01-2006; 96.7 MHz FM; 50 kw; 413 ft.; N46 32 2 W85 35 24
Mailing Address: US
Second Address: 210 W. John St., Newberry, MI 49868-1125
(906) 293-1400; *Fax:* (906) 293-5161
www.radioeagle.com
License: McMillan, Luce County, MI held by David L. Smith.
Arbitron Metro Market: McMillan, MI; *Format:* Adult Contemp
Dave Smith, President
Chip Arledge, Programming Director
Teri Petrie, General Manager and General Sales Manager

Menominee

WAGN
11-14-1952; 1340 kHz AM; *Hrs Open:* 24; 1 kw-U; N45 06 27 W87 36 25
413 10th Ave., Menominee, MI 49858
(715) 735-6631
License: Menominee, Menominee County, MI held by Armada Media - Menominee Inc.
Group Owner: Armada Media Corp.; (acq 12-19-2006; grpsl)
Nat'l Network: CBS Radio; Marketwatch; *Regional Network:* Wisconsin Radio Net.; Michigan Radio Network; *Wire Services:* AP
Population Served: 55,000 *Hrs. of News Programming:* news progmg 15 hrs wkly; *No. News Employees:* 1; *Target Audience:* 30 plus; older, affluent adults
Jim Callow, Operations Dir
Chris Bernier, General Manager
Barb Vandehei, General Sales Mgr
Jim Callow, Programming Director
Ken Conners, News Director
Jim Callow, Chief Engineer

WHYB
10-24-1984; 103.7 MHz FM; *Hrs Open:* 24; 7 kw; 299 ft.; N45 4 0 W87 39 55
413 10th Ave., Menominee, MI 49858 US
(715) 735-6631
www.baycitiesradio.net
jimcallow@baycitiesradio.net
License: Menominee, Menominee County, MI held by Armada Media-Menominee Inc.
Group Owner: Armada Media Corp.
Nat'l Network: CBS Radio; *Regional Network:* Wisconsin Radio Net.; *Wire Services:* AP
Format: Oldies; *Hrs. of News Programming:* news progmg 5 hrs wkly; *No. News Employees:* 1; *Target Audience:* 35+
Jim Callow, Operations Dir
Mike Peot, General Manager
Ken Conners, News Director
Chris Johnson, Sports Director
Nicole Kelsey, Account Executive

Michigamme

*WKPK
01-01-2009; 88.3 MHz FM; 15 kw vert; 827 ft.; N46 36 14 W87 37 15
2628 Howard Rd, Petdskey, MI 49770 US
(517) 381-0573
www.smile.fm
License: Michigamme, Marquette County, MI held by Northland Community Broadcasters.
Arbitron Metro Market: Anchorage, AK; *Format:* Christian
Edward Czelada, President
Jennifer Czelada, General Manager

Midland

WKQZ
12-14-1976; 93.3 MHz FM; 39 kw; 554 ft.; N43 50 46 W84 05 32
1740 Champagne Dr. N, Saginaw, MI 48604 US
(989) 776-2100
www.therockstationz93.com
julia.richardson@cumulus.com
License: Midland, MI held by Radio License Holding CBC, LLC
Group Owner: Cumulus Media Inc.; (acq 2-8-99; grpsl).
Nat'l Reps: McGavren Guild
Arbitron Metro Market: Saginaw-Bay City-Midland, MI; *Format:* Rock/AOR
Julia Richardson, General Sales Mgr
Stan Parman, Programming Director

WMPX
09-11-1948; 1490 kHz AM; *Hrs Open:* 24; 1 kw-U, ND1; N43 36 48 W84 13 17
Mailing Address: 1510 Bayliss Street, Midland, MI 48640 US
Second Address: 1510 Bayliss St., Midland, MI 48640
(989) 631-1490; *Fax:* (989) 631-6357
www.wmpxwmrx.com
admin@wmpxwmrx.com
License: Midland, MI held by Steel Broadcasting Inc.
Nat'l Network: ABC; *Nat'l Reps:* Patt
Arbitron Metro Market: Saginaw-Bay City-Midland, MI; *Format:* Oldies, Adult Contemp *Special Programming:* Sounds of Sinatra 2 hrs wkly, relg 3 hrs wkly; *Hrs. of News Programming:* news progmg 9 hrs wkly *No. NewsEmployees:* 1; *Target Audience:* General.
Thomas Steel, Sales

*WUGN
12-02-1973; 99.7 MHz FM; 100 kw; 997 ft.; N43 30 56 W84 32 49
7355 N. Oracle, #200, Tucson, AZ 85704 US
(989) 631-7060; *Fax:* (989) 631-4825
License: Midland, Midland County, MI held by Family Life Communications System.
Group Owner: Family Life Communications Inc.; (acq 1996).
Nat'l Network: Salem Radio Network
Arbitron Metro Market: Midland, MI; *Format:* Christian, Religious; *Hrs. of News Programming:* News progmg 8 hrs wkly; *Target Audience:* 35-54; female with young children
Peter Brooks, General Manager

Mio

WAVC
10-01-1994; 93.9 MHz FM; 50 kw; 433 ft.; N44 43 40 W84 21 35
Rebroadcasts: Rebroadcasts WMKC(FM) Saint Ignace 100%
232 Front Street, No. 2, Traverse City, MI 49684 US
(231) 922-4981
License: Mio, Oscoda County, MI held by Northern Star Broadcasting L.L.C.
Group Owner: Northern Star Broadcasting L.L.C.; (acq 9-11-98; grpsl)
Arbitron Metro Market: Calico Rock AR; *Format:* News, News/Talk, 86; *Hrs. of News Programming:* news progmg 29 hrs/week; *No. News Employees:* 1
Scott Gray, CEO, General Manager
Kim Szecksi, News Director
Mike Wiseman, Engineering Dir
Dale Hoffman, Host, Producer
Roy Roane, Sales Representative

Monroe

*WYDM
11-01-1978; 97.5 MHz FM; 0.049 kw; 135 ft.; N41 55 7 W83 26 12
1275 Macomb Street, Monroe, MI 48161 US
(734) 265-3550
License: Monroe, Monroe County, MI held by Monroe Public Schools
Arbitron Metro Market: Monroe, MI; *Format:* Variety/Diverse; *Target Audience:* 15-24.
Mike Brandt, General Manager
Wendy Sherrod, General Sales Mgr

WRDT
07-12-1956; 560 kHz AM; *Hrs Open:* 24
12300 Radio Place, Detroit, MI 48228 US
(313) 272-3434; *Fax:* (313) 272-5045
www.wrdt560.com
station@wmuz.com
License: Monroe, MI held by WMUZ Radio Inc.
Group Owner: Crawford Broadcasting Co.; (acq 6-16-97; $3.15 million).
Nat'l Reps: McGavren Guild
Arbitron Metro Market: Detroit; *Format:* Christian, Religious, 86
Rich Hanovich, Operations Dir
Frank Franciosi, General Manager

*WSMF
01-01-2003; 88.1 MHz FM; 910 w; Ant 144 ft; N41 55 08 W83 22 34 *Rebroadcasts:* rebroadcast of WHYT(FM) Imlay city 100%
Box 388, Williamston, MI 49770
(810) 721-0891; *Fax:* (413) 410-9708
License: Monroe, Monroe County, MI held by Northland Community Broadcasters.
Jenn Czelada, General Manager

Mount Clemens

WPZR
11-06-1960; 102.7 MHz FM; *Hrs Open:* 24; 50 kw; 499 ft; N42 32 39 W82 54 09
3250 Franklin, Detroit, MI 48207 US
(313) 259-2000; *Fax:* (313) 259-7011
www.praise1027detroit.com
License: Mount Clemens, Macomb County, MI held by Radio One of Detroit LLC.
Group Owner: Radio One Inc.; (acq 1999; $27 million).
Nat'l Network: ABC; *Nat'l Reps:* D & R Radio
Arbitron Metro Market: Detroit; *Format:* Gospel; *Target Audience:* 25-49; rock and rollers of all ages
Alfred Liggins, President/CEO

Mount Pleasant

*WCMU-FM
04-06-1964; 89.5 MHz FM; *Hrs Open:* 24; 100 kw; 420 ft.; N43 34 24 W84 46 21
3965 Broomfield Road, Mt. Pleasant, MI 48859 US
(989) 774-3105; *Fax:* (989) 774-4427
www.wcmu.org
schud1ra@cmich.edu
License: Mount Pleasant, Isabella County, MI held by Central Michigan University.
Nat'l Network: NPR; PRI
Arbitron Metro Market: Michigan, Upper Peninsula, MS *TV Affiliate:* *WCMU-TV affil; *Format:* Jazz, News; *Hrs. of News Programming:* news progmg 30 hrs wkly; *No. News Employees:* 2; *Target Audience:* General.
Ed Grant, General Manager

WCZY-FM
08-20-1991; 104.3 MHz FM; *Hrs Open:* 24; 3 kw; 328 ft.; N43 35 39 W84 49 26
4095 E. Wing Rd, Mt. Pleasant, MI 48858 US
(989) 772-9664; *Fax:* (989) 773-5000
www.wczy.net
License: Mount Pleasant, Isabella County, MI held by Central Michigan Communications Inc.
Nat'l Network: Jones Radio Networks; *Nat'l Reps:* Michigan Spot Sales *Regional Reps:* Patt.
Arbitron Metro Market: Mt. Pleasant, MI; *Format:* Adult Contemp, Easy Listening; *Hrs. of News Programming:* news progmg 6 hrs wkly; *No. News Employees:* 1; *Target Audience:* 25-54.; *Adv. Rates:* 18; 18; 18; 18
Mike Carey, President
Bob Peters, General Sales Mgr
Tina Sawyer, News Director
Lisa Johnson, Traffic Manager

*WMHW-FM
11-20-1972; 91.5 MHz FM; *Hrs Open:* 24; 9.1 kw; 538 ft.; N43 34 33 W84 46 29
US
(989) 774-7287; *Fax:* (989) 774-2426
www.wmhw.org
wmhw@mail.cmich.edu
License: Mount Pleasant, Isabella County, MI held by Board of Trustees, Central Michigan University.
Regional Network: Mich. Radio
Arbitron Metro Market: Mount Pleasant, MI; *Format:* Alternative; *Hrs. of News Programming:* News progmg 10 wkly; *Target Audience:* 12-34.
Meghan Binion, Production Director
Randy Kapenga, Chief Engineer

Munising

*WSHN
01-01-2000; 89.7 MHz FM; *Hrs Open:* 24; kw
US
(506) 646-5161
License: Munising, Northampton County, MI held by Delmarva Educational Association.
Nat'l Network: K-Love
Arbitron Metro Market: Saint John NB; *Format:* News, News/Talk, 86
Rael Merson, President
Jim Hamm, General Manager

WQXO
09-20-1955; 1400 kHz AM; *Hrs Open:* 24; 1 kw-U, ND1; N46 24 30 W86 38 22
101 E. Munising Ave., Marquette, MI 49862 US
(906) 387-1400; *Fax:* (906) 387-4000
wqxo.com
contact@wqxo.com
License: Munising, MI held by Great Lakes Radio Inc.
Group Owner: Great Lakes Radio Inc.; (acq 11-30-99; grpsl).
Nat'l Reps: Patt
Format: Oldies; *Target Audience:* 25-54.
Todd Noordyk, General Manager

Muskegon

WGVS
01-01-1926; 850 kHz AM; *Hrs Open:* 24; 1 kw-U, DA1; N43 8 5 W86 15 41 *Rebroadcasts:* Rebroadcasts WGVU(AM) Kentwood 100%
301 West Fulton, Grand Rapids, MI 49504 US
(616) 331-6666; *Fax:* (616) 331-6625
www.wgvu.org
wgvu@gvsu.edu
License: Muskegon, MI held by Grand Valley State University.
Nat'l Network: NPR; PRI
Arbitron Metro Market: Muskegon, MI; *Format:* News
Ken Kolbe, Operations Dir
Michael Walenta, General Manager
Gary Hunt, General Sales Mgr
Scott Vander Werf, Programming Director
Pamela Holtz, Promotions Manager
Fred Martino, News Director
Bob Lumbert, Engineering Dir
Ed Spier,Traffic Manager

WKBZ
06-15-1947; 1090 kHz AM; *Hrs Open:* 6 AM-2 hrs past sunset
3565 Green St., Muskegon, MI 49444 US
(231) 733-2600; *Fax:* (231) 733-7461
www.newstalk1090.com
License: Muskegon, MI held by CC Licenses LLC.
Group Owner: iHeartMedia; (acq 1-17-2001; grpsl).
Nat'l Reps: D & R Radio
Arbitron Metro Market: Muskegon, MI; *Format:* News, News/Talk, 86; *No. News Employees:* 1; *Target Audience:* 25-54 primary; 35-64 secondary
Doug Montgomery, Operations Manager
Tim Feagan, General Manager
Kelly Norton, Director of Sales
Samantha Bennett, Promotions Manager
Matt Benson, Digital Sales Manager
Laura Murdoch, Business Manager

WOOD-FM
01-01-1962; 106.9 MHz FM; *Hrs Open:* 24; 50 kw; Ant 479 ft; N43 13 48 W86 05 03
77 Monroe Center Ave. N.W., Suite 1000, Grand Rapids, MI 49503 US
(616) 459-1919; *Fax:* (616) 723-3303
www.woodradio.com
License: Muskegon, Muskegon County, MI held by CC Licenses LLC.
Group Owner: iHeartMedia
Population Served: 160,000; *Arbitron Metro Market:* Muskegon, MI; *Format:* News, News/Talk, 86
Doug Montgomery, Operations Manager
Tim Feagan, General Manager
Henry Capogna, General Sales Mgr
Phil Tower, Programming Director
Samantha Bennett, Promotions Manager
Matt Benson, Digital Sales Manager
Laura Murdoch, BusinessManager
Kelly Norton, Director of Sales

WMUS
02-01-1990; 107.9 MHz FM; *Hrs Open:* 24; 15 kw; 348 ft; N43 17 41 W86 13 12
3565 Green St., Muskegon, MI 49512
(231) 733-2600; *Fax:* (231) 739-7461
www.107mus.com
License: Muskegon, Muskegon County, MI held by CC Licenses LLC.
Group Owner: iHeartMedia; (acq 1-17-2001; grpsl).
Population Served: 350,000; *Arbitron Metro Market:* Muskegon, MI; *Format:* Country; *Target Audience:* 18-49.
Doug Montgomery, Operations Manager
Tim Feagan, General Manager
Travis Piccard, General Sales Mgr
Mark Dixon, Programming Director
Samantha Bennett, Promotions Manager
Kelly Norton, Director of Sales
Matt Benson, Digital SalesManager
Laura Murdoch, Business Manager

WSNX-FM
11-18-1971; 104.5 MHz FM; *Hrs Open:* 24; 32 kw; 620 ft.; N43 12 16 W86 1 45
77 Monroe Center Ave. N.W., Suite 1000, Grand Rapids, MI 49503 US
(616) 459-1919; *Fax:* (616) 235-9104
www.1045snx.com
License: Muskegon, Muskegon County, MI held by CC Licenses LLC.
Group Owner: iHeartMedia; (acq 9-30-99)
Nat'l Network: ABC; *Nat'l Reps:* Clear Channel
Arbitron Metro Market: Grand Rapids, MI; *Format:* Urban Contemporary, Contemporary Hits/Top 40; *Hrs. of News Programming:* news progrmg one hr wkly; *No. News Employees:* 1; *Target Audience:* 18-34; women
Doug Montgomery, Operations Manager
Tim Feagan, General Manager
Ron Clement, General Sales Mgr
Samantha Bennett, Promotions Manager
Kelly Norton, Director of Sales
Matt Benson, Digital Sales Manager
Laura Murdoch, BusinessManager

***WMCQ**
03-31-2005; 91.7 MHz FM; 6 kw; 328 ft.; N43 18 37 W85 54 44
P.O. Box 334, Stanwood, MI 49346 US
(662) 844-8888; *Fax:* (662) 842-6791
www.afr.net
faq@afa.net
License: Muskegon, Muskegon County, MI held by American Family Association.
Group Owner: American Family Radio; (acq 12-20-2002).
Arbitron Metro Market: Tupelo, MS; *Format:* Christian
Tim Wildmon, President
Donald Wildmon, Founder
Buddy Smith, Sr VP
Ed Vitagliano, Exec VP
Randy Sharp, Director Of Special Projects
Meeke Addison, Director Of Communications
Abraham Hamilton III, General Counsel

Muskegon Heights

WMRR
03-29-1974; 101.7 MHz FM; *Hrs Open:* 24; 12 kw; 476 ft.; N43 16 38 W86 20 5
3565 Green St., Muskegon, MI 49444 US
(231) 733-2600; *Fax:* (231) 733-7461
www.rock1017fm.com
License: Muskegon Heights, Muskegon County, MI held by CC Licenses LLC.
Group Owner: iHeartMedia; (acq 1-17-2001; grpsl).
Nat'l Network: Westwood One; *Wire Services:* UPI
Arbitron Metro Market: Grand Rapids, MI; *Format:* Classic Rock; *Target Audience:* 25-54; male
Doug Montgomery, Operations Manager
Tim Feagan, General Manager
Travis Piccard, General Sales Mgr
Samantha Bennett, Promotions Manager
Kelly Norton, Director of Sales
Matt Benson, Digital Sales Manager
Laura Murdoch, BusinessManager

Negaunee

WKQS-FM
01-05-1998; 101.9 MHz FM; 13 kw; 938 ft.; N46 36 14 W87 37 15
3060 US 41 W., Marquette, MI 49855 US
(906) 228-6800, (906) 227-7777; *Fax:* (906) 228-8128
sunny.fm
License: Negaunee, Marquette County, MI held by Great Lakes Radio Inc.
Group Owner: Great Lakes Radio Inc.
Format: Contemporary Hits/Top 40, Oldies

WNGE
01-01-2001; 99.5 MHz FM; 3.6 kw; 430 ft.; N46 30 51 W87 28 58
1009 W. Ridge St., Suite A, Marquette, MI 49855 US
(906) 225-1313; *Fax:* (906) 225-1492
License: Negaunee, Marquette County, MI held by Sovereign Communications LLC
Group Owner: Sovereign Communications LLC
Arbitron Metro Market: Negaunee, MI; *Format:* Oldies
Coral Howe, Chief Engineer

Newaygo

WLAW
07-29-2005; 92.5 MHz FM; 2.25 kw; 541 ft.; N43 18 35 W85 54 45
3375 Merriam, Suite 201, Muskegon Heights, MI 49444 US
(231) 830-0176; *Fax:* (231) 830-0104
www.muskegonnashicon.com
ronald.gates@cumulus.com
License: Newaygo, MI held by Radio License Holding CBC, LLC
Group Owner: Cumulus Media Inc.; (acq 7-8-2005).
Arbitron Metro Market: Newaygo, MI; *Format:* Country
Jon Russell, Operations Dir
Ron Gates, General Manager
Rich Berry, VP/Market Manager

Newberry

***WIHC**
04-24-1989; 97.9 MHz FM; *Hrs Open:* 24; 50 kw; 492 ft.; N46 26 58 W85 6 4 *Rebroadcasts:* WGCP(FM) Cadillac, MI 100%
Box 567, Cadillac, MI 49601 US
(231) 468-2087
www.strongtowerradio.com
License: Newberry, Luce County, MI held by West Central Michigan Media Minstries
Format: Classic Rock; *Target Audience:* 18-44.
David Bodluc, President

WNBY
05-16-1966; 1450 kHz AM
Mailing Address: P.O. Box 501, Newberry, MI 49868 US
Second Address: Hwy. S. M-123, Newberry, MI 49868
(906) 293-3221
www.1450wnby.com
License: Newberry, MI held by Sovereign Communications LLC
Nat'l Reps: Patt
Arbitron Metro Market: Newberry, MI; *Format:* Country *Special Programming:* Polka 2 hrs wkly; *Target Audience:* 35 plus.

WNBY-FM
01-01-1977; 93.9 MHz FM; 50 kw; 443 ft.; N46 26 58 W85 6 4
P.O. Box 1230, Sault Ste. Marie, MI 49783 US
(906) 293-3221
www.oldies93fm.com
License: Newberry, Luce County, MI held by Sovereign Communications LLC
Group Owner: Sovereign Communications
Arbitron Metro Market: Newberry, MI; *Format:* Oldies; *Target Audience:* 25-45.

***WUMI**
90.3 MHz FM; kw
Box 567, Cadillac, MI 49601 US
(231) 468-2087
License: Newberry, Luce County, MI held by West Central Michigan Media Ministries
Arbitron Metro Market: Newberry, MI
David Bodluc, President

Niles

WRSW
09-13-1968; 107.3 Hz FM; *Hrs Open:* 24; 3.3 kw; 298 ft; N41 49 22 W86 17 03
216 West Market Street, Warsaw, IN 46580
(888) 333-6133
www.1073wrsw.com
ddaggett@lakecitymediagroup.com
License: Niles, Berrien County, MI held by Pathfinder Communications Corp.
Group Owner: Federated Media
Nat'l Reps: Christal
Population Served: 500,000; *Arbitron Metro Market:* South Bend, IN; *Format:* Classic Rock; *Hrs. of News Programming:* News progmg 5 hrs wkly; *Target Audience:* 25-54; predominantly male, socially active, economicallysecure; *Adv. Rates:* 70; 70; 70; 70
Brad Williams, General Manager
Mike Ragozino, Promotions Manager

WOWO
12-06-1956; 1290 kHz AM; *Hrs Open:* 24; 0.5 kw-D, ND2; 0.044 kw-N, ND2; N41 49 22 W86 17 3
P.O. Box 487, Elkhart, IN 46515 US
(616) 683-6123
www.wowo.com
License: Niles, MI held by Pathfinder Communications Corp.
Group Owner: Federated Media; (acq 7-21-99; $2 million with co-lo
Nat'l Network: Salem Radio Network
Arbitron Metro Market: Berrien, IN; *Format:* Religious, Talk
Special Programming: Relg 6 hrs wkly; *Hrs. of News*

Programming: News progmg 5 hrs wkly; *Target Audience:* 35-54; adult, pro-active, community-involvedpeople; *Adv. Rates:* 15; 15; 15; 15
Clint Marsh, Operations Dir
Brad Williams, General Manager

North Muskegon

WLCS
11-01-1983; 98.3 MHz FM; *Hrs Open:* 24; 1.6 kw; 456 ft.; N43 18 50 W86 9 17
3375 Merriam, Suite 201, Muskegon Heights, MI 49444 US
(231) 830-0176; *Fax:* (231) 830-0104
www.983wlcs.com
License: North Muskegon, MI held by Radio License Holding CBC, LLC
Group Owner: Cumulus Media Inc.; (acq 9-28-2005; grpsl).
Format: Adult Contemp; *Target Audience:* 35-54; general
Jon Russell, Operations Dir
Ron Gates, General Manager
Rich Berry, VP/Market Manager

***WHEY**
88.9 MHz FM; 1 kw; 157 ft.; N43 16 45 W86 20 32
PO Box 1511, Muskegon, MI 49443 US
(231) 744-6940
License: North Muskegon, Muskegon County, MI held by Muskegon Community Radio Broadcast Co.
Arbitron Metro Market: North Muskegon, MI; *Format:* Christian
William Erickson, President

Norway

WZNL
03-15-1990; 94.3 MHz FM; 2.4 kw; 650 ft.; N45 49 15 W88 2 25
1411 Ashmun St., Sault Ste. Marie, MI 49783 US
(906) 774-4321
www.wznl.net
License: Norway, Dickinson County, MI held by Sovereign Communications
Group Owner: Sovereign Communications
Arbitron Metro Market: Iron Mountain, MI; *Format:* Adult Contemp; *Target Audience:* 18-54.

Novi

***WOVI**
09-04-1978; 89.5 MHz FM; *Hrs Open:* 24; 0.1 kw; 105 ft.; N42 27 49 W83 29 28
25345 Taft Road, Novi, MI 48375 US
(248) 449-1526; *Fax:* (248) 449-1519
License: Novi, Oakland County, MI held by Board of Education Novi School District.
Format: Alternative, Classic Rock; *Target Audience:* General.
Dave Legg, General Manager

Okemos

***KTGG**
08-15-1985; 1540 kHz AM; *Hrs Open:* Sunrise-sunset; 0.185 kw-C, NDD; 0.45 kw-D, NDD; N42 9 13 W84 32 57
106 E. Main Street, Spring Arbor, MI 49283 US
(517) 750-9723; *Fax:* (517) 750-6619
www.home.fm
info@home.fm
License: Okemos, MI held by Spring Arbor University.
Format: Religious; *Target Audience:* 18-49; rural to urban
Hal Munn, President
Carl Fletcher, General Manager
Rachel Buchanan, Programming Director

Olivet

***WOCR**
04-22-1975; 89.1 MHz FM; 0.5 kw; 82 ft.; N42 26 31 W84 55 30
320 S. Main St, Olivet, MI 49076 US
(269) 749-7598; *Fax:* (269) 749-7695
wocr@olivetcollege.edu
License: Olivet, Eaton County, MI held by Olivet College.
TV Affiliate: CHR *Special Programming:* News progmg one hr wkly; *No. News Employees:* College; high school and

Onaway

WWMK
09-01-1997; 106.3 MHz FM; *Hrs Open:* 24; 21 kw; 738 ft.; N44 49 16 W85 59 47
1356 Mackinaw Ave., Traverse City, MI 49721 US
(231) 627-2341; *Fax:* (231) 627-7000
1063macfm.com
License: Onaway, MI held by Black Diamond Broadcast Holdings, LLC
Group Owner: Black Diamond Broadcast Group, LLC; (acq 01-01-2017; grpsl)
Arbitron Metro Market: Onaway, MI; *Format:* Rock/AOR

Ontonagon

***WOAS**
11-15-1978; 88.5 MHz FM; *Hrs Open:* 8 AM-10 PM (M-F); 10 w; 124 ft; N46 52 30 W89 18 00
701 Parker, Ontonagon, MI 49953
(906) 884-4433; *Fax:* (906) 884-2742
www.woas-fm.org
ken@oasd.k12.mi.us
License: Ontonagon, Ontonagon County, MI held by Ontonagon Area School District.
Population Served: 1,000 *Target Audience:* General; local residents of the area
Ken Raisanen, General Manager

WUPY
01-01-1987; 101.1 MHz FM; *Hrs Open:* 24; 100 kw; 696 ft.; N46 45 1.4 W89 10 46.2
622 River Street, Ontonagon, MI 49953 US
(906) 884-9668; *Fax:* (906) 884-4985
www.wupy101.com
wupy@jamadots.com
License: Ontonagon, Ontonagon County, MI held by SNRN Broadcasting Inc.
Nat'l Network: ABC
Arbitron Metro Market: Ontonagon, MI; *Format:* Country *Special Programming:* relg 3 hrs, polka 1 hr wkly; *Hrs. of News Programming:* news progmg 13 hrs wkly; *No. News Employees:* 2; *Target Audience:* 25 plus.
Kenny Lee, General Manager
Jay Nix, General Sales Mgr
Jackie Dobbins, Programming Director
Ted.K.Frantz, Chief Engineer
Bob Peltola, Sports Director

Orchard Lake

***WBLD**
05-28-1974; 89.3 MHz FM; *Hrs Open:* 2; 0.015 kw horiz; 161 ft.; N42 33 56 W83 21 32
4925 Orchard Lake Road, West Bloomfield, MI 48323 US
(248) 865-6754; *Fax:* (248) 865-6756
www.wbldradio.tripod.com/
wbld_fm@hotmail.com
License: Orchard Lake, Oakland County, MI held by West Bloomfield Board of Education.
Arbitron Metro Market: West Bloomfield, MI; *Format:* Variety/Diverse
Paul Townley, Station Manager
Randy Long, Chief Engineer

Oscoda

WWTH
08-29-1992; 100.7 MHz FM; *Hrs Open:* 24; 20.5 kw; 361 ft.; N44 34 42 W83 22 40
1491 M-32 W., Alpena, WI 49707 US
(989) 354-4611; *Fax:* (989) 354-4014
www.truenorthradionetwork.com
thebay@truenorthradionetwork.com
License: Oscoda, Iosco County, MI held by Edwards Communications LC.
Group Owner: Edwards Communications L.C.; (acq 12-21-2004; grpsl).
Nat'l Reps: Roslin *Regional Reps:* Michigan.
Arbitron Metro Market: Alpena, MI; *Format:* Classic Rock; *Hrs. of News Programming:* news progmg 4 hrs wkly; *No. News Employees:* 1; *Target Audience:* 25-54.; *Adv. Rates:* 15; 15; 15; 10
Darrel Kelly, General Manager
Phil Heimerl, News Director

***WCMB-FM**
06-01-1998; 95.7 MHz FM; *Hrs Open:* 24; 25 kw; 699 ft.; N44 40 29 W83 31 6 *Rebroadcasts:* Rebroadcasts WCMU-FM Mount Pleasant 100%
1999 East Campus Drive, Mt. Pleasant, MI 48859 US
(989) 774-3105; *Fax:* (989) 774-4427
www.wcmu.org
schud1ra@cmich.edu
License: Oscoda, Iosco County, MI held by Central Michigan University.
Nat'l Network: NPR; PRI; *Regional Network:* Mich. Radio; *Wire Services:* AP
Arbitron Metro Market: Michigan, Upper Peninsula, MS; *Format:* Jazz, News; *Hrs. of News Programming:* news progmg 45 hrs wkly; *No. News Employees:* 2
John Sheffler, Director of Radio

Otsego

WAKV
01-01-1958; 980 kHz AM; *Hrs Open:* 24; 1 kw-D; N42 27 33 W85 43 58
213 Gilkey St., Plainwell, MI 49080
(269) 685-2438
980am@net-link.net
License: Otsego, Allegan County, MI held by Vintage Radio Enterprises L.L.C.
Wire Services: AP
Population Served: 300,000; *Arbitron Metro Market:* Kalamazoo, MI; *Target Audience:* 50 plus; adults
Jim Higgs, President/General Manager/News Director

WQXC-FM
04-17-1981; 100.9 MHz FM; 3 kw; 299 ft; N42 30 31 W85 46 08
Mailing Address: Box 80, Otsego, MI 49078
Second Address: 706 E. Allegan St., Otsego, MI 49078
(269) 343-1717; *Fax:* (269) 692-6861
www.wqxc.com
tflynn@wqxc.com
License: Otsego, Allegan County, MI held by Forum Communications Inc.
Population Served: 300,000; *Arbitron Metro Market:* Kalamazoo, MI
Todd Overhuel, Programming Director

Ovid-Elsie

***WOES**
03-21-1978; 91.3 MHz FM; 0.55 kw horiz; 171 ft.; N43 2 44 W84 23 14
8989 Colony Road, Elsie, MI 48831 US
517-371-2642; *Fax:* 517-862-4463
License: Ovid-Elsie, Clinton County, MI held by Ovid-Elsie Area Schools.
TV Affiliate: Variety

Owosso

WOAP
01-01-1948; 1080 kHz AM; 1 kw-D, NDD; N43 1 51 W84 10 41
2391 Briarwood Dr., Owosso, MI 48867 US
989-472-4104; *Fax:* 989-472-4106
License: Owosso, MI held by 1090 Investments L.L.C.
TV Affiliate: Hits of the 40s, 50s & 60s

WRSR
12-02-1965; 103.9 MHz FM; 2.85 kw; 482 ft.; N42 59 44 W83 59 33
G-4511 Miller Road, Flint, MI 48507 US
(810) 720-9510
www.classicfox.com
License: Owosso, Shiawassee County, MI held by Cumulus Licensing Corp.
Group Owner: Cumulus Media Inc.; (acq 3-15-00; grpsl).
Arbitron Metro Market: Flint, MI; *Format:* Classic Rock *Special Programming:* Class one hr, relg one hr, sports 4 hrs wkly; *Target Audience:* 25-54.
Scott Meier, General Manager
Jeff Wade, Programming Director
Les Root, News Director
Dan Greer, Chief Engineer

Palmer

WRUP
06-21-1974; 98.3 MHz FM; *Hrs Open:* 24; 2.6 kw; 1018 ft.; N46 36 14 W87 37 15
3060 US 41 W., Marquette, MI 49855 US
(906) 228-6800
wrup.com
License: Palmer, Alger County, MI held by Great Lakes Radio Inc.
Group Owner: Great Lakes Radio Inc.
Nat'l Network: Westwood One; *Nat'l Reps:* Patt
Format: Classic Rock; *Target Audience:* 18-54.

Paradise

WUPN
95.1 MHz FM; 25 kw; 233 ft.; N46 27 57.6 W84 43 9.9 US
(989) 732-2341; *Fax:* (989) 732-6202
License: Paradise, Chippewa County, MI held by Darby Advertising Inc.
Group Owner: Darby Advertising Inc.
Arbitron Metro Market: Paradise, MI
Kent Smith, President

Pentwater

WMOM
09-26-1999; 102.7 MHz FM; 6 kw; 328 ft.; N43 52 10 W86 21 32
4359 South Howell Ave, Suite 106, Milwaukee, WI 53207 US
(231) 845-9666; *Fax:* (231) 845-9322
www.wmom.fm
License: Pentwater, Oceana County, MI held by Bay View Broadcasting Inc.
Arbitron Metro Market: Pentwater, MI; *Format:* Adult Contemp
Patrick Lopeman, General Manager
Brian Renchler, News Director

Petoskey

WJML
12-06-1966; 1110 kHz AM; *Hrs Open:* 24; 10 kw-D, DA; N45 20 05 W84 55 34
2175 Click Rd., Petoskey, MI 49770
(231) 348-5000
www.wjml.com
talk@wjml.com
License: Petoskey, Emmet County, MI held by Stone Communications Inc.
Nat'l Network: CBS; *Regional Network:* Mich. Talk
Population Served: 415,627; *Arbitron Metro Market:* Traverse City-Petoskey, MI *Special Programming:* Loc professional and college sports, relg 4 hrs wkly; *Hrs. of News Programming:* news progmg 72 hrs wkly *No. NewsEmployees:* 1; *Target Audience:* 25 plus.; *Adv. Rates:* 20; 20; 20; 18
Richard Stone, President
Philip Clever, Station Manager

WARD
06-16-2000; 750 kHz AM; *Hrs Open:* 24 *Rebroadcasts:* Rebroadcasts WLDR-FM Traverse City 100%
2175 Click Road, Petoskey, MI 49770 US
(231) 947-3220; *Fax:* (231) 947-7201
License: Petoskey, MI held by Roy E. Henderson.
Group Owner: Fort Bend Broadcasting Co.; (acq 4-25-2007; swap with WJNL(AM) Kingsley)
Arbitron Metro Market: Traverse City-Petoskey, MI; *Format:* Country
Roy Henderson, General Manager

WKLZ-FM
12-07-1965; 98.9 MHz FM; *Hrs Open:* 24; 100 kw; 801 ft.; N45 28 40 W84 57 4 *Rebroadcasts:* Rebroadcasts WKLT(FM) Kalkaska 85%
2215 Oak Indust. Dr. N.E, Grand Rapids, MI 49505 US
(231 947-0003; *Fax:* (231) 947-7002
www.wklt.com
License: Petoskey, Emmet County, MI held by Northern Radio of Petoskey Inc.
Nat'l Network: ABC; *Nat'l Reps:* Christal
Arbitron Metro Market: Traverse City-Petoskey, MI; *Format:* Rock/AOR; *Hrs. of News Programming:* News progmg 2 hrs wkly; *Target Audience:* 18-49; baby boomers
Charlie Ferguson, General Manager
Greg Marsh, General Sales Mgr
Terri Ray, Programming Director
Kristal Flateau, News Director
Dennis Murray, Chief Engineer

WLXT
01-01-1967; 96.3 MHz FM; 100 kw; 981 ft.; N45 19 17 W84 52 33
2095 US 131, South Petoskey, MI 49770 US
(231) 941-0963; *Fax:* (231) 941-9626
www.lite96.com
License: Petoskey, Emmet County, MI held by MacDonald Garber Broadcasting Inc
Group Owner: MacDonald Garber Broadcasting Co.
Arbitron Metro Market: Traverse City, MI; *Format:* Adult Contemp; *No. News Employees:* 4
Trish Garber, President
Kerry Davis, General Sales Mgr

WMBN
05-01-1946; 1340 kHz AM; *Hrs Open:* 24; 1 kw-U, ND1; N45 20 50 W84 58 1
2095 US 131, Petoskey, MI 49770 US
(231) 347-8713; *Fax:* (231) 347-8782
www.1340amwmbn.com
License: Petoskey, MI held by MacDonald Garber Broadcasting Inc.
Group Owner: MacDonald Garber Broadcasting Co.; acq 11-17-98; grpsl).
Nat'l Reps: D & R Radio
Arbitron Metro Market: Traverse City, MI; *Format:* Sports; *Hrs. of News Programming:* news progmg 2 hrs wkly; *No. News Employees:* 2; *Target Audience:* 35 plus.
Trish Garber, General Manager
Kerry Davis, General Sales Mgr

Pickford

WMKD
12-22-2000; 105.5 MHz FM; 100 kw; 253 ft.; N46 23 48 W84 23 52
P.O. Box 1230, Sault Ste. Marie, MI 49783 US
(877) 448-1055
www.country105fm.net
License: Pickford, Chippewa County, MI held by Sovereign Communications
Group Owner: Sovereign Communications
Arbitron Metro Market: Pickford, MI; *Format:* Religious

Pinconning

WLUN
11-15-1983; 100.9 MHz FM; *Hrs Open:* 24; 2.6 kw; 495 ft.; N43 50 46 W84 5 32
825 East Main Street, Midland, MI 48648 US
(989) 837-6169
License: Pinconning, Bay County, MI held by The Last Bastion Station Trust LLC, as Trustee
Nat'l Network: ESPN Radio
Arbitron Metro Market: Pinconning, MI; *Format:* Sports, Talk; *Target Audience:* 25-54; general
Paul Barbeau, General Manager
Brad Golder, Programming Director

Pittsford

***WPCJ**
10-23-1985; 91.1 MHz FM; *Hrs Open:* 16; 0.27 kw; 184 ft.; N41 53 4 W84 28 15
9400 Beecher Road, Pittsford, MI 49271 US
(517) 523-3427; *Fax:* (517) 523-3427
www.freedomfarm.info
wpcj@freedomfarm.info
License: Pittsford, Hillsdale County, MI held by Pittsford Educational Broadcasting Foundation.
Nat'l Network: Moody
Format: Christian, Religious; *Hrs. of News Programming:* News progmg 10 hrs wkly; *Target Audience:* General; rural
Tim Neinas, Station Manager
Ed Trombley, Chief Engineer

Plymouth

***WSDP**
02-14-1972; 88.1 MHz FM; *Hrs Open:* 24; 0.2 kw; 72 ft.; N42 20 50 W83 29 51
46181 Joy Road, Canton, MI 48187 US
(734) 416-7732; *Fax:* (734) 416-7732
881ThePark@gmail.com
License: Plymouth, Wayne County, MI held by Plymouth Canton Community Schools.
Arbitron Metro Market: Detroit; *Format:* Contemporary Hits/Top 40; *Hrs. of News Programming:* News progmg 2 hrs wkly; *Target Audience:* General.
Bill Keith, Station Manager
Dallas Haselhuhn, Programming Director
Lillian Thompson, Promotions Manager
Archana Sondor, News Director

Port Huron

WGRT
12-01-1991; 102.3 MHz FM; *Hrs Open:* 24; 3 kw; 318 ft; N43 04 08 W82 28 48
624 Grand River Ave., Port Huron, MI 48060
(810) 987-3200; *Fax:* (810) 987-3325
www.wgrt.com
License: Port Huron, St. Clair County, MI held by Port Huron Family Radio Inc.
Nat'l Network: ABC
Population Served: 200,000; *Arbitron Metro Market:* Detroit; *No. News Employees:* 1; *Target Audience:* General.
Martin Doorn, President
Martin Doorn, General Manager
Bruce Peterson, General Sales Mgr
Cathie Martin, News Director
Susan Doorn, Promotions/Sales Manager
George Van Camp, Production Manager
Martha Van Camp, Client ServicesManager

WHLS
08-08-1938; 1450 kHz AM; *Hrs Open:* 24; 1 kw-U, ND1; N42 58 37 W82 27 52
808 Huron Ave., Port Huron, MI 48060 US
(810) 982-9000; *Fax:* (810) 987-9380
License: Port Huron, MI held by Liggett Communications LLC.
Group Owner: Liggett Communications LLC.; (acq 1-1-56)
Nat'l Reps: Michigan Spot Sales
Arbitron Metro Market: Detroit; *Format:* Rock/AOR; *Target Audience:* 18-50; middle class
Robert Liggett, President

***WNFA**
05-15-1986; 88.3 MHz FM; *Hrs Open:* 24; 1.3 kw; 200 ft.; N42 59 36 W82 28 6 *Rebroadcasts:* Rebroadcasts WNFR(FM) Sandusky 100%
2865 Maywood Drive, Port Huron, MI 48060 US
(810) 985-3260
www.power883.com
info@power883.com
License: Port Huron, St. Clair County, MI held by Ross Bible Church.
Nat'l Network: Moody; USA
Arbitron Metro Market: Port Huron, MI; *Format:* Religious; *Hrs. of News Programming:* News progmg 14 hrs wkly; *Target Audience:* 25-44; females
Lori McNaughton, Operations Dir
Brian Smith, Programming Director
Ellyn Davey, Music Director

***WORW**
05-31-1973; 91.9 MHz FM; 0.18 kw horiz; 20 ft.; N43 1 30 W82 26 10
1799 Krafft Road, Port Huron, MI 48060 US
(810) 984-2675; *Fax:* (810) 984-2747
www.port-huron.k12.mi.us/ourschools/highschools/phn/actclubs/worwradiostation/
License: Port Huron, St. Clair County, MI held by Port Huron Area School District.
TV Affiliate: var

WPHM
12-06-1947; 1380 kHz AM; *Hrs Open:* 24; 5 kw-D, DA2; 5 kw-N, DA2; N42 51 50 W82 29 40
808 Huron Ave., Port Huron, MI 48060 US
(810) 982-9000; *Fax:* (810) 987-9380
www.wphm.net
License: Port Huron, MI held by Liggett Communications LLC.
Group Owner: Liggett Communications LLC.; (acq 5-1-2000; grpsl).
Nat'l Reps: Michigan Spot Sales; *Wire Services:* NWS (National Weather Service)
Arbitron Metro Market: Detroit; *Format:* News/Talk, Sports; *Target Audience:* 25-54.
Scott Shigley, General Manager

WSAQ
08-07-1964; 107.1 MHz FM; *Hrs Open:* 24; 6 kw; 299 ft.; N42 58 37 W82 27 52
808 Huron Ave., Port Huron, MI 48061 US
(810) 982-9000; *Fax:* (810) 987-9380
www.wsaq.com
csantoni@radiofirst.net
License: Port Huron, St. Clair County, MI held by Liggett Communications LLC.
Group Owner: Liggett Communications LLC.
Arbitron Metro Market: Detroit; *Format:* Country; *Target Audience:* 25-55.
Alisa Milano, Director of Sales
Chuck Santoni, Programming Director

***WSGR-FM**
10-01-1971; 91.3 MHz FM; 0.12 kw; 43 ft.; N42 58 43 W82 25 45
323 Erie Street, P.O. Box 5015, Port Huron, MI 48061 US
(313) 989-5646; *Fax:* (313) 984-2852
License: Port Huron, St. Clair County, MI held by St. Clair County Community College.
Format: Jazz *Special Programming:* Metal-hard rock 12 hrs, urban 6 hrs wkly; *Target Audience:* General; all age groups
John Hill, General Manager

Portage

WZOX
06-01-1992; 96.5 MHz FM; 6 kW; 249 ft; N42 12 55 W85 36 37
4200 W Main St, Kalamazoo, MI 49006 USA
(269) 345-7121; *Fax:* (269) 345-1436
z965fm.com
License: Portage, Kalamazoo County, MI held by Midwest Communications Inc.
Group Owner: Midwest Communications Inc.
Nat'l Reps: Christal
Arbitron Metro Market: Kalamazoo, MI; *Format:* Alternative
Mark Hamlin, Brand Manager

WNWN-AM
07-25-1986; 1560 kHz AM; 4.1 kW; N42 10 59 W85 35 30
4200 W Main St, Kalamazoo, MI 49006 USA
(269) 345-7121; *Fax:* (269) 345-1436
go955.com
License: Portage, MI held by Midwest Communications Inc.
Group Owner: Midwest Communications Inc.; acq 1995; grpsl)
Nat'l Reps: Christal
Arbitron Metro Market: Kalamazoo, MI; *Format:* Urban Contemporary *Special Programming:* news progmg 5 hrs wkly; *Hrs. of News Programming:* 2; *No. News Employees:* 25-54; emphasis on 35-50
Troy Robertson, Brand Manager

WRKR
10-13-1988; 107.7 MHz FM; *Hrs Open:* 24; 50 kw; 486 ft.; N42 7 44 W85 20 22
4154 Jennings Drive, Kalamazoo, MI 49048 US
(269) 987-1077
www.wrkr.com
radio@wrkr.com
License: Portage, Kalamazoo County, MI held by Cumulus Licensing Corp.
Group Owner: Cumulus Media Inc.; (acq 5-26-98; grpsl)
Arbitron Metro Market: Kalamazoo, MI; *Format:* Classic Rock, Rock/AOR *Special Programming:* Blues 5 hrs, jazz 4 hrs wkly; *Hrs. of News Programming:* news progmg 4 hrs wkly; *No. News Employees:* 2; *Target Audience:* 25-54.
Mike McKelly, Director of Sales

Powers

WUPF
01-01-2008; 107.3 MHz FM; 50 kw; 318 ft.; N45 42 39 W87 20 49
524 Ludington St., Suite 300, Escanaba, MI 49829 US
(906) 789-9700
www.radioresultsnetwork.com
License: Powers, Menominee County, MI held by Radioactive LLC.
Group Owner: Radioactive LLC
Arbitron Metro Market: Powers, MI; *Format:* Classic Rock
Kent Smith, General Manager

Raco

***WJOH**
01-01-2006; 91.5 MHz FM; 5.5 kw; 328 ft.; N46 23 28 W84 27 52 *Rebroadcasts:* simulcasts WJOM (FM) Eagle 100%
P.O. Box 388, Williamston, MI 48895 US
(888) 887-7140
www.smile.fm
Jennc@smile.fm
License: Raco, Chippewa County, MI held by Michigan Community Radio.
Arbitron Metro Market: Raco, MI; *Format:* Christian
Ed Czelada, President
Ed Czelada, Administration, Programming & Engineering
Clayton Hewitt, Administration and Engineering
Aaron Burrell, Administration
Dale Mazzoline, Production

Reed City

WDEE-FM
08-16-1997; 97.3 MHz FM; 2.85 kw; 479 ft.; N43 46 53 W85 36 58
P.O. Box 722, Big Rapids, MI 49307 US
(231)796-9730; *Fax:* (231) 796-9738
sunny@sunny973.com
License: Reed City, Osceola County, MI held by Steven V. Beilfuss.
Arbitron Metro Market: Reed City, MI; *Format:* Oldies; *Target Audience:* 35 plus; anyone who likes oldies
Steven Beilfuss, General Manager
Scott Roman, News Director

Republic

WUPG
01-01-2008; 96.7 MHz FM; 50 kw; 351 ft.; N46 30 29.2 W87 58 6.5
714 West Washington Street, Marquette, WI 49855 US
(906) 225-0656; *Fax:* (906) 225-0607
www.radioeaglemarquette.com
License: Republic, Marquette County, MI held by Radioactive LLC.
Group Owner: Radioactive LLC
Arbitron Metro Market: Republic, MI
Kent Smith, General Manager
Chip Arledge, Programming Director

Richland

***WMJC**
01-01-2008; 91.9 MHz FM; 6 kw vert; Ant 221 ft; N42 27 13 W85 20 39
150 West Lincolnway, Suite 2001, Valparaiso, IN 46383 US
(219) 548-5800
License: Richland, Kalamazoo County, MI held by Calvary Radio Network Inc.
Group Owner: Calvary Radio Network Inc.
Format: Christian, Religious

Riverside

***WSIS**
01-01-2008; 88.7 MHz FM; 6 kw; 384 ft.; N42 15 14 W86 20 9
Rebroadcasts: Rebroadcasts WHYT(FM) Goodland Township 100%
3302 N Van Dyke, Imlay City, MI 48444 US
(912) 961-9000; *Fax:* (912) 961-7070
www.smile.fm
411@smile.fm
License: Riverside, Missaukee County, MI held by Smile FM.
Group Owner: Superior Communications
Arbitron Metro Market: Riverside, MI; *Format:* Christian
Jenn Czelada, General Manager
Aaron Burrell, Administration
Clayton Hewitt, Administration and Engineering
Ed Czelada, Administration, Programming & Engineering
Dale Mazzoline, Production

Rockford

WMJH
01-01-1965; 810 kHz AM; 3.6 kw-D, NDD; N43 7 5 W85 34 46
6272 28th St. S.E., Grand Rapids, MI 49546 US
(616) 451-0551; *Fax:* (616) 451-0565
www.birach.com
sima@birach.com
License: Rockford, Kent County, MI held by Birach Broadcasting Corp.
Group Owner: Birach Broadcasting Corp.; (acq 11-6-2001; $1.9 million with WMFN(AM) Zeeland).
Nat'l Network: CBS; Westwood One
Arbitron Metro Market: Grand Rapids, MI; *Format:* Tejano; *Target Audience:* 30 plus.
Sima Birach, President

Rogers City

WHAK
05-01-1949; 960 kHz AM; 5 kw-D, ND1; 0.136 kw-N, ND1; N45 23 53 W83 55 19
1491 M -32, West, Alpena, MI 49707 US
(517) 354-4611
License: Rogers City, MI held by Edwards Communications LC
Group Owner: Edwards Communications L.C.
Nat'l Reps: Michigan Spot Sales
Format: Country; *Target Audience:* 18-75.
Darrell Kelly, Programming Director
Mary Garrow, News Director

WHAK-FM
04-01-1994; 99.9 MHz FM; 50 kw; 476 ft.; N45 23 53 W83 55 19
1491 M-32 W., Alpena, MI 49707 US
(989) 354-4611; *Fax:* (989) 354-4014
www.truenorthradionetwork.com
thebay@truenorthradionetwork.com
License: Rogers City, Presque Isle County, MI held by Edwards Communications LC
Group Owner: Edwards Communications LC.; (acq 12-21-2004; grpsl).
Format: Adult Contemp
Darrel Kelly, General Manager
Phil Heimerl, News Director

WRGZ
06-16-1984; 96.7 MHz FM; 42 kw; 531 ft.; N45 21 2 W83 46 59
Rebroadcasts: Simulcast with WATZ-FM Alpena, MI 100%
123 Prentiss St., Alpena, MI 49707 US
(989) 354-8400; *Fax:* (989) 354-3436
www.watz.com
License: Rogers City, Presque Isle County, MI held by WATZ Radio Inc.
Group Owner: Midwestern Broadcasting Co.; (acq 5-26-2006; $411,000).
Arbitron Metro Market: Alpena, MI; *Format:* Country; *No. News Employees:* 1
Mike Centala, General Sales Mgr
Steve Wright, Programming Director
Bruce Johnson, News Director
Mary Thurston, Production Director

Roscommon

WGRY-FM
03-01-1990; 101.1 MHz FM; *Hrs Open:* 24; 3.4 kw; 443 ft.; N44 34 15 W84 41 33
6514 Old Lake Rd., Grayling, MI 49738 US
(989) 348-6171; *Fax:* (989) 348-6181
www.gannonbroadcasting.com
License: Roscommon, Roscommon County, MI held by Blarney Stone Broadcasting Inc.
Group Owner: Blarney Stone Broadcasting Inc.
Nat'l Reps: Michigan Spot Sales
Format: Adult Contemp; *Hrs. of News Programming:* news progmg 16 hrs wkly; *No. News Employees:* 1; *Target Audience:* 25 plus.
Pete Michaels, Operations Dir
William Gannon, General Manager

Rose Township

***WMSD**
08-11-2000; 90.9 MHz FM; *Hrs Open:* 24; 5 kw vert; Ant 69 ft; N44 25 58 W84 00 33
2906 E Heath Rd., Lupton, MI 48635
(989) 473-4616
www.wmsdradio.com
License: Rose Township, Ogemaw County, MI held by Bible Baptist Church.
Population Served: 90,000
Paul Heaton, President
Paul Heaton, Programming Director
Dan Karbginsky, Chief Engineer
Tony Madaj, Assistant Programming Director
Kim Landenberg, Office Manager

Royal Oak

WEXL
10-01-1923; 1340 kHz AM; *Hrs Open:* 24; 1 kw-D, DAD; 1 kw-N, DAD; N42 28 10 W83 6 54
12300 Radio Place, Detroit, MI 48228 US
(313) 272 -1340; *Fax:* (313) 272-5045
www.wexl1340.com
station@wmuz.com
License: Royal Oak, MI held by WMUZ Radio Inc.
Group Owner: Crawford Broadcasting Co.; (acq 4-18-97; $3.5 million)
Arbitron Metro Market: Royal Oak, MI; *Format:* Gospel, Religious, 20; *Target Audience:* General.
Rich Hanovich, Operations Dir
Frank Franciosi, General Manager

Rust Township

***WJOJ**
12-01-2001; 89.7 MHz FM; 0.001 kw horiz, 31 kw vert; 469 ft.; N44 42 12 W83 31 27
2628 Howard Road, Petoskey, MI 49770 US
(810) 721-0891
License: Rust Township, Alcona County, MI held by Northland Community Broadcasters.
Arbitron Metro Market: Harrisville, MI; *Format:* Christian
Jenn Czelada, General Manager
Ed Czelada, Programming Director

Saginaw

WGER
02-19-1969; 106.3 MHz FM; 4.4 kw; 381 ft.; N43 28 36 W83 57 6
1795 Tittabawassee Road, Saginaw, MI 48604 US
(989) 752-3456; *Fax:* (989)754-5046
www.mix1063fm.com
License: Saginaw, Saginaw County, MI
Arbitron Metro Market: Saginaw-Bay City-Midland, MI; *Format:* Adult Contemp; *Target Audience:* 25-54; upscale, mid/high level income
Brian ""Fig"" Figula, Programming Director

WILZ
01-01-1992; 104.5 MHz FM; 2.9 kw; 413 ft.; N43 23 34 W83 55 27
1740 Champagne Dr. N., Saginaw, MI 48604 US
(989) 776-2100
www.wheelz1045.com
License: Saginaw, Saginaw County, MI held by Radio License Holding CBC, LLC
Group Owner: Cumulus Media Inc.; (acq 2-8-99).
Nat'l Reps: McGavren Guild
Arbitron Metro Market: Saginaw-Bay City-Midland, MI; *Format:* Classic Rock
Julia Richardson, General Sales Mgr

WKCQ
01-01-1947; 98.1 MHz FM; 50 kW; 492 ft.; N43 25 4 W83 55 6
PO Box 1776, Saginaw, MI 48605 USA
(989) 752-8161; *Fax:* (989) 752-8102
www.98fmkcq.com
License: Saginaw, Saginaw County, MI held by The MacDonald Broadcasting Company
Group Owner: MacDonald Broadcasting
Nat'l Reps: Eastman Radio *Regional Reps:* Eastman Radio; *Wire Services:* AP
Arbitron Metro Market: Flint-Saginaw-Bay City; *Format:* Country; *No. News Employees:* 1; *Target Audience:* Adults 25-54; 46% Male, 54% Female
Ken MacDonald Jr., CEO
Duane Alverson, President
Cindy Tuck, Operations Dir
Mary Yearham, General Sales Mgr
Jim Kramer, Operations Manager

WSAM
01-01-1940; 1400 kHz AM; 1 kW; N43 25 0 W83 55 5
2000 Whittier St, Saginaw, MI 48601 USA
(989) 752-8161; *Fax:* (989) 752-8102
thebay104fm.com
License: Saginaw, MI held by The MacDonald Broadcasting Company
Group Owner: MacDonald Broadcasting; acq 12-20-2001; grpsl
Nat'l Reps: Eastman Radio *Regional Reps:* Eastman Radio
Arbitron Metro Market: Flint-Saginaw-Bay City; *Format:* Easy Listening, Adult Contemp; *No. News Employees:* 1; *Target Audience:* Adults 25-54; 37% Male, 63% Female
Ken MacDonald Jr., CEO
Duane Alverson, President
Jim Kramer, Operations Dir
Mary Yearham, General Sales Mgr
Cindy Tuck, Vice President

WSGW
08-11-1950; 790 kHz AM; *Hrs Open:* 24; 5 kw-D, DA2; 1 kw-N, DA2; N43 27 40 W83 48 48
US
www.wsgw.com
License: Saginaw, MI held by NM Licensing LLC.
Group Owner: NextMedia Group Inc.; (acq 12-30-2002; grpsl).
Nat'l Network: CBS; *Regional Network:* Mich. Farm
Arbitron Metro Market: Saginaw-Bay Cit; *Format:* News, News/Talk, 86 *Special Programming:* Farm 10 hrs wkly; *Hrs. of News Programming:* news progmg 40 hrs wkly; *No. News Employees:* 5; *Target Audience:* 35-54;general
Dave Maurer, Operations Dir
Shannone Dunlap, General Manager

WTLZ
11-15-1968; 107.1 MHz FM; *Hrs Open:* 24; 4.9 kw; 361 ft.; N43 21 14 W83 55 6
1795 Titttabawassee Road, Saginaw, MI 48604 US
(989) 752-3456
www.kisswtlz.com
License: Saginaw, Saginaw County, MI held by NM Licensing LLC.
Group Owner: NextMedia Group Inc.; (acq 12-30-02).
Nat'l Network: American Urban
Arbitron Metro Market: Saginaw, MI; *Format:* Blues *Special Programming:* Gospel 6 hrs wkly; *Hrs. of News Programming:* News progmg 6 hrs wkly; *Target Audience:* 18-49; upscale, Blacks, women
Shannone Dunlap, General Manager
Yvonne Daniels, Programming Director

Salem Township

WSDS
01-01-1962; 1480 kHz AM; *Hrs Open:* 24; 0.75 kw-D, DA2; 3.8 kw-N, DA2; N42 15 42 W83 37 10
580 W. Clark Rd., Ypsilanti, MI 48197 US
(734) 484-1480
www.explosiva1480.com
License: Salem Township, Washtenaw County, MI held by Vazquez Broadcasting Corp.
Group Owner: Vazquez Broadcasting Corp.; (acq 7-1-2013; $1.45 million).
Arbitron Metro Market: Ann Arbor, MI; *Format:* Spanish *Special Programming:* Mexican Regional Music and Latin; *Hrs. of News Programming:* top at hour 8am-8pm; *No. News Employees:* 1; *Target Audience:* 25 plus. *Adv. Rates:* 55x60sec - 45x30sec
Alex Resendez, General Manager and Program Director

Saline

WLBY
01-01-1958; 1290 kHz AM; *Hrs Open:* Sunrise-sunset; 0.5 kw-D, DA2; 0.026 kw-N, DA2; N42 12 17 W83 47 19
1100 Victors Way, Suite 100, Ann Arbor, MI 48108 US
(734) 302-8100; *Fax:* (734) 213-7508
www.1290wlby.com
programming@1290wlby.com
License: Saline, MI held by Cumulus Licensing LLC
Group Owner: Cumulus Media Inc.; (acq 2006)
Nat'l Reps: Cumulus Radio Sales; *Wire Services:* AP
Arbitron Metro Market: Ann Arbor, MI; *Format:* Talk; *Hrs. of News Programming:* news progmg 15 hrs wkly; *No. News Employees:* 1
Matt Spaulding, Vice President/Market Manager

Sandusky

WMIC
06-27-1968; 660 kHz AM; 1 kw-D, DAD; N43 23 34 W82 49 57
19 South Elk Street, Sandusky, MI 48471 US
(810) 648-2700; *Fax:* (810) 648-3242
www.sanilacbroadcasting.com
License: Sandusky, MI held by Sanilac Broadcasting Co.
Regional Network: Mich. Farm
Arbitron Metro Market: Sandusky, MI; *Format:* Country, News, 62, Talk *Special Programming:* Farm 12 hrs, Pol 5 wkly; *Hrs. of News Programming:* news progmg 20 hrs wkly; *No. News Employees:* 2 *Target Audience:* 25 plus; general; *Adv. Rates:* 13; 13; 13; 13
George Benko, President

***WNFR**
02-14-1994; 90.7 MHz FM; 42 kw; 492 ft.; N43 10 27 W82 36 1
Rebroadcasts: Rebroadcasts WNFA(FM) Port Huron 100%
2865 Maywood Drive, Port Huron, MI 48060 US
(810) 985-3260
www.wnradio.com
License: Sandusky, Sanilac County, MI held by Ross Bible Church.
Nat'l Network: Moody; USA
Arbitron Metro Market: Sandusky, MI; *Format:* Religious; *Target Audience:* 25-44; females
Lori McNaughton, Operations Dir
Brian Smith, Station Manager
Ellyn Davey, Programming Director
Jana Simpson, News Director
Ed Czelada, Chief Engineer

WTGV-FM
08-16-1971; 97.7 MHz FM; *Hrs Open:* 24; 3 kw; 325 ft.; N43 23 34 W82 50 6
19 South Elk Street, Sandusky, MI 48471 US
(810) 648-2700; *Fax:* (810) 648-3242
www.sanilacbroadcasting.com
boba@sanilacbroadcasting.com
License: Sandusky, Sanilac County, MI held by Sanilac Broadcasting Co
Arbitron Metro Market: Sandusky, MI; *Format:* Adult Contemp; *Adv. Rates:* 13; 13; 13; 13
George Benko, President

Saugatuck

WYVN
07-04-1987; 92.7 MHz FM; *Hrs Open:* 24; 3.3 kW; 374 ft.; N42 41 10 W86 10 5
87 Central Ave, Holland, MI 49423 USA
(616) 392-3121; *Fax:* (616) 392-8066
927thevan.com
License: Saugatuck, Allegan County, MI held by Midwest Communications Inc.
Group Owner: Midwest Communications Inc.; (acq 9-5-2001)
Nat'l Reps: Christal
Arbitron Metro Market: Holland, MI; *Format:* Contemporary Hits/Top 40; *Hrs. of News Programming:* news progmg one hr wkly; *No. News Employees:* 1; *Target Audience:* 25-54.
Brent Alan, Brand Manager

Sault Sainte Marie

WKNW
08-25-1990; 1400 kHz AM; *Hrs Open:* 24; 1 kw-D, ND1; 0.95 kw-N, ND1; N46 29 18 W84 19 45
P.O. Box 1230, Sault Ste. Marie, MI 49783 US
(906) 632-1400; *Fax:* (906) 635-1216
License: Sault Sainte Marie, MI held by Sovereign Communications
Group Owner: Sovereign Communications
Format: News, News/Talk, 84, Talk

Sault Ste. Marie

***WCMZ-FM**
07-13-1990; 98.3 MHz FM; *Hrs Open:* 24; 25 kw; 328 ft.; N46 29 10 W84 13 49 *Rebroadcasts:* Rebroadcasts WCMU-FM Mount Pleasant 100%
3965 E. Broomfield Road, Mt. Pleasant, MI 48859 US
(989) 774-3105; *Fax:* (989) 774-4427
www.wcmu.org
schud1ra@cmich.edu
License: Sault Ste. Marie, Chippewa County, MI held by Central Michigan University.
Nat'l Network: NPR; PRI; *Regional Network:* Mich. Radio; *Wire Services:* AP
Arbitron Metro Market: Michigan, Upper Peninsula,MS; *Format:* Jazz, News; *Hrs. of News Programming:* news progmg 45 hrs wkly; *No. News Employees:* 2; *Target Audience:* General.
John Sheffler, General Manager

***WLSO**
01-01-1995; 90.1 MHz FM; 0.1 kw; 98 ft.; N46 29 31 W84 21 48
680 West Easterday Avenue, Sault Sainte Marie, MI 49783 US
(906) 635-7504
www.lssu.edu/wlso
wlso@gw.lssu.edu
License: Sault Ste. Marie, Chippewa County, MI held by Lake Superior State University.
Format: Variety/Diverse
Scott Korb, General Sales Mgr

WSOO
06-01-1940; 1230 kHz AM; 1 kw-U, ND1; N46 26 16 W84 22 42
1411 Ashmun St., Sault Ste. Marie, MI 49783 US
(906) 632-2231
License: Sault Ste. Marie, MI held by Sovereign Communications LLC
Group Owner: Sovereign Communications; (acq 12-18-03; $2.6 million with co-located FM).
Nat'l Network: ABC; ESPN Radio; *Nat'l Reps:* Michigan Spot Sales
Format: Adult Contemp

WSUE
01-01-1978; 101.3 MHz FM; 100 kw; 220 ft.; N46 26 16 W84 22 42
1411 Ashmun St., Sault Ste. Marie, MI 49783 US
(855) 876-2536
www.rock101.net
theresa@sovcomm.net
License: Sault Ste. Marie, Chippewa County, MI held by Sovereign Communications, LLC
Group Owner: Sovereign Communications
Format: Classic Rock
Theresa Henderson, General Sales Mgr

WYSS
07-12-1972; 99.5 MHz FM; 100 kw; 253 ft.; N46 23 48 W84 23 52
P.O. Box 1230, Sault Ste. Marie, MI 49783 US
(906) 632-2231; *Fax:* (906) 632-4411
www.yesfm.net
License: Sault Ste. Marie, Chippewa County, MI held by Sovereign Communications
Group Owner: Sovereign Communications
Arbitron Metro Market: Altoona, PA; *Format:* Contemporary Hits/Top 40; *Target Audience:* 18-49.

***WTHN**
01-29-2005; 102.3 MHz FM; *Hrs Open:* 24; 22.5 kw; 344 ft.; N46 29 8 W84 13 49 *Rebroadcasts:* WPHN (FM) Gaylord 100%
P.O. Box 695, Gaylord, MI 49734 US
(800) 545-8857
promisefm.com
info@thepromisefm.com
License: Sault Ste. Marie, Chippewa County, MI held by Northern Christian Radio Inc.
Group Owner: Northern Christian Radio Inc.
Arbitron Metro Market: Gaylord, MI; *Format:* Christian, Religious

Schoolcraft

***WOFR**
05-01-2003; 89.5 MHz FM; *Hrs Open:* 24; 10 kw; 138 ft.; N42 6 38 W85 37 57
290 Hegenberger Road, Oakland, CA 94621 US
(800) 543-1495; *Fax:* (916) 641-8238
www.familyradio.com
international@familyradio.com
License: Schoolcraft, Kalamazoo County, MI held by Family Stations Inc.
Group Owner: Family Stations Inc.
Arbitron Metro Market: Oakland, CA; *Format:* Christian, Religious

John Rorvik, Operations Dir
Harold Camping, General Manager
Craig Hulsebos, Programming Director

Scottville

WKZC
02-16-1983; 94.9 MHz FM; *Hrs Open:* 24; 17 kw; 400 ft.; N44 3 27 W86 24 58
PO Box 855, Ludington, MI 49431 US
(231) 843-3438; *Fax:* (231) 843-1886
License: Scottville, Mason County, MI held by Synergy Media, Inc.
Group Owner: Synergy Broadcast Group
Nat'l Network: ABC; *Nat'l Reps:* Patt
Format: Country; *Hrs. of News Programming:* news progmg 5 hrs wkly; *No. News Employees:* 1; *Target Audience:* 25-54.; *Adv. Rates:* 22; 18; 20; 10
Lynn Baerwolf, President
Jason Wilder, Operations Dir

Shepherd

WMMI
02-02-1987; 830 kHz AM; *Hrs Open:* Daytime; 1 kw-D, NDD; N43 33 42 W84 45 0
4065 East Wing Rd, Mount Pleasant, MI 48858 US
(989) 772-9664; *Fax:* (989) 773-5000
www.wczy.net
wczy@wczy.net
License: Shepherd, MI held by Central Michigan Communications Inc.
Regional Network: Mich. Talk; *Nat'l Reps:* Michigan Spot Sales
Regional Reps: Patt.; *Wire Services:* AP
Arbitron Metro Market: Shepherd, MI; *Format:* Talk; *Hrs. of News Programming:* news progmg 6 hrs wkly; *No. News Employees:* 1; *Target Audience:* 25-54; general; *Adv. Rates:* 18; 18; 18; N/A
Mike Carey, President
John Sebastian, Programming Director
Tina Sawyer, News Director
Lisa Johnson, Traffic Manager

South Haven

WCSY
03-01-1996; 103.7 MHz FM; *Hrs Open:* 24; 3 kW; 328 ft.; N42 18 2 W86 15 3
580 E Napier Ave, Benton Harbor, MI 49022 USA
(269) 637-6397; *Fax:* (269) 637-2675
www.wcsy.com
License: South Haven, Van Buren County, MI held by WSJM, Inc.
Group Owner: Mid-West Family Broadcasting; (acq 4-96; grpsl)
Nat'l Network: ABC; *Nat'l Reps:* Rgnl Reps; *Wire Services:* AP
Arbitron Metro Market: South Haven, MI; *Format:* Oldies
Gayle Olson, Chairman
Dave Doetsch, President & General Manager
Paul Layendecker, Operations Dir
Bob Bucholtz, General Sales Mgr

Southfield

*WSHJ
02-28-1967; 88.3 MHz FM; *Hrs Open:* 7:30 AM-10 PM; 0.105 kw; 69 ft.; N42 28 12 W83 15 51
24675 Lahser Road, Southfield, MI 48034 US
(248) 746-8500
www.southfield.k12.mi.us
License: Southfield, Oakland County, MI held by Board of Education Southfield Public Schools.
Arbitron Metro Market: Detroit; *Format:* Oldies; *Target Audience:* General; students & families
Jamie Rudolph, General Manager

Spring Arbor

*WJKN-FM
01-01-2005; 89.3 MHz FM; 2.5 kw vert; 272 ft.; N42 9 13 W84 32 57
106 E Main Street, Spring Arbor, MI 49283 US
(517) 750-6540; *Fax:* (517) 750-6619
info@893themessage.com
License: Spring Arbor, Jackson County, MI held by Spring Arbor University.
Arbitron Metro Market: Spring Arbor, MI; *Format:* Christian
Malachi Crane, General Manager
Tonya Hernandez, Programming Director
Rachel Ryder, Promotions Manager
Dave Benson, Chief Engineer
Malachi Crane, Executive Director

Springfield

*WCFG
90.9 MHz FM; *Hrs Open:* 24; 0.7 kw; 351 ft.; N42 21 20 W85 20 28 *Rebroadcasts:* Rebroadcasts WCSG(FM) Grand Rapids 100%
1159 E. Beltline Ave. N.E., Grand Rapids, MI 49525 US
(616) 942-1500; *Fax:* (616) 942-7078
www.wcsg.org
wcsg@wcsg.org
License: Springfield, Calhoun County, MI held by Cornerstone University.
Arbitron Metro Market: Springfield, MI; *Format:* Christian; *Target Audience:* 35-49.
Chris Lemke, General Manager

St. Ignace

WIDG
06-07-1966; 940 kHz AM; *Hrs Open:* Sunrise-sunset
P.O. Box 1109, Indian River, MI 49749 US
(231) 238-0811; *Fax:* (231) 238-0803
www.baragabroadcasting.com
Christine@baragamail.com
License: St. Ignace, MI held by Baraga Broadcasting Inc.
Format: Christian
Harry Speckman, Chaplain
Christine Schicker, General Manager
Brian Brachel, Chief Engineer
Bob Fraiser, Controller

St. Johns

WQTX
07-15-1972; 92.1 MHz FM; *Hrs Open:* 24; 4 kW; 400 ft; N42 53 30 W84 34 31
2495 Cedar St, Holt, MI 48842 USA
(517) 699-0111; *Fax:* (517) 699-1880
team921fm.com
License: St. Johns, Clinton County, MI held by Midwest Communications Inc.
Group Owner: Midwest Communications Inc.
Nat'l Network: Jones Radio Networks; *Nat'l Reps:* Katz Radio; *Wire Services:* AP
Population Served: 397,000; *Arbitron Metro Market:* Lansing, MI; *Format:* Sports
Joe Cassady, Brand Manager

WWSJ
09-23-1959; 1580 kHz AM; *Hrs Open:* 24; 1 kw-D, DA2; 0.003 kw-N, DA2; N42 58 14 W84 32 59
P.O. Box 451, 1363 West Partes Road, St. Johns, MI 48879 US
(989) 224-7911; *Fax:* (989) 224-4683
www.joy1580.com
License: St. Johns, MI held by L. Harp, H. Harp, W. Hill, Elmira Hill.
Nat'l Network: American Urban
Arbitron Metro Market: Lansing, MI; *Format:* Gospel; *Adv. Rates:* 20; 20; 20; 10
Larry Harp, President
Helen Harp, Programming Director
Danielle Beckley, Promotions Manager
Ed Czelada, Chief Engineer
Dione Harp, Music Director

St. Joseph

WIRX
06-20-1966; 107.1 MHz FM; *Hrs Open:* 24; 1.2 kW; 499 ft.; N42 4 19 W86 22 14
PO Box 107, St. Joseph, MI 49085 USA
(269) 925-1111; *Fax:* (269) 925-1011
www.wirx.com
License: St. Joseph, Berrien County, MI held by WSJM, Inc.
Group Owner: Mid-West Family Broadcasting
Wire Services: AP
Arbitron Metro Market: St. Joseph, MI; *Target Audience:* 18-49.
Gayle Olson, Chairman
Dave Doetsch, President & General Manager
Paul Layendecker, Operations Manager
Bob Bucholtz, General Sales Mgr
Zack East, Programming Director
Lindsay Kay, Promotions Director
Ray Gustafson, NewsDirector
Terry Green, Technical Director

St. Louis

WMLM
12-15-1977; 1520 kHz AM; *Hrs Open:* 24
Mailing Address: P.O. Box 17, St. Louis, MI 48880 US
Second Address: 4170 N. State Rd., Alma, MI 48801
(989) 463-4013; *Fax:* (989) 463-4014
wmlm@cmsinter.net
License: St. Louis, MI held by Siefker Broadcasting Corp.
Nat'l Network: ABC
Format: Country *Special Programming:* Farm 5 hrs, gospel 2 hrs wkly; *Target Audience:* 35 plus.; *Adv. Rates:* 12.50; 11.00; 12.50.
Gregory Siefker, President

Standish

*WWCM
01-01-1990; 96.9 MHz FM; *Hrs Open:* 24; 3 kw; 328 ft.; N44 2 8 W84 0 31 *Rebroadcasts:* Rebroadcasts WCMU-FM Mount Pleasant 100%
7585 Pigeon Road, Pigeon, MI 48755 US
(989) 774-3105; *Fax:* (989) 774-4427
www.wcmu.org
License: Standish, Arenac County, MI held by Central Michigan University
Format: Jazz, News; *Target Audience:* General.
Ed Grant, General Manager

Stephenson

WMXG
01-01-1999; 106.3 MHz FM; 50 kw; 492 ft.; N45 38 36 W87 22 37
1101c Ludington St., Escanaba, WI 49829 US
(906) 786-0060; *Fax:* (906) 786-2990
License: Stephenson, Menominee County, MI held by Pacer Radio of the Near-North.
Arbitron Metro Market: Stephenson, MI; *Format:* Contemporary Hits/Top 40
Mike DuBord, General Manager

Sterling Heights

*WUFL
10-26-1988; 1030 kHz AM; *Hrs Open:* Daytime
Mailing Address: 7355 N. Oracle, #200, Tucson, AZ 85740 US
Second Address: 42669 Garfield Rd., Suite 328, Clinton Township, MI 48038
(586) 263-1030; *Fax:* (586) 228-1030
www.myflr.org
License: Sterling Heights, MI held by Family Life Broadcasting System.
Group Owner: Family Life Communications Inc.; acq 10-25-88)
Nat'l Network: USA
Arbitron Metro Market: Detroit, MI; *Format:* Christian, Religious; *Hrs. of News Programming:* 45 min news progmg wkly; *Target Audience:* 35-54; Women
Dr. Randy L.ÿCarlson, President
Adam Nash, Programming Director
Alonzo Williams, Evan Carlson
Executive Director of Marketing and Community Tran, Rod Robison
Vice President of Development

Sturgis

WBET
01-01-1951; 1230 kHz AM; 1 kw-U, DA-1; N41 46 11 W85 25 09
7080 South Nottawa Rd., Sturgis, MI 49091
(269) 651-9238
www.wmshradio.com
wmsh@wmshradio.com
License: Sturgis, St. Joseph County, MI held by Lake Cities Broadcasting Corp.
Group Owner: Lake Cities Broadcasting Corp.; acq 1-12-98; $600,000 with co-located FM)
Nat'l Network: ABC; ESPN Radio; *Nat'l Reps:* Michigan Spot Sales
Population Served: 100,000 *Target Audience:* 25-54.
Carter Snider, General Manager
Mike Stiles, News Director

WBET-FM
01-01-1951; 99.3 MHz FM; 2.15 kw; Ant 390 ft; N41 46 11 W85 25 09
7080 South Nottawa Rd., Sturgis, MI 49091
(269) 651-9238
License: Sturgis, St. Joseph County, MI held by Lake Cities Broadcasting Corp.
Group Owner: Lake Cities Broadcasting Corp.

Tom Crawford, General Manager

Tawas City

***WHST**
11-01-1972; 106.1 MHz FM; *Hrs Open:* 24; 25 kw; 305 ft.; N44 16 25 W83 39 48 *Rebroadcasts:* Rebroadcasts WPHN(FM) Gaylord 100%
P.O. Box 695, Gaylord, MI 49734 US
(800) 545-8857
promisefm.com
License: Tawas City, Iosco County, MI held by Northern Christian Radio Inc.
Group Owner: Northern Christian Radio Inc.; acq 7-19-01).
Format: Christian, Religious; *Target Audience:* 25-54.

WKJC-FM
10-01-1979; 104.7 MHz FM; 50 kw; 492 ft.; N44 24 48 W83 37 14
PO Box 549, 523 Meadow Rd., Tawas City, MI 48764 US
(989) 362-3417; *Fax:* (989) 362-4544
www.wkjc.com
License: Tawas City, Iosco County, MI held by Carroll Enterprises Inc.
Group Owner: Carroll Enterprises Inc.
Format: Country
John Carroll Jr., General Manager
Tim Carroll, Sales Manager

WQLB
07-09-1997; 103.3 MHz FM; 25 kw; 423 ft.; N44 24 48 W83 37 14
523 Meadow Rd., Tawas City, MI 48764 US
(989) 362-3417; *Fax:* (989) 362-4544
www.hitsfm.net
License: Tawas City, Iosco County, MI held by Carroll Broadcasting Inc.
Group Owner: Carroll Enterprises Inc.; (acq 12-1-97)
Regional Network: Minn. News Net.
Format: Variety/Diverse
John Carroll Jr., General Manager
Tim Carroll, General Sales Mgr
Deb Michaels, Programming Director
Mary Hill, News Director

Tawas City-East Tawas

WIOS
09-27-1958; 1480 kHz AM; 1 kw-D, DAD; 0.109 kw-N, DA2; N44 15 48 W83 32 42
PO Box 549, Tawas City, MI 48764 US
(989) 362-3417; *Fax:* (989) 362-4544
www.wiosradio.com
License: Tawas City-East Tawas, MI held by Carroll Enterprises Inc.
Group Owner: Carroll Enterprises Inc.; (acq 5-1-69)
Regional Network: Mich. Farm; *Nat'l Reps:* Michigan Spot Sales
Format: Talk, Big Band *Special Programming:* Big band 6 hrs wkly; *Target Audience:* 25 plus; general
John Carroll Sr., Chairman
John Carroll Jr., CEO
Tim Carroll, General Sales Mgr

Taylor

WCHB
01-01-1990; 1200 kHz AM
3250 Franklin St., Detroit, MI 48207 US
(313) 259-2000; *Fax:* (313) 259-7011
www.wchbnewsdetroit.com
License: Taylor, MI held by Radio One of Detroit LLC.
Group Owner: Radio One Inc.; (acq 6-19-98; $34.2 million with WDTJ(FM) Detroit)
Arbitron Metro Market: Detroit,MI; *Format:* News/Talk; *Target Audience:* Adults 25-54.
Alfred Liggins, President/CEO

Three Rivers

WRCI
05-03-1962; 1520 kHz AM; *Hrs Open:* 24
59750 Constantine Road, Three Rivers, MI 49093 US
(269) 278-1815; *Fax:* (269) 273-7975
www.wlkm.com
info@wlkm.com
License: Three Rivers, MI held by Impact Radio LLC
Group Owner: Impact Radio LLC; (acq 8-1-2002; grpsl)
Nat'l Network: AP Radio; Jones Radio Networks; *Regional Network:* Mich. Radio *Regional Reps:* Patt Media Sales
Format: Country; *Hrs. of News Programming:* news progmg 14 hrs wkly; *No. News Employees:* 1; *Target Audience:* General.
Dennis Rumsey, President
Pat Holtz, Operations Dir
Kathy Loker, General Sales Mgr
Walker Sisson, Engineering Dir

WLKM-FM
03-01-1975; 95.9 MHz FM; *Hrs Open:* 24; 3.6 kw; 425 ft.; N41 53 51 W85 33 51
59750 Constantine Road, Three Rivers, MI 49093 US
(269) 278-1815; *Fax:* (269) 273-7975
www.wlkm.com
info@wlkm.com
License: Three Rivers, St. Joseph County, MI held by Impact Radio LLC
Group Owner: Impact Radio LLC
Nat'l Network: CNN Radio *Regional Reps:* Patt Media Sales;
Wire Services: AP
Format: Contemporary Hits/Top 40, Adult Contemp; *Hrs. of News Programming:* news progmg 2 hrs wkly; *No. News Employees:* 1; *Target Audience:* 25-54.
Pat Holtz, Operations Dir
Dennis Rumsey, General Manager
Kathy Loker, General Sales Mgr
Walker Sisson, Engineering Dir

Traverse City

WCCW
07-15-1960; 1310 kHz AM; 15 kw-D, DA2; 7.5 kw-N, DA2; N44 40 38 W85 39 56
300 E. Front St., Suite 450, Traverse City, MI 49684 US
(231) 946-6211; *Fax:* (231) 946-1914
www.1310thescore.com
License: Traverse City, Grand Traverse County, MI held by WCCW Radio Inc.
Group Owner: Midwestern Broadcasting Co.; (acq 9-16-96; $2.2 million with co-located FM)
Nat'l Reps: Michigan Spot Sales; Katz Radio
Arbitron Metro Market: Traverse City-Petoskey, MI; *Format:* Sports
Brian Hale, Programming Director
Chris Davis, Marketing Director
Courtney Rehmer, News Director
Jordan Anderson, Production Manager
George Bliss, Account Manager
Linda Francomb, Account Manager
Judy Gill, Account Manager
Heather Barelmay, Account Manager

WCCW-FM
11-08-1967; 107.5 MHz FM; 50 kw; 492 ft.; N44 46 2 W85 41 26
300 E. Front St., Suite 450, Traverse City, MI 49684 US
(231) 946-6211; *Fax:* (231) 946-1914
www.wccw.fm
License: Traverse City, Grand Traverse County, MI held by WCCW Radio Inc.
Group Owner: Midwestern Broadcasting Co.
Arbitron Metro Market: Traverse City-Petoskey, MI; *Format:* Oldies
Ross Biederman, President
Dave Gauthier, Programming Director
Chris Davis, Marketing Director
Courtney Rehmer, News Director
Jordan Anderson, Production Manager
George Bliss, Account Manager
Linda Francomb, Account Manager
JudyGill, Account Manager
Heather Bartelmay, Account Manager

***WICA**
09-13-2000; 91.5 MHz FM; *Hrs Open:* 24; 4 kw; 748 ft.; N44 45 22 W85 40 42
US
License: Traverse City, Grand Traverse County, MI held by Interlochen Center for the Arts.
Wire Services: AP
Arbitron Metro Market: Traverse City-Petoskey, MI; *Format:* News, Talk; *Hrs. of News Programming:* news progmg 168 hrs wkly; *No. News Employees:* 4; *Target Audience:* 25-80.
Thom Paulson, Operations Dir

WLDR-FM
07-17-1966; 101.9 MHz FM; *Hrs Open:* 24; 100 kw; 630 ft.; N44 46 13 W85 41 43
13999 S.W. Bayshore Drive, Traverse City, MI 49684 US
(231) 947-3220
License: Traverse City, Grand Traverse County, MI held by Great Northern Broadcasting System Inc.
Group Owner: Fort Bend Broadcasting Co.; (acq 4-10-2001; $3.6 million for stock)
Arbitron Metro Market: Traverse City-Petoskey, MI; *Format:* Country; *No. News Employees:* 1; *Target Audience:* 25-54.; *Adv. Rates:* 25; 30; 25; 14
Roy Henderson, CEO
Steve Smith, CFO

***WLJN-FM**
10-01-1989; 89.9 MHz FM; *Hrs Open:* 24; 39 kw vert; 554 ft.; N44 46 36 W85 39 43
P.O. Box 1408, Traverse City, MI 49685 US
(231) 946-1400; *Fax:* (231) 946-3959
www.wljn.com
info@wljn.com
License: Traverse City, Grand Traverse County, MI held by Good News Media Inc.
Group Owner: Good News Media Inc.
Arbitron Metro Market: Traverse City-Petoskey, MI; *Format:* Christian, Religious; *Hrs. of News Programming:* News progmg 4 hrs wkly; *Target Audience:* General.
Brian Harcey, General Manager
Pete Lathrop, Programming Director

***WNMC-FM**
10-01-1967; 90.7 MHz FM; *Hrs Open:* 8 AM-2 AM; 0.6 kw; 538 ft.; N44 46 36 W85 41 2
1701 E, Front St., Traverse City, MI 49686 US
(231) 995-2562
www.wnmc.org
License: Traverse City, Grand Traverse County, MI held by Northwestern Michigan College.
Arbitron Metro Market: Traverse City, MI; *Format:* Blues, Jazz, 94 *Special Programming:* American Indian one hr, Black 20 hrs, folk 11 hrs,
Eric Hines, Station Manager

WTCM
01-01-1941; 580 kHz AM; *Hrs Open:* 24; 50 kw-D, DA2; 1.1 kw-N, DA2; N44 43 18 W85 42 18
314 E. Front St., P.O. Box 472, Traverse City, MI 49684 US
(231) 947-7675; *Fax:* (231) 929-3988
www.wtcmradio.com
License: Traverse City, Grand Traverse County, MI held by WTCM Radio Inc.
Group Owner: Midwestern Broadcasting Co.
Arbitron Metro Market: Traverse City, MI; *Format:* News, News/Talk, 86 *Special Programming:* Farm 5 hrs wkly; *Hrs. of News Programming:* news progmg 12 hrs wkly; *No. News Employees:* 4; *Target Audience:* 25-54.
Ross Biederman, President
Chris Warren, General Manager
Paul Binsfeld, General Sales Mgr
Jack O'Malley, Programming Director
Joel Franck, News Director
Steve Cook, Production Manager

WTCM-FM
12-13-1965; 103.5 MHz FM; *Hrs Open:* 24; 100 kw; 991 ft.; N44 27 31 W85 42 2
314 E. Front St., P.O. Box 472, Traverse City, MI 49684 US
(231) 947-7675; *Fax:* (231) 929-3988
www.wtcmi.com
wtcm@wtcmradio.com
License: Traverse City, Grand Traverse County, MI held by WTCM Radio Inc.
Group Owner: Midwestern Broadcasting Co.
Arbitron Metro Market: Traverse City, MI; *Format:* Country; *Target Audience:* 25-54.
Ross Biederman, President
Chris Warren, General Manager
Paul Binsfeld, General Sales Mgr
Jack O'Malley, Programming Director
Joel Franck, News Director
Steve Cook, Production Manager

Trout Lake

***WHWG**
01-01-1999; 89.9 MHz FM; 1 kw; 390 ft.; N46 11 17 W84 56 46
Rebroadcasts: Rebroadcasts WHWL(FM) Marquette 100%
130 Carmen Drive, Marquette, MI 49855 US
(906) 249-1423; *Fax:* (906) 249-4042
www.whwl.net
whwl@whwl.net
License: Trout Lake, Chippewa County, MI held by Gospel Opportunities Inc.
Format: Religious
W. Curtis Marker, General Manager

Tuscarora Township

WWSS
95.3 MHz FM; 3.3 kw; Ant 447 ft; N44 52 43 W84 40 50
(877) 732-2360
License: Tuscarora Township, Crawford County, MI held by Darby Advertising Inc.

Group Owner: Darby Advertising Inc.

Kent Smith, President

Tuscola

WWBN

09-14-1987; 101.5 MHz FM; *Hrs Open:* 24; 1.8 kw; 489 ft.; N43 12 0 W83 33 30
G-3338 East Bristol Road, Burton, MI 48529 US
(810) 742-1470; *Fax:* (810) 742-5170
www.banana1015.com
info@banana1015.com
License: Tuscola, Tuscola County, MI
Group Owner: Townsquare Media; (acq 12-19-97; grpsl).
Nat'l Reps: Katz Radio
Arbitron Metro Market: Flint, MI; *Format:* Rock/AOR; *Hrs. of News Programming:* news progmg 20 hrs wkly; *No. News Employees:* 1; *Target Audience:* 18-49; men; *Adv. Rates:* 50; 50; 50; 50
Tony LaBrie, Programming Director

Twin Lake

*WBLV

07-03-1982; 90.3 MHz FM; *Hrs Open:* 24; 100 kw; 607 ft.; N43 33 0 W86 2 34 *Rebroadcasts:* Rebroadcasts WBLU-FM Grand Rapids 100%
300 East Crystal, Twin Lake, MI 49457 US
(231) 894-1966; *Fax:* (231) 893-2457
www.bluelake.org
radio@bluelake.org
License: Twin Lake, Muskegon County, MI held by Blue Lake Fine Arts Camp.
Nat'l Network: PRI; NPR; *Regional Network:* Minn. Pub. Radio
Arbitron Metro Market: Twin Lake, MI; *Format:* Jazz, News *Special Programming:* Folk 5 hrs wkly; *Hrs. of News Programming:* News progmg 20 hrs wkly; *Target Audience:* Adult.
Heidi Stansell, Vice President

Vassar

WOWE

07-01-1990; 98.9 MHz FM; 3 kw; 328 ft.; N43 17 56 W83 30 34
107 South Main Street, Vassar, MI 48768 US
(810) 234-4335; *Fax:* (810) 234-7286
License: Vassar, Tuscola County, MI held by Praestantia Broadcasting Inc.
Arbitron Metro Market: Flint, MI; *Format:* Urban Contemporary
Michael Shumpert, President

Walker

WTRV

06-15-1993; 100.5 MHz FM; *Hrs Open:* 24; 3 kw; 328 ft.; N43 0 59 W85 44 24
50 Monroe Avenue N.W., Grand Rapids, MI 49503 US
(616) 451-4800; *Fax:* (616) 451-0113
www.theriver-fm.com
Tom.Cook@townsquaremedia.com
License: Walker, Kent County, MI
Group Owner: Townsquare Media; (acq 8-7-00; grpsl).
Nat'l Reps: Katz Radio
Arbitron Metro Market: Grand Rapids, MI; *Format:* Adult Contemp; *Target Audience:* 35-64.
Russ Hines, General Manager
Tom Cook, Programming Director

Walled Lake

WPON

12-01-1954; 1460 kHz AM; *Hrs Open:* 24; 1 kw-D, DA2; 0.76 kw-N, DA2; N42 32 38 W83 29 58
21700 Northwestern Hwy., Suite 1190, Tower 14, Southfield, MI 48075 US
(248) 557-3500; *Fax:* (248) 557-2950
www.wpon.com
wpon@wpon.com
License: Walled Lake, Oakland County, MI held by Birach Broadcasting Corp.
Group Owner: Birach Broadcasting Corp.; acq 5-25-2004; $800,000).
Arbitron Metro Market: Detroit; *Format:* Oldies, Talk; *Target Audience:* 35-65; 35 and above; *Adv. Rates:* 40; 40; 40; 40
Sima Birach, Operations Manager

Warren

*WPHS

03-20-1964; 89.1 MHz FM; *Hrs Open:* 6:30 AM-8:30 PM; 0.1 kw; 98 ft.; N42 31 0 W83 0 36
Mailing Address: 3033 Hoover Road, Warren, MI 48093 US
Second Address: Warren Consolidated Schools, 31300 Anita, Warren, MI 48093
(586) 698-4501
www.wphs.com
License: Warren, Macomb County, MI held by Warren Consolidated Schools.
Format: Urban Contemporary *Special Programming:* Blues 3 hrs, Pol 2 hrs, news 5 hrs, country 4 hrs, Christian rock 4 hrs wkly; *Hrs. of News Programming:* news progmg 10 hrs wkly; *No. News Employees:* 2 *TargetAudience:* 12-27; males
Jenny Stanczyk, General Manager

West Branch

WBMI

11-07-1977; 105.5 MHz FM; 6 kw; 299 ft.; N44 17 57 W84 15 54
3275 West M-55, West Branch, MI 48661 US
(989) 345-4269; *Fax:* (989) 345-3996
License: West Branch, Ogemaw County, MI held by Peggy R. Warner
Nat'l Network: Jones Radio Networks
Format: Oldies *Special Programming:* Pol 6 hrs wkly; *Target Audience:* 25-54.
Charlie Cobb, General Manager
Mike McCall, Programming Director

White Star

*WEJC

07-01-2001; 88.3 MHz FM; 0.001 kw horiz, 55 kw vert; 374 ft.; N43 41 40 W84 5 3
3302 N Van Dyke, Imlay City, MI 48444 US
(517) 381-0573; *Fax:* (877) 850-0881
www.positivehits.com
info@positivehits.com
License: White Star, Gladwin County, MI held by Superior Communications.
Group Owner: Superior Communications
Arbitron Metro Market: White Star, MI; *Format:* Christian
Jenn Czelada, General Manager
Ed Czelada, Programming Director

Whitehall

WWSN

04-01-1991; 97.5 MHz FM; *Hrs Open:* 24; 1.7 kw; Ant 426 ft; N43 23 04 W86 19 30
3375 Merriam St, Suite 201, Muskegon Heights, MS 60005
(616) 774-8461; *Fax:* (616) 774-2491
www.975thechamp.com
License: Whitehall, Muskegon County, MI held by Radio License Holding CBC LLC
Nat'l Network: Westwood One
Hrs. of News Programming: News progmg one hr wkly; *Target Audience:* 25-49; male and female
Jon Russell, Operations Dir
Jeff Morton, General Manager
Renee Dudek, General Sales Mgr
John Alan, Chief Engineer

WGVS-FM

01-01-1975; 95.3 MHz FM; 2 kw; 361 ft.; N43 21 14 W86 19 38
Rebroadcasts: Rebroadcasts WGVU-FM Allendale 100%
301 West Fulton, Grand Rapids, MI 49504 US
(616) 331-6666; *Fax:* (616) 331-6625
www.wgvu.org
wgva@gvsu.edu
License: Whitehall, Muskegon County, MI
Arbitron Metro Market: Muskegon, MI; *Format:* Jazz, News
Ed Spier, News Director

WKLQ

04-25-1979; 1490 kHz AM; 1 kw-U, ND1; Ant 492 ft; N43 23 4 W86 19 30
3375 Merriam, Suite 201, Muskegon Heights, MI 49444 US
(231) 830-0176
www.bigtalk1490.com
ronald.gates@cumulus.com
License: Whitehall, MI held by Radio License Holding CBC, LLC
Group Owner: Cumulus Media Inc.; (acq 5-30-2000; grpsl).
Arbitron Metro Market: Grand Rapids, M; *Format:* Talk
Jon Russell, Operations Dir
Ron Gates, General Sales Mgr
Rich Berry, VP/Director of Sales

Wixom

*WSHM

88.3 MHz FM; kw
US
(313) 755-5163
License: Wixom, Oakland County, MI held by By Grace Through Faith.
Arbitron Metro Market: Wixom, MI
Mark Ramseyer, General Manager

Wyoming

*WYCE

11-01-1983; 88.1 MHz FM; *Hrs Open:* 24; 10 kw; 164 ft.; N42 54 43 W85 41 0
711 Bridge Street, NW, Grand Rapids, MI 49504 US
(616) 742-9923; *Fax:* (616) 742-0599
www.grcmc.org
comment@wyce.org
License: Wyoming, Kent County, MI held by Grand Rapids Cable Access Center Inc.
Arbitron Metro Market: Wyoming, MI; *Format:* Alternative *Special Programming:* Folk one hr, Sp 10 hrs; *Target Audience:* 25-54; general; *Adv. Rates:* 25; 18; 25; 15
Kevin Murphy, Station Manager
Pete Bruinsma, Programming Director

WYGR

11-14-1964; 1530 kHz AM; 0.25 kw-C, NDD; 0.5 kw-D, NDD; N42 55 38 W85 44 50
P. O. Box 9591, Wyoming, MI 49509 US
(616) 452-8589; *Fax:* (616) 248-0176
www.wygr.net
License: Wyoming, MI held by WYGR Broadcasting.
Nat'l Reps: Patt
Arbitron Metro Market: Wyoming, MI; *Format:* Spanish *Special Programming:* Polka pops 3 hrs wkly; *Target Audience:* Sp speaking Hispanics.
Robert Womack, Station Manager
Roland Rusticus, Business Manager

Ypsilanti

*WEMU

12-08-1965; 89.1 MHz FM; *Hrs Open:* 24; 15.5 kw; 289 ft.; N42 15 48 W83 37 34
P.O. Box 980350, Ypsilanti, MI 48197 US
(734) 487-2229; *Fax:* (734) 487-1015
www.wemu.org
wemu@emich.edu
License: Ypsilanti, Washtenaw County, MI held by Eastern Michigan University.
Nat'l Network: NPR; *Wire Services:* AP
Arbitron Metro Market: Ypsilanti, MI; *Format:* Blues, Jazz, 60; *Hrs. of News Programming:* news progmg 39 hrs wkly; *No. News Employees:* 4; *Target Audience:* General.
Patrick Campion, Programming Director

WDEO

11-16-1962; 990 kHz AM; *Hrs Open:* 24; 9.2 kw-D, DA2; 0.25 kw-N, DA2; N42 15 53 W83 36 47; N42 15 55 W83 36 42
P.O. Box 504, Ann Arbor, MI 48106 US
(734) 930-5200; *Fax:* (734) 930-3179
www.avemariaradio.net
License: Ypsilanti, MI held by Word Broadcasters Inc.
Arbitron Metro Market: Ann Arbor, MI; *Format:* Christian, Talk; *Hrs. of News Programming:* News progmg 9 hrs wkly; *Target Audience:* 21 plus; adult Christian; *Adv. Rates:* 45; 45; 65; 45
Al Kresta, CEO
Steve Clarke, Operations Dir
Michael Jones, General Manager

Zeeland

*WGNB

01-21-1989; 89.3 MHz FM; *Hrs Open:* 24; 30 kW; 499 ft.; N42 50 14 W85 59 17
3764 84th Ave, Zeeland, MI 49464 USA
(616) 772-7300
www.moodyradio.org/stations/grand-rapids
License: Zeeland, Ottawa County, MI held by The Moody Bible Institute of Chicago
Group Owner: The Moody Bible Institute of Chicago; acq 2-5-91;
Nat'l Network: Salem Radio Network; Moody
Arbitron Metro Market: Grand Rapids, MI; *Format:* Christian; *Hrs. of News Programming:* News progmg 15 hrs wkly; *Target Audience:* 35-54; Evangelical Christians

WJQK

08-23-1971; 99.3 MHz FM; *Hrs Open:* 24; 4.7 kw; 371 ft.; N42 48 59 W85 57 24
425 Centerstone Court, Zeeland, MI 94964 US
(616) 931-9930; *Fax:* (616) 931-1280
www.jq99.com
traffic@jq99.com
License: Zeeland, Ottawa County, MI held by Lanser Broadcasting Corp.

Nat'l Network: Fox News Radio; *Nat'l Reps:* Salem *Regional Reps:* Mich Spot Sales; *Wire Services:* Metro Weather Service Inc.
Arbitron Metro Market: Grand Rapids, MI; *Format:* Christian; *Hrs. of News Programming:* News progmg 7 hrs wkly; *Target Audience:* 25-49.; *Adv. Rates:* 49; 42; 49; 42
Les Lanser, President
Brad Lanser, Operations Dir
Troy West, Station Manager

WMFN
02-01-1990; 640 kHz AM; *Hrs Open:* 24; 1.2 kw-D, ND1; 0.23 kw-N, ND1; N42 48 59 W85 57 24
2422 Burton S.E., Grand Rapids, MI 49546 US
(616) 949-8585; *Fax:* (616) 949-9262
www.birach.com
sima@birach.com
License: Zeeland, Ottawa County, MI held by Birach Broadcasting Corp.
Group Owner: Birach Broadcasting Corp.; acq 11-6-01; $1.9 million with WMJH(AM) Rockford).
Nat'l Network: CBS
Arbitron Metro Market: Grand Rapids, MI; *Format:* Tejano; *Target Audience:* 25-54.
Sima Birach, President

WPNW
11-02-1956; 1260 kHz AM; *Hrs Open:* 24; 10 kw-D, DA2; 1 kw-N, DA2; N42 43 56 W86 6 6
425 Centerstone Court, Zeeland, MI 49464 US
(616) 931-6620; *Fax:* (616) 931-1280
www.1260thepledge.com
traffic@jq99.com
License: Zeeland, MI held by Lanser Broadcasting Corp.
Nat'l Network: CNN Radio; *Nat'l Reps:* Salem
Arbitron Metro Market: Zeeland, MI; *Format:* News, Talk *Special Programming:* Sp 2 hrs, farm one hr wkly; *Hrs. of News Programming:* news progmg 9 hrs wkly; *No. News Employees:* 1; *Target Audience:* 35 plus;mature adults; *Adv. Rates:* 18; 18; 18; 18
Leslie Lanser, President
Troy West, Station Manager
Chad Millard, General Sales Mgr
Jason Cramer, Programming Director
Bradley Lanser, Executive Vice President

Minnesota

Ada

KRJB
09-01-1985; 106.5 MHz FM; 100 kw; 452 ft.; N47 18 41 W96 31 13
312 West Main Street, Ada, MN 56510 US
(218) 784-2844; *Fax:* (218) 784-3749
www.krjbradio.com
krjbada@loretel.net
License: Ada, Norman County, MN held by R & J Broadcasting.
Regional Network: MNN
Arbitron Metro Market: Fargo-Moorhead; *Format:* Country; *Adv. Rates:* 18; 18; 17; 10
Jim Birkemeyer, General Manager
Woody Roux, Programming Director
Heather Krogstadt, Traffic Manager

Aitkin

KKIN
06-01-1961; 930 kHz AM; *Hrs Open:* 24; 2.5 kw-D, ND1; 0.36 kw-N, ND1; N46 32 26 W93 39 22
Mailing Address: PO Box 140, Aitkin, MN 56431 US
Second Address: 305 W. Washington St., Brainerd, MN 56401
(218) 828-9994; *Fax:* (218) 927-4090
www.kkinradio.com
kkinradio@embarqmail.com
License: Aitkin, MN held by Red Rock Radio Corp.
Group Owner: Red Rock Radio Corp.; (acq 9-1-2006; grpsl)
Nat'l Network: Jones Radio Networks
Arbitron Metro Market: Saint Cloud, MN; *Format:* Sports; *No. News Employees:* 1; *Target Audience:* General.; *Adv. Rates:* 9.50; 9.50; 9.50; 9.50
Tom Martin, Station Manager
Pete Vukelich, Sports Dir./News Dir.

KKIN-FM
01-03-1972; 94.3 MHz FM; *Hrs Open:* 24; 14 kw; 436 ft.; N46 41 18 W93 35 58
Mailing Address: PO Box 140, Aitkin, MN 56431 US
Second Address: 305 W. Washington St., Brainerd, MN 56401
(218) 828-9994; *Fax:* (218) 927-4090
www.kkinradio.com
kkinradio@embarqmail.com
License: Aitkin, Aitkin County, MN held by Red Rock Radio Corp.
Group Owner: Red Rock Radio Corp.
Arbitron Metro Market: Duluth, MN; *Format:* Country; *Hrs. of News Programming:* news progmg 5 hrs wkly; *No. News Employees:* 1; *Target Audience:* 35 plus.; *Adv. Rates:* Same as AM
Tom Martin, Station Manager
Pete Vukelich, Sports Dir./News Dir.

Albany

KASM
11-20-1950; 1150 kHz AM; 2.1 kw-D, ND1; 0.021 kw-N, ND1; N45 37 53 W94 36 0
35223 238th Avenue, Albany, MN 56307 US
(320) 845-2184; *Fax:* (320) 845-2187
www.kasmwqpm.com
License: Albany, MN held by Starcom LLC
Regional Reps: Hyett/Ramsland.
Arbitron Metro Market: Albany, MN; *Format:* Country, News, 66 *Special Programming:* Oldies, Ger mus 2 hrs, farm 6 hrs wkly; *Hrs. of News Programming:* news progmg 2 hrs wkly; *No. News Employees:* 1 *TargetAudience:* 36 plus.
Randy Rothstein, General Manager
Mark Sprint, Programming Director

KDDG
10-01-1993; 105.5 MHz FM; 6 kw; 328 ft.; N45 37 53 W94 36 0
35223 238th Avenue, Albany, MN 56307 US
(320) 845-2184; *Fax:* (320) 845-2187
kddg1150fm@albanytel.com
License: Albany, Stearns County, MN held by Starcom LLC
Arbitron Metro Market: St. Cloud, MN; *Format:* Adult Contemp
Randy Rothstein, Station Manager
Mark Sprint, Programming Director

Albert Lea

KATE
01-01-1986; 1450 kHz AM; *Hrs Open:* 24; 1 kw-U, ND1; N43 38 0 W93 22 15
1633 W. Main St., Albert Lea, MN 56007 US
(507) 373-2338; *Fax:* (507) 373-4736
www.myalbertlea.com
949thebreeze@digity.me
License: Albert Lea, MN held by Digity 3E License, LLC.
Group Owner: Digity, LLC
Arbitron Metro Market: Albert Lea, MN; *Format:* News/Talk; *Target Audience:* 12 plus; general; *Adv. Rates:* 22; 22; 22; 22
Paul Shea, Programming Director
Pete Leisen, News Director
Darrel Amundson, Production Dir.

KCPI
07-01-1974; 94.9 MHz FM; *Hrs Open:* 24; 5 kw; 295 ft.; N43 38 0 W93 22 15
1633 W. Main St., Albert Lea, MN 56007 US
(507) 373-2338
www.myalbertlea.com
949thebreeze@digity.me
License: Albert Lea, Freeborn County, MN held by Digity 3E License, LLC.
Group Owner: Digity, LLC
Nat'l Network: ABC
Arbitron Metro Market: Albert Lea, MN; *Format:* Adult Contemp; *Hrs. of News Programming:* news progmg 12 hrs wkly; *No. News Employees:* 1; *Target Audience:* 25-54.; *Adv. Rates:* 16; 16; 16; 16
Paul Shea, Programming Director
Pete Leisen, News Director
Darrel Amundson, Production Dir.

KQPR
08-14-1990; 96.1 MHz FM; *Hrs Open:* 24; 25 kw; 308 ft.; N43 36 58 W93 12 47 109
US
(507) 373-9401; *Fax:* (507) 373-9045
www.power96rocker.com
kqpr@power96rocker.com
License: Albert Lea, Freeborn County, MN held by Hometown Broadcasting Inc.
Nat'l Network: Jones Radio Networks; *Regional Network:* Linder Farm; *Nat'l Reps:* Hyett/Ramsland
Arbitron Metro Market: Albert Lea-Austin; *Format:* Light Rock; *No. News Employees:* 1; *Target Audience:* General.
Greg Jensen, CEO
Anna Rahn, General Manager
Ron Hunter, Programming Director
Jim Pilgrim, News Director
Marv Olson, Chief Engineer
Stephen Helleksen, Information Technology
Kristi Swalve, Traffic Manager

Alexandria

***KBHG**
89.5 MHz FM; kw
515 Pike Street East, Alexandria, MN 56360 US
(320) 859-3000; *Fax:* (320) 859-3010
david@praisefm.org
License: Alexandria, Douglas County, MN held by Christian Heritage Broadcasting Inc.
Arbitron Metro Market: Alexandria, MN; *Format:* Christian
David McIver, General Manager

KULO
01-01-1976; 94.3 MHz FM; *Hrs Open:* 24; 12 kw; 466 ft.; N45 56 25 W95 28 3
Mailing Address: PO Box 1024, 105 2nd Ave Ne, Glenwood, MN 56334 US
Second Address: P.O. Box 1024, Alexandria, MN 56308
(320) 762-2154; *Fax:* (320) 762-2156
cool943.com
100.7@kikvfm.com
License: Alexandria, Douglas County, MN held by BDI Broadcasting Inc.
Group Owner: Omni Broadcasting Co.; (acq 12-31-2001; $700,000).
Nat'l Network: ABC
Format: Oldies; *Hrs. of News Programming:* news progmg 12 hrs wkly; *No. News Employees:* 1; *Target Audience:* 35-64; adults
Mary Campbell, CFO

KXRZ
04-02-1984; 99.3 MHz FM; *Hrs Open:* 24; 6 kw; Ant 285 ft; N45 52 47 W95 18 35
1312 Broadway, Alexandria, MN 56308
(320) 763-3131
www.voiceofalexandria.com/z99
thefolks@kxra.com
License: Alexandria, Douglas County, MN held by Paradis Broadcasting of Alexandria Inc.
Group Owner: Paradis Broadcasting of Alexandria Inc.; acq 5-1-00; $900,000).
Nat'l Network: Dial Global Hot AC *Regional Reps:* Midwest Radio.
Population Served: 40,000 *Special Programming:* Relg 3 hrs wkly; *Hrs. of News Programming:* news progmg 5 hrs wkly; *No. News Employees:* 1; *Target Audience:* 18-40; young adults; *Adv. Rates:* 20; 18; 20; 10.

KXRA
07-27-1949; 1490 kHz AM; *Hrs Open:* 24; 1 kw-U; N45 52 05 W95 21 47
1312 Broadway, Alexandria, MN 56308
(320) 763-3131
www.voiceofalexandria.com/kxra
thefolks@kxra.com
License: Alexandria, Douglas County, MN held by Paradis Broadcasting of Alexandria Inc.
Group Owner: Paradis Broadcasting of Alexandria Inc.; (acq 10-1-88).
Nat'l Network: NBC Radio; *Regional Network:* MNN *Regional Reps:* Midwest Radio.
Population Served: 40,000 *Special Programming:* Farm 5 hrs, relg 2 hrs wkly; *Hrs. of News Programming:* news progmg 25 hrs wkly; *No. News Employees:* 1; *Target Audience:* 35-64.; *Adv. Rates:* 20; 18; 15; 12

KXRA-FM
05-01-1968; 92.3 MHz FM; *Hrs Open:* 24; 13.5 kw; 446 ft; N45 52 30 W95 21 30
1312 Broadway, Alexandria, MN 56308
(320) 763-3131
www.voiceofalexandria.com
License: Alexandria, Douglas County, MN
Group Owner: Paradis Broadcasting of Alexandria Inc.
Population Served: 50,000 *Hrs. of News Programming:* news progmg 5 hrs wkly; *No. News Employees:* 1; *Target Audience:* 25-45; young adults, dual income households; *Adv. Rates:* 20; 18; 20; 15

Anoka

KQQL
08-01-1968; 107.9 MHz FM; 96 kw; 1093 ft.; N45 20 20 W93 23 27
60 South 6th Street, Suite 930, Minneapolis, MN 55402 US
(952) 417-3000; *Fax:* (952) 417-3001
www.kool108.com
info@kqql.com

License: Anoka, Anoka County, MN held by AMFM Broadcasting Licenses LLC.
Group Owner: iHeartMedia; (acq 8-30-2000; grpsl).
Nat'l Reps: Clear Channel
Arbitron Metro Market: Minneapolis-St. Paul; *Format:* Oldies; *Target Audience:* 25-54.
Jeff Tyler, Market President
Greg Alexander, Vice President of Sales
Ellie Tungseth, Promotions Director

Appleton

*KRSU
02-01-1997; 88.5 MHz FM; 100 kw; 984 ft; N45 10 03 W96 00 02
480 Cedar Street, Saint Paul, MN 55101
(651) 290-1500
License: Appleton, Swift County, MN held by Minnesota Public Radio.

William Kling, CEO
Steve Griffith, Operations Dir
Jon Gossett, General Sales Mgr
Eric Nycklemoe, Programming Director
Bill Wareham, News Director
Mark Alfuth, CFO
Dianne Krizan, Development Director
Deborah Brown, DevelopmentDirector
Thomas Kigin, Executive Vice President

*KNCM
10-25-1989; 91.3 MHz FM; *Hrs Open:* 24; 75 kw; 1,158 ft; N45 10 03 W96 00 02 *Rebroadcasts:* Rebroadcast of KSJN(FM) Minneapolis-St. Paul
P.O. Box 7011, Collegeville, MN 56231
info@mpr.org
License: Appleton, Swift County, MN held by Minnesota Public Radio Inc.
Nat'l Network: NPR; PRI; *Regional Network:* Minn. Pub. Radio

Chris Cross, Regional Network Manager
Mark Steil, Reporter

Atwater

KKLN
11-26-1988; 94.1 MHz FM; *Hrs Open:* 24; 6 kw; 328 ft.; N45 4 24 W94 45 19
1605 South 1st Street, Wilmar, MN 56201 US
(320) 235-1194; *Fax:* (320) 235-6894
www.kkln.com
info@kkln.com
License: Atwater, Kandiyohi County, MN held by Flagship Broadcasting.
Arbitron Metro Market: Saint Cloud, MN; *Format:* Rock/AOR
Special Programming: NASCAR Sprint Cup Races; *No. News Employees:* 1; *Target Audience:* General.; *Adv. Rates:* 20; 15; 15; 10
John Jennings, President
Nate Thomas, Operations Dir
Melanie Eckhart, News Director
Justin Klinghagen, Operating Partner

Austin

KAUS
05-30-1948; 1480 kHz AM; *Hrs Open:* 24; 1 kw-D, DA2; 1 kw-N, DA2; N43 37 20 W92 59 26
18431 State Hwy 105, Austin, MN 55912 US
(507) 437-7666
www.myaustinminnesota.com
rmithuen@digity.me
License: Austin, MN held by Digity 3E License, LLC
Group Owner: Digity, LLC
Nat'l Network: NBC; *Regional Network:* MNN
Arbitron Metro Market: Austin, MN; *Format:* News/Talk; *No. News Employees:* 2; *Target Audience:* 25-54.
Scott Muller, Operations Mgr
Bob Mithuen, General Manager
Jason Brandt, News Director
Clint Narramore, Sports

KAUS-FM
01-01-1987; 99.9 MHz FM; *Hrs Open:* 24; 100 kw; 928 ft.; N43 37 42 W93 9 12
18431 State Hwy 105, Austin, MN 55912 US
(507) 434-3699
www.kaus.itmwpb.com
rmithuen@digity.me
License: Austin, Mower County, MN held by Digity 3E License, LLC
Group Owner: Digity, LLC
Arbitron Metro Market: Austin, MN; *Format:* Country; *Hrs. of News Programming:* news progmg 12 hrs wkly; *No. News Employees:* 2; *Target Audience:* 25-54.
Bob Mithuen, General Manager
Scott Fuller, Programming Director

*KMSK
01-12-1981; 91.3 MHz FM; *Hrs Open:* 24; 0.135 kw; 194 ft.; N43 40 39 W93 0 4 *Rebroadcasts:* Rebroadcasts KMSU(FM) Mankato 100%
Msu 153, P. O. Box 8400, Mankato, MN 56002 US
(507) 389-5678; *Fax:* (507) 389-1705
www.kmsu.org
info@kmsu.org
License: Austin, Mower County, MN held by Mankato State University.
Nat'l Network: NPR
Format: Public Affairs *Special Programming:* Drama 3 hrs, folk/ethnic 5 hrs, new age 5 hrs wkly; *Hrs. of News Programming:* news progmg 50 hrs wkly; *No. News Employees:* 1; *Target Audience:* General; upscale,educated
Jim Gullickson, General Manager

KQAQ
04-16-1960; 970 kHz AM; *Hrs Open:* 5 AM-midnight; 5 kw-D, DA2; 0.5 kw-N, DA2; N43 42 27 W92 56 45
109 East Clark Street, P.O. Box 1106, Albert Lea, MN 56607 US
(507) 373-9600; *Fax:* (507) 373-9045
www.classiccountrylegends.com
License: Austin, MN held by Hometown Broadcasting Inc.
Nat'l Network: Fox News Radio; Motor Racing Net; Jones Radio Networks; *Regional Network:* Linder Farm
Format: Country
Anna Rahn, General Manager

*KNSE
90.1 MHz FM; *Hrs Open:* summer 2003; 6 kw; 318 ft.; N43 38 27 W93 8 51
45 East Seventh Street, Saint Paul, MN 55101 US
(651) 290-1500; *Fax:* (651) 290-1224
www.mpr.org
newsroom@mpr.org
License: Austin, Mower County, MN held by Minnesota Public Radio.
Arbitron Metro Market: Mason City, IA; *Format:* News
Chuck Lantz, Chairman
Chris Cross, Regional Network Manager
Dennis Brooks, Account Executive

Babbitt

KAOD
01-01-1999; 106.7 MHz FM; 33 kw; 430 ft.; N47 41 18 W91 54 21 *Rebroadcasts:* Rebroadcast of KQDS-FM Duluth 100%
501 Lake Ave. S., Suite 200, Duluth, MN 55802 US
(218) 728-9500
www.95kqds.com
License: Babbitt, St. Louis County, MN held by Red Rock Radio Corp.
Group Owner: Red Rock Radio Corp.; acq 1-10-00; grpsl).
Arbitron Metro Market: Duluth, MN; *Format:* Classic Rock
Shawn Skramstad, General Manager
Jim Payne, General Sales Mgr

Bagley

KKCQ-FM
10-01-1997; 96.7 MHz FM; *Hrs Open:* 24; 25 kw; 328 ft.; N47 36 12 W95 32 40
P.O. Box 606, Fosston, NM 56542 US
(218) 435-1071; *Fax:* (218) 435-1480
www.kkcqradio.com
License: Bagley, Clearwater County, MN held by Pine to Prairie Broadcasting Inc.
Nat'l Network: ABC
Arbitron Metro Market: Grand Forks, ND; *Format:* Country
Special Programming: Farm 10 hrs, relg 9 hrs wkly; *No. News Employees:* 1; *Adv. Rates:* 14; 11; 12.50; 9
Phil Ehlke, General Manager
Don Brinkman, General Sales Mgr
Laura Hamilton, News Director
Jim Offerdahl, Chief Engineer
Jamie Nesvold, Music Director
Karen Bingham, Office Manager
Tom Lano, Sports Director

Barnesville

KBVB
01-02-1976; 95.1 MHz FM; *Hrs Open:* 24; 100 kw; 384 ft.; N46 49 9 W96 45 56
Mailing Address: 1020 25th Street South, Fargo, ND 58108 US
Second Address: Box 10097, Fargo, ND 58106
(701) 237-5346; *Fax:* (701) 237-0980
www.bob95fm.com
studio@bob95fm.com
License: Barnesville, Clay County, MN held by Radio Fargo-Moorhead Inc.
Group Owner: Radio Fargo-Moorhead Inc.
Nat'l Reps: Eastman Radio
Arbitron Metro Market: Fargo-Moorhead, ND-MN; *Format:* Country; *Target Audience:* Adults 18 - 54
Nancy Odney, COO
John Austin, Operations Dir

Baxter

WWWI
08-29-1987; 1270 kHz AM; *Hrs Open:* 24; 5 kw-D, DAN; 5 kw-N, DAN; N46 17 55 W94 16 42
305 West Washington St, PO Box 783, Brainerd, MN 56401 US
(218) 828-9994; *Fax:* (218) 828-8327
www.3wiradio.com
talk@3wiradio.com
License: Baxter, MN held by Tower Broadcasting Corp.
Nat'l Network: CBS
Arbitron Metro Market: Baxter, MN; *Format:* News, News/Talk, 86; *Target Audience:* 25 plus.; *Adv. Rates:* 12; 12; 12; 12
James Pryor, President
Lon Schmidt, News Director
Mary Pryor, Office Manager/Co-Owner
Steve Foy, Sales Executive
Stephanie Palmer, Office Assistant

Bemidji

KBHP
08-03-1972; 101.1 MHz FM; *Hrs Open:* 24; 100 kw; 522 ft.; N47 22 11 W94 52 54
P.O. Box 1656, Bemidji, MN 56619 US
(218) 444-1500; *Fax:* (218) 759-0345
www.kb101fm.com
phanson@pbbroadcasting.com
License: Bemidji, Beltrami County, MN held by Paul Bunyan Broadcasting Co.
Group Owner: Omni Broadcasting Co.
Nat'l Network: ABC; *Regional Network:* MNN
Arbitron Metro Market: Bemidji, MN; *Format:* Country; *Hrs. of News Programming:* news progmg 12 hrs wkly; *No. News Employees:* 1; *Target Audience:* 25-54.
Mary Campbell, CFO
Todd Haugen, Operations Dir
Lou Buron, General Manager
Peggy Hanson, General Sales Mgr
Mardy Karger, News Director
Mark Anderson, Chief Engineer

*KBSB
01-19-1970; 89.7 MHz FM; *Hrs Open:* 24; 0.12 kw horiz; 125 ft.; N47 29 0 W94 52 27
1500 Birchmont Dr, Bemidji, MN 56601 US
(218) 755-4120; *Fax:* (218) 755-4119
www.fm90.org
License: Bemidji, Beltrami County, MN held by Bemidji State University.
Format: Contemporary Hits/Top 40 *Special Programming:* American Indian 3 hrs, folk 3 hrs wkly; *Target Audience:* 12-28; teens to young adults; *Adv. Rates:* 3; 3; 3; 3
Nick Stroltman, Station Manager

KBUN
01-01-1946; 1450 kHz AM; *Hrs Open:* 24
Mailing Address: P.O. Box 1656, Bemidji, MN 56619 US
Second Address: 502 Beltrami Ave. N.W., Bemidji, MN 56601
(218) 444-1500; *Fax:* (218) 751-8091
phanson@pbbroadcasting.com
License: Bemidji, MN held by Paul Bunyan Broadcasting Co.
Group Owner: Omni Broadcasting Co.; (acq 6-22-89;
Nat'l Network: ESPN Radio; Westwood One; *Regional Network:* MNN
Format: Sports, Talk; *Hrs. of News Programming:* news progmg 12 hrs wkly; *No. News Employees:* 1; *Target Audience:* 18-54.
Lou Buron, CEO
Peggy Hanson, General Sales Mgr
Mardy Karger, News Director
Mary Campbell, CFO
Kevin Jackson, Operations Manager

*KCRB-FM
12-22-1982; 88.5 MHz FM; *Hrs Open:* 24; 83 kw; 988 ft.; N47 42 21 W94 29 9 *Rebroadcasts:* Rebroadcast of KSJN(FM) Minneapolis-St. Paul

Minnesota Public Radio, 480 Cedar Street, Saint Paul, MN 55101 US
(651) 290-1500; *Fax:* (651) 290-1243
www.mpr.org
info@mpr.org
License: Bemidji, Beltrami County, MN held by Minnesota Public Radio Inc.
Nat'l Network: PRI; NPR; *Regional Network:* Minn. Pub. Radio
Arbitron Metro Market: St. Paul, MN; *Format:* Talk; *Hrs. of News Programming:* news progmg 25 hrs wkly; *No. News Employees:* 1
Ian R Friendly, Chairman
Jon MacTaggart, President
Randy Hogan, Vice Chair
Bradbury H. Anderson, Secretary

KKBJ
10-31-1977; 1360 kHz AM; *Hrs Open:* 24; 5 kw-D, DAN; 2.5 kw-N, DAN; N47 26 32 W94 51 57
2115 Washington Avenue, Bemidji, MN 56601 US
(218) 751-7777; *Fax:* (218) 759-0658
www.kkbj.com
License: Bemidji, MN held by R.P. Broadcasting Corp.
Nat'l Network: AP Radio; *Wire Services:* AP
Arbitron Metro Market: Fargo, ND; *Format:* Talk; *Hrs. of News Programming:* news progmg 15 hrs wkly; *No. News Employees:* 1; *Target Audience:* 25-54.
Troy Paskvan, Owner
Roger Paskvan, President
Daniel Voss, General Manager
Mark Ricci, Programming Director
Rocky Coffin, Religion Ed

KKBJ-FM
08-08-1983; 103.7 MHz FM; *Hrs Open:* 24; 100 kw; 479 ft.; N47 33 21 W94 48 4
3516 Mill St., Bemidji, MN 56601 US
(218)751-7777; *Fax:* (218) 759-0658
www.kkbj.com
License: Bemidji, Beltrami County, MN held by R.P. Broadcasting Corp.
Wire Services: AP
Arbitron Metro Market: Fargo, ND; *Format:* Adult Contemp; *Hrs. of News Programming:* news progmg 20 hrs wkly; *No. News Employees:* 1; *Target Audience:* 18-49; 40% male & 60% female; *Adv. Rates:* 21; 21; 21; 18
Daniel Voss, General Sales Mgr
Tracy Bailey, Promotions Manager

KKZY
05-07-1999; 95.5 MHz FM; *Hrs Open:* 24; 100 kw; 423 ft.; N47 22 12 W94 52 54
502 Beltrami Avenue N.W., Bemidji, MN 56601 US
(218) 444-4955
www.kzyfm955.com
License: Bemidji, Beltrami County, MN held by BG Broadcasting Inc.
Group Owner: Omni Broadcasting Co.; (acq 6-22-98)
Nat'l Network: ABC
Arbitron Metro Market: Fargo, MD; *Format:* Adult Contemp; *Hrs. of News Programming:* news progmg 12 hrs wkly; *No. News Employees:* 1; *Target Audience:* 25-54; adults
Lou Buron, CEO
Peggy Hanson, General Sales Mgr
Mardy Karger, News Director
Mary Campbell, CFO

***KNBJ**
07-01-1994; 91.3 MHz FM; *Hrs Open:* 24; 65 kw; 988 ft.; N47 42 21 W94 29 9 *Rebroadcasts:* Rebroadcasts KNOW-FM Minneapolis-St. Paul 90%
P.O. Box 578, Bemidji, MN 56619 US
(218) 751-8864; *Fax:* (218) 751-8640
minnesota.publicradio.org/radio/stations/knbjkerb/
License: Bemidji, Beltrami County, MN held by Minnesota Public Radio.
Nat'l Network: PRI; NPR; *Regional Network:* Minn. Pub. Radio
Format: News
John McTaggard, Chairman
William Kling, General Manager
Jim McGuinn, Station Manager
Timothy Roesler, General Manager of Classical Music
Chris Worthington, News Director
Kristi Booth, Regional Network Director
Barb Treat, AccountExecutive

Benson

KBMO
12-01-1956; 1290 kHz AM; *Hrs Open:* 24
105 13th Street, N, Benson, MN 56215 US
(320) 843-3290; *Fax:* (320) 843-3955
License: Benson, MN held by Quest Broadcasting Inc.
Nat'l Network: Jones Radio Networks; *Regional Network:* MNN
Arbitron Metro Market: Benson, MN; *Format:* Contemporary Hits/Top 40 *Special Programming:* Farm 10 hrs wkly; *Hrs. of News Programming:* news progmg 25 hrs wkly; *No. News Employees:* 1; *Target Audience:* 40plus.
John Jennings, Co-Owner
Justin Klinghagen, Co-Owner
Jolen Moreland, Traffic/Office Manager
Maynard Meyer, Chief Engineer

KSCR-FM
04-26-1968; 93.5 MHz FM; *Hrs Open:* 24; 25 kw; 328 ft.; N45 19 6 W95 33 48
105 13th Street, N., Benson, MN 56215 US
(320) 843-3290; *Fax:* (320) 843-3955
License: Benson, Swift County, MN held by Quest Broadcasting Inc.
Arbitron Metro Market: Benson, MN; *Format:* Contemporary Hits/Top 40, Adult Contemp; *Target Audience:* 18-54.
Sabrina Pack, General Manager
Ted Tucker, Programming Director

Blackduck

WBJI
01-01-1991; 98.3 MHz FM; *Hrs Open:* 24; 100 kw; 479 ft.; N47 33 21 W94 48 4
2115 Washington Avenue South, Bemidji, MN 56601 US
(218) 751-7777
www.wbji.com
License: Blackduck, Beltrami County, MN held by R.P. Broadcasting Inc.
Nat'l Network: ABC
Arbitron Metro Market: Bemidji, MN; *Format:* Sports *Special Programming:* NASCAR 4 hrs wkly; *Hrs. of News Programming:* news progmg 8 hrs wkly; *No. News Employees:* 1; *Target Audience:* 35-64; adults with aboveaverage income
Roger Paskvan, CEO
Marla Weckman, President
Dan Voss, General Manager
Jeff Halverson, General Sales Mgr
Mark Ricci, Programming Director
Tracy Bailey, Promotions Manager
Brian Schultz, News Director
Tracy Bailey, TrafficManager
Marla Weckman, Business Manager

WMIS-FM
01-01-2007; 92.1 MHz FM; 36 kw; 577 ft.; N47 33 26 W94 48 4
2115 Washington Avenue South, Bemidji, MN 56601 US
(218) 751-7777
www.wmisfm.com
License: Blackduck, Beltrami County, MN held by Paskvan Media Inc.
Arbitron Metro Market: Blackduck, MN; *Format:* Rock/AOR
Troy Paskvan, President

WQXJ
01-01-2008; 104.5 MHz FM; 8.5 kw; 486 ft.; N47 33 26 W94 48 4
US
(218) 444-1500
www.trueoldies1045.com
License: Blackduck, Beltrami County, MN held by BG Broadcasting Inc.
Group Owner: Omni Broadcasting Co.
Nat'l Network: ABC
Arbitron Metro Market: Blackduck, MN; *Format:* Oldies
Mary Campbell, CFO
Lou Buron, General Manager
Peggy Hanson, General Sales Mgr
Mardy Karger, News Director

***WYNJ**
89.5 MHz FM; 0.8 kw; 328 ft.; N47 44 21 W94 41 10
Mailing Address: Life Talk Radio, P.O. Box 500, Simi Valley, CA 93062 US
Second Address: 101 W. Cochran Street, Simi Valley, CA 93065
(800) 775-4673
www.lifetalk.net
License: Blackduck, Beltrami County, MN held by We Have This Hope Christian Radio Inc.
Arbitron Metro Market: Blackduck, MN; *Format:* Christian
Vern Erickson, President
John Geli, Program Manager
Marcelo Vallado, Chief Engineer
Debby Wade, Administration/Station Relations Director
Deloris Trujillo, HR Director

Blooming Prairie

KOWZ-FM
09-01-1995; 100.9 MHz FM; 100 kw; 620 ft.; N44 2 44 W93 23 2
255 Cedardale Dr., Owatonna, MN 55060 US
(507) 444-9224; *Fax:* (507) 444-9080
www.kowzfm.com
kowz@kowzonline.com
License: Blooming Prairie, Steele County, MN held by Blooming Prairie Farm Radio Inc.
Group Owner: Linder Broadcasting Group
Format: Adult Contemp
Jeff Seaton, General Manager
Craig Stevens, Programs Director

Blue Earth

KBEW
08-29-1963; 1560 kHz AM; 1 kw-D; N43 38 48 W95 33 48
705 Leland Parkway, Blue Earth, MN 55987
(507) 526-2181; *Fax:* (507) 526-7468
kbew@bevcomm.net
License: Blue Earth, Faribault County, MN held by KBEW Radio Inc.
Group Owner: The Result Radio Group; (acq 2-1-81)
Nat'l Network: CBS; *Regional Network:* Linder Farm; *Nat'l Reps:* Katz Radio; *Wire Services:* AP
Population Served: 50,000 *Special Programming:* Farm 15 hrs wkly; *Hrs. of News Programming:* news progmg 17 hrs wkly; *No. News Employees:* 1; *Target Audience:* Farming community.; *Adv. Rates:* 15.30; 13.50;15.30; 13.50
Jerry Papenfuss, President
Kevin Benson, Station Manager
Randy Allen, Programming Director
Norm Hall, News Director
Jeff Vriesen, Chief Engineer

KBEW-FM
01-01-1993; 98.1 MHz FM; *Hrs Open:* 24; 25 kw; 328 ft; N43 38 44 W94 05 33
Box 278, Blue Earth, MN 55987
(507) 526-2181; *Fax:* (507) 526-7468
kbew@bevcomm.net
License: Blue Earth, Faribault County, MN held by KBEW Radio Inc.
Group Owner: The Result Radio Group
Regional Network: Linder Farm; *Nat'l Reps:* Katz Radio; *Wire Services:* AP
Population Served: 50,000 *Hrs. of News Programming:* news progmg 3 hrs wkly; *No. News Employees:* 1; *Target Audience:* 18-54.; *Adv. Rates:* Same as AM
Kevin Benson, General Manager
Randy Allen, Programming Director
Norm Hall, News Director
Jeff Vriesen, Chief Engineer

***KJLY**
11-01-1983; 104.5 MHz FM; 50 kw; 492 ft.; N43 54 38 W94 3 9
Mailing Address: P.O. Box 72, Blue Earth, MN 56013 US
Second Address: 12089 380th Ave., Blue Earth, MN 56013
(507) 526-3233; *Fax:* (507) 526-3235
www.kjly.com
License: Blue Earth, Faribault County, MN held by Minn-Iowa Christian Broadcasting Inc.
Group Owner: Minn-Iowa Christian Broadcasting Inc.
Nat'l Network: Moody; Salem Radio Network
Format: Religious *Special Programming:* Farm 5 hrs, children 4 hrs wkly; *Hrs. of News Programming:* News progmg 21 hrs wkly; *Target Audience:* 45-65.
Matt Dorfner, Executive Director
Jay Rudolph, Operations Dir
Steve Ware, Programming Director
Mark Bohnett, Chief Engineer

Brainerd

***KBPR**
02-01-1988; 90.7 MHz FM; *Hrs Open:* 24; 34 kw; 679 ft.; N46 25 21 W94 27 41 *Rebroadcasts:* Rebroadcast of KSJN(FM) Minneapolis-St. Paul
480 Cedar Street, St. Paul, MN 55101 US
(651) 290-1500; *Fax:* (651) 290-1188
www.mpr.org
License: Brainerd, Crow Wing County, MN held by Minnesota Public Radio.
Nat'l Network: PRI; NPR; *Regional Network:* Minn. Pub. Radio
Format: Talk; *No. News Employees:* 2; *Target Audience:* General.
Jon McTaggart, President
David W. Kansas, Operations Officer

KUAL-FM
06-03-1994; 103.5 MHz FM; 20 kw; 279 ft.; N46 19 56 W94 10 26
Mailing Address: P.O. Box 746, Brainerd, MN 56401 US
Second Address: 13225 Dogwood Drive South, Baxter, MN 56425
(218) 828-7625; (218) 822-7655; *Fax:* (218) 828-1119
www.cool1035.com
License: Brainerd, Crow Wing County, MN
Group Owner: Omni Broadcasting Co.
Nat'l Network: ABC
Arbitron Metro Market: Brainerd, MN; *Format:* Oldies; *Hrs. of News Programming:* news progmg 12 hrs wkly; *No. News Employees:* 1; *Target Audience:* 25-54; adults
Tess Taylor, Operations Dir
Billy Holiday, Programming Director

KLIZ
08-06-1946; 1380 kHz AM; *Hrs Open:* 24; 5 kw-D, DAN; 5 kw-N, DAN; N46 19 55 W94 10 26
Mailing Address: 602 Laurel Street, Brainerd, MN 56401 US
Second Address: 13225 Dogwood Dr., Baxter, MN 56425-8613
(218) 828-1244; *Fax:* (218) 828-1119
www.kliz.com
License: Brainerd, MN held by BL Broadcasting Inc.
Group Owner: Omni Broadcasting Co.; (acq 4-1-2004; grpsl).
Nat'l Network: Sporting News Radio Network
Arbitron Metro Market: Saint Cloud, MN; *Format:* Sports, Talk; *Hrs. of News Programming:* news progmg 12 hrs wkly; *No. News Employees:* 1; *Target Audience:* 25-64; adults
Lou Buron, CEO
G. Michael Boen, General Manager
Jeff Hilborn, General Sales Mgr
Tess Taylor, News Director
Mary Campbell, CFO
Danny Wild

KLIZ-FM
05-23-1960; 107.5 MHz FM; 100 kw; 351 ft.; N46 19 56 W94 10 26
Mailing Address: P.O. Box 746, Brainerd, MN 56401 US
Second Address: 13225 Dogwood Dr., Baxter, MN 56425
(218) 828-1244; *Fax:* (218) 828-1119
License: Brainerd, Crow Wing County, MN
Group Owner: Omni Broadcasting Co.
Nat'l Network: ABC; *Regional Network:* Minn. News Net.
Arbitron Metro Market: Saint Cloud, MN; *Format:* Classic Rock; *Hrs. of News Programming:* news progmg 12 hrs wkly; *No. News Employees:* 1; *Target Audience:* 18-54; adults
Brad Hollstrom, Operations Dir
Mike Boen, General Manager
Janice Degner, General Sales Mgr
Kelly Klaas, Farm Director

KVBR
05-16-1964; 1340 kHz AM; *Hrs Open:* 24; 1 kw-U, ND1; N46 20 51 W94 10 52
Mailing Address: P.O. Box 980, Brainerd, MN 56401 US
Second Address: 13225 Dogwood Dr., Baxter, MN 56425-8613
(218) 828-1244; *Fax:* (218) 828-1119
brainerdradio.net
production@brainerd.net
License: Brainerd, MN held by BL Broadcasting Inc.
Group Owner: Omni Broadcasting Co.; (acq 4-1-2004; grpsl).
Nat'l Network: ABC; USA; Westwood One; *Regional Network:* MNN
Arbitron Metro Market: Brainerd, MN; *Format:* Sports; *Hrs. of News Programming:* news progmg 12 hrs wkly; *No. News Employees:* 1; *Target Audience:* 25-54; adults
Lou Buron, CEO
G. Michael Boen, General Manager
Jeff Hilborn, General Sales Mgr
Tess Taylor, News Director
Mary Campbell, CFO
Danny Wild, Operations Director

WJJY-FM
07-21-1978; 106.7 MHz FM; *Hrs Open:* 24; 100 kw; 558 ft.; N46 26 34 W94 22 55
Mailing Address: P.O. Box 746, Brainerd, MN 56401 US
Second Address: 13225 Dogwood Dr., Baxter, MN 56425-8613
(218) 828-1119; *Fax:* (218) 828-1119
brainerdradio.net
License: Brainerd, Crow Wing County, MN held by BL Broadcasting Inc.
Group Owner: Omni Broadcasting Co.; (acq 3-2-94; $900,000;
Nat'l Network: ABC
Format: Adult Contemp; *Hrs. of News Programming:* news progmg 20 hrs wkly; *No. News Employees:* 1; *Target Audience:* 25-54; adults
Lou Buron, CEO
Michael Boen, General Manager
Jeff Hillborn, General Sales Mgr
Tess Taylor, News Director
Mary Campbell, CFO
Mark Hegstrom, Operations Manager

***KBPN**
07-01-2003; 88.3 MHz FM; *Hrs Open:* 24; 5 kw; 669 ft.; N46 25 21 W94 27 41
Mailing Address: P.O. Box 578, Bemidji, MN 56619 US
Second Address: Minnesota Public Radio, 45 E. 7th St., Saint Paul, MN 55101
(218) 829-1072; *Fax:* (218) 751-8640
www.mpr.org
kbooth@mpr.org
License: Brainerd, Crow Wing County, MN held by Minnesota Public Radio.
Arbitron Metro Market: Bemidji, MN; *Format:* News
Kristi Booth, Station Manager
Barb Treat, General Sales Mgr
Tim Post, News Director
Kristi Booth, Regional Network Director
Tom Robertson, Reporter
Natalie Grosfield, Regional Office Coordinator
Barb Treat, Account Executive
Tom Robertson, Reporter

Breckenridge

KBMW
08-28-1948; 1450 kHz AM
605 Dakota Avenue, Wahpeton, ND 58075 US
(701) 642-8747; *Fax:* (701) 642-9501
www.kbmwam.com
studio@kbmwam.com
License: Breckenridge, MN held by Radio Fargo-Moorhead Inc.
Group Owner: Radio Fargo-Moorhead
Format: Country; *Hrs. of News Programming:* news progmg 18 hrs wkly; *No. News Employees:* 1; *Target Audience:* 25-54; general
Bill Dadlow, Station Manager

KQWB-FM
02-17-1970; 105.1 MHz FM; *Hrs Open:* Monday- Friday 8-5pm; 100 kw; 659 ft.; N46 32 46 W96 37 39
Mailing Address: Post Office Box 1248, Minnetonka, MN 55345 US
Second Address: 2720 7th Ave. S., Fargo, ND 58103
(701) 237-4500; *Fax:* (701) 235-9082
www.fm1051.net
License: Breckenridge, Wilkin County, MN held by Radio Fargo-Moorhead Inc.
Group Owner: Radio Fargo-Moorhead Inc.
Nat'l Reps: Christal; *Wire Services:* AP
Arbitron Metro Market: Fargo; *Format:* Variety/Diverse; *Target Audience:* 25-54; skews female
Tom Douglas, CEO
David Benjamin, President
Nancy Odney, General Manager
Jessica Benson, General Sales Mgr

Breezy Point

WZFJ(FM)
06-14-1984; 104.3 MHz FM; *Hrs Open:* 24; 50 kw; 492 ft.; N46 36 13 W94 15 4
P.O. Box 409, Pequot Lakes, MN 56472 US
(866) 568-4422
License: Breezy Point, Crow Wing County, MN held by Lakes Broadcasting Group Inc.
Arbitron Metro Market: Saint Cloud, MN; *Format:* Big Band, Adult Contemp; *Hrs. of News Programming:* news progmg 25 hrs wkly; *No. News Employees:* 2; *Target Audience:* 40 plus.
Bob Bundgaard, CEO
Mike Heuberger, General Manager
Tim Norton, Programming Director
Adam Hannan, Music Director
Diane Anderson, CFO
Carol Bundgaard

Brooklyn Park

KMNQ
04-15-1956; 1470 kHz AM; *Hrs Open:* 24; 5 kw-D, DA2; 5 kw-N, DA2; N45 5 17 W93 22 59
444 Cedar St. Suite 1900, St. Paul, MN 55101 US
(612) 354-3282; *Fax:* (612) 729-5999
www.laraza1400.com
License: Brooklyn Park, MN held by Davidson Media Station KLBP Licensee LLC.
Group Owner: Davidson Media Group LLC; (acq 9-7-2005; $5.2 million with KMNV(AM) Saint Paul)
Nat'l Network: Westwood One; *Regional Network:* MNN
Arbitron Metro Market: Minneapolis-St. Paul, MN
Ricardo Manjarrez, General Manager

Browerville

KXDL
05-15-1992; 99.7 MHz FM; *Hrs Open:* 24; 6 kw; 312 ft.; N46 3 12 W94 50 46
221 Central Avenue, P.O. Box 187, Long Prairie, MN 56347 US
(320) 732-2164; *Fax:* (320) 732-2284
kxdlhotrodradio.com
License: Browerville, Todd County, MN held by Prairie Broadcasting Co.
Regional Reps: O'Malley.
Format: Adult Contemp *Special Programming:* Sports 2 hrs wkly; *Hrs. of News Programming:* News progmg 4 hrs wkly; *Target Audience:* 18-44; female
Gene Sullivan, President
Clif Cline, Operations Dir
Todd Jensen, General Sales Mgr

Buffalo

KRWC
11-16-1971; 1360 kHz AM; *Hrs Open:* 24; 0.5 kw-D, ND1; 0.027 kw-N, ND1; N45 10 0 W93 55 11
Mailing Address: PO Box 267, Buffalo, MN 55313 US
Second Address: 1472 10th St. N.W., Buffalo, MN 55313
(763) 682-4444; *Fax:* (763) 682-3542
www.krwc1360.com
info@krwc1360.com
License: Buffalo, MN held by Donnell Inc.
Nat'l Network: CNN Radio; *Regional Network:* MNN
Arbitron Metro Market: Buffalo, MN; *Format:* Adult Contemp, Country, 60, News/Talk, Oldies, Talk; *Hrs. of News Programming:* news progmg 16 hrs wkly; *No. News Employees:* 1; *Target Audience:* 25 plus.
Joe Carlson, President
Tim Matthews, Operations Dir
John George, Chief Engineer

Buhl

***WIRN**
01-01-1997; 92.5 MHz FM; 26 kw; 558 ft.; N47 29 46 W92 47 5
45 East Seventh St, Saint Paul, MN 55101 US
(651) 291-1500; *Fax:* (651) 222-7795
www.mpr.org
info@mpr.org
License: Buhl, St. Louis County, MN held by Minnesota Public Radio.
Regional Network: Minn. Pub. Radio
Format: News
William Kling, President
Kat Eldred, General Manager
Cynthia Johnson, General Sales Mgr
Bob Kelleher, News Director
Doug Thompson, Engineering Dir

Caledonia

KCLH
11-14-1994; 94.7 MHz FM; *Hrs Open:* 24; 2.1 kW; 561 ft.; N43 41 24 W91 30 9
201 State St, La Crosse, WI 54601 USA
(608) 782-1230; *Fax:* (608) 782-1170
classichits947.com
email@classichits947.com
License: Caledonia, Houston County, MN held by Family Radio Inc.
Group Owner: Mid-West Family Broadcasting; (acq 7-19-01; grpsl).
Wire Services: AP
Arbitron Metro Market: La Crosse, WI; *Format:* Oldies *Special Programming:* Christmas; *Hrs. of News Programming:* news progmg one hr wkly; *No. News Employees:* 4; *Target Audience:* General; 25-54; *Adv. Rates:* 72; 39; 42; 3 0

Cambridge

WRXP
05-05-1973; 105.3 MHz FM; *Hrs Open:* 24; 25 kw; 299 ft.; N45 34 40 W93 12 56 *Rebroadcasts:* Rebroadcasts WGVX(FM) Lakeville
2000 SE Elm St., Minneapolis, MN 55414 US
(612) 617-4000; *Fax:* (612) 676-8292
www.105thevibe.com
License: Cambridge, MN held by Radio License Holdings LLC
Group Owner: Cumulus Media Inc.; (acq 6-12-2007; grpsl)

Nat'l Network: ABC; *Nat'l Reps:* Interep
Arbitron Metro Market: Minneapolis, MN; *Format:* Urban Contemporary
Shelly Wilkes, VP/Market Mgr

Cass Lake

*KOJB
90.1 MHz FM; 18 kw; 459 ft.; N47 20 4 W94 12 43
6530 US Highway 2 NW, Cass Lake, US
(218) 339-5652; *Fax:* (218) 335-7288
www.kojb.org
brad.walhof@llojibwe.org
License: Cass Lake, Cass County, MN held by Leech Lake Band of Ojibwe.
Nat'l Network: NPR
Arbitron Metro Market: Cass Lake, MN; *Format:* Native American
Arthur La Rose, Chairman
Brad Walhof, Station Manager
Marie Rock, Program Manager

Chatfield

KFIL-FM
09-01-1970; 103.1 MHz FM; 3.5 kw; 159.1 meters; N43 43 59 W92 05 08
Mailing Address: Box 370, Preston, MN 55965 US
Second Address: 300 St. Paul St. S.W., Preston, MN 55965
(507) 765-3856; *Fax:* (507) 765-2738
License: Chatfield, Fillmore County, MN held by KFIL Inc.
Group Owner: Cumulus Media Inc.
Arbitron Metro Market: Preston, MN; *Format:* Country
Robin Wade, Programming Director

Cloquet

WKLK
01-31-1950; 1230 kHz AM; *Hrs Open:* 24; 0.72 kw-U, ND1; N46 44 58 W92 25 17
1104 Cloquet Avenue, Cloquet, MN 55720 US
(218) 879-4534; *Fax:* (218) 879-1962
License: Cloquet, MN held by QB Broadcasting Ltd.
Group Owner: Quarnstrom Media Group LLC; (acq 5-12-92; $200,000 with co-located FM;
Format: Contemporary Hits/Top 40; *Hrs. of News Programming:* news progmg 16 hrs wkly; *No. News Employees:* 1; *Target Audience:* Community oriented.
Mark Senarighi, General Manager
Jake Kachinske, Programming Director
Bill Meyes, Chief Engineer

WKLK-FM
04-30-1992; 96.5 MHz FM; *Hrs Open:* 24; 25 kw; 315 ft.; N46 44 58 W92 25 17
1104 Cloquet Avenue, Cloquet, MN 55720 US
(218) 879-4534; *Fax:* (218) 879-1962
www.wklk-fm.com
License: Cloquet, Carlton County, MN held by QB Broadcasting Ltd.
Group Owner: Quarnstrom Media Group LLC
Format: Adult Contemp
Kevin Callahan, Operations Dir
Dan Austin, General Manager
Suzette Anthony, General Sales Mgr
Jay Scott, Programming Director
Jillian Shuhart, Promotions Manager
Mike Carey, News Director

*WSCN
11-17-1975; 100.5 MHz FM; *Hrs Open:* 24; 97 kw; 876 ft.; N46 47 21 W92 6 51
207 West Superior Street, Duluth, MN 55802 US
(218) 722-9411; *Fax:* (218) 720-4900
www.minnesotapublicradio.org
info@minnesotapublicradio.org
License: Cloquet, Carlton County, MN held by Minnesota Public Radio.
Nat'l Network: PRI; NPR; *Regional Network:* Minn. Pub. Radio
Format: News
Patty Mester, Regional Network Manager
Cynthia Johnson, Development Coordinator

*WGZS
89.1 MHz FM; 50 kw; 443 ft.; N46 50 11 W92 42 8
US
(218) 878-7292
www.wgzs89.net
WGZS@fdlrez.com
License: Cloquet, Carlton County, MN held by Fond du Lac Band of Lake Superior Chippewa.
Arbitron Metro Market: Cloquet, MN
Dan Huculak, Operations Dir
Karen Diver, General Manager
Dan Huculak, Station Manager

Cold Spring

KMXK
08-30-1968; 94.9 MHz FM; *Hrs Open:* 24; 50 kw; 492 ft.; N45 23 53 W94 25 15
640 SE Lincoln Avenue, St. Cloud, MN 56301 US
(320) 251-4422; *Fax:* (320) 251-1855
www.mix949.com
License: Cold Spring, Stearns County, MN
Group Owner: Townsquare Media; (acq 5-1-99; grpsl)
Arbitron Metro Market: St. Cloud, MN; *Format:* Adult Contemp; *Target Audience:* 35-54.
David Engberg, General Manager
Steve Lahr, Director of Sales
Chad Taylor, Programming Director

Coleraine

KGPZ
07-01-1995; 96.1 MHz FM; *Hrs Open:* 24; 100 kw; 577 ft.; N47 19 31 W93 16 18
PO Box 9115, Fargo, ND 58106-9115 US
(701) 277-1515
License: Coleraine, Itasca County, MN held by Red Rock Radio Corp.
Group Owner: Red Rock Radio.
Nat'l Network: ABC
Format: Country; *Target Audience:* 35-64.

WDKE
09-12-1996; 96.1 MHz FM; 100 kW; 577 ft; N47 19 31 W93 16 18
807 West 37th St, Hibbing, MN 55746
877-747-3853
961dukefm.com
License: Coleraine, MN held by Midwest Communications Inc.
Group Owner: Midwest Communications Inc.
Nat'l Reps: Christal
Arbitron Metro Market: Hibbing, MN; *Format:* Country; *Target Audience:* 35-54.; *Adv. Rates:* 20; 20; 20; 15
Scott Hanson, Brand Manager

Collegeville

*KNSR
08-29-1988; 88.9 MHz FM; *Hrs Open:* 24; 100 kw; 728 ft.; N45 29 52 W94 32 14
PO Box 711, Collegeville, MN 56321 US
(320) 363-7702; *Fax:* (320) 363-4948
www.minnesotapublicradio.org
License: Collegeville, Stearns County, MN held by Minnesota Public Radio.
Nat'l Network: PRI; NPR; *Regional Network:* Minn. Pub. Radio
Format: News; *No. News Employees:* 2; *Target Audience:* General.
William Kling, President
Kat Eldred, General Manager
Chris Cross, Regional Network Manager

*KSJR-FM
01-21-1967; 90.1 MHz FM; *Hrs Open:* 24; 100 kw; 846 ft.; N45 29 52 W94 32 14 *Rebroadcasts:* Rebroadcast of KSJN(FM) Minneapolis
PO Box 7011, Collegeville, MN 56321 US
(651) 290-1500; *Fax:* (651) 290-1224
www.mpr.org
info@mpr.org
License: Collegeville, Stearns County, MN held by Minnesota Public Radio.
Nat'l Network: PRI; *Regional Network:* Minn. Pub. Radio
Arbitron Metro Market: St. Paul, MN; *Format:* Talk; *No. News Employees:* 2; *Target Audience:* General.
Ian R Friendly, Chairman
John Mc Taggart, President
Chris Cross, Regional Network Manager

Cook

*WQRN
88.9 MHz FM; 16 kw; 230 ft.; N47 53 9 W92 39 47
3434 West Kilbourn Avenue, Milwaukee, WI 53208 US
(800) 729-9829
www.vcyamerica.org
vcy@vcyamerica.org
License: Cook, St. Louis County, MN held by VCY America Inc.
Group Owner: VCY America Inc.
Arbitron Metro Market: Cook, MN; *Format:* Christian
Jeff Fitzgerald, Operations Dir
Vic Eliason, General Manager
Wayne Fisk, Programming Director
Andrew Kalb, Executive Director, Programming

Coon Rapids

WTMY(FM)
09-01-1968; 107.1 MHz FM; *Hrs Open:* 24; 22 kw; Ant 587 ft; N45 03 45 W93 08 21
3415 University Ave., Minneapolis, MN 55414
(651) 642-4107; *Fax:* (651) 647-2932
www.fm107.fm
info@fm107.fm
License: Coon Rapids, Anoka County, MN held by WFMP-FM LLC.
Group Owner: Hubbard Broadcasting Inc.; (acq 12-21-2000; $27 million)
Nat'l Reps: Christal; *Wire Services:* Wheeler News Service
Arbitron Metro Market: Minneapolis-St. Paul, MN
Dan Seeman, General Manager
Sonia Ungerman, Sales Manager
Amy Daniels, Programming Director
Jeremy Sinon, Webmaster

Crookston

KQHT
03-01-1986; 96.1 MHz FM; 100 kw; 413 ft.; N47 50 43 W96 50 22
4701 East Lake Harriet Pkwy, Minneapolis, NM 55409 US
(701) 775-0575; *Fax:* (701) 746-1410
www.961thefox.com
License: Crookston, Polk County, MN held by Citicasters Licenses Inc.
Group Owner: iHeartMedia; (acq 10-26-99; grpsl).
Regional Reps: Hyett/Ramsland.
Arbitron Metro Market: Grand Forks, ND; *Format:* Contemporary Hits/Top 40; *Target Audience:* 18-49.
Richard J. Bressler, President

KROX
04-01-1948; 1260 kHz AM; *Hrs Open:* 5:30 AM To midnight; 1 kw-D, 500 w-N, DA-N; N47 47 20 W96 35 40
Mailing Address: 208 S. Main St., Crookston, MN 56716
Second Address: PO Box 620, Crookston, MN 56716
(218) 281-1140; *Fax:* (218) 281-5036
www.kroxam.com
krox@rrv.net
License: Crookston, Polk County, MN held by Gopher Communications Co.
Nat'l Network: CNN Radio; *Regional Network:* MNN; *Wire Services:* AP
Arbitron Metro Market: Grand Forks, ND-MN *Special Programming:* Farm 10 hrs wkly; *Hrs. of News Programming:* one.; *No. News Employees:* 1; *Target Audience:* 35 plus; general
Chris Fee, President
Jeanette Fee, Operations Dir
Chris Fee, Station Manager
Chris Fee, General Sales Mgr
Chris Fee, Programming Director
Maryann Simmons, News Director
Stan Mueller, Chief Engineer
Jacob Fee, Music Director

KYCK
03-04-1980; 97.1 MHz FM; *Hrs Open:* 24; 100 kw; 372 ft.; N47 49 20 W96 49 13
1186 9th Street NE, Thompson, ND 58278 US
(701) 775-4611; *Fax:* (701) 772-0540
www.97kyck.com
live@97kyck.com
License: Crookston, Polk County, MN held by Leighton Enterprises Inc.
Group Owner: Leighton Enterprises Inc.
Arbitron Metro Market: Thompson, ND; *No. News Employees:* 2
Jarrod Thomas, Operations Dir
Jack Hansen, General Manager
Phil O'Reilley, Programming Director

Crosby

KFGI
10-10-1990; 101.5 MHz FM; 25 kw; 328 ft.; N46 33 52 W93 57 3
PO Box 9115, Fargo, ND 58106-9115 US
(701) 277-1515
License: Crosby, Crow Wing County, MN held by Red Rock Radio Corp.
Group Owner: Red Rock Radio Corp.; (acq 9-1-2006; grpsl)
Nat'l Network: Jones Radio Networks
Arbitron Metro Market: Aitkin, MN; *Format:* Variety/Diverse

Tom Martin, General Manager
Pete Vukelich, News Dir/Sports Dir

Dassel

KARP-FM
06-06-1968; 106.9 MHz FM; *Hrs Open:* 24; 7 kw; 554 ft.; N45 2 43 W94 33 32
20132 Highway 15 North, Hutchinson, MN 55350 US
(320) 587-2140; *Fax:* (320) 587-5158
www.karpradio.com
License: Dassel, Meeker County, MN held by Iowa City Broadcasting Co. Inc.
Group Owner: Tom Ingstad Broadcasting Group
Wire Services: AP
Arbitron Metro Market: Saint Cloud, MN; *Format:* Country; *Hrs. of News Programming:* news progmg 3 hrs wkly; *No. News Employees:* 2; *Target Audience:* 18 plus.
Mike Novak, President
Dale Koktan, General Manager
Darla Kramer, Office Manager
Randy Asplund, Administrative Assistant

Deer River

KBAJ
01-01-2000; 105.5 MHz FM; 100 kw; 509 ft.; N47 20 22 W93 23 48 *Rebroadcasts:* Rebroadcasts KQDS-FM Duluth 100%
501 Lake Ave. S., Suite 200, Duluth, MN 55802 US
(218) 728-9500
www.95kqds.com
License: Deer River, Itasca County, MN held by Red Rock Radio Corp.
Group Owner: Red Rock Radio Corp.; acq 1-10-00; grpsl).
Arbitron Metro Market: Duluth, MN; *Format:* Classic Rock
Shawn Skramstad, General Manager
Jim Payne, General Sales Mgr

Detroit Lakes

KDLM
10-01-1951; 1340 kHz AM; *Hrs Open:* 24; 1 kw-U, ND1; N46 50 14 W95 50 17
P. O. Box 1458, St. Cloud, MN 56302 US
(218) 847-5624; *Fax:* (218) 847-7657
www.1340kdlm.com
kdlmkbot@lakesnet.net
License: Detroit Lakes, MN held by Leighton Enterprises Inc.
Group Owner: Leighton Enterprises Inc.
Nat'l Network: CBS; *Regional Network:* MNN; *Wire Services:* AP
Arbitron Metro Market: Detroit Lakes, MN; *Format:* Adult Contemp, News, 62, Sports, Talk *Special Programming:* Farm one hr, relg 8 hrs wkly; *Hrs. of News Programming:* news progmg 10 hrs wkly; *No. News Employees:* 1 *Target Audience:* 30 plus.; *Adv. Rates:* 19.50; 19.50; 19.50; 19.50
Alver Leighton, Chairman
John Sowada, President
Denny Niess, Operations Dir
Jeff Leighton, General Manager
Andy Lia, Operations Manager

KRCQ
07-04-1994; 102.3 MHz FM; *Hrs Open:* 24; 50 kw; 413 ft.; N46 43 19 W95 50 37
1340 Richwood Road, Detroit Lakes, MN 56501 US
(218) 847-5624; *Fax:* (218) 847-2271
www.realcountry102.com
krcq@lakesnet.net
License: Detroit Lakes, Becker County, MN held by Detroit Lakes Broadcasting Co. Inc.
Wire Services: AP
Format: Country; *Hrs. of News Programming:* news progmg 10 hrs wkly; *No. News Employees:* 1; *Target Audience:* General.; *Adv. Rates:* 15; 14; 15; 14
Jeff Leighton, General Manager
Deb Olson, General Sales Mgr
Travis McGinnis, Webmaster

Dilworth

WZFG
01-01-2007; 1100 kHz AM
Mailing Address: US
Second Address: 64 Broadway, Fargo, ND 58102
(701) 664-3322; *Fax:* (701) 356-5111
www.am1100.tv/
License: Dilworth, MN held by SMAHH Communications Inc.
Arbitron Metro Market: Dilworth, MN; *Format:* Talk
J. Scott Hennen, President
Jill Renee Helm, Operations Dir
Greg Burd, General Sales Mgr
Dustin Moore, Programming Director

Duluth

KDAL-AM
11-26-1936; 610 kHz AM; 5 kW; N46 43 15 W92 07 21
11 E Superior St, Suite 380, Duluth, MN 55802 USA
(218) 722-4321; *Fax:* (218) 722-5423
kdal610.com
License: Duluth, MN held by Midwest Communications Inc.
Group Owner: Midwest Communications Inc.; (acq 8-1-2001; grpsl)
Nat'l Network: CBS; Westwood One; Jones Radio Networks; *Regional Network:* MNN *Regional Reps:* Hyett/Ramsland.; *Wire Services:* AP
Arbitron Metro Market: Duluth, MN - Superior, WI; *Format:* News/Talk; *No. News Employees:* 3; *Target Audience:* 35-64.; *Adv. Rates:* 30; 22; 22; 18.
Tom Roubik, Brand Manager

KDAL-FM
07-01-1985; 95.7 MHz FM; 100 kW; 725 ft.; N46 47 15 W92 7 21
11 E Superior St, Suite 380, Duluth, MN 55802 USA
(218) 722-4321; *Fax:* (218) 722-5423
my957.com
License: Duluth, St. Louis County, MN held by Midwest Communications Inc.
Group Owner: Midwest Communications Inc.
Wire Services: AP
Arbitron Metro Market: Duluth, MN - Superior, WI; *Format:* Contemporary Hits/Top 40; *Target Audience:* 25-49.
Rich Canatta, Brand Manager

*KDNI
04-16-1983; 90.5 MHz FM; *Hrs Open:* 24; 2 kw; 728 ft.; N46 47 21 W92 6 51
Mailing Address: 3003 North Snelling Ave, St. Paul, MN 55113 US
Second Address: Northwestern College, 3003 N. Snelling Ave. N., Roseville, MN 55811
(218) 722-6700; *Fax:* (218) 722-1092
License: Duluth, St. Louis County, MN held by Northwestern College Radio Network.
Group Owner: Northwestern College & Radio; (acq 12-18-92).
Nat'l Network: AP Radio; *Wire Services:* AP
Arbitron Metro Market: Duluth-Superior, MN-WI; *Format:* Talk; *Hrs. of News Programming:* News progmg 5 hrs wkly; *Target Audience:* 25-54; baby boomers
Paul Virts, Operations Dir
Paul Harkness, Station Manager

*KDNW
12-01-1993; 97.3 MHz FM; *Hrs Open:* 24; 72 kw; 551 ft.; N46 47 20 W92 7 4
1101 East Central Entrance, Duluth, MN 55811 US
(218) 722-6700; *Fax:* (218) 722-1092
www.kdnw.fm
kdnw@kdnw.fm
License: Duluth, St. Louis County, MN held by Northwestern College.
Group Owner: Northwestern College & Radio; (acq 12-4-91; $20,000;
Nat'l Network: AP Radio; *Wire Services:* AP
Arbitron Metro Market: Duluth-Superior, MN-WI; *Format:* Christian; *Target Audience:* 25-54.
Paul Virts, Operations Dir
Paul Harkness, Station Manager

KKCB
01-01-1966; 105.1 MHz FM; 100 kw; Ant 789 ft; N46 47 21 W92 06 51
14 E. Central Entrance, Duluth, MN 47732
(218) 727-4500; *Fax:* (218) 727-9356
www.kkcb.com
License: Duluth, St. Louis County, MN held by Townsquare Media Duluth License LLC
Group Owner: Townsquare Media
Arbitron Metro Market: Duluth-Superior, MN-WI; *Target Audience:* General.
David Drew, Operations Dir
Merry Wallin, General Manager
Derek Falter, General Sales Mgr
Kimberly Carr, Promotions Manager

KLDJ
01-01-1994; 101.7 MHz FM; *Hrs Open:* 24; 18.5 kw; 823 ft.; N46 47 13 W92 7 17
14 East Central Entrance, Duluth, MN 47732 US
(218) 727-4500; *Fax:* (218) 727-9356
www.kool1017.com
License: Duluth, St. Louis County, MN held by Townsquare Media Duluth License LLC
Group Owner: Townsquare Media; (acq 2-13-2008; grpsl)
Nat'l Reps: Christal
Arbitron Metro Market: Duluth, MN; *Format:* Oldies; *Target Audience:* 25-54; general
Merry Wallin, Operations Dir
Debbi Passo, General Sales Mgr
Kimberly Carr, Promotions Manager
Mark Marette, News Director
David Drew, Operations Manager

KQDS
04-01-1976; 94.9 MHz FM; *Hrs Open:* 24; 100 kW; 846 ft.; N46 47 37 W92 07 03
11 E Superior St, Suite 380, Duluth, MN 55802 USA
95kqds.com
License: Duluth, St. Louis County, MN held by Midwest Communications Inc.
Group Owner: Midwest Communications Inc.
Nat'l Reps: McGavren Guild *Regional Reps:* O'Malley.
Arbitron Metro Market: Duluth, MN; *Format:* Classic Rock; *Target Audience:* 25-54.; *Adv. Rates:* 40; 56; 40; 20
Jason Manning, Brand Manager

KTCO
06-14-1972; 98.9 MHz FM; *Hrs Open:* 24; 100 kW; 600 ft.; N46 47 27 W92 6 59
11 E Superior St, Suite 380, Duluth, MN 55802 USA
(218) 722-4321; *Fax:* (218) 722-5423
katcountry989.com
License: Duluth, St. Louis County, MN held by Midwest Communications Inc.
Group Owner: Midwest Communications Inc.; acq 8-1-01; grpsl).
Regional Reps: Hyett/Ramsland.
Arbitron Metro Market: Duluth, MN - Superior, WI *TV Affiliate:* CMT; *Format:* Country; *Target Audience:* 25-49.

*KUMD-FM
05-26-1971; 103.3 MHz FM; *Hrs Open:* 5 AM-3 AM (M-F); 6 AM-11 PM (Su); 95 kw; 820 ft.; N46 47 31 W92 7 21
10 University Drive, Duluth, MN 55812 US
(218) 726-7181; *Fax:* (218) 726-6571
www.kumd.org
kumd@kumd.org
License: Duluth, St. Louis County, MN held by Board of Regents of University of Minnesota.
Nat'l Network: PRI
Arbitron Metro Market: Duluth, MN; *Format:* Triple A; *Hrs. of News Programming:* News progmg 12 hrs wkly; *Target Audience:* 25-45.
Vicki Jacoba, Station Manager
Maija Jenson, Programming Director
Kirk Kersten, Chief Engineer
Christine Dean, Music Director/Webmaster
Donna Neveau, Office Administrator
Christopher Harwood, Production Director
Ira Salmela,Development Director

WEBC
06-01-1924; 560 kHz AM; 5 kw-D, DA2; 5 kw-N, DA2; N46 38 37 W91 59 9
P.O. Box 3355, Evansville, IN 47732 US
(218) 727-4500; *Fax:* (218) 727-9356
www.560webc.com
merrywallin@townsquaremedia.com
License: Duluth, MN held by Townsquare Media Duluth License LLC
Group Owner: Townsquare Media; (acq 2-13-2008; grpsl)
Nat'l Network: ESPN Radio; *Nat'l Reps:* Christal
Arbitron Metro Market: Duluth, MN; *Format:* News, News/Talk, 84, Talk
Erik Hellum, President
Merry Wallin, Operations Dir
Merry Wallin, General Manager
Kristine Jensen, Director of Sales
Corey Carter, Programming Director
Randy Wabik, Chief Engineer
David Drew, Operations Manager

*WJRF
10-22-1982; 89.5 MHz FM; *Hrs Open:* 24; 0 kw horiz, 2.85 kw vert; 512 ft.; N46 47 21 W92 7 9
4604 Airpark Boulevard, Duluth, MN 55811 US
(218) 722-2727; *Fax:* (218) 722-1650
www.refugeradio.com
airstaff@refugeradio.com
License: Duluth, St. Louis County, MN held by Refuge Media Group.
Arbitron Metro Market: Duluth, MN; *Format:* Christian; *Target Audience:* 18-34; female
Mike Morrone, President
Paulette Kutzler, General Manager

***WSCD-FM**
01-01-1975; 92.9 MHz FM; 70 kw; 607 ft.; N46 47 20 W92 7 4
207 West Superior, Duluth, MN 55802 US
(218) 722-9411; *Fax:* (218) 720-4900
www.mpr.org
info@mpr.org
License: Duluth, St. Louis County, MN held by Minnesota Public Radio.
Regional Network: Minn. Pub. Radio
Arbitron Metro Market: Duluth-Superior, MN-WI; *Format:* Classical
Jim McTaggard, Chairman
William Kling, President
Patty Meester, Regional Network Manager
Kat Eldred, General Manager
John McGuinn, Station Manager
Timothy Roesler, General Manager of Classical Music
Chris Worthington, NewsDirector

WWJC
04-26-1963; 850 kHz AM; 10 kw-D; N46 39 19 W92 12 40
1120 E. McCuen St., Duluth, MN 55808
(218) 626-2738; *Fax:* (603) 907-7881
www.wwjc.com
radio@wwjc.com
License: Duluth, St. Louis County, MN held by WWJC Inc.
Nat'l Network: USA
Population Served: 225,000; *Arbitron Metro Market:* Duluth-Superior
Ted Elm, General Manager
Taylor Elm, Traffic Manager

Eagle Lake

KXLP
01-01-2007; 94.1 MHz FM; 3.7 kw; 397 ft.; N44 8 31 W94 0 5
59346 Madison Ave., Mankato, MN 56001 US
(507) 345-4537
www.94kxlp.com
License: Eagle Lake, Blue Earth County, MN held by Minnesota Valley Broadcasting Co.
Group Owner: Linder Broadcasting Group
Arbitron Metro Market: Eagle Lake, MN; *Format:* Classic Rock
Special Programming: Oldies 15 hrs wkly; *Target Audience:* 25-54.
Jo Bailey, General Manager
Deb Armstrong, General Sales Mgr

East Grand Forks

KGFK
08-14-1959; 95.7 kHz FM; *Hrs Open:* 24; 5 kw-D, 1 kw-N, DA-2; N47 52 41 W97 00 24
Mailing Address: 667 Demers Avenue, Grand Forks, ND 58201
Second Address: 1185 9th St. N.E., Thompson, ND 58278
(701) 772-2204; *Fax:* (701) 772-0540
www.957theforks.com
License: East Grand Forks, Polk County, MN held by Leighton Enterprises Inc.
Group Owner: Leighton Enterprises Inc.; (acq 11-14-2003;. $2.5 million)
Nat'l Network: CBS; CNN Radio; *Wire Services:* AP
Population Served: 100,000; *Arbitron Metro Market:* Grand Forks, ND-MN *Special Programming:* Farm 6 hrs wkly; *Hrs. of News Programming:* 2; *Target Audience:* 25-60.
Jarrod Thomas, Operations Dir
Jeff Hoberg, General Manager
Linn Hodgson, General Sales Mgr
Doug Barrett, News Director

KZLT-FM
04-01-1975; 104.3 MHz FM; 100 kw; 458 ft.; N47 48 49 W96 55 48
1185 9th Street NE, Thompson, ND 58278 US
(701) 775-4611; *Fax:* (701) 772-0540
www.1043kzlt.com
License: East Grand Forks, Polk County, MN held by Leighton Enterprises Inc.
Group Owner: Leighton Enterprises Inc.
Arbitron Metro Market: Grand Forks, ND-MN; *Format:* Adult Contemp
Matt Opsahl, Programming Director

Eden Prairie

WGVZ
03-01-1993; 105.7 MHz FM; *Hrs Open:* 24; 0.95 kw; 833 ft.; N44 58 34 W93 16 20 *Rebroadcasts:* Rebroadcasts WGVX(FM) Lakeville
2000 SE Elm St., Minneapolis, MN 55414 US
(612) 617-4000; *Fax:* (612) 676-8292
www.105thevibe.com
License: Eden Prairie, MN held by Radio License Holdings LLC
Group Owner: Cumulus Media Inc.; (acq 6-12-2007; grpsl)
Nat'l Network: ABC; *Nat'l Reps:* Katz Radio
Arbitron Metro Market: Minneapolis, MN; *Format:* Urban Contemporary; *Adv. Rates:* 85; 70; 70; 30
Shelly Wilkes, VP/Market Mgr

Edina

KTWN-FM
09-23-1993; 96.3 MHz FM; *Hrs Open:* 24; 100 kw; Ant 577 ft; N44 56 25 W93 55 43
420 North 5th Street, Minneapolis, MN 55401
(952) 842-7200; *Fax:* (952) 842-1048
License: Edina, McLeod County, MN held by Northern Lights Broadcasting LLC
No. News Employees: 1; *Target Audience:* 18-34; adults; *Adv. Rates:* 19; 15; 19; 12.50
Steve Woodbury, Operations Dir
John McMonagle, General Sales Mgr

Elk River

KLCI
12-01-1974; 106.1 MHz FM; *Hrs Open:* 24; 9.1 kw; 538 ft.; N45 14 20 W93 41 14
Mailing Address: 14443 Armstrong Boulevard, Ramsey, MN 55303 US
Second Address: 32215 124th St., Elk River, MN 55271
(763) 450-7777
License: Elk River, Sherburne County, MN
Arbitron Metro Market: Minneapolis, MN; *Format:* Country; *Hrs. of News Programming:* News progmg 7 hrs wkly
George Pelletier, Operations Dir
Don Kliewer, General Manager
Jim Alan, News Director
Mike Laughter, Chief Engineer
Tom Hughes, Operations Director

Ely

WELY
10-02-1954; 1450 kHz AM
133 East Chapman Street, Ely, MN 55731 US
(218) 365-4444; *Fax:* (218) 365-3657
www.wely.com
License: Ely, MN held by Bois Forte Tribal Council
Arbitron Metro Market: Ely, MN; *Format:* Variety/Diverse; *Target Audience:* General; senior citizens
Bill Roloff, General Manager
Brett Ross, Programming Director
Joany Haag, News Director

WELY-FM
07-25-1992; 94.5 MHz FM; 6 kw; 328 ft.; N47 53 40 W91 51 50
133 East Chapman Street, Ely, MN 55731 US
(218) 365-4444; *Fax:* (218) 365-3657
www.wely.com
welydj@wely.com
License: Ely, St. Louis County, MN
Arbitron Metro Market: Ely, MN
Anthony Gonzales, Programming Director

***WIRC**
89.3 MHz FM; 18.5 kw; 381 ft.; N47 53 1 W91 50 31
US
(651) 290-1500; *Fax:* (651) 290-1243
www.mpr.org
info@mpr.org
License: Ely, St. Louis County, MN held by Minnesota Public Radio.
Arbitron Metro Market: Ely, MN; *Format:* News
Mark Alfuth, Chief Executive Officer
Jon McTaggart, President
Daniel Gilliam, Programming Director
Mike Edgerly, News Director
Chandra Kavati, Development Director
Eugene Cha, Associate Producer
JJ Yore, Vice President,Programming

Eveleth

KRBT
12-01-1948; 1340 kHz AM; *Hrs Open:* 24; 1 kw-U, ND1; N47 28 40 W92 32 0
PO Box 650, Eveleth, MN 55734 US
(218) 741-5922; *Fax:* (218) 741-7302
www.redrockradioeveleth.com
License: Eveleth, MN held by Red Rock Radio Corp.
Group Owner: Red Rock Radio; (acq 5-1-78)
Arbitron Metro Market: Iron Range; *Format:* Sports *Special Programming:* Finnish one hr, polka 3 hrs wkly; *Target Audience:* 25-54.; *Adv. Rates:* 12; 10; 10; 10
Dennis Jerrold, General Manager
Steve Carlson, News Dir./Sports Dir.

WEVE
06-26-1978; 97.9 MHz FM; *Hrs Open:* 24; 100 kW; 518 ft.; N47 35 53 W92 13 26
807 West 37th St, Hibbing, MN 55746 USA
(218) 263-7531; *Fax:* (218) 263-6112
979weve.com
License: Eveleth, Saint Louis County, MN held by Midwest Communications Inc.
Group Owner: Midwest Communications Inc.
Arbitron Metro Market: Hibbing, MN; *Format:* Adult Contemp; *Hrs. of News Programming:* news progmg one hr wkly; *No. News Employees:* 1; *Adv. Rates:* 18; 18; 15; 15
Sean Mull, Brand Manager

Eyota

KDCZ
01-01-2008; 103.9 MHz FM; 1.3 kw; Ant 566 ft; N44 02 25 W92 13 05
122 4th St. S.W., Rochester, MN
(507) 286-1010; *Fax:* (507) 286-9370
www.klcxfm.com
License: Eyota, Olmsted County, MN held by Cumulus Licensing LLC.
Group Owner: Cumulus Media Inc.
Nat'l Network: Westwood One; *Nat'l Reps:* Christal; *Wire Services:* AP
Arbitron Metro Market: Rochester, MN; *Hrs. of News Programming:* news progmg 2 hrs wkly; *No. News Employees:* 1; *Target Audience:* 25-49.
Brett Ackerman, Operations Manager
Shannon Knoepke, General Manager
Terry Lee, General Sales Mgr
Jeff Cecil, Programming Director
Kim David, News Director
Bill Davis, Chief Engineer

Fairmont

KFMC-FM
07-31-1978; 106.5 MHz FM; *Hrs Open:* 24; 100 kw; 371 ft.; N43 37 45 W94 29 0
Mailing Address: 1371 W. Lair Rd. Box 491, Fairmont, MT 56031 US
Second Address: 1371 W. Lair Rd., Fairmont, MN 56031
(507) 235-5595; *Fax:* (507) 235-5973
www.ksum.com
License: Fairmont, Martin County, MN
Arbitron Metro Market: Fairmont, MN; *Format:* Classic Rock
Special Programming: 2 hrs agriculture wkly; *No. News Employees:* 1; *Target Audience:* 25-54.
Dan Brookens, Programming Director
Rob Halvorsen, News Director
Lynn Yuen, Research Director

KSUM
01-01-1949; 1370 kHz AM; 1 kw-D, DA2; 1 kw-N, DA2; N43 37 45 W94 29 0
Mailing Address: P.O. Box 491, 1371 W. Lair Road, Fairmont, MN 56031 US
Second Address: 1371 W. Lair Rd., Fairmont, MN 56031
(507) 235-5595; *Fax:* (507) 235-5973
www.ksum.com
classics@kfmc.com
License: Fairmont, MN held by Woodward Broadcasting Inc.
Nat'l Reps: Hyett/Ramsland
Arbitron Metro Market: Fairmont, MN; *Format:* Agriculture, News, 84; *Target Audience:* General.
Charles Woodward, General Manager
Stan Brookens, Programming Director
Rod Halverson, News Director
Ethan V-production director

***KRLP**
01-01-2008; 88.1 MHz FM; 0.04 kw; 387 ft.; N43 53 3 W95 10 56 *Rebroadcasts:* Rebroadcasts KLVR(FM) Middletown, CA 100%
P. O. Box 1452, Washington, DC 20013 US
(916) 251-1600; *Fax:* (916) 251-1650
www.klove.com
klove@klove.com
License: Fairmont, Cottonwood County, MN held by Educational Media Foundation.
Group Owner: EMF Broadcasting; (acq 3-23-2007; grpsl)
Nat'l Network: K-Love
Arbitron Metro Market: Fairmont, MN; *Format:* Christian

Darrell Chambliss, Chairman
Alan Mason, CEO/COO
Mike Novak, CEO
David Pierce, Chief Creative Officer
Dan Antonelli, Chief Business Development Officer
Eric Moser, Chief Financial Officer
Brian Burger, Vice President of HumanResources
D. Kevin Blair, Secretary and General Counsel

Faribault

KBGY
10-01-2001; 107.5 MHz FM; *Hrs Open:* 24; 48 kw; 394 ft.; N44 12 42 W93 20 18
857 Payne Avenue, St. Paul, MN 55130 US
(952) 435-5777; *Fax:* (952) 435-3181
License: Faribault, Rice County, MN held by Milestone Radio II LLC
Arbitron Metro Market: Fairbault, MN; *Format:* Christian; *Hrs. of News Programming:* news progmg 10 hrs wkly; *No. News Employees:* 1; *Target Audience:* General; 25-54
Gilberto Neco, Programming Director
Mary Bello, Sales Representative

KDHL
01-10-1948; 920 kHz AM; *Hrs Open:* 24; 5 kw-D, DA2; 5 kw-N, DA2; N44 15 47 W93 16 29
330 East Kilbourn Avenue, Suite 250, Milwaukee, WI 53202 US
(507) 334-0061; *Fax:* (507) 334-7057
www.kdhlradio.com
info@kdhlradio.com
License: Faribault, MN held by Cumulus Licensing Corp.
Group Owner: Cumulus Media Inc.; (acq 7-21-98; grpsl)
Regional Network: MNN
Arbitron Metro Market: Faribault, MN; *Format:* News, Sports; *Hrs. of News Programming:* news progmg 8 hrs wkly; *No. News Employees:* 1; *Target Audience:* 35 plus.
Paul Benzick, Operations Manager
John Anderson, Programming Director
Gordy Kosfeld, News Director
Shannon Knoepke, Market Manager
Jerry Groskreutz, Farm Director

KQCL
01-10-1968; 95.9 MHz FM; 3 kw; 328 ft.; N44 21 25 W93 11 31
601 Central Avenue N, Fairbault, MN 55021 US
(507) 334-0061; *Fax:* (507) 334-7057
www.power96radio.com
License: Faribault, Rice County, MN held by Cumulus Licensing Corp.
Group Owner: Cumulus Media Inc.
Format: Light Rock; *Target Audience:* 18-49.
Kris Lake, Director of Sales
Mike Eiler, Programming Director
Shannon Knoepke, Promotions Manager

Fergus Falls

KBRF
10-20-1926; 1250 kHz AM; *Hrs Open:* 24; 5 kw-D, DAN; 2.2 kw-N, DAN; N46 16 22 W96 2 41
Mailing Address: P.O. Box 767, Winona, MN 55987 US
Second Address: 728 Western Ave. N., Fergus Falls, MN 56537
(218) 736-7596; *Fax:* (218) 736-2836
www.lakesradio.net
lakesradio@lakesradio.net
License: Fergus Falls, MN held by Result Radio Inc.
Group Owner: The Result Radio Group; (acq 1-30-78).
Nat'l Network: Westwood One; *Nat'l Reps:* Hyett/Ramsland; *Wire Services:* AP
Format: News, News/Talk, 86 *Special Programming:* Farm 15 hrs, relg 5 hrs wkly; *Hrs. of News Programming:* news progmg 20 hrs wkly; *No. News Employees:* 2; *Target Audience:* Adults 35+.; *Adv. Rates:* 33; 30;33; 25
Jerry Papenfuss, CEO
Greg Brady, Operations Dir
Doug Gray, General Manager
Brian Lokken, News Director

KJJK
12-01-1986; 1020 kHz AM; *Hrs Open:* 24; 2 kw-D, DAN; 0.37 kw-N, DAN; N46 14 43 W95 58 46
Mailing Address: P.O. Box 5767, Winona, MN 55987 US
Second Address: 728 Western Ave. N., Fergus Falls, MN 56537
(218) 736-7596; *Fax:* (218) 736-2836
www.lakesradio.net
lakesradio@lakesradio.net
License: Fergus Falls, MN held by Result Radio Inc.
Group Owner: The Result Radio Group; (acq 3-27-97; $1.1 million with co-located FM)
Nat'l Network: ABC; Westwood One; *Nat'l Reps:* Hyett/Ramsland
Format: Oldies *Special Programming:* Relg 3 hrs wkly; *Hrs. of News Programming:* news progmg one hr wkly; *No. News Employees:* 2; *Target Audience:* 35 plus; family, home owners, execs, mgrs, dual house income *Adv. Rates:* 16; 12; 12; 7.50
Jerry Papenfuss, CEO
Greg Brady, Operations Dir
Doug Gray, General Manager
Jeff Swedberg, Programming Director
Brian Lokken, News Director

KJJK-FM
10-14-1981; 96.5 MHz FM; *Hrs Open:* 24; 100 kw; 561 ft.; N46 14 43 W95 58 46
Mailing Address: P.O. Box 5767, Winona, MN 55982 US
Second Address: 728 Western Ave. N., Fergus Falls, MN 56537
(218) 736-7596; *Fax:* (218) 736-2836
www.lakesradio.net
lakesradio@lakesradio.net
License: Fergus Falls, Otter Tail County, MN held by Result Radio Inc.
Group Owner: The Result Radio Group
Nat'l Network: ABC; *Nat'l Reps:* Hyett/Ramsland
Format: Country; *Hrs. of News Programming:* news progmg 3 hrs wkly; *No. News Employees:* 2; *Target Audience:* 21-54; today's country music fans; *Adv. Rates:* 32.00; 23.00; 23.00; 17.50
Jerry Papenfuss, CEO
Greg Brady, Operations Dir
Doug Gray, General Manager
Jeff Swedberg, Programming Director

KZCR
01-19-1968; 103.3 MHz FM; *Hrs Open:* 24; 100 kw; 650 ft.; N46 28 6 W96 11 54
Mailing Address: Box 495, Fergus Falls, MN 56537 US
Second Address: 728 Western Ave, Fergus Falls, MN 56537
(218) 736-7596; *Fax:* (218) 736-2836
www.lakesradio.net
lakesradio@lakesradio.net
License: Fergus Falls, Otter Tail County, MN held by Result Radio Inc.
Group Owner: The Result Radio Group
Nat'l Reps: Hyett/Ramsland *Regional Reps:* Hyett/Ramsland
Arbitron Metro Market: Fergus Falls, MN; *Hrs. of News Programming:* news progmg 10 hrs wkly; *No. News Employees:* 2; *Target Audience:* Adults 25-49.; *Adv. Rates:* 27.00; 21.00; 21.00; 12.50
Jerry Papenfuss, CEO
Susan Kay, Operations Dir
Doug Gray, General Manager
Greg Brady, Programming Director

*KNWF
04-01-2003; 91.5 MHz FM; 2.7 kw; 217 ft.; N46 19 12 W96 5 32
Rebroadcasts: Rebroadcast of KNOW-FM Minneapolis-St. Paul
901 S 8th Street, Moorhead, MN 56562 US
(218) 287-0666
www.mpr.org
newsroom@mpr.org
License: Fergus Falls, Otter Tail County, MN held by Minnesota Public Radio.
Arbitron Metro Market: St. Paul, MN; *Format:* News
William Kling, General Manager
Mike Edgerly, News Director
Kristi Booth, Regional Network Director
Larissa Anderson, Assistant Producer
Valerie Arganbright, Managing Director, Membership
Sarah Ashworth, Producer, MPR MorningEdition
Sasha Aslanian, Producer/Reporter
Robert Boos, Associate Editor, Online News
Linda Fantin, Director, Public Insight Journalism

*KCMF
06-06-2003; 89.7 MHz FM; 2.7 kw; 217 ft.; N46 19 12 W96 5 32
Rebroadcasts: Rebroadcasts KSJN(FM) Minneapolis
45 East Seventh Street, Saint Paul, MN 55101 US
(651) 290-1500; *Fax:* (651) 290-1224
www.mpr.org
newsroom@mpr.org
License: Fergus Falls, Otter Tail County, MN held by Minnesota Public Radio.
Arbitron Metro Market: St. Paul, MN; *Format:* Talk
Mark Alfuth, Chief Executive Officer
Mike Edgerly, News Director
Larissa Anderson, Assistant Producer
Chandra Kavati, Development Director
Sarah Ashworth, Producer, MPR Morning Edition
Sasha Aslanian, Producer/Reporter
RobertBoos, Associate Editor, Online News
Linda Fantin, Director, Public Insight Journalism

Fisher

KSNR
05-01-1976; 100.3 MHz FM; *Hrs Open:* 24; 100 kw; 564 ft.; N47 58 38 W96 36 42
P.O. Box 1248, Minnetonka, MN 55345 US
(701) 746-1417; *Fax:* (701) 746-1410
www.thecatfm.com
License: Fisher, Pennington County, MN held by Citicasters Licenses Inc.
Group Owner: iHeartMedia; (acq 10-26-99; grpsl).
Arbitron Metro Market: Grand Forks, ND; *Format:* Country *Special Programming:* Farm one hr wkly; *Hrs. of News Programming:* news progmg 10 hrs wkly; *No. News Employees:* 1; *Target Audience:* 25-54; boomers &kids
Richard J. Bressler, President

Forest Lake

WLKX-FM
10-28-1978; 95.9 MHz FM; *Hrs Open:* 24; 3 kw; 299 ft.; N45 17 40 W93 4 22
15226 West Freeway Drive, Forest Lake, MN 55025 US
(651) 464-6796; *Fax:* (651) 464-3638
www.spirit.fm
tom@spirit.net
License: Forest Lake, Washington County, MN held by Lakes Broadcasting Co. Inc.
Arbitron Metro Market: Minneapolis-St. Paul, MN; *Format:* Adult Contemp, Christian *Special Programming:* Auction show 9 hrs, relg 6 hrs wkly; *Hrs. of News Programming:* news progmg 20 hrs wkly *No. News Employees:* 1; *Target Audience:* 25-54; general
Howard Johnson, Group General Manager
John Engen, Station Manager
Mike Wagoneer, Sales Director
Jim Erickson, Sport Director

Fosston

KKCQ
12-12-1966; 1480 kHz AM; *Hrs Open:* 24
Mailing Address: P. O. Box 606, Fosston, MN 56542 US
Second Address: 35006 Hwy. 2 E., Fosston, MN 56542
(218) 435-1919; *Fax:* (218) 435-1480
www.kkcqradio.com
License: Fosston, MN held by Pine to Prairie Broadcasting Inc.
Regional Network: MNN
Arbitron Metro Market: Grand Forks, ND; *Format:* Oldies, Talk *Special Programming:* Farm 5 hrs, relg 4 hrs wkly; *Hrs. of News Programming:* news progmg 4 hrs wkly; *No. News Employees:* 1 *Target Audience:* 25-54; family-oriented adults
Bob Overmoe, President
Phil Ehlke, General Manager
Don Brinkman, General Sales Mgr
Laura Hamilton, News Director
Jim Offerdahl, Chief Engineer
Jamie Nesvold, Music Director
Karen Bingham, Office Manager
Tom Lano, SportsDirector

Glencoe

KGLB
08-05-1957; 1310 kHz AM; *Hrs Open:* 24; 1 kw-D, 343 w-N, DA-1; N44 19 51 W93 58 19
5300 Edina Industrial Blvd., Suite 200, Edina, MN 56082
(952) 842-7200; *Fax:* (952) 842-1048
License: Glencoe, Nicollet County, MN held by Iowa City Broadcasting Co. Inc.
Population Served: 71,000; *Arbitron Metro Market:* Mankato-New Ulm-St. Peter, MN
Steve Woodbury, General Manager

Glenwood

KMGK
03-11-1983; 107.1 MHz FM; *Hrs Open:* 24; 3.3 kw; 299 ft.; N45 36 53 W95 23 28
PO Box 241, 105 2nd Ave, Ne, Glenwood, MN 56334 US
(320) 634-5358; *Fax:* (320) 634-5359
www.kmgk1071.com
traffic@kmgk1071.com
License: Glenwood, Pope County, MN held by Branstock Communications Inc.
Regional Network: Minn. News Net.
Arbitron Metro Market: St. Cloud, MN; *Format:* Classic Rock; *Hrs. of News Programming:* news progmg 13 wkly; *No. News Employees:* 1; *Target Audience:* 25-54.; *Adv. Rates:* 12; 12; 12; 12
Steven Nestor, CEO
Paul Rykhus, General Sales Mgr

Dave McClurg, Promotions Manager
Rockland DeBoer, News Director

***KRFG**
90.5 MHz FM; kw *Rebroadcasts:* WJRF/Duluth, MN
US
(218) 722-2727; *Fax:* (218) 722-1650
www.refugeradio.com
airstaff@refugeradio.com
License: Glenwood, Pope County, MN held by Refuge Media Group.
Arbitron Metro Market: Duluth, MN; *Format:* Christian; *Target Audience:* 18-34 female
Daniel Hatifeld, Programming Director

Golden Valley

KDIZ
05-13-1948; 1440 kHz AM; *Hrs Open:* 24; 5 kw-D, DAN; 0.5 kw-N, DAN; N44 59 20 W93 21 6
77 W 66th St., 16th Fl., New York, NY 10023 USA
(612) 617-4000; *Fax:* (612) 676-8292
www.radiodisney.com
License: Golden Valley, MN held by RD Minneapolis Assets LLC
Group Owner: Disney Channels Worldwide; Sale to Salem Media Group pending
Nat'l Network: Radio Disney; *Nat'l Reps:* ABC Radio Sales
Arbitron Metro Market: Minneapolis-St. Paul, MN; *Format:* Children; *No. News Employees:* 1
Gary Marsh, President & Chief Creative Officer

KQRS
09-01-1962; 92.5 MHz FM; *Hrs Open:* 24; 100 kw; 1033 ft.; N45 3 30 W93 7 27
2000 SE Elm St., Minneapolis, MN 55414 US
(612) 617-4000; *Fax:* (612) 676-8292
www.92kqrs.com
License: Golden Valley, MN held by Radio License Holdings LLC
Group Owner: Cumulus Media Inc.; (acq 6-12-2007; grpsl)
Nat'l Network: ABC; *Nat'l Reps:* ABC Radio Sales
Arbitron Metro Market: Minneapolis-St. Paul; *Format:* Classic Rock
Scott Jameson, Operations Dir
Mark Ellis, General Sales Mgr
Scott Jameson, Programming Director
Cassie Hilke, Promotions Manager

KYCR
10-27-1961; 1570 kHz AM; *Hrs Open:* 24; 3.8 kw-D, ND1; 0.23 kw-N, ND1; N44 57 39 W93 21 25
4880 Santa Rosa Road, Suite 300, Camarillo, CA 93012 US
(651) 405-8800; *Fax:* (651) 405-8222
www.kycr.com
License: Golden Valley, MN held by Common Ground Broadcasting Co. Inc.
Group Owner: Salem Communications Corp.; (acq 7-2-98; $2.7 million with KTEK(AM) Alvin, TX)
Arbitron Metro Market: Eagan, MN; *Format:* Religious, Talk
Special Programming: Sp 14 hrs wkly; *Hrs. of News Programming:* News progmg 6 hrs wkly; *Target Audience:* 25-49; 60% female, 40% male
Lee Michaels, Operations Dir
Nick Novak, Programming Director
Kate Fisher, Promotions Manager
Steve Smit, Chief Engineer
Nic Anderson, General Sales Manager
Cindy Bohm, Traffic Director
Ross Brendel, Producer
Eric Emery,Productionn/ Imaging Director
Steve Smit, Engineer
Mike Murphy, Account Executive

Grand Marais

***WTIP**
07-01-1998; 90.7 MHz FM; *Hrs Open:* 5 AM-3 AM; 25 kw; 584 ft.; N47 46 9 W90 20 49 *Rebroadcasts:* Rebroadcasts KUMD-FM Duluth 70%
Mailing Address: P.O. Box 1005, Grand Marais, MN 55604 US
Second Address: 55 W. 5th St., Grand Marais, MN 55604
(218) 387-1070; *Fax:* (218) 387-1120
www.wtip.org
License: Grand Marais, Cook County, MN held by Cook County Community Radio Corp.
Arbitron Metro Market: Grand Marais, MN; *Format:* Adult Contemp, Triple A *Special Programming:* Blues 15 hrs, AOR 15 hrs, progsv rock 15 hrs wkly; *Hrs. of News Programming:* News progmg 15 hrs wkly; *Target Audience:* General.
Ann Possis, President
Deb Benedict, Executive Director
Kelly Schoenfelder, Programming Director
Barbara Jean Meyers, News Director
Jeff Nemitz, Engineering Dir
Cathy Quinn, Music Director
Jana Kokemiller-Berka, DevelopmentAssistant
Melanie Steele, Development Director

WXXZ
01-01-1999; 95.3 MHz FM; 63 kw; 686 ft.; N47 39 55 W90 42 22
Rebroadcasts: Rebroadcasts KQDS-FM Duluth 100%
501 Lake Ave. S., Suite 200, Duluth, MN 55802 US
(218) 728-9500; *Fax:* (218) 723-1499
www.95kqds.com
License: Grand Marais, Cook County, MN held by Red Rock Radio Corp.
Group Owner: Red Rock Radio Corp.; acq 1-10-00; grpsl).
Arbitron Metro Market: Grand Marais, MN; *Format:* Classic Rock
Shawn Skramstad, General Manager
Jim Payne, General Sales Mgr

***WLSN**
01-01-2005; 89.7 MHz FM; 6 kw; 636 ft.; N47 46 4 W90 20 47
480 Cedar Street, Saint Paul, MN 55101 US
(651) 290-1500; *Fax:* (651) 290-1224
www.mpr.org
newsroom@mpr.org
License: Grand Marais, Cook County, MN held by Minnesota Public Radio.
Regional Network: Minn. Pub. Radio
Arbitron Metro Market: St. Paul, MN; *Format:* News
Jon McTaggart, President
Nick Kereakos, Vice President of Technology & Operations
Tim Roesler, Vice President/General Manager
Chandra Kavati, Director of Development Services
Craig Curtis, Vice President of Programming
ChrisWorthington, News Director
Melanie Walker, Music Director

***WMLS**
88.7 MHz FM; 6 kw; 636 ft.; N47 46 4 W90 20 47
480 Cedar Street, Saint Paul, MN 55101 US
(651) 290-1500; *Fax:* (651) 290-1224
www.mpr.org
newsroom@mpr.org
License: Grand Marais, Cook County, MN held by Minnesota Public Radio.
Regional Network: Minn. Pub. Radio
Arbitron Metro Market: St. Paul, MN; *Format:* Classical
Jon McTaggart, President
Nick Kereakos, Vice President of Technology & Operations
Tim Roesler, Senior Vice President/General Manager
Chandra Kavati, Director Of Development Services
Craig Curtis, Vice President of Programming
ChrisWorthington, News Director
Melanie Walker, Music Director

Grand Rapids

***KAXE**
04-23-1976; 91.7 MHz FM; kw
260 NE 2nd Street, Grand Rapids, MN 55744 US
(218) 326-1234; *Fax:* (218) 326-1235
www.kaxe.org
shall@kaxe.org
License: Grand Rapids, Itasca County, MN held by Northern Community Radio Inc.
Nat'l Network: NPR; PRI
Arbitron Metro Market: Grand Rapids, MN; *Format:* Variety/Diverse; *Target Audience:* General.
Maggie Montgomery, General Manager
John Bauer, Development Director
Heidi Holtan, Programming Director
Dan Houg, Engineering Dir
Maddi Frick, Music Director

KMFY
12-05-1975; 96.9 MHz FM; *Hrs Open:* 24; 100 kw; 479 ft.; N47 15 17 W93 26 3
Mailing Address: 507 Southeast 11th St, P O Box 597, Grand Rapids, MN 55744 US
Second Address: 507 11th St. S.E., Grand Rapids, MN 55744
(218) 999-5639; *Fax:* (218) 990-5609
License: Grand Rapids, Itasca County, MN
Arbitron Metro Market: Duluth, MN; *Format:* Adult Contemp; *No. News Employees:* 1; *Target Audience:* 35-54.
Jim Lamke, President/General Manager/Sales Manager
Kathy Lynn, Programming Director
Michael Davis, News Director
Jason Groth, Sports Director
Tim Edwards, Chief Engineer

KOZY
01-29-1948; 1320 kHz AM; *Hrs Open:* 24; 5 kw-D, DAN; 5 kw-N, DAN; N47 10 22 W93 27 10
Mailing Address: P.O. Box 597, Grand Rapids, MN 55744 US
Second Address: 507 11th St. S.E., Grand Rapids, MN 55744
(218) 999-5699; *Fax:* (218) 990-5609
jimlamke@kozyradio.com
License: Grand Rapids, MN held by Lamke Broadcasting
Nat'l Network: ABC; *Regional Network:* MNN
Format: Classic Rock; *No. News Employees:* 1; *Adv. Rates:* 12.75; 12.75; 12.75; 12.75
Jim Lamke, President/General Manager/Sales Manager
Kathy Lynn, Programming Director
Michael Davis, News Director
Jason Groth, Sports Director
Tim Edwards, Chief Engineer

***KGRP**
01-01-2007; 89.7 MHz FM; kw
US
(707) 528-4434; *Fax:* (707) 527-8216
www.k1063.fm
License: Grand Rapids, Sonoma County, MN held by Redwood Empire Stereocasters
Group Owner: Minnesota Public Radio
Nat'l Reps: McGavren Guild; *Wire Services:* AP
Arbitron Metro Market: Cazadero, CA; *Format:* Country
Jon McTaggart, President
Nick Kereakos, Vice President of Technology & Operations
Tim Roesler, Senior Vice President/General Manager
Chandra Kavati, Director of Development Services
Craig Curtis, Vice President of Programming
ChrisWorthington, News Director
Melanie Walker, Music Director

Granite Falls

KKRC
10-05-1993; 93.9 MHz FM; *Hrs Open:* 24; 6 kw; 262 ft.; N44 51 24 W95 37 46
P.O. Box 513, Montevideo, MN 56265 US
(320) 269-8815; *Fax:* (320) 269-8449
www.kdmanews.com
dwight@kdmanews.com
License: Granite Falls, Yellow Medicine County, MN held by Iowa City Broadcasting Co.
Group Owner: Tom Ingstad Broadcasting Group
Nat'l Network: ABC; *Regional Network:* Minn. News Net; *Nat'l Reps:* Katz Radio
Arbitron Metro Market: Saint Cloud, MN; *Format:* Oldies; *Adv. Rates:* 20; 16; 16; 12
Dwight Mulder, Operations Dir
Roger Hill, General Manager
Andy Coulter, General Sales Mgr

Gunflint Lake

***WKEK**
06-28-2011; 89.1 MHz FM; 1000 w; 259 ft; N48 04 40 W90 45 34
1712 W. Highway 61, PO Box 1005, Grand Marais, MN
(218)387-1070; *Fax:* (218)387-1120
www.wtip.org
wtip@boreal.org
License: Gunflint Lake, Cook County, MN held by Cook County Community Radio Corporation

Ann Possis, President
Executive Director, General Sales Mgr
Kelly Schoenfelder, Programming Director
Melanie Steele, Development Director
Barbara Jean Johnson, News Director

Hastings

KDWA
10-24-1963; 1460 kHz AM; *Hrs Open:* 24
514 Vermillion Street, PO Box 215, Hastings, MN 55033 US
(651) 437-1460; *Fax:* (651) 438-3042
www.kdwa.com
dan@kdwa.com
License: Hastings, MN held by K & M Broadcasting Inc.
Nat'l Network: CNN Radio; *Regional Network:* MNN
Arbitron Metro Market: Minneapolis-St. Paul, MN; *Format:* News, Sports, 86; *Hrs. of News Programming:* news progmg 18 hrs wkly; *No. News Employees:* 15; *Target Audience:* 25-65; general
Dan Massman, General Manager
Ben Parks, News Director

Hermantown

WWAX
06-17-1996; 92.1 MHz FM; 5.4 kw; 705 ft.; N46 47 41 W92 7 5
501 Lake Ave. S., Suite 200, Duluth, MN 55802 US

(218) 728-9500
www.921thefan.com
License: Hermantown, St. Louis County, MN held by Red River Broadcasting
Group Owner: Red Rock Radio Corp.; acq 1-10-00; grpsl).
Arbitron Metro Market: Duluth, MN; *Format:* Sports; *Target Audience:* 18-35; general
Romeo Grignon, CEO/COO
Shawn Skramstad, President

Hibbing

WMFG-AM
01-01-1935; 1240 kHz AM; *Hrs Open:* 24; 1 kW; N47 24 30 W92 57 04
807 West 37th St, Hibbing, MN 55746
(218) 263-7531; *Fax:* (218) 263-6112
License: Hibbing, Saint Louis County, MN held by Midwest Communications Inc.
Group Owner: Midwest Communications Inc.; (acq 5-10-2004; grpsl).
Regional Network: MNN
Population Served: 70,000 *Format:* Oldies; *Target Audience:* Adults 35-64
Doug Diedrich, Brand Manager

WMFG-FM
01-01-1971; 106.3 MHz FM; *Hrs Open:* 24; 25 kW; 252 ft.; N47 24 30 W92 57 5
807 West 37th St, Hibbing, MN 55746 USA
(218) 263-7531; *Fax:* (218) 263-6112
License: Hibbing, Saint Louis County, MN held by Midwest Communications Inc.
Group Owner: Midwest Communications Inc.
Arbitron Metro Market: Hibbing, MN; *Format:* Classic Rock; *Target Audience:* 25-54.

WTBX
12-31-1980; 93.9 MHz FM; 100 kW; 531 ft.; N47 22 24 W93 0 48
807 West 37th St, Hibbing, MN 55746 USA
(218) 263-7531; *Fax:* (218) 263-6112
wtbx.com
License: Hibbing, Saint Louis County, MN held by Midwest Communications Inc.
Group Owner: Midwest Communications Inc.
Arbitron Metro Market: Hibbing, MN; *Format:* Contemporary Hits/Top 40; *Target Audience:* 18-40.
Craig Holgate, Brand Manager

*KADU
07-18-1994; 90.1 MHz FM; 1.5 kw; 338 ft.; N47 24 10 W92 57 50 *Rebroadcasts:* Simulcast with KBHW(FM) International Falls 100%
12104 Old Highway 169, Hibbing, MN 55746 US
(218) 285-7398
License: Hibbing, St. Louis County, MN held by Heartland Christian Broadcasters Inc.
Group Owner: Heartland Christian Broadcasters Inc.; (acq 4-22-2005; $30,000).
Arbitron Metro Market: Hibbing, MN; *Format:* Christian
Bruce Christopherson, Station Manager
Gene Gee, Programming Director

Hinckley

*WGRH
88.5 MHz FM; 3.8 kw; 422 ft.; N46 1 28.2 W93 1 21.3
480 Cedar Street, St. Paul, MN 55101 US
(651) 290-1500; *Fax:* (651) 290-1243
www.mpr.org
info@mpr.org
License: Hinckley, Pine County, MN held by Minnesota Public Radio.
Arbitron Metro Market: Hinckley, MN; *Format:* News
Jon McTaggart, President
Nick Kereakos, Vice President of Technology & Operations
Tim Roesler, Senior Vice President/General Manager
Chandra Kavati, Director of Development Services
Craig Curtis, Vice President of Programming
ChrisWorthington, News Director
Melanie Walker, Music Director

Hutchinson

KDUZ
09-16-1953; 1260 kHz AM; *Hrs Open:* 24; 1 kw-D, ND1; 0.064 kw-N, ND1; N44 54 24 W94 21 59
20132 Hwy 15 North, Hutchinson, MN 55350 US
(320) 587-2140; *Fax:* (320) 587-5158
www.kduz.com
info@kduz.com
License: Hutchinson, MN held by Iowa City Broadcasting Co. Inc.
Group Owner: Tom Ingstad Broadcasting Group; (acq 4-1-2000; grpsl)
Regional Network: Minn. News Net.; Minn. Farm *Regional Reps:* Hyett/Ramsland.; *Wire Services:* AP
Arbitron Metro Market: Hutchinson, MN; *Format:* News, Oldies, 84 *Special Programming:* Farm 18 hrs, gospel 3 hrs, polka 8 hrs, Sp one hr wkly; *Hrs. of News Programming:* news progmg 21 hrs wkly *No. News Employees:* 2; *Target Audience:* 30 plus; general; *Adv. Rates:* 37; 31; 37; 20
Tor Ingstag, Chairman
John Mons, Operations Dir
Jim Bartells, General Manager
Adam Buboltz, Sales Manager
Jon Carrigan, Programming Director
Mark Wodarczyk, News Director
Duane Wawyrzniak, Chief Engineer
Darla Kramer, OfficeManager
Randy Asplund, Administrative Assistant

International Falls

*KBHW
01-04-1983; 99.5 MHz FM; *Hrs Open:* 24; 100 kw; 561 ft.; N48 33 45 W93 49 21
P. O. Box 433, International Falls, MN 56649 US
(218) 285-7398; *Fax:* (218) 285-7419
www.psalm995.org
connect@psalmfm.org
License: International Falls, Koochiching County, MN held by Heartland Christian Broadcasters.
Group Owner: Heartland Christian Broadcasters Inc.; (acq 7-23-99; $1 with KXBR(FM) International Falls)
Nat'l Network: USA; Moody
Arbitron Metro Market: International Falls, MN; *Format:* Christian; *Hrs. of News Programming:* News progmg 15 hrs wkly; *Target Audience:* General.
Gene Gee, Operations Dir
Bruce Christopherson, General Manager

*KXBR
06-01-2000; 91.9 MHz FM; 1.5 kw; 128 ft.; N48 34 15 W93 26 19
P.O. Box 433, International Falls, MN 56649 US
(218) 285-9190; *Fax:* (218) 285-7419
License: International Falls, Koochiching County, MN held by Heartland Christian Broadcasters.
Group Owner: Heartland Christian Broadcasters Inc.; (acq 7-23-99; $1 with KBHW(FM) International Falls)
Format: Christian
Gene Gee, Operations Dir
Bruce Christopherson, General Manager

KGHS
09-01-1959; 1230 kHz AM; *Hrs Open:* 24; 0.46 kw-D, ND2; 0.23 kw-N, ND2; N48 35 29 W93 22 54
519 Third St., International Falls, MN 56649 US
(218) 283-3481; *Fax:* (218) 283-3087
www.ksdmradio.com
dennis@ksdmradio.com
License: International Falls, MN held by Red Rock Radio Corp.
Group Owner: Red Rock Radio Corp.; (acq 9-1-2006; grpsl)
Nat'l Network: Jones Radio Networks; *Regional Network:* MNN
Format: Oldies; *Hrs. of News Programming:* news progmg 10 hrs wkly; *No. News Employees:* 1; *Adv. Rates:* 19; 18; 16; 10
Dennis Martin, General Manager
Jerry Franzen, Programming Director

KSDM
03-17-1979; 104.1 MHz FM; *Hrs Open:* 24; 8.5 kw; Ant 200 ft; N48 35 39 W93 22 56
519 3rd St., International Falls, MN 56649 US
(218) 283-3481; *Fax:* (218) 283-3087
www.ksdmradio.com
dennis@ksdmradio.com
License: International Falls, Koochching County, MN held by Red River Broadcasting
Group Owner: Red Rock Radio Corp.
Nat'l Network: AP
Population Served: 30,000 *Format:* Country; *Hrs. of News Programming:* news progmg 20 hrs wkly; *No. News Employees:* 1; *Adv. Rates:* 19; 18; 16; 10
Dennis Martin, General Manager
Jerry Franzen, News Director

*KITF
88.3 MHz FM; 5.75 kw; Ant 154 ft; N48 28 24 W93 20 00
480 Cedar St., Saint Paul, MN
(651) 290-1259
www.mpr.org
License: International Falls, Koochching County, MN held by Minnesota Public Radio.
Regional Network: Minn. Pub. Radio
Jon McTaggart, President
Nick Kereakos, Vice President of Technology & Operations
Tim Roesler, Senior Vice President/General Manager
Chandra Kavati, Director of Development Services
Craig Curtis, Vice President of Programming
ChrisWorthington, News Director
Melanie Walker, Music Director

Jackson

KKOJ
07-10-1980; 1190 kHz AM; *Hrs Open:* Sunrise-sunset; 5 kw-D, DAD; N43 31 45 W95 0 5
Mailing Address: P.O. Box 29, Jackson, MN 56143 US
Second Address: 71991 US Hwy. 71, Jackson, MN 56143
(507) 847-5400; *Fax:* (507) 847-5745
www.kkoj.com
info@kkoj.com
License: Jackson, MN held by Kleven Broadcasting Co. of Minnesota.
Regional Network: Linder Farm; *Wire Services:* AP
Arbitron Metro Market: Mankato, MN; *Format:* Country *Special Programming:* Farm 15 hrs wkly; *Hrs. of News Programming:* news progmg 20 hrs wkly; *No. News Employees:* 1; *Target Audience:* General.; *Adv. Rates:* 19.80; 19.80; 19.80; 13.50
Doug Johnson, President
Dave Maschoff, News Director
Lee Larson, Sports Commentator
Jerrie Johnson, Traffic Manager
Lee Larson

KRAQ
04-25-1994; 105.7 MHz FM; *Hrs Open:* 24; 25 kw; 328 ft.; N43 36 54 W94 57 48
Mailing Address: Post Office Box 29, Jackson, MN 56143 US
Second Address: 71991 US Hwy. 71, Jackson, MN 56143
(507) 847-5400; *Fax:* (507) 847-5745
www.kkoj.com
info@kkoj.com
License: Jackson, Jackson County, MN held by Kleven Broadcasting Co. of Minnesota.
Nat'l Network: AP Radio; *Wire Services:* AP
Format: Oldies; *Hrs. of News Programming:* new progmg 18 hrs wkly; *No. News Employees:* 1; *Adv. Rates:* 18.90; 18.90; 18.90; 13.50
Doug Johnson, President
Dave Maschoff, News Director
Jerrie Johnson, Traffic Manager

Kelliher

KKWB
01-01-2008; 102.5 MHz FM; 50 kw; 472 ft.; N47 44 21 W94 41 10
Mailing Address: 17340 State Highway 34, PO Box 49, Park Rapids, MN 56470 US
Second Address: 324 Beltrami Ave. N.W., Bemidji, MN 56601-3105
(218) 732-3306; *Fax:* (218) 732-3307
kprmkdkk@unitelc.com
License: Kelliher, Beltrami County, MN held by Bemidji Radio Inc.
Arbitron Metro Market: Kelliher, MN; *Format:* Country
Edward De La Hunt, General Manager

La Crescent

KQEG
04-05-1989; 102.7 MHz FM; *Hrs Open:* 24; 4 kw; 702 ft.; N43 43 17 W91 17 24
1407 2nd Ave. N., Onalaska, WI 54650 US
(608) 782-8335; *Fax:* (608) 782-8340
www.eagle1027.com
License: La Crescent, Houston County, MN held by White Eagle Broadcasting Inc.
Group Owner: La Crosse Radio Group; (acq 2-4-2000; $2 million).
Regional Reps: O'Malley.
Arbitron Metro Market: La Crosse, WI; *Format:* Oldies; *Hrs. of News Programming:* News progmg 4 hrs wkly; *Target Audience:* 25-54.
Pat Smith, General Manager
Erik Sjolander, Sales Manager
Dave Kennedy, Programming Director
Heidi Hanse, Promotions Director
Caroline Grosvold, Business Manager
JoAnn Steffes, HR Director
Laurie Lane, Traffic Director
LoisLosby, Public Service
Isaac Wenzel, Director of Interactive Media

***KXLC**
11-24-1991; 91.1 MHz FM; *Hrs Open:* 24; 0.23 kw; 843 ft.; N43 48 16.1 W91 22 19.3
480 Cedar Street, St. Paul, MN 55101 US
(507) 282-0910; *Fax:* (507) 282-2107
www.mpr.org
License: La Crescent, Houston County, MN held by Minnesota Public Radio.
Nat'l Network: NPR; PRI; *Regional Network:* Minn. Pub. Radio
Arbitron Metro Market: Rochester, MN; *Format:* News; *Hrs. of News Programming:* news progmg 24 hrs wkly; *No. News Employees:* 1; *Target Audience:* General.
Chris Cross, General Manager
Stacy Davis, Traffic Manager
Dennis Brooks, Account Executive
Elizabeth Baier, News Director

Lake City

KMFX-FM
02-14-1991; 102.5 MHz FM; 9.4 kw; 528 ft.; N44 16 45 W92 23 38
1530 Greenview Drive SW, Suite 200, Rochester, MN 55902 US
(507) 288-3888; *Fax:* (507) 288-7815
www.1025thefox.com
License: Lake City, Wabasha County, MN held by CC Licenses LLC.
Group Owner: iHeartMedia; (acq 10-2000; grpsl).
Nat'l Reps: D & R Radio
Arbitron Metro Market: Rochester, MN; *Format:* Country
Craig Erpestad, Operations Manager/Programming Director
Mary Anne Nonn, Vice President of Sales
Jessica Pustelnik, Digital Content Manager/Sales Manager

KLCH
12-01-2001; 94.9 MHz FM; *Hrs Open:* 24; 5 kw; 328 ft.; N44 29 15 W92 13 55
122 SW Forth Street, Rochester, MN 55901 US
(651) 388-7151; *Fax:* (651) 388-7153
www.lakehits95.com
news@kwng.com
License: Lake City, Wabasha County, MN held by Q Media Group LLC
Arbitron Metro Market: Rochester, MN; *Format:* Adult Contemp; *No. News Employees:* 2; *Target Audience:* 25-54.; *Adv. Rates:* 23.50; 19.50; 23.50; 19.50
Tom Hughes, Operations Dir
Don Kliewer, General Manager
Craig Livingstone, Chief Engineer
Ronnie Stockwell, Business Manager
Erika Duxbury, Traffic Manager
Tom Hughes, Operations Manager
Jack Colwell, Sports Director
DawnLaffey, Account Executive
Jodie Schultz, Account Executive

Lake Crystal

KMKO-FM
01-01-2005; 95.7 MHz FM; 6 kw; Ant 328 ft; N44 03 06 W94 17 59
1807 Lee Blvd, N. Mankato, MN 56003 US
(507) 345-4646; *Fax:* (507) 345-3299
www.957therockstation.com
ddose@digity.me
License: Lake Crystal, Blue Earth County, MN held by Digity 3E License, LLC
Group Owner: Digity, LLC
Nat'l Reps: Katz Radio
Format: Rock/AOR; *No. News Employees:* 1
Denise Dose, General Manager
Kathy Varva, Station Manager
Jeff Spence, Programming Director

Lakeville

WGVX
01-01-1992; 105.1 MHz FM; *Hrs Open:* 24; 2.6 kw; 499 ft.; N44 42 5 W93 9 2
2000 SE Elm St., Minneapolis, MN 55414 US
(612) 617-4000; *Fax:* (612) 676-8292
www.105thevibe.com
License: Lakeville, MN held by Radio License Holdings LLC
Group Owner: Cumulus Media Inc.; (acq 6-12-2007; grpsl)
Nat'l Network: ABC; *Nat'l Reps:* Interep
Arbitron Metro Market: Minneapolis, MN; *Format:* Urban Contemporary
Shelly Wilkes, VP/Market Mgr
Mark Ellis, General Sales Mgr

Litchfield

KLFD
01-02-1959; 1410 kHz AM; *Hrs Open:* 24; 0.5 kw-D, ND1; 0.045 kw-N, ND1; N45 7 2 W94 33 13
234 N. Sibley Avenue, Litchfield, MN 55355 US
(320) 693-3281; *Fax:* (320) 693-3283
www.klfd1410.com
pam@klfd1410.com
License: Litchfield, MN held by Mid-Minnesota Broadcasting Co.
Arbitron Metro Market: Saint Cloud, MN; *Format:* Variety/Diverse *Special Programming:* Farm 20 hrs, relg 3 hrs wkly; *Hrs. of News Programming:* news progmg 10 hrs wkly; *No. News Employees:* 1 *Target Audience:* 25-54.
Steve Gretsch, President
Jennifer Flynn, General Sales Mgr
Aaron Imholte, Programming Director
Tim Bergstrom, News Director

Little Falls

KFML
11-01-1988; 94.1 MHz FM; *Hrs Open:* 24; 6 kw; 328 ft.; N46 0 15 W94 19 40
16405 Haven Road, Little Falls, MN 56345 US
(320) 632-2992; *Fax:* (320) 632-2571
www.fallsradio.com
License: Little Falls, Morrison County, MN held by Little Falls Radio Corp.
Group Owner: Little Falls Radio Corp.; (acq 6-28-2004)
Nat'l Network: CNN Radio; *Regional Network:* Minn. News Net.
Arbitron Metro Market: Little Falls, MN; *Format:* Adult Contemp; *Hrs. of News Programming:* news progmg 3 hrs wkly; *No. News Employees:* 1; *Target Audience:* 25-54.
Tim McCoy, General Manager
Belinda Beninger, General Sales Mgr
Steve Sunshine, Programming Director

KLTF
10-01-1950; 960 kHz AM; *Hrs Open:* 24; 5 kw-D, ND1; 0.038 kw-N, ND1; N46 0 16 W94 19 42
16405 Haven Road, Little Falls, MN 56345 US
(320) 632-2992; *Fax:* (320) 632-2571
www.fallsradio.com
ads@fallsradio.com
License: Little Falls, MN held by Little Falls Radio Corp.
Group Owner: Little Falls Radio Corp.; acq 6-28-2004; grpsl).
Nat'l Network: Fox News Radio; ABC; Fox Sports; Westwood One; *Regional Network:* MNN; Linder Farm
Arbitron Metro Market: Morrison County, MN; *Format:* News, News/Talk, 86 *Special Programming:* Farm 8 hrs, relg 4 hrs, polka 2 hrs, party line 5; *Hrs. of News Programming:* news progmg 24 hrs wkly; *No. News Employees:* 1; *Target Audience:* 35-65; loc audience who listen for news & info
Rod Grams, President
Chris Grams, General Manager
Melanie Lintner, General Sales Mgr
Lacey Welle, News Director
Al Windsperger, Sports Commentator

WYRQ-FM
05-19-1980; 92.1 MHz FM; *Hrs Open:* 24; 3 kw; 299 ft; N45 56 57 W94 17 48
16405 Haven Rd., Little Falls, MN 56345
(320) 632-2992; *Fax:* (320) 632-2571
www.fallsradio.com
License: Little Falls, Morrison County, MN held by Little Falls Radio Corp.
Group Owner: Little Falls Radio Corp.; acq 6-28-2004; grpsl).
Nat'l Network: NBC; *Regional Network:* MNN; Minn. Farm; *Wire Services:* UPI
Population Served: 50,000 *Hrs. of News Programming:* news progmg 20 hrs wkly; *No. News Employees:* 1; *Target Audience:* 25-54; farmers & working people
Rod Grams, President
Chris Grams, General Manager
Rod Grams, Station Manager
Chris Grams, General Sales Mgr
Al Windsperger, Programming Director
Larry Bargardt, Promotions Manager
Corey Fink, News Director
Doug Thompson, ChiefEngineer

Long Prairie

KEYL
09-15-1959; 1400 kHz AM; *Hrs Open:* 24; 1 kw-U, ND1; N45 57 45 W94 52 9
P.O. Box 187, Long Prairie, MN 56347 US
(320) 732-2164; *Fax:* (320) 732-2284
www.kxdlhotrodradio.com/keyl_1400am.htm
License: Long Prairie, MN held by Prairie Broadcasting Co.
Nat'l Network: ABC
Arbitron Metro Market: Long Prairie, MN; *Format:* Country *Special Programming:* Farm 5 hrs, sports 10 hrs, relg 4 hrs wkly; *Hrs. of News Programming:* News progmg 15 hrs wkly; *Target Audience:* 25 plus.
Gene Sullivan, President
Todd Jensen, General Sales Mgr

Luverne

KLQL
11-24-1971; 101.1 MHz FM; *Hrs Open:* 24; 100 kw; 531 ft.; N43 48 24 W96 12 23
1140 150th Avenue, Luverne, MN 56156 US
(507) 283-4444; *Fax:* (507) 283-4445
License: Luverne, Rock County, MN
Arbitron Metro Market: Mankato, MN; *Format:* Country *Special Programming:* Farm 10 hrs, gospel 4 hrs wkly; *Hrs. of News Programming:* News progmg 4 hrs wkly; *Target Audience:* 25-54.
Steve Graphenteen, General Manager
Matt Crosby, General Sales Mgr
Bruce Thalhuber, Programming Director/Operations Manager
Andy Gott, News Director
Angie Gangestad, Traffic Manager

KQAD
03-01-1971; 800 kHz AM; *Hrs Open:* 24; 0.5 kw-D, DA2; 0.08 kw-N, DA2; N43 39 1 W96 10 19
1140 150th Ave., Luverne, MN 56156 US
(507) 283-4444
www.k101fm.net
sg@digity.me
License: Luverne, MN held by Digity 3E License, LLC
Group Owner: Digity, LLC
Nat'l Reps: Hyett/Ramsland
Arbitron Metro Market: Luverene-Rock Rapids; *Format:* Adult Contemp; *No. News Employees:* 1
Bruce Thalhuber, Operations Dir
Steve Graphenteen, General Manager
Travis Kriens, News Director

Madison

KLQP
01-31-1983; 92.1 MHz FM; *Hrs Open:* 24; 25 kw; 300 ft; N45 01 37 W96 11 15
Box 70, 623 W. 3rd St., Madison, MN 56256
(320) 598-7301; *Fax:* (320) 598-7955
www.klqpfm.com
klqpfm@farmerstel.net
License: Madison, Lac Qui Parle County, MN held by Lac Qui Parle Broadcasting Co. Inc.
Nat'l Network: CNN Radio; *Regional Network:* Minn. News Net.
Population Served: 40,000 *Special Programming:* Farm 5 hrs wkly; *Hrs. of News Programming:* News progmg 18 hrs wkly; *Target Audience:* General.; *Adv. Rates:* 7; 7; 7; 3.50
Maynard Meyer, General Manager
Terry Overlander, General Sales Mgr
Kris Kuechenmeister, Office Manager

Mahnomen

KRJM
08-27-2001; 101.5 MHz FM; *Hrs Open:* 24; 25 kw; 328 ft.; N47 27 23 W96 7 57
AF 205-MSU, Ada, MN 56510 US
(218) 935-5355; *Fax:* (218) 935-9020
www.krjmradio.com
krjm@arvig.net
License: Mahnomen, Mahnomen County, MN held by R & J Broadcasting.
Arbitron Metro Market: Mahnomen, MN; *Format:* Oldies
Jim Birkemeyer, General Manager

Mankato

KEEZ-FM
01-01-1974; 99.1 MHz FM; *Hrs Open:* 24; 100 kw; 784 ft.; N44 3 6 W94 17 59
1807 Lee Blvd., North Mankato, MN 56003 US
(507) 345-4646
www.myz99.com
License: Mankato, Blue Earth County, MN held by Digity 3E License, LLC
Group Owner: Digity, LLC
Nat'l Network: Westwood One; *Nat'l Reps:* Katz Radio
Arbitron Metro Market: Mankato-New Ulm-St. Peter, MN; *Format:* Contemporary Hits/Top 40; *No. News Employees:* 1; *Target Audience:* 18-49; *Adv. Rates:* 25; 30; 25; 18
Denise Dose, General Manager
Kelly Marks, Station Manager
Brad Steele, Programming Director

***KMSU**
01-07-1963; 89.7 MHz FM; *Hrs Open:* 24; 17 kw; 436 ft.; N44 8 31 W94 0 6
Msu 153, P.O. Box 8400, Mankato, MN 56002 US
(507) 389-5678; *Fax:* (507) 389-1705
www.kmsu.org
License: Mankato, Blue Earth County, MN held by Mankato State University.
Nat'l Network: PRI
Arbitron Metro Market: Mankato, MN; *Format:* Public Affairs *Special Programming:* Drama 3 hrs, folk/ethnic 5 hrs, new age 5 hrs wkly; *Hrs. of News Programming:* news progmg 50 hrs wkly; *No. News Employees:* 1 *Target Audience:* General; upscale, educated
Karen Wright, Operations Dir
Jim Gullickson, General Manager

KTOE
01-01-1950; 1420 kHz AM; *Hrs Open:* 24; 5 kw-D, DAN; 5 kw-N, DAN; N44 10 6 W93 54 37
59346 Madison Ave., Mankato, MN 56001 US
(507) 345-4537; *Fax:* (507) 345-5364
www.ktoe.com
License: Mankato, MN held by Minnesota Valley Broadcasting Co.
Group Owner: Linder Broadcasting Group
Arbitron Metro Market: Mankato-New Ulm-St. Peter, MN; *Format:* News/Talk; *Hrs. of News Programming:* news progmg 21 hrs wkly; *No. News Employees:* 3; *Target Audience:* 25-54.
Jo Bailey, General Manager
Deb Armstrong, General Sales Mgr

KFSP
07-25-1938; 1230 kHz AM; *Hrs Open:* 24
59346 Madison Ave., Mankato, MN 56001 US
(507) 388-2900; *Fax:* (507) 345-4657
www.thefan1230.com/
jobailey@radiomankato.com
License: Mankato, MN held by Minnesota Valley Broadcasting Co.
Group Owner: Linder Broadcasting Group; (acq 12-31-2007; $700,000)
Arbitron Metro Market: Mankato, MN; *Format:* Sports
Jo Bailey, General Manager
Deb Armstrong, General Sales Mgr

KYSM-FM
08-01-1997; 103.5 MHz FM; *Hrs Open:* 24; 100 kw; 541 ft.; N44 10 20 W94 2 23
1807 Lee Blvd., N. Mankato, MN 56003 US
(507) 345-4646; *Fax:* (507) 345-4675
www.1035kysm.com
ddose@digity.me
License: Mankato, Blue Earth County, MN held by Digity 3E License, LLC
Group Owner: Digity, LLC
Nat'l Reps: Katz Radio; *Wire Services:* AP
Arbitron Metro Market: Mankato, MN; *Format:* Country; *No. News Employees:* 2; *Target Audience:* 25-54.; *Adv. Rates:* 75; 75; 75; 25
Denise Dose, General Manager
Kathy Varva, Station Mgr/Sales Mgr
Jess McGraw, Programming Director

Maplewood

WCTS
08-01-1964; 1030 kHz AM; *Hrs Open:* 24; 50 kw-D, DA2; 1 kw-N, DA2; N44 52 1 W92 54 2
1250 West Broadway, Minneapolis, MN 55411 US
(763) 417-8270; *Fax:* (763) 417-8278
www.wctsradio.com
info@wctsradio.com
License: Maplewood, MN held by Central Baptist Theological Seminary of Plymouth.
Nat'l Network: Moody; *Wire Services:* AP
Arbitron Metro Market: Minneapolis-Saint Paul, MN; *Format:* Christian, Religious; *Hrs. of News Programming:* News progmg 3 hrs wkly; *Target Audience:* 30 plus; Christian
Stephen Davis, General Manager

Marshall

KARZ
07-07-1985; 107.5 MHz FM; 15 kw; 430 ft.; N44 19 32 W95 52 19
1414 E. College Dr., Marshall, MN 56258 US
(507) 532-2282
License: Marshall, Lyon County, MN held by KMHL Broadcasting Company.
Group Owner: Linder Broadcasting Group; (acq 5-6-97; $450,000)
Arbitron Metro Market: Marshall, MN; *Format:* Classic Rock; *Target Audience:* 25-54.; *Adv. Rates:* 10.50; 10.50; 10.50; 8.25
Keith Petermeier, Operations Dir
Brad Strootman, General Manager

KKCK
12-13-1967; 99.7 MHz FM; *Hrs Open:* 24; 100 kw; 925 ft.; N44 16 56 W96 19 5
P.O. Box 1420, Mankato, MN 56001 US
(507) 532-2282; *Fax:* (507) 532-3739
marshallradio.net
info@marshallradio.net
License: Marshall, Lyon County, MN
Arbitron Metro Market: Mankato, MN; *Format:* Adult Contemp; *Hrs. of News Programming:* news progmg 8 hrs wkly; *No. News Employees:* 1; *Target Audience:* 21-39.; *Adv. Rates:* 19.50; 16.25; 16.25; 12
Keith Petermierer, Operations/Programming Director
Brad Strootman, General Manager
Russ Berreth, Music Director
Aaron Ziemer, News Director

KMHL
11-30-1946; 1400 kHz AM; *Hrs Open:* 24; 1 kw-U, ND1; N44 26 59 W95 45 43
1414 E. College Dr., Marshall, MN 56258 US
(507) 532-2282
License: Marshall, MN held by KMHL Broadcasting Co.
Group Owner: Linder Broadcasting Group
Nat'l Network: ABC; *Regional Network:* Linder Farm; MNN; *Nat'l Reps:* Katz Radio
Format: News/Talk, Country *Special Programming:* Relg 7 hrs wkly; *Hrs. of News Programming:* news progmg 20 hrs wkly; *No. News Employees:* 1; *Target Audience:* 27 plus.; *Adv. Rates:* 23; 13.50; 13.50; 11.25
Brad Strootman, General Manager

***KOMH**
90.7 MHz FM; kw
US
(910) 368-1581
License: Marshall, Lyon County, MN held by Shining Light Ministries.
Arbitron Metro Market: Marshall, MN
Joshua Hawkins, President

***KRGM**
89.9 MHz FM; 4 kw; 535 ft.; N44 29 3 W95 29 27
4604 Airpark Boulevard, Duluth, MN 55811 US
(218) 722-2727; *Fax:* (218) 279-5010
www.refugeradio.com
License: Marshall, Lyon County, MN held by Refuge Media Group.
Arbitron Metro Market: Duluth, MN
Mike Marrone, President
Paulette Kutzler, General Manager

Minneapolis

***KBEM-FM**
10-04-1970; 88.5 MHz FM; *Hrs Open:* 24; 2.9 kw; 479 ft.; N44 59 54 W93 11 18
1555 James Avenue North, Minneapolis, MN 55411 US
(612) 668-1735; *Fax:* (612) 668-1766
jazz88.mpls.k12.mn.us
studio@jazz88fm.com
License: Minneapolis, Hennepin County, MN held by Special School District No. 1, Board of Education.
Nat'l Network: PRI
Arbitron Metro Market: Minneapolis, MN; *Format:* Jazz *Special Programming:* Bluegrass 4 hrs, Sp 4 hrs wkly; *Hrs. of News Programming:* news progmg 14 hrs wkly; *No. News Employees:* 1; *Target Audience:* 35 plus;jazz/progsv adults, club/audiophiles
Michele Jansen, Station Manager
Jen Odden, Programming Director
Kevin O'Connor, Music Director
Ted Allison, Promotions Director
Ed Jones, News Director
Michael Jamnick, Engineering Dir

***KFAI**
05-01-1978; 90.3 MHz FM; *Hrs Open:* 24; 0.9 kw; 791 ft.; N44 58 34 W93 16 21
1808 Riverside Avenue, Minneapolis, MN 55454 US
(612) 341-3144; *Fax:* (612) 341-4281
www.kfai.org
janislaneewart@kfai.org
License: Minneapolis, Hennepin County, MN held by Fresh Air Inc.
Arbitron Metro Market: Minneapolis-St. Paul, MN; *Format:* Variety/Diverse *Special Programming:* Black 10 hrs, folk 6 hrs, Fr 2 hrs, jazz 12 hrs, Sp 8 hrs wkly; *Hrs. of News Programming:* news progmg 7 hrs wkly *No.News Employees:* 1; *Target Audience:* General; underserved, under-represented communities
Willie Dean, Executive Director
Miguel Vargas, Programming Director
Dale Connelly, News Director
Dan Zimmerman, Chief Engineer
Jason Buck, Marketing & Underwriting Director

KFXN
04-05-1962; 690 kHz AM; 0.5 kw-D, DA2; 0.004 kw-N, DA2; N45 1 25 W93 22 58
1088 Payne Ave., St. Paul, MN 55130 US
(612) 810-6412
www.hmongradioam690.com
License: Minneapolis, Hennepin County, MN held by Asian American Broadcasting LLC
Group Owner: Asian American Broadcasting LLC
Arbitron Metro Market: Minneapolis, MN; *Format:* Ethnic *Special Programming:* Cultural Talk 10 hrs wkly; *Target Audience:* 25-54, Asian Adults
Xeng Xiong, General Manager

***KMOJ**
09-15-1978; 89.9 MHz FM; *Hrs Open:* 24; 6.2 kw; 394 ft.; N45 4 7 W93 10 34
501 Bryant Avenue North, Minneapolis, MN 55405 US
(612) 377-0594; *Fax:* (612) 377-3990
License: Minneapolis, Hennepin County, MN held by Center for Communication & Development.
Arbitron Metro Market: Minneapolis, MN; *Format:* Urban Contemporary; *Hrs. of News Programming:* news progmg 4 hrs wkly; *No. News Employees:* 2; *Target Audience:* General.
Kelvin Quarles, General Manager
Candice Breedlove, Programming Director

KSJN
01-01-1956; 99.5 MHz FM; 100 kw; 1033 ft.; N45 3 30 W93 7 27
480 Cedar Street, St. Paul, MN 55101 US
(651) 290-1500; *Fax:* (651) 290-1224
www.mpr.org
info@mpr.org
License: Minneapolis, Hennepin County, MN held by Minnesota Public Radio Inc.
Wire Services: Reuters
Arbitron Metro Market: St. Paul, MN; *Format:* Talk
Jon McTaggart, President
Randi Yoder, Senior Vice President of Development
Chandra Kavati, Director of Development
Mary Ladner, Promotions Manager
Nick Kereakos, Vice President of Technology & Operations
Chris Worthington, NewsDirector
Jim McGuinn, Programming Director

KTCZ-FM
01-01-1956; 97.1 MHz FM; *Hrs Open:* 24; 100 kw; 1033 ft.; N45 3 30 W93 7 27
1600 Utica Avenue South, Suite 500, Minneapolis, MN 55431 US
(952) 417-3000; *Fax:* (952) 417-3001
www.cities97.com
info@cities97.com
License: Minneapolis, Hennepin County, MN held by AMFM Broadcasting Licenses LLC.
Group Owner: iHeartMedia
Arbitron Metro Market: Minneapolis-St. Paul, MN; *Format:* Adult Contemp
Jeff Tyler, Market President
Greg Alexander, Vice President of Sales

***KTIS**
02-07-1949; 900 kHz AM; *Hrs Open:* 24
3003 North Snelling Ave, Roseville, MN 55113 US
(651) 631-5000; *Fax:* (651) 631-5084
www.ktis.fm
info@ktis.fm
License: Minneapolis, MN held by Northwestern College.
Group Owner: Northwestern College & Radio
Arbitron Metro Market: Minneapolis-St. Paul, MN; *Format:* Christian, News, 74; *Hrs. of News Programming:* news progmg 20 hrs wkly; *No. News Employees:* 2; *Target Audience:* 35-45.
Paul Virts, President
Marilyn Ryan, Operations Dir
Jason Sharp, Station Manager

***KTIS-FM**
05-01-1949; 98.5 MHz FM; *Hrs Open:* 24; 100 kw; 1033 ft.; N45 3 30 W93 7 27
3003 North Snelling Ave, St. Paul, MN 55113 US

(651) 631-5000; *Fax:* (651) 631-5084
www.ktis.fm
info@ktis.fm
License: Minneapolis, Hennepin County, MN held by Northwestern College.
Group Owner: Northwestern College & Radio
Nat'l Network: AP Network News
Arbitron Metro Market: Minneapolis-St. Paul, MN; *Format:* Religious; *Hrs. of News Programming:* news progmg 20 hrs wkly; *No. News Employees:* 1; *Target Audience:* 25-45.
Alan Cureton, President
Harv Hendrickson, Operations Dir
Jason Sharp, Station Manager
Dr. Paul Virts, Executive Vice President

***KUOM**
01-13-1922; 770 kHz AM; *Hrs Open:* Sunrise-sunset; 5 kw-D, NDD; N44 59 54 W93 11 18
330 21st. Avenue, South, Minneapolis, MN 55455 US
(612) 625-3500; *Fax:* (612) 625-2112
www.radiok.org
request@radiok.org
License: Minneapolis, MN held by University of Minnesota
Wire Services: AP
Arbitron Metro Market: Minneapolis, MN; *Format:* Rock/AOR; *Target Audience:* 18-34
Sara Miller, Station Manager/Department Director

KTLK
12-23-1923; 1130 kHz AM; 50 kw-D, DA2; 25 kw-N, DA2; N44 38 48 W93 23 31
1600 Utica Ave. S., Suite 500, St. Louis Park, MN 55416 US
(952) 417-3000; *Fax:* (952) 417-3001
www.twincitiesnewstalk.com
License: Minneapolis, Hennepin County, MN held by AMFM Broadcasting Licenses LLC
Group Owner: iHeartMedia
Arbitron Metro Market: Minneapolis, MN; *Format:* News, News/Talk, 86
Greg Alexander, Senior Vice President of Sales

KXXR
10-01-1960; 93.7 MHz FM; *Hrs Open:* 24; 100 kw; 1033 ft.; N45 3 30 W93 7 27
2000 SE Elm St., Minneapolis, MN 55414 US
(612) 617-4000; *Fax:* (612) 676-8292
www.93x.com
License: Minneapolis, MN held by Radio License Holdings LLC
Group Owner: Cumulus Media Inc.; (acq 6-12-2007; grpsl)
Nat'l Reps: Interep
Arbitron Metro Market: Minneapolis-St. Paul, MN; *Format:* Rock/AOR; *Target Audience:* 18-54.
Scott Jameson, Operations Manager
Mark Ellis, General Sales Mgr
Derek Madden, Programming Director
Graham Swart, Promotions Dir
Shelly Malecha Wilkes, VP/Market Mgr

WCCO
10-02-1924; 830 kHz AM; *Hrs Open:* 24; 50 kW; N45 10 40 W93 20 55
625 2nd Ave. South, Minneapolis, MN 55402 USA
(612) 370-0611
www.wccoradio.com
License: Minneapolis, MN held by CBS Radio Media Corporation
Group Owner: CBS Radio; (acq 11-13-98; grpsl).
Nat'l Network: CBS; *Nat'l Reps:* Interep
Arbitron Metro Market: Minneapolis-St. Paul, MN; *Format:* News/Talk, News, 86; *Hrs. of News Programming:* news progmg 25 hrs wkly; *No. News Employees:* 7; *Target Audience:* General

KMNB
12-26-2011; 102.9 MHz FM; *Hrs Open:* 24; 100 kW; 1037 ft.; N45 03 30 W93 07 27
625 2nd Ave. South, Minneapolis, MN 55402 USA
(612) 370-0611
www.buzn1029.com
License: Minneapolis, Hennepin County, MN held by CBS Radio Media Corporation
Group Owner: CBS Radio
Arbitron Metro Market: Minneapolis-St. Paul, MN; *Format:* Country; *Hrs. of News Programming:* News progmg 5 hrs wkly; *Target Audience:* 25-54
Lara Engh, Promotions Manager

WLOL
01-01-1939; 1330 kHz AM; *Hrs Open:* 24; 9.7 kw-D, DA2; 5.1 kw-N, DA2; N44 47 2 W93 20 38
1496 Bellevue Street, Suite 202, Green Bay, WI 54311 US
(612)643-4119; *Fax:* (763)546-4444
www.relevantradio.com
info@relevantradio.com
License: Minneapolis, MN held by Starboard Media Foundation Inc.
Group Owner: Relevant Radio; (acq 3-16-2004; $6.75 million)
Arbitron Metro Market: Minneapolis, MN; *Format:* Christian; *Hrs. of News Programming:* 3 hrs news progmg wkly
Thomas Vorpahl, Chairman
Francis J. Hoffman, Executive Director
Bob Benes, General Sales Mgr
Mike Kendall, Programming Director

KFXN-FM
06-26-1965; 100.3 MHz FM; *Hrs Open:* 24; 97 kw; 905 ft; N45 20 12 W93 23 28
1600 Utica Ave. S., Suite 500, St. Louis Park, MN 55416 US
(952) 417-3000; *Fax:* (952) 417-3001
www.kfan.com
License: Minneapolis, Hennepin County, MN held by AMFM Broadcasting Licenses LLC.
Group Owner: iHeartMedia; (acq 8-30-2000; grpsl).
Nat'l Network: Fox News Radio; *Nat'l Reps:* Clear Channel
Population Served: 2,500,000; *Arbitron Metro Market:* Minneapolis-St. Paul, MN; *Format:* Sports, Talk; *No. News Employees:* 3; *Target Audience:* Adults 25-54; adults
Gregg Swedberg, Operations Manager
Jeff Tyler, General Manager
Tom Bourassa, Sales Manager
Chad Abbott, Programming Director
Ellie Tungseth, Promotions Director
Veronica Rodriguez, Chief Engineer

WWTC
08-10-1925; 1280 kHz AM
8910 University Center Lane, #130, San Diego, CA 92122 US
(651) 405-8800; *Fax:* (651) 405-8222
www.am1280thepatriot.com
comments@am1280thepatriot.com
License: Minneapolis, MN held by Salem Media Group LLC.
Group Owner: Salem Communications Corp.; (acq 12-18-2000; $7 million with WAUK(AM) Jackson, WI)
Arbitron Metro Market: Egan, MN; *Format:* News, News/Talk, 86; *Target Audience:* 18-54.; *Adv. Rates:* 100; 75; 100; 50
Lee Michaels, Operations Dir
Nic Anderson, General Manager
Nick Novak, Programming Director
Steve Smit, Chief Engineer
Cindy Bohm, Traffic Director
Eric Emery, Production/Imaging Director
Desta Kraft, Administrative Assistant
Laurie Krier, Business Manager
Kirsten Aura, Account Executive

Minneapolis-St. Paul

***KNOW-FM**
07-01-1967; 91.1 MHz FM; 100 kw; 1275 ft.; N45 3 44 W93 8 21
480 Cedar Street, St. Paul, MN 55101 US
(651) 290-1500; *Fax:* (651) 290-1224
www.mpr.org
info@mpr.org
License: Minneapolis-St. Paul, Hennepin County, MN held by Minnesota Public Radio.
Wire Services: Reuters
Arbitron Metro Market: Minneapolis-St. Paul, MN; *Format:* News
Jon McTaggart, President
Nick Kereakos, Vice President of Operations
Jim McGuinn, Station Manager
Timothy Roesler, General Manager of Classsical Music
Chris Worthington, News Director

Montevideo

***KBPG**
07-01-2002; 89.5 MHz FM; 0.5 kw; 151 ft.; N44 54 50 W95 44 10
P.O. Box 3206, Tupelo, MS 38803 US
(662) 844-8888; *Fax:* (662) 842-6791
www.afr.net
faq@afa.net
License: Montevideo, Chippewa County, MN held by American Family Association.
Group Owner: American Family Radio; (acq 11-26-99).
Nat'l Network: USA
Format: Religious
Tim Wildmon, President
Donald Wildmon, Founder
Buddy Smith, Sr VP
Ed Vitagliano, Executive VP
Randy Sharp, Director Of Special Projects
Meeke Addison, Director Of Communications
Abraham Hamilton III, General Counsel &ÆPublicPolicy Analyst

KDMA
12-21-1951; 1460 kHz AM; *Hrs Open:* 24
Box 513, Montevideo, MN 55409 US
(320) 269-8815(320) 269-5131; *Fax:* (320) 269-8449
www.kdmanews.com
License: Montevideo, MN held by Iowa City Broadcasting Co.
Group Owner: Tom Ingstad Broadcasting Group; (acq 10-21-97; grpsl)
Regional Network: Linder Farm *Regional Reps:* O'Malley.; *Wire Services:* Weather Wire
Format: News/Talk *Special Programming:* Farm 7 hrs wkly; *No. News Employees:* 1; *Adv. Rates:* 19.25; 15.75; 15.75; 12
Dwight Mulder, Operations Dir
Roberta Kuno, Station Manager
Roger Hill, General Sales Mgr
Lynn Ketelson, Farm Director

KMGM
10-01-1982; 105.5 MHz FM; *Hrs Open:* 24; 3 kw; 295 ft.; N44 51 24 W95 37 46
4454 Highway 212 West, Montevideo, MN 56265 US
(320) 269-8815; *Fax:* (320) 269-8449
dwight@kdmanews.com
License: Montevideo, Chippewa County, MN held by Iowa City Broadcasting Co.
Group Owner: Tom Ingstad Broadcasting Group
Wire Services: Weather Wire
Format: Classic Rock; *Target Audience:* 25-54.
Roger Hill, General Manager
Roger Hill, General Sales Mgr
Dwight Mulder, Programming Director
Andy Coulter, Sales Manager
Ashley Flinn, Traffic Manager

Moorhead

***KCCD**
06-01-1992; 90.3 MHz FM; *Hrs Open:* 24; 100 kw vert; 495 ft.; N46 45 35 W96 36 26
480 Cedar Street, Saint Paul, MN 55101 US
(651) 290-1500
www.mpr.org
License: Moorhead, Clay County, MN held by Minnesota Public Radio.
Nat'l Network: NPR; PRI; *Regional Network:* Minn. Pub. Radio
Arbitron Metro Market: Saint Paul, MN; *Format:* News; *No. News Employees:* 2; *Target Audience:* General.
Jon McTaggart, President
Randi Yoder, Senior Vice President of Development
Chandra Kavati, Director of Development
Nick Kereakos, Vice President of Technology & Operations
Jim McGuinn, Programming Director
Chris Worthington, NewsDirector

***KCCM-FM**
10-23-1971; 91.1 MHz FM; *Hrs Open:* 24; 67 kw; 659 ft.; N46 45 35 W96 36 26
480 Cedar Street, St. Paul, MN 55101 US
(651) 290-1500; *Fax:* (218) 299-3418
www.mpr.org
License: Moorhead, Clay County, MN held by Minnesota Public Radio Inc.
Nat'l Network: NPR; PRI; *Regional Network:* Minn. Pub. Radio
Arbitron Metro Market: Saint Paul, MN; *Format:* Ethnic; *Hrs. of News Programming:* news progmg one hr wkly; *No. News Employees:* 2; *Target Audience:* General.
Jon McTaggart, President
Randi Yoder, Senior Vice President of Development
Chandra Kavati, Director of Development
Nick Kereakos, Vice President of Technology & Operations
Jim McGuinn, Programming Director
Chris Worthington, NewsDirector

KLTA-FM
11-01-1966; 98.7 MHz FM; 100 kw; 581 ft.; N46 45 35 W96 36 26
Mailing Address: 301 8th Street South, Fargo, ND 58103 US
Second Address: 2720 7th Ave. S., Fargo, ND 58103
(701) 237-4500; *Fax:* (701) 235-9082
License: Moorhead, Clay County, MN held by Radio Fargo-Moorhead Inc.
Group Owner: Radio Fargo-Moorhead Inc.
Nat'l Reps: Christal
Arbitron Metro Market: Fargo-Moorhead, ND-MN; *Format:* Classic Rock; *Target Audience:* 18-49; men
David Benjamin, President
John Austin, Operations Dir
Nancy Odney, General Manager
Jessica Benson, Sales Manager
Gunner, Programming Director
Bonita Baker, Traffic Manager

John Austin, Operations Director
Anne Phibian,Operations Manager

KVXR
11-30-1937; 1280 kHz AM; *Hrs Open:* 24
P.O. Box 13703, Grand Forks, ND 58208 US
(701) 795-0122
License: Moorhead, MN held by Voice of Reason Radio
Arbitron Metro Market: Fargo-Moorhead, ND-MN; *Format:* Christian
Robert Schumacher, President

KVOX-FM
11-30-1966; 99.9 MHz FM; *Hrs Open:* 24; 100 kW; 381 ft.; N46 49 9 W96 45 56
1020 S 25th Street, Fargo, ND 58103 USA
(701) 237-5346; *Fax:* (701) 237-0980
froggyweb.com
License: Moorhead, Clay County, MN held by Midwest Communications Inc.
Group Owner: Midwest Communications Inc.
Nat'l Reps: Christal; *Wire Services:* AP
Arbitron Metro Market: Fargo-Moorhead; *Format:* Country; *Hrs. of News Programming:* News progmg 7 hrs wkly; *Target Audience:* 25-54; female skew
Dan Cash, Sales Manager
Chris Daniels, Brand Manager

Moose Lake

WMOZ
01-01-2001; 106.9 MHz FM; 6 kw; 164 ft.; N46 30 20 W92 40 45
1104 Cloquet Avenue, Cloquest, MN 55720 US
(218) 879-4534; *Fax:* (218) 879-1962
www.wmoz-fm.com
License: Moose Lake, Carlton County, MN held by QB Broadcasting Ltd.
Group Owner: Quarnstrom Media Group LLC
Arbitron Metro Market: Moose Lake, MN; *Format:* Oldies
Mark Senarighi, General Manager

Mora

KBEK
05-12-1995; 95.5 MHz FM; *Hrs Open:* 24; 25 kw; 328 ft.; N45 44 33 W93 22 48
PO Box 136, 1947 Dennis Road, Mora, MN 55051 US
(320) 679-6955; *Fax:* (320) 679-2348
www.kbek.com
kbek@besttimes.com
License: Mora, Kanabec County, MN held by Colleen McKinney, personal representative
Arbitron Metro Market: Mora, MN; *Format:* Oldies; *Hrs. of News Programming:* News progmg 8 hrs wkly; *Target Audience:* General.
Colleen McKinney, General Manager
Scott McKenney, Programming Director
Diana Wilson, Promotions Manager
Dave Bailey, Chief Engineer
Webster Ford, Sports Director
Lloyd Falk, Traffic Manager

Morris

KKOK-FM
09-16-1976; 95.7 MHz FM; 100 kw; 361 ft.; N45 36 11 W95 53 14
1020 25th Street South, Fargo, ND 58108 US
(320) 589-3131; *Fax:* (320) 589-2715
www.kmrskkok.com
kmrskkok@fedtel.net
License: Morris, Stevens County, MN
Arbitron Metro Market: Saint Cloud, MN; *Format:* Country
Deborah Driggins-Mattheis, General Manager
Bill Eckersen, Programming Director
Katie McKenzie, News Director
Paul McDonald, Sports Director
Krystal Dohlen, Marketing Consultant
Aileen Sperr, Marketing Consultant
Milissa Bjorge,Traffic Manager

KMRS
09-16-1956; 1230 kHz AM; *Hrs Open:* 19; 1 kw-U, ND1; N45 36 11 W95 53 14
1020 25th Street South, Fargo, ND 58108 US
(320) 589-3131; *Fax:* (320) 589-2715
www.kmrskkok.com
kmrskkok@fedtel.net
License: Morris, MN held by Iowa City Broadcasting Co.
Group Owner: Tom Ingstad Broadcasting Group; (acq 1-11-2000; with co-located FM).
Nat'l Reps: McGavren Guild
Format: Adult Contemp, News, 62, Talk; *Hrs. of News Programming:* news progmg 80 hrs wkly; *No. News Employees:* 1; *Target Audience:* 35-64; farmers & agri-business people
Deb Mattheis, General Manager
Deb Mattheis, General Sales Mgr
Bill Eckersen, Programming Director
Katie McKenzie, News Director
Ken Bartz, Chief Engineer

***KUMM**
09-17-1970; 89.7 MHz FM; *Hrs Open:* 24; 0.7 kw; 125 ft.; N45 35 11 W95 53 57
600 East 4th Street, Morris, MN 56267 US
(320) 589-6076; *Fax:* (320) 589-6084
www.kumm.org
bark0293@morris.umn.edu
License: Morris, Stevens County, MN held by University of Minnesota.
Wire Services: AP
Arbitron Metro Market: Morris, MN; *Format:* Alternative; *Hrs. of News Programming:* News progmg 3 hrs wkly; *Target Audience:* 18-30; primarily college students; *Adv. Rates:* 6; 4; 6; 3.
Ross Penning, Station Manager
Marco Riley, Programming Director
Alyssa Powell, Publicity Director
Torri Jordan, Training Director

Nashwauk

WNMT
06-02-1975; 650 kHz AM; 10 kW; N47 22 31 W93 0 56
807 West 37th St, Hibbing, MN 55746 USA
(218) 263-7531; *Fax:* (218) 263-6112
wnmtradio.com
License: Nashwauk, MN held by Midwest Communications Inc.
Group Owner: Midwest Communications Inc.; acq 5-10-2004; grpsl).
Arbitron Metro Market: Hibbing, MN; *Format:* News/Talk *Special Programming:* Pol 2 hrs wkly; *Target Audience:* 35 plus.
Craig Holgate, Brand Manager

New Prague

KCHK
09-22-1969; 1350 kHz AM; *Hrs Open:* 24; 0.5 kw-D, DA2; 0.07 kw-N, DA2; N44 34 39 W93 30 16
25821 Langford Avenue, New Prague, MN 56071 US
(952) 758-2571; *Fax:* (952) 758-3170
www.kchkradio.net
kchkamfm@beucomm.net
License: New Prague, MN held by Ingstad Brothers Broadcasting LLC
Group Owner: Ingstad Brothers Broadcasting LLC; acq 5-1-2004; grpsl).
Nat'l Network: ABC; *Regional Network:* MNN; *Wire Services:* NWS (National Weather Service)
Arbitron Metro Market: Minneapolis-St. Paul, MN; *Format:* News, News/Talk, 86 *Special Programming:* Sp. 6 hrs, Pol, Czch, Ger 40 hrs wkly; *Hrs. of News Programming:* News progmg 50 hrs wkly; *Target Audience:* 35-59. *Adv. Rates:* 10; 10; 10; 10
Tom Goetzinger, General Manager
Sam O'Byrne, General Sales Mgr
Dave Douglas, Engineering Dir

KCHK-FM
12-01-1990; 95.5 MHz FM; *Hrs Open:* 24; 6 kw; 328 ft.; N44 27 40 W93 35 8
207 Textile Bldg., 119 North 4th Street, Minneapolis, MN 55401 US
(952) 758-2571; *Fax:* (952) 758-3170
www.kchkradio.net
License: New Prague, Le Sueur County, MN held by Ingstad Brothers Broadcasting LLC
Group Owner: Ingstad Brothers Broadcasting LLC
Wire Services: NWS (National Weather Service)
Arbitron Metro Market: Minneapolis-St. Paul, MN; *Format:* Oldies; *Hrs. of News Programming:* news progmg 7 hrs wkly; *No. News Employees:* 3; *Target Audience:* 25-64; general
Mike Nolen, General Manager
Lynn Nolen, Station Manager

New Ulm

KNUJ
05-01-1949; 860 kHz AM; *Hrs Open:* 24; 1 kw-D, ND1; 0.005 kw-N, ND1; N44 17 10 W94 25 50
317 North Minnesota Street, New Ulm, MN 56073 US
(507) 359-2921; *Fax:* (507) 359-4520
www.knuj.net
knuj@knuj.net
License: New Ulm, MN held by Ingstad Brothers Broadcasting LLC
Group Owner: Ingstad Brothers Broadcasting LLC; acq 5-1-2004; grpsl).
Arbitron Metro Market: Mankato-New Ulm; *Format:* Country *Special Programming:* Old-time 8 hrs wkly; *Hrs. of News Programming:* news progmg 30 hrs wkly; *No. News Employees:* 2; *Target Audience:* 30 plus.
Jim Bartels, General Manager
Brian Filzen, Programming Director

KATO-FM
11-21-1966; 93.1 MHz FM; 100 kw; 489 ft.; N44 7 44 W94 11 15
59346 Madison Ave., Madison, WI 56001 US
(507) 345-4537; *Fax:* (507) 345-5364
www.minnesota93.com/
jobailey@radiomankato.com
License: New Ulm, Brown County, MN held by Minnesota Valley Broadcasting Co.
Group Owner: Linder Broadcasting Group; (acq 9-1-2007; $3.13 million)
Arbitron Metro Market: Mankato, MN; *Format:* Country
Jo Bailey, General Manager
Deb Armstrong, General Sales Mgr

Nisswa

KBLB
01-01-2002; 93.3 MHz FM; *Hrs Open:* 24; 100 kw; 558 ft.; N46 26 34 W94 22 55
Mailing Address: P.O. Box 746, Brainerd, MN 56401-0746 US
Second Address: 13225 Dogwood Drive South, Baxter, MN 56425-8613
(218) 828-1244; *Fax:* (218) 828-1119
brainerdradio.net
production@brainerd.net
License: Nisswa, Crow Wing County, MN held by BL Broadcasting Inc.
Group Owner: Omni Broadcasting Co.; (acq 12-11-2000).
Nat'l Network: ABC; *Regional Network:* Minn. News Net.
Format: Country; *Hrs. of News Programming:* news progmg 12 hrs wkly; *No. News Employees:* 1; *Target Audience:* 25-54; adults
Lou Buron, CEO
G. Michael Boen, General Manager
Al Davison, Programming Director
Tess Taylor, News Director
David Cox, Chief Engineer
Mary Campbell, CFO

North Branch

***KMKL**
10-06-2001; 90.3 MHz FM; *Hrs Open:* 24; 15 kw vert; 397 ft.; N45 32 36 W92 58 24
, North Branch, MN US
(800) 525-5683; *Fax:* (916) 251-1650
www.klove.com
klove@klove.com
License: North Branch, Chisago County, MN held by Educational Media Foundation.
Group Owner: EMF Broadcasting
Nat'l Network: K-Love
Arbitron Metro Market: North Branch, MN; *Format:* Christian; *No. News Employees:* 3; *Target Audience:* 25-44; Judeo Christian, female
Darrell Chambliss, Chairman
Mike Novak, President and CEO
John Clements, Operations Dir
David Pierce, Programming Director
Ed Lenane, News Director
Sam Wallington, Engineering Dir
Scott Smith, Music Director
Marya Morgan, NewsReporter
Richard Hunt, News Reporter
Tracy Butler, Traffic Manager
Laura Daniels, News Reporter
Tim Luttrell, News Reporter

North Mankato

KDOG
04-01-1985; 96.7 MHz FM; 4 kw; 650 ft.; N44 13 20 W94 7 3
59346 Madison Ave., Mankato, MN 56001 US
(507) 345-4537
www.hot967.fm
License: North Mankato, Blue Earth County, MN held by Minnesota Valley Broadcasting Co.
Group Owner: Linder Broadcasting Group
Arbitron Metro Market: Mankato-New Ulm-St. Peter, MN; *Format:* Contemporary Hits/Top 40; *Hrs. of News Programming:* news progmg 4 hrs wkly; *No. News Employees:* 1
Jo Bailey, General Manager
Deb Armstrong, General Sales Mgr

Northfield

***KRLX**
01-25-1975; 88.1 MHz FM; 0.1 kw; 16 ft.; N44 27 39 W93 9 21
300 North College Street, Northfield, MN 55057 US
(507) 646-4102
License: Northfield, Rice County, MN held by Carleton College.
Arbitron Metro Market: Northfield, MN; *Format:* Talk; *Target Audience:* General; college-associated people and rural
Don Cumming, Communications Director
Steven Reid, Media Relations Officer

KYMN-AM
09-27-1968; 1080 kHz AM; *Hrs Open:* 24; 1 kW-D; N44 29 12 W93 06 20
200 Division St, Suite 260, Northfield, MN 55057 USA
(507) 645-5695; *Fax:* (507) 645-9768
contact@kymnradio.net
License: Northfield, Rice County, MN held by Northfield Media Inc.
Group Owner: Northfield Media; acq 1-1-2009; grpsl).
Nat'l Network: Westwood One; *Regional Network:* Minnesota Twins Radio Network; Minnesota News Network
Population Served: 100,000 *Special Programming:* Eclectic music, local news and talk, Spanish language 2 hrs; *No. News Employees:* 1; *Target Audience:* 35-54; parents with school-age children, well-educated *Adv.Rates:* 18; 16; 14; 10
Jeff Johnson, CEO/COO
Jeff Johnson, President
Jeff Johnson, General Manager
Jeff Johnson, General Sales Mgr
Teri Knight, News Director
Tim Valley, Chief Engineer

***KCMP**
04-04-1968; 89.3 MHz FM; *Hrs Open:* 24; 97.6 kw; 768 ft.; N44 41 21 W93 4 21
480 Cedar Street, St. Paul, MN 55101 US
(651) 290-1500; *Fax:* (651) 290-1295
www.mpr.org
License: Northfield, Rice County, MN held by Minnesota Public Radio
Arbitron Metro Market: Saint Paul, MN; *Format:* Triple A
Jon McTaggart, President
Nick Kereakos, Vice President of Technology & Operations
Tim Roesler, Senior Vice President/General Manager
Chandra Kavati, Director of Development Services
Craig Curtis, Vice President of Programming
ChrisWorthington, News Director
Melanie Walker, Music Director

KYMN-FM
09-27-1968; 95.1 MHz FM; *Hrs Open:* 24; 1 kW-D; N44 29 12 W93 06 20
200 Division St, Suite 260, Northfield, MN 55057 USA
(507) 645-5695; *Fax:* (507) 645-9768
contact@kymnradio.net
License: Northfield, Rice County, MN held by Northfield Media Inc.
Group Owner: Northfield Media; acq 1-1-2009; grpsl).
Nat'l Network: Westwood One; *Regional Network:* Minnesota Twins Radio Network; Minnesota News Network
Population Served: 100,000 *Special Programming:* Eclectic music, local news and talk, Spanish language 2 hrs; *No. News Employees:* 1; *Target Audience:* 35-54; parents with school-age children, well-educated *Adv.Rates:* 18; 16; 14; 10
Jeff Johnson, CEO/COO
Jeff Johnson, President
Jeff Johnson, General Manager
Jeff Johnson, General Sales Mgr
Teri Knight, News Director
Tim Valley, Chief Engineer

Olivia

KOLV
06-27-1983; 100.1 MHz FM; 50 kw; 466 ft.; N44 58 14 W95 14 59
1340 7th St NW., PO Box 838, Willmar, MN 56201 US
(320) 235-1342
www.willmarradio.com
License: Olivia, Renville County, MN held by Bold Radio Inc.
Group Owner: Linder Broadcasting Group; (acq 3-18-98; $335,000).
Regional Network: Linder Farm; *Nat'l Reps:* Keystone (unwired net)
Format: Country *Special Programming:* Big band, adult contemp, oldies, Top-40
MaryElin Macht, Programming/Operations Director

Ortonville

***KCGN-FM**
09-23-1983; 101.5 MHz FM; *Hrs Open:* 24; 98 kw; 1001 ft.; N45 22 29 W97 2 20
402 Pike Street East, Osakis, MN 56360 US
(320) 859-3000; *Fax:* (320) 859-3010
www.praisefm.org
License: Ortonville, Big Stone County, MN held by Praise Broadcasting Inc.
Format: Adult Contemp, Christian; *Target Audience:* 25-44; middle-aged women; *Adv. Rates:* 14; 11; 14; 11
Dave Hartman, Operations Dir
David McIver, General Manager
Matt Brown, Marketing
Jack Zitzmann, Programming Director
Steve Kneprath, Chief Engineer
Sherrie McIver, Music Director
Michelle Anderson, Traffic Manager

KDIO
07-23-1956; 1350 kHz AM
47 2nd Street NW, Ortonville, MN 56278 US
(320) 839-2581; *Fax:* (320) 839-2571
bigstoneradio.com
kdio@bigstoneradio.com
License: Ortonville, MN held by Armada Media-Watertown Inc.
Group Owner: Armada Media Corp.; (acq 8-3-2007; grpsl)
Nat'l Network: ABC; *Regional Network:* Linder Farm; Minn. News Net.
Arbitron Metro Market: Ortonville, MN; *Format:* Country *Special Programming:* Farm 18 hrs, relg 5 hrs wkly
Jeff Kurtz, President
Joan Lien, General Sales Mgr
Julie Anne French, Programming Director

KPHR
01-01-1996; 106.3 MHz FM; 100 kw; 955 ft.; N45 6 17 W96 59 17
232 Third Street, Ne, Valley City, ND 58072 US
(605) 884-1000; *Fax:* (605) 884-3549
www.bigstoneradio.com
License: Ortonville, Big Stone County, MN held by Armada Media-Watertown Inc.
Group Owner: Armada Media Corp.
Arbitron Metro Market: Watertown, SD; *Format:* Classic Rock
Jeff Kurtz, Operations Dir
Kim Krause, News Director

Osakis

***KBHL**
03-11-1985; 103.9 MHz FM; 6 kw; 328 ft.; N45 50 24 W95 5 56
402 Pike St. E., Osakis, MN 56360 US
(320) 859-3000; *Fax:* (320) 859-3010
www.praisefm.org
mail@praisefm.org
License: Osakis, Douglas County, MN held by Christian Heritage Broadcasting Inc.
Nat'l Network: Moody
Arbitron Metro Market: Osakis, MN; *Format:* Christian
Dave Hartman, Operations Dir
David McIver, General Manager
Matt Brown, Marketing Director

Owatonna

KRFO
01-01-1950; 1390 kHz AM; *Hrs Open:* 5 AM-midnight; 0.5 kw-D, ND1; 0.094 kw-N, ND1; N44 4 29 W93 10 46
245 18th Street SE, Owatonna, MN 55060 US
(507) 451-2250; *Fax:* (507) 451-8837
www.krforadio.com
License: Owatonna, MN held by Cumulus Licensing Corp.
Group Owner: Cumulus Media Inc.; (acq 7-21-98; grpsl)
Format: Oldies *Special Programming:* Sp 2 hrs wkly; *Hrs. of News Programming:* news progmg 18 hrs wkly; *No. News Employees:* 1; *Target Audience:* 35 plus.
John Connor, General Sales Mgr
Loren Hart, Programming Director
Gary Schmidt, Chief Engineer
Shannon Knoepke, Marketing Manager
Paul Benzick, Business Manager
Missi Jensen, Traffic Manager

KRFO-FM
12-29-1966; 104.9 MHz FM; *Hrs Open:* 18; 4.7 kw; 174 ft.; N44 4 29 W93 10 46
245 18th Street SE, Owatonna, WI 55060 US
(507) 451-2250; *Fax:* (507) 451-8837
www.krforadio.com
License: Owatonna, Steele County, MN
Format: Country; *Hrs. of News Programming:* news progmg 12 hrs wkly; *No. News Employees:* 1; *Target Audience:* 25-54.
John Connor, General Sales Mgr
Loren Hart, Programming Director
Gary Schmidt, Chief Engineer
Shannon Knoepke, Marketing Manager
Paul Benzick, Business Manager
Missi Jensen, Traffic Manager

Park Rapids

KDKK
12-01-1967; 97.5 MHz FM; 100 kw; 636 ft.; N46 55 51 W95 0 27
P.O. Box 49, Highway 34 East, Park Rapids, MN 65470 US
(218) 732-3306
www.kkradionetwork.com
kprmkdkk@unitelc.com
License: Park Rapids, Hubbard County, MN
Wire Services: Weather Wire
Arbitron Metro Market: Park Rapids, MN; *Format:* Contemporary Hits/Top 40; *Target Audience:* 40 plus.
E.P. De La Hunt, General Manager
Bernie Schumacher, Women's Int Ed

KPRM
12-01-1962; 870 kHz AM; 25 kw-D, DAN; 1 kw-N, DAN; N46 55 42 W95 0 22; N46 54 18 W95 1 4
P.O. Box 49, Highway 34 East, Park Rapids, MN 56470 US
(218) 732-3306; *Fax:* (218) 732-3307
www.kkradionetwork.com
kprmkdkk@unitelc.com
License: Park Rapids, MN held by De La Hunt Broadcasting Corp.
Nat'l Network: CBS
Format: Country; *Target Audience:* 25 plus.
Ed DeLa Hunt, General Manager
Bernie Schumacher, General Sales Mgr
David De La Hunt, Chief Engineer

KXKK
01-01-1998; 92.5 MHz FM; 10 kw; 584 ft.; N46 55 51 W95 0 27
17340 State Highway 34, PO Box 49, Park Rapids, MN 56470 US
(218) 732-3306; *Fax:* (218) 732-3307
License: Park Rapids, Hubbard County, MN held by Bernadine A. Schumacher.
Arbitron Metro Market: Park Rapids, MN; *Format:* Country
Bernadine Schumacher, General Manager

Paynesville

KZPK
12-01-1995; 98.9 MHz FM; *Hrs Open:* 24; 47 kw; 499 ft.; N45 34 3 W94 30 43
22184 Fairmont Road, St. Cloud, MN 56301 US
(320) 251-1450; *Fax:* (320) 251-8952
www.wildcountry99.com
License: Paynesville, Stearns County, MN held by Leighton Enterprises Inc.
Group Owner: Leighton Enterprises Inc.; acq 4-15-97; $1 million)
Arbitron Metro Market: St. Cloud, MN; *Format:* Country
Bob Leighton, CEO
John Sowada, President/General Manager
Matt Senne, Operations Dir
Denny Niess, Vice President
Matt Senne, Programming Director/Operations Manager
Melissa Malat, Promotions Manager
Cassie Hart, News Director
Dale Daley, Chief Engineer
Denise Prozinski, General Sales Manager
Kathy Carton, Traffic Manager
Cindy Niess, Traffic Manager

Pelican Rapids

KBOT
06-01-1994; 104.1 MHz FM; *Hrs Open:* 24; 50 kw; 456 ft.; N46 43 19 W95 50 37
1340 Richwood Road, Detroit Lakes, MN 56501 US
(218) 847-5624; *Fax:* (218) 847-7657
www.wild1041.com
kdlmkbot@lakesnet.net
License: Pelican Rapids, Otter Tail County, MN held by Leighton Enterprises Inc.
Group Owner: Leighton Enterprises Inc.; (acq 9-24-96; $700,000).
Regional Reps: O'Malley.
Arbitron Metro Market: Fargo-Moorhead, ND-MN; *Format:* Country; *Hrs. of News Programming:* news progmg one hr wkly; *No. News Employees:* 1; *Target Audience:* 25-54; Fargo-Moorhead, metro & TSA listeners *Adv.Rates:* 19.50; 19.50; 19.50; 19.50

Bob Leighton, CEO
John Sowada, President/General Manager
Denny Niess, Operations Dir
Jeff Leighton, General Manager
Kevin Flynn, Programming Director
Deb Olson, Sales Manager

Pequot Lakes

*KTIG

04-30-1978; 102.7 MHz FM; *Hrs Open:* 24; 40 kw; 541 ft.; N46 40 48 W94 25 2
P.O. Box 409, Pequot Lakes, MN 56472 US
(218) 568-4422; *Fax:* (218) 568-5950
theword.mn/
License: Pequot Lakes, Crow Wing County, MN held by Minnesota Christian Broadcasters Inc.
Nat'l Network: Moody; USA
Arbitron Metro Market: Minneapolis-St. Paul, MN; *Format:* Religious; *Target Audience:* 35-55; general
Mike Heuberger, General Manager
Phil Kvamme, Programming Director
Randy Kennedy, News Director
Aaron Pearson, Chief Engineer

*KLKS

01-01-2002; 100.1 MHz FM; 3.9 kw; Ant 407 ft; N46 40 48 W94 25 02
Box 409, Pequot Lakes, MN 56472
(866) 568-4422; *Fax:* (218) 568-5950
License: Pequot Lakes, Crow Wing County, MN held by Minnesota Christian Broadcasters Inc.
Nat'l Network: Moody; USA

Mike Heuberger, General Manager
Tim Norman, Programming Director
Aaron Pearson, News Director
Dwayne Walker, Chief Engineer

Perham

KPRW

08-26-1996; 99.5 MHz FM; *Hrs Open:* 24; 6 kw; 328 ft.; N46 33 16 W95 27 24
728 Western Avenue, Fergus Falls, MN 56537 US
(218) 346-4800; *Fax:* (218) 346-7595
License: Perham, Otter Tail County, MN held by Jerry Papenfuss.
Group Owner: The Result Radio Group
Nat'l Reps: Hyett/Ramsland
Arbitron Metro Market: Perham, MN, Fergus Falls, Detroit Lakes; *Format:* Triple A; *Hrs. of News Programming:* news progmg 10 hrs wkly; *No. News Employees:* 1; *Target Audience:* 25-54.; *Adv. Rates:* 24; 18; 18;12
Jerry Pappenfuss, CEO
Doug Gray, General Manager
David Howey, Programming Director

Pillager

WWWI-FM

01-01-2000; 95.9 MHz FM; 6 kw; 240 ft.; N46 15 3 W94 19 30
PO Box 140, Aitkin, MN 56431 US
(218) 828-9994; *Fax:* (218) 828-8327
www.3wiradio.com
talK@3wiradio.com
License: Pillager, Cass County, MN held by Tower Broadcasting Corp.
Arbitron Metro Market: Brainerd, MN; *Format:* News, News/Talk, 86
Tom Martin, General Manager
Pete Vukelich, News Director

Pine City

WCMP

06-13-1957; 1350 kHz AM; *Hrs Open:* 24; 1 kw-D, ND1; 0.052 kw-N, ND1; N45 49 10 W92 59 45
15429 Pokegama Lake Road, Pine City, MN 55063 US
(715)-825-4240; *Fax:* (715)-825-4244
www.redrockonair.com
jesselogan@redrockonair.com.
License: Pine City, MN held by Quarnstrom Media Group LLC
Group Owner: Quarnstrom Media Group LLC; acq 9-22-03).
Regional Network: MNN
Arbitron Metro Market: Sebring, FL; *Format:* News *Special Programming:* Farm 6 hrs wkly; *Hrs. of News Programming:* News progmg 25 hrs wkly; *Target Audience:* 30 plus; farmers, commuters, homemakers; *Adv. Rates:* 25; 20; 25; 15
Al Quarnstrom, President
Mike Hughes, Operations Dir
Jennifer Thorson, General Manager
Gail Smetana, News Director
Laura Cort, Office/Traffic Manager
Bill Mayes, Chief Engineer
Jesse Logan, News/Sports Director

WCMP-FM

10-15-1977; 100.9 MHz FM; *Hrs Open:* 24; 25 kw; 276 ft.; N45 54 7 W92 57 25
US
(715)-825-4240; *Fax:* (715)-825-4244
www.redrockonair.com
License: Pine City, Pine County, MN held by Quarnstrom Media Group LLC
Group Owner: Quarnstrom Media Group LLC; acq 8-23-01; $1.2 million with co-located AM including five-year noncompete agreement).
Arbitron Metro Market: Sebring, FL; *Format:* News, Sports; *Target Audience:* 18 plus; commuters, working adults with families
Mike Hughes, Operations Manager

Pipestone

KISD

11-20-1968; 98.7 MHz FM; *Hrs Open:* 24; 100 kw; 1014 ft.; N43 53 52 W95 56 50
Mailing Address: West Highway 30, Box 456, Pipestone, MN 56164 US
Second Address: 608 W. Hwy. 30, Pipestone, MN 56164
(507) 825-4282; *Fax:* (507) 825-3364
kisdradio.com
kloh@klohradio.com
License: Pipestone, Pipestone County, MN
Nat'l Network: ABC; *Wire Services:* AP
Format: Oldies; *Target Audience:* 18-65.; *Adv. Rates:* Same as AM
Collin Christensen, General Manager
Carmen Christensen, General Sales Mgr

KLOH

06-01-1955; 1050 kHz AM; *Hrs Open:* 24
Mailing Address: West Highay 30, Box 456, Pipestone, MN 56164 US
Second Address: 608 W. Hwy. 30, Pipestone, MN 56164
(507) 825-4282; *Fax:* (507) 825-3364
www.klohradio.com
kloh@klohradio.com
License: Pipestone, MN held by Wallace Christensen.
Nat'l Network: ABC; *Regional Network:* Linder Farm; *Wire Services:* AP
Arbitron Metro Market: Mankato, MN; *Format:* News, Talk
Special Programming: Relg 5 hrs, Sp 2 hrs wkly; *Adv. Rates:* 18; 18; 18; 15
Diane Carlson, Operations Dir
Collin Christensen, General Manager
Carmen Christensen, General Sales Mgr
Mylan Ray, Programming Director
Bernie Wieme, News Director
Honee Longstreet, Traffic Manager

Preston

KFIL

05-21-1966; 1060 kHz AM
300 St. Paul Street SW, Preston, MN 55965 US
(507) 765-3856; *Fax:* (507) 765-2738
License: Preston, MN held by KFIL Inc.
Group Owner: Cumulus Media Inc.; (acq 3-30-2004; grpsl)
Regional Network: MNN
Arbitron Metro Market: Preston, MN; *Format:* Country
Shannon Knoepke, General Manager
Bruce Fishbaugher, General Sales Mgr
Bryan Dawson, Programming Director

Princeton

WQPM

02-01-1967; 1300 kHz AM; *Hrs Open:* 24
14443 Armstrong Boulevard, Ramsey, MN 55303 US
(763) 389-1300; *Fax:* (763) 389-1359
wqpmradio@yahoo.com
License: Princeton, MN held by Milestone Radio L.L.C.
Nat'l Network: ABC; *Regional Network:* Minn. Pub. Radio
Format: Country *Special Programming:* Farm 2 hrs wkly; *Hrs. of News Programming:* news progmg 20 hrs wkly; *No. News Employees:* 1; *Target Audience:* 25-54.
Dennis Carpenter, President
Neil Freeman, General Manager
Howard Johnson, General Sales Mgr
Neil Freedman, Programming Director

*KPCS

04-23-2010; 89.7 MHz FM; 50 kw vert; Ant 105 ft; N45 35 54 W93 33 18
Box 18000, Pensacola, FL 32523
(850) 479-6570; *Fax:* (850) 969-1638
www.rejoice.org
rbn@rejoice.org
License: Princeton, Mille Lacs County, MN held by Pensacola Christian College Inc.

Troy Shoemaker, President
Caleb Keener, Station Manager
Tonita Ohman, Promotions Manager

Proctor

KBMX

01-01-1994; 107.7 MHz FM; *Hrs Open:* 24; 7.7 kw; 912 ft.; N46 47 13 W92 7 17
100 Elizabeth Street, Duluth, MN 55803 US
(218) 727-4500; *Fax:* (218) 727-9356
www.mix108.com
MerryWallin@townsquaremedia.com
License: Proctor, St. Louis County, MN held by Townsquare Media Duluth License LLC.
Group Owner: Townsquare Media; (acq 2-13-2008; grpsl)
Arbitron Metro Market: Proctor, MN; *Format:* Adult Contemp; *Hrs. of News Programming:* News progmg one hr wkly; *Target Audience:* 25-54; working adults & families
Merry Wallin, Operations Dir
Merry Wallin, General Manager
Kristine Jensen, Digital Sales Manager
Laura Peterson, Programming Director
Kariana Bite, Promotions Manager
Randy Wabik, Chief Engineer
David Drew, OperationsManager
Derek Falter, Director of Sales

Red Wing

KCUE

01-29-1949; 1250 kHz AM; *Hrs Open:* 24; 1 kw-D, ND1; 0.11 kw-N, ND1; N44 32 14 W92 31 21
474 Guernsey Lane, Red Wing, MN 55066 US
(651) 388-7151; *Fax:* (651) 388-7153
www.1250kcue.com
traffic@kwng.com
License: Red Wing, MN held by Q-Media.
Group Owner: Quarnstrom Media Group LLC; (acq 6-81; $1.1 million with co-located FM;
Regional Network: MNN
Arbitron Metro Market: Red Wing, MN; *Format:* Country; *Hrs. of News Programming:* news progmg 7 hrs wkly; *No. News Employees:* 2; *Target Audience:* 35 plus; information consumer; *Adv. Rates:* 33; 29; 33; 29
Erika Duxbury, Traffic Manager
Jack Colwell, Sports/News Director
Dawn Laffey, Account Executive
Jodie Schultz, Account Executive
Craig Livingstone, Account Executive

KWNG

08-26-1965; 105.9 MHz FM; *Hrs Open:* 24; 12 kw; 328 ft.; N44 32 14 W92 31 21
474 Guernsey Lane, Red Wing, MN 55066 US
(651) 388-7151; *Fax:* (651) 388-7153
www.kwng.com
news@kwng.com
License: Red Wing, Goodhue County, MN held by Q-Media.
Group Owner: Quarnstrom Media Group LLC
Nat'l Network: ABC Information & Entertainment
Arbitron Metro Market: Red Wing, MN; *Format:* Contemporary Hits/Top 40, Adult Contemp; *Hrs. of News Programming:* news progmg one hr wkly; *No. News Employees:* 2; *Target Audience:* 25-44; family & yuppie *Adv.Rates:* 33; 29; 33; 29
Alan Quarnstrom, CEO
Tom Hughes, Operations Dir
Donald Kliewer, General Manager
Ronnie Stockwell, Business Manager
Erika Duxbury, Triffic Manager
Jack Colwell, Sports Director
Dawn Laffey, Account Executive
Jodie Schultz,Account Executive
Craig Livingstone, Account Executive

Redwood Falls

KLGR

11-01-1954; 1490 kHz AM; 1 kw-U, ND1; N44 32 33 W95 7 57
PO Box 65, Redwood Falls, MN 56283 US

(507) 637-2989; *Fax:* (507) 637-5347
www.myklgr.com
klgr@mchsi.com
License: Redwood Falls, MN held by Digity 3E License, LLC
Group Owner: Digity, LLC
Regional Network: MNN
Arbitron Metro Market: Mankato, MN; *Format:* Country; *Target Audience:* General.
Mike Neudecker, General Manager
Laura Olson, Programming Director

*KRFI
88.1 MHz FM; 0.36 kw; 168 ft.; N44 32 28 W95 10 58
480 Cedar Street, St. Paul, MN 55101 US
(651) 290-1259
www.mpr.org
License: Redwood Falls, Redwood County, MN held by Minnesota Public Radio.
Regional Network: Minn. Pub. Radio
Arbitron Metro Market: Redwood Falls, MN; *Format:* News
Jon McTaggart, President
Nick Kereakos, Vice President of Technolgoy & Operations
Tim Roesler, Senior Vice President/General Manager
Chandra Kavati, Director of Development Services
Craig Curtis, Vice President of Programming
ChrisWorthington, News Director
Melanie Walker, Music Director

Richfield

KDWB-FM
01-01-1969; 101.3 MHz FM; *Hrs Open:* 24; 100 kw; 1,033 ft.; N45 3 30 W93 7 27
1600 Utica Ave. S., Suite 500, Minneapolis, MN 55416 US
(651) 989-5392
www.kdwb.com
License: Richfield, Hennepin County, MN held by AMFM Radio Licenses LLC.
Group Owner: iHeartMedia; (acq 8-30-00; grpsl).
Nat'l Reps: Clear Channel
Arbitron Metro Market: Minneapolis-St. Paul, MN; *Format:* Contemporary Hits/Top 40; *No. News Employees:* 1; *Target Audience:* 18-34; women
Gregg Swedberg, Vice President of Programming
Ben Taylor, Vice President of Sales
Barb Neren, Director of Events

KKMS
10-18-1949; 980 kHz AM; *Hrs Open:* 24
4880 Santa Rosa Road, Suite 300, Camarillo, CA 93012 US
(651) 405-8800; *Fax:* (651) 405-8222
www.kkms.com
License: Richfield, MN held by Common Ground Broadcasting Inc.
Group Owner: Salem Communications Corp.; (acq 9-27-96; $3 million)
Arbitron Metro Market: Minneapolis, MN; *Format:* Christian, Talk; *Target Audience:* 18-50.; *Adv. Rates:* 73; 58; 73
Lee Michaels, Operations Dir
Nic Anderson, General Manager/Sales Manager
Desta Kraft, Office Manager
Nick Novak, Programming Director
Ross Brendel, Promotions Manager
Steve Smit, Chief Engineer
Gary Borgendale, Local MinistryDirector
Laurie Krier, Business Manager
Cindy Bohm, Traffic Manager

Rochester

*KFSI
04-28-1981; 92.9 MHz FM; 6 kw; 318 ft.; N44 1 27 W92 32 36
4016 28th Street, S.E., Rochester, MN 55904 US
(507) 289-8585; *Fax:* (507) 529-4017
www.kfsi.org
shine@kfsi.org
License: Rochester, Olmsted County, MN held by Faith Sound Inc.
Nat'l Network: Moody
Arbitron Metro Market: Rochester, MN; *Format:* Adult Contemp, Christian *Special Programming:* Youth 2 hrs wkly
Ray Logan, President
Paul Logan, Operations Dir
Steve Schuh, Engineering Dir
Mike Anderson, Music Director

*KZSE
12-17-1974; 91.7 MHz FM; *Hrs Open:* 24; 100 kw; Ant 953 ft; N44 02 26 W92 20 28
480 Cedar Street, St. Paul, MN 55101
(507) 282-0910; *Fax:* (507) 282-2107
www.mpr.org
License: Rochester, Olmsted County, MN held by Minnesota Public Radio Inc.
Nat'l Network: NPR; PRI; *Regional Network:* Minn. Pub. Radio
Population Served: 463,000; *Arbitron Metro Market:* Rochester, MN; *No. News Employees:* 1
John McTaggard, Chairman
Nick Kereakos, Vice President of Technology & Operations
Tim Roesler, Senior Vice President/General Manager
Craig Curtis, Vice President of Programming
Chris Worthington, News Director
Melanie Walker, MusicDirector
Chandra Kavati, Director of Development Services

*KMSE
08-01-1998; 88.7 MHz FM; *Hrs Open:* 24; 0.85 kw; 561 ft.; N44 2 28.1 W92 20 25.4
480 Cedar Street, St. Paul, MN 55101 US
(507) 282-0910; *Fax:* (507) 282-2107
www.mpr.org
License: Rochester, Olmsted County, MN held by Minnesota Public Radio
Arbitron Metro Market: Rochester, MN; *Format:* Triple A; *No. News Employees:* 1
John McTaggard, Chairman
Nick Kereakos, Vice President of Technology & Operations
Tim Roesler, Senior Vice President/General Manager
Craig Curtis, Vice President of Programming
Chris Worthington, News Director
Melanie Walker, MusicDirector
Chandra Kavati, Director of Development Services

KNXR
12-24-1965; 97.5 MHz FM; 100 kw; 1,040 ft; N44 02 28 W92 20 25
1620 Greenview Dr. S.W., Rochester, MN 55902
(507) 288-7700; *Fax:* (507) 288-4531
www.knxr.com
License: Rochester, Olmsted County, MN held by United Audio Corp.
Nat'l Network: CBS; Wall Street; *Nat'l Reps:* McGavren Guild; *Wire Services:* AP
Population Served: 225,000; *Arbitron Metro Market:* Rochester, MN *Special Programming:* Class 4 hrs, talk 2 hrs wkly; *Target Audience:* 35 plus.
Thomas Jones, President

KOLM
11-01-1963; 1520 kHz AM; *Hrs Open:* 24
1220 4th Ave., S.W., Rochester, MN 55902 US
(507) 286-1010; *Fax:* (507) 286-9370
www.1520theticket.com
info@1520theticket.com
License: Rochester, MN held by Cumulus Licensing LLC.
Group Owner: Cumulus Media Inc.; (acq 3-31-2004; grpsl)
Nat'l Network: Westwood One; *Regional Network:* Linder Farm;
Nat'l Reps: Christal
Arbitron Metro Market: Rochester, MN; *Format:* Sports; *Hrs. of News Programming:* news progmg 3 hrs wkly; *No. News Employees:* 2; *Target Audience:* 35-64; male 55%, female 45%
Shannon Knoepke, General Manager
Terry Lee, General Sales Mgr
Brent Ackerman, Programming Director
Kim David, News Director
Bill Davis, Chief Engineer

KRCH
01-01-1972; 101.7 MHz FM; *Hrs Open:* 24; 39 kw; 554 ft.; N44 6 59 W92 41 22
1530 Greenview Drive SW, Rochester, MN 55902 US
(507) 288-3888; *Fax:* (507) 288-7815
www.laser1017.net
License: Rochester, Olmsted County, MN held by CC Licenses LLC
Group Owner: iHeartMedia
Arbitron Metro Market: Rochester, MN; *Format:* Classic Rock; *Target Audience:* 25-54.
Craig Erpestad, Operations Manager
Mary Anne Nonn, Vice President of Sales
Mark Clark, Program Manager
Jessica Pustelnik, Digital Content/Sales Manager

KROC
10-01-1935; 1340 kHz AM; *Hrs Open:* 24; 1 kw-U, ND1; N44 1 47 W92 29 31
122 Sw 4th Street, Rochester, MN 55902 US
(507) 286-1010; *Fax:* (507) 280-0000
www.krocam.com
brent@kroc.com
License: Rochester, MN held by Cumulus Licensing LLC.
Group Owner: Cumulus Media Inc.; (acq 3-29-2004; grpsl)
Nat'l Reps: Hyett/Ramsland
Arbitron Metro Market: Rochester, MN; *Format:* News, News/Talk, 86 *Special Programming:* Farm 12 hrs wkly; *Hrs. of News Programming:* news progmg 42 hrs wkly; *No. News Employees:* 3; *Target Audience:* 30-64.
Shannon Knoepke, General Manager
Terry Lee, General Sales Mgr
Brent Ackerman, Programming/Operations Manager
Kim David, News Director
Bill Davis, Chief Engineer

KROC-FM
07-01-1965; 106.9 MHz FM; 100 kw; 1109 ft.; N43 34 15 W92 25 37
122 Sw 4th Street, Rochester, MN 55902 US
(507) 286-1010; *Fax:* (507) 280-0000
www.kroc.com
License: Rochester, Olmsted County, MN
Group Owner: Cumulus Media Inc.
Arbitron Metro Market: Rochester-Austin-Mason City; *Format:* Contemporary Hits/Top 40; *Target Audience:* 18-54.
Shannon Knoepke, General Manager
Terry Lee, General Sales Mgr
Brent Ackerman, Programming Director/Operations Manager
Kim David, News Director
Bill Davis, Chief Engineer

*KRPR
01-01-1976; 89.9 MHz FM; *Hrs Open:* 24; 3.2 kw; Ant 590 ft; N44 02 28 W92 20 25
Rochester Public Radio, 1620 Greenview Dr. S.W., Rochester, MN 55902
(507) 288-2376; *Fax:* (507) 288-4531
www.krpr.org
License: Rochester, Olmsted County, MN held by Rochester Public Radio
Nat'l Network: USA
Population Served: 100,000; *Arbitron Metro Market:* Rochester, MN; *Target Audience:* General.
Thomas Jones, President
Todd Brakke, General Manager
Aaron Manthei, Chief Engineer

KFAN
11-27-1957; 1270 kHz AM; 5 kw-D, 1 kw-N, DA-2; N43 58 47 W92 26 51
1530 Greenview Dr. S.W., Suite 200, Rochester, MN 53202
(507) 288-3888; *Fax:* (507) 288-7815
www.fan1270.com
License: Rochester, Olmsted County, MN held by CC Licenses LLC.
Group Owner: iHeartMedia; (acq 9-25-2000; grpsl).
Nat'l Network: CBS; *Regional Network:* MNN; *Nat'l Reps:* D & R Radio
Population Served: 75,000; *Arbitron Metro Market:* Rochester, MN; *Format:* Sports, Talk; *Target Audience:* Men.
Craig Erpestad, Operations Manager
Mary Anne Nonn, Vice President of Sales
Greg Henn, Program Director/Sports Director
Jessica Pustelnik, Digital Content/Sales Manager

KWWK
07-04-1967; 96.5 MHz FM; *Hrs Open:* 24; 43 kw; 528 ft.; N44 1 59 W92 36 10
122 4th Street S.W., Rochester, MN 55902 US
(507) 286-1010; *Fax:* (507) 286-9370
www.quickcountry.com
License: Rochester, Olmsted County, MN
Group Owner: Cumulus Media Inc.
Nat'l Reps: Christal
Arbitron Metro Market: Rochester, MN; *Format:* Country; *Hrs. of News Programming:* News progmg 2 hrs wkly; *Target Audience:* 25-54; male & female 18-49, 25-54, 35-54
Shannon Knoepke, General Manager
Terry Lee, Sales Manager
Jas Caffrey, Programming Manager
Bill Davis, Chief Engineer

*KLSE
02-01-1989; 90.7 MHz FM; *Hrs Open:* 24; 1.38 kw; Ant 259 ft; N44 02 26 W92 20 28
480 Cedar Street, St. Paul, MN 55101
(507) 282-0910; *Fax:* (507) 282-2107
www.mpr.org
License: Rochester, Olmsted County, MN held by Minnesota Public Radio Inc.
Nat'l Network: NPR; PRI; *Regional Network:* Minn. Pub. Radio
Arbitron Metro Market: Rochester, MN; *No. News Employees:* 1
Jon McTaggart, President
Nick Kereakos, Vice President of Technology & Operations
Tim Roesler, Senior Vice President/General Manager
Craig Curtis, Vice President of Programming
Chris Worthington, News Director

Melanie Walker, MusicDirector
Chandra Kavati, Director of Development Services

Rockville

KYES
1180 kHz AM
Mailing Address: US
Second Address: 1310 2nd St. N., Sauk Rapids, MN 56379-2532
(320) 257-9700; *Fax:* (320) 257-1624
www.kyesradio.com
License: Rockville, MN held by Gabriel Media
Arbitron Metro Market: Sauk Rapids, MN; *Format:* Christian
Andrew Hilger, President
Deb Huschle, General Manager
Mike Van Vooren, Programming Coordinator
Denise Gill, Donor Relations
Sheri Moran, Development Director

Roseau

KCAJ-FM
06-01-1996; 102.1 MHz FM; *Hrs Open:* 24; 50 kw; 285 ft.; N48 38 50 W95 44 10
107 Center Street W, Roseau, MN 56751 US
(218) 463-3360; *Fax:* (218) 463-1977
wild102fm.com
info@wild102fm.com
License: Roseau, Roseau County, MN held by Jack J. Swanson.
Nat'l Network: CNN Radio; *Regional Network:* Minn. News Net.
Arbitron Metro Market: Roseau, MN; *Format:* Contemporary Hits/Top 40; *Hrs. of News Programming:* news progmg 10 hrs wkly; *No. News Employees:* 1; *Target Audience:* General.
Jack Swanson, General Manager
Jack McDonald, General Sales Mgr
Justin Gallo, Promotions Manager

KRWB
04-05-1963; 1410 kHz AM; *Hrs Open:* 24
Route 5, Box 9, Langdon, ND 58249 US
(218) 463-1410; *Fax:* (218) 463-3778
www.1410krwb.com
License: Roseau, MN held by Border Broadcasting L.P.
Nat'l Network: ABC
Arbitron Metro Market: Warraod, MN; *Format:* Classic Rock; *No. News Employees:* 1; *Target Audience:* 25-54; general; *Adv. Rates:* 15; 13; 10; 8
Mike Pederson, General Manager

*KRXW
01-01-2008; 103.5 MHz FM; 48 kw; 493 ft.; N48 54 10 W95 22 38.1
480 Cedar Street, St. Paul, MN 55101 US
(651) 290-1500; *Fax:* (651) 290-1224
www.mpr.org
License: Roseau, Roseau County, MN held by Minnesota Public Radio.
Arbitron Metro Market: Roseau, MN; *Format:* News
Jon McTaggart, President
Nick Kereakos, Vice President of Technology & Operations
Tim Roesler, Senior Vice President/General Manager
Craig Curtis, Vice President of Programming
Chris Worthington, News Director
Melanie Walker, MusicDirector
Chandra Kavati, Director of Development Services

Rushford

KWNO-FM
12-18-1991; 99.3 MHz FM; *Hrs Open:* 24; 11 kw; 495 ft.; N43 56 32 W91 43 9
Mailing Address: Box 767, 752 Bluffview Cir., Winona, MN 55947 US
Second Address: 752 Bluffview Cir., Winona, MN 55987
(507) 452-4000; (800) 584-6782; *Fax:* (507) 452-9494
www.winonaradio.com
License: Rushford, Fillmore County, MN held by KAGE Inc.
Group Owner: The Result Radio Group; (acq 6-19-95; $1 million with KWNO(AM) Winona)
Wire Services: AP
Arbitron Metro Market: Winona, MN; *Format:* Country; *Hrs. of News Programming:* news progmg one hr wkly; *No. News Employees:* 1; *Target Audience:* 18-49; active young students & working persons
Jerry Papenfuss, CEO
Pat Papenfuss, President
Les Guderian, General Sales Mgr
Aaron Taylor, Programming Director
Darryl Smelser, News Director
Bob Sebo, Public Affairs Director

Saint Peter

*KNGA
03-29-1985; 90.5 MHz FM; *Hrs Open:* 24; 75 kw; 708 ft; N44 13 20 W94 07 03
480 Cedar Street, St. Paul, MN 55101
(651) 290-1500; *Fax:* (651) 290-1224
www.mpr.org
mail@mpr.org
License: Saint Peter, Nicollet County, MN held by Minnesota Public Radio Inc.
Nat'l Network: PRI; *Regional Network:* Minn. Pub. Radio
Population Served: 200,000; *Arbitron Metro Market:* Mankato-New Ulm-St. Peter, MN *Special Programming:* Folk var 17 hrs wkly; *No. News Employees:* 2; *Target Audience:* General.
Jon McTaggart, President
Nick Kereakos, Vice President of Technology & Operations
Tim Roesler, Senior Vice President/General Manager
Craig Curtis, Vice President of Programming
Chris Worthington, News Director
Melanie Walker, MusicDirector
Chandra Kavati, Director of Development Services

*KGAC
03-01-1992; 91.5 MHz FM; *Hrs Open:* 24; 8.5 kw; 600 ft; N44 13 20 W94 07 03 *Rebroadcasts:* Rebroadcasts KNOW-FM Minneapolis-St. Paul
Minnesota Public Radio, 480 Cedar St., Saint Paul, MN 55101
(800) 228-7123; *Fax:* (507) 651-1295
www.mpr.org
mail@mpr.org
License: Saint Peter, Nicollet County, MN held by Minnesota Public Radio.
Nat'l Network: NPR; PRI; *Regional Network:* Minn. Pub. Radio
Population Served: 150,000; *Arbitron Metro Market:* Mankato-New Ulm-St. Peter, MN; *No. News Employees:* 2; *Target Audience:* General.
Jon McTaggart, President
Nick Kereakos, Vice President of Technology & Operations
Tim Roesler, Vice President/General Manager
Craig Curtis, Vice President of Programming
Chris Worthington, News Director
Melanie Walker, MusicDirector
Chandra Kavati, Director of Development Services

Sartell

KZRV
08-26-1988; 96.7 MHz FM; *Hrs Open:* 24; 50 kw; 453 ft.; N45 46 3 W94 8 4
640 SE Lincoln Avenue, St. Cloud, MN 56304 US
(320) 251-4422; *Fax:* (320) 251-1855
www.kiss96.com
studio@kiss96.com
License: Sartell, Stearns County, MN
Group Owner: Townsquare Media; (acq 5-8-2001; grpsl)
Arbitron Metro Market: St. Cloud, MN; *Format:* Rock/AOR; *No. News Employees:* 1
Dave Engberg, General Manager
Steve Lahr, Director of Sales
Lee Voss, News Director
Mark Young, Chief Engineer

Sauk Centre

KIKV-FM
12-25-1970; 100.7 MHz FM; *Hrs Open:* 24; 100 kw; 791 ft.; N45 41 10 W95 8 3
Mailing Address: P.O. Box 1656, Bemidji, MN 56619 US
Second Address: 604 Third Ave. W., Alexandria, MN 56308
(320) 762-2154; *Fax:* (320) 762-2156
kikvradio.com
100.7@kikvfm.com
License: Sauk Centre, Douglas County, MN held by BDI Broadcasting Inc.
Group Owner: Omni Broadcasting Co.; (acq 9-25-89; $855,000;
Nat'l Network: ABC; *Regional Network:* Linder Farm
Format: Country *Special Programming:* Farm 20 hrs wkly; *Hrs. of News Programming:* news progmg 12 hrs wkly; *No. News Employees:* 1; *Target Audience:* 25-54; adults
Lou Buron, CEO
Dave Vagle, General Manager
Trudy Blanshan, General Sales Mgr
Rick Blanshan, Programming Director
Jim Rohn, News Director
Mary Campbell, CFO

Sauk Rapids

WBHR
08-03-1963; 660 kHz AM; *Hrs Open:* 24
1010 2nd Street North, Sauk Rapids, MN 56739 US
(320) 257-6403; *Fax:* (320) 252-9367
www.660wbhr.com
mail@660wbhr.com
License: Sauk Rapids, MN held by Tri-County Broadcasting Inc.
Group Owner: Tri-County Broadcasting Inc.
Nat'l Network: Radio Disney
Arbitron Metro Market: Sauk Rapids, MN; *Format:* Sports
Herb Hoppe, President
Gary Hoppe, Operations Dir
Doug Kurtz, General Sales Mgr

WHMH-FM
10-31-1975; 101.7 MHz FM; *Hrs Open:* 24; 50 kw; 476 ft.; N45 30 2 W94 14 31
1010 2nd St. North, Sauk Rapids, MN 56379 US
(320) 252-6200; *Fax:* (320) 252-9367
www.rockin101.com
License: Sauk Rapids, Benton County, MN
Group Owner: Tri-County Broadcasting Inc.
Arbitron Metro Market: St. Cloud, MN
Herb Hoppe, President
Gary Hoppe, Operations Dir
Doug Kurtz, General Sales Mgr

WVAL
03-01-1999; 800 kHz AM; 2.6 kw-D, DA2; 0.85 kw-N, DA2; N45 36 18 W94 8 21
Mailing Address: 1010 2nd St South, Sauk Rapids, MN 56379 US
Second Address: 1010 2nd St. N., Sauk Rapids, MN 56379
(320) 252-6200; *Fax:* (320) 252-9367
www.800wval.com
License: Sauk Rapids, MN held by Tri-County Broadcasting Inc.
Group Owner: Tri-County Broadcasting Inc.
Arbitron Metro Market: Sauk Rapids, MN; *Format:* Classical, Country
Herb Hoppe, President
Gary Hoppe, Operations Dir
Doug Kurtz, General Sales Mgr

WMIN
01-01-2008; 1010 kHz AM
US
(320) 252-6200; *Fax:* (320) 252-9367
License: Sauk Rapids, MN held by Herbert M. Hoppe.
Arbitron Metro Market: Evanston, WY; *Format:* Adult Contemp
Herb Hoppe, General Manager
Doug Kertz, General Sales Mgr

WXYG
540 kHz AM; 250 w-U, DA-2; N45 36 18 W94 08 21
Box 366, Sauk Rapids, MN
(320) 252-6200; *Fax:* (320) 252-9367
License: Sauk Rapids, Benton County, MN held by Herbert M. Hoppe.

Herbert Hoppe, President
Gary Hoppe, Operations Dir
Doug Kurtz, General Sales Mgr

Sebeka

*KOPJ
89.3 MHz FM; *Hrs Open:* 24; 100 kw; Ant 872 ft; N46 40 35.9 W94 43 02
PO Box 481, Park Rapids, MN 98901
(218) 237-4673
www.wehavethishoperadio.org
sserickson@hotmail.com
License: Sebeka, Menahga County, MN held by We Have This Hope Inc.
Nat'l Network: LifeTalk Radio Network

Sharon Erickson, President
Sharon Erickson, General Manager

Shakopee

KQSP
10-06-1963; 1530 kHz AM; *Hrs Open:* 24; 8.6 kw-D, DA2; 0.01 kw-N, DA2; N44 48 26 W93 33 25
919 Lilac Drive N, Minneapolis, MN 55422 US
(847) 687-6550
License: Shakopee, MN held by Broadcast One Inc.

Yong Kim, President

Slayton

KJOE
01-01-1993; 106.1 MHz FM; *Hrs Open:* 24; 13 kw; 971 ft.; N43 53 52 W95 56 50

West Highway 30, Pipestone, MN 56164 US
(507) 836-6125,(507) 836-6126; *Fax:* (507) 836-6537
www.kjoeradio.com
kjoe@kjoeradio.com
License: Slayton, Murray County, MN held by Wallace Christensen.
Format: Country
Wallace Christensen, President
Diane Marie, Operations Dir
Collin Christensen, General Manager
Carmen Christensen, General Sales Mgr
Mylan Ray, Programming Director
Bernard Wieme, Promotions Manager
Joel Herrig, News Director
Honee Longstreet, Traffic Manager

Sleepy Eye

KNUJ-FM
06-01-1995; 107.3 MHz FM; *Hrs Open:* 24; 4 kw; 407 ft.; N44 19 38 W94 43 41 *Rebroadcasts:* Rebroadcasts KNUJ(AM) New Ulm 70%
317 North Minnesota Street, New Ulm, MN 56073 US
(507) 359-2921; *Fax:* (507) 359-4520
www.knuj.net
knuj@knuj.net
License: Sleepy Eye, Brown County, MN held by Ingstad Brothers Broadcasting LLC
Group Owner: Ingstad Brothers Broadcasting LLC; acq 5-1-2004; grpsl).
Format: Adult Contemp; *Hrs. of News Programming:* news progmg 20 hrs wkly; *No. News Employees:* 1; *Target Audience:* 18-49; slightly more females than males
Jim Bartels, Operations Dir
Janine Enter, General Sales Mgr
Brian Filzen, Programming Director
Mike Lemmer, News Director
Greg Brandt, Chief Engineer

Spring Grove

KQYB
08-02-1980; 98.3 MHz FM; *Hrs Open:* 24; 33 kW; 607 ft.; N43 40 53 W91 45 28
201 State St, La Crosse, WI 54601 USA
(608) 782-1230; *Fax:* (608) 782-1170
kq98.com
contactus@kq98.com
License: Spring Grove, Houston County, MN held by Family Radio Inc.
Group Owner: Mid-West Family Broadcasting; (acq 7-19-01; grpsl).
Wire Services: AP
Arbitron Metro Market: LaCrosse, WI; *Format:* Country; *Hrs. of News Programming:* news progmg one hr wkly; *No. News Employees:* 1; *Target Audience:* General.; *Adv. Rates:* 50; 45; 47; 35

Spring Valley

KVGO
01-01-1993; 104.3 MHz FM; 10 kw; 512 ft.; N43 38 23 W92 38 30
300 St. Paul Street SW, Preston, MN 55965 US
(507) 765-3856; *Fax:* (507) 765-2738
License: Spring Valley, Fillmore County, MN held by KVGO Inc.
Group Owner: Cumulus Media Inc.; (acq 3-30-2004; grpsl).
Nat'l Reps: D & R Radio
Arbitron Metro Market: Preston, MN; *Format:* Oldies
Bruce Fishbaugher, General Manager
John Milne, Programming Director

*KVCS
89.1 MHz FM; 12 kw; Ant 138 meters; N43 38 34 W92 31 35
3434 W. Kilbourn Ave., Milwaukee, WI
(414) 935-3000; *Fax:* (414) 935-3015
www.vcyamerica.org
KVCS@vcyamerica.org
License: Spring Valley, Fillmore County, MN held by VCY America Inc.
Group Owner: VCY America Inc.

Vic Eliason, General Manager
Jim Schneider, Programming Director
Andy Eliason, Chief Engineer

Springfield

KNSG
01-01-1995; 94.7 MHz FM; *Hrs Open:* 24; 50 kw; 472 ft.; N44 21 54 W95 19 27
110 West Central Street, Springfield, MN 56087 US
(507) 532-2282; *Fax:* (507) 532-3739
marshallradio.net
info@marshallradio.net
License: Springfield, Brown County, MN held by Springfield Radio Inc.
Nat'l Network: Westwood One; *Regional Network:* Linder Farm; Minn. News Net; *Nat'l Reps:* Katz Radio; *Wire Services:* AP
Format: Adult Contemp *Special Programming:* Farm 15 hrs, women 3 hrs wkly; *Target Audience:* 30 plus; women; *Adv. Rates:* 10.50; 10.50; 10.50; 8.25
Heath Radke, Operations Dir
Brad Strootman, General Manager

St. Charles

KDZZ
04-18-1998; 107.7 MHz FM; *Hrs Open:* 24; 1.95 kw; 571 ft.; N44 2 25 W92 13 5
1220 4th Avenue Sw, Rochester, MN 55902 US
(507) 286-1010; *Fax:* (507) 286-9370
www.zrock1077.com
License: St. Charles, Winona County, MN held by Cumulus Licensing LLC.
Group Owner: Cumulus Media Inc.; (acq 3-31-2004; grpsl)
Nat'l Reps: Christal
Arbitron Metro Market: Rochester, MN
Brent Ackerman, Operations Dir
Shannon Knoepke, General Manager
Terry Lee, Sales Manager
Jeff Cecil, Programming Director

St. Cloud

*KCFB
11-17-1986; 91.5 MHz FM; *Hrs Open:* 24; 15 kw; 348 ft.; N45 30 2 W94 14 31 *Rebroadcasts:* Rebroadcasts KTIG(FM) Pequot Lakes 100%
P.O. Box 409, Pequot Lakes, MN 56472 US
(320) 252-4214; *Fax:* (218) 568-5950
License: St. Cloud, Stearns County, MN held by Minnesota Christian Broadcasters Inc.
Nat'l Network: Moody; *Wire Services:* AP
Arbitron Metro Market: St. Cloud, MN; *Format:* Religious; *Hrs. of News Programming:* news progmg 14 hrs wkly; *No. News Employees:* 1; *Target Audience:* General.
Mike Heuberger, General Manager
Jim Park, Programming Director

KCLD-FM
05-01-1948; 104.7 MHz FM; 100 kw; 984 ft.; N45 34 3 W94 30 43
619 W. St. Germain Street, St. Cloud, MN 56302 US
(320) 251-1047; *Fax:* (320) 251-8952
www.1047kcld.com
License: St. Cloud, Stearns County, MN held by Leighton Enterprises Inc.
Group Owner: Leighton Enterprises Inc.
Arbitron Metro Market: St. Cloud, MN; *Format:* Contemporary Hits/Top 40
Bob Leighton, General Sales Mgr
J.J. Holiday, Programming Director
Matt Senne, Operations

KNSI
06-01-1938; 1450 kHz AM; 1 kw-U, ND1; N45 32 21 W94 10 5
619 W. St. Germain Street, St. Cloud, MN 56302 US
(320) 251-1450; *Fax:* (320) 251-8952
www.1450knsi.com
info@1450knsi.com
License: St. Cloud, MN held by Leighton Enterprises Inc.
Group Owner: Leighton Enterprises Inc.; acq 9-15-75)
Regional Reps: O'Malley.
Arbitron Metro Market: St. Cloud, MN; *Format:* News, News/Talk, 86; *Target Audience:* 35 plus; males
Bob Leighton, General Sales Manager
Matt Stone, Operations
J.J. Holiday, Programming Director

*KVSC
05-10-1967; 88.1 MHz FM; *Hrs Open:* 20-24; 16.5 kw vert; 446 ft.; N45 31 0 W94 13 52
720 Fourth Avenue South, 27 Stewart Hall, St. Cloud, MN 56301 US
(320) 308-5872; *Fax:* (320) 308-5337
www.kvsc.org
info@kvsc.org
License: St. Cloud, Stearns County, MN held by St. Cloud State University.
Nat'l Network: PRI; *Wire Services:* AP
Arbitron Metro Market: St. Cloud, MN; *Format:* Alternative *Special Programming:* jazz, indie, folk, americana, MN music; *Hrs. of News Programming:* news progmg 12 hrs wkly; *No. News Employees:* 2.5 *TargetAudience:* 17-60; educated, progsv; *Adv. Rates:* 15; 15; 15; 15
Jim Grey, Operations Dir
Roya Majid, General Manager
Jo McMullen-Boyer, Station Manager
Cheyenne Malcolm, Programming Director
Amelia Rowland, News Director
Jett Carmack, Arts and Cultural Heritage Producer
Alex Hartman, ProjectAnalyst
Conrad Magalis, Marketing / Sales Director
James Tollefson, Music Director
Nick Hendrickson, Production Director
Dave Overlund, Sports Director

WJON
09-01-1950; 1240 kHz AM; *Hrs Open:* 24
640 SE Lincoln Avenue, St. Cloud, MN 56304 US
(320) 251-4422
www.wjon.com
License: St. Cloud, MN
Group Owner: Townsquare Media; (acq 5-1-99; grpsl)
Nat'l Network: CBS; *Regional Network:* MNN
Arbitron Metro Market: St. Cloud, MN; *Format:* News, News/Talk, 86; *Hrs. of News Programming:* news progmg 30 hrs wkly; *No. News Employees:* 3; *Target Audience:* 25 plus.
Dave Engberg, General Manager
Steve Lahr, Director of Sales
Jay Caldwell, Programming Director
Lee Voss, News Director
Mark Young, Chief Engineer

WWJO
01-01-1975; 98.1 MHz FM; 97 kw; 1001 ft.; N45 48 52 W94 1 38 US
(320) 251-4422
www.98country.com
License: St. Cloud, Stearns County, MN
Group Owner: Townsquare Media
Arbitron Metro Market: St. Cloud, MN; *Format:* Country; *Target Audience:* 18 plus.
Steven Price, Chief Executive Officer
David Engberg, General Manager
Steve Lahr, Director of Sales
Chad Taylor, Programming Director
Dave McCord, Brand Manager

St. James

KRRW
07-24-1983; 101.5 MHz FM; *Hrs Open:* 24; 14 kw; 446 ft.; N43 52 27 W94 36 0
816 N 2nd St., Mankato, MN 56001 US
(507) 345-1282; *Fax:* (507) 345-7689
www.katoinfo.com
katoinfo@katoinfo.com
License: St. James, Watonwan County, MN held by Minnesota Valley Broadcasting Co.
Group Owner: Linder Broadcasting Group; (acq 1996; $800,000 with KXAC(FM) St)
Regional Network: Linder Farm
Format: Country *Special Programming:* Sp one hr wkly; *Hrs. of News Programming:* news progmg 16 hrs wkly; *No. News Employees:* 1; *Target Audience:* 25-54.
Charlie Voda, Programming Director

KXAC
11-01-1992; 100.5 MHz FM; *Hrs Open:* 24; 34 kw; 591 ft.; N43 57 3 W94 23 25
59346 Madison Ave., Mankato, MN 56002 US
(507) 345-4537; *Fax:* (507) 345-5364
jobailey@radiomankato.com
License: St. James, Watonwan County, MN held by Minnesota Valley Broadcasting Co.
Group Owner: Linder Broadcasting Group; (acq 1996; $800,000 with KXAX(FM) St)
Regional Network: MNN
Format: Oldies; *Target Audience:* 25-58.
Jo Bailey, General Manager
Deb Armstrong, General Sales Mgr

St. Joseph

KCML
01-01-1998; 99.9 MHz FM; 2.9 kw; 476 ft.; N45 32 21 W94 10 5
619 W. St. Germain Street, St. Cloud, MN 56302 US
(320) 251-1450; *Fax:* (320) 251-8952
www.lite999.com
License: St. Joseph, Stearns County, MN held by Leighton Enterprises Inc.
Group Owner: Leighton Enterprises Inc.

Arbitron Metro Market: St. Cloud, MN; *Format:* Contemporary Hits/Top 40
Al Leighton, CEO
John Sowada, General Manager
Denny Niess, General Sales Mgr
Ron Linder, Programming Director
Cindy Niess, News Director
Dale Daley, Chief Engineer
Denise Prozinski, General Sales Manager

KKJM
05-07-1996; 92.9 MHz FM; *Hrs Open:* 24; 25 kw; 328 ft.; N45 38 19 W94 22 23
640 Lincoln Ave., Se, Box 220, St. Cloud, MN 56302 US
(320) 251-1780; *Fax:* (320) 257-1624
www.spirit929.com
friends@spirit929.com
License: St. Joseph, Stearns County, MN held by Gabriel Communications Co., St. Cloud.
Wire Services: AP
Arbitron Metro Market: St. Cloud, MN; *Format:* Adult Contemp, Christian; *Hrs. of News Programming:* News progmg 5 hrs wkly; *Target Audience:* 25-54; females; *Adv. Rates:* 18; 18; 18; 18
Deb Huschle, General Manager
Jessica Hart, Programming Director
Michelle Crabb, News Director
Denise Gill, Donor Relations
Mike Van Vooren, Music Director

St. Louis Park

***KDXL**
03-17-1977; 106.5 MHz FM; *Hrs Open:* 7:30 AM-10 PM (M-F); 0.008 kw; 85 ft.; N44 56 36 W93 21 39
6425 W. 33rd Street, St. Louis Park, MN 55426 US
(612) 928-6149; *Fax:* (612) 928-6206
License: St. Louis Park, Hennepin County, MN held by Independent School District 283.
Arbitron Metro Market: Minneapolis-St. Paul, MN; *Format:* Classic Rock, Rock/AOR; *Target Audience:* 15-30; high school students & loc residents
Charlie Fiss, Station Manager

KTNF
05-13-1958; 950 kHz AM; *Hrs Open:* 24; 1 kw-D, DA2; 1 kw-N, DA2; N44 52 8 W93 25 11
11320 Valley View Road, Eden Prairie, MN 55344 US
(952) 946-8885; *Fax:* (952) 946-0888
www.am950ktnf.com
traffic@am950ktnf.com
License: St. Louis Park, MN held by JR Broadcasting LLC
Nat'l Network: Air America; CNN Radio; Jones Radio Networks;
Wire Services: AP
Arbitron Metro Market: Eden Prair, MN; *Format:* Talk; *Target Audience:* 35+.
Janet Robert, President

KZJK
05-10-2005; 104.1 MHz FM; 100 kW; 1037 ft.; N45 3 30 W93 7 27
625 2nd Ave. South, Minneapolis, MN 55402 USA
(612) 370-0611
www.1041jackfm.com
License: St. Louis Park, Hennepin County, MN held by The Audio House Inc.
Group Owner: CBS Radio
Arbitron Metro Market: St. Louis Park, MN; *Format:* Adult Contemp
Lara Engh, Promotions Manager

***KUOM-FM**
02-17-2003; 106.5 MHz FM; *Hrs Open:* 4:30 PM-8 AM M-F; 24 S-S; 0.006 kw; 208 ft.; N44 56 47.4 W93 19 24.1 *Rebroadcasts:* Rebroadcasts KUOM(AM) Minneapolis 100%
US
(612) 625-3500; *Fax:* (612) 625-2112
www.radiok.org
request@radiok.org
License: St. Louis Park, Hennepin County, MN held by Regents of the University of Minnesota.
Wire Services: AP
Arbitron Metro Market: Saint Louis Park, MN; *Format:* Rock/AOR; *Target Audience:* 18-34
Sara Milller, Station Manager/Department Director

St. Paul

KEEY-FM
06-01-1969; 102.1 MHz FM; *Hrs Open:* 24; 100 kw; 1,033 ft.; N45 3 30 W93 7 27
1600 Utica Ave. S., Suite 500, St. Louis Park, MN 55416 US
(952) 417-3000; *Fax:* (612) 417-3001
www.k102.com
License: St. Paul, Ramsey County, MN held by AMFM Broadcasting Licenses LLC.
Group Owner: iHeartMedia
Nat'l Reps: Clear Channel
Arbitron Metro Market: Minneapolis-St. Paul, MN; *Format:* Country; *Hrs. of News Programming:* news progmg 2 hrs wkly; *No. News Employees:* 40; *Target Audience:* 25-54; women
Gregg Swedberg, Vice President of Programming
Ben Taylor, Vice President of Sales
Matt Tell, Promotions Director
Cathy Maness, Traffic Manager

KMNV
01-01-1936; 1400 kHz AM; *Hrs Open:* 24; 1 kw-U, ND1; N44 57 28 W93 12 23
611 Frontenac Place, St. Paul, MN 55104 US
(612) 729-5900; *Fax:* (612) 729-5999
www.laraza1400.com
License: St. Paul, MN held by Davidson Media Station KLBB Licensee LLC.
Group Owner: Davidson Media Group LLC; (acq 9-7-2005; $5.2 million with KMNQ(AM) Brooklyn Park)
Regional Network: ABN Radio
Arbitron Metro Market: Minneapolis, MN
Tim Dennis, General Manager

KNOF
04-10-1960; 95.3 MHz FM; *Hrs Open:* 6 AM-10 PM; 6 kw; 249 ft.; N44 56 48 W93 9 26
402 Pike Street East, Osakis, MN 56360 US
(651) 645-8271; *Fax:* (651) 645-4593
License: St. Paul, Ramsey County, MN held by Selby Gospel Broadcasting Co.
Nat'l Network: Salem Radio Network
Arbitron Metro Market: Minneapolis, MN; *Format:* Gospel *Special Programming:* Black 5 hrs, Sp one hr, Russian one hr wkly; *Hrs. of News Programming:* News progmg 2 hrs wkly; *Target Audience:* All ages.
Paul Freitag, President
Phil Mullen, Operations Dir

KSTP
04-01-1924; 1500 kHz AM
3415 University Ave, St. Paul, MN 55114 US
(651) 647-1500; *Fax:* (651) 649-1515
www.am1500.com
info@kstp.com
License: St. Paul, MN held by KSTP-AM L.L.C., a Delaware L.L.C.
Group Owner: Hubbard Broadcasting Inc.
Nat'l Reps: Christal; *Wire Services:* AP
Arbitron Metro Market: Minneapolis-St. Paul, MN *TV Affiliate:* KSTP-TV affil.; *Format:* Talk; *Hrs. of News Programming:* news progmg 5 hrs wkly; *No. News Employees:* 3; *Target Audience:* 25-54; adults
Stanley Hubbard, CEO
Virginia Morris, President
Alan DeFlorio, Sales Manager
Brad Lane, Programming Director
Mel Miltz, Promotions Manager
Bernie Laur, Online Sales Manager

KSTP-FM
11-01-1965; 94.5 MHz FM; 95 kw; 1220 ft.; N45 3 45 W93 8 22
3415 University Avenue, St Paul, MN 55114 US
(651) 642-4141; *Fax:* (651) 642-4239
www.ks95.com
License: St. Paul, Ramsey County, MN held by KSTP-FM L.L.C. a Delaware L.L.C.
Group Owner: Hubbard Broadcasting Inc.
Nat'l Network: ABC; *Nat'l Reps:* Christal; *Wire Services:* AP
Arbitron Metro Market: Minneapolis-St. Paul, MN *TV Affiliate:* KSTP-TV affil; *Format:* Adult Contemp; *No. News Employees:* 1; *Target Audience:* 25-54; female
Virginia Morris, President
Dave Bestler, Executive Vice President/Chief Financial Officer
John Seidl, General Sales Mgr
Leighton Peck, Programming Director
Mel Miltz, Promotions Director

WREY
09-19-1959; 630 kHz AM
205 Cesar Chavez Street, St. Paul, MN 55107 US
(612) 729-3776; *Fax:* (612) 724-0437
www.radiorey630am.com
License: St. Paul, MN held by 630 Radio Inc.
Arbitron Metro Market: Minneapolis-St. Paul, MN; *Format:* Spanish
Felicia Ortega, General Manager

***WMCN**
09-15-1979; 91.7 MHz FM; *Hrs Open:* 8 AM-4 AM (M-F); 11 AM-4 AM (S, Su); 0.005 kw; 161 ft.; N44 56 19 W93 10 4
1600 Grand Ave, St. Paul, MN 55105 US
(651) 696-6082; *Fax:* (651) 696-6689
www.macalester.edu/wmcn
wmcn@macalester.edu
License: St. Paul, Ramsey County, MN held by Macalester College.
Arbitron Metro Market: Minneapolis, MN; *Format:* Variety/Diverse *Special Programming:* Country 2 hrs, Latin 6 hrs, multicultural 10 hrs,; *Target Audience:* General, students
John Kreitzberg, General Manager
Will Kent-Daggett, Chief Engineer

St. Peter

KRBI-FM
09-01-1966; 105.5 MHz FM; *Hrs Open:* 24; 25 kw; 222 ft.; N44 10 20 W94 2 23
1807 Lee Blvd., Mankato, MN 56003 US
(507) 345-4646; *Fax:* (507) 345-3299
www.river105.com
License: St. Peter, Nicollet County, MN held by Digity 3E License, LLC
Group Owner: Digity, LLC
Nat'l Reps: Katz Radio
Arbitron Metro Market: Mankato, MN; *Format:* Adult Contemp; *No. News Employees:* 1; *Adv. Rates:* 26; 26; 26; 26
Denise Dose, General Manager
Kelly Marks, Station Manager
Brad Steele, Programming Director

Staples

KNSP
06-03-1982; 1430 kHz AM; *Hrs Open:* 24; 1 kw-D, ND1; 0.199 kw-N, ND1; N46 21 34 W94 46 55
201 1/2 Jefferson Street S, Wadena, MN 56482 US
(218) 631-1803; *Fax:* (218) 631-4557
kwadknsp.com
rick@kwadknsp.com
License: Staples, MN held by BL Broadcasting Inc.
Group Owner: Omni Broadcasting Co.; (acq 4-1-2004; grpsl).
Nat'l Network: ABC; *Regional Network:* Minn. Farm; Minn. News Net.
Format: Country *Special Programming:* Farm 10 hrs wkly; *Hrs. of News Programming:* news progmg 20 hrs wkly; *No. News Employees:* 1; *Target Audience:* 25-54; adults
Lou Buron, CEO
Rick Youngbauer, General Manager
Kyle Gylsen, Programming Director
Sherry Linnes, Promotions Manager
Mary Campbell, CFO

KSKK
08-01-1994; 94.7 MHz FM; *Hrs Open:* 24; 50 kw; 469 ft; N46 33 08 W94 39 03
11 S.E. Bryant Ave., Wadena, MN 56470
(218) 631-3441; *Fax:* (218) 631-3414
kskk@eot.com
License: Staples, Todd County, MN held by NorMin Broadcasting Co.
Nat'l Network: CBS
Hrs. of News Programming: News progmg 20 hrs wkly; *Target Audience:* 30 plus.; *Adv. Rates:* 12; 12; 12; 12
David De LaHunt, CEO
Joleen De LaHunt, Operations Dir
Gene Marie Kanten, General Manager
Heidi Hutson, General Sales Mgr

Starbuck

KRVY-FM
01-01-2001; 97.3 MHz FM; *Hrs Open:* 24; 50 kw; 492 ft.; N45 31 42 W95 32 52
Mailing Address: P.O. Box 380/730 NE Hwy 71-Service Dr., Willmar, MN 56201 US
Second Address: MN 56201
(320) 231-1600; *Fax:* (320) 235-7010
www.k-musicradio.com
License: Starbuck, Pope County, MN held by Iowa City Broadcasting Co.
Group Owner: Tom Ingstad Broadcasting Group; (acq 7-19-99; $200,000 for stock).
Wire Services: UPI
Format: Adult Contemp, Light Rock; *Hrs. of News Programming:* news progmg 8 hrs wkly; *No. News Employees:* 1; *Target Audience:* 25-54; male & female; *Adv. Rates:* 16.25; 16.25; 16.25; 16.25

Doug Hanson, General Manager
Beverley Ahlquist, News Director
Rob Ryan, Programming Director
Jessie Holmstrom, Traffic Manager
Aaron Buttenhoff, Sports Director

Stewartville

KYBA

02-01-1993; 105.3 MHz FM; 50 kw; 492 ft.; N43 40 23 W92 41 54
122 4th Street SW, Rochester, MN 55902 US
(507) 286-1010; *Fax:* (507) 286-9370
www.y105fm.com
License: Stewartville, Olmsted County, MN held by Cumulus Licensing LLC
Group Owner: Cumulus Media Inc.; (acq 3-29-2004; grpsl).
Nat'l Network: ABC; *Nat'l Reps:* Christal *Regional Reps:* Christal Radio
Arbitron Metro Market: Rochester, MN; *Format:* Adult Contemp; *Target Audience:* 25-54.; *Adv. Rates:* 26; 26; 26; 22
Brent Ackerman, Operations Dir
Shannon Knoepke, General Manager
Terry Lee, Sales Manager
Tom Garrett, Program Diretor
Kim David, News Director
Bill Davis, Chief Engineer

Stillwater

KLBB

03-13-1949; 1220 kHz AM; *Hrs Open:* 24; 5 kw-D, ND1; 0.254 kw-N, ND1; N45 3 15 W92 49 42
104 North Main Street, Stillwater, MN 55082 US
(651) 439-5006; *Fax:* (651) 439-5015
www.klbbradio.com
License: Stillwater, MN held by Endurance Broadcasting LLC
Nat'l Network: ABC; Westwood One; *Regional Network:* Minn. News Net.
Arbitron Metro Market: Stillwater, MN; *Format:* Adult Contemp; *No. News Employees:* 1; *Target Audience:* 35-64.; *Adv. Rates:* 25; 20; 25; 15
Daniel Smith, CEO
Scott Murray, General Manager
Reed Hagen, Programming Director

Sunburg

KLFN

01-01-2003; 106.5 MHz FM; 6 kw; 328 ft.; N45 22 14 W95 8 28
601 15th Avenue Ne, Waseca, MN 56093 US
(320) 235-1342; *Fax:* (320) 235-9111
www.willmarradio.com
License: Sunburg, Kandiyohi County, MN held by Lakeland Broadcasting Co.
Arbitron Metro Market: Willmar, MN; *Format:* Classic Rock
Doug Loy, General Manager
Maryelin Macht, Programming Director
J.P. Cola, News Director

Thief River Falls

KKAQ

11-02-1979; 1460 kHz AM; *Hrs Open:* 24; 2.5 kw-D, ND1; 0.15 kw-N, ND1; N48 7 25 W96 8 31
P.O. Box 218, Thief River Falls, MN 56701 US
(218) 681-4900; *Fax:* (218) 681-3717
www.trfradio.com
info@trradio.com
License: Thief River Falls, MN held by Iowa City Broadcasting Co. Inc.
Group Owner: Tom Ingstad Broadcasting Group; (acq 11-19-99; $620,000 with co-located FM).
Arbitron Metro Market: Grand Forks, ND; *Format:* News, Sports; *No. News Employees:* 1; *Target Audience:* 25-54.
John Praska, General Manager
Davin Halvorson, Programming Director
Key Teeters, News Director
Stan Mueller, Chief Engineer
Sheila Strange, Traffic Manager

KKDQ

11-01-1989; 99.3 MHz FM; *Hrs Open:* 24; 18 kw; 387 ft.; N48 3 22 W96 22 23
P. O. Box 218, Thief River Falls, MN 56701 US
(218) 681-4900; *Fax:* (218) 681-3717
www.trfradio.com
info@trradio.com
License: Thief River Falls, Pennington County, MN held by Iowa City Broadcasting Co. Inc.
Arbitron Metro Market: Grand Forks, ND; *Format:* Country, Sports
John Praska, General Manager
Matt Gillon, General Sales Mgr
Greg Chance, Programming Director
Sean Cage, Music Director

KNTN

12-13-1991; 102.7 MHz FM; *Hrs Open:* 24; 100 kw; 538 ft.; N47 58 38 W96 36 32
Minnesota Public Radio, 480 Cedar Street, St. Paul, MN 55101 US
(218) 299-3666; *Fax:* (218) 299-3418
www.mpr.org
License: Thief River Falls, Pennington County, MN held by Minnesota Public Radio Inc.
Nat'l Network: NPR; PRI; *Regional Network:* Minn. Pub. Radio
Format: News; *No. News Employees:* 2; *Target Audience:* General.
Jon McTaggart, President
Nick Kereakos, Vice President of Technology & Operations
Tim Roesler, Senior Vice President/General Manager
Craig Curtis, Vice President of Programming
Chris Worthington, News Director
Melanie Walker, MusicDirector
Chandra Kavati, Director of Development Services

*KQMN

11-26-1990; 91.5 MHz FM; *Hrs Open:* 24; 84 kw; 653 ft.; N47 58 38 W96 36 32
Minnesota Public Radio, 480 Cedar Street, St. Paul, MN 55101 US
(651) 290-1500; *Fax:* (218) 299-3418
www.mpr.org
License: Thief River Falls, Pennington County, MN held by Minnesota Public Radio.
Nat'l Network: NPR; PRI
Arbitron Metro Market: Grand Forks, ND; *Format:* News/Talk, Classical; *No. News Employees:* 2
Jon McTaggart, President
Nick Kereakos, Vice President of Technology & Operations
Tim Roesler, Senior Vice President/General Manager
Craig Curtis, Vice President of Programming
Chris Worthington, News Director
Melanie Walker, MusicDirector
Chandra Kavati, Director of Development Services

*KSRQ

11-15-1971; 90.1 MHz FM; *Hrs Open:* 24; 24 kw; 335 ft.; N48 1 19 W96 22 12
1101 Hwy One East, Thief River Falls, MN 56701 US
(218) 681-0791(800) 959-6282; *Fax:* (218) 681-0774
www.pioneer90.org
License: Thief River Falls, Pennington County, MN held by Northland Community & Technical College
Regional Reps: Jim Lowe; Independent Community Media; *Wire Services:* AP
Arbitron Metro Market: Thief River Falls, MN; *Format:* Alternative, Triple A *Special Programming:* Sp one hr, adult standards 5 hrs wkly; *Hrs. of News Programming:* News progmg 10 hrs wkly; *Target Audience:* 18-54;professionals; *Adv. Rates:* 10; 10; 10; 10
Anne Temte, President
Ben Kosharek, Operations Dir
Travis Ryder, General Manager
Stan Mueller, Chief Engineer

KTRF

01-30-1947; 1230 kHz AM; *Hrs Open:* 24; 1 kw-U, ND1; N48 7 47 W96 11 11
P.O. Box 1248, Minnetonka, MN 55345 US
(218) 681-4900; *Fax:* (218) 681-3717
www.trfradio.com
ktrf@mncable.net
License: Thief River Falls, MN held by Iowa City Broadcasting Co.
Nat'l Network: CBS; *Regional Network:* MNN
Arbitron Metro Market: Thief River Falls, MN; *Format:* Adult Contemp, News *Special Programming:* Farm 12 hrs wkly; *Hrs. of News Programming:* news progmg 35 hrs wkly; *No. News Employees:* 2 *Target Audience:* General; 25 plus
Jon Praska, General Manager
Mark Allen, Programming Director
Key Teters, News Director

Tracy

KARL

07-19-1994; 105.1 MHz FM; *Hrs Open:* 24; 45 kw; 502 ft.; N44 19 32 W95 52 19
1414 E. College Dr., Marshall, MN 56258 US
(507) 532-2282; *Fax:* (507) 532-3739
License: Tracy, Lyon County, MN held by KMHL Broadcasting Co.
Group Owner: Linder Broadcasting Group; (acq 12-17-92; $22,100;
Nat'l Network: ABC; *Regional Network:* Linder Farm
Arbitron Metro Market: Tracy, MN; *Format:* Country *Special Programming:* Farm 15 hrs wkly; *Hrs. of News Programming:* News progmg 3 hrs wkly; *Target Audience:* General.; *Adv. Rates:* 12.75; 12.75; 12.75; 9.25
Brad Strootman, General Manager

Two Harbors

KZIO

09-01-1995; 104.3 MHz FM; 50 kw; 397 ft.; N46 56 28 W91 58 58
PO Box 9115, Fargo, ND 58106-9115 US
(701) 277-9115
www.94xrocks.com
License: Two Harbors, Lake County, MN held by Red Rock Radio Corp.
Group Owner: Red Rock Radio Corp.; acq 1-10-00; grpsl).
Arbitron Metro Market: Two Harbors, MN; *Format:* Rock/AOR
Jim Payne, General Sales Mgr

Verndale

KVKK

01-01-2005; 1070 kHz AM
11 SE Bryant Avenue, Wadena, MN 56482 US
(218) 631-3441; *Fax:* (218) 631-3414
License: Verndale, MN held by DJ Broadcasting Corp.
Arbitron Metro Market: Verndale, MN; *Format:* Country
Edward DeLaHunt Sr., General Manager

Virginia

WUSZ

06-02-1971; 99.9 MHz FM; *Hrs Open:* 24; 100 kW; 531 ft.; N47 22 24 W93 0 48
807 West 37th St, Hibbing, MN 55746 USA
(218) 263-7531; *Fax:* (218) 263-6112
radiousa.com
License: Virginia, Saint Louis County, MN held by Midwest Communications Inc.
Group Owner: Midwest Communications Inc.; acq 5-10-2004; grpsl).
Nat'l Network: USA; *Regional Network:* MNN
Arbitron Metro Market: Hibbing, MN; *Format:* Country; *Hrs. of News Programming:* News progmg one hr wkly; *Target Audience:* 25-49; blue and white collar workers and families
Scott Hanson, Brand Manager

Virginia-Hibbing

*WIRR

12-01-1985; 90.9 MHz FM; *Hrs Open:* 24; 21 kw; 551 ft.; N47 29 46 W92 47 5
207 West Superior Street, Duluth, MN 55802 US
(218) 722-9411; *Fax:* (218) 720-4900
www.mpr.org
info@mpr.org
License: Virginia-Hibbing, St. Louis County, MN held by Minnesota Public Radio Inc.
Nat'l Network: PRI; NPR; *Regional Network:* Minn. Pub. Radio
Format: Talk; *No. News Employees:* 3; *Target Audience:* General.
William Kling, President
Kat Eldred, General Manager
Patty Mester, Regional Network Manager

Wabasha

WBHA

04-01-1976; 1190 kHz AM; *Hrs Open:* 6 AM-sunset; 1 kw-D; N44 20 44 W91 58 28 *Rebroadcasts:* Rebroadcasts KMFX-FM Lake City 90%
474 Guernsey Lane, Red Wing, MN 55066
(507) 288-3888; *Fax:* (507) 288-7815
www.1025thefox.com
License: Wabasha, Wabasha County, MN held by CC Licenses LLC.
Group Owner: Q Media Group LLC
Regional Network: MNN
Target Audience: 18-54.
Tom Hughes, Operations Manager
Donald Kliewer, General Manager
Ronnie Stockwell, Business Manager
Craig Livingstone, Account Executive

Wadena

KKWS
09-23-1968; 105.9 MHz FM; *Hrs Open:* 24; 100 kw; 561 ft.; N46 35 59 W94 54 4
Mailing Address: P.O. Box 980, Brainerd, MN 56401 US
Second Address: 201 1/2 Jefferson St. S., Wadena, MN 56482
(218) 631-1803; *Fax:* (218) 631-4557
www.superstationk106.com
License: Wadena, Wadena County, MN
Group Owner: Omni Broadcasting Co.
Nat'l Network: ABC
Arbitron Metro Market: Saint Cloud, MN; *Format:* Country; *Hrs. of News Programming:* news progmg 12 hrs wkly; *No. News Employees:* 1; *Target Audience:* 25-54; adults
Rick Youngbauer, General Manager
Danny Wild, Programming Director

KWAD
04-24-1948; 920 kHz AM; *Hrs Open:* 24
201 1/2 Jefferson Street South, Wadena, MN 56482 US
(218) 631-1803; *Fax:* (218) 631-4557
www.kwadknsp.com
License: Wadena, MN held by BL Broadcasting Inc.
Group Owner: Omni Broadcasting Co.; (acq 4-1-2004; grpsl).
Nat'l Network: ABC; *Regional Network:* Minn. Farm; Minn. News Net.
Format: Country *Special Programming:* Farm 10 hrs wkly; *Hrs. of News Programming:* news progmg 20 hrs wkly; *No. News Employees:* 1; *Target Audience:* 25-54; adults
Lou Buron, CEO
Rick Youngbauer, General Manager
Kyle Gylsen, Programming Director
Sherry Linnes, Promotions Manager
Mary Campbell, CFO

Waite Park

KLZZ
07-01-1989; 103.7 MHz FM; 9 kw; 413 ft.; N45 30 2 W94 14 31
640 SE Lincoln Avenue, St. Cloud, MN 56304 US
(320) 251-4422; *Fax:* (320) 251-1855
www.1037theloon.com
License: Waite Park, Stearns County, MN
Group Owner: Townsquare Media
Arbitron Metro Market: St. Cloud, MN; *Format:* Classic Rock
David Engberg, General Manager
Steve Lahr, Director of Sales
Pete Hanson, Programming Director

KXSS
01-01-1981; 1390 kHz AM; 2.5 kw-D, DA2; 1 kw-N, DA2; N45 32 31 W94 15 41
640 SE Lincoln Avenue, St. Cloud, MN 56304 US
(320) 251-4422; *Fax:* (320) 251-1855
www.1390thefan.com
License: Waite Park, MN
Group Owner: Townsquare Media; (acq 5-8-2001; grpsl).
Arbitron Metro Market: St. Cloud, MN; *Format:* Sports; *Target Audience:* 18-49.
David Engberg, General Manager
Jay Caldwell, Programming Director
Lee Voss, News Director
Mark Young, Chief Engineer
Steve Lahr, Director of Sales
Jay Cladwell, Brand Manager

Walker

KAKK
07-11-1970; 1570 kHz AM; *Hrs Open:* 24
P.O. Box 980, Brainerd, MN 56401 US
(218) 732-3306; *Fax:* (218) 547-4001
License: Walker, MN held by Edward De La Hunt
Regional Network: MNN
Arbitron Metro Market: Fargo, MD; *Format:* Oldies; *Target Audience:* General.
Tammy De La Hunt, General Manager
Marcus Mitchell, News Director
Bernie Schumacher, Account Executive

KLLZ-FM
05-06-1984; 99.1 MHz FM; *Hrs Open:* 24; 100 kw; 505 ft.; N47 12 52 W94 55 18
Mailing Address: P.O. Box 980, Brainerd, MN 56401 US
Second Address: 502 Beltrami Ave. N.W., Bemidji, MN 56601
(218) 444-1500; *Fax:* (218) 751-8091
License: Walker, Cass County, MN held by BG Broadcasting Inc.
Group Owner: Omni Broadcasting Co.; (acq 10-24-2000).
Nat'l Network: ABC
Arbitron Metro Market: Fargo, MD; *Format:* Classic Rock; *Hrs. of News Programming:* news progmg 12 hrs wkly; *No. News Employees:* 1; *Target Audience:* 25-54; adults
Lou Buron, CEO
Peggy Hanson, General Sales Mgr
Mardy Karger, News Director
Mary Campbell, CFO

KQKK
05-01-1999; 101.9 MHz FM; *Hrs Open:* 5:30 AM-Midday; 50 kw; 390 ft.; N47 3 14 W94 15 32
P.O. Box 49, Hwy 34 East, Park Rapids, MN 56470 US
(218) 547-4000; *Fax:* (218) 547-4001
www.kkradionetwork.com
kqkkkakk@eot.com
License: Walker, Cass County, MN held by CJ Broadcasting.
Nat'l Network: CBS Radio; *Wire Services:* AP
Format: Adult Contemp
Tammy De La Hunt, General Manager
Marcus Mitchell, News Director
Bernie Schumacher, Account Executive

Warroad

KKWQ
08-01-1989; 92.5 MHz FM; *Hrs Open:* 24; 100 kw; 463 ft.; N48 49 41 W95 23 16
501 East Lake Street, Box 69, Warroad, MN 56763 US
(218) 386-3024; *Fax:* (218) 386-3090
www.kq92.com
License: Warroad, Roseau County, MN held by Border Broadcasting LP
Nat'l Network: ABC; Jones Radio Networks; *Regional Network:* Minn. News Net.
Arbitron Metro Market: Grand Forks, ND; *Format:* Country; *Target Audience:* 25-54.; *Adv. Rates:* 24; 24; 24; 24
Mike Pederson, President

*KOLJ-FM
91.7 MHz FM; 0.25 kw; -230 ft.; N48 54 26 W95 18 58
PO Box 500, Simi Valley, CA 93062 US
(940) 663-5711; *Fax:* (940) 663-2125
www.lifetalk.net
License: Warroad, Roseau County, MN held by We Have This Hope Christian Radio Inc.
Arbitron Metro Market: Warroad, MN
Vern Erickson, President

Waseca

KRUE
12-22-1971; 1170 kHz AM; *Hrs Open:* 24; 2.5 kw-D, 60 w-N, 1 kw-CH; N44 02 45 W93 23 08 (D), N44 04 45 W93 30 24 (N)
255 Cedardale Dr., Owatonna, MN 55060 US
(507) 444-9224; *Fax:* (507) 444-9080
www.krue92.com
booth@krue92.com
License: Waseca, Waseca County, MN held by Main Street Broadcasting Inc.
Group Owner: Linder Broadcasting Group; (acq 12-26-01; with co-located FM).
Regional Network: MNN
Population Served: 65,000 *Format:* Country; *Hrs. of News Programming:* news progmg 12 hrs wkly; *No. News Employees:* 2; *Target Audience:* 30-65; general, farm
Matt Kelelsen, Sales Manager
Craig Stevens, Programming Director

KRUE
06-01-1972; 92.1 MHz FM; *Hrs Open:* 24; 25 kw; 286 ft; N44 02 45 W93 23 08
255 Cedardale Dr., Owatonna, MN 55060 US
(507) 444-9224; *Fax:* (507) 444-9080
www.krue92.com
booth@krue92.com
License: Waseca, Waseca County, MN held by Main Street Broadcasting, Inc.
Group Owner: Linder Broadcasting Group
Nat'l Network: ABC
Format: Country; *Hrs. of News Programming:* news progmg 4 hrs wkly; *No. News Employees:* 1; *Target Audience:* 25-54.
Andy Gott, Brand Mgr

Watertown

KPNP
05-16-1996; 1600 kHz AM; *Hrs Open:* 24; 5 kw-U, DA1; N44 55 23 W93 46 56
6500 Brooklyn Boulevard, Brooklyn Center, MN 55429 US
(763) 585-1600
www.kpnp1600.com
peter@kpnp1600.com
License: Watertown, MN held by Self Retire Inc.
Arbitron Metro Market: Brooklyn Center, MN; *Format:* Ethnic
Peter Phia Xiong, General Manager

Willmar

*KBHZ
02-16-1996; 91.9 MHz FM; 25 kw; 328 ft.; N45 0 40 W94 53 56
5402 Pike Street East, Osakis, MN 56360 US
(320) 859-3000; *Fax:* (320) 859-3010
www.praisefm.org
mail@praisefm.org
License: Willmar, Kandiyohi County, MN held by Christian Heritage Broadcasting Inc.
Arbitron Metro Market: Osakis, MN; *Format:* Religious
Dave Hartman, Operations Dir
David McIver, General Manager

KDJS
03-02-1981; 1590 kHz AM; *Hrs Open:* 24; 1 kw-D, 89 w-N, DA-2; N45 05 07 W95 00 19
Mailing Address: Box 380, Willmar, MN 56201
Second Address: 730 N.E. Hwy. 71, Willmar, MN 56201
(320) 231-1600; *Fax:* (320) 235-7010
www.k-musicradio.com
spots@k-musicradio.com
License: Willmar, Kandiyohi County, MN held by Iowa City Broadcasting Inc.
Population Served: 100,000 *Special Programming:* Farm 5 hrs wkly; *No. News Employees:* 1; *Target Audience:* 25-54.; *Adv. Rates:* 10; 10; 10; 2
Doug Hanson, General Manager
Doug Hanson, General Sales Mgr
Rob Ryan, Programming Director
Bev Ahlquist, News Director
Steve Youngberg, Chief Engineer
Jeremy Goulet, Traffic/Office Manager
Aaron Buttenhoff, Sports Director

KDJS-FM
05-17-1993; 95.3 MHz FM; *Hrs Open:* 24; 50 kw; 436 ft; N45 01 23 W95 15 57
Mailing Address: Box 380, Willmar, MN 56201
Second Address: 730 N.E. Hwy. 71, Willmar, MN 56201
(320) 231-1600; *Fax:* (320) 235-7010
www.k-musicradio.com
spots@k-musicradio.com
License: Willmar, Kandiyohi County, MN held by Iowa City Broadcasting Inc.
Regional Reps: Tacher
Population Served: 100,000; *No. News Employees:* 1
Doug Hanson, General Manager/General Sales Manager
Bob Ryan, Programming Director
Bev Ahlquist, News Director
Steve Youngberg, Engineering Dir
Steve Youngberg, Chief Engineer
Aaron Buttenhoff, Sports Director
Jeremy Goulet,Traffic/Office Manager

KQIC
07-01-1965; 102.5 MHz FM; 100 kw; 830 ft.; N45 11 40 W95 5 1
Mailing Address: US
Second Address: 1340 N. 7th St., Willmar, MN 56201
(320) 235-1340; *Fax:* (320) 235-9111
www.1025fm.com
License: Willmar, Kandiyohi County, MN
Format: Adult Contemp; *Target Audience:* 18-49.; *Adv. Rates:* 31.25; 30; 31.25; 25
Steve Linder, President
Mary Elin Macht, Operations Dir
Doug Loy, General Manager
Bob Thompson, Programming Director
J.P. Cola, News Director
Mary Overman, Business Manager

KWLM
01-01-1940; 1340 kHz AM; *Hrs Open:* 24; 1 kw-U, ND1; N45 8 0 W95 2 35
Mailing Address: US
Second Address: 1340 N. 7th St., Willmar, MN 56201
(320) 235-1340; *Fax:* (320) 235-9111
www.kwlm.com
askus@kwlm.com
License: Willmar, MN held by Steven W. Linder.
Regional Network: Linder Farm
Arbitron Metro Market: Willmar, MN; *Format:* News, News/Talk, 86 *Special Programming:* Farm 8 hrs wkly; *Hrs. of News Programming:* news progmg 30 hrs wkly; *No. News Employees:* 3; *Target Audience:* General. *Adv. Rates:* 30.50; 29; 30.50; 24.50
Steve Linder, President
Mary Elin Macht, Operations Dir
Doug Loy, General Manager

Bob Thompson, Programming Director
J.P. Cola, News Director
Mary Overman, Business Manager

***KKLW**
01-29-2004; 90.9 MHz FM; *Hrs Open:* 24; 0.4 kw; 423 ft.; N45 11 52 W94 56 58
1425 N. Market Blvd, Suite 9, Sacramento, CA 95834 US
(800) 525-5683; *Fax:* (916) 251-1650
www.klove.com
klove@klove.com
License: Willmar, Kandiyohi County, MN held by Educational Media Foundation.
Group Owner: EMF Broadcasting
Nat'l Network: K-Love
Arbitron Metro Market: Willmar, MN; *Format:* Christian; *No. News Employees:* 3; *Target Audience:* 25-44; Judeo Christian, female
Darrell Chambliss, Chairman
Mike Novak, President and CEO
John Clements, Operations Dir
David Pierce, Programming Director
Ed Lenane, News Director
Sam Wallington, Engineering Dir
Marya Morgan, News Reporter
Richard Hunt, NewsReporter
Laura Daniels, News Reporter
Tim Luttrell, News Reporter
Kenny Noble Cortes, News Reporter
Darren Vinson, News Reporter

Wilton

WBKK
820 kHz AM; 15 kw-D, 750 w-N, DA-2; N47 23 29 W95 04 40
Box 49, Park Rapids, MN 56470
(218) 732-3306
kprmkdkk@unitelc.com
License: Wilton, Beltrami County, MN held by Bemidji Radio Inc

Edward De La Hunt Sr., General Manager

Windom

KDOM
12-28-1958; 1580 kHz AM; *Hrs Open:* 24; 1 kw-D, DA2; 0.002 kw-N, DA2; N43 51 41 W95 5 50
Box 218, Windom, MN 56101 US
(507) 831-3908; *Fax:* (507) 831-3913
www.kdomradio.com
kdomnew@windomnet.com
License: Windom, MN held by Windom Radio Inc.
Group Owner: The Result Radio Group; (acq 4-89; with co-located FM;
Regional Network: MNN
Arbitron Metro Market: Windom, MN; *Format:* Country, News, 62, Sports, Talk; *Hrs. of News Programming:* news progmg 21 hrs wkly; *No. News Employees:* 1; *Target Audience:* General; farm audience, housewives, businessowners & laborers; *Adv. Rates:* 31; 31; 27; 27
Dave Cory, General Manager
Judi Cory, General Sales Mgr
Dirk Abraham, News Director

KDOM-FM
12-08-1976; 94.3 MHz FM; *Hrs Open:* 6 AM-midnight; 5.7 kw; 335 ft.; N43 53 6 W95 10 56
Box 218, Windom, MN 56101 US
(507) 831-3908; *Fax:* (507) 831-3913
www.kdomradio.com
kdomnew@windomnet.com
License: Windom, Cottonwood County, MN held by Windom Radio Inc.
Group Owner: The Result Radio Group
Arbitron Metro Market: Windom, MN; *Format:* Country, News, 62, Sports, Talk; *Adv. Rates:* 31; 31; 27; 27
Jo Bailey, Operations Dir
Dave Cory, General Manager
Judi Cory, General Sales Mgr

***KJWR**
01-01-2008; 90.9 MHz FM; *Hrs Open:* 24; 25 kw; 328 ft.; N44 0 22 W95 12 9 *Rebroadcasts:* Rebroadcasts KJIA(FM) Spirit Lake, IA 100%
PO Box 125, Windom, MN 56101 US
(800) 810-5559; *Fax:* (712) 332-2428
www.kjwrradio.com
kjwr@kjwrradio.com
License: Windom, Cottonwood County, MN held by Minn-Iowa Christian Broadcasting Inc.
Group Owner: Minn-Iowa Christian Broadcasting Inc.
Arbitron Metro Market: Windom, MN; *Format:* Christian
Eugene Stallkamp, President
Matt Dorfner, General Manager
Steve Ware, Programming Director
Mark Bohnett, Chief Engineer
Matt Dorfner, Executive Director
Doug Johnson, Program Coordinator

Winona

KAGE
02-17-1957; 1380 kHz AM; *Hrs Open:* Sunrise-sunset
752 Bluffview Circle, Winona, MN 55987 US
(507) 452-4000; *Fax:* (507) 452-9494
www.winonaradio.com
jpapenfuss@winonradio.com
License: Winona, MN held by KAGE Inc.
Group Owner: The Result Radio Group; (acq 1-73)
Wire Services: AP
Arbitron Metro Market: Winona, MN; *Format:* Country *Special Programming:* Farm, relg; *Hrs. of News Programming:* news progmg 7 hrs wkly; *No. News Employees:* 1; *Target Audience:* 35 plus; general
Pat Papenfuss, President
Jerry Papenfuss, General Manager
Les Guderian, General Sales Mgr
Darryl Smelser, News Director
Steve Schuh, Chief Engineer
Paul Van Beck, Sports Commentator

KAGE-FM
08-14-1971; 95.3 MHz FM; *Hrs Open:* 24; 11 kw; 495 ft.; N44 2 31 W91 40 47
752 Bluffview Circle, Winona, MN 55987 US
(507) 452-4000; *Fax:* (507) 452-9494
www.winonaradio.com
jristow@winonaradio.com
License: Winona, Winona County, MN held by KAGE Inc.
Group Owner: The Result Radio Group
Wire Services: AP
Arbitron Metro Market: Winona, MN; *Format:* Adult Contemp; *Hrs. of News Programming:* news progmg 14 hrs wkly; *No. News Employees:* 1; *Target Audience:* 25-54.
Jerry Papenfuss, CEO
Aaron Taylor, Programming Director

KHME
06-04-1992; 101.1 MHz FM; *Hrs Open:* 24; 5 kw; 741 ft.; N44 4 26 W91 34 38
752 Bluffview Circle, Winona, MN 55987 US
(507) 452-4000; *Fax:* (507) 452-9494
www.winonaradio.com
jristow@winonaradio.com
License: Winona, Winona County, MN held by KAGE Inc.
Group Owner: The Result Radio Group; (acq 10-19-01; $1 million).
Wire Services: AP
Format: Classic Rock; *Hrs. of News Programming:* news progmg 20 hrs wkly; *No. News Employees:* 2; *Target Audience:* 25-54; women
Pat Papenfuss, Operations Dir
Jerry Papenfuss, General Manager
Les Guderian, General Sales Mgr

***KQAL**
12-12-1975; 89.5 MHz FM; *Hrs Open:* 24; 2.5 kw; 690 ft.; N44 4 26 W91 34 38
Mailing Address: P.O. Box 5838, Winona, MN 55987 US
Second Address: 175 W. Mark St., Winona, MN 55987
(507) 453-2222; *Fax:* (507) 457-5226
www.kqal.org
kqal@kqal.org
License: Winona, Winona County, MN held by Winona State University.
Nat'l Network: AP Radio; *Wire Services:* AP
Format: Variety/Diverse *Special Programming:* Class 14 hrs, pub affrs 10 hrs wkly; *Hrs. of News Programming:* News progmg 5 hrs wkly; *Target Audience:* General.
Mike Martin, Operations Dir
Mike Martin, General Manager
Doug Westerman, General Sales Mgr
Teri Tenseth, Programming Director
Nate Siems, News Director

***KSMR**
11-01-1978; 92.5 MHz FM; 0.004 kw; -141 ft.; N44 2 47 W91 41 43
700 Terrace Heights, Box 29, Winona, MN 55987 US
(507) 457-1613; *Fax:* (507) 457-1439
www.smumn.edu
License: Winona, Winona County, MN held by St. Mary's University
Arbitron Metro Market: Winona, MN; *Format:* Rock/AOR; *Target Audience:* 18-24.
Dean Beckman, General Manager

KWNO
01-01-1938; 1230 kHz AM; *Hrs Open:* 24
752 Bluffview Circle, Winona, MN 55987 US
(507) 452-4000; (800) 584-6782; *Fax:* (507) 452-9494
www.winonaradio.com
jristow@winonaradio.com
License: Winona, MN held by KAGE Inc.
Group Owner: The Result Radio Group; (acq 6-19-95; $1 million with KWNO-FM Rushford)
Regional Network: MNN; *Wire Services:* AP
Arbitron Metro Market: Winona, MN; *Format:* News, News/Talk, 64, Sports, Talk *Special Programming:* Polka 5 hrs wkly; *Hrs. of News Programming:* news progmg 21 hrs wkly; *No. News Employees:* 1; *Target Audience:* 35 plus; Sports fans
Pat Papenfuss, Chairman
Jerry Papenfuss, CEO

Winthrop

KHRS
07-01-2008; 105.9 MHz FM; 23 kw; 344 ft.; N44 28 25 W94 28 15 *Rebroadcasts:* Simulcast with KXLP(FM) Eagle Lake 100%
511 3rd Street N., New Ulm, MN 56073 US
(507) 345-4537; *Fax:* (507) 345-5364
License: Winthrop, Sibley County, MN held by Ketelsen Radio Inc.
Arbitron Metro Market: Winthrop, MN; *Format:* Classic Rock
Jo Bailey, Operations Dir

Worthington

KITN
11-01-1994; 93.5 MHz FM; *Hrs Open:* 24; 50 kw; 466 ft.; N43 31 31 W95 24 47
28779 Co. Highway 35, Worthington, MN 56187 US
(507) 376-6165; *Fax:* (507) 376-5071
info@myradioworks.net
License: Worthington, Nobles County, MN
Regional Network: MNN
Format: Adult Contemp
Gary Buchanan, CFO
Tom Mulso, General Manager
Jerry Mason, Programming Director
Darrell Stitt, News Director
Bob Cook, Chief Engineer

***KRSW**
12-01-1973; 89.3 MHz FM; 100 kw; 554 ft.; N43 53 1 W95 55 44
1450 College Way, Worthington, MN 56187 US
(605) 335-6666(651) 290-1259; *Fax:* (605) 335-1259
License: Worthington, Nobles County, MN held by Minnesota Public Radio Inc.
Nat'l Network: PRI; NPR
Arbitron Metro Market: St.Paul,MN; *Format:* Talk
Marty Mahowald, Chairman
Chris Cross, Network Manager
Debbie Erickson, Vice Chair

KWOA
10-11-1947; 730 kHz AM; *Hrs Open:* 24; 1 kw-D, ND1; 0.159 kw-N, ND1; N43 37 48 W95 40 32
28779 Co. Highway 35, Worthington, MN 56197 US
(507) 376-6165; *Fax:* (507) 376-5071
www.kwoa.com
contactus@935thebreeze.com
License: Worthington, MN
Nat'l Network: CBS; Fox Sports; *Nat'l Reps:* Hyett/Ramsland
Regional Reps: Midwest Radio.
Arbitron Metro Market: Worthington, MN; *Format:* News, News/Talk, 86 *Special Programming:* Farm; *Hrs. of News Programming:* news progmg 18 hrs wkly; *No. News Employees:* 2; *Target Audience:* 35 plus.
Todd Mejia, General Manager
Barry Roberts, Programming Director

KUSQ-FM
05-03-1961; 95.1 MHz FM; *Hrs Open:* 20; 100 kw; Ant 660 ft; N43 37 48 W95 40 32
28779 County Hwy. 35, Worthington, MN 56187
(507) 376-6165; *Fax:* (507) 376-5071
License: Worthington, Nobles County, MN
Population Served: 103,500 *Hrs. of News Programming:* news progmg 10 hrs wkly; *No. News Employees:* 1
Todd Mejia, General Manager
Barry Roberts, Programming Director

KUSQ
01-01-2008; 95.1 MHz FM; 100 kw; 650 ft.; N43 37 48 W95 40 32
28779 Country Highway 35, Worthington, MN 56187 US
(507) 376-6165; *Fax:* (507) 376-5071
License: Worthington, Osceola County, MN held by Absolute Communications L.L.C.
Arbitron Metro Market: Worthington, MN; *Format:* Christian
Todd Mejia, General Manager
Barry Roberts, Programming Director

Worthington-Marshall

***KNSW**
01-01-1979; 91.7 MHz FM; 99 kw; 797 ft.; N43 53 1 W95 55 44
Minnesota Public Radio, 480 Cedar Street, St. Paul, MN 55101 US
(651) 290-1500; *Fax:* (651) 290-1224
www.mpr.org
newsroom@mpr.org
License: Worthington-Marshall, Nobles County, MN held by Minnesota Public Radio.
Arbitron Metro Market: Worthington, MN; *Format:* News, News/Talk, 86
Jon McTaggart, President
Nick Kereakos, Vice President of Tecnhology & Operations
Tim Roesler, Vice President/General Manager
Craig Curtis, Vice President of Programming
Chris Worthington, News Director
Melanie Walker, MusicDirector
Chandra Kavati, Director of Development Services

Mississippi

Aberdeen

WWZQ
02-01-1952; 1240 kHz AM; 1 kw-U, ND1; N33 48 32 W88 32 33
P.O. Box 458, Amory, MS 38821 USA
(662) 256-9726; *Fax:* (662) 256-9725
www.fm95radio.com
fm95@fm95radio.com
License: Aberdeen, MS held by Stanford Communications Inc.
Group Owner: Stanford Communications Inc.; acq 12-2-99; $51,000)
Nat'l Network: USA
Arbitron Metro Market: Tupelo, MS; *Format:* Oldies *Special Programming:* Gospel 8 hrs wkly

Ackerman

WFCA
01-01-1986; 107.9 MHz FM; *Hrs Open:* 24; 100 kw; 1,007 ft; N33 25 25 W89 24 13
40 Mecklin Ave., French Camp, MS 39745
(662) 547-6414; *Fax:* (662) 547-9451
www.wfcafm108.com
sales@wfcafm108.com
License: Ackerman, Choctaw County, MS held by French Camp Radio Inc.
Regional Network: Miss. News Net.
Target Audience: General.
Carol Prewiit, Operations Dir
Charles Carroll, Station Manager
H Glen Barlow, General Sales Mgr
Ron Linkins, Programming Director

Amory

WAFM
01-01-1974; 95.7 MHz FM; *Hrs Open:* 24; 6 kw; 274 ft.; N33 58 33 W88 29 29
P.O. Box 458, Amory, MS 38821 USA
(662) 256-9726; *Fax:* (662) 256-9725
www.fm95radio.com
fm95@fm95radio.com
License: Amory, Monroe County, MS held by Stanford Communications Inc.
Group Owner: Stanford Communications Inc.; 9/21/1992
Nat'l Network: ABC
Arbitron Metro Market: Amory-Monroe County, MS; *Format:* Oldies *Special Programming:* Relg 2 hrs wkly

WAMY
10-23-1955; 1580 kHz AM; *Hrs Open:* 6 AM-10PM; 1 kw-D, ND1; 0.018 kw-N, ND1; N33 58 33 W88 29 29 *Rebroadcasts:* Rebroadcasts WWZQ(AM) Aberdeen 75%
P.O. Box 458, Amory, MS 38821 US
(662) 256-9726; *Fax:* (662) 256-9725
fm95radio.com
fm95@fm95radio.com
License: Amory, MS held by Stanford Communications Inc.
Group Owner: Stanford Communications Inc.; acq 9-21-92; $85,000 with co-located FM;
Nat'l Network: USA
Arbitron Metro Market: Tupelo, MS; *Format:* News, Sports, 86
Special Programming: Relg 6 hrs, Gospel 6 hrs wkly; *No. News Employees:* 1; *Target Audience:* Genral.

Artesia

WSMS
01-01-1985; 99.9 MHz FM; *Hrs Open:* 24; 47 kw; 505 ft.; N33 39 14 W88 37 15
200 6th Street N., Suite 205, Columbus, MS 39701 US
(662) 327-1183; *Fax:* (662) 654-6510
www.999thefoxrocks.com
License: Artesia, Lowndes County, MS held by Cumulus Licensing Corp.
Group Owner: Cumulus Media Inc.; (acq 9-99; grpsl).
Arbitron Metro Market: Artesia, MS; *Format:* Rock/AOR; *Target Audience:* 18-49.
Greg Benefield, General Manager
Chris Stryker, Programming Director

Baldwyn

WESE
10-01-1980; 92.5 MHz FM; *Hrs Open:* 24; 12 kw; 472 ft.; N34 21 46 W88 35 28
5026 Cliff Gookin Boulevard, Tupelo, MS 38801 US
(662) 842-1067
License: Baldwyn, Lee County, MS held by Capstar TX LLC
Group Owner: iHeartMedia; (acq 12-19-2000; grpsl)
Nat'l Network: ABC; *Nat'l Reps:* Interep
Arbitron Metro Market: Baldwyn, MS; *Format:* Urban Contemporary *Special Programming:* Gospel 6 hrs, Blues 6 hrs wkly; *Target Audience:* 18-54.
Richard J. Bressler, President

Batesville

WBLE
08-01-1978; 100.5 MHz FM; 50 kw; 492 ft.; N34 22 44 W89 45 57
P.O. Box 1528, Batesville, MS 38606 US
(662) 563-4664; *Fax:* (662) 563-9002
www.wble101.com/
advertising@wble101.com
License: Batesville, Panola County, MS held by Batesville Broadcasting Co. Inc.
Arbitron Metro Market: Batesville, MS; *Format:* Country; *Target Audience:* 25 plus.
J. Boyd Ingram, General Manager

WJBI
06-19-1953; 1290 kHz AM; 0.73 kw-D, ND1; 0.091 kw-N, ND1; N34 18 13 W89 58 59
P. O. Box 1528, Batesville, MS 38606 US
(662) 563-1290; *Fax:* (662) 563-9002
License: Batesville, MS held by Batesville Broadcasting Co. Inc.
Format: Adult Contemp; *Target Audience:* 30 plus.
J. Boyd Ingram, General Manager

Bay Springs

WIZK
1570 kHz AM; *Hrs Open:* 12; 3.2 kw-D, NDD; N31 57 56 W89 18 3
27 Kings Highway N., Westport, CT 06880 US
(601) 764-9888; *Fax:* (601) 764-9887
License: Bay Springs, MS held by Sage Communications LLC
Arbitron Metro Market: Laurel-Hattiesburg, MS; *Format:* Country; *Target Audience:* 25-54; baby boomers & older consumers; *Adv. Rates:* 25; 20; 25; na
Tom Diaz, Chief Engineer

Bay St. Louis

WZKX
03-13-1987; 107.9 MHz FM; 100 kW; 1509 ft.; N30 45 5.7 W89 3 24.2
PO Box 2639, Gulfport, MS 39505-2639 USA
(228) 896-5500; *Fax:* (228) 896-0458
www.kicker108.com
rhodes@kicker108.com
License: Bay St. Louis, Hancock County, MS held by Dowdy & Dowdy Partnership
Group Owner: Dowdy & Dowdy Partnership
Arbitron Metro Market: Bay Saint Louis, MS; *Format:* Country
Morgan Dowdy, General Manager
Steve Spillmann, General Sales Mgr
Dennis Warren, Local Sales Manager
Bryan Rhodes, Operations Manager

WMEJ
1190 kHz AM; 5 kw-D; N30 19 25 W89 21 03
204 Courthouse Road, Suite 1, Gulfport, MS 39520
(504)233-0091
License: Bay St. Louis,
Group Owner: Hancock Broadcasting Corporation

Belzoni

WBYP
01-01-1986; 107.1 MHz FM; *Hrs Open:* 24; 9.4 kw; 531 ft.; N33 3 4 W90 37 51
Mailing Address: P.O. Box 130, Yazoo City, MS 39194 US
Second Address: 611 Center Park Ln., Yazoo City, MS 39194
(662) 746-7676; *Fax:* (662) 746-1525
License: Belzoni, Humphreys County, MS held by Zoo-Bel Broadcasting LLC.
Nat'l Network: ABC; *Regional Network:* Miss. News Net; *Nat'l Reps:* Rgnl Reps
Arbitron Metro Market: Yazoo City, MS; *Format:* Country, Gospel; *Hrs. of News Programming:* news progmg 18 hrs wkly; *No. News Employees:* 3; *Target Audience:* 18-65; Adults
Colon Johnston, General Manager
Brenda Johnston, News Director

WELZ
01-01-1959; 1460 kHz AM; 1 kw-D, NDD; N33 10 24 W90 28 51
Mailing Address: 8 Southwood Blvd., Clinton, MS 39056 US
Second Address: 204 Church St., Belzoni, MS 39038
(662) 746-7676; *Fax:* (662) 746-1525
License: Belzoni, MS held by Zoo-Bel Broadcasting LLC.
Regional Network: Miss. News Net.
Arbitron Metro Market: Belzoni, MS; *Format:* Black, Blues, 44; *Hrs. of News Programming:* 5 Hours Per Week; *No. News Employees:* 1; *Target Audience:* 25 - 65
Colon Johnston, General Manager

Benton

WXTN
10-23-1959; 1000 kHz AM
100 Radio Rd., PO Box 369, Lexington, MS 39095 US
(662) 834-1106; *Fax:* (662) 834-1254
License: Benton, MS held by Brad Maurice Cothran
Arbitron Metro Market: Lexington, MS; *Format:* Christian, Gospel
Brad Cothran, General Manager

***WYAD**
88.3 MHz FM; 0.1 kw; 33 ft.; N32 50 37 W90 14 26 US
(662) 571-2987
License: Benton, Yazoo County, MS held by Bountiful Blessings Broadcasting Inc.
Arbitron Metro Market: Benton, MS
Joseph Thomas, General Manager

Bentonia

***WJNS-FM**
12-13-1968; 92.1 MHz FM; 4.8 kw; 365 ft.; N32 33 25 W90 20 14
645 Church St, Ste 400, Norfolk, VA 23510 US
(662) 746-5921; *Fax:* (662) 746-5996
License: Bentonia, Yazoo County, MS held by Family Worship Center Church Inc.
Group Owner: Family Worship Center Church Inc.; acq 6-16-2004; $350,000).
Format: Religious *Special Programming:* Farm 16 hrs, weather 16 hrs wkly; *Target Audience:* 25-54.
Bruce Grassman, President
Keith Huotari, Operations Dir
Trisha Peterson, General Manager
Aaron Harper, News Director
Walt Baldwin, Chief Engineer

Biloxi

***WMAH-FM**
12-01-1983; 90.3 MHz FM; *Hrs Open:* 24; 100 kw; 1414 ft.; N30 45 18 W88 56 44
3825 Ridgewood Road, Jackson, MS 39211 US
(601) 432-6800; *Fax:* (601) 432-6806
www.mpbonline.org
License: Biloxi, Harrison County, MS held by Mississippi Authority for Educational Television.
Nat'l Network: PRI; NPR; *Wire Services:* AP

Arbitron Metro Market: Biloxi, MI *TV Affiliate:* WMAH-TV; *Format:* News; *Hrs. of News Programming:* news progmg 100 hrs wkly; *No. News Employees:* 7; *Target Audience:* General.
Ronnie Agnew, Executive Director
Paul Moore, Deputy Administrator

WMJY

07-11-1966; 93.7 MHz FM; *Hrs Open:* 24; 100 kw horiz, 98.3 kw vert; 984 ft.; N30 29 9 W88 42 53
286 DeBuys Road, Biloxi, MS 39531 US
(228) 388-2323; *Fax:* (228) 388-2362
www.magic937.com
License: Biloxi, Harrison County, MS held by CC Licenses LLC.
Group Owner: iHeartMedia; (acq 2-2-2004; grpsl).
Nat'l Reps: Clear Channel; *Wire Services:* AP
Arbitron Metro Market: Biloxi, MS; *Format:* Adult Contemp; *Hrs. of News Programming:* news progmg 5 hrs wkly; *No. News Employees:* 1; *Target Audience:* 25-54.
James Wynne, Senior Account Executive
Kristan Saucier, Digital Content Director

WXBD

05-01-1948; 1490 kHz AM; *Hrs Open:* 24; 1 kw-U, ND1; N30 23 38 W88 59 58
9471 Three Rivers Rd., Suite A, Gulfport, MS 39503 US
(228) 388-2001; *Fax:* (228) 896-9114
www.1640thechamp.com
License: Biloxi, Harrison County, MS held by Alpha Media Licensee LLC
Group Owner: Alpha Media LLC
Nat'l Network: ESPN Radio
Arbitron Metro Market: Biloxi, MS; *Format:* Sports
Kenny Vest, Operations Manager
Ricky Mitchell, General Manager
Jesse Alvarez, Sales Manager
Kyle Curley, Programming Director
Mindy Patton, Promotions/New Media Director
Michelle Shortridge, Business Manager

WTNI

01-01-2003; 1640 kHz AM; 10 kw-D, ND2; 1 kw-N, ND2; N30 28 27 W88 51 23
9471 Three Rivers Rd., Suite A, Gulfport, MS 39503 US
(228) 388-2001; *Fax:* (228) 896-9114
www.1640thechamp.com
License: Biloxi, Harrison County, MS held by Alpha Media Licensee LLC
Group Owner: Alpha Media LLC
Nat'l Network: ESPN Radio; *Wire Services:* AP
Arbitron Metro Market: Gulfport, MS; *Format:* Sports
Kenny Vest, Operations Manager
Ricky Mitchell, General Manager
Jesse Alvarez, Sales Manager
Kyle Curley, Programming Director
Mindy Patton, Promotions/New Media Director
Michelle Shortridge, Business Manager

Booneville

WBIP

09-01-1950; 1400 kHz AM; *Hrs Open:* 24; 1 kw-U; N34 38 21 W88 34 33
Mailing Address: Box 356, Booneville, MS 38829
Second Address: 1100 So. Second St., Booneville, MS 38829-2572
(662) 728-0200; *Fax:* (662) 728-2572
WBIPAM@YAHOO.COM
License: Booneville, Prentiss County, MS held by Community Broadcasting Services of Mississippi Inc
Regional Network: Miss. News Net.
Population Served: 50,000; *Arbitron Metro Market:* Tupelo, MS; *Hrs. of News Programming:* News progmg 7 hrs wkly; *Target Audience:* 24-54.; *Adv. Rates:* 5; 5; 5; 5
Larry Melton, President
Jerry Thornton, Operations Dir
Larry Hill, General Manager
Marty Williams, Station Manager

*WMAE-FM

12-01-1983; 89.5 MHz FM; *Hrs Open:* 24; 85 kw; 653 ft.; N34 40 0 W88 45 5
3825 Ridgewood Road, Jackson, MS 39211 US
(601) 432-6565; *Fax:* (601) 432-6806
www.mpbonline.org
License: Booneville, Prentiss County, MS held by Mississippi Authority for Educational Television.
Nat'l Network: PRI; NPR; *Wire Services:* AP
Arbitron Metro Market: Tupelo, MS *TV Affiliate:* WMAE-TV; *Format:* News; *Hrs. of News Programming:* news progmg 100 hrs wkly; *No. News Employees:* 7; *Target Audience:* General.
Jason Klein, Operations Dir
Jay Woods, General Manager
Marie Antoon, General Sales Mgr

Brandon

WRBJ

12-01-1974; 97.7 MHz FM; *Hrs Open:* 24; 6 kw; 328 ft.; N32 10 31 W89 56 10
1408 N. Kingshighway, Suite 300, St. Louis, MO 63113 USA
(314) 367-4600
www.thebeatofthecapital.com
License: Brandon, MS held by Roberts Radio Broadcasting, LLC
Group Owner: Roberts Radio Broadcasting, LLC
Arbitron Metro Market: Jackson, MS; *Format:* Urban Contemporary; *Target Audience:* 18-34.
Tambra Cherie, Promotions Manager

WFQY

06-01-1967; 970 kHz AM; 1 kw-D, DA; N32 17 20 W89 59 50
209 Commerce Dr., Suite D, Brandon, MS 39043
(601) 825-2970; *Fax:* (601) 825-0339
License: Brandon, Rankin County, MS held by Jackson Radio LLC
Population Served: 500,000; *Arbitron Metro Market:* Jackson, MS
Gerald Smith, General Manager
Joann Bell, Sales Executive

Brookhaven

WBKN

07-29-1976; 92.1 MHz FM; *Hrs Open:* 24; 3.4 kw; 302 ft.; N31 33 48 W90 26 27
Mailing Address: P.O. Box 711, Brookhaven, MS 39601 US
Second Address: 911 Hwy. 550, Brookhaven, MS 39602
(601) 833-9210; *Fax:* (601) 833-6221
brookhavenbroadcast@yahoo.com
License: Brookhaven, Lincoln County, MS held by Brookhaven Broadcasting Inc.
Regional Network: Miss. News Net.
Arbitron Metro Market: Brookhaven, MS; *Format:* Country
Special Programming: Gospel 3 hrs wkly; *Hrs. of News Programming:* News progmg 5 hrs wkly; *Target Audience:* 25-54.; *Adv. Rates:* 13.85; 13.85; 13.85;13.85
C. Wayne Dowdy, President
Tyler Bridge, Operations Dir
Ken Hollingsworth, General Manager
Robbie Hamilton, General Sales Mgr
Gaye Laird, Programming Director
Jamey Lambert, Min Affairs Director

WCHJ

08-15-1955; 1470 kHz AM; *Hrs Open:* 24 hrs
Mailing Address: 210 West Corut St., Brookhaven, MS 39601 US
Second Address: 983 Sawmill Ln., Brookhaven, MS 39601
(601) 823-9006; *Fax:* (601) 823-0503
victory1470wchj@birch.net
License: Brookhaven, MS held by Tillman Broadcasting Network Inc.
Nat'l Network: USA
Arbitron Metro Market: Brookhaven, MS; *Format:* Black, Gospel; *Hrs. of News Programming:* News progmg one hr wkly; *Target Audience:* 25-54.; *Adv. Rates:* 10; 10; 10; 10 (60 sec spot)
Charles Tillman, CEO
Joe Segura, Assistant Operations Director

Brooksville

WAJV

08-01-1995; 98.9 MHz FM; *Hrs Open:* 24; 5.8 kw; 676 ft.; N33 20 40 W88 32 47
P.O. Box 707, Columbus, MS 39703 US
(662) 338-5424; *Fax:* (662) 338-5436
www.joy989.com
wmsuproduction@urbanradio.fm
License: Brooksville, Noxubee County, MS held by Urban Radio Licenses LLC
Group Owner: Urban Radio Licenses LLC; (acq 4-20-2001).
Arbitron Metro Market: Columbus, MS; *Format:* Gospel; *Hrs. of News Programming:* News progmg 14 hrs wkly; *Target Audience:* General.
Kevin Wagner, President
James Alexander, Operations Dir
Ron Davis, Programming Director

Bude

*WMAU-FM

12-01-1983; 88.9 MHz FM; *Hrs Open:* 24; 100 kw; 961 ft.; N31 22 22 W90 45 4
3825 Ridgewood Road, Jackson, MS 39211 US
(601) 432-6565; *Fax:* (601) 432-6806
www.mpbonline.org
mpbinfo@mpbonline.org
License: Bude, Franklin County, MS held by Mississippi Authority for Educational Television.
Nat'l Network: NPR; PRI; *Wire Services:* AP
Arbitron Metro Market: Bude, MS *TV Affiliate:* WMAU-TV; *Format:* News; *Hrs. of News Programming:* news progmg 100 hrs wkly; *No. News Employees:* 7; *Target Audience:* General.
Jason Klein, Operations Dir
Jay Woods, General Manager
Marie Antoon, General Sales Mgr
Ron Davis, Closed Captioning

WMJU

08-30-1999; 104.3 MHz FM; *Hrs Open:* 24; 25 kw; 328 ft.; N31 33 33 W90 40 26
Mailing Address: 104 N. First Street, Brookhaven, MS 39601 US
Second Address: 911 Hwy. 550, Brookhaven, MS 39601
(601) 833-9210; *Fax:* (601) 833-6221
brookhavenbroadcast@yahoo.com
License: Bude, Franklin County, MS held by Brookhaven Broadcasting Inc.
Arbitron Metro Market: Bude, MS; *Format:* Adult Contemp; *Hrs. of News Programming:* news progmg 10 hrs wkly; *No. News Employees:* 1; *Target Audience:* 25-49; adults who are middle income & above
C. Wayne Dowdy, President
Ken Hollingsworth, General Manager
Robbie Hamilton, General Sales Mgr
Gaye Laird, Programming Director

Burnsville

*WOWL

01-01-2000; 91.9 MHz FM; 18 kw; 548 ft.; N34 55 47 W88 24 37
121 Front Street, Luka, MS 38852 US
(662) 423-9919; *Fax:* (662) 423-9333
License: Burnsville, Tishomingo County, MS held by Southern Community Services Inc.
Nat'l Reps: Rgnl Reps
Format: Adult Contemp
Rick Biddle, President
Brian Biddle, General Manager
Mike Canon, Programming Director

Byhalia

*WMSB

01-04-1971; 88.9 MHz FM; *Hrs Open:* 24; 52 kw vert; 476 ft.; N34 39 30 W89 37 32
P.O. Box 241880, Memphis, TN 38124 US
(662) 844-8888; *Fax:* (662) 842-6791
www.afr.net
faq@afa.net
License: Byhalia, Marshall County, MS held by American Family Association.
Group Owner: American Family Radio; (acq 4-13-2007; $2 million)
Nat'l Network: American Family Radio
Format: Christian
Tim Wildmon, President
Donald Wildmon, Founder
Buddy Smith, Sr VP
Ed Vitagliano, Exec VP
Randy Sharp, Director Of Special Projects
Meeke Addison, Director Of Communications
Abraham Hamilton, General Counsel

Canton

WMGO

12-09-1954; 1370 kHz AM; *Hrs Open:* 24; 1 kw-D, ND1; 0.028 kw-N, ND1; N32 37 36 W90 1 47
360 North Liberty Street, Canton, MS 39046 US
(601) 859-2373; *Fax:* (601) 859-2664
www.wmgoradio.com
admin@wmgo.com
License: Canton, MS held by WMGO Broadcasting Corp. Inc.
Regional Network: Miss. News Net.
Arbitron Metro Market: Jackson, MS; *Format:* Variety/Diverse; *Hrs. of News Programming:* news progmg 12 hrs wkly; *No. News Employees:* 1; *Target Audience:* 25-54; upscale & involved adults; *Adv. Rates:* 14.50;9.50; 10.50; 3.50
Jerry Lousteau, President
John Woods, Programming Director

WONG

04-01-1989; 1150 kHz AM; 0.5 kw-D, ND1; 0.019 kw-N, ND1; N32 32 35 W90 3 36
210 S. Philip Rd., P.O. Box 213, Niles, MI 49120 USA
(269) 683-4343

License: Canton, MS held by Marion R. Williams.
Group Owner: Marion R. Williams Stns; (acq 7-26-99; $50,000)
Nat'l Network: American Urban
Arbitron Metro Market: Jackson, MS *TV Affiliate:* Gospel, blues; *No. News Employees:* 25 plus.

Carthage

WKOZ-FM
04-01-1979; 98.3 MHz FM; 20 kw; Ant 328 ft; N32 43 29 W89 32 44
Mailing Address: Box 1700, Kosciusko, MS 39051
Second Address: 1 Golf Course Rd., Kosciusko, MS 39039
(601) 267-7098; *Fax:* (662) 289-7907
www.kicks98.com
License: Carthage, Leake County, MS held by Johnny Boswell Radio LLC
Nat'l Network: USA; *Wire Services:* NOAA Weather

Johnny Boswell, CEO
Eric Matthews, Operations Dir
Lora Bain, General Manager

Centreville

*WPAE
01-01-1997; 89.7 MHz FM; *Hrs Open:* 24; 70 kw; 298 ft; N31 05 56 W91 02 27 *Rebroadcasts:* Rebroadcasts KPAE(FM) Erwinville, L
Mailing Address: Box 1390, Centreville, MS 70767
Second Address: 122 E. Main St., Centreville, MS 39631
(601) 645-6515
License: Centreville, Amite County, MS held by Port Allen Educational Broadcasting Foundation.
Nat'l Network: Moody
Population Served: 1,000,000 *Special Programming:* Children 5 hrs, Gospel 15 hrs wkly; *Adv. Rates:* none
Willie Kennedy, General Manager
Willie Kennedy, Station Manager
Willie Kennedy, Programming Director
Willie Kennedy, Promotions Manager
Bo Hoover, Chief Engineer

WKJN
11-21-1977; 104.9 MHz FM; 3 kw; 299 ft.; N31 6 7 W91 2 27
PO Box 30, Magnolia, MS 39652 US
(601) 783-6600
License: Centreville, Amite County, MS held by Charles W. Dowdy, Debtor-In-Possession
Group Owner: Charles W. Dowdy
Arbitron Metro Market: Centreville, MS; *Format:* Country
Charles W. Dowdy, Owner/General Manager

Charleston

*WTGY
04-01-1986; 95.7 MHz FM; *Hrs Open:* 18; 6 kw; 328 ft.; N33 53 28 W90 3 9
PO Box 9, Charleston, MS 38921 US
(621) 647-5600; *Fax:* (225) 768-3729
sonlifetv.com
License: Charleston, Tallahatchie County, MS held by Family Worship Center Church Inc.
Group Owner: Family Worship Center Church Inc.; acq 7-15-02; $300,000).
Arbitron Metro Market: Charleston, MS; *Format:* Religious
David Whitelaw, COO
Jimmy Swaggart, President
John Santiago, Programming Director

Clarksdale

WAID
07-01-1978; 106.5 MHz FM; *Hrs Open:* 24; 50 kw; 295 ft.; N34 9 22 W90 37 52
P.O. Box 780, Cleveland, MS 38732 US
(662) 627-2281; *Fax:* (662) 624-2900
License: Clarksdale, Coahoma County, MS held by Radio Cleveland Inc.
Group Owner: Radio Cleveland Inc.; acq 8-2-83; $185,000;
Nat'l Network: USA
Arbitron Metro Market: Cleveland, MS; *Format:* Urban Contemporary; *Hrs. of News Programming:* news progmg 2 hrs wkly; *No. News Employees:* 1; *Target Audience:* General.
Clint Webster, General Manager
Greg Shurden, General Sales Mgr
Jim Thomas, Programming Director
Houston McDavid, Chief Engineer

WKDJ-FM
11-01-1988; 96.5 MHz FM; 6 kw; 328 ft.; N34 9 22 W90 37 52
P.O. Box 780, Cleveland, MS 38732 US
(601) 627-2281; *Fax:* (601) 624-2900
License: Clarksdale, Coahoma County, MS held by Clint Webster.
Format: Country; *Target Audience:* 25-55.
Clint Webster, General Manager
Greg Shurden, Station Manager
Jim Thomas, Programming Director

WROX
01-01-1944; 1450 kHz AM; *Hrs Open:* 24; 1 kw-U; N34 12 40 W90 34 42
628 Desoto Avenue, Clarksdale, MS 38732
(662) 627-1450; *Fax:* (662) 621-1176
License: Clarksdale, Coahoma County, MS held by LL James Medua LLC
Group Owner: Contemporary Communications
Population Served: 65,000 *Special Programming:* Blues Saturday nights; *Hrs. of News Programming:* news progmg 3 hrs wkly; *No. News Employees:* 1; *Target Audience:* General; *Adv. Rates:* 6; 5; 5.50; 4.50
Paul Wilson, Co-Owner
Bobbie Wilson, Co-Owner
Tim Brown, Afternoons

Cleveland

WCLD
01-01-1949; 1490 kHz AM; *Hrs Open:* 24; 1 kw-U, ND1; N33 44 1 W90 42 50
P.O. Box 780, Cleveland, MS 38732 US
(601) 843-4091; *Fax:* (601) 843-9805
License: Cleveland, MS held by Radio Cleveland Inc.
Group Owner: Radio Cleveland Inc.; acq 1957)
Arbitron Metro Market: Cleveland, MS; *Format:* Black, Gospel; *Target Audience:* 18 plus.
Jim Thomas, Operations Dir
Clint Webster, General Manager
Kevin Cox, General Sales Mgr
Houston McDavitt, Chief Engineer
Vicky Lowry, Traffic Manager

WCLD-FM
01-01-1972; 103.9 MHz FM; *Hrs Open:* 24; 24.5 kw; 315 ft.; N33 44 1 W90 42 50
P. O. Box 780, Cleveland, MS 38732 US
(601) 843-4091; *Fax:* (601) 843-9805
License: Cleveland, Bolivar County, MS
Arbitron Metro Market: Cleveland, MS; *Format:* Urban Contemporary; *Target Audience:* 18 plus.
Vicky Lowry, News Director

*WDFX
01-01-1993; 98.3 MHz FM; 25 kw; 328 ft.; N33 52 47 W90 42 32
P.O. Box 3206, Tupelo, MS 38803 US
(662) 844-8888; *Fax:* (662) 842-6791
www.afr.net
faq@afa.net
License: Cleveland, Bolivar County, MS held by American Family Association.
Group Owner: American Family Radio; (acq 5-3-93; $6,150;
Nat'l Network: USA
Arbitron Metro Market: Cleveland, MS; *Format:* Christian
Tim Wildmon, President
Donald Wildmon, Founder
Buddy Smith, Sr VP
Ed Vitagliano, Exec VP
Randy Sharp, Director Of Special Projects
Meeke Addison, Director Of Communications
Abraham Hamilton III, General Counsel

Clinton

WHJT
01-01-1974; 93.5 MHz FM; *Hrs Open:* 24; 6 kw; 328 ft.; N32 20 15 W90 19 47
Mailing Address: 100 S. Jefferson Street, Clinton, MS 39058 US
Second Address: 100 S. Jefferson, Clinton, MS 39058
(601) 925-3458; *Fax:* (601) 925-3337
www.star93fm.com
License: Clinton, Hinds County, MS held by Mississippi College.
Wire Services: NOAA Weather
Arbitron Metro Market: Jackson, MS; *Format:* Contemporary Hits/Top 40 *Special Programming:* Relg 6 hrs wkly; *Hrs. of News Programming:* News progmg 7 hrs wkly; *Target Audience:* 18-54; upper & middle class Christianlisteners
Billy Lytal, President
Russ Robinson, Station Manager

WTWZ
10-10-1982; 1120 kHz AM; *Hrs Open:* Sunrise-sunset
4611 Terry Road, Jackson, MS 39212 US
(601) 346-0074; *Fax:* (601) 346-0896
am1120@wtwzradio.com
License: Clinton, MS held by Terry E. Wood.
Nat'l Network: USA; *Regional Network:* Miss. News Net.
Arbitron Metro Market: Jackson, MS; *Format:* Blues; *Hrs. of News Programming:* News progmg 7 hrs wkly; *Target Audience:* 18-50; 50% men & 50% women; *Adv. Rates:* 10; 10; 10; 10
Terry Wood, President

Coldwater

WEBL
01-01-1976; 95.3 MHz FM; *Hrs Open:* 24; 3.4 kw; 440 ft.; N34 48 22 W89 59 47
5555 McCracken Road, Hernando, MS 38632 US
(662) 349-0826; *Fax:* (662) 349-9255
License: Coldwater, Tate County, MS held by Memphis First Ventures L.P.
Arbitron Metro Market: Southaven, MS; *Format:* Country; *Target Audience:* 25-54.; *Adv. Rates:* 25; 25; 25; 15
Chip Miller, President
Paul Pesce, Station Manager

Collins

*WLVZ
08-15-1978; 107.1 MHz FM; *Hrs Open:* 24; 2.25 kw; 541 ft.; N31 31 47 W89 30 30 *Rebroadcasts:* Rebroadcasts KLVR(FM) Middletown, CA 100%
37 South High Ave, Columbia, MS 39429 US
(800) 525-5683; *Fax:* (916) 251-1650
www.klove.com
License: Collins, Covington County, MS held by Educational Media Foundation.
Group Owner: EMF Broadcasting; (acq 7-15-2005; $700,000)
Nat'l Network: K-Love
Arbitron Metro Market: Laurel-Hattiesburg, MS; *Format:* Christian
Mike Novak, President

Collinsville

WZKR
01-01-2001; 103.3 MHz FM; *Hrs Open:* 24; 13 kw; 347 ft.; N32 20 39 W88 42 40
6311 Ridgewood Road, Jackson, MS 39211 US
(601) 957-1700; *Fax:* (601) 956-5228
License: Collinsville, Newton County, MS held by Morning Star Media LLC
Nat'l Network: Salem Radio Network; *Nat'l Reps:* Salem
Arbitron Metro Market: Collinsville, MS; *Format:* Country; *Target Audience:* 25-54.
Ron Harper, General Manager

Columbia

WCJU
12-20-1946; 1450 kHz AM; *Hrs Open:* 24; 1 kw-U, ND1; N31 14 14 W89 50 24
P. O. Box 472, Columbia, MS 39429 US
(601) 736-2616; *Fax:* (601) 736-2617
www.wcjuam.com
wcju@wcjufm.com
License: Columbia, MS held by WCJU Inc.
Nat'l Network: ABC; *Nat'l Reps:* Keystone (unwired net)
Arbitron Metro Market: Columbia, MS; *Format:* News, News/Talk, 84, Talk *Special Programming:* Gospel 4 hrs wkly; *Hrs. of News Programming:* news progmg 30 hrs wkly; *No. News Employees:* 2 *Target Audience:* 18-54.
T. McDaniel, President
Steve Mercier, Operations Dir
John Pittman Jr., Programming Director
Pam Ball, Regional Sales Manager

WFFF
04-14-1961; 1360 kHz AM; *Hrs Open:* 24; 1 kw-D, ND1; 0.159 kw-N, ND1; N31 15 44 W89 50 41
PO Box 550, Columbia, MS 39429 US
(601) 736-1360; *Fax:* (601) 736-1361
wfffradio@zzip.cc
License: Columbia, MS held by Haddox Enterprises Inc.
Nat'l Network: ABC; *Regional Network:* Miss. News Net.
Arbitron Metro Market: Columbia, MS; *Format:* Gospel, Country; *Hrs. of News Programming:* news progmg 8 hrs wkly; *No. News Employees:* 4; *Target Audience:* General.
Ronnie Geiger, President
Terri Geiger, Operations Dir

WFFF-FM
10-01-1966; 96.7 MHz FM; *Hrs Open:* 24; 6 kw; 299 ft.; N31 15 44 W89 50 41
PO Box 550, Columbia, MS 39429 US

(601) 736-1360; *Fax:* (601) 736-1361
License: Columbia, Marion County, MS
Regional Network: Miss. News Net.
Arbitron Metro Market: Columbia, MS; *Format:* Adult Contemp; *Hrs. of News Programming:* news progmg 8 hrs wkly; *No. News Employees:* 4; *Target Audience:* 25-54.
Ronnie Geiger, Operations Dir
Terri Geiger, News Director

***WPRG**
89.5 MHz FM; 0.25 kw; 207 ft.; N31 15 44 W89 51 41
P.O. Box 3206, Tupelo, MS 38803 US
(662) 844-8888; *Fax:* (662) 842-6791
www.afr.net
faq@afa.net
License: Columbia, Marion County, MS held by American Family Association.
Group Owner: American Family Radio; (acq 10-1-01).
Nat'l Network: USA
Arbitron Metro Market: Tupelo, MS; *Format:* Christian
Tim Wildmon, President
Donald Wildmon, Founder
Buddy Smith, Sr VP
Ed Vitagliano, Exec VP
Randy Sharp, Director Of Special Projects
Meeke Addison, Director Of Communications
Abraham Hamilton III, General Counsel

Columbus

WTWG
01-01-1950; 1050 kHz AM; 1 kw-D, ND1; 0.048 kw-N, ND1; N33 30 36 W88 24 46
Mailing Address: 1910 14th Ave, N., Columbus, MS 39701 US
Second Address: 1910 14th Ave. N., Columbus, MS 39703
(662) 328-1050
wtwg1050@yahoo.com
License: Columbus, MS held by T & W Communications Inc.
Arbitron Metro Market: Paragould AR; *Format:* Adult Contemp; *No. News Employees:* 1; *Target Audience:* 45 plus; adults
Rob Bye, General Manager
Marlow Weldon, News Director
Pam Doherty, Traffic Manager

WJWF
11-01-1969; 1400 kHz AM; 1 kw-U, ND1; N33 29 30 W88 24 14
420 20th Street North, Suite 1600, Birmingham, AL 35203 US
(662) 327-1183; *Fax:* (662) 328-1122
License: Columbus, MS held by Cumulus Licensing Corp.
Group Owner: Cumulus Media Inc.; (acq 2-14-2002; with co-located FM)
Nat'l Network: ESPN Radio
Arbitron Metro Market: Columbus-Starkville-West Point, MS; *Format:* Sports
C.J. Jones, Operations Dir

WKOR-FM
12-16-1992; 94.9 MHz FM; *Hrs Open:* 24; 50 kw; 492 ft.; N33 28 38 W88 16 25
200 6th Street North, Suite 205, Columbus, MS 39702 US
(662) 327-1183; *Fax:* (662) 328-1122
www.k949.net
License: Columbus, Lowndes County, MS held by Cumulus Licensing Corp.
Group Owner: Cumulus Media Inc.; (acq 2-14-02; grpsl).
Nat'l Network: ABC
Arbitron Metro Market: Columbus-Starkville-West Point, MS; *Format:* Country; *Target Audience:* 18-54.
Chris Stryker, Programming Director
Greg Benefield, Market Manager

WNMQ
11-01-1969; 103.1 MHz FM; 22 kw; 755 ft.; N33 20 40 W88 32 47
200 6th Street North, Suite 205, Columbus, MS 39702 US
(662) 327-1183; *Fax:* 662-328-1122
www.1031theteam.com/
greg.benefield@cumulus.com
License: Columbus, Lowndes County, MS held by Cumulus Licensing LLC.
Group Owner: Cumulus Media Inc.
Arbitron Metro Market: Columbus, MS; *Format:* Sports
Chris Stryker, Programming Director
Greg Benefield, Market Manager

***WCSO**
01-01-2006; 90.5 MHz FM; 10 kw vert; 530 ft.; N33 20 44 W88 14 6 *Rebroadcasts:* Rebroadcasts WAFR(FM) Tupelo MS 100%
P.O. Box 3206, Tupelo, MS 38803 US
(662) 844-8888; *Fax:* (662) 842-6791
www.afr.net
faq@afa.net
License: Columbus, Lowndes County, MS held by American Family Association.
Group Owner: American Family Radio
Arbitron Metro Market: Columbus, MS; *Format:* Christian
Tim Wildmon, President
Donald Wildmon, Founder
Buddy Smith, Sr VP
Ed Vitagliano, Exec VP
Randy Sharp, Director Of Special Projects
Meeke Addison, Director Of Communications
Abraham Hamilton III, General Counsel

***WMUW**
02-22-2008; 88.5 MHz FM; *Hrs Open:* 24/7; 1,000 w EH Rad; Ant 89 ft; N33 29 23 W88 25 18
Mississippi University for Women, 1100 College St. - MUW - 1619, Columbus, MS 39701
(662) 329-4750; *Fax:* (662) 329-7250
www.muw.edu/wmuw
wmuw@muw.edu
License: Columbus, Lowndes County, MS held by Mississippi University for Women.
Population Served: 30,000; *Arbitron Metro Market:* Columbus-Starkv; *Hrs. of News Programming:* News progmg 2.5 hrs wkly; *Target Audience:* College students and those that like music
Timothy Etheridge, Operations Dir
Eric Harlan, General Manager
Timothy Etheridge, Programming Director
Hilary Jasain, Music Director
Alonzo Bouldin, Music Director

Columbus Afb

WACR-FM
06-01-1975; 105.3 MHz FM; 50 kw; 352 ft.; N33 40 9 W88 40 8
608 Yellowjacket Drive, Starkville, MS 39759 US
(662) 338-5424; *Fax:* (662) 338-5436
www.wacr1053.com
wmsuproduction@urbanradio.fm
License: Columbus Afb, Lowndes County, MS held by Urban Radio Licenses LLC.
Group Owner: Urban Radio Licenses LLC; (acq 7-13-2005; $1.1 million)
Arbitron Metro Market: Aberdeen, MS; *Format:* Black, Blues
Pamela Hancock, General Manager
Jeffrey Hedgemon, Marketing
Aubra Turner, Advertising Contact

Como

WRBO
09-28-1966; 103.5 MHz FM; *Hrs Open:* 24; 100 kw; 587 ft.; N34 51 44 W89 52 42
5629 Murray Rd., Memphis, TN 38119 US
(901) 682-1106
www.1035wrbo.com
License: Como, MS held by Radio License Holding CBC, LLC
Group Owner: Cumulus Media Inc.; (acq 3-23-2004; grpsl).
Nat'l Network: ABC; Westwood One; *Nat'l Reps:* Katz Radio
Arbitron Metro Market: Memphis, TN; *Format:* Christian, Urban Contemporary; *Target Audience:* 25-54.
DeSean Grayson, General Sales Mgr
Earle Augustus, Programming Director

Corinth

WADI
10-26-1968; 95.3 MHz FM; 2.6 kw; 472 ft.; N34 55 47 W88 24 37
121 Front Street, Iuka, MS 39211 US
(662) 423-9533
License: Corinth, Alcorn County, MS held by Power Valley Communications Inc.
Arbitron Metro Market: Dubuque IA; *Format:* News
Rita Ray, General Manager
Marilyn DeVita, General Sales Mgr
James Muhammad, Programming Director
Greg Collard, News Director
Jack Wells, Chief Engineer
Teresa Wills, Traffic Manager

WTKN
03-01-1946; 1230 kHz AM; 1 kw-U, ND1; N34 57 27 W88 31 17
1608 John Street, Corinth, MS 38834 US
(662) 423-9533; *Fax:* (662) 423-9333
newstalk1230.iheart.com
License: Corinth, MS held by Perihelion Global Inc.
Arbitron Metro Market: Corinth, MS
Rick Biddle, General Manager

WKCU
10-24-1965; 1350 kHz AM; *Hrs Open:* 24
6311 Ridgewood Rd., Jackson, MS 39211 US
(601) 957-1700
License: Corinth, MS held by TeleSouth Communications Inc.
Group Owner: TeleSouth Communications Inc.; acq 12-20-02; $350,000 with co-located FM).
Regional Network: Miss. News Net.; *Wire Services:* NWS (National Weather Service)
Format: Christian *Special Programming:* Black 2 hrs wkly; *Hrs. of News Programming:* News progmg 12 hrs wkly; *Target Audience:* 25-54; female; *Adv. Rates:* 5; 5; 5; 3

WXRZ
01-01-1967; 94.3 MHz FM; *Hrs Open:* 24; 25 kw; 328 ft.; N34 48 36 W88 34 45
6311 Ridgewood Rd., Jackson, MS 39211 US
(601) 957-1700
www.supertalk.fm
feedback@supertalk.fm
License: Corinth, Alcorn County, MS held by TeleSouth Communications Inc.
Group Owner: TeleSouth Communications Inc.
Wire Services: NWS (National Weather Service)
Arbitron Metro Market: Corinth, MS; *Format:* Talk; *Adv. Rates:* 7; 7; 7; 6

Crenshaw

WHKL
03-01-1997; 106.9 MHz FM; 6 kw; 328 ft.; N34 26 51 W90 6 25
P.O. Box 1528, Batesville, MS 38606 US
(662) 563-4664; *Fax:* (662) 563-9008
country101radio@yahoo.com
License: Crenshaw, Panola County, MS held by Batesville Broadcasting Co. Inc.
Format: Oldies
John Ingram, General Manager

D'Iberville

WCPR-FM
12-01-1992; 97.9 MHz FM; *Hrs Open:* 24; 50 kw; 466 ft.; N30 37 2 W89 8 3
9471 Three Rivers Rd., Suite A, Gulfport, MS 39503 US
(228) 388-2001; *Fax:* (228) 896-9114
www.979cprrocks.com
License: D'Iberville, Harrison County, MS held by Alpha Media Licensee LLC
Group Owner: Alpha Media LLC
Nat'l Network: ABC
Arbitron Metro Market: Biloxi-Gulfport, MS; *Format:* Alternative, Rock/AOR
Kenny Vest, Operations Manager
Ricky Mitchell, General Manager
Jesse Alvarez, Sales Manager
Mindy Patton, Promotions/New Media Director
Scot Fox, Music Director
Michelle Shortridge, Business Manager

De Kalb

WJXM
01-01-1999; 105.7 MHz FM; 50 kw; 384 ft.; N32 38 37 W88 40 29
P.O. Box 1699, Meridian, MS 39302 US
(601) 693-2661; *Fax:* (601) 483-0826
www.1057thebeat.com
wjxm@wokk.com
License: De Kalb, Kemper County, MS held by Mississippi Broadcasters L.L.C.
Group Owner: Mississippi Broadcasters L.L.C.
Arbitron Metro Market: Meridian, MS; *Format:* Urban Contemporary
Clay Holladay, President
Scott Stevens, Operations Dir
Georgia Edmiston, General Manager
Diane Horton, Sales Manager
Dee Williams, Traffic Manager

Decatur

***WSQH**
01-01-2005; 91.7 MHz FM; 18 kw; 476 ft.; N32 23 57 W89 5 2
P.O. Box 3206, Tupelo, MS 38803 US
(662) 844-8888; *Fax:* (662) 842-6791
www.afr.net
faq@afa.net
License: Decatur, Newton County, MS held by American Family Association.
Group Owner: American Family Radio
Nat'l Network: USA

Arbitron Metro Market: Decatur, MS; *Format:* Christian, Talk
Tim Wildmon, President
Donald Wildmon, Founder
Buddy Smith, Sr VP
Ed Vitagliano, Exec VP
Randy Sharp, Director Of Special Projects
Meeke Addison, Director Of Communications
Abraham Hamilton III, General Counsel

Duck Hill

***WAUM**
01-01-1998; 91.9 MHz FM; 2.5 kw; 512 ft.; N33 38 34 W89 29 59
P.O. Box 3206, Tupelo, MS 38803 US
(662) 844-8888; *Fax:* (662) 842-6791
www.afr.net
faq@afa.net
License: Duck Hill, Montgomery County, MS held by American Family Association.
Group Owner: American Family Radio
Nat'l Network: USA
Format: Christian, Talk
Tim Wildmon, President
Donald Wildmon, Founder
Buddy Smith, Sr VP
Ed Vitagliano, Exec VP
Randy Sharp, Director Of Special Projects
Meeke Addison, Director Of Communications
Abraham Hamilton III, General Counsel

Durant

WLIN-FM
01-01-1997; 101.1 MHz FM; 4.8 kw horiz, 4.6 kw vert; 371 ft.; N33 3 51 W89 36 12
P.O. Box A, Kosciusko, MS 39090 US
(662) 289-1050; *Fax:* (662) 289-7907
www.breezynews.com
breezy@boswellmedia.net
License: Durant, Holmes County, MS held by Boswell Radio LLC.
Format: Adult Contemp
Johnny Boswell, General Manager
Ann Steen, Station Manager
Jerry Price, General Sales Mgr
Eric Matthews, Programming Director

Ellisville

WJKX
10-05-1973; 102.5 MHz FM; *Hrs Open:* 24; 50 kw; 492 ft.; N31 46 5 W89 10 12
2018 Highway 15 North, Laurel, MS 39441 US
(601) 296-9800; *Fax:* (601) 296-9838
www.102jkx.com
License: Ellisville, Jones County, MS held by CC Licenses LLC.
Group Owner: iHeartMedia; (acq 12-19-2000; grpsl)
Arbitron Metro Market: Laurel-Hattiesburg, MS; *Format:* Urban Contemporary
Mike Comfort, Market President
Jackson Walker, Senior Vice President of Programming

Eupora

WLZA
09-01-1978; 96.1 MHz FM; *Hrs Open:* 24; 40 kw; 500 ft; N33 32 51 W89 03 22
P.O. Box 884, Starkville, MS 39760
(662) 324-9601; *Fax:* (662) 324-7400
www.961wlza.com
wlza@961wlza.com
License: Eupora, Webster County, MS held by Metro Radio Inc.
Group Owner: Air South Radio Inc.
Arbitron Metro Market: Columbus-Starkville-West Point, MS; *Format:* Adult Contemp; *Target Audience:* General.
Carolyn Jackson, Station Manager
Bill Thurlow, Sales Director
Bill Thurlow, Programming Director

Fayette

WTYJ
10-17-1983; 97.7 MHz FM; 6 kw; 500 ft; N31 40 32 W91 06 18
20 E. Franklin St., Natchez, MS 39120
(601) 442-2522; *Fax:* (601) 446-9918
wmiswtyj@bellsouth.net
License: Fayette, Jefferson County, MS held by Natchez Broadcasting Inc.
Nat'l Network: American Urban; *Regional Network:* Miss. News Net.
Population Served: 100,000 *Target Audience:* Black.
James Nutter, President
Calvin Butler, Operations Dir
LlJuna Weir, Station Manager
Diana Nutter, Secretary/Treasurer

Flora

WFMN
07-07-1997; 97.3 MHz FM; *Hrs Open:* 24; 19.5 kw; 367 ft.; N32 27 21 W90 15 32
6311 Ridgewood Rd., Jackson, MS 32911 US
(601) 957-1700
www.supertalkms.com
feedback@supertalk.fm
License: Flora, Madison County, MS held by TeleSouth Communications Inc.
Group Owner: TeleSouth Communications Inc.; acq 9-8-97; $700,000)
Nat'l Network: ABC
Arbitron Metro Market: Jackson, MS; *Format:* Sports, Talk; *Adv. Rates:* 25; 20; 22; 16

WYAB
08-01-1997; 103.9 MHz FM; *Hrs Open:* 24; 5 kw; 325 ft.; N32 26 49 W90 18 8
740 US Highway 49 N, Flora, MS 39071 US
(601) 879-0093; *Fax:* (601) 879-9003
www.wyab.com
matt@wyab.com
License: Flora, Madison County, MS held by SSR Communications Inc.
Arbitron Metro Market: Flora, MS; *Format:* Talk; *No. News Employees:* 1; *Target Audience:* 25-64.; *Adv. Rates:* 17.50; 12.50; 15.50; 8.50
Matthew Wesolowski, CEO

Flowood

WPBQ
01-01-1995; 1240 kHz AM; *Hrs Open:* 24; 0.88 kw-U, ND1; N32 18 3 W90 8 12
1240 Old Pearl Levy Road, Flowood, MS 39209 US
(601) 355-1240; *Fax:* (601) 355-1069
License: Flowood, MS held by PDB Corp.
Arbitron Metro Market: Jackson, MS; *Format:* Sports; *Target Audience:* 25-54.
Derrel Palmer, General Manager

Forest

***WMBU**
10-03-1997; 89.1 MHz FM; *Hrs Open:* 24; 10 kW horiz, 100 kW vert; 640 ft.; N32 18 54 W89 21 12 *Rebroadcasts:* Rebroadcasts WMBV(FM) Dixons Mills, AL 95%
5710 Watermelon Rd, Suite 316, Northport, AL 35473 USA
Fax: (205) 758-0059
www.moodyradiosouth.fm
License: Forest, Scott County, MS held by The Moody Bible Institute of Chicago
Group Owner: The Moody Bible Institute of Chicago
Nat'l Network: Moody; *Wire Services:* AP
Arbitron Metro Market: Lake, MS; *Format:* Christian *Special Programming:* Children 2 hrs wkly; *Target Audience:* 35-54.

***WQST**
92.5 MHz FM; 97 kw; 991 ft.; N32 21 48 W89 25 29
P.O. Box 3206, Tupelo, MS 38803 US
(662) 844-8888; *Fax:* (662) 842-6791
www.afr.net
faq@afa.net
License: Forest, Scott County, MS held by American Family Association.
Group Owner: American Family Radio
Arbitron Metro Market: Forest, MS; *Format:* Christian
Tim Wildmon, President
Donald Wildmon, Founder
Buddy Smith, Sr VP
Ed Vitagliano, Exec VP
Randy Sharp, Director Of Special Projects
Meeke Addison, Director Of Communications
Abraham Hamilton III, General Counsel

Friar's Point

***WWUN-FM**
101.5 MHz FM; 14 kw; 395 ft.; N34 34 2 W90 37 37
P.O. Box 391, Twin Falls, ID 83303 US
(800) 357-4226
www.csnradio.com/stations/studiowaivered/WWUN.php
License: Friar's Point, Coahoma County, MS held by CSN International.
Group Owner: CSN International; (acq 8-27-2001)
Arbitron Metro Market: Clarksdale, MS; *Format:* Christian, Religious
Kelly Carlson, Engineering Dir

Friars Point

WNEV
98.7 MHz FM; 6 kw; 328 ft.; N34 21 56 W90 38 14
700 MLK Drive, Helena-West, Helena, AR 72390 US
(870) 572-9506; *Fax:* (870) 572-1845
www.force3radio.com
force2@sbcglobal.net
License: Friars Point, Coahoma County, MS held by L.T. Simes II & Raymond Simes.
Arbitron Metro Market: Friars Point, MS; *Format:* Blues, Gospel
Raymond Simes, General Manager
Elaine Simes, Advertising Manager
Earnest Simes, Music Director

Fulton

WFTA
08-19-1976; 101.9 MHz FM; *Hrs Open:* 24; 50 kw; 479 ft.; N34 15 46 W88 32 24
1241 Cliff Gookin Blvd., Tupelo, MS 38801 US
(662) 842-7625
www.tupeloradio.com
License: Fulton, Itawamba County, MS held by Air South Radio Inc.
Group Owner: Air South Radio Inc.
Arbitron Metro Market: Tupelo, MS; *Format:* Adult Contemp; *Hrs. of News Programming:* News progmg 4 hrs wkly; *Target Audience:* 14-44.
Olvie E. Sisk, General Manager

Gluckstadt

WYOY
01-07-1976; 101.7 MHz FM; *Hrs Open:* 24; 50 kw; 456 ft.; N32 25 36 W90 12 20
3436 Highway 45 North, Meridian, MS 39301 US
(601) 956-0102; *Fax:* (601) 978-3980
www.y101.com
frontdesk@us963.com
License: Gluckstadt, Madison County, MS held by New South Radio Inc.
Group Owner: New South Communications Inc.; (acq 11-10-94; $750,000 with WLRM(AM) Ridgeland;
Nat'l Reps: McGavren Guild
Arbitron Metro Market: Jackson, MS; *Format:* Contemporary Hits/Top 40; *Target Audience:* 18-49.
Gwen Rakestraw, General Manager
Bill Rakestraw, General Sales Mgr
John Anthony, Programming Director

Greenville

WLTM
05-01-1970; 97.9 MHz FM; *Hrs Open:* 5:30 AM-midnight; 48 kw horiz; Ant 502 ft; N33 23 51 W91 00 35
Mailing Address: 1383 Pickett Street, Greenville, MS 38703
Second Address: 800 Hwy 1 South, Delta Plaza, Ste #39, Greenville, MS 38701
(662) 378-2617; *Fax:* (662) 378-8341
info@wbaq.com
License: Greenville, Washington County, MS held by Debut Broadcasting Mississippi Inc.
Group Owner: Debut Broadcasting Corp. Inc.; (acq 6-19-2007; grpsl)
Nat'l Network: ABC; *Regional Network:* Miss. News Net.
Population Served: 75,000 *Special Programming:* Farm one hr, btfl sacred music 4 hrs wkly; *Hrs. of News Programming:* News progmg 14 hrs wkly; *Target Audience:* 25-54; quality-conscious adults with spendable income
Linda McKee, Office Manager
Michelle Nicholson, Sales Manager
D.K. Pierce, Programming Director/Operations Manager

WDMS
12-01-1967; 100.7 MHz FM; 100 kw; 443 ft.; N33 25 20 W91 1 41
1383 Pickett Street, Greenville, MS 38703 US
(662) 334-4559; *Fax:* (662) 332-1315
wdms@bellsouth.net
License: Greenville, Washington County, MS
Regional Network: Miss. News Net.
Arbitron Metro Market: Greenville, MI; *Format:* Country
D.K. Pierce, Operations Manager/Programming Director
Steve Shelton, General Manager
Michelle Nicholson, Sales Manager
Linda McKee, Traffic Manager

WGVM
01-01-1948; 1260 kHz AM; 2.4 kw-D, NDD; N33 25 20 W91 1 41
Mailing Address: 1383 Pickett Street, Greenville, MS 38703 US
Second Address: 1383 Pickett St., Greenville, MS 38701
(662) 334-4550; *Fax:* (662) 332-1315
wdms@bellsouth.net
License: Greenville, MS held by WDMS Inc.
Target Audience: General.
D.K. Pierce, Operations Manager/Programming Director
Steve Shelton, General Manager
Michelle Nicholson, Sales Manager
Linda McKee, Traffic Manager

WNIX
08-01-1937; 1330 kHz AM; *Hrs Open:* 24; 1 kw-D, DAN; 0.5 kw-N, DAN; N33 24 36 W91 1 3
1399 East Reed Road, Greenville, MS 38703 US
(662) 378-2617; *Fax:* (888) 704-4762
www.wnixradio.com
info@deltaradio.net
License: Greenville, MS held by Delta Radio LLC
Arbitron Metro Market: Greenville, MS; *Format:* Oldies
John Nichols, Station Manager
Douglas Johnson, Marketing Manager/Director of Sales

***WLRK**
01-01-2006; 91.5 MHz FM; 50 kw vert; 322 ft.; N33 32 25 W91 22 39
US
(800) 525-5683; *Fax:* (916) 251-1650
www.klove.com
klove@klove.com
License: Greenville, Washington County, MS held by Educational Media Foundation.
Group Owner: EMF Broadcasting; (acq 1-23-2008; $320,000 with KAKV(FM) El Dorado, AR)
Nat'l Network: K-Love
Arbitron Metro Market: Greenville, MS; *Format:* Christian; *No. News Employees:* 13
Darrell Chambliss, Chairman
Mike Novak, President and CEO
Chip Bailey, Operations Dir
David Pierce, Chief Creative Officer and Programming Director
Ed Lenane, News Director
Sam Wallington, Engineering Dir
Alan Mason, ChiefOperating Officer
Dan Antonelli, Chief Business Development Officer
Eric Moser, Chief Financial Officer
Brian Burger, Vice President of Human Resources
D. Kevin Blair, Secretary and General Counsel
Tim Luttrell, News Reporter

WJIW
104.7 MHz FM; 31 kw; 620 ft.; N33 28 10 W90 50 30
830 Main Street, Greenville, MS 38701 US
(662) 332-5701; *Fax:* (870) 334-9049
www.wjiwfm.com
License: Greenville, Washington County, MS held by Mondy-Burke Broadcasting Network.
Arbitron Metro Market: Greenville, MS; *Format:* Gospel
April Mondy, Operations Dir
Elijah Mondy, General Manager
Belinda Mondy, General Sales Mgr
Elijah Mondy Jr., Co-Owner
Darren Smith, Co-Owner
Kirkland Burke, Co-Owner
Belinda Mondy, Exec. Administrator
Glenda Smith, Exec.Administrator
Zipporah Mondy, Sales/Music Director

***WDSV**
91.9 MHz FM; 1.5 kw horiz, 1.35 kw vert; 344 ft.; N33 24 21 W90 59 30
US
(662) 537-4939; *Fax:* (662) 335-5295
www.wdsv919fm.org
License: Greenville, Washington County, MS held by Delta Foundation Inc.
Arbitron Metro Market: Greenville, MS; *Format:* Talk
Spencer Nash, CEO
Mashondia Redmond, Executive Director

Greenwood

WABG
02-01-1950; 960 kHz AM; *Hrs Open:* 6 AM-1 PM
68322 Money Road, Greenwood, MS 38930 US
(662) 455-1688; *Fax:* (281 540-2198
www.ksbj.org
thejamespoe@yahoo.com
License: Greenwood, MS
Arbitron Metro Market: Benton AR; *Format:* Christian
Bill Luckett, Vice President
James Poe, General Manager

WGNL
12-01-1989; 104.3 MHz FM; *Hrs Open:* 24; 50 kw; 299 ft.; N33 40 45 W90 4 7
Mailing Address: Box 1801, 503 Ione St., Greenwood, MS 38930 US
Second Address: 503 Ione St., Greenwood, MS 38930
(662) 453-1646; *Fax:* (662) 453-7002
www.broadcasturban.net
wgnlbooth@bellsouth.net
License: Greenwood, Leflore County, MS held by Team Broadcasting Co. Inc.
Nat'l Reps: Dora-Clayton
Format: Adult Contemp *Special Programming:* Jazz 6 hrs wkly; *Hrs. of News Programming:* news progmg 12 hrs wkly; *No. News Employees:* 1; *Target Audience:* 18 plus.
Maxine Hughes, Operations Dir
Ruben Hughes, General Manager

WGRM
01-01-1937; 1240 kHz AM; 0.72 kw-U, ND1; N33 32 2 W90 11 42
645 Church Street, Suite 400, Norfolk, VA 23510 US
(662) 453-1240; *Fax:* (662) 453-1241
wgrmradiostation@bellsouth.net
License: Greenwood, MS held by Christian Broadcasting of Greenwood Inc.
Group Owner: Willis Broadcasting Corp.; (acq 2-22-99; $500,000 with co-located FM)
Format: Gospel *Special Programming:* Black 2 hrs wkly; *Target Audience:* 25-45.
Lee Hall, General Manager
Gwen Riley, Music Director
Gwen Rilley, Traffic Manager

WGRM-FM
07-17-1989; 93.9 MHz FM; *Hrs Open:* 24; 12 kw; 295 ft.; N33 32 2 W90 11 42
645 Church Street, Suite 400, Norfolk, VA 23510 US
(662) 453-1240; *Fax:* (662) 453-1241
License: Greenwood, Leflore County, MS
Group Owner: Willis Broadcasting Corp.
Format: Gospel
Lee Hall, General Manager
Gwen Riley, Music Director/Traffic Manager

WKXG
01-01-1987; 1540 kHz AM; *Hrs Open:* 6 AM-10 PM
Mailing Address: 6310 I-55 North, Jackson, MS 39211 US
Second Address: 3192 Browning Rd., Greenwood, MS 38935
(662) 453-2174; *Fax:* (662) 455-5733
License: Greenwood, MS held by Joy Christian Communications Inc.
Group Owner: Joy Christian Communications Inc.; (acq 12-8-2010)

Charlotte Michael, General Manager

***WMAO-FM**
12-01-1983; 90.9 MHz FM; *Hrs Open:* 24; 100 kw; 879 ft.; N33 22 34 W90 32 32
3825 Ridgewood Road, Jackson, MS 39211 US
(601) 432-6119; *Fax:* (601) 432-6806
www.mpbonline.org
License: Greenwood, Leflore County, MS held by Mississippi Authority for Educational Television.
Nat'l Network: PRI; NPR; *Wire Services:* AP
Arbitron Metro Market: Greenwood, MS *TV Affiliate:* WMAO-TV; *Format:* News; *Hrs. of News Programming:* news progmg 100 hrs wkly; *No. News Employees:* 7; *Target Audience:* General.
Jason Klein, Operations Dir
Ronnie Agnew, Executive Director
Shirley Mixon, Programming Director
Mari Irby, Communications Director
Teresa Collier, News Director
Cy Vance, Director of Technical Services
Bill Ellison, MusicDirector
LaSharne Patton, Traffic Manager

WYMX
06-15-1965; 99.1 MHz FM; *Hrs Open:* 24/7; 100 kw; Ant 1,029 ft; N33 31 12 W90 08 28
6311 Ridgewood Rd., Jackson, MS 39211
(601) 957-1700; *Fax:* (601) 956-5228
telesouth.com
License: Greenwood, Leflore County, MS held by TeleSouth Communications Inc.
Group Owner: TeleSouth Communications Inc.
Population Served: 315,000 *Adv. Rates:* Call for rate information

WBZL(FM)
103.3 MHz FM; 6 kw; Ant 328 ft; N33 32 21 W90 02 08
6311 Ridgewood Rd., Jackson, MS 39211 USA
(601) 957-1700; *Fax:* (601) 956-5228
telesouth.com
License: Greenwood, Leflore County, MS held by TeleSouth Communications Inc.
Group Owner: TeleSouth Communications Inc.
Population Served: 6,639; *Arbitron Metro Market:* Mount Vernon, IN

Grenada

WQXB
10-16-1970; 100.1 MHz FM; 48 kw; 503 ft.; N33 51 24 W89 55 15
P.O. Box 946, Grenada, MS 38901 US
(601) 226-1400; *Fax:* (601) 226-1464
License: Grenada, Grenada County, MS held by Chatterbox Inc.
Format: Country
Bob Adams, General Manager

WOHT
01-01-2003; 92.3 MHz FM; 4.1 kw; 397 ft.; N33 51 33 W89 55 13
P.O. Box 1438, Cleveland, MS 38732 US
(662) 846-0929; *Fax:* (662) 843-1410
License: Grenada, Grenada County, MS held by Century Broadcasting L.L.C.
Format: Oldies
Will Stammerjohan, General Manager

WMUT
01-01-2004; 101.3 MHz FM; 6 kw; 328 ft.; N33 49 20 W89 55 40
Mailing Address: 188 South Bellevue, Suite 222, Memphis, TN 28104 US
Second Address: 157 Dowdle Rd., Grenada, MS 38901
(662) 832-8023; *Fax:* (662) 226-3233
License: Grenada, Grenada County, MS held by George S. Flinn Jr.
Nat'l Network: CNN Radio; Westwood One
Arbitron Metro Market: Tupelo, MS; *Format:* Sports, Talk; *Target Audience:* 18-54.; *Adv. Rates:* 180; 180; 180; 120
Will Stammerjohan, General Manager
Connie Stammerjohan, General Sales Mgr

Gulfport

***WAOY**
01-01-1999; 91.7 MHz FM; 78 kw; 1089 ft.; N30 42 29 W89 5 6
Rebroadcasts: Rebroadcasts WAFR(FM) Tupelo 80%
P.O. Box 3206, Tupelo, MS 38803 US
(601) 844-8888; *Fax:* (601) 842-6791
www.afr.net
faq@afa.net
License: Gulfport, Harrison County, MS held by American Family Association.
Group Owner: American Family Radio
Nat'l Network: USA
Arbitron Metro Market: Gulfport, MS; *Format:* Christian; *Target Audience:* General.
Tim Wildmon, President
Donald Wildmon, Founder
Buddy Smith, Sr VP
Ed Vitagliano, Exec VP
Randy Sharpn, Meeke Addison
Director Of Communications, Abraham Hamilton III
General Sounsel & Public Policy Analyst, General Sales Mgr

WGCM
01-01-1928; 1240 kHz AM; *Hrs Open:* 24; 1 kw-U, ND1; N30 25 45 W89 1 10
P.O. Box 2639, Gulfport, MS 39505 US
(228) 896-5500; *Fax:* (228) 896-0458
www.coast102.com
pat@coast102.com
License: Gulfport, MS held by Coast Radio Group
Arbitron Metro Market: Biloxi-Gulfport-Pascagoula, MS; *Format:* Country; *Target Audience:* 35 plus.
Morgan Dowdy, President
Bryan Rhodes, Operations Dir
Lisa Stiglets, Station Manager
Steve Spillman, General Sales Mgr
Pat McGowan, Programming Director
Dave Melton, Chief Engineer
Dennis Warren, Local Sales Manager

WGCM-FM
11-14-1969; 102.3 MHz FM; *Hrs Open:* 24; 50 kw; 394 ft.; N30 20 44 W89 11 47

P.O. Box 2639, Gulfport, MS 39505 US
(228) 896-5500; *Fax:* (228) 896-0458
www.coast102.com
pat@coast102.com
License: Gulfport, Harrison County, MS held by Coast Radio Group
Arbitron Metro Market: Biloxi-Gulfport-Pascagoula, MS; *Format:* Easy Listening; *Target Audience:* 25-54.
Morgan Dowdy, President
Bryan Rhodes, Operations Dir
Lisa Stiglets, Station Manager
Steve Spillman, General Sales Mgr
Pat McGowan, Programming Director
Dennis Warren, Local Sales Manager

WGBL
07-13-1977; 96.7 MHz FM; *Hrs Open:* 24; 4.3 kw; 390 ft.; N30 27 31 W89 4 46
9471 Three Rivers Rd., Suite A, Gulfport, MS 39503 US
(228) 388-2001; *Fax:* (228) 896-9114
License: Gulfport, Harrison County, MS held by Alpha Media Licensee LLC
Group Owner: Alpha Media LLC
Arbitron Metro Market: Biloxi-Gulfport-Pascagoula, MS; *Format:* Country
Kenny Vest, Operations Manager
Ricky Mitchell, General Manager
Jesse Alvarez, Sales Manager
Mindy Patton, Promotions/New Media Director
Michelle Shortridge, Business Manager

WQFX
05-07-1975; 1130 kHz AM
336 Rodenberg Avd, Biloxi, MS 39531 US
(228) 374-9739; *Fax:* (228) 374-9739
www.wqfx.net
wqfxradio@aol.com
License: Gulfport, MS held by Walking by Faith Ministries Inc.
Group Owner: Walking by Faith Ministries Inc.; (acq 1994)
Arbitron Metro Market: Biloxi-Gulfport-Pascagoula, MS; *Format:* Gospel
James Black, General Manager

WROA
02-27-1955; 1390 kHz AM; 5 kw-D, DA2; 5 kw-N, DA2; N30 27 30 W89 4 45
P.O.Box 2639, Gulfport, MS 39503 US
(228) 896-5500; *Fax:* (228) 896-0458
License: Gulfport, MS held by Coast Radio Group
Arbitron Metro Market: Biloxi-Gulfport-Pascagoula, MS; *Format:* Contemporary Hits/Top 40 *Special Programming:* Farm one hr wkly
Morgan Dowdy, President
Bryan Rhodes, Operations Dir
Lisa Stiglets, Station Manager
Pat McGowan, Programming Director
Dave Melton, Chief Engineer
Dennis Warren, Local Sales Manager

WXYK
01-01-1964; 107.1 MHz FM; *Hrs Open:* 24; 2.8 kw; 400 ft.; N30 27 31 W89 4 46
9471 Three Rivers Rd., Suite A, Gulfport, MS 39503 US
(228) 388-2001; *Fax:* (228) 896-9114
www.1071themonkey.net
License: Gulfport, Harrison County, MS held by Alpha Media Licensee LLC
Group Owner: Alpha Media LLC
Nat'l Network: ABC
Arbitron Metro Market: Gulfport-Biloxi-Pascagoula, MS; *Format:* Contemporary Hits/Top 40
Kenny Vest, Operations Manager
Ricky Mitchell, General Manager
Jesse Alvarez, Sales Manager
Lucas Lloyd, Programming Director
Mindy Patton, Promotions/New Media Director
Michelle Shortridge, Business Manager

Guntown

WBVV
01-15-1976; 99.3 MHz FM; *Hrs Open:* 24; 15.5 kw; 420 ft.; N34 21 46 W88 35 28
P.O. Box 356, Booneville, MS 38829 US
License: Guntown, Lee County, MS held by CC Licenses LLC.
Group Owner: Urban Radio Communications Inc.; (acq 9-27-2001; $700,000 including 5-year noncompete agreement)
Nat'l Network: USA; Reach Satellite; *Regional Network:* Miss. News Net.
Arbitron Metro Market: Booneville, MS; *Format:* Religious
Kevin Wagner, President

Hattiesburg

***WAII**
01-01-1998; 89.3 MHz FM; 1 kw; 269 ft.; N31 16 59 W89 21 1
933 Richburg Rd., Hattiesburg, MS 39402 US
(601) 268-2825
www.afr.net
License: Hattiesburg, Forrest County, MS held by American Family Association.
Group Owner: American Family Radio
Nat'l Network: USA
Arbitron Metro Market: Laurel, MS; *Format:* Religious
Tim Wildman, President
Donald Wildmon, Founder
Buddy Smith, Sr VP
Ed Vitagliano, Executive VP
Randy Sharp, Director Of Special Projects
Meeke Addison, Director Of Communications
Abraham Hamilton III, General Counsel &ÆPublicPolicy Analyst

WHSY
09-01-1954; 950 kHz AM; *Hrs Open:* 24; 5 kw-D, ND2; 0.064 kw-N, ND2; N31 22 33 W89 19 49
PO Box 15216, Hattiesburg, MS 39401 US
(601) 582-7078; *Fax:* (601) 582-7122
whsy950@yahoo.com
License: Hattiesburg, MS held by Gulf South Communications LLC
Nat'l Network: CBS Radio
Arbitron Metro Market: Laurel-Hattiesburg, MS; *Format:* News, Talk
Charlie Holt, President

WFOR
05-01-1924; 1400 kHz AM; *Hrs Open:* 24
6555 Highway 98 West, Suite 8, Hattiesburg, MS 39402 US
(601) 296-9800; *Fax:* (601) 296-9838
www.1400thescore.com
License: Hattiesburg, MS held by CC Licenses LLC.
Group Owner: iHeartMedia; (acq 12-19-2000; grpsl).
Arbitron Metro Market: Laurel-Hattiesburg, MS; *Format:* Sports; *Target Audience:* 35 plus.
Mike Comfort, Market President
Jackson Walker, Senior Vice President of Programming

WJMG
05-10-1982; 92.1 MHz FM; *Hrs Open:* 24; 6 kw; 299 ft.; N31 20 33 W89 17 53
1204 Graveline Street, Hattiesburg, MS 39401 US
(601) 544-1941; *Fax:* (601) 544-1947
License: Hattiesburg, Forrest County, MS held by Vernon C. Floyd dba Circuit Broadcasting of Hattiesburg
Arbitron Metro Market: Laurel-Hattiesburg, MS; *Format:* Urban Contemporary
Vernon Floyd, General Manager

WORV
06-07-1969; 1580 kHz AM; 1 kw-D, ND1; 0.088 kw-N, ND1; N31 20 33 W89 17 53
1204 Graveline St., Hattiesburg, MS 39401 US
(601) 544-1941; *Fax:* (601) 544-1947
License: Hattiesburg, MS held by Vernon C. Floyd dba Circuit Broadcasting of Hattiesburg.
Nat'l Network: American Urban; *Nat'l Reps:* Dora-Clayton
Arbitron Metro Market: Laurel-Hattiesb *TV Affiliate:* Relg

***WUSM-FM**
05-10-1973; 88.5 MHz FM; 3 kw; 424 ft.; N31 18 25.6 W89 24 47.2
Box 10045 S. Station, Hattiesburg, MS 39406* US
(601) 266-4287
wusm@usm.edu
License: Hattiesburg, Forrest County, MS held by University of Southern Mississippi.
Arbitron Metro Market: Hattiesburg, MS; *Format:* Triple A, Variety/Diverse; *Hrs. of News Programming:* news progmg 22 hrs wkly; *No. News Employees:* 4; *Target Audience:* General; college students & upper income univ& community listeners
Justin Martin, General Manager
Leslie Sanders-Wood, Business Manager

WFFX
07-01-1966; 103.7 MHz FM; *Hrs Open:* 24; 100 kw; Ant 1,056 ft; N31 31 37 W89 08 07
6555 Hwy. 98 W., Suite 8, Hattiesburg, MS 53202
(601) 296-9800; *Fax:* (601) 296-9838
www.1037wffx.com
License: Hattiesburg, Forrest County, MS held by CC Licenses LLC.
Group Owner: iHeartMedia

Population Served: 500,000; *Arbitron Metro Market:* Laurel-Hattiesburg, MS; *Format:* Rock/AOR; *Target Audience:* 25-54.
Mike Comfort, Vice President/Market Manager

WXRR
07-01-1967; 104.5 MHz FM; *Hrs Open:* 24; 100 kw; 981 ft.; N31 25 52 W89 8 51
Box 16596, Hattiesburg, MS 39404 US
(601) 544-0095; *Fax:* (601) 649-8199
www.rock104fm.com
rock104@rock104fm.com
License: Hattiesburg, Forrest County, MS held by Blakeney Communications Inc.
Group Owner: Blakeney Communications Inc.; acq 8-30-94; $450,000 with co-located AM;
Arbitron Metro Market: Hattiesburg, MS; *Format:* Classic Rock; *Target Audience:* General.
Larry Blakeney, President/CEO
Debbie Blakeney, General Manager

Hazlehurst

WDXO
12-24-1970; 92.9 MHz FM; *Hrs Open:* 24; 2.7 kw; 497 ft.; N31 53 33 W90 24 8
110 W. Monticello St., Brookhaven, MS 39601 US
(601) 835-5005; *Fax:* (601) 835-5415
myespn929.com
License: Hazlehurst, Copiah County, MS held by TeleSouth Communications Inc.
Group Owner: TeleSouth Communications Inc.
Nat'l Network: ABC
Arbitron Metro Market: Hazlehurst, MS; *Format:* Sports; *Target Audience:* 18-50.

WOEG
06-01-1953; 1220 kHz AM
6311 Ridgewood Rd., Jackson, MS 39211 US
(601) 957-1700; *Fax:* (601) 956-5228
License: Hazlehurst, MS held by TeleSouth Communications Inc.
Group Owner: TeleSouth Communications Inc.; (acq 6-20-2006; grpsl).
TV Affiliate: Black; *No. News Employees:* General; Black

Heidelberg

WLAU
05-01-1980; 99.3 MHz FM; *Hrs Open:* 24; 50 kw; 492 ft.; N31 49 17 W89 18 37
6311 Ridgewood Rd., Jackson, MS 39211 US
(601) 957-1700
www.supertalk.fm
feedback@supertalk.fm
License: Heidelberg, Jasper County, MS held by TeleSouth Communications Inc.
Group Owner: TeleSouth Communications Inc.; (acq 12-19-2000; grpsl).
Regional Network: Miss. News Net.
Population Served: 350,000; *Arbitron Metro Market:* Laurel-Hattiesburg, MS; *Format:* News, News/Talk, 86; *Target Audience:* General.

Holly Springs

WKRA
09-02-1966; 1110 kHz AM; *Hrs Open:* Sunrise-sunset; 1 kw-D, NDD; N34 47 11 W89 25 0
145 Memphis St, Holly Springs, MS 38635 US
(662) 252-1110; *Fax:* (662) 252-2739
power927fm.com
wkraradio@gmail.com
License: Holly Springs, MS held by Bill Autry.
Regional Network: Miss. News Net.
Arbitron Metro Market: Memphis, TN; *Format:* Ethnic *Special Programming:* Gospel 12 hrs wkly; *Hrs. of News Programming:* news progmg 9 hrs wkly; *No. News Employees:* 1; *Target Audience:* 25-55.
Deirdra Autry, General Manager

WKRA-FM
06-30-1976; 92.7 MHz FM; *Hrs Open:* 24; 3 kw; 299 ft.; N34 47 11 W89 25 0
P.O. Box 398, Holly Springs, MS 38635 US
(662) 252-1810; *Fax:* (662) 252-2739
power927@gmail.com
License: Holly Springs, Marshall County, MS
Arbitron Metro Market: Memphis, TN; *Format:* Adult Contemp; *No. News Employees:* 1; *Target Audience:* General; Black community

Ederic Kerney, Chief Executive Officer
Charles Boyd, Sales Manager
Annette Kerney, Programming Director

***WURC**
10-14-1988; 88.1 MHz FM; 3 kw; 272 ft.; N34 46 53 W89 26 49
150 Rust Avenue, Holly Springs, MS 38635 US
(662) 252-5881; *Fax:* (662) 252-8869
www.wurc.org
wurc@wurc.org
License: Holly Springs, Marshall County, MS held by Rust College Inc.
Nat'l Network: NPR
Arbitron Metro Market: Holly Springs, MS; *Format:* Blues, Gospel, 52, News, News/Talk, Talk; *Target Audience:* General; alternative seekers and minority listeners
David Beckley, President
Debayo Moyo, General Manager
Wayne.A.Fiddis, Station Manager
Jerald White, Broadcast Engineer
Sharron Goodman-Hill, Instructor & Music Director

Horn Lake

WHAL-FM
07-26-1994; 95.7 MHz FM; *Hrs Open:* 24; 6 kw; 289 ft.; N35 8 9 W89 58 17
2650 Thousand Oaks Boulevard, Suite 4100, Memphis, TN 38118 US
(901) 259-1300; *Fax:* (901) 259-6434
www.hallelujahfm.com
License: Horn Lake, DeSoto County, MS held by CC Licenses LLC.
Group Owner: iHeartMedia; (acq 1996; grpsl).
Nat'l Reps: Clear Channel
Arbitron Metro Market: Memphis, TN; *Format:* Gospel; *Hrs. of News Programming:* News progmg 3 hrs wkly; *Target Audience:* 35-54; baby boomers
Morgan Bohannon, Regional Market President

Houston

WCPC
10-21-1955; 940 kHz AM; *Hrs Open:* 5 AM-9:15 PM; 31 kw; N33 55 43 W89 00 35
1189 N. Jackson St., Houston, MS 38851 US
(662) 456-3071
www.wilkinsradio.com
denise@wilkinsradio.com
License: Houston, MS held by Cajun Radio Corp.
Group Owner: Wilkins Communications Network Inc.; (acq 6-1-2007; $200,000)
Nat'l Network: USA; *Regional Network:* Miss. News Net.
Arbitron Metro Market: Tupelo, MS; *Format:* Christian, Gospel; *Hrs. of News Programming:* news progmg 14 hrs wkly; *No. News Employees:* 1; *Target Audience:* Adults; *Adv. Rates:* 7; 7; 7; 7
Chris Hester, Station Manager

WSYE
09-19-1968; 93.3 MHz FM; *Hrs Open:* 24; 100 kw; 1804 ft.; N33 45 6 W88 52 40
2214 S. Gloster, Tupelo, MS 38802 US
(662) 842-0197
License: Houston, Chickasaw County, MS held by JMD Inc.
Nat'l Reps: Christal
Arbitron Metro Market: Tupelo, MS; *Format:* Adult Contemp; *Hrs. of News Programming:* news progmg 2 hrs wkly; *No. News Employees:* 1; *Target Audience:* 25-54.; *Adv. Rates:* 36; 36; 36; 28
Steve Drunam, Operations Dir
Brenda Bebout, Station Manager
Scott Bebout, Promotions Manager

Indianola

WNLA
05-01-1953; 1380 kHz AM; *Hrs Open:* 12; 0.5 kw-D, ND1; 0.044 kw-N, ND1; N33 28 41 W90 38 28; N33 27 32 W90 37 45
P.O. Box 667, Indianola, MS 38751 US
(662) 887-1380; *Fax:* (662) 887-6006
www.wnlaradio.com
wnlaamfm@bellsouth.net
License: Indianola, MS held by Delta Radio LLC
Group Owner: Delta Radio LLC; (acq 6-7-2007; $300,000 with co-located FM)
Regional Network: Miss. News Net.
Arbitron Metro Market: Greenville, MS; *Format:* Black, Gospel; *Target Audience:* 21-55; Black
Larry Fuss, President
Recardo Thomas, Station Manager
Douglas Johnson, Market Manager
Paul Coates, Senior Marketing Consultant

WIBT
09-01-1969; 105.5 MHz FM; *Hrs Open:* 24; 4.4 kw; 200 ft; N33 28 41 W90 38 28
P.O. Box 667, Indianola, MS 38751
(662) 887-1380; *Fax:* (662) 887-6006
wnlaamfm@bellsouth.net
License: Indianola, Sunflower County, MS held by Delta Radio LLC
Group Owner: Delta Radio LLC; (acq 6-7-2007; $300,000 with co-located FM)
Hrs. of News Programming: News progmg 21 hrs wkly; *Target Audience:* 21-55.; *Adv. Rates:* 8; 8; 8; na
Larry Fuss, President
Recardo Thomas, Station Manager
Douglas Johnson, Market Manager
Paul Coates, Marketing Consultant

WTCD
05-01-1990; 96.9 MHz FM; *Hrs Open:* 24; 40 kw; 548 ft.; N33 34 34 W90 22 33
6311 Ridgewood Rd., Jackson, MS 39211 US
(601) 957-1700
www.supertalk.fm
feedback@supertalk.fm
License: Indianola, Sunflower County, MS held by TeleSouth Communications Inc.
Group Owner: TeleSouth Communications Inc.; acq 5-28-97; $325,000)
Nat'l Network: USA; *Regional Network:* Miss. News Net.
Arbitron Metro Market: Indianola, MS; *Format:* News, News/Talk, 86 *Special Programming:* Farm 5 hrs, relg 11 hrs, talk 10 hrs wkly; *Hrs. of News Programming:* news progmg 20 hrs wkly; *No. News Employees:* 1 *Target Audience:* 35-64; strong family orientation, middle to upper incomes

***WYTF**
08-26-2004; 88.7 MHz FM; 100 kw vert; 636 ft.; N33 35 3 W90 36 13
P.O. Box 3206, Tupelo, MS 38803 US
(662) 844-8888; *Fax:* (662) 842-6791
www.afr.net
faq@afa.net
License: Indianola, Sunflower County, MS held by American Family Association.
Group Owner: American Family Radio
Nat'l Network: USA
Arbitron Metro Market: Indianola, MS; *Format:* Christian
Tim Wildmon, President
Donald Wildmon, Founder
Buddy Smith, Sr VP
Ed Vitagliano, Exec VP
Randy Sharp, Director Of Special Projects
Meeke Addison, Director Of Communications
Abraham Hamilton III, General Counsel

Itta Bena

***WVSD**
06-23-1991; 91.7 MHz FM; *Hrs Open:* 6 AM-midnight; 3 kw; 292 ft.; N33 31 5 W90 20 38
14000 Hwy 82, Box 7221, Itta Bena, MS 38941 US
(662) 254-3612; *Fax:* (662) 254-3611
License: Itta Bena, Leflore County, MS held by Mississippi Valley State University.
Arbitron Metro Market: Itta Bena, MS; *Format:* Gospel, Jazz *Special Programming:* Oldies 10 hrs, reggae/Latin 3 hrs, comedy 2 hrs wk
Wanda Young, Programming Director of Campus Radio Operations
Debra Harmon, Programming Director

Iuka

WKZU
11-05-1970; 104.9 MHz FM; *Hrs Open:* 24/7; 50 kw; 443 ft.; N34 46 35 W88 23 40
311 W. Eastport, St. Iuka, MS 38852 US
(662) 837-1023; *Fax:* (662) 837-2994
classicradiofm@aol.com
License: Iuka, Tishomingo County, MS held by Kudzu Communications Inc.
Arbitron Metro Market: Tupelo, MS; *Format:* Country *Special Programming:* Bluegrass, Bluegrass Gospel; *Target Audience:* 25-54; 50% men & 50% women
Joan Peters, General Manager
Lisa Yates, General Sales Mgr
Sarah Shelton, Account Manager

Jackson

WJDX
01-01-1929; 620 kHz AM; *Hrs Open:* 24; 5 kw-D, DAN; 1 kw-N, DAN; N32 22 56 W90 11 26
1375 Beasley Road, Jackson, MS 39206 US
(601) 982-1062; *Fax:* (601) 362-1905
www.wjdx.com
License: Jackson, MS held by Capstar TX LLC
Group Owner: iHeartMedia; (acq 8-30-2000; grpsl)
Nat'l Reps: McGavren Guild
Arbitron Metro Market: Jackson, MS; *Format:* News, News/Talk, 84, Talk *Special Programming:* Farm 2 hrs wkly; *Hrs. of News Programming:* news progmg 10 hrs wkly; *No. News Employees:* 1; *Target Audience:* 25-54;middle to upper income contemp adults
Todd Berry, Operations Manager
Kenny Windham, Vice President/General Manager
Doug Jones, Director of Sales
Randy Bell, Programming Director
Jan Michaels, Marketing Director
Rick Adams, Public Service Director

WJMI
01-01-1967; 99.7 MHz FM; *Hrs Open:* 24; 98 kw; 1,060 ft.; N32 12 28 W90 24 50
731 S. Pear Orchard Rd., Suite 27, Ridgeland, MS 39157 US
(601) 957-1300; *Fax:* (601) 956-0516
www.wjmi.com
License: Jackson, Hinds County, MS held by Alpha Media Licensee LLC
Group Owner: Alpha Media LLC
Arbitron Metro Market: Jackson, MS; *Format:* Urban Contemporary; *No. News Employees:* 1; *Target Audience:* 18-49.
Kevin Webb, Senior Vice President and Market Manager
Stan Branson, Program Director and Operations Manager

***WJSU-FM**
08-01-1975; 88.5 MHz FM; 24.5 kw; 200 ft.; N32 17 47 W90 12 23
P.O. Box 18450, Jackson, MS 39217 US
(601) 979-2285; *Fax:* (601) 979-2878
License: Jackson, Hinds County, MS held by Jackson State University.
Nat'l Network: NPR
Arbitron Metro Market: Jackson, MS; *Format:* Jazz, News; *Hrs. of News Programming:* news prgmg 36 hrs wkly; *No. News Employees:* 2; *Target Audience:* 25-54; middle-class multiracial who prefer jazz
Gina Carter-Simmers, General Manager
Dale Morris, Station Engineer

WHLH
11-19-1973; 95.5 MHz FM; 100 kw; 1480 ft.; N32 14 26 W90 24 15
1375 Beasley Road, Jackson, MS 39206 US
(601) 982-1062; *Fax:* (601) 362-1905
www.hallelujah955.com
License: Jackson, Hinds County, MS held by Capstar TX LLC
Group Owner: iHeartMedia; (acq 8-30-00; grpsl).
Nat'l Network: CBS; *Nat'l Reps:* D & R Radio
Arbitron Metro Market: Jackson, MS; *Format:* Gospel; *Target Audience:* 18-34; female
Todd Berry, Operations Manager
Kenny Windham, Vice President/General Manager
Doug Jones, Director of Sales
Torrez Harris, Programming Director
Jan Michaels, Marketing Director
Rick Adams, Public Service Director

WJQS
01-01-1947; 1400 kHz AM; *Hrs Open:* 24; 1 kw-U, ND1; N32 19 12 W90 11 25
840 E. River Pl., Jackson, MS 39202 US
(601) 965-2001; *Fax:* (601) 961-3042
License: Jackson, Hinds County, MS held by Alpha Media Licensee LLC
Group Owner: Alpha Media LLC; (acq 9-24-2013; grpsl).
Arbitron Metro Market: Jackson, MS; *Format:* Oldies
Kevin Webb, Senior Vice President and Market Manager
Stan Branson, Program Director and Operations Manager

***WMPN-FM**
11-01-1984; 91.3 MHz FM; *Hrs Open:* 24; 45 kw; 1388 ft.; N32 11 29 W90 24 22
3825 Ridgewood Road, Jackson, MS 39211 US
(601) 432-6565; *Fax:* (601) 432-6806
www.mpbonline.org
License: Jackson, Hinds County, MS held by Mississippi Authority for Educational Television.
Nat'l Network: PRI; NPR; *Wire Services:* AP

Arbitron Metro Market: Jackson, MS; *Format:* News; *Hrs. of News Programming:* news progmg 100 hrs wkly; *No. News Employees:* 7; *Target Audience:* General.
Robert Sawyer, Chairman
Jason Holland, Operations Dir
Jay Woods, General Manager
Mari Irby, Promotions Manager

***WMPR**
01-01-1983; 90.1 MHz FM; 100 kw; 449 ft.; N32 11 33 W90 5 28
1018 Pecan Park Circle, Jackson, MS 39209 US
(601) 948-5837; *Fax:* (601) 948-6162
License: Jackson, Hinds County, MS held by J.C. Maxwell Broadcasting Group Inc.
Arbitron Metro Market: Jackson, MS; *Format:* Variety/Diverse
Charles Evers, General Manager

WMSI-FM
01-01-1948; 102.9 MHz FM; *Hrs Open:* 24; 100 kw; 1886 ft.; N32 12 49 W90 22 56
1375 Beasley Road, Jackson, MS 39206 US
(601) 982-1062; *Fax:* (601) 362-1905
www.miss103.com
info@miss103.com
License: Jackson, Hinds County, MS held by Capstar TX LLC
Group Owner: iHeartMedia
Arbitron Metro Market: Jackson, MS; *Format:* Country *Special Programming:* Farm one hr wkly; *Hrs. of News Programming:* News progmg 4 hrs wkly; *Target Audience:* 25 plus.
Todd Berry, Operations Manager
Kenny Windham, Vice President/General Manager
Doug Jones, Director of Sales
Rick Adams, Programming Director
Jan Michaels, Marketing Director

WOAD
01-01-1929; 1300 kHz AM; 5 kw-D, ND1; 1 kw-N, ND1; N32 23 12 W90 9 47
731 S. Pear Orchard Rd., Suite 27, Ridgeland, MS 39157 US
(601) 995-1400
www.woad.com
License: Jackson, Hinds County, MS held by Alpha Media Licensee LLC
Group Owner: Alpha Media LLC; (acq 9-24-2013; grpsl).
Nat'l Network: American Urban; ABC; *Wire Services:* Weather Wire
Arbitron Metro Market: Jackson, MS *TV Affiliate:* Gospel; *Format:* Gospel; *No. News Employees:* 25-54.
Kevin Webb, Senior Vice President and Market Manager
Stan Branson, Program Director and Operations Manager

WSFZ
09-01-1938; 930 kHz AM; *Hrs Open:* 24
Mailing Address: 301 Congress Ave, Suite 410, Austin, TX 78701 US
Second Address: 574 Highway 51 North, Suite F, Ridgeland, MS 39157
(601) 605-6656; *Fax:* (601) 605-6646
beubank@jacksonacademy.org
License: Jackson, MS held by Sportsrad Inc.
Nat'l Network: Westwood One; Sporting News Radio Network
Arbitron Metro Market: Jackson, MS; *Format:* Sports
Bryan Eubank, General Manager
Bo Bounds, General Sales Mgr

***WJLV**
08-10-1971; 94.7 MHz FM; *Hrs Open:* 24; 97 w; 1,168 ft; N32 16 53 W90 17 41
5700 West Oaks Boulevard, Rocklin, CA 95765 US
(916) 251-1600; *Fax:* (916) 251-1650
www.klove.com
License: Jackson, Hinds County, MS held by Educational Media Foundation
Group Owner: EMF Broadcasting
Population Served: 330,000; *Arbitron Metro Market:* Jackson, MS; *Target Audience:* 25-54.
Mike Novak, President

Kosciusko

WJDX-FM
06-25-1965; 105.1 MHz FM; *Hrs Open:* 24; 100 kw; 981 ft; N32 41 25 W89 52 06
1375 Beasley Road, Jackson, MS 39206 US
(601) 982-1062; *Fax:* (601) 362-1905
www.1051theriver.com
License: Kosciusko, Attala County, MS held by Capstar TX LLC
Group Owner: iHeartMedia; (acq 8-30-00; grpsl)
Population Served: 450,000; *Arbitron Metro Market:* Jackson, MS; *Format:* Oldies; *Target Audience:* 35-64.; *Adv. Rates:* 18; 15; 18; 15
Todd Berry, Operations Manager
Kenny Windham, Vice President/General Manager
Doug Jones, Director of Sales
Jan Michaels, Program Director/Marketing Director

Laurel

WAML
10-20-1932; 1340 kHz AM; *Hrs Open:* 24; 1 kw-U, ND1; N31 40 1 W89 8 59
1425 Ellisville Boulevard, Laurel, MS 39440 US
(601) 425-0011; *Fax:* (601) 425-0016
License: Laurel, MS held by Walking by Faith Ministries Inc.
Group Owner: Walking by Faith Ministries Inc.; (acq 10-1-99)
Arbitron Metro Market: Laurel, MS; *Format:* Sports, Talk; *Target Audience:* General.
James Black, General Manager

***WATP**
01-01-1998; 90.9 MHz FM; 69 kw; 723 ft.; N31 52 39 W88 52 44
P.O. Box 3206, Tupelo, MS 38803 US
(662) 844-8888; *Fax:* (662) 842-6791
www.afr.net
faq@afa.net
License: Laurel, Jones County, MS held by American Family Association.
Group Owner: American Family Radio
Nat'l Network: USA
Arbitron Metro Market: Laurel, MS; *Format:* Religious
Tim Wildmon, President
Donald Wildmon, Founder
Buddy Smith, Sr VP
Ed Vitagliano, Exec VP
Randy Sharp, Director Of Special Projects
Meeke Addison, Director Of Communications
Abraham Hamilton III, General Sales Mgr

WHJA
02-27-1957; 890 kHz AM; *Hrs Open:* Sunrise-sunset; 10 kw-C, NDD; 10 kw-D, NDD; N31 31 29 W89 14 31
3201 Sheffield Drive, Emmaus, PA 18049 US
(601) 296-9800; *Fax:* (601) 296-9838
License: Laurel, MS
Group Owner: Donald H. Pugh
Arbitron Metro Market: Laurel, MS; *Format:* Blues; *Hrs. of News Programming:* news progmg 4 hrs wkly; *No. News Employees:* 1; *Target Audience:* General.
Donald H. Pugh, President

WMXI
04-01-1989; 98.1 MHz FM; 2.55 kw; 512 ft.; N31 33 22 W89 9 9
7501 U.S. Highway 49, Hattiesburg, MS 39403 US
(601) 261-0898
www.wmxi.com
zoo107@bellsouth.net
License: Laurel, Jones County, MS held by Rainey Broadcasting Inc.
Nat'l Network: Premiere Radio Networks
Arbitron Metro Market: Laurel, MS; *Format:* News, News/Talk, 86 *Special Programming:* sports; *Hrs. of News Programming:* 24; *Target Audience:* adults 25 plus; *Adv. Rates:* $25.00
Ted Tibbett, General Manager

WNSL
03-10-1959; 100.3 MHz FM; 100 kw; 1063 ft.; N31 31 37 W89 8 7
6555 Highway 98 West, Suite 8, Hattiesburg, MS 39402 US
(601) 296-9800; *Fax:* (601) 296-9838
www.sl100.com
contact@sl100.com
License: Laurel, Jones County, MS held by CC Licenses LLC
Group Owner: iHeartMedia
Nat'l Network: ABC
Arbitron Metro Market: Laurel, MS; *Format:* Contemporary Hits/Top 40; *Target Audience:* 18-49.; *Adv. Rates:* 42; 42; 42; 28
Jackson Walker, Senior Vice President of Programming
Don King, Account Executive

Leland

WBAD
01-01-1973; 94.3 MHz FM; *Hrs Open:* 19; 50 kw; 289 ft.; N33 24 55 W90 59 18
Mailing Address: P.O. Box 4426, Greenville, MS 38701 US
Second Address: 126 Seven Oaks Rd., Greenville, MS 38701
Fax: (208) 734-6633
www.csnradio.com
License: Leland, Washington County, MS held by Interchange Communications Inc.
Nat'l Network: American Urban
Arbitron Metro Market: Junction City OR; *Format:* Christian
Mike Stocklin, General Manager

WESY
04-08-1957; 1580 kHz AM; *Hrs Open:* 24; 1 kw-D, ND1; 0.048 kw-N, ND1; N33 22 46 W90 55 47
Mailing Address: P.O. Box 4426, Greenville, MS 38701 US
Second Address: 126 Seven Oaks Rd., Greenville, MS 38701
(662) 378-9405; *Fax:* (662) 335-5538
wbad@tecinfo.com
License: Leland, MS held by East Delta Communications Inc.
Nat'l Network: American Urban
Arbitron Metro Market: Leland, MS; *Format:* Blues, Gospel, 74; *Target Audience:* 18-54.
William Jackson, President
Stanley Sherman, Executive Vice President

WIQQ
09-01-1985; 102.3 MHz FM; *Hrs Open:* 24; 1.65 kw; 446 ft.; N33 23 51 W91 0 35
1399 East Reed Road, Greenville, MS 38703 US
(662) 378-2617; *Fax:* (662) 378-8341
License: Leland, Washington County, MS held by Debut Broadcasting Mississippi Inc.
Group Owner: Debut Broadcasting Corp. Inc.; (acq 6-19-2007; grpsl)
Nat'l Network: USA; Jones Radio Networks; *Regional Network:* Ark. Radio Net; *Nat'l Reps:* McGavren Guild
Format: Adult Contemp *Special Programming:* Farm 6 hrs, relg 6 hrs wkly; *Hrs. of News Programming:* news progmg 4 hrs wkly; *No. News Employees:* 1; *Target Audience:* 18-49; multi-paycheck & spendable income
Larry Fuss, President
John Nichols, Station Manager
Douglas Johnson, Market Manager
Paul Coates, Senior Marketing Consultant

Lexington

WAGR-FM
06-01-1990; 102.5 MHz FM; 6 kw; 328 ft.; N33 9 6 W90 7 45
100 Radio Rd, PO Box 369, Lexington, MS 39095 US
(662) 834-1025(662) 834-1254; *Fax:* (662) 834-1254
License: Lexington, Holmes County, MS held by Brad Maurice Cothran
Arbitron Metro Market: Lexington, MS; *Format:* Country, Oldies
Brad Cothran, General Manager

Liberty

WAZA
01-01-1998; 107.7 MHz FM; 25 kw; 328 ft.; N31 17 12 W90 47 53
PO Box 30, Magnolia, MS 39652 US
(601) 783-6600
License: Liberty, Amite County, MS held by Charles W. Dowdy, Debtor-In-Possession
Group Owner: Charles W. Dowdy
Arbitron Metro Market: East Wenatchee WA; *Format:* Contemporary Hits/Top 40, Urban Contemporary
Charles W. Dowdy, Debtor-In-Possession, President

Long Beach

WJZD-FM
03-20-1994; 94.5 MHz FM; *Hrs Open:* 24; 6 kw; 322 ft.; N30 26 0 W89 2 10
10211 Southpark Drive, Gulfport, MS 39503 US
(228) 896-5307; *Fax:* (228) 896-5703
www.wjzd.com
info@wjzd.com
License: Long Beach, Harrison County, MS held by WJZD Inc.
Nat'l Network: ABC; *Wire Services:* AP
Arbitron Metro Market: Biloxi-Gulfport-Pascagoula, MS; *Format:* Adult Contemp, News, 62, Talk *Special Programming:* American Blues Network; *Hrs. of News Programming:* news progmg 2 hrs wkly; *No. News Employees:* 2 *Target Audience:* P 18-54; *Adv. Rates:* 75; 60; 60; 50
Rip Daniels, CEO
Danielle Jewett, Operations Dir

Lorman

***WPRL**
10-12-1987; 91.7 MHz FM; *Hrs Open:* 6 AM-2 AM (M-F); 6 AM-midnight (S,; 3 kw; 299 ft.; N31 53 37 W91 8 54
Mailing Address: 1000 Asu Drive, Box #269, Lorman, MS 39096 US
Second Address: Alcorn State Univ., 1000 Alcorn Dr., Lorman, MS 39096
(601) 877-6290,(601) 877-6613; *Fax:* (601) 877-2213
lljunag@hotmail.com
License: Lorman, Jefferson County, MS held by Alcorn State University.
Nat'l Network: PRI; NPR; AP Radio

Format: Variety/Diverse; *Hrs. of News Programming:* news progmg 23 hrs wkly; *No. News Employees:* 1; *Target Audience:* General; African-American, rural, University faculty & students
Lijuana Weir, Operations Dir
Charles Edmond, Operational Manager
Dr. Jerry Domatch, General Manager

Louisville

WLSM-FM
04-22-1966; 107.1 MHz FM; *Hrs Open:* 24; 12.5 kw; 466 ft.; N33 7 20 W89 1 7
2142 Highway 14 East, Louisville, MS 39339 US
(662) 773-3481; *Fax:* (662) 773-3482
License: Louisville, Winston County, MS held by Harrison Communications Inc.
Nat'l Network: ABC; Jones Radio Networks; *Regional Network:* Miss. News Net.
Format: Adult Contemp; *Target Audience:* 18-54.
Phillip Harrison, President
Stacy Harrison, Station Manager

*KOUI
90.7 MHz FM; kw
US
License: Louisville, Winston County, MS held by Ron Elmore Ministries Inc.
Arbitron Metro Market: Louisville, MS
Ron Elmore, President

Lucedale

WVGG
09-03-1960; 1440 kHz AM; 5 kw-D; N30 56 00 W88 36 20
Mailing Address: Box 827, Lucedale, MS 39355
Second Address: 3276 Hwy. 198 W., Lucedale, MS 39452
(601) 947-8151; *Fax:* (601) 947-8152
License: Lucedale, George County, MS held by JDL Corp.
Nat'l Reps: Dora-Clayton; Keystone (unwired net)
Population Served: 35,000 *Target Audience:* General.
Larry Shirley, President
Lillian Hodgel, General Sales Mgr
Bob Bonnell, Farm Director

WRBE-FM
04-01-1993; 106.9 MHz FM; 6 kw; 259 ft.; N30 55 58 W88 36 21
Mailing Address: 129 Long Blvd., Quitman, MS 39355 US
Second Address: 3276 Hwy. 198 W., Lucedale, MS 39452
(601) 947-8151; *Fax:* (601) 947-8152
License: Lucedale, George County, MS held by JDL Corp.
Nat'l Network: Jones Radio Networks; Westwood One; *Regional Network:* Miss. News Net.
Format: Country
Larry Shirley, General Manager
Anthony Pugh, General Sales Mgr
Bob Bonnell, Farm Director

Lumberton

WZNF
03-22-2002; 95.3 MHz FM; *Hrs Open:* 24; 100 kW; 1410 ft.; N30 45 5 W89 3 24
1025 Lorraine Road, Gulfport, MS 39503 USA
www.953gorilla.com
License: Lumberton, Lamar County, MS held by JMD, Inc.
Group Owner: JMD, Inc.
Arbitron Metro Market: Biloxi-Gulfport-Pascagoula, MS; *Format:* Contemporary Hits/Top 40
Morgan Dowdy, CEO
Buddy Baylor, General Manager

Madison

WUSJ
09-16-1966; 96.3 MHz FM; 100 kw; 1284 ft.; N32 11 29 W90 24 22
265 Highpoint Drive, Ridgeland, MS 39157 US
(601) 956-0102; *Fax:* (601) 978-3890
www.us963.com
gwenr@radiopeople.net
License: Madison, Madison County, MS held by New South Communications Inc.
Group Owner: New South Communications Inc.; acq 8-24-99; $5 million)
Arbitron Metro Market: Jackson, MS; *Format:* Country
Gwen Rakestraw, General Manager
Nancy Fletcher, Sales Manager
Russ Williams, Programming Director

*WQVI
07-20-2004; 90.5 MHz FM; 60 kw vert; 430 ft.; N32 42 51 W89 49 19
P.O. Box 3206, Tupelo, MS 38803 US
(662) 844-8888; *Fax:* (662) 842-6791
www.afr.net
faq@afa.net
License: Madison, Madison County, MS held by American Family Association.
Group Owner: American Family Radio
Nat'l Network: USA
Arbitron Metro Market: Madison, MS; *Format:* Christian
Tim Wildmon, President
Donald Wildmon, Founder
Buddy Smith, Sr VP
Ed Vitagliano, Exec VP
Randy Sharp, Director Of Special Projects
Meeke Addison, Director Of Communications
Abraham Hamilton III, General Counsel

Magee

WKXI-FM
04-11-1970; 107.5 MHz FM; 98 kw; 951 ft.; N32 15 29 W89 47 22
731 S. Pear Orchard Rd., Suite 27, Ridgeland, MS 39157 US
(601) 957-1300; *Fax:* (601) 956-0516
www.wkxi.com
License: Magee, Simpson County, MS held by Alpha Media Licensee LLC
Group Owner: Alpha Media LLC; (acq 9-24-2013; grpsl).
Arbitron Metro Market: Jackson, MS; *Format:* Urban Contemporary; *Target Audience:* 25-54.
Kevin Webb, Senior Vice President and Market Manager
Stan Branson, Program Director and Operations Manager

WSJC
07-05-1957; 810 kHz AM; 50 kw-D, DAN; 0.5 kw-N, DAN; N31 52 0 W89 41 35
P.O. Box 107, Keene, TX 76059 US
wsjcradio.com
License: Magee, MS held by Witko Broadcasting L.L.C.
Format: Religious
Norm Wick, General Manager

Mantee

WKBB
04-14-1974; 100.9 MHz FM; 47 kw; 510 ft.; N33 40 43 W88 48 18
6311 Ridgewood Road, Jackson, MS 39211 US
(662) 494-1450; *Fax:* (662) 494-9762
www.supertalk.fm
License: Mantee, Clay County, MS
Arbitron Metro Market: Columbus-Starkville-West Point, MS; *Format:* News, News/Talk, 86; *Target Audience:* 35-54.
William Miller, General Manager

Marietta

WXWX
01-01-2008; 96.3 MHz FM; 3.9 kw; 410 ft.; N34 24 33 W88 32 24
US
(662) 680-1606
License: Marietta, Prentiss County, MS held by George S. Flinn Jr.
Nat'l Network: ESPN Radio
Arbitron Metro Market: Marietta, MS; *Format:* Sports
Russ Wilson, General Manager

Marion

WKZB
03-15-1990; 95.1 MHz FM; 50 kw; 606 ft; N32 26 08 W88 36 24
3436 Highway 45 North, Meridian, MS 39301
(601) 693-2381; *Fax:* (601) 485-2972
License: Marion, Lauderdale County, MS held by New South Communications Inc.
Group Owner: New South Communications Inc.; (acq 3-16-2001; grpsl).
Population Served: 45,083; *Arbitron Metro Market:* Meridian, MS; *Target Audience:* 25-54.
Clay Holladay, President

McComb

WAKH
10-15-1978; 105.7 MHz FM; *Hrs Open:* 24; 100 kw; 489 ft; N31 16 50 W90 27 05
206 N. Front St., McComb, MS 39648 US
(601) 684-4116; *Fax:* (601) 684-4654
www.k106country.wordpress.com
License: McComb, Pike County, MS held by Charles W. Dowdy, Debtor-In-Possession
Group Owner: Charles W. Dowdy
Format: Country; *Target Audience:* General.
Charles W. Dowdy, President/General Manager

WAPF
04-25-1975; 1140 kHz AM; 1 kw-D, NDD; N31 14 51 W90 25 14
PO Box 30, Magnolia, MS 39652 US
(601) 783-6600
License: McComb, MS held by Charles W. Dowdy, Debtor-In-Possession
Group Owner: Charles W. Dowdy; (acq 8-5-93; $600,000;
Regional Network: Miss. News Net.
Arbitron Metro Market: Baton Rouge LA; *Format:* Sports; *Target Audience:* General.
Wayne Dowdy, President/General Manager

WAKK
04-18-1948; 980 kHz AM; 5 kw-D, ND1; 0.152 kw-N, ND1; N31 12 51 W90 27 42
PO Box 30, Magnolia, MS 39652 US
(601) 783-6600
License: McComb, MS held by Charles W. Dowdy, Debtor-In-Possession
Group Owner: Charles W. Dowdy; (acq 9-86; $600,000 with co-located FM;
Nat'l Network: ABC
Arbitron Metro Market: Mccomb, MS; *Format:* Gospel; *Target Audience:* General.
Charles W. Dowdy, President/General Manager

*WAQL
01-01-1999; 90.5 MHz FM; 30 kw; 534 ft.; N31 26 1 W90 34 45
P.O. Box 3206, Tupelo, MS 38803 US
(662) 844-8888; *Fax:* (662) 842-6791
www.afr.net
faq@afa.net
License: McComb, Pike County, MS held by American Family Association.
Group Owner: American Family Radio
Nat'l Network: USA
Arbitron Metro Market: McComb, MS; *Format:* Religious
Tim Wildmon, President
Donald Wildmon, Founder
Buddy Smith, Sr VP
Ed Vitagliano, Exec VP
Randy Sharp, Director Of Special Projects
Meeke Addison, Director Of Communications
Abraham Hamilton III, General Counsel

Meridian

WALT
01-01-1946; 910 kHz AM; *Hrs Open:* 24; 5 kw-D, ND1; 1 kw-N, ND1; N32 23 37 W88 40 8
4307 Highway 39 North, Meridian, MS 39301 US
(601) 693-3434; *Fax:* (601) 483-0826
michelle@910talkradio.com
License: Meridian, MS held by New South Communications Inc.
Group Owner: New South Communications L.L.C; (acq 2-26-93; $243,500)
Nat'l Reps: McGavren Guild
Arbitron Metro Market: Meridian, MS; *Format:* News, News/Talk, 86; *Target Audience:* 35-64.; *Adv. Rates:* 12; 12; 12; 8
Ron Harper, General Manager/Sales Manager
Marty Williams, Programming Director
Joyce Franklin, Traffic Manager

WYHL
12-01-1957; 1450 kHz AM; *Hrs Open:* 24/7; 1 kw-U, ND1; N32 23 9 W88 41 36
3436 Highway 45 North, Meridian, MS 39301 US
(601) 693-2381; *Fax:* (601) 485-2972
License: Meridian, MS held by New South Communications Inc.
Group Owner: New South Communications Inc.; (acq 3-16-2001; grpsl)
Arbitron Metro Market: Meridian, MS; *Format:* Gospel
Bryan Holladay, General Manager
Diane Horton, Sales Manager
Lee Taylor, Programming Director
Denise Williams, Traffic Manager

WJDQ
02-01-1968; 101.3 MHz FM; 99 kw; Ant 581 ft; N32 18 43 W88 41 33
3436 Highway 45 North, Meridian, MS 39301
(601) 693-2381; *Fax:* (601) 485-2972
License: Meridian, Lauderdale County, MS

Group Owner: New South Communications Inc.; (acq 3-16-2001; grpsl).
Population Served: 101,300; *Arbitron Metro Market:* Meridian, MS
Bryan Holladay, General Manager
Diane Horton, Sales Manager
Lee Taylor, Programming Director
Denise Williams, Traffic Manager

***WMAW-FM**
12-01-1983; 88.1 MHz FM; *Hrs Open:* 24; 100 kw; 1050 ft.; N32 8 18 W89 5 36
3825 Ridgewood Road, Jackson, MS 39211 US
(601) 432-6565; *Fax:* (601) 432-6806
www.mpbonline.org
License: Meridian, Lauderdale County, MS held by Mississippi Authority for Educational Television.
Nat'l Network: PRI; NPR; *Wire Services:* AP
Arbitron Metro Market: Meridian, MS *TV Affiliate:* WMAW-TV;
Format: News; *Hrs. of News Programming:* news progmg 100 hrs wkly; *No. News Employees:* 7; *Target Audience:* General.
Jason Klein, Operations Dir
Jay Woods, General Manager

WMER
10-16-1973; 1390 kHz AM; *Hrs Open:* 19; 5 kw-D, ND1; 0.101 kw-N, ND1; N32 20 41 W88 41 32
1413 Rubush Avenue, Meridian, MS 39301 US
(601) 693-9637; *Fax:* (601) 693-9637
License: Meridian, MS held by Michael H. Glass.
Nat'l Network: USA
Arbitron Metro Market: Meridian, MS; *Format:* Gospel; *Target Audience:* 25-54; upscale, young families, non-working mothers
Michael C. Glass, President

WALT-FM
01-01-1994; 102.1 MHz FM; 800 w; Ant 610 ft; N32 21 51 W88 38 34
4307 Highway 39 North, Meridian, MS 39301
(601) 693-3434; *Fax:* (601) 483-0826
wmmz@wokk.com
License: Meridian, Lauderdale County, MS held by Mississippi Broadcasters L.L.C.
Group Owner: New South Communications L.L.C; (acq 2-26-93; $243,500;
Arbitron Metro Market: Meridian, MS
Ron Harper, General Manager/Sales Manager
Marty Williams, Programming Director
Joyce Franklin, Traffic Manager

WMOX
12-01-1945; 1010 kHz AM; *Hrs Open:* 24; 10 kw-D, DA2; 1 kw-N, DA2; N32 23 42 W88 39 28
PO Box 5184, Meridian, MS 39302 US
(601) 693-1891; *Fax:* (601) 483-1010
www.wmox.net
wmoxradio@wmox.net
License: Meridian, MS held by Magnolia State Broadcasting Inc.
Regional Network: Miss. News Net; *Nat'l Reps:* Dora-Clayton
Arbitron Metro Market: Meridian, MS; *Format:* News, Sports, 86
Special Programming: Relg 8 hrs wkly; *No. News Employees:* 1; *Target Audience:* 25 plus; College educated with 30k plus annual income; *Adv. Rates:* 20; 16; 16; 10
Eddie Smith, President
William Smith, Operations Dir

WNBN
11-01-1987; 1290 kHz AM; *Hrs Open:* 18
1290 Hawkins Crossing Rd, Meridian, MS 39301 US
(601) 286-7030; *Fax:* (601) 286-3070
License: Meridian, MS held by Frank Rackley Jr.
Arbitron Metro Market: Meridian, MS; *Format:* Blues, Gospel
Special Programming: Black, women's, business, inspirational;
Hrs. of News Programming: News progmg 61 hrs wkly; *Target Audience:* 18-54.; *Adv. Rates:* 10; 10; 10; 9.50.
Frank Rackley Jr., General Manager

WOKK
08-01-1967; 97.1 MHz FM; 100 kw; 600 ft.; N32 19 30 W88 41 17
3436 Highway 45n, Meridian, MS 39301 US
601-693-2661; *Fax:* (601) 693-3439
www.wokk.com
michelle@910talkradio.com
License: Meridian, Lauderdale County, MS
Arbitron Metro Market: Meridian, MS *TV Affiliate:* Country; *No. News Employees:* 25-54.
Georgia Edmiston, General Manager
Diane Horton, General Sales Mgr
Scott Stevens, Programming Director/Operations Manager
Dee Williams, Traffic Director
Operations Manager

Merigold

WKXY
01-01-2003; 92.1 MHz FM; 6 kw; 328 ft.; N33 52 49 W90 42 24
P.O. Box 905, Cleveland, MS 38732 US
(662) 843-3392; *Fax:* (888) 704-4762
www.kix921.com
info@deltaradio.net
License: Merigold, Bolivar County, MS held by Delta Radio LLC.
Group Owner: Contemporary Communications
Arbitron Metro Market: Merigold, MS; *Format:* Country
Shawn McIntire, General Manager
Dan Hawthorne, News Director

Mississippi State

***WMAB-FM**
12-01-1983; 89.9 MHz FM; *Hrs Open:* 24; 64.3 kw; 1061 ft.; N33 21 14 W89 9 0
3825 Ridgewood Road, Jackson, MS 39211 US
(601) 432-6565; *Fax:* (601) 432-6806
www.mpbonline.org
communications@mpbonline.org
License: Mississippi State, Oktibbeha County, MS held by Mississippi Authority for Educational Television.
Nat'l Network: PRI; NPR; *Wire Services:* AP
Arbitron Metro Market: MS State, MS *TV Affiliate:* WMAB-TV;
Format: News; *Hrs. of News Programming:* news progmg 100 hrs wkly; *No. News Employees:* 7; *Target Audience:* General.
Jay Woods, General Manager
Jason Klein, Programming Director

Monticello

WRQO
11-19-1990; 102.1 MHz FM; *Hrs Open:* 24; 50 kw; 433 ft.; N31 36 13 W90 12 26
6311 Ridgewood Rd., Jackson, MS 39211 US
(601) 957-1700
www.supertalk.fm
feedback@supertalk.fm
License: Monticello, Lawrence County, MS held by TeleSouth Communications Inc.
Group Owner: TeleSouth Communications Inc.; (acq 6-20-2006; grpsl).
Nat'l Network: CBS; *Regional Network:* Miss. News Net.
Format: Talk *Special Programming:* Farm one hr, relg 10 hrs wkly; *Hrs. of News Programming:* News progmg 15 hrs wkly; *Target Audience:* 25-54.

WMLC
01-01-1969; 1270 kHz AM; 1 kw-D, ND2; 0.053 kw-N, ND2; N31 33 24 W90 8 6
Rt.1, Box 293, Monticello, MS 39654 US
(601) 587-1270; *Fax:* (601) 587-2119
wmlc@bellsouth.net
License: Monticello, MS held by Walking by Faith Ministries Inc.
Group Owner: Walking by Faith Ministries Inc.; (acq 6-28-2006; $50,000)
Nat'l Network: ESPN Radio
Arbitron Metro Market: Monticello, MS; *Format:* Sports
Will Watson, General Manager

Moss Point

WBUV
06-01-1964; 104.9 MHz FM; *Hrs Open:* 24; 16 kw; 879 ft.; N30 29 9 W88 42 53
286 DeBuys Road, Biloxi, MS 39531 US
(228) 388-2323; *Fax:* (228) 388-2362
www.newstalk1049.com
License: Moss Point, Jackson County, MS held by CC Licenses LLC.
Group Owner: iHeartMedia; (acq 12-7-98; $1.4 million swap with WYOK(FM) Atmore, AL).
Nat'l Network: Fox News Radio; Fox Sports; Premiere Radio Networks; *Nat'l Reps:* Clear Channel; *Wire Services:* AP
Arbitron Metro Market: Moss Point, MS; *Format:* News, News/Talk, 86; *No. News Employees:* 4; *Target Audience:* 25-54; men
James Wynne, Senior Account Executive
Jim Fisher, Programming Director
Kristan Saucier, Digital Content Director
Kelly Bennett, News Director

Natchez

***WASM**
01-01-2001; 91.1 MHz FM; 1 kw; 193 ft.; N31 33 24 W91 23 0
P.O. Box 3206, Tupelo, MS 38803 US
(662) 844-8888; *Fax:* (662) 842-6791
www.afr.net
faq@afa.net
License: Natchez, Adams County, MS held by American Family Association.
Group Owner: American Family Radio
Nat'l Network: USA
Arbitron Metro Market: Natchez, MS; *Format:* Religious
Tim Wildmon, President
Donald Wildmon, Founder
Buddy Smith, Sr VP
Ed Vitagliano, Exec VP
Randy Sharp, Director Of Special Projects
Meeke Addison, Director Of Communications
Abraham Hamilton III, General Counsel

WMIS
05-18-1941; 1240 kHz AM; *Hrs Open:* 24; 1 kw-U; N31 31 14 W91 23 09
Mailing Address: Box 1248, Natchez, MS 39121
Second Address: 20 E. Franklin St., Natchez, MS 39120
(601) 442-2522; *Fax:* (601) 446-9918
wmiswtyj@bellsouth.net
License: Natchez, Adams County, MS held by Natchez Broadcasting Co.
Nat'l Network: American Urban; *Regional Network:* Miss. News Net.
Population Served: 100,000; *Arbitron Metro Market:* Jackson, MS; *Target Audience:* General; Black; *Adv. Rates:* 16; 16; 16; 16
Diana Nutter, President
Calvin Butler, Operations Dir
James Nutter, General Manager
Lijuna Weir, Station Manager

WNAT
12-04-1949; 1450 kHz AM; *Hrs Open:* 24; 1 kw-U, ND1; N31 33 33 W91 23 30
2 O'Ferral St., Natchez, MS 39121 USA
(601) 442-4895; *Fax:* (601) 446-8260
www.listenupyall.com
License: Natchez, MS held by First Natchez Radio Group
Group Owner: First Natchez Radio Group; (acq 11-28-58).
Regional Network: Miss. News Net.
Arbitron Metro Market: Natchez, MS; *Format:* News, News/Talk, 84, Talk *Special Programming:* Gospel 18 hrs wkly; *No. News Employees:* 2; *Target Audience:* 25-54.; *Adv. Rates:* 16; 18; 16; 10

WQNZ
03-01-1968; 95.1 MHz FM; *Hrs Open:* 24; 100 kw; 719 ft.; N31 30 33.4 W91 24 18.6
2 O'Ferrall St., Natchez, MS 39120 USA
(601) 442-4895; *Fax:* (601) 446-8260
listenupyall.com
License: Natchez, Adams County, MS held by First Natchez Radio Group
Group Owner: First Natchez Radio Group
Regional Network: La. Net.
Format: Country; *Hrs. of News Programming:* news progmg 7 hrs wkly; *No. News Employees:* 2; *Target Audience:* 25 plus.; *Adv. Rates:* 18.50; 16.50; 18.50; 16.50

WKSO
03-01-1993; 97.3 MHz FM; 1.45 kw; 686 ft.; N31 30 33 W91 24 19
2 O'Ferrall St., Natchez, MS 39120 US
(601) 442-4895; *Fax:* (601) 446-8260
listenupyall.com
License: Natchez, Adams County, MS held by First Natchez Radio Group
Group Owner: First Natchez Radio Group; (acq 8-31-92; $36,000;
Nat'l Network: ABC
Arbitron Metro Market: Natchez, MS; *Format:* Adult Contemp;
Adv. Rates: 8; 7; 8; 7

New Albany

WNAU
03-27-1955; 1470 kHz AM
PO Box 808, New Albany, MS 38652 US
(662) 534-8133; *Fax:* (662) 538-4183
www.wnau1470.com
info@wnau1470.com
License: New Albany, MS held by MPM Investment Group
Regional Network: Miss. News Net.
Arbitron Metro Market: Tupelo, MS; *Format:* News, Oldies, 84
Special Programming: Gospel; *Target Audience:* 25-54.
Terry Cook, President
Ricky McCollum, Executive Vice President

RADIO - U.S.

WWZD-FM
03-03-1986; 106.7 MHz FM; *Hrs Open:* 24; 28 kw; 656 ft.; N34 29 6 W88 54 2
5026 Cliff Gookin Boulevard, Tupelo, MS 38803 US
(662) 842-1067; *Fax:* (662) 842-0725
www.wizard106.com
markmaharrey@iheartmedia.com
License: New Albany, Union County, MS held by Urban Radio Broadcasting Licenses Inc.
Nat'l Network: ABC; *Nat'l Reps:* Interep
Arbitron Metro Market: Tupelo, MS; *Format:* Country *Special Programming:* Southern gospel 4 hrs wkly; *No. News Employees:* 1; *Target Audience:* 25-54.
Rick Stevens, Operations Manger/Programming Director
Rebecca Yarbrough, General Sales Mgr
Melanie Kieght, Promotions Manager
Andrew Fuller, Traffic Manager
Mark Maharrey, Market Manager

WTPO
101.5 MHz FM; kw
, New Albany, MS US
(512) 329-5843
License: New Albany, Union County, MS held by Ace Radio Corp.
Group Owner: Ace Radio Corp.
Arbitron Metro Market: New Albany, MS
Stephen Hackerman, President

New Augusta

WZHL
101.7 MHz FM; 5 kw; 312 ft.; N31 13 0.5 W89 10 56.8
, New Augusta, MS US
(713) 528-2517
License: New Augusta, Perry County, MS held by Ace Radio Corp.
Group Owner: Ace Radio Corp.
Arbitron Metro Market: New Augusta, MS
Stephen Hackerman, President

New Hebron

***WSMP**
91.9 MHz FM; 0.75 kw; 194 ft.; N31 40 36 W89 52 36
, New Hebron, MS US
(601) 849-9111; *Fax:* (601) 849-0582
License: New Hebron, Lawrence County, MS held by Church Alive Inc.
Arbitron Metro Market: New Hebron, MS
Gene Amason II, General Manager

Newton

WUCL
04-17-1975; 97.9 MHz FM; *Hrs Open:* 24; 11 kw; Ant 492 ft; N32 29 16 W89 01 23
4307 Hwy. 39 N., Meridian, MS 39301
(601) 485-0979; *Fax:* (601) 485-2972
License: Newton, Newton County, MS held by CC Licenses LLC.
Group Owner: New South Communications Inc.; (acq 3-16-2001; grpsl)

Ron Harper, General Manager/Sales Manager
Marty Williams, Programming Director
Joyce Franklin, Traffic Manager

Ocean Springs

WOSM
02-12-1971; 103.1 MHz FM; *Hrs Open:* 24; 50 kw; 459 ft.; N30 24 34 W88 42 23
4720 Radio Road, Ocean Springs, MS 39564 US
(228) 875-9031; *Fax:* (228) 875-6461
License: Ocean Springs, Jackson County, MS held by Charles H. Cooper.
Nat'l Network: AP Radio; Salem Radio Network; *Wire Services:* AP
Arbitron Metro Market: Biloxi-Gulfport-Pascagoula, MS; *Format:* Gospel; *Hrs. of News Programming:* News progmg 14 hrs wkly; *Target Audience:* 18-54; family
Phil Moss, Operations Dir
Charles Cooper, General Manager
Margaret Cooper, Programming Director

WQYZ
09-01-1992; 92.5 MHz FM; *Hrs Open:* 24; 6 kw; 322 ft.; N30 27 9 W88 51 21
286 DeBuys Road, Biloxi, MS 39531 US
(228) 388-2323; *Fax:* (228) 388-2362
www.925fmthebeat.com
License: Ocean Springs, Jackson County, MS held by Capstar TX LLC
Group Owner: iHeartMedia; (acq 7-5-2005; $1,287,200)
Nat'l Reps: Clear Channel; *Wire Services:* AP
Arbitron Metro Market: Biloxi-Gulfport-Pascagoula, MS; *Format:* Blues; *Hrs. of News Programming:* News progmg one hr wkly; *Target Audience:* 28-42; adult families/singles; *Adv. Rates:* 20; 20; 20; 10
Walter Brown, Operations Dir
James Wynne, Senior Account Executive
Kristan Saucier, Digital Content Director

Okolona

WWKZ
12-15-1978; 103.9 MHz FM; *Hrs Open:* 24; 50 kw; 394 ft.; N34 12 18 W88 41 49
5026 Cliff Gookin Boulevard, Tupelo, MS 38801 US
(662) 842-1067
www.kz103.com
License: Okolona, Lowndes County, MS held by Citicasters Licenses Inc.
Group Owner: iHeartMedia; (acq 7-13-2005; $2.2 million)
Nat'l Network: American Urban
Arbitron Metro Market: Tupelo, MS; *Format:* Contemporary Hits/Top 40
Melonie Kight, General Sales Mgr

Olive Branch

KJMS
03-10-1965; 101.1 MHz FM; *Hrs Open:* 24; 100 kw; 561 ft.; N35 13 22 W90 2 36
2650 Thousand Oaks Blvd., Suite 4100, Memphis, TN 38118 US
(901) 259-1300; *Fax:* (901) 259-6456
www.myv101.com
License: Olive Branch, DeSoto County, MS held by CC Licenses LLC.
Group Owner: iHeartMedia
Arbitron Metro Market: Memphis, TN; *Format:* Urban Contemporary; *Target Audience:* 18-49.
Morgan Bohannon, Regional Market President
Frank Gilbert, Promotions Manager
Alonzo Pendleton, Chief Engineer

Oxford

***WAVI**
01-01-2002; 91.5 MHz FM; 8.13 kw vert; 574 ft.; N34 11 57 W89 49 9
P.O. Box 3206, Tupelo, MS 38803 US
(662) 844-8888; *Fax:* (662) 842-6791
www.afr.net
faq@afa.net
License: Oxford, Lafayette County, MS held by American Family Association.
Group Owner: American Family Radio
Nat'l Network: USA
Format: Religious
Tim Wildmon, President
Donald Wildmon, Founder
Buddy Smith, Sr VP
Ed Vitagliano, Exec VP
Randy Sharp, Director Of Special Projects
Meeke Addison, Director Of Communications
Abraham Hamilton III, General Counsel

***WMAV-FM**
12-01-1983; 90.3 MHz FM; *Hrs Open:* 24; 100 kw vert; 1240 ft.; N34 17 28 W89 42 21
3825 Ridgewood Road, Jackson, MS 39211 US
(601) 432-6565; *Fax:* (601) 432-6806
License: Oxford, Lafayette County, MS held by Mississippi Authority for Educational Television.
Nat'l Network: PRI; NPR; *Wire Services:* AP
Arbitron Metro Market: Oxford, MS *TV Affiliate:* WMAV-TV; *Format:* News; *Hrs. of News Programming:* news progmg 100 hrs wkly; *No. News Employees:* 7; *Target Audience:* General.
Jason Klein, Operations Dir
Jay Woods, General Manager

WOXD
10-01-1988; 95.5 MHz FM; *Hrs Open:* 24; 6 kw; 328 ft.; N34 18 10 W89 31 25
302 Highway 7, South, Oxford, MS 38655 US
(662) 533-4487,(662) 234-9631; *Fax:* (662) 236-5390
www.bullseye955.com
production@bullseye955.com
License: Oxford, Lafayette County, MS held by Taylor Communications.
Nat'l Reps: Rgnl Reps
Format: Contemporary Hits/Top 40, Adult Contemp *Special Programming:* Gospel 12 hrs wkly; *Target Audience:* 25-54.; *Adv. Rates:* 14; 14; 14; 14
Jason Plunk, President
Ron Cox, General Manager

WQLJ
12-31-1984; 93.7 MHz FM; *Hrs Open:* 24; 13 kw; 456 ft.; N34 20 5 W89 43 29
P.O. Box 1077, Oxford, MS 38655 US
(662) 234-5107
theq105.com
rmize@telesouth.com
License: Oxford, Lafayette County, MS held by TeleSouth Communications Inc.
Group Owner: TeleSouth Communications Inc.; acq 11-30-99; $1.4 million)
Regional Network: Miss. News Net.
Format: Adult Contemp *Special Programming:* Contemp Christian 9 hrs wkly; *Hrs. of News Programming:* news progmg one hrs wkly; *No. News Employees:* 1; *Target Audience:* 18-45.; *Adv. Rates:* 19; 19; 19; 10

WWMS
01-01-1969; 97.5 MHz FM; 100 kw; 981 ft.; N34 10 5 W89 9 23
Mailing Address: P.O. Box 2639, Gulfport, MS 39505 US
Second Address: 2214 S. Gloster St., Tupelo, MS 38801
(662) 842-7658; *Fax:* (662) 842-0197
www.miss98.net
License: Oxford, Lafayette County, MS held by San-Dow Broadcasting Inc.
Arbitron Metro Market: Tupelo, MS; *Format:* Country *Special Programming:* Farm 2 hrs wkly; *Target Audience:* General.
Brenda Bebout, General Manager
Scott Bebout, Promotions Manager

Pascagoula

WKNN-FM
12-01-1964; 99.1 MHz FM; *Hrs Open:* 24; 99 kw horiz, 97.3 kw vert; 984 ft.; N30 29 9 W88 42 53
286 DeBuys Road, Biloxi, MS 39531 US
(228) 388-2323; *Fax:* (228) 388-2362
www.k99fm.com
License: Pascagoula, Jackson County, MS held by CC Licenses LLC.
Group Owner: iHeartMedia; (acq 2-2-2004; grpsl).
Nat'l Reps: Clear Channel; *Wire Services:* AP
Arbitron Metro Market: Biloxi-Gulfport-Pascagoula, MS; *Format:* Country; *Hrs. of News Programming:* news progmg 6 hrs wkly; *No. News Employees:* 1; *Target Audience:* 25-54.
James Wynne, Advertising
Bill Black, Programming Director
Stance Bingham, Music Director
Kristan Saucier, Digital Content Director

***WPAS**
03-25-2004; 89.1 MHz FM; 60 kw; 574 ft.; N30 33 3 W88 27 6
P.O. Box 3206, Tupelo, MS 33880 US
(662) 844-8888; *Fax:* (662) 842-6791
www.afr.net
faq@afa.net
License: Pascagoula, Jackson County, MS held by American Family Association.
Group Owner: American Family Radio
Nat'l Network: USA
Arbitron Metro Market: Pascagoula, MS; *Format:* Christian
Tim Wildmon, President
Donald Wildmon, Founder
Buddy Smith, Sr VP
Ed Vitagliano, Exec VP
Randy Sharp, Director Of Special Projects
Meeke Addison, Director Of Communications
Abraham Hamilton III, General Counsel

WQBB
01-01-1976; 105.9 MHz FM; 25 kw; 312 ft.; N30 24 19 W88 47 26
9471 Three Rivers Rd., Suite A, Gulfport, MS 39503 US
(228) 388-2001; *Fax:* (228) 896-9114
www.bob1059.com
License: Pascagoula, Jackson County, MS held by Alpha Media Licensee LLC
Group Owner: Alpha Media LLC
Arbitron Metro Market: Biloxi-Gulfport-Pascagoula, MS; *Format:* Contemporary Hits/Top 40
Kenny Vest, Operations Manager
Ricky Mitchell, General Manager
Jesse Alvarez, Sales Manager
Wayne Watkins, Programming Director
Mindy Patton, Promotions/New Media Director
Michelle Shortridge, Business Manager

Pascagoula-Moss Point

WPMO
09-01-1951; 1580 kHz AM; *Hrs Open:* 24; 5 kw-D, 51 w-N, DA-2; N30 23 01 W88 32 07
5115 Telephone Rd., Pascagoula, MS 39567
(228) 762-5683; *Fax:* (228) 762-1222
License: Pascagoula-Moss Point, Jackson County, MS held by Flagship Radio Group Inc.
Arbitron Metro Market: Biloxi-Gulfport-Pascagoula, MS
Henry Hoot, General Manager

Pearl

WJNT
10-28-1980; 1180 kHz AM; *Hrs Open:* 24; 10 kw-C, DAN; 50 kw-D, DAN; 0.5 kw-N, DA; N32 17 43 W90 6 54
P.O. Box 9446, Jackson, MS 39286-9446 US
(601) 957-1300; *Fax:* (601) 956-0516
www.wjnt.com
License: Pearl, Rankin County, MS held by Alpha Media Licensee LLC
Group Owner: Alpha Media LLC; (acq 9-24-2013; grpsl)
Nat'l Network: Premiere Radio Networks; ABC; Talk Radio Network; Westwood One; *Nat'l Reps:* D & R Radio
Arbitron Metro Market: Jackson, MS; *Format:* News, News/Talk, 86; *Hrs. of News Programming:* news progmg 28 hrs wkly; *Target Audience:* 35 plus; high income, college educated, home owners
Kevin Webb, Senior Vice President and Market Manager
Stan Branson, Program Director and Operations Manager

*WJAI
11-07-1994; 93.9 MHz FM; *Hrs Open:* 24; 25 kw; 328 ft; N32 14 06 W89 53 46 *Rebroadcasts:* Rebroadcasts KLRD(FM) Yucaipa, CA 100%
5700 West Oaks Boulevard, Rocklin, CA 95765 US
(916) 251-1600; *Fax:* (916) 251-1650
www.air1.com
License: Pearl, Rankin County, MS held by Educational Media Foundation
Group Owner: EMF Broadcasting
Nat'l Network: Air 1
Population Served: 250,000; *Arbitron Metro Market:* Jackson, MS; *Target Audience:* 35 plus.
Mike Novak, President

Petal

WZLD
01-01-1986; 106.3 MHz FM; *Hrs Open:* 24; 10.5 kw; 1063 ft.; N31 31 37 W89 8 7
6555 Highway 98 West, Suite 8, Hattiesburg, MS 39402 US
(601) 296-9800; *Fax:* (601) 296-9838
www.wild1063.com
contact@wild1063.com
License: Petal, Forrest County, MS held by CC Licenses LLC.
Group Owner: iHeartMedia; (acq 12-19-2000; grpsl)
Nat'l Network: CNN Radio; *Regional Network:* Miss. News Net.
Arbitron Metro Market: Hattiesburg, MI; *Format:* Urban Contemporary *Special Programming:* Sports 3 hrs wkly; *Hrs. of News Programming:* News progmg 4 hrs wkly; *Target Audience:* 25-54; upscale, educated &professional
Mike Comfort, Market President
Jackson Walker, Senior Vice President of Programming
Devin Cole, Programming Director

Philadelphia

WHOC
07-31-1948; 1490 kHz AM; 1 kw-U, ND1; N32 45 52 W89 7 48
1016 West Beacon Street, Philadelphia, MS 39350 US
(601) 656-1490; *Fax:* (601) 656-1491
wwslfm@yahoo.com
License: Philadelphia, MS held by WHOC Inc.
Regional Network: Miss. News Net.
Format: Talk, Adult Contemp *Special Programming:* Farm 2 hrs wkly; *Target Audience:* General.
Joe Vines, Operations Dir
Leah Jarrell, General Manager
Rex Smith, Chief Engineer

WWSL
01-01-1981; 102.3 MHz FM; 4.9 kw; 364 ft.; N32 43 35 W89 5 56
Mailing Address: P.O. Box 26, Philadelphia, MS 39350 US
Second Address: 1016 W. Beacon St., Philadelphia, MS 39350
(601) 656-7102; *Fax:* (601) 656-1491
License: Philadelphia, Neshoba County, MS held by H & GC Inc.
Nat'l Network: Westwood One; *Regional Network:* Miss. News Net.
Arbitron Metro Market: Philadelphia, MS; *Format:* Adult Contemp, Classical
Nick Ferrara, General Manager

Picayune

WZRH
01-01-1991; 106.1 MHz FM; *Hrs Open:* 24; 28 kw; 659 ft.; N30 31 17 W90 01 12
201 St. Charles Avenue, Suite 201, New Orleans, LA 70170 US
(504) 581-7002
License: Picayune, MS held by Radio License Holding CBC, LLC
Group Owner: Cumulus Media Inc.; (acq 1-3-2006; $7 million)
Arbitron Metro Market: New Orleans, LA; *Format:* Alternative; *Hrs. of News Programming:* news progmg 2 hrs wkly; *No. News Employees:* 2; *Target Audience:* 18-45; young professionals; *Adv. Rates:* 45; 35; 40; 25.
Greg Benefeld, General Manager
Ray Mariner, Programming Director
Gus Kattengell, Sports Director

WRJW
10-01-1949; 1320 kHz AM; *Hrs Open:* 5a-10p; 5 kw-D, 75 kw-N; N30 31 06 W89 38 41
Mailing Address: Box 907, Picayune, MS 39466
Second Address: 2438 Hwy. 43 S., Picayune, MS 39466
(601) 798-4835; *Fax:* (601) 798-9755
www.wrjwradio.com
License: Picayune, Pearl River County, MS held by Pearl River Communications Inc.
Nat'l Network: ABC; *Regional Network:* Miss. News Net.
Population Served: 48,000 *Special Programming:* Black 8 hrs, farm 6 hrs, relg 16 hrs, sports 4 hrs; *Hrs. of News Programming:* news progmg 10 hrs wkly; *No. News Employees:* 2; *Target Audience:* 18-54; contempcountry listeners
Denise Wilson, Operations Dir
Delores Wood, General Manager
Roy Bunales, Programming Director
Dusty Dearman, News Director
Phil Moss, Music Director

Pickens

WRKS
01-01-1980; 105.9 MHz FM; 23 kw; 735 ft.; N32 38 53 W89 59 20
731 S. Pear Orchard Rd., Suite 27, Ridgeland, MS 39157 US
(601) 957-1300; *Fax:* (601) 956-0516
www.thezone1059.com
License: Pickens, Holmes County, MS held by Alpha Media Licensee LLC
Group Owner: Alpha Media LLC
Arbitron Metro Market: Jackson, MS; *Format:* Sports
Kevin Webb, Senior Vice President and Market Manager
Stan Branson, Program Director and Operations Manager

Pontotoc

WSEL
11-30-1962; 1440 kHz AM; 1 kw-D, ND1; 0.066 kw-N, ND1; N34 15 10 W88 57 36
P.O. Box 3788, Tupelo, MS 38803 US
(662) 489-0297; *Fax:* (662) 488-9735
License: Pontotoc, MS held by Ollie Collins Jr.
Arbitron Metro Market: Tupelo, MS; *Format:* Religious
Ollie Collins Jr., General Manager
Jerry Campbell, Chief Engineer

WSEL-FM
01-01-1966; 96.7 MHz FM; 3 kw horiz; 299 ft.; N34 15 10 W88 57 36
P.O. Box 3788, Tupelo, MS 38803 US
(662) 489-0297; *Fax:* (662) 488-9735
License: Pontotoc, Pontotoc County, MS
Arbitron Metro Market: Tupelo, MS; *Format:* Religious
Ollie Collins, Jr., General Manager

Poplarville

WRPM
01-01-1963; 1170 kHz AM; *Hrs Open:* 6 AM-6 PM; 1 kw-C, NDD; N30 48 55 W89 30 24
P.O. Box 2639, Poplarville, MS 39505 US
(601) 795-4900; *Fax:* (601) 795-0277
wrpm@wrpm.com
License: Poplarville, MS held by Dowdy & Dowdy Partnership

Thomas Vaughn, General Manager

Port Gibson

*WATU
01-01-1999; 89.3 MHz FM; 24.5 kw; 384 ft.; N32 7 56 W90 45 29
P.O. Box 3206, Tupelo, MS 38803 US
(662) 844-8888; *Fax:* (662) 842-6791
www.afr.net
faq@afa.net
License: Port Gibson, Claiborne County, MS held by American Family Association.
Group Owner: American Family Radio
Nat'l Network: USA
Arbitron Metro Market: Port Gibson, MS; *Format:* Religious
Tim Wildmon, President
Donald Wildmon, Founder
Buddy Smith, Sr VP
Ed Vitagliano, Exec VP
Randy Sharp, Director Of Special Projects
Meeke Addison, Director Of Communications
Abraham Hamilton III, General Counsel

Potts Camp

WCNA
10-01-1995; 95.9 MHz FM; *Hrs Open:* 24; 14 kw; 436 ft.; N34 35 51 W89 6 12
P.O. Box 2116, Tupelo, MS 38803 US
(662) 842-7625; *Fax:* (662) 842-9568
www.max959.com
License: Potts Camp, Marshall County, MS held by Air South Radio Inc.
Group Owner: Air South Radio Inc.
Arbitron Metro Market: Tupelo, MS; *Format:* Adult Contemp, Oldies; *Hrs. of News Programming:* News progmg 14 hrs wkly
Gene Sisk, Station Manager
Ivous Sisk, News Director

Prentiss

WCJU-FM
01-01-2002; 104.9 MHz FM; 2.8 kw; Ant 436 ft; N31 31 56 W89 56 17
37 S. High School Ave., Columbia, MS 39429
(601) 736-2616; *Fax:* (601) 736-2617
www.wcjufm.com
wcju@wcjufm.com
License: Prentiss, Jefferson Davis County, MS held by Sunbelt Broadcasting Corp.
Group Owner: Sunbelt Broadcasting Corp.

Caston Countz, Operations Dir
Megan Brown, General Manager
Pam Ball, Promotions Manager
Debbie Beets, Office Manager

WJDR
06-01-1982; 98.3 MHz FM; *Hrs Open:* 24; 6 kw; 328 ft.; N31 29 37 W89 53 33
MS US
License: Prentiss, Jefferson Davis County, MS held by Sunbelt Broadcasting Corp.
Group Owner: Sunbelt Broadcasting Corp.; acq 12-1-85)
Nat'l Network: ABC; *Regional Network:* Miss. News Net.
Format: Country *Special Programming:* Black 5 hrs wkly; *Hrs. of News Programming:* News progmg 20 hrs wkly; *Target Audience:* 25-54.

Quitman

WQMS
02-02-1968; 1500 kHz AM; 1 kw-D, NDD; N32 3 51 W88 43 27
Po Drawer 70, Quitman, MS 39355 US
(601) 557-4710
info@wqmsradio.com
License: Quitman, MS held by Stephen C. Hellinger
Arbitron Metro Market: Quitman, MS; *Format:* Sports
Simcha Hellinger, General Manager

*WMSO
07-31-1981; 98.9 MHz FM; *Hrs Open:* 24; 25 kw; Ant 315 ft; N32 03 51 W88 43 27 *Rebroadcasts:* Rebroadcasts KLVR(FM) Santa Rosa, CA 100%
2351 Sunset Blvd., Suite 170-218, Rocklin, CA 39355
(916) 251-1600; *Fax:* (916) 251-1650
www.klove.com
License: Quitman, Clarke County, MS held by Educational Media Foundation.
Group Owner: EMF Broadcasting; (acq 4-29-2005; $500,000)
Nat'l Network: K-Love

Mike Novak, President
Chip Bailey, Operations Dir
David Pierce, Programming Director
Ed Lenane, News Director
Sam Wallington, Engineering Dir
Marya Morgan, News Reporter
Richard Hunt, News Reporter

Redwood

WVBG-FM
01-01-2005; 105.5 MHz FM; 1.95 kw; 430 ft.; N32 23 22 W90 48 34
P.O. Box 46, Vicksburg, MS 39181 US
(601) 883-0848
www.vicksburgv105.com
mark@vicksburgv105.com
License: Redwood, Warren County, MS held by Lendsi Radio LLC.
Arbitron Metro Market: Redwood, MS; *Format:* Oldies
Mark Jones, CEO/COO
Dailon Huskey, Operations Dir
Lina Jones, General Manager
Stephen Donovan, Engineering Dir
Karen Kirk, Traffic Manager

Richton

WXHB
01-01-1995; 96.5 MHz FM; 5.7 kw; 574 ft.; N31 28 9 W88 45 53
Box 6408, 4580 Hwy. 15 N., Laurel, MS 39441 US
(601) 649-0095; *Fax:* (601) 649-8199
www.wxhbfm.com
wxhb@wxhbfm.comÿ
License: Richton, Perry County, MS held by Blakeney Communications Inc.
Group Owner: Blakeney Communications Inc.; acq 3-27-03; $650,000).
Arbitron Metro Market: Richton, MS; *Format:* Gospel
Larry Blakeney, President/CEO
Debbie Blakeney, General Manager

Ridgeland

WIIN
12-01-1984; 780 kHz AM; *Hrs Open:* Sunrise-sunset; 5 kw-D, NDD; N32 25 36 W90 12 19
3436 Highway 45 North, Meridan, MS 39302 US
(601) 956-0102; *Fax:* (601) 978-3980
frontdesk@us963.com
License: Ridgeland, MS held by New South Radio Inc.
Group Owner: New South Communications Inc.; (acq 11-10-94; $750,000 with WLIN(FM) Gluckstadt;
Nat'l Reps: McGavren Guild
Arbitron Metro Market: Jackson, MS; *Format:* Oldies; *Target Audience:* General; Adult professionals
Gwen Rakestraw, General Manager
Bill Rakestraw, General Sales Mgr
Russ Williams, Programming Director

Ripley

WCSA
01-01-1995; 1260 kHz AM; 0.5 kw-D, NDD; N34 43 15 W88 56 40
, Ripley, MS US
(601) 837-2816
License: Ripley, MS held by Keyboard Broadcasting Communication.
Arbitron Metro Market: Memphis, TN
Michael Powell, General Manager

WSKK
06-01-1979; 102.3 MHz FM; *Hrs Open:* 24; 3.5 kw; 433 ft.; N34 42 35 W88 50 36
107 East Spring Street, P O Box 572, Ripley, MS 38663 US
(662) 837-1023; *Fax:* (662) 837-2994
classicradiofm@aol.com
License: Ripley, Tippah County, MS held by Kudzu Communications Inc.
Arbitron Metro Market: Tupelo, MS; *Format:* Contemporary Hits/Top 40, Adult Contemp *Special Programming:* Religious 1 hrs, gospel 3 hrs, bluegrass 3 hrs wkl; *Hrs. of News Programming:* News programming 1 hrs wkly *Target Audience:* 25-54 male/felmale
Scott Peters, President

Rosedale

WMJW
01-01-1993; 107.5 MHz FM; *Hrs Open:* 24; 25 kw; 328 ft.; N33 56 48 W90 50 58
, Rosedale, MS US
(662) 843-4091; *Fax:* (662) 843-9805
License: Rosedale, Bolivar County, MS held by Radio Cleveland Inc.
Group Owner: Radio Cleveland Inc.; acq 7-18-95).
Arbitron Metro Market: Cleavland, MS; *Format:* Country; *Hrs. of News Programming:* News progmg 8 hrs wkly; *Target Audience:* 25-54; adults
Clint Webster, President
Kevin Cox, Operations Dir
Vickie Lowery, News Director
Jim Thomas, Operations Manager
Jim Gregory, Public Affairs Director

Saltillo

WWMR
01-01-2008; 102.9 MHz FM; 12.5 kw; 466 ft.; N34 24 33 W88 32 24
306 Troy Street, Tupelo, MS 38804 US
(662) 680-1606; *Fax:* (662) 680-8604
www.supertalk.fm
License: Saltillo, Lee County, MS held by George S. Flinn III.
Arbitron Metro Market: Saltillo, MS; *Format:* Talk
Russ Wilson, General Manager

Sandersville

WKZW
07-07-1975; 94.3 MHz FM; 50 kw; 492 ft.; N31 25 50 W89 8 51
Box 6408, Laurel, MS 39441 US
(601) 649-0095; *Fax:* (601) 649-8199
www.kz943.com
kz943@kz943.com
License: Sandersville, Jasper County, MS held by Blakeney Communications Inc.
Group Owner: Blakeney Communications Inc.; acq 3-25-98; $553,000 for stock)
Arbitron Metro Market: Laurel-Hattiesburg, MS; *Format:* Adult Contemp; *Target Audience:* 18-60; average working people; *Adv. Rates:* 28; 26; 26; 24
Larry Blakeney, President/CEO
Debbie Blakeney, General Manager

Sardis

KBUD
01-01-2005; 102.1 MHz FM; 4 kw; 404 ft.; N34 22 33 W89 45 52
Rebroadcasts: Simulcast with WHBQ-FM Germantown, TN 100%
6080 Mount Moriah Road, Memphis, TN 38115 US
(901) 375-9324; *Fax:* (901) 375-0041
www.flinn.com
mail@flinn.com
License: Sardis, Panola County, MS held by George S. Flinn Jr.
Arbitron Metro Market: Memphis, TN; *Format:* Contemporary Hits/Top 40
Keith Parnell, General Manager
Edrick Kearney, Station Manager

Senatobia

WSAO
08-08-1962; 1140 kHz AM; *Hrs Open:* 5 AM-5 PM; 5 kw-D, NDD; N34 36 56 W89 56 9
Mailing Address: PO Box 190, Senatobia, MS 38668 US
Second Address: 15763 Hwy. 4 E., Senatobia, MS 38668
(662) 562-4445; *Fax:* (662) 562-4445
License: Senatobia, MS held by Jesse C. Ross and Earnestine A. Ross.
Regional Network: Miss. News Net.
Format: Religious; *No. News Employees:* 1; *Target Audience:* General.
Jesse Ross, General Manager

Sharon

WRTM-FM
07-16-1999; 100.5 MHz FM; *Hrs Open:* 24; 6 kw; Ant 328 ft.; N31 31 20 W90 04 36
Mailing Address: Box 9734, Jackson, MS 39286
Second Address: 855 S. Pear Orchard Dr., Suite 204, Ridgeland, MS 39157
(601) 956-1937; *Fax:* (601) 856-1937
www.smoothsoul1005.com
smoothsoul1005@bellsouth.net
License: Sharon, Madison County, MS held by Commander Communications Corp.
Arbitron Metro Market: Jackson, MS; *Target Audience:* 25-54.
Marty Hart, Operations Dir
Carl Haynes, General Manager
Carl Haynes, General Sales Mgr
Emmette Rushing, Chief Engineer

Southaven

WAVN
06-04-1990; 1240 kHz AM; *Hrs Open:* 24; 0.58 kw-U, ND1; N34 58 57 W90 0 45
1336 Brookhaven Drive, Southaven, MS 38671 US
(601) 393-8056; *Fax:* (601) 393-8066
License: Southaven, MS held by Arlington Broadcasting Co. Inc.
Regional Network: Miss. News Net.
Format: Oldies
Colleen Barill, General Manager

Starkville

***WJZB**
01-01-1999; 88.7 MHz FM; 1 kw; 243 ft.; N33 27 47 W88 49 1
P.O. Box 3206, Tupelo, MS 38803 US
(662) 844-8888; *Fax:* (662) 842-6791
www.afr.net
faq@afa.net
License: Starkville, Oktibbeha County, MS held by American Family Association.
Group Owner: American Family Radio; (acq 10-8-97)
Nat'l Network: USA
Arbitron Metro Market: Columbus-Starkville-West Point, MS; *Format:* Religious
Tim Wildmon, President
Donald Wildmon, Founder
Buddy Smith, Sr VP
Ed Vitagliano, Exec VP
Randy Sharp, Director Of Special Projects
Meeke Addison, Director Of Communications
Abraham Hamilton III, General Counsel

WMSU
09-13-1979; 92.1 MHz FM; 1.1 kw; 499 ft.; N33 25 49 W88 45 17
608 Yellowjacket Drive, Starkville, MS 39759 US
(662) 338-5424; *Fax:* (662) 338-5436
www.power92jamz.net
wmsuproduction@urbanradio.fm
License: Starkville, Oktibbeha County, MS held by Urban Radio Licenses LLC.
Group Owner: Urban Radio Licenses LLC; (acq 12-7-2000).
Arbitron Metro Market: Columbus, MS; *Format:* Urban Contemporary; *Target Audience:* 25-54.
Kevin Wagner, President
James Alexander, Operations Dir
Jeffrey Hedgeman, Marketing

***WMSV**
03-01-1994; 91.1 MHz FM; 14 kw; 456 ft.; N33 25 56 W88 45 0
P.O. Box 6210, Mississippi State, MS 39762 US
(662) 325-8034; *Fax:* (662) 325-8037
www.wmsv.msstate.edu
wmsv@msstate.edu
License: Starkville, Oktibbeha County, MS held by Mississippi State University.
Arbitron Metro Market: Columbus, MS; *Format:* Alternative
Steve Ellis, General Manager
Anthony Craven, News Director

WMXU
07-15-1968; 106.1 MHz FM; *Hrs Open:* 24; 40 kw; 502 ft.; N33 17 38 W88 39 27
601 2nd Avenue North, Columbus, MS 39701 US
(662) 327-1183; *Fax:* (662) 328-1122
License: Starkville, Oktibbeha County, MS
Group Owner: Cumulus Media Inc.
Arbitron Metro Market: Columbus, MS; *Format:* Urban Contemporary
Chris Stryker, Programming Director
Greg Benefield, Market Manager

WSSO
11-08-1948; 1230 kHz AM; 1 kw-U, ND1; N33 27 9 W88 49 15
601 2nd Avenue North, Columbus, MS 39701 US
(662) 327-1183; *Fax:* (662) 328-1122
License: Starkville, MS held by Cumulus Licensing Corp.
Group Owner: Cumulus Media Inc.; (acq 1998; grpsl)
Regional Network: Miss. News Net; *Nat'l Reps:* Keystone (unwired net) *Regional Reps:* Allied Radio Partners.
Arbitron Metro Market: Columbus-Starkville-West Point, MS; *Format:* Sports *Special Programming:* Black 12 hrs wkly
Chris Stryker, Programming Director
Greg Benefield, Market Manager

State College

WQJB
104.5 MHz FM; 12 kw; 476 ft.; N33 22 4 W88 41 39
188 South Bellevue, Suite 222, Memphis, TN 38104 US
(901) 375-9324; *Fax:* (901) 375-0041
www.flinn.com
mail@flinn.com
License: State College, Oktibbeha County, MS held by George S. Flinn Jr.
Arbitron Metro Market: Memphis, TN; *Format:* Country
Melanie Henkin-Booth, General Manager

Stonewall

WEXR
01-01-1998; 106.9 MHz FM; *Hrs Open:* 24; 2.55 kw; 508 ft; N32 10 48 W88 40 22
910 Highway 19 North, Meridian, MS 39307
(601) 693-2661; *Fax:* (601) 483-0826
wmlv@wokk.com
License: Stonewall, Clarke County, MS held by Meridian Community College
Group Owner: Meridian Community College
Arbitron Metro Market: Meridian, MS; *Target Audience:* 25-54.
Robby Atkinson, Operations Dir
Edward Bishop, Sales Manager

Strasburg

WZEC
01-01-1987; 104.9 MHz FM; *Hrs Open:* 24; 3 kw; Ant 219 ft; N39 01 22 W78 25 35 *Rebroadcasts:* Simulcast with WWRE(FM) Berryville 100%
Mailing Address: Box 3300, Winchester, VA
Second Address: 520 N. Pleasant Valley Rd., Winchester, VA 22601
(540) 667-2224; *Fax:* (540) 722-3295
www.everythingthatrocks.fm
License: Strasburg, Shenandoah County, VA held by Mid Atlantic Network Inc.
Group Owner: Mid Atlantic Network; (acq 7-8-97; $850,000 with WWRE(FM) Berryville).
Arbitron Metro Market: Winchester, VA; *Target Audience:* 18 plus.
Allen Shaw, President
Jeff Adams, Operations Dir
Kathie Flerx, General Manager
Ron Baker, Programming Director
Robert Allen, News Director

Sumrall

WFMM
01-01-1998; 97.3 MHz FM; 6 kw; 328 ft.; N31 21 18 W89 31 19
Rebroadcasts: Rebroadcasts WFMN(FM) Flora 100%.
6311 Ridgewood Rd., Jackson, MS 39211 US
(601) 957-1700
www.supertalkms.com
feedback@supertalk.fm
License: Sumrall, Lamar County, MS held by TeleSouth Communications Inc.
Group Owner: TeleSouth Communications Inc.; acq 1999; $200,000)
Format: News, News/Talk, 86

WGDQ
01-01-2005; 93.1 MHz FM; 25 kw; 302 ft.; N31 22 58 W89 23 43
1204 Gravelline Street, Hattiesburg, MS 39401 US
(601) 544-1941; *Fax:* (601) 544-1947
License: Sumrall, Lamar County, MS held by Unity Broadcasters.
Arbitron Metro Market: Hattiesburg, MS; *Format:* Oldies
Victor Floyd, General Manager

Taylorsville

WBBN
03-20-1985; 95.9 MHz FM; 100 kw; 732 ft.; N31 38 3 W89 28 35
Box 6408, 4580 Hwy. 15 N., Laurel, MS 39441 US
(601) 649-0095; *Fax:* (601) 649-8199
www.b95country.com
b95@b95country.com
License: Taylorsville, Smith County, MS held by Blakeney Communications Inc.
Group Owner: Blakeney Communications Inc.
Arbitron Metro Market: Eureka CA; *Format:* Country
Larry Blakeney, President/CEO
Debbie Blakeney, General Manager

Tchula

WGNG
01-01-2001; 106.3 MHz FM; 7.1 kw; 499 ft.; N33 18 6 W90 7 31
503 lone Street, Greenwood, MS 38930 US
(662) 453-1646; *Fax:* (662) 453-7002
wgnlbooth@bellsouth.net
License: Tchula, Holmes County, MS held by Team Broadcasting Co. Inc.
Format: Urban Contemporary
Reuben Hughes, General Manager

Tunica

WIVG
01-01-1998; 96.1 MHz FM; 4.1 kw; 807 ft.; N34 43 36 W90 9 43
6080 Mount Moriah Road, Memphis, TN 38115 US
(901) 454-9948; *Fax:* (901) 454-1027
www.q1075.com/
License: Tunica, Tunica County, MS held by Flinn Broadcasting Corp.
Arbitron Metro Market: Memphis, TN; *Format:* Contemporary Hits/Top 40
Carmen Reyes, General Manager

Tupelo

*WAFR
08-31-1991; 88.3 MHz FM; *Hrs Open:* 24; 75 kw; 492 ft.; N34 28 28 W88 43 41
P.O. Box 3206, Tupelo, MS 38803 US
(662) 844-8888; *Fax:* (662) 842-6791
www.afr.net
faq@afa.net
License: Tupelo, Lee County, MS held by American Family Association.
Group Owner: American Family Radio
Nat'l Network: American Family Radio
Arbitron Metro Market: Tupelo, MS; *Format:* Christian; *Hrs. of News Programming:* news progmg 3 hrs wkly; *No. News Employees:* 1; *Target Audience:* 30-60; conservative Christian
Tim Wildman, President
Donald Wildman, Founder
Buddy Smith, Sr VP
Ed Vitagliano, Exec VP
Randy Sharp, Director Of Special Projects
Meeke Addison, Abraham Hamilton III

*WAJS
01-01-1996; 91.7 MHz FM; 23 kw; 505 ft.; N33 55 35 W88 39 46
107 Park Gate Dr., Tupelo, MS 38801 US
(662) 844-9090
www.afr.net
License: Tupelo, Lee County, MS held by American Family Association.
Group Owner: American Family Radio
Nat'l Network: USA
Arbitron Metro Market: Tupelo, MS.; *Format:* Christian, Talk
Tim Wildmon, President
Donald Wildmon, Founder
Buddy Smith, Ed Vitagliano
Randy Sharp, Director Of Special Projects
Meeke Addison, Director Of Communications
Abraham Hamilton III, General Counsel & Public Policy Analyst

*WAQB
01-01-1997; 90.9 MHz FM; 35 kw; 427 ft.; N34 28 28 W88 43 41
P.O. Box 3206, Tupelo, MS 38803 US
(662) 844-8888; *Fax:* (662) 842-6791
www.afr.net
faq@afa.net
License: Tupelo, Lee County, MS held by American Family Association.
Group Owner: American Family Radio
Nat'l Network: USA
Arbitron Metro Market: Tupelo, MS; *Format:* Christian
Tim Wildmon, President
Donald Wildmon, Founder
Buddy Smith, Sr VP
Ed Vitagliano, Exec VP
Randy Sharp, Director Of Special Projects
Meeke Addison, Director Of Communications
Abraham Hamilton III, General Counsel

WELO
05-15-1944; 580 kHz AM; *Hrs Open:* 24
2214 South Gloster, PO Box 410, Tupelo, MS 38802 US
(662) 842-7658; *Fax:* (662) 842-0197
msradiogroup.com/
License: Tupelo, MS held by JMD Inc.
Arbitron Metro Market: Tupelo, MS; *Format:* Big Band *Special Programming:* Farm one hr wkly; *Target Audience:* 45 plus.
Dave Dunaway, Operations Dir
Brenda Bebout, General Manager
Scott Kelly, Programming Director
Cathy Williams, Public Service Director

WKMQ
08-25-1972; 1060 kHz AM; *Hrs Open:* 24
5026 Cliff Gookin Boulevard, Tupelo, MS 38801 US
(662) 842-1067; *Fax:* (662) 842-0725
rickstevens@clearchannel.com
License: Tupelo, MS held by Capstar TX L.P.
Group Owner: Urban Radio Broadcasting; (acq 12-19-2000; grpsl)
Arbitron Metro Market: Tupelo, MS; *Format:* Talk; *Target Audience:* 35-54.
Rick Stevens, Operations/Programming Director
Mark Maharrey, General Manager/Market Manager
Rebecca Yarbrough, General Sales Mgr
Allison Fuller, Traffic Manager
Jerry Mathis, Chief Engineer

WTUP
10-01-1953; 1490 kHz AM; *Hrs Open:* 24
5026 Cliff Gookin Boulevard, Tupelo, MS 38801 US
(662) 842-1067; *Fax:* (662) 842-0725
urbanradio.fm
License: Tupelo, MS held by Capstar TX L.P.
Group Owner: Urban Radio Broadcasting; (acq 12-19-2000; grpsl)
Regional Network: Miss. News Net; *Nat'l Reps:* Interep
Arbitron Metro Market: Tupelo, MS; *Format:* Sports; *Hrs. of News Programming:* news progmg 12 hrs wkly; *No. News Employees:* 1; *Target Audience:* 25-54; men
Rick Stevens, Operations/Programming Director
Rebecca Yarbrough, General Sales Mgr
Melanie Knight, Promotions Director
Allison Fuller, Traffic Manager
Jerry Mathis, Chief Engineer
Mark Maharrey, General Manager/Market Manager

WZLQ
09-01-1968; 98.5 MHz FM; 100 kw; 981 ft.; N34 10 5 W89 9 23
2214 S. Gloster, PO Box 410, Tupelo, MS 38802 US
(662) 842-7658; *Fax:* (662) 842-0197
www.z985.net
License: Tupelo, Lee County, MS
Arbitron Metro Market: Tupelo, MS; *Format:* Adult Contemp; *Target Audience:* 25-54.
Steve Drumm, Programming Director

Tylertown

WTYL
02-08-1969; 1290 kHz AM; *Hrs Open:* 11; 1 kw-D, NDD; N31 7 50 W90 8 13
930 Union Road, Tylertown, MS 39667 US
(601) 876-2105; *Fax:* (601) 876-9551
License: Tylertown, MS held by Tylertown Broadcasting Co.
Arbitron Metro Market: Tylertown, MS; *Format:* Country *Special Programming:* Farm 6 hrs wkly
Carolyn Dillon, President
Gail Ratcliff, Programming Director

WTYL-FM
04-09-1970; 97.7 MHz FM; *Hrs Open:* 24; 3 kw; 144 ft.; N31 7 50 W90 8 13
930 Union Road, Tylertown, MS 39667 US
(601) 876-2105; *Fax:* (601) 876-9551
License: Tylertown, Walthall County, MS
Arbitron Metro Market: Tylertown, MS
Gail Ratcliff, News Director

WFCG
01-01-2005; 107.3 MHz FM; 3.2 kw; Ant 457 ft; N31 04 39 W90 04 46
PO Box 30, Magnolia, MS 39652 US
(601) 783-6600
License: Tylertown, Walthall County, MS held by Charles W. Dowdy, Debtor-In-Possession
Group Owner: Charles W. Dowdy, Debtor-In-Possession
Format: Gospel
Charles Wayne Dowdy, President

Union

WZKS
10-01-1995; 104.1 MHz FM; 19 kw; 535 ft.; N32 29 53 W88 53 20
3436 Highway 45 N, Meridian, MS 39301 US

RADIO - U.S.

(601) 693-2661
www.1041kissfm.com
License: Union, Walthall County, MS
Group Owner: Mississippi Broadcasters LLC; (acq 3-16-2001; grpsl).
Arbitron Metro Market: Union, MS; *Format:* Urban Contemporary
Scott Stevens, Operations/Programming Director
Georgia Edwards, General Manager
Diane Horton, Sales Manager
Dee Williams, Traffic Director
Sam Weaver, Program Director

University

WUMS
04-10-1989; 92.1 MHz FM; *Hrs Open:* 24; 2.9 kw; 476 ft.; N34 24 12 W89 24 13
Farley Hall, Room 231, University, MS 38677 US
(662) 915-5503; *Fax:* (662) 915-5703
myrebelradio.com/
manager@myrebelradio.com
License: University, Lafayette County, MS held by Student Media Center of the University of Mississippi.
Nat'l Network: Premiere Radio Networks; CNN Radio; *Wire Services:* AP
Arbitron Metro Market: Oxford, MS; *Format:* Adult Contemp, Alternative *Special Programming:* International 2 hrs, women one hr, the 80s 2 hrs wkly; *Hrs. of News Programming:* News progmg 2 hrs wkly; *Target Audience:* 18-24.
Jason Caviness, General Manager
Stephen Goforth, Programming Director

Utica

WJXN-FM
08-28-1990; 100.9 MHz FM; *Hrs Open:* 24; 39 kw; 551 ft.; N32 3 13 W90 20 23
US
(800) 434-8400; *Fax:* (800) 372-0888
www.1009thelegend.com
License: Utica, Hinds County, MS held by Flinn Broadcasting Corp.
Nat'l Network: USA; *Wire Services:* NWS (National Weather Service)
Arbitron Metro Market: Jackson, MS; *Format:* Christian; *Target Audience:* 25 plus.
George Flinn, President
Karen Porter, Station Manager
Steve Poston, Programming Director

Vicksburg

WBBV
08-21-1989; 101.3 MHz FM; 13 kw; 394 ft.; N32 20 42 W90 52 55
1601 E North Frontage Rd, Vicksburg, MS 39180 US
(416) 213-1035; *Fax:* (416) 233-8617
delo@bayou.com
License: Vicksburg, Warren County, MS held by Debut Broadcasting Mississippi Inc.
Group Owner: Debut Broadcasting Corp. Inc.; (acq 8-27-2008; $900,000)
Arbitron Metro Market: San Angelo TX; *Format:* Contemporary Hits/Top 40; *Adv. Rates:* 20; 17; 17; 14
Al Erickson, President
Ray Lawson, Station Manager
Deloris Evans, Sales

WJKK
03-19-1966; 98.7 MHz FM; *Hrs Open:* 24; 52 kw; 1284 ft.; N32 11 29 W90 24 22
265 High Point Drive, Ridgeland, MS 39157 US
(601) 956-0102; *Fax:* (601) 978-3980
www.mix987.com/
frontdesk@us963.com
License: Vicksburg, Warren County, MS held by New South Radio Inc.
Group Owner: New South Communications Inc.; (acq 1-89; $1.1 million;
Arbitron Metro Market: Jackson, MS; *Format:* Adult Contemp; *Hrs. of News Programming:* news progmg one hr wkly; *No. News Employees:* 1; *Target Audience:* 18-49; upper income & educ
Gwen Rakestraw, General Manager
Bill Rakestraw, General Sales Mgr
John Anthony, Programming Director

WQBC
01-01-1931; 1420 kHz AM; *Hrs Open:* 24; 1 kw-D, ND1; 0.5 kw-N, ND1; N32 19 56 W90 51 0
Mailing Address: P.O.Box 8082, Vicksburg, MS 39181 US
Second Address: Box 820483, Vicksburg, MS 39182
(601) 636-1108; *Fax:* (601) 631-0087
License: Vicksburg, MS held by Grace Media International LLC
Nat'l Network: ESPN Radio
Format: Sports, Talk
Mike Corley, President
Jerry Rushins, General Manager

WVBG
01-01-1948; 1490 kHz AM; *Hrs Open:* 24
801 Clay Street, Vicksburg, MS 39183 US
(601) 883-0848
www.vicksburgv105.com/index.html
mark@vicksburgv105.com
License: Vicksburg, MS held by Commander Communications Corp.
Format: Contemporary Hits/Top 40, Adult Contemp; *Hrs. of News Programming:* 168 hrs. News progmg wkly; *Target Audience:* 25 plus.
Erin Buckner, Account Executive
Mark Jones, General Manager
Stephen Donovan, Engineering Dir

WSTZ-FM
06-01-1968; 106.7 MHz FM; 85 kw; 1886 ft.; N32 12 49 W90 22 56
1375 Beasley Road, Jackson, MS 39206 US
(601) 982-1062; *Fax:* (601) 362-1905
www.z106.com
License: Vicksburg, Warren County, MS held by Capstar TX LLC
Group Owner: iHeartMedia; (acq 8-30-00; grpsl).
Nat'l Reps: D & R Radio
Arbitron Metro Market: Jackson, MS; *Format:* Classic Rock; *Target Audience:* 25-54.
Todd Berry, Operations Manager
Kenny Windham, General Manager
Doug Jones, Director of Sales
Mike Bridges, Programming Director
Jan Michaels, Marketing Director
Rick Adams, Public Service Director

Walnut

WLRC
06-21-1982; 850 kHz AM; 0.94 kw-D, NDD; N34 56 46 W88 52 44
Mailing Address: 190 Luna Street, P.O. Box 142, Walnut, MS 38683 US
Second Address: 7760 Hwy. 72 E., Walnut, MS 38683
(662) 223-4071; *Fax:* (662) 223-4072
www.wlrcradio.com
License: Walnut, MS held by B.R. & Martha S. Clayton.
Regional Network: Miss. News Net.
Format: Christian; *Hrs. of News Programming:* News progmg 14 hrs wkly
Don Davis, President
Mike Weaver, Operations/Programming Director
Vanessa Wetterling, General Manager

Washington

WWUU
103.9 MHz FM; 450 watts; 175 meters; N31 30 16 W91 21 06
740 Highway 49 North, Suite R, Flora, MS
(601) 201-2789; *Fax:* (601) 427-0088
License: Washington, Adams County, MS held by SSR Communications Inc

Brad Hunstable, President

Water Valley

WTNM
08-01-1996; 105.5 MHz FM; *Hrs Open:* 24; 4.7 kw; 371 ft.; N34 12 45 W89 44 49
6311 Ridgewood Rd., Jackson, MS 39211 US
(601) 957-1700
www.supertalk.fm
feedback@supertalk.fm
License: Water Valley, Yalobusha County, MS held by TeleSouth Communications Inc.
Group Owner: TeleSouth Communications Inc.; acq 3-17-00).
Regional Network: Miss. News Net.
Format: Talk *Special Programming:* Christian, contemp 4 hrs wkly; *Hrs. of News Programming:* news progmg 3 hrs wkly; *No. News Employees:* 1; *Target Audience:* 25 plus.; *Adv. Rates:* 10; 10; 10; 5

Waynesboro

WABO
09-11-1954; 990 kHz AM; 1 kw-D, ND2; 0.1 kw-N, ND2; N31 40 48 W88 40 34
Mailing Address: P. O. Box 507, Waynesboro, MS 39367 US
Second Address: 6746 Hwy. 184 W., Waynesboro, MS 39367
(601) 735-4331; *Fax:* (601) 735-4332
wabo@c-gate.net
License: Waynesboro, MS held by Martin Broadcasting Inc.
Arbitron Metro Market: Albuquerque NM; *Format:* Ethnic
Shushma Datt, CEO
Sudhir Datta, General Manager

WABO-FM
06-13-1973; 105.5 MHz FM; 6 kw; 144 ft.; N31 40 40 W88 40 13
Mailing Address: P. O. Box 507, Waynesboro, MS 39367 US
Second Address: 6746 Hwy. 184 W., Waynesboro, MS 39367
(601) 735-4331; *Fax:* (601) 735-4332
License: Waynesboro, Wayne County, MS
Arbitron Metro Market: Belcourt ND; *Format:* Alternative, Christian
Mike Novak, President

Winona

WONA
10-25-1958; 1570 kHz AM; 1 kw-D, ND1; 0.025 kw-N, ND1; N33 27 52 W89 44 11
P. O. Box 746, Winona, MS 38967 US
(601) 283-1570; *Fax:* (601) 283-1571
hawg95@cablesouthmedia.net
License: Winona, MS held by Southern Electronics Co.
TV Affiliate: Country
Operations Manager

WONA-FM
01-04-1976; 95.1 MHz FM; 10 kw; 515 ft.; N33 34 56 W89 44 52
P. O. Box 746, Winona, MS 38967 US
(662) 283-1570; *Fax:* (662) 283-1520
http://www.hawg95.com/
License: Winona, Montgomery County, MS held by Southern Electronics Co.
TV Affiliate: Country
Scott Kent, General Manager

Yazoo City

***WYAZ**
01-01-2005; 89.5 MHz FM; 85 kw; 531 ft.; N32 48 4 W89 56 32
P.O. Box 3206, Tupelo, MS 38803 US
(662) 844-8888; *Fax:* (662) 842-6791
www.afr.net
faq@afa.net
License: Yazoo City, Yazoo County, MS held by American Family Association.
Group Owner: American Family Radio; (acq 5-13-2004).
Arbitron Metro Market: Yazoo City, MS; *Format:* Christian
Tim Wildmon, President
Donald Wildmon, Founder
Buddy Smith, Sr VP
Ed Vitagliano, Executive VP
Randy Sharp, Director Of Special Projects
Meeke Addison, Director Of Communications
Abraham Hamilton III, General Counsel

Missouri

Adrian

***KYLF**
05-11-2012; 88.9 MHz FM; 30 kw; 452 ft.; N38 12 3.7 W94 16 11.6 *Rebroadcasts:* Rebroadcasts KSIV-FM St. Louis, MO.
10550 Barkley St., Suite 100, Overland Park, KS 66212 US
(913) 642-7770
www.bottradionetwork.com
comments@bottradionetwork.com
License: Adrian, Bates County, MO held by Community Broadcasting Inc.
Group Owner: Bott Radio Network
Arbitron Metro Market: Adrian, MO; *Format:* Christian, Talk
Richard Bott Sr., President & CEO
Eben Fowler, Operations Dir
Monna Stafford, Regional Manager
Pat Rulon, Director of National Sales
Candy Green, Program Services Manager
Rachel Launius, Marketing Manager
Jason Potocnik, Directorof Traffic Operations

Albany

***KGTR**
89.9 MHz FM; kw
US
(580) 653-2777
License: Albany, Gentry County, MO held by Ron Elmore Ministries Inc.

Arbitron Metro Market: Larned, KS
Ron Elmore, President

Arcadia

KTNX
01-01-2006; 103.9 MHz FM; 0.45 kw; 932 ft.; N37 34 23 W90 41 35
900 East Karsch Boulevard, Farmington, MO 63640 US
(573) 701-9590; *Fax:* (573) 701-9696
License: Arcadia, Iron County, MO held by Southern Star Broadcasting of Missouri LLC.
Group Owner: Southern Star Broadcasting of Missouri LLC; (acq 5-8-2008; grpsl)
Arbitron Metro Market: Arcadia, MO; *Format:* Contemporary Hits/Top 40
Chip Miller, President
Joel Jordan, Operations Dir

Arnold

*KGNA-FM
03-26-1987; 89.9 MHz FM; *Hrs Open:* 24; 0.15 kw horiz, 0.084 kw vert; 131 ft.; N38 26 14 W90 23 24 *Rebroadcasts:* Rebroadcasts KGNV(FM) Washington 100%
P.O. Box 187, Washington, MO 63090 US
(636) 239-0400; *Fax:* (636) 239-4448
www.goodnewsvoice.org
info@goodnewsvoice.org
License: Arnold, Jefferson County, MO held by Missouri River Christian Broadcasting Inc.
Group Owner: Missouri River Christian Broadcasting Inc.; (acq 10-5-99).
Nat'l Network: Moody; Salem Radio Network
Arbitron Metro Market: Arnold, MO; *Format:* Gospel, News, 62, Religious, Talk; *Hrs. of News Programming:* News progmg 14 hrs wkly; *Target Audience:* 20-70:; inquisitive, conservative, liberal, philosophical; *Adv. Rates:* 8; 8; 8; 8
James C. Goggan, President
James Goggan, General Manager
Marilyn Goggan, Programming Director

Asbury

KWXD
10-01-1993; 103.5 MHz FM; 16 kw; 413 ft.; N37 23 44 W94 40 42
412 N. Locust St., Pittsburg, KS 66762 US
(620) 232-5993
www.1035x.net
License: Asbury, Jasper County, MO held by Southeast Kansas Broadcasting Co. Inc.
Group Owner: MyTown Media, Inc.
Arbitron Metro Market: Pittsburg, KS; *Format:* Rock/AOR; *Adv. Rates:* 100; 80; 80; 80
Mike Snow, Programming Director

Ash Grove

KSGF-FM
03-01-1994; 104.1 MHz FM; 21.5 kw; 354 ft.; N37 15 22 W93 41 14
US
(417) 447-5743
www.ksgf.com
nreed@jrn.com
License: Ash Grove, Greene County, MO held by Journal Broadcast Corp.
Group Owner: Journal Communications Inc.; (acq 11-26-2003; $5 million with KZRQ-FM Mount Vernon).
Arbitron Metro Market: Ash Grove, MO; *Format:* News, Talk
Nick Reed, Programming Director

Ashland

KOQL
10-01-1993; 106.1 MHz FM; *Hrs Open:* 24; 69 kw; 958 ft.; N38 45 1 W92 33 31
503 Old Hwy. 63 North, Columbia, MO 65201 US
(573) 449-4141; *Fax:* (573) 449-7770
www.q1061.com
License: Ashland, Boone County, MO held by Cumulus Licensing LLC.
Group Owner: Cumulus Media Inc.; (acq 4-26-2004; grpsl).
Nat'l Reps: Katz Radio
Arbitron Metro Market: Columbia, MO; *Format:* Contemporary Hits/Top 40
Kevin Joyce, Vice President/General Manager
D. Larimer, Programming Director
Nick Snyder, Promotions Director

Aurora

KSWF
02-19-1968; 100.5 MHz FM; 33 kw; 600 ft.; N37 5 39 W93 31 5
1856 S. Glenstone, Springfield, MO 65804 US
(417) 890-5555
www.1005thewolf.com
License: Aurora, Lawrence County, MO held by Clear Channel Broadcasting Licenses Inc.
Group Owner: iHeartMedia; (acq 10-10-2000; grpsl).
Arbitron Metro Market: Springfield, MO; *Format:* Country *Special Programming:* discover and uncover 2 hrs wkly; *Target Audience:* 18-54; general
Matt Saunders, Market President

KSWM
10-19-1961; 940 kHz AM; *Hrs Open:* 24; 1 kw-D, ND2; 0.025 kw-N, NDD; N36 59 39 W93 42 58
126 South Jefferson Avenue, Aurora, MD 65605 US
(417) 678-0416; *Fax:* (417) 678-4111
kswm@radiotalon.com
License: Aurora, MO held by Falcon Broadcasting Inc.
Nat'l Network: CNN Radio; USA; *Regional Network:* Missourinet
Arbitron Metro Market: Aurora, MO; *Format:* News, News/Talk, 86; *Hrs. of News Programming:* news progmg 168 hrs wkly; *No. News Employees:* 2; *Target Audience:* General.
DeWayne Gandy, President
Bill Lewis, Operations Manager
Lance Matlock, General Manager/General Sales Manager
Dan Kesterson, Programming Director

Ava

KKOZ
01-01-1968; 1430 kHz AM; 0.5 kw-D, ND1; 0.02 kw-N, ND1; N36 55 48 W92 39 19
P.O. Box 386, Ava, MO 65608 US
(417) 683-4191
www.kkoz.com
news@kkoz.com
License: Ava, MO held by Corum Industries Inc.
Arbitron Metro Market: Springfield, MO
Art Corum, Operations Dir
Joe Corum, General Manager
Chantelle Emmerson, General Sales Mgr
Heather Lee, Programming Director
Rob Strand, News Director
Jeanette Gooden, Office Manager
Vickie Corum, Bids for Bargains Mgr
TimLandsdown, Sports

KKOZ-FM
01-01-1990; 92.1 MHz FM; *Hrs Open:* 6 AM-10 PM; 4.5 kw; 381 ft.; N36 55 48 W92 39 19
P. O. Box 386, Ava, MO 65608 US
(417) 683-4191
www.kkoz.com
news@kkoz.com
License: Ava, Douglas County, MO held by Corum Industries Inc.
Regional Network: Missourinet
Arbitron Metro Market: Springfield, MO; *Format:* News, News/Talk, 86; *Hrs. of News Programming:* News progmg 15 hrs wkly; *Target Audience:* 45 plus; farm oriented
Art Corum, Operations Dir
Joe Corum, General Manager
Chantelle Emmerson, General Sales Mgr
Vickie Corum, News Director
Jeanette Gooden, Office Manager
Vickie Corum, Bids for Bargains Mgr
Tim Landsdown, Sports

Ballwin

*KGNX
02-01-1978; 89.7 MHz FM; 120 w; Ant 171 ft; N38 37 23 W90 32 01
P.O. Box 187, Washington, MO 63090
(636) 239-0400
ymcastlouis.org
License: Ballwin, St. Louis County, MO held by YMCA of Greater St. Louis-W. County Branch.
Arbitron Metro Market: St. Louis, MO
Kent Frandsen, President
Jay Eubanks, General Manager
Lori Gill, News Director
Paul Anderson, Chief Engineer

Bethany

KAAN
12-03-1983; 870 kHz AM; *Hrs Open:* Sunrise-sunset; 0.93 kw-D, NDD; N40 15 23 W94 9 23
P.O. Box 447, Bethany, MO 64424
(660) 425-6380; *Fax:* (660) 425-8148
www.northwestmoinfo.com
stuartj@regionalradio.com
License: Bethany, MO held by Cameron/Bethany License Co. LLC.
Group Owner: GoodRadio.TV; (acq 8-8-2007; grpsl)
Regional Network: Missourinet
Arbitron Metro Market: Bethany, MO; *Format:* Country, News *Special Programming:* Farm 10 hrs, relg one hr wkly; *Hrs. of News Programming:* news progmg 10 hrs wkly; *No. News Employees:* 3; *Target Audience:* 25plus.; *Adv. Rates:* 25; 21; 19; 18
Connie Querry, Operations Dir
Doug Schmitz, General Manager
Mike Mattson, Station Manager
Denise Fritzel, General Sales Mgr
Stuart Johnson, Programming Director
Stuart Johnson, News Director
Gregg Richwine, Engineering Dir

KAAN-FM
10-27-1978; 95.5 MHz FM; *Hrs Open:* 19; 50 kw; 354 ft.; N40 15 23 W94 9 23
P.O. Box 447, Bethany, MO 64424
(660) 425-6380; *Fax:* (660) 425-8148
www.northwestmoinfo.com
stuartj@regionalradio.com
License: Bethany, Harrison County, MO held by Cameron/Bethany License Co. LLC
Group Owner: GoodRadio.TV
Arbitron Metro Market: Bethany, MO; *No. News Employees:* 3
Doug Schmitz, General Manager

Birch Tree

KBMV-FM
01-01-1983; 107.1 MHz FM; *Hrs Open:* 24; 25 kw; 328 ft.; N36 56 3 W91 43 7
204 East Washington, Doniphan, MO 63935 US
(417) 255-0427; *Fax:* (417) 255-2907
www.threeriversdailynews.com
thepoint@centurytel.net
License: Birch Tree, Shannon County, MO held by E-Communications LLC
Group Owner: E-Communications LLC; (acq 9-8-2003;
Regional Reps: True Media; Regional Reps
Format: Adult Contemp; *No. News Employees:* 1; *Target Audience:* 18-54
Connie Feifer, General Manager

Bismarck

KHCR
01-01-2005; 99.5 MHz FM; 4.2 kw; 798 ft.; N37 38 52 W90 37 33
627 Stte Highway 47, Bonne Terre, MO 63628 US
(573) 431-9000; *Fax:* (573) 358-0010
License: Bismarck, St. Francois County, MO held by Joseph W. & Donna M. Bollinger.
Arbitron Metro Market: Bismarck, MO; *Format:* Christian, Religious
Sandi Brown, General Manager
Nick Spiniolas, Promotions Manager
Kelly Corday, News & Traffic Director
Greg Cassidy, Music Director
Kim Underwood, Social Media Director
Ryan Wiggins, Production Director
Jill Willis,Concerts/Events Manager
Jill Holt, Bookkeeper
Amy Strong, Donor Relations

Bloomfield

*KAIA
91.5 MHz FM; 49 kw vert; 417 ft.; N36 40 31 W89 46 19
P O Drawer 2118, Omaha, NE 68103 US
(888) 937-2471; *Fax:* (916) 251-1650
www.air1.com
info@air1.com
License: Bloomfield, Stoddard County, MO held by Educational Media Foundation.
Group Owner: EMF Broadcasting; (acq 3-23-2007; grpsl)
Nat'l Network: Air 1
Arbitron Metro Market: Bloomfield, MO; *Format:* Alternative, Christian
Darrell Chambliss, Chairman
Alan Mason, COO
Mike Novak, President and CEO
Ed Lenane, News Director
Sam Wallington, Engineering Dir
Dan Antonelli, Chief Business Development Officer

Eric Moser, Chief Financial Officer
BrianBurger, Vice President of Human Resources
D. Kevin Blair, Secretary and General Counsel
Larry Moody, Director
Mitch Barnhart, Director

Blue Springs

KCWJ

02-02-1984; 1030 kHz AM; *Hrs Open:* 24; 200 ft. haat
18920 East Valley View Parkway, Independence, MO 64055 US
(816) 795-6826
www.kcwj.org
info@kcwj.org
License: Blue Springs, MO held by KCWJ Inc./dba Christian Broadcasting Associates L.P.
Nat'l Network: Salem Radio Network; *Nat'l Reps:* Salem
Regional Reps: PioneerSports Sales; *Wire Services:* Metro Weather Service Inc.
Arbitron Metro Market: Kansas City, MO-KS; *Format:* Christian, Gospel *Special Programming:* local and regional sports; *Hrs. of News Programming:* News progmg 5 hrs wkly; *Target Audience:* 18-49; family orientedChristian audience; *Adv. Rates:* 60;25 60;25 60;25 60;25
Ken Ball, General Manager
Jason Friedline, General Sales Mgr
Ed Treese, Chief Engineer
Jeff Henderson, Sales Account Executive
Willie Williams, Public Relations and Sales

Bolivar

KYOO

11-01-1961; 1200 kHz AM; 1 kw-D, NDD; N37 37 16 W93 24 6
304 E. Jackson, Bolivar, MO 65613 US
(417) 326-5259(417) 326-5257; *Fax:* (417) 326-5900
www.kyooradio.com/
kyooradio@aol.com
License: Bolivar, MO held by KYOO Communications
Nat'l Network: ABC; *Wire Services:* NWS (National Weather Service)
Arbitron Metro Market: Bolivar, MO; *Format:* Country, News *Special Programming:* Farm 3 hrs, gospel 2 hrs wkly; *Hrs. of News Programming:* news progmg 12 hrs. wkly; *No. News Employees:* 1 *Target Audience:* 10-72 yrs.; *Adv. Rates:* 22.50; 9; 6
Stephen Paris, President
Ann Paris, Operations Dir

Bonne Terre

KDBB

09-01-1989; 104.3 MHz FM; *Hrs Open:* 24; 1.65 kw; 663 ft.; N37 48 1 W90 33 47
P O Box 36, Park Hills, MO 63601 US
(573) 431-1000; *Fax:* (573) 431-0850
www.b104fm.com
radio@b104fm.com
License: Bonne Terre, St. Francois County, MO held by MKS Broadcasting Inc.
Nat'l Network: Westwood One
Arbitron Metro Market: Park Hills, MO; *Hrs. of News Programming:* news progmg 20 hrs wkly; *No. News Employees:* 1; *Target Audience:* 25-55.
Ann DeBold, Business Manager
Larry D. Joseph, General Manager
Kelly Valle, General Sales Mgr
Jason Loughary, Programming Director
Erik Hanson, News Director

Boonville

KWJK

09-15-1999; 93.1 MHz FM; *Hrs Open:* 24; 7.2 kw; 413 ft.; N38 56 31 W92 34 32
1600 Radio Hill Road, Boonville, MO 65233 US
(573) 441-9310; *Fax:* (660) 882-6688
kwrt@classicnet.net
License: Boonville, Cooper County, MO held by Bittersweet Broadcasting Inc.
Arbitron Metro Market: Columbia, MO; *Format:* Adult Contemp
William Glynn Jr., President
Matt Billings, Advertising

KCLR-FM

10-01-1974; 99.3 MHz FM; *Hrs Open:* 24; 33 kw; 591 ft.; N38 46 34 W92 32 45
3215 Lemone Industrial Blvd., Columbia, MO 65201 US
(800) 449-5257
www.clear99.com
License: Boonville, Cooper County, MO held by Zimmer Radio of Mid-Missouri, Inc.
Group Owner: Zimmer Radio of Mid-Missouri, Inc.
Nat'l Reps: Christal
Arbitron Metro Market: Columbia, MO; *Format:* Country; *Hrs. of News Programming:* news progmg 3 hrs wkly; *No. News Employees:* 3; *Target Audience:* 25-54.
James Zimmer, President

KWRT

08-11-1953; 1370 kHz AM; *Hrs Open:* 24; 1 kw-D, ND1; 0.084 kw-N, ND1; N38 56 44 W92 46 14
1600 Radio Hill Rd, Boonville, MO 65233 US
(660) 882-6686; *Fax:* (660) 882-6688
www.1370kwrt.com
kwrt@classicnet.net
License: Boonville, MO held by Big Country of Missouri Inc.
Nat'l Network: Jones Radio Networks; *Regional Network:* Missourinet
Arbitron Metro Market: Boonville, MO; *Format:* Country *Special Programming:* Farm 5 hrs wkly; *Hrs. of News Programming:* news progmg 5 hrs wkly; *No. News Employees:* 1; *Target Audience:* 35 plus; general
Dick Billings, President
Pat Billings, Operations Dir
Matt Billings, General Manager
Ted Bleil, News Director
Mike Mcgowan, Chief Engineer
Sharon Korte, Sports Commentator

Bourbon

KZOC

94.1 MHz FM; 6 kw; 328 feet; N38 05 00 W91 15 00
, Bourbon, MO
(202) 251-7589
License: Bourbon, MO held by Alma Corporation

Dennis Wallace, President

Bowling Green

KPVR

08-01-1975; 94.1 MHz FM; *Hrs Open:* 24; 7.5 kw; 592 ft.; N39 15 45 W91 4 9
30 Tower Street, Moscow Mills, MO 63362 US
(314) 909-8569; *Fax:* (314) 835-9739
www.joyfmonline.org
info@joyfmonline.org
License: Bowling Green, Pike County, MO held by Four Him Enterprises L.L.C.
Format: Christian
Sandi Brown, General Manager
Greg Cassidy, Programming Director

Branson

*KLFC

07-01-1988; 88.1 MHz FM; *Hrs Open:* 24; 1.8 kw; Ant 199 ft; N36 33 06 W93 14 17
205 W. Atlantic, Branson, MO 65616 USA
(417) 334-5532
www.klfcradio.com
881fm@klfcradio.com
License: Branson, Taney County, MO held by Mountaintop Broadcasting Inc.
Nat'l Network: USA
Population Served: 50,000 *Hrs. of News Programming:* news progmg 7 hrs wkly; *No. News Employees:* 1; *Target Audience:* Adults 25-50.
Herb Smith, President
Vicky Smith, Operations Dir
Darin Ahrends, Station Manager
Krista Ahrends, Programming Director

KOMC

12-21-1956; 1220 kHz AM; *Hrs Open:* 24; 1 kw-D, 53 w-N; N36 37 12 W93 12 40 *Rebroadcasts:* Rebroadcasts KDMC-FM Kimberling City 95%
202 Courtney St., Branson, MO 65616
(417) 334-6003,(417) 334-6012; *Fax:* (417) 334-7141
License: Branson, Taney County, MO held by KOMC-KRZX LLC.
Group Owner: Earls Broadcasting Co.; (acq 11-21-86; $335,000).
Nat'l Network: CBS; *Regional Network:* Missourinet
Population Served: 42,000 *Hrs. of News Programming:* news progmg 10 hrs wkly; *No. News Employees:* 3; *Target Audience:* 40 plus.; *Adv. Rates:* 17; 13; 16; 11
Charles Earls, President
Scottie Earls, General Manager
Steve Willoughby, Station Manager
Scott McCaulley, Programming Director
Kristen Clemmens, Promotions Manager
Sally Kaucher, News Director
Greg Pyron, Chief Engineer

*KOZO

01-01-1998; 89.7 MHz FM; *Hrs Open:* 24; 0.15 kw horiz, 20 kw vert; 427 ft.; N36 33 4 W93 14 36
P.O. Box 1924, Tulsa, OK 74101 US
(918) 455-5693,(417) 339-3388; *Fax:* (417) 339-3410
www.oasisnetwork.org
mail@oasisnetwork.org
License: Branson, Taney County, MO held by Creative Educational Media Corp. Inc.
Nat'l Network: USA *Regional Reps:* Rgnl Reps
Format: Religious; *Target Audience:* General.
David Ingles, President

KRZK

03-01-1971; 106.3 MHz FM; *Hrs Open:* 24; 5.7 kw; 672 ft; N36 43 52 W93 10 03
202 Courtney St., Branson, MO 65616
(417) 334-6003,(417) 334-6012; *Fax:* (417) 334-7141
www.krzk.com
krzk@krzk.com
License: Branson, Taney County, MO
Group Owner: Earls Broadcasting Co.
Nat'l Network: ABC
Hrs. of News Programming: news progmg 7 hrs wkly; *No. News Employees:* 3; *Target Audience:* 25-54; Branson & loc tourists; *Adv. Rates:* 40; 30; 40; 20
Charles Earles, CEO
Scottie Earles, General Manager
Steve Willoughby, Station Manager
Kristen Clemmens, Programming Director
Greg Pyron, Chief Engineer

Bridgeton

KMJM-FM

11-15-2010; 100.3 mhz; 17000 w; 150 m; N38 41 07 W90 22 54
1001 Highland Plaza Drive West, Suite 200, St. Louis, MO 63110 US
(314) 333-8000
www.1003thebeat.com
License: Bridgeton, St. Louis County, MO held by Citicasters Licenses Inc.
Group Owner: iHeartMedia
Format: Urban Contemporary
Beth Davis, Regional Market President

Brookfield

KFMZ

02-14-1956; 1470 kHz AM; *Hrs Open:* 24; 0.5 kw-D, DA2; 0.02 kw-N, DA2; N39 50 26 W93 4 52 *Rebroadcasts:* Rebroadcasts KZBK-FM Brookfield
107 S. Main St., Brookfield, MO 64628 US
(660) 258-3383; *Fax:* (660) 258-7307
www.bestbroadcastgroup.com/kfmz.htm
gm@bestbroadcastgroup.com
License: Brookfield, MO held by Best Broadcasting Inc.
Group Owner: Best Broadcast Group; (acq 6-14-93; $70,000 with co-located FM;
Nat'l Network: ABC
Arbitron Metro Market: Brookfield, MO; *Format:* Adult Contemp; *Hrs. of News Programming:* News progmg 4 hrs wkly; *Target Audience:* 18-49; men & women with spendable income
Dale Palmer, General Manager

KZBK

09-01-1981; 96.9 MHz FM; *Hrs Open:* 24; 50 kw; 492 ft.; N39 54 32 W93 4 34
107 S. Main, Brookfield, MO 64628 US
(660) 258-3383; *Fax:* (660) 258-7307
www.kzbkradio.com
kzbk@shighway.com
License: Brookfield, Linn County, MO held by Best Broadcasting Inc.
Group Owner: Best Broadcast Group
Arbitron Metro Market: Brookfield, MO; *Format:* Adult Contemp
Dale Palmer, General Manager

Brookline

KQRA

05-28-2002; 102.1 MHz FM; *Hrs Open:* 24; 4.9 kW; 361 ft.; N37 12 39 W93 13 42
2453 E Elm St, Springfield, MO 65802 USA
(417) 886-5677; *Fax:* (417) 886-2155
www.q1021.fm
License: Brookline, Greene County, MO held by MW SpringMo Inc.
Group Owner: The Mid-West Family Broadcast Group
Nat'l Reps: Eastman Radio
Arbitron Metro Market: Springfield, MO; *Format:* Rock/AOR; *Target Audience:* Persons 21-49; *Adv. Rates:* 40; 45; 45; 25

Brian Tyndall, General Sales Mgr
Valerie Rogers, Programming Director

Buffalo

KBFL-FM

01-01-1965; 99.9 MHz FM; *Hrs Open:* 24; 3.1 kW; 476 ft.; N37 31 14 W93 6 14
3000 E Chestnut Expy, Springfield, MO 65802 USA
(417) 862-3751; *Fax:* (417) 869-7675
kbflam.com
License: Buffalo, Dallas County, MO held by Meyer-Baldridge Inc.
Group Owner: Meyer Communications Inc.; (acq 6-1-2000; $550,000).
Nat'l Network: NBC Radio; *Regional Network:* Missourinet
Arbitron Metro Market: Springfield, MO; *Format:* Oldies *Special Programming:* Gospel 3 hrs wkly; *Hrs. of News Programming:* news progmg 15 hrs wkly; *No. News Employees:* 1; *Target Audience:* 34-54; male-femaleadults

Butler

KMAM

05-11-1962; 1530 kHz AM; *Hrs Open:* 16; 0.5 kw-D, NDD; N38 14 56 W94 19 18
Mailing Address: 800 East Nursery Street, Butler, MO 64730 US
Second Address: none, none, none, none
(660) 679-4191; *Fax:* (660) 679-4193
License: Butler, MO held by Bates County Broadcasting Co.
Nat'l Network: ABC; *Regional Network:* Brownfield
Format: Country *Special Programming:* Farm/Abc World News/ Local News; *Hrs. of News Programming:* news progmg 15 hrs wkly; *No. News Employees:* 1; *Target Audience:* General; family; *Adv. Rates:* 16; 16; 16; 16
Melody Thornton, President

KMOE

01-15-1975; 92.1 MHz FM; *Hrs Open:* 16; 4.7 kw; 148 ft.; N38 14 56 W94 19 18
800 East Nursery Street, Butler, MO 64730 US
(660) 679-4191; *Fax:* (660) 679-4193
License: Butler, Bates County, MO

Keith Sanderson, Station Manager
Daniel Boyd, Programming Director
Delvin Kinser, News Director

Cabool

KOZX

05-01-1978; 98.1 MHz FM; 3 kw; 220 ft.; N37 7 58 W92 8 3
P.O. Box 514, Cabool, MO 65689 US
(417) 962-4380; *Fax:* (417) 962-3303
License: Cabool, Texas County, MO held by Ozark Media Inc.
Group Owner: Ozark Media Inc.; (acq 5-1-2007; $625,000 with KELE-FM Mountain Grove)
Format: Contemporary Hits/Top 40, Adult Contemp *Special Programming:* Farm 2 hrs wkly
Tracy O'Quinn, General Sales Mgr
Shawn Anthony, Programming Director
Jim Morris, News Director
Tonya Shannon, Traffic Manager

*KCVY

01-01-2003; 89.9 MHz FM; *Hrs Open:* 24; 10.5 kw; 495 ft.; N37 5 32 W92 3 10 *Rebroadcasts:* Rebroadcasts KCVO-FM Camdenton 100%.
P.O. Box 800, Camdenton, MO 65020 US
(573) 346-3200; *Fax:* (573) 346-1010
www.spiritfm.org
License: Cabool, Texas County, MO held by Lake Area Educational Broadcasting Foundation.
Nat'l Network: Salem Radio Network
Arbitron Metro Market: Camdenton, MO; *Format:* Christian; *Hrs. of News Programming:* News progmg one hr wkly; *Target Audience:* 25-45.
James McDermott, President

*KZGM

01-01-2009; 88.1 MHz FM; 12.5 kw vert; 443 ft.; N37 7 15 W92 0 9
1211 Ozark Avenue, Cabool, MO 65689 US
(417) 200-0522; *Fax:* (206) 202-1735
www.kz88.org
radio@kz88.org
License: Cabool, Texas County, MO held by Real Community Radio Network Inc.
Arbitron Metro Market: Cabool, MO; *Format:* Talk
Kazie Perkins, Operations Dir
Gene Colliflower, News Director

California

KATI

05-18-1982; 94.3 MHz FM; *Hrs Open:* 19; 50 kw; 492 ft.; N38 31 25 W92 24 25
3109 S. Ten Mile Dr., Jefferson City, MO 65109 US
(573) 893-5696
www.kat943.com
kati@zrgmail.com
License: California, Moniteau County, MO held by Zimmer Radio of Mid-Missouri Inc.
Group Owner: Zimmer Radio; (acq 11-19-99; grpsl)
Arbitron Metro Market: Jefferson City, MT; *Format:* Country
James Zimmer, President

KRLL

07-27-1984; 1420 kHz AM; *Hrs Open:* 18; 0.5 kw-D, ND1; 0.225 kw-N, ND1; N38 38 12 W92 35 0
P.O. Box 307, 100 a E Buchanan, California, MO 65018 US
(573) 796-3139; *Fax:* (573) 796-4131
krll01@embarqmail.com
License: California, MO held by Moniteau Communications Inc.
Format: Country *Special Programming:* Farm 5 hrs, gospel 3 hrs wkly; *Hrs. of News Programming:* news progmg 19 hrs wkly; *No. News Employees:* 1; *Target Audience:* 20 plus.
Jeffrey Shackleford, President

Camdenton

*KCVO-FM

09-23-1985; 91.7 MHz FM; *Hrs Open:* 24; 10 kw; 436 ft.; N38 1 13 W92 45 27
Mailing Address: P.O. Box 800, Camdenton, MO 65020 US
Second Address: 128 Possom Hollow Dr, Camdenton, MO 65020
(573) 346-3200; *Fax:* (573) 346-1010
www.spiritfm.org
License: Camdenton, Camden County, MO held by Lake Area Educational Broadcasting Foundation.
Nat'l Network: Salem Radio Network
Arbitron Metro Market: Camdenton, MO; *Format:* Christian; *Hrs. of News Programming:* News progmg one hr wkly; *Target Audience:* 25-45.
Alice McDermott, CFO
James McDermott, President
Jim McDermott, General Manager
Alice McDermott, Financial Director

Cameron

KMRN

02-01-1971; 1360 kHz AM; *Hrs Open:* 5:30 AM-7 PM; 500 w-D, 25 w-N; N39 41 05 W94 14 22
P.O. Box 643, Cameron, MO 65279
(816) 632-6661; *Fax:* (816) 632-1334
www.northwestmoinfo.com
dschmitz@regionalradio.com
License: Cameron, Clinton County, MO held by Cameron/Bethany License Co. LLC.
Group Owner: GoodRadio.TV; (acq 8-8-2007; grpsl)
Nat'l Network: Fox News Radio; *Regional Network:* Missourinet; Brownfield
Population Served: 50,000; *Arbitron Metro Market:* Kansas City, MO-KS *Special Programming:* Local News, Talk & Farm; *Hrs. of News Programming:* 5 hrs; *No. News Employees:* 9; *Target Audience:* General. *Adv.Rates:* 12; 10; 11; na
Dean Goodman, Chairman
George Pelletier Jr, CEO/COO
Doug Schmitz, General Manager
Chris Ward, Programming Director
Chris Ward, Promotions Manager
Chris Ward, News Director
Lloyd Collins, Engineering Dir
Gregg Richwine, ChiefEngineer

KKWK

04-05-1995; 100.1 MHz FM; 50 kw; 492 ft; N39 57 28 W94 06 55
P.O. Box 643, Cameron, MO 65279
(816) 632-6661; *Fax:* (816) 632-1334
www.northwestmoinfo.com
License: Cameron, Clinton County, MO
Group Owner: GoodRadio.TV
Nat'l Network: Fox News Radio; *Regional Network:* Brownfield
Population Served: 250,000 *Special Programming:* Community Affairs; *No. News Employees:* 2; *Target Audience:* 25-49.; *Adv. Rates:* 29.50; 23; 23; 14
Dean Goodman, Chairman
George Pelletier Jr, CEO/COO
Doug Schmitz, General Manager
Doug Schmitz, Station Manager
Doug Schmitz, General Sales Mgr
Chris Ward, News Director
Gregg Richwine, Engineering Dir
Lloyd Collins, ChiefEngineer
Ruth Hammontree, Traffic Manager

*WRVX

91.7 MHz FM; 20 kw; Ant 321 ft; N39 52 42 W94 05 33
3434 West Kilbourn Avenue, Milwaukee, WI 53208
(706) 965-2355; *Fax:* (706) 965-3755
License: Cameron, Clinton County, MO held by Victor Broadcasting Inc.

James Price III, President

Campbell

KFEB

10-01-1998; 107.5 MHz FM; 17.5 kw; 390 ft.; N36 29 55 W89 51 16
932 County Rd. 448, Poplar Bluff, MO 63901 US
(573) 686-3700
www.foxradionetwork.com
info@foxradionetwork.com
License: Campbell, Dunklin County, MO held by Eagle Bluff Enterprises.
Group Owner: Eagle Bluff Enterprises.
Arbitron Metro Market: Poplar Bluff, MO; *Format:* Contemporary Hits/Top 40
Steven Fuchs, President

Canton

KRRY

05-04-1971; 100.9 MHz FM; *Hrs Open:* 24; 28 kw; 656 ft.; N39 53 9 W91 36 38
119 North 3rd St, Box 711, Hannibal, MO 63401 US
(217) 223-5292; *Fax:* (217) 223-5299
www.y101radio.com
Ed.Foxall@townsquaremedia.com
License: Canton, Lewis County, MO held by Townsquare Media Quincy-Hannibal License LLC
Group Owner: Townsquare Media; (acq 2-29-2012; grpsl)
Nat'l Reps: McGavren Guild
Arbitron Metro Market: Quincy, IL-Hannibal, MO; *Format:* Contemporary Hits/Top 40; *Adv. Rates:* 19.52; 16.51; 18.02; 7.50
Ed Foxall, General Manager
Jeff Asmussen, General Sales Mgr
Dennis Oliver, Programming Director
Ed Foxall, Promotions Manager
Gary Glaenzer, Chief Engineer

Cape Girardeau

KAPE

01-01-1951; 1550 kHz AM
901 S. Kings Highway, Cape Girardeau, MO 63703 US
(573) 339-7000; *Fax:* (573) 651-4100
www.kaperadio1550.com
License: Cape Girardeau, MO held by Withers Broadcasting Co. of Missouri LLC.
Group Owner: Withers Broadcasting Co.; (acq 6-72).
Nat'l Network: Westwood One; Fox Sports; *Nat'l Reps:* Katz Radio; *Wire Services:* AP
Arbitron Metro Market: Cape-Girardeau, MT; *Format:* News, Sports, 86; *Target Audience:* 25-54; active, aware adults
Scott Stone, Production Director
Rick Lambert, General Manager
Kevin Casey, Programming Director
Smokey King, Chief Engineer

KEZS-FM

12-10-1970; 102.9 MHz FM; *Hrs Open:* 24; 100 kw; 948 ft.; N37 24 23 W89 33 44
324 Broadway, Cape Girardeau, MO 63701 US
(573) 335-8291; *Fax:* (573) 335-4806
www.k103fm.com
License: Cape Girardeau, Cape Girardeau County, MO held by MRR License LLC
Group Owner: MAX Media L.L.C.; (acq 6-2-2004; grpsl).
Arbitron Metro Market: Cape Girardeau, MO; *Format:* Country; *No. News Employees:* 1; *Target Audience:* 25-54.
Whitney Thomas, Programming Director

KGIR

06-10-1966; 1220 kHz AM; *Hrs Open:* 24; 0.25 kw-D, ND2; 0.137 kw-N, ND2; N37 18 0 W89 29 24
324 Broadway, Cape Girardeau, MO 63701 US
(573) 335-8291; *Fax:* (573) 335-4806
www.semoespn.com
License: Cape Girardeau, Cape Girardeau County, MO held by MRR License LLC.
Group Owner: MAX Media L.L.C.; (acq 6-2-2004; grpsl)

Nat'l Network: ESPN Radio
Arbitron Metro Market: Cape Girardeau, MO *TV Affiliate:* ESPN; *Format:* Sports, Talk; *Target Audience:* 18 plus; men
Ronnie Glover, General Manager
Todd Bonacki, Programming Director
Hunter Hendricks, Promotions Director
Faune Riggin, News Director
Sherry Crider, Traffic Manager

KGMO
03-17-1969; 100.7 MHz FM; 100 kw; 991 ft.; N37 21 45 W89 31 19
901 South Kings Highway, Cape Girardeau, MO 63703 US
(573) 651-4100
www.kgmo.com
rlambert@withersradio.net
License: Cape Girardeau, Cape Girardeau County, MO held by Withers Broadcasting Co. of Missouri LLC
Group Owner: Withers Broadcasting Co.
Nat'l Reps: Katz Radio
Format: Classic Rock; *Hrs. of News Programming:* news progmg 10 hrs wkly; *Target Audience:* 25-54
Rick Lambert, General Manager
Kevin Casey, Station Manager
Chris Cook, Promotions Manager
Jared Smith, Production Director

***KRCU**
03-03-1976; 90.9 MHz FM; 6.5 kw vert; 696 ft.; N37 24 17 W89 34 6
One University Plaza, Cape Girardeau, MO 63701 US
(573) 651-5070; *Fax:* (573) 651-5071
www.semo.edu
comments@krcu.org
License: Cape Girardeau, Cape Girardeau County, MO held by Board of Regents of Southeast Missouri State University.
Nat'l Network: NPR; PRI
Arbitron Metro Market: Cape Girardeau, Sikeston/MO's Parkland; *Format:* Classical, Jazz, 60; *Target Audience:* General.
Jason Brown, Operations Dir
Dan Woods, General Manager
Amanda Lincoln, General Sales Mgr
Jacob McCleland, Programming Director
Allen Lane, Chief Engineer

KZIM
01-01-1925; 960 kHz AM; *Hrs Open:* 24; 5 kw-D, DAN; 0.5 kw-N, DAN; N37 18 59 W89 29 6
324 Broadway, Cape Girardeau, MO 63701 US
(573) 355-8291; *Fax:* (573) 355-4806
www.960kzim.com
License: Cape Girardeau, Cape Girardeau County, MO held by MRR License LLC
Group Owner: MAX Media L.L.C.
Nat'l Network: CBS
Arbitron Metro Market: Cape Girardeau, MO; *Format:* News, News/Talk, 86; *Target Audience:* 35-64.
Ronnie Glover, General Manager
Todd Bonacki, Programming Director
Hunter Hendricks, Promotions Director
Faune Riggin, News Director
Sherry Crider, Traffic Manager

Carrollton

KAOL
04-18-1959; 1430 kHz AM; *Hrs Open:* 24; 0.5 kw-D, ND1; 0.027 kw-N, ND1; N39 19 58 W93 32 15
102 North Mason, Carrollton, MO 64633 US
(660) 542-0404; *Fax:* (660) 542-0420
www.kmzu.com
License: Carrollton, MO held by Kanza Inc.
Nat'l Reps: McGavren Guild
Arbitron Metro Market: Carrollton, MT; *Format:* Country *Special Programming:* Sp 3 hrs wkly; *Hrs. of News Programming:* news progmg 10 hrs wkly; *No. News Employees:* 2; *Target Audience:* 25-54; farm families &those with agricultural backgrounds
Miles Carter, General Manager
Rick Barton, General Sales Mgr
Scott Powell, Programming Director
Chastity Anderson, News Director
Jim Woods, Music Director
Sue Lightfoot, Traffic Manager

KMZU
07-13-1962; 100.7 MHz FM; 99 kw; 991 ft.; N39 21 59 W93 24 12 *Rebroadcasts:* Rebroadcasts WHB(AM) Kansas City 95%
102 North Mason, Carrollton, MO 64633 US
(660) 542-0404; *Fax:* (660) 542-0420
www.kmzu.com
License: Carrollton, Carroll County, MO held by Kanza Inc.

Don Sibley, Programming Director

Carthage

KDMO
06-03-1947; 1490 kHz AM; *Hrs Open:* 24; 1 kw-U; N37 10 58 W94 21 43
221 East 4th Street, Carthage, MO 64836
(417) 358-6054
modulation45@yahoo.com
License: Carthage, Jasper County, MO held by Ronald L. Petersen
Nat'l Network: NBC News Radio; *Nat'l Reps:* In house
Population Served: 397,000; *Arbitron Metro Market:* Joplin, MO
Special Programming: Sp 10 hrs wkly; *Hrs. of News Programming:* news progmg 10 hrs wkly; *No. News Employees:* 1; *Target Audience:* 55 plus.
Ronald Petersen, President

KMXL
01-10-1972; 95.1 MHz FM; *Hrs Open:* 24; 50 kw; 472 ft; N37 10 58 W94 21 35
221 East 4th Street, Carthage, MO 64836
(417) 358-6054
www.951mikefm.com
mike@951mikefm.com
License: Carthage, Jasper County, MO held by Ronald L. Petersen Sr.
Nat'l Network: NBC Radio; *Nat'l Reps:* In house
Population Served: 775,000; *Arbitron Metro Market:* Joplin, MO; *Hrs. of News Programming:* news progmg one hr wkly; *No. News Employees:* 1; *Target Audience:* 25-54; young adults & baby-boomers
Ronald Petersen Sr., President
Ronald Petersen Jr., Station Manager

Caruthersville

KCRV-AM
02-22-1950; 1370 kHz AM; 1 kW; N36 12 50 W89 41 25
5500 Poplar Ave, Suite 1, Memphis, TN 38119 USA
(901) 685-3993; *Fax:* (901) 685-3995
kcrvradio.com
License: Caruthersville, MO held by Pollack Broadcasting Co.
Group Owner: Pollack Broadcasting Co.; (acq 9-21-99; with co-located FM)
Nat'l Network: Moody; *Regional Network:* Brownfield
Arbitron Metro Market: Caruthersville-Hayti, MO; *Format:* Country
Special Programming: Relg 20 hrs wkly; *Target Audience:* General; residents of Pemiscot county

KCRV-FM
04-28-1975; 105.1 MHz FM; 4.8 kW; 328 ft.; N36 12 50 W89 41 25
5500 Poplar Ave, Suite 1, Memphis, TN 38119 USA
(901) 685-3993; *Fax:* (901) 685-3995
www.kcrvradio.com
info@kcrvradio.com
License: Caruthersville, Pemiscot County, MO held by Pollack Broadcasting Co.
Group Owner: Pollack Broadcasting Co.
Arbitron Metro Market: Caruthersville-Hayti, MO; *Format:* Oldies

Cassville

KRMO
08-01-1950; 990 kHz AM; *Hrs Open:* 24; 2.5 kw-D, ND1; 0.047 kw-N, ND1; N36 56 15 W93 55 30
126 South Jefferson, Aurora, MO 65605 US
(417) 235-6041; *Fax:* (417) 235-6388
www.krmo.com
License: Cassville, MO held by Eagle Broadcasting Inc.
Regional Network: Brownfield; Missourinet
Arbitron Metro Market: Joplin, MO; *Format:* Country; *Hrs. of News Programming:* news progmg 10 hrs wkly; *No. News Employees:* 1; *Target Audience:* 35 plus; business professionals, farmers, elderly *Adv. Rates:* 12; 12; 12; 12
DeWayne Gandy, President
Bill Lewis, Operations Dir
Janet Gandy, General Manager
Lance Mettlach, General Sales Mgr
Dan Kesterson, Programming Director
Sam Clapper, Sports Director

Cedar Hill

***KNLH**
10-01-1998; 89.5 MHz FM; 0.068 kw; 699 ft.; N38 21 40 W90 32 54
1411 Locust Street, St. Louis, MO 63103 US
(314) 436-2424; *Fax:* (314) 436-2434
www.hereshelpnet.org
larryr@hereshelpnet.org
License: Cedar Hill, Jefferson County, MO held by New Life Evangelistic Center Inc.
Format: Adult Contemp, Gospel, 86
Victor Anderson, General Manager

Centralia

KMFC
02-03-1986; 92.1 MHz FM; *Hrs Open:* 24; 1.85 kw; Ant 418 ft; N39 09 58 W92 09 52
1249 E. Hwy. 22, Centralia, MO 65240
(573) 682-5525; *Fax:* (573) 682-2744
License: Centralia, Boone County, MO held by Clair Broadcasting Co.
Nat'l Network: USA
Population Served: 260,000; *Arbitron Metro Market:* Columbia, MO *Special Programming:* Black 3 hrs, gospel 2 hrs, Sp one hr wkly; *Target Audience:* 25-50.; *Adv. Rates:* 15; 11.25; 14.25; 8.25
Jerry Clair, General Manager
Sharon Dollens, Station Manager
Tonya Beamer, General Sales Mgr
Deanna Arnold, Promotions Manager
Sharon Dollens, News Director

Chaffee

KREZ
07-01-1990; 104.7 MHz FM; 7.7 kw; 585 ft.; N37 9 46 W89 28 59
901 South Kings Highway, Cape Girardeau, MO 63701 US
(573) 339-7000; *Fax:* (573) 651-4100
rlambert@withersradio.net
License: Chaffee, Scott County, MO held by Dana R. Withers
Nat'l Reps: Katz Radio
Arbitron Metro Market: Cape Girardeau, MO; *Format:* Adult Contemp; *Target Audience:* 18-49.
Rick Lambert, General Manager
Steve Thomas, Programming Director
Rebecca Thomas, Promotions Manager

Charleston

KCHR
01-01-1953; 1350 kHz AM; *Hrs Open:* 24; 1 kw-D, ND1; 0.079 kw-N, ND1; N36 55 30 W89 17 45
P. O. Box 432, Charleston, MO 63834 US
(573) 683-6044
License: Charleston, MO held by South Missouri Broadcasting Co. Inc.
Arbitron Metro Market: Charleston, MO; *Format:* Oldies, Talk
Special Programming: Oldies about 3 hrs; *Hrs. of News Programming:* News progmg 21 hr per day; *Target Audience:* General.
James Byrd, III, President
Danny Adams, General Manager
Pam Haws, Programming Director
Charlie Lampe, Chief Engineer

KWKZ
02-01-1993; 106.1 MHz FM; *Hrs Open:* 24; 34 kw; 584 ft.; N37 3 38 W89 37 27
753 Enterprise, Cape Girardeau, MO 63703 US
(573) 334-7800; *Fax:* (573) 334-7440
www.kwkz.com
License: Charleston, Mississippi County, MO held by Anderson Broadcasting Co. Inc.
Arbitron Metro Market: Cape Giradeau, MO; *Format:* Country; *Target Audience:* 18-44; 35-55 male, 30-45 female
Ann Anderson, Chairman
Bill Anderson, CEO
Susan Bell, Programming Director
Palmer Johnson, Engineering Dir

Chillicothe

KCHI
03-03-1950; 1010 kHz AM; 0.25 kw-D, ND1; 0.037 kw-N, ND1; N39 45 51 W93 33 21
421 Washington, Chillicothe, MO 64601 US
(660) 646-4173; *Fax:* (660) 646-2868
www.kchi.com
kchi@greenhills.net
License: Chillicothe, MO held by Leatherman Communications Inc.
Regional Network: Missourinet
Arbitron Metro Market: Chillicothe, MO; *Format:* News; *Target Audience:* 35-49.

Dan Leatherman, Owner/General Manager
Tom Tingerthal, News Director

KCHI-FM
10-01-1976; 98.5 MHz FM; 3.2 kw; 453 ft.; N39 44 50 W93 38 38
421 Washington, Chillicothe, MO 64601 US
(660) 646-4173; *Fax:* (660) 646-2868
www.kchi.com
kchi@greenhills.net
License: Chillicothe, Livingston County, MO held by Leatherman Communications Inc.
Arbitron Metro Market: Chillicothe, MO
Dan Leatherman, Owner/General Manager
Tom Tingerthal, News Director

***KRNW**
08-30-1993; 88.9 MHz FM; *Hrs Open:* 24; 38 kw; 512 ft.; N39 48 48 W93 35 26
800 University Drive, Maryville, MO 64468 US
(660) 562-1163; *Fax:* (660) 562-1832
www.kxcv.org
kxcv@nwmissouri.edu
License: Chillicothe, Livingston County, MO held by Northwest Missouri State University.
Format: News, News/Talk, 86; *Hrs. of News Programming:* news progmg 39 hrs wkly; *No. News Employees:* 2; *Target Audience:* General.
John Jasinski, President
Patty Andrews Holley, Operations Dir
Rodney Harris, General Manager
Patty Holley, Programming Director
Darren Perkins, Chief Engineer
John Coffey, Sports Director

***KLWL**
88.1 MHz FM; 50 kw vert; 75 m; N39 54 35 W93 21 42
Box 391, Twin Falls, ID 83303
(208)733-3133; *Fax:* (208) 736-1958
www.csnradio.com
License: Chillicothe, Livingston County, MO held by Calvary Chapel of Twin Falls Inc
Group Owner: CSN International
Format: Christian, Religious

Clayton

***KFUO**
12-14-1924; 850 kHz AM; *Hrs Open:* Sunrise-sunset; 5 kw-D, NDD; N38 38 20 W90 18 57
85 Founders Lane, St. Louis, MO 63105 US
(314) 965-9000; *Fax:* (314) 725-3801
www.kfuoam.org
worldwide@kfuo.org
License: Clayton, MO held by Lutheran Church-Missouri Synod
Nat'l Network: AP Network News
Arbitron Metro Market: St. Louis, MO; *Format:* Religious, Talk; *Target Audience:* General.
Gary Duncan, Operations Dir
Dennis Stortz, General Manager
Paul Clayton, Programming Director
Chuck Rathert, Promotions Manager

KLJY
01-01-1948; 99.1 MHz FM; *Hrs Open:* 24; 100 kw; 1,026 ft; N38 39 08 W90 17 03
85 Founders Ln., St. Louis, MO 63105
(314) 725-0099; *Fax:* (314) 725-3801
License: Clayton, St. Louis County, MO held by Lutheran Church-Missouri Synod
Nat'l Network: Wall Street; CNN Radio; *Nat'l Reps:* McGavren Guild
Arbitron Metro Market: St. Louis, MO *Special Programming:* Metrpolitan Opera; *Target Audience:* General; upscale, educated
Dennis Stortz, General Manager
Oliver Trittler, General Sales Mgr
Jim Connett, Programming Director

KSIV
1320 kHz AM; *Hrs Open:* 24; 4.6 kw-D, DAN; 0.27 kw-N, DAN; N38 36 26 W90 21 14
1750 S. Brentwood Blvd., Suite 811, St. Louis, MO 63144 US
(314) 961-1320; *Fax:* (314) 961-7562
www.bottradionetwork.com
comments@bottradionetwork.com
License: Clayton, St. Louis County, MO held by Bott Communications Inc.
Group Owner: Bott Radio Network; acq 2-25-82;
Nat'l Network: USA
Arbitron Metro Market: St. Louis, MO; *Format:* Christian, Talk; *Target Audience:* 25-54; family-oriented
Richard Bott Sr., President & CEO
Eben Fowler, Operations Dir
Fred Zielonko, Regional Manager
Pat Rulon, Director of National Sales
Candy Green, Program Services Manager
Rachel Launius, Marketing Manager

***KWUR**
07-04-1976; 90.3 MHz FM; *Hrs Open:* 24; 0.009 kw; 95 ft.; N38 38 55 W90 18 28
1 Brookings Drive, Campus Box 1205, Clayton, MO 63130 US
(314) 935-5952; *Fax:* (314) 935-8833
www.kwur.com
License: Clayton, St. Louis County, MO held by Washington University.
Arbitron Metro Market: St. Louis, MO; *Format:* Alternative, Variety/Diverse; *Target Audience:* 18 plus; those seeking alternative radio

Cleveland

KCTO
11-08-2007; 1160 kHz AM
310 South La Frenz Road, Liberty, MO 64068 US
(816) 792-1140; *Fax:* (816) 792-8258
www.kcxl.com
davekcxl@yahoo.com
License: Cleveland, MO held by Alpine Broadcasting Corp.
Nat'l Network: AP Network News
Arbitron Metro Market: Cleveland, MO; *Format:* Talk; *Adv. Rates:* 30; 30; 25; 20
Peter Schartel, President
David Brewer, Station Manager
Jonne Santoli, Programming Director

Clinton

KDKD
01-01-1951; 1280 kHz AM; *Hrs Open:* 24
Mailing Address: P.O. Box 448, Clinton, MO 64735 US
Second Address: 2201 N. Antioch Rd., Clinton, MO 64735
(660) 885-6141; *Fax:* (660) 885-4801
www.mykdkd.com
bob@kdkd.net
License: Clinton, MO held by GoodRadio.TV
Group Owner: GoodRadio.TV; (acq 10-7-2003; with co-located FM)
Nat'l Network: ABC Information & Entertainment; *Regional Network:* Missourinet; *Nat'l Reps:* Rgnl Reps
Arbitron Metro Market: Clinton, MO; *Format:* Oldies; *Hrs. of News Programming:* news progmg 10 hrs wkly; *No. News Employees:* 1; *Target Audience:* 25-55.
Dave Young, Programming Director
David Lee, News Director
Jennifer Schlagle, Traffic Manager

KDKD-FM
01-01-1975; 95.3 MHz FM; *Hrs Open:* 24; 14.5 kw; 433 ft.; N38 22 18 W93 55 6
Mailing Address: P.O. Box 448, Clinton, MO 64735 US
Second Address: 2201 N. Antioch Rd., Clinton, MO 64735
(660) 885-6141; *Fax:* (660) 885-4801
License: Clinton, Henry County, MO held by GoodRadio.TV
Group Owner: GoodRadio.TV; (acq 5-28-1985)
Nat'l Network: Fox News Radio; Motor Racing Net; *Regional Network:* Missourinet; *Nat'l Reps:* Rgnl Reps
Arbitron Metro Market: Clinton, MO; *Format:* Country *Special Programming:* NASCAR - MRN + PRN; *Hrs. of News Programming:* 10+; *No. News Employees:* 1; *Target Audience:* 25-55.
Jennifer Schlagle, Business Manager
Bob May, General Manager
Bob May, General Sales Mgr
Dave Young, Assistant Programming Director
Larry Moffitt, Programming Director
David Lee, Sports Director
Barry Wilson, Engineering Dir
David Lee, News Director

***KLRQ**
10-05-1990; 96.1 MHz FM; *Hrs Open:* 24; 100 kw; 988 ft.; N38 28 27 W93 30 28 *Rebroadcasts:* Rebroadcasts KLVR(FM) Santa Rosa, CA 100%
702 E. Ohio, Box 446, Clinton, MO 64735 US
(660) 885-7517
www.klove.com
License: Clinton, Henry County, MO held by Educational Media Foundation.
Group Owner: EMF Broadcasting; (acq 12-23-2003; $1.9 million).
Nat'l Network: K-Love
Format: Christian
Mike Novak, President
Glenn Goodwin, Operations Dir
Eric Allen, General Sales Mgr
David Pierce, Programming Director
Ed Lenane, News Director
Sam Wallington, Engineering Dir
Scott Smith, Music Director
Marya Morgan, ScottSmith
Richard Hunt, News Reporter
Tracy Butler, Traffic Manager

Columbia

***KBIA**
01-01-1972; 91.3 MHz FM; *Hrs Open:* 24; 100 kw; 610 ft.; N38 53 16 W92 15 48
401 S 9th St., Columbia, MO 65201 US
(573) 882-3431; *Fax:* (573) 882-2636
www.kbia.org
kbia@kbia.org
License: Columbia, Boone County, MO held by Board of Curators, University of Missouri.
Group Owner: The Curators of the University of Missouri
Nat'l Network: NPR; PRI; Harvest Public Media; Side Effects
Arbitron Metro Market: Columbia, MO; *Format:* News; *Hrs. of News Programming:* news progmg 55 hrs wkly; *No. News Employees:* 2; *Target Audience:* 25-64.; *Adv. Rates:* 30; 20; 30; 10
Karen Walker Seeger, Operations Dir
Michael Dunn, General Manager
Roger Karwoski, Station Manager
Robert Wells, General Sales Mgr
Kyle Felling, Programming Director
Janet Saidi, News Director

KBXR
11-11-1994; 102.3 MHz FM; *Hrs Open:* 24; 3.5 kw; 856 ft.; N39 0 52 W92 16 32
503 Old Highway 63 North, Columbia, MO 65201 US
(573) 874-1023; *Fax:* (573) 449-7770
www.bxr.com
1023bxr@gmail.com
License: Columbia, Boone County, MO held by Cumulus Licensing LLC.
Group Owner: Cumulus Media Inc.; (acq 4-26-2004; grpsl).
Nat'l Reps: Katz Radio
Arbitron Metro Market: Columbia, MO; *Format:* Rock/AOR; *Hrs. of News Programming:* news progmg one hr wkly; *No. News Employees:* 3; *Target Audience:* 29-59; educated professional/technical
Kevin Joyce, Vice President/Market Manager
Greg Renoe, General Sales Mgr
Chris Kellogg, Programming Director
Nick Snyder, Promotions Manager
Tom Holmes, Chief Engineer

KCMQ
12-03-1967; 96.7 MHz FM; *Hrs Open:* 24; 99.1 kw; 912 ft.; N38 41 30 W92 5 44
3215 Lemone Industrial Boulevard, Columbia, MO 65201 US
(573) 875-1099; *Fax:* (573) 875-2439
www.kcmq.com
License: Columbia, Boone County, MO held by Zimmer Radio of Mid-Missouri Inc.
Arbitron Metro Market: Columbia, MO; *Format:* Rock/AOR; *Hrs. of News Programming:* News progmg one hr wkly; *Target Audience:* 25-54; male
John Zimmer, Chairman
Carla Leible, General Manager
Dave Wisniewski, General Sales Mgr
Nicci Garmon, Programming Director
Shelley Tucker, News Director
Drew Haigh, Chief Engineer

***KCOU**
10-31-1973; 88.1 MHz FM; *Hrs Open:* 24; 0.43 kw; 144 ft.; N38 56 24 W92 19 16
2500 M.U. Student Center, Columbia, MO 65211 US
(573) 882-7820; *Fax:* (573) 882-6262
www.kcou.mu.org
comments@kcou.fm
License: Columbia, Boone County, MO held by The Curators of the University of Missouri.
Arbitron Metro Market: Columbia, MO; *Format:* Alternative, Rock/AOR; *Target Audience:* 18-22; students & community members
Carson Cornelius, General Manager
Dustion Rios, Business Manager

KFRU
10-10-1925; 1400 kHz AM; *Hrs Open:* 24
503 Old Highway 63 North, Columbia, MO 65201 US

(573) 449-4141; *Fax:* (573) 449-7770
www.kfru.com
License: Columbia, MO held by Cumulus Licensing LLC.
Group Owner: Cumulus Media Inc.; (acq 4-26-2004; grpsl).
Regional Network: Missourinet
Arbitron Metro Market: Columbia, MO; *Format:* News, News/Talk, 86 *Special Programming:* The Woman show 2 hrs wkly, pets 1 hr wkly, gardening 1 hr wkly; *Hrs. of News Programming:* news progmg 140 hrs wkly *No. NewsEmployees:* 9; *Target Audience:* General.
Kevin Joyce, Vice President/Marketing Manager
Greg Renoe, General Sales Mgr
Chris Kellogg, Programming Director
Nick Snyder, Promotions Manager

***KOPN**
03-01-1973; 89.5 MHz FM; *Hrs Open:* 24; 36 kw; 236 ft.; N38 59 53 W92 11 48
915 E. Broadway, Columbia, MO 65201 US
(573) 874-1139; *Fax:* (573) 499-1662
www.kopn.org
mail@kopn.org
License: Columbia, Boone County, MO held by New Wave Corp.
Nat'l Network: NPR; PRI
Arbitron Metro Market: Columbia, MO; *Format:* News, News/Talk, 86 *Special Programming:* Blues 13 hrs, Black 10 hrs, AAA 10 hrs, Grateful Dead 6 hrs, jazz 4 hrs, gospel 3 hrs, bluegrass 6 hrs, folk 2 hrs wkly *Hrs. of NewsProgramming:* News progmg 40 hrs wkly; *Target Audience:* 25-54; well educated, upwardly mobile
David Owens, General Manager
Steve Jerrett, Music Director
Rich Winkel, Chief Engineer

KPLA
02-23-1983; 101.5 MHz FM; *Hrs Open:* 24; 41 kw; 1063 ft.; N39 0 52 W92 16 32
503 Old Highway 63 North, Columbia, MO 65201 US
(573) 449-4141; *Fax:* (573) 449-7770
www.kpla.com
License: Columbia, Boone County, MO held by Cumulus Licensing LLC.
Group Owner: Cumulus Media Inc.; (acq 4-26-2004; grpsl).
Arbitron Metro Market: Columbia, MO; *Format:* Adult Contemp; *Hrs. of News Programming:* news progmg one hr wkly; *No. News Employees:* 2; *Target Audience:* 25-54.
Chris Kellogg, Programming Director
Nick Snyder, Promotions

KTGR
01-01-1955; 1580 kHz AM
3215 Lemone Industrial Boulevard, Columbia, MO 65201 US
(573) 875-1099; *Fax:* (573) 875-2439
ktgr.com
License: Columbia, MO held by Zimmer Radio of Mid-Missouri Inc.
Nat'l Network: ABC; ESPN Radio
Arbitron Metro Market: Columbia, MO; *Format:* Sports; *Target Audience:* 18-34; male
Cosmo, Programming Director

***KWWC-FM**
02-02-1965; 90.5 MHz FM; *Hrs Open:* 24; 1.25 kw; 131 ft.; N38 57 12 W92 19 5
1200 East Broadway, Columbia, MO 65201 US
(573) 442-2211
www.stephens.edu/campuslife/kwwc/
info@stephens.edu
License: Columbia, Boone County, MO held by Stephens College.
Arbitron Metro Market: Columbia, MO; *Format:* Jazz, Oldies; *Target Audience:* 25-60; college educated, professional or retired with middle upper income
Jonna Wiseman, General Manager
Max Ornles, Chief Engineer

***KCIU**
01-01-1972; 88.1 MHz FM; *Hrs Open:* 24; 100 kw; 610 ft.; N38 53 16 W92 15 48
401 S 9th St., Columbia, MO 65201 US
(573) 882-7820
www.kcou.org
pd@kcou.fm
License: Columbia, Boone County, MO held by Board of Curators, University of Missouri.
Group Owner: The Curators of the University of Missouri
Nat'l Network: NPR; PRI; Harvest Public Media; Side Effects
Arbitron Metro Market: Columbia, MO; *Format:* News; *Hrs. of News Programming:* news progmg 55 hrs wkly; *No. News Employees:* 2; *Target Audience:* 25-64.; *Adv. Rates:* 30; 20; 30; 10
Evan Campbell, Program Director
Zach Gee, Sports Content Director
Jim Jung, Assistant Music Director
Ashwini Mantrala, Assistant Music Director
Brett Stover, News Director
Carter Woodiel, Sports Director
Pierce Portfield, GeneralManager
Annabelle Ludwig, Business Director
Mark Johnson, Coordinator

Concordia

***KYRV**
01-01-1998; 88.1 MHz FM; 1 kw vert; 213 ft.; N38 52 10 W93 32 58
712 Chaucer Lane, Warrensburg, MO 64093 US
(660) 747-4155; *Fax:* (660) 747-4155
License: Concordia, Lafayette County, MO held by Full Smile Inc.
Arbitron Metro Market: Concordia, MO; *Format:* Gospel
Jim McCollum, General Manager

Country Club

***KJCV-FM**
01-01-2005; 89.7 MHz FM; 25 kw; 347 ft.; N39 44 42 W94 45 6
Rebroadcasts: Rebroadcasts KSIV-FM St. Louis, MO
10550 Barkley St., Suite 100, Overland Park, KS 64052 US
(913) 642-7770
www.bottradionetwork.com
comments@bottradionetwork.com
License: Country Club, Andrew County, MO held by Community Broadcasting Inc.
Group Owner: Bott Radio Network
Nat'l Network: USA
Arbitron Metro Market: St. Joseph, MO; *Format:* Christian, Talk
Richard Bott Sr., President & CEO
Eben Fowler, Operations Dir
Pat Rulon, Regional Manager
Candy Green, Program Services Manager
Rachel Launius, Marketing Manager
Jason Potocnik, Director of Traffic Operations

Crestwood

KSHE
02-11-1961; 94.7 MHz FM; *Hrs Open:* 24; 100 kw; 1027 ft.; N38 34 24 W90 19 30
401 S 18th St., St. Louis, MO 63103 USA
(314) 621-0095; *Fax:* (314) 621-3428
www.kshe95.com
info@kshe95.com
License: Crestwood, St. Louis County, MO held by Emmis Radio License LLC
Group Owner: Emmis Communications Corp.
Nat'l Reps: D & R Radio
Arbitron Metro Market: St. Louis, MO; *Format:* Rock/AOR; *Hrs. of News Programming:* news progmg one hr wkly; *No. News Employees:* 1; *Target Audience:* 18-40.
Jeff Smulyan, Chairman & CEO

Cuba

***KGNN-FM**
01-26-1997; 90.3 MHz FM; *Hrs Open:* 24; 6.3 kw; 325 ft.; N38 5 11 W91 18 30 *Rebroadcasts:* Rebroadcasts KGNV(FM) Washington 100%
P.O. Box 87, Washington, MO 63090 US
(636) 385-3787; *Fax:* (636) 239-4448
goodnewsvoice.org
info@goodnewsvoice.org
License: Cuba, Crawford County, MO held by Missouri River Christian Broadcasting Inc.
Group Owner: Missouri River Christian Broadcasting Inc.
Nat'l Network: Moody; Salem Radio Network
Format: Gospel, News, 62, Talk *Special Programming:* Children 7 hrs wkly; *Hrs. of News Programming:* News progmg 14 hrs wkly; *Target Audience:* 20-70; inquisitive, conservative, philosophical, liberal *Adv. Rates:* 8; 8; 8; 8
James Goggan, President/General Manager
Kerry Messer, Network Director
Rob Allyn, Engineering Dir
Marilyn Goggan, Program Director

***KNLQ**
01-01-2004; 91.9 MHz FM; 5 kw; 249 ft.; N38 2 14 W91 23 4
1411 Locust Street, St. Louis, MO 63103 US
(314) 421-3020; *Fax:* (314) 421-1702
www.hereshelpnet.org
License: Cuba, Crawford County, MO held by New Life Evangelistic Center Inc.
Arbitron Metro Market: Cuba, MO; *Format:* Gospel
Rick Jesse, Station Manager

De Soto

***KDJR**
01-29-1991; 100.1 MHz FM; 2 kw; 348 ft.; N38 1 25 W90 34 2
8919 World Ministry Avenue, Baton Rouge, LA 70810 US
(225) 768-3688(225) 766-8300; *Fax:* (225) 768-3729
www.jsm.org
kawikfish@yahoo.com
License: De Soto, Jefferson County, MO held by Family Worship Center Church Inc.
Group Owner: Family Worship Center Church Inc.; (acq 9-27-2005; $1.25 million).
Arbitron Metro Market: St. Louis, MO; *Format:* Religious
David Whitelaw, COO
Jimmy Swaggart, President
John Santiago, Programming Director

Dexter

KDEX
02-01-1956; 1590 kHz AM; *Hrs Open:* 5 AM-midnight; 0.62 kw-D, NDD; N36 47 20 W89 54 28
Mailing Address: P.O. Box 249, Dexter, MO 63841 US
Second Address: 20487 State Hwy 114, Dexter, MO 63841
(573) 624-3545; *Fax:* (573) 624-9926
www.kdexfm.com
kdex1@dexter.net
License: Dexter, MO
Nat'l Network: ABC; Jones Radio Networks
Arbitron Metro Market: Dexter, MO; *Format:* Country
Tony James, Operations Dir
Walter Turner, General Manager
Joeli Barbour, Station Manager
Walt Turner, General Sales Mgr
Dave Obergoenner, Chief Engineer

KDEX-FM
07-17-1969; 102.3 MHz FM; *Hrs Open:* 24; 5.9 kw; 279 ft.; N36 47 20 W89 54 28
P.O. Box 249, Dexter, MO 63841 US
(573) 624-3545; *Fax:* (573) 624-9926
kdex1@dexter.net
License: Dexter, Stoddard County, MO held by Dexter Broadcasting Inc.
Regional Network: Yancey AG Network
Arbitron Metro Market: Dexter, MO; *Format:* Country; *Hrs. of News Programming:* news progmg 5 hrs wkly; *No. News Employees:* 2; *Target Audience:* 25-54.
Tony James, Operations Dir
Walt Turner, General Manager
Dave Obergoenner, Chief Engineer
Joeli Barbour, National Sales Manager

Dixon

***KCVZ**
05-01-2003; 92.1 MHz FM; *Hrs Open:* 24; 6 kw; 328 ft.; N37 57 59 W92 10 3 *Rebroadcasts:* Rebroadcasts KCVO-FM Camdenton 100%
P.O. Box 800, Camdenton, MO 65020 US
(573) 346-3200; *Fax:* (573) 346-1010
www.spiritfm.org
License: Dixon, Pulaski County, MO held by Lake Area Educational Broadcasting Foundation
Nat'l Network: Salem Radio Network
Arbitron Metro Market: Camdenton, MO; *Format:* Christian; *Hrs. of News Programming:* News progmg one hr wkly; *Target Audience:* 25-45.
Alice McDermott, CFO
James McDermott, President
Jim McDermott, General Manager
Alice McDermott, Financial Director

***KFCV**
90.5 MHz FM; 3.3 kw; 514 ft.; N37 50 1.2 W92 0 59
Rebroadcasts: Rebroadcasts KSIV-FM Saint Louis 100%
10550 Barkley St., Suite 100, Overland Park, US
(913) 642-7770
www.bottradionetwork.com
comments@bottradionetwork.com
License: Dixon, Pulaski County, MO held by Community Broadcasting Inc.
Group Owner: Bott Radio Network
Arbitron Metro Market: Dixon, MO; *Format:* Christian, Talk
Eben Fowler, Operations Dir
Sue Stoltz, Regional Manager
Pat Rulon, Director of National Sales
Candy Green, Program Services Manager
Rachel Launius, Marketing Manager
Jason Potocnik, Director of Traffic Operations

Doniphan

KDFN
02-04-1963; 1500 kHz AM
932 County Rd. 448, Poplar Bluff, MO 63901 US
(573) 686-3700
www.foxradionetwork.com
info@foxradionetwork.com
License: Doniphan, MO held by Eagle Bluff Enterprises.
Group Owner: Eagle Bluff Enterprises; (acq 9-8-99; grpsl)
Regional Network: Missourinet
Format: Oldies *Special Programming:* Farm 5 hrs wkly; *Target Audience:* General.
Steven Fuchs, President

KOEA
04-11-1975; 97.5 MHz FM; 40 kw; 577 ft.; N36 35 20 W90 49 10
204 E. Washington St., Doniphan, MO 63935 US
(573) 686-3700
www.foxradionetwork.com
info@foxradionetwork.com
License: Doniphan, Ripley County, MO held by Eagle Bluff Enterprises.
Group Owner: Eagle Bluff Enterprises
Format: Country
Steven Fuchs, President

Doolittle

KUMR
104.5 MHz FM; 3.9 kw; 407 ft.; N37 56 21.3 W91 56 44.9
1051 Kings Highway, Rolla, MO 65401 US
(573) 308-1045; *Fax:* (573) 341-3443
www.mysunny1045.com
License: Doolittle, Phelps County, MO held by Alma Corp.
Group Owner: Alma Corp.
Arbitron Metro Market: Doolittle, MO; *Format:* Easy Listening
Dennis Wallace, President
Keith Stephenson, General Manager

East Prairie

KYMO
11-15-1965; 1080 kHz AM; 0.5 kw-D, NDD; N36 47 49 W89 21 19
Mailing Address: P.O. Box 130, East Prairie, MO 63845 US
Second Address: 390 S. Hwy. 102, East Prairie, MO 63845
(573) 649-3597; *Fax:* (573) 649-3983
License: East Prairie, MO held by Usher Broadcasting Inc.
Arbitron Metro Market: Marion IL; *Format:* Easy Listening
Barney Webster, President
Michael Bennett, Operations Dir
Reid Howell, Programming Director

El Dorado Springs

KESM-FM
06-01-1965; 105.5 MHz FM; 6 kw; 187 ft.; N37 51 51 W94 0 54
200 Radio Lane, El Dorado Springs, MO 64744 US
(417) 876-2741; *Fax:* (417) 876-2743
www.kesmradio.com
kesm@kesmradio.com
License: El Dorado Springs, Cedar County, MO held by Wildwood Communications Inc.
Arbitron Metro Market: El Dorado, AR
Andy Taylor, President

Eldon

KLOZ
92.7 MHz FM; *Hrs Open:* 24; 31 kw; 620 ft.; N38 20 27 W92 35 33
160 Highway 42, Kaiser, MO 65047 US
(573) 348-1958; *Fax:* (573) 348-1923
www.mix927.com
mike@mix927.com
License: Eldon, Miller County, MO held by Benne Broadcasting Co. L.L.C.
Nat'l Network: ABC; Cumulus
Arbitron Metro Market: Columbia, MO; *Format:* Adult Contemp; *Target Audience:* 25-54; 70% female/30% male with average or above income
Denny Benne, General Manager
Greg Sullens, Station Manager
Mike Clayton, Programming Director
Dan Yeager, Engineering Dir

KZWV
01-01-2006; 101.9 MHz FM; *Hrs Open:* 24; 43 kw; 528 ft.; N38 16 46 W92 35 6
1081 Osage Beach Road, Osage Beach, MO 65065 US
(573) 746-7873; *Fax:* (573) 746-7874
www.1019thewave.com
thewave@1019thewave.com
License: Eldon, Miller County, MO held by Randall C. Wright.
Arbitron Metro Market: Osage Beach, MO; *Format:* Adult Contemp, Jazz, 80; *Target Audience:* 25 plus; affluent adults
John Caran, General Manager
Steve Richards, Programming Director
Stacy Johnson, News Director
Jessica Brink, Traffic Manager

Eldorado Springs

KESM
07-18-1961; 1580 kHz AM; 0.5 kw-D, ND1; 0.032 kw-N, ND1; N37 51 51 W94 0 54
200 Radio Lane, El Dorado Springs, MO 64744 US
(417) 876-2741; *Fax:* (417) 876-2743
www.kesmradio.com
kesm@kesmradio.com
License: Eldorado Springs, MO held by Wildwood Communications Inc.
Arbitron Metro Market: El Dorado, AR; *Format:* Oldies, Country; *Target Audience:* General.
Donald Kohn, President
Jena Worthington, Station Manager

Ellington

KDKN
01-01-1999; 106.7 MHz FM; 3 kw; 298 ft; N37 13 58 W90 51 08
900 East Karsch Boulevard, Farmington, MO 63640
(573) 701-9590; *Fax:* (573) 701-9696
www.hereshelpnet.org
larryr@hereshelpnet.org
License: Ellington, Reynolds County, MO held by New Life Evangelistic Center.
Larry Rice, General Manager
Judy Redlich, General Sales Mgr

Excelsior Springs

***KEXS**
08-01-1968; 1090 kHz AM
201 Industrial Park Road, Excelsior Springs, MO 64024 US
(816) 630-1090
www.thecatholicradionetwork.com
kccatholic@aol.com
License: Excelsior Springs, MO held by Catholic Radio Network Inc.
Group Owner: Catholic Radio Network Inc.; (acq 5-17-2004; $825,000)
Nat'l Network: USA
Arbitron Metro Market: Excelsior Springs, MO; *Format:* Christian; *Target Audience:* 25-54.
James O'Laughlin, General Manager

Fairview Heights

KQQZ
11-01-1968; 1190 kHz AM; *Hrs Open:* Sunrise-sunset; 10 kw-D, 22 w-N, DA-2; N38 42 25 W90 03 10
8045 Big Bend Blvd., St. Louis, MO 65201
(314) 962-0590; *Fax:* (314) 962-7576
www.kfns.com
License: Fairview Heights, St. Clair County, IL held by Big Stick Three LLC.
Group Owner: Big League Broadcasting LLC; (acq 7-13-2004; grpsl).
Nat'l Network: ESPN Radio
Arbitron Metro Market: St. Louis, MO; *Target Audience:* 25-64; sports fans, men 25-54
Mike Phares, General Manager

Farmington

KREI
12-07-1947; 800 kHz AM; *Hrs Open:* 24; 1 kw-D, ND2; 0.15 kw-N, ND2; N37 47 32 W90 24 36
Box 461, Farmington, MO 63640 US
(573) 756-6476; *Fax:* (573) 756-1110
www.myMOinfo.com
j98@j98.com
License: Farmington, MO held by Festus/Farmington License Co. LLC.
Group Owner: GoodRadio.TV; (acq 8-8-2007; grpsl)
Nat'l Network: ABC; Premiere Radio Networks; Talk Radio Network; Westwood One; NBC Radio; *Regional Network:* Missourinet
Format: News, News/Talk, 86; *Hrs. of News Programming:* news progmg 40 hrs wkly; *No. News Employees:* 12; *Target Audience:* General.
Dean Goodman, President
Richard Womack, General Manager
Kimberly Long, Station Manager
Scott Kubala, Programming Director
Kevin Brooks, Chief Engineer

KTJJ
06-05-1977; 98.5 MHz FM; *Hrs Open:* 24; 100 kw; 1040 ft.; N37 43 7 W90 33 1
P.O. Box 461, Farmington, MO 63640 US
(573) 756-6476; *Fax:* (573) 756-1110
www.myMOinfo.com
License: Farmington, St. Francois County, MO held by Festus/Farmington License Co. LLC.
Group Owner: GoodRadio.TV
Nat'l Network: ABC
Arbitron Metro Market: Farmington, MO; *Format:* Country; *Hrs. of News Programming:* news progmg 16 hrs wkly; *No. News Employees:* 12; *Target Audience:* General.
Dean Goodman, President
Richard Womack, General Manager
Kim Long, Station Manager
Scott Kubala, Programming Director
Kevin Brooks, Chief Engineer
Tami Propst, Office Manager

Fayette

KSSZ
07-15-1994; 93.9 MHz FM; *Hrs Open:* 24; 25 kw; 328 ft.; N39 3 28 W92 28 49
3215 Lemone Industrial Boulevard, Columbia, MO 65201 US
(573) 875-1099; *Fax:* (573) 875-2439
www.939theeagle.com
eagle939@zrgmail.com
License: Fayette, Howard County, MO held by Zimmer Radio of Mid-Missouri Inc.
Nat'l Network: ABC; Jones Radio Networks; Westwood One; *Wire Services:* AP
Arbitron Metro Market: Columbia, MO; *Format:* News, News/Talk, 86; *Hrs. of News Programming:* news progmg 4 hrs wkly; *No. News Employees:* 2; *Target Audience:* 25-54; adults
Jennifer Herrin, Operations Dir
Carla Lieble, General Manager
Cynthia Schreen, General Sales Mgr
Nicci Garmon, Programming Director
Shelley Tucker, News Director
Drew Haines, Chief Engineer

Ferguson

***KCFV**
04-17-1972; 89.5 MHz FM; *Hrs Open:* 16; 0.1 kw; 161 ft.; N38 46 7 W90 17 16
3400 Pershall Road, Ferguson, MO 63135 US
(314) 513-4472,(314) 513-4478; *Fax:* (314) 513-4217
www.stlcc.edu/fv/kcfv
tgorry@stlcc.edu
License: Ferguson, St. Louis County, MO held by St. Louis Community College District.
Arbitron Metro Market: St. Louis, MO; *Format:* Adult Contemp *Special Programming:* Jazz 8 hrs, Black 4 hrs, hard rock 4 hrs wkly; *Hrs. of News Programming:* News progmg 2 hrs wkly; *Target Audience:* General.
Paul Huddleston, General Manager
Sabrina Reitmeyer, Programming Director

Festus

KJFF
05-10-1951; 1400 kHz AM; *Hrs Open:* 24; 1 kw-U, ND1; N38 13 56 W90 23 50
P.O. Box 461, Farmington, MO 63640 US
(636) 937-7642; *Fax:* (636) 937-3636
www.kjff.com
License: Festus, MO held by Festus/Farmington License Co. LLC.
Group Owner: GoodRadio.TV; (acq 8-8-2007; grpsl)
Nat'l Network: ABC; *Regional Network:* Missourinet
Arbitron Metro Market: St. Louis, MO; *Format:* News, News/Talk, 86; *Hrs. of News Programming:* news progmg 30 hrs wkly; *No. News Employees:* 4; *Target Audience:* General.
Dean Goodman, President
Dick Womack, General Manager
Kirk Mooney, Station Manager
Matt West, Programming Director
Kevin Brooks, Chief Engineer

***KTBJ**
01-01-1998; 89.3 MHz FM; 25 kw; 371 ft.; N38 9 16 W90 2 7
Mailing Address: P.O. Box 391, Twin Falls, ID 83303 US
Second Address: 4002 North 3300 East, Twin Falls, ID 83301
(800) 357-4226; *Fax:* (208) 736-1958
www.csnradio.com
License: Festus, Jefferson County, MO held by CSN International
Group Owner: CSN International; acq 6-17-98; $100,000).
Arbitron Metro Market: Festus, MO; *Format:* Christian, Talk
Mike Kestler, President
Daniel Davidson, Operations Dir
Don Mills, Network Programming Director
Mike Stocklin, Underwriting Director
Kelly Carlson, Engineering Dir

Florissant

KFTK
04-15-1977; 97.1 MHz FM; *Hrs Open:* 24; 100 kw; 561 ft.; N38 46 45 W90 43 43
401 S 18th St., St. Louis, MO 63103 USA
(314) 231-9710; *Fax:* (314) 621-3000
www.971talk.com
License: Florissant, St. Louis County, MO held by Emmis Radio License LLC
Group Owner: Emmis Communications Corp.
Nat'l Reps: McGavren Guild
Arbitron Metro Market: St. Louis, MO; *Format:* News/Talk
Libby Nolan, General Sales Mgr
Jeff Allen, Programming Director
Tony Colombo, Promotions Manager

Fredericktown

KYLS
06-29-1963; 1450 kHz AM; *Hrs Open:* 24; 1 kw-U, ND1; N37 35 0 W90 17 31
540 Maple Valley Drive, Farmington, MO 63640 US
(573) 701-9590; *Fax:* (573) 701-9696
License: Fredericktown, MO held by Southern Star Broadcasting of Missouri LLC.
Group Owner: Southern Star Broadcasting of Missouri LLC; (acq 5-8-2008; grpsl)
Nat'l Network: ESPN Radio
Arbitron Metro Market: Farmington, MO; *Format:* Sports; *Target Audience:* 24-55; Men
Chip Miller, President
Joel Jordan, Operations Dir

Fulton

KFAL
11-14-1950; 900 kHz AM; *Hrs Open:* 19; 1 kw-D, ND1; 0.135 kw-N, ND1; N38 51 58 W91 57 15
1805 Westminster, Fulton, MO 65251 US
(800) 455-1099
www.kfalthebig900.com/?page_id=3
License: Fulton, MO held by Zimmer Radio of Mid-Missouri Inc.
Nat'l Network: Motor Racing Net; *Regional Network:* Missourinet
Arbitron Metro Market: Columbia, MO; *Format:* Country *Special Programming:* Other 6 hrs wkly; *Hrs. of News Programming:* news progmg 3 hrs wkly; *No. News Employees:* 1; *Target Audience:* 35 plus.; *Adv. Rates:* 14; 14; 14; 12
John Zimmer, Chairman
Jerry Zimmer, CEO
Don Zimmer, President
Jeremiah Washington, General Manager
Steve Mallinkrott, General Sales Mgr

KTGR-FM
01-01-1970; 100.5 MHz FM; *Hrs Open:* 24; 6 kw; Ant 300 ft; N38 51 58 W91 57 15
3215 Industrial Boulevard, Columbia, MO 65201
(573) 875-1099
License: Fulton, Callaway County, MO held by Zimmer Radio of Mid-Missouri Inc.
Nat'l Network: ABC; Westwood One; Jones Radio Networks
Population Served: 12,248 *Hrs. of News Programming:* news progmg 2 hrs wkly; *No. News Employees:* 1; *Target Audience:* 25-54.; *Adv. Rates:* 13; 13; 13; 5
Howard Kalmenson, President
Mike Ginsburg, General Manager

Gainesville

KBOD
03-17-1994; 99.7 MHz FM; *Hrs Open:* 24; 50 kw; Ant 492 ft; N36 36 06 W92 25 48
Mailing Address: P.O. Box 2010, Mountain Home, AR 72654 US
Second Address: 620 Hwy 5 N., Mountain Home, AR 72653
(870) 425-3101; *Fax:* (870) 424-4314
www.ktlo.com
License: Gainesville, Ozark County, MO held by KTLO LLC
Group Owner: KTLO LLC; (acq 12-19-94; $150,000;
Format: Country; *Target Audience:* General.
Brad Haworth, Operations Manager
Bob Knight, General Manager
Danny Ward, Station Manager
Heather Loftis, Sales Manager
Sonny Elliot, News Director
Patty Sindlinger, Traffic Director
Tim Tibbs, Production Manager

Gallatin

KGOZ
06-01-1994; 101.7 MHz FM; *Hrs Open:* 24; 15 kw; 423 ft.; N39 53 14 W93 43 24
P.O. Box 217, Trenton, MO 64683 US
(660) 359-2727; *Fax:* (660) 359-4126
http://www.parbroadcastgroup.com/kgoz.htm
john@kttn.com
License: Gallatin, Daviess County, MO held by PAR Broadcasting Co. Inc.
Nat'l Network: Jones Radio Networks; *Nat'l Reps:* Rgnl Reps
Format: Country; *Hrs. of News Programming:* News progmg 2 hrs wkly; *No. News Employees:* 1; *Target Audience:* 14-50.; *Adv. Rates:* 25; 20; 15; 15
John Ausberger, President
John Anthony, General Manager
Jeanette Houck, General Sales Mgr
Dave Counsell, News Director

Garden City

KCJK
01-01-2001; 105.1 MHz FM; *Hrs Open:* 24; kw
5800 Foxridge Drive, 6th Floor, Mission, KS 66202 US
(913) 514-3000; *Fax:* (913) 514-3002
www.1051jackfm.com
jared.robb@cumulus.com
License: Garden City, Cass County, MO held by CMP Houston-KC LLC.
Group Owner: Cumulus Media Inc.
Nat'l Reps: Katz Radio
Arbitron Metro Market: KS City, MO; *Format:* Adult Contemp; *Hrs. of News Programming:* News progmg 10.5 hrs wkly; *Target Audience:* 25-54.
Chris Hoffman, Operations Dir
Mark Sullivan, Senior Vice President/General Manager
Jared Robb, General Sales Mgr
Dan Persigehl, Programming Director
Ashley Coppock, Promotions Manager
Biran Goeke, Director of Marketing
JonAnthony, Music Director

Gideon

KGLU
103.9 MHz FM; 2.5 kw; 400 ft.; N36 25 31 W89 41 29
, Gideon, MO US
(901) 685-0882
License: Gideon, New Madrid County, MO held by Pollack Steel Supply Inc.
Arbitron Metro Market: Gideon, MO; *Format:* Adult Contemp
Sydney Pollack, President

Gladstone

KGGN
11-18-1996; 890 kHz AM; 0.96 kw-D, DAD; N39 11 4 W94 27 28
1734 East 63rd Street, Kansas City, MO 64110 US
(816) 333-0092; *Fax:* (816) 363-8120
www.kggnam.com
kggnproduction@aol.com
License: Gladstone, MO held by Mortenson Broadcasting Co.
Group Owner: Mortenson Broadcasting Co.; acq 12-24-96; $450,000)
Arbitron Metro Market: KS City, MO; *Format:* Gospel *Special Programming:* Ministry 5 hrs wkly; *Target Audience:* 25-54, Christian
Rita Berry, General Manager
Reggie Brown, Programming Director

Gordonville

KCGQ-FM
01-01-1978; 99.3 MHz FM; *Hrs Open:* 24; 5 kw; 358 ft.; N37 21 34 W89 37 16
324 Broadway, Cape Girardeau, MO 63701 US
(573) 335-8291; *Fax:* (573) 335-4806
www.realrock993.com
License: Gordonville, Cape Girardeau County, MO held by MRR License LLC.
Group Owner: MAX Media L.L.C.
Arbitron Metro Market: Gordonville, MO; *Format:* Rock/AOR; *Target Audience:* 18-49; general
Ronnie Glover, General Manager
Kirby Ray, Programming Director
Hunter Hendricks, Promotions Director
Faune Riggin, News Director

Grandin

KCBW
104.5 MHz FM; 6 kw; 328 feet; N36 48 15 W90 43 12
932 County Road 448, Poplar Bluff, MO
(573) 686-3700; *Fax:* (573) 686-1713
www.foxradionetwork.com
License: Grandin, MO held by Fox Radio Network LLC

Steve Fuchs, President

Half Way

KYOO-FM
04-01-1995; 99.1 MHz FM; 25 kw; 328 ft.; N37 45 41 W93 15 42
304 E. Jackson, Bolivar, MO 65613 US
(417) 326-5259(417) 326-5257; *Fax:* (417) 326-5900
www.kyooradio.com/
License: Half Way, Polk County, MO held by KYOO Communications.
Nat'l Network: ABC
Arbitron Metro Market: Bolivar, MO; *Format:* Adult Contemp; *Hrs. of News Programming:* news progmg 5 hrs wkly; *No. News Employees:* 1; *Target Audience:* 10-72.; *Adv. Rates:* 20.50; 9; 6; na
Stephen Paris, President
Ann Paris, Operations Dir

Hannibal

KGRC
11-28-1968; 92.9 MHz FM; 100 kw; 502 ft.; N39 43 48 W91 24 19
329 Maine, Quincy, IL 62301 US
(217) 224-4102; *Fax:* (217) 224-4133
www.real929.com
License: Hannibal, Marion County, MO held by STARadio Corp.
Group Owner: STARadio Corp.; acq 12-2-98; $2.1 million with KZZK(FM) New London)
Nat'l Network: Westwood One; *Nat'l Reps:* Katz Radio
Format: Contemporary Hits/Top 40; *Hrs. of News Programming:* news progmg one hr wkly; *No. News Employees:* 1; *Target Audience:* 18-49; women
Michael Moyers, Vice President
Brenda Park, Sales Manager
Phil Reilly, Chief Engineer
Samantha Barnes, Music/Production Director

KHMO
04-01-1941; 1070 kHz AM; *Hrs Open:* 24
119 N. Third St. Box 711, Hannibal, MO 63401 US
(573) 221-3450; *Fax:* (573) 221-5331
www.khmoradio.com
harold.smith@townsquaremedia.com
License: Hannibal, MO held by Townsquare Media Quincy-Hannibal License LLC
Group Owner: Townsquare Media; (acq 2-29-2012;grpsl)
Nat'l Reps: McGavren Guild; *Wire Services:* Weather Wire
Format: News, News/Talk, 84, Talk *Special Programming:* Agriculture 5 hrs wkly; *Hrs. of News Programming:* news progmg 100 hrs wkly; *No. News Employees:* 2
Ed Foxall, General Manager
Jeff Asmussen, General Sales Mgr
Jeff Dorsey, Programming Director
John Hanvelt, News Director
Gary Glaenzer, Chief Engineer
Harold Smith, Program Director

***KJIR**
04-01-2000; 91.7 MHz FM; *Hrs Open:* 24; 12 kw; 570 ft.; N39 41 54 W91 29 48
222 North 6th Street, Quincy, IL 62301 US
(217) 221-9410; *Fax:* (217) 228-0966
thecross@kjir.org
License: Hannibal, Marion County, MO held by Believers Broadcasting Corp.
Format: Gospel; *Hrs. of News Programming:* News progmg 7.5 hrs wkly; *Target Audience:* Christian; 30-70
I. Carl Geisendorfer, General Manager
Michael Wartman, Programming Director

Harrisonville

KCFX
07-19-1974; 101.1 MHz FM; 97 kw; 1099 ft.; N39 1 20 W94 30 49
5800 Foxridge Drive, 6th Floor, Mission, MD 66202 US
(913) 514-3000; *Fax:* (913) 514-3001
www.101thefox.net
License: Harrisonville, Cass County, MO held by CMP Houston-KC LLC
Group Owner: Cumulus Media Inc.
Nat'l Reps: Katz Radio
Arbitron Metro Market: Kansas City, MO-KS; *Format:* Classic Rock; *Target Audience:* 25-54; baby boomers
Mark Sullivan, Senior Vice President/General Manager
Kristi Goodloe, Sales Manager
Brian Goeke, Promotions Director

Hazelwood

WHHL
10-10-1967; 104.1 MHz FM; *Hrs Open:* 24; 50 kw; 459 ft.; N38 39 8 W90 17 3
9666 Olive Blvd., Suite 610, St. Louis, MO 63132 US
(314) 989-9550; *Fax:* (314) 989-9551
www.hot1041stl.com
License: Hazelwood, Jersey County, MO held by Radio One Licenses LLC.
Group Owner: Radio One Inc.; (acq 12-19-2005; $20 million).
Arbitron Metro Market: St. Louis, MO; *Format:* Urban Contemporary; *No. News Employees:* 1; *Target Audience:* 25-54; families with children, singles
Gary Gunter, General Manager
Nate Dixon, General Sales Mgr
Boogie D, Programming Director
James Perry, Promotions Manager
Gary Benett, Chief Engineer

Hermann

KQQX
09-01-1985; 93.3 MHz FM; 10.25 kw; 1050 ft.; N38 6 16 W91 2 30
3418 Douglas Road, Florissant, MO 63034 US
(314) 921-9330
License: Hermann, Gasconade County, MO held by Broadcast Communications Inc.
Format: Alternative
Ruth Choate, General Manager

High Point

***KMCV**
01-01-2001; 89.9 MHz FM; 50 kw; 316 ft.; N38 35 48 W92 32 17
3732 W. Truman Blvd., Jefferson City, MO 65109 US
(573) 893-8990; *Fax:* (573) 893-8991
www.bottradionetwork.com
comments@bottradionetwork.com
License: High Point, Moniteau County, MO held by Community Broadcasting Inc.
Group Owner: Bott Radio Network; (acq 2-7-01; $1.25 million with KSCV(FM) Springfield).
Nat'l Network: USA
Arbitron Metro Market: Jefferson City, MO; *Format:* Christian, Talk
Richard Bott Sr., President & CEO
Eben Fowler, Operations Dir
Sue Stoltz, Regional Manager
Pat Rulon, Director of National Sales
Candy Green, Program Services Manager
Rachel Launius, Marketing Manager
Jason Potocnik, Director ofTraffic Operations

Hollister

KBCV
01-01-2004; 1570 kHz AM; 5 kw-D, DA2; 3 kw-N, DA2; N36 36 51 W93 12 50
500 W. Main St., Suite 103A, Branson, MO 65616 US
(417) 336-1570
www.bottradionetwork.com
comments@bottradionetwork.com
License: Hollister, Taney County, MO held by Bott Communications Inc.
Group Owner: Bott Radio Network
Nat'l Network: USA
Arbitron Metro Market: Branson, MO; *Format:* Christian, Talk
Richard Bott Sr., President & CEO
Eben Fowler, Operations Dir
Monna Stafford, Regional Manager
Pat Rulon, Director of National Sales
Candy Green, Program Services Manager
Rachel Launius, Marketing Manager
Jason Potocnik, Directorof Traffic Operations

Houston

KBTC
06-28-1962; 1250 kHz AM; 1 kw-D, ND1; 0.051 kw-N, ND1; N37 19 45 W91 53 55
PO Box 230, Houston, MO 65483 US
(417) 217-1404
License: Houston, MO held by Media Professional, LLC
Group Owner: Media Professional, Inc.
Arbitron Metro Market: Houston, TX; *Format:* Sports, Talk

KUNQ
05-01-1965; 99.3 MHz FM; *Hrs Open:* 24; 30 kw; 604 ft.; N37 5 21 W92 3 24
PO Box 230, Houston, MO 65483 US
(417) 217-1404
www.bigcountry99.com
License: Houston, Texas County, MO held by Media Professionals, LLC.
Group Owner: Media Professionals, Inc.; (acq 6-22-2000; $150,000 with co-located AM)
Arbitron Metro Market: Houston, MO; *Format:* Country *Special Programming:* Farm 2 hrs, gospel 10 hrs wkly; *Hrs. of News Programming:* news progmg 12 hrs wkly; *No. News Employees:* 1; *Target Audience:* 25-69;blue collar
Shelly Adams, Station Manager
Max Owens, General Sales Mgr
Cynthia Spratt, News Director

Independence

KCTE
01-01-1947; 1510 kHz AM; *Hrs Open:* Sunrise-sunset; 10 kw-D, DAD; N39 4 14 W94 26 58
20285 Mission Road, Stilwell, KS 66085 US
(913) 344-1500; *Fax:* (913) 344-1599
www.1510.com
License: Independence, MO held by Union Broadcasting Inc.
Nat'l Network: CBS Radio; ESPN Radio; Sporting News Radio Network
Arbitron Metro Market: Independence, MO; *Format:* Sports, Talk; *No. News Employees:* 2; *Target Audience:* Adults.
Nick McCabe, Operations Dir
Chad Boeger, General Manager
Gary Hailes, General Sales Mgr
Dennis Rooney, News Director

Ironton

KYLS-FM
01-06-1984; 95.9 MHz FM; *Hrs Open:* 24; 3.1 kw; 650 ft.; N37 40 2 W90 34 38
900 East Karsch Boulevard, Farmington, MO 63640 US
(573) 701-9590; *Fax:* (573) 701-9696
www.froggy96.com
License: Ironton, Iron County, MO held by Dockings Communications Inc.
Group Owner: Southern Star Broadcasting of Missouri LLC; (acq 5-8-2008; grpsl)
Arbitron Metro Market: Farmington, MO; *Format:* Country; *Target Audience:* 18-54.
Fred Dockins, President/General Manager
Aaron Cox, Operations Dir
Brad Dockins, Programming Director
M.J. Benz, Production Director
Dustin Kopp, Director of Web Development

Jackson

KJXX
03-01-1972; 1170 kHz AM; *Hrs Open:* 24
P.O. Box 558, Cape Girardeau, MO 63701 US
(573) 339-7000; *Fax:* (573) 651-4100
www.1170kjxx.com
rlambert@withersradio.net
License: Jackson, MO held by W. Russell Withers Jr.
Group Owner: Withers Broadcasting Co.; (acq 6-28-2005; $150,000)
Nat'l Network: Fox News Radio
Arbitron Metro Market: Jackson, MO; *Format:* Religious *Special Programming:* Parenting and family talk; *Target Audience:* General.
Rick Lambert, General Manager
Steve Thomas, Operations Manager and Program Director

***KHIS**
07-19-2010; 89.9 MHz FM; 12500 w; 466 ft; N37 22 40 W89 56 05
P.O. Box 1030, Cape Girardeau, MO 63702
(573) 651-0899
www.khisradio.org
License: Jackson, Cape Girardeau County, MO
Group Owner: Pure Word Communications
Glen Cantrell, Music Director
Ben Crass, General Manager

Jefferson City

***KJLU**
08-01-1973; 88.9 MHz FM; *Hrs Open:* 6 AM-midnight; 29.5 kw; 604 ft.; N38 27 29 W92 13 32
820 Chestnut Street, Jefferson City, MO 65102 US
(573) 681-5301,(573) 681-5296; *Fax:* (573) 681-5299
www.lincolnu.edu/~kjlu/
info@kjlu.com
License: Jefferson City, Cole County, MO held by Board of Curators of Lincoln University.
Format: Jazz; *Target Audience:* 18-54.
Michael Downey, General Manager
Dan Turner, Programming Director
LaVaughn Wilson, Promotions Manager
Leslie Taylor, News/Development Director

KBBM
01-01-1974; 100.1 MHz FM; *Hrs Open:* 24; 33 kw; 600 ft.; N38 31 25 W92 24 25
1002 Diamond Ridge, Suite 400, Jefferson City, MO 65109 US
(573) 893- 5100; *Fax:* (573) 893-8330
www.buzz.fm
buzz@buzz.fm
License: Jefferson City, Cole County, MO
Group Owner: Cumulus Media Inc.
Format: Rock/AOR; *No. News Employees:* 2; *Target Audience:* 18-34.
Kevin Joyce, Vice President/Marketing Manager
Darryl Burnett, Sales Manager
Leslie Scott, Programming Director

KWOS
02-01-1954; 950 kHz AM; 5 kw-D, DAN; 0.5 kw-N, DAN; N38 31 13 W92 10 42
3109 S. 10 Mile Drive, Jefferson City, MO 65109 US
(573) 893-5696; *Fax:* (573) 893-4137
www.kwos.com
kati@zrgmail.com
License: Jefferson City, MO held by Zimmer Radio of Mid-Missouri Inc.
Arbitron Metro Market: Columbia, MO; *Format:* News, News/Talk, 86 *Special Programming:* Farm 12 hrs wkly
John Zimmer, Chairman
Carla Leible, General Manager
Russ Davis, General Sales Mgr
Warren Krech, Programming Director
John Marsh, News Director
Jeff Studley, Chief Engineer

KTXY
12-01-1969; 106.9 MHz FM; 96 kw; 1250 ft.; N38 38 16 W92 29 34
3215 Lemone Industrial Boulevard, Columbia, MO 65201 US
(573) 875-1099; *Fax:* (573) 875-2439
www.y107.com
y107@zrgmail.com
License: Jefferson City, Cole County, MO
Arbitron Metro Market: Jefferson City, MO; *Format:* Adult Contemp
Dave Wisniewski, General Sales Mgr

KLIK
01-01-1937; 1240 kHz AM; *Hrs Open:* 24; 1 kw-U, ND1; N38 33 50 W92 11 21
503 Old Highway 63 N, Columbia, MO 65201 US
(573) 893-5100; *Fax:* (573) 893-8330
www.klik1240.com
License: Jefferson City, MO held by Cumulus Licensing LLC.
Group Owner: Cumulus Media Inc.; (acq 4-26-2004; grpsl).
Arbitron Metro Market: Jefferson City, MO; *Format:* News, News/Talk, 86; *Hrs. of News Programming:* news progmg 39 hrs wkly; *No. News Employees:* 4; *Target Audience:* 35 plus; mid to upper income-well informed
Lew Dickey, President
Kevin Joyce, VP/ General Manager
Darryl Burnett, General Sales Mgr
Brian Wilson, Programming Director
Nick Snyder, Promotions Manager
Chris Kellogg, Operations Manager

KZJF
01-01-2000; 104.1 MHz FM; *Hrs Open:* 24; 5.3 kw; 348 ft.; N38 33 50 W92 11 21

1002 Diamond Ridge, Suite 400, Jefferson City, MO 65109 US
(573) 893-5100; *Fax:* (573) 893-8330
www.jeffcountry.com
License: Jefferson City, Cole County, MO held by Cumulus Licensing LLC.
Group Owner: Cumulus Media Inc.; (acq 4-26-2004; grpsl).
Nat'l Reps: Katz Radio
Arbitron Metro Market: Jefferson City, MO; *Format:* Country
Kevin Joyce, VP/General Manager
Darryl Burnett, General Sales Mgr
Tim Murphy, KZJF Programming
Nick Snyder, KZJF Promotions/Webmaster

Joplin

KIXQ
01-01-1981; 102.5 MHz FM; *Hrs Open:* 24; 100 kw; 912 ft.; N37 5 49 W94 34 25
2702 E. 32nd St., Joplin, MO 64804 US
(417) 624-1025
www.kix1025.com
chade@zrgmail.com
License: Joplin, Jasper County, MO held by Zimmer Radio, Inc.
Group Owner: Zimmer Radio, Inc.
Nat'l Reps: Christal
Arbitron Metro Market: Joplin, MO; *Format:* Country; *No. News Employees:* 4; *Target Audience:* 25-54.
Chad Elliot, Dir. of Operations
Larry Boyd, Dir. of Sales
Randy Brooks, Programming Director

*KOBC
03-17-1969; 90.7 MHz FM; *Hrs Open:* 18; 60 kw; 495 ft.; N37 3 8 W94 23 20
1111 N. Main Street, Joplin, MO 64801 US
(417) 781-6401; *Fax:* (417) 782-1841
www.klove.com
License: Joplin, Jasper County, MO held by Educational Media Foundation.
Group Owner: EMF Broadcasting; (acq 10-1-2008; $1 million)
Nat'l Network: K-Love
Arbitron Metro Market: Joplin, MO; *Format:* Christian
Mike Novak, President

KZRG
01-01-1943; 1310 kHz AM; *Hrs Open:* 24 hrs; 5 kw-D, 1 kw-N, DA-2; N37 07 03 W94 32 41
2702 E. 32nd St., Joplin, MO 64804 US
(417) 624-1025; *Fax:* (417) 781-6842
www.newstalkkzrg.com
info@zrgmail.com
License: Joplin, Jasper County, MO held by Zimmer Radio Inc.
Group Owner: Zimmer Radio Inc.; (acq 11-15-2005; $350,100)
Nat'l Network: Fox News Radio; *Nat'l Reps:* Christal; *Wire Services:* AP
Arbitron Metro Market: Joplin, MO; *Format:* News/Talk; *Hrs. of News Programming:* 5; *No. News Employees:* 4
Chad Elliot, Operations Dir
James Zimmer, General Manager
Larry Boyd, General Sales Mgr

WMBH
05-25-1962; 1560 kHz AM; *Hrs Open:* 6 AM-9 PM; 0.25 kw-D, ND1; 0.009 kw-N, ND1; N37 4 10 W94 32 49
611 Main Street, Joplin, MO 64801 US
(417) 623-4011; *Fax:* (417) 624-1568
License: Joplin, MO held by Hardman Broadcasting Inc.
Arbitron Metro Market: Joplin, MO; *Format:* Urban Contemporary
Dave Clemons, General Sales Mgr

KSYN
12-19-1960; 92.5 MHz FM; *Hrs Open:* 24 hrs; 100 kw; 984 ft.; N37 5 49 W94 34 25
325 S. Kingshighway St., Suite B, Cape Girardeau, MO 63703-5701 US
(417) 578-9292
www.ksyn925.com
License: Joplin, Jasper County, MO held by Zimmer Radio Inc.
Group Owner: Zimmer Radio Inc.
Arbitron Metro Market: Joplin, MO; *Format:* Contemporary Hits/Top 40; *Target Audience:* 18-34.
James Zimmer, President

KZYM
06-01-1946; 1230 kHz AM; *Hrs Open:* 24; 0.56 kw-DU, 0.6 kw-N; N37 4 48 W94 33 10
2702 E. 32nd St., Joplin, MO 64804 US
(417) 624-1025; *Fax:* (417) 781-6842
www.1230thetalker.com
License: Joplin, MO held by Zimmer Radio Inc.
Group Owner: Zimmer Radio Inc.; (acq 9-30-2005; $300,000)
Nat'l Network: Salem Radio Network; *Regional Network:* Missourinet; *Nat'l Reps:* Christal; *Wire Services:* AP
Arbitron Metro Market: Joplin, MO; *Format:* News/Talk; *No. News Employees:* 30; *Target Audience:* General.
James Zimmer, General Manager
Larry Boyd, General Sales Mgr
Brett James, Programming Director
Mel Williams, Engineering Dir

*KXMS
04-05-1986; 88.7 MHz FM; 10 kw vert; 184 ft.; N37 5 57 W94 27 46
3650 E. Newman Rd., Joplin, MO 64801 US
(417) 625-9356; *Fax:* (417) 625-9742
License: Joplin, Jasper County, MO held by Board of Governors— Missouri Southern State College
Arbitron Metro Market: Joplin, MO; *Format:* Variety/Diverse
Special Programming: Big band 2 hrs wkly
Jeffrey Skibbe, General Manager
Jeffrey Scibbe, Programming Director

Kansas City

KBEQ-FM
11-01-1960; 104.3 MHz FM; *Hrs Open:* 24; 99 kw; 988 ft.; N39 4 59 W94 28 49
508 Westport Road, Suite 202, Kansas City, MO 64111 US
(816) 753-4000; *Fax:* (816) 753-4045
www.q104kc.com
License: Kansas City, Jackson County, MO held by Wilks License Co.-Kansas City LLC.
Group Owner: Wilks Broadcast Group LLC; (acq 1-10-2007; grpsl)
Arbitron Metro Market: KS City, MO; *Format:* Country; *Hrs. of News Programming:* news progmg 6 hrs wkly; *No. News Employees:* 1; *Target Audience:* 18-54; women
Mike Rowen, Vice President/Market Manager
Mike Kennedy, Programming Director
Cherie Ramirez, Promotions Director
Ben Weiss, Chief Engineer

KCMO
03-01-1922; 710 kHz AM; *Hrs Open:* 24; 10 kw-D, DA2; 5 kw-N, DA2; N39 19 8 W94 29 48
5800 Foxridge Drive, 6th Floor, Mission, KS 66202 US
(913) 514-3000; *Fax:* (913) 514-3004
www.710kcmo.com
bill.ryan@cumulus.com
License: Kansas City, MO held by CMP Houston-KC LLC
Group Owner: Cumulus Media Inc.
Nat'l Reps: Katz Radio
Arbitron Metro Market: Kansas City, MO; *Format:* Talk *Special Programming:* Pub affrs one hrs wkly; *Hrs. of News Programming:* news progmg 30 hrs wkly; *No. News Employees:* 3; *Target Audience:* 35-64.
Mark Sullivan, Senior Vice President, General Manager
Bill Ryan, General Sales Mgr
Dan McClintock, Programming Director/Operations Manager
Tom Bamford, Producer / PSA Director
Brian Goeke, Director of Marketing & Online

*KCUR-FM
10-01-1957; 89.3 MHz FM; *Hrs Open:* 24; 100 kw; 820 ft.; N39 4 59 W94 28 49
4825 Troost, Suite 202, Kansas City, MO 64110 US
(816) 235-1551; *Fax:* (816) 235-2864
www.kcur.org
kcur@umkc.edu
License: Kansas City, Jackson County, MO held by Curators of the University of Missouri.
Group Owner: The Curators of the University of Missouri
Nat'l Network: NPR; PRI
Arbitron Metro Market: Kansas City, MO-KS; *Format:* News
Special Programming: Sp 2 hrs wkly; *Hrs. of News Programming:* news progmg 50 hrs wkly; *No. News Employees:* 3; *Target Audience:* General; educated
Nico Leone, General Manager
Parker Van Hecke, General Sales Mgr
Bill Anderson, Programming Director
Frank Morris, News Director
Robin Cross, Engineering Dir
Robert Moore, Music Director
Steve Bell, Reporter

*KKFI
02-28-1988; 90.1 MHz FM; *Hrs Open:* 24; 100 kw; 423 ft.; N39 5 5 W94 28 47
Mailing Address: PO Box 32250, Kansas City, MO 64171 US
Second Address: 3901 Main Street, Kansas City, MO 64111
(816) 931-3122; *Fax:* (816) 931-7078
www.kkfi.org
info@kkfi.org
License: Kansas City, Jackson County, MO held by Mid-Coast Radio Project Inc.
Arbitron Metro Market: Kansas City, MO; *Format:* News, Talk
Special Programming: Jazz 10 hrs, blues 9 hrs, Sp 16 hrs, folk 4 hrs, A; *Hrs. of News Programming:* News progmg 10 hrs wkly; *Target Audience:* General;women & minorities; *Adv. Rates:* 32.50; 28.50; 32.50; 12.50
Dorothy Hawkins, General Manager

*KJNW
08-09-1970; 88.5 MHz FM; *Hrs Open:* 24; 100 kw; 745 ft.; N39 4 24 W94 29 6
15800 Calvary Road, Kansas City, MO 64147 US
(816) 331-8700; *Fax:* (816) 331-3497
License: Kansas City, Jackson County, MO held by Northwestern College
Group Owner: Northwestern College & Radio
Nat'l Network: Salem Radio Network
Arbitron Metro Market: Kansas City, MO; *Format:* Christian; *Hrs. of News Programming:* News progmg 6 hrs wkly; *Target Audience:* 25-54.
Elwood Chipchase, President
Michael Griman, Programming Director
Glenn Williams, Chief Engineer

KMBZ
01-01-1921; 980 kHz AM; 5 kw-D, DAN; 5 kw-N, DAN; N39 2 17 W94 36 55
7000 Squibb Road, Mission, KS 66202 US
(913) 677-8998; *Fax:* (913) 677-8901
www.kmbz.com
License: Kansas City, MO held by Entercom Kansas City News License L.L.C.
Group Owner: Entercom Communications Corp.; (acq 3-6-97; grpsl)
Arbitron Metro Market: Kansas City, MO; *Format:* News
Dave Alpert, Vice President/General Manager
Rich Deutsch, General Sales Mgr
Jack Landreth, Programming Director
Lisa Carter, News Director
Mike Cooney, Chief Engineer
Megan Wilson, Traffic Manager

KMXV
03-03-1958; 93.3 MHz FM; *Hrs Open:* 24; 100 kw; 1066 ft.; N39 0 57 W94 30 24
Mailing Address: 600 New Hampshire Ave., N.W. Suite 1200, Washington, DC 20037 US
Second Address: 508 Westport Road, Suite 202, Kansas City, MO 64111
(816) 756-5698; *Fax:* (816) 931-8540
www.mix93.com
info@mix93.com
License: Kansas City, Jackson County, MO held by Wilks License Co.-Kansas City LLC.
Group Owner: Wilks Broadcast Group LLC; (acq 1-10-2007; grpsl)
Arbitron Metro Market: Kansas City, MO; *Format:* Contemporary Hits/Top 40; *No. News Employees:* 1; *Target Audience:* 18-49; women
Mike Kennedy, Operations Dir
Mike Rowen, Vice President/General Manager
Mark Herrell, General Sales Mgr
Teresa Maxwell, News Director
Ben Weiss, Chief Engineer

KPHN
09-01-1971; 1190 kHz AM; *Hrs Open:* 24
1212 Baltimore, Kansas City, KS 64105 US
(816) 421-1900; *Fax:* (816) 471-1320
www.radiodisney.com
License: Kansas City, MO held by Radio Disney Group LLC.
Group Owner: ABC Inc.; (acq 7-19-2002; $3.8 million)
Nat'l Network: Radio Disney
Arbitron Metro Market: KS City, MO; *Format:* Children
Robert Hill, Promotions Manager
Sean Cocchia, Sr. VP & General Mngr
Ray de la Garza, VP Programming
Phil Guerini, VP Marketing

KPRS
01-01-1963; 103.3 MHz FM; *Hrs Open:* 24; 100 kw; 994 ft.; N39 0 57 W94 30 24
11131 Colorado Ave., Kansas City, MO 64137 US
(816) 763-2040; *Fax:* (816) 966-1055
www.kprs.com
License: Kansas City, Jackson County, MO held by Carter Broadcast Group Inc.
Group Owner: Carter Broadcast Group Inc.
Nat'l Reps: Eastman Radio

Arbitron Metro Market: Kansas City, MO-KS; *Format:* Urban Contemporary; *Hrs. of News Programming:* News progmg one hr wkly; *Target Audience:* 18-34 and 25-54; mid-upper income
Todd Fries, General Sales Mgr
Myron Fears, Programming Director
Rich McCauley, Promotions Manager
Mark Leaver, Chief Engineer

KPRT
01-01-1950; 1590 kHz AM; *Hrs Open:* 24; 1 kw-D, ND1; 0.047 kw-N, ND1; N39 4 5 W94 32 10
11131 Colorado Ave., Kansas City, MO 64137 US
(816) 763-2040; *Fax:* (816) 966-1055
www.kprs.com
License: Kansas City, MO held by Carter Broadcast Group Inc.
Group Owner: Carter Broadcast Group Inc.
Nat'l Reps: Eastman Radio
Arbitron Metro Market: Kansas City, MO-KS; *Format:* Urban Contemporary; *Target Audience:* 25-54
Myron Fears, Operations Dir
Todd Fries, General Sales Mgr
Rich McCauley, Promotions Manager
Mark Leaver, Chief Engineer

KCKC
03-05-1961; 102.1 MHz FM; 100 kw; 1119 ft.; N39 5 26 W94 28 18
5098 Westport Road, Kansas City, MO 64111 US
(816) 576-7102; *Fax:* (816) 531-6547
info@ksrh.com
License: Kansas City, Jackson County, MO held by Wilks License Co.-Kansas City LLC.
Group Owner: Wilks Broadcast Group LLC; (acq 1-10-2007; grpsl)
Wire Services: UPI
Arbitron Metro Market: Kansas City, MO-KS; *Format:* Adult Contemp
Mike Rowen, Vice President/Market Manager
Mike Kennedy, Programming Director
Cherie Ramirez, Promotions Director

KRBZ
01-01-1959; 96.5 MHz FM; *Hrs Open:* 24; 98.5 kw; 1099 ft.; N39 1 20 W94 30 49
7000 Squibb Road, Mission, KS 66202 US
(913) 576-7965; *Fax:* (913) 677-7520
www.965thebuzz.com
bedwards@entercom.com
License: Kansas City, Jackson County, MO held by Entercom Kansas City License L.L.C.
Group Owner: Entercom Communications Corp.; (acq 7-14-00; grpsl)
Arbitron Metro Market: Mission, KS; *Format:* Rock/AOR; *Target Audience:* 25 plus; adults with above-average disposable income
Dave Alpert, Vice President/General Manager
Frank Flores, General Sales Mgr
Sammy Jo Gibson, Promotions/Marketing Director

KZPT
10-01-1962; 99.7 MHz FM; 100 kw; Ant 1,010 ft; N39 05 01 W94 30 57
7000 Squibb Rd., Mission, KS 66202
(913) 744-3600
www.997theboulevard.com
License: Kansas City, Jackson County, MO held by Entercom Kansas City License L.L.C.
Group Owner: Entercom Communications Corp.
Arbitron Metro Market: Kansas City, MO-KS; *Format:* Adult Contemp, Contemporary Hits/Top 40
Dave Alpert, Vice President/Market Manager
Joanne Raines, Sales Manager
Tony Lo, Programming Director
Jennifer Nagel, Promotions Director
Stephanie Curren, Webmaster

KCSP
02-16-1922; 610 kHz AM; *Hrs Open:* 24
7000 Squibb Road, Mission, KS 66202 US
(913) 744-3624; *Fax:* (913) 677-8061
www.610sports.com
jhanson@entercom.com
License: Kansas City, MO held by Entercom Kansas City License L.L.C.
Group Owner: Entercom Communications Corp.; (acq 10-17-97; grpsl).
Nat'l Network: Sporting News Radio Network; *Nat'l Reps:* D & R Radio
Arbitron Metro Market: Kansas City, MO; *Format:* Sports; *Hrs. of News Programming:* News progmg 8 hrs wkly; *Target Audience:* 25-54; general
Dave Alpert, Vice President/General Manager
Wayne Walker, General Sales Mgr
John Hanson, Programming Director
Dustin Boehm, Promotions Manager

WHB
06-10-1936; 810 kHz AM; *Hrs Open:* 24; 50 kw-D, DAN; 5 kw-N, DAN; N39 18 21 W94 34 30
102 North Mason, Carrollton, MO 64633 US
(913) 344-1500; *Fax:* (913) 344-1599
License: Kansas City, MO held by Union Broadcasting Inc.
Nat'l Network: ESPN Radio; Sporting News Radio Network
Arbitron Metro Market: KS City, MO; *Format:* Sports, Talk
Special Programming: Sp 2 hrs wkly; *Hrs. of News Programming:* news progmg 19 hrs wkly; *No. News Employees:* 2; *Target Audience:* Males: 18 plus.
Jason Justice, Operations Dir
Chad Boeger, President/General Manager
Sandy Cohen, General Sales Mgr
Craig Brenner, Chief Engineer
Natalie Vizcarra, Director of Marketing

Kennett

***KAUF**
06-01-1998; 89.9 MHz FM; 1 kw; 164 ft.; N36 14 32 W90 3 54
P.O. Box 3206, Tupelo, MS 38803 US
(662) 844-8888; *Fax:* (662) 842-6791
www.afr.net
faq@afa.net
License: Kennett, Dunklin County, MO held by American Family Association.
Group Owner: American Family Radio
Arbitron Metro Market: Tupelo, MS; *Format:* Christian, Religious
Tim Wildmon, President
Donald wildmon, Founder
Buddy Smith, Sr. VP
Ed Vitagliano, Exec. VP
Randy Sharp, Director Of Special Projects
Meeke Addison, Director Of Communications
Abraham Hamilton III, General Counsel & PublicPolicy

KBOA-AM
01-01-1963; 1540 kHz AM; 1 kW-D, 0.001 kW-N, 0.5 kW-C; N36 15 11 W90 2 56
5500 Poplar Ave, Suite 1, Memphis, TN 38119 USA
(901) 685-3993; *Fax:* (901) 685-3995
kboaradio.com
License: Kennett, MO held by Pollack Broadcasting Co.
Group Owner: Pollack Broadcasting Co.
Arbitron Metro Market: New Madrid-Kennett, MO; *Format:* Adult Contemp

KXOQ
12-13-1995; 104.3 MHz FM; 6 kw; 328 ft.; N36 21 58 W90 5 36
Mailing Address: Hc 1 Box 14, Williamsville, MO 63967 US
Second Address: 700 N. Bypass, Kennett, MO 63857
(573) 686-3700; *Fax:* (573) 686-6116
www.foxradionetwork.com
kotc@sheltonbbs.com
License: Kennett, Dunklin County, MO
Format: Oldies
Blake Brewer, President
Gabe Ednay, Chief Engineer

Kimberling City

KOMC-FM
01-01-1992; 100.1 MHz FM; *Hrs Open:* 24; 36 kw; Ant 577 ft; N36 31 58 W93 19 43
202 Courtney St., Branson, MO 65616
(417) 334-6003; *Fax:* (417) 334-7141
www.mykomc.com
krzk@krzk.com
License: Kimberling City, Stone County, MO held by KOMC-KRZK LLC.
Group Owner: Earls Broadcasting Co.; (acq 6-27-97; $1,064,919).
Nat'l Network: ABC; CBS
Population Served: 70,000 *Hrs. of News Programming:* news progmg 11 hrs wkly; *No. News Employees:* 2; *Target Audience:* 45 plus; Branson & local tourists; *Adv. Rates:* 40; 36; 38; 22
Charles Earls, President
Scottie Earls, General Manager
Steve Willoughby, Station Manager
Eric Marshall, Programming Director
Kristen Clemmens, Promotions Manager
Sally Kaucher, News Director
Greg Pyron, Chief Engineer

Kirksville

***KKTR**
01-01-2002; 89.7 MHz FM; 3.5 kw; Ant 197 ft; N40 10 40 W92 34 40
409 Jesse Hall, Columbia, MO 63501
(573) 882-3431; *Fax:* (573) 882-2636
www.kbia.org
License: Kirksville, Adair County, MO held by Truman State University.

Mike Dunn, General Manager
Sally Jameson, Station Manager
Robert Wells, General Sales Mgr
Kyle Felling, Programming Director
Roger Karowski, Chief Engineer

***KVSR**
10-06-1997; 90.7 MHz FM; *Hrs Open:* 24; 32.5 kw; 325 ft; N40 13 46 W92 32 38
Mailing Address: Box 500, Kirksville, MO 63501
Second Address: RR5, Box 14AB, Kirksville, MO 63501
(660) 665-0466; *Fax:* (660) 665-7304
www.khgn.org
License: Kirksville, Adair County, MO held by Care Broadcasting Inc.
Nat'l Network: Moody
Target Audience: 30 plus; general
Dennis Phelps, President
Tom Lloyd, Chief Engineer

KIRX
10-17-1947; 1450 kHz AM; *Hrs Open:* 24; 1 kw-U, ND1; N40 12 24 W92 34 31
P.O.Box 130, 1308 N. Baltimore St., Kirksville, MO 63501 US
(660) 665-3781; *Fax:* (660) 665-0711
www.1450kirx.com
kirx@cableone.net
License: Kirksville, MO held by KIRX Inc.
Regional Network: Brownfield
Format: Oldies *Special Programming:* Farm 10 hrs wkly; *Hrs. of News Programming:* news progmg 40 hrs wkly; *No. News Employees:* 2; *Target Audience:* 25-54; general
David Nelson, President
Steven Lloyd, Executive Vice President

KLTE
05-20-1991; 107.9 MHz FM; *Hrs Open:* 24; 97 kw; 981 ft.; N39 57 23 W92 58 29
3 Crown Dr., Suite 100, Kirksville, MO 63501 US
(660) 627-5583; *Fax:* (660) 665-8900
www.bottradionetwork.com
comments@bottradionetwork.com
License: Kirksville, Adair County, MO held by Bott Communications Inc.
Group Owner: Bott Radio Network
Nat'l Network: USA; *Nat'l Reps:* Salem
Arbitron Metro Market: Columbia, MO; *Format:* Christian, Talk; *Hrs. of News Programming:* News progmg 3 hrs wkly; *Target Audience:* 35 plus.; *Adv. Rates:* 204; 168; 180; 84
Richard Bott Sr., President & CEO
Ebel Fowler, Operations Dir
Paul Shipman, General Manager
Pat Rulon, Director of National Sales
Candy Green, Program Services Manager
Rachel Launius, Marketing Manager
Jason Potocnik, Director ofTraffic Operations

KRXL
09-01-1967; 94.5 MHz FM; *Hrs Open:* 24; 90 kw; 1010 ft.; N40 14 34 W92 25 42
Mailing Address: P.O. Box 130, Kirksville, MO 63501 US
Second Address: 1308 N. Baltimore, Kirksville, MO 63501
(660) 665-9828; *Fax:* (660) 665-0711
www.945thex.com
krxl@cableone.net
License: Kirksville, Adair County, MO held by KIRX Inc.
Nat'l Network: ABC
Arbitron Metro Market: Kirksville, MO; *Format:* Classic Rock; *Hrs. of News Programming:* News progmg 2 hrs wkly; *Target Audience:* 25-54.
Steve Lloyd, General Manager

***KTRM**
02-10-1998; 88.7 MHz FM; *Hrs Open:* 7 AM-2 AM; 3.5 kw; 197 ft.; N40 10 40 W92 34 40
East Normal Street, Kirksville, MO 63501 US
(660) 785-4000; *Fax:* (660)785-4506
ktrm.truman.edu
ktrmtheedge@hotmail.com
License: Kirksville, Adair County, MO held by Truman State University.

Arbitron Metro Market: Kirksville, MO; *Format:* Alternative; *Hrs. of News Programming:* News progmg 3 hrs wkly
Geoffrey Woehlk, Station Manager
Brooke Giddens, Programming Director
Jessica McMichael, News Director

KTUF
02-14-1983; 93.7 MHz FM; *Hrs Open:* 24; 50 kw; 492 ft.; N40 11 16 W92 31 32
Mailing Address: P.O. Box 130, 1308 N. Baltimore, Kirksville, MO 63501 US
Second Address: 1308 N. Baltimore Rd., Kirksville, MO 63501
(660) 627-5883; *Fax:* (660) 665-0711
www.937ktuf.com
ktuf@cableone.net
License: Kirksville, Adair County, MO held by KIRX Inc.
Nat'l Network: ABC
Arbitron Metro Market: Kirksville, MO; *Format:* Country; *Hrs. of News Programming:* news progmg 40 hrs wkly; *No. News Employees:* 2; *Target Audience:* 18-44.
David Nelson, President
Duncan Miller, Operations Dir
Steve Lloyd, General Manager
Steven Lloyd, Executive Vice President

***KCKV**
91.9 MHz FM; *Hrs Open:* 24; 1 kw; 308 ft.; N40 13 46 W92 32 38
P O Box 467, Quincy, IL 62306 US
(573) 346-3200; *Fax:* (573) 346-1010
www.lifechangingradio.org
License: Kirksville, Adair County, MO held by Lake Area Educational Broadcasting Foundation
Arbitron Metro Market: Kirksville, MO; *Format:* Religious; *Target Audience:* 45+
Alice McDermott, CFO
James McDermott, President

Knob Noster

***KCVQ**
07-01-1998; 89.7 MHz FM; *Hrs Open:* 24; 7.7 kw; 230 ft.; N38 52 10 W93 32 58 *Rebroadcasts:* Rebroadcasts KCVO-FM Camdenton 100%
P.O. Box 800, Camdenton, MO 65020 US
(573) 346-3200; *Fax:* (573) 346-1010
www.spiritfm.org
email@spiritfm.org
License: Knob Noster, Johnson County, MO held by Lake Area Educational Broadcasting Foundation.
Nat'l Network: Salem Radio Network
Arbitron Metro Market: Camdenton, MO; *Format:* Christian; *Hrs. of News Programming:* One; *Target Audience:* 25-45.
Alice McDermott, CFO
James McDermott, President
Jim McDermott, General Manager
Alice McDermott, Financial Director

KXKX
06-24-1983; 105.7 MHz FM; *Hrs Open:* 24; 38 kw; 446 ft.; N38 45 34 W93 25 32
119 N. Third St, Box 711, Hannibal, MO 63401 US
(660) 826-1050; *Fax:* (660) 827-5072
www.kxkx.com
License: Knob Noster, Johnson County, MO held by Townsquare Media Sedalia License LLC
Group Owner: Townsquare Media; (acq 2-29-2012; grpsl)
Arbitron Metro Market: Sedalia, MO; *Format:* Country; *Hrs. of News Programming:* news progmg 5 hrs wkly; *No. News Employees:* 1; *Target Audience:* 25-54.
Dennis Polk, General Manager
Doug Sokolowski, Programming Director
Danny Hampton, News Director
Carl Zimmerschied, Chief Engineer
Dee Johnson, Traffic Manager

La Monte

KPOW-FM
11-18-1998; 97.7 MHz FM; *Hrs Open:* 24; 100 kw; 981 ft.; N39 3 10 W93 16 1
P. O. Box 1546, 906 Thompson Blvd., Sedalia, MO 65302 US
(660) 826-5005; *Fax:* (660) 826-5557
www.power977.com
sales@bennemedia.com
License: La Monte, Pettis County, MO held by Sedalia Investment Group L.L.C.
Nat'l Network: CNN Radio
Arbitron Metro Market: Columbia, MO, parts of KS City; *Format:* Talk *Special Programming:* Blues 6 hrs wkly; *Hrs. of News Programming:* news progmg 2 hrs wkly; *No. News Employees:* 1; *Target Audience:* 25-54. *Adv. Rates:* 19.55; 16.24; 19.55; 9.83
Stuart Steinmetz, General Manager
Sally Altena, General Sales Mgr

Lake Ozark

KQUL
05-09-1994; 102.7 MHz FM; *Hrs Open:* 24; 6 kw; 328 ft.; N38 2 6 W92 34 31
209 E. 2nd Street, Eldon, MO 65026 US
(573) 348-1958; *Fax:* (573) 348-1923
mike@mix927.com
License: Lake Ozark, Camden County, MO held by Benne Broadcasting of Lake Ozark Inc.
Format: Oldies; *Target Audience:* 35-60.
Denny Benne, General Manager
Greg Sullens, Station Manager
Mike Clayton, Programming Director

Lamar

KHST
05-01-1992; 101.7 MHz FM; 22 kw; 328 ft.; N37 25 27 W94 16 11
412 N. Locust, Pittsburg, KS 66762 US
(620) 232-5993
www.mycountry1017.com
License: Lamar, Barton County, MO held by My Town Media, Inc.
Group Owner: MyTown Media, LLC.; (acq 9-22-98; $330,000)
Arbitron Metro Market: Joplin, MO; *Format:* Country; *Target Audience:* 25-54.; *Adv. Rates:* 100; 80; 80; 80
Dave Lee, Operations Dir

Lebanon

KBNN
10-20-1973; 750 kHz AM; *Hrs Open:* 6 AM-sunset
P.O.Box 1112, Lebanon, MO 65536 US
(417) 532-9111; *Fax:* (417) 532-3989
www.regionalradio.com
kjel@regionalradio.com
License: Lebanon, MO held by Waynesville/Lebanon License Co. LLC.
Group Owner: GoodRadio.TV; (acq 8-8-2007; grpsl)
Regional Network: Missourinet
Format: Talk *Special Programming:* News, farm 8 hrs wkly; *Hrs. of News Programming:* news progmg 35 hrs wkly; *No. News Employees:* 5; *Target Audience:* 35-64; middle America; *Adv. Rates:* 40; 38; 24; 24
Theresa Nixon, Operations Dir
Mike Edwards, General Manager
Marcy Todd, News Director

KCLQ
05-18-1979; 107.9 MHz FM; *Hrs Open:* 24; 19 kw; 669 ft.; N37 48 11 W92 33 1
18785 Finch Rd, Lebanon, MO 65536 US
(417) 532-2962; *Fax:* (417) 532-5184
www.1079thecoyote.com
License: Lebanon, Laclede County, MO
Arbitron Metro Market: Lebanon, MO; *Format:* Country; *Hrs. of News Programming:* news progmg 3 hrs wkly; *No. News Employees:* 3; *Target Audience:* 25-54; female; *Adv. Rates:* 23.25; 20.25; 21.75; 11.25
Wilburn Luna, CFO
Fred Key, President
Audrey Luna, General Manager
Doug Smith, General Sales Mgr
Juan Vela, Programming Director
Freddy Maskill, Promotions Manager
Jeff Rottman, News Director

KJEL
10-20-1973; 103.7 MHz FM; *Hrs Open:* 24; 100 kw; 984 ft.; N37 49 10 W92 44 51
P.O. Box 430, Moberly, MO 65270 US
(417) 532-9111; *Fax:* (417) 532-3989
License: Lebanon, Laclede County, MO held by Waynesville/Lebanon License Co. LLC.
Group Owner: GoodRadio.TV
Nat'l Network: ABC
Format: Country; *Hrs. of News Programming:* news progmg 45 hrs wkly; *No. News Employees:* 5; *Target Audience:* 25-65; equal Male/Female; *Adv. Rates:* 44; 38; 28; 25
Teresa Nixon, Operations Dir
Mike Edwards, General Manager
Mary Todd, News Director
Bob Moore, Chief Engineer
Marcy Todd, Office Manager

KLWT
07-04-1948; 1230 kHz AM; *Hrs Open:* 24; 1 kw-U, ND1; N37 40 40 W92 41 16
18785 Finch Road, Lebanon, MO 65536 US
(417) 532-2962; *Fax:* (417) 532-5184
www.klwt1230.com
klwt@klwt1230.com
License: Lebanon, MO held by Pearson Broadcasting of Lebanon Inc.
Format: Country, News, 62, Sports, Talk; *Hrs. of News Programming:* news progmg 10 hrs wkly; *No. News Employees:* 3; *Target Audience:* 30 plus; adults; *Adv. Rates:* 15.75; 12.75; 14.25; 9
Kit Caldwell, Operations Dir
Dan Caldwell, General Manager
Brian McClendon, General Sales Mgr
Jannise Restivo, News Director

***KTTK**
01-01-1992; 90.7 MHz FM; *Hrs Open:* 5 AM-midnight; 11 kw; 476 ft.; N37 37 58 W92 45 22
221 East Commercial St., Lebanon, MO 65536 US
(417) 588-1435; *Fax:* (417) 532-3055
License: Lebanon, Laclede County, MO held by Lebanon Educational Broadcasting Foundation.
Nat'l Network: USA
Arbitron Metro Market: Lebanon, MO; *Format:* Christian *Special Programming:* Gospel 7 hrs wkly
Max Rhoades, General Manager
Dave Hutton, Programming Director

Lee's Summit

***KLRX**
01-01-1998; 97.3 MHz FM; 55 kw; 1171 ft.; N39 5 26 W94 28 18
P.O. Box 219, Moberly, MO 65270 US
(913) 344-1500; *Fax:* (913) 344-1599
www.klove.com
info@klove.com
License: Lee's Summit, Jackson County, MO held by Union First Broadcasting LLC
Nat'l Network: K-Love
Arbitron Metro Market: Kansas City, MO-KS; *Format:* Christian
Chad Boeger, General Manager

Lexington

KLEX
04-19-1956; 1570 kHz AM; *Hrs Open:* 24; 0.25 kw-D, ND1; 0.04 kw-N, ND1; N39 11 14 W93 50 03 *Rebroadcasts:* Rebroadcasts KAYX(FM) Richmond 100%
10550 Barkley St., Suite 100, Overland Park, KS 66212 US
(816) 470-9925; *Fax:* (816) 470-8925
www.bottradionetwork.com
comments@bottradionetwork.com
License: Lexington, Lafayette County, MO held by Bott Communications Inc.
Group Owner: Bott Radio Network; (acq 1994; with KAYX(FM) Richmond)
Nat'l Network: USA
Population Served: 50,000; *Arbitron Metro Market:* Lexington, MO; *Format:* Christian, Talk; *Target Audience:* 25-54.
Richard Bott Sr., President & CEO
Eben Fowler, Operations Dir
Pat Rulon, Director of National Sales
Candy Green, Program Services Manager
Rachel Launius, Marketing Manager
Jason Potocnik, Director of Traffic Operations
JulieWhite, Officer Manager

Liberty

KCXL
02-14-1967; 1140 kHz AM
310 South La Frenz Road, Liberty, MO 64068 US
(816) 792-1140; *Fax:* (816) 792-8258
www.kcxl.com
kcxl11140@yahoo.com
License: Liberty, MO held by Alpine Broadcasting Corp.
Nat'l Network: AP Network News; Jones Radio Networks
Arbitron Metro Market: Liberty, MO; *Format:* Adult Contemp, Talk *Special Programming:* News 4 hrs, Sp 5 hrs, relg 3 hrs, health 17 hrs wkly; *Target Audience:* 25-54; baby boomers; *Adv. Rates:* 25; 20; 25; 15
Peter Schartel, President
David Brewer, Operations Dir
David Brewer, Station Manager
Jonne Santoli, General Sales Mgr
John Christopher, Chief Engineer

***KWJC**
04-14-1974; 91.9 MHz FM; *Hrs Open:* 24; 7 kw; 623 ft.; N39 7 23 W94 23 24
Div/DBA: Dpeartment of Communication
Dept. of Communication, 500 College Hill, Liberty, MO 64068 US
(816) 415-7594; *Fax:* (816) 415-5027
www.air1.com
License: Liberty, Clay County, MO held by William Jewell College.
Arbitron Metro Market: Kansas City, MO-KS; *Format:* Contemporary Hits/Top 40 *Special Programming:* Class 10 hrs, Christian 10 hrs wkly; *Hrs. of News Programming:* News progmg 5 hrs wkly; *Target Audience:* 12-34; men& women; *Adv. Rates:* 10; 10; 10; 8
Paul Worstell, General Manager

Licking

***KIKG**
91.1 MHz FM; kw
US
License: Licking, Texas County, MO held by Ron Elmore Ministries Inc.
Arbitron Metro Market: Licking, MO
Ron Elmore, President

Linn

KJMO
01-01-2006; 97.5 MHz FM; 6 kw; 328 ft.; N38 29 56.9 W91 53 0.4
1002 Diamond Ridge, Suite 400, Jefferson, MO 65109 US
(573) 893-5100; *Fax:* (573) 893-8330
www.kjmo.com
License: Linn, Osage County, MO held by Cumulus Licensing LLC.
Group Owner: Cumulus Media Inc.
Arbitron Metro Market: Jefferson City, MO; *Format:* Oldies
Kevin Joyce, VP
Darryl Burnett, General Sales Mgr
Chris Kellogg, Programming Director
Nick Snyder, Promotions Manager

Louisiana

KJFM
09-04-1984; 102.1 MHz FM; 3.7 kw; 387 ft.; N39 26 29 W91 2 19
Mailing Address: P.O. Box 438, Louisiana, MO 63353 US
Second Address: 615 Georgia St., Louisiana, MO 63353
(573) 754-5102; *Fax:* (573) 754-5544
kjfmradio@yahoo.com
License: Louisiana, Pike County, MO held by Foxfire Communications Inc.
Nat'l Network: ABC Information & Entertainment; *Regional Network:* Missourinet
Format: Country; *Hrs. of News Programming:* 27 hrs news progmg wkly; *Target Audience:* 25-54.; *Adv. Rates:* 22.5; 20; 20; 17.50
Marianne Everhart, Operations Dir
Thom T. Sanders, General Manager

Lutesville

KMHM
08-04-1995; 104.1 MHz FM; *Hrs Open:* 24; 2.5 kw; 509 ft.; N37 22 40 W89 56 4
R R 1 Box 266E, Marble Hill, MO 63764 US
(573) 238-1041; *Fax:* (573) 238-0104
www.kmhm.net
kmhm1041@clas.net
License: Lutesville, Bollinger County, MO held by Southern Gospetality LLC.
Nat'l Network: Salem Radio Network
Format: Gospel; *Hrs. of News Programming:* News progmg 14 hrs wkly; *Target Audience:* 30-55; Christians and family-oriented listeners; *Adv. Rates:* 12; 11:50; 12; 11:50
Harold Lawder, CEO
Will Stephens, General Manager
James Aaron, Station Manager
Joy Duprey, Programming Director
Tom Beattie, Chief Engineer
Sheila Kirkpatrick, Traffic Director

Macon

KIRK
01-01-1998; 99.9 MHz FM; *Hrs Open:* 24; 12.5 kw; 463 ft.; N39 36 2 W92 34 24
Mailing Address: 300 West Reed Street, P.O Box 619, Moberly, MO 65270 US
Second Address: 300 W. Reed St., Moberly, MO 65270
(660) 263-6999; *Fax:* (660) 263-2300
License: Macon, Macon County, MO held by Moberly/Macon License Co. LLC.
Group Owner: GoodRadio.TV; (acq 8-8-2007; grpsl)
Format: Adult Contemp
Terry Strickland, General Manager

KLTI
01-30-1966; 1560 kHz AM; *Hrs Open:* 24
32968 US Hwy 63 S., Macon, MO 63552 US
(660) 385-1560; *Fax:* (660) 385-7090
www.kltiradio.com
klti@mcmsys.com
License: Macon, MO held by Chirillo Electronics Inc.
Group Owner: Best Broadcast Group
Format: Country; *Target Audience:* 25-44.
Dale Palmer, General Manager

Madison

KTCM
97.3 MHz FM; 25 kw; Ant 328 ft; N39 28 52 W92 10 13
525 S. Flagler Dr., # 21-A, West Palm Beach, FL
(561) 515-6142
License: Madison, Monroe County, MO held by Christine Radio LLC.
Group Owner: GoodRadio.TV; (acq 10-4-2007)

Trace Michaels, General Manager
Brad Elliott, Programming Director
Chris Andrews, Chief Engineer

Malden

KLSC
11-23-1979; 92.9 MHz FM; *Hrs Open:* 6 AM-midnight; 50 kw; 476 ft.; N36 40 31 W89 46 19
324 Broadway, Cape Girardeau, MO 63702 US
(573) 335-8291
www.semoespn.com
License: Malden, Dunklin County, MO held by MRR License LLC.
Group Owner: MAX Media L.L.C.
Nat'l Network: ESPN Radio
Arbitron Metro Market: Sikeston, MO; *Format:* Sports; *Hrs. of News Programming:* news progmg 30 hrs wkly; *No. News Employees:* 2; *Target Audience:* General.
Ronnie Glover, General Manager
Hunter Hendricks, Promotions Director
Sherry Crider, Traffic Manager

KMAL
09-15-1954; 1470 kHz AM; *Hrs Open:* 6 AM-sunset; 1 kw-D, NDD; N36 33 8 W89 58 42 *Rebroadcasts:* Simulcasts KSIM (Sikeston)
324 Broadway, Cape Girardeau, MO 63701 US
(573) 335-8291
www.semoespn.com
License: Malden, Dunklin County, MO held by MRR License LLC.
Group Owner: MAX Media L.L.C.; (acq 6-2-2004; grpsl).
Arbitron Metro Market: Cape Girardeau, MO; *Format:* Sports; *No. News Employees:* 3; *Target Audience:* 35 plus.
Ronnie Glover, General Manager
Todd Bonacki, Programming Director
Hunter Hendricks, Promotions Director
Sherry Crider, Traffic Manager

Malta Bend

KRLI
10-28-1996; 103.9 MHz FM; *Hrs Open:* 24; 12 kw; 879 ft.; N39 21 59 W93 24 12
203 North Mason Street, Carrollton, MO 64633 US
(660) 542-0404; *Fax:* (660) 542-3152
License: Malta Bend, Saline County, MO held by Kanza Inc.
Format: Big Band, Jazz, 64; *Hrs. of News Programming:* news progmg 6 hrs wkly; *No. News Employees:* 2; *Target Audience:* 45 plus; baby boomers; *Adv. Rates:* 96; 96; 96; 42
Miles Carter, CEO

Mansfield

KTRI-FM
01-01-1978; 95.9 MHz FM; *Hrs Open:* 24; 8.9 kw; 541 ft.; N37 17 10 W92 36 55
7450 Midlothian Pike, Richmond, VA 23225 US
(417) 235-6041; *Fax:* (417) 235-6388
www.buzz959.com/index.php?option=com_content&view=article&id=52&Itemid=43
License: Mansfield, Wright County, MO held by Thirteen Forty Productions Inc.
Arbitron Metro Market: Monett, MO; *Format:* Adult Contemp
Gary Snadon, President

Marble Hill

KYRX
12-01-1999; 97.3 MHz FM; 3.6 kw; 427 ft.; N37 22 49 W90 4 49
P O Box 818, Benton, IL 62812 US
(573) 339-7000; *Fax:* (573) 651-4100
License: Marble Hill, Bollinger County, MO held by Dana R. Withers.
Nat'l Reps: Katz Radio
Format: Oldies
Rick Lambert, General Manager

Marshall

KMMO
05-29-1949; 1300 kHz AM; *Hrs Open:* 24; 1 kw-D, ND1; 0.068 kw-N, ND1; N39 8 3 W93 13 19
P. O. Box 128, Marshall, MO 63540 US
(660) 886-7422; *Fax:* (660) 886-6291
License: Marshall, MO held by Missouri Valley Broadcasting Inc.

Eric Strobel, General Manager
Carl Raida, Programming Director

KMMO-FM
12-01-1968; 102.9 MHz FM; *Hrs Open:* 24; 100 kw; 381 ft.; N39 8 3 W93 13 19
1190 N. Highway 65, Marshall, MO 65340 US
(660) 886-7422; *Fax:* (660) 886-6291
License: Marshall, Saline County, MO held by Missouri Valley Broadcasting Inc.
Nat'l Network: CBS
Format: Country; *Target Audience:* General.; *Adv. Rates:* 30; 28; 30; 20
John Wilson, General Manager
Peter Hollabaugh, General Sales Mgr
Ken Lewellen, News Director
Debbie Bowlen, Office Manager
Melinda Mueller, Webmaster
Brian Sowers, Agricultural Director
Velda Ellison, Traffic Manager

***KMVC**
11-01-1968; 91.7 MHz FM; *Hrs Open:* 7 AM-11 PM (M-F); 9 AM-11 PM (S); n; 0.1 kw vert; 62 ft.; N39 6 31 W93 11 29
500 East College Street, Marshall, MO 65340 US
(660) 831-4193; *Fax:* (660) 886-9818
License: Marshall, Saline County, MO held by Missouri Valley College.
Format: Alternative, Blues *Special Programming:* Black 10 hrs, progsv 10 hrs, relg 16 hrs, classic; *Hrs. of News Programming:* News progmg 3 hrs wkly; *Target Audience:* 17-26; pre-, current & post-college age
Brent Foster, General Manager
Josh Branch, Station Manager

Marshfield

KKLH
06-01-1982; 104.7 MHz FM; *Hrs Open:* 24; 34 kW; 594 ft.; N37 12 21 W92 54 20
2453 E Elm St, Springfield, MO 65802 USA
(417) 886-5677; *Fax:* (417) 886-2155
www.1047thecave.com
info@1047thecave.com
License: Marshfield, Webster County, MO held by MW SpringMo Inc.
Group Owner: The Mid-West Family Broadcast Group; (acq 1996; $1.8 million).
Nat'l Reps: Eastman Radio
Arbitron Metro Market: Springfield, MO; *Format:* Classic Rock; *Target Audience:* Persons 35-54; *Adv. Rates:* 30; 35; 35; 15
Brian Tyndall, General Sales Mgr
Mike Holmes, Programming Director

KMRF
11-01-1969; 1510 kHz AM; *Hrs Open:* Sunrise-sunset
1411 Locust Street, St Louis, MO 63103 US
(417) 468-6188; *Fax:* (417) 859-2916
License: Marshfield, MO held by New Life Evangelistic Center Inc.
Nat'l Network: USA; *Regional Network:* Missourinet; Brownfield
Arbitron Metro Market: Springfield, MO; *Format:* Gospel; *Hrs. of News Programming:* news progmg 6 hrs wkly; *No. News Employees:* 1; *Target Audience:* General.

Larry Rice, President
Ed Moore, Operations Dir
Hank Zenicwicz, Programming Director

*KQOH

91.9 MHz FM; 1.75 kw; 249 ft.; N37 19 1 W92 57 51
Rebroadcasts: Rebroadcasts KNLG(FM) New Bloomfield 100%
1411 Locust Street, St. Louis, MO 63103 US
(417) 468-6188; *Fax:* (417) 859-2916
License: Marshfield, Webster County, MO
Format: Christian; *Target Audience:* General.
Marvin Sanders, General Manager

Maryville

KNIM

01-01-1953; 1580 kHz AM; *Hrs Open:* 24; 0.7 kw-D, ND1; 0.007 kw-N, ND1; N40 19 3 W94 52 14
Mailing Address: P.O. Box 278, Maryville, MO 64468 US
Second Address: 1618 S. Main, Maryville, MO 64468
(660) 582-2151; *Fax:* (660) 582-3211
knimmaryville.com
License: Maryville, MO held by Nodaway Broadcasting Corp.
Nat'l Network: CNN Radio; *Nat'l Reps:* Keystone (unwired net)
Format: News, Sports *Special Programming:* Farm 5 hrs wkly; *No. News Employees:* 1; *Target Audience:* 25-54.
Joyce Cronin, President
Jim Cronin, Executive Vice President

KVVL

09-01-1972; 97.1 MHz FM; *Hrs Open:* 24; 21.5 kw; Ant 354 ft; N40 23 31 W94 58 04
Mailing Address: Box 278, Maryville, MO 64468
Second Address: 1618 S. Main, Maryville, MO 64468
(660) 582-2151; *Fax:* (660) 582-3211
www.knimmaryville.com
License: Maryville, Nodaway County, MO
Wire Services: AP
Population Served: 120,000 *Hrs. of News Programming:* news progmg 25 hrs wkly; *No. News Employees:* 1
Mike Robbins, General Manager
Dan Thomas, Programming Director

*KXCV

01-01-1971; 90.5 MHz FM; *Hrs Open:* 24; 100 kw; 634 ft.; N40 24 9 W94 53 16
800 University Drive, Maryville, MO 64468 US
(660) 562-1163(660) 562-1164; *Fax:* (660) 562-1832
www.kxcv.org
kxcv@nwmissouri.edu
License: Maryville, Nodaway County, MO held by Northwest Missouri State University.
Nat'l Network: NPR; PRI
Arbitron Metro Market: Maryville, MO; *Format:* Jazz, News; *Hrs. of News Programming:* news progmg 39 hrs wkly; *No. News Employees:* 2; *Target Audience:* General.
John Jasinski, President
Patty Holley, Operations Dir
Rodney Harris, General Manager
Patty Andrews Holley, Programming Director
Venus Brown, Promotions Manager
Kirk Wayman, News Director
Darren Perkins, Chief Engineer
JohnCoffey, Sports Director
Marcia Fish, Traffic Manager
Venus Brown, Membership Development/ Events Coordinator

Memphis

KMEM-FM

03-29-1982; 100.5 MHz FM; *Hrs Open:* 24; 25 kw; 299 ft.; N40 29 59 W92 9 58
Mailing Address: P.O. Box 121, Memphis, MO 63555 US
Second Address: 650 N. Clay, Memphis, MO 63555
(660) 465-7225; *Fax:* (660) 465-2626
www.kmemfm.com
mdenney@kmemfm.com
License: Memphis, Scotland County, MO held by Boyer Broadcasting Co. Inc.
Regional Network: Missourinet; Brownfield
Format: Country *Special Programming:* Farm 8 hrs, relg 4 hrs wkly; *Hrs. of News Programming:* news progmg 15 hrs wkly; *No. News Employees:* 1; *Target Audience:* General; adult audience 30+; *Adv. Rates:* 16.50;16.50; 16.50; 12.50
Mark McVey, President
Karen McVey, Operations Dir
Mark Denney, General Manager

Mexico

*KJAB-FM

10-09-1985; 88.3 MHz FM; *Hrs Open:* 24; 4.8 kw vert; 272 ft.; N39 6 13 W91 53 35
621 West Monroe, Mexico, MO 65265 US
(573) 581-8606; *Fax:* (573) 581-9655
www.kjab.com
kjab@kjab.com
License: Mexico, Audrain County, MO held by Mexico Educational Broadcasting Foundation.
Nat'l Network: USA
Format: Gospel *Special Programming:* Gospel 20 hrs, relg 20 hrs wkly; *Hrs. of News Programming:* news progmg 2 hrs wkly; *No. News Employees:* 1; *Target Audience:* General.
Kevin Weber, President
Daniel Taylor, Programming Director
Tim Knight, Underwriting Director

KWWR

12-14-1966; 95.7 MHz FM; *Hrs Open:* 24; 91 kw; 1181 ft.; N39 15 49 W92 8 6
Mailing Address: 1705 E. Liberty, P.O. Box 475, Mexico, MO 65265 US
Second Address: 1705 E. Liberty St., Mexico, MO 65265-3537
(573) 581-5500; *Fax:* (573) 581-1801
info.kwwr.com
production@radiogetsresults.net
License: Mexico, Audrain County, MO held by KXEO Radio Inc.
Nat'l Network: CNN Radio; Westwood One; *Wire Services:* NWS (National Weather Service); AP
Arbitron Metro Market: Mexico, MO; *Format:* Country *Special Programming:* Farm, News, Sports; *No. News Employees:* 21; *Target Audience:* 24-54.; *Adv. Rates:* 57; 45; 57; 29
Anne Johnson, President
Gary Leonard, Operations Dir
Michael Daugherty, General Manager
David Moser, General Sales Mgr
Matt Bingham, Programming Director
Chris Newbrough, News Director
Penny Daugherty, Traffic Manager

KXEO

12-03-1948; 1340 kHz AM; *Hrs Open:* 24
Mailing Address: P.O. Box 475, Mexico, MO 65265 US
Second Address: 1705 E. Liberty St., Mexico, MO 65265-0475
(573) 581-5500; *Fax:* (573) 581-1801
www.kxeo.com
License: Mexico, MO held by KXEO Radio Inc.
Nat'l Network: CNN Radio; Westwood One; *Regional Network:* Missourinet; Brownfield; *Wire Services:* AP
Arbitron Metro Market: Mexico, MO; *Format:* Adult Contemp, News, 84; *Hrs. of News Programming:* News progmg 4 hrs wkly; *Target Audience:* 25-54.; *Adv. Rates:* 24; 20; 24; 20
Gary Leonard, General Manager
Chris Newbrough, News Director

*KAUD

90.5 MHz FM; 0.45 kw; 158 ft.; N39 10 36 W91 47 41.9
University of Missouri, 409 Jesse Hall, Columbia, MO 65211 US
(573) 882-3431; *Fax:* (573) 882-2636
www.kbia.org
kbia@kbia.org
License: Mexico, Audrain County, MO held by The Curators of the University of Missouri.
Group Owner: The Curators of the University of Missouri
Nat'l Network: NPR; PRI
Arbitron Metro Market: Columbia, MO; *Format:* Classical
Karen Walker Seeger, Operations and Music Director
Mike Dunn, General Manager
Robert Wells, General Sales Mgr
Kyle Felling, Programming Director
Janet Saidi, News Director
Scott Pham, Web Content Director
Roger Karwoski, WebContent Director
Sally Jameson, Business Manager
Ryan Famuliner, Asst. News Director
Nathan Anderson, Development
Shannon Watkins, Membership Coordinator
Pat Akers, Operations Manager

Miner

KBHI

01-01-2001; 107.1 MHz FM; 3.7 kw; 420 ft.; N36 56 33 W89 41 47
P O Box 818, Benton, IL 62812 US
(573) 471-2000; *Fax:* (573) 471-8525
www.star1071.com
License: Miner, Scott County, MO held by Dana R. Withers.
Nat'l Reps: Katz Radio
Arbitron Metro Market: Sikeston, MO; *Format:* Oldies
Rick Lambert, General Manager
Joe Bill Davis, Station Manager
C.J. Cruze, Programming Director

Mission

WDAF-FM

11-09-1979; 106.5 MHz FM; 100 kw; 981 ft.; N39 4 24 W94 29 6
7000 Squibb Rd., Mission, KS 66202 US
(913) 677-8998; *Fax:* (913) 677-8061
www.1065thewolf.com
info@1065thewolf.com
License: Mission, KS held by Entercom Kansas City License LLC.
Group Owner: Entercom Communications Corp.; (acq 7-14-00; grpsl).
Nat'l Reps: D & R Radio
Arbitron Metro Market: Kansas City, MO; *Format:* Jazz, Smooth Jazz; *Target Audience:* 18-34.
Herndon Hasty, General Manager
Joanne Raines, General Sales Mgr
Wes Poe, Program Director and Music Director
Natalie Puhr, Program Director and Music Director
Kelsey Nelson, Promotions Coordinator
Justin Neighbor, PromotionsAssistant

Moberly

*KBKC

01-01-2004; 90.1 MHz FM; 0.33 kw; 253 ft.; N39 24 39 W92 26 46
P O Drawer 2440, Tupelo, MS 38803 US
(314) 752-7000
www.covenantnet.net
office@covenantnet.net
License: Moberly, Randolph County, MO held by Covenant Network.
Group Owner: Covenant Network; (acq 3-30-2004; $112,500 with WHOJ(FM) Terre Haute, IN)
Arbitron Metro Market: St. Louis, MO; *Format:* Christian
Tony Holman, General Manager
Jim Schaper, Programming Director

KRES

10-01-1966; 104.7 MHz FM; 100 kw; 1020 ft.; N39 27 35 W92 42 7
Mailing Address: P.O. Box 619, Moberly, MO 65270 US
Second Address: 300 West Reed, Moberly, MO 65270
(660) 263-1600; *Fax:* (660) 269-8811
www.centralmoinfo.com
kresnews@regionalradio.com
License: Moberly, Randolph County, MO
Group Owner: GoodRadio.TV
Nat'l Network: ABC
Format: Country
George Pelletier, COO
Dean Goodman, President
Stephanie Ross, Operations Dir
Terry Strickland, General Manager
Brad Boyer, Programming Director
Mike Lear, News Director

KWIX

06-17-1950; 1230 kHz AM; *Hrs Open:* 24; 0.49 kw-D, ND1; 1 kw-N, ND1; N39 24 11 W92 25 57
Mailing Address: 300 West Reed Street, Moberly, MO 65270 US
Second Address: 300 West Reed, Moberly, MO 65270
(660) 263-1600; *Fax:* (660) 269-8811
www.centralmoinfo.com
kresnews@regionalradio.com
License: Moberly, MO held by Moberly/Macon License Co. LLC.
Group Owner: GoodRadio.TV; (acq 8-8-2007; grpsl)
Nat'l Network: CBS; *Wire Services:* NOAA Weather
Arbitron Metro Market: Moberly, Mo; *Format:* Talk; *Hrs. of News Programming:* news progmg 30 hrs wkly; *No. News Employees:* 4; *Target Audience:* General.
George Pelletier, COO
Terry Strickland, General Manager
Brad Boyer, Programming Director
Mike Lear, News Director
Lloyd Collins, Chief Engineer
Stephanie Ross, Webmaster

KZZT

04-10-1987; 105.5 MHz FM; *Hrs Open:* 24; 50 kw; 492 ft.; N39 26 2 W92 14 24
Mailing Address: PO Box 128, Moberly, MO 65270 US
Second Address: 107 S. Main, Brookfield, MO 64628
(660) 263-9390; *Fax:* (660) 263-8800
www.kzztradio.com
kzzt@mcmsys.com

License: Moberly, Randolph County, MO held by FM-105 Inc.
Group Owner: Best Broadcast Group; (acq 7-9-97; $200,000 for 43%).
Nat'l Network: ABC
Arbitron Metro Market: Columbia, MO; *Format:* Classic Rock; *Hrs. of News Programming:* News progmg 5 hrs wkly; *Target Audience:* 25-54; men & women with spendable income
Dale Palmer, General Manager

***KSDQ**
88.7 MHz FM; 17 kw vert; 187 ft.; N39 14 40 W92 12 40
US
(573) 682-5887
www.ksdqradio.net
mickeyburkett@gmail.com
License: Moberly, Randolph County, MO held by Sunnydale Seventh-Day Adventist Church.
Arbitron Metro Market: Moberly, MO
Micky Burkett, Operations Dir
Erving Bales, General Manager

Monett

KKBL
12-01-1977; 95.9 MHz FM; *Hrs Open:* 24; 6 kw; 269 ft.; N36 56 15 W93 55 30
1569 N. Central St., Monett, MO 65708 US
(417) 235-6041; *Fax:* (417) 235-6388
info@buzz959.com
License: Monett, Barry County, MO
Arbitron Metro Market: Joplin, MO; *Format:* Rock/AOR; *Hrs. of News Programming:* news progmg 4 hrs wkly; *No. News Employees:* 1; *Target Audience:* General; young, adults, families; *Adv. Rates:* 12; 12; 12; 12
Daniel Voss, General Sales Mgr
Tracy Bailey, Promotions Manager

Monroe City

KWBZ
07-04-1981; 107.5 MHz FM; 10 kw; 328 ft.; N39 35 12 W91 47 57
1645 Highway 104, Quincy, IL 62305 US
(217) 885-3222(217) 224-4653; *Fax:* (217) 885-3233
wpwqfm.com
wpwq106@adams.net
License: Monroe City, Monroe County, MO held by WPW Broadcasting Inc.
Group Owner: Prairie Radio Communications; (acq 8-17-2000)
Arbitron Metro Market: Quincy, IL; *Format:* Oldies
Larry Bostwick, General Manager
Kim Beaty, Sales Consultant

Montgomery City

KMCR
08-15-1977; 103.9 MHz FM; *Hrs Open:* 24; 6 kw; 299 ft.; N38 59 10 W91 30 39
Mailing Address: 205 E. Norman, Montgomery City, MO 63361 US
Second Address: 107 S. Main, Brookfield, MO 64628
(573) 564-2275; *Fax:* (573) 564-8026
www.kmcrradio.com
kmcr@socket.net
License: Montgomery City, Montgomery County, MO held by Chirillo Electronics Inc.
Group Owner: Best Broadcast Group; (acq 1994).
Regional Network: Missourinet
Format: Adult Contemp *Special Programming:* Farm 2 hrs, relg 2 hrs wkly; *Hrs. of News Programming:* news progmg 3 hrs wkly; *No. News Employees:* 1; *Target Audience:* 25-60; male/female
Dale Palmer, General Manager

Mount Vernon

KRVI
07-29-1993; 106.7 MHz FM; 25 kw; 328 ft; N37 09 16 W93 36 58
2330 W. Grand St., Springfield, MO 59937
(417) 865-6614; *Fax:* (417) 865-9643
www.2rocks.com
ccannon@journalbroadcastgroup.com
License: Mount Vernon, Lawrence County, MO held by Journal Broadcast Corp.
Group Owner: Journal Communications Inc.; (acq 11-26-2003; $5 million with KSGF-FM Ash Grove).

Chris Cannon, Operations Dir
Rex Hansen, General Manager
Janelle Carter, General Sales Mgr

Mountain Grove

KELE
11-16-1954; 1360 kHz AM; *Hrs Open:* 24; 1 kw-D, NDD; 0.06 kw-N, ND1; N37 8 7 W92 14 59
800 North Hubbard, Mountain Grove, MO 65711 US
(417) 926-4650; *Fax:* (417) 926-7604
tonya@925thegrove.com
License: Mountain Grove, MO held by Quorum Radio Partners Inc.
Nat'l Network: USA; *Regional Network:* Brownfield
Format: Country; *Hrs. of News Programming:* news progmg 10 hrs wkly; *No. News Employees:* 1; *Adv. Rates:* 5; 5; 5; 5
Tracy O'Quinn, General Manager
Shaun Anthony, Programming Director
Jim Morris, News Director
Terry Dobson, Sports Commentator
Perry Dobson, Sports Commentator
Tonya Shannon, Traffic Manager

KELE-FM
01-01-1977; 92.5 MHz FM; 3 kw; 300 ft.; N37 8 7 W92 14 59
800 N. Hubbard, Mountain Grove, MO 65711 US
(417) 926-4650; *Fax:* (417) 926-7604
License: Mountain Grove, Wright County, MO held by Ozark Media Inc.
Group Owner: Ozark Media Inc.; (acq 5-1-2007; $625,000 with KOZX(FM) Cabool)
Format: Country *Special Programming:* Relg 3 hrs wkly; *Hrs. of News Programming:* news progmg 8 hrs wkly; *No. News Employees:* 1; *Target Audience:* 24-59; general; *Adv. Rates:* 13.75; 9.25; 11.75; 8
Tracy O'Quinn, General Manager
Shaun Anthony, Programming Director
Jim Morris, News Director
Perry Dobson, Sports Commentator
Terry Dobson, Sports Commentator
Tonya Shannon, Traffic Manager

Mountain View

KUPH
07-31-1998; 96.9 MHz FM; *Hrs Open:* 24; 50 kw; 492 ft.; N36 59 29 W91 47 41
983 East U.W. Hwy 160, West Plains, MO 65775 US
(417) 967-3353; *Fax:* (417) 967-2281
www.thefox969.com
License: Mountain View, Howell County, MO held by Central Ozark Radio Network Inc.
Arbitron Metro Market: Mountain View, MO; *Format:* Adult Contemp; *Hrs. of News Programming:* News progmg 2 hrs wkly; *Target Audience:* 25-54; upscale, mature individuals; *Adv. Rates:* 10.50; 10.50; 10.50; na
Tom Marhefka, CEO
Bob Eckman, General Manager
Jonathon Bergman, General Sales Mgr
Gary Lee, Programming Director
Mike Robertson, News Director
Jim White, Chief Engineer

Naylor

KZMA
01-01-2005; 99.9 MHz FM; 4.2 kw; 387 ft.; N36 39 43 W90 29 16
20001 Pa Ave NW, Suite 400, Washington, DC 20006 US
(573) 778-0142; *Fax:* (573) 686-2377
jhborders@yahoo.com
License: Naylor, Ripley County, MO held by Daniel S. Stratemeyer
Arbitron Metro Market: Naylor, MO; *Format:* Adult Contemp
Jim Borders, General Manager

Neosho

KBTN
02-01-1954; 1420 kHz AM; *Hrs Open:* 5 AM-midnight; 1 kw-D, DAN; 0.5 kw-N, DAN; N36 50 52 W94 19 12
Mailing Address: P. O. Box K, Neosho, MO 64850 US
Second Address: 216 W. Spring, Neosho, MO 64850
(417) 781-1313; *Fax:* (417) 781-1316
www.kbtnradio.com
License: Neosho, MO held by American Media Investments Inc.
Group Owner: American Media Investments Inc.; (acq 2-17-2009; grpsl)
Nat'l Network: ABC; CNN Radio
Arbitron Metro Market: Joplin, MO; *Format:* Country *Special Programming:* Farm 6 hrs wkly; *Hrs. of News Programming:* news progmg 14 hrs wkly; *No. News Employees:* 2; *Target Audience:* 18-54.
Gail Johnson, General Manager
Monica Blain, Programming Director
David Horvath, News Director
Art Morris, Chief Engineer

KBTN-FM
01-01-1995; 99.7 MHz FM; *Hrs Open:* 24; 16.5 kw; 404 ft.; N36 54 33 W94 27 40
P.O. Box K, Neosho, MO 64850 US
(417) 781-1313; *Fax:* (417)781-1316
www.kbtnradio.com
License: Neosho, Newton County, MO held by American Media Investments Inc.
Group Owner: American Media Investments Inc.; (acq 2-17-2009; grpsl)
Arbitron Metro Market: Joplin, MO; *Format:* Country; *Hrs. of News Programming:* news progmg 9 hrs wkly; *No. News Employees:* 2; *Target Audience:* 18 plus.
Warren McDonald, Operations Dir
Jennifer Isom, General Manager
Dave Clemons, General Sales Mgr
Steve Smith, Programming Director

***KNEO**
10-01-1986; 91.7 MHz FM; *Hrs Open:* 24; 14.0 kw; 374 ft; N36 52 49 W94 26 59
10827 E. Hwy. 86, Neosho, MO 64850
(417) 451-5636; *Fax:* (417) 451-1891
www.kneo.org
License: Neosho, Newton County, MO held by Sky High Broadcasting Corp.
Nat'l Network: USA; Moody
Population Served: 650,000 *Hrs. of News Programming:* News progmg 10 hrs wkly; *Target Audience:* 30-65.; *Adv. Rates:* Sponsorship rates available
Mark Taylor, President
Adam Winkler, Operations Dir
Mark Taylor, General Manager
Mark Taylor, Programming Director
Andy Farmer, Production Director
Clark Matthews, Website Development

Nevada

KNEM
01-01-1949; 1240 kHz AM; *Hrs Open:* 24; 0.5 kw-U, ND1; N37 51 37 W94 22 54
P.O. Box 447, Nevada, MO 64772 US
(417) 667-3113; *Fax:* (417) 667-9797
www.knemknmo.com
mharbit@knemknmo.com
License: Nevada, MO held by Harbit Communications Inc.
Regional Network: Brownfield; Missourinet
Format: Country *Special Programming:* Farm one hr, Christian 5 hrs wkly; *Hrs. of News Programming:* news progmg 30 hrs wkly; *No. News Employees:* 1; *Target Audience:* General.; *Adv. Rates:* 15.19; 14; 15.19;10
Mike Harbit, President
Russ Warren, News Director
Daryl Nickolaus, Chief Engineer

KNMO-FM
09-10-1984; 97.5 MHz FM; *Hrs Open:* 24; 6 kw; 281 ft.; N37 52 45 W94 20 15
P.O. Box 447, Nevada, MO 64772 US
(417) 667-3113; *Fax:* (417) 667-9797
www.knemknmo.com
License: Nevada, Vernon County, MO
Adv. Rates: Same as AM
Darren Nez, General Manager

New Bloomfield

***KNLG**
07-20-1997; 90.3 MHz FM; *Hrs Open:* 24; 0.15 kw; 217 ft.; N38 42 16 W92 5 20
1411 Locust Street, St Louis, MO 63103 US
(573) 896-5945; *Fax:* (573) 896-4376
License: New Bloomfield, Callaway County, MO held by New Life Evangelistic Center Inc.
Format: Gospel; *Hrs. of News Programming:* News progmg 9 hrs wkly; *Target Audience:* General.
Rev. Larry Rice, President
John Shepard, Programming Director

New London

KZZK
04-01-1996; 105.9 MHz FM; *Hrs Open:* 24; 10 kw; 515 ft.; N39 43 48 W91 24 19
2 Dearborn Square, Kankakee, IL 60901 US
(217) 224-4102; *Fax:* (217) 224-4133
www.kzzk.com
kzzk@staradio.com

License: New London, Ralls County, MO held by STARadio Corp.
Group Owner: STARadio Corp.; acq 12-2-98; $2.1 million with KGRC(FM) Hannibal)
Arbitron Metro Market: New London, MO; *Format:* Alternative, Classic Rock; *Hrs. of News Programming:* News progmg 2 hrs wkly; *Target Audience:* 18-49; skews male
Howard Doss, President
Mike Moyers, General Manager
Brenda Park, General Sales Mgr
Quaid, Programming Director
Phil Reilly, Chief Engineer

New Madrid

KTMO
01-31-1976; 106.5 MHz FM; *Hrs Open:* 24; 50 kW; 469 ft.; N36 25 31 W89 41 29
5500 Poplar Ave, Suite 1, Memphis, MO 38119 USA
(901) 685-3993; *Fax:* (901) 685-3995
pollackcompanies.net
License: New Madrid, New Madrid County, MO held by Pollack Broadcasting Co.
Group Owner: Pollack Broadcasting Co.
Nat'l Network: ABC
Format: Country; *No. News Employees:* 1; *Target Audience:* 18-49 adults; males

Nixa

KGBX-FM
12-01-1989; 105.9 MHz FM; *Hrs Open:* 24; 38 kw; 558 ft.; N37 17 41 W93 9 10
1856 S. Glenstone, Springfield, MO 65804 US
(417) 890-5555
www.kgbx.com
kgbx@kgbx.com
License: Nixa, Christian County, MO held by Clear Channel Broadcasting Licenses Inc.
Group Owner: iHeartMedia
Arbitron Metro Market: Springfield, MO; *Format:* Adult Contemp
Special Programming: 70's Saturday; *Hrs. of News Programming:* news progmg 5 hrs wkly; *No. News Employees:* 1; *Target Audience:* 25-54; educated,high income, women
Matt Saunders, Sales Manager
Matt Parrish, Programming Director
Sarah Green, Promotions Manager
Lynne Strickland, Webmaster

North Kansas City

KMJK
09-11-1969; 107.3 MHz FM; *Hrs Open:* 24; 100 kw; 299 meters; N39 05 40 W94 05 47
5800 Foxridge Dr, Suite 600, Mission, KS 64133
(913) 514-3000; *Fax:* (816) 353-2300
magic@1073.com
License: North Kansas City, Lafayette County, MO held by A R Licensing LLC.
Population Served: 2,000,000; *Arbitron Metro Market:* Kansas City, MO-KS; *Hrs. of News Programming:* news progmg 5 hrs wkly; *No. News Employees:* 1; *Target Audience:* 25-54.
Lewis Dickey, CEO
Mark Sullivan, Senior Vice President/General Manager
Jared Robb, General Sales Mgr
Jerold Jackson, Programming Director
Ashley Coppock, Promotions Manager
Dennis Ebersoll, Chief Engineer
Brian Goeke,Marketing/Online Director

Oran

*KCGR
01-01-2008; 90.5 MHz FM; 2.1 kw; 241 ft.; N36 59 52 W89 38 52 *Rebroadcasts:* Rebroadcasts KSIV-FM Saint Louis 100%
10550 Barkley St., Suite 100, Overland Park, KS 66212 US
(913) 642-7770
www.bottradionetwork.com
comments@bottradionetwork.com
License: Oran, Scott County, MO held by Community Broadcasting Inc.
Group Owner: Bott Radio Network
Arbitron Metro Market: Oran, MO; *Format:* Christian, Talk
Eben Fowler, Operations Dir
Sue Stoltz, Regional Manager
Pat Rulon, Director of National Sales
Candy Green, Program Services Manager
Rachel Launius, Marketing Manager
Jason Potocnik, Director of Traffic Operations

Osage Beach

KRMS
12-01-1952; 1150 kHz AM; *Hrs Open:* 24; 840 W Day, 55 W Night
PO Box 225, Osage Beach, MO 65065 USA
(573) 348-2772; *Fax:* (573) 348-2779
www.krmsradio.com
info@krmsradio.com
License: Osage Beach, MO held by Viper Communications Inc.
Group Owner: Viper Communications Inc.; (acq 11-97; $500,000 with co-located FM).
Regional Network: Missourinet
Arbitron Metro Market: Lake of the Ozarks; *Format:* News, News/Talk, 86

KMYK
04-12-1964; 93.5 MHz FM; 39 kW; 469 ft.; N38 9 52 W92 36 12
PO Box 225, 5715 Osage Beach Pkwy, Osage Beach, MO 65065 USA
(573) 348-2772; *Fax:* (573) 348-2779
www.935rocksthelake.com
License: Osage Beach, Camden County, MO held by Viper Communications Inc.
Group Owner: Viper Communications Inc.
Arbitron Metro Market: Lake of the Ozarks; *Format:* Light Rock

*KIRL
89.3 MHz FM; 0 kw horiz, 0.3 kw vert; 210 ft.; N38 7 20 W92 40 42
US
(660) 238-1024
License: Osage Beach, Camden County, MO held by Full Smile Inc.
Arbitron Metro Market: Osage Beach, MO
Joey Anderson, Operations Dir

Osceola

*KCVJ
06-29-1990; 100.3 MHz FM; *Hrs Open:* 24; 6 kw; 282 ft.; N38 3 43 W93 33 24 *Rebroadcasts:* Rebroadcasts KCVO-FM Camdenton 100%
P.O. Box 800, Camdenton, MO 65020 US
(573) 346-3200; *Fax:* (573) 346-1010
www.spiritfm.org
License: Osceola, St. Clair County, MO held by Lake Area Educational Broadcasting Foundation
Nat'l Network: Salem Radio Network
Arbitron Metro Market: Osceola, MO; *Format:* Christian; *Hrs. of News Programming:* 1; *Target Audience:* 25-45.
Alice McDermott, CFO
James McDermott, President
Jim McDermott, General Manager
Alice McDermott, Financial Director

Otterville

*KCVK
01-01-2001; 107.7 MHz FM; *Hrs Open:* 24; 3.7 kw; 410 ft.; N38 40 26 W92 51 44 *Rebroadcasts:* Rebroadcasts KCVO-FM Camdenton 100%
185 Commerce Center, Greenville, SC 29615 US
(573) 346-3200; *Fax:* (573) 346 1010
www.spiritfm.org
License: Otterville, Cooper County, MO held by Lake Area Educational Broadcasting Foundation
Nat'l Network: Salem Radio Network
Format: Christian; *Hrs. of News Programming:* News progmg one hr wkly; *Target Audience:* 25-45.
Alice McDermott, CFO
James McDermott, President
James McDermott, Programming Director

Overland

*KRHS
11-07-1977; 90.1 MHz FM; 0.014 kw horiz; 144 ft.; N38 42 38 W90 21 22
2420 Woodson, Overland, MO 63114 US
(314) 429-7111; *Fax:* (314) 429-6725
http://www.edline.net/pages/Ritenour_High_School/News___Media/KRHS_90_1_FM_Radioactiv
License: Overland, St. Louis County, MO held by Ritenour Consolidated School District.
Target Audience: General.
Jane Bannester, General Manager

Owensville

KXMO
01-01-2001; 95.3 MHz FM; *Hrs Open:* 24; 37 kW; 459 ft.; N38 8 8 W91 24 0
PO Box 727, Rolla, MO 65402 USA
(573) 364-2525; *Fax:* (573) 364-5161
resultsradioonline.com
License: Owensville, MO held by Results Radio
Group Owner: Results Radio
Arbitron Metro Market: Rolla, MO; *Format:* Oldies; *Target Audience:* 35-64; male & female

Ozark

KOSP
01-01-1995; 92.9 MHz FM; *Hrs Open:* 24; 50 kW; Ant 492 ft; N36 58 26 W93 25 37
2453 E Elm St, Springfield, MO 65802 USA
(417) 886-5677; *Fax:* (417) 886-2155
www.929thebeat.com
License: Ozark, Christian County, MO held by MW Springmo Inc.
Group Owner: The Mid-West Family Broadcast Group; (acq 12-15-99).
Nat'l Network: NBC Radio; *Nat'l Reps:* Eastman Radio
Population Served: 295,300; *Arbitron Metro Market:* Springfield, MO; *Format:* Contemporary Hits/Top 40, Urban Contemporary; *Target Audience:* Women 18-49; *Adv. Rates:* 30; 33; 33; 15.
Brian Tyndall, General Sales Mgr
Bailey, Programming Director

Palmyra

KICK-FM
09-01-1981; 97.9 MHz FM; *Hrs Open:* 24; 43 kw; 531 ft.; N39 45 26 W91 29 58
P.O. Box 711, 119 North 3rd, Hannibal, MO 63401 US
(217) 223-5292; *Fax:* (573) 221-5331
www.979kickfm.com
License: Palmyra, Marion County, MO held by Townsquare Media Quincy-Hannibal License LLC
Group Owner: Townsquare Media
Nat'l Reps: McGavren Guild
Format: Country; *No. News Employees:* 2; *Target Audience:* 25-54; mainstream adults
Ed Foxall, General Manager
Jeff Asmussen, General Sales Mgr
Brian Myles, Programming Director
John Hanvelt, News Director
Gary Glaenzer, Chief Engineer

Park Hills

*KBGM
01-01-2001; 91.1 MHz FM; 8 kw; 620 ft.; N37 48 4 W90 33 51
P.O. Box 3206, Tupelo, MS 38803 US
(662) 844-8888; *Fax:* (662) 842-6791
www.afr.net
faq@afa.net
License: Park Hills, St. Francois County, MO held by American Family Association.
Group Owner: American Family Radio
Arbitron Metro Market: Park Hills, MO; *Format:* Christian, Religious
Tim Wildmon, President
Donald Wildmon, Founder
Buddy Smith, Sr VP
Ed Vitagliano, Executive VP
Randy Sharp, Director Of Special Projects
Meeke Addison, Director Of Communications
Abraham Hamilton III, General Counsel & PublicPolicy Analyst

KFMO
07-01-1947; 1240 kHz AM; 1 kw-U, ND1; N37 51 10 W90 31 13
Mailing Address: P.O. Box 36, Park Hills, MO 63601 US
Second Address: 804 St. Joe Dr., Park Hills, MO 63601
(573) 431-2000; *Fax:* (573) 431-0850
www.kfmo.com
License: Park Hills, MO held by MKS Broadcasting Inc.
Nat'l Network: Westwood One
Arbitron Metro Market: Flat River, MO; *Format:* News, News/Talk, 84, Talk; *Hrs. of News Programming:* news progmg 150 hrs wkly; *Target Audience:* 25-54
M.L. Steinmetz, President
Larry Joseph, Operations Dir
Kelly Valle, General Sales Mgr
Greg Camp, Programming Director
Gib Collins, News Director

Parkville

*KGSP
04-01-1972; 90.5 MHz FM; *Hrs Open:* 6 AM-midnight (M-F); 9 AM-midnight; 0.099 kw; 59 ft.; N39 11 24 W94 40 49
Box 2 8700 River Park Dr, Parkville, MO 64152 US
(816) 741-2000; *Fax:* (816) 741-4911
License: Parkville, Platte County, MO held by Board of Trustees of Park College.
Format: Alternative *Special Programming:* Jazz 14 hrs, gospel 3 hrs, blues 12 hrs wkly; *Hrs. of News Programming:* News progmg 6 hrs wkly; *Target Audience:* General; college students
Steve Youngblood, General Manager

Perryville

KBDZ
01-30-1990; 93.1 MHz FM; *Hrs Open:* 24; 1.6 kw; 623 ft.; N37 38 56 W89 56 21
Mailing Address: P.O. Box 428, Ste. Genevieve, MO 63670 US
Second Address: Box 428, Radio Hill, Ste. Genevieve, MO 63670
(573) 547-8005; *Fax:* (573) 883-2866
License: Perryville, Perry County, MO held by Donze Communications Inc.
Arbitron Metro Market: Perryville, MO; *Format:* Country, News *Special Programming:* Sports 5 hrs, relg 5 hrs, farm 2 hrs wkly; *Hrs. of News Programming:* news progmg 5 hrs wkly; *No. News Employees:* 3 *TargetAudience:* 25-54.
Elmo Donze, President
Bob Scott, General Sales Mgr
Don Pritchard, News Director
Brian Snider, Reporter

Piedmont

KPWB
05-16-1966; 1140 kHz AM; 1 kw-D, NDD; N37 8 29 W90 42 11
204 Washington, Doniphan, MO 63935 US
(573) 223-4218; *Fax:* (573) 223-2351
License: Piedmont, MO held by Southern Star Broadcasting of Missouri LLC.
Group Owner: Southern Star Broadcasting of Missouri LLC; (acq 5-8-2008; grpsl)
Nat'l Network: USA; *Regional Network:* Missourinet
Format: Gospel; *Target Audience:* 18 plus; Christians; *Adv. Rates:* 3.60; 3; 3; na
Wanda Emert, General Manager

KPWB-FM
09-05-1985; 104.9 MHz FM; 3.7 kw; 856 ft.; N37 11 35 W90 39 49
204 East Washington, Doniphan, MO 63935 US
(573) 223-4218; *Fax:* (573) 223-2351
License: Piedmont, Wayne County, MO held by Southern Star Broadcasting of Missouri LLC.
Group Owner: Southern Star Broadcasting of Missouri LLC; (acq 5-8-2008; grpsl)
Nat'l Network: USA
Format: Country; *Target Audience:* General.; *Adv. Rates:* 7; 7; 7; 7
Wanda Emert, Operations Dir
Fred Dockins, Chief Engineer

Pleasant Hope

KTOZ-FM
05-01-1993; 95.5 MHz FM; 44 kw; 522 ft.; N37 13 25 W93 14 30
1856 South Glenstone, Springfield, MO 65804 US
(417) 890-5555; *Fax:* (417) 890-5050
www.alice955.com
alice955@alice955.com
License: Pleasant Hope, Polk County, MO held by Clear Channel Broadcasting Licenses Inc.
Group Owner: iHeartMedia; (acq 10-10-00; grpsl).
Arbitron Metro Market: Springfield, MO; *Format:* Adult Contemp; *Target Audience:* 18-34; young adults, 60/40 female/male split
Matt Saunders, Sales Manager
Clint Girlie, Programming Director
Sarah Green, Promotions Manager

Point Lookout

*KCOZ
01-01-1995; 91.7 MHz FM; 0.2 kw; 187 ft.; N36 36 39 W93 14 23
College of the Ozarks, Point Lookout, MO 65726 US
(417) 334-6411; *Fax:* (417) 335-2618
www.cofo.edu
License: Point Lookout, Taney County, MO held by College of the Ozarks.
Nat'l Network: PRI; NPR
Arbitron Metro Market: Point Lookout, MO; *Format:* Blues, Jazz, 60, News/Talk, Talk *Special Programming:* Folk 10 hrs, new age 10 hrs wkly; *Target Audience:* Older & educated.
Jae Jones, General Manager

*KSMS-FM
02-12-1962; 90.5 MHz FM; 8.5 kw; 771 ft.; N36 33 44 W93 15 35 *Rebroadcasts:* Rebroadcasts KSMU(FM) Springfield 100%
901 S. National Ave, Springfield, MO 65804 US
(417) 836-5878; *Fax:* (417) 836-5889
www.ksmu.org
ksmu@missouristate
License: Point Lookout, Taney County, MO held by Board of Governors, Southwest Missouri State University
Arbitron Metro Market: Springfield, MO; *Format:* Classical, News; *Target Audience:* 25-54.
Tammy Wiley, General Manager

Poplar Bluff

KAHR
03-03-1985; 96.7 MHz FM; 6 kw; 328 ft.; N36 45 59 W90 28 52
932 Coutny Rd. 448, Poplar Bluff, MO 63901 US
(573) 686-3700
www.foxradionetwork.com
License: Poplar Bluff, Butler County, MO held by Eagle Bluff Enterprises
Group Owner: Eagle Bluff Enterprises; (acq 8-3-93; $350,000;
Arbitron Metro Market: Poplar Bluff, MT; *Format:* Adult Contemp; *Target Audience:* 18-54; listeners living in the middle-class strata
Steven Fuchs, President

KJEZ
08-20-1977; 95.5 MHz FM; *Hrs Open:* 24; 100 kw; 410 ft.; N36 50 50 W90 19 52
1015 West Pine, Poplar Bluff, MO 63901 US
(573) 785-0881; *Fax:* (573) 785-0646
www.z95thebone.net
z95@riverradio.net
License: Poplar Bluff, Butler County, MO held by MRR License LLC.
Group Owner: MAX Media L.L.C.; (acq 6-2-2004; grpsl).
Nat'l Network: Westwood One
Arbitron Metro Market: Poplar Bluff, MO; *Format:* Classic Rock; *Hrs. of News Programming:* News progmg 10 hrs wkly; *Target Audience:* 18-49; general
John Rice, General Manager
Katie Ray, General Sales Mgr
Randy Bailey, Programming Director
Charlie Lampe, Chief Engineer

KKLR-FM
01-01-1952; 94.5 MHz FM; *Hrs Open:* 24; 100 kw; 807 ft.; N36 45 46 W90 26 3
1015 West Pine, Poplar Bluff, MO 63901 US
(573) 785-0881; *Fax:* (573) 785-0646
www.clear94.com
clear94@riverradio.net
License: Poplar Bluff, Butler County, MO held by MRR License LLC.
Group Owner: MAX Media L.L.C.
Arbitron Metro Market: Jonesboro, AR; *Format:* Country; *Target Audience:* 18-49.
John Rice, General Manager
Galen Stevens, Programming Director

KLID
05-22-1961; 1340 kHz AM; *Hrs Open:* 24; 1 kw-U, ND1; N36 46 3 W90 22 11
102 N. 11th Street, Poplar Bluff, MO 63901 US
(573) 686-1600; *Fax:* (573) 785-9844
License: Poplar Bluff, MO held by Browning Skidmore Broadcasting Inc.
Arbitron Metro Market: Jonesboro, AR; *Format:* Oldies, Sports, 86 *Special Programming:* Relg 2 hrs, Black 2 hrs wkly; *Hrs. of News Programming:* News progmg 15 hrs wkly; *Target Audience:* 18-54; upper class,professionals; *Adv. Rates:* 9; 7; 9; 6
Chris Browning, President
Dolores Skidmore, General Manager
Palmer Johnson, Chief Engineer
Paul White, Disc Jockey
Alverna Skidmore, Paul White
Nick Novak, Sports Commentator

*KLUH
10-08-1988; 90.3 MHz FM; *Hrs Open:* Monday- Friday 9-5pm; 25 kw; 253 ft.; N36 43 8 W90 23 48
Kluh Radio Lone Star Rd, Route 8 Box 14, Poplar Bluff, MO 63901 US
(573) 686-1663; *Fax:* (573) 686-7703
www.dcmliferadio.org
info@dcmliferadio.org
License: Poplar Bluff, Butler County, MO held by David Craig Ministries
Format: Religious; *Target Audience:* General.
David Craig, General Manager
Harriet Craig, General Sales Mgr
John Moore, Programming Director

*KOKS
10-02-1988; 89.5 MHz FM; *Hrs Open:* 24; 100 kw; 423 ft; N36 48 40 W90 27 50
2773 Barron Road, Poplar Bluff, MO 63901
(573) 686-5080; *Fax:* (573) 686-5544
koksradio@mycitycable.com
License: Poplar Bluff, Butler County, MO held by Calvary Educational Broadcasting Network
Population Served: 1,000,000 *Hrs. of News Programming:* News progmg 14 hrs wkly; *Target Audience:* General.
Nina Stewart, Station Manager
Charley Lampe, Chief Engineer
Ben Stewart, Music Director

KWOC
05-10-1938; 930 kHz AM; *Hrs Open:* 24; 5 kw-D, DAN; 0.5 kw-N, DAN; N36 43 15 W90 22 4
1015 West Pine, Poplar Bluff, MO 63901 US
(573) 785-0881; *Fax:* (573) 785-0646
www.kwoc.com
kwoc@riverradio.net
License: Poplar Bluff, Butler County, MO held by MRR License LLC.
Group Owner: MAX Media L.L.C.; (acq 6-2-2004; grpsl).
Regional Network: Missourinet; Brownfield
Arbitron Metro Market: Poplar Bluff, MO; *Format:* News, News/Talk, 86; *Hrs. of News Programming:* news progmg 5 hrs wkly; *No. News Employees:* 2; *Target Audience:* 25-54; adults with middle to upper income
Ronnie Glover, General Manager
Rick Carl, Programming Director

KLUE
01-01-1995; 103.5 MHz FM; *Hrs Open:* 24; 50 kw; 325 ft.; N36 50 50 W90 19 52
P.O. Box 558, Metropolis, IL 62960 US
(618) 564-9836; *Fax:* (618) 564-3202
klue1035.bizland.com/
jhborders@yahoo.com
License: Poplar Bluff, Butler County, MO held by Benjamin Stratemeyer
Arbitron Metro Market: Poplar Bluff, MO; *Format:* Variety/Diverse
Willie Kerns, Operations Dir
Samuel Stratemeyer, General Manager

KPPL
01-01-2003; 92.5 MHz FM; 25 kw; 328 ft.; N36 50 59 W90 22 20
Route #2, Box 496, Portageville, MO 63873 US
(573) 686-3700; *Fax:* (573) 686-1713
License: Poplar Bluff, Butler County, MO held by George S. Flinn Jr.
Arbitron Metro Market: Poplar Bluff, MO; *Format:* Country
Steven Fuchs, General Manager
Shelly Fuchs, Programming Director
Palmer Johnson, Chief Engineer

*KPBR
03-15-2006; 91.7 MHz FM; *Hrs Open:* 24; 1.9 kw; 249 ft.; N36 49 2.7 W90 27 20.2
US
(406) 248-7777
License: Poplar Bluff, Carbon County, MO held by Community Broadcasting Inc.
Arbitron Metro Market: Poplar Bluff, MO; *Format:* Country
Cam Maxwell, General Manager
Willy Tyler, Programming Director

Portageville

KMIS-AM
09-01-1960; 1050 kHz AM; *Hrs Open:* 24; 0.6 kW; N36 25 31 W89 41 29
5500 Poplar Ave, Suite 1, Memphis, TN 38119 USA
(901) 685-3993; *Fax:* (901) 685-3995
kmisradio.com
License: Portageville, MO held by Pollack Broadcasting Co.
Group Owner: Pollack Broadcasting Co.
Regional Network: Missourinet
Arbitron Metro Market: Portageville, MO; *Format:* Sports *Special Programming:* Relg gospel 5 hrs wkly; *No. News Employees:* 1; *Target Audience:* General.

Potosi

KHZR
04-17-1997; 97.7 MHz FM; *Hrs Open:* 24; 26.5 kw; 679 ft.; N37 57 31 W90 45 47
1800 State Hwy. 47, Bonne Terre, MO 63628 US
(314) 909-8569; *Fax:* (314) 835-9739
www.joyfmonline.org
info@joyfmonline.org
License: Potosi, Washington County, MO held by Four Him Enterprises L.L.C.
Format: Christian; *Target Audience:* Christian Adults
Sandi Brown, General Manager
Brenda Pacini, Office Assistant

*KNLP
04-01-1998; 89.7 MHz FM; 2.3 kw; 262 ft.; N37 55 42 W90 46 2
1411 Locust Street, St. Louis, MO 63103 US
(314) 436-2424; *Fax:* (314) 436-2434
www.hereshelpnet.org
larryr@hereshelpnet.org
License: Potosi, Washington County, MO held by New Life Evangelistic Center Inc.
Format: Adult Contemp, Gospel, 86
Larry Rice, General Manager

Ravenwood

*KEXS-FM
01-01-2008; 106.1 MHz FM; 50 kw; 423 ft.; N40 25 15 W94 43 20
US
(816) 630-1090
www.thecatholicradionetwork.com
catholicradionetwork@gmail.com
License: Ravenwood, Nodaway County, MO held by Catholic Radio Network Inc.
Group Owner: Catholic Radio Network Inc.
Arbitron Metro Market: Excelsior Springs, MO; *Format:* Religious
James O'Laughlin, General Manager

Republic

KADI-FM
06-18-1990; 99.5 MHz FM; *Hrs Open:* 24; 6 kw; 328 ft.; N37 9 54 W93 23 44
1601 W Sunshine Rd # P, Springfield, MO 65807 US
(417) 831-0995; *Fax:* (417) 831-4026
www.99hitfm.com
License: Republic, Greene County, MO held by Vision Communications Inc.
Arbitron Metro Market: Brookline Station, MT; *Format:* Adult Contemp, Christian; *Hrs. of News Programming:* News progmg 8 hrs wkly; *Target Audience:* General; adults in their mid 30s
R.C. Amer, General Manager
Mark Hill, General Sales Mgr
Rod Kettleman, Programming Director

Richmond

KAYX
08-01-1990; 92.5 MHz FM; 2.35 kw; 535 ft.; N39 11 14 W93 50 3 *Rebroadcasts:* Rebroadcasts KCCV(AM) Overland Park, KS 85%
111 W. Main St., Richmond, MO 64085 US
(816) 470-9925; *Fax:* (816) 470-8925
www.bottradionetwork.com
comments@bottradionetwork.com
License: Richmond, Ray County, MO held by Bott Communications, Inc.
Group Owner: Bott Radio Network; (acq 1996)
Nat'l Network: USA
Arbitron Metro Market: Kansas City, MO; *Format:* Christian, Talk
Eben Fowler, Operations Dir
Pat Rulon, Director of National Sales
Candy Green, Program Services Manager
Rachel Launius, Marketing Manager
Jason Potocnik, Director of Traffic Operations
Julie White, Office Manager

Rolla

KDAA
11-20-1964; 103.1 MHz FM; *Hrs Open:* 24; 2.05 kW; 394 ft.; N37 52 39 W91 44 45
PO Box 727, Rolla, MO 65402 USA
(573) 364-2525; *Fax:* (573) 364-5161
www.resultsradioonline.com
License: Rolla, Phelps County, MO held by Results Radio
Group Owner: Results Radio
Arbitron Metro Market: Rolla, MO; *Format:* Contemporary Hits/Top 40, Adult Contemp; *Target Audience:* 18-44.

*KMNR
01-01-1974; 89.7 MHz FM; 0.45 kw; 325 ft.; N37 57 7 W91 46 12
218 Havener Center, 1346 N. Bishop Avenue, Rolla, MO 65409-1440 US
(573) 341-4272
www.kmnr.org
stationmanager@kmnr.org
License: Rolla, Phelps County, MO held by Curators of the University of Missouri.
Group Owner: The Curators of the University of Missouri
Nat'l Network: AP Radio
Format: Variety/Diverse; *Target Audience:* 18-25; college community
Brandon Kane, Station Manager
Lauren Cockrum, Program Director
Alex Richter, Chief Engineer
Mark Farmer, Music Director
Taylor Schubert, Personnel Manager
Danny Massa, Public Relations
Caleb Wilczynski, Business Manager
JoelThorne, Roadshow Director
Judah Schad, Productions

KMOZ
08-19-1960; 1590 kHz AM; 1 kw-D, ND2; 0.085 kw-N, ND2; N37 56 41 W91 48 42
1701 N. Bishop Ave., Suite 15, Rolla, MO 65401 US
(573) 308-1616
www.bottradionetwork.com
comments@bottradionetwork.com
License: Rolla, Phelps County, MO held by Community Broadcasting Inc.
Group Owner: Bott Radio Network; (acq 5-5-2006; $40,000).
Nat'l Network: USA
Arbitron Metro Market: Rolla, MO; *Format:* Christian, Talk; *Target Audience:* 50 plus; mature adults
Eben Fowler, Operations Dir
Sue Stoltz, Regional Manager
Pat Rulon, Director of National Sales
Candy Green, Program Services Manager
Rachel Launius, Marketing Manager
Jason Potocnik, Director of Traffic Operations

KTTR AM
09-30-1947; 1490 kHz AM; *Hrs Open:* 24; 1 kW; N37 56 42 W91 44 46
PO Box 727, Rolla, MO 65402 USA
(573) 364-2525; *Fax:* (573) 364-5161
resultsradioonline.com
License: Rolla, MO held by Results Radio
Group Owner: Results Radio
Arbitron Metro Market: Phelps Cty., MO; *Format:* Contemporary Hits/Top 40; *No. News Employees:* 1; *Target Audience:* General.; *Adv. Rates:* 39; 31; 37; 28

*KMST
01-01-1964; 88.5 MHz FM; *Hrs Open:* 24; 100 kw; 479 ft.; N37 47 56 W91 43 28
400 W 14th St, Rolla, MO 65409 US
(573) 341-4386; *Fax:* (573) 341-4889
www.kmst.org
kmst@mst.edu
License: Rolla, Phelps County, MO held by The Curators of the University of Missouri.
Group Owner: The Curators of the University of Missouri
Nat'l Network: NPR; PRI; *Wire Services:* AP
Arbitron Metro Market: Rolla, MO *TV Affiliate:* *KOMU-TV affil.; *Format:* News, Variety/Diverse *Special Programming:* Bluegrass 5 hrs, jazz 3 hrs, folk 5 hrs wkly; *Hrs. of News Programming:* News progmg 35 hrs wkly *Target Audience:* General.
Wayne Bledsoe, General Manager
John Francis, Programming Director
Charles Knapp, Chief Engineer
Joel Goodridge, Marketing Manager
Norm Movitz, Producer
Jim Graham, Underwriting Coordinator
Sandy Ray, Administrative Assistant
Katie Lacewell, Secretary

KZNN
02-12-1973; 105.3 MHz FM; 100 kW; 456 ft.; N37 52 39 W91 44 45
PO Box 727, Rolla, MO 65402 USA
(573) 364-2525; *Fax:* (573) 364-5161
resultsradioonline.com
License: Rolla, Phelps County, MO held by Results Radio
Group Owner: Results Radio
Arbitron Metro Market: Rolla, MO; *Format:* Country

Saint Joseph

*KSJI
91.1 MHz FM; 50 kw; Ant 492 ft; N39 40 51 W94 46 47
2414 S. Leonard Rd., Saint Joseph, MO 64503
(816) 233-2577; *Fax:* (816) 233-2374
License: Saint Joseph, Buchanan County, MO held by Good News Ministries Inc.
Chris Meikel, General Manager
Chris Meikel, General Sales Mgr
James Schumaker, Programming Director
Jeff Landers, Engineering Dir
Jeff Landers, Chief Engineer

Saint Louis

*KDHX
10-14-1987; 88.1 MHz FM; *Hrs Open:* 24; 42 kw; 738 ft.; N38 25 1 W90 25 59
3504 Magnolia, St Louis, MO 63113 US
(314) 664-3955; *Fax:* (314) 664-1020
www.kdhx.org
License: Saint Louis, St. Louis County, MO held by Double Helix Corp.
Nat'l Network: PRI
Arbitron Metro Market: St. Louis, MO; *Format:* Variety/Diverse; *Target Audience:* General.
Beverly Hacker, Executive Director
Andrew Scavatto, President
Paul Dever, Vice President
Tim Yeaglin, Treasurer
Matthew Potter, Secretary

KXFN
01-01-1927; 1380 kHz AM; *Hrs Open:* 24; 5 kw-D, 1 kw-N, DA-3; N38 31 27 W90 14 17
12250 Webber Hill Rd., Suite 125, St. Louis, MO 63127 USA
(314) 270-0670
theanswerstl.com
lvernier@salemstl.com
License: Saint Louis, St. Louis County, MO held by Salem Radio License, LLC
Group Owner: Salem Media Group
Population Served: 504,000; *Arbitron Metro Market:* St. Louis, MO; *Hrs. of News Programming:* News progmg 168 hrs wkly; *Target Audience:* 25-54; men and women; *Adv. Rates:* 45; 30; 45; 25
Lori Vernier, General Sales Mgr

Salem

KKID
01-01-1971; 92.9 MHz FM; *Hrs Open:* 6 AM-midnight; 21 kw; 361 ft.; N37 43 45 W91 28 23
P.O. Box 650, Salem, MO 65560 US
(573) 364-4433; *Fax:* (573) 364-8385
929fm@kkid929fm.com
License: Salem, Dent County, MO held by Ultra-Sonic Broadcast Stations Inc.
Nat'l Network: USA
Arbitron Metro Market: Columbia, MO; *Format:* Country; *Hrs. of News Programming:* news progmg 20 hrs wkly; *No. News Employees:* 1; *Target Audience:* 30-49.
David Wheeler, President
Steve Wheeler, General Sales Mgr
Al Martia, Programming Director

KSMO
11-01-1953; 1340 kHz AM; *Hrs Open:* 24; 1 kw-U, ND1; N37 37 36 W91 32 9
800 South Main, Salem, MO 65560 US
(573) 729-6117; *Fax:* (573) 729-7337
www.ksmoradio.com
License: Salem, MO held by KSMO Enterprises.
Nat'l Network: AP Network News; *Regional Network:* Missourinet; Brownfield; *Nat'l Reps:* Commercial Media Sales; *Wire Services:* The Sports Network; AP
Arbitron Metro Market: Salem. MO; *Format:* Country, News, 62, Sports, Talk *Special Programming:* Farm 18 hrs wkly; *Hrs. of News Programming:* news progmg 40 hrs wkly; *No. News Employees:* 1 *Target Audience:* General; middle class; *Adv. Rates:* 16; 13; 15; 10
Stanley Podorski, President
Stan Podorski, General Manager
Melba Hendrick, General Sales Mgr
Stan Stevens, News Director

*KCVX
02-01-2004; 91.7 MHz FM; *Hrs Open:* 24; 40 kw; 210 ft.; N37 36 16 W91 32 46 *Rebroadcasts:* Rebroadcasts KCVO(FM) Campenton 100%

PO Box 800, Camdenton, MO 65020 US
(573) 346-3200; *Fax:* (573) 346-1010
www.spiritfm.org
License: Salem, Dent County, MO held by Lake Area Educational Broadcasting Foundation
Nat'l Network: Salem Radio Network
Arbitron Metro Market: Camdenton, MO; *Format:* Christian; *Hrs. of News Programming:* News progmg one hr wkly; *Target Audience:* 25-45; primarily females, married with children
Alice McDermott, CFO
James McDermott, President

Sarcoxie

*KCKJ

89.5 MHz FM; 31 kw; Ant 328 ft; N37 04 34 W93 55 27
PO Box 800, Camdenton, MO 65020
(417) 782-2141; *Fax:* (417) 782-9141
www.spiritfm.org
License: Sarcoxie, Jasper County, MO held by Calvary Chapel of Joplin.

Jeffery Kingery, President

Savannah

KSJQ

09-01-1991; 92.7 MHz FM; *Hrs Open:* 24; 50 kw; 492 ft.; N39 58 34 W94 58 37
4104 Country Lane, St. Joseph, MO 64506 US
(816) 233-8881
www.myqcountry.com
License: Savannah, Andrew County, MO held by Eagle Communications Inc.
Group Owner: Eagle Communications Group; (acq 1993; $450,000;
Nat'l Reps: Katz Radio; *Wire Services:* AP
Arbitron Metro Market: St. Joseph, MO; *Format:* Country; *Hrs. of News Programming:* news progmg 3 hrs wkly; *No. News Employees:* 2; *Adv. Rates:* 29; 24; 26; 20
Gary Exline, Operations Dir
Travis Dodge, Programming Director
Mark Goff, Chief Engineer

Scott City

KGKS

01-01-1998; 93.9 MHz FM; 16.5 kw; 407 ft.; N37 21 34 W89 37 16
324 Broadway, Cape Girardeau, MO 63701 US
(573) 335-8291; *Fax:* (573) 335-4806
License: Scott City, Scott County, MO held by MRR License LLC.
Group Owner: MAX Media L.L.C.; (acq 6-2-2004; grpsl).
Arbitron Metro Market: Scott City, MO; *Format:* Contemporary Hits/Top 40
Ronnie Glover, General Manager
Mike Renick, Programming Director
Hunter Hendricks, Promotions Director
Faune Riggin, News Director
Sherry Crider, Traffic Manager

Sedalia

KDRO

09-13-1939; 1490 kHz AM; *Hrs Open:* 24; 0.78 kw-U, ND1; N38 40 35 W93 15 18
301 S. Ohio St., Sedalia, MO 65301 US
(660) 826-5005; *Fax:* (660) 826-5557
www.kdro.com
License: Sedalia, MO held by Mathewson Broadcasting Co.
Nat'l Network: CBS; *Regional Network:* Brownfield; Missourinet
Arbitron Metro Market: Sedalia, MO; *Format:* Country *Special Programming:* Farm 6 hrs, Black one hr, relg 3 hrs wkly; *Hrs. of News Programming:* news progmg 11 hrs wkly; *No. News Employees:* 2; *Target Audience:* General.; *Adv. Rates:* 19.55; 16.24; 19.55; 9.83
Stu Steinmetz, General Manager/Station Manager
Beau Matthews, Programming Director
Jeff Spalding, News Director
Susan Daniels, Traffic Manager

KSDL

05-11-1964; 92.3 MHz FM; *Hrs Open:* 24; 6 kw; 292 ft.; N38 44 3 W93 13 31
119 North 3rd, Box 711, Hannibal, MO 63401 US
(660) 826-1050; *Fax:* (660) 827-5072
www.ksdl.com
License: Sedalia, Pettis County, MO held by Townsquare Media Sedalia License LLC
Group Owner: Townsquare Media
Wire Services: U.S. Weather Service
Arbitron Metro Market: Sedalia, MO; *Format:* Adult Contemp; *No. News Employees:* 2; *Target Audience:* 12-40; women
Peggy Gordon-Miller, President
Jay Buchholz, General Manager

KSIS

02-18-1954; 1050 kHz AM; *Hrs Open:* 24
119 North 3rd, Box 711, Hannibal, MO 63401 US
(660) 826-1050; *Fax:* (660) 827-5072
www.ksisradio.com
License: Sedalia, MO held by Townsquare Media Sedalia License LLC
Group Owner: Townsquare Media; (acq 2-29-2012; grpsl)
Wire Services: U.S. Weather Service
Arbitron Metro Market: Sedalia, MO; *Format:* News, News/Talk, 86; *No. News Employees:* 2; *Target Audience:* 25-54.
Dennis Polk, General Manager
Julie Hoffert, General Sales Mgr
Doug Sokolowski, Programming Director

Seligman

KIGL

08-01-1986; 93.3 MHz FM; *Hrs Open:* 24; 100 kw; 492 ft.; N36 28 3 W94 10 25
2049 E. Joyce Blvd., Suite 101, Fayetteville, AR 72703 US
(479) 521-0104; *Fax:* (479) 587-8255
www.933theeagle.com
License: Seligman, Barry County, MO held by Capstar TX LLC
Group Owner: iHeartMedia; (acq 8-30-00; grpsl).
Nat'l Network: USA
Arbitron Metro Market: Fayetteville (Northwest Arkansas), AR; *Format:* Classic Rock; *Hrs. of News Programming:* news progmg 7 hrs wkly; *No. News Employees:* 1; *Target Audience:* 35 plus; mature, upscale professionals *Adv. Rates:* 55; 50; 50; 25
Dave Ashcraft, Senior Vice President of Programming
Judy Hudson, Business Manager

Shelbina

*KKWW

03-16-2012; 89.1 MHz FM; 12.5 kw; 325 ft; N39 40 21 W91 58 34
1411 Locust Street, St. Louis, MO
chale@nlecstl.org
License: Shelbina, Shelby County, MO
Group Owner: New Life Evangelistic Center Inc.

Lawrence W. Rice Jr, Chairman

Shell Knob

KQMO

07-16-1999; 97.7 MHz FM; *Hrs Open:* 24; 2.1 kw; 558 ft.; N36 44 55 W93 39 32
109 Monet, Aurora, MO 65708 US
(417) 235-6041; *Fax:* (417) 235-6388
www.kqmo977.com
kqmo@radiotalon.com
License: Shell Knob, Barry County, MO held by Falcon Broadcasting Inc.
Format: News; *Hrs. of News Programming:* news progmg 21 hrs wkly; *No. News Employees:* 1; *Target Audience:* Mexican-Hispanic.
Dewayne Gandy, General Manager

Sikeston

KBXB

09-12-1968; 97.9 MHz FM; *Hrs Open:* 24; 50 kw; 469 ft.; N36 59 52 W89 38 52
125 South Kings Highway, Sikeston, MO 63801 US
(573) 471-2000; *Fax:* (573) 471-8525
www.b979.net
License: Sikeston, Scott County, MO
Group Owner: Withers Broadcasting Co.
Nat'l Reps: Katz Radio
Arbitron Metro Market: Sikeston, MO; *Format:* Country; *Target Audience:* 18-49.
Rick Lambert, General Manager
Joe Bill Davis, General Sales Mgr
George Davis, Programming Director
John Steeke, News Director
Smokey King, Chief Engineer

KRHW

03-17-1966; 1520 kHz AM
125 South Kings Highway, Sikeston, MO 63801 US
(573) 471-2000; *Fax:* (573) 471-8525
License: Sikeston, MO held by Withers Broadcasting Co. of Southeast Missouri LLC.
Group Owner: Withers Broadcasting Co.; (acq 4-96; with co-located FM).
Arbitron Metro Market: MO Bootheel; *Format:* Country *Special Programming:* Farm 6 hrs wkly; *Target Audience:* 45 plus.
Rick Lambert, General Manager
Joe Bill Davis, General Sales Mgr
George Davis, Programming Director
John Steeke, News Director
Smokey King, Chief Engineer

KSIM

07-17-1948; 1400 kHz AM; 1 kw-U, ND1; N36 52 12 W89 36 32
324 Broadway, Cape Girardeau, MO 63701 US
(573) 335-8291; *Fax:* (573) 335-4806
www.kzimksim.com
License: Sikeston, Scott County, MO held by MRR License LLC.
Group Owner: MAX Media L.L.C.; (acq 6-2-2004; grpsl)
Nat'l Reps: Christal
Arbitron Metro Market: Cape Girardeau, MO; *Format:* News, News/Talk, 86 *Special Programming:* Loc sports, news, Paul Harvey, various features; *No. News Employees:* 4; *Target Audience:* 25-54.
Ronnie Glover, General Manager
Hunter Hendricks, Promotions Director
Faune Riggin, News Director
Sherry Crider, Traffic Manager

Sparta

KSPW

03-01-1989; 96.5 MHz FM; *Hrs Open:* 24; 50 kw; 492 ft.; N36 57 16 W93 17 22
2330 West Grand Street, Springfield, MO 65802 US
(417) 865-6614; *Fax:* (417) 865-9643
www.power965.com
License: Sparta, Christian County, MO held by Journal Broadcast Corp.
Group Owner: Journal Communications Inc.; (acq 6-11-99; grpsl)
Nat'l Reps: Christal
Arbitron Metro Market: Springfield, MO; *Format:* Contemporary Hits/Top 40; *No. News Employees:* 6; *Target Audience:* 18-34; young active adults; *Adv. Rates:* 20; 25; 30; 20
Valorie Rogers, Operations Dir
Rex Hansen, General Manager
Natalie Randall, Programming Director

Springfield

*KSCV

04-03-2001; 90.1 MHz FM; *Hrs Open:* 24; 11 kw; 492 ft.; N37 17 41 W93 9 10 *Rebroadcasts:* Rebroadcasts KCCV(FM) Overland Park, KS 90%
1111 S. Glenstone Ave., Suite 3-102, Springfield, MO 65804 US
(417) 864-0901
www.bottradionetwork.com
comments@bottradionetwork.com
License: Springfield, Greene County, MO held by Community Broadcasting Inc.
Group Owner: Bott Radio Network; (acq 2-7-01; 1.25 million with KMCV(FM) High Point).
Nat'l Network: USA
Arbitron Metro Market: Springfield, MO; *Format:* Christian, Talk; *Hrs. of News Programming:* News progmg 4 hrs wkly; *Target Audience:* 25-54 plus; women 60%, men 40%; *Adv. Rates:* 19; 17; 18; 10
Eben Fowler, Operations Dir
Monna Stafford, Regional Manager
Candy Green, Program Services Manager
Rachel Launius, Marketing Manager

KGMY

10-31-1926; 1400 kHz AM; 1 kw-U, ND1; N37 11 46 W93 19 21
1856 S. Glenstone, Springfield, MO 65804 US
(417) 890-5555
www.espn1400.com
License: Springfield, Greene County, MO held by Clear Channel Broadcasting Licenses Inc.
Group Owner: iHeartMedia; (acq 10-10-2000; grpsl)
Nat'l Network: Fox Sports Radio
Arbitron Metro Market: Springfield, MO; *Format:* Sports; *Target Audience:* 35 plus; affluent, educated white-collar skewing 35 plus year olds
Matt Saunders, Market President
Sarah Green, Promotions Manager

KADI

07-29-1949; 1340 kHz AM
5431 West Sunshine, Springfield, MO 65619 US
(417) 831-0995; *Fax:* (417) 831-4026
License: Springfield, MO held by Vision Communications Inc.

RADIO - U.S.

Arbitron Metro Market: Springfield, MO; *Format:* Talk *Special Programming:* Shopping 6 hrs wkly, local business 2 hr wkly; *Hrs. of News Programming:* news progmg 120 hrs wkly
R.C. Amer, General Manager
Mark Hill, General Sales Mgr
Jason Worth, Programming Director

KLFJ
11-01-1974; 1550 kHz AM; *Hrs Open:* 24; 5 kw-D, ND1; 0.028 kw-N, ND1; N37 11 45 W93 19 7
430-C Highway 165 South, Branson, MO 65616 US
(417) 831-1550
License: Springfield, MO held by 127 Inc.
Arbitron Metro Market: Springfield, MO; *Format:* News; *Adv. Rates:* 20; 18; 15; 8
Kent Emmons, General Manager
Shelly O'Brien, Station Manager
Patricia Pugh, Promotions Manager

***KSMU**
05-07-1974; 91.1 MHz FM; *Hrs Open:* 24; 40 kw; 410 ft.; N37 10 14 W93 19 25
901 South National, Springfield, MO 65804 US
(417) 836-5878; *Fax:* (417) 836-5889
www.ksmu.org
ksmu@missouristate
License: Springfield, Greene County, MO held by Board of Governors, Southwest Missouri State University
Nat'l Network: NPR
Arbitron Metro Market: Springfield, MO; *Format:* Classical, News *Special Programming:* Jazz 10 hrs wkly; *Hrs. of News Programming:* news progmg 54 hrs wkly; *No. News Employees:* 1; *Target Audience:* 25-54.
Tammy Wiley, General Manager
Lori Street, Membership Manager
Doug Waugh, Chief Engineer

KBFL-AM
01-01-1972; 1060 kHz AM; *Hrs Open:* 6 AM-sunset + 2 hrs; 0.47 kW; N37 13 33 W93 21 33
3000 E Chestnut Expy, Springfield, MO 65802 USA
(417) 862-3751; *Fax:* (417) 869-7675
kbflam.com
License: Springfield, MO held by Meyer-Baldridge Inc.
Group Owner: Meyer Communications Inc.; (acq 2-27-2006; $275,000)
Arbitron Metro Market: Springfield, MO; *Format:* Oldies *Special Programming:* Jazz 12 hrs, blues 4 hrs, 50s mus 4 hrs wkly; *Target Audience:* General.; *Adv. Rates:* 21.00; 21.00; 21.00; 21.00

KSGF
01-01-1926; 1260 kHz AM; *Hrs Open:* 24; 5 kw-D, DAN; 5 kw-N, DAN; N37 15 51 W93 19 4 *Rebroadcasts:* Rebroadcast KSGF-FM Ash Grove
2330 West Grand, Springfield, MO 65802 US
(417) 865-6614; *Fax:* (417) 865-9643
www.ksgf.com
nreed@jrn.com
License: Springfield, MO held by Journal Broadcast Corp.
Group Owner: Journal Communications Inc.; (acq 6-11-99; grpsl).
Regional Network: Missourinet; *Nat'l Reps:* Christal
Arbitron Metro Market: Springfield, MO; *Format:* News, News/Talk, 86; *Hrs. of News Programming:* news progmg 30 hrs wkly; *No. News Employees:* 4; *Target Audience:* 35-54.; *Adv. Rates:* 25; 30; 35; 10
Nick Reed, Programming Director
Kortni Tucker, Asisstant Programming Director
Jason Rima, Traffic Director

KTTS-FM
08-01-1948; 94.7 MHz FM; *Hrs Open:* 24; 98 kw; 1102 ft.; N37 10 30 W93 2 35
2330 West Grand, Springfield, MO 65802 US
(417) 865-6614; *Fax:* (417) 865-9643
www.ktts.com
news@ktts.com
License: Springfield, Greene County, MO held by Journal Broadcast Corp.
Group Owner: Journal Communications Inc.
Nat'l Reps: Christal
Arbitron Metro Market: Springfield, MO; *Format:* Country; *Hrs. of News Programming:* news progmg 5 hrs wkly; *No. News Employees:* 4; *Target Audience:* 25-54; adults; *Adv. Rates:* 140; 130; 120; 30
Rex Hansen, General Manager
Chris Michaels, Programming Director

KTXR
06-12-1962; 101.3 MHz FM; *Hrs Open:* 24; 97.8 kW; 1486 ft.; N37 11 41 W92 56 7
3000 E Chestnut Expy, Springfield, MO 65802 USA
(417) 862-3751; *Fax:* (417) 869-7675
1013theoutlaw.com
License: Springfield, Greene County, MO held by Stereo Broadcasting Inc.
Group Owner: Meyer Communications Inc.
Arbitron Metro Market: Springfield, MO; *Format:* Easy Listening *Special Programming:* MSU Bears sports, St. Louis Cardinals baseball; *Hrs. of News Programming:* 21; *No. News Employees:* 2; *Target Audience:* 35plus; female

***KWFC**
04-17-1985; 89.1 MHz FM; *Hrs Open:* 24; 98 kw; 1122 ft.; N37 12 6 W92 56 33
Mailing Address: P.O. Box 8900, Springfield, MO 65801 US
Second Address: 2316 N. Benton, Springfield, MO 65801
(417) 869-0891; *Fax:* (417) 866-7525
www.kwfc.org
info@kwfc.org
License: Springfield, Greene County, MO held by Baptist Bible College Inc.
Nat'l Network: USA; *Wire Services:* AP
Arbitron Metro Market: Springfield, MO; *Format:* Christian, Religious; *Hrs. of News Programming:* news progmg 17 hrs wkly; *No. News Employees:* 1; *Target Audience:* General; conservative, church-oriented *Adv.Rates:* 216; 216; 216; 216;
Gary Longstaff, General Manager
Kyle Dowden, Programming Director
Brady Shoemaker, News Director
Vickie Hawkins, Traffic Manager

***KWND**
07-12-1993; 88.3 MHz FM; *Hrs Open:* 24; 35 kw horiz, 34.9 kw vert; 633 ft.; N37 10 30 W93 2 35
25505 Campbell Avenue, Springfield, MO 65807 US
(417) 889-0883; *Fax:* (417) 886-8656
License: Springfield, Greene County, MO held by The Radio Training Network.
Arbitron Metro Market: Springfield, MO; *Format:* Adult Contemp, Christian *Special Programming:* Gospel 3 hrs wkly; *Target Audience:* 25-49.
Ben Birdsong, General Manager
Chalmer Harper, Station Manager
Jeremy Morris, Programming Director
Johanna Antes, Director Of Support
Kathleen Birdsong, Office Manager
Keith Stafford, Underwriter
Lowell Hamilton, BusinessRepresentative
Mike Russel, Program Director
Sue Bowen, Administrative Assistant

KWTO-AM
12-25-1933; 560 kHz AM; 5 kW; N36 56 40 W93 13 17
3000 E Chestnut Expy, Springfield, MO 65802 USA
(417) 862-3751; *Fax:* (417) 869-7675
radiospringfield.com
License: Springfield, MO held by KWTO Inc.
Group Owner: Meyer Communications Inc.; (acq 3-20-95; $1.88 million with co-located FM;
Arbitron Metro Market: Springfield, MO; *Format:* News/Talk *Special Programming:* Farm 20 hrs, relg one hr wkly; *Hrs. of News Programming:* News progmg one hr wkly; *Target Audience:* 25-55; male

KWTO-FM
11-23-1967; 98.7 MHz FM; *Hrs Open:* 24; 96 kW; 551 ft.; N37 4 6 W93 18 31
3000 E Chestnut Expy, Springfield, MO 65802 USA
(417) 862-3751; *Fax:* (417) 869-7675
radiospringfield.com
License: Springfield, Greene County, MO held by KWTO Inc.
Group Owner: Meyer Communications Inc.
Arbitron Metro Market: Springfield, MO; *Format:* Sports, Talk; *Target Audience:* 25-45; male dominant middle class
Bonnie Bell, Operations Dir
Lewis Miller, General Sales Mgr
Susie Proffitt, News Director
R.J. McAllister, Reporter

KXUS
04-17-1969; 97.3 MHz FM; *Hrs Open:* 24; 100 kw; 581 ft.; N37 11 10 W93 1 23
1856 South Glenstone, Springfield, MO 65804 US
(417) 890-5555; *Fax:* (417) 823-8506
www.us97.com
request@us97.com
License: Springfield, Greene County, MO held by Clear Channel Broadcasting Licenses Inc.
Group Owner: iHeartMedia; (acq 10-10-00; grpsl).
Arbitron Metro Market: Springfield, MO; *Format:* Classic Rock; *Hrs. of News Programming:* news progmg 5 hrs wkly; *No. News Employees:* 1; *Target Audience:* 25-54; males -75%
Matt Saunders, General Manager
George Spankmeister, Programming Director
Sarah Green, Promotions Director

St. Charles

***KCLC**
10-01-1968; 89.1 MHz FM; *Hrs Open:* 24; 50 kw; 239 ft.; N38 47 13.5 W90 30 27.9
209 S. Kingshighway, St. Charles, MO 63301 US
(636) 949-4891; *Fax:* (636) 949-4111
www.891thewood.com
fm891@lindenwood.edu
License: St. Charles, St. Charles County, MO held by Lindenwood University.
Arbitron Metro Market: St. Louis, MO; *Format:* Triple A; *Target Audience:* 18-34; young adults
Mike Wall, General Manager

KHOJ
04-13-1958; 1460 kHz AM
3713 Highway 94 North, St. Charles, MO 63366 US
(314) 752-7000
www.covenantnet.net
covenantnetwork@juno.com
License: St. Charles, MO held by Covenant Network.
Group Owner: Covenant Network; (acq 5-13-2005; $730,000)
Arbitron Metro Market: St. Louis, MO
Tony Holman, General Manager
Jim Schaper, Programming Director

St. James

KTTR FM
01-01-1994; 99.7 MHz FM; *Hrs Open:* 24; 12 kW; 466 ft.; N38 4 15 W91 39 52
PO Box 727, Rolla, MO 65402 USA
(573) 364-2525; *Fax:* (573) 364-5161
resultsradioonline.com
License: St. James, Phelps County, MO held by Results Radio
Group Owner: Results Radio
Nat'l Network: Fox Sports Radio; Premiere Networks
Arbitron Metro Market: Rolla-Cuba-Owensville, MO; *Format:* News, News/Talk, 86; *Hrs. of News Programming:* news progmg 20 hrs wkly; *No. News Employees:* 1; *Target Audience:* 25-54.

St. Joseph

KFEQ
02-16-1926; 680 kHz AM; *Hrs Open:* 24
4104 Country Lane, St. Joseph, MO 64506 US
(816) 233-8881
www.680kfeq.com
gary.exline@eagleradio.net
License: St. Joseph, MO held by Eagle Communications Inc.
Group Owner: Eagle Communications Group; (acq 3-20-69; grpsl;
Nat'l Network: ABC; *Nat'l Reps:* Katz Radio; *Wire Services:* AP
Arbitron Metro Market: Saint Joseph, MO; *Format:* News/Talk, Sports *Special Programming:* Farm 20 hrs wkly; *Hrs. of News Programming:* news progmg 50 hrs wkly; *No. News Employees:* 4; *Target Audience:* 18 plus;adults; *Adv. Rates:* 65, 26, 28, 23
Gary Exline, General Manager
Gregg Lynn, Programming Director
Barry Birr, News Director
Mark Goff, Chief Engineer

KGNM
11-01-1985; 1270 kHz AM; *Hrs Open:* 24; 1 kw-D, ND1; 0.036 kw-N, ND1; N39 44 39 W94 47 16
2414s. Leonard Road, St. Joseph, MO 64503 US
(816) 233-2577; *Fax:* (816) 233-2374
kgnm@stjoelive.com
License: St. Joseph, MO held by Orama Inc.
Nat'l Network: USA
Format: Adult Contemp, Christian; *Target Audience:* 30-55; conservative; *Adv. Rates:* $12 per :60/$10 per; 30
Rory Pullen, President
Greg Glauser, Operations Dir
Chris Meikel, General Manager
Marci Meikel, Programming Director

KKJO-FM
09-01-1962; 105.5 MHz FM; *Hrs Open:* 24; 100 kw; 981 ft.; N39 42 35 W95 2 33
4104 Country Lane., St. Joseph, MO 64506 US
(816) 233-8881
www.kjo1055.com
gary.exline@eagleradio.net
License: St. Joseph, Buchanan County, MO held by Eagle Communications, Inc.
Group Owner: Eagle Communications Group

Arbitron Metro Market: Kansas City, MO; *Format:* Contemporary Hits/Top 40; *Hrs. of News Programming:* news progmg 2 hrs wkly; *No. News Employees:* 2; *Target Audience:* 18-49.; *Adv. Rates:* 37; 32; 35; 29
Gary Exline, General Manager
Greg Lynn, Programming Director
Mark Goff, Chief Engineer

KESJ
06-01-1946; 1550 kHz AM; *Hrs Open:* 24; 5 kw-U, DA-N; N39 42 23 W94 44 36
4104 Country Lane, St. Joseph, MO 64506 US
(816) 233-8881
www.1550espn.com
License: St. Joseph, Buchanan County, MO held by Eagle Communications Inc.
Group Owner: Eagle Communications Group; (acq 3-1-99; $4 million with co-located FM).
Population Served: 150,000; *Arbitron Metro Market:* Saint Jose, MO; *Format:* Sports; *Hrs. of News Programming:* News progmg 5 hrs wkly; *Target Audience:* 45-64.; *Adv. Rates:* 15; 14; 15; 11
Gary Exline, General Manager
Mark Goff, Chief Engineer

*KSRD
01-01-2004; 91.9 MHz FM; 10 kw; 492 ft.; N39 42 35 W95 2 33
1215 Jules Street, St. Joseph, MO 64501 US
(816) 233-5773; *Fax:* (816) 233-5777
www.air1.com
License: St. Joseph, Buchanan County, MO held by Educational Media Foundation
Group Owner: EMF Broadcasting
Arbitron Metro Market: Kansas City, KS; *Format:* Christian
Brian Jones, General Manager

St. Louis

KATZ
01-03-1955; 1600 kHz AM; *Hrs Open:* 24; 6 kw-D, DA2; 3.5 kw-N, DA2; N38 37 2 W90 4 58
1001 Highlands Plaza Dr. W., Suite 200, St. Louis, MO 63110 US
(314) 333-8000; *Fax:* (314) 333-8311
www.hallelujah1600.com
katzam@iheartmedia.com
License: St. Louis, MO held by Citicasters Licenses Inc.
Group Owner: iHeartMedia; (acq 5-4-99; grpsl).
Nat'l Network: American Urban
Arbitron Metro Market: St. Louis, MO; *Format:* Gospel; *Target Audience:* 25-54; Adults
Beth Davis, Regional Market President
Andre Carson, Programming Director

KEZK
01-29-1991; 102.5 MHz FM; *Hrs Open:* 24; 100 kW; 1066 ft.; N38 34 27.7 W90 19 31.5
1220 Olive St., 3rd Fl., St. Louis, MO 63103 USA
(314) 621-2345; *Fax:* (314) 969-7638
www.kezk.com
License: St. Louis, St. Louis County, MO held by CBS Radio Stations Inc.
Group Owner: CBS Radio; (acq 11-13-98; grpsl)
Arbitron Metro Market: St. Louis, MO; *Format:* Adult Contemp; *Target Audience:* 25-54; high average household income
Dave Cooper, General Sales Mgr
Marty Linck, Programming Director
Lisa Letterman, Digital Sales Manager
Tim Burt, Commercial Production Director

KNOU
12-22-1959; 96.3 MHz FM; 80 kw; 1027 ft.; N38 34 24 W90 19 30
One EMMIS Plaza, 40 Monument Circle, Suite 700, Indianapolis, IN 46204-3011 USA
(314) 621-4106; *Fax:* (314) 621-3000
now963.com
License: St. Louis, St. Louis County, MO held by Emmis Radio License LLC
Group Owner: Emmis Communications Corp.
Arbitron Metro Market: St. Louis, MO; *Format:* Contemporary Hits/Top 40, Adult Contemp; *Target Audience:* 25-54.
Jeff Smulyan, Chairman & CEO

*KYFI
09-19-1938; 630 kHz AM; *Hrs Open:* 24; 5 kw-D, DA2; 5 kw-N, DA2; N38 40 18 W90 6 52
Mailing Address: P.O. Box 7300, Charlotte, NC 28241 US
Second Address: 11530 Carmel Commons Blvd., Charlotte, NC 28226
(800) 888-7077
www.bbnradio.org
bbn@bbnmedia.org
License: St. Louis, MO held by Bible Broadcasting Network Inc.
Group Owner: Bible Broadcasting Network; (acq 9-20-2013; $2 million)
Arbitron Metro Market: St. Louis, MO; *Format:* Christian, Talk; *Target Audience:* 30-60.
Jason Padgett, Operations Manager

KLOU
11-01-1962; 103.3 MHz FM; *Hrs Open:* 24; 90 kw; 1027 ft.; N38 34 24 W90 19 30
1001 Highlands Plaza Drive West, Suite 200, St. Louis, MO 63110 US
(314) 333-8000; *Fax:* (314) 333-8314
www.klou.com
License: St. Louis, St. Louis County, MO held by Citicasters Licenses Inc.
Group Owner: iHeartMedia; (acq 5-4-99; grpsl)
Arbitron Metro Market: St. Louis, MO; *Format:* Oldies; *No. News Employees:* 1; *Target Audience:* 25-54.
Beth Davis, Regional Market President
Dave Adams, Programming Director
Chelsey Childress, Promotions Director
Matt Saunders, Director of Sales

KMOX
12-24-1925; 1120 kHz AM; *Hrs Open:* 24; 50 kW; N38 43 21 W90 3 18
1220 Olive St., 3rd Fl., St. Louis, MO 63103 USA
(314) 621-2345; *Fax:* (314) 588-1234
www.kmox.com
kmoxnews@kmox.com
License: St. Louis, St. Louis County, MO held by CBS Radio East Inc.
Group Owner: CBS Radio; (acq 11-13-98; grpsl)
Nat'l Network: CBS
Arbitron Metro Market: St. Louis, MO; *Format:* News/Talk, News, 86, Talk *Special Programming:* Jazz 4 hrs, relg one hr wkly; *Hrs. of News Programming:* news progmg 60 hrs wkly; *No. News Employees:* 16 *TargetAudience:* 25 plus

KSD
11-01-1954; 93.7 MHz FM; *Hrs Open:* 24; 74 kw; 1027 ft.; N38 34 24 W90 19 30
1001 Highlands Plaza Drive West, Suite 200, St. Louis, MO 63110 US
(314) 333-8000; *Fax:* (314) 333-8332
www.937thebull.com
ksd@iheartmedia.com
License: St. Louis, St. Louis County, MO held by Citicasters Licenses Inc.
Group Owner: iHeartMedia; (acq 5-4-99; grpsl).
Arbitron Metro Market: St. Louis, MO; *Format:* Country; *No. News Employees:* 1; *Target Audience:* 18-34; adults
Beth Davis, Regional Market President

*KSIV-FM
04-13-1950; 91.5 MHz FM; 85 kw; 1,014 ft.; N38 34 27.7 W90 19 31.5
1750 S. Brentwood Blvd., Suite 811, St. Louis, MO 63144 US
(314) 961-1320; *Fax:* (314) 961-7562
www.bottradionetwork.com
comments@bottradionetwork.com
License: St. Louis, St. Louis County, MO held by Community Broadcasting Inc.
Group Owner: Bott Radio Network; (acq 1996; $1.625 million)
Arbitron Metro Market: St. Louis, MO; *Format:* Christian, Religious, 86
Richard Bott Sr., President & CEO
Eben Fowler, Operations Dir
Fred Zielonko, Regional Manager
Pat Rulon, Director of National Sales
Candy Green, Program Services Manager
Rachel Launius, Marketing Manager

KSLZ
09-28-1972; 107.7 MHz FM; *Hrs Open:* 24; 100 kw; 1027 ft.; N38 34 24 W90 19 30
1001 Highlands Plaza Drive West, Suite 200, St. Louis, MO 63110 US
(314) 333-8000; *Fax:* (314) 333-8312
www.z1077.com
License: St. Louis, St. Louis County, MO held by Citicasters Licenses Inc.
Group Owner: iHeartMedia; (acq 5-4-99; grpsl).
Arbitron Metro Market: St. Louis, MO; *Format:* Contemporary Hits/Top 40; *Target Audience:* 18-34; adults
Beth Davis, Regional Market President

KSTL
01-01-1948; 690 kHz AM; *Hrs Open:* 18; 1 kw-D, ND1; 0.0179 kw-N, ND1; N38 37 1 W90 10 17
10845 Olive Boulevard, Suite 160, Creve Coeur, MO 63141 US
(314) 878-3600; *Fax:* (314) 656-3608
www.jubilee690.com
jubilee690@gmai.com
License: St. Louis, MO held by WMUZ Radio Inc.
Group Owner: Crawford Broadcasting Co.; (acq 1994)
Arbitron Metro Market: Creve Coeur, MO; *Format:* Gospel, Christian, 74; *Adv. Rates:* 420; 420; 420; na
Katrina Chase, General Manager
Linda Galloway, Operations Manager
Hernandes Union, Program Director
Milton Green, Board Operator
William Foster, Account Executive
Richard Johnson, Account Executive
Alvin Rooks, AccountExecutive

KTRS
02-14-1922; 550 kHz AM; *Hrs Open:* 24
638 West Port Plaza, St Louis, MO 63146 US
(314) 453-5500; *Fax:* (314) 453-9704
www.ktrs.com
info@ktrs.com
License: St. Louis, MO held by KTRS-AM License L.L.C.
Nat'l Network: ABC; *Nat'l Reps:* Christal; *Wire Services:* AP
Arbitron Metro Market: St. Louis, MO; *Format:* News, News/Talk, 84, Talk; *No. News Employees:* 40; *Target Audience:* 35-64.
Tim Dorsey, President
Geoff Witt, General Sales Mgr

*KWMU
06-02-1972; 90.7 MHz FM; 100 kw; 948 ft.; N38 34 50 W90 19 45
3651 Olive Street, St. Louis, MO 63108 US
(314) 516-5968; *Fax:* (314) 516-5993
www.stlpublicradio.org
amcneil@stlpublicradio.org
License: St. Louis, St. Louis County, MO held by The Curators of the University of Missouri.
Group Owner: The Curators of the University of Missouri
Nat'l Network: NPR; PRI; *Wire Services:* AP
Arbitron Metro Market: St. Louis, MO; *Format:* News; *Hrs. of News Programming:* news progmg 40 hrs wkly; *No. News Employees:* 5; *Target Audience:* 27-45; upscale
Patricia Wente, General Manager
Shelly Kerley, Station Manager
Shelley Kerley, General Sales Mgr
Mike Schrand, Programming Director
Phil Donato, Promotions Manager
Bill Raack, News Director

KXEN
05-10-1951; 1010 kHz AM; *Hrs Open:* 24
5615 Pershing Avenue, St. Louis, MO 63112 US
(314) 454-0400; *Fax:* (618) 797-2293
License: St. Louis, MO held by BDJ Radio Enterprises LLC
Arbitron Metro Market: St. Louis, MO; *Format:* Religious
Dirk Hallemeier, General Manager
Jay Madas, Programming Director

KYKY
07-22-1986; 98.1 MHz FM; *Hrs Open:* 24; 90 kW; 1066 ft.; N38 34 27.7 W90 19 31.5
1220 Olive St., 3rd Fl., St. Louis, MO 63103 USA
(314) 621-2345; *Fax:* (314) 531-9855
www.y98.com
License: St. Louis, St. Louis County, MO held by CBS Radio Stations Inc.
Group Owner: CBS Radio; (acq 11-13-98; grpsl)
Nat'l Network: Westwood One
Arbitron Metro Market: St. Louis, MO; *Format:* Adult Contemp; *Target Audience:* 25-54
John Sheehan, Senior Vice President/Market Manager
Dave Cooper, General Sales Mgr
Marty Linck, Programming Director

WEW
04-26-1921; 770 kHz AM; *Hrs Open:* 2 hrs past sunset (pssa); 1 kw-D, NDD; N38 37 18 W90 4 34
2740 Hampton Ave., St. Louis, MO 63139 US
(314) 781-9397; *Fax:* (314) 781-8545
www.wewradio.com
wewradio@aol.com
License: St. Louis, MO held by Birach Broadcasting Corp.
Group Owner: Birach Broadcasting Corp.; acq 1-6-2004; $1.35 million).
Nat'l Network: CBS Radio; CNN Radio
Arbitron Metro Market: St. Louis, MO; *Format:* Variety/Diverse
Special Programming: Ger 2 hrs, Pol 2 hrs wkly; *Target Audience:* 35-64; Mature audience/older; *Adv. Rates:* 20; 20; 20; 15
Sima Birach, President

WIL-FM
07-15-1962; 92.3 MHz FM; 99 kw; 984 ft.; N38 28 56 W90 23 53
11647 Olive Blvd., St. Louis, MO 63141 US
(314) 983-6000
www.wil92.com
webmaster@wil92.com
License: St. Louis, MO held by St. Louis FCC License Sub LLC
Group Owner: Hubbard Broadcasting Inc.
Arbitron Metro Market: St. Louis, MO; *Format:* Country
Keith Kraus, Director of Sales
Greg Mozingo, Programming Director
Kelly Rebal, Promotions Director
Danny Montana, Music Director
Kim Grant, Digital Media Director
Jerry England, Human Resources Director

KZQZ
02-09-1922; 1430 kHz AM; *Hrs Open:* 24; 5 kw-D, DA2; 5 kw-N, DA2; N38 32 9 W90 11 26
, St. Louis, MO US
(314) 983-6000; *Fax:* (314) 994-9421
kzqz1430am.com
info@kzqz1430am.com
License: St. Louis, MO held by Entertainment Media Trust, Dennis J. Watkins, trustee
Nat'l Network: Westwood One
Arbitron Metro Market: St. Louis, MO; *Format:* Oldies; *No. News Employees:* 1; *Target Audience:* 35 plus; affluent, mature baby boomers
John Kijowski, General Manager
Keith Kraus, General Sales Mgr
Greg Mozingo, Programming Director
Tom Ennis, News Director
Marshall Rice, Chief Engineer

St. Robert

KFLW
03-22-1994; 98.9 MHz FM; *Hrs Open:* 24; 6.7 kw; 627 ft.; N37 52 42 W92 1 4
555 Marshall Drive, St. Robert, MO 65584 US
(573) 336-5359; *Fax:* (573) 336-7619
www.kflw989.com
License: St. Robert, Pulaski County, MO held by Ozark Media Inc.
Group Owner: Ozark Media Inc.; (acq 2-21-2002; $575,000)
Arbitron Metro Market: Saint Robert, MO; *Format:* Adult Contemp; *Hrs. of News Programming:* News progmg 3 hrs wkly; *Target Audience:* 25-55.
Dalton Wright, President
Tracey O'Quinn, General Manager

Ste. Genevieve

***KSEF**
09-14-2006; 88.9 MHz FM; 20 kw vert; 673 ft.; N37 47 58 W90 33 44 *Rebroadcasts:* Rebroadcasts KRCU(FM) Cape Girardeau 100%
One University Plaza, Cape Girardeau, MO 63701 US
(573) 651-5070; *Fax:* (573) 651-5071
comments@krcu.org
License: Ste. Genevieve, St. Francois County, MO held by Board of Regents, Southeast Missouri State University.
Nat'l Network: NPR; PRI
Arbitron Metro Market: Sainte Genevieve, MO; *Format:* Classical, Jazz, 60
Jason Brown, Operations Dir
Dan Woods, General Manager
Jacob McCleland, Programming Director
Allen Lane, Chief Engineer
Samantha Power, Web Producer/Reporter
Jeanette Lawson, Office Manager
Alex Jackson, Development Director

Steelville

KLPW-FM
08-01-1966; 107.3 MHz FM; *Hrs Open:* 24; 6.7 kw; 627 ft.; N37 55 17 W91 26 36
6531 Highway BB, Washington, MO 63090 US
(636) 583-5155; *Fax:* (636) 583-1644
License: Steelville, Lincoln County, MO held by Marathon Media Group L.L.C.
Arbitron Metro Market: St. Louis, MO; *Format:* Country; *Hrs. of News Programming:* news progmg 16.5 hrs wkly; *No. News Employees:* 2; *Target Audience:* 18-49.
Tim McDonald, General Manager
Steve Leslie, Programming Director
Marcy Frankenberg, News Director
John Covington, Local News Editor

Stockton

KRWP
01-20-1999; 107.7 MHz FM; *Hrs Open:* 24; 11.7 kw; Ant 479 ft; N37 31 24 W93 52 40
Box 1070, 1225 South St., Suite B, Stockton, MO 65785
(417) 276-5253; *Fax:* (417) 276-2255
License: Stockton, Cedar County, MO held by Cumulus Licensing LLC.
Group Owner: Cumulus Media Inc.; (acq 4-27-2004; $825,000).
Nat'l Network: Jones Radio Networks; *Regional Network:* Missourinet
Population Served: 79,000 *Special Programming:* Local news, weather, farm 8 hrs wkly; *Hrs. of News Programming:* News progmg 16 hrs wkly; *Target Audience:* 25-54; male & female
Lance Beamer, General Manager
Ed Koca, Programming/News Director
Ed Koka, News Director
Lee Reisinger, Chief Engineer

Sullivan

KTUI
02-14-1966; 1560 kHz AM; *Hrs Open:* 6 AM-sunset; 1 kw-D, NDD; N38 11 42 W91 11 12
PO Box 99, 229 Bud Street, Sullivan, MO 63080 US
(573) 468-5101; *Fax:* (573) 468-5440
www.ktui.com
custserv@fidelitycommunications.com
License: Sullivan, MO held by Fidelity Broadcasting Inc.
Regional Network: Missourinet
Arbitron Metro Market: St. Louis, MO; *Format:* News, News/Talk, 86; *No. News Employees:* 1; *Target Audience:* General.
John Rice, General Manager
Sam Scott, Programming Director
Steve Jesse, Sales
Linda Vickers, Sales
Wilma Scott, Traffic Manager

KTUI-FM
01-01-1981; 102.1 MHz FM; 6 kw; 276 ft.; N38 11 42 W91 11 12
P. O. Box 99, 299 Bud Street, Sullivan, MO 63080 US
(573) 468-5101; *Fax:* (573) 468-5440
www.ktui.com
custserv@fidelitycommunications.com
License: Sullivan, Franklin County, MO held by Fidelity Broadcasting Inc.
Regional Network: Missourinet
Arbitron Metro Market: St. Louis, MO; *Format:* Country, Sports; *Target Audience:* General.
John Rice, Operations Dir
Sales, Programming Director
Linda Vickers, Sales

Sunrise Beach

***KCRL**
09-01-1998; 90.3 MHz FM; *Hrs Open:* 24; 25 kw; 197 ft.; N38 14 21 W92 45 56
Mailing Address: 10550 Barkley St., Suite 100, Overland Park, KS 66212 US
Second Address: 30690 Gray Eagle Rd., Gravois Mills, MO 65037
(913) 693-5807
www.bottradionetwork.com
comments@bottradionetwork.com
License: Sunrise Beach, Camden County, MO held by Community Broadcasting Inc.
Group Owner: Bott Radio Network
Nat'l Network: USA
Arbitron Metro Market: Sunrise Beach, MO; *Format:* Christian, Talk; *Target Audience:* 25-55.
Richard Bott Sr., President & CEO
Eben Fowler, Operations Dir
Pat Rulon, Regional Manager
Candy Green, Program Services Manager
Rachel Launius, Marketing Manager
Jason Potocnik, Director of Traffic Operations

Tarkio

KRSS
08-22-1977; 93.5 MHz FM; *Hrs Open:* 24; 11 kw; 489 ft.; N40 31 11 W95 11 3
1500 South 14th St, Clarinda, IA 51632 US
(660) 736-4321; *Fax:* (660) 736-5789
www.krss.me/index.php?option=com_contact&view=category&catid=0&Itemid=56
License: Tarkio, Atchison County, MO held by Radio Free Ministries, Inc.
Group Owner: Radio Free Ministries, Inc.
Arbitron Metro Market: Tarkio,MO; *Format:* Christian, Religious; *Target Audience:* 25+, Christian

Thayer

KALM
12-11-1953; 1290 kHz AM; *Hrs Open:* 6 AM-sunset
P.O. Box 15, Thayer, MO 65791 US
(417) 264-7211; *Fax:* (417) 264-7212
www.AM1290TheGift.com
peggy@kkountry.com
License: Thayer, MO held by E-Communications LLC
Group Owner: E-Communications LLC; (acq 4-24-2008; $830,000 with KAMS(FM) Mammoth Spring, AR)
Regional Network: Brownfield; Missourinet *Regional Reps:* Regional Reps
Arbitron Metro Market: Thayer, MO; *Format:* Gospel; *Hrs. of News Programming:* news progmg 70 hrs wkly; *No. News Employees:* 1; *Target Audience:* 18 plus; farmers, ranchers, rural families *Adv. Rates:* :60-$14.00—:30-$12.25
Robert Eckman, President

KSAR
92.3 MHz FM; *Hrs Open:* 24; 50 kw; 427 ft.; N36 21 58 W91 28 35
Mailing Address: 909 Cherokee Village, Salem, AR 72575 US
Second Address: 352 Hwy. 62/412, Salem, AR 72576
(870) 856-3240; *Fax:* (870) 856-4408
www.myhometownradiostations.com/ksar___92_3_fm
hometownradio@centurytel.net
License: Thayer, Oregon County, MO held by Bragg Broadcasting Corp.
Regional Network: Ark. Radio Net.
Arbitron Metro Market: Cherokee Village, AR; *Format:* Country, News, 84 *Special Programming:* Farm 4 hrs wkly; *Target Audience:* 25-54.
James Bragg, General Manager

Trenton

KTTN
04-17-1955; 1600 kHz AM; *Hrs Open:* 24; 0.5 kw-D, ND1; 0.033 kw-N, ND1; N40 5 0 W93 33 30
Mailing Address: 804 Main Street, Box 307, Trenton, MO 64683 US
Second Address: 804 Main St., Trenton, MO 64683
(660) 359-2261; *Fax:* (660) 359-4126
www.kttn.com
john@kttn.com
License: Trenton, MO held by Luehrs Broadcasting Co.
Nat'l Network: AP Radio; Jones Radio Networks
Arbitron Metro Market: Trenton, MO; *Format:* Adult Contemp; *Hrs. of News Programming:* News progmg 8 hrs wkly; *Target Audience:* 35 plus; general; *Adv. Rates:* 5; 4; 4; na
David Pridemore, General Manager
Ken Berry, Station Manager
Traffic Director, Michelle Shaw
Sales account executives, Jerry Shirley
Sales account executives

KTTN-FM
09-15-1978; 92.3 MHz FM; *Hrs Open:* 24; 18.5 kw; 381 ft.; N40 5 0 W93 33 30
Mailing Address: 804 Main Street, Trenton, MO 64683 US
Second Address: 804 Main St., Trenton, MO 64683
(660) 359-2261; *Fax:* (660) 359-4126
www.kttn.com
john@kttn.com
License: Trenton, Grundy County, MO held by Luehrs Broadcasting Co.
Nat'l Network: AP Radio; *Regional Network:* Brownfield; Missourinet *Regional Reps:* Rgnl Reps
Arbitron Metro Market: Trenton, MO; *Format:* Country, News, 84 *Special Programming:* Gospel 6 hrs wkly; *Hrs. of News Programming:* news progmg 15 hrs wkly; *No. News Employees:* 2; *Target Audience:* General. *Adv. Rates:* 25; 20; 15; 15
John Ausberger, President
John Anthony, General Manager
Traffic Director, Michelle Shaw
Sales account executives, Jerry Shirley
Sales account executives

Troy

KYRO
02-22-1959; 1280 kHz AM; *Hrs Open:* 24; 660 w-D, 45 w-N; N37 58 28 W90 45 44
P.O. Box 280, Potosi, MO 63664
License: Troy, Lincoln County, MO held by JLF Communications LLP.
Group Owner: The RAFTT Corp.
Nat'l Network: ABC; *Regional Network:* Missourinet

Population Served: 30,000 *Hrs. of News Programming:* news progmg 12 hrs wkly; *No. News Employees:* 1; *Target Audience:* 25 plus; general; *Adv. Rates:* 9; 8; 9; 7
James Porter, President
Debra Porter, Operations Dir

KFNS-FM
11-29-1993; 100.7 MHz FM; 6 kw; 328 ft.; N39 3 13 W90 59 47
Rebroadcasts: Simulcast with KFNS(AM) Wood River, IL 100%
1000 Lake St. Louis Boulevard, Lake St. Louis, MO 63367 US
(636) 356-4487; *Fax:* (636) 356-4363
www.westplexradio.com/
kfns@kfns.com
License: Troy, Lincoln County, MO held by Big Stick Two LLC.
Group Owner: Big League Broadcasting LLC; (acq 7-13-2004; grpsl).
Arbitron Metro Market: Troy, MO; *Format:* Sports
Dave Greene, General Manager
James Oelklaus, General Sales Mgr

Union

KLPW
08-18-1954; 1220 kHz AM; *Hrs Open:* 24; 1 kw-D, ND1; 0.126 kw-N, ND1; N38 28 57 W91 2 39
PO Box 623, Washington, MO 63090 US
(636) 583-5155; *Fax:* (636) 583-1644
timjones@klpw.com
License: Union, MO held by Broadcast Properties Inc.
Arbitron Metro Market: St. Louis, MO; *Format:* Talk *Special Programming:* Relg 6 hrs wkly; *Hrs. of News Programming:* news progmg 40 hrs wkly; *No. News Employees:* 2; *Target Audience:* 25-54; male
Ray Heller, Operations Dir
Tim McDonald, General Manager
Dee Coppeans, General Sales Mgr
Greg Marshall, Programming Director
Diana Stanley, Promotions Manager
John Covington, News Director
Tom Lyons, Chief Engineer
MarcyFrankenberg, Traffic Manager

Van Buren

*KBIY
01-01-2001; 91.3 MHz FM; 100 kw horiz, 98 kw vert; 492 ft.; N37 6 25 W90 59 30
1411 Locust Street, St. Louis, MO 63103 US
(314) 421-3020; *Fax:* (314) 421-1702
www.hereshelpnet.org
larryr@hereshelpnet.org
License: Van Buren, Carter County, MO held by New Life Evangelistic Center Inc.
Arbitron Metro Market: Saint Louis, MO; *Format:* Adult Contemp, Gospel
Larry Rice, President

Vandalia

KKAC
104.3 MHz FM; 11.38 kw; 486 ft.; N39 25 4 W91 27 26
319 West Church Street, Bowling Green, MO 63334 US
(573) 594-6000; *Fax:* (314) 594-2100
License: Vandalia, Lincoln County, MO held by Broadcast Associates Inc.
Arbitron Metro Market: Vandalia, MO; *Format:* Country
Joe Baker, Operations Dir
Chuck Branstetter, General Sales Mgr

Versailles

KTKS
06-16-1989; 95.1 MHz FM; *Hrs Open:* 24; 12.5 kw; 463 ft.; N38 24 32 W92 45 42
Mailing Address: P. O. Box 409, Versailles, MO 65084 US
Second Address: 16875 Hwy 52, Barnett, MO 65011
(573) 378-5669; *Fax:* (573) 378-6640
lakeradio.com
License: Versailles, Morgan County, MO held by Twin Lakes Communications Inc.
Nat'l Network: CNN Radio; *Wire Services:* AP
Arbitron Metro Market: Versailles, MO; *Format:* Country *Special Programming:* Farm 2 hrs, relg 3 hrs wkly; *Hrs. of News Programming:* news progmg 23 hrs wkly; *No. News Employees:* 1; *Target Audience:* 25-54;loc rural audience & transient tourist population
Douglas Fisher, Chairman
James Fisher, President
Sheryl Lehman, General Sales Mgr
J.T. Gerlt, Programming Director

Vienna

*KNLN
90.9 MHz FM; 10 kw; 328 ft.; N38 11 27 W92 7 22
1411 Locust Street, St. Louis, MO 63103 US
(314) 421-3020; *Fax:* (314) 421-1702
www.hereshelpnet.org
larryr@hereshelpnet.org
License: Vienna, Maries County, MO held by New Life Evangelistic Center Inc.
Arbitron Metro Market: St. Louis, MO; *Format:* Religious
Larry Rice, General Manager
Larry Rice, Founder and Director

Warrensburg

*KTBG
04-01-1962; 90.9 MHz FM; 97 kw; 443 ft.; N38 55 54 W93 49 6
125 East 31st Street, Kansas City, MO 64108
(660) 543-4130; *Fax:* (660) 543-8863
www.ktbg.fm
License: Warrensburg, Johnson County, MO held by Central Missouri State University Board of Regents.
Nat'l Network: NPR; PRI
Arbitron Metro Market: Warrensburg, MO; *Format:* Triple A; *Target Audience:* General.
Jon Hart, Music & Programming
Sarah Bradshaw, Music & Programming
Bob Garrett, Underwriting

KOKO
12-01-1953; 1450 kHz AM; *Hrs Open:* 24; 1 kw-U, ND1; N38 46 32 W93 43 12
119 North Third Street, Hannibal, MO 63401 US
(660) 747-9191; *Fax:* (660) 747-5611
www.warrensburgradio.com
License: Warrensburg, MO held by D & H Media L.L.C.
Nat'l Network: ABC; *Regional Network:* Missourinet
Format: Oldies, Sports; *Hrs. of News Programming:* news progmg 20 hrs wkly; *No. News Employees:* 1; *Target Audience:* 25-54; educated-mainly female & sports enthusiasts; *Adv. Rates:* 13; 12; 13; 12
Vance Delozier, President
Greg Hassler, General Manager

Warrenton

KFAV
11-01-1991; 99.9 MHz FM; *Hrs Open:* 24; 10.5 kw; 512 ft.; N38 50 20 W91 2 40
P. O. Box 220, Warrenton, MO 63383 US
(636) 456-3311; *Fax:* (636) 978-4710
www.kfav.com
kwreksava@socket.net
License: Warrenton, Warren County, MO
Group Owner: Kaspar Broadcasting Group
Arbitron Metro Market: St. Louis, MO; *Format:* Country; *Hrs. of News Programming:* news progmg 2 hrs wkly; *No. News Employees:* 3; *Target Audience:* 20-49; general; *Adv. Rates:* Same as AM
Vern Kaspar, General Manager
Marty Becker, Sales Manager
Mike Thomas, Programming Director
Debbie Groeper, Traffic Manager

KWRE
03-09-1949; 730 kHz AM; *Hrs Open:* 5 AM-11 PM; 1 kw-D, ND1; 0.12 kw-N, ND1; N38 49 20 W91 8 15
P.O. Box 220, Warrenton, MO 63383 US
(636) 377-2300; *Fax:* (636) 456-8767
www.kwre.com
kwrekfav@socket.net
License: Warrenton, MO held by Kaspar Broadcasting Co.
Group Owner: Kaspar Broadcasting Group
Arbitron Metro Market: Warrenton, MO; *Format:* Country *Special Programming:* Farm one hr wkly; *Hrs. of News Programming:* news progmg 3 hrs wkly; *No. News Employees:* 3; *Target Audience:* 35 plus. *Adv.Rates:* 36; 19.50; 24; 7.50
Vern Kaspar, General Manager
Mark Becker, Sales Manager
Mike Thomas, Programming Director
Debbie Groeper, Traffic Manager

Warsaw

KAYQ
03-10-1980; 97.1 MHz FM; *Hrs Open:* 24; 6 kw; 240 ft.; N38 17 19 W93 18 32
Box 1420, Warsaw, MO 65355 US
(660) 438-7343; *Fax:* (660) 438-7159
kayqtraffic@embarqmail.com
License: Warsaw, Benton County, MO held by Valkyrie Broadcasting Co. Inc.
Nat'l Network: AP Radio
Arbitron Metro Market: Warsaw, MO; *Format:* Country; *Hrs. of News Programming:* news progmg 5 hrs wkly; *No. News Employees:* 1
Jim McCollum, President
Joey Anderson, General Manager
Glenna Thrasher, News Director

Washington

*KGNV
12-25-1990; 89.9 MHz FM; *Hrs Open:* 24; 1 kw; 213 ft.; N38 35 49 W91 6 17
P. O. Box 87, Washington, MO 63090 US
(636) 385-3787; *Fax:* (636) 293-4448
goodnewsvoice.org
License: Washington, Franklin County, MO held by Missouri River Christian Broadcasting Inc.
Group Owner: Missouri River Christian Broadcasting Inc.
Nat'l Network: Moody; Salem Radio Network
Format: Gospel, News, 62, Talk *Special Programming:* Class 5 hrs, children 6 hrs, teen 5 hrs wkly; *Hrs. of News Programming:* News progmg 14 hrs wkly; *Target Audience:* 20-70; inquisitive, conservative, liberal,philosophical; *Adv. Rates:* 8; 8; 8; 8
James Goggan, President
Marilyn Groggan, Programming Director
Kerry Messer, Network Director

KSLQ-FM
11-21-1989; 104.5 MHz FM; *Hrs Open:* 24; 3 kw; 328 ft.; N38 36 3 W90 56 4
511 West 5th Street, Washington, MO 63090 US
(636) 239-6800; *Fax:* (636) 239-0364
www.kslq.co
brad@kslq.com
License: Washington, Franklin County, MO held by Y2K Inc.
Nat'l Network: USA; *Regional Network:* Missourinet
Arbitron Metro Market: Washington, MO; *Format:* Adult Contemp; *Target Audience:* 25-54.
Robert Eurich, President

KWMO
10-19-1985; 1350 kHz AM; 0.5 kw-D, DA2; 0.084 kw-N, DA2; N38 34 44 W90 59 57
8604 Hedgebur, St. Louis, MO 63114 US
(636) 239-5432; *Fax:* (636) 239-0364
www.themouth.info
License: Washington, MO held by Computraffic Inc.
Nat'l Network: USA; *Regional Network:* Missourinet
Arbitron Metro Market: Washington, MO; *Format:* Talk; *Target Audience:* 35-54.
Waldo Zimarskie, General Manager
Chris Dieckhause, News Director

Waynesville

KFBD-FM
12-09-1964; 97.9 MHz FM; *Hrs Open:* 5 AM-midnight; 10 kw; 515 ft.; N37 56 50 W92 21 18
PO Box 583, 104 Peggy Ave, Waynesville, MO 65583 US
(314) 336-3133; *Fax:* (314) 336-3133
www.myozarksonline.com
License: Waynesville, Pulaski County, MO
Group Owner: Lebanon License Co.
Arbitron Metro Market: Waynesville, MO; *Format:* Adult Contemp
Mike Edwards, General Manager
Sue Jones, Business Manager

KJPW
04-03-1962; 1390 kHz AM; *Hrs Open:* 19; 5 kw-D, ND1; 0.111 kw-N, ND1; N37 49 9 W92 9 6
Mailing Address: P. O. Box D, Waynesville, MO 65583 US
Second Address: 313 Old Rte 66, St. Robert, MO 65583-0480
(573) 336-4913; *Fax:* (573) 336-2222
www.myozarksonline.com
kjpw@regionalradio.com
License: Waynesville, MO held by Waynesville/Lebanon License Co. LLC.
Group Owner: GoodRadio.TV; (acq 8-8-2007; grpsl)
Nat'l Network: Fox News Radio; *Regional Network:* Missourinet
Format: Talk *Special Programming:* Relg 2 hrs wkly; *Hrs. of News Programming:* news progmg 14 hrs wkly; *No. News Employees:* 1; *Target Audience:* General.; *Adv. Rates:* 22; 18; 16; 13.
Mike Edwards, General Manager
Gary Knehans, Station Manager
Warren Goforth, News Director
Bob Moore, Chief Engineer
Sue Jones, Business Manager

KOZQ-FM
05-02-1968; 102.3 MHz FM; *Hrs Open:* 19; 2.65 kw; Ant 492 ft; N37 49 09 W92 09 06
PO Box 1112, Lebanon, MO 65536
(417) 532-9111
mike.edwards@digity.me
License: Waynesville, Pulaski County, MO held by Waynesville/Lebanon License Co. LLC.
Group Owner: GoodRadio.TV
Nat'l Network: Fox News Radio
Population Served: 60,000 *Hrs. of News Programming:* news progmg 7 hrs wkly; *No. News Employees:* 1; *Target Audience:* General.; *Adv. Rates:* 17; 13; 17; 13
Sue Jones, Business Manager
Mike Edwards, General Manager

KIIK
05-09-1968; 1270 kHz AM; 500 w-D; N37 49 42 W92 10 27
Mailing Address: PO Box 583, Waynesville, MO 65583
Second Address: 313 Old Rte. 66, Waynesville, MO 65584
(573) 336-4913; *Fax:* (573) 336-2222
License: Waynesville, Pulaski County, MO held by Waynesville/Lebanon License Co. LLC.
Group Owner: GoodRadio.TV; (acq 8-8-2007; grpsl)
Population Served: 100,000 *Target Audience:* 40 plus.
Mike Edwards, General Manager

Webb City

KJMK
01-01-1984; 93.9 MHz FM; *Hrs Open:* 24 hrs; 48 kw; 505 ft; N37 14 34 W94 30 21
2702 E. 32nd St., Joplin, MO 64804 US
(417) 624-1025; *Fax:* (417) 781-6842
www.939classichits.com
chade@zrgmail.com
License: Webb City, Jasper County, MO held by Zimmer Radio Inc.
Group Owner: Zimmer Radio Inc.; (acq 6-17-97; grpsl)
Nat'l Reps: Christal
Arbitron Metro Market: Joplin, MO; *Format:* Adult Contemp; *Target Audience:* 25-54.
Chad Elliott, Operations Dir
Larry Boyd, Dir. of Sales
Rob Meyer, Programming Director

KKLL
03-10-1984; 1100 kHz AM; 2.5 kw-C, NDD; 5 kw-D, NDD; N37 6 23 W94 16 50
1411 Locust Street, St. Louis, MO 63103 US
(417) 781-1100; *Fax:* (417) 781-1100
License: Webb City, MO held by New Life Evangelistic Center Inc.
Arbitron Metro Market: Joplin, MO; *Format:* Christian
Charlie Hale, Operations Dir

KXDG
01-01-1997; 97.9 MHz FM; *Hrs Open:* 24; 15.5 kw; 417 ft.; N37 14 34 W94 30 21
2702 E. 32nd St., Joplin, MO 64804 US
(417) 624-1025; *Fax:* (417) 781-6842
www.bigdog979.com
kxdg@zrgmail.com
License: Webb City, Jasper County, MO held by Zimmer Radio Inc.
Group Owner: Zimmer Radio Inc.; (acq 6-17-97; grpsl).
Nat'l Reps: Christal
Arbitron Metro Market: Joplin, MO; *Format:* Classic Rock; *No. News Employees:* 4; *Target Audience:* General.
Chad Elliott, Operations Dir
Larry Boyd, General Sales Mgr
Chris Hayes, Programming Director

West Plains

KKDY
03-31-1984; 102.5 MHz FM; *Hrs Open:* 24; 50 kw; 486 ft.; N36 41 22 W91 53 45
983 East Us Highway 160, West Plains, MO 65775 US
(417) 256-1025; *Fax:* (417) 256-2208
www.kkdy.com
news@ozarkradionetwork.com
License: West Plains, Howell County, MO held by Central Ozark Radio Network Inc.
Nat'l Network: CNN Radio
Arbitron Metro Market: Springfield, MO; *Format:* Country *Special Programming:* Contemp Christian 3 hrs wkly; *Hrs. of News Programming:* news progmg 10 hrs wkly; *No. News Employees:* 2; *Target Audience:* 18-49.
Harlin Hutchison, Programming Director
Ed Button, News
Brett Stevens, Music

KSPQ
01-01-1951; 93.9 MHz FM; 100 kw; 650 ft.; N37 0 12 W91 54 24
983 Us Hwy 160 East, West Plains, MO 65775 US
(417) 256-2322; *Fax:* (417) 256-2208
www.ozarkareanetwork.com
hotcountrykdy@kkdy.com
License: West Plains, Howell County, MO
Arbitron Metro Market: West Plains, MO; *Format:* Classic Rock; *Target Audience:* 45-65 plus.
Crystal Cook, Sales
Jim Lambert, Programming Director

KWPM
01-01-1947; 1450 kHz AM; *Hrs Open:* 24; 1 kw-U, ND1; N36 44 28 W91 50 1
983 Us Hwy. 160 E., West Plains, MO 65775 US
(417) 256-1025; *Fax:* (417) 256-2208
www.ozarkradionetwork.com
news@ozarkradionetwork.com
License: West Plains, MO held by Missouri Ozarks Radio Network.
Regional Network: Brownfield; Missourinet
Arbitron Metro Market: West Plains, MO; *Format:* News, News/Talk, 86; *No. News Employees:* 4; *Target Audience:* 25-54.
Tom Marheska, Operations Dir
Gerry Elan, General Manager
Jonathan Bergman, General Sales Mgr
Bobby Helm, News Director
Bill Martin, Chief Engineer
Crystal Cook, Traffic Manager

***KSMW**
90.3 MHz FM; 0.8 kw; 394 ft.; N36 44 48.4 W91 49 55.8
901 South National Ave, Springfield, MO 65804 US
(417) 836-5878; *Fax:* (417) 836-5889
www.ksmu.org
License: West Plains, Howell County, MO held by Board of Governors, Southwest Missouri State University.
Arbitron Metro Market: Springfield, MO; *Format:* News
Tammy Wiley, General Manager
Scott Harvey, News Director
Doug Waugh, Chief Engineer
Rachel Knight, Assistant to the General Manager
Lori Street, Membership Manager
Sue Camp, Membership Coordinator
Jamie Miller, MembershipCoordinator
Liz Malarkey, Traffic Coordinator
Barb McMeekin, Corporate Support Manager

Wheeling

KULH
05-03-1999; 105.9 MHz FM; *Hrs Open:* 24; 6 kw; 328 ft.; N39 54 25 W93 20 28
802 Calhoun Street, Chillicothe, MO 64601 US
(660) 646-2255; *Fax:* (660) 646-2242
www.1059thewave.com
ean1059@sbcglobal.net
License: Wheeling, Livingston County, MO held by Resources Management Unlimited, Inc.
Nat'l Network: USA
Arbitron Metro Market: Wheeling, MO; *Format:* Adult Contemp, Christian; *Target Audience:* General.; *Adv. Rates:* 15; 15; 15; 15
Ean Leppin, General Manager
Holly Mosier, Traffic Manager
Rod Tompkins, Sports Director and Sales Rep.

Willow Springs

KUKU
10-01-1957; 1330 kHz AM; *Hrs Open:* Sunrise-sunset; 1 kw-D, ND1; 0.052 kw-N, ND1; N36 58 47 W91 59 29 *Rebroadcasts:* Rebroadcasts KWPM(AM) West Plains 100%
Box 250, Willow Springs, MO 65793 US
(417) 469-2500; *Fax:* (417) 934-2565
www.ozarknewstalkradio.com
License: Willow Springs, MO held by Missouri Ozarks Radio Network.
Nat'l Network: ABC
Arbitron Metro Market: Willow Springs, MO; *Format:* News, News/Talk, 86
Tove Sorensen, Operations Dir
Roe Edmons, Production Director

KUKU-FM
06-15-1985; 100.3 MHz FM; *Hrs Open:* 24; 50 kw; 492 ft.; N37 3 49 W92 1 39
Box 250, Willow Springs, MO 65793 US
(417) 256-1025
www.kukuradio.com
License: Willow Springs, Howell County, MO
Arbitron Metro Market: Willow Springs, MO; *Format:* Oldies; *Hrs. of News Programming:* news progmg 27 hrs wkly; *No. News Employees:* 2; *Target Audience:* 29 plus.
Gary Taylor, Programming Director
Harlin Hutchinson, News Director

Windsor

KWKJ
02-21-2002; 98.5 MHz FM; *Hrs Open:* 24; 9 kw; 535 ft.; N38 35 37 W93 31 26
398 Warrensburg, Springfield, MO 64093 US
(660) 747-9191; *Fax:* (660) 747-5611
www.warrensburgradio.com
ghassler@kwkj.com
License: Windsor, Henry County, MO held by D & H Media LLC
Wire Services: AP
Arbitron Metro Market: Warrensburg, MO; *Format:* Country; *Hrs. of News Programming:* news progmg 1 hr wkly; *No. News Employees:* 1; *Target Audience:* Students; Central MO State Univ. Students and like age group *Adv. Rates:* 14;13;14;13
Vance DeLozier, President
Greg Hassler, Operations Dir

Montana

Alberton

KOYT(FM)
105.5 MHz FM; 1.1 kw; Ant 787 ft; N47 02 05 W114 41 11
Box 4106, Missoula, MT 59806
(406) 728-5000; *Fax:* (406) 721-3020
License: Alberton, Mineral County, MT held by CCR-Missoula IV LLC.
Group Owner: Cherry Creek Radio LLC; (acq 10-31-2006; grpsl)
Population Served: 1,359,758; *Arbitron Metro Market:* San Antonio, TX
Chad Parrish, General Manager

Anaconda

KGLM-FM
01-18-1974; 97.7 MHz FM; *Hrs Open:* 24; 2.75 kw; 984 ft.; N46 6 4 W112 56 59
P.O. Box 811, Deer Lodge, MT 59722 US
(406) 563-8011; *Fax:* (406) 563-8259
www.magic97.net
License: Anaconda, Deer Lodge County, MT held by Butte Broadcasting Inc.
Format: Adult Contemp; *Target Audience:* 18 plus.
Ron Davis, President
Joe Frankland, Operations Dir
Paula Carriger, General Manager

KANA
08-01-1947; 580 kHz AM; *Hrs Open:* 24
P.O. Box 580, Anaconda, MT 59711 US
(406) 563-8011; *Fax:* (406) 563-8259
www.kana580.com
License: Anaconda, MT held by Butte Broadcasting Inc.
Nat'l Network: ABC
Arbitron Metro Market: Great Falls, MT; *Format:* Oldies; *Hrs. of News Programming:* News progmg one hr wkly; *Target Audience:* 40+.
Ron Davis, President
Joe Frankland, Operations Dir
Paula Carriger, General Manager

Arlee

***KJFT**
90.3 MHz FM; 0.4 kw; 1906 ft.; N47 1 4 W114 0 49
Rebroadcasts: Rebroadcasts KAWZ (FM)
P.O. Box 391, Twin Falls, ID 83303 US
(800) 357-4226; *Fax:* (208) 736-1958
www.csnradio.com
csn@csnradio.com
License: Arlee, Lake County, MT held by CSN International
Group Owner: CSN International
Arbitron Metro Market: Arlee-Missoula, MT; *Format:* Christian, Religious
Mike Kestler, President
Daniel Davidson, Operations Dir
Don Mills, Network Programming Director
Mike Stocklin, Underwriting Director
Kelly Carlson, Engineering Dir

Baker

KFLN
07-14-1964; 960 kHz AM; 5 kw-D, ND1; 0.091 kw-N, ND1; N46 22 31 W104 16 25
P. O. Box 790, Baker, MT 59313 US
(406) 778-3371; *Fax:* (406) 778-3373
http://www.newellbroadcasting.com/
kfln@midrivers.com
License: Baker, MT held by Newell Broadcasting Corp.
Nat'l Network: ABC; *Regional Network:* Agrinet; *Wire Services:* AP
Arbitron Metro Market: Baker, MT; *Format:* Classic Rock *Special Programming:* Farm 5 hrs wkly, Sports 5 hrs wkly; *Hrs. of News Programming:* news progmg 10 hrs wkly; *Target Audience:* 18-64
Russ Newell, Owner
Devin Bannister, General Sales Mgr
Russ Newell

KJJM
05-26-2001; 100.5 MHz FM; *Hrs Open:* 24; 7.4 kw; 610 ft.; N46 30 20 W104 12 36
Mailing Address: P O Box 790, Baker, MT 59313 US
Second Address: 3600 Hwy. 7, Baker, MT 59313
(406) 778-3371; *Fax:* (406) 778-3373
www.newellbroadcasting.com
License: Baker, Fallon County, MT held by Newell Broadcasting Corp.
Format: Classic Rock
Russ Newell, General Manager
Vaughn Zenko, Programming Director

Belgrade

KISN
11-01-1963; 96.7 MHz FM; 18.5 kw; 814 ft.; N45 40 24 W110 52 2
101 West Grand Avenue, Chicago, IL 60610 US
(406) 586-2343; *Fax:* (406) 587-2202
www.bozemanskissfm.com
ksen@townsquaremedia.com
License: Belgrade, Gallatin County, MT held by Townsquare Media Bozeman License LLC
Group Owner: Townsquare Media; (acq 2-13-2008; grpsl)
Arbitron Metro Market: Bozeman, MT; *Format:* Contemporary Hits/Top 40; *Target Audience:* 25-54; women
Julie Martin, General Manager
Anne James, Brand Manager
Julie Martin, Director Of Sales
Wendy Nielson, Digital Managing Editor

KCMM
01-01-2001; 99.1 MHz FM; 25 kw; 203 ft.; N45 46 15 W111 13 26
201 West Madison, Belgrade, MT 59714 US
(406) 813-8364; *Fax:* (406) 813-8368
info@kcmmtheone.com
License: Belgrade, Gallatin County, MT held by Gallatin Valley Witness Inc.
Arbitron Metro Market: Belgrade, MT; *Format:* Christian
Phil Lang, CFO
Bryan Brucks, General Manager
Mark Brashear, General Sales Mgr
Dale Heidner, Chief Engineer

***KGCM**
01-01-2006; 90.9 MHz FM; 5.5 kw vert; 623 ft.; N45 57 25 W111 22 11
PO Box 2426, 317 1st Street, Havre, MT 59501 US
(800) 442-9222; *Fax:* (916) 251-1650
www.ynop.org
ynop@ynop.org
License: Belgrade, Gallatin County, MT held by Educational Media Foundation.
Group Owner: EMF Broadcasting
Arbitron Metro Market: Eureka, CA; *Format:* Country, Gospel
Mike Novak, President

Belt

***KGFJ**
88.1 MHz FM; 0.73 kw; 1960 ft.; N47 9 34 W111 0 39
Rebroadcasts: Rebroadcasts KAWZ (FM), Twin Falls, ID 100%
Mailing Address: P.O. Box 391, Twin Falls, ID 83303 US
Second Address: 4002 North 3300 East, Twin Falls, ID 83301
(800) 357-4226; *Fax:* (208) 736-1958
www.csnradio.com
License: Belt, Cascade County, MT held by Calvary Chapel of Twin Falls Inc.
Group Owner: CSN International
Arbitron Metro Market: Belt, MT; *Format:* Christian
Mike Kestler, President
Daniel Davidson, Operations Dir
Joe Jennings, Station Manager & Program Director
Mike Stocklin, Underwriting Director
Kelly Carlson, Engineering Dir

Big Sky

KBZM
07-31-1998; 104.7 MHz FM; *Hrs Open:* 24; 5 kw; 3337 ft.; N45 16 41 W111 26 57 *Rebroadcasts:* Simulcast on KKQX(FM) Manhattan
8274 Huffine Lane, Bozeman, MT 59718 US
(406) 582-1045; *Fax:* (406) 582-0388
www.montanassuperstation.com
jbalding@kbzm.com
License: Big Sky, Gallatin County, MT held by Orion Media LLC.
Nat'l Reps: Interep *Regional Reps:* Local Focus 310-441-8188
Arbitron Metro Market: Bozeman, MT; *Format:* Classic Rock
Special Programming: 6a-10a; 3p-6p; *No. News Employees:* 2; *Target Audience:* Adults; 25-54
Jeff Balding, General Manager
Susan Balding, General Sales Mgr
Kim Noyes, Programming Director

Big Timber

***KYPB**
89.3 MHz FM; 0.5 kw; 413 ft.; N45 45 1 W109 57 16
1500 University Drive, Billings, MT 59101 US
(406) 657-2941; *Fax:* (406) 657-2977
www.yellowstonepublicradio.org
mail@ypradio.org
License: Big Timber, Sweet Grass County, MT held by Montana State University - Billings.
Arbitron Metro Market: Big Timber, MT; *Format:* Variety/Diverse
Dennis Hall, President
Ken Siebert, General Manager / Media Services Director
Jackie Yamanaka, News Director
Jim Nichols, Chief Engineer
Barbara Bernheim, Development and Listener Support Manager
Alicia Lee, Underwriting Manager /Public Information Manager
Ana Henrickson, Business & Finance Manager
Art Hooker, Control Room Operator / Production Assistant
Merry Ann Peters, Control Room Operator
Wesley Jessen, Media Services Assistant / Control Room Operator

Bigfork

KIBG
01-01-2001; 100.7 MHz FM; 85 kw; 2119 ft.; N47 46 25 W114 16 4
36581 N. Roservior Rd., Polson, MT 59860 US
(406) 883-5255; *Fax:* (406) 883-4441
www.thebig100.com
License: Bigfork, Flathead County, MT held by Anderson Radio Broadcasting Inc.
Group Owner: Anderson Radio Broadcasting Inc.; (acq 9-22-2003; grpsl)
Arbitron Metro Market: Polson, MT

Billings

KMHK
12-06-1987; 103.7 MHz FM; *Hrs Open:* 24; 100 kw; 480 ft; N45 46 00 W108 27 27
27 N. 27th St., 23rd Fl. Crowne Plaza, Billings, MT 59101
(406) 248-7827; *Fax:* (406) 252-9577
www.kmhk.com
bobfreeman@townsquaremedia.com
License: Billings, Yellowstone County, MT held by Townsquare Media Billings License LLC
Group Owner: Townsquare Media
Nat'l Reps: Tacher
Arbitron Metro Market: Billings, MT; *Format:* Adult Contemp; *Target Audience:* 25-54; general
Mike Sutton, Market President
Abella Sutton, Director Of Sales
Kris Edwards, Brand Manager
Cindy Uken, Digital Managing Editor

KYSX
03-04-2011; 105.1 MHz FM; *Hrs Open:* 24; 6 kW; 95 ft.; N45 45 54 W108 27 20
222 N. 32nd St., 10th Fl., Billings, MT 59101 USA
(406) 238-1098
License: Billings, Yellowstone County, MT held by Radio Billings, LLC
Group Owner: Radio Billings, LLC
Arbitron Metro Market: Billings, MT; *Format:* Rock/AOR; *Target Audience:* 25-54.; *Adv. Rates:* 15; 15; 15; 5

KBLG
09-25-1955; 910 kHz AM; *Hrs Open:* 24
North 1212 Washington, Suite 307, Spokane, WA 99201 US
(406) 248-7777; *Fax:* (406) 652-4899
www.kblg910.com
License: Billings, MT held by Connoisseur Media Licenses LLC
Group Owner: Connoisseur Media LLC
Nat'l Network: CBS
Arbitron Metro Market: Billings, MT; *Format:* News, News/Talk, 84, Talk; *Hrs. of News Programming:* news progmg 46 hrs wkly; *No. News Employees:* 1; *Target Audience:* 35-64; upscale executives
Cal Hunter, General Manager

KBUL
03-20-1951; 970 kHz AM; *Hrs Open:* 24
Mailing Address: City Center West, 7201 W. Lake Mead Blvd, Las Vegas, NV 89128 US
Second Address: 27 N. 27th St., 23rd Fl., Billings, MT 59101
(406) 294-0970; *Fax:* (406) 252-9577
www.newsradio970.com
bobfreeman@townsquaremedia.com
License: Billings, MT held by Townsquare Media Billings License LLC
Group Owner: Townsquare Media; (acq 2-13-2008; grpsl)
Nat'l Reps: Christal
Arbitron Metro Market: Billings, MT; *Format:* News; *Hrs. of News Programming:* news progmg 2 hrs wkly; *No. News Employees:* 1; *Target Audience:* 25-54.
Dennis Coffman, President
Bob Freeman, General Manager
Roy Brown, General Sales Mgr
Pat Stinson, Programming Director
Stacy Ulstad, News Director
Dick Jones, Chief Engineer

KRZN
01-01-1998; 96.3 MHz FM; 100 kw; 696 ft.; N45 45 37 W108 27 9
N. 1212 Washington, Suite 307, Spokane, WA 99201 US
(406) 248-7777; *Fax:* (406) 652-4899
License: Billings, Yellowstone County, MT held by Connoisseur Media Licenses LLC
Group Owner: Connoisseur Media LLC
Arbitron Metro Market: Billings, MT; *Format:* Rock/AOR
Cam Maxwell, General Manager
Dan Reese, Station Manager
Scott Fredricks, Sales Manager

KCTR-FM
08-14-1979; 102.9 MHz FM; 100 kw; 499 ft.; N45 45 59 W108 27 19
Mailing Address: City Center West, 7201 W. Lake Mead Blvd, Las Vegas, NV 89128 US
Second Address: 27 N. 27th St., 23rd Fl., Billings, MT 59101
(406) 248-7827; *Fax:* (406) 252-9577
www.kctr.com
mike.sutton@townsquaremedia.com
License: Billings, Yellowstone County, MT held by Townsquare Media Billings License LLC
Group Owner: Townsquare Media; (acq 2-13-2008; grpsl)
Arbitron Metro Market: Billings, MT; *Format:* Country
Mike Sutton, General Manager
Kris Edwards, Brand Manager
Adella Sutton, Director Of Sales
Cindy Uken, Digital Managing Editor

***KEMC**
04-25-1973; 91.7 MHz FM; *Hrs Open:* 24; 100 kw; 518 ft.; N45 39 31 W108 34 14
1500 North 30th Street, Billings, MT 59101 US
(406) 657-2941; *Fax:* (406) 657-2977
www.yellowstonepublicradio.org
mail@yellowstonepublicradio.org
License: Billings, Yellowstone County, MT held by Montana State University/Billings.
Nat'l Network: NPR; AP Radio
Arbitron Metro Market: Billings, MT; *Format:* Jazz, News *Special Programming:* Folk 5 hrs wkly; *Hrs. of News Programming:* news progmg 24 hrs wkly; *No. News Employees:* 1; *Target Audience:* General.
Dennis Hall, President
Ken Siebert, General Manager
Jackie Yamanaka, News Director
Jim Nichols, Chief Engineer

***KBZR**
05-02-1965; 88.5 MHz FM; kw
, Billings, MT US

RADIO - U.S.

(402) 571-0200; *Fax:* (402) 571-0833
www.kvss.com
kvss@kvss.com
License: Billings, Lancaster County, MT held by VSS Catholic Communications Inc.
Arbitron Metro Market: Billings, NE; *Format:* Christian *Special Programming:* Live Mass 2 hrs wkly, business 1 hr wkly; *Target Audience:* Christian Families
John Soukup, Station Manager
Mark Voris, Chief Engineer

KGHL
06-08-1928; 790 kHz AM; *Hrs Open:* 24; 5 kW-D, 1.8 kW-N; N45 49 29 W108 24 38
PO Box 1742, Billings, MT 59103-1742 USA
(406) 252-6661; *Fax:* (406) 238-1038
www.mighty790.com
License: Billings, Yellowstone County, MT held by KGHL Radio, LLC
Group Owner: Northern Broadcasting System
Nat'l Network: CBS; *Wire Services:* AP
Population Served: 166,855; *Arbitron Metro Market:* Billings, MT; *Format:* Country *Special Programming:* Three hrs of ag news daily; *Hrs. of News Programming:* news progmg 4 hrs wkly; *No. News Employees:* 1 *Target Audience:* 35-64
Nick Tyler, Programming Director

KGHL(FM)
08-01-1978; 98.5 MHz FM; 85 kw; Ant 370 ft; N45 45 51 W108 27 18
222 N. 32nd St., Billings, MT 59101
(406) 238-1000; *Fax:* (406) 238-1038
www.985thewolf.com
streaming@benedettimedia.com
License: Billings, Yellowstone County, MT held by BMG Billings, LLC
Group Owner: New Northwest Broadcasters LLC
Population Served: 192,800; *Arbitron Metro Market:* Billings, MT; *Format:* Country; *Target Audience:* 18-54.
Terry Strickland, General Manager
Nick Tyler, Programming Director

KKBR
12-17-1963; 97.1 MHz FM; *Hrs Open:* 24; 28 kw; 400 ft.; N45 45 59 W108 27 19
City Center West, 7201 W. Lake Mead Blvd, Las Vegas, NV 89128 US
(406) 248-7827; *Fax:* (406) 252-9577
www.kbear.com
mike.sutton@townsquaremedia.com
License: Billings, Yellowstone County, MT held by Townsquare Media Billings License LLC
Group Owner: Townsquare Media; (acq 2-13-2008; grpsl)
Arbitron Metro Market: Billings, MT; *Format:* Oldies
Mike Sutton, General Manager
Kris Edwards, Brand Manager
Adella Sutton, Director Of Sales
Jordan Dawson, Digital Managing Editor

KMHK
01-01-1975; 103.7 MHz FM; 100 kw; 479 ft.; N45 46 0 W108 27 27
City Center West, 7201 W. Lake Mead Blvd., Las Vegas, NV 89128 US
(406) 248-7827; *Fax:* (406) 252-9577
www.kmhk.com
mike.sutton@townsquaremedia.com
License: Billings, Big Horn County, MT held by Townsquare Media Billings License LLC
Group Owner: Townsquare Media; (acq 2-13-2008; grpsl)
Arbitron Metro Market: Billings, MT; *Target Audience:* 18-34; general
Mike Sutton, Market President
Adella Sutton, Director Of Sales
Kris Edwards, Brand Manager
Cindy Uken, Digital Managing Editor

KRKX
07-01-1989; 94.1 MHz FM; *Hrs Open:* 24; 100 kw; 591 ft.; N45 45 37 W108 27 9
North 1212 Washington, Suite 124, Spokane, WA 99201 US
(406) 248-7777; *Fax:* (406) 652-4899
www.941ksky.com
License: Billings, Yellowstone County, MT held by Connoisseur Media Licenses LLC
Group Owner: Connoisseur Media LLC
Arbitron Metro Market: Billings Metro area; *Format:* Country; *Target Audience:* 25-54; affluent; *Adv. Rates:* 60; 60; 60; 60
Terry Keys, Operations Dir
Debbie Sundberg, General Manager
Augie Aga, General Sales Mgr

KYYA
10-15-1959; 730 kHz AM; *Hrs Open:* 24; 5 kw-D, 236 w-N; N45 45 29 W108 29 53
Mailing Address: Box 30315, Billings, MT 99201
Second Address: 636 Haugen, Billings, MT 59101
(406) 245-3121; *Fax:* (406) 245-0822
www.kurlradio.com
genmgr@kurlradio.com
License: Billings, Yellowstone County, MT held by Connoisseur Media Licenses LLC
Group Owner: Connoisseur Media LLC
Nat'l Network: Salem
Population Served: 125,000; *Arbitron Metro Market:* Billings, MT; *Target Audience:* 35-64.
Herm Elenbaas, President

KURL(FM)
04-05-1969; 93.3 MHz FM; *Hrs Open:* 24; 60 kw; 700 ft; N45 45 37 W108 27 09
2075 Central Ave., PO Box 31038, Billings, MT 59102
(406) 652-8400; *Fax:* (406) 652-4899
www.newstalk730.com
License: Billings, Yellowstone County, MT held by CCR-Billings IV LLC.
Group Owner: Cherry Creek Radio LLC; (acq 10-31-2006; grpsl)
Nat'l Network: ABC
Population Served: 105,636; *Arbitron Metro Market:* Billings, MT; *Format:* Classic Rock; *Hrs. of News Programming:* news progmg 2 hrs wkly; *No. News Employees:* 1; *Target Audience:* 18-49; women; *Adv. Rates:* 35; 35; 30; 25
Steve Aga, General Manager
Dave Wood, Programming Director
Michael Lyon, News Director
Bruce Faulkner, Chief Engineer

KRPM
107.5 MHz FM; 100 kW; 210 ft.; N45 45 48 W108 27 20
222 N. 32nd St., 10th Fl., Billings, MT 59101 USA
(406) 238-1098
License: Billings, Yellowstone County, MT held by Radio Billings, LLC
Group Owner: Radio Billings, LLC
Arbitron Metro Market: Billings, MT; *Format:* Country; *Target Audience:* 25-54
Pete Benedetti, CEO
Kyle McCoy, General Manager

***KBLW**
08-01-2002; 90.1 MHz FM; *Hrs Open:* 24; 0.45 kw; 449 ft.; N45 45 37 W108 27 9 *Rebroadcasts:* Rebroadcasts KXEI(FM) Havre 100%.
317 First Street, Havre, MT 59501 US
(800) 442-9222
www.ynop.org
ynop@ynop.org
License: Billings, Yellowstone County, MT held by Hi-Line Radio Fellowship Inc.
Nat'l Network: Moody; Salem Radio Network; *Wire Services:* AP
Arbitron Metro Market: Billings, MT; *Format:* Religious; *Target Audience:* General; those looking for Christian inspirational music & progmg
Brenda Boyum, KXEI Station Manager
Clark Berg, KALS Sales Manager
David Brown, YNOP Program Director
Nicholas Tobiason, Music/IT Director
Ron Huckeby, Chief Engineer
Crystal MacInnes, Production Assistant
Elizabeth McClenahan,Office Manager at KXEI/Webmaster
Joe McGee, KALS Account Executive
Carlene Prince, YNOP Associate Network Manager
Dan Shepherd, KALS Account Executive

***KLMT**
12-18-2002; 89.3 MHz FM; *Hrs Open:* 24; 0.35 kw horiz, 0.98 kw vert; 528 ft.; N45 45 48 W108 27 20
6363 Highway 50 E., Carson City, NV 89701-1410 US
(775) 883-5647
www.pilgrimradio.com
info@pilgrimradio.com
License: Billings, MT held by Western Inspirational Broadcasters Inc.
Group Owner: Western Inspirational Broadcasters Inc.
Arbitron Metro Market: Billings, MT; *Format:* Christian; *No. News Employees:* 1
Tom Hesse, General Manager

***KLRV**
01-01-2005; 90.9 MHz FM; 7.5 kw vert; 593 ft.; N45 45 54 W108 27 19 *Rebroadcasts:* Rebroadcasts KLVR(FM) Santa Rosa, CA).
188 South Bellevue, Suite 222, Memphis, TN 38104 US
(800) 525-5683; *Fax:* (916) 251-1650
www.klove.com
klove@klove.com
License: Billings, Yellowstone County, MT held by Educational Media Foundation.
Group Owner: EMF Broadcasting; (acq 12-8-2004; $100,000 for CP with CP for KLWC(FM) Casper, WY).
Nat'l Network: K-Love
Arbitron Metro Market: Billings, MT; *Format:* Christian
Darrell Chambliss, Chairman
Mike Novak, President and CEO
Mike Lee, Operations Dir
David Pierce, Programming Director
Ed Lenane, News Director
Sam Wallington, Engineering Dir
Marya Morgan, News Reporter
Richard Hunt, NewsReporter
Tracy Butler, Traffic Manager
Laura Daniels, News Reporter
Tim Luttrell, News Reporter
Kenny Noble Cortes, News Reporter

KEWF
03-08-2011; 98.5 MHz FM; 100 kW; 164 ft.; N45 45 51 W108 27 18
222 N. 32nd St., Billings, MT 59101 USA
(406) 238-1000
985thewolf.com
License: Billings, Yellowstone County, MT held by BMG Billings, LLC
Group Owner: BMG Billings, LLC
Format: Country
Terry Strickland, General Manager
Scott Phillips, Programming Director

Bozeman

***KBMC**
10-01-1991; 102.1 MHz FM; 20.5 kw; 728 ft.; N45 38 18 W111 16 5 *Rebroadcasts:* Rebroadcasts KEMC(FM) Billings 100%
1500 North 30th Street, Billings, MT 59101 US
(406) 657-2941; *Fax:* (406) 657-2977
www.ypradio.org
License: Bozeman, Gallatin County, MT held by Montana State University/Billings.
Arbitron Metro Market: Billings, MT; *Format:* Jazz, News
Ken Siebert, General Manager
Jim Nichols, Chief Engineer

KBOZ
12-19-1975; 1090 kHz AM; 5 kw-D, DAN; 5 kw-N, DAN; N45 36 58 W111 5 16
Mailing Address: P.O. Box 519, Bozeman, MT 59771 US
Second Address: 5445 Johnson Rd., Bozeman, MT 59715
(406) 587-9999; *Fax:* (406) 587-5855
www.kboz.com
License: Bozeman, MT held by Reier Broadcasting Co. Inc.
Group Owner: Reier Broadcasting Co. Inc.; acq 10-18-96; grpsl).
Nat'l Network: CBS; Jones Radio Networks
Format: Talk; *Target Audience:* 25-64.
Bill Reier, General Manager
Eric Reier, General Sales Mgr
Brian Bennett, Programming Director
Les Clay, News Director
Dick Jones, Chief Engineer
Diane Stovall, Traffic Manager

***KGLT**
12-01-1963; 91.9 MHz FM; 12000 kw; 365 ft; N45 41 35 W110 59 00
Montana State Univ., Bozeman, MT 59717
(406) 994-3001; *Fax:* (406) 994-1987
www.kglt.net
License: Bozeman, Gallatin County, MT held by Montana State University.
Population Served: 67,000 *Target Audience:* General.
Ellen King Rodgers, General Manager
Jim Kehoe, Music Director
Brodie Cates, Production Director

KMMS
10-15-1939; 1450 kHz AM
125 W. Mendenhall, Bozeman, IL 59715 US
(406) 586-2343; *Fax:* (406) 587-2202
www.kmmsam.com
scott.souharada@townsquaremedia.com
License: Bozeman, MT held by Townsquare Media Bozeman License LLC
Group Owner: Townsquare Media; (acq 2-13-2008; grpsl)
Nat'l Network: ABC; *Nat'l Reps:* Clear Channel
Format: News, News/Talk, 84, Talk; *Hrs. of News Programming:* News progmg one hr wkly; *Target Audience:* 35-64.

Scott Souhrada, General Manager
Chris Griffin, Brand Manager
Devon Doers, Director Of Sales
Erin Schattauer, Digital Managing Editor

KMMS-FM
08-14-1986; 95.1 MHz FM; *Hrs Open:* 24; 94 kw; 781 ft.; N45 40 24 W110 52 2
101 West Grand Avenue, Chicago, IL 60610 US
(406) 586-2343; *Fax:* (406) 587-2202
www.mooseradio.com
scott.souharda@townsquaremedia.com
License: Bozeman, Gallatin County, MT held by Townsquare Media Bozeman License LLC
Group Owner: Townsquare Media; (acq 2-13-2008; grpsl)
Format: Triple A; *Adv. Rates:* 33; 30; 32; 22
Michelle Wolfe, Programming Director

KOBB
05-22-1950; 1230 kHz AM; *Hrs Open:* 24; 1 kw-U, ND1; N45 39 33 W111 3 22
Mailing Address: PO Box 20, Bozeman, MT 59715 US
Second Address: 5445 Johnson Rd., Bozeman, MT 59718
(406) 587-9999; *Fax:* (406) 587-5855
reier@bigsky.net
License: Bozeman, MT held by Reier Broadcasting Co. Inc.
Group Owner: Reier Broadcasting Co. Inc.; (acq 2-19-93; $125,000;
Nat'l Network: ABC; *Regional Network:* Agrinet *Regional Reps:* Tacher.
Format: Adult Contemp; *Hrs. of News Programming:* News progmg 15 hrs wkly; *Target Audience:* 30 plus; affluent adults
William Reier Sr., President
Eric Reier, General Sales Mgr
Diane Stovall, News Director
Dick Jones, Chief Engineer

KOBB-FM
11-01-1980; 93.7 MHz FM; 51 kw; -128 ft.; N45 36 58 W111 5 16
P.O. Box 20, Bozeman, MT 59715 US
(406) 587-9999; *Fax:* (406) 587-5855
less@kboz.com
License: Bozeman, Gallatin County, MT held by Reier Broadcasting Co. Inc.
Group Owner: Reier Broadcasting Co. Inc.
Format: Oldies; *Target Audience:* 25-54.
William Reier Sr., President
Eric Reier, General Sales Mgr
Diane Stovall, News Director
Dick Jones, Chief Engineer

KBOZ-FM
01-01-1983; 99.9 MHz FM; 19 kw; -184 ft.; N45 36 58 W111 5 16
Mailing Address: P.O. Box 20, Bozeman, MT 59715 US
Second Address: 5445 Johnson Rd., Bozeman, MT 59718
(406) 587-9999; *Fax:* (406) 587-5855
www.kboz.com/
License: Bozeman, Gallatin County, MT
Group Owner: Reier Broadcasting Co. Inc.
Arbitron Metro Market: Bozeman, MT; *Format:* Country
Terry Michaels, Programming Director
Diane Stovall, News Director

KZMY
01-01-2004; 103.5 MHz FM; *Hrs Open:* 24; 100 kw; 948 ft.; N45 57 25 W111 22 11
3610 Broadwater Street, Bozeman, MT 59715 US
(406) 556-0123; *Fax:* (406) 587-2202
my1035.com
License: Bozeman, Gallatin County, MT held by Townsquare Media Bozeman License LLC
Group Owner: Townsquare Media; (acq 2-13-2008; grpsl)
Arbitron Metro Market: Great Falls, MT; *Format:* Adult Contemp
Scott Souhara, General Manager
Devon Doers, Director Of Sales
Erin Schattauer, Digital Managing Editor
Erin Phillips, Brand Manager
Dick Loughney, Director of Sales

***KLBZ**
01-01-2007; 89.3 MHz FM; 7 kw vert; 679 ft.; N45 57 25 W111 22 11 *Rebroadcasts:* Rebroadcasts KLVR(FM) Middletown, CA 100%
1425 N Market Blvd., Suite 9, Sacramento, CA 95834 US
(505) 533-6100; *Fax:* (916) 251-1650
www.klove.com
License: Bozeman, Gallatin County, MT held by Educational Media Foundation.
Group Owner: EMF Broadcasting
Nat'l Network: K-Love
Arbitron Metro Market: Bozeman, MT; *Format:* Christian
Darrell Chambliss, Chairman
Mike Novak, CEO, President
Mike Lee, Operations Dir
Dr. David R. Ferry, Chief Engineer
Mitch Barnhart, Director
Larry Moody, Director

Butte

KAAR
11-01-1988; 92.5 MHz FM; *Hrs Open:* 24; 4.5 kw; 1804 ft.; N46 0 29 W112 26 30
Box 3788, Butte, WA 59702 US
(406) 494-1030; *Fax:* (406) 494-6020
www.925kaar.com
License: Butte, Silver Bow County, MT held by CCR-Butte IV LLC.
Group Owner: Cherry Creek Radio LLC; (acq 10-31-2006; grpsl)
Nat'l Reps: McGavren Guild
Arbitron Metro Market: Butte, MT; *Format:* Country; *Hrs. of News Programming:* News progmg 8 hrs wkly; *Target Audience:* General.
Jeff Gray, Operations Dir
Chris Ackerman, General Manager
Rene Wimberley, General Sales Mgr

***KAPC**
01-01-1999; 91.3 MHz FM; 0.8 kw; 1873 ft.; N46 0 27 W112 26 30
Partv Building, Rm 180, Missoula, MT 59812 US
(406) 243-4931; *Fax:* (406) 243-3299
www.mtpr.org
License: Butte, Silver Bow County, MT held by University of Montana.
Nat'l Network: NPR; *Wire Services:* AP
Arbitron Metro Market: Missoula, MT; *Format:* Classical, Jazz, 60; *Hrs. of News Programming:* News progmg 2 hrs wkly
William Marcus, General Manager
Michael Marsolek, Programming Director
Edward O'Brien, Assistant News Director

KBOW
02-14-1947; 550 kHz AM; 5 kw-D, DAN; 1 kw-N, DAN; N45 58 30 W112 34 18
Mailing Address: 190 Kossuth, Butte, MT 59701 US
Second Address: 660 Dewey Blvd., Butte, MT 59702
(406) 494-7500; *Fax:* (406) 494-5534
kbow550.net
License: Butte, MT held by Butte Broadcasting Inc.
Nat'l Network: CBS
Format: Sports *Special Programming:* Farm 5 hrs, relg 2 hrs wkly; *Target Audience:* 25 plus; general
Ron Davis, President
Fran Workman, Operations Dir
Paul Panisko, Programming Director
Mike Beckworth, Promotions Manager
Pat Schulte, News Director
Chuck Beardslee, Engineering Dir
Araka Williams, Traffic Manager

KMBR
02-07-1980; 95.5 MHz FM; 50 kw; 1821 ft.; N46 0 29 W112 26 30
750 Dewey Boulevard, Butte, MT 59702 US
(406) 494-5895; *Fax:* (406) 494-6020
www.955kmbr.com
jgray@cherrycreekradio.com
License: Butte, Silver Bow County, MT
Group Owner: Cherry Creek Radio LLC
Nat'l Reps: McGavren Guild
Format: Classic Rock
John Klapperich, CEO
Terri Bush, General Sales Mgr
Roxi Lennox, Programming Director
Van Craft, Chief Engineer

***KMSM-FM**
01-01-1975; 103.9 MHz FM; *Hrs Open:* 24; 0.74 kw; -223 ft.; N46 0 44 W112 33 26
Kmsm-Fm/Montana Tech, 1300 West Park Street, Butte, MT 59701 US
(406) 496-4601; *Fax:* (406) 496-4389
www.mtech.edu/kmsm
kmsm@mtech.edu
License: Butte, Silver Bow County, MT held by Associated Students of Montanta Tech.
Arbitron Metro Market: Great Falls, MT; *Format:* Alternative, Variety/Diverse *Special Programming:* Jazz 5 hrs, relg 3 hrs, class 2 hrs wkly; *Hrs. of News Programming:* News progmg 2 hrs wkly *Target Audience:* General; very diversified group
Wendy Dyer, General Manager
Ben Carter, Station Manager

KOPR
10-26-1972; 94.1 MHz FM; *Hrs Open:* 24; 58 kw; 1857 ft.; N46 0 23 W112 26 28
P.O. Box 3389, Butte, MT 59702 US
(406) 494-7777; *Fax:* (406) 494-5534
www.kopr94.net
License: Butte, Silver Bow County, MT held by Butte Broadcasting Inc.
Format: Adult Contemp; *Hrs. of News Programming:* news progmg 5 hrs wkly; *No. News Employees:* 2; *Target Audience:* 25-45; women
Fran Workman, Operations Dir

KXTL
01-01-1927; 1370 kHz AM; *Hrs Open:* 24
Mailing Address: 4135 Northgate Boulevard, Sacramento, CA 95834 US
Second Address: North 1212 Washington, Suite 307, Spokane, WA 99201
(406) 494-4442; *Fax:* (406) 494-6020
www.kxtl.com
License: Butte, MT held by CCR-Butte IV LLC.
Group Owner: Cherry Creek Radio LLC; (acq 10-31-2006; grpsl)
Nat'l Reps: McGavren Guild
Format: Oldies *Special Programming:* Relg one hr wkly; *Hrs. of News Programming:* News progmg 14 hrs wkly; *Target Audience:* 25-54.
Jeff Gray, Operations Dir
Chris Ackerman, General Manager
Roger Bennett, Chief Engineer
Tammy Gordon, Traffic Manager

***KEDR(FM)**
01-01-2003; 88.1 MHz FM; 850 w vert; Ant 1,729 ft; N46 00 27 W112 26 30 *Rebroadcasts:* Rebroadcasts KUFR(FM) Salt Lake City, UT 100%
Family Stations Inc., 290 Hegenberger Rd., Oakland, CA 94621
(800) 543-1495
www.familyradio.com
info@familyradio.com
License: Butte, Silver Bow County, MT held by Family Stations Inc.
Group Owner: Family Stations Inc.
Nat'l Network: Family Radio
Population Served: 17,663; *Arbitron Metro Market:* Bay City, TX;
Format: Christian, Religious
Harold Camping, President/General Manager

***KFRD**
01-01-2006; 88.9 MHz FM; 2.8 kw vert; 1729 ft.; N46 0 27 W112 26 30 *Rebroadcasts:* Rebroadcasts KUFR(FM) Salt Lake City, UT 100%
4135 Northgate Blvd, Suite 1, Sacramento, CA 95834 US
1-800-543-1495; *Fax:* (801) 359-8112
www.familyradio.com
info@familyradio.com
License: Butte, Silver Bow County, MT held by Family Stations Inc.
Group Owner: Family Stations Inc.
Arbitron Metro Market: Butte, MT; *Format:* Christian, Religious
Harold Camping, General Manager

***KJLF**
01-01-2008; 90.5 MHz FM; 1 kw vert; 1739 ft.; N46 0 22 W112 26 33 *Rebroadcasts:* Rebroadcasts KXEI(FM) Havre 100%
P.O. Box 2426, Havre, MT 59501 US
(406) 265-5845; *Fax:* (406) 265-8860
www.ynopradio.org
License: Butte, Silver Bow County, MT held by Hi-Line Radio Fellowship Inc.
Nat'l Network: Salem Radio Network
Arbitron Metro Market: Butte, MT; *Format:* Christian, Religious; *Target Audience:* General; those looking for inspirational Christian music & programming
Roger Lonnquist, General Manager
Brenda Boyum, Station Manager
Clark Berg, General Sales Mgr
David Brown, Programming Director
Ron Huckeby, Chief Engineer

Cascade

KIKF
01-01-2002; 104.9 MHz FM; 94 kw; 2037 ft.; N47 9 34 W111 0 39
1300 Central Avenue W., Grat Falls, MT 59404 US
(406) 761-2800; *Fax:* (406) 727-7218
www.1049wolf.com
tjlee@mykikfm.com

License: Cascade, Cascade County, MT held by Fisher Radio Regional Group Inc.
Group Owner: Fisher Communications Inc.; (acq 3-12-01).
Nat'l Reps: McGavren Guild
Arbitron Metro Market: Great Falls, MT; *Format:* Country
Jim Senst, General Manager
Jane Fischer, General Sales Mgr
T.J. Lee, Operations Manager and Programn Director

Chinook

KRYK
11-19-1983; 101.3 MHz FM; *Hrs Open:* 5 a.m. - midnight; 100 kw; 679 ft.; N48 23 29 W109 17 50
2210 31st Street, North Havre, MT 59501 US
(406) 265-7841; *Fax:* (406) 265-8855
www.kryk.com
nmb@nmbi.com
License: Chinook, Blaine County, MT held by New Media Broadcasters Inc.
Group Owner: New Media Broadcasters Inc.; (acq 12-30-2002: grpl)
Nat'l Network: ABC
Arbitron Metro Market: Havre, MT; *Format:* Adult Contemp; *Hrs. of News Programming:* News progmg 10 hrs wkly; *No. News Employees:* 3; *Target Audience:* 18-49.
C. David Leeds, President
Marlys Flathers, General Manager
Geoff Cole, Programming Director
Kyke Leeds, Promotions Manager
Justin Krezelak, News Director
Bruce Faulkner, Engineering Dir
Ron Bruschi, Sports Director

Choteau

*KUDI
88.7 MHz FM; 0.11 kw; -118 ft.; N47 48 24 W112 10 43
Mailing Address: US
Second Address: 414 S. Main St., Choteau, MT 59422
(406) 467-2303
www.kudifm.com
License: Choteau, Teton County, MT held by New Life Assembly Church.
Arbitron Metro Market: Choteau, MT; *Format:* Christian
Mike Manuel, President

Circle

*KMGT
90.3 MHz FM; kw
Mailing Address: US
Second Address: 1105 F Ave., Circle, MT 59215
(406) 696-8555; *Fax:* (406) 485-2332
License: Circle, McCone County, MT held by Circle Community Radio Association.
Arbitron Metro Market: Circle, MT
Jerrod Williams, General Manager

Colstrip

*KMCJ
08-01-2001; 99.5 MHz FM; *Hrs Open:* 24; 100 kw; 801 ft.; N46 10 32 W106 24 21 *Rebroadcasts:* Rebroadcasts KXEI(FM) Havre 100%
317 First Street, Havre, MT 59501 US
(406) 265-5845; *Fax:* (406) 265-8860
www.ynopradio.org
info@ynop.org
License: Colstrip, Rosebud County, MT held by Hi-Line Radio Fellowship Inc.
Nat'l Network: Salem Radio Network; *Wire Services:* AP
Arbitron Metro Market: Havre, MT; *Format:* Christian, Religious; *Target Audience:* General:; those looking for inspirational Christian music & programming
Roger Lonnquist, YNOP General Manager
Brenda Boyum, KXEI Station Manager
Clark Berg, KALS Sales Manager
David Brown, YNOP Program Director
Ron Huckeby, Chief Engineer
MarySue Amundgaard, KALS Office Staff
Joanna Baer,Announcer/Office Assistant
Earl Houtz, Announcer
Dave Kirby, Announcer
Crystal MacInnes, Production Assistant
Elizabeth McClenahan, Office Manager at KXEI/Webmaster

*KYPC
89.9 MHz FM; 3.5 kw; 1171 ft.; N45 50 17 W106 54 16
1500 University Drive, Billings, MT 59101 US
(406) 657-2941; *Fax:* (406) 657-2977
www.yellowstonepublicradio.org
mail@ypradio.org
License: Colstrip, Rosebud County, MT held by Montana State University - Billings.
Arbitron Metro Market: Colstrip, MT; *Format:* Variety/Diverse
Dennis Hall, President
Ken Siebert, General Manager
Jim Nichols, Chief Engineer
Barbara Bernheim, Development and Listener Support Manager

Columbia Falls

KHNK
11-17-1998; 95.9 MHz FM; *Hrs Open:* 24; 55 kw horiz, 5.6 kw vert; 2287 ft.; N48 30 42 W114 22 16
2432 Hwy 2 E., Box 5409, Kalispell, MT 59903 US
(406) 755-8700; *Fax:* (406) 755-8770
www.beebroadcasting.com
License: Columbia Falls, Flathead County, MT held by Bee Broadcasting Inc.
Group Owner: Bee Broadcasting Inc.; (acq 12-31-97; $337,500)
Format: Country
Benny Bee Sr., President
Mark Wagner, General Sales Mgr

KRVO
01-01-2006; 103.1 MHz FM; 8 kw; 2362 ft.; N48 30 43 W114 22 13
, Columbia Falls, MT US
(406) 755-8700; *Fax:* www.1031theriver.com
kdbr@beebroadcasting.com
License: Columbia Falls, Flathead County, MT held by Cathleen R. Bee.
Arbitron Metro Market: Columbia Falls, MT; *Format:* Alternative
Cathleen Bee, General Manager

Conrad

KTZZ
07-01-1997; 93.7 MHz FM; *Hrs Open:* 24; 100 kw; 558 ft.; N47 49 13 W111 47 56
Mailing Address: P. O. Box F, Black Eagle, MT 59414 US
Second Address: 3313 15th St. N.E., PO Box F, Black Eagle, MT 59414
(406) 761-1310; *Fax:* (406) 454-3775
License: Conrad, Pondera County, MT held by Jeannine M. Mason.
Nat'l Network: ABC
Format: Classic Rock; *Hrs. of News Programming:* news progmg 5 hrs wkly; *No. News Employees:* 1; *Target Audience:* 25-54; general
Steven Dow, President
Laurie Vosberg, General Sales Mgr

Darby

KHDV
01-01-2007; 107.9 MHz FM; 14 kw; 361 ft.; N46 13 46 W114 14 1
US
(406) 542-1025; *Fax:* (406) 721-1036
www.moclub.com
info@mtnbdc.com
License: Darby, Ravalli County, MT held by Sheila Callahan and Friends Inc.
Group Owner: Sheila Callahan and Friends Inc.
Arbitron Metro Market: Darby, MT
Sheila Callahan, General Manager
Kris Hardy, Traffic Director
Marsha Davis, Executive Assistant

Deer Lodge

KBCK
01-01-1963; 1400 kHz AM
P. O. Box 580, Anaconda, MT 59711 US
License: Deer Lodge, MT held by Robert Cummings Toole
Target Audience: 18 plus.
Chuck Schwartz, General Manager

KQRV
07-04-1997; 96.9 MHz FM; 20 kw; 984 ft.; N46 6 3 W112 57 0
774 Eastside Road, Deer Lodge, MT 59722 US
(406) 846-1100; *Fax:* (406) 846-1100
License: Deer Lodge, Powell County, MT held by Robert Cummings Toole.
Arbitron Metro Market: Butte, MT; *Format:* Country
Robert Toole, General Manager
Karen Toole, General Sales Mgr

Dillon

KBEV-FM
08-01-1972; 98.3 MHz FM; 10.5 kw; 495 ft; N45 14 22 W112 40 03
610 N. Montana St., Dillon, MT 69725
(406) 683-2800; *Fax:* (406) 683-9480
License: Dillon, Beaverhead County, MT held by Dead-Air Broadcasting Co. Inc.

Jo Ann Juliano, President
Jo Ann Juliano, Owner
John B Schuyler, Jr, Programming Director
Ron Huckeby, Chief Engineer

KDBM
01-01-1957; 1490 kHz AM
P.O. Box 546, Dillon, MT 69725 US
(406) 683-2800(406) 683-6171; *Fax:* (406) 683-9480
License: Dillon, MT held by Dead-Air Broadcasting Co. Inc.
Arbitron Metro Market: Dillon, MT; *Format:* Country
Jo Ann Juliano, President
Kathy Wise, General Manager
Kasey Briggs, General Sales Mgr
John Schuyler, Programming Director
Ron Huckaby, Chief Engineer
Jo An Juliano, Owner
John Schuyler, Vice President
Rick Kuntz, SportsTeam
John Jorey, Sports Team

*KDWG
90.9 MHz FM; *Hrs Open:* 24; 0.85 kw; -236 ft.; N45 12 33 W112 38 14
Campus Box 119, 710 S Atlantic St, Dillion, MT 59725 US
(406) 683-7156
www.my.umwestern.edu/kdwg
License: Dillon, Beaverhead County, MT held by Western Montana College University of Montana.
Arbitron Metro Market: Dillon, MT; *Format:* Rock/AOR
Cory Craden, Programming Director

Dutton

KVVR
08-07-2001; 97.9 MHz FM; 100 kw; 715 ft.; N47 36 52 W111 20 51
20 3rd Street N, Great Falls, MT 59340 US
(406) 761-7600; *Fax:* (406) 761-5511
License: Dutton, Teton County, MT held by CCR-Great Falls IV LLC.
Group Owner: Cherry Creek Radio LLC; (acq 12-19-2003; grpsl)
Arbitron Metro Market: Great Falls, MT; *Format:* Adult Contemp
Ron Korb, General Manager

East Helena

KBMI-FM
04-13-1989; 104.1 MHz FM; 5 kw; 653 ft.; N46 46 11 W112 1 25
P.O. Box 4111, Helena, MT 59604 US
(406) 442-4490; *Fax:* (406) 442-7356
info@khkr.com
License: East Helena, Lewis and Clark County, MT held by CCR-Helena IV LLC.
Group Owner: Cherry Creek Radio LLC; (acq 2-3-2004; grpsl).
Format: Country; *Target Audience:* 25-54.
Dewey Bruce, General Manager

KKGR
05-26-1988; 680 kHz AM
1400 Eleventh Avenue, Helena, MT 59601 US
(406) 443-5237
License: East Helena, MT held by KKGR Inc.
Arbitron Metro Market: Great Falls, MT; *Format:* Oldies
Jim Schaffer, General Manager
Ron Davidson, General Manager

East Missoula

KMPT
06-27-1959; 930 kHz AM; *Hrs Open:* 24; 5 kw-D, DAN; 1 kw-N, DAN; N46 51 57 W114 4 57
980 North Michigan Ave., Suite 1880, Chicago, IL 60611 US
(406) 728-9300; *Fax:* (406) 542-2329
scott.richman@townsquaremedia.com
License: East Missoula, MT held by Townsquare Media Missoula License LLC
Group Owner: Townsquare Media; (acq 2-13-2008; grpsl)
Format: Alternative, Talk; *Hrs. of News Programming:* News progmg 14 hrs wkly; *Target Audience:* 35-54; adult spenders

Scott Richman, General Manager
Robert Gibbons, Director Of Sales
Tan Curtis, Digital Managing Editor

Eureka

KZXT
93.5 MHz FM; 2 kw; -689 ft.; N48 54 0.7 W115 1 20.7
36581 N. Reservoir Rd., Polson, MT 59860 US
(406) 883-5255; *Fax:* (406) 883-4441
www.kzxt93.com
License: Eureka, Lincoln County, MT held by Anderson Radio Broadcasting Inc.
Group Owner: Anderson Radio Broadcasting Inc.; (acq 6-6-2008; $140,406 for CP)
Arbitron Metro Market: Eureka, MT

Evergreen

KYWL
01-01-2008; 97.9 kHz FM
120 3rd St. E., Kalispell, MT 59901 US
(406) 257-9430; *Fax:* (406) 752-0313
License: Evergreen, MT held by Anderson Radio Broadcasting Inc.
Group Owner: Anderson Radio Broadcasting Inc.; (acq 2-29-2008; $200,000)
Arbitron Metro Market: Evergreen, MT; *Format:* Jazz, Smooth Jazz

Florence

KDTR
01-01-2005; 103.3 MHz FM; 1.84 kw; 2083 ft.; N46 48 6 W113 58 22
2425 West Central Avenue, Missoula, MT 59801 US
(406) 721-6800; *Fax:* (406) 329-1850
www.trail1033.com
rharsell@simmonsmedia.com
License: Florence, Ravalli County, MT held by Spanish Peaks Broadcasting Inc.
Group Owner: Spanish Peaks Broadcasting Inc.
Nat'l Reps: Interep
Arbitron Metro Market: Florence, MT; *Format:* Triple A; *No. News Employees:* 1; *Target Audience:* 25-54; adults; *Adv. Rates:* 27; 24; 27; 15
Rod Harsell, General Manager
Robert Chase, Programming Director

Forsyth

KIKC
10-10-1975; 1250 kHz AM; *Hrs Open:* 24; 5 kw-D, ND2; 0.132 kw-N, ND2; N46 15 30 W106 41 21
Mailing Address: P.O. Box 1140, Forsyth, MT 59327 US
Second Address: 210 W. Front St., Forsyth, MT 59327
(406) 346-2711; *Fax:* (406) 346-2712
www.kikcradio.com
kikc@rangeweb.net
License: Forsyth, MT held by Mile City, Forsyth Broadcasting Inc.
Wire Services: AP
Format: Oldies; *Target Audience:* 18-35; general; *Adv. Rates:* 9; 9; 9; 9
Stephen Marks, President

KIKC-FM
09-01-1980; 101.3 MHz FM; *Hrs Open:* 24; 100 kw; 1010 ft.; N46 10 32 W106 24 21
Mailing Address: P.O. Box 1140, Forsyth, MT 59327 US
Second Address: 210 W. Front St., Forsyth, MT 59327
(406) 346-2711; *Fax:* (406) 346-2712
www.kikcradio.com
kikc@rangeweb.net
License: Forsyth, Rosebud County, MT held by Miles City, Forsyth Broadcasting Inc.
Nat'l Network: CNN Radio; *Nat'l Reps:* Interep *Regional Reps:* Allied Radio Partners; *Wire Services:* AP
Format: Country; *Hrs. of News Programming:* News progmg 4 hrs wkly; *Target Audience:* 18 plus; general; *Adv. Rates:* 18; 18; 18; 18
Steve Marks, CEO
Dick Haugen, Operations Dir
Grant West, Programming Director
Patti Haugen, Operations Manager

Fort Belknap Agency

*KGVA
10-01-1996; 88.1 MHz FM; 95 kw; 797 ft.; N48 11 18 W108 42 36
P.O. Box 159, Harlem, MT 59526 US
(406) 353-4656; *Fax:* (406) 353-2898
www.kgvafm.org
kgvaradiostation@yahoo.com
License: Fort Belknap Agency, Blaine County, MT held by Fort Belknap College.
Nat'l Network: NPR
Format: News, News/Talk, 86 *Special Programming:* American Indian 60 hrs wkly; *Target Audience:* General.
Gerald Stiffarm, Operations Dir
Will Gray Jr., General Manager

Fort Benton

KVMO
01-01-2008; 95.9 MHz FM; 0.1 kw horiz; 13 ft.; N47 50 8 W110 39 10
US
(406) 442-2655
License: Fort Benton, Chouteau County, MT held by The Montana Radio Company LLC
Group Owner: The Montana Radio Company LLC; (acq 11-6-2008)
Arbitron Metro Market: Fort Benton, MT; *Format:* Adult Contemp
Kevin Terry, Manager

Four Corners

KSCY
03-01-2008; 106.9 MHz FM; 4 kw; 646 ft.; N45 38 20 W111 15 56
8274 Huffine Lane, Bozeman, MT 59718 US
(406) 582-1045; *Fax:* (406) 582-0388
License: Four Corners, Gallatin County, MT held by Radick Construction Inc.
Arbitron Metro Market: Dallas-Fort Worth; *Format:* Country
Jeff Balding, General Manager
Susan Balding, General Sales Mgr

Frenchtown

KGVO-FM
01-01-2007; 101.5 MHz FM; 3.4 kw; Ant 2,089 ft; N46 48 08 W113 58 21
3250 S. Reserve St., Suite 200, Missoula, MT 59801-8236
(406) 728-9300; *Fax:* (406) 363-6436
www.1015theview.com
scott.richman@townsquaremedia.com
License: Frenchtown, Missoula County, MT held by Townsquare Media Missoula License LLC
Group Owner: Townsquare Media; (acq 2-13-2008; $500,000)
Population Served: 67,290; *Arbitron Metro Market:* Missoula, MT; *Format:* Classic Rock
Scott Richman, General Manager
Billy Jenkins, Brand Manager
Robert Gibbons, Director Of Sales
Tan Curtis, Digital Managing Editor

Glasgow

KLAN
03-01-1983; 93.5 MHz FM; 3 kw; 299 ft.; N48 5 42 W106 37 8
P.O. 671, Glasgow, MT 59230 US
(406) 228-9336; *Fax:* (406) 228-9338
www.kltz.com
kltz@kltz.com
License: Glasgow, Valley County, MT held by Glasgow Broadcasting Corp.
Arbitron Metro Market: Billings, MT; *Format:* Adult Contemp
Shirley Trang, General Manager
Leila J., General Sales Mgr
Tim Phillips, Programming Director
Stan Ozark, News Director
Lori Mason, Music Director
Gwen Page, Traffic Manager
Annette Vegge, Office Manager
Mary Nyquist,Production

KLTZ
08-14-1954; 1240 kHz AM; 1 kw-U, ND1; N48 13 9 W106 38 54
P.O. Box 671, Glasgow, MT 59230 US
(406) 228-9336; *Fax:* (406) 228-9338
www.kltz.com
License: Glasgow, MT held by Glasgow Broadcasting Inc.
Regional Network: Agrinet
Format: Country; *Target Audience:* 25 plus.
Shirley Trang, General Manager
Tim Phillips, Programming Director
Stan Ozark, News Director
Gwen Page, Traffic Manager
Annette Vegge, Office Manager

Glendive

KDZN
12-21-1969; 96.5 MHz FM; *Hrs Open:* 24; 90 kw horiz; 489 ft.; N47 5 15 W104 48 4
210 South Douglas, Glendive, MT 59330 US
(406) 377-3377; *Fax:* (406) 365-2181
www.kxgn.com
kxgnkdzn@midrivers.com
License: Glendive, Dawson County, MT held by Magic Air Communications Co.
Nat'l Network: CBS Radio; Westwood One; *Wire Services:* AP
Arbitron Metro Market: Glendive, MT; *Format:* Country; *Hrs. of News Programming:* News progmg 4 hrs wkly; *Target Audience:* 25-54.
Steven Marks, President
Paul Sturlaugson, General Manager
Marcy Copp, Programming Director
Ed Agre, News Director

KGLE
08-22-1962; 590 kHz AM; *Hrs Open:* 24; 1 kw-D, ND2; 0.111 kw-N, ND2; N47 5 50 W104 47 9
86 Seven Mile Drive, Glendive, MT 59330 US
(406) 377-3331; *Fax:* (406) 377-3332
www.kgle.org
kgle@midrivers.com
License: Glendive, MT held by Friends of Christian Radio Inc.
Nat'l Network: Salem Radio Network; *Wire Services:* AP
Format: Religious; *Hrs. of News Programming:* news 20 hrs wkly; *Target Audience:* 35-64; general; *Adv. Rates:* 6; 6; 6; 6
Tom Fatzinger, President
Jim McBride, General Manager
Diane Odenbach, Station Manager

KXGN
09-23-1948; 1400 kHz AM; *Hrs Open:* 24; 1 kw-U, ND1; N47 5 40 W104 42 50
210 South Douglas, Glendive, MT 59330 US
(406) 377-3377; *Fax:* (406) 365-2181
www.glendivebroadcasting.com
kxgnkdzn@midrivers.com
License: Glendive, MT held by Glendive Broadcasting Corp.
Nat'l Network: ABC; *Wire Services:* NWS (National Weather Service)
TV Affiliate: KXGN-TV affil; *Format:* Adult Contemp, Oldies
Special Programming: Derry Brownfield 5 hrs, farm 2 hrs wkly; *Hrs. of News Programming:* news progmg 6 hrs wkly; *No. News Employees:* 1 *Adv. Rates:* 15.50; 15.50; 5.50; na
Stephen Marks, President
Paul Sturlaugson, General Manager
Paul Strulaugson, Executive Vice President

Great Falls

KAAK
06-19-1972; 98.9 MHz FM; *Hrs Open:* 24; 100 kw; 482 ft.; N47 32 23 W111 17 6
1300 Central Avenue West, PO Box 3129, Great Falls, MT 59403
(406) 761-7600; *Fax:* (406) 761-5511
License: Great Falls, Cascade County, MT held by CCR-Great Falls IV LLC.
Group Owner: Fisher Radio Regional Group
Arbitron Metro Market: Great Falls, MT; *Format:* Adult Contemp; *Target Audience:* 25-44.
Ron Korb, General Manager

KEIN
07-01-1922; 1310 kHz AM; *Hrs Open:* 24; 5 kw-D, ND2; 1 kw-N, ND2; N47 31 20 W111 23 18
Mailing Address: 3313 15th Street N.E., Box F, Black Eagle, MT 59414 US
Second Address: 3313 15th St. N.E., Black Eagle, MT 59414
(406) 761-1310; *Fax:* (406) 454-3775
License: Great Falls, MT held by Munson Radio Inc.
Format: Adult Contemp; *Hrs. of News Programming:* news progmg 5 hrs wkly; *No. News Employees:* 1; *Target Audience:* 35 plus.; *Adv. Rates:* 17.50; 17.50; 16.50; 15.00
Steven Dow, President

*KGFC
01-01-1996; 88.9 MHz FM; *Hrs Open:* 24; 6 kw; 243 ft.; N47 27 52.4 W111 21 17.8 *Rebroadcasts:* Rebroadcasts KXEI(FM) Havre 100%.
P.O. Box 2426, Havre, MT 59501 US
1 (800) 442-9222; *Fax:* (406) 265-8860
www.ynop.org
info@ynop.org
License: Great Falls, Cascade County, MT held by Hi-Line Radio Fellowship Inc.
Wire Services: AP

Format: Christian, Religious; *Target Audience:* General; those looking for inspirational Christian music & progmg
Roger Lonnquist, General Manager
Brenda Boyum, Station Manager
David Brown, Programming Director
Nicholas Tobiason, Music/IT Director

***KGPR**
04-01-1984; 89.9 MHz FM; *Hrs Open:* 24; 9.5 kw; 295 ft.; N47 32 23 W111 17 6 *Rebroadcasts:* Rebroadcasts KUFM(FM) Missoula 100%
2100 16th Avenue S., Great Falls, MT 59406 US
(406) 268-3739; *Fax:* (406) 268-3736
www.kgpr.org
info@kgpr.org
License: Great Falls, Cascade County, MT held by Great Falls Public Radio Association.
Nat'l Network: PRI; NPR
Format: News; *Hrs. of News Programming:* News progmg 44 hrs wkly; *Target Audience:* General.
Joseph Duffy, President
Bill Tacke, Operations Dir
Tom Halverson, Station Manager
Carol Spahr, General Sales Mgr

KLFM
02-14-1982; 92.9 MHz FM; *Hrs Open:* 24; 98 kw; 410 ft.; N47 32 19 W111 15 41
P.O. Box 3309, Great Falls, MT 59403 US
(406) 761-7600; *Fax:* (406) 761-5511
License: Great Falls, Cascade County, MT held by CCR-Great Falls IV LLC.
Group Owner: CCR-Great Falls LV, LLC
Arbitron Metro Market: Great Falls, MT; *Format:* Oldies; *Target Audience:* 25-54.
Ron Korb, General Manager

KMON
05-30-1947; 560 kHz AM; *Hrs Open:* 24
20 3rd Street N., Great Falls, MT 59401 US
(406) 453-1554
www.kmon.com
License: Great Falls, MT held by CCR-Great Falls IV LLC.
Group Owner: Cherry Creek Radio LLC; (acq 12-19-2003; grpsl)
Format: Country *Special Programming:* Sports 5 hrs wkly; *Hrs. of News Programming:* news progmg 20 hrs wkly; *No. News Employees:* 1; *Target Audience:* 35-64.
Ron Korb, General Manager
Melissa Horton, General Sales Mgr
Skip Walters, Programming Director
Ken Eklund, Chief Engineer
Angie Depping, Research Director

KMON-FM
10-01-1972; 94.5 MHz FM; *Hrs Open:* 24; 98 kw; 495 ft.; N47 32 19 W111 15 41
P.O. Box 3309, Great Falls, MT 59403 US
(406) 761-7600; *Fax:* (406) 761-5511
License: Great Falls, Cascade County, MT
Group Owner: Cherry Creek Radio LLC
Wire Services: U.S. Weather Service
Format: Country; *Hrs. of News Programming:* news progmg 5 hrs wkly; *No. News Employees:* 1; *Target Audience:* 25-54.
Ron Korb, General Sales Mgr
Scott Hershey, Programming Director

KQDI
01-01-1955; 1450 kHz AM; 0.72 kw-U, ND1; N47 27 56 W111 19 22
N. 1212 Washington, Suite 307, Spokane, WA 99201 US
(406) 761-2800; *Fax:* (406) 727-7218
www.newstalk1450.com
License: Great Falls, MT held by Staradio Corp.
Group Owner: Staradio Corp.
Nat'l Reps: Christal
Arbitron Metro Market: Great Falls area; *Format:* News, News/Talk, 86; *Target Audience:* 25-54.
Dave France, Operations Dir
Terry Strickland, General Manager
Anna Palagi, General Sales Mgr
Pam Bennett, News Director
Joe Bower, Chief Engineer

KXGF
01-01-1987; 1400 kHz AM; 1 kw-U; N47 27 56 W111 20 22
Mailing Address: Box 3129, Great Falls, MT 99201
Second Address: 1300 Central Ave. W., Great Falls, MT 59403
(406) 761-2800; *Fax:* (406) 727-7218
License: Great Falls, Cascade County, MT held by Staradio Corp
Group Owner: Staradio Corp; (acq 12-28-94; grpsl, including co-
Nat'l Reps: Katz

Population Served: 86,000 *Special Programming:* Farm 2 hrs wkly; *Target Audience:* 35-64.
TJ Lee, Operations Dir
Jane Fischer, General Sales Mgr
Evin Thomas, Programming Director
Phil O'Reilly, Chief Engineer

KLSK
01-01-2003; 100.3 MHz FM; 100 kw; 495 ft.; N47 15 57 W111 8 39
188 South Bellevue, Suite 222, Memphis, TN 38104 US
(800) 525-5683; *Fax:* (916) 251-1650
www.klove.com
klove@klove.com
License: Great Falls, Cascade County, MT held by Flinn Broadcasting Corp.
Arbitron Metro Market: Great Falls, MT; *Format:* Urban Contemporary
Darrell Chambliss, Chairman
Mike Novak, President and CEO
Karen Wheatley, General Manager
David Pierce, Programming Director
Ed Lenane, News Director
Sam Wallington, Engineering Dir
Scott Smith, Music Director
Marya Morgan,News Reporter
Richard Hunt, News Reporter
Tracy Butler, Traffic Manager
Laura Daniels, News Reporter
Tim Luttrell, News Reporter

***KGFA**
01-01-2006; 90.7 MHz FM; 2.3 kw; 299 ft.; N47 31 57 W111 16 38
P.O. Drawer 2440, Tupelo, MS 38803 US
(888) 937-2471; *Fax:* (916) 251-1650
www.air1.com
info@air1.com
License: Great Falls, Cascade County, MT held by Educational Media Foundation.
Group Owner: EMF Broadcasting; (acq 3-23-2007; grpsl)
Nat'l Network: Air 1
Arbitron Metro Market: Great Falls, MT; *Format:* Alternative, Christian
Darrell Chambliss, Chairman
Alan Mason, COO
Mike Novak, President and CEO
Ed Lenane, News Director
Sam Wallington, Engineering Dir
Eric Moser, Chief Financial Officer
Brian Burger, Vice President of Human Resources
D. KevinBlair, Secretary and General Counsel
Larry Moody, Director
Mitch Barnhart, Director

***KFRW**
01-01-2007; 91.9 MHz FM; 50 kw; 466 ft.; N47 49 13 W111 47 56 *Rebroadcasts:* Rebroadcasts KUFR(FM) Salt Lake City, UT 100%
4135 Northgate Blvd., Great Falls, MT 95834 US
(800) 543-1495; *Fax:* (916) 641-8238
www.familyradio.com
info@familyradio.com
License: Great Falls, Cascade County, MT held by Family Stations Inc.
Group Owner: Family Stations Inc.
Arbitron Metro Market: Great Falls, MT; *Format:* Christian, Religious
Harold Camping, General Manager

***KAFH**
01-01-2006; 91.5 MHz FM; 1 kw; 298 ft.; N47 31 57 W111 16 38
Rebroadcasts: Rebroadcasts WAFR(FM) Tupelo, MS 100%
P.O. Box 3206, Tupelo, MS 38803 US
(662) 844-8888; *Fax:* (662) 842-6791
www.afr.net
faq@afa.net
License: Great Falls, Cascade County, MT held by American Family Association.
Group Owner: American Family Radio
Arbitron Metro Market: Great Falls, MT; *Format:* Christian
Tim Wildmon, President
Donald Wildmon, Founder
Buddy Smith, Sr VP
Ed Vitagliano, Exec VP
Randy Sharp, Director Of Special Projects
Meeke Addison, Director Of Communications
Abraham Hamilton III, General Counsel

Hamilton

KBAZ
02-11-1969; 96.3 MHz FM; *Hrs Open:* 24; 50 kw; 2090 ft.; N46 48 8 W113 58 21
101 West Grand, Suite 600, Chicago, IL 60610 US
(406) 728-9300; *Fax:* (406) 363-6436
www.963theblaze.com
License: Hamilton, Ravalli County, MT held by Townsquare Media Missoula License LLC
Group Owner: Townsquare Media; (acq 2-13-2008; grpsl)
Format: Alternative
Scott Richman, General Manager
Angel, Brand Manager
Robert Gibbons, Director Of Sales
Tan Curtis, Digital Managing Editor

KLYQ
02-03-1961; 1240 kHz AM; *Hrs Open:* 5:30 AM-midnight; 1 kw-U, ND1; N46 15 22 W114 9 45
101 West Grand, Suite 600, Chicago, IL 60610 US
(406) 363-3010; *Fax:* (406) 363-6436
www.klyq.com
contact@klyq.com
License: Hamilton, MT held by Townsquare Media Missoula License LLC
Group Owner: Townsquare Media; (acq 2-13-2008; grpsl)
Arbitron Metro Market: Great Falls, MT; *Format:* News, News/Talk, 86; *Hrs. of News Programming:* news progmg 25 hrs wkly; *No. News Employees:* 1; *Target Audience:* 25-54; adults
Scott Richman, General Manager
Steve Fullerton, Brand Manager
Robert Gibbons, Director Of Sales
Tan Curtis, Digital Managing Editor

***KUFN**
10-01-1998; 91.9 MHz FM; 0.9 kw; 427 ft.; N46 13 46 W114 14 1
Broadcast Media Center, Missoula, MT 59812 US
(406) 243-4931; *Fax:* (406) 243-3299
www.kufm.org
License: Hamilton, Ravalli County, MT held by The University of Montana.
Nat'l Network: NPR; *Wire Services:* AP
Arbitron Metro Market: Hamilton, MT; *Format:* Classical, Jazz, 60; *Hrs. of News Programming:* News progmg 2 hrs wkly
William Marcus, General Manager
Michael Marsolek, Programming Director
Saxon Holbrook, Technical Director
Sue Ginn, Business Manager
Edward F. O'Brien, Assistant News Director
Linda Talbott, Development Director
Kathy Woodford,Director of Corporate Support

***KMZO**
90.7 MHz FM; *Hrs Open:* 24; 5 kw; 331 ft.; N46 13 46 W114 14 1
2201 South 6th St., Las Vegas, NV 89104 US
(208) 734-5777; *Fax:* (702) 731-1992
www.sosradio.net
scott@sosradio.net
License: Hamilton, Ravalli County, MT held by Faith Communications Corp.
Group Owner: Faith Communications Corp.
Arbitron Metro Market: Great Falls, MT; *Format:* Christian; *Hrs. of News Programming:* News progmg 5 hrs wkly
Brad Staley, President and General Manager
Scott Herrold, Programming Director
Robert Forbes, Promotions Manager
Tim Hunt, Network Director of Engineering
Gary Thompson, Creative Services Director
Mike Mead, Donor Relations
Marney Domeraski, Donor Relations
Dawn Vincent, Listener Services
Rick Hall, Music Director
Chris Staley, Vice-President of Programming & Administration

Hardin

KHDN
12-28-1962; 1230 kHz AM; *Hrs Open:* 24; 1 kw-U, ND1; N45 42 55 W107 35 59
PO Box 230, Hardin, MT 59034 US
(406) 665-2828; *Fax:* (406) 665-2131
www.bigskyradio.net
rich@bigskyradio.net
License: Hardin, MT held by Sun Mountain Inc.
Group Owner: Sun Mountain Inc.; (acq 11-30-2000)
Nat'l Network: ABC
Format: Adult Contemp, News; *Hrs. of News Programming:* News progmg 24 hrs wkly; *Target Audience:* 25-54.

Richard Solberg, President

Havre

*KNMC
02-01-1979; 90.1 MHz FM; 0.38 kw; -112 ft.; N48 32 31 W109 41 17
PO Box 7751, Havre, MT 59501 US
(406) 657-2941; *Fax:* (406) 657-2977
License: Havre, Hill County, MT held by Northern Montana College
Format: Jazz *Special Programming:* Class 10 hrs wkly
Marvin Granger, General Manager

KOJM
10-31-1947; 610 kHz AM; *Hrs Open:* 5 a.m.-midnight; 1 kw-D, DA2; 1 kw-N, DA2; N48 34 48 W109 38 54
2210 31st Street N., Havre, MT 59501 US
(406) 265-7841; *Fax:* (406) 265-8855
www.kojm.com
nmb@nmbi.com
License: Havre, MT held by New Media Broadcasters Inc.
Group Owner: New Media Broadcasters Inc.; (acq 12-30-2002; grpsl)
Nat'l Network: ABC; *Wire Services:* AP
Format: Adult Contemp *Special Programming:* Agriculture 4 hrs wkly; *Hrs. of News Programming:* news progmg 20 wkly; *No. News Employees:* 3; *Target Audience:* 30-64; boomer generation
C. David Leeds, President
Marlys Flathers, General Manager
Geoff Cole, Programming Director
Kyle Leeds, Promotions Manager
Justin Krezelak, News Director
Bruce Faulkner, Chief Engineer
Ron Bruschi, Sports Director

KPQX
03-08-1975; 92.5 MHz FM; *Hrs Open:* 5 a.m.-midnight; 96 kw; 1788 ft.; N48 10 55 W109 41 1
2210 31st Street N., Havre, MT 59501 US
(406) 265-7841; *Fax:* (406) 265-8855
www.kpqx.com
nmb@nmbi.com
License: Havre, Hill County, MT held by New Media Broadcasters Inc.
Group Owner: New Media Broadcasters Inc.; (acq 12-30-2002; grpsl)
Nat'l Network: ABC; *Wire Services:* AP
Format: Country *Special Programming:* Farm 10 hrs wkly; *Hrs. of News Programming:* News progmg 20 hrs wkly; *No. News Employees:* 3; *Target Audience:* 25-54.
C. David Leeds, President
Marlys Flathers, General Manager
Geoff Cole, Programming Director
Kyle Leeds, Promotions Manager
Justin Krezelak, News Director
Bruce Faulkner, Chief Engineer
Ron Bruschi, Sports Director

*KXEI
07-28-1983; 95.1 MHz FM; *Hrs Open:* 24; 98 kw; 1699 ft.; N48 10 42 W109 41 21
Mailing Address: P.O. Box 2426, Havre, MT 59501 US
Second Address: 317 First St., Havre, MT 59501
(406) 265-5845; *Fax:* (406) 265-8860
www.ynopradio.org
info@ynop.org
License: Havre, Hill County, MT held by Hi-Line Radio Fellowship Inc.
Nat'l Network: Moody; Salem Radio Network; *Wire Services:* AP
Arbitron Metro Market: Havre, MT; *Format:* Christian, Religious *Special Programming:* C&W one hr, farm one hr wkly; *Target Audience:* General; those looking for Christian inspirational music & progmg
Roger Lonnquist, General Manager
Brenda Jackson, Station Manager
Brian Jackson, Programming Director
Elizabeth McClenahan, Office Manager

Helena

KBLL
09-01-1937; 1240 kHz AM
Mailing Address: PO Box 4111, Helena, MT 59604 US
Second Address: 110 E. Broadway St., Helena, MT 59601
(406) 442-4490
www.kbllradio.com
License: Helena, MT held by CCR-Helena IV LLC
Group Owner: Cherry Creek Radio LLC; (acq 6-30-2004; $2.8 million with co-located FM)
Arbitron Metro Market: Helena, MT; *Format:* News, News/Talk, 86; *Target Audience:* 29-54; high buying power
Dewey Bruce, General Manager
Chris McCarthy, General Sales Mgr
Stan Evans, Programming Director
Cato Butler, News Director
Ken Eklund, Chief Engineer
Michele McAlister, Traffic Manager

KBLL-FM
08-01-1979; 99.5 MHz FM; 12 kw; 1932 ft.; N46 44 51.8 W112 19 47.6
1400 11th Avenue, Helena, MT 59601 US
(406) 442-6620; *Fax:* (406) 442-6161
License: Helena, Lewis and Clark County, MT held by CCR-Helena IV LLC.
Group Owner: Cherry Creek Radio LLC
Arbitron Metro Market: Helena, MT; *Format:* Country
Kurt Kittelson, Programming Director

KCAP
10-01-1949; 1340 kHz AM; 1 kw-U, ND1; N46 36 43 W112 3 13
Mailing Address: 110 Broadway St., Helena, MT 59601 US
Second Address: 110 E. Broadway St., Helena, MT 59601
(406) 442-4490; *Fax:* (406) 442-7356
License: Helena, MT held by CCR-Helena IV LLC.
Group Owner: Cherry Creek Radio LLC; (acq 2-3-2004; grpsl)
Nat'l Network: CBS; Moody; Fox Sports
Arbitron Metro Market: Helena, MT; *Format:* News, News/Talk, 84, Talk; *Target Audience:* 25-54.
Dewey Bruce, General Manager
Jim Willard, General Sales Mgr
Stan Evans, Programming Director
Cato Butler, News Director
Ken Eklund, Chief Engineer
Michele McAlister, Traffic Manager

KMTX
11-01-1976; 950 kHz AM; *Hrs Open:* 25.?AÝ?; 5 kw-D, DAN; 5 kw-N, DAN; N46 40 28 W112 1 5
Mailing Address: 1300 North 17th Street, 11th Floor, Rosslyn, VA 22209 US
Second Address: 516 Fuller, Helena, MT 59601
(406) 442-0400; *Fax:* (406) 442-0491
License: Helena, MT held by The Montana Radio Company LLC
Group Owner: The Montana Radio Company LLC
Nat'l Network: AP Radio
Format: Oldies
Kevin Terry, President
Kevin Skaalure, General Manager

KMTX-FM
01-19-1985; 105.3 MHz FM; 87 kw horiz, 58 kw vert; 1946 ft.; N46 44 52 W112 19 47
Mailing Address: 1300 North 17th Street, 11th Floor, Rosslyn, VA 22209 US
Second Address: 516 Fuller, Helena, MT 59601
(406) 443-1053
License: Helena, Lewis and Clark County, MT held by The Montana Radio Company LLC
Group Owner: The Montana Radio Company LLC
Nat'l Network: ABC
Format: Adult Contemp
Kevin Skaalure, General Manager
Steve Phillips, Promotions Manager
Karen Feldner, News Director
Shawn Ketchum, Chief Engineer

*KUHM
01-01-2000; 91.7 MHz FM; 0.91 kw; 761 ft.; N46 46 11 W112 1 22 *Rebroadcasts:* Rebroadcasts KUFM(FM) Missoula 100%
Partv Building, Room 180, Missoula, MT 59812 US
(406) 243-4931; *Fax:* (406) 243-3299
www.mtpr.org
License: Helena, Lewis and Clark County, MT held by The University of Montana.
Nat'l Network: NPR; *Wire Services:* AP
Arbitron Metro Market: Helena, MT; *Format:* Classical, Jazz, 60; *No. News Employees:* 2
William Marcus, General Manager
Michael Marsolek, Programming Director
Saxon Holbrook, Technical Director
Sue Ginn, Business Manager
Jerri Balsam, Administrative Associate
Edward F. O'Brien, Assistant News Director
Linda Talbott,Associate Director
Kathy Woodford, Director of Corporate Support

*KVCM
08-02-1993; 103.1 MHz FM; *Hrs Open:* 24; 30 kw; 771 ft.; N46 46 7 W112 1 21 *Rebroadcasts:* Rebroadcasts KXEI(FM) Havre 100%.
PO Box 2426, Havre, MT 59501 US
(406) 265-5845; *Fax:* (406) 265-8860
www.ynopradio.org
info@ynop.org
License: Helena, Lewis and Clark County, MT held by Hi-Line Radio Fellowship Inc.
Nat'l Network: Moody; Salem Radio Network; *Wire Services:* AP
Arbitron Metro Market: Helena, MT; *Format:* Christian, Religious; *Target Audience:* General:; those looking for inspirational Christian music & progmg
Roger Lonnquist, General Manager
Brenda Boyum, Station Manager
David Brown, Programming Director
Nicholas Tobiason, Music/IT Director
Ron Huckeby, Chief Engineer
Joanna Baer, Office Assistant
Crystal MacInnes, ProductionAssistant

KZMT
01-01-1975; 101.1 MHz FM; 90.5 kw; 1991 ft.; N46 44 51.8 W112 19 47.6
101 West Grand, Chicago, IL 60610 US
(406) 442-4490; *Fax:* (406) 442-7356
License: Helena, Lewis and Clark County, MT held by CCR-Helena IV LLC.
Group Owner: Cherry Creek Radio LLC
Arbitron Metro Market: Helena, MT; *Format:* Classic Rock; *Target Audience:* 18-54; upscale, entrepreneurial, adults
Michele McAlister, News Director

*KHLV
01-01-2005; 90.1 MHz FM; *Hrs Open:* 24; 0.001 kw horiz, 3.5 kw vert; 662 ft.; N46 46 7 W112 1 21 *Rebroadcasts:* Rebroadcasts KLVR(FM) Santa Rosa, CA 100%
1425 N Market Blvd., Suite 9, Sacramento, CA 95834 US
(800) 525-5683; *Fax:* (916) 251-1650
www.klove.com
klove@klove.com
License: Helena, Lewis and Clark County, MT held by Educational Media Foundation.
Group Owner: EMF Broadcasting
Nat'l Network: K-Love
Arbitron Metro Market: Helena, MT; *Format:* Christian; *No. News Employees:* 13; *Target Audience:* 25-44; Judeo Christian, female
Darrell Chambliss, Chairman
Mike Novak, President and CEO
Mike Lee, Operations Dir
David Pierce, Chief Creative Officer and Programming Director
Ed Lenane, News Director
Sam Wallington, Engineering Dir
Marya Morgan, NewsReporter
Richard Hunt, News Reporter
Alan Mason, Chief Operating Officer
Dan Antonelli, Chief Business Development Officer
Eric Moser, Chief Financial Officer
Brian Burger, Vice President of Human Resources

Helena Valley NE

KMXM(FM)
01-01-2008; 101.7 MHz FM; 100 kw; Ant 895 ft; N47 36 24 W111 21 31
118 6th St. S., Great Falls, MT 59401-3625
(406) 761-8816; *Fax:* (406) 454-3484
License: Helena Valley NE, Chouteau County, MT held by The Montana Radio Company LLC
Group Owner: The Montana Radio Company LLC
Population Served: 189; *Arbitron Metro Market:* Highwood, MT; *Format:* Contemporary Hits/Top 40
Kevin Terry, President
Darnell Washington, General Manager

Helena Valley SE

KIMO
02-04-2002; 107.3 MHz FM; 86 kw horiz; 896 ft.; N47 36 24 W111 21 31
US
(406) 452-1073; *Fax:* (406) 727-7218
mail@1073.com
License: Helena Valley SE, Cascade County, MT held by The Montana Radio Company LLC
Group Owner: The Montana Radio Company LLC
Nat'l Reps: McGavren Guild
Arbitron Metro Market: Fairfield, MT; *Format:* Variety/Diverse; *Target Audience:* 25-54.
Terry Strickland, General Manager
Troy Mellinger, Programming Director
Courteney McKinnon, Asst. Program Director

Highwood

KQDI-FM
12-31-1963; 106.1 MHz FM; 100 kw; 276 ft; N47 32 23 W111 17 06
Box 3129, Great Falls, MT 99201
(406) 761-2800; *Fax:* (406) 727-7218
License: Highwood, Cascade County, MT
Group Owner: Staradio Corp.
Population Served: 65,000 *Target Audience:* 18-49.
Howard Doss, President
T J Lee, Operations Dir
Jim Senst, General Manager
Tonya Jorgensen, General Sales Mgr
Jared Walker, Programming Director
Greg Miller, Chief Engineer

Joliet

KWMY
02-15-2006; 105.9 MHz FM; *Hrs Open:* 24; 100 kw; 440 ft.; N45 39 31 W108 34 14
US
(406) 248-7777; *Fax:* (406) 248-857
planet@planet1067.com
License: Joliet, Stillwater County, MT held by Connoisseur Media Licenses LLC
Group Owner: Connoisseur Media LLC
Arbitron Metro Market: Billings, MT; *Format:* Contemporary Hits/Top 40, Adult Contemp
Cam Maxwell, General Manager

Kalispell

KALS
11-01-1974; 97.1 MHz FM; 26.5 kw; 2487 ft.; N48 0 48 W114 21 55
PO Box 2426, 317 1st Street, Havre, MT 59501 US
(406) 752-5257; *Fax:* (406) 752-3416
www.ynop.org
info@ynop.org
License: Kalispell, Flathead County, MT held by Kalispell Christian Radio Fellowship Inc.
Arbitron Metro Market: Kalispell, MT; *Format:* Adult Contemp, Christian *Special Programming:* Class one hr wkly; *Target Audience:* 25-54
Brad Rauch, General Manager

KBBZ
09-12-1983; 98.5 MHz FM; 61 kw horiz, 6.1 kw vert; 2379 ft.; N48 30 42 W114 22 14
Box 5409, Kalispell, MT 59903 US
(406) 755-8700; *Fax:* (406) 755-8770
www.kbbz.com
License: Kalispell, Flathead County, MT held by Bee Broadcasting Inc.
Group Owner: Bee Broadcasting Inc.; acq 6-12-83; $315,000;
Arbitron Metro Market: Kalispell, MT; *Format:* Classic Rock
Benny Bee Sr., President
Mark Wagner, General Sales Mgr

KDBR
11-01-1993; 106.3 MHz FM; 59 kw horiz, 5.9 kw vert; 2365 ft.; N48 30 42 W114 22 16
2432 Hwy 2 E., Box 5409, Kalispell, MT 59903 US
(406) 755-8770; *Fax:* (406) 755-8770
www.kdbr.com
License: Kalispell, Flathead County, MT held by Bee Broadcasting Inc.
Group Owner: Bee Broadcasting Inc.
Arbitron Metro Market: Kalispell, MT; *Format:* Country
Benny Bee Sr., President
Mark Wagner, General Sales Mgr

KGEZ
03-24-1927; 600 kHz AM; *Hrs Open:* 24; 5 kw-D, DA2; 1 kw-N, DA2; N48 9 40 W114 16 51
2295 Highway 93 S, Kalispell, MT 59901 US
(406) 752-2600; *Fax:* (406) 257-0459
www.kgez.com
License: Kalispell, MT held by Skyline Broadcasters Inc.
Nat'l Network: USA
Format: News, News/Talk, 84, Talk; *Target Audience:* 25-60.; *Adv. Rates:* 18; 18; 18; 18
John Stokes, General Manager

KOFI
11-11-1955; 1180 kHz AM; *Hrs Open:* 24; 50 kw-D, DAN; 10 kw-N, DAN; N48 11 52 W114 15 3
Mailing Address: 317 First Avenue, East, Kalispell, MT 59901 US
Second Address: 317 First Ave. E., Kalispell, MT 59901
(406) 755-6690; *Fax:* (406) 752-5078
www.kofiradio.com
kofi@kofiradio.com
License: Kalispell, MT held by KOFI Inc.
Nat'l Network: ABC; CNN Radio
Format: News, News/Talk, 64, Talk; *Hrs. of News Programming:* news progmg 35 hrs wkly; *No. News Employees:* 2; *Target Audience:* 25-54.; *Adv. Rates:* 26.50; 21.50; 26.50; 21.50
Dave Rae, General Manager

KZMN
06-10-1988; 103.9 MHz FM; *Hrs Open:* 24; 100 kw horiz, 43 kw vert; 571 ft.; N48 5 39 W114 16 11
317 First Avenue E., Kalispell, MT 59901 US
(406) 755-6690,(406) 752-5078
www.monster1039.com
traffic@monster1039.com
License: Kalispell, Flathead County, MT
Nat'l Network: CNN Radio
Format: Classic Rock; *Hrs. of News Programming:* News progmg 3 hrs wkly; *Target Audience:* 18-49.
Dave Rae, President
Mike Jorgensen, Operations Dir

*KSPL
02-01-1997; 90.9 MHz FM; *Hrs Open:* 24 hours; 0.25 kW; 2529 ft; N48 30 22 W114 20 49 *Rebroadcasts:* Rebroadcasts KMBI-FM Spokane, WA 100%
5408 S Freya St, Spokane, WA 99223 USA
(509) 448-2555; *Fax:* (509) 448-6855
www.moodyradio.org/stations/northwest
License: Kalispell, Flathead County, MT held by The Moody Bible Institute of Chicago
Group Owner: The Moody Bible Institute of Chicago
Arbitron Metro Market: Kalispell, MT; *Format:* Christian; *Target Audience:* 35-54; Christian men & women

*KUKL
10-01-1998; 90.1 MHz FM; 1.83 kw; 2579 ft.; N48 30 22 W114 20 49
Broadcast Media Center, Partv Building, Room 180, Missoula, MT 59812 US
(406) 243-4931; *Fax:* (406) 243-3299
www.mtpr.org
License: Kalispell, Flathead County, MT held by University of Montana.
Nat'l Network: NPR; *Wire Services:* AP
Arbitron Metro Market: Kalispell, MT; *Format:* Classical, Jazz, 60; *Hrs. of News Programming:* News progmg 2 hrs wkly
William Marcus, General Manager
Michael Marsolek, Programming Director
Sue Ginn, Accounting Associate
Jerri Balsam, Administrative Associate
Edward F. O'Brien, Assistant News Director
Linda Talbott, Associate Director
KathyWoodford, Director of Corporate Support

*KLKM
01-01-2006; 88.7 MHz FM; 3.3 kw; 2575 ft.; N48 0 48 W114 21 55 *Rebroadcasts:* Rebroadcasts KLVR(FM) Santa Rosa, CA 100%
188 S. Bellevue, Suite 222, Memphis, TN 38104 US
(800) 525-5683; *Fax:* (916) 251-1650
www.klove.com
klove@klove.com
License: Kalispell, Flathead County, MT held by Educational Media Foundation.
Group Owner: EMF Broadcasting; (acq 1-11-2005; $95,000 for CP).
Nat'l Network: K-Love
Arbitron Metro Market: Kalispell, MT; *Format:* Christian; *No. News Employees:* 13
Darrell Chambliss, Chairman
Mike Novak, President and CEO
Mike Lee, Operations Dir
Eric Allen, General Sales Mgr
David Pierce, Chief Creative Officer and Programming Director
Ed Lenane, News Director
Sam Wallington, EngineeringDir
Marya Morgan, News Reporter
Richard Hunt, News Reporter
Alan Mason, Chief Operating Officer
Dan Antonelli, Chief Business Development Officer
Eric Moser, Chief Financial Officer
Brian Burger, Vice President of Human Resources

Laurel

KBSR
09-01-1979; 1490 kHz AM; *Hrs Open:* 24; 1 kw-U, ND1; N45 39 11 W108 45 9
PO Box 230, Hardin, MT 59034 US
(406) 665-2828; *Fax:* (406) 665-2131
www.bigskyradio.net
rich@bigskyradio.net
License: Laurel, MT held by Sun Mountain Inc.
Group Owner: Sun Mountain Inc.; (acq 11-30-2000)
Nat'l Network: ABC
Arbitron Metro Market: Billings, MT; *Format:* News, Talk; *Hrs. of News Programming:* News prgmg 24 hrs wkly; *Target Audience:* 35 plus; professional, business people
Richard Solberg, President

KRSQ
04-01-1994; 101.9 MHz FM; 100 kW; 131 ft.; N45 45 48 W108 27 20
4915 Vine St., Cherry Hills Village, CO 80113 USA
(425) 466-4628
hot1019.com
License: Laurel, Yellowstone County, MT held by BMG Billings, LLC
Group Owner: BMG Billings, LLC
Arbitron Metro Market: Billings, MT; *Format:* Rock/AOR; *Target Audience:* 18-49
Pete Benedetti, CEO
Terry Strickland, General Manager
Emily Petroff, General Sales Mgr
Kyle McCoy, Programming Director

Lewistown

KLCM
04-01-1975; 95.9 MHz FM; 3 kw; -230 ft.; N47 4 16 W109 24 32
P.O. Box 620, Lewistown, MT 59457 US
(406) 707-5275; *Fax:* (406) 538-3495
www.kxlo-klcm.com
License: Lewistown, Fergus County, MT held by Montana Broadcast Communications Inc.
Arbitron Metro Market: Great Falls, MT; *Format:* Contemporary Hits/Top 40, Adult Contemp; *Target Audience:* 18-54.
Fred Lark, President
Phyllis Hall, Station Manager
Joe Zahler, News Director

KXLO
01-01-1947; 1230 kHz AM
P. O. Box 620, Lewistown, MT 59457 US
(406) 707-5275; *Fax:* (406) 538-3495
www.kxlo-klcm.com
kxlo@lewistown.net
License: Lewistown, MT held by KXLO Broadcast Inc.
Nat'l Network: CBS
Arbitron Metro Market: Lewistown, MT; *Format:* Country *Special Programming:* Farm; *Target Audience:* General.
Fred Lark, President
Phyllis Hall, Station Manager

*KLEU
10-21-2003; 91.1 MHz FM; *Hrs Open:* 24; 4 kw; 1877 ft.; N47 10 39.4 W109 32 5.6 *Rebroadcasts:* Rebroadcasts KXEI(FM) Havre 100%
PO Box 2426, 317 1st Street, Havre, MT 59501 US
(406) 265-5845; *Fax:* (406) 265-8860
www.ynopradio.org
info@ynop.org
License: Lewistown, Fergus County, MT held by Hi-Line Radio Fellowship Inc.
Nat'l Network: Moody; Salem Radio Network; *Wire Services:* AP
Arbitron Metro Market: Havre, MT; *Format:* Christian, Religious
Roger Lonnquist, YNOP General Manager
Brenda Boyum, KXEI Station Manager
Clark Berg, KALS Sales Manager
David Brown, YNOP Program Director
Ron Huckeby, Chief Engineer
MarySue Amundgaard, KALS Office Staff
Joanna Baer,Announcer/Office Assistant
Earl Houtz, Announcer
Dave Kirby, Announcer
Crystal MacInnes, Production Assistant
Elizabeth McClenahan, Office Manager at KXEI/Webmaster

Libby

KLCB
12-23-1950; 1230 kHz AM; *Hrs Open:* 16; 1 kw-U, ND1; N48 22 14 W115 32 19
251 West Cedar Street, PO Box 730, Libby, MT 59923 US
(406) 293-6234; *Fax:* (406) 293-6235
www.klcb-ktny.com
License: Libby, MT held by Lincoln County Broadcasters Inc.
Nat'l Network: ABC

Arbitron Metro Market: Great Falls, MT; *Format:* Country; *Hrs. of News Programming:* news progmg 13 hrs wkly; *No. News Employees:* 1; *Target Audience:* 25-54.
Duane Williams, CEO

KTNY
04-05-1986; 101.7 MHz FM; *Hrs Open:* 16; 3 kw; -1017 ft.; N48 22 14 W115 32 19
P.O. Box 730, 251 West Cedar Street, Libby, MT 59923 US
(406) 293-6234; *Fax:* (406) 293-6235
www.klcb-ktny.com
License: Libby, Lincoln County, MT held by Lincoln County Broadcasters Inc.
Nat'l Network: ABC
Arbitron Metro Market: Libby, MT; *Format:* Oldies; *Hrs. of News Programming:* news progmg 16 hrs wkly; *No. News Employees:* 1; *Target Audience:* 35-54.
Duane Williams, CEO

*KVRZ
88.9 MHz FM; 0.085 kw; 1247 ft.; N48 29 13 W115 47 39 US
(406) 293-6551
www.kvrz.net
lpshowkvrz@gmail.com
License: Libby, Lincoln County, MT held by Troy Fine Arts Council.
Arbitron Metro Market: Libby, MT
Scott Curry, President
Brian Sherry, Station Manager
John Herrmann, Vice President

*KUFL
90.5 MHz FM; 1 kw; -1043 ft.; N48 22 45 W115 33 29
University of Montana, 32 Campus Drive, Missoula, MT 59812 US
(406) 243-4931; *Fax:* (406) 243-3299
www.mtpr.org
License: Libby, Lincoln County, MT held by The University of Montana.
Arbitron Metro Market: Libby, MT; *Format:* Public Affairs; *No. News Employees:* 6
William Marcus, General Manager
Michael Marsolek, Programming Director
Doug Drader, Chief Engineer
Beth Anne Austein, Production
Anne Hosler, Membership Manager
Kathy Woodford, Director of Corporate Support
Jeff Croonenberghs,Chief Operator
Saxon Holbrook, Technical Director

Livingston

KOZB
12-01-1977; 97.5 MHz FM; *Hrs Open:* 24; 100 kw; 246 ft.; N45 39 26 W110 58 22 US
(406) 587-9999; *Fax:* (406) 587-5855
License: Livingston, Park County, MT held by Reier Broadcasting Co. Inc.
Group Owner: Reier Broadcasting Co. Inc.; acq 10-18-96; grpsl).
Arbitron Metro Market: Bozemon, MT; *Format:* Classic Rock; *No. News Employees:* 2; *Target Audience:* 18-44.
Bill Reier, General Manager

KPRK
01-10-1947; 1340 kHz AM; *Hrs Open:* 5:30 AM-midnight; 1 kw-U, ND1; N45 40 21 W110 32 21
980 North Michigan Ave, Suite 1880, Chicago, IL 60611 US
(406) 222-2841; *Fax:* (406) 222-1341
License: Livingston, MT held by Townsquare Media Bozeman License LLC
Group Owner: Townsquare Media; (acq 2-13-2008; grpsl)
Nat'l Network: AP Radio
Arbitron Metro Market: Bozemon, MT; *Format:* Talk *Special Programming:* Oldies 5 hrs, big band 4 hrs wkly; *Hrs. of News Programming:* News progmg 15 hrs wkly; *Target Audience:* 25-64; general
Dave Cowan, General Manager
Courtney Lehman, Station Manager
Kaye Rugh, General Sales Mgr
Gary Weiss, News Director
Ron Huckeby, Chief Engineer

KXLB
100.7 MHz FM; 94 kw; 814 ft.; N45 40 24 W110 52 2
980 Norht Michigan Avenue, Suite 1880, Chicago, IL 60611 US
(406) 586-2343
www.xlcountry.com
License: Livingston, Park County, MT held by Townsquare Media Bozeman License LLC
Group Owner: Townsquare Media; (acq 2-13-2008; grpsl)
Arbitron Metro Market: Bozeman, MT; *Format:* Country
Scott Souhara, General Manager
Dave Wooten, Brand Manager
Devon Doers, Director Of Sales
Erin Schattauer, Digital Managing Editor

*KYPM
89.9 MHz FM; 0.44 kw; 869 ft.; N45 35 51 W110 32 45 US
(406) 657-2941; *Fax:* (406) 657-2977
www.yellowstonepublicradio.org
License: Livingston, Park County, MT held by Montana State University -Billings.
Arbitron Metro Market: Livingston, MT
Dennis Hall, President
Ken Siebert, Media Services Director
Jackie Yamanaka, News Director
Jim Nichols, Chief Engineer
Barbara Bernheim, Development and Listener Support Manager
Alicia Lee, Underwriting Manager / Public InformationManager
Ana Henrickson, Business & Finance Manager
Brad Edwards Jazz, Programmer / Announcer
Wesley Jessen, Media Services Assistant / Control Room Operator

Lockwood

*KYWH
05-26-1999; 88.9 MHz FM; 1.9 kw vert; 452 ft; N45 51 12 W108 45 50
120 - 2nd St East, Kalispell, MT 59901 US
(406) 257-3339
www.freshliferadio.com
info@freshliferadio.com
License: Lockwood, Yellowstone County, MT held by Fresh Life Church Inc.
Group Owner: Fresh Life Radio
Arbitron Metro Market: Billings, MT; *Format:* Christian

KYLW
01-01-2005; 1450 kHz AM; *Hrs Open:* 24
PO Box 230, Hardin, MT 59034 US
(406) 665-2828; *Fax:* (406) 665-2131
www.bigskyradio.net
rich@bigskyradio.net
License: Lockwood, MT held by Sun Mountain Inc.
Group Owner: Sun Mountain Inc.; (acq 7-7-2005; $26,000 for CP)
Nat'l Network: ABC
Arbitron Metro Market: Lockwood, MT; *Target Audience:* General.
Richard Solberg, General Manager

KPLN
03-01-2006; 106.7 MHz FM; 100 kw; 512 ft.; N45 45 54 W108 27 19 US
(406) 248-7777; *Fax:* (406) 248-8577
www.planet1067.com
License: Lockwood, Yellowstone County, MT held by Connoisseur Media LLC.
Group Owner: Connoisseur Media Licenses LLC
Arbitron Metro Market: Lockwood, MT; *Format:* Adult Contemp, Contemporary Hits/Top 40
Cam Maxwell, General Manager

Lolo

KDXT
01-01-2008; 97.9 MHz FM; 10 kw; 417 ft.; N46 30 37 W113 58 48
2600 Garfield Street, Missoula, MT 59601 US
(406) 541-1071; *Fax:* (406) 721-1036
www.107theranch.com
License: Lolo, Missoula County, MT held by Sheila Callahan and Friends Inc.
Group Owner: Sheila Callahan and Friends Inc.
Arbitron Metro Market: Lolo, MT; *Format:* Country
Sheila Callahan, General Manager
Chad Parrish, Sales

Malta

KMMR
09-09-1980; 100.1 MHz FM; *Hrs Open:* 6 AM-11 PM; 2.25 kw; 377 ft.; N48 15 17 W107 49 18
PO Box 1073, Malta, MT 59538 US
(406) 654-2472; *Fax:* (406) 654-2506
www.kmmrfm.com
kmmrfm@itstriangle.com
License: Malta, Phillips County, MT held by KMMR Radio Inc.
Nat'l Network: ABC
Format: Adult Contemp, Country; *Hrs. of News Programming:* news progmg 3 hrs wkly; *No. News Employees:* 1; *Target Audience:* 18-65; general, rural; *Adv. Rates:* 7.50; 7.50; 7.50; 7.50
Gregory Kielb, President
Claudette Kielb, Operations Dir
Valene Kielb, Programming Director
Joyce Robinson, Operations Director

Manhattan

KKQX
11-01-2005; 105.7 MHz FM; *Hrs Open:* 24; 12.3 kw; 682 ft.; N45 38 16 W111 16 5 *Rebroadcasts:* Simulcast on KBZM (FM) Big Sky
8274 Huffine Lane, Bozeman, MT 59718 US
(406) 582-1045; *Fax:* (406) 582-0388
www.montanasuperstation.com
sbalding@kbzm.com
License: Manhattan, Gallatin County, MT held by Radick Construction Inc.
Regional Reps: Local Focus 310-441-8188
Arbitron Metro Market: Rocklin, CA; *Format:* Classic Rock, Adult Contemp; *No. News Employees:* 2; *Target Audience:* 25-54.
Jeff Balding, General Manager
Susan Balding, Sales Manager

Miles City

KATL
09-04-1941; 770 kHz AM; *Hrs Open:* 24; 10 kw-D, DAN; 1 kw-N, DAN; N46 23 46 W105 46 44
Mailing Address: P. O. Box 700, Miles City, MT 59301 US
Second Address: 818 Main St., Miles City, MT 59301
(406) 234-7700; *Fax:* (406) 234-7783
www.katlradio.com
katlradio@katlradio.com
License: Miles City, MT held by Star Printing Co.
Nat'l Network: Westwood One; ABC; *Wire Services:* AP
Arbitron Metro Market: Miles City, MT; *Format:* Adult Contemp; *Hrs. of News Programming:* news progmg 17 hrs wkly; *No. News Employees:* 8; *Target Audience:* 25-54; Adults; *Adv. Rates:* 12.50, 12.50; 12.50
John Sullivan, President
Donald Richard, General Manager
Mark Waddington, General Sales Mgr

*KYPR
11-17-1988; 90.7 MHz FM; *Hrs Open:* 24; 0.5 kw; 502 ft.; N46 23 22 W105 45 22 *Rebroadcasts:* Rebroadcasts KEMC(FM) Billings 100%
1500 N. 30th Street, Billings, MT 59101 US
(406) 657-2941; *Fax:* (406) 657-2977
www.yellowstonepublicradio.org
License: Miles City, Custer County, MT held by Montana State University-Billings.
Nat'l Network: NPR; PRI
Arbitron Metro Market: Billings, MT; *Format:* Variety/Diverse; *Hrs. of News Programming:* News progmg 39 hrs wkly; *Target Audience:* General.
Dennis Hall, President
Ken Siebert, General Manager
Jackie Yamanaka, News Director
Jim Nichols, Chief Engineer
Barbara Bernheim, Development Manager

KYUS-FM
11-08-1984; 92.3 MHz FM; *Hrs Open:* 24; 100 kw; 984 ft.; N46 24 4 W105 39 6
508 Main Street, Miles City, MT 59301 US
(406) 234-5626; *Fax:* (406)-874-7000
terry@kyuskmta.com
License: Miles City, Custer County, MT held by Marks Radio Group.
Nat'l Network: USA
Arbitron Metro Market: Billings, MT; *Format:* Adult Contemp *Special Programming:* Farm one hr wkly; *Hrs. of News Programming:* news progmg 3 hrs wkly; *No. News Employees:* 1; *Target Audience:* 18-54; programmedfor general audience appeal
Terry Virag, General Manager
Lee Akers, Announcer
Charice Virag, Office Manager
Paul Grutkowski, Chief Engineer
C.W. Wilcox, Sports Commentator
Charice Virag, Traffic Manager

KMTA
10-01-1986; 1050 kHz AM; *Hrs Open:* 24; 10 kw-D, ND2; 0.136 kw-N, ND2; N46 24 4 W105 39 6
508 Main Street, Miles City, MT 59301 US

(406) 234-5626; *Fax:* (406) 874-7000
www.kyuskmta.com
License: Miles City, MT held by Marks Radio Group.
Nat'l Network: USA
Format: Classic Rock; *Hrs. of News Programming:* news progmg 6 hrs wkly; *No. News Employees:* 1; *Target Audience:* 25-54.

Missoula

*KBGA
08-24-1996; 89.9 MHz FM; 1 kw; -262 ft.; N46 52 56 W113 59 8
Office of President, University Hall, Missoula, MT 59812 US
(406) 243-6758; *Fax:* (406) 243-6428
www.kbga.org
gm@kbga.org
License: Missoula, Missoula County, MT held by The University of Montana.
Arbitron Metro Market: Missoula, MT; *Format:* Talk; *Hrs. of News Programming:* 10; *No. News Employees:* 2
Chris Justice, General Manager

KGGL
04-29-1977; 93.3 MHz FM; 43 kw; 2549 ft.; N47 1 57 W113 59 31
1600 N. Avenue W., Missoula, MT 59801 US
(406) 728-9399; *Fax:* (406) 721-3020
www.eagle93.com
thill@cherrycreekradio.com
License: Missoula, Missoula County, MT held by CCR-Missoula IV LLC.
Group Owner: Cherry Creek Radio LLC
Nat'l Reps: McGavren Guild
Arbitron Metro Market: Missoula, MT; *Format:* Country; *Target Audience:* 25-54.
Scott Richards, Operations Dir
Chad Parrish, General Manager
Bill McPherson, General Sales Mgr
Samantha Honold, News Director
Joe Bowers, Chief Engineer
Michelle Weber, Business Manager

KGRZ
01-01-1947; 1450 kHz AM; *Hrs Open:* 24; 1 kw-U, ND1; N46 52 39 W114 2 36
N. 1212 Washington, Suite 307, Spokane, WA 99201 US
(406) 728-1450; *Fax:* (406) 721-3020
License: Missoula, MT held by CCR-Missoula IV LLC.
Group Owner: Cherry Creek Radio LLC; (acq 10-31-2006; grpsl)
Nat'l Reps: McGavren Guild
Format: Sports, Talk; *Target Audience:* 25-54; male, sports orientated
Scott Richards, Operations Dir
Chad Parrish, General Manager
Bill McPherson, General Sales Mgr
Samantha Honold, News Director
Joe Bowers, Chief Engineer
Michelle Weber, Business Manager

KGVO
01-18-1931; 1290 kHz AM; 5 kw-U, DA-N; N46 49 47 W114 04 45
3250 S. Reserve St., Suite 200, Missoula, MT 60611
(406) 728-9300; *Fax:* (406) 542-2329
www.kgvo1290.com
scott.richman@townsquaremedia.com
License: Missoula, Missoula County, MT held by Townsquare Media Missoula License LLC
Group Owner: Townsquare Media; (acq 2-13-2008; grpsl)
Nat'l Network: Fox News Radio
Population Served: 90,000 *Target Audience:* General.
Scott Richman, General Manager
Billy Jenkins, Brand Manager
Robert Gibbons, Director Of Sales
Tan Curtis, Digital Managing Editor

KMSO
02-09-1985; 102.5 MHz FM; *Hrs Open:* 24; 29 kw; 1752 ft.; N46 48 30 W113 58 38
Mailing Address: P.O. Box 309, Missoula, MT 59806 US
Second Address: 725 Strand Ave., Missoula, MT 59801
(406) 542-1025; *Fax:* (406) 721-1036
www.mountain1025.com
info@mtnbdc.com
License: Missoula, Missoula County, MT held by Sheila Callahan & Friends Inc.
Group Owner: Sheila Callahan and Friends Inc.
Nat'l Network: AP Radio *Regional Reps:* Tacher; Portland; *Wire Services:* AP
Format: Adult Contemp *Special Programming:* Relg one hr wkly; *Hrs. of News Programming:* News progmg 6 hrs wkly; *Target Audience:* 25-54; upscale professional, well-educated mgmt level; *Adv. Rates:* 34; 34; 34; 22
Sheila Callahan, General Manager
Diana Helms, General Sales Mgr
Dale Desmond, Programming Director
Kris Hardy, News Director

*KMZL
01-01-1998; 91.1 MHz FM; *Hrs Open:* 24; 2.2 kw; 2054 ft.; N46 48 9 W113 58 21
2201 South 6th Street, Las Vegas, NV 89104 US
(800) 804-5452
sosradio.net
info@sosradio.net
License: Missoula, Missoula County, MT held by Faith Communications Corp.
Group Owner: Faith Communications Corp.
Format: Adult Contemp, Christian; *Hrs. of News Programming:* News progmg 5 hrs wkly; *Target Audience:* 25-44.
Brad Staley, General Manager
Scott Herald, Programming Director
Robert Forbes, Promotions Director

*KUFM
01-31-1965; 89.1 MHz FM; 14.5 kw; 2474 ft.; N47 1 58 W113 59 29
Broadcast Media Center, Partv Building, Room 180, Missoula, MT 59812 US
(406) 243-4931; *Fax:* (406) 243-3299
www.mtpr.org
License: Missoula, Missoula County, MT held by University of Montana.
Nat'l Network: NPR; *Wire Services:* AP
Arbitron Metro Market: Missoula, MT; *Format:* Jazz; *No. News Employees:* 2
William Marcus, General Manager
Michael Marsolek, Programming Director
Saxon Holbrook, Technical Director
William Marcus, Director of UM Broadcast Media Center
Sue Ginn, Accounting Associate
Jerri Balsam, AdministrativeAssociate
Edward F. O'Brien, Assistant News Director
Linda Talbott, Associate Director
Kathy Woodford, Director of Corporate Support

KYLT
07-15-1955; 1340 kHz AM; *Hrs Open:* 24; 1 kw-U, ND1; N46 52 56 W113 59 8
Mailing Address: N. 1212 Washington, Suite 307, Spokane, WA 99201 US
Second Address: 1600 North Ave. W., Suite 101, Missoula, MT 59801-5500
(406) 721-9300; *Fax:* (406) 721-3020
www.1340kylt.com
kylt@1340kylt.com
License: Missoula, MT held by CCR-Missoula IV LLC.
Group Owner: Cherry Creek Radio LLC; (acq 10-31-2006; grpsl)
Nat'l Network: Fox Sports; *Nat'l Reps:* McGavren Guild
Arbitron Metro Market: Missoula, MT; *Format:* Sports; *Target Audience:* 35-55.
Scott Richards, Operations Dir
Chad Parrish, General Manager
Bill McPherson, General Sales Mgr
Samantha Honold, News Director
Joe Bowers, Chief Engineer
Michelle Weber, Business Manager

KYSS-FM
05-11-1969; 94.9 MHz FM; *Hrs Open:* 24; 63 kw; 2392 ft.; N47 1 57 W113 59 30
980 North Michigan Ave., Suite 1880, Chicago, IL 60611 US
(406) 543-9500; *Fax:* (406) 542-2329
www.kyssfm.com
scott.richman@townsquaremedia.com
License: Missoula, Missoula County, MT held by Townsquare Media Missoula License LLC
Group Owner: Townsquare Media; (acq 2-13-2008; grpsl)
Arbitron Metro Market: Missoula,MT; *Format:* Country; *Hrs. of News Programming:* News progmg 12 hrs wkly; *Target Audience:* 25-54; adults
Scott Richman, General Manager
Billy Jenkins, Brand Manager
Robert Gibbons, Director Of Sales
Digital Managing Editor, Tan Curtis

KZOQ-FM
07-29-1974; 100.1 MHz FM; *Hrs Open:* 24; 13.5 kw; Ant 2,102 ft; N46 48 09 W113 58 21
Box 4106, 1600 North Ave. W., Missoula, MT 99201
(406) 728-5000; *Fax:* (406) 721-3020
www.z100missoula.com
thill@cherrycreekradio.com
License: Missoula, Missoula County, MT
Group Owner: Cherry Creek Radio LLC
Nat'l Reps: Tacher
Target Audience: 25-54.
Tom Anthony, Operations Dir
Bob Breck, General Manager
Dan Buchta, General Sales Mgr
Eric Wolfermann, Programming Director
Angel Hughes, Promotions Manager
Lauri Pulley, News Director
Joe Bowers, Chief Engineer
Rose Ramer,Business Manager

KYJK
07-01-2005; 105.9 MHz FM; *Hrs Open:* 25.?Â ?; 1.84 kw; 2083 ft.; N46 48 6 W113 58 22
2425 West Central Avenue, Missoula, MT 59801 US
(406) 721-6800; *Fax:* (406) 329-1850
www.jackfmmissoula.com
rharsell@simmonsmedia.com
License: Missoula, Missoula County, MT held by Spanish Peaks Broadcasting Inc.
Group Owner: Spanish Peaks Broadcasting Inc.
Nat'l Reps: Interep
Arbitron Metro Market: Missoula, MT; *Format:* Adult Contemp; *Target Audience:* 25-54; adults; *Adv. Rates:* 18; 15; 18; 9
Rod Harsell, General Manager

*KJCG
88.3 MHz FM; 1 kW; 2034 ft.; N46 48 6 W113 58 22
PO Box 2426, Havre, MT 59501 USA
(800) 442-9222
www.ynop.org
ynop@ynop.org
License: Missoula, Missoula County, MT held by Hi-Line Radio Fellowship, Inc.
Group Owner: Hi-Line Radio Fellowship, Inc.
Arbitron Metro Market: Missoula, MT; *Format:* Christian

Montana City

KOYT(FM)
01-01-2007; 98.5 MHz FM; 6 kw; Ant -108 ft; N46 33 25.8 W111 55 01.4
License: Montana City, Jefferson County, MT held by Cherry Creek Radio LLC.
Group Owner: Cherry Creek Radio LLC
Population Served: 28,592; *Arbitron Metro Market:* Helena, MT
Dewey Bruce, General Manager

Pablo

KQRK
01-01-2006; 99.7 MHz FM; 1.8 kw; 2113 ft.; N47 46 25 W114 16 4
36581 N. Reservoir Rd., Polson, MT 59860 US
(406) 883-5255; *Fax:* (406) 883-4441
www.qcountry997.com
License: Pablo, Lake County, MT held by Anderson Radio Broadcasting Inc.
Group Owner: Anderson Radio Broadcasting Inc.
Arbitron Metro Market: Pablo, MT; *Format:* Adult Contemp, Contemporary Hits/Top 40

Park City

*KBIL
01-01-2006; 89.7 MHz FM; *Hrs Open:* 24; 2.7 kw vert; 525 ft.; N45 51 12 W108 45 50 *Rebroadcasts:* Rebroadcasts KLRD(FM) Yucaipa, CA 100%
16075 W Belleview Ave, Morrison, CO 80465 US
(888) 937-2471; *Fax:* (916) 251-1650
www.air1.com
info@air1.com
License: Park City, Stillwater County, MT held by Educational Media Foundation.
Group Owner: EMF Broadcasting; (acq 10-2-2003; grpsl).
Nat'l Network: Air 1
Arbitron Metro Market: Billings, MT; *Format:* Alternative, Christian; *No. News Employees:* 3; *Target Audience:* 25-44; Judeo Christian female
Darrell Chambliss, Chairman
Alan Mason, COO
Mike Novak, President and CEO
Mike Lee, Operations Dir
David Pierce, Programming Director
Ed Lenane, News Director
Sam Wallington, Engineering Dir
Marya Morgan, News Reporter
Richard Hunt, News Reporter
Larry Moody, Director
Mitch Barnhart, Director
David R. Ferry, Director
Walter Golembeski, Director

Pinesdale

KXDR
07-16-1999; 106.7 MHz FM; *Hrs Open:* 24; 38 kw; 2090 ft.; N46 48 9 W113 58 19
1600 North Avenue, Missoula, MT 59803 US
(406) 728-5000; *Fax:* (406) 721-3020
www.1067starfm.com
License: Pinesdale, Ravalli County, MT held by CCR-Missoula IV LLC.
Group Owner: Cherry Creek Radio LLC; (acq 10-31-2006; grpsl)
Nat'l Reps: McGavren Guild
Arbitron Metro Market: Missoula, MT; *Format:* Contemporary Hits/Top 40
Scott Richards, Operations Dir
Chad Parrish, General Manager
Bill McPherson, General Sales Mgr
Samantha Honold, News Director
Michelle Weber, Business Manager

KXDR(FM)
01-01-2003; 106.7 MHz FM; 13 kw; Ant 2,089 ft; N46 48 09 W113 58 19
Cherry Creek Radio, 1600 North Ave., Missoula, MT 59801
(406) 728-5000; *Fax:* (406) 721-3020
www.1067starfm.com
License: Pinesdale, Ravalli County, MT held by CCR-Missoula IV LLC.
Group Owner: Cherry Creek Radio LLC; (acq 10-31-2006; grpsl)
Nat'l Reps: McGavren Guild
Population Served: 58,950; *Arbitron Metro Market:* Great Falls, MT; *Format:* Oldies
Scott Richards, Operations Dir
Chad Parrish, General Manager
Bill McPherson, General Sales Mgr
Samantha Honold, News Director
Joe Bowers, Chief Engineer
Michelle Weber, Business Manager

Plains

*KPLG
01-01-1998; 91.5 MHz FM; *Hrs Open:* 24; 1.8 kw; 4042 ft.; N47 22 22 W114 51 31 *Rebroadcasts:* Rebroadcasts KXEI(FM) Havre 100%
P O Box 2426, Havre, MT 59501 US
(406) 265-5845; *Fax:* (406) 265-8860
www.ynop.org
ynop@ynop.org
License: Plains, Sanders County, MT held by Hi Line Radio Fellowship Inc.
Nat'l Network: Moody; Salem Radio Network; *Wire Services:* AP
Format: Religious; *Target Audience:* General; those who are looking for Christian progmg
Roger Lonnquist, General Manager
Brenda Boyum, Station Manager
Clark Berg, General Sales Mgr
David Brown, Programming Director
Ron Huckeby, Chief Engineer

Plentywood

KATQ
1070 kHz AM; *Hrs Open:* 6 AM-6 PM
112 Third Ave., East, Plentywood, MT 59254 US
(406) 765-1480; *Fax:* (406) 765-2357
www.katqradio.com
katq@nemont.net
License: Plentywood, MT held by Radio International-KATQ Broadcast Association Inc.
Nat'l Network: ABC
Arbitron Metro Market: Plentywood, MT; *Format:* Country *Special Programming:* Top-40, farm 5 hrs, relg 6 hrs wkly; *Target Audience:* 18-54.; *Adv. Rates:* 9.50; 9; 8.50; na
Bonnie Simon, General Manager
Bonnie Simon, Station Manager
Bonnie Simon, General Sales Mgr
Bonnie Simon, Programming Director
Bonnie Simon, Promotions Manager
Bruce Lapke, News Director
Bruce Lapke, Engineering Dir
ArtGehnert, Chief Engineer

KATQ-FM
06-01-1962; 100.1 MHz FM; *Hrs Open:* 24; 3 kw horiz; 33 ft.; N48 47 6 W104 32 0
112 Third Ave., East, Plentywood, MT 59254 US
(406) 765-1480; *Fax:* (406) 765-2357
www.katqradio.com
License: Plentywood, Sheridan County, MT held by Radio International-KATQ Broadcast Association Inc.
Nat'l Network: ABC; AP Radio
Arbitron Metro Market: Plentywood, MT; *Format:* Country; *Adv. Rates:* Same as AM
Bruce Lapke, Music Director
Bonnie Simon, General Manager

Polson

KERR
03-22-1976; 750 kHz AM; 50 kw-D, DAN; 1 kw-N, DAN; N47 38 34 W114 7 25
36581 N. Reservoir Rd., Polson, MT 59860 US
(406) 883-5255; *Fax:* (406) 883-4441
www.750kerr.com
License: Polson, MT held by Anderson Radio Broadcasting Inc.
Group Owner: Anderson Radio Broadcasting Inc.; acq 9-22-2003; grpsl).
Arbitron Metro Market: Polson, MT; *Format:* Country; *Target Audience:* General.

*KPJH
89.5 MHz FM; 0.13 kw; 1870 ft.; N47 46 25 W114 16 5
32 Campus Drive, Missoula, MT 59812 US
(406) 243-4931; *Fax:* (406) 243-3299
www.mtpr.org
License: Polson, Lake County, MT held by The University of Montana.
Nat'l Network: NPR
Arbitron Metro Market: Polson, MT; *Format:* Public Affairs; *No. News Employees:* 6
William Marcus, General Manager
Michael Marsolek, Programming Director
Doug Drader, Chief Engineer
Beth Anne Austein, Production
Anne Hosler, Membership Manager
Kathy Woodford, Director of Corporate Support
Jeff Croonenberghs,Chief Operator
Saxon Holbrook, Technical Director

*KMBM
90.7 MHz FM; 1.95 kw; 135 ft.; N47 40 37 W114 8 33 US
(406) 883-7252
License: Polson, Lake County, MT held by Divine Mercy Apostolate.
Nat'l Network: EWTN Radio
Arbitron Metro Market: Polson, MT; *Format:* Religious
Jeffrey Devlin, President

Pryor

*KPGB
88.3 MHz FM; 0.1 kw vert; -325 ft.; N45 26 6 W108 32 9
P O Box 24, Pryor, MT 59066 US
(406) 861-7560
www.kpgbfaithbaptistchurch.com
ronvicky01@hughes.net
License: Pryor, Big Horn County, MT held by Faith Baptist Church.
Arbitron Metro Market: Pryor, MT; *Format:* Religious
Ronnie Henderson, General Manager

Red Lodge

KMXE-FM
01-24-1994; 99.3 MHz FM; *Hrs Open:* 24; 30 kw; 1211 ft.; N45 11 39 W109 20 30
P.O. Box 1678, Red Lodge, MT 59068 US
(406) 446-1199; *Fax:* (406) 446-9178
fm99mtn@starband.net
License: Red Lodge, Carbon County, MT held by Silver Rock Communications Inc.
Format: Oldies; *Hrs. of News Programming:* news progmg one hr wkly; *No. News Employees:* 1; *Target Audience:* 25-49; upwardly mobile; *Adv. Rates:* 15; 15; 15; 15
Leslie Brent-Oliphant, President
Jeffrey Oliphant, Executive Vice President

Rocky Boy's Reserv.

*KHEW
88.5 MHz FM; 16 kw; 1579 ft.; N48 10 42 W109 41 21 US
(406) 395-4396; *Fax:* (406) 395-4497
License: Rocky Boy's Reserv., Hill County, MT held by Chippewa Cree Tribe of the Rocky Boy's Reservation.
Arbitron Metro Market: Rocky Boy's Reservation, MT; *Format:* Native American
Dustin White, Programming Director

Ronan

KKMT
10-04-1981; 92.3 MHz FM; *Hrs Open:* 24; 60 kw; 2320 ft.; N47 46 25 W114 16 4
36581 N. Reservoir Rd., Polson, MT 59860 US
(406) 883-5255; *Fax:* (406) 883-4441
www.star92hits.com
License: Ronan, Lake County, MT held by Anderson Radio Broadcasting Inc.
Group Owner: Anderson Radio Broadcasting Inc.; (acq 9-22-2003; grpsl).
Arbitron Metro Market: Kalispell-Flathead Valley, MT; *Format:* Rock/AOR; *Target Audience:* 25-49.

Roundup

*KLMB
88.3 MHz FM; 0.25 kw vert; 79 ft.; N46 27 58 W108 33 20 US
(406) 323-1861
License: Roundup, Musselshell County, MT held by Roundup Community Radio Association.
Arbitron Metro Market: Roundup, MT
Bill Edwards, President

KZMO
100.1 MHz FM; 100 w; 17 meters; N46 27 58 W108 33 20
100 West Lyndale Avenue, Suite B, Helena, MT 59601
(406) 442-6645
License: Roundup, MT held by The Montana Radio Company LLC
Group Owner: The Montana Radio Company LLC

Kevin Terry, Manager

Scobey

KCGM
06-21-1971; 95.7 MHz FM; *Hrs Open:* 16; 52 kw; 659 ft.; N48 48 3 W105 21 0
20 Main St. PO Bx 220, Scobey, MT 59263 US
(406) 487-2293; *Fax:* (406) 487-5933
www.kcgmradio.com
License: Scobey, Daniels County, MT held by Prairie Communications Inc.
Nat'l Network: USA *Regional Reps:* Taylor Brown; *Wire Services:* AP
Format: Country *Special Programming:* Farm 6 hrs wkly; *Hrs. of News Programming:* news progmg 8 hrs wkly; *No. News Employees:* 2; *Adv. Rates:* 8.60; 8.60; 8.60; 8.60
Dixie Halverson, CEO

Shelby

KSEN
08-11-1947; 1150 kHz AM; *Hrs Open:* 19
830 Oilfield Ave, Shelby, MT 59474 US
(406) 434-5241; *Fax:* (406) 434-2122
www.ksenam.com
scott.richman@townsquaremedia.com
License: Shelby, MT held by Townsquare Media Shelby License LLC
Group Owner: Townsquare Media
Arbitron Metro Market: Shelby, MT; *Format:* Oldies *Special Programming:* Farm 8 hrs wkly; *Hrs. of News Programming:* news progmg 15 hrs wkly; *No. News Employees:* 1; *Target Audience:* 25-59.
Scott Richman, General Manager
Billy Jenkins, Brand Manager
Robert Gibbons, Director Of Sales
Tan Curtis, Digital Managing Editor
Anne James, Brand Manager
Wendy Nielsen, Digital Managing Editor

KZIN-FM
12-09-1978; 96.7 MHz FM; *Hrs Open:* 24; 100 kw; 551 ft.; N48 19 42 W112 2 3
830 Oilfield Avenue, Shelby, MT 59474 US
(406) 434-5241; *Fax:* (406) 434-2122
www.k96fm.com
ksen@townsquaremedia.com
License: Shelby, Toole County, MT held by Townsquare Media Shelby License LLC
Group Owner: Townsquare Media
Arbitron Metro Market: Shelby, MT; *Format:* Country; *Hrs. of News Programming:* news progmg 6 hrs wkly; *No. News Employees:* 1; *Target Audience:* 18-49.
Julie Martin, General Manager
Anne James, Brand Manager
Julie Martin, Director Of Sales
Wendy Nielsen, Digital Managing Editor

Sidney

KTHC
12-01-1996; 95.1 MHz FM; 100 kw; 719 ft.; N48 2 52 W103 59 1
120 East Main Street, Sidney, MT 59270 US
(406) 433-5090; *Fax:* (406) 433-5095
power95@midrivers.com
License: Sidney, Richland County, MT held by CCR-Williston IV LLC.
Group Owner: Cherry Creek Radio LLC; (acq 12-19-2003; grpsl).
Arbitron Metro Market: Sidney, MT; *Format:* Adult Contemp;
Target Audience: General.
Larry Timpe, Operations Dir

KGCX
06-01-2004; 93.1 MHz FM; *Hrs Open:* 24; 55 kw; Ant 499 ft; N47 45 02 W104 18 22
213 2nd Ave. S.W., Sidney, MT 85377
(406) 433-5429; *Fax:* (406) 433-5430
www.kgcx.com
kgcxeagle@midrivers.com
License: Sidney, Richland County, MT held by Sidney Community Broadcasting Corp.
Nat'l Network: Fox News Radio; *Nat'l Reps:* The Teacher Company
Hrs. of News Programming: News progmg 15 hrs wkly; *Adv. Rates:* 7.50; 7.50; 7.50; 6.50
Stephen Marks, President
Andrew Sturlaugson, Operations Manager
Paul Sturlaugson, Vice President/General Manager
Paul Sturlaugson, Vice President/General Manager
Melissa Quilling, Sales Manager
Andrew Sturlaugson, ProgrammingDirector
Andrew Sturlaugson, Promotions Manager
Emilie Boyles, News Director
Wayne Harbig, Engineering Dir
Wayne Harbig, Chief Engineer
Staci Smith, Office Manager

Somers

***KFLF**
91.3 MHz FM; 1 kw; 259 ft.; N48 4 7 W114 2 20
US
(703) 812-0415
www.freshliferadio.com
License: Somers, Flathead County, MT held by Fresh Life Church Inc.
Arbitron Metro Market: Somers, MT
Levi Lusko, President

St. Regis

KZJZ
99.1 MHz FM; 0.93 kw; 2844 ft.; N47 22 20 W114 51 28
36581 N. Reservoir Rd., Polson, MT 59860 US
(406) 883-5255; *Fax:* (406) 883-4441
www.991theriver.com
License: St. Regis, Mineral County, MT held by Anderson Radio Broadcasting Inc.
Group Owner: Anderson Radio Broadcasting Inc.; (acq 6-6-2008; $75,000 for CP)
Arbitron Metro Market: Saint Regis, MT; *Format:* Easy Listening

Stanford

***KYPF**
89.5 MHz FM; 4 kw; 1890 ft.; N47 10 39 W109 32 9
1500 University Drive, Billings, MT 59101 US
(406) 657-2941; *Fax:* (406) 657-2977
www.yellowstonepublicradio.org
mail@ypradio.org
License: Stanford, Judith Basin County, MT held by Montana State University - Billings.
Arbitron Metro Market: Standford/Lewistown, MT; *Format:* News
Ken Siebert, General Manager / Media Services Director
Jackie Yamanaka, News Director
Jim Nichols, Chief Engineer
Barbara Bernheim, Development and Listener Support Manager
Alicia Lee, Underwriting Manager / Public InformationManager
Ana Henrickson, Business & Finance Manager
Art Hooker, Control Room Operator / Production Assistant
Merry Ann Peters, Control Room Operator
Wesley Jessen, Media Services Assistant / Control Room Operator

Stevensville

KKVU
07-16-2005; 104.5 MHz FM; 14.15 kw; 2083 ft.; N46 48 6 W113 58 22
2425 West Central Avenue, Missoula, MT 59801 US
(406) 721-6800; *Fax:* (406) 329-1850
www.u1045.com
tanthony@simmonsmedia.com
License: Stevensville, Ravalli County, MT held by Spanish Peaks Broadcasting Inc.
Group Owner: Spanish Peaks Broadcasting Inc.
Nat'l Reps: Interep
Arbitron Metro Market: Stevensville, MT; *Format:* Adult Contemp;
No. News Employees: 1; *Target Audience:* Adults 18-49.; *Adv. Rates:* 18; 15; 18; 9
Rod Harsell, General Manager

Superior

KENR
10-01-1999; 107.5 MHz FM; 100 kw horiz; 945 ft.; N47 1 45 W114 41 18
6807 Foxglove Drive, Cheyenne, WY 82009 US
(406) 728-9300; *Fax:* (406) 542-2329
www.1075zoofm.com
shawnabatt@townsquaremedia.com
License: Superior, Mineral County, MT held by Townsquare Media Missoula License LLC
Group Owner: Townsquare Media; (acq 2-13-2008; grpsl)
Arbitron Metro Market: Missoula, MT; *Format:* Contemporary Hits/Top 40
Scott Ruchman, General Manager
Billy Jenkins, Brand Manager
Robert Gibbons, Director Of Sales
Tan Curtis, Digital Managing Editor

Three Forks

KMTZ
107.7 MHz FM; 23 kw; 846 ft.; N45 38 20 W111 15 56
1336 Stoneridge, Bozeman, MT 59718 US
(406) 542-1025; *Fax:* (406) 721-1036
License: Three Forks, Gallatin County, MT held by Sheila Callahan and Friends Inc.
Group Owner: Sheila Callahan and Friends Inc.
Arbitron Metro Market: Three Forks, MT
M. Sheila Murphy, President

West Yellowstone

KEZQ
06-01-1996; 92.9 MHz FM; 46 kw; 2733 ft.; N44 33 41 W111 26 32
US
(203) 912-3761
License: West Yellowstone, Gallatin County, MT held by Chapavral Broadcasting, Inc.
Arbitron Metro Market: Westport, CT; *Format:* Adult Contemp
Scott Parker, General Manager

KWYS
12-20-1967; 920 kHz AM; 1 kw-D, ND2; 0.038 kw-N, ND2; N44 38 56 W111 5 50
P.O. Box 2158, Ketchum, ID 83340 US
(406) 646-7361
www.kwys920.com
License: West Yellowstone, MT held by Radio West LLC
Nat'l Network: CNN Radio
Arbitron Metro Market: West Yellowstone; *Format:* Oldies
Scott Anderson, General Manager

Whitefish

KJJR
02-14-1979; 880 kHz AM; 10 kw-D, ND1; 0.5 kw-N, ND1; N48 23 44 W114 19 11
2432 US Hwy 2 E., Kalispell, MT 59903 US
(406) 755-8700; *Fax:* (406) 755-8770
www.kjjr.com
License: Whitefish, MT held by Bee Broadcasting Inc.
Group Owner: Bee Broadcasting Inc.
Format: News/Talk
Benny Bee Sr., President
Mark Wagner, General Sales Mgr

KWOL-FM
01-01-2005; 105.1 MHz FM; 62 kw; 2405 ft.; N48 30 43 W114 22 13
2432 US Highway 2 E, Kalispell, MT 59901 US
(406) 755-8700; *Fax:* (406) 755-8770
www.1051cool.com
info@1051cool.com
License: Whitefish, Flathead County, MT held by Cathleen R. Bee dba Rose Communications.
Arbitron Metro Market: Whitefish, MT; *Format:* Oldies
Cassie Bee, General Manager

KSAM
01-01-2006; 1240 kHz AM
2432 Hwy 2 E., Kalispell, MT 59903 US
(406) 755-8700; *Fax:* (406) 755-8770
www.sam1240.com
License: Whitefish, MT held by Bee Broadcasting Inc.
Group Owner: Bee Broadcasting Inc.
Arbitron Metro Market: Whitefish, MT; *Format:* Sports
Benny Bee Sr., President
Mark Wagner, General Sales Mgr

Whitehall

***KQLR**
01-01-2007; 89.7 MHz FM; 1.45 kw vert; 1795 ft.; N46 0 22 W112 26 33 *Rebroadcasts:* Rebroadcasts KLVR(FM) Santa Rosa, CA 100%
US
(800) 877-5600; *Fax:* (916) 251-1650
www.klove.com
License: Whitehall, Jefferson County, MT held by Educational Media Foundation.
Group Owner: EMF Broadcasting; (acq 12-2-2005; $28,450 for CP)
Nat'l Network: K-Love
Arbitron Metro Market: Whitehall, MT; *Format:* Christian
Mike Novak, President
Mike Lee, Operations Dir

KKRK
106.5 MHz FM; 2.8 kw horiz; -50 meters; N46 04 54 W112 06 53
100 West Lyndale Avenue, Suite B, Helena, MT 59601 US
(406) 438-6353
License: Whitehall, MT

Kevin Terry, Manager

Wolf Point

KVCK
09-01-1957; 1450 kHz AM; *Hrs Open:* 24; 1 kw-U, ND1; N48 5 18 W105 39 22
324 Main Street, Wolf Point, MT 59201 US
(406) 653-1900; *Fax:* (406) 653-1909
www.kuckradio.com
License: Wolf Point, MT held by Wolf Town Wireless Inc.
Nat'l Network: ABC
Arbitron Metro Market: Wolf Point, MT; *Format:* Oldies *Special Programming:* Farm 6 hrs wkly; *Hrs. of News Programming:* News progmg 15 hrs wkly; *Target Audience:* General.
Larry Corns, Programming Director

KVCK-FM
09-01-1981; 92.7 MHz FM; *Hrs Open:* 24; 11.5 kw; 499 ft.; N48 11 9 W105 40 8
324 Main Street, Wolf Point, MT 59201 US
(406) 653-1900; *Fax:* (406) 653-1909
License: Wolf Point, Roosevelt County, MT
Arbitron Metro Market: Wolf Point, MT; *Format:* Country *Special Programming:* Farm 6 hrs wkly; *Hrs. of News Programming:* News progmg 15 hrs wkly
Susan Allmer, General Manager

***KYPW**
88.3 MHz FM; 0.73 kw; 194 ft.; N48 2 8 W105 31 13
1500 University Drive, Billings, MT 59101 US
(406) 657-2941; *Fax:* (406) 657-2977
www.yellowstonepublicradio.org
mail@ypradio.org
License: Wolf Point, Roosevelt County, MT held by Montana State University - Billings.
Arbitron Metro Market: Wolf Point, MT
Dennis Hall, President
Ken Siebert, General Manager / Media Services Director
Jackie Yamanaka, News Director
Jim Nichols, Chief Engineer
Barbara Bernheim, Development and Listener Support Manager
Alicia Lee, Underwriting Manager /Public Information Manager
Ana Henrickson, Business & Finance Manager
Art Hooker, Control Room Operator / Production Assistant
Merry Ann Peters, Control Room Operator
Wesley Jessen, Media Services Assistant / Control Room Operator

Worden

KCHH
95.5 MHz FM; 100 kw; 300 meters; N45 44 29 W108 08 19
27 North 27th Street, 23rd Floor Crowne Plaza, Billings, MT 59101 US

(406) 248-7827; *Fax:* (406) 252-9577
www.newstalk955.com
mike.sutton@townsquaremedia.com
License: Worden, Yellowstone County, MT held by Townsquare Media Billings License LLC
Group Owner: Townsquare Media

Mike Sutton, General Manager
Kris Edwards, Brand Manager
Adella Sutton, Director Of Sales
Cindy Uken, Digital Managing Editor

Wyola

***KZXZ**
90.9 MHz FM; kw
US
(479) 646-6700; *Fax:* (479) 646-1373
License: Wyola, Big Horn County, MT held by 1 A Chord Inc.
Arbitron Metro Market: Wyola, MT
Mary Fay Jackson, President

Nebraska

Ainsworth

KBRB
02-06-1968; 1400 kHz AM; *Hrs Open:* 24; 1 kw-U, ND1; N42 33 16 W99 49 52
PO Box 285, Ainsworth, NE 69210 US
(402) 387-1400; *Fax:* (402) 387-2624
kbrbradio.com
kbrb@sscg.net
License: Ainsworth, NE held by K.B.R. Broadcasting Co.
Nat'l Network: ABC; *Regional Network:* Brownfield; *Wire Services:* AP
Format: Adult Contemp, Country; *Hrs. of News Programming:* News progmg 30 hrs wkly; *Target Audience:* General.; *Adv. Rates:* 8.25; 8.25; 8.25; 8.25
Lorris Rice, President
Graig Kinzie, General Manager
Angie Von Heeder, Sales
Randy Brudigan, Chief Engineer

KBRB-FM
05-30-1983; 92.7 MHz FM; 4.5 kw; 331 ft.; N42 33 16 W99 49 52
PO Box 285, Ainsworth, NE 69210 US
(402) 387-1400; *Fax:* (402) 387-2624
License: Ainsworth, Brown County, NE held by K.B.R. Broadcasting Co.
Nat'l Network: ABC; *Regional Network:* Brownfield; *Wire Services:* AP
Format: Adult Contemp; *Adv. Rates:* Same as AM
Lorris Rice, President
Graig Kinzie, General Manager
Angie Von Heeders, Sales
Randy Brudigan, Chief Engineer

Albion

KUSO
05-10-2000; 92.7 MHz FM; *Hrs Open:* 24; 50 kw; 492 ft.; N41 49 50 W97 41 12
Mailing Address: PO Box 747, West Point, NE 68788 US
Second Address: 214 N. 7th St., Norfolk, NE 68701
(402) 371-0100; *Fax:* (402) 371-0050
www.us92.com
dave@us92.com
License: Albion, Boone County, NE held by Flood Communications L.L.C.
Arbitron Metro Market: Norfolk, NE; *Format:* Country *Special Programming:* Farm 10 hrs wkly; *Hrs. of News Programming:* news progmg 3 hrs wkly; *No. News Employees:* 1; *Target Audience:* General.; *Adv. Rates:* 264; 225; 264; 216
Michael Flood, General Manager
Lee Terry, Operations Dir
Angie Stenger, Sales Manager

Allen

KHSK
100.9 MHz FM; 10 kw horiz, 0 kw vert; N42 30 29 W96 56 1
US
(312) 204-9900
License: Allen, Dixon County, NE held by College Creek Media LLC.
Group Owner: College Creek Media LLC
Arbitron Metro Market: Allen, NE
Neal Robinson, President

Alliance

KAAQ
09-30-1985; 105.9 MHz FM; *Hrs Open:* 24; 100 kw; 705 ft.; N41 50 29 W103 5 7
2703 Hall St., Suite 15, Hays, KS 67601
(785) 625-4000
www.panhandlepost.com
License: Alliance, Box Butte County, NE held by Eagle Communications Inc.
Group Owner: Eagle Communications Group
Nat'l Network: ABC Information & Entertainment; ABC Music Radio; *Nat'l Reps:* Interep; *Wire Services:* NWS (National Weather Service); AP
Arbitron Metro Market: Denver-Boulder, CO; *Format:* Country *Special Programming:* Farm 4 hrs wkly; *Hrs. of News Programming:* news progmg 15 hrs wkly; *No. News Employees:* 2; *Target Audience:* 18-54. *Adv.Rates:* 45; 45; 45; 30.
Scott Boomer, Operations Dir
Travis Kohlrus, General Manager
Mark Goff, Chief Engineer

KCOW
02-15-1949; 1400 kHz AM; *Hrs Open:* 24 (M-S); 1 kw-U, ND1; N42 6 26 W102 53 15
2703 Hall St., Suite 15, Hays, KS 67601 US
(785) 625-4000
www.panhandlepost.com
License: Alliance, NE held by Eagle Communications Inc.
Group Owner: Eagle Communications Group; (acq 1965)
Nat'l Network: ABC Information & Entertainment; ABC Music Radio; *Nat'l Reps:* Interep; *Wire Services:* NWS (National Weather Service); AP
Arbitron Metro Market: Alliance, NE; *Format:* Oldies *Special Programming:* Farm 18 hrs wkly; *Hrs. of News Programming:* news progmg 22 hrs wkly; *No. News Employees:* 2; *Target Audience:* 25-54.; *Adv. Rates:* 27.50; 27.50; 15; 15
Scott Boomer, Operations Dir
Travis Kohlrus, General Manager
Mark Goff, Chief Engineer

***KPNY**
01-01-1978; 102.1 MHz FM; *Hrs Open:* 24; 100 kw; 522 ft.; N42 7 1 W103 7 9
P.O. Box 1153, Scottsbluff, NE 69361 US
(402) 845-6595
www.mybridgeradio.net
email@mybridgeradio.net
License: Alliance, Box Butte County, NE held by My Bridge Radio
Group Owner: My Bridge Radio
Format: Religious; *Target Audience:* 18-35.
Stan Parker, General Manager

***KTNE-FM**
05-01-1990; 91.1 MHz FM; *Hrs Open:* 24; 92 kw; Ant 1,325 ft; N41 50 24 W103 03 18 *Rebroadcasts:* Rebroadcasts KUCV(FM) Lincoln 100%
PO Box 83111, Lincoln, NE 68501
(402) 472-3611; *Fax:* (402) 472-2403
netnebraska.org/radio
radio@netnebraska.org
License: Alliance, Box Butte County, NE held by Nebraska Educational Telecommunications Commission
Nat'l Network: NPR; APM; PRI; *Regional Network:* NET Radio
Hrs. of News Programming: news progmg 45 hrs wkly; *No. News Employees:* 8; *Target Audience:* 35 plus; general
Rod Bates, General Manager
Nancy Finken, Station Manager
Susan Dinsmore, General Sales Mgr
Nancy Finken, Programming Director
Mary Jane Winquest, Promotions Manager
Stacey Decker, News Director
William Stibor, Music Director
Jeff Smith, Operations

Auburn

KNCY-FM
09-18-1981; 103.1 MHz FM; *Hrs Open:* 24; 14 kw; 436 ft.; N40 27 57 W95 45 38
814 Central Avenue, Nebraska City, NE 68410 US
(402) 873-3348; *Fax:* (402) 873-7882
kncycountry.com
License: Auburn, Nemaha County, NE held by Riverfront Broadcasting LLC
Nat'l Network: ABC; *Wire Services:* AP
Format: Country, News; *Hrs. of News Programming:* news progmg 30 hrs wkly; *No. News Employees:* 2; *Adv. Rates:* 19; 19; 19; 19

Scott Kooistra, General Manager
Chris Yates, General Sales Mgr
Doug Jennings, Programming Director

Aurora

KRGY
03-01-1980; 97.3 MHz FM; *Hrs Open:* 24; 50 kw; 348 ft.; N40 52 44 W98 5 36
P.O. Box 4907, Aurora, NE 68802 US
(308) 381-1430; *Fax:* (308) 382-6701
www.thewolf973fm.com
License: Aurora, Hamilton County, NE held by Legacy Communications LLC
Group Owner: Legacy Communications LLC; (acq 5-17-2004; grpsl).
Nat'l Network: ABC
Arbitron Metro Market: Lincoln, NE; *Format:* Adult Contemp; *Hrs. of News Programming:* news progmg 2 hrs wkly; *No. News Employees:* 2; *Target Audience:* 18-49.
Jim Davis, Operations Dir
Lyle Nelson, General Manager

***KJGS**
10-12-2011; 91.9 MHz FM; kw
US
(760)375-2355
ejwitzel@mchsi.com
License: Aurora, Hamilton County, NE
Group Owner: Radio 74 Internationale
Format: Religious
Ron Myers, Founder

Bassett

***KMNE-FM**
06-01-1991; 90.3 MHz FM; *Hrs Open:* 24; 92.3 kw; 1,292 ft; N42 20 05 W99 29 01 *Rebroadcasts:* Simulcasts KUCV(FM) Lincoln 100%
1800 N. 33rd St., Lincoln, NE 68501
(402) 472-3611; *Fax:* (402) 472-2403
netnebraska.org/radio
radio@netnebraska.org
License: Bassett, Rock County, NE held by Nebraska Educational Telecommunications Commission
Nat'l Network: NPR; APM; PRI; *Regional Network:* NET Radio
Hrs. of News Programming: news progmg 45 hrs wkly; *No. News Employees:* 8; *Target Audience:* General.
Mark Leonard, Chief Executive Officer/General Manager
Nancy Finken, Station Manager
Susan Dinsmore, Marketing Specialist
Nancy Finken, Programming Director
Mary Jane Winquest, Promotions Manager
Dennis Kellogg, News Director
Stacey Decker, Engineering Dir
Jenny Herstein, Development Director
Jeff Smith, Operations Coordinator

Beatrice

KTGL
11-26-1962; 92.9 MHz FM; *Hrs Open:* 24; 100 kw; 810 ft.; N40 31 6 W96 46 7
3800 Cornhusker Hwy., Lincoln, NE 68504 US
(402) 466-1234
www.ktgl.com
programming@ktgl.com
License: Beatrice, Gage County, NE held by Digity 3E License, LLC
Group Owner: Digity, LLC
Arbitron Metro Market: Lincoln, NE; *Format:* Classic Rock; *Hrs. of News Programming:* news progmg 3 hrs wkly; *No. News Employees:* 1; *Target Audience:* 18-49.
Joy Patten, General Manager
Katie Philippi, General Sales Mgr
Scott Kaye, Programming Director
Jill Marshall, News Director

KWBE
06-12-1949; 1450 kHz AM; *Hrs Open:* 24; 0.53 kw-U, ND1; N40 15 49 W96 46 27
200 Sherman Street, Beatrice, NE 68310 US
(402) 228-5923; *Fax:* (402) 228-3704
www.kwbe.com
License: Beatrice, NE held by NRG License Sub. LLC.
Group Owner: Siebert Communications Inc.
Nat'l Network: CBS; Westwood One *Regional Reps:* Howard Anderson.
Arbitron Metro Market: Beatrice, NE; *Format:* Adult Contemp, News, 62, Talk *Special Programming:* Farm 14 hrs wkly; *Hrs. of News Programming:* news progmg 25 hrs wkly; *No. News*

Employees: 1 *Target Audience:* 24-54; mature, affluent adults; *Adv. Rates:* 17.50; 16.50; 17.50; 15.50
Brad Achtemeier, General Manager
Rick Siebert, Owner
Dave Niedfeldt, Programming Director
Tyler Bursobsky, Promotions Director
Doug Kennedy, News Director
Tom Russell, Engineer
Bryan Cook, Sports Director

***KNBE**
01-01-2008; 88.9 MHz FM; 7.5 kw vert; 479 ft.; N40 33 3 W96 38 45
PO Box 262550, Baton Rouge, LA 70826 US
(225) 768-3102; *Fax:* (225) 768-3729
www.jsm.org
kawikfish@yahoo.com
License: Beatrice, Gage County, NE held by Family Worship Center Church Inc.
Group Owner: Family Worship Center Church Inc.; (acq 10-12-2006; grpsl)
Arbitron Metro Market: El Dorado, AR; *Format:* Christian, Religious
David Whitelaw, COO

Bellevue

KOZN
06-01-1999; 1620 kHz AM; *Hrs Open:* 24
1001 Farnam-On-The-Mall, Omaha, NE 68102 US
(402) 342-2000; *Fax:* (402) 346-5748
www.1620thezone.com
nnelkin@nrgmedia.com
License: Bellevue, NE held by Waitt Omaha LLC.
Group Owner: Waitt Omaha LLC; (acq 1-7-2002; grpsl)
Nat'l Network: ESPN Radio; Westwood One; *Nat'l Reps:* Katz Radio
Arbitron Metro Market: Omaha, NB; *Format:* Sports; *Target Audience:* 25-54; men
Andy Ruback, General Manager
Stacie McElligott, General Sales Mgr
Neil Nelkin, Programming Director
Brandon Pappas, Promotions Manager
Becca Sautter, Traffic Manager

KZOT
03-19-1987; 1180 kHz AM; *Hrs Open:* 24; 25 kw-D, 1 kw-N, DA-2; N41 16 12 W95 47 10
5011 Capitol Ave., Omaha, NE 68102
(402) 342-2000; *Fax:* (402) 346-5748
License: Bellevue, Sarpy County, NE held by Waitt Omaha LLC.
Group Owner: Waitt Omaha LLC; (acq 1-7-2002; grpsl)
Population Served: 350,000; *Arbitron Metro Market:* Omaha-Council Bluffs, NE-IA; *Target Audience:* 18+; General
Andy Ruback, General Manager
Stacie McElligott, General Sales Mgr
Becca Sautter, Traffic Manager

Bennington

KFFF
06-10-1991; 93.3 MHz FM; 6 kw; Ant 350 ft; N41 22 57 W96 07 57
5010 Underwood Ave., Omaha, NE 78701 US
(402) 561-2000; *Fax:* (402) 556-8937
www.wolfradio933.com
License: Bennington, Douglas County, NE held by Capstar TX LLC
Group Owner: iHeartMedia; (acq 8-30-2000; grpsl)
Arbitron Metro Market: Omaha-Council Bluffs, NE-IA; *Format:* Country
Taylor Walet, Regional Market President
Erik Johnson, Programming Director
Heath Hedstrom, Promotions Manager

Blair

KBLR-FM
09-10-2002; 97.3 MHz FM; 25 kw horiz, 24.5 kw vert; 302 ft.; N41 38 21 W96 12 31
118 East 5th Street, Fremont, NE 68026 US
(402) 721-1340; *Fax:* (402) 721-5023
www.kblr-fm.com
License: Blair, Washington County, NE held by Waitt Omaha LLC.
Group Owner: Waitt Omaha LLC; (acq 1-7-2002; grpsl)
Arbitron Metro Market: Omaha, NE; *Format:* Country
Chris Waltz, General Manager
Theron Hayse, General Sales Mgr
Matt Price, Programming Director
Connie Green, News Director
Del Meyer, Account Executive
Barry C. Reker, Sales & Promotions Director
Earnie Parker, AdvertisingConsultant

Bridgeport

KOZY-FM
01-01-2001; 101.3 MHz FM; 100 kw; Ant 1,112 ft; N41 50 23 W103 49 36
Box 1263, Scottsbluff, NE 69363
(308) 632-5667; *Fax:* (308) 635-1905
info@hometownfamilyradio.com
License: Bridgeport, Morrill County, NE held by Legacy Communications LLC.
Group Owner: Armada Media LLC
No. News Employees: 2; *Target Audience:* 25-54; general
Chris Bernier, President/Chief Executive Officer
Rob Mandeville, General Manager

Broken Bow

KBBN-FM
06-15-1982; 95.3 MHz FM; *Hrs Open:* 6 AM-11 PM; 30 kw; 574 ft.; N41 23 14 W99 49 15
P. O. Box 409, Broken Bow, NE 68822 US
(308) 872-5881; *Fax:* (308) 872-3284
www.kbbn.com
info@sandhillexpress.com
License: Broken Bow, Custer County, NE held by Custer County Broadcasting Co.
Arbitron Metro Market: Broken Bow, NB; *Format:* Classic Rock; *Hrs. of News Programming:* news progmg 10 hrs wkly; *No. News Employees:* 1; *Target Audience:* 24-45; baby boomers & on either edge of age breakdown
David Birnie, General Manager
Jeff Bailey, Programming Director
Colleen Warwick, Sales Executive

KCNI
09-28-1949; 1280 kHz AM; *Hrs Open:* 6 AM-6 PM; 1 kw-D, NDD; N41 24 31 W99 40 28
Box 409, Broken Bow, NE 68822 US
(308) 872-5881; *Fax:* (308) 872-3284
www.kbbn.com
License: Broken Bow, NE held by Custer County Broadcasting Co.
Arbitron Metro Market: Broken Bow, NE; *Format:* Country; *Hrs. of News Programming:* news progmg 24 hrs wkly; *No. News Employees:* 1; *Target Audience:* 25-65; focus on rural audience
David Birnie, Owner/GM/Operations Manager/Sales Manager
Jeff Bailey, Programming Director
Julie Toline, News Director
Bob Bowles, Copy Writer/Commercial Production
Cynthia Huhman, Office Manager/Commercial Traffic Manager
ColleenWarwick, Sales Executive

Central City

KZEN
07-22-1985; 100.3 MHz FM; *Hrs Open:* 24; 100 kw; 1844 ft.; N41 32 28 W97 40 45
1418 - 25th St., Columbus, NE 68601 US
(402) 564-2866; *Fax:* (402) 564-2867
www.mycentralnebraska.com
lcherry@digity.me
License: Central City, Merrick County, NE held by Digity 3E License, LLC
Group Owner: Digity, LLC
Nat'l Reps: Interep; *Wire Services:* AP
Arbitron Metro Market: Columbus, NE; *Format:* Country; *Hrs. of News Programming:* news progmg 18 hrs wkly; *No. News Employees:* 2; *Target Audience:* 25-54; rgnl, rural & small town audience
David Gustafson, Operations Dir
Lisa Cherry, General Manager
David Gustafson, Programming Director
Ryan Kumpf, News Director

Chadron

***KCNE-FM**
08-29-1991; 91.9 MHz FM; *Hrs Open:* 24; 8.4 kw; 338 ft; N42 48 47 W103 00 22 *Rebroadcasts:* Rebroadcasts KUCV(FM) Lincoln 100%
Mailing Address: 68501
Second Address: 1800 N. 33rd St., Lincoln, NE 68503
(402) 472-3611; *Fax:* (402) 472-2403
netnebraska.org/radio
radio@netnebraska.org
License: Chadron, Dawes County, NE held by Nebraska Educational Telecommunications Commission
Nat'l Network: NPR; APM; PRI; *Regional Network:* NET Radio
Hrs. of News Programming: news progmg 45 hrs wkly; *No. News Employees:* 8; *Target Audience:* General.
Mark Leonard, Chief Executive Officer/General Manager
Nancy Finken, Station Manager/Programming Director
Susan Dinsmore, Marketing Specialist
Jenny Herstein, Development Director
Mary Jane Winquest, Promotions Manager
DennisKellogg, News Director
Jeff Smith, Operations Coordinator

KCSR
05-09-1954; 610 kHz AM; *Hrs Open:* 24; 1 kw-D, ND1; 0.118 kw-N, ND1; N42 49 56 W103 1 0
226 Bordeaux St, Chadron, NE 69337 US
(308) 432-5545(308) 432-2233; *Fax:* (308) 432-5601
www.chadrad.com
kcsr@chadrad.com
License: Chadron, NE held by Chadrad Communications Inc.
Nat'l Network: AP Radio; *Regional Network:* Mid-America Ag; Brownfield; *Wire Services:* AP
Arbitron Metro Market: Chadron, NE; *Format:* Country *Special Programming:* Farm 6 hrs wkly; *Hrs. of News Programming:* news progmg 20 hrs wkly; *No. News Employees:* 2; *Target Audience:* 25-54; people in theranch, farm & agricultural industry; *Adv. Rates:* 18; 18; 18; 8
Kathi Brown, General Sales Mgr
Joe Lowery, Music Director
Mike Trueblood, Senior Account Executive

KQSK
06-01-1983; 97.5 MHz FM; *Hrs Open:* 24; 100 kw; Ant 840 ft; N42 38 06 W103 06 12 *Rebroadcasts:* Simulcast with KAAQ(FM) Alliance 95%
1210 West 10th St., P.O. Box 600, Alliance, NE 67601
(308) 762-1400; *Fax:* (308) 762-7804
www.doubleqcountry.com
License: Chadron, Dawes County, NE held by Eagle Communications Inc.
Nat'l Network: ABC Information & Entertainment; ABC Music Radio; *Nat'l Reps:* Regional Reps; *Wire Services:* AP; NWS (National Weather Service)
Population Served: 65,000 *Special Programming:* Farm 4 hrs wkly; *Hrs. of News Programming:* news progmg 15 hrs wkly; *No. News Employees:* 2; *Target Audience:* 18-54.; *Adv. Rates:* 45; 45; 45; 30
Michael Glesinger, Operations Dir
Terri Friesen, General Manager
Jason Wentworth, Programming Director
John Axtell, News Director
Tony Cuesto, Chief Engineer

KCNB
02-28-2008; 94.7 MHz FM; *Hrs Open:* 24; 100 kw; 472 ft.; N42 39 5.1 W102 41 49.3
2703 Hall St., Suite 15, Hays, KS 67601 US
(785) 625-4000
www.panhandlepost.com
License: Chadron, Dawes County, NE held by Eagle Communications Inc.
Group Owner: Eagle Communications Group
Arbitron Metro Market: Chadron, NE; *Format:* Contemporary Hits/Top 40; *No. News Employees:* 1; *Target Audience:* 18-54.
Scott Boomer, Operations Dir
Travis Kohlrus, General Manager
Mark Goff, Chief Engineer

Columbus

KJSK
04-28-1948; 900 kHz AM; *Hrs Open:* 24; 1 kw-D, ND1; 0.065 kw-N, ND1; N41 26 12 W97 23 47
1418 - 25th St., Columbus, NE 68601 US
(402) 564-2866; *Fax:* (402) 564-2867
www.mycentralnebraska.com
lcherry@digity.me
License: Columbus, NE held by Digity 3E License, LLC
Group Owner: Digity, LLC
Nat'l Network: CBS Radio; *Wire Services:* AP
Arbitron Metro Market: Lincoln, NE; *Format:* News/Talk; *No. News Employees:* 1; *Target Audience:* General.
Davis Gustafson, Operations Dir
Lisa Cherry, General Manager
James Nickel, Programming Director
Ryan Kumpf, News Director
Bob Cook, Chief Engineer

KKOT
11-25-1969; 93.5 MHz FM; *Hrs Open:* 24; 100 kw; 981 ft.; N41 32 28 W97 40 45
1418 - 25th St., Columbus, NE 68601 US

(402) 564-2866; *Fax:* (402) 564-2867
www.mycentralnebraska.com
lcherry@digity.me
License: Columbus, Platte County, NE held by Digity 3E License, LLC
Group Owner: Digity, LLC
Nat'l Reps: McGavren Guild
Arbitron Metro Market: Lincoln, NE; *Format:* Oldies *Special Programming:* 0; *No. News Employees:* 2
David Gustafson, Operations Dir
Lisa Cherry, General Manager
Ryan Kumpf, News Director

KLIR

08-01-1964; 101.1 MHz FM; 100 kw; 761 ft.; N41 16 55 W97 24 30
1418 - 25th St., Columbus, NE 68601 US
(402) 564-2866; *Fax:* (402) 564-2867
lcherry@digity.me
License: Columbus, Platte County, NE held by Digity 3E License, LLC
Group Owner: Digity, LLC
Nat'l Network: CNN Radio; *Wire Services:* AP
Arbitron Metro Market: Lincoln, NE; *Format:* Adult Contemp
Special Programming: Oldies 12 hrs wkly; *No. News Employees:* 1; *Target Audience:* General.
David Gustafson, Operations Dir
Lisa Cherry, General Manager
Lu Zehr, Programming Director
Ryan Kumpf, News Director

*KTLX

07-01-1974; 91.3 MHz FM; 0.1 kw; 52 ft.; N41 26 26 W97 21 14
2200 - 25th Street, Columbus, NE 68601 US
(402) 564-8548; *Fax:* (402) 562-6003
ktlx@megavision.com
License: Columbus, Platte County, NE held by TLC Educational Corp.
Arbitron Metro Market: Columbus, NE; *Format:* Religious
Gary Spuit, President
Russ Rote, General Manager

KTTT

12-02-1962; 1510 kHz AM; 0.5 kw-D, NDD; N41 27 14 W97 24 20
1418 25th St., Columbus, NE 68601 US
(402) 564-2866; *Fax:* (402) 564-2867
www.mycentralnebraska.com
lcherry@digity.me
License: Columbus, NE held by Digity 3E License, LLC
Group Owner: Digity, LLC
Nat'l Reps: McGavren Guild
Arbitron Metro Market: Columbus, NE; *Format:* News/Talk; *Hrs. of News Programming:* news progmg 10 hrs wkly; *No. News Employees:* 1; *Target Audience:* 25-65.
David Gustafson, Operations Dir
Lisa Cherry, General Manager
Ryan Kumpf, News Director

Cozad

*KAMI

11-01-1965; 1580 kHz AM; *Hrs Open:* 8 AM-5 PM; 1 kw-D, ND2; 0.017 kw-N, ND2; N40 50 16 W99 56 20
P.O. Box F, Lexington, NE 68850 US
(308) 325-2247; *Fax:* (308) 324-52786
License: Cozad, Dawson County, NE held by Nebraska Rural Radio Association
Group Owner: Nebraska Rural Radio Foundation
Nat'l Network: USA
Arbitron Metro Market: Cozad, NE; *Format:* Country; *Target Audience:* 25-54; adults
Eric Brown, Executive Director
Barb Bierman Batie, Director of Marketing

*KCVN

08-04-1983; 104.5 MHz FM; *Hrs Open:* 24; 100 kw; 985 ft.; N40 41 48 W99 47 18
10550 Barkley St., Suite 100, Overland Park, KS 66212 US
(402) 465-8850
www.bottradionetwork.com
comments@bottradionetwork.com
License: Cozad, Dawson County, NE held by Community Broadcasting Inc.
Group Owner: Bott Radio Network; (acq 7-9-2004; $365,000 with co-located AM).
Nat'l Network: USA
Arbitron Metro Market: Lexington, NE; *Format:* Christian, Talk; *Target Audience:* 25-54; adults
Richard Bott Sr., President & CEO
Richard Bott II, Executive Vice President
Eben Fowler, Operations Dir
Tom Millett, Nebraska Area Manager
Pat Rulon, Director of National Sales
Candy Green, Program Services Manager
RachelLaunius, Marketing Manager
Jason Potocnik, Director of Traffic Operations

Crawford

*KCFD

88.1 MHz FM; 1.5 kw; 659 ft.; N42 45 38 W103 39 26 US
(256) 497-4502
southcultural@yahoo.com
License: Crawford, Dawes County, NE held by Southern Cultural Foundation.
Arbitron Metro Market: Crawford, NE; *Format:* Classic Rock
Richard Dabney, General Manager

Crete

*KDNE

08-30-1993; 91.9 MHz FM; 0.2 kw; 66 ft.; N40 37 16 W96 57 4
1014 Boswell Avenue, Crete, NE 68333 US
(402) 826-8677; *Fax:* (402) 826-8634
www.doaneline.com/kdne/
kdne@doane.edu
License: Crete, Saline County, NE held by Doane College Board of Trustees.
Arbitron Metro Market: Crete, NE; *Format:* Alternative; *Target Audience:* General; males & females between the ages of 12 to 34
Jonathan Brand, President
Lee Thomas, General Manager
John Thayer, Station Manager
Corey Rotschafer, Programming Director
Tyler Weihe, Editor In Chief
Erin Bell, Managing Director
Alyssa Bouc, News Editor
Richard Creeger,Sports Editor

KIBZ

03-02-1992; 104.1 MHz FM; *Hrs Open:* 24; 31 kw; 614 ft.; N40 31 6 W96 46 7
3800 Cornhusker Hwy., Lincoln, NE 68504 US
(402) 466-1234
www.kibz.com
License: Crete, Saline County, NE held by Digity 3E License, LLC
Group Owner: Digity, LLC
Arbitron Metro Market: Lincoln, NE; *Format:* Rock/AOR; *No. News Employees:* 1; *Target Audience:* 18-34.
Jaren Alled, Programming Director

Crookston

KINI

01-01-1978; 96.1 MHz FM; *Hrs Open:* 24; 90 kw; 499 ft.; N43 7 50 W100 54 2
P.O. Box 419, St. Francis, SD 57572 US
(605) 747-2291; *Fax:* (605) 747-5791
kinifm@gwtc.net
License: Crookston, Cherry County, NE held by Rosebud Educational Society Inc.
Wire Services: AP
Format: Adult Contemp, Native American *Special Programming:* American Indian 15 hrs, gospel 6 hrs, relg 6 hrs wkly; *Hrs. of News Programming:* news progmg 12 hrs wkly; *No. News Employees:* 1 *Target Audience:* General; Indian & white
Fr. John Hatcher, President
Richard Iyotte, Station Manager
Marcy VanWinkle, Executive Vice President

Dakota City

KTFJ

01-01-1991; 1250 kHz AM; *Hrs Open:* 24; 0.5 kw-D, DA2; 0.7 kw-N, DA2; N42 26 33 W96 15 41 *Rebroadcasts:* Rebroadcasts KTFC(FM) Sioux City, IA.
1534 Buchanan Ave, Sioux City, IA 51106 US
(712) 252-4621
www.bottradionetwork.com
License: Dakota City, NE held by Donald A. Swanson.
Nat'l Network: USA
Arbitron Metro Market: Sioux City, IA; *Format:* Gospel
Richard (Dick) Bott Sr., Chairman
Richard (Rich) Bott, CEO/COO
Richard(Rich) Bott, President
Eben Fowler, Operations Dir
Kim Cotter, General Manager

Emerson

KCTY

10-19-1975; 104.9 MHz FM; *Hrs Open:* 24; 25 kw; 302 ft.; N42 14 4 W97 3 20
PO Box 413, Wayne, NE 68787 US
(402) 375-3700
www.ktch.com
info@ktch.com
License: Emerson, Wayne County, NE held by Wayne Radio Work LLC.
Arbitron Metro Market: Wayne, NE; *Format:* Oldies; *No. News Employees:* 1; *Target Audience:* General.
David Kelly, General Manager
Mick Kemp, General Sales Mgr
Dan Baddorf, Programming Director
Joel Janecek, News Director
Tony Wortman, Chief Engineer

Fairbury

KGMT

06-13-1960; 1310 kHz AM; *Hrs Open:* 6 AM-6 PM; 0.5 kw-D, ND2; 0.095 kw-N, ND2; N40 6 58 W97 9 5
414 Fourth St., Fairbury, NE 68352 US
(402) 729-3382; *Fax:* (402) 729-3446
kutt@diodecom.net
License: Fairbury, NE held by Siebert Communications Inc.
Nat'l Reps: Farmakis
Format: News, Oldies *Special Programming:* Farm 18 hrs wkly; *Hrs. of News Programming:* News progmg 10 hrs wkly; *No. News Employees:* 2; *Target Audience:* 25-52.
Rick Siebert, President
Randy Bauer, General Manager
Brad Achtemeier, General Sales Mgr
Randy Bauer, Program Director

Falls City

KLZA-FM

07-07-1998; 101.3 MHz FM; 25 kw; 328 ft.; N40 6 54 W95 39 6
1602 Stone St., Falls City, NE 68355 US
(402) 245-6010; *Fax:* (402) 245-6040
www.sunny1013.com
sunny1013fm@hotmail.com
License: Falls City, Richardson County, NE held by KNZA Inc.
Group Owner: KNZA Inc.
Format: Adult Contemp; *No. News Employees:* 3
Robert Hilton, Operations Dir
Mike Gilmore, Station Manager
Mike Slocum, Chief Engineer

KTNC

08-03-1957; 1230 kHz AM; *Hrs Open:* 24; 0.5 kw-D, ND1; 1 kw-N, ND1; N40 3 57 W95 36 55
1602 Stone St., Falls City, NE 68355 US
(402) 245-2453; *Fax:* (402) 245-6040
www.ktncradio.com
ktnc@sentco.net
License: Falls City, NE held by KNZA Inc.
Group Owner: KNZA Inc.; (acq 9-7-2007; $330,000)
Nat'l Network: ABC; *Regional Network:* Brownfield
Arbitron Metro Market: Falls City, NE; *Format:* Oldies *Special Programming:* Christian mus one hr wkly; *Hrs. of News Programming:* news progmg 23 hrs wkly; *No. News Employees:* 1; *Target Audience:* 25 plus;farmers, businessmen, employees, retirees; *Adv. Rates:* 15; 14.70; 15; 14.40
Jackie Johnson, Operations Dir
Aaron J. Wisdom, News Director

Firth

KNTK

93.7 MHz FM; 6 kw; Ant 226 ft; N40 34 57.4 W96 37 15.2
5829 N. 60th St., Omaha, NE
(402) 464-5611
www.theticketfm.com
info@theticketfm.com
License: Firth, Lancaster County, NE held by VSS Catholic Communications Inc.
Arbitron Metro Market: Lincoln, NE
Jim Carroll, General Manager

Fremont

KFMT-FM

07-01-1972; 105.5 MHz FM; *Hrs Open:* 5 AM-midnight; 1.2 kw; 449 ft.; N41 24 40 W96 31 53
P.O. Box 669, Fremont, NE 68026 US
(402) 721-1340; *Fax:* (402) 721-5023
kfmt@midia.com

License: Fremont, Dodge County, NE held by R&R Broadcasting Inc.
Group Owner: R&R Broadcasting Inc.
Arbitron Metro Market: Fremont, NE; *Format:* Classic Rock; *Target Audience:* 25-54.
Chris Walz, General Manager
Theron Hayse, Sales Manager
Patt Price, Programming Director
Connie Green, News Director
Emily Peck, Traffic Manager

KHUB
12-01-1939; 1340 kHz AM; *Hrs Open:* 5 AM-midnight; 0.5 kw-D, ND1; 0.25 kw-N, ND1; N41 25 58 W96 27 16
P.O. Box 669, Fremont, NE 68026 US
(402) 721-1340; *Fax:* (402) 721-5023
www.khubradio.com
License: Fremont, NE held by R&R Broadcasting Inc.
Group Owner: R&R Broadcasting Inc.
Format: News, News/Talk, 86 *Special Programming:* Farm 6 hrs wkly; *Hrs. of News Programming:* news progmg 25 hrs wkly; *No. News Employees:* 1; *Target Audience:* 35 plus; mature adults
Chris Walz, General Manager
Theron Hayse, Sales Manager
Matt Price, Programming Director
Connie Green, News Director
Emily Peck, Traffic Manager
Barry Reker, General Sales Manager

Gering

KMOR
08-01-1996; 93.3 MHz FM; 100 kw; Ant 1,020 ft; N41 50 23 W103 49 36
Box 1263, Scottsbluff, NE 69363
(308) 632-5667; *Fax:* (308) 635-1905
info@hometownfamilyradio.com
License: Gering, Scotts Bluff County, NE held by Legacy Communications LLC.
Group Owner: GI Hometown Family Radio
Population Served: 125,000
Alan Usher, President/Chief Executive Officer
Dan Zabka, Sales Manager

Gibbon

KMTY
10-01-1970; 97.7 MHz FM; *Hrs Open:* 24; 55 kw; 253 ft.; N40 26 26 W99 23 59
Mailing Address: P.O. Box 465, Holdrege, NE 68949 US
Second Address: 613 4th Ave., Holdrege, NE 68949
(308) 995-4020; *Fax:* (308) 995-2202
kmtyfm.com
License: Gibbon, Phelps County, NE
Nat'l Network: ABC
Format: Adult Contemp; *Target Audience:* 20-45.
Alan Usher, President/Chief Executive Officer
Dan Zabka, Sales Manager

Goodland

***KVAM**
88.3 MHz FM; 510 w; Ant 282 ft; N41 11 36 W103 31 45
87 Jasper Lake Rd., Loveland, CO 80537 US
(970) 669-9200
License: Goodland, KS held by Kona Coast Radio, LLC.
Group Owner: Kona Coast Radio, LLC.
Format: Oldies

Gordon

KSDZ
05-19-1979; 95.5 MHz FM; *Hrs Open:* 24; 60 kw; 312 ft.; N42 47 56 W102 15 40
PO Box 390, Gordon, NE 69343 US
(308) 282-2500; *Fax:* (308) 282-0061
www.ksdzfm.com
thetwister@ksdzfm.com
License: Gordon, Sheridan County, NE held by DJ Broadcasting Inc.
Nat'l Network: ABC; *Wire Services:* AP
Arbitron Metro Market: Gordon, NE; *Format:* Oldies, Country; *Target Audience:* 25-54.; *Adv. Rates:* 35; 35; 35; 35
Jim Lambley, President

Grand Island

KMMJ
11-01-1925; 750 kHz AM; *Hrs Open:* Sunrise-sunset
Mailing Address: P.O. Box 404, Shenandoah, IA 51601 US
Second Address: Box 4907, Grand Island, NE 68802
(308) 382-2800; *Fax:* (308) 382-6701
missionnebraska.org/thebridge/
ausher@krgi.com
License: Grand Island, NE held by Mission Nebraska Inc.
Group Owner: Mission Nebraska Inc.; (acq 5-1-2006; $825,000)
Format: Christian
Alan Usher, President/Chief Executive Officer
Dan Zabka, Sales Manager

KRGI
04-01-1953; 1430 kHz AM; 5 kw-D, DAN; 1 kw-N, DAN; N40 52 17 W98 16 27
Mailing Address: P.O. Box 404, Shenandoah, IA 51601 US
Second Address: 3205 W. N. Front St., Grand Island, NE 68803
(308) 381-1430; *Fax:* (308) 382-6701
www.krgi.com
License: Grand Island, NE held by GI Hometown Family Radio
Group Owner: GI Hometown Family Radio
Nat'l Reps: Christal
Arbitron Metro Market: Grand Island-Kearney; *Format:* News, News/Talk, 86; *Target Audience:* 25-54.
Alan Usher, President/Chief Executive Officer
Dan Zabke, General Sales Mgr

KRGI-FM
10-30-1975; 96.5 MHz FM; *Hrs Open:* 24; 100 kw; 420 ft.; N40 51 53 W98 23 47
Mailing Address: P.O. Box 404, Shenandoah, IA 51601 US
Second Address: 3205 W. N. Front St., Grand Island, NE 68803
(308) 381-1430; *Fax:* (308) 382-6701
www.nebraskasbestcountry.com
ausher@krgi.com
License: Grand Island, Hall County, NE held by GI Hometown Family Radio
Group Owner: GI Hometown Family Radio
Nat'l Network: ABC
Arbitron Metro Market: Grand Island-Kearney; *Format:* Country
Alan Usher, President/Chief Executive Officer
Dan Zabka, Sales Manager

***KROA**
08-11-1967; 95.7 MHz FM; *Hrs Open:* 24; 100 kw; 459 ft.; N40 47 11 W98 22 0
P.O. Box 495, Doniphan, NE 68832 US
(402) 845-6595; *Fax:* (402) 845-6597
www.mybridgeradio.net
email@mybridgeradio.net
License: Grand Island, Hall County, NE held by My Bridge Radio
Group Owner: My Bridge Radio
Nat'l Network: Moody
Arbitron Metro Market: Grand Island-Kearney; *Format:* Religious
Dave Chally, Chairman
Stanley A. Parker, President
Gordon Wheeler, Station Manager
Taryn Julane, Programming Director

KSYZ-FM
11-01-1982; 107.7 MHz FM; *Hrs Open:* 24; 100 kw; 899 ft; N40 51 53 W98 23 47
Mailing Address: 3532 W. Captial Ave., Grand Island, NE 68508
Second Address: Box 5108, Grand Island, NE 68802
(308) 381-1077; *Fax:* (308) 384-8900
www.ksyz.com
ksyzprod@nrgmedia.com
License: Grand Island, Hall County, NE held by NRG Media LLC.
Group Owner: NRG Media LLC; (acq 10-31-2005; $5.28 million)
Target Audience: 25-49; adults; *Adv. Rates:* 30; 25; 25; 16
Jim Cartwright, Operations Dir
Tim Marshall, General Manager

***KLNB**
01-01-2005; 88.3 MHz FM; *Hrs Open:* 24; 1.7 kw; 147 ft.; N40 54 50 W98 23 52
P. O. Box 2098, Omaha, NE 68103 US
(800) 525-5683; *Fax:* (916) 251-1650
www.klove.com
klove@klove.com
License: Grand Island, Hall County, NE held by Educational Media Foundation.
Group Owner: EMF Broadcasting; (acq 3-11-2003; grpsl).
Nat'l Network: K-Love
Arbitron Metro Market: Grand Island, NE; *Format:* Christian; *No. News Employees:* 13; *Target Audience:* 25-44; Judeo Christian, female
Darrell Chambliss, Chairman
Mike Novak, President and CEO
Jennifer Lohman, Operations Dir
David Pierce, Chief Creative Officer and Programming Director
Ed Lenane, News Director
Sam Wallington, Engineering Dir
Marya Morgan, NewsReporter
Richard Hunt, News Reporter
Alan Mason, Chief Operating Officer
Dan Antonelli, Chief Business Development Officer
Eric Moser, Chief Financial Officer
Brian Burger, Vice President of Human Resources

***KNFA**
01-01-2008; 90.7 MHz FM; 1.3 kw; 191 ft.; N40 54 50 W98 23 52
Mailing Address: P O Box 1452, Washington, DC 20013 US
Second Address: 8919 World Ministry Ave., Baton Rouge, NE 70810
(225) 768-3102; *Fax:* (225) 768-3729
www.jsm.org
kawikfish@yahoo.com
License: Grand Island, Hall County, NE held by Family Worship Center Church Inc..
Group Owner: Family Worship Center Church Inc.; (acq 10-12-2006; grpsl)
Arbitron Metro Market: Grand Island, NE; *Format:* Christian, Religious
David Whitelaw, COO

Hastings

KLIQ
01-01-2001; 94.5 MHz FM; *Hrs Open:* 24; 97.7 kw; 948 ft.; N40 36 8 W98 50 21
1001 Farnum-On-The-Mall, Omaha, NE 68102 US
(402) 461-4922; *Fax:* (402) 461-3866
www.kliqfm.com
thebreeze@kliqfm.com
License: Hastings, Adams County, NE held by Platte River Radio Inc.
Group Owner: Platte River Radio Inc.; (acq 2-1-2006; $700,000).
Nat'l Network: ABC; *Wire Services:* AP
Arbitron Metro Market: Hastings, NB; *Format:* Adult Contemp *Special Programming:* News & special community interest; *No. News Employees:* 1; *Target Audience:* 25-54.
Jim Stevens, Operations Dir
Craig Eckert, General Manager
Brad Beahm, Programming Director
Kevin Michaelson, News Director

***KCNT**
02-22-1971; 88.1 MHz FM; *Hrs Open:* 24; 2.3 kw horiz; 180 ft.; N40 34 52 W98 19 58
P.O. Box 1024, Hastings, NE 68902 US
(402) 463-9811; *Fax:* (402) 461-2454
www.cccneb.edu/programs/mart/kcnt/index.html
rglenn@cccneb.edu
License: Hastings, Adams County, NE held by Central Community College.
Arbitron Metro Market: Hastings, NE; *Format:* Contemporary Hits/Top 40
John Brooks, General Manager
Dr. Deb Brennan, Executive Vice President
Marni Nelson-Snyde, Grants Manager
Heidi Farrall, Grants Development Coordinator
Michelle Setlik, Grants Compliance Officer
Christopher Waddle, JD, ExecutiveDirector
Tom Peters, ITS Manager

***KFKX**
90.1 MHz FM; 0.78 kw vert; 223 ft.; N40 34 27 W98 22 19
700 Turner Street, Hastings, NE 68901 US
(402) 461-7367; *Fax:* (402) 461-7442
License: Hastings, Adams County, NE held by Hastings College.
Wire Services: AP
Arbitron Metro Market: Hastings, NE; *Format:* Urban Contemporary; *Target Audience:* General.
Phillip Dudley, President
Bart Jones, Operations Dir
Sharon Behl Brooks, General Manager
Stefan Welsh, Station Manager

KHAS
09-30-1940; 1230 kHz AM; *Hrs Open:* 24; 1 kw-U, ND1; N40 34 40 W98 24 17
Mailing Address: 902 W. 2nd St, # 200, Hastings, NE 68901 US
Second Address: 500 East J St., Hastings, NE 68901
(402) 462-5101; *Fax:* (402) 461-3866
hastingslink.com
License: Hastings, NE held by Platte River Radio Inc.
Group Owner: Platte River Radio Inc.; (acq 2-1-2006; $560,000 with KICS(AM) Hastings).
Nat'l Network: CBS; *Regional Network:* Brownfield *Regional Reps:* Howard Anderson; *Wire Services:* AP
Format: Adult Contemp *Special Programming:* Farm 2 hrs, class 2 hrs wkly; *Hrs. of News Programming:* news progmg 20 hrs wkly; *No. News Employees:* 1; *Target Audience:* 35 plus; general

Craig Eckert, General Manager
Brad Beatim, Programming Director
Brandon Peoples, News Director
Mike Will, Sports Director

***KHNE-FM**
06-01-1990; 89.1 MHz FM; *Hrs Open:* 24; 64.3 kw; 328 ft; N40 46 17 W98 05 22 *Rebroadcasts:* Rebroadcasts KUCV(FM) Lincoln 100%.
1800 N. 33rd St., Lincoln, NE 68501
(402) 472-3611; *Fax:* (402) 472-2403
netnebraska.org/radio
radio@netnebraska.org
License: Hastings, Adams County, NE held by Nebraska Educational Telecommunications Commission
Nat'l Network: NPR; APM; PRI; *Regional Network:* Net Radio *Hrs. of News Programming:* news progmg 45 hrs wkly; *No. News Employees:* 8; *Target Audience:* General.
Mark Leonard, General Manager
Nancy Finken, Station Manager
Susan Dinsmore, Marketing Specialist
Nancy Finken, Programming Director
Dennis Kellogg, News Director
Stacey Decker, Engineering Dir
William Stibor, Music Director
Jeff Smith, Operations Coordinator

KICS
04-15-1964; 1550 kHz AM; *Hrs Open:* 24; 0.5 kw-D, ND1; 0.027 kw-N, ND1; N40 34 3 W98 22 31
PO Box 726, Hastings, NE 68902 US
(402) 462-5101; *Fax:* (402) 461-3866
www.espnsuperstation.com
License: Hastings, NE held by Platte River Radio Inc.
Group Owner: Platte River Radio Inc.; (acq 2-1-2006; $560,000 with KHAS(AM) Hastings).
Nat'l Network: ESPN Radio *Regional Reps:* Howard Anderson *TV Affiliate:* ESPN; *Format:* Sports *Special Programming:* College football 8 hrs wkly; *Hrs. of News Programming:* news progmg 12 hrs wkly; *No. News Employees:* 1; *Target Audience:* 18-54; males

KROR
02-01-1965; 101.5 MHz FM; *Hrs Open:* 24; 100 kw; Ant 1,004 ft; N40 39 28 W98 52 04
3532 W. Capital Ave., Grand Island, NE 68803
(308) 381-1077; *Fax:* (308) 384-8900
www.rock1015.com
ksyzprod@nrgmedia.com
License: Hastings, Adams County, NE held by NRG License Sub LLC.
Group Owner: NRG Media LLC; (acq 1-31-2006; swap for KLIQ(FM) Hastings)
Population Served: 250,000 *Target Audience:* 25-54.; *Adv. Rates:* 30; 24; 24; 16
Jim Cartwright, Operations Dir
Dallas Nau, General Manager

Hershey

KNPQ
01-01-2008; 107.3 MHz FM; *Hrs Open:* 24; 25 kw; 226 ft.; N41 9 14 W100 46 22.4
2703 Hall St., Suite 15, Hays, KS 67601 US
(785) 625-4000
www.northplattepost.com
License: Hershey, Lincoln County, NE held by Eagle Communications Inc.
Group Owner: Eagle Communications Group
Arbitron Metro Market: Hershey, NE; *Format:* Country; *Hrs. of News Programming:* news prgmg one hour wkly; *No. News Employees:* 1; *Target Audience:* 18-44.; *Adv. Rates:* same as KOOQ
Jerome Gilg, General Manager/Sales Manager

Holdrege

KUVR
10-20-1956; 1380 kHz AM
Mailing Address: 613 4th Avenue, Holdrege, NE 68949 US
Second Address: 613 4th Ave., Holdrege, NE 68949
(308) 995-4020; *Fax:* (308) 345-4720
www.plainsreporter.com
bryan@highplainsradio.net?subject=Email%20for%20further%20details%20here
License: Holdrege, NE held by Armada Media-McCook Inc.
Group Owner: Armada Media Corp.; (acq 5-16-2008; grpsl)
Arbitron Metro Market: Holdrege, NE; *Format:* Oldies *Special Programming:* Farm 5 hrs, big band 5 hrs, contemp gospel 5 hrs wkly; *Target Audience:* 35-54.
Andrew Stossmeister, Operations Dir
Bryan Loker, General Manager

Jim Conner, General Sales Mgr
Val Lane, Chief Engineer
Randy Issler, Music Director

Hubbard

***KAYA**
01-01-1998; 91.3 MHz FM; 5.1 kw; 377 ft.; N42 21 10 W96 31 32
P.O. Box 3206, Tupelo, MS 38803 US
(662) 844-8888; *Fax:* (662) 842-6791
www.afr.net
faq@afa.net
License: Hubbard, Dakota County, NE held by American Family Association.
Group Owner: American Family Radio
Arbitron Metro Market: Tupelo, MS; *Format:* Christian, Religious
Tim Wildmon, President
Donald Wildmon, Founder
Buddy Smith, Sr VP
Ed Vitagliano, Exec VP
Randy Sharp, Director Of Special Projects
Meeke Addison, Director Of Communications
Abraham Hamiltin III, General Counsel & Public PolicyAnalyst

Humboldt

***KNIT**
90.1 MHz FM; 6.1 kw horiz; Ant 607 ft; N40 13 11 W95 39 55
License: Humboldt, Richardson County, NE held by Kona Coast Radio, LLC.
Group Owner: Kona Coast Radio, LLC.
Format: Adult Contemp

Imperial

KADL
01-01-2003; 102.9 MHz FM; 300 w; Ant 223 ft; N40 30 45 W101 38 39
Mailing Address: PO Box 333, McCook, NE 69001
Second Address: 824 Douglas St., Imperial, NE 69033
(308) 345-5400,(308) 882-4209; *Fax:* (308) 345-4720,(308) 882-4319
www.kadlimperial.com
License: Imperial, Chase County, NE held by Armada Media - McCook Inc.
Group Owner: Armada Media Corp.; (acq 1-17-2007; grpsl)

Bryan Loker, General Manager/General Sales Manager
Cyndi Stratton, Programming Director
Tara O'Dell, Traffic Manager

Kearney

KGFW
01-01-1927; 1340 kHz AM; *Hrs Open:* 24
Mailing Address: P.O. Box 669, Tri-Cities, NE 66848 US
Second Address: 2223 Central Ave., Kearney, NE 68847
(308) 698-2131; *Fax:* (308) 237-0312
www.kgfw.com
swhite@nrgmedia.com
License: Kearney, NE held by NRG License Sub. LLC.
Group Owner: NRG Media LLC; (acq 10-31-2005; grpsl)
Nat'l Network: Westwood One; *Regional Network:* Waitt Farm Net.; Brownfield; *Nat'l Reps:* Christal; *Wire Services:* AP
Format: News, News/Talk, 86 *Special Programming:* Farm 8 hrs, sports 10 hrs wkly; *Hrs. of News Programming:* news progmg 25 hrs wkly; *No. News Employees:* 2; *Target Audience:* 25 plus; adults in central Nebraska
Mary Quass, President
Mark Reid, Operations Dir
Sharron White, General Manager
Andrew Mihm, Programming Director

KXPN
12-05-1956; 1460 kHz AM; *Hrs Open:* 24; 5 kw-D, ND1; 0.056 kw-N, ND1; N40 42 45 W99 10 15
Mailing Address: PO Box 130, Kearney, NE 68848 US
Second Address: 403 E. 25th St., Kearney, NE 68848
(308) 236-9900; *Fax:* (308) 234-6781
www.espnsuperstation.com
generalmanager@espnsuperstation.com
License: Kearney, NE held by Platte River Radio Inc.
Group Owner: Platte River Radio Inc.; (acq 1-1-94; $750,000 with co-located FM;
Nat'l Network: ESPN Radio
Arbitron Metro Market: Lincoln, NE; *Format:* Sports; *Hrs. of News Programming:* news progmg 2 hrs wkly; *No. News Employees:* 1; *Target Audience:* 25-54; men; *Adv. Rates:* 27; 19; 27; 12
Craig Eckert, General Manager

KKPR-FM
11-01-1962; 98.9 MHz FM; *Hrs Open:* 24; 100 kw; 627 ft.; N40 48 53 W98 46 12
PO Box 130, Kearney, NE 68848 US
(308) 236-9900; *Fax:* (308) 234-6781
generalmanager@kkpr.com
License: Kearney, Buffalo County, NE
Group Owner: Platte River Radio Inc.
Arbitron Metro Market: Lincoln, NE; *Format:* Oldies; *Hrs. of News Programming:* news progmg 3 hrs wkly; *No. News Employees:* 1; *Target Audience:* 35-64.; *Adv. Rates:* 27; 19; 27; 12.
Dan Beck, Operations Dir
Johnnie McCann, General Sales Mgr

***KLPR**
03-08-1968; 91.1 MHz FM; *Hrs Open:* 6 AM-midnight; 1 kw; 102 ft.; N40 42 30 W99 5 45
109 Thomas Hall, Kearney, NE 68849 US
(308) 865-8217
klpr.unk.edu
License: Kearney, Buffalo County, NE held by University of Nebraska at Kearney.
Arbitron Metro Market: Lincoln, NE; *Format:* Jazz, Rock/AOR
Special Programming: Class 18 hrs wkly
Elle Scholwin, General Manager

KQKY
10-01-1979; 105.9 MHz FM; *Hrs Open:* 24; 97.6 kw; 1204 ft.; N40 36 8 W98 50 21
Mailing Address: P.O. Box 669, Tri-Cities, NE 68848 US
Second Address: 2223 Central Ave., Kearney, NE 68847
(308) 698-2100; *Fax:* (308) 237-0312
www.kqky.com
License: Kearney, Buffalo County, NE held by NRG License Sub. LLC.
Group Owner: NRG Media LLC
Nat'l Network: Fox News Radio; Superadio; *Nat'l Reps:* Christal; *Wire Services:* AP
Arbitron Metro Market: Grand Island-Kearney; *Format:* Contemporary Hits/Top 40; *Target Audience:* 18-49.
Mary Quass, President
Mark Reid, Operations Dir
Sharon White, Station Manager
Jason Murphy, Programming Director

KRNY
01-01-1987; 102.3 MHz FM; *Hrs Open:* 24; 77.1 kw; 1086 ft.; N40 36 8 W98 50 21
Mailing Address: P.O. Box 669, Tri-Cities, NE 68848 US
Second Address: 2223 Central Ave., Kearney, NE 68847
(308) 698-2100; *Fax:* (308) 237-0312
www.krny.com
License: Kearney, Buffalo County, NE held by NRG License Sub. LLC.
Group Owner: NRG Media LLC; (acq 10-31-2005; grpsl)
Nat'l Network: Fox News Radio; Premiere Radio Networks; *Nat'l Reps:* Christal; *Wire Services:* AP
Arbitron Metro Market: Tri Cities, NB (Kearney, Grand Island, Hastings); *Format:* Country; *Hrs. of News Programming:* News progmg 2 hrs wkly; *Target Audience:* 25 plus.
Mary Quass, President
Mark Reid, Operations Dir
Sharon White, Station Manager
Scott O'Rourke, Programming Director
Dave Jenner, Sports Director

Kimball

KIMB
01-01-1958; 1260 kHz AM; 1 kw-D, ND1; 0.112 kw-N, ND1; N41 15 42 W103 40 6
213 S. Chestnut St., Kimball, NE 69145 US
(970) 867-7271; *Fax:* (970) 867-2676
License: Kimball, NE held by Laramie Mountain Broadcasting LLC
Target Audience: General.
Alec Creighton, General Manager

La Vista

KOOO
06-22-1958; 101.9 MHz FM; *Hrs Open:* 24; 100 kw; Ant 1,132 ft; N40 47 09 W96 23 07
5011 Capitol Ave., Omaha, NE 68102
(402) 342-2000; *Fax:* (402) 346-5748
thebigo1019.com
info@thebigo1019.com
License: La Vista, Sarpy County, NE held by Waitt Omaha LLC.
Group Owner: Waitt Omaha LLC; (acq 1-7-2002; grpsl)
Nat'l Reps: Katz Radio

Population Served: 2,120,000; *Arbitron Metro Market:* Omaha-Council Bluffs, NE-IA; *Target Audience:* 25-54; general
Mary Quass, President/Chief Executive Officer
Jeff Lynn, Operations Dir
Stacie McElligott, General Sales Mgr
Ken Kohls, Programming Director
Chris Pflaum, Promotions Manager
Cynthia Wallace, News Director
Becca Sautter, TrafficManager

Lexington

*KLNE-FM
05-04-1990; 88.7 MHz FM; *Hrs Open:* 24; 43.8 kw; 938 ft; N40 23 05 W99 27 30 *Rebroadcasts:* Rebroadcasts KUCV(FM) Lincoln 100%
1800 N. 33rd St., Lincoln, NE 68501
(402) 472-3611; *Fax:* (402) 472-2403
netnebraska.org/radio
radio@netnebraska.org
License: Lexington, Dawson County, NE held by Nebraska Educational Telecommunications Commission
Nat'l Network: NPR; APM; PRI; *Regional Network:* Nebraska Public Radio
Hrs. of News Programming: news progmg 45 hrs wkly; *No. News Employees:* 8; *Target Audience:* General
Mark Leonard, General Manager
Susan Dinsmore, Marketing Specialist
Nancy Finken, Programming Director
Dennis Kellogg, News Director
William Stibor, Music Director
Jeff Smith, Operations Coordinator

KRVN
02-01-1951; 880 kHz AM; *Hrs Open:* 24; 50 kw-U, DA-N; N40 31 03 W99 23 20
Box 880, 1007 Plum Creek Pkwy., Lexington, NE 68850
(308) 324-2371; *Fax:* (308) 324-5786
www.krvn.com
krvnam@krvn.com
License: Lexington, Dawson County, NE held by Nebraska Rural Radio Assn.
Group Owner: Nebraska Rural Radio Association; (acq 2-1-51)
Nat'l Network: Fox News Radio; *Nat'l Reps:* Katz Radio; *Wire Services:* AP
Special Programming: Relg 12 hrs wkly; *Hrs. of News Programming:* news progmg 30 hrs wkly; *No. News Employees:* 4; *Target Audience:* General; Nebraska farm/ranch families & consumers; *Adv. Rates:* 230; 230; 136; 90
Craig Larson, General Manager
Dwight Lane, Station Manager
Amy Biehl-Owens, General Sales Mgr
Adam Smith, Programming Director
Beth Rogers, Promotions Manager
Frank Snyder, News Director
Rod Zeigler, Engineering Dir
MikeLePorte, Farm Director
Don Norman, Internet Sales Manager

KRVN-FM
11-01-1962; 93.1 MHz FM; *Hrs Open:* 24; 100 kw; 890 ft; N40 41 48 W99 47 18
Box 880, 1007 Plum Creek Pkwy., Lexington, NE 22203
(308) 324-2371; *Fax:* (308) 324-5786
License: Lexington, Dawson County, NE
Group Owner: Nebraska Rural Radio Association
Nat'l Network: Fox News Radio; *Nat'l Reps:* Katz Radio
Population Served: 125,000 *Special Programming:* Farm 10 hrs wkly; *Hrs. of News Programming:* news prog 20 hrs wkly; *No. News Employees:* 1; *Target Audience:* Contemp young adults; *Adv. Rates:* 50; 50; 35; 25
Craig Larson, General Manager
Dwight Lane, Station Manager
Amy Biehl-Owens, General Sales Mgr
Adam Smith, Programming Director
Beth Rogers, Promotions Manager/Webmaster
Frank Snyder, News Director
Rod Zeigler, Engineering Dir
Mike LePorte, Farm Director
Don Norman, Internet Sales Manager

Lincoln

KBBK
09-01-1968; 107.3 MHz FM; *Hrs Open:* 24; 100 kw; 551 ft.; N40 43 38 W96 36 51
P. O. Box 30181, Lincoln, NE 68503 US
(402) 475-4567; *Fax:* (402) 479-1411
www.b1073.com
news@broadcasthouse.com
License: Lincoln, Lancaster County, NE held by NRG License Sub. LLC.
Group Owner: NRG Media LLC; (acq 12-28-2007; grpsl)
Arbitron Metro Market: Lincoln, NE; *Format:* Adult Contemp; *Target Audience:* 25-54; middle-to-upper income, households, in-office & in-store lstng
Mary Quass, President
Ami Graham, Market Manager
Tina Segerstrom, General Sales Mgr
Steve Albertsen, Programming Director

KFOR
03-04-1924; 1240 kHz AM; *Hrs Open:* 24; 1 kw-U, ND1; N40 49 12 W96 39 29
3800 Cornhusker Hwy, Lincoln, NE 68504 US
(402) 466-1234; *Fax:* (402) 467-4095
www.kfor1240.com
License: Lincoln, NE held by Digity 3E License, LLC
Group Owner: Digity, LLC
Arbitron Metro Market: Lincoln, NE; *Format:* News/Talk; *No. News Employees:* 6; *Target Audience:* 25-54.
Joy Patten, General Sales Mgr
Dale Johnson, News Director

KFRX
02-23-1973; 106.3 MHz FM; *Hrs Open:* 24; 100 kw; 702 ft.; N40 43 40 W96 36 50
701 Northpoint Pkwy., 5th Floor, West Palm Beach, FL 33407 US
(561) 616-4777
www.kfrxfm.com
License: Lincoln, Lancaster County, NE held by Digity 3E License, LLC
Group Owner: Digity, LLC
Arbitron Metro Market: Lincoln, NE; *Format:* Contemporary Hits/Top 40
Matt McKay, Programming Director

KLNC
01-01-1992; 105.3 MHz FM; 3.2 kw; 453 ft.; N40 43 38 W96 36 51
P.O. Box 30181, Lincoln, NE 68503 US
(402) 475-4567; *Fax:* (402) 479-1411
1053wow.com
news@broadcasthouse.com
License: Lincoln, Lancaster County, NE held by NRG License Sub. LLC.
Group Owner: NRG Media LLC; (acq 12-28-2007; grpsl)
Arbitron Metro Market: Lincoln, NE; *Format:* Oldies
Mary Quass, President/Chief Executive Officer
Mark Halverson, Operations Dir
Ami Graham, General Manager/General Sales Manager
Lester St. James, Programming Director
Steve Looney, Chief Engineer

*KLCV
01-01-1996; 88.5 MHz FM; *Hrs Open:* 8 AM-5 PM (M-F); 46 kw; 1,255 ft.; N40 47 10 W96 23 10
233 S. 13th St., Suite 1520, Lincoln, NE 68508 US
(402) 465-8850; *Fax:* (402) 465-8852
www.bottradionetwork.com
comments@bottradionetwork.com
License: Lincoln, Lancaster County, NE held by Community Broadcasting Inc.
Group Owner: Bott Radio Network
Nat'l Network: USA
Arbitron Metro Market: Lincoln-Omaha, NE; *Format:* Christian, Talk; *Target Audience:* 25 plus; Christian families
Richard Bott Sr., President & CEO
Eben Fowler, Operations Dir
Tom Millett, Nebraska Area Manager
Pat Rulon, Director of National Sales
Candy Green, Program Services Manager
Rachel Launius, Marketing Manager
Jason Potocnik,Director of Traffic Operations

KLIN
08-01-1947; 1400 kHz AM; *Hrs Open:* 24
4343 O Street, Lincoln, NE 68510 US
(402) 475-4567; *Fax:* (402) 479-1411
www.klin.com
news@broadcasthouse.com
License: Lincoln, NE held by NRG License Sub. LLC.
Group Owner: NRG Media LLC; (acq 12-28-2007; grpsl)
Nat'l Network: Fox News Radio
Arbitron Metro Market: Lincoln, NE; *Format:* News, News/Talk, 86; *Hrs. of News Programming:* news progmg 80 hrs wkly; *No. News Employees:* 4; *Target Audience:* 35-64; upper income, business owner, educated with highdisposable income
Ami Elizabeth Graham, General Manager
Kevin Thomas, Programming Director
Bill Frost, Chief Engineer

Chris Whitney, Sports Director
Tina Segerstrom, Sales Manager

KLMS
10-01-1949; 1480 kHz AM; 1 kw-D, DA2; 0.75 kw-N, DA2; N40 47 47 W96 34 56
3800 Cornhusker Hwy., Lincoln, NE 68504 US
(402) 466-1234
www.espn1480.com
License: Lincoln, NE held by Digity 3E License, LLC
Group Owner: Digity Media, LLC; (acq 1996; grpsl)
Arbitron Metro Market: Lincoln, NE; *Format:* Sports
Chris Goforth, Programming Director

*KRNU
02-23-1970; 90.3 MHz FM; *Hrs Open:* 24; 0.1 kw; 125 ft.; N40 49 11 W96 42 11
206 Avery Hall, Lincoln, NE 68508 US
(402) 472-3054; *Fax:* (402) 472-8403
krnu@unl.edu
License: Lincoln, Lancaster County, NE held by University of Nebraska.
Nat'l Network: ABC
Arbitron Metro Market: Lincoln, NE *TV Affiliate:* *KUON-TV affil.; *Format:* Rock/AOR *Special Programming:* Hip-hop 2 hrs, electronic 4 hrs, gospel 2 hrs, ja; *Hrs. of News Programming:* News progmg 5 hrs wkly
Rick Alloway, General Manager
Ford Clark, Station Manager

*KUCV-FM
01-01-1968; 91.1 MHz FM; *Hrs Open:* 24; 19.5 kw horiz, 100 kw ver; Ant 689 ft; N40 31 06 W96 46 06
1800 N. 33rd St., Lincoln, NE 68503
(402) 472-3611; *Fax:* (402) 472-2403
www.netNebraska.org/radio
radio@Netnebraska.org
License: Lincoln, Lancaster County, NE held by Nebraska Educational Telecommunications Commission
Nat'l Network: NPR; APM; PRI; *Regional Network:* NET Radio
Population Served: 1,100,000; *Arbitron Metro Market:* Lincoln, NE; *Hrs. of News Programming:* news progmg 45 hrs wkly; *No. News Employees:* 8; *Target Audience:* General.
Jeff Smith, Operations Coordinator
Mark Leonard, General Manager
Susan Dinsmore, Marketing Specialist
Nancy Finken, Programming Director
Dennis Kellogg, News Director
William Stibor, Music Director

*KZUM
01-01-1978; 89.3 MHz FM; *Hrs Open:* 6 AM-2 AM; 1.5 kw; 102 ft.; N40 48 47 W96 42 24
3534 S. 48th Street, Lincoln, NE 68508 US
(402) 474-5086; *Fax:* (402) 474-5091
www.kzum.org
gm@kzum.org
License: Lincoln, Lancaster County, NE held by Sunrise Communications Inc.
Arbitron Metro Market: Lincoln, NE; *Format:* Jazz, Variety/Diverse *Special Programming:* Sp 4 hrs, rock/progsv 15 hrs, new age 8 hrs, blues 13 hrs, folk 8 hrs, gospel 3 hrs wkly; *Hrs. of News Programming:* News progmg 11hrs wkly; *Target Audience:* General; the unserved & underserved population; *Adv. Rates:* 15; 15; 15; 15

Loup City

*KSRC
88.1 MHz FM; kw
US
(918) 333-8700
License: Loup City, Sherman County, NE held by Pearl Communications Group.
Arbitron Metro Market: Kansas City, MO; *Format:* Adult Contemp
Danny Hester, President

Maxwell

KHAQ
01-01-2000; 98.5 MHz FM; *Hrs Open:* 24; 85 kw; Ant 371 ft; N41 12 49 W100 43 49
Mailing Address: 1811 West D Street, McCook, NE 69001
Second Address: 1811 W. O St., McCook, NE 69001
(308) 345-5400; *Fax:* (308) 345-4720
www.kicx.net
bryan@highplainsradio.net
License: Maxwell, Lincoln County, NE held by Armada Media - McCook Inc.
Group Owner: Armada Media Corp.; (acq 3-31-2007; grpsl)
Population Served: 40,000 *Target Audience:* 18-54.

Chris Bernier, President
Rob Mandeville, General Manager

McCook

KBRL
09-26-1947; 1300 kHz AM; 5 kw-D, DA2; 0.136 kw-N, DA2; N40 11 31 W100 39 6
1811 West O Street, McCook, NE 69001 US
(308) 345-5400; *Fax:* (308) 345-4720
www.kicx.net
bryan@highplainsradio.net
License: McCook, NE held by Armada Media - McCook Inc.
Group Owner: Armada Media Corp.; (acq 3-31-2007; grpsl)
Format: Oldies; *Target Audience:* 35-64.
Chris Bernier, President
Rob Mandeville, General Manager

KICX-FM
01-31-1979; 96.1 MHz FM; *Hrs Open:* 24; 55 kw; 295 ft.; N40 10 17 W100 41 4
1811 West O Street, McCook, NE 69001 US
(705) 722-5429; *Fax:* (308) 345-4720
www.kicx106.com
License: McCook, Red Willow County, NE held by Armada Media - McCook Inc.
Group Owner: Armada Media Corp.; (acq 3-31-2007; grpsl)
Nat'l Network: ABC
Format: Country; *No. News Employees:* 1; *Target Audience:* 25-64.
Chris Bernier, President
Rob Mandeville, General Manager

KIOD
05-01-1981; 105.3 MHz FM; *Hrs Open:* 24; 100 kw; Ant 591 ft; N40 11 27 W100 48 29
Mailing Address: Box 939, McCook, NE 69001
Second Address: 106 W. 8th St., McCook, NE 69001
(308) 345-1981; *Fax:* (308) 345-7202
coyote105.com
info@hometownfamilyradio.com
License: McCook, Red Willow County, NE held by Legacy Communications LLC.
Group Owner: Legacy Communications LLC; (acq 10-13-2005; $1.3 million with
Population Served: 40,000 *Special Programming:* Sports 10 hrs, farm 6 hrs wkly; *Hrs. of News Programming:* news progmg 5 hrs wkly; *No. News Employees:* 1; *Target Audience:* 25-54.; *Adv. Rates:* 15; 15; 15; 8
Alan Usher, CEO/COO
Jesse Stevens, Programming Director
Ann Doyle, News Director
Derek Beck, Music Director

*KNGN
06-23-1961; 1360 kHz AM; *Hrs Open:* 6 AM-2 hrs past sunset
38005 Road 717, McCook, NE 69001 US
(308) 345-2006; *Fax:* (308) 345-2052
www.kngn.org
License: McCook, NE held by Kansas Nebraska Good News Broadcasting Corp.
Format: Religious; *Hrs. of News Programming:* News progmg 7 hrs wkly; *Target Audience:* 35 plus; family oriented
Greg Stuekwiseh, President
Mike Nielsen, General Manager

KSWN
09-17-1998; 93.9 MHz FM; *Hrs Open:* 24; 50 kw; 492 ft.; N40 11 27 W100 48 29
P O Box 939, 106 Wesst 8th St, McCook, NE 69001 US
(308) 345-1100; *Fax:* (308) 345-7202
License: McCook, Red Willow County, NE held by Legacy Communications LLC.
Group Owner: Legacy Communications LLC; (acq 10-13-2005; $1.3 million with KIOD(FM) McCook)
Nat'l Network: ESPN Radio
Arbitron Metro Market: McCook, NE; *Format:* Adult Contemp, Sports; *Target Audience:* 25-54.; *Adv. Rates:* 10; 10; 10; 6.50
Eileen Austin, Operations Dir
Jay Austin, General Manager
Jesse Stevens, Programming Director

KNAX
700 kHz AM
US
(308) 345-5400; *Fax:* (308) 345-4720
License: McCook, NE held by McCook Radio Group L.L.C.
Arbitron Metro Market: McCook, NE
David Stout, General Manager
Connie Stout, General Sales Mgr
Rich Barnett, News Director

KZMC
10-25-2006; 102.1 MHz FM; 100 kw; Ant 590 ft; N40 11 27 W100 48 29
Mailing Address: Box 939, McCook, NE
Second Address: 106 W. 8th St., McCook, NE 69001-3508
(308) 345-1981; *Fax:* (308) 345-7202
www.hometownfamilyradio.com/Z/index.php
info@hometownfamilyradio.com
License: McCook, Red Willow County, NE held by Legacy Communications LLC.
Group Owner: Legacy Communications LLC

Jesse Stevens, Operations Manager

KQHK
01-01-2008; 103.9 MHz FM; 50 kw; 371 ft.; N40 10 19 W100 41 5
US
(308) 345-5400; *Fax:* (308) 345-4720
www.kicx.net
License: McCook, Red Willow County, NE held by Armada Media - McCook Inc.
Group Owner: Armada Media Corp.; (acq 3-31-2007; grpsl)
Arbitron Metro Market: McCook, NE; *Format:* Classic Rock
Andrew Stossmeister, Operations Dir
Bryan Loker, General Manager

Merriman

*KRNE-FM
08-29-1991; 91.5 MHz FM; *Hrs Open:* 24; 92 kw; 964 ft; N42 40 38 W101 42 36 *Rebroadcasts:* Rebroadcasts KUCV(FM) Lincoln 100%
1800 N. 33rd St., Lincoln, NE 68501
(402) 472-3611; *Fax:* (402) 472-2403
netnebraska.org/radio
radio@netnebraska.org
License: Merriman, Cherry County, NE held by Nebraska Educational Telecommunications Commission
Nat'l Network: NPR; APM; PRI; *Regional Network:* NET Radio
Hrs. of News Programming: news progmg 45 hrs wkly; *No. News Employees:* 8; *Target Audience:* General.
Mark Leonard, General Manager
Nancy Finken, Station Manager
Susan Dinsmore, Marketing Specialist
Nancy Finken, Programming Director
Dennis Kellogg, News Director
Bill Stibor, Music Director
Jeff Smith, Operations Coordinator

Milford

KFGE
01-01-1996; 98.1 MHz FM; 100 kw; 981 ft.; N40 51 52 W97 16 14
4343 O St., Lincoln, NE 68510 US
(402) 475-4567; *Fax:* (402) 479-1411
www.froggy981.com
License: Milford, Seward County, NE held by NRG License Sub. LLC.
Group Owner: NRG Media LLC; (acq 12-28-2007; grpsl)
Arbitron Metro Market: Lincoln, NE; *Format:* Country
Mark Halverson, Operations Dir
Ami Graham, General Manager
Steve Albertson, Programming Director

Minatare

KHYY
01-01-2008; 106.9 MHz FM; 25 kw; 92 ft.; N41 51 50 W103 42 20
Mailing Address: US
Second Address: 2002 Char Ave., Scottsbluff, NE 69361
(308) 632-5667; *Fax:* (308) 635-1905
License: Minatare, Scotts Bluff County, NE held by Armada Media
Group Owner: Armada Media LLC
Arbitron Metro Market: Centennial, CO; *Format:* Country
Chris Bernier, President/Chief Executive Officer
Rob Mandeville, General Manager

Mitchell

KETT
01-01-2008; 99.3 MHz FM; 0.95 kw; 817 ft.; N41 50 23 W103 49 35
Mailing Address: US
Second Address: 2002 Char Ave., Scottsbluff, NE 69361
(308) 632-5667; *Fax:* (308) 635-1905
License: Mitchell, Scotts Bluff County, NE held by Armada Media
Group Owner: Armada Media LLC
Arbitron Metro Market: Glen Elder, KS

Chris Bernier, President/Chief Executive Officer
Scott Mandeville, General Manager

Nebraska City

KNCY
06-29-1959; 1600 kHz AM; *Hrs Open:* 24; 0.5 kw-D, DA2; 0.031 kw-N, DA2; N40 40 27 W95 53 8
814 Central Avenue, Nebraska City, NE 68410 US
(402) 873-3348; *Fax:* (402) 873-7882
www.kncycountry.com
kncy@kncycountry.com
License: Nebraska City, NE held by Riverfront Broadcasting LLC
Nat'l Network: ABC
Format: Variety/Diverse *Special Programming:* Farm 3 hrs, sports 6 hrs wkly; *Hrs. of News Programming:* news progmg 21 hrs wkly; *No. News Employees:* 2; *Target Audience:* 18-80; local residents, farmers, businessowners, workers, students; *Adv. Rates:* 10; 10; 10; 5
Scott Kooistra, General Manager
Chris Yates, General Sales Mgr

KBBX-FM
02-01-1995; 97.7 MHz FM; *Hrs Open:* 24; 99 kw; 978 ft.; N40 53 27 W96 9 11
1128 John Galt Boulevard, Suite 025, Omaha, NE 68137 US
(402) 884-0968; *Fax:* (402) 884-4754
info@z92.com
License: Nebraska City, Otoe County, NE held by Connoisseur Media Licenses LLC
Group Owner: Connoisseur Media LLC; (acq 9-25-2006; $7.5 million).
Nat'l Network: ABC; *Regional Network:* Southwest Agri-Radio
Arbitron Metro Market: Omaha-Lincoln; *Format:* Tejano; *Target Audience:* 25-54.
Jim Timm, General Manager/General Sales Manager
Valentin Maldonado, Programming Director
Melissa Schoonover, Promotions Manager

Norfolk

KQKX
08-01-1971; 106.7 MHz FM; *Hrs Open:* 24; 100 kw; Ant 1,027 ft; N41 55 59 W97 40 49
Mailing Address: Box 789, Norfolk, NE 68701
Second Address: 309 Braasch Ave., Norfolk, NE 68701
(402) 371-0780; *Fax:* (402) 371-6303
www.106kix.com
License: Norfolk, Madison County, NE held by WJAG Inc.
Group Owner: WJAG Inc.
Nat'l Network: Fox News Radio; Westwood One; *Wire Services:* AP
Population Served: 100,000 *Hrs. of News Programming:* news progmg 6 hrs wkly; *No. News Employees:* 2; *Target Audience:* 18-49; full service FM adults; *Adv. Rates:* 25; 23; 25; 20
Bradley Hughes, Operations Dir
Sally Lewis, General Sales Mgr
Michael Nissen, Programming Director
Jim Curry, News Director
Susan Risinger, Farm Director
Jeffrey Steffen, Operations Manager
Joe Tjaden, Sports Commentator
DeniseReikofski, Traffic Manager

KNEN
04-06-1979; 94.7 MHz FM; 100 kw; 539 ft.; N41 55 28 W97 36 22
214 N. 7th Street, PO Box 747, Norfolk, NE 68701 US
(402) 371-0100; *Fax:* (402) 371-0050
www.94rock.fm
License: Norfolk, Madison County, NE held by Red Beacon Communications LLC.
Format: Classic Rock *Special Programming:* Farm 10 hrs wkly; *Hrs. of News Programming:* news progmg 15 hrs wkly; *No. News Employees:* 2; *Target Audience:* 25-54; young to middle-aged; *Adv. Rates:* 19.50;19.50; 19.50; 18.50
Andy Stenger, General Manager

*KPNO
09-23-1992; 90.9 MHz FM; *Hrs Open:* 24; 100 kw; 338 ft.; N42 6 16 W97 20 11
128 S. 4th Street, O'Neill, NE 68763 US
(402) 336-3886
License: Norfolk, Madison County, NE held by The Praise Network Inc.
Nat'l Network: Moody; USA
Format: Religious; *Hrs. of News Programming:* News progmg 14 hrs wkly; *Target Audience:* 25-54; family-oriented adults
Herb Roszhart Jr., CEO
Jon Shipman, General Manager
Brian Gall, Station Manager

***KXNE-FM**
05-29-1990; 89.3 MHz FM; *Hrs Open:* 24; 42.3 kw; 984 ft; N42 14 15 W97 16 41 *Rebroadcasts:* Rebroadcasts KUCV(FM) Lincoln 100%
1800 N. 33rd St., Lincoln, NE 68501
(402) 472-3611; *Fax:* (402) 472-2403
netnebraska.org/radio
radio@netnebraska.org
License: Norfolk, Madison County, NE held by Nebraska Educational Telecommunications Commission
Nat'l Network: NPR; APM; PRI; *Regional Network:* NET Radio
Hrs. of News Programming: news progmg 45 hrs wkly; *No. News Employees:* 8; *Target Audience:* General.
Mark Leonard, General Manager
Nancy Finken, Station Manager/Programming Director
Susan Dinsmore, Marketing Specialist
Dennis Kellogg, News Director
Stacey Decker, Engineering Dir
William Stibor, Music Director
Jeff Smith,Operations Coordinator

WJAG
07-27-1922; 780 kHz AM; *Hrs Open:* Sunrise-sunset; 1 kw-D, NDD; N42 1 54 W97 29 47
Mailing Address: P. O. Box 789, 309 Braasch Avenue, Norfolk, NE 68701 US
Second Address: 309 Braasch Ave., Norfolk, NE 68701
(402) 371-0780; *Fax:* (402) 371-6303
www.wjag.com
License: Norfolk, NE held by WJAG Inc.
Group Owner: WJAG Inc.
Nat'l Network: ABC; ESPN Radio; *Wire Services:* AP
Format: News, News/Talk, 84, Talk; *Hrs. of News Programming:* news progmg 10 hrs wkly; *No. News Employees:* 2; *Target Audience:* 35-64; info-oriented
Bradley Hughes, Operations Dir
Sally Lewis, General Sales Mgr
Michael Nissen, Programming Director
Stephanie Hoff, Promotions Manager
Jim Curry, News Director
Susan Risinger, Farm Director
Jeffrey Steffen, Operations Manager
Joe Tjaden, Sports Commentator

***KLSB**
91.7 MHz FM; 8 kw; Ant 454 ft; N42 04 54 W97 48 55
Box 159, Rural Hall, NC
(605) 868-0525
License: Norfolk, Madison County, NE held by Church Planters of America.

Danny Hawkins, President

North Platte

KELN
02-01-1979; 97.1 MHz FM; *Hrs Open:* 24; 100 kw; 459 ft.; N41 14 20 W100 41 43
2703 Hall St., Suite 13, Hays, KS 67601 US
(785) 625-4000
www.northplattepost.com
License: North Platte, Lincoln County, NE held by Eagle Communications Inc.
Group Owner: Eagle Communications Group; (acq 1982)
Wire Services: AP
Arbitron Metro Market: North Platte, NE; *Format:* Contemporary Hits/Top 40; *Hrs. of News Programming:* news progmg one hr wkly; *No. News Employees:* 1; *Target Audience:* 21-44; Young adults; *Adv. Rates:* same asKOOQ
Scott Boomer, Operations Dir
Travis Kohlrus, General Manager
Mark Goff, Chief Engineer

***KJLT**
07-01-1957; 970 kHz AM; *Hrs Open:* Sunrise-sunset
Mailing Address: P. O. Box 709, North Platte, NE 69103 US
Second Address: 201 S. Bailey Ave., North Platte, NE 69101
(308) 532-5515
www.kjlt.org
kjlt@kjlt.org
License: North Platte, NE held by Tri-State Broadcasting Assn. Inc.
Nat'l Network: Moody; Salem Radio Network; *Wire Services:* NOAA Weather; AP
Format: Christian *Special Programming:* Sp one hr wkly; *Target Audience:* General; families
John Townsend, President
John L. Townsend, Programming Director
Gary Hofer, Chief Engineer

***KJLT-FM**
09-24-1979; 94.9 MHz FM; *Hrs Open:* 24; 100 kw; 755 ft.; N40 59 49 W100 52 47
Mailing Address: P.O. Box 709, North Platte, NE 69103 US
Second Address: 201 S. Bailey Ave., North Platte, NE 69101
(308) 532-5515
www.kjlt.org
License: North Platte, Lincoln County, NE held by Tri-State Broadcasting Assn. Inc.
Nat'l Network: Moody; Salem Radio Network; *Wire Services:* AP
Format: Adult Contemp, Gospel, 74; *Target Audience:* General; young adults
John Townsend, President
Todd Nelson, General Manager

KODY
07-05-1930; 1240 kHz AM; 1 kw-U, ND1; N41 9 14 W100 46 23
1001 Farnum-On-The-Mall, Omaha, NE 69102 US
(308) 532-3344; *Fax:* (308) 534-6651
info@kodyradio.com
License: North Platte, NE held by Armada Media-McCook Inc.
Group Owner: Armada Media Corp.; (acq 5-16-2008; grpsl)
Nat'l Network: CBS; Moody; Westwood One; *Nat'l Reps:* Katz Radio
Format: News, News/Talk, 86; *Target Audience:* 25 plus; middle to upper income
Chris Bernier, President/Chief Executive Officer
Rob Mandeville, General Manager/General Sales Manager

KOOQ
01-01-1966; 1410 kHz AM; *Hrs Open:* 24; 5 kw-D, DAN; 0.5 kw-N, DAN; N41 10 30 W100 45 7
2703 Hall St., Suite 13, Hays, KS 67601 US
(785) 625-4000
www.northplattepost.com
License: North Platte, NE held by Eagle Communications Inc.
Group Owner: Eagle Communications Group
Nat'l Network: ESPN Radio
Format: Sports; *Hrs. of News Programming:* news prmrg one hour/week; *No. News Employees:* 1; *Target Audience:* 18-45; males; *Adv. Rates:* 16; 15; 15; 12
Scott Boomer, Travis Kohlrus
Mark Goff, Chief Engineer

***KPNE-FM**
07-01-1991; 91.7 MHz FM; *Hrs Open:* 24; 16.5 kw horiz, 81 kw vert; 843 ft; N41 01 21 W101 09 13 *Rebroadcasts:* Rebroadcasts KUCV(FM) Lincoln 100%
Mailing Address: 1800 N. 33rd St., Lincoln, NE 68501
Second Address: NE
(402) 472-3611; *Fax:* (402) 472-2403
netnebraska.org
radio@netnebraska.org
License: North Platte, Lincoln County, NE held by Nebraska Educational Telecommunications Commission
Nat'l Network: NPR; APM; PRI; *Regional Network:* NET Radio
Hrs. of News Programming: 45 hrs wkly; *No. News Employees:* 8; *Target Audience:* General
Rod Bates, General Manager
Nancy Finken, Station Manager
Susan Dinsmore, General Sales Mgr
Nancy Finken, Programming Director
Mary Jane Winquest, Promotions Manager
Dennis Kellogg, News Director
Stacey Decker, Engineering Dir
William Stibor, Music Director
Jeff Smith, Operations

KXNP
06-07-1982; 103.5 MHz FM; *Hrs Open:* 24; 100 kw; 479 ft.; N41 12 49 W100 43 48
305 E 4th Street, PO Box 1085, Omaha, NE 68101 US
(308) 532-3344; *Fax:* (308) 534-6651
www.tlama.com
License: North Platte, Lincoln County, NE held by Armada Media-McCook Inc.
Group Owner: Armada Media Corp.; (acq 5-16-2008; grpsl)
Nat'l Network: Jones Radio Networks
Arbitron Metro Market: North Platte, NE; *Format:* Country
Robert Mandeville, General Manager

***KFJS**
07-16-2012; 90.1 MHz FM; 1400 w; 421 ft; N41 12 13 W100 43 58
13326 A Street, Omaha, NE
(402) 571-0200
www.spiritcatholicradio.com
kvss@kvss.com
License: North Platte, Lincoln County, NE
Group Owner: Vss Catholic Communications
Jim Carroll, Executive Director
Bruce McGregor, Program Director
Bernie Schaefer, Development Director

O'Neill

KBRX
11-01-1955; 1350 kHz AM; *Hrs Open:* 24; 1 kw-D, ND2; 0.044 kw-N, ND2; N42 27 34 W98 39 23
Mailing Address: 250 North Jefferson St., PO Box 150, O'Neill, NE 68763 US
Second Address: 251 N. Jefferson St., O'Neill, NE
(402) 336-1612; *Fax:* (402) 336-3585
www.kbrx.com
License: O'Neill, NE held by Ranchland Broadcasting Co. Inc.
Nat'l Network: ABC; *Regional Network:* Brownfield; *Wire Services:* AP
Format: Classic Rock *Special Programming:* Farm 12 hrs, Ger 6 hrs wkly; *Hrs. of News Programming:* news progmg 25 hrs wkly; *No. News Employees:* 1; *Target Audience:* 25-65.; *Adv. Rates:* 14; 14; 14; 14
Gilbert Poese, President
Scott Poese, General Manager

KBRX-FM
12-01-1973; 102.9 MHz FM; *Hrs Open:* 24; 100 kw; Ant 500 ft; N42 26 06 W98 33 39
Box 150, 251 N. Jefferson, O'Neill, NE 68763
(402) 336-1612; *Fax:* (402) 336-3585
www.kbrx.com
scott@kbrx.com
License: O'Neill, Holt County, NE held by Ranchland Broadcasting Co. Inc.
Nat'l Network: ABC; *Regional Network:* Brownfield; *Wire Services:* AP
Population Served: 45,000; *No. News Employees:* 1; *Target Audience:* 25-60.; *Adv. Rates:* 17; 17; 17; 13
Gil Poese, President
Scott Poese, General Manager
Scott Poese, General Sales Mgr

Ogallala

KMCX-FM
01-01-1975; 106.5 MHz FM; *Hrs Open:* 24; 100 kw; 315 ft.; N41 8 2 W101 41 42
113 W. 4th St., Ogallala, NE 69153 US
(308) 284-3633; *Fax:* (308) 284-3517
License: Ogallala, Keith County, NE held by Capstar TX LLC
Group Owner: iHeartMedia; (acq 8-30-2000; grpsl).
Arbitron Metro Market: Ogallala, NE; *Format:* Country *Special Programming:* Farm 2 hrs wkly; *Hrs. of News Programming:* news progmg 10 hrs wkly; *No. News Employees:* 1; *Target Audience:* 25-54; general
Susan Jones, Traffic Manager

KOGA
01-23-1955; 930 kHz AM; 5 kw-D, DA2; 0.5 kw-N, DA2; N41 8 32 W101 42 48
Mailing Address: P.O. Box 509, Ogallala, NE 69153 US
Second Address: 113 W. 4th St., Ogallala, NE 69153
(308) 284-3633; *Fax:* (308) 284-3517
www.930koga.com
License: Ogallala, NE held by Capstar TX LLC
Group Owner: iHeartMedia; (acq 8-30-00; grpsl).
Arbitron Metro Market: Ogallala, NE; *Format:* Oldies *Special Programming:* Farm 10 hrs wkly
Taylor Walet, Regional Market President

KOGA-FM
11-01-1978; 99.7 MHz FM; *Hrs Open:* 24; 100 kw; 804 ft.; N41 3 50 W101 20 16
113 West 4th Street, Ogallala, NE 69153 US
(308) 284-3633; *Fax:* (308) 284-3517
www.997thelake.com
License: Ogallala, Keith County, NE held by Capstar TX LLC
Group Owner: iHeartMedia
Arbitron Metro Market: Ogallala, NE; *Format:* Rock/AOR
Taylor Walet, Regional Market President

Omaha

KOTK
03-02-1957; 1420 kHz AM; 1 kw-D, DA2; 0.33 kw-N, DA2; N41 11 59 W95 54 34
P.O. Box 693, Milwaukee, WI 53201 US
(402) 422-1600; *Fax:* (402) 422-1602
www.salem.cc
License: Omaha, NE held by Pennsylvania Media Associates Inc.
Group Owner: Salem Communications Corp.; (acq 12-7-2005; $900,000)

Nat'l Reps: Salem
Arbitron Metro Market: Omaha, NB; *Format:* Religious
Mike Shane, Operations Dir
Greg Vogt, General Manager
Jim Leedham, Chief Engineer

KCRO
03-01-1922; 660 kHz AM
11717 Burt Street, Omaha, NE 68154 US
(402) 422-1600; *Fax:* (402) 422-1602
www.kcro.com
License: Omaha, NE held by Salem Media of Illinois LLC.
Group Owner: Salem Communications Corp.; (acq 9-1-2005; $3.1 million).
Nat'l Network: Salem Radio Network; *Nat'l Reps:* Salem
Arbitron Metro Market: Omaha-Council Bluffs, NE-IA; *Format:* Christian, Talk
Greg Vogt, General Manager
Sue Garrett, General Sales Mgr
Jim Leedham, Chief Engineer
Peggy Holzapfel, Business Manager

KISO
10-21-1983; 96.1 MHz FM; *Hrs Open:* 24; 82 kw; 1,086 ft.; N41 18 32 W96 1 33
5010 Underwood Ave., Omaha, NE 68132 US
(402) 561-2000
www.961kissonline.com
License: Omaha, Douglas County, NE held by Clear Channel Broadcasting Licenses Inc.
Group Owner: iHeartMedia; (acq 10-9-2003; $10.5 million).
Population Served: 537,700; *Arbitron Metro Market:* Omaha, NE; *Format:* Contemporary Hits/Top 40; *Hrs. of News Programming:* news progmg one hr wkly; *No. News Employees:* 1
Taylor Walet, Regional Market President
Erik Johnson, Programming Director

KEZO-FM
05-15-1961; 92.3 MHz FM; 95 kw; 1184 ft.; N41 18 16 W96 1 41
11128 John Galt Blvd., Suite 192, Omaha, NE 68137 US
(402) 592-5300; *Fax:* (402) 592-6605
www.z92.com
info@z92.com
License: Omaha, Douglas County, NE held by Journal Broadcast Corp.
Group Owner: Journal Communications Inc.; (acq 11-29-94; $9 million with co-located AM;
Arbitron Metro Market: Omaha-Council Bluffs, NE-IA; *Format:* Rock/AOR
Rob Burton, General Manager
Ros Mercio, Sales Manager
Jim Spector, Programming Director
Brian Delehant, Promotions Director
Susie Copenhaver, News Director

KFAB
01-01-1924; 1110 kHz AM; *Hrs Open:* 24; 50 kw-D, DAN; 50 kw-N, DAN; N41 7 11 W96 0 6
5010 Underwood Ave., Omaha, NE 68132 US
(402) 561-2000
www.kfab.com
License: Omaha, Douglas County, NE held by Capstar TX LLC
Group Owner: iHeartMedia; (acq 8-30-2000; grpsl)
Nat'l Network: ABC; *Nat'l Reps:* Christal
Arbitron Metro Market: Omaha-Council Bluffs, NE-IA; *Format:* News, News/Talk, 86 *Special Programming:* Farm 5 hrs wkly; *Hrs. of News Programming:* news progmg 6 hrs wkly; *No. News Employees:* 3; *Target Audience:* 35-64.
Taylor Walet, Regional Market President
Gary Sadlemyer, Programming Director
Tom Stanton, News Director

KGBI-FM
05-17-1966; 100.7 MHz FM; *Hrs Open:* 24; 100 kw; 1014 ft.; N41 18 40 W96 1 37
11717 Burt Street, Omaha, NE 68514 US
(402) 422-1600; *Fax:* (402) 422-1602
www.thefishomaha.com
License: Omaha, Douglas County, NE held by Pennsylvania Media Associates Inc.
Group Owner: Salem Communications Corp.; (acq 1-31-2005; $8 million).
Nat'l Reps: Salem
Arbitron Metro Market: Omaha,NE; *Format:* Christian; *Hrs. of News Programming:* news progmg 28 hrs wkly; *No. News Employees:* 1; *Target Audience:* 25-54; conservative, Evangelical
Mike Shane, Operations Dir
Greg Vogt, General Manager
Jim Leedham, Chief Engineer

KGOR
01-01-1959; 99.9 MHz FM; *Hrs Open:* 24; 110 kw; 1,214 ft.; N41 18 24.6 W96 1 36.6
5010 Underwood Ave., Omaha, NE 68132 US
(402) 561-2000
www.kgor.com
License: Omaha, Douglas County, NE held by Capstar TX LLC
Group Owner: iHeartMedia
Arbitron Metro Market: Omaha-Council, NE; *Format:* Contemporary Hits/Top 40; *No. News Employees:* 1; *Target Audience:* 35-54.
Rad Messick, Programming Director
Tom Stanton, News Director

***KIOS-FM**
09-15-1969; 91.5 MHz FM; 55 kw; 554 ft.; N41 17 15 W95 59 37
3230 Burt Street, Omaha, NE 68131 US
(402) 557-2777; *Fax:* (402) 557-2559
www.kios.org
License: Omaha, Douglas County, NE held by Douglas County School District 001.
Nat'l Network: NPR; PRI; *Wire Services:* AP
Arbitron Metro Market: Omaha-Council Bluffs, NE-IA; *Format:* Jazz, News *Special Programming:* Local Jazz 15 hrs wkly; *No. News Employees:* 1
Molly Nicklin, Operations Dir
Bob Coate, Station Manager
Edward McGrath, General Sales Mgr
Katie Knapp, News Director
Richard Dennis, Chief Engineer
Mike Jacobs, Music Director

KOIL
03-01-1925; 1290 kHz AM; *Hrs Open:* 24; 5 kw-U, DA-N; N41 11 20 W96 00 21
5011 Capitol Ave., Omaha, NE 68102
(402) 342-2000; *Fax:* (402) 346-5748
www.mighty1290koil.com
License: Omaha, Douglas County, NE held by Waitt Omaha LLC.
Group Owner: Waitt Omaha LLC; (acq 1-7-2002; grpsl)
Nat'l Network: ABC; Fox News Radio; Jones Radio Networks; Premiere Radio Networks; Talk Radio Network; *Nat'l Reps:* Katz Radio
Population Served: 346,929; *Arbitron Metro Market:* Omaha-Council Bluffs, NE-IA; *Target Audience:* General.; *Adv. Rates:* 100; 100; 100; 45
Mark Todd, Operations Dir
Jim McKernan, General Manager
Rhonda Gerrard, General Sales Mgr
Neil Nelkin, Programming Director
Terry Leahy, News Director
Darwin Stinton, Chief Engineer
Tim Marshall, Sales Manager
Lori Storz,Traffic Manager

KKCD
08-11-1990; 105.9 MHz FM; *Hrs Open:* 24; 50 kw; 479 ft.; N41 12 4 W95 57 12
1074 Mockingbird Drive, Omaha, NE 68127 US
(402) 592-5300; *Fax:* (402) 331-1348
www.cd1059.com
info@cd1059.com
License: Omaha, Douglas County, NE held by Journal Broadcast Corp.
Group Owner: Journal Communications Inc.; (acq 2-95; $3.55 million;
Nat'l Network: AP Network News
Arbitron Metro Market: Omaha, NE; *Format:* Classic Rock *Special Programming:* Jazz 4 hrs, blues one hr, reggae one hr wkly; *Hrs. of News Programming:* news progmg 10 hrs wkly; *No. News Employees:* 1 *TargetAudience:* 25-54.
Chris Sehring, Vice President/General Manager
Ros Mercio, General Sales Mgr
Jim Spector, Programming Director
Brian Delehant, Promotions Manager
John Gaeta, Chief Engineer

KOMJ
03-01-1942; 1490 kHz AM; *Hrs Open:* 24
P.O. Box 693, Milwaukee, WI 53201 US
(402) 592-5300,(402) 898-5300; *Fax:* (402) 331-1348
License: Omaha, NE held by Cochise Broadcasting LLC.
Group Owner: Cochise Broadcasting LLC; (acq 3-27-2007; $500,000)
Arbitron Metro Market: Omaha-Council Bluffs, NE-IA; *Format:* Adult Contemp; *No. News Employees:* 1; *Target Audience:* 18-49.

KSRZ
05-12-1972; 104.5 MHz FM; 98 kw; 1088 ft.; N41 18 16 W96 1 41
P.O. Box 693, Milwaukee, WI 53201 US
(402) 592-5300; *Fax:* (402) 592-6605
www.104star.com
info@104star.com
License: Omaha, Douglas County, NE held by Journal Broadcast Corp.
Group Owner: Journal Communications Inc.; (acq 1-98; $5.475 million with co-located AM)
Arbitron Metro Market: Omaha, NE; *Format:* Adult Contemp
Steve Wexler, Vice President of Operations
Jim Timm, Station Manager
Kris Christiansen, General Sales Mgr
Kurt Owens, Programming Director
Brian Delehant, Promotions Manager
Kathi Knutson, News Director
John Gaeta, ChiefEngineer
Dave Swan, Music Director

***KVNO**
08-27-1972; 90.7 MHz FM; *Hrs Open:* 24; 8.9 kw; 646 ft.; N41 18 25 W96 1 37
60th and Dodge Street, Engg 202, Omaha, NE 68182 US
(402) 559-5866; *Fax:* (402) 554-2440
www.kvno.org
License: Omaha, Douglas County, NE held by University of Nebraska Board of Regents.
Arbitron Metro Market: Omaha-Council Bluffs, NE-IA; *Format:* Talk; *Hrs. of News Programming:* news progmg 2.5 hrs wkly; *No. News Employees:* 1; *Target Audience:* General.
Chris Hopp, Operations Dir
Robert Franklin, General Manager/Director of Media Operations
James Arey, Programming Director
Ben Rasmussen, Music Director
Dave Kline, Chief Engineer
Dana Buckingham, Assistant General Manager
FrankVacek, Engineering Services Manager
Gina Saitta, Membership Manager
Ja'Nel Johnson, News Director
Kim Balkovec, Marketing Specialist

KXSP
04-02-1923; 590 kHz AM; *Hrs Open:* 24; 5 kw-U, ND1; N41 19 0 W95 59 52
10714 Mockingbird Drive, Omaha, NE 68127 US
(402) 592-5300; *Fax:* (402) 331-1348
www.bigsports590.com
info@bigsports590.com
License: Omaha, NE held by Journal Broadcast Corp.
Group Owner: Journal Communications Inc.; (acq 10-26-98 with co-located FM).
Arbitron Metro Market: Omaha-Council Bluffs, NE-IA; *Format:* Sports; *No. News Employees:* 4; *Target Audience:* General.
Steve Wexler, Vice President of Operations
Ros Mercio, General Sales Mgr
Bill Jensen, News Director
John Gaeta, Chief Engineer
Cheryl Brye, Traffic Manager

KQCH
01-01-1959; 94.1 MHz FM; *Hrs Open:* 24; 95 kw; 1184 ft.; N41 18 16 W96 1 41
10714 Mockingbird Drive, Omaha, NE 68127 US
(402) 592-5300; *Fax:* (402) 331-1348
License: Omaha, Douglas County, NE
Group Owner: Journal Communications Inc.
Wire Services: Weather Wire; Reuters
Arbitron Metro Market: Omaha-Council Bluffs, NE-IA; *Format:* Adult Contemp; *Target Audience:* 25-54.
Kris Christiansen, Sales Manager
Mark Todd, Programming Director
Brian Delehant, Promotions Manager
Peter Shinn, Farm Director
Bill Jensen, News Reporter

***KYFG**
88.9 MHz FM; 0.085 kw horiz, 1.5 kw vert; 482 ft.; N41 18 47 W96 0 36 *Rebroadcasts:* Rebroadcasts WYFQ(AM) Charlotte 100%
P.O. Box 7300, Charlotte, NC 28241
(800) 888-7077
www.bbnradio.org
bbn@bbnmedia.org
License: Omaha, Douglas County, NE held by Bible Broadcasting Network Inc.
Group Owner: Bible Broadcasting Network
Population Served: 168,528; *Arbitron Metro Market:* Omaha, NE; *Format:* Christian, Religious
Lowell Davey, President
Jason Padgett, Operations Manager

Orchard

*KGRD

06-14-1987; 105.3 MHz FM; *Hrs Open:* 24; 100 kw; 502 ft.; N42 20 45 W98 25 5
128 S. 4th Street, O'Neill, NE 68763 US
(402) 336-3886
www.kgrd.org
License: Orchard, Antelope County, NE held by The Praise Network Inc.
Nat'l Network: Salem Radio Network; *Wire Services:* AP
Format: Christian, Religious; *Hrs. of News Programming:* News progmg 10 hrs wkly; *Target Audience:* 35-54.
Lloyd Mintzmeyer, President
Todd Gunnarson, Station Manager
Bill Taylor, Programming Director

Ord

KNLV

07-15-1965; 1060 kHz AM; *Hrs Open:* 24
205 South 16th Street, Ord, NE 68862 US
(308) 728-3263; *Fax:* (308) 728-3264
www.knlvradio.com
knlv@yahoo.com
License: Ord, NE held by Sandhills Advertising Corp.
Nat'l Network: ABC; *Wire Services:* AP
Format: Oldies *Special Programming:* Farm 8 hrs, Pol/Czeck/Bohemian 4 hrs wkly; *Target Audience:* 25-64.
Johnnie James, General Manager
Gene McCoy, General Sales Mgr
Jeannie Neidhardt, Promotions Manager
Johnnie James, News Director
Randy Faaborg, Chief Engineer
Kristen Miller, Traffic Manager

KNLV-FM

07-10-1981; 103.9 MHz FM; *Hrs Open:* 24; 30 kw; Ant 638 ft; N41 34 17 W98 55 21
205 S. 16th St., Ord, NE 68862
(308) 728-3263; *Fax:* (308) 728-3264
www.knlvradio.com
License: Ord, Valley County, NE held by Sandhills Advertising Corp.
Nat'l Network: ABC; *Wire Services:* AP
Population Served: 7,200 *Special Programming:* Farm 8 hours; *Target Audience:* 18-54.; *Adv. Rates:* 14; 14; 13; 6
Johnnie James, Station Manager
Gene McCoy, General Sales Mgr
Johnnie James rdt, Promotions Manager
Val Lane, Chief Engineer
Amber Whited, Traffic Manager

Overton

*KHZY

01-01-2007; 99.3 MHz FM; 100 kw; 751 ft.; N40 41 49 W99 47 16 *Rebroadcasts:* Rebroadcasts KROA(FM) Grand Island 100%
US
(816) 233-5773; *Fax:* (816) 233-5777
www.mybridgeradio.net
License: Overton, Dawson County, NE held by My Bridge Radio
Group Owner: My Bridge Radio
Arbitron Metro Market: Overton, NE; *Format:* Christian
Stanley A. Parker, President
Brian KC Jones, General Manager

Papillion

*KVSS

01-09-1999; 102.7 MHz FM; *Hrs Open:* 24; 46.1 kw; 1,343 ft.; N41 4 15.9 W96 13 31.2
13326 A St., Omaha, NE 68144
(402) 571-0200; *Fax:* (402) 571-0833
www.spiritcatholicradio.com
License: Papillion, Sarpy County, NE held by VSS Catholic Communications Inc.
Group Owner: Spirit Catholic Radio
Arbitron Metro Market: Omaha-Lincoln, NE; *Format:* Christian; *Target Audience:* General.
Bruce McGregor, Programming Director
Kelly Miller, Marketing and Promotions Manager
Mark Voris, Chief Engineer
Jim Carroll, Executive Director
Bernie Schaefer, Development Director
Mary Jorgensen, Director of Underwriting
MattWillkom, Program Producer

Paxton

KZTL

01-01-2007; 93.5 MHz FM; 100 kw; 753 ft.; N41 3 50 W101 20 16
305 East 4th Street, North Platte, NE 69101 US
(308) 534-0935; *Fax:* (308) 535-9100
License: Paxton, Keith County, NE held by Legacy Communications LLC.
Group Owner: Legacy Communications LLC; (acq 8-14-2007; $475,000 for CP with CP for KRNP(FM) Sutherland)
Arbitron Metro Market: Paxton, NE; *Format:* Country
Chris Bernier, President/Chief Executive Officer
Rob Mandeville, General Manager

Pierce

KEXL

11-05-2009; 97.5 MHz FM; 6.5 kw; 463 ft.; N42 19 17 W97 25 40
3009 Braasch Avenue, PO Box 789, Norfolk, NE 68702 US
(402)371-0780; *Fax:* (402)371-6303
www.literock97.com
License: Pierce, Pierce County, NE held by WJAG Inc
Group Owner: WJAG Inc.
Format: Light Rock
Bradley Hughes, General Manager

Plattsmouth

KMMQ

10-26-1970; 1020 kHz AM; *Hrs Open:* Sunrise-sunset
5011 Capitol Avenue, Omaha, NE 68132 US
(402) 977-9267; *Fax:* (402) 342-2000
License: Plattsmouth, NE held by Waitt Omaha LLC.
Group Owner: NRG Media
Nat'l Network: Radio Disney
Arbitron Metro Market: Omaha-Council Bluffs, NE-IA; *Format:* Children
Mary Quass, President/Chief Executive Officer
Andy Ruback, General Manager
Stacie McElligott, Sales Manager
Jose Munoz, Programming Director
Becca Sautter, Traffic Manager

KOPW

07-01-1993; 106.9 MHz FM; *Hrs Open:* 24; 25 kw; 328 ft.; N41 9 18 W95 45 42
5011 Capitol Avenue, Omaha, NE 68132 US
(402) 342-2000; *Fax:* (402) 346-5748
power1069fm.com
License: Plattsmouth, Cass County, NE held by Platte Broadcasting Co. Inc.
Group Owner: Waitt Omaha LLC
Nat'l Reps: Katz Radio
Arbitron Metro Market: Omaha-Council Bluffs, NE-IA; *Format:* Contemporary Hits/Top 40; *Target Audience:* 18-34; gen
Mary Quass, President/Chief Executive Officer
Andy Ruback, General Manager
Stacie McElligott, General Sales Mgr
Greg Lemons, Programming Director
Becca Sautter, Traffic Manager

Ponca

*KFHC

01-01-2008; 88.1 MHz FM; 2.28 kw horiz, 8.8 kw vert; 417 ft.; N42 27 48 W96 37 1.9
705 Douglas Street, Sioux City, IA 51101 US
(712) 224-5342; *Fax:* (712) 224-5345
www.fhcradio.com
License: Ponca, Dixon County, NE held by St. Gabriel Communications Ltd.
Nat'l Network: EWTN Radio
Arbitron Metro Market: Sioux City, IA; *Format:* Christian
John Fitzsimmons, President
James Cameron, Operations Dir
Ted Warren, General Manager
Renee Gonzalez, General Sales Mgr
John Wolpert, Vice-President
Paul Wolpert, Treasurer/Secretary

Ralston

*KMLV

07-21-2001; 88.1 MHz FM; *Hrs Open:* 24; 59 kw; 1280 ft.; N41 18 40 W96 1 37 *Rebroadcasts:* Rebroadcasts KLVR(FM) Middletown, CA 100%
1425 N. Market Blvd, Suite 9, Sacramento, CA 95834 US
(916) 251-1600; *Fax:* (916) 251-1650
www.klove.com
klove@klove.com
License: Ralston, Douglas County, NE held by Educational Media Foundation.
Group Owner: EMF Broadcasting
Nat'l Network: K-Love
Arbitron Metro Market: Omaha, NE; *Format:* Christian; *Target Audience:* 25-44; Judeo Christian, female
Mike Novak, President
Jennifer Lohman, Operations Dir

Ravenna

KKJK

06-01-2006; 103.1 MHz FM; 100 kw; 640 ft.; N40 48 57 W98 46 18
Mailing Address: US
Second Address: 3205 W. North Front St., Grand Island, NE 68803
(308) 381-1430; *Fax:* (308) 382-6701
www.2dayfm1031.com
License: Ravenna, Buffalo County, NE held by Community Radio Inc.
Arbitron Metro Market: Ravenna, NE; *Format:* Rock/AOR
Alan Usher, General Manager
Adam Jurgens, Programming Director

Sargent

KBRY

01-01-2008; 92.1 MHz FM; 0.11 kw; 52 ft.; N41 38 29 W99 22 12
1309 Road 11, York, NE 68467 US
(402) 362-4433; *Fax:* (402) 362-6501
License: Sargent, Custer County, NE held by Mid Nebraska Broadcasting LLC
Arbitron Metro Market: Sargent, NE; *Format:* Christian
Mark G. Jensen, President

Scottsbluff

KNEB

01-01-1948; 960 kHz AM; *Hrs Open:* 5 AM-1 AM
P.O. Box 239, Scottsbluff, NE 69363 US
(308) 632-7121; *Fax:* (308) 635-1079
www.kneb.com
License: Scottsbluff, NE held by Nebraska Rural Radio Association.
Group Owner: Nebraska Rural Radio Association; (acq 8-1-84)
Format: News, News/Talk, 86, Country *Special Programming:* Farm 18 hrs, Sp 5 hrs wkly; *No. News Employees:* 2; *Target Audience:* 18 plus.; *Adv. Rates:* 70; 70; 50; 25
Bill Boyer, Operations Dir
Craig Larson, General Manager
Kendra Feather, General Sales Mgr
Dennis Ernest, Programming Director
Les Proctor, Chief Engineer
Leslie Smith, Farm Director

KNEB-FM

12-25-1960; 94.1 MHz FM; *Hrs Open:* 5 AM-1 AM; 100 kw; 679 ft.; N41 42 4 W103 40 49
P.O. Box 239, Scottsbluff, NE 69363 US
(308) 632-7121; *Fax:* (308) 635-1079
License: Scottsbluff, Scotts Bluff County, NE
Group Owner: Nebraska Rural Radio Association
Format: Country, Agriculture; *Adv. Rates:* Same as AM
Bill Boyer, Operations Dir
Craig Larson, General Manager
Kendra Feather, General Sales Mgr
Dennis Ernest, Programming Director
Les Proctor, Chief Engineer
Leslie Smith, Farm Director

KOLT

02-15-1930; 1320 kHz AM; *Hrs Open:* 24; 5 kw-D, 1 kw-N, DA-N; N41 51 37 W103 41 53
Mailing Address: Box 1263, Scottsbluff, NE 69363
Second Address: 2002 Char Ave., Scottsbluff, NE 69361
(308) 632-5667; *Fax:* (308) 635-1905
www.koltam.com
License: Scottsbluff, Scotts Bluff County, NE held by Armada Media
Group Owner: Armada Media
Nat'l Network: ESPN Radio
Population Served: 15,000
Chris Bernier, President/Chief Executive Officer
Rob Mandeville, General Manager

*KLJV

02-20-2003; 88.3 MHz FM; *Hrs Open:* 24; 0.39 kw; 781 ft.; N41 50 21 W103 49 53
US

(800) 525-5683; *Fax:* (916) 251-1650
www.klove.com
klove@klove.com
License: Scottsbluff, Scotts Bluff County, NE held by Educational Media Foundation.
Group Owner: EMF Broadcasting
Nat'l Network: K-Love
Arbitron Metro Market: Scottsbluff, NE; *Format:* Christian; *No. News Employees:* 13; *Target Audience:* 25-44.
Darrell Chambliss, Chairman
Mike Novak, President and CEO
Jennifer Lohman, Operations Dir
David Pierce, Chief Creative Officer and Programming Director
Ed Lenane, News Director
Sam Wallington, Engineering Dir
Marya Morgan, NewsReporter
Richard Hunt, News Reporter
Alan Mason, Chief Operating Officer
Dan Antonelli, Chief Business Development Officer
Eric Moser, Chief Financial Officer
Brian Burger, Vice President of Human Resources

*KDAI

01-01-2008; 89.1 MHz FM; 1.4 kw; 781 ft.; N41 50 21 W103 49 53 *Rebroadcasts:* Rebroadcasts KLRD(FM) Yucaipa, CA 100%
US
(800) 877-5600; *Fax:* (916) 251-1650
www.air1.com
info@air1.com
License: Scottsbluff, Scotts Bluff County, NE held by Educational Media Foundation.
Group Owner: EMF Broadcasting; (acq 7-23-2007; grpsl)
Nat'l Network: Air 1
Arbitron Metro Market: Scottsbluff, NE; *Format:* Alternative, Christian
Mike Novak, President

Seward

KZKX

11-12-1976; 96.9 MHz FM; 100 kw; 610 ft; N41 07 26 W96 50 03
3800 Cornhusker Hwy., Lincoln, NE 68504-1533 US
(402) 466-1234; *Fax:* (402) 467-4095
www.kzkc.com
jp@kzkc.com
License: Seward, Seward County, NE held by Digity 3E License, LLC
Group Owner: Digity Media, LLC
Population Served: 262,341; *Arbitron Metro Market:* Lincoln, NE; *Format:* Country; *Target Audience:* 25-54.
Joy Patten, General Manager
Katie Philippi, General Sales Mgr
Scott Kaye, Programming Director

Sidney

KSID

06-02-1952; 1340 kHz AM; *Hrs Open:* 24; 1 kw-U, ND1; N41 7 50 W102 58 15
P. O. Box 37, Sidney, NE 69162 US
(308) 254-5803; *Fax:* (308) 254-5901
www.ksibradio.com
License: Sidney, NE held by KSID Radio Inc.
Arbitron Metro Market: Sidney, NE; *Format:* Country *Special Programming:* Farm 5 hrs wkly; *Target Audience:* General.; *Adv. Rates:* 15; 15; 15; na
Suzy Ernest, General Manager
Lana Butts, General Sales Mgr

KSID-FM

09-13-1974; 98.7 MHz FM; 62 kw; 371 ft.; N41 11 3 W103 11 37
P. O. Box 37, Sidney, NE 69162 US
(308) 254-5803; *Fax:* (308) 254-5901
www.ksibradio.com
License: Sidney, Cheyenne County, NE
Arbitron Metro Market: Sidney, NE; *Format:* Adult Contemp
Suzy Ernest, General Manager
Lana Butts, General Sales Mgr
Dave Collins, News Director

South Sioux City

KSFT-FM

01-01-1997; 107.1 MHz FM; *Hrs Open:* 24; 2.3 kw; 325 ft.; N42 32 16 W96 26 58
1113 Nebraska Street, Sioux City, IA 51102 US
(712) 258-6740; *Fax:* (712) 252-2430
www.1071kissfm.com
License: South Sioux City, Dakota County, NE held by AMFM Radio Licenses LLC.
Group Owner: iHeartMedia; (acq 10-1-2002; grpsl)
Nat'l Reps: Katz Radio
Arbitron Metro Market: Sioux City, IA; *Format:* Contemporary Hits/Top 40; *Target Audience:* 12-35.
Rob Powers, Senior Vice President of Operations
Kelli Erickson, Market President

Superior

KRFS

03-17-1959; 1600 kHz AM; *Hrs Open:* 6 AM-sunset; 0.5 kw-D, ND1; 0.044 kw-N, ND1; N40 1 30 W98 4 38
630 West 8th Street, Superior, NE 68978 US
(402) 879-4741; *Fax:* (402) 879-4741
www.krfsfm.com
krfsfm@yahoo.com
License: Superior, NE held by CK Broadcasting Inc.
Regional Network: Brownfield
Format: Adult Contemp *Special Programming:* Farm 5 hrs, gospel 3 hrs, relg 3 hrs wkly; *Hrs. of News Programming:* News progmg 11 hrs wkly; *Target Audience:* 25-55; general; *Adv. Rates:* 6; 6; 6; na
Cory Kopsa, General Manager
Marvin Hoffman, Chief Engineer

KRFS-FM

02-25-1977; 103.9 MHz FM; *Hrs Open:* 24; 6 kw; 220 ft.; N40 6 20 W98 6 20
630 West 8th Street, Superior, NE 68978 US
(402) 879-4741; *Fax:* (402) 879-4741
www.krfsfm.com
krfs@yahoo.com
License: Superior, Nuckolls County, NE
Regional Network: Brownfield
Format: Country
Cory Kopsa, News Director

Sutherland

KRNP

01-01-2007; 100.7 MHz FM; 100 kw; 753 ft.; N41 3 50 W101 20 16
305 East 4th Street, North Platte, NE 69101 US
(308) 532-5767; *Fax:* (308) 535-9100
License: Sutherland, Lincoln County, NE held by Armada Media
Group Owner: Armada Media
Arbitron Metro Market: Sutherland, NE
Chris Bernier, President/Chief Executive Officer
Rob Mandeville, General Manager

Terrytown

KCMI

03-01-1981; 96.9 MHz FM; *Hrs Open:* 24; 100 kw; 692 ft.; N41 42 8 W103 41 0
209 East 15th Street, Scottsbluff, NE 69361 US
(308) 632-5264; *Fax:* (308) 635-0104
www.kcmifm.org
info@kcmifm.org
License: Terrytown, Scotts Bluff County, NE held by Christian Media Inc.
Nat'l Network: USA; *Regional Network:* Brownfield
Arbitron Metro Market: Terrytown, NE; *Format:* Religious *Special Programming:* Class 4 hrs wkly; *Hrs. of News Programming:* News progmg 12 hrs wkly; *Target Audience:* 25 plus.; *Adv. Rates:* 9; 9; 9; 9
Glenn Hascall, General Manager
Gary Almquist, General Sales Mgr
Lorraine Brown, News Director
Sherry Kaiser, Clerk/librarian, Cross Times content editor and co
Lorraine Brown, Office Staff
Elnora Bauer, Office Staff

KOAQ

06-15-1961; 690 kHz AM; *Hrs Open:* 24; 1 kw-D, DA2; 0.065 kw-N, DA2; N41 50 55 W103 40 2
US
(308) 532-5767; *Fax:* (308) 635-1905
info@hometownfamilyradio.com
License: Terrytown, NE held by Armada Media
Group Owner: Armada Media
Format: Oldies; *Target Audience:* 25-54; Baby Boomers
Chris Bernier, President/Chief Executive Officer
Rob Mandeville, General Manager

Valentine

KVSH

03-06-1961; 940 kHz AM; *Hrs Open:* 16; 5 kw-D, ND1; 0.019 kw-N, ND1; N42 51 54 W100 31 7
126 W. 3rd Street, Valentine, NE 69201 US
(402) 376-2400; *Fax:* (402) 376-2402
www.kvsh.com
License: Valentine, NE held by Heart City Radio Corp.
Wire Services: AP
Arbitron Metro Market: Valentine, NE; *Format:* Country; *Hrs. of News Programming:* news progmg 24 hrs wkly; *No. News Employees:* 1; *Target Audience:* 35-60; general
Dave Otradovsky, President/General Manager
Mike Burge, Programming Director
Kerri, Traffic

*KKNL

89.3 MHz FM; 0.25 kw; 184 ft.; N42 53 22 W100 33 15
P.O. Box 3206, Tupelo, MS 38803 US
(662) 844-8888; *Fax:* (662) 842-6791
www.afr.net
faq@afa.net
License: Valentine, Cherry County, NE held by American Family Association.
Group Owner: American Family Radio
Arbitron Metro Market: Valentine, NE; *Format:* Christian
Tim Wildmon, President
Donald Wildmon, Founder
Buddy Smith, Sr VP
Ed Vitagliano, Exec VP
Randy Sharp, Director Of Special Projects
Meeke Addison, Director Of Communications
Abraham Hamilton III, General Counsel

*KMBV

90.7 MHz FM; 0.68 kw; 105 ft.; N42 53 17 W100 33 11
Rebroadcasts: Rebroadcasts KROA(FM) Grand Island 100%
US
(402) 477-1090
www.mybridgeradio.net
License: Valentine, Cherry County, NE held by My Bridge Radio
Group Owner: My Bridge Radio
Arbitron Metro Market: Valentine, NE; *Format:* Country
Stanley Parker, General Manager

Waverly

*KRKR

03-06-1975; 95.1 MHz FM; *Hrs Open:* 24; 50 kw; 276 ft.; N40 58 48 W96 41 46 *Rebroadcasts:* Rebroadcasts KROA(FM) Grand Island 100%
Box 30345, Lincoln, NE 68503 US
(402) 770-4616
License: Waverly, Douglas County, NE held by My Bridge Radio
Group Owner: My Bridge Radio
Arbitron Metro Market: Lincoln, NE; *Format:* Adult Contemp, Christian; *Hrs. of News Programming:* news progmg 2 hrs wkly; *No. News Employees:* 1; *Target Audience:* 25-54.
Stanley A. Parker, President
Rob Powers, Operations/Programming Director
Kevin Wolf, Promotions Manager
Kelli Erickson, Market Manager

Wayne

KCTY

03-18-1968; 1590 kHz AM; *Hrs Open:* 24; 2.5 kw-D, 47 w-N, DA-2 & 250 w FM; 300 ft.; N42 14 03 W97 03 19
P.O. Box 413, Wayne, NE 68787
(402) 375-3700; *Fax:* (402) 375-5402
www.waynedailynews.com
dkelly@sio.midco.net
License: Wayne, Wayne County, NE held by Wayne Radio Works LLC.
Group Owner: David M. Kelly; (acq 5-30-2008; $450,000 with KCTY(FM) Wayne)
Nat'l Network: Townhall (SRN); *Nat'l Reps:* Regional Reps; *Wire Services:* AP
Population Served: 40,000 *Special Programming:* Farm 5 hrs wkly; *Hrs. of News Programming:* news progmg 15 hrs wkly; *No. News Employees:* 1; *Target Audience:* 30-64.; *Adv. Rates:* 8; 8; 8; 7
David M. Kelly, Owner
David Kelly, General Sales Mgr
Dan Baddorf, Programming Director
Aaron Sheffler, News Director
Tony Wortman, Chief Engineer

*KWSC

10-13-1971; 91.9 MHz FM; 0.32 kw horiz; 95 ft.; N42 14 30 W97 0 48
1111 Main Street, Wayne, NE 68787 US
(402) 375-7561
License: Wayne, Wayne County, NE held by Wayne State College.
Nat'l Network: Westwood One

Format: Alternative, Rock/AOR *Special Programming:* Black 4 hrs, jazz 2 hrs, heavy metal 2 hrs, blues 2 hrs wkly; *Target Audience:* 18 plus.
Frank Venturo, General Manager

West Point

KTIC
03-17-1985; 840 kHz AM; *Hrs Open:* Sunrise-sunset; 5 kw-D, NDD; N41 47 6 W96 40 39
1011 North Lincoln Street, West Point, NE 68788 US
(402) 372-5423; *Fax:* (402) 372-5425
www.kticam.com
jayt@kticradio.com
License: West Point, NE held by Nebraska Rural Radio Association.
Group Owner: Nebraska Rural Radio Association; (acq 8-1-97; $1.5 million with co-located FM)
Nat'l Network: ABC; *Regional Network:* Nebraska Public Radio; *Nat'l Reps:* Katz Radio *Regional Reps:* Neb. Pub.; *Wire Services:* AP
Arbitron Metro Market: West Point, NE; *Format:* Country, News; *Hrs. of News Programming:* news progmg 20 hrs wkly; *No. News Employees:* 1; *Target Audience:* General; farmers, ranchers, stockmen and all involved inagri-business; *Adv. Rates:* 70; 70; 70; na
Craig Larson, Chief Executive Officer
Jay Thouvenell, General Manager
Judy Mauch, General Sales Mgr
J.D. Gibbs, Programming Director
Rick Vincent, News Director
Rod Zeigler, Engineering Dir
Chad Moyer, Farm Director
RichardSterling, Music Director
Tom McMahon, Sports Director
Jodi Frye, Traffic Manager

KTIC-FM
08-01-1988; 107.9 MHz FM; *Hrs Open:* 18; 33 kw; 597 ft.; N41 52 53 W97 0 58
1011 North Lincoln Street, West Point, NE 68788 US
(402) 372-5423; *Fax:* (402) 372-5425
www.kticradio.com
License: West Point, Cuming County, NE
Group Owner: Nebraska Rural Radio Association; (Acq 1997)
Nat'l Network: ABC
Arbitron Metro Market: West Point, NE; *Format:* Country *Special Programming:* Farm 10 hrs wkly; *Hrs. of News Programming:* news progmg 12 hrs wkly; *No. News Employees:* 1; *Target Audience:* 25-49; generalaudience, adults; *Adv. Rates:* 21; 21; 21; 8
Craig Larson, Chief Executive Officer
Jay Thouvenell, General Manager
Randy Koenen, General Sales Mgr
Chris Recker, Programming Director
Rick Vincent, News Director
Rod Zeigler, Engineering Dir
Tom McMahon, Sports Director
Karen Benne, Traffic Manager
Judy Mauch, Sales Manager
Tom Goodwin, Production/ Continuity Director

Wilber

***KFLV**
03-01-2001; 89.9 MHz FM; *Hrs Open:* 24; 5.8 kw; 515 ft.; N40 31 6 W96 46 6
1425 N Market Blvd., Suite 9, Sacramento, CA 95834 US
(707) 538-9236; *Fax:* (707) 538-9246
www.klove.com
klove@klove.com
License: Wilber, Saline County, NE held by Educational Media Foundation.
Group Owner: EMF Broadcasting
Nat'l Network: K-Love
Arbitron Metro Market: Wilber, NE; *Format:* Christian; *No. News Employees:* 2; *Target Audience:* 25-44; Judeo-Christian, female
Darrell Chambliss, Chairman
Mike Novak, President/CEO
Alan Mason, COO
Eric Moser, CFO
David Pierce, Chief Creative Officer
D. Kevin Blair, Secretary/General Counsel

Winnebago

KSUX
06-01-1990; 105.7 MHz FM; *Hrs Open:* 24; 50 kw; 463 ft.; N42 20 33 W96 31 13
2000 Indian Hills Drive, Sioux City, IA 51104 US
(712) 274-1057
www.ksux.com
License: Winnebago, Thurston County, NE held by Powell Broadcasting Co.
Group Owner: Powell Broadcasting Co. Inc.; (acq 1996; $3.8 million with KSCJ(AM) Sioux City, IA)
Arbitron Metro Market: Sioux City, IA; *Format:* Country; *No. News Employees:* 2; *Target Audience:* 25-54; female average to above average income, secondary male; *Adv. Rates:* 30; 30; 30; 25
Dennis Bullock, General Manager
Dave Grosenheider, General Sales Mgr
Tony Michaels, Programming Director
Tony Michaels, Promotions Manager

York

KAWL
09-01-1954; 1370 kHz AM; *Hrs Open:* 24; 0.5 kw-D, ND1; 0.176 kw-N, ND1; N40 50 30 W97 35 16
1309 Road 11, York, NE 68467 US
(402) 362-4433; *Fax:* (402) 362-6501
www.ktmxfm.com
License: York, NE held by MWB Broadcasting LLC
Nat'l Network: ABC; *Regional Network:* Mid-America Ag; *Nat'l Reps:* Interep; *Wire Services:* AP
Arbitron Metro Market: York, NB; *Format:* Oldies, Talk *Special Programming:* Farm 7 hrs, women 3 hrs wkly; *Hrs. of News Programming:* news progmg 10 hrs wkly; *No. News Employees:* 1; *Target Audience:* 20 plus;general; *Adv. Rates:* 20; 16; 18; 10
Mark Jensen, General Manager
Donna Panritz, General Sales Mgr
Bob Bedient, News Director
Linda Korbelik, Sales
Brenda Janzen, Traffic Manager

KTMX
09-01-1970; 104.9 MHz FM; *Hrs Open:* 24; 13 kw; 974 ft.; N40 45 7 W97 27 4
1309 Road 11, York, NE 68467 US
(402) 362-4433; *Fax:* (402) 362-6501
www.ktmxfm.com
License: York, York County, NE held by MWB Broadcasting LLC
Nat'l Network: ABC; *Nat'l Reps:* McGavren Guild
Arbitron Metro Market: York, NE; *Format:* Adult Contemp; *Hrs. of News Programming:* news progmg 3 hrs wkly; *No. News Employees:* 1; *Target Audience:* 25-54; general; *Adv. Rates:* Same as AM
Mary Fay Jackson, President

***KEIS**
90.3 MHz FM; 1.6 kw; 217 ft.; N40 49 41.8 W97 42 59.1
US
(864) 297-0216; *Fax:* (864) 297-0344
networkofglory.com
info@networkofglory.org
License: York, York County, NE held by Network of Glory Inc.
Arbitron Metro Market: York, NE; *Format:* Christian, Gospel
Lola Richey, President

Nevada

Amargosa Valley

KPKK
01-01-2003; 101.1 MHz FM; 51 kw horiz; -49 ft.; N36 38 33 W116 23 53
2570 S Eastern Avenue, Las Vegas, NV 89109 US
(312) 204-9900; *Fax:* (312) 587-9466
License: Amargosa Valley, Nye County, NV held by Sky Media L.L.C.
Arbitron Metro Market: Chicago, IL
Bruce Buzil, General Manager

Boulder City

KCYE
04-01-1989; 102.7 MHz FM; *Hrs Open:* 24; 96 kw; 1978 ft.; N35 56 46 W115 2 34
2920 S. Durango Dr., Las Vegas, NV 89117 US
(702) 730-0300; *Fax:* (702) 736-8447
www.1027thecoyote.com
License: Boulder City, Clark County, NV held by Beasley Media Group LLC
Group Owner: Beasley Broadcast Group Inc.; (acq 1-31-2001; grpsl).
Arbitron Metro Market: Las Vegas, NV; *Format:* Country; *Hrs. of News Programming:* News progmg one hr wkly; *Target Audience:* 35-64.; *Adv. Rates:* 100; 110; 100; 75
Tom Humm, General Manager
Lee Grau, General Sales Mgr
Kris Daniels, Programming Director
Shayla Martinez, Promotions and Marketing Manager
Lamar Smith, Chief Engineer
Cory Cuddeback, Director of Sales/National Sales Manager
SandyEllis, Digital Director
Jesus Novo, Director of Business Affiars/Human Resources

Bunkerville

KYLI
96.7 MHz FM; 93 kw; Ant 1,886 ft; N36 49 53 W114 26 12
980 N. Michigan Ave., Suite 1880, Chicago, IL
(312) 204-9900
License: Bunkerville, Clark County, NV held by LKCM RG Licenses LLC
Group Owner: LKCM Radio Group LP; (acq 9-1-2010; $2 million)
Arbitron Metro Market: Las Vegas, NV
Bruce Buzil, General Manager

Cal-Nev-Ari

KVAL
01-01-2008; 104.9 MHz FM; 0.1 kw; 2372 ft.; N35 15 8 W114 44 58
US
(928) 855-1051; *Fax:* (928) 855-7996
www.maddogwireless.net
License: Cal-Nev-Ari, Clark County, NV held by Smoke and Mirrors LLC.
Group Owner: Smoke and Mirrors LLC
Arbitron Metro Market: Cal-Nev-Ari, NV; *Format:* Adult Contemp
Kim Turner, Operations Manager
Scott Gosselin, Vice President

Carlin

KHIX
03-01-2001; 96.7 MHz FM; *Hrs Open:* 24; 12.6 kw; 1598 ft.; N40 55 18 W115 50 58
1750 Manzanita Drive, Elko, NV 89801 US
(775) 777-1196; *Fax:* (775) 777-9587
ken@rubyradio.fm
License: Carlin, Elko County, NV held by Ruby Radio Corp.
Group Owner: Ruby Radio Corp.; (acq 6-15-2003; $475,000 for CP)
Format: Adult Contemp
Scott Gosselin, Vice President
Kim Turner, Operations Dir
Alene Sutherland, Vice President

Carson City

KBUL
01-01-1985; 98.1 MHz FM; *Hrs Open:* 24; 72 kw; 2293 ft.; N39 15 32 W119 42 6
595 E. Plumb Ln., Reno, NV 89502 US
(775) 789-6700; *Fax:* (775) 789-6767
www.nashfm981.com
License: Carson City, NV held by Radio License Holding CBC, LCC
Group Owner: Cumulus Media Inc.; (acq 5-29-92).
Arbitron Metro Market: Reno, Nevada; *Format:* Country; *Hrs. of News Programming:* news progmg 4 hrs wkly; *No. News Employees:* 1; *Target Audience:* 25-54.
Jennifer Odom, General Sales Mgr
Bob Richards, Programming Director
Jay Schell, Promotions Manager

***KNIS**
10-15-1989; 91.3 MHz FM; *Hrs Open:* 24; 67 kw; 2165 ft.; N39 15 30 W119 42 36
PO Box 21888, Carson City, NV 89721 US
(775) 883-5647
www.pilgrimradio.com
License: Carson City, NV held by Western Inspirational Broadcasters Inc.
Group Owner: Western Inspirational Broadcasters Inc.; (acq 10-15-89).
Arbitron Metro Market: Reno, NV; *Format:* Christian; *No. News Employees:* 1
Tom Hesse, General Manager

KCMY
05-14-1955; 1300 kHz AM; 5 kw-D, DAN; 0.5 kw-N, DAN; N39 9 59 W119 43 37
1960 Idaho Street, Carson City, NV 89701 US
(775) 884-8000; *Fax:* (775) 882-3961
License: Carson City, NV held by The Evans Broadcast Co. Inc.
Nat'l Network: Fox News Radio
Arbitron Metro Market: Carson City; *Format:* Country; *Hrs. of News Programming:* news progmg 16 hrs wkly; *No. News Employees:* 2; *Target Audience:* 35-54.; *Adv. Rates:* 18; 16; 18; 8
Jerry Evans, General Manager

KOLC
06-27-1972; 97.3 MHz FM; *Hrs Open:* 24; 87 kw; 2,112 ft; N39 15 21 W119 42 37
961 Matley Lane, Suite 120, Reno, NV 89502
(775) 829-1964; *Fax:* (775) 825-3183
www.tencountry.com
info@tencountry.com
License: Carson City, Carson City County, NV held by Americom Limited Partnership
Group Owner: Americom Broadcasting; (acq 4-27-98; grpsl).
Population Served: 285,000; *Arbitron Metro Market:* Reno, NV; *Format:* Country; *Hrs. of News Programming:* news progmg 2 hrs wkly; *No. News Employees:* 1; *Target Audience:* 18-34; women
Tom Quinn, President
Lori Heeren, Vice President and General Manager
Heather Forcier, National Regional Sales Director
Carrie Carano, Local Sales Manager
Teresa Estabrook, Local Sales Manager

Crystal

KHWG-FM
100.1 MHz FM; 4 kw; Ant 827 ft; N36 27 45 W116 03 33
250 W. Nopah Vista Ave., Pahrump, NV 89060
License: Crystal, Nye County, NV held by President of the Liberty Church and His Successors
Population Served: 8,777; *Arbitron Metro Market:* Crystal, NV
Keily Miller, General Manager

Dayton

KTHX-FM
06-10-1983; 100.1 MHz FM; *Hrs Open:* 24; 12 kw; 2162 ft.; N39 15 34 W119 42 21
300 E Second Street, Reno, NV 89501 US
(775) 333-0123; *Fax:* (775) 322-7361
www.myradiox.com
License: Dayton, Lyon County, NV held by Wilks License Co.-Reno LLC.
Group Owner: Wilks Broadcast Group LLC; (acq 9-29-2005; grpsl).
Nat'l Network: ABC
Arbitron Metro Market: Reno, NV; *Format:* Triple A; *Hrs. of News Programming:* News progmg 2 hrs wkly; *Target Audience:* 18-49; upscale, high income & educated
Dave Herold, Music Director

Elko

KELK
12-07-1948; 1240 kHz AM; *Hrs Open:* 24; 1 kw-U, ND1; N40 50 37 W115 44 58
1800 Idaho Street, Elko, NV 89801 US
(775) 738-1240; *Fax:* (775) 753-5556
elkoradio.com
elkoradio@elkoradio.com
License: Elko, NV held by Elko Broadcasting Co.
Arbitron Metro Market: Elko, NV; *Format:* Adult Contemp; *Hrs. of News Programming:* news progmg 25 hrs wkly; *No. News Employees:* 1; *Target Audience:* 25-54; upscale, family oriented, white collar workforce *Adv.Rates:* 18; 18; 18; 18
Paul Gardner, President
Tyler Gunter, General Manager

KLKO
05-01-1982; 93.7 MHz FM; 4.5 kw; Ant 1,538 ft; N40 55 20 W115 50 56
1800 Idaho St., Elko, NV 89802
(775) 738-1240; *Fax:* (775) 753-5556
elkoradio.com
License: Elko, Elko County, NV held by Elko Broadcasting Co.
Population Served: 35,000 *Hrs. of News Programming:* news progmg 5 hrs wkly; *No. News Employees:* 1; *Adv. Rates:* 20; 20; 20; na
Paul Gardner, President
Lori Gilbert, News Director
Eric Allen, National Sales Manager
Marya Morgan, News Reporter
Richard Hunt, News Reporter
Karen Johnson, News Reporter

***KNCC**
01-01-1992; 91.5 MHz FM; *Hrs Open:* 24; 0.054 kw; 2041 ft.; N40 53 41 W115 37 44 *Rebroadcasts:* Rebroadcasts *KUNR(FM) Reno
University of Nv, Reno, Kunr, Mail Stop 294, Reno, NV 89557 US
(775) 327-5867; *Fax:* (775) 738-8771
www.kunr.org
License: Elko, Elko County, NV held by Great Basin College.
Format: Big Band, Jazz, 60 *Special Programming:* Public radio
Dave Stipech, General Manager
Ahh Gray, News Producer
AJ Kenneson, Office Manager

KRJC
10-01-1981; 95.3 MHz FM; *Hrs Open:* 24; 25 kw; 774 ft.; N40 54 35 W115 49 5
1250 Lamoille Highway, Elko, NV 89801 US
(775) 738-9895; *Fax:* (775) 753-8085
www.krjc.com
License: Elko, Elko County, NV held by Holiday Broadcasting of Elko.
Group Owner: Carlson Communications International
Nat'l Network: AP Network News; *Wire Services:* AP
Format: Country; *Hrs. of News Programming:* news progmg 4 hrs wkly; *No. News Employees:* 1; *Target Audience:* 25-54.; *Adv. Rates:* 15; 15; 15; 13
Jennifer Sprout, Station Manager
Julie Hughes, Programming Director

KTSN
11-01-1996; 1340 kHz AM; 1 kw-U, ND1; N40 52 8 W115 43 9
1859 Manzanita Drive, Elko, NV 89801 US
(775) 738-9895; *Fax:* (775) 753-9895
License: Elko, NV held by Humboldt Broadcasting LLC.
Group Owner: Carlson Communications International
Arbitron Metro Market: Elko, NV; *Format:* News, Sports, 86
Jennifer Sprout, Station Manager
Kristi Agenbroad, General Sales Mgr

KZBI
01-01-2005; 94.5 MHz FM; 36 kw; Ant 1,519 ft; N40 55 18 W115 50 58
1750 Manzanita Drive, Suite 1, Elko, NV
(775) 777-1196; *Fax:* (775) 777-9587
License: Elko, Elko County, NV held by Ruby Radio Corp.
Group Owner: Ruby Radio Corp.; (acq 10-25-2005; exchange for KCLS(
Ken Sutherland, President
Alene Sutherland, Operations Dir
Ken Sutherland, General Manager
Ken Sutherland, Programming Director

KZMG
97.5 MHz FM; 85 kw horiz; 1558 ft.; N40 55 18 W115 50 58
100 W. Lyndale Avenue, Suite B, Helena, MY 59601 US
(406) 438-6353
License: Elko, Elko County, NV held by JLD Media LLC
Arbitron Metro Market: Elko, NV
Kevin Terry, Manager

***KTQQ**
88.1 MHz FM; 230 w; 1811 ft; N40 42 01 W115 54 07
PO Box 716, Ridgecrest, CA 93556
(760)375-2355
www.radio74.net
ejwitzel@mchsi.com
License: Elko, Elko County, NV held by Radio 74 Internationale
Ron Myers, Founder

Ely

KDSS
12-22-1984; 92.7 MHz FM; *Hrs Open:* 24; 32 kw; 961 ft.; N39 14 46 W114 55 39
501 Aultman St., # 208, Ely, NV 89301 US
(775) 289-6474; *Fax:* (775) 289-6531
License: Ely, White Pine County, NV held by Coates Broadcasting Inc.
Nat'l Network: Jones Radio Networks
Format: Country *Special Programming:* Nashville News, fishing, outdoor; *Hrs. of News Programming:* News progmg 10 hrs wkly; *Target Audience:* 18-64; older demographics, new & classic C&W listeners
Samantha Coates, President
Karen Livingston, General Manager
Jim Liebsack, Chief Engineer

KELY
07-08-1950; 1230 kHz AM; *Hrs Open:* 24; 0.25 kw-U, ND1; N39 15 45 W114 51 46
807 Avenue F, Ely, NV 89301 US
(775) 289-2077; *Fax:* (775) 289-6997
www.kely1230.com
License: Ely, NV held by Ely Radio LLC.
Group Owner: Ely Radio LLC; (acq 3-21-2006; $140,000)
Arbitron Metro Market: Ely, NV; *Format:* Talk *Special Programming:* Local High School Sports; *Hrs. of News Programming:* 5; *No. News Employees:* 1; *Target Audience:* 35 plus.; *Adv. Rates:* 20; 10; 10; 11
Wyatt Cox, General Manager

Fallon

KRNG
07-04-1997; 101.3 MHz FM; *Hrs Open:* 24; 1.65 kw; Ant 2,207 ft; N39 42 30 W119 10 16
Mailing Address: Box 490, Wadsworth, NV 89442
Second Address: 360 Pyramid St., Wadsworth, NV 89442
(775) 575-7777
www.renegaderadio.org
email@renegaderadio.org
License: Fallon, Churchill County, NV held by Sierra Nevada Christian Music Association Inc.
Nat'l Reps: McGavren Guild
Population Served: 200,000; *Arbitron Metro Market:* Reno, NV; *Target Audience:* 12-35; youth, young adults; *Adv. Rates:* 9.33; 9.33; 9.33; 5
Rev. Karry Crites, President
William Bauer PhD., Operations Dir

KVLV
05-09-1957; 980 kHz AM; *Hrs Open:* 6 AM-sunset; 5 kw-D, NDD; N39 29 47 W118 48 50
1155 Gummow Drive, Fallon, NV 89406 US
(702) 423-2243; *Fax:* (702) 423-8889
www.kvlvradio.com
kvlv@phonewave.net
License: Fallon, NV held by Lahontan Valley Broadcasting LLC.
Nat'l Network: ABC
Arbitron Metro Market: Fallon, NV; *Format:* Country; *Hrs. of News Programming:* News progmg 10 hrs wkly; *Target Audience:* 25 plus.; *Adv. Rates:* 15; 15; 15; na.
Mike McGinness, General Manager

KKTV
11-26-1966; 99.5 MHz FM; *Hrs Open:* 24; 6 kw; Ant 250 ft; N39 29 47 W118 48 50
1155 Gummow Dr., Fallon, NV 89406
(775) 423-2243; *Fax:* (775) 423-8889
www.kvlvradio.com
License: Fallon, Churchill County, NV held by Lahontan Valley Broadcasting LLC.
Nat'l Network: AP Radio
Population Served: 40,000 *Hrs. of News Programming:* News progmg 10 hrs wkly; *Adv. Rates:* 15; 15; 15; 15
Mike McGinness, General Manager
Lynn Pearce, Chief Operator

KHWG
06-01-2005; 750 kHz AM
US
(775) 428-1764; *Fax:* (775) 428-1765
License: Fallon, NV held by Media Enterprises Inc.
Arbitron Metro Market: Fallon, NV; *Format:* Country
Keily Miller, President
Dee Gregory, General Manager
Bill Kling, Station/Production Manager
Lisa DeWitt, Sales Manager
Dizzy Don Roberts, Music Director

***KQNV**
89.9 MHz FM; 0.6 kw; 33 ft.; N39 27 42 W118 42 38
US
(702) 731-5588; *Fax:* (702) 731-5851
License: Fallon, Churchill County, NV held by American Educational Broadcasting Inc.
Arbitron Metro Market: Fallon, NV
Carl Auel, President

KKTU-FM
99.3 MHz FM; 6000 w; 249 ft; N39 29 26 W118 49 08
1155 Gummow Drive, Fallon, NV 89406
(775) 423-2243
License: Fallon, Churchill County, NV
Group Owner: Lahontan Valley Broadcasting Company LLC

Gardnerville-Minden

KKFT
09-19-1985; 99.1 MHz FM; *Hrs Open:* 24; 410 w; Ant 2,006 ft; N39 15 34 W119 42 21
1960 Idaho St., Carson City, NV 89423
(775) 884-8000; *Fax:* (775) 882-3961
www.991fmtalk.com
info@991fmtalk.com
License: Gardnerville-Minden, Douglas County, NV held by Jerry Evans
Nat'l Network: Fox News Radio

RADIO - U.S.

Population Served: 600,000 *Hrs. of News Programming:* news progmg 24 hrs wkly; *No. News Employees:* 2; *Target Audience:* 25-54; btfl people; *Adv. Rates:* 32; 30; 32; 14
Jerry Evans, CEO
David Reichert, General Sales Mgr
Jen Austin, Assistant

Gerlach

*KLAP
89.5 MHz FM; 0.13 kw; -325 ft.; N40 39 6 W119 21 14
PO Box 181, Cedarville, CA 96104 US
(775) 279-6677
info@kdup.org
License: Gerlach, Washoe County, NV held by OpenSkyRadio Corp.
Arbitron Metro Market: Gerlach, NV; *Format:* Country
Jeffrey Cotton, General Manager

*KFBR
01-20-2011; 91.5 MHz FM; 600 w; 46 ft; N40 39 07 W119 21 25
320 Main Street, PO Box 224, Gerlach, NV
(775)557-2900
www.blackrockdesert.org
info@blackrockdesert.org
License: Gerlach, Washoe County, NV
Group Owner: Friends Of Black Rock High Rock Inc.

Stephanie McKnight, Program Volunteer and Manager
Michael Myers, Information Center Manager

Hawthorne

*KQMC
90.1 MHz FM; 0.48 kw vert; 3140 ft.; N38 27 28 W118 45 52
401 Spring Street, Nevada City, CA 95959 US
(702) 731-5588
www.kqmc.com
License: Hawthorne, Mineral County, NV held by American Educational Broadcasting Inc.
Arbitron Metro Market: Hawthorne, NV; *Format:* Classical
Lee Amundsen, General Manager

*KAVB
12-01-2007; 98.7 MHz FM; *Hrs Open:* 24; 0.1 kw; -853 ft.; N38 31 26.6 W118 37 18
PO Box 26590, Santa Ana, CA 92799 US
(213) 627-8711; *Fax:* (213) 627-8712
www.almavision.com
info@almavision.com
License: Hawthorne, Mineral County, NV held by Alma Vision Hispanic Network Inc.
Arbitron Metro Market: Hawthorne, NV; *Format:* Spanish
Juan Caamano, President

*KELC
91.9 MHz FM; 0.5 kw; -853 ft.; N38 31 26.6 W118 37 18 US
(702) 731-5588; *Fax:* (702) 731-5851
License: Hawthorne, Mineral County, NV held by American Educational Broadcasting Inc.
Arbitron Metro Market: Hawthorne, NV
Carl Auel, President

Henderson

KQLL
05-01-1956; 1280 kHz AM; *Hrs Open:* 24; 5 kw-D, 28 w-N; N36 03 13 W114 58 30
150 Spectrum Blvd., Las Vegas, NV 89104
(702) 258-0285; *Fax:* (702) 732-3060
License: Henderson, Clark County, NV held by S & R Broadcasting Inc.
Nat'l Reps: Lotus Entravision Reps LLC
Population Served: 160,000; *Arbitron Metro Market:* Las Vegas, NV; *Target Audience:* General; Hispanic, above-average income, high home ownership; *Adv. Rates:* 40; 40; 40; 40
Paul Ruttan, President
Scott Gentry, General Manager
Eric Bonnici, General Sales Mgr
David Allen, Programming Director
Jeremy Dawes, News Director
Marcus Dayley, Web Manager

KMXB
07-01-1996; 94.1 MHz FM; 100 kW; 95 ft.; N36 0 30 W115 0 20
7255 S Tenaya Way, Suite 100, Las Vegas, NV 89113 USA
(702) 257-9400; *Fax:* (702) 257-2936
www.mix941.fm
License: Henderson, Clark County, NV held by CBS Radio Stations Inc.
Group Owner: CBS Radio; (acq 11-13-98; grpsl)
Nat'l Network: CBS Radio
Arbitron Metro Market: Las Vegas, NV; *Format:* Adult Contemp; *No. News Employees:* 1; *Target Audience:* 18-49; female; *Adv. Rates:* 300; 275; 260; 100
Tony Perlongo, General Sales Mgr
Cat Thomas, VP of Programming
Katrina Llapitan, Promotions Manager

KXNT-FM
11-28-1982; 100.5 MHz FM; *Hrs Open:* 24; 100 kw; 1,105 ft; N36 00 28 W115 00 20
7255 South Tenaya Way, Suite 100, Las Vegas, NV 89113
(702) 889-5100; *Fax:* (702) 257-2936
jack@jackbaby.com
License: Henderson, Clark County, NV held by Infinity Radio Inc.
Group Owner: CBS Radio; (acq 11-13-98; grpsl).
Nat'l Network: CBS Radio; *Nat'l Reps:* Katz Radio
Arbitron Metro Market: Las Vegas, NV; *Hrs. of News Programming:* News progmg one hr wkly; *Target Audience:* 25-54.; *Adv. Rates:* 180; 180; 180; 65
Dan Mason, Chief Executive Officer
Chad Forster, Operations Dir
Brenda Brown, General Sales Mgr
Andrew Paul, Programming Director
Kyle Helmick, Promotions Manager
Jerry McKenna, Senior Vice President/Market Manager

KWNR
07-18-1972; 95.5 MHz FM; 92 kw; 1161 ft.; N36 0 31 W115 0 22
2880 Meade Avenue, Suite 250, Las Vegas, NV 89102 US
(702) 238-7300; *Fax:* (702) 732-4890
www.955thebull.com
License: Henderson, Clark County, NV held by Citicasters Licenses Inc.
Group Owner: iHeartMedia; (acq 1999; grpsl).
Arbitron Metro Market: Henderson, NV; *Format:* Country; *Target Audience:* 18-54.
Chris Pickett, Senior Vice President of Programming
Glynn Alan, Regional Market President
Joel Gable, Senior Vice President of Sales
Jojo Turnbeaugh, Programming Director
Joanna DiNatale, Director of Marketing and Public Relations

KXQQ
09-28-2015; 100.5 MHz FM; 100 kW; 105 ft.; N36 0 30 W115 0 20
NV USA
www.q100vegas.com
License: Henderson, Clark County, NV held by CBS Radio Stations Inc.
Group Owner: CBS Radio
Arbitron Metro Market: Las Vegas, NV; *Format:* Adult Contemp; *Target Audience:* 25-54

Incline Village

KRNO
07-01-1974; 106.9 MHz FM; *Hrs Open:* 24; 35 kw; 2989 ft.; N39 18 38 W119 53 1
961 Matley Lane, Suite 120, Reno, NV 89502 US
(775) 829-1964; *Fax:* (775) 825-3183
www.1069morefm.com
info@1069morefm.com
License: Incline Village, Washoe County, NV held by Americom Limited Partnership
Group Owner: Americom Broadcasting; (acq 4-16-98; grpsl).
Arbitron Metro Market: Reno, NV; *Format:* Adult Contemp; *Hrs. of News Programming:* news progmg 18 hrs wkly; *No. News Employees:* 1; *Target Audience:* 25-54; women; *Adv. Rates:* 12; 12; 12; na
Tom Quinn, President
Lori Heeren, Vice President and General Manager
Heather Forcier, National Regional Sales Director
Carrie Carano, Local Sales Manager
Teresa Estabrook, Local Sales Manager

Indian Springs

KRGT
11-22-2002; 99.3 MHz FM; *Hrs Open:* 24; 31 kw; 2,264 ft.; N36 19 28 W115 33 58
6767 W. Tropicana Ave., Suite 102, Las Vegas, NV 89103 US
(702) 284-6400; *Fax:* (702) 284-6403
www.univision.com
License: Indian Springs, Clark County, NV held by Univision Radio License Corp.
Group Owner: Univision Radio; (acq 9-22-2003; grpsl).
Arbitron Metro Market: Las Vegas, NV; *Format:* Spanish
Rene Morales, Vice President and General Manager
Mauricio Palacios, Local Sales Manager
Ratael Miramontes, Programming Director
Manny Garcia, Chief Engineer
Joe Reynolds, National Sales Manager

KUDD
01-01-2007; 105.1 MHz FM; 100 kw; 1952 ft.; N36 50 49 W113 29 28
50 W. Broadway, Suite 200, Salt Lake City, UT 84101 US
(801) 524-2600, (844) 649-1051
mix1051utah.com
mj@bwaymedia.com
License: Indian Springs, Washington County, NV held by Broadway Media LS, LLC
Group Owner: Broadway Media Group
Arbitron Metro Market: Hurricane, UT
Erik Goddard, General Sales Mgr
MJ, Programming Director

Jackpot

*KBSJ
91.3 MHz FM; 3.7 kw; 2464 ft.; N41 47 8 W114 50 22
1910 University Drive, Boise, ID 83725 US
(208) 426-3663; *Fax:* (208) 344-6631
www.boisestatepublicradio.org
boisestatepublicradio@boisestate.edu
License: Jackpot, Elko County, NV held by Idaho State Board of Education.
Arbitron Metro Market: Boise, OD; *Format:* Classical, Jazz
Erik Jones, Membership Manager
John Hess, General Manager
Kelly Balmer, Associate GM
Kira Parker, Senior Broadcast Engineer
Krista Doble, Business Manager

Las Vegas

KBAD
06-01-1953; 920 kHz AM
8755 West Flamingo Road, Las Vegas, NV 89147 US
(702) 876-1460; *Fax:* (702) 876-6685
www.lvsportsnetwork.com
lotussignup@yahoo.com
License: Las Vegas, NV held by Lotus Broadcasting Corp.
Group Owner: Lotus Communications Corp.; (acq 11-4-92; $1.42 million with co-located FM;
Nat'l Network: Fox Sports; *Nat'l Reps:* Interep
Arbitron Metro Market: Las Vegas, NV; *Format:* Sports; *Target Audience:* 18 plus.
Tony Bonnici, General Manager
Jesse Leeds, General Sales Mgr
Mitch Moss, Programming Director

*KCEP
10-01-1973; 88.1 MHz FM; *Hrs Open:* 24; 9.8 kw; 1194 ft.; N36 0 31 W115 0 22
330 West Washington Avenue, Las Vegas, NV 89106 US
(702) 648-0104; *Fax:* (702) 647-0803
License: Las Vegas, Clark County, NV held by Economic Opportunity Board of Clark County.
Arbitron Metro Market: Las Vegas, NV; *Format:* Black, Blues
Special Programming: Gospel 14 hrs, Jazz 12 hrs wkly; *Hrs. of News Programming:* News progmg 11 hrs wkly; *Target Audience:* 12-55; African-Americans
Diane Lubak, Business Manager
Craig Knight, Programming Director

KDWN
04-07-1975; 720 kHz AM; *Hrs Open:* 24; 50 kw-D, 50 kw-N
2920 S. Durango Dr., Las Vegas, NV 89117 US
(702) 730-0300; *Fax:* (702) 736-8447
www.kdwn.com
License: Las Vegas, Clark County, NV held by Beasley Media Group LLC
Group Owner: Beasley Broadcast Group Inc.; (acq 8-7-2006; $17 million).
Nat'l Network: Fox News Radio
Arbitron Metro Market: Las Vegas, NV *TV Affiliate:* .; *Format:* News, News/Talk, 86; *Target Audience:* 35-54.; *Adv. Rates:* 39; 33; 39; 22
Tom Humm, General Manager
Lee Grau, General Sales Mgr
John Shaffer, Programming Director
Shayla Martinez, Promotions and Marketing Manager
John Shaffer, News Director
Lamar Smith, Chief Engineer
Cory Cuddeback, Director ofSales
Sandy Ellis, Digital Director
Craig Davis, Local Sales Manager
Jesus Novo, Director of Business Affairs/Human Resources

KENO
01-01-1940; 1460 kHz AM; 10 kw-D, DA2; 0.62 kw-N, DA2; N36 11 25 W115 10 35
US
(702) 876-1460; *Fax:* (702) 876-6685
License: Las Vegas, NV held by Lotus Broadcasting Corp.
Group Owner: Lotus Communications Corp.; (acq 6-1-65)
Nat'l Network: ESPN Deportes; *Nat'l Reps:* Interep
Arbitron Metro Market: Las Vegas, NV; *Format:* Sports
Tony Bonnici, Vice President/General Manager
Jesse Leeds, General Sales Mgr

KWID
03-22-1963; 101.9 MHz FM; 47 kw; 1900 ft.; N35 56 44 W115 2 31
8755 West Flamingo Road, Las Vegas, NV 89147 US
(702) 876-1460; *Fax:* (702) 792-9018
License: Las Vegas, Clark County, NV held by Texas Lotus Corp.
Group Owner: Lotus Communications Corp.; (acq 7-29-2008; with KVMX(FM) Bakersfield, CA in exchange for KZEP-FM San Antonio, TX)
Arbitron Metro Market: Las Vegas, NV; *Format:* Spanish; *Target Audience:* 25-49.
Tony Bonnici, Vice President/General Manager
Jesse Leeds, General Sales Mgr

***KSOS**
07-18-1972; 90.5 MHz FM; *Hrs Open:* 24; 100 kw; 1270 ft.; N36 0 29 W115 0 20
2201 South 6th Street, Las Vegas, NV 89103 US
(702) 731-5452; *Fax:* (702) 731-1992
www.sosradio.net
info@sosradio.net
License: Las Vegas, Clark County, NV held by Faith Communications Corp.
Group Owner: Faith Communications Corp.; (acq 12-31-71).
Arbitron Metro Market: Las Vegas, NV; *Format:* Religious; *Hrs. of News Programming:* News progmg 5 hrs wkly; *Target Audience:* 25-44; young families
Brad Staley, CEO
Brad Staley, General Manager
Duane Luchsinger, Station Manager
Scott Herrold, Programming Director
Tim Hunt, Director of Network Engineering

KISF
03-01-1989; 103.5 MHz FM; 100 kw; 1,158 ft.; N36 0 29 W115 0 20
6767 W. Tropicana Ave., Suite 102, Las Vegas, NV 89103 US
(702) 284-6400; *Fax:* (702) 284-6403
www.univision.com
License: Las Vegas, Clark County, NV held by Univision Radio License Corp.
Group Owner: Univision Radio; (acq 9-22-2003; grpsl).
Arbitron Metro Market: Las Vegas, NV; *Format:* Tejano
Rene Morales, Vice President and General Manager
Manny Garcia, Chief Engineer
Joe Reynolds, National Sales Manager
Luis Zuniga, Sales

KKLZ
01-26-1984; 96.3 MHz FM; *Hrs Open:* 24; 100 kw; 1175 ft.; N36 0 29 W115 0 20
2920 S. Durango Dr., Las Vegas, NV 89117 US
(702) 730-0300; *Fax:* (702) 736-8447
www.963kklz.com
License: Las Vegas, Clark County, NV held by Beasley Media Group LLC
Group Owner: Beasley Broadcast Group Inc.; (acq 2-1-2001; grpsl)
Arbitron Metro Market: Las Vegas, NV; *Format:* Contemporary Hits/Top 40, Adult Contemp; *No. News Employees:* 1; *Target Audience:* 25-44; baby boomers
Tom Humm, General Manager
Lee Grau, General Sales Mgr
Mike O'Brian, Programming Director
Shayla Martinez, Promotions and Marketing Manager
Lamar Smith, Chief Engineer
Cory Cuddeback, Director of Sales/National Sales Manager
SandyEllis, Digital Director
Jesus Novo, Director of Business Affiars/Human Resources

KKVV
05-01-1990; 1060 kHz AM; *Hrs Open:* 24; 5 kw-D, ND1; 0.043 kw-N, ND1; N36 9 22 W115 15 24
3185 South Highland Drive, Suite 13, Las Vegas, NV 89109 US
(702) 731-5588; *Fax:* (702) 731-5851
www.kkvv.com
License: Las Vegas, NV held by Las Vegas Broadcasters Inc.
Nat'l Network: Salem Radio Network; *Nat'l Reps:* Salem
Arbitron Metro Market: Las Vegas, NV; *Format:* Adult Contemp, Talk, 74 *Special Programming:* Sp christian 20 hrs wkly; *Hrs. of News Programming:* 2 hrs news progmg wkly min; *No. News Employees:* 2 *TargetAudience:* General; General; *Adv. Rates:* 18; 18; 18; 18
Carl Auel, President
Jane Filler, Operations Dir
Fred Hodges, General Manager

KLAV
06-01-1947; 1230 kHz AM; *Hrs Open:* 24
6055 West Sahara Avenue, Las Vegas, NV 89146 US
(702) 796-1230; *Fax:* (702) 853-2599
www.klav1230am.com
License: Las Vegas, NV held by Burken Broadcasting LLC
Arbitron Metro Market: Las Vegas, NV; *Format:* Sports, Talk
Special Programming: Relg 3 hrs, Indian one hr, Hawaiian 4 hrs, Arabic; *Target Audience:* 25-54.
Robin Covey, Operations Dir
Jon Lindquist, Production Manager

KLUC
08-15-1989; 98.5 MHz FM; 97 kW; 121 ft.; N36 0 29 W115 0 20
7255 S Tenaya Way, Suite 100, Las Vegas, NV 89113 USA
(702) 253-9800; *Fax:* (702) 889-7373
www.kluc.com
info@kluc.com
License: Las Vegas, Clark County, NV held by CBS Radio Stations Inc.
Group Owner: CBS Radio; (acq 12-14-00; grpsl).
Arbitron Metro Market: Las Vegas, NV; *Format:* Contemporary Hits/Top 40; *No. News Employees:* 1; *Target Audience:* 18-34
Gina Massenzi, General Sales Mgr
Cat Thomas, VP of Programming

***KCNV**
03-24-1980; 89.5 MHz FM; *Hrs Open:* 24; 98 kw; Ant 1,532 ft; N35 56 50 W115 03 01
1289 S. Torrey Pines, Las Vegas, NV 89146
(702) 258-9895; *Fax:* (702) 258-5646
www.knpr.org
info@knpr.org
License: Las Vegas, Clark County, NV held by Nevada Public Radio Corp.
Population Served: 1,200,000; *Arbitron Metro Market:* Las Vegas, NV; *Target Audience:* 35-54.
Flo Rogers, President/General Manager
Phil Burger, Operations Dir
Melanie Canon, Director of Development
Adam Burke, News Director
Joe Sands, Chief Engineer
Jay Bartos, Public Affairs Director

KOMP
09-01-1966; 92.3 MHz FM; 25 kw; 3688 ft.; N35 57 57 W115 30 3
6290 Sunset Boulevard, Suite 1600, Los Angeles, CA 90028 US
(702) 876-1460; *Fax:* (702) 876-6685
www.komp.com
License: Las Vegas, Clark County, NV held by Lotus Broadcasting Corp.
Group Owner: Lotus Communications Corp.
Nat'l Reps: Interep; *Wire Services:* UPI
Arbitron Metro Market: Las Vegas, NV; *Format:* Rock/AOR
Jesse Leeds, General Sales Mgr
John Griffin, Programming Director

KPLV
09-01-1977; 93.1 MHz FM; 24 kw; 3743 ft.; N35 58 2 W115 30 6
2880 Meade Avenue, Suite #250 (2nd Floor), Las Vegas, NV 89102 US
(702) 238-7300; *Fax:* (702) 732-4890
www.931theparty.com
License: Las Vegas, Clark County, NV held by Citicasters Licenses Inc.
Group Owner: iHeartMedia; (acq 1999)
Arbitron Metro Market: Las Vegas, NV; *Format:* Contemporary Hits/Top 40
Chris Pickett, Senior Vice President of Programming
Glynn Alan, Regional Market President
Joel Gable, Sales and Advertising

KRLV
01-01-1947; 1340 kHz AM; *Hrs Open:* 24; 1 kw-U, ND1; N36 9 22 W115 15 24
6655 West Sahara Avenue, Las Vegas, NV 89146 US
(702) 796-1230; *Fax:* (702) 853-2597
generalmanager@krlv.net
License: Las Vegas, NV held by Burken Broadcasting LLC
Arbitron Metro Market: Las Vegas Valley; *Format:* Tejano; *Hrs. of News Programming:* news progmg 12 hrs wkly; *No. News Employees:* 3; *Target Audience:* 25-54.; *Adv. Rates:* 30; 30; 25; 25
Jon Lindquist, Production Manager
Robin Covey, Operations Manager

KSNE-FM
08-18-1987; 106.5 MHz FM; *Hrs Open:* 24; 100 kw; 1155 ft.; N36 0 30 W115 0 20
2880 Meade Ave., Suite 250, Las Vegas, NV 89102 US
(702) 238-7300; *Fax:* (702) 732-4890
www.sunny1065.com
License: Las Vegas, Clark County, NV held by Citicasters Licenses Inc.
Group Owner: iHeartMedia; (acq 1999; grpsl).
Arbitron Metro Market: Las Vegas, NV; *Format:* Adult Contemp
Special Programming: Relg one hr, pub affrs one hr wkly; *Hrs. of News Programming:* News progmg 4 hrs wkly; *Target Audience:* 25-54; emphasis on women
Glynn Alan, Regional Market President
Joel Gable, Senior Vice President/Sales

***KUNV**
04-21-1981; 91.5 MHz FM; *Hrs Open:* 24; 15 kw; 1099 ft.; N36 0 28 W115 0 20
2601 Enterprise Road, Reno, NV 89512 US
(702) 895-0065; *Fax:* (702) 895-0068
www.kunv.org
frank.mueller@kunv.org
License: Las Vegas, Clark County, NV held by University of Nevada Board of Regents.
Nat'l Network: NPR
Arbitron Metro Market: Las Vegas, NV; *Format:* Jazz *Special Programming:* Sp 5 hrs, electronic 2 hrs, community affrs 4 hrs, Ger one hr wkly; *Target Audience:* General.; *Adv. Rates:* 50; 50; 50; 50
Frank Mueller, General Manager
Kim Linzy, Programming Director
Richard Regal, News and Community Partnership Manager
Dave Nourse, Operations Manager
Kim Linzy, Music Director & Asst. Operations Manager
Gretchen Rexroad, BusinessManager
Steven Zeller, Production Engineer
Vanessa Thill, Marketing Manager/Membership Director

KQRT
11-29-1989; 105.1 MHz FM; *Hrs Open:* 24; 50 kw; 62 ft.; N36 20 0 W115 21 41
500 Pilot Rd., Suite D, Las Vegas, NV 89119 US
(702) 597-3070; *Fax:* (702) 507-1084
www.tricolor1051.com
License: Las Vegas, Clark County, NV held by Entravision Holdings LLC.
Group Owner: Entravision Communications Corp.; (acq 3-14-2000; grpsl).
Nat'l Reps: Lotus Entravision Reps LLC
Arbitron Metro Market: Las Vegas, NV; *Format:* Tejano
Jose Monreal, Senior Operations Manager
Javier Ortiz, Station Manager
Fabian Saldivar, Promotions Manager
John Garcia, Engineering Dir

KXPT
11-29-1961; 97.1 MHz FM; 25 kw; 3675 ft.; N35 58 2 W115 30 6
6290 Sunset Blvd., Suite 1600, Los Angeles, CA 90028 US
(702) 876-1460; *Fax:* (702) 876-6685
www.point97.com
LOTUSSIGNUP@YAHOO.COM
License: Las Vegas, Clark County, NV held by Lotus Broadcasting Corp.
Group Owner: Lotus Communications Corp.
Nat'l Reps: Interep
Arbitron Metro Market: Las Vegas, NV; *Format:* Contemporary Hits/Top 40, Adult Contemp; *Target Audience:* 35-49.
Tony Bonnici, President
John Griffin, Operations Dir
Jesse Leeds, General Sales Mgr

***KNPR**
10-31-2003; 88.9 MHz FM; 24.5 kw; Ant 3,680 ft; N35 58 02 W115 30 06
1289 S. Torrey Pines Dr., Las Vegas, NV 89122
(702) 258-9895; *Fax:* (702) 258-5646
www.knpr.org
info@knpr.org
License: Las Vegas, Clark County, NV held by Nevada Public Radio.
Nat'l Network: NPR; PRI
Population Served: 1,800,000; *Arbitron Metro Market:* Las Vegas, NV
Flo Rogers, President/General Manager
Phil Burger, Operations Dir
Christine Kiely, General Sales Mgr

Dave Becker, Programming Director
Adam Burke, News Director
Joe Sands, Chief Engineer

KWWN
01-01-2007; 1100 kHz AM
8755 West Flamingo Road, Las Vegas, NV 89147 US
(702) 876-1460; *Fax:* (702) 876-6685
www.espn1100.com
License: Las Vegas, NV held by Lotus Broadcasting Corp.
Group Owner: Lotus Communications Corp.
Nat'l Network: ESPN Radio; *Nat'l Reps:* Interep
Arbitron Metro Market: Las Vegas, NV; *Format:* Sports
Tony Bonnici, General Manager
Jessee Leeds, General Sales Mgr
Mitch Moss, Programming Director
Andy Kaye, News Director

***KVKL**
01-01-2006; 91.1 MHz FM; 41 kw; 1066 ft.; N35 37 41 W115 16 24
1601 Belvedere Rd, 204 E, West Palm Beach, FL 33406 US
(702) 731-5588
License: Las Vegas, Clark County, NV held by Southern Nevada Educational Broadcasters.
Arbitron Metro Market: Farmington, NM
Carl Auel, CEO
Fred Hodges, General Manager

KMZQ
01-01-2008; 670 kHz AM
US
(702) 736-6161; *Fax:* (702) 385-6001
www.670theq.com
License: Las Vegas, NV held by Kemp Communications Inc.
Group Owner: Kemp Communications Inc.
Arbitron Metro Market: Las Vegas, NV; *Format:* Talk
Will Kemp, President
Dierdre Palmer, General Manager
Gary Cox, Executive Vice Presdient/Market Manager

Laughlin

KJJJ
05-24-1994; 102.3 MHz FM; 17 kw; 1890 ft.; N35 1 58 W114 21 57
1845 McCulloch Boulevard, Lake Havasu City, AZ 86405 US
(928) 855-9336; *Fax:* (928) 855-9333
www.kjjjfm.com
steve@kjjjfm.com
License: Laughlin, Mohave County, NV held by Steven M. Greeley.
Format: Country
Steve Greeley, CEO
Traceye Jones, General Manager

Logandale

KADD
09-01-1997; 93.5 MHz FM; 93 kw horiz; 2090 ft.; N36 38 7 W114 7 18
P.O. Box 67, Santa Clara, CA 95052 US
(928) 855-4560; *Fax:* (928) 855-7996
www.klove.com
License: Logandale, Clark County, NV held by M&M Broadcasting LLC
Group Owner: M&M Broadcasting; (acq 5-11-2001; $150,000)
Arbitron Metro Market: Las Vegas, NV; *Format:* Adult Contemp
Chris Rolando, General Manager

Lovelock

KWNZ
01-01-2008; 106.3 MHz FM; 3 kw horiz; Ant 2,106 ft; N40 07 05.2 W118 43 35.5
510 East Plumb Lane, Reno, NV 89502
(570) 348-9103; *Fax:* (570) 348-9109
www.1063popfm.com
License: Lovelock, Pershing County, NV held by Shamrock Communications Inc.
Group Owner: Shamrock Communications Inc.; (acq 9-19-2007; $500,000 for CP)

Willobee Carlan, Programming Director
Kara Brown, Director of Sales
John Burkavage, General Manager

Lund

***KWPR**
09-01-2000; 88.7 MHz FM; *Hrs Open:* 24; 3 kw; 2201 ft.; N39 18 54 W115 5 19 *Rebroadcasts:* Rebroadcasts KNPR(FM) Las Vegas 100%
1289 S. Torrey Pines Dr., Las Vegas, NV 89146 US
(702) 258-9895; *Fax:* (702) 258-5646
www.nevadapublicradio.org
reception@knpr.org
License: Lund, White Pine County, NV held by Nevada Public Radio.
Arbitron Metro Market: Henderson, NV; *Format:* News, Variety/Diverse
Lamar Marchese, General Manager

Mesquite

KVEG
07-23-2001; 97.5 MHz FM; *Hrs Open:* 24; 100 kw; 1969 ft.; N36 35 6 W114 36 1
3999 Las Vegas Boulevard South, Suite K, Las Vegas, NV 89119 US
(702) 736-6161; *Fax:* (702) 736-2986
www.kvegas.com
lapablaza@kvegas.com
License: Mesquite, Clark County, NV held by Kemp Broadcasting Inc.
Group Owner: Kemp Communications Inc.
Arbitron Metro Market: Las Vegas, NV; *Format:* Contemporary Hits/Top 40; *Target Audience:* 25-39.
Gary Cox, Executive Vice President/Market Manager
Dierdre Palmer, General Manager
Sherita Saulsberry, Programming Director

***KAIZ**
01-01-2005; 90.9 MHz FM; *Hrs Open:* 24; 0.5 kw; 761 ft.; N36 53 48 W114 17 23 *Rebroadcasts:* Rebroadcasts KLRD(FM) Yucaipa, CA 100%
PO Box 2118, Omaha, NE 68103 US
(888) 937-2471; *Fax:* (916) 251-1650
www.air1.com
info@air1.com
License: Mesquite, Clark County, NV held by Educational Media Foundation.
Group Owner: EMF Broadcasting
Nat'l Network: Air 1
Arbitron Metro Market: Mesquite, NV; *Format:* Alternative, Christian; *No. News Employees:* 3; *Target Audience:* 18-35; Judeo-Christian, female
Darrell Chambliss, Chairman
Alan Mason, COO
Mike Novak, President and CEO
Dan Beck, Operations Dir
Eric Allen, General Sales Mgr
David Pierce, Programming Director
Ed Lenane, News Director
Sam Wallington, Engineering Dir
Larry Moody, Director
Mitch Barnhart, Director
David R. Ferry, Director
Walter Golembeski, Director
David Pierce, Chief Creative Officer

***KAER**
01-01-2006; 89.3 MHz FM; *Hrs Open:* 24; 0.74 kw; 784 ft.; N36 53 48 W114 17 23 *Rebroadcasts:* Rebroadcasts KLRD(FM) Yucaipa, CA 100%
PO Box 2118, Omaha, NE 68103 US
(888) 937-2471; *Fax:* (916) 251-1650
www.air1.com
info@air1.com
License: Mesquite, Washington County, NV held by Educational Media Foundation.
Group Owner: EMF Broadcasting
Nat'l Network: Air 1
Arbitron Metro Market: Mesquite, NV; *Format:* Alternative, Christian; *No. News Employees:* 3; *Target Audience:* 19-35; Judeo Christian female
Darrell Chambliss, Chairman
Alan Mason, COO
Mike Novak, President and CEO
Mike Lee, Operations Dir
Eric Allen, General Sales Mgr
David Pierce, Programming Director
Ed Lenane, News Director
Sam Wallington, Engineering Dir

***KEKL**
01-01-2005; 88.5 MHz FM; 20.5 kw; 489 ft.; N36 41 0 W114 30 48
1601 Belverdera Rd, 204 E., West Palm Beach, FL 33406 US
(800) 525-5683; *Fax:* (916) 251-1650
www.klove.com
klove@klove.com
License: Mesquite, Clark County, NV held by Southern Nevada Educational Broadcasters.
Arbitron Metro Market: Mesquite, NV; *Format:* Christian, Gospel; *No. News Employees:* 13
Darrell Chambliss, Chairman
Carl Auel, CEO
Mike Novak, President and CEO
Fred Hodges, General Manager
David Pierce, Programming Director
Ed Lenane, News Director
Sam Wallington, Engineering Dir
Dan Antonelli, Chief BusinessDevelopment Officer
Eric Moser, Chief Financial Officer
Brian Burger, Vice President of Human Resources
D. Kevin Blair, Secretary and General Counsel
Tim Luttrell, News Reporter

Moapa

KXLI
01-01-2008; 94.5 MHz FM; 93 kw horiz; Ant 2,089 ft; N36 38 07 W114 07 18
2100 S. Eastern Avenue, Las Vegas, NV 89104
(702) 432-3022
www.exafm.com
License: Moapa, Clark County, NV held by Aurora Media LLC.
Arbitron Metro Market: Las Vegas, NV
Scott Mahalick, General Manager

Moapa Valley

KJUL
07-01-2001; 104.7 MHz FM; *Hrs Open:* 24; 100 kw; 604 ft.; N36 41 0 W114 30 48
150 Spectrum Boulevard, Las Vegas, NV 89101 US
(702) 258-0285; *Fax:* (702) 258-7570
www.kjul1047.com
scott@smiradio.com
License: Moapa Valley, Clark County, NV held by Summit American Inc.
Wire Services: AP
Arbitron Metro Market: Las Vegas, NV; *Format:* Adult Contemp, Country; *Target Audience:* 25-54.; *Adv. Rates:* 5; 5; 5; na
Scott Gentry, General Manager
Kurt Gentry, Station Manager
Scott Gentry, Programming Director

KRRN
01-01-1989; 92.7 MHz FM; 100 kw horiz; 1926 ft.; N36 36 4 W114 35 6
500 Pilot Rd., Suite D, Las Vegas, NV 89119 US
(702) 434-0015
www.superestrella927.com
License: Moapa Valley, Mohave County, NV held by Entravision Holdings LLC.
Group Owner: Entravision Communications Corp.; (acq 8-29-02; $12.43 million).
Nat'l Network: ABC
Arbitron Metro Market: Moapa Valley-Las Vegas, NV Dolan Springs, AZ; *Format:* Spanish, Contemporary Hits/Top 40
Javier Ortiz, Senior VP

North Las Vegas

KXST
01-02-2013; 1140 kHz AM; *Hrs Open:* 24 hrs; 10 kW; N36 16 5 W115 2 41
7255 S Tenaya Way, Suite 100, Las Vegas, NV 89113 USA
(702) 889-7300; *Fax:* (702) 889-7373
www.cbssportsradio1140.com
License: North Las Vegas, NV held by CBS Radio Stations Inc.
Group Owner: CBS Radio
Arbitron Metro Market: Las Vegas, NV; *Format:* Sports
Maureen Pulicella, General Sales Mgr
Kyle Helmick, Promotions Manager

KSHP
01-01-1954; 1400 kHz AM; *Hrs Open:* 24; 1 kW; N36 12 39 W115 9 47
5500 Poplar Ave, Suite 1, Memphis, TN 38119 USA
(901) 685-3993; *Fax:* (901) 685-3995
www.kshp.com
mail@kshp.com
License: North Las Vegas, NV held by Las Vegas Broadcasting LLC
Group Owner: Pollack Broadcasting; 2016
Arbitron Metro Market: Las Vegas, NV; *Format:* Sports; *Adv. Rates:* 40; 25; 40; 25

KFRH
09-01-1982; 104.3 MHz FM; *Hrs Open:* 24; 24.5 kw; 3701 ft.; N35 58 2 W115 30 6
6725 Via Austi Parkway, 2nd Floor, Las Vegas, NV 89119 US
(702) 730-0300; *Fax:* (702) 736-8447
www.1027fresh.fm
License: North Las Vegas, Clark County, NV held by KJUL License LLC.
Group Owner: Royce International Broadcasting Corp.
Arbitron Metro Market: Las Vegas, NV; *Format:* Adult Contemp
Edward Morawski, General Manager
Debbie McKay, General Sales Mgr
James Palomares, Programming Director

KXNT
12-16-1996; 840 kHz AM; *Hrs Open:* 24; 50 kW; N36 23 53 W114 54 57
7255 S Tenaya Way, Suite 100, Las Vegas, NV 89113 USA
(702) 889-7300; *Fax:* (702) 889-7555
www.kxnt.com
License: North Las Vegas, NV held by CBS Radio Stations Inc.
Group Owner: CBS Radio; (acq 11-13-98; grpsl).
Nat'l Network: CBS Radio
Arbitron Metro Market: Las Vegas, NV; *Format:* News/Talk, News, 86; *Target Audience:* 35-64; upscale adults; *Adv. Rates:* 140; 175;140; 20

Overton

KVGQ
106.9 MHz FM; 92 kw; Ant 2,043 ft; N36 50 55 W114 28 23
3999 Las Vegas Boulevard, Las Vegas, NV 89119
Fax: (702) 736-6161
www.1069theq.com
License: Overton, Clark County, NV held by Kemp Communications Inc.
Group Owner: Kemp Communications Inc.
Arbitron Metro Market: Las Vegas, NV
Will Kemp, President

Pahrump

KXTE
08-12-1996; 107.5 MHz FM; *Hrs Open:* 24; 24.5 kW; 85 ft.; N35 57 57 W115 30 3
7255 S Tenaya Way, Suite 100, Las Vegas, NV 89113 USA
(702) 257-1075; *Fax:* (702) 889-7575
www.x1075lasvegas.com
License: Pahrump, Nye County, NV held by CBS Radio Stations Inc.
Group Owner: CBS Radio; (acq 11-13-98; grpsl).
Arbitron Metro Market: Las Vegas, NV; *Format:* Alternative; *Target Audience:* 18-49
Maureen Pulicella, General Sales Mgr
Cat Thomas, Programming Director
Katrina Llapitan, Promotions Manager

KNYE
11-19-2001; 95.1 MHz FM; *Hrs Open:* 24; 6 kw; -93 ft.; N36 11 52 W116 2 8
1230 Dutch Ford Street, Pahrump, NV 89048 US
(775) 751-6100; *Fax:* (775) 751-6193
www.knye.com
karen@knye.com
License: Pahrump, Nye County, NV held by Pahrump Radio Inc.
Arbitron Metro Market: Las Vegas, NV; *Format:* Oldies
Karen Jackson, President
Joe Sands, Chief Engineer

Panaca

***KLNR**
05-01-1989; 91.7 MHz FM; *Hrs Open:* 24; 1 kw; 3425 ft.; N37 53 38 W114 34 40 *Rebroadcasts:* Rebroadcasts KNPR(FM) Las Vegas 100%
1289 S. Torrey Pines Dr., Las Vegas, NV 89102 US
(702) 258-9895; *Fax:* (702) 258-5646
reception@knpr.org
License: Panaca, Lincoln County, NV held by Nevada Public Radio.
Nat'l Network: NPR
Arbitron Metro Market: Las Vegas, NV; *Format:* News
Florence Rogers, President/General Manager
Dave Becker, Programming Director
Adam Burke, News Director
Melanie Connor, Director of Development
Phil Burger, Director of Broadcast Operations
Christine Kiely, Marketing Manager
Michelle LaBonney, Business Manager

Paradise

KNIH
02-21-1962; 970 kHz AM; *Hrs Open:* 24
4800 North Central Ave, Phoenix, AZ 85012 US
(702) 735-8644; *Fax:* (702) 734-4755
www.knews970.com
License: Paradise, NV held by BTR West Inc.
Group Owner: BusinessTalkRadio.Net Inc.; (acq 11-13-2006; $3.9 million)
Nat'l Network: Wall Street; ABC; CNN Radio
Arbitron Metro Market: Las Vegas, NV; *Format:* News, News/Talk, 86; *Hrs. of News Programming:* news progmg 154 hrs wkly; *No. News Employees:* 8; *Target Audience:* 35 plus.
Michael Metter, President
Jim Servino, General Manager

Reno

KSGG
10-30-1963; 1230 kHz AM; *Hrs Open:* 24; 1.0 kw-U, ND1; N39 30 50 W119 42 54
961 Matley Lane, Suite 120, Reno, NV 89502 US
(775) 829-1964; *Fax:* (775) 825-3183
www.969therodeo.com
info@969therodeo.com
License: Reno, Washoe County, NV held by Americom Limited Partnership
Group Owner: Americom Broadcasting
Arbitron Metro Market: Reno, Nevada; *Format:* Country; *Target Audience:* 35 plus.
Tom Quinn, President
Lori Heeren, Vice President and General Manager
Heather Forcier, National Regional Sales Director
Carrie Carano, Local Sales Manager
Teresa Estabrook, Local Sales Manager

KDOT
10-12-1966; 104.5 MHz FM; *Hrs Open:* 24; 25 kw; 2930 ft.; N39 18 48 W119 52 59
2900 Sutro Street, Reno, NV 89512 US
(775) 329-9261; *Fax:* (775) 323-1450
www.kdot.com
javet@kdot.com
License: Reno, Washoe County, NV held by Lotus Radio Corp.
Group Owner: Lotus Communications Corp.; (acq 3-30-93; $600,000 with KIRS(AM) Sun Valley;
Nat'l Reps: D & R Radio
Arbitron Metro Market: Reno, NV; *Format:* Rock/AOR; *Hrs. of News Programming:* news progmg 3 hrs wkly; *No. News Employees:* 1; *Target Audience:* 18-49; young active adults that like today's lifestyle
Dane Wilt, General Manager Of Advertising
Paul Kriegler, Operations Manager
Dee Kane, Regional/National Sales Manager
Donna Lewis, PSA Announcement Director

KHIT
01-29-1955; 1450 kHz AM; *Hrs Open:* 24
C/O Jerome S. Boros, Esq, 1290 Ave of the Americas, New York, NY 10104 US
(775) 329-9261; *Fax:* (775) 323-1450
kena@kozzradio.com
License: Reno, NV held by Lotus Radio Corp.
Group Owner: Lotus Communications Corp.; (acq 9-67)
Nat'l Network: Fox Sports; *Nat'l Reps:* D & R Radio
Arbitron Metro Market: Reno, NV *TV Affiliate:* ESPN; *Format:* Sports; *Target Audience:* 25-49.
Jim McClain, Operations Dir
Dane Wilt, General Manager
Raina Weathers, General Sales Mgr
Ken Allen, Promotions Manager
Steve Diamond, News Director
Mike Weaver, Chief Engineer
Dawn Keeble, Traffic Manager

***KIHM**
01-01-1984; 920 kHz AM; *Hrs Open:* 24
3256 Penryn Road, Loomis, CA 95650 US
(916) 535-0500; *Fax:* (916) 535-0504
www.ihradio.org
License: Reno, NV held by IHR Educational Broadcasting
Group Owner: IHR Educational Broadcasting; acq 8-24-2000).
Arbitron Metro Market: Reno, NV; *Format:* Christian
Doug Pearson, Station Manager

KKOH
01-01-1971; 780 kHz AM; *Hrs Open:* 24; 50 kw-D, 50 kw-N; N39 40 41 W119 48 6
595 E. Plumb Ln., Reno, NV 89502 US
(775) 789-6700; *Fax:* (775) 789-6767
www.kkoh.com
License: Reno, NV held by Radio License Holding CBC, LLC
Group Owner: Cumulus Media Inc.; (acq 5-18-92; $12.5 million; grpsl;).
Nat'l Reps: McGavren Guild
Arbitron Metro Market: Reno, NV; *Format:* News/Talk; *No. News Employees:* 4; *Target Audience:* 35-64.
Jon Sanchez, Advertising Sales

KNEV
12-25-1953; 95.5 MHz FM; 60 kw; 2280 ft.; N39 15 34 W119 42 16
595 East Plumb Ln., Reno, NV 89502 US
(775) 789-6700; *Fax:* (775) 789-6767
www.955thevibe.com
License: Reno, NV held by Radio License Holding CBC, LLC
Group Owner: Cumulus Media Inc.; (acq 4-13-93; $500,000;)
Arbitron Metro Market: Reno, NV; *Format:* Urban Contemporary; *Target Audience:* General.
Ryan Nutter, Programming Director
Jay Schell, Promotions Manager

KURK
11-01-1994; 92.9 MHz FM; 48 kw; 502 ft.; N39 35 3 W119 48 6
City Center West, 7201 W. Lake Mead Blvd, Las Vegas, NV 89128 US
(775) 333-0123; *Fax:* (775) 322-7361
License: Reno, Washoe County, NV held by Wilks License Co.-Reno LLC.
Group Owner: Wilks Broadcast Group LLC; (acq 9-29-2005; grpsl)
Arbitron Metro Market: Reno, NV; *Format:* Classic Rock
Andrew Perini, General Manager
Rob Brooks, Programming/Operations Manager
Jay Davis, News Director

KOZZ-FM
09-01-1969; 105.7 MHz FM; *Hrs Open:* 24; 25 kw; 2930 ft.; N39 18 48 W119 52 59
Mailing Address: 690 East Plumb Lane, Reno, NV 89502 US
Second Address: 2900 Sutro St., Reno, NV 89512
(775) 329-9261; *Fax:* (775) 323-1450
www.kozzradio.com
paulk@lotusradio.com
License: Reno, Washoe County, NV held by Lotus Radio Corp.
Group Owner: Lotus Communications Corp.; (acq 1-1-78)
Arbitron Metro Market: Reno, NV; *Format:* Classic Rock
Paul Kriegler, Operations Manager
Max Volume, Music Director
Dee Kane, Regional/National Sales Manager
Donna Lewis, Public Service Announcement Director
Dane Wilt, General Manager

KPLY
10-25-1928; 630 kHz AM
US
(775) 329-9261; *Fax:* (775) 323-1450
www.espn945.com
dane@lotusradio.com
License: Reno, NV held by Lotus Radio Corp.
Group Owner: Lotus Communications Corp.; (Acq 1995; $325,000)
Arbitron Metro Market: Reno, NV; *Format:* Sports; *Target Audience:* 25-54.
Jave Patterson, Operations Dir
Dane Wilt, General Manager
Chip Cooper, General Sales Mgr
Ken Allen, Programming Director

KRNV-FM
01-01-1983; 102.1 MHz FM; *Hrs Open:* 24; 11 kw; 492 ft.; N39 35 3 W119 47 52
300 S. Well Ave., Suite 12, Reno, NV 89502 US
(775) 333-1017
www.tricolor1021.com
License: Reno, NV held by Entravision Communications
Group Owner: Intermountain West Communications; (acq 3-14-00; grpsl).
Arbitron Metro Market: Reno, NV; *Format:* Tejano; *Target Audience:* 18-49; adults
Walter Ulloa, CEO

***KUNR**
10-07-1963; 88.7 MHz FM; 20 kw; 2169 ft.; N39 15 34 W119 42 16
Kunr, Mail Stop 294, Reno, NV 89557 US
(775) 327-5867; *Fax:* (775) 327-5386
www.kunr.org
feedback@kunr.org
License: Reno, Washoe County, NV held by University of Nevada Board of Regents.

Nat'l Network: NPR; PRI
Arbitron Metro Market: Reno, NV; *Format:* Jazz, News; *Target Audience:* General.
David Stipech, General Manager
Albert "AJ" Kenneson, Business Manager

KXEQ
07-01-1946; 1340 kHz AM; 0.9774 kw-U, ND1; N39 31 5 W119 44 29
323 E. San Joaquin St., Tulare, CA 93274 US
(775) 827-1111; *Fax:* (775) 827-2082
License: Reno, NV held by Azteca Broadcasting Corp.
Group Owner: Azteca Broadcasting Corp.; acq 10-16-91; $30,000;
Nat'l Network: AP Radio
Arbitron Metro Market: Reno, NV; *Format:* Tejano
Jose Mares, Programming Director

KXTO
02-03-2003; 1550 kHz AM; *Hrs Open:* 24; 2.5 kw-D, ND1; 0.094 kw-N, ND1; N39 34 39 W119 50 52
Mailing Address: Box 1290, Weslaco, TX 78596 US
Second Address: 5301 Longley Ln., Unit 19, Reno, NV 89511
(956) 969-9623
www.radiovidareno.com
License: Reno, NV held by Christian Ministries of the Valley Inc.
Group Owner: Christian Ministries of the Valley Inc.
Arbitron Metro Market: Reno, NV; *Format:* Religious
Eduardo Luevano, General Manager

***KJIV**
89.5 MHz FM; kw
Meadows Community Colleg, 7000 Dandini Blvd., Reno, NV 89512 US
(775) 824-8611
www.tmcc.edu
License: Reno, Washoe County, NV held by Board of Regents of the Nevada System of Higher Education.
Arbitron Metro Market: Reno, NV
Michael Rainey, General Manager

Smith

KSVL
01-01-1999; 92.3 MHz FM; 0.49 kw; 2073 ft.; N38 41 6 W119 11 4
P.O. Box 123, Smith, NV 89430 US
(775) 465-2200
www.ksvl92.com
ksvl92@yahoo.com
License: Smith, Lyon County, NV held by Donegal Enterprises.
Arbitron Metro Market: Smith, NV; *Format:* Talk
Wayne Donegal, General Manager

Sparks

KBZZ
08-09-1960; 1270 kHz AM; *Hrs Open:* 24; 13 kw-D, 5 kw-N; N39 32 1 W119 39 48
961 Matley Lane, Suite 120, Reno, NV 89502 US
(775) 829-1964; *Fax:* (775) 825-3183
info@renosportsradio.com
License: Sparks, Washoe County, NV held by Americom Limited Partnership
Group Owner: Americom Broadcasting; (acq 1996; grpsl)
Nat'l Network: CBS; Westwood One
Arbitron Metro Market: Reno, NV; *Format:* News, News/Talk, 84, Talk; *Target Audience:* 25-54; primarily men who are interested in sports
Tom Quinn, President
Lori Heeren, Vice President and General Manager
Heather Forcier, National Regional Sales Director
Carrie Carano, Local Sales Manager
Teresa Estabrook, Local Sales Manager

KMXW
07-01-1983; 100.9 MHz FM; *Hrs Open:* 24; 2.9 kw; 203 ft; N39 22 04 W119 47 07
300 E. 2nd St. 14th Floor, Reno, NV 89512
(775) 333-0123; *Fax:* (775) 333-0110
License: Sparks, Washoe County, NV held by Wilks License Co.-Reno LLC.
Group Owner: Wilks Broadcast Group LLC; (acq 9-29-2005; grpsl).
Nat'l Network: ABC
Arbitron Metro Market: Reno, NV; *Target Audience:* 18-54; general
Jeff Wilks, President/Chief Executive Officer
Jeff Sanders, Executive Vice President

KWFP
01-01-1993; 92.1 MHz FM; *Hrs Open:* 24; 8.9 kw; Ant 502 ft; N39 35 03 W119 48 06
300 E. Second St. 14 th Fl., Reno, NV 89502
(775) 333-0123
www.smoothjazzreno.com
License: Sparks, Washoe County, NV held by Wilks License Co.-Reno LLC.
Group Owner: Wilks Broadcast Group LLC; (acq 9-29-2005; grpsl).
Population Served: 300,000; *Arbitron Metro Market:* Reno, NV
Jeff Wilks, President/Chief Executive Officer
Jeff Sanders, Executive Vice President

KNNR
01-01-2002; 1400 kHz AM; 600 w-U; N39 34 10 W119 45 03
1085 E. 2nd St., Suite 1, Reno, NV 38104
(775) 786-2900; *Fax:* (775) 348-5865
License: Sparks, Washoe County, NV held by George S. Flinn Jr.
George Flinn, President
Ruben Villalobos, General Manager

***KLRH**
88.3 MHz FM; 2.95 kw; 2877 ft.; N39 45 38 W119 27 59
PO Box 2098, Omaha, NE 68103 US
(800) 525-5683; *Fax:* (916) 251-1650
www.klove.com
klove@klove.com
License: Sparks, Washoe County, NV held by Educational Media Foundation.
Group Owner: EMF Broadcasting
Nat'l Network: K-Love
Arbitron Metro Market: Sparks, NV; *Format:* Christian; *No. News Employees:* 13; *Target Audience:* 25-44; Judeo Christian female
Darrell Chambliss, Chairman
Mike Novak, President and CEO
Dan Beck, Operations Dir
David Pierce, Programming Director
Ed Lenane, News Director
Sam Wallington, Engineering Dir
Richard Hunt, News Reporter
Marya Morgan, NewsReporter
Dan Antonelli, Chief Business Development Officer
Eric Moser, Chief Financial Officer
Brian Burger, Vice President of Human Resources
D. Kevin Blair, Secretary and General Counsel

Spring Creek

KBGZ
11-18-2007; 103.9 MHz FM; 12.6 kw; Ant 1,597 ft; N40 55 18 W115 50 58
c/o Ruby Radio Corp., 1750 Manzanita, Suite 1, Elko, NV
(775) 777-1196; *Fax:* (775) 777-9587
www.bigcountry.fm
License: Spring Creek, Elko County, NV held by Ruby Radio Corp.
Group Owner: Ruby Radio Corp.
Population Served: 25,000 *Target Audience:* 18-54; men & women
Ken Sutherland, President
Alene Sutherland, Vice President

Sun Valley

KZTQ
01-01-2002; 93.7 MHz FM; 3.6 kw; Ant 423 ft; N39 35 02 W119 47 54
961 Matley Lane, Reno, NV 89502
(775) 789-6700; *Fax:* (775) 789-6767
www.bob937.com
License: Sun Valley, Washoe County, NV held by Flinn Broadcasting Corp.
Arbitron Metro Market: Reno, NV
Scott Seidensticker, Sales Manager

KUUB
01-01-1999; 94.5 MHz FM; 50 kw; 459 ft.; N39 35 2 W119 47 53
8755 West Flamingo Road, Las Vegas, NV 89147 US
(775) 329-9261; *Fax:* (775) 323-1450
www.espn945.com
License: Sun Valley, Washoe County, NV held by Lotus Radio Corp.
Group Owner: Lotus Communications Corp.
Arbitron Metro Market: Reno, NV *TV Affiliate:* ESPN; *Format:* Sports, Talk
Dane Wilt, General Manager
Chip Cooper, General Sales Mgr
Chuck Short, News Director
Mike Weaver, Chief Engineer

***KXNV**
89.1 MHz FM; kw
US
(775) 348-7557
License: Sun Valley, NV held by Progressive Leadership Alliance of Nevada
Bob Fulkerson, Station Manager

Tonopah

***KTPH**
10-01-1988; 91.7 MHz FM; *Hrs Open:* 24; 1 kw; 1411 ft.; N38 3 7 W117 13 30 *Rebroadcasts:* Rebroadcasts KNPR(FM) Las Vegas 100%
1289 S. Torrey Pines Dr., Las Vegas, NV 89102 US
(702) 258-9895; *Fax:* (702) 258-5646
www.knpr.org
reception@knpr.org
License: Tonopah, Nye County, NV held by Nevada Public Radio.
Nat'l Network: NPR
Arbitron Metro Market: Las Vegas, NV; *Format:* Classical, News
Florence Rogers, President
David Stipech, General Manager
Paul Cashin, Programming Director
Adam Burke, News Director
Stefanie Givens, Development Director

Tucsun

KLPX
01-01-2007; 91.6 kHz FM
3871 N Commerce Dr., Tuscon, AZ 85705 US
(520) 880-5579
www.klpx.com
kkwilosz@azlotus.com
License: Tucsun, AZ held by Lotus Broadcasting Corp.
Group Owner: Lotus Communications Corp.
Nat'l Reps: Interep
Arbitron Metro Market: Tucson, AZ; *Format:* Classic Rock, Rock/AOR
Ken Kwilosz, General Manager
Larry Mac, Operations Manager
Scott Romero, Local Sales Manager
Razor, Programming Director
Sherm, The Frank Show Producer
Cindy Glysson, Marketing Director
Jessica Allen, Promotions Coordinator

Wendover

KVUW
01-01-2006; 102.3 MHz FM; 3 kw; 26 ft.; N40 44 30 W114 2 10
218 N Wolcott, Wendover, NV 82601 US
(435) 665-0600; *Fax:* (435) 665-0600
License: Wendover, Elko County, NV held by Murray Grey Broadcasting Inc.
Group Owner: Northeast Broadcasting Company Inc.; (acq 12-21-2005; $750,000 with KRQU(FM) Laramie, WY)
Arbitron Metro Market: Wendover, NV
Steven Silberberg, President

Whitney

KLSQ
08-15-1986; 870 kHz AM; *Hrs Open:* 24; 5 kw-D, DAN; 0.43 kw-N, DAN; N35 58 35 W114 57 3
6767 W. Tropicana Ave., Suite 102, Las Vegas, NV 89103 US
(702) 284-6400; *Fax:* (702) 284-6403
www.univision.com
License: Whitney, Clark County, NV held by KLSQ-AM License Corp.
Group Owner: Univision Radio; (acq 9-22-2003; grpsl).
Arbitron Metro Market: Las Vegas, NV; *Format:* Spanish; *Target Audience:* 35 plus.
Rene Morales, Vice President and General Manager
Manny Garcia, Chief Engineer
Mauricio Palacios, Local Sales Manager

Winnemucca

KWNA
01-28-1955; 1400 kHz AM; *Hrs Open:* 24; 1 kw-U, ND1; N40 57 23 W117 42 48
Mailing Address: P. O. Box 1400, Winnemucca, NV 89445 US
Second Address: 335 West 4th Street, Winnemucca, NV 89445
(775) 623-3926
www.kwnaradio.net
ghorky1400@gmail.com
License: Winnemucca, NV held by Ely Radio LLC.

Group Owner: Ely Radio LLC; (acq 11-6-2006; $500,000 with co-located FM)
Nat'l Network: ABC
Arbitron Metro Market: Winnemucca, NV; *Format:* News, News/Talk, 86 *Special Programming:* Farm 2 hrs wkly; *Hrs. of News Programming:* news progmg 12 hrs wkly; *No. News Employees:* 2; *Target Audience:* General.
Bob Bolton, General Manager
Rodd Stowell, Programming Director
Rachael Marie, News Director
Sandy Crownover, Traffic Manager

KWNA-FM
04-03-1982; 92.7 MHz FM; *Hrs Open:* 24; 0.47 kw; 2116 ft.; N41 0 40 W117 45 59
P.O. Box 1400, Winnemucca, NV 89445 US
(775) 623-3926; *Fax:* y
ghorky1400@gmail.com
License: Winnemucca, Humboldt County, NV
Group Owner: Ely Radio LLC
Nat'l Network: ABC
Arbitron Metro Market: Winnemucca, NV; *Format:* Country; *Target Audience:* 25-54.
Sandy Crownover, Operations Dir
Bob Bolton, General Manager
Rodd Stowell, Programming Director

*KWNM
89.7 MHz FM; kw
PO Box 7150, Riverside, CA 92513 US
(615) 469-5122; *Fax:* (615) 216-7266
www.lifetalk.net
License: Winnemucca, Humboldt County, NV held by Life Talk Radio Inc.
Arbitron Metro Market: Hurley, NM
John Geli, Manager
Randy Schornstein, Engineer

New Hampshire

Bedford

WMLL
06-01-1996; 96.5 MHz FM; 0.73 kw; 935 ft.; N42 59 2 W71 35 22
500 Commercial Street, Manchester, NH 03101 US
(603) 669-7979,(603) 669-5777; *Fax:* (603) 669-4641
www.965themill.com
License: Bedford, Hillsborough County, NH held by Saga Communications of New England LLC.
Group Owner: Saga Communications Inc.; (acq 9-29-97; $3.3 million).
Nat'l Reps: Katz Radio
Arbitron Metro Market: Manchester, NH; *Format:* Classic Rock; *Target Audience:* 35-54; baby boomers
Edward Christian, CEO
Raymond Garon, President/General Manager
Steven Goldstein, Executive Vice President/Group Program Director
Andy Orcutt, Director of Sales
Samuel Bush, CFO

Belmont

WNHW
05-08-1994; 93.3 MHz FM; 0.3 kw; 1020 ft.; N43 23 52 W71 33 3
P.O. Box 1923, Concord, NH 03302 US
(603) 224-8486; *Fax:* (603) 528-5185
www.933thewolf.com
License: Belmont, Belknap County, NH held by WBIN Media Co. Inc.
Group Owner: WBIN Media Co. Inc.
Arbitron Metro Market: Concord, NH; *Format:* Country
Mike Trombly, General Manager
AJ Dukette, Programming Director/Operations Manager
Kim Terbrack, Promotions Manager
Steve Ordinetz, Engineering Dir

Berlin

WMOU
01-01-1947; 1230 kHz AM; *Hrs Open:* 24
38 Glen Avenue, Box 489, Berlin, NH 03570 US
(603) 752-1230; *Fax:* (603) 788-3536
www.kiss1023fm.com
wmou@ncia.net
License: Berlin, NH held by Barry P. Lunderville.
Group Owner: Barry P. Lunderville Stns; (acq 11-11-2003; $75,000)
Nat'l Network: Westwood One
Arbitron Metro Market: Berlin, NH; *Format:* Adult Contemp
Special Programming: Fr 3 hrs, talk 2 hrs, swap shop 3 hrs wkly; *Hrs. of News Programming:* news progmg 6 hrs wkly; *No. News Employees:* 1 *TargetAudience:* 25-54; local residents of northern New Hampshire
Barry Lunderville, President
Bob Barbin, Operations Dir
Randy Frank, General Sales Mgr
Brian Lunderville, Chief Engineer

WKDR
1490 kHz AM
US
(603) 752-1230; *Fax:* (603) 752-3117
License: Berlin, NH held by Barry P. Lunderville.
Group Owner: Barry P. Lunderville Stns
Arbitron Metro Market: Berlin, NH; *Format:* Adult Contemp
Barry Lunderville, General Manager

Campton

WLKC
01-01-1997; 105.7 MHz FM; *Hrs Open:* 24; 4.1 kw; 390 ft.; N43 45 45 W71 39 0 *Rebroadcasts:* Rebroadcasts WXRU(FM) Wolfeboro 100%
288 South River Road, Bedford, NH 03110 US
(802) 288-1033; *Fax:* (802) 288-8134
nebco231@hotmail.com
License: Campton, Grafton County, NH held by Devon Broadcasting Co. Inc.
Format: Triple A; *Target Audience:* 25-54.
Steve Young, General Manager
Dana Marshall, Programming Director
Stephanie Battaglia, News Director
Lou Muise, Chief Engineer

Claremont

WHDQ
01-01-1948; 106.1 MHz FM; 1.6 kw; 2247 ft.; N43 26 15 W72 27 8
Box 1230, Claremont, NH 03743 US
(603) 298-0332; *Fax:* (603) 727-0134
www.q106rock.com
info@q106rock.com
License: Claremont, Sullivan County, NH
Group Owner: Great Eastern Radio LLC
Format: Classic Rock
Gene Purcell, General Manager
Phil Corrivean, Station Manager

WTSV
01-01-1948; 1230 kHz AM; 1 kw-U, ND1; N43 22 15 W72 19 42
P. O. Box 1230, Claremont, NH 03743 US
(603) 542-7735; *Fax:* (603) 542-8721
License: Claremont, NH held by Great Eastern Radio LLC
Group Owner: Great Eastern Radio LLC
Nat'l Network: ABC; ESPN Radio *Regional Reps:* Roslin.
Arbitron Metro Market: Lebanon, NH; *Format:* Sports; *Target Audience:* 35 plus.
Jeffrey Shapiro, President
Shirley Clark, General Manager

Concord

*WEVO(FM)
08-04-1981; 89.1 MHz FM; *Hrs Open:* 24; 50 kw; 380 ft; N43 12 53 W71 34 28
2 Pillsbury Street, 6th Floor, Concord, NH 3301
(603) 228-8910; *Fax:* (603) 224-6052
www.nhpr.org
admin@nhpr.org
License: Concord, Merrimack County, NH held by New Hampshire Public Radio Inc.
Nat'l Network: NPR; PRI; *Wire Services:* AP
Population Served: 42,733; *Arbitron Metro Market:* Concord, NH; *Format:* News, News/Talk, 86 *Special Programming:* Folk 3 hrs wkly; *Hrs. of News Programming:* news progmg 42 hrs wkly; *No. News Employees:* 9 *Target Audience:* 25-54; well educated adults
Elizabeth Gardella, President & CEO
Dan Colgan, Operations Manager
Michael Rathke, Programming Director
Sarah Ashworth, News Director
Alexandra Urbanowski, Vice President of Development & Marketing
Todd Bookman, Health Reporter
R.J. Perkins, Broadcast Engineer
Scott McPherson, Vice President of Operations & Finance

WJYY
09-15-1983; 105.5 MHz FM; *Hrs Open:* 24; 1.55 kw; 456 ft.; N43 16 46 W71 30 15
Box 7326, Gilford, NH 03249 US
(603) 225-1160; *Fax:* (603) 224-7280
www.wjyy.com
License: Concord, Merrimack County, NH held by WBIN Media Co. Inc.
Group Owner: WBIN Media Co. Inc.
Format: Contemporary Hits/Top 40; *Hrs. of News Programming:* news progmg 6 hrs wkly; *No. News Employees:* 1; *Target Audience:* 25-54.
AJ Dukette, Operations Manager
Mike Trombly, General Manager

WKXL
06-15-1946; 1450 kHz AM; *Hrs Open:* 24; 1 kw-U, ND1; N43 11 39 W71 33 17
P. O. Box 875, Concord, NH 03301 US
(603) 225-5521; *Fax:* (603) 224-6400
www.wkxl1450.com
License: Concord, NH held by New Hampshire Family Radio LLC
Nat'l Network: AP Radio; *Wire Services:* AP
Arbitron Metro Market: Concord (Lake Regions), NH; *Format:* News, News/Talk, 86; *Hrs. of News Programming:* news progmg 36 hrs wkly; *No. News Employees:* 2; *Target Audience:* 35 plus; adults in Concord, Hillsboro,Manchester & contiguous towns; *Adv. Rates:* 15; 7.50; 15; 5
Anthony Schilella, Station Manager

WWHK
03-07-1972; 102.3 MHz FM; *Hrs Open:* 24; 3 kw; 285 ft.; N43 13 0 W71 34 34
3140 Williamsburg Court, State College, PA 16801 US
(603) 225-1160; *Fax:* (603) 225-8935
www.thehawkrocks.com
License: Concord, Merrimack County, NH held by Birch Broadcasting Inc.
Group Owner: Birch Broadcasting Inc.
Target Audience: 25-54; adult audience in Merrimack county - south central NH
Andrew Sumereau, President

*WSPS
01-01-1974; 90.5 MHz FM; *Hrs Open:* 24; 0.2 kw; -59 ft.; N43 11 37 W71 34 29
325 Pleasant Street, Concord, NH 03301 US
(603) 228-4810,(603) 230-5810; *Fax:* (603) 229-4891
wsps.sps.edu
wsps@sps.edu
License: Concord, Merrimack County, NH held by St. Paul's School.
Format: Variety/Diverse; *Target Audience:* General.
Glenn Reider, Faculty Station Manager

*WVNH
03-07-1999; 91.1 MHz FM; 0.65 kw vert; 331 ft.; N43 23 54 W71 25 24
37 Redington Road, Concord, NH 03301 US
(603) 227-0911
www.nhgr.org
info@nhgr.org
License: Concord, Merrimack County, NH held by New Hampshire Gospel Radio Inc.
Arbitron Metro Market: Concord, NH; *Format:* Christian
Peter Stohrer, Station Manager & President
John Loker, Vice President
George Dyksta, Treasurer
Janice Cyr, Office Administrator

*WEVO
08-04-1981; 89.1 MHz FM; *Hrs Open:* 24; 50 kw; 381 ft; N43 12 53 W71 34 28 *Rebroadcasts:* Rebroadcasts WEVO(FM) Concord 100%
2 Pillsbury St., 6th Floor, Concord, NH 03301
(603) 228-8910; *Fax:* (603) 224-6052
www.nhpr.org
admin@nhpr.org
License: Concord, Merrimack County, NH held by New Hampshire Public Radio Inc.
Nat'l Network: NPR; PRI; APM; *Wire Services:* AP
Special Programming: Folk 3 hrs wkly; *Hrs. of News Programming:* news progmg 42 hrs wkly; *No. News Employees:* 9; *Target Audience:* 25-54.
Elizabeth Gardella, President & CEO
Scott McPherson, Vice President, Operations & Finance
Jim McCann, Director of Corporate Support
Abby Goldstein, Vice President, Programming
Sarah Ashworth, News Director
Michael Saffell, Directorof Technology
Alexandra Urbanowski, Vice President of Development &

Marketing
Michael Rathke, Programming Director

Conway

WVMJ
10-23-1995; 104.5 MHz FM; *Hrs Open:* 24; 1.85 kw; 429 ft.; N43 56 48 W71 8 24
Mailing Address: P.O. Box 2008, Conway, NH 03818 US
Second Address: 2 Common Court, Unit A30, N. Conway, NH 3860
(603) 356-8870; *Fax:* (603) 356-8875
www.conwaymagic.com
lucia@wmwv.com
License: Conway, Carroll County, NH held by Mt. Washington Radio & Gramophone L.L.C.
Group Owner: Mt. Washington Radio & Gramophone L.L.C.; acq 10-15-01; grpsl).
Arbitron Metro Market: Conway, NH; *Format:* Adult Contemp; *Adv. Rates:* 25; 25; 25; 17.50
Lucia Seavey, Vice President of Operations
Greg Frizzell, General Manager/Chief Executive Officer
Christoper McNevich, VP of Sales/Marketing
Cooper Fox, Programming Director
Gair MacKenzie, News Director

WMWV
06-23-1967; 93.5 MHz FM; 1.85 kw; 423 ft.; N43 56 48 W71 8 24
Mailing Address: P. O. Box 2008, Conway, NH 03818 US
Second Address: 2 Common Court, Unit A30, North Conway, NH 3860
(603) 356-8870; *Fax:* (603) 356-8875
www.wmwv.com
office@wmwv.com
License: Conway, Carroll County, NH held by Mt. Washington Radio & Gramophone L.L.C.
Group Owner: Mt. Washington Radio & Gramophone L.L.C.; acq 9-27-01; grpsl).
Nat'l Reps: Roslin
Arbitron Metro Market: Conway, NH; *Format:* Triple A
Lucia Seavey, Vice President of Operations
Greg Frizzell, General Manager/Chief Executive Officer
Mark Johnson, Programming Director
Gair MacKenzie, News Director
Christopher McNevish, Vice President of Sales & Marketing

Derry

WDER
10-01-1983; 1320 kHz AM; *Hrs Open:* 24; 10 kw-D, DA2; 1 kw-N, DA2; N42 51 59 W71 17 14
8 Lawrence Rd., Derry, NH 03038 US
(603) 437-9337; *Fax:* (603) 434-1035
www.lifechangingradio.com
License: Derry, Rockingham County, NH held by Blount Communications Inc. of NH.
Group Owner: Blount Communications Group; (acq 9-5-00; $793,000)
Nat'l Network: Salem Radio Network
Arbitron Metro Market: Manchester, NH; *Format:* Religious, Talk; *Target Audience:* 25-54; male & female
William Blount, President
Steve Sobozenski, Director

Dover

WOKQ
08-01-1970; 97.5 MHz FM; 50 kw; 492 ft.; N43 13 26 W70 58 18
Mailing Address: PO Box 576, Dover, NH 03821-0576 US
Second Address: 292 Middle Rd., Dover, NH 03820
(603) 749-9750
www.wokq.com
License: Dover, NH held by Townsquare Media Portsmouth License, LLC
Group Owner: Townsquare Media; (acq 9-1-99; grpsl).
Arbitron Metro Market: Portsmouth-Dove; *Format:* Country
Brian Lang, General Manager
Paul Kelley, Director of Sales
Mark Jennings, Brand Manager

WTSN
08-01-1956; 1270 kHz AM; *Hrs Open:* 24; 5 kw-D, DA2; 5 kw-N, DA2; N43 11 1 W70 51 14
P. O. Box 400, Back Rd., Dover, NH 03820 US
(603) 742-0987; *Fax:* (603) 742-0448
www.987thebay.com
License: Dover, NH held by Garrison City Broadcasting Inc.
Nat'l Reps: McGavren Guild
Arbitron Metro Market: Dover, NH; *Format:* News, News/Talk, 84, Talk; *No. News Employees:* 3; *Target Audience:* 35-64; very affluent; *Adv. Rates:* 50, 40, 40, 20
Bob Demers, CEO
Susan Demers Weigold, Senior Vice President
Sarah Sullivan, Operations/Programming Director
Rick Bean, General Manager
Mike Pomp, News Director
Carole Lanctot, Business Manager

Durham

***WUNH**
07-15-1963; 91.3 MHz FM; *Hrs Open:* 24; 1.45 kw horiz, 6 kw vert; 256 ft.; N43 9 23 W70 56 26
Memorial Union Building, Durham, NH 03824 US
(603) 862-2541; *Fax:* (603) 862-2543
gm@wunh.unh.edu
License: Durham, Strafford County, NH held by University of New Hampshire.
Nat'l Network: AP Radio
Arbitron Metro Market: Dover, NH; *Format:* Alternative *Special Programming:* Black 4 hrs, blues 3 hrs, jazz 5 hrs, Pol 2 hrs,; *Hrs. of News Programming:* News progmg 7 hrs wkly; *Target Audience:* Diverse.
Ian Chase, General Manager
Charlie MacCall, Programming Director
Alicia Jacobs, Promotions Manager
Daniel Day, News Director
Peter Geremia, Chief Engineer
Hannah DeBenedictis, Production Director
Scott Higgins, BusinessManager
Matt Walsh, Sports Director
Joey Rowell, Webmaster
Amanda Mead, Secretary
Sean Riley, Music Director

Exeter

WERZ
09-21-1972; 107.1 MHz FM; 5.2 kw; 348 ft.; N43 1 38 W70 52 51
815 Lafayette Rd., Portsmouth, NH 03801 US
(603) 436-7300; *Fax:* (603) 430-9415
www.werz.com
info@werz.com
License: Exeter, Rockingham County, NH held by Capstar TX LLC
Group Owner: iHeartMedia
Arbitron Metro Market: Exeter, NH; *Format:* Contemporary Hits/Top 40
Jadd Naamani, Programming Director
Marc Provenzano, Promotions Director

WXEX
06-04-1966; 1540 kHz AM; 2.5 kw-C, ND3; 5 kw-D, ND3; ND3; 0.003 k; N42 59 23 W70 56 14
US
(603) 583-4767; *Fax:* (603) 430-9415
info@WXEXradio.com
License: Exeter, NH held by Aruba Capital Holdings LLC
Nat'l Reps: McGavren Guild
Arbitron Metro Market: Portsmouth-Dover-Rochester, NH; *Format:* News, News/Talk, 84, Talk

***WPEA**
01-01-1964; 90.5 MHz FM; 0.1 kw; 33 ft.; N42 58 44 W70 57 0
20 Main Street, Exeter, NH 03833 US
(603) 777-4414
www.exeter.edu
WPEA@exeter.edu
License: Exeter, Rockingham County, NH held by Trustees of Phillips Exeter Academy.
Format: Variety/Diverse; *Target Audience:* General; students
Alex Snipes, General Manager
Tersa Haire, General Sales Mgr
Tony Gee, Programming Director

Farmington

***WNHI**
07-09-1999; 106.5 MHz FM; *Hrs Open:* 24; 2.9 kw; 486 ft.; N43 24 1 W71 9 27 *Rebroadcasts:* Rebroadcasts KLVR(FM) Middletown, CA 100%
19 Boas Lane, Wilton, CT 06897 US
(916) 251-1600; *Fax:* (916) 251-1650
www.klove.com
License: Farmington, Strafford County, NH held by Educational Media Foundation.
Group Owner: EMF Broadcasting; (acq 6-2-2008; $1 million)
Nat'l Network: Air 1
Arbitron Metro Market: Portsmouth-Dove; *Format:* Christian
Mike Novak, President

Fitzwilliam Depot

WZNH
870 kHz AM
US
(845) 356-9613
License: Fitzwilliam Depot, NH held by Steven Wendell.
Arbitron Metro Market: Fitzwilliam Depot, NH
Steven Wendell, General Manager

Franklin

WFTN
10-30-1966; 1240 kHz AM; 1 kw-U, ND1; N43 27 16 W71 38 33
PO Box 99, Babbit Rd, Franklin, NH 03235 US
(603) 934-2500; *Fax:* (603) 934-2933
License: Franklin, NH held by Northeast Communications Corp.
Group Owner: Northeast Communications Corp.; acq 9-30-74)
Format: Contemporary Hits/Top 40
Jeff Fisher, President
Fred Caruso, Operations Dir
Jeff Levitan, General Sales Manager/Vice President
Amy Bates, News Director
Gary Ford, Music Director
Cathy Keyser, Traffic Manager

WFTN-FM
04-10-1987; 94.1 MHz FM; 6 kw; 328 ft.; N43 28 23 W71 36 20
P.O.Box 99, Franklin, NH 03235 US
(603) 934-2500; *Fax:* (603) 934-2933
License: Franklin, Merrimack County, NH
Format: Adult Contemp
Amy Bates, News Director
Fred Caruso, Programming Director

Hampton

WSAK
08-01-1992; 102.1 MHz FM; *Hrs Open:* 24; 3 kw; 328 ft.; N42 53 51 W70 53 2 *Rebroadcasts:* Rebroadcasts WSHK-FM Kittery
292 Middle Rd., Dover, NH 03820 US
(603) 749-9750
www.shark1053.com
License: Hampton, NH held by Townsquare Media Portsmouth License, LLC
Group Owner: Townsquare Media; (acq 7-7-99; grpsl).
Arbitron Metro Market: Hampton, NH; *Format:* Adult Contemp
Brian Lang, General Manager
Paul Kelley, Director of Sales
Jonathan Smith, Brand Manager
Rob Michaelson, Digital Managing Editor

Hanover

***WEVH**
10-01-1993; 91.3 MHz FM; 0.175 kw; 1181 ft.; N43 42 30 W72 9 16 *Rebroadcasts:* Rebroadcasts WEVO(FM) Concord 100%
207 North Main Street, Concord, NH 03301 US
(603) 228-8910; *Fax:* (603) 224-6052
www.nhpr.org
License: Hanover, Grafton County, NH held by New Hampshire Public Radio Inc.
Nat'l Network: NPR; PRI; *Wire Services:* AP
Arbitron Metro Market: Hanover, NH; *Format:* News, News/Talk, 86 *Special Programming:* Folk 3 hrs wkly; *Hrs. of News Programming:* news progmg 42 hrs wkly; *No. News Employees:* 9; *Target Audience:* 25-54.
Elizabeth Gardella, President & CEO
Dan Colgan, Operations Manager
Michael Rathke, Programming Director
Sarah Ashworth, News Director
Scott McPherson, Vice President of Operations & Finance
Alexandra Urbanowski, Vice President ofDevelopment & Marketing
Jim McCann, Director of Corporate Support

WFRD
02-19-1976; 99.3 MHz FM; *Hrs Open:* 24; 6 kw; Ant 328 ft; N43 39 14 W72 17 44.2
Mailing Address: 6176 Robinson Hall, Dartmouth College, Hanover, NH 03755
Second Address: 3rd Fl., Robinson Hall, Dartmouth College, Hanover, NH 3826
(603) 646-3313; *Fax:* (603) 643-7655
www.wfrd.com
License: Hanover, Grafton County, NH
Population Served: 150,000; *No. News Employees:* 2; *Target Audience:* 18-45.
Heath Cole, Operations Dir
Kathryn MacNaughton, General Manager
Isa Ford, Marketing Director

WGXL
01-12-1987; 92.3 MHz FM; 6 kw; 325 ft.; N43 39 17 W72 17 41
31 Hanover St, Suite 4, Lebanon, NH 03766 US
(603) 448-1400; *Fax:* (603) 448-1755
www.wgxl.com
License: Hanover, Grafton County, NH held by Great Eastern Radio LLC.
Group Owner: Great Eastern Radio LLC; (acq 10-30-2007; grpsl)
Format: Adult Contemp; *Target Audience:* 25-49.
Justin Tyler, Programming Director
Nicole Romano, General Manager

WTSL
10-01-1950; 1400 kHz AM; *Hrs Open:* 24; 1 kw-U, ND1; N43 41 3 W72 17 46
106 North Main Street, West Lebanon, NH 03784 US
(603) 298-0332; *Fax:* (603) 448-1755
www.wtsl.com
License: Hanover, NH held by Great Eastern Radio LLC.
Group Owner: Great Eastern Radio LLC; (acq 10-30-2007; grpsl)
Nat'l Network: CBS
Arbitron Metro Market: Lebanon, NH; *Format:* News, News/Talk, 84, Talk; *Hrs. of News Programming:* news progmg 25 hrs wkly; *No. News Employees:* 2; *Target Audience:* 35 plus.
Michael Barrett, Operations Dir
Tim Plant, General Manager
Nichole Romano, Sales Manager
Gary Laperle, Chief Engineer
Christopher Olsen, General Manager

Haverhill

WYKR-FM
02-19-1990; 101.3 MHz FM; *Hrs Open:* 6 AM-10 PM; 3 kw; 39 ft.; N44 6 49 W71 58 54
Mailing Address: P.O. Box 675, Wells River, VT 05081 US
Second Address: Box 1013, Woodsville, NH 3785
(802) 757-2773; *Fax:* (802) 757-2774
www.wykr.com
License: Haverhill, Grafton County, NH held by Puffer Broadcasting Inc.
Nat'l Network: Westwood One; NBC; Jones Radio Networks; *Nat'l Reps:* Roslin
Arbitron Metro Market: Haverhill, NH; *Format:* Country; *Target Audience:* 25 plus.
Stephen Puffer, President
Teresa Puffer, Operations Dir
Don Smith, Chief Engineer

Henniker

***WNEC-FM**
02-09-1971; 91.7 MHz FM; *Hrs Open:* 17; 0.12 kw; -210 ft.; N43 10 34 W71 49 22
98 Bridge Street, Henniker, NH 03242 US
(603) 428-2000; *Fax:* (603) 428-7230
www.nec.edu
wnec@nec.edu
License: Henniker, Merrimack County, NH held by New England College.
Arbitron Metro Market: Henniker, NH; *Format:* Adult Contemp, Black, 52 *Special Programming:* Blues 4 hrs, country 3 hrs, American Indian 18 hrs; *Hrs. of News Programming:* News progmg one hr wkly *Target Audience:* 18-25; college students
Ambrose Metzegen, CEO
Meghan Stone, Station Manager
Justin McDougall, Programming Director
Dale Carlow, Engineering Dir
Kristen Westhoven, Music Director

WNNH
11-17-1989; 99.1 MHz FM; *Hrs Open:* 24; 2.8 kw; 479 ft.; N43 12 49 W71 41 19
25 Country Club Road, Gilford, NH 03249 US
ÿ(603)ÿ224-8486ÿ; *Fax:* (603) 528-5185
www.wjyy.com
License: Henniker, Merrimack County, NH held by WBIN Media Co. Inc.
Group Owner: WBIN Media Co. Inc.
Nat'l Reps: McGavren Guild
Arbitron Metro Market: Henniker, NH; *Format:* Talk; *Hrs. of News Programming:* news progmg 20 hrs wkly; *No. News Employees:* 2; *Target Audience:* 25-54; mass appeal
Mike Trombly, General Sales Mgr
AJ Dukette, Programming Director
Kim Kessler, Promotions Manager
Sara Rine, News Director

Hillsboro

WTPL
10-01-1989; 107.7 MHz FM; *Hrs Open:* 24; 1.25 kw horiz, 1.22 kw vert; 712 ft.; N43 9 17 W71 47 44
501 South Street, Bow, NH 03304 US
(603) 545-0777; *Fax:* (603) 545-0781
www.wtplfm.com
License: Hillsboro, Hillsborough County, NH held by Great Eastern Radio LLC.
Group Owner: Great Eastern Radio LLC; (acq 6-3-2004; $1.5 million)
Nat'l Network: CBS Radio; ESPN Radio
Arbitron Metro Market: Manchester, NH; *Format:* News, News/Talk, 84, Talk; *Hrs. of News Programming:* news progmg 50 hrs wkly; *No. News Employees:* 2; *Target Audience:* 35 plus; adult audience in Merrimack &Hillsborough counties
Bob Lipman, Operations Dir
Justin Tyler, Director of Programming
Courtney Galluzzo, Market Manager

Hinsdale

WYRY
06-30-1987; 104.9 MHz FM; *Hrs Open:* 24; 4.1 kw; 400 ft.; N42 46 33 W72 27 17
30-10 Warwick Rd., Winchester, NH 03470 US
(877) 444-1049; *Fax:* (603) 239-6203
www.wyry.com
License: Hinsdale, Cheshire County, NH held by Tri-Valley Broadcasting Corp.
Nat'l Network: Jones Radio Networks
Arbitron Metro Market: Hinsdale, NH; *Format:* Country; *Hrs. of News Programming:* news progmg 10 hrs wkly; *No. News Employees:* 3; *Target Audience:* 25-49; upscale adults & business decision makers
Brian McCormick, Operations Dir
Sean Patrik, Programming Director
Dan Guy, Chief Engineer

Jackson

***WEVJ**
08-02-2009; 99.5 MHz FM; *Hrs Open:* 24; 4.7 kw; 171 ft.; N44 10 30 W71 10 7 *Rebroadcasts:* Rebroadcasts WEVO(FM) Concord 100%
207 N Main Street, Concord, NH 03301 US
(603) 228-8910; *Fax:* (603) 224-6052
www.nhpr.org
License: Jackson, Carroll County, NH held by New Hampshire Public Radio.
Nat'l Network: NPR; PRI; *Wire Services:* AP
Arbitron Metro Market: Lewiston, ME; *Format:* News, News/Talk, 86; *No. News Employees:* 9; *Target Audience:* 25-54.
Elizabeth Gardella, President/Chief Executive Officer
Dan Colgan, Operations Manager
Michael Rathke, Programming Director
Sarah Ashworth, News Director
Michael Saffrel, Chief Engineer
Alexandra Urbanowski, Vice President ofDevelopment & Marketing
Donna Hiltz, Traffic Manager
Scott McPherson, Vice President of Operations & Finance
Jim McCann, Director of Corporate Support

Keene

***WEVN**
04-01-1994; 90.7 MHz FM; *Hrs Open:* 24; 1.5 kw; 938 ft.; N43 2 0 W72 22 4 *Rebroadcasts:* Rebroadcasts WEVO(FM) Concord 100%
207 North Main Street, Concord, NH 03301 US
(603) 228-8910; *Fax:* (603) 224-6052
www.nhpr.org
admin@nhpr.org
License: Keene, Cheshire County, NH held by New Hampshire Public Radio Inc.
Nat'l Network: NPR; PRI; *Wire Services:* AP
Arbitron Metro Market: Keene, NH; *Format:* News, News/Talk, 86 *Special Programming:* Folk 3 hrs wkly; *Hrs. of News Programming:* news progmg 42 hrs wkly; *No. News Employees:* 9; *Target Audience:* 25-54.
Elizabeth Gardella, President & CEO
Dan Colgan, Operations Manager
Michael Rathke, Programming Director
Sarah Ashworth, News Director
Michael Saffrel, Chief Engineer
Donna Hiltz, Traffic Manager
Scott McPherson, Vice President ofOperations & Finance
Jim McCann, Director of Corporate Support

WSNI
01-01-1983; 97.7 MHz FM; *Hrs Open:* 24; 2.15 kw; 554 ft.; N42 54 57 W72 19 53
69 Stanhope Avenue, Keene, NH 03431 US
(603) 352-9230; *Fax:* (603) 357-3926
www.sunnykeene.com
License: Keene, Cheshire County, NH held by Saga Communications of New England LLC.
Group Owner: Saga Communications Inc.; (acq 4-1-2003; $400,000)
Nat'l Network: ABC
Format: Adult Contemp; *Hrs. of News Programming:* news progmg 7 hrs wkly; *No. News Employees:* 2; *Target Audience:* 25-54; 60% female, 40% male; *Adv. Rates:* 30; 20; 30; 12
Robert Cox, General Manager
Susan Wells, General Sales Mgr
Vicki Lenahan, Promotions Manager
Steve Hamel, Operations Manager

WZBK
05-01-1959; 1220 kHz AM
69 Stanhope Avenue, Keene, NH 03431 US
(603) 352-9230; *Fax:* (603) 357-3926
www.wkbkradio.com
info@wkbkam.com
License: Keene, NH held by Saga Communications of New Hampshire LLC.
Group Owner: Saga Communications Inc.; (acq 7-1-2002; $2.63 million with WOQL(FM) Winchester)
Format: News, News/Talk, 86; *Target Audience:* 25-54; general
Bruce Lyons, Station Manager
Susan Wells, General Sales Mgr
Dan Mitchell, Programming Director
Paul Scheuring, News Director
Ira Wilner, Chief Engineer
Jennifer Bond, Traffic Manager

WKBK
06-02-1927; 1290 kHz AM
Mailing Address: US
Second Address: 69 Stanhope Ave., Keene, NH 3431
(603) 352-9230; *Fax:* (603) 357-3926
www.wkbkam.com
License: Keene, NH held by Saga Communications of New England LLC.
Group Owner: Saga Communications Inc.; (acq 5-1-02; grpsl).
Nat'l Network: CBS; *Nat'l Reps:* McGavren Guild
Format: News, Talk; *Target Audience:* 25 plus.
Steve Hamel, Operations Dir
Bob Cox, General Manager
Susan Wells, General Sales Mgr
Dan Mitchell, Programming Director
Vicki Lenahan, Promotions Manager
Paul Scheuring, News Director
Ira Wilner, Chief Engineer
Jennifer Bond,Traffic Manager

WKNE
05-01-1964; 103.7 MHz FM; 12 kw; 991 ft.; N43 2 0 W72 22 4
P.O. Box 466, Keene, NH 03431 US
(603) 352-9230; *Fax:* (603) 357-3926
www.wkne.com
info@wkne.com
License: Keene, Cheshire County, NH held by Saga Communications of New England LLC.
Group Owner: Saga Communications Inc.
Format: Contemporary Hits/Top 40, Adult Contemp; *Target Audience:* 18-49.
Steve Hamel, Operations Dir
Bob Cox, General Manager
Susan Wells, General Sales Mgr
Dan Mitchell, Programming Director
Vicki Lenahan, Promotions Director
Paul Scheuring, News Director
Ira Wilner, Chief Engineer
Jennifer Bond,Traffic Manager

***WKNH**
11-01-1975; 91.3 MHz FM; *Hrs Open:* 24; 0.275 kw; -387 ft.; N42 55 36 W72 16 54
229 Main Street, Keene, NH 03435 US
(603) 358-2420; *Fax:* (603) 358-2417
www.wknh.org
wknhinfo@aol.com
License: Keene, Cheshire County, NH held by Board of Trustees University System of New Hampshire.
Format: Alternative *Special Programming:* Class 4 hrs, folk 6 hrs, jazz 3 hrs, blues 3 hrs,; *Hrs. of News Programming:* news progmg 3 hrs wkly; *No. News Employees:* 2; *Target Audience:* General.
James McCluskey, General Manager

Laconia

WEMJ
04-09-1961; 1490 kHz AM; 1 kw-U, ND1; N43 32 29 W71 27 45
1921 Gallows Rd, #850, Vienna, VA 22182 US
(603) 524-1323; *Fax:* (603) 528-5185
www.1490wemj.com/
License: Laconia, NH held by WBIN Media Co. Inc.
Group Owner: WBIN Media Co. Inc.
Nat'l Network: CBS; *Nat'l Reps:* D & R Radio
Arbitron Metro Market: Laconia, NH; *Format:* Talk
Mike Trombly, General Manager/General Sales Manager
Pat Kelly, Programming Director
Sara Rine, News Director

WEZS
08-22-1922; 1350 kHz AM; 5 kw-D, ND1; 0.112 kw-N, ND1; N43 30 27 W71 31 0
277 Union Avenue, Laconia, NH 03246 US
(603) 524-6288; *Fax:* (603) 528-1638
www.wezs.com
staff@wezs.com
License: Laconia, NH held by Gary W. Hammond.
Nat'l Network: USA
Arbitron Metro Market: Laconia, NH; *Format:* Oldies; *Target Audience:* 45 plus.; *Adv. Rates:* 15; 14; 14; 6
Gary Hammond, General Manager

WLNH-FM
11-22-1965; 98.3 MHz FM; *Hrs Open:* 24 hrs; 15.5 kw; 407 ft.; N43 35 46 W71 29 55
25 Country Club Road, Village West, Building 1, Gilford, NH 03247 US
(603) 524-1323; *Fax:* (603) 528-5185
www.wlnh.com
info@wlnh.com
License: Laconia, Belknap County, NH held by WBIN Media Co. Inc.
Group Owner: WBIN Media Co. Inc.
Format: Adult Contemp; *Target Audience:* 25-54.
Molly King, Programming Director
Kim Kessler, Promotions Manager

Lancaster

WXXS
01-01-1998; 102.3 MHz FM; *Hrs Open:* 24; 1.5 kw; 965 ft.; N44 23 39 W71 39 20
Mailing Address: 195 Main Street, Lancaster, NH 03584 US
Second Address: 195 Main St., Lancaster, NH 3584
(603) 444-4102; *Fax:* (603) 788-3536
www.kiss1023fm.com
kiss102@together.net
License: Lancaster, Coos County, NH held by Radio New England Broadcasting LLC
Group Owner: Barry P. Lunderville Stns
Nat'l Network: CBS
Arbitron Metro Market: Lancaster, NH; *Format:* Adult Contemp
Brian Lunderville, Operations Dir
Barry Lunderville, General Manager
Danielle Corbiel, News Director

Lebanon

KIXX
12-18-1990; 100.5 MHz FM; *Hrs Open:* 24; 22 kw; 325 ft.; N43 39 18 W72 17 42
31 Hanover Street, Suite 4, Lebanon, NH 03766 US
(603) 448-1400; *Fax:* (603) 448-1755
www.kixx.com
JTYLER@GREATEASTERNRADIO.COM
License: Lebanon, Grafton County, NH held by Great Eastern Radio LLC.
Group Owner: Great Eastern Radio LLC; (acq 10-30-2007; grpsl)
Nat'l Network: Westwood One; CNN Radio
Arbitron Metro Market: Lebanon, NH; *Format:* Country; *Hrs. of News Programming:* news progmg 20 hrs wkly; *No. News Employees:* 3; *Target Audience:* 25-54.
Kenny Michaels, Operations Dir
Nichole Romano, General Manager
Justin Tyler, Vice President of Programming
Matt Cross, News Director
Lori Richardson, Traffic Director

***WVFA**
02-06-2004; 90.5 MHz FM; *Hrs Open:* 24; 0.012 kw; 614 ft.; N43 36 56 W72 10 24
Mailing Address: PO Box 126, Hartford, VT 05047 US
Second Address: 48 Wescott Rd., Enfield, NH 3748
(802) 295-9683; *Fax:* (802) 295-9683
www.wvfaradio.com
vtpreacher@aol.com
License: Lebanon, Grafton County, NH held by Green Mountain Educational Fellowship Inc.
Wire Services: AP
Arbitron Metro Market: Hartford, VT; *Format:* Religious; *Hrs. of News Programming:* News progmg 11 hrs wkly; *Target Audience:* 25-49; primary
William Wittik, President
Betsy Murray, Operations Dir
Elmer Murray, Operations Manager

WUVR
01-01-2004; 1490 kHz AM
P.O. Box 2295, New London, NH 03257 US
(603) 526-9464; *Fax:* (603) 448-0500
www.wntk.com
admin@wntk.com
License: Lebanon, NH held by KOOR Communications Inc.
Group Owner: KOOR Communications Inc.
Arbitron Metro Market: Lebanon, NH; *Format:* News, News/Talk, 86
Matt Cross, General Manager

Lisbon

WLTN-FM
09-01-1991; 96.7 MHz FM; *Hrs Open:* 24; 6 kw; 295 ft.; N44 13 11 W71 52 7
15 Main Street, Littleton, NH 03561 US
(603) 444-3911; *Fax:* (603) 444-7186
mix967@roadrunner.com
License: Lisbon, Grafton County, NH held by Barry P. Lunderville L.L.C.
Group Owner: Barry P. Lunderville Stns
Nat'l Network: Westwood One
Arbitron Metro Market: Littleton, NH; *Format:* Adult Contemp; *Hrs. of News Programming:* news progmg 7 hrs wkly; *No. News Employees:* 1; *Target Audience:* 25-54.; *Adv. Rates:* Same as AM
Ray Garon, President/General Manager
Pat McKay, Operations Manager/Programming Director
Andy Orcutt, Director of Sales
Shannon Stephens, Promotions & Marketing Coordinator

Littleton

WLTN
10-10-1963; 1400 kHz AM; *Hrs Open:* 24; 1 kw-U, ND1; N44 18 47 W71 46 8
15 Main Street, Littleton, NH 03561 US
(603) 444-3911; *Fax:* (603) 444-7186
www.wltnradio.com
mix967@roadrunner.com
License: Littleton, NH held by Barry P. Lunderville L.L.C.
Group Owner: Barry P. Lunderville Stns; (acq 6-30-2005; with WLTN-FM Lisbon)
Arbitron Metro Market: Littleton, NH; *Format:* Oldies; *Hrs. of News Programming:* news progmg 40 hrs wkly; *No. News Employees:* 1; *Target Audience:* 21-65.; *Adv. Rates:* 21; 14; 14; 14
Barry Lunderville, General Manager
Christina Brooks, General Sales Mgr
Phil Rivera, Programming Director
Jim Clothey, News Director
Brian Lunderville, Chief Engineer
Danielle Corbiel, Traffic Manager

WMTK
02-23-1985; 106.3 MHz FM; *Hrs Open:* 24; 0.39 kw; 1257 ft.; N44 21 14 W71 44 23
PO Box 106, Littleton, NH 03561 US
(603) 444-5106; *Fax:* (603) 444-1205
www.notchfm.com
License: Littleton, Grafton County, NH held by Vermont Broadcast Associates Inc.
Group Owner: Vermont Broadcast Associates Inc.; (acq 8-2000; $250,000)
Arbitron Metro Market: Littleton, NH; *Format:* Contemporary Hits/Top 40; *No. News Employees:* 1; *Target Audience:* 30-50; slightly more males, active lifestyles; *Adv. Rates:* 30; 30; 30; 20
Bruce James, General Manager
Steve Nichols, General Sales Mgr
Todd Wellington, News Director
Don Smith, Chief Engineer

Madbury

WWNH
05-20-1989; 1340 kHz AM; *Hrs Open:* 24
Mailing Address: P.O.Box 69, Dover, NH 03820 US
Second Address: 284 Rt. 155, Dover, NH 3821
(603) 742-8575; *Fax:* (603) 743-6444
www.loveradio.net
info@loveradio.net
License: Madbury, NH held by Harvest Broadcasting.
Nat'l Network: USA
Arbitron Metro Market: Portsmouth-Dove; *Format:* Adult Contemp
Special Programming: Family 24 hrs wkly; *Hrs. of News Programming:* News progmg 3 hrs wkly; *Target Audience:* General; 29 plus
Patti Smith, CEO
Ernie Jenkins, Operations Dir
Steve Donnell, Chief Engineer

Manchester

WFEA
03-08-1932; 1370 kHz AM
500 Commercial Street, Manchester, NH 03101 US
(603) 669-5777; *Fax:* (603) 669-4641
www.wfea1370.com
raydionh@wzid.com
License: Manchester, NH held by Saga Communications of New England LLC.
Group Owner: Saga Communications Inc.; (acq 6-2-92; grpsl, including co-located FM).
Regional Reps: Katz.
Arbitron Metro Market: Manchester, NH; *Format:* Adult Contemp
Special Programming: Fr 3 hrs, Sp 2 hrs wkly; *Target Audience:* 50 plus; Modern Maturity market
Ray Garon, President/General Manager
Ray Garon, General Manager
Andy Orcutt, Director of Sales
Pat Mckay, Operations Manager & Program Director
Shannon Stephens, Operations Manager & Program Director
Peter Stohrer, EngineeringDir

WGIR
10-01-1941; 610 kHz AM; *Hrs Open:* 24; 5 kw-D, DA2; 1 kw-N, DA2; N43 0 57 W71 28 48
195 McGregor Street, Suite 810, Manchester, NH 03103 US
(603) 625-6915; *Fax:* (603) 625-9255
www.nhnewsnetwork610.com
info@wgiram.com
License: Manchester, NH held by Capstar TX LLC
Group Owner: iHeartMedia; (acq 8-30-00; grpsl)
Nat'l Network: Fox News Radio; Westwood One
Format: News, News/Talk, 84, Talk; *Hrs. of News Programming:* news progmg 38 hrs wkly; *No. News Employees:* 2; *Target Audience:* 35-54.
Joseph Graham, Market President
Tim Moore, Programming Director
Adam Furious, Promotions Manager

WGIR-FM
06-05-1963; 101.1 MHz FM; 11.5 kw; 1027 ft.; N42 58 54 W71 35 21
195 McGregor Street, Suite 810, Manchester, NH 03103 US
(603) 625-6915; *Fax:* (603) 669-0610
www.rock101fm.com
info@rock101fm.com
License: Manchester, Hillsborough County, NH held by Capstar TX LLC
Group Owner: iHeartMedia
Format: Rock/AOR
Joseph Graham, Market President
Tim Moore, Programming Director
Adam Furious, Promotions Manager

WGAM
10-01-1946; 1250 kHz AM; *Hrs Open:* 5 AM-11 PM; 5 kw-D, DA2; 5 kw-N, DA2; N43 0 40 W71 30 19
288 South River Road, Bedford, NH 03110 US
(603) 880-9001; *Fax:* (603) 577-8682
www.wgamradio.com
info@wgamradio.com
License: Manchester, NH held by Absolute Broadcasting LLC.
Group Owner: Absolute Broadcasting LLC; (acq 11-21-2006; $1.6 million)
Nat'l Network: Fox Sports
Arbitron Metro Market: Manchester, NH; *Format:* Sports
Matt Perrault, General Manager

***WLMW**
09-01-1997; 90.7 MHz FM; *Hrs Open:* 24; 15 w; 869 ft; N42 58 59 W71 35 25
Mailing Address: Box 366, Auburn, NH 03060
Second Address: 134 Hollis Rd., Amherst, NH 3031
(603) 672-0573; *Fax:* (603) 672-0573
www.nhfamilyradio.org
jim@nhfamilyradio.org

License: Manchester, Hillsborough County, NH held by Knowledge For Life.

Jim Phelan, General Manager
Jim Phelan, Station Manager

WZID
01-01-1948; 95.7 MHz FM; 14.5 kw; 925 ft.; N42 59 2 W71 35 22
500 Commercial Ave, Manchester, NH 03101 US
(603) 669-5777; *Fax:* (603) 669-4641
www.wzid.com
radionh@wzid.com
License: Manchester, Hillsborough County, NH
Group Owner: Saga Communications Inc.
Arbitron Metro Market: Manchester, NH; *Format:* Adult Contemp; *Target Audience:* 25-54.
Ray Garon, President/General Manager
Pat McKay, Operations Manager
Andy Orcutt, General Sales Mgr
Bob Bronson, Programming Director
Shannon Stevens, Promotions Coordinator

WGAM(AM)
1250 kHz AM; 1 kw-D, 670 w-N; N44 30 00 W71 33 50
Mailing Address: 149 Main Street, Suite 210, Nashua, NH 03060
Second Address: 195 Main St., Lancaster, NH 03060
(603) 444-4102; *Fax:* (603) 788-3536
kiss102@together.net
License: Manchester, Coos County, NH held by Absolute Broadcasting
Group Owner: Barry P. Lunderville Stns
Population Served: 109,830; *Arbitron Metro Market:* Manchester, NH
Matt Perrault, General Manager

Meredith

WZEI
11-16-1988; 101.5 MHz FM; 6 kw; 328 ft.; N43 35 46 W71 29 55
20 Guest Street, 3rd Floor, Brighton, MA 02135 US
(617) 779-3500
www.thehawkrocks.com
Zack@TheHawkRocks.com
License: Meredith, Belknap County, NH held by Great Eastern Radio LLC
Group Owner: Great Eastern Radio LLC
Arbitron Metro Market: Gilford, NH; *Format:* Classic Rock
David Field, President/Chief Executive Officer
Jeff Brown, General Manager
Dana Panepinto, Sales Manager
Jason Wolfe, Programming Director

***WANH**
91.5 MHz FM; 1.7 kw horiz; 26 ft.; N43 41 25 W71 22 34
37 Reddington Road, Concord, NH 03301 US
(603) 227-0911
License: Meredith, Belknap County, NH held by New Hampshire Gospel Radio Inc.
Arbitron Metro Market: Meredith, NH
Janice Cyr, General Manager

Moultonborough

WSCY
05-31-1993; 106.9 MHz FM; 0.13 kw; 2096 ft.; N43 46 9 W71 18 52
P.O. Box 99, Franklin, NH 03235 US
(603) 253-8080; *Fax:* (603) 934-2933
www.wscy.com
License: Moultonborough, Carroll County, NH held by Northeast Communications Corp.
Group Owner: Northeast Communications Corp.; acq 5-4-93; $399,072;
Format: Country
Jeff Fisher, President
Jeff Fisher, General Manager
Jeff Levitan, General Sales Mgr
Joyce Danas, Programming Director
Amy Bates, News Director
Jeff Levitan, Vice President

Mount Washington

WHOM
07-09-1958; 94.9 MHz FM; 50 kw; 3743 ft.; N44 16 11 W71 18 15
One City Ctr., 3rd Floor, Portland, ME 04101 US
(207) 774-6364
www.949whom.com
brian.lang@townsquaremedia.com
License: Mount Washington, NH held by Townsquare Media Portland License, LLC
Group Owner: Townsquare Media; (acq 7-7-99; grpsl).
Nat'l Reps: Christal
Arbitron Metro Market: Portland, ME; *Format:* Adult Contemp; *Target Audience:* 35-64; professionals with active lifestyles
Brian Lang, General Manager
Mike Marcello, Director of Sales
AJ Dukette, Brand Manager
Stephen Lenz, Digital Managing Editor

Nashua

WFNQ
10-19-1987; 106.3 MHz FM; *Hrs Open:* 24; 0.95 kw; 541 ft.; N42 44 7 W71 23 37
20 Industrial Park Drive, 1st Floor, Unit 2, Nashua, NH 03062 US
(603) 889-1063; *Fax:* (603) 882-0688
www.1063frankfm.com
License: Nashua, Hillsborough County, NH held by WBIN Media Co. Inc.
Group Owner: WBIN Media Co. Inc.
Format: Adult Contemp; *Hrs. of News Programming:* news progmg 5 hrs wkly; *No. News Employees:* 1; *Target Audience:* 18-49.
Chris Garrett, General Manager
Paul Seccareccio, General Sales Mgr
Bethany Moore, Promotions Director
Brian Battle, Production Director

WGHM
01-01-1991; 900 kHz AM; *Hrs Open:* 6 AM-6 PM (Oct-Apr); 6 AM-10 PM (Ma
Longmeadow Way, Box 403, Hamilton, MA 01936 US
(603) 880-9001; *Fax:* (603) 577-8682
info@wgamradio.com
License: Nashua, NH held by Absolute Broadcasting LLC.
Group Owner: Absolute Broadcasting LLC; (acq 11-2-2005; $925,000)
Nat'l Network: Fox Sports
Arbitron Metro Market: Nashua, NH; *Format:* Sports; *Target Audience:* 35 plus.
Matt Perrault, General Manager

WSMN
03-09-1958; 1590 kHz AM; *Hrs Open:* 18; 5 kw-U, DA1; N42 44 40 W71 29 52
502 West Hollis St., P.O. Box 548, Nashua, NH 03061 US
(603) 880-9001; *Fax:* (603) 577-8682
www.wsmnradio.com
License: Nashua, NH held by Absolute Broadcasting LLC.
Group Owner: Absolute Broadcasting LLC; (acq 11-10-2005; $250,000)
Nat'l Network: ESPN Radio
Format: News, News/Talk, 84, Talk
Matt Perrault, General Manager

***WEVS**
01-01-2005; 88.3 MHz FM; 3.5 kw horiz, 5 kw vert; 69 ft.; N42 45 0 W71 28 47 *Rebroadcasts:* Rebroadcasts WEVO(FM) Concord 100%
207 N. Main St., Concord, NH 03301 US
(603) 228-8910; *Fax:* (603) 224-6052
www.nhpr.org
License: Nashua, Hillsborough County, NH held by New Hampshire Public Radio Inc.
Nat'l Network: NPR; PRI
Arbitron Metro Market: Nashua, NH; *Format:* News, News/Talk, 86
Elizabeth Gardella, President/Chief Executive Officer
Dan Colgan, Operations Manager
Michael Rathke, Programming Director
Donna Hiltz, Traffic Manager
Michael Saffel, Chief Engineer
Alexandria Urbanowski, Vice President ofDevelopment & Marketing
Scott McPherson, Vice President of Operations & Finance
Jim McCann, Director of Corporate Support

New London

WNTK-FM
11-30-1992; 99.7 MHz FM; *Hrs Open:* 24; 1.45 kw; 676 ft.; N43 26 52 W72 2 4 *Rebroadcasts:* Rebroadcasts WNTK(AM) Newport 50%
P.O. Box 2295, New London, NH 03257 US
(603) 526-9464; *Fax:* (603) 448-0500
www.wntk.com
admin@wntk.com
License: New London, Merrimack County, NH held by Koor Communications Inc.
Group Owner: KOOR Communications Inc.
Arbitron Metro Market: Newport, NH; *Format:* News, Talk; *No. News Employees:* 2; *Target Audience:* 24-54.; *Adv. Rates:* 19; 19; 19; 19
Matt Cross, General Manager

***WSCS**
02-01-1996; 90.9 MHz FM; 0.063 kw horiz, 0.25 kw vert; 299 ft.; N43 24 41 W71 58 33
541 Main Street, New London, NH 03257 US
(603) 526-3493; *Fax:* (603) 526-3452
www.colby-sawyer.edu/wscs
wscs@colby-sawyer.edu
License: New London, Merrimack County, NH held by Colby-Sawyer College.

Pat Gamble, Station Manager

Newport

WCNL
08-11-1960; 1010 kHz AM; *Hrs Open:* 24
11 Main St., Newport, NH 03773 US
(603) 863-0080
www.country1010.com
info@country1010.com
License: Newport, NH held by KOOR Communications.
Group Owner: KOOR Communications Inc.; (acq 8-88; $250,000;
Arbitron Metro Market: Newport, NH; *Format:* Country; *Target Audience:* 25-54; informed adults
Steve Smith, General Manager

North Conway

WPKQ
03-01-1952; 103.7 MHz FM; *Hrs Open:* 24; 21.5 kw; 3802 ft.; N44 16 13 W71 18 17
One City Center, Portland, ME 04101 US
(207) 774-6364
www.1037thepeak.com
brian.lang@townsquaremedia.com
License: North Conway, NH held by Townsquare Media Portsmouth License, LLC
Group Owner: Townsquare Media; (acq 7-7-99; grpsl).
Arbitron Metro Market: Concord (Lake Regions), NH; *Format:* Country
Brian Lang, General Manager
Mike Marcello, Director of Sales
Herb Ivy, Brand Manager
Stephen Lenz, Digital Managing Editor

Peterborough

WDER-FM
06-01-1971; 92.1 MHz FM; *Hrs Open:* 24; 0.17 kw; Ant 1,332 ft; N42 51 41 W71 52 45 *Rebroadcasts:* Rebroadcasts WFNX(FM) Lynn, MA 80%
P.O. Box 1923, 7 Perley St., Concord, NH 03302
(603) 437-9337; *Fax:* (603) 434-1035
www.lifechangingradio.com
License: Peterborough, Hillsborough County, NH held by Blount Communications Inc. of NH.
Group Owner: Blount Communications Group; (acq 11-29-99).
Wire Services: AP
Population Served: 511,000; *Arbitron Metro Market:* Manchester, MA; *Format:* Religious *Special Programming:* Jazz 6 hrs wkly; *Hrs. of News Programming:* news progmg 2 hrs wkly; *No. News Employees:* 1 *TargetAudience:* Adults 18-44; young, educated white collar professionals with extremely active lifestyles
William Blount, President

Plymouth

***WPCR-FM**
09-29-1974; 91.7 MHz FM; *Hrs Open:* 24; 0.215 kw; -377 ft.; N43 45 25 W71 41 23
19 Highland Avenue, Plymouth, NH 03264 US
(603) 535-2242; *Fax:* (603) 535-2783
www.wpcr.org
License: Plymouth, Grafton County, NH held by Plymouth State College.
Nat'l Network: AP Radio
Format: Rock/AOR *Special Programming:* Class 3 hrs, jazz 3 hrs, reggae 3 hrs, blues 3 hrs, comedy 3 hrs wkly; *Target Audience:* 15-35; college students & those interested in progressive alternative music
Nick Landry, General Manager
Miles Winzeler, Assistant GM

WPNH
11-10-1965; 1300 kHz AM; *Hrs Open:* 24; 5 kw-D, NDD; 0.082 kw-N, ND1; N43 46 32 W71 42 20

P.O. Box 941, Franklin, NH 03235 US
(603) 536-2500,(603) 536-2501; *Fax:* (603) 934-2933
info@mix941fm.com
License: Plymouth, NH held by Northeast Communications Corp.
Group Owner: Northeast Communications Corp.; acq 2-9-99; with co-located FM)
Format: Big Band *Special Programming:* Breakfast with the bands 6 hrs wkly; *Target Audience:* 35 plus.; *Adv. Rates:* 118; 18; 18; 18
Fred Caruso, Operations/Programming Director
Jeff Fisher, President/General Manager
Jeff Levitan, General Sales Mgr
Amy Bates, News Director
Tim Martin, Traffic Manager

WPNH-FM
10-01-1975; 100.1 MHz FM; 0.41 kw; 1234 ft.; N43 44 21 W71 47 27
Box 941, Franklin, NH 03235 US
(603) 536-2500,(603) 536-2501; *Fax:* (603) 934-2933
www.wpnhfm.com
info@mix941fm.com
License: Plymouth, Grafton County, NH held by Northeast Communications Corp.
Format: Alternative
Jeff Fisher, President/General Manager
Jeff Levitan, General Sales Mgr
Annie Biello, Programming Director
Amy Bates, News Director
Tim Martin, Traffic Manager

Portsmouth

WHEB
01-14-1964; 100.3 MHz FM; 50 kw; 459 ft.; N43 3 11 W70 46 4
815 Lafayette Road, Portsmouth, NH 03801 US
(603) 436-7300; *Fax:* (603) 430-9415
www.wheb.com
info@wheb.com
License: Portsmouth, Rockingham County, NH held by Capstar TX LLC
Group Owner: iHeartMedia; (acq 8-30-00; grpsl).
Arbitron Metro Market: Portsmouth-Dover-Rochester, NH; *Format:* Rock/AOR; *Target Audience:* 18-49.
Tim Moore, Programming Director
Kayla Winsor, Promotions Director
Matt Provost, Digital Content Director

WMYF
12-05-1960; 1380 kHz AM; *Hrs Open:* 24; 1 kw-D, DAN; 1 kw-N, DAN; N43 3 48 W70 47 9
815 Lafayette Road, Portsmouth, NH 03801 US
(603) 436-7300; *Fax:* (603) 430-9415
www.wmyf.com
License: Portsmouth, NH held by Capstar TX LLC
Group Owner: iHeartMedia
Arbitron Metro Market: Portsmouth, NH; *Format:* Country; *Target Audience:* 25-54.
Tim Moore, Programming Director
Marc Provenzano, Promotions Manager
Matt Provost, Digital Content Director

Rochester

WPKX
01-01-1947; 930 kHz AM; *Hrs Open:* 24; 5 kw-U, DA-N; N43 17 13 W70 56 55
815 Lafayette Rd., Portsmouth, NH 3801
(603) 436-7300; *Fax:* (603) 430-9415
www.foxsports930.com
License: Rochester, Strafford County, NH held by Capstar TX LLC
Group Owner: iHeartMedia
Population Served: 310,000; *Arbitron Metro Market:* Portsmouth-Dover-Rochester, NH; *Format:* News, News/Talk, 84, Talk; *Target Audience:* 25-64; decision-makers, heads of businesses, households
Joseph Graham, Market President
Tim Moore, Programming Director
Marc Provenzano, Promotions Manager

WQSO
10-21-1979; 96.7 MHz FM; *Hrs Open:* 24; 3 kw; 328 ft.; N43 17 14 W70 56 49
815 Lafayette Road, Portsmouth, NH 03801 US
(603) 436-7300; *Fax:* (603) 430-9415
www.newsradio967.com
License: Rochester, Strafford County, NH held by Capstar TX LLC
Group Owner: iHeartMedia; (acq 8-30-00; grpsl).
Arbitron Metro Market: Portsmouth-Dover-Rochester, NH; *Format:* News, News/Talk, 86; *Hrs. of News Programming:* news progmg 12 hrs wkly; *No. News Employees:* 3; *Target Audience:* 25-54.
Tim Moore, Programming Director
Adam Furious, Promotions Director
Matt Provost, Digital Content Director

Salem

WMVX
01-10-1977; 1110 kHz AM; 5 kw-D, DAD; N42 45 42 W71 16 13
462 Merrimack St., Methuen, MA 01844 US
(978) 686-9966
License: Salem, NH held by Costa-Eagle Radio Ventures L.P.
Group Owner: Costa-Eagle Radio Ventures L.P.; (acq 1996)
Nat'l Reps: Roslin
Arbitron Metro Market: Portsmouth, MA; *Format:* News, News/Talk, 86; *Hrs. of News Programming:* news progmg 25 hrs wkly; *No. News Employees:* 2; *Target Audience:* General.
Pat Costa, General Manager

Somersworth

WBYY
01-25-1995; 98.7 MHz FM; *Hrs Open:* 24; 6 kw; 315 ft.; N43 14 11 W70 53 37
P.O. Box 400, Dover, NH 03820 US
(603) 742-0987; *Fax:* (603) 742-0448
www.987thebay.com
susan@987thebay.com
License: Somersworth, Strafford County, NH held by Garrison City Broadcasting Inc.
Arbitron Metro Market: Dover, NH; *Format:* Adult Contemp; *No. News Employees:* 2; *Target Audience:* 25-54.; *Adv. Rates:* 60; 50; 50; 30
Bob Demers Sr., CEO
Sarah Sullivan, Operations Dir
Jeff Rosenberg, Chief Engineer
Susan Demers Weigold, Senior Vice President

Swanzey

WEEY
01-01-1972; 93.5 MHz FM; 2 kw; 574 ft.; N42 54 57 W72 19 52
52 Main Street, West Lebanon, NH 03784 US
(617) 779-3500; *Fax:* (617) 779-3557
www.weei.com
License: Swanzey, Windsor County, NH held by Great Eastern Radio LLC.
Group Owner: Great Eastern Radio LLC; (acq 10-30-2007; grpsl)
Arbitron Metro Market: Brighton, MA; *Format:* Sports; *Target Audience:* 25-54.
Jeff Brown, General Manager
Ian Carerra, General Sales Mgr
Dayna Thurston, Programming Director

Walpole

WFYX
11-01-2000; 96.3 MHz FM; 0.32 kw; 407 ft.; N43 8 14 W72 25 59 *Rebroadcasts:* Rebroadcasts WWOD(FM) Hartford, VT 100%
106 North Main Street, West Lebanon, NH 03784 US
(603) 298-0332; *Fax:* (603) 727-0134
www.bestoldies104.com
License: Walpole, Cheshire County, NH held by Great Eastern Radio LLC
Group Owner: Great Eastern Radio LLC
Arbitron Metro Market: Walpole, NH; *Format:* Oldies
Nichole Romano, General Manager
Justin Tyler, Vice President of Programming

Whitefield

WNYN-FM
01-01-2007; 99.1 MHz FM; 0.46 kw; 1135 ft.; N44 21 10 W71 44 15
US
(802) 223-2396; *Fax:* (802) 223-1520
www.free991.com
License: Whitefield, Coos County, NH held by White Park Broadcasting Inc.
Group Owner: Northeast Broadcasting Company Inc.
Arbitron Metro Market: Whitefield, NH; *Format:* Adult Contemp
Steven Silberberg, President
Ed Flanagan, General Manager

Winchester

WINQ
10-15-1991; 98.7 MHz FM; *Hrs Open:* 24; 2.15 kw; 554 ft.; N42 54 57 W72 19 53
69 Stanhope Avenue, Keene, NH 03431 US
(603) 352-9230; *Fax:* (603) 357-3926
www.987wink.com
License: Winchester, Cheshire County, NH held by Saga Communications of New Hampshire LLC.
Group Owner: Saga Communications Inc.; (acq 7-1-2002; $2.63 million with WZBK(AM) Keene).
Nat'l Network: ABC; Jones Radio Networks
Arbitron Metro Market: Winchester, NH; *Format:* Country; *Hrs. of News Programming:* news progmg 8 hrs wkly; *No. News Employees:* 4; *Target Audience:* 25-54.
Bob Cox, General Manager/Operations Director
Susan Wells, General Sales Mgr
Mark Heasley, Assistant Programming Director/Brand Manager
Vicki Lenahan, Promotions Manager

Wolfeboro

WASR
04-01-1970; 1420 kHz AM; *Hrs Open:* 5 AM-8 PM
Mailing Address: P. O. Box 900, Wolfeboro, NH 03894 US
Second Address: 73 Varney Rd., Wolfeboro, NH 03894-0900
(603) 569-1420; *Fax:* (603) 569-1900
www.wasr.net
mail@wasr.net
License: Wolfeboro, NH held by Winnipesaukee Network Inc.
Arbitron Metro Market: Wolfeboro, NH; *Format:* Adult Contemp, News; *Hrs. of News Programming:* news progmg 35 hrs wkly; *No. News Employees:* 4; *Target Audience:* 25-54.
Grant Hatch, President
Gary Hammond, Engineering Dir

WLKZ
02-01-1985; 104.9 MHz FM; *Hrs Open:* 24; 0.56 kw; 1065 ft.; N43 32 45.3 W71 22 42.8
Mailing Address: 21 Production Place, #15, Gilford, NH 03246 US
Second Address: 25 Country Club Rd., Bldg. One, Gilford, NH 3249
(603) 524-1323; *Fax:* (603) 528-5185
License: Wolfeboro, Carroll County, NH held by Great Eastern Radio
Group Owner: Great Eastern Radio; (acq 3-16-2004; grpsl).
Nat'l Reps: McGavren Guild
Format: Contemporary Hits/Top 40, Adult Contemp; *Hrs. of News Programming:* News progmg 5 hrs wkly; *Target Audience:* 25-54; baby boomers; *Adv. Rates:* 32; 32; 32; na
Rob Fulmer, General Manager
Justin Tyler, Programming Director
Dirk Nadon, Chief Engineer
Pete Detone, Market Manager
Jim Whedon, Sales Manager
Kelly Kowalski, Brnad Manager

New Jersey

Asbury Park

WADB(AM)
01-01-1926; 1310 kHz AM; 2.5 kw-D, 1 kw-N, DA-2; N40 13 47 W74 05 27
2351 Sunset Blvd., Suite 170-218, Rocklin, CA 95765
(916) 251-1600; *Fax:* (916) 251-1650
www.air1.com
info@air1.com
License: Asbury Park, Monmouth County, NJ held by Townsquare Media Monmouth-Ocean License LLC
Group Owner: Townsquare Media; (acq 6-11-2002; grpsl)
Nat'l Network: Fox Sports
Population Served: 8,383; *Arbitron Metro Market:* Denison IA; *Format:* Alternative, Christian
Mike Novak, President

WJLK
11-20-1947; 94.3 MHz FM; 1.3 kw; 499 ft.; N40 13 45 W74 5 25
619 Alexander Road, 3rd Floor, Princeton, NJ 08540 US
(732) 897-8282; *Fax:* (732) 897-8283
License: Asbury Park, Monmouth County, NJ held by Townsquare Media Monmouth-Ocean License LLC
Group Owner: Townsquare Media
Arbitron Metro Market: New York; *Format:* Adult Contemp
Lou Russo, Operations Dir
Tara Hessline, News Director
Debbie Mazzella, Music Director

***WYGG**
88.1 MHz FM; 0.001 kw horiz, 0.92 kw vert; 112 ft.; N40 13 2 W74 0 38
1488 New York Avenue, Brooklyn, NY 11210 US
(908) 775-0821
www.goodnewsradiofm.com

License: Asbury Park, Monmouth County, NJ held by Minority Business & Housing Development, Inc.
Arbitron Metro Market: Asbury Park, NJ; *Format:* Religious
Ethel Huff, Chairman
Gene Huff, General Manager

Atlantic City

*WAJM
01-01-1997; 88.9 MHz FM; 0.15 kw vert; 102 ft.; N39 21 54 W74 28 31
Mailing Address: 1809 Pacific Avenue, Atlantic City, NJ 08401 US
Second Address: 1809 Pacific Ave., Atlantic City, NJ 8402
(609) 343-7300; *Fax:* (609) 343-7347
wajm@comcast.net
License: Atlantic City, Atlantic County, NJ held by Atlantic City Board of Education.
Arbitron Metro Market: Atlantic City, NJ; *Format:* Variety/Diverse
Pamela Lewis, General Manager
Albert Horner, Station Manager

WAYV
04-01-1961; 95.1 MHz FM; *Hrs Open:* 24; 50 kw; 331 ft.; N39 22 51 W74 27 3 *Rebroadcasts:* Simulcast with WAIV(FM) Cape May 100%
8025 Black Horse Pike, Suite 100-102, W. Atlantic City, NJ 08232 US
(609) 484-8444; *Fax:* (609) 646-6331
951wayv.com
gfisher@equitycommunications.net
License: Atlantic City, Atlantic County, NJ held by Equity Communications L.P.
Group Owner: Equity Communications LP; (acq 6-21-96; $3.1 million).
Nat'l Reps: Katz Radio
Arbitron Metro Market: Selma AL; *Format:* Religious; *Adv. Rates:* 200; 200; 200; 50
Gary Fisher, General Sales Mgr
Rob Garcia, Programming Director
Shannon Wray, Promotions Manager

WPGG
01-01-1940; 1450 kHz AM; *Hrs Open:* 24; 1 kw-U, ND1; N39 22 42 W74 26 53
950 Tilton Road, Suite 200, Northfield, NJ 08225 US
(609) 645-9797; *Fax:* (609) 272-9228
www.literock969.com
mike.ruble@mrgnj.com
License: Atlantic City, NJ held by Townsquare Media Atlantic City License LLC
Group Owner: Townsquare Media; (acq 5-11-2001; grpsl).
Nat'l Network: CBS
Arbitron Metro Market: Atlantic City-Cape May, NJ; *Format:* Talk; *Hrs. of News Programming:* news progmg 24 hrs wkly; *No. News Employees:* 1; *Target Audience:* 25 plus; the population of South Jersey
Dan Sullivan, General Manager
Gary Guida, Programming Director
Jennifer Smith, Promotions Manager
Tom McNally, Chief Engineer
Greg Janoff, Regional Market Manager
Mike Ruble, Market Manager
Joe Mitchell, Local Sales Manager
Chris Coleman, Production Director

WFPG
09-01-1962; 96.9 MHz FM; *Hrs Open:* 24; 50 kw; 361 ft.; N39 22 42 W74 26 53
950 Tilton Road, Suite 200, Northfield, NJ 08225 US
(609) 645-9797; *Fax:* (609) 272-9228
www.literock969.com
License: Atlantic City, Atlantic County, NJ held by Townsquare Media Atlantic City License LLC
Group Owner: Townsquare Media
Arbitron Metro Market: Atlantic City-Cape May, NJ; *Format:* Adult Contemp, Light Rock; *No. News Employees:* 1; *Target Audience:* 25-54.
Gary Guida, Programming Director
Jennifer Smith, Promotions Manager
Tom McNally, Chief Engineer
Greg Janoff, Regional Market Manager
Mike Ruble, Market Manager/General Sales Manager
Joe Mitchell, Local Sales Manager
ChrisColeman, Production Director

WMGM
06-14-1961; 103.7 MHz FM; *Hrs Open:* 24; 50 kw; 348 ft.; N39 23 24 W74 30 45
1601 New Rd., Linwood, NJ 08221 US
(609) 653-1400; *Fax:* (609) 601-0450
www.1037wmgm.com
License: Atlantic City, Atlantic County, NJ held by Longport Media LLC
Group Owner: Longport Media LLC; (acq 8-2-2011)
Nat'l Reps: McGavren Guild
Arbitron Metro Market: Atlantic City, NJ; *Format:* Rock/AOR; *Target Audience:* 25-54; men
Dave Coskey, President
Paul Kelly, VP of Operations
Joe Croce, VP of Sales

WMID
05-30-1947; 1340 kHz AM; *Hrs Open:* 24; 0.89 kw-U, ND1; N39 22 35 W74 27 8
8025 Black Horse Pike, Suite 100-102, W. Atlantic City, NJ 08232 US
(609) 484-8444; *Fax:* (609) 646-6331
www.classicoldieswmid.com
rgarcia@equitycommunications.net
License: Atlantic City, NJ held by Equity Communications L.P.
Group Owner: Equity Communications LP; (acq 3-29-2002; grpsl).
Nat'l Reps: Katz Radio
Arbitron Metro Market: Atlantic City, NJ; *Format:* Oldies; *Target Audience:* 35-64; adults; *Adv. Rates:* 50; 50; 50; 50
Rob Garcia, Programming Director
Shannon Wray, Promotions Manager

*WNJN-FM
09-01-1996; 89.7 MHz FM; 0.025 kw horiz, 6 kw vert; 276 ft.; N39 27 40 W74 41 6
150 N 6th Street, Philadelphia, PA 19106 US
(215) 351-1200; *Fax:* (215) 351-0398
www.whyy.org
talkback@whyy.org
License: Atlantic City, Atlantic County, NJ held by New Jersey Public Broadcasting Authority.
Nat'l Network: NPR; PRI
Arbitron Metro Market: Atlantic City, PA; *Format:* News, News/Talk, 86; *Target Audience:* General.
William Marrazzo, CEO/COO
Kyra McGrath, Operations Dir
Pharoah Cranston, Station Manager
Chris Satullo, News Director

WPUR
06-01-1998; 107.3 MHz FM; 25 kw; 308 ft.; N39 22 42 W74 26 53
950 Tilton Road, Suite 200, Northfield, NJ 08225 US
(609) 645-9797; *Fax:* (609) 272-9224
www.catcountry1073.com
License: Atlantic City, Atlantic County, NJ held by Townsquare Media Atlantic City License LLC
Group Owner: Townsquare Media; (acq 5-11-01; grpsl).
Nat'l Reps: McGavren Guild
Arbitron Metro Market: Atlantic City-Cape May, NJ; *Format:* Country; *Target Audience:* 25-54.
Mike Ruble, General Sales Mgr
Joe Kelly, Programming Director
Hank Weisbecher, News Director
Tom McNally, Chief Engineer
Joe Mitchell, Director of Sales

Avalon

WIBG-FM
03-29-1976; 94.3 MHz FM; *Hrs Open:* 24; 3 kw; 300 ft; N39 07 48 W74 47 20
3328 Simpson Avenue, Ocean City, NJ 08226
(609) 398-7575; *Fax:* (609) 522-3666
www.wilw.com
wilwradio@mac.com
License: Avalon, Cape May County, NJ
Population Served: 43,114; *Arbitron Metro Market:* Atlantic City-Cape May, NJ; *Format:* Oldies
Rick Brancadora, President/General Manager

Barnegat

*WBNJ
91.9 MHz FM; 0 kw horiz, 4.5 kw vert; 226 ft.; N39 45 54 W74 19 12
PO Box 446, Waretown, NJ 08758 US
(609) 660-2028
www.wbnj.org
License: Barnegat, Ocean County, NJ held by WWN Educational Radio Corp.
Arbitron Metro Market: Barnegat, NJ; *Format:* Oldies
William Clanton Jr., President

Beach Haven West

*WVBH
01-01-2003; 88.3 MHz FM; 0.001 kw horiz, 0.1 kw vert; 427 ft.; N39 42 56 W74 17 32 *Rebroadcasts:* Simulcast of WXHL (FM) Christiana 100%
12 Oak Glen Lane, Colts Neck, NJ 07722 US
(302) 731-0690; *Fax:* (302) 738-3090
www.thereachfm.com
listenercare@myreachradio.com
License: Beach Haven West, Ocean County, NJ held by Priority Radio Inc.
Group Owner: Priority Radio Inc.; (acq 11-14-2003; $400,000).
Arbitron Metro Market: Newark, DE; *Format:* Adult Contemp
Dan Edwards, Operations Dir
Steve Hare, General Manager

Belvidere

WWYY
10-15-1992; 107.1 MHz FM; 1.2 kw; 719 ft.; N40 56 53 W75 9 38
11 Skyline Drive, Hawthorne, NJ 10532 US
(570) 421-2100; *Fax:* (570) 421-2040
License: Belvidere, Warren County, NJ held by Connoisseur Media Licences LLC
Group Owner: Connoisseur Media LLC
Nat'l Network: ABC
Arbitron Metro Market: Allentown-Bethlehem-Easton, PA
Maureen Barth, Operations Dir

Berlin

*WNJS-FM
08-21-1992; 88.1 MHz FM; 0.001 kw horiz, 0.08 kw vert; 942 ft.; N39 43 41 W74 50 39
150 N. 6th Street, Philadelphia, PA 19106 US
(215) 351-1200; *Fax:* (215) 351-0398
www.whyy.org
talkback@whyy.org
License: Berlin, Camden County, NJ held by New Jersey Public Broadcasting Authority
Nat'l Network: NPR; PRI
Arbitron Metro Market: Berlin, PA; *Format:* News, News/Talk, 86; *Target Audience:* General.
William Marrazzo, CEO/COO
Kyra McGrath, Operations Dir
Anthony Fleury, General Sales Mgr
Chris Satullo, News Director

Blackwood

*WDBK
06-07-1979; 91.5 MHz FM; 0.1 kw; 82 ft.; N39 47 6 W75 2 19
P. O. Box 200, Blackwood, NJ 08012 US
(856) 227-7200; *Fax:* (856) 374-4969
www.camdencc.edu/studentlife/WDBK-Radio.cfm
JMyerson@camdencc.edu
License: Blackwood, Camden County, NJ held by Camden County College.
Arbitron Metro Market: Blackwood, New Jersey; *Format:* Alternative
Chris Passanante, Station Manager

Blairstown

WHCY
10-21-1973; 106.3 MHz FM; *Hrs Open:* 24; 0.43 kw; 860 ft.; N41 2 53 W74 58 21
45 Ed Mitchell Avenue, Franklin, NJ 07416 US
(973) 827-2525; *Fax:* (973) 827-2135
www.max1063.com
License: Blairstown, Warren County, NJ held by CC Licenses LLC
Group Owner: iHeartMedia; (acq 2-13-2001).
Nat'l Reps: Katz Radio
Arbitron Metro Market: Wilkes Barre-Scranton, PA; *Format:* Contemporary Hits/Top 40 *Special Programming:* Public Affairs one hr wkly; *Target Audience:* 18-49; Women
Chuck Benfer, Market President
Gary Cee, Senior Vice President of Programming
Ricky Hoffend, Promotions Director

Bridgeton

*WNJB-FM
01-01-1998; 89.3 MHz FM; *Hrs Open:* 5 AM-midnight; 0.001 kw horiz, 2.5 kw vert; 220 ft.; N39 27 35 W75 9 28
150 N. 6th Street, Philadelphia, PA 19106 US
(215) 351-1200; *Fax:* (215) 351-0398
www.whyy.org
talkback@whyy.org

License: Bridgeton, Cumberland County, NJ held by New Jersey Public Broadcasting Authority.
Nat'l Network: NPR; PRI
Arbitron Metro Market: Bridgeton, PA; *Format:* News, News/Talk, 86; *Target Audience:* General.
William Marrazzo, CEO/COO
Kyra McGrath, Operations Dir
Pharoah Cranston, Station Manager
Steve Prido, General Sales Mgr
Chris Satullo, News Director
Bill Schorbus, Engineering Dir

WSNJ
08-01-1937; 1240 kHz AM; *Hrs Open:* 5:30 AM-midnight
P.O. Box 69, 1771 South Burlington Rd, Bridgeton, NJ 08302 US
(856) 451-2930; *Fax:* (856) 453-9440
wsnjam.com
License: Bridgeton, NJ held by Quinn Broadcasting Inc.
Format: Variety/Diverse *Special Programming:* Big band, MOR, news/talk, farm 10 hrs wkly; *Hrs. of News Programming:* news progmg 10 hrs wkly; *No. News Employees:* 1; *Target Audience:* 25 plus.
Toni Coogan, CFO
James Quinn, President
Greg Hennis, General Manager
Fred Sharkey, Programming Director
Richard Arsenault, Chief Engineer
John Casey, Music Director

Bridgewater

WWTR
12-23-1971; 1170 kHz AM; *Hrs Open:* 6am - 8pm
55 Horsehill Road, Cedar Knolls, NJ 07927 US
(732) 821-6009; *Fax:* (732) 821-6003
www.ebcmusic.com
info@ebcmusic.com
License: Bridgewater, NJ held by The Sentinel Publishing Co.
Group Owner: Beasley Broadcast Group; (acq 7-12-2001; grpsl)
Arbitron Metro Market: Monmouth Junction, NJ; *Format:* Ethnic; *Hrs. of News Programming:* new progmg one hr wkly; *No. News Employees:* 5; *Target Audience:* Indian; *Adv. Rates:* 30; 20; 30; 20
Arvind Agarwal, CEO/COO
Kulraaj Anand, Programming Director
Neal Newman, Chief Engineer
Alka Agrawal, COO

Brigantine

***WWFP**
01-01-2006; 90.5 MHz FM; 0.077 kw vert; 307 ft.; N39 22 46 W74 25 45
55 East Main St, Marlton, NJ 08053 US
(856) 983-1662
www.hopefm.net
info@hopefm.net
License: Brigantine, Atlantic East County, NJ held by Hope Christian Church of Marlton, Inc.
Group Owner: Hope Christian Church of Marlton
Arbitron Metro Market: Brigantine, NJ; *Format:* Christian

Burlington

WPEN-FM
01-19-1949; 97.5 MHz FM; 26 kw; Ant 682 ft; N40 04 57 W75 10 53
One Bala Plaza, Mail Stop 429, Bala Cynwyd, PA 19004
(610) 771-9750
www.975thefanatic.com
License: Burlington, Burlington County, NJ held by Greater Philadelphia Radio Inc.
Group Owner: Beasley Broadcast Group; (acq 11-15-2006; exchange for WCRB(FM) Lowell, MA)
Population Served: 500,000; *Arbitron Metro Market:* Philadelphia
Peter Smyth, Chairman
John Fullam, General Manager
Jim Brown, Station Manager
Don Gosselin, Programming Director
Chrissy Sirianni, Promotions Manager
Margo Marano, Music Director

Camden

***WKVP**
07-23-1968; 106.9 MHz FM; 38 kw; 600 ft; N39 54 33 W75 06 00 *Rebroadcasts:* Rebroadcasts KLVR(FM) Middletown, CA 100%
5700 West Oaks Boulevard, Rocklin, CA 95765 US
(916) 251-1600; *Fax:* (916) 251-1650
www.klove.com
License: Camden, Camden County, NJ held by Educational Media Foundation
Group Owner: EMF Broadcasting; (acq 11-19-2013; $1,012,500)
Arbitron Metro Market: Philadelphia
Mike Novak, President/CEO

WEMG
09-01-1925; 1310 kHz AM; *Hrs Open:* 24; 1 kw-D, ND2; 0.25 kw-N, ND2; N39 57 28 W75 6 54
8121 Georgia Ave 10th Fl, Silver Spring, MD 20910 US
(856) 963-5194; *Fax:* (215) 426-1550
http://mega1310am.com
License: Camden, NJ held by Davidson Media Station WEMG Licensee LLC.
Group Owner: Davidson Media Group LLC; (acq 1-31-2006; $8.75 million)
Nat'l Reps: Interep
Arbitron Metro Market: Philadelphia; *Hrs. of News Programming:* news in am/pm drive; *No. News Employees:* 1
Marc Taub, General Manager
Yesenia Torres, General Sales Mgr
Jorge Melendez, Programming Director

WTMR
11-01-1948; 800 kHz AM; 5 kw-D, DA2; 0.5 kw-N, DA2; N39 54 33 W75 6 0
2775 Mount Ephraim Ave., Camden, NJ 08104 US
(856) 962-8000; *Fax:* (856) 962-8004
www.wtmrradio.com
License: Camden, Camden County, NJ held by Beasley Media Group LLC
Group Owner: Beasley Broadcast Group Inc.; (acq 9-4-98; $8 million).
Arbitron Metro Market: Camden, NJ; *Format:* Religious, Talk
Louise Bessler, General Manager

Canton

WJKS
01-15-1972; 101.7 MHz FM; 3 kw; 263 ft; N39 25 51 W75 20 13
704 King Street, Suite 604, Wilmington, DE 19801
(302) 622-8895; *Fax:* (302) 622-8678
www.wjks1017.com
License: Canton, Salem County, NJ held by QC Communication Inc.
Population Served: 700,000; *Arbitron Metro Market:* Wilmington, DE; *Target Audience:* 18-44.
Mel Brittingham, Operations Dir
Steven Chanin, General Manager
Maria Sylvanus, General Sales Mgr
Jeff DePaulo, Chief Engineer

Cape May

WGBZ
06-03-1967; 102.3 MHz FM; 3.2 kw; 292 ft.; N39 0 33 W74 52 13 *Rebroadcasts:* Simulcast with WAYV(FM) Atlantic City 100%
8025 Black Horse Pike, Suite 100-102, W. Atlantic City, NJ 08232 US
(609) 484-8444; *Fax:* (609) 646-6331
www.993thebuzz.com
gfisher@equitycommunications.net
License: Cape May, Cape May County, NJ held by Equity Communications L.P.
Group Owner: Equity Communications LP; (acq 3-29-2002; grpsl).
Nat'l Reps: Katz Radio
Arbitron Metro Market: Atlantic City-Cape May, NJ; *Format:* Adult Contemp; *Target Audience:* 18-49; adults; *Adv. Rates:* 200; 200; 200; 50
Rob Garcia, Programming Director

***WWCJ**
09-01-1999; 89.1 MHz FM; *Hrs Open:* 24; 8.2 kw horiz, 13.5 kw vert; 385 ft.; N39 7 27.6 W74 45 56.4 *Rebroadcasts:* Rebroadcasts WWFM(FM) Trenton 100%
PO Box 17202, Trenton, NJ 08690 US
(609) 570-3189; *Fax:* (609) 570-3863
www.jazzon2.org
License: Cape May, Cape May County, NJ held by Mercer County Community College.
Nat'l Network: NPR
Arbitron Metro Market: Cape May, NJ; *Format:* Classical
Peter Fretwell, General Manager

Cape May Court House

***WNJZ**
08-01-1999; 90.3 MHz FM; 6 kw; 236 ft.; N39 6 18 W74 48 6
150 N. 6th Street, Philadelphia, PA 19106 US
(215) 351-1200; *Fax:* (215) 351-0398
www.whyy.org
talkback@whyy.org
License: Cape May Court House, Cape May County, NJ held by New Jersey Public Broadcasting Authority.
Nat'l Network: NPR; PRI
Arbitron Metro Market: Berlin, PA; *Format:* News, News/Talk, 86
William Marrazzo, CEO/COO
Kyra McGrath, Operations Dir
Pharoah Cranston, Station Manager
Chris Satullo, News Director

WAIV
09-05-1985; 105.5 MHz FM; *Hrs Open:* 24; 3.3 kw; 295 ft.; N39 7 32 W74 49 26 *Rebroadcasts:* Simulcast with WZBZ(FM) Atlantic City 100%
8025 Black Horse Pike, Suite 100-102, W. Atlantic City, NJ 08401 US
(609) 484-8444; *Fax:* (609) 646-6331
www.951wayv.com
License: Cape May Court House, Cape May County, NJ held by Equity Communications L.P.
Group Owner: Equity Communications LP; (acq 5-31-2002; grpsl)
Nat'l Reps: Katz Radio
Arbitron Metro Market: Atlantic City-C; *Format:* Contemporary Hits/Top 40; *Target Audience:* 18-49; adults; *Adv. Rates:* 200; 200; 200; 50
Rob Garcia, Programming Director
Shannon Wray, Promotions Manager

***WJPG**
01-01-2004; 88.1 MHz FM; 0 kw horiz, 0.55 kw vert; 213 ft.; N39 7 32 W74 49 27
950 Tilton Road, Suite 101, Northfield, NJ 08225 US
(877) 300-8105; *Fax:* (609) 861-3730
www.praise899.org
letters@praise899.org
License: Cape May Court House, Cape May County, NJ held by Maranatha Ministries.
Arbitron Metro Market: Cape May, NJ; *Format:* Religious *Special Programming:* Gospel one hr wkly; *Hrs. of News Programming:* News progmg 10 hrs wkly; *Target Audience:* 25-54; women

Cherry Hill

***WYPA**
01-07-1985; 89.5 MHz FM; *Hrs Open:* 24; 1.9 kw vert; 200 ft.; N39 54 43 W74 59 21 *Rebroadcasts:* Rebroadcasts KLVR(FM) Santa Rosa, CA 100%
P.O. Box 895, Cherry Hill, NJ 08003 US
(800) 525-5683; *Fax:* (916) 251-1650
www.klove.com
License: Cherry Hill, Camden County, NJ held by Educational Media Foundation.
Group Owner: EMF Broadcasting; (acq 1-10-2007; $2.45 million)
Nat'l Network: K-Love
Arbitron Metro Market: Philadelphia; *Format:* Religious
Darrell Chambliss, Chairman
Alan Mason, COO
Mike Novak, President
Glenn Goodwin, Operations Dir

Delaware Township

***WDVR**
02-19-1990; 89.7 MHz FM; *Hrs Open:* 24; 0.006 kw horiz, 3.8 kw vert; 725 ft.; N40 30 36 W74 57 34
P.O. Box 191, Sergeantsville, NJ 08557 US
(609) 397-1620; *Fax:* (609) 397-5991
www.wdvrfm.org
webmaster@wdvrfm.org
License: Delaware Township, Hunterdon County, NJ held by Penn-Jersey Educational Radio Corp.
Nat'l Network: ABC
Arbitron Metro Market: Delaware, NJ; *Format:* Variety/Diverse *Special Programming:* Folk 6 hrs, relg 6 hrs, jazz 11 hrs, oldies 13 hrs, bluegrass 6 hrs, country classic, 12 hrs; Americana country 6 hrs wkly. *Hrs. of NewsProgramming:* News progmg 2 hrs wkly; *Target Audience:* 30 plus.
Frank Napurano, General Manager
Victoria Davis, Office Manager

Dover

WDHA-FM
02-22-1961; 105.5 MHz FM; *Hrs Open:* 24; 1 kw; 574 ft.; N40 51 19 W74 30 42
55 Horsehill Road, Cedar Knolls, NJ 07927 US
(973) 538-1250(973) 455-1055; *Fax:* (973) 538-3060
www.wdhafm.com
ckay@greatermedianj.com

License: Dover, Morris County, NJ held by The Sentinel Publishing Co.
Group Owner: Beasley Broadcast Group; (acq 7-6-01; grpsl).
Nat'l Reps: Katz Radio
Arbitron Metro Market: New Jersey; *Format:* Classic Rock;
Target Audience: 18-49.; *Adv. Rates:* 250; 250; 250; 75
Nancy McKinley, Station Manager
Matt DeVoti, General Sales Mgr
Curtis Kay, Programming/Music Director
Scott Kohlhepp, Promotions Director

East Orange

*WFMU

01-01-1958; 91.1 MHz FM; *Hrs Open:* 24; 1.25 kw; 495 ft.; N40 47 19 W74 15 20
P.O. Box 2011, Jersey City, NJ 07303 US
(201) 521-1416
www.wfmu.org
wfmu@wfmu.org
License: East Orange, Essex County, NJ held by Auricle Communications.
Arbitron Metro Market: New York; *Format:* Variety/Diverse
Special Programming: International 15 hrs wkly; *Target Audience:* General.
Ken Freedman, General Manager
Ken Freedman, Station Manager
Ken Freedman, Programming Director
John Fogarazzo, Chief Engineer
Liz Berg, Assistant General Manager
Brian Turner, Music Director
Scott William, Public ServiceAnnouncement Dorector
Joe McGasko, Listener Service Director
Mike Adler, Technology Director
Jason Sigal, Free Music Achieve Managing Director

Eatontown

WHTG

11-01-1957; 1410 kHz AM; 0.5 kw-D, ND1; 0.126 kw-N, ND1; N40 16 10 W74 4 19
1129 Hope Road, Asbury Park, NJ 07712 US
(732) 774-4755; *Fax:* (732) 774-4974
www.1410amradio.com
License: Eatontown, NJ held by Press Communications L.L.C.
Group Owner: Press Communications L.L.C.; (acq 11-4-2000; $15 million with co-located FM)
Nat'l Reps: Christal
Arbitron Metro Market: New York; *Format:* Contemporary Hits/Top 40 *Special Programming:* Baseball 20 hrs, football 3 hrs, basketball 6 hrs; *Target Audience:* 35 plus; general
Josh Gertzog, General Sales Mgr

WKMK

10-11-1961; 106.3 MHz FM; 1.1 kw; Ant 528 ft; N40 16 41 W74 04 51
2355 W. Bangs Ave., Neptune, NJ 07712
(732) 774-4755; *Fax:* (732) 774-4974
g1063@g1063.com
License: Eatontown, Monmouth County, NJ held by Press Communications L.L.C.
Group Owner: Press Communications L.L.C.
Arbitron Metro Market: New York; *Target Audience:* 18-34.; *Adv. Rates:* 100; 100; 100; 55
Rich Morena, General Manager
John Furno, General Sales Mgr
Marty Mitchell, Programming Director
Diana Pellegrino, Marketing & Promotions Director
Brian Phillips, Music Director

Egg Harbor City

WSJO

09-23-1971; 104.9 MHz FM; 10 kw; 509 ft.; N39 32 49 W74 38 19
950 Tilton Road, Suite 200, Northfield, NJ 08225 US
(609) 645-9797; *Fax:* (609) 272-9224
www.sojo1049.com
jennifersmith@townsquaremedia.com
License: Egg Harbor City, Atlantic County, NJ held by Townsquare Media Atlantic City III License LLC
Group Owner: Townsquare Media
Nat'l Network: AP Radio
Arbitron Metro Market: Egg Harbor City, NJ; *Format:* Adult Contemp *Special Programming:* Relg 4 hrs wkly; *Target Audience:* 35 plus.
Joe Kelly, Programming Director
Jennifer Smith, Promotions Manager
Tom McNally, Chief Engineer
Greg Janoff, Regional Market Manager
Mike Ruble, Market Manager/General Sales Manager
Joe Mitchell, Local Sales Manager

Elizabeth

WJDM

03-11-1970; 1530 kHz AM; 0.67 kw-C, NDD; 1 kw-D, NDD; N40 41 25 W74 15 40
27 William St., 11th Floor, New York, NY 10005 US
(212) 966-1059; *Fax:* (212) 625-2894
www.radiocanticonuevo.com
License: Elizabeth, NJ held by Multicultural Radio Broadcasting Licensee LLC.
Group Owner: Multicultural Radio Broadcasting Inc.; (acq 2-4-2004; grpsl).
Arbitron Metro Market: New York; *Format:* Spanish
Andrew Liu, CEO/COO

Ewing

WIMG

01-01-1923; 1300 kHz AM; *Hrs Open:* 24; 3.2 kw-D, DA2; 1.3 kw-N, DA2; N40 17 16 W74 52 23
Mailing Address: PO Box 9078, Trenton, NJ 08650 US
Second Address: 1842 S. Broad St., Trenton, NJ 8610
(609) 695-1300; *Fax:* (609) 278-1588
www.wimg1300.com
wimg1300@aol.com
License: Ewing, NJ held by Morris Broadcasting Co. of New Jersey Inc.
Nat'l Network: American Urban; NBC; Westwood One; *Nat'l Reps:* Williams Radio Sales
Arbitron Metro Market: Trenton, NJ; *Format:* Adult Contemp, Gospel; *Hrs. of News Programming:* News progmg 6 hrs wkly;
Target Audience: 25-54.
Louise Morris, Chairman
Johnny Morris, CEO
Michael Morris, President
Felicia Brannon, Operations Dir
Pamela Pruitt, General Sales Mgr
Maggie Guzzardo, Executive Vice President

Flemington

*WCVH

04-01-1974; 90.5 MHz FM; *Hrs Open:* 25.?Â ?; 0.078 kw; 449 ft.; N40 33 25 W74 54 18
State Hwy. 31, Flemington, NJ 08822 US
(908) 782-9595; *Fax:* (908) 284-7109
License: Flemington, Hunterdon County, NJ held by Hunterdon Central Board of Education.
Arbitron Metro Market: Flemington, NJ; *Format:* Country; *Target Audience:* 18-54.; *Adv. Rates:* 5; 4; 5; 2
Chris Puorro, General Manager
Nick Biando, Promotions Manager
Bryan Leoni, News Director
John Anastasio, Chief Engineer
Ryan Gill, Music Director
Travis Rainey, Music Director

WCHR

01-05-1998; 1040 kHz AM; *Hrs Open:* 24 *Rebroadcasts:* Rebroadcasts WEPN(AM) New York, NY 100%
449 Broadway, New York, NY 10013 US
(212) 613-3800; *Fax:* (212) 613-3861
www.1050espnradio.com
License: Flemington, NJ held by Connoisseur Media Licenses LLC
Group Owner: Connoisseur Media Licenses LLC
Nat'l Network: ESPN Radio
Format: Sports
Tim McCarthy, General Manager

Florence

WIFI

01-01-1985; 1460 kHz AM; *Hrs Open:* 24; 5 kw-D, 500 w-N, DA-2; N40 04 53 W74 47 41
2025 Burllington-Columbus Rd., Burlington, NJ 08016
(609) 499-4800; *Fax:* (609) 499-4905
www.wifiam1460.com
License: Florence, Burlington County, NJ held by Real Life Broadcasting.
Nat'l Network: USA
Population Served: 2,000,000; *Arbitron Metro Market:* Philadelphia
Stanley Jordan, General Manager
Mark Emanuele, Chief Engineer

Franklin

WSUS

02-28-1965; 102.3 MHz FM; 0.59 kw; 715 ft.; N41 8 36 W74 32 21
45 Mitchell Avenue, Franklin, NJ 07416 US
(973) 827-2525; *Fax:* (973) 827-2135
www.wsus1023.com
info@wsus1023.com
License: Franklin, Sussex County, NJ held by CC Licenses LLC.
Group Owner: iHeartMedia; (acq 2-15-2001; grpsl).
Nat'l Reps: Katz Radio; *Wire Services:* AP
Arbitron Metro Market: Sussex, NJ; *Format:* Adult Contemp; *Hrs. of News Programming:* news progmg 10 hrs wkly; *Target Audience:* 18-54; Adults & Families
Chuck Benfer, Market President

Freehold

*WFJS-FM

89.3 MHz FM
Domestic Church Media, PO Box 7509, Trenton, NJ
(609)882-9357; *Fax:* (609)403-2908
www.domesticchurchmedia.org
info@domesticchurchmedia.org
License: Freehold, Monmouth County, NJ

Jim Manfredonia, President
Cheryl Manfredonia, General Manager

Freehold Township

*WRDR

02-20-1997; 89.7 MHz FM; *Hrs Open:* 24; 0.001 kw horiz, 1.6 kw vert; 328 ft.; N40 7 49 W74 7 19
127 White Oak Lane, Old Bridge, NJ 08857 US
(732) 901-9953; *Fax:* (732) 679-1030
www.bridgefm.org
License: Freehold Township, Monmouth County, NJ held by Bridgelight LLC
Format: Christian *Special Programming:* Relg 6 hrs wkly; *Target Audience:* 25-62.
Brian J. Rechton, General Manager
John Gates, Programming Director

Glassboro

*WGLS-FM

01-01-1964; 89.7 MHz FM; *Hrs Open:* 24; 0.75 kw; 489 ft.; N39 41 41 W75 17 55
201 Mullica Hill Road, Glassboro, NJ 08028 US
(856) 863-9457; *Fax:* (856) 256-4704
wgls.rowan.edu
wgls@rowan.edu
License: Glassboro, Gloucester County, NJ held by Rowan University.
Nat'l Network: ABC
Arbitron Metro Market: Philadelphia; *Format:* Variety/Diverse
Special Programming: Black 10 hrs wkly; *Hrs. of News Programming:* one; *No. News Employees:* 1; *Target Audience:* 18-45; general
Mandy Rippert, Operations Dir
Frank J. Hogan, General Manager
Derek Jones, Station Manager
Frank Sippel, Chief Engineer

Hackensack

WNYM

01-01-1921; 970 kHz AM
777 Terrace Avenue, Suite 602, Hasbrouck Heights, NJ 07604 US
(201) 298-9700; *Fax:* (201) 298-5797
www.am970theanswer.com
contact@nycradio.com
License: Hackensack, NJ held by Salem Media of New York LLC.
Group Owner: Salem Communications Corp.; (acq 8-3-94)
Arbitron Metro Market: Hackensack, NJ; *Format:* News, News/Talk, 86; *Target Audience:* 25-44.
Joe Davis, Chief Operating Officer
Edward Atsinger III, Chief Executive Officer
Jerry Crowley, Vice President/General Manager

Hackettstown

*WNTI

12-05-1957; 91.9 MHz FM; *Hrs Open:* 24; 5.5 kw horiz, 5.6 kw vert; 509 ft.; N40 51 7 W74 52 35
400 Jefferson Street, Hackettstown, NJ 07840 US
(908) 852-4545; *Fax:* (908) 852-8515
www.wnti.org
License: Hackettstown, Warren County, NJ held by Centenary College.
Nat'l Network: PRI
Arbitron Metro Market: Warren, NJ; *Format:* Variety/Diverse
Special Programming: Big band 4 hrs, blues 11 hrs, heavy metal

6 hrs, r; *Hrs. of News Programming:* News progmg 2 hrs wkly; *Target Audience:* 15 plus.
John Del Re, Operations Dir
Paul Massen, General Manager
Melanie Thiel, Donations

WRNJ
01-01-1996; 1510 kHz AM
P.O. Box 1000, Hackettstown, NJ 07840 US
(908) 850-1000; *Fax:* (908) 852-8000
www.wrnj.com
License: Hackettstown, NJ held by WRNJ Radio Inc.
Nat'l Network: ABC; *Wire Services:* AP
Format: News, News/Talk, 64, Talk *Special Programming:* Talk 10 hrs wkly; *Hrs. of News Programming:* news progmg 10 hrs wkly; *No. News Employees:* 3; *Target Audience:* 25-50 plus; upwardly mobile *Adv. Rates:* 55; 40; 50; 30
L.J. Tighe, President
Russ Long, Operations Dir
Norman Worth, President/General Manager
Chuck Reiger, Programming Director
Pat Layton, Office/Traffic Manager
Larry Tighe, Chief Engineer
Tom DuHamel, Account Manager
SteveRandolph, Account Manager
Joyce Estey, News Director

Hammonton

WGYM
05-11-1961; 1580 kHz AM; 1 kw-D, ND1; 0.006 kw-N, ND1; N39 37 33 W74 47 44 *Rebroadcasts:* Rebroadcasts WOND(AM) Atlantic City 100%
1601 New Road, Linwood, NJ 08221 US
(609) 601-1100; *Fax:* (609) 601-0450
License: Hammonton, NJ
Group Owner: Domesitic Church Media Foundation; (acq 11-17-2003; grpsl).
Nat'l Network: Westwood One; *Nat'l Reps:* McGavren Guild
Arbitron Metro Market: Atlantic City-C *TV Affiliate:* Talk; *No. News Employees:* Adults 35+.; *Target Audience:* Sydney Small

Hazlet

***WPDI**
05-24-1979; 103.9 MHz FM; 10 w; Ant 125 ft; N40 25 37 W74 11 40
49 Briscoe Terr., Hazlet, PA 07730
(732) 452-0777
License: Hazlet, Monmouth County, NJ held by WVRM Inc.

James Manfredonia, President

Hopatcong

***WDNJ**
01-01-2009; 88.1 MHz FM; 0.5 kw vert; 387 ft.; N40 56 25 W74 36 48
99 Clinton Road, West Caldwell, NJ 07006 US
(888) 776-9365; *Fax:* (804) 353-8549
www.wdnjfm.com
License: Hopatcong, Sussex County, NJ held by Youngshine Media Inc.
Arbitron Metro Market: Hopatcong, NJ; *Format:* Christian, Spanish
Sun Young Joo, General Manager

Jersey City

WSNR
12-01-1948; 620 kHz AM; 3 kw-D, DA2; 7.6 kw-N, DA2; N40 47 53 W74 6 24
1935 Techny Rd, Suite18, Northbrook, IL 60062 US
(847) 509-1661; *Fax:* (646) 424-2232
www.sportingnews.com
License: Jersey City, NJ held by Rose City Radio Corp.
Group Owner: Rose City Radio Corp.; acq 3-23-01; grpsl).
Nat'l Network: CBS; *Wire Services:* CBS
Arbitron Metro Market: New York; *Format:* Sports; *Target Audience:* General.
Clancy Woods, President
Colleen Mamzella, News Director

WWRU
12-08-1995; 1660 kHz AM
27 William St., 11th Floor, New York, NY 10005 US
(212) 966-8700; *Fax:* (212) 966-9580
www.nyradiokorea.com
License: Jersey City, NJ held by Multicultural Radio Broadcasting Licensee LLC.
Group Owner: Multicultural Radio Broadcasting Inc.; (acq 2-4-2004; grpsl).
Arbitron Metro Market: Jersey City, NJ; *Format:* Korean
Arthur Liu, CEO/COO

Lakehurst

***WLNJ**
91.7 MHz FM; *Hrs Open:* 24; 3.5 kw; 49 m HAAT 160 ft/32 m AGL; N40 04 07 W74 28 09 *Rebroadcasts:* WYRS 90.7
Box 730, Manahawkin, NJ 08050
(609) 978-1678; *Fax:* (609) 597-4146
www.wyrs.org
info@wyrs.org
License: Lakehurst, Ocean County, NJ held by WYRS Broadcasting.
Nat'l Network: IRN/USA News
Arbitron Metro Market: Monmouth/Ocgan
Nancy Wick, Operations Manager
Bob Wick, General Manager

Lakewood Township

WOBM
11-20-1970; 1160 kHz AM; 5 kw-D, DA2; 8.9 kw-N, DA2; N40 8 9 W74 13 48
P O Box 927, Toms River, NJ 08754 US
848-221-8000; *Fax:* (732) 269-9292
www.wobmam.com
Brad.Burascano@townsquaremedia.com
License: Lakewood Township, NJ held by Townsquare Media Monmouth-Ocean License LLC
Group Owner: Townsquare Media; (acq 5-14-02; grpsl).
Nat'l Network: AP Radio; *Nat'l Reps:* Katz Radio
TV Affiliate: Oldies; *Format:* Talk *Special Programming:* news progmg 14 hrs wkly; *Hrs. of News Programming:* 5; *No. News Employees:* 45 plus; educated
General Sales Manager, Steve Ardolina
Program Director, Brad Burascano
Promotions Director, Promotions Manager

Lawrenceville

***WRRC**
09-23-1989; 107.7 MHz FM; *Hrs Open:* 16; 0.02 kw; 36 ft.; N40 16 44 W74 44 15
2083 Lawrenceville Rd., Lawrenceville, NJ 08648 US
(609) 896-5369; *Fax:* (609) 219-4724
www.1077thebronc.com
License: Lawrenceville, Mercer County, NJ held by Rider University Board of Trustees.
Format: Variety/Diverse *Special Programming:* Black 10 hrs, heavy metal 10 hrs wkly; *Hrs. of News Programming:* news progmg 4 hrs wkly; *No. News Employees:* 3; *Target Audience:* 16-21; high school & collegestudents
Charles Benfer, General Manager

Lincroft

***WBJB-FM**
01-13-1975; 90.5 MHz FM; *Hrs Open:* 24; 0.9 kw; 371 ft.; N40 19 19 W74 7 57
765 Newman Springs Road, Lincroft, NJ 07738 US
(732) 224-2252; *Fax:* (732) 224-2494
www.wbjb.org
License: Lincroft, Monmouth County, NJ held by Board of Trustees of Brookdale Community College.
Nat'l Network: NPR
Arbitron Metro Market: Lincroft, NJ; *Format:* News, Triple A
Special Programming: Haitian 3 hrs, pub affrs 5 hrs, bluegrass 3 hrs, Sp 4 hrs, blues 4 hrs wkly; *Hrs. of News Programming:* News progmg 16 hrs wkly *TargetAudience:* ages 25-54.
Michelle McBride, Operations Dir
Tom Brennan, Station Manager
Jeff Raspe, Programming Director
George Marshall, Chief Engineer

Lindenwold

WTTM
05-01-1999; 1680 kHz AM
3573 Bristol Pike, Suite 102, Bansalem, PA 19020 US
(267) 527-9886; *Fax:* (267) 527-1684
www.radiowttm1680.com
wttm1680@yahoo.com
License: Lindenwold, NJ held by Multicultural Radio Broadcasting Licensee LLC.
Group Owner: Multicultural Radio Broadcasting Inc.; (acq 5-24-2002; grpsl).
Arbitron Metro Market: Philadelphia, PA; *Format:* Ethnic
Arthur Liu, CEO/COO

Long Branch

WWZY
06-01-1960; 107.1 MHz FM; 5 kw; 361 ft.; N40 18 17 W73 59 8
2355 West Bangs Avenue, Neptune, NJ 07753 US
(732) 774-4755; *Fax:* (732) 774-7315
www.1071radio.com
License: Long Branch, Monmouth County, NJ held by Press Communications LLC
Group Owner: Press Communications L.L.C.; acq 6-18-2003; $20 million).
Nat'l Reps: Eastman Radio; *Wire Services:* AP
Arbitron Metro Market: Long Branch, NJ; *Format:* Adult Contemp; *Target Audience:* Women; 25-54
Rich Morena, General Manager
Matt Rosenberg, Programming Director
Diana Pellegrino, Promotions Manager

Mahwah

***WRPR**
07-15-1980; 90.3 MHz FM; *Hrs Open:* 18; 0.1 kw horiz; -66 ft.; N41 4 51 W74 10 34
505 Ramapo Valley Rd., Mahwah, NJ 07430 US
(201) 825-1234,(201) 825-7998; *Fax:* (201) 327-9036
wrpr@ramapo.edu
License: Mahwah, Bergen County, NJ held by Ramapo College of New Jersey.
Format: Contemporary Hits/Top 40 *Special Programming:* Pub affrs 12 hrs wkly; *Hrs. of News Programming:* news progmg 10 hrs wkly; *No. News Employees:* 4; *Target Audience:* 18-24; college students
Craig Homa, General Manager

Manahawkin

WCHR-FM
01-01-2002; 105.7 MHz FM; 13 kw; 459 ft.; N39 42 56 W74 17 31
P.O. Box 658, Union, NJ 07083 US
(848)221-8000; *Fax:* (732) 269-9292
www.1057thehawk.com
Wendy.Wesley@townsquaremedia.com
License: Manahawkin, Ocean County, NJ held by Townsquare Media Monmouth-Ocean License LLC
Group Owner: Townsquare Media; (acq 3-15-2004; $12 million).
Arbitron Metro Market: Atlantic City, NJ; *Format:* Classic Rock
Phil LoCascio, Operations Dir
Bill Saurer, General Manager
Russ DelCore, General Sales Mgr
Steve Ardolina, Programming Director
Brad Burascano, Promotions Manager
Tom Monzeli, News Director
Jay Pierce, Engineering Dir
TomDunphy, Digital Managing Editor
Zoe Burdine-Fly, Regional Vice President
Andy Chase, Music Director/APD
James Thomas, Director of Digital Sales
Wendy Wesley, Director of Live Events & Non-Traditional Revenue
Mario Forcellati, ProductionDirector

WJRZ-FM
07-04-1976; 100.1 MHz FM; *Hrs Open:* 24; 1.7 kw; 436 ft.; N39 47 54 W74 12 10
Mailing Address: PO Box 1000, Manahawkin, NJ 08050 US
Second Address: 610 Main Street, Belmar, NJ 7719
(732) 681-9591; *Fax:* (609) 597-4400
www.wjrz.com
License: Manahawkin, Ocean County, NJ held by Jersey Shore Broadcasting Corp.
Group Owner: Beasley Broadcast Group; (acq 7-19-02).
Nat'l Network: AP Radio; *Nat'l Reps:* Katz Radio
Format: Contemporary Hits/Top 40, Adult Contemp; *Hrs. of News Programming:* news progmg 4 hrs wkly; *No. News Employees:* 1; *Target Audience:* 35-54.
Glenn Kalina, Program Director
Marge Guglielmo, General Sales Mgr
Marie Senkeleski, Promotions Director

***WNJM**
08-01-1999; 89.9 MHz FM; 0.001 kw horiz, 0.2 kw vert; 259 ft.; N39 41 57 W74 14 5
150 N. 6th Street, Philadelphia, NJ 19106 US
(215) 351-1200; *Fax:* (215) 351-0398
www.whyy.org
talkback@whyy.org
License: Manahawkin, Ocean County, NJ held by New Jersey Public Broadcasting Authority.
Nat'l Network: NPR; PRI
Arbitron Metro Market: Bridgeton, PA; *Format:* News, News/Talk, 86

William Marrazzo, CEO/COO
Kyra McGrath, Operations Dir
Pharoah Cranston, Station Manager
Chris Satullo, News Director

***WYRS**
03-27-1995; 90.7 MHz FM; *Hrs Open:* 24; 0.001 kw horiz, 15 kw vert; 262 ft.; N39 38 24 W74 17 32
150 N. 6th Street, Philadelphia, PA 19106 US
(609) 978-1678; *Fax:* (609) 597-4146
www.wyrs.org
info@wyrs.org
License: Manahawkin, Ocean County, NJ held by WYRS Broadcasting
Nat'l Network: USA
Arbitron Metro Market: Manahawkin, NJ; *Format:* Children; *Target Audience:* General.
Bob Wick, CEO

Margate City

WTTH
11-19-1991; 96.1 MHz FM; *Hrs Open:* 24; 2.8 kw; 400 ft.; N39 21 2 W74 26 55 *Rebroadcasts:* Simulcast with WDTH(FM) Wildwood Crest 100%
8025 Black Horse Pike, Suite 100-102, W. Atlantic City, NJ 08232 US
(609) 484-8444; *Fax:* (609) 646-6331
www.961wtth.com
License: Margate City, Atlantic County, NJ held by Equity Communications L.P.
Group Owner: Equity Communications LP; (acq 5-30-2003; grpsl).
Nat'l Reps: Katz Radio
Arbitron Metro Market: Atlantic City-C; *Format:* Adult Contemp *Special Programming:* Gospel 5 hrs, relg one hr wkly; *Target Audience:* 18-49; adults; *Adv. Rates:* 200; 200; 200; 50
Rob Garcia, Programming Director
Shannon Wray, Promotions Manager

Medford Lakes

***WVBV**
01-01-2005; 90.5 MHz FM; *Hrs Open:* 24; 0 kw horiz, 21 kw vert; 453 ft.; N39 33 20 W74 44 48
55 East Main Street, Marlton, NJ 08053 US
(856) 983-1662; *Fax:* (856) 983-1814
www.hopefm.net
info@hopefm.net
License: Medford Lakes, Burlington County, NJ held by Hope Christian Church of Marlton Inc.
Arbitron Metro Market: Medford Lakes, NJ; *Format:* Christian, Talk
William Luebkemann Jr., President

Millville

WMVB
12-01-1953; 1440 kHz AM; *Hrs Open:* 24; 1 kw-D, DA2; 0.065 kw-N, DA2; N39 25 19 W75 1 14 *Rebroadcasts:* Simulcast with WSNJ(AM) Bridgeton
4369 South Lincoln Avenue, Vineland, NJ 08361 US
(856) 327-8800; *Fax:* (856) 327-0408
information@wsnjam.com
License: Millville, NJ held by Quinn Broadcasting Inc
Arbitron Metro Market: Millville, NJ; *Format:* Variety/Diverse *Special Programming:* Sp 2 hrs, gospel 8 hrs, children 3 hrs wkly; *No. News Employees:* 4; *Target Audience:* 25-54; general public *Adv. Rates:* 23; 23; 23; 23
Jim Quinn, President
Carl Elwood, General Manager
Richard Hoch, General Sales Mgr

WENJ
02-02-1962; 97.3 MHz FM; 50 kw; 142 meters; N39 19 13.9 W74 46 17.6
950 Tilton Road, Suite 200, Northfield, NJ 08225
(609) 645-9797; *Fax:* (609) 272-9224
www.973espn.com
License: Millville, Cumberland County, NJ held by Townsquare Media Atlantic City II License LLC
Group Owner: Townsquare Media
Nat'l Network: ESPN Radio

Greg Janoff, Regional Market Manager

Morristown

***WJSV**
02-22-1971; 90.5 MHz FM; *Hrs Open:* 8 AM-10 PM (M-F); 0.125 kw; 16 ft.; N40 50 10 W74 29 16
50 Early Street Rm. 163, Morristown, NJ 07960 US
(973) 292-2168; *Fax:* (973) 539-5573
www.wjsv.org
norman.wallerstein@msdk12.net
License: Morristown, Morris County, NJ held by Morris School District Board of Education.
Format: Rock/AOR *Special Programming:* News/talk 3 hrs, sports 3 hrs wkly; *Hrs. of News Programming:* news progmg 3 hrs wkly; *No. News Employees:* 1; *Target Audience:* General.
Norman Wallerstein, General Manager
Dame Mallan, Station Manager
Michael O'Brien, Programming Director
Ryan Whitenack, Promotions Manager
Lee Tyler, Promotions Director

WMTR
12-12-1948; 1250 kHz AM
55 Horsehill Road, Cedar Knolls, NJ 07927 US
(973) 538-1250; *Fax:* (973) 538-3060
www.wmtram.com
cedwards@greatermedianj.com
License: Morristown, NJ held by The Sentinel Publishing Co.
Group Owner: Beasley Broadcast Group; (acq 7-6-01; grpsl).
Arbitron Metro Market: Morristown, NJ; *Format:* Oldies *Special Programming:* Community connection 5 hrs wkly; *Target Audience:* 35 plus.
Dan Finn, Senior Vice President/General Manager
Chris Edwards, Operations Dir
Matt DeVoti, General Sales Mgr
Chris Edwards, Programming Director
Scott Kohlhepp, Promotions Manager

Mount Holly

WWJZ
11-01-1992; 640 kHz AM
50 Tensaw Drive, Browns Mills, NJ 08015 US
(215) 591-0100; *Fax:* (215) 591-4527
www.radiodisney.com/philadelphia
License: Mount Holly, NJ held by Radio Disney Group LLC.
Group Owner: ABC Inc.; (acq 12-30-99).
Arbitron Metro Market: Philadelphia, PA; *Format:* Children; *Target Audience:* 45 plus.; *Adv. Rates:* 35; 25; 35; 20
Phil Guerini, Vice President and General Manager
Ray De La Garza, VP of Programming
Rita Ferro, Executive Vice President, Disney Media Sales and M
Kelly Edwards, Executive Director Music & Programming, Radio Disn
Ivan Heredia, VP,Marketing
Anne Sweeney, Co-Chair

Netcong

***WNJY**
01-01-2008; 89.3 MHz FM; 0.001 kw horiz, 0.52 kw vert; 430 ft.; N40 53 14 W74 41 55 *Rebroadcasts:* Rebroadcasts WNJT-FM Trenton 100%
160 Varick Street, New York, NY 10013 US
(609) 777-5000; *Fax:* (609) 777-5217
www.njpublicradio.com
License: Netcong, Morris County, NJ held by New Jersey Public Broadcasting Authority.
Regional Network: NJN Public Radio
Arbitron Metro Market: Netcong, NJ; *Format:* News, News/Talk, 86
Josh Weston, Chairman
Pharoah Cranston, Station Manager
Andre Butts, Programming Director

New Brunswick

WCTC
12-12-1946; 1450 kHz AM; *Hrs Open:* 24; 0.25 kw-U, ND1; 1 kw-U, ND1; N40 28 33 W74 29 34; N40 29 32 W74 25 11
78 Veronica Avenue, Somerset, NJ 08873 US
(732) 249-2600; *Fax:* (732) 545-9282
www.wctcam.com
License: New Brunswick, NJ held by The Sentinel Publishing Co.
Group Owner: Beasley Broadcast Group; (acq 5-1-57)
Arbitron Metro Market: New York; *Format:* Oldies *Special Programming:* Rutgers Univ. & high school sports; *Hrs. of News Programming:* news progmg 15 hrs wkly; *No. News Employees:* 6; *Target Audience:* 35-54. *Adv. Rates:* 125; 90; 90; 30
Dan Finn, Operations Dir
Frank Calderaro, General Manager
John Ford, Station Manager
Jack Cahill, General Sales Mgr
Dave Kirby, Promotions Manager
Keith Smeal, Chief Engineer
Bruce Johnson, Operations Manager
Susan Young,Traffic Manager

WMGQ
01-01-1947; 98.3 MHz FM; *Hrs Open:* 24; 1.2 kw; 518 ft.; N40 28 37 W74 29 33
78 Veronica Avenue, Somerset, NJ 08873 US
(732) 249-2600; *Fax:* (732) 249-9010
www.magic983.com
License: New Brunswick, Middlesex County, NJ
Group Owner: Beasley Broadcast Group
Arbitron Metro Market: New York, NY; *Format:* Adult Contemp; *Hrs. of News Programming:* News progmg 3 hrs wkly; *Target Audience:* 25-54.
Dan Henrickson, Station Manager
Ed Silver, General Sales Mgr
Jeff Rafter, Programming Director
Dave Kirby, Promotions Manager
Chris McCoy, News Director
Keith Smeal, Engineering Dir

***WRSU-FM**
04-01-1974; 88.7 MHz FM; *Hrs Open:* 24; 1.35 kw; 125 ft.; N40 28 0 W74 26 15
126 College Avenue, New Brunswick, NJ 08901 US
(732) 932-7800; *Fax:* (732) 932-1768
www.wrsu.org
wrsu@wrsu.rutgers.edu
License: New Brunswick, Middlesex County, NJ held by Board of Governors Rutgers University.
Wire Services: AP
Format: Variety/Diverse; *Hrs. of News Programming:* News progmg 6 hrs wkly; *Target Audience:* 15-30; college students, div group of young adults
Tim Espar, Broadcast Administrator
Dave Pilmenstein, General Manager
Ryan Downey, Programming Director

Newark

***WBGO**
02-07-1948; 88.3 MHz FM; *Hrs Open:* 24; 2.5 kw; 883 ft.; N40 45 22 W73 59 12
54 Park Place, Newark, NJ 07102 US
(973) 624-8880; *Fax:* (973) 824-8888
www.wbgo.org
jazz88@wbgo.org
License: Newark, Essex County, NJ held by Newark Public Radio Inc.
Nat'l Network: NPR; *Wire Services:* AP
Arbitron Metro Market: New York; *Format:* Jazz; *Hrs. of News Programming:* news progmg 5 hrs wkly; *No. News Employees:* 2; *Target Audience:* General.
Tim Porter, Chairman
David Tallacksen, Operations Dir
Cephas Bowles, General Manager
Amy Niles, General Sales Mgr
Thurston Briscoe, Programming Director
Brandy Wood, Promotions Manager
Doug Doyle, News Director
David Antoine,Chief Engineer
Stevan Smith, Traffic Manager
Brandy Wood, Marketing Manager
David Tallacksen, Vice President, Operations and Engineering

WQXR-FM
08-01-1992; 105.9 MHz FM; 0.61 kw; 1,365 ft.; N40 44 54 W73 59 10
160 Varick St., New York, NY 10013 US
(646) 829-4400
www.wqxr.org
License: Newark, Essex County, NJ held by New York Public Radio
Group Owner: New York Public Radio; (acq 7-14-2009).
Population Served: 18,000,000; *Arbitron Metro Market:* New York, NY; *Format:* Classical
Graham Parker, General Manager
Matt Abramovitz, Programming Director

WNSH
01-01-1947; 94.7 MHz FM; *Hrs Open:* 24; 23.5 kw; 679 ft.; N40 47 17 W74 15 19
2 Pennsylvania Plaza, 17th Floor, New York, NY 10121 US
(212) 613-8900; *Fax:* (212) 613-8956
www.nashfm947.com
License: Newark, Essex County, NJ held by Radio License Holdings LLC
Group Owner: Cumulus Media Inc.; (acq 3-10-66).
Arbitron Metro Market: New York; *Format:* Country; *Target Audience:* General.
Kim Bryant, General Manager

WHTZ
06-01-1961; 100.3 MHz FM; 6 kw; 1362 ft.; N40 44 54 W73 59 10
32 Avenue of the Americas, New York, NY 10013 US
(212) 239-2300; *Fax:* (212) 239-2308
www.z100.com
License: Newark, Essex County, NJ held by AMFM Radio Licenses L.L.C.
Group Owner: iHeartMedia; (acq 8-30-00; grpsl)
Nat'l Reps: Christal
Arbitron Metro Market: New York; *Format:* Contemporary Hits/Top 40
Scott Hopeck, Market President
Tom Poleman, Senior Vice President of Programming
Josh Hadden, Engineering Dir

WNSW
01-01-1947; 1430 kHz AM; *Hrs Open:* 24
499 Broadway, New York, NY 10013 US
(212) 966-1059; *Fax:* (212) 966-9580
License: Newark, NJ held by Multicultural Radio Broadcasting Licensee LLC.
Group Owner: Multicultural Radio Broadcasting Inc.; (acq 1-30-98; grpsl)
Nat'l Reps: Katz Radio
Arbitron Metro Market: New York, NY; *Format:* Christian
Gene Heinemeyer, General Manager
Harold Chou, Chief Engineer

Newton

WTOC
12-15-1953; 1360 kHz AM; *Hrs Open:* 24
P.O. Box 2908, Paterson, NJ 07509 US
(973) 881-8700; *Fax:* (973) 881-8324
www.radiovision.net
License: Newton, NJ held by Centro Biblico of NJ Inc.
Nat'l Reps: Katz Radio; *Wire Services:* AP
Arbitron Metro Market: Sussex, NJ; *Format:* Spanish *Special Programming:* Relg half hr, pub affrs one hr wkly; *Hrs. of News Programming:* news progmg 5 hrs wkly; *Target Audience:* 35 plus; mature adults with highincomes
Delia Goldschmidt, General Manager

WNNJ
10-15-1961; 103.7 MHz FM; *Hrs Open:* 24; 2.3 kw; 892 ft.; N41 11 12 W74 46 4
45 Ed Mitchell Avenue, Franklin, NJ 07416 US
(973) 827-2525; *Fax:* (973) 827-2135
www.wnnj.com
License: Newton, Sussex County, NJ held by CC Licenses LLC
Group Owner: iHeartMedia
Arbitron Metro Market: Sussex, NJ; *Format:* Rock/AOR; *Target Audience:* 18-54; adults and families
Chuck Benfer, Market President
Gary Cee, Senior Vice President of Programming
Ricky Hoffend, Promotions Director

North Cape May

WJSE
01-01-1993; 106.3 MHz FM; 6 kw; 80 m; N38 57 32 W74 55 23
3208 Pacific Ave., Wildwood, NJ 08210
(609) 522-3666,(609) 522-1987
www.wjserocks.com
License: North Cape May, Cape May County, NJ held by Coastal Broadcasting Systems Inc.
Group Owner: Coastal Broadcasting Systems Inc.; (acq 11-1-2004; $700,000)
Nat'l Network: USA; Moody
Arbitron Metro Market: Atlantic City-Cape May, NJ *Special Programming:* Class 3 hrs wkly
Bob Maschio, President
Scott Wahl, Vice President

Oakland

WVNJ
12-13-1993; 1160 kHz AM; *Hrs Open:* 24; 20 kw-D, DA2; 2.5 kw-N, DA2; N41 3 23 W74 14 58
1086 Teaneck Road, Ste 4f, Teaneck, NJ 07666 US
(201) 837-0400; *Fax:* (201) 837-9664
www.wvnj.com
advertising@wvnj.com
License: Oakland, NJ held by Universal Broadcasting of New York Inc.
Group Owner: Universal Broadcasting of New York Inc.; acq 3-24-94; $12,050,000. with WTHE(AM) Mineola, NY;
Nat'l Reps: Universal Broadcasting Inc *Regional Reps:* Universal Broadcasting Inc
Arbitron Metro Market: Oakland, NJ; *Format:* News, Talk *Special Programming:* Health related; *Hrs. of News Programming:* news progmg 8 hrs wkly; *No. News Employees:* 1; *Target Audience:* 35-64; upscale *Adv.Rates:* 100; 100; 100; 40
Miriam Warshaw, President
Howard Warshaw, Vice President
Abe Warshaw, Vice President
Dave Margalotti, Program & Production Director
Howard Warshaw, Vice President

Ocean Acres

WBBO(FM)
01-01-1992; 98.5 MHz FM; *Hrs Open:* 24; 6 kw; Ant 328 ft; N39 45 06 W74 15 39
2355 W. Bangs Ave., Neptune, NJ 7753
(732) 774-4755; *Fax:* (732) 774-7315
www.b985radio.com
License: Ocean Acres, Ocean County, NJ held by Press Communications LLC.
Group Owner: Press Communications L.L.C.; (acq 8-9-2004; $17 million)
Nat'l Reps: Eastman Radio
Population Served: 400,000 *Target Audience:* 25-55; women
Richard Morena, General Manager
Diana Pellegrino, Promotions Manager

Ocean City

WWAC
08-01-1991; 102.7 MHz FM; *Hrs Open:* 24; 4.1 kw; Ant 399 ft; N39 21 4 W74 26 54
1601 New Rd., Linwood, NJ 08221
(609) 653-1400
www.ac1027.com
License: Ocean City, Cape May County, NJ held by Longport Media LLC
Group Owner: Longport Media LLC
Population Served: 325,000; *Arbitron Metro Market:* Atlantic City-Cape May, NJ; *Format:* Contemporary Hits/Top 40
Dave Coskey, President
Paul Kelly, VP of Broadcast Operations
Joe Croce, VP of Sales

***WRTQ**
09-27-1994; 91.3 MHz FM; *Hrs Open:* 24; 1.36 kw horiz, 13.5 kw vert; 394 ft.; N39 19 14 W74 46 18 *Rebroadcasts:* Rebroadcasts WRTI(FM) Philadelphia 100%
1509 Cecil B Moore Avenue, 3rd Floor, Philadelphia, PA 19121 US
(215) 204-8405; *Fax:* (215) 204-7027
www.wrti.org
comments@wrti.org
License: Ocean City, Cape May County, NJ held by Temple University of the Commonwealth System of Higher Education.
Nat'l Network: NPR; AP Radio
Format: Jazz; *Hrs. of News Programming:* news progmg 15 hrs wkly; *No. News Employees:* 1; *Target Audience:* 30-65.
Dave Conant, General Manager
William Johnson, Station Manager
Jack Moore, Programming Director
Lorna Dixon, Traffic Director
Jeff DePolo, Chief Engineer

Ocean City/Somers Po

WIBG
10-01-1992; 1020 kHz AM; *Hrs Open:* Sunrise-sunset
3328 Simpson Avenue, Ocean City, NJ 08226 US
(609) 398-7575; *Fax:* (609) 398-3736
www.wibg.am
License: Ocean City/Somers Po, NJ held by Enrico S. Brancadora.
Arbitron Metro Market: Atlantic City-Cape May, NJ; *Format:* Christian, News, 86; *Hrs. of News Programming:* news progmg 7 hrs wkly; *No. News Employees:* 1; *Target Audience:* 25-45; young urban-suburban professional *Adv. Rates:* 30; 30; 30; 30
Rick Brancadora, CEO
Josh Hennig, Operations Dir

Parsippany-Troy Hill

WXMC
01-13-1973; 1310 kHz AM; *Hrs Open:* 24; 1 kw-D, DA1; 0.088 kw-N, DA1; N40 51 51 W74 21 6
76 National Road, Edison, NJ 08817 US
(732) 609-8420; *Fax:* (732) 650-1112
www.radioasiafm.com
License: Parsippany-Troy Hill, NJ held by James Chladek
Arbitron Metro Market: Parsippany, NJ; *Format:* Religious; *Hrs. of News Programming:* news progmg 4 hrs wkly; *No. News Employees:* 1; *Target Audience:* 25 plus; young upper middle class business professionals
H.R. Shah, CEO
Mr. Paul Suri, Programming Director

Paterson

WPAT
05-03-1941; 930 kHz AM; 5 kw-D, DA2; 5 kw-N, DA2; N40 50 59 W74 10 59
27 William St., 11th Floor, New York, NY 10005 US
(212) 966-1059; *Fax:* (212) 966-9580
www.wpat930am.com
License: Paterson, NJ held by Multicultural Radio Broadcasting Licensee LLC.
Group Owner: Multicultural Radio Broadcasting Inc.; (acq 7-22-98).
Arbitron Metro Market: New York; *Format:* Ethnic
Arthur Liu, CEO/COO

WPAT-FM
03-29-1957; 93.1 MHz FM; 5.4 kw; 1421 ft.; N40 42 43 W74 0 49
26 West 56th Street, New York, NY 10019 US
(212) 246-9393 ext. 7646; *Fax:* (212) 664-1922
www.931amor.com
info@931amor.com
License: Paterson, Passaic County, NJ held by WPAT Licensing Inc.
Group Owner: Spanish Broadcasting System Inc.; (acq 1996; $83.5 million)
Arbitron Metro Market: New York; *Format:* Adult Contemp
Roberto Castillo, Chairman
Jose Garcia, CFO

Pemberton

***WBZC**
01-24-1995; 88.9 MHz FM; *Hrs Open:* 24; 0.47 kw horiz, 10 kw vert; 220 ft.; N39 50 34 W74 32 40
601 Pemberton-Browns Mill Road, Pemberton, NJ 08068 US
(609) 894-9311 EXT. 1189; *Fax:* (609) 894-9440
www.z889.org
License: Pemberton, Burlington County, NJ held by Burlington County College.
Arbitron Metro Market: Pemberton, NJ; *Format:* Adult Contemp *Special Programming:* Folk 4 hrs, jazz 4 hrs, bluegrass 4 hrs, reggae 4 hrs,; *Hrs. of News Programming:* News progmg 4 hrs wkly; *Target Audience:* 18-35.
Rick Ayala, Assistant Programming Direcotr
Jason ""Jaybird"" Varga, Production Director

Pennsauken

WPHI-FM
11-01-1982; 107.9 MHz FM; *Hrs Open:* 24; 0.78 kw; 906 ft.; N39 57 9 W75 10 5
Two Bala Plaza, Suite 700, Bala Cynwyd, PA 19004 US
(610) 538-1100
www.boomphilly.com
License: Pennsauken, Delaware County, NJ held by Radio One Licenses LLC.
Group Owner: Radio One Inc.; (acq 11-8-2001; grpsl).
Arbitron Metro Market: Philadelphia; *Format:* Urban Contemporary; *No. News Employees:* 1; *Target Audience:* 18-44; savvy suburban educated professional
Catherine Nye, General Sales Mgr
Darrick Williams, Programming Director

Petersburg

WTKU-FM
04-01-1983; 98.3 MHz FM; *Hrs Open:* 24; 6 kw; 328 ft.; N39 12 18 W74 39 33
1601 New Rd., Linwood, NJ 08221 US
(609) 653-1400; *Fax:* (609) 601-0450
www.kool983.com
License: Petersburg, Cape May County, NJ held by Longport Media LLC
Group Owner: Longport Media LLC; (acq 8-2-2011)
Nat'l Reps: McGavren Guild
Arbitron Metro Market: Atlantic City, NJ; *Format:* Oldies; *Hrs. of News Programming:* News progmg 5 hrs wkly; *Target Audience:* 25-64.
Dave Coskey, President
Paul Kelly, VP of Operations
Joe Croce, VP of Sales

Piscataway

***WVPH**
05-01-1976; 90.3 MHz FM; 0.1 kw; 254 ft.; N40 31 21 W74 25 52.5
84 Joyce Kilmer Avenue, Piscataway, NJ 08854 US

(732) 445-4100
www.thecore.fm
news@thecore.fm
License: Piscataway, Middlesex County, NJ held by Board of Education Piscataway High School.
Arbitron Metro Market: Middlesex, NJ; *Format:* News, Talk; *No. News Employees:* 1
Andrew Sadowski, General Manager
Danielle Bruno, Programming Director
Samantha Shaw, Promotions Manager
John Cronin, Business Director

Pleasantville

WBSS(AM)
01-01-1955; 1490 kHz AM; *Hrs Open:* 24 hrs; 400 w-U; N39 23 24 W74 30 45
1601 New Rd., Linwood, NJ 8221
(609) 653-1400; *Fax:* (609) 601-0450
www.kool983.com
License: Pleasantville, Atlantic County, NJ held by Long Port Media
Group Owner: Long Port Media
Nat'l Network: La Gran D; *Nat'l Reps:* McGavren Guild
Population Served: 27,000; *Arbitron Metro Market:* Atlantic City-Cape May, NJ
Dave Corskey, CEO
Paul Kelly, Programming Director

WOND
07-01-1950; 1400 kHz AM; 1 kw-U, ND1; N39 23 24 W74 30 45
Rebroadcasts: Rebroadcasts WGYM(AM) Hammonton 100%
1601 New Rd., Linwood, NJ 08221 US
(609) 653-1400; *Fax:* (609) 601-0450
www.wondradio.com
License: Pleasantville, Atlantic County, NJ held by Longport Media LLC
Group Owner: Longport Media LLC; (acq 8-2-2011)
Nat'l Network: Westwood One; *Nat'l Reps:* McGavren Guild
Arbitron Metro Market: Atlantic City, NJ; *Format:* News, News/Talk, 86; *No. News Employees:* Adults 35 +.
Dave Coskey, President
Paul Kelly, VP of Broadcast Operations
Joe Croce, VP of Sales

WBSS
03-30-1992; 1490 kHz AM; *Hrs Open:* 24; 0.4 kw-D, ND2; 0.4 kw-N, ND2; Ant 1,440 ft; N39 23 24 W74 30 45
1601 New Rd., Linwood, NJ 08221 US
(609) 653-1400; *Fax:* (609) 601-0450
www.longportmedia.com
License: Pleasantville, NJ held by Longport Media LLC
Group Owner: Longport Media LLC; (acq 3-13-2002; $620,000)
Nat'l Reps: Dome
Format: Sports; *No. News Employees:* 1; *Adv. Rates:* 16; 14; 16; 12
Dave Coskey, President
Paul Kelly, VP of Operations
Joe Croce, VP of Sales

WZBZ
01-01-1974; 99.3 MHz FM; *Hrs Open:* 24; 3 kw; 328 ft.; N39 22 35 W74 27 8 *Rebroadcasts:* Simulcast with WGBZ(FM) Cape May Court House 100%
8025 Black Horse Pike, Suite 100-102, W. Atlantic City, NJ 08232 US
(609) 484-8444; *Fax:* (609) 646-6331
993thebuzz.com
License: Pleasantville, Atlantic County, NJ held by Equity Communications L.P.
Group Owner: Equity Communications LP; acq 5-31-2002; grpsl).
Nat'l Reps: Katz Radio
Arbitron Metro Market: Atlantic City-C; *Format:* Urban Contemporary; *Target Audience:* 18-49; adults; *Adv. Rates:* 200; 200; 200; 50
Rob Garcia, Programming Director
Shannon Wray, Promotions Manager

Point Pleasant

WRAT
10-04-1968; 95.9 MHz FM; *Hrs Open:* 24; 4 kw; 240 ft.; N40 10 15 W74 1 42
Mailing Address: 1731 Main Street, Lake Romo, NJ 07719 US
Second Address: 610 Main St., Belmar, NJ 7719
(732) 681-9591
www.wrat.com
License: Point Pleasant, Ocean County, NJ held by The Sentinel Publishing Co.
Group Owner: Beasley Broadcast Group; (acq 7-6-01; grpsl).
Nat'l Reps: Katz Radio
Target Audience: 21-44; men 25-54
Peter H. Smyth, CEO/COO
Dan Finn, Operations Dir

Pomona

***WLFR**
10-16-1984; 91.7 MHz FM; *Hrs Open:* 6 AM-2 AM; 0.82 kw; 148 ft.; N39 28 34.3 W74 32 20.3
Richard Stockton College of NJ, 101 Vera King Drive, Galloway, NJ 08205 US
(609) 652-4781; *Fax:* (609) 652-4958
www.wlfr.fm
License: Pomona, Atlantic County, NJ held by Stockton State College
Format: Alternative *Special Programming:* Folk 3 hrs, class 4 hrs, jazz 10 hrs wkly; *Hrs. of News Programming:* News progmg one hr wkly; *Target Audience:* General.
Christine Farina, General Manager

Pompton Lakes

WGHT
10-03-1964; 1500 kHz AM; *Hrs Open:* Sunrise-sunset; 1 kw-D, DAD; N40 58 51 W74 17 6
1878 Lincoln Ave., PO Box 316, Pompton Lakes, NJ 07442 US
(973) 839-1500; *Fax:* (973) 839-2400
www.ghtradio.com
livestudio@ghtradio.com
License: Pompton Lakes, NJ held by Mariana Broadcasting Inc.
Nat'l Network: AP Radio
Arbitron Metro Market: New York; *Format:* Oldies, Talk *Special Programming:* Relg 2 hrs, polka one hr, loc sports 3 hrs wkly; *Hrs. of News Programming:* news progmg 10 hrs wkly; *No. News Employees:* 3 *TargetAudience:* 25-54; general
Tom Niven, Operations Dir
John Silliman, General Manager
Mary Hamilton, General Sales Mgr
Jimmy Howes, Programming Director
Deborah Valentine, News Director
Tom Niven, Chief Engineer
Greta Latona, Assistant Program Director
Carmela Minervini, Office Manager
Mary Hamilton, Sales Director

Port Republic

***WEHA(FM)**
01-01-2003; 88.7 MHz FM; 760 w vert; Ant 131 ft; N39 35 34 W74 26 15
P.O. Box 1674, Pleasantville, NJ 08232
(609) 377-8612; *Fax:* (609) 377-8591
info@wehagospel887.com
License: Port Republic, Atlantic County, NJ held by WXXY Broadcasting Inc.
Arbitron Metro Market: Little Egg Harbor, NJ; *Format:* Gospel
Priscilya M. Hawkes, General Manager

Princeton

WHWH
09-07-1963; 1350 kHz AM; *Hrs Open:* 24; 5 kw-D, DA2; 5 kw-N, DA2; N40 22 0 W74 44 38
27 William St., 11th Floor, New York, NY 10005 US
(212) 966-1059; *Fax:* (212) 625-2894
www.radiowttm1680.com
License: Princeton, NJ held by Multicultural Radio Broadcasting Licensee LLC.
Group Owner: Multicultural Radio Broadcasting Inc.; (acq 5-24-2002; grpsl)
Arbitron Metro Market: Trenton, NJ *TV Affiliate:* *KHIZ-TV; *Format:* Christian, Spanish
Arthur Liu, CEO/COO

WPRB
10-01-1955; 103.3 MHz FM; *Hrs Open:* 24; 14 kw; 728 ft.; N40 16 58 W74 41 11
30 Bloomberg Hall, Princeton, NJ 08544 US
(609) 258-3655; *Fax:* (609) 258-1806
www.wprb.com
manager@wprb.com
License: Princeton, Mercer County, NJ held by Princeton Broadcasting Service Inc.
Arbitron Metro Market: Trenton, NJ; *Format:* Jazz *Special Programming:* Asian Indian 6 hrs wkly; *Target Audience:* 13-60.; *Adv. Rates:* 22; 22; 22; 22
Chester Dubon, General Manager

Princeton Junction

***WWPH**
11-01-1975; 107.9 MHz FM; 0.017 kw horiz; 36 ft.; N40 18 20 W74 37 16
346 Clarksville Road, Princeton Junction, NJ 08550 US
(609) 716-5145
www.wwph1079fm.com
License: Princeton Junction, Mercer County, NJ held by West Windsor Plainsboro Regional Board of Education.
Arbitron Metro Market: Princeton Junction, NJ *TV Affiliate:* WWPH-TV; *Format:* Variety/Diverse; *Target Audience:* 14-30; West Windsor & Plainsboro residents interested in their community

Salem

WFAI
09-01-1966; 1510 kHz AM; *Hrs Open:* 6 AM-6 PM; 2.5 kw-D, DAD; N39 34 58 W75 27 39
704 King Street, Suite 604, Wilmington, DE 19801 US
(302) 622-8895; *Fax:* (302) 622-8678
www.faith1510.com
License: Salem, NJ held by QC Communication Inc.
Arbitron Metro Market: Wilmington, DE; *Format:* Gospel *Special Programming:* Farm 8 hrs wkly; *Hrs. of News Programming:* news progmg 3 hrs wkly; *No. News Employees:* 2; *Target Audience:* 18 plus.
Steven Chanin, General Manager
James Himmons, Programming Director

Somers Point

***WXGN**
01-01-2000; 90.5 MHz FM; *Hrs Open:* 24; 350 w; 32 meters; N39 16 47 W74 34 30
1102 New Road, Northfield, NJ 08225 US
(609) 938-0012; *Fax:* (609) 926-5185
www.wxgnradio.org
wxgn90.5fm@gmail.com
License: Somers Point, Atlantic County, NJ held by Joy Broadcasting Inc.
Arbitron Metro Market: Egg Harbor City, NJ; *Format:* Christian; *Target Audience:* Teens - Young Adults
Bill Link, Station Manager
Bob Green, License Holder

South Orange

***WSOU**
04-14-1948; 89.5 MHz FM; *Hrs Open:* 24; 2.4 kw; 312 ft.; N40 44 28 W74 14 42
400 South Orange Avenue, South Orange, NJ 07079 US
(973) 761-9768; *Fax:* (973) 761-7593
www.wsou.net
License: South Orange, Essex County, NJ held by Seton Hall University.
Wire Services: AP
Arbitron Metro Market: New York; *Format:* Rock/AOR *Special Programming:* Pol 2 hrs, Ethnic 10 hrs, pub affrs 5 hrs, relg 5 hrs wkly; *Hrs. of News Programming:* News progmg 7 hrs wkly; *Target Audience:* 18-34.
Mark Maben, General Manager
Steve Varsanyi, Programming Director
Rohit Ravi, Promotions Manager
Caroline Ramos-Pinsky, News Director
Tommy Willert, Music Director
Vincent Coughlin, Sports Director

Stirling

WKMB
02-01-1972; 1070 kHz AM; *Hrs Open:* Sunrise-sunset; 0.25 kw-D, NDD; N40 40 35 W74 28 36
120 West 7th Street, Suite 201, Plainfield, NJ 07980 US
(908) 822-1515
License: Stirling, NJ held by World Harvest Communications Inc.
Arbitron Metro Market: New York; *Format:* Christian, Talk
Gary Kirkwood Sr., CEO

Sussex

***WNJP**
01-01-1998; 88.5 MHz FM; 0.45 kw; 636 ft.; N41 8 37 W74 32 18
160 Varick Street, New York, NY 10013 US
(646) 829-4000
www.wnyc.org
License: Sussex, Sussex County, NJ held by New Jersey Public Broadcasting Authority.
Nat'l Network: NPR; PRI

Arbitron Metro Market: Sussex, NJ; *Format:* News, News/Talk, 86; *Target Audience:* General.
Laura Walker, President/CEO

Teaneck

*WFDU

08-30-1971; 89.1 MHz FM; *Hrs Open:* 1:15 AM-3:45 PM (M-F); 24 (S, Su); 550 w; 550 ft; N40 57 39 W73 55 23
1000 River Rd., Teaneck, NJ 07666
(201) 692-2806; *Fax:* (201) 692-2807
www.wfdu.fm
duff@fdu.edu
License: Teaneck, Bergen County, NJ held by Fairleigh Dickinson University.
Wire Services: AP
Population Served: 18,000,000; *Arbitron Metro Market:* New York
Special Programming: Sp 3 hrs hrs wkly; *Hrs. of News Programming:* News progmg 2 hrs wkly; *Target Audience:* General.
Wender Tartaglia, Operations Dir
Duff Sheffield, General Manager

Toms River

WOBM-FM

03-01-1968; 92.7 MHz FM; 1.4 kw; 486 ft.; N39 52 31 W74 9 57.3
P. O. Box 927, Toms River, NJ 08754 US
848-221-8000; *Fax:* (732) 269-9292
www.wobmam.com
Brad.Burascano@townsquaremedia.com
License: Toms River, Ocean County, NJ held by Townsquare Media Monmouth-Ocean License LLC
Group Owner: Townsquare Media; (acq 5-14-02; grpsl).
TV Affiliate: Adult contemp
General Sales Manager, Steve Ardolina
Program Director, Brad Burascano
Promotions Director, Promotions Manager

*WNJO

01-01-2008; 90.3 MHz FM; 0.001 kw horiz, 4 kw vert; 121 ft.; N39 54 52 W74 4 58 *Rebroadcasts:* Rebroadcasts WNJT-FM Trenton 100%
US
(646) 829-4000
www.wnyc.org
License: Toms River, Ocean County, NJ
Group Owner: New York Public Radio
Nat'l Network: NPR; *Regional Network:* NJN Public Radio
Arbitron Metro Market: Toms River, NJ; *Format:* Jazz
Laura Walker, CEO/President

Toms River Township

*WWNJ

12-01-1991; 91.1 MHz FM; *Hrs Open:* 24; 0.05 kw horiz, 50 kw vert; 151 ft.; N39 58 7 W74 4 19 *Rebroadcasts:* Rebroadcasts WWFM(FM) Trenton 100%
1200 Old Trenton Road, West Windsor, NJ 08690 US
(609) 587-8989; *Fax:* (609) 570-3863
www.wwfm.org
info@wwfm.org
License: Toms River Township, Ocean County, NJ held by Mercer County Community College Board of Trustees.
Nat'l Network: NPR
Arbitron Metro Market: Toms River, NJ; *Format:* Classical; *Target Audience:* General.
Peter Fretwell, General Manager
Alice Weiss, Programming Director
David Osenberg, Music Director
Diane Guvenis, Development Director
Marcia Galambos, Membership Coordinator

Trenton

WFJS

01-20-1947; 1260 kHz AM
Domestic Church Media, P.O. Box 7509, Trenton, NJ 08628 US
(609)882-9357; *Fax:* (609)403-2908
www.wfjs.org
License: Trenton, NJ held by Domestic Church Media Foundation
Nat'l Network: EWTN Radio
Arbitron Metro Market: Trenton, NJ; *Format:* Christian
James Manfredonia, President

WNJE

04-11-1941; 920 kHz AM; *Hrs Open:* 24
224 Maugers Mill Road, Pottstown, PA 19464 US
(609)454-4185; *Fax:* (215) 321-5583
www.wchram.net
License: Trenton, NJ held by Connoisseur Media Licenses LLC
Group Owner: Connoisseur Media Licenses LLC
Arbitron Metro Market: Trenton, NJ; *Format:* Religious; *Target Audience:* General; relg adults; *Adv. Rates:* 40; 40; 40; 20
Curt Simpson, Operations Dir
John White, General Manager
John White, Station Manager
Chuck Zulker, General Sales Mgr
Dwain Decker, Programming Director

WKXW

08-27-1962; 101.5 MHz FM; 15.5 kw; 902 ft.; N40 16 58 W74 41 11
Mailing Address: 1350 Campus Parkway, Suite 106, Wall, NJ 07753 US
Second Address: 109 Walters Ave., Trenton, NJ 8638
(609) 771-8181; *Fax:* (609) 406-7956
www.nj1015.com
jason.finkelberg@townsquaremedia.com
License: Trenton, Mercer County, NJ held by Townsquare Media Trenton License LLC
Group Owner: Townsquare Media
Nat'l Reps: Christal
Arbitron Metro Market: Trenton, NJ; *Format:* Talk; *Hrs. of News Programming:* news progmg 75 hrs wkly; *No. News Employees:* 15; *Target Audience:* General; New Jersey residents
Jason Finkelberg, General Manager
Joe Limardi, Brand Manager
Jason Pugliese, Director Of Sales
Jackie Corley, Digital Managing Editor

WPST

08-07-1965; 94.5 MHz FM; 50 kw horiz, 48 kw vert; 492 ft.; N40 11 22 W74 50 47
224 Maugers Mill Road, Pottstown, PA 19464 US
(609) 419-0300; *Fax:* (609) 419-0143
www.wpst.com
dmckay@wpst.com
License: Trenton, Mercer County, NJ held by Connoisseur Media Licenses LLC
Group Owner: Connoisseur Media LLC
Arbitron Metro Market: Trenton, NJ; *Format:* Contemporary Hits/Top 40
Jim Spector, Programming Director
Angela Hartman, News Director
Randy Ellis, Music Director

*WNJT-FM

05-20-1991; 88.1 MHz FM; 0.11 kw vert; 689 ft.; N40 16 58 W74 41 11
160 Varick Street, New York, NY 10013 US
(646) 829-4000
www.wnyc.org
License: Trenton, Mercer County, NJ
Group Owner: New York Public Radio
Nat'l Network: NPR; PRI
Arbitron Metro Market: Trenton, NJ; *Format:* News, News/Talk, 86; *Target Audience:* General.
Graham Parker, General Manager
Aaron Cohen, Director of Programming Operations

*WTSR

09-01-1966; 91.3 MHz FM; *Hrs Open:* 24; 1.5 kw; 36 ft.; N40 16 17 W74 46 55
College of New Jersey, P.O Box 7718, Ewing, NJ 08628 US
(609) 771-3200; *Fax:* (609) 637-5113
www.wtsr.org
License: Trenton, Mercer County, NJ held by The College of New Jersey Radio System.
Arbitron Metro Market: Trenton, NJ; *Format:* Alternative *Special Programming:* Gospel 6 hrs, pub affrs 8 hrs, folk 4 hrs, jazz 4; *Hrs. of News Programming:* News progmg 15 hrs wkly; *Target Audience:* 13-40; peoplewho listen to div mus formats
Nick Dolce, Operations Dir
Kevin Potucek, General Manager
Mary Jo Lambino, Station Manager
Conor Sheehan, News Director
Madison Quellette, Music Director
Kyle Newins, Production Director
Thomas Moore, PR Director
Paul Mitchell,Sports Director

*WWFM

09-06-1982; 89.1 MHz FM; *Hrs Open:* 24; 1.15 kw; 292 ft.; N40 15 30 W74 38 59
1200 Old Trenton Rd., Trenton, NJ 08550 US
(609) 587-8989; *Fax:* (609) 570-3863
www.wwfm.org
info@wwfm.org
License: Trenton, Mercer County, NJ held by Mercer County Community College
Nat'l Network: NPR; PRI
Arbitron Metro Market: Trenton, NJ; *Format:* Classical; *Hrs. of News Programming:* 3.5 hrs wkly
Alice Weiss, Operations Dir
Peter Fretwell, General Manager
Alice Weiss, Programming Director
David Osenberg, Music Director
Diane Guvenis, Development Director
Marcia Galambos, Membership Coordinator
Rachel Katz, ProductionManager

Tuckerton

WBHX

01-01-1999; 99.7 MHz FM; 5.6 kw; 108 ft.; N39 33 41 W74 14 27
2355 West Bangs Avenue, Neptune, NJ 07753 US
(732) 774-4755; *Fax:* (732) 774-7315
www.1071radio.com
License: Tuckerton, Ocean County, NJ held by Press Communications L.L.C.
Group Owner: Press Communications L.L.C.; acq 9-18-02; $1.15 million).
Arbitron Metro Market: Neptune, N.J.; *Format:* Adult Contemp
Rich Morena, General Manager
Josh Gertzog, General Sales Mgr
Matt Rosenberg, Programming Director
Diana Pellegrino, Promotions Manager

Union Township

*WKNJ-FM

01-01-1980; 90.3 MHz FM; *Hrs Open:* 24/7; 0.009 kw; 16 ft.; N40 40 35 W74 14 2
1000 Morris Avenue, Union, NJ 07083 US
(908) 737-5326; *Fax:* (908) 737-0445
www.wknj903.com
License: Union Township, Union County, NJ held by Kean University.
Format: Rock/AOR *Special Programming:* Rock block, sports, classic times, Irish; *Target Audience:* University students/administration; music lovers
Scott McHugh, General Manager

Upper Montclair

*WMSC

12-09-1974; 90.3 MHz FM; *Hrs Open:* 7 AM-1 AM; 0.001 kw; 673 ft.; N40 51 53 W74 12 3
Schmitt Hall, Room 389, 3891 Normal Avenue, Montclair, NJ 07043 US
(973) 655-3135
www.wmscradio.com
License: Upper Montclair, Essex County, NJ held by Montclair State University.
Arbitron Metro Market: Montclair, NJ; *Format:* Variety/Diverse *Special Programming:* Black 4 hrs, gospel 2 hrs, jazz 2 hrs, Sp 2 hrs, s; *Hrs. of News Programming:* News progmg 5 hrs wkly; *Target Audience:* Under 35.
Silas Kezengust, Programming Director
Brianna Oshin, Promotions Manager
Joey Vecchione, Music Director
Lisa Hresko, Music Director

Villas

WCZT

02-01-1992; 98.7 MHz FM; *Hrs Open:* 24; 6 kw; 328 ft.; N38 59 45 W74 50 19
1602 Route 47 2nd Floor, Rio Grande, NJ 08242 US
(609) 522-1987; *Fax:* (609) 522-3666
www.987thecoast.com
bob@coastalbroadcasting.com
License: Villas, Cape May County, NJ held by Coastal Broadcasting Systems Inc.
Group Owner: Coastal Broadcasting Systems Inc.; (acq 5-21-2001; $1.4 million for stock)
Arbitron Metro Market: Villas, NJ; *Format:* Adult Contemp
Bob Maschio, President /General Manager
Scott Wahl, Vice President/ News Director

Vineland

WMIZ

08-19-1959; 1270 kHz AM; 0.36 kw-D, DA1; 0.21 kw-N, DA1; N39 29 53 W75 4 31
632 Maurice River Parkway, Vineland, NJ 08360 US
(856) 692-8888; *Fax:* (856) 696-2568
www.wmizradio.com
License: Vineland, NJ held by Clear Communications Inc.
Arbitron Metro Market: Vineland, NJ; *Format:* Spanish; *Target Audience:* Hispanic.

Bob Maschio Jr., President
Scott Wahl, News Director

WNJC

07-29-1946; 1360 kHz AM; *Hrs Open:* 6 AM-midnight
123 Egg Harbor Road, #302, Sewell, NJ 08080 US
(856) 227-1360; *Fax:* (856) 232-9093
www.wnjc1360.com
missradiochick@hotmail.com
License: Vineland, NJ held by Forsyth Broadcasting LLC
Arbitron Metro Market: Sewell, NJ; *Format:* Gospel, Talk *Special Programming:* Relg 6 hrs wkly; *Hrs. of News Programming:* news progmg 20 hrs wkly; *No. News Employees:* 3; *Target Audience:* 30 plus; 52% women,upper income
John Forsythe, President
Al Jones, General Manager

WVLT

10-01-1968; 92.1 MHz FM; 6 kw; 328 ft.; N39 29 53 W75 4 31
632 Maurice River Parkway, Vineland, NJ 08360 US
(856) 692-8888; *Fax:* (856) 696-2568
www.wvlt.com
chemple@aol.com
License: Vineland, Cumberland County, NJ held by Clear Communications Inc.
Nat'l Network: ABC; Jones Radio Networks
Arbitron Metro Market: Vineland, NJ; *Format:* Oldies; *Target Audience:* 25-54; baby boomers; *Adv. Rates:* 30; 27; 30; 22
Carl Hemple Sr., CEO/General Manager

Wayne

*WPSC-FM

11-01-1988; 88.7 MHz FM; *Hrs Open:* 9 am-3 am M-F; 6 am-3 am S-S; 0.2 kw; 259 ft.; N40 59 46 W74 16 51
300 Pompton Road, Wayne, NJ 07470 US
(973) 720-2000; *Fax:* (973) 720-2454
License: Wayne, Passaic County, NJ held by William Paterson University of New Jersey.
Format: Alternative *Special Programming:* Punk 3 hrs, hip hop 18 hrs, metal 18 hrs, classic rock 12 hrs, jazz 12 hrs wkly; *Target Audience:* 18-35; independent thinking
Rob Quickie, General Manager

West Long Branch

*WMCX

05-02-1974; 88.9 MHz FM; *Hrs Open:* 24; 1 kw; 118 ft; N40 16 44 W74 00 26
Monmouth Univ., 400 Cedar Ave., West Long Branch, NJ 07764
(732) 571-3493; *Fax:* (732) 263-5145
www.wmcx.com
afurguse@monmouth.edu
License: West Long Branch, Monmouth County, NJ held by Monmouth University.
Nat'l Network: AP Radio
Population Served: 200,000 *Special Programming:* Sports 11 hrs, jazz 3 hrs, changes w/semester; *Hrs. of News Programming:* News progmg 2.5 hrs wkly; *Target Audience:* 18-25; college students, recent grads, young adults
Danielle Gertz, General Manager

Wildwood

WCMC

11-25-1951; 1230 kHz AM; *Hrs Open:* 24; 1 kw-U, ND1; N39 0 9 W74 48 46
8025 Black Horse Pike, Suite 100-102, W. Atlantic City, NJ 08232 US
(609) 484-8444; *Fax:* (609) 646-6331
www.classicoldieswmid.com
License: Wildwood, NJ held by Equity Communications L.P.
Group Owner: Equity Communications LP; (acq 11-4-97; $7.1 million with co-located FM).
Nat'l Network: ABC; *Nat'l Reps:* Katz Radio
Arbitron Metro Market: Atlantic City-Cape May, NJ; *Format:* Adult Contemp; *Target Audience:* Adults 35-64.; *Adv. Rates:* 50; 50; 50; 50
Rob Garcia, Programming Director
Shannon Wray, Promotions Manager

WZXL

12-17-1959; 100.7 MHz FM; *Hrs Open:* 24; 38 kw; 331 ft.; N39 7 28 W74 45 56
8025 Black Horse Pike, Suite 100-102, W. Atlantic City, NJ 08232 US
(609) 484-8444; *Fax:* (609) 646-6331
www.wzxl.com
License: Wildwood, Cape May County, NJ
Group Owner: Equity Communications LP
Nat'l Reps: Katz Radio
Arbitron Metro Market: West Atlantic City, NJ; *Format:* Classic Rock; *Target Audience:* Adults 18-49.; *Adv. Rates:* 200; 200; 200; 50
Rob Garcia, Programming Director
Shannon Wray, Promotions Manager

Wildwood Crest

WEZW

08-15-1993; 93.1 MHz FM; *Hrs Open:* 24; 4.1 kw; 223 ft.; N38 59 34 W74 48 48 *Rebroadcasts:* Simulcast with WTTH(FM) Margate City 100%
8025 Black Horse Pike, Suite 100-102, W. Atlantic City, NJ 08232 US
(609) 484-8444; *Fax:* (609) 646-6331
www.easy931.com
rgarcia@equitycommunications.net
License: Wildwood Crest, Cape May County, NJ held by Equity Communications L.P.
Group Owner: Equity Communications LP; (acq 5-30-2003; grpsl).
Nat'l Reps: Katz Radio
Arbitron Metro Market: Gibsland,La; *Format:* Adult Contemp; *Target Audience:* 18-49; adults; *Adv. Rates:* 200; 200; 200; 50
Rob Garcia, Programming Director
Shannon Wray, Promotions Manager

Woodbine

*WJPG

02-16-1999; 89.9 MHz FM; *Hrs Open:* 24; 1 kw; 105 ft.; N39 16 51 W74 51 11
950 Tilton Road, Suite 101, Northfield, NJ 08225 US
(877) 300-8105
www.praise899.org
letters@praise899.org
License: Woodbine, Cape May County, NJ held by Maranatha Ministries/Joy Communications Inc.
Format: Religious *Special Programming:* Gospel one hr wkly; *Hrs. of News Programming:* News progmg 10 hrs wkly; *Target Audience:* 25-54; women
Kenneth Manri, President

Zarephath

WAWZ

08-22-1954; 99.1 MHz FM; *Hrs Open:* 24; 50,000 watts; Ant 656 ft; N40 36 41 W74 34 12
Box 9058, Zarephath, NJ 08890
(732) 469-0991
www.star991fm.com
info@star991fm.com
License: Zarephath, Somerset County, NJ held by Pillar of Fire Inc.
Group Owner: Pillar of Fire Inc.
Arbitron Metro Market: New York; *Target Audience:* 25-54.; *Adv. Rates:* 160; 160; 160; 75
Scott Taylor, Station Manager
Therese Romano, Programming Director

New Mexico

Alamo

*KYGR

88.1 MHz FM; 400 w; Ant -195 ft; N34 25 01 W107 30 04
Box 907, Magdalena, NM
(505) 854-2543
License: Alamo, Magdalena County, NM held by Alamo Navajo School Board Inc.

Alamo Community

*KABR

107.5 MHz FM; 10000 w; -41 m; N34 25 01 W107 30 04
PO Box 907, Magdalena, NM
(575) 854-2525
www.ansbi.org
License: Alamo Community, Socorro County, NM
Group Owner: Alamo Navajo School Board Inc.

Steve Guerro, President
Stanley Herrera, Vice President

Alamogordo

KINN

06-10-1957; 1270 kHz AM; *Hrs Open:* 24; 1 kw-D, ND2; 0.08 kw-N, ND2; N32 53 13 W105 57 4
501 S. Florida Ave., Alamogordo, NM 88310 US
(505) 434-1414
License: Alamogordo, NM held by Burt Broadcasting Inc.
Group Owner: Burt Broadcasting Inc.; (acq 4-1-2001; with co-located FM)
Format: News/Talk; *Hrs. of News Programming:* News progmg 22 hrs wkly; *Target Audience:* 24-50; military & civil service personnel employed in high-tech jobs
Paula Maes, President

KRSY

01-01-1954; 1230 kHz AM; *Hrs Open:* 24; 1 kw; 150 ft; N33 10 45 W105 53 53
Mailing Address: 119 N. Canyon Road, Alamogordo, NM 88310
Second Address: 119 N. Canyon Rd., Alamogordo, NM 88310
(575) 437-1505; *Fax:* (575) 437-5566
www.snmradio.com
Lhenke@snmradio.com
License: Alamogordo, Otero County, NM held by WP Broadcasting LLC.
Group Owner: Westburg Media Capital LP; (acq 5-19-2006; grpsl).
Nat'l Network: ESPN Radio

Sunny Aris, Chairman
Les Henke, General Manager

KNMZ

01-01-1997; 103.7 MHz FM; *Hrs Open:* 24; 6 kw; 1,338 ft; N33 10 45 W105 53 53
119 N. Canyon Road, Alamogordo, NM 88310
(575) 437-1505; *Fax:* (575) 437-5566
www.snmradio.com
License: Alamogordo, Otero County, NM held by WP Broadcasting LLC.
Group Owner: Westburg Media Capital LP; (acq 5-19-2006; grpsl).
Nat'l Network: ESPN

Sunny Aris, Chairman
Les Henke, General Manager

*KLAG

10-14-2000; 91.7 MHz FM; *Hrs Open:* 24; 1.4 kw; 1680 ft.; N32 49 47 W105 53 10
5700 West Oaks Boulevard, Rocklin, CA 95765 US
(916) 251-1600; *Fax:* (916) 251-1650
www.klove.com
License: Alamogordo, Otero County, NM held by Educational Media Foundation
Group Owner: EMF Broadcasting
Arbitron Metro Market: Alamogordo, NM; *Format:* Country, Gospel; *Target Audience:* 25-60; adults
Mike Novak, President

KYEE

07-21-1980; 94.3 MHz FM; *Hrs Open:* 24; 3 kw; -384 ft.; N32 56 42 W105 56 47
PO Box 1848, Alamogordo, NM 88310 US
(505) 434-1414; *Fax:* (505) 434-2213
www.totacc.com/94Key
License: Alamogordo, Otero County, NM held by Burt Broadcasting Inc.
Group Owner: Burt Broadcasting Inc.; acq 11-88; $230,000;
Arbitron Metro Market: Alamogordo, NM; *Format:* Contemporary Hits/Top 40; *Target Audience:* 18-44; young adults
Paula Maes, President

KZZX

01-01-1979; 105.3 MHz FM; *Hrs Open:* 24; 0.91 kw; 1614 ft.; N32 49 48 W105 53 12
501 S. Florida, Alamogordo, NM 88311-1414 US
(575) 434-1414
License: Alamogordo, Otero County, NM held by Burt Broadcasting Inc.
Group Owner: Burt Broadcasting Inc.
Arbitron Metro Market: Alamogordo, NM; *Format:* Country; *Hrs. of News Programming:* News progmg 22 hrs wkly; *Target Audience:* 20-55.
Paula Maes, President

KQEL

01-01-2006; 107.9 MHz FM; *Hrs Open:* 24; 3 kw; -594 ft.; N32 53 13 W105 57 4
501 S. Florida, Alamogordo, NM 88311 US
(505) 434-1414; *Fax:* (505) 434-2213
License: Alamogordo, Otero County, NM held by Burt Broadcasting Inc.
Group Owner: Burt Broadcasting Inc.; (acq 10-29-2003; $93,000 for CP).
Arbitron Metro Market: Alamogordo, NM; *Format:* Oldies
Paula Maes, President/CEO

***KYCM**
01-01-2006; 89.9 MHz FM; 0.8 kw; 1631 ft.; N32 49 47 W105 53 13 *Rebroadcasts:* Rebroadcasts KYCC(FM) Stockton, CA 100%
9019 West Lane, Stockton, CA 95210 US
(209) 477-3690; *Fax:* (209) 477-2762
www.kycc.org
kycc@kycc.org
License: Alamogordo, Otero County, NM held by Your Christian Companion Network Inc.
Arbitron Metro Market: Alamogordo, NM; *Format:* Adult Contemp, Gospel, 74
Shirley Garner, General Manager
Vanessa Kudenox, Office Manager
John Ramos, Outside Promotions
Gary Harding, Evening Host

Albuquerque

KABQ
01-01-1947; 1350 kHz AM; *Hrs Open:* 8am - 5:30pm; 5 kw-D, DAN; 0.5 kw-N, DAN; N35 6 2 W106 40 34
5411 Jefferson Ave., Suite 100, Albuquerque, NM 87109 US
(505) 830-6400
www.abqtalk.com
License: Albuquerque, Bernalillo County, NM held by Clear Channel Broadcasting Licenses Inc.
Group Owner: iHeartMedia; (acq 3-01-00; grpsl)
Nat'l Reps: Lotus Entravision Reps LLC
Arbitron Metro Market: Albuquerque, NM; *Format:* Talk; *Target Audience:* General.
Chuck Hammond, Regional Market President
Bev Rainey, Programming Director
Ryan Safford, Promotions Director
John White, Sales Manager
Hope Romero, Sales Manager

***KANW**
10-01-1950; 89.1 MHz FM; *Hrs Open:* 24; 17 kw; 4154 ft.; N35 12 44 W106 26 57
2020 Coal Ave Se, Albuquerque, NM 87106 US
(505) 242-7163
www.kanw.com
License: Albuquerque, Bernalillo County, NM held by Board of Education of the City of Albuquerque.
Nat'l Network: NPR; PRI
Arbitron Metro Market: Albuquerque, NM; *Hrs. of News Programming:* News progmg 20 hrs wkly
Michael Brasher, General Manager

KDAZ
01-01-1969; 730 kHz AM; *Hrs Open:* 24; 1 kw-D, DA2; 0.076 kw-N, DA2; N35 0 31 W106 42 52
Mailing Address: P.O. Box 4338, Albuquerque, NM 87196 US
Second Address: 5010 4th St. N.W., Albuquerque, NM 87107
(505) 345-1991; *Fax:* (505) 345-5669
www.kdaz.org
birga@kdaz.org
License: Albuquerque, NM held by Pan American Broadcasting Inc.
Nat'l Network: USA
Arbitron Metro Market: Albuquerque, NM; *Format:* Variety/Diverse; *Target Audience:* 25-54.; *Adv. Rates:* 16.50;16.50;16.50;16.50
Annette Garcia, Operations Dir
Jim Sandell, Programming Director
Vickie Archiveque, CFO

KDEF
09-01-1953; 1150 kHz AM; 5 kw-D, DAN; 0.5 kw-N, DAN; N35 12 6 W106 35 54
2900 Louisiana N.E., Suite 250, Albuquerque, NM 87110 US
(505) 265-0991
License: Albuquerque, NM held by RAMH Corp.
Nat'l Network: CNN Radio
Arbitron Metro Market: Albuquerque, NM; *Format:* News, Sports, 2; *Target Audience:* General.
Henry Tafoya, General Manager

KIVA
05-14-1956; 1600 kHz AM; *Hrs Open:* 24; 10 kw-D, 128 w-N; N35 10 14 W106 37 51
1213 San Pedro Drive NE, Albuquerque, NM 87110
(505) 550-5500; *Fax:* (505) 899-6865
rockoftalk@me.com
License: Albuquerque, Bernalillo County, NM held by Vanguard Media LLC
Nat'l Network: CNN Radio; *Nat'l Reps:* Christal
Population Served: 600,000; *Arbitron Metro Market:* Albuquerque, NM; *Target Audience:* 30-50.
Nick Govatski, CEO

***KFLQ**
02-20-1983; 91.5 MHz FM; *Hrs Open:* 24; 20 kw; 4042 ft.; N35 12 51 W106 27 2
P.O. Box 35300, Tucson, AZ 85704 US
Fax: (800) 776-1070
www.myflr.org
License: Albuquerque, Bernalillo County, NM held by Family Life Broadcasting System.
Group Owner: Family Life Communications Inc.; (acq 1982).
Nat'l Network: Moody; USA
Arbitron Metro Market: Albuquerque, NM; *Format:* Religious, Christian *Special Programming:* Children's stories 10 hrs wkly.; *No. News Employees:* 2; *Target Audience:* Christian families
Randy Carlson, President

KBZU
11-01-1954; 96.3 MHz FM; *Hrs Open:* 24; 17.5 kw; 4134 ft.; N35 12 44 W106 26 58
City Center West, 7201 W. Lake Mead Blvd, Las Vegas, NV 89128 US
(505) 767-6700; *Fax:* (505) 767-6767
License: Albuquerque, Bernalillo County, NM held by Radio License Holding CBC LLC
Group Owner: Cumulus Media Inc.
Nat'l Network: ESPN Deportes; *Nat'l Reps:* McGavren Guild
Arbitron Metro Market: Albuquerque, NM; *Format:* Sports
Eddie Haskell, Operations Dir
Jeff Berry, General Sales Mgr
Bill Harris, Engineering Dir
Art Ortega, Public Affairs Director

KNML
01-01-1994; 610 kHz AM; *Hrs Open:* 24; 5 kw
500 4th St. NW, 5th Floor, Albuquerque, NM 87102 US
(505) 767-6700; *Fax:* (505) 767-6711
www.610knml.com
License: Albuquerque, NM held by Radio License Holding CBC, LLC
Group Owner: Cumulus Media Inc.; (acq 3-23-00; swap with KSVA(AM) Albuquerque).
Arbitron Metro Market: Albuquerque, NM; *Format:* Sports, Talk; *Target Audience:* 25-54.
Pat Frisch, Programming Director

KKIM
04-15-1972; 1000 kHz AM; 10 kw-D, ND1; 0.038 kw-N, ND1; N35 10 14 W106 37 51
P.O. Box 444, Spartanburg, SC 29304 US
(888) 989-2299
www.wilkinsradio.com
denise@wilkinsradio.com
License: Albuquerque, NM held by Wild West Radio Corp.
Group Owner: Wilkins Communications Network Inc.; (acq 12-22-97; grpsl)
Arbitron Metro Market: Albuquerque, NM; *Format:* Christian, Talk *Special Programming:* Black 2 hrs wkly; *Target Audience:* 25-54.
Robert Wilkins, CEO/COO

KKOB
04-05-1922; 770 kHz AM; *Hrs Open:* 24; 50 kw-D, 50 kw-N
500 4th St. NW, Suite 500, Albuquerque, NM 87102 US
(505) 767-6700; *Fax:* (505) 767-6767
www.770kkob.com
770@cumulus.com
License: Albuquerque, NM held by Radio License Holding CBC, LLC
Group Owner: Cumulus Media Inc.; (acq 3-15-94; $7.8 million with co-located FM;).
Nat'l Reps: McGavren Guild
Arbitron Metro Market: Albuquerque, NM; *Format:* News/Talk
Pat Frisch, Programming Director

KKOB
08-01-1967; 93.3 MHz FM; *Hrs Open:* 24; 21.5 kw; 4150 ft.; N35 12 42 W106 26 59
500 4th St. NW, Suite 500, Albuquerque, NM 87102 US
(404) 949-0700
www.kobfm.com
License: Albuquerque, NM held by Radio License Holding CBC, LLC
Group Owner: Cumulus Media Inc.
Arbitron Metro Market: Albuquerque, NM; *Format:* Contemporary Hits/Top 40
Kris Abrams, Operations Manager

***KLYT**
09-11-1976; 88.3 MHz FM; *Hrs Open:* 24; 4.1 kw; 4245 ft.; N35 12 49 W106 27 1
4001 Osuna Road NE, Albuquerque, NM 87109 US
(505) 344-9146; *Fax:* (505) 344-9193
License: Albuquerque, Bernalillo County, NM held by Calvary Chapel of Albuquerque, Inc.
Arbitron Metro Market: Albuquerque, NM; *Format:* Christian
Maria Guy, General Manager
Daniel Davidson, Station Manager
Steve Reimann, General Sales Mgr

KPEK
12-01-1974; 100.3 MHz FM; *Hrs Open:* 8am - 5:30pm; 22.5 kw; 4111 ft.; N35 12 51 W106 27 2
5411 Jefferson Avenue, Suite 100, Albuquerque, NM 87109 US
(505) 830-6400; *Fax:* (505) 830-6543
www.1003thepeak.com
info@1003thepeak.com
License: Albuquerque, Bernalillo County, NM held by Citicasters Licenses Inc.
Group Owner: iHeartMedia; (acq 9-28-99; grpsl).
Arbitron Metro Market: Albuquerque, NM; *Format:* Adult Contemp; *Target Audience:* 25-54; adults, high income professional and technical
Chuck Hammond, Vice President/Market Manager
John White, General Sales Mgr
Bev Rainey, Programming Director
Ryan Safford, Promotions Director

KKRG
10-01-1994; 105.1 MHz FM; *Hrs Open:* 24; 100 kw; 1,896 ft.; N35 46 49 W106 31 34
8009 Marble Ave. N.E., Albuquerque, NM 87110 US
(505) 254-7100
www.univision.com
License: Albuquerque, Bernalillo County, NM held by Univision Radio License Corp.
Group Owner: Univision Radio; (acq 9-22-2003; grpsl).
Arbitron Metro Market: Albuquerque, NM; *Format:* Urban Contemporary; *Target Audience:* 35-54.
Larry Lemanski, Vice President and General Manager

KRST
09-15-1965; 92.3 MHz FM; *Hrs Open:* 24; 22 kw; 4160 ft.; N35 12 55 W106 27 2
500 4th St. NW, Albuquerque, NM 87102 US
(505) 767-6700; *Fax:* (505) 767-6767
www.nashfm923krst.com
License: Albuquerque, NM held by Radio License Holding CBC, LLC
Group Owner: Cumulus Media Inc.; (acq 9-30-96; grpsl).
Arbitron Metro Market: Albuquerque, NM; *Format:* Country; *Adv. Rates:* 150; 140; 140; 100
Jason Martinez, General Sales Mgr
Kris Abrams, Programming Director
Mandi Vaquera, Promotions Director

KRZY
06-01-1956; 1450 kHz AM; *Hrs Open:* 24; 1 kw-U, ND1; N35 7 56 W106 37 18
2725 Broadbent Parkway NE, Suite F, Albuqurque, NM 87107 US
(505) 342-4141; *Fax:* (505) 344-8714
www.espndeportes1450.com
rmather@entravision.com
License: Albuquerque, NM held by Entravision Holdings LLC.
Group Owner: Entravision Communications Corp.; (acq 3-14-2000; grpsl).
Arbitron Metro Market: Albuquerque, NM; *Format:* Sports, Spanish
Carlos Fourzan, General Manager
Esmeralda Ruiz, General Sales Mgr
Francisco Gutierrez, Promotions Manager

KSVA
03-28-1998; 920 kHz AM; *Hrs Open:* 24; 1 kw-D, ND1; 0.13 kw-N, ND1; N35 7 56 W106 37 18
P.O. Box 500, Simi Valley, CA 93062 US
(800) 775-4673
www.lifetalk.net
License: Albuquerque, NM held by Lifetalk Radio Inc.
Nat'l Network: USA
Arbitron Metro Market: Corrales, NM; *Format:* Christian, Religious *Special Programming:* Sp 4 hrs wkly; *Hrs. of News Programming:* News progmg 2 hrs wkly; *Target Audience:* 35 plus; Christians
Warren Judd, Administrator
Robert Hardy, Operations Dir
John Geli, Station Manager
Debby Wade, General Sales Mgr
Marcelo Vallado, Chief Engineer

KDRF
04-20-1988; 103.3 MHz FM; *Hrs Open:* 24; 20 kw; 4242 ft.; N35 12 50 W106 27 1
500 4th St. NW, 5th Floor, Albuquerque, NM 87102 US

(505) 767-6700
www.ed.fm
License: Albuquerque, NM held by Radio License Holding CBC, LLC
Group Owner: Cumulus Media Inc.; (acq 1996; $5 million).
Nat'l Reps: Christal
Arbitron Metro Market: Albuquerque, NM; *Format:* Adult Contemp; *Target Audience:* 18-49.
Jason Martinez, Sales Manager
Kris Abrams, Programming Director
Alison Page Atwood, Promotions Director

KBQI
04-27-1979; 107.9 MHz FM; *Hrs Open:* 24; 22.5 kw; 4131 ft.; N35 12 43 W106 26 57
5411 Jefferson Avenue, Suite 100, Albuquerque, NM 87109 US
(505) 875-1079; *Fax:* (505) 830-6543
www.bigi1079.com
info@bigi1079.com
License: Albuquerque, Bernalillo County, NM held by Citicasters Licenses Inc.
Group Owner: iHeartMedia; (acq 9-28-99; grpsl).
Arbitron Metro Market: Albuquerque, NM; *Format:* Country; *Target Audience:* 18-49.
Chuck Hammond, Vice President/Market Manager
John White, General Sales Mgr
Ryan Safford, Promotions Director

***KUNM**
10-17-1966; 89.9 MHz FM; *Hrs Open:* 24; 18.5 kw; 4108 ft.; N35 12 44 W106 26 57
1 University of New Nexico, Albuquerque, NM 87131 US
(505) 277-4806
www.kunm.org
kunm@kunm.org
License: Albuquerque, Bernalillo County, NM held by Regents of the University of New Mexico.
Nat'l Network: NPR; PRI
Arbitron Metro Market: Albuquerque, NM; *Format:* News, News/Talk, 86, Variety/Diverse *Special Programming:* Class 12 hrs, Sp 9 hrs, Indian 9 hrs wkly; *Hrs. of News Programming:* news progmg 50 hrs wkly *No. NewsEmployees:* 3; *Target Audience:* 25-54; those who enjoy NPR and diverse community-produced programs; *Adv. Rates:* 45; 30; 45; 30
Scott MacNicholl, Operations Dir
Richard Towne, General Manager
Tristan Clum, Programming Director
Elaine Baumgartel, News Director
Matthew Finch, Music Director
Nicole Candelaria, Production Assistant
Melissa Rios, ManagementAssistant
Matthew Finch, Music Director

KXKS
12-16-1969; 1190 kHz AM; *Hrs Open:* 24; 10 kw-D, ND2; 0.024 kw-N, ND2; N35 3 4 W106 38 34
P.O. Box 444, Spartanburg, SC 29304 US
(864) 585-1885; *Fax:* (864) 597-0687
www.wilkinsradio.com
denise@wilkinsradio.com
License: Albuquerque, NM held by Wild West Radio Corp.
Group Owner: Wilkins Communications Network Inc.; (acq 12-16-2004; $775,000).
Arbitron Metro Market: Spartanburg, SC; *Format:* Christian, Talk; *Target Audience:* 35 plus.
Robert Wilkins, CEO/COO

KZRR
06-25-1961; 94.1 MHz FM; *Hrs Open:* 24; 19.5 kw; 4131 ft.; N35 12 44 W106 26 58
5411 Jefferson Avenue, Suite 100, Albuquerque, NM 87109 US
(505) 830-6400; *Fax:* (505) 830-6543
www.94rock.com
kzrr@94rock.com
License: Albuquerque, Bernalillo County, NM held by Clear Channel Broadcasting Licenses Inc.
Group Owner: iHeartMedia; (acq 9-28-99; grpsl)
Nat'l Network: Westwood One
Arbitron Metro Market: Albuquerque, NM; *Format:* Rock/AOR
Chuck Hammond, Vice President/Market Manager
John White, Sales Manager
Ryan Safford, Promotions Director

Angel Fire

KKTC
01-15-1990; 99.9 MHz FM; *Hrs Open:* 24; 1.75 kw; 2119 ft.; N36 33 30 W105 11 38
125A Camino de la Merced, Taos, NM 87571-5119 US
(505) 758-4491
License: Angel Fire, Colfax County, NM held by DMC Broadcasting Inc.
Group Owner: DMC Broadcasting Inc.; (acq 3-19-2003; $645,000 with KXMT(FM) Taos).
Nat'l Network: ABC
Format: Country *Special Programming:* Jazz 4 hrs, relg 8 hrs wkly; *Hrs. of News Programming:* news progmg 7 hrs wkly; *No. News Employees:* 1; *Target Audience:* 25-54; adults middle-upper-income residents & tourists *Adv. Rates:* 15; 15; 15; 10
Roy Seale, Web Administrator

Armijo

KNKT
12-17-1991; 107.1 MHz FM; *Hrs Open:* 24; 17.5 kw; 705 ft.; N35 3 15 W106 51 31
4001 Osuna Road, Albuquerque, NM 87109 US
(505) 338-5790; *Fax:* (505) 344-9193
www.knkt.com
knkt@calvaryabq.org
License: Armijo, Bernalillo County, NM held by Calvary Chapel of Albuquerque Inc.
Arbitron Metro Market: Albuquerque, NM; *Format:* Religious; *Hrs. of News Programming:* News progmg 4 hrs wkly; *Target Audience:* 25-54.
Brian Nixon, General Manager

Arroyo Seco

***KRRT**
04-03-2008; 90.9 MHz FM; 5.1 kw horiz; -610 ft.; N36 23 52 W105 32 36 *Rebroadcasts:* Rebroadcasts KUNM(FM) Albuquerque 100%
Room 326 Onate Hall, University of New Mexico, Albuquerque, NM 87131 US
(505) 277-4806
www.kunm.org
kunm@kunm.org
License: Arroyo Seco, Taos County, NM held by Regents of the University of New Mexico.
Arbitron Metro Market: Albuquerque, NM; *Format:* News, News/Talk, 86, Variety/Diverse
Richard Towne, General Manager

Artesia

KSVP
11-14-1946; 990 kHz AM; *Hrs Open:* 24; 1 kw-D, ND1; 0.25 kw-N, ND1; N32 49 29 W104 23 59
317 West Quay, Artesia, NM 88210 US
(575) 746-2751; *Fax:* (575) 748-3748
www.ksvpradio.com
License: Artesia, NM held by Pecos Valley Broadcasting Co.
Group Owner: Pecos Valley Broadcasting Co.; (acq 1993; $150,000 with co-located FM;
Nat'l Network: CBS
Arbitron Metro Market: Artesia, NM; *Format:* Talk; *Hrs. of News Programming:* news progmg 18 hrs wkly; *No. News Employees:* 1; *Target Audience:* General.; *Adv. Rates:* 11.45; 11.45; 11.45; 11.45
Gene Dow, General Manager
Thomas Beard, General Sales Mgr
Mike Jaxon, News Director
Mike Montgomery, Chief Engineer

KTZA
05-09-1969; 92.9 MHz FM; *Hrs Open:* 24; 100 kw; 1089 ft.; N32 47 38 W104 12 29
Dave Oakley Building, 121 South Canal Street, #C, Carlsbad, NM 88220 US
(575) 628-8402; *Fax:* (575) 941-3000
www.kz93.com
License: Artesia, Eddy County, NM
Group Owner: Pecos Valley Broadcasting Co.
Nat'l Network: ABC
Arbitron Metro Market: Artesia, NM; *Format:* Country; *Hrs. of News Programming:* News progmg 3 hrs wkly; *Target Audience:* 25-54.
Gene Dow, Operations Dir
Gene Dow, Vice President & General Manager
Thomas Beard, Sales Manager
Mike Jaxson, News Director
Mike Montgomery, Chief Engineer
Shea Waller, Traffic Director
Marlee Smith, Traffic Assistant
MikeWinters, Operations Manager
Lauren Romero, Account Executive

Aztec

KCQL
09-04-1959; 1340 kHz AM; *Hrs Open:* 24; 1 kw-U, ND1; N36 49 17 W107 59 58
200 E. Broadway, Farmington, NM 87401 US
(505) 325-1716; *Fax:* (505) 325-6797
www.sports1340.com
License: Aztec, San Juan County, NM held by Capstar TX LLC
Group Owner: iHeartMedia; (acq 8-30-2000; grpsl).
Nat'l Network: Fox Sports; *Wire Services:* UPI
Arbitron Metro Market: Farmington, NM; *Format:* Sports *Special Programming:* Sp 6 hrs wkly; *Hrs. of News Programming:* News progmg 14 hrs wkly; *Target Audience:* 18-54.
Chuck Hammond, Vice President/Market Manager

KWYK-FM
01-02-1978; 94.9 MHz FM; *Hrs Open:* 24; 100 kw; 433 ft.; N36 41 54 W108 13 18
1515 West Main Street, Farmington, NM 87401 US
(505) 325-1996; *Fax:* (505) 327-2019
www.kwykradio.com
productionroom@basinbroadcasting.com
License: Aztec, San Juan County, NM held by Basin Broadcasting Co.
Arbitron Metro Market: Farmington, NM; *Format:* Adult Contemp; *Hrs. of News Programming:* News progmg 15 hrs wkly; *Target Audience:* 25-54; mainstream population; *Adv. Rates:* 19; 17; 19; 16
Bill O'Brien, Programming Director

Bayard

KNFT
07-04-1968; 950 kHz AM
1560 North Corbin, Silver City, NM 88061 US
(575) 383-3396; *Fax:* (575) 388-1759
www.silvercityradio.com
events@silvercityradio.com
License: Bayard, NM held by SkyWest Licenses New Mexico LLC.
Group Owner: SkyWest Media L.L.C.; (acq 6-1-2006; grpsl).
Format: Sports, Talk
Matthew Runnell, General Manager
Anna Gallegos, News Director
Rita Niccum, Chief Engineer

KNFT-FM
06-15-1981; 102.9 MHz FM; 5.1 kw; 1578 ft.; N32 51 49 W108 14 27
1560 North Corbin, Silver City, NM 88061 US
(575) 538-3396; *Fax:* (575) 388-1759
www.silvercityradio.com
License: Bayard, Grant County, NM
Group Owner: SkyWest Media L.L.C.
Format: Country
Tim Brown, CEO
David Bach, Operations Dir
Colleen Barill, General Manager
Dave Rogers, CFO

Belen

KARS
10-07-1961; 840 kHz AM; *Hrs Open:* 24; 1.8 kw D, 0.03 kw N, ND2; N35 00 31 W106 42 52
P.O. Box 2700, Bakersfield, CA 93303 US
(505) 864-3024; *Fax:* (505) 864-2719
www.americangeneralmedia.com
rbrandon@americangeneralmedia.com
License: Belen, Valencia County, NM held by AGM-Nevada L.L.C.
Group Owner: American General Media; (acq 12-22-97; grpsl)
Nat'l Reps: Lotus Entravision Reps LLC
Arbitron Metro Market: Belen, NM; *Format:* Country *Special Programming:* Relg; *Hrs. of News Programming:* news progmg 30 hrs wkly; *No. News Employees:* 1; *Target Audience:* 25 plus.
Rogers Brandon, General Manager
Dewey Moede, Station Manager
Ron Travis, Programming Director
Bob Picknell, Chief Engineer
Russ Ortego, Disc Jockey

KLVO
01-01-1982; 97.7 MHz FM; *Hrs Open:* 24; 98.4 kw; N34 47 55 W106 48 59
4125 Carlisle NE, Albuquerque, NM 93303
(505) 878-0980; *Fax:* (505) 878-0098
www.radiolobo.net
License: Belen, Valencia County, NM held by AGM Nevada, LLC
Group Owner: American General Media
Arbitron Metro Market: Albuquerque, NM; *Format:* Adult Contemp; *Target Audience:* Hispanic Adults 18-49
William Kruger, General Manager

RADIO - U.S.

Bloomfield

KKFG

01-01-1988; 104.5 MHz FM; 100 kw; 1086 ft.; N36 38 33 W107 46 54
5411 Jefferson Avenue, Suite 100, Albuquerque, NM 87109 US
(505) 325-1716; *Fax:* (505) 325-6797
www.kool1045.com
License: Bloomfield, San Juan County, NM held by Capstar TX LLC
Group Owner: iHeartMedia; (acq 8-30-2000; grpsl).
Arbitron Metro Market: Santa Fe, NM; *Format:* Oldies
Dave Schaefer, Operations Manager

Bosque Farms

KABQ-FM

07-01-1987; 104.7 MHz FM; 100 kw; 843 ft.; N34 46 12 W106 51 42
5411 Jefferson Avenue, Suite 100, Albuquerque, NM 87109 US
(505) 830-6400; *Fax:* (505) 830-6543
www.classiccountry1047.com
License: Bosque Farms, Valencia County, NM held by Aloha Station Trust LLC, as Trustee
Arbitron Metro Market: Albuquerque, NM; *Format:* Country; *No. News Employees:* 1; *Target Audience:* 25-54.
Chuck Hammond, General Manager
John White, General Sales Mgr
Bev Rainey, Programming Director
Ryan Safford, Promotions Director
Dave Shelton, Chief Engineer

*KQLV(FM)

11-16-2001; 105.5 MHz FM; *Hrs Open:* 24; 22 kw; Ant 745 ft; N34 47 55 W106 48 59
6401 Richards Avenue, Santa Fe, NM 87505
(800) 525-5683; *Fax:* (916) 251-1650
www.klove.com
klove@klove.com
License: Bosque Farms, Valencia County, NM held by Educational Media Foundation.
Group Owner: EMF Broadcasting
Nat'l Network: K-Love
Format: Christian; *No. News Employees:* 3; *Target Audience:* 25-44; Judeo-Christian, female
Mitch Barnhart, Director
Dr. David R. Ferry, Director
Walter Golembeski, Director
Mark Voltmann, Director
Dan Antonelli, Director
Marya Morgan, News Reporter
Richard Hunt, News Reporter

*KQRI

01-01-2004; 105.5 MHz FM; 97.58 kw; 745 ft.; N34 47 55 W106 48 59 *Rebroadcasts:* Rebroadcasts KLRD(FM) Yucaipa, CA 100%
Air 1, P.O. Box 2118, Omaha, NE 68103-2118 US
(888) 937-2471; *Fax:* (916) 251-1650
www.air1.com
License: Bosque Farms, Valencia County, NM held by Educational Media Foundation.
Group Owner: EMF Broadcasting
Nat'l Network: Air 1
Arbitron Metro Market: Bosque Farms, NM; *Format:* Christian
Darrell Chambliss, Chairman
Alan Mason, COO
Mike Novak, President and CEO
Dan Antonelli, Chief Business Development Officer
Eric Moser, Chief Financial Officer
D. Kevin Blair, Secretary and General Counsel
Larry Moody,Director
Mitch Barnhart, Director

Cannon Afb

*KKCJ

90.7 MHz FM; 25 kw; 194 ft.; N34 26 58 W103 37 3
4001 Osuna Rd NE, Albuquerque, NM 87109 US
(505) 250-7742
License: Cannon Afb, Curry County, NM held by Calvary Chapel of Albuquerque
Group Owner: Calvary Chapel of Albuquerque
Nat'l Network: CSN
Arbitron Metro Market: Canon, NM; *Format:* Christian, Religious

Carlsbad

KAMQ

06-10-1938; 1240 kHz AM; 1 kw-D, ND1; 1 kw-N, ND1; N32 23 43 W104 14 48
P. O. Box 1538, Carlsbad, NM 88220 US
(575) 887-7563; *Fax:* (575) 887-7000
www.carlsbadradio.com
don@carlsbadradio.com
License: Carlsbad, NM held by KAMQ Inc.
Arbitron Metro Market: Carlsbad, NM; *Format:* Adult Contemp, Christian
Don Hughes, General Manager
Frank Nymeyer, Chief Engineer

KATK

05-17-1950; 740 kHz AM; 1 kw-D, ND1; 0.5 kw-N, ND1; N32 27 2 W104 12 47
Mailing Address: 539 Radio Boulevard, Carlsbad, NM 88220 US
Second Address: P.O. Box 1538, Carlsbad, NM 87221
(575) 887-5323
www.carlsbadradio.com
don@carlsbadradio.com
License: Carlsbad, NM held by Stubbs Broadcasting Co. Inc.
Arbitron Metro Market: Carlsbad, NM; *Format:* Adult Contemp *Special Programming:* Gospel 2 hrs wkly; *Hrs. of News Programming:* News progmg 70 hrs wkly; *Target Audience:* 50 plus; bilingual Hispanics; *Adv. Rates:* 8; 8; 8
Don Hughes, General Manager/General Sales Manager

KATK-FM

09-15-1966; 92.1 MHz FM; 6 kw; 190 ft.; N32 27 2 W104 12 47
Mailing Address: 539 Radio Boulevard, Carlsbad, MN 88220 US
Second Address: P.O. Box 1538, Carlsbad, NM 87221
(575) 887-7563; *Fax:* (575) 887-7000
www.carlsbadradio.com
don@carlsbadradio.com
License: Carlsbad, Eddy County, NM held by Stubbs Broadcasting Co. Inc.
Arbitron Metro Market: Carlsbad, NM; *Format:* Country; *Hrs. of News Programming:* News progmg 70 hrs wkly; *Target Audience:* 18-54.
Don Hughes, General Sales Mgr

KPZE-FM

01-01-2000; 106.1 MHz FM; *Hrs Open:* 24; 39 kw; 558 ft.; N32 34 22 W104 5 32
105 West 3rd Street, #228, Roswell, NM 88202 US
(575) 578-1198; *Fax:* (575) 578-1197
www.kpze.com
License: Carlsbad, Eddy County, NM held by Pecos Valley Broadcasting Co.
Group Owner: Pecos Valley Broadcasting Co.; (acq 2005; $475,000).
Arbitron Metro Market: Artesia, NM; *Format:* Tejano; *Hrs. of News Programming:* news progmg one hr wkly; *No. News Employees:* 1; *Adv. Rates:* 12; 12; 12; 10
Gene Dow, General Manager

KCCC

07-01-1966; 930 kHz AM; *Hrs Open:* 24; 1 kw-D, ND1; 0.06 kw-N, ND1; N32 24 20 W104 11 21
930 N. Canal, Carlsbad, NM 88220 US
(505) 887-5521; *Fax:* (505) 885-5481
License: Carlsbad, NM held by Compass Enterprises Inc.
Arbitron Metro Market: Carlsbad, NM; *Format:* Oldies
Nick Jenkins, President
Michelle McCutcheon, Operations Dir
Phil Tozier, News Director
Frank Nymeyer, Chief Engineer

KCDY

07-01-1989; 104.1 MHz FM; 100 kw; 676 ft.; N32 34 22 W104 5 32
P. O. Box 1538, Carlsbad, NM 88220 US
(575) 887-7563; *Fax:* (505) 887-7000
License: Carlsbad, Eddy County, NM held by KAMQ Inc.
Format: Adult Contemp
Don Hughes, Sales Manager

Chama

KZRM

10-08-1999; 96.1 MHz FM; *Hrs Open:* 24; 25 kw; 302 ft.; N36 53 56 W106 36 6
2202 State Road 17, Chama, NM 87520 US
(575) 756-1617; *Fax:* (575) 756-1317
www.kzrmradio.com
License: Chama, Rio Arriba County, NM held by Lance Broadcasting LLC
Arbitron Metro Market: Chama, NM; *Format:* Classic Rock
Uncle Ralphie, Chief Engineer

Church Rock

KYVA-FM

08-07-1997; 103.7 MHz FM; *Hrs Open:* 24; 100 kw; 1378 ft.; N35 36 22 W108 41 26
300 West Aztec Avenue, Suite 200, Gallup, NM 87301 US
(505) 863-6851; *Fax:* (505) 863-2429
www.gallupradio.com
sammychioda@gmail.com
License: Church Rock, Cibola County, NM held by Millennium Media Inc.
Nat'l Network: ABC
Arbitron Metro Market: Church Rock, NM; *Format:* Oldies *Special Programming:* American Indian 10 hrs, Sp 4 hrs wkly.; *Hrs. of News Programming:* news progmg 12 hrs wkly; *No. News Employees:* 1; *Target Audience:* 25+. 0
George Malti, CEO
Sammy Chioda, General Manager
Thomas Devlin, General Sales Mgr
John McBreen, News Director
Keith Desautels, Chief Engineer

Clayton

KLMX

11-10-1949; 1450 kHz AM; 1 kw-U, ND1; N36 26 39 W103 11 24
P.O. Box 547, Clayton, NM 88415 US
(505) 374-2555; *Fax:* (505) 374-2557
www.klmx.us
License: Clayton, NM held by Johnson County Broadcasters Inc.
Arbitron Metro Market: Santa Fe NM; *Format:* Country *Special Programming:* Sp 2 hrs wkly
Jimmy N. Bear, Owner
Melba Mcollum, Owner
Jeremy Cook, General Manager
Louanne Snedden, Programming Director
Henry Walker, Chief Engineer

*KUHC

90.5 MHz FM
PO Box 8088, Amarillo, TX 79114 US
(806) 359-8855; *Fax:* (806) 354-2039
www.kingdomkeysradio.org
License: Clayton, Union County, NM held by Top O' Texas Educational Broadcasting Foundation
Group Owner: Top O' Texas Educational Broadcasting Foundation

Cloudcroft

*KHII

01-01-2004; 88.9 MHz FM; *Hrs Open:* 24; 0.1 kw; 1188 ft.; N32 59 48 W105 42 38 *Rebroadcasts:* Rebroadcasts KUPR(FM) Alamogordo 80%
3001 North Florida Avenue, Alamogordo, NM 88310 US
(575) 437-0917; *Fax:* (575) 437-9917
kupr917@yahoo.com
License: Cloudcroft, Otero County, NM held by Southern New Mexico Radio Foundation.
Format: Gospel
Bob Flotte, President

KNMB

96.7 MHz FM; 25 kw; 2881 ft.; N33 24 14 W105 46 56
1086 Mechem, Ruidoso, NM 88346 US
(576) 258-9922
mymtdradio.com
sales@mtdradio.com
License: Cloudcroft, Otero County, NM held by MTD Inc.
Group Owner: MTD Inc.
Arbitron Metro Market: Ruidoso Downs, NM; *Format:* Country

Clovis

*KAQF

03-01-1998; 91.1 MHz FM; 0.45 kw; 174 ft.; N34 26 19.8 W103 12 38.1
P.O. Box 3206, Tupelo, MS 38803 US
(662) 844-8888; *Fax:* (662) 842-6791
www.afr.net
faq@afa.net
License: Clovis, Curry County, NM held by American Family Association.
Group Owner: American Family Radio
Arbitron Metro Market: Tupelo, MO; *Format:* Christian, Religious
Tim Wildmon, President
Donald Wildmon, Founder
Buddy Smith, Sr. VP
Ed Vitagliano, Randy Sharp
Director Of Special Projects, Meeke Addison
Director Of Communications, Abraham Hamilton III
General Counsel & Public Policy, GeneralSales Mgr

KCLV
02-01-1953; 1240 kHz AM; *Hrs Open:* 24; 1 kw-U, ND1; N34 22 40 W103 12 17
2112 Thornton Street, Clovis, NM 88101 US
(575) 763-4401
www.kclvsports.com
License: Clovis, NM held by Zia Broadcasting Co.
Group Owner: Zia Broadcasting Co.; (Acq 7-1-71)
Nat'l Network: ESPN Radio
Arbitron Metro Market: Clovis, NM; *Format:* Sports; *Adv. Rates:* 6.50; 6.50; 6.50; 6.50
Lonnie Allsup, President
Rick Keefer, Genral Manager and General Sales Manager

KCLV-FM
01-08-1970; 99.1 MHz FM; *Hrs Open:* 24; 74 kw; 230 ft.; N34 23 18 W103 11 7
Mailing Address: P.O. Box 1907, Clovis, NM 88101 US
Second Address: 2112 Thornton St., Clovis, NM 88101
(505) 763-4401; *Fax:* (505) 769-2564
www.kclvsports.com
kclv@allsups.com
License: Clovis, Curry County, NM held by Zia Broadcasting Co.
Group Owner: Zia Broadcasting Co.; (acq 11-12-81)
Nat'l Network: ABC
Arbitron Metro Market: Clovis, NM; *Format:* Country; *Target Audience:* 30 plus.; *Adv. Rates:* 8.50; 8.50; 8.50; 8.50
Lonnie Allsup, President
Rick Keefer, Genral Manager and General Sales Manager
Lorraine Weingates, News Director
Gary Jackson, Chief Engineer

KICA
01-01-1933; 980 kHz AM; *Hrs Open:* 24
1000 Sycamore Street, Clovis, NM 88101 US
(505) 762-6200
License: Clovis, NM held by Tallgrass Broadcasting LLC.
Group Owner: Tallgrass Broadcasting LLC; (acq 4-2-2007; grpsl)
Nat'l Network: USA
Format: Talk *Special Programming:* Farm 5 hrs, high school sports 4 hrs wkly; *Target Audience:* 30 plus.
Dana Taylor, Operations Dir

KKYC
01-01-1993; 102.3 MHz FM; *Hrs Open:* 24; 25 kw horiz; 177 ft.; N34 24 31 W103 11 15
1000 Sycamore Street, Clovis, NM 88101 US
(575) 762-6200
License: Clovis, NM held by Tallgrass Broadcasting LLC.
Group Owner: Tallgrass Broadcasting LLC; (acq 4-2-2007; grpsl)
Arbitron Metro Market: Sante Fe, NM; *Format:* Contemporary Hits/Top 40; *Hrs. of News Programming:* news progmg 2 hrs wkly; *No. News Employees:* 1; *Target Audience:* 25-54.

KSMX-FM
11-01-1982; 107.5 MHz FM; 100 kw; 541 ft.; N34 11 34 W103 16 44
Mailing Address: 208 East Grand Avenue, Clovis, NM 88101 US
Second Address: 42437 U.S. 70, Portales, NM 88130
(505) 763-0338
www.heymix.com
info@heymix.com
License: Clovis, Curry County, NM held by Rooney Moon Broadcasting Inc.
Group Owner: Rooney Moon Broadcasting Inc.; (acq 7-15-2002; grpsl)
Arbitron Metro Market: Clovis, NM; *Format:* Adult Contemp
Steve Rooney, President
Duffy Moon, Operations Dir

KTQM-FM
03-01-1963; 99.9 MHz FM; *Hrs Open:* 24; 100 kw; 299 ft.; N34 21 48 W103 13 5
Mailing Address: P.O. Box 1907, Clovis, NM 88101 US
Second Address: 710 Curry Rd. K, Clovis, NM 88101
(575) 762-4411; *Fax:* (575) 769-0197
www.ktqmclovis.com
ktqm@plateautel.net
License: Clovis, Curry County, NM held by Curry County Broadcasting, Inc.
Nat'l Network: ABC
Arbitron Metro Market: Clovis, NM; *Format:* Adult Contemp; *Hrs. of News Programming:* News progmg 3 hrs wkly; *Target Audience:* 25-54; young affluent; *Adv. Rates:* 17; na; 16; 10
Hewel Jones, President

KWKA
01-01-1971; 680 kHz AM; *Hrs Open:* 24; 0.5 kw-U, DA1; N34 21 48 W103 13 5
710 Curry Road K, Clovis, NM 88101 US
(575) 769-0197
License: Clovis, NM held by Curry County Broadcasting Inc.
Nat'l Network: CNN Radio *Regional Reps:* Rgnl Reps.
Arbitron Metro Market: Clovis, NM; *Format:* News, News/Talk, 86 *Special Programming:* Sean Hannity Talk Show; *Hrs. of News Programming:* News progmg 3 hrs wkly; *Target Audience:* 35 - 64;; *Adv. Rates:* 11:25;8; 9:35; 6.50
Hewel Jones, President

KRMQ-FM
01-01-2003; 101.5 MHz FM; 100 kw; 453 ft.; N34 15 8 W103 14 21
Box 4937, Casper, WY 82604 US
(575) 763-0338
q1015.com
License: Clovis, Curry County, NM held by Rooney Moon Broadcasting Inc.
Group Owner: Rooney Moon Broadcasting Inc.; (acq 1-13-2006; $595,000)
Arbitron Metro Market: Clovis, NM; *Format:* Oldies
Steve Rooney, President

***KELU**
01-01-2006; 90.3 MHz FM; 14 kw; 397 ft.; N34 26 21 W103 12 22 *Rebroadcasts:* Rebroadcasts KLVR(FM) Middletown, CA 100%
1750 Saratoga Drive, Rio Rancho, NM 87144 US
(505) 352-4028
www.klove.com
License: Clovis, Curry County, NM held by Educational Media Foundation.
Group Owner: EMF Broadcasting; (acq 9-22-2005; $40,000 for CP)
Nat'l Network: K-Love
Arbitron Metro Market: Clovis, NM; *Format:* Christian; *No. News Employees:* 13
Darrell Chambliss, Chairman
Mike Novak, President and CEO
David Pierce, Chief Creative Officer
Dan Antonelli, Director
Eric Moser, Chief Financial Officer
D. Kevin Blair, Secretary and General Counsel

Corrales

KKNS
07-15-1985; 1310 kHz AM; *Hrs Open:* 24; 5 kw-D, DAN; 0.5 kw-N, DAN; N35 12 0 W106 35 59 *Rebroadcasts:* 95.9FM Simulcast
1606 Central Avenue SE, Suite 104, Albuquerque, NM 87106 US
(505) 255-5015; *Fax:* (505) 262-4792
License: Corrales, NM held by El Camino Communications LLC
Arbitron Metro Market: Albuquerque, NM; *Format:* Tejano; *Target Audience:* H-18-49
Victor Camino, President

KLQT
04-27-1996; 95.1 MHz FM; *Hrs Open:* 24; 3 kw; Ant -531 ft; N35 14 42 W106 36 18
5411 Jefferson St. N.E., Suite 100, Albuquerque, NM 60559
(505) 830-6400; *Fax:* (505) 830-6517
www.hotabq.com
License: Corrales, Sandoval County, NM held by Clear Channel Broadcasting Licenses Inc.
Group Owner: iHeartMedia; (acq 9-28-99)
Arbitron Metro Market: Albuquerque, NM; *Format:* Adult Contemp
Chuck Hammond, Vice President/Market Manager

Deming

KDEM
04-15-1977; 94.3 MHz FM; 3 kw; 194 ft.; N32 15 5 W107 45 28
1700 S. Gold Avenue, P.O. Box 470, Deming, NM 88031 US
(505) 546-9011
www.demingradio.com
radio@demingradio.com
License: Deming, Luna County, NM
Nat'l Network: Westwood One; *Wire Services:* AP
Arbitron Metro Market: Deming, NM; *Format:* Adult Contemp; *Hrs. of News Programming:* news progmg 5 hrs wkly; *No. News Employees:* 1; *Target Audience:* 18-54.; *Adv. Rates:* Same as AM
Candie Sweetser, General Manager

KOTS
03-10-1954; 1230 kHz AM; *Hrs Open:* 24; 1 kw-U, ND1; N32 15 5 W107 45 28
1700 S. Gold Avenue, P.O. Box 470, Deming, NM 88031 US
(575) 546-9011; *Fax:* (575) 546-9342
www.demingradio.com
radio@demingradio.com
License: Deming, NM held by Luna County Broadcasting Co.
Nat'l Network: Westwood One; *Wire Services:* AP
Format: Country *Special Programming:* Farm 5 hrs, Sp 8 hrs wkly; *Hrs. of News Programming:* news progmg 13 hrs wkly; *No. News Employees:* 1; *Target Audience:* General.; *Adv. Rates:* 10; 10; 10; 10
Candie Sweetser, General Manager

Des Moines

***KENU**
10-04-2012; 88.5 MHz FM; 0.24 kw; 2011 ft.; N36 42 20 W103 52 36 *Rebroadcasts:* KENW-FM
Eastern New Mexico University, 1500 South Avenue K, Portales, NM 88130-9989 US
(575) 562-2112; *Fax:* (575) 562-2590
www.kenw.org
kenwfm@enmu.edu
License: Des Moines, Union County, NM held by Eastern New Mexico University.
Nat'l Network: NPR; BSN; APM; PRX
Arbitron Metro Market: Des Moines, NM
Dr. Steven G. Gamble, President
Duane Ryan, General Manager
Janet Lyn Bresenham, News Director
Jeff Burmeister, Engineering Dir
Rena Garrett, Development Director
Don Criss, Production/Community Services Director, TV
Duane W.Ryan, Director of Broadcasting
Karen Leonhardt', Accountant
Mickey Morgan, Audio Engineer

Dexter

KALN
01-01-2009; 96.1 MHz FM; 50 kw; 453 ft.; N33 23 57 W104 22 30
500 North Main Street, Suite 904, Roswell, NM 88201 US
(575) 623-3914
License: Dexter, Chaves County, NM held by Hispanic Target Media Inc.
Group Owner: Hispanic Target Media Inc.
Arbitron Metro Market: Dexter, NM; *Format:* Tejano
Francisco San Millan, President

Dulce

***KCIE**
12-03-1990; 90.5 MHz FM; *Hrs Open:* 24; 0.1 kw horiz, 0.093 kw vert; 1535 ft.; N36 59 0 W106 58 12
Aie Bldg/Narrow Gauge Rd, P.O. Box 603, Dulce, NM 87528 US
(505) 759-3681; *Fax:* (505) 759-9140
www.nv1.org/kcie.html
kcie@zianet.com
License: Dulce, Rio Arriba County, NM held by Jicarilla Apache Tribe.
Arbitron Metro Market: Dulce, NM; *Format:* Variety/Diverse; *Hrs. of News Programming:* news progmg 2 hrs wkly; *No. News Employees:* 1; *Target Audience:* General.
Lisa Vigil-Gomez, General Manager/Station Manager
Romaine Wood, Programming Director
Annette Martinez, News Director
William Vicente, Engineering Tech
Jordan Vigil, Computer Tech
Donna Shorty, Secretary
Carlos Davis, ProductionAssistant
Rita King, Custodian

Encino

***KXNM**
88.7 MHz FM; kw
P.O. Box 174, McIntosh, NM 87032 US
(505) 886-0605; *Fax:* (505) 886-0610
www.tcponm.com
License: Encino, Torrance County, NM held by Torrance County.
Arbitron Metro Market: Encino, NM

Espanola

KDCE
01-01-1963; 950 kHz AM; 4.2 kw-D, ND1; 0.08 kw-N, ND1; N36 0 8 W106 3 59
403 West Pueblo Dr., Espanola, NM 87533 US
(505) 753-2201
License: Espanola, NM held by Richard L. Garcia Broadcasting Inc.
Arbitron Metro Market: Espanola, NM
Richard Garcia, President

RADIO - U.S.

KYBR
07-06-1981; 92.9 MHz FM; 15.5 kw; 417 ft.; N36 5 52 W106 7 18
403 West Pueblo Road, Espanola, NM 87532 US
(505) 753-2201
www.radiooso.com
License: Espanola, Rio Arriba County, NM held by Rio Chama Broadcasting Co.
Arbitron Metro Market: Espanola, NM
Efrem Galindo, Programming Director

***KRAR**
04-01-2008; 91.9 MHz FM; 5.9 kw; 530 ft.; N36 9 8 W106 2 21
Rebroadcasts: Rebroadcasts KUNM(FM) Albuquerque 100%
403 West Pueblo Drive, Espanola, NM 87532 US
(505) 277-4806
www.kunm.org
kunm@kunm.org
License: Espanola, Rio Arriba County, NM held by Regents of the University of New Mexico
Arbitron Metro Market: Espanola, NM; *Format:* Public Affairs, Variety/Diverse
Richard Towne, General Manager

Eunice

KEJL
01-01-1996; 100.9 MHz FM; *Hrs Open:* 24; 50 kw; 364 ft.; N32 28 5 W103 9 27
Mailing Address: 511 S. 93rd Street, Omaha, NE 68114 US
Second Address: 1423 W. Bender, Hobbs, NM 88240
(505) 393-1551
www.hobbsradio.com/eagle/
License: Eunice, Lea County, NM held by FiveStar Enterprises L.C.
Nat'l Network: Jones Radio Networks
Arbitron Metro Market: Eunice, NM; *Format:* Classic Rock; *No. News Employees:* 1; *Target Audience:* 18-49.; *Adv. Rates:* 12; 12; 12; 12
Larry Philpot, General Manager
Al Lobeck, General Sales Mgr

Farmington

KDAG
09-01-1969; 96.9 MHz FM; *Hrs Open:* 24; 100 kw; 994 ft.; N36 48 52 W107 53 32
200 E. Broadway, Farmington, NM 87401 US
(505) 325-1716; *Fax:* (505) 325-6797
www.969thedogrocks.com
License: Farmington, San Juan County, NM held by Capstar TX LLC
Group Owner: iHeartMedia; (acq 8-30-2000; grpsl).
Arbitron Metro Market: Farmington, NM; *Format:* Rock/AOR; *Target Audience:* 18-49.
Dave Schaefer, Operations Manager

KENN
11-01-1951; 1390 kHz AM; 5 kw-D, DAN; 1.3 kw-N, DAN; N36 42 27 W108 8 50
212 West Apache, Farmington, NM 87401 US
(505) 325-3541; *Fax:* (505) 327-5796
www.kennradio.com
License: Farmington, NM held by Winton Road Broadcasting Co. LLC
Group Owner: Winton Road Broadcasting Co. LLC; (acq 5-3-2001; grpsl)
Arbitron Metro Market: Farmington, NM; *Format:* News, News/Talk, 84, Talk; *Target Audience:* 25-54; upper middle class
Bill Kruger, General Manager
Randy Klock, General Sales Mgr

KNDN
08-01-1957; 960 kHz AM; *Hrs Open:* 6 AM-10 PM; 5 kw-D, ND1; 0.163 kw-N, ND1; N36 43 48 W108 13 47
1515 West Main, Farmington, NM 87401 US
(505) 325-1996
License: Farmington, NM held by Basin Broadcasting Co.
Format: Native American; *Target Audience:* General; Navajo Indian reservation; all Navajo language
Jim Gober, General Manager
Kerwin Gober, General Sales Mgr
Judy Yancey, Traffic
Jim Burt, Chief Engineer

***KNMI**
03-18-1980; 88.9 MHz FM; *Hrs Open:* 24; 27 kw vert; 663 ft.; N36 40 16 W108 13 54
2103 West Main Street, Farmington, NM 87401 US
(505) 327-4357
www.verticalradio.org
music@verticalradio.org
License: Farmington, San Juan County, NM held by Navajo Missions Inc.
Nat'l Network: USA
Format: Christian, Talk; *Hrs. of News Programming:* News progmg 9 hrs wkly; *Target Audience:* 24-40; general
Emmet Fowler, General Manager

***KPCL**
12-14-1988; 95.7 MHz FM; *Hrs Open:* 24; 80 kw; 1040 ft.; N36 48 53 W107 53 31
Box 232, Farmington, NM 87499 US
(505) 327-7202
www.kpcl.org
License: Farmington, San Juan County, NM held by Voice Ministries of Farmington Inc.
Nat'l Network: Salem Radio Network
Format: Christian *Special Programming:* Class one hr, Navajo 7 hrs wkly; *Hrs. of News Programming:* news progmg 3 hrs wkly; *No. News Employees:* 1; *Target Audience:* General; relg audience
Fareed Ayoub, President

KRWN
01-01-1974; 92.9 MHz FM; *Hrs Open:* 24; 62 kw; 394 ft.; N36 41 45 W108 13 23
212 West Apache, Farmington, NM 87401 US
(505) 325-3541
www.krwn.com
License: Farmington, San Juan County, NM held by Winton Road Broadcasting Co. LLC.
Group Owner: Winton Road Broadcasting Co. LLC
Arbitron Metro Market: Farmington, NM; *Format:* Classic Rock; *Target Audience:* 18-49.
Dan Buchta, General Manager
Randy Klock, General Sales Mgr

***KSJE**
11-01-1990; 90.9 MHz FM; *Hrs Open:* 24; 15 kw; 390 ft.; N36 41 52 W108 13 14
4601 College Boulevard, Farmington, NM 87401 US
(505) 566-3517; *Fax:* (505) 566-3377
www.ksje.com
michlins@sanjuancollege.edu
License: Farmington, San Juan County, NM held by San Juan College.
Nat'l Network: PRI
Arbitron Metro Market: Framington, NM; *Format:* Classical, Jazz, 60 *Special Programming:* Jazz 15 hrs, folk 15 hrs wkly; *Hrs. of News Programming:* news progmg 15 hrs wkly; *No. News Employees:* 1; *Target Audience:* 25-65.
Scott Michlin, General Manager

KTRA-FM
02-19-1987; 102.1 MHz FM; *Hrs Open:* 24; 100 kw; 994 ft.; N36 48 52 W107 53 32
200 East Broadway, P.O. Box 6030, Farmington, NM 87490 US
(505) 325-1716; *Fax:* (505) 325-6797
www.102ktra.com
License: Farmington, San Juan County, NM held by Capstar TX LLC
Group Owner: iHeartMedia; (acq 8-30-2000; grpsl)
Nat'l Network: ABC
Arbitron Metro Market: Farmington, NM; *Format:* Country; *Target Audience:* 25-54.
Dave Schaefer, Programming Director

***KUUT**
01-01-2008; 89.7 MHz FM; 1.35 kw vert; 663 ft.; N36 40 16 W108 13 54 *Rebroadcasts:* Rebroadcasts KUTE(FM) Ignacio, CO 100%
P.O. Box 737, Ignacio, CO 81137 US
(970) 563-0255
www.ksut.org
License: Farmington, San Juan County, NM held by KUTE Inc.
Group Owner: KUTE Inc.
Arbitron Metro Market: Hobbs, NM; *Format:* Triple A
Bruce Campbell, Development Director
Ken Brott, Operations Dir

Flora Vista

***KUSW**
01-01-2008; 88.1 MHz FM; 4.1 kw vert; 663 ft.; N36 40 16 W108 13 54 *Rebroadcasts:* Rebroadcasts KUTE(FM) Ignacio, CO 100%
US
(970) 563-0255
www.ksut.org
License: Flora Vista, San Juan County, NM held by KUTE Inc.
Group Owner: KUTE Inc.; (acq 6-7-2006)
Arbitron Metro Market: Flora Vista, NM; *Format:* News, Native American
Richard Hoehlein, President
Rob Rawls, Adminstrative Director
Jim Belcher, Programming Director

Fruitland

***KTGW**
91.7 MHz FM; *Hrs Open:* 24; 12.5 kw; 394 ft.; N36 41 46 W108 13 13
P.O. Box 232, Farmington, NM 87499 US
(505) 327-2163
www.kpcl.org
kpcl@kpcl.org
License: Fruitland, San Juan County, NM held by Native American Christian Voice Inc.
Arbitron Metro Market: Farmington, NM; *Format:* Christian, Talk
Fareed Ayoub, President
Annette Ayoub, Executive Vice President

Gallup

KFMQ
01-01-1996; 106.1 MHz FM; 100 kw; 187 ft.; N35 29 39 W108 44 32
1632 S. 2nd St., Gallup, NM 87301 US
(505) 863-9391
www.kfmqrock1061.com
License: Gallup, McKinley County, NM held by Clear Channel Broadcasting Licenses Inc.
Group Owner: iHeartMedia; (acq 4-17-97)
Arbitron Metro Market: Gallup, NM; *Format:* Rock/AOR
Chuck Hammond, Vice President/Market Manager
Sylvester Paquin, Advertising Executive

KGAK
02-09-1945; 1330 kHz AM; *Hrs Open:* 5am-10pm; 5 kw-D, DAN; 1 kw-N, DAN; N35 32 34 W108 44 11
401 East Coal Avenue, Gallup, NM 87301 US
(505) 863-4444
License: Gallup, NM held by KRJG Inc.
Nat'l Network: CBS
Arbitron Metro Market: Gallup, NM; *Format:* Native American; *Target Audience:* 30-55.

***KGLP**
09-01-1992; 91.7 MHz FM; *Hrs Open:* 24; 0.88 kw; 1147 ft.; N35 36 13 W108 40 45 *Rebroadcasts:* Rebroadcasts KSUT(FM) Ignacio, CO 50%
Board of Directors, 200 College Road, Gallup, NM 87301 US
(505) 863-7626; *Fax:* (505) 863-7633
www.kglp.org
kglpradio@kglp.org
License: Gallup, McKinley County, NM held by Gallup Public Radio.
Nat'l Network: NPR
Format: News, Variety/Diverse *Special Programming:* 3 hrs jazz, 2 hrs latin; *Hrs. of News Programming:* News progmg 40 hrs wkly; *Target Audience:* General; adult professional, academic, business community
David Pracy, Operations Dir
Rachel Kaub, Station Manager

KGLX
03-01-1989; 99.1 MHz FM; *Hrs Open:* 24; 51 kw; 1,250 ft.; N35 36 18 W108 41 11
1632 S. 2nd St., Gallup, NM 87301 US
(505) 863-9391
www.991kglx.com
License: Gallup, McKinley County, NM held by Clear Channel Broadcasting Licenses Inc.
Group Owner: iHeartMedia; (acq 8-18-00; grpsl).
Arbitron Metro Market: Gallup, NM; *Format:* Country *Special Programming:* American Indian 3 hrs wkly; *Hrs. of News Programming:* news progmg 14 hrs wkly; *No. News Employees:* 2; *Target Audience:* 25-54.
Chuck Hammond, Vice President/Market Manager

KYAT
10-06-1974; 94.5 MHz FM; *Hrs Open:* 24; 100 kw; 1,388 ft; N35 28 03 W108 14 25
Box 420, Gallup, NM 87305
(505) 863-6851; *Fax:* (505) 863-2429
www.gallupradio.com
License: Gallup, McKinley County, NM
Population Served: 180,000; *No. News Employees:* 1; *Target Audience:* 25-44; young families with buying power
Sammy Chioda, President
Tom Devin, General Sales Mgr

KYVA
07-15-1959; 1230 kHz AM; *Hrs Open:* 24
P.O. Box 420, Gallup, NM 87305 US

(505) 863-6851; *Fax:* (505) 863-2429
www.gallupradio.com
License: Gallup, NM held by Millennium Media Inc.
Nat'l Network: ABC
Arbitron Metro Market: Gallup, NM; *Format:* Country; *Hrs. of News Programming:* news progmg 12 hrs wkly; *No. News Employees:* 1; *Target Audience:* 35-54; mature, with buying power
Sammy Chioda, President
Sammy Chioda, General Manager
Tom Devlin, General Sales Mgr
Brian Smith, Promotions Manager
John McBreen, News Director
Keith Desautels, Engineering Dir
Keith DeSautels, Chief Engineer

KXXI

08-15-1975; 93.7 MHz FM; *Hrs Open:* 24; 100 kw; 1378 ft.; N35 36 22 W108 41 26
Mailing Address: P.O. Box 420, Gallup, NM 87305 US
Second Address: 300 W. Aztec, Suite 200, Gallup, NM 87301
(505) 863-6851; *Fax:* (505) 863-2429
www.gallupradio.com
sammychioda@gmail.com
License: Gallup, McKinley County, NM held by Millennium Media Inc.
Nat'l Network: ABC
Arbitron Metro Market: Gullap, NM; *Format:* Classic Rock; *Target Audience:* 25-44.
Sammy Chioda, President
Thomas Devlin, General Sales Mgr
John McBreen, News Director
Keith Desautles, Engineering Dir
Tom Devlin, Sales Manager
Deni Gonzales, Marketing

*KGGA

01-01-2008; 88.1 MHz FM; 1 kw; 16 ft.; N35 32 27 W108 44 36
Rebroadcasts: Rebroadcasts KLRD(FM) Yucaipa, CA 100%
188 South Bellevue, Suite 222, Memphis, TN 38104 US
(800) 877-5600; *Fax:* (916) 251-1650
www.air1.com
info@air1.com
License: Gallup, McKinley County, NM held by Educational Media Foundation.
Group Owner: EMF Broadcasting; (acq 7-23-2007; grpsl)
Nat'l Network: Air 1
Arbitron Metro Market: Sioux Falls, SD; *Format:* Alternative, Christian
Mike Novak, President

*KLLU

01-01-2008; 88.9 MHz FM; 0.65 kw; 1165 ft.; N35 36 15 W108 41 10 *Rebroadcasts:* Rebroadcasts KLVR(FM) Middletown, CA 100%
1425 North Market Blvd, Suite 9, Sacramento, CA 95834 US
(800) 877-5600; *Fax:* (916) 251-1650
www.klove.com
License: Gallup, McKinley County, NM held by Educational Media Foundation.
Group Owner: EMF Broadcasting
Nat'l Network: K-Love
Arbitron Metro Market: El Paso, TX; *Format:* Christian
Mike Novak, President

Grants

KDSK-FM

06-01-1997; 92.7 MHz FM; *Hrs Open:* 24; 26 kw; 171 ft.; N35 7 9 W107 54 8
P.O. Box 11102, Albuquerque, NM 87192 US
(505) 285-5598; *Fax:* (505) 285-5575
License: Grants, Cibola County, NM held by KD Radio Inc.
Group Owner: KD Radio Inc.; (acq 11-16-00; with KMIN(AM) Grants).
Arbitron Metro Market: Albuquerque, NM; *Format:* Oldies; *Target Audience:* 30-50; earning boom
Derek Underhill, President
Debbie Anderson, General Sales Mgr
Tom Anderson, Promotions Manager

KMIN

09-01-1956; 980 kHz AM; *Hrs Open:* 24; 1 kw-D, 250 kw-N; N35 09 05 W107 52 31
733 Roosevelt, Grants, NM 84103
(505) 285-5598; *Fax:* (505) 285-5575
www.kdsk.com
License: Grants, Cibola County, NM held by KD Radio Inc.
Group Owner: KD Radio Inc.; (acq 1-2-01; $145,000 with KDSK(FM) Grants).
Population Served: 25,000; *Arbitron Metro Market:* Albuquerque, NM; *Target Audience:* 25-54; active, working adults
Derek Underhill, President
Debbie Anderson, General Sales Mgr

*KDRI

01-01-2006; 90.3 MHz FM; 1 kw; Ant 2,713 ft; N35 15 08 W107 35 45 *Rebroadcasts:* Rebroadcasts KLVR(FM) Santa Rosa, CA 100%
2351 Sunset Blvd., Suite 170-218, Rocklin, CA 95834
(916) 251-1600; *Fax:* (916) 251-1650
www.air1.com
License: Grants, Cibola County, NM held by Educational Media Foundation.
Group Owner: EMF Broadcasting
Nat'l Network: Air 1

Mike Novak, President

*KIDS

88.1 MHz FM; 100 w; Ant 162 ft; N35 07 09 W107 54 02
2020 Coal Ave. S.E., Albuquerque, NM 87106
(505) 242-7163
www.kanw.com
brasher@aps.edu
License: Grants, Cibola County, NM held by Board of Education of the City of Albuquerque, NM.
Population Served: 30,000
Michael Brasher, General Manager

Hatch

KVLC

04-01-1994; 101.1 MHz FM; *Hrs Open:* 24; 100 kw; 1033 ft.; N32 41 35 W107 4 6
101 Perkins Drive, Las Cruces, NM 88005 US
(505) 527-1111
www.101gold.com
License: Hatch, Dona Ana County, NM held by Bravo Mic Communications LLC.
Group Owner: Bravo Mic Communications LLC; (acq 1-7-2005; $1.3 million)
Arbitron Metro Market: Albuquerque, NM *TV Affiliate:* KVLC-TV; *Format:* Oldies *Special Programming:* Bi-lingual Sp/English 6 hrs wkly; *Hrs. of News Programming:* news progmg 3 hrs wkly; *No. News Employees:* 1 *Target Audience:* 25-54.
Mike McKay, Executive Vice President
Michael Smith, General Manager
K.C. Counts, Programming Director

Hobbs

KHOB

08-07-1954; 1390 kHz AM; *Hrs Open:* 24; 5 kw-D, DAN; 0.5 kw-N, DAN; N32 44 21 W103 10 48
1000 East Sanger, Hobbs, NM 88240 US
(505) 392-9292; *Fax:* (505) 392-7579
License: Hobbs, NM held by American Asset Management Inc.
TV Affiliate: ESPN; *Format:* Sports; *Hrs. of News Programming:* news progmg 48 hrs wkly; *No. News Employees:* 2; *Target Audience:* Males 18-45
Tommy Basberry, Sales

KIXN

02-01-1996; 102.9 MHz FM; *Hrs Open:* 24; 100 kw; 387 ft.; N32 47 12 W103 7 3
619 N. Turner Street, Hobbs, NM 88240 US
(505) 397-4969
www.kix103fm.com
License: Hobbs, Lea County, NM held by Noalmark Broadcasting Corp.
Group Owner: Noalmark Broadcasting Corp.; acq 1995; $53,000 for CP).
Format: Country; *Hrs. of News Programming:* news progmg 5 hrs wkly; *No. News Employees:* 1; *Target Audience:* Adults 18-49.; *Adv. Rates:* 16; 14; 16; 12.
William Nolan, CEO
Paul Starr, Operations Dir
Harry Harlan, General Sales Mgr
Dawn Morgan, News Director
Ken Bass, Engineering Dir
Edwin Alderson, Executive Vice President
Cathy Cox, Traffic Manager

KLMA

11-01-1993; 96.5 MHz FM; *Hrs Open:* 24; 100 kw; 377 ft.; N32 28 5 W103 9 27
108 S. Willow, P.O. Box 457, Hobbs, NM 88240 US
(575) 391-9650; *Fax:* (575) 397-9373
www.klmaradio.com
License: Hobbs, Lea County, NM held by Ojeda Broadcasting Inc.
Arbitron Metro Market: El Paso, TX; *Format:* Spanish; *Target Audience:* Hispanic.; *Adv. Rates:* 12; 12; 12; 12
Hermilo Ojeda, CEO

KPER

08-01-1965; 95.7 MHz FM; *Hrs Open:* 24; 25 kw; 328 ft.; N32 43 27 W103 9 4
Mailing Address: 1423 W. Bader, Hobbs, NM 88240 US
Second Address: 1423 W. Bender St., Hobbs, NM 88240
(575) 393-1551
www.hobbsradio.com
License: Hobbs, Lea County, NM held by Noalmark Broadcasting Corp.
Group Owner: Noalmark Broadcasting Corp.; acq 1-99)
Format: Country; *No. News Employees:* 1; *Target Audience:* 25-54.
Al Lobeck, General Manager
Tyler Robinson, News Director
Ken Fine, Chief Engineer

*KOBH

91.7 MHz FM; 0.25 kw; 157 ft.; N32 42 48 W103 5 28
P.O. Box 3206, Tupelo, MS 38803 US
(662) 844-8888; *Fax:* (662) 842-6791
www.afr.net
faq@afa.net
License: Hobbs, Lea County, NM held by American Family Association.
Group Owner: American Family Radio; (acq 8-27-2007)
Nat'l Network: American Family Radio
Arbitron Metro Market: Hobbs, NM; *Format:* Christian
Tim Wildmon, President
Donald Wildmon, Founder
Buddy Smith, Sr VP
Ed Vitagliano, Exec VP
Randy Sharp, Director Of Special Projects
Meeke Addison, Director Of Communications
Abraham Hamilton III, General Counsel

Humble City

KYKK

07-17-1971; 1110 kHz AM; *Hrs Open:* 6 AM-sunset; 2.5 kw-C, NDD; 5 kw-D, NDD; N32 48 59 W103 13 56
Mailing Address: P.O. Box 5967, Hobbs, NM 88241-5967 US
Second Address: 1423 W. Bender Blvd., Hobbs, NM 88240
(575) 393-1551; *Fax:* (575) 397-6088
License: Humble City, NM held by Noalmark Broadcasting Corp.
Group Owner: Noalmark Broadcasting Corp.; acq 8-8-77).
Nat'l Network: Premiere Radio Networks; Sporting News Radio Network; ABC Information & Entertainment
Arbitron Metro Market: Hobbs, NM; *Format:* News, News/Talk, 84, Talk; *Hrs. of News Programming:* news progmg 10 hrs wkly; *No. News Employees:* 1; *Target Audience:* 25-54; men & women
Al Lobeck, General Manager
Tyler Robinson, News Director
Ken Fine, Chief Engineer

Hurley

*KOOT

88.1 MHz FM; 2 kw vert; 167 ft.; N32 49 29 W108 14 54
213 North Bullard Street, Silver City, NM 88061 US
(505) 534-0130
www.catsilver.org
catstv@comcast.net
License: Hurley, Grant County, NM held by Community Access Television of Silver.
Arbitron Metro Market: Hurley, NM; *Format:* Variety/Diverse
Trent Petty, President
Lori Ford, Executive Director

Isleta

KOAZ

08-01-1983; 1510 kHz AM; 5 kw-D, 25 w-N, 4.2 kw-CH; N34 25 01 W107 30 04
Box 907, Magdalena, NM 87825
(505) 854-2632,(505) 854-2641, Ext 1600-01; *Fax:* (505) 854-2545
info@kabram.com
License: Isleta, Bernalillo County, NM held by Martha Whitman dba Isleta Radio Co.
Special Programming: American Indian 10 hrs wkly; *Target Audience:* General; Native Americans, loc ranchers, tourists, teachers & health professionals; *Adv. Rates:* 55; 55; 55; na
Ann Kerr, President
Sarah Apache, General Manager

Jal

KPZA-FM

11-01-1998; 103.7 MHz FM; *Hrs Open:* 24; 100 kw; 371 ft.; N32 25 53 W103 9 8

619 North Turner, Hobbs, NM 88240 US
(505) 397-4969; *Fax:* (505) 393-4310
www.1radiosquare.com
License: Jal, Lea County, NM held by Noalmark Broadcasting Corp.
Group Owner: Noalmark Broadcasting Corp.; (acq 5-29-98; $10,000 for CP).
Format: News, Sports; *Hrs. of News Programming:* news progmg 5 hrs wkly; *No. News Employees:* 1; *Target Audience:* Hispanic.; *Adv. Rates:* 14; 12; 14; 10.
William Nolan, CEO

Kirtland

KAZX
01-01-1999; 102.9 MHz FM; 100 kw; 994 ft.; N36 48 52 W107 53 32
200 E. Broadway, P.O. Box 87499, Farmington, NM 87401 US
(505) 325-1716; *Fax:* (505) 325-6797
www.star1029.com
License: Kirtland, San Juan County, NM held by Capstar TX LLC
Group Owner: iHeartMedia; (acq 12-19-00; $1.26 million).
Arbitron Metro Market: Farmington, NM; *Format:* Contemporary Hits/Top 40
Chuck Hammond, Vice President/Market Manager

La Luz

KRSY-FM
01-17-1987; 92.7 MHz FM; *Hrs Open:* 24; 6 kw; -217 ft.; N32 58 13 W105 59 21
119 North Canyon Road, Alamogordo, NM 88310 US
(575) 437-1505; *Fax:* (575) 437-5566
www.snmradio.com
lhenke@snmradio.com
License: La Luz, Otero County, NM held by WP Broadcasting LLC.
Group Owner: Westburg Media Capital LP
Nat'l Network: ABC
Format: Country *Special Programming:* NASCAR; *Hrs. of News Programming:* news progmg 2 hrs wkly; *No. News Employees:* 2; *Target Audience:* 18-34; active adults, young adults
Les Henke, General Manager

Las Cruces

*KMBN
01-01-2000; 89.7 MHz FM; 0.5 kW; 171 ft.; N32 16 41 W106 54 39
PO Box 16691, Las Cruces, NM 88004 USA
(575) 521-8053
moodyradiolascruces.fm
License: Las Cruces, Dona Ana County, NM held by The Moody Bible Institute of Chicago
Group Owner: The Moody Bible Institute of Chicago
Arbitron Metro Market: Las Cruces, NM; *Format:* Christian

KSNM
12-15-1955; 570 kHz AM; *Hrs Open:* 24; 5 kw-D, ND1; 0.155 kw-N, ND1; N32 18 33 W106 49 24
Mailing Address: PO Box 968, Las Cruces, NM 88004 US
Second Address: 1355 E. California Ave., Las Cruces, NM 88001
(575) 525-9298; *Fax:* (575) 525-9419
www.ksnm570.am
radiolc@kgrt.com
License: Las Cruces, NM held by Sunrise Broadcasting Inc.
Group Owner: Adams Radio Group
Nat'l Network: CNN Radio
Arbitron Metro Market: Las Cruces, NM; *Format:* News, Sports, 86; *Hrs. of News Programming:* news progmg 15 hrs wkly; *No. News Employees:* 2; *Target Audience:* 25 plus; adults
Ron Stone, President

KGRT-FM
09-08-1966; 103.9 MHz FM; *Hrs Open:* 24; 6 kw; 151 ft.; N32 18 33 W106 49 24
Mailing Address: PO Box 968, Las Cruces, NM 88004 US
Second Address: 1355 E. California Ave., Las Cruces, NM 88001
(575) 525-9298; *Fax:* (575) 525-9419
www.kgrt.com
License: Las Cruces, Dona Ana County, NM held by Sunrise Broadcasting Inc.
Group Owner: Adams Radio
Nat'l Network: CNN Radio
Arbitron Metro Market: Las Cruces, NM; *Format:* Country; *No. News Employees:* 2; *Target Audience:* 25-54; adults
Ron Stone, President

KOBE
04-01-1947; 1450 kHz AM; *Hrs Open:* 24; 1 kw-U, ND1; N32 18 7 W106 48 8
Mailing Address: P.O. Drawer 1838, Las Cruces, NM 88004 US
Second Address: 1832 W. Amador, Las Cruces, NM 88005
(575) 527-1111; *Fax:* (575) 527-1100
License: Las Cruces, NM held by Bravo Mic Communications II LLC.
Group Owner: Bravo Mic Communications LLC; (acq 1-24-2007; $1.9 million with KMVR(FM) Mesilla Park)
Nat'l Network: CBS
Format: News, News/Talk, 84, Talk; *Hrs. of News Programming:* news progmg 25 hrs wkly; *No. News Employees:* 1; *Target Audience:* 25 plus.
Mike McKay, Executive VP
Michael Smith, VP/General Manager
K.C. Counts, Programming Director
Keith Lamonica, Chief Engineer

KXPZ
05-01-1994; 99.5 MHz FM; *Hrs Open:* 24; 100 kw; 1024 ft.; N32 41 35 W107 4 6
P.O. Box Drawer 1838, Las Cruces, NM 88004 US
(575) 527-1111; *Fax:* (575) 527-1100
www.rocket995.com
License: Las Cruces, Dona Ana County, NM held by Bravo Mic Communications LLC.
Group Owner: Bravo Mic Communications LLC; (acq 4-18-2006; $1.4 million)
Arbitron Metro Market: Las Cruses and southern NM; *Format:* Rock/AOR
Michael Smith, General Manager
K.C. Counts, Programming Director
Glen Leffler, Chief Engineer

*KRUC
03-01-1998; 88.9 MHz FM; *Hrs Open:* 24; 0.5 kw; 197 ft.; N32 16 41 W106 54 39
Box 3765, McAllen, TX 78502 US
(956) 787-9788
www.worldradionetwork.org
License: Las Cruces, Dona Ana County, NM held by World Radio Network Inc.
Group Owner: World Radio Network Inc.
Arbitron Metro Market: El Paso, TX; *Format:* Religious
Neil Torquiano, Station Manager

*KRUX
09-20-1989; 91.5 MHz FM; *Hrs Open:* 7 AM-2 AM; 1 kw; -194 ft.; N32 17 3 W106 45 0
Corbett Center, Student Union, Las Cruces, NM 88003 US
(575) 646-2453
www.kruxradio.com
License: Las Cruces, Dona Ana County, NM held by Board of Regents New Mexico State University.
Arbitron Metro Market: Las Cruces, NM; *Format:* Variety/Diverse; *Hrs. of News Programming:* news progmg 2 hrs wkly; *No. News Employees:* 1; *Target Audience:* General.
Robert Palacios, General Manager
Joe Pestovich, Programming Director
Abdul Alyami, Chief Engineer

*KRWG
10-03-1964; 90.7 MHz FM; *Hrs Open:* 24; 100 kw; 351 ft.; N32 15 24 W106 58 34
KRWG-TV/FM, New Mexico State University, P.O. Box 30001, Las Cruces, NM 88003 US
(575) 646-2222; *Fax:* (575) 646-1974
krwg.org
krwgfm@nmsu.edu
License: Las Cruces, Dona Ana County, NM held by Regents of New Mexico State University.
Nat'l Network: NPR; PRI; *Wire Services:* AP
Arbitron Metro Market: Las Cruces, NM *TV Affiliate:* *KRWG-TV affil; *Format:* Jazz, News *Special Programming:* Sp 10 hrs, bluegrass/folk 8 hrs wkly; *Hrs. of News Programming:* news progmg 39 hrs wkly *No. NewsEmployees:* 4; *Target Audience:* 18-60.
Carrie Hamblen, Operations Dir
Edmundo Resendez, Station Manager
Fred Martino, Content Director
Anthony Moreno, News Director

KHQT
12-12-1974; 103.1 MHz FM; *Hrs Open:* 24; 1 kw; 551 ft.; N32 24 18 W106 45 41
1355 East California Avenue, Las Cruces, NM 88001 US
(575) 525-9298; *Fax:* (575) 525-9419
www.hot103.fm
License: Las Cruces, Dona Ana County, NM held by Richardson Commercial Corp.
Arbitron Metro Market: Las Cruces, NM *TV Affiliate:* KHQT-TV aff.; *Format:* Contemporary Hits/Top 40; *No. News Employees:* 2; *Target Audience:* 18-34; adult
Ernesto Garcia, Operations Dir
Damien Willis, Program Director
Ernesto Garcia, Operations Manager
Veronica Vaillancourt-Test, Market Manager

Las Vegas

KBAC
11-10-1989; 98.1 MHz FM; *Hrs Open:* 24; 100 kw; 1037 ft.; N35 22 20 W105 22 2
2502 Camino Entrada, Suite C, Santa Fe, NM 87507 US
(505) 471-1067
www.santefe.com/kbac
info@kbacfm.com
License: Las Vegas, San Miguel County, NM held by Hutton Broadcasting LLC.
Group Owner: Hutton Broadcasting LLC; (acq 10-16-2007; $650,000)
Arbitron Metro Market: Santa Fe, NM
Scott Hutton, General Manager
Ira Gordon, Programming Director
Eric Davis, Promotions Director

*KEDP
09-01-1968; 91.1 MHz FM; 1.32 kw horiz; -199 ft.; N35 35 39 W105 13 15
Mass Communication Depar, Las Vegas, NM 87701 US
(505) 454-3238
www.nmhu.edu/kedp
martinezda@nmhu.edu
License: Las Vegas, San Miguel County, NM held by Board of Regents, New Mexico Highlands University.
Arbitron Metro Market: Las Vegas, NM; *Format:* Oldies
Donna Martinez, General Manager
Doyle Hanschulz, Engineering Dir

KFUN
12-25-1941; 1230 kHz AM; *Hrs Open:* 24; 1 kw-U, ND1; N35 35 48 W105 12 21
255 King Street North, Suite 207, Waterloo, ON N2S 4V2 Canada
(519) 884-4470
www.kfun995.com
License: Las Vegas, NM held by Meadows Media LLC.
Arbitron Metro Market: Las Vegas, NV; *Format:* Country *Special Programming:* Spanish 20 hrs wkly, Oldies 7 hrs wkly; *Target Audience:* General.; *Adv. Rates:* 7.50; 7.50; 7.50; 7.50
Paul Fisher, General Manager
Brian Bourke, News Director

KLVF
06-19-1973; 100.7 MHz FM; *Hrs Open:* 24; 10 kw; -75 ft.; N35 35 48 W105 12 21 *Rebroadcasts:* (CP: COL Pecos. 3.7 kw horiz, ant 686 ft. TL: N35 39 06 W105 33 15)
P.O. Box 700, Radio Heights, Las Vegas, NM 87701 US
(505) 425-6766; *Fax:* (505) 425-6767
jpbaca1946@yahoo.com
License: Las Vegas, San Miguel County, NM held by Baca Broadcasting
Format: Adult Contemp; *Target Audience:* 17-40.; *Adv. Rates:* 7.50; 7.50; 7.50; 7.50
Georgia Carrera, Operations Dir
Bill Shadorf, General Sales Mgr
Jose Santos, Programming Director

KNMX
10-01-1980; 540 kHz AM; *Hrs Open:* Sunrise-sunset; 5 kw-D, DA1; 0.02 kw-N, DA1; N35 34 25 W105 10 17
300 S. Grand Ave., Los Vegas, NM 87701 US
(505) 425-3555; *Fax:* (505) 425-3557
www.lvnmradio.com
License: Las Vegas, NM held by Sangre de Cristo Broadcasting Co.
Format: News, News/Talk, 86; *Hrs. of News Programming:* news progmg 15 hrs wkly; *No. News Employees:* 1; *Target Audience:* 25-55; Hispanic, Anglo
Matt Martinez, President

KMDZ
01-01-2000; 96.7 MHz FM; *Hrs Open:* 24; 4.4 kw; 381 ft.; N35 36 16 W105 15 35
300 S. Grand, Las Vegas, NM 87701 US
(505) 425-5669; *Fax:* (505) 425-3557
mattmartinez@knmx.com
License: Las Vegas, San Miguel County, NM held by Sangre de Cristo Broadcasting Co.
Arbitron Metro Market: Las Vegas, NM; *Format:* Classic Rock
Matt Martinez, General Manager

***KRRE**
01-01-2008; 91.9 MHz FM; 0.1 kw; -38 ft.; N35 37 59 W105 14 10 *Rebroadcasts:* Rebroadcasts KUNM(FM) Albuquerque 100%
US
(505) 277-4806
www.kunm.org
kunm@kunm.org
License: Las Vegas, San Miguel County, NM held by Regents of the University of New Mexico.
Nat'l Network: NPR
Arbitron Metro Market: Las Vegas, NM; *Format:* Public Affairs, Variety/Diverse
Richard Towne, General Manager

KBQL
92.7 MHz FM; 23 kw; 341 ft.; N35 34 23 W105 10 16
304 S. Grand Avenue, Las Vegas, NM 87701 US
(505) 425-3555; *Fax:* (505) 425-3557
License: Las Vegas, San Miguel County, NM held by Matias C. Martinez.
Arbitron Metro Market: Las Vegas, NM
Matt Martinez, General Manager

Lordsburg

KPSA-FM
07-04-1986; 97.9 MHz FM; *Hrs Open:* 24; 0.25 kw; -135 ft.; N32 20 57 W108 42 18
P.O Box 720, Alamogordo, NM 88310 US
(575) 538-3396; *Fax:* (575) 388-1759
www.silvercityradio.com
License: Lordsburg, Hidalgo County, NM held by Silver City Radio
Group Owner: Silver City Radio
Format: Classic Rock

Los Alamos

KABG
06-01-1956; 98.5 MHz FM; 100 kw; 1906 ft.; N35 46 49 W106 31 37
4125 Carlisle Boulevard NE, Albuqurque, NM 87107 US
(505) 878-0980; *Fax:* (505) 878-0098
www.big985.com
License: Los Alamos, Los Alamos County, NM held by AGM Nevada LLC
Group Owner: American General Media
Arbitron Metro Market: Albuquerque, NM; *Format:* Adult Contemp, Oldies; *Target Audience:* 25-54
William Kruger, Regional Director

KAGM
03-19-1987; 106.7 MHz FM; *Hrs Open:* 24; 43 kw; N35 46 50 W106 31 35
4125 Carlisle N.E., Albuqerque, NM 87107
(505) 878-0980; *Fax:* (505) 878-0098
www.theriver1067.com
License: Los Alamos, Los Alamos County, NM held by AGM Nevada, LLC
Group Owner: American General Media; (acq 8-9-2000; grpsl)
Arbitron Metro Market: Santa Fe, NM; *Format:* Contemporary Hits/Top 40; *Hrs. of News Programming:* News progmg 7 hrs wkly; *Target Audience:* Adults 18-49
Scott Hutton, General Manager

KQBA
03-01-1998; 107.5 MHz FM; *Hrs Open:* 12a-12a; 100 kw; 797 ft.; N36 5 21 W106 1 41
2502 Camino Entrada, Suite C, Santa Fe, NM 87507 US
(505) 471-1067
www.santafe.com
License: Los Alamos, Los Alamos County, NM held by Hutton Broadcasting LLC.
Group Owner: Hutton Broadcasting LLC; (acq 12-4-2000; $1 million)
Nat'l Network: Jones Radio Networks
Arbitron Metro Market: Santa Fe, NM; *Format:* Country; *Target Audience:* 18-49; male
Lisa Clanc, Operations Manager
Chris Destler, Programming Director
Eric Davis, Promotions Manager

KRSN
12-09-1946; 1490 kHz AM; *Hrs Open:* 24; 1 kw-U, ND1; N35 53 46 W106 17 21
3801 Arkansas, Suite E, Los Alamos, NM 87544 US
(505) 663-1490; *Fax:* (505) 663-0011
www.krsnam1490.com
License: Los Alamos, NM held by Gillian Sutton
Nat'l Network: CBS; Westwood One
Arbitron Metro Market: Santa Fe, NM; *Format:* News, Sports
Special Programming: hs sports, interviews on hot topics; *Hrs. of News Programming:* news progmg 20 hrs wkly; *No. News Employees:* 1; *Target Audience:* 35 plus; well educated, affluent; *Adv. Rates:* 16;16;16;
Gillian Sutton, CEO
David Sutton, Operations Dir

Los Lunas

KIOT
07-06-1981; 102.5 MHz FM; *Hrs Open:* 24; 21 kw; 4,075 ft.; N35 12 47 W106 26 59
8009 Marble Ave. N.E., Albuquerque, NM 87110 US
(505) 254-7100; *Fax:* (505) 254-7106
www.coyote1025.com
License: Los Lunas, Valencia County, NM held by Univision Radio License Corp.
Group Owner: Univision Radio; (acq 10-3-2007)
Arbitron Metro Market: Albuquerque, NM; *Format:* Rock/AOR
Special Programming: Gospel 4 hrs wkly; *No. News Employees:* 1; *Target Audience:* 25-49; hip adults who like diversity & have disposable income
Larry Lemanski, General Manager
Jeff Joerg, Sales Manager
Homie Marco, Brand Manager
Raul Faz, Digital Content Manager

KDLW
01-01-1995; 106.3 MHz FM; *Hrs Open:* 24; 98.1 kw; N34 47 55 W106 48 59
4125 Carlisle Boulevard NE, Albuquerque, NM 87107 US
(505) 878-0980; *Fax:* (505) 878-0098
www.z1063.com
License: Los Lunas, Valencia County, NM held by AGM Nevada LLC
Group Owner: American General Media; (acq 12-22-97; grpsl).
Arbitron Metro Market: Los Lunas, NM; *Format:* Contemporary Hits/Top 40 *Special Programming:* Club mix 18 hrs wkly; *Target Audience:* Adults 18-34.
Rogers Brandon, President
William Kruger, General Manager

Los Ranchos

KTBL
12-16-1987; 1050 kHz AM; 1 kw-D, DA1; 1 kw-N, DA1; N34 58 46 W106 44 13
500 4th Street NW, Albuqurque, NM 87102 US
(505) 767-6700; *Fax:* (505) 767-6767
www.1050talk.com
pat.frisch@cumulus.com
License: Los Ranchos, NM
Group Owner: Cumulus Media Inc.; (acq 6-28-96; $5.725 million with KBZU(FM) Albuquerque).
Arbitron Metro Market: Albuquerque, NM; *Format:* News/Talk, 86; *Target Audience:* 25-54.
Pat Frisch, Programming Director

Los Ranchos De Albuquerque

KDSK
01-01-1982; 1240 kHz AM; *Hrs Open:* 24
P.O. Box 6492, 2505 6th St., NW, Albuquerque, NM 87197 US
(505) 244-1100; *Fax:* (505) 244-0612
www.radiodisney.com
License: Los Ranchos De Albuquerque, NM
Group Owner: KD Radio Inc.; (acq 10-16-2012; $225,000)
Arbitron Metro Market: Albuquerque, NM; *Format:* Children; *Target Audience:* 25-49.
Lynn Southard, General Manager

Lovington

KLEA
12-25-1952; 630 kHz AM; *Hrs Open:* 24; 0.5 kw-D, ND1; 0.069 kw-N, ND1; N32 56 30 W103 19 12
P.O. Box 877, Lovington, NM 88260 US
(575) 396-2244; *Fax:* (575) 396-3355
www.107oldies.com
oldies1017@gmail.com
License: Lovington, NM held by Lea County Broadcasting Co.
Arbitron Metro Market: El Paso, TX; *Format:* Sports, Contemporary Hits/Top 40 *Special Programming:* Relg 3 hrs wkly; *Hrs. of News Programming:* news progmg 12 hrs wlky; *No. News Employees:* 1 *Target Audience:* 25-54.
Susan Coe, General Manager

KLEA-FM
10-01-1965; 101.7 MHz FM; *Hrs Open:* 24; 25 kw; 289 ft.; N32 56 30 W103 19 12
P. O. Box 877, Lovington, NM 88260 US
(505) 396-2244; *Fax:* (505) 396-3355
License: Lovington, Lea County, NM
Arbitron Metro Market: El Paso, TX; *Format:* Oldies; *Hrs. of News Programming:* news progmg 10 hrs wkly; *No. News Employees:* 1
Susan Coe, President

Maljamar

***KMTH**
02-14-1985; 98.7 MHz FM; *Hrs Open:* 24; 100 kw; 709 ft.; N32 54 55 W103 46 31 *Rebroadcasts:* Rebroadcasts KENW-FM Portales 100%
Eastern N.M University, 52 Broadcast Street, Portales, NM 88130 US
(575) 562-2112; *Fax:* (575) 562-2590
kenw.org
License: Maljamar, Lea County, NM held by Eastern New Mexico University.
Nat'l Network: NPR; PRI; *Wire Services:* AP
Format: News; *Hrs. of News Programming:* news progmg 41 hrs wkly; *No. News Employees:* 1; *Target Audience:* General.
Jane Christensen, President
Ronnie Birdsong, Operations Dir
Duane Ryan, General Manager

KWMW
01-17-1990; 105.1 MHz FM; 100 kw; 925 ft.; N32 52 50 W103 41 1
1086 Mechem, Ruidoso, NM 88346 US
(575) 258-9922
mymtdradio.com
sales@mtdradio.com
License: Maljamar, Lea County, NM held by MTD Inc.
Group Owner: MTD Inc.
Arbitron Metro Market: Ruidoso Downs, NM; *Format:* Country
Will Rooney, Station Manager

Mentmore

***KPKJ**
88.5 MHz FM; 1.45 kw; 489 ft.; N35 33 36 W109 6 30
4001 Osuna Rd NE, Albuquerque, NM 87109 US
(505) 344-0880; *Fax:* (505) 345-9140
License: Mentmore, McKinley County, NM held by Calvary Chapel of Albuquerque
Group Owner: Calvary Chapel of Albuquerque
Format: Christian

Mesilla Park

KMVR
06-01-1974; 104.9 MHz FM; *Hrs Open:* 24; 3 kw; -33 ft.; N32 18 7 W106 48 8
401 Spring Street, Nevada City, CA 95959 US
(530) 265-9073; *Fax:* (575) 527-1100
office@kvmr.org
License: Mesilla Park, Dona Ana County, NM held by Bravo Mic Communications II LLC.
Group Owner: Bravo Mic Communications LLC; (acq 1-24-2007; $1.9 million with KOBE(AM) Las Cruces)
Format: Adult Contemp; *Target Audience:* 18-54.
David Levin, General Manager

Mesquite

***KELP-FM**
02-01-2004; 89.3 MHz FM; *Hrs Open:* 24; 3 kw; 184 ft.; N32 5 5 W106 44 1
6900 Commerce Avenue, El Paso, TX 79912 US
(915) 779-0016; *Fax:* (915) 779-6641
www.kelpradio.com
License: Mesquite, Dona Ana County, NM held by Sky High Broadcasting Inc.
Nat'l Network: Salem Radio Network
Arbitron Metro Market: El Paso, TX; *Format:* Christian; *Target Audience:* 25-55 plus.
Tina Casano, Office Manager
Arniold McClatchey, Owner, General Manager
Steve Barker, Programming Director

Milan

KRKE
09-01-1989; 1100 kHz AM; *Hrs Open:* 24; 250 w-D, 20 w-N; N35 05 51 W107 52 19
809 Wellesly N.E., Albuqueque, NM 98901
(505) 899-5029; *Fax:* (505) 899-6865
License: Milan, Cibola County, NM held by Cibola Radio Co.
Population Served: 22,000 *Target Audience:* 25-54; upscale men; *Adv. Rates:* 7; 7; 7; 3
Don Davis, President

KQNM
02-22-1971; 1090 kHz AM; *Hrs Open:* 24
P.O. Box 1675, 211 W. Sabte Fe Ave, Grants, NM 87020 US
(505) 899-5029
www.nmtruth.com
License: Milan, NM held by Vanguard Media L.L.C.
Arbitron Metro Market: Albuquerque, NM; *Format:* Adult Contemp; *Hrs. of News Programming:* News progmg 5 hrs wkly; *Target Audience:* 35-64; mature upscale adults; *Adv. Rates:* 20; 20; 20; 5
Don Davis, CEO
Craig Collins, Operations Dir
Josie Bunch, Station Manager
Crystal Felice, Promotions Manager

***KXXQ**
06-01-1991; 100.7 MHz FM; *Hrs Open:* 24; 100 kw; 1362 ft.; N35 28 7 W108 14 24
3256 Penryn Road, Suite 100, Loomis, CA 95650 US
(916) 535-0500; *Fax:* (916) 535-0504
www.ihradio.org
info@ihradio.org
License: Milan, Cibola County, NM held by IHR Educational Broadcasting.
Group Owner: IHR Educational Broadcasting; (acq 5-31-2005; $450,000).
Format: Christian
Douglas Sherman, President

***KVLK**
01-01-2007; 89.5 MHz FM; *Hrs Open:* 24; 0.11 kw; 2625 ft.; N35 15 12 W107 35 50 *Rebroadcasts:* Rebroadcasts KLVR(FM) Santa Rosa, CA 100%
US
(800) 525-5683
www.klove.com
License: Milan, Socorro County, NM held by Educational Media Foundation.
Group Owner: EMF Broadcasting
Nat'l Network: K-Love
Arbitron Metro Market: Socorro, NM; *Format:* Christian; *No. News Employees:* 13
Darrell Chambliss, Chairman
Mike Novak, President and CEO
David Pierce, Creative Director

Pecos

KLBU
08-01-2001; 102.9 MHz FM; 3.7 kw horiz, 0 kw vert; N35 39 6 W105 33 15
2502 Camino Entrada, Suite C, Santa Fe, NM 87507 US
(505) 471-1067; *Fax:* (505) 473-2667
www.blu1029.com
License: Pecos, San Miguel County, NM held by Hutton Broadcasting LLC.
Group Owner: Hutton Broadcasting LLC; (acq 10-16-2007; $450,000)
Arbitron Metro Market: Santa Fe, NM; *Format:* Adult Contemp
Edward Hutton, President
Scott Hutton, General Manager

KVSF-FM
01-01-2004; 101.5 MHz FM; 25 kw horiz; -92 ft.; N35 34 57 W105 46 34
2502 Camino Entrada, Suite C, Santa Fe, NM 87507 US
(505) 471-1067; *Fax:* (505) 473-2667
www.santafe.com/
License: Pecos, San Miguel County, NM held by Hutton Broadcasting LLC.
Group Owner: Hutton Broadcasting LLC; (acq 10-16-2007; $700,000)
Arbitron Metro Market: Santa Fe, NM; *Format:* Variety/Diverse
Scott Hutton, General Manager

Portales

***KENW-FM**
10-01-1968; 89.5 MHz FM; *Hrs Open:* 24; 100 kw; Ant 590 ft; N34 15 08.11 W103 14 20.63
Mailing Address: Eastern New Mexico Univ., 52 Broadcast Center, Portales, NM 88130
Second Address: Eastern New Mexico Univ., 1500 S. Ave. K, Portales, NM 88130
(575) 562-2112; *Fax:* (575) 562-2590
www.kenw.org
kenwfm@enmu.edu
License: Portales, Roosevelt County, NM held by Eastern New Mexico University.
Nat'l Network: NPR; BSN
Population Served: 350,000 *TV Affiliate:* *KENW-TV affil; *Hrs. of News Programming:* news progmg 41 hrs wkly; *No. News Employees:* 1; *Target Audience:* General.
Jane Christensen, President
Chad Lydick, Vice President
Duane Ryan, General Manager

KSEL
02-01-1950; 1450 kHz AM; *Hrs Open:* 24
42437 US 70, Portales, NM 88130 US
(505) 359-1759
License: Portales, NM held by Rooney Moon Broadcasting Inc.
Group Owner: Rooney Moon Broadcasting Inc.; (acq 7-15-2002; grpsl)
Nat'l Network: CNN Radio
Arbitron Metro Market: Portales, NM; *Format:* News, News/Talk, 86; *Hrs. of News Programming:* News progmg 168 hrs wkly; *Target Audience:* 35+.
Steve Rooney, President
Duffy Moon, Operations Dir

KSEL-FM
03-01-1980; 105.9 MHz FM; 100 kw; 463 ft.; N34 15 8 W103 14 21
P.O. Box 886, Portales, MN 88130 US
(505) 359-4649; *Fax:* (505) 359-0724
License: Portales, Roosevelt County, NM held by Rooney Moon Broadcasting Inc.
Group Owner: Rooney Moon Broadcasting Inc.
Nat'l Network: CNN Radio
Arbitron Metro Market: Portales, NM; *Format:* Country *Special Programming:* Farm 4 hrs wkly; *Target Audience:* 18-54.
Lisa Schmidt, News Director

***KPCV**
02-01-2005; 91.7 MHz FM; *Hrs Open:* 24; 9 kw; 315 ft.; N34 8 6 W103 36 58 *Rebroadcasts:* Rebroadcasts KPCC(FM) Pasadena 100%
474 S. Raymond Avenue, Pasadena, CA 91105 US
(866) 893-5720
www.scpr.org
License: Portales, Riverside County, NM held by American Public Media Group
Nat'l Network: NPR; PRI
Arbitron Metro Market: Portales, NM; *Format:* Talk; *Target Audience:* General.
Bill Davis, President and CEO
Mark Crowley, Vice President and General Manager
Jon Cohn, Programming Director
Lance Harper, Chief Engineer
Mark Crowley, Vice President, Content
Melanie Sill, Executive Editor

Questa

KLNN
01-01-2006; 103.7 MHz FM; 51 kw horiz; -211 ft.; N36 39 23 W105 37 57
P.O. Box 1844, Taas, NM 87571 US
(575) 758-5826
www.luna1037.com
comeot@luna1037.com
License: Questa, Taos County, NM held by West Waves Inc.
Arbitron Metro Market: Questa, NM; *Format:* Adult Contemp

Ramah

***KTDB**
04-24-1972; 89.7 MHz FM; *Hrs Open:* 5 AM-11 PM; 15 kw; 289 ft.; N34 57 59 W108 25 31
P. O. Box 40, Pine Hill, NM 87357 US
(505) 775-3215; *Fax:* (505) 775-3551
www.ktdbfm.com
License: Ramah, McKinley County, NM held by Ramah Navajo School Board Inc.
Nat'l Network: NPR
Arbitron Metro Market: Pine Hill, NM; *Format:* Country *Special Programming:* Navajo; *Target Audience:* General; Native American
Barbara Maria, General Manager
Irene Beaver, Programming Director
Earl Ericcho, News Director
Bernard Bustos, Chief Engineer

Ranchos De Taos

***KCEY**
89.5 MHz FM; 9000 w; 2877 ft; N36 14 54 W105 39 19
HC 78, Box 10731, Ranchos de Taos, NM 87557
(575)758-9791
www.culturalenergy.org
License: Ranchos De Taos, Taos County, NM
Group Owner: Cultural Energy
Robin Collier, Production, Outreach & Member Station Devlopment
Ernie Atencio, Earth Beat
Roberta Salazar, Farming
Lisa Fox, Native Momentum

Raton

KBKZ
12-20-2001; 96.5 MHz FM; 5.4 kw; 968 ft.; N36 59 33 W104 28 24
100 Fisher Drive, Trinidad, CO 81082 US
(719) 846-3355
www.kcrtradio.com
kcrt@comcast.net
License: Raton, Colfax County, NM held by Phillips Broadcasting Co. Inc.
Group Owner: Phillips Broadcasting Inc.
Arbitron Metro Market: Trinidad, CO; *Format:* Country
Lory Phillips, General Manager

KRTN
01-01-1948; 1490 kHz AM; *Hrs Open:* 24
1128 State Street, Raton, NM 87740 US
(575) 445-3652
www.krtnradio.com
krtn@bacavalley.com
License: Raton, NM held by Enchanted Air Inc.
Arbitron Metro Market: Raton, NM; *Format:* Adult Contemp; *Target Audience:* General.
Jim Veltri, Station Manager/Chief Engineer
Marty Mayfield, News Director

KRTN-FM
04-01-1982; 93.9 MHz FM; *Hrs Open:* 24; 26 kw; 1447 ft.; N36 40 59 W104 24 50
P.O Box 638, Raton, NM 87740 US
(505) 445-3652; *Fax:* (505) 445-2911
License: Raton, Colfax County, NM
Arbitron Metro Market: Raton, NM; *Format:* Oldies
Robbie Ley, Programming Director
Mike Higgins, Disc Jockey
Billy Donoti, Disc Jockey

Red River

***KCEI**
01-01-2002; 90.1 MHz FM; 3.2 kw vert; Ant 718 ft; N36 41 25 W105 33 43
HC 78, Box 10731, Ranchos de Taos, NM 87557
(575) 758-9791
www.culturalenergy.org
License: Red River, Taos County, NM held by Red River Radio Inc.

Robin Collier, General Manager

Rincon

KSIL
01-01-2002; 105.5 MHz FM; *Hrs Open:* 24; 11 kw; 1063 ft.; N32 50 40 W108 14 19
13915 Lakeview Dr, Austin, TX 78732 US
(505) 534-1055; *Fax:* (505) 534-1400
www.ksilradio.com
License: Rincon, Grant County, NM held by James S. Bumpous dba Yellow Dog Radio.
Arbitron Metro Market: Rincon, NM; *Format:* Variety/Diverse; *Hrs. of News Programming:* News progmg 5 hrs wkly; *Target Audience:* 25-54.
Steve Bumpous, General Manager

Rio Rancho

KQTM
11-02-1984; 101.7 MHz FM; 3 kw; 98 ft.; N35 11 35 W106 28 15
4131 Barbora Loop SE, Rio Rancho, NM 87124 US
(505) 994-1017
www.1017theteam.com
License: Rio Rancho, Sandoval County, NM held by Team Broadcasting Inc.
Nat'l Network: Fox Sports; *Nat'l Reps:* Christal
Arbitron Metro Market: Albuquerque, NM; *Format:* Sports
Joe O'Neill, President

Roswell

KBCQ-FM
10-15-1977; 97.1 MHz FM; *Hrs Open:* 24; 100 kw; 361 ft.; N33 24 5 W104 22 45

P.O. Box 670, Roswell, NM 88202 US
(575) 622-6450
License: Roswell, Chaves County, NM held by Roswell Radio Inc.
Group Owner: Roswell Radio Inc./Quay Broadcasters Inc.; (acq 11-2000; grpsl)
Arbitron Metro Market: Roswell, NM; *Format:* Contemporary Hits/Top 40; *No. News Employees:* 1; *Target Audience:* 18-49.; *Adv. Rates:* 25; 20; 22; 20

KBIM
05-01-1953; 910 kHz AM; *Hrs Open:* 24; 5 kw-D, DAN; 0.5 kw-N, DAN; N33 26 26 W104 31 35
P.O. Box 1953, Roswell, NM 88202 US
(575) 623-9100
kevin@kbimradio.com
License: Roswell, NM held by Noalmark Broadcasting Corp.
Group Owner: Noalmark Broadcasting Corp.; (acq 11-30-2007; $1.5 million with co-located FM)
Nat'l Network: ABC
Arbitron Metro Market: Roswell, NM; *Format:* News, News/Talk, 86; *Hrs. of News Programming:* News progmg 16 hrs wkly; *Target Audience:* 25-54; upscale male & active working female; *Adv. Rates:* 16; 15; 14; 12
Don Niccum, Operations Dir
Kevin Bonner, General Manager
Darryl Burkfield, General Sales Mgr
Richard Morris, News Director

KBIM-FM
06-01-1959; 94.9 MHz FM; *Hrs Open:* 24; 100 kw; 1880 ft.; N33 3 20 W103 49 12
P.O.Box 1953, Roswell, NM 88202 US
(575) 623-9100
License: Roswell, Chaves County, NM held by Noalmark Broadcasting Corp.
Group Owner: Noalmark Broadcasting Corp.
Arbitron Metro Market: Roswell, NM; *Format:* Adult Contemp; *Hrs. of News Programming:* News progmg 16 hrs wkly; *Target Audience:* 25-54.; *Adv. Rates:* Same as AM
Kevin Bonner, General Manager
Darryl Burkfield, General Sales Mgr
Richard Morris, News Director
John King, General Sales Manager

KCKN
12-20-1965; 1020 kHz AM; *Hrs Open:* 24
P.O. Box 220, Rosewell, NM 88202 US
(575) 622-0658; *Fax:* (505) 622-0852
License: Roswell, NM
Group Owner: Radio Vision Cristiana Subsidiary Corp.; (acq 2000; $2.5 million).
Nat'l Network: AP Network News; Jones Radio Networks
Arbitron Metro Market: Kansas City, KS; *Format:* Country, Religious *Special Programming:* local news 6 X daily; *Hrs. of News Programming:* news progmg 5 hrs wkly; *No. News Employees:* 2 *Target Audience:* 25-54; adult professionals
Jim Hilliard, President
Don Niccum, Operations Dir
Jerry Kiefer, General Manager
Bob Souza, General Sales Mgr
Don Nicuum, News Director
Bob Williams, Regional Sales Manager
Kathi Silvas, Traffic Manager

KEND
05-30-1990; 106.5 MHz FM; *Hrs Open:* 24; 65 kw; 135 ft.; N33 23 5 W104 43 22
105 W. 3rd Street, #228, Roswell, NM 88202 US
(575) 578-1198; *Fax:* (575) 578-1197
www.roswelljackfm.com
License: Roswell, Chaves County, NM held by Pecos Valley Broadcasting Co.
Group Owner: Pecos Valley Broadcasting Co.; (acq 4-1-2007; $500,000)
Arbitron Metro Market: Roswell, NM; *Format:* Rock/AOR; *Hrs. of News Programming:* News progmg 6 hrs wkly; *Target Audience:* 18-34; upscale adults
Gene Dow, General Manager
Thomas Bad, General Sales Mgr

KMOU
08-01-1992; 104.7 MHz FM; *Hrs Open:* 24; 100 kw; 328 ft.; N33 24 49 W104 22 49
Mailing Address: 5206 West 2nd Street, Roswell, NM 88201 US
Second Address: 5206 W. 2nd St., Roswell, NM 88203
(575) 622-6450
License: Roswell, Chaves County, NM held by Roswell Radio Inc.
Group Owner: Roswell Radio Inc./Quay Broadcasters Inc.; (acq 11-22-2000; $750,000).
Format: Country; *Hrs. of News Programming:* news progmg 12 hrs wkly; *No. News Employees:* 2; *Adv. Rates:* 25; 20; 22; 20
Jim Matteucci Jr., Owner/CEO

KRDD
01-01-1963; 1320 kHz AM; 1 kw-D, ND2; 0.188 kw-N, ND2; N33 24 14 W104 28 12
P.O. Box 3, Santa Cruz, NM 87576 US
(575) 448-1110
krddam@yahoo.com
License: Roswell, NM held by Media Mining Group LLC
Carlos Espinoza, President

KBCQ
05-01-1947; 1230 kHz AM; *Hrs Open:* 24
5206 West Second Street, Roswell, NM 88201 US
(575) 622-6450
License: Roswell, NM held by Roswell Radio Inc.
Group Owner: Roswell Radio Inc./Quay Broadcasters Inc.; (acq 2-28-2003)
Nat'l Network: CNN Radio
Arbitron Metro Market: Roswell, NM; *Format:* Oldies *Special Programming:* Talk 15 hrs wkly; *Target Audience:* 35-75.; *Adv. Rates:* 98; 115; 115; 98
Jim Matteucci, Owner
J.R. Law, Station Manager

KSFX
03-15-1991; 100.5 MHz FM; *Hrs Open:* 24; 100 kw; 121 ft.; N33 23 37 W104 36 16
Mailing Address: 5206 W. 2nd Street, Roswell, New Mexico, NY 88201 US
Second Address: 5206 W. 2nd St., Roswell, NM 88201
(575) 623-4000
www.1005ksfx.com/
License: Roswell, Chaves County, NM held by Roswell Radio Inc.
Group Owner: Roswell Radio Inc./Quay Broadcasters Inc.; (acq 11-2000; grpsl)
Arbitron Metro Market: Rosewell, NM; *Format:* Contemporary Hits/Top 40, Adult Contemp; *Hrs. of News Programming:* news progmg 12 hrs wkly; *No. News Employees:* 2; *Target Audience:* 25-49; mainstream upscale *Adv.Rates:* 25; 20; 22; 20
Jim Matteucci, Owner
J.R. Law, Station Manager

***KWFL**
12-21-1989; 99.3 MHz FM; *Hrs Open:* 24; 16.5 kw; 436 ft.; N33 21 47 W104 38 11
7355 N. Oracle Road, Tuscan, AZ 85704 US
(800) 776-1070
www.myflr.org
License: Roswell, Chaves County, NM held by Family Life Broadcasting System.
Group Owner: Family Life Communications Inc.; (acq 5-24-2004; $1)
Nat'l Network: Moody
Arbitron Metro Market: Albuqerque, NM; *Format:* Religious, Christian; *Target Audience:* Christian community.
Randy Carlson, President

***KRLU**
01-01-2004; 90.1 MHz FM; *Hrs Open:* 24; 2.4 kw vert; 394 ft.; N33 21 47 W104 38 11 *Rebroadcasts:* Rebroadcasts KLVR(FM) Middletown, CA 100%
US
(800) 525-5683
www.klove.com
License: Roswell, Chaves County, NM held by Educational Media Foundation.
Group Owner: EMF Broadcasting
Nat'l Network: K-Love
Arbitron Metro Market: Roswell, NM; *Format:* Christian; *No. News Employees:* 13; *Target Audience:* 25-44; Judeo Christian, female
Darrell Chambliss, Chairman
Mike Novak, President and CEO
David Pierce, Programming Director
Eric Moser, Chief Financial Officer
Brian Burger, Vice President of Human Resources

***KQAI**
01-01-2007; 89.1 MHz FM; 2 kw vert; 207 ft.; N33 23 36 W104 37 27 *Rebroadcasts:* Rebroadcasts KLRD(FM) Yucaipa, CA 100%
P.O. Box 2118, Omaha, NE 68103-2118 US
(888) 946-2471
www.air1.com
License: Roswell, Chaves County, NM held by Educational Media Foundation.
Group Owner: EMF Broadcasting; (acq 9-22-2005; $40,000 for CP)
Nat'l Network: Air 1
Arbitron Metro Market: Roswell, NM; *Format:* Alternative, Christian
Darrell Chambliss, Chairman
Mike Novak, President and CEO
Brian Burger, Vice President of Human Resources
D. Kevin Blair, Secretary and General Counsel
Larry Moody, Director

***KGCN**
91.7 MHz FM; 3.5 kw vert; 394 ft.; N33 21 47 W104 38 11
188 South Bellevue, Suite 222, Memphis, TN 38104 US
(916) 251-1600; *Fax:* (916) 251-1650
www.nuevavida.com
info@nuevavida.com
License: Roswell, Chaves County, NM held by Educational Media Foundation.
Group Owner: EMF Broadcasting; (acq 7-23-2007; grpsl)
Arbitron Metro Market: Roswell, NM; *Format:* Christian, Spanish
Mike Novak, President

Ruidoso

KBUY
11-01-1959; 1360 kHz AM; *Hrs Open:* 24
1096 Mechen Drive, Suite 230, Ruidoso, NM 88345 US
(575) 258-2222; *Fax:* (575) 258-2224
www.kwes.net
License: Ruidoso, NM held by Walton Stations New Mexico Inc.
Group Owner: Walton Stns; (acq 10-22-82; $475,000 with co-located FM;
Nat'l Network: Fox News Radio
Arbitron Metro Market: Ruidoso, NM; *Format:* Oldies *Special Programming:* Sp 4 hrs wkly; *Hrs. of News Programming:* news progmg 14 hrs wkly; *No. News Employees:* 1; *Target Audience:* 38 plus; 25-54 females *Adv. Rates:* 10; 10; 10; 10

KWES-FM
01-01-1982; 93.5 MHz FM; *Hrs Open:* 24; 25 kw; 187 ft.; N33 23 12 W105 40 14
P.O. Box 39, Ruidoso, NM 88355 US
(505) 258-2222; *Fax:* (505) 258-2224
www.kwes.net
License: Ruidoso, Lincoln County, NM held by Walton Stations New Mexico Inc.
Group Owner: Walton Stns
Nat'l Network: Jones Radio Networks
Arbitron Metro Market: Ruidoso, NM; *Format:* Country; *Hrs. of News Programming:* news progmg 17 hrs wkly; *No. News Employees:* 1; *Target Audience:* 18-54.; *Adv. Rates:* Same as AM
Steve Swayze, General Manager
Juanita, General Sales Mgr
Steve Swayze, Programming Director
Kelly Capece, Promotions Manager
Gary Herron, News Director

KIDX
01-01-2000; 101.5 MHz FM; 0.92 kw; 2851 ft.; N33 24 14 W105 46 56
1086 Mechem Dr., Ruidoso, NM 88346 US
(575) 258-9922
mymtdradio.com
sales@mtdradio.com
License: Ruidoso, Lincoln County, NM held by MTD Inc.
Group Owner: MTD Inc.
Arbitron Metro Market: Ruidoso, NM; *Format:* Classic Rock

***KKLB**
91.3 MHz FM; 0.235 kw; 2894 ft.; N33 24 15.2 W105 46 54.7
Rebroadcasts: Rebroadcasts KLVR(fM) Middletown, CA 100%
5700 West Oaks Boulevard, Rocklin, CA 95765 US
(916) 251-1600; *Fax:* (916) 251-1650
www.klove.com
License: Ruidoso, Lincoln County, NM held by Educational Media Foundation
Group Owner: EMF Broadcasting
Arbitron Metro Market: Ruidoso, NM; *Format:* Adult Contemp, Gospel, 74
Mike Novak, President

KWES
01-01-2008; 1450 kHz AM
US
(575) 258-2222; *Fax:* (575) 258-2224
www.kwes.net/foxsports1450am.html
License: Ruidoso, NM held by Walton Stations New Mexico Inc.
Group Owner: Walton Stns
Nat'l Network: Fox Sports
Arbitron Metro Market: Ruidoso, NM; *Format:* Sports

Juanita Jones, General Sales Mgr

Ruidoso Downs

KRUI

04-01-1984; 1490 kHz AM; *Hrs Open:* 24; 1 kw-U, ND1; N33 19 17 W105 35 24
1086 Mechem, Ruidoso, NM 88346 US
(575) 258-9922
mymtdradio.com
sales@mtdradio.com
License: Ruidoso Downs, NM held by MTD Inc.
Group Owner: MTD Inc.; acq 12-88; $20,000;
Nat'l Network: Westwood One
Arbitron Metro Market: Ruidoso, NM; *Format:* News, Sports, 86; *Hrs. of News Programming:* News progmg 14 hrs wkly; *Adv. Rates:* 20; 10; 10; 5

Santa Clara

KNUW

01-01-1996; 95.1 MHz FM; *Hrs Open:* 24; 7.7 kw; 1549 ft.; N32 51 47 W108 14 28
106 South Bullard Street, Silver City, NM 88061 US
(505) 534-8700; *Fax:* (505) 534-8702
knuw@zianet.com
License: Santa Clara, Grant County, NM held by Duran-Hill, Inc.
Target Audience: General; Hispanic
George Mesa, President
Cecilia Soza, General Sales Mgr
Ken Bass, Engineering Dir

Santa Fe

KJFA-FM

09-28-1985; 101.3 MHz FM; 3.7 kw; 420 ft.; N35 4 4 W106 46 47
8009 Marble Ave. N.E., Albuquerque, NM 87110 US
(505) 254-7100; *Fax:* (505) 254-7106
www.univision.com
License: Santa Fe, Santa Fe County, NM held by Univision Radio License Corp.
Group Owner: Univision Radio; (acq 9-22-2003; grpsl)
Arbitron Metro Market: Albuquerque, NM; *Format:* Tejano; *Target Audience:* 35-54.
Larry Lemanski, Vice President and General Manager

KKOB Exp S

01-01-1986; 770 kHz AM; 230 w-U; N35 40 56 W105 58 21
Rebroadcasts: Rebroadcasts KKOB(AM) Albuquerque 100%
500 4th St. N.W., Suite 500, Albuquerque, NM 87102
(505) 243-3333
www.770kkob.com
License: Santa Fe, Santa Fe County, NM held by Citadel Broadcasting Co.
Nat'l Reps: McGavren Guild
Format: Adult Contemp
Pat Frisch, Operations Dir
Pam Gutierrez, General Sales Mgr
Pat Frish, Programming Director

KKSS

03-01-1969; 97.3 MHz FM; *Hrs Open:* 24; 94 kw; 1,877 ft.; N35 46 50 W106 31 35
8009 Marble Ave. N.E., Albuquerque, NM 87110 US
(505) 254-7100
www.mykiss973.com
License: Santa Fe, Santa Fe County, NM held by Univision Radio License Corp.
Group Owner: Univision Radio; (acq 9-22-2003; grpsl).
Nat'l Reps: D & R Radio
Arbitron Metro Market: Albuquerque, NM; *Format:* Contemporary Hits/Top 40; *Target Audience:* 18-34; Hispanic females
Larry Lemanski, General Manager
Jeff Joerg, Sales Manager
Homie Marco, Brand Manager
Raul Faz, Digital Content Manager
Sam Newton, Community Affairs

KTEG

11-24-1983; 104.1 MHz FM; *Hrs Open:* 24; 100 kw; 1877 ft.; N35 46 50 W106 31 35
5411 Jefferson Street SE, Suite 100, Albuquerque, NM 87109 US
(505) 830-6400; *Fax:* (505) 830-6599
www.1041theedge.com
License: Santa Fe, Santa Fe County, NM held by Citicasters Licenses Inc.
Group Owner: iHeartMedia; (acq 1-27-2009)
Arbitron Metro Market: Albuquerque, NM; *Format:* Alternative
Chuck Hammond, Vice President/Market Manager

KHFM

08-15-1965; 95.5 MHz FM; *Hrs Open:* 24; 17.5 kw; 1791 ft.; N35 46 49 W106 31 37
4125 Carlisle Boulevard NE, Albuquerque, NM 87107 US
(505) 878-0980; *Fax:* (505) 878-0098
www.classicalkhfm.com
brent@classicalkhfm.com
License: Santa Fe, Santa Fe County, NM held by AGM Nevada LLC
Group Owner: American General Media
Arbitron Metro Market: Albuquerque, NM; *Format:* Classical; *Target Audience:* Adults 35+
William Kruger, Regional Director
Brent Stevens, Programming Director

KRZY-FM

11-02-1983; 105.9 MHz FM; *Hrs Open:* 24; 100 kw; 1919 ft.; N35 46 49 W106 31 34
2725 Broadbent Pkwy NE, Suite F, Albuquerque, NM 87107 US
(505) 342-4141; *Fax:* (505) 344-8714
www.jose1059.com
rmather@entravision.com
License: Santa Fe, Santa Fe County, NM held by Entravision Holdings LLC.
Group Owner: Entravision Communications Corp.; (acq 3-14-2000; grpsl).
Arbitron Metro Market: Albuquerque, NM; *Target Audience:* 18-34.
Carlos Fourzan, General Manager
Esmeralda Ruiz, General Sales Mgr
Francisco Gutierrez, Promotions Manager

KSWV

06-01-1966; 810 kHz AM
120 Taos Street, Santa Fe, NM 87505 US
(505) 989-7441
License: Santa Fe, NM held by La Voz Broadcasting Co.
Arbitron Metro Market: Santa Fe, NM; *Format:* Spanish; *Target Audience:* 25-54.
Celine Gonzales, President
George Gonzales, General Manager

KVSF

02-20-1947; 1400 kHz AM; 1 kw-U, ND1; N35 40 56 W105 58 21
2502 Camino Entrada, Suice C, Santa Fe, NM 87507 US
(505) 471-1067
www.espnsantafe.com
scott@huttonbroadcasting.com
License: Santa Fe, NM held by Hutton Broadcasting LLC.
Group Owner: Hutton Broadcasting LLC; (acq 6-5-2006; $350,000) .
Nat'l Network: ESPN Radio
Arbitron Metro Market: Santa Fe, NM; *Format:* Sports
Edward Hutton, President
Scott Hutton, General Manager

KTRC

01-01-1935; 1260 kHz AM; *Hrs Open:* 12a-12a; 5 kw-D, ND1; 1 kw-N, ND1; N35 40 56 W105 58 21
2502 Camino Entrada, Suice C, Santa Fe, NM 87507 US
(505) 471-1067; *Fax:* (505) 473-2667
www.santafe.com/ktrc
License: Santa Fe, NM held by Hutton Broadcasting L.L.C.
Group Owner: Hutton Broadcasting LLC; acq 11-2008
Nat'l Network: Air America; CNN Radio
Arbitron Metro Market: Santa Fe, NM; *Format:* Alternative, News, 86; *Target Audience:* 35-64; involved affluent adults
Edward Hutton, President
Scott Hutton, General Manager
Ira Gordon, Programming Director
Eric Davis, Promotions Manager

KLBU

01-01-2000; 94.7 MHz FM; 100 kw; 797 ft.; N36 5 21 W106 1 41
4125 Carlisle Boulevard NE, Albuquerque, NM 87107 US
(505) 878-0980; *Fax:* (505) 878-0098
www.mykkim.com/
License: Santa Fe, Santa Fe County, NM held by Hutton Broadcasting, LLC
Group Owner: Hutton Broadcasting, LLC; (acq 1996; $96,250)
Arbitron Metro Market: Santa Fe, NM; *Format:* Christian, News, 62, Talk
Michael Benge, General Sales Mgr

Santa Rosa

KSSR-FM

01-01-2001; 95.9 MHz FM; 1.5 kw; Ant 118 ft; N34 56 47 W104 39 10 *Rebroadcasts:* Rebroadcasts KSSR(AM) Santa Rosa 100%
P.O. Box 333 South, Rosa, NM 88435
(575) 472-5777
License: Santa Rosa, Guadalupe County, NM held by Cibola Radio Co.

Luisa Chappell, General Manager

*KNLK

01-01-2004; 91.9 MHz FM; 0.1 kw; -26 ft.; N34 57 20 W104 40 53
2020 Coal Ave., S.E., Albuquerque, NM 87106 US
(505) 242-7163
www.kanw.com
brasher@aps.edu
License: Santa Rosa, Guadalupe County, NM held by Board of Education of the City of Albuquerque, NM.
Arbitron Metro Market: Santa Rosa, NM
Michael Brasher, General Manager

Shiprock

*KFDC

90.5 MHz FM; kw
US
(505) 368-1028
License: Shiprock, San Juan County, NM held by Dine Agriculture Inc.
Arbitron Metro Market: Shiprock, NM
Gilbert Yazzie, General Manager

Silver City

KSCQ

11-28-1989; 92.9 MHz FM; *Hrs Open:* 24; 11.5 kw; 1024 ft.; N32 50 40 W108 14 18
1560 North Corbin Street, Silver City, NM 88061 US
(575) 538-3396; *Fax:* (575) 388-1759
www.silvercityradio.com
License: Silver City, Grant County, NM held by Skywest Media LLC
Group Owner: SkyWest Media L.L.C.; (acq 10-31-2005; $330,000).
Arbitron Metro Market: Silver City, NM; *Format:* Adult Contemp; *Hrs. of News Programming:* News progmg 3 hrs wkly; *Target Audience:* 25-55; baby boomers, generation X; *Adv. Rates:* 10; 10; 10; 10
Sabrina Pack, General Manager
Ted Tucker, Programming Director

Socorro

KMXQ

01-22-1995; 92.9 MHz FM; *Hrs Open:* 24; 0.137 kw; -177 ft.; N34 2 43 W106 54 21
Mailing Address: P.O. Box 30570, Albuquerque, NM 87190 US
Second Address: 834 Hwy. 60 W., Socorro, NM 87801
(505) 835-1286; *Fax:* (505) 835-2015
License: Socorro, Socorro County, NM held by Lakeshore Media L.L.C.
Format: Country *Special Programming:* Farm 2 hrs, talk one hr wkly; *Hrs. of News Programming:* 167 hrs wkly; *No. News Employees:* 4; *Target Audience:* 12 plus.; *Adv. Rates:* 14; 14; 14; 14
Virgil Vigil, General Manager
George Funkhoustol, News Director
Deb Hoyland, News Commentator
John Gonzales

*KXFR

01-01-2008; 91.9 MHz FM; 25 kw; 243 ft.; N34 23 44 W107 0 42
Rebroadcasts: Rebroadcasts KUFR(FM) Salt Lake City, UT 100%
US
(855) 613-8319; *Fax:* (510) 568-6200
www.familyradio.com
License: Socorro, Socorro County, NM held by Family Stations Inc.
Group Owner: Family Stations Inc.
Nat'l Network: Family Radio
Arbitron Metro Market: Socorro, NM; *Format:* Christian
Harold Egbert, President
Jennifer Grant, Operations Dir

*KBOM

02-15-2008; 88.7 MHz FM; 0.1 kw; 1877 ft.; N34 4 17 W106 57 44 *Rebroadcasts:* Rebroadcasts KUNM(FM) Albuquerque 100%
1 University of New Mexico, Aluquerque, NM 87131 US
(505) 277-4806
www.kunm.org
kunm@kunm.org
License: Socorro, Socorro County, NM held by Regents of the University of New Mexico.

Arbitron Metro Market: Socorro, NM; *Format:* Public Affairs, Variety/Diverse
Richard Towne, General Manager
Tristan Clum, Programming Director

KYRN
01-01-2009; 102.1 MHz FM; 0.25 kw; -476 ft.; N34 4 35 W106 54 29
US
www.minecountry1021.com
License: Socorro, Socorro County, NM held by Sovereign City Radio Services LLC.
Arbitron Metro Market: Socorro, NM
Scott Krusinski, Operations Dir

Taos

KXMT
12-01-2000; 99.1 MHz FM; 60 kw; 2136 ft.; N36 51 32 W106 0 28
Mailing Address: P.O. Box 2158, Ketchum, ID 83340 US
Second Address: 125A Camino de la Merced, Taos, NM 87571-5119
(575) 758-4491; *Fax:* (505) 758-4452
www.kxmt.com
License: Taos, Taos County, NM held by DMC Broadcasting Inc.
Group Owner: DMC Broadcasting Inc.; (acq 3-19-2003; $645,000 with KKTC(FM) Angel Fire).
Format: Tejano; *Target Audience:* Locals, Spanish speakers
Darren Cordova, President
Jeff Singer, Operations Dir
Jojo Valdez, General Sales Mgr
Jennifer Trujillo, News Director
Darren Lee Cordova, Vice President
Brenda Cordova, VP Human Resources
Andrew Alaniz, Web Administrator

KTAO
01-01-1978; 101.9 MHz FM; *Hrs Open:* 6 AM-2 AM; 1.2 kw; 2795 ft.; N36 14 48 W105 39 15
P.O. Box 1844, Taos, NM 87571 US
(575) 758-5826
www.ktao.com
info@ktaos.com
License: Taos, Taos County, NM held by Taos Communications Corp.
Arbitron Metro Market: Taos, NM; *Format:* Triple A *Special Programming:* Jazz 3 hrs, Roots & Wires, 5 hrs; maccasin wire, 3 hrs; world on tour, 2 hrs; celtic 4 hrs; Sonido del sol, 3 hrs.; *Hrs. of News Programming:* newsprogmg 7 hrs wkly; *No. News Employees:* 2; *Target Audience:* 25-49; educated, responsive, upwardly mobile; *Adv. Rates:* 18; 18; 18; 5
Kate, President/Production Director
Aldan, Co-Owner/Engineer
Brian, Chief Engineer
Paddy Mac, Music Director

KKIT
01-01-2005; 95.9 MHz FM; *Hrs Open:* 24; 4 kw; -630 ft.; N36 23 22 W105 35 9
125A Camino de la Merced, Taos, NM 87571-5119 US
(575) 737-5548
www.kkitthemountain.com
License: Taos, Taos County, NM held by DMC Broadcasting Inc.
Group Owner: DMC Broadcasting Inc.
Nat'l Network: ABC
Format: Adult Contemp

KVOT
01-01-2005; 1340 kHz AM; *Hrs Open:* 25.?Â ?
125A Camino de la Merced, Taos, NM 87571-5119 US
(575) 758-5868
License: Taos, NM held by DMC Broadcasting Inc.
Group Owner: DMC Broadcasting Inc.; (acq 12-20-2005)
Nat'l Network: ABC
Arbitron Metro Market: Tucson, AZ; *Format:* Talk

Tatum

KTUM
01-01-2003; 107.1 MHz FM; 100 kw; 919 ft.; N32 52 50 W103 41 1
916 W. Ave. D, Lovington, NM 88260 US
(505) 396-0499
mymtdradio.com
sales@mtdradio.com
License: Tatum, Lea County, NM held by MTD Inc.
Group Owner: MTD Inc.
Arbitron Metro Market: Ruidoso, NM; *Format:* Classic Rock
Will Rooney, Station Manager

Thoreau

KXTC
10-21-1991; 99.9 MHz FM; *Hrs Open:* 24; 100 kw; 1211 ft.; N35 36 13 W108 40 45
1632 South Second Street, Gallup, NM 87301 US
(505) 863-9391; *Fax:* (505) 863-9393
www.999xtc.com
License: Thoreau, McKinley County, NM held by Clear Channel Broadcasting Licenses Inc.
Group Owner: iHeartMedia; (acq 9-7-2000)
Arbitron Metro Market: Gallup, NM; *Format:* Contemporary Hits/Top 40 *Special Programming:* American Indian one hr, Sp 8 hrs wkly; *Hrs. of News Programming:* news progmg 2 hrs wkly; *No. News Employees:* 2 *TargetAudience:* 18-44; Women; *Adv. Rates:* 14; 14; 14; 8
Tony Manero, Senior Vice President of Programming

Truth or Consequence

***KLCF**
01-01-1938; 91.1 MHz FM; *Hrs Open:* 24; kw
5700 West Oaks Boulevard, Rocklin, CA 95765 US
(916) 251-1600; *Fax:* (916) 251-1650
License: Truth or Consequence, Sacramento County, NM held by Educational Media Foundation
Group Owner: EMF Broadcasting; (acq 11-19-2004; $3 million)
Arbitron Metro Market: Sacramento, CA; *Format:* Gospel; *Target Audience:* 18 plus.
Mike Novak, President

Truth or Consequences

KCHS
09-01-1944; 1400 kHz AM; *Hrs Open:* 6am-11pm 7days a wk; 1 kw-U; N33 08 26 W107 13 55
1747 East Third Avenue, Truth or Consequences, NM 87901
(575) 894-2400
www.gpkmedia.com
License: Truth or Consequences, Sierra County, NM held by Myrna Baird-Kohs dba GPK Media LLC
Nat'l Network: AP Radio
Population Served: 13,000; *No. News Employees:* 4; *Target Audience:* General; area residents & visitors at lake
Frances Luna, Co-Owner/General Sales Manager

KKVS
11-01-1984; 98.7 MHz FM; *Hrs Open:* 24; 49 kw; Ant 2,644 ft; N32 58 15 W107 13 26
Mailing Address: P.O. Box 968, Las Cruces, NM 88004
Second Address: 1355 E. California Ave., Las Cruces, NM 88001
(575) 525-9298; *Fax:* (575) 525-9419
www.vista.fm
radiolc@kgrt.com
License: Truth or Consequences, Sierra County, NM held by Richardson Commercial Corp.
Nat'l Network: La Gran D
Population Served: 174,100; *Arbitron Metro Market:* Las Cruces, NM; *No. News Employees:* 1; *Target Audience:* 25-54; Hispanic
Allen Lumeyer, Operations Dir
Veronica Vaillancourt-Test, General Sales Mgr
Ernesto Garcia, Programming Director
Tamara Blaeser, National Sales Manager

Tse Bonito

KHAC
03-21-1967; 880 kHz AM; 10 kw-D, ND1; 0.43 kw-N, ND1; N35 38 41 W109 1 13
P.O. Box 9090, Window Rock, AZ 86515 US
(505) 371-5587; *Fax:* (505) 371-5588
www.westernindian.net
khac@westernindian.org
License: Tse Bonito, NM held by Western Indian Ministries.
Format: Christian *Special Programming:* children's 8 hrs wkly; *No. News Employees:* 1; *Target Audience:* American Indian
Greg Lewis, Station Manager
Scott Hill, Chief Engineer

Tucumcari

KQAY-FM
01-19-1968; 92.7 MHz FM; 3 kw; 412 ft.; N35 8 23 W103 44 35
P.O. Box 668, Tucumcari, NM 88401 US
(505) 461-0522; *Fax:* (505) 461-0092
ktmnkqay@yahoo.com
License: Tucumcari, Quay County, NM
Group Owner: Roswell Radio Inc./Quay Broadcasters Inc.
Format: Country
Mike Martin, General Manager

KTNM
01-01-1941; 1400 kHz AM; 1 kw-U, ND1; N35 10 15 W103 42 25
P.O. Box 668, Tucumcari, NM 88202 US
(505) 461-0522(505) 461-1400; *Fax:* (505) 461-0092
www.tucumcari.ws
ktnmkqay@yahoo.com
License: Tucumcari, NM held by Quay Broadcasters Inc.
Group Owner: Roswell Radio Inc./Quay Broadcasters Inc.; (acq 1-10-2003; with co-located FM)
Nat'l Network: ABC
Arbitron Metro Market: Tucumcari, NM; *Format:* Country *Special Programming:* Sp 18 hrs wkly; *Target Audience:* General.
Diane Paris, General Manager
Greg Carnefix, Programming Director

***KVLP**
01-01-2009; 91.7 MHz FM; 0.57 kw; 312 ft.; N35 8 23 W103 44 35 *Rebroadcasts:* Rebroadcasts KLVR(FM) Middletown, CA 100%
P. O. Box 1458, Washington, DC 20013 US
(916) 251-1600; *Fax:* (916) 251-1650
www.klove.com
klove@klove.com
License: Tucumcari, Quay County, NM held by Educational Media Foundation.
Group Owner: EMF Broadcasting; (acq 3-23-2007; grpsl)
Nat'l Network: K-Love
Arbitron Metro Market: Tucumcari, NM; *Format:* Christian
Darrell Chambliss, Chairman
Alan Mason, CEO/COO
Mike Novak, CEO
David Pierce, Chief Creative Officer
Dan Antonelli, Chief Business Development Officer
Eric Moser, Chief Financial Officer
Brian Burger, Vice President of HumanResources
D. Kevin Blair, Secretary and General Counsel

***KENM**
09-03-2011; 88.9 MHz FM; 3 kw; 869 ft.; N35 8 3 W103 41 53
Rebroadcasts: KENW-FM
US
(575) 562-2112; *Fax:* (575) 562-2590
www.kenw.org
kenwfm@enmu.edu
License: Tucumcari, Quay County, NM held by Eastern New Mexico University.
Nat'l Network: NPR; BSN; APM; PRX
Arbitron Metro Market: Tucumcari, NM; *No. News Employees:* 2
Orlando Ortega, Operations Dir
Duane Ryan, General Manager
Jenifer Baca, Programming Director
Rena Garrett, Promotions Manager
James Lee, News Director
Jeff Burmeister, Engineering Dir
Martin Quintero, Chief Engineer
CarlaChacon, Development Director, FM
Don Criss, Production/Community Services Director

Tularosa

***KNMA**
05-05-2008; 88.1 MHz FM; 7 kw vert; 1900 ft.; N32 49 49 W105 53 25 *Rebroadcasts:* Rebroadcasts KAWZ(FM) Twin Falls, ID 100%
Mailing Address: P.O. Box 391, Twin Falls, ID 83303 US
Second Address: 4002 North 3300 East, Twin Falls, ID 83301
(800) 357-4226
www.csnradio.com
License: Tularosa, Otero County, NM held by Calvary Chapel of Twin Falls Inc.
Group Owner: CSN International
Format: Christian, Religious
Mike Kestler, President
Daniel Davidson, Operations Dir
Don Mills, Network Programming Director
Mike Stocklin, Underwriting Director
Kelly Carlson, Engineering Dir

White Rock

KSFR
01-01-1991; 101.1 MHz FM; *Hrs Open:* 24; 2.5 kw; Ant 1,863 ft; N35 53 09 W106 23 16
P.O. Box 31366, Santa Fe, NM 87504
(505) 428-1527; *Fax:* (505) 424-8938
www.ksfr.org
info@ksfr.org
License: White Rock, Los Alamos County, NM held by Santa Fe Community College

Population Served: 147,000; *Arbitron Metro Market:* Santa Fe, NM *Special Programming:* American Indian 4 hrs, Sp 4 hrs wkly; *Hrs. of News Programming:* news progmg 14 hrs wkly; *No. News Employees:* 1 *TargetAudience:* General.
George Weston, Operations Dir
Ma LeBlanc, General Manager

Zuni

***KSHI**
04-06-1978; 90.9 MHz FM; *Hrs Open:* 8am - 5pm; 0.1 kw; -249 ft.; N35 5 18 W108 47 22
P.O. Box 339, Zuni, NM 87327 US
(505) 782-4144
zuniradio@gmail.com
License: Zuni, McKinley County, NM held by Zuni Communications Authority.
Special Programming: Indian 20 hrs wkly; *Target Audience:* 18-34; primarily Indian
Duane Chimoni, General Manager

New York

Acra

***WGXC**
90.7 MHz FM; 0.125 kw horiz, 3.3 kw vert; 312 ft.; N42 19 43 W73 58 15
US
(518) 622-2598
www.wgxc.org
License: Acra, Greene County, NY held by free103point9
Arbitron Metro Market: Acra, NY; *Format:* Reggae
Lyn Sloneker, Station Manager
Katy Donnelly, Programming Director

Albany

***WAMC**
01-01-1934; 1400 kHz AM *Rebroadcasts:* wamc(FM) 97%
Mailing Address: 12 Dennis Terrace, Schenectady, NY 12303 US
Second Address: 318 Central Ave., Albany, NY 12206
(800) 323-9262
www.wamc.org
License: Albany, NY held by WAMC.
Group Owner: WAMC/Northeast Public Radio; (acq 4-24-03; $500,000).
Nat'l Network: NPR; PRI; *Wire Services:* AP
Arbitron Metro Market: Tyler-Longview TX; *Format:* Christian
Toni Brandy, General Manager

***WAMC-FM**
10-01-1958; 90.3 MHz FM; *Hrs Open:* 24; 10 kw; 1969 ft.; N42 38 14 W73 10 7
Mailing Address: 12 Dennis Terrace, Schenectady, NY 12303 US
Second Address: 318 Central Avenue, Albany, NY 12206
(800) 323-9262
www.wamc.org
mail@wamc.org
License: Albany, Albany County, NY held by WAMC.
Group Owner: WAMC/Northeast Public Radio; (acq 7-1-82)
Nat'l Network: NPR; PRI; *Wire Services:* AP
Arbitron Metro Market: Albany NY; *Format:* News, Talk *Special Programming:* Jazz 18 hrs, folk 7 hrs; *Hrs. of News Programming:* news progmg 48 hrs wkly; *No. News Employees:* 11; *Target Audience:* General.
Toni Brandy, General Manager

***WCDB**
03-01-1978; 90.9 MHz FM; *Hrs Open:* 24; 0.1 kw; 210 ft.; N42 41 16 W73 49 19
University of Albany Campus Center 316, Albany, NY 12222 US
(518) 442-5234;(518) 442-5262; *Fax:* (518) 442-4366
www.wcdbfm.com
License: Albany, Albany County, NY held by State University of New York.
Arbitron Metro Market: Albany, NY; *Format:* Rock/AOR, Variety/Diverse *Special Programming:* Gospel 3 hrs, Sp 3 hrs, dance 3 hrs, jazz 10 hrs, metal 10 hrs wkly; *Hrs. of News Programming:* News progmg 15 hrs wkly *Target Audience:* 15-55; students & surrounding community
Robby Yuskevich, General Manager

WDDY
06-14-1924; 1460 kHz AM; *Hrs Open:* 24; 5 kw-D, DAN; 5 kw-N, DAN; N42 37 21 W73 48 9
600 Congress Ave., Suite 1400, Austin, TX 78701 US
(518) 464-1311; *Fax:* (518) 464-4185
www.radiodisney.com
License: Albany, NY held by Radio Disney Group LLC.
Group Owner: ABC Inc.; (acq 2-12-02; $2 million).
Nat'l Network: ABC; *Nat'l Reps:* Katz Radio
Arbitron Metro Market: Albany-Schenectady-Troy, NY; *Format:* Children; *No. News Employees:* 1; *Target Audience:* 25-54; general
Rob Thomson, General Manager
Sarah Wiseman, Promotions Manager

WGNA-FM
12-01-1973; 107.7 MHz FM; 12.5 kw; 984 ft.; N42 38 13 W73 59 51
1241 Kings Road, Schenectady, NY 12303 US
(518) 476-1077
www.wgna.com
matty.jeff@townsquaremedia.com
License: Albany, Albany County, NY
Group Owner: Townsquare Media; (acq 8-24-2001; grpsl).
Arbitron Metro Market: Albany-Schenectady-Troy, NY; *Format:* Country
Matty Jeff, Brand Manager
Ariana Sheehan, Digital Managing Editor

WGY-FM
09-01-1966; 103.1 MHz FM; 6 kw; 328 ft; N42 39 46 W73 40 37
1203 Troy-Schenectady Rd., Latham, NY 17106 US
(518) 452-4800; *Fax:* (518) 452-4813
www.wgy.com
jeff@wgy.com
License: Albany, Albany County, NY held by CC Licenses LLC.
Group Owner: iHeartMedia; (acq 8-5-98; grpsl)
Nat'l Reps: Clear Channel
Population Served: 114,873; *Arbitron Metro Market:* Albany-Schenectady-Troy, NY; *Format:* News, News/Talk, 86; *Target Audience:* 21-54; upscale arrivers; *Adv. Rates:* 50; 45; 45; 35
Kristen Delaney, Regional Market President
John Cooper, Senior Vice President of Programming
Cliff Wohl, Sales Manager
Jeff Wolf, Program Director/News Director
Jill Manti, Marketing Director
David Abdoo, Chief Engineer
BJRagone, Online Content Director

WKLI-FM
01-01-1972; 100.9 MHz FM; *Hrs Open:* 24; 6 kw; 299 ft.; N42 43 54 W73 52 56
6 Johnson Road, Latham, NY 12110 US
(518) 786-6747
www.albanymagic.com
jscott@albanybroadcasting.com
License: Albany, Albany County, NY held by 6 Johnson Road Licenses Inc.
Group Owner: Pamal Broadcasting Ltd.; (acq 10-9-2001).
Nat'l Network: CBS Radio
Arbitron Metro Market: Albany-Schenectady-Troy, NY; *Format:* Adult Contemp; *Target Audience:* 25-54; upscale women; *Adv. Rates:* 150; 140; 140; 50
Kevin Callahan, Operations Dir
Dan Austin, General Manager
Merret Price, General Sales Mgr

WPYX
09-16-1980; 106.5 MHz FM; *Hrs Open:* 24; 15.5 kw; 902 ft.; N42 38 9 W74 0 5
1203 Troy-Schenectady Road, Latham, NY 12110 US
(518) 452-4800; *Fax:* (518) 452-4813
www.pyx106.com
License: Albany, Albany County, NY held by Capstar TX LLC
Group Owner: iHeartMedia; (acq 8-30-00; grpsl).
Arbitron Metro Market: Albany-Schenectady-Troy, NY; *Format:* Classic Rock; *Target Audience:* 25-54.
Kristen Delaney, Regional Market President
John Cooper, Senior Vice President of Programming
Cliff Wohl, Senior Vice President of Sales
Jill Manti, Marketing Director
BJ Ragone, Online Content Director

WROW
09-30-1947; 590 kHz AM; *Hrs Open:* 24; 5 kw-D, DA2; 1 kw-N, DA2; N42 34 25 W73 47 12
6 Johnson Road, Latham, NY 12110 US
(518) 786-6747
www.wrow.com
jscott@albanybroadcasting.com
License: Albany, NY held by 6 Johnson Road Licenses Inc.
Group Owner: Pamal Broadcasting Ltd.; (acq 10-19-2001; grpsl).
Nat'l Network: CBS; *Nat'l Reps:* McGavren Guild; *Wire Services:* AP
Arbitron Metro Market: Albany-Schenectady-Troy, NY; *Format:* News, News/Talk, 86 *Special Programming:* Gospel 3 hrs wkly; *Hrs. of News Programming:* news progmg 8 hrs wkly; *No. News Employees:* 3; *Target Audience:* 35 plus; affluent, educated, white collar, upwardly mobile, homeowners
Kevin Callahan, Operations Dir

WYJB
10-01-1966; 95.5 MHz FM; 12 kw; 1024 ft.; N42 38 11 W74 0 0
6 Johnson Road, Latham, NY 12110 US
(518) 786-6600
www.b95.com
mprice@albanybroadcasting.com
License: Albany, Albany County, NY
Group Owner: Pamal Broadcasting Ltd.
Nat'l Reps: McGavren Guild
Arbitron Metro Market: Albany, NY; *Format:* Adult Contemp; *No. News Employees:* 3; *Target Audience:* 25-54.; *Adv. Rates:* 275; 275; 250; 75
Kevin Callahan, Operations Dir

Albion

***WJCA**
12-27-2001; 102.1 MHz FM; 3.7 kw; 423 ft.; N43 11 19 W78 8 53
8919 World Ministry Avenue, Baton Rouge, LA 70810 US
(225) 768-8300
www.jsm.org
License: Albion, Orleans County, NY held by Family Worship Center Church Inc.
Group Owner: Family Worship Center Church Inc.; (acq 1-30-2006; $950,000).
Arbitron Metro Market: Baton Rouge, LA; *Format:* Christian
Jimmy Swaggart, President

Alfred

***WALF**
01-01-1971; 89.7 MHz FM; 0.2 kw; -20 ft.; N42 15 17 W77 47 13
C/O Dr. Joseph Gow, Alfred University, 1 Saxon Drive, Alfred, NY 14802 US
(607) 871-2287
www.walf.fm
lej1@alfred.edu
License: Alfred, Allegany County, NY held by Alfred University.
Nat'l Network: NPR
Arbitron Metro Market: Alfred, NY; *Format:* Variety/Diverse
Luke Jaeger, General Manager

***WETD**
03-19-1973; 90.7 MHz FM; *Hrs Open:* 24; 3.2 kw; 299 ft.; N42 15 37 W77 47 51
Alfred State University, Student Leadership Center, Room 401/Media Suite, 10 Upper College Drive, Alfred, NY 14802 US
(607) 587-2907
www.wetd.fm
wetd@alfredstate.edu
License: Alfred, Allegany County, NY held by State University of New York.
Arbitron Metro Market: Alfred, NY; *Format:* Rock/AOR; *Target Audience:* 18-22; college students
Logan Merrill, General Manager/Chief Webmaster
Dale Burns, Chief Engineer
Peter Brendel, Treasurer
Josh Cook, Production
Tiffany Wagner, Public Relations

WZKZ
02-28-1999; 101.9 MHz FM; *Hrs Open:* 24; 1 kw; 801 ft.; N42 11 25 W77 49 17
1705 Lake Road, Elmira, NY 14901 US
(585) 593-9553; *Fax:* (585) 593-9554
License: Alfred, Allegany County, NY held by Pembrook Pines Inc.
Group Owner: Pembrook Pines Media Group
Nat'l Network: Jones Radio Networks; *Nat'l Reps:* Interep; *Wire Services:* AP
Arbitron Metro Market: Alfred, NY; *Format:* Country; *Hrs. of News Programming:* news progmg 10 hrs wkly; *No. News Employees:* 2; *Target Audience:* 18-54.; *Adv. Rates:* 10; 10; 10; 10
Robert Pfuntner, CEO
Bob Weigand, Operations Dir
Rod Biehler, General Manager
Jim Davison, Programming Director

WZKZ(FM)
101.9 MHz FM; 1000 watts; 845 meters; 42 11 25N 77 49 17W
Mailing Address: 1705 Lake Road, Elmira, NY 14901 USA
Second Address: 3012 Eastside Avenue, Wellsville, NY 14895
(585) 593-9553; *Fax:* (585) 593-9554
License: Alfred, Allegany County, NY held by Pembrook Pines Inc
Group Owner: Pembrook Pines Inc
Target Audience: Adults 25-54

Robert J Pfuntner, President

Altamont

WZMR
06-26-1968; 104.9 MHz FM; *Hrs Open:* 24; 0.53 kw; 932 ft.; N42 38 11 W74 0 2
6 Johnson Road, Latham, NY 12110 US
(518) 786-6747
albanyedge.com
mprice@albanybroadcasting.com
License: Altamont, Albany County, NY held by 6 Johnson Road Licenses Inc.
Group Owner: Pamal Broadcasting Ltd.; (acq 10-19-2001; grpsl).
Arbitron Metro Market: Altamont, NY; *Format:* Rock/AOR; *Target Audience:* 18-44; men; *Adv. Rates:* 50; 50; 50; 25
Kevin Callahan, Operations Dir

Amherst

WUFO
01-01-1948; 1080 kHz AM; *Hrs Open:* Sunrise-sunset; 1 kw-D, NDD; N42 56 46 W78 49 43
143 Broadway Avenue, Buffalo, NY 14203 US
(716) 834-1080; *Fax:* (716) 837-1438
www.wufoam.com
sbrown@wufoam.com
License: Amherst, NY held by McL/McM New York LLC.
Group Owner: Sheridan Broadcasting Corp.; (acq 3-1-72)
Nat'l Network: American Urban
Arbitron Metro Market: Buffalo, NY; *Format:* Gospel *Special Programming:* Talk 8 hrs wkly; *Hrs. of News Programming:* News progmg 5 hrs wkly; *Target Audience:* 25-54; Black adults, relg foundation, strong workethics
Sheila L. Brown, Station Manager/CEO
Lee Pettigrew, Program/Music Director
Lee Ann Carr, Account Executive/HR

Amsterdam

***WEXT**
08-01-1975; 97.7 MHz FM; 1.6 kw; 623 ft.; N42 59 5 W74 10 49
4 Global Way, Troy, NY 12180 US
(518) 880-3400
www.exit977.org
feedback@exit977.org
License: Amsterdam, Montgomery County, NY held by WMHT Educational Telecommunications
Arbitron Metro Market: Troy, NY; *Format:* Classical
Dave Michaels, President

WVTL
08-16-1961; 10MHz FM; *Hrs Open:* 24; 1 kw-D, ND1; 0.204 kw-N, ND1; N42 54 38 W74 13 4
5816 State Highway 30, Amsterdam, NY 12010 US
(314) 734-9245
www.wvtlfm.com
grant@rosergroup.com
License: Amsterdam, NY held by Roser Communications Network Inc.
Group Owner: Roser Communications Network Inc.; (acq 10-21-94; $400,000 with WBUG-FM Fort Plain;
Arbitron Metro Market: Amsterdam, NY; *Format:* News, Sports, 86; *Hrs. of News Programming:* news progmg 10 hrs wkly; *No. News Employees:* 2; *Target Audience:* 25 -54
Grant Roser, General Sales Mgr

WCSS
04-08-1948; 1490 kHz AM; *Hrs Open:* 24; 1 kw-U; N42 57 40 W74 10 35
Box 1250 Riverfront Ctr., Amsterdam, NY 12010
(518) 684-6260; (518) 684-6091
www.wcss1490.com
wcss@cranesville.com
License: Amsterdam, Montgomery County, NY held by Cranesville Block Co.
Nat'l Network: ABC/Classic Hits
Population Served: 800,000; *Arbitron Metro Market:* Albany-Schenectady-Troy, NY *Special Programming:* Local progmg & talk 20 hrs wkly; *Hrs. of News Programming:* news progmg 20 hrs wkly; *No. News Employees:* 1 *Target Audience:* 25 plus; adults interested in loc, community info & mus; *Adv. Rates:* 15; 10; 12; 8
Joseph Isabel, Operations Dir

Arcade

***WCOF**
01-01-2005; 89.5 MHz FM; 1 kw; 593 ft.; N42 27 41 W78 18 26
Rebroadcasts: Rebroadcasts WCIK(FM) Bath 100%
Mailing Address: PO Box 506, Bath, NY 14810 US
Second Address: , Bath, NY 14810
(607) 776-4151
www.fln.org
License: Arcade, Wyoming County, NY held by Family Life Ministries Inc.
Group Owner: Family Life Network
Nat'l Network: Salem Radio Network; *Wire Services:* Metro Weather Service Inc.
Arbitron Metro Market: Bath, NY; *Format:* Christian; *Hrs. of News Programming:* news progmg 14 hrs wkly; *No. News Employees:* 3; *Target Audience:* 30-54; general
Dave Margalotti, Operations Dir
Terese Main, Programming Director
Bob Price, News Director

Argyle

***WNGN**
08-01-1994; 91.9 MHz FM; *Hrs Open:* 24; 2 kw; 571 ft.; N43 13 33 W73 26 34
4880 Santa Rosa Road, Camarillo, CA 93012 US
(805) 987-0400
License: Argyle, Washington County, NY held by Northeast Gospel Broadcasting Inc.
Nat'l Network: Moody
Arbitron Metro Market: Buskirk, NY; *Format:* Christian, Religious; *Hrs. of News Programming:* News progmg one hr wkly; *Target Audience:* 35-54; general
Stuart Epperson, President

Arlington

WRRB
12-01-1989; 96.9 MHz FM; *Hrs Open:* 24; 0.31 kw; 1007 ft.; N41 43 9 W73 59 47 *Rebroadcasts:* Rebroadcasts WDST(FM) Woodstock 100%
Mailing Address: P.O. Box 416, Poughkeepsie, NY 12602 US
Second Address: 2 Pendell Rd., Poughkeepsie, NY 12602
(845) 471- 1500; *Fax:* (845) 454-1204
www.wrrv.com
jason.finkelberg@townsquaremedia.com
License: Arlington, Dutchess County, NY held by Peak Broadcasting of Fresno Licenses LLC
Group Owner: Townsquare Media; (acq 1-23-02; grpsl).
Arbitron Metro Market: Arlington, NY; *Format:* Alternative; *Hrs. of News Programming:* News progmg 5 hrs wkly; *Target Audience:* 25-54; upscale professionals
Jason Finkelberg, General Manager
Bill Dunn, Brand Manager
Jason Pugliese, Director Of Sales
Jackie Corley, Digital Managing Editor

Attica

***WCOU**
12-14-1992; 88.3 MHz FM; 11 kw; 535 ft.; N42 49 36 W78 12 25
Rebroadcasts: Rebroadcasts WCIK(FM) Bath 100%
Mailing Address: PO Box 506, Bath, NY 14810 US
Second Address: 7634 Campbell Creek Rd., Bath, NY 14810
(607) 776-4151; *Fax:* (607) 776-6929
www.fln.org
License: Attica, Wyoming County, NY held by Family Life Ministries Inc.
Group Owner: Family Life Network
Nat'l Network: Salem Radio Network; *Wire Services:* Metro Weather Service Inc.
Arbitron Metro Market: Bath,NY; *Format:* Christian; *Hrs. of News Programming:* news progmg 14 hrs wkly; *No. News Employees:* 3; *Target Audience:* 30-54; general
Dave Margalotti, Operations Dir
Terese Main, Programming Director
Bob Price, News Director

Au Sable

WZXP
97.9 MHz FM; 18 kw; Ant 830 ft; N44 46 30 W73 36 48
P.O. Box 9, Bristol, UT 05443
(802) 759-4000
www.musicheads.us
License: Au Sable, Clinton County, NY held by Radioactive LLC.
Group Owner: Radioactive LLC
Arbitron Metro Market: Burlington-Plattsburgh, VT-NY

Auburn

WAUB
12-24-1959; 1590 kHz AM
3568 Lenox Rd., Geneva, NY 14456 US
(315) 781-7000; *Fax:* (315) 781-7077
www.flradiogroup.com
tbaker@flradiogroup.com
License: Auburn, NY held by Auburn Broadcasting Inc.
Group Owner: Finger Lakes Radio Group; (acq 7-2-97; $70,000 plus additonal consideration)
Nat'l Network: CBS
Arbitron Metro Market: Fargo-Moorhead, ND-MN; *Format:* Talk, News; *Target Audience:* General.
Frank Lischak, General Sales Mgr
Ted Baker, Programming Director
Joe Nittler, News Director

***WDWN**
10-31-1972; 89.1 MHz FM; 3 kw; 102 ft; N42 56 40 W76 32 33
197 Franklin St., Auburn, NY 13021
(315) 255-1743
www.wdwn.fm
License: Auburn, Cayuga County, NY held by Cayuga County Community College.
Population Served: 250,000; *Arbitron Metro Market:* Syracuse, NY; *Target Audience:* 18-25; high school & college students, young adults
Steven Keeler, General Manager

WMBO
01-26-1927; 1340 kHz AM; 1 kw-U, ND1; N42 57 5 W76 35 5
401 W. Kirkpatrick Street, Syracuse, NY 13204 US
(315) 472-0222; *Fax:* (315) 478-7745
www.radiodisney.com
info@radiodisney.com
License: Auburn, NY held by WOLF Radio Inc.
Group Owner: WOLF Radio Inc.; acq 6-26-98; $103,000).
Nat'l Network: Radio Disney
Format: Children
Sam Furco, General Manager
Becky Mullen, Promotions Manager

Avon

WYSL
01-23-1987; 1040 kHz AM; *Hrs Open:* 24
5620 South Lima Road, Avon, NY 14414 US
(585) 346-3000; *Fax:* (585) 346-0450
www.wysl1040.com
info@wysl1040.com
License: Avon, NY held by Radio Livingston Ltd.
Nat'l Network: ABC; Westwood One
Arbitron Metro Market: Avon, NY; *Format:* News, Sports *Special Programming:* Relg 4 hrs wkly; *Hrs. of News Programming:* news progmg 160 hrs wkly; *No. News Employees:* 3; *Target Audience:* 35 plus; general
Robert Savage, CEO
J.C. Delass, Station Manager

Babylon

WBAB
08-27-1958; 102.3 MHz FM; *Hrs Open:* 24; 6 kw; 269 ft.; N40 47 58 W73 20 8
555 Sunrise Highway, West Babylon, NY 11704 US
(631) 587-1023; *Fax:* (631) 587-1282
www.wbab.com
wbab@wbab.com
License: Babylon, Suffolk County, NY held by Cox Radio Inc.
Group Owner: Cox Radio Inc.; (acq 5-22-98; grpsl)
Nat'l Reps: Christal
Format: Oldies
John Shea, General Manager
Chris Lloyd, Program Director
Jason Steinberg, Director Of Marketing & Promotion

Baldwinsville

***WBXL**
01-29-1975; 90.5 MHz FM; *Hrs Open:* 7 AM-11 PM; 0.175 kw; 207 ft.; N43 9 47 W76 18 47
E. Oneida Street Complex, Baldwinsville, NY 13027 US
(315) 638-6010
License: Baldwinsville, Onondaga County, NY held by Baldwinsville Central School District.
Arbitron Metro Market: Baldwinsville, NY; *Format:* Contemporary Hits/Top 40; *Target Audience:* Family of school district students
Peter Hunn, General Manager

WSEN
02-25-1959; 1050 kHz AM; *Hrs Open:* 24; 2.5 kw-D, DA2; 0.019 kw-N, DA2; N43 10 46 W76 20 19 *Rebroadcasts:* Rebroadcasts WSEN-FM Baldwinsville
8456 Smokey Hollow Rd., P.O. Box 1050, Baldwinsville, NY 13027 US
(315) 635-3971; *Fax:* (315) 635-3490
www.cnyoldiesradio.com
License: Baldwinsville, Onondaga County, NY held by Leatherstocking Media Group Inc.

Group Owner: Leatherstocking Media Group Inc.
Nat'l Network: CBS; *Nat'l Reps:* McGavren Guild
Arbitron Metro Market: Syracuse, NY; *Format:* Oldies; *Target Audience:* 35 plus; well-educated professionals with disposable income
Dan Elliott, General Manager
Krista Galster, General Sales Mgr
Paul DeLaubell, Sales Representative

WSEN-FM
11-10-1967; 92.1 MHz FM; *Hrs Open:* 24; 25 kw; 299 ft.; N43 10 46 W76 20 19
8456 Smokey Hollow Rd., P.O. Box 1050, Baldwinsville, NY 13027 US
(315) 635-3971; *Fax:* (315) 635-3490
www.wsenfm.com
License: Baldwinsville, Onondaga County, NY held by Leatherstocking Media Group Inc.
Group Owner: Leatherstocking Media Group Inc.
Nat'l Reps: McGavren Guild
Arbitron Metro Market: Syracuse, NY; *Format:* Adult Contemp, Contemporary Hits/Top 40; *Target Audience:* 35-64; well-educated professionals with disposable income
Dan Elliott, General Manager
Krista Galster, General Sales Mgr
Paul DeLaubell, Sales Representative

Ballston Spa

WKKF
05-27-1968; 102.3 MHz FM; *Hrs Open:* 24; 4.1 kw; 387 ft.; N42 52 44 W73 51 47
1203 Troy-Schenectady Road, Latham, NY 12110 US
(518) 452-4800; *Fax:* (518) 452-4813
www.kiss1023.com
License: Ballston Spa, Saratoga County, NY held by CC Licenses LLC.
Group Owner: iHeartMedia; (acq 3-6-97)
Nat'l Reps: Clear Channel
Arbitron Metro Market: Ballstone Spa, NY; *Format:* Contemporary Hits/Top 40; *Target Audience:* 18-34; upscale, hip women
Kristen Delaney, Regional Market President
John Cooper, Senior Vice President of Programming
Cliff Wohl, Senior Vice President of Sales
Randy McCarten, Program/News Director
Jill Manti, Marketing Director
BJ Ragone, Online ContentDirector

Batavia

WBTA
02-06-1941; 1490 kHz AM; *Hrs Open:* 24
113 Main Street, Batavia, NY 14020 US
(585) 344-1490; *Fax:* (585) 344-1441
www.wbta1490.com
License: Batavia, NY held by HPL Communications Inc.
Nat'l Reps: Rgnl Reps
Arbitron Metro Market: Batavia, NY; *Format:* News, News/Talk, 86 *Special Programming:* Sports 9 hrs wkly; *Hrs. of News Programming:* news progmg 10 hrs wkly; *No. News Employees:* 2; *Target Audience:* PrimaryDemographic: Adults 25-54;Secondary Demographic: 35-64; *Adv. Rates:* 14; 14; 14; 8
Daniel Fischer, President
Lorne Way, General Sales Mgr

***WGCC-FM**
11-13-1985; 90.7 MHz FM; *Hrs Open:* 6 AM-1 AM; 0.88 kw; 164 ft.; N43 1 3 W78 8 18
1 College Road, Batavia, NY 14020 US
(585) 343-9422
wgccradio@gmail.com
License: Batavia, Genesee County, NY held by Genesee Community College Board of Trustees.
Format: Rock/AOR; *Hrs. of News Programming:* news progmg 5 hrs wkly; *No. News Employees:* 1; *Target Audience:* 13-30; high school & college youth
Steve Smith, Co-Station Manager
Joseph Shepard, Co-Station Manager
Tom Martel, Music Director

Bath

WABH
11-02-1962; 1380 kHz AM; *Hrs Open:* 19
7035 East Washington Street Extension, Bath, NY 14810 US
(607) 776-3326; *Fax:* (607) 776-6161
www.1380wabh.com
License: Bath, NY held by Pembrook Pines Mass Media Inc.
Group Owner: Pembrook Pines Media Group; (acq 4-13-90; with co-located FM;
Nat'l Network: CBS
Arbitron Metro Market: Texarkana TX-AR; *Format:* Christian
Rick Snavely, General Manager

WVIN-FM
10-10-1971; 98.3 MHz FM; *Hrs Open:* 19; 4.5 kw; 367 ft.; N42 19 6 W77 21 27
1705 Lake Road, Elmira, NY 14902 US
(607) 776-3326; *Fax:* (607) 776-6161
wvinbath.com
License: Bath, Steuben County, NY
Arbitron Metro Market: Bath, NY; *Format:* Adult Contemp *Special Programming:* Jazz 2 hrs wkly
Robert Pfuntner, Station Manager

Bay Shore

WBZO
02-01-1993; 103.1 MHz FM; *Hrs Open:* 24; 3 kw; 141 meters; N40 45 04 W73 12 52
234 Airport Plaza Blvd., Suite 5, Farmingdale, NY 11747
(631) 770-4200; *Fax:* (631) 770-0101
www.b103.com
webmaster@b103.com
License: Bay Shore, Suffolk County, NY held by Connoisseur Media Licenses LLC
Group Owner: Connoisseur Media LLC
Nat'l Reps: D & R Radio
Population Served: 8,219; *Arbitron Metro Market:* Farmingdale, NY; *Hrs. of News Programming:* news progmg 25 hrs wkly; *No. News Employees:* 1; *Target Audience:* General.
Dave Widmer, General Manager
Bill Wise, Programming Director
Frank Brinka, News Director
Michael Glaser, Chief Engineer

Beacon

WBNR
12-17-1959; 1260 kHz AM; *Hrs Open:* 24; 1 kw-D, DA2; 0.4 kw-N, DA2; N41 29 32 W73 58 43 *Rebroadcasts:* Simulcast with WLNA(AM) Peekskill 100%
715 Route 52, Beacon, NY 12508 US
(845) 838-6000; *Fax:* (845) 838-2109
www.realcountryhv.com
License: Beacon, NY held by 6 Johnson Road Licenses Inc.
Group Owner: Pamal Broadcasting Ltd.; (acq 10-19-2001; grpsl).
Nat'l Network: ABC
Arbitron Metro Market: Beacon, NY; *Format:* Classic Rock
Special Programming: Relg 5 hrs wkly; *Hrs. of News Programming:* news progmg 2 hrs wkly; *No. News Employees:* 2; *Target Audience:* 35 plus. *Adv.Rates:* 35; 25; 15; 10
Don Verity, Station Manager

Big Flats

WENI-FM
04-01-1989; 97.7 MHz FM; *Hrs Open:* 24; 0.61 kw; 722 ft.; N42 8 31 W77 4 40 *Rebroadcasts:* Simulcast With WENY-FM Elmire 100%
21 East Market Street, Suite 101, Corning, NY 14830-2650 US
(607) 937-8181; *Fax:* (607) 962-1138
www.magic927977.net
License: Big Flats, Chemung County, NY held by Sound Communications LLC
Group Owner: Sound Communications LLC; (acq 7-14-2008; grpsl)
Nat'l Network: ABC; *Nat'l Reps:* Roslin
Arbitron Metro Market: Elmira-Corning, NY; *Format:* Oldies; *Target Audience:* 25-54.
Jamie Evans, General Manager
Scott Benjamin, General Sales Mgr
Frank Acomb, Programming Director
Betty Coccho, Traffic Manager

Binghamton

WAAL
03-01-1954; 99.1 MHz FM; *Hrs Open:* 24; 8.7 kw; 955 ft.; N42 3 31 W75 57 6
Mailing Address: 405 Park Avenue, Suite 702, New York, NY 10022 US
Second Address: 59 Court St., Binghamton, NY 13901
(662) 844-8888; *Fax:* (662) 842-6791
www.afr.net
License: Binghamton, Broome County, NY held by Citadel Broadcasting Co.
Arbitron Metro Market: El Dorado AR; *Format:* Christian

***WHRW**
03-01-1966; 90.5 MHz FM; *Hrs Open:* 24; 1.45 kw horiz, 0 kw vert; N42 5 24 W75 58 5
P.O. Box 2000, Binghamton, NY 13902 US
(607) 777-2139; *Fax:* (607) 777-6501
www.whrwfm.org
gm@whrwfm.org
License: Binghamton, Broome County, NY held by State University of New York.
Wire Services: UPI
Arbitron Metro Market: Binghamton, NY; *Format:* Variety/Diverse
Special Programming: It 3 hrs, Jazz 9 hrs, Pol 3 hrs, Relg 6 hrs, Sp 9; *Hrs. of News Programming:* News progmg 5 hrs wkly; *Target Audience:* General.
Dan Spaventa, General Manager
Evan Flury, Programming Director

WHWK
09-01-1956; 98.1 MHz FM; 6.7 kw; 1296 ft.; N42 3 40 W75 56 45
140 S. Ash Ave., Tempe, AZ 85281 US
(607) 772-8400; *Fax:* (607) 772-9806
www.981thehawk.com
License: Binghamton, Broome County, NY held by Townsquare Media Binghamton License LLC
Group Owner: Townsquare Media
Arbitron Metro Market: Binghamton, NY; *Format:* Country; *Target Audience:* 25-54.
Barbara Meaney, General Manager
John Davison, Brand Manager

WINR
01-01-1946; 680 kHz AM; *Hrs Open:* 24
320 N. Jensen Road, Vestal, NY 13850 US
(607) 584-5800; *Fax:* (607) 584-5900
www.us969.com
License: Binghamton, NY held by AMFM Radio Licenses LLC.
Group Owner: iHeartMedia; (acq 2-13-2001; $1 million).
Nat'l Network: CBS
Arbitron Metro Market: Binghamton, NY; *Format:* Country; *Hrs. of News Programming:* news progmg 10 hrs wkly; *No. News Employees:* 1; *Target Audience:* 35 plus.
Jim Free, Operations Manager

WYOS
06-01-1947; 1360 kHz AM; *Hrs Open:* 24
59 Court Street, Binghamton, NY 13901 US
(607) 772-8850; *Fax:* (607) 772-9806
www.wnbf.com
License: Binghamton, NY held by Townsquare Media Binghamton License LLC
Group Owner: Townsquare Media; (acq 6-9-99; grpsl)
Nat'l Network: ESPN Radio; *Nat'l Reps:* McGavren Guild
Arbitron Metro Market: Binghamton, NY; *Format:* Sports
Barbara Meaney, General Manager
Roger Neel, Brand Manager

WNBF
01-01-1928; 1290 kHz AM
59 Court Street, Binghamton, NY 13901 US
(607) 772-8400; *Fax:* (607) 772-9806
www.wnbf.com
barbara.meaney@townsquaremedia.com
License: Binghamton, NY held by Townsquare Media Binghamton License LLC
Group Owner: Townsquare Media; (acq 6-9-99; grpsl).
Arbitron Metro Market: Binghamton, NY; *Format:* News, News/Talk, 86; *Target Audience:* 35-64.
Barbara Meaney, General Manager
Roger Neel, Brand Manager

***WSKG-FM**
10-22-1975; 89.3 MHz FM; *Hrs Open:* 24; 11.5 kw; 1040 ft.; N42 3 40 W75 56 46
PO Box 3000, Binghamton, NY 13902 US
(607) 729-0100; *Fax:* (607) 729-7328,
www.wskg.com
wskg_mail@wskg.pbs.org
License: Binghamton, Broome County, NY held by WSKG Public Telecommunications Council.
Nat'l Network: NPR; PRI
Arbitron Metro Market: Binghamton, NY *TV Affiliate:* *WSKG-TV affil.; *Format:* News *Special Programming:* Jazz, folk 5 hrs wkly; *Hrs. of News Programming:* news progmg 33 hrs wkly; *No. News Employees:* 1 *Target Audience:* General.
Brian Sickora, President/Chief Executive Officer
Gregory Keeler, Programming/Operations Director
Matt Richmond, News Director
Dave Fulton, Engineering Dir
Caroline Basso, Director of Development & Marketing

***WSQX-FM**
01-17-1995; 91.5 MHz FM; *Hrs Open:* 24; 3.5 kw; 381 ft.; N42 7 54 W75 55 56
PO Box 3000, Binghamton, NY 13902 US

(607) 729-0100; *Fax:* (607) 729-7328
www.wskg.com
License: Binghamton, Broome County, NY held by WSKG Public Telecommunications Council.
Nat'l Network: NPR; PRI
Arbitron Metro Market: Binghamton, NY *TV Affiliate:* *WSKG-TV affil; *Format:* Jazz, News *Special Programming:* Talk 10 hrs wkly; *Target Audience:* General.
Brian Sickora, President/Chief Executive Officer
Gregory Keeler, Programming/Operations Director
Matt Richmond, News Director
Dave Fulton, Engineering Dir
Caroline Basso, Director of Development & Marketing

Black River

WBLH

08-11-2008; 92.5 MHz FM; 6 kw; Ant 328 ft; N44 03 17.8 W75 57 15.3
223 J.B. Wise Pl., Suite 10, Watertown, NY
(315) 786-0925; *Fax:* (315) 786-0920
License: Black River, Jefferson County, NY held by Radioactive LLC.
Group Owner: Radioactive LLC
Arbitron Metro Market: Watertown, NY; *No. News Employees:* 5-11; *Adv. Rates:* 10-12 dollars primetime
Michael Stapleford, CEO/COO
Benjamin Homel, President
Johnny Keagan, Operations Dir
Tim Sweeney, General Manager
Tim Sweeney, Station Manager
Tim Sweeney, General Sales Mgr
Robert Shackley, Programming Director
Dale Hobson, WebManager

Blue Mountain Lake

*WXLH

11-01-1992; 91.3 MHz FM; *Hrs Open:* 24; 0.078 kw; 1729 ft.; N43 52 18 W74 24 2 *Rebroadcasts:* Rebroadcasts WSLU(FM) Canton 100%
N. Country Public Radio, St. Lawrence University, Canton, NY 13617 US
(315) 229-5356; *Fax:* (315) 229-5373
www.ncpr.org
info@ncpr.org
License: Blue Mountain Lake, Hamilton County, NY held by St. Lawrence University.
Arbitron Metro Market: Blue Mountain Lake, NY; *Format:* Talk *Special Programming:* Gospel, jazz, class, folk, pub affrs; *Hrs. of News Programming:* news progmg 35 hrs wkly; *No. News Employees:* 4; *Target Audience:* General.
Shelly Pike, Operations Dir
Ellen Rocco, Station Manager
Jacqueline Sauter, Programming Director
Martha Foley, News Director
Bob Sauter, Chief Engineer
Joel Hurd, Production Manager
June Peoples, Membership Director
NaomiWeller, Office Managerÿ
Dale Hobson, Web Manager
Sandy Demarest, Development Director

Boonville

WBRV

06-22-1955; 900 kHz AM; *Hrs Open:* 24; 1 kw-D, ND1; 0.052 kw-N, ND1; N43 30 47 W75 21 46 *Rebroadcasts:* Rebroadcasts WLLG(FM) Lowville 50%
7607 North State Street, Lowville, NY 13367 US
(315) 376-7500; *Fax:* (315) 376-8549
www.themoose.net
sales@themoose.net
License: Boonville, NY held by Flack Broadcasting Group L.L.C.
Nat'l Network: USA
Arbitron Metro Market: Lowville, NY; *Format:* Country; *Hrs. of News Programming:* News progmg 18 hrs wkly; *Target Audience:* General.
William Flack, President
Sara Flack, Operations Dir
Brian Best, News Director
Dana Crouse, Disc Jockey

WBRV-FM

01-31-1989; 101.3 MHz FM; *Hrs Open:* 24; 4.7 kw; 374 ft.; N43 26 52 W75 20 50 *Rebroadcasts:* Rebroadcasts WLLG (FM) Lowville 50%
3399 Moose River Road, Boonville, NY 13309 US
(315) 376-7500; *Fax:* (315) 376-8549
www.themoose.net
sales@themoose.net
License: Boonville, Oneida County, NY
Arbitron Metro Market: Lowville, NY *Special Programming:* Farm 3 hrs, relg 3 hrs wkly; *Hrs. of News Programming:* News progmg 10 hrs wkly; *Target Audience:* General.
Jon Zucker, General Manager
Marianna Faircloth, Station Manager
Mark Stackowski, General Sales Mgr
Chris Novello, Programming Director
Olivia Hoffman, Promotions Manager
Kaitlyn Laabs, News Director

*WXLB

01-01-2009; 91.7 MHz FM; 0.1 kw; 351 ft.; N43 26 53 W75 20 48 *Rebroadcasts:* Rebroadcasts WSLU(FM) Canton 100% US
(315) 229-5356; *Fax:* (315) 229-5373
www.northcountrypublicradio.org
radio@ncpr.org
License: Boonville, Oneida County, NY held by The St. Lawrence University.
Nat'l Network: NPR; PRI
Arbitron Metro Market: Boonville, NY; *Format:* Talk
Shelly Pike, Operations Dir
Ellen Rocco, General Manager
Jackie Sauter, Programming Director
Martha Foley, News Director
Bob Sauter, Chief Engineer
Joel Hurd, Production Manager

Brentwood

*WXBA

06-21-1975; 88.1 MHz FM; *Hrs Open:* 24; 0.18 kw; 95 ft.; N40 46 19 W73 15 19
52 Third Avenue, Brentwood, NY 11717 US
(631) 434-2123; *Fax:* (631) 273-6572
License: Brentwood, Suffolk County, NY held by Brentwood Public School District.
Arbitron Metro Market: Brentwood, NY; *Format:* Christian *Special Programming:* Black 5 hrs wkly; *Hrs. of News Programming:* news progmg 3 hrs wkly; *No. News Employees:* 2; *Target Audience:* 18-54; general
Jaime Lane, Station Manager
Frank Lapple, Chief Engineer
Pete Mandzych, Sports Commentator

Brewster

WPUT

07-03-1958; 1510 kHz AM; 1 kw-D, NDD; N41 24 34 W73 37 29
1004 Federal Road, Brookfield, CT 06804 US
(203) 775-1212; *Fax:* (203) 775-6452
License: Brewster, NY held by Cumulus Licensing Corp.
Group Owner: Cumulus Media Inc.
Nat'l Network: ESPN Radio
Arbitron Metro Market: New York; *Format:* Sports
Ann McManus, Regional Vice President
Miranda Goodspeed, Sales Manager
Tim Sheehan, Programming Director
Tarryn Donnarummo, Promotions Director

Briarcliff Manor

WXPK

04-08-1960; 107.1 MHz FM; *Hrs Open:* 24; 1.9 kw; 591 ft.; N41 4 49 W73 48 26
56 Lafayette Avenue, Suite 370, White Plains, NY 10603 US
(845) 838-6000; *Fax:* (848) 838-2109
www.1071thepeak.com
info@1071thepeak.com
License: Briarcliff Manor, Westchester County, NY held by 6 Johnson Road Licenses Inc.
Group Owner: Pamal Broadcasting Ltd.; (acq 11-5-2004; $18.4 million).
Arbitron Metro Market: New York; *Format:* Triple A; *No. News Employees:* 1; *Target Audience:* 18-44; upscale, young, suburban
Rob DellaGreca, Sales Manager
Chris Hermann, Programming Director
Katarina Suda, Promotions Director
Bruce Feniger, National Advertising Manager
Rob Arrow, Music Director/Assistant Programming Director

Bridgehampton

WBAZ

01-01-1996; 102.5 MHz FM; *Hrs Open:* 24; 4.8 kw; 348 ft.; N40 53 58 W72 23 6
Mailing Address: P.O. Box 157, Watermill, NY 11976 US
Second Address: 760 Montauk Hwy., Suice 1C, Watermill, NY 11976
(631) 267-7800; *Fax:* (631) 267-1018
www.wbaz.com
License: Bridgehampton, Suffolk County, NY held by AAA Licensing LLC.
Group Owner: Long Island Radio Broadcasting LLC; (acq 8-22-2000; $2.75 million with WBEA(FM) Southold).
Arbitron Metro Market: Watermill, NY; *Format:* Adult Contemp *Special Programming:* News, sports; *Target Audience:* 25-44; adults with active lifestyles
Mike Raye, President/General Manager
Hedy Krebs-DeMaio, General Manager
Susan Wolfson, Sales Manager
Jaime Emerson, Programming Director
Rebecca Campbell, Traffic Manager

Bridgeport

WTKW

11-09-1992; 99.5 MHz FM; *Hrs Open:* 24; 5.7 kw; 338 ft.; N43 9 24 W75 57 25
235 Walton St., Syracuse, NY 13202 US
(315) 472-9111; *Fax:* (315) 472-1888
www.tk99.net
asktk@tk99.net
License: Bridgeport, Madison County, NY held by Galaxy Syracuse Licensee LLC.
Group Owner: Galaxy Communications L.P.; (acq 4-6-2000; grpsl)
Arbitron Metro Market: Syracuse, NY; *Format:* Classic Rock; *Hrs. of News Programming:* news progmg 3 hrs wkly; *No. News Employees:* 1; *Target Audience:* 25-54 plus; stable, peak-earning adults

Brighton

WZNE

11-01-1996; 94.1 MHz FM; *Hrs Open:* 24; 1.8 kw; 407 ft.; N43 8 7 W77 35 7
28 East Main Street, Rochester, NY 14614 US
(585) 399-5700; *Fax:* (585) 399-5750
www.thezone941.com
License: Brighton, Monroe County, NY held by Stephens Media Group-Rochester LLC.
Group Owner: Stephens Family L.P.; (acq 7-14-2008; grpsl)
Nat'l Network: CNN Radio; *Nat'l Reps:* Christal
Arbitron Metro Market: Moca, PR; *Format:* Alternative; *Target Audience:* Men 18-34; affluent fans of alternative rock music
Michael Ninnie, General Manager
Laurie Zsedely, Director of Sales
Nik Rivers, Programming Director
Scott Hixson, Promotions Manager

Brockport

WASB

02-15-1970; 1590 kHz AM; *Hrs Open:* 24; 1 kw-D, DA2; 1 kw-N, DA2; N43 11 44 W77 57 5
6675 4th Section Road, Brockport, NY 14420 US
(585) 637-7040
www.theteam.fm
License: Brockport, NY held by David L. Wolfe
Arbitron Metro Market: Brockport, NY; *Format:* Christian; *Target Audience:* All ages; rural audience, western Rochester & suburbs
Daniel Wolfe, General Manager
Gail Reed, Programming Director

*WBSU

01-14-1981; 89.1 MHz FM; *Hrs Open:* 24; 7.33 kw; 160 ft; N43 12 45 W77 57 17
135 Seymour Union, Brockport, NY 14420
(585) 395-2580; *Fax:* (585) 395-5334
www.891thepoint.com
wkozires@brockport.edu
License: Brockport, Monroe County, NY held by State University of New York.
Nat'l Network: AP Radio; *Wire Services:* AP
Population Served: 500,000; *Arbitron Metro Market:* Rochester, NY *Special Programming:* Pub affrs 6 hrs wkly; *Hrs. of News Programming:* News progmg 3 hrs wkly; *Target Audience:* 17-34; college & young professional
Dr. John Halstead, President
Warren Kozireski, General Manager
Dean King, Chief Engineer

*WKDL-FM

01-01-1999; 104.9 MHz FM; 6 kw; 328 ft.; N43 9 51 W77 47 2
P.O. Box 2098, Omaha, NE 68103 US
(800) 525-5683
www.klove.com
License: Brockport, Monroe County, NY held by Brockport Licenses LLC.
Group Owner: EMF Broadcasting; (acq 1-27-2006; $4 million)
Nat'l Network: K-Love
Format: Christian

Mike Novak, President

Bronxville

WFAS-FM

09-01-1947; 103.9 MHz FM; 0.6 kw; 667 ft.; N41 1 32 W73 49 39
365 Secor Road, Hartsdale, NY 10530 US
(914) 693-2400; *Fax:* (914) 693-0000
www.wfasfm.com
License: Bronxville, Westchester County, NY
Group Owner: Cumulus Media Inc.
Arbitron Metro Market: Bronxville, NY; *Format:* Adult Contemp; *Hrs. of News Programming:* News progmg one hr wkly; *Target Audience:* 25-54.
Ann McManus, Regional Vice President
Joan Franzino, Operations Dir
Marty Sheehan, General Sales Mgr
Jolana Smith, Programming Director
Jeremiah Johnsen, Marketing & Promotions Director
Pam Puso, News Director

Brooklyn

*WKRB

05-28-1978; 90.3 MHz FM; *Hrs Open:* 24; 0.01 kw; 134 ft.; N40 34 36 W73 56 4
2001 Oriental Boulevard, Brooklyn, NY 11235 US
(718) 368-5817; *Fax:* (718) 368-4776
www.wkrb.org
gm@wkrb.org
License: Brooklyn, Kings County, NY held by Kingsborough Community College.
Arbitron Metro Market: New York; *Format:* Variety/Diverse; *Target Audience:* General; young adults
Regina Peruggi, President
Rob Herklotz, General Manager
Cliff Hesse, Director of Broadcasting

Brookville

*WCWP

04-01-1965; 88.1 MHz FM; *Hrs Open:* 24; 0.1 kw; 190 ft.; N40 49 0 W73 35 49 *Rebroadcasts:* Rebroadcasts WLIU(FM) Southampton 85%
700 Northern Blvd, University Center, Brookville, NY 11548 US
(516) 299-2683(516) 299-2626; *Fax:* (516) 299-2767
www.wcwp.org
License: Brookville, Nassau County, NY held by Long Island University.
Nat'l Network: NPR
Arbitron Metro Market: Nassau County, NY; *Format:* Jazz, News; *Hrs. of News Programming:* news progmg 15 hrs wkly; *No. News Employees:* 1; *Target Audience:* General
Dan Cox, General Manager/Director of Broadcasting
Joseph Manfredi, Instructor/Radio Station Manager

Buffalo

WBEN

09-08-1930; 930 kHz AM; *Hrs Open:* 24; 5 kw-D, DAN; 5 kw-N, DAN; N42 58 42 W78 57 27
500 Corporate Parkway, Suite 200, Buffalo, NY 14226 US
(716) 803-0930; *Fax:* (716) 832-3080
www.wben.com
newsroom@wben.com
License: Buffalo, NY held by Entercom Buffalo License L.L.C.
Group Owner: Entercom Communications Corp.; (acq 1999)
Nat'l Network: CBS; *Nat'l Reps:* D & R Radio
Arbitron Metro Market: Buffalo, NY; *Format:* News, News/Talk, 84, Talk *Special Programming:* Buffalo Bills football; *Hrs. of News Programming:* news progmg 20 hrs wkly; *No. News Employees:* 10; *Target Audience:* 35-64; general
Tim Wenger, Operations Dir
Greg Reid, General Manager/Vice President
Tim Holly, Sales Director
Tim Wenger, Programming Director
John Zach, News Director
Dennis Kavanaugh, Engineering Dir
Kevin Sylvester, Sports Commentator
Susan Rose, Morning Anchor
Dave Debo, Anchor/Reporter/wben.com Editor

*WBFO

01-07-1959; 88.7 MHz FM; *Hrs Open:* 24; 50 kw; 384 ft.; N43 0 12 W78 45 56
Horizons Plaza, P.O. Box 1263, Buffalo, NY 14240 US
(716) 845-7040; *Fax:* (716)-845-7036
www.wbfo.org
License: Buffalo, Erie County, NY held by State University of New York.
Nat'l Network: NPR
Arbitron Metro Market: Buffalo, NY; *Format:* Jazz *Special Programming:* Blues 8 hrs, bluegrass 3 hrs, class one hr, Pol 3 hrs wkly; *Hrs. of News Programming:* news progmg 50 hrs wkly; *No. News Employees:* 2 *Target Audience:* General; educated professionals
Donald K. Boswell, President/CEO
Mary Wozniak, Operations Dir
Jim Ranney, News Director/Station Manager
Joan Wilson, Director of Communications & Marketing

*WBNY

01-01-1982; 91.3 MHz FM; *Hrs Open:* 24; 0.1 kw; 112 ft.; N42 55 59 W78 52 59
1300 Elmwood Avenue, Campbell Student Union 220, Buffalo, NY 14222 US
(716) 878-3080
www.buffalostate.edu/wbny/
wbnyprogram@gmail.com
License: Buffalo, Erie County, NY held by State University of New York.
Arbitron Metro Market: Buffalo, NY; *Format:* Alternative *Special Programming:* Black 12 hrs, jazz 3 hrs, reggae 3 hrs, heavy metal 3 hrs, folk 3 hrs wkly; *Hrs. of News Programming:* News progmg 6 hrs wkly *TargetAudience:* 18-25; college student
Tom Calderone, General Manager
Thomas Scott Reuther, News Director

WDCX-FM

02-01-1963; 99.5 MHz FM; *Hrs Open:* 24; 110 kw; 640 ft.; N42 38 7 W78 46 5
625 Delaware Avenue, Suite 308, Buffalo, NY 14202 US
(716) 883-3010; *Fax:* (716) 883-3606
www.wdcxfm.com
License: Buffalo, Erie County, NY held by Kimtron Inc.
Group Owner: Crawford Broadcasting Co.
Arbitron Metro Market: Buffalo-Niagara Falls, NY; *Format:* Christian, Talk, 74; *Target Audience:* General.
Steven Napoli, Operations Manager (FM Radio)
Brett Larson, General Manager
Peter Tasca, General Sales Mgr
Keri Cardinale, Programming Director
Brian Cunningham, Chief Engineer
Brandon Grinder, Production Manager
Lesvia Diaz,Office Manager
Earl Schillinger, Operations Manager (AM Radio)

WEDG

01-01-1947; 103.3 MHz FM; 49 kw; 348 ft.; N42 55 34 W78 50 28
50 James E. Casey Dr., Buffalo, NY 14206 US
(716) 881-4555; *Fax:* (716) 884-2931
www.wedg.com
steve.bearance@cumulus.com
License: Buffalo, Erie County, NY held by Radio License Holding CBC, LLC
Group Owner: Cumulus Media Inc.; (acq 2-23-00; grpsl).
Nat'l Reps: Eastman Radio
Arbitron Metro Market: Buffalo, NY; *Target Audience:* 18-44
Steve Bearance, General Manager
Rose Porter, General Sales Mgr

*WFBF

01-01-1989; 89.9 MHz FM; 16 kw; 295 ft.; N42 41 19 W78 45 15
Mailing Address: 4135 Northgate Blvd., Suite 1, Sacramento, CA 95834 US
Second Address: 290 Hegenberger Rd., Oakland, CA 94621
(800) 543-1495; *Fax:* (916) 641-8238
www.familyradio.com
info@familyradio.com
License: Buffalo, Erie County, NY held by Family Stations Inc.
Group Owner: Family Stations Inc.
Arbitron Metro Market: Buffalo-Niagara Falls, NY; *Format:* Christian, Religious
Harold Camping, President
Tim Evans, Vice President

WGR

05-22-1922; 550 kHz AM; *Hrs Open:* 24
500 Corporate Parkway, Suite 200, Buffalo, NY 14226 US
(716) 843-0600; *Fax:* (716) 843-0250
www.wgr550.com
info@wgr550.com
License: Buffalo, NY held by Entercom Buffalo License LLC.
Group Owner: Entercom Communications Corp.; (acq 12-13-99; grpsl).
Nat'l Network: ESPN Radio
Arbitron Metro Market: Buffalo-Niagara Falls, NY; *Format:* Sports; *Target Audience:* 25-54; men
Greg Reid, Vice President/General Manager
Jill Kowalski, Local Sales Manager
Allan Davis, Programming Director
Samantha Ogrodnik, Promotions Director
Tim Wenger, Operations Manager

WGRF

09-14-1959; 96.9 MHz FM; 24 kw; 712 ft.; N42 57 13 W78 52 36
50 James E. Casey Dr., Buffalo, NY 14206 US
(716) 881-4555
www.97rock.com
License: Buffalo, Erie County, NY held by Radio License Holding CBC, LLC
Group Owner: Cumulus Media Inc.; (acq 2-23-00; grpsl).
Arbitron Metro Market: Buffalo-Niagara Falls, NY; *Format:* Classic Rock; *Target Audience:* 25-49; classic rock listeners
Steve Bearance, General Manager
Rose Porter, General Sales Mgr
John Hager, Programming Director

WHTT

10-03-1954; 104.1 MHz FM; *Hrs Open:* 24; 50 kw; 387 ft.; N42 49 50 W78 48 1
50 James E. Casey Dr., Buffalo, NY 14206 US
(716) 881-4555; *Fax:* (716) 885-6104
www.whtt.com
whtt@whtt.com
License: Buffalo, NY held by Radio License Holding CBC, LLC
Group Owner: Cumulus Media Inc.; (acq 2-23-2000; grpsl).
Nat'l Network: ABC; *Nat'l Reps:* Eastman Radio
Arbitron Metro Market: Buffalo-Niagara Falls, NY; *Format:* Adult Contemp
Rose Porter, General Sales Mgr

WJYE

11-11-1966; 96.1 MHz FM; *Hrs Open:* 24; 47 kw; 505 ft.; N42 53 10 W78 52 25
(716) 856-3550; *Fax:* (716) 852-0537
www.961joyfm.com
bob.richards2@townsquaremedia.com
License: Buffalo, Erie County, NY
Group Owner: Townsquare Media; (acq 12-15-2006; grpsl)
Nat'l Reps: Christal
Arbitron Metro Market: Buffalo-Niagara Falls, NY; *Format:* Adult Contemp *Special Programming:* Pub affrs 2 hrs wkly; *Hrs. of News Programming:* news progmg 23 hrs wkly; *No. News Employees:* 1 *Target Audience:* 25-54.
Bob Richards, Brand Manager
David Crumb, Director Of Sales
Amanda Tunis, Digital Sales Manager
Melissa Kory, Digital Managing Editor
Andrea Kallivrousis, Digital Sales Manager

WBUF

01-01-1947; 92.9 MHz FM; 76 kw; 640 ft.; N42 57 13 W78 52 36
14 Lafayette Square, Buffalo, NY 14203 US
(716) 852-9292; *Fax:* (716) 852-9290
www.wbuf.com
joe.covlin@townsquaremedia.com
License: Buffalo, Erie County, NY
Group Owner: Townsquare Media; (acq 12-15-2006; grpsl)
Nat'l Network: CBS Radio; CNN Radio; *Nat'l Reps:* Christal
Arbitron Metro Market: Buffalo-Niagara Falls, NY; *Format:* Talk; *Target Audience:* 18-34; men
Joe Colvin, Brand Manager
David Crumb, Director Of Sales
Amanda Tunis, Digital Sales Manager
Melissa Kory, Digital Managing Editor

WTSS

11-11-1946; 102.5 MHz FM; *Hrs Open:* 24; 110 kw; 1,340 ft; N42 39 33 W78 37 33
500 Corporate Pkwy., Suite 200, Buffalo, NY 14226
(716) 843-0600; *Fax:* (716) 832-2872
www.star1025.com
License: Buffalo, Erie County, NY
Nat'l Reps: Katz
Arbitron Metro Market: Buffalo-Niagara Falls, NY; *Target Audience:* 18-49.
Michael Doyle, Regional President
Sue O'Neil, Operations Dir
Tim Holly, Sales Manager

WBBF

09-01-1947; 1120 kHz AM; 1 kw-D, NDD; N42 49 50 W78 48 1
3280 Peachtree Rd. NW, Suite 2300, Atlanta, GA 30305 US
(404) 949-0700
License: Buffalo, NY held by Radio License Holding CBC, LLC
Group Owner: Cumulus Media Inc.
Arbitron Metro Market: Buffalo, NY; *Format:* Spanish
Steve Bearance, Vice President/Marketing Manager
Natalie Hutchen, Operations Dir
Juan Carlos Rivera, Programming Director

WDCZ
10-14-1924; 970 kHz AM; *Hrs Open:* 24; 5 kw-U, DA1; N42 44 41 W78 53 13
Mailing Address: 625 Delaware Avenue, Suite 308, Buffalo, NY 14202 US
Second Address: 140 Lower Terr., Buffalo, NY 14202
(716) 845-7000; *Fax:* (716) 845-7043
info@wdcxradio.com
License: Buffalo, NY held by Crawford Broadcasting Company
Nat'l Network: PRI; NPR
Arbitron Metro Market: Buffalo, NY; *Format:* News, News/Talk, 86 *Special Programming:* Pub affrs; *No. News Employees:* 8; *Target Audience:* 35 plus.
Steven Napoli, Operations Manager (FM Radio)
Brett Larson, General Manager
Peter Tasca, Sales Manager
Keri Cardinale, Programming Director
Brian Cunningham, Chief Engineer
Brandon Grinder, Production Manager
Lesvia Diaz, OfficeManager
Earl Schillinger, Operations Manager (AM Radio)

WNED-FM
06-06-1960; 94.5 MHz FM; 105 kw; 709 ft.; N42 38 13 W78 46 5
P.O. Box 1263, Buffalo, NY 14240 US
(716) 845-7000; *Fax:* (716) 845-7043
www.wned.org
info@wned.org
License: Buffalo, Erie County, NY held by Western New York Public Broadcasting Assoc.
Nat'l Network: PRI
Arbitron Metro Market: Buffalo, NY *TV Affiliate:* *WNED-TV affil; *Format:* Talk
Donald K. Boswell, President/CEO
Ron Santoria, Vice President of Broadcasting/Station Manager
Gordon Bayless, Vice President of Sales & Marketing
Gabe DiMaio, Programming Director
Jim Ranney, News Director
Sylvia Bennett, SVP ofDevelopment & Corporate Communications
Nathen Schneekloth, Webmaster

WWKB
01-01-1925; 1520 kHz AM; *Hrs Open:* 24; 50 kw-U, DA1; N42 46 10 W78 50 34
500 Corporate Parkway, Suite 500, Buffalo, NY 14226 US
(716) 843-0600; *Fax:* (716) 832-3323
www.espn1520.com
License: Buffalo, NY held by Entercom Buffalo License LLC.
Group Owner: Entercom Communications Corp.; (acq 12-13-99; grpsl)
Nat'l Reps: D & R Radio
Arbitron Metro Market: Buffalo, NY; *Format:* Sports, Talk; *Hrs. of News Programming:* news progmg 20 hrs wkly; *No. News Employees:* 4; *Target Audience:* 25-54.
Tim Wenger, Operations Dir
Gregory Reid, General Manager
Tim Wenger, Programming Director
Samantha Ogrodnik, Promotions Manager
Kevin Carr, Assistant Program Director
Tim Holly, Sales Director
Tell Vickers, Web Developer

WWWS
01-01-1934; 1400 kHz AM
500 Corporate Parkway, Suite 200, Buffalo, NY 14226 US
(716) 843-0600; *Fax:* (716) 843-3323
www.am1400solidgoldsoul.com
License: Buffalo, NY held by Entercom Buffalo License LLC.
Group Owner: Entercom Communications Corp.; (acq 12-13-99; grpsl)
Nat'l Reps: Katz Radio
Arbitron Metro Market: Buffalo, NY; *Format:* Oldies; *Target Audience:* 35-54.
Greg Reid, General Manager
Tim Holly, Sales Director
Sue O'Neil, Programming Director
Samantha Ogrodnik, Promotions Director
Tom Karvelis, Chief Engineer
TellyVickers, Web Developer
Matt Giansante, Internet Sales

WYRK
11-14-1962; 106.5 MHz FM; 50 kw; 466 ft.; N42 53 10 W78 52 25
14 Lafayette Square, Buffalo, NY 14203 US
(716) 852-7444; *Fax:* (716) 852-5683
www.wyrk.com
License: Buffalo, Erie County, NY
Group Owner: Townsquare Media; (acq 12-15-2006; grpsl)
Nat'l Reps: Katz Radio; *Wire Services:* UPI
Arbitron Metro Market: Buffalo-Niagara; *Format:* Country; *Target Audience:* 25-54; adults
Jeff Silver, Operations Dir
Ross DiFranco, Director of Sales
Wendy Lynn, Programming Director
Dean Sarago, Promotions Manager
Bob Hill, News Director

Calcium

WOTT
01-01-2009; 94.1 MHz FM; 21.5 kw; 354 ft.; N43 58 0 W75 48 11
199 Wealtha Avenue, Watertown, NY 13601-1837 US
(315) 786-9552; *Fax:* (315) 782-0312
www.94rockwott.com
lancer.rockradio@gmail.com
License: Calcium, Jefferson County, NY held by Community Broadcasters LLC.
Group Owner: Community Broadcasters LLC; (acq 1-8-2009; $200,000 for CP)
Arbitron Metro Market: Calcium, NY
James Leven, President
Jim Leven, General Manager
Lance Hale, Programming Director

Calverton-Roanoke

WPTY
05-27-1998; 105.3 MHz FM; *Hrs Open:* 24; 0.66 kw; Ant 607 ft.; N40 51 18 W72 46 12
3075 Veterans Memorial Hwy., Suite 201, Ronkonkoma, NY 11779
(631) 648-2500; *Fax:* (631) 648-2510
www.party105.com
License: Calverton-Roanoke, Suffolk County, NY held by JVC Media LLC
Group Owner: JVC Broadcasting; (acq 10-2-98).
Nat'l Reps: Christal
Arbitron Metro Market: New York; *Format:* Contemporary Hits/Top 40
Bruce Shepard, Director of Sales

Canajoharie

***WCAN**
10-01-1988; 93.3 MHz FM; *Hrs Open:* 24; 6 kw; 269 ft.; N42 53 46 W74 35 45 *Rebroadcasts:* Rebroadcasts WAMC-FM Albany 100%
318 Central Avenue, Albany, NY 12206 US
(518) 465-5233(800) 323-9262; *Fax:* (518) 432-6974
www.wamc.org
mail@wamc.org
License: Canajoharie, Montgomery County, NY held by WAMC.
Group Owner: WAMC/Northeast Public Radio
Nat'l Network: PRI; NPR; *Wire Services:* AP
Arbitron Metro Market: Albany, NY; *Format:* News, Talk *Special Programming:* Jazz 17 hrs, folk 7 hrs wkly; *Hrs. of News Programming:* News progmg 48 hrs wkly; *Target Audience:* General.
Alan Chartock, President/CEO
Selma Kaplan, Operations Dir
Stefanie Abel, Sales & Development Manager
Katie Britton, Programming Director
Ian Pickus, News Director
Joe Donahue, Vice President of News & Programming

Canandaigua

WCGR
04-05-1961; 1550 kHz AM; *Hrs Open:* 6 AM-6 PM; 0.25 kw-D, NDD; N42 52 52 W77 15 2
P.O. Box 155, Canandaigua, NY 14424 US
(315) 781-7000; *Fax:* (315) 781-7700
www.k1017.com/Home.html
License: Canandaigua, NY
Arbitron Metro Market: Geneva, NY; *Format:* News, News/Talk, 86; *Hrs. of News Programming:* news progmg 10 hrs wkly; *No. News Employees:* 1; *Target Audience:* General.
George Kimble, President
Alan Bishop, General Manager
Mike Smith, Programming Director
Ted Baker, News Director

***WCIY**
12-14-1992; 88.9 MHz FM; 0.68 kw; 1063 ft.; N42 44 44 W77 25 34 *Rebroadcasts:* Rebroadcasts WCIK(FM) Bath 100%
Mailing Address: PO Box 506, Bath, NY 14810 US
Second Address: 7634 Campbell Creek Rd., Bath, NY 14810
(607) 776-4151
www.fln.org
License: Canandaigua, NY held by Family Life Ministries Inc.
Group Owner: Family Life Network
Nat'l Network: Salem Radio Network; *Wire Services:* Metro Weather Service Inc.
Arbitron Metro Market: Bath, NY; *Format:* Christian; *Hrs. of News Programming:* news progmg 14 hrs wkly; *No. News Employees:* 3; *Target Audience:* 30-54.
Dave Margalotti, Operations Dir
Terese Main, Programming Director
Bob Price, News Director

WVOR
07-16-1974; 102.3 MHz FM; *Hrs Open:* 24; 3.4 kw; 282 ft.; N42 51 47 W77 19 22
100 Chestnut Street, Suite 1200, Rochester, NY 14604 US
(585) 393-1240; *Fax:* (585) 454-5081
www.radiosunny.com
License: Canandaigua, Ontario County, NY held by Citicasters Licenses Inc.
Group Owner: iHeartMedia; (acq 5-4-99; grpsl).
Arbitron Metro Market: Rochester, NY; *Format:* Adult Contemp; *Hrs. of News Programming:* News progmg 3 hrs wkly; *Target Audience:* 25-54.
Robert Morgan, Regional Market President
JP Hastings, Programming Director
Bonnie Porter, Sales Manager
Becki Efing, Sales Manager

WRSB
04-05-1997; 1310 kHz AM; 1 kw-D, DA2; 1 kw-N, DA2; N42 53 20 W77 19 9 *Rebroadcasts:* Rebroadcasts WASB(AM) Brockport 100%
20 Office Park Way, Pittsford, NY 14534 US
(877) 970-1310
sports@theteam.fm
License: Canandaigua, NY held by David Wolfe
Nat'l Network: ABC
Arbitron Metro Market: Rochester, NY; *Format:* Christian; *Target Audience:* Everyone; all ages
Dr. David Wolfe, General Manager
Gail Reed, Programming Director

Canton

WRCD
01-01-1997; 101.5 MHz FM; *Hrs Open:* 24; 50 kw; 453 ft.; N44 35 56 W74 46 24
P.O. Box 210, 2155 State Highway 420, Massena, NV 13662 US
(315) 769-3333; *Fax:* (315) 769-3299
www.1015thefox.com
studio@1015thefox.com
License: Canton, St. Lawrence County, NY held by Stephens Media Group-Massena LLC.
Group Owner: Stephens Family L.P.
Hrs. of News Programming: news progmg 7 hrs wkly; *No. News Employees:* 2; *Target Audience:* 30-50; country fans
Mark F. Gaines, General Manager

***WSLU**
12-01-1964; 89.5 MHz FM; *Hrs Open:* 24; 40 kw; 299 ft.; N44 32 1 W75 5 50
North Country Public Rad, Canton, NY 13617 US
(315) 229-5356; *Fax:* (315) 229-5373
www.ncpr.org
radio@ncpr.org
License: Canton, St. Lawrence County, NY held by St. Lawrence University.
Nat'l Network: NPR; PRI
Format: Variety/Diverse *Special Programming:* Gospel, jazz, class, folk, pub affrs, Black; *Hrs. of News Programming:* news progmg 35 hrs wkly; *No. News Employees:* 2; *Target Audience:* General.
Gary Knell, President/CEO
Shelly Pike, Operations Manager
Ellen Rocco, Station Manager
Jacqueline Sauter, Programming Director
Martha Foley, News Director
Robert Sauter, Chief Engineer
Sandra Demarest, Underwriting Director
Joel Hurd, Production Manager
Dale Hobson, Webmaster

WNCQ-FM
07-01-1984; 102.9 MHz FM; *Hrs Open:* 24; 23.5 kw; Ant 338 ft; N44 32 10 W75 05 46
1 Bridge Plaza, Suite 204, Ogdensburg, NY 89451
(315) 393-1220; *Fax:* (315) 393-3974
www.q1029.com
john@q1029.com
License: Canton, St. Lawrence County, NY held by Stephens Media Group-Ogdensburg LLC.

Group Owner: Stephens Family L.P.
Population Served: 100,000 *Target Audience:* 25-54; adults; *Adv. Rates:* 26; 22; 26; 22
John Winter, General Manager/Sales Manager
Dave Merz, Programming Director

***WREM**
88.7 MHz FM; 2.6 kw; Ant 233 ft; N44 32 01 W75 05 50
North Country Public Radio, St. Lawrence University, Canton, NY
(315) 229-5356; *Fax:* (315) 229-5373
www.northcountrypublicradio.org
License: Canton, St. Lawrence County, NY held by The St. Lawrence University.

Gary Knell, President/CEO
Shelly Pike, Operations Manager
Jackie Sauter, Programming Director
Martha Foley, News Director
Bob Sauter, Chief Engineer
Sandy Demarest, Development Director
Dale Hobson, Web Manager
Naomi Weller,Office Manager

Cape Vincent

WLYK
04-21-1997; 102.7 MHz FM; *Hrs Open:* 24; 6 kw; 328 ft.; N44 6 58 W76 20 21
3434 West Kilbourn Avenue, Milwaukee, WI 53208 US
(414) 935-3000; *Fax:* (414) 935-3015
www.vcyamerica.org
vcy@vcyamerica.org
License: Cape Vincent, Jefferson County, NY held by Border International Broadcasting Inc.
Group Owner: Clancy-Mance Communications; (acq 10-15-98; $50,000)
Nat'l Reps: Roslin
Arbitron Metro Market: Colorado Springs CO; *Format:* Christian, Religious
Vic Eliason, Operations Dir
Jim Schneider, Programming Director

***WMHI**
10-01-1990; 94.7 MHz FM; *Hrs Open:* 24; 6 kW; 331 ft; N44 02 42 W76 15 26 *Rebroadcasts:* Rebroadcasts WMHR(FM) Syracuse 98%
4044 Makyes Rd, Syracuse, NY 13215 USA
(315) 469-5051
www.marshillnetwork.org
info@marshillnetwork.org
License: Cape Vincent, Jefferson County, NY held by Mars Hill Broadcasting Co. Inc.
Group Owner: Mars Hill Network
Nat'l Network: Moody; Salem Radio Network; *Wire Services:* AP
Arbitron Metro Market: Cape Vincent, NY; *Format:* Christian; *Hrs. of News Programming:* News progmg 6 hrs wkly; *Target Audience:* General; Christian families
Wayne Taylor, General Manager
Mike Dwinell, Chief Engineer

***WSLZ**
88.1 MHz FM; 2 kw; 302 ft.; N44 6 58 W76 20 21 US
(315) 229-5356; *Fax:* (315) 229-5373
www.ncpr.org
radio@ncpr.org
License: Cape Vincent, Jefferson County, NY held by The St. Lawrence University.
Arbitron Metro Market: Cape Vincent, NY; *No. News Employees:* 4
Shelly Pike, Operations Dir
Ellen Rocco, General Manager
Ellen Rocco, Station Manager
Jackie Sauter, Programming Director
Martha Foley, News Director
Bob Sauter, Chief Engineer
Sandy Demarest, Development Director
Joel Hurd,Production Manager
June Peoples, Membership Director
Naomi Weller, Office Manager

Carthage

WTOJ
11-01-1984; 103.1 MHz FM; *Hrs Open:* 24; 1.8 kw; 594 ft.; N43 57 15 W75 43 45
199 Wealtha Ave., Watertown, NY 13601 US
(315) 782-1240; *Fax:* (315) 782-0312
www.magic103.com
jim_leven@commbroadcasters.com
License: Carthage, Jefferson County, NY held by Community Broadcasters LLC.
Group Owner: Community Broadcasters LLC; (acq 2-8-2007; grpsl)
Nat'l Reps: Roslin
Arbitron Metro Market: Watertown, NY; *Format:* Adult Contemp; *Target Audience:* 25-54.
James Leven, President/CEO
Kevin Keefe, General Manager
Ken Martin, Programming Director

Catskill

WCKL
02-06-1970; 560 kHz AM; *Hrs Open:* 24; 1 kw-D, DA2; 0.043 kw-N, DA2; N42 12 3 W73 50 9
P.O. Box 1345, Hudson, NY 12534 US
www.familybroadcasting.net
License: Catskill, NY held by Family Broadcasting And Media LLC
Arbitron Metro Market: Mid-Hudson Region; *Format:* Talk
Tim Allen, General Manager

WCTW
09-01-1990; 98.5 MHz FM; *Hrs Open:* 24; 4.7 kw; 374 ft.; N42 12 3 W73 50 9
5620 Route 9g, Hudson, NY 12534 US
(518) 828-5006; *Fax:* (518) 828-1080
www.985thecat.com
billwilliams@iheartmedia.com
License: Catskill, Greene County, NY held by CC Licenses LLC.
Group Owner: iHeartMedia; (acq 1-17-2002; grpsl)
Nat'l Network: Fox News Radio; *Nat'l Reps:* Katz Radio; *Wire Services:* AP
Arbitron Metro Market: Hudson, NY; *Format:* Adult Contemp; *Hrs. of News Programming:* news progmg 7 hrs wkly; *No. News Employees:* 1; *Target Audience:* 25-44; female
Chris Marino, Senior Vice President of Programming
Chuck Benfer, Market President
Rob VanDerbeck, Senior Vice President of Sales
Bill Williams, Programming Director
Elise Penge, Promotions Director
Deirdre Burns, Digital ContentDirector

Cazenovia

***WITC**
04-01-1978; 88.9 MHz FM; *Hrs Open:* Noon-midnight; 0.13 kw; 33 ft.; N42 55 53 W75 51 15
22 Sullivan Street, Cazenovia, NY 13035 US
(315) 655-7154; *Fax:* (315) 655-7208
License: Cazenovia, Madison County, NY held by Cazenovia College.
Format: Alternative *Special Programming:* News/talk 3 hrs, div 10 hrs wkly; *Hrs. of News Programming:* News progmg 3 hrs wkly; *Target Audience:* 15-35; college & young area residents
Wayne Westervelt, Director of Communications

Center Moriches

WJVC
03-03-1997; 96.1 MHz FM; *Hrs Open:* 24; 2.65 kw; Ant 499 ft; N40 51 08 W72 45 55
3075 Veterans Memorial Hwy., Suite 201, Ronkonkoma, NY 11779
(631) 648-2500; *Fax:* (631) 648-2510
www.licountry.com
License: Center Moriches, Suffolk County, NY held by JVC Media LLC
Group Owner: JVC Broadcasting; acq 1-13-2004; $3.75 million).
Format: Country
John Caracciolo, President
Bruce Shepard, Director of Sales
Ron Reeve, Chief Engineer

Champlain

WCHP
08-20-1985; 760 kHz AM; *Hrs Open:* Sunrise-sunset
137 Rapids Road, Champlain, NY 12919 US
(518) 298-2800; *Fax:* (518) 298-2604
www.wchp.com
wchp@primelink1.net
License: Champlain, NY held by Champlain Radio Inc.
Arbitron Metro Market: Detroit, MI; *Format:* Talk, Religious
Special Programming: Fr, Sp; *Target Audience:* 25 plus.
Tonya Billiter, Operations Dir
Teri Billiter, General Manager
Brandi Lloyd, Programming Director

Chateaugay

WYUL
04-15-1997; 94.7 MHz FM; *Hrs Open:* 24; 50 kW; 449 ft.; N44 46 56 W74 13 9
86 Porter Rd, Malone, NY 12953 USA
(800) 947-0947
www.947hits.com
License: Chateaugay, Franklin County, NY held by Cartier Communications Inc.
Group Owner: Martz Communications Group
Arbitron Metro Market: Chateaugay, NY; *Format:* Contemporary Hits/Top 40, Urban Contemporary
Tim Martz, CEO/COO
Michael Boldt, General Manager
Kim Kiser, General Sales Mgr
Jonathan Steele, Programming Director
Marty Lamarre, Promotions Manager

Cheektowaga

WECK
08-01-1956; 1230 kHz AM; 1 kw-D, ND1; 1 kw-N, ND1; N42 55 27 W78 46 41
2900 Genesee Street, Buffalo, NY 14225 US
(716) 783-9120; *Fax:* (716) 783-9121
www.breezebuffalo.com/
License: Cheektowaga, NY held by Culver Communications II Inc.
Nat'l Network: Westwood One; *Nat'l Reps:* Christal
Arbitron Metro Market: Buffalo, NY; *Format:* Talk *Special Programming:* Pol 2 hrs wkly; *Target Audience:* 35-64.
Richard Greene, President
Tom Schuh, Marketing Specialist

Chenango Bridge

WWYL
07-01-1996; 104.1 MHz FM; 0.93 kw; 833 ft.; N42 3 29 W75 57 15
59 Court Street, Binghamton, NY 13901 US
(607) 772-8400; *Fax:* (607) 772-9806
www.wild104fm.com
License: Chenango Bridge, Broome County, NY held by Townsquare Media Binghamton License LLC
Group Owner: Townsquare Media; (acq 6-9-99; grpsl).
Arbitron Metro Market: Binghamton, NY; *Format:* Contemporary Hits/Top 40
Mary Beth Walsh, General Manager
Eric Donaldson, General Sales Mgr
Randy Horton, Programming Director
Holly Fey, Promotions Manager
Heather Barrows, Traffic Manager

Cherry Valley

WJIV
01-01-1949; 101.9 MHz FM; *Hrs Open:* 24; 11.5 kw; 1024 ft.; N42 47 36 W74 41 41
1668 County Highway 50, Cherry Valley, NY 13320 US
(607) 264-3062; *Fax:* (607) 264-8277
www.wjivradio.com
wjiv@cbslradio.com
License: Cherry Valley, Otsego County, NY held by Christian Broadcasting System Ltd.
Group Owner: Christian Broadcasting System Ltd.; acq 6-5-00; $1.3 million).
Wire Services: UPI
Format: Talk, Religious; *Target Audience:* 25-54.
Alfin Maynor, Station Manager
Mark Zimmerman, Programming Director
Antoniette Parson, Business Manager

Clayton

***WRVH**
08-16-1989; 89.3 MHz FM; *Hrs Open:* 24; 7.9 kw; 86 ft.; N44 15 3 W76 1 50.6
7060 State Route 104, Oswego, NY 13126 US
(570) 312-3690; *Fax:* (315) 312-3174
www.wrvo.org
License: Clayton, Lycoming County, NY held by State University of New York
Group Owner: WRVO Public Media; (acq 12-1-2002; grpsl)
Nat'l Network: NPR
Arbitron Metro Market: Williamsport, P; *Format:* Adult Contemp; *Target Audience:* 25-54.
Michael S. Smeigh, General Manager
Jeff Windsor, Programming Director/Technical Operations Director
Catherine Loper, News Director

Bonnie Prime, Underwriting Manager
Pam Cantine, Business Operations Manager

Clifton Park

WDCD-FM

11-01-1985; 96.7 MHz FM; *Hrs Open:* 24; 4.7 kw; 328 ft; N42 52 44 W73 51 47
4243 Albany St., Albany, NY 19422
(518) 862-1540; *Fax:* (518) 862-1545
www.newlight967.com
info@crawfordbroadcasting.com
License: Clifton Park, Saratoga County, NY held by Kimtron Inc.
Group Owner: Crawford Broadcasting Co.; (acq 1996; $820,000).
Population Served: 850,000; *Arbitron Metro Market:* Albany-Schenectady-Troy, NY; *Format:* Christian, Religious; *Target Audience:* 30-64; financially capable
Donald Crawford, Jr., President
Kenneth Burns, Operations Dir
Nanette Foster, General Sales Mgr
Peter Kaye, Programming Director
David Groth, Chief Engineer

Clinton

*WHCL-FM

02-18-1963; 88.7 MHz FM; *Hrs Open:* 24; 0.27 kw; 95 ft.; N43 3 4 W75 24 24
% Office of Student Act., 198 College Hill Rd, Clinton, NY 13323 US
(315) 859-4200
www.whcl.org
mngrwhcl@hamilton.edu
License: Clinton, Oneida County, NY held by The Trustees of Hamilton College.
Format: Rock/AOR, Variety/Diverse *Special Programming:* Class 9 hrs, jazz 9 hrs, relg 2 hrs wkly; *Target Audience:* General.
Noelle Niznik, Station Manager

Clyde

*WCOV-FM

12-05-1995; 93.7 MHz FM; 3.8 kw; 328 ft.; N42 59 38 W76 51 59 *Rebroadcasts:* Rebroadcasts WCIK(FM) Bath 100%
Mailing Address: PO Box 506, Bath, NY 14810 US
Second Address: 7634 Campbell Creek Rd., Bath, NY 14810
(607) 776-4151
www.fln.org
License: Clyde, Wayne County, NY held by Family Life Ministries Inc.
Group Owner: Family Life Network; (acq 10-3-00).
Nat'l Network: Salem Radio Network; *Wire Services:* Metro Weather Service Inc.
Format: Christian; *Hrs. of News Programming:* news progmg 14 hrs wkly; *No. News Employees:* 3; *Target Audience:* 30-54.
Dave Margalotti, Operations Dir
Terese Main, Programming Director
Bob Price, News Director

Cobleskill

WQBJ

09-01-1986; 103.5 MHz FM; 50 kw; 492 ft.; N42 58 21 W74 29 30 *Rebroadcasts:* Rebroadcasts WQBK-FM Rensselaer 100%
1241 Kings Road, Schenectady, NY 12303 US
(518) 881-1515; *Fax:* (518) 881-1516
www.wqbk.com
License: Cobleskill, Schoharie County, NY
Group Owner: Townsquare Media; (acq 8-7-2000; grpsl)
Arbitron Metro Market: Albany-Schenectady-Troy, NY; *Format:* Rock/AOR; *Target Audience:* 18-49; general
Dan Austin, General Manager
Wes Styles, Programming Director
Bob O'Neal, Chief Engineer
Jennifer Moen, Digital Sales Manager

WSDE

07-01-1981; 1190 kHz AM; *Hrs Open:* 6 AM-sunset
813 East Main Street, #5, Cobbleskill, NY 12043 US
(518) 234-3400; *Fax:* (518) 234-4567
www.1190wsde.com
License: Cobleskill, NY held by Viva Communications Group LLC
Nat'l Network: CNN Radio
Arbitron Metro Market: Cobleskill, NY; *Format:* Classic Rock; *Target Audience:* General.
Ed Sherlock, President/General Manager
Bob Taylor, Operations/Traffic
Alla Horak, Office Manager

Cold Brook

*WMHU

91.1 MHz FM; 560 W; 470 ft.; N43 12 01 W74 53 17
4044 Makyes Rd, Syracuse, NY 13215 USA
(800) 677-1881
www.marshillnetwork.org
License: Cold Brook, Herkimer County, NY held by Mars Hill Broadcasting Co. Inc.
Group Owner: Mars Hill Network
Arbitron Metro Market: Cold Brook, NY; *Format:* Christian
Wayne Taylor, General Manager
Mike Dwinell, Chief Engineer

Conklin

WKGB-FM

02-11-1989; 92.5 MHz FM; *Hrs Open:* 24; 1.45 kw; 676 ft.; N42 6 48 W75 51 9
Suite 200, 776 Conklin Rd., Binghamton, NY 13903 US
(607) 584-5800; *Fax:* (607) 584-5900
www.925kgb.com
info@925kgb.com
License: Conklin, Broome County, NY held by CC Licenses LLC.
Group Owner: iHeartMedia; (acq 4-14-2000; grpsl)
Nat'l Reps: D & R Radio
Arbitron Metro Market: Binghamton, NY; *Format:* Classic Rock, Rock/AOR *Special Programming:* Jazz 2 hrs, farm one hr wkly; *Hrs. of News Programming:* News progmg one hr wkly; *Target Audience:* 25-49; baby boomerswho grew up with rock and roll of the 60s & 70s
Tom Barney, Market President
Jim Free, Operations Manager
Lisa Doyle, Promotions Director

Copenhagen

WBDR

01-01-1994; 106.7 MHz FM; *Hrs Open:* 24; 1.8 kw; 1191 ft.; N43 52 47 W75 43 11
199 Wealtha Ave, Watertown, NY 13601 US
(315) 782-1240; *Fax:* (315) 782-0312
License: Copenhagen, Lewis County, NY held by Community Broadcasters LLC.
Group Owner: Community Broadcasters LLC; (acq 2-8-2007; grpsl)
Nat'l Reps: Roslin
Arbitron Metro Market: Watertown, NY; *Format:* Contemporary Hits/Top 40
James Leven, President/CEO
Todd Dalesandro, Operations Dir
Kevin Keefe, General Manager

Corinth

WFFG-FM

06-26-1967; 107.1 MHz FM; *Hrs Open:* 24; 2.85 kw; 482 ft.; N43 14 40 W73 46 18
89 Everts Avenue, Queensbury, NY 12804 US
(518) 793-7733; *Fax:* (518) 793-0838
www.froggy107.com
License: Corinth, Saratoga County, NY held by 6 Johnson Road Licenses Inc.
Group Owner: Pamal Broadcasting Ltd.; (acq 4-1-2004; grpsl).
Format: Country; *Hrs. of News Programming:* news progmg 2 hrs wkly; *No. News Employees:* 1; *Target Audience:* 18-54.; *Adv. Rates:* 30; 28; 30; 15.
Tom Jacobson, General Manager/Sales Manager
Chris O'Neil, Programming Director

Corning

WCBA

11-01-1948; 1350 kHz AM; *Hrs Open:* 24; 1 kw-D, ND1; 0.037 kw-N, ND1; N42 6 59 W77 2 24
21 East Market Street, Suite 101, Corning, NY 14830-2650 US
(607) 937-8181; *Fax:* (607) 962-1138
License: Corning, NY held by Great Radio LLC
Nat'l Network: Westwood One; *Nat'l Reps:* Roslin
Arbitron Metro Market: Corning, NY; *Format:* Sports; *Target Audience:* 50 plus.
Frank Acomb, Operations Dir
Jamie Evans, General Manager
Scott Benjamin, Sales Manager
James Bogart, Production Director
Betty Coccho, Business Manager

WGMM

02-01-1989; 98.7 MHz FM; *Hrs Open:* 24; 1.2 kw; 722 ft.; N42 8 31 W77 4 40 *Rebroadcasts:* Rebroadcasts WENY-FM Elmira 100%
21 East Market Street, Suite 101, Corning, NY 14830-2650 US
(607) 937-8181; *Fax:* (607) 962-1138
www.987gemfm.com/
wenyfranklyspeaking@gmail.com
License: Corning, Steuben County, NY held by Sound Communications LLC
Group Owner: Sound Communications LLC; (acq 7-14-2008; grpsl)
Nat'l Network: ABC; *Nat'l Reps:* McGavren Guild
Arbitron Metro Market: Corning, NY; *Format:* Adult Contemp
Frank Acomb, Operations Dir
Jamie Evans, General Manager
Scott Benjamin, Sales Manager
Betty Coccho, Business Manager
James Bogart, Production Director

WENI

11-01-1949; 1450 kHz AM; 1 kw-D, ND1; 0.93 kw-N, ND1; N42 6 59 W77 2 24 *Rebroadcasts:* Rebroadcasts WENY(AM) Elmira 100%.
21 East Market Street, Suite 101, Corning, NY 14830-2650 US
(607) 962-4646; *Fax:* (607) 962-1138
cnj@route81radio.com
License: Corning, NY held by Uound Communications LLC
Group Owner: Sound Communications LLC; (acq 7-14-2008; grpsl)
Nat'l Network: USA; *Nat'l Reps:* McGavren Guild
Arbitron Metro Market: Corning, NY; *Format:* News, News/Talk, 86; *Target Audience:* 25-64.
Frank Acomb, Operations Dir
Jamie Evans, General Manager
Scott Benjamin, Sales Manager
Betty Coccho, Business Manager
James Bogart, Production Director

WNKI

05-01-1947; 106.1 MHz FM; 40 kw; 531 ft.; N42 9 43 W77 2 15
1685 Four Mile Drive, Williamsport, PA 17701 US
(607) 732-4400; *Fax:* (607) 732-7774
www.wink106.com
License: Corning, Steuben County, NY held by Community Broadcasters LLC
Group Owner: Community Broadcasters LLC; (acq 12-1-02; grpsl).
Nat'l Reps: Christal
Arbitron Metro Market: Elmira, NY; *Format:* Adult Contemp; *Hrs. of News Programming:* news progmg one hr wkly; *No. News Employees:* 1; *Target Audience:* 25-54; women
Scott Free, Operations Dir
Smitty O'Loughlin, General Manager
Brian Povancher, General Sales Mgr
Scott Free, Programming Director

*WSQE

01-01-1995; 91.1 MHz FM; *Hrs Open:* 24; 3.6 kw; 653 ft.; N42 6 20 W76 52 17 *Rebroadcasts:* Rebroadcasts WSKG-FM Binghamton 100%
P.O. Box 3000, Binghamton, NY 13902 US
(607) 729-0100
www.wskg.com
License: Corning, Steuben County, NY held by WSKG Public Telecommunications Council.
Nat'l Network: NPR; PRI; AP Radio
Arbitron Metro Market: Elmira-Corning, NY; *Format:* News *Special Programming:* Jazz, folk 5 hrs wkly; *Hrs. of News Programming:* news progmg 33 hrs wkly; *No. News Employees:* 1; *Target Audience:* General.
Brian Sickora, President/CEO
Gregory Keeler, Programming/Operations Director
Matt Richmond, News Director
Caroline Basso, Director of Development
Joshua B. Ludzki, Manager of Marketing & Promotions

Cornwall

WWLE

11-22-1969; 1170 kHz AM; 0.8 kw-D, DAD; N41 26 24 W74 4 25
Mailing Address: 1153 Route 44-55, Clintondale, NY 12515 US
Second Address: P.O. Box 2130, Newburgh, NY 12550
(845) 569-7010; *Fax:* (845) 562-1348
License: Cornwall, NY held by 1170 Broadcast Radio Inc.
Nat'l Network: USA
Arbitron Metro Market: Newburgh-Middletown, NY; *Format:* News, News/Talk, 86 *Special Programming:* Farm one hr wkly
Charles Stewart, General Manager

Cortland

WIII

11-15-1947; 99.9 MHz FM; *Hrs Open:* 24; 26 kw; 682 ft.; N42 33 23 W76 9 19
1751 Hanshaw Road, Ithaca, NY 14850 US

(607) 257-6400; *Fax:* (607) 257-6497
www.i100rocks.com
i100@wiii.com
License: Cortland, Cortland County, NY held by Saga Communications of New England LLC.
Group Owner: Saga Communications Inc.; (acq 9-1-2007; $4 million with co-located AM)
Nat'l Reps: Katz Radio
Arbitron Metro Market: Ithaca, NY; *Format:* Classic Rock; *Hrs. of News Programming:* news progmg one hr wkly; *No. News Employees:* 1; *Target Audience:* 25-54; men
Chris Allinger, Operations Manager/Programming Director
Chet Osadchey, General Manager
Connie Fairfax-Ozmun, Promotions/Marketing Director
Brian Kerkan, Chief Engineer
Kat Walters, Production Director

***WYBY**
11-15-1947; 920 kHz AM; *Hrs Open:* 24; 1 kw-D, DAN; 0.5 kw-N, DAN; N42 33 22 W76 9 18
1064 James St., Syracuse, NY 13203 US
(800) 888-7077
www.bbnradio.org
bbn@bbnmedia.org
License: Cortland, Cortland County, NY held by Bible Broadcasting Network Inc.
Group Owner: Bible Broadcasting Network; (acq 9-1-2007; donation)
Arbitron Metro Market: Ithaca, NY; *Format:* Religious
Lowell Davey, President
Jason Padgett, Operations Manager

***WSUC-FM**
11-17-1976; 90.5 MHz FM; *Hrs Open:* 24; 0.21 kw; -59 ft.; N42 35 48 W76 11 23
Graham Ave Brockway Hall, Cortland, NY 13045 US
(607) 753-2936; *Fax:* (607) 753-2807
License: Cortland, Cortland County, NY held by State University of New York.
Nat'l Network: AP Radio
Format: Variety/Diverse; *Target Audience:* 12-50.

Dannemora

***WKVJ**
01-01-2005; 89.7 MHz FM; *Hrs Open:* 24; 4.4 kw; 1096 ft.; N44 34 24 W73 40 31
Mailing Address: 1601 Belvedere Road, 204 E, West Palm Beach, FL 33406 US
Second Address: Box 888, Studio, Champlain, NY 12919
(800) 525-5683; *Fax:* (916) 251-1650
www.klove.com
klove@klove.com
License: Dannemora, Clinton County, NY held by American Educational Broadcasting Inc.
Arbitron Metro Market: Dannemora, NY; *Format:* Christian
Darrell Chambliss, Chairman
Mike Novak, President and CEO
Fred Hodges, General Manager
Eric Allen, General Sales Mgr
David Pierce, Chief Creative Officer and Programming Director
Ed Lenane, News Director
Sam Wallington,Engineering Dir
Marya Morgan, News Reporter
Richard Hunt, News Reporter
Alan Mason, Chief Operating Officer
Dan Antonelli, Chief Business Development Officer
Eric Moser, Chief Financial Officer
Brian Burger, Vice President of HumanResources

WNMR
01-01-2008; 107.1 MHz FM; 1 kw; 276 ft.; N44 43 15.8 W73 44 10.5 *Rebroadcasts:* Simulcast with WCLX(FM) Westport 100% US
(804) 759-4000
License: Dannemora, Clinton County, NY held by Radioactive LLC.
Group Owner: Radioactive LLC
Arbitron Metro Market: Dannemora, NY; *Format:* Classic Rock
Benjamin Homel, President

Dansville

WDNY
10-20-1978; 1400 kHz AM; *Hrs Open:* 19; 0.88 kw-D, ND1; 1 kw-N, ND1; N42 32 19 W77 40 57
195 Main Street, Dansville, NY 14437 US
(585) 335-9369; *Fax:* (585) 335-9677
www.wdnyradio.com
License: Dansville, NY held by Genesee Media Corp.
Nat'l Network: Jones Radio Networks; Westwood One
Arbitron Metro Market: Rochester, NY; *Format:* Contemporary Hits/Top 40; *Hrs. of News Programming:* news progmg 8 hrs wkly; *No. News Employees:* 1; *Adv. Rates:* 21; 12; 12; 12.
Brian McGlynn, President
Ed Trefzger, Vice President/General Manager

WMRV
03-01-1990; 93.9 MHz FM; *Hrs Open:* 24; 0.57 kw; 741 ft.; N42 30 45 W77 38 7
195 Main St., Dansville, NY 14437 US
(585) 335-9369; *Fax:* (585) 335-9677
www.wdnyradio.com
License: Dansville, Livingston County, NY held by Genesee Media Corp.
Nat'l Network: Jones Radio Networks; Westwood One
Arbitron Metro Market: Rochester, NY; *Format:* Adult Contemp *Special Programming:* Relg one hr, big band 3 hrs, sports 4 hrs wkly; *Hrs. of News Programming:* news progmg 8 hrs wkly; *No. News Employees:* 1 *TargetAudience:* 25-54.; *Adv. Rates:* 21; 14; 14; 12
Brian McGlynn, President
Ed Trefzger, Vice President/General Manager

DeRuyter

WOLF-FM
01-01-1948; 105.1 MHz FM; 42 kw; Ant 541 ft; N42 46 58 W75 50 28
500 Plum St., Suite 400, Syracuse, NY 13204
(315) 472-9797; *Fax:* (315) 472-2323
License: DeRuyter, Madison County, NY held by Foxfur Communications LLC
Population Served: 145,151; *Arbitron Metro Market:* Syracuse, NY; *Format:* Country; *Target Audience:* 18-40; general
Sam Furco, General Manager
John Hunt, Director of Sales
Skip Clark, Programming Director

WOLF-FM
105.1 MHz FM; 33000 w; 607 ft; N42 46 58 W75 50 28
401 W. Kirkpatrick Street, Syracuse, NY 13204
(315)472-0222; *Fax:* (315)478-7745
www.1051thewolf.com
License: DeRuyter, Madison County, NY
Group Owner: Foxfur Communications LLC

Sam Furco, Station Manager
John Hunt, Sales Manager
Skip Clark, Programming Director
Taylor Smith, Promotions Director

Delhi

WDHI
03-16-1992; 100.3 MHz FM; *Hrs Open:* 16; 1.6 kw; 643 ft.; N42 22 43 W74 50 22
34 Chestnut Street, Oneonta, NY 13820 US
(607) 432-1030; *Fax:* (607) 432-6909
www.wdhifm.com
George.Wells@townsquaremedia.com
License: Delhi, Delaware County, NY held by Townsquare Media Oneonta License LLC
Group Owner: Townsquare Media; (acq 10-22-2004; grpsl)
Nat'l Network: USA
Arbitron Metro Market: Delhi, NY; *Format:* Contemporary Hits/Top 40
Wade Lott, General Manager
Eric Malanoski, Brand Manager

WTBD-FM
01-01-2008; 97.5 MHz FM; 6 kw; 328 ft.; N42 14 9 W74 57 12
34 Chestnut Street, Oneonta, NY 13820 US
(607) 432-1030; *Fax:* (607) 432-6909
www.wtbdfm.com
License: Delhi, Delaware County, NY held by Townsquare Media Oneonta License LLC
Group Owner: Townsquare Media
Arbitron Metro Market: Delhi, NY
George Wells, General Manager/Programming Director
Charlene Sugihara, Director of Sales

Depew

WBLK
12-01-1964; 93.7 MHz FM; 47 kw; 505 ft.; N42 53 10 W78 52 25
14 Lafayette Square, Buffalo, NY 14203 US
(716) 852-9393; *Fax:* (716) 852-9390
www.wblk.com
License: Depew, Erie County, NY
Group Owner: Townsquare Media; (acq 12-15-2006; grpsl)
Nat'l Network: CBS Radio; *Nat'l Reps:* Katz Radio
Arbitron Metro Market: Buffalo, NY; *Format:* Urban Contemporary; *Target Audience:* General.
Chris Reynolds, Brand Manager
David Crumb, Director Of Sales
Amanda Tunis, Digital Sales Manager
Melissa Kory, Digital Managing Editor

Deposit

WIYN
01-16-1991; 94.7 MHz FM; *Hrs Open:* 16; 0.77 kw; 643 ft.; N42 1 44 W75 28 25
34 Chestnut Street, Oneonta, NY 13820 US
(607) 432-1030; *Fax:* (607) 432-6909
info@centralnewyorkradio.com
License: Deposit, Broome County, NY held by Townsquare Media Oneonta License LLC
Group Owner: Townsquare Media; (acq 10-22-2004; grpsl)
Arbitron Metro Market: Binghamton, NY; *Format:* Oldies; *Target Audience:* 28-55.
George Wells, General Manager/Programming Director
Charlene Sugihara, Director of Sales

Dundee

WFLR
10-01-1956; 1570 kHz AM; *Hrs Open:* 24; 5 kw-D, ND1; 0.442 kw-N, ND1; N42 32 40 W76 59 35
3568 Lenox Rd., Geneva, NY 14456 US
(607) 243-7158; *Fax:* (607) 243-7662
www.flradiogroup.com
License: Dundee, NY held by Finger Lakes Radio Group Inc.
Group Owner: Finger Lakes Radio Group; (acq 3-5-2004; $600,000 with co-located FM)
Nat'l Network: Motor Racing Net
Format: Country *Special Programming:* Relg 5 hrs wkly; *Hrs. of News Programming:* news progmg 40 hrs wkly; *No. News Employees:* 1; *Target Audience:* 25-55.
Frank Lischak, General Sales Mgr
Mike Smith, Programming Director
Joe Nittler, News Director

Dunkirk

WDOE
12-24-1949; 1410 kHz AM
4561 Willow Road, Dunkirk, NY 14048 US
(716) 366-1410(716) 366-8580; *Fax:* (716) 366-1416
www.wdoe1410.com
community@wdoe1410.com
License: Dunkirk, NY held by Chadwick Bay Broadcasting Corp.
Nat'l Network: ABC
Arbitron Metro Market: Dunkirk, NY; *Format:* News, News/Talk, 64, Talk *Special Programming:* Pol 6 hrs, Sp 2 hrs wkly; *Hrs. of News Programming:* News progmg 12 hrs wkly; *Target Audience:* 45-65.
John Bulmer, President
Mark James, Operations Dir
Patti Pritchard, General Manager/Sales Manager
Dave Rowley, News Director

E. Syracuse

WSIV
12-06-1955; 1540 kHz AM; *Hrs Open:* 24; 1 kw-D, ND2; N43 5 40 W76 2 0
7095 Myers Road East, Syracuse, NY 13057 US
(315) 656-2231; *Fax:* (315) 656-2259
www.wsiv1540.com
info@wsiv1540.com
License: E. Syracuse, NY held by CRAM Communications L.L.C.
Group Owner: Cram Communications LLC; (acq 1-6-97; $900,000 with WVOA(FM) DeRuyter)
Arbitron Metro Market: Syracuse, NY; *Format:* Religious *Special Programming:* Black 20 hrs, Gospel music; *Adv. Rates:* 6; 6; 6; 4
Charles Cannon, Radio Host

East Hampton

WEHN
03-01-1993; 96.9 MHz FM; *Hrs Open:* 24; 4.3 kw; 384 ft.; N40 59 37 W72 10 19 *Rebroadcasts:* Simulcast with WEHM(FM) Southampton 100%
P.O. Box 157, Water Mill, NY 11976 US
(631) 267-7800; *Fax:* (631) 267-1018
www.wehm.com
License: East Hampton, Suffolk County, NY held by AAA Licensing LLC.
Group Owner: Long Island Radio Broadcasting LLC; (acq 5-31-2000; grpsl).
Nat'l Network: CNN Radio

Arbitron Metro Market: Water Mill, NY; *Format:* Alternative; *Target Audience:* 24-54; upscale Hamptons residents and NYC second homeowners
Mike Raye, President/General Manager
Suzanne Wolfson, Sales Manager
Harry Wareing, Programming Director
Rebecca Cambell, Traffic Manager

Ellenville

WJIP
12-01-1964; 1370 kHz AM; 5 kw-D; N41 44 19 W74 23 48
20 Tucker Dr., Poughkeepsie, NY 12603
(845) 471-2300; *Fax:* (845) 471-2683
www.1450wkip.com
License: Ellenville, Ulster County, NY held by CC Licenses LLC.
Group Owner: iHeartMedia; (acq 7-14-2000; grpsl)
Nat'l Network: Fox News Radio; ABC News/Talk; Premiere Radio Networks; Talk Radio Network; *Nat'l Reps:* Katz Radio; *Wire Services:* AP
Population Served: 50,000 *Format:* News, News/Talk, 86; *Hrs. of News Programming:* 12 hours; *No. News Employees:* 1; *Target Audience:* 30-64.
Chris Marino, Senior Vice President of Programming
Chuck Benfer, Market President
Rob VanDerbeck, Senior Vice President of Sales
Cameron Hendrix, Programming Director
Elise Penge, Promotions Director
Dierdre Burns, Digital ContentDirector

WRWB-FM
08-01-1970; 99.3 MHz FM; *Hrs Open:* 24; 115 w; Ant 1,630 ft; N41 41 06 W74 21 23 *Rebroadcasts:* Simulcast with WRWD-FM Highland
20 Tucker Dr., Poughkeepsie, NY 12603 US
(845) 453-9734
www.wrwdcountry.com
License: Ellenville, Ulster County, NY held by CC Licenses LLC
Group Owner: iHeartMedia
Nat'l Network: Fox News Radio; *Nat'l Reps:* Katz Radio
Population Served: 400,000; *Arbitron Metro Market:* Newburgh-Middletown, NY (Mid-Hudson Valley); *Format:* Country; *Hrs. of News Programming:* 7 hours; *No. News Employees:* 1
Chuck Benfer, Market President
Chris Marino, Senior Vice President of Programming
Rob VanDerbeck, Senior Vice President of Sales
Marty Mitchell, Programming Director
Elise Penge, Promotions Director
Deirdre Burns, Digital ContentDirector

Elma

WLOF
11-09-1977; 101.7 MHz FM; 2.8 kw; 486 ft.; N42 46 58 W78 27 28
6325 Sheridan Drive, Williamsville, NY 14221 US
(716) 839-6117; *Fax:* (716) 839-0400
www.wlof.net
info@thestationofthecross.com
License: Elma, Wyoming County, NY held by Holy Family Communications Inc.
Group Owner: Holy Family Communications; acq 12-20-99; $655,000).
Arbitron Metro Market: Elma, NY; *Format:* Religious; *Target Audience:* 25-54; blue collar, housewives
Jim Wright, President/General Manager
Bill Havas, Technical Operations Manager
Kevin Spears, Station Manager
Gina Zanicky, Programming Director
Zach Krajacic, Vice President of Development, Marketing, and PR
Rick Paolini, BusinessManager
Sarah Buttino, Executive Assistant
Debbie Daigler, Administrative Assistant

Elmira

*WCIH
07-31-1989; 90.3 MHz FM; *Hrs Open:* 24; 4 kw; 527 ft.; N41 53 39 W76 51 32 *Rebroadcasts:* Rebroadcasts WCIK(FM) Bath 100%
Mailing Address: Box 506, Bath, NY 14810 US
Second Address: 7634 Campbell Creek Rd., Bath, NY 14810
(607) 776-4151
www.fln.org
License: Elmira, Chemung County, NY held by Family Life Ministries Inc.
Group Owner: Family Life Network
Nat'l Network: Salem Radio Network; *Wire Services:* Metro Weather Service Inc.
Arbitron Metro Market: Elmira-Corning, NY; *Format:* Christian; *Hrs. of News Programming:* news progmg 14 hrs wkly; *No. News Employees:* 3; *Target Audience:* 30-54
Dave Margalotti, Operations Dir
Terese Main, Programming Director
Bob Price, News Director

*WECW
01-19-1959; 107.7 MHz FM; 0.009 kw; -338 ft.; N42 5 48 W76 49 0
One Park Place, Elmira, NY 14901 US
(607) 735-1800
wecw@elmira.edu
License: Elmira, Chemung County, NY held by Elmira College.
Arbitron Metro Market: Elmira, NY; *Format:* Classic Rock, Contemporary Hits/Top 40; *Target Audience:* 18-30.
Mary Swasta, Station Manager

WELM
04-01-1947; 1410 kHz AM; *Hrs Open:* 24; 5 kw-D, DAN; 1 kw-N, DAN; N42 7 11 W76 48 37
1705 Lake Street, Elmira, NY 14901 US
(607) 733-5626(607) 732-1400; *Fax:* (607) 733-5627
www.welm1410.com/
License: Elmira, NY held by Pembrook Pines Elmira Ltd.
Group Owner: Pembrook Pines Media Group; (acq 10-1-77).
Nat'l Network: CBS; ESPN Radio
Arbitron Metro Market: Elmira, NY; *Format:* Sports *Special Programming:* Relg one hr wkly; *Hrs. of News Programming:* news progmg 10 hrs wkly; *No. News Employees:* 1; *Target Audience:* 25-54.
Robert Pfuntner, CEO/General Manager
Steve Mills, Operations Dir
Henry Stoll, Sales Manager
Shelly Rich, Programming Director

WENY
01-01-1939; 1230 kHz AM; *Hrs Open:* 24 *Rebroadcasts:* Rebroadcasts WENI(AM) Corning 100%
21 East Market Street, Suite 101, Elmira, NY 14803 US
(607) 937-8181; *Fax:* (607) 962-1138
License: Elmira, NY held by Sound Communications LLC
Group Owner: Sound Communications LLC; (acq 7-14-2008; grpsl)
Nat'l Reps: McGavren Guild
Arbitron Metro Market: Elmira, NY; *Format:* News, News/Talk, 86; *Target Audience:* 30 plus.
Frank Acomb, Operations Manager
Jamie Evans, General Manager
Scott Benjamin, Sales Manager
Betty Coccho, Business Manager

WENY-FM
08-15-1965; 92.7 MHz FM; *Hrs Open:* 24; 1.2 kw; 715 ft.; N42 1 55 W76 47 2 *Rebroadcasts:* Simulcast With WENI-FM Big Flats 100%
21 East Market Street, Suite 101, Corning, NY 14830-2650 US
(607) 937-8181; *Fax:* (607) 962-1138
www.magic927977.net
cnj@route81radio.com
License: Elmira, Chemung County, NY held by Sound Communications LLC
Group Owner: Sound Communications LLC; (acq 7-14-2008; grpsl)
Nat'l Network: ABC
Arbitron Metro Market: Elmira, NY; *Format:* Adult Contemp

WLVY
08-01-1966; 94.3 MHz FM; 1.15 kw; 745 ft.; N42 7 51 W76 47 26
1705 Lake Road, Elmira, NY 14901 US
(607) 733-5626; *Fax:* (607) 733-5627
www.94rockfm.com
License: Elmira, Chemung County, NY
Group Owner: Pembrook Pines Media Group
Nat'l Network: Westwood One *Regional Reps:* Pembrook Pines
Arbitron Metro Market: Elmira, NY; *Format:* Adult Contemp, Contemporary Hits/Top 40; *Hrs. of News Programming:* news progmg 5 hrs wkly; *No. News Employees:* 1; *Target Audience:* 18-36; young vibrant adults
Robert Pfunter, CEO/General Manager
Michele Monks, General Sales Mgr
Steven Mills, Programming Director
Donna Bogart, News Director

Elmira Hts-Horsehds

WEHH
07-04-1956; 1600 kHz AM; *Hrs Open:* 24
1705 Lake Road, Elmira, NY 14901 US
(607) 733-5626; *Fax:* (607) 733-5627
wehhelmira.com
License: Elmira Hts-Horsehds, NY held by Pembrook Pines Elmira Ltd.
Group Owner: Pembrook Pines Media Group; (acq 5-19-99).
Nat'l Network: CBS Radio
Arbitron Metro Market: Elmira Heights, NY; *Format:* Adult Contemp; *Hrs. of News Programming:* News progmg 2 hrs wkly; *Target Audience:* 45 plus; upscale adults
Robert Pfuntner, CEO/General Manager
Michele Monks, General Sales Mgr
Steven Mills, Programming Director

Endicott

WENE
09-01-1947; 1430 kHz AM; *Hrs Open:* 24; 5 kw-D, DAN; 5 kw-N, DAN; N42 4 56 W76 1 53
320 North Jensen Road, Vestal, NY 13850 US
(607) 584-5800; *Fax:* (607) 584-5900
www.foxsports1430.com
License: Endicott, NY held by CC Licenses LLC.
Group Owner: iHeartMedia; (acq 4-14-2000; grpsl)
Nat'l Network: Westwood One; *Nat'l Reps:* McGavren Guild
Arbitron Metro Market: Endicott, NY; *Format:* Sports, Talk; *Hrs. of News Programming:* news progmg 28 hrs wkly; *No. News Employees:* 2; *Target Audience:* 35 plus.; *Adv. Rates:* 20; 15; 15; 5
Tom Barney, Market President
Jon Scaptura, Chief Engineer

WBNW-FM
01-01-1969; 105.7 MHz FM; *Hrs Open:* 24; 35 kw; 571 ft.; N42 8 17 W75 59 59
320 N. Jensen Rd., Vestal, NY 13850 US
(607) 584-5800; *Fax:* (607) 584-5900
www.radionow1057.com
matt@radionow1057.com
License: Endicott, Broome County, NY held by CC Licenses LLC
Group Owner: iHeartMedia
Arbitron Metro Market: Binghamton, NY; *Format:* Contemporary Hits/Top 40; *Target Audience:* 18-34.; *Adv. Rates:* 35; 25; 25; 10
Jim Free, Operations Manager
Tom Barney, General Manager
Matt Gapske, Programming Director

Endwell

WBBI
01-01-1998; 107.5 MHz FM; 2.2 kw; 545 ft.; N42 8 17 W75 59 59
320 North Jensen Road, Vestal, NY 13850 US
(607) 584-5800; *Fax:* (607) 584-5900
www.b1075country.com
License: Endwell, Broome County, NY held by CC Licenses LLC.
Group Owner: iHeartMedia; (acq 4-14-2000; grpsl)
Format: Country; *No. News Employees:* 1; *Target Audience:* 20-55.
Jim Free, Operations Manager
Tom Barney, General Sales Mgr
Tom Scott, Programming Director

Essex

WCPV
10-01-1994; 101.3 MHz FM; 1 kw; 797 ft.; N44 24 12 W73 26 2
265 Hegeman Avenue, Colchester, VT 05446 US
(802) 654-0093; *Fax:* (802) 655-0478
www.1013espn.com
License: Essex, Essex County, NY held by Vox AM/FM LLC.
Group Owner: Vox AM/FM LLC; (acq 7-25-2008; grpsl)
Arbitron Metro Market: Burlington-Plattsburgh, VT-NY; *Format:* Classic Rock
Chris Villani, Operations/Programming Director
Ken Barlow, General Manager
Brian Crogan, General Sales Mgr

Fairport

WFKL
01-01-1993; 93.3 MHz FM; *Hrs Open:* 24; 4.4 kw; 384 ft.; N43 10 37 W77 28 39
28 East Main Street, 8th Floor, Rochester, NY 14614 US
(585) 399-5700; *Fax:* (585) 325-5139
License: Fairport, Monroe County, NY held by Stephens Media Group-Rochester LLC.
Group Owner: Stephens Family L.P.; (acq 7-14-2008; grpsl)
Nat'l Reps: Katz Radio
Arbitron Metro Market: Rochester, NY; *Format:* Oldies; *No. News Employees:* 1; *Target Audience:* 25-54; upscale
Mike Ninnie, General Manager
Laurie Zsedely, Director of Sales
Nik Rivers, Programming Director

Scott Hixson, Promotions/Marketing Director
Zack Schaefer, Promotions Coordinator

Fenner

*WXXE
12-21-1998; 90.5 MHz FM; 0.049 kw; 413 ft.; N42 58 12 W75 47 7
826 Euclid Avenue, Syracuse, NY 13210 US
(315) 863-6013
License: Fenner, Madison County, NY held by Syracuse Community Radio Inc.
Arbitron Metro Market: Syracuse, NY; *Format:* Variety/Diverse
Kendric Bedell, Chairman
Dana Bonn, President
Danny Danhauser, General Manager

Fort Plain

WBUG-FM
03-01-1990; 101.1 MHz FM; *Hrs Open:* 24; 1.25 kw; 719 ft.; N42 52 44 W74 47 7
185 Genesee Street, Suite 1601, Utica, NY 13504 US
(315) 734-9245; *Fax:* (315) 624-9245
www.bugcountry.com
License: Fort Plain, Montgomery County, NY held by Roser Communications Network Inc.
Group Owner: Roser Communications Network Inc.; (acq 10-21-94; $400,000 with WVTL(AM) Amsterdam;
Nat'l Network: ABC
Arbitron Metro Market: Utica, NY; *Format:* Country; *Hrs. of News Programming:* news progmg 10 hrs wkly; *No. News Employees:* 2; *Target Audience:* 25 plus.; *Adv. Rates:* 20; 15; 15; 15
Dave Silvers, Operations/Programming Director
Ken Roser, General Manager
Grant Roser, General Sales Mgr
Tony Saponaro, Webmaster

Frankfort

WKLL
02-12-1990; 94.9 MHz FM; 34 kw; 568 ft.; N43 8 40 W75 10 32
235 Walton St., Syracuse, NY 13202 US
(315) 472-9111; *Fax:* (315) 472-1888
www.krock.com
askus@krock.com
License: Frankfort, Herkimer County, NY held by Galaxy Communications L.P.
Group Owner: Galaxy Communications L.P.; (acq 4-6-2000; grpsl).
Nat'l Network: ABC; *Nat'l Reps:* D & R Radio
Arbitron Metro Market: Utica-Rome, NY; *Format:* Rock/AOR

Fredonia

WBKX
04-01-1989; 96.5 MHz FM; *Hrs Open:* 24; 1.4 kw; 686 ft.; N42 22 2 W79 23 12
4561 Willow Road, Dunkirk, NY 14048 US
(716) 366-8580(716) 366-1410; *Fax:* (716) 366-1416
www.wbkxcountry.com
License: Fredonia, Chautauqua County, NY held by Chadwick Bay Broadcasting Corp.
Nat'l Network: ABC
Arbitron Metro Market: New York,Jamestown, NY; *Format:* Country; *Hrs. of News Programming:* News progmg 12 hrs wkly; *No. News Employees:* 1; *Target Audience:* 25-54.
Patti Pritchard, Vice President/General Manager
Mark James, Programming/Operations Manager
Dave Rowley, News Director
Dan Palmer, Sports Director
Alexandra Sherwood, Business Office Manager

*WCVF-FM
07-06-1978; 88.9 MHz FM; *Hrs Open:* 24; 0.13 kw; -115 ft.; N42 27 8 W79 20 14
Svny Fredonia, 115 McEwen Hall, Fredonia, NY 14063 US
(716) 673-3420; *Fax:* (716) 673-3427
www.fredoniaradio.com
wcvf@fredoniaradio.com
License: Fredonia, Chautauqua County, NY held by State University of New York.
Nat'l Network: NPR; *Wire Services:* UPI
Arbitron Metro Market: Fredonia, NY; *Format:* Variety/Diverse
Special Programming: Reggae 4 hrs, folk 4 hrs, world 4 hrs, spanish 4 hrs, new age 4 hrs, polka 3 hours weekly; *Hrs. of News Programming:* News progmg 28 hrswkly; *Target Audience:* All ages of campus & community of Fredonia
Jeff Wick, Operations Dir

Freeport

WGBB
08-01-1924; 1240 kHz AM; 1 kw-D, ND1; 1 kw-N, ND1; N40 38 44 W73 34 39
404 Route 109, West Babylon, NY 11704 US
(516) 623-1240; *Fax:* (516) 623-1240
www.am1240wgbb.com
support@am1240wgbb.com
License: Freeport, NY held by WGBB-AM Inc.
Group Owner: Cox Radio Inc.; (acq 5-22-98; grpsl)
Arbitron Metro Market: New York; *Format:* Variety/Diverse
Special Programming: Relg 6 hrs, Sp 2 hrs wkly; *Target Audience:* 25-65.
Josephine Chain, President
Jeff Lo, Operations Dir
Josephine Chain, General Manager
Jeff Lo, Station Manager
Tom Ross, Programming Director
Neil Newman, Chief Engineer
Robert Kowal, Sports Director
Robert Kowal, AccountExecutive
Trevor Vassell, Sound Engineer
Adam Kern, Sound Engineer

Friendship

*WCID
01-01-1989; 89.1 MHz FM; *Hrs Open:* 24; 7 kw; 492 ft.; N42 7 7 W78 10 43 *Rebroadcasts:* Rebroadcasts WCIK(FM) Bath 100%
PO Box 506, Bath, NY 14810 US
(607) 776-4151
www.fln.org
License: Friendship, Allegany County, NY held by Family Life Ministries Inc.
Group Owner: Family Life Network
Nat'l Network: Salem Radio Network; *Wire Services:* Metro Weather Service Inc.
Arbitron Metro Market: Bath, NY; *Format:* Christian; *Hrs. of News Programming:* news progmg 14 hrs wkly; *No. News Employees:* 3; *Target Audience:* 30-54; general
Dave Margalotti, Operations Dir
Terese Main, Programming Director
Bob Price, News Director

Fulton

WBBS
08-01-1961; 104.7 MHz FM; 50 kw; 492 ft.; N43 12 50 W76 23 47
500 Plum St., Suite 400, Syracuse, NY 13204 US
(315) 472-9797; *Fax:* (315) 472-2323
www.b1047.net
License: Fulton, Oswego County, NY held by Citicasters Licenses Inc.
Group Owner: iHeartMedia; (acq 5-4-99; grpsl).
Arbitron Metro Market: New York, NY; *Format:* Country
Rick Yacobush, Market President
Barbara Meaney, General Sales Mgr
Rich Lauber, Programming Director

WOSW
08-19-1949; 1300 kHz AM; *Hrs Open:* 24; 1 kw-D; N43 17 41 W76 26 35
401 W. Kirkpatrick St., Syracuse, NY 13069
(315) 472-0222; *Fax:* (315) 478-7745
License: Fulton, Oswego County, NY held by Cram Communications LLC.
Group Owner: Cram Communications LLC; (acq 11-14-2007)
Nat'l Network: ABC
Population Served: 300,000; *Arbitron Metro Market:* Syracuse, NY *Special Programming:* It 2 hrs, Pol 5 hrs wkly; *Target Audience:* 35 plus; hometown listeners, county coverage; *Adv. Rates:* 15; 15; 12; 8
Sam Furco, Vice President

Garden City

*WHPC
10-12-1972; 90.3 MHz FM; *Hrs Open:* 24; 0.5 kw; 213 ft.; N40 43 47 W73 35 33
One Education Drive, Garden City, NY 11530 US
(516) 572-7501; *Fax:* 516) 572-7831
www.ncc.edu/studentlife/whpcradiostation/
WHPC@ncc.edu
License: Garden City, Nassau County, NY held by Nassau Community College Board of Trustees.
Format: Adult Contemp, Variety/Diverse; *Hrs. of News Programming:* news progmg 5 hrs wkly; *No. News Employees:* 2; *Target Audience:* 20-65; general
Jack Ostling, President
Jim Green, Operations Dir

WQBU-FM
01-01-1988; 92.7 MHz FM; 2 kw; 522 ft.; N40 45 26 W73 42 52
1103 Stewart Ave., Garden City, NY 11530 US
(212) 310-6036; *Fax:* (212) 888-3694
www.univision.com
License: Garden City, Nassau County, NY held by Univision Radio License Corp.
Group Owner: Univision Radio; (acq 1-12-2004; $60 million)
Arbitron Metro Market: New York, NY; *Format:* Tejano
Ramon Pineda, General Manager
Karima Khawja, Director of Sales

Geneseo

*WGSU
02-18-1963; 89.3 MHz FM; *Hrs Open:* 24; 1.8 kw horiz; 10 ft.; N42 47 51 W77 49 13
State University College, 1 College Circle, Geneseo, NY 14454 US
(585) 245-5486
www.geneseo.edu/~wgsu/
wgsu@geneseo.com
License: Geneseo, Livingston County, NY held by State University of New York.
Format: Alternative, News; *Hrs. of News Programming:* News progmg 7 hrs wkly; *Target Audience:* 12-55; college, immediate community
Katy Boland, General Manager

Geneva

*WEOS
03-30-1971; 89.7 MHz FM; *Hrs Open:* 24; 4 kw; 312 ft.; N42 48 32 W77 5 12
Mailing Address: 300 Pulteney Street, Geneva, NY 14456 US
Second Address: 113 Hamilton St., Geneva, NY 14456
(315) 781-3456(315) 781-3897; *Fax:* (315) 781-3916
www.weos.org
underwriting@wxxi.org
License: Geneva, Ontario County, NY held by The Colleges of the Seneca.
Nat'l Network: NPR; PRI; *Wire Services:* AP
Arbitron Metro Market: Geneva, NY; *Format:* Jazz, News, 62, Talk *Special Programming:* AAA 12 hrs, world 10 hrs, metal 6 hrs, gospel 3 hrs, reggae 3 hrs wkly; *Hrs. of News Programming:* news progmg 40 hrs wkly *No.News Employees:* 1; *Target Audience:* 18-plus.; *Adv. Rates:* 13; 1113; 13; 7.50
Greg Cotterill, General Manager
Michael Black, Radio Program Manager
Hazel Moellering, Music Director
Alison Jones, Underwriting

WFLK
01-01-1974; 101.7 MHz FM; *Hrs Open:* 24; 5.4 kw; 125 ft.; N42 51 34 W77 0 29
3568 Lenox Rd., Geneva, NY 14456 US
(315) 781-1101
www.k1017.com
License: Geneva, Ontario County, NY held by RSK Communications, Inc.
Group Owner: RSK Communications, Inc.; (acq 1993)
Arbitron Metro Market: Rochester, NY; *Format:* Country; *Hrs. of News Programming:* news progmg 10 hrs wkly; *No. News Employees:* 2; *Target Audience:* 25-49.; *Adv. Rates:* 12; 12; 12; 12
Frank Lischak, VP of Sales
Paul Szmal, Programming Director
Joe Nittler, News Director

WGVA
01-01-1947; 1240 kHz AM; *Hrs Open:* 24; 1 kw-U, ND1; N42 51 37 W77 0 59
3568 Lenox Road, Geneva, NY 14456 US
(315) 781-1240; *Fax:* (315) 781-7700
www.fingerlakesdailynews.com
info@fingerlakesdailynews.com
License: Geneva, NY held by Geneva Broadcasting Inc.
Arbitron Metro Market: Rochester, NY; *Format:* News, News/Talk, 86; *Hrs. of News Programming:* news progmg 10 hrs wkly; *No. News Employees:* 1; *Target Audience:* General.; *Adv. Rates:* 15; 12; 15; 10
Alan Bishop, President
Frank Lischak, Vice President of Sales
Ted Baker, Programming Director
Joe Nittler, News Director
Jack Anderson, Chief Engineer

Glens Falls

*WGFR
01-01-1977; 92.7 MHz FM; 0.013 kw horiz; 49 ft.; N43 18 44 W73 38 58

640 Bay Road, Queensbury, NY 12804 US
(518) 743-2200; *Fax:* (518) 745-1433
www.wgfr.org
jimfree@clearchannel.com
License: Glens Falls, Warren County, NY held by Board of Trustees of Adirondack Community College.
Format: Triple A; *Target Audience:* 18 plus; adults
Kevin Ankeny, General Manager
Mary Howard, Station Manager

WMML
05-28-1959; 1230 kHz AM; *Hrs Open:* 24; 1 kw-U, ND1; N43 19 43 W73 38 58
89 Everts Avenue, Queensbury, NY 12804 US
(518) 793-7733; *Fax:* (518) 793-0838
License: Glens Falls, NY held by 6 Johnson Road Licenses Inc.
Group Owner: Pamal Broadcasting Ltd.; (acq 4-1-2004; grpsl).
Nat'l Network: ESPN Radio
Arbitron Metro Market: Glenn Falls, NY; *Format:* Sports *Special Programming:* Relg 3 hrs wkly; *Hrs. of News Programming:* news progmg 6 hrs wkly; *No. News Employees:* 1; *Target Audience:* 18-54 plus. *Adv.Rates:* 10; 10; 10; 2.
Tom Jacobsen, General Manager/Sales Manager
John Lawrence, Programming Director

WWSC
12-18-1946; 1450 kHz AM; *Hrs Open:* 24
238 Bay Road, Queensbury, NY 12804 US
(518) 761-9890; *Fax:* (518) 761-9893
www.radiowins.com
License: Glens Falls, NY held by Regional Radio Group LLC.
Group Owner: Regional Radio Group LLC; (acq 9-10-2008; grpsl)
Nat'l Network: ABC; Wall Street; Westwood One
Arbitron Metro Market: Glens Falls, NY; *Format:* News, News/Talk, 84, Talk; *Hrs. of News Programming:* news progmg 166 hrs wkly; *No. News Employees:* 15; *Target Audience:* 12 plus; people who want full news radio &talk
Clay Ashworth, General Manager
Dan Miner, Station Manager
Alan Doane, Programming Director
Pete Cloutier, Promotions Manager
Ken Leccese, Sports Director
Jenelle Lapointe, Traffic Director

Gloversville

WENT
07-01-1944; 1340 kHz AM; *Hrs Open:* 5:30 AM-midnight; 1 kw-U; N43 01 30 W74 21 10
Box 831, 138 Harrison St. Ext., Gloversville, NY 12078
(518) 725-7175; *Fax:* (518) 725-7177
www.am1340went.com
went@capital.net
License: Gloversville, Fulton County, NY held by Whitney Radio Broadcasting Inc.
Nat'l Network: CNN Radio; ESPN Radio; *Wire Services:* AP
Population Served: 102,000 *Special Programming:* Talk one hr wkly; *Hrs. of News Programming:* news progmg 14 hrs wkly; *No. News Employees:* 2; *Target Audience:* 30 plus.
Jack Scott, President
Jon Clark, Operations Dir
Tim Murphy, Promotions Manager
Tom Roehl, News Director
Lloyd Smith, Chief Engineer
Shirley Clark, Traffic Manager

WFNY
03-01-2003; 1440 kHz AM
US
(518) 725-1108; *Fax:* (518) 773-3349
am1440wfny@gmail.com
License: Gloversville, NY held by Michael A. Sleezer.
Arbitron Metro Market: Gloversville, NY
Michael A. Sleezer, Owner and General Manager

Gouverneur

WLFK
12-05-1967; 95.3 MHz FM; *Hrs Open:* 24; 6 kw; Ant 328 ft; N44 20 22 W75 24 00
199 Wealther Avenue, Watertown, NY 13669
(315) 393-1100; *Fax:* (315) 393-6673
License: Gouverneur, St. Lawrence County, NY held by Community Broadcasters LLC.
Group Owner: Community Broadcasters LLC; (acq 2-8-2007; grpsl)
Population Served: 120,000 *Hrs. of News Programming:* news progmg 7 hrs wkly; *No. News Employees:* 3; *Target Audience:* 35-54.
James Leven, President

***WSLG**
90.5 MHz FM; 2 kw; 207 ft.; N44 15 32 W75 34 40
St. Lawrence University, Canton, NY 13617 US
(315) 229-5356; *Fax:* (315) 229-5373
www.ncpr.org
radio@ncpr.org
License: Gouverneur, St. Lawrence County, NY held by The St. Lawrence University.
Arbitron Metro Market: Gouverneur, NY; *Format:* Public Affairs
Shelly Pike, Operations Dir
Ellen Rocco, General Manager
Jackie Sauter, Programming Director
Martha Foley, News Director
Bob Sauter, Chief Engineer
Naomi Weller, Office Manager
Joel Hurd, Production Manager
Sandy Demarest,Development Director

Grand Gorge

***WGKR**
11-01-1997; 105.3 MHz FM; 0.06 kw; 1358 ft.; N42 23 55 W74 35 23 *Rebroadcasts:* Rebroadcasts WFGB(FM) Kingston 100%.
Mailing Address: Post Office Box 777, Lake Katrine, NY 12449 US
Second Address: 199 Tuytenbridge Rd., Lake Katrine, NY 12449
(800) 724-8518
www.soundoflife.org
email@soundoflife.org
License: Grand Gorge, Delaware County, NY held by Sound of Life Inc.
Format: Christian
Tom Michaels Zahradnik, CEO
Joe Hunter, Programming Director

***WLJH**
01-01-2001; 90.7 MHz FM; 0.04 kw vert; 1325 ft.; N43 25 12 W73 45 37 *Rebroadcasts:* Rebroadcasts WFGB(FM) Kingston 100%
Mailing Address: P O Box 777, Lake Katrine, NY 12449 US
Second Address: 199 Tuytenbridge Road, Lake Katrine, NY 12449
(845) 336-6199; *Fax:* (845) 336-7205
www.soundoflife.org
email@soundoflife.org
License: Grand Gorge, Warren County, DE held by Sound of Life Inc.
Format: Christian
Jay Cookingham, Chairman
Tom Michaels Zahradnik, CEO
Bob Conti, Operations Dir
Tom Zahradnik, General Manager
Joe Hunter, Programming Director
Paul Grimsland, Production Director
Connie van Kleeck, Assistant Program Director
Donna Quiles, Office Administrator

Greece

***WGMC**
11-11-1973; 90.1 MHz FM; *Hrs Open:* 24; 15 kw; 138 ft.; N43 14 40 W77 41 36
1139 Maiden Lane, Rochester, NY 14615 US
(585) 966-2660; *Fax:* (585) 581-8185
www.jazz901.org
jazzinfo@jazz901.org
License: Greece, Monroe County, NY held by Greece Central School District.
Arbitron Metro Market: Rochester, NY; *Format:* Jazz *Special Programming:* Pol 2 hrs, Sp 10 hrs, Lithuanian one hr, Turkish o; *Target Audience:* 25-50; upscale, educated, mus lovers
Jack Mindy, Operations Dir
Rob Linton, Station Manager
Derrick Lucas, Music Director
Laurylann Romneo, Development Director
Joelle VanBuren, Production Director
Jack Mindy, Community Calendar Coordinator

Hamilton

***WRCU-FM**
03-22-1970; 90.1 MHz FM; 1.9 kw; 154 ft.; N42 48 38 W75 31 58
Student Activites Office, Hamilton, NY 13346 US
(315) 228-7901; *Fax:* (315) 228-7028
License: Hamilton, Madison County, NY held by Colgate University.
Format: Jazz, Variety/Diverse *Special Programming:* Jazz 12 hrs, class 4 hrs, Black 10 hrs wkly

Lydia Gulick, General Manager
Tracy Hoole, Programming Director
Paul Osmolskis, News Director

Hempstead

WHLI
07-22-1947; 1100 kHz AM; *Hrs Open:* Sunrise-sunset; 10 kw-D, DAD; N40 41 6 W73 36 36
234 Airport Plaza Boulevard, Farmingdale, NY 11735 US
(631) 770-4200; *Fax:* (631) 770-0101
www.whli.com
info@whli.com
License: Hempstead, NY held by Connoisseur Media Licenses LLC
Group Owner: Connoisseur Media LLC
Nat'l Reps: Katz Radio
Arbitron Metro Market: New York; *Format:* Adult Contemp
Special Programming: Black one hr wkly; *Hrs. of News Programming:* news progmg 2 hrs wkly; *No. News Employees:* 1; *Target Audience:* 35-64; adults
Dave Widmer, President
Janine John, General Sales Mgr
Paul Richards, Programming Director
Frank Campanella, Promotions Director
Frank Brinka, News Director
Mike Glaser, Chief Engineer
Antoinette Rodriguez, Traffic Manager

WKJY
07-22-1947; 98.3 MHz FM; *Hrs Open:* 24; 3 kw; 328 ft.; N40 41 8 W73 36 37
234 Airport Plaza Boulevard, Farmingdale, NY 11735 US
(631) 770-4200; *Fax:* (631) 770-0090
www.whli.com
info@whli.com
License: Hempstead, Nassau County, NY held by Connoisseur Media Licenses LLC
Group Owner: Connoisseur Media LLC
Nat'l Reps: Katz Radio
Arbitron Metro Market: New York; *Format:* Adult Contemp
Special Programming: Black one hr wkly; *No. News Employees:* 1; *Target Audience:* 25-54.
Janine John, General Sales Mgr
Steve Harper, Programming Director
Frank Campanella, Promotions Director
Frank Brinka, News Director
Mike Glaser, Chief Engineer
Antoinette Rodriguez, Traffic Manager

***WRHU**
06-09-1959; 88.7 MHz FM; *Hrs Open:* 24; 0.47 kw; 180 ft.; N40 43 3 W73 36 12
900 Fulton Avenue, Hempstead, NY 11549 US
(516) 463-5667
www.wrhu.org
License: Hempstead, Nassau County, NY held by Hofstra University.
Wire Services: AP
Format: Variety/Diverse; *Hrs. of News Programming:* News progmg 11 hrs wkly; *Target Audience:* General.
Dan Savarino, Station Manager

Henderson

WEFX
01-01-1991; 100.7 MHz FM; 6 kw; 328 ft.; N43 49 13 W76 5 29
199 Wealtha Ave., Watertown, NY 13601 US
(203) 845-3030; *Fax:* (203) 845-3097
License: Henderson, Jefferson County, NY held by Community Broadcasters LLC.
Group Owner: Community Broadcasters LLC; (acq 2-8-2007; grpsl)
Nat'l Reps: Roslin
Arbitron Metro Market: Watertown, NY; *Format:* Rock/AOR
James Leven, President

Henrietta

***WITR**
03-07-1975; 89.7 MHz FM; *Hrs Open:* 24; 0.91 kw; 125 ft.; N43 5 8 W77 40 5
32 Lomb Memorial Drive, Rochester, NY 14623 US
(585) 475-2000; *Fax:* (585) 475-4988
www.witr.rit.edu
License: Henrietta, Monroe County, NY held by Rochester Institute of Technology.
Format: Contemporary Hits/Top 40 *Special Programming:* Reggae 5 hrs, jazz 8 hrs, contemp Christian rock 1; *Target Audience:* General.
Joe Makowski, General Manager
Eta Santoro, Programming Director

Zoe Rabinowitz, News Director
Vlad Ionescu, Chief Engineer
AJ Colosimo, Development Director
Mitch Bennett, Production Director
Emily Kvale, Business Director
RyanAquilino, Webmaster
Jake Walsh, Music Director

Herkimer

WNRS

10-01-1956; 1420 kHz AM; *Hrs Open:* 24; 1 kw-D, ND2; 0.064 kw-N, ND2; N43 3 40 W75 1 44
1900 Genesee Street, Utica, NY 13502 US
(315) 797-9270
License: Herkimer, NY held by Arjuna Broadcasting Corp.
Nat'l Network: ESPN Radio; *Nat'l Reps:* Roslin
Arbitron Metro Market: Herkimer, NY; *Format:* Sports; *No. News Employees:* 1; *Target Audience:* 18 plus; men; *Adv. Rates:* 30; 25; 25; 20
Tim Barstein, General Sales Mgr
Tom Davenport, Chief Engineer

*WVHC

10-01-1993; 91.5 MHz FM; *Hrs Open:* 24; 0.35 kw vert; -115 ft.; N43 1 58 W75 0 31
100 Reservoir Road, Herkimer, NY 13350 US
(315) 574-3997
www.herkimer.edu
License: Herkimer, Herkimer County, NY held by Herkimer County Community College.
Arbitron Metro Market: Herkimer, NY; *Format:* Jazz; *Hrs. of News Programming:* News progmg 5 hrs wkly; *Target Audience:* General; residents of southern Herkimer county & college community

WXUR

04-28-1979; 92.7 MHz FM; *Hrs Open:* 24; 6.4 kw; 659 ft.; N43 8 38 W75 10 40
1900 Genesee Street, Suite 205, Utica, NY 13502 US
(315) 866-9700; *Fax:* (315) 733-5438
www.927thedrive.net
License: Herkimer, Herkimer County, NY held by Arjuna Broadcasting Corp.
Nat'l Network: Westwood One
Arbitron Metro Market: Utica-Rome, NY; *Format:* Contemporary Hits/Top 40, Adult Contemp; *No. News Employees:* 1; *Adv. Rates:* 35; 30; 30; 25
Jack Moran, Operations/Business Manager
Mindy Barstein, General Manager/Sales Manager
Tom Starr, Programming Director

Highland

WRWD-FM

10-03-1989; 107.3 MHz FM; 0.33 kw; 968 ft.; N41 41 58 W74 0 11
20 Tucker Drive, Poughkeepsie, NY 12603 US
(845) 471-2300; *Fax:* (845) 471-2683
www.wrwdcountry.com
License: Highland, Ulster County, NY held by AMFM Radio Licenses LLC.
Group Owner: iHeartMedia; (acq 12-10-97; $7.5 million with WBWZ(FM) New Paltz).
Nat'l Network: Jones Radio Networks; *Nat'l Reps:* Katz Radio
Arbitron Metro Market: Poughkeepsie, N; *Format:* Country
Special Programming: Farm one hr wkly; *Target Audience:* 18 plus.; *Adv. Rates:* 80; 65; 75; 35
Chuck Benfer, Market President
Chris Marino, Senior Vice President of Programming
Rob VanDerbeck, Senior Vice President of Sales
Elise Penge, Promotions Director
Dierdre Burns, Digital Content Director

Homer

WXHC

01-01-1991; 101.5 MHz FM; *Hrs Open:* 24; 1.3 kw; 495 ft.; N42 41 12 W76 11 54
P.O. Box 386, 12 South Main Street, Homer, NY 13077 US
(607) 749-9942; *Fax:* (607) 749-2374
www.wxhc.com
johneves@wxhc.com
License: Homer, Cortland County, NY held by John Eves.
Nat'l Reps: Roslin
Arbitron Metro Market: Homer, NY; *Format:* Oldies; *Hrs. of News Programming:* news progmg 10 hrs wkly; *No. News Employees:* 1; *Target Audience:* 25-54.
John Eves, General Manager
Bruce Eves, General Sales Mgr
Bobby Comstock Jr., Programming Director

Eric Mulvihill, News Director
Mike Eves, Traffic / Office Manager

Honeoye Falls

WAIO

01-01-1948; 95.1 MHz FM; *Hrs Open:* 24; 50 kw; Ant 479 ft; N43 02 01 W77 25 18
100 Chestnut Street, 17th Floor, Rochester, NY 14604 US
(585) 454-4884; *Fax:* (585) 454-5081
www.radio951.com
License: Honeoye Falls, Monroe County, NY held by Citicasters Licenses Inc.
Group Owner: iHeartMedia; (acq 1999; grpsl).
Population Served: 120,000; *Arbitron Metro Market:* Rochester, NY; *Format:* Classic Rock; *Target Audience:* 25-54.
Robert Morgan, Regional Market President
Becki Efing, General Sales Manager
Bonnie Porter, General Sales Manager

Hoosick Falls

WHAZ-FM

07-04-1991; 97.5 MHz FM; 0.42 kw; 1184 ft.; N42 51 49 W73 13 59
30 Park Ave, Cohoes, NY 12047-3330 US
(518) 237-1330; *Fax:* (518) 235-4468
www.aliveradionetwork.com
events@aliveradionetwork.com
License: Hoosick Falls, Rensselaer County, NY held by Capital Media Corp.
Group Owner: Capital Media Corp.; (acq 7-19-2005; $1.1 million)
Arbitron Metro Market: Albany-Schenectady, NY; *Format:* Christian, Religious
Paul Lotters, President
Steve Klob, Operations Director/Sales Manager

Hornell

WCKR

06-01-1981; 92.1 MHz FM; *Hrs Open:* 24; 2.55 kw; 509 ft.; N42 20 38 W77 37 36
5942 Ashbaugh Hill Rd, Hornell, NY 14843 US
(607) 324-1480; *Fax:* (607) 324-5415
kpd@wlea.net
License: Hornell, Steuben County, NY held by PMJ Communications Inc.
Nat'l Network: USA; *Wire Services:* AP
Arbitron Metro Market: Elmira-Corning, NY; *Format:* Country; *Hrs. of News Programming:* news progmg 11 hrs wkly; *No. News Employees:* 2; *Target Audience:* 21 plus.
Kevin P. Doran, President
Glenn Lee, Operations Dir
Tom Booth, General Sales Mgr
Brian O'Neil, News Director

WKPQ

01-01-1946; 105.3 MHz FM; *Hrs Open:* 24; 43 kw; 531 ft.; N42 17 32 W77 40 27
112 Main Street, Hornell, NY 14843 US
(607) 324-1596; *Fax:* (877) 575-1320
www.kickincountry1053.com
License: Hornell, Steuben County, NY held by Sound Communications LLC
Group Owner: Sound Communications LLC
Arbitron Metro Market: Elmira-Corning, NY; *Format:* Adult Contemp; *Target Audience:* Adult 25-54
Kevin White, General Manager

WLEA

09-01-1951; 1480 kHz AM; *Hrs Open:* 24; 2.5 kw-D, ND1; 0.019 kw-N, ND1; N42 17 15 W77 38 47
5940 County Route 64, Hornell, NY 14843 US
(607) 324-1480; *Fax:* (607) 324-5415
www.wlea.net
License: Hornell, NY held by PMJ Communications Inc.
Wire Services: AP
Arbitron Metro Market: Elmira-Corning, NY; *Format:* News, News/Talk, 86; *Hrs. of News Programming:* news progmg 16 hrs wkly; *No. News Employees:* 2; *Target Audience:* 35 plus.
Tom Booth, General Manager
Brian O'Neil, News Director

*WSQA

01-01-2000; 88.7 MHz FM; 4.5 kw; 495 ft.; N42 16 2 W77 37 55
PO Box 3000, Binghamton, NY 13902 US
(607) 729-0100; *Fax:* (607) 729-7328
www.wskg.com
wskg_mail@wskg.pbs.org
License: Hornell, Steuben County, NY held by WSKG Public Telecommunications Council.
Format: Jazz, News

Brian Sickora, President
Gregory Keeler, Programming Director/Operations Manager
Matt Richmond, News Director

Horseheads

WLNL

05-07-1967; 1000 kHz AM; *Hrs Open:* Sunrise-sunset; 2.5 kw-C, NDD; 5 kw-D, NDD; N42 9 14 W76 50 47
3134 Lake Road, Horseheads, NY 14845 US
(607) 737-9208; *Fax:* (607) 737-9210
www.wlnlradio.com
License: Horseheads, NY held by Trinity Media Ltd.
Nat'l Network: USA; Salem Radio Network
Arbitron Metro Market: Elmira-Corning, NY; *Format:* Religious
Special Programming: Country/bluegrass one hr wkly; *Target Audience:* 25-54; Christian families, women/mothers who work at home
Jesse Pierce, General Manager

WPGI

07-04-1970; 100.9 MHz FM; 3.8 kw; 246 ft.; N42 12 0 W76 51 30
2205 College Avenue, Elmira, NY 14903 US
(607) 732-4400; *Fax:* (607) 732-7774
License: Horseheads, Chemung County, NY held by Community Broadcasters LLC
Group Owner: Community Broadcasters LLC
Arbitron Metro Market: Elmira-Corning, NY; *Format:* Country; *Target Audience:* General.
Scott Free, Operations Dir
Smitty O'Loughlin, General Manager/Sales Manager
Ally Payne, Webmaster

WWLZ

04-01-1966; 820 kHz AM; 4.1 kw-D, DAN; 0.85 kw-N, DAN; N42 9 14 W76 50 47
1685 Four Mile Drive, Williamsport, PA 17701 US
(607) 732-4400; *Fax:* (607) 732-7774
www.wwlzam820.com
License: Horseheads, NY held by Community Broadcasters LLC
Group Owner: Community Broadcasters LLC; (acq 12-1-2002; grpsl).
Arbitron Metro Market: Horseheads, NY; *Format:* News, News/Talk, 86; *Target Audience:* 25-54; baby boomers
Scott Free, Operations Dir
Smitty O' Loughlin, General Manager
Ally Payne, Webmaster

Houghton

*WXXY

08-02-1957; 90.3 MHz FM; *Hrs Open:* 24; 6 kw; 217 ft.; N42 22 39 W78 10 45
280 State Street, Rochester, NY 14614 US
(585) 325-7500
License: Houghton, Kent County, NY held by WXXI Public Broadcasting Council
Format: Black, Gospel
Norm Silverstein, President
Jeanne Fisher, Vice President, Radio
Susan Rogers, Executive Vice President/General Manager
Julie Philipp, News Director

Hudson

WHUC

01-01-1947; 1230 kHz AM; *Hrs Open:* 24; 1 kw-U, ND1; N42 15 13 W73 45 45
5620 Route 9G, Hudson, NY 12534 US
(518) 828-5006; *Fax:* (518) 828-1080
www.wrwdcountry.com
License: Hudson, NY held by CC Licenses LLC.
Group Owner: iHeartMedia; (acq 1-17-2002; grpsl)
Nat'l Network: Jones Radio Networks; *Nat'l Reps:* Katz Radio
Format: Adult Contemp; *Hrs. of News Programming:* news progmg 4 hrs wkly; *No. News Employees:* 1; *Target Audience:* 35 plus; loc people in Columbia & Greene counties
Chuck Benfer, Market President
Chris Marino, Senior Vice President of Programming
Rob VanDerbeck, Senior Vice President of Sales
Marty Mitchell, Programming Director
Elise Penge, Promotions Director
Deirdre Burns, Digital ContentDirector

*WHVP

05-01-1998; 91.1 MHz FM; 0.22 kw vert; 1043 ft.; N42 18 28 W73 29 35 *Rebroadcasts:* Rebroadcasts WFGB(FM) Kingston 100%
P.O. Box 777, Lake Katrine, NY 12449 US

(845) 336-6199; *Fax:* (845) 336-7205
www.soundoflife.org
email@soundoflife.org
License: Hudson, Columbia County, NY held by Sound of Life Inc.
Format: Christian
Tom Zahradink, CEO/General Manager
Joe Hunter, Programming Director

WZCR

01-20-1969; 93.5 MHz FM; *Hrs Open:* 24; 5.8 kw; -16 ft.; N42 15 13 W73 45 45
5620 Route 9G, Hudson, NY 12534 US
(518) 828-5006; *Fax:* (518) 828-1080
www.oldies935.com
License: Hudson, Columbia County, NY held by CC Licenses LLC.
Group Owner: iHeartMedia
Nat'l Network: Westwood One; *Nat'l Reps:* Katz Radio
Arbitron Metro Market: Hudson, NY; *Format:* Oldies; *Hrs. of News Programming:* News progmg 3 hrs wkly; *Target Audience:* General; adults 35-54
Chuck Benfer, Market President
Chris Marino, Senior Vice President of Programming
Rob VanDerbeck, Senior Vice President of Sales
Bill Williamsÿ, Programming Director
Elise Penge, Promotions Director
Deirdre Burns, Digital ContentDirector

Hudson Falls

WNYQ

09-19-1983; 101.7 MHz FM; *Hrs Open:* 24; 4.6 kw; 180 ft.; N43 22 40 W73 39 56
89 Everts Avenue, Queensbury, NY 12804 US
(518) 793-7733; *Fax:* (518) 793-0838
www.classichitswnyq.com/
jdonovan@adirondackbroadcasting.com
License: Hudson Falls, Washington County, NY held by 6 Johnson Road Licenses Inc.
Group Owner: Pamal Broadcasting Ltd.; (acq 4-1-2004; grpsl).
Arbitron Metro Market: Hudson Falls, NY; *Format:* Adult Contemp; *No. News Employees:* 1; *Target Audience:* 35-64.
Mike Thompson, General Manager
Jackie Donovan, Programming Director

Huntington

WNYH

09-01-1951; 740 kHz AM; *Hrs Open:* 24; 25 kw-D, DA2; 0.043 kw-N, DA2; N40 51 4 W73 26 16
P.O. Box 12, Brooklyn, NY 11220 US
(980) 558-1430
www.radiocanticonuevo.com
ericksalgado1430@hotmail.com
License: Huntington, NY held by Win Radio Broadcasting Corp.
Arbitron Metro Market: New York; *Format:* Alternative
Richard Yoon, President

Hyde Park

WCZX

08-18-1970; 97.7 MHz FM; *Hrs Open:* 24; 0.3 kw; 1030 ft.; N41 43 11 W73 59 45
2 Pendell Road, Poughkeepsie, NY 12601 US
(845) 471-1500; *Fax:* (845) 454-1204
www.mix97fm.com
jason.finkelberg@townsquaremedia.com
License: Hyde Park, Dutchess County, NY held by Peak Broadcasting of Fresno Licenses LLC
Group Owner: Townsquare Media; (acq 1-23-02; grpsl).
Nat'l Reps: Katz Radio
Arbitron Metro Market: Hudson Valley, NY; *Format:* Adult Contemp; *Hrs. of News Programming:* news progmg 10 hrs wkly; *No. News Employees:* 1; *Target Audience:* 25-54.
Jason Finkelberg, General Manager
Reggie Osterhoudt, Brand Manager
Jason Pugliese, Director Of Sales
Jackie Corley, Digital Managing Editor

WHVW

07-04-1963; 950 kHz AM; *Hrs Open:* 24; 0.5 kw-D, ND1; 0.057 kw-N, ND1; N41 44 46 W73 54 46
316 Main Mall, Poughkeepsie, NY 12601 US
(845) 431-6524
www.whvw.com
whvw@whvw.net
License: Hyde Park, NY held by Joseph-Paul Ferraro.
Arbitron Metro Market: Poughkeepsie, NY; *Format:* Oldies *Special Programming:* Ger one hr, It one hr, Irish one hr wkly; *Target Audience:* 25-54.; *Adv. Rates:* 30; 20
J.P. Ferraro, President

Irondequoit

WKGS

03-01-1992; 106.7 MHz FM; *Hrs Open:* 24; 4.6 kw horiz, 4.51 kw vert; 374 ft.; N43 8 5 W77 35 7
100 Chestnut St., 17th Floor, Rochester, NY 14604 US
(585) 454-4884; *Fax:* (585) 454-5081
www.kiss1067.com
License: Irondequoit, Monroe County, NY held by Citicasters Licenses Inc.
Group Owner: iHeartMedia; (acq 1999; grpsl).
Arbitron Metro Market: Rochester, NY; *Format:* Contemporary Hits/Top 40; *Target Audience:* 18-34.
Tias Schuster, Programming Director
Bonnie Porter, Sales Manager
Becki Efing, Sales Manager

Islip

WLIE

01-01-1960; 540 kHz AM; *Hrs Open:* 24
900 Motor Parkway, Central Islip, NY 11722 US
(631) 580-0540; *Fax:* (631) 471-5401
License: Islip, NY held by Stuart Henry
Nat'l Network: USA; Jones Radio Networks
Arbitron Metro Market: Islip, NY; *Format:* Ethnic *Special Programming:* Relg 3 hrs wkly; *Hrs. of News Programming:* News progmg 10 hrs wkly; *Target Audience:* 45 plus.; *Adv. Rates:* 55; 55; 55; 40
Stuart Henry, President

Ithaca

WHCU

01-23-1923; 870 kHz AM; *Hrs Open:* 24
1751 Hanshaw Road, Ithaca, NY 14850 US
(607) 257-6400; *Fax:* (607) 257-6497
www.whcu870.com
info@whcu870.com
License: Ithaca, NY held by Saga Communications of New England LLC.
Group Owner: Saga Communications Inc.; (acq 5-31-2005; grpsl)
Nat'l Network: CBS; Westwood One; AP Radio; *Nat'l Reps:* Christal
Arbitron Metro Market: Ithaca, NY; *Format:* News, News/Talk, 84, Talk; *Hrs. of News Programming:* news progmg 40 hrs wkly; *No. News Employees:* 3; *Target Audience:* 25-64.
Edward Christian, President/CEO
Chris Allinger, Operations Dir
Chet Osadchey, General Manager
Connie Fairfax-Ozmun, Promotions/Marketing Director
Greg Fry, News Director
Brian Kerkan, Chief Engineer
Jeffrey Probert, Webmaster

*WICB

01-14-1947; 91.7 MHz FM; *Hrs Open:* 24; 4.1 kw; 135 ft.; N42 25 7 W76 29 39
118 Park Hall, Ithaca, NY 14850 US
(607) 274-3217; (607)-274-1040
www.wicb.org
License: Ithaca, Tompkins County, NY held by Ithaca College.
Nat'l Network: ABC
Arbitron Metro Market: Ithaca, NY; *Format:* Rock/AOR, Urban Contemporary *Special Programming:* Jazz 13 hrs, folk 2 hrs, blues 2 hrs, reggae 2 hrs; *Hrs. of News Programming:* News progmg 6 hrs wkly *Target Audience:* 18-34; young audience with taste for innovative mus
Christopher Wheatley, General Manager

WQNY

01-01-1948; 103.7 MHz FM; *Hrs Open:* 24; 16.5 kw; 863 ft.; N42 23 10 W76 40 9
1751 Hanshaw Rd, Ithaca, NY 14850 US
(607) 257-6400; *Fax:* (607) 257-6497
License: Ithaca, Tompkins County, NY held by Saga Communications of New England LLC
Group Owner: Saga Communications Inc.
Arbitron Metro Market: Ithaca, NY; *Format:* Country; *No. News Employees:* 3; *Target Audience:* 25-54.
Edward Christian, President/CEO
Chris Allinger, Operations/Programming Director
Chet Osadchey, General Manager
Connie Fairfax-Ozmun, Promotions/Marketing Director
George Fry, News Director
Brian Kerkan, Chief Engineer
JefreyProbert

*WSQG-FM

01-01-1988; 90.9 MHz FM; *Hrs Open:* 24; 5 kw; 325 ft.; N42 34 55 W76 33 22 *Rebroadcasts:* Rebroadcasts WSKG-FM Binghamton 100%
P.O. Box 3000, Binghamton, NY 13902 US
(607) 729-0100; *Fax:* (607) 729-7328
www.wskg.com
wskg_mail@wskg.pbs.org
License: Ithaca, Tompkins County, NY held by WSKG Public Telecommunications Council.
Nat'l Network: NPR; PRI
Arbitron Metro Market: Ithaca, NY; *Format:* News *Special Programming:* Jazz 7 hrs, folk/bluegrass 5 hrs wkly; *Hrs. of News Programming:* news progmg 33 hrs wkly; *No. News Employees:* 1 *Target Audience:* General.
Brian Sickora, President/CEO
Gregory Keeler, Operations/Programming Director
Ken Campbell, Programming Director
Joshua B. Ludzki, Promotions Manager
Matt Richmond, News Director
Caroline Basson, Director of Development

WNYY

04-01-1956; 1470 kHz AM; *Hrs Open:* 24; 5 kw-D, DAN; 1 kw-N, DAN; N42 23 32 W76 28 29
1751 Hanshaw Road, Ithaca, NY 14850 US
(607) 257-6400; *Fax:* (607) 257-6497
www.1470wnyy.com
cosadchey@cyradiogroup.com
License: Ithaca, NY held by Saga Communications of New England LLC.
Group Owner: Saga Communications Inc.; (acq 5-31-2005; grpsl)
Nat'l Network: Westwood One; *Nat'l Reps:* Christal
Arbitron Metro Market: Ithaca, NY; *Format:* Alternative, Talk; *No. News Employees:* 3; *Target Audience:* 35-54.
Edward Christian, President/CEO
Chris Allinger, Operations/Programming Director
Chet Osadchey, General Manager
Connie Fairfax-Ozmun, Promotions/Marketing Director
Greg Fry, News Director
Brian Kerkan, Chief Engineer
JeffreyProbert, Webmaster

WVBR-FM

06-07-1958; 93.5 MHz FM; *Hrs Open:* 24; 3 kw; 249 ft.; N42 25 42 W76 26 57
227 Linden Avenue, Ithaca, NY 14850 US
(607) 273-4000; *Fax:* (607) 273-4069
www.wvbr.com
concert@wvbr.com
License: Ithaca, Tompkins County, NY held by Cornell Radio Guild Inc.
Nat'l Network: Westwood One; *Nat'l Reps:* Eastman Radio; Katz Radio
Arbitron Metro Market: Ithaca, NY; *Format:* Rock/AOR *Special Programming:* Oldies 5 hrs, heavy metal 6 hrs, folk 8 hrs,blues; *Hrs. of News Programming:* News progmg 10 hrs wkly; *Target Audience:* 18-49; highlyeducated listeners
Robert Schur, Assistant General Manager
Dan Cole, Programming Director

WYXL

09-01-1947; 97.3 MHz FM; 26 kw; 879 ft.; N42 27 54 W76 22 23
1751 Hanshaw Rd, Ithaca, NY 14850 US
(607) 257-6400; *Fax:* (607) 257-6497
License: Ithaca, Tompkins County, NY held by Saga Communications of New England LLC.
Group Owner: Saga Communications Inc.
Arbitron Metro Market: Ithaca, NY; *Format:* Adult Contemp; *Target Audience:* 25-54.
Edward Christian, President/CEO
Chris Allinger, Operations/Programming Director
Chet Osadchey, General Manager
Connie Fairfax-Ozmun, Promotions/Marketing Director
Greg Fry, News Director
Brian Kerkan, Chief Engineer
JeffreyProbert, Webmaster

*WITH

90.1 MHz FM; 1 kw; 286 ft.; N42 34 55 W76 33 22
300 Pulteney Street, Geneva, NY 14456 US
(315) 781-3456; *Fax:* (315) 781-3916
www.weos.org
weos@hws.edu
License: Ithaca, Tompkins County, NY held by The Colleges of the Seneca.
Arbitron Metro Market: Ithaca, NY
Greg Cotterill, General Manager
Michael Black, Programming Director
Allison Jones, Underwriting Director

RADIO - U.S.

Jamestown

*WCOT
12-14-1992; 90.9 MHz FM; 12 kw; 653 ft.; N42 0 6 W79 3 19
Rebroadcasts: Rebroadcasts WCIK(FM) Bath 100%
PO Box 506, Bath, NY 14810 US
(607) 776-4151
www.fln.org
License: Jamestown, Chautauqua County, NY held by Family Life Ministries Inc.
Group Owner: Family Life Network
Nat'l Network: Salem Radio Network; *Wire Services:* Metro Weather Service Inc.
Arbitron Metro Market: Bath,NY; *Format:* Christian; *Hrs. of News Programming:* news progmg 14 hrs wkly; *No. News Employees:* 3; *Target Audience:* 30-54.
Dave Margalotti, Operations Dir
Terese Main, Programming Director
Bob Price, News Director

WHUG
02-01-1965; 101.9 MHz FM; 6 kw; 328 ft.; N42 7 53 W79 13 13
2 Orchard Road, Jamestown, NY 14701 US
(716) 487-1151; *Fax:* (716) 644-9326
www.whug.com
License: Jamestown, Chautauqua County, NY
Group Owner: Media One Group
Format: Country; *Hrs. of News Programming:* news progmg 2 hrs wkly; *No. News Employees:* 2
Andrew Hill, Operations Manager/Programming Director
Jeff Storey, General Manager/Vice President
Jim Yezzi, Sales Manager
Kathy Roselle, News Director

WJTN
12-01-1924; 1240 kHz AM; *Hrs Open:* 24
2 Orchard Road, Jamestown, NY 14701 US
(716) 487-1151; *Fax:* (716) 664-9326
www.wjtn.com
License: Jamestown, NY held by Media One Group LLC
Group Owner: Media One Group; (acq 8-30-2002; $5.05 million with co-located FM)
Nat'l Network: Westwood One; *Nat'l Reps:* Rgnl Reps; *Wire Services:* AP
Format: News, Sports, 86 *Special Programming:* It one hr, Sp one hr, Swedish one hr, farm one hr; *Hrs. of News Programming:* news progmg 16 hrs wkly; *No. News Employees:* 3; *Target Audience:* 35 plus; adultsseeking full service progmg; *Adv. Rates:* 26; 26; 26; 26
Andrew Hill, Operations Manager/Programming Director
Jeff Storey, General Manager/Vice President
Larry Saracki, General Sales Mgr
Kathy Roselle, News Director
Terry Frank, Local News Editor
Jason Sample, News Reporter

WKSN
01-26-1948; 1340 kHz AM
2 Orchard Road, Jamestown, NY 14701 US
(716) 487-1151; *Fax:* (716) 664-9326
www.wksn.com
License: Jamestown, NY held by Media One Group II LLC.
Group Owner: Media One Group; (acq 5-31-2005; grpsl)
Format: Oldies *Special Programming:* Relg 2 hrs, Swedish one hr wkly; *Hrs. of News Programming:* news progmg 3 hrs wkly; *No. News Employees:* 2
Andrew Hill, Operations Manager/Programming Director
Jeff Storey, General Manager/Vice President
Larry Saracki, General Sales Mgr
Kathy Roselle, News Director
Terry Frank, Local News Editor
Jason Sample, News Reporter

*WNJA
01-01-1991; 89.7 MHz FM; *Hrs Open:* 24; 6 kw; 755 ft.; N42 2 48 W79 5 26
Mailing Address: P.O. Box 1263, Buffalo, NY 14240 US
Second Address: 140 Lower Terr., Buffalo, NY 14202-1263
(716) 845-7000; *Fax:* (716) 845-7043
www.wned.org
License: Jamestown, Chautauqua County, NY held by Western New York Public Broadcasting Association.
Arbitron Metro Market: Buffalo, NY; *Format:* Talk; *Target Audience:* 35 plus.
Donald Boswell, President/CEO
Ron Santora, Station Manager/Vice President
Sylvia Bennett, Senior Vice President of Development
Gabe DiMaio, Programming Director
Jim Ranney, News Director
Michael Sutton, Executive VP/COO
GordonBayliss, Vice President of Sales & Marketing

*WUBJ
07-11-1994; 88.1 MHz FM; *Hrs Open:* 24; 2.7 kw; 499 ft.; N42 10 47 W79 20 29 *Rebroadcasts:* Rebroadcasts WBFO(FM) Buffalo 100%
Mailing Address: P.O. Box 1263, Buffalo, NY 14240 US
Second Address: 140 Lower Terrace, Buffalo, NY 14202-1263
(716) 845-7000; *Fax:* (716) 845-7036
www.wbfo.org
mail@wbfo.org
License: Jamestown, Chautauqua County, NY held by State University of New York.
Nat'l Network: NPR
Arbitron Metro Market: Jamestown, NY; *Format:* Jazz, News *Special Programming:* Blues 8 hrs, bluegrass music 3 hrs, Pol 3 hrs wkly; *Hrs. of News Programming:* news progrmg 50 hrs wkly; *No. News Employees:* 2 *Target Audience:* General; educated professional
Donald Boswell, CEO/President
Ron Santora, Station Manager/Vice President
Sylvia Bennett, Senior Vice President of Development
Gabe DiMaio, Programming Director
Jim Ranney, News Director
Gordon Bayliss, Vice President of Sales &Marketing
Michael Sutton, EVP/COO

WWSE
10-01-1947; 93.3 MHz FM; *Hrs Open:* 24; 26.5 kw; 643 ft.; N42 5 6 W79 17 22
2 Orchard Road, Jamestown, NY 14701 US
(716) 487-1151; *Fax:* (716) 664-9326
www.se933.com
License: Jamestown, Chautauqua County, NY held by Media One Group LLC.
Group Owner: Media One Group
Arbitron Metro Market: Jamestown, NY; *Format:* Adult Contemp; *Hrs. of News Programming:* news progmg 7 hrs wkly; *No. News Employees:* 3; *Target Audience:* 12554; female; *Adv. Rates:* 32; 32; 32; 32
Andrew Hill, Operations Manager/Programming Director
Jeff Storey, General Manager/Vice President
Larry Saracki, General Sales Mgr
Nick Keefe, Programming Director
Kathy Roselle, News Director
Terry Frank, Local News Editor
JasonSample, News Reporter

Jeffersonville

*WJFF
02-12-1990; 90.5 MHz FM; *Hrs Open:* 24; 3.7 kw; 630 ft.; N41 48 58 W74 47 15
Rte 52 , Box 797, Jeffersonville, NY 12748 US
(845) 482-4141; *Fax:* (845) 482-WJFF
www.wjffradio.org
wjff@wjffradio.org
License: Jeffersonville, Sullivan County, NY held by Radio Catskill.
Nat'l Network: NPR; PRI
Format: News, News/Talk, 86; *Hrs. of News Programming:* News progmg 75 hrs wkly; *Target Audience:* 16-60; general
Sonja Hedlund, President
Adam Weinreich, Station Manager

WPDA
01-01-1993; 106.1 MHz FM; 1.6 kw; 627 ft.; N41 48 57 W74 45 42 *Rebroadcasts:* Rebroadcasts WPDH(FM) Poughkeepsie 100%
2 Pendell Road, Poughkeepsie, NY 12601 US
(845) 471-1500; *Fax:* (845) 454-1204
www.wpdh.com
License: Jeffersonville, Sullivan County, NY held by Peak Broadcasting of Fresno Licenses LLC
Group Owner: Townsquare Media; (acq 1-23-02; grpsl).
Nat'l Reps: Katz Radio
Format: Rock/AOR
Jay Pugliese, General Manager/Sales Manager
Andrew Boris, Programming Director
Anthony Verano, Director of Marketing & Promotions
Jillian Price, Traffic Manager/Promotions Coordinator
Kathy Butsko, Business Manager

WDNB
11-15-1999; 102.1 MHz FM; *Hrs Open:* 24; 6 kw; 253 ft.; N41 44 30 W74 51 23
198 Bridgeville Rd., Monticello, NY 12701 US
(845) 974-9898; *Fax:* (845) 794-0125
www.boldgoldnewyork.com
pciliberto@boldgoldmedia.com
License: Jeffersonville, Sullivan County, NY held by Bold Gold Media Group L.P.
Group Owner: Bold Gold Media Group LP; (acq 5-23-2005; grpsl).
Arbitron Metro Market: Liberty, NY; *Format:* Country; *Hrs. of News Programming:* news progmg 5 hrs wkly; *No. News Employees:* 1; *Target Audience:* 25 plus; male & female general high school education plus *Adv.Rates:* 20; 15; 18; 12
Paul Ciliberto, General Manager
Dawn Ciorciari, Director of Sales
Jennifer Desrochers, Promotions Manager
Mike Sakell, News Director

Johnson City

WLTB
09-03-1972; 101.7 MHz FM; 0.58 kw; 1024 ft.; N42 3 22 W75 56 39
3215 East Main Street, 2nd Floor, Endwell, NY 13760 US
(607) 748-9131; *Fax:* (607) 748-0061
www.magic1017fm.com
info@magic1017fm.com
License: Johnson City, Broome County, NY held by GM Broadcasting Inc.
Nat'l Network: CNN Radio; *Nat'l Reps:* Christal
Arbitron Metro Market: Binghamton, NY; *Format:* Adult Contemp; *Target Audience:* 25 - 54; emphasis on females
Thomas Mollen, President
Steve Gilinsky, General Manager

Johnstown

WIZR
01-01-1964; 930 kHz AM; *Hrs Open:* 24; 1 kw-D, ND1; 0.028 kw-N, ND1; N42 59 54 W74 21 31
309 West Montomery Street, Johnstown, NY 12095 US
(518) 762-4631; *Fax:* (518) 762-0105
License: Johnstown, NY held by 6 Johnson Road Licenses Inc.
Group Owner: Pamal Broadcasting Ltd.; (acq 10-19-2001; grpsl).
Arbitron Metro Market: Albany-Schenectady-Troy, NY; *Format:* Adult Contemp *Special Programming:* It one hr, Pol one hr, Sp one hr wkly; *Hrs. of News Programming:* news progmg 6 hrs wkly; *No. News Employees:* 1 *Target Audience:* 25-54.; *Adv. Rates:* 10; 10; 10; 10
Tom Kuettel, President/General Manager
Mike Swain, Operations Manager/Programming Director
Joey Fisk, Directo4r of Sales Marketing

Kingston

*WAMK
03-01-1988; 90.9 MHz FM; *Hrs Open:* 24; 0.94 kw; 1486 ft.; N42 4 35 W74 6 26 *Rebroadcasts:* Rebroadcasts WAMC-FM Albany 100%
P.O. Box 66600, Albany, NY 12206 US
(518) 465-5233; *Fax:* (518) 432-0991
www.wamc.org
mail@wamc.org
License: Kingston, Ulster County, NY held by WAMC.
Group Owner: WAMC/Northeast Public Radio
Nat'l Network: PRI; NPR; *Wire Services:* AP
Arbitron Metro Market: Poughkeepsie NY; *Format:* News, News/Talk, 86 *Special Programming:* Jazz 13 hrs, folk 7 hrs; *Hrs. of News Programming:* News progmg 77 hrs wkly; *Target Audience:* General.
Alan Chartock, CEO
Ian Lect, Vice President

WKXP
12-13-1965; 94.3 MHz FM; *Hrs Open:* 24; 2.25 kw; 545 ft.; N41 53 44 W73 59 32
2 Pendell Road, Poughkeepsie, NY 12602 US
(845) 471-1500; *Fax:* (845) 454-1204
www.hudsonvalleycountry.com
jason.finkelberg@townsquaremedia.com
License: Kingston, Ulster County, NY held by Peak Broadcasting of Fresno Licenses LLC
Group Owner: Townsquare Media; (acq 2-11-2004; $3.5 million).
Arbitron Metro Market: Poughkeepsie, NY; *Format:* Country; *Target Audience:* 18-49; women; *Adv. Rates:* 35; 25; 30; na
Jason Finklelberg, General Manager
Beth Christy, Brand Manager
Jason Pugliese, Director Of Sales
Jackie Corley, Digital Managing Editor

*WFGB
01-01-1985; 89.7 MHz FM; *Hrs Open:* 24; 3.1 kw; 1486 ft.; N42 4 35 W74 6 26
P.O. Box 777, Lake Katrine, NY 12449 US
(800) 724-8518; *Fax:* (845) 336-7205
www.soundoflife.org
email@soundoflife.org
License: Kingston, Ulster County, NY held by Sound of Life Inc.

Arbitron Metro Market: Kingston, NY; *Format:* Christian; *Hrs. of News Programming:* News progmg 3 hrs wkly; *Target Audience:* General.
Tom Michaels Zahradnik, CEO
Tom Zahradnik, General Manager
Joe Hunter, Programming Director
Donna Quiles, Office Administrator/Director of Partner Relations
Connie Van Kleeck, Assistant Program Director
Derek Duncan, BusinessPartnership Representative
Paul Grimsland, Production Director
Tim Millard, Secretary

***WFRH**
09-01-1993; 91.7 MHz FM; *Hrs Open:* 24; 1.2 kw vert; 325 ft.; N41 59 14 W74 1 13
4135 Northgate Blvd., Suite 1, Sacramento, CA 95834 US
(315) 331-7482; *Fax:* (410) 268-0931
www.familyradio.com
info@familyradio.com
License: Kingston, Ulster County, NY held by Family Stations Inc.
Group Owner: Family Stations Inc.
Format: Religious
Harold Camping, President
Don Evans, Operations Manager/Vice President

WGHQ
03-04-1956; 920 kHz AM; *Hrs Open:* 24; 5 kw-D, DA1; 0.078 kw-N, DA1; N41 53 9 W73 58 15
427 Bedford Road, Suite 300, Pleasantville, NY 10570 US
(845) 838-6000; *Fax:* (845) 838-6088
License: Kingston, NY held by 6 Johnson Road Licenses Inc.
Format: News, News/Talk, 86 *Special Programming:* Relg 3 hrs wkly; *No. News Employees:* 1; *Target Audience:* 30 plus.
Walter Maxwell, General Manager

WKNY
08-01-1939; 1490 kHz AM; *Hrs Open:* 24; 1 kw-U, ND1; N41 56 11 W74 0 30
Mailing Address: 718 Broadway, Kingston, NY 12401 US
Second Address: Box 1398, Kingston, NY 12402
(845) 331-1490; *Fax:* (845) 331-9569
www.1490wkny.com
jason.finkelberg@townsquaremedia.com
License: Kingston, NY held by Peak Broadcasting of Fresno Licenses LLC
Group Owner: Townsquare Media; (acq 1-23-02; grpsl).
Nat'l Network: CBS; *Nat'l Reps:* Katz Radio; *Wire Services:* AP
Format: Adult Contemp *Special Programming:* Ger one hr, Pol one hr, Irish one hr wkly; *Hrs. of News Programming:* news progmg 26 hrs wkly; *No. News Employees:* 2; *Target Audience:* 25-54; 60% female; *Adv. Rates:* 28; 22; 24; 20
Jay Pugliese, General Sales Mgr
Warren Lawrence, Brand Manager
Jason Finkelberg, General Manager
Jackie Corley, Digital Managing Editor

Lake George

WCKM-FM
04-21-1994; 98.5 MHz FM; *Hrs Open:* 24; 0.37 kw; 1289 ft.; N43 25 12 W73 45 37
38 Bay Road, Queensberry, NY 12845 US
(518) 761-9890; *Fax:* (518) 761-9893
www.radiowins.com
License: Lake George, Warren County, NY held by Regional Radio Group LLC.
Group Owner: Regional Radio Group LLC; (acq 9-10-2008; grpsl)
Nat'l Network: ABC
Arbitron Metro Market: Albany-Schenectady-Troy, NY; *Format:* Oldies *Special Programming:* Interviews; *Hrs. of News Programming:* news progmg 7 hrs wkly; *No. News Employees:* 15; *Target Audience:* 25-54; upscalebaby boomers; *Adv. Rates:* 37; 25; 30; 15
Steve Babson, Operations Dir
Clay Ashworth, General Manager
Dan Miner, Station Manager/Programming Director
Pete Cloutier, Promotions Manager
Robin Truax, News Director
Ken Leccese, Sports Director

Lake Luzerne

WBAR-FM
06-30-1992; 94.7 MHz FM; *Hrs Open:* 24; 1.25 kw; 722 ft.; N43 18 16.7 W73 45 6.6 *Rebroadcasts:* Rebroadcasts WHAZ(AM) Troy 100%
30 Park Ave, Cohoes, NY 12047 US
(518) 237-1330; *Fax:* (518) 235-4468
events@aliveradionetwork.com
License: Lake Luzerne, Warren County, NY held by Capital Media Corp.
Group Owner: Capital Media Corp.; (acq 10-1-92)
Arbitron Metro Market: Tylertown, MS; *Format:* Religious
Paul Lotters, President/General Manager
Steve Klob, Operations Director/Sales Manager

Lake Placid

WIRD
11-21-1961; 920 kHz AM; *Hrs Open:* 24; 5 kw-D, ND1; 0.087 kw-N, ND1; N44 15 36 W74 1 22
159 Santanoni Avenue, Saranac Lake, NY 12983 US
(518) 891-1544; *Fax:* (518) 891-1545
brandy@mtnradio.com
License: Lake Placid, NY held by Radio Lake Placid Inc.
Group Owner: Mountain Communications; (acq 1-10-2005)
Nat'l Network: ESPN Radio
Format: Sports; *Hrs. of News Programming:* news progmg 20 hrs wkly; *No. News Employees:* 2; *Target Audience:* 25-54; working blue collar/college educated
Todd Morgan, President/General Manager

WLPW
10-01-1979; 105.5 MHz FM; *Hrs Open:* 24; 3 kw; -236 ft.; N44 15 36 W74 1 22
159 Santanoni Avenue, Saranac Lake, NY 12983 US
(518) 891-1544; *Fax:* (518) 891-1545
brandy@mtnradio.com
License: Lake Placid, Essex County, NY held by Radio Lake Placid Inc.
Group Owner: Mountain Communications
Format: Classic Rock
Ted Morgan, President/General Manager

Lake Ronkonkoma

***WSHR**
01-01-1966; 91.9 MHz FM; *Hrs Open:* 24; 6 kw; 177 ft.; N40 50 10 W73 5 59
212 Smith Road, Lake Ronkonkoma, NY 11779 US
(631) 471-1472
License: Lake Ronkonkoma, Suffolk County, NY held by Board of Education Sachem Central School District at Holbrook.
Format: Variety/Diverse; *Target Audience:* General.
Mark Laura, General Manager
Isaic Ramaswamy, Station Manager

Lake Success

WKTU
01-01-1940; 103.5 MHz FM; *Hrs Open:* 24; 6 kw; 1362 ft.; N40 44 54 W73 59 10
32 Avenue of the Americas, New York, NY 10013 US
(201) 420-3700; *Fax:* (201) 420-3737
www.ktu.com
License: Lake Success, Nassau County, NY held by AMFM Radio Licenses LLC.
Group Owner: iHeartMedia; (acq 8-30-2000; grpsl)
Nat'l Reps: D & R Radio
Arbitron Metro Market: New York; *Format:* Adult Contemp; *No. News Employees:* 1; *Target Audience:* 18-54.
Scott Hopeck, Market President
Jennifer Breault, General Sales Mgr
Rob Miller, Programming Director

Lakewood

WKZA
03-01-2001; 106.9 MHz FM; 5.1 kw; 738 ft.; N41 57 31 W79 16 11
106 West 3rd Street, #106, Jamestown, FL 14701 US
(716) 487-1106; *Fax:* (716) 488-2169
www.1069kissfm.com
sherriewkza@hotmail.com
License: Lakewood, Chautauqua County, NY held by Cross Country Communications LLC.
Arbitron Metro Market: Jamestown, NY; *Format:* Contemporary Hits/Top 40; *Target Audience:* 25-54.
John Newman, General Manager
Sherrie Brookmire, Sales Manager
Steve Rockford, Programming Director
Megan Arnone, Media Consultant
Jamie Trusler, Media Consultant
Jerod Zahn, Media Consultant
Bill Dorrion, Media Consultant

***WYRR**
88.9 MHz FM; 0.42 kw horiz, 0.336 kw vert; 335 ft.; N42 10 33 W79 19 2
US
(225)768-8300
www.jsm.org
onair@jsm.org
License: Lakewood, Chautauqua County, NY held by Muncy Hills Broadcasting Inc.
Arbitron Metro Market: Baton Rouge, LA; *Format:* Religious
Van Michael, President

Lancaster

WXRL
01-01-1964; 1300 kHz AM; *Hrs Open:* 24
P.O. Box 170, Lancaster, NY 14086 US
(716) 681-1313
www.wxrl.com
info@wxrl.com
License: Lancaster, NY held by Dome Broadcasting Inc.
Nat'l Network: CNN Radio
Arbitron Metro Market: Buffalo, NY; *Format:* Country *Special Programming:* German one hr, Polish 19 hrs wkly; *Target Audience:* 35 plus; Mature men & women 35 and older; *Adv. Rates:* 40; 40; 45; 30
Louis Schriver, President

Liberty

***WGWR**
11-01-1997; 88.1 MHz FM; *Hrs Open:* 24; 0.06 kw; 561 ft.; N41 48 55 W74 45 48 *Rebroadcasts:* Rebroadcasts WFGB(FM) Kingston 100%
P O Box 777, Lake Katrine, NY 12449 US
(845) 336-6199; *Fax:* (845) 336-7205
www.soundoflife.org
wmial@soundoflife.org
License: Liberty, Sullivan County, NY held by Sound of Life Inc.
Format: Christian
Tom Zahradnik, General Manager
Joe Hunter, Programming Director

WVOS
01-01-1947; 1240 kHz AM; *Hrs Open:* 5 AM-11 PM; 1 kw-U, ND1; N41 46 54 W74 43 49
198 Bridgeville Rd., Monticello, NY 12701 US
(845) 794-9898; *Fax:* (845) 794-0125
www.boldgoldnewyork.com
License: Liberty, NY held by Bold Gold Media Group LP
Group Owner: Bold Gold Media Group LP; (acq 11-2-2005; $1.7 million with co-located FM)
Arbitron Metro Market: Liberty, NY; *Format:* Country
Paul Ciliberto, General Manager
Dawn Ciorciari, Director of Sales
Jennifer Desrochers, Promotions Manager
Mike Sakell, News Director

WVOS-FM
12-01-1964; 95.9 MHz FM; *Hrs Open:* 24; 6 kw; 328 ft.; N41 45 9 W74 43 1
198 Bridgeville Road, Monticello, NY 12701 US
(845) 794-9898; *Fax:* (845) 794-0125
www.wvosfm.com
mail@wVOSFM.comÿ
License: Liberty, Sullivan County, NY
Arbitron Metro Market: Liberty, NY; *Format:* Oldies; *Target Audience:* 25-54.
Helena Manzione, General Manager
John Moultrie, Programming Director
Bill James, News Director

Little Falls

WIXT
06-10-1952; 1230 kHz AM; *Hrs Open:* 24; 1 kw-U, ND1; N43 2 33 W74 51 31
235 Walton St., Syracuse, NY 13202 US
(315) 797-1330; *Fax:* (315) 738-1073
www.espnur.com
pscibilia@galaxycommunications.com
License: Little Falls, NY held by Galaxy Utica Licensee LLC.
Group Owner: Galaxy Communications L.P.; (acq 10-24-2007; grpsl)
Arbitron Metro Market: Utica-Rome, NY; *Format:* Sports *Special Programming:* Farm one hr, relg one hr wkly; *Hrs. of News Programming:* news progmg 16 hrs wkly; *No. News Employees:* 1; *Target Audience:* 25-54.

WSKU
01-03-1991; 105.5 MHz FM; *Hrs Open:* 24; 2.25 kw; 528 ft.; N42 59 27 W74 55 6
185 Genesee Street, Suite 1601, Utica, NY 13501 US
(315) 734-9245; *Fax:* (315) 624-9245
www.cnykiss.com

License: Little Falls, Herkimer County, NY held by Roser Communications Network Inc.
Group Owner: Roser Communications Network Inc.; (acq 10-24-2007; grpsl)
Nat'l Reps: Roslin
Arbitron Metro Market: Utica-Rome, NY; *Format:* Contemporary Hits/Top 40; *Hrs. of News Programming:* news progmg one hr wkly; *No. News Employees:* 1; *Target Audience:* 25-54.
Dave Silvers, Operations Dir
Grant Roser, General Manager/Sales Manager
Shaun Andrews, Programming Director

Lockport

WLVL
05-08-1947; 1340 kHz AM
Mailing Address: P.O. Box 477, 320 Michigan Street, Lockport, NY 14095 US
Second Address: 320 Michigan St., Lockport, NY 14094
(716) 433-5944; *Fax:* (716) 433-6588
www.wlvl.com
wlvl@wlvl.com
License: Lockport, NY held by Culver Communications Inc.
Nat'l Network: Westwood One
Arbitron Metro Market: Lockport, NY; *Format:* News, News/Talk, 84, Talk *Special Programming:* Farm one hr, lt 2 hrs, Pol one hr, relg 3 hrs wkly; *Target Audience:* 25-64; adult Lockport area citizens
Richard Greene, President

Loudonville

*WVCR-FM
04-26-1963; 88.3 MHz FM; *Hrs Open:* 24; 2.8 kw; 840 ft.; N42 38 13 W74 0 5
515 Loudon Road/Route 9, Loudonville, NY 12211 US
(518) 782-6750
www.wvcr.com
dkibbey@siena.edu
License: Loudonville, Albany County, NY held by Siena College.
Arbitron Metro Market: Loudonville, NY; *Format:* Variety/Diverse *Special Programming:* Pol 3 hrs, Sp 3 hrs, gospel 3 hrs, Irish 3 hrs; *Target Audience:* 12-34; female; *Adv. Rates:* 20; 20; 20; 20
Darrin Kibbey, General Manager
John F. Kelly, Director

Lowville

WLLG
04-01-1987; 99.3 MHz FM; *Hrs Open:* 24; 1 kw; 561 ft.; N43 45 12 W75 33 50
7606 North State Street, Lowville, NY 13367 US
(315) 376-7500; *Fax:* (315) 376-8549
www.themoose.net
sales@themoose.net
License: Lowville, Lewis County, NY held by The Flack Broadcasting Group L.L.C.
Nat'l Network: USA
Format: Country, News *Special Programming:* Farm 3 hrs, relg 2 hrs wkly; *Hrs. of News Programming:* news progmg 18 hrs wkly; *No. News Employees:* 1; *Target Audience:* General.
William Flack, President
Brian Best, News Director
Ken Ruhlend, Chief Engineer

Malone

WICY
11-04-1946; 1500 kHz AM; *Hrs Open:* 18; 1 kW; N44 50 46 W74 16 7
86 Porter Rd, Malone, NY 12953 USA
(518) 483-1100; *Fax:* (518) 483-1382
www.1027wicy.com
License: Malone, NY held by Cartier Communications Inc.
Group Owner: Martz Communications Group; (acq 6-30-97; $761,000 with co-located FM)
Nat'l Reps: Rgnl Reps
Arbitron Metro Market: Malone, NY; *Format:* Oldies *Special Programming:* Farm one hr wkly; *Hrs. of News Programming:* news progmg 15 hrs wkly; *No. News Employees:* 2; *Target Audience:* 25-54.
Matt Maneely, Operations Dir
Michael Boldt, General Manager
Kim Kiser, General Sales Mgr
Jonathan Steele, Programming Director

*WSLO
02-01-1989; 90.9 MHz FM; *Hrs Open:* 24; 0.2 kw; 348 ft.; N44 49 46 W74 22 31 *Rebroadcasts:* Rebroadcasts WSLU(FM) Canton 100%
N. Country Public Radio, Canton, NY 13617 US
(315) 229-5356; *Fax:* (315) 229-5373
www.ncpr.org
radio@ncpr.org
License: Malone, Franklin County, NY held by St. Lawrence University.
Format: Variety/Diverse; *Hrs. of News Programming:* news progmg 35 hrs wkly; *No. News Employees:* 2; *Target Audience:* General.
Shelly Pike, Operations Dir
Ellen Rocco, General Manager/Station Manager
Jackie Sauter, Programming Director
Martha Foley, News Director
Robert Sauter, Chief Engineer
Sandra Demarest, Development Director

WVNV
05-01-1993; 96.5 MHz FM; *Hrs Open:* 20; 16 kW; 400 ft.; N44 46 56 W74 13 9
86 Porter Rd, Malone, NY 12953 USA
(518) 483-1100; *Fax:* (518) 483-1382
www.country965.com
License: Malone, Franklin County, NY held by Cartier Communications Inc.
Group Owner: Martz Communications Group
Arbitron Metro Market: Malone, NY; *Format:* Country; *Hrs. of News Programming:* news progmg 2 hrs wkly; *No. News Employees:* 2; *Target Audience:* 18-54.
Michael Boldt, General Manager
Kim Kiser, General Sales Mgr
Jonathan Steele, Programming Director

*WMHQ
12-03-2003; 90.1 MHz FM; *Hrs Open:* 24; 2.7 kW; 354 ft.; N44 49 41 W74 22 43 *Rebroadcasts:* Rebroadcasts WMHR(FM) Syracuse 99%
4044 Makyes Rd, Syracuse, NY 13215 USA
(800) 677-1881
www.marshillnetwork.org
info@marshillnetwork.org
License: Malone, Franklin County, NY held by Mars Hill Broadcasting Co. Inc.
Group Owner: Mars Hill Network
Nat'l Network: Moody; Salem Radio Network; *Wire Services:* AP
Arbitron Metro Market: Malone, NY; *Format:* Christian; *Hrs. of News Programming:* News progmg 6 hrs wkly; *Target Audience:* General; Christian families
Wayne Taylor, General Manager
Mike Dwinell, Chief Engineer

Malta

WQSH
10-01-1996; 105.7 MHz FM; 7.1 kw; Ant 613 ft; N42 47 09 W73 37 43
1241 Kings Rd., Schenectady, NY 12804
(518) 881-1515; *Fax:* (518) 881-1516
www.buzz1057.com
License: Malta, Saratoga County, NY
Group Owner: Townsquare Media; (acq 1-4-2007; $4.9 million)
Population Served: 275,000; *Arbitron Metro Market:* Albany-Schenectady-Troy, NY; *Target Audience:* 18-54; general; *Adv. Rates:* 30; 28; 30; 15
Dan Austin, General Manager

Manlius

WAQX
08-23-1978; 95.7 MHz FM; *Hrs Open:* 24; 25 kw; 300 ft; N43 00 25 W76 05 38
1064 James St., Syracuse, NY 13203 US
(315) 472-0200; *Fax:* (315) 472-1146
www.95x.com
License: Manlius, NY held by Radio License Holding CBC, LLC
Group Owner: Cumulus Media Inc.; (acq 4-26-01; grpsl).
Nat'l Network: ABC; *Nat'l Reps:* D & R Radio
Arbitron Metro Market: Syracuse, NY; *Format:* Rock/AOR *Special Programming:* Pub service one hr wkly; *Hrs. of News Programming:* News progmg 3 hrs wkly; *Target Audience:* 19-49; male
Joe DeTomaso, Programming Director
Janice Cole, Promotions Director

Manorville

WEHM
07-21-2003; 92.9 MHz FM; 6 kw; Ant 276 ft; N40 52 10 W72 34 37
Mailing Address: PO Box 157, Water Mill, NY 11976
Second Address: 249 Montauk Hwy., Amagansett, NY 11930
(631) 267-7800; *Fax:* (631) 267-1018
www.wehm.com
info@wehm.com
License: Manorville, Suffolk County, NY held by AAA Licensing LLC.
Group Owner: Long Island Radio Broadcasting LLC; (acq 4-30-2003).
Mike Raye, President/General Manager
Suzanne Wolfson, Sales Manager
Harry Wareing, Programming Director
Rebecca Campbell, Traffic Manager

Massena

WMSA
10-12-1945; 1340 kHz AM; *Hrs Open:* 5:30 AM-10:15 PM
2155 State Highway 420, Massena, NY 13662 US
(315) 769-3333; *Fax:* (315) 769-3299
www.1340wmsa.com
info@1340wmsa.com
License: Massena, NY held by Stephens Media Group-Massena LLC.
Group Owner: Stephens Family L.P.
Arbitron Metro Market: Massena, NY; *Format:* Adult Contemp; *Hrs. of News Programming:* news progmg 16 hrs wkly; *No. News Employees:* 1; *Target Audience:* 18 plus.
Chuck Poirier, Operations Manager/Programming Director
Mark F. Gaines, General Manager
Bob LaRue, News Director

WYBG
08-18-1958; 1050 kHz AM; *Hrs Open:* 6 AM-7 PM; 1 kw-D, 500 w-N; N44 53 42 W74 56 05
Box 298, 24 Andrews St., Massena, NY 13662
(315) 764-0554
License: Massena, St. Lawrence County, NY held by Wade Communications Inc.
Nat'l Network: USA; *Nat'l Reps:* Commercial Media Sales
Population Served: 295,000 *Special Programming:* American Indian, children, farm, folk; *Hrs. of News Programming:* news progmg 14 hrs wkly; *No. News Employees:* 2; *Target Audience:* 25-65; baby boomers & seniors *Adv. Rates:* 15; 15; 15; 15
Curran Wade, President
Dorothy Wade, Operations Dir

Mechanicville

WTMM-FM
01-04-1993; 104.5 MHz FM; *Hrs Open:* 24; 5 kw; 351 ft.; N42 52 44 W73 51 47
1241 Kings Road, Schenectady, NY 12303 US
(805) 240-2070
www.1045theteam.com
License: Mechanicville, Rensselaer County, NY
Group Owner: Townsquare Media; (acq 8-24-2001; grpsl)
Nat'l Network: ESPN Radio
Arbitron Metro Market: Duluth-Superior MN-WI
Steven Price, CEO
Dan Austin, General Manager
Stephen Guittari, Programming Director

Medford

WNYG
01-01-1958; 1440 kHz AM; *Hrs Open:* 24; 1 kw-D, 38 w-N; N40 42 32 W73 21 53
404 Rt. 109, West Babylon, NY 11704
(631) 321-9694; *Fax:* (631) 321-9693
License: Medford, Suffolk County, NY held by Multicultural Radio Broadcasting Licensee LLC.
Group Owner: Multicultural Radio Broadcasting Inc.; (acq 6-14-00; $850,000).
Population Served: 2,500,000; *Arbitron Metro Market:* New York; *Hrs. of News Programming:* news progmg 3 hrs wkly; *No. News Employees:* 1; *Target Audience:* 25-64.; *Adv. Rates:* 600; 300; 600; 240
Phyllis Rose, General Manager
Doug Edwards, Programming Director

Medina

*WFWO
89.7 MHz FM; 0.4 kw; 131 ft.; N43 14 33 W78 18 27
P.O. Box 287, Freeport, ME 04032 US
(207) 865-3448; *Fax:* (207) 865-1763
www.positive.fm
info@positive.fm
License: Medina, Orleans County, NY held by The Positive Radio Network.
Arbitron Metro Market: Freeport, ME; *Format:* Gospel
Mie Stoddard, Chairman
Suzanne Happs, General Manager
Kenny Robinson, Programming Director
Mark Marston, Office Manager

Shawn Katzback, Business Development Representative
Holly Norburg, Administrative Assistant / VolunteerCoordinator

Mexico

WNDR-FM
01-01-1997; 103.9 MHz FM; 3 kw; 292 ft; N43 28 36 W76 16 44
Renard Communications Corp., 401 W. Kirkpatrick St., Syracuse, NY 13215
(315) 472-0222; *Fax:* (315) 478-7745
WVOARadio.com
programming@WVOARadio.com
License: Mexico, Oswego County, NY held by Renard Communications Corp.
Special Programming: Ger 2 hrs, It 2 hrs, Pol 4 hrs , Sp 15 hrs wkly
Sam Furco, General Manager

Middletown

WALL
08-06-1942; 1340 kHz AM; *Hrs Open:* 24
2 Pendell Road, Middletown, NY 12602 US
(845) 471-1500; *Fax:* (845)-454-1204
License: Middletown, NY held by Peak Broadcasting of Fresno Licenses LLC
Group Owner: Townsquare Media; (acq 1-23-02; grpsl).
Arbitron Metro Market: Middletown, NY; *Format:* Children; *Hrs. of News Programming:* news progmg 30 hrs wkly; *No. News Employees:* 2; *Target Audience:* 35-64; educated, upscale families

***WOSR**
02-03-1992; 91.7 MHz FM; *Hrs Open:* 24; 1.8 kw; 630 ft.; N41 36 4 W74 33 17 *Rebroadcasts:* Rebroadcasts WAMC-FM Albany 100%
Mailing Address: 318 Central Avenue, Albany, NY 12206 US
Second Address: 318 Central Ave., Middletown, NY 12206-6600
(518) 465-5233,(800) 323-9262; *Fax:* (518) 432-6974
www.wamc.org
mail@wamc.org
License: Middletown, Orange County, NY held by WAMC.
Group Owner: WAMC/Northeast Public Radio
Nat'l Network: NPR; PRI; *Wire Services:* AP
Arbitron Metro Market: Newburgh-Middletown, NY (Mid-Hudson Valley); *Format:* News, Talk *Special Programming:* Folk 7 hrs, jazz 13 hrs wkly; *Hrs. of News Programming:* News progmg 77 hrs wkly *Target Audience:* General.
Alan Chartock, CEO
Selma Kaplan, Operations Director/Senior Vice President

WRRV
11-11-1966; 92.7 MHz FM; *Hrs Open:* 24; 6 kw; 269 ft.; N41 27 25 W74 26 24
Mailing Address: . Pendell Road, Poughkeepsie, NY 12601 US
Second Address: W
(845) 471-1500
www.wrrv.com
License: Middletown, Orange County, NY held by Peak Broadcasting of Fresno Licenses LLC
Group Owner: Townsquare Media
Arbitron Metro Market: Newburgh-Middletown, NY (Mid-Hudson Valley); *Format:* Alternative *Special Programming:* New mus 2 hrs wkly; *Hrs. of News Programming:* news progmg 3 hrs wkly; *No. News Employees:* 1 *TargetAudience:* 18-44; younger, mobile, upscale families
Jay Pugliese, General Manager
Andrew Boris, Programming Director
Anthony Verano, Director of Marketing & Promotions
Bill Dunn, Music Director

Milford

WYNY(AM)
1400 kHz AM; 1 kw-U, DA-D; N41 28 26 W74 27 01
2927 US Route 6, Slate Hill, NY 10973
(845) 355-4001; *Fax:* (845) 355-4002
License: Milford, PA held by Digital Radio Broadcasting Inc.
Group Owner: Digital Radio Broadcasting Inc.
Arbitron Metro Market: Newburgh-Middletown, NY (Mid-Hudson Valley)
Bud Williamson, President

***WUOW**
88.5 MHz FM; 0.1 kw vert; 732 ft.; N42 35 44 W74 51 53 US
License: Milford, Otsego County, NY
Group Owner: State University of New York College at Oneonta

Mineola

WTHE
01-01-1964; 1520 kHz AM; 0.347 kw-C, NDD; 1 kw-D, NDD; N40 44 45 W73 37 29
260 East Second Street, Mineola, NY 11501 US
(516) 742-1520; *Fax:* (516) 742-2878
www.wthe1520am.com
nygospelradio@aol.com
License: Mineola, NY held by Universal Broadcasting of New York Inc.
Group Owner: Universal Broadcasting of New York Inc.; acq 7-10-69; $235,000).
Arbitron Metro Market: Mineola, NY; *Format:* Black, Gospel, 74; *Hrs. of News Programming:* news progmg 10 hrs wkly; *No. News Employees:* 1; *Target Audience:* General.; *Adv. Rates:* 30;30;30;30
Darren Greggs, Programming Director

Minetto

WKRH
10-01-1996; 106.5 MHz FM; 5 kw; 328 ft.; N43 25 4 W76 27 54
235 Walton St., Syracuse, NY 13202 US
(315) 472-9111; *Fax:* (315) 472-1888
www.krock.com
askus@krock.com
License: Minetto, Oswego County, NY held by Galaxy Syracuse Licensee LLC.
Group Owner: Galaxy Communications L.P.; (acq 8-31-2000).
Arbitron Metro Market: Syracuse, NY; *Format:* Alternative; *Hrs. of News Programming:* news progmg 2 hrs wkly; *No. News Employees:* 1; *Target Audience:* 18-49; men

Monroe

***WLJP**
05-01-1991; 89.3 MHz FM; 0.2 kw; 1040 ft.; N41 22 38 W74 7 55 *Rebroadcasts:* Rebroadcasts WFGB(FM) Kingston 100%
PO Box 777, 199 Tuyten Bridge, Lake Katrine, NY 12449 US
(800) 724-8518; *Fax:* (845) 336-7205
www.soundoflife.org
License: Monroe, Orange County, NY held by Sound of Life Inc.
Format: Christian; *Target Audience:* General.
Tom Zahradnik, General Manager
Joe Hunter, Programming Director

Montauk

WELJ
02-19-1993; 104.7 MHz FM; *Hrs Open:* 24; 6 kw; Ant 328 ft; N41 01 57 W71 58 31
7 Governor Winthrop Blvd., New London, CT 06320 US
(860) 443-1980
www.1047nashicon.com
danny.lyons@cumulus.com
License: Montauk, NY held by Joule Broadcasting, LLC
Group Owner: Cumulus Media Inc.; (acq 4-3-2003)
Arbitron Metro Market: New York; *Format:* Country
Jessica Vargas, General Sales Mgr
Danny Lyons, Programming Director

***WEER**
01-01-2004; 88.7 MHz FM; 8 w horiz, 2.7 kw vert; Ant 226 ft; N41 01 53 W71 58 32 *Rebroadcasts:* Rebroadcasts WPKN(FM) Bridgeport, CT 100%
244 Myrtle Avenue, Bridgeport, CT 06604
(203) 331-9756
www.wpkn.org
wpkn@wpkn.org
License: Montauk, Suffolk County, NY held by WPKN Inc.

Steve di Costanzo, General Manager

Monticello

***WJUX**
11-01-1994; 99.7 MHz FM; *Hrs Open:* 24; 6 kw; 299 ft.; N41 45 9 W74 43 1
127 White Oak Lane, Old Bridge, NJ 08857 US
(888) 861-6100; *Fax:* (732) 679-030
www.bridgefm.org
info@bridgefm.org
License: Monticello, Sullivan County, NY held by Bridgelight LLC
Format: Religious; *Target Audience:* 35-54.
Rob Taylor, General Manager
Patti Gates, General Sales Mgr

WSUL
04-16-1977; 98.3 MHz FM; *Hrs Open:* 24; 2.2 kw; 535 ft.; N41 39 38 W74 41 14
198 Bridgeville Rd., Monticello, NY 12701 US
(845) 794-9898; *Fax:* (845) 794-0125
www.wsul.com
pciliberto@boldgoldmedia.com
License: Monticello, Sullivan County, NY held by Bold Gold Media Group LP
Group Owner: Bold Gold Media Group LP; (acq 3-17-2005; $2.5 million).
Format: Adult Contemp; *No. News Employees:* 2; *Target Audience:* 25-54.; *Adv. Rates:* 42; 36; 42; 26
Helena Manzione, General Manager

Montour Falls

WNGZ
06-01-1973; 104.9 MHz FM; *Hrs Open:* 24; 1 kw; 479 ft.; N42 15 5 W76 52 53
2205 College Avenue, Elmira, NY 14903 US
(607) 732-4400; *Fax:* (607) 732-7774
www.wngz.com
smitty.oloughlin@bybradio.com
License: Montour Falls, Schuyler County, NY held by Community Broadcasters LLC
Group Owner: Community Broadcasters LLC; (acq 12-1-02; grpsl).
Arbitron Metro Market: Elmira, NY; *Format:* Classic Rock; *No. News Employees:* 1; *Target Audience:* 20-49; baby boomers, young adults
Scott Free, Operations Dir
Smitty O'Loughlin, General Manager
Ally Payne, Webmaster

Morristown

WYSX
11-01-1998; 96.7 MHz FM; *Hrs Open:* 24; 17 kw; 354 ft.; N44 34 43 W75 30 51
1 Bridge Plaza, Suite 204, Ogdensburg, NY 13669 US
(315) 393-1220; *Fax:* (315) 393-3974
www.yesfm.com
john@q1029.com
License: Morristown, St. Lawrence County, NY held by Stephens Media Group-Ogdensburg LLC.
Group Owner: Stephens Family L.P.
Arbitron Metro Market: Morristown, NY; *Format:* Contemporary Hits/Top 40; *Target Audience:* 18-34.; *Adv. Rates:* 25; 25; 25; 25
Mark Gaines, General Manager
Dawn Merz, Sales Manager
Dave Merz, Programming Director
Ethan Shantie, News Director
Kelly Lustyik, Office/Traffic Manager

Mount Hope

***WMFU(FM)**
09-01-1994; 90.1 MHz FM; *Hrs Open:* 24; 1.1 kw; Ant 600 ft; N41 25 36 W74 34 54
Mailing Address: Box 2011, Jersey City, NJ 07303-2011
Second Address: 4th Floor, 43 Montgomery St., Jersey City, NJ 7302
(201) 521-1416; *Fax:* (201) 521-1286
www.wfmu.org
License: Mount Hope, Orange County, NY held by Auricle Communications.
Population Served: 7,018; *Arbitron Metro Market:* Mount Hope, NY; *Format:* Variety/Diverse; *Target Audience:* General.
Ken Freedman, Station Manager & Program Director
Brian Turner, Music Director
John Fogarazzo, Chief Engineer
Jeff Moore, Technology Director
Brian Turner, Music Director
Liz Berg, Assistant General Manager
Joe McGasko,Underwriting Director

Mount Kisco

WRVP
10-27-1957; 1310 kHz AM; *Hrs Open:* 6 AM-6 PM
P.O. Box 2908, Patterson, NJ 07509 US
(973) 881-8700; *Fax:* (973) 881-8324
www.radiovision.net
License: Mount Kisco, NY held by Radio Vision Cristiana Management Corp.
Arbitron Metro Market: Paterson, NJ; *Format:* Christian; *No. News Employees:* 3; *Target Audience:* General.; *Adv. Rates:* 40; 30; 40; na
Delia Goldschmidt, Station Manager

***WFME**
01-15-1964; 106.3 MHz FM; 1.4 kw; Ant 440 ft; N41 11 56 W73 41 37 *Rebroadcasts:* Rebroadcasts KEAR(AM) San Francisco, CA 100%
4135 Northgate Boulevard, Suite 1, Sacramento, CA 95834

(916) 641-8191; *Fax:* (916) 736-4832
www.familyradio.com
License: Mount Kisco, Westchester County, NY held by Family Stations Inc.
Group Owner: Family Stations Inc.
Population Served: 150,000 *Format:* Christian, Religious
Charlie Menut, Station Manager

***WWES**
88.9 MHz FM; 0.2 kw vert; 115 ft.; N41 14 20 W73 42 48
318 Central Avenue, Albany, NY 12206 US
(518) 465-5233; *Fax:* (518) 432-6974
www.wamc.org
License: Mount Kisco, Westchester County, NY held by WAMC.
Group Owner: WAMC/Northeast Public Radio
Arbitron Metro Market: Mount Kisco, NY
Alan Chartock, CEO
Katie Britton, Programming Director
Ian Pickus, News Director
Joe Donahue, Vice President, News and Programming

Napeague

***WEGB**
90.7 MHz FM; 4.6 kw; 262 ft.; N41 1 56 W71 58 30
2837 Noyac Road, Sagharbor, NJ 11963 US
(631) 725-4155; *Fax:* (631) 725-4155
cbchamptons.com
office@cbchamptons.com
License: Napeague, Suffolk County, NY held by Community Bible Church.
Arbitron Metro Market: Napeague, NY
Doug Kinney, President

New City

WRKL
07-04-1964; 910 kHz AM; *Hrs Open:* 24; 1 kw-D, 0.8 kw-N
3656 W. Belmont Ave., Chicago, IL 60618 US
(773) 588-6300; *Fax:* (773) 588-0834
www.polskieradio.com
License: New City, NY held by Polnet Communications Ltd.
Group Owner: Polnet Communications Ltd.
Arbitron Metro Market: New York; *Format:* Ethnic, Polish; *Hrs. of News Programming:* news progmg 50 hrs wkly; *No. News Employees:* 1; *Target Audience:* 18-54; Polish language audience; *Adv. Rates:* 60; 60; 60;30
Walter Kotaba, President

New Paltz

WBWZ
11-19-1992; 93.3 MHz FM; *Hrs Open:* 24; 0.33 kw; 968 ft.; N41 41 58 W74 0 11
20 Tucker Drive, Poughkeepsie, NY 12603 US
(845) 471-2300; *Fax:* (845) 471-2683
www.rock933.com
License: New Paltz, Ulster County, NY held by AMFM Radio Licenses LLC.
Group Owner: iHeartMedia; (acq 12-22-2000; with WRWD-FM Highland).
Nat'l Network: Fox News Radio; *Nat'l Reps:* Katz Radio; *Wire Services:* AP
Arbitron Metro Market: Poughkeepsie, NY; *Format:* Classic Rock; *Hrs. of News Programming:* news progmg 7 hrs wkly; *No. News Employees:* 1; *Target Audience:* 25-54; baby boomers
Chuck Benfer, Market President
Chris Marino, Senior Vice President of Programming
Rob VanDerbeck, Senior Vice President of Sales
Jaleel Williams, Programming Director
Elise Penge, Promotions Director
Deirdre Burns, Digital ContentDirector

New Rochelle

WVIP
01-01-1953; 93.5 MHz FM; *Hrs Open:* 24; 1.75 kw; 433 ft.; N40 52 48 W73 52 40
1 Broadcast Forum, New Rochelle, NY 10801 US
(914) 636-1460; *Fax:* (914) 636-2900
don@wvox.com
License: New Rochelle, Westchester County, NY held by Hudson-Westchester Radio, Inc.
Nat'l Network: Fox News Radio; Music of Your Life
Arbitron Metro Market: New York; *Format:* Variety/Diverse; *Hrs. of News Programming:* 12; *No. News Employees:* 2; *Target Audience:* 18 plus; adults
William O'Shaughnessy, Chairman
Cindy Gallagher, Vice Chairman
David O'Shaughnessy, President
Don Stevens, Vice President of Operations
Judy Fremont, Station Manager
Maggie Hernandez, Office/Marketing Manager
Ari Brown, WebOperations Manager

WVOX
01-01-1950; 1460 kHz AM; *Hrs Open:* 24; 0.5 kw-D, ND1; 0.122 kw-N, ND1; N40 55 42 W73 46 30
Mailing Address: 411 5th Avenue, New Rochelle, NY 10801 US
Second Address: Broadcast Forum, New Rochelle, NY 10801
(914) 636-1460; *Fax:* (914) 636-2900
www.wvox.com
don@wvox.com
License: New Rochelle, NY held by Hudson-Westchester Radio Inc.
Nat'l Network: Fox News Radio; Music of Your Life
Arbitron Metro Market: Westchester, NY; *Format:* Variety/Diverse; *Hrs. of News Programming:* 6 hours daily; *No. News Employees:* 4; *Target Audience:* 24 plus; community minded; *Adv. Rates:* 110; 90; 72; na
Cindy Hall Gallagherÿ, Vice Chairman
William O'Shaughnessy, President
David O'Shaughnessy, Operations Dir
Judy Fremontÿ, Station Manager
Maggie Hernandez, Office & Marketing Manager
Kevin Elliott, Director Of InformationalServices

New York

WADO
03-12-1934; 1280 kHz AM; *Hrs Open:* 24; 50 kw-D, DA2; 7.2 kw-N, DA2; N40 49 36 W74 4 32
485 Madison Ave., 3rd Fl., New York, NY 10022 US
(212) 310-6000; *Fax:* (212) 310-6095
www.univision.com
License: New York, NY held by WADO-AM License Corp.
Group Owner: Univision Radio; (acq 9-22-2003; grpsl).
Nat'l Reps: Katz Radio
Arbitron Metro Market: New York, NY; *Format:* News, News/Talk, 82, Talk; *Hrs. of News Programming:* news progmg 7 hrs wkly; *No. News Employees:* 1; *Target Audience:* 25 plus.
Ramon Pineda, General Manager
Peter Tran, National Sales Manager
Nomar Vizcarrondo, Programming Director
Luis Antonio Valera, Director of Marketing and Promotions
Donovan Welsh, Sales Manager
Karima Khawja, Director of Sales
RossDaron, Digital Sales Manager

WAXQ
12-01-1956; 104.3 MHz FM; 6 kw; 1362 ft.; N40 44 54 W73 59 10
32 Ave. of the Americas, New York, NY 10013 US
(212) 377-7900
www.q1043.com
License: New York, New York County, NY held by AMFM Radio Licenses LLC.
Group Owner: iHeartMedia; (acq 8-30-2000; grpsl).
Arbitron Metro Market: New York, NY; *Format:* Classic Rock
Scott Hopeck, Market President
Thea Mitchem, Senior Vice President of Programming

WBAI
01-01-1960; 99.5 MHz FM; *Hrs Open:* 24; 4.3 kw; 1362 ft.; N40 44 54 W73 59 10
388 Atlantic Avenue, Brooklyn, NY 11217 US
(800) 877-5600; *Fax:* (916) 251-1650
www.air1.com
info@air1.com
License: New York, New York County, NY held by Pacifica Foundation.
Group Owner: Pacifica Foundation Inc.; (acq 1-9-60)
Arbitron Metro Market: Scottsbluff NE; *Format:* Alternative, Christian
Tony Ryan, Operations Dir
Berthold Reimers, General Manager
Andrew Phillips, Programming Director
Andrea Katz, Development Director

WBBR
02-13-1991; 1130 kHz AM; 50 kw-D, DAN; 50 kw-N, DAN; N40 48 39 W74 2 24
731 Lexington Avenue, New York, NY 10022 US
(212) 318-2000; *Fax:* (212) 893-5637
License: New York, NY held by Bloomberg Communications Inc.
Format: Christian
Al Mayers, General Manager
Anthony Mancini, Promotions Manager
Mark Mills, News Director

WBLS
09-15-1965; 107.5 MHz FM; *Hrs Open:* 24; 4.2 kw; 1362 ft.; N40 44 54 W73 59 10
3 Park Ave., 40th Fl., New York, NY 10016 USA
(212) 447-1000; *Fax:* (212) 447-5193
www.wbls.com
Deon@wbls.com
License: New York, New York County, NY held by WBLS-WLIB License LLC
Group Owner: Emmis Communications Corp.
Population Served: 2,300,000; *Arbitron Metro Market:* New York; *Format:* Black; *Target Audience:* 25-54; upscale, urban
Deon Levingston, VP & General Manager
Skip Dillard, Program Director & Operations Manager
Bethany Kent, Promotions Director

WCBS
01-01-1924; 880 kHz AM; *Hrs Open:* 24; 50 kW; N40 51 35 W73 47 9
345 Hudson St., New York, NY 10014 USA
www.wcbs880.com
License: New York, NY held by CBS Radio East Inc.
Group Owner: CBS Radio; (acq 11-13-98; grpsl)
Nat'l Network: CBS
Arbitron Metro Market: New York, NY; *Format:* News; *Target Audience:* 25-54
Tim Scheld, News Director

WCBS-FM
07-27-1979; 101.1 MHz FM; 6.7 kW; 1335 ft.; N40 44 54 W73 59 10
345 Hudson St., 10th Fl., New York, NY 10014 USA
(800) 367-1101
www.wcbsfm.com
License: New York, New York County, NY held by CBS Radio East Inc.
Group Owner: CBS Radio
Arbitron Metro Market: New York, NY; *Format:* Oldies

WEPN
08-28-1922; 1050 kHz AM; *Hrs Open:* 24; 50 kw-U; N40 48 26 W74 04 11
2 Penn Plaza, 17th Fl., New York, NY 10001 USA
(212) 613-3800; *Fax:* (212) 613-3861
espndeportes.espn.go.com
License: New York, New York County, NY held by New York AM Radio LLC
Group Owner: ESPN Inc.
Nat'l Network: ESPN Deportes
Population Served: 15,340,000; *Arbitron Metro Market:* New York; *Format:* Sports, Spanish; *No. News Employees:* 2; *Target Audience:* Men 25-54.

WFAN
10-07-1988; 660 kHz AM; *Hrs Open:* 24; 50 kW; N40 51 35 W73 47 9
345 Hudson St., New York, NY 10014 USA
(212) 314-9200
www.wfan.com
License: New York, NY held by CBS Radio East Inc.
Group Owner: CBS Radio; (acq 2-25-92; $70 million;
Nat'l Network: CBS; *Nat'l Reps:* CBS Radio; *Wire Services:* SportsTicker; Sports Wire
Arbitron Metro Market: New York, NY; *Format:* Sports; *No. News Employees:* 34; *Target Audience:* 25-54; sports fans
Mark Chernoff, VP, Programming

***WFUV**
07-01-1947; 90.7 MHz FM; *Hrs Open:* 24; 46 kw; 509 ft.; N40 52 48 W73 52 40
Keating Hall, Bronx, NY 10458 US
(718) 817-4550; *Fax:* (718) 365-9815
www.wfuv.org
thefolks@wfuv.org
License: New York, Bronx County, NY held by Fordham University, Executive Committee, Board of Trustees.
Nat'l Network: NPR; PRI; *Wire Services:* AP
Arbitron Metro Market: New York; *Format:* News, Sports, 90, Variety/Diverse *Special Programming:* Irish 10 hrs wkly; *Hrs. of News Programming:* news progmg 8 hrs wkly; *No. News Employees:* 2 *Target Audience:* 25 plus; intelligent & sophisticated mus listeners
Joseph McShane, President
John Hollwitz, Operations Dir
Chuck Singleton, General Manager
Cara Tobin, Membership Director
Rita Houston, Programming Director
John Platt, Director of Communications
Julianne Welby, News Director
Joey Delvecchio, Traffic Director
George Evans, Operations Director
Janeen Shaitelman, Promotions/Marketing Director
George Bodarky, Public Affairs Director
Russ Borris, Music Director
Claudia DeVivo, Disc Jockey

***WHCR-FM**
02-01-1985; 90.3 MHz FM; *Hrs Open:* 24; 0.008 kw; 266 ft.; N40 49 9 W73 56 59
160 Convent Avenue, New York City, NY 10031 US
(212) 650-7481; *Fax:* (212) 650-7480
www.whcr.org
info@whcr.org
License: New York, New York County, NY held by City College of New York.
Arbitron Metro Market: New York; *Format:* Black, Jazz; *Hrs. of News Programming:* News progmg 70 hrs wkly; *Target Audience:* Community of Harlem.
Angela Harden, General Manager
Tina Dixon, Production Manager
Daycia Bowman, Webmaster

WINS
01-01-1924; 1010 kHz AM; *Hrs Open:* 24; 50 kW; N40 48 14 W74 6 24
345 Hudson St., New York, NY 10014 USA
www.1010wins.com
License: New York, NY held by CBS Radio East Inc.
Group Owner: CBS Radio
Nat'l Network: ABC; CNN Radio; *Nat'l Reps:* CBS Radio; *Wire Services:* AP
Arbitron Metro Market: New York *TV Affiliate:* WCBS-TV affil.; *Format:* News; *Hrs. of News Programming:* news progmg 168 hrs wkly; *No. News Employees:* 50; *Target Audience:* General
Ely Izakson, General Sales Mgr
Ben Mevorach, News Director

***WKCR-FM**
10-01-1941; 89.9 MHz FM; *Hrs Open:* 24; 1.35 kw; 932 ft.; N40 45 22 W73 59 12
535 West 116th Street, 313 Low Library, New York, NY 10027 US
(212) 854-9920; *Fax:* (212) 854-9296
www.wkcr.org
bored@wkcr.org
License: New York, New York County, NY held by Trustees of Columbia University.
Arbitron Metro Market: New York; *Format:* Jazz, Variety/Diverse *Special Programming:* Country 6 hrs, news/sports 6 hrs, international 8; *Hrs. of News Programming:* News progmg 3 hrs wkly; *Target Audience:* General.
Ben Young, Station Manager/Programming Director

WKDM
01-01-1927; 1380 kHz AM; 5 kw-U, DA1; N40 49 13 W74 4 9
27 William St., 11th Floor, New York, NY 10005 US
(212) 966-1059; *Fax:* (212) 625-2894
www.wkdm1380am.com
License: New York, NY held by Multicultural Radio Broadcasting Licensee LLC.
Group Owner: Multicultural Radio Broadcasting Inc.; (acq 6-30-2003; $37 million)
Arbitron Metro Market: New York; *Format:* Chinese, Spanish
Arthur Liu, CEO/COO

WLIB
01-01-1942; 1190 kHz AM; *Hrs Open:* 24; 10 kw-D, DA2; 30 kw-N, DA2; N40 47 48 W74 6 6
3 Park Ave., 41st Fl., New York, NY 10016 USA
(212) 447-1000
www.wlib.com
License: New York, NY held by WBLS-WLIB License LLC
Group Owner: Emmis Communications Corp.
Nat'l Reps: McGavren Guild
Arbitron Metro Market: New York; *Format:* Gospel
Deon Levingston, VP & General Manager
Doug James, Director of Sales
Skip Dillard, Program Director & Operations Manager
Bethany Kent, Promotions Director

WLTW
01-26-1961; 106.7 MHz FM; 6 kw; 1362 ft.; N40 44 54 W73 59 10
32 Avenue of the Americas, New York, NY 10013 US
(212) 377-7900; *Fax:* (212) 603-4602
www.1067litefm.com
License: New York, New York County, NY held by AMFM Radio Licenses LLC.
Group Owner: iHeartMedia; (acq 8-30-2000; grpsl).
Nat'l Network: AP Radio; *Nat'l Reps:* Katz Radio
Arbitron Metro Market: New York, NY; *Format:* Adult Contemp
Scott Hopeck, Market President
Thea Mitchem, Senior Vice President of Programming
Bernie Weiss, Senior Vice President of Sales
Chris Conley, Programming Director

WMCA
01-01-1925; 570 kHz AM; *Hrs Open:* 24; 5 kw-U, DA1; N40 45 10 W74 6 15
777 Terrace Avenue, Suite 602, Hasbrouck Heights, NJ 07604 US
(201) 298-5700; *Fax:* (201) 298-5757
www.wmca.com
contact@nycradio.com
License: New York, NY held by Salem Media of New York LLC.
Group Owner: Salem Communications Corp.; (acq 9-15-89; $13 million;
Arbitron Metro Market: New York, NY; *Format:* Christian, Talk *Special Programming:* Jewish 9 hrs wkly; *Hrs. of News Programming:* News progmg 5 hrs wkly; *Target Audience:* General.
Edward Atsinger III, President
Mark de Boer, Operations Dir
Jerry Crowley, Vice President/General Manager
Steve Viehmeyer, General Sales Mgr
Peter Thiele, Programming Director
Peter Thiele, Operations Manager
Nick Brino, Directorof Minority Relations/Sales Manager

***WNYC**
07-08-1924; 820 kHz AM; 10 kw-D, DA2; 1 kw-N, DA2; N40 45 10 W74 6 15
160 Varick St., New York, NY 10013 US
(646) 829-4400
www.wnyc.org
newsroom@wnyc.org
License: New York, NY held by New York Public Radio
Group Owner: New York Public Radio; (acq 10-3-96; $20 million with co-located FM)
Nat'l Network: PRI; NPR
Arbitron Metro Market: New York, NY *TV Affiliate:* Public radio; *Format:* Big Band; *No. News Employees:* General.
Laura R. Walker, President & CEO

WNYC-FM
09-21-1943; 93.9 MHz FM; 5.2 kw; 1,362 ft.; N40 44 54 W73 59 10
160 Varick St., New York, NY 10013 US
(646) 829-4400
www.wnyc.org
newsroom@wnyc.org
License: New York, NY held by New York Public Radio
Group Owner: New York Public Radio
Arbitron Metro Market: New York, NY *TV Affiliate:* Public radio; *Format:* Jazz *Special Programming:* News progmg 35 hrs wkly
Laura R. Walker, President & CEO
Michele Rusnak, Vice President of Finance and Business Affairs

***WNYE**
11-01-1938; 91.5 MHz FM; *Hrs Open:* WNYE-TV affil; 2 kw; 922 ft.; N40 45 22 W73 59 12
Fordham University, Bronx, NY 10458-8111 US
(718) 250-5800; *Fax:* (718) 855-8863
http://www.nyc.gov/html/media/html/radio/radio.shtml
License: New York, Kings County, NY held by New York City Dept. of Info Technology & Telecommunications.
Nat'l Network: NPR; PRI
Arbitron Metro Market: New York *TV Affiliate:* Public radio; *No. News Employees:* General.
George Evans, Operations Manager
Chuck Singleton, General Manager
Laura Fedele, News Media Director

***WNYU-FM**
05-03-1973; 89.1 MHz FM; 8.3 kw; 256 ft.; N40 51 26 W73 54 48
5-11 University Plaza, New York, NY 10003 US
(212) 998-1660; *Fax:* (212) 998-1652
www.wnyu.org
License: New York, New York County, NY held by New York University.
Nat'l Network: ABC
Arbitron Metro Market: New York *TV Affiliate:* College; *Format:* Black, Reggae *Special Programming:* News progmg 4 hrs wkly
Barney Canson, General Manager
Zane Brzezinski, Programming Director
Jamie Dinsmoor, Promotions Director
Zoe Rosenberg, News Director
Aldona Watts, Engineering Dir
Pier Harrison, Business Director

WOR
02-22-1922; 710 kHz AM; *Hrs Open:* 24; 50 kw-U, DA-1; N40 47 50 W74 05 24
32 Avenue of the Americas, New York, NY 10013 US
(212) 377-7900; *Fax:* (212) 642-4486
www.wor710.com
License: New York, New York County, NY held by AMFM Radio Licenses LLC
Group Owner: iHeartMedia; (acq 12-89; $25.1 million;
Nat'l Network: NBC Radio News; *Nat'l Reps:* Eastman Radio
Population Served: 18,000,000; *Arbitron Metro Market:* New York; *Format:* News, News/Talk, 84, Talk *Special Programming:* Relg 4 hrs wkly; *Hrs. of News Programming:* news progmg 4 hrs wkly *No. News Employees:* 5; *Target Audience:* 35-64.
Scott Hopeck, Market President
Bernie Weiss, Senior Vice President of Sales

WPLJ
01-18-1960; 95.5 MHz FM; *Hrs Open:* 24; 6.7 kw; 1339 ft.; N40 44 54 W73 59 10
2 Pennsylvania Plaza, 17th Floor, New York, NY 10121 US
(212) 613-8900; *Fax:* (212) 613-8956,(212) 613-8950
www.plj.com
License: New York, NY held by Radio License Holdings LLC
Group Owner: Cumulus Media Inc.
Arbitron Metro Market: New York; *Format:* Adult Contemp
Mary-Jo Vetrano, General Sales Mgr
Theresa Angela, Promotions Manager

WFAN-FM
11-02-2012; 101.9 MHz FM; *Hrs Open:* 24; 6.2 kW; 1352 ft.; N40 44 54 W73 59 10
345 Hudson St., 10th Fl., New York, NY 10014 USA
(212) 314-9200
www.wfan.com
License: New York, New York County, NY held by CBS Radio East Inc.
Group Owner: CBS Radio; (acq 12-10-2012; $75 million)
Nat'l Reps: CBS Radio
Population Served: 1,245,000; *Arbitron Metro Market:* New York; *Format:* Sports; *Target Audience:* 25-54 Sports Fans
Mark Chernoff, VP, Programming

WQEW
12-03-1936; 1560 kHz AM
2 Penn Plaza, 17th Floor, New York, NY 10117 US
(212) 613-3800; *Fax:* (212) 613-3823
www.radiodisney.com
Jospeh.M.Weinholtz@radiodisney.com
License: New York, NY held by Radio Disney New York LLC.
Group Owner: ABC Inc.; (acq 5-24-2007; $40 million)
Wire Services: Reuters
Arbitron Metro Market: New York; *Format:* Children; *Target Audience:* 25-64; educated & affluent
Timothy McCarthy, General Manager

WQHT
01-01-1940; 97.1 MHz FM; *Hrs Open:* 24; 6.7 kw; 1,338 ft.; N40 44 54 W73 59 10
395 Hudson St., 7th Fl., New York, NY 10014 USA
(212) 229-9797; *Fax:* (212) 929-8559
www.hot97.com
License: New York, New York County, NY held by Emmis License Corp. of New York
Group Owner: Emmis Communications Corp.
Nat'l Reps: Katz Radio
Population Served: 2,000,000; *Arbitron Metro Market:* New York; *Format:* Urban Contemporary; *Target Audience:* General.
Deon Livingston, VP & General Manager
Doug James, Director of Sales
Pio Ferro, Programming Director
Bethany Kent, Promotions Director

WXNY-FM
11-08-1939; 96.3 MHz FM; *Hrs Open:* 24; 6 kw; 1,361 ft.; N40 44 54 W73 59 10
485 Madison Ave., 3rd Fl., New York, NY 10022
(212) 310-6000; *Fax:* (212) 888-3694
www.univision.com
License: New York, New York County, NY held by WADO-AM License Corp.
Group Owner: Univision Radio; (acq 2-1-44)
Wire Services: Reuters
Arbitron Metro Market: New York, NY; *Format:* Spanish
Ramon Pineda, General Manager
Peter Tran, National Sales Manager
Nomar Vizcarrondo, Programming Director
Luis Antonio Valera, Director of Marketing and Promotions
Donovan Welsh, Sales Manager
Karima Khawja, Director of Sales
RossDaron, Digital Sales Manager

WEPN-FM
01-01-1941; 98.7 MHz FM; *Hrs Open:* 24; 6 kw; 1,361 ft.; N40 44 54 W73 59 10
2 Penn Plaza, 17th Floor, New York, NY 10121

(212) 613-3800; *Fax:* (212) 613-3868
License: New York, New York County, NY held by Emmis New York Radio License LLC
Group Owner: Emmis Communications Corp.
Nat'l Network: ESPN Radio; *Nat'l Reps:* Katz Radio
Population Served: 2,500,000; *Arbitron Metro Market:* New York; *Format:* Sports; *No. News Employees:* 1
Jeff Smulyan, Chairman & CEO

WSKQ-FM
01-01-1950; 97.9 MHz FM; 6 kw; 1362 ft.; N40 44 54 W73 59 10
26 West 56th Street, New York, NY 10019 US
(212) 541-9200; *Fax:* (212) 541-9408
www.lamega.com
License: New York, New York County, NY held by WSKQ Licensing Inc.
Group Owner: Spanish Broadcasting System Inc.; (acq 2-1-89; $55 million)
Nat'l Reps: McGavren Guild
Arbitron Metro Market: New York; *Target Audience:* 18-49; Hispanic
Marko Radlovic, SVP/Market Manager
Frank Flores, General Manager
Bill Kehlbeck, Sales Manager
George Mier, Programming Director
Jose Garcia, CFO

WWPR-FM
12-14-1953; 105.1 MHz FM; *Hrs Open:* 24; 6 kw; 1362 ft.; N40 44 54 W73 59 10
1120 Avenue of the Americas, 18th Floor, New York, NY 10036 US
(212) 377-7900; *Fax:* (212) 398-3299
www.power1051fm.com
License: New York, New York County, NY held by AMFM Radio Licenses LLC.
Group Owner: iHeartMedia; (acq 8-30-00; grpsl).
Arbitron Metro Market: New York, NY; *Format:* Urban Contemporary; *No. News Employees:* 1; *Target Audience:* 25-54.
Scott Hopeck, Market President
Ray Tejeda, Vice President of Sales
Thea Mitchem, Senior Vice President of Programming

WWRL
08-26-1926; 1600 kHz AM
333 Seventh Avenue, New York, NY 10001 US
(212) 631-0800; *Fax:* (212) 239-7203
License: New York, NY held by NJ Broadcasting, LLC.
Group Owner: Nimisha Shukla & Jeetendra Shukla; (acq 9-28-89; $1.98 million;
Nat'l Network: Air America; ABC; Fox News Radio; Westwood One
Arbitron Metro Market: New York, NY; *Format:* Alternative, Talk
Adriane Gaines, President/General Managerÿ
Anthony Small, Sr. Vice President, Operations
Adriane Gaines, General Manager
Michael Hill, General Sales Mgr
Rennie Bishop, Programming Director
Jeffrey Haveson, ExecutiveProducerÿÿÿÿÿ
John Campanario, Digital Media/Sr. Account Executive
Shevette Watson-Brunn, Office Manager

***WWRV**
05-01-1972; 1330 kHz AM; *Hrs Open:* 24
Mailing Address: 419 Broadway, Paterson, NJ 07501 US
Second Address: 419 Broadway, Paterson, NJ 7501
(973) 881-8700; *Fax:* (973) 881-8324
www.radiovision.net
License: New York, NY held by Radio Vision Christiana Management Corp.
Arbitron Metro Market: New York, NY; *Format:* Christian, Religious; *No. News Employees:* 1; *Target Audience:* General.
Rev. Milton Donato, President
Jose Lastra, Operations Dir
Julio Carbrera, Station Manager

WZRC
01-01-1925; 1480 kHz AM; 5 kw-D, DA2; 5 kw-N, DA2; N40 50 42 W74 1 12
27 William St., 11th Floor, New York, NY 10005 US
(212) 966-1059; *Fax:* (212) 625-2894
www.nyam1480.com
License: New York, NY held by Multicultural Radio Broadcasting Licensee LLC.
Group Owner: Multicultural Radio Broadcasting Inc.; (acq 1-30-98; grpsl).
Arbitron Metro Market: New York, NY; *Format:* Chinese; *Target Audience:* 12-34.
Arthur Liu, CEO/COO

WBMP
06-23-2014; 92.3 MHz FM; 6 kW; 1355 ft.; N40 44 54 W73 59 10
NY USA
www.923ampradio.com
License: New York, NY held by CBS Radio East Inc.
Group Owner: CBS Radio
Arbitron Metro Market: New York, NY; *Format:* Contemporary Hits/Top 40

New York City

WABC
10-01-1921; 770 kHz AM; 50 kw
2 Pennsylvania Plaza, 17th Floor, New York, NY 10001 US
(212) 613-3800
www.wabcradio.com
comments@wabcradio.com
License: New York City, NY held by Radio License Holdings LLC
Group Owner: Cumulus Media Inc.; (acq 6-12-2007; grpsl)
Nat'l Reps: Interep
Arbitron Metro Market: Lafayette LA; *Format:* News/Talk
Jonathan Mason, General Sales Mgr
Tony Mascaro, Programming Director
Leslie Slender, Promotions Director
Kim Bryant, Market Manager

Newark

WACK
10-19-1957; 1420 kHz AM; *Hrs Open:* 24; 5 kw-D, DA2; 0.5 kw-N, DA2; N43 1 8 W77 4 41
PO Box 292, Newark, NY 14513 US
(585) 482-9667; *Fax:* (315) 331-1420
License: Newark, NY held by Waynco Radio Inc.
Nat'l Network: CNN Radio; Motor Racing Net; Westwood One
Arbitron Metro Market: De Queen AR; *Adv. Rates:* 25; 20; 25; 15
John Tickner, General Manager
John Derletti, Sales Manager
Dick Reeves, Programming Director

Newburgh

WGNY
02-25-1933; 1220 kHz AM; *Hrs Open:* 24; 5 kw-D, DA; N41 29 57 W74 03 54
661 Little Britain Road, New Windsor, NY 12553
(845) 561-2131; *Fax:* (845) 561-2138
www.foxradio.net
License: Newburgh, Orange County, NY held by Sunrise Broadcasting Corp.
Group Owner: Sunrise Broadcasting Corp.; (acq 8-90; $10,000 with co-located FM;
Nat'l Reps: Katz Radio
Arbitron Metro Market: Newburgh-Middletown, NY (Mid-Hudson Valley) *Special Programming:* Relg 4 hrs, Sp one hr wkly; *Target Audience:* General.
Joerg Klebe, President
Robert Maines, Operations Dir

WJGK(FM)
10-29-1966; 103.1 MHz FM; 6 kW; 275 ft; N41 28 22 W74 08 22
661 Little Britain Road, Newburgh, NY 12553
(845) 561-2131,(845) 561-2132; *Fax:* (845) 561-2138
www.wgnyfm.com
License: Newburgh, Orange County, NY
Group Owner: Sunrise Broadcasting Corp.
Arbitron Metro Market: Newburgh-Middletown, NY (Mid-Hudson Valley); *Adv. Rates:* 50; 50; 50; 35
Bob DeFelice, Market Manager

Newport Village

WBGK
01-01-2001; 99.7 MHz FM; 1.4 kw; 676 ft.; N43 8 28 W75 1 49
185 Genesee Street, Suite 1601, Utica, NY 13501-3413 US
(315) 734-9245; *Fax:* (315) 624-9245
www.bugcountry.com
License: Newport Village, Herkimer County, NY held by Roser Communications Network Inc.
Group Owner: Roser Communications Network Inc.; (acq 5-29-2001; $575,000)
Nat'l Network: ABC
Arbitron Metro Market: Utica-Rome, NY; *Format:* Country
Dave Silvers, Operations Dir
Ken Roser, General Manager
Roxanne Roser, Station Manager
Grant Roser, General Sales Mgr

Niagara Falls

WHLD
01-01-1941; 1270 kHz AM; *Hrs Open:* 19; 5 kw-D, 1 kw-N; N42 44 41 W78 53 13
50 James E. Casey Dr., Buffalo, NY 14206 US
(716) 881-4555
www.sportsradio1270.com
steve.bearance@cumulus.com
License: Niagara Falls, NY held by Radio License Holding CBC, LLC
Group Owner: Cumulus Media Inc.
Arbitron Metro Market: Buffalo-Niagara Falls, NY; *Format:* Sports
Rose Porter, General Sales Mgr
Steve Bearance, Market Manager

WJJL
12-21-1947; 1440 kHz AM; *Hrs Open:* 24; 1 kw-D, ND1; 0.055 kw-N, ND1; N43 4 43 W79 0 40
Mailing Address: 976 B Union Road, West Seneca, NY 14224 US
Second Address: portage&pine, Niagara Falls, NY 14304
(716) 674-9555; *Fax:* (716) 674-0400
www.wjjl.com
License: Niagara Falls, NY held by M.J. Phillips Communications Inc.
Arbitron Metro Market: Buffalo-Niagara Falls, NY; *Format:* Rock/AOR, Oldies *Special Programming:* Black 2 hrs, It 4 hrs, news/talk 5 hrs wkly, gospe; *Hrs. of News Programming:* news progmg 3 hrs wkly *No. NewsEmployees:* 1; *Target Audience:* 25-54; baby boomers
Earl Morgan, Chairman
Mark Phillips, CEO
John Phillips, President
M.J. Phillips, Operations Dir
Dennis Westberg, CFO

WKSE
01-01-1946; 98.5 MHz FM; *Hrs Open:* 24; 46 kw; 420 ft.; N43 0 18 W78 59 34
500 Corporate Parkway, Suite 200, Buffalo, NY 14226 US
(716) 843-0600; *Fax:* (716) 843-0250
www.kiss985.com
Info@kiss985.com
License: Niagara Falls, Niagara County, NY held by Entercom Buffalo License LLC.
Group Owner: Entercom Communications Corp.; (acq 12-13-99; grpsl).
Nat'l Network: ABC; *Nat'l Reps:* D & R Radio
Arbitron Metro Market: Buffalo-Niagara Falls, NY; *Format:* Contemporary Hits/Top 40; *No. News Employees:* 3; *Target Audience:* 12-49.
Greg Ried, Vice President/General Manager
Tim Holly, Director of Sales
Sue O'Neil, Programming Director

North Creek

***WXLG**
01-01-1995; 89.9 MHz FM; *Hrs Open:* 24; 0.2 kw; 1995 ft.; N43 40 22 W74 2 58 *Rebroadcasts:* Rebroadcasts WSLU(FM) Canton 100%
N. Country Public Radio, Canton, NY 13617 US
(315) 229-5356; *Fax:* (315) 229-5373
www.ncpr.org
radio@ncpr.org
License: North Creek, Warren County, NY held by St. Lawrence University.
Arbitron Metro Market: North Creek, NY; *Format:* Talk; *Hrs. of News Programming:* news progmg 35 hrs wkly; *No. News Employees:* 4; *Target Audience:* General.
Shelly Pike, Operations Dir
Ellen Rocco, Station Manager
Martha Foley, News Director
Joel Hurd, Production Manager
Dale Hobson, Web Manager
Sandy Demarest, Development Director

North Salem

***WJZZ**
90.1 MHz FM; 0.44 kw; -43 ft.; N41 23 3 W73 34 35 US
(404) 765-9750; *Fax:* (404) 688-7686
www.majicatl.com
Jhavis@radio-one.com
License: North Salem, Westchester County, NY held by Foothills Public Radio Inc.
Arbitron Metro Market: North Salem, NY
Dennis Jackson, President

***WJZZ(FM)**
90.1 MHz FM; 4.3 kw; Ant 232 ft; N42 58 47 W76 32 40
16 Walker Avenue, Westfield, MA 30309
(413) 572-4864
www.vivaatlanta.com
License: North Salem, Cayuga County, NY held by Quaboag Hills Public Radio
Population Served: 432,427; *Arbitron Metro Market:* Atlanta, GA
Aaron Read, General Manager
Justin Schaflander, General Sales Mgr
Raffy Contigo, Programming Director
Liz Leos, Promotions Manager

North Syracuse

WKRL-FM
03-01-1972; 100.9 MHz FM; 6 kw; 164 ft.; N43 9 6 W76 7 58
235 Walton St., Syracuse, NY 13202 US
(315) 472-9111; *Fax:* (315) 472-1888
www.krock.com
askus@krock.com
License: North Syracuse, Onondaga County, NY held by Galaxy Communicatons L.P.
Group Owner: Galaxy Communications L.P.
Nat'l Network: ABC
Arbitron Metro Market: Syracuse, NY; *Format:* Rock/AOR; *Target Audience:* 18-34; upscale, educated

WTLA
08-01-1959; 1200 kHz AM; *Hrs Open:* 24; 1 kw-D, DAN; 1 kw-N, DAN; N43 9 6 W76 7 58
235 Walton St., Syracuse, NY 13202 US
(315) 472-9111; *Fax:* (315) 472-1888
www.espncny.com
License: North Syracuse, NY held by Galaxy Syracuse Licensee LLC.
Group Owner: Galaxy Communications L.P.; (acq 4-6-2000; grpsl)
Nat'l Network: Jones Radio Networks
Arbitron Metro Market: Syracuse, NY; *Format:* Sports *Special Programming:* Ger 2 hrs, Pol 2 hrs, relg 2 hrs wkly; *Hrs. of News Programming:* news progmg 2 hrs wkly; *No. News Employees:* 1 *Target Audience:* 35-64; white collar executives

Norwich

WBKT
06-01-1997; 95.3 MHz FM; *Hrs Open:* 24; 0.47 kw; 841 ft.; N42 26 8 W75 30 47
36 Chestnut Street, Oneonta, NY 13820 US
(607) 432-1030; *Fax:* (607) 432-6909
www.wbktfm.com
wade.lott@townsquaremedia.com
License: Norwich, Chenango County, NY held by Townsquare Media Oneonta License LLC
Group Owner: Townsquare Media; (acq 10-22-2004; grpsl)
Nat'l Network: ABC
Arbitron Metro Market: Oneonta, NY; *Format:* Country; *No. News Employees:* 2; *Target Audience:* 25-54; general
Wade Lott, General Manager
Charlene Sugihara, Director of Sales
Eric Malanoski, Brand Manager
Bud Williamson, Chief Engineer

WCHN
01-01-1953; 970 kHz AM; *Hrs Open:* 24
36 Chestnut Street, Oneonta, NY 13820 US
(607) 334-2218; *Fax:* (607) 334-9867
License: Norwich, NY held by Townsquare Media Oneonta License LLC
Group Owner: Townsquare Media; (acq 10-22-2004; grpsl)
Nat'l Network: ABC
Format: Classic Rock; *Hrs. of News Programming:* News progmg 20 hrs wkly; *Target Audience:* 35-65; mature
George Wells, General Manager/Programming Director
Charlene Sugihara, Director of Sales
Bud Williamson, Chief Engineer

WKXZ
01-01-1961; 93.9 MHz FM; *Hrs Open:* 5 AM-1 AM; 26 kw; 676 ft.; N42 32 51 W75 27 9
36 Chestnut Street, Oneonta, NY 13820 US
(607) 334-2218; *Fax:* (607) 334-9867
www.wkxzfm.com
License: Norwich, Chenango County, NY held by Townsquare Media Oneonta License LLC
Group Owner: Townsquare Media
Nat'l Network: ABC
Format: Adult Contemp; *Hrs. of News Programming:* News progmg 10 hrs wkly; *Target Audience:* 25-54; growing families

Norwood

WVLF
01-01-2001; 96.1 MHz FM; 25 kw; 328 ft.; N44 54 11 W74 53 2
2155 State Highway 420, Massena, NY 13662 US
(315) 769-3333; *Fax:* (315) 769-3299
www.mymix961.com
License: Norwood, St. Lawrence County, NY held by Stephens Media Group-Massena LLC.
Group Owner: Stephens Family L.P.
Arbitron Metro Market: Odessa-Midland
Matt George, Operations Manager/Programming Director
Tami Gormley, Sales Manager

Noyack

***WSUF**
09-15-1996; 89.9 MHz FM; *Hrs Open:* 24; 1.9 kw horiz, 12 kw vert; 358 ft.; N41 6 35 W72 22 5 *Rebroadcasts:* Rebroadcasts WSHU(FM) Fairfield, CT 30%
5151 Park Avenue, Fairfield, CT 06432 US
(203) 365-6604
www.wshu.org
License: Noyack, Suffolk County, NY held by Sacred Heart University Inc.
Nat'l Network: NPR; PRI; *Wire Services:* AP
Format: News, News/Talk, 86 *Special Programming:* Folk 5 hrs, new age 6 hrs wkly; *Hrs. of News Programming:* news progmg 45 hrs wkly; *No. News Employees:* 4; *Target Audience:* General.
Barbara Bashar, Operations Dir
George Lombardi, General Manager
Gillian Anderson, Director of Development

Nyack

***WNYK**
05-05-1982; 88.7 MHz FM; 0.01 kw; 56 ft.; N41 4 59 W73 55 45
One South Blvd, Nyack, NY 10960 US
(845) 358-1710
wnyk@nyack.edu
License: Nyack, Rockland County, NY held by Nyack College.
TV Affiliate: College; *Format:* Black, Religious; *No. News Employees:* 18-35; 60%/40% -F/M, well

Odessa

WFIZ
08-20-1968; 95.5 MHz FM; *Hrs Open:* 24; 0.85 kw; 869 ft.; N42 23 13 W76 40 11
1751 Hanshaw Road, Ithaca, NY 14850 US
(607) 257-6400; *Fax:* (607) 257-6495
www.z955.net
cosadchey@cyradiogroup.com
License: Odessa, Schuyler County, NY held by Saga Communications of New England, LLC
Group Owner: Saga Communications, Inc.; (acq 3-5-2004; $600,000 with co-located AM)
Arbitron Metro Market: Ithaca, NY; *Format:* Contemporary Hits/Top 40
Chris Allinger, Operations Manager
Chet Osadchey, General Manager
Gabe Carrillo, Brand Manager
Connie Fairfax-Ozmun, Promotions/Marketing
Bryan Agnello, Chief Engineer/IT
Alan Bishop, Managing Partner
John Wiedemer, MarketingConsultant
Gina Lamannis, Senior Marketing Consultant

***WINO**
89.9 MHz FM; 0.25 kw; 341 ft.; N42 18 7 W76 48 1
103 West Seneca Street, Suite 305, Ithaca, NY 14850 US
(607) 441-9734
www.wino.com
License: Odessa, Schuyler County, NY held by Ithaca Community Radio Inc.
Arbitron Metro Market: Washington, DC
Danila Apasov, President

Ogdensburg

WQTK
07-01-1981; 92.7 MHz FM; 3 kw; 312 ft.; N44 42 21 W75 27 55
2315 Knox Street, Ogdensburg, NY 13669 US
(315) 393-1100; *Fax:* (315) 393-6673
License: Ogdensburg, St. Lawrence County, NY held by Community Broadcasters LLC.
Group Owner: Community Broadcasters LLC; (acq 2-8-2007; grpsl)
Nat'l Network: CNN Radio; *Nat'l Reps:* Eastman Radio; Katz Radio; *Wire Services:* AP
Format: Talk; *Hrs. of News Programming:* News progmg 10 hrs wkly; *Target Audience:* 25-49; community connected, active, mature, responsible & responsive
Jim Leven, President/CEO
Michael R. Guimond, General Manager

WSLB
01-01-1940; 1400 kHz AM; *Hrs Open:* 24; 1 kw-U, ND1; N44 42 21 W75 27 55
2315 Knox Street, Box 239, Ogdensburg, NY 13669 US
(315) 393-1100; *Fax:* (315) 393-6673
burgproduction@commbroadcasters.com
License: Ogdensburg, NY held by Community Broadcasters LLC.
Group Owner: Community Broadcasters LLC; (acq 2-8-2007; grpsl)
Nat'l Network: ESPN Radio; *Nat'l Reps:* Eastman Radio; Katz Radio; *Wire Services:* AP
Format: Sports
James Leven, President/CEO
Michael R. Guimond, General Manager/Sales Manager
Ray Knight, Programming Director

WPAC
06-01-1998; 98.7 MHz FM; *Hrs Open:* 24; 3 kw; Ant 92 ft; N44 43 41 W75 26 36
1 Bridge Plaza, Suite 204, Ogdensburg, NY 89451
(315) 393-1220; *Fax:* (315) 393-3974
License: Ogdensburg, St. Lawrence County, NY held by Stephens Media Group-Ogdensburg LLC.
Group Owner: Stephens Family L.P.
Population Served: 112,000; *No. News Employees:* 1; *Adv. Rates:* 20; 20; 20; 20
Mark F. Gaines, General Manager

Olean

WHDL
02-01-1929; 1450 kHz AM; *Hrs Open:* 24; 1 kw-U, ND1; N42 4 39 W78 28 32
199 Wealtha Avenue, Watertown, NY 13601 US
(716) 372-0161; *Fax:* (716) 372-0164
wpig.production@bybradio.com
License: Olean, NY held by Community Broadcasters LLC
Group Owner: Community Broadcasters LLC; (acq 12-1-2002; grpsl).
Regional Reps: Rgnl Reps.
Format: Oldies; *Hrs. of News Programming:* news progmg 6 hrs wkly; *No. News Employees:* 2; *Target Audience:* 25-54.
James Levin, President/CEO

WOEN
05-20-1957; 1360 kHz AM; *Hrs Open:* 24; 1 kw-D, ND1; 0.03 kw-N, ND1; N42 6 18 W78 23 25
231 North Union Street, Olean, NY 14760 US
(716) 375-1015; *Fax:* (716) 375-7705
traffic@mix101.com
License: Olean, NY held by Pembrook Pines Inc.
Group Owner: Pembrook Pines Media Group; (acq 2-22-2005; $950,000 with co-located FM).
Nat'l Network: CBS; Westwood One; *Nat'l Reps:* Dome
Arbitron Metro Market: Olean, NY; *Format:* News, News/Talk, 86; *No. News Employees:* 1; *Target Audience:* 45-65.
Robert Pfuntner, President/CEO
Tami Dunlavey, General Manager
Steve Mills, Programming Director
Tom Power, Chief Engineer

WMXO
11-01-1978; 101.5 MHz FM; 4 kw; 404 ft.; N42 6 18 W78 23 25
231 North Union Street, Olean, NY 14760 US
(716) 375-1015; *Fax:* (716) 375-7705
www.themixwmxo.com
traffic@mix101.com
License: Olean, Cattaraugus County, NY held by Pembroke Pines Inc.
Group Owner: Pembrook Pines Media Group
Nat'l Network: CBS; Westwood One
Arbitron Metro Market: Olean, NY; *Format:* Adult Contemp; *Target Audience:* 18-49.; *Adv. Rates:* 13; 13; 13; 9
Robert Pfunter, President/CEO
Tami Dunlavey, General Manager
Steve Mills, Programming Director
Tom Power, Chief Engineer

***WOLN**
03-01-1993; 91.3 MHz FM; 1 kw; 656 ft.; N42 2 8 W78 26 47
Rebroadcasts: Rebroadcasts WBFO(FM) Buffalo 100%
3435 Main Street, Buffalo, NY 14214 US
716-845-7000; *Fax:* 716-845-7036
www.wbfo.org
mail@wbfo.org

License: Olean, Cattaraugus County, NY held by State University of New York.
Nat'l Network: NPR
TV Affiliate: Public *Special Programming:* news progmg 50 hrs wkly; *Hrs. of News Programming:* 2; *No. News Employees:* General; educated profess
Donald K. Boswell, President/CEO
Michael J. Sutton, EVP/COO
Ron Santora, Vice President/Station Manager
Gordon Bayliss, Vice President of Sales & Marketing
Jim Ranney, News Director

WPIG
02-01-1949; 95.7 MHz FM; *Hrs Open:* 24; 43 kw; 741 ft.; N42 2 8 W78 26 47
3163 NYS Route 417, Olean, NY 14760-1853 US
(716) 372-0161; *Fax:* (716) 372-0164
www.wpig.com
License: Olean, Cattaraugus County, NY held by Community Broadcasters LLC
Group Owner: Community Broadcasters LLC
Nat'l Network: ABC
Format: Country
John Morton, General Manager
Mark Thompson, Programming Director
Gary Nease, News/Sports Director
Brenda Nease, Traffic Manager

Olivebridge

***WFSO**
12-27-1996; 88.3 MHz FM; *Hrs Open:* 27/7; 80 W Circular; Ant 195 ft; N41 54 30 W74 14 46
PO Box 1520, Olivebridge, NY 12572
(888) 724-4427
www.redeemerbroadcasting.org
ministry@redeemerbroadcasting.org
License: Olivebridge, Ulster County, NY held by Redeemer Broadcasting Inc.
Population Served: 120,000; *Arbitron Metro Market:* Hudson Valley *Special Programming:* Classic Christian
Dan Elmendorf, President/Operations Director/General Manager

Oneida

WMCR
09-26-1956; 1600 kHz AM; *Hrs Open:* 16; 1 kw-D, ND1; 0.02 kw-N, ND1; N43 5 4 W75 41 35
8456 Smokey Hollow Rd., Baldwinsville, NY 13027 US
(315) 635-3971; *Fax:* (315) 635-3490
License: Oneida, Madison County, NY held by Leatherstocking Media Group Inc.
Group Owner: Leatherstocking Media Group Inc.
Arbitron Metro Market: Syracuse, NY; *Format:* News, News/Talk, 86; *Target Audience:* General.
Dan Elliott, General Manager
Krista Galster, General Sales Mgr
Paul DeLaubell, Sales Representative

WMCR-FM
09-01-1972; 106.3 MHz FM; 1.25 kw; 719 ft.; N43 2 48 W75 39 58
8456 Smokey Hollow Rd., Baldwinsville, NY 13027 US
(315) 635-3971; *Fax:* (315) 635-3490
License: Oneida, Madison County, NY held by Leatherstocking Media Group Inc.
Group Owner: Leatherstocking Media Group Inc.
Arbitron Metro Market: Syracuse, NY; *Format:* Contemporary Hits/Top 40
Dan Elliott, General Manager
Krista Galster, General Sales Mgr
Paul DeLaubell, Sales Representative

Oneonta

WDOS
12-01-1947; 730 kHz AM
34 Chestnut Street, Oneonta, NY 13820 US
(607) 432-1030; *Fax:* (607) 432-6909
cnynews.com/
info@centralnewyorkradio.com
License: Oneonta, NY held by Townsquare Media Oneonta License LLC
Group Owner: Townsquare Media; (acq 11-4-2005; $3.8 million with co-located FM)
Arbitron Metro Market: Oneonta, NY; *Format:* Country *Special Programming:* Big band 7 hrs, nostalgia 2 hrs, relg 7 hrs wkly; *Target Audience:* General; adult
George Wells, Market Manager
Steve Dillon, Director of Sales
Daniel Cassavaugh, Programming Director

***WONY**
01-01-1975; 90.9 MHz FM; 0.18 kw horiz; -72 ft.; N42 28 2 W75 3 40
State University Plaza, Albany, NY 12246 US
(607) 436-2711
www.wonyfm.com
License: Oneonta, Otsego County, NY held by State University of New York.
TV Affiliate: Educ, div; *No. News Employees:* General.

***WRHO**
01-01-1970; 89.7 MHz FM; *Hrs Open:* 18; 0.27 kw; -13 ft.; N42 27 24 W75 4 28
Radio Station Wrho, Oneonta, NY 13820 US
(607) 431-4555,(607) 431-4556; *Fax:* (607) 431-4064
License: Oneonta, Otsego County, NY held by Hartwick College.
Nat'l Network: AP Radio
Format: Classic Rock, Rock/AOR *Special Programming:* Folk 5 hrs, jazz 4 hrs, Sp 2 hrs, world beat 2 hrs, children's 2 hrs wkly; *Hrs. of News Programming:* News progmg 4 hrs wkly; *Target Audience:* General; teenagers,college students & young adults
Valerie Herz, General Manager
Hilary Fiona, Programming Director

***WSQC-FM**
01-01-1992; 91.7 MHz FM; *Hrs Open:* 24; 0.57 kw horiz, 2.3 kw vert; 528 ft.; N42 25 27 W75 2 33 *Rebroadcasts:* Rebroadcasts WSKG-FM Binghamton 100%
P. O. Box 3000, Binghamton, NY 13902 US
(607) 729-0100; *Fax:* (607) 729-7328
www.wskg.com
wskg_mail@wskg.pbs.org
License: Oneonta, Otsego County, NY held by WSKG Public Telecommunications Council.
Nat'l Network: NPR; PRI
Format: News *Special Programming:* Jazz, folk 5 hrs wkly; *Hrs. of News Programming:* news progmg 33 hrs wkly; *No. News Employees:* 1; *Target Audience:* General.
Brian Sickora, President
Gregory Keeler, Operations Director/Programming Director
Matt Richmond, News Director
Caroline Basso, Director of Development
Teresa Peltier, Digital Content Manager

WSRK
01-26-1970; 103.9 MHz FM; *Hrs Open:* 5 AM-midnight; 1.4 kw; 591 ft.; N42 25 26 W75 2 33
34 Chestnut Street, Oneonta, NY 13820 US
(607) 432-1030; *Fax:* (607) 432-6909
www.wsrk.com
License: Oneonta, Otsego County, NY held by Townsquare Media Oneonta License LLC
Group Owner: Townsquare Media
Format: Adult Contemp *Special Programming:* Class 2 hrs wkly; *Hrs. of News Programming:* News progmg 5 hrs wkly; *Target Audience:* 25-54; adult males & females
George Wells, General Manager/Programming Director
John Hayen, General Sales Mgr

WZOZ
11-28-1972; 103.1 MHz FM; *Hrs Open:* 24; 2 kw; 361 ft.; N42 25 28 W75 4 36
P.O. Box 552, Norwich, NY 13815 US
(607) 432-1030; *Fax:* (607) 432-6909
www.wzozfm.com
George.Wells@townsquaremedia.com
License: Oneonta, Otsego County, NY held by Townsquare Media Oneonta License LLC
Group Owner: Townsquare Media; (acq 10-22-2004; grpsl)
Arbitron Metro Market: Oneonta, NY; *Format:* Oldies *Special Programming:* Jazz 2 hrs, blues 2 hrs, oldies 2 hrs wkly; *Hrs. of News Programming:* news progmg 8 hrs wkly; *No. News Employees:* 2 *Target Audience:* 25-54.
Steven Price, CEO
George Wells, General Manager
George Wells, Programming Director
Steven Dillon, Director of Sales

Ontario

WYNY(AM)
1450 kHz AM; 1 kw-D, 2 kw-N, DA-2; N43 10 49 W77 18 15
Mailing Address: 15 Neversink Drive, Port Jervis, NY 12771
Second Address: PO Box 920, Port Jervis, NY 12771
(845) 856-6000; *Fax:* (845) 856-4757
bud@dre.cc
License: Ontario, Wayne County, NY held by Digital Radio Broadcasting Inc.
Group Owner: Digital Radio Broadcasting Inc.
Arbitron Metro Market: Rochester, NY
Bud Williamson, President/General Manager
Doug Beck, Sales Director
Rick Knight, Programming Director

Ossining

***WQXW**
07-15-1995; 90.3 MHz FM; *Hrs Open:* 24; 0.25 kw; 476 ft.; N41 09 07 W73 47 10
160 Varick St., New York, NY 10013 US
(646) 829-4400
www.wqxr.org
License: Ossining, Westchester County, NY held by New York Public Radio
Group Owner: New York Public Radio
Population Served: 625,000; *Arbitron Metro Market:* Ossining, NY; *Format:* Classical *Special Programming:* Pub affrs 20 hrs wkly; *Target Audience:* 18+
Graham Parker, General Manager
Matt Abramovitz, Programming Director

***WOSS**
02-22-1972; 91.1 MHz FM; *Hrs Open:* 24; 0.015 kw horiz; 69 ft.; N41 9 36 W73 51 38
Mailing Address: 190 Croton Avenue, Ossining, NY 10562 US
Second Address: 29 S. Highland Ave., Ossining, NY 10562
(914) 762-5760 x370; (914) 941-3512
License: Ossining, Westchester County, NY held by Board of Education Union Free School District 1.
Format: Contemporary Hits/Top 40; *No. News Employees:* 3; *Target Audience:* General.
Martin McDonald, Station Manager

Oswego

***WNYO**
01-01-1993; 88.9 MHz FM; 0.1 kw; 10 ft.; N43 27 7 W76 32 40
State University Plaza, Albany, NY 12246 US
(315) 312-2101; *Fax:* (315) 312-3542
http://www.wnyo.org/
wnyo@wnyo.org
License: Oswego, Oswego County, NY held by State University of New York.
TV Affiliate: Variety; *Format:* News, News/Talk, 86; *No. News Employees:* 13-34.
Andrew Nicholson, General Manager

WWLF-FM
07-01-1990; 96.7 MHz FM; *Hrs Open:* 24; 3 kw; Any 328 ft; N43 29 12 W76 23 10
401 W. Kirkpatrick St., Syracuse, NY 13024
(315) 472-0222
movin100.com
jhunt@movin100.com
License: Oswego, Oswego County, NY held by WOLF Radio Inc.
Group Owner: WOLF Radio Inc.; (acq 8-4-97; $65,000)
Regional Reps: Rgnl Reps
Population Served: 140,000; *Arbitron Metro Market:* Syracuse, NY
Sam Furco, General Manager

***WRVO**
01-06-1969; 89.9 MHz FM; *Hrs Open:* 24; 50 kw horiz, 49.01 kw vert; 440 ft.; N43 25 14 W76 32 39
Lanigan Hall, Oswego, NY 13126 US
(315) 312-3690; *Fax:* (315) 312-3174
www.wrvo.fm
feedback@wrvo.fm
License: Oswego, Oswego County, NY held by State University of New York.
Nat'l Network: NPR; *Wire Services:* AP
Arbitron Metro Market: Syracuse, NY; *Format:* Variety/Diverse; *Hrs. of News Programming:* news progmg 140 hrs wkly; *No. News Employees:* 4; *Target Audience:* 25-55.; *Adv. Rates:* 60; 50; 60; 10
Michael Ameigh, General Manager
Jeff Windsor, Programming Director
Lee Mitchell, Chief Engineer
Bonnie Prime, Financial Resource Manager

WSGO
01-01-1960; 1440 kHz AM; *Hrs Open:* 24; 1 kw-D, ND1; 0.045 kw-N, ND1; N43 24 56 W76 28 0 *Rebroadcasts:* Rebroadcasts WTLA(AM) North Syracuse 100%
235 Walton St., Syracuse, NY 13202 US
(315) 472-9111; *Fax:* (315) 472-1888
www.espnsyracuse.com
askespn@espncny.com
License: Oswego, NY held by Galaxy Syracuse Licensee LLC.
Group Owner: Galaxy Communications L.P.; (acq 4-6-2000; grpsl)
Nat'l Network: Jones Radio Networks

Arbitron Metro Market: Syracuse, NY; *Format:* Sports *Special Programming:* Ger 2 hrs, Pol 2 hrs wkly; *Hrs. of News Programming:* News progmg one hr wkly; *Target Audience:* 40 plus; retired & mobile

WTKV
03-15-1973; 105.5 MHz FM; *Hrs Open:* 24; 4 kw; 397 ft.; N43 24 56 W76 27 54 *Rebroadcasts:* Rebroadcasts WTKW(FM) Bridgeport 100%
235 Walton St., Syracuse, NY 13202 US
(325) 472-9111; *Fax:* (315) 472-1888
tk99.net
asktk@tk99.net
License: Oswego, Oswego County, NY
Group Owner: Galaxy Communications L.P.
Arbitron Metro Market: Syracuse, NY; *Format:* Classic Rock *Special Programming:* Folk 3 hrs, blues one hr wkly; *Hrs. of News Programming:* news progmg 2 hrs wkly; *No. News Employees:* 1 *Target Audience:* 25-54.

Owego

WEBO
07-27-1957; 1330 kHz AM; *Hrs Open:* 5 AM-10 PM
Mailing Address: Executive Inn, Bldg 3 #2, 1 Delaware Ave., Endicott, NY 13760 US
Second Address: 60 North Avenue, Owego, NY 13327
(607) 687-9933; *Fax:* (607) 687-9033
www.newsradiowebo.com/
License: Owego, NY held by Tioga Media Inc.
Nat'l Network: USA; *Nat'l Reps:* D & R Radio
Arbitron Metro Market: Owego, NY; *Format:* News, Talk *Special Programming:* NASCAR racing 16 hrs, relg 6 hrs wkly; *No. News Employees:* 2; *Target Audience:* 35 plus.
Dave Radigan, General Manager

Palmyra

***WZXV**
05-01-1993; 99.7 MHz FM; *Hrs Open:* 24; 2.8 kw; 486 ft.; N43 2 0 W77 25 17
Mailing Address: P.O. Box 25099, Farmington, NY 14425 US
Second Address: 1777 Rt. 332, Farmington, NY 14425
(315) 597-9574;; *Fax:* (585) 398-3250
www.wzxv.org
License: Palmyra, Wayne County, NY held by Calvary Chapel of the Finger Lakes Inc.
Arbitron Metro Market: Farmington, NY; *Format:* Christian
Jeff Gallatin, General Manager

Patchogue

WALK
05-20-1952; 1370 kHz AM; *Hrs Open:* 24; 0.5 kw-D, ND1; 0.102 kw-N, ND1; N40 45 14 W72 59 14
234 Airport Plaza, Suite 5, Farmingdale, NY 11735 US
(631) 770-4200; *Fax:* (631) 770-0101
www.whli.com
webmaster@connoisseurli.com
License: Patchogue, NY held by Connoisseur Media Licenses LLC
Group Owner: Connoisseur Media LLC; (acq 5-15-2014).
Arbitron Metro Market: Long Island, NY; *Format:* Adult Contemp; *Hrs. of News Programming:* News progmg 15 hrs wkly; *Target Audience:* 50 plus.
Darren DiPrima, Director of Sales

WALK-FM
12-01-1952; 97.5 MHz FM; 39 kw; 554 ft.; N40 50 41 W73 2 1
66 Colonial Dr, Parchogue, NY 11772 US
(631) 475-5200; *Fax:* (631) 475-9016
walkradio.com
psa@walkradio.com
License: Patchogue, Suffolk County, NY
Arbitron Metro Market: Long Island, NY; *Format:* Adult Contemp *Special Programming:* Hits of the 70s, love songs; *Target Audience:* 25-54.
Patrick Shea, Programming Director

WBLI
12-01-1958; 106.1 MHz FM; *Hrs Open:* 24; 49 kw; 499 ft.; N40 50 32 W73 2 25
555 Sunrise Highway, West Babylon, NY 11704 US
(631) 669-9254; *Fax:* (631) 376-0569
www.wbli.com
requests@wbli.com
License: Patchogue, Suffolk County, NY held by Cox Medai Group
Group Owner: Cox Media Group; (acq 5-22-98; grpsl)
Nat'l Network: AP Radio; *Nat'l Reps:* Christal
Arbitron Metro Market: West Babylon, NY; *Format:* Contemporary Hits/Top 40; *Hrs. of News Programming:* news progmg 5 hrs wkly; *No. News Employees:* 1; *Target Audience:* 18-34; women
John Shea, General Manager
Jeremy Rice, Programming Director
Nancy Cambino, Operations Manager/Marketing Director

WLIM
12-01-1951; 1580 kHz AM; *Hrs Open:* 24
3656 W. Belmont Ave., Chicago, IL 60618 US
(773) 588-6300; *Fax:* (773) 588-0834
www.polskieradio.com
License: Patchogue, NY held by Polnet Communications Ltd.
Group Owner: Polnet Communications Ltd.
Arbitron Metro Market: New York; *Format:* Polish, Ethnic; *Hrs. of News Programming:* news progmg 20 hrs wkly; *No. News Employees:* 1; *Target Audience:* 18-54; Polish language audience; *Adv. Rates:* 54; 54; 52;50
Walter Kotaba, President

WBLI
12-13-1957; 106.1 kHz FM; 1 kw-D, ND1; 1 kw-N, ND1; N40 50 32 W73 02 25
555 Sunrise Highway, West Babylon, NY 11704 US
(631) 669-9254; *Fax:* (631) 373-0569
www.am1240wgbb.com
License: Patchogue, NY held by Cox Ration Inc.
Group Owner: Cox Radio Inc.; (acq 5-22-98; grpsl)
Arbitron Metro Market: New York; *Format:* Contemporary Hits/Top 40; *Target Audience:* 25-45
John Shae, General Manager
Jeremy Rice, Program Director
Nancy Cambino, Operations Manager/Marketing Director

Patterson

WDBY
01-17-1982; 105.5 MHz FM; *Hrs Open:* 24; 0.9 kw; 610 ft.; N41 31 18 W73 38 6
1004 Federal Road, Brookfield, CT 06804 US
(203) 775-1212; *Fax:* (203) 775-6452
www.air1.com
info@air1.com
License: Patterson, Putnam County, NY held by Cumulus Licensing Corp.
Group Owner: Cumulus Media Inc.; (acq 1-23-2002; grpsl).
Nat'l Network: Westwood One
Arbitron Metro Market: Nanty Glo PA; *Format:* Alternative, Christian
Miranda Goodspeed, Sales Manager
Tim Sheehan, Programming Director
Taryn Donnarummo, Promotions Director
Ann McManus, Regional Vice President

Pattersonville

***WPGL**
08-15-1994; 90.7 MHz FM; *Hrs Open:* 24; 0.03 kw; 653 ft.; N42 51 0 W74 3 58 *Rebroadcasts:* Rebroadcasts WFGB(FM) Kingston 95%
Mailing Address: P.O. Box 777, Lake Katrine, NY 12449 US
Second Address: 199 Tuytenbridge Rd., Lake Katrine, NY 12449
(800) 724-8518; *Fax:* (845) 336-7205
www.soundoflife.org
License: Pattersonville, Schenectady County, NY held by Sound of Life Inc.
Format: Christian; *Hrs. of News Programming:* News progmg 3 hrs wkly; *Target Audience:* General.
Bob Conti, Operations Dir
Tom Zahradnik, General Manager
Joe Hunter, Programming Director

Peekskill

WHUD
10-24-1958; 100.7 MHz FM; 50 kw; 499 ft.; N41 20 18 W73 53 41
6 Johnson Road, Latham, NY 12110 US
(914) 838-6000; *Fax:* (914) 838-2109
www.whud.com
info@whud.com
License: Peekskill, Westchester County, NY held by 6 Johnson Road Licenses Inc.
Group Owner: Pamal Broadcasting Ltd.
Nat'l Network: ABC
Arbitron Metro Market: New York; *Format:* Adult Contemp; *Target Audience:* Upscale adults.
Jason Finkleburg, General Manager
Bruce Feniger, General Sales Mgr
Steven Petrone, Programming Director/Vice President of Operations

Penn Yan

WYLF
01-01-1988; 850 kHz AM; *Hrs Open:* 24; 1 kw-D, ND1; 0.045 kw-N, ND1; N42 39 41 W77 7 14
100 Main Street, Penn Yan, NY 14527 US
(315) 536-0850
www.wylf.com
License: Penn Yan, NY held by M.B. Communications.
Group Owner: M.B. Communications; (acq 10-88)
Arbitron Metro Market: Penn Yan, NY; *Format:* Adult Contemp; *No. News Employees:* 2; *Target Audience:* 35 plus.
Jeff Pearce, Owner
Philip Mann, General Manager/Sales Manger
Sandy Sommers, Productions Manager

Peru

***WXLU**
01-01-1991; 88.1 MHz FM; *Hrs Open:* 24; 1 kw; 1119 ft.; N44 34 25 W73 40 29 *Rebroadcasts:* Rebroadcasts WSLU(FM) Canton 100%
N Country Public Radio, Canton, NY 13617 US
(315) 229-5356
www.ncpr.org
License: Peru, Clinton County, NY held by St. Lawrence University.
Arbitron Metro Market: Burlington, NY; *Format:* Talk; *Hrs. of News Programming:* news progmg 35 hrs wkly; *No. News Employees:* 4; *Target Audience:* General.
Shelly Pike, Operations Dir
Ellen Rocco, General Manager
Jacqueline Sauter, Programming Director
Martha Foley, News Director
Joel Hurd, Production Manager
June Peoples, Membership Director
Naomi Weller, Office Managerÿ
DaleHobson, Web Manager
Sandy Demarest, Development Director

Phoenix

WZUN
05-22-1995; 102.1 MHz FM; *Hrs Open:* 24; 6 kw; 266 ft.; N43 6 4 W76 16 58
235 Walton St., Syracuse, NY 13202 US
(315) 472-9111; *Fax:* (315) 472-1888
www.thesunnyspot.com
License: Phoenix, Oswego County, NY held by Galaxy Syracuse Licensee LLC.
Group Owner: Galaxy Communications L.P.; (acq 12-15-2000; $3.75 million).
Arbitron Metro Market: Syracuse, NY; *Format:* Adult Contemp; *Target Audience:* 25-54; general

Plainview

***WPOB**
09-01-1973; 88.5 MHz FM; 0.125 kw; 259 ft.; N40 47 48 W73 27 44
Jfk Bldg., 50 Kennedy Dr, Plainview, NY 11803 US
(516) 937-6373; *Fax:* (516) 937-6344
License: Plainview, Nassau County, NY held by Plainview-Old Bethpage Central School District.
Format: Rock/AOR; *Target Audience:* General.
Joe Genero, General Manager
Adam Weinstock, General Manager

Plattsburgh

WBTZ
02-03-1960; 99.9 MHz FM; *Hrs Open:* 24; 100 kw; 984 ft.; N44 46 13.9 W73 36 48.49
450 Weaver Street, Winooski, VT 05404 US
(802) 860-2440; *Fax:* (802) 860-1818
License: Plattsburgh, Clinton County, NY held by Hall Communications Inc.
Group Owner: Hall Communications Inc.; (acq 7-31-2006; $2.5 million)
Arbitron Metro Market: Winooski, VT; *Format:* Alternative; *Target Audience:* 18-44.
Dan Dubonnet, General Manager
Candis Leopold, General Sales Mgr
Matt Grasso, Programming Director

***WCEL**
01-14-1991; 91.9 MHz FM; *Hrs Open:* 24; 0.38 kw; 853 ft.; N44 46 27 W73 36 48 *Rebroadcasts:* Rebroadcasts WAMC-FM Albany 100%
Mailing Address: 318 Central Ave., Albany, Ny, NY 12206 US
Second Address: 318 Central Ave., Albany, NY 12206

(518) 465-5233(800) 323-9262; *Fax:* (518) 432-6974
www.wamc.org
License: Plattsburgh, Clinton County, NY held by WAMC.
Group Owner: WAMC/Northeast Public Radio; (acq 1996; $160,000)
Nat'l Network: PRI; NPR; *Wire Services:* AP
Format: News, Talk *Special Programming:* Folk 7 hrs, jazz 13 hrs wkly; *Hrs. of News Programming:* News progmg 77 hrs wkly; *Target Audience:* General.
Shelly Pike, Operations Dir
Ellen Rocco, General Manager
Jacqueline Sauter, Programming Director
Martha Foley, News Director
Joel Hurd, Production Manager
June Peoples, Membership Director
Naomi Weller, Office Manager
DaleHobson, Web Manager
Sandy Demarest, Development Director

WTWK
01-01-1998; 1070 kHz AM; 5 kw-D, NDD; N44 36 14 W73 27 18
P.O. Box 8260, Essex, VT 05451 US
(802) 863-1010
www.wtwk1070.com/
License: Plattsburgh, NY held by Champlain Communications Corp.
Group Owner: Northeast Broadcasting Company Inc.; (acq 1-11-2002; $150,000)
Nat'l Network: Air America
Arbitron Metro Market: Plattsburgh, NY; *Format:* Talk; *Target Audience:* 25-54; women
Richard DeLancey Sr., General Manager
J.J. Prieve, Programming Director

WEAV
02-03-1935; 960 kHz AM
63 Maple Street, Marbleworks #9, Middlebury, VT 05753 US
(802) 655-0093; *Fax:* (802) 654-9376
www.thezone960am.com/
jamiedennis@thezone960am.com
License: Plattsburgh, NY held by Vox AM/FM LLC.
Group Owner: Vox AM/FM LLC; (acq 7-25-2008; grpsl)
Arbitron Metro Market: Plattsburgh, NY; *Format:* Sports, Talk; *Target Audience:* General.
Bruce Zeman, General Manager/Programming Director
Nicole Daigle, Sales Manager
Jamie Dennis, News Director

WIRY
01-30-1950; 1340 kHz AM; *Hrs Open:* 24 hours; 1 kw-D, 940 w-N; N44 40 12 W73 26 41
4712 State Route 9, Plattsburgh, NY 12901
(518) 563-1340; *Fax:* (518) 563-1343
www.wiry.com
wiry@wiry.com
License: Plattsburgh, Clinton County, NY held by Hometown Radio Inc.
Nat'l Network: NBC News Radio; Dial Global Radio Network;
Nat'l Reps: Roslin
Population Served: 25,000 *Hrs. of News Programming:* news progmg 14 hrs wkly; *No. News Employees:* 2; *Target Audience:* 18 plus.
William Santa, President/General Manager
Bob Pooler, Vice President
Bob Pooler, Vice President/Programming & Music Director
Alan Drake, News/Sports Director
Linda Whalen, Business Manager

WKOL
08-22-1994; 105.1 MHz FM; *Hrs Open:* 24; 23.5 kw; 338 ft.; N44 31 31 W73 31 7
Mailing Address: P.O. Box 4489, Burlington, VT 05403 US
Second Address: 70 Joy Dr., South Burlington, VT 5403
(802) 658-1230; *Fax:* (802) 862-0786
www.wkol.com
kool105@hallradio.com
License: Plattsburgh, Clinton County, NY held by Hall Communications Inc.
Group Owner: Hall Communications Inc.; acq 6-13-95; $1.1 million)
Nat'l Reps: D & R Radio; *Wire Services:* AP
Arbitron Metro Market: Burlington-Plattsburgh, VT-NY; *Format:* Contemporary Hits/Top 40, Adult Contemp; *Target Audience:* 25-54.
Bonnie Rowbotham, Chairman
Arthur Rowbotham, President
Dan Dubonnet, General Manager
Lee Boudette, General Sales Mgr
Rod Hill, Programming Director
Bill Baldwin, Executive Vice President

*WQKE
04-01-1979; 93.9 MHz FM; *Hrs Open:* 7 AM-2:30 PM; 0.009 kw; 26 ft.; N44 41 40 W73 28 0
101 Broad Street, Kehoe 202, Plattsburgh, NY 12901 US
(518) 564-2727
License: Plattsburgh, Clinton County, NY held by State University of N.Y.
Format: Alternative *Special Programming:* Heavy metal 10 hrs, classic rock 12 hrs, Black 9 hrs, relg 3 hrs wkly; *Target Audience:* 18-24.
Kyle Rando, Operations Dir
Dan Krenske, Programming Director

Plattsburgh West

WPLB
100.7 MHz FM; 2.3 kw; 221 meters; N43 47 14 W73 58 53
1080 Military Turnpike, Suite 6, Plattsburgh, NY 12901
(518) 825-0010
License: Plattsburgh West, Essex County, NY held by Westport Radio Partners
Group Owner: Radioactive LLC

Jim Williams, Vice President/General Manager/Sales Manager
Paul Varga, Programming Director
Sandy Caligiore, News Director
James Horton, Traffic Director/Information Technologies Manager

Port Chester

WKLV-FM
10-18-1974; 96.7 MHz FM; *Hrs Open:* 24; 3 kw; Ant 328 ft; N41 02 49 W73 31 36
PO Box 2098, Highway 40 South, Omaha, NE 68103
(800) 525-5683
www.klove.com
info@967thecoast.com
License: Port Chester, Fairfield County, NY held by Cox Radio Inc.
Group Owner: Cox Radio Inc.; (acq 8-25-2000; grpsl).
Nat'l Reps: Katz Radio
Population Served: 123,000; *Arbitron Metro Market:* New York; *Format:* Adult Contemp; *Target Audience:* 25-54; upscale
Parrell Chambliss, President

Port Dickinson

WCDW
01-01-2006; 106.7 MHz FM; *Hrs Open:* 24; 1.2 kw; 725 ft.; N42 3 22 W75 56 39
101 Main Street, Johnson City, NY 13790 US
(607) 772-1005; *Fax:* (607) 772-2945
License: Port Dickinson, Broome County, NY held by Equinox Broadcasting Corp.
Group Owner: Equinox Broadcasting Corp.
Nat'l Reps: Katz Radio
Arbitron Metro Market: Port Dickinson, NY; *Format:* Adult Contemp; *Target Audience:* 18-45.
George Hawras, President/General Manager
Steve Shimer, Operations Manager
Tom Shiptenko, Station Manager
Joyce Knapik, Sales Manager

Port Henry

WVTK
09-05-1982; 92.1 MHz FM; *Hrs Open:* 24; 18 kw; 10 ft.; N44 1 38 W73 28 54
63 Maple Street, Marbleworks #9, Middlebury, VT 05753 US
(802) 655-0093; *Fax:* (802) 655-0478
www.trueoldieschannel.com
info@trueoldieschannel.com
License: Port Henry, Essex County, NY held by Vox AM/FM LLC.
Group Owner: Vox AM/FM LLC; (acq 7-25-2008; grpsl)
Arbitron Metro Market: Burlington, VT; *Format:* Oldies; *Hrs. of News Programming:* News progmg one hr wkly; *Target Audience:* 25-54.

Port Jervis

WDLC
07-04-1953; 1490 kHz AM; *Hrs Open:* 24; 1 kw-U, ND1; N41 21 49 W74 40 41
P.O. Box 920, Port Jervis, NY 12771 US
(845) 856-5185; *Fax:* (845) 856-4757
www.country1077.com
info@foxcountry.us
License: Port Jervis, NY held by PJ Radio L.L.C.
Arbitron Metro Market: Sussex, NJ; *Format:* Country
James Morley, General Manager

*WRPJ
10-01-1992; 88.9 MHz FM; 0.5 kw; 591 ft.; N41 25 36 W74 34 54 *Rebroadcasts:* Rebroadcasts WFGB(FM) Kingston 100%
Mailing Address: Post Office Box 777, Lake Katrine, NY 12449 US
Second Address: 199 Tuytenbridge Rd., Lake Katrine, NY 12449
(845) 336-6199,(800) 724-8518; *Fax:* (845) 336-7205
www.soundoflife.org
email@soundoflife.org
License: Port Jervis, Orange County, NY held by Sound of Life Inc.
Format: Christian; *Target Audience:* General.
Bob Conti, Operations Dir
Tom Zahradnik, General Manager
Joe Hunter, Programming Director

Portville

WVTT
96.7 MHz FM; 460 w; 509 ft; N42 03 04 W78 25 11
1 Bluebird Square, Olean, NY 14760
www.colonial.cc/WVTT
License: Portville, Cattaraugus County, NY
Group Owner: Colonial Media & Entertainment

Jeff Andrulonis, CEO
Steve Douglas, Operations Manager

Potsdam

*WAIH
09-10-1998; 90.3 MHz FM; 0.1 kw; -16 ft.; N44 39 43 W74 58 26 US
(315) 267-4888
www2.potsdam.edu/waih
License: Potsdam, St. Lawrence County, NY held by State University of New York.
Arbitron Metro Market: Potsdam, NY; *Format:* Talk
Dan Laskaris, General Manager

WPDM
04-30-1955; 1470 kHz AM; 1 kw-D, ND1; 0.044 kw-N, ND1; N44 38 38 W75 3 32
86 Porter Road, Malone, NY 12953 US
(518) 483-1100; *Fax:* (315) 265-4040
License: Potsdam, NY held by Martz Communications Group
Format: Adult Contemp; *Hrs. of News Programming:* news progmg 5 hrs wkly; *No. News Employees:* 1; *Target Audience:* 25 plus; div audience; *Adv. Rates:* 20; 13; 16; 13
Tim Martz, President/CEO
Mike Boldt, General Manager
Drew Scott, Programming Director

WSNN
10-15-1968; 99.3 MHz FM; *Hrs Open:* 6 AM-midnight; 3 kw; 154 ft.; N44 38 38 W75 3 32
86 Porter Road, Malone, NY 12953 US
(518) 483-1100; *Fax:* (315) 265-4040
License: Potsdam, St. Lawrence County, NY held by Martz Communications Group
Format: Country; *Hrs. of News Programming:* news progmg 5 hrs wkly; *No. News Employees:* 1; *Target Audience:* 25-54.; *Adv. Rates:* 19.80; 13; 15.65; 13
Tim Martz, President/CEO
Mike Boldt, General Manager
Drew Scott, Programming Director

*WTSC-FM
11-03-1963; 91.1 MHz FM; *Hrs Open:* 24 hrs a day; 0.7 kw horiz; 135 ft.; N44 39 45 W75 0 7
10 Clarkson Avenue, Box 8743, Potsdam, NY 13699 US
(315) 268-7657; (312) 268-7658
radio.clarkson.edu
radio@clarkson.edu
License: Potsdam, St. Lawrence County, NY held by Clarkson University.
Arbitron Metro Market: Potsdam, NY; *Format:* Alternative
Kurtis Lanning, General Manager
Austin Lund, Chief Engineer
Ben Morton-Black, Sports Director

WSNN
99.3 MHz FM; 3 kW; N44 38 38 W75 03 28
5 Beal St, Potsdam, NY 13676 USA
(315) 265-5510
www.b993.fm
License: Potsdam, NY held by Waters Communications Inc.
Group Owner: Martz Communications Group
Arbitron Metro Market: Potsdam, NY; *Format:* Contemporary Hits/Top 40
Chris Engel, Sports Director

Poughkeepsie

WEOK
10-01-1949; 1390 kHz AM; *Hrs Open:* 24; 5 kw-D, DA2; 0.106 kw-N, DA2; N41 43 14 W73 54 29
Mailing Address: P.O. Box 416, Poughkeepsie, NY 12602 US
Second Address: 2 Pendell Rd., Poughkeepsie, NY 12602-0416
(845) 471-1500
www.cumulus.com
License: Poughkeepsie, NY held by Peak Broadcasting of Fresno Licenses LLC
Group Owner: Townsquare Media; (acq 1-23-2002).
Arbitron Metro Market: Poughkeepsie, NY *Special Programming:* Farm 2 hrs, Pol one hr, relg 2 hrs, talk 5 hrs, Sinatra 2 hrs wkly; *No. News Employees:* 3; *Target Audience:* 35 plus.
Jay Pugliese, General Manager
Anthony Verano, Promotions Director

WKIP
06-01-1940; 1450 kHz AM; 1 kw-D, DAD; 1 kw-N, DAD; N41 42 18 W73 53 16
20 Tucker Drive, Poughkeepsie, NY 12603 US
(845) 471-2300; *Fax:* (845) 471-2683
www.1450wkip.com
chuckbenfer@iheartmedia.com
License: Poughkeepsie, NY held by CC Licenses LLC.
Group Owner: iHeartMedia; (acq 7-12-2000; grpsl)
Nat'l Network: ABC News/Talk; Fox News Radio; Premiere Radio Networks; Talk Radio Network; *Nat'l Reps:* Katz Radio; *Wire Services:* AP
Arbitron Metro Market: Poughkeepsie, NY; *Format:* News, News/Talk, 86; *Hrs. of News Programming:* news progmg 24 hrs wkly; *No. News Employees:* 1; *Target Audience:* 35-64.
Chuck Benfer, Market President
Chris Marino, Senior Vice President of Programming
Rob VanDerbeck, Senior Vice President of Sales
Cameron Hendrix, Programming Director
Elise Penge, Promotions Director
Deirdre Burns, Digital ContentDirector

WPDH
12-01-1962; 101.5 MHz FM; *Hrs Open:* 24; 4.4 kw; 1539 ft.; N41 43 9 W73 59 47
2 Pendell Road, Poughkeepsie, NY 12601 US
(845) 471-1500; *Fax:* (845) 454-1204
www.wpdh.com
License: Poughkeepsie, Dutchess County, NY held by Peak Broadcasting of Fresno Licenses LLC
Group Owner: Townsquare Media
Arbitron Metro Market: Poughkeepsie, NY; *Format:* Classic Rock
Special Programming: Blues deluxe, flashback 4 hrs wkly
Jay Pugliese, General Manager/Sales Manager
Andrew Boris, Programming Director
Anthony Verano, Director of Marketing & Promotions
Jillian Price, Traffic Manager/Promotions Coordinator
Kathy Busko, Business Manager

*WRHV
09-05-1990; 88.7 MHz FM; 0.23 kw vert; 1289 ft.; N41 43 9 W73 59 47 *Rebroadcasts:* Rebroadcasts Wmht-FM Schenectady 60%
4 Global View, Troy, NY 12180 US
(518) 880-3400
www.wmht.org
License: Poughkeepsie, Dutchess County, NY held by WMHT Educational Telecommunications.
Nat'l Network: PRI
Arbitron Metro Market: Poughkeepsie, NY; *Format:* Talk *Special Programming:* Jazz 2 hrs, ethnic one hr wkly; *Target Audience:* 35-54; class mus lovers
Deborah Onslow, President
Dave Nicosia, Chief Engineer

WRNQ
06-30-1989; 92.1 MHz FM; *Hrs Open:* 24; 0.52 kw; 1030 ft.; N41 43 9 W73 59 47
20 Tucker Drive, Poughkeepsie, NY 12603 US
(845) 471-2300; *Fax:* (845) 471-2683
www.q92hv.com
License: Poughkeepsie, Dutchess County, NY held by CC Licenses LLC.
Group Owner: iHeartMedia
Nat'l Network: Fox News Radio; *Nat'l Reps:* Katz Radio; *Wire Services:* AP
Arbitron Metro Market: Poughkeepsie, NY; *Format:* Adult Contemp; *Hrs. of News Programming:* news progmg 7 hrs wkly; *No. News Employees:* 1; *Target Audience:* 35-54; primary market is women
Chuck Benfer, Market President
Chris Marino, Senior Vice President of Programming
Rob VanDerbeck, Senior Vice President of Sales
Elise Penge, Promotions Director
Deirdre Burns, Digital Content Director

WSPK
12-07-1947; 104.7 MHz FM; *Hrs Open:* 24; 7.4 kw; 1250 ft.; N41 29 19 W73 56 52
P.O. Box 310, Beacon, NY 12508 US
(845) 838-8600,(845) 838-6000; *Fax:* (845) 838-2109
www.k104online.com
License: Poughkeepsie, Dutchess County, NY held by 6 Johnson Road Licenses Inc.
Group Owner: Pamal Broadcasting Ltd.; (acq 10-19-2001; grpsl).
Nat'l Network: Westwood One; ABC; *Nat'l Reps:* Katz Radio
Arbitron Metro Market: Poughkeepsie, NY; *Format:* Contemporary Hits/Top 40; *No. News Employees:* 1; *Target Audience:* 18-49.
Jason Finkelberg, General Manager
Bruce Feniger, General Sales Mgr
Megan Denaut, Promotions Director
Jessica Meyrowitz, National Sales Manager

WPKF
01-01-1996; 96.1 MHz FM; *Hrs Open:* 24; 4.4 kw; 184 ft.; N41 44 25 W73 54 17
20 Tucker Drive, Poughkeepsie, NY 12603 US
(845) 471-2300; *Fax:* (845) 471-2683
www.kissfmhv.com
License: Poughkeepsie, Dutchess County, NY held by CC Licenses LLC.
Group Owner: iHeartMedia; (acq 7-14-2000; grpsl).
Nat'l Network: Fox News Radio; *Nat'l Reps:* Clear Channel; Katz Radio; *Wire Services:* AP
Arbitron Metro Market: Poughkeepsie, NY; *Format:* Contemporary Hits/Top 40
Chuck Benfer, Market President
Chris Marino, Senior Vice President of Programming
Rob VanDerBeck, Senior Vice President of Sales
Elise Penge, Promotions Director
Deirdre Burns, Digital Content Director

*WVKR-FM
01-01-1976; 91.3 MHz FM; *Hrs Open:* 24; 3.7 kw horiz; 820 ft.; N41 38 25 W74 1 16
124 Raymond Avenue, Box 726, Poughkeepsie, NY 12604 US
(845) 437-5475; *Fax:* (845) 437-7656
www.wvkr.org
License: Poughkeepsie, Dutchess County, NY held by Vassar College.
Arbitron Metro Market: Poughkeepsie, NY; *Format:* Variety/Diverse; *Hrs. of News Programming:* news progmg 5 hrs wkly; *No. News Employees:* 4; *Target Audience:* General.
William Jay Lancaster, General Manager

Pulaski

*WGKV
01-01-1987; 101.7 MHz FM; 5 kw; 358 ft.; N43 36 28 W75 58 23
5090 Us Rt #11, P.O. Box 640, Pulaski, NY 13142 US
(800) 525-5683
www.klove.com
klove@klove.com
License: Pulaski, Oswego County, NY held by Educational Media Foundation.
Group Owner: EMF Broadcasting; (acq 7-6-2007; grpsl)
Nat'l Network: K-Love
Format: Religious
Darrell Chambliss, Chairman
Alan Mason, COO
Mike Novak, President

Queensbury

WCQL
09-01-1967; 95.9 MHz FM; *Hrs Open:* 24; 0.38 kw; 1273 ft.; N43 25 12 W73 45 37
238 Bay Road, Queensbury, NY 12804 US
(518) 761-9890; *Fax:* (518) 761-9893
www.radiowins.com
cashworth@rrggf.com
License: Queensbury, Warren County, NY held by Regional Radio Group LLC.
Group Owner: Regional Radio Group LLC; (acq 9-10-2008; grpsl)
Nat'l Network: Jones Radio Networks
Arbitron Metro Market: Saratoga, NC; *Hrs. of News Programming:* news progmg 3 hrs wkly; *No. News Employees:* 15; *Target Audience:* 18-49.; *Adv. Rates:* 32; 25; 28; 15
Clay Ashworth, General Manager
Dan Miner, Station Manager
Colleen O'Sick, Sales Manager
Pete Cloutier, Promotions Manager
Jason Ross, Digital Media Manager

Ramapo

WRCR
09-15-1977; 1700 kHz AM; *Hrs Open:* 24; 0.5 kw-D, DA2; 0.083 kw-N, DA2; N41 5 48 W74 0 18
5 Provident Bank Park Drive, Pomona, NY 10970 US
(845) 362-5070; *Fax:* (845) 362-5073
www.wrcr.com
info@wrcr.com
License: Ramapo, NY held by Alexander Broadcasting Inc.
Nat'l Network: USA
Arbitron Metro Market: New York; *Format:* Adult Contemp, News; *Hrs. of News Programming:* news progmg 18 hrs wkly; *No. News Employees:* 2; *Target Audience:* 25-54; upscale
Alexander Medakovic, President
Alexander Madakovic, Programming Director

Rapids

*WLNF
02-08-2012; 90.5 MHz FM; 250 w; Ant 74 ft; N43 05 12 W78 37 59
293 Niagara St., Lockport, NY 14094
(716) 434-1733; *Fax:* (716) 434-2837
www.lctv.net
lctv@lctv.net
License: Rapids, Niagara County, NY held by Lockport Community Television.

Tom Riley, General Manager
Rich Zapp, Programming Director

Ravena

*WYKV
01-01-1991; 94.5 MHz FM; *Hrs Open:* 24; 3 kw; 328 ft.; N42 33 23 W73 52 5
12 Dennis Terrace, Schenectady, NY 12303 US
(817) 641-3495
License: Ravena, Albany County, NY held by Educational Media Foundation.
Group Owner: EMF Broadcasting; (acq 7-6-2007; grpsl)
Nat'l Network: K-Love
Arbitron Metro Market: Windom MN
Linda De Romanett, President

Remsen

WRCK
12-12-1966; 1480 kHz AM; *Hrs Open:* 24; 5 kw-D; N43 19 31 W75 10 29 *Rebroadcasts:* Rebroadcasts WRNY(AM) Rome 100%
239 Genesee St., Suite 500, Utica, NY 17110
(315) 797-0803; *Fax:* (315) 797-7813
License: Remsen, Oneida County, NY held by Roser Communications Network Inc.
Group Owner: Roser Communications Network Inc.; (acq 10-24-2007; grpsl)
Nat'l Network: Westwood One; *Nat'l Reps:* Christal
Population Served: 175,000; *Arbitron Metro Market:* Utica-Rome, NY; *Hrs. of News Programming:* News progmg 3 hrs wkly; *Target Audience:* 35 plus; 60% female, 40% male
Brian Delaney, General Manager
Gene Conte, Programming Director
Joe Petro, Chief Engineer

*WOKR
12-01-1982; 93.5 MHz FM; *Hrs Open:* 24; 2.1 kw; 564 ft.; N43 16 51 W75 18 14
US
(888) 946-2471
www.air1.com
License: Remsen, Oneida County, NY held by Educational Media Foundation.
Group Owner: EMF Broadcasting; (acq 10-24-2007; $350,000)
Arbitron Metro Market: Utica-Rome, NY; *Format:* Country, Gospel
Mike Novak, President

*WRUN
12-16-2008; 90.3 MHz FM; 1.2 kw; Ant 669 ft; N43 20 47.8 W75 13 58.8 *Rebroadcasts:* Rebroadcasts WAMC-FM Albany 100%
318 Central Avenue, Albany, NY 12206
(518) 465-5233; *Fax:* (518) 432-6974
www.wamc.org
License: Remsen, Oneida County, NY held by WAMC.
Group Owner: WAMC/Northeast Public Radio
Population Served: 507; *Arbitron Metro Market:* Remsen, NY
Alan Chartock, President/CEO
Katie Britton, Programming Director
Ian Pickus, News Director
Joe Donahue, Vice President, News and Programming

Rensselaer

WQBK-FM
12-01-1972; 103.9 MHz FM; *Hrs Open:* 24; 6 kw; 302 ft.; N42 35 6 W73 46 29
1241 Kings Road, Schenectady, TX 12303 US
(518) 881-1515; *Fax:* (518) 881-1516
www.wqbk.com
License: Rensselaer, Rensselaer County, NY
Group Owner: Townsquare Media; (acq 2000; grpsl)
Arbitron Metro Market: Albany-Schenectady-Troy, NY
Wes Styles, Programming Director
Dan Austin, Market Manager

WGDJ
12-03-1961; 1300 kHz AM; *Hrs Open:* 24
51 South Pearl Street, Albany, NY 12207 US
(518) 813-4975; *Fax:* (518) 813-9025
www.talk1300.com
License: Rensselaer, NY held by Capital Broadcasting Inc.
Nat'l Network: ABC; *Nat'l Reps:* Interep
Arbitron Metro Market: Albany, NY; *Format:* Talk; *Target Audience:* 35-64.
Paul Vandenburgh, President & General Manager
Mike Carey, News Director
Angela Rosetti, Executive Producer/Traffic

Riverhead

WRCN-FM
08-14-1962; 103.9 MHz FM; 1.4 kw; 486 ft.; N40 51 8 W72 45 55
3075 Veterans Memorial Hwy., Suite 201, Ronkonkoma, NY 11779 US
(631) 648-2500; *Fax:* (631) 648-2510
www.linewsradio.com
License: Riverhead, Suffolk County, NY held by JVC Media LLC
Group Owner: JVC Broadcasting; (acq 10-1-97; grpsl).
Nat'l Reps: Katz Radio
Arbitron Metro Market: New York; *Format:* News, News/Talk, 86; *Target Audience:* 18-49.
John Caracciolo, President
Bruce Shepard, Director of Sales
Matthew Goldapper, Programming Director

WFTU
08-08-1963; 1570 kHz AM; 1 kw-D, DA2; 0.5 kw-N, DA2; N40 54 48 W72 39 16
305 North Service Road, Dix Hills, NY 11746 US
(631) 424-7000,(631) 656-3192
License: Riverhead, NY held by Five Towns College
Arbitron Metro Market: New York; *Format:* Talk
Eugene Free, General Manager

WRIV
06-01-1955; 1390 kHz AM; *Hrs Open:* 6 AM-midnight; 1 kw-D, ND1; 0.064 kw-N, ND1; N40 54 55 W72 39 28
Mailing Address: PO Box 1390, Riverhead, NY 11901 US
Second Address: 40 W. Main St., Riverhead, NY 11901
(631) 727-1390; *Fax:* (631) 369-WRIV (9748)
www.1390wriv.com
License: Riverhead, NY held by Crystal Coast Communications.
Arbitron Metro Market: New York; *Format:* Adult Contemp
Special Programming: Farm 8 hrs, Pol 4 hrs wkly; *Hrs. of News Programming:* news progmg 14 hrs wkly; *No. News Employees:* 1; *Target Audience:* 35-64.
Bruce Tria, General Manager

Rochester

WBZA
01-01-1939; 98.9 MHz FM; *Hrs Open:* 24; 37 kw; 564 ft.; N43 10 14 W77 40 23
70 Commercial Street, Rochester, NY 14614 US
(585) 423-2900
www.rochesterbuzz.com
License: Rochester, Monroe County, NY held by Entercom Rochester Inc.
Group Owner: Entercom Communications Corp.; (acq 4-23-98; grpsl)
Nat'l Network: Westwood One; *Nat'l Reps:* Katz Radio
Arbitron Metro Market: Tri-Cities WA (Richland-Kennewick-Pasco); *Format:* Classic Rock
Bob Barnett, Operations Manager
Sue Munn, Vice President/General Manager
Mike Johnson, Director of Sales
Mike Danger, Programming Director

WBEE-FM
02-01-1961; 92.5 MHz FM; *Hrs Open:* 24; 50 kw; 499 ft.; N43 10 37 W77 28 39
70 Commercial Street, Rochester, NY 14614 US
(585) 423-2900
www.wbee.org
License: Rochester, Monroe County, NY held by Entercom Rochester License LLC
Group Owner: Entercom Communications Corp.; (acq 4-23-98; grpsl).
Nat'l Network: Westwood One
Arbitron Metro Market: Bakersfield CA; *Format:* News, News/Talk, 86 *Special Programming:* Haitian 3 hrs wkly; *Hrs. of News Programming:* news progmg 111 hrs wkly; *No. News Employees:* 7 *Target Audience:* General; well educated, moderate to high income bracket
Bob Barnett, Operations Manager
Steve Munn, Vice President/General Manager
Mike Johnson, Director of Sales
Mike Danger, Programming Director

*WBER
01-01-1974; 90.5 MHz FM; *Hrs Open:* 24; 2.5 kw; 417 ft.; N43 2 0 W77 25 11
2596 Baird Road, Penfield, NY 14526 US
(585) 419-8190; *Fax:* (585) 419-8191
wber@monroe.edu
License: Rochester, Monroe County, NY held by Monroe B.O.C.E.S #1.
Arbitron Metro Market: Rochester, NY; *Format:* Alternative; *Target Audience:* 25-34; male & female
Joey Guisto, General Manager

WCMF-FM
06-09-1960; 96.5 MHz FM; *Hrs Open:* 24; 48 kw; 466 ft.; N43 8 5.17 W77 35 6.6
70 Commercial Street, Rochester, NY 14614 US
(585) 423-2900; *Fax:* (585) 325-5139
www.wcmf.com
smunn@entercom.com
License: Rochester, Monroe County, NY held by Entercom Rochester License LLC.
Group Owner: Entercom Communications Corp.; (acq 11-30-2007; grpsl)
Arbitron Metro Market: Rochester, NY; *Format:* Classic Rock; *Hrs. of News Programming:* news progmg 10 hrs wkly; *No. News Employees:* 1
Bob Barnett, Operations Dir
Sue Munn, General Manager/Vice President
Mike Johnson, Director of Sales
Chris Crowley, Programming Director

WDCX
02-01-1947; 990 kHz AM; *Hrs Open:* 24; 5 kw-D, DA2; 2.5 kw-N, DA2; N43 13 54 W77 52 0
625 Delaware Avenue, Suite 308, Buffalo, NY 14202 US
(716) 883-3010; *Fax:* (716) 883-3606
www.wdcxam.com
info@wdcxradio.com
License: Rochester, Monroe County, NY held by Crawford Broadcasting Co.
Group Owner: Crawford Broadcasting Co.; (acq 6-5-97; $650,000)
Arbitron Metro Market: Rochester, NY; *Format:* Christian, Religious, 86
Earl Schillinger, Operations Manager
Brett Larson, General Manager
Peter Tasca, Sales Manager
Keri Cardinale, Programming Director
Nevin Larson, Director of Christian Programming
Lesvia Diaz, Office Manager

WDKX
04-06-1974; 103.9 MHz FM; *Hrs Open:* 24; 0.8 kw; 541 ft.; N43 9 17 W77 36 16
683 East Main Street, Rochester, NY 14605 US
(585) 222-1039
www.wdkx.com
License: Rochester, Monroe County, NY held by Monroe County Broadcasting Co. Ltd.
Arbitron Metro Market: Rochester, NY; *Format:* Urban Contemporary *Special Programming:* Jazz 4 hrs, gospel 7 hrs wkly; *Hrs. of News Programming:* news progmg 6 hrs wkly; *No. News Employees:* 2; *Target Audience:* General.
Andrew Langston, CEO
Camilla Maas, Operations Dir
Gloria Langston, Station Manager
Marietta Avery, CFO
Andre Langston, Operations Director

WROC
01-01-1947; 950 kHz AM; *Hrs Open:* 24; 1 kw-D, DA2; 1 kw-N, DA2; N43 6 25 W77 35 51
70 Commercial Street, Rochester, NY 14614 US
(585) 423-2900; *Fax:* (585) 325-5139
www.espnrochester.com
smunn@entercom.com
License: Rochester, NY held by Entercom Rochester License LLC.
Group Owner: Entercom Communications Corp.
Nat'l Network: ESPN Radio
Arbitron Metro Market: Rochester, NY; *Format:* Sports
Bob Barnett, Operations Dir
Sue Munn, VP/General Manager
Mike Johnson, Director of Sales
Chris Crowley, Programming Director

WHAM
07-11-1922; 1180 kHz AM; *Hrs Open:* 24; 50 kw-U, ND1; N43 4 55 W77 43 30
1700 HSBC Plaza, 100 Chestnut St., Rochester, NY 14604 US
(585) 454-4884
www.wham1180.com
License: Rochester, Monroe County, NY held by Citicasters Licenses L.P.
Group Owner: iHeartMedia; (acq 3-7-97; grpsl).
Nat'l Network: CBS
Arbitron Metro Market: Rochester, NY; *Format:* News, News/Talk, 86; *No. News Employees:* 6; *Target Audience:* Adults: 25-54.
Joe Bonadonna, Programming Director
Shari Smith, News Director
Becki Efing, Sales Manager
Bonnie Porter, Sales Manager
John DiTullio, Sports Director

WHTK
11-22-1947; 1280 kHz AM; *Hrs Open:* 24; 5 kw-D, DAN; 5 kw-N, DAN; N43 5 54 W77 35 1
1700 HSBC Plaza, 100 Chestnut Street, Rochester, NY 14604 US
(585) 454-4884; *Fax:* (585) 262-2334
www.foxsports1280.com
License: Rochester, NY held by Citicasters Licenses Inc.
Group Owner: iHeartMedia; (acq 5-4-99; grpsl).
Nat'l Reps: McGavren Guild
Arbitron Metro Market: Rochester, NY; *Format:* Sports; *Target Audience:* 25-54; men
JP Hastings, Programming Director
Bonnie Porter, Sales Manager
Becki Efing, Sales Manager
John DiTullio, Sports Director

*WIRQ
01-01-1960; 90.9 MHz FM; *Hrs Open:* 1 PM-8 PM (M-F); Sept-June; 19 w; 35 meters; N43 12 59 W77 35 51
260 Cooper Rd., Rochester, NY 14617
(585) 336-0740
License: Rochester, Monroe County, NY held by Board of Education West, Irondequoit Central School District.
Population Served: 600,000; *Arbitron Metro Market:* Rochester, NY *Special Programming:* Top-35 countdown 3 hrs, Progressive Pioneers 3 hrs; *Hrs. of News Programming:* News progmg one hr wkly *Target Audience:* 13-45.
Hannah Jacobs, General Manager
Ty McHugh, Station Manager
Josh Deutsch, Programming Director
Dave Desilet, Music Director
Jake Bigenwald, Webmaster

WJZR
01-22-1993; 105.9 MHz FM; *Hrs Open:* 24; 3 kw; 180 ft.; N43 9 35 W77 34 44
1237 East Main Street, Rochester, NY 14609 US
(585) 288-5020
License: Rochester, Monroe County, NY held by North Coast Radio Inc.
Nat'l Network: AP Radio
Arbitron Metro Market: Rochester, NY; *Format:* Blues, Jazz
Special Programming: News review one hr wkly; *Hrs. of News Programming:* News progmg 14 hrs wkly; *Target Audience:* 25 plus.
Lee Rust, President
Barry Vee, General Sales Mgr

WPXY-FM
09-14-1959; 97.9 MHz FM; 50 kw; 466 ft.; N43 8 5.17 W77 35 6.6
70 Commercial Street, Rochester, NY 14614 US
(585) 423-2900; *Fax:* (585) 325-5139
www.98pxy.com
License: Rochester, Monroe County, NY held by Entercom Rochester License LLC.
Group Owner: Entercom Communications Corp.; (acq 11-30-2007; grpsl)

Arbitron Metro Market: Rochester, NY; *Format:* Contemporary Hits/Top 40
Bob Barnett, Operations Manager
Sue Munn, Vice President/General Manager
Mike Johnson, Director of Sales
Mike Danger, Programming Director

WRMM-FM
11-14-1966; 101.3 MHz FM; 27 kw; 640 ft.; N43 10 13 W77 40 23
28 East Main Street, 8th Floor, Rochester, NY 14614 US
(585) 399-5700; *Fax:* (585) 399-5750
www.warm1013.com
info@warm1013.com
License: Rochester, Monroe County, NY held by Stephens Media Group-Rochester LLC.
Group Owner: Stephens Family L.P.; (acq 7-14-2008; grpsl)
Nat'l Reps: Christal
Arbitron Metro Market: Rochester, NY; *Format:* Adult Contemp; *Target Audience:* 25-54; baby boomers
Michael Ninnie, General Manager
Laurie Zsedely, Director of Sales
Stan Main, Programming Director
Scott Hixon, Marketing Director

***WRUR-FM**
03-06-1966; 88.5 MHz FM; *Hrs Open:* 24; 15.1 kw; 378 ft.; N43 8 7 W77 35 3
280 State Street, Rochester, NY 14627 US
(585) 325-7500
www.wrur.org
License: Rochester, Monroe County, NY held by University of Rochester Broadcasting Corp.
Arbitron Metro Market: Rochester, NY; *Format:* Variety/Diverse
Special Programming: Jazz, gospel 3 hrs, relg one hr, world 10 hrs, fol; *Hrs. of News Programming:* News progmg 4 hrs wkly; *Target Audience:* General.
Paul Szymanski, Operations Dir

WDVI
01-01-1962; 100.5 MHz FM; *Hrs Open:* 24; 50 kw; 479 ft.; N43 2 1 W77 25 18
1700 HSBC Plaza, 100 Chestnut Street, Rochester, NY 14604 US
(585) 454-4884; *Fax:* (585) 454-5081
www.mydrivefm.com
License: Rochester, Monroe County, NY held by Citicasters Licenses Inc.
Group Owner: iHeartMedia
Arbitron Metro Market: Rochester, NY; *Format:* Adult Contemp; *Target Audience:* 25-54.
Robert Morgan, Regional Market President
Tias Schuster, Programming Director
Bonnie Porter, Sales Manager
Becki Efing, Sales Manager
Scott Brooks, Digital Program Director

WHIC
09-11-1925; 1460 kHz AM; *Hrs Open:* 24
Station of the Cross, 6325 Sheridan Drive, Williamsville, NY 14221 US B4618
(877) 888-6279
www.whicradio.com
info@thestationofthecross.com
License: Rochester, NY held by Holy Family Communications
Group Owner: Holy Family Communications; acq 7-1-2003; $300,000).
Arbitron Metro Market: Rochester, NY; *Format:* Christian
James Wright, President

***WXXI**
01-01-1936; 1370 kHz AM; *Hrs Open:* 24; 5 kw-U, DA-N; N43 06 01 W77 34 23
280 State St., Rochester, NY 14601
(585) 325-7500; *Fax:* (585) 258-0339
www.wxxi.org
radio@wxxi.org
License: Rochester, Monroe County, NY held by WXXI Public Broadcasting Council.
Nat'l Network: NPR; *Wire Services:* AP
Population Served: 941,600; *Arbitron Metro Market:* Rochester, NY
Norm Silverstein, President
Susan Rogers, EVP/General Manager
Jeanne Fisher, Vice President/Station Manager
Alison Jones, General Sales Mgr
Michael Black, Programming Director
Julie Phillip, News Director
Kent Hatfield,Engineering Dir
Bud Lowell, Reporter

***WXXI-FM**
12-01-1974; 91.5 MHz FM; *Hrs Open:* 24; 45 kw; 440 ft.; N43 8 7 W77 35 3
280 State St., Box 21, Rochester, NY 14601 US
(585) 258-0200
www.wxxi.org
radio@wxxi.org
License: Rochester, Monroe County, NY held by WXXI Public Broadcasting Council
Nat'l Network: PRI
Arbitron Metro Market: Rochester, NY *TV Affiliate:* *WXXI-TV affil.; *Format:* Talk
Norm Silverstein, President
Julia Figueras, Music Director

Rome

WODZ-FM
08-01-1968; 96.1 MHz FM; 7.4 kw; 604 ft.; N43 8 39 W75 10 45
9418 River Road, Marcy, NY 13502 US
(315) 768-9500; *Fax:* (315) 736-0720
http://961wodz.com
License: Rome, Oneida County, NY
Group Owner: Townsquare Media; (acq 11-5-99; grpsl)
Arbitron Metro Market: Utica-Rome, NY *TV Affiliate:* Oldies
Karen Casey, General Manager
Tracy DeCarr, Director of Sales
Dave Wheeler, Programming Director

WRNY
10-12-1959; 1350 kHz AM; *Hrs Open:* 24; 0.5 kw-D, ND1; 0.057 kw-N, ND1; N43 12 18 W75 29 8
520 Seneca St., Suite 101, Utica, NY 13502 US
(315) 797-1330; *Fax:* (315) 797-1073
www.espnur.com
pscibilia@galaxycommunications.com
License: Rome, NY held by Galaxy Utica Licensee LLC.
Group Owner: Galaxy Communications L.P.; (acq 10-24-2007; grpsl)
Arbitron Metro Market: Utica-Rome, NY; *Format:* Sports *Special Programming:* Black 3 hrs wkly; *No. News Employees:* 1; *Target Audience:* 25 plus.

WUMX
05-01-1983; 102.5 MHz FM; *Hrs Open:* 24; 27 kw; 650 ft.; N43 2 14 W75 26 40
520 Seneca St., Suite 101, Utica, NY 13502 US
(315) 797-1330; *Fax:* (315) 738-1073
mix1025.com
askmix@mix1025.com
License: Rome, Oneida County, NY
Group Owner: Galaxy Communications Inc.
Arbitron Metro Market: Utica-Rome, NY; *Format:* Variety/Diverse
Special Programming: Pub affrs one hr wkly; *No. News Employees:* 1; *Target Audience:* 18-49.

WKAL
09-01-1946; 1450 kHz AM; *Hrs Open:* 24; 1 kw-D, ND2; 1 kw-N, ND2; N43 12 18 W75 28 48
1721 Black River Blvd., Rome, NY 13440
(315) 533-2795
www.wkal1450.com
traffic@wkal1450.com
License: Rome, Oneida County, NY held by Tune In Broadcasting LLC
Group Owner: Tune In Broadcasting LLC; (acq 2011).
Population Served: 275,000; *Arbitron Metro Market:* Utica-Rome, NY; *Format:* News, News/Talk, 84, Talk
Ron Frisch, General Manager

Rosendale

***WFNP**
09-05-1990; 88.7 MHz FM; *Hrs Open:* 7 PM-5 AM; 0.23 kw vert; 1289 ft.; N41 43 9 W73 59 47
State University Plaza, Albany, NY 12246 US
(845) 257-3090
www.wfnp.org
wfnp.sm@gmail.com
License: Rosendale, Ulster County, NY held by State University of New York, Albany.
Nat'l Network: ABC; AP Radio
Format: Talk *Special Programming:* Black 14 hrs, jazz 4 hrs, Sp 3 hrs, news/talk 5 hr; *Hrs. of News Programming:* News progmg 3 hrs wkly; *Target Audience:* General; demographic-specific programs

Rotterdam

WTRY-FM
12-15-1986; 98.3 MHz FM; *Hrs Open:* 24; 6 kw; 318 ft.; N42 44 43 W74 4 10
1203 Troy-Schenectady Road, Latham, NY 12110 US
(518) 452-4800; *Fax:* (518) 452-4813
www.983try.com
License: Rotterdam, Schenectady County, NY held by Capstar TX LLC
Group Owner: iHeartMedia; (acq 8-30-00; grpsl).
Nat'l Reps: Clear Channel
Arbitron Metro Market: Albany, NY; *Format:* Oldies; *Hrs. of News Programming:* news progmg 20 hrs wkly; *No. News Employees:* 1; *Target Audience:* 35-54.
Kristen Delaney, Regional Market President
Cliff Wohl, General Sales Mgr
John Cooper, Programming Director
Jill Manti, Marketing Director
BJ Ragone, Online Content Director

Rouses Point

***WKYJ**
01-01-2005; 88.7 MHz FM; 0.42 kw vert; 13 ft.; N44 56 44 W73 25 41
1601 Belvedere Rd, 204e, West Palm Beach, FL 33406 US
(800) 525-5683; *Fax:* (916) 251-1650
www.klove.com
klove@klove.com
License: Rouses Point, Clinton County, NY held by American Educational Broadcasting Inc.
Arbitron Metro Market: Rouses Point, NY; *Format:* Christian, Gospel; *No. News Employees:* 13
Darrell Chambliss, Chairman
Carl Auel, CEO
Mike Novak, President and CEO
Fred Hodges, General Manager
David Pierce, Programming Director
Ed Lenane, News Director
Sam Wallington, Engineering Dir
Dan Antonelli, Chief BusinessDevelopment Officer
Eric Moser, Chief Financial Officer
Brian Burger, Vice President of Human Resources
D. Kevin Blair, Secretary and General Counsel
Tim Luttrell, News Reporter

Roxbury

***WIOX**
91.3 MHz FM; 3.3 kw; -600 ft.; N42 16 13 W74 34 16
Mailing Address: 2335 County Highway 41, Roxbury, NY 12474 US
Second Address: PO Box 100, Roxbury, NY 12474
(607) 326-3900
www.wioxradio.org
License: Roxbury, Delaware County, NY held by Town of Roxbury.
Arbitron Metro Market: Roxbury, NY
Thomas Hynes, General Manager

Sag Harbor

WLNG
04-13-1969; 92.1 MHz FM; 5.3 kw; 350 ft; N40 58 19 W72 20 54
Mailing Address: Box 2000, Sag Harbor, NY 11963
Second Address: 23 Redwood Road, Sag Harbor, NY 11963
(631) 725-2300; *Fax:* (631) 725-5897
www.wlng.com
info@wlng.com
License: Sag Harbor, Suffolk County, NY held by Mainstreet Broadcasting Co.
Arbitron Metro Market: New York
Gary Sapiane, President
Gary Sapiane, Operations Dir
Rusty Potz, EVP/General Sales Manager
David Kline, Promotions Manager
Brian Bannon, Engineering Dir
Gary Sapiane, Vice President

Salamanca

WGGO
06-18-1957; 1590 kHz AM; 5 kw-D, ND2; 0.014 kw-N, ND2; N42 10 24 W78 41 7
Mailing Address: P.O. Box 62, Salamanca, NY 14779 US
Second Address: 4104 Killbuck Rd., Salamanca, NY 14779
(716) 945-1590; *Fax:* (716) 945-1515
wgrt983@direcway.com
License: Salamanca, NY held by Pembrook Pines Inc.
Group Owner: Pembrook Pines Media Group; (acq 6-9-2006; $1.25 million with co-located FM).
Nat'l Network: ESPN Radio
Format: Sports *Special Programming:* Country 5 hrs, Pol one hr wkly; *Target Audience:* General.
Robert Pfuntner, President
Tami Dunlavey, General Manager

Tami Dunlavey, General Sales Mgr
Jessica Wilson, Traffic Manager
Tom Power, Chief Engineer

WQRS
10-15-1988; 98.3 MHz FM; 3.2 kw; 443 ft.; N42 6 32 W78 36 28
Mailing Address: P.O. Box 62, Salamanca, NY 14779 US
Second Address: 4104 Killbuck Rd., Salamanca, NY 14779
(716) 945-1590; *Fax:* (716) 945-1515
License: Salamanca, Cattaraugus County, NY
Group Owner: Pembrook Pines Media Group
Format: Classic Rock
Tami Dunlavey, General Manager
Jessica Wilson, Traffic Manager

Sandy Creek-Pulaski

WSCP
08-08-1974; 1070 kHz AM; 2.5 kw-D, NDD; N43 36 19 W76 7 48
520 Seneca St., Suite 101, Utica, NY 13502 US
(315) 797-1330; *Fax:* (315) 738-1073
www.espnur.com
pscibilia@galaxycommunications.com
License: Sandy Creek-Pulaski, NY held by Galaxy Syracuse Licensee LLC.
Group Owner: Galaxy Communications L.P.; (acq 7-17-2001; $400,000 with WSCP-FM Pulaski).
Nat'l Network: Jones Radio Networks
Arbitron Metro Market: Syracuse, NY; *Format:* Sports; *Hrs. of News Programming:* news progmg one hr wkly; *No. News Employees:* 1; *Target Audience:* 35 plus.

Saranac

WYZY
07-12-1989; 106.3 MHz FM; *Hrs Open:* 24; 1.47 kw; 2316 ft.; N44 41 43 W73 53 0
60 Smithfield Boulevard, Plattsburgh, NY 12901 US
(518) 561-1063
License: Saranac, Franklin County, NY held by Saranac Lake Radio LLC
Group Owner: Mountain Communications
Format: Contemporary Hits/Top 40; *Hrs. of News Programming:* news progmg 10 hrs wkly; *No. News Employees:* 2; *Target Audience:* 18-49; adults; *Adv. Rates:* Same as AM
Crystal Tatro, Operations Dir
Ted Morgan, Office Manager

Saranac Lake

WNBZ
09-11-1927; 1240 kHz AM; *Hrs Open:* 24; 1 kw-U, ND1; N44 18 58 W74 7 8
Mailing Address: 159 Santanani Avenue, Saranac Lake, NY 12983 US
Second Address: , Baranac Lake,
(518) 891-1544; *Fax:* (518) 891-1545
www.wnbz.com
License: Saranac Lake, NY held by Saranac Lake Radio L.L.C.
Group Owner: Mountain Communications; (acq 6-1-98; $397,500 with co-located FM)
Arbitron Metro Market: Sarnak Lake, NY; *Format:* News, News/Talk, 86; *Hrs. of News Programming:* news progmg 36 hrs wkly; *No. News Employees:* 1; *Target Audience:* 35 plus; loc community; *Adv. Rates:* 20; 20;20; 15
Ted Morgan, President
John Gagnon, Operations Dir

*WSLL
07-01-1989; 90.5 MHz FM; 0.6 kw; 351 ft.; N44 20 28 W74 7 43
Rebroadcasts: Rebroadcasts WSLU(FM) Canton 100%
N. Country Public Radio, Canton, NY 13617 US
(315) 229-5356; *Fax:* (315) 229-5373
www.ncpr.org
radio@ncpr.org
License: Saranac Lake, Franklin County, NY held by St. Lawrence University.
Format: Variety/Diverse; *Target Audience:* General.
Ellen Rocco, General Manager
Jackie Sauter, Programming Director
Martha Foley, News Director
Robert Sauter, Chief Engineer
Sandra Demarest, Underwriting Director

WSLP
01-01-2007; 93.3 MHz FM; 11 kw; -207 ft.; N44 15 36 W74 1 22
2302 Saranac Avenue, Lake Placid, NY 12946 US
(518) 523-4900; *Fax:* (518) 523-4290
www.wslpfm.com
License: Saranac Lake, Franklin County, NY held by North Country Radio Inc.
Nat'l Network: CNN Radio
Arbitron Metro Market: Saranac Lake, NY; *Format:* Adult Contemp; *Target Audience:* 25-54.
Jim Williams, General Sales Manager/Vice President

Saratoga Springs

*WSPN
09-09-1974; 91.1 MHz FM; *Hrs Open:* 24; 0.25 kw horiz; 98 ft.; N43 5 55 W73 47 10
815 North Broadway, Saratoga Springs, NY 12866 US
(518) 580-5783
www.skidmore.edu/studentorgs/wspn
License: Saratoga Springs, Saratoga County, NY held by Skidmore College.
Nat'l Network: AP Radio
Format: Talk *Special Programming:* Folk 3 hrs, Pol 3 hrs, Sp 3 hrs, blues 9 hrs, world mus 3 hrs wkly; *Hrs. of News Programming:* News progmg 5 hrs wkly; *Target Audience:* All ages.
Gretchen Schaub, General Manager
Lena Bilik, Programming Director

*WSSK
01-01-2001; 89.7 MHz FM; 0.05 kw vert; 430 ft.; N43 11 35 W73 45 25
P.O. Box 777, Lake Katrine, NY 12449 US
(845) 336-6199; *Fax:* (845) 336-7205
www.soundoflife.org
info@soundoflife.org
License: Saratoga Springs, Saratoga County, NY held by Sound of Life Inc.
Format: Christian
Bob Conti, Operations Dir
Tom Zahradnik, General Manager
Joe Hunter, Programming Director

Saugerties

WBPM
01-01-1999; 92.9 MHz FM; *Hrs Open:* 24; 6 kw; 289 ft.; N41 59 20 W74 1 8
12 Tucker Drive, Poughkeepsie, NY 12603 US
(845) 838-6000; *Fax:* (845) 838-6088
www.wbpmfm.com
License: Saugerties, Ulster County, NY held by 6 Johnson Road Licenses Inc.
Group Owner: Pamal Broadcasting Ltd.; (acq 4-1-2007; grpsl)
Arbitron Metro Market: Poughkeepsie, NY; *Format:* Contemporary Hits/Top 40, Adult Contemp
Jason Finkelberg, Market Manager
Don Verity, Station Manager
Bruce Feniger, General Sales Mgr
Randy Turner, Programming/Music Director
Jessica Meyrowitz, National Sales Manager

Schenectady

WGY
02-01-1922; 810 kHz AM; *Hrs Open:* 24; 50 kw-U, ND1; N42 47 37 W74 0 36
1203 Troy-Schenectady Road, Latham, NY 12110 US
(518) 452-4800; *Fax:* (518) 452-4855
www.wgy.com
jeff@wgy.com
License: Schenectady, NY held by CC Licenses LLC
Group Owner: iHeartMedia; (acq 8-5-98; grpsl)
Nat'l Network: Fox News Radio; Premiere Radio Networks; *Nat'l Reps:* Clear Channel; *Wire Services:* AP
Arbitron Metro Market: Albany-Schenectady-Troy, NY; *Format:* News, News/Talk, 86; *Hrs. of News Programming:* news progmg 23 hrs wkly; *No. News Employees:* 12; *Target Audience:* 25-54; college graduate, married,homeowner
Kristen Delaney, Regional Market President
John Cooper, Senior Vice President of Programming
Cliff Wohl, Sales Manager
Jeff Wolf, Program Director/News Director
Jill Manti, Marketing Director
Dave Abdoo, Chief Engineer
BJ Ragone,Online Content Director

*WMHT-FM
06-08-1972; 89.1 MHz FM; 11 kw; 928 ft.; N42 38 13 W74 0 6
17 Fern Avenue, P.O. Box 17, Schenectady, NY 12301 US
(518) 880-3400; *Fax:* (518) 880-3409
www.wmht.org
info@wmht.org
License: Schenectady, Schenectady County, NY held by WMHT Educational Telecommunications.
Arbitron Metro Market: Albany, NY *TV Affiliate:* WMHT-TV.;
Format: Talk *Special Programming:* Jazz one hr wkly
Robert Altman, President/CEO
Bill Winans, Operations Manager
Paul Hoagland, SVP/Station Manager
Derek van Rijsewijk, Chief Engineer
Chris Wienk, Vice President of Radio

*WRUC
05-09-1975; 89.7 MHz FM; 0.1 kw; -89 ft.; N42 49 4 W73 55 45
807 Nion Street, Schenectady, NY 12308 US
(518) 388-6154
http://wruc.union.edu/wruc/
wruc@union.edu
License: Schenectady, Schenectady County, NY held by Trustees of Union College.
Nat'l Network: AP Radio
Arbitron Metro Market: Albany-Schenect; *Format:* Rock/AOR
Special Programming: It one hr, Sp 3 hrs, jazz 15 hrs, sports 4 hrs wkl; *Target Audience:* 18 plus; general
Kris Hammer, General Manager
Valerie Commerford, Promotions Manager

WRVE
04-01-1940; 99.5 MHz FM; *Hrs Open:* 24; 14.5 kw; 925 ft.; N42 38 13 W73 59 45
1203 Troy-Schenectady Road, Latham, NY 12110 US
(518) 452-4800; *Fax:* (518) 452-4855
www.995theriver.com
License: Schenectady, Schenectady County, NY held by CC Licenses LLC
Group Owner: iHeartMedia
Nat'l Network: Premiere Radio Networks
Arbitron Metro Market: Albany-Schenect; *Format:* Adult Contemp; *Hrs. of News Programming:* news progmg 3 hrs wkly; *No. News Employees:* 1; *Target Audience:* 25-54.
Kristen Delaney, Regional Market President
John Cooper, Senior Vice President of Programming
Cliff Wohl, General Sales Mgr
Randy McCarten, Programming Director
Jill Manti, Marketing Director
BJ Ragone, Online Content Director

WPTR
04-15-1942; 1240 kHz AM; *Hrs Open:* 24; 1 kw-U; N42 48 37 W73 59 04
100 Saratoga Village Blvd., Suite 21, Ballston Spa, NY 12020
(518) 899-3000; *Fax:* (518) 899-3057
www.sporty1240.com
License: Schenectady, NY held by Empire Broadcasting Corp.
Group Owner: Empire Broadcasting Corp.; (acq 4-10-2000; $137,500).
Population Served: 97,660; *Arbitron Metro Market:* Albany, NY; *Format:* Sports; *No. News Employees:* 1; *Target Audience:* 45 plus.
Scott Collins, President
John Meaney, Station Manager
Amanda Albright, Promotions Manager

Schoharie

WMYY
01-01-1990; 97.3 MHz FM; *Hrs Open:* 24; 0.8 kw; 896 ft.; N42 37 51 W74 16 1 *Rebroadcasts:* Rebroadcasts WHAZ(AM) Troy 100%
30 Park Ave, Cohoes, NY 12047 US
(518) 237-1330; *Fax:* (518) 235-4468
www.aliveradionetwork.com
events@aliveradionetwork.com
License: Schoharie, Schoharie County, NY held by Capital Media Corp.
Group Owner: Capital Media Corp.; (acq 2-14-92)
Arbitron Metro Market: Albany, NY; *Format:* Christian, Religious; *Target Audience:* 25-75
Paul Lotters, President
Steven Klob, Operations Dir

Schuyler Falls

*WOXR
01-01-2004; 90.9 MHz FM; 2.7 kw; 1073 ft.; N44 34 24 W73 40 31
P O Box 583, Essex Jct, VT 05453 US
(802) 655-9451; *Fax:* (802) 655-2799
www.vpr.net
vermontedition@vpr.net
License: Schuyler Falls, Clinton County, NY held by Vermont Public Radio
Regional Network: Vermont Public Radio
Arbitron Metro Market: Schuyler Falls, NY; *Format:* Classical
Robin Turnau, President & CEO
Victoria St. John, Operations Dir
Rich Parker, Engineering Dir
Mike Seguin, Engineering Dir
Tim Johnson, Online Producer
Brian Tagliaferro, Manager Of Special Giving

Ty Robertson, Coordinator ofCommunity Engagement
Leslie Blount, Director of Corporate Support

Scotia

***WYAI**
12-01-1981; 93.7 MHz FM; 1.25 kw; 705 ft.; N42 51 24 W74 4 3
89 Everts Avenue, Queensbury, NY 12804 US
(888) 937-2471; *Fax:* (916) 251-1650
www.air1.com
info@air1.com
License: Scotia, Schenectady County, NY held by Educational Media Foundation.
Group Owner: EMF Broadcasting; (acq 7-6-2007; grpsl)
Nat'l Network: Air 1
Arbitron Metro Market: Omaha, NE; *Format:* Alternative, Christian; *Target Audience:* 18-35; Judeo-Christian, female
Darrell Chambliss, Chairman
Mike Novak, President & CEO
Larry Moody, Director
Mitch Barnhart, Director
David R. Ferry, Director
Walter Golembeski, Director
David Pierce, Chief Creative Officer
Alan Mason, Chief OperatingOfficer

Seneca Falls

***WSFW**
1110 kHz AM; *Hrs Open:* Sunrise-sunset; 1 kw, NDD; N42 54 55 W76 46 28
P.O. Box 391, Twin Falls, ID 83303 US
(800) 357-4226; *Fax:* (208) 736-1958
www.csnradio.com
License: Seneca Falls, NY held by Calvary Chapel of Twin Falls, Inc.
Group Owner: CSN International
Format: Christian, Religious *Special Programming:* Irish 2 hrs, It 2 hrs, jazz one hr, oldies 3 hrs,; *Hrs. of News Programming:* news progmg 24 hrs wkly; *No. News Employees:* 1; *Target Audience:* 25-54.

WLLW
11-01-1968; 99.3 MHz FM; *Hrs Open:* 24; 5 kw; 358 ft.; N42 59 38 W76 51 59
3568 Lenox Rd., Geneva, NY 14456 US
(315) 781-7000; *Fax:* (315) 781-7700
www.flradiogroup.com
License: Seneca Falls, Seneca County, NY held by Auburn Broadcasting Inc.
Group Owner: Finger Lakes Radio Group
Format: Classic Rock; *Adv. Rates:* 14; 12; 14; 10
Frank Lischak, VP of Sales
Paul Szmal, Programming Director
Joe Nittler, News Director

Sidney

WCDO
01-01-1983; 1490 kHz AM; 1 kw-U, ND1; N42 19 24 W75 22 57
75 Main Street, Sidney, NY 13838 US
(607) 563-3588; *Fax:* (607) 563-7805
www.wcdoonline.com
wcdo@wcdofm.com
License: Sidney, NY held by CDO Broadcasting Inc.
Group Owner: CDO Broadcasting Inc.
Format: Adult Contemp; *Target Audience:* 25-54.
Craig Stevens, General Manager

WCDO-FM
05-01-1982; 100.9 MHz FM; 1.9 kw; 577 ft.; N42 17 33 W75 22 3
75 Main Street, Sidney, NY 13838 US
(607) 563-3588; *Fax:* (607) 563-7805
www.wcdoonline.com
wcdo@wcdofm.com
License: Sidney, Delaware County, NY held by CDO Broadcasting Inc.
Group Owner: CDO Broadcasting Inc.
Format: Adult Contemp, Oldies; *Target Audience:* 25-54.
Craig Stevens, General Manager
Greg Davie, General Sales Mgr

Silver Creek

***WCOM-FM**
89.3 MHz FM; 8 kw; 272 ft.; N42 34 41 W78 57 47
PO Box 506, Bath, NY 14810 US
(602) 776-4151
www.fln.org
License: Silver Creek, Chautauqua County, NY held by Family Life Ministries, Inc.
Group Owner: Family Life Ministries Inc.
Format: Christian
Dave Margalotti, Operations Dir
Terese Main, Programming Director
Bob Price, News Director

Smithtown

***WFRS**
10-17-1988; 88.9 MHz FM; *Hrs Open:* 24; 1.5 kw horiz, 1.45 kw vert; 433 ft.; N40 48 27 W73 10 48
4135 Northgate Blvd. #1, Sacramento, CA 95834 US
(631) 234-4151; *Fax:* (631) 234-4628
www.familyradio.com
License: Smithtown, Suffolk County, NY held by Family Stations Inc.
Group Owner: Family Stations Inc.; acq 9-27-83)
Nat'l Network: Family Radio
Format: Christian; *Hrs. of News Programming:* News progmg 5 hrs wkly; *Target Audience:* General.
Harold Camping, President

WWSK
05-21-1957; 94.3 MHz FM; *Hrs Open:* 24; 2.6 kw; Ant 315 ft; N40 48 08 W73 17 12
234 Airport Plaza Blvd., Suite 5, Farmingdale, NY 11747
(631) 770-4200; *Fax:* (631) 770-0101
License: Smithtown, Suffolk County, NY held by Connoisseur Media Licenses LLC
Group Owner: Connoisseur Media LLC
Nat'l Network: AP Radio; *Wire Services:* Standard Broadcast Wire
Population Served: 2,000,000; *Arbitron Metro Market:* New York, NY; *Hrs. of News Programming:* news progmg 2 hrs wkly; *No. News Employees:* 1; *Target Audience:* 25-54; men & women; *Adv. Rates:* 45; 50; 45; 40
Dave Widmer, General Manager

Sodus

WUUF
01-01-1991; 103.5 MHz FM; *Hrs Open:* 24; 6 kw; 243 ft.; N43 16 5 W77 9 40
187 Vienna Road, PO Box 292, Newark, NY 14513 US
(315) 331-9667; *Fax:* (315) 331-7101
bigdogfm@rochester.rr.com
License: Sodus, Wayne County, NY held by Waynco Radio
Nat'l Network: Motor Racing Net; Westwood One
Arbitron Metro Market: Rochester, NY; *Format:* Country; *Hrs. of News Programming:* news progmg one hr wkly; *No. News Employees:* 1; *Target Audience:* 25-54.; *Adv. Rates:* 30; 25; 30; 20
John Tickner, President
Jim Hill, Operations Dir
Rus Jeffrey, News Director

Solvay

WSYR
106.9 MHz FM; 9 kw; N43 0 10 W76 11 58
500 Plum Street, Suite 400, Syracuse, NY 13204 US
(315) 472-9797; *Fax:* (315) 472-2323
www.wsyr.com
License: Solvay, Onondaga County, NY held by CC Licenses LLC.
Group Owner: iHeartMedia
Arbitron Metro Market: Syracuse, NY; *Format:* News, News/Talk, 86
Rick Yacobush, Market President
Rich Lauber, Senior Vice President of Programming
Barbara Meaney, General Sales Mgr

South Bristol Township

WNBL
01-22-1996; 107.3 MHz FM; *Hrs Open:* 24; 650 w; Ant 994 ft; N42 44 47 W77 25 35
1700 HSBC Plaza, 100 Chestnut Street, Rochester, NY 41011 US
(585) 454-4884; *Fax:* (585) 454-5081
www.1073thebull.com
License: South Bristol Township, Ontario County, NY held by Citicasters Licenses Inc.
Group Owner: iHeartMedia; (acq 1999; grpsl)
Arbitron Metro Market: Rochester, NY; *Format:* Country; *Target Audience:* 25-54.
JP Hastings, Programming Director
Bonnie Porter, Sales Manager
Becki Efing, Sales Manager

South Glen Falls

WENU
09-01-1988; 1410 kHz AM; *Hrs Open:* 24
89 Everts Avenue, Queensbury, NY 12804 US
(518) 793-7733; *Fax:* (518) 793-0838
License: South Glen Falls, NY held by 6 Johnson Road Licenses Inc.
Group Owner: Pamal Broadcasting Ltd.; (acq 4-1-2004; grpsl).
Nat'l Network: Westwood One
Arbitron Metro Market: Queensbury, NY; *Format:* Contemporary Hits/Top 40; *No. News Employees:* 1; *Target Audience:* 35 plus.; *Adv. Rates:* 15; 15; 15; 5
James Morrell, President
Steven Petrone, Vice President of Operations

Southampton

WHFM
10-01-1971; 95.3 MHz FM; 5 kw; 354 ft.; N40 56 5 W72 23 15
555 Sunrise Highway West, Babylon, NY 11704 US
(631) 587-1023; *Fax:* (631) 283-9506
www.wbab.com
License: Southampton, Suffolk County, NY held by Cox Radio Inc.
Group Owner: Cox Radio Inc.; (acq 5-22-98; grpsl)
Nat'l Reps: Christal
Arbitron Metro Market: New York; *Format:* Adult Contemp, Rock/AOR; *Target Audience:* 25-49; upscale
John Shea, General Manager
Dain Alaia, Sales Manager
Chris Lloyd, Programming Director
Jason Steinberg, Director of Marketing & Promotions

***WPPB**
03-03-1979; 88.3 MHz FM; *Hrs Open:* 24; 5.9 kw horiz, 25 kw vert; 217 ft; N40 53 17 W72 26 43
Box 1410, Southhampton, NY 11548
(631) 591-7000; *Fax:* (631) 591-7080
www.peconicpublicbroadcasting.org
wally@peconicpublicbroadcasting.org
License: Southampton, Suffolk County, NY held by Peconic Public Broadcasting
Nat'l Network: PRI; NPR; *Wire Services:* AP
Population Served: 115,000 *Special Programming:* Pub affrs one hr wkly; *Hrs. of News Programming:* news progmg 34 hrs wkly; *No. News Employees:* 2; *Target Audience:* 34-55; upscale, educ, public radio listeners
Paula Jean Hinck, Director of Underwriting/Operations
Dr. Wallace Smith, General Manager
Nancye Simpson, Programming Director
Brian Cosgrove, Music Director

***WRLI-FM**
07-01-1999; 91.3 MHz FM; 10 kw; 312 ft.; N40 56 5 W72 23 15
Rebroadcasts: Rebroadcasts WPKT(FM) Meriden 100%
240 New Britain Avenue, Hartford, CT 06106 US
(860) 278-5310; *Fax:* (860) 244-9624
www.wnpr.org
info@wnpr.org
License: Southampton, Suffolk County, NY held by Connecticut Public Television & Radio.
Nat'l Network: NPR; PRI
Format: News, News/Talk, 86
Jerry Franklin, CEO
Kim Grehn, Vice President/Operations Director
Nancy Bauer, Vice President of Sales/Corporate Sponsorships

Southold

WBEA
07-03-1985; 101.7 MHz FM; *Hrs Open:* 24; 6 kw; 283 ft.; N40 52 10 W72 34 37
760 Montauk Highway, Suite 1C, Water Mill, NY 11976 US
(631) 267-7800
License: Southold, Suffolk County, NY held by AAA Licensing LLC.
Group Owner: Long Island Radio Broadcasting LLC; (acq 8-22-2000; $2.75 million with WBAZ(FM) Bridgehampton).
Nat'l Network: Westwood One
Arbitron Metro Market: Omaha-Council Bluffs NE-IA
Danny Manciu, President

Southport

WOKN
09-15-1993; 99.5 MHz FM; 1.25 kw; 725 ft.; N42 7 51 W76 47 26
1705 Lake Street, Elmira, NY 14901 US
(607) 733-5626; *Fax:* (607) 733-5627
http://995woknelmira.com/

License: Southport, Chemung County, NY held by Pembrook Pines Elmira Ltd.
Group Owner: Pembrook Pines Media Group
Nat'l Network: Jones Radio Networks
Arbitron Metro Market: Elmira-Corning, *TV Affiliate:* Country
Special Programming: news progmg 2 hrs wkly; *Hrs. of News Programming:* 1; *No. News Employees:* 18-49; female; *Adv. Rates:* 25; 25; 25; 20
Robert Pfunter, President/CEO
Michael Williams, Programming Director

Spectacular

WYVS

96.5 MHz FM; 2.6 kw; 152 m; N43 31 26 W74 21 39
1250 Riverfront Center, Amsterdam, NY
(518) 684-6260
www.wyvs965.com
wess@cranesville.com
License: Spectacular, Hamilton County, NY
Group Owner: Tesiero, Joseph C.

Joseph C. Tesiero, CEO/COO

Spencer

*WCII

10-01-1989; 88.5 MHz FM; *Hrs Open:* 24; 17 kw; 591 ft.; N42 0 50 W76 15 53 *Rebroadcasts:* Rebroadcasts WCIK(FM) Bath 100%
PO Box 506, Bath, NY 14810 US
(607) 776-4151
www.fln.org
License: Spencer, Tioga County, NY held by Family Life Ministries Inc.
Group Owner: Family Life Network
Nat'l Network: Salem Radio Network; *Wire Services:* Metro Weather Service Inc.
Arbitron Metro Market: Bath, NY; *Format:* Christian *Special Programming:* News 14 hrs wkly; *Hrs. of News Programming:* news progmg 14 hrs wkly; *No. News Employees:* 3; *Target Audience:* 30-54; general public
Dave Margalotti, Operations Dir
Terese Main, Programming Director
Bob Price, News Director

Springville

WSPQ

04-20-1986; 1330 kHz AM; *Hrs Open:* 24; 1 kw-D, DA2; 1 kw-N, DA2; N42 29 53 W78 41 10
51 Franklin Street, Springville, NY 14141 US
(716) 592-1330
wspq1330@yahoo.com
License: Springville, NY held by Hawk Communications Ltd.
Nat'l Network: CNN Radio; ESPN Radio; Motor Racing Net
Arbitron Metro Market: Buffalo-Niagara Falls, NY; *Format:* Adult Contemp, Country, 84, Variety/Diverse *Special Programming:* Farm 5 hrs, relg 2 hrs wkly; *Hrs. of News Programming:* news progmg 10 hrs wkly *No. NewsEmployees:* 1; *Target Audience:* 25-54.; *Adv. Rates:* 20; 18; 20; 15
Fred Haier, General Manager

Staten Island

*WSIA

08-31-1981; 88.9 MHz FM; *Hrs Open:* 24; 0.011 kw; 630 ft.; N40 35 51 W74 6 53
2800 Victory Blvd, Building 1C, Suite 106, Staten Island, NY 10314 US
(718) 982-3050; *Fax:* (718) 982-3052
www.wsia.fm
music@wsia.fm
License: Staten Island, Richmond County, NY held by College of Staten Island.
Arbitron Metro Market: New York; *Format:* Triple A; *Target Audience:* General.
Philip Masciantonio, General Manager
John Ladley, Chief Engineer

Stillwater

WJKE

10-03-1988; 101.3 MHz FM; *Hrs Open:* 24; 2.9 kw; 470 ft; N43 00 42 W73 41 01
100 Saratoga Village Blvd., Ste. 21, Ballston Spa, NY 12020 US
(518) 899-3000; *Fax:* (518) 899-3057
License: Stillwater, Saratoga County, NY held by Empire Broadcasting Corp
Group Owner: Empire Broadcasting Corp.; acq 9-4-98; $900,000).

Arbitron Metro Market: Albany-Schenectady-Troy, NY; *Format:* Adult Contemp; *Hrs. of News Programming:* news progmg 6 hrs wkly; *No. News Employees:* 1; *Target Audience:* 25-54; upscale
Robert Kieve, President

Stony Brook

*WUSB

06-27-1977; 90.1 MHz FM; *Hrs Open:* 24; 3.6 kw; 531 ft.; N40 50 32 W73 2 23
2nd Floor, Union Building, Stony Brook University, Stony Brook, NY 11794 US
(631) 632-6501; *Fax:* (631) 632-7182
www.wusb.fm
md@wusb.fm
License: Stony Brook, Suffolk County, NY held by State University of New York.
Wire Services: AP
Arbitron Metro Market: Stony Brook, NY; *Format:* News, News/Talk, 86, Variety/Diverse *Special Programming:* Black 12 hrs, Pol one hr, Sp 3 hrs, Chinese one hr; *Hrs. of News Programming:* News progmg 20 hrs wkly *TargetAudience:* 18-49; progsv & musically adventurous
Marko Srdanovic, Operations Dir
Norman Prusslin, General Manager

Sylvan Beach

WMVN

04-01-1999; 100.3 MHz FM; 6 kw; Ant 328 ft; N43 14 46 W75 46 25
401 W. Kirkpatrick St., Syracuse, NY 13476
(315) 476-9653; *Fax:* (315) 478-7745
www.movin100.com
License: Sylvan Beach, Oswego County, NY held by WOLF Radio Inc.
Group Owner: WOLF Radio Inc.; (acq 2-28-2002; $350,000)
Population Served: 145,151; *Arbitron Metro Market:* Syracuse, NY
Sam Furco, General Manager/Station Manager
John Hunt, General Sales Mgr

Syosset

*WKWZ

07-24-1973; 88.5 MHz FM; 0.125 kw; 259 ft.; N40 47 48 W73 27 44
Pell Lane, Syosset, NY 11791 US
www.wkwz.org
License: Syosset, Nassau County, NY held by Syosset Central School District.
Format: Variety/Diverse *Special Programming:* C&W 6 hrs, class 6 hrs, jazz 12 hrs wkly
Cord Lehman, General Manager
Sarah Lim, Station Manager

Syracuse

*WAER

04-01-1947; 88.3 MHz FM; *Hrs Open:* 24; 50 kw; 276 ft.; N43 2 1 W76 7 53
7095 Ostrom Avenue, Syracuse, NY 13210 US
(315) 443-4021
www.waer.org
waer@waer.org
License: Syracuse, Onondaga County, NY held by Syracuse University.
Nat'l Network: NPR
Arbitron Metro Market: Syracuse NY; *Format:* Jazz, News, 84 *Special Programming:* Gospel 3 hrs, blues 3 hrs, world mus 4 hrs, new age 3 hrs wkly; *Hrs. of News Programming:* news progmg 20 hrs wkly; *No. News Employees:* 3; *Target Audience:* 25-49.
Joe Lee, General Manager
Ron Ockert, Programming Director
Eric Cohen, Music Director

*WCNY-FM

12-04-1971; 91.3 MHz FM; *Hrs Open:* 5 AM-midnight; 18.5 kw; 741 ft.; N42 56 42 W76 1 28
415 West Fayette Street, Syracuse, NY 13204 US
(315) 453-2424; *Fax:* (315) 451-8824
www.wcny.org
wcny-fm@wcny.org
License: Syracuse, Onondaga County, NY held by Public Broadcasting Council of Central New York.
Nat'l Network: NPR
Arbitron Metro Market: Syracuse, NY *TV Affiliate:* *WCNY-TV affil; *Format:* Classical *Special Programming:* Bluegrass 3 hrs, jazz 7 hrs wkly; *Target Audience:* General.
Colleen Edwards, CFO
Richard A. Sullivan, COO
Robert J. Daino, President/CEO
Jim Aroune, Vice President of Operations
Peter Hirsch, Director of Marketing
John Duffy, Chief Engineer

WFBL

02-04-1922; 1390 kHz AM; 5 kw-D, DA2; 5 kw-N, DA2; N43 9 10 W76 11 35
8456 Smokey Hollow Rd., Baldwinsville, NY 13027 US
(315) 635-3971; *Fax:* (315) 635-3490
www.wfbl.com
License: Syracuse, Onondaga County, NY held by Leatherstocking Media Group Inc.
Group Owner: Leatherstocking Media Group Inc.; (acq 11-10-2003; $1.2 million)
Arbitron Metro Market: Syracuse, NY; *Format:* Talk
Dan Elliott, General Manager
Krista Galster, General Sales Mgr
Paul DeLaubell, Sales Representative

WHEN

04-14-1941; 620 kHz AM; *Hrs Open:* 24; 5 kw-D, DAN; 1 kw-N, DAN; N43 5 32 W76 11 22; N43 5 34 W76 11 17
Bridgewater Place, 500 Plum Street, Suite 400, Syracuse, NY 13204 US
(315) 472-9797; *Fax:* (315) 472-1904
www.power620.com
License: Syracuse, NY held by CC Licenses LLC.
Group Owner: iHeartMedia; (acq 1999)
Arbitron Metro Market: Syracuse, NY; *Format:* Urban Contemporary *Special Programming:* Syracuse Chiefs, Buffalo Bills, Syracuse Crunch
Rick Yacobush, Market President
Rich Lauber, Senior Vice President of Programming
Barbara Meaney, General Sales Mgr
Kenny Dees, Programming Director

*WJPZ-FM

01-30-1985; 89.1 MHz FM; *Hrs Open:* 24; 0.1 kw; 121 ft.; N43 2 1 W76 7 53
316 Waverly Avenue, Syracuse, NY 13244 US
(315) 443-4689; *Fax:* (315) 443-4379
www.z89.com
License: Syracuse, Onondaga County, NY held by WJPZ Radio Inc.
Arbitron Metro Market: Syracuse, NY; *Format:* Contemporary Hits/Top 40 *Special Programming:* Black 12 hrs, pub service 13 hrs wkly; *Target Audience:* 12-34; women & teenagers
Scott Purdy, Operations Dir
Corey Crockett, General Manager
Louise Vazquez, General Sales Mgr
Marie Strycharz, Business/Promotions Manager

WXTL

04-08-1996; 105.9 MHz FM; *Hrs Open:* 24; 4 kw; 200 ft; N43 03 30 W76 10 00
1064 James St., Syracuse, NY 13203 US
(315) 472-0200
www.therebelrocks.com
jaime.lawlor@cumulus.com
License: Syracuse, NY held by Radio License Holding CBC, LLC
Group Owner: Cumulus Media Inc.; (acq 2000; grpsl).
Nat'l Network: CBS Radio
Population Served: 536,300; *Arbitron Metro Market:* Syracuse, NY; *Format:* Classic Rock; *Target Audience:* 25-54; general
Jaime Lawlor, General Sales Mgr

*WMHR

03-09-1969; 102.9 MHz FM; *Hrs Open:* 24; 20 kW; 784 ft.; N42 58 1 W76 12 0
4044 Makyes Rd, Syracuse, NY 13215 USA
(800) 677-1881
www.marshillnetwork.org
info@marshillnetwork.org
License: Syracuse, Onondaga County, NY held by Mars Hill Broadcasting Co. Inc.
Group Owner: Mars Hill Network
Nat'l Network: Moody; Salem Radio Network; *Wire Services:* AP
Arbitron Metro Market: Syracuse, NY; *Format:* Christian *Special Programming:* Children 11 hrs wkly; *Hrs. of News Programming:* News progmg 6 hrs wkly; *Target Audience:* General; Christian families
Wayne Taylor, General Manager
Mike Dwinell, Chief Engineer

WSKO

01-01-1946; 1260 kHz AM; *Hrs Open:* 24; 5 kw-U, DA-2; N43 09 10 W76 11 35
1064 James St., Syracuse, NY 13203 US
(315) 472-0200
www.thescore1260.com
License: Syracuse, NY held by Radio License Holding CBC, LLC

Group Owner: Cumulus Media Inc.
Nat'l Network: ESPN Radio
Population Served: 536,300; *Arbitron Metro Market:* Syracuse, NY; *Format:* Sports, Talk; *Target Audience:* 25-54; men
Shane Bogardus, Vice President/Market Manager

WNTQ
01-01-1945; 93.1 MHz FM; *Hrs Open:* 24; 97 kw; 659 ft.; N42 56 48 W76 1 28
1064 James St., Syracuse, NY 13203 US
(315) 472-0200
www.93q.com
License: Syracuse, NY held by Radio License Holding CBC, LLC
Group Owner: Cumulus Media Inc.; (acq 4-26-01; grpsl).
Nat'l Reps: McGavren Guild
Arbitron Metro Market: Syracuse, NY; *Format:* Contemporary Hits/Top 40
Frank Hammon, Programming Director

WOLF
04-27-1940; 1490 kHz AM; 1 kw-D, DAD; 1 kw-N, DAD; N43 3 30 W76 10 0
401 West Kirkpatrick St., Syracuse, NY 13204 US
(315) 472-0222; *Fax:* (315) 478-7745
www.radiodisney.com
License: Syracuse, NY held by WOLF Radio Inc.
Group Owner: WOLF Radio Inc.; acq 10-5-82).
Nat'l Network: Radio Disney
Arbitron Metro Market: Syracuse, NY *TV Affiliate:* Children
Craig L. Fox, President

***WRVD**
06-01-1999; 90.3 MHz FM; *Hrs Open:* 24; 0.28 kw; 43 ft.; N43 2 27 W76 8 22 *Rebroadcasts:* Rebroadcasts WRVO(FM) Oswego 100%
7060 State Route 104, Oswego, NY 13126 US
(315) 312-3690; *Fax:* (315) 312-3174
wrvo.fm
feedback@wrvo.fm
License: Syracuse, Onondaga County, NY held by State University of New York.
Nat'l Network: NPR
Arbitron Metro Market: Syracuse, NY; *Format:* Variety/Diverse; *Hrs. of News Programming:* news progmg 140 hrs wkly; *No. News Employees:* 4; *Target Audience:* 35-54.; *Adv. Rates:* 60, 50, 60, 40
Lee Mitchell, Operations Manager
Michael S. Ameigh, General Manager
Catherine Loper, News Director
Jeff Windsor, Chief Engineer
Pam Cantine, Business Manager

WSYR
01-01-1922; 570 kHz AM; *Hrs Open:* 24; 5 kw-D, DA2; 5 kw-N, DA2; N42 59 13 W76 9 9
500 Plum Street, Suite 400, Syracuse, NY 13204 US
(315) 472-9797; *Fax:* (315) 472-1904
www.wsyr.com
License: Syracuse, NY held by CC Licenses LLC.
Group Owner: iHeartMedia
Nat'l Network: PRI
Arbitron Metro Market: Syracuse, NY; *Format:* News, News/Talk, 86; *Hrs. of News Programming:* News progmg 35 hrs wkly; *Target Audience:* 25-54.
Rick Yacobush, Market President
Rich Lauber, Senior Vice President of Programming
Barbara Meaney, General Sales Mgr

WWHT
09-01-1958; 107.9 MHz FM; *Hrs Open:* 24; 50 kw; 499 ft.; N42 57 21 W76 6 36
500 Plum Street, Suite 400, Syracuse, NY 13204 US
(315) 472-9797; *Fax:* (315) 472-2323
www.hot1079.com
License: Syracuse, Onondaga County, NY held by CC Licenses LLC.
Group Owner: iHeartMedia
Arbitron Metro Market: Syracuse, NY; *Format:* Contemporary Hits/Top 40
Rick Yacobush, Market President
Rich Lauber, Senior Vice President of Programming
Barbara Meaney, General Sales Mgr

WYYY
01-01-1946; 94.5 MHz FM; 100 kw; 650 ft.; N42 56 46 W76 7 7
500 Plum Street, Suite 400, Syracuse, NY 13204 US
(315) 472-9797; *Fax:* (315) 472-2323
www.y94fm.com
License: Syracuse, Onondaga County, NY held by CC Licenses LLC
Group Owner: iHeartMedia
Arbitron Metro Market: Syracuse, NY; *Format:* Adult Contemp
Rick Yacobush, Market President
Rich Lauber, Senior Vice President of Programming
Barbara Meaney, General Sales Mgr
Kathy Rowe, Programming Director

Ticonderoga

***WANC**
09-06-1982; 103.9 MHz FM; *Hrs Open:* 24; 1.55 kw; 381 ft.; N43 49 55 W73 24 28 *Rebroadcasts:* Rebroadcasts WAMC-FM Albany 100%
318 Central Avenue, Albany, NY 12206 US
(518) 465-5233(800) 323-9262; *Fax:* (518) 432-6974
www.wamc.org
mail@wamc.org
License: Ticonderoga, Essex County, NY held by WAMC.
Group Owner: WAMC/Northeast Public Radio; (acq 8-90; $400,000;
Nat'l Network: NPR; PRI; *Wire Services:* AP
Arbitron Metro Market: Ticonderoga, NY; *Format:* News, Talk
Special Programming: Folk 6 hrs, jazz 17 hrs wkly; *Target Audience:* General.
Alan Chartock, CEO
Selma Kaplan, SVP/Operations Director
Joe Donohue, Vice President of News and Programming

Troy

WFLY
08-01-1948; 92.3 MHz FM; *Hrs Open:* 24; 17 kw; 850 ft.; N42 38 16 W73 59 55
6 Johnson Road, Latham, NY 12110 US
(518) 786-6600; *Fax:* (518) 786-6610
www.fly92.com
ally@fly92.com
License: Troy, Rensselaer County, NY held by 6 Johnson Road Licenses Inc.
Group Owner: Pamal Broadcasting Ltd.; (acq 10-19-2001; grpsl)
Nat'l Network: ABC; *Nat'l Reps:* McGavren Guild
Arbitron Metro Market: Albany-Schenectady-Troy, NY; *Format:* Contemporary Hits/Top 40; *Hrs. of News Programming:* news progmg 5 hrs wkly; *No. News Employees:* 1; *Target Audience:* 18-49.; *Adv. Rates:* 175; 150;175; 100
Kevin Callahan, Operations Dir
Bob Ausfeld, General Manager
Ally Reid, Programming Director
Gioanna Sasso, Promotions Manager

WHAZ
08-01-1922; 1330 kHz AM; *Hrs Open:* 24; 1 kw-D, ND1; 0.049 kw-N, ND1; N42 46 35 W73 41 10
30 Park Ave, Cohoes, NY 12047 US
(518) 237-1330; *Fax:* (518) 235-4468
www.aliveradionetwork.com
events@aliveradionetwork.com
License: Troy, NY held by Capital Media Corporation
Group Owner: Capital Media Corp.; (acq 9-24-87)
Arbitron Metro Market: Albany-Schenectady-Troy, NY; *Format:* Christian, Religious; *Target Audience:* 25-75
Paul Lotters, President
Steven Klob, Operations Dir

***WRPI**
11-01-1957; 91.5 MHz FM; *Hrs Open:* 6 AM-2 AM; 10 kw; 371 ft.; N42 41 14 W73 42 22
1 WRPI Plaza, Troy, NY 12180 US
(518) 276-6248; *Fax:* (518) 276-2360
www.wrpi.org
License: Troy, Rensselaer County, NY held by Rensselaer Polytechnic Institute.
Arbitron Metro Market: Albany-Schenectady-Troy, NY; *Format:* Variety/Diverse; *Hrs. of News Programming:* News progmg 5 hrs wkly; *Target Audience:* General; open minded, educated listeners
Dennis Conley, President
Johnny Greeman, General Manager

WOFX
04-15-1940; 980 kHz AM; 5 kw-D, DAN; 5 kw-N, DAN; N42 46 56 W73 50 7
1203 Troy-Schenectady Road, Latham, NY 12110 US
(518) 452-4800; *Fax:* (518) 452-4813
www.foxsports980.com
License: Troy, NY held by Capstar TX LLC
Group Owner: iHeartMedia; (acq 8-30-00; grpsl).
Nat'l Reps: Clear Channel
Arbitron Metro Market: Albany, NY; *Format:* Sports, Talk; *Target Audience:* 18-49.
Kristen Delaney, Regional Market President
Jeff Wolf, Programming Director
Jill Manti, Marketing Director
BJ Ragone, Online Content Director

Trumansburg

WPIE
01-15-1990; 1160 kHz AM; *Hrs Open:* 24; 5 kw-D, DA2; 0.31 kw-N, DA2; N42 32 42 W76 42 39
3100 North Triphammer Road, Suite 100, Lansing, NY 14882 US
(607) 533-0057
License: Trumansburg, NY held by Taughannock Media LLC
Nat'l Network: ESPN Radio
Arbitron Metro Market: Ithaca, NY; *Format:* Sports; *Hrs. of News Programming:* news progmg 18 hrs wkly; *No. News Employees:* 1; *Target Audience:* 25-54; mature, upscale adults
Jeremy Menard, Operations Manager
Todd Mallinson, General Manager
Ed White, Account Manager
Eric Silverman, Account Manager
Nick Karski, Traffic Manager/Reporter
Tina Mallinson, Business Manager

Tupper Lake

WRGR
02-29-1980; 102.1 MHz FM; *Hrs Open:* 24; 0.14 kw; 1447 ft.; N44 9 35 W74 28 34 *Rebroadcasts:* Rebroadcasts WLPW(FM) Lake Placid 100%
P.O. Box 831, Lake Placid, NY 12946 US
(518) 891-1544; *Fax:* (518) 891-1545
sales@wnbz.com
License: Tupper Lake, Franklin County, NY held by Radio Lake Placid Inc.
Group Owner: Mountain Communications; (acq 2003; grpsl)
Nat'l Network: ABC; *Wire Services:* UPI
Format: Adult Contemp, Classic Rock *Special Programming:* Relg one hr, big band 2 hrs wkly; *Hrs. of News Programming:* news progmg 2 hrs wkly; *No. News Employees:* 2; *Target Audience:* 25-54; men
Ted Morgan, President

***WXLS**
88.3 MHz FM; 0.11 kw; 1421 ft.; N44 9 34 W74 28 34 US
(315) 229-5356; *Fax:* (315) 229-5373
www.ncpr.org
radio@ncpr.org
License: Tupper Lake, Franklin County, NY held by The St. Lawrence University.
Arbitron Metro Market: Tupper Lake, NY; *Format:* Public Affairs; *No. News Employees:* 3
Shelly Pike, Operations Dir
Ellen Rocco, General Manager
Jackie Sauter, Programming Director
Martha Foley, News Director
Bob Sauter, Chief Engineer
Bill Haenel, New Media Developer
Joel Hurd, Production Manager
Naomi Weller,Office Manager
Dale Hobson, Web Manager

Unadilla

***WCIJ**
88.9 MHz FM; 5 kw vert; 791 ft.; N42 23 27 W75 19 41
PO Box 506, Bath, NY 14810 US
(607) 776-4151
www.fln.org
License: Unadilla, Sullivan County, NY held by Family Life Ministries Inc.
Group Owner: Family Life Network
Arbitron Metro Market: Unadilla, NY; *Format:* Christian
Dave Margalotti, Operations Dir
Terese Main, Programming Director
Bob Price, News Director

Utica

WFRG-FM
10-10-1948; 104.3 MHz FM; 100 kw; 456 ft.; N43 3 22.9 W75 25 2
9418 River Road, Marcy, NY 13403 US
(315) 768-9500; *Fax:* (315) 736-3311
www.bigfrog104.com
info@bigfrog104.com
License: Utica, Oneida County, NY
Group Owner: Townsquare Media; (acq 11-5-99; grpsl)
Arbitron Metro Market: Utica-Rome, NY; *Format:* Country; *Target Audience:* 25-54.
Karen Carey, General Manager
Bill McAdams, Brand Manager
Tracey DeCarr, Director Of Sales
Paige Cummings, Digital Sales Manager
Stacey McAdams, Digital Managing Editor

WIBX
12-05-1925; 950 kHz AM; *Hrs Open:* 24; 5 kw-U, DA1; N43 6 12 W75 20 31
9418 River Road, Marcy, NY 13403 US
(315) 768-9500; *Fax:* (315) 736-0720
www.wibx950.com
karen.carey@townsquaremedia.com
License: Utica, NY
Group Owner: Townsquare Media; (acq 2-11-2000; grpsl)
Nat'l Network: CBS
Arbitron Metro Market: Utica-Rome, NY; *Format:* News, News/Talk, 84, Talk *Special Programming:* Pol 3 hrs, farm 14 hrs wkly; *No. News Employees:* 5; *Target Audience:* 35-64; middle to upper income adults
Karen Carey, General Manager
Jeff Monaski, Brand Manager
Tracey DeCarr, Director Of Sales
Paige Cummings, Digital Sales Manager
Phillip Creighton, Digital Managing Editor

WLZW
01-01-1972; 98.7 MHz FM; *Hrs Open:* 24; 25 kw; 659 ft.; N43 8 39 W75 10 45
9418 River Road, Marcy, NY 13403 US
(315) 768-9500; *Fax:* (315) 736-0720
www.lite987.com
eric.meier@townsquaremedia.com
License: Utica, Oneida County, NY
Group Owner: Townsquare Media
Arbitron Metro Market: Utica-Rome, NY; *Format:* Adult Contemp; *No. News Employees:* 6; *Target Audience:* 25-54; middle to upper income & educ levels
Karen Carey, General Manager
Tracy DeCarr, General Sales Mgr
Eric Meier, Programming Director

WOUR
06-01-1967; 96.9 MHz FM; 19.5 kw; 791 ft.; N43 8 46 W75 10 40
520 Seneca St., Suite 101, Utica, NY 13502 US
(315) 797-1330; *Fax:* (315) 738-1073
www.wour.com
askwour@wour.com
License: Utica, Oneida County, NY held by Galaxy Utica Licensee LLC.
Group Owner: Galaxy Communications L.P.; (acq 9-21-2007; grpsl)
Arbitron Metro Market: Utica-Rome, NY; *Format:* Rock/AOR; *Target Audience:* 25-49; adults

***WPNR-FM**
11-01-1977; 90.7 MHz FM; 0.43 kw; -141 ft.; N43 5 47 W75 16 19
US
(860) 275-7550
www.wnpr.org
wnprinfo@wnpr.org
License: Utica, Oneida County, NY held by Utica College.
Arbitron Metro Market: Utica-Rome, NY; *Format:* Rock/AOR, Variety/Diverse *Special Programming:* Class 10 hrs, jazz 14 hrs, reggae 5 hrs wkly
Todd Hutton, President

***WKVU**
04-23-1962; 107.3 MHz FM; 50 kw; Ant 499 ft; N43 08 40 W75 10 32
2351 Sunset Blvd., Suite 170-218, Rocklin, CA 13039
(916) 251-1600; *Fax:* (916) 251-1650
www.air1.com
info@air1.com
License: Utica, Oneida County, NY held by Educational Media Foundation.
Group Owner: EMF Broadcasting; (acq 10-24-2007; $1,224,000)
Nat'l Network: Air 1
Population Served: 8,500; *Arbitron Metro Market:* Utica-Rome, NY
Mike Novak, President

WUTI
04-24-1948; 1150 kHz AM; 5 kw-D, 1 kw-N, DA-2; N43 10 31 W75 21 03
318 Central Ave., Albany, NY 16648
(518) 465-5233; *Fax:* (518) 432-6974
www.wamc.org
mail@wamc.org
License: Utica, Oneida County, NY held by WAMC.
Group Owner: WAMC/Northeast Public Radio; (acq 7-6-2005; $275,000)
Nat'l Network: NPR; PRI; *Wire Services:* AP
Population Served: 91,611; *Arbitron Metro Market:* Utica-Rome, NY
Alan Chartock, CEO
Selma Kaplan, Operations Director/SVP

***WRVN**
06-04-1986; 91.9 MHz FM; 1.9 kw; -62 ft.; N43 8 31 W75 13 36
Rebroadcasts: Rebroadcasts WRVO(FM) Oswego 100%
7060 State Route 104, Oswego, NY 13126 US
(315) 312-3690; *Fax:* (315) 312-3174
www.wrvo.fm
feedback@wrvo.fm
License: Utica, Oneida County, NY held by State University of New York.
Nat'l Network: NPR; PRI; *Wire Services:* AP
Arbitron Metro Market: Utica-Rome, NY; *Format:* Variety/Diverse; *Hrs. of News Programming:* news progmg 140 hrs wkly; *No. News Employees:* 3; *Adv. Rates:* 60; 50; 60; 40
Michael S. Ameigh, General Manager
Thomas Herbert, General Sales Mgr
Catherine Loper, News Director
Jeff Windsor, Chief Engineer
Pam Cantine, Business Manager
Thomas Herbert, Underwriting Manager

WTLB
01-01-1946; 1310 kHz AM; *Hrs Open:* 24; 5 kw-D, DA2; 0.5 kw-N, DA2; N43 3 24 W75 16 42
520 Seneca St., Suite 101, Utica, NY 13502 US
(315) 797-1330; *Fax:* (315) 738-1073
wour.com
askwour@wour.com
License: Utica, NY held by Galaxy Communications L.P.
Group Owner: Galaxy Communications L.P.; (acq 4-6-2000; grpsl)
Arbitron Metro Market: Utica, NY; *Format:* Adult Contemp; *Hrs. of News Programming:* News progmg one hr wkly; *Target Audience:* 55 plus.

***WUNY**
10-30-1985; 89.5 MHz FM; *Hrs Open:* 5 AM-midnight; 6.3 kw; 778 ft.; N43 8 38 W75 10 40
P.O. Box 2400, 506 Old Liverpool Rd, Syracuse, NY 13220 US
(315) 453-2424; *Fax:* (315) 451-8824
www.wcny.org
wcny—online@wcny.org
License: Utica, Oneida County, NY held by Public Broadcasting Council of Central New York.
Nat'l Network: NPR
Arbitron Metro Market: Utica, NY; *Format:* Talk *Special Programming:* Bluegrass 3 hrs, jazz 7 hrs wkly; *Target Audience:* General.
Colleen Edwards, CFO
Robert Daino, President/CEO
Peter Hirsch, Director of Marketing
Peter Spartano, Vice President of Broadcasting

WUSP
01-29-1962; 1550 kHz AM; *Hrs Open:* 24; 1 kw-D; N43 06 48 W75 15 25 *Rebroadcasts:* Rebroadcasts WRNY(AM) Rome 100%
185 Genesee Street, Suite 1501, Utica, NY 13501
(315) 797-0803; *Fax:* (315) 797-7813
License: Utica, Oneida County, NY held by Good Guys Broadcasting
Nat'l Network: Westwood One; *Nat'l Reps:* Christal
Population Served: 91,611; *Arbitron Metro Market:* Utica-Rome, NY *Special Programming:* It 2 hrs, Pol 4 hrs wkly; *Target Audience:* 35 plus; 60% female, 40% male
Frank Abbdessa, Owner/General Sales Manager
Tom Coyne, Owner/Programming Director
Carleen Battisa, Traffic Manager

WUTQ-FM
07-11-1994; 100.7 MHz FM; *Hrs Open:* 24; 1.2 w; 551 ft; N43 09 12 W75 09 32
185 Genesee Street, Suite 1601, Utica, NY 13501
(315) 734-9245; *Fax:* (315) 624-9245
www.klove.com
License: Utica, Oneida County, NY held by Roser Communications Network
Group Owner: EMF Broadcasting; (acq 6-7-01; $1.25 million).
Nat'l Network: K-Love
Arbitron Metro Market: Utica-Rome, NY; *Target Audience:* 25-45.
Dave Silvers, Operations Manager
Grant Roser, Sales Manager
Jason Aiello, Programming Director
Tony Saponaro, Webmaster

Valhalla

***WARY**
10-03-1973; 88.1 MHz FM; *Hrs Open:* 10 AM-10 PM (M-F); 0.042 kw horiz, 0.039 kw vert; 404 ft.; N41 4 13 W73 47 25
75 Grasslands Road, Valhalla, NY 10595 US
(914) 606-6752(914) 606-6753; *Fax:* (914) 606-6260
radprime1@aol.com
License: Valhalla, Westchester County, NY held by Westchester Community College.
Arbitron Metro Market: New York; *Format:* Rock/AOR *Special Programming:* Pub svc 10 hrs wkly; *Target Audience:* 12-24.
Radames Ocasio, General Manager

Vestal

WMXW
06-02-1989; 103.3 MHz FM; *Hrs Open:* 24; 0.52 kw; 1099 ft.; N42 3 40 W75 56 45
320 North Jensen Road, Vestal, NY 13850 US
(607) 584-5800; *Fax:* (607) 584-5900
www.mix1033fm.com
License: Vestal, Broome County, NY held by CC Licenses LLC.
Group Owner: iHeartMedia; (acq 9-2000; grpsl)
Nat'l Reps: Katz Radio
Arbitron Metro Market: Binghamton, NY; *Format:* Adult Contemp; *No. News Employees:* 1; *Target Audience:* 25-54.
Jim Free, Operations Manager
Tom Barney, General Manager

Voorheesville

WAJZ
05-24-1991; 96.3 MHz FM; *Hrs Open:* 24; 0.47 kw; 961 ft.; N42 38 11 W74 0 2
6 Johnson Road, Latham, NY 12110 US
(518) 786-6624; *Fax:* (518) 786-6610
www.jamz963.com
pryan@albanybroadcasting.com
License: Voorheesville, Albany County, NY held by 6 Johnson Road Licenses Inc.
Group Owner: Pamal Broadcasting Ltd.; (acq 10-19-2001; grpsl).
Nat'l Reps: McGavren Guild
Arbitron Metro Market: Voorheesville, NY; *Format:* Christian *Special Programming:* Relg one hr wkly; *Hrs. of News Programming:* news progmg 3 hrs wkly; *No. News Employees:* 2; *Target Audience:* 18-49. *Adv.Rates:* 100; 100; 125; 75
Bob Ausfeld, General Manager
Erin Buchwald, Programming Director

Walton

WDLA
05-30-1951; 1270 kHz AM; 5 kw-D, ND1; 0.089 kw-N, ND1; N42 8 10 W75 4 48
34 Chestnut Street, Oneonta, NY 13820 US
(607) 432-1030; *Fax:* (607) 865-4189
www.cnynews.com
George.Wells@townsquaremedia.com
License: Walton, NY held by Townsquare Media Oneonta License LLC
Group Owner: Townsquare Media; (acq 10-22-2004; grpsl)
Arbitron Metro Market: Walton, NY; *Format:* Oldies *Special Programming:* When Radio Was; *Target Audience:* 28-55; general
Donald L. Perkins, Operations Dir
George Wells, General Manager/Programming Director
Steven Dillon, Director of Sales

WDLA-FM
11-16-1973; 92.1 MHz FM; 0.69 kw; 656 ft.; N42 8 10 W75 4 48
34 Chestnut Street, Oneonta, NY 13820 US
(607) 432-1030
www.wdlafm.com
eric.malanoski@townsquaremedia.com
License: Walton, Delaware County, NY held by Townsquare Media Oneonta License LLC
Group Owner: Townsquare Media
Arbitron Metro Market: Walton, NY
Wade Lott, General Manager
Eric Malanoski, Brand Manager

Warrensburg

WKBE
01-01-1990; 100.3 MHz FM; *Hrs Open:* 24; 1.45 kw; 1312 ft.; N43 25 12 W73 45 39
89 Everts Avenue, Queensbury, NY 12804 US
(518) 786-6600; *Fax:* (518) 786-6610
License: Warrensburg, Warren County, NY held by 6 Johnson Road Licenses Inc.

Group Owner: Adirondack Broadcasting; (acq 10-9-2001).
Format: Contemporary Hits/Top 40; *Hrs. of News Programming:* news progmg 10 hrs wkly; *No. News Employees:* 1; *Target Audience:* 18-34; women
John Reilly, Operations Manager
Thomas Jacobsen, General Manager/Sales Manager
Jackie Powell, Programming Director
Tim Celeste, News Director

Warsaw

WCJW
05-16-1973; 1140 kHz AM; *Hrs Open:* Sunrise-sunset
3258 Merchant Rd., Warsaw, NY 14569 US
(585) 786-8131; *Fax:* (585) 786-2241
www.wcjw.com
wcjw@wcjw.com
License: Warsaw, NY held by Lloyd Lane Inc.
Nat'l Network: USA *Regional Reps:* Regional Reps
Arbitron Metro Market: Warsaw, NY; *Format:* Agriculture, Country, 60, Sports *Special Programming:* Farm 11 hrs wkly; *Hrs. of News Programming:* news progmg 20 hrs wkly; *No. News Employees:* 1 *Target Audience:* 25-54; adults; *Adv. Rates:* 16; 16; 16; na
Lloyd Lane, President
RJ Jordan, Programming Director
Steve Weber, News Director

Warwick

WTBQ
07-24-1969; 1110 kHz AM; *Hrs Open:* Sunrise-sunset
179 Sanford Road, Warwick, NY 10990 US
(845) 651-1110; *Fax:* (845) 651-1025
www.wtbq.com
License: Warwick, NY held by FST Broadcasting Corp.
Nat'l Network: ABC; Jones Radio Networks
Arbitron Metro Market: Florida, NY; *Format:* Oldies, Talk *Special Programming:* Folk one hr, Irish 2 hrs wkly; *Hrs. of News Programming:* news progmg 10 hrs wkly; *No. News Employees:* 2 *Target Audience:* 24-55; affluent Orange County-New York City commuters; *Adv. Rates:* 20; 20; 20; 20
Frank Truatt, President
Rob McLean, General Sales Mgr
Richard Bak, Programming Director
Rich Ball, Programming Director

Waterloo

WNYR
04-19-1989; 98.5 MHz FM; 3.2 kw; 446 ft.; N42 48 22 W76 50 47
3568 Lenox Rd., Geneva, NY 14456 US
(315) 781-7000; *Fax:* (315) 781-7700
License: Waterloo, Seneca County, NY held by Lake Country Broadcasting, Inc.
Group Owner: Finger Lakes Radio Group
Arbitron Metro Market: Rochester, NY *TV Affiliate:* Adult Contemp; *Format:* Adult Contemp *Special Programming:* news progmg 5 hrs wkly; *Hrs. of News Programming:* 1; *No. News Employees:* 25-54.; *Adv. Rates:* 18; 15; 18; 12
Frank Lischak, VP of Sales
Jim Schreck, Programming Director
Joe Nittler, News Director

Watertown

WATN
02-03-1941; 1240 kHz AM; *Hrs Open:* 24; 1 kw-U, ND1; N43 58 49 W75 56 12
199 Wealtha Ave., Watertown, NY 13601 US
(315) 782-1240; *Fax:* (315) 782-0312
www.gisco.net/watn/
License: Watertown, NY held by Community Broadcasters LLC.
Group Owner: Community Broadcasters LLC; (acq 2-8-2007; grpsl)
Nat'l Reps: Roslin
Arbitron Metro Market: Watertown, NY; *Format:* Talk
James Leven, President
Todd Dalesandro, Operations Dir
Kevin Keefe, General Manager

WCIZ-FM
08-25-1986; 93.3 MHz FM; *Hrs Open:* 24; 6 kw; 328 ft.; N43 57 23 W75 50 45
134 Mullin Street, Watertown, NY 13601 US
(315) 788-0790; *Fax:* (315) 788-4379
www.z93.fm
License: Watertown, Jefferson County, NY held by Stephens Media Group-Watertown LLC.
Group Owner: Stephens Family L.P.
Arbitron Metro Market: Watertown, NY; *Format:* Oldies; *Hrs. of News Programming:* news progmg 2 hrs wkly; *No. News Employees:* 3; *Target Audience:* 35-54.
Dick Snavely, CFO
Rick Snavely, President
John Owens, Programming Director
Jim Travis, Chief Engineer

WFRY-FM
11-22-1968; 97.5 MHz FM; 97 kw; 476 ft.; N43 57 23 W75 50 45
134 Mullin Street, Watertown, NY 13601 US
(315) 788-0790; *Fax:* (315) 788-4379
www.froggy97.com
eliva.gaines@smgny.com
License: Watertown, Jefferson County, NY held by Stephens Media Group-Watertown LLC.
Group Owner: Stephens Family L.P.
Arbitron Metro Market: Watertown, NY; *Format:* Country
Mark Gaines, General Manager

*WJNY
07-24-1986; 90.9 MHz FM; *Hrs Open:* 5 AM-midnight; 7.1 kw; 449 ft.; N43 51 44 W75 43 40 *Rebroadcasts:* Rebroadcasts WCNY-FM Syracuse
Mailing Address: 506 Old Liverpool Rd, PO Box 2400, Syracuse, NY 13220 US
Second Address: 506 Old Liverpool Pl., Syracuse, NY 13220
(315) 453-2424; *Fax:* (315) 451-8824
www.wcny.org
wcny-online@wcny.org
License: Watertown, Jefferson County, NY held by Public Broadcasting Council of Central New York Inc.
Nat'l Network: NPR
Arbitron Metro Market: Watertown, NY; *Format:* Talk *Special Programming:* Bluegrass 3 hrs, jazz 5 hrs wkly
Coleen Edwards, CFO
Robert Daino, President/CEO
Peter Spartano, Vice President of Broadcasting
Peter Hirsch, Director of Marketing

*WRVJ
07-01-1989; 91.7 MHz FM; *Hrs Open:* 24; 1.6 kw; 443 ft.; N43 51 44 W75 43 40 *Rebroadcasts:* Rebroadcasts WRVO(FM) Oswego 100%
7060 State Route 104, Oswego, NY 13126 US
(315) 312-3690; *Fax:* (315) 312-3174
www.wrvo.com
feedback@wrvo.fm
License: Watertown, Jefferson County, NY held by State University of New York.
Nat'l Network: NPR; PRI; *Wire Services:* AP
Arbitron Metro Market: Watertown, NY; *Format:* Variety/Diverse; *Hrs. of News Programming:* news progmg 140 hrs wkly; *No. News Employees:* 4; *Target Audience:* 25-55.; *Adv. Rates:* 60; 50; 60; 40
Lee Mitchell, Operations Dir
Michael S. Ameigh, General Manager
Jeff Windsor, Chief Engineer
Pam Cantine, Business Manager

*WSLJ
01-01-1992; 88.9 MHz FM; *Hrs Open:* 24; 0.2 kw; 453 ft.; N43 57 23 W75 50 28 *Rebroadcasts:* Rebroadcasts WSLU(FM) Canton 100%
North Country Public Rad, Canton, NY 13617 US
(315) 229-5356; *Fax:* (315) 229-5373
www.ncpr.org
radio@ncpr.org
License: Watertown, Jefferson County, NY held by St. Lawrence University.
Arbitron Metro Market: Watertown, NY; *Format:* Variety/Diverse; *Hrs. of News Programming:* news progmg 35 hrs wkly; *No. News Employees:* 2; *Target Audience:* General.
Shelly Pike, Operations Dir
Ellen Rocco, General Manager
Jacqueline Sauter, Programming Director
Martha Foley, News Director
Robert Sauter, Chief Engineer
Sandra Demarest, Underwriting Director

WTNY
04-29-1941; 790 kHz AM; *Hrs Open:* 24; 1 kw-D, DAN; 1 kw-N, DAN; N43 56 44 W75 56 54
134 Mullin Street, Watertown, NY 13601 US
(315) 788-0790; *Fax:* (315) 788-4379
www.production@790wtny.com
eliva.gaines@smgny.com
License: Watertown, NY held by Stephens Media Group-Watertown LLC.
Group Owner: Stephens Family L.P.
Nat'l Network: CBS
Arbitron Metro Market: Watertown, NY; *Format:* News *Special Programming:* Farm 3 hrs wkly; *Hrs. of News Programming:* news progmg 20 hrs wkly; *No. News Employees:* 3; *Target Audience:* 25 plus.
Mark Gaines, General Manager
Laurie Zsedely, Director of Sales

WNER
11-02-1959; 1410 kHz AM
134 Mullin Street, Watertown, NY 13601 US
(315) 788-0790; *Fax:* (315) 788-4379
www.wner1410.com
License: Watertown, NY held by Stephens Media Group-Watertown LLC.
Group Owner: Stephens Family L.P.
Nat'l Network: ESPN Radio
Arbitron Metro Market: Watertown, NY; *Format:* Sports; *Target Audience:* 35-64.
Mark Gaines, General Manager
Laurie Zsedely, Director of Sales

*WKWV
06-26-2000; 90.1 MHz FM; *Hrs Open:* 24; 0.4 kw; 679 ft.; N43 57 15 W75 43 45 *Rebroadcasts:* Rebroadcasts KLVR(FM) Santa Rosa, CA 100%
Network Inc, 17102 Cty Rt 53 Pob 563, Dexter, NY 13634 US
(800) 525-5683; *Fax:* (916) 251-1650
klove@klove.com
License: Watertown, Jefferson County, NY held by Educational Media Foundation.
Group Owner: EMF Broadcasting; (acq 1-13-2006; $300,000)
Nat'l Network: K-Love
Arbitron Metro Market: Omaha, NE; *Format:* Christian; *No. News Employees:* 13
Darrell Chambliss, Chairman
Mike Novak, President & CEO
David Pierce, Programming Director
Ed Lenane, News Director
Sam Wallington, Engineering Dir
Marya Morgan, News Reporter
Richard Hunt, News Reporter
Laura Daniels, NewsReporter
Tim Luttrell, News Reporter
Kenny Noble Cortes, News Reporter
Darren Vinson, News Reporter

Watervliet

WUAM
03-23-1964; 900 kHz AM; *Hrs Open:* 24
100 Saratoga Village Boulevard, Suite 21, Malta, NY 12020 US
(518) 899-3000; *Fax:* (518) 899-3057
wabymoon@aol.com
License: Watervliet, NY held by Empire Broadcasting Corp.
Group Owner: Empire Broadcasting Corp.; (acq 9-99; $100,000)
Arbitron Metro Market: Albany-Schenectady-Troy, NY; *Format:* News; *Target Audience:* 25 plus.
John Meaney, Operations Manager
Fran Dingeman, General Manager/Sales Manager
Amanda Allbright, Traffic Manager

WABY
01-01-1964; 900 kHz AM; *Hrs Open:* 24; 0.4 kw-D, 0.07 kw-N; N43 04 24 W73 48 07
100 Saratoga Village Blvd., Suite 21, Ballston Spa, NY 12020 US
(518) 899-3000
www.wabyalbany.com
License: Watervliet, NY held by Empire Broadcasting Corp.
Group Owner: Empire Broadcasting Corp.; (acq 12-7-00; $280,000).
Nat'l Network: ABC
Arbitron Metro Market: Albany, NY; *Format:* Adult Contemp; *Hrs. of News Programming:* news progmg 50 hrs wkly; *No. News Employees:* 1; *Target Audience:* 40 plus; adults, male & female; *Adv. Rates:* 35; 30; 30;10
John Meaney, Operations Dir
Fran Dingeman, General Manager

Watkins Glen

WRCE
06-22-1968; 1490 kHz AM
Mailing Address: 1685 Four Mile Drive, Williamsport, PA 17701 US
Second Address: 1685 Four Mile Dr., Williamsport, PA 17701
(607) 732-4400; *Fax:* (607) 732-7774
License: Watkins Glen, NY held by Community Broadcasters LLC
Group Owner: Community Broadcasters LLC; (acq 12-1-2002; grpsl)
Nat'l Reps: D & R Radio

RADIO - U.S.

Format: Country; *Target Audience:* 20-49; baby boomers
Scott Free, Operations Dir
Margaret Tollner, General Manager
Brian Povancher, General Sales Mgr

***WRFI**
91.9 MHz FM; 0.42 kw; -374 ft.; N42 23 20 W76 53 27
103 West Seneca Street, Suite 305, Ithaca, NY 14850 US
(607) 319-5445
www.wrfi.org
License: Watkins Glen, Schuyler County, NY held by Ithaca Community Radio Inc.
Arbitron Metro Market: Watkins Glen, NY
Danila Apasou, President
Nicholas Hill, General Manager

Waverly

WAVR
10-01-1974; 102.3 MHz FM; 4.1 kw; 400 ft.; N42 3 48 W76 31 28 *Rebroadcasts:* Rebroadcasts WATS(AM) Sayre 100%
106 N. First Street, Saratoga, NY 82331 US
(307) 326-8642; *Fax:* (307) 326-8340
www.bigfoot99.com
bigfoot@bigfoot99.com
License: Waverly, Tioga County, NY held by Wats Broadcasting Inc.
Arbitron Metro Market: Saratoga WY; *Format:* Country; *No. News Employees:* 3; *Adv. Rates:* 21; 16; 20; 12
Jim O'Reilly, General Manager

Webster

WLGZ-FM
08-23-1991; 102.7 MHz FM; *Hrs Open:* 24; 6 kw; 328 ft.; N43 10 14 W77 40 23
2494 Brown Croft Boulevard, Rochester, NY 14625 US
(585) 264-1027; *Fax:* (585) 264-1165
www.legends1027.com
info@legends1027.com
License: Webster, Monroe County, NY held by Kimtron Inc.
Group Owner: Crawford Broadcasting Co.; (acq 11-25-92; $950,000;
Arbitron Metro Market: Rochester, NY; *Format:* Oldies, Classic Rock, 76
Don Crawford Jr., General Manager
Mark Shuttleworth, Programming Director
Brian Cunningham, Chief Engineer

***WKEL**
10-01-1988; 88.1 MHz FM; *Hrs Open:* 24; 11 kw horiz, 8.5 kw vert; 338 ft.; N43 4 18 W77 5 35
5700 West Oaks Boulevard, Rocklin, CA 95765 US
(916) 251-1600; *Fax:* (916) 251-1650
www.klove.com
klove@klove.com
License: Webster, Monroe County, NY held by Educational Media Foundation
Group Owner: EMF Broadcasting
Format: Religious; *Target Audience:* General.
Mike Novak, President

***WMHN**
02-29-1988; 89.3 MHz FM; *Hrs Open:* 24; 1 kW; 144 ft; N43 13 45 W77 26 52 *Rebroadcasts:* Rebroadcasts WMHR(FM) Syracuse 99%
4044 Makyes Rd, Syracuse, NY 13215 USA
(315) 469-5051
www.marshillnetwork.org
info@marshillnetwork.org
License: Webster, Monroe County, NY held by Mars Hill Broadcasting Co. Inc.
Group Owner: Mars Hill Network
Nat'l Network: Moody; Salem Radio Network; *Wire Services:* AP
Population Served: 1,000,000; *Arbitron Metro Market:* Webster, NY; *Format:* Christian *Special Programming:* Children 11 hrs wkly; *Hrs. of News Programming:* News progmg 13 hrs wkly; *Target Audience:* Christianfamilies
Wayne Taylor, General Manager
Mike Dwinell, Chief Engineer

Wellsville

WJQZ
02-03-1986; 103.5 MHz FM; 1.75 kw; 620 ft.; N42 3 24 W78 0 34
82 Railroad Avenue, Wellsville, NY 14985 US
(585) 593-6070; *Fax:* (585) 593-6212
oldiesz103.topcities.com
oldiesz103@yahoo.com
License: Wellsville, Allegany County, NY held by DBM Communications Inc.
Format: Oldies; *Target Audience:* 25-54.
Robert Mangels, Programming Director

WLSV
10-31-1955; 790 kHz AM; 1 kw-D, ND1; 0.041 kw-N, ND1; N42 4 37 W77 55 47
2 Green Acres Court, Ellenville, NY 12428 US
(585) 593-6070
www.wlsv.com
License: Wellsville, NY held by DBM Communications Inc.
Format: Country; *Target Audience:* General.
Richard Mangels, President
Bob Mangels, News Director

WQRW
02-14-2007; 93.5 MHz FM; 1.1 kw; 768 ft.; N42 11 25 W77 49 17
100 Railroad Avenue, Wellsville, NY 14895 US
(585) 593-9553; *Fax:* (585) 593-9554
License: Wellsville, Allegany County, NY held by Pembrook Pines Mass Media N.A. Corp.
Group Owner: Pembrook Pines Media Group
Arbitron Metro Market: Wellsville, NY; *Format:* Contemporary Hits/Top 40
Robert Pfuntner, President
Jeff Wilson, Operations/Programming Director
Rod Biehler, General Manager/Sales Manager

Westhampton

WBON
11-18-1993; 98.5 MHz FM; *Hrs Open:* 24; 0.95 kw; 525 ft.; N40 51 18 W72 46 11
3075 Veterans Memorial Hwy., Suite 201, Ronkonkoma, NY 11779 US
(631) 648-2500; *Fax:* (631) 648-2510
www.lafiestali.com
License: Westhampton, Suffolk County, NY held by JVC Media LLC
Group Owner: JVC Broadcasting
Nat'l Reps: Christal
Arbitron Metro Market: Westhampton, NY; *Format:* Spanish
John Caracciolo, President
Bruce Shepard, Director of Sales
Ron Reeve, Chief Engineer

Westport

WCLX
01-01-1995; 102.9 MHz FM; *Hrs Open:* 24; 6 kw; Ant 312 ft; N44 13 15 W73 24 41
PO Box 114, Birdport, VT 05734
(802) 758-5000; *Fax:* (802) 758-5000
www.farmfreshradio.com
License: Westport, Essex County, NY held by Westport Broadcasting.
Population Served: 150,000; *Arbitron Metro Market:* Burlington-Plat; *Target Audience:* 25-54.
Dennis Jackson, CEO
Chip Morgan, General Manager
Kathy Morgan, Programming Director
Chip Morgan, Chief Engineer

Wethersfield Twnshp

WLKK
01-01-1948; 107.7 MHz FM; *Hrs Open:* 24; 19.5 kw; 801 ft.; N42 37 23 W78 17 16
500 Corporate Parkway, Suite 200, Buffalo, NY 14226 US
(716) 843-0600; *Fax:* (716) 832-3323
www.1077thelake.com
License: Wethersfield Twnshp, Wyoming County, NY held by Entercom Buffalo License LLC.
Group Owner: Entercom Communications Corp.; (acq 5-5-2004; $9 million).
Nat'l Network: Westwood One
Arbitron Metro Market: Buffalo, NY; *Format:* Rock/AOR; *Target Audience:* 25-54; adults
Tim Wenger, Operations Dir
Greg Ried, General Manager
Tim Holly, Sales Director
Hank Dole, Programming Director
Samantha Ogrodnick, Promotions Director

White Plains

WFAS
08-11-1932; 1230 kHz AM; 1 kw-U, ND1; N41 1 32 W73 49 39
365 Secor Road, Hartsdale, NY 10530 US
(914) 693-2400; *Fax:* (914) 693-0000
www.wfasam.com
Marty.Sheehan@cumulus.com
License: White Plains, NY held by Cumulus Licensing Corp.
Group Owner: Cumulus Media Inc.; (acq 1-23-2002; grpsl)
Nat'l Network: AP Radio; *Nat'l Reps:* McGavren Guild
Arbitron Metro Market: White Plains, NY; *Format:* Adult Contemp
Special Programming: Sports progmg 8 hrs wkly; *Hrs. of News Programming:* news progmg 5 hrs wkly; *No. News Employees:* 2
Target Audience: General.
Rod Colarco, General Manager
Marty Sheehan, General Sales Mgr
Jolana Smith, Programming Director
Jeremiah Johnsen, Marketing/Promotions Director
Ann McManus, Regional Vice President

Whitehall

WNYV
07-14-1990; 94.1 MHz FM; 3 kw; 328 ft.; N43 28 37 W73 26 56
Mailing Address: PO Box 568, East Poultney, VT 05741 US
Second Address: Box 568, East Poultney, VT 5741
(802) 287-9031
License: Whitehall, Washington County, NY held by Pine Tree Broadcasting.
Nat'l Reps: Commercial Media Sales
TV Affiliate: Adult contemp; *Format:* Big Band, Religious *Special Programming:* news progmg 3 hrs wkly; *Hrs. of News Programming:* 1; *No. News Employees:* 25-55; active community o
Judy Leech, Vice President/General Manager

Whitesboro

WSKS
01-01-1994; 97.9 MHz FM; 1.5 kw; 669 ft; N43 02 14 W75 26 40
Rebroadcasts: Rebroadcasts WOWB(FM) Little Falls 100%
185 Genesee St., Suite 1601, Utica, NY 13502
Fax: (315) 624-9245
www.cnykiss.com
License: Whitesboro, Oneida County, NY held by Roser Communications Network Inc.
Group Owner: Roser Communications Network Inc.; (acq 10-24-2007; grpsl)
Arbitron Metro Market: Utica-Rome, NY
Ken Roser, President
Dave Silvers, Operations Dir
Granty Roser, General Sales Mgr
Shaun Andrews, Programming Director
Sean Morelle, Promotions Manager
Ken Ruhland, Chief Engineer

Willsboro

WXZO
01-01-1997; 96.7 MHz FM; *Hrs Open:* 24; 1 kw; 797 ft.; N44 24 12 W73 26 2
265 Hegeman Avenue, Colchester, VT 05446 US
(802) 655-0093; *Fax:* (802) 655-0478
www.theplanet967.com
Slater@theplanet967.com
License: Willsboro, Essex County, NY held by Vox AM/FM LLC.
Group Owner: Vox AM/FM LLC; (acq 7-25-2008; grpsl)
Arbitron Metro Market: Willsboro, NY; *Format:* Talk
Rob Ryan, Operations Manager

Windham

WRIP
08-05-1999; 97.9 MHz FM; *Hrs Open:* 24; 580 w; Ant 1,056 ft; N42 17 06 W74 15 52
134 South St., PO Box 979, Windham, NY 12496-0979
(518) 734-4747; *Fax:* (518) 734-9147
www.wripfm.com
wrip@mhcable.com
License: Windham, Greene County, NY held by Rip Radio LLC.
Nat'l Network: AP Network News *Regional Reps:* Local Focus - NYC
Population Served: 125,000; *Arbitron Metro Market:* Albany-Schenectady-Troy, NY *Special Programming:* AAA 5 hours, Classic Hits 4 hrs, Jazz 2 hrs, Christian contemp 2 hrs wkly; *Hrs. of News Programming:* Approx 6 hrswkly (Net); *Target Audience:* 25 plus; mass appeal; *Adv. Rates:* 25; 18; 18; 15
Dennis Jackson, CEO
Jay Fink, Vice President/General Manager

Windsor

***WIFF**
01-01-1995; 90.1 MHz FM; *Hrs Open:* 24; 0.1 kw; 686 ft.; N42 3 10 W75 42 7 *Rebroadcasts:* Rebroadcasts KAWZ (FM)
P.O.Box 391, Twin Falls, ID 83303 US
(607) 732-2484; *Fax:* (607) 732-8704
www.csnradio.com

License: Windsor, Broome County, NY held by CSN International
Group Owner: CSN International; (acq 5-30-2003; $67,000).
Arbitron Metro Market: Binghamton, NY; *Format:* Religious; *Hrs. of News Programming:* news progmg 8 hrs wkly; *No. News Employees:* 2; *Target Audience:* General.

Woodstock

WDST
04-29-1980; 100.1 MHz FM; *Hrs Open:* 24; 3 kw; 315 ft.; N41 59 24 W74 1 7
Mailing Address: 118 Tinker Street, P.O Box 367, Woodstock, NY 12498 US
Second Address: 293 Tinker St., Woodstock, NY 12498
(845) 679-7266(845) 679-7600; *Fax:* (845) 679-5395
www.radiowoodstock.com
live@radiowoodstock.com
License: Woodstock, Ulster County, NY held by CHET-5 Broadcasting L.P.
Nat'l Network: CBS Radio; *Nat'l Reps:* Katz Radio
Arbitron Metro Market: Woodstock, NY; *Format:* Alternative; *Hrs. of News Programming:* news progmg 5 hrs wkly; *No. News Employees:* 1; *Target Audience:* 24-55; upscale professionals
Gary Chetkof, President/General Manager
Mike Tuttle, Operations Dir
Jimmy Buff, Programming Director
Katie DiMartile, Promotions Manager
Ike Phillips, Vice President of Sales/Marketing
Cynthia Huggins, Business Manager
RichardFusco, Digital Media Director

Wurtsboro

WZAD
09-01-1990; 97.3 MHz FM; *Hrs Open:* 24; 0.62 kw; 719 ft.; N41 36 4 W74 33 17
2 Pendell Road, Poughkeepsie, NY 12601 US
(845) 471-1500; *Fax:* (845) 454-1204
License: Wurtsboro, Sullivan County, NY held by Peak Broadcasting of Fresno Licenses LLC
Group Owner: Townsquare Media; (acq 1-23-2002; grpsl).
Arbitron Metro Market: Newburgh-Middle; *Format:* Country; *Hrs. of News Programming:* news progmg 5 hrs wkly; *No. News Employees:* 1; *Target Audience:* 25-54; upscale, educated
Charles Benfer, General Manager
Jay Pugliese, General Sales Mgr
Beth Christy, Programming Director
Anthony Verano, Director of Marketing/Promotions

Youngstown

WTOR
05-06-1998; 770 kHz AM; 13 kw-D, DAD; N43 13 5 W78 56 53
21700 Northwestern Hwy., Suite 1190, Tower 14, Southfield, MI 48075 US
(716) 791-4926; *Fax:* (248) 557-2950
www.birach.com
sima@birach.com
License: Youngstown, Niagara County, NY held by Birach Broadcasting Corp.
Group Owner: Birach Broadcasting Corp.; (acq 1996; $409,000 less land cost for CP)
Arbitron Metro Market: Southfield, MI; *Format:* Ethnic; *Target Audience:* Ethnic, Serbian, Lithuanian, Sp, Pol, Macedonian
Sima Birach, President

North Carolina

Ahoskie

*WBKU
01-01-2002; 91.7 MHz FM; 87 kw; 430 ft.; N36 5 45 W77 12 30
P.O. Box 3206, Tupelo, MS 38803 US
(662) 844-8888; *Fax:* (662) 842-6791
www.afr.net
faq@afa.net
License: Ahoskie, Hertford County, NC held by American Family Association.
Group Owner: American Family Radio
Arbitron Metro Market: Ahoskie, NC; *Format:* Christian, Religious
Tim Wildmon, President
Donald Wildmon, Founder
Buddy Smith, Sr VP
Ed Vitagliano, Exec VP
Randy Sharp, Director Of Special Projects
Meeke Addison, Director Of Communications
Abraham Hamilton III, General Counsel

WRCS
04-25-1948; 970 kHz AM; *Hrs Open:* 24; 1 kw-D, ND2; 0.08 kw-N, ND2; N36 16 46 W77 1 59
443 NC Highway 42W, Ahoskie, NC 27910 US
(252) 332-3101; *Fax:* (252) 332-3103
wrcs@gate811.net
License: Ahoskie, NC held by WRCS-AM 970 Inc.
Format: Gospel; *Target Audience:* 12-70.; *Adv. Rates:* 10; 10; 10; 10

Albemarle

WSPC
07-01-1947; 1010 kHz AM; *Hrs Open:* 24; 1 kw-D, ND2; 0.064 kw-N, ND2; N35 22 40 W80 11 38
Mailing Address: P.O. Box 550, Albemarle, NC 28002 US
Second Address: 1234 Magnolia St., Albemarle, NC 28001
(704) 983-1580; *Fax:* (704) 983-1436
1010wspc.com
wspc@ctc.net
License: Albemarle, NC held by Stanly Communications Inc.
Format: News, News/Talk, 86; *No. News Employees:* 1; *Target Audience:* General.; *Adv. Rates:* 18,18,18,10
Matt Smith, General Manager
Kristi Johnson, Marketing Specialist

WZKY
07-09-1956; 1580 kHz AM; *Hrs Open:* 24; 1 kw-D, ND1; 0.012 kw-N, ND1; N35 21 38 W80 10 39
Post Office Box 550, Albemarle, NC 28001 US
(704) 983-1580; *Fax:* (704) 983-1436
mattsmith@1010wspc.com
License: Albemarle, NC held by Stanly Communications Inc.
Regional Network: N.C. News Net.
Arbitron Metro Market: Albemarle, NC; *Format:* News, Oldies, 84; *Target Audience:* 30 plus.
Matt Smith, President
Kristi Johnson, Marketing Specialist

Asheboro

WKRR
11-01-1948; 92.3 MHz FM; *Hrs Open:* 24; 100 kw; 1289 ft.; N35 49 59 W79 50 2
192 East Lewis Street, Greensboro, NC 27406 US
(336) 274-8042; *Fax:* (336) 274-1629
www.rock92.com
jgoodman@dbcradio.com
License: Asheboro, Randolph County, NC held by Dick Broadcasting Co. Inc. of Tennessee
Arbitron Metro Market: Greensboro-Winston Salem-High Point, NC; *Format:* Classic Rock; *Target Audience:* 18-49.; *Adv. Rates:* 175; 125; 125; 30
Dick Harlow, General Manager
Jason Goodman, Programming Director

WKXR
05-24-1947; 1260 kHz AM; *Hrs Open:* 24; 5 kw-D, DA2; 0.5 kw-N, DA2; N35 43 26 W79 48 21
1119 Eastview Drive, Asheboro, NC 27203 US
(336) 625-2187; *Fax:* (336) 626-9292
www.wkxr.com
wkxr@atomic.net
License: Asheboro, NC held by Randolph Broadcasting Inc.
Nat'l Network: AP Network News; Jones Radio Networks;
Regional Network: N.C. News Net.
Arbitron Metro Market: Greensboro-Winston Salem-High Point, NC; *Format:* Country *Special Programming:* Farm one hr, gospel 10 hrs wkly; *Hrs. of News Programming:* News progmg 8 hrs wkly; *Target Audience:* 18 plus.
Edward Swicegood II, President
Ted Swicegood, Operations Dir
Larry Reid, Promotions Manager

*WTJY
06-30-1999; 89.5 MHz FM; *Hrs Open:* 24; 9.7 kw horiz, 7.8 kw vert; 535 ft.; N35 36 55 W79 53 28 *Rebroadcasts:* Rebroadcasts WXRI(FM) Winston-Salem Joy FM Network
P.O. Box 889, Blacksburg, VA 24063 US
(336) 788-1155; *Fax:* (336) 788-7199
www.joyfm.org
office@joyfm.org
License: Asheboro, Randolph County, NC held by Positive Alternative Radio Inc.
Group Owner: Positive Alternative Radio Inc.
Nat'l Network: Salem Radio Network
Arbitron Metro Market: Asheboro, NC; *Format:* Gospel
Daniel Britt, General Manager
Candi Payne, Production Director
Katie Harmon, Office Manager

WZOO
05-03-1971; 710 kHz AM; 1 kw-D, DAD; N35 45 50 W79 50 4
2641 Lazy Pine Road, Asheboro, NC 27204 US
(336) 672-0944
www.wzooradio.com
info@wzooradio.com
License: Asheboro, NC held by Faith Enterprises Inc.
Format: Gospel
Huey Turner, General Manager

Asheville

*WCQS
01-01-1975; 88.1 MHz FM; *Hrs Open:* 24; 1.6 kw; 1168 ft.; N35 35 23 W82 40 26
73 Broadway, Asheville, NC 28801 US
(828) 210-4800; *Fax:* (828) 210-4801
www.wcqs.org
info@wcqs.org
License: Asheville, Buncombe County, NC held by Western N.C. Public Radio Inc.
Nat'l Network: NPR; PRI
Arbitron Metro Market: Asheville, NC; *Format:* Jazz, News
Special Programming: Folk 9 hrs wkly; *Hrs. of News Programming:* news progmg 35 hrs wkly; *No. News Employees:* 1; *Target Audience:* 25 plus. *Adv.Rates:* 36; 24; 36; 18
Jody Evans, President/CEO
Lee Wilcher, Operations Dir
Ed Subkis, General Manager
Barbara Sayer, Programming Director
David Hurand, News Director
Tom Spaight, Chief Engineer
Michelle Keenan, Membership Director
Myra Fuller,Customer Support
Richard Kowal, Music Director
Steve Busey, Director of Underwriting

WISE
01-01-1939; 1310 kHz AM; *Hrs Open:* 24; 5 kw-D, DAN; 1 kw-N, DAN; N35 37 9 W82 34 21
P.O. Box 607, 401 Sawmill Road, Burnsville, NC 28714 US
(816) 226-4576
www.wise-radio.com
wise-radio@hotmail.com
License: Asheville, NC held by Saga Communications of North Carolina, LLC
Nat'l Network: ESPN Radio
Arbitron Metro Market: Asheville, NC; *Format:* Sports; *Hrs. of News Programming:* news progmg 15 hrs wkly; *No. News Employees:* 1; *Target Audience:* 35 plus; mature upscale audience; *Adv. Rates:* 36; 25; 30; 21
Randy Cable, General Manager

*WLFA
01-01-1975; 91.3 MHz FM; 440 w; 3,340 ft; N35 36 02 W82 39 07
2420 Wade Hampton Blvd., Greenville, SC 28802
(864) 292-6040
www.hisradio.com
comments@hisradio.com
License: Asheville, Buncombe County, NC held by Asheville Educational Association Inc.
Arbitron Metro Market: Asheville, NC
Ken Brantley, General Manager

WSKY
04-11-1947; 1230 kHz AM; *Hrs Open:* 20; 1 kw-U, ND1; N35 37 08 W82 34 19
22 Thompson Rd., Asheville, NC 28806 US
(828) 458-9551
www.wilkinsradio.com
denise@wilkinsradio.com
License: Asheville, NC held by Macon Media Inc.
Group Owner: Wilkins Communications Network Inc.; (acq 1996).
Nat'l Network: CBS; Salem Radio Network
Arbitron Metro Market: Asheville, NC; *Format:* Christian, Talk; *Target Audience:* 35 plus.; *Adv. Rates:* 30; 30; 30; 30
Ruthie Spears, Station Manager

WWNC
02-22-1927; 570 kHz AM; *Hrs Open:* 24
13 Summerlin Road, Asheville, NC 28806 US
(828) 257-2700; *Fax:* (828) 255-7850
www.wwnc.com
info@wwnc.com
License: Asheville, NC held by Capstar TX LLC
Group Owner: iHeartMedia; (acq 8-30-2000; grpsl)
Nat'l Network: Motor Racing Net; *Nat'l Reps:* McGavren Guild
Arbitron Metro Market: Asheville, NC; *Format:* News, News/Talk, 86 *Special Programming:* Farm one hr, gospel 3 hrs, relg 3 hrs wkly; *Hrs. of News Programming:* news progmg 30 hrs wkly; *No. News Employees:* 3 *Target Audience:* 25-54.
Gene Austin, Sales Manager
Brian Hall, Programming Director

Skip Wilson, Digital Sales Manager
Jessica Lee, Digital Content Director

Atlantic

WTKF

05-01-1992; 107.1 MHz FM; 46 kw; 625 ft.; N34 53 1 W76 30 22.3
Mailing Address: P.O. Box 70, Newport, NC 28570 US
Second Address: 5447 Hwy. 70, Morehead City, NC 28557
(252) 247-6343; *Fax:* (252) 247-7343
www.wtkf107.com
mail@thetalkstation.com
License: Atlantic, Carteret County, NC held by Atlantic Ridge Telecasters Inc.
Nat'l Network: Westwood One; Motor Racing Net; USA; *Regional Network:* N.C. News Net.
Arbitron Metro Market: Morehead City, NC; *Format:* News, News/Talk, 84, Talk; *Target Audience:* 25 plus; educated, informed

Lockwood Phillips, CEO
Shane Willis, Operations Dir
Ben Ball, Station Manager

Atlantic Beach

*WBJD

01-01-1999; 91.5 MHz FM; *Hrs Open:* 24; 85 kw; 384 ft.; N34 45 34 W76 51 16
800 College Court, New Bern, NC 28562 US
(252) 638-3434; *Fax:* (252) 638-3538
www.publicradioeast.org
jmcguire@publicradioeast.org
License: Atlantic Beach, Carteret County, NC held by Craven Community College.
Arbitron Metro Market: New Bern, NC; *Format:* News

Kelly Batchelor, Operations Dir
Charles Wethington, General Manager
Chris Wethington, Station Manager
Jill McGuire, Programming Director
George Olsen, News Director
J. Howard Jones, Chief Engineer
Kathleen Beal, ExecutiveDirector
Jill McGuire, Assistant General Manager

Aurora

WSTK

104.5 MHz FM; 4.2 kw; 393 ft.; N35 18 9 W76 34 0
4998 NC Highway 222, Fountain, NC 27829 US
(252) 341-8327
www.yourchristianradio.com
office@yourchristianradio.com
License: Aurora, Beaufort County, NC held by Media East LLC.
Group Owner: Conner Media Corp.; (acq 1-15-2003)

Ronald Benfield, President

*WZGO

08-01-2006; 91.1 MHz FM; *Hrs Open:* 24; 40 kw; 351 ft.; N35 18 9 W76 34 0 *Rebroadcasts:* Rebroadcasts WAGO(FM) Snow Hill
PO Box 1895, Goldsboro, NC 27533 US
(252) 747-8887; *Fax:* (252) 747-7888
www.gomixradio.org
wago@gomixradio.org
License: Aurora, Beaufort County, NC held by Pathway Christian Academy Inc.
Nat'l Network: Moody; Salem Radio Network
Arbitron Metro Market: Aurora, NC; *Format:* Christian; *Hrs. of News Programming:* news progmg 14 hrs wkly; *No. News Employees:* 1; *Target Audience:* General.

T.D. Worthington, President
Keith Aycock, Programming Director
Ashley Lovett, Promotions Manager
Joe Patton, Chief Engineer
Tiffany Johnson, Music Director

Banner Elk

WZJS

08-05-1989; 100.7 MHz FM; *Hrs Open:* 24; 0.15 kw; 1946 ft.; N36 11 3 W81 52 48
738 Blowing Rock Road, Boone, NC 28607 US
(828) 264-2411; *Fax:* (828) 264-2412
www.goblueridge.com
License: Banner Elk, Avery County, NC held by High Country Adventures LLC.
Group Owner: Curtis Media Group; (acq 3-3-2009; grpsl)
Nat'l Network: Motor Racing Net
Arbitron Metro Market: Banner Elk, NC; *Format:* Classic Rock; *Target Audience:* 18-44, Men.; *Adv. Rates:* 15; 15; 15; 7.50

Andy Glass, Operations Dir
Robin Wohlbruck, Market Manager

Bath

*WZPE

01-01-2005; 90.1 MHz FM; *Hrs Open:* 24; 4.5 kw; 128 ft.; N35 28 32 W76 48 44
Box 897, Wake Forest, NC 27588 US
(919) 556-5178; *Fax:* (919) 556-9273
www.wcpe.org
music@TheClassicalStation.org
License: Bath, Beaufort County, NC held by Educational Information Corp.
Arbitron Metro Market: Bath, NC; *Format:* Classical

Deborah Proctor, General Manager & Chief Engineer
Dick Storck, Programming Director
John Graham, Engineering Dir
Will Woltz, Music Director
John Graham, Engineering Services
Peter Blume, Business Development Director

Bayboro

WNBB

01-01-2001; 97.9 MHz FM; *Hrs Open:* 24; 50 kw; 433 ft.; N35 0 2 W76 49 58
702 Hartness Road, Statesville, NC 28677 US
(800)608-9798; *Fax:* (252) 638-8597
www.bear979.com
License: Bayboro, Pamlico County, NC held by Coastal Carolina Radio LLC
Nat'l Network: Fox News Radio; *Nat'l Reps:* Rgnl Reps
Arbitron Metro Market: New Bern, NC; *Format:* Country; *Target Audience:* 35-64; adults; *Adv. Rates:* 27; 27; 27; 5

Dann Miller, General Manager

Beaufort

*WXBE

01-01-2005; 88.3 MHz FM; 1 kw; 180 ft.; N34 43 26 W76 43 18
P.O. Box 3206, Tupelo, MS 38803 US
(662) 844-8888; *Fax:* (662) 842-6791
www.afr.net
faq@afa.net
License: Beaufort, Carteret County, NC held by American Family Association.
Group Owner: American Family Radio
Arbitron Metro Market: Beaufort, NC; *Format:* Christian, Religious

Tim Wildmon, President
Donald Wildmon, Founder
Buddy Smith, Sr VP
Ed Vitagliano, Exec VP
Randy Sharp, Director Of Special Projects
Meeke Addison, Director Of Communications
Abraham Hamilton III, General Counsel

Beech Mountain

WECR-FM

01-01-1996; 102.3 MHz FM; *Hrs Open:* 24; 0.15 kw; 1957 ft.; N36 11 3 W81 52 48
1281 Newland Hwy, Newland, NC 28657 US
(828) 733-0188; *Fax:* (828) 733-0189
www.wecr1023.com
License: Beech Mountain, Watauga County, NC held by High Country Adventures LLC.
Group Owner: Curtis Media Group; (acq 3-3-2009; grpsl)
Nat'l Network: CBS Radio
Arbitron Metro Market: Beech Mountain, NC; *Format:* Adult Contemp; *Hrs. of News Programming:* news progmg 2 hrs wkly; *No. News Employees:* 2; *Target Audience:* 25-54.; *Adv. Rates:* 14; 14; 14; 14

Donald W. Curtis, Chairman/CEO
Phil Zachary, President/COO
Robin Wohlbruck, Market Manager

Belhaven

WQZL

10-15-1980; 101.1 MHz FM; *Hrs Open:* 24; 50 kw; 463 ft.; N35 28 30 W76 51 51 *Rebroadcasts:* Rebroadcasts WQSL(FM) Jacksonville 100%
1361 Colony Drive, New Bern, NC 28562 US
(252) 639-7900; *Fax:* (252) 639-7976
www.carolinatouch.com
License: Belhaven, Beaufort County, NC held by NM Licensing LLC.
Group Owner: NextMedia Group Inc.; (acq 11-26-2001; grpsl)
Nat'l Reps: Eastman Radio
Arbitron Metro Market: Belhaven, NC; *Format:* Blues; *Hrs. of News Programming:* News progmg 3 hrs wkly; *Target Audience:* 25-54

Larry Weiss, General Manager

Belmont

WCGC

12-11-1954; 1270 kHz AM; *Hrs Open:* 24
P.O. Box 18614, Charlotte, NC 28210 US
(704) 596-1240; *Fax:* (704) 825-2127
www.heavenradio.org
wcgc1270am@yahoo.com
License: Belmont, NC held by WHVN Inc.
Group Owner: GHB Radio Group; (acq 4-17-98; $250,000)
Nat'l Network: Westwood One
Arbitron Metro Market: Charlotte, NC; *Format:* Talk, Religious; *Hrs. of News Programming:* news progmg 8 hrs wkly; *No. News Employees:* 2; *Target Audience:* General.

Brant Hart, Operations Manager
Tom Gentry, General Manager
Jim Mintzer, Sales Manager
Gary Hattaway, Chief Engineer
Dave Hodges, Production Manager

Benson

WPYB

09-01-1961; 1130 kHz AM
2234 Hodges Chapel Road, Benson, NC 27504 US
(919) 894-1130; *Fax:* (919) 894-1530
wpyb@dockpoint.net
License: Benson, NC held by Benson-Dunn Broadcasting Inc.
Arbitron Metro Market: Raleigh-Durham, NC; *Format:* Country, Gospel; *Target Audience:* General.

Jasper Tart, President
Mable Sue Tart, Executive Vice President

Bethel

WNBR-FM

12-05-1988; 98.9 MHz FM; *Hrs Open:* 24; 11.2 kw; Ant 489 ft; N35 47 29 W77 22 54
Drawer L, New Bern, NC 28563
(800) 608-9798
License: Bethel, Pitt County, NC held by Coastal Carolina Radio LLC
Nat'l Network: Fox News Radio; *Nat'l Reps:* Rgnl Reps
Population Served: 697; *Arbitron Metro Market:* Greenville-New Bern-Jacksonville, NC; *Target Audience:* 35-64; Adults; *Adv. Rates:* 27; 27; 27; 5

Dann Miller, General Manager

Biltmore Forest

WOXL-FM

01-01-2002; 96.5 MHz FM; 2.1 kw; 1112 ft.; N35 36 4 W82 39 7
1190 Patton Avenue, Asheville, NC 28806 US
(828) 259-9695; *Fax:* (828) 253-5619
www.theriverasheville.com
gbrown@avlradio.com
License: Biltmore Forest, Buncombe County, NC held by Saga Communications of North Carolina LLC.
Group Owner: Saga Communications Inc.; (acq 1-31-2008; $8 million)
Arbitron Metro Market: Asheville, NC; *Format:* Light Rock

Chris Wheat, General Manager
Garry Brown, General Sales Mgr
Neal Sharpe, Brand Manager
Bill McClement, News Director

Black Mountain

WKJW

05-27-1962; 1010 kHz AM; *Hrs Open:* 24; 19 kw-C, DA3; 50 kw-D, DA3; 0.5 kw-; N35 36 19 W82 21 0
P.O. Box 159, Black Mountain, NC 28711 US
(828) 669-8477; *Fax:* (828) 298-0017
www.wfgw.org
thankyou@brb.org
License: Black Mountain, NC held by International Baptist Outreach Missions Inc.
Nat'l Network: Salem Radio Network
Arbitron Metro Market: Black Mountain, NC; *Format:* Christian, Talk *Special Programming:* Black one hr wkly; *Hrs. of News Programming:* News progmg 3 hrs wkly; *Target Audience:* 35 plus.

Billy Graham, Chairman
Dr. David Bruce, President
Jim Kirkland, General Manager
Wayne Roper, General Sales Mgr
Tom Greene, Programming Director

Keith Pittman, News Director
Paul Zettle, Engineering Dir

WMIT
06-01-1942; 106.9 MHz FM; *Hrs Open:* 24; 36 kw; 3091 ft.; N35 44 6 W82 17 10
P.O. Box 159, 1330 U.S. Highway 70, Black Mountain, NC 28711 US
(828) 669-8477; *Fax:* (828) 298-0117
www.1069thelight.org
License: Black Mountain, Buncombe County, NC held by Blue Ridge Broadcasting Corp.
Group Owner: Blue Ridge Broadcasting Corp.; (Acq 1963).
Nat'l Network: Fox News Radio
Arbitron Metro Market: Asheville, NC; *Format:* Christian; *Target Audience:* 35-54; women
Jim Kirkland, Programming Director

WZGM
02-26-1966; 1350 kHz AM; *Hrs Open:* 24
109 Charlotte Street, Black Mountain, NC 28711 US
(828) 505-8439
License: Black Mountain, NC held by HRN Broadcasting Inc.
Group Owner: HRN Broadcasting Inc.; (acq 4-28-2005; $850,000)
Arbitron Metro Market: Asheville, NC; *Format:* Gospel; *Target Audience:* General.
Matt Mittan, Owner
Leslie Godbold, Operations Manager

***WKJW**
1010 kHz AM; 50,000 watts; 35 36 19 N 82 21 0 W
1010 WFGW Faith and Freedom, P.O. Box 159, Black Mountain, NC 28711 US
(828) 285-8477; *Fax:* (828) 298-0017
License: Black Mountain, NC
Group Owner: Blue Ridge Broadcasting Corp.

Bladenboro

***WRDK**
90.7 MHz FM; 0.16 kw; 190 ft.; N34 32 59 W78 48 30
P.O. Box 15, Chester, SC 29706 US
(803) 581-9030; *Fax:* (803) 581-9932
License: Bladenboro, Bladen County, NC held by Richburg Educational Broadcasters Inc.
Arbitron Metro Market: Bladenboro, NC
Jeff Sigmon, General Manager

Blowing Rock

WXIT
01-01-1983; 1200 kHz AM
738 Blowing Rock Road, Boone, NC 28607 US
(828) 264-2411; *Fax:* (828) 264-2412
www.goblueridge.net
robinwohlbruck@gmail.com
License: Blowing Rock, NC held by High Country Adventures LLC.
Group Owner: Curtis Media Group; (acq 3-3-2009; grpsl)
Nat'l Network: CBS
Arbitron Metro Market: Blowing Rock, NC; *Format:* News, News/Talk, 86 *Special Programming:* Relg 8 hrs, big band 4 hrs wkly; *No. News Employees:* 1; *Target Audience:* 25-60; professionals *Adv. Rates:* 14;14;14;14
Tom Lanier, General Manager
Steve Frank, News Director
Andy Zlass, Operations Manager
Robin Wohlbruck, Market Manager

Boiling Spring Lakes

WKXB
12-13-1964; 99.9 MHz FM; *Hrs Open:* 24; 26 kw; 581 ft.; N34 5 51.7 W77 58 18.2
25 N. Kerr Ave., Wilmington, NC 28405 US
(910) 791-3088; *Fax:* (910) 791-0112
www.jammin999fm.com
stanleyb@jammin999fm.com
License: Boiling Spring Lakes, Brunswick County, NC held by Sunrise Broadcasting LLC.
Group Owner: Capitol Broadcasting Co. Inc.; (acq 11-18-2008; grpsl)
Nat'l Reps: McGavren Guild
Arbitron Metro Market: Wilmington, NC; *Format:* Oldies; *Hrs. of News Programming:* news progmg 3 hrs wkly; *No. News Employees:* 1; *Target Audience:* 25-54.
Brian Schimmel, General Manager
Josh Lee, Sales
Erika Burns, Sales
Kristine Smith, Sales
Veronica Banning, Sales
Holly Shaw, Sales

Boiling Springs

***WGWG**
01-22-1974; 88.3 MHz FM; *Hrs Open:* 24; 50 kw; 302 ft.; N35 13 52 W81 42 57
106 Emily Lane, Boiling Springs, NC 28017 US
(704) 406-3525; *Fax:* (704) 434-4338
www.wgwg.org
info@wgwg.org
License: Boiling Springs, Cleveland County, NC held by Gardner-Webb University.
Format: Triple A *Special Programming:* Gospel 15 hrs wkly; *Hrs. of News Programming:* News progmg one hr wkly; *Target Audience:* General.; *Adv. Rates:* 10; 10; 10; 10
Noel Manning, General Manager
Jeff Powell, Programming Director

Bolivia

WUDE
09-20-1986; 106.3 MHz FM; *Hrs Open:* 24; 6 kw; 305 ft.; N34 2 50 W78 16 12
1410 Commonwealth Dr., Suite 102A, Wilmington, NC 28403 US
(910) 772-6300
portcitydaily.com
thedude@localvoicemedia.com
License: Bolivia, Brunswick County, NC held by Local Voice Media Group
Group Owner: Local Voice Media Group
Arbitron Metro Market: Wilmington, NC; *Format:* News, News/Talk, 86 *Special Programming:* Beach mus 6 hrs wkly; *Target Audience:* 25 plus; mature professionals

Boone

WMMY
10-01-1999; 106.1 MHz FM; 10.5 kw; 509 ft.; N36 19 53 W81 35 17
738 Blowing Rock Road, Boone, NC 28607 US
(828) 264-2411; *Fax:* (828) 264-2412
www.GoBlueRidge.net
License: Boone, Watauga County, NC held by High Country Adventures LLC.
Group Owner: Curtis Media Group; (acq 3-3-2009; grpsl)
Arbitron Metro Market: Jefferson, NC; *Format:* Country *Special Programming:* Southern Fried Friday Night; Mountainhome Music Live Bluegrass Saturday Nights; *Target Audience:* 18-49; adults
Robert Zurowesti, Operations Dir
Jeff Stevens, Operations Manager

***WASU-FM**
05-18-1972; 90.5 MHz FM; 0.14 kw; 1251 ft.; N36 13 59 W81 41 55
Director of B/Cg Speech, Wey Hall, Boone, NC 28608 US
(828) 262-3170; *Fax:* (828) 262-6521
www.wasuradio.com
License: Boone, Watauga County, NC held by Appalachian State University.
Arbitron Metro Market: Boone, NC.; *Format:* Alternative *Special Programming:* Urban contemp 6 hrs, blues 2 hrs, Christian rock 3 hrs, country 8 hrs wkly; *Hrs. of News Programming:* News progmg 2 hrs wkly *TargetAudience:* 18-30; college students & area residents
Caleb Day, Station Manager
Lindsey Adorjan, Programming Director

WATA
09-01-1950; 1450 kHz AM; *Hrs Open:* 5 AM-midnight (M-S); 6 AM-midnight; 1 kw-U, ND1; N36 12 59 W81 42 6
738 Blowing Rock Road, Boone, NC 28607 US
(828) 264-2411; *Fax:* (828) 264-2412
www.wataradio.com
tom@wecr1023.com
License: Boone, NC held by High Country Adventures LLC.
Group Owner: Curtis Media Group; (acq 3-3-2009; grpsl)
Nat'l Network: ABC
Arbitron Metro Market: Boone, NC.; *Format:* News *Special Programming:* Gospel 5 hrs, Paul Harvey 2.5 hrs.,Watauga High sports wkly; *Hrs. of News Programming:* news progmg 4 hrs wkly; *No. News Employees:* 1 *TargetAudience:* 25-54.; *Adv. Rates:* 15; 15; 15; 15
Andy Glass, Operations Dir
Tom Lanier, General Manager
Steve Frank, News Director
Robin Wohlbruck, Market Manager

Brevard

WSQL
07-06-1950; 1240 kHz AM; 1 kw-U, ND1; N35 13 23 W82 42 20
1361 Colony Drive, New Bern, NC 28562 US
(828) 877-5252; *Fax:* (828) 877-5253
License: Brevard, NC held by A & L Broadcasting Inc.
Nat'l Network: CBS
Format: Adult Contemp, Talk *Special Programming:* Jazz 10 hrs, gospel 8 hrs, relg 4 hrs wkly; *Target Audience:* General.
Larry Weiss, General Manager
Tony Denton, Director of Sales

Bryson City

WBHN
10-01-1967; 1590 kHz AM; 0.5 kw-D, ND1; 0.037 kw-N, ND1; N35 25 41 W83 26 18
P.O. Box 1309, Bryson City, NC 28713 US
(708) 488-2682; *Fax:* (708) 488-3594
wbhn@verizon.net
License: Bryson City, NC held by Starcast South Inc.
Format: Contemporary Hits/Top 40, Adult Contemp
Jack Mullen Jr., President
Jason Nations, General Manager
J.B. Jacobs, Chief Engineer

Buies Creek

***WCCE**
10-07-1974; 90.1 MHz FM; *Hrs Open:* 24; 0 kw horiz, 15 kw vert; 302 ft.; N35 12 39 W78 50 1
7610 Falls of Neuse Road, Suite 155, Raleigh, NC 27615 US
(919)256-9787; *Fax:* (919)256-9559
www.hisradiowrtp.com
Management@hisradiowrtp.com
License: Buies Creek, Harnett County, NC held by Campbell University.
Arbitron Metro Market: Raleigh, NC; *Format:* Jazz, Smooth Jazz, 74 *Special Programming:* Bluegrass 3 hrs, big band 4 hrs wkly; *Hrs. of News Programming:* News progmg 10 hrs wkly; *Target Audience:* General.
Carolyn Bowden, Operations Dir
Travis Autry, General Manager

Bunn

WFXK
09-01-1952; 104.3 MHz FM; *Hrs Open:* 24; 100 kw; 987 ft; N35 48 40 W77 44 33 *Rebroadcasts:* 100% Simulcast with WFXC. WFXC, Durham, NC, 100%
www.foxync.com
License: Bunn, Franklin County, NC held by Radio One Licenses LLC.
Group Owner: Radio One Inc.; (acq 11-8-01; grpsl).
Population Served: 870,000; *Arbitron Metro Market:* Raleigh-Durham, NC; *Format:* Urban Contemporary *Special Programming:* Gospel 3 hrs, jazz 4 hrs wkly; *Hrs. of News Programming:* news progmg 3 hrs wkly *No. NewsEmployees:* 1; *Target Audience:* 25-54.
Alfred Liggins, President/CEO

Burgaw

WVBS
06-21-1963; 1470 kHz AM; *Hrs Open:* Sunrise-sunset; 0.88 kw-D, ND1; 0.093 kw-N, ND1; N34 31 22 W77 54 17
520 Roberts Road, Newport, NC 28570 US
(252) 223-6088
www.fbnradio.com
fbn@fbnradio.com
License: Burgaw, NC held by Grace Christian School.
Arbitron Metro Market: Wilmington, NC; *Format:* Christian
Carl Gibbs, General Manager
Dick Jones, Station Manager

Burlington

WYMY
12-01-1946; 101.1 MHz FM; *Hrs Open:* 24; 100 kw; 1176 ft.; N35 56 15 W79 26 30
3012 Highwoods Blvd., Suite 201, Raleigh, NC 27604 US
(336) 584-0126; *Fax:* (336) 854-0739
www.laleync.com
sdavenport@curtismedia.com
License: Burlington, Alamance County, NC held by Carolina Radio Group Inc.
Group Owner: Curtis Media Group
Arbitron Metro Market: Greensboro-Winston Salem-High Point, NC; *Format:* Talk, Spanish *Special Programming:* Hispanic Programming; *Target Audience:* 25-54.

David Stuckey, Vice President/General Manager
Lisa McKay, Programming Director
Rick Martinez, News Director

Burlington-Graham

WBAG

01-01-1946; 1150 kHz AM; *Hrs Open:* 24; 1 kw-D, 48 w-N; N36 06 48 W79 27 00
Mailing Address: Box 2450, Burlington, NC 27253
Second Address: 1745 Burch Bridge Rd., Burlington-Graham, NC 27217
(336) 226-1150; *Fax:* (336) 226-1180
www.wbag1150.com
wbag@bellsouth.net
License: Burlington-Graham, Alamance County, NC held by Gray Broadcasting LLC
Regional Network: N.C. News Net.
Population Served: 108,000; *Arbitron Metro Market:* Greensboro-Winston Salem-High Point, NC *Special Programming:* Relg 5 hrs wkly; *Hrs. of News Programming:* news progmg 25 hrs wkly; *No. News Employees:* 2 *TargetAudience:* 25-54; general

Harry Myers, Operations Dir
Joe Gray, General Manager
Gailes Stuckey, General Sales Mgr
Harry Myers, News Director
Tim Walker, Chief Engineer

WPCM

09-01-1941; 920 kHz AM; 5 kw-D, ND1; 0.055 kw-N, ND1; N36 5 50 W79 29 3
Mailing Address: 3012 Highwoods Blvd., Suite 201, Raleigh, NC 27604 US
Second Address: 1109 Tower Dr., Burlington, NC 27215
(336) 584-0126; *Fax:* (336) 584-0739
www.920wpcm.com
License: Burlington-Graham, NC held by Carolina Radio Group Inc.
Group Owner: Curtis Media Group; (acq 3-1-90).
Arbitron Metro Market: Greensboro-Winston Salem-High Point, NC; *Format:* Oldies; *Target Audience:* 25 plus; upscale; *Adv. Rates:* 10; 10; 10; 10

Byron Tucker, General Manager
Carson Johnson, Operations Manager
John Brockwell, News Director

Burnsville

WKYK

05-28-1967; 940 kHz AM; *Hrs Open:* 24; 4.6 kw-D, DAN; 0.25 kw-N, DAN; N35 55 32 W82 16 20
Mailing Address: P. O. Box 744, Burnsville, NC 28714 US
Second Address: 749 Sawmill Road, Burnsville, NC 28714
(828) 682-3510; *Fax:* (828) 682-6227
www.wkyk.com
940@wkyk.com
License: Burnsville, NC held by Mark Media Inc.
Group Owner: Mark Media Group; (acq 4-10-69)
Nat'l Network: ABC; *Regional Network:* N.C. News Net.
Format: Country *Special Programming:* Gospel 12 hrs wkly; *Hrs. of News Programming:* news progmg 10 hrs wkly; *No. News Employees:* 1; *Target Audience:* 18-55.; *Adv. Rates:* 20; 17; 20; 12

J. Ardell Sink, CEO
Michael Sink, President/General Manager
David Grindstaff, News Director
Remelle Sink, Executive Vice President/CFO
Holly Hall, Vice President of Marketing/Administration

Buxton

*WBUX

01-01-1999; 90.5 MHz FM; 5.9 kw; 154 ft.; N35 16 1 W75 32 38
Rebroadcasts: Rebroadcasts WCPE(FM) Wake Forest 99.9%
Box 0915, Chapel Hill, NC 27599 US
(919) 445-9150; *Fax:* (919) 966-5955
www.wunc.org
wunc@wunc.org
License: Buxton, Dare County, NC held by Board of Trustees/University of North Carolina at Chapel Hill.
Nat'l Network: NPR; PRI; CBC Radio One
Arbitron Metro Market: Buxton, NC; *Format:* Classical *Special Programming:* Folk 20 hrs wkly; *Hrs. of News Programming:* news progmg 124 hrs wkly; *No. News Employees:* 7

Bob Levin, COO
Deborah Proctor, General Manager
Dick Stork, Programming Director
Nandini Sen, Director of Technologies & Engineering
Regina Yeager, Director of Development
Susan Anderson, Accounting Coordinator
JacquelineEdwards, Business Assistant
Nathan Olawsky, Business Services Coordinator
Jennifer Bowling, Corporate Support Associate
Nancy Brookshire, Corporate Support Manager

WHDX

01-01-2008; 99.9 MHz FM; 0.11 kw; 56 ft.; N35 15 43 W75 31 23
US
(703) 527-1434
www.whdzx.com
radiobuxton@yahoo.com
License: Buxton, Dare County, NC held by David Wilson

David Wilson, General Manager

WHDZ

01-01-2008; 101.5 MHz FM; 0.11 kw; 66 ft.; N35 15 43 W75 31 23
US
(703) 527-1434
www.whdzx.com
radiobuxton@yahoo.com
License: Buxton, Dare County, NC held by David Wilson

David Wilson, General Manager

Calabash

WYNA

06-01-1964; 104.9 MHz FM; 15 kw; 338 ft.; N33 49 19 W78 46 18
4841 Highway 17 Bypass S., Myrtle Beach, SC 29577 US
(843) 293-0107; *Fax:* (843) 293-1717
www.1049bobfm.com
License: Calabash, Brunswick County, NC held by AMFM Radio Licenses LLC.
Group Owner: iHeartMedia
Arbitron Metro Market: Calabash, NC; *Format:* Urban Contemporary; *Target Audience:* 25-54; adults

Jimmy Feuger, Market President
Ron Roberts, Senior Vice President of Programming
Denise Atkins, Senior Vice President of Sales
Jennifer Habib, Business Manager

Camp Lejeune

WSME

09-08-1980; 1120 kHz AM
410 New Bridge St., Suite 3B, Jacksonville, NC 28450 US
(910) 346-2248
wsme1120@yahoo.com
License: Camp Lejeune, NC held by B&M Broadcasting LLC
Group Owner: B&M Broadcasting LLC
Arbitron Metro Market: New Bern, NC; *Format:* Country

Ashley Moseley, General Manager

Canton

WPTL

08-03-1963; 920 kHz AM; *Hrs Open:* 6 AM-6:30 PM; 0.5 kw-D, ND2; 0.038 kw-N, ND2; N35 31 15 W82 48 24
P.O. Box 909, Canton, NC 28716 US
(828) 648-3576,(828) 648-3577; *Fax:* (828) 648-3577
www.wptlradio.net
admin@wptlradio.net
License: Canton, NC held by Skycountry Broadcasting Inc.
Nat'l Network: AP Radio; Jones Radio Networks
Arbitron Metro Market: Asheville, NC; *Format:* Religious, Country; *Hrs. of News Programming:* News progmg 8 hrs wkly; *Target Audience:* 25 plus; adult family; *Adv. Rates:* 10 10 10 na

William Reck, President
Linda Reck, Operations Dir

WYSE

07-12-1954; 970 kHz AM; 5 kw-D, ND1; 0.03 kw-N, ND1; N35 31 58 W82 51 58
1190 Patton Avenue, Asheville, NC 28806 US
(828) 259-9695; *Fax:* (828) 253-5619
www.1310bigwise.com
License: Canton, NC held by Saga Communications of North Carolina LLC.
Group Owner: Saga Communications Inc.; (acq 3-11-2003).
Nat'l Network: ESPN Radio
Arbitron Metro Market: Asheville, NC; *Format:* Sports

Ed Christian, President/CEO
Bob Bolak, General Manager
Ken Carson, Programming Director
Nikki Mitchell, Promotions Manager
Bill McClement, News Director

Carolina Beach

WMYT

10-01-1996; 106.7 MHz FM; *Hrs Open:* 24; 5.6 kw; Ant 341 ft; N34 03 02 W77 57 20 *Rebroadcasts:* Simulcast with WPPG(FM) Fair Bluff.
311 Judges Road, Wilmington, NC 28405
(910) 772-6300
www.carolinapenguin.com
License: Carolina Beach, New Hanover County, NC held by Ocean Broadcasting II LLC

George Bell, General Manager/Sales Director
Curtis Wright, Programming Director

Carrboro

WQOK

10-01-1960; 97.5 MHz FM; *Hrs Open:* 24; 50 kw; 479 ft.; N35 58 39 W78 48 58
(919) 848-9736; *Fax:* (919) 848-4724
www.hiphopnc.com
License: Carrboro, South Boston City County, NC held by Radio One Licenses LLC.
Group Owner: Radio One Inc.; (acq 11-8-01; grpsl).
Nat'l Network: ABC; *Nat'l Reps:* Christal
Arbitron Metro Market: Raleigh-Durham, NC; *Format:* Urban Contemporary; *Hrs. of News Programming:* news progmg 20 hrs wkly; *No. News Employees:* 1; *Target Audience:* 25-54; upwardly mobile with discretionary income

Alfred Liggins, President/CEO

Cary

WNCB

01-01-1946; 93.9 MHz FM; 100 kw; 1486 ft.; N35 42 50 W78 49 4
3100 Smoketree Court, 7th Floor, Raleigh, NC 27604 US
(919) 877-0939; *Fax:* (919) 876-2929
www.b939country.com
License: Cary, Wake County, NC held by Capstar TX LLC
Group Owner: iHeartMedia; (acq 8-30-2000; grpsl)
Arbitron Metro Market: Raleigh-Durham, NC; *Format:* Country; *Target Audience:* 25-49; men

George Allen, Market President
Todd Nixon, Programming Director
Nathan James, Director of Integrated Media
Melody Mechanic, Digital Program Director

Chadbourn

WVOE

04-23-1962; 1590 kHz AM; 1 kw-D, NDD; N34 21 5 W78 50 38
1528 Old 74 Highway West, Chadbourn, NC 28431 US
(910) 654-5621; *Fax:* (910) 654-4385
License: Chadbourn, NC held by Ebony Enterprises Inc.
Arbitron Metro Market: Chadbourn, NC; *Format:* Gospel; *Target Audience:* General; white & blue collar workers, housewives, students, sr citizens

Willie Walls, President
Willie Walls, General Manager

Chapel Hill

WCHL

01-25-1953; 1360 kHz AM; *Hrs Open:* 24; 5 kw-D, DAN; 1 kw-N, DAN; N35 56 18 W79 1 36
88 Vilcom Center Drive, Suite 130, Raleigh, NC 27514 US
(919) 933-4165; *Fax:* (919) 968-3748
www.chapelboro.com
cdixon@wchl.com
License: Chapel Hill, NC held by Vilcom Interactive Media LLC
Nat'l Network: ABC; CBS Radio; Jones Radio Networks;
Regional Network: N.C. News Net.; *Wire Services:* AP
Arbitron Metro Market: Raleigh-Durham, NC; *Format:* News, News/Talk, 86; *Hrs. of News Programming:* news progmg 25 hrs wkly; *No. News Employees:* 3; *Target Audience:* 25-54; educated adults with high median incomes

Barry Leffler, CEO
Christy Dixon, Station Manager
Ron Stutts, Programming Director

WLLQ

12-01-1973; 1530 kHz AM; *Hrs Open:* Sunrise-sunset; 10 kw-D, DAD; N35 58 7 W79 0 10
P.O. Box 15400, Durham, NC 27704 US
(202) 638-1959; *Fax:* (202) 638-6127
estuardovaldemar@hotmail.com
License: Chapel Hill, NC held by Estuardo Valdemar Rodriguez and Leonor Rodriguez.
Group Owner: Radio La Grande; (acq 2-2-2005; grpsl)

Arbitron Metro Market: Raleigh-Durham,; *Target Audience:* Spanish young adult.
Estuardo Rodriguez, General Manager

***WUNC**
11-03-1952; 91.5 MHz FM; *Hrs Open:* 24; 100 kw; 1362 ft.; N35 51 59 W79 10 0
120 Friday Center Drive, Chapel Hill, NC 27517 US
(919) 445-9150; *Fax:* (919) 966-5955
www.wunc.org
wunc@wunc.org
License: Chapel Hill, Orange County, NC held by University of North Carolina at Chapel Hill.
Nat'l Network: NPR; PRI; CBC Radio One
Arbitron Metro Market: Chapel Hill, NC; *Format:* News *Special Programming:* Folk 20 hrs wkly; *Hrs. of News Programming:* news progmg 124 hrs wkly; *No. News Employees:* 7; *Target Audience:* 25-54; highlyeducated, pro-active in the community, concerned about local issues
Kevin Wolf, Operations Dir
Connie Walker, General Manager
David Brower, Programming Director
Regina Yeager, Director of Development
Jacqueline Edwards, Business Assistant
Robin Copley, Audio Manager
Laura Shaffer, DevelopmentAssistant

***WXYC**
03-18-1977; 89.3 MHz FM; *Hrs Open:* 24; 400 w; 280 ft; N35 54 15 W79 02 50
CB 5210, Carolina Union, Chapel Hill, NC 27599
(919) 962-8989
www.wxyc.org
info@wxyc.org
License: Chapel Hill, Orange County, NC held by Student Educational Broadcasting Inc.
Population Served: 25,000; *Arbitron Metro Market:* Raleigh-Durham, NC; *Hrs. of News Programming:* News progmg 3 hrs wkly; *Target Audience:* General.
Olivia Branscam, Station Manager
Anne Symons, Programming Director
Cozy Brents, Promotions Manager

Charlotte

WBCN
12-01-2003; 1660 kHz AM; 10 kw-D, 1 kw-N; N35 14 56 W80 51 44
1520 South Blvd., Suite 300, Charlotte, NC 28203
(704) 319-9369; *Fax:* (704) 319-3934
www.americaspulse1660.com
License: Charlotte, Mecklenburg County, NC held by WKIS License Limited Partnership
Group Owner: Beasley Broadcast Group Inc.
Nat'l Network: CBS Sports Radio; *Nat'l Reps:* D & R Radio; Katz Radio
Population Served: 751,087; *Arbitron Metro Market:* Charlotte,NC; *Format:* Sports, Talk
Robin Colfax, General Sales Mgr
DJ Stout, Programming Director
Chele Fassig, Promotions Manager
Bill Schoening, Senior Vice President/Market Manager
Jenna Land, Digital Sales Manager
Amanda Knepp, Marketing Director

WBT
04-10-1922; 1110 kHz AM; *Hrs Open:* 24; 50 kw-D, DAN; 50 kw-N, DAN; N35 7 56 W80 53 23
One Julian Price Place, Charlotte, NC 28208 US
(704) 570-1110
www.wbt.com
tsavery@wbt.com
License: Charlotte, NC held by Greater Media of Charlotte Inc.
Group Owner: Greater Media Inc.; (acq 1-31-2008; grpsl)
Nat'l Network: CBS
Arbitron Metro Market: Charlotte, NC; *Format:* News, News/Talk, 86; *Hrs. of News Programming:* news progmg 20 hrs wkly; *No. News Employees:* 5; *Target Audience:* 35-54; men
Trip Savery, Vice President/General Manager
Terry Mace, General Sales Mgr
Jason Furst, Programming Director
Matt Dubois, Promotions Manager/Marketing Director
Marshall Adams, News Director
Jerry Dowd, Chief Engineer
Zach Simpson,Webmaster
Matt DuBois, Marketing Director
Jessica ""Reeves"" RoBards, Marketing Administrator

***WFAE**
06-29-1981; 90.7 MHz FM; *Hrs Open:* 24; 100 kw; 1086 ft.; N35 17 14 W80 41 45
8801 Jm Keynes Dr, Suite 91, Charlotte, NC 28262 US
(704) 549-9323; *Fax:* (704) 547-8851
www.wfae.org
wfae@wfae.org
License: Charlotte, Mecklenburg County, NC held by University Radio Foundation Inc.
Nat'l Network: NPR; PRI
Arbitron Metro Market: Charlotte, NC; *Format:* News, News/Talk, 86; *Hrs. of News Programming:* news progmg 42 hrs wkly; *No. News Employees:* 4; *Target Audience:* 35-49; professionals
Roger Sarow, President and General Manager
Dale Spear, Director of Programming
Debra Peterson, Business Manager

WFNZ
01-01-1941; 610 kHz AM; 5 kw-D, 1 kw-N; N35 18 3 W80 53 18
1520 South Blvd., Suite 300, Charlotte, NC 28203 US
(704) 319-9369; *Fax:* (704) 319-3934
www.wfnz.com
License: Charlotte, Mecklenburg County, NC held by WXTU License Limited Partnership
Group Owner: Beasley Broadcast Group Inc.; (acq 11-13-98; grpsl).
Arbitron Metro Market: Charlotte-Gastonia-Rock Hill, NC; *Format:* Sports, Talk; *Target Audience:* 18 plus; male, sports oriented
Jenna Land, Digital Sales Manager/General Sales Manager
DJ Stout, Programming Director
Chele Fassig, Promotions Manager
Bill Schoening, Senior Vice President/Market Manager
Amanda Knepp, Marketing Director

WGFY
01-18-1955; 1480 kHz AM; *Hrs Open:* 24
1100 S Tryon Street, Charlotte, NC 28203 US
(704) 377-2223; *Fax:* (704) 373-2245
www.radiodisney.com
info@radiodisney.com
License: Charlotte, NC held by Radio Disney Group LLC.
Group Owner: ABC Inc.; (acq 8-22-00; grpsl).
Arbitron Metro Market: Charlotte-Gastonia-Rock Hill, NC-SC; *Format:* Children; *Hrs. of News Programming:* news progmg 25 hrs wkly; *No. News Employees:* 6; *Target Audience:* Under 12; kids, mothers, families

WGSP
08-23-1958; 1310 kHz AM
645 Church St, Suite 400, Norfolk, VA 23510 US
(704) 442-7277; *Fax:* (704) 442-9518
www.pepecharlotte.com
License: Charlotte, NC held by Norsan Consulting and Management Inc.
Group Owner: Norsan Consulting and Management Inc.; (acq 12-13-2004; $2 million).
Arbitron Metro Market: Charlotte-Gastonia-Rock Hill, NC-SC; *Format:* Spanish
Norberto Sanchez, President
Javier Placencia, Programming Director

WHVN
01-01-1958; 1240 kHz AM; 1 kw-D, ND2; 1 kw-N, ND2; N35 12 0 W80 48 39
5732 N. Tryon Street, Charlotte, NC 28213 US
(704) 596-1240; *Fax:* (704) 596-6939
www.heavenradio.org
License: Charlotte, NC held by WHVN Inc.
Group Owner: GHB Radio Group; (acq 7-11-83)
Arbitron Metro Market: Charlotte-Gastonia-Rock Hill, NC-SC; *Format:* Religious; *Target Audience:* 35 plus; Christian
Tom Gentry, General Manager

WLNK
08-15-1962; 107.9 MHz FM; *Hrs Open:* 24; 100 kw; 1693 ft.; N35 21 51 W81 11 13
One Julian Price Place, Charlotte, NC 28208 US
(704) 374-3500; *Fax:* (704) 338-3062
www.1079wnct.com
License: Charlotte, Mecklenburg County, NC held by Greater Media of Charlotte Inc.
Group Owner: Beasley Broadcast Group; (acq 1-31-2008; grpsl)
Arbitron Metro Market: Charlotte-Gastonia-Rock Hill, NC-SC; *Format:* Adult Contemp
Trip Savery, Vice President/General Manager
Tony Sciotto, Programming Director
Matt DuBois, Promotions/Marketing Manager
Derek James, Music Director

WNKS
07-21-1962; 95.1 MHz FM; 100 kw; 1542 ft.; N35 21 44 W81 9 19
1520 South Blvd., Suite 300, Charlotte, NC 28203 US
(704) 522-1103; *Fax:* (704) 344-8237
www.kiss951.com
License: Charlotte, Mecklenburg County, NC held by WPOW License Limited Partnership
Group Owner: Beasley Broadcast Group Inc.
Arbitron Metro Market: Charlotte, NC; *Format:* Contemporary Hits/Top 40
Jenna Land, General Sales Mgr
John Reynolds, Programming Director
Stacey Canady, Promotions Manager
Bill Schoening, Senior Vice President/Market Manager
Amanda Knepp, Marketing Director

WOGR
05-07-1964; 1540 kHz AM
Mailing Address: P.O. Box 16408, Charlotte, NC 28297 US
Second Address: 1501 N. Carrier Dr., Charlotte, NC 28216
(704) 393-1540; *Fax:* (704) 393-1527
wordnet.org
info@wordnet.org
License: Charlotte, NC held by Victory Christian Center Inc.
Nat'l Network: Salem Radio Network
Arbitron Metro Market: Charlotte-Gasto *TV Affiliate:* Relg; *No. News Employees:* General.
Programming Manager, Operations Dir
Music Director, Programming Director

WSOC-FM
01-01-1947; 103.7 MHz FM; 100 kw; 1348 ft.; N35 15 6 W80 41 12
1520 South Blvd., Suite 300, Charlotte, NC 28203 US
(704) 522-1103
www.thenew1037.com
License: Charlotte, Mecklenburg County, NC held by WXTU License Limited Partnership
Group Owner: Beasley Broadcast Group Inc.; (acq 11-13-98; grpsl).
Arbitron Metro Market: Charlotte-Gastonia-Rock Hill, NC-SC; *Format:* Country; *Target Audience:* 25-54.
Robin Colfax, General Sales Mgr
D.J. Stout, Programming Director
Chele Fassig, Promotions Manager
Bill Schoening, Senior Vice President/Market Manager
Amanda Knepp, Marketing Director
Jenna Land, Digital Sales Manager

WKQC
01-01-1972; 104.7 MHz FM; *Hrs Open:* 24; 96 kw; 1211 ft.; N35 15 6 W80 41 12
1520 South Blvd., Suite 300, Charlotte, NC 28203 US
(704) 522-1103; *Fax:* (704) 344-8237
www.k1047.com
License: Charlotte, Mecklenburg County, NC held by WKIS License Limited Partnership
Group Owner: Beasley Broadcast Group Inc.; (acq 11-13-98; grpsl).
Arbitron Metro Market: Charlotte-Gastonia-Rock Hill, NC-SC; *Format:* Adult Contemp; *No. News Employees:* 2; *Target Audience:* 25-54.
Robin Colfax, General Sales Mgr
John Reynolds, Programming Director
Stacey Canady, Promotions Manager
Bill Schoening, Senior Vice President/Market Manager
Amanda Knepp, Marketing Director
Jenna Land, Digital Sales Manager

***WYFQ**
10-14-1933; 930 kHz AM; *Hrs Open:* 24; 5 kw-D, DAN; 1 kw-N, DAN; N35 16 5 W80 54 11
P.O. Box 7300, Charlotte, NC 28241 US
(800) 888-7077
www.bbnradio.org
bbn@bbnmedia.org
License: Charlotte, Mecklenburg County, NC held by Bible Broadcasting Network Inc.
Group Owner: Bible Broadcasting Network; acq 2-6-92; $475,000;
Arbitron Metro Market: Charlotte, NC; *Format:* Christian; *Hrs. of News Programming:* News progmg 3 hrs wkly; *Target Audience:* General.
Jason Padgett, Operations Manager
Ron Muffley, Chief Engineer

Cherryville

WCSL
06-28-1967; 1590 kHz AM; *Hrs Open:* 24
1416 Shelby Highway 150, Cherryvillle, NC 28021 US
(704) 732-8011; *Fax:* (704) 732-9567
www.ktcbroadcasting.com
License: Cherryville, NC held by HRN Broadcasting Inc.
Group Owner: HRN Broadcasting Inc.; (acq 4-14-2004; $500,000 with WLON(AM) Lincolnton)

Nat'l Network: Westwood One; *Regional Network:* N.C. News Net.
Arbitron Metro Market: Charlotte, NC; *Format:* Christian *Special Programming:* Loc sports 3 hrs wkly; *Target Audience:* General.
Josh Collins, Sales
Andrey Bush, Art Director

China Grove

WRNA

11-17-1980; 1140 kHz AM; *Hrs Open:* 6 AM-2 hrs past sunset; 0.25 kw-C, DAD; 1 kw-D, DAD; N35 34 20 W80 35 21
P. O. Box 1388, Kannapolis, NC 28082 US
(704) 857-1101; *Fax:* (704) 857-0680
www.fordbroadcasting.com
carl@fordbroadcasting.com
License: China Grove, NC held by South Rowan Broadcasting Co.
Nat'l Network: USA
Arbitron Metro Market: Charlotte-Gastonia-Rock Hill, NC-SC; *Format:* Gospel; *Target Audience:* General.
Carl Ford, President
Angela Ford, Operations Dir
Taylor Ford, Executive Vice President

Claremont

WCXN

09-05-1985; 1170 kHz AM; 1 kw-C, NDD; 7.7 kw-D, NDD; N35 43 34 W81 8 52
P.O. Box 909, Claremont, NC 28610-0909 US
(828) 459-9803
www.birach.com
sima@birach.com
License: Claremont, Catawba County, NC held by Birach Broadcasting Corp.
Group Owner: Birach Broadcasting Corp.; (acq 8-1-2007; $800,000 with KXLQ(AM) Indianola, IA)
Nat'l Network: USA
Arbitron Metro Market: Claremont, NC; *Format:* Tejano; *Target Audience:* General.
Sima Birach, President

Clayton

WHPY

01-01-1974; 1590 kHz AM; *Hrs Open:* Sunrise-sunset; 5 kw-D, ND1; 0.025 kw-N, ND1; N35 38 49 W78 30 21
P.O. Box 535, Clayton, NC 27520 US
(919) 553-6774; *Fax:* (919) 359-0016
www.whpyradio.com
License: Clayton, NC held by Fellowship Baptist Church Inc. dba Fellowship Christian Academy.
Arbitron Metro Market: Raleigh-Durham, NC; *Format:* Christian
Charles Ennis, President
Keith Holland, General Manager

Clemmons

WMKS

05-03-1947; 105.7 MHz FM; *Hrs Open:* 24; 30 kw; 1549 ft.; N36 22 36.4 W80 22 8.6
2-B PAI Park, Greensboro, NC 27409 US
(336) 822-2000; *Fax:* (336) 887-0104
www.1003kissfm.com
License: Clemmons, Forsyth County, NC held by Capstar TX LLC
Group Owner: iHeartMedia; (acq 9-12-2006;. $15.65 million)
Arbitron Metro Market: Greensboro-Winston Salem-High Point, NC; *Format:* Contemporary Hits/Top 40
Bobby Tatum, Sales Manager
Keith Allen, Programming Director
Kelly Hildebrandt, Director of Marketing and Promotions
Dennis Elliott, Digital Content Director
Andie Cooper, Internship Director

Clinton

WCLN

09-27-1975; 1170 kHz AM; *Hrs Open:* Sunrise-sunset; 1 kw-C, NDD; 5 kw-D, NDD; N35 1 21 W78 20 58
118 East Main Street, Clinton, NC 28328 US
(910) 592-8949; *Fax:* (910) 592-3732
www.oldies1170.com
grandpas@oldies1170.com
License: Clinton, NC held by CLINTON SAMPSON RADIO CO INC
Nat'l Network: ABC; *Regional Network:* N.C. News Net.
Arbitron Metro Market: Clinton, NC; *Format:* Oldies *Special Programming:* Community, gospel 8 hrs wkly; *Hrs. of News Programming:* news progmg 4.5 hrs. wkly; *No. News Employees:* 7; *Target Audience:* 35 PLUS *Adv. Rates:* 10.35; 10.35; 10.35.; 10.35
Joyce Dixon, Vice President
Pat "Grandpa" Dixon, GM
-, General Sales Mgr
Nolan Wiggins, Programming Director
Don Smith, News Director
Nicole Nelson, Music Director

WCLN-FM

06-11-1967; 107.3 MHz FM; *Hrs Open:* 24; 9.2 kw; 535 ft.; N35 7 37 W78 35 19
996 Helen Street, Fayetteville, NC 28303 US
(910) 864-5028; *Fax:* (910) 864-6270
www.christian107.com
License: Clinton, Sampson County, NC held by Christian Listening Network Inc.
Group Owner: Christian Listening Network Inc.; (acq 7-94).
Arbitron Metro Market: Fayetteville, NC; *Format:* Christian, Religious
George Wilson, President
Dan DeBruler, General Manager
Steve Turley, Programming Director
Cindy Long, Promotions Manager
Van Clough, Chief Engineer

WRRZ

04-05-1947; 880 kHz AM; 1 kw-D, NDD; N34 58 40 W78 18 15
2164 SE Boulevard, Clinton, NC 28238 US
(910) 592-1285; *Fax:* (910) 592-8556
License: Clinton, NC held by Sanchez Broadcasting Corp.
Regional Network: N.C. News Net.
Special Programming: Black 5 hrs, relg 6 hrs, Sp 5 hrs wkly; *Target Audience:* 25 plus.; *Adv. Rates:* 8.75; 8.25; 8.75; 8.25
Victor Sanchez, President
Martha Sanchez, General Manager

Columbia

WERX-FM

03-14-1983; 102.5 MHz FM; *Hrs Open:* 24; 64 kw; 689 ft.; N35 55 5 W76 20 48
Mailing Address: P.O. Box 1017, Edenton, NC 27932 US
Second Address: 2422 S. Wrightsville Ave., Nags Head, NC 27959
(252) 441-1024; *Fax:* (252) 441-2109
www.1025theshark.com
marko@ecri.net
License: Columbia, Tyrrell County, NC held by East Carolina Radio of Elizabeth City Inc.
Group Owner: East Carolina Radio Group
Arbitron Metro Market: Columbia, NC; *Format:* Oldies *Special Programming:* Flashback, in concert, off the record, BBC classic tracks; *Target Audience:* 18-49; moderate to high income, mobile professionals & families withchildren
Rick Loesch, President
Tom Charity, Operations Dir
R. Loesch, General Manager
Rick Loesch, General Sales Mgr

WRSF

06-13-1983; 105.7 MHz FM; *Hrs Open:* 24; 100 kw; 614 ft.; N35 53 18 W76 13 50
Mailing Address: P.O. Box 1800, Raleigh, NC 27602 US
Second Address: 2422 S. Wrightsville Ave., Nags Head, NC 27959
(252) 449-8331; *Fax:* (252) 449-8354
www.dixie1057.com
License: Columbia, Tyrrell County, NC held by East Carolina Radio of Elizabeth City Inc.
Group Owner: East Carolina Radio Group; (acq 1996).
Format: Country; *Hrs. of News Programming:* news progmg 5 hrs wkly; *No. News Employees:* 1; *Target Audience:* 18-54; young & mid-range adults
Rick Loesch, General Manager
Ray Turner, Programming Director

Concord

WPEG

06-15-1962; 97.9 MHz FM; 95 kw horiz, 71.7 kw vert; 1611 ft.; N35 21 44 W81 9 19
1520 South Blvd., Suite 300, Charlotte, NC 28203 US
(704) 522-1103
www.power98fm.com
License: Concord, Cabarrus County, NC held by WPOW License Limited Partnership
Group Owner: Beasley Broadcast Group Inc.; (acq 11-13-98; grpsl).
Nat'l Network: Westwood One; *Nat'l Reps:* Katz Radio
Arbitron Metro Market: Charlotte-Gastonia-Rock Hill, NC-SC; *Format:* Urban Contemporary *Special Programming:* Gospel 6 hrs, mix show 8 hrs wkly; *Hrs. of News Programming:* news progmg 20 hrs wkly; *No. News Employees:* 1; *Target Audience:* 12 plus; Black
Jacque Freeman, Sales Manager
Jamillah Muhammad, Program Director/Promotions Manager
Bill Schoening, Senior Vice President/Market Manager
Amanda Knepp, Marketing Director
Jenna Land, Digital Sales Manager

Cramerton

WZGV

08-21-1946; 730 kHz AM; *Hrs Open:* 24; 1 kw-D, 168 w-N; N35 17 27 W81 34 05
1511 W. Dixon Blvd., Shelby, NC 28021
(704) 482-4510,(704) 487-6313; *Fax:* (704) 482-4680
www.espn730.com
License: Cramerton, Gaston County, NC held by HRN Broadcasting Inc.
Group Owner: HRN Broadcasting Inc.; (acq 10-6-2006; $1.5 million with WGNC(AM) Gastonia)
Nat'l Network: ABC; *Regional Network:* N.C. News Net.
Regional Reps: T-N.
Population Served: 500,000; *Arbitron Metro Market:* Charlotte-Gastonia-Rock Hill, NC-SC; *No. News Employees:* 2; *Target Audience:* General.
Lanny Ford, General Manager
Bobby Rosinski, Assistant Programming Director

Creedmore

WDRU

09-01-1989; 1030 kHz AM; *Hrs Open:* Daytime; 50 kw-D, DA; N36 10 43 W78 45 30 *Rebroadcasts:* Simulcast with WTRU(AM) Kernersville
4601 Six Forks Rd., Suite 520, Raleigh, NC 27609 US
(336) 759-0363; *Fax:* (336) 759-0366
www.truthnetwork.com
mcarbone@truthnetwork.com
License: Creedmore, Granville County, NC held by Truth Broadcasting Corp.
Group Owner: Truth Broadcasting Corp.; (acq 5-2-2005; swap for WWBG(AM) Greensboro and WTOB(AM) Winston-Salem).
Nat'l Network: Salem Radio Network
Arbitron Metro Market: Raleigh-Durham, NC; *Format:* Christian; *Target Audience:* 25-54; middle-class families; *Adv. Rates:* 356; 35; 35; 30
Stuart Epperson Jr., General Manager

Cullowhee

*WWCU

01-15-1977; 90.5 MHz FM; *Hrs Open:* 24; 0.24 kw horiz, 0.23 kw vert; 948 ft.; N35 26 23 W83 7 11
Western Carolina University, Cullowhee, NC 28723 US
(828) 227-7454; *Fax:* (828) 227-7099
www.wwcufm.com
info@wwcufm.com
License: Cullowhee, Jackson County, NC held by Western Carolina University.
Nat'l Network: ABC; *Wire Services:* Reuters
Arbitron Metro Market: Cullowhee, NC; *Format:* Sports; *Target Audience:* 25-54; univ students & faculty, general public
David McWhirter, Program Coordinator
Bradley Lucore, General Manager

Dallas

WCRU

01-01-1963; 960 kHz AM; *Hrs Open:* 6 AM-midnight
PO Box 477, 407 Robinson-Clemmer Rd., Dallas, NC 28034 US
(336) 480-2038; *Fax:* (336) 759-0366
www.truthnetwork.com
mcarbone@truthnetwork.com
License: Dallas, NC held by Truth Broadcasting Corp.
Group Owner: Truth Broadcasting Corp.; (acq 6-30-2004; $775,000)
Arbitron Metro Market: Charlotte, NC; *Format:* Religious; *Hrs. of News Programming:* News progmg 10 hrs wkly; *Target Audience:* Male 25-59; college educ, income 50K; *Adv. Rates:* 180; 180; 180; 180
Stuart Epperson, President
Monty Monaghan, Station Manager

*WSGE

10-27-1980; 91.7 MHz FM; *Hrs Open:* 24; 7.5 kw; 853 ft.; N35 24 26 W81 7 48
201 Highway 321 South, Dallas, NC 28034 US
(704) 922-4286; *Fax:* (704) 922-2347
www.wsge.org
hall.cathis@gaston.edu

License: Dallas, Gaston County, NC held by Gaston College Board of Trustees.
Format: Triple A; *Hrs. of News Programming:* News progmg 5 hrs wkly; *Target Audience:* General.
Cathis Hall, Station Manager
Ben Dungan, Membership Coordinator

Davidson

*WDAV

09-01-1973; 89.9 MHz FM; *Hrs Open:* 24; 100 kw; 807 ft.; N35 26 54 W80 50 23
423 N. Main Street, PO Box 8990, Davidson, NC 20836 US
(877) 333-8990; *Fax:* (704) 894-2997
www.wdav.org
wdav@davidson.edu
License: Davidson, Mecklenburg County, NC held by Trustees of Davidson College.
Nat'l Network: PRI; NPR
Arbitron Metro Market: Charlotte, NC; *Format:* Talk; *Hrs. of News Programming:* News progmg 2 hrs wkly; *Target Audience:* General.
Joe Brant, Operations Dir
Scott Nolan, General Manager
Frank Dominguez, Programming Director
Larry Schropp, Chief Engineer
Kim Cline, Assistant General Manager
Ted Weiner, Music Director
Joe Brant, On-Air Host
Jennifer Foster,On-Air Host
Mike McKay, On-Air Host
Ted Weiner, Music Director

Dobson

WYZD

10-10-1978; 1560 kHz AM
P.O. Box 797, Dobson, NC 27017 US
(336) 356-1560
License: Dobson, NC held by Gospel Broadcasting Inc.
Regional Network: N.C. News Net.
Arbitron Metro Market: Dobson, NC; *Format:* Gospel
Ricky Cothren, General Manager

Dunn

WCKB

12-07-1946; 780 kHz AM; *Hrs Open:* Sunrise-sunset
Mailing Address: P. O. Box 789, Dunn, NC 28335 US
Second Address: 17336 US Hwy 421 S., Dunn, NC 28334
(910) 892-3133; *Fax:* (910) 892-3135
www.wckb780.com
wckb@wckb780.com
License: Dunn, NC held by N.C. Central Broadcasters Inc.
Regional Network: N.C. News Net.
Arbitron Metro Market: Dunn, NC; *Format:* Gospel, Religious
Special Programming: Good Morning, Charlie,Southern Gospel Concert Update,Hymnal Harmony; *Hrs. of News Programming:* News progmg 6 hrs wkly; *Target Audience:* 25 plus; Christian, family-oriented with regional interests; *Adv. Rates:* 11; 11; 11; 11; na
Charles Fowler, President
Ronald Tart, General Manager
Lottie Squires, Programming Director
Neal Wood, Assistant Music Director

WRCQ

05-17-1971; 103.5 MHz FM; *Hrs Open:* 24; 48 kw; 502 ft.; N35 3 9 W78 38 54
1009 Drayton Road, Fayetteville, NC 28303 US
(910) 864-5222; *Fax:* (910) 864-3065
www.rock103rocks.com
License: Dunn, Harnett County, NC held by Cumulus Licensing Corp.
Group Owner: Cumulus Media Inc.; (acq 3-12-01; grpsl).
Nat'l Network: ABC
Arbitron Metro Market: Fayetteville, NC; *Format:* Rock/AOR; *Hrs. of News Programming:* news progmg one hr wkly; *No. News Employees:* 1; *Target Audience:* 18-49.
Richard Stadlen, Operations Manager
Kevin Culbreth, Programming/Music Director
Patrick Jackson, Marketing/Promotions Director
Stephen Roberts, Vice President/Market Manager

Durham

WDCG

02-28-1948; 105.1 MHz FM; 73 kw; 1112 ft.; N35 42 50 W78 49 4
3100 Smoketree Court, Raleigh, NC 27604 US
(919) 878-1500; *Fax:* (919) 876-8578
www.g105.com
License: Durham, Durham County, NC held by Capstar TX LLC
Group Owner: iHeartMedia; (acq 8-30-00; grpsl).
Nat'l Network: ABC
Arbitron Metro Market: Raleigh-Durham, NC; *Format:* Contemporary Hits/Top 40; *Target Audience:* 18-49.
Chris Edge, Programming Director
Nathan James, Director of Integrated Media
Melody Mechanic, Digital Program Director

WDNC

04-09-1934; 620 kHz AM; *Hrs Open:* 24
3100 Highwoods Boulevard, Raleigh, NC 27604 US
(919) 890-6290; *Fax:* (919) 890-6146
www.wralsportsfan.com
contact@999thefan.com
License: Durham, NC held by WCHL-WDNC Inc.
Group Owner: Curtis Media Group; (acq 12-30-86)
Nat'l Network: Sporting News Radio Network; *Nat'l Reps:* McGavren Guild; *Wire Services:* AP
Arbitron Metro Market: Raleigh-Durham, NC; *Format:* Sports; *Adv. Rates:* 30; 26; 30; 18
Brian Maloney, General Manager
Dennis Glasgow, Programming Director
Luanne Lane, Promotions Manager

WDUR

01-01-1947; 1490 kHz AM; *Hrs Open:* 24; 1 kw-U, ND1; N35 58 3 W78 53 18
US
(919) 878-1500; *Fax:* (919) 876-2929
www.prietobroadcasting.com
License: Durham, NC held by Arohi Media LLC
Group Owner: Arohi Media LLC
Nat'l Network: ESPN Radio
Arbitron Metro Market: Durham, NC; *Format:* Sports
Filiberto Prieto, President

WFXC

05-15-1971; 107.1 MHz FM; *Hrs Open:* 24; 8 kw; 479 ft.; N35 58 39 W78 48 58
US
(919) 848-9736; *Fax:* (919) 863-4859
www.foxync.com
License: Durham, Durham County, NC held by Radio One Licenses LLC.
Group Owner: Radio One Inc.; (acq 11-8-2001; grpsl).
Wire Services: UPI
Arbitron Metro Market: Raleigh-Durham, NC; *Format:* Urban Contemporary *Special Programming:* Gospel 4 hrs wkly; *Hrs. of News Programming:* news progmg 5 hrs wkly; *No. News Employees:* 1 *Target Audience:* 25-54; African American
Alfred Liggins, President/CEO

*WNCU

08-01-1995; 90.7 MHz FM; *Hrs Open:* 24; 50 kw; 433 ft.; N36 3 33 W78 57 14
Post Office Box 19875, Durham, NC 27702 US
(919) 530-7445; *Fax:* (919) 530-5031
www.wncu.org
lsykes@nccu.edu
License: Durham, Durham County, NC held by North Carolina Central University.
Nat'l Network: NPR; PRI
Arbitron Metro Market: Durham, NC; *Format:* Jazz, News, 62, Talk; *Hrs. of News Programming:* news progmg 33 hrs wkly; *No. News Employees:* 1; *Target Audience:* 25-54; middle class/middle age
Chris Whitfield, Operations Dir
Lackisha Freeman, General Manager
Uchenna Johnson, General Sales Mgr
Kimberley Pierce, News Director
James Davis, Chief Engineer
B.H. Hudson, Music Director

WRJD

10-14-1954; 1410 kHz AM; *Hrs Open:* 24
645 Church St, Suite 400, Norfolk, VA 23510 US
(919) 220-3226; *Fax:* (919) 220-0006
License: Durham, NC held by Davidson Media Station WSRC Licensee LLC.
Group Owner: Davidson Media Group LLC; (acq 3-20-2006; $1.2 million).
Arbitron Metro Market: Raleigh-Durham, NC; *Format:* Gospel, Talk; *No. News Employees:* 5; *Target Audience:* 25-54.
Linda Greenwood, General Manager

WTIK

01-01-1945; 1310 kHz AM; *Hrs Open:* 24; 5 kw-D, DA2; 1 kw-N, DA2; N36 1 30 W78 54 8
707 Leon Street, Durham, NC 27704 US
(704) 987-3585
www.lameganc.com
info@wtik.com
License: Durham, NC held by Davidson Media Carolinas Stations LLC.
Group Owner: Davidson Media Group LLC; (acq 5-10-2004; grpsl).
Arbitron Metro Market: Durham, NC; *Format:* Spanish
Peter Davidson, President

*WXDU

11-01-1983; 88.7 MHz FM; *Hrs Open:* 24; 2.15 kw; 253 ft.; N36 2 8 W79 4 48
P.O. Box 90834, Durham, NC 27708 US
(919) 684-2957; *Fax:* (919) 684-3260
www.wxdu.org
wxdu@duke.edu
License: Durham, Durham County, NC held by Duke University.
Arbitron Metro Market: Durham, NC; *Format:* Variety/Diverse
Special Programming: Jazz 18 hrs, urban sound & hip hop 12 hrs wkly; *Target Audience:* General.
Sharla, General Manager
Adrienne, Programming Director
Dave, Promotions Manager
Jim Davis, Chief Engineer
Ross, Local Music Director
Georg, World Music Director

East Fayetteville

*WWFJ

88.1 MHz FM; 0.13 kw; 117 ft.; N35 0 4.4 W78 48 33.2
US
(910) 693-7729
License: East Fayetteville, Cumberland County, NC held by Highland Baptist Church.
Arbitron Metro Market: East Fayetteville, NC; *Format:* Christian
Bill Vaughn, President

Eden

WCLW

08-16-1970; 1130 kHz AM; 1 kw-D; N36 31 21 W79 45 55
116 S. Franklin St., Reidsville, NC 27320
(336) 634-1774; *Fax:* (336) 342-6497
www.reidsvillebaptist.org
License: Eden, Rockingham County, NC held by Dr. Jerry L. Carter dba Reidsville Baptist Church.
Target Audience: all
Dr. Jerry Carter, General Manager
Aaron Shelton, Producer

WLOE

12-20-1946; 1490 kHz AM; *Hrs Open:* 5 AM-10 PM; 1 kw-U, ND1; N36 30 21 W79 46 18 *Rebroadcasts:* Rebroadcasts WMYN Mayodan NC 100%.
P. O. Box 279, Mayodan, NC 27027 US
(336) 427-9696; *Fax:* (336) 548-4636
www.wloewmyn.com
License: Eden, NC held by Mayo Broadcasting Corp.
Nat'l Network: Salem Radio Network; USA
Format: Talk, Religious; *Hrs. of News Programming:* news progmg 30 hrs wkly; *No. News Employees:* 1; *Target Audience:* 25 plus; general; *Adv. Rates:* 25; 25; 25; 25
Richard Hall, President
Mike Moore, General Manager
Annette Moore, Station Manager

WPTI

03-20-1949; 94.5 MHz FM; 100 kw; Ant 981 ft; N36 20 48 W79 54 30
2-B PAI Park, Greensboro, NC 27409 US
(336) 822-2000; *Fax:* (336) 887-0104
www.945wpti.com
License: Eden, Rockingham County, NC held by Clear Channel Broadcasting Licenses Inc.
Group Owner: iHeartMedia; (acq 1996; grpsl).
Nat'l Reps: Clear Channel
Population Served: 15,871; *Arbitron Metro Market:* Greensboro-Winston Salem-High Point, NC; *Format:* Talk
Rich McMillan, Senior Vice President of Programming
Bobby Tatum, Sales Manager
Jason Newton, Director of Marketing and Promotions
Dennis Elliott, Digital Content Director

Edenton

WBXB

06-18-1976; 100.1 MHz FM; *Hrs Open:* 24; 50 kw; 302 ft.; N36 7 11 W76 35 29

Mailing Address: C/O Putbrese Hunsaker, P. O. Box 217, Sterling, VA 20167 US
Second Address: 1900 Paradise Rd., Edenton, NC 27932
(252) 482-8680; *Fax:* (252) 482-4260
License: Edenton, Chowan County, NC held by Willis Family Broadcasting Inc.
Group Owner: Willis Broadcasting Corp.; acq 3-4-92; grpsl;
Nat'l Network: American Urban
Arbitron Metro Market: Sterling, VA; *Format:* Gospel; *Hrs. of News Programming:* News progmg 8 hrs wkly; *Target Audience:* General.; *Adv. Rates:* 15; 12; 15; 12
Bishop L.E. Willis Sr., President
Toina Willis, General Manager

WZBO
11-01-1955; 1260 kHz AM; 1 kw-D, ND2; 0.034 kw-N, ND2; N36 5 0 W76 36 0
911 Parsonage Street, Elizabeth City, NC 27909 US
(252) 335-4379; *Fax:* (252) 338-5275
www.ecri.net
License: Edenton, NC held by East Carolina Radio of Elizabeth City Inc.
Group Owner: East Carolina Radio Group; (acq 3-12-90; $400,000 with co-located FM;
Arbitron Metro Market: Edenton, NC; *Format:* Tejano
Rick Loesch, President
Tom Charity, Operations Dir
Sam Walker, Programming Director

Elizabeth City

WCNC
09-01-1939; 1240 kHz AM; *Hrs Open:* 24; 1 kw-U, ND1; N36 18 38 W76 13 56
Mailing Address: 911 Parsonage Street, Elizabeth City, NC 27909 US
Second Address: 911 Parsonage St. Ext., Elizabeth City, NC 27909
(252) 335-4379; *Fax:* (252) 338-5275
www.ecri.net
psa@ecri.net
License: Elizabeth City, NC held by East Carolina Radio of Elizabeth City Inc.
Group Owner: East Carolina Radio Group; (acq 10-29-98; $230,000)
Arbitron Metro Market: Elizabeth City-Nags Head, NC; *Format:* Tejano
Rick Loesch, President
Cuervo Curtis, Operations Dir
Tom Charity, General Sales Mgr
Sam Walker, Programming Director

WGAI
11-02-1947; 560 kHz AM; *Hrs Open:* 24; 1 kw-D, DA2; 0.5 kw-N, DA2; N36 20 16 W76 14 49
444 N.W. Backwoods Rd., Moyock, NC 27958 US
(252) 435-2176
www.gregorygospel.com
License: Elizabeth City, Pasquotank County, NC held by Gregory Communications License Inc.
Group Owner: Gregory Communications License Inc.; (acq 9-25-2014).
Regional Network: Agrinet
Arbitron Metro Market: Elizabeth City, NC; *Format:* Gospel *Special Programming:* Relg 4 hrs, farm 7 hrs, Black 4 hrs, relg 4 hrs wk; *Hrs. of News Programming:* news progmg 30 hrs wkly; *No. News Employees:* 3 *Target Audience:* General.
George Gregory, General Manager

WKJX
08-21-1984; 96.7 MHz FM; *Hrs Open:* 24; 50 kw; 407 ft.; N36 12 10 W75 52 23
911 Parsonage Street Ext., Elizabeth City, NC 27909 US
(252) 338-0196; *Fax:* (252) 338-5275
www.ecri.net
pas@ecri.net
License: Elizabeth City, Pasquotank County, NC held by East Carolina Radio of Elizabeth City Inc.
Group Owner: East Carolina Radio Group; (acq 5-21-98; $475,000).
Nat'l Network: NBC Radio; Westwood One; *Regional Network:* N.C. News Net.
Format: Adult Contemp; *Hrs. of News Programming:* news progmg one hr wkly; *No. News Employees:* 1; *Target Audience:* 18-55.; *Adv. Rates:* 15; 15; 15; 12
Rick Loesch, President
Cuervo Curtis, Operations Dir
Tom Charity, General Sales Mgr
Sam Walker, Programming Director

*WRVS-FM
03-18-1986; 89.9 MHz FM; *Hrs Open:* 24; 41 kw; 230 ft.; N36 16 55 W76 12 44
1704 Weedsville Road, Campus Box 790, Elizabeth City, NC 27909 US
(252) 335-3400; *Fax:* (252) 335-3745
www.ecsu.edu/wrvs/
mybrown@mail.ecsu.edu
License: Elizabeth City, Pasquotank County, NC held by Elizabeth City State University.
Nat'l Network: NPR; PRI
Format: Variety/Diverse *Special Programming:* Jazz 6 hrs, Black 20 hrs, gospel 20; *Hrs. of News Programming:* news progmg 5 hrs wkly; *No. News Employees:* 1; *Target Audience:* 18-24; young adult, college
Willie Gilchnist, CEO
Melba Smith, General Manager
Ben Shaner, Chief Engineer

*WVRL
01-01-2003; 88.3 MHz FM; 50 kw; 446 ft; N36 18 40 W76 17 34
3700 Candlers Mountain Rd, Suite F, Lynchburg, VA 24502
(434) 582-3688; *Fax:* (434) 582-9594
www.myjourneyfm.com
License: Elizabeth City, Pasquotank County, NC held by Liberty University, Inc.
Group Owner: Liberty University, Inc.
Format: Christian
Chris Wygal, Operations Manager
Barry Armstrong, General Manager
Mike Weston, Programming Director

Elizabethtown

WBLA
08-03-1956; 1440 kHz AM; *Hrs Open:* 24
Mailing Address: 512 Peanuts Road, Elizabethtown, NC 28337 US
Second Address: Box 28, Clinton, NC 28329
(910) 862-2000; *Fax:* (910) 872-0100
www.wgqr1057.com
wgqr1057@carolina.net
License: Elizabethtown, NC held by Sound Business of Elizabethtown Inc.
Regional Network: N.C. News Net.
Format: Oldies *Special Programming:* Black gospel/relg 8 hrs wkly; *Hrs. of News Programming:* News progmg 5 hrs wkly;
Target Audience: 25-54.
Lee Hauser, President
Bruce Dickerson, Operations Dir
Patrick Dixon, General Manager
Al Radlein, Programming Director
Buddy Wommack, Chief Engineer
Paul Reese, Disc Jockey
Bill Monroe, Disc Jockey
Don Arnsan, Disc Jockey

Elkin

WIFM-FM
01-01-1949; 100.9 MHz FM; *Hrs Open:* 24; 600 w; 709 ft; N36 11 33 W80 50 59
Mailing Address: Box 1038, Elkin, NC 20120
Second Address: 813 N. Bridge St., Elkin, NC 28621
(336) 835-2511; *Fax:* (336) 835-5248
www.wifmradio.com
wifm@wifmradio.com
License: Elkin, Surry County, NC held by Yadkin Valley Broadcasting Corp.
Nat'l Network: ABC
No. News Employees: 1; *Target Audience:* 25-45.; *Adv. Rates:* 24; 22.25; 24; 19.50
Gary York, CEO

Elm City

WRSV
01-01-1949; 92.1 MHz FM; *Hrs Open:* 24; 2.35 kw; 531 ft.; N35 48 40 W77 44 33
P.O. Box 2665, Rocky Mount, NC 27802 US
(252) 937-7400; *Fax:* (252)443-5977
www.soul92jams.com
soul92_2000@yahoo.com
License: Elm City, Nash County, NC
Nat'l Network: Premiere Radio Networks
Arbitron Metro Market: Rocky Mount-Wil; *Format:* Urban Contemporary; *Hrs. of News Programming:* news progmg 3 hrs wkly; *No. News Employees:* 25; *Target Audience:* General; African American consumers of all age groups *Adv. Rates:* Call for rates

Sonya Johnson, Operations Dir
Charles Johnson, II, General Manager
Chuck Johnson, Music Director

Elon College

*WSOE
11-01-1978; 89.3 MHz FM; 0.5 kw; 121 ft.; N36 6 25 W79 30 22
100 Campus Drive, 6000 Campus Box, Elon College, NC 27244 US
(336) 278-7210; *Fax:* (336) 278-7298
www.wsoeelon.com
wsoe@elon.edu
License: Elon College, Alamance County, NC held by Elon University.
Format: Alternative
Mack White, General Manager
Cat Hollister, Programming Director
Caroline Arnold, Promotions Director

Enfield

WVRA
07-14-2007; 107.3 MHz FM; *Hrs Open:* 24; 4.1 kw; 278 ft; N36 09 59 W77 46 46
3700 Candlers Mountain Rd, Suite F, Lynchburg, VA
(800) 424-9594
www.myjourneyfm.com
License: Enfield, Halifax County, NC held by Liberty University, Inc.
Group Owner: Liberty University, Inc.
Arbitron Metro Market: Rocky Mount-Wilson, NC; *Format:* Christian

Erwin

*WUAW
05-11-1990; 88.3 MHz FM; *Hrs Open:* 24; 3 kw; 207 ft.; N35 20 15 W78 39 49
215 Maynard Lake Road, Erwin, NC 28339 US
(910) 897-8070; *Fax:* (910) 897-3148
www.wuawfm.com
wuaw883fm@gaggle.net
License: Erwin, Harnett County, NC held by Central Carolina Community College.
Arbitron Metro Market: Fayetteville, NC; *Format:* Variety/Diverse
Matt Garrett, President
Ron McLamb, General Manager
Dr. Jim Davis, Chief Engineer

Fair Bluff

WQTM
07-01-1988; 1480 kHz AM; *Hrs Open:* 24; 1 kw-D, 48 w-N; N34 19 23 W79 00 07
Mailing Address: Box 424, Cerrogordo, NC 28439
Second Address: 12045 Andrew Jackson Hwy., Fair Bluff, NC 28439
(910) 649-1480; *Fax:* (910) 649-7266
License: Fair Bluff, Columbus County, NC held by Rama Radio of North Carolina Inc.
Population Served: 250,000
Anthony Lee, Station Manager

WODR
01-01-2003; 105.3 MHz FM; 11 kw; 492 ft.; N34 17 1 W78 48 9
126 Memory Plaza, Whiteville, NC 28472 US
(910) 642-2013; *Fax:* (910) 642-2019
License: Fair Bluff, Columbus County, NC held by The Padner Group LLC
Arbitron Metro Market: Whiteville, NC; *Format:* Oldies
William Polk, General Manager

Fairmont

WFMO
07-13-1953; 860 kHz AM; 1 kw-D, ND1; 0.012 kw-N, ND1; N34 31 3 W79 6 19
5448 N Carolina 41, Fairmont, NC 28340 US
(910) 486-9438; *Fax:* (910) 484-4040
License: Fairmont, NC held by Pro Media Inc.
Regional Network: N.C. News Net.
Arbitron Metro Market: Fayetteville, NC; *Format:* Black, Gospel, 74 *Special Programming:* Farm 5 hrs wkly; *Target Audience:* 25-54.
James Clark, President

WSTS
08-01-1975; 100.9 MHz FM; 50 kw; 489 ft.; N34 16 17 W78 56 24
5448 N Carolina 41, Fairmont, NC 28340 US

(910) 628-6781; *Fax:* (910) 628-6648
wstf@carolina.net
License: Fairmont, Robeson County, NC held by Davidson Media Station WSTS Licensee LLC.
Group Owner: Davidson Media Group LLC; (acq 10-31-2005)
Regional Network: N.C. News Net.
Arbitron Metro Market: Fayetteville, NC; *Format:* Gospel
James Clark, General Manager
Shanna Todd, Programming Director

Fairview

WPEK

07-04-1997; 880 kHz AM
13 Summerlin Road, Asheville, NC 28806 US
(828) 257-2700; *Fax:* (828) 255-7850
www.880therevolution.com
brianhall@iheartmedia.com
License: Fairview, NC held by Clear Channel Broadcasting Licenses Inc.
Group Owner: iHeartMedia; (acq 3-21-01; grpsl).
Nat'l Network: CBS
Arbitron Metro Market: Asheville, NC; *Format:* Talk; *Target Audience:* 25-64; generally upscale adults
Gene Austin, Sales Manager
Brian Hall, Programming Director
Skip Wilson, Digital Sales Manager
Jessica Lee, Digital Content Director

Farmville

WGHB

12-12-1959; 1250 kHz AM; *Hrs Open:* 24; 5 kw-D, DA2; 2.5 kw-N, DA2; N35 36 17 W77 34 29
PO Box 3333, Greenville, NC 27836 US
(252) 317-1250; *Fax:* (252) 317-1255
www.pirateradio1250.com
License: Farmville, NC held by Pirate Media Group LLC
Nat'l Network: USA
Arbitron Metro Market: Greenville-New Bern-Jacksonville, NC; *Format:* Sports, Talk; *Hrs. of News Programming:* News progmg 8 hrs wkly; *Target Audience:* 25-54.
Troy Dreyfus, Owner
Jonathan Ellerbe, Owner

WRHD

03-24-1974; 94.3 MHz FM; *Hrs Open:* 24; 3.9 kw; Ant 407 ft; N35 36 25 W77 28 05
211 Commerce St., Suite C, Greenville, NC 27834
(252) 355-1037; *Fax:* (252) 355-2234
License: Farmville, Pitt County, NC held by Inner Banks Media LLC.
Group Owner: Inner Banks Media LLC; (acq 3-12-2007; grpsl)
Regional Network: N.C. News Net.
Population Served: 100,000; *Arbitron Metro Market:* Greenville-New Bern-Jacksonville, NC; *Hrs. of News Programming:* News progmg 3 hrs wkly; *Target Audience:* 25-54.
Henry Hinton, General Manager

Fayetteville

WAZZ

01-01-1947; 1490 kHz AM; *Hrs Open:* 24; 1 kw-D, 1 kw-N
508 Person St., Fayetteville, NC 28301 US
(910) 486-2000
www.sunny943.com
License: Fayetteville, Cumberland County, NC held by Beasley Media Group LLC
Group Owner: Beasley Broadcast Group Inc.; (acq 1996; $228,635).
Nat'l Reps: D & R Radio
Arbitron Metro Market: Charleston WV; *Format:* Adult Contemp
Mac Edwards, Vice President/Market Manager
Tricia Gallenbeck, Director of Sales
Danny Highsmith, Regional Vice President
Katy Lollis, General Sales Manager
Angela Godwin, General Sales Manager
Curt Nunnery, Sales Manager
InaCartrette, Advertising

WFAY

01-01-1947; 1230 kHz AM; *Hrs Open:* 24 *Rebroadcasts:* Simulcast with WCIE(AM) Spring Lake 100%
346 Wagoner Drive, Fayetteville, NC 28303 US
(910) 867-4129; *Fax:* (704) 537-9735
www.espnfay.com
wfayespnradio@gmail.com
License: Fayetteville, NC held by Norsan Consulting and Management Inc.
Group Owner: Norsan Consulting and Management Inc.; (acq 5-25-2006; $850,000)
Nat'l Network: ESPN Radio
Arbitron Metro Market: Fayetteville, NC; *Format:* Sports
Norberto Sanchez, CEO
Paul Lawing, General Manager

WFNC

01-01-1940; 640 kHz AM; *Hrs Open:* 24; 10 kw-D, ND1; 1 kw-N, ND1; N35 4 46 W78 55 58
1009 Drayton Road, Fayetteville, NC 28303 US
(910) 864-5222; *Fax:* (910) 864-3065
www.wfnc640am.com
jimcooke@cumulus.com
License: Fayetteville, NC held by Cumulus Licensing Corp.
Group Owner: Cumulus Media Inc.; (acq 3-12-2001; grpsl)
Nat'l Network: CBS; *Wire Services:* AP
Arbitron Metro Market: Fayetteville, NC; *Format:* News, News/Talk, 86; *Hrs. of News Programming:* news progmg 20 hrs wkly; *No. News Employees:* 4; *Target Audience:* 35 plus.
Cheryl Canders, General Manager
Jim Cooke, Programming Director
Brittany Barley, Promotions Manager

*WFSS

12-07-1977; 91.9 MHz FM; *Hrs Open:* 24; 100 kw; 351 ft.; N35 4 22 W78 53 27
1200 Murchison Road, Fayetteville, NC 28301 US
(910) 672-2650; *Fax:* (910) 672-1964
wfss.org
wfss@uncfsu.edu
License: Fayetteville, Cumberland County, NC held by Fayetteville State University Board of Trustees.
Nat'l Network: NPR; PRI; *Wire Services:* AP
Arbitron Metro Market: Fayetteville, NC; *Format:* Jazz, News *Special Programming:* Gospel 2 hrs, African rhythms 2 hrs, class 5 hrs,; *Hrs. of News Programming:* news progmg 38 hrs wkly; *No. News Employees:* 1 *Target Audience:* 18 plus; general
Dr. Marsha McLean, General Manager
Janet Wright, Programming Director
Kathy Klaus, News Director
Jimmy Miller, Music Director

WIDU

01-20-1958; 1600 kHz AM; *Hrs Open:* 24; 5 kw-D, DA2; 0.147 kw-N, DA2; N35 5 54 W78 53 12
Mailing Address: P. O. Box 2247, Fayetteville, NC 28302 US
Second Address: 1338 Bragg Blvd., Fayetteville, NC 28301
(910) 483-6111; *Fax:* (910) 483-6601
widu1600@aol.com
License: Fayetteville, NC held by Charles W. Cookman
Arbitron Metro Market: Fayetteville, NC; *Format:* Black, Gospel, 60, News/Talk, Talk
Wes Cookman, Owner
Sandra Cookman, Owner

WQSM

01-01-1947; 98.1 MHz FM; 100 kw; 830 ft.; N35 4 46 W78 55 58
1009 Drayton Road, Fayetteville, NC 28303 US
(910) 864-5222; *Fax:* (910) 864-3065
www.q98fm.com
jeffdavis@cumulus.com
License: Fayetteville, Cumberland County, NC
Arbitron Metro Market: Fayetteville, NC; *Format:* Contemporary Hits/Top 40; *Target Audience:* General.
Jeff Davis, Programming Director

*WYBH

01-01-2008; 91.1 MHz FM; 0.255 kw; 640 ft.; N35 3 35 W78 59 24 *Rebroadcasts:* Rebroadcasts WYFQ(AM) Charlotte 100%
P.O. Box 7300, Charlotte, NC 28241 US
(800) 888-7077
www.bbnradio.org
bbn@bbnmedia.org
License: Fayetteville, Cumberland County, NC held by Bible Broadcasting Network Inc.
Group Owner: Bible Broadcasting Network
Nat'l Network: Bible Bcstg Net
Arbitron Metro Market: Fayetteville, NC; *Format:* Christian
Lowell Davey, President
Jason Padgett, Operations Manager

Fletcher

WQNQ

02-05-1991; 104.3 MHz FM; *Hrs Open:* 24; 0.47 kw; 1145 ft.; N35 31 39 W82 29 49
13 Summerlin Road, Asheville, NC 28806 US
(828) 257-2700; *Fax:* (828) 255-7850
www.star1043.com
info@star1043.com
License: Fletcher, Henderson County, NC held by Clear Channel Broadcasting Licenses Inc.
Group Owner: iHeartMedia; (acq 3-21-2001; grpsl).
Arbitron Metro Market: Asheville, NC; *Format:* Contemporary Hits/Top 40 *Special Programming:* Relg 2 hrs, news/talk 5 hrs wkly; *Hrs. of News Programming:* news progmg 10 hrs wkly; *No. News Employees:* 2 *TargetAudience:* 25-54.; *Adv. Rates:* 40; 30; 40; 15
Caroline Earley, Sales Manager
Josh Michael, Programming Director
Skip Wilson, Digital Sales Manager
Jessica Lee, Digital Content Director

Forest City

WTPT

09-10-1947; 93.3 MHz FM; 93 kw; 2031 ft.; N35 16 19 W82 14 0
25 Garlington Road, Greenville, SC 29615 US
(864) 271-9200; *Fax:* (864) 242-1567
www.newrock933.com
License: Forest City, Rutherford County, NC held by Entercom Greenville License LLC.
Group Owner: Entercom Communications Corp.; (acq 10-7-2005; grpsl).
Arbitron Metro Market: Greenville, SC; *Format:* Rock/AOR; *No. News Employees:* 1
Randy Cables, General Sales Mgr
Mark Hendrix, Programming Director
Roy Hummers, Promotions

WWOL

09-10-1947; 780 kHz AM; *Hrs Open:* Sunrise-sunset; 10 kw-D, NDD; N35 21 2 W81 54 4
1381 West Main Street, Forest City, NC 28043 US
(828) 245-0078; *Fax:* (828) 245-8528
www.wwol780.com
wwol@wwol780.com
License: Forest City, NC held by Holly Springs Baptist Church.
Nat'l Network: USA
Arbitron Metro Market: Forest City, NC; *Format:* Gospel, Religious *Special Programming:* Our community forum, NC family policy issues; *No. News Employees:* 3; *Target Audience:* General.
Wade Huntley, President
Ray Davis, Operations Dir
Terri Frashier, General Sales Mgr
Jean Bruce, News Director

WAGY

10-15-1958; 1320 kHz AM; 1 kw-D, DAN; 0.5 kw-N, DAN; N35 21 19 W81 52 52
P. O. Box 280, Forest City, NC 28043 US
(828) 245-9887; *Fax:* (828) 245-9880
License: Forest City, NC held by WAGY Inc.
Arbitron Metro Market: Forest City, NC; *Format:* Country
Malcolm Watson, General Manager

Fort Dodge

*KWOP(FM)

88.7 MHz FM; 200 watts; 37.8 meters; N42 33 18.1 W94 07 46.6
6704 NC Highway 8 South, Germantown, NC 27019 USA
(336) 591-9076
License: Fort Dodge, IA held by Church Planters of America
Arbitron Metro Market: Fort Dodge, IA
William Danny Hawkins, President

Franklin

*WFQS

03-31-1989; 91.3 MHz FM; *Hrs Open:* 24; 0.265 kw horiz, 0.255 kw vert; 2303 ft.; N35 10 24 W83 34 52 *Rebroadcasts:* Rebroadcasts WCQS(FM) Asheville 100%
73 Broadway, Asheville, NC 28801 US
(828) 210-4800; *Fax:* (828) 210-4801
www.wcqs.org
info@wcqs.org
License: Franklin, Macon County, NC held by Western N.C. Public Radio Inc.
Nat'l Network: NPR; PRI
Format: Jazz, News *Special Programming:* Folk 9 hrs wkly; *Hrs. of News Programming:* news progmg 35 hrs wkly; *No. News Employees:* 1; *Target Audience:* 25 plus.
Lee Wilcher, Operations Dir
Edward Subkis, General Manager
Steve Busey, General Sales Mgr
Barbara Sayer, Programming Director
David Hurand, News Director
Tom Spaight, Chief Engineer
Richard Kowal, Music Director
Vicky Gerald,Taffic Manager
Trent Henley, Public Service Announcements Producer
Michelle Keenan, Membership Director
Dick Kowal, Director of Music Programming

WFSC
05-05-1957; 1050 kHz AM; *Hrs Open:* 24/7; 5 kw-D, 0.153 kw-N, ND2; N35 12 40 W83 22 07
Mailing Address: P. O. Box 470, Franklin, NC 28744 US
Second Address: 180 Radio Hill Rd., Franklin, NC 28734
(828) 524-4418; *Fax:* (828) 524-2788
www.1050wfsc.com
gyoung@gacaradio.com
License: Franklin, Macon County, NC held by Sutton Radiocasting Corp.
Group Owner: Georgia-Carolina Radiocasting Companies; (acq 12-14-2001; grpsl).
Nat'l Network: CBS; ABC
Format: News, Oldies; *Hrs. of News Programming:* Local news progmg 12 hrs wkly; *No. News Employees:* 1; *Target Audience:* 35 plus.
Douglas M. Sutton Jr., President
George Young, Operations Manager
Sean Gibson, Vice President & General Manager
Dustin Short, News Director
Benita Snyder, Office Manager

WPFJ
05-24-1979; 1480 kHz AM; *Hrs Open:* 24
106 Palmer Street, Franklin, NC 28734 US
(828) 369-5033; *Fax:* (828) 369-3197
www.wpfj.com
License: Franklin, NC held by Drake Enterprises Ltd.
Nat'l Network: Salem Radio Network
Format: Religious; *Hrs. of News Programming:* News progmg 12 hrs wkly; *Target Audience:* 25-54.
Johnny Lee, General Sales Mgr
Brenda Wooten, Promotions Manager
Rick Cruse, Chief Engineer

WNCC
09-01-1965; 104.1 MHz FM; *Hrs Open:* 24; 0.115 kw; N35 19 38 W83 20 9
Mailing Address: P.O. Box 470, Franklin, NC 28744 US
Second Address: 180 Radio Hill Rd., Franklin, NC 28734
(828) 524-4418; *Fax:* (828) 524-2788
1041wncc.com
gyoung@gacaradio.com
License: Franklin, Macon County, NC held by Sutton Radiocasting Corporation
Group Owner: Georgia-Carolina Radiocasting Companies
Nat'l Network: ABC; *Regional Network:* Jones Radio Network
Format: Country *Special Programming:* NASCAR, Local Sports; *Hrs. of News Programming:* news progmg 6 hrs wkly; *No. News Employees:* 1; *Target Audience:* 25 plus.
Douglas M. Sutton, Jr., President
George Young, Operations Manager
Sean Gibson, VP/General Manager
Keith Giles, Programming Director
Dustin Short, News Director

Franklinton

*WRTP
07-04-1994; 88.5 MHz FM; *Hrs Open:* 24; 24 kw; 479 ft.; N36 17 44 W78 6 21
7610 Falls of Neuse Road, Raleigh, NC 27615 US
(919) 256-9787; *Fax:* (919) 256-9559
www.hisradiowrtp.com
Management@hisradiowrtp.com
License: Franklinton, Halifax County, NC held by Radio Training Network Inc.
Nat'l Network: Salem Radio Network; *Nat'l Reps:* Salem
Arbitron Metro Market: Raleigh, NC; *Format:* Christian; *Hrs. of News Programming:* News progmg 14 hrs wkly; *Target Audience:* 25-54; Christian
Mark Parker, General Manager
Charlyne Laudrille, Underwriting Representative
Donna C, Public Service Director
Johanna, Director Of Support

Fuquay-Varina

WNNL
12-01-1980; 103.9 MHz FM; *Hrs Open:* 24; 7.9 kw; 577 ft.; N35 35 47 W78 45 18
US
(919) 848-9736
www.thelightnc.com
mmarinaro@radio-one.com
License: Fuquay-Varina, Wake County, NC held by Radio One Licenses LLC.
Group Owner: Radio One Inc.; (acq 11-8-01; grpsl).
Nat'l Network: ABC; *Nat'l Reps:* Christal
Arbitron Metro Market: Raleigh, NC; *Format:* Gospel; *Hrs. of News Programming:* News progmg 20 hrs wkly; *Target Audience:* 25-54; educated, upper income, professionals
Alfred Liggins, President/CEO

Garner

WRTG
08-11-1969; 1000 kHz AM; *Hrs Open:* Daytime Only; 1 kw-D, NDD; N35 43 50 W78 36 12 *Rebroadcasts:* Rebroadcasts WRTP(AM) Chapel Hill 100%
P.O. Box 15400, Durham, NC 27704 US
(919) 477-7222; *Fax:* (919) 477-4424
estuardovaldemar@hotmail.com
License: Garner, NC held by Estuardo Valdemar Rodriguez and Leonor Rodriguez.
Group Owner: Radio La Grande; (acq 2-2-2005; grpsl)
Nat'l Network: USA
Arbitron Metro Market: Raleigh-Durham,
Leonor Rodriguez, President
Estuardo Rodriguez, General Manager

Garysburg

*WZRU
12-08-1972; 90.1 MHz FM; *Hrs Open:* 24; 11 kw; 505 ft.; N36 14 39 W77 34 40
P.O. Box 2061, Bristol, TN 37621 US
(252) 308-0885; *Fax:* (252) 537-3333
www.wzru.org
License: Garysburg, Halifax County, NC held by Roanoke Valley Communications Inc.
Nat'l Network: NPR
Format: Adult Contemp *Special Programming:* Gospel 6 hrs, jazz 6 hrs, folk 5 hrs, oldies 4 hrs; *Hrs. of News Programming:* news progmg 30 hrs wkly; *No. News Employees:* 2; *Target Audience:* 35 plus; communityoriented, above-average education
Allen Garrett, General Manager

Gaston

WTRG
11-28-1988; 97.9 MHz FM; *Hrs Open:* 24; 1.35 kw; 489 ft.; N36 27 38 W77 33 52
Mailing Address: PO Box 910, Roanoke Rapids, NC 27870 US
Second Address: 3 E. First St., Weldon, NC 27850
(252) 578-3867
www.thegreat98fm.com
License: Gaston, Northampton County, NC held by First Media Radio LLC.
Group Owner: First Media Radio LLC; (acq 7-22-2003; grpsl)
Regional Network: N.C. News Net.; Va. News Net.
Format: Oldies; *Hrs. of News Programming:* News progmg 2 hrs wkly; *Target Audience:* 21-54.
Cody Clark, Operations Dir
Al Haskins, General Manager

Gastonia

WBAV-FM
09-01-1947; 101.9 MHz FM; 99 kw; 988 ft.; N35 13 57 W81 16 35
1520 South Blvd., Suite 300, Charlotte, NC 28203 US
(704) 522-1103
www.v1019.com
License: Gastonia, Gaston County, NC held by WKIS License Limited Partnership
Group Owner: Beasley Broadcast Group Inc.; (acq 11-13-98; grpsl).
Nat'l Reps: Christal
Arbitron Metro Market: Charlotte, NC; *Format:* Adult Contemp
Jacque Freeman, Sales Manager
Jamillah Muhammad, Program Director and Promotions Manager
Bill Schoening, Senior Vice President/Market Manager
Amanda Knepp, Marketing Director
Jenna Land, Digital Sales Manager

WGNC
03-01-1939; 1450 kHz AM; *Hrs Open:* 24; 1 kw-U, ND1; N35 16 32 W81 12 4
405 Neisler Drive, Kings Mountain, NC 28086 US
(704) 460-6049
1450am@gmail.com
License: Gastonia, NC held by SN Radio
Group Owner: SN Radio; (acq 10-6-2006; $1.5 million with WOHS(AM) Shelby)
Nat'l Network: ABC; CBS Radio; Westwood One; *Regional Network:* N.C. News Net.
Arbitron Metro Market: Charlotte-Gastonia-Rock Hill, NC-SC; *Format:* Oldies, Sports; *Hrs. of News Programming:* news progmg 5 hrs wkly; *No. News Employees:* 1; *Target Audience:* 18-49.; *Adv. Rates:* 14.20;14.20; 14.20; 14.20
D. Mark Boyd III, President
Terresa Hastings, Operations Dir
Calvin Hastings, General Manager
Harold Watson, General Sales Mgr
Mike Slade, Programming Director
Lori Deitz, Promotions Manager
Anna McGinnis, News Director
AndyFoster, Music Director

Gatesville

WQDK
09-02-1968; 99.3 MHz FM; *Hrs Open:* 24; 3.7 kw; 420 ft.; N36 16 29 W76 43 17
443 Hwy. 42 W., Ahoskie, NC 27910 US
(252) 332-7993; *Fax:* (252) 332-6887
License: Gatesville, Gates County, NC held by Icon Broadcasting Inc.
Group Owner: Icon Broadcasting Inc.; (acq 10-22-2015).
Regional Network: Agrinet
Arbitron Metro Market: Elizabeth City-Nags Head, NC; *Format:* Country *Special Programming:* Farm 7 hrs wkly
Amy Bristle, Sales Executive

Goldsboro

WFMC
11-11-1951; 730 kHz AM; *Hrs Open:* 24; 1 kw-D, 98 w-N; N35 22 25 W78 00 41
2581 Highway 70 West, Goldsboro, NC 27530
(919) 734-4211; *Fax:* (919) 736-3876
tdenton@curtismedia.com
License: Goldsboro, Wayne County, NC held by New Age Communications Inc.
Group Owner: Curtis Media Group; (acq 6-95; $300,000)
Population Served: 120,000; *Arbitron Metro Market:* Raleigh-Durham, NC; *Hrs. of News Programming:* news progmg 10 hrs wkly; *No. News Employees:* 1; *Target Audience:* 25+.
Donald Curtis, President
Bill Johnston, General Manager
Averill Williams, Programming Director
Robyn Wade, News Director

WGBR
01-01-1939; 1150 kHz AM; *Hrs Open:* 24
2581 US Highway 70W, Goldsboro, NC 27530 US
(919) 734-3336; *Fax:* (919) 736-3876
www.wgbr.com
License: Goldsboro, NC held by New Age Communications L.P.
Group Owner: Curtis Media Group; (acq 2-15-89; $2.2 million with co-located FM;
Nat'l Network: CNN Radio; *Regional Network:* N.C. News Net.; *Wire Services:* AP
Format: News, News/Talk, 86; *Hrs. of News Programming:* news progmg 11 hrs wkly; *No. News Employees:* 1; *Target Audience:* 25 plus.
Donald Curtis, President
Kari DelaCruz, Operations Dir
Bill Johnston, General Manager
Wayne Alley, Programming Director
Robyn Wade, News Director

WBZJ
01-01-1946; 96.9 MHz FM; *Hrs Open:* 24; 100 kw; 984 ft.; N35 23 52 W78 8 7
3012 Highwoods Blvd, Raleigh, NC 27604 US
(919) 790-9392; *Fax:* (919) 736-3876
License: Goldsboro, Wayne County, NC
Group Owner: Curtis Media Group
Regional Network: N.C. News Net.; *Wire Services:* AP
Arbitron Metro Market: Raleigh-Durham, NC; *Format:* Tejano, Spanish; *Hrs. of News Programming:* News progmg 2 hrs wkly; *Target Audience:* 25-54.
Jon Bloom, General Manager

WSSG
10-22-1955; 1300 kHz AM; 1 kw-D, ND1; 0.049 kw-N, ND1; N35 24 8 W78 1 20
P. O. Box 1141, Goldsboro, NC 27530 US
(919) 734-1300
License: Goldsboro, NC held by Robert Swinson
Arbitron Metro Market: Goldsboro, NC; *Format:* Christian
Reginald Swinson, General Manager

Graham

WSML
12-02-1967; 1200 kHz AM; *Hrs Open:* 24 *Rebroadcasts:* Rebroadcasts WSJS-AM 600, Winston-Salem NC 90%
3012 Highwoods Blvd., Suite 201, Raleigh, NC 27604 US

(336) 777-3900; *Fax:* (336) 777-3915
www.triadsports.com
License: Graham, NC held by Crescent Media Group LLC.
Group Owner: Curtis Media Group; (acq 2-14-2007; grpsl)
Arbitron Metro Market: Greensboro-Winston Salem-High Point, NC; *Format:* News, News/Talk, 86 *Special Programming:* Black 18 hrs wkly; *Adv. Rates:* 15; 15; 15; 12
Tom Hamilton, General Manager
Larry Ingold, Programming Director
George Newman, Chief Engineer

Granite Falls

WYCV

02-22-1963; 900 kHz AM; *Hrs Open:* 5 AM-11 PM (M-S); 6 AM-9 PM (Su)
P. O. Box 486, Granite Falls, NC 28630 US
(828) 396-3361; *Fax:* (828) 396-9193
www.gospel9.com
License: Granite Falls, NC held by Freedom Broadcasting Corp.
Nat'l Network: USA; AP Radio
Arbitron Metro Market: Granite Falls, NC; *Format:* Gospel, Religious *Special Programming:* Gospel; *Hrs. of News Programming:* news progmg 2 hrs wkly; *No. News Employees:* 1; *Target Audience:* 3-100.
Marvin Sizemore, President
Buddy Sizemore, General Manager
Clyde Smith, General Sales Mgr
Teresa Sizemore, News Director
Ted Fuller, Engineering Dir

Greensboro

WCOG

05-22-1948; 1320 kHz AM; *Hrs Open:* 24; 5 kw-D, DA2; 5 kw-N, DA2; N36 9 1 W79 54 48
875 W. 5th Street, Winston Salem, NC 27101 US
(336) 777-3900; *Fax:* (336) 777-3915
www.triadsports.com
comments@triadsports.com
License: Greensboro, NC held by Radio Disney Group LLC.
Group Owner: ABC Inc.; (acq 5-6-2005; $1.675 million)
Arbitron Metro Market: Winston Salem, NC; *Format:* Children; *Target Audience:* General.
Gerry Franzer., Station Manager
Chris Nowak, Promotions Manager

WEAL

10-05-1962; 1510 kHz AM; *Hrs Open:* Sunrise-sunset
7819 National Service Road, Greensboro, NC 27409 US
(336) 605-5200; *Fax:* (336) 605-0138
www.1510weal.com/
License: Greensboro, NC held by Entercom Greensboro License LLC
Group Owner: Entercom Communications Corp.
Nat'l Reps: McGavren Guild
Arbitron Metro Market: Greensboro, NC; *Format:* Gospel; *Target Audience:* 25-54; North Carolina A&T State Univ
Shilynne Cole, Programming Director

WKEW

02-16-1942; 1400 kHz AM; *Hrs Open:* 24 hrs 7 days; 1 kw-U, ND1; N36 4 0 W79 47 49
4405 Providence Ln., Winston-Salem, NC 27106 US
(336) 759-0363; *Fax:* (336) 759-0366
www.lightthetriad.com
License: Greensboro, NC held by Truth Broadcasting Corp.
Group Owner: Truth Broadcasting Corp.; acq 8-9-00; $800,000)
Arbitron Metro Market: Greensboro-Winston Salem-High Point, NC; *Format:* Gospel; *Target Audience:* 35 plus; African-American; *Adv. Rates:* 206; 206; 20; 20
Stuart Epperson, General Manager

WSMW

01-09-1958; 98.7 MHz FM; *Hrs Open:* 24; 100 kw; 1230 ft.; N35 56 42 W79 51 45
7819 National Service Road, Suite 401, Greensboro, NC 27409 US
(336) 605 5200; *Fax:* (336) 387-7206
www.987simon.com
mcassady@intercom.com
License: Greensboro, Guilford County, NC held by Entercom Greensboro License LLC.
Group Owner: Entercom Communications Corp.
Arbitron Metro Market: Greensboro-Winston Salem-High Point, NC; *Format:* Adult Contemp; *Target Audience:* 18-49.
Travis Moore, General Sales Mgr
Sean Sellers, Programming Director
Brent Millar, Vice President/Market Manager

*WNAA

01-01-1979; 90.1 MHz FM; *Hrs Open:* 24; 10 kw; 433 ft.; N36 4 58 W79 46 8
1601 East Market Street, Greensboro, NC 27411 US
(336) 334-7936; *Fax:* (336) 334-7960
wnaamail@gmail.com
License: Greensboro, Guilford County, NC held by North Carolina Agricultural & Technical State University.
Arbitron Metro Market: Greensboro, NC; *Format:* Gospel, Jazz *Special Programming:* Blues 4 hrs, Reggae 5 hrs, Gospel Hip Hop 3 hrs; *Hrs. of News Programming:* News prog 5 hrs wkly; *Target Audience:* 35-45; general
D. Cherie Lofton, Operations Dir
Tony Welborne, General Manager
Cherie Lofton, Programming Director
Larry Allen, Chief Engineer

WPET

01-01-1954; 950 kHz AM
7819 National Service Road, Suite 401, Greensboro, NC 27409 US
(336) 605-5200; *Fax:* (336) 387-7206
www.wpetam950.com
License: Greensboro, NC held by Entercom Greensboro License LLC.
Group Owner: Entercom Communications Corp.; (acq 1-28-2002; $20.5 million with co-located FM).
Arbitron Metro Market: Greensboro-Winston Salem-High Point, NC; *Format:* Gospel; *Target Audience:* 25-54.
Travis Moore, General Sales Mgr
Sean Sellers, Programming Director
Brent Millar, Vice President/Market Manager

*WQFS

01-01-1970; 90.9 MHz FM; *Hrs Open:* 24; 1.9 kw; 200 ft.; N36 5 39 W79 53 21
5800 W. Friendly Avenue, Greensboro, NC 27410 US
(336) 316-2352,(336) 316-2444; *Fax:* (336) 316-2949
www.guilford.edu
License: Greensboro, Guilford County, NC held by Guilford College Board of Trustees.
Arbitron Metro Market: Greensboro-Winston Salem-High Point, NC; *Format:* Variety/Diverse; *Hrs. of News Programming:* news progmg 4 hrs wkly; *No. News Employees:* 1; *Target Audience:* 15-50.
Elizabeth Bass, General Manager

WQMG

07-08-1962; 97.1 MHz FM; *Hrs Open:* 24; 100 kw; 1073 ft.; N35 56 42 W79 51 45
7819 National Service Road, Greensboro, NC 27409 US
(336) 605-5200; *Fax:* (336) 605-0138
www.wqmg.com
info@wqmg.com
License: Greensboro, Guilford County, NC held by Entercom Greensboro License LLC
Group Owner: Entercom Communications Corp.; (acq 12-13-99; grpsl).
Nat'l Network: ABC; *Nat'l Reps:* McGavren Guild
Arbitron Metro Market: Greensboro-Winston Salem-High Point, NC; *Format:* Black, Blues; *No. News Employees:* 1; *Target Audience:* 18-49; Black
Shilynne Cole, Programming Director

*WUAG

07-20-1964; 103.1 MHz FM; *Hrs Open:* 24; 18.1 w; 230 ft; N36 03 51 W79 48 37
402 Tate Street,Brown Building Room 210, UNCG, Greensboro, NC 27412
(336) 334-5450
www.wuag.net
wuag@uncg.edu
License: Greensboro, Guilford County, NC held by University of North Carolina at Greensboro Board of Trustees.
Population Served: 273,425; *Arbitron Metro Market:* Greensboro, NC *Special Programming:* Hip hop 6 hrs, world music 2 hrs, bluegrass 2 hrs,; *Hrs. of News Programming:* news progmg 2 hrs wkly; *No. News Employees:* 4 *Target Audience:* 12-40; high school & college students; *Adv. Rates:* 10; 10; 10; 10
Randall Quillian, General Manager
Gabrielle McNair, Programming Director

WWBG

01-01-1998; 1470 kHz AM
PO Box 690036, Charlotte, NC 28227 US
(704) 634-6706; *Fax:* (704) 634-6706
www.radioadoracion.com
radioadoracion@hotmail.com
License: Greensboro, NC held by Davidson Media Station WWBG Licensee LLC.
Group Owner: Davidson Media Group LLC; (acq 3-25-2005; swap with WTOB(AM) Winston-Salem for WDRU(AM) Wake Forest).
Nat'l Reps: Salem
Arbitron Metro Market: Greensboro, NC; *Format:* Tejano
Jose Isasiÿ, President & CEO
Roger Martinez, General Manager
Hernando Santos Ramirez, Executive Editor
German Navy, Commercial Director
Roberto Aisenberg, Commercial Manager

Greenville

WNCT

01-01-1940; 1070 kHz AM; *Hrs Open:* 24; 50 kw-D, 10 kw-N; N35 36 8 W77 25 35
207 Glenburnie Dr., New Bern, NC 28560 US
(252) 757-0011
www.beachboogieandblues.com
License: Greenville, Pitt County, NC held by Beasley Media Group LLC
Group Owner: Beasley Broadcast Group Inc.; (acq 1996)
Arbitron Metro Market: Greenville, NC; *Format:* Blues; *Target Audience:* General.
Brad Hood, General Manager
John Sheftic, Regional/National Sales

WNCT-FM

12-22-1963; 107.9 MHz FM; *Hrs Open:* 24; 100 kw; 1699 ft.; N35 21 55 W77 23 38
2929 Radio Station Rd., Greenville, NC 27834 US
(252) 757-0011; *Fax:* (252) 757-0286
www.1079wnct.com
License: Greenville, Pitt County, NC held by Beasley Media Group LLC
Group Owner: Beasley Broadcast Group Inc.
Arbitron Metro Market: Greenville, NC *TV Affiliate:* WNCT-TV affil.; *Format:* Oldies
Brad Hood, General Manager
Richard Banks, Chief Engineer
Bruce Simel, Market Manager
John Sheftic, Director of Sales

*WZMB

02-02-1982; 91.3 MHz FM; *Hrs Open:* 8am - 5pm; 0.28 kw; 135 ft.; N35 36 1 W77 21 53
Mendenhall Student Ctr., Greenville, NC 27858 US
(252) 328-4751; *Fax:* (252) 328-4773
www.ecu.edu/cs-studentaffairs/wzmb
wzmb@ecu.edu
License: Greenville, Pitt County, NC held by East Carolina University Media Board.
Nat'l Network: ABC
Arbitron Metro Market: Greenville, NC; *Format:* Alternative, Variety/Diverse; *Hrs. of News Programming:* News progmg 12 hrs wkly; *Target Audience:* 18-24; univ students
Michael Crenshaw, General Manager
Rashaad Toney, Music Manager
Jared Roach, Production Manager

Grifton

WXNR

09-11-1989; 99.5 MHz FM; *Hrs Open:* 24; 16.5 kw; 843 ft.; N35 12 7 W77 11 15
207 Glenburnie Dr., New Bern, NC 28560 US
(252) 633-1500; *Fax:* (252) 633-6546
License: Grifton, Pitt County, NC held by Beasley Media Group LLC
Group Owner: Beasley Broadcast Group Inc.
Nat'l Reps: D & R Radio
Arbitron Metro Market: Greenville, NC; *Format:* Rock/AOR; *Target Audience:* 18-34.
Bruce Simel, Market Manager
John Sheftic, Director of Sales
Cindy Miller, Programming Director

Hamlet

WJSG

08-25-1991; 104.3 MHz FM; 6 kw; 489 ft.; N34 48 39 W79 43 38
180 Airport Rd, Rockingham, NC 28379 US
(910) 895-3787; *Fax:* (910) 895-8811
www.g104fm.com
License: Hamlet, Richmond County, NC held by Jackson Broadcasting Co.
Format: Christian, Country
Sherrell Jackson, General Manager
Jerry Stout, News Director

WKDX
06-30-1957; 1250 kHz AM; 1 kw-D, ND1; 0.08 kw-N, ND1; N34 53 6 W79 40 50
208 South Rutherford St., Wadesboro, NC 28170 US
(910) 582-1997; *Fax:* (910) 582-1920
www.wkdx.net
wkdx@carolina55.com
License: Hamlet, NC held by The McLaurin Group
Format: Gospel
Howard McLaurin Jr., President

Harrisburg

WQNC
02-01-1958; 100.9 MHz FM; *Hrs Open:* 24; 5.2 kw; 107 meters; N35 22 40 W80 11 38
8809 Lenox Pointe Dr., Suite A, Charlotte, NC 28273 US
(704) 548-7800; *Fax:* (704) 548-7810
www.927theblock.com
License: Harrisburg, NC held by Radio One of North Carolina LLC.
Group Owner: Radio One Inc.; (acq 11-12-2004; $11.5 million).
Population Served: 4,646; *Arbitron Metro Market:* Windom MN;
Format: Urban Contemporary
Gary Weiss, General Manager

WPZS
01-01-1995; 100.9 MHz FM; 6 kw; Ant 328 ft; N35 16 20 W80 45 54
8809 Lenox Pointe Dr., Charlotte, PA 28273 US
(704) 548-7800; *Fax:* (704) 548-7810
www.praisecharlotte.com
License: Harrisburg, Cabarrus County, NC held by Radio One of North Carolina LLC.
Group Owner: Radio One Inc.; (acq 6-7-2000)
Nat'l Reps: McGavren Guild
Population Served: 751,087; *Arbitron Metro Market:* Charlotte-Gastonia-Rock Hill, NC-SC; *Format:* Gospel; *Target Audience:* Adults 25-54.
Gary Weiss, General Manager

Hatteras

WCMS-FM
05-01-1999; 94.5 MHz FM; *Hrs Open:* 24; 100 kw; 981 ft.; N35 29 10 W75 59 58
103-D W. Wood Hill Dr., Nags Head, NC 27959 US
(252) 480-4655; *Fax:* (252) 441-8063
www.wcms.com
License: Hatteras, Dare County, NC held by Max Radio of the Carolinas Licenses LLC.
Group Owner: MAX Media L.L.C.; (acq 11-12-2002; grpsl)
Nat'l Network: Jones Radio Networks
Arbitron Metro Market: Hatteras, NC; *Format:* Country; *No. News Employees:* 2; *Adv. Rates:* 35; 35; 35; 35
Bob Davis, Sales Manager

WYND-FM
03-01-1995; 97.1 MHz FM; *Hrs Open:* 24; 59 kw; 558 ft.; N35 27 48 W76 2 7
637 Harbor Road, Wanohese, NC 27981 US
(252) 475-1888; *Fax:* (252) 475-1881
www.klove.com
License: Hatteras, Dare County, NC held by CapSan Media LLC.
Group Owner: CapSan Media LLC; (acq 6-30-2006; grpsl)
Nat'l Network: Westwood One
Arbitron Metro Market: Hatteras, NC; *Format:* Country
William Whitlow, President
Hunt Thomas, Operations Dir

Havelock

WANG
06-16-1962; 1330 kHz AM; *Hrs Open:* Sunrise-sunset; 1 kw-D; N34 55 24 W76 56 37 *Rebroadcasts:* Rebroadcasts WSSM-FM Morehead City 100%
1361 Colony Dr., New Bern, NC 75050
(252) 639-7900; *Fax:* (252) 639-7979
License: Havelock, Craven County, NC held by NM Licensing LLC.
Group Owner: NextMedia Group Inc.; (acq 11-26-2001; grpsl)
Nat'l Reps: Eastman Radio
Population Served: 5,283; *Arbitron Metro Market:* Greenville-New Bern-Jacksonville, NC; *Target Audience:* 25-54
Larry Weiss, General Manager

***WLVG**
11-12-1971; 105.1 MHz FM; 18.5 kw; Ant 384 ft; N34 45 07 W76 52 57 *Rebroadcasts:* Rebroadcasts KLVR(FM) Middletown, CA 100%
1705 West NW Highway, Grapevine, TX 76051
(916) 251-1600; *Fax:* (916) 251-1650
www.klove.com
License: Havelock, Craven County, NC held by Educational Media Foundation
Group Owner: NextMedia Group Inc.; (acq 5-27-2010)
Population Served: 17,035; *Arbitron Metro Market:* Greenville-New Bern-Jacksonville, NC
Mike Novak, President
Larry Weiss, Operations Dir

Henderson

WHNC
06-20-1945; 890 kHz AM; *Hrs Open:* Sunrise-sunset
Rebroadcasts: Rebroadcasts WCBQ(AM) Oxford 100%
Mailing Address: 1 Alvin Augustus Jones Way, Oxford, NC 27565 US
Second Address: 1 Alvin Augustus Jones Way, Oxford, NC 27565
(919) 693-3540; *Fax:* (919) 693-9054
www.dralvinjones.com
License: Henderson, NC held by The Paradise Network Of North Carolina (TPN)
Nat'l Reps: Keystone (unwired net) *Regional Reps:* T-N.
Format: Gospel, Talk; *Hrs. of News Programming:* news progmg 7 hrs wkly; *No. News Employees:* 1; *Target Audience:* 18 plus.
Alvin Jones, CEO

WIZS
05-01-1955; 1450 kHz AM; *Hrs Open:* 24; 1 kw-U, ND1; N36 19 31 W78 24 36
Box 1299, Henderson, NC 27536 US
(252) 492-3001; *Fax:* (252) 492-3002
www.wizs.com
wizs@vance.net
License: Henderson, NC held by Rose Farm and Rentals Inc.
Regional Network: N.C. News Net.
Format: Country, Oldies, 86 *Special Programming:* TownTalk, Tradio, Sports Mayhem; *Hrs. of News Programming:* news proraming 6 hrs wkly; *No. News Employees:* 2; *Target Audience:* 25 plus; fans of Country, Oldiesand Beach music; *Adv. Rates:* 22.50; 22.50; 22.50; 22.50
George Rush, General Manager
Don Simmons, Programming Director
John Rose III, Chief Engineer
Dan Simmons, Programming Director

***WYFL**
01-01-1948; 92.5 MHz FM; 100 kw; 1020 ft.; N36 13 30 W78 12 10
120 E. Belle St., Henderson, NC 27536 US
(252) 492-9511
www.bbnradio.org
bbn@bbnmedia.org
License: Henderson, Vance County, NC held by Bible Broadcasting Network Inc.
Group Owner: Bible Broadcasting Network; acq 10-3-81; $335,000;
Arbitron Metro Market: Henderson, NC; *Format:* Religious; *Target Audience:* General.
Jason Padgett, Operations Manager

Hendersonville

WHKP
10-24-1946; 1450 kHz AM; *Hrs Open:* 25.?Â ?
P.O. Box 2470, Hendersonville, NC 28793 US
(828) 693-9061; *Fax:* (828) 696-9329
www.whkp.com
1450@whkp.com
License: Hendersonville, NC held by Radio Hendersonville Inc.
Nat'l Network: ABC Information & Entertainment
Format: Variety/Diverse *Special Programming:* Var 18 hrs wkly; *Hrs. of News Programming:* 10 hrs news progmg wkly; *No. News Employees:* 10; *Target Audience:* 25 plus; middle to upper income; *Adv. Rates:* 22;22; 22; 11
Art Cooley, General Manager
Larry Freeman, Programming Director
Larry Freeman, News Director
Marge Duncan, Traffic Director

WMYI
04-15-1958; 102.5 MHz FM; *Hrs Open:* 24; kw
Mailing Address: P.O. Box 100, Greenville, SC 29602 US
Second Address: 101 N. Main St., Suite 1000, Greenville, SC 29601
(864) 235-1025; *Fax:* (864) 242-2536
www.my1025.com
License: Hendersonville, Henderson County, NC held by Capstar TX LLC
Group Owner: iHeartMedia; (acq 8-30-00; grpsl).
Arbitron Metro Market: Greenville, SC; *Format:* Adult Contemp; *No. News Employees:* 1
Chris Leavitt, Senior Vice President of Sales
Josh Michael, Programming Director
Joshua Hipp, Promotions Director
Lizz Ryals, Public Affairs Director
Carole Sloan, Market Controller
Raquel Ponce, Digital Content Coordinator

WTZQ
12-25-1964; 1600 kHz AM; *Hrs Open:* 24; 1 kw-D, ND1; 0.012 kw-N, ND1; N35 18 53 W82 25 58
418 Duncan Road, Hendersonville, NC 28793 US
(828) 692-1600; *Fax:* (828) 697-1416
www.wtzq.com
1600@wtzq.com
License: Hendersonville, NC held by Houston Broadcasting Inc.
Group Owner: Mark Media Group; (acq 5-3-2008)
Nat'l Network: ABC; *Regional Network:* N.C. News Net.
Arbitron Metro Market: Hendersonville, NC; *Format:* Classic Rock
Special Programming: Gospel 4 hrs wkly; *Hrs. of News Programming:* news progmg 8 hrs wkly; *No. News Employees:* 1; *Target Audience:* 35 plus;mature upscale audiences; *Adv. Rates:* 36; 20; 24; 10
Mark Warwick, General Manager
George Henry, Programming Director
Paige Posey, Traffic Coordinator
Tom Brown, Engineer

Hertford

WFMZ
12-01-1997; 104.9 MHz FM; *Hrs Open:* 24; 50 kw; 492 ft.; N36 5 59 W76 28 31
637 Harbor Road, Wanchese, NC 27981 US
(252) 475-1888; *Fax:* (252) 475-1881
www.yourclassicrock.com
License: Hertford, Perquimans County, NC held by CapSan Media LLC.
Group Owner: CapSan Media LLC; (acq 6-30-2006; grpsl).
Nat'l Network: USA
Format: Contemporary Hits/Top 40, Adult Contemp; *Target Audience:* 25-54.
William Whitlow, President
Hunt Thomas, Operations Dir
William Whitlow, General Manager

***WHGO**
06-01-1976; 91.3 MHz FM; *Hrs Open:* 24; kw
US
(252) 747-8887; *Fax:* (252) 747-7888
www.gomixradio.org
License: Hertford, Jackson County, NC held by Pathway Christian Academy Inc.
Nat'l Network: ABC; *Nat'l Reps:* Katz Radio
Arbitron Metro Market: Biloxi-Gulfport, MS; *Format:* Contemporary Hits/Top 40, Adult Contemp; *Target Audience:* 25-54; male/female
T.D. Worthington, President

Hickory

***WFHE**
08-31-1995; 90.3 MHz FM; *Hrs Open:* 24; 4 kw; 417 ft.; N35 50 59 W81 26 40 *Rebroadcasts:* Rebroadcasts WFAE(FM) Charlotte 100%
8801 J.M. Keynes Drive, Charlotte, NC 28262 US
(704) 549-9323; *Fax:* (704) 547-8851
www.wfae.org
wfae@wfae.org
License: Hickory, Catawba County, NC held by University Radio Foundation Inc.
Arbitron Metro Market: Hickory, NC; *Format:* News/Talk, Variety/Diverse
Roger Sarow, President and General Manager
Catherine Little, Development Director

WHKY
06-10-1940; 1290 kHz AM; *Hrs Open:* 24
P.O. Box 1059, Hickory, NC 28603 US
(828) 322-1290; *Fax:* (828) 322-8256
www.whky.com
whky@whky.com
License: Hickory, NC held by Long Communications LLC
Nat'l Network: ABC; ESPN Radio; *Regional Network:* N.C. News Net; *Nat'l Reps:* Rgnl Reps *Regional Reps:* Rgnl Reps
TV Affiliate: WHKY-TV affil.; *Format:* News, News/Talk, 86; *Hrs. of News Programming:* news progmg 50 hrs wkly; *No. News Employees:* 4; *Target Audience:* 35-54.
Thomas Long, General Manager
Jeff Long, Station Manager

Patty Guthrie, General Sales Mgr
Heather Isenhour, News Director

WAIZ
12-05-1948; 630 kHz AM; *Hrs Open:* 24 hrs; 1 kw-D, ND1; 0.057 kw-N, ND1; N35 43 22 W81 16 41
P.O. Box 940, Newton, NC 28658 US
(828) 322-9472; *Fax:* (828) 464-9662
www.mytotalradio.com
waiz@mytotalradio.com
License: Hickory, NC held by Newton-Conover Communications Inc.
Nat'l Network: ABC
Format: Oldies; *Target Audience:* 25 plus.; *Adv. Rates:* 30; 15; 15; 10.75
Dave Lingafelt, President
Jim Turner, General Sales Mgr
Karol Lowery, News Director

WLKO
01-20-1959; 102.9 MHz FM; 31 kw; 1,545 ft; N35 24 26 W81 07 47
801 Wood Ridge Center Dr., Charlotte, NC 28217 US
(704) 714-9444; *Fax:* (704) 332-8805
License: Hickory, Catawba County, NC held by Capstar TX LLC
Group Owner: iHeartMedia; (acq 8-30-00; grpsl).
Population Served: 150,000; *Arbitron Metro Market:* Charlotte, NC; *Format:* Adult Contemp; *Target Audience:* 25-54.
Keith Hotchkiss, Market President
Keith Cornwell, General Sales Mgr
Anthony Testa, Promotions Director
Benjamin Brinitzer, Chief Engineer

***WPIR**
12-03-1985; 88.1 MHz FM; *Hrs Open:* 24; 26.5 kw horiz, 21 kw vert; 253 ft.; N35 43 34 W81 8 52 *Rebroadcasts:* Rebroadcasts WXRI(FM) East Bend 60%
PO Box 25775, Winston-Salem, NC 27114 US
(828) 459-2772; *Fax:* (828) 459-9805
www.joyfm.org
office@joyfm.org
License: Hickory, Catawba County, NC held by Positive Alternative Radio Inc.
Group Owner: Positive Alternative Radio Inc.
Format: Gospel
Brian Sanders, General Manager

WXRC
12-07-1962; 95.7 MHz FM; *Hrs Open:* 24; 100 kw; 1,276 ft; N35 42 32 W81 31 32
PO Box 430, Newton, NC 28658
(704) 527-0957; *Fax:* (704) 527-2720
957theride.com
totalradio@aol.com
License: Hickory, Catawba County, NC held by Pacific Broadcasting Group Inc.
Nat'l Reps: McGavren Guild
Arbitron Metro Market: Charlotte-Gasto; *Target Audience:* 25-54.
Dave Lingafelt, General Manager
Karol Lowery, Traffic

***WRYN**
89.1 MHz FM; 0.85 kw; 295 ft.; N35 41 23 W81 25 16
P.O. Box 3206, Tupelo, MS 38803 US
(662) 844-8888; *Fax:* (662) 842-6791
www.afr.net
faq@afa.net
License: Hickory, Catawba County, NC held by American Family Association.
Group Owner: American Family Radio
Arbitron Metro Market: Hickory, NC; *Format:* Christian
Tim Wildmon, President
Donald Wildmon, Founder
Buddy Smith, Sr VP
Ed Vitagliano, Exec VP
Randy Sharp, Director Of Special Projects
Meeke Addison, Director Of Communications
Abraham Hamilton III, General Counsel

High Point

WGOS
07-01-1947; 1070 kHz AM; *Hrs Open:* Sunrise-sunset; 1 kw-D, NDD; N35 54 58 W80 1 0
6223 Old Menden Hall Rd., High Point, NC 27263 US
(336) 434-5024; *Fax:* (336) 434-6018
www.wgos.net
License: High Point, NC held by Iglesia Nueva Vida of High Point Inc.
Nat'l Network: USA
Arbitron Metro Market: Greensboro-Winston Salem-High Point, NC; *Format:* Talk *Special Programming:* Loc college sports 10 hrs wkly; *Hrs. of News Programming:* News progmg 2 hrs wkly; *Target Audience:* General. *Adv. Rates:* 25; 20; 25; na
Javier Fernandez, President
Lynn Ritchy, General Manager
Max Parrish, Station Manager
Simon Ritchy, Programming Director

***WHPE-FM**
11-01-1947; 95.5 MHz FM; *Hrs Open:* 24; 100 kw; 522 ft.; N35 55 10 W80 1 47
1714 Tower Ave., High Point, NC 27260 US
(336) 889-9473
www.bbnradio.org
bbn@bbnmedia.org
License: High Point, Guilford County, NC held by Bible Broadcasting Network Inc.
Group Owner: Bible Broadcasting Network; (acq 10-74)
Nat'l Network: USA
Arbitron Metro Market: Greensboro-Winston Salem-High Point, NC; *Format:* Religious
Lowell Davey, President
Jason Padgett, Operations Manager

WVBZ
06-01-1953; 105.7 MHz FM; *Hrs Open:* 24; 100 kw; 1037 ft.; N35 58 9 W79 49 29
2 - B PAI Park, Greensboro, NC 27409 US
(336) 822-2000; *Fax:* (336) 887-0104
www.1057manup.com
License: High Point, Guilford County, NC held by Clear Channel Broadcasting Licenses Inc.
Group Owner: iHeartMedia; (acq 8-30-00; grpsl).
Arbitron Metro Market: Greensboro-Winston Salem-High Point, NC; *Format:* Rock/AOR; *Target Audience:* 25-54.
Bobby Tatum, Sales Manager
Keith Allen, Programming Director
Alan Chapman, Director of Marketing and Promotions
Dennis Elliott, Digital Content Director

WMAG
01-01-1946; 99.5 MHz FM; *Hrs Open:* 24; 100 kw; 1496 ft.; N35 52 13 W79 50 25
2-B PAI Park, Greensboro, NC 27409 US
(336) 822-2000; *Fax:* (336) 887-0104
jeffcushman@iheartmedia.com
License: High Point, Guilford County, NC held by Capstar TX LLC
Group Owner: iHeartMedia; (acq 8-30-00; grpsl).
Arbitron Metro Market: Greensboro, NC; *Format:* Adult Contemp; *Target Audience:* 25-54.
Bobby Tatum, Sales Manager
Jeff Cushman, Programming Director
Jason Newton, Director of Marketing and Promotions
Dennis Elliott, Digital Content Director

WMFR
10-15-1935; 1230 kHz AM; *Hrs Open:* 5:30 AM-1 AM; 1 kw-U, ND1; N35 57 20 W80 0 22
875 West 5th Street, Winston-Salem, NC 27101 US
(336) 777-3900; *Fax:* (336) 885-3915
www.triadsports.com
mclark@curtismedia.com
License: High Point, NC held by Crescent Media Group LLC.
Group Owner: Curtis Media Group; (acq 2-14-2007; grpsl)
Arbitron Metro Market: Greensboro, NC; *Format:* Sports
Tom Hamilton, Operations Dir
Marty Holbrook, Promotions Manager
Bob Costner, News Director
George Newman, Chief Engineer

WYSR
06-01-1953; 1590 kHz AM
327 North Main Street, High Point, NC 27260 US
(336) 883-8852; *Fax:* (336) 882-1594
wysr@northstate.net
License: High Point, NC held by Latino Broadcasting LLC
Arbitron Metro Market: Greensboro-Wins *TV Affiliate:* Talk, sports; *No. News Employees:* General.

Highlands

WHLC
07-01-1993; 104.5 MHz FM; *Hrs Open:* 24; 0.46 kw; 1158 ft.; N35 3 40 W83 11 5
Mailing Address: P.O. Box 1889, Highlands, NC 28741 US
Second Address: 2420 Hwy. 64 E., Highlands, NC 28741
(828) 526-1045; *Fax:* (828) 526-4900
www.whlc.com
info@whlc.com
License: Highlands, Macon County, NC held by Charisma Radio Corp.
Arbitron Metro Market: Greenville-Spartanburg, SC; *Format:* Easy Listening; *Target Audience:* 35 plus.
Charles Cooper, President
Will Amari, Operations Dir

Hillsborough

WPLW
12-05-1989; 102.5 MHz FM; *Hrs Open:* 24; 1.5 kw; 203.8 m; N36 07 12 W78 22 48
3012 Highwoods Boulevard, Suite 201, Raleigh, NC 27604
(919) 790-9392; *Fax:* (919) 882-1746
info@curtismedia.com
License: Hillsborough, Orange County, NC held by New Century Media Group LLC
Group Owner: Curtis Media Group
Arbitron Metro Market: Raleigh-Durham, NC *Special Programming:* News, birthday celebration, country exchange, sports; *Hrs. of News Programming:* News progmg 6 hrs wkly
Jackie Ayscue, News Director

Holly Springs

WCMC-FM
02-01-1993; 99.9 MHz FM; *Hrs Open:* 24; 26.5 kw; 676 ft.; N35 40 35 W78 32 8
Mailing Address: P.O. Box 12000, Raleigh, NC 27605 US
Second Address: 2619 Western Blvd., Raleigh, NC 27606
(919) 821-8555; *Fax:* (919) 821-8541
www.wralsportsfan.com
License: Holly Springs, Wake County, NC held by WCMC-FM LLC
Group Owner: Capitol Broadcasting Co. Inc.; (acq 4-22-2005; $7.25 million)
Nat'l Network: ESPN Radio; *Nat'l Reps:* Katz Radio; *Wire Services:* AP
Arbitron Metro Market: Raleigh-Durham, NC; *Format:* Sports, Talk
Brian Maloney, General Manager
Alex McTighe, Local Sales Manager
Brian Grube, National Sales Manager
Haki Dennis, Account Executive
Barbara Purtee, Account Executive
Dorian Baldwin, Traffic Manager

Hope Mills

WCCG
07-01-1997; 104.5 MHz FM; 6 kw; 276 ft.; N34 56 34 W78 51 41
115 Gillespie Street, Fayetteville, NC 28301 US
(910) 484-4932; *Fax:* (910) 485-5192
www.wccg1045fm.com/
ccg1045@aol.com
License: Hope Mills, Cumberland County, NC held by James E. Carson.
Arbitron Metro Market: Fayetteville, NC; *Format:* Oldies, Blues
James Carson, General Manager
Anthony Carson

Jacksonville

WJCV
10-10-1968; 1290 kHz AM; *Hrs Open:* 24; 5 kw-D, 47 w-N; N34 45 58 W77 23 28
Box 1216, Jacksonville, NC 28541
(910) 347-6141; *Fax:* (910) 347-1290
www.wjcv.com
License: Jacksonville, Onslow County, NC held by Down East Broadcasting Co. Inc.
Nat'l Network: USA; *Nat'l Reps:* Salem
Population Served: 250,000; *Arbitron Metro Market:* Greenville-New; *Target Audience:* 25-54; general; *Adv. Rates:* 12; 10; 12; 5
Michael Bland, President

WJNC
10-16-1945; 1240 kHz AM; 1 kw-U, ND1; N34 44 56 W77 24 51
PO Box 70, Newport, NC 28570 US
(252) 247-6343; *Fax:* (252) 247-7343
www.wtkf107.com
news@thetalkstation.com
License: Jacksonville, NC held by Heritage Broadcasting LLC.
Group Owner: Conner Media Corp.; (acq 8-10-2001; $358,500)
Nat'l Network: Westwood One
Arbitron Metro Market: Greenville-New Bern-Jacksonville, NC; *Format:* News, News/Talk, 84, Talk; *Target Audience:* 18-45 plus.
Ben Ball, General Manager
Dave Gremoske, Chief Engineer

RADIO - U.S.

WRMR
04-28-1965; 98.7 MHz FM; *Hrs Open:* 24; 100 kw; 974 ft.; N34 29 41 W77 29 19
25 N. Kerr Ave., Wilmington, NC 28405 US
(910) 791-3088; *Fax:* (910) 791-0112
www.modernrock987.com
License: Jacksonville, Onslow County, NC held by Sunrise Broadcasting LLC.
Group Owner: Capitol Broadcasting Co. Inc.; (acq 11-18-2008; grpsl)
Population Served: 1,000,000; *Arbitron Metro Market:* Greenville-New Bern-Jacksonville, NC; *Format:* Rock/AOR
Brian Schimmel, General Manager
Ross Mahoney, Programming Director
Lauren LaMothe, Promotions Director

WLGP
08-01-1996; 100.3 MHz FM; *Hrs Open:* 24; 100 kw; 486 ft.; N34 48 17 W76 54 23
P.O. Box 510, Appling, GA 30802 US
(800) 926-4669
www.gnnradio.org
brian@gnnradio.org
License: Jacksonville, NC held by Barinowski Investment Co.
Group Owner: Good News Network
Format: Christian

WQSL
11-01-1993; 92.3 MHz FM; *Hrs Open:* 24; 22.5 kw; 725 ft.; N34 31 10 W77 26 52
1361 Colony Drive, New Bern, NC 28562 US
(252) 639-7900; *Fax:* (252) 639-7979
www.wqsl.com
License: Jacksonville, Onslow County, NC held by NM Licensing LLC.
Group Owner: NextMedia Group Inc.; (acq 11-26-2001; grpsl)
Nat'l Reps: Eastman Radio
Arbitron Metro Market: Greenville-New Bern-Jacksonville, NC; *Format:* Adult Contemp
Larry Weiss, General Manager
Tony Denton, Director of Sales

WSRP
06-21-1954; 910 kHz AM; *Hrs Open:* 24
702 Hartness Road, Statesville, NC 28677 US
(910) 455-2202; *Fax:* (910) 355-2203
License: Jacksonville, NC held by Estuardo Valdemar Rodriguez & Leonor Rodriguez.
Group Owner: Radio La Grande; (acq 6-30-2006; $475,000)
Arbitron Metro Market: Greenville-New Bern-Jacksonville, NC
Henry Gonzalez, Station Manager

WXQR-FM
03-14-1966; 105.5 MHz FM; *Hrs Open:* 24; 19 kw; 794 ft.; N34 31 10 W77 26 52
1361 Colony Drive, New Bern, NC 28562 US
(252) 639-7900; *Fax:* (252) 639-7979
www.myrock105.com
License: Jacksonville, Onslow County, NC held by NM Licensing LLC.
Group Owner: NextMedia Group Inc.; (acq 11-26-2001; grpsl)
Nat'l Reps: Eastman Radio
Arbitron Metro Market: Greenville-New Bern, NC; *Format:* Rock/AOR
Larry Weiss, VP/GM
Tina Smash, Programming Director

***WJKA**
01-01-2008; 90.1 MHz FM; 17 kw vert; 281 ft.; N34 38 52 W77 37 28 *Rebroadcasts:* Rebroadcasts WAFR(FM) Tupelo, MS 100%
P.O. Box 3206, Tupelo, MS 38803 US
(662) 844-8888; *Fax:* (662) 842-6791
www.afr.net
faq@afa.net
License: Jacksonville, Onslow County, NC held by American Family Association.
Group Owner: American Family Radio
Nat'l Network: American Family Radio
Arbitron Metro Market: Eagle Pass, TX; *Format:* Christian
Tim Wildmon, President
Donald Wildmon, Founder
Buddy Smith, Sr VP
Ed Vitagliano, Exec VP
Randy Sharp, Director Of Special Projects
Meeke Addison, Director Of Communications
Abraham Hamilton III, General Counsel

WAVQ
01-01-2008; 1400 kHz AM
US
(910) 219-0455
License: Jacksonville, NC held by Conner Media Corp.
Group Owner: Conner Media Corp.
Arbitron Metro Market: Jacksonville, NC; *Format:* Sports, Talk
Ronald Benfield, President

Kannapolis

WRFX
10-01-1964; 99.7 MHz FM; 84 kw; 1056 ft.; N35 17 14 W80 41 45
801 Wood Ridge Center Drive, Charlotte, NC 28217 US
(704) 714-9444; *Fax:* (704) 371-3238
www.997thefox.com
License: Kannapolis, Cabarrus County, NC held by Capstar TX LLC
Group Owner: iHeartMedia; (acq 8-30-2000; grpsl)
Arbitron Metro Market: Charlotte-Gastonia-Rock Hill, NC-SC; *Format:* Classic Rock, Rock/AOR *Special Programming:* Talk 3 hrs wkly; *Target Audience:* 25-54; male
Keith Hotchkiss, Market President
Keith Cornwell, General Sales Mgr
Jeff Kent, Programming Director
Anthony Testa, Promotions Director
Benjamin Brinitzer, Chief Engineer
Jodi Phillips, Digital Program Director

WRKB
12-11-1960; 1460 kHz AM; *Hrs Open:* 24 *Rebroadcasts:* Rebroadcasts WRNA(AM) China Grove 90%
P.O. Box 1388, Kannapolis, NC 28082 US
(704) 857-1101; *Fax:* (704) 938-1460
www.fordbroadcasting.com
carl@fordbroadcasting.com
License: Kannapolis, NC held by Ford Broadcasting Inc.
Nat'l Network: USA
Arbitron Metro Market: Charlotte-Gastonia-Rock Hill, NC-SC; *Format:* Gospel
Carl Ford, President
Angela Ford, Operations Dir
Taylor Ford, Executive Vice President

Kernersville

WTRU
08-16-1970; 830 kHz AM; *Hrs Open:* 24; 50 kw-D, DA2; 10 kw-N, DA2; N36 11 58 W80 12 25
4405 Providence Ln., Suite D, Winston-Salem, NC 27106 US
(336) 759-0363; *Fax:* (336) 759-0366
www.truthnetwork.com
mcarbone@truthnetwork.com
License: Kernersville, NC held by Truth Broadcasting Corp.
Group Owner: Truth Broadcasting Corp.; (acq 7-20-2000; $3.5 million with WGTK(AM) Louisville, KY)
Nat'l Network: Salem Radio Network
Arbitron Metro Market: Greensboro, NC; *Format:* Christian; *Hrs. of News Programming:* News progmg 24 hrs wkly; *Target Audience:* General.; *Adv. Rates:* 306; 306; 30; 20
Stuart Epperson, General Manager

Kill Devil Hills

WCXL
01-01-1993; 104.1 MHz FM; *Hrs Open:* 24; 100 kw; 971 ft.; N36 8 8 W75 49 28
103 West Woodhill Dr., Nags Head, NC 27959 US
(252) 480-4655; *Fax:* (252) 441-4827
www.beach104.com
info@beach104.com
License: Kill Devil Hills, Dare County, NC held by Max Radio of the Carolinas Licenses LLC.
Group Owner: MAX Media L.L.C.; (acq 11-12-2002; grpsl).
Arbitron Metro Market: Hampton Roads, Outer Banks, NC; *Format:* Adult Contemp *Special Programming:* Farm 2 hrs wkly; *No. News Employees:* 2; *Target Audience:* 18-54.; *Adv. Rates:* 75; 45; 75; 35.
Michael Smith, Regional Vice President/General Manager
Bob Davis, Director of Sales

King

WKTE
12-04-1963; 1090 kHz AM; 1 kw-D, NDD; N36 17 48 W80 22 18
118 WKTE Drive, King, NC 27021 US
(336) 983-3111; *Fax:* (336) 368-1090
License: King, NC held by Booth-Newsom Broadcasting Inc.
Regional Network: Southern Farm
Arbitron Metro Market: Greensboro-Winston Salem-High Point, NC; *Format:* Country, Gospel *Special Programming:* Farm 2 hrs wkly
Rodney Booth, General Manager

Kings Mountain

WDYT
03-12-1953; 1220 kHz AM; *Hrs Open:* 5 AM-midnight
P.O. Box 1220, Kings Mountain, NC 28086 US
(704) 295-7901; *Fax:* (704) 295-7919
License: Kings Mountain, NC held by CRN Communications LLC
Arbitron Metro Market: Charlotte-Gastonia-Rock Hill, NC-SC
Deanna Greco, General Manager

Kinston

WELS
09-01-1950; 1010 kHz AM; *Hrs Open:* 8 AM-5 PM; 1 kw-D, ND1; 0.078 kw-N, ND1; N35 17 3 W77 39 53
Mailing Address: 645 Church Street, Suite 400, Norfolk, VA 23510 US
Second Address: 313 N. Queen St., Kinston, NC 28501
(252) 523-5151; *Fax:* (252) 523-9357
welsradio@juno.com
License: Kinston, NC held by Eastern Air Waves LLC
Regional Network: N.C. News Net; *Nat'l Reps:* Clayton-Davis
Arbitron Metro Market: Kinston, NC; *Format:* Gospel; *Target Audience:* 25-54; middle income
Anthony Gonzales, General Manager

WELS-FM
11-21-1990; 102.9 MHz FM; *Hrs Open:* 24; 3 kw; 295 ft.; N35 17 3 W77 39 53
Mailing Address: 2581 US Highway 70 W, Goldsboro, NC 27530 US
Second Address: 313 N. Queen St., Kinston, NC 28501
(252) 523-5151; *Fax:* (252) 523-9357
License: Kinston, Lenoir County, NC held by Eastern Airwaves LLC
Nat'l Network: ABC
Arbitron Metro Market: Kinston, NC *Special Programming:* East Carolina Univ. sports, Kinston Indians baseball; *Target Audience:* General; middle to upper income, married, working, college grads
Anthony Gonzales, Programming Director

***WKNS**
03-26-1977; 90.3 MHz FM; 35 kw horiz, 34 kw vert; 322 ft.; N35 25 1 W77 48 57 *Rebroadcasts:* Rebroadcasting WTEB(FM) New Bern 100%
800 College Ct, New Bern, NC 28562 US
(252) 638-3434; *Fax:* (252) 638-3538
www.publicradioeast.org
License: Kinston, Lenoir County, NC held by Craven Community College.
Format: Public Affairs, News *Special Programming:* Jazz 6 hrs wkly
Kelly Batchlor, Operations Dir
Charles Wethington, Station Manager
Kathleen Beal, General Sales Mgr
Jill McGuire, Programming Director
George Olsen, News Director
J. Howard Jones, Chief Engineer

WLNR
05-01-1954; 1230 kHz AM; *Hrs Open:* 24; 1 kw-U, ND1; N35 15 31 W77 36 33
1223 West New Bern Rd, Kinston, NC 28504 US
(252) 522-9567
estuardovaldemar@hotmail.com
License: Kinston, NC held by Estuardo Valdemar Rodriguez & Leonor Rodriguez.
Group Owner: Radio La Grande; (acq 1-2004; $315,000)
Arbitron Metro Market: Greenville-New Bern-Jacksonville, NC
Estuardo Rodriguez, General Manager

WRNS
02-28-1937; 960 kHz AM; *Hrs Open:* 24; 5 kw-D, DAN; 1 kw-N, DAN; N35 16 57 W77 39 9
1705 W. Northwest Hwy, Ste 275, Grapevine, TX 76051 US
(252) 639-7900; *Fax:* (252) 639-7979
www.wrns.com
mail@wrns.com
License: Kinston, NC held by NM Licensing LLC
Group Owner: NextMedia Group Inc.
Arbitron Metro Market: Greenville-New Bern-Jacksonville, NC; *Format:* Country; *Target Audience:* 25-64.
Wayne Carlyle, Programming Director

WRNS-FM
10-12-1968; 95.1 MHz FM; *Hrs Open:* 24; 100 kw; 1506 ft.; N35 6 15 W77 20 12
1361 Colony Drive, New Bern, NC 28562 US
(252) 639-7900; *Fax:* (252) 639-7979
www.wrns.com
License: Kinston, Lenoir County, NC held by NM Licensing LLC

Group Owner: NextMedia Group Inc.; (acq 11-26-01; grpsl).
Nat'l Reps: Eastman Radio
Arbitron Metro Market: Greenville-New Bern-Jacksonville, NC; *Format:* Country *Special Programming:* NASCAR racing 6 hrs wkly; *No. News Employees:* 1; *Target Audience:* 25-54.; *Adv. Rates:* 1440; 1440; 1440; 600
Larry Weiss, General Manager
Tommy Garrett, Programming Director

Knightdale

WTKK
03-01-1961; 106.1 MHz FM; *Hrs Open:* 24; 27.5 kw; 1604 ft.; N35 40 28 W78 31 40
3100 Smoketree Court, Suite 700, Raleigh, NC 27604 US
(919) 878-1500; *Fax:* (919) 876-8578
www.1061fmtalk.com
License: Knightdale, Wilson County, NC held by Capstar TX LLC
Group Owner: iHeartMedia; (acq 8-30-2000; grpsl).
Arbitron Metro Market: Raleigh-Durham, NC; *Format:* Talk; *Hrs. of News Programming:* news progmg 3 hrs wkly; *No. News Employees:* 1
Brian Taylor, Programming Director
Nathan James, Director of Integrated Media
Melody Mechanic, Digital Program Director

La Grange

WZUP
01-01-1993; 104.7 MHz FM; 25 kw; 249 ft.; N35 15 31 W77 36 33
1223 West New Bern Road, Kinston, NC 28504 US
(252) 753-3202; *Fax:* (910) 355-2203
www.lainvasora1047fm.com
License: La Grange, Lenoir County, NC held by Conner Media Corp.
Group Owner: Conner Media Corp.
Arbitron Metro Market: Farmville, NC; *Format:* Spanish
Rodney Rainey, General Manager

Laurinburg

WEWO
09-01-1947; 1460 kHz AM; *Hrs Open:* 24; 5 kw-D, DA2; 5 kw-N, DA2; N34 47 0 W79 30 40
1338 Bragg Blvd., Fayetteville, NC 28301 US
(910) 486-9438; *Fax:* (910) 484-4040
www.widuradio.com
wewo1460@aol.com
License: Laurinburg, NC held by Service Media Inc.
Arbitron Metro Market: Laurinburg, NC; *Format:* Gospel; *Target Audience:* 25-54.
Westley Johnson, General Manager

WFLB
05-01-1951; 96.5 MHz FM; *Hrs Open:* 24; 100 kw; 1043 ft.; N34 46 49 W79 2 45
508 Person St., Fayetteville, NC 28301 US
(910) 486-2000; *Fax:* (910) 486-2109
www.965bobfm.com
License: Laurinburg, Scotland County, NC held by Beasley Media Group LLC
Group Owner: Beasley Broadcast Group Inc.; (acq 7-31-96; $4.2 million with co-owned AM).
Nat'l Reps: D & R Radio
Arbitron Metro Market: Fayetteville, NC; *Format:* Adult Contemp *Special Programming:* University of North Carolina football & basketball; *Target Audience:* 25-54; affluent men & women in their peak earning years *Adv.Rates:* 65; 85; 65; 30
Tricia Gallenbeck, Director of Sales
Mac Edwards, Vice President/Market Manager
Danny Highsmith, Regional Vice President
Katy Lollis, General Sales Manager
Angela Godwin, General Sales Manager
Ina Cartrette, Advertising

WLNC
01-02-1962; 1300 kHz AM; *Hrs Open:* sunrise-sunset; 0.5 kw-D, ND2; 0.074 kw-N, ND2; N34 47 0 W79 26 22
1011 Lila Drive, Laurinburg, NC 28352 US
(910) 276-1300
www.wlncradio.com
contact@wlncradio.com
License: Laurinburg, NC held by Fox Broadcasting Inc.
Format: Adult Contemp *Special Programming:* Gospel 4 hrs wkly; *Target Audience:* General.
Fred Fox, General Manager

Leland

WAAV
12-20-1957; 980 kHz AM; *Hrs Open:* 24; 5 kw-D, DAN; 5 kw-N, DAN; N34 14 54 W78 0 6
3233 Burnt Mill Road, Wilmington, NC 28403 US
(620) 665-5758; *Fax:* (620) 665-6655
www.980waav.com
License: Leland, NC held by Cumulus Licensing Corp.
Group Owner: Cumulus Media Inc.; (acq 7-2-97; $1.6 million with co-located FM)
Nat'l Reps: McGavren Guild; *Wire Services:* AP
Arbitron Metro Market: Dallas-Fort Worth; *Format:* Oldies; *Hrs. of News Programming:* news progmg 2 hrs wkly; *No. News Employees:* 1
Mike Farrow, Programming Director

WKXS-FM
12-10-1994; 94.5 MHz FM; *Hrs Open:* 24; 3.8 kw; 416 ft.; N34 12 35 W77 56 53
111 East Kilbourn Ave, Suite 2700, Milwaukee, WI 53202 US
(505) 242-7163
www.kanw.com
brasher@aps.edu
License: Leland, Brunswick County, NC
Arbitron Metro Market: San Francisco
Michael Brasher, General Manager

Lenoir

WJRI
03-15-1947; 1340 kHz AM; *Hrs Open:* 24; 1 kw-U, ND1; N35 53 39 W81 33 30
827 S. Fairview Dr., Lenoir, NC 28645 US
(828) 758-1033; *Fax:* (828) 757-3300
www.gofoothills.com
al@gofoothills.com
License: Lenoir, NC held by Foothills Radio Group LLC
Group Owner: Foothills Radio Group LLC; acq 11-28-01).
Regional Network: N.C. News Net.
Format: News, News/Talk, 86; *Hrs. of News Programming:* news progmg 14 hrs wkly; *No. News Employees:* 1; *Target Audience:* 20-45.
Al Bunch, President
Steve Zushin, Operations Dir
Jon Blair, General Manager

WKGX
02-13-1969; 1080 kHz AM; *Hrs Open:* 12; 2.5 kw-C, NDD; 5 kw-D, NDD; N35 54 38 W81 33 35
827 S. Fairview Dr., Lenoir, NC 28645 US
(828) 758-1033; *Fax:* (828) 757-3300
www.gofoothills.com
al@gofoothills.com
License: Lenoir, NC held by Foothills Radio Group LLC
Group Owner: Foothills Radio Group LLC; acq 11-28-01).
Format: Adult Contemp *Special Programming:* Trading post show 16 hrs wkly; *Hrs. of News Programming:* news progmg 6 hrs wkly; *No. News Employees:* 1; *Target Audience:* 24-55; older, mature wise spenders
Steve Zushin, Operations Dir
Jon Blair, General Manager

WKVS
09-27-1993; 103.3 MHz FM; 0.91 kw; 843 ft.; N35 58 30 W81 33 7
827 S. Fairview Dr., Lenoir, NC 28645 US
(828) 758-1033; *Fax:* (828) 757-3300
al@gofoothills.com
License: Lenoir, Caldwell County, NC held by Foothills Radio Group LLC.
Group Owner: Foothills Radio Group LLC; (acq 11-28-2001)
Format: Country; *Target Audience:* 18-54.
Steve Zushin, Operations Dir
Jon Blair, General Manager

Lewisville

WSGH
01-01-1986; 1040 kHz AM; *Hrs Open:* 24; 9.1 kw-D, DA2; 0.182 kw-N, DA2; N36 8 6 W80 30 14
Box 889, Blacksburg, VA 24060 US
(336) 768-0050; *Fax:* (336) 768-0032
www.radiolamovidita.com
License: Lewisville, NC held by Davidson Media Carolinas Stations LLC.
Group Owner: Davidson Media Group LLC; (acq 5-10-2004; grpsl).
Nat'l Network: USA
Arbitron Metro Market: Greensboro-Wins; *Target Audience:* 17-28.
Marco Antonio Saucedo, President
Lucy Saucedo, Operations Dir
Samuel Saucedo, General Manager

Lexington

WLXN
09-22-1946; 1440 kHz AM; *Hrs Open:* 24
200 Radio Drive, Lexington, NC 27292 US
(336) 242-1440; *Fax:* (336) 248-2800
www.wlxn.com
License: Lexington, NC held by Davidson County Broadcasting Co. Inc.
Regional Network: N.C. News Net.
Arbitron Metro Market: Greensboro, NC; *Format:* News, News/Talk, 84, Talk; *Hrs. of News Programming:* news progmg 30 hrs wkly; *No. News Employees:* 1; *Target Audience:* 35 plus; those interested in news & sports
Greeley Hilton Jr., President
Tom Collins, Operations Dir
Harold Bowen, Programming Director
Willie Edwards, Promotions Manager
Bob Mahoney, News Director
Hal McGee, Engineering Dir

WWLV(FM)
08-24-1949; 94.1 MHz FM; *Hrs Open:* 24; 100 kw; 1,014 ft; N35 55 02 W80 17 37
200 Radio Dr., Lexington, NC 27292
(336) 248-2716; *Fax:* (336) 248-2800
www.klove.com
License: Lexington, Davidson County, NC held by Davidson County Broadcasting Co. Inc.
Regional Reps: T-N.
Population Served: 273,425; *Arbitron Metro Market:* Greensboro, NC; *Format:* Adult Contemp; *Hrs. of News Programming:* news progmg one hr wkly; *No. News Employees:* 1; *Target Audience:* General; 25-49
Greeley Hilton Jr., President
Bob Campbell, Programming Director
Hal McGee, Chief Engineer

Lillington

*WLLN
02-12-1979; 1370 kHz AM; *Hrs Open:* Day time; 5 kw-D, DA2; 0.049 kw-N, DA2; N35 23 16 W78 48 22
Mailing Address: P.O. Box 1166, Dunn, NC 28335 US
Second Address: 910 E. McNeil St., Lillington, NC 27546
(910) 893-2811; *Fax:* (910) 893-2811
License: Lillington, NC held by Estuardo Valdemar Rodriguez
Format: Spanish; *Target Audience:* General.
Estuardo Rodriguez, Chairman
Leonor Rodriguez, President
Helen Hernandez, Station Manager
Orlando Henao, Programming Director

Lincolnton

WLON
08-28-1953; 1050 kHz AM; *Hrs Open:* 24; 1 kw-D, ND1; 0.231 kw-N, ND1; N35 29 28 W81 16 3 *Rebroadcasts:* Rebroadcasts WCSL(AM) Cherryville 80%
P.O. Box 730, Cherryville, NC 28021 US
(704) 735-8071; *Fax:* (704) 732-9567
www.hrnb.com
info@hrnb.com
License: Lincolnton, NC held by HRN Broadcasting Inc.
Group Owner: HRN Broadcasting Inc.; (acq 4-14-2004; $500,000 with WCSL(AM) Cherryville).
Nat'l Network: Westwood One; *Regional Network:* N.C. News Net.
Arbitron Metro Market: Charlotte-Gastonia-Rock Hill, NC-SC; *Format:* Oldies, Sports *Special Programming:* Gospel 5 hrs wkly; *Target Audience:* 25 plus.
Mark Boyd, President
Milton Baker, Operations Dir
Lanny Ford, General Manager

Lockwoods Folly Town

*WGHW
01-01-2006; 88.1 MHz FM; 10 kw vert; 311 ft.; N34 3 48 W78 5 32
520 Roberts Rd, New Port, NC 28570 US
(910) 253-6593
www.kjbbfm.com
License: Lockwoods Folly Town, Brunswick County, NC held by Church Planters of America
Arbitron Metro Market: Modesto, CA; *Format:* Christian
Danny Hawkins, President

RADIO - U.S.

Louisburg

WYRN
09-12-1958; 1480 kHz AM; *Hrs Open:* 24; 0.5 kw-D, ND1; 0.035 kw-N, ND1; N36 6 46 W78 16 50
495 NC 561 Highway, Louisburg, NC 27549 US
(919) 496-3105; *Fax:* (919) 496-5864
License: Louisburg, NC held by New Century Media Group LLC.
Group Owner: Curtis Media Group; (acq 6-1-2003; $2.8 million with co-located FM)
Regional Network: N.C. News Net.
Arbitron Metro Market: Raleigh-Durham,; *Format:* Talk *Special Programming:* Black; *Hrs. of News Programming:* news progmg 20 hrs wkly; *No. News Employees:* 1; *Target Audience:* Adults 25-54. *Adv. Rates:* 25; 23; 25; 15
William McClatchey Jr., President
Randy Jordan, General Manager
Jackie Ayscue, News Director

Lumberton

WAGR
11-27-1954; 1340 kHz AM; *Hrs Open:* 24; 1 kw-U, ND1; N34 35 58 W79 0 33
Mailing Address: 145 Rowan Street A-3, Fayetteville, NC 28301 US
Second Address: 145 Rowen Street A-3, Fayetteville, NC 28301
(910)486-9438; *Fax:* (910) 739-1349
License: Lumberton, NC held by WAGR Broadcasting Inc.
Regional Reps: Williams
Arbitron Metro Market: Fayetteville, NC; *Format:* Gospel; *Hrs. of News Programming:* News progmg 4 hrs wkly; *Target Audience:* 25-54.; *Adv. Rates:* 19; 17; 19; 14
Wes Cookman, Manager
Redean Cotton, Assistant Manager

WFVL
07-19-1964; 102.3 MHz FM; *Hrs Open:* 24; 6 kw; 85.1 meters; N34 35 58 W79 00 33
2700 West Paks Blvd, Rocklin, CA 28303
(916) 251-1600; *Fax:* (916) 251-1650
License: Lumberton, Robeson County, NC held by Educational Media Foundation
Population Served: 103,000; *Arbitron Metro Market:* Fayetteville, NC
Mike Novak, President

WKML
12-01-1960; 95.7 MHz FM; *Hrs Open:* 24; 100 kw; 1043 ft.; N34 46 49 W79 2 45
508 Person St., Fayetteville, NC 28301 US B8301
(910) 486-2000; *Fax:* (90) 486-2109
www.wkml.com
License: Lumberton, Robeson County, NC held by Beasley Media Group LLC
Group Owner: Beasley Broadcast Group Inc.; (acq 1981).
Nat'l Reps: D & R Radio
Arbitron Metro Market: Fayetteville, NC; *Format:* Country; *Hrs. of News Programming:* news progmg 5 hrs wkly; *No. News Employees:* 1; *Target Audience:* 25-54.
Mac Edwards, VP/Market Manager
Tricia Gallenbeck, Director of Sales
Danny Highsmith, Regional Vice President
Katy Lollis, General Sales Manager
Angela Godwin, General Sales Manager
Ina Cartrette, Advertising

***WLPS-FM**
89.5 MHz FM; 2 kw vert; 440 ft.; N34 42 2 W79 6 32
3463 Oak Grove Church Rd, Lumberton, NC 28358 US
(910) 521-3101
License: Lumberton, Robeson County, NC held by Billy Ray Locklear Evangelistic Association.
Arbitron Metro Market: Lumberton,NC; *Format:* Gospel
Billy Ray Locklear, Chairman

Manteo

WOBX-FM
01-01-2001; 98.1 MHz FM; *Hrs Open:* 24; 40 kw; 233 ft.; N35 51 52 W75 39 1
Mailing Address: 2401 S. Croatan Highway, Nags Head, NC 27959 US
Second Address: 2422 S. Wrightsville Ave., Nags Head, NC 27959
(252) 441-1024; *Fax:* (252) 449-8354
License: Manteo, Dare County, NC held by East Carolina Radio of Elizabeth City Inc.
Arbitron Metro Market: Nags Head, NC; *Format:* News, Talk
Rick Loesch, President
Cliff Curtis, Operations Dir
R. Loesch, General Manager
Rick Loesch, General Sales Mgr

WVOD
03-28-1986; 99.1 MHz FM; *Hrs Open:* 24; 50 kw; 492 ft.; N35 50 44 W75 38 50
637 Harbor Road, Wanchese, NC 28971 US
(252) 475-1888; *Fax:* (252) 475-1881
www.991thesound.com
matt@maxradionc.com
License: Manteo, Dare County, NC held by CapSan Media LLC.
Group Owner: CapSan Media LLC; (acq 6-30-2006; grpsl)
Arbitron Metro Market: Manteo, NC; *Format:* Triple A *Special Programming:* Class 6 hrs, blues 2 hrs, reggae 2 hrs wkly; *No. News Employees:* 1; *Target Audience:* 25-49.
Hunt Thomas, Operations Dir
William Whitlow, General Manager
Matt Cooper, Programming Director
Sharon Pro, News Director
Andy Booth, Chief Engineer
Tad Abbey, Music Director

***WURI**
01-01-1999; 90.9 MHz FM; *Hrs Open:* 24; 3.9 kw; 187 ft.; N35 54 28 W75 40 26 *Rebroadcasts:* Rebroadcasts WCPE(FM) Wake Forest 99.9%
Campus Box 0915, Chapel Hill, NC 27599 US
(919) 445-9150; *Fax:* (919) 966-5955
www.theclassicalstation.com
License: Manteo, Dare County, NC held by Board of Trustees/University of North Carolina at Chapel Hill.
Nat'l Network: CBC Radio One; NPR; PRI
Arbitron Metro Market: Chapel Hill, NC; *Format:* Classical *Special Programming:* Folk 20 hrs wkly.
Bob Levin, COO
Kevin Wolf, Operations Dir
Connie Walker, General Manager
David Brower, Programming Director
Nandini Sen, Director of Technologies & Engineering
Regina Yeager, Director of Development
Susan Anderson, AccountingCoordinator
Jacqueline Edwards, Business Assistant
Nathan Olawsky, Business Services Coordinator
Jennifer Bowling, Corporate Support Associate

***WUND-FM**
01-01-2004; 88.9 MHz FM; *Hrs Open:* 24; 50 kw horiz, 47 kw vert; 1371 ft.; N35 54 0 W76 20 45 *Rebroadcasts:* Rebroadcasts WUNC(FM) Chapel Hill 99.9%
Campus Boc 0915, Chapel Hill, NC 27599 US
(919) 445-9150; *Fax:* (919) 966-5955
www.wunc.org
wunc@wunc.org
License: Manteo, Dare County, NC held by Board of Trustees of the University of North Carolina at Chapel Hill.
Nat'l Network: NPR; PRI
Arbitron Metro Market: Elizabeth City, NC; *Format:* News *Special Programming:* Folk 20 hrs wkly; *Hrs. of News Programming:* news progmg 124 hrs wkly; *No. News Employees:* 7
Bob Levin, COO
Connie Walker, General Manager
David Brower, Programming Director
Nandini Sen, Director of Technologies & Engineering
Regina Yeager, Director of Development
Susan Anderson, Accounting Coordinator
JacquelineEdwards, Business Assistant
Nathan Olawsky, Business Services Coordinator
Jennifer Bowling, Corporate Support Associate
Nancy Brookshire, Corporate Support Manager

Marion

WBRM
05-09-1949; 1250 kHz AM; *Hrs Open:* 24
147 North Garden Street, Marion, NC 28752 US
(828) 652-9500
info@wbrmradio.com
License: Marion, NC held by WBRM Inc.
Arbitron Metro Market: Marion, NC; *Format:* Country *Special Programming:* Gospel 5 hrs, relg 7 hrs wkly; *Hrs. of News Programming:* news progmg 9 hrs wkly; *No. News Employees:* 1; *Target Audience:* 25-55; youngadult to mature; *Adv. Rates:* 12.50; 12,50; 12.50; na
Annette Bryant, CEO
Kevin Estes, Operations Dir

Mars Hill

***WYQS**
01-01-1974; 90.5 MHz FM; *Hrs Open:* 24; 0.25 kw; 1276 ft.; N35 53 12 W82 33 23
73 Broadway, Asheville, NC 28801 US
(828) 210-4800; *Fax:* (828) 210-4801
www.wcqs.org
info@wcqs.org
License: Mars Hill, Madison County, NC held by Western North Carolina Public Radio Inc.
Nat'l Network: NPR
Arbitron Metro Market: Asheville, NC; *Format:* News, News/Talk, 86; *Hrs. of News Programming:* news progmg 7 hrs wkly; *No. News Employees:* 3; *Target Audience:* 14-30; college students & college community
Lee Wilcher, Operations Dir
Ed Subkis, General Manager
Steve Busey, General Sales Mgr
Barbara Sayer, Programming Director
David Hurand, News Director
Tom Spaight, Chief Engineer
Lee Wilcher, Operations Manager
Vicky Gerald,Traffic Manager
Jody Evans, Executive Director
Jessica Frantz, Membership Associate

Marshall

WHBK
09-20-1956; 1460 kHz AM; *Hrs Open:* 24; 5 kw-D, ND1; 0.139 kw-N, ND1; N35 48 4 W82 40 48
351 Skyway Drive, Marshall, NC 28753 US
(828) 649-3914; *Fax:* (828) 649-2869
www.1460whbk.com
1460whbk@gmail.com
License: Marshall, NC held by Southern Broadcasting Inc.
Arbitron Metro Market: Asheville, NC; *Format:* Gospel *Special Programming:* Farm 3 hrs wkly
Ricky Seay, General Manager
Ricky West, Disc Jockey

Mayodan

WMYN
07-15-1957; 1420 kHz AM; *Hrs Open:* 5 AM-10 PM
Rebroadcasts: Rebroadcasts WLOE(AM) Eden 100%
PO Box 279, Mayodan, NC 27027 US
(336) 427-9696; *Fax:* (336) 548-4636
www.wloewmyn.com
info@rockinghamcountyradio.com
License: Mayodan, NC held by Mayo Broadcasting Corp.
Nat'l Network: Salem Radio Network; USA
Arbitron Metro Market: Mayodan, NC; *Format:* Talk, Religious; *Hrs. of News Programming:* news progmg 30 hrs wkly; *No. News Employees:* 1; *Target Audience:* 25 plus; general; *Adv. Rates:* 25; 25; 25; 25
Richard Hall, President
Mike Moore, General Manager
Annette Moore, Station Manager

Mebane

WGSB
12-07-1973; 1060 kHz AM; *Hrs Open:* Sunrise-sunset; 0.5 kw-C, DAD; 1 kw-D, DAD; N36 3 28 W79 16 36 *Rebroadcasts:* Rebroadcasts WRTP(AM) Chapel Hill 100%
7610 Falls of Neuse Road, Raleigh, NC 27615 US
(202) 638-1959; *Fax:* (202) 638-6127
www.hisradiowrtp.com
estuardovaldemar@hotmail.com
License: Mebane, NC held by Estuardo Valdemar Rodriguez and Leonor Rodriguez.
Group Owner: Radio La Grande; (acq 2-2-2005; grpsl)
Arbitron Metro Market: Raleigh-Durham, NC
Estuardo Valdemar Rodriguez, General Manager

Mint Hill

WNOW
08-01-1987; 1030 kHz AM; *Hrs Open:* Sunrise-sunset
4321 E-Stuart Andrew Boulevard, Charlotte, VA 28217 US
(704) 831-2465
License: Mint Hill, NC held by Davidson Media Carolinas Stations LLC.
Group Owner: Davidson Media Group LLC; (acq 5-10-2004; grpsl)
Arbitron Metro Market: Charlotte, NC
Peter Davidson, President
Russ Douglass Jones, General Manager
Aura Gavilan, Promotions Manager
Maria Zarate, News Director
Winston Hawkins, Chief Engineer

Mocksville

WDSL
10-01-1964; 1520 kHz AM; 1 kw-C, NDD; 5 kw-D, NDD; N35 52 50 W80 32 26
431 Eaton Road, Mocksville, NC 27028 US
(336) 751-9375
www.wdsl1520.com/
wdsl1520am@yahoo.com
License: Mocksville, NC held by Davie Broadcasting Inc.
Arbitron Metro Market: Mocksville, NC; *Format:* Country, Gospel; *Target Audience:* 25-80; general
Craig Dalla Riva, General Manager
Sherry Miller, General Sales Mgr

Monroe

WDEX
12-01-1983; 1430 kHz AM; *Hrs Open:* 24; 2.5 kw-D, DA2; 2.5 kw-N, DA2; N34 59 4 W80 36 14
Mailing Address: P.O. Box 8146, Kannapolis, NC 22028 US
Second Address: Weddington Rd., Monroe, NC 28110
(704) 289-9444; *Fax:* (704) 857-0680
wdex1430am@yahoo.com
License: Monroe, NC held by New Life Community Temple of Faith Inc.
Arbitron Metro Market: Charlotte, NC; *Format:* Gospel; *Target Audience:* 25-55.
Ella Hood, CEO
Sharon Talford, General Manager

WIXE
05-03-1968; 1190 kHz AM; *Hrs Open:* 24
Mailing Address: P. O. Box 1007, 1700 Buena Vista Rd, Monroe, NC 28112 US
Second Address: 1700 Buena Vista Dr., Monroe, NC 28112
(704) 289-2525; *Fax:* (704) 289-1416
www.wixe.com
wixeradio@carolina.rr.com
License: Monroe, NC held by Monroe Broadcasting Co.
Regional Network: N.C. News Net.
Arbitron Metro Market: Charlotte-Gastonia-Rock Hill, NC-SC; *Format:* Gospel, Talk, 30 *Special Programming:* Beach & oldies 5 hrs wkly; *Hrs. of News Programming:* News progmg 8 hrs wkly; *Target Audience:* 18-55. *Adv. Rates:* 21.25; 21.25; 21.25; na
Archie Morgan, President

WXNC
07-01-1947; 1060 kHz AM
506 South Church Street, Monre, NC 28110 US
(704) 442-7277; *Fax:* (704) 442-9518
License: Monroe, NC held by Norsan Consulting and Management Inc.
Group Owner: Norsan Consulting and Management Inc.; (acq 8-3-2005; $1.15 million).
Nat'l Network: CNN Radio
Arbitron Metro Market: Charlotte-Gastonia-Rock Hill, NC-SC; *Hrs. of News Programming:* news progmg 5 hrs wkly; *No. News Employees:* 1
Kris Phillips, CFO
Norberto Sanchez, President
Cheri Moore, News Director

Mooresville

WHIP
01-01-1950; 1350 kHz AM; *Hrs Open:* 6 AM-6:30 PM; 1 kw-D, 670 w-N; N35 36 04 W80 48 51
Box 600, 2432 Statesville Hwy., Mooresville, NC 82115
(704) 664-9447; *Fax:* (704) 664-5551
License: Mooresville, Iredell County, NC held by Mooresville Media Inc.
Nat'l Network: USA
Population Served: 225,000 *Special Programming:* Black 6 hrs, relg 6 hrs wkly; *Hrs. of News Programming:* News progmg 13 hrs wkly; *Target Audience:* 25-45.; *Adv. Rates:* 10; 10; 10
Glenn Hamrick, President
Martha Hamrick, Operations Dir
Norman Tindal, General Sales Mgr
Harrill Hamrick, Chief Engineer
Vivian Brandon, Disc Jockey
Kevin Burchett, Sports Commentator
Gary Trexler, Sports Commentator

Morehead City

*WOTJ
12-12-1988; 90.7 MHz FM; *Hrs Open:* 24; 24 kw; 466 ft.; N34 46 41 W76 52 42
520 Roberts Road, Newport, NC 28570 US
(252) 223-4600/223-6088; *Fax:* (252) 223-2201
www.fbnradio.com
fbn@fbnradio.com
License: Morehead City, Carteret County, NC held by Grace Christian School.
Nat'l Network: USA
Format: Religious; *Hrs. of News Programming:* News progmg 8 hrs wkly; *Target Audience:* General; family
Michael Ebron, General Manager

WRHT
12-20-1972; 96.3 MHz FM; *Hrs Open:* 24; 100 kw; 492 ft.; N34 45 7 W76 52 57 *Rebroadcasts:* Rebroadcasts WCBZ(FM) Williamston 100%
P.O. Box 1019, Morehead City, NC 28557 US
(252) 672-5900; *Fax:* (252) 637-6872
License: Morehead City, Carteret County, NC held by Inner Banks Media LLC.
Group Owner: Inner Banks Media LLC; (acq 3-12-2007; grpsl)
Arbitron Metro Market: Greenville-New Bern-Jacksonville, NC; *Format:* Contemporary Hits/Top 40; *Hrs. of News Programming:* news progmg 7 hrs wkly; *No. News Employees:* 1; *Target Audience:* 18-49; young active adults& military personnel
Henry Hinton, President
Christine Cashwell, Business Manager

Morganton

WCIS
03-01-1988; 760 kHz AM; *Hrs Open:* Day station
PO Box 1806, Morganton, NC 28655 US
(828) 584-3076; *Fax:* (828) 433-1498
powerhouse76@aol.com
License: Morganton, NC held by W.F.M. Inc.
Nat'l Network: USA
Arbitron Metro Market: Morganton, NC; *Format:* Gospel
John Whisnant Sr., General Manager
Bob Clark, News Director

WMNC
09-23-1947; 1430 kHz AM; *Hrs Open:* 24; 2.7 kw-D, ND1; 0.046 kw-N, ND1; N35 45 9 W81 43 19
1103 N. Green Street, Morganton, NC 28655 US
(828) 437-0521; *Fax:* (828) 433-8855
www.bigdawg92fm.com
wmnc@bellsouth.net
License: Morganton, NC held by Cooper Broadcasting Co.
Nat'l Network: CNN Radio
Arbitron Metro Market: Morganton, NC; *Format:* Country
Joe Cooper, Station Manager
Cindy Byas, Programming Director
C.J. Stancil, News Director

WMNC-FM
08-03-1963; 92.1 MHz FM; *Hrs Open:* 24; 25 kw; 328 ft.; N35 45 9 W81 43 19
1103 N. Green Street, Morganton, NC 28655 US
(828) 437-0521; *Fax:* (828) 433-8855
www.bigdawg92fm.com
wmnc@bellsouth.net
License: Morganton, Burke County, NC held by Cooper Broadcasting Co.
Arbitron Metro Market: Charlotte, NC; *Format:* Country

Mount Airy

WPAQ
02-01-1948; 740 kHz AM; *Hrs Open:* 6 AM-6:15 PM winter, loc sunset sum; 1 kw-C, ND1; 10 kw-D, ND1; ND1; 0.007 kw; N36 32 4 W80 35 48
P.O. Box 907, Mount Airy, NC 27030 US
(336) 786-6111; *Fax:* (336) 789-7792
www.wpaq740.com
info@wpaq740.com
License: Mount Airy, NC held by WPAQ Radio Inc.
Group Owner: Blue Ridge Radio Inc.
Format: Big Band *Special Programming:* Farm one hr, community affrs one hr, old time string mus 15 hrs wkly; *Hrs. of News Programming:* news progmg 13 hrs wkly; *No. News Employees:* 1; *Target Audience:* 25-64. *Adv. Rates:* 8.50; 8.50; 8.50; 8.50
Mary Branch, Sales
John Mullins, Chief Engineer

WSYD
10-04-1951; 1300 kHz AM; *Hrs Open:* 24; 5 kw-D, DAN; 1 kw-N, DAN; N36 30 12 W80 35 35
Box 1678, Mt Airy, NC 27030 US
(336) 786-2147; *Fax:* (336) 789-9858
License: Mount Airy, NC held by Granite City Broadcasters Inc.
Group Owner: Blue Ridge Radio Inc.; (acq 1996)
Format: Gospel; *Hrs. of News Programming:* news progmg 8 hrs wkly; *No. News Employees:* 1; *Target Audience:* General.
Kelly Epperson, President
Deborah Cochran, Programming Director
Bernie Phillips, News Director
John Mullins, Chief Engineer

Mount Olive

WDJS
12-27-1961; 1430 kHz AM
Mailing Address: P.O. Box 479, Mount Olive, NC 28365 US
Second Address: 990 N. Center St., Ext., Mount Olive, NC 28365
(919) 658-9751; *Fax:* (919) 658-4894
License: Mount Olive, NC held by The Mount Olive Broadcasting Co.
Arbitron Metro Market: Fayetteville, NC; *Format:* Christian, Religious *Special Programming:* Black 5 hrs, gospel 5 hrs, Sp 5 hrs wkly
Ann Mayo, CEO
Nancy West, Programming Director

Moyock

WHBT-FM
10-17-1974; 92.1 MHz FM; 18 kw; Ant 384 ft; N36 41 39 W76 02 57
1003 Norfolk Sq., Norfolk, VA 23502-4948 US
(757) 466-0009; *Fax:* (757) 466-7043
www.thebeatva.com
License: Moyock, Currituck County, NC held by CC Licenses LLC.
Group Owner: iHeartMedia
Population Served: 1,700,000; *Arbitron Metro Market:* Norfolk-Virginia Beach-Newport News, VA; *Format:* Urban Contemporary; *Target Audience:* 18-34; males 18-49
Derrick Martin, Market President
Matt Derrick, Senior Vice President of Programming
Marlon George, Senior Vice President of Sales
Mike Street, Programming Director
Nathan James, Promotions Manager
Jay Flanagan, Digital ContentDirector

Murfreesboro

WDLZ
10-11-1970; 98.3 MHz FM; 3 kw; 328 ft.; N36 26 24 W77 8 10
306 Port St., Easton, MD 21601 US
(410) 822-3301; *Fax:* (410) 822-0576
www.firstmediaradio.com
License: Murfreesboro, Hertford County, NC held by First Media Radio
Group Owner: First Media Radio LLC
Arbitron Metro Market: Elizabeth City-Nags Head, NC; *Format:* Adult Contemp
Alex Kolobielski, President/CEO

WWDR
03-20-1965; 1080 kHz AM
306 Port St., Easton, MD 21601 US
(410) 822-3301; *Fax:* (410) 822-0576
www.firstmediaradio.com
License: Murfreesboro, NC held by First Media Radio LLC.
Group Owner: First Media Radio LLC; (acq 1-7-2003; grpsl)
Nat'l Network: Moody; *Regional Network:* N.C. News Net.
Arbitron Metro Market: Murfreesboro, NC; *Format:* Gospel
Special Programming: Farm 10 hrs wkly
Alex Kolobielski, President/CEO

Murphy

WCNG
10-23-1990; 102.7 MHz FM; *Hrs Open:* 5 AM-midnight; 3 kw; 236 ft.; N35 4 0 W83 59 58
P. O. Box 280, Murphy, NC 28906 US
704) 837-9264
info@wcng.com
License: Murphy, Cherokee County, NC held by Cherokee Broadcasting Company
Arbitron Metro Market: Murphy,NC; *Format:* Classic Rock
Dennis Gene, General Manager

WCVP
10-12-1958; 600 kHz AM; *Hrs Open:* 5 AM-10 PM; 1 kw-D, ND1; 0.02 kw-N, ND1; N35 4 0 W83 59 58
P. O. Box 280, Murphy, NC 28906 US
(823) 837-9264
info@wcvp.com
License: Murphy, NC held by Cherokee Broadcasting Co.

Arbitron Metro Market: Knoxville, TN; *Format:* Adult Contemp, Gospel, 60 *Special Programming:* Farm 3 hrs, class 20 hrs, C&W 12 hrs wkly; *Target Audience:* All ages.
Allan Blakemore, President
Jane Blakemore, General Manager
Dennis Blakemore, General Sales Mgr
Skip Ballard, Music Director

WKRK

08-08-1958; 1320 kHz AM; *Hrs Open:* 24; 5 kw-D, ND1; 0.062 kw-N, ND1; N35 6 42 W84 0 31
90 Tennessee Street, Murphy, NC 28906 US
(828) 837-1320; *Fax:* (828) 837-8610
www.1320am.com
License: Murphy, NC held by Radford Communications Inc.
Nat'l Network: Jones Radio Networks; *Nat'l Reps:* Rgnl Reps
Regional Reps: Commercial Media Sales; *Wire Services:* AP
Arbitron Metro Market: Chattanooga, TN; *Format:* Country
Special Programming: Pub affrs 3 hrs wkly; *Hrs. of News Programming:* AP Radio News, 2 minutes an hour; *Target Audience:* 35-64; *Adv. Rates:* 17; 15;17; 8
Tim Radford, President
Ab Radford, Operations Dir
Larry Nelson, Programming Director
Emma Ramsey, Promotions Manager
Bill Yonce, Disc Jockey
Marty Montell, Disc Jockey
John St. John, Disc Jockey

Nags Head

WZPR

04-04-1990; 92.3 MHz FM; *Hrs Open:* 24; 10 kw; 384 ft.; N35 50 49 W75 37 20
637 Harbor Road, Wanchese, NC 27981 US
(252) 475-1888; *Fax:* (252) 475-1881
www.yourclassicrock.com
License: Nags Head, Dare County, NC held by CapSan Media LLC.
Group Owner: CapSan Media LLC; (acq 6-30-2006; grpsl)
Nat'l Network: ESPN Radio
Arbitron Metro Market: Wanchese, NC; *Format:* Contemporary Hits/Top 40
William Whitlow, President
Hunt Thomas, Operations Dir

Nashville

WZAX

02-01-1997; 99.3 MHz FM; *Hrs Open:* 24; 6 kw; 328 ft.; N35 57 1 W77 57 26
306 Port St., Easton, MD 21601 US
(410) 822-3301; *Fax:* (410) 822-0576
www.993rockcity.com
License: Nashville, Nash County, NC held by First Media Radio LLC
Group Owner: First Media Radio LLC; (acq 7-22-2003; grpsl)
Nat'l Reps: Interep
Arbitron Metro Market: Rocky Mount-Wil; *Format:* Classic Rock
Steve Roberts, General Manager

New Bern

*WAAE

01-01-1997; 91.9 MHz FM; *Hrs Open:* 24 hours; 1.35 kw; 164 ft.; N35 8 14 W77 0 22 *Rebroadcasts:* Rebroadcasts WAFR(FM) Tupelo 100%
P.O. Box 3206, Tupelo, MS 38803 US
(662) 844-8888; *Fax:* (662) 842-6791
www.afr.net
faq@afa.net
License: New Bern, Craven County, NC held by American Family Association.
Group Owner: American Family Radio
Nat'l Network: American Family Radio
Arbitron Metro Market: New Bern, NC; *Format:* Religious
Time Wildmon, President
Donald Wildmon, Founder
Buddy Smith, Sr VP
Ed Vitagliano, Exec VP
Randy Sharp, Director Of Special Projects
Meeke Addison, Director Of Communications
Abraham Hamilton III, General Sounsel & Public PolicyAnalyst

WIKS

08-01-1977; 101.9 MHz FM; *Hrs Open:* 24; 100 kw; 981 ft.; N35 12 7 W77 11 15
207 Glenburnie Dr., New Bern, NC 28560 US
(252) 633-1500; *Fax:* (252) 633-0718
www.1019online.com
License: New Bern, Craven County, NC held by Beasley Media Group LLC
Group Owner: Beasley Broadcast Group Inc.
Nat'l Reps: D & R Radio
Arbitron Metro Market: Greenville-New Bern-Jacksonville, NC; *Format:* Adult Contemp *Special Programming:* Gospel 4 hrs, jazz 2 hrs wkly
Jay Blaze, Programming Director
John Sheftic, Director of Sales
Bruce Simel, Market Manager

WNOS

04-23-1942; 1450 kHz AM; *Hrs Open:* 24; 1 kw-U, ND1; N35 6 3 W77 4 33
1331 South Glenburnie, New Bern, NC 28562 US
(252) 633-1490; *Fax:* (888) 878-5251
License: New Bern, NC held by CTC Media Group Inc.
Group Owner: CTC Media Group Inc.; acq 7-1-00; $65,000).
Nat'l Network: Fox Sports; Westwood One; *Regional Network:* N.C. News Net.
Arbitron Metro Market: Greenville, NC; *Format:* Sports, Talk; *Target Audience:* 12+, Male 12-45
Lee Afflerbach, President
Mike Afflerbach, General Manager

WSFL-FM

07-20-1968; 106.5 MHz FM; *Hrs Open:* 24; 100 kw; 915 ft.; N35 2 27 W77 21 11
207 Glenburnie Dr., New Bern, NC 28560 US
(252) 633-1500; *Fax:* (252) 633-6546
www.wsfl.com
cindymiller@wsfl.com
License: New Bern, Craven County, NC held by Beasley Media Group LLC
Group Owner: Beasley Broadcast Group Inc.; (acq 7-10-91; $500,000 with co-located AM;
Nat'l Reps: D & R Radio
Arbitron Metro Market: Greenville-New; *Format:* Classic Rock, Rock/AOR; *Target Audience:* 18-54.
Bruce Simel, General Manager/Market Manager
John Sheftic, Director of Sales
Cindy Miller, Programming Director
Beth McCall, Production Director

*WTEB

06-04-1984; 89.3 MHz FM; *Hrs Open:* 24; 99 kw; 482 ft.; N35 6 32 W77 6 10
800 College Court, New Bern, NC 28562 US
(800) 222-9832; *Fax:* (252) 638-3538
www.publicradioeast.org
hsegar@publicradioeast.org
License: New Bern, Craven County, NC held by Board of Trustees, Craven Community College.
Nat'l Network: NPR; PRI
Arbitron Metro Market: Greenville-New Bern, NC; *Format:* News
Special Programming: Jazz 4 hrs wkly; *Hrs. of News Programming:* News progmg 44 hrs wkly; *Target Audience:* 35 plus; highly educated professionals
Kelly Batchelor, Operations Dir
Charles Wethington, General Manager
Kathleen Beal, General Sales Mgr
Jill McGuire, Programming Director
George Olsen, News Director
J. Howard Jones, Chief Engineer
Michael.R.Foster, BusinessAccount Executive

WWNB

07-05-1953; 1490 kHz AM; *Hrs Open:* 24; 1 kw-U, ND1; N35 7 59 W77 3 56
114 S. Business Plaza, New Bern, NC 28562 US
(252) 633-1490; *Fax:* (888) 878-5251
www.rfenc.com
info@rfenc.com
License: New Bern, NC held by CTC Media Group Inc.
Group Owner: CTC Media Group Inc.; acq 11-15-90; $75,000).
Nat'l Network: ESPN Radio; Westwood One
Arbitron Metro Market: Greenville, NC; *Format:* Sports; *Target Audience:* Men 12-54; general
Mike Afflerbach, General Manager
Chris Butler, General Sales Mgr

*WZNB

01-01-2006; 88.5 MHz FM; 0.3 kw; 121 ft.; N35 6 32 W77 6 10
800 College Court, New Bern, NC 28562 US
(800) 222-9832; *Fax:* (252) 638-3538
www.publicradioeast.org
License: New Bern, Craven County, NC held by Craven Community College.
Arbitron Metro Market: Greenville, NC; *Format:* Public Affairs, News
Kelly Batchelor, Operations Dir
Charles Wethington, Station Manager
Kathleen Beal, General Sales Mgr
Jill McGuire, Programming Director
George Olsen, News Director
J. Howard Jones, Chief Engineer
Kelly Batchelor, BroadcastSupervisor
Jared Brumbaugh, Announcer / Reporter and Producer

New Hope

WAUG

07-20-1987; 750 kHz AM; 0.5 kw-D, NDD; N35 47 28 W78 37 10
1315 Oakwood Avenue, Raleigh, NC 97610 US
(919) 516-4750
License: New Hope, NC held by Saint Augustine's College.
Nat'l Network: American Urban
Format: Gospel, News, 62, Talk, Religious; *Target Audience:* 18 plus; Black adults
Diane Suber, President
Frank Butler, Operations Dir
Alan Riggs, Station Manager
John Hardee, Chief Engineer

Newland

WECR

08-14-1978; 1130 kHz AM; 1 kw-D, NDD; N36 4 39 W81 54 59
1281 Newland Hwy, Newland, NC 28657 US
(828) 733-0188; *Fax:* (828) 733-0189
www.wecglory1130.wordpress.com
wecr@bellsouth.net
License: Newland, NC held by High Country Adventures LLC.
Group Owner: Curtis Media Group; (acq 3-3-2009; grpsl)
Arbitron Metro Market: Newland, NC; *Format:* Country, Gospel
Special Programming: Gospel 10 hrs, relg 5 hrs, bluegrass 2 hrs wkly; *Target Audience:* 25-54; middle class, blue collar; *Adv. Rates:* 11.40; 11.40;11.40; na
Phillip Greene, Station Manager

Newport

WMGV

09-04-1983; 103.3 MHz FM; *Hrs Open:* 24; 100 kw; 981 ft.; N35 7 55 W76 52 32
207 Glenburnie Dr., New Bern, NC 28560 US
(252) 633-1500; *Fax:* (252) 633-0718
www.v1033.com
webmaster@v1033.com
License: Newport, Carteret County, NC held by Beasley Media Group LLC
Group Owner: Beasley Broadcast Group Inc.; (acq 2-3-2000; grpsl)
Nat'l Reps: D & R Radio
Arbitron Metro Market: Greenville, NC; *Format:* Adult Contemp; *Target Audience:* 18-54.
Bruce Simel, General Manager
Colleen Jackson, Programming Director
John Grant, Public Affairs Director

Newton

WNNC

06-18-1948; 1230 kHz AM; *Hrs Open:* 24; 1 kw-U, ND1; N35 40 20 W81 14 12
P.O. Box 940, Newton, NC 28658 US
(828) 464-4041; *Fax:* (828) 464-9662
www.mytotalradio.com
wnnc@mytotalradio.com
License: Newton, NC held by Newton-Conover Communications Inc.
Arbitron Metro Market: Newton, NC; *Format:* Adult Contemp
Special Programming: Black 2 hrs, jazz 3 hrs wkly; *No. News Employees:* 1; *Target Audience:* 25-49.; *Adv. Rates:* 30; 15; 15; 12
Dave Lingafelt, President
Jim Turner, General Sales Mgr
Karol Lowery, News Director

Newton Grove

*WYBJ

01-01-2007; 90.7 MHz FM; 3 kw; 354 ft.; N35 13 54 W78 22 11
2630 Mirror Lake Drive, Fayetteville, NC 28303 US
(252) 223-4600; *Fax:* (252) 223-2201
www.fbnradio.com
License: Newton Grove, Sampson County, NC held by Grace Missionary Baptist Church Inc.
Arbitron Metro Market: Newton Grove, NC
Michael Ebron, General Manager

Norlina

*WVRH
01-01-2001; 94.3 MHz FM; *Hrs Open:* 24; 6 kw; Ant 328 ft; N36 29 46 W78 11 14 *Rebroadcasts:* Rebroadcasts WRVL(FM)
3700 Candlers Mountain Rd, Lynchburg, VA 24502
(434) 582-3688; *Fax:* (434) 582-2994
www.myjourneyfm.com
License: Norlina, Warren County, NC held by Liberty University, Inc.
Group Owner: Liberty University, Inc.
Format: Christian, Religious
Chris Wygal, Operations Manager & Host
Barry Armstrong, General Manager
Mike Weston, Programming Director
Mark Edwards, Production Director

*WZRN
90.5 MHz FM; 2.3 kw; Ant 298 ft; N36 29 38 W78 11 23
PO Box 1895, Goldsboro, NC 27533
(252) 308-0885; *Fax:* (252) 537-3333
www.gomixradio.org
wago@gomixradio.com
License: Norlina, Warren County, NC held by Roanoke Valley Communications Inc.
Nat'l Network: WZRU
Target Audience: 23 and older
Dr. T.D. Worthington, President
Allen Garrett, General Manager
Glenda Browder, General Sales Mgr
Rusty Draper, Chief Engineer

North Wilkesboro

WKBC
06-01-1947; 800 kHz AM; *Hrs Open:* 24; 1 kw-D, ND1; 0.308 kw-N, ND1; N36 11 16 W81 8 30
Box 938, 400 C Street, North Wilkesboro, NC 28659 US
(336) 667-2221; *Fax:* (336) 667-3677
License: North Wilkesboro, NC held by Wilkes Broadcasting Co. Inc.
Nat'l Network: CBS Radio; *Wire Services:* AP
Format: Country; *No. News Employees:* 1; *Adv. Rates:* 22; 14; 18; 12
Robert Brown, President
Ed Racey, News Director

WKBC-FM
07-01-1962; 97.3 MHz FM; *Hrs Open:* 24; 100 kw horiz, 92 kw vert; 1322 ft.; N36 4 34 W81 7 43
P.O. Box 938, North Wilkesboro, NC 28659 US
(336) 667-2221; *Fax:* (336) 667-3677
License: North Wilkesboro, Wilkes County, NC held by Wilkes Broadcasting Co. Inc.
Format: Contemporary Hits/Top 40; *Adv. Rates:* 48; 40; 44; 30
Robert Brown, General Manager
Bob Brown, Programming Director
Ed Racey, Chief Engineer

Oak Island

WUIN
07-01-2000; 98.3 MHz FM; *Hrs Open:* 24; 18.5 kw; 381 ft.; N33 57 40 W78 01 37
1410 Commonwealth Dr., Suite 102A, Wilmington, NC 28403 US
(910) 772-6300
portcitydaily.com/983thepenguin
thepenguin@localvoicemedia.com
License: Oak Island, Brunswick County, NC held by Local Voice Media Group
Group Owner: Local Voice Media Group; (acq 9-2014)
Arbitron Metro Market: Wilmington, NC; *Format:* Triple A

Ocean Isle Beach

WLQB
01-01-1999; 93.5 MHz FM; 6 kw; 328 ft.; N33 55 37 W78 23 48
Rebroadcasts: Simulcast with WGTR(FM) Bucksport, SC 100%
4841 Highway 17 Bypass South, Myrtle Beach, SC 29577 US
(843) 293-0107; *Fax:* (843) 293-1717
www.b935fm.com
License: Ocean Isle Beach, Brunswick County, NC held by AMFM Radio Licenses LLC.
Group Owner: iHeartMedia
Arbitron Metro Market: Ocean Isle Beach, NC; *Format:* Adult Contemp
Jimmy Feuger, Market President
Ron Roberts, Senior Vice President of Programming
Denise Atkins, Senior Vice President of Sales
Jennifer Habib, Business Manager

Ocracoke

*WOVV
90.1 MHz FM; 0.65 kw; 62 ft.; N35 6 43 W75 58 38.2
PO Box 1447, Ocracoke, NC 27960 US
(252) 921-0365
www.wovv.org
info@wovv.org
License: Ocracoke, Hyde County, NC held by Ocracoke Foundation.
Arbitron Metro Market: Ocracoke, NC; *Format:* Variety/Diverse
Robin Payne, President

Old Fort

WKSF
08-01-1947; 99.9 MHz FM; *Hrs Open:* 24; 48 kw; 2621 ft.; N35 25 32 W82 45 25
13 Summerlin Road, Asheville, NC 28806 US
(828) 257-2700; *Fax:* (828) 255-7850
www.99kisscountry.com
info@99kisscountry.com
License: Old Fort, Buncombe County, NC held by Capstar TX LLC
Group Owner: iHeartMedia
Arbitron Metro Market: Asheville, NC; *Format:* Country; *Hrs. of News Programming:* News progmg 3 hrs wkly; *Target Audience:* 25-44.
Caroline Earley, Sales Manager
Jeff Davis, Programming Director
Skip Wilson, Digital Sales Manager
Jessica Lee, Digital Content Director

Oriental

WNBU(FM)
03-18-1993; 94.1 MHz FM; *Hrs Open:* 24; 11 kw; Ant 485 ft; N35 00 02 W76 49 58
1884 West Arlington Boulevard, Greenville, NC 29834
(252) 355-1037; *Fax:* (252) 355-2234
www.wnbufm.com
dmckay@ibxmedia.com
License: Oriental, Pamlico County, NC held by Inner Banks Media LLC.
Group Owner: Inner Banks Media LLC; (acq 3-12-2007; grpsl)
Population Served: 250,000; *Arbitron Metro Market:* Greenville, NC; *Format:* Talk; *Target Audience:* 25 plus; adults with disposable incomes
Henry Hinton, General Manager
Bill Poole, Sales Manager
Hank Hinton, General Sales Mgr

Oxford

WCBQ
06-09-1949; 1340 kHz AM; *Hrs Open:* 18; 1 kw-U, ND1; N36 18 27 W78 34 37 *Rebroadcasts:* Rebroadcasts WHNC(AM) Henderson 100%
Mailing Address: P. O. Box 336, Oxford, NC 27565 US
Second Address: 1 Alvin Augustus Jones Way, Oxford, NC 27565
(919) 693-3540(919) 693-1340; *Fax:* (919) 693-9054
www.dralvinjones.com
alvin@dralvinjones.com
License: Oxford, NC held by The Paradise Network Of North Carolina (TPN)
Format: Gospel, Talk *Special Programming:* Farm, professional & college sports, news/talk; *Hrs. of News Programming:* News progmg 10 hrs wkly; *Target Audience:* General.
Dr. Alvin Jones, CEO

Pilot Mountain

*WGIW
01-01-2008; 89.7 MHz FM; 0.43 kw vert; 373 ft.; N36 25 23.6 W80 37 52.6
US
(605) 868-0525
License: Pilot Mountain, Surry County, NC held by Church Planters of America.
Arbitron Metro Market: Pilot Mountain, NC; *Format:* Gospel
Danny Hawkins, President

Pine Knoll Shores

WBNK
01-01-2009; 92.7 MHz FM; *Hrs Open:* 24 7; 11.5 kw; 748 ft.; N34 53 0.4 W76 30 21.3
224 South Front Street, New Bern, NC 28560 US
(252) 636-3333
License: Pine Knoll Shores, Carteret County, NC held by Tower Investment Trust Inc.
Group Owner: Tower Investment Trust Inc.
Arbitron Metro Market: Pine Knoll Shores, NC; *Format:* Christian; *Target Audience:* w 25 -54 w 18 - 34
William Brothers, President

Pinehurst

WIOZ
03-25-1980; 550 kHz AM; *Hrs Open:* 24; 1 kw-D, DA2; 0.26 kw-N, DA2; N35 09 04 W79 28 40
200 Short Rd., Southern Pines, NC 28387 US
(910) 692-2107; *Fax:* (910) 692-6849
www.wioz.com
License: Pinehurst, NC held by Muirfield Broadcasting Inc.
Group Owner: Muirfield Broadcasting Inc.
Format: Adult Contemp; *Hrs. of News Programming:* news progmg 5 hrs wkly; *No. News Employees:* 1; *Target Audience:* General.
Walker Morris, President
Tiffany Hewitt, General Manager

Pinetops

WPWZ
12-02-1996; 95.5 MHz FM; *Hrs Open:* 24; 12.5 kw; 459 ft.; N35 56 45 W77 39 37
306 Port St., Easton, MD 21601 US
(410) 822-3301
License: Pinetops, Edgecombe County, NC held by First Media Radio LLC.
Group Owner: First Media Radio LLC; (acq 12-3-2003; grpsl)
Nat'l Reps: Interep
Arbitron Metro Market: Rocky Mount-Wilson, NC; *Format:* Urban Contemporary; *No. News Employees:* 1; *Target Audience:* 24-54.
Steve Roberts, General Manager

Pineville

WGIV
03-08-1948; 1370 kHz AM *Rebroadcasts:* Rebroadcasts WRNA(AM) China Grove 90%
P.O. Box 861, Rock Hill, SC 29731 US
(803) 329-2760; *Fax:* (803) 329-3317
License: Pineville, NC held by Wisdom LLC.
Group Owner: Wisdom LLC; (acq 2-2-2009; grpsl)
Nat'l Network: USA
Arbitron Metro Market: Charlotte-Gastonia-Rock Hill, NC-SC; *Format:* Blues; *Target Audience:* 30 plus Black
Emma Neely, Operations Dir
Frank Neely, General Manager
Frankie Hemphill, Station Manager

Pisgah Forest

WGCR
09-16-1985; 720 kHz AM
3232 Hendersonville Highway, Pisgah Forest, NC 28768 US
(828) 884-9427; *Fax:* (828) 883-9427
www.wgcr.net
License: Pisgah Forest, NC held by Anchor Baptist Broadcasting Association.
Nat'l Network: USA; *Regional Network:* N.C. News Net.
Format: News, Religious *Special Programming:* Gospel; *Target Audience:* General.
Randy Barton, President
Shanna Barton, Promotions Manager
Shamma Barton, News Director
Lamar Owen, Chief Engineer

Plymouth

WPNC-FM
12-01-1979; 95.9 MHz FM; *Hrs Open:* 24; 2.6 kw; 331 ft.; N35 50 48 W76 45 22
930 Highway 32 South, Plymouth, NC 27962 US
(252) 793-9995; *Fax:* (252) 793-4673
www.magic959online.com
magic959production@yahoo.com
License: Plymouth, Washington County, NC held by Durlyn Broadcasting Inc.
Nat'l Network: CBS Radio; *Regional Network:* N.C. News Net.
Format: Adult Contemp; *Target Audience:* 25-54.; *Adv. Rates:* 10; 10; 10; 10.
Bill Benjamin, Owner
Christy Tucker, Sales Manager
Alex Rains, Operations Manager

Raeford

WMFA
04-25-1963; 1400 kHz AM; *Hrs Open:* 6 AM-10 PM; 1 kw-U, ND1; N34 58 43 W79 12 32

1085 E. Central Ave., Raeford, SC 28376 US
(910) 875-6225; *Fax:* (910) 875-3220
wmfa1400@yahoo.com
License: Raeford, NC held by W & V Broadcasting Enterprises Inc.
Arbitron Metro Market: Raeford, NC; *Format:* Gospel *Special Programming:* Sp 6 hrs wkly; *Target Audience:* General. Black
William Hollingsworth, CEO
Jeremy Hollingsworth, General Manager
Vera Hollingsworth, CFO

***WRAE**
01-01-2006; 88.7 MHz FM; 6 kw; 472 ft.; N34 54 57 W79 7 28
Rebroadcasts: Rebroadcasts WAFR(FM) Tupelo, MS 100%
P.O. Box 3206, Tupelo, MS 38803 US
(662) 844-8888; *Fax:* (662) 842-6791
www.afr.net
faq@afa.net
License: Raeford, Hoke County, NC held by American Family Association.
Group Owner: American Family Radio
Arbitron Metro Market: Raeford, NC; *Format:* Christian
Tim Wildmon, President
Donald Wildmon, Founder
Buddy Smith, Sr VP
Ed Vitagliano, Exec VP
Randy Sharp, Director Of Special Projects
Meeke Addison, Director Of Communications
Abraham Hamilton III, General Counsel

Raleigh

WBBB
01-01-1947; 96.1 MHz FM; *Hrs Open:* 24; 98 kw; 984 ft.; N35 41 7 W78 43 14
3012 Highwoods Blvd., Suite 201, Raleigh, NC 27604 US
(413) 597-3265; *Fax:* (413) 597-2259
www.radio961.com
info@curtismedia.com
License: Raleigh, Wake County, NC held by Carolina Media Group Inc.
Group Owner: Curtis Media Group; (acq 1996; $16 million)
Nat'l Reps: McGavren Guild
Arbitron Metro Market: Twin Falls ID; *Format:* Adult Contemp, Classic Rock, 76
Adam Ain, General Manager

WCLY
08-15-1962; 1550 kHz AM
2619 Western Boulevard, Raleigh, NC 27606 US
(919) 890-6299; *Fax:* (919) 890-6146
www.wral.com
License: Raleigh, NC held by Triangle Broadcast Associates LLC.
Group Owner: Curtis Media Group; (acq 4-5-99)
Arbitron Metro Market: Raleigh-Durham, NC; *Format:* Sports, Talk; *Target Audience:* 25-65;
Rick Heilmann, General Manager

***WCPE**
07-17-1978; 89.7 MHz FM; *Hrs Open:* 24; 96.7 kw; 1178 ft.; N35 56 25 W78 28 45
P.O. Box 897, Wake Forest, NC 27588 US
(800) 556-5178; *Fax:* (919) 556-9273
theclassicalstation.org
webmaster@TheClassicalStation.org
License: Raleigh, Wake County, NC held by Educational Information Corp.
Arbitron Metro Market: Raleigh-Durham, NC; *Format:* Classical *Special Programming:* Sacred music, Opera; *Target Audience:* 35 plus; class mus listeners
Deborah Proctor, CEO
Dick Storck, Programming Director
Deborah Proctor, Chief Engineer
Will Woltz, Music Director

***WKNC-FM**
10-09-1966; 88.1 MHz FM; *Hrs Open:* 24/7/365; 25 kw; 259 ft; N35 47 15 W78 40 14
343 Witherspoon Student Ctr., Campus Box 8607, Raleigh, NC 27695
(919) 515-2401; *Fax:* (919) 515-5333
www.wknc.org
gm@wknc.org
License: Raleigh, Wake County, NC held by North Carolina State University.
Population Served: 1,000,000; *Arbitron Metro Market:* Raleigh-Durham, NC *Special Programming:* South Asian, A capella, Americana, Punk; *Hrs. of News Programming:* 4 hrs wkly; *Target Audience:* 18-59; adults & highschool & college students of all demographics; *Adv. Rates:* 40; 30; 40; 30

John Kovalchik, General Manager
Walt Lilly, Program Director
Phian Tran, Promotions Director

WPJL
03-01-1939; 1240 kHz AM; *Hrs Open:* 5:30 AM-midnight; 1 kw-U, ND1; N35 46 25 W78 37 9
P. O. Box 27946, 515 Bart Street, Raleigh, NC 27611 US
(919) 834-6401
License: Raleigh, NC held by WPJL Inc.
Nat'l Network: USA
Arbitron Metro Market: Raleigh-Durham, NC; *Format:* Christian *Special Programming:* Black gospel; *Hrs. of News Programming:* News progmg 10 hrs wkly; *Target Audience:* 25-54; Evangelical Christian community ofgreater Raleigh area; *Adv. Rates:* 30; 25; 30; 20
William Suttles, President
LaRue Porter, Operations Dir
Jon Hardee, Chief Engineer

WPTF
09-22-1924; 680 kHz AM; *Hrs Open:* 24; 50 kw-N, DAN; N35 47 38 W78 45 41
3012 Highwoods Blvd #201, Raleigh, NC 27604 US
(919) 790-9392; *Fax:* (919) 882-1746
www.wptf.com
License: Raleigh, NC held by First State Communications.
Group Owner: Curtis Media Group
Nat'l Network: CBS; *Regional Network:* Southern Farm; *Nat'l Reps:* McGavren Guild
Arbitron Metro Market: Raleigh-Durham, NC; *Format:* News, News/Talk, 86 *Special Programming:* Farm 10 hrs wkly; *Hrs. of News Programming:* News progmg 20 hrs wkly; *Target Audience:* 35-64.
David Stuckey, General Manager

WQDR-FM
08-01-1949; 94.7 MHz FM; *Hrs Open:* 24; 96 kw; 1,679 ft; N35 40 35 W78 32 09
3012 Highwoods Blvd., Suite 200, Raleigh, NC 27604
(919) 790-9392; *Fax:* (919) 882-1746
www.wqdr.net
info@curtismedia.com
License: Raleigh, Wake County, NC held by Carolina Media Group Inc.
Group Owner: Curtis Media Group
Regional Network: Southern Farm
Population Served: 1,000,000; *Arbitron Metro Market:* Raleigh-Durham, NC *Special Programming:* NASCAR racing, bluegrass; *Hrs. of News Programming:* news progmg 2 hrs wkly; *No. News Employees:* 1; *Target Audience:* 25-54.
Trip Savery, General Manager

WRAL
01-01-1947; 101.5 MHz FM; *Hrs Open:* 24; 96 kw; 1,821 ft.; N35 40 35 W78 32 8
3100 Highwoods Blvd., Suite 140, Raleigh, NC 27604 US
(919) 890-6101; *Fax:* (919) 890-6146
www.wralfm.com
License: Raleigh, Wake County, NC held by WRAL-FM Inc.
Group Owner: Capitol Broadcasting Co. Inc.; (acq 1946)
Regional Network: N.C. News Net; *Nat'l Reps:* Katz Radio; *Wire Services:* AP
Arbitron Metro Market: Raleigh-Durham, NC *TV Affiliate:* WRAL-TV affil.; *Format:* Adult Contemp *Special Programming:* Public Afffairs Block - 6:30-8:00am Sundays; *Hrs. of News Programming:* 7 hrs wkly news progmg *Target Audience:* 25-54.
James F. Goodmon, President
Katie Phillips, General Manager
Alex McTighe, Local Sales Manager
Patrick McMahon, Programming Director
Brian Grube, National Sales Manager
Haki Dennis, Account Executive
Barbara Purtee, AccountExecutive
Dorian Baldwin, Traffic Manager

WPTK(AM)
01-01-1947; 850 kHz AM; *Hrs Open:* 24; 10 kw-D, 5 kw-N, DA-N; N35 48 04 W78 48 51
3012 Highwoods Boulevard, Raliegh, NC 27604
(919) 875-9100; *Fax:* (919) 510-6990
www.wptf.com
License: Raleigh, Wake County, NC held by McClatchey Broadcasting Co. LLC
Nat'l Network: Westwood One; Fox Sports; *Nat'l Reps:* McGavren Guild; *Wire Services:* AP
Population Served: 1,490,000; *Arbitron Metro Market:* Raleigh-Durham, NC; *Hrs. of News Programming:* News progmg 5 hrs wkly; *Target Audience:* 25-54.
Brian Maloney, General Manager
Adam Gold, Programming Director

Mike Stangl, Promotions Manager
Ted Sawyer, News Director

WFNL
12-01-1981; 570 kHz AM; *Hrs Open:* 24; 500 w-D, 54 w-N; N35 45 37 W78 39 27
3012 Highwoods Blvd., Raleigh, NC 27604
(919) 855-9383; *Fax:* (919) 790-6654
License: Raleigh, Wake County, NC held by Triangle Broadcast Associates LLC.
Group Owner: Curtis Media Group; (acq 6-1-99).
Nat'l Network: ABC; *Nat'l Reps:* McGavren Guild
Population Served: 600,000; *Arbitron Metro Market:* Raleigh-Durham, NC; *Format:* News/Talk, News, 86; *Adv. Rates:* 18; 15; 24; 15
Rick Heilmann, General Manager
Peter Richon, Programming Director

***WSHA**
11-18-1968; 88.9 MHz FM; *Hrs Open:* 24; 50 kw; 456 ft.; N35 45 5 W78 36 1
118 East South Street, Raleigh, NC 27602 US
(919) 546-8430; *Fax:* (919) 546-8315
www.shawu.edu/wsha
License: Raleigh, Wake County, NC held by Shaw University.
Nat'l Network: NPR
Arbitron Metro Market: Raleigh-Durham,; *Format:* Jazz *Special Programming:* Sp 3 hrs, African 3 hrs, Caribbean 3 hrs, blues 8; *Hrs. of News Programming:* News progmg 13.5 hrs wkly; *Target Audience:* 25-55; highincome, well educated
Dr. Emeka Emekauwa, General Manager
Sharon Berry-Vivian, Programming Director
Jim Davis, Chief Engineer
Rashad Mulhaimin, Assistant General Manager
Michael Rochelle, Senior Underwriting

WKIX-FM
01-01-2000; 102.9 MHz FM; 1.7 kw; Ant 620 ft; N35 47 38 W78 45 41
3012 Highwoods Blvd., Suite 201, Raleigh, NC 27604
(919) 790-6961; *Fax:* (919) 790-8369
www.kix1029.com
License: Raleigh, Wake County, NC held by WWND LLC.
Group Owner: Curtis Media Group; (acq 10-2-98; $495,000 for stock)
Nat'l Reps: McGavren Guild
Population Served: 1,100,000; *Arbitron Metro Market:* Raleigh-Durham, NC; *Format:* Adult Contemp, Classic Rock
Mike Hartel, General Manager
Bill Campbell, Programming Director
Shalon Lenfestry, Promotions Manager
Ali Diatta, News Director
Allen Sherrill, Chief Engineer

Reidsville

WJMH
09-06-1948; 102.1 MHz FM; *Hrs Open:* 24; 99 kw; 1204 ft.; N36 16 33 W79 56 26
7819 National Service Road, Greensboro, NC 27409 US
(336) 605-5200; *Fax:* (336) 605-5219
www.102jamz.com
info@102jamz.com
License: Reidsville, Rockingham County, NC held by Entercom Greensboro License LLC.
Group Owner: Entercom Communications Corp.; (acq 12-13-99; grpsl)
Nat'l Reps: McGavren Guild
Arbitron Metro Market: Greensboro-Winston Salem-High Point, NC; *Format:* Adult Contemp; *Target Audience:* 16-35; 65% Black, 35% white
Brian Douglas, Programming Director
Travis Moore, Advertising

WREV
01-01-1948; 1220 kHz AM; 1 kw-D, NDD; N36 23 19 W79 38 51
Rebroadcasts: Rebroadcasts WRTP(AM) Chapel Hill 100% US
(202) 638-1959; *Fax:* (202) 638-6127
estuardovaldemar@hotmail.com
License: Reidsville, NC held by Estuardo Valdemar Rodriguez and Leonor Rodriguez.
Group Owner: Radio La Grande; (acq 8-5-2004; $125,000).
Format: Tejano
Estuardo Valdemar Rodriguez, General Manager

Rennert

WGQR
12-01-1989; 105.7 MHz FM; *Hrs Open:* 24; 7.7 kw; 583 ft.; N34 44 5 W78 47 25

Mailing Address: 1602 Greenwood Street, Elizabethtown, NC 28337 US
Second Address: Box 28, Elizabethtown, NC 28329
(910) 488-7729
www.wgqr1057.com
License: Rennert, Bladen County, NC
Arbitron Metro Market: Fayetteville, NC; *Format:* Gospel; *Hrs. of News Programming:* News progmg 6 hrs wkly
Paul Brian, Programming Director
Al Radlein, News Director
Dan Arnsan, Disc Jockey
Buddy Edwards, Disc Jockey
K.C Evers, Disc Jockey

Roanoke Rapids

WCBT
11-01-1940; 1230 kHz AM; *Hrs Open:* 24; 1 kw-U, ND1; N36 26 45 W77 39 51
P.O. Box 910, Roanoke Rapids, NC 27870 US
(919) 537-4184; *Fax:* (919) 535-2686
haskinsal@yahoo.com
License: Roanoke Rapids, NC
Nat'l Network: ABC; ESPN Radio; *Regional Network:* N.C. News Net.
Format: Sports
John Green, Operations Dir
Al Haskin, General Manager
Allen Garrett, Programming Director
Frank White, Chief Engineer

WPTM
01-01-1973; 102.3 MHz FM; *Hrs Open:* 24; 6 kw; 317 ft.; N36 30 13 W77 44 20
Mailing Address: PO Box 910, Roanoke Rapids, NC 27870 US
Second Address: 3 E. Forst St., Weldon, NC 27890
(252) 536-3115; *Fax:* (252) 538-0378
www.1023wptm.com
License: Roanoke Rapids, Halifax County, NC held by First Media Radio LLC.
Group Owner: First Media Radio LLC; (acq 7-22-2003; grpsl)
Regional Network: Southern Farm; *Wire Services:* UPI
Format: Country *Special Programming:* Farm15 hrs, relg 3 hrs wkly; *Hrs. of News Programming:* news progmg 14 hrs wkly; *No. News Employees:* 3; *Target Audience:* 25-54; females with spendable income, decision-makers
Cody Clark, Operations Dir
Al Haskins, General Manager

*WVRP
91.1 MHz FM; 2 kw; 69 ft; N36 28 08 W77 39 02 *Rebroadcasts:* Rebroadcasts WVRL(FM)
3700 Candler's Mountain Rd, Suite F, Lynchburg, VA 24502 US
(800) 424-9594
www.myjourneyfm.com
License: Roanoke Rapids, Halifax County, NC held by Liberty University, Inc.
Group Owner: Liberty University, Inc.
Format: Adult Contemp, Christian; *Hrs. of News Programming:* News progmg one hr wkly

Robbins

WLHC
06-02-2003; 103.1 MHz FM; *Hrs Open:* 24; 6 kw; 328 ft.; N35 26 33 W79 26 37
Box 1963, Pinehurst, NC 28370 US
(919) 775-1031; *Fax:* (919) 775-1397
www.life1031.com
License: Robbins, Moore County, NC held by Woolstone Corporation
Nat'l Network: ABC; *Regional Network:* N.C. News Net.
Arbitron Metro Market: Robbins, NC; *Format:* Adult Contemp
Special Programming: Jazz 2 hrs, Christian 5 hrs, bluegrass 5 hrs wkly; *No. News Employees:* 1; *Adv. Rates:* 30; 26; 29; 20
-, Chief Engineer
Mary Button, Marketing/Sales Staff
Patrick Neal, Marketing/Sales Staff
Pete Saunders, Marketing/Sales Staff

Robbinsville

WCVP-FM
01-01-1987; 95.9 MHz FM; *Hrs Open:* 5:30 AM-10 PM (M-F); 6 AM-10 PM (S); 0.12 kw; 2008 ft.; N35 15 28 W83 47 44
P.O. Box 280, Murphy, NC 28906 US
(828) 4798080
info@wcvp.com
License: Robbinsville, Graham County, NC held by Cherokee Broadcasting Co.
Arbitron Metro Market: Knoxville, TN; *Format:* Country; *Target Audience:* General.

Dennis Blakemore, President
Penny Wade, Operations Dir

Rockingham

WAYN
09-01-1946; 900 kHz AM; *Hrs Open:* 6 AM-10 PM; 1 kw-D, ND1; 0.297 kw-N, ND1; N34 55 30 W79 44 35
Mailing Address: P.O. Box 519, Rockingham, NC 28379 US
Second Address: 1223 Rockingham Rd., Rockingham, NC 28380
(406) 721-6800; *Fax:* (406) 329-1850
License: Rockingham, NC held by WAYN Inc.
Regional Network: N.C. News Net.
Arbitron Metro Market: Missoula MT; *Format:* Adult Contemp; *Target Audience:* 25-54; adults
Rod Harsell, General Manager

WLWL
10-27-1969; 770 kHz AM; 5 kw-D, NDD; N34 55 30 W79 47 11
Mailing Address: P.O. Box 1536, Rockingham, NC 28379 US
Second Address: 275 River Rd., Rockingham, NC 28379
(910) 895-9595
bigwaveradio@gmail.com
License: Rockingham, NC held by Sandhills Broadcasting Co. Inc.
Regional Network: N.C. News Net.
Arbitron Metro Market: Rockingham, NC; *Format:* Oldies; *Target Audience:* 25-60.
Keith Davis, Operations Dir
Beth Ballard, General Manager

*WRSH
05-01-1973; 91.1 MHz FM; 0.34 kw; 161 ft.; N34 56 59 W79 42 52
Mailing Address: P.O. Box 1259, Hamlet, NC 28345 US
Second Address: Richmond Sr. High School, 838 N. US Hwy. 1, Rockingham, NC 28379
(910) 997-9812; *Fax:* (910) 997-9816
License: Rockingham, Richmond County, NC held by Richmond County Board of Education.

Kim Newton, General Manager

Rocky Mount

WEED
09-10-1933; 1390 kHz AM; *Hrs Open:* 24
Mailing Address: P.O. Box 2666, Rocky Mounty, NC 27802 US
Second Address: 115 N. Church St., Rocky Mount, NC 27802
(252) 443-5976; *Fax:* (252) 443-5977
License: Rocky Mount, NC held by Northstar Broadcasting Corp.
Nat'l Network: Premiere Radio Networks
Arbitron Metro Market: Rocky Mount, NC; *Format:* Religious; *Hrs. of News Programming:* news progmg 14 hrs wkly; *No. News Employees:* 10; *Target Audience:* Males; 18+
Sonya Johnson, Operations Dir
Charles Johnson II, General Manager
Charles Johnson, II, Programming Director
Ethan Arrington, Music Director

WRMT
12-15-1958; 1490 kHz AM; *Hrs Open:* 24; 1 kw-U, ND1; N35 55 57 W77 49 49
306 Port St., Easton, MD 21601 US
(410) 822-3301; *Fax:* (410) 822-0576
www.firstmediaradio.com
License: Rocky Mount, NC held by First Media Radio LLC
Group Owner: First Media Radio LLC; (acq 1-7-2003; grpsl)
Regional Network: N.C. News Net; *Nat'l Reps:* Interep
Arbitron Metro Market: Rocky Mount-Wilson, NC; *Format:* Sports; *Target Audience:* 30 plus.
Alex Kolobielski, President/CEO

*WRQM
04-01-1996; 90.9 MHz FM; *Hrs Open:* 24; 7.5 kw; 627 ft.; N35 48 40 W77 44 33 *Rebroadcasts:* Rebroadcasts WUNC(FM) Chapel Hill 99.9%
434 Falls Road, Rocky Mount, NC 27803 US
(919) 966-5454; *Fax:* (919) 966-5955
www.wunc.org
wunc@unc.edu
License: Rocky Mount, Edgecombe County, NC held by The Board of Trustees of the University of NC at Chapel Hill
Nat'l Network: NPR; PRI; CBC Radio One
Format: News; *Hrs. of News Programming:* news progmg 124 hrs wkly; *No. News Employees:* 7; *Target Audience:* 35 plus; educated, successful, community active
Kevin Wolf, Operations Dir
Joan Rose, General Manager

WDWG
12-18-1989; 98.5 MHz FM; 16 kw; 410 ft.; N35 54 43 W77 50 6
306 Port St., Easton, MD 21601 US
(410) 822-3301; *Fax:* (410) 822-0576
www.firstmediaradio.com
License: Rocky Mount, Nash County, NC held by First Media Radio LLC
Group Owner: First Media Radio LLC
Nat'l Reps: Interep
Arbitron Metro Market: Rocky Mount-Wil; *Format:* Country; *Target Audience:* 18 plus.
Alex Kolobielski, President/CEO

Rose Hill

WEGG
01-01-1971; 710 kHz AM; *Hrs Open:* Sunrise-sunset
Mailing Address: 1223 West New Bern Rd, Kinston, NC 28504 US
Second Address: 3228 U.S. Hwy. 117, Rose Hill, NC 28458
(252) 341-8327; *Fax:* (252) 497-2486
License: Rose Hill, NC held by Conner Media Corp.
Group Owner: Conner Media Corp.
Regional Network: Southern Farm; *Nat'l Reps:* Keystone (unwired net)
Arbitron Metro Market: Rose Hill, NC; *Format:* Black, Gospel, 74
Special Programming: Farm 9 hrs, bluegrass gospel 10 hrs wkly
Suzanne Wilson, General Manager
Don Brown, Chief Engineer
C.D. Melvin, Religion Ed

Roxboro

WKRX
01-01-1958; 96.7 MHz FM; *Hrs Open:* 5:30 AM-11 PM; 3 kw; 299 ft.; N36 22 4 W78 59 58
P. O. Box 1176, Roxboro, NC 27573 US
(336) 599-0266; *Fax:* (336) 599-9411
www.radioroxboro.com
License: Roxboro, Person County, NC held by Roxboro Broadcasting Co.
Nat'l Network: ABC; *Regional Network:* N.C. News Net.
Hrs. of News Programming: news progmg 7 hrs wkly; *No. News Employees:* 1; *Target Audience:* 18-49.; *Adv. Rates:* Same as AM
David Bradsher, Promotions Manager
David Ramsey, Disc Jockey
Bill Lester, Disc Jockey
Don Carroll, Disc Jockey

WRXO
01-01-1949; 1430 kHz AM; *Hrs Open:* 6 AM-sunset; 1 kw-D, NDD; N36 22 4 W78 59 58 *Rebroadcasts:* Simulcast with WKRX(FM) Roxboro
P. O. Box 1176, Roxboro, NC 27573 US
(336) 599-0266; *Fax:* (336) 599-9411
www.radioroxboro.com
radiod@aol.com
License: Roxboro, NC held by Roxboro Broadcasting Co.
Nat'l Network: ABC; *Regional Network:* N.C. News Net.
Arbitron Metro Market: Raleigh-Durham,; *Format:* Country
Special Programming: Black 4 hrs, farm 5 hrs, Southern gospel 5 hrs wkl; *Hrs. of News Programming:* news progmg 7 hrs wkly; *No. News Employees:* 1 *TargetAudience:* 18-49.; *Adv. Rates:* 9.40; 9.40; 9.40; 9.40
David Bradsher, President
Wayne Tuck, News Director
Conrad Kimbrough, Chief Engineer
Don Carroll, Disc Jockey
Bill Lester, Disc Jockey
David Ramsey, Disc Jockey

Rutherfordton

WCAB
10-19-1966; 590 kHz AM; *Hrs Open:* 24
191 White Sides, Rutherfordton, NC 28139 US
(828) 287-3356; *Fax:* (828) 287-7182
www.wcab59.com
License: Rutherfordton, NC held by Isothermal Broadcasting Corp.
Regional Network: N.C. News Net.
Arbitron Metro Market: Rutherfordton, NC; *Format:* Country, News, 62, Sports, Talk; *Hrs. of News Programming:* News progmg 25 hrs wkly; *Target Audience:* 25 plus; adult consumers; *Adv. Rates:* 12.70; 11.70; 12.70;11.70
James Bishop, President
Lou Gilliam, News Director

Salisbury

WEND
03-16-1946; 106.5 MHz FM; *Hrs Open:* 24; 84 kw; 1047 ft.; N35 35 32 W80 37 44
10828 Lockland Road, Potomac, MD 20854 US
(704) 376-1065; *Fax:* (704) 334-9525
www.1065.com
jackdaniel@1065.com
License: Salisbury, Rowan County, NC held by Capstar TX LLC
Group Owner: iHeartMedia; (acq 3-12-01).
Nat'l Reps: McGavren Guild
Arbitron Metro Market: Salisbury, NC; *Format:* Alternative; *Target Audience:* 18-34.
Keith Cornwell, Sales Manager
Jack Daniel, Programming Director
Phillip Higginbotham, Promotions Director
Jodi Phillips, Webmaster

***WOGR-FM**
11-01-1996; 93.3 MHz FM; 0.01 kw; 180 ft.; N35 40 3 W80 28 13 *Rebroadcasts:* Rebroadcasts WOGR(AM) Charlotte 100%
Box 16408, Charlotte, NC 28297 US
(704) 393-1540; *Fax:* (704) 393-1527
www.wordnet.org
info@wordnet.org
License: Salisbury, Rowan County, NC held by Victory Christian Center Inc.
TV Affiliate: Relg
Maceo Harris, Operations Manager
Andrea Ingram, Music Director

WSAT
06-01-1947; 1280 kHz AM; *Hrs Open:* 24; 1 kw-D, DAN; 1 kw-N, DAN; N35 40 30 W80 30 30
1525 Jake Alex. Blvd. W, Salisbury, NC 28144 US
(704) 633-0621; *Fax:* (704) 636-2955
www.1280wsat.com
License: Salisbury, NC held by Cap Communications Inc.
Nat'l Network: Motor Racing Net
Arbitron Metro Market: Charlotte-Gasto; *Format:* Oldies; *Target Audience:* 25-64; people that can afford high ticket items
Charles Poole, President
Bubby Poole, Programming Director
Ted Fuller, Chief Engineer
Eddie Fuller, Disc Jockey
Buddy Poole, Disc Jockey
Lance Anderson, Disc Jockey

WSTP
01-01-1939; 1490 kHz AM; *Hrs Open:* 24; 1 kw-U, ND1; N35 41 18 W80 29 44
1105 Statesville Boulevard, Salisbury, NC 28144 US
(704) 636-3811; *Fax:* (704) 637-1490
newsradio1490@yahoo.com
License: Salisbury, NC held by Rowan Media INC.
Nat'l Network: Fox News Radio; Talk Radio Network; Jones Radio Networks; *Regional Network:* N.C. News Net. *Regional Reps:* Capital Radio
Arbitron Metro Market: Charlotte-Gastonia-Rock Hill, NC-SC; *Format:* News, News/Talk, 86; *Hrs. of News Programming:* News progmg 24 hrs daily; *Target Audience:* 25-59.; *Adv. Rates:* 22; 15; 22; 12
Timothy Coates, President
Mike Mangan, Operations Dir
Nicole Brown, Programming Director
Mark Brown, News Director
Hal McGee, Chief Engineer

Sanford

***WDCC**
01-01-1971; 90.5 MHz FM; *Hrs Open:* 24; 2 kw; 236 ft.; N35 28 22.7 W79 8 32
1105 Kelly Drive, Sanford, NC 27330 US
(919) 718-7257
www.wdccfm.com
wdcc@cccc.edu
License: Sanford, Lee County, NC held by Central Carolina Community College.
Arbitron Metro Market: Sanford, NC; *Format:* Alternative, Contemporary Hits/Top 40
Bill Freeman, General Manager

WFJA
01-01-1950; 105.5 MHz FM; *Hrs Open:* 24; 2.3 kw; 486 ft.; N35 26 34 W79 18 41
Box 3457, Sanford, NC 27331 US
(919) 775-3525; *Fax:* (919) 775-4503
www.classichitsandoldies.com
License: Sanford, Lee County, NC held by WWGP Broadcasting Corp.
Format: Oldies; *No. News Employees:* 1; *Target Audience:* 25-54.; *Adv. Rates:* 19; 18; 19; 17
Richard Feindel, President & General Manager
Cindy Johnson, Sales

WWGP
01-01-1946; 1050 kHz AM; *Hrs Open:* 6 AM-1 AM
P.O. Box 3457, Sanford, NC 27330 US
(919) 775-3525; *Fax:* (919) 775-4503
www.wwgp1050.com
production@wfjaradio.com
License: Sanford, NC held by Richard K. Feindel.
Arbitron Metro Market: Sanford, NC; *Format:* Country *Special Programming:* Farm 7 hrs wkly; *Hrs. of News Programming:* news progmg 7 hrs wklyone; *No. News Employees:* 1; *Target Audience:* 18-54.; *Adv. Rates:* 18; 17; 18; 16
Richard Feindel, President
Jessica Osborne, Operations Dir
Cindy Johnson, General Sales Mgr
Margaret Murchison, News Director

WXKL
10-02-1952; 1290 kHz AM; *Hrs Open:* 6 AM-8 PM; 1 kw-D, ND1; 0.04 kw-N, ND1; N35 27 1 W79 9 30
P. O. Box 25488, Raleigh, NC 27611 US
(919) 774-1080; *Fax:* (919) 774-1118
License: Sanford, NC held by Thomas Broadcasting Inc.
Nat'l Network: NBC
Arbitron Metro Market: Sanford, NC; *Format:* Christian, Gospel; *Hrs. of News Programming:* News progmg 6 hrs wkly; *Target Audience:* 25 plus; general
James Thomas, President
Amos Marks, Programming Director
Tommy Mack, Disc Jockey
Marilyn Cross, Disc Jockey
Danny Davis, Disc Jockey

Scotland Neck

WYAL
04-03-1960; 1280 kHz AM; 5 kw-D, NDD; N36 8 9 W77 26 9
Highway 125, Weldon Road, Scotland Neck, NC 27874 US
(252) 826-3866
License: Scotland Neck, NC held by Sky City Communications Inc.
Regional Network: N.C. News Net.
Arbitron Metro Market: Scotland Neck, NC; *Format:* Gospel, Religious *Special Programming:* Farm 2 hrs wkly
Richard Petway, President

Scotts Hill

***WZDG**
03-23-2007; 88.5 MHz FM; 8.9 kw vert; 545 ft.; N34 30 7 W78 4 58
3305 Burnt Mill Dr., Wilmington, NC 28403 US
(910) 763-2452; *Fax:* (910) 763-6578
www.theword885.com
info@carolinachristianradio.com
License: Scotts Hill, Pender County, NC held by Carolina Christian Radio Inc.
Group Owner: Carolina Christian Radio
Arbitron Metro Market: Wilmington, NC; *Format:* Alternative, Christian

Selma

WTSB
08-04-1964; 1090 kHz AM; *Hrs Open:* Sunrise-sunset
Post Office Box 1, Selma, NC 27567 US
(919) 934-6789; *Fax:* (919)934-6824
www.wtsbradio.com
info@wtsbradio.com
License: Selma, NC held by Lamm Media Group LLC
Arbitron Metro Market: Smithfield, NC; *Format:* Country
Mickey Lamm, General Manager

Semora

***WKVK**
03-01-1996; 106.7 MHz FM; 50 kw; 492 ft.; N36 25 7 W79 11 49 US
(916) 251-1600, (843) 267-0036; *Fax:* (916) 251-1650, (843) 399-9031
www.klove.com
License: Semora, Caswell County, NC held by Educational Media Foundation.
Group Owner: EMF Broadcasting
Nat'l Network: K-Love
Format: Christian
Mike Novak, President
Len Bagwell, Operations Dir

Shallotte

WVCB
06-11-1964; 1410 kHz AM; 0.5 kw-D, ND1; 0.168 kw-N, ND1; N33 58 20 W78 23 2
Mailing Address: Hwy. 17, Main St., Shallotte, NC 28459 US
Second Address: 4640 Main St., Shallotte, NC 28459
(910) 754-4512; *Fax:* (910) 754-3461
wvcb@atmc.net
License: Shallotte, NC held by John G. Worrell.
Regional Network: N.C. News Net.
Arbitron Metro Market: Shallotte, NC; *Format:* Gospel, Religious; *Target Audience:* General.
Rhonda Worrell, Station Manager

Sharpsburg

WLQC
103.1 MHz FM; 6 kw; Ant 295 ft; N35 57 01 W77 57 26
3048 Zebulon Road, Rocky Mount, NC 27804 US
(252) 937-1031
www.life1031fm.com
License: Sharpsburg, Nash County, NC held by Pinestone Media Corp.
Arbitron Metro Market: Rocky Mount-Wilson, NC
Alan L. Button, President

Shelby

WOHS
07-09-1958; 1390 kHz AM; *Hrs Open:* 24; 1 kw-D, 500 w-N, DA-N; N35 19 28 W81 32 00
Mailing Address: 1366 Startown Rd, Lincolnton, NC 29340
Second Address: Box 2266, Shelby, NC 28151-2266
(704) 482-1390; *Fax:* (704) 481-9007
www.site.realcountry1390.com
info@hrnb.com
License: Shelby, Cleveland County, NC held by HRN Broadcasting Inc.
Group Owner: HRN Broadcasting Inc.; (acq 2006; $350,000).
Nat'l Network: ABC
Population Served: 250,000 *Target Audience:* 25-54; middle and older
D. Mark Boyd III, President
Joe Martin, Station Manager
Andy Johnson, General Sales Mgr

WHQC
01-01-1948; 96.1 MHz FM; *Hrs Open:* 24; 100 kw; 1,738 ft; N35 21 44 W81 09 19
801 Wood Ridge Center Dr., Charlotte, NC 28217 US
(704) 714-9444; *Fax:* (704) 334-9525
www.channel961.com
License: Shelby, Cleveland County, NC held by Clear Channel Broadcasting Licenses Inc.
Group Owner: iHeartMedia; (acq 10-18-2000).
Nat'l Reps: McGavren Guild
Population Served: 2,000,000; *Arbitron Metro Market:* Charlotte-Gastonia-Rock Hill, NC-SC; *Format:* Contemporary Hits/Top 40; *Hrs. of News Programming:* news progmg 4 hrs wkly; *No. News Employees:* 1 *TargetAudience:* 25-54.
Keith Hotchkiss, Market President
Della Pizzati, Sales Manager
Anna Nyeste, Promotions Director
Benjamin Brinitzer, Chief Engineer
Jodi Phillips, Digital Program Director

Siler City

WNCA
08-19-1952; 1570 kHz AM; *Hrs Open:* 6am - midnight
P. O. Box 429, Siler City, NC 27344 US
(919) 742-2135; *Fax:* (919) 663-2843
License: Siler City, NC held by Chatham Broadcasting Co. Inc. of Siler City.
Regional Network: N.C. News Net.
Arbitron Metro Market: Siler City, NC; *Format:* Christian, News, 62, Talk *Special Programming:* Gospel 5 hrs, relg 12 hrs, loc sports 6 hrs & Span; *Hrs. of News Programming:* news progmg 15+ hrs wkly *No. NewsEmployees:* 2; *Target Audience:* 25-55; rural, agri-oriented, blue-collar, growing spanish community; *Adv. Rates:* 12; 10; 10; 8
Barry Hayes, President
Renee Kennedy, Station Manager
Dacia Hayes, General Sales Mgr
Jose Alvarado, Spanish Director
Debbie Applewhite, Traffic Manager

Smithfield

WWPL
02-02-1972; 102.3 MHz FM; *Hrs Open:* 24; 2.6 kw; Ant 561 ft; N35 23 54 W78 00 38 *Rebroadcasts:* Simulcast with WWMY(FM) Raleigh 100%
3012 Highwoods Blvd., Suite 201, Raleigh, NC 27604
(919) 860-1102; *Fax:* (919) 892-1746
www.pulse102.com
bcampbell@curtismedia.com
License: Smithfield, Johnston County, NC held by New Age Communications Inc.
Group Owner: Curtis Media Group; (acq 7-1-96; $550,000)
Population Served: 120,000; *No. News Employees:* 4
Don Curtis, President
Mike Hartel, General Manager

WMPM
01-01-1950; 1270 kHz AM; 5 kw-D, ND2; 0.145 kw-N, ND2; N35 31 33 W78 20 1
P. O. Box 57, Smithfield, NC 27577 US
(919) 934-2434; *Fax:* (919) 989-6388
www.1270wmpm.com
lynda@1270wmpm.com
License: Smithfield, NC held by Family Media Group LLC
Nat'l Network: CBS
Arbitron Metro Market: Raleigh, NC; *Format:* Christian *Special Programming:* Farm 2 hrs, relg 8 hrs, news/talk 12 hrs wkly; *Target Audience:* 30 plus; general
Lynda Carroll, Sales

Snow Hill

***WAGO**
07-01-1998; 88.7 MHz FM; *Hrs Open:* 24; 17 kw; 292 ft.; N35 26 49 W77 39 20
P. O. Box 1895, Goldsboro, NC 27533 US
(252) 747-8887; *Fax:* (252) 747-7888
www.gomixradio.org
wago@gomixradio.org
License: Snow Hill, Greene County, NC held by Pathway Christian Academy Inc.
Nat'l Network: Moody; Salem Radio Network
Arbitron Metro Market: Greenville NC; *Format:* Christian; *Hrs. of News Programming:* news progmg 14 hrs wkly; *No. News Employees:* 1; *Target Audience:* General.
T.D. Worthington, President
Keith Aycock, Programming Director
Ashley Worthington, Promotions Manager
Joe Patton, Chief Engineer
Tim Sutton, Music Director

South Gastonia

***WGAS**
08-14-1959; 1420 kHz AM *Rebroadcasts:* Rebroadcasts WOGR(AM) Charlotte
P.O. 16408, Charlotte, NC 28297 US
(704) 393-1540; *Fax:* (704) 393-1527
www.wordnet.org
info@wordnet.org
License: South Gastonia, NC held by Victory Christian Center Inc.
Arbitron Metro Market: Charlotte-Gastonia-Rock Hill, NC-SC *TV Affiliate:* WGTB- TV; *Format:* Gospel; *Target Audience:* General.
Maceo Harris, Operations Manager

Southern Pines

WEEB
11-15-1947; 990 kHz AM; *Hrs Open:* 24; 5 kw-C, ND1; 10 kw-D, ND1; ND1; 0.026 kw; N35 11 37 W79 24 42
Box 1855, Midland Rd., Southern Pines, NC 28388 US
(910) 692-7440; *Fax:* (888) 390-5186
www.weeb990.com
steve@weeb990.com
License: Southern Pines, NC held by Pinehurst Broadcasting Corp.
Nat'l Network: ABC; Fox News Radio; Salem Radio Network;
Regional Network: N.C. News Net.
Arbitron Metro Market: Southern Pines, NC; *Format:* News, News/Talk, 86 *Special Programming:* High school & college sports, gospel 6 hrs wkly; *Hrs. of News Programming:* news progmg 26 hrs wkly *No. News Employees:* 3; *Target Audience:* 25 plus; business professionals, CEOs, retirees; *Adv. Rates:* $12,00 per spot
Charles Bennett, General Sales Mgr
Steve Leader, Programming Director
Al Mangum, News Director

WIOZ
01-01-1995; 102.5 MHz FM; 3.4 kw; 436 ft.; N35 04 04 W79 28 40
200 Short Rd., Southern Pines, NC 28387 US
(910) 692-2107; *Fax:* (910) 692-6849
www.star1025fm.com
License: Southern Pines, Moore County, NC held by Meridian Communications LLC.
Group Owner: Muirfield Broadcasting Inc.; (acq 6-17-97; $316,500)
Format: Adult Contemp
Walker Morris, President
Tiffany Hewitt, General Manager

WMGU
08-14-1973; 106.9 MHz FM; *Hrs Open:* 24; 50 kw; 469 ft.; N34 59 53 W79 15 47
1009 Drayton Road, Fayetteville, NC 28303 US
(910) 864-5222; *Fax:* (910) 864-3065
www.magic1069.com
License: Southern Pines, Moore County, NC held by Cumulus Licensing Corp.
Group Owner: Cumulus Media Inc.; (acq 3-12-2001; $6.15 million)
Arbitron Metro Market: Fayetteville, NC; *Format:* Urban Contemporary; *Hrs. of News Programming:* news progmg 18 hrs wkly; *No. News Employees:* 2; *Target Audience:* 35 plus.
Richard Stadlen, Operations Manager
Vic Jackson, Programming Director
Steven Roberts, VP/Market Manager/Director of Sales

Southern Shores

WFMI
01-01-2003; 100.9 MHz FM; 39 kw; 486 ft.; N36 12 10 W75 52 23
P.O. Box 539, McLean, VA 22101 US
(757) 774-7148; *Fax:* (757) 490-2524
www.rejoice1009.com
rejoice@rejoice100point9.com
License: Southern Shores, Dare County, NC held by Communications Systems Inc.
Arbitron Metro Market: Virginia Beach, VA; *Format:* Gospel, Talk
Mike Chandler, General Manager
Karol Scott, Station Manager

Southport

WAZO
04-15-1978; 107.5 MHz FM; *Hrs Open:* 24; 21 kw; 768 ft.; N34 14 37 W78 7 24
25 N. Kerr Ave., Wilmington, NC 28405 US
(910) 791-3088; *Fax:* (910) 791-0112
www.z1075.com
requests@z1075.com
License: Southport, Brunswick County, NC held by Sunrise Broadcasting LLC.
Group Owner: Capitol Broadcasting Co. Inc.; (acq 11-18-2008; grpsl)
Nat'l Reps: McGavren Guild
Arbitron Metro Market: Wilmington, NC; *Format:* Contemporary Hits/Top 40; *Hrs. of News Programming:* news progmg one hr wkly; *No. News Employees:* 1; *Target Audience:* 18-49; young, upwardly mobile professionals
Brian Schimmel, General Manager
Lauren LaMothe, Promotions Director
Josh Lee, Sales
Erika Burns, Sales
Kristine Smith, Sales
Veronica Banning, Sales
Holly Shaw, Sales

Sparta

WCOK
04-01-1967; 1060 kHz AM
P. O. Box 637, Sparta, NC 28675 US
(336) 372-5700; *Fax:* (336) 372-5863
www.wyzdradio.org
wcoksparta@yahoo.com
License: Sparta, NC held by Mountain Empire Broadcasting Inc.
Arbitron Metro Market: Piedmont Triad, NC; *Format:* Religious, Country; *Target Audience:* General.
Bro. Ricky Cothren, President
Jos Reynoso, General Manager
Bro. Jake Easter, Programming Director
Johnathan Johnson, Disc Jockey
Michael Sexton, Disc Jockey

Spindale

WGMA
10-01-1982; 1520 kHz AM; *Hrs Open:* Sunrise-sunset; 500 w-D; N35 21 00 W81 56 18
Box 805, 301 W. Main St., Spindale, NC 28160
(828) 287-5151; *Fax:* 1-828-287-0081
WGMA1520AM@BellSouth.Net
License: Spindale, Rutherford County, NC held by Blue Mountain Braodcasting LLC
Population Served: 35,000 *Hrs. of News Programming:* news progmg 20 hrs wkly; *No. News Employees:* 1; *Target Audience:* 30-50; adults; *Adv. Rates:* 3.90; 3.90; 3.90; 3.90
Jesse A. Cowan, Owner
Barbara Martin, President
Andy Foster, Operations Dir
Kaye Cantrell, General Manager
Neil Murray, Programming Director
Jerrell Bedford, Engineering Dir

***WNCW**
10-13-1989; 88.7 MHz FM; *Hrs Open:* 24; 17 kw horiz, 9.6 kw vert; 3028 ft.; N35 44 6 W82 17 11
Post Office Box 804, Spindale, NC 28160 US
(828) 287-8000; *Fax:* (828) 287-8012
www.wncw.org
info@wncw.org
License: Spindale, Rutherford County, NC held by Isothermal Community College.
Nat'l Network: PRI; NPR
Arbitron Metro Market: Spindale, NC; *Format:* News, Triple A *Special Programming:* Blues 4 hrs, jazz 5 hrs, folk 12 hrs, drama 3 hrs,; *Hrs. of News Programming:* news progmg 31 hrs wkly; *No. News Employees:* 1 *Target Audience:* 35-49; anyone interested in diverse info & culture
Dave Kester, Director of Programming
Martin Anderson, Music Director
Terri Frashier, Director of Business Operations

Spring Lake

WFBX
05-22-1963; 1450 kHz AM; *Hrs Open:* 24 *Rebroadcasts:* Simulcast with WFAY(AM) Fayetteville 100%
5600 Cliffdale Road, Fayetteville, NC 28314 US
(910) 867-4129; *Fax:* (910) 223-1451
www.espnfay.com/
wfayespnradio@gmail.com
License: Spring Lake, NC held by WCIE-AM Inc.
Nat'l Network: ESPN Radio
Arbitron Metro Market: Fayetteville, NC; *Format:* Sports
JoAnn Germers Hausen, Operations Dir
Kevin Fennessy, General Manager

***WZRI**
01-01-2005; 89.3 MHz FM; *Hrs Open:* 24; 2 kw vert; 179 ft.; N35 10 14 W78 57 44
2630 Mirror Lake Drive, Fayetteville, NC 28303 US
(888) 937-2471; *Fax:* (916) 251-1650
www.air1.com
info@air1.com
License: Spring Lake, Cumberland County, NC held by Educational Media Foundation.
Group Owner: EMF Broadcasting; (acq 11-12-2002).
Nat'l Network: Air 1
Arbitron Metro Market: Spring Lake, NC; *Format:* Alternative, Christian; *No. News Employees:* 3; *Target Audience:* 18-35; Judeo-Christian, female
Darrell Chambliss, Chairman
Alan Mason, COO
Mike Novak, President and CEO
Len Bagwell, Operations Dir
Paul Goldsmith, Programming Director
Ed Lenane, News Director
Sam Wallington, Engineering Dir
Richard Hunt, News Reporter
Marya Morgan, News Reporter
Dan Antonelli, Chief Business Development Officer
Eric Moser, Chief Financial Officer
Brian Burger, Vice President of Human Resources
D. Kevin Blair, Secretary and General Counsel

Spruce Pine

WTOE
12-24-1955; 1470 kHz AM; *Hrs Open:* 24; 5 kw-D, ND1; 0.103 kw-N, ND1; N35 54 24 W82 6 21
Mailing Address: P.O. Box 744, Burnsville, NC 28714 US
Second Address: 749 Sawmill Road, Burnsville, NC 28714
(828) 765-7441; *Fax:* (828) 682-6227
www.wtoe.com
1470@wtoe.com

License: Spruce Pine, NC held by Mountain Valley Media Inc.
Group Owner: Mark Media Group; (acq 9-27-91)
Nat'l Network: ABC; *Regional Network:* N.C. News Net.
Arbitron Metro Market: Burnsville, NC; *Format:* Oldies *Special Programming:* Relg 8 hrs wkly; *Hrs. of News Programming:* news progmg 10 hrs wkly; *No. News Employees:* 1; *Target Audience:* 25 plus. *Adv.Rates:* 18; 16; 18; 10
Remelle Sink, Vice President
J. Ardell Sink, President and General Manager

St. Pauls

WUKS
10-16-1994; 107.7 MHz FM; 5.2 kw; 656 ft.; N34 52 17 W79 8 49
508 Person St., Fayetteville, NC 28301 US
(910) 486-2000; *Fax:* (910) 486-2109
www.1077jamz.com
License: St. Pauls, Robeson County, NC held by Beasley Media Group LLC
Group Owner: Beasley Broadcast Group Inc.; (acq 6-12-97; $1.2 million with WTEL(AM) Red Springs).
Nat'l Network: ABC; *Nat'l Reps:* D & R Radio
Arbitron Metro Market: Fayetteville, NC; *Format:* Urban Contemporary; *Target Audience:* 25-54.
Tricia Gallenbeck, Director of Sales
Mac Edwards, Vice President/Market Manager
Danny Highsmith, Regional Vice President
Katy Lollis, General Sales Manager
Angela Godwin, General Sales Manager
Ina Cartrette, Advertising

Statesville

WAME
10-07-1957; 550 kHz AM; *Hrs Open:* 24
212 Signal Hill Drive, Statesville, NC 28625 US
(704) 872-0550; *Fax:* (704) 872-5547
www.realcountry929.com
License: Statesville, NC held by Statesville Family Radio Corp.
Group Owner: GHB Radio Group; (acq 4-22-86; $210,000;
Arbitron Metro Market: Charlotte-Gastonia-Rock Hill, NC-SC;
Format: Country; *Target Audience:* Adults 25- 54, Adults 35+
Jeff Davis, Production Director
Walter Sterling, Marketing Consultant

WKKT
03-16-1961; 96.9 MHz FM; *Hrs Open:* 24; 100 kw; 1549 ft.; N35 31 57 W80 47 47
801 Wood Ridge Center Drive, Charlotte, NC 28217 US
(704) 714-9444; *Fax:* (704) 332-8805
www.969thekat.com
License: Statesville, Iredell County, NC held by Capstar TX LLC
Group Owner: iHeartMedia; (acq 8-30-00; grpsl).
Arbitron Metro Market: Charlotte-Gastonia-Rock Hill, NC-SC;
Format: Country; *Target Audience:* 25-54; middle to upper income adults
Keith Hotchkiss, Market President
Ryan Petrosso, Sales Manager
Anna Nyeste, Promotions Director
Benjamin Brinitzer, Chief Engineer
Jodi Phillips, Digital Program Director

WSIC
05-03-1947; 1400 kHz AM; *Hrs Open:* 24; 1 kw-D, ND2; 1 kw-N, ND2; N35 48 9 W80 53 30
1117 Radio Road, Statesville, NC 28679 US
(704) 872-6345; *Fax:* (704) 873-6921
www.wsicweb.com
License: Statesville, NC held by Iredell Broadcasting Inc.
Nat'l Reps: Rgnl Reps *Regional Reps:* T-N.
Format: News, Sports; *Hrs. of News Programming:* news progmg 21 hrs wkly; *No. News Employees:* 1; *Target Audience:* 35 plus; upscale
KC Kena Cooper, Executive Producer
Mark Sanger, President/CEO
Brian Weiss, General Manager

Swansboro

***WKGV**
09-12-1993; 104.1 MHz FM; *Hrs Open:* 24; 5.4 kw; 345 ft.; N34 43 26 W77 14 57 *Rebroadcasts:* Rebroadcasts KLVR(FM) Middletown, CA 100%
4309 West Ocean Avenue, Emerald Isle, NC 28554 US
(800) 525-5683; *Fax:* (916) 251-1650
www.klove.com
klove@klove.com
License: Swansboro, Onslow County, NC held by Educational Media Foundation.
Group Owner: EMF Broadcasting; (acq 11-29-2007)
Nat'l Network: K-Love
Arbitron Metro Market: Omaha, NE; *Format:* Christian; *No. News Employees:* 13
Darrell Chambliss, Chairman
Mlke Novak, President & CEO
Laura Daniels, News Reporter
Tim Luttrell, News Reporter
Kenny Noble Cortes, News Reporter
Darren Vinson, News Reporter

Sylva

WRGC
540 kHz AM; 5 kw-D, 0.14 kw-N, ND2; N35 23 35 W83 11 38
1846 Skyland Dr, P.O. Box 1044, Sylva, NC 28779 US
(828) 586-2221; *Fax:* (828) 586-6834
www.wrgc.com
info@wrgc.com
License: Sylva, Jackson County, NC held by Five Forty Broadcasting Company, Llc
Group Owner: Five Forty Broadcasting Companies; (acq. from Georgia-Carolina Radiocasting Companies)
Nat'l Network: NBC; NCNN; CNBC; *Regional Network:* Atlanta Braves Radio Network; North Carolina News Network; Southern Farm Network
Format: Variety/Diverse *Special Programming:* NASCAR, Local Sports; *Hrs. of News Programming:* news progmg 14 hrs wkly; *No. News Employees:* 1; *Target Audience:* General.
Roy Burnette, Managing Member

Tabor City

WTAB
07-01-1954; 1370 kHz AM; *Hrs Open:* 6 AM-midnight; 5 kw-D, ND1; 0.109 kw-N, ND1; N34 9 0 W78 51 40
Mailing Address: Avon and 701 Bypass, Tabor City, NC 28463 US
Second Address: 210 Avon St., Tabor City, NC 28463
(910) 653-2131; *Fax:* (910) 653-5146
www.wtabradio.com
wtab@wtabradio.com
License: Tabor City, NC held by WTAB Inc.
Regional Network: N.C. News Net.
Arbitron Metro Market: Myrtle Beach, SC; *Format:* Country, Gospel *Special Programming:* Swap shop, 12hrs wkly; *Hrs. of News Programming:* News progmg 7 hrs wkly; *Target Audience:* General.; *Adv. Rates:* 12
Jack Miller, President
Bobby Pait, Programming Director
Bob Gause, Engineering Dir
Bonnie Miller, Executive Vice President
Benny Miller, Webmaster

Tarboro

WCPS
01-01-1947; 760 kHz AM; *Hrs Open:* Sunrise-sunset; 1 kw-D; N35 55 40 W77 34 15
Mailing Address: Box 1202, Tarboro, NC 27604
Second Address: 1406 St Andrew St., Tarboro, NC 27886
(252) 824-7878; *Fax:* (252) 824-7818
jjwcpsam@embarqmail.com
License: Tarboro, Edgecombe County, NC held by Johnson Broadcast Ventures Ltd.
Regional Network: N.C. News Net.
Population Served: 13,000; *Arbitron Metro Market:* Rocky Mount-Wilson, NC; *Target Audience:* General.; *Adv. Rates:* 20 ROS
Jimmy Johnson, President
Stephanie Randolph, Station Manager

Taylorsville

WACB
05-02-1964; 860 kHz AM; *Hrs Open:* 24; 1 kw-D; N35 55 57 W81 10 19
133 E. Main Ave., Taylorsville, NC 28681
(828) 632-4621; *Fax:* (828) 632-9081
www.860wacb.com
License: Taylorsville, Alexander County, NC held by Apple City Broadcasting Co. Inc.
Regional Network: N.C. News Net.
Population Served: 500,000 *Special Programming:* Gospel 12 hrs wkly; *Hrs. of News Programming:* news progmg 4 hrs wkly; *No. News Employees:* 2; *Target Audience:* General.
Roger Brown, CEO
Norris Keever, President
Mary Brown, Operations Dir
Joyce Brown, General Sales Mgr
Lonnie Carrigan, Programming Director
Lisa McLain, Promotions Manager
Pete Ray, Assistant Music Director

WTLK
06-17-1962; 1570 kHz AM
239 E. Main St., Taylorsville, NC 28681 US
(828) 632-4621; *Fax:* (828) 632-9081
License: Taylorsville, NC held by Apple City Broadcasting Co. Inc.
Regional Network: N.C. News Net.
Arbitron Metro Market: Taylorsville, NC; *Format:* Gospel
Roger Brown, CEO
Norris Keever, President
Joyce Brown, General Sales Mgr
Lisa McLain, Promotions Manager
Jeff Watts, Chief Engineer
Mary Alice Brown, Executive Vice President

Thomasville

WBLO
09-01-1947; 790 kHz AM; *Hrs Open:* 24 hrs
1607 Country Club Drive, High Point, NC 27262 US
(336) 887-0983; *Fax:* (336) 887-3055
License: Thomasville, NC held by GHB Radio Inc.
Group Owner: GHB Radio Group; (acq 4-3-2001; $350,000).
Nat'l Network: Fox Sports
Arbitron Metro Market: Charlotte, NC; *Format:* Sports, Talk; *Target Audience:* Men 25-54
Edgar Saucedo, General Manager
Sergio Garcia, Programming Director
Don West, Regional Sales
Koji Kryzwosz, Local Sales

Topsail Beach

WNTB
11-27-2000; 93.7 MHz FM; *Hrs Open:* 24; 6 kw; 328 ft.; N34 18 4 W77 48 7
1410 Commonwealth Dr., Suite 102A, Wilmington, NC 28403 US
(910) 772-6300
portcitydaily.com/thedude
thedude@localvoicemedia.com
License: Topsail Beach, New Hanover County, NC held by Local Voice Media Group
Group Owner: Local Voice Media Group; (acq 6-30-2000; $1.2 million for CP)
Arbitron Metro Market: Wilmington, NC; *Format:* Classic Rock

Troy

WJRM
12-08-1961; 1390 kHz AM; *Hrs Open:* 5 AM-9 PM
401 Troy-Candor Road, Albenare, NC 28002 US
(910) 576-1390; *Fax:* (910) 576-1393
www.wjrm.com
License: Troy, NC held by Family Worship Ministries Inc.
Format: Christian, Gospel; *No. News Employees:* 1
Harold Pope, President
Jeffrey Pope, Operations Dir

Tryon

WJFJ
10-01-1954; 1160 kHz AM; *Hrs Open:* 24; 10 kw-D, DAN; 0.5 kw-N, DAN; N35 14 7 W82 14 27
1950 Old Hendersonville, Hwy, Pisgah Forest, NC 28768 US
(828) 894-5858; *Fax:* (828) 894-2957
www.wjfjradio.com
wjfjradio@wjfjradio.com
License: Tryon, NC held by Columbus Broadcast Corp. Inc.
Nat'l Network: USA
Format: Christian; *Hrs. of News Programming:* news progmg 25 hrs wkly; *No. News Employees:* 1; *Target Audience:* 25 plus; middle-to-upper income; *Adv. Rates:* 9.50; 9:50; 9:50; 9:50
John Owens, General Manager

Valdese

WSVM
10-06-1961; 1490 kHz AM; *Hrs Open:* 24; 1 kw-U, ND1; N35 44 3 W81 34 4
P. O. Box 99, Valdese, NC 28690 US
(828) 874-0000; *Fax:* (828) 874-2123
License: Valdese, NC held by GHB of Waxhaw Inc.
Group Owner: GHB Radio Group; (acq 10-28-2002; $450,000 with WEGO(AM) Concord).
Format: Talk; *No. News Employees:* 4; *Target Audience:* 25+
Jerry Clegg, General Manager

Wadesboro

WADE
07-23-1947; 1340 kHz AM; *Hrs Open:* 24; 1 kw-U, ND1; N34 57 9 W80 3 0
P.O. Box 416, Waxhaw, NC 28173 US
License: Wadesboro, NC held by Inspirational Deliverance Center Inc.

***WYFQ-FM**
01-01-1994; 93.5 MHz FM; *Hrs Open:* 24; 8.7 kw; 554 ft.; N35 2 57 W80 18 38
P.O. Box 7300, Charlotte, NC 28241 US
(800) 888-7077
www.bbnradio.org
bbn@bbnmedia.org
License: Wadesboro, Anson County, NC held by Bible Broadcasting Network Inc.
Group Owner: Bible Broadcasting Network; acq 1996; $2,425,000)
Arbitron Metro Market: Wadesboro, NC; *Format:* Religious; *Target Audience:* 18-55.
Lowell Davey, President
Jason Padgett, Operations Manager

Wake Forest

WRDU
11-01-1947; 100.7 MHz FM; 100 kw; 1969 ft.; N35 49 53 W78 8 50
3100 Smoketree Court, Suite 700, Raleigh, NC 27604 US
(919) 878-1500; *Fax:* (919) 876-8578
www.wrdu.com
License: Wake Forest, Edgecombe County, NC held by Capstar TX LLC
Group Owner: iHeartMedia; (acq 8-30-2000; grpsl).
Nat'l Network: ABC
Arbitron Metro Market: Raleigh, NC; *Format:* Classic Rock; *Target Audience:* 25-54; upscale adults
Brian Taylor, Programming Director
Nathan James, Director of Integrated Media
Melody Mechanic, Digital Program Director

Walnut Creek

WEQR
09-15-1976; 97.7 MHz FM; *Hrs Open:* 24; 2.65 kw; 501 ft.; N35 17 28 W77 49 25
2581 US Highway 70 W, Goldsboro, NC 27530 US
(919) 736-1150; *Fax:* (919) 736-3876
License: Walnut Creek, Wayne County, NC held by New Age Communications Inc.
Group Owner: Curtis Media Group; (acq 8-30-2004; $875,000)
Wire Services: AP
Arbitron Metro Market: Walnut Creek, NC; *Format:* Adult Contemp; *Hrs. of News Programming:* 3 hrs/week; *No. News Employees:* 1
Donald Curtis, President
Bill Johnston, General Manager
Jeff Farrow, Programming Director
Robyn Wade, News Director

Wanchese

WOBX
05-29-1970; 1530 kHz AM; 1 kw-D, DAD; N35 51 52 W75 39 1
Mailing Address: 1331 Paradise Road, Edenton, NC 17932 US
Second Address: 3855 Mill Landing Rd., Hwy. 345, Wanchese, NC 27981
(252) 473-5402; *Fax:* (252) 473-5838
License: Wanchese, NC held by East Carolina Radio Inc.
Group Owner: East Carolina Radio Group; (acq 8-82; $110,000;
TV Affiliate: Relg; *No. News Employees:* Christian.

WOBR-FM
06-01-1973; 95.3 MHz FM; 25 kw; 295 ft.; N35 51 52 W75 39 1
1331 Paradise Rd, Edemtpm, NC 27932 US
(252) 441-1024; *Fax:* (252) 441-2109
www.ecri.net
License: Wanchese, Dare County, NC held by East Carolina Radio Inc.
Group Owner: East Carolina Radio Group
Nat'l Network: ABC
TV Affiliate: Rock; *Hrs. of News Programming:* 1; *No. News Employees:* 25-54; upscale, affluent

Warrenton

WARR
01-01-1970; 1520 kHz AM; *Hrs Open:* sun up-sun down; 1 kw-C, NDD; 5 kw-D, NDD; N36 24 18 W78 8 9
PO Box 611, Warrenton, NC 27589 US
(252) 257-5557/257-9277
www.warr1520.com
License: Warrenton, NC held by Quad Divisions Inc. dba Darensburg Broadcasting
Regional Network: N.C. News Net.
Arbitron Metro Market: Warrenton, NC; *Format:* Black, Gospel; *Hrs. of News Programming:* News progmg 5 hrs wkly; *Target Audience:* 25-56.
Reverend Dr. Liliplana D. Darensburg, President/CEO
Logan Darensburg, Vice President

Washington

WLGT
12-01-1988; 98.3 MHz FM; *Hrs Open:* 24; 1.35 kw; 489 ft.; N35 29 14 W77 2 42
P.O. Box 874, Greenville, NC 27834 US
(252) 446-9262; *Fax:* (252) 446-9261
License: Washington, Beaufort County, NC held by Media East LLC
Arbitron Metro Market: Greenville-New Bern-Jacksonville, NC; *Format:* Gospel; *Target Audience:* 25-54; upscale, affluent audience
Wesley Hines, General Manager

WDLX
03-03-1942; 930 kHz AM
Mailing Address: 1705 W. Northwest Hwy, Ste 275, Grapevine, TX 76051 US
Second Address: 525 S. Evans St., Greenville, NC 27858
(252) 317-1250; *Fax:* (252) 317-1255
www.pirateradio930.com
troy@pirateradio1250.com
License: Washington, NC held by Pirate Media Group LLC
Regional Network: N.C. News Net.
Arbitron Metro Market: Greenville-New Bern-Jacksonville, NC; *Format:* Talk; *Target Audience:* 35 plus.
Troy Dreyfus, General Manager
Troy Dreyfus, Owner
Jonathan Ellerbe, Owner

WERO
01-20-1961; 93.3 MHz FM; *Hrs Open:* 24; 100 kw; 1781 ft.; N35 21 55 W77 23 38
1361 Colony Drive, New Bern, NC 28562 US
(252) 639-7900; *Fax:* (252) 639-7979
www.bob933.com
hollywood@bob933.com
License: Washington, Beaufort County, NC held by NM Licensing LLC.
Group Owner: NextMedia Group Inc.; (acq 11-26-2001; grpsl)
Nat'l Reps: Eastman Radio
Arbitron Metro Market: Washington, NC; *Format:* Contemporary Hits/Top 40; *Hrs. of News Programming:* news progmg 12 hrs wkly; *No. News Employees:* 1; *Target Audience:* 18-49
Chris "Hollywood" Mann, Programming Director
Chelsea DeMonch, Promotions Manager
Gina Gray, Assistant Program Director

Waxhaw

WOLS
03-01-1995; 106.1 MHz FM; *Hrs Open:* 24; 21 kw; 617 ft.; N34 53 1 W80 47 37
4801 East Independence Boulevard, Charlotte, NC 28212 US
(704) 405-3172; *Fax:* (704) 405-3174
www.larazalaraza.com
License: Waxhaw, Union County, NC held by GHB of Waxhaw Inc.
Group Owner: GHB Radio Group; (acq 6-95; $325,000)
Arbitron Metro Market: Charlotte, NC
George Buck Jr., President
Julian Miguel, Operations Dir
Edgar Saucedo, General Manager
Ronnie Coates, General Sales Mgr
Sergio Garcia, Programming Director

Waynesville

WMXF
08-01-1947; 1400 kHz AM; *Hrs Open:* 24; 1 kw-U, ND1; N35 30 14 W82 58 25
13 Summerlin Road, Asheville, NC 28806 US
(828) 257-2700; *Fax:* (828) 281-3299
www.wwnc.com
License: Waynesville, NC held by Clear Channel Broadcasting Licenses Inc.
Group Owner: iHeartMedia; (acq 3-21-2001; grpsl)
Nat'l Reps: Keystone (unwired net)
Format: Adult Contemp *Special Programming:* Relg 3 hrs wkly; *No. News Employees:* 1; *Target Audience:* General.; *Adv. Rates:* 12; 12; 12; 10
Gene Austin, Sales Manager
Brian Hall, Programming Director
Skip Wilson, Digital Sales Manager
Jessica Lee, Digial Content Director

WQNS
10-01-1979; 105.1 MHz FM; *Hrs Open:* 24; 0.245 kw; 1581 ft.; N35 34 7 W82 54 27
13 Summerlin Road, Asheville, NC 28806 US
(828) 257-2700; *Fax:* (828) 281-3299
www.1051rocks.com
License: Waynesville, Buncombe County, NC held by Clear Channel Broadcasting Licenses Inc.
Group Owner: iHeartMedia
Arbitron Metro Market: Asheville, NC; *Format:* Classic Rock; *Target Audience:* General.; *Adv. Rates:* 14; 14; 14; 12
Gene Austin, Sales Manager
Rick Rice, Programming Director
Skip Wilson, Digital Sales Manager
Jessica Lee, Digital Content Director

Weaverville

WTMT
10-01-1989; 105.9 MHz FM; *Hrs Open:* 24; 9.5 kw; 1112 ft.; N35 36 4 W82 39 7
1190 Patton Avenue, Asheville, NC 28806 US
(828) 259-9695; *Fax:* (828) 253-5619
1059themountain.com
gbrown@avlradio.com
License: Weaverville, Buncombe County, NC held by Saga Communications of North Carolina LLC.
Group Owner: Saga Communications Inc.; (acq 8-7-2006; $650,000)
Arbitron Metro Market: Asheville, NC
Neal Sharpe, Brand Manager
Nikki Mitchell, Promotions Director
Chris Wheat, General Managers

Weldon

WSMY
01-01-1957; 1400 kHz AM; *Hrs Open:* 24; 1 kw-U, ND1; N36 24 43 W77 37 6
306 Port St., Easton, MD 21601 US
(410) 822-3301; *Fax:* (410) 822-0576
www.firstmediaradio.com
License: Weldon, NC held by First Media Radio LLC.
Group Owner: First Media Radio LLC; (acq 7-22-2003; grpsl)
Format: Sports; *Target Audience:* 18 plus; affluent adults
Alex Kolobielski, CEO/President

Wendell-Zebulon

WETC
06-16-1959; 540 kHz AM; *Hrs Open:* 24
P.O. Box 58246, Raleigh, NC 27658 US
(919) 772-9540; *Fax:* (770) 246-0054
www.vision540.com
vision540am@gmail.com
License: Wendell-Zebulon, NC held by Prieto Broadcasting Inc.
Group Owner: Prieto Broadcasting Inc.; (acq 6-1-2004; $1.8 million)
Arbitron Metro Market: Wendell, NC
Everado Morales, Station Manager

West Jefferson

WKSK
05-27-1959; 580 kHz AM; *Hrs Open:* 24 hours a day; 5 kw-D, 34 w-N; N36 24 39 W81 29 46
Box 729, West Jefferson, NC 28694
(336) 846-9575
www.580wksk.com
wksk@skybest.com
License: West Jefferson, Ashe County, NC held by Caddell Broadcasting, Inc.
Nat'l Network: AP Radio; *Wire Services:* AP
Population Served: 80,000 *Special Programming:* Farm 3 hrs, gospel 5 hrs, Sp one hr wkly; *Hrs. of News Programming:* news progmg 16 hrs wkly; *No. News Employees:* 1; *Target Audience:* General. *Adv. Rates:* 15; 15; 15; 12
Graham Caddell, Sales

Whiteville

WENC
07-14-1946; 1220 kHz AM; *Hrs Open:* 6 AM-10 PM; 5 kw-D, ND1; 0.152 kw-N, ND1; N34 18 30 W78 43 0

108 Radio Station Road, Whiteville, NC 28472 US
(910) 642-2133; *Fax:* (910) 642-5981
www.power1220am.com
aneshia@embarqmail.com
License: Whiteville, NC held by DHA Communications.
Regional Network: N.C. News Net.
Format: Blues, Gospel *Special Programming:* Farm 5 hrs, relg 4 hrs, talk 5 hrs wkly; *Hrs. of News Programming:* news progmg 10 hrs wkly; *No. News Employees:* 1; *Target Audience:* 25-54; women; *Adv. Rates:* 12;12; 12; 12;
Jesse Lee Godwin, General Manager
Bob Gause, Engineering Dir

WTXY
01-01-1976; 1540 kHz AM; *Hrs Open:* Sunrise-sunset; 1 kw-D, NDD; N34 19 23 W78 42 47
P.O. Box 1038, Whiteville, NC 28472 US
(910) 212-7202
www.wtxy1540.com
License: Whiteville, NC held by Stanley Broadcasting System Inc.
Nat'l Network: Westwood One; Motor Racing Net; *Regional Network:* Tenn. Agri-Net
Arbitron Metro Market: Whiteville, NC; *Format:* News, News/Talk, 86 *Special Programming:* Farm 2 hrs, relg 10 hrs wkly; *Hrs. of News Programming:* news progmg 84 hrs wkly; *No. News Employees:* 2; *Target Audience:* General.; *Adv. Rates:* 15; 13.50; 15; 8.50
Thomas Stanley Jr., President
Robby Kendall, Owner & Operations
Jason Dozier, Owner & Operations
Franklin Davis, Advertising Sales Contact
Suzanne King, Advertising Sales Contact

WZFX
02-21-1962; 99.1 MHz FM; 100 kw; 981 ft.; N34 44 5 W78 47 25
508 Person St., Fayetteville, NC 28301 US
(910) 486-2000; *Fax:* (910) 486-2109
www.foxy99.com
License: Whiteville, Columbus County, NC held by Beasley Media Group LLC
Group Owner: Beasley Broadcast Group Inc.; (acq 5-8-97; $11.5 million)
Nat'l Reps: Katz Radio
Arbitron Metro Market: Fayetteville, NC; *Format:* Urban Contemporary; *Target Audience:* 18-49.
Tricia Gallenbeck, Director of Sales
Mac Edwards, Vice President/Market Manager
Danny Highsmith, Regional Vice President
Katy Lollis, General Sales Manager
Angela Godwin, General Sales Manager
Ina Cartrette, Advertising

Wilkesboro

***WSIF**
04-06-1977; 90.9 MHz FM; *Hrs Open:* 24; 1 kw; -171 ft.; N36 8 12 W81 11 2
Mailing Address: P.O. Box 120, Wilkesboro, NC 28697 US
Second Address: 1328 S. Collegiate Dr., Wilkesboro, NC 28697
(336) 838-6179; *Fax:* (336) 838-6277
www.wncw.org
al.delachica@wilkescc.edu
License: Wilkesboro, Wilkes County, NC held by Wilkes Community College.
Format: Triple A
Brenda Gray, Marketing Manager
Carol Rifkin, Music Director

WWWC
01-26-1970; 1240 kHz AM; 1 kw-U; N36 09 00 W81 09 42
Mailing Address: Box 580, Wilkesboro, NC 28697
Second Address: 413 Wilkesboro Blvd., Wilkesboro, NC 28697
(336) 838-1241/838-9992; *Fax:* (336) 838-9040
www.12403wc.com
onair@12403wc.com
License: Wilkesboro, Wilkes County, NC held by Foothills Media Inc.
Nat'l Network: USA; *Regional Network:* N.C. News Net.
Population Served: 60,000 *Target Audience:* General.
John Wishon, President
Petrice Edwards, General Sales Mgr
Angela Henley, News Director
Stoney Owen, Chief Engineer

Williamston

WTIB
08-01-1962; 103.7 MHz FM; *Hrs Open:* 24; 100 kw; Ant 981 ft; N35 53 47 W76 58 58 *Rebroadcasts:* Rebroadcasts WRHT(FM) Morehead City 100%
408 W. Arlington Blvd., Suite 101-C, Greenville, NC 28557
(252) 355-1037; *Fax:* (252) 355-2234
www.wtibfm.com
License: Williamston, Martin County, NC held by Inner Banks Media LLC.
Group Owner: Inner Banks Media LLC; (acq 3-12-2007; grpsl)
Population Served: 300,000; *Arbitron Metro Market:* Greenville-New Bern-Jacksonville, NC; *Target Audience:* 18-49; young adults
Henry Hinton, President
Christine Cashwell, Business Manager
Dylan McKay, Business Manager

WIAM
03-01-1951; 900 kHz AM; *Hrs Open:* 24; 1 kw-D, ND1; 0.258 kw-N, ND1; N35 51 27 W77 2 34
P.O. Box 590, Williamston, NC 27892 US
(252) 792-4161; *Fax:* (252) 809-0039
www.opendoorradio.com
bryant@opendoorradio.com
License: Williamston, NC held by Lifeline Ministries Inc.
Regional Network: N.C. News Net.
Format: Gospel, Religious; *Target Audience:* General.
Johnny Bryant, President

Wilmington

WLSG
12-24-1946; 1340 kHz AM; *Hrs Open:* 24
410 New Bridge St., Suite 3B, Jacksonville, NC 28450 US
(910) 632-0766; *Fax:* (910) 346-2248
941thebeach.com
wsme1120@yahoo.com
License: Wilmington, NC held by B&M Broadcasting LLC
Group Owner: B&M Broadasting LLC
Arbitron Metro Market: Wilmington, NC; *Format:* Gospel, Religious; *Target Audience:* 30 plus.
Ashley Moseley, General Manager

***WDVV**
01-01-1999; 89.7 MHz FM; 13.5 kw vert; 348 ft.; N34 10 52 W78 2 33
3305 Burnt Mill Dr., Wilmington, NC 28403 US
(910) 763-2452; *Fax:* (910) 763-6578
www.thedoveonline.org
info@carolinachristianradio.com
License: Wilmington, New Hanover County, NC held by Carolina Christian Radio Inc.
Group Owner: Carolina Christian Radio; (acq 2-16-2001; $100,000 with WMYT(AM) Carolina Beach)
Nat'l Network: USA
Arbitron Metro Market: Wilmington, NC; *Format:* Christian

WGNI
03-01-1970; 102.7 MHz FM; *Hrs Open:* 24; 100 kw; 981 ft.; N34 3 6 W78 4 57
3233 Burnt Mill Road, Wilmington, NC 28403 US
(910) 763-9977; *Fax:* (910) 762-0456
www.wgni.com
gmail@wgni.com
License: Wilmington, New Hanover County, NC held by Cumulus Licensing LLC.
Group Owner: Cumulus Media Inc.
Nat'l Reps: McGavren Guild; *Wire Services:* AP
Arbitron Metro Market: Wilmington, NC; *Format:* Adult Contemp; *No. News Employees:* 2
Jackie Jordan, Programming Director
Pamela Heider, Promotions Director

***WHQR**
04-24-1984; 91.3 MHz FM; *Hrs Open:* 24; 100 kw; 1142 ft.; N34 7 53 W78 11 17
254 North Front Street, Wilmington, NC 28401 US
(910) 343-1640; *Fax:* (910) 251-8693
www.whqr.org
whqr@whqr.org
License: Wilmington, New Hanover County, NC held by Friends of Public Radio Inc.
Nat'l Network: NPR; PRI *Regional Reps:* Megan Gorham; *Wire Services:* AP
Arbitron Metro Market: Wilmington, NC; *Format:* News; *Hrs. of News Programming:* news progmg 63 hrs wkly; *No. News Employees:* 3; *Target Audience:* 35 plus.
George Scheibner, Operations Dir
John Milligan, General Manager
Bob Klorkmon, Programming Director
Ann Berry, Promotions Manager
Catherine Welch, News Director

WMFD
04-15-1935; 630 kHz AM; *Hrs Open:* 24; 0.8 kw-D, DA2; 1 kw-N, DA2; N34 16 19 W77 58 28
25 N. Kerr Ave., Wilmington, NC 28405 US
(910) 791-3088
www.am630.net
ben@am630.net
License: Wilmington, New Hanover County, NC held by Sunrise Broadcasting LLC.
Group Owner: Capitol Broadcasting Co. Inc.; (acq 11-18-2008; grpsl)
Nat'l Network: ESPN Radio
Arbitron Metro Market: Wilmington, NC; *Format:* Sports; *Hrs. of News Programming:* news progmg 3 hrs wkly; *No. News Employees:* 1; *Target Audience:* 30 plus; upscale audience
Brian Schimmel, General Manager
Ben Darnell, Programming Director

WMNX
02-24-1970; 97.3 MHz FM; *Hrs Open:* 24; 100 kw; 884 ft.; N34 3 6 W78 4 57
1890 Dawson Street, Wilmington, NC 28403 US
(910) 763-9977; *Fax:* (910) 762-0456
www.coast973.com
info@coast973.com
License: Wilmington, New Hanover County, NC held by Cumulus Licensing Corp.
Group Owner: Cumulus Media Inc.; (acq 3-12-2001; grpsl)
Nat'l Reps: McGavren Guild; *Wire Services:* AP
Arbitron Metro Market: Wilmington, NC; *Format:* Urban Contemporary; *No. News Employees:* 1; *Target Audience:* 18-49; general
Perry Stone, Operations Dir
Jim Principi, General Manager

WILT
02-01-1994; 104.5 MHz FM; 3.1 kw; 449 ft.; N34 10 0 W77 56 40
25 N. Kerr Ave., Wilmington, NC 28405 US
(910) 791-3088; *Fax:* (910) 791-0112
www.1045sunnyfm.com
License: Wilmington, New Hanover County, NC held by Sunrise Broadcasting LLC.
Group Owner: Capitol Broadcasting Co. Inc.; (acq 11-18-2008; grpsl)
Arbitron Metro Market: Wilmington, NC; *Format:* Adult Contemp; *Target Audience:* 25-54.
Brian Schimmel, General Manager
Mike Edwards, Programming Director

WWIL
08-25-1963; 1490 kHz AM; *Hrs Open:* 24; 1 kw-U, ND1; N34 13 52 W77 57 18
3305 Burnt Mill Road, Wilmington, NC 28403 US
(910) 763-2452; *Fax:* (910) 763-6578
www.life905.com
info@carolinachristianradio.com
License: Wilmington, NC held by Carolina Christian Radio Inc.
Group Owner: Carolina Christian Radio; (acq 10-28-92; $35,000;
Nat'l Network: USA
Arbitron Metro Market: Wilmington, NC; *Format:* Black, Gospel; *Target Audience:* 25-49.

***WWIL-FM**
12-01-1995; 90.5 MHz FM; *Hrs Open:* 24; 1 kw horiz, 20 kw vert; 328 ft.; N34 10 52 W78 2 33
3305 Burnt Mill Dr., Wilmington, NC 28403 US
(910) 763-2452; *Fax:* (910) 763-6578
www.life905.com
info@carolinachristianradio.com
License: Wilmington, New Hanover County, NC
Group Owner: Carolina Christian Radio; (Acq 6-95;
Nat'l Network: USA
Arbitron Metro Market: Wilmington, NC; *Format:* Adult Contemp, Christian; *Target Audience:* 25-54.

WWQQ-FM
03-31-1969; 101.3 MHz FM; *Hrs Open:* 24; 40 kw; 545 ft.; N34 3 2 W77 57 20
US
(910) 763-9977; *Fax:* (910) 762-0456
www.wwqq101.com
Joyce.Thomas@cumulus.com
License: Wilmington, New Hanover County, NC held by Cumulus Licensing Corp.
Group Owner: Cumulus Media Inc.; (acq 7-3-97;
Nat'l Reps: McGavren Guild; *Wire Services:* AP
Arbitron Metro Market: Wilmington, NC; *Format:* Country; *No. News Employees:* 1; *Target Audience:* 25-54.; *Adv. Rates:* 60; 50; 55; 40
Perry Stone, Operations Dir
Jim Principi, General Manager
Robin Batson, General Sales Mgr
Brian Sims, Programming Director
Kerry Hinshaw, Promotions Manager

Tim Nelson, Chief Engineer
Joyce Thomas, Assistant Business Manager

Wilson

WVOT
06-01-1948; 1420 kHz AM; *Hrs Open:* 24; 1 kw-D, DAN; 0.5 kw-N, DAN; N35 44 8 W77 53 2
2108 Beekman Place N.W., Wilson, NC 27896 US
(252) 243-5157; *Fax:* (252) 291-5000
License: Wilson, NC held by Kingdom Expansion Corp.
Arbitron Metro Market: Wilson, NC; *Format:* Christian, Sports; *Hrs. of News Programming:* News progmg 25 hrs wkly; *Target Audience:* 25-55.; *Adv. Rates:* 20; 15; 20; 15
Pastor MK Smith, CEO/COO
M.K. Smith, President
Noel Johnson, Operations Dir
Joyce Farmer, Station Manager
Geri Kidd Brown, Programming Director

WLLY
01-01-1961; 1350 kHz AM; *Hrs Open:* Daylight; 1 kw-D, ND1; 0.079 kw-N, ND1; N35 43 24 W77 55 16
7354 Lindley Mill Road, Graham, NC 27253 US
(252) 237-5171; *Fax:* (252) 237-5172
License: Wilson, NC held by Estuardo Valdemar Rodriguez and Leonor Rodriguez, joint tenants.
Group Owner: Radio La Grande; (acq 10-11-2002; $255,000)
Nat'l Network: USA; *Regional Network:* N.C. News Net.
Format: Gospel; *Target Audience:* General.
Vivien Ogburn, Station Manager

Windsor

WBTE
01-01-1969; 990 kHz AM; 1 kw-D, ND2; 0.025 kw-N, ND2; N35 58 0 W76 56 54
US
(252) 582-8680; *Fax:* (252)482-4260
wbte@earthlink.net
License: Windsor, NC held by Dr. Tine Hicks & Associate
Arbitron Metro Market: Norfolk, VA; *Format:* Gospel
Arbutis Walston, General Manager

Winfall

*WGTI
01-01-1980; 97.7 MHz FM; *Hrs Open:* 24; 31 kw; 157 m; N36 04 06 W76 58 35
Box 590, Williamston, NC 23510
(252) 792-4161; *Fax:* (252) 809-0039
www.air1.com
License: Winfall, Perquimans County, NC held by Lifeline Ministries Inc.

Johnny Bryant, President

Wingate

*WRCM
06-14-1993; 91.9 MHz FM; *Hrs Open:* 24; 30 kw; 495 ft.; N35 3 34 W80 40 14
1092 Radio Drive, Indian Trail, NC 28079 US
(704) 821-9293,(704) 570-9200
www.newlife919.com
info@newlife919.com
License: Wingate, Union County, NC held by Columbia Bible College Broadcasting Co.
Nat'l Network: Salem Radio Network; *Wire Services:* UPI
Format: Adult Contemp, Christian; *Target Audience:* 25-44; female
Renee Gleason, Office Manager
Leigh Anderson, Director of Marketing
Gary Morland, Director of Operations

Winston-Salem

WEGO(AM)
10-28-1950; 980 kHz AM; 1.3 kw-D, 49 w-N; N36 06 40 W80 14 36
4405 Providence Lane, Winston-Salem, NC 27106
(336) 887-0983; *Fax:* (336) 887-3055
License: Winston-Salem, Forsyth County, NC held by GHB Radio Inc.
Group Owner: GHB Radio Group; (acq 3-6-2006; $235,000)
Nat'l Network: ESPN Radio
Population Served: 150,000; *Arbitron Metro Market:* Greensboro-Winston Salem-High Point, NC; *Target Audience:* Men 25-54
George Buck Jr., President
Wes Jones, Operations Dir
Susan Childress, General Manager
Gary Hattaway, Engineering Dir

WBFJ
10-01-1960; 1550 kHz AM; *Hrs Open:* Sunrise-sunset; 1 kw-D, NDD; N36 6 33 W80 14 44
1249 Trade Street, Winston Salem, NC 27101 US
(336) 721-1560
www.wbfj.fm
live@wbfjfm.com
License: Winston-Salem, NC held by Word of Life Broadcasting Inc.
Nat'l Network: USA
Arbitron Metro Market: Winston Salem, NC; *Format:* Christian, Talk; *Target Audience:* 29-54; general; *Adv. Rates:* 15; 15; 15; na
Philip Watson, President
Wally Decker, General Manager
John Hill, Programming Director
Larry Schropp, Chief Engineer
Bonnie Hilton, Volunteer Coordinator
Cindy Davis, Donor Services
Jeff Foster, Production/Web/On-Air

*WBFJ-FM
09-01-1994; 89.3 MHz FM; *Hrs Open:* 24; 2.5 kw; 423 ft.; N36 5 56 W80 15 0
1249 Trade Street, Winston-Salem, NC 27101 US
(336) 721-1560
www.wbfj.fm
License: Winston-Salem, Forsyth County, NC held by Triad Family Network Inc.
Nat'l Network: USA
Arbitron Metro Market: Winston Salem, NC; *Format:* Christian; *Target Audience:* 25-49.
Wally Decker, General Manager
Kurt Myers, Promotions Manager
Verne Hill, News Director
Larry Shropp, Chief Engineer
Bonnie Hilton, Volunteer Coordinator
Cindy Davis, Donor Services
Jeff Foster, Production/Web/On-Air

*WFDD
03-13-1961; 88.5 MHz FM; *Hrs Open:* 24; 60 kw; 935 ft.; N35 55 2 W80 17 37
1834 Wake Forest Road, Winston-Salem, NC 27109 US
(336) 758-8850; *Fax:* (336) 758-5193
www.wfdd.org
wfdd@wfu.edu
License: Winston-Salem, Forsyth County, NC held by Trustees of Wake Forest University.
Nat'l Network: PRI; NPR *Regional Reps:* Public Radio Adv. Alliance
Arbitron Metro Market: Winston-Salem, NC; *Format:* News
Special Programming: Jazz 16 hrs wkly; *Hrs. of News Programming:* news progmg 29 hrs wkly; *No. News Employees:* 3; *Target Audience:* General;educated/public radio
Marian Wilson Reich, Operations / Production / Webmaster
Tom Dollenmayer, General Manager
Denise Franklin, News Director
ShaDonna Crosby, Listener Services and Volunteer Coordinator
Molly Davis, Marketing & Community Outreach
Audrey Fannin, Multimedia Producer
Eddie Garcia, Operations Technician
Karen Davis Kantziper, Account Manager
Greg Keener, Membership Operations Coordinator

WKZL
01-01-1972; 107.5 MHz FM; 100 kw; 994 ft.; N36 16 33 W79 56 27
192 E. Lewis St, Greensboro, NC 27406 US
(336) 274-8042; *Fax:* (336) 274-1629
www.1075kzl.com
dharlow@dbcradio.com
License: Winston-Salem, Forsyth County, NC held by Dick Broadcasting Co. Inc. of Tennessee
Arbitron Metro Market: Greensboro-Winston Salem-High Point, NC; *Format:* Contemporary Hits/Top 40; *Target Audience:* 25-49; women; *Adv. Rates:* 175; 125; 125; 30
Jennifer Harden, Business Manager
Dick Harlow, General Manager
Jason Goodman, Programming Director
Lauren McCombs, Promotions Manager

WPAW
04-01-1947; 93.1 MHz FM; *Hrs Open:* 24; 99 kw; 1099 ft.; N36 16 33 W79 56 26
7819 National Service Road, Greensboro, NC 27409 US
(336) 605-5200
www.931wolfcountry.com
License: Winston-Salem, Forsyth County, NC held by Entercom Greensboro License LLC.
Group Owner: Entercom Communications Corp.; (acq 12-13-99; grpsl)
Nat'l Network: CBS; *Nat'l Reps:* McGavren Guild
Arbitron Metro Market: Greensboro,NC; *Format:* Country; *Target Audience:* General
Randall Bliss, Program Director
Randy Bliss, Programming Director
Jill Dyson, Promotions Manager
Leanne Petty, Events/PSA Announcer

WPIP
06-01-1995; 880 kHz AM; *Hrs Open:* Sunrise-sunset
4135 Thomasville Road, Winston Salem, NC 27107 US
(336) 785-0527
wpip880am@triad.rr.com
License: Winston-Salem, NC held by Berean Baptist Church.
Nat'l Network: USA
Arbitron Metro Market: Greensboro-Winston Salem-High Point, NC; *Format:* Christian
Jeff Baity, Operations Dir
Ron Baity, General Manager

WPOL
03-25-1937; 1340 kHz AM; *Hrs Open:* 24; 1 kw-U, ND1; N36 4 26 W80 15 19
4405 Providence Ln., Suite D, Winston-Salem, NC 27106 US
(336) 759-0363; *Fax:* (336) 759-0366
www.lightthetriad.com
License: Winston-Salem, NC held by Truth Broadcasting Corp.
Group Owner: Truth Broadcasting Corp.; (acq 5-10-2000)
Arbitron Metro Market: Greensboro-Winston Salem-High Point, NC; *Format:* Gospel; *Hrs. of News Programming:* News progmg one hr wkly; *Target Audience:* Relg; *Adv. Rates:* 206; 20; 20; 20
Stuart Epperson Jr., General Manager

WSJS
04-17-1930; 600 kHz AM; 5 kw-D, DA2; 5 kw-N, DA2; N36 7 0 W80 21 26
875 West 5th Street, Winston-Salem, NC 27101 US
(336) 777-3900; *Fax:* (336) 777-3915
www.wsjs.com
License: Winston-Salem, NC held by Crescent Media Group LLC.
Group Owner: Mediaspan X Network
Nat'l Network: Wall Street; *Nat'l Reps:* Clear Channel
Arbitron Metro Market: Greensboro-Wins; *Format:* News; *Target Audience:* 25-64.
David Stuckey/Alex McTighe, General Manager
Lisa Mckay, Programming Director

WSMX
10-01-1964; 1500 kHz AM; *Hrs Open:* Sunrise-sunset
P.O. Box 16056, Winston-Salem, NC 27115 US
(336) 724-6336; *Fax:* (336) 724-6368
wsmxradio@aol.com
License: Winston-Salem, NC held by Gospel Media Inc.
Arbitron Metro Market: Greensboro-Winston Salem-High Point, NC; *Format:* Gospel; *Hrs. of News Programming:* News progmg 12 hrs wkly; *Target Audience:* 30-50 plus; blue collar, minorities, church members *Adv. Rates:* 10.00 per min
Joe Watson, President

*WSNC
01-01-1982; 90.5 MHz FM; *Hrs Open:* 24; 10 kw; 194 ft.; N36 5 24 W80 13 20
601 S. MLK Jr. Drive, 105B Hall-Patterson, Winston-Salem, NC 27110 US
(336) 750-2321; *Fax:* (336) 750-2329
www.wsncradio.org
WSNCFM@wssu.edu
License: Winston-Salem, Forsyth County, NC held by Winston-Salem State University.
Nat'l Network: NPR; PRI
Arbitron Metro Market: Greensboro-Winston Salem-High Point, NC; *Format:* Jazz, News; *Target Audience:* 30-70; African-Americans; *Adv. Rates:* 10; 35; 35; 20
Ben Donnelly, Operations Dir
Elvin Jenkins, General Manager

WTOB
04-22-1947; 1380 kHz AM; *Hrs Open:* 18; 5 kw-D, DA2; 2.5 kw-N, DA2; N36 8 53 W80 19 11
3789 Will Scarlet Road, Winston-Salem, NC 27104 US
(336) 815-8240
www.wtob1380.com
goodguys@wtob1380.com
License: Winston-Salem, NC held by Davidson Media Station WTOB Licensee LLC.

Group Owner: Davidson Media Group LLC; (acq 3-25-2005; swap with WWBG(AM) Greensboro for WDRU(AM) Wake Forest).
Regional Network: N.C. News Net.
Arbitron Metro Market: Greensboro, NC; *Target Audience:* 35 plus; affluent audience
Roger Martinez, General Manager

WTQR
12-01-1947; 104.1 MHz FM; *Hrs Open:* 24; 99 kw; 1732 ft.; N36 22 36.4 W80 22 8.6
2-B PAI Park, Greensboro, NC 27409 US
(336) 822-2000; *Fax:* (336) 887-0104
www.newcountryq1041.com
License: Winston-Salem, Forsyth County, NC held by Clear Channel Broadcasting Licenses Inc.
Group Owner: iHeartMedia; (acq 1996; grpsl).
Arbitron Metro Market: Greensboro, NC; *Format:* Country *Special Programming:* NASCAR, bluegrass 2 hrs wkly; *Target Audience:* 25-54.
Bobby Tatum, Sales Manager
Todd Nixon, Programming Director
Jason Newton, Director of Marketing and Promotions
Dennis Elliott, Digital Content Director
Andie Cooper, Internship Director

***WXRI**
05-17-1997; 91.3 MHz FM; *Hrs Open:* 24; 50 kw; 217 ft.; N36 8 6 W80 30 14
PO Box 25775, Winston-Salem, NC 27114 US
(336) 788-1155; *Fax:* (336) 788-7199
www.joyfm.org
office@joyfm.org
License: Winston-Salem, Forsyth County, NC held by Positive Alternative Radio Inc.
Group Owner: Positive Alternative Radio Inc.; (acq 5-21-92)
Nat'l Network: Salem Radio Network
Arbitron Metro Market: Greensboro, NC; *Format:* Gospel; *Target Audience:* Female; middle-aged
Candi Payne, Production Manager
Daniel Britt, General Manager

Winterville

WECU
02-07-2006; 1570 kHz AM; *Hrs Open:* 24
US
(773) 752-1570
License: Winterville, NC held by CTC Media Group.
Group Owner: CTC Media Group Inc.
Arbitron Metro Market: Winterville, NC; *Format:* Gospel
Edwin Afflerbach, President
Michael Afflerbach, Station Manager

Wrightsville Beach

WILT
10-31-1977; 103.7 MHz FM; *Hrs Open:* 24; 35 kw; 510 ft.; N34 3 2 W77 57 20
25 N. Kerr Ave., Wilmington, NC 28405 US
(910) 791-3088
www.sunny1037.com
License: Wrightsville Beach, Brunswick County, NC held by Capitol Broadcasting Company Inc.
Group Owner: Capitol Broadcasting Company Inc.
Arbitron Metro Market: Wilmington, NC; *Format:* Classic Rock; *Hrs. of News Programming:* news progmg 7 hrs wkly; *No. News Employees:* 1; *Target Audience:* 25-54; upscale female

Yadkin

***WWQY**
90.3 MHz FM; 1.6 kw; 105 ft.; N35 48 13 W80 17 42
PO Box 52, Greenville, SC 29602 US
(888) 500-8047
www.thelifefm.com
License: Yadkin, Yadkin County, NC
Group Owner: The Power Foundation

Yanceyville

WYNC
11-09-1979; 1540 kHz AM; *Hrs Open:* sun up-sun down; 1 kw-C, NDD; 2.5 kw-D, NDD; N36 24 52 W79 20 6
545 Firetower Road, Yanceyville, NC 27379 US
(336) 694-7343; *Fax:* (336) 694-7514
embarqmail.com
License: Yanceyville, NC held by Semora Broadcasting Inc.
Nat'l Network: Westwood One
Arbitron Metro Market: Yanceyville, NC; *Format:* Gospel *Special Programming:* Gospel 16 hrs wkly; *Target Audience:* General; rural Caswell county & Danville, VA
George Thaxton, Station Manager
Leroy Connally, Chief Engineer

Zebulon

***WVRD**
05-01-1990; 90.5 MHz FM; *Hrs Open:* 24; 1.2 kw; Ant 210 ft; N35 49 19 W78 18 36 *Rebroadcasts:* Rebroadcasts WVRL (FM)
3700 Candler's Mountain Rd, Suite F, Lynchburg, VA 24502 Us
(434) 582-3688
www.myjourneyfm.com
License: Zebulon, Wake County, NC held by Liberty University, Inc.
Group Owner: Liberty University, Inc.
Population Served: 416,468; *Arbitron Metro Market:* Raleigh, NC; *Format:* Christian, Religious
Chris Wygal, Operations Manager & Host
Barry Armstrong, General Manager
Mike Weston, Programming Director
Mark Edwards, Production Director

North Dakota

Arthur

KVMI
04-01-1994; 103.9 MHz FM; 25 kw; 328 ft.; N47 7 20 W97 19 29
PO Box 52, Casselton, ND 58012 US
(701) 347-5005; *Fax:* (218) 347-5508
www.1039thetruck.com
License: Arthur, Cass County, ND held by Vision Media Inc.
Nat'l Network: Westwood One
Arbitron Metro Market: Fargo-Moorhead, ND-MN; *Format:* Country
Angela Babbitt, Account Executive

Belcourt

***KEYA**
10-01-1975; 88.5 MHz FM; *Hrs Open:* 19; 19 kw; 361 ft.; N48 50 37 W99 45 2
P.O. Box 190, Belcourt, ND 58316 US
(701) 477-5686(701) 477-5687; *Fax:* (701) 477-3252
keya.utma.com/885
keya@utma.com
License: Belcourt, Rolette County, ND held by KEYA Inc.
Nat'l Network: NPR; *Wire Services:* AP
Arbitron Metro Market: Belcourt, ND; *Format:* Oldies, Rock/AOR, 30 *Special Programming:* American Indian 6 hrs, relg 10 hrs, old-time fiddle mus 4 hrs, Chippewa 3 hrs wkly; *Hrs. of News Programming:* news progmg 7 hrswkly; *Target Audience:* General; members of the Turtle Mountain Band of Chippewa Indians
Kimberly Thomas, General Manager
Jarle Kvale, Programming Director
Janice Keplin, Chief Engineer
Jarle Kvale, Programming Director

***KSIH**
90.1 MHz FM; kw
US
(888) 408-0201; *Fax:* (318) 449-9954
www.radiomaria.us
License: Belcourt, Rolette County, ND held by Friends of Radio Maria Inc.
Arbitron Metro Market: Belcourt, ND
Florinda Iannace, President
Robert Young, General Manager

Belfield

KXDI
93.9 MHz FM; 100 kw; 253.6 m; N46 43 31 W102 55 0.4
127 1st Street West, Dickinson, ND 58601
(701) 483-5547; *Fax:* (701) 483-5548
License: Belfield, Stark County, ND held by Williston Community Broadcasting Corp.

Stephen A. Marks, President

Beulah

KDKT
10-05-1978; 1410 kHz AM; *Hrs Open:* 24; 1 kw-D, 180 w-N; N47 17 15 W101 45 46
Mailing Address: 547 S. 7th Street, Bismarck, ND 58523
Second Address: 850 County 21, Bevlah, ND 58504
(701) 873-2215
www.kdktsports.com
info@dsnradio.com
License: Beulah, Mercer County, ND held by Digital Syndicate Network LLC
Nat'l Network: Fox Sports; *Regional Network:* American Ag
Population Served: 83,000; *Arbitron Metro Market:* Bismarck, ND; *Hrs. of News Programming:* news progmg 14 hrs wkly; *No. News Employees:* 35; *Target Audience:* 22-54; general
Guy Giuliano, President
Derek Stacklie, Station Manager

KQLZ
01-01-2008; 95.7 MHz FM; 700 w; Ant 610 ft; N46 27 48 W102 58 46
5331 Mt. Alifan Dr., San Diego, CA
(858) 277-4991; *Fax:* (858) 277-1365
License: Beulah, Hettinger County, ND held by Synergy Broadcast North Dakota LLC

Mike MacIntosh, President

Bismarck

KACL
04-22-1997; 98.7 MHz FM; *Hrs Open:* 24; 100 kw; 837 ft.; N46 35 24 W100 47 46
330 East Kilbourn Avenue, Suite 250, Milwaukee, WI 53202 US
(701) 250-6602; *Fax:* (701) 250-6632
www.cool987fm.com
License: Bismarck, Burleigh County, ND held by Townsquare Media Bismarck License LLC
Group Owner: Townsquare Media; (acq 5-11-98; grpsl)
Arbitron Metro Market: Bismarck, ND; *Format:* Oldies
Syd Stewart, General Manager
Mark Wishnia, Brand Manager
Bill Schmid, Director Of Sales
Lauren Bjork, Digital Managing Editor

KBMR
08-15-1958; 1130 kHz AM; *Hrs Open:* 24; 10 kw-D, NDD; 0.024 kw-N, ND2; N46 48 37 W100 44 10
3500 E. Rosser Ave., Bismarck, ND 58501 US
(701) 255-1234; *Fax:* (701) 222-1131
www.kbmr.com
License: Bismarck, Burleigh County, ND held by CC Licenses LLC.
Group Owner: iHeartMedia; (acq 2-13-2004;. grpsl).
Nat'l Reps: McGavren Guild
Arbitron Metro Market: Bismarck, ND; *Format:* Country *Special Programming:* Farm 6 hrs wkly; *Target Audience:* 25 plus.
Neil Cary, General Manager
Jim Klundt, Sales Manager
Rick Anthony, Programming Director

KBYZ
06-01-1985; 96.5 MHz FM; 100 kw; 963 ft.; N46 35 24 W100 47 46
4303 Memorial Highway, Bismarck, ND 58554 US
(701) 663-9600; *Fax:* (701) 663-8790
www.965thefox.com
kbyz@cumulus.com
License: Bismarck, Burleigh County, ND held by Townsquare Media Bismarck License LLC
Group Owner: Townsquare Media
Arbitron Metro Market: Bismarck, ND; *Format:* Classic Rock; *No. News Employees:* 1; *Target Audience:* 25-54.; *Adv. Rates:* 25; 25; 25; 25
Syd Stewart, General Manager
Larry Leblanc, Brand Manager
Bill Schmid, Director Of Sales
Lauren Bjork, Digital Managing Editor

***KCND**
09-01-1981; 90.5 MHz FM; *Hrs Open:* 24; 50 kw; 1217 ft.; N46 35 23 W100 48 2
P.O. Box 3240, Fargo, ND 58108 US
(701) 241-6900; *Fax:* (701) 239-7650
www.prairiepublic.org
info@prairiepublic.org
License: Bismarck, Burleigh County, ND held by Prairie Public Broadcasting Inc.
Nat'l Network: PRI; NPR
Arbitron Metro Market: Bismarck, ND *TV Affiliate:* *KBME-TV affil.; *Format:* Jazz, News *Special Programming:* American Indian 2 hrs, folk 6 hrs, blues 2 hrs wkly; *Hrs. of News Programming:* news progmg 40 hrs wkly; *No. News Employees:* 2; *Target Audience:* General.
Bill Thomas, General Sales Mgr
David Thompson, News Director

KFYR
01-01-1925; 550 kHz AM; 5 kw-D, DAN; 5 kw-N, DAN; N46 51 12 W100 32 37
Mailing Address: P.O. Box 2156, Bismarck, ND 58502 US
Second Address: 3500 E. Rosser Ave., Bismarck, ND 58501
(701) 255-1234; *Fax:* (701) 222-1131
www.kfyr.com
License: Bismarck, Burleigh County, ND held by Citicasters Licenses Inc.
Group Owner: iHeartMedia; (acq 5-4-99; grpsl)
Arbitron Metro Market: Bismarck, ND; *Format:* News, News/Talk, 86 *Special Programming:* Oldies 6 hrs wkly
Todd Mitchell, Senior Vice President of Programming
Neil Cary, General Manager
Jim Klundt, Sales Manager

KKCT
01-01-1994; 97.5 MHz FM; 100 kw; 837 ft.; N46 35 24 W100 47 46
330 East Kilbourn Ave., Suite 250, Milwaukee, WI 53202 US
(701) 250-6602; *Fax:* (701) 250-6632
www.hot975fm.com
syd.stewart@townsquaremedia.com
License: Bismarck, Burleigh County, ND held by Townsquare Media Bismarck License LLC
Group Owner: Townsquare Media; (acq 5-11-98; grpsl)
Arbitron Metro Market: Bismarck, ND; *Format:* Contemporary Hits/Top 40
Syd Stewart, General Manager
Jax, Brand Manager
Bill Schmid, Director Of Sales
Bill Schmid, Director Of Sales
Digital Managing Editor, General Manager

KQDY
09-13-1968; 94.5 MHz FM; *Hrs Open:* 24; 100 kw; 1119 ft.; N46 56 31 W100 41 38
3500 East Rosser Avenue, Bismarck, ND 58501 US
(701) 255-1234; *Fax:* (701) 222-1131
www.kqdy.com
License: Bismarck, Burleigh County, ND held by CC Licenses LLC.
Group Owner: iHeartMedia; (acq 2-13-2004; grpsl).
Arbitron Metro Market: Bismarck-Mandan; *Format:* Country; *Hrs. of News Programming:* News progmg 4 hrs wkly; *Target Audience:* 18-49.
Todd Mitchell, Senior Vice President of Programming
Neil Cary, General Manager
Jim Klundt, Sales Manager

KSSS
08-01-1994; 101.5 MHz FM; *Hrs Open:* 24; 100 kw; 988 ft.; N46 56 31 W100 41 37
3500 East Rosser Avenue, Bismarck, ND 58501 US
(701) 255-1234; *Fax:* (701) 222-1131
www.1015.fm
rock101@clearchannel.com
License: Bismarck, Burleigh County, ND held by CC Licenses LLC.
Group Owner: iHeartMedia; (acq 2-13-2004; grpsl).
Arbitron Metro Market: Bismarck, ND; *Format:* Classic Rock
Neil Cary, General Manager
Jim Klundt, Sales Manager

KXMR
03-20-1999; 710 kHz AM; *Hrs Open:* 24
3500 East Rosser Avenue, Bismarck, ND 58501 US
(701) 255-1234; *Fax:* (701) 222-1131
www.foxsports710.com
License: Bismarck, ND held by CC Licenses LLC.
Group Owner: iHeartMedia; (acq 12-10-2003).
Arbitron Metro Market: Bismarck, ND; *Format:* Sports
Neil Cary, General Manager
Rick Anthony, Programming Director
Corey Wickham, Public Service Announcements

KYYY
08-15-1966; 92.9 MHz FM; 100 kw; 988 ft.; N46 56 31 W100 41 37
Mailing Address: P.O. Box 2156, Bismarck, ND 58502 US
Second Address: 3500 E. Rosser Ave., Bismarck, ND 58501
(701) 255-1234; *Fax:* (701) 222-1131
www.y93.com
y93@y93.fm
License: Bismarck, Burleigh County, ND held by Citicasters Licenses Inc.
Group Owner: iHeartMedia
Arbitron Metro Market: Bismarck, ND; *Format:* Adult Contemp
Neil Cary, General Manager
Jim Klundt, Sales Manager
Curtis Booker, Programming Director

***KBFR**
10-01-2003; 91.7 MHz FM; *Hrs Open:* 24; 0.78 kw; 348 ft.; N46 49 38 W100 46 28
Mailing Address: 4135 Northgate Blvd., Suite 1, Sacramento, CA 95834 US
Second Address: 290 Hegenberger Rd., Oakland, CA 94621
(800) 543-1495
www.familyradio.org
info@familyradio.com
License: Bismarck, Burleigh County, ND held by Family Stations Inc.
Group Owner: Family Stations Inc.
Arbitron Metro Market: Bismarck, ND; *Format:* Christian, Religious
Harold Camping, President
Don Horton, Operations Dir

***KBMK**
01-01-2006; 88.3 MHz FM; 8.5 kw vert; 381 ft.; N46 49 38 W100 46 28 *Rebroadcasts:* Rebroadcasts KLVR(FM) Santa Rosa, CA 100%.
188 South Bellevue, Suite 222, Memphis, TN 38104 US
(800) 525-5683; *Fax:* (916) 251-1650
www.klove.com
klove@klove.com
License: Bismarck, Burleigh County, ND held by Educational Media Foundation
Group Owner: EMF Broadcasting
Nat'l Network: K-Love
Arbitron Metro Market: Bismarck, ND; *Format:* Christian; *No. News Employees:* 13
Darrell Chambliss, Chairman
Mike Novak, President and CEO
John Clements, General Sales Mgr
David Pierce, Chief Creative Officer and Programming Director

***KNRI**
01-01-2006; 89.7 MHz FM; *Hrs Open:* 24; 1.3 kw; 361 ft.; N46 49 38 W100 46 28
PO Box 12118, Omaha, NE 68105 US
(888) 937-2471
www.air1.com
info@air1.com
License: Bismarck, Burleigh County, ND held by Educational Media Foundation.
Group Owner: EMF Broadcasting
Nat'l Network: Air 1
Arbitron Metro Market: Bismarck, ND; *Format:* Alternative, Christian; *No. News Employees:* 3; *Target Audience:* 18-35; Judeo Christian female
Darrell Chambliss, Chairman
Alan Mason, COO
Mike Novak, President and CEO
David Pierce, Chief Creative Officer
Eric Moser, Chief Financial Officer

Bismarck-Mandan

KLXX
01-01-1925; 1270 kHz AM; *Hrs Open:* 24; 1 kw-D, ND1; 0.25 kw-N, ND1; N46 48 37 W100 50 10
4303 Memorial Highway, Mandan, ND 58554 US
(701) 663-6411; *Fax:* (701) 663-8790
supertalk1270.com
License: Bismarck-Mandan, ND held by Townsquare Media Bismarck License LLC
Group Owner: Townsquare Media; (acq 5-11-98; grpsl)
Nat'l Network: CNN Radio; *Nat'l Reps:* Katz Radio
Arbitron Metro Market: Bismarck, ND; *Format:* News, News/Talk, 84, Talk *Special Programming:* Sports 6 hrs wkly; *Hrs. of News Programming:* news progmg 90 hrs wkly; *No. News Employees:* 1; *Target Audience:* 35plus.; *Adv. Rates:* 15; 15; 15; 15
Syd Stewart, General Manager
Larry LeBlanc, Brand Manager
Bill Schmid, Director Of Sales
Lauren Bjork, Digital Managing Editor

Bottineau

KBTO
11-09-1980; 101.9 MHz FM; *Hrs Open:* 24; 94 kw; 489 ft.; N48 51 10 W100 20 1
1120 Highway SNE, Bottineau, ND 58318 US
(701) 228-5151; *Fax:* (701) 228-2483
rickgust@vtma.com
License: Bottineau, Bottineau County, ND held by Programmers Broadcasting Inc.
Group Owner: Programmers Broadcasting Inc.; (acq 1-2-2002; $595,000).
Nat'l Network: ABC; *Regional Network:* American Ag
Arbitron Metro Market: Bottineau, ND; *Format:* Country; *Hrs. of News Programming:* News progmg 15 hrs wkly; *Adv. Rates:* 11.88; 9.90; 9.90; 9.90
Rick Gustafson, President

Bowman

KPOK
08-09-1980; 1340 kHz AM; *Hrs Open:* 24; 1 kw-U, ND1; N46 10 48 W103 22 12
PO Box 829, Bowman, ND 58623 US
(701) 523-3883; *Fax:* (701) 523-3885
www.kpokradio.com
kpok@ndsupernet.com
License: Bowman, ND held by Tri-State Communications Inc.
Nat'l Network: Westwood One
Format: Country *Special Programming:* Farm 2 hrs wkly; *Hrs. of News Programming:* news progmg 14 hrs wkly; *No. News Employees:* 1; *Target Audience:* 25-54.
Larry Kemnitz, President
Richard Peterson, Operations Dir
Brian Fischer, General Manager

Burlington

KWGO
01-01-2005; 102.9 MHz FM; *Hrs Open:* 24; 98 kw; 512 ft.; N48 3 4 W101 20 23
US
(701) 852-7449
www.1029wgo.com
License: Burlington, Ward County, ND held by Programmers Broadcasting Inc.
Group Owner: Programmers Broadcasting Inc.
Arbitron Metro Market: Burlington, ND; *Format:* Adult Contemp; *Hrs. of News Programming:* News progmg 5 hrs wkly; *Target Audience:* 18-49.
John Kircher, President

Cannon Ball

KXRV
107.5 MHz FM; 100 kw; 778 ft.; N46 34 19 W100 47 42
409 North 4th Street, Bismarck, ND 58501 US
(701) 751-4757; *Fax:* (701) 751-4312
www.mojo1075.com
License: Cannon Ball, Sioux County, ND held by World Radio Link Inc.
Group Owner: World Radio Link Inc.
Arbitron Metro Market: Bismarck, ND; *Format:* Contemporary Hits/Top 40, Adult Contemp
Bob Denver, Owner/General Manager

Carrington

KDAK
10-16-1961; 1600 kHz AM; *Hrs Open:* 24; 0.5 kw-D, ND1; 0.09 kw-N, ND1; N47 25 43 W99 5 3
2625 8th Avenue, Jamestown, ND 58401 US
(701) 252-1400
www.newsdakota.com
License: Carrington, ND held by Two Rivers Broadcasting Inc.
Group Owner: Robert Ingstad Broadcast Properties; (acq 7-1-94)
Nat'l Network: ABC; *Regional Network:* N.D. News Net.
Format: Country, News; *Target Audience:* 30 plus.

KXGT
01-01-1997; 98.3 MHz FM; 100 kw; 866 ft.; N47 5 38 W99 2 11
1211 SW 5th Avenue, 6th Floor, Portland, OR 97204 US
(503) 517-6000
www.750thegame.com
License: Carrington, Foster County, ND held by Two Rivers Broadcasting Inc.
Group Owner: Alpha Media
Arbitron Metro Market: Portland, OR; *Format:* Adult Contemp
Dave Reed, General Manager
Bill Ashenden, Director of Sales
Scott Mahalick, Programming Director

Cavalier

KAOC
09-29-1998; 105.1 MHz FM; *Hrs Open:* 24; 100 kw; 764 ft.; N48 38 38 W97 58 46
PO Box 30, Langdon, MO 58249 US
(701) 256-1080; *Fax:* (701) 256-1081
www.maverick105fm.com
knakmw@utma.com
License: Cavalier, Pembina County, ND held by Simmons Broadcasting Inc.
Group Owner: Simmons Broadcasting Inc.; (acq 9-7-2004; $1).
Arbitron Metro Market: Langdon, ND; *Format:* Country

Mike Walsh, Operations Dir
Bob Simmons, General Manager

Devils Lake

KDLR
01-25-1925; 1240 kHz AM; 1 kw-U, ND1; N48 6 42 W98 50 43 US
(701) 662-7563; *Fax:* (701) 662-7564
kdlrkdvl@gondtc.com
License: Devils Lake, ND held by Double Z Broadcasting Inc.
Group Owner: Lake Region Radio Works; (acq 1-1-2003; $820,000 with KDVL(FM) Devils Lake)
Arbitron Metro Market: Devils Lake, ND; *Format:* Country, News
Special Programming: Minnesota Twins baseball, Vikings football; *Target Audience:* 25 plus; general
Curt Teigen, President

KDVL
01-01-1967; 102.5 MHz FM; *Hrs Open:* 24; 100 kw; 469 ft.; N47 59 16 W98 55 59
Mailing Address: 400 12th Ave., Devils Lake, ND 58301 US
Second Address: 400 12 Ave., Devils Lake, ND 58301
(701) 662-7563; *Fax:* (701) 662-7564
lrradioworks.com
kdlrkdvl@stellarnet.com
License: Devils Lake, Ramsey County, ND held by Double Z Broadcasting Inc.
Group Owner: Lake Region Radio Works; (acq 1-1-2003; $820,000 with KDLR(AM) Devils Lake).
Arbitron Metro Market: Devil's Lake, ND; *Format:* Oldies; *No. News Employees:* 1; *Target Audience:* 18-54.
Curt Teigen, President
Roger Mertens, General Sales Mgr
Bob Gunderson, Programming Director
Eric Arndt, News Director
Kara Danelle, Disc Jockey
Mark Beighley, Sports Commentator
Paul Clementich, Traffic Manager

KQZZ
08-01-1996; 96.7 MHz FM; *Hrs Open:* 24; 38 kw; 561 ft.; N47 58 49 W99 3 11
232 Third Street, Ne, Valley City, ND 58072 US
(701) 662-7563; *Fax:* (701) 662-7564
www.lrradioworks.com
License: Devils Lake, Ramsey County, ND held by Two Rivers Broadcasting Inc.
Group Owner: Robert Ingstad Broadcast Properties; (acq 3-11-99; $250,000)
Format: Adult Contemp
Curt Teigen, General Manager

KZZY
03-01-1984; 103.5 MHz FM; *Hrs Open:* 24; 100 kw; 453 ft.; N47 58 49 W99 3 11
C/O Fisher Wayland: Ddo, 2001 Penn Ave NW Ste 400, Washington, DC 20006 US
(701) 662-7563; *Fax:* (701) 662-7564
www.lrradioworks.com
tradio@lrradioworks.com
License: Devils Lake, Ramsey County, ND held by Double Z Broadcasting Inc.
Group Owner: Lake Region Radio Works; (acq 4-11-90).
Arbitron Metro Market: Devils Lake, ND; *Format:* Country; *No. News Employees:* 1
Curt Teigen, General Manager

*KDVI
01-01-2007; 89.9 MHz FM; 0.25 kw; 171 ft.; N48 8 5 W98 46 20
Rebroadcasts: Rebroadcasts WAFR(FM) Tupelo, MS 100%
P.O. Box 3206, Tupelo, MS 38803 US
(662) 844-8888; *Fax:* (662) 842-6791
www.afr.net
faq@afa.net
License: Devils Lake, Ramsey County, ND held by American Family Association.
Group Owner: American Family Radio; (acq 6-9-2006)
Nat'l Network: American Family Radio
Arbitron Metro Market: Devils Lake, ND; *Format:* Christian
Tim Wildmon, President
Donald Wildmon, Founder
Buddy Smith, Sr VP
Ed Vitagliano, Exec VP
Randy Sharp, Director Of Special Projects
Meeke Addison, Director Of Communications
Abraham Hamilton III, General Counsel

*KPPD
91.7 MHz FM; 24 kw; 703 ft.; N48 3 47.8 W99 20 8.7
207 North Street, Fargo, ND 58102 US
(701) 241-6900; *Fax:* (701) 239-7650
www.prairiepublic.org
info@prairiepublic.org
License: Devils Lake, Ramsey County, ND held by Prairie Public Broadcasting Inc.
Arbitron Metro Market: Devils Lake, ND; *Format:* Jazz, Triple A
John Harris, President & CEO
John Harris, General Manager
Dave Thompson, News Director
Jack Anderson, Engineering Dir

Dickinson

KCAD
11-20-1996; 99.1 MHz FM; *Hrs Open:* 24; 100 kw; 400 ft.; N46 56 9 W102 43 55
11291 39th St. S.W., Dickinson, ND 58601 US
(701) 227-1876; *Fax:* (701) 227-1959
www.kc99country.com
License: Dickinson, Stark County, ND held by CC Licenses LLC
Group Owner: iHeartMedia; (acq 9-1-2000; grpsl).
Nat'l Network: AP Radio; Jones Radio Networks
Arbitron Metro Market: Dickinson, ND; *Format:* Country; *Target Audience:* 16-50; general
Neil Cary, General Manager

KDIX
01-01-1947; 1230 kHz AM; *Hrs Open:* 24
119 Second Avenue, West, Dickinson, ND 58601 US
(701) 225-5133; *Fax:* (701) 225-4136
www.kdix.net
kdix@kdix.net
License: Dickinson, ND held by Starrdak Inc.
Nat'l Network: CBS
Arbitron Metro Market: Dickinson, ND; *Format:* Adult Contemp, Oldies *Special Programming:* College sports; *Hrs. of News Programming:* news progmg 6 hrs wkly; *No. News Employees:* 8; *Target Audience:* 35-60. *Adv. Rates:* 10.85; 10.85; 10.85; 8.85
Lee Leiss, Chairman
Rod Kleinjan, Operations Dir

*KDPR
10-12-1987; 89.9 MHz FM; *Hrs Open:* 24; 12.5 kw; 492 ft.; N46 43 34 W102 54 56 *Rebroadcasts:* Rebroadcast KCND(FM) Bismark 100%
207 North 5th Street, Fargo, ND 58102 US
(701) 241-6900; *Fax:* (701) 239-7650
www.prairiepublic.org
License: Dickinson, Stark County, ND held by Prairie Public Broadcasting Inc.
Nat'l Network: PRI; NPR
Arbitron Metro Market: Bismarck, ND; *Format:* Jazz, News
Special Programming: American Indian 2 hrs, folk 6 hrs wkly; *Hrs. of News Programming:* news progmg 40 hrs wkly; *No. News Employees:* 2; *Target Audience:* General.
John Harris, CEO/COO
John Harris, President
John Peterson, Engineering/Operations Director
Bill Thomas, General Manager
Steve Wennblom, Programming Director
Dave Thompson, News Director

KLTC
07-04-1978; 1460 kHz AM; *Hrs Open:* 24; 5 kw-D, DAN; 5 kw-N, DAN; N46 50 54 W102 49 49
1129 I-39th Street SW, Dickinson, SD 58601 US
(701) 483-1876
www.1460kltc.com
License: Dickinson, ND held by CC Licenses LLC
Group Owner: iHeartMedia
Nat'l Reps: Hyett/Ramsland
Arbitron Metro Market: Dickinson, ND; *Format:* Country; *Target Audience:* General.
Neil Cary, General Manager
Jeff Glaser, Business Manager

KZRX
08-15-1983; 92.1 MHz FM; *Hrs Open:* 5 AM-midnight; 17 kw; 400 ft.; N46 56 9 W102 43 55
427 Bedford Road, Suite 300, Pleasantville, NY 10570 US
(701) 483-1876
www.kzrx921.com
License: Dickinson, Stark County, ND held by CC Licenses LLC.
Group Owner: iHeartMedia; (acq 9-1-2000; grpsl).
Nat'l Reps: Hyett/Ramsland
Arbitron Metro Market: Dickinson, ND; *Format:* Rock/AOR; *No. News Employees:* 1; *Target Audience:* 18-45.
Richard J. Bressler, President
Jeff Glaser, Business Manager/Sales

Fargo

*KDSU
01-17-1966; 91.9 MHz FM; *Hrs Open:* 24; 100 kw; 991 ft.; N47 0 48 W97 11 37
PO Box 5347, Fargo, ND 58105 US
(701) 241-6900; *Fax:* (701) 231-8899
www.prairiepublic.org
License: Fargo, Cass County, ND held by North Dakota State University.
Nat'l Network: NPR; PRI; *Wire Services:* AP
Arbitron Metro Market: Fargo-Moorhead, ND-MN; *Format:* Variety/Diverse; *Hrs. of News Programming:* news progmg 45 hrs wkly; *No. News Employees:* 3; *Target Audience:* 24 plus; general
John Harris, CEO/COO
John Harris, President
John Peterson, Operations Dir
Bill Thomas, General Manager
Nancy Wood, General Sales Mgr
Steve Wennblom, Programming Director

*KFBN
12-08-1997; 88.7 MHz FM; 30 kw horiz, 100 kw vert; 869 ft.; N47 0 48 W97 11 37
PO Box 107, Fargo, ND 58107 US
(701) 298-8877
www.kfbn.org
License: Fargo, Cass County, ND held by Fargo Baptist Church.
Arbitron Metro Market: Fargo-Moorhead, ND-MN; *Format:* News
T.C. Scheving, President
Michael Jordahl, Operations Dir
T.C. Scheving, General Manager
Tim Schaefer, Station Manager

KFGO
03-14-1948; 790 kHz AM; 5 kW; N46 43 5 W96 48 5
1020 S 25th Street, Fargo, ND 58103 USA
(701) 237-5346; *Fax:* (701) 237-0980
kfgo.com
License: Fargo, ND held by Midwest Communications Inc.
Group Owner: Midwest Communications Inc.; (acq 1-19-2007; grpsl)
Nat'l Network: CBS Radio; *Regional Network:* MNN; *Nat'l Reps:* Eastman Radio; *Wire Services:* AP
Arbitron Metro Market: Fargo-Moorhead; *Format:* News/Talk; *No. News Employees:* 4; *Target Audience:* 25+
Dan Cash, Sales Manager
Jack Sunday, Brand Manager

KRWK
02-23-1984; 101.9 MHz FM; 96 kW; 1001 ft.; N47 0 36 W97 11 41
1020 S 25th Street, Fargo, ND 58103 USA
(701) 237-5346; *Fax:* (701) 237-0980
jackfmfargo.com
License: Fargo, Cass County, ND held by Midwest Communications Inc.
Group Owner: Midwest Communications Inc.
Nat'l Reps: Eastman Radio
Arbitron Metro Market: Fargo-Moorhead; *Format:* Adult Contemp, Classic Rock; *Target Audience:* Men 25 - 54
Dan Cash, Sales Manager
Chris Daniels, Brand Manager

*KFNW-FM
03-12-1965; 97.9 MHz FM; *Hrs Open:* 24; 100 kw; 1001 ft.; N47 0 36 W97 11 41
3003 Snelling Ave.North, Roseville, MN 55113 US
(701) 282-5910; *Fax:* (701) 282-5781
www.kfnw.org
License: Fargo, Cass County, ND held by Northwestern College.
Group Owner: Northwestern College & Radio
Arbitron Metro Market: Fargo-Moorhead, ND-MN; *Format:* Christian; *Target Audience:* 25-54.
Desiree Smith, General Manager

KPFX
01-04-1993; 107.9 MHz FM; *Hrs Open:* 24; 100 kw; 659 ft.; N46 32 46 W96 37 39
Mailing Address: P.O. Box 9439, Fargo, ND 58103 US
Second Address: 2720 Seventh Ave. S., Fargo, ND 58103
(701) 237-4500; *Fax:* (701) 235-9082
www.1079thefox.com/
studio@1079thefox.com
License: Fargo, Cass County, ND held by Radio Fargo-Moorhead Inc.
Group Owner: Radio Fargo-Moorhead Inc.; (acq 8-18-99; grpsl).
Nat'l Reps: Christal

Arbitron Metro Market: Fargo-Moorhead, ND-MN; *Format:* Classic Rock; *No. News Employees:* 4; *Target Audience:* 25-54; skews male
Micheal Kapel, Operations Dir
Micheal Brooks, General Manager
David Howland, General Sales Mgr
Moose Johnson, Programming Director
Dave Jacobs, Mornings Host

WDAY
05-22-1922; 970 kHz AM; *Hrs Open:* 24
301 8th Street South, Fargo, ND 58103 US
(701) 237-6500; *Fax:* (701) 241-5358
www.wday.com
License: Fargo, ND held by Forum Communications Co. Inc.
Group Owner: Forum Communications Co.
Nat'l Network: ABC; *Regional Network:* American Ag; *Nat'l Reps:* Christal; *Wire Services:* NWS (National Weather Service)
Arbitron Metro Market: Fargo-Moorhead, ND-MN; *Format:* News, News/Talk, 84, Talk; *Hrs. of News Programming:* news progmg 35 hrs wkly; *No. News Employees:* 3; *Target Audience:* 35-64.
Lori Becker, Operations Manager of Traffic
Mari Ossenfort, General Manager
Sue Eider, Television Operations Manager
Jen Gion, National Sales Assistant
Dave Johnson, Chief Engineer

KNFL
01-01-2007; 740 kHz AM; 50 kW; N46 58 29 W96 30 12
1020 S 25th Street, Fargo, ND 58103 USA
(701) 237-5346; *Fax:* (701) 237-0980
740thefan.com
License: Fargo, ND held by Midwest Communications Inc.
Group Owner: Midwest Communications Inc.; (acq 7-31-2007)
Nat'l Network: Fox Sports; *Nat'l Reps:* Eastman Radio
Arbitron Metro Market: Fargo-Moorhead; *Format:* Sports; *Target Audience:* Men 25-54
Dan Cash, Sales Manager
Chase Miller, Brand Manager

KOYY
93.7 MHz FM; 100 kW; 1007 ft.; N47 0 36 W97 11 41
1020 S 25th Street, Fargo, ND 58103 USA
(701) 237-5346; *Fax:* (701) 237-0980
y94.com
License: Fargo, Cass County, ND held by Midwest Communications Inc.
Group Owner: Midwest Communications Inc.
Arbitron Metro Market: Fargo-Moorhead; *Format:* Contemporary Hits/Top 40
Dan Cash, Sales Manager
Jack Spade, Brand Manager

Flasher

KKBO
01-01-2008; 105.9 MHz FM; 100 kw; 912 ft.; N46 35 23 W100 47 39
US
(701) 751-8000
License: Flasher, Morton County, ND held by Radio Bismarck Mandan LLC
Arbitron Metro Market: Flasher, ND; *Format:* Adult Contemp
Michael Driscoll, General Manager

Fort Totten

***KABU**
03-15-1999; 90.7 MHz FM; 28 kw; 397 ft.; N47 59 31 W98 56 53
7889 Highway 57, South St. Michael, ND 58370 US
(701) 766-4095; *Fax:* (701) 766-4068
nv1.org/kabu.html
License: Fort Totten, Benson County, ND held by Dakota Circle Tipi Inc.
Arbitron Metro Market: Fort Totten, ND; *Format:* Public Affairs, Variety/Diverse *Special Programming:* American Indian 19 hrs, children 12 hrs, gospel 7; *Target Audience:* General; community on Spirit Lake Nation &surrounding areas to reach all age groups; *Adv. Rates:* 55; 55; 55; na
John Chaske, General Manager
Candice Anderson, Reception/Broadcaster
Ken Chaske, Maintenance Tech Broadcaster

Four Bears

***KMHA**
03-01-1984; 91.3 MHz FM; *Hrs Open:* 24; 97 kw; 449 ft.; N47 44 23 W102 43 24
603 Lodge Road, New Town, ND 58763 US
(701) 627-3333
kmha_fm@restel.net
License: Four Bears, McKenzie County, ND held by Fort Berthold Communications Enterprise.
Format: Variety/Diverse *Special Programming:* American Indian-Mandan/Hidatsa/Arikara 4 hrs, coun; *No. News Employees:* 1; *Target Audience:* Ranchers, farmers, Native Americans.
Tilden Bird, General Manager

Georgetown

KLJA(FM)
107.7 MHz FM; 10,500 watts; 154.8 meters; N46 26 43 W97 39 07
599 Center Drive, Los Angeles, CA 90045
(310) 348-3434
License: Georgetown, TX held by Jose J. Garcia Jr.
Population Served: 820,611; *Arbitron Metro Market:* Austin, TX
Dan Wilson, General Manager
Andrew E. Olivera, General Sales Mgr
Claudia Talamantez, Programming Director
Karem Hocking, National Sales Manager

Grafton

KXPO
07-12-1958; 1340 kHz AM; *Hrs Open:* 6 AM-midnight; 1 kw-U, ND1; N48 23 53 W97 26 56
856 West 12th Street, Grafton, ND 58237 US
(701) 352-0431; *Fax:* (701) 352-0436
www.walshcountydailynews.com
kxpoaj@polarcomm.com
License: Grafton, ND held by KGPC Co.
Nat'l Network: ABC; *Regional Network:* American Ag; N.D. News Net.; *Wire Services:* AP
Arbitron Metro Market: Grafton, ND; *Format:* Country *Special Programming:* Farm 18 hrs, gospel 5 hrs, relg 4 hrs wkly; *Hrs. of News Programming:* news progmg 15 hrs wkly; *No. News Employees:* 2; *Target Audience:* 30-70.
Del Nygard, President
Andrea Johnston, General Manager
Todd Ingstad, General Sales Mgr
Sean Ford, Sports Director
Jesse Forster, Marketing Consultant/ CRMC
Nicki Larson, Adminsitrative Assistant/ RMP

KAUJ
09-17-1984; 100.9 MHz FM; *Hrs Open:* 24; 3 kw; 125 ft.; N48 23 53 W97 26 56
856 West 12th Stret, Grafton, ND 58237 US
(701) 352-0431
www.walshcountydailynews.com
License: Grafton, Walsh County, ND
Format: Oldies; *Hrs. of News Programming:* news progmg 2 hrs wkly; *No. News Employees:* 1; *Target Audience:* 18-60.
Nick Amico, News Director

Grand Forks

***KFJM**
03-06-1995; 90.7 MHz FM; *Hrs Open:* 24; 4 kw; 112 ft.; N47 54 17 W97 6 53
207 North 5th Street, Fargo, ND 58102 US
(701) 241-6900; *Fax:* (701) 239-7650
http://www.prairiepublic.org/radio/roots-rock-and-jazz/
License: Grand Forks, Grand Forks County, ND held by University of North Dakota.
Nat'l Network: NPR; PRI
Arbitron Metro Market: Grand Forks, ND; *Format:* Jazz, Triple A *Special Programming:* Blues 3 hrs wkly, car talk 1 hr wkly,; *Hrs. of News Programming:* news progmg 15 hrs wkly; *No. News Employees:* 3 *TargetAudience:* 25-44; well-educated
Bill Thomas, Operations Dir
Michael Olson, General Manager
Dave Thompson, News Director

KJKJ
08-01-1985; 107.5 MHz FM; *Hrs Open:* 24; 100 kw; 456 ft.; N47 57 52 W97 1 46
505 University Ave., Grand Forks, ND 58203 US
(701) 775-7625
www.kjkj.com
License: Grand Forks, Grand Forks County, ND held by Citicasters Licenses Inc.
Group Owner: iHeartMedia; (acq 10-26-99; grpsl).
Arbitron Metro Market: Grand Forks, ND; *Format:* Rock/AOR; *Hrs. of News Programming:* News progmg 5 hrs wkly; *Target Audience:* 18-49.
Richard J. Bressler, President

KKXL
01-01-1941; 1440 kHz AM; *Hrs Open:* 24; 0.6 kw-D, ND1; 0.3 kw-N, ND1; N47 57 52 W97 1 46
1600 Utica Avenue South, Suite 500, Minneapolis, MN 55416 US
(800) 989-5326
www.kfan.com
License: Grand Forks, ND held by Citicasters Licenses Inc.
Group Owner: iHeartMedia; (acq 10-26-99; grpsl).
Nat'l Network: Jones Radio Networks
Arbitron Metro Market: Grand Forks, ND; *Format:* Sports; *Hrs. of News Programming:* news progmg 10 hrs wkly; *No. News Employees:* 1; *Target Audience:* 25-54; farm community
Richard J. Bressler, President

KKXL-FM
03-01-1975; 92.9 MHz FM; 100 kw; 358 ft.; N47 57 52 W97 1 46
Mailing Address: 505 University Avenue, Grand Forks, ND 58203 US
Second Address: 505 University Ave., Grand Forks, ND 58203
(701) 746-9393
www.xl93.com
suzijohnson@clearchannel.com
License: Grand Forks, Grand Forks County, ND
Arbitron Metro Market: Grand Forks, ND; *Format:* Contemporary Hits/Top 40; *Target Audience:* 18-34.

KNOX
09-07-1947; 1310 kHz AM; *Hrs Open:* 24; 5 kw-D, DAN; 5 kw-N, DAN; N47 50 39 W97 1 30
1185 9th Street NE, Thompson, ND 58278 US
(701) 775-4611; *Fax:* (701) 772-0540
www.knoxradio.com
License: Grand Forks, ND held by Leighton Enterprises Inc.
Group Owner: Leighton Enterprises Inc.; acq 10-23-96; $1.1 million with co-located FM)
Nat'l Network: ABC; *Regional Network:* MNN; *Wire Services:* AP
Arbitron Metro Market: Grand Forks, ND; *Format:* News, News/Talk, 86; *Hrs. of News Programming:* news progmg 80 hrs wkly; *No. News Employees:* 3; *Target Audience:* 35 plus.
Jarrod Thomas, Operations Dir
Jack Hansen, General Manager
Lynn Hodgson, General Sales Mgr
Doug Barrett, News Director

KZGF
02-04-1967; 94.7 MHz FM; *Hrs Open:* 24; 100 kw; Ant 325 ft; N48 00 20 W97 04 18
1185 9th St. N.E., Thompson, ND 56301
(701) 775-4611; *Fax:* (701) 772-0540
www.z947.com
License: Grand Forks, Grand Forks County, ND held by Leighton Enterprises Inc.
Group Owner: Leighton Enterprises Inc.
Nat'l Network: ABC
Population Served: 43,765; *Arbitron Metro Market:* Grand Forks, ND-MN; *Target Audience:* 18-45.
Jarrod Thomas, Operations Dir

***KWTL**
10-22-1923; 1370 kHz AM; *Hrs Open:* 24
216 Belmont Road, Grand Forks, ND 58202 US
(877) 795-0122
License: Grand Forks, ND held by Real Presence Radio
Arbitron Metro Market: Grand Forks, ND; *Format:* Christian
Steve Splonskowski, Executive Director

***KUND-FM**
05-30-1976; 89.3 MHz FM; 50 kw; 292 ft.; N48 11 39.8 W97 11 28.4
Box 8117, Grand Forks, ND 58202 US
(701) 241-6900; *Fax:* (701) 239-7650
www.prairiepublic.org
info@prairiepublic.org
License: Grand Forks, Grand Forks County, ND held by University of North Dakota.
Arbitron Metro Market: Grand Forks, ND; *Format:* Talk *Special Programming:* New age 5 hrs wkly
John Harris, President & CEO
John Peterson, Operations Dir
Mike Olson, Station Manager
Steve Wennblom, Program Manager
Dave Thompson, News Director
Jack Anderson, Engineering Dir
Beth Bradley, Business DevelopmentRepresentative
Ann Clark, Director of Development
Troy Davis, Membership Manager
John Gast, Director of Finance
Barbara Gravel, Production Manager

Harvey

KHND
07-21-1981; 1470 kHz AM; 1 kw-D, ND1; 0.161 kw-N, ND1; N47 45 23 W99 55 6

Mailing Address: 718 Lincoln Avenue, Harvey, ND 59341 US
Second Address: 718 Lincoln Ave., Harvey, ND 58341
(701) 324-4848; *Fax:* (701) 324-2043
studio@khnd1470.com
License: Harvey, ND held by Three Way Broadcasting Inc.
Nat'l Network: ABC
Format: Adult Contemp *Special Programming:* weather, news, talk, classic rock programs, polka; *Hrs. of News Programming:* 15 hrs News Programing wkly; *Target Audience:* 12 -85.
Sheila Jensen, General Manager
Rick Jensen, Producer
Kyle Dean, Sports Director

Harwood

*KKLQ
01-01-2001; 100.7 MHz FM; 40 kw; 328 ft.; N47 8 43 W96 58 18
PO Box 298, Omaha, NE 68103-2098 US
(800) 525-5683
www.klove.com
klove@klove.com
License: Harwood, Cass County, ND held by Educational Media Foundation.
Group Owner: EMF Broadcasting; (acq 1-8-2004; $750,000).
Nat'l Network: K-Love
Arbitron Metro Market: Fargo-Moorhead; *Format:* Christian
Mike Novak, President
David Pierce, Chief Compliance Officer

Hazelton

KUSB
01-01-2006; 103.3 MHz FM; 100 kw; 965 ft.; N46 35 23.8 W100 47 46.2
US
(701) 250-6602; *Fax:* (701) 250-6632
License: Hazelton, Emmons County, ND held by Townsquare Media Bismarck License LLC
Group Owner: Townsquare Media
Arbitron Metro Market: Hazelton, ND; *Format:* Country
Syd Stewart, General Manager
Mike Rose, Programming Director
Elliott Davidson, Chief Engineer

Hettinger

KNDC
03-01-1954; 1490 kHz AM; *Hrs Open:* 12:ooam -11:59pm; 1 kw-U, ND1; N46 1 11 W102 41 33
Box 151, Hettinger, ND 58639 US
(701) 567-2421; *Fax:* (701) 567-4636
kndc1490@ndsupernet.com
License: Hettinger, ND held by Schweitzer Media Inc.
Nat'l Network: ABC News/Talk; *Regional Network:* N.D. News Net.; S.D. News Net.
Format: Country *Special Programming:* Farm; *Hrs. of News Programming:* News progmg 24 hrs wkly; *Target Audience:* 24-52; rural residents
Mike Schweitzer, President
Nolan Dix, General Manager

KNDH
102.3 MHz FM; 51 kw; 59 meters; N46 09 12.97 W102 46 24.4
8515 Georgia Avenue, 9th Floor, Siver Spring, MD 20910
(815) 346-2657; *Fax:* (301) 645-1426
aleinwind@radio-one.com
License: Hettinger, Adams County, ND held by Midnation Media LLC
Group Owner: Alma Corp.

Alan Leinwind, General Manager

Hope

KMJO
01-01-2002; 104.7 MHz FM; *Hrs Open:* 24; 100 kW; 702 ft.; N47 3 15 W97 24 44
1020 S 25th Street, Fargo, ND 58103 USA
(701) 237-5346; *Fax:* (701) 237-0980
dukefmfargo.com
License: Hope, Steele County, ND held by Midwest Communications Inc.
Group Owner: Midwest Communications Inc.; (acq 1-19-2007; grpsl)
Nat'l Reps: Eastman Radio
Arbitron Metro Market: Fargo-Moorhead; *Format:* Country; *Target Audience:* Adults 25-64
Dan Cash, Sales Manager
Chris Daniels, Brand Manager

Jamestown

*KPRJ
01-01-1993; 91.5 MHz FM; *Hrs Open:* 24; 18.5 kw; 354 ft.; N46 46 36 W98 31 20 *Rebroadcasts:* Rebroadcasts KCND(FM) Bismarck 100%
P.O. Box 3240, Fargo, ND 58108 US
(701) 241-6900; *Fax:* (701) 239-7650
www.prairiepublic.org
info@prairiepublic.org
License: Jamestown, Stutsman County, ND held by Prairie Public Broadcasting Inc.
Nat'l Network: NPR; PRI
Format: Jazz, News *Special Programming:* American Indian 2 hrs, folk 6 hrs wkly; *No. News Employees:* 3; *Target Audience:* General.
John Harris, CEO
Duane Lee, Operations Dir
Bill Thomas, General Sales Mgr
David Thompson, News Director

KQDJ
08-12-1954; 1400 kHz AM; *Hrs Open:* 24; 1 kw-U, ND1; N46 53 37 W98 41 20
Mailing Address: 232 Third St, Ne, Valley City, ND 58072 US
Second Address: 2625 8th Ave. S.W., Jamestown, ND 58401
(701) 252-1400
www.newsdakota.com
License: Jamestown, ND held by Two Rivers Broadcasting Inc.
Group Owner: Robert Ingstad Broadcast Properties; (acq 1994; $600,000)
Nat'l Network: Fox Sports
Format: Contemporary Hits/Top 40
Dave Reed, General Manager

KSJB
01-01-1937; 600 kHz AM; *Hrs Open:* 24; 5 kw-U, DA1; N46 49 3 W98 42 34
Mailing Address: 4700 South Lewis Blvd, Sioux City, IA 51106 US
Second Address: 2400 8th Ave. S. W., Jamestown, ND 58402-1840
(701) 252-3570
www.ksjbam.com
License: Jamestown, ND held by Chesterman Communications Inc.
Arbitron Metro Market: Jamestown, ND; *Format:* Country *Special Programming:* Farm 12 hrs wkly; *Hrs. of News Programming:* news progmg 13 hrs wkly; *No. News Employees:* 1; *Target Audience:* 25 plus.
Patrick Pfieffer, General Manager
Patrick Pfeiffer, General Sales Mgr
Curt Sayler, Senior Account Executive

KSJZ
01-01-1968; 93.3 MHz FM; *Hrs Open:* 6 AM-midnight; 100 kw; 449 ft.; N46 49 6.6 W98 42 38.7
2400 8th Avenue SW, Jamestown, ND 58402 US
(701) 252-3570; *Fax:* (701) 252-1277
www.mixjamestown.com
License: Jamestown, Stutsman County, ND
Arbitron Metro Market: Jamestown, ND; *Format:* Adult Contemp; *Target Audience:* 28-52; 60% male, 40% female
Marvin Sanders, General Manager
Bonnie Weatherly, Office Manager

KYNU
08-25-1984; 95.5 MHz FM; *Hrs Open:* 24; 100 kw; 646 ft.; N46 56 21 W98 18 30
Mailing Address: 136 Central Avenue N., Valley City, ND 58072 US
Second Address: 2625 8th Ave. S.W., Jamestown, ND 58402
(701) 252-1400
www.newsdakota.com
License: Jamestown, Stutsman County, ND held by Two Rivers Broadcasting Inc.
Group Owner: Robert Ingstad Broadcast Properties
Nat'l Network: ABC
Format: Country; *Target Audience:* 18-65.
Dave Reed, General Manager

*KLUU
01-01-2008; 89.1 MHz FM; 1.7 kw vert; 285 ft.; N46 50 5 W98 41 31 *Rebroadcasts:* Rebroadcasts KLVR(FM) Middletown, CA 100%
1425 North Market Blvd, Suite 9, Sacramento, CA 95834 US
(800) 877-5600; *Fax:* (916) 251-1650
www.klove.com
License: Jamestown, Stutsman County, ND held by Educational Media Foundation.
Group Owner: EMF Broadcasting
Nat'l Network: K-Love
Arbitron Metro Market: Tulsa, OK; *Format:* Christian
Mike Novak, President

*KJTW
89.9 MHz FM; 0.4 kw; 154 ft.; N46 53 30 W98 42 46
P.O. Box 3206, Tupelo, MS 38803 US
(662) 844-8888; *Fax:* (662) 842-6791
www.afr.net
faq@afa.net
License: Jamestown, Stutsman County, ND held by American Family Association.
Group Owner: American Family Radio; (acq 8-27-2007)
Nat'l Network: American Family Radio
Arbitron Metro Market: Jamestown, ND; *Format:* Christian
Tim Wildmon, President
Donald Wildmon, Founder
Buddy Smith, Sr VP
Ed Vitagliano, Executive VP
Randy Sharp, Director Of Special Projects
Meeke Addison, Director Of Communications
Abraham Hamilton III, General Counsel

Kindred

KFNL
06-06-1986; 92.7 MHz FM; *Hrs Open:* 24; 25 kw; 328 ft.; N46 39 37 W96 43 1
1020 25th Street South, Fargo, ND 58108 US
(651) 631-5000; *Fax:* (612) 631-5086
License: Kindred, Cass County, ND held by Northwestern College.
Group Owner: Northwestern College & Radio; (acq 1-19-2007; donation)
Arbitron Metro Market: Fargo-Moorhead, ND-MN; *Format:* Rock/AOR
Robert Ingstad, President

Langdon

KNDK
06-27-1967; 1080 kHz AM; *Hrs Open:* 16
PO Box 30, Langdon, ND 58249 US
(701) 256-1080; *Fax:* (701) 256-1881
kndk1080@utma.com
License: Langdon, ND held by KNDK Inc.
Group Owner: Simmons Broadcasting Inc.; (acq 12-1-87).
Nat'l Network: CBS
Format: Country, News, 62, Talk *Special Programming:* Farm 12 hrs, relg 4 hrs wkly; *Hrs. of News Programming:* news progmg 42 hrs wkly; *No. News Employees:* 3; *Target Audience:* 25 plus.
Bob Simmons, President
Mike Walsh, Operations Dir
Courtney Bodnar, Traffic Manager
Diane Simmons, CFO

KNDK-FM
01-15-1992; 95.7 MHz FM; *Hrs Open:* 24; 6 kw; 328 ft.; N48 45 18 W98 21 38
Route 5, P.O. Box 9, Langdon, ND 58249 US
(701) 256-1080; *Fax:* (701) 256-1081
www.kndkradio.com
kndk1080@utma.com
License: Langdon, Cavalier County, ND
Group Owner: Simmons Broadcasting Inc.; (Acq 11-20-91; $90,000;
Format: Adult Contemp
Bob Simmons, President
Brain Matthews, Operations Dir
Courtney Bodnar, Traffic Manager
Diane Simmons, CFO

Lisbon

KQLX
11-01-1984; 890 kHz AM
64 Broadway, Fargo, ND 58102 US
(701) 356-1156; *Fax:* (701) 356-1155
www.agnews890.com
License: Lisbon, ND held by Loomis Broadcasting Inc.
Regional Network: Agrinet
Arbitron Metro Market: Fargo-Moorhead; *Format:* Agriculture, News, 62, Talk *Special Programming:* Farm 18 hrs, Gospel 6 hrs wkly; *Hrs. of News Programming:* news progmg 5 hrs wkly; *No. News Employees:* 1 *TargetAudience:* 18-65; farmers; *Adv. Rates:* 22; 22; 17; 12
Terry Loomis, President
Rita Loomis, Operations Dir
Lisa Nelson, General Manager
Dave Baxter, Programming Director

KQLX-FM
10-24-1986; 106.1 MHz FM; 100 kw; 715 ft.; N46 44 39 W97 25 38
64 Broadway, Fargo, ND 58102 US
(701) 356-1156; *Fax:* (701) 356-1155
www.thunder1061.com
thunderstudio@thunder1061.com
License: Lisbon, Ransom County, ND held by Sheyenne Valley Broadcasting Inc.
Nat'l Network: CNN Radio
Arbitron Metro Market: Fargo-Moorhead; *Format:* Country; *Hrs. of News Programming:* news progmg 5 hrs wkly; *No. News Employees:* 1; *Target Audience:* 18-54; general; *Adv. Rates:* 18; 18; 14; 10
Terry Loomis, President
Rita Loomis, Operations Director
Lisa Nelson, General Manager
Dave Baxter, Programming Director

Mandan

KNDR
06-19-1977; 104.7 MHz FM; *Hrs Open:* 24; 100 kw; 853 ft.; N46 35 11 W100 48 20
Mailing Address: 1400 3rd Street SE, Mandan, ND 58554 US
Second Address: ND
(701) 663-2345; *Fax:* (701) 663-2347
www.kndr.fm
kndr@midconetwork.com
License: Mandan, Morton County, ND held by Central Dakota Enterprise Inc.
Wire Services: AP
Arbitron Metro Market: Bismarck, ND; *Format:* Adult Contemp, Christian; *Target Audience:* 25-54; women and famlies (with children)
Brad Bales, General Manager

Mayville

KMSR
10-20-1967; 1520 kHz AM; *Hrs Open:* Sunrise-sunset; 2.5 kw-D; N47 29 45 W97 21 03
1000 Main Street West, PO Box 216, Mayville, ND 58257
(701) 786-2335; *Fax:* (701) 786-2268
www.kmav.com
craig@kmav.com
License: Mayville, Traill County, ND held by KMSR Inc.
Nat'l Network: ESPN Radio; *Regional Network:* N.D. News Net.
Population Served: 150,000 *Target Audience:* 25-55.; *Adv. Rates:* 14; 14; 14; 10
Dan Keating, General Manager
Mary Keating, General Sales Manager/Sports Director
Greg Keating, Weather

KMAV-FM
01-10-1977; 105.5 MHz FM; *Hrs Open:* 24; 25 kw; Ant 328 ft; N47 29 45 W97 21 03
1000 Main Street West, PO Box 216, Mayville, ND 58257
(701) 786-2335; *Fax:* (701) 786-2268
www.kmav.com
craig@kmav.com
License: Mayville, Traill County, ND held by KMSR Inc.
Nat'l Network: CBS; ESPN; Premiere; Dial Global; *Regional Network:* Red River Farm Network; Dakota News Network; American DC Network
Population Served: 150,000 *Target Audience:* 18-54; *Adv. Rates:* $7.00 30s; $11.00 60s
Dan Keating, General Manager
Mary Keating, General Sales Manager/Sports Director
Greg Keating, Weather

Minot

KCJB
09-01-1950; 910 kHz AM; 5 kw-D, DA2; 5 kw-N, DA2; N48 12 9 W101 20 54
1000 20th Ave. S.W., Minot, ND 58701 US
(701) 852-4646; *Fax:* (701) 852-1390
www.kcjb910.com
License: Minot, Ward County, ND held by CC Licenses LLC.
Group Owner: iHeartMedia; (acq 1-12-2000; grpsl).
Nat'l Network: Fox News Radio
Arbitron Metro Market: Bismarck, ND; *Format:* Country *Special Programming:* Loc sports, various loc talk segments, farm 4 hrs wkly; *Target Audience:* 25 plus.
Richard J. Bressler, President

KHRT
11-17-1957; 1320 kHz AM; *Hrs Open:* 24; 2.5 kw-D, ND1; 0.31 kw-N, ND1; N48 11 48 W101 14 0
P.O. Box 1210, Minot, ND 58702 US
(701) 852-3789; *Fax:* (701) 852-8498
www.khrt.com
office@khrt.com
License: Minot, ND held by Faith Broadcasting Inc.
Format: Gospel, News, 62, Talk, Religious *Special Programming:* Family 10 hrs wkly; *Hrs. of News Programming:* news progmg 10 hrs wkly; *No. News Employees:* 1; *Target Audience:* 25-54; large families, loyal,upper-income professionals
Richard Leavitt, President
Roy Leavitt, General Manager
John Kennedy, News Director
John McCann, Chief Engineer
Johas Nelson, Music Director
Marcia Leavitt, Traffic Manager

KIZZ
09-07-1968; 93.7 MHz FM; *Hrs Open:* 24; 100 kw; 554 ft.; N48 3 11 W101 26 4
1000 20th Ave. S.W., Minot, ND 58701 US
(701) 852-4646; *Fax:* (701) 852-1390
www.z94radio.com
License: Minot, Ward County, ND held by CC Licenses LLC.
Group Owner: iHeartMedia; (acq 9-1-2000; grpsl).
Arbitron Metro Market: Minot, ND; *Format:* Contemporary Hits/Top 40; *Hrs. of News Programming:* news progmg 3 hrs wkly; *No. News Employees:* 1; *Target Audience:* 25-54.
Richard J. Bressler, President

***KMPR**
11-23-1983; 88.9 MHz FM; *Hrs Open:* 24; 50 kw; 928 ft.; N48 3 3 W101 23 24 *Rebroadcasts:* Rebroadcasts KCND(FM) Bismarck 100%
P.O. Box 3240, Fargo, ND 58108 US
(701) 224-1700; *Fax:* (701) 224-0555
www.prairiepublic.org
info@prairiepublic.org
License: Minot, Ward County, ND held by Prairie Public Broadcasting Inc.
Nat'l Network: PRI; NPR
TV Affiliate: *KSRE(TV) affil.; *Format:* Jazz, News *Special Programming:* American Indian 2 hrs, folk 6 hrs wkly; *Hrs. of News Programming:* news progmg 40 hrs wkly; *No. News Employees:* 2 *Target Audience:* General.
John Harris, CEO
Duane Lee, Operations Dir
Bill Thomas, General Sales Mgr
David Thompson, News Director

KMXA-FM
04-01-1984; 99.9 MHz FM; *Hrs Open:* 24; 100 kw; 466 ft.; N48 10 57 W101 31 57
1000 20th Avenue SW, Minot, ND 58701 US
(701) 852-4646; *Fax:* (701) 852-1390
www.mix999fm.com
License: Minot, Ward County, ND held by CC Licenses LLC.
Group Owner: iHeartMedia; (acq 1-12-2000; grpsl).
Arbitron Metro Market: Minot, ND; *Format:* Adult Contemp; *Hrs. of News Programming:* News progmg 4 hrs wkly; *Target Audience:* 25-54; adult upper middle class with teens at home
Richard J. Bressler, President

KRRZ
10-28-1929; 1390 kHz AM; 5 kw-D, ND1; 1 kw-N, ND1; N48 12 45 W101 14 30
1000 20th Avenue SW, Minot, ND 58701 US
(701) 852-4646; *Fax:* (701) 852-1390
www.oldies1390.com
License: Minot, ND held by Aloha Station Trust
Regional Network: N.D. News Net; *Nat'l Reps:* Roslin
Format: Adult Contemp *Special Programming:* Sports; *Target Audience:* 25-54.
Rick Stensby, General Manager

KYYX
11-15-1966; 97.1 MHz FM; *Hrs Open:* 24; 95 kw; 984 ft.; N48 3 2 W101 20 29
1000 20th Avenue SW, Minot, ND 58701 US
(701) 839-5999
www.97kicksfm.com
License: Minot, Ward County, ND held by CC Licenses LLC.
Group Owner: iHeartMedia
Arbitron Metro Market: Minot, ND; *Format:* Country; *Hrs. of News Programming:* news progmg 6 hrs wkly; *No. News Employees:* 1; *Target Audience:* 18-49; young families
Richard J. Bressler, President

KZPR
07-08-1985; 105.3 MHz FM; *Hrs Open:* 24; 100 kw; 554 ft.; N48 3 11 W101 26 4
1000 20th Avenue SW, Minot, ND 58701 US
(701) 852-4646; *Fax:* (701) 852-1390
www.1053thefox.com
License: Minot, Ward County, ND held by CC Licenses LLC
Group Owner: iHeartMedia
Arbitron Metro Market: Minot, ND; *Format:* Classic Rock *Special Programming:* Farm 4 hrs wkly; *Hrs. of News Programming:* News progmg 4 hrs wkly
Richard J. Bressler, President

KHRT-FM
01-01-1992; 106.9 MHz FM; 50 kw; 344 ft.; N48 9 48 W101 17 55
Mailing Address: P.O. Box 1210, Minot, ND 58702 US
Second Address: 3600 County Rd. 195 S., Minot, ND 58702
(701) 852-3789; *Fax:* (701) 852-8498
www.khrt.com
khrt@srt.com
License: Minot, Ward County, ND held by Faith Broadcasting Inc.
Arbitron Metro Market: Minot, ND; *Format:* Christian
Johas Nelson, Programming Director

Oakes

KDDR
07-31-1959; 1220 kHz AM; 1 kw-D, ND1; 0.327 kw-N, ND1; N46 7 23 W98 5 21 *Rebroadcasts:* Rebroadcast KOVC(AM) Valley City
136 Central Avenue N., Valley City, ND 58072 US
(701) 845-1490
License: Oakes, ND held by Sioux Valley Broadcasting Co.
Group Owner: Robert Ingstad Broadcast Properties; (acq 2-1-93; $85,000;
Regional Network: N.D. News Net.
Format: Country, News; *Target Audience:* 28-59; farm/agriculture

Rugby

KZZJ
08-21-1961; 1450 kHz AM; *Hrs Open:* 24; 1 kw-U, ND1; N48 21 14 W99 59 31
230 Highway 2 SE, Rugby, ND 58368 US
(701) 776-5254; *Fax:* (701) 776-6154
www.kzzj.com
kzzj@kzzj.com
License: Rugby, ND held by Rugby Broadcasters Inc.
Arbitron Metro Market: Rugby, ND; *Format:* Country; *No. News Employees:* 1; *Target Audience:* 25-65.; *Adv. Rates:* 8; 7; 6; 5
Lila D. Harstad, General Manager
Bruce Allen, News Director
Dee Dee Bishoff, Traffic Manager

South Heart

KDXN
11-01-2008; 105.7 MHz FM; 100 kw; 545 ft.; N46 56 53 W102 59 25
26 West Villard Street, Dickinson, ND 58601 US
(701) 225-1057
www.themix1057.com
studio@themix1057.com
License: South Heart, Stark County, ND held by Western Edge Media LLC
Arbitron Metro Market: South Heart, ND; *Format:* Country

Tioga

KTGO
02-27-1966; 1090 kHz AM; 1 kw-D, NDD; N48 23 30 W102 56 12
Mailing Address: Box 457, Tioga, ND 58852 US
Second Address: 301 S.E. 2nd St., Tioga, ND 58852
(701) 664-5846; *Fax:* (701) 664-3322
gary@bakkenbeacon.com
License: Tioga, ND held by Tioga Broadcasting Corp.
Nat'l Network: CBS
Arbitron Metro Market: Tioga, ND; *Format:* Country *Special Programming:* Gospel 11 hrs wkly; *Target Audience:* 18-55.
George Emineth, General Manager
Dustin Moore, Programming Director
Cristi Trulson, Management

KZTW
104.1 MHz FM; 100 kw; 116 m; N48 20 40 W103 12 27
3325 Conservancy Lane, Middleton, WI
(608) 831-8708
License: Tioga, Williams County, ND held by L. Topaz Enterprises Inc.

Dale A. Ganske, President

Valley City

KOVC
10-19-1936; 1490 kHz AM; *Hrs Open:* 19; 1 kw-U, ND1; N46 54 48 W98 1 2
136 Central Avenue N., Valley City, ND 58072 US
(701) 845-1490
www.newsdakota.com
License: Valley City, ND held by Sioux Valley Broadcasting Co.
Group Owner: Robert Ingstad Broadcast Properties
Format: Country, News, 84; *Hrs. of News Programming:* News progmg 7 hrs wkly; *Target Audience:* 25 plus.

KQDJ-FM
08-01-1983; 101.1 MHz FM; *Hrs Open:* 19; 100 kw; 646 ft.; N46 56 21 W98 18 30
232 3rd Street, Ne, Valley City, ND 58072 US
(701) 845-1490; *Fax:* (701) 845-1245
www.newsdakota.com
License: Valley City, Barnes County, ND
Arbitron Metro Market: Jamestown-Valley City; *Format:* Contemporary Hits/Top 40; *Target Audience:* 25-54.
Dave Reed, Programming Director

Velva

KTZU
01-01-2005; 94.9 MHz FM; *Hrs Open:* 24; 98 kw; 512 ft.; N48 3 4 W101 20 23
624 21st Avenue SW, Minot, ND 58101 US
(701) 838-0949
www.949thezoo.com
pbiminot@srt.com
License: Velva, McHenry County, ND held by Programmers Broadcasting Inc.
Group Owner: Programmers Broadcasting Inc.
Arbitron Metro Market: Velva, ND; *Format:* Classic Rock; *Hrs. of News Programming:* News progmg 5 hrs wkly; *Target Audience:* 25-54.

Wahpeton

KEGK
05-21-1989; 106.9 MHz FM; *Hrs Open:* 24; 41 kw; 538 ft.; N46 32 46 W96 37 39
64 Broadway, Fargo, ND 58102 US
(701) 356-1069; *Fax:* (701) 346-1155
www.youreagle1069.com
License: Wahpeton, Richland County, ND held by Guderian Broadcasting Inc.
Nat'l Reps: Midwest Radio *Regional Reps:* Quest Marketing.
Format: Oldies; *Hrs. of News Programming:* news progmg 5 hrs wkly; *No. News Employees:* 1; *Target Audience:* 25-54.
Broadway Boe, Operations Dir
Lisa Hook, General Manager

Walhalla

KYTZ
09-01-1998; 106.7 MHz FM; *Hrs Open:* 24; 16 kw; 837 ft.; N48 38 38 W97 58 46
P. O. Box 30, Langdon, ND 58249 US
(701) 256-1080; *Fax:* (701) 256-1081
www.thevalleysbiggesthits.com
kndkkicksbs@utma.com
License: Walhalla, Pembina County, ND held by Simmons Broadcasting Inc.
Group Owner: Simmons Broadcasting Inc.; (acq 9-7-2004).
Arbitron Metro Market: Langdon, ND; *Format:* Adult Contemp
Bob Simmons, CEO
Mike Walsh, Operations Dir

West Fargo

*KFNW
10-28-1955; 1200 kHz AM; *Hrs Open:* 24
5702 52nd Avenue South, Fargo, ND 58104 US
(701) 282-5910; *Fax:* (701) 282-5781
www.life979.com
License: West Fargo, ND held by Northwestern College.
Group Owner: Northwestern College & Radio
Arbitron Metro Market: Fargo-Moorhead, ND-MN; *Format:* Religious; *Hrs. of News Programming:* news progmg 6 hrs wkly; *No. News Employees:* 1; *Target Audience:* 25-54.
Tim Unsinn, Station Manager

KQWB
09-01-2000; 1660 kHz AM
2001 Penn. Ave., NW, Ste 400 Dms, Washington, DC 20006 US
(701) 237-4500; *Fax:* (701) 235-9082
www.123fargo.com
info@123fargo.com
License: West Fargo, ND held by Radio Fargo-Moorhead Inc.
Group Owner: Radio Fargo-Moorhead Inc.; (acq 8-18-99; grpsl)
Nat'l Network: Westwood One; *Nat'l Reps:* Christal
Arbitron Metro Market: Fargo-Moorhead; *Format:* Oldies; *Target Audience:* 35 plus.
Tom Douglas, CFO
David Benjamin, President
Anne Phibian, Operations Dir
Nancy Odney, General Manager
John Austin, Programming Director

Williston

KDSR
02-28-1985; 101.1 MHz FM; *Hrs Open:* 18; 98 kw; 801 ft.; N48 3 30 W104 0 0
723 15th Street West, Williston, ND 58801 US
(309) 691-0101
www.jack1011.com
mrea@ampillinois.com
License: Williston, Williams County, ND held by Williston Community Broadcasting Corp. dba KDSR(FM)
Nat'l Network: CNN Radio
Hrs. of News Programming: News progmg 7 hrs wkly

KEYZ
01-01-1948; 660 kHz AM; *Hrs Open:* 24; 5 kw-D, DA2; 5 kw-N, DA2; N48 14 20 W103 39 1
Mailing Address: PO Box 2048, Williston, ND 58801 US
Second Address: 410 E. 6th, Williston, ND 58801
(701) 572-5371; *Fax:* (701) 572-7511
www.keyzradio.com
License: Williston, ND held by CCR-Williston IV LLC.
Group Owner: Cherry Creek Radio LLC; (acq 12-19-2003; grpsl)
Nat'l Network: ABC; *Regional Network:* American Ag
Arbitron Metro Market: Williston, ND; *Format:* Country, News, 62, Talk *Special Programming:* Relg 5 hrs wkly; *No. News Employees:* 1; *Target Audience:* 25-54.; *Adv. Rates:* 15; 15; 15; 8.25
Jamey Parsons, Sales Manager

*KPPR
11-20-1986; 89.5 MHz FM; *Hrs Open:* 24; 10.5 kw; 492 ft.; N48 8 30 W103 53 34 *Rebroadcasts:* Rebroadcasts KCND(FM) Bismarck 100%
207 N 5th Street, Fargo, ND 58102 US
(701) 241-6900; *Fax:* (701) 239-7650
www.prairiepublic.org
info@prairiepublic.org
License: Williston, Williams County, ND held by Prairie Public Broadcasting.
Nat'l Network: PRI; NPR
TV Affiliate: KWSE(TV) affil; *Format:* Triple A *Special Programming:* American Indian 2 hrs, folk 6 hrs wkly; *Hrs. of News Programming:* news progmg 40 hrs wkly; *No. News Employees:* 2 *Target Audience:* General.
John Harris, President/CEO
Bill Thomas, Director of Radio
Dave Thompson, News Director
Jack Anderson, Engineering Dir

KYYZ
12-01-1979; 96.1 MHz FM; *Hrs Open:* 24; 100 kw; 869 ft.; N48 2 52 W103 59 1
Mailing Address: P.O. Box 2048, Williston, ND 58802 US
Second Address: 410 E. 6th, Williston, ND 58801
(701) 572-5371; *Fax:* (701) 572-7511
License: Williston, Williams County, ND held by CCR-Williston IV LLC.
Group Owner: Cherry Creek Radio LLC
Nat'l Network: Fox News Radio
Arbitron Metro Market: Williston, ND; *Format:* Country; *No. News Employees:* 1; *Target Audience:* 25-54.
Joe Schwartz, Corporate President

*KNDW
91.7 MHz FM; 0.25 kw; 118 ft.; N48 10 45 W103 33 54
PO Box 3206, Tupelo, MS 38803 US
(662) 844-8888
www.afr.net
comments@afr.net
License: Williston, Williams County, ND held by Salt & Light Communications Inc.
Arbitron Metro Market: Williston, ND; *Format:* Christian
Jim Stanley, Operations

*KJND-FM
12-05-2011; 90.7 MHz FM; *Hrs Open:* 24; 2 kw; 574 ft.; N48 8 30 W103 53 34
PO Box 2426, 317 First Street, Havre, MT 59501 US
(800) 442-9222
www.ynopradio.org
info@ynop.org
License: Williston, Williams County, ND held by Hi-Line Radio Fellowship Inc.
Arbitron Metro Market: Havre, MT; *Adv. Rates:* Non-comm
Roger Lonnquist, General Manager
Brenda Boyum, KXEI Station Manager
Clark Berg, KALS Sales Manager
David Brown, YNOP Program Director
Nicholas Tobiason, Music/IT Director
Ron Huckeby, Chief Engineer
Crystal MacInnes, ProductionAssistant
Joe McGee, KALS Account Executive
Carlene Prince, YNOP Associate Network Manager

Wimbledon

KRVX
01-01-2005; 103.1 MHz FM; 99 kw; 472 ft.; N46 56 21 W98 18 30
Mailing Address: US
Second Address: 2625 8th Ave. S.W., Jamestown, ND 58402
(701) 252-1400; *Fax:* (701) 252-1402
www.newsdakota.com
License: Wimbledon, Barnes County, ND held by James River Broadcasting Inc.
Group Owner: Robert Ingstad Broadcast Properties
Nat'l Network: NBC Radio
Arbitron Metro Market: Lubbock, TX; *Target Audience:* 18-54.

Ohio

Ada

*WONB
10-18-1991; 94.9 MHz FM; 3 kw; 328 ft.; N40 45 58 W83 50 14
525 South Main Street, Ada, OH 45810 US
(419) 772-1194; *Fax:* (419) 772-2794
www.wonbradio.net
wonb@onu.edu
License: Ada, Hardin County, OH held by Ohio Northern University.
Nat'l Network: CNN Radio; *Wire Services:* CNN
Arbitron Metro Market: Lima, OH *TV Affiliate:* var/div *Special Programming:* News progmg 8 hrs wkly; *No. News Employees:* 18-49; general
General Manager, Nichole Tebbe
Station Manager, Station Manager
News Director, News Director

Akron

WAKR
10-16-1940; 1590 kHz AM; *Hrs Open:* 24; 5 kw-D, DAN; 5 kw-N, DAN; N41 1 14 W81 30 20
1795 West Market Street, Akron, OH 44333 US
(330) 869-9800; *Fax:* (330) 864-6799
www.wakr.net
License: Akron, OH held by Rubber City Radio Group Inc.
Group Owner: Rubber City Radio Group Inc.; acq 10-6-93; $9.3 million with co-located FM;
Nat'l Network: ABC; *Nat'l Reps:* Christal; *Wire Services:* AP
Arbitron Metro Market: Akron, OH; *Format:* News, Oldies, 84; *Hrs. of News Programming:* news progmg 40 hrs wkly; *No. News Employees:* 10; *Target Audience:* 35 plus.
Thomas Mandel, CEO
Chuck Collins, Operations Dir
Dominic Rizzo, General Sales Mgr
Joyce Lagios, Promotions Manager
Ed Esposito, News Director
Henry Zelman, CFO
Al Hruska, Chief of Operations
Chuck Collins, OperationsDirector
Mark Biviano, Senior Vice President

*WAPS
10-04-1955; 91.3 MHz FM; *Hrs Open:* 24; 800 w; Ant 151 ft; N41 03 18 W81 31 35
65 Steiner Ave., Akron, OH 44301
(330) 761-3099; *Fax:* (330) 761-3240
www.913thesummit.com
tommybruno@913thesummit.com
License: Akron, Summit County, OH held by Board of Education, Akron City School District.
Population Served: 300,000; *Arbitron Metro Market:* Akron, OH *Special Programming:* Ger 2 hrs, It 2 hrs, Hungarian one hr, Slovenian 2 hrs, Latin 2 hrs wkly; *Target Audience:* 25-54; college educated adults

Andrew James, Operations Dir
Tommy Bruno, General Manager
Garrett Hart, Director of Creative Content
Jim Chenot, General Sales Mgr
Bill Gruber, Programming Director
Liz Mozzocco, Music Director
Jim Morgan, Chief Engineer

WHLO
10-01-1944; 640 kHz AM; *Hrs Open:* 24; 5 kw-D, DA2; 0.5 kw-N, DA2; N41 4 47 W81 38 45
7755 Freedom Ave., North Canton, OH 44720 US
(330) 492-4700; *Fax:* (330) 492-1350
www.640whlo.com
news@640whlo.com
License: Akron, OH held by CC Licenses LLC.
Group Owner: iHeartMedia; (acq 12-31-2001; $4.5 million).
Arbitron Metro Market: Akron, OH; *Format:* News, News/Talk, 86
Keith Kennedy, Director of Programming Operations
Greg Ausham, Programming Director

WAKS
01-01-1950; 96.5 MHz FM; 31 kw; 620 ft.; N41 16 50 W81 37 22
6200 Oak Tree Blvd., 4th Floor, Independence, OH 44131 US
(216) 520-2600; *Fax:* (216) 981-8167
www.kisscleveland.com
License: Akron, Summit County, OH held by Capstar TX LLC.
Group Owner: iHeartMedia; (acq 7-30-2008; grpsl)
Arbitron Metro Market: Akron, OH; *Format:* Contemporary Hits/Top 40
Richard J. Bressler, President
Sharon Moses, General Sales Manager
Maureen Esposito, General Sales Manager

WONE-FM
10-01-1947; 97.5 MHz FM; 12 kw; 889 ft.; N41 3 53 W81 34 59
1795 West Market Street, Akron, OH 44333 US
(330) 869-9800; *Fax:* (330) 864-6799,
www.wone.net
License: Akron, Summit County, OH
Group Owner: Rubber City Radio Group Inc.
Arbitron Metro Market: Akron, OH *TV Affiliate:* Rock; *No. News Employees:* 18-49.
Disc Jockey, Sandra Miller
Disc Jockey, Dana Durban
News Reporter

WARF
01-01-1926; 1350 kHz AM; 5 kw-U, DA1; N41 10 5 W81 30 45
1867 W. Market Street, Akron, OH 44313 US
(330) 492-4700; *Fax:* (330) 492-1350
www.sportsradio1350.com
info@sportsradio1350.com
License: Akron, OH held by Capstar TX LLC
Group Owner: iHeartMedia; (acq 2000; grpsl)
Nat'l Network: Sporting News Radio Network
Arbitron Metro Market: Akron, OH; *Format:* Sports, Talk
Mark Boarman, Market Manager
Keith Kennedy, Senior Vice President of Programming

***WZIP**
12-10-1962; 88.1 MHz FM; *Hrs Open:* 24; 7.5 kw; 820 ft.; N41 4 58 W81 38 2
1004 Guzzetta, Akron, OH 44325 US
(330) 972-7105; *Fax:* (330) 972-5521
www.wzip.fm
wzip@uakron.edu
License: Akron, Summit County, OH held by University of Akron.
Nat'l Network: AP Network News; *Wire Services:* AP
Arbitron Metro Market: Akron, OH; *Format:* Rock/AOR, Contemporary Hits/Top 40 *Special Programming:* Polka 4 hrs, pub affrs 11 hrs, sports talk 3 hrs w; *Target Audience:* 18-34.
Thomas Beck, General Manager
Blake Thompson, Chief Engineer

Alliance

WDPN
09-02-1953; 1310 kHz AM; *Hrs Open:* 24; 1 kw-D, DA2; 0.48 kw-N, DA2; N40 55 34 W81 7 41
Mailing Address: 393 Smyth Ave Ne, Po2356, Alliance, OH 44601 US
Second Address: 392 Smyth Ave., Alliance, OH 44601
(330) 821-1111; *Fax:* (330) 821-0379
www.1310wdpn.com/
License: Alliance, OH held by D.A. Peterson Inc.
Arbitron Metro Market: Alliance, OH; *Format:* Urban Contemporary *Special Programming:* Relg 4 hrs wkly; *Hrs. of News Programming:* news progmg 21 hrs wkly; *No. News Employees:* 2; *Target Audience:* 35-64.
Doug Lane, Programming Director
Rex Coombs, News Director

***WRMU-FM**
10-17-1970; 91.1 MHz FM; *Hrs Open:* 24/7; 2.8 kw horiz; 190 ft.; N40 54 16 W81 6 45
1972 Clark Avenue, Alliance, OH 44601 US
(330) 823-2414,(330) 823-3777; *Fax:* (330) 829-4913
License: Alliance, Stark County, OH held by Mount Union College.
Wire Services: AP
Arbitron Metro Market: Canton, OH; *Format:* Jazz, Oldies, 76, Smooth Jazz *Special Programming:* Gospel 2 hrs, news/talk 5 hrs wkly; *Hrs. of News Programming:* news progmg 8 hrs wkly; *No. News Employees:* 1
Richard Giese, President
Mark Bergmann, General Manager
William Weisinger, Chief Engineer

WDJQ
04-01-1947; 92.5 MHz FM; *Hrs Open:* 24; 50 kw horiz, 49.7 kw vert; 499 ft.; N40 47 25 W81 6 26
Mailing Address: 393 Smyth Ave, Ne, PO Box 2356, Alliance, OH 44601 US
Second Address: 392 Smyth Ave., Alliance, OH 44601
(330) 450-9250; *Fax:* (330) 821-0379
www.q92radio.com
License: Alliance, Stark County, OH held by D.A. Peterson Inc.
Arbitron Metro Market: Alliance, OH; *Format:* Adult Contemp; *Hrs. of News Programming:* news progmg 4 hrs wkly; *No. News Employees:* 2; *Target Audience:* 25-54.
Don Peterson, General Manager
Mark O'Brian, General Sales Mgr
John Stewart, Programming Director
Clint M, News Director
Steve Hundt, Chief Engineer
Mark O'Brien, General Sales Manager
Dee Zink, Traffic Manager

Anna

***WHJM**
06-01-2006; 88.7 MHz FM; 1 kw vert; 318 ft.; N40 28 1.8 W84 11 24.2
352 West 44th Street, New York, NY 10036 US
(888) 333-6279; *Fax:* (318) 449-9954
www.radiomaria.us
info.usa@radiomaria.org
License: Anna, Shelby County, OH held by Friends of Radio Maria Inc.
Group Owner: Radio Maria Inc.
Arbitron Metro Market: Anna, OH; *Format:* Christian
Father Duane Stenzel, Operations Dir

Archbold

***WBCY**
89.5 MHz FM; 20 kw; 315 ft.; N41 28 59 W84 16 58
Rebroadcasts: Rebroadcasts WBCL (FM)
1115 W. Rudisill Blvd., Fort Wayne, IN 46807 US
(260) 745-0576; *Fax:* (260) 456-2913
www.wbcl.org
License: Archbold, Fulton County, OH held by Taylor University Broadcasting Inc.
Group Owner: Taylor University Broadcasting, Inc.; (acq 6-24-92)
Arbitron Metro Market: Portales, NM; *Format:* Adult Contemp, Christian

WMTR-FM
03-01-1968; 96.1 MHz FM; *Hrs Open:* 24; 3.8 kw; Ant 400 ft; N41 33 29 W84 11 08
303 1/2 N. Defiance St., Archbold, OH 43502
(419) 445-9050; *Fax:* (419) 445-3531
www.961wmtr.com
wmtr@rtecexpress.net
License: Archbold, Fulton County, OH held by Nobco Inc.
Nat'l Network: Westwood One; *Nat'l Reps:* Rgnl Reps
Population Served: 125,000; *Arbitron Metro Market:* Toledo, OH; *Hrs. of News Programming:* news progmg 8 hrs wkly; *No. News Employees:* 1; *Target Audience:* 25-54.
Max Smith Sr., President
Max Smith Jr., General Manager
Mark Knapp, Programming Director
Larry Christy, News Director

Ashland

WNCO
01-01-1949; 1340 kHz AM; *Hrs Open:* 24; 1 kw-U, ND1; N40 50 25 W82 21 26
1400 Radio Lane, Mansfield, OH 44906 US
(419) 529-2211; *Fax:* (419) 529-2516
www.wncoam.com
License: Ashland, OH held by Capstar TX LLC
Group Owner: iHeartMedia; (acq 2-12-01; grpsl).
Nat'l Reps: Rgnl Reps
Arbitron Metro Market: Mansfield, OH; *Format:* Sports *Special Programming:* Farm 3 hrs wkly; *Hrs. of News Programming:* news progmg 20 hrs wkly; *No. News Employees:* 2; *Target Audience:* 35 plus.
Keith Kennedy, Senior Vice President of Programming
Margie Tasseff, General Sales Mgr

WNCO-FM
05-01-1947; 101.3 MHz FM; *Hrs Open:* 24; 50 kw; 499 ft.; N40 50 25 W82 21 26
1400 Radio Lane, Mansfield, OH 44906 US
(419) 529-2211; *Fax:* (419) 529-2516
www.1013wnco.com
License: Ashland, Ashland County, OH held by Capstar TX LLC
Group Owner: iHeartMedia
Arbitron Metro Market: Ashland, OH; *Format:* Country; *Hrs. of News Programming:* news progmg 14 hrs wkly; *No. News Employees:* 3; *Target Audience:* 25 plus.
Keith Kennedy, Senior Vice President of Programming
Margie Tasseff, General Sales Mgr

***WRDL**
08-24-1967; 88.9 MHz FM; *Hrs Open:* 6 AM-1 AM; 3 kw; 171 ft.; N40 51 41 W82 19 11
401 College Avenue, Ashland, OH 44805 US
(419) 289-5678,(419) 289-5311; *Fax:* (419) 289-5329
License: Ashland, Ashland County, OH held by Ashland University.
Format: Rock/AOR *Special Programming:* Christian contemp 7 hrs, jazz 5 hrs, oldies 4 hrs wkly; *Hrs. of News Programming:* News progmg 7 hrs wkly; *Target Audience:* 18-35; general
Dr. G. William Benz, President
Tom Griffiths, General Manager

Ashtabula

WFUN
11-01-1937; 970 kHz AM; *Hrs Open:* 24; 5 kw-D, DA2; 1 kw-N, DA2; N41 48 52 W80 46 45
P. O. Box 738, Ashtabula, OH 44004 US
(440) 993-2126; *Fax:* (440) 992-2658
License: Ashtabula, OH held by Sweet Home Ashtabula LLC.
Group Owner: Sweet Home Ashtabula LLC; (acq 9-17-2007; grpsl)
Nat'l Network: ESPN Radio
Format: Sports; *Target Audience:* General.
Dana Schulte, Operations Dir
Dennis Brockman, Operations Director

WREO-FM
01-01-1949; 97.1 MHz FM; 50 kw; 499 ft.; N41 48 58 W80 46 52
P. O. Box 738, Ashtabula, OH 44004 US
(440) 993-2126; *Fax:* (440) 992-2658
License: Ashtabula, Ashtabula County, OH
Group Owner: Sweet Home Ashtabula LLC
Format: Adult Contemp; *Target Audience:* 25-54; professionals
Dennis O'Brien, Programming Director

WYBL
01-01-2005; 98.3 MHz FM; 5.3 kw; 344 ft.; N41 50 23 W80 44 36
P O Box 738, Ashtabula, OH 44004 US
(440) 993-2126; *Fax:* (440) 992-2658
www.983thebull.com
rogermccoy@983thebull.com
License: Ashtabula, Ashtabula County, OH held by Sweet Home Ashtabula LLC.
Group Owner: Sweet Home Ashtabula LLC; (acq 9-17-2007; grpsl)
Arbitron Metro Market: Ashtabula, OH; *Format:* News
Dana Schulte, General Manager
Kim Frustere, Sales Manager
Roger McCoy, Programming Director
Roger McCoy, Internet Content Manager

WOHA
96.1 MHz FM; 0.5 kw; 41-48-58.0 N 80-46-52.0 W
P.O. Box 158, Fitzgerald, GA 31750 USA
(912) 381-9395
License: Ashtabula, OH held by Madison Media Partners LLC
Group Owner: Madison Media Partners LLC
Format: Variety/Diverse

***WVMU**
91.7 MHz FM; 3.2 kW; 342 ft.; N41 51 13.8 W80 41 20.7
9756 Barr Rd, Cleveland, OH 44141 USA

RADIO - U.S.

(440) 526-1111
www.moodyradio.org/stations/cleveland
License: Ashtabula, OH held by The Moody Bible Institute of Chicago
Group Owner: The Moody Bible Institute of Chicago
Arbitron Metro Market: Ashtabula, OH; *Format:* Christian

Ashville

WODC
07-01-1961; 93.3 MHz FM; *Hrs Open:* 24; 50 kw; 335 ft; N39 19 52 W82 59 49
2323 W. Fifth Ave., Suite 200, Columbus, OH 43204 US
(614) 486-6101; *Fax:* (614) 487-2559
www.933odc.com
License: Ashville, Ross County, OH held by CC Licenses LLC.
Group Owner: iHeartMedia; (acq 4-11-2003).
Nat'l Network: ABC
Population Served: 100,000; *Arbitron Metro Market:* Columbus, OH; *Format:* Oldies; *No. News Employees:* 3; *Target Audience:* 24-54.; *Adv. Rates:* 35; 35; 35; 35
Brian Dytko, President/Market Manager
Michael McCoy, Programming Director

Athens

WATH
10-25-1950; 970 kHz AM; *Hrs Open:* 24; 1 kw-D, ND1; 0.026 kw-N, ND1; N39 20 40 W82 6 21
Mailing Address: 300 N. Columbus Rd., Athens, OH 45701 US
Second Address: 300 Columbus Rd., Athens, OH 45701
(740) 593-6651(740) 593-7982 (News); *Fax:* (740) 594-3488
www.970wath.com
palmerd@wxtq.com
License: Athens, OH held by WATH Inc.
Nat'l Network: CBS Radio; *Regional Network:* Ohio News Network; *Nat'l Reps:* Rgnl Reps *Regional Reps:* Rgnl Reps.; *Wire Services:* AP
Arbitron Metro Market: Athens,OH; *Format:* Adult Contemp, News, 62, Sports, Talk *Special Programming:* Big band 15 hrs wkly; *Hrs. of News Programming:* 25 hrs wkly; *No. News Employees:* 3; *Target Audience:* 40+
David Palmer, President
Bob Stilson, Operations Dir
Thom Williams, General Manager
Thom Williams, Station Manager
Marianne Williams, General Sales Mgr
Bob Beyette, Programming Director
Zahid Mumtaz, Chief Engineer
SallieSauber, Production Director
Robin Barnes, Public Service Director
Caleb Troop, Sports Director
Angie Marks, Traffic Director

WJKW
09-01-1998; 95.9 MHz FM; *Hrs Open:* 24; 5.5 kw; 341 ft.; N39 14 10 W82 4 16
P.O. Box 247, Castalia, OH 44824 US
(740) 592-9879; *Fax:* (740) 592-9952
www.wjkw.net
wjkw@cfbroadcast.net
License: Athens, Athens County, OH held by Christian Faith Broadcast Inc.
Group Owner: Christian Faith Broadcasting Inc.
Format: Adult Contemp, Christian; *Target Audience:* 25-44.
Rusty Yost, General Manager
Kevin Ingle, Station Manager

*WOUB
09-14-1957; 1340 kHz AM; *Hrs Open:* 24; 0.5 kw-D, ND2; 1 kw-N, ND2; N39 19 45 W82 5 29
9 South College Street, Athens, OH 45701 US
(740) 593-4554; *Fax:* (740) 593-0240
www.woub.org
woub@woub.org
License: Athens, OH held by Ohio University.
Nat'l Network: NPR; PRI
Format: News, News/Talk, 86 *Special Programming:* Black 8 hrs wkly; *No. News Employees:* 3
David Wiseman, Operations Dir
Carolyn Lewis, General Manager
Tim Myers, Programming Director
Doug Partusch, Promotions Manager
Tim Sharp, News Director
Ted Ross, Engineering Director
Steve Skidmore, Operations Director
ScottMartin, Operations Manager
Bryan Gibson, Programming Director

*WOUB-FM
12-13-1949; 91.3 MHz FM; *Hrs Open:* 24; 50 kw; 492 ft.; N39 18 52 W82 8 59
9 South College Street, Athens, OH 45701 US
(740) 593-4554; *Fax:* (740) 593-0240
www.woub.org
woub@woub.org
License: Athens, Athens County, OH held by Ohio University
Wire Services: UPI
TV Affiliate: *WOUB-TV affil.; *Format:* Adult Contemp; *No. News Employees:* 3
Rusty Smith, Programming Director
Mark Hellenberg, Assistant Music Director
Jan Sole, Assistant Music Director

WXTQ
09-16-1964; 105.5 MHz FM; *Hrs Open:* 24; 6 kw; 312 ft.; N39 21 18 W82 5 32
Mailing Address: 300 North Columbus Road, Athens, OH 45701 US
Second Address: 300 Columbus Rd., Athens, OH 45701
(740) 593-6651; *Fax:* (740) 594-3488
www.wxtq.com
palmerd@wxtq.com
License: Athens, Athens County, OH held by WATH Inc.
Nat'l Network: Superadio; *Regional Network:* Ohio News Network; *Nat'l Reps:* Rgnl Reps *Regional Reps:* Rgnl Reps; *Wire Services:* AP
Arbitron Metro Market: Athens, OH; *Format:* Adult Contemp *Special Programming:* Ohio University Sports; *Hrs. of News Programming:* news progmg 5 hrs wkly; *No. News Employees:* 2; *Target Audience:* 18-34.
Dave Palmer, President
Robin Barnes, Operations Dir
Thom Williams, Station and General Sales Manager
Thom Williams, Station Manager
Bob Beyette, Programming Director
Bob Beyette, News Director
Zahid Mumtaz, Chief Engineer
Sallie Sauber, Production Director
Marianne Williams, National Sales Manager
Caleb Troop, Sports Director
Angie Marks, Traffic Director
Scott Dailey, Account Executive
Maryjane Burch, Account Executive

Bainbridge

*WKHR
05-06-1977; 91.5 MHz FM; 0.75 kw; 463 ft.; N41 27 49 W81 17 38
17419 Snyder Road, Chagrin Falls, OH 44023 US
(440) 543-9646; *Fax:* (440) 543-9012
www.wkhr.org
License: Bainbridge, Ross County, OH held by Kenston Local School District.
Arbitron Metro Market: Cleveland, OH; *Format:* Big Band; *Target Audience:* 55 plus; well established, mature
Chris Kofron, General Manager

Baltimore

WWCD
07-08-1924; 1240 kHz AM; *Hrs Open:* 24; 1 kw-U; 130 meters; N39 46 14.8 w82 44 25.3
503. South Front Street, Suite 101, Columbus, OH 43701
(614) 221-9923; *Fax:* (614) 227-0021
www.whizamfmtv.com
License: Baltimore, Muskingum County, OH held by Southeastern Ohio Broadcasting System Inc.
Nat'l Reps: Roslin; Rgnl Reps
Population Served: 33,045 *Special Programming:* Farm progmg 2 hrs wkly; *Hrs. of News Programming:* news progmg 30 hrs wkly; *No. News Employees:* 10; *Target Audience:* 25-54; general
N.J. Littick, Chairman
Henry Littick, President
Van Vannelli, Operations Dir
Jay Benson, General Sales Mgr
George Hiotis, News Director
Ken Cash, Chief Engineer
Brian Wagner, Operations Director

Barnesville

WBNV
07-01-1991; 93.5 MHz FM; *Hrs Open:* 24; 2.5 kw; 489 ft.; N39 54 10 W81 12 37
Mailing Address: 63021 Ridgewood Drive, Cambridge, OH 43725 US
Second Address: Box 293, 175 E. Main St., Barnesville, OH 43713-0293
(740) 432-5605; *Fax:* (740) 432-1991
www.yourradioplace.com
webmaster@yourradioplace.com
License: Barnesville, Belmont County, OH held by W. Grant Hafley.
Nat'l Network: USA; *Nat'l Reps:* Rgnl Reps
Arbitron Metro Market: Cambridge, Oh; *Format:* Adult Contemp; *Hrs. of News Programming:* News progmg 15 hrs wkly; *Target Audience:* 25-54.
Grant Hafley, CEO/COO
Grant Hafley, President
Dave Wilson, Operations Dir
Joel Losego, General Manager

Batavia

*WOBO
07-30-1981; 88.7 MHz FM; 15.5 kw horiz, 12.5 kw vert; 466 ft.; N39 3 43 W84 5 50
P. O. Box 338, Owensville, OH 45160 US
(513) 724-3939
www.wobofm.com
df1littman@cs.com
License: Batavia, Clermont County, OH held by Educational Community Radio Inc.
Arbitron Metro Market: Cincinnati, OH *TV Affiliate:* Var/div; *Format:* Ethnic; *No. News Employees:* 35 plus.

Beach City

*WOFN
09-27-2000; 88.7 MHz FM; 3.5 kw horiz, 22.5 kw vert; 344 ft.; N40 35 41 W81 34 39
Mailing Address: P.O. Box 1924, Tulsa, OK 74101 US
Second Address: 4916 Spruce Hill Dr., Suite 400, Canton, OH 44617
(330) 244-9151; *Fax:* 330-244-9153
www.oasisnetwork.org
mail@oasisnetwork.org
License: Beach City, Stark County, OH held by Creative Educational Media Corp. Inc.
Arbitron Metro Market: Canton, OH *TV Affiliate:* Relg; *No. News Employees:* General.

Beavercreek

WZDA
06-18-1972; 103.9 MHz FM; *Hrs Open:* 24; 2.9 kw; 479 ft.; N39 43 19 W84 12 33
101 Pine Street, Dayton, OH 45402 US
(937) 224-1137; *Fax:* (937) 224-3667
www.altdayton.com
License: Beavercreek, Greene County, OH held by Citicasters Licenses Inc.
Group Owner: iHeartMedia; (acq 1999; grpsl).
Arbitron Metro Market: Dayton, OH; *Format:* Alternative; *No. News Employees:* 1; *Target Audience:* 18-34.
Dave Litteral, Senior Vice President of Sales

Bellaire

WOMP
12-02-1947; 1290 kHz AM; 1 kw-D, ND1; 0.033 kw-N, ND1; N40 2 9 W80 46 16
2 Robinson Plaza, Suite 410, Pittsburgh, PA 15205 US
(412) 275-3393; *Fax:* (412) 275-3165
kool105@hotmail.com
License: Bellaire, OH held by FM Radio Licenses, LLC.
Group Owner: Keymarket Communications LLC; (acq 1-15-93; $575,000 with co-located FM;
Nat'l Network: ESPN Radio; *Nat'l Reps:* Rgnl Reps
Arbitron Metro Market: Wheeling, WV *TV Affiliate:* Sports; *Format:* Ethnic *Special Programming:* news progmg 20 hrs wkly; *Hrs. of News Programming:* 2

WRQY-FM
01-01-1947; 96.5 MHz FM; *Hrs Open:* 24; 48 kw; Ant 518 ft; N40 02 09 W80 46 16
56325 High Ridge Rd., Bellaire, OH 43906 US
(740) 676-5661; *Fax:* (740) 676-2742
www.rocky965.com
License: Bellaire, Belmont County, OH held by FM Radio Licenses, LLC.
Group Owner: Keymarket Communications LLC
Wire Services: AP
Arbitron Metro Market: Wheeling, WV; *Format:* Sports, Rock/AOR; *No. News Employees:* 1; *Target Audience:* 18-44; educated adults
Gerald Getz, CEO

Bellefontaine

WBLL
01-01-1951; 1390 kHz AM; *Hrs Open:* 24; 0.5 kw-D, ND1; 0.081 kw-N, ND1; N40 22 5 W83 44 2

1501 Road 235, Bellefontaine, OH 43311 US
(937) 592-1045; *Fax:* (937) 592-3299
www.peakofohio.com
License: Bellefontaine, OH held by V-Teck Communications Inc.
Nat'l Network: ABC; ESPN Radio; *Regional Network:* ABN Radio; *Nat'l Reps:* Rgnl Reps; *Wire Services:* AP
Arbitron Metro Market: Bellefontaine, OH; *Format:* News, News/Talk, 84, Talk *Special Programming:* Relg 6 hrs wkly; *Hrs. of News Programming:* news progmg 126 hrs wkly; *No. News Employees:* 2 *Target Audience:* General.
Lou Vito, President
Chad Wilkinson, Operations Dir
Sheryl Godwin, General Sales Mgr
Ken Keller, Promotions Manager
Bill Tipple, News Director
Bill Bowin, Chief Engineer
Amie Huffman, Advertising Director

WPKO-FM
07-15-1969; 98.3 MHz FM; *Hrs Open:* 24; 1.75 kw; 430 ft.; N40 22 5 W83 44 2
1501 Road 235, Bellefontaine, OH 43311 US
(937) 592-1045; *Fax:* (973) 592-3299
www.wpko.com
cwilkinson@wpko.com
License: Bellefontaine, Logan County, OH
Format: Adult Contemp; *No. News Employees:* 2; *Target Audience:* 12 plus.
Chad Wilkinson, Programming Director
Pam Allen, Promotions Manager
Bill Bowin, Engineering Dir
Louie Vito, Assistant Music Director
Matt Hull, Disc Jockey
Mark Brake, Disc Jockey
Ken Keller, Disc Jockey

Bellevue

WOHF
04-04-1973; 92.1 MHz FM; *Hrs Open:* 24; 6 kw; 328 ft.; N41 14 19 W82 50 16
107 1/2 East Main Street, Bellevue, OH 44811 US
(419) 332-8218; *Fax:* (419) 333-8226
jonkerns@basbroadcasting.com
License: Bellevue, Huron County, OH held by BAS Broadcasting Inc.
Group Owner: BAS Broadcasting Inc.; (acq 10-1-2003; $550,000)
Nat'l Network: ABC; *Regional Network:* ABN Radio *Regional Reps:* Rgnl Reps
Arbitron Metro Market: Fremont, OH; *Format:* Contemporary Hits/Top 40; *Hrs. of News Programming:* news progmg 5 hrs wkly; *No. News Employees:* 1; *Adv. Rates:* 20; 20; 20; 15
Tom Klein, CEO
Jim Lorenzen, President
Jon Kerns, Programming Director

Belpre

***WCVV**
01-01-1986; 89.5 MHz FM; *Hrs Open:* 24; 4.4 kw; 384 ft.; N39 19 27 W81 37 33
P.O. Box 405, Belpre, OH 45714 US
(740) 423-5895; *Fax:* (740) 423-9951
License: Belpre, Washington County, OH held by Belpre Educ. Broadcasting Foundation.
Arbitron Metro Market: Parkersburg-Marietta, WV-OH; *Format:* Christian, News; *Target Audience:* General.
Clay Sloan, General Manager
Ralph Matheny, Chief Engineer

***WLKP**
05-01-1991; 91.9 MHz FM; 5.2 kw; 325 ft.; N39 20 46 W81 29 55
PO Box 568, 2411 1/2 Washington Blv, Belpre, OH 45714 US
(800) 525-5683; *Fax:* (916) 251-1650
www.klove.com
License: Belpre, Washington County, OH held by Educational Media Foundation.
Group Owner: EMF Broadcasting; (acq 3-31-2005; $700,000 with WLKV(FM) Ripley, WV).
Nat'l Network: K-Love
Arbitron Metro Market: Rocklin, CA; *Format:* Christian
Mike Novak, President
David Pierce, Programming Director
Ed Lenane, News Director
Sam Wallington, Engineering Dir
Marya Morgan, News Reporter
Richard Hunt, News Reporter

WNUS
09-12-1981; 107.1 MHz FM; *Hrs Open:* 24; 4.7 kw; 351 ft.; N39 18 36 W81 35 49
6006 Grand Central Ave., Parkersburg, WV 26105 US
(304) 295-6070; *Fax:* (304) 295-4389
www.107nus.com
roadcrew@wnus.com
License: Belpre, Washington County, OH held by CC Licenses LLC.
Group Owner: iHeartMedia; (acq 4-17-2001; grpsl).
Nat'l Reps: Clear Channel
Arbitron Metro Market: Parkersburg, WV; *Format:* Country; *Hrs. of News Programming:* news progmg 2 hrs wkly; *No. News Employees:* 2; *Target Audience:* 18 plus.; *Adv. Rates:* 37.50; 35; 20; 16
Rodney Ortiz, Programming Director

Berea

***WBWC**
03-02-1958; 88.3 MHz FM; *Hrs Open:* 19; 4 kw; 256 ft.; N41 25 5 W81 54 3
275 Eastland Road, Berea, OH 44017 US
(440) 826-2145; *Fax:* (440) 826-3426
www.wbwc.com
License: Berea, Cuyahoga County, OH held by Baldwin-Wallace College.
Nat'l Network: AP Radio
Arbitron Metro Market: BEREA, OH; *Format:* Rock/AOR; *Target Audience:* 12-25; alternative mus listeners
Allen Thompson, Operations Dir
Alex Hooper, General Sales Mgr
Amy Popik, Programming Director
Anthony Hrestak, Promotions Manager
Danielle Schwinn, News Director
Eddy Janson, Sports Director

Bowling Green

***WBGU**
11-01-1951; 88.1 MHz FM; *Hrs Open:* 24; 0.45 kw; 177 ft.; N41 22 33 W83 38 34
West Hall, Bowling Green, OH 43403 US
(419) 372-8657; *Fax:* (419) 372-0202
www.wbgufm.com
smerril@bgsu.edu
License: Bowling Green, Wood County, OH held by Bowling Green State University.
Arbitron Metro Market: Bowling Green,OH *TV Affiliate:* *WBGU-TV affil.; *Format:* Black, Jazz, 94 *Special Programming:* Country 4 hrs, class 3 hrs, folk 4 hrs, Sp 4 hrs wkly; *Hrs. of News Programming:* News progmg 7hrs wkly; *Target Audience:* General.
Ron Tolbert, Operations Dir
Rebecca Priebe, General Manager
Paige Dunham, Programming Director
Neil Carrier, Promotions Manager
Jim Davis, Chief Engineer
Chris Cedar, Music Director
Josh Clay, Production Director

WJYM
12-01-1964; 730 kHz AM; *Hrs Open:* 6 AM-midnight; 1 kw-D, DA2; 0.359 kw-N, DA2; N41 31 57 W83 33 55
8761 Freemont Pike, Perrysburg, OH 43551 US
(225) 768-3202; *Fax:* (225) 768-3729
www.jsm.org
kawikfish@yahoo.com
License: Bowling Green, OH held by Family Worship Center Church Inc.
Group Owner: Family Worship Center Church Inc.; acq 12-15-99).
Nat'l Network: USA
Arbitron Metro Market: Toledo, OH; *Format:* Religious; *Hrs. of News Programming:* News progmg 3 hrs wkly; *Target Audience:* 25-49.
David Whitelaw, COO

WRQN
06-01-1964; 93.5 MHz FM; 7 kw; 397 ft.; N41 27 28 W83 39 33
111 East Kilbourn Ave., Suite 2700, Milwaukee, WI 53202 US
(419) 725-5700; *Fax:* (419) 385-2902
www.935wrqn.com
License: Bowling Green, Wood County, OH held by Cumulus Licensing Corp.
Group Owner: Cumulus Media Inc.; (acq 9-11-97; grpsl)
Arbitron Metro Market: Toledo, OH; *Format:* Oldies *Special Programming:* Pub service one hr wkly; *Target Audience:* 25-54.
Skip Schmidt, General Manager
Ron Finn, Programming Director

***WNOC**
89.7 MHz FM; 5.3 kw; 288 ft.; N41 25 39 W83 36 30 US
(419) 754-1009
www.annunciationradio.com
License: Bowling Green, Wood County, OH held by Ministry to Catholic Charismatic Renewal.
Arbitron Metro Market: Bowling Green, OH; *Format:* Religious
Roy Handy, General Manager

Brunswick

***WKJA**
91.9 MHz FM; 25 kw; 318 ft.; N40 54 56 W81 55 56
P.O. Box 890820, Temecula, CA 99258 US
(855) 500-3759
wkja.krtmradio.org
License: Brunswick, Medina County, OH held by Penfold Communications, Inc.
Group Owner: Penfold Communications, Inc
Arbitron Metro Market: Brunswick, OH; *Format:* Christian, Religious

Bryan

WBNO-FM
06-30-1966; 100.9 MHz FM; *Hrs Open:* 24; 6 kw; 299 ft.; N41 28 44 W84 34 50
P.O. Box 603, Bryan, OH 43506 US
(419) 636-3175; *Fax:* (419) 636-4570
www.wbno-wqct.com/WBNO
wbno@wbno-wqct.com
License: Bryan, Williams County, OH held by Impact Radio LLC
Group Owner: Impact Radio LLC; (acq 8-1-2002; grpsl).
Nat'l Network: ABC *Regional Reps:* Rgnl Reps; *Wire Services:* AP
Arbitron Metro Market: Toledo, OH; *Format:* Contemporary Hits/Top 40, Adult Contemp; *Hrs. of News Programming:* news progmg 27 hrs wkly; *No. News Employees:* 1; *Target Audience:* 25-54; loc oriented; *Adv. Rates:* 10; 9; 9; na
Dennis Rumsey, President
Andy Brigle, Programming Director
Sports Director

***WGBE**
01-01-1996; 90.9 MHz FM; *Hrs Open:* 24; 0.85 kw; 394 ft.; N41 28 47 W84 35 50 *Rebroadcasts:* Rebroadcasts WGTE-FM Toledo 100%
136 N Huron Street, Toledo, OH 43697 US
(419) 380-4600; *Fax:* (419) 380-4710
www.wgte.org
info@wgte.com
License: Bryan, Williams County, OH held by The Public Broadcasting Foundation of Northwest Ohio.
Nat'l Network: NPR; PRI
TV Affiliate: WGTE-TV; *Format:* News *Special Programming:* Jazz 16 hrs wkly; *Hrs. of News Programming:* News progmg 23 hrs wkly; *Target Audience:* General.
George Jones, Chairman
Marlon Kiser, CEO
Chris Pfeiffer, Operations Dir
Ross Pfeiffer, General Sales Mgr

WQCT
12-01-1962; 1520 kHz AM; *Hrs Open:* 24
P.O. Box 603, Bryan, OH 43506 US
(419) 636-3175; *Fax:* 419) 636-4570
License: Bryan, OH held by Impact Radio LLC
Group Owner: Impact Radio LLC; .
Regional Reps: Rgnl Reps
Arbitron Metro Market: Toledo, OH; *Format:* Oldies; *Hrs. of News Programming:* news progmg 3 hrs wkly; *No. News Employees:* 1; *Target Audience:* 35-65; general
Dennis Rumsey, President

Buchtel

WAIS
12-03-1984; 770 kHz AM; *Hrs Open:* Sunrise-sunset; 1 kw-D, NDD; N39 25 56 W82 12 2
15751 Us Route 33, Nelsonville, OH 45764 US
(740) 753-4094; *Fax:* (740) 753-4965
License: Buchtel, OH held by Nelsonville TV Cable Inc.
Nat'l Network: ABC
Arbitron Metro Market: Buchtel, OH; *Format:* News, News/Talk, 86 *Special Programming:* Farm 5 hrs, gospel 3 hrs wkly; *Hrs. of News Programming:* news progmg 21 hrs wkly; *No. News Employees:* 3; *Target Audience:* 35 plus.
Eugene Edwards, President
Sharon Elliott, Station Manager

Bucyrus

WBCO
12-22-1962; 1540 kHz AM
403 East Rensselaer St., P.O. Box 1140, Bucyrus, OH 44820 US
(530) 257-6100; *Fax:* (530) 257-6107
dennis@jackfm963.com
License: Bucyrus, OH held by Franklin Communications Inc.
Group Owner: Saga Communications Inc.; (acq 12-1-2003; $2.2 million with co-located FM).
Nat'l Network: CBS; *Nat'l Reps:* Rgnl Reps
Arbitron Metro Market: Yakima WA; *Format:* Adult Contemp
Gary Katz, President
Dennis Carlson, General Manager

WQEL
09-05-1964; 92.7 MHz FM; *Hrs Open:* 24; 3 kw; 305 ft.; N40 45 49 W82 56 0
403 East Rensselaer St, Post Office Box 1140, Bucyrus, OH 44820 US
(419) 562-2222; *Fax:* (419) 562-0520
License: Bucyrus, Crawford County, OH
Group Owner: Saga Communications Inc.
Nat'l Network: CBS; *Nat'l Reps:* Rgnl Reps
Format: Classic Rock, Sports; *Hrs. of News Programming:* news progmg 10 hrs wkly; *No. News Employees:* 2; *Target Audience:* 25-54.
Will Beard, Programming Director
Jim Hahn, Disc Jockey

Byesville

WILE-FM
10-29-1994; 97.7 MHz FM; *Hrs Open:* 24; 1.8 kw; 413 ft.; N40 2 24 W81 38 50
Mailing Address: 114 North Sixth Street, Coshocton, OH 43812 US
Second Address: 4988 Skyline Dr., Cambridge, OH 43725
(740) 432-5605; *Fax:* (740) 432-1991
www.yourradioplace.com
License: Byesville, Guernsey County, OH held by AVC Communications Inc.
Group Owner: AVC Communications Inc.; acq 7-13-00).
Format: Adult Contemp
W. Grant Hafley, CEO
Dave Wilson, Operations Dir
Joel Losego, General Manager

Cadiz

WCDK
08-28-1985; 106.3 MHz FM; *Hrs Open:* 24; 2.7 kw; 495 ft.; N40 15 14 W80 50 35
2307 Pennsylvania Ave., Weirton, WV 26062 US
(304) 723-1444; *Fax:* (304) 723-1688
www.1063theriver.com
deedee@1063theriver.com
License: Cadiz, Harrison County, OH held by Priority Communications Ohio, LLC.
Group Owner: Priority Communications Ohio, LLC; (acq 12-98; $475,000 with WEIR(AM) Weirton, WV)
Nat'l Network: Jones Radio Networks; *Nat'l Reps:* Dome
Arbitron Metro Market: Weirton, WV; *Format:* Contemporary Hits/Top 40 *Special Programming:* OSU football, Cleveland Browns football, high school football; *Hrs. of News Programming:* news progmg 5 hrs wkly *No. NewsEmployees:* 1; *Target Audience:* 25-54; general
Dee Dee Dupre, General Manager
Cindy Taylor, Programming Director

Caldwell

WWKC
07-01-1989; 104.9 MHz FM; *Hrs Open:* 24; 3 kw; 328 ft.; N39 48 47 W81 36 38
Mailing Address: 63021 Ridgewood Drive, Cambridge, OH 43725 US
Second Address: Box 19, Caldwell, OH 43724
(740) 432-5605; *Fax:* (740) 432-1991
www.yourradioplace.com
info@yourradioplace.com
License: Caldwell, Noble County, OH held by W. Grant Hafley.
Nat'l Reps: Rgnl Reps
Arbitron Metro Market: Caldwell, OH; *Format:* Country; *Target Audience:* 25-54.
Grant Hafley, President & CEO
David Wilson, Operations Dir
Joel Losego, General Manager
Dave Wilson, Operations Manager

Caledonia

WYNT
10-01-1986; 95.9 MHz FM; *Hrs Open:* 19; 4.6 kw; 374 ft.; N40 40 55 W83 0 27
1330 N. Main St., Marion, OH 43302 US
(740) 383-1131; *Fax:* (740) 387-3697
www.majic959.com
License: Caledonia, Wyandot County, OH held by CC Licenses LLC.
Group Owner: iHeartMedia; (acq 4-2-2002; $825,000).
Arbitron Metro Market: Caledonia, OH; *Format:* Adult Contemp
Special Programming: Farm 3 hrs wkly; *Target Audience:* 27 plus; general
Matt Bell, Market President
Jordan Treadway, Vice President of Sales

Cambridge

WCMJ
10-01-1964; 96.7 MHz FM; 2.3 kw; 367 ft.; N40 2 24 W81 38 50
Mailing Address: P.O. Box 338, Cambridge, OH 43725 US
Second Address: 4988 Skyline Dr., Cambridge, OH 43725
(740) 432-5605; *Fax:* (740) 432-1991
www.yourradioplace.com
webmaster@yourradioplace.com
License: Cambridge, Guernsey County, OH held by AVC Communications Inc.
Group Owner: AVC Communications Inc.; (acq 5-5-83)
Regional Reps: Rgnl Reps
Arbitron Metro Market: Cambridge, Oh; *Format:* Adult Contemp; *Hrs. of News Programming:* 2; *Target Audience:* 18-49.
Grant Hafley, CEO
Dave Wilson, Operations Dir
Joel Losego, General Manager

WILE
04-09-1948; 1270 kHz AM; 1 kw-D, ND2; 0.035 kw-N, ND2; N40 2 24 W81 38 50
4988 Skyline Drive, PO Box 338, Cambridge, OH 43725 US
(419) 946-0016
www.yourradioplace.com
License: Cambridge, OH held by St. Gabriel Radio Inc.
Nat'l Network: ESPN Radio
Format: Sports; *Target Audience:* 25-54.
Christopher Gabrelcik, President

*WOUC-FM
05-11-1987; 89.1 MHz FM; *Hrs Open:* 24; 5 kw; 499 ft.; N40 5 32 W81 17 19 *Rebroadcasts:* Rebroadcasts WOUB-FM Athens 100%
9 South College Street, Athens, OH 45701 US
(740) 593-4554; *Fax:* (740) 593-0240
www.woub.org
woub@woub.org
License: Cambridge, Guernsey County, OH held by Ohio University.
Nat'l Network: PRI; NPR
TV Affiliate: *WOUC-TV affil; *Format:* News, News/Talk, 86; *No. News Employees:* 3
David Wiseman, Operations Dir
Carolyn Lewis, General Manager
Steve Skidmore, Operations Director
Scott Martin, Operations Manager

*WYFY
88.1 MHz FM; 1.5 kw; 144 ft.; N40 1 37 W81 33 9
Rebroadcasts: Rebroadcasts WYFQ(AM) Charlotte 100%
P.O. Box 7300, Charlotte, NC 28241 US
(800) 888-7077
www.bnbradio.org
bbn@bbnmedia.org
License: Cambridge, Guernsey County, OH held by Bible Broadcasting Network Inc.
Group Owner: Bible Broadcasting Network
Format: Christian, Religious, 86
Lowell Davey, President
Jason Padgett, Operations Manager

Campbell

WGFT
10-16-1955; 1330 kHz AM
401 North Blair Ave., Youngstown, OH 44505 US
(330) 744-5115; *Fax:* (330) 744-4020
Savannah@ytownradio.com
License: Campbell, OH held by Bernard of Ohio LLC.
Group Owner: Bernard Radio LLC; (acq 1-22-2007; grpsl)
Nat'l Network: CNN Radio
Arbitron Metro Market: Campbell, OH; *Format:* Talk; *Target Audience:* General; family
Skip Bednarczyk, General Manager
Tiffany Allen, Promotions Manager

Canton

WHBC
03-09-1925; 1480 kHz AM; 15 kw-D, DA2; 5 kw-N, DA2; N40 53 51 W81 19 10; N40 43 15 W81 26 28
P.O. Box 9917, Canton, OH 44711 US
(330) 456-7166; *Fax:* (330) 456-7199
www.whbc.com
pcook@whbc.com
License: Canton, OH held by NM Licensing LLC.
Group Owner: NextMedia Group Inc.; (acq 9-30-2000; with WHBC-FM Canton)
Nat'l Reps: Christal
Arbitron Metro Market: Canton, OH; *Format:* Oldies *Special Programming:* Farm one hr wkly; *Target Audience:* 25 plus.
Richard Bossler, General Manager

WHBC-FM
02-02-1948; 94.1 MHz FM; 45 kw; 515 ft.; N40 53 53 W81 19 7
P.O. Box 9917, Canton, OH 44711 US
(330) 456-7166; *Fax:* (330) 456-7199
www.mix941.com
pcook@whbc.com
License: Canton, Stark County, OH held by NM Licensing LLC.
Group Owner: NextMedia Group Inc.; (acq 9-30-2000; with WHBC(AM) Canton)
Arbitron Metro Market: Canton, OH; *Format:* Adult Contemp; *Target Audience:* 25-54.
Terry Simmons, Programming Director

WINW
04-14-1966; 1520 kHz AM; *Hrs Open:* Sunrise-sunset; 1 kw-D, DAD; N40 50 41 W81 21 2
P.O. Box 616, Cuyahoga Falls, OH 44222 US
(330) 453-1520; *Fax:* (330) 454-3030
License: Canton, OH held by Pinebrook Corp.
Nat'l Reps: Rgnl Reps
Arbitron Metro Market: Canton, OH; *Format:* Gospel; *Target Audience:* 35-54; professionals
Patrick Barb, President
Curtis Perry, General Manager

WILB
08-11-1946; 1060 kHz AM
4601 Hills and Dale Rdnw, Canton, OH 44718 US
(330) 966-2903; *Fax:* (330) 966-3177
www.livingbreadradio.com
License: Canton, OH held by Living Bread Radio Inc.
Arbitron Metro Market: Canton, OH; *Format:* Talk, Christian
Barbara Gaskell, President
Dan Clark, Operations Dir
Kate Sell, Station Manager

WRQK-FM
03-01-1961; 106.9 MHz FM; *Hrs Open:* 24; 27.5 kw; 338 ft.; N40 49 22 W81 25 40
7755 Freedom Ave. N.W., North Canton, OH 44720 US
(330) 492-5630; *Fax:* (330) 492-5633
www.wrqk.com
wrqk@wrqk.com
License: Canton, Stark County, OH held by Capstar TX LLC
Group Owner: iHeartMedia; (acq 3-15-00; grpsl).
Arbitron Metro Market: Canton, OH; *Format:* Rock/AOR; *Hrs. of News Programming:* News progmg one hr wkly; *Target Audience:* 18-49; emphasis on men
Mark Boarman, Market President
Keith Kennedy, Senior Vice President of Programming

Carrollton

*WJDD
90.9 MHz FM; 0.27 kw horiz, 0 kw vert; 318 ft.; N40 34 15 W81 10 48
US
(330) 875-7181
License: Carrollton, Carroll County, OH held by Denny and Marge Hazen Ministries Inc.
Arbitron Metro Market: Carrollton, OH
Denny Hazen, President

Castalia

WGGN
01-01-1975; 97.7 MHz FM; *Hrs Open:* 24; 0.64 kw; 725 ft.; N41 23 48 W82 47 31
Mailing Address: 3809 Maple Avenue, Castalia, OH 44824 US
Second Address: P. O. Box 247, Castalia, OH 44824

(419) 684-5311; *Fax:* (419) 684-5378
www.fm977.net
fm977@cfbroadcast.net
License: Castalia, Erie County, OH held by Christian Faith Broadcasting Inc.
Group Owner: Christian Faith Broadcasting Inc.
Nat'l Network: USA
Format: Adult Contemp, Christian; *Target Audience:* 25-49; general
Shelby Gillam, President
Rusty Yost, General Manager
Jeff Ferback, General Sales Mgr
Dave Yost, Programming Director

Cedarville

*WKDC-FM
12-01-1962; 90.3 MHz FM; *Hrs Open:* 24; 30 kw; 354 ft; N39 45 46 W83 53 05
Box 601, Cedarville, OH 45314-0601
(937) 766-7815; *Fax:* (937) 766-7927
www.thepath.fm
info@thepath.fm
License: Cedarville, Greene County, OH held by The Cedarville University.
Nat'l Network: AP Radio; CNN Radio; Moody
Population Served: 400,000 *Special Programming:* Black 2 hrs wkly; *Hrs. of News Programming:* news progmg 16 hrs wkly; *No. News Employees:* 1; *Target Audience:* 35-54.
William Brown, President
Martin Clark, Operations Dir
Paul Gathany, General Manager
Keith Hamer, Operations Manager

Celina

WCSM
09-11-1963; 1350 kHz AM; *Hrs Open:* 24; 0.5 kw-D, DA2; 0.011 kw-N, DA2; N40 32 17 W84 35 20
P. O. Box 492, Celina, OH 45822 US
(419) 586-5133; *Fax:* (419) 586-3814
www.wcsmradio.com
wcsm@bright.net
License: Celina, OH held by Hayco Broadcasting Inc.
Regional Network: Agrinet
Arbitron Metro Market: Lima, OH; *Hrs. of News Programming:* news progmg 20 hrs wkly; *No. News Employees:* 1; *Target Audience:* 18-49.; *Adv. Rates:* 12.75; 12.75; 12.75; 12.75
John Coe, President
Sue Heiser, General Sales Mgr
Jim Hyatt, Programming Director
Kevin Sandler, News Director

WCSM-FM
01-01-1968; 96.7 MHz FM; *Hrs Open:* 24; 2.2 kw; 384 ft.; N40 33 10 W84 31 2
P. O. Box 492, Celina, OH 45822 US
(419) 586-5133; *Fax:* (419) 586-3814
www.wcsmradio.com
wcsm@bright.net
License: Celina, Mercer County, OH
Nat'l Network: ABC; Jones Radio Networks; *Regional Network:* Agrinet
Arbitron Metro Market: Lima, OH; *Format:* Sports; *Adv. Rates:* Same as AM
Jeff Hall, Station Manager

WKKI
12-18-1960; 94.3 MHz FM; *Hrs Open:* 24; 2.2 kw; 448 ft; N40 33 08 W84 30 46
126 W. Fayette St., Celina, OH 45822
(419) 586-7715; *Fax:* (419) 586-1074
License: Celina, Mercer County, OH held by The Sonshine Communications Corp.
Rgnl Reps
Population Served: 250,000; *Arbitron Metro Market:* Lima, OH
Special Programming: Contemp Christian 2 hrs wkly; *Target Audience:* 25-54.
Paul Schmitmeyer, President
Dan Dietz, Operations Dir

Centerville

*WCWT-FM
09-20-1971; 107.3 MHz FM; 0.023 kw; 190 ft.; N39 37 38 W84 8 54
111 Virginia Avenue, Centerville, OH 45459 US
(937) 439-3558(937) 439-3557; *Fax:* (937) 439-3574
wcwt@centerville.k12.oh.us
License: Centerville, Montgomery County, OH held by Centerville City Board of Education.
Arbitron Metro Market: Centerville, Oh; *Format:* Classic Rock; *Target Audience:* General.
Bob Romond, General Manager

Chillicothe

WBEX
09-01-1947; 1490 kHz AM; *Hrs Open:* 24; 1 kw-U, ND1; N39 19 52 W82 59 49
Mailing Address: 50 East River Center Blvd., Covington, KY 41011 US
Second Address: 45 W. Main St., Chillicothe, OH 45601
(740) 773-3000; *Fax:* (740) 774-4494
www.wbex.com
newsroom@wkkj.com
License: Chillicothe, OH held by Citicasters Licenses Inc.
Group Owner: iHeartMedia; (acq 1999; grpsl).
Nat'l Network: CBS; Westwood One; *Nat'l Reps:* Katz Radio
Arbitron Metro Market: Chillicothe, OH; *Format:* News, News/Talk, 86; *Hrs. of News Programming:* news progmg 10 hrs wkly; *No. News Employees:* 3; *Target Audience:* 30-50.
Dan Latham, Market President
Jim Davis, Regional Senior Vice President of Programming
Joshua Koch, Sales Manager
Dan Ramey, Programming Director
Mike Smith, News Director/Sports Director

WCHI
10-01-1951; 1350 kHz AM; *Hrs Open:* 24
45 W. Main Street, PO Box 94, Chillicothe, OH 45601 US
(740) 773-3000
www.easy1350.com
License: Chillicothe, OH held by CC Licenses LLC.
Group Owner: iHeartMedia; (acq 10-19-99; $4 million with co-located FM).
Nat'l Network: ABC; *Nat'l Reps:* Katz Radio
Arbitron Metro Market: Chillicothe, OH; *Format:* Oldies; *No. News Employees:* 2; *Target Audience:* 25-65.; *Adv. Rates:* 10; 10; 10; 10
Dan Latham, Market President
Joshua Koch, Sales Manager
Dan Ramey, Programming Director

WKKJ
12-22-1978; 94.3 MHz FM; *Hrs Open:* 24; 19 kw; 353 ft.; N39 19 52 W82 59 49
45 W. Main St., Chillicothe, OH 45601 US
(740) 773-3000; *Fax:* (740) 774-4494
www.wkkj.com
newsroom@wkkj.com
License: Chillicothe, Ross County, OH held by CC Licenses LLC
Group Owner: iHeartMedia
Nat'l Network: ABC
Arbitron Metro Market: Chillicothe, OH; *Format:* Country; *Hrs. of News Programming:* news progmg 14 hrs wkly; *No. News Employees:* 3; *Adv. Rates:* 60; 50; 50; 50
Jim Davis, Regional Senior Vice President of Programming
Dan Latham, Market President
Joshua Koch, Sales Manager
Christina Wolford, Programming Director
Mike Smith, News Director/Sports Director

*WOHC
05-01-1992; 90.1 MHz FM; 2 kw vert; 394 ft.; N39 20 45 W83 11 15 *Rebroadcasts:* Rebroadcasts WCDR(FM) Cedarville 100%
PO Box 2118, Omaha, NE 68103-2118 US
(888) 937-2471
www.air1.com
License: Chillicothe, Ross County, OH held by Educational Media Foundation
Nat'l Network: AP Radio; CNN Radio; Moody
TV Affiliate: Relg; *Format:* Black *Special Programming:* news progmg 16 hrs wkly; *Hrs. of News Programming:* 1; *No. News Employees:* 35-54; information-orient
Darrell Chambliss, Chairman
Mike Novak, President/CEO
David Pierce, Chief Creative Officer
Alan Mason, COO
Eric Moser, CFO
D. Kvin Blair, Secretary/General Counsel

*WOUH-FM
10-01-1992; 91.9 MHz FM; *Hrs Open:* 24; 0.75 kw; 650 ft.; N39 19 46 W82 48 8 *Rebroadcasts:* Rebroadcasts WOUB-FM Athens 100%
35 S. College Street, Athens, OH 45701 US
(740) 593-1771; *Fax:* (800) 546-2044
www.woub.org
woub@woub.org
License: Chillicothe, Ross County, OH held by Ohio University.
Format: News, News/Talk, 86; *No. News Employees:* 3
Jeannie Jeffers, Development Director
Thomas Hodson, Director/General Manager
Mark Brewer, Chief Content Officer
Joan Butcher, Programming Director
Kathy Malesick, Director of Corporate Support
Rusty Smith, Chief Engineer
MikeRodriguez, Director of Production Serices
Tim Myers, Director of Digital Delivery
Allison Hunter, News Director
Ted Ross, Engineering Director
Steve Skidmore, CTO
Sue Cyram, Director oF Business Operations

*WZCP
01-15-1988; 89.3 MHz FM; *Hrs Open:* 24; 2.5 kw vert; 351 ft.; N39 20 45 W83 11 15
881 East Johnstown Road, Gahanna, OH 43230 US
614-289-5704
www.893theriver.com
theriver@893theriver.com
License: Chillicothe, Ross County, OH held by One Connection Media Group
Group Owner: Christian Voice of Central Ohio Inc.; (acq 5-15-2007; grpsl)
Arbitron Metro Market: Chillicothe, OH; *Format:* Christian
Dan Baughman, General Manager
Olivia Lomeli, Director of Socal Media
Mike Dorsey, Director of Community Relations
Matt Levin, Director of Community Relations
Bill Montogomery, Chief Sales Officer
Jon Dennings, TrafficCoordinator
Eric Faulds, Music Director
Andy Meyer, Director of Brand Development
Todd Stach, Chief Creative Officer
Josh Hooper, Director of Brand Audio

WQLX
106.5 MHz FM; 4.8 kw; N39 19 52 W82 59 49
45 W. Main St., Chillicothe, OH 45601 US
(740) 773-3000; *Fax:* (740) 774-4494
www.mix1065.com
License: Chillicothe, Ross County, OH held by CC Licenses LLC
Group Owner: iHeartMedia
Arbitron Metro Market: Chillicothe, OH; *Format:* Adult Contemp
Jim Davis, Regional Senior Vice President of Programming
Joshua Koch, Sales Manager
Christina Wolford, Programming Director
Mike Smith, News Director/Sports Director

Cincinnati

WAKW
11-21-1961; 93.3 MHz FM; *Hrs Open:* 24; 50 kw horiz, 49 kw vert; 492 ft.; N39 12 19 W84 33 23
Mailing Address: 6275 Collegevue Place, Cincinnati, OH 45224 US
Second Address: PO Box 24126, Cincinnati, OH 45224
(513) 542-9259; *Fax:* (513) 542-9333
www.mystar933.com
License: Cincinnati, Hamilton County, OH held by Pillar of Fire Inc.
Group Owner: Pillar of Fire Inc.
Nat'l Network: Moody
Arbitron Metro Market: Cincinnati, OH; *Format:* Christian; *No. News Employees:* 1; *Target Audience:* General; families; *Adv. Rates:* 90; 75; 75; 56
Gerald Croucher, General Manager
Jeff, Programming Director
Julie, Promotions Director

WSAI
06-07-1923; 1360 kHz AM; *Hrs Open:* 24; 5 kw-D, DAN; 5 kw-N, DAN; N39 14 51 W84 31 52
5044 Montgomery Road, Suite 650, Cincinnati, OH 45236 US
(513) 686-8300
www.foxsports1360.com
scottreinhart@clearchannel.com
License: Cincinnati, OH held by Citicasters Licenses Inc.
Group Owner: iHeartMedia; (acq 4-29-99; grpsl)
Nat'l Network: ESPN Radio
Arbitron Metro Market: Cincinnati, OH; *Format:* Sports
Chuck Fredrick, President/Market Manager
Joe Fredrick, Sales Manager/Director of Sports Marketing
Scott Reinhart, Programming Director
Matt Overla, Promotions Director
Dave Abbott, Chief Engineer
Dan Gialluca, Director ofMarketing
Alethea Marshall, Community Engagement Director

WEBN
08-27-1967; 102.7 MHz FM; 16 kw; 866 ft.; N39 6 59 W84 30 7
8044 Montgomery Road, Suite 650, Cincinnati, OH 45236 US

(513) 686-8300
www.webn.com
License: Cincinnati, Hamilton County, OH held by Citicasters Licenses Inc.
Group Owner: iHeartMedia; (Acq 2-86; $8 million;
Arbitron Metro Market: Cincinnati, OH; *Format:* Rock/AOR
Chuck Fredrick, President/Market Manager
DJ Hodge, Local Sales Manager
Bo Matthews, Programming Director
Justin Tabias, Promotions Director
Dave Abbott, Chief Engineer
Alethea Marshall, Community Engagement Director
James Brooks,Digital Program Director

***WGUC**
09-21-1960; 90.9 MHz FM; *Hrs Open:* 24; 18.5 kw; 686 ft.; N39 7 29.9 W84 29 56.2
1223 Central Parkway, Cincinnati, OH 45214 US
(513) 241-8282
www.wguc.org
wguc@wguc.org
License: Cincinnati, Hamilton County, OH held by Cincinnati Public Radio, Inc.
Nat'l Network: PRI
Arbitron Metro Market: Cincinnati, OH; *Format:* Talk; *Target Audience:* 35 plus; well-educated
Richard Eiswerth, General Manager
Christine Trenholm, CFO
Jessica Lorey, Music Director
Bruce Ellis, Production Director
Sherri Mancini, VP, Development
Pete Pickering, General Sales Mgr
Robin Gehl, Programming Director
ChrisPhelps, VP, Content
Maryane Zekzrik, News Director
Don Danko, VP, Engineering
Barry Weinstein, CFO
David Schackmann, Corporate Sales Manager
Gordon Bayliss, Sales VP

WKRC
01-01-1922; 550 kHz AM; 5 kw-D, DA2; 1 kw-N, DA2; N39 0 29 W84 26 39
8044 Montgomery Road, Suite 650, Cincinnati, OH 45236 US
(513) 686-8300
www.55krc.com
info@55krc.com
License: Cincinnati, OH held by Citicasters Licenses Inc.
Group Owner: iHeartMedia; (acq 5-4-99; grpsl).
Nat'l Network: Westwood One; CBS
Arbitron Metro Market: Cincinnati, OH; *Format:* News, News/Talk, 86; *Target Audience:* 35-64; adult, affluent, conservative
Chuck Fredrick, President/Market Manager
Bo Matthews, Senior Vice President of Programming
Bill Mountel, Sales Manager
Scott Reinhart, Programming Director
Dave Abbott, Chief Engineer
Alethea Marshall, Community EngagementDirector

WKRQ
01-01-1947; 101.9 MHz FM; 16 kw; 866 ft.; N39 6 59 W84 30 7
2060 Reading Rd., Cincinnati, OH 45202 US
(513) 699-5102; *Fax:* (513) 699-5000
www.wkrq.com
License: Cincinnati, Hamilton County, OH held by Cincinnati FCC License Sub LLC
Group Owner: Hubbard Broadcasting Inc.
Nat'l Reps: Katz Radio
Arbitron Metro Market: Cincinnati, OH; *Format:* Contemporary Hits/Top 40
Jim Bryant, Vice President and Market Manager
Lisa Thal, General Sales Mgr

WLW
03-22-1922; 700 kHz AM; 50 kw-U, ND1; N39 21 11 W84 19 30
8044 Montgomery Road, Suite 650, Cincinnati, OH 45236 US
(513) 749-7000
www.700wlw.com
License: Cincinnati, OH held by Citicasters Licenses Inc.
Group Owner: iHeartMedia; (acq 4-99; grpsl).
Arbitron Metro Market: Cincinnati, OH; *Format:* News, News/Talk, 86
Chuck Fredrick, President/Market Manager
Joe Fredrick, Sales Manager/Director of Sports Marketing
Scott Reinhart, Programming Director
Dave Abbott, Chief Engineer
James Brooks, Digital Program Director
Alethea Marshall, CommunityEngagement Director

WOFX-FM
08-19-1964; 92.5 MHz FM; 16 kw; 866 ft.; N39 6 59 W84 30 7
4805 Montgomery Road, Suite 300, Cincinnati, OH 45212 US
(513) 241-9898; *Fax:* (513) 241-6689
www.foxcincinnati.com
License: Cincinnati, Hamilton County, OH held by Cumulus Licensing LLC.
Group Owner: Cumulus Media Inc.; (acq 4-10-2009; grpsl)
Arbitron Metro Market: Cincinnati, OH *TV Affiliate:* Classic rock;
No. News Employees: 25-54.
John Laing, Sales Manager
Chris Geisen, Programming Director
Vincent Moses, Promotions Director

WRRM
10-01-1959; 98.5 MHz FM; 17.5 kw; 807 ft.; N39 7 19 W84 32 52
4805 Montgomery Rd., Suite 300, Cincinnati, OH 45212 US
(513) 241-9898; *Fax:* (513) 241-6689
www.warm98.com
tim.toelke@cumulus.com
License: Cincinnati, OH held by Radio License Holding SRC, LLC
Group Owner: Cumulus Media Inc.; (acq 1-72)
Arbitron Metro Market: Cincinnati, OH; *Format:* Adult Contemp
Tim Toelke, Sales Manager
Greg Dunkin, Programming Director
Vincent Moses, Promotions Director
Tina Klemann, HR/Market Controller

WCKY
09-16-1929; 1530 kHz AM; 50 kw-D, DAN; 50 kw-N, DAN; N39 4 7 W84 36 20; N39 3 55 W84 36 27
8044 Montgomery Road, Suite 650, Cincinnati, OH 45236 US
(513) 686-8300; *Fax:* (513) 333-4269
www.espn1530.com
License: Cincinnati, OH held by Citicasters Licenses Inc.
Group Owner: iHeartMedia
Nat'l Network: ESPN Radio; Fox Sports; Westwood One
Arbitron Metro Market: Cincinnati, OH; *Format:* Sports; *Target Audience:* 35 plus; special focus on ages 35-64
Chuck Fredrick, President/Market Manager
Bo Matthews, Senior Vice President of Programming
Joe Fredrick, Sales Manager
Scott Reinhart, Programming Director
Dave Abbott, Chief Engineer
Alethea Marshall, Community EngagementDirector

WGRI
01-01-1947; 1050 kHz AM; *Hrs Open:* 24; 1 kw-D, ND1; 0.279 kw-N, ND1; N39 4 50 W84 31 18
635 W. 7th St., Suite 400, Cincinnati, OH 45203 US
(513) 533-2500; *Fax:* (513) 579-2528
inspiration1050.com
License: Cincinnati, OH held by Christian Broadcasting System Ltd.
Group Owner: Christian Broadcasting System Ltd.; (acq 2-10-2006; swap of WCVX(AM) and WDJO(AM) Florence, KY plus $6.75 million cash for WLQV(AM) Detroit, MI)
Nat'l Network: Salem Radio Network
Arbitron Metro Market: Cincinnati, OH; *Format:* Talk, Religious
Special Programming: Gospel 15 hrs, Sp 3 hrs wkly; *Hrs. of News Programming:* News progmg 10 hrs wkly; *Target Audience:* 24-54; family oriented youngadults

WDBZ
01-01-1927; 1230 kHz AM; *Hrs Open:* 24
1 Centennial Plaza, 705 Central Ave Suite 200, Cincinnati, OH 45202 US
(513) 679-6000; *Fax:* (513) 679-6014
www.thebuzzcincy.com
jtolliver@radio-one.com
License: Cincinnati, OH held by Blue Chip Broadcasting Licenses Ltd.
Group Owner: Radio One Inc.; (acq 7-20-2007; $2.69 million)
Nat'l Reps: Christal
Arbitron Metro Market: Cincinnati, OH; *Format:* Gospel, Talk; *No. News Employees:* 1; *Target Audience:* 25-54.
Mitch Galvin, Station Manager
Jeri Tolliver, Programming Director

WUBE-FM
07-20-1949; 105.1 MHz FM; 14.5 kw; 915 ft.; N39 7 30 W84 29 56
2060 Reading Rd., Cincinnati, OH 45202 US
(513) 699-5105; *Fax:* (513-) 699-5000
www.b105.com
License: Cincinnati, Hamilton County, OH held by Cincinnati FCC License Sub LLC
Group Owner: Hubbard Broadcasting Inc.; (acq 1-19-2011).
Arbitron Metro Market: Cincinnati, OH; *Format:* Country
Mike Fredrick, Vice President and Market Manager
Christine Mello, General Sales Mgr
Kehra Woolfolk, Account Executive

WNNF
01-01-1955; 94.1 MHz FM; *Hrs Open:* 24; 16 kw; 866 ft.; N39 6 59 W84 30 7
4805 Montgomery Road, Suite 300, Cincinatti, OH 45212 US
(513) 241-9898; *Fax:* (513) 241-6689
www.radio941.com
License: Cincinnati, Hamilton County, OH held by Cumulus Licensing LLC.
Group Owner: Cumulus Media Inc.; (acq 4-10-2009; grpsl)
Arbitron Metro Market: Cincinnati, OH; *Format:* Adult Contemp;
No. News Employees: 1; *Target Audience:* 25-54.
John Laing, Sales Manager
Mike Scott, Programming Director

***WVXU**
10-01-1971; 91.7 MHz FM; 26 kw; 682 ft.; N39 7 31 W84 29 57
1223 Central Parkway, Cincinnati, OH 45214 US
(513) 352-9170; *Fax:* (513) 241-8456
www.wvxu.org
wvxu@wvxu.org
License: Cincinnati, Hamilton County, OH held by Cincinnati Public Radio, Inc.
Nat'l Network: PRI; NPR
Arbitron Metro Market: Cincinnati, OH; *Format:* News; *Hrs. of News Programming:* 107 hrs wkly; *No. News Employees:* 6; *Target Audience:* 35 yrs plus; well educated
Mr.William Fee, Chairman
Barry Weinstein, CFO
Richard Eiswerth, General Manager
Sherri Mancini, General Sales Mgr
Robin Gehl, Programming Director
Chris Phelps, Promotions Manager
Maryanne Zeleznik, News Director
Don Danko,Engineering Dir
David Schackmann, Corporate Sales Manager

Circleville

WHOK-FM
10-01-1965; 107.1 MHz FM; 3 kw; 328 ft.; N39 39 52 W82 51 4
600 New Hampshire Ave., NW, Suite 1200, Washington, DC 20037 US
(956) 686-6382; *Fax:* (956) 686-2999
License: Circleville, Pickaway County, OH held by Wilks License Co.-Columbus LLC.
Group Owner: Radio One.; (acq 1-10-2007; grpsl)
Nat'l Reps: Christal
Format: Gospel
Alfred Liggins, President/CEO

Cleveland

WWGK
01-01-1947; 1540 kHz AM; 1 kw-D, NDD; N41 30 10 W81 37 57
1301 E. 9th St., Cleveland, OH 44114 US
(216) 583-9901; *Fax:* (216) 583-9550
www.espn.com/cleveland
spines@goodkarmabrands.com
License: Cleveland, OH held by Good Karma Broadcasting L.L.C.
Group Owner: Good Karma Broadcasting L.L.C.; (acq 10-27-2006; $2.5 million)
Nat'l Network: ESPN Radio; Fox Sports; Premiere Radio Networks
Arbitron Metro Market: Altus OK
Sam Pines, General Sales Mgr
Nick Bartram, Promotions Manager
Mike Bloomstine, Creative Services Director

WFHM-FM
04-01-1960; 95.5 MHz FM; *Hrs Open:* 24; 31 kw; 620 ft.; N41 26 32 W81 29 28
4 Summit Park Drive, Suite 150, Cleveland, OH 44131 US
(216) 901-0921
www.955thefish.com
License: Cleveland, Cuyahoga County, OH held by Salem Media Group LLC.
Group Owner: Salem Communications Corp.; (acq 12-22-2000; grpsl)
Nat'l Reps: Salem
Arbitron Metro Market: Cleveland, OH; *Format:* Adult Contemp, Christian; *Hrs. of News Programming:* News progmg one hr wkly; *Target Audience:* 25-54; female
Willie Adams, Business Manager
Mark Jaycox, General Manager
Tim Vaughan, General Sales Mgr
Len Howser, Programming Director

***WCPN**
09-08-1984; 90.3 MHz FM; *Hrs Open:* 24; 47 kw; 509 ft.; N41 22 18 W81 42 48

1375 Euclid Avenue, Cleveland, OH 44115-1335 US
(216) 916-6100; *Fax:* (817) 399-3307
www.wcpn.org
License: Cleveland, Cuyahoga County, OH held by Ideastream
Nat'l Network: PRI; NPR
Arbitron Metro Market: Cleveland, OH; *Format:* Jazz, News, 86
Special Programming: Ger one hr, Hungarian one hr, Lithuanian one hr, Pol one hr, Slovak one hr wkly; *Hrs. of News Programming:* news progmg 50 hrs wkly; *No. News Employees:* 16; *Target Audience:* General.
Jerry Wareham, CEO
Maxie C. Jackson III, President/General Manager
Kit Jensen, COO
Mary Grace Herrington, COO
John Phillips, CFO
Tom Purnas, Senior Director of Technology
Linda J. Williams, Senior Director of Education

***WCRF**
11-23-1958; 103.3 MHz FM; *Hrs Open:* 24; 25.5 kW; 659 ft.; N41 17 48 W81 39 27
9756 Barr Rd, Cleveland, OH 44141 USA
(440) 526-1111; *Fax:* (440) 526-1319
www.moodyradio.org/stations/cleveland
License: Cleveland, Cuyahoga County, OH held by The Moody Bible Institute of Chicago
Group Owner: The Moody Bible Institute of Chicago
Nat'l Network: Moody; Salem Radio Network; *Wire Services:* AP
Arbitron Metro Market: Cleveland, OH; *Format:* Christian; *Target Audience:* 25-55.

***WCSB**
05-10-1976; 89.3 MHz FM; *Hrs Open:* 24; 0.63 kw; 203 ft.; N41 30 12 W81 40 30
3100 Chester Avenue, 4th Floor, Cleveland, OH 44115 US
(216) 687-3515
www.wcsb.org
gm@wcsb.org
License: Cleveland, Cuyahoga County, OH held by Cleveland State University.
Arbitron Metro Market: Cleveland, OH; *Format:* Alternative; *Hrs. of News Programming:* News progmg 7 hrs wkly; *Target Audience:* General.
Monica Jordan, Development Director
Graham Beck, General Manager
Mark Manolio, Chief Engineer
Auduman Dowling, Programming Director
Chris Connelly, Music Director
Joel Greenlee, Promotions Director

WDOK
04-30-1950; 102.1 MHz FM; 12 kW; 850 ft.; N41 22 58 W81 42 7
1041 Huron Rd., Cleveland, OH 44115 USA
(216) 861-0100
www.new102.com
License: Cleveland, Cuyahoga County, OH held by CBS Radio Stations Inc.
Group Owner: CBS Radio; (acq 2000; grpsl).
Arbitron Metro Market: Cleveland, OH; *Format:* Adult Contemp; *Target Audience:* 25-54; general
Dave Popovich, Programming Director
Vincent Ing, Advertising/Sales

WENZ
07-14-1959; 107.9 MHz FM; *Hrs Open:* 24; 16 kw horiz, 15 kw vert; 892 ft.; N41 27 54 W81 17 13
6555 Carnegie Ave., Suite 100, Cleveland, OH 44103 US
(216) 579-1111; *Fax:* (216) 771-4164
www.zhiphopcleveland.com/
License: Cleveland, Cuyahoga County, OH held by Blue Chip Broadcasting Licenses Ltd.
Group Owner: Radio One Inc.; (acq 11-8-01; grpsl).
Nat'l Reps: Christal
Arbitron Metro Market: Cleveland, OH; *Format:* Urban Contemporary; *No. News Employees:* 1; *Target Audience:* 18-34.
Bill Black, Operations Dir
Elisabeth Logan, General Sales Mgr

WJMO
07-06-1949; 1300 kHz AM; *Hrs Open:* 24; 5 kw-U, DA1; N41 20 28 W81 44 30
6555 Carnegie Ave., Suite 100, Cleveland, OH 44103 US
(216) 579-1111; *Fax:* (216) 432-1625
www.praisecleveland.com
elogan@radio-one.com
License: Cleveland, OH held by Blue Chip Licenses LLC.
Group Owner: Radio One Inc.; (acq 11-8-2001; grpsl)
Nat'l Reps: Christal
Arbitron Metro Market: Cleveland, OH; *Format:* Gospel; *Hrs. of News Programming:* news progmg 4 hrs wkly; *No. News Employees:* 2; *Target Audience:* 25-54; Black adults
Bill Black, Operations Manager
Elisabeth Logan, General Sales Mgr

WGAR-FM
07-01-1948; 99.5 MHz FM; *Hrs Open:* 24; 50 kw; 499 ft.; N41 22 18 W81 43 4
6200 Oak Tree Boulevard, 4th Floor, Independence, OH 44131-2510 US
(216) 520-2600
www.wgar.com
feedback@wgar.com
License: Cleveland, Cuyahoga County, OH held by Citicasters Licenses Inc.
Group Owner: iHeartMedia; (acq 5-4-99; grpsl).
Nat'l Network: AP Radio; *Nat'l Reps:* Christal
Arbitron Metro Market: Cleveland, OH; *Format:* Country; *No. News Employees:* 2; *Target Audience:* 25-54.
Richard J. Bressler, President
Cindy Hunter, General Sales Manager
Nick Myers, General Sales Manager

WHK
07-28-1921; 1420 kHz AM; 5 kw-D, DAN; 5 kw-N, DAN; N41 21 30 W81 40 3
4 Summit Park Drive, Suite 150, Independence, OH 44131 US
(216) 525-1818
www.whkradio.com
License: Cleveland, OH held by Common Ground Broadcasting, Inc.
Group Owner: Salem Communications Corp.; (acq 9-1-2004; $10 million).
Nat'l Network: Salem Radio Network; *Wire Services:* AP
Arbitron Metro Market: Cleveland, OH; *Format:* Talk; *Target Audience:* 25-54; male & female
Len Howser, Programming Director

WHKW
12-01-1930; 1220 kHz AM; 50 kw-U, DA1; N41 18 26 W81 41 21
4 Summit Park Drive, Suite 150, Cleveland, OH 44131 US
(216) 901-0921; *Fax:* (216) 901-5517
www.whkwradio.com
License: Cleveland, OH held by Caron Broadcasting Inc.
Group Owner: Salem Communications Corp.; (acq 8-24-2000; grpsl).
Arbitron Metro Market: Cleveland, OH; *Format:* Christian, Talk
Mark Jaycox, General Manager
Len Howser, Programming Director
Willie Adams, Business Manager
Brett Crow, Operations Supervisor
Tim Vaughan, General Sales Manager

WMJI
12-06-1948; 105.7 MHz FM; *Hrs Open:* 24; 16 kw; 1129 ft.; N41 23 2 W81 41 44
6200 Oak Tree Boulevard, Independence, OH 44131 US
(216) 520-2600; *Fax:* (216) 524-3200
www.wmji.com
feedback@wmji.com
License: Cleveland, Cuyahoga County, OH held by Citicasters Licenses Inc.
Group Owner: iHeartMedia; (acq 5-4-99; grpsl).
Nat'l Network: AP Radio; *Nat'l Reps:* Christal; *Wire Services:* UPI
Arbitron Metro Market: Cleveland, OH; *Format:* Contemporary Hits/Top 40; *Hrs. of News Programming:* news progmg 5 hrs wkly; *No. News Employees:* 4; *Target Audience:* 25-54.
Gary Mincer, Market President
Keith Abrams, Senior Vice President of Programming
Sharon Moses, General Sales Mgr

WMMS
11-11-1948; 100.7 MHz FM; 34 kw; 600 ft.; N41 21 30 W81 40 3
6200 Oak Tree Boulevard, 4th Floor, Independence, OH 44131-2510 US
(216) 986-8899; *Fax:* (216) 901-8166
www.wmms.com
feedback@wmms.com
License: Cleveland, Cuyahoga County, OH held by Citicasters Licenses Inc.
Group Owner: iHeartMedia; (acq 1999; grpsl).
Arbitron Metro Market: Cleveland, OH; *Format:* Rock/AOR; *Target Audience:* 18-34.
Gary Mincer, Market President
Sharon Moses, General Sales Manager
Maureen Esposito, General Sales Manager

WHLK
05-04-1960; 106.5 MHz FM; *Hrs Open:* 24; 11.3 kw; 1,036 ft; N41 22 45 W81 43 12
6200 Oak Tree Blvd., 4th Fl., Independence, OH 44131 US
(216) 520-2600; *Fax:* (216) 520-3008
www.1065thelake.com
feedback@1065thelake.com
License: Cleveland, Cuyahoga County, OH held by Citicasters Licenses Inc.
Group Owner: iHeartMedia
Population Served: 2,200,000; *Arbitron Metro Market:* Cleveland, OH; *Format:* Adult Contemp; *Adv. Rates:* 240; 240; 240; 75
Keith Abrams, Senior Vice President of Programming
Cindy Hunter, General Sales Manager
Nick Myers, General Sales Manager

WNCX
10-22-1986; 98.5 MHz FM; *Hrs Open:* 24; 31 kW; 480 ft.; N41 20 28 W81 44 24
1041 Huron Rd., Cleveland, OH 44115 USA
(216) 861-0100; *Fax:* (216) 696-0385
www.wncx.com
info@wncx.com
License: Cleveland, Cuyahoga County, OH held by CBS Radio Stations Inc.
Group Owner: CBS Radio
Nat'l Network: ABC; Westwood One
Arbitron Metro Market: Cleveland, OH; *Format:* Classic Rock; *Target Audience:* 25-54; adults; *Adv. Rates:* 300; 250; 250; 75
Linda Rodriguez, Sales Director
Marshall Goudy, Promotions Director

WQAL
01-01-1948; 104.1 MHz FM; *Hrs Open:* 24; 12 kW; 745 ft.; N41 20 28 W81 44 24
1041 Huron Rd., Cleveland, OH 44115 USA
(216) 861-0100; *Fax:* (216) 348-0107
www.q104.com
License: Cleveland, Cuyahoga County, OH held by CBS Radio Stations Inc.
Group Owner: CBS Radio; (acq 12-14-00; grpsl).
Arbitron Metro Market: Cleveland, OH; *Format:* Adult Contemp; *No. News Employees:* 1; *Target Audience:* 25-49; women
Linda Rodriguez, Advertising/Sales
Dave Popovich, Programming Director

WKNR
01-01-1926; 850 kHz AM; *Hrs Open:* 24; 50 kw-D, DA2; 4.7 kw-N, DA2; N41 19 0 W81 43 51
1301 E. 9th St., Suite 252, Cleveland, OH 44114 US
(216) 583-9901; *Fax:* (216) 583-9550
www.espn.com/cleveland
spines@goodkarmabrands.com
License: Cleveland, OH held by Good Karma Broadcasting LLC.
Group Owner: Good Karma Broadcasting L.L.C.; (acq 2-7-2007; $7 million)
Nat'l Network: ESPN Radio
Arbitron Metro Market: Cleveland, OH; *Format:* Sports; *Target Audience:* 25-54; male sports fans
Sam Pines, General Sales Mgr
Nick Bartram, Promotions Manager
Mike Bloomstine, Creative Services Director

***WRUW-FM**
02-26-1967; 91.1 MHz FM; *Hrs Open:* 24; 15 kw; 292 ft.; N41 31 14 W81 35 3
2040 Adelbert Road, Cleveland, OH 44106 US
(216) 368-2207,
www.wruw.org
gm@wruw.org
License: Cleveland, Cuyahoga County, OH held by Case Western Reserve University.
Arbitron Metro Market: Cleveland, OH; *Format:* Variety/Diverse; *Target Audience:* General; Cleveland & CWRU community
Tessa Greene, Operations Dir
Dan Janini, General Manager
Bethany Kaufman, Business Manager
Laura Childers, Programming Director
Roger Ganley, Promotions Manager
Ed Zeitz, Production Director
Charlie Topel, PR Director
DavidCaban, Technical Director
Roger Weist, Music Director

WTAM
01-01-1923; 1100 kHz AM; *Hrs Open:* 24; 50 kw-U, ND1; N41 16 50 W81 37 22
6200 Oak Tree Boulevard, 4th Floor, Independence, OH 44131 US
(216) 520-2600
www.wtam.com
feedback@wtam.com
License: Cleveland, OH held by Citicasters Licenses Inc.
Group Owner: iHeartMedia; (acq 5-4-99; grpsl)

Arbitron Metro Market: Cleveland, OH; *Format:* News, News/Talk, 84, Talk; *Hrs. of News Programming:* news progmg 25 hrs wkly; *No. News Employees:* 14; *Target Audience:* 25-54.; *Adv. Rates:* 250; 250; 375; 150
Ray Davis, Programming Director
Sharon Moses, General Sales Manager
Maureen Esposito, General Sales Manager

WWMK
04-03-1950; 1260 kHz AM; *Hrs Open:* 24; 10 kw-D, DA2; 5 kw-N, DA2; N41 17 10 W81 38 34
77 W. 66th St., 16th Fl, Attn: Sam Antar, New York, NY 10023 US
(818) 460-7477; *Fax:* (440) 746-1720
www.radiodisney.com
License: Cleveland, OH held by Radio Disney Group LLC.
Group Owner: ABC Inc.; (acq 8-26-98; $3.9 million).
Nat'l Network: USA
Arbitron Metro Market: Cleveland, OH; *Format:* Children; *Target Audience:* 3-12, women 21-44; children & families; *Adv. Rates:* 80; 80; 80; 45
Michelle Kulball, Station Manager
Jeniffer Hansen, General Sales Mgr

WZAK
05-26-1963; 93.1 MHz FM; *Hrs Open:* 24; 27.5 kw; 620 ft.; N41 16 50 W81 37 22
6555 Carnegie Ave., Suite 100, Cleveland, OH 44103 US
(216) 579-1111; *Fax:* (216) 771-4164
www.wzakcleveland.com
License: Cleveland, Cuyahoga County, OH held by Blue Chip Broadcasting
Group Owner: Radio One Inc.; (acq 11-8-01; grpsl).
Nat'l Reps: Christal
Arbitron Metro Market: Cleveland, OH; *Format:* Urban Contemporary; *No. News Employees:* 1; *Target Audience:* 25-54 Black adults
Bill Black, Operations Dir
Elisabeth Logan, General Sales Mgr
Rohnesha Horne, Promotions Manager

Cleveland Heights

WERE
01-01-1947; 1490 kHz AM; *Hrs Open:* 24; 1 kw-D, ND2; 1 kw-N, ND2; N41 30 48 W81 36 5
6555 Carnegie Ave., Suite 100, Cleveland, OH 44103 US
(216) 579-1111; *Fax:* (216) 771-4164
www.newstalkcleveland.com
License: Cleveland Heights, OH held by Blue Chip Broadcasting
Group Owner: Radio One Inc.; (acq 8-7-2000; grpsl)
Nat'l Reps: Christal
Arbitron Metro Market: Cleveland, OH; *Format:* News/Talk; *Hrs. of News Programming:* news progmg 30 hrs wkly; *No. News Employees:* 4
Bill Black, Operations Dir
Elisabeth Logan, General Sales Mgr

WKRK-FM
10-03-2007; 92.3 MHz FM; *Hrs Open:* 24; 40 kW-Horiz, 36 kW-Vert; 390 ft.; N41 26 32 W81 29 28
1041 Huron Rd., Cleveland, OH 44115 USA
(216) 861-0100; *Fax:* (216) 696-0385
www.923thefan.com
License: Cleveland Heights, Cuyahoga County, OH held by CBS Radio Stations Inc.
Group Owner: CBS Radio; (acq 12-14-2000; grpsl)
Nat'l Network: ABC
Arbitron Metro Market: Cleveland, OH; *Format:* Sports; *Target Audience:* 18-34; mass appeal, young adults
Jeff Miller, General Sales Mgr
Andy Roth, Programming Director
Marshall Goudy, Promotions Director

Clyde

WMJK
07-16-1981; 100.9 MHz FM; *Hrs Open:* 24; 3 kw; 299 ft.; N41 14 57 W82 54 47
50 East Rivercenter Blvd., Suite 1200, Covington, KY 41011 US
(419) 625-1010; *Fax:* (419) 625-1348
www.coast1009.com
randyhugg@basbroadcasting.com
License: Clyde, Sandusky County, OH held by BAS Broadcasting Inc.
Group Owner: BAS Broadcasting Inc.; (acq 6-30-2008; grpsl)
Nat'l Network: ABC; *Nat'l Reps:* Katz Radio *Regional Reps:* Rgnl Reps.
Arbitron Metro Market: Sandusky/Port Clinton, Ohio; *Format:* Country; *Hrs. of News Programming:* news progmg 4 hrs wkly; *No. News Employees:* 2; *Target Audience:* 18-34 and 25-54; *Adv. Rates:* 20; 20; 20; 14
Randy Hugg, Operations Dir
Lisa Rich, General Manager
Adam Klein, Director of Sales
Steve Shoffner, News Director
Gary Homza, Chief Engineer

***WHVT**
12-01-1986; 90.5 MHz FM; 2.7 kw; 154 ft.; N41 17 45 W82 58 26
1022 S. Main Street, PO Box 273, Cldye, OH 43410 US
(877) 444-4046; *Fax:* (567) 855-0001
www.cleanair.fm
License: Clyde, Sandusky County, OH held by Clyde Educ. Broadcasting Foundation.
Format: Religious
Pastor Lewis, Station Manager
Pastor Mott, Disc Jockey

Coal Grove

WBVB
02-01-1990; 97.1 MHz FM; 3 kw; 472 ft; N38 25 27 W82 32 04
Mailing Address: Box 2288, Huntington, WV 78701
Second Address: 134 4th Ave., Coal Grove, OH 25701
(304) 525-7788; *Fax:* (304) 525-6281
www.b97fm.com
License: Coal Grove, Lawrence County, OH held by Capstar TX LLC
Group Owner: iHeartMedia; (acq 8-30-00; grpsl)
Arbitron Metro Market: Huntington-Ashland, WV-KY; *Format:* Oldies *Special Programming:* Winston Cup racing; *Target Audience:* 18-34.
Judy Jennings, Market President
Jim Davis, Regional Senior Vice President of Programming
Mark Wood, Programming Director

Columbus

WBNS
01-01-1922; 1460 kHz AM; *Hrs Open:* 24; 5 kw-D, DAN; 1 kw-N, DAN; N39 57 6 W82 54 23
605 South Fron Street, Columbus, OH 43215 US
(614) 460-3850; *Fax:* (614) 460-3757
www.971thefan.com
License: Columbus, OH held by RadiOhio Incorporated
Group Owner: Dispatch Broadcast Group; (acq 1933).
Nat'l Network: ESPN Radio; *Regional Network:* Ohio News Network; *Nat'l Reps:* Christal; *Wire Services:* AP
Arbitron Metro Market: Columbus, OH; *Format:* Sports, Talk; *Target Audience:* Men 25-54.
Dave VanStone, General Manager
Todd Markiewicz, Director of Sales
Jay Taylor, Director of Operations
Emily Spehek, Promotions Director

WBNS-FM
06-01-1959; 97.1 MHz FM; *Hrs Open:* 24; 20.5 kw; Ant 781 ft; N39 58 16 W83 01 40
605 S. Front St., Suite 300, Columbus, OH 43215
(614) 460-3850; *Fax:* (614) 460-3757
www.971thefan.com
License: Columbus, Franklin County, OH held by RadiOhio Incorporated
Group Owner: Dispatch Broadcast Group
Regional Network: Ohio News Network; *Nat'l Reps:* Christal; *Wire Services:* AP
Population Served: 1,773,120; *Arbitron Metro Market:* Columbus, OH; *Format:* Sports, Talk; *Target Audience:* Adults 25-54.
Jay Taylor, Operations Dir
Dave Van Stone, President/General Manager
Todd Markiewicz, Sales Director

WRKZ
04-26-1962; 99.7 MHz FM; *Hrs Open:* 24; 20 kw; 784 ft.; N39 58 16 W83 1 40
1458 Dublin Rd., Columbus, OH 43215 US
(614) 481-7800; *Fax:* (614) 486-9970
www.theblitz.com
License: Columbus, Franklin County, OH held by North American Broadcasting Co. Inc.
Group Owner: North American Broadcasting Co. Inc.
Nat'l Reps: D & R Radio; *Wire Services:* AP
Arbitron Metro Market: Columbus, OH; *No. News Employees:* 5; *Target Audience:* 18-49.
Ronni Hunter, Music Director

***WCBE**
09-26-1956; 90.5 MHz FM; *Hrs Open:* 24; 11 kw; 531 ft.; N39 57 48 W83 0 17
540 Jack Gibbs Boulevard, Columbus, OH 43215 US
(614) 365-5555; *Fax:* (614) 365-5060
www.wcbe.org
License: Columbus, Franklin County, OH held by Board of Education, City School District of Columbus, Ohio.
Nat'l Network: NPR; PRI; *Wire Services:* AP
Arbitron Metro Market: Columbus, OH; *Format:* News *Special Programming:* Jazz 4 hrs, blues 3 hrs, Celtic 4 hrs wkly; *Hrs. of News Programming:* news progmg 37 hrs wkly; *No. News Employees:* 3 *Target Audience:* 35-54.
Dan Mushalko, General Manager
Maggie Brennan, Music Director

WCKX
02-01-1996; 107.5 MHz FM; *Hrs Open:* 24; 1.9 kw; 413 ft.; N39 57 46 W82 59 46
350 East 1st Ave., Suite 100, Columbus, OH 43201 US
(614) 487-1444; *Fax:* (614) 487-5862
www.mycolumbuspower.com
License: Columbus, Franklin County, OH held by Blue Chip Broadcasting Licenses Ltd.
Group Owner: Radio One Inc.; (acq 4-30-01; grpsl).
Nat'l Network: ABC; *Nat'l Reps:* D & R Radio
Arbitron Metro Market: Columbus, OH; *Format:* Urban Contemporary; *Hrs. of News Programming:* News progmg one hr wkly
Eddie Harrell, General Manager
Theodore Turner, Programming Director

WCOL-FM
01-01-1947; 92.3 MHz FM; *Hrs Open:* 24; 22 kw; 755 ft.; N39 58 16 W83 1 40
2323 W. 5th Avenue, Suite 200, Columbus, OH 43204 US
(614) 486-6101; *Fax:* (614) 487-2559
www.wcol.com
daveman@iheartmedia.com
License: Columbus, Franklin County, OH held by Citicasters Licenses Inc.
Group Owner: iHeartMedia; (acq 5-4-99; grpsl)
Arbitron Metro Market: Columbus, OH; *Format:* Country; *No. News Employees:* 1; *Target Audience:* 18-49.
Michael McCoy, Operations Manager
Dan E. Zuko, Program Director
Dave Man, Digital Program Director

WYTS
01-01-1922; 1230 kHz AM; 1 kw-U, ND1; N39 56 31 W83 1 20
50 East Rivercenter Boulevard, Suite 1200, Covington, KY 41011 US
(614) 487-2470
www.am1230wyts.com
License: Columbus, OH held by Citicasters Licenses Inc.
Group Owner: iHeartMedia
Nat'l Network: Fox Sports
Arbitron Metro Market: Columbus, OH; *Format:* Sports; *Target Audience:* 35 plus; general
Brian Dytko, President/Market Manager
Jeff Rehl, General Sales Mgr
Michael McCoy, Programming Director
Erin Rafferty, Marketing and Promotion Director

WLVQ
04-01-1959; 96.3 MHz FM; *Hrs Open:* 24; 18 kw; 751 ft.; N39 58 16 W83 1 40
2400 Corporate Exchange Drve, Suite 200, Columbus, OH 43231 US
(614) 227-9696
www.qfm96.com
ccassidy@wilkscolumbus.com
License: Columbus, Franklin County, OH held by Wilks License Co.-Columbus LLC.
Group Owner: Wilks Broadcast Group LLC; (acq 1-10-2007; grpsl)
Nat'l Reps: Christal
Arbitron Metro Market: Columbus, OH; *Format:* Classic Rock; *Hrs. of News Programming:* news progmg 2 hrs wkly; *No. News Employees:* 1; *Target Audience:* 25-54.
Carolyn Cassidy, General Sales Mgr
Ross Wagner, Programming Director
Megan Slater, Program Director
Mike Dorsey, Promotions Director

WMNI
04-26-1958; 920 kHz AM; *Hrs Open:* 24; 1 kw-D, DA2; 0.5 kw-N, DA2; N39 53 32 W83 2 51
1458 Dublin Rd., Columbus, OH 43215 US
(614) 481-7800
www.wmni.com
License: Columbus, OH held by North American Broadcasting Inc.
Group Owner: North American Broadcasting Co. Inc.
Nat'l Network: AP Network News; *Wire Services:* AP
Arbitron Metro Market: Columbus, OH; *Format:* News *Special Programming:* Relg 4 hrs wkly; *Hrs. of News Programming:* news

progmg 20 hrs wkly; *No. News Employees:* 5; *Target Audience:* 35 plus.

WNCI
07-01-1961; 97.9 MHz FM; *Hrs Open:* 24; 175 kw horiz, 105 kw vert; 561 ft.; N39 58 10 W83 0 10
2323 W. 5th Avenue, Suite 200, Columbus, OH 43204 US
(614) 486-6101; *Fax:* (614) 487-2559
www.wnci.com
License: Columbus, Franklin County, OH held by Citicasters Licenses Inc.
Group Owner: iHeartMedia; (acq 1999; grpsl).
Arbitron Metro Market: Columbus, OH; *Format:* Contemporary Hits/Top 40; *Hrs. of News Programming:* news progmg 4 hrs wkly; *No. News Employees:* 1; *Target Audience:* 18-49.
Rob O'Boyle, Director of Sales
Michael McCoy, Vice President of Programming
Erin Rafferty, Assistant Program Director

***WVSG**
04-24-1922; 820 kHz AM; *Hrs Open:* 24; 5 kw-D, 790 w-N (L-WBAP Ft. Worth, Tex.); N40 01 44 W82 03 22
2400 Olentangy River Rd., Columbus, OH 43210
(614) 292-9678; *Fax:* (614) 292-0513
www.wosu.org
License: Columbus, Franklin County, OH held by St. Gabriel Radio, Inc.
Nat'l Network: NPR; PRI; *Wire Services:* AP
Population Served: 1,200,000; *Arbitron Metro Market:* Columbus, OH *Special Programming:* Black one hr, bluegrass 12 hrs wkly; *Hrs. of News Programming:* news progmg 114 hrs wkly; *No. News Employees:* 9 *TargetAudience:* 35 plus; general
Thomas Rieland, General Manager
David Carwile, Director of Planning/Initiatives
Brent Davis, Sr. Content Director
Beverly Ervine, Music Director
Mary Alice Akins, Sr. Director of Operations

***WOSU-FM**
12-13-1949; 89.7 MHz FM; *Hrs Open:* 24; 40 kw; 552 ft.; N40 1 2 W83 1 11
2400 Olentangy River Road, Columbus, OH 43210 US
(614) 292-9678; *Fax:* (614) 292-0513
www.wosu.org
License: Columbus, Franklin County, OH held by Ohio State University
Nat'l Network: PRI; *Wire Services:* AP
Arbitron Metro Market: Columbus, OH *TV Affiliate:* *WOSU-TV affil.; *Format:* Contemporary Hits/Top 40; *Target Audience:* 25 plus.
Karen Olstad, COO
David Carwile, Director of Planning/Initiatives
Brent Davis, Sr. Content Director
Beverly Ervine, Music Director
Mary Alice Akins, Senior Director of Operations

WSNY
08-12-1982; 94.7 MHz FM; 22 kw; 755 ft.; N39 58 16 W83 1 40
4401 Carriage Hill Lane, Columbus, OH 43220 US
(614) 451-2191; *Fax:* (614) 451-1831
www.sunny95.com
License: Columbus, Franklin County, OH held by Franklin Communications Inc.
Group Owner: Saga Communications Inc.; (acq 9-86).
Nat'l Reps: Christal; Katz Radio; *Wire Services:* AP
Arbitron Metro Market: Columbus, OH; *Format:* Adult Contemp; *Hrs. of News Programming:* news progmg 3 hrs wkly; *No. News Employees:* 1; *Target Audience:* 25-64; women, upscale families
Alan Goodman, President
Katie Cyr, General Sales Mgr
Michelle Hurley, Promotions Manager
Jill McCarron, National Sales Manager

WTVN
01-01-1924; 610 kHz AM; *Hrs Open:* 24
2323 W. 5th Avenue, Suite 200, Columbus, OH 43204 US
(614) 486-6101; *Fax:* (614) 487-2559
www.610wtvn.com
License: Columbus, OH held by Citicasters Licenses Inc.
Group Owner: iHeartMedia; (acq 1999; grpsl).
Arbitron Metro Market: Columbus, OH; *Format:* News, News/Talk, 86; *Target Audience:* 25-54; leaning male
Michael McCoy, Senior Vice President of Programming
Jeff Rehl, General Sales Mgr
Mike Elliott, Programming Director
Joe Bradley, Producer
Tom Schmid, Producer
Matt McCoy, Sports Director

***WUFM**
03-22-1996; 88.7 MHz FM; *Hrs Open:* 24; 5 kw; 774 ft.; N39 56 16 W83 1 16
P.O. Box 1887, Westerville, OH 43086 US
(614) 839-7100
www.radiou.com
License: Columbus, Franklin County, OH held by Spirit Communications Inc.
Arbitron Metro Market: Westerville, OH; *Format:* Contemporary Hits/Top 40; *Target Audience:* 12-24; Male
John Shumate Sr., President
Kathy Shumate, Operations Dir
Michael Buckingham, General Manager
Nikki Cantu, Programming Director
Cole Drake, Promotions Manager

WVKO
11-21-1951; 1580 kHz AM; *Hrs Open:* 24
4673 Winterset Drive, Columbus, OH 43220 US
(614) 489-4820
www.stgabrielradio.com
info@stgabrielradio.com
License: Columbus, OH held by Bernard Ohio LLC.
Group Owner: Bernard Radio LLC; (acq 1-22-2007; grpsl)
Nat'l Network: EWTN Radio
Arbitron Metro Market: Columbus, OH; *Format:* Christian
Marc Hawk, President
Bill Messerly, Executive Director
Dave Orsborn, Production Manager

***WHKC**
09-01-2007; 91.5 MHz FM; 15 kw; Ant 689 ft; N39 56 14 W83 01 16
1630 Strathshire Hall Pl., Powell, OH 43065
(740) 548-5919; *Fax:* (740) 548-5911
License: Columbus, Franklin County, OH held by Christian Broadcasting Services Inc.
Arbitron Metro Market: Columbus, OH
Penny Neilsen, CEO
Nate Adams, Operations Dir
John Malone, General Manager
Nate Adams, General Sales Mgr
Don Roden, Chief Engineer

Columbus Grove

WBKS
01-01-2003; 93.9 MHz FM; 14 kw; Ant 436 ft; N40 57 21 W84 07 59
667 W. Market St., Lima, OH 45801
(419) 223-2060; *Fax:* (419) 229-3888
www.kisslima.com
License: Columbus Grove, Putnam County, OH held by CC Licenses LLC.
Group Owner: iHeartMedia; (acq 8-10-2000).
Format: Contemporary Hits/Top 40; *Hrs. of News Programming:* News progmg one hr wkly
Matt Bell, Market President

Columbus-Worthington

WRFD
09-27-1947; 880 kHz AM; *Hrs Open:* Sunrise-sunset; 6.1 kw-C, NDD; 23 kw-D, NDD; N39 56 31 W83 1 20
8101 N. High Street, Suite 360, Columbus, OH 43235 US
(614) 885-0880; *Fax:* (614) 885-6322
www.wrfd.com
mail@wrfd.com
License: Columbus-Worthington, OH held by Salem Media of Ohio
Group Owner: Salem Communications Corp.
Nat'l Network: Salem Radio Network; *Nat'l Reps:* Christal; Salem
Arbitron Metro Market: Columbus, OH; *Format:* Talk, Religious; *Hrs. of News Programming:* News progmg one hr wkly; *Target Audience:* 30-60; conservatives, Christians, farmers
Bekki Spencer, Traffic Director
Tom Heyl, General Manager
Aaron Light, Program Producer
Ryan Moran, Operations Manager
Jason Whitt, Promotions Director
Ryan Moran, Operations Manager

Conneaut

WGOJ
105.5 MHz FM; *Hrs Open:* 24; 6 kw horiz, 5.8 kw vert; 295 ft.; N41 51 42 W80 31 1
235 Mill Street, Conneaut, OH 44030 US
(440) 599-1055
www.wgoj-christian-radio.com
wgoj@suite224.net
License: Conneaut, Ashtabula County, OH held by Bible Brodcasting Inc.
Format: Christian; *Target Audience:* General.
Dr. Roger Hogle, General Manager
Floyd Huston, Chief Engineer

WWOW
10-25-1959; 1360 kHz AM; *Hrs Open:* 24
239 Broad Street, Conneaut, OH 44030 US
(440) 593-2233
www.1360wwow.com
wshanleaf@aol.com
License: Conneaut, OH held by Cause Plus Marketing LLC
Arbitron Metro Market: Conneaut, OH; *Format:* News, News/Talk, 86
Bill Shannon, Owner

Cortland

WKTX
04-01-1985; 830 kHz AM; 1 kw-D; N41 24 56 W80 43 49
11906 Madison Ave., Lakewood, OH 44140
(216) 221-0330; *Fax:* (216) 221-3638
License: Cortland, Trumbull County, OH held by Miklos Kossanyi, Maria Kossanyi
Nat'l Network: USA
Arbitron Metro Market: Youngstown-Warren, OH *Special Programming:* Slovenian 2 hrs, Greek 2 hrs, Pol one hr, German 5 hrs wkly; *Target Audience:* 35 plus; homeowners
Attila Kossanyl, President
Jim Georgiades, General Manager
Jack Cory, Programming Director
Tom Derrit, Promotions Manager
Andrew Huston, News Director
Jim Gorgiades, Engineering Dir

Coshocton

***WOSE**
01-01-1996; 91.1 MHz FM; 6 kw; 322 ft.; N40 20 30 W81 57 56
Rebroadcasts: Rebroadcasts WOSU-FM Columbus 100%
2400 Olentangy River Rd, Columbus, OH 43210 US
(614) 292-9678; *Fax:* (614) 292-7625
www.wosu.org
wosu@osu.edu
License: Coshocton, Coshocton County, OH held by The Ohio State University.
Nat'l Network: PRI; NPR; *Wire Services:* AP
Format: Talk
Kevin Petrilla, Operations Dir
Thomas Rieland, General Manager
Tim Eby, Station Manager

WTNS
11-09-1947; 1560 kHz AM; 1 kw-D; N40 16 30 W81 49 37
114 N. 6th St., Coshocton, OH 43812
(740) 622-1560; *Fax:* (740) 622-7940
www.mywtnsradio.com
License: Coshocton, Coshocton County, OH held by Coshocton Broadcasting Co.
Group Owner: Coshocton Broadcasting Co.; acq 9-86; $560,653;
Population Served: 13,747 *Format:* Country
Bruce Wallace, President
Tom Thompson, General Sales Mgr
Mike Bechtol, Programming Director
Ken Smailes, News Director
John Hartmeyer, Chief Engineer

WTNS-FM
04-25-1968; 99.3 MHz FM; 1.2 kw; 440 ft.; N40 16 30 W81 49 37
114 North 6th Street, Coshocton, OH 43812 US
(740) 622-1560; *Fax:* (740) 622-7940
www.mywtnsradio.com
License: Coshocton, Coshocton County, OH held by Cochocton Broadcasting Co.
Arbitron Metro Market: Coshocton, OH; *Format:* Adult Contemp
Flo Murdock, Programming Director
Brad Haynes, Disc Jockey
Tom Thompson, Disc Jockey
Jim Parr, Disc Jockey

Crestline

***WYKL**
12-10-1990; 98.7 MHz FM; *Hrs Open:* 24; 1.8 kw; 400 ft.; N40 46 13 W82 45 23
PO Box 2098, Omaha, NE 68103 US
(800) 525-5683
www.klove.com
License: Crestline, Crawford County, OH held by Educational Media Foundation.
Group Owner: EMF Broadcasting; (acq 12-18-03; $900,000).
Nat'l Network: K-Love

RADIO - U.S.

Arbitron Metro Market: Crestline, OH; *Format:* Christian; *Target Audience:* 25-44; Judeo Christian female
Darrell Chambliss, Chairman
Mike Novak, President/CEO
Eric Moser, CFO
Allen Mason, COO
David Pierce, Chief Creative Officer
D. Kevin Blair, Secretary/General Counsel

Cridersville

WVLO
99.3 MHz FM; 6 kw; 74 meters; n40 45 19 w84 05 20
5700 West Oaks Blvd, Rocklin, CA 95765
(916) 251-1600; *Fax:* (916) 251-1650
www.emfbroadcasting.com
info@emfbroadcasting.com
License: Cridersville, OH held by Educational Media Foundation
Group Owner: EMF Broadcasting

Mike Novak, President/CEO

Crooksville

WYBZ
10-26-1990; 107.3 MHz FM; *Hrs Open:* 24; 3 kw; 328 ft; N39 47 23 W82 05 39
2895 A Maysville Pike, Zanesville, OH 43701
(740) 453-6004; *Fax:* (740) 453-5865
www.wybz.com
License: Crooksville, Perry County, OH held by Y Bridge Broadcasting Inc.
Nat'l Network: NBC
Hrs. of News Programming: news progmg 9 hrs wkly; *No. News Employees:* 1; *Target Audience:* 35-64.
Rick Sabine, President
Jenny McCloy, Operations Dir
Jenny McCloy, Station Manager
Monica Martinelli, General Sales Mgr
Ron Strong, Programming Director
Mark Hiner, Chief Engineer

Cuyahoga Falls

*WCUE
01-01-1950; 1150 kHz AM; *Hrs Open:* 24
290 Hegenberger Road, Oakland, CA 94621 US
(800)-543-1495
www.familyradio.com
License: Cuyahoga Falls, OH held by Family Stations Inc.
Group Owner: Family Stations Inc.; acq 10-22-86)
Arbitron Metro Market: Akron, OH; *Format:* Religious *Special Programming:* Class 2 hrs wkly; *Hrs. of News Programming:* News progmg 4 hrs wkly; *Target Audience:* 25 plus; Christians
Harold Camping, President

Dayton

WDAO
03-01-1955; 1210 kHz AM; 1 kw-D, NDD; N39 43 36 W84 12 23
1012 W. 3rd Street, Dayton, OH 45402 US
(937) 222-9326; *Fax:* (937) 461-6100
www.wdaoradio.com
wdao1210@aol.com
License: Dayton, OH held by Johnson Communications Inc.
Nat'l Reps: Christal
Arbitron Metro Market: Dayton, OH; *Format:* Blues
Jim Johnson, President/General Manager
Sophia Carr, General Sales Mgr

*WDPR
04-09-1977; 88.1 MHz FM; *Hrs Open:* 24; 0.6 kw; 781 ft.; N39 43 16 W84 15 0
126 N. Main St., Dayton, OH 45402 US
(937) 496-3850; *Fax:* (937) 496-3852
www.discoverclassical.org
dpr@dpr.org
License: Dayton, Montgomery County, OH held by Dayton Public Radio Inc.
Nat'l Network: USA
Arbitron Metro Market: Dayton, OH; *Format:* Talk; *Target Audience:* 24-50.
Shaun Yu, President/CEO
Rosemary Bradley, Development Director
Cheryl Dring, Programming Director

*WDPS
01-01-1976; 89.5 MHz FM; *Hrs Open:* 9:15 AM-4:30 PM; 6 kw horiz, 5.8 kw vert; 210 ft.; N39 45 28 W84 11 36
741 Washington Street, Dayton, OH 45402 US
(937) 542-7182; *Fax:* (937) 542-6714
www.dps.k12.oh.us/departments/PIO/wdps-fm.html
License: Dayton, Montgomery County, OH held by Dayton City Schools
Arbitron Metro Market: Dayton, OH; *Format:* Jazz, Triple A
P.R. Frank, Operations Dir
Ken Kreitzer, General Manager
Christopher Hartley, Programming Director
Tom Nornhold, Chief Engineer
Jennifer Bryant, Assistant Music Director

WHIO
02-09-1935; 1290 kHz AM *Rebroadcasts:* Simulcast with WHIO-FM Piqua 100%
1611 S. Main Street, Dayton, OH 45409 US
(937) 259-9871
www.whio.com
fantine.kerckaert@cmgohio.com
License: Dayton, OH held by Cox Radio Inc.
Group Owner: Cox Radio Inc.
Nat'l Reps: D & R Radio
Arbitron Metro Market: Dayton, OH *TV Affiliate:* WHIO-TV affil.; *Format:* News, News/Talk, 86 *Special Programming:* Relg 2 hrs wkly; *Hrs. of News Programming:* news progmg 30 hrs wkly; *No. News Employees:* 4 *Target Audience:* 35-54.
Fantine Kerckaert, Program Director
Ashley Long, Program Director

WHKO
01-01-1946; 99.1 MHz FM; 50 kw; 1066 ft.; N39 44 2 W84 14 53
1611 S. Main Street, Dayton, OH 45409 US
(937) 259-9871; *Fax:* (937) 259-2168
www.whio.com
liz.goshert@coxinc.com
License: Dayton, Montgomery County, OH held by Cox Radio Inc.
Group Owner: Cox Radio Inc.
Nat'l Reps: Christal
Arbitron Metro Market: Dayton, OH *TV Affiliate:* WHIO-TV affil.; *Format:* Country
Nancy Wilson, Music Radio Program Director
Nick Roberts, Operations Dir
Sheila McCune, Programming Director

WING
05-24-1921; 1410 kHz AM; 5 kw-D, DAN; 5 kw-N, DAN; N39 40 56 W84 9 33
717 E. David Rd., Kettering, OH 45429 US
(937) 457-9464
www.wingam.com
License: Dayton, Montgomery County, OH held by Alpha Media Licensee LLC
Group Owner: Alpha Media LLC; (acq 4-17-2014; grpsl).
Nat'l Network: ESPN Radio; *Nat'l Reps:* Katz Radio
Arbitron Metro Market: Dayton, OH; *Format:* Sports, Talk; *Target Audience:* 25-54; well educated
John King, General Manager

WMMX
09-01-1964; 107.7 MHz FM; *Hrs Open:* 24; 28 kw; 656 ft.; N39 43 19 W84 12 33
101 Pine Street, Dayton, OH 45402 US
(937) 224-1137; *Fax:* (937) 224-5015
www.mix1077.com
License: Dayton, Montgomery County, OH held by Citicasters Licenses Inc.
Group Owner: iHeartMedia; (acq 1999; grpsl).
Arbitron Metro Market: Dayton, OH; *Format:* Adult Contemp; *Target Audience:* 25-54.
Dave Litteral, Senior Vice President of Sales

WONE
03-20-1949; 980 kHz AM; 5 kw-D, DAN; 5 kw-N, DAN; N39 40 3 W84 10 1
101 Pine Street, Dayton, OH 45402 US
(937) 224-1137; *Fax:* (937) 224-5015
www.wone.com
License: Dayton, OH held by Citicasters Licenses Inc.
Group Owner: iHeartMedia; (acq 5-4-99; grpsl).
Arbitron Metro Market: Dayton, OH *TV Affiliate:* Sports; *Format:* Sports *Special Programming:* news progmg 18 hrs wkly; *Hrs. of News Programming:* 3; *No. News Employees:* 35-64.
Dave Litteral, Senior Vice President of Sales

*WQRP
01-01-1976; 89.5 MHz FM; 6 kw; 210 ft.; N39 45 28 W84 11 36
PO Box 2098, Omaha, NE 68103 US
(800) 525-5683
www.klove.com
License: Dayton, Montgomery County, OH held by Educational Media Foundation.
Group Owner: EMF Broadcasting; (acq 7-9-2008; $350,000)
Nat'l Network: K-Love
Arbitron Metro Market: Dayton, OH; *Format:* Christian
Darrell Chambliss, Chairman
Mike Novak, President/CEO
David Pierce, Chief Creative Officer
Eric Moser, CFO
Alan Mason, COO
D. Kevin Blair, Secretary/General Counsel

WTUE
01-01-1959; 104.7 MHz FM; *Hrs Open:* 24; 28 kw; 656 ft.; N39 43 19 W84 12 33
101 Pine Street, Dayton, OH 45402 US
(937) 224-1137; *Fax:* (937) 224-5015
www.wtue.com
License: Dayton, Montgomery County, OH held by Citicasters Licenses Inc.
Group Owner: iHeartMedia
Arbitron Metro Market: Dayton, OH; *Format:* Rock/AOR; *Hrs. of News Programming:* news progmg 2 hrs wkly; *No. News Employees:* 1; *Target Audience:* 18-49.
Dave Litteral, Senior Vice President of Sales

*WUDR
01-01-2003; 98.1 MHz FM; 0.013 kw; 90 ft.; N39 47 14 W84 14 23
300 College Park Drive, Dayton, OH 45469 US
(937) 229-1000
info@udayton.edu
License: Dayton, Montgomery County, OH held by University of Dayton.
Arbitron Metro Market: Dayton, OH; *Format:* Variety/Diverse
Roy Flynn, Operations Dir
Carson Smith, General Manager
Keith Raad, Sports Director
Bobby Beebe, Program Manager
Liz Rosevear, Promotions Manager

De Graff

*WDEQ-FM
09-01-1967; 91.7 MHz FM; 0.1 kw; 10 ft.; N40 18 54 W83 55 23
2096 County Road 245, Degraff, OH 43318 US
(937) 585-5981; *Fax:* (937) 585-4599
www.riverside.k12.oh.us
License: De Graff, Logan County, OH held by Riverside Local Board of Education.
Arbitron Metro Market: De Graff, Ohio
Gene Kirby, General Manager
Steve Webb, Station Manager

Defiance

WDFM
06-25-1985; 98.1 MHz FM; *Hrs Open:* 24; 50 kw; 499 ft.; N41 17 28 W84 32 17
709 North Perry Street, Napoleon, OH 43545 US
(419) 782-9336; *Fax:* (419) 784-0306
www.mix981fm.com
ricksmall@iheartmedia.com
License: Defiance, Defiance County, OH held by Citicasters Licenses Inc.
Group Owner: iHeartMedia; (acq 5-4-99; grpsl).
Nat'l Network: CNN Radio; *Nat'l Reps:* Katz Radio
Arbitron Metro Market: Defiance, Oh; *Format:* Adult Contemp *Special Programming:* Relg 3 hrs wkly; *Hrs. of News Programming:* news progmg 7 hrs wkly; *No. News Employees:* 1; *Target Audience:* 25-54. *Adv.Rates:* 35; 20; 30; 12
Rick Small, Operations Manager/Programming Director
Bob McLimans, Market President
John Schuette, Sales Manager

*WGDE
03-14-1999; 91.9 MHz FM; *Hrs Open:* 24; 6 kw; 305 ft.; N41 17 41 W84 23 24 *Rebroadcasts:* Rebroadcasts WGTE-FM Toledo 100%
1270 S. Detroit Avenue, PO Box 30, Toledo, OH 43614 US
(419) 380-4600; *Fax:* (419) 380-4710
www.wgte.org
License: Defiance, Defiance County, OH held by Public Broadcasting Foundation of NW Ohio
Format: News *Special Programming:* Jazz 16 hrs, new age 4 hrs wkly; *Hrs. of News Programming:* News progmg 23 hrs wkly; *Target Audience:* General.
Daniel T. Anderson, Chairman
Marlon Kiser, President/General Manager
Darren LaShelle, Director of Content/Creative Services
Dan Niedzwicki, Director of Engineering

WONW
01-01-1949; 1280 kHz AM; *Hrs Open:* 24; 1 kw-D, 500 w-N, DA-N; N41 16 44 W84 23 50
2110 Radio Drive, Defiance, OH 43512 US

(419) 782-8126; *Fax:* (419) 784-4154
www.wonw1280.com
License: Defiance, Defiance County, OH held by CC Licenses LLC.
Group Owner: iHeartMedia; (acq 11-5-99; grpsl)
Nat'l Network: ABC Radio; *Nat'l Reps:* Katz Radio; *Wire Services:* AP
Format: News, News/Talk, 84, Talk *Special Programming:* Rush Limbaugh; *No. News Employees:* 1; *Target Audience:* General.; *Adv. Rates:* 25; 15; 20; 8
Bob McLimans, Market President
Josh Busch, Senior Vice President of Programming
John Schuette, Sales Manager

WZOM
08-25-1989; 105.7 MHz FM; *Hrs Open:* 24; 6 kw; 328 ft.; N41 13 23 W84 22 36
2110 Radio Drive, Defiance, OH 43512 US
(419) 782-8126; *Fax:* (419) 784-4154
www.1057thebull.com
License: Defiance, Defiance County, OH held by CC Licenses LLC.
Group Owner: iHeartMedia; (acq 1-1-2000; grpsl)
Nat'l Reps: Katz Radio *Regional Reps:* Rgnl Reps.
Arbitron Metro Market: Defiance, OH; *Format:* Country *Special Programming:* Relg 6 hrs wkly; *Hrs. of News Programming:* news progmg 4 hrs wkly; *No. News Employees:* 1; *Target Audience:* 25-54.; *Adv. Rates:* 30; 20; 25; 10
Bob McLimans, Market President
Josh Busch, Senior Vice President of Programming
John Schuette, General Sales Mgr

Delaware

WDLR
01-18-1961; 1550 kHz AM; *Hrs Open:* 24; 0.5 kw-D, DA2; 0.029 kw-N, DA2; N40 17 56 W83 2 46
501 Bowtown Road, Delaware, OH 43015 US
(937) 644-1270
License: Delaware, OH held by ICS Holdings Inc.
Arbitron Metro Market: Columbus, OH
Mike Schnell, General Sales Mgr

***WJJE**
01-01-2005; 89.1 MHz FM; 6 kw vert; 328 ft.; N40 24 2 W82 46 43
#102, 320 London Rd., Delaware, OH 43015-6401 US
(740) 363-9553
www.afr.net
License: Delaware, Delaware County, OH held by American Family Association.
Group Owner: American Family Radio; (acq 12-15-2003; $10 for CP).
Arbitron Metro Market: Delaware, OH; *Format:* Religious
Tim Wildmon, President
Donald Wildmon, Founder
Buddy Smith, Sr VP
Ed Vitagliano, Exec VP
Randy Sharp, Director Of Special Projects
Meeke Addison, Director Of Communications
Abraham Hamilton III, General Sales Mgr

Delhi Hills

WNLT
09-01-1991; 104.3 MHz FM; 2 kw; 175 meters; N39 6 18 W84 33 25
8686 Michael Lane, Fairfield, OH 45014
(707) 528-9236; *Fax:* (707) 528-9246
License: Delhi Hills, Hamilton County, OH held by Vernon R. Baldwin Inc.
Group Owner: Vernon R Baldwin Inc.
Population Served: 2,000,000; *Arbitron Metro Market:* Cincinnati, OH; *Format:* Christian
Marcella Baldwin, President

Delphos

***WBIE**
01-01-2001; 91.5 MHz FM; 5.5 kw; 322 ft.; N40 56 48 W84 15 24
P.O. Box 3206, Tupelo, MS 38803 US
(662) 844-8888; *Fax:* (662) 842-6791
www.afr.net
faq@afa.net
License: Delphos, Allen County, OH held by American Family Association.
Group Owner: American Family Radio
Arbitron Metro Market: Delphos, OH; *Format:* Christian, Religious
Tim Wildmon, President
Donald Wildmon, Founder
Buddy Smith, Sr VP
Ed Vitagliano, Exec VP
Randy Sharp, Director Of Special Projects
Meeke Addison, Director Of Communications
Abraham Hamilton III, General Counsel

WDOH
12-16-1972; 107.1 MHz FM; 3.3 kw; 299 ft.; N40 49 55 W84 21 11
P.O. Box 100, Delphos, OH 45833 US
(419) 331-1600; *Fax:* (419) 228-5085
License: Delphos, Allen County, OH held by Childers Media Group LLC
Group Owner: Childers Media Group LLC; (acq 11-15-2004; $1.15 million).
Nat'l Network: CBS
Arbitron Metro Market: Delphos, OH; *Format:* Classic Rock *Special Programming:* Farm 8 hrs wkly; *Hrs. of News Programming:* news progmg 7 hrs wkly; *No. News Employees:* 1; *Target Audience:* 25 plus. *Adv.Rates:* 10; 8; 10; 8
Gary Rozynek, President
Deb Klaus, Operations Dir
David Roach, General Manager
Tiffany Kayser, Director of Sales
Phil Austin, Programming Director
Bob Ulm, News Director

Delta

WLQR-FM
09-01-1994; 106.5 MHz FM; 3 kw; 328 ft; N41 35 13 W83 54 11
3225 Arlington Ave., Toledo, OH 43614
(419) 725-5700; *Fax:* (419) 725-5805
www.1065thezone.com
matt.spaulding@cumulus.com
License: Delta, Fulton County, OH held by Cumulus Licensing Corp.
Group Owner: Cumulus Media Inc.; (acq 11-18-99; $4,925,000).
Population Served: 286,038; *Arbitron Metro Market:* Toledo, OH; *Format:* Alternative; *Target Audience:* 18-34; male
Cody Welling, General Sales Mgr
Norm Wamer, Programming Director
Ryan Young, Director of Marketing & Promotions
Dave Fuller, Chief Engineer
John Gallagher, Market Manager

Dover-New Philadelphia

WJER
02-10-1950; 1450 kHz AM; *Hrs Open:* 24; 1 kw-U; N40 30 46 W81 27 24
646 Boulevard, Dover, OH 44622
(330) 343-7755; *Fax:* (330) 364-4538
www.wjer.com
wjer@wjer.com
License: Dover-New Philadelphia, Tuscarawas County, OH held by WJER Radio LLC
Nat'l Network: A.P; *Nat'l Reps:* Rgnl Reps
Population Served: 86,000; *No. News Employees:* 3; *Target Audience:* Adult
Gary Petricola, President
Bob Scanlon, General Manager
Jennifer Clark, News Director
Bruce Willis, Chief Engineer
Michael Roberts, Operations Manager

Dublin

WZCB
04-01-1953; 106.7 MHz FM; 7.3 kw; Ant 590 ft; N40 09 33 W82 55 23
2323 W. 5th Ave., Suite 200, Columbus, OH 41011 US
(614) 486-6101; *Fax:* (614) 487-3575
www.thebeat1067.com
License: Dublin, Franklin County, OH held by Citicasters Licenses Inc.
Group Owner: iHeartMedia; (acq 1999; grpsl)
Arbitron Metro Market: Columbus, OH; *Format:* Urban Contemporary
Brian Dytko, Market Manager
Michael McCoy, Programming Director
Erin Rafferty, Marketing and Promotion Director

East Liverpool

WOHI
12-01-1949; 1490 kHz AM; 1 kw-U, ND1; N40 37 47 W80 36 9
123 Blaine Rd., Brownsville, PA 15417 US
(724) 378-1271; *Fax:* (724) 378-4653
www.picklefm.com
License: East Liverpool, OH held by FM Radio Licenses, LLC
Group Owner: Keymarket Communications LLC; (acq 2000; grpsl).
Nat'l Network: Jones Radio Networks; *Nat'l Reps:* Rgnl Reps
TV Affiliate: Adult Contemp; *No. News Employees:* General.
Kerby Confer, President

Eaton

WEDI
01-01-1979; 1130 kHz AM; 0.25 kw-D, DAD; N39 44 55 W84 35 2 *Rebroadcasts:* Rebroadcasts WBZI(AM) Xenia 80%
23 East 2nd Street, Xenia, OH 45385 US
(888) 740-9444
www.myclassiccountry.com
cds@myclassiccountry.com
License: Eaton, OH held by Town and Country Broadcasting Inc.
Group Owner: Town and Country Broadcasting Inc.; (acq 1-4-2005; $175,000).
Nat'l Network: Fox News Radio; *Regional Network:* Agrinet; *Nat'l Reps:* Rgnl Reps; *Wire Services:* AP
Arbitron Metro Market: Dayton, OH; *Format:* Country *Special Programming:* Gospel 5 hrs., Farm 2 hrs. wkly; *Hrs. of News Programming:* news progmg 3 hrs wkly; *No. News Employees:* 2; *Target Audience:* 35-64;adults; *Adv. Rates:* 18; 18; 18; na
Joe Mullins, President
Roy Hatfield, Programming Director
Darrin Johnston, News Director
Bucks Braun, Morning Host
Megan Brugger, Traffic Manager

WGTZ
11-28-1960; 92.9 MHz FM; *Hrs Open:* 24; 40 kw; 551 ft.; N39 50 10 W84 24 16
717 E. David Rd., Kettering, OH 45429 US
(937) 294-5858; *Fax:* (937) 297-5233
www.softrock929.com
License: Eaton, Preble County, OH held by Alpha Media Licensee LLC
Group Owner: Alpha Media LLC; (acq 4-17-2014; grpsl).
Nat'l Reps: Katz Radio
Arbitron Metro Market: Dayton, OH; *Format:* Adult Contemp; *Target Audience:* 18-49; contemp middle America
Keith Wright, Director of Sales
Brad Waldo, Programming Director
Andrea Scott, Market Manager
Sue Killinen, Business Manager

Edgewood

WZOO-FM
01-23-1989; 102.5 MHz FM; *Hrs Open:* 24; 5.8 kw; 328 ft.; N41 49 44 W80 49 28
P.O. Box 102, Ashtabula, OH 44004 US
(440) 993-2126; *Fax:* (440) 992-2658
License: Edgewood, Ashtabula County, OH held by Sweet Home Ashtabula LLC.
Group Owner: Sweet Home Ashtabula LLC; (acq 9-17-2007; grpsl)
Arbitron Metro Market: Ashtabula, OH; *Format:* Oldies; *No. News Employees:* 3; *Target Audience:* General.
Dana Schulte, Vice President/General Manager/Operations Director
Dennis O'Brien, Operations Manager
Roger McCoy, Internet Content Manager

Elyria

WEOL
10-17-1948; 930 kHz AM; *Hrs Open:* 24; 1 kw-D, 1 kw-N
538 Broad St., 4th Floor, Elyria, OH 44035 USA
(440) 322-3761; *Fax:* (440) 284-3189
weol.northcoastnow.com
bvandyke@weol.com
License: Elyria, OH held by Elyria-Lorain Broadcasting Co.
Group Owner: Elyria-Lorain Broadcasting Co.
Nat'l Network: ABC; *Nat'l Reps:* McGavren Guild *Regional Reps:* Rgnl Reps.; *Wire Services:* AP
Arbitron Metro Market: Elyria, OH; *Format:* News/Talk, Sports *Special Programming:* Sp 2 hrs wkly; H.S. Sports; *No. News Employees:* 4; *Target Audience:* 35 plus.
Bruce Van Dyke, Operations Dir
Craig Adams, News Director

WNWV
10-18-1948; 107.3 MHz FM; 20 kw; 781 ft.; N41 16 10 W82 0 16
6133 Rockside Rd., Suite 102, Independence, OH 44131 USA
(216) 828-1073
www.1073thewave.net
mribbins@rcrg.net
License: Elyria, OH held by Rubber City Radio Group, Inc.
Group Owner: Rubber City Radio Group, Inc.
Nat'l Reps: McGavren Guild *Regional Reps:* Regional Reps; *Wire Services:* AP

Arbitron Metro Market: Cleveland, OH *TV Affiliate:* Jazz; *Format:* Adult Contemp *Special Programming:* News progmg 4 hrs wkly; *No. News Employees:* 25 plus; upscale
Mark Ribbins, Operations Mgr/Program Dir
Logan Rice, Promotions Manager

Englewood

WYDB
02-20-1962; 94.5 MHz FM; *Hrs Open:* 24; 3.6 kw; 427 ft.; N39 49 3 W84 14 53
50 East Rivercenter Boulevard, Suite 1200, Covington, KY 41011 US
(937) 224-1137; *Fax:* (937) 224-3667
www.hotcountryb945.com
License: Englewood, Montgomery County, OH held by Aloha Station Trust LLC
Arbitron Metro Market: Dayton, OH; *Format:* Adult Contemp; *Target Audience:* 35-64; persons 35-64
Robert Zurowesti, Operations Dir
Karrie Sudbrack, General Manager
Jeff Stevens, Operations Manager

Enon

WCLI-FM
08-01-1965; 101.5 MHz FM; *Hrs Open:* 24; 6 kw; 328 ft.; N39 53 02 W84 04 17
717 E. David Rd., Kettering, OH 45429 US
(937) 294-5858
www.1015hankfm.com
License: Enon, Clark County, OH held by Alpha Media Licensee LLC
Group Owner: Alpha Media LLC; (acq 4-17-2014; grpsl).
Population Served: 250,000; *Arbitron Metro Market:* Dayton, OH; *Format:* Country; *Target Audience:* 25-54; above-average income, blue-collar; *Adv. Rates:* 30; 26; 26; 22
John King, General Manager
Keith Wright, Director of Sales
Andy Lawrence, Account Executive

Fairborn

WGNZ
09-01-1968; 1110 kHz AM
Mailing Address: 8010 North Main, Dayton, OH 45415 US
Second Address: PO Box 1100, Dayton, OH 45405
(937) 454-9000; *Fax:* (937) 454-1980
www.wgnz.com
License: Fairbom, OH held by L & D Broadcasters Inc.
Nat'l Network: Salem Radio Network
Arbitron Metro Market: Dayton, OH; *Format:* Gospel, Religious; *Target Audience:* General; listeners who like family radio
Tim Livingston, President

*WWSU
04-04-1977; 106.9 MHz FM; *Hrs Open:* 24; 0.02 kw; 210 ft.; N39 46 57.2 W84 3 42
Office of General Counse, 120g Allyn Hall -, Dayton, OH 45435 US
(937) 775-5554; *Fax:* (937) 775-5553
www.listen.to/wwsu
wwsugeneralmanager@yahoo.com
License: Fairbom, Montgomery County, OH held by Wright State University.
Arbitron Metro Market: Dayton, OH; *Format:* Variety/Diverse *Special Programming:* Black 12 hrs, relg 11 hrs, gospel 3 hrs, jazz 3 hr; *Target Audience:* 15-26; college & high school students
Shannon McGrath, General Manager
Alexandra Simmons, Programming Director
Effamarie Valdez, Chief Engineer
Taylor Dicus, Music Director
Matthew Schirtzinger, Production/Training Director
Kristin Henshaw, Marketing Director
KennethBolton, Sports Director

Fairfield

WCNW
02-14-1964; 1560 kHz AM; 1 kw-C, DA2; 5 kw-D, DA2; N39 20 20 W84 31 30
8686 Michael Lane, Fairfield, OH 45014 US
(513) 829-7700; *Fax:* (513) 829-1560
License: Fairfield, OH held by Vernon R. Baldwin Inc.
Group Owner: Vernon R Baldwin Inc.; acq 6-11-84; $700,000;
Arbitron Metro Market: Cincinnati, OH; *Format:* Gospel, Religious
Marcella Baldwin, President

Findlay

WFIN
12-15-1941; 1330 kHz AM; *Hrs Open:* 24
Mailing Address: 551 Lake Cascade Parkway, Findlay, OH 45839 US
Second Address: 551 Lake Cascades Pkwy., Findlay, OH 45840
(419) 422-4545; *Fax:* (419) 422-6736
www.wfin.com
wfin@wfin.com
License: Findlay, OH held by Blanchard River Broadcasting Co.
Group Owner: The Findlay Publishing Co.; (acq 1949).
Nat'l Network: ABC; *Regional Network:* ABN Radio *Regional Reps:* Rgnl Reps.
Arbitron Metro Market: Findlay, OH; *Format:* News, News/Talk, 86 *Special Programming:* Farm 7 hrs, sports 12 hrs wkly; *No. News Employees:* 2; *Target Audience:* 45 plus.
David Glass, President
Kurt Heminger, Operations Dir
Mike Holman, General Manager
Bill Rice, Programming Director
Doug Jenkins, News Director
Dennis Rund, Chief Engineer
Vaun Wickerham, Agricultural Services Director
RogerKranz, Production Director
Chris Miller, Sports Director

WKXA-FM
01-01-1948; 100.5 MHz FM; *Hrs Open:* 24; 20 kw; 440 ft.; N40 55 0 W83 35 45
Mailing Address: 551 Lake Cascade Parkway, Findlay, OH 45840 US
Second Address: 551 Lake Cascades Pkwy., Findlay, OH 45840
(415) 422-4545; *Fax:* (419) 422-6736
www.wkxa.com
License: Findlay, Hancock County, OH held by Blanchard River Broadcasting Co.
Group Owner: The Findlay Publishing Co.
Regional Reps: Regional Reps
Format: Contemporary Hits/Top 40, Adult Contemp; *No. News Employees:* 2; *Target Audience:* 25-54.
Dave Glass, President
Kurt Heminger, Operations Dir
Mike Holman, General Manager
Meg Stevens, Programming Director
Chris Miller, News Director
Dennis Rund, Chief Engineer
Vaun Wickerham, Agricultural Services Director
ShirleyNebergall, Business Manager
Roger Kranz, Production Director

*WTKC
07-01-2006; 89.7 MHz FM; 0.2 kw; 85 ft.; N41 3 11 W83 39 13
701 N. Main Street, PO Box 1212, Findley, OH 45840 US
(419) 423-3285
www.wtkc897.com
wtkc89.7@sbcglobal.net
License: Findlay, Hancock County, OH held by Church of the Living God Ministries.
Arbitron Metro Market: Findlay, OH; *Format:* Christian, Talk
Juan Salinas, General Manager
Richard Lugo, Programming Director

Fort Shawnee

WZRX-FM
01-01-1991; 107.5 MHz FM; *Hrs Open:* 24; 1.35 kw; 495 ft.; N40 39 50 W84 5 7
667 West Market Street, Lima, OH 45801 US
(419) 223-2060; *Fax:* (419) 229-3888
www.1075wzrx.com
License: Fort Shawnee, Allen County, OH held by Citicasters Licenses Inc.
Group Owner: iHeartMedia; (acq 5-4-99; grpsl).
Nat'l Reps: Clear Channel
Arbitron Metro Market: Lima, OH; *Format:* Rock/AOR; *Hrs. of News Programming:* News progmg one hr wkly; *Target Audience:* 18-49; male dominated; *Adv. Rates:* 28; 22; 25; 11
Matt Bell, Market President
Jordan Treadway, Vice President of Sales

Fostoria

WBVI
01-01-1946; 96.7 MHz FM; *Hrs Open:* 24; 3 kw; 289 ft.; N41 6 0 W83 28 32
Mailing Address: 1800 Tiffin Avenue, Findlay, OH 45840 US
Second Address: Box 1624, Findlay, OH 45839
(419) 422-9284; *Fax:* (419) 425-8019
www.wbvi.com
License: Fostoria, Seneca County, OH held by TCB Holdings Inc.
Nat'l Network: Westwood One *Regional Reps:* OAB
Arbitron Metro Market: Findlay, OH; *Format:* Adult Contemp; *No. News Employees:* 1; *Target Audience:* 18-50.; *Adv. Rates:* 18; 18; 18; 18
Josh Hohman, General Manager
Trisha Meier, Promotions Director
Jim Duggan, News Director
Todd Groves, Account Executive
Amy Masterlasco, Account Executive
Deanna White, Traffic Manager

WFOB
12-09-1952; 1430 kHz AM; *Hrs Open:* 25.?Â ?; 1 kw-D, DA2; 1 kw-N, DA2; N41 6 6 W83 23 59
Mailing Address: P.O. Box 1157, 101 N. Main Street, Fostoria, OH 44883 US
Second Address: Box 1624, Findlay, OH 45840
(419) 435-1430; *Fax:* (419) 435-6611
www.wfob.com
production@wfob.com
License: Fostoria, OH held by TCB Holdings Inc. c/o Roppe Corp.
Nat'l Network: CBS; *Nat'l Reps:* Rgnl Reps
Format: Sports *Special Programming:* Sp 3 hrs wkly; *Target Audience:* General.
Josh Hohman, General Manager/Programming Director
Trisha Meier, Promotions Director
Amy Masterlasco, Account Executive
Deanna White, Traffic and Billing
Karen Waltermeyer, Administrative Assistant
Todd Groves, Account Executive

Fredericktown

WMAN-FM
09-14-1987; 98.3 MHz FM; *Hrs Open:* 24; 1.8 kw; Ant 423 ft; N40 34 27 W82 30 27 *Rebroadcasts:* Rebroadcasts WFXN-FM Galion 100%
1400 Radio Lane, Mansfield, OH 44906 US
(419) 529-2211; *Fax:* (419) 529-2516
www.wmanfm.com
License: Fredericktown, Knox County, OH held by Capstar TX LLC
Group Owner: iHeartMedia; (acq 2-12-2001; grpsl).
Nat'l Network: Fox News Radio
Format: News, News/Talk, 86 *Special Programming:* Underground Garage, House of Hair; *Target Audience:* 25-54; Male
Margie Tasseff, General Sales Mgr
Rusty Cates, Programming Director

Fremont

WFRO-FM
12-15-1946; 99.1 MHz FM; *Hrs Open:* 24; 11.5 kw; 364 ft.; N41 21 58 W83 5 20
1281 North River Road, Fremont, OH 43420 US
(419) 332-8218; *Fax:* (419) 333-8226
www.wfroradio.com
jonkerns@basbroadcasting.com
License: Fremont, Sandusky County, OH held by BAS Broadcasting Inc.
Group Owner: BAS Broadcasting Inc.; (acq 9-11-2002; $1.3 million)
Nat'l Network: ABC; *Regional Network:* Agrinet *Regional Reps:* Rgnl Reps
Format: Adult Contemp; *Hrs. of News Programming:* news progmg 5 hrs wkly; *No. News Employees:* 2; *Target Audience:* 25-54; adults; *Adv. Rates:* 20; 20; 20; 15
Tom Klein, CEO
Jim Lorenzen, President
Dave Campbell, Operations Dir
Jon Kerns, Programming Director
Tom Fullen, News Director
Adam Klien, Sales Representative
Russ Rutherford, Production Manager
Beverly Klein, BusinessManager

Gahanna

WCVO
10-13-1972; 104.9 MHz FM; *Hrs Open:* 24; 6 kw; 313 ft.; N40 4 4 W82 51 38
Mailing Address: P.O. Box 7, New Albany, OH 43054 US
Second Address: 4400 Reynoldsburg-New Albany Road, New Albany, OH 43054
(614) 289-5700; *Fax:* (614) 289-5796
www.1049theriver.com
theriver@1049theriver.com
License: Gahanna, Franklin County, OH held by Christian Voice of Central Ohio Inc.
Group Owner: Christian Voice of Central Ohio Inc.
Arbitron Metro Market: Columbus, Oh; *Format:* Adult Contemp, Christian; *Hrs. of News Programming:* 1.5; *Target Audience:* 25-54; Christian, politically aware, female, middle aged professionals

Dan Baughman, President
Todd Stack, Programming Director
Mike Russell, Music Director

Galion

WFXN-FM
11-08-1974; 102.3 MHz FM; *Hrs Open:* 24; 3.5 kw; 430 ft.; N40 45 26 W82 47 23
1400 Radio Lane, Mansfield, OH 44906 US
(416) 529-2211
www.wfxnthefox.com
License: Galion, Crawford County, OH held by Capstar TX LLC
Group Owner: iHeartMedia; (acq 2-12-2001; grpsl).
Nat'l Network: Fox News Radio
Format: Classic Rock *Special Programming:* Underground Garage 2hrs, House of Hair 2hrs; *Target Audience:* 25-54; Male
Margie Tasseff, General Sales Mgr

Gallipolis

WJEH
06-19-1950; 990 kHz AM; *Hrs Open:* 24
Mailing Address: 117 Portsmouth Road, Gallipolis, OH 45631 US
Second Address: 117 Portsmouth Rd., Gallipolis, OH 45631
(740) 446-3543; *Fax:* (740) 446-3001
License: Gallipolis, OH held by Sunny Broadcasting LLC
Nat'l Reps: Rgnl Reps
Format: Contemporary Hits/Top 40; *Hrs. of News Programming:* news progmg 10 hrs wkly; *No. News Employees:* 1; *Target Audience:* 35 plus.
Dave Diddle, General Manager
Tina Merry, Programming Director
Bob Triplett, Chief Engineer

WXBW
12-15-1961; 101.5 MHz FM; *Hrs Open:* 24; 50 kw; 492 ft.; N38 48 19 W82 13 36
Mailing Address: 555 Fifth Avenue, Suite K, Huntington, WV 25701 US
Second Address: 919 Fifth Ave., Suite 210, Huntington, WV 25701
(304) 523-8401; *Fax:* (304) 523-8045
www.bigbuck1015.com
License: Gallipolis, Gallia County, OH held by Kindred Communications Inc.
Group Owner: Kindred Communications Inc.; (acq 6-21-2006; $3.1 million)
Nat'l Network: Westwood One; *Nat'l Reps:* McGavren Guild
Arbitron Metro Market: Huntington-Ashl; *Format:* Adult Contemp; *Target Audience:* 24-49.
Mike Kirtner, Chief Executive Officer
Reeves Kirtner, Operations Manager
Rich Myhrwold, General Sales Mgr
Teresa Robinson, Traffic Manager
Jim Kowalski, Chief Engineer

Gambier

*WKCO
01-01-1975; 91.9 MHz FM; *Hrs Open:* 19; 0.265 kw horiz; 190 ft.; N40 22 25 W82 23 45
P.O. Box 312, Gambier, OH 43022 US
(740) 427-5412
wkco@kenyon.edu
License: Gambier, Knox County, OH held by Kenyon College.
Format: Variety/Diverse; *Hrs. of News Programming:* News progmg 8 hrs wkly; *Target Audience:* 18-25; college population
Kelsey Vogt, Co-General Manager/Webmaster
Hugh Wilikofsky, Co-General Manager
John Ciecka, Co-Programming Director
Taylor Cornelius, Co-Programming Director
Lucie Levine, Co-Programming Director
Teddy Farkas, Music Director

Geneva

WKKY
11-02-1987; 104.7 MHz FM; *Hrs Open:* 24; 6 kw; 328 ft; N41 47 30 W81 05 31
95 W. Main St., Geneva, OH 44041
(440) 466-9559; *Fax:* (440) 466-3138
www.wkky.com
wkky@wkky.com
License: Geneva, Ashtabula County, OH held by Music Express Broadcasting Corp. of Northeast Ohio
Nat'l Network: ABC
Population Served: 128,000 *Special Programming:* Pub affrs 2 hrs wkly; *Hrs. of News Programming:* News progmg 6 hrs wkly; *Target Audience:* 25-54.

Warren Jones, President
Gary Hayes, General Manager
Clarence Bucaro, General Sales Mgr
Garth Cornell, Programming Director
Jim Pogras, Chief Engineer

Georgetown

WRAC
12-15-1981; 103.1 MHz FM; *Hrs Open:* 24; 6 kw; 328 ft.; N38 52 14 W83 45 55
114 South Manchester Ave., West Union, OH 45693 US
www.c103.fm
License: Georgetown, OH held by DreamCatcher Communications Inc.
Group Owner: DreamCatcher Communications Inc.; (acq 9-21-81; $4,820;)
Nat'l Reps: Rgnl Reps
Format: Country; *Target Audience:* General.
Don Bowles, President
Venita Bowles, Operations Dir
Ted Foster, Station Manager

Gibsonburg

WIMX
01-24-1989; 95.7 MHz FM; *Hrs Open:* 24; 3.5 kw; 433 ft.; N41 28 19 W83 25 5
720 Water Street, 4th Floor, Toledo, OH 43604 US
(419) 244-6354; *Fax:* (419) 244-8261
www.mix957.net
brandibrown@urbanradio.fm
License: Gibsonburg, Sandusky County, OH held by Urban Radio Licenses LLC.
Group Owner: Urban Radio Licenses LLC; (acq 5-13-2005; $2 million)
Nat'l Reps: Interep *Regional Reps:* Regional Reps
Arbitron Metro Market: Toledo, OH; *Format:* Adult Contemp
Special Programming: 0; *Target Audience:* 20-40.
Brandi Brown, Programming Director
Curtis Downey, Promotions Manager
John Guzan, Market Director of Sales
Kevin Hemmings, Market Manager

Granville

*WDUB
02-07-1962; 91.1 MHz FM; *Hrs Open:* 24; 0.1 kw; 171 ft.; N40 4 16 W82 31 24
Denison University, Slayter Union, Granville, OH 43023 US
(740) 587-9382
www.911wdub.com/
License: Granville, Licking County, OH held by Denison University.
Nat'l Network: USA; *Wire Services:* UPI
Arbitron Metro Market: Granville, OH.; *Format:* Classic Rock
Special Programming: Black 9 hrs, reggae 2 hrs, Sp 2 hrs, Swedish 2 hrs wkly; *No. News Employees:* 3; *Target Audience:* General; college students,faculty & loc residents

Greenfield

WVNU
05-01-1994; 97.5 MHz FM; *Hrs Open:* 24; 2.3 kw; 538 ft.; N39 24 26.6 W83 21 14
321 Jefferson Street, Greenfield, OH 45123 US
(937) 981-5050; *Fax:* (937) 981-2107
wvnu.com
License: Greenfield, Highland/Fayette County, OH held by Southern Ohio Broadcasting Inc.
Nat'l Network: Jones Radio Networks; CNN Radio; *Regional Network:* ABN Radio
Arbitron Metro Market: Cincinnati, OH; *Format:* Adult Contemp; *Target Audience:* 24-54.
Patrick Hays, President
Jody Wilson, Sales Manager
Nelson Eads, Programming Director
Elaine Hays, Promotions Manager
Christian Wheel, Chief Engineer

Greenville

WDSJ
10-26-1990; 106.5 MHz FM; *Hrs Open:* 24; 50 kw; 479 ft.; N40 8 49 W84 36 36
101 Pine Street, Dayton, OH 45402 US
(937) 224-1137; *Fax:* (937) 224-5015
www.big1065.com
TonyTilford@clearchannel.com
License: Greenville, Darke County, OH held by Aloha Station Trust LLC, as Trustee
Nat'l Network: Jones Radio Networks
Arbitron Metro Market: Dayton, OH; *Format:* Country; *Target Audience:* 25-54.
Tony Tilford, Operations Dir
Marvin Kopman, Director of Sales
Tony Tilford, Programming Director
Tom Doran, Market Manager

*WDPG
02-01-1994; 89.9 MHz FM; *Hrs Open:* 24; 50 kw; 403 ft; N40 08 49 W84 36 36 *Rebroadcasts:* Rebroadcasts WDPR(FM) West Carrollton 100%
126 N. Main St., Dayton, OH 45402
(937) 496-3850; *Fax:* (937) 496-3852
www.dpr.org
dpr@dpr.org
License: Greenville, Darke County, OH held by Dayton Public Radio Inc.

Shaun Yu, President/CEO/Programming Director
Larry Coressel, Operations Dir
Stephanie Llacuna, Promotions Manager
Jim Stitt, Chief Engineer
Nick Wilson, Corporate Support Coordinator
Zach Kramer, Music Director

Grove City

WOSA
08-21-1990; 101.1 MHz FM; *Hrs Open:* 24; 6 kw; 328 ft; N39 48 50 W83 03 19
2400 Olentangy River Road, Columbus, OH 43215
(614) 292-9678; *Fax:* (614) 292-0513
License: Grove City, Franklin County, OH held by The Ohio State University
Arbitron Metro Market: Columbus, OH; *Target Audience:* 21-40; well educated, upscale professionals with discretionary income;
Adv. Rates: 95; 95; 95; 45
Tom Rieland, General Manager

*WWGV
01-01-2008; 88.1 MHz FM; 5.4 kw vert; 272 ft.; N39 43 16 W83 8 36 *Rebroadcasts:* Rebroadcasts WAFR(FM) Tupelo, MS 100%
P.O. Box 3206, Tupelo, MS 38803 US
(662) 844-8888; *Fax:* (662) 842-6791
www.afr.net
faq@afa.net
License: Grove City, Franklin County, OH held by American Family Association.
Group Owner: American Family Radio
Nat'l Network: American Family Radio
Arbitron Metro Market: Grove City, OH; *Format:* Christian, Talk
Tim Wildmon, President
Donald Wildmon, Founder
Buddy Smith, Sr VP
Ed Vitagliano, Exec VP
Randy Sharp, Director Of Special Projects
Meeke Addison, Director Of Communications
Abraham Hamilton III, General Counsel

Hamilton

WGRR
02-09-1959; 103.5 MHz FM; *Hrs Open:* 24; 11 kw; 1037 ft.; N39 12 1 W84 31 22
4805 Montgomery Rd., Cincinnati, OH 45212 US
(513) 241-9898; *Fax:* (513) 241-6689
www.wgrr.com
info@cumulus.com
License: Hamilton, Butler County, OH held by Radio License Holding SRC, LLC
Group Owner: Cumulus Media Inc.; (acq 11-29-2007; exchange for WSWD-FM Fairfield)
Arbitron Metro Market: Cincinnati, OH; *Format:* Adult Contemp
Mike Combs, General Sales Mgr
Keith Mitchell, Programming Director
Nakia Fowler, Promotions Manager

*WHSS
05-12-1975; 89.5 MHz FM; *Hrs Open:* Midnight-noon; 190 w; 282 ft; N39 25 51 W84 37 40
5440 Moeller Avenue, Cincinnati, OH 45212
(513) 731-7740; *Fax:* (513) 731-6465
www.sacredheartradio.com
info@sacredheartradio.com
License: Hamilton, Butler County, OH held by Sacred Heart Radio Inc.
Population Served: 432,000 *Target Audience:* 12 plus; general
Bill Leavitt, Station Manager

WMOH
08-15-1944; 1450 kHz AM; *Hrs Open:* 24; 1 kw-U; N39 24 12 W84 31 50

2081 Fairgrove Ave., Hamilton, OH 45011 US
(513) 863-1111; *Fax:* (513) 863-6856
www.wmoh.com
License: Hamilton, Butler County, OH held by Vernon R. Baldwin Inc.
Group Owner: Vernon R Baldwin Inc.; acq 1-7-03; $950,000).
Nat'l Network: ESPN Radio; *Nat'l Reps:* Rgnl Reps
Arbitron Metro Market: Cincinnati, OH; *Format:* News, News/Talk, 84, Talk; *Hrs. of News Programming:* news progmg 25 hrs wkly; *No. News Employees:* 5; *Target Audience:* 35-64; adults above medium income *Adv.Rates:* 22; 18; 20; 12
Chris Theiss, Station Manager
Brian Kauffmann, Sales Manager
Steve Vaughn, News Director
Susan Theiss, Business Manager

Harrison

*WORI

07-01-1998; 90.1 MHz FM; *Hrs Open:* 24; 15 kw; Ant 335 ft; N39 13 34 W84 42 59
Box 2118, Omaha, NE 68103-2118
(888) 937-2471
www.air1.com
License: Harrison, Hamilton County, OH held by Educational Media Foundation.
Group Owner: EMF Broadcasting; (acq 10-2-2003; grpsl)
Nat'l Network: Air 1
Arbitron Metro Market: Cincinnati, OH; *Target Audience:* 18-35; Judeo Christian, female
Darrell Chambliss, Chairman
Mike Novak, President/CEO
Alan Mason, COO
Eric Moser, CFO
David Pierce, Chief Creative Officer
D. Kevin Blair, Secretary/General Counsel

Heath

WHTH

10-16-1970; 790 kHz AM; *Hrs Open:* 24; 1 kw-D, DA-1; N40 03 05 W82 28 08
Mailing Address: Box 1057, Newark, OH 43058
Second Address: 1000 N. 40th Street, Newark, OH 43058
(740) 522-8171; *Fax:* (740) 522-8174
www.wnko.com
studio@wnko.com
License: Heath, Licking County, OH held by Runnymede Corp.
Nat'l Network: CNN Radio; *Wire Services:* AP
Population Served: 140,000; *Arbitron Metro Market:* Columbus, OH; *Target Audience:* 35-54.; *Adv. Rates:* 15; 12; 15; 10
John Franks, President
J. Thomas Swank, General Manager
Ben E. Krooze, Programming Director
Dave Doney, News Director

Hicksville

WFGA

01-01-2002; 106.7 MHz FM; 2.8 kw; 492 ft.; N41 25 24 W84 51 36
2915 Maples Road, Fort Wayne, IN 46816 US
(260) 471-5100; *Fax:* (260) 920-3604
feedback@thefanfortwayne.com
License: Hicksville, Defiance County, OH held by Federated Media
Arbitron Metro Market: Fort Wayne, IN; *Format:* Variety/Diverse
John Dill III, President/CEO
Joel Pyle, Director of Sales
Nikki Jasperson, Promotions Manager

Hilliard

WBWR

02-06-1991; 105.7 MHz FM; *Hrs Open:* 24; 2.4 kw; 522 ft.; N39 58 10 W83 0 10
2323 West Fifth Avenue, Columbus, OH 43204 US
(614) 486-6101; *Fax:* (614) 487-2559
www.thexcolumbus.com
License: Hilliard, Franklin County, OH held by Citicasters Licenses Inc.
Group Owner: iHeartMedia; (acq 1999; grpsl).
Nat'l Network: ABC
Arbitron Metro Market: Columbus, OH; *Format:* Alternative; *No. News Employees:* 1; *Target Audience:* 18-34.
Michael McCoy, Senior Vice President of Programming
Eric Feucht, General Sales Mgr
Mike Elliot, Programming Director
Chad Highland, Promotions Director

Hillsboro

WSRW

07-15-1956; 1590 kHz AM; 500 w-D; N39 09 58 W83 36 25
1535 N. North Street, Washington Court House, OH 43160 US
(740) 335-0941
www.buckeyecountry105.com
License: Hillsboro, Highland County, OH held by CC Licenses LLC.
Group Owner: iHeartMedia; (acq 10-26-99; $2.5 million with WSRW-FM Hillsboro)
Nat'l Network: Jones Radio Networks; *Nat'l Reps:* Katz Radio
Population Served: 75,000 *Format:* Country; *Hrs. of News Programming:* News progmg 3 hrs wkly; *Target Audience:* 35-54; general; *Adv. Rates:* 10; 10; 10; 10
Dan Latham, Market President

Holland

*WPOS-FM

09-01-1966; 102.3 MHz FM; *Hrs Open:* 24; 6 kw; 312 ft.; N41 37 32 W83 42 41
Mailing Address: PO Box 457, Holland, OH 43528 US
Second Address: 7112 Angola Rd., Holland, OH 43528
(419) 865-5551; *Fax:* (419) 865-0112
www.wposfm.com
radio@wposfm.com
License: Holland, Lucas County, OH held by Maumee Valley Broadcasting Association.
Format: Christian *Special Programming:* Gospel 20 hrs wkly; *Hrs. of News Programming:* News progmg 10 hrs wkly
Craig Magrum, General Manager
Cliff Smithers, Programming Director
Tim Hauenstein, Music Director
Linda Lingo, Traffic Manager

Huron

WKFM

01-13-1995; 96.1 MHz FM; *Hrs Open:* 24; 3.4 kw; 436 ft.; N41 18 5 W82 29 16
10327 Milan Rd., US Route 250, Milan, OH 44846 USA
(419) 609-5961; *Fax:* (419) 609-2679
wkfm.northcoastnow.com
bforthofer@wkfm.com
License: Huron, Erie County, OH held by Elyria-Lorain Broadcasting Co.
Group Owner: Elyria-Lorain Broadcasting Co.; (acq 7-1-96; $450,000)
Nat'l Network: Westwood One; *Regional Network:* ABN Radio; *Nat'l Reps:* McGavren Guild
Arbitron Metro Market: Cleveland, OH; *Format:* Country; *Hrs. of News Programming:* news progmg one hr wkly; *No. News Employees:* 1; *Target Audience:* General.
Bill Forthofer, Stations Mgr
Kami Moon, Promotions Dir/Program Dir
Carol Walters, Office Manager

Ironton

WLRX

07-01-1973; 107.1 MHz FM; *Hrs Open:* 18; 3.1 kw; Ant 449 ft; N38 31 23 W82 39 11
8044 Montgomery Road, Suite 650, Cincinnati, OH 45236 US
(304) 525-7788; *Fax:* (304) 525-3299
kiss107fm@clearchannel.com
License: Ironton, Lawrence County, OH held by Clear Channel Media and Entertainment
Arbitron Metro Market: Huntington-Ashland, WV-KY *Special Programming:* Relg 2 hrs wkly; *Hrs. of News Programming:* News progmg 3 hrs wkly; *Target Audience:* 35 plus; affluent, middle-aged
Chuck Fredrick, President/Marketing Manager
Paul Frodge, Local Sales Manager
Jare, Programming Director
Dave Abbott, Chief Engineer
Dan Gialluca, Marketing Director

WIRO

09-01-1951; 1230 kHz AM; *Hrs Open:* 24; 1 kw-U, ND1; N38 32 22 W82 40 17
134 4th Avenue, Huntington, WV 25701 US
(304) 525-7788; *Fax:* (304) 525-6281
www.800wvhu.com
paulswann@clearchannel.com
License: Ironton, OH held by Aloha Station Trust LLC
Nat'l Reps: Keystone (unwired net); Rgnl Reps
Arbitron Metro Market: Huntington-Ashland, WV-KY; *Format:* News, News/Talk, 86 *Special Programming:* Relg 7 hrs wkly; *Hrs. of News Programming:* News progmg 5 hrs wkly; *Target Audience:* 21-49.
Judy Jennings, General Manager
Jim Davis, Programming Director
Bill Cornwell, News Director

*WOUL-FM

10-12-1987; 89.1 MHz FM; *Hrs Open:* 24; 50 kw; 400 ft.; N38 31 23 W82 39 20 *Rebroadcasts:* Rebroadcasts WOUB-FM Athens 100%
9 South College Street, Athens, OH 45701 US
(740) 593-4554; *Fax:* (740) 593-0240
www.woub.org
woub@woub.org
License: Ironton, Lawrence County, OH held by Ohio University.
Nat'l Network: PRI; NPR
Format: News, News/Talk, 86; *No. News Employees:* 3
Terry Douds, Operations Dir
Thomas Hodson, Director/General Manager
Joan Butcher, Programming Director
Tim Sharp, News Director
Jeannie Jeffers, Development Director

Jackson

WCJO

01-01-1971; 97.7 MHz FM; *Hrs Open:* 24; 3 kw; 299 ft.; N39 1 45 W82 35 51
Mailing Address: 235 Water Street, Jackson, OH 45640 US
Second Address: 295 E. Main St., Jackson, OH 45640
(740) 286-3023; *Fax:* (740) 286-6679
jmossbarger@jcbiradio.com
License: Jackson, Jackson County, OH held by Jackson County Broadcasting Inc.
Group Owner: Jackson County Broadcasting Inc.; (acq 6-15-99; grpsl).
Nat'l Network: Westwood One
Arbitron Metro Market: Jackson, Oh; *Format:* Country; *Hrs. of News Programming:* news progmg 8 hrs wkly; *No. News Employees:* 1; *Target Audience:* General; current-country music lovers; *Adv. Rates:* 17; 14; 17;9
Jerry Mossbarger, General Manager
Ron Speakman, General Sales Mgr
John Pelletier, Programming Director

Jefferson

*WCVJ

01-01-1978; 90.9 MHz FM; 1.85 kw; 643 ft.; N41 37 50 W80 45 36
4422 Lenox New Lyme Road, Jefferson, OH 44047 US
(888) 937-2471; *Fax:* (916) 251-1650
www.air1.com
info@air1.com
License: Jefferson, Ashtabula County, OH held by Educational Media Foundation.
Group Owner: EMF Broadcasting; (acq 10-14-2005; $650,000)
Nat'l Network: Air 1
Arbitron Metro Market: Jefferson, Oh; *Format:* Alternative, Christian
Alan Mason, COO
Mike Novak, President
David Pierce, Chief Creative Officer
Ed Lenane, News Director
Sam Wallington, Engineering Dir
Chuck Pryor, Director of Programming
Richard Hunt, News Reporter

Johnstown

WVKO-FM

06-16-1975; 103.1 MHz FM; 1.6 kw; 443 ft.; N40 13 44 W82 39 35.8
3360 East Livingston, Sutie 2A, Columbus, OH 43227 US
(614) 824-2550; *Fax:* (614) 224-2139
wvko1580am@gmail.com
License: Johnstown, Licking County, OH held by Gold Chip Communication
Group Owner: Bernard Radio LLC; (acq 1-22-2007; grpsl)
Nat'l Reps: D & R Radio
Arbitron Metro Market: Columbus, OH; *Format:* Tejano; *Target Audience:* 18-54; upscale, professional; homeowners with disposable incomes; *Adv. Rates:* 34; 25; 34; 22
Alvis Moore, Operations Dir
Wayne Dandridge, Music Director

Kent

WJMP

03-01-1964; 1520 kHz AM; 1 kw-D, DAD; N41 9 37 W81 18 16
Mailing Address: Box 2170, Akron, OH 44309 US
Second Address: 2449 S.R. 59, Kent, OH 44240
(330) 673-2323; *Fax:* (330) 673-0301
License: Kent, OH held by Media-Com Inc.

Arbitron Metro Market: Akron, OH; *Format:* Sports; *Target Audience:* 18 plus.
William Klaus, CEO/Station Manager
Robert Klaus, President/General Sales Manager
Phil Ferguson, News Director
Dan Mammone, Chief Engineer
Cathy Heavner, Traffic Manager

***WKSU-FM**
01-01-1950; 89.7 MHz FM; *Hrs Open:* 24; 14.5 kw; Ant 909 ft; N41 04 58 W81 38 02
Mailing Address: Box 5190, Kent, OH 44242
Second Address: 1613 E. Summit St., Kent, OH 44242-0001
(330) 672-3114; *Fax:* (330) 672-4107
www.wksu.org
letters@wksu.org
License: Kent, Portage County, OH held by Kent State University.
Nat'l Network: PRI; NPR; AP Radio
Population Served: 2,650,000; *Arbitron Metro Market:* Akron, OH *Special Programming:* Folk 12 hrs wkly; *Hrs. of News Programming:* news progmg 35 hrs wkly; *No. News Employees:* 5; *Target Audience:* 35-65;college grad, professional & upper income
Kandy Neal, Operations Coordinator
Dan Skinner, Executive Director/General Manager
M L Schutlze, Web Content Director
Ronald Bartlebaugh, Engineering Dir
Ruth Krise, Senior Development Associate

WNIR
02-19-1962; 100.1 MHz FM; 4.2 kw; 394 ft.; N41 6 28 W81 21 19
Mailing Address: P. O. Box 2170, Akron, OH 44309 US
Second Address: 2449 S.R. 59, Kent, OH 44240
(330) 673-2323; *Fax:* (330) 673-0301
www.wnir.com
bobklaus@wnir.com
License: Kent, Portage County, OH held by Media-Com Inc.
Wire Services: AP
Arbitron Metro Market: Akron, OH; *Format:* Talk; *Target Audience:* General.
Bill Klaus, CEO/COO
Bob Klaus, President/General Sales Manager
Phil Ferguson, News Director
Dan Mammone, Chief Engineer

Kenton

WKTN
06-20-1963; 95.3 MHz FM; *Hrs Open:* 5 AM-midnight; 3.5 kw; 276 ft.; N40 38 41 W83 33 59
112 North Detroit Street, Kenton, OH 43326 US
(419) 675-2355; *Fax:* (419) 673-1096
www.wktn.com
License: Kenton, Hardin County, OH held by Radio General Ltd.
Format: Adult Contemp *Special Programming:* Farm 2 hrs wkly; *Hrs. of News Programming:* news progmg 10 hrs wkly; *No. News Employees:* 1; *Target Audience:* 25-54.
Keith Gensheimer, President/General Manager
Barb Scott, Sales Director
Amy Chiles, Programming Director
Dennis Beverly, News Director
Andrew Flynn, Webmaster

Kettering

***WKET**
05-05-1975; 98.3 MHz FM; 0.013 kw horiz; 249 ft.; N39 41 46 W84 9 43
3301 Shroyer Road, Kettering, OH 45429 US
(937) 499-1688; *Fax:* (937) 297-7435
www.fairmontmediaproductions.com/wket-radio
License: Kettering, Montgomery County, OH held by Kettering City School District.
Arbitron Metro Market: Dayton, OH; *Format:* Classic Rock, Rock/AOR; *Target Audience:* 13-18; high school students
Laura Hutchens/Scott Leo, General Manager

WCHD
01-01-1962; 99.9 MHz FM; 28 kw; N39 43 19 W84 12 33
101 Pine Street, Dayton, OH 45402 US
(937) 224-1137; *Fax:* (937) 224-5015
www.channeldayton.com
License: Kettering, Montgomery County, OH held by Citicasters Licenses Inc.
Group Owner: iHeartMedia
Arbitron Metro Market: Dayton, OH; *Format:* Contemporary Hits/Top 40
Dave Litteral, Senior Vice President of Sales

Lancaster

***WFCO**
08-01-1988; 90.9 MHz FM; *Hrs Open:* 24; 0 kw horiz, 1.2 kw vert; 256 ft.; N39 40 49 W82 35 51
201 South Broad Street, Suite 303, Lancaster, OH 43130 US
(740) 689-0909; (866) 430-0909; *Fax:* (740) 654-8581
wfcofm.com
wfco@wfcofm.com
License: Lancaster, Fairfield County, OH held by Lancaster Educational Broadcasting Foundation.
Nat'l Network: Salem Radio Network
Arbitron Metro Market: Lancaster, OH; *Format:* Christian, News, 62, Talk *Special Programming:* Live coverage of sports & community events; *Hrs. of News Programming:* news progmg one hr wkly; *No. News Employees:* 1 *Target Audience:* 30 plus; Christian audience & those interested in community events
John Hablitzel, Operations Dir
Steve Rauch, General Manager
Steve Rauch, Station Manager
Mark Linn, Sales and Marketing Manager
Josh Messerly, News and Production Director
Andy Smeltzer, Sports Director
Amy Fratturo, OfficeManager
Andy Smeltzer, Sports Assistant

WZOH-FM
12-01-1958; 95.5 MHz FM; *Hrs Open:* 24; 21 kw; 761 ft.; N39 40 32 W82 40 34
350 E. 1st Ave., Suite 100, Columbus, OH 43201 US
(614) 487-1444; *Fax:* (614) 487-5862
www.mycolumbusmagic.com
License: Lancaster, Fairfield County, OH held by Wilks License Co.-Columbus LLC.
Group Owner: Radio One.; (acq 1-10-2007; grpsl)
Nat'l Reps: Christal
Arbitron Metro Market: Columbus, OH; *Format:* Urban Contemporary; *Hrs. of News Programming:* news progmg 2 hrs wkly; *No. News Employees:* 1; *Target Audience:* 25-54.
Randy Hershoff, General Manager
Mat Myers, Programming Director

WLOH
10-01-1948; 1320 kHz AM; *Hrs Open:* 24
PO Box 116, Lancaster, OH 43130 US
(740) 653-4373; *Fax:* (740) 653-0702
www.wloh.net
community@wloh.net
License: Lancaster, OH
Nat'l Reps: D & R Radio
Arbitron Metro Market: Columbus, OH; *Format:* Talk *Special Programming:* Farm one hr wkly; *Hrs. of News Programming:* news progmg 24 hrs wkly; *No. News Employees:* 2; *Target Audience:* General; Fairfield,Franklin & surrounding county residents
Mark Bohach, Operations Dir
Arlene Bohach, General Manager
Anne Darling, News Director
JR Smith, Sports Director

Lebanon

WFTK
05-26-1958; 96.5 MHz FM; *Hrs Open:* 24; 19.5 kw; 810 ft.; N39 21 11 W84 19 30
4805 Montgomery Rd., Suite 300, Cincinnati, OH 45212 US
(513) 241-9898; *Fax:* (513) 241-6689
www.purerock96.com
jon.laing@cumulus.com
License: Lebanon, OH held by Radio License Holding SRC, LLC
Group Owner: Cumulus Media Inc.
Arbitron Metro Market: Lebanon, OH; *Format:* Rock/AOR
John Laing, Sales Manager
Vinny Moses, Promotions Manager

Lexington

***WFOT**
02-01-2007; 89.5 MHz FM; 0.36 kw vert; 304 ft.; N40 43 36 W82 36 59
4673 Winterset Rive, Columbus, OH 93220 US
(614) 489-4820
www.stgabrielradio.com
info@stgabrielradio.com
License: Lexington, Richland County, OH held by Our Lady of Guadalupe Radio, Inc.
Nat'l Network: EWTN Radio
Arbitron Metro Market: Lexington, OH; *Format:* Christian
Bill Messerly, Executive Director
Dave Orsborn, Production Manager

Lima

WEGE
11-25-1970; 104.9 MHz FM; *Hrs Open:* 24; 3 kw; 220 ft.; N40 43 21 W84 5 4
57 Town Square, Lima, OH 45801 US
(419) 331-1600; *Fax:* (419) 228-5085
www.1049theeagle.com/
License: Lima, Allen County, OH held by Childers Media Group LLC
Group Owner: Childers Media Group LLC; (acq 12-4-2003; grpsl)
Nat'l Network: ABC; *Nat'l Reps:* Christal
Arbitron Metro Market: Allen County, OH; *Format:* Classic Rock; *Target Audience:* 25-54; affluent, community involved
Matthew Childers, President
Tiffany Kayser, Sales Manager
Phil Austin, Programming Director
Dave Woodward, Promotions Director
Deb Klaus, Business Manager

***WGLE**
12-02-1981; 90.7 MHz FM; *Hrs Open:* 24; 50 kw horiz, 46 kw vert; 420 ft.; N40 39 15 W84 6 36 *Rebroadcasts:* Rebroadcasts WGTE-FM Toledo 100%
1270 South Detroit Avenue, Toledo, OH 43614 US
(419) 380-4600; *Fax:* (419) 380-4710
www.wgte.org
info@wgte.org
License: Lima, Allen County, OH held by The Public Broadcasting Foundation of Northwest Ohio.
Nat'l Network: PRI; NPR
Arbitron Metro Market: Lima, OH *TV Affiliate:* *WGTE-TV affil.; *Format:* News, Public Affairs *Special Programming:* Jazz 16 hrs, new age/eclectic 4 hrs wkly; *Hrs. of News Programming:* News progmg 23 hrs wkly *Target Audience:* General.
George Jones, Chairman
Marlon Kiser, CEO
Chris Pfeiffer, Operations Dir

WIMA
12-05-1948; 1150 kHz AM; *Hrs Open:* 24; 1 kw-D, DAN; 1 kw-N, DAN; N40 40 47 W84 6 34
667 West Market Street, Lima, OH 45801 US
(419) 223-2060; *Fax:* (419) 229-3888
www.1150wima.com
comments@1150wima.com
License: Lima, OH held by Citicasters Licenses Inc.
Group Owner: iHeartMedia; (acq 5-4-99; grpsl)
Nat'l Network: Fox News Radio; Fox Sports; *Nat'l Reps:* Clear Channel; *Wire Services:* AP
Arbitron Metro Market: Lima, OH; *Format:* News, News/Talk, 84, Talk *Special Programming:* Farm 5 hrs wkly; *Hrs. of News Programming:* news progmg 20 hrs wkly; *No. News Employees:* 1; *Target Audience:* 35 plus. *Adv. Rates:* 35; 32; 28; 12
Matt Bell, Market President
Jason Aldrich, Programming Director

WIMT
12-01-1948; 102.1 MHz FM; *Hrs Open:* 24; 11 kw; 1060 ft.; N40 38 3 W84 12 29
667 West Market Street, Lima, OH 45801 US
(419) 223-2060; *Fax:* (419) 229-3888
www.t102.com
comments@t102.com
License: Lima, Allen County, OH held by Citicasters Licenses Inc.
Group Owner: iHeartMedia; (acq 5-4-99)
Wire Services: AP
Arbitron Metro Market: Lima, OH; *Format:* Country; *Hrs. of News Programming:* news progmg one hr wkly; *No. News Employees:* 1; *Target Audience:* 25-54.; *Adv. Rates:* 55; 45; 50; 15
Matt Bell, Market President

WCIT(AM)
08-22-1963; 940 kHz AM; *Hrs Open:* 24; 250 w-D, DA-2; N40 43 21 W84 05 04
57 Town Square, Lima, OH 45801 US
(419) 331-1600; *Fax:* (419) 228-5085
License: Lima, Allen County, OH held by Childers Media Group LLC
Group Owner: Childers Media Group LLC; (acq 12-4-2003; grpsl)
Nat'l Reps: Christal; Rgnl Reps
Population Served: 220,000; *Arbitron Metro Market:* Lima, OH; *Format:* Urban Contemporary *Special Programming:* Jazz 2 hrs, relg 11 hrs wkly; *Hrs. of News Programming:* news progmg 20 hrs wkly; *No. News Employees:* 2; *Target Audience:* 35-54; affluent, community involved
Matthew Childers, President
Tiffany Kayser, Sales Manager
Phil Austin, Programming Director

RADIO - U.S.

Dave Woodward, Promotions Manager
Deb Klaus, Business Manager

***WTGN**
09-27-1966; 97.7 MHz FM; 6 kw; 299 ft.; N40 45 23 W84 8 0
1600 Elida Road, Lima, OH 45805 US
(419) 227-2525; *Fax:* (419) 222-5438
www.wtgn.org
wtgn@wcoil.com
License: Lima, Allen County, OH held by Associated Christian Broadcasters Inc.
Arbitron Metro Market: Lima, OH; *Format:* Christian
Wesley Lytle, President
Scott Young, General Manager
Dave Morris, Engineering Dir
Judi Skonieczny, Administrative Assistant

WWSR
07-01-1964; 93.1 MHz FM; *Hrs Open:* 24; 3 kw; 318 ft.; N40 45 47 W84 10 59
57 Town Square, Lima, OH 45801 US
(419) 331-1600; *Fax:* (419) 228-5085
www.931thefan.com
sportstalkwithkoza@wcoil.com
License: Lima, Auglaize County, OH held by Childers Media Group LLC
Group Owner: Childers Media Group LLC; (acq 12-4-2003; grpsl).
Nat'l Reps: Christal *Regional Reps:* Rgnl Reps.
Arbitron Metro Market: Lima, OH; *Format:* Contemporary Hits/Top 40; *Hrs. of News Programming:* news progmg 6 hrs wkly; *No. News Employees:* 1; *Target Audience:* 18-49; young, affluent women; *Adv. Rates:* 30; 25;27; 18
Matthew Childers, President
Phil Austin, Operations Manager
Aaron Matthews, Programming Director
Dave Woodward, Promotions Director
Robin Palmer, Traffic Director
Mark Gierhart, Chief Engineer
Vince Koza, Sports MarketingDirector
Deb Klaus, Business Manager
Tiffany Kayser, Director of Sales

***WYSM**
01-01-2001; 89.3 MHz FM; 3 kw; Ant 220 ft; N40 39 15 W84 06 36
5105 Glendale Ave., Suite C, Toledo, OH 43537
(419) 389-0893; *Fax:* (419) 381-0731
www.yeshome.com
yesfm@yeshome.com
License: Lima, Allen County, OH held by Side by Side Inc.
Arbitron Metro Market: Lima, OH
J. Todd Hostetler, General Manager
Jeff Howe, Programming Director
Janet Yonke, Underwriting Manager

Logan

WLGN
12-01-1967; 1510 kHz AM; *Hrs Open:* Sunrise-sunset; 0.25 kw-C, 1 kw-D
Mailing Address: P.O. Box 889, Blacksburg, VA 24063 US
Second Address: 1 Radio Lane, Logan, OH 43138
(540) 951-9791; *Fax:* (540) 961-2021
License: Logan, Hocking County, OH held by WLGN LLC.
Group Owner: Baker Family Stations; (acq 1-4-2005; $675,000 with co-located FM)
Nat'l Network: ABC; *Nat'l Reps:* Rgnl Reps
Format: Oldies; *Target Audience:* 18-54.
Scott Blazer, General Manager
Vicky Lutz, Creative Services

WKNA
12-10-1965; 98.3 MHz FM; *Hrs Open:* 24; 6 kw; 220 ft.; N39 31 43 W82 23 6
1 Radio Lane, Logan, OH 43138 US
(740) 380-9546; *Fax:* (740) 385-4022
www.983samfm.com
License: Logan, Hocking County, OH held by WLGN LLC.
Group Owner: Baker Family Stations
Format: Adult Contemp; *Hrs. of News Programming:* news progmg 25 hrs wkly; *No. News Employees:* 1
Scott Blazer, General Manager
Vicky Lutz, Creative Services
Scott Vermillion, Sports Services

London

WXMG
01-01-1965; 106.3 MHz FM; *Hrs Open:* 24; 6 kw; 328 ft; N39 53 05 W83 25 23
350 E. 1st Ave., Suite 100, Columbus, OH 45237 US
License: London, Franklin County, OH held by Blue Chip Broadcasting Licenses Ltd.
Group Owner: Radio One Inc.; (acq 4-30-01; grpsl).
Nat'l Network: ABC; *Nat'l Reps:* D & R Radio
Population Served: 1,603,000; *Arbitron Metro Market:* Columbus, OH; *Format:* Urban Contemporary; *No. News Employees:* 3; *Target Audience:* 18-34.
Alfred Liggins, President/CEO

Lorain

WDLW
12-01-1969; 1380 kHz AM; *Hrs Open:* 24; 0.5 kw-D, ND1; 0.057 kw-N, ND1; N41 25 48 W82 9 7
Mailing Address: PO Box 277, Oberlin, OH 44074 US
Second Address: 45624 State Rt. 20, Oberlin, OH 44047
(440) 774-1320; *Fax:* (440) 774-1336
www.woblwdlw.com
dwilber@woblwdlw.com
License: Lorain, OH held by WDLW Radio Inc.
Wire Services: AP
Arbitron Metro Market: Cleveland, OH; *Format:* Oldies; *Hrs. of News Programming:* news progmg 10 hrs wkly; *No. News Employees:* 3; *Target Audience:* 35-64.; *Adv. Rates:* 22.50; 21.50; 22.50; 19.50
Doug Wilber, President/General Manager

***WNZN**
01-01-1992; 89.1 MHz FM; 2.2 kw; 374 ft.; N41 18 34 W82 26 31
511 West 26th Street, Lorain, OH 44052 US
(419) 588-3700
License: Lorain, Lorain County, OH held by Spanish Cultural Network.
Arbitron Metro Market: Cleveland, OH *TV Affiliate:* Sp
William Sanchez, General Manager

WCLV
04-01-1961; 104.9 MHz FM; *Hrs Open:* 24; 6 kw; 328 ft.; N41 28 32 W81 59 24
50 E. Rivercenter Blvd., #1200, Covington, KY 41011 US
(216) 464-0900; *Fax:* (216) 464-2206
wclv@wclv.com
License: Lorain, Lorain County, OH held by Radio Seaway Inc.
Nat'l Reps: D & R Radio; Interep; *Wire Services:* AP
Arbitron Metro Market: Lorain, OH; *Format:* Classical *Special Programming:* Jazz 5 hrs, financial news one hr wkly; *Hrs. of News Programming:* News progmg 5 hrs wkly; *Target Audience:* 35-64; high-income, collegegraduates & professionals; *Adv. Rates:* 80; 80; 80; 80
Jerry Wareham, President/CEO
Jeff Carlton, Operations & Traffic Manger
Bill O'Connell, Programming Director
Dave Rodriguez, Chief Engineer
Robert Conrad, Co-Founder
John Simna, Music Director
Kent Geist, Senior Director,Development & Communications
Jerry Northern, Senior Director
John Phillips, Chief Financial Officer
Jim Mehrling, Technical Producer

Loudonville

WXXF
03-01-1990; 107.7 MHz FM; *Hrs Open:* 24; 6 kw; 328 ft.; N40 36 58 W82 5 34 *Rebroadcasts:* Rebroadcasts WFXN-FM Galion 100%
Suite 2, 115 S. Water St., Loudonville, OH 44842 US
(419) 529-2211; *Fax:* (419) 529-2516
www.wfxnthefox.com
License: Loudonville, Ashland County, OH held by Capstar TX LLC
Group Owner: iHeartMedia; (acq 2-12-2001; grpsl).
Nat'l Network: Fox News Radio
Arbitron Metro Market: Mansfield, OH; *Format:* Classic Rock *Special Programming:* Underground Garage, House of Hair; *Target Audience:* 25-54; Male
Keith Kennedy, Senior Vice President of Programming
Margie Tasseff, General Sales Mgr

Luckey

WPFX-FM
07-30-1990; 107.7 MHz FM; 5.2 kw; 350 ft; N41 07 04 W83 32 38
720 Water Street, 4th Floor, Toledo, OH 41011
(419) 255-0107; *Fax:* (419) 241-1077
www.1077wolf.com
License: Luckey, Wood County, OH held by Toledo Radio LLC
Group Owner: BAS Broadcasting Inc.; (acq 6-30-2008; grpsl)
Arbitron Metro Market: Toledo, OH
Daniel Dudley, President
Laura Hart, General Manager
Rusty Walker, Programming Director

Manchester

WAGX
10-26-1992; 101.3 MHz FM; *Hrs Open:* 24; 3 kw; 299 ft; N38-36-03, W83-40-22
Mailing Address: PO Box 492, Manchester, OH 41001
Second Address: 9503 Mason Lewis Road, Maysville, KY 41056
(606) 564-8474; *Fax:* (606) 564-8383
License: Manchester, Adams County, OH held by Jewell Schaeffer Broadcasting Inc.
Population Served: 125,000; *Arbitron Metro Market:* Cincinnati, OH; *Hrs. of News Programming:* local, 7 hrs per week; *Target Audience:* 25-54; upscale adults; *Adv. Rates:* upon request
James Wagner, President

Mansfield

WMAN
12-04-1939; 1400 kHz AM; *Hrs Open:* 24; 0.92 kw-U, ND1; 0.958 kw-U, ND1; N40 46 13 W82 32 36; N40 46 0 W82 32 48
1400 Radio Lane, Mansfield, OH 44901 US
(419) 529-2211; *Fax:* (419) 529-2516
www.wmanfm.com
rustycates@iheartmedia.com
License: Mansfield, OH held by Capstar TX LLC
Group Owner: iHeartMedia; (acq 8-7-00; grpsl).
Nat'l Network: CBS; Westwood One
Arbitron Metro Market: Mansfield, OH; *Format:* News, News/Talk, 86; *Hrs. of News Programming:* news progmg 30 hrs wkly; *No. News Employees:* 3; *Target Audience:* 35 plus; upscale, active mgmt/exec
Margie Tasseff, General Sales Mgr
Rusty Cates, Programming Director

***WOSV**
06-27-1989; 91.7 MHz FM; *Hrs Open:* 24; 0.75 kw; 449 ft.; N40 42 33 W82 29 11 *Rebroadcasts:* Rebroadcasts WOSU-FM Columbus 100%
2400 Olentangy River Rd, Columbus, OH 43210 US
(614) 292-9678; *Fax:* (614) 292-7625
www.wosu.org
wosu@osu.edu
License: Mansfield, Richland County, OH held by The Ohio State University.
Nat'l Network: PRI; NPR; *Wire Services:* AP
Format: Classical; *Hrs. of News Programming:* News progmg 28 hrs wkly; *Target Audience:* 35 plus.
Kevin Petrilla, Operations Dir
Thomas Rieland, General Manager
Michael Thompson, News Director
Mike Meadows, Chief Engineer
Beverly Ervine, Music Director
Meredith Hart, Director of Marketing & Communications
Nick Houser, DigitalMedia Director
Christine Sadic, Manager of Underwriting

***WVMC-FM**
03-01-1979; 90.7 MHz FM; *Hrs Open:* 24; 170 w; 100 ft; N40 43 19 W82 31 52
500 Logan Rd., Mansfield, OH 44907
(419) 744-9862; *Fax:* (419) 756-7470
www.wvmcfm.com
License: Mansfield, Richland County, OH held by Mansfield Christian School.
Population Served: 35,000 *Target Audience:* 18-34; middle income adults, mostly female
Scott Saunders, General Manager

WMFD
08-11-1962; 106.1 MHz FM; 40 kw; 545 ft.; N40 45 50 W82 37 4
2900 Park Avenue West, Mansfield, OH 44906 US
(419) 529-5900
www.wmfd.com
comments@wmfd.com
License: Mansfield, Richland County, OH held by Johnny Appleseed Broadcasting Co.
Regional Reps: Rgnl Reps
Arbitron Metro Market: Mansfield, OH; *Format:* Adult Contemp; *Hrs. of News Programming:* news progmg 10 hrs wkly; *No. News Employees:* 5; *Target Audience:* 25-54; female

WYHT
10-18-1962; 105.3 MHz FM; 50 kw; 371 ft.; N40 46 9 W82 32 23
1400 Radio Lane, Mansfield, OH 44906 US
(419) 529-2211; *Fax:* (419) 529-2516
www.wyht.com

License: Mansfield, Richland County, OH held by Capstar TX LLC
Group Owner: iHeartMedia
Arbitron Metro Market: Mansfield, OH; *Format:* Adult Contemp
Margie Tasseff, General Sales Mgr

Marietta

*WCMO
10-01-1960; 98.5 MHz FM; 0.004 kw; 105 ft.; N39 25 7 W81 26 32
215 Fifth Street, Marietta, OH 45750 US
(740) 376-3345; *Fax:* (740) 376-4807
www.marietta.edu
License: Marietta, Washington County, OH held by Marietta College.
Arbitron Metro Market: Marietta, Oh; *Format:* Rock/AOR
Marilee Morrow, General Manager

WMOA
09-08-1946; 1490 kHz AM; *Hrs Open:* 24
925 Lancaster Street, Marietta, OH 45750 US 45750
(740) 373-1490; *Fax:* (740) 373-1717
www.wmoa1490.com
jwharff@wmoa1490.com
License: Marietta, OH held by JAWCO Inc.
Nat'l Network: ABC Information & Entertainment; *Regional Network:* Ohio News Network
Arbitron Metro Market: Parkersburg, OH; *Format:* Adult Contemp, News, 84 *Special Programming:* Farm one hr, relg one hr, sports 15 hrs wkly; *Hrs. of News Programming:* news progmg 5 hrs wkly; *No. News Employees:* 1 *Target Audience:* 35 plus; mature, middle-class to affluent
John Wharff, President/Promotions Director
Stephanie Wiles, Station Manager
Andy Rex, Production Director
Kyle Wenzel, Public Service Director

*WMRT
11-13-1975; 88.3 MHz FM; 9.2 kw; 203 ft.; N39 25 7 W81 26 32
211 Fifth Street, Marietta, OH 45750 US
(740) 376-4800; *Fax:* (740) 376-4807
www.marietta.edu/~wmrt
License: Marietta, Washington County, OH held by Marietta College.
Arbitron Metro Market: Parkersburg, OH; *Format:* Jazz, News, 62, Talk
David St Peter, Station Manager

WRVB
12-01-1964; 102.1 MHz FM; *Hrs Open:* 24; 11 kw; 492 ft.; N39 19 27 W81 37 33
6006 Grand Central Ave., Parkersburg, WV 26105 US
(304) 295-6070
www.102theriver.com
License: Marietta, Washington County, OH held by CC Licenses LLC.
Group Owner: iHeartMedia; (acq 4-17-2001; grpsl).
Arbitron Metro Market: Parkersburg-Mar; *Format:* Contemporary Hits/Top 40; *Target Audience:* 25-54; general; *Adv. Rates:* 14; 12; 14; 12
Rodney Ortiz, Programming Director

WLTP
05-08-1996; 910 kHz AM; *Hrs Open:* 24
6006 Grand Central Avenue, Parkersburg, WV 26105 US
(304) 295-6070
www.newstalk910wltp.com
talk@wltp.com
License: Marietta, OH held by CC Licenses LLC.
Group Owner: iHeartMedia; (acq 9-4-2002).
Nat'l Network: CBS; Westwood One; AP Radio
Arbitron Metro Market: Marietta, OH; *Format:* News, News/Talk, 86; *Hrs. of News Programming:* news progmg 8 hrs wkly; *No. News Employees:* 1; *Target Audience:* 18-54; males
Rodney Ortiz, Senior Vice President of Programming
Jon Chalfant, Programming Director

Marion

WMRN-FM
02-27-1975; 94.3 MHz FM; *Hrs Open:* 24; 3 kw; 299 ft.; N40 36 27 W83 14 14
1330 North Main Street, Marion, OH 43302 US
(740) 383-1131; *Fax:* (740) 387-3697
www.buckeyecountry943.com
License: Marion, Marion County, OH held by Citicasters Licenses Inc.
Group Owner: iHeartMedia; (acq 1999; grpsl)
Nat'l Reps: Rgnl Reps
Arbitron Metro Market: Upper Sandusky- Marion- Bucyrus, Oh; *Format:* Country; *Target Audience:* 25-54.
Scott Shawver, Operations Manager

WMRN
12-23-1940; 1490 kHz AM
1330 North Main Street, Marion, OH 43302 US
(740) 383-1131; *Fax:* (740) 387-3697
www.wmrn.com
License: Marion, OH held by Citicasters Licenses Inc.
Group Owner: iHeartMedia; (acq 1999; grpsl)
Arbitron Metro Market: Marion, OH; *Format:* News, News/Talk, 86 *Special Programming:* Farm 5 hrs wkly; *Target Audience:* 35-65
Matt Bell, Market President
Jordan Treadway, Vice President of Sales

*WOSB
04-14-1998; 91.1 MHz FM; 2.5 kw horiz, 6.8 kw vert; 285 ft.; N40 41 4 W83 15 24 *Rebroadcasts:* Rebroadcasts WOSU-FM Columbus
2400 Olentagy River Rd, Columbus, OH 43210 US
(614) 292-9678; *Fax:* (614) 292-7625
www.wosu.org
License: Marion, Marion County, OH held by The Ohio State University.
Nat'l Network: NPR; *Wire Services:* AP
TV Affiliate: var
David Carville, Director of Planning
Mary Alice Akins, Senior Director of Operations
Brent Davis, Senior Content Director
Karen Olstad, COO
Thomas Rieland, General Manager
Beverly Ervine, Music Director

*WXMF
91.9 MHz FM; 6 kw; 305 ft.; N40 36 51 W83 12 56
Mailing Address: PO Box 158, Upper Sandusky, OH 43351 US
Second Address: 1800 East Wyandot Avenue, Upper Sandusky, OH 43351
(419) 294-2900
www.wxml.cc
contactus@newvision.fm
License: Marion, Marion County, OH held by Kayser Broadcast Ministries Inc.
Arbitron Metro Market: Marion, OH; *Format:* Christian, Religious
Daniel Kayser, President/General Manager
Jon & Carla Bowlus, Programming Director

Marysville

WQTT
12-01-1983; 1270 kHz AM; *Hrs Open:* 24; 500 w-U, DA-2; N40 14 46 W83 19 50
113 South Main Street, Marysville, OH 43040
(937) 644-1270
License: Marysville, Union County, OH held by ICS Communications Inc.
Population Served: 40,000; *Arbitron Metro Market:* Columbus, OH
Chris Gabrelcik, President
Gary Rivers, General Manager
Mike Schnell, General Sales Mgr
Farris Wilhite, Engineering Dir

Mason

WOXY
12-24-1959; 97.7 MHz FM; *Hrs Open:* 24; 3.5 kw; 436 ft.; N39 20 56.8 W84 12 8.2
4412 Carver Woods Drive, Cincinnati, OH 45242 US
(513) 891-1000; *Fax:* (513) 523-1412
License: Mason, Butler County, OH held by TSJ Media
Group Owner: TSJ Media; (acq 3-17-2004; $5.64 million).
Wire Services: AP
Arbitron Metro Market: Cincinnati, OH; *Format:* Alternative; *Target Audience:* 18-34.; *Adv. Rates:* 50; 50; 50; 50
Josh Guttman, General Sales Mgr
Claudia De Leon, Market Manager

Massillon

WTIG
08-01-1957; 990 kHz AM; *Hrs Open:* 24; 0.25 kw-D, DA2; 0.112 kw-N, DA2; N40 49 56 W81 33 40
P.O. Box 38, Massillon, OH 44648 US
(330) 837-9900
www.espn990.com
espn990@gmail.com
License: Massillon, OH held by WTIG Inc.
Arbitron Metro Market: Massillon, OH; *Format:* Sports *Special Programming:* Loc church svcs 6 hrs wkly; *Target Audience:* 25-54; male
Ray Jeske, President
Donovan Resh, Operations Dir

Maumee

*WYSZ
11-14-1992; 89.3 MHz FM; *Hrs Open:* 24; 2.45 kw horiz, 1.85 kw vert; 305 ft.; N41 38 55 W83 42 22
Mailing Address: 9035 Salisbury Road, Mouclova, OH 43542 US
Second Address: 501 Glendale Avenue, Suite C, Toledo, OH 43614
(419) 389-0893; *Fax:* (419) 381-0731
www.yeshome.com
yesfm@yeshome.com
License: Maumee, Lucas County, OH held by Side By Side Inc.
Arbitron Metro Market: Toledo, OH; *Format:* Christian; *Target Audience:* 15-25.
Jeff Howe, Station Manager/COO
Jamey Schmitz, CEO/General Manager
April O'Brien, Programming Director
Cindy Ulsell, VP

McArthur

WYRO
01-01-1994; 98.7 MHz FM; *Hrs Open:* 24; 5.4 kw; 344 ft.; N39 9 18 W82 35 49
Mailing Address: P.O. Box 606, Jackson, OH 45640 US
Second Address: 295 E. Main St., Jackson, OH 45640
(740) 286-3023; *Fax:* (740) 286-6679
License: McArthur, Vinton County, OH held by Davis Broadcasting Media Inc.
Nat'l Network: Westwood One *Regional Reps:* Rgnl Reps.
Format: Classic Rock; *No. News Employees:* 1; *Target Audience:* 18-65.; *Adv. Rates:* 18; 14; 18; 10
Jerry Mossbarger, General Manager
Ron Speakman, General Sales Mgr
John Pelletier, Programming Director

McConnelsville

WJAW-FM
10-01-1992; 100.9 MHz FM; *Hrs Open:* 24; 0.93 kw; 577 ft.; N39 33 24 W81 51 6
925 Lancaster Street, Marietta, OH 45750 US
(740) 373-1490; *Fax:* (740) 373-1717
www.wmoa1490.com
License: McConnelsville, Morgan County, OH held by Quiet Radio Inc. DIB/A WJAW Radio
Nat'l Network: ESPN Radio; *Regional Network:* Ohio News Network
Arbitron Metro Market: Columbus, OH; *Format:* Sports; *No. News Employees:* 1; *Target Audience:* 18-34; male
John Wharff III, Owner/President/Promotions
Bryon Sunderman, Chief Operator
Jamey Styer, Operations Dir
Andy Rex, Production Director

Medina

WQMX
01-01-1960; 94.9 MHz FM; *Hrs Open:* 24; 16 kw; 879 ft.; N41 4 58 W81 38 0
1795 West Market Street, Akron, OH 44313 US
(330) 869-9800; *Fax:* (330) 864-6799
wqmx.com
thom@wakr.net
License: Medina, Medina County, OH held by Rubber City Radio Group Inc.
Group Owner: Rubber City Radio Group Inc.; (acq 1988)
Nat'l Network: ABC; *Nat'l Reps:* Christal; *Wire Services:* AP
Arbitron Metro Market: Akron, OH; *Format:* Country; *Hrs. of News Programming:* news progmg 10 hrs wkly; *No. News Employees:* 10; *Target Audience:* 25-54; adults
Thomas Mandel, CEO
Nick Anthony, Operations Dir
Paul Christopherson, General Sales Mgr
Sue Wilson, Programming Director
Jody Wheatley, Promotions Manager
Ed Esposito, News Director
Al Hruska, COO
Ken Steel, Music Director
Mark Biviano, Senior Vice President

Miamisburg

WFCJ
01-07-1961; 93.7 MHz FM; *Hrs Open:* 24; 50 kw; 492 ft.; N39 39 35 W84 18 53

Mailing Address: P.O. Box 93.7, Dayton, OH 45449 US
Second Address: 7333 Manning Rd., Miamisburg, OH 45342
(937) 866-2471; *Fax:* (937) 866-2062
www.wfcj.com
inspiration@wfcj.com
License: Miamisburg, Montgomery County, OH held by Miami Valley Christian Broadcasting Association Inc.
Nat'l Network: USA; Salem Radio Network; *Nat'l Reps:* Salem; *Wire Services:* AP
Arbitron Metro Market: Miamisburg, OH; *Format:* Christian, Religious *Special Programming:* Black 3 hrs, children 2 hrs wkly; *Hrs. of News Programming:* News progmg 10 hrs wkly; *Target Audience:* 35-64; EvangelicalChristians; *Adv. Rates:* 25; 21; 25; 21
Bud Schindler, President
Jeff Jacobsen, Operations Dir
Bill Nance, Programming Director
John Nole, Traffic Manager
John Graham, Chief Engineer
Diane Akers, Office Manager

Miamitown

*WMWX
08-05-2006; 88.9 MHz FM; *Hrs Open:* 24; 4.6 kw; 374 ft.; N39 19 18 W84 57 33
5114 Princeton Glendale, Hamilton, OH 45011 US
(513) 436-0089
classxradio.com
classx@classxradio.com
License: Miamitown, Hamilton County, OH held by Spry Group Multimedia, LLC
Arbitron Metro Market: Miamitown, OH; *Format:* Classic Rock; *Target Audience:* 30-58.
Bill Spry, Founder, General Manager and Programming Director
Alex O'Bryan, Station Manager
Melodi C. Moon, Creative Content Coordinator

Middleport

WYVK
08-27-1973; 92.1 MHz FM; *Hrs Open:* 19; 4.7 kw; 364 ft.; N39 3 30 W82 2 31
39520 Bradbury Road, Middleport, OH 45760 US
(740) 992-6485; *Fax:* (740) 992-6486
www.wyvk.com
office@wyvk.com
License: Middleport, Meigs County, OH held by Positive Radio Group Inc. of Ohio
Arbitron Metro Market: Middleport, OH; *Format:* Contemporary Hits/Top 40; *Hrs. of News Programming:* News progmg 3 hrs wkly; *Target Audience:* 25-54.
Brenda Merritt, General Manager

Middleport-Pomeroy

WMPO
08-28-1959; 1390 kHz AM; 5 kw-D, 0.12 kw-N; N39 0 37 W82 3 58
P.O. Box 889, Blacksburg, VA 24063 US
(540) 951-9791; *Fax:* (540) 961-2021
License: Middleport-Pomeroy, Meigs County, OH held by Positive Radio Group Inc. of Ohio.
Group Owner: Baker Family Stations; (acq 1999; $492,000 with WYVK(FM) Middleport)
Nat'l Network: ESPN Radio; *Nat'l Reps:* Rgnl Reps
Arbitron Metro Market: Middleport, OH; *Format:* Sports *Special Programming:* Relg 6 hrs, farm one hr, gospel 18 hrs wkly; *Target Audience:* 35 plus.
Edward A. Baker, President

Middletown

WPFB
09-01-1947; 910 kHz AM; *Hrs Open:* 24
4505 Central Avenue, Middletown, OH 45044 US
(513) 422-3625; *Fax:* (513) 424-9732
www.wpfb.com
info@wpfb.com
License: Middletown, OH held by Northern Kentucky University
Nat'l Reps: Roslin
Arbitron Metro Market: Dayton, OH; *Format:* Country *Special Programming:* Radio Movie of the Week 2 hrs wkly; *Hrs. of News Programming:* news progmg 26 hrs wkly; *No. News Employees:* 2
Chuck Miller, General Manager

WNKN
07-01-1959; 105.9 MHz FM; *Hrs Open:* 24; 34 kw; 590 ft; N39 30 57 W84 21 05
4505 Central Ave., Middletown, OH 45044
(513) 422-3625; *Fax:* (513) 424-9732
License: Middletown, Butler County, OH
Population Served: 48,767; *Arbitron Metro Market:* Dayton, OH; *Target Audience:* 25-54.

Milford

WKFS
08-01-1969; 107.1 MHz FM; 2.8 kw; 866 ft.; N39 6 59 W84 30 7
8044 Montgomery Road, Suite 650, Cincinnati, OH 45236 US
(513) 686-8300
www.kiss107.com
License: Milford, Clermont County, OH held by Citicasters Licenses Inc.
Group Owner: iHeartMedia; (acq 5-4-99; grpsl)
Arbitron Metro Market: Cincinnati, OH; *Format:* Contemporary Hits/Top 40
Chuck Fredrick, President/Market Manager
Bo Matthews, Senior Vice President of Programming
DJ Hodge, Local Sales Manager
James Brooks, Digital Program Director
Brieann Sherlock, Promotions Director
Dave Abbott, Chief Engineer
Alethea Marshall, Community Engagement Director

Millersburg

WKLM
01-01-1988; 95.3 MHz FM; *Hrs Open:* 5:30 AM-midnight; 3 kw; 328 ft.; N40 29 9 W81 50 45
59750 Constantine Road, Three Rivers, MI 49093 US
(269) 278-1815; *Fax:* (269) 273-7975
www.wlkm.com
wklmradio@earthlink.net
License: Millersburg, Holmes County, OH held by WKLM Radio, Inc.
Group Owner: Coshocton Broadcasting Co.; acq 7-10-90; $490,000;
Nat'l Network: ABC
Format: Adult Contemp *Special Programming:* Loc sports; *Hrs. of News Programming:* news progmg 12 hrs wkly; *No. News Employees:* 1; *Target Audience:* General.
Bruce Wallace, President
Tom Thompson, General Sales Mgr
Matt Croy, Programming Director

*WVML
06-01-2004; 90.5 MHz FM; *Hrs Open:* 24; 15 kW; 367 ft.; N40 36 8 W81 44 32 *Rebroadcasts:* Rebroadcasts WCRF(FM) Cleveland 100%
9756 Barr Rd, Cleveland, OH 44141 USA
(440) 526-1111; *Fax:* (440) 526-1319
www.moodyradio.org/stations/cleveland
License: Millersburg, Holmes County, OH held by The Moody Bible Institute of Chicago
Group Owner: The Moody Bible Institute of Chicago
Wire Services: AP
Arbitron Metro Market: Millersburg, OH; *Format:* Christian; *Target Audience:* 25-55; Adults

Mount Gilead

WVXG
03-01-1994; 95.1 MHz FM; 6 kw; 328 ft.; N40 35 15 W82 48 20
501 Bowtown Road, Delaware, OH 43015 US
(614) 935-1038
www.951rocks.com
mschnell@icsohio.com
License: Mount Gilead, Morrow County, OH held by ICS Holdings Sub 1 Inc.
Arbitron Metro Market: Mount Gilead, OH; *Format:* Classic Rock
Gary Rivers, General Manager
Mike Schnell, General Sales Mgr

Mount Vernon

WMVO
11-26-1953; 1300 kHz AM; 0.41 kw-D, DA2; 0.051 kw-N, DA2; N40 24 17 W82 26 23
17421 Coshocton Road, Mt. Vernon, OH 43050 US
(740) 397-1000; *Fax:* (740) 392-9300
www.wmvo.com
License: Mount Vernon, OH held by BAS Broadcasting Inc.
Group Owner: BAS Broadcasting Inc.; (acq 10-1-2005; $2 million with WQIO(FM) Mount Vernon)
Nat'l Network: ABC; *Nat'l Reps:* Rgnl Reps; *Wire Services:* AP
Arbitron Metro Market: Mt. Vernon, OH; *Format:* News, News/Talk, 86 *Special Programming:* Relg 7 hrs wkly
Curtis Newland, Operations Manager
Doug Berg, General Manager
Tina Davis, Local Sales Manager

*WNZR
05-01-1986; 90.9 MHz FM; *Hrs Open:* 24; 1300 w; 300 ft; N40 22 14 W82 28 05
800 Martinsburg Rd., Mount Vernon, OH 43050
(740) 392-9090; *Fax:* (740) 392-9155
www.wnzr.fm
wnzr@mvnu.edu
License: Mount Vernon, Knox County, OH held by Mt. Vernon Nazarene University.
Nat'l Network: AP Radio; *Wire Services:* AP
Population Served: 61,275 *Hrs. of News Programming:* News progmg 5 hrs wkly; *Target Audience:* 25-54; Christian adults
Marcy Rinehart, Station Manager
Chris Runion, Sports Director
Zach Roys, Production Director
Jomar Shaffer, Promotions Director
Emily Blazek, Music Director
Joe Rineharf, Director of Broadcasting

WQIO
05-26-1951; 93.7 MHz FM; *Hrs Open:* 24; 37 kw; 564 ft.; N40 24 18 W82 26 20
17421 Coshocton Road, Mt. Vernon, OH 43050 US
(740) 397-1000; *Fax:* (740) 392-9300
info@ohioradio.com
License: Mount Vernon, Knox County, OH held by BAS Broadcasting Inc.
Group Owner: BAS Broadcasting Inc.; (acq 10-1-2005; $2 million with WMVO(AM) Mount Vernon)
Arbitron Metro Market: Columbus, OH; *Format:* Adult Contemp *Special Programming:* Hit mus 4 hrs, gospel 2 hrs wkly; *No. News Employees:* 1; *Target Audience:* 35-54.
Curtis Newland, Operations Dir
Tina Davis, Local Sales Manager

Munroe Falls

WKDD
11-19-1961; 98.1 MHz FM; *Hrs Open:* 24; 50 kw; 453 ft.; N41 12 0 W81 31 23
7755 Freedom Avenue, North Canton, OH 44720 US
(330) 492-4700; *Fax:* (330) 492-1350
www.wkdd.com
info@wkdd.com
License: Munroe Falls, Stark County, OH held by Citicasters Licenses Inc.
Group Owner: iHeartMedia; (acq 12-22-2000; grpsl).
Arbitron Metro Market: Canton, OH; *Format:* Contemporary Hits/Top 40
Mark Boarman, Market President
Keith Kennedy, Senior Vice President of Programming

Napoleon

WNDH
06-01-1972; 103.1 MHz FM; *Hrs Open:* 24; 3.3 kw; 300 ft; N41 18 00 W84 09 22
709 N. Perry St., Napoleon, OH 43545 US
(419) 592-8060; *Fax:* (419) 592-1085
www.wndh1031.com
License: Napoleon, Henry County, OH held by CC Licenses LLC.
Group Owner: iHeartMedia; (acq 1-1-2000; grpsl)
Nat'l Network: CBS *Regional Reps:* Rgnl Reps; *Wire Services:* AP
Format: Oldies; *No. News Employees:* 1; *Target Audience:* General.; *Adv. Rates:* 30; 25; 28; 12
Bob McLimans, Market President
John Schuette, General Sales Mgr
Judy Damman, Business Manager

Nelsonville

WSEO
09-01-1990; 107.7 MHz FM; *Hrs Open:* 24; 3 kw; 328 ft.; N39 27 38 W82 13 9
15751 U.S. Rt 33 South, Nelsonville, OH 45764 US
(740) 753-4094; *Fax:* (740) 753-4965
License: Nelsonville, Athens County, OH held by Nelsonville TV Cable Inc.
Format: Country *Special Programming:* Farm; *Hrs. of News Programming:* news progmg 15 hrs wkly; *No. News Employees:* 3; *Target Audience:* 25-49.
Eugene Edwards, President
Nick Brooks, Programming Director

New Albany

WNKO
12-08-1972; 101.7 MHz FM; *Hrs Open:* 24; 22 kw; 351 ft.; N40 8 38 W82 38 20
Mailing Address: P. O. Box 1057, Newark, OH 43058 US
Second Address: 1000 N. 40th Street, Newark, OH 43058

(740) 522-8171; *Fax:* (740) 522-8174
www.wnko.com
License: New Albany, Licking County, OH held by Runnymede Corp.
Nat'l Network: CNN Radio; *Wire Services:* AP
Arbitron Metro Market: Columbus, OH; *Format:* Contemporary Hits/Top 40; *No. News Employees:* 2; *Target Audience:* 25-54.; *Adv. Rates:* 25; 20; 23; 18
Ben Krooze, Programming Director
Dave Doney, News Director

New Boston

WIOI
09-02-1959; 1010 kHz AM; 1 kw-D, ND1; 0.022 kw-N, ND1; N38 43 48 W82 57 10
PO Box 1233, Portsmouth, OH 45662 US
(606) 932-4796; *Fax:* (606) 932-4796
www.wioiradio.com
License: New Boston, OH held by Maillet Media Inc.
Format: Adult Contemp
Chip Maillet, General Manager

WNKE
06-15-1948; 104.1 MHz FM; 100 kw; Ant 1,486 ft; N38 41 00 W83 00 46
4505 Central Avenue, Middletown, OH 45044
(513) 422-3625
License: New Boston, Scioto County, OH held by Northern Kentucky University
Nat'l Network: CBS
Population Served: 88,500
Chuck Miller, General Manager

New Concord

***WMCO**
01-28-1961; 90.7 MHz FM; *Hrs Open:* 6 AM-midnight; 1.3 kw; 85 ft.; N39 59 46 W81 43 18
163 Stormont St, Muskingum College, New Concord, OH 43762 US
(740) 826-8189
www.muskingum.edu
lisam@muskingum.edu
License: New Concord, Muskingum County, OH held by Muskingum College.
Arbitron Metro Market: New Concord, OH; *Format:* Variety/Diverse *Special Programming:* Class 4 hrs, jazz 10 hrs, relg 2 hrs wkly; *Hrs. of News Programming:* News progmg 10 hrs wkly; *Target Audience:* General,students
Lisa Marshall, Station Manager
Dr. Jeff Harmon, Director of Broadcasting

New Lexington

WWJM
05-01-1978; 106.3 MHz FM; *Hrs Open:* 24; 1.7 kw; 627 ft.; N39 46 37 W82 9 54
Mailing Address: 210 South Jackson St., New Lexington, OH 43764 US
Second Address: 247 Market St., Zanesville, OH 43701
(740) 342-1988; *Fax:* (740) 342-1036
wwjm.com
wwjm@aol.com
License: New Lexington, Perry County, OH held by Perry County Broadcasting Co.
Nat'l Network: Westwood One
Arbitron Metro Market: New Lexington, OH; *Format:* Adult Contemp; *Hrs. of News Programming:* news progmg 2 hrs wkly; *No. News Employees:* 1; *Target Audience:* 18-54; young to middle-aged *Adv. Rates:* 16,16,16,16
Charles Edwards, President/General Manager
Tina Edwards, Vice President
Cheyenne Campbellÿ, General Sales Mgr
Bill O'Reed, Operations Manager

New Philadelphia

***WKRJ**
07-12-1994; 91.5 MHz FM; 2 kw; 240 ft.; N40 33 50 W81 31 5
Rebroadcasts: Rebroadcasts WKSU-FM Kent 100%
Mailing Address: 1613 East Summit Street, Kent, OH 44242 US
Second Address: 1613 E. Summit St, Kent, OH 44242-0001
(330) 672-3114; *Fax:* (330) 672-4107
www.wksu.org
letters@wksu.org
License: New Philadelphia, Tuscarawas County, OH held by Kent State University.
Nat'l Network: NPR; PRI
Format: News; *Hrs. of News Programming:* news progmg 35 hrs wkly; *No. News Employees:* 5; *Target Audience:* 35-65; college grad, professional & upper income
Daniel E. Skinner, General Manager
David Roden, Programming Director
David Fuente, Promotions Coordinator
Amanda Rabinowitz, News Director
Ronald Bartlebaugh, Engineering Dir

WNPQ
02-02-1969; 95.9 MHz FM; *Hrs Open:* 24; 3 kw; 400 ft; N40 35 51 W81 29 32
3969 Convenience Cir. N.W., Suite 205, Canton, OH 44718
(330) 492-9590
www.thelight959.com
License: New Philadelphia, Tuscarawas County, OH held by Tuscarawas Broadcasting Co.
Nat'l Network: SRN Radio
Population Served: 300,000; *Arbitron Metro Market:* Canton, OH *Special Programming:* Black 4 hrs, southern gospel 4 hrs wkly; *Target Audience:* 18-49; family oriented; *Adv. Rates:* 15; 13; 15; 10.
James Natoli Jr., President
Tom Bishop, General Manager
Jan Markowitz, Programming/Promotions Diretor

Newark

WCLT
01-04-1949; 1430 kHz AM; *Hrs Open:* 24; 0.5 kw-D, ND1; 0.048 kw-N, ND1; N40 2 2 W82 24 8
Mailing Address: PO Box 5150, Newark, OH 43058 US
Second Address: 674 Jacksontown Rd. S.E., Heath, OH 43056
(740) 345-4004; *Fax:* (740) 345-5775
www.wclt.com
wclt@wclt.com
License: Newark, OH held by WCLT Radio Inc.
Nat'l Network: AP Radio; Fox News Radio; *Wire Services:* AP
Arbitron Metro Market: Columbus, OH; *Format:* News, News/Talk, 86; *Hrs. of News Programming:* news progmg 12 hrs wkly; *No. News Employees:* 2; *Target Audience:* General.
Douglas Pricer, President/General Manager
Tom Bunyard, General Sales Mgr
Walley Schneider, Programming Director
Jim Ferguson, Chief Engineer
Dave Johnson, Business Manager

WCLT-FM
08-07-1947; 100.3 MHz FM; *Hrs Open:* 24; 50 kw; 390 ft; N40 02 02 W82 24 08
Mailing Address: Box 5150, Newark, OH 43055
Second Address: 674 Jacksontown Rd. S.E., Newark, OH 43056
(740) 345-4004; *Fax:* (740) 345-5775
www.wclt.com
License: Newark, Licking County, OH
Nat'l Network: ABC; *Wire Services:* AP
Arbitron Metro Market: Columbus, OH; *Target Audience:* 25-54.
Douglas C. Pricer, President/General Manager
Tom Bunyard, General Sales Mgr
Walley Schneider, Programming Director
Jim Fergusen, Chief Engineer
Dave Johnson, Business Manager

***WZNP**
01-01-2008; 89.3 MHz FM; 4.5 kw vert; 325 ft.; N39 58 45 W82 12 7
881 East Johnstown Road, Gahanna, OH 43230 US
(614) 289-5700
www.893theriver.com
License: Newark, Licking County, OH held by One Connection Media Group
Arbitron Metro Market: Newark, OH; *Format:* Christian
Dan Baughman, CEO
Dan Baughman, General Manager
Craig Bennington, General Sales Mgr
Matt Levin, Chief Engineer
Scott Thompson, Chief Financial Officer
Todd Stach, Chief Creative Officer
Bill Montgomery, Chief Sales Officer

Niles

WBBG
05-15-1988; 106.1 MHz FM; 3 kw; 328 ft.; N41 15 52 W80 45 35
7461 South Avenue, Youngstown, OH 44512 US
(330) 729-2577; *Fax:* (330) 729-9991
www.big1061.com
License: Niles, Trumbull County, OH held by Citicasters Licenses Inc.
Group Owner: iHeartMedia; (acq 5-4-99; grpsl).
Arbitron Metro Market: Youngstown, OH; *Format:* Oldies; *Target Audience:* 18-49.
Bill Kelly, Regional President
Steve Granato, Senior Vice President of Programming
Karl Brandt, General Sales Mgr
Jeff Kelly, Programming Director
Thomas John, Digital Content Director
Jim Davis, Regional Senior Vice President ofProgramming
Bob Hotchkiss, Director of Sales

WYCL
11-10-1976; 1540 kHz AM; *Hrs Open:* 24; 0.5 kw-D, DAD; Ant 1,407 ft; N41 7 56 W80 45 40
534 East Pleasant Street, Corry, PA 16407 US
(816) 664-4115
www.my107.com
License: Niles, OH held by Group Radio LLC
Group Owner: Group Radio LLC; (acq 9-30-2003; $2.2 million).
Nat'l Reps: McGavren Guild
Arbitron Metro Market: Pensacola, FL; *Format:* Classic Rock; *Hrs. of News Programming:* news progmg 15 hrs wkly; *No. News Employees:* 2; *Target Audience:* 25-54.
Chris Lash, President/General Manager

North Baltimore

***WLFC**
11-01-1973; 88.3 MHz FM; *Hrs Open:* 24 hours; 4.6 kw; 328 ft.; N41 7 4 W83 32 38
1000 North Main St., Findlay, OH 45840 US
(419) 434-4747; *Fax:* (419) 434-4305
www.myspace.com/wlfc88_3
wlfc@findlay.edu
License: North Baltimore, Hancock County, OH held by University of Findlay
Wire Services: AP
Arbitron Metro Market: Toledo, OH; *Format:* Rock/AOR *Special Programming:* AOR/metal, Saturday; Christian/jazz Sunday; *Hrs. of News Programming:* News progmg hourly; *Target Audience:* 18-40. *Adv. Rates:* underwriting only
Miranda Rife, General Manager
Alli McMann, Programming Director

North Canton

WHOF
08-29-1968; 101.7 MHz FM; *Hrs Open:* 24; 6 kw; 266 ft.; N40 49 22 W81 25 41
7755 Freedom Avenue NW, North Canton, OH 44720 US
(330) 492-4700
www.my1017.com
License: North Canton, Stark County, OH held by CC Licenses LLC.
Group Owner: iHeartMedia; (acq 1-30-2004; $4.3 million with WJER(AM) Dover-New Philadelphia)
Arbitron Metro Market: Canton, OH; *Format:* Adult Contemp *Special Programming:* Farm 2 hrs wkly
Mark Boarman, Vice President/Market Manager
Keith Kennedy, Senior Vice President of Programming

North Kingsville

WFXJ-FM
04-08-2002; 107.5 MHz FM; 3.6 kw; 427 ft.; N41 53 4 W80 38 28
3226 Jefferson Road, Ashtabula, OH 44004 US
(440) 998-1075; *Fax:* (440) 992-2658
www.thefox1075.com
hunter@thefox1075.com
License: North Kingsville, Ashtabula County, OH held by Sweet Home Ashtabula LLC.
Group Owner: Sweet Home Ashtabula LLC; (acq 9-17-2007; grpsl)
Arbitron Metro Market: Ashtabula, OH; *Format:* Classic Rock; *Target Audience:* 18-54; males
Dana Schulte, General Manager
Kid Mitchell, Programming Director
Dennis O'Brien, Operations Director
Paula Taylor, Advertising Manager

North Ridgeville

WJTB
09-16-1984; 1040 kHz AM; 2.5 kw-C, NDD; 5 kw-D, NDD; N41 22 37 W82 0 27
612 Wayne St, Elyria, OH 44035 US
(440) 327-1844
wjtb.njit.edu
License: North Ridgeville, OH held by Taylor Broadcasting Co.
Arbitron Metro Market: Cleveland, OH; *Format:* Gospel
James Taylor, President
Henry Dunn, Operations Dir

Norwalk

WLKR
09-17-1962; 95.3 MHz FM; *Hrs Open:* 24; 3.3 kw; 299 ft.; N41 16 49 W82 39 27
10327 Milan Rd., Milan, OH 44846 USA
(419) 609-5961; *Fax:* (419) 609-2679
wlkr.northcoastnow.com
wlkr@wlkrradio.com
License: Norwalk, Huron County, OH held by Elyria-Lorain Broadcasting Co.
Group Owner: Elyria-Lorain Broadcasting Co.
Nat'l Reps: McGavren Guild
Arbitron Metro Market: Cleveland, OH; *Format:* Adult Contemp, Sports; *No. News Employees:* 1; *Target Audience:* General; residents of Huron & Erie counties; *Adv. Rates:* 21; 21; 21; 21
Bill Forthofer, Station/Sales Manager
Melissa Sharp, Program Dir/Production Dir
Kami Moon, Promotions Manager
Scott Truxell, News Director

WLKR
03-18-1968; 1510 kHz AM; *Hrs Open:* Sunrise-sunset; 0.5 kw-D, DAD; N41 16 45 W82 39 23
10327 Milan Rd., Milan, OH 44846 USA
(419) 609-5961; *Fax:* (419) 609-2679
www.northcoastnow.com
wlkr@wlkrradio.com
License: Norwalk, OH held by Elyria-Lorain Broadcasting Co.
Group Owner: Elyria-Lorain Broadcasting Co.; (acq 4-9-02; with co-located FM).
Nat'l Network: Westwood One; ESPN Radio
Arbitron Metro Market: Milan, OH; *Format:* Adult Contemp, Oldies; *Hrs. of News Programming:* news progmg 2 hrs wkly; *No. News Employees:* 1; *Target Audience:* 40 plus.; *Adv. Rates:* 12; 12; 12; 12
Bill Forthofer, Station Mgr

*WNRK
01-01-2004; 90.7 MHz FM; *Hrs Open:* 24; 4 kw; Ant 407 ft; N41 10 50 W82 23 21 *Rebroadcasts:* Rebroadcasts WKSU-FM Kent 100%
Mailing Address: c/o WKSU-FM, Box 5190, Kent, OH 44242
Second Address: 1613 E. Summit St., Kent, OH 44242-0001
(330) 672-3114; *Fax:* (330) 672-4107
www.wksu.org
letters@wksu.org
License: Norwalk, Huron County, OH held by Kent State University.
Nat'l Network: AP Radio; NPR; PRI

Daniel E. Skinner, General Manager
David Roden, Programming Director
David Fuente, Promotions Coordinator
Amanda Rabinowitz, News Director
Ronald Bartlebaugh, Engineering Dir
Kerry Kurchak, Assistant General Manager

Norwood

WOSL
02-27-1948; 100.3 MHz FM; *Hrs Open:* 24; 3.1 kw; 463 ft.; N39 7 19 W84 32 52
1 Centennial Plaza, 705 Central Avenue, Suite 200, Cincinnati, OH 45202 US
(513) 679-6000; *Fax:* (513) 679-6014
www.oldschoolcincy.com
info@wmoj.com
License: Norwood, Fayette County, OH held by Blue Chip Broadcasting Licenses Ltd.
Group Owner: Radio One Inc.; (acq 9-21-2006; $18 million)
Format: Oldies
Mitch Galvin, Station Manager
Chris Coleman, Programming Director

Oak Harbor

WJZE
08-01-1993; 97.3 MHz FM; *Hrs Open:* 24; 4.3 kw; 387 ft.; N41 28 19 W83 25 5
720 Water Street, 4th Floor, Toledo, OH 43604 US
(419) 244-6354; *Fax:* (419) 244-8261
www.hot973.net
brandibrown@urbanradio.fm
License: Oak Harbor, Ottawa County, OH held by Urban Radio Licenses LLC.
Group Owner: Urban Radio Licenses LLC; (acq 6-30-2005; $2.6 million)
Nat'l Reps: Interep *Regional Reps:* Regional Reps
Arbitron Metro Market: Toledo, OH; *Format:* Contemporary Hits/Top 40; *No. News Employees:* 1; *Target Audience:* Adults 18-34; *Adv. Rates:* 25; 25; 25; 15
Brandi Brown, Programming Director
John Guzan, Market Director of Sales
Kevin Hemmings, Market Manager

Oberlin

*WOBC-FM
11-01-1951; 91.5 MHz FM; 1 kw; 135 ft.; N41 17 38 W82 13 20
Wilder Hall, Room 319, 135 West Lorain Street, Oberlin, OH 44074 US
(440) 775-8107; *Fax:* (440) 775-6678
www.wobc.org
License: Oberlin, Lorain County, OH held by Oberlin College Student Network Inc.
TV Affiliate: College; *Format:* Jazz *Special Programming:* News progmg 5 hrs wkly; *No. News Employees:* General.
Katie Thornton, Operations Dir
Brian Becker, General Manager
Arielle Edelman, Programming Director

WOBL
12-24-1971; 1320 kHz AM; 1 kw-D, DA2; 1 kw-N, DA2; N41 16 5 W82 12 40
P.O. Box 277, Oberlin, OH 44074 US
(440) 774-1320; *Fax:* (440) 774-1336
woblwdlw@earthlink.net
License: Oberlin, OH held by WOBL Inc.
Wire Services: AP
Arbitron Metro Market: Cleveland, OH *TV Affiliate:* Country
Special Programming: news progmg 14 hrs wkly; *Hrs. of News Programming:* 3; *No. News Employees:* 35-55.; *Adv. Rates:* 22.50; 20.50; 22.50; 16.50
Doug Wilber, President/General Manager

Ontario

WRGM
07-17-1987; 1440 kHz AM; *Hrs Open:* 24; 1 kw-D, DA2; 0.028 kw-N, DA2; N40 46 5 W82 37 4
2900 Park Ave West, Mansfield, OH 44906 US
(419) 529-5900; *Fax:* (419) 529-2319
www.wrgm.com
License: Ontario, OH held by GSM Media Corp.
Nat'l Network: ESPN Radio; *Nat'l Reps:* Rgnl Reps
Format: Sports *Special Programming:* High school football & basketball, NASCAR races; *Hrs. of News Programming:* 10 hrs news progmg wkly; *No. News Employees:* 5; *Target Audience:* 25 plus.
Beth Tappan, Sales Manager
Matt Weinberger, Sports Director
Rick Healy, Programming Director

Ottawa

WBUK
02-04-1977; 106.3 MHz FM; *Hrs Open:* 24; 1.4 kw; 489 ft.; N40 57 21 W83 54 42
PO Box 1507, Findlay, OH 45839 US
(419) 422-4545
www.1063thefox.com
info@wbuk.com
License: Ottawa, Putnam County, OH held by The Blanchard River Broadcasting Co.
Group Owner: The Findlay Publishing Co.; (acq 12-3-2008; $500,000)
Format: Classic Rock *Special Programming:* Farm 5 hrs, sports 2 hrs, MOR 4 hrs wkly; *Hrs. of News Programming:* news progmg 3 hrs wkly; *No. News Employees:* 1; *Target Audience:* 18-49; affluent, upscale adults
Mike Holman, General Manager

Oxford

*WMUB
01-01-1950; 88.5 MHz FM; *Hrs Open:* 24; 24.5 kw; 505 ft.; N39 33 26 W84 47 35
1223 Central Parkway, Cincinnati, OH 45214 US
(513) 352-9170; *Fax:* (513) 241-8456
www.wmub.org
WMUB@WMUB.org
License: Oxford, Butler County, OH held by President & Trustees of Miami University.
Nat'l Network: NPR; PRI; *Regional Network:* Ohio Educ. Telecommunications; *Wire Services:* AP
Arbitron Metro Market: Dayton, OH; *Format:* Jazz, News, 62, Talk; *Target Audience:* General.
Richard Eisworth, President/General Manager
Maryanne Zeleznik, News Director
Claire Wagner, Director: Miami University
Chris Phelps, Vice President of Programming
Jessica Lorey, Classical Music Director

Painesville

WABQ
04-25-1956; 1460 kHz AM; *Hrs Open:* 24; 1 kw-D, DA2; 0.5 kw-N, DA2; N41 44 20 W81 14 9
One Radio Place, Painesville, OH 44077 US
(440) 352-1460
www.talk1460wabq.com
License: Painesville, OH held by Radio Advantage One LLC
Arbitron Metro Market: Cleveland, OH; *Format:* Gospel
Danelle Caldwell, Programming Director
Janet Lynn Skinner, Director of Marketing
Tina Farmer, Director of Promotions
Dionne Edwards, Director of Sports
Almira Byrd, Executive Vice President

Parma

WCCD
01-09-1973; 1000 kHz AM; 0.5 kw-D, DAD; N41 19 11 W81 46 7
3130 Mayfield Road, Cleveland, OH 44118 US
(216) 320-0000; *Fax:* (216) 321-9878
www.radio1000.org
License: Parma, OH held by New Spirit Revival Center Ministries, Inc.
Arbitron Metro Market: Cleveland, OH; *Format:* Christian, Gospel, 86 *Special Programming:* Black 3 hrs, Greek 2 hrs, Ukrainian one hr wkly; *Target Audience:* 52.2% Female, 47.8% Male MEDIAN HOUSEHOLD INCOME:$35,236-$46,879; *Adv. Rates:* 30; 30; 30; 20
Dr. Belinda Scott, President

Paulding

WKSD
08-14-1989; 99.7 MHz FM; *Hrs Open:* 24; 3 kw; 328 ft.; N41 3 32 W84 35 30
9070 Mendon Road, Van Wert, OH 45891 US
(419) 238-1220
www.wert1220.com
wert@bright.net
License: Paulding, Paulding County, OH held by First Family Broadcasting Inc.
Nat'l Network: ESPN Radio; *Nat'l Reps:* Rgnl Reps
Format: Oldies, Sports; *Adv. Rates:* 20; 10; 12; 8
Chris Roberts, President
Mona Kennedy, General Sales Mgr

Pemberville

WCKY-FM
07-11-1963; 103.7 MHz FM; 50 kw; 430 ft.; N41 8 20 W83 14 45
125 South Superior Street, Toledo, OH 43604 US
(419) 244-8321; *Fax:* (419) 244-7631
www.1037wcky.com
wcky@1037wcky.com
License: Pemberville, Seneca County, OH held by Citicasters Licenses Inc.
Group Owner: iHeartMedia
Arbitron Metro Market: Toledo, OH; *Format:* Country
Nathan Reed, Operations Manager
Kristy Beebe, Local Sales Manager
Jodi Szczublewski, Promotions Director

Pickerington

WNND
10-07-1989; 103.5 MHz FM; *Hrs Open:* 24; 4 kw; 435 ft; N39 51 52 W82 38 19
4401 Carriage Hill Ln., Columbus, OH 43017
(614) 451-2191; *Fax:* (614) 451-1831
www.wjza.com
License: Pickerington, Fairfield County, OH held by Franklin Communications Inc.
Group Owner: Saga Communications Inc.; (acq 10-1-2003; $13 million)
Nat'l Reps: Christal; *Wire Services:* AP
Population Served: 1,500,000; *Arbitron Metro Market:* Columbus, OH *Special Programming:* Various 15 hrs wkly; *Hrs. of News Programming:* News progmg 2 hrs wkly; *Target Audience:* 25-54.
Alan Goodman, President
Jimmy Steele, Programming Director
Michelle Hurley, Marketing Director
Steve Goldstein, Executive Vice President

Piketon

WXZQ
12-01-1997; 100.1 MHz FM; *Hrs Open:* 24; 6 kw; 328 ft.; N39 5 53 W82 57 20
P. O. Box 820, Piketon, OH 45661 US

(740) 947-0059; *Fax:* (740) 947-4600
wxiz@roadrunner.com
License: Piketon, Pike County, OH held by Crystal Communications
Arbitron Metro Market: Piketon, OH; *Format:* Contemporary Hits/Top 40; *Target Audience:* 18-49.
Gerald Davis, President/General Manager
Tim Hughes, Operations/Sales Manager

Piqua

WPTW
11-01-1947; 1570 kHz AM; *Hrs Open:* 24; 0.25 kw-U, ND1; N40 8 25 W84 16 7
1625 Covington Ave., Piqua, OH 45356 US
(937) 773-3513
www.981wptw.com
rick@muzzybroadcasting.net
License: Piqua, Miami County, OH held by Muzzy Broadcasting, LLC
Group Owner: Muzzy Broadcasting L.L.C.; (acq 7-1-2008)
Nat'l Network: ABC; *Regional Network:* ABN Radio
Arbitron Metro Market: Dayton, OH; *Format:* Oldies *Special Programming:* Farm 2 hrs, sports 30 hrs wkly; *Hrs. of News Programming:* news progmg 8 hrs wkly; *No. News Employees:* 1; *Target Audience:* 35 plus. *Adv. Rates:* 14; 11; 14; 6.25
Richard Muzzy, President
Becky Smith, General Sales Mgr

Pleasant City

WBIK
01-01-2002; 92.1 MHz FM; *Hrs Open:* 24; 6 kw; 169 ft.; N40 1 37 W81 33 9
4988 Skyline Drive, Cambridge, OH 43725 US
(740) 432-5605; *Fax:* (740) 432-1991
yourradioplace.com/wbik/
webmaster@yourradioplace.com
License: Pleasant City, Guernsey County, OH held by David L. Wilson
Regional Reps: Rgnl Reps
Arbitron Metro Market: Cambridge, Oh; *Format:* Classic Rock
Dave Wilson, President/General Manager

Pleasant Hill

WHIO-FM
11-30-1960; 95.7 MHz FM; *Hrs Open:* 24; 50 kw; Ant 476 ft; N40 13 02 W84 17 35 *Rebroadcasts:* Simulcast with WHIO(AM) Dayton 100%
1611 South Main Street, Dayton, OH 45409 US
(937) 259-2111; *Fax:* (937) 259-2168
1290whio.com
License: Pleasant Hill, Miami County, OH held by Cox Radio Inc.
Group Owner: Cox Media Group; (acq 1998; grpsl)
Population Served: 1,463,000; *Arbitron Metro Market:* Dayton, OH; *Target Audience:* 35-54.
Rob Rohr, Senior VP/General Manager
Kathy Eagle, General Sales Mgr
Jennifer Perkins, Promotions Director
Allen Willis, Local Sales Manager
Chip Beale, Digital Sales Manager
Chris Hartley, Assistant Programming Director
NickRoberts, Vice President of Marketing

Port Clinton

WXKR
10-04-1961; 94.5 MHz FM; *Hrs Open:* 24; 30 kw; 617 ft.; N41 30 3 W83 16 16
3225 Arlington Avenue, Toledo, OH 43614 US
(419) 725-5700; *Fax:* (419) 385-2902
www.wxkr.com
info@wxkr.com
License: Port Clinton, Ottawa County, OH held by Cumulus Licensing Corp.
Group Owner: Cumulus Media Inc.; (acq 12-18-97; $5 million cash)
Nat'l Network: ABC
Arbitron Metro Market: Toledo, OH; *Format:* Classic Rock
Special Programming: Sp one hr wkly; *Hrs. of News Programming:* news progmg one hr wkly; *No. News Employees:* 1; *Target Audience:* 25-49.
Cody Welling, General Sales Mgr
Brent Alberts, Programming Director
Ryan Young, Promotions Manager
London Mitchell, News Director
Dave Fuller, Chief Engineer
Debbie Calevro, Traffic Manager
John Gallagher, Market Manager

Portsmouth

WNXT
08-30-1951; 1260 kHz AM; 5 kw-D, DA2; 1 kw-N, DA2; N38 48 38 W82 59 21
P.O. Box 1228, Portsmouth, OH 45662 US
(740) 353-1161; *Fax:* (740) 353-8080
www.wnxtradio.com
wnxtradio@yahoo.com
License: Portsmouth, OH held by Hometown Broadcasting of Portsmouth Inc.
Nat'l Network: ABC; ESPN Radio; *Nat'l Reps:* Rgnl Reps
TV Affiliate: ESPN sports radio/talk *Special Programming:* news progmg 35 hrs wkly; *Hrs. of News Programming:* 1; *No. News Employees:* Adult males; 25-54
Steve Hayes, Operations Manager
Rick Mayne, General Manager
Roger Gray, Sales Manager/Sports Director
Chris Smith, Programming Director

WNXT-FM
09-15-1965; 99.3 MHz FM; 2.55 kw; 512 ft.; N38 43 22 W82 59 56
P.O. Box 1228, Portsmouth, OH 45662 US
(740) 353-1161; *Fax:* (740) 353-3191
www.wnxtradio.com
wnxtradio@yahoo.com
License: Portsmouth, Scioto County, OH
TV Affiliate: Variety *Special Programming:* news progmg one hr wkly; *Hrs. of News Programming:* 1; *No. News Employees:* 25-54.
Steve Hayes, Operations Manager
Rick Mayne, General Manager
Roger Gray, Sales Manager/Sports Director
Chris Smith, Programming Director

***WUKV**
02-18-1992; 88.3 MHz FM; *Hrs Open:* 24; 1 kw; 643 ft; N38 43 20 W83 00 05 *Rebroadcasts:* Rebroadcasts WCDR-FM Cedarville 100%
Box 601, 251 N. Main St., Cedarville, OH 45314
(937) 766-7815; *Fax:* (937) 766-7927
www.thepath.fm
License: Portsmouth, Scioto County, OH held by Educational Media Foundation
Population Served: 100,000 *Special Programming:* Black 2 hrs wkly; *Hrs. of News Programming:* news progmg 16 hrs wkly; *No. News Employees:* 1; *Target Audience:* 35-54; church oriented audience
Mike Novak, President
Terra Seidel, Regional Manager

***WOSP**
05-25-1993; 91.5 MHz FM; *Hrs Open:* 24; 0.11 kw; 1207 ft.; N38 45 42 W83 3 41 *Rebroadcasts:* Rebroadcasts WOSU-FM Columbus 100%
2400 Olentangy River Rd., Columbus, OH 43210 US
(614) 292-9678; *Fax:* (614) 292-7625
www.wosu.org
wosu@osu.edu
License: Portsmouth, Scioto County, OH held by The Ohio State University.
Nat'l Network: PRI; NPR; AP Radio; *Wire Services:* AP
TV Affiliate: *WPBO-TV affil.; *Format:* Classical; *Target Audience:* 35 plus.
Kevin Petrilla, Operations Dir
Thomas Rieland, General Manager
Michael Thompson, News Director
Meredith Hart, Director of Marketing & Communications
Christine Sadic, Manager of Underwriting
Beverly Ervine, Music Director

WZZZ
01-01-2003; 107.5 MHz FM; *Hrs Open:* 24; 2.6 kw; 495 ft.; N38 43 22 W82 59 56
Mailing Address: P.O. Box 1228, Portsmouth, OH 45662 US
Second Address: 602 Chillicothe St., Portsmouth, OH 45662
(740) 353-1979; *Fax:* (740) 353-8080
www.wzzz.com
classicrock1075thebreeze@yahoo.com
License: Portsmouth, Scioto County, OH held by Hometown Broadcasting of Portsmouth 2 Inc.
Regional Reps: Rgnl Reps
Arbitron Metro Market: Portsmouth, OH; *Format:* Classic Rock; *Hrs. of News Programming:* news progmg .25 hrs wkly; *No. News Employees:* 1; *Target Audience:* 35-54; working class & professional adults
Steve Hayes, Operations Dir
Rick Mayne, General Manager
Bill Murphy, Programming Director

Sam McKibbin, News Director
Tyrone Henry, Chief Engineer

Proctorville

***WHKU**
01-25-1986; 91.9 MHz FM; *Hrs Open:* 24; 3 kw; 299 ft.; N38 27 14 W82 25 5
P.O. Box 2098, Omaha, NE 68103 US
(800) 525-5683
www.klove.com
License: Proctorville, Lawrence County, OH held by Educational Media Foundation.
Group Owner: EMF Broadcasting; (acq 2-29-2008; $900,000 with WCKU(FM) Clarksburg, WV)
Nat'l Network: K-Love
Arbitron Metro Market: Proctorville, CA; *Format:* Christian; *Target Audience:* General.
Darrell Chambliss, Chairman
Michael Novak, President/CEO
David Pierce, Chief Creative Officer
Alan Mason, COO
Eric Moser, CFO
D. Kevin Blair, Secretary/General Counsel

Racine

WNTO
07-15-1996; 93.1 MHz FM; 4.1 kw; 397 ft.; N38 56 56 W82 3 2
Mailing Address: P.O. Box 667, Ravenswood, WV 26164 US
Second Address: 117 Portsmouth Rd., Gallipolis, OH 45631
(740) 446-3543; *Fax:* (740) 446-3001
dave@sunny93.net
License: Racine, Meigs County, OH held by Sunny Boradcasting LLC
Arbitron Metro Market: Racine, OH; *Format:* Adult Contemp
Special Programming: American Indian one hr, Black one hr, farm one hr,; *Target Audience:* 18-50; general
Dave Diddle, Station Manager
Jerry Barkey, General Sales Mgr
Tina Merry, Programming Director

Reading

***WMKV**
01-01-1995; 89.3 MHz FM; *Hrs Open:* 24; 0.41 kw; 236 ft.; N39 13 23 W84 25 56
11100 Springfield Pike, Springdale, OH 45246 US
(513) 782-2427; *Fax:* (513) 782-2720
www.wmkvfm.org
License: Reading, Hamilton County, OH held by Lifesphere.
Arbitron Metro Market: Cincinnati, OH; *Format:* Big Band; *Target Audience:* 40 plus.
Dave Schram, Operations Dir
George Zahn, Station Manager
Bob Hannerken, Development Director

Republic

***WYOR**
09-01-1999; 88.5 MHz FM; 0.1 kw; 105 ft.; N41 6 32 W83 0 11 US
(540) 582-9700
License: Republic, Laurens County, OH held by Smile FM
Group Owner: Smile FM; (acq 11-6-2006; $800,000 with WCRS(AM) Greenwood)
Arbitron Metro Market: Saint George UT; *Format:* Blues
Ed Czelada, President

Richwood

WNNP
11-30-1995; 104.3 MHz FM; *Hrs Open:* 24; 3.4 kw; Ant 436 ft; N40 21 52 W83 15 34
4401 Carriage Hill Ln., Columbus, OH 43017
(614) 451-2191; *Fax:* (614) 451-1831
License: Richwood, Union County, OH held by Franklin Communications Inc.
Group Owner: Saga Communications Inc.; (acq 10-1-2003; $13 million with WJZA(FM) Lancaster).
Nat'l Reps: Christal; *Wire Services:* AP
Population Served: 1,500,000; *Arbitron Metro Market:* Columbus, OH *Special Programming:* Various 15 hrs wkly; *Hrs. of News Programming:* News progmg 2 hrs wkly; *Target Audience:* 25-54.
Chris Forgy, General Manager
Patrick Foy, General Sales Mgr
Jimmy Steele, Programming Director
Michelle Hurley, Promotions/Marketing Director
Rob Gaier, Chief Engineer

Ripley

WAOL
01-01-1993; 99.5 MHz FM; 13 kw; 459 ft.; N38 38 55 W84 0 42
777 Willits Street, Birmingham, MI 48009 US
(937) 378-6151; *Fax:* (937) 377-2200
info@waol.com
License: Ripley, Brown County, OH held by Queeb Cities Broadcasting LLC
Arbitron Metro Market: Cincinnati, OH; *Format:* Adult Contemp

Rossford

WNWT
11-28-1966; 1520 kHz AM
PO Box 2098, Omaha, NE 68103 US
(800) 525-5683
www.klove.com
License: Rossford, OH held by Educational Media Foundation.
Group Owner: EMF Broadcasting; (acq 4-21-2009; $2,825,000 with WNKL(FM) Wauseon)
Nat'l Network: K-Love
Arbitron Metro Market: Toledo, OH; *Format:* Christian
Darrell Chambliss, Chairman
Alan Mason, COO
Mike Novak, President/CEO
Eric Moser, CFO
D. Kevin Blair, Secretary/General Counsel

Rushville

*WLRY
12-01-1998; 88.9 MHz FM; *Hrs Open:* 24; 1.1 kw vert; 299 ft.; N39 46 41 W82 25 26
P.O. Box 220, Rushville, OH 43150 US
(740) 536-0885
www.wlry.org
mikewlry@gmail.com
License: Rushville, Fairfield County, OH held by Arcangel Broadcasting Foundation.
Nat'l Network: USA
Format: Christian *Special Programming:* Issues talk 16 hrs wkly; *Hrs. of News Programming:* News progmg 40 hrs wkly; *Target Audience:* 15-55; youth & adult mentors
Richard Finke, General Manager

Salem

WQXK
11-25-1958; 105.1 MHz FM; 88 kw; 446 ft.; N40 53 8 W80 49 55
4040 Simon Road, Youngstown, OH 44515 US
(330) 783-1000
www.k105country.com
win@k105country.com
License: Salem, Columbiana County, OH held by Cumulus Licensing, LLC
Arbitron Metro Market: Youngstown-Warren, OH; *Format:* Country; *Target Audience:* 25-54.
Brian Schimmel, General Manager

WSOM
06-02-1965; 600 kHz AM
4040 Simon Road, Youngstown, OH 44515 US
(330) 783-1000
www.600wsom.com
License: Salem, OH held by Cumulus Licensing Corp.
Group Owner: Cumulus Media Inc.; (acq 3-15-00; grpsl).
Arbitron Metro Market: Youngstown-Warren, OH; *Format:* Oldies *Special Programming:* Farm 2 hrs wkly; *Target Audience:* 35 plus.
Lou Dickey, CEO
Brian Schimmel, General Manager
Wes Boyd, Chief Engineer

Sandusky

WLEC
12-07-1947; 1450 kHz AM; *Hrs Open:* 24; 1 kw-U, ND1; N41 26 28 W82 41 14
50 East Rivercenter Blvd., Suite 1200, Covington, KY 41011 US
(419) 625-1010; *Fax:* (419) 625-1348
www.wlec.com
License: Sandusky, OH held by BAS Broadcasting Inc.
Group Owner: BAS Broadcasting Inc.; (acq 6-30-2008; grpsl)
Regional Reps: Rgnl Reps.
Format: Sports; *Hrs. of News Programming:* News progmg 2 hrs wkly
Tom Booth, General Manager
Brian O'Neil, News Director

WCPZ
08-15-1959; 102.7 MHz FM; 50 kw; 135 ft.; N41 26 28 W82 41 14
50 East Rivercenter Blvd., Suite 1200, Covington, KY 41011 US
(419) 625-1010; *Fax:* (419) 625-1348
www.mix1027.com
randyhugg@basbroadcasting.com
License: Sandusky, Erie County, OH held by BAS Broadcasting Inc.
Group Owner: BAS Broadcasting Inc.; (acq 6-30-2008; grpsl)
Arbitron Metro Market: Cleveland, OH; *Format:* Adult Contemp; *Hrs. of News Programming:* News progmg 2 hrs wkly; *Target Audience:* 18-54.
Paul Mize, General Manager
Randy Hugg, Programming Director
Tammy Harrison, News Director

*WVMS
12-01-1993; 89.5 MHz FM; *Hrs Open:* 24; 5.5 kW; 98 ft.; N41 26 29 W82 48 20 *Rebroadcasts:* Rebroadcasts WCRF(FM) Cleveland 100%
9576 Barr Rd, Cleveland, OH 44141 USA
(440) 526-1111; *Fax:* (440) 526-1319
www.moodyradio.org/stations/cleveland
License: Sandusky, Erie County, OH held by The Moody Bible Institute of Chicago
Group Owner: The Moody Bible Institute of Chicago
Wire Services: AP
Arbitron Metro Market: Sandusky, OH; *Format:* Christian, Religious; *Target Audience:* 25-55; Adults

Shadyside

WVKF
09-01-1990; 95.7 MHz FM; *Hrs Open:* 24; 6.8 kw horiz, 6.67 kw vert; 627 ft.; N40 3 41 W80 45 9
C/O Gene McCoy, P.O. Box 30, Arlington, VA 22210 US
(304) 232-1170; *Fax:* (304) 234-0067
www.kisswheeling.com
License: Shadyside, Belmont County, OH held by Capstar TX LLC
Group Owner: iHeartMedia; (acq 2-26-2004; $930,000).
Nat'l Reps: Christal
Arbitron Metro Market: Wheeling, WV; *Format:* Contemporary Hits/Top 40
Bill Kelly, Regional President
Jim Davis, Regional Senior Vice President of Programming
Chuck Poet, Market President
Scott Deel, Director of Sales
Jim Elliott, Programming Director
Ken Andrews, Production Director

Shelby

*WAUI
11-01-1998; 88.3 MHz FM; 0.7 kw; 456 ft.; N40 45 50 W82 37 4
P.O. Box 3206, Tupelo, MS 38803 US
(662) 844-8888; *Fax:* (662) 842-6791
www.afr.net
faq@afa.net
License: Shelby, Richland County, OH held by American Family Association.
Group Owner: American Family Radio
Format: Christian, Religious
Tim Wildmon, President
Donald Wildmon, Founder
Buddy Smith, Dr VP
Ed Vitagliano, Exec VP
Randy Sharp, Director Of Special Projects
Meeke Addison, Director Of Communications
Abraham Hamilton III, General Counsel

WSWR
12-01-1981; 100.1 MHz FM; 3 kw; 299 ft.; N40 56 42 W82 39 42
400 Radio Lane, Mansfield, OH 44906 US
(419) 529-2211; *Fax:* (419) 529-2516
www.my100fm.com
License: Shelby, Richland County, OH held by Capstar TX LLC
Group Owner: iHeartMedia; (acq 8-24-2000; grpsl).
Format: Oldies
Richard J. Bressler, President

Sidney

WMVR-FM
11-28-1963; 105.5 MHz FM; *Hrs Open:* 24; 6 kw; 154 ft.; N40 18 4 W84 12 21
2929 West Russell Road, Sidney, OH 45365 US
(937) 492-1270; *Fax:* (937) 498-2277
www.hits1055.com
loretta@hits1055.com
License: Sidney, Shelby County, OH held by Dean Miller Broadcasting Corp.
Regional Network: ABN Radio; Ohio News Network; *Nat'l Reps:* Rgnl Reps; ABN Radio & TV
Arbitron Metro Market: Sidney, OH; *Format:* Adult Contemp; *No. News Employees:* 6; *Target Audience:* 18-54; women
Julie Burns, Operations Dir
Loretta Kinney, General Manager
Scott Foxx, Programming Director
Becca Woolley, Promotions Manager
Joe Laber, Music Director

South Vienna

*WOAR
01-01-2006; 88.3 MHz FM; 1 kw vert; 278 ft.; N39 55 54 W83 36 36
P. O. Box 2098, Omaha, NE 68103 US
(800) 525-5683
www.air1.com
License: South Vienna, Clark County, OH held by Educational Media Foundation.
Group Owner: EMF Broadcasting; (acq 3-23-2007; grpsl)
Nat'l Network: Air 1
Arbitron Metro Market: South Vienna, OH; *Format:* Alternative, Christian
Darrell Chambliss, Chairman
Mike Novak, President/CEO
Alan Mason, COO
Eric Moser, CFO
David Pierce, Chief Creative Officer
D. Kevin Blair, Secretary/General Counsel

South Webster

*WEKV
01-01-1996; 94.9 MHz FM; *Hrs Open:* 24; 2.2 kw; 459 ft.; N38 42 30 W82 40 15
PO Box 2098, Omaha, NE 68103 US
(800) 525-5683
www.klove.com
License: South Webster, Scioto County, OH held by Educational Media Foundation.
Group Owner: EMF Broadcasting; (acq 12-30-2005; $450,000).
Nat'l Network: K-Love
Arbitron Metro Market: South Webster, OH; *Format:* Christian
Darrell Chambliss, Chairman
Mike Novak, President/CEO
Alan Mason, COO
Eric Moser, CFO
D. Kevin Blair, Secretary/General Counsel
David Pierce, Chief Creative Officer

South Zanesville

*WHIZ(FM)
01-05-1983; 92.7 MHz FM; *Hrs Open:* 24; 16 kw; Ant 407 ft; N39 42 52 W82 04 10
Mailing Address: 629 Downard Road, South Zanesville, OH 43701-4626 US
Second Address: Box 3208, Zanesville, OH 43701
(740) 452-5431; *Fax:* (740) 452-6553
www.whiznews.com/fm/
License: South Zanesville, Muskingum County, OH held by Southeastern Ohio Broadcasting Systems Inc.
Nat'l Network: USA
Population Served: 250,000 *Hrs. of News Programming:* News progmg 10 hrs wkly; *Target Audience:* General; young children 5-10 to senior citizens
Henry Littick II, President/General Manager
Brian Wagner, Operations/Programming Director
Jay Benson, Sales Manager
George Hiotis, News Director

WHIZ-FM
12-16-1961; 92.7 MHz FM; *Hrs Open:* 24; 16 kw; 407 ft.; N39 42 52 W82 4 10
629 Downard Road, New Albany, OH 43054 US
(740) 452-5431; *Fax:* (740) 452-6553
www.whizamfmtv.com
License: South Zanesville, Muskingum County, OH held by Southeastern Ohio Broadcasting System Inc.
TV Affiliate: WHIZ-TV affil.; *Format:* Adult Contemp *Special Programming:* Relg one hr, sports 3 hrs wkly; *Hrs. of News Programming:* News progmg 12 hrs wkly; *Target Audience:* 25 plus; general
Henry Littick II, President/General Manager
Brian Wagner, Operations/Programming Director
Jay Benson, Sales Manager
George Hiotis, News Director

Spencerville

*WBCJ
88.1 MHz FM; 3.1 kw; 469 ft.; N40 42 41 W84 23 1
Rebroadcasts: Rebroadcasts WBCL (FM)
1115 W. Rudisill Boulevard, Fort Wayne, IN 46807 US
(260) 745-0576; *Fax:* (260) 456-2913
www.wbcl.org
License: Spencerville, Allen County, OH held by Taylor University Broadcasting Inc.
Group Owner: Taylor University Broadcasting
Arbitron Metro Market: Tulsa OK; *Format:* Adult Contemp, Christian

Springfield

WULM
01-01-1947; 1600 kHz AM; *Hrs Open:* 24; 1 kw-D, ND1; 0.034 kw-N, ND1; N39 57 11 W83 52 7
601 Washington Street, Alexandria, LA 74301 US
(888)408-0201; *Fax:* (318)449-9954
www.radiomaria.us/
info.usa@radiomaria.org
License: Springfield, OH held by Radio Maria Inc.
Group Owner: Radio Maria Inc.; (acq 5-30-2008; $225,000)
Arbitron Metro Market: Alexandria, LA; *Format:* Christian
Father Robert Young, Director

*WEEC
12-15-1961; 100.7 MHz FM; *Hrs Open:* 24; 50 kw; 469 ft.; N39 57 42 W83 52 5
1205 Whitefield Circle, Xenia, OH 45885 US
(937) 424-1640
www.weec.org
info@weec.org
License: Springfield, Clark County, OH held by World Evangelistic Enterprise Corp.
Nat'l Network: USA; Moody; AP Radio; *Wire Services:* AP
Arbitron Metro Market: Springfield, OH; *Format:* Christian, Talk
Special Programming: Black one hr, farm one hr wkly; *Hrs. of News Programming:* news progmg 16 hrs wkly; *No. News Employees:* 1; *Target Audience:* 40 plus; general
Claude (Bud) Schindler, Chairman
Tracy Figley, President
Andrew Fessler, Vice Chairman
Clair Miller, Vice President

WIZE
11-01-1940; 1340 kHz AM; *Hrs Open:* 24; 1 kw-D, ND2; 1 kw-N, ND2; N39 56 33 W83 47 15 *Rebroadcasts:* Simulcasts WONE(AM) Dayton 100%
101 Pine Street, Dayton, OH 45402 US
(937) 224-1137; *Fax:* (937) 224-5015
www.wizeam.com
License: Springfield, OH held by Citicasters Licenses Inc.
Group Owner: iHeartMedia; (acq 5-4-99; grpsl).
Regional Reps: Rgnl Reps.
Arbitron Metro Market: Dayton, OH; *Format:* Country; *Hrs. of News Programming:* news progmg 14 hrs wkly; *No. News Employees:* 1; *Target Audience:* 25 plus; upper income, businesses, offices; *Adv. Rates:* 20; 18;20; 12
Richard J. Bressler, President

*WUSO
02-20-1966; 89.1 MHz FM; *Hrs Open:* 24; 0.1 kw vert; 85 ft.; N39 56 9 W83 48 41
C/O Wittenberg Universit, Box 720, P.O. Box 6100, Springfield, OH 45501 US
(937) 327-7026; *Fax:* (937) 327-6340
wuso.org
wusoprogrock@yahoo.com
License: Springfield, Clark County, OH held by Wittenberg University.
Arbitron Metro Market: Springfield, OH; *Format:* Alternative, Rock/AOR *Special Programming:* Jazz 6 hrs, class 3 hrs, blues 3 hrs, urban contem; *No. News Employees:* 1; *Target Audience:* General; liberal artsstudents & residents of Springfield, OH
Andrew Jajack, General Manager
Andrew Bowen, Programming Director
Amber Reyes, Promotions Manager
Nishant Makhija, News Director
Sven Isaacson, Engineering Dir
Caity Valley, Head Music Director
Adam Markinsÿ, Treasurer
NateDorowÿ, Secretary

St. Marys

WMLX
01-01-1998; 103.3 MHz FM; *Hrs Open:* 24; 1.95 kw; 558 ft.; N40 38 3 W84 12 29
667 West Market Street, Lima, OH 45801 US
(419) 223-2060; *Fax:* (419) 229-3888
www.mix1033.com
License: St. Marys, Auglaize County, OH held by Citicasters Licenses Inc.
Group Owner: iHeartMedia; (acq 5-4-99; grpsl)
Arbitron Metro Market: St. Marys, OH; *Format:* Adult Contemp; *Hrs. of News Programming:* News progmg 2 hrs wkly; *Target Audience:* 18-49; women; *Adv. Rates:* 30; 25; 28; 13
Matt Bell, Market President
Jordan Treadway, Vice President of Sales

Steubenville

*WBJV
01-01-2002; 88.9 MHz FM; 0.125 kw; 256 ft.; N40 21 56 W80 43 36
P.O. Box 3206, Tupelo, MS 38803 US
(662) 844-8888; *Fax:* (662) 842-6791
www.afr.net
faq@afa.net
License: Steubenville, Jefferson County, OH held by American Family Association.
Group Owner: American Family Radio
Arbitron Metro Market: Steubenville, OH; *Format:* Christian
Tim Wildmon, President
Donald Wildmon, Founder
Buddy Smith, Sr VP
Ed Vitagliano, Exec VP
Randy Sharp, Director Of Special Projects
Meeke Addison, Director Of Communications
Abraham Hamilton III, General Counsel

WDIG
09-25-1973; 950 kHz AM; *Hrs Open:* 24; 1 kw-D, DA2; 0.035 kw-N, DA2; N40 26 49 W80 34 6
500 North 5th Street, Steubenville, OH 43952 US
(740) 264-1760; *Fax:* (740) 264-5035
License: Steubenville, OH held by World Witness For Christ Ministries Inc.
Nat'l Network: ABC
Arbitron Metro Market: Wheeling, WV; *Format:* Oldies *Special Programming:* Gospel; *Target Audience:* 25-54; general
Roy Dawkins, CEO
Del King, General Manager

Streetsboro

*WSTB
09-01-1973; 88.9 MHz FM; *Hrs Open:* 7 AM-midnight; 0.68 kw; 373 ft.; N41 9 4 W81 20 13
1900 Annalane Drive, Streetsboro, OH 44241 US
(330) 626-4906; *Fax:* (330) 626-4906
www.rock889.com
mail@rock889.com
License: Streetsboro, Portage County, OH held by Streetsboro City Schools.
Format: Rock/AOR; *Hrs. of News Programming:* news progmg 4 hrs wkly; *No. News Employees:* 1; *Target Audience:* 16-34.
Matthew Kolke, Operations Dir
Robert Long, General Manager

Struthers

*WKTL
09-06-1965; 90.7 MHz FM; 13.5 kw; 23 ft.; N41 3 6 W80 35 56
65 Steiner Avenue, Akron, OH 44301 US
(330) 761-3099; *Fax:* (330) 761-3103
www.913thesummit.com
License: Struthers, Mahoning County, OH held by Struthers Board of Education.
Format: Adult Contemp, Classic Rock
Andrew James, Operations/Membership Manager
Tommy Bruno, General Manager
Bill Gruber, Programming Director
Garrett Hart, Creative Content Director

Swanton

WJUC
02-27-1997; 107.3 MHz FM; *Hrs Open:* 24; 3 kw; 328 ft.; N41 38 30 W83 54 3
Mailing Address: P.O. Box 351450, Toledo, OH 43635 US
Second Address: 5902 Southwyck Blvd., Toledo, OH 43614
(419) 861-9582; *Fax:* (419) 861-2866
www.thejuice1073.com
wcharleswelch@aol.com
License: Swanton, Fulton County, OH held by Welch Communications Inc.
Regional Reps: Interep; *Wire Services:* AP
Arbitron Metro Market: Toledo, OH; *Format:* Adult Contemp, Blues *Special Programming:* Blues, gospel; *Target Audience:* 18-54; African Americans 70%, others 30%; *Adv. Rates:* 65; 65; 75; 60
W. Charles Welch, CEO/General Manager
Rich Hogan, Sales Manager
Charlie Mack, Programming Director
Martini Rox, Promotions Coordinator
Tisha Lee, Production Director

Sylvania

WWWM-FM
11-29-1968; 105.5 MHz FM; *Hrs Open:* 24; 4.3 kw; 389 ft.; N41 38 49 W83 36 18
Mailing Address: 3225 Arlington Avenue, Toledo, OH 43614 US
Second Address: 2965 Pickle Rd., Oregon, OH 43616
(419) 725-5700; *Fax:* (419) 385-2902
www.star105toledo.com
License: Sylvania, Lucas County, OH held by Cumulus Licensing Corp.
Group Owner: Cumulus Media Inc.; (acq 9-11-97; $10 million with WLQR(AM) Toledo)
Nat'l Reps: D & R Radio
Arbitron Metro Market: Toledo, OH; *Format:* Adult Contemp; *Target Audience:* 25-54.
Cody Welling, General Sales Mgr
Nikki Landy, Programming Director
Ryan Young, Promotions Manager
London Mitchell, News Director
Dave Fuller, Chief Engineer
John Gallagher, Market Manager
Deb Piechocki, Business Manager

Thompson

*WKSV
06-01-1997; 89.1 MHz FM; *Hrs Open:* 24; 50 kw; Ant 472 ft; N41 41 34 W81 02 51 *Rebroadcasts:* Rebroadcasts WKSU-FM Kent 100%
Mailing Address: c/o WKSU-FM, Box 5190, Kent, OH 44242
Second Address: 1613 E.Summit St, Kent, OH 44242-0001
(330) 672-3114; *Fax:* (330) 672-4107
www.wksu.org
letters@wksu.org
License: Thompson, Geauga County, OH held by Kent State University.
Nat'l Network: NPR; PRI; AP Radio
Population Served: 191,723; *Arbitron Metro Market:* Cleveland, OH; *Hrs. of News Programming:* news progmg 35 hrs wkly; *No. News Employees:* 5; *Target Audience:* 35-65; college grad, professional & upper income
Kandy Neal, Operations Coordinator
Daniel Skinner, General Manager
Amanda Rabinowitz, News Director
Ronald Bartlebaugh, Engineering Dir
Kerry Kurchak, Assistant General Manager
M L Shultze, Web Editor

Tiffin

WTTF
12-19-1959; 1600 kHz AM; *Hrs Open:* 6 AM-10 PM; 500 w-D, 20 w-N, DA-1; N41 07 32 W83 13 45
Mailing Address: PO Box 309, Tiffin, OH 44883
Second Address: 167 Main Street, Tiffin, OH 44883
(419) 427-2212; *Fax:* (419) 422-2954
www.wttf.com
License: Tiffin, Seneca County, OH held by Tiffen Broadcasting II LLC
Group Owner: BAS Broadcasting Inc.; (acq 10-15-2008)
Population Served: 65,000 *Hrs. of News Programming:* news progmg 18 hrs wkly; *No. News Employees:* 2; *Target Audience:* General.
John Spahr, Operations/Program Manager
Jon Kerns, Sports Director
Steve Shoffner, News Director
Billy Hassinger, Sports/Production Director

Toledo

WCWA
04-10-1938; 1230 kHz AM; 1 kw-U, ND1; N41 38 13 W83 33 52
125 South Superior Street, Toledo, OH 43604 US
(419) 244-8321; *Fax:* (419) 244-7631
www.1230foxsports.com
wcwa@wcwa.com
License: Toledo, OH held by Citicasters Licenses Inc.
Group Owner: iHeartMedia; (acq 1999; grpsl)
Nat'l Reps: Clear Channel
Arbitron Metro Market: Toledo, OH; *Format:* Sports *Special Programming:* Ger one hr, Pol one hr, relg 3 hrs, sports 15 hrs wkly; *Target Audience:* 25-54; male; *Adv. Rates:* 20; 125; 25; 10

Nathan Reed, Operations Manager
Kellie Holeman-Szenderski, Regional Market Manager
Kristy Beebe, Local Sales Manager

***WGTE-FM**
05-02-1976; 91.3 MHz FM; *Hrs Open:* 24; 13.5 kw; 948 ft.; N41 39 27 W83 25 55
136 N Huron St PO Box 30, Toledo, OH 43692 US
(419) 380-4600; *Fax:* (419) 380-4710
www.wgte.org
License: Toledo, Lucas County, OH held by The Public Broadcasting Foundation of Northwest Ohio.
Nat'l Network: NPR; PRI
Arbitron Metro Market: Toledo, OH *TV Affiliate:* *WGTE-TV affil.; *Format:* News, Public Affairs *Special Programming:* Jazz 16 hrs, new age 4 hrs wkly; *Hrs. of News Programming:* News progmg 23 hrs wkly *TargetAudience:* General.
Marlon Kiser, CEO
Darren LaShelle, Director of Content
Lindsay Eberly, Director of Development

WIOT
10-01-1949; 104.7 MHz FM; *Hrs Open:* 24; 50 kw; 541 ft.; N41 40 23 W83 25 31
125 South Superior Street, Toledo, OH 43604 US
(419) 244-8321; *Fax:* (419) 244-7631
www.wiot.com
wiot@wiot.com
License: Toledo, Lucas County, OH held by Citicasters Licenses Inc.
Group Owner: iHeartMedia; (Acq 1997).
Arbitron Metro Market: Toledo, OH; *Format:* Rock/AOR *Special Programming:* Progsv rock 2 hrs, metal 2 hrs wkly
Kellie Holeman, Regional Market Manager
Nathan Reed, Operations Manager
Rob Crider, General Sales Mgr
Scott Sands, Programming Director
Jodi Szczublewski, Promotions Director

WKKO
12-07-1956; 99.9 MHz FM; *Hrs Open:* 24; 50 kw; 500 ft.; N41 40 5 W83 27 11
3225 Arlington Avenue, Toledo, OH 43614 US
(419) 725-5700; *Fax:* (419) 385-2902
www.k100country.com
License: Toledo, Lucas County, OH
Nat'l Network: ABC
Arbitron Metro Market: Toledo, OH
Cody Welling, General Sales Mgr
Gary Shores, Programming Director
Ryan Young, Director of Promotions/Marketing
Dave Fuller, Chief Engineer
John Gallagher, Market Manager

WLQR
10-01-1954; 1470 kHz AM; 1 kw-D, DA2; 1 kw-N, DA2; N41 37 54 W83 28 38
3225 Arlington Avenue, Toledo, OH 43614 US
(419) 725-5700; *Fax:* (419) 385-2902
www.1470theticket.com
License: Toledo, OH held by Cumulus Licensing Corp.
Group Owner: Cumulus Media Inc.; (acq 9-11-97; $10 million with WWWM-FM Sylvania)
Arbitron Metro Market: Toledo, OH; *Format:* Sports; *Target Audience:* 25-54.
Cody Welling, General Sales Mgr
Norm Wamer, Programming Director
Ryan Young, Director of Promotions/Marketing
Dave Fuller, Chief Engineer
John Gallagher, Market Manager

***WOTL**
03-24-1988; 90.3 MHz FM; 0.7 kw; 377 ft.; N41 38 48 W83 36 22
Mailing Address: 4135 Northgate Blvd, Suite 1, Sacramento, CA 95834 US
Second Address: 716 N. Westwood Ave., Toledo, OH 43607
(815) 725-1331
www.familyradio.com
License: Toledo, Lucas County, OH held by Family Stations Inc.
Group Owner: Family Stations Inc.
Arbitron Metro Market: Toledo, OH; *Format:* Religious; *Target Audience:* General.
Harold Camping, President/General Manager
John Rorvik, General Manager

WRVF
08-11-1946; 101.5 MHz FM; 33 kw; 538 ft.; N41 40 23 W83 25 31
125 South Superior Street, Toledo, OH 43604 US
(419) 244-8321; *Fax:* (419) 244-7631
www.1015theriver.com
License: Toledo, Lucas County, OH held by Citicasters Licenses Inc.
Group Owner: iHeartMedia
Nat'l Reps: Clear Channel
Arbitron Metro Market: Toledo, OH; *Format:* Adult Contemp
Special Programming: Jazz 6 hrs wkly; *Target Audience:* 25-54; mostly female; *Adv. Rates:* 175; 250; 225; 50
Kristy Beebe, Local Sales Manager
Jodi Szczublewski, Promotions Director

WSPD
04-15-1921; 1370 kHz AM; 5 kw-D, DAN; 5 kw-N, DAN; N41 36 3 W83 32 11
125 South Superior Street, Toledo, OH 43604 US
(419) 244-8321; *Fax:* (419) 244-7631
www.wspd.com
news@wspd.com
License: Toledo, OH held by Citicasters Licenses Inc.
Group Owner: iHeartMedia; (acq 5-4-99; grpsl).
Regional Reps: Rgnl Reps.
Arbitron Metro Market: Toledo, OH; *Format:* News, News/Talk, 86 *Special Programming:* Relg 5 hrs, farm 3 hrs wkly; *Target Audience:* 25-54; mostly males
Kristy Beebe, Local Sales Manager
Scott Sands, Programming Director

WWYC
06-16-1946; 1560 kHz AM; 5 kw-D, DA; N41 36 59 W83 37 22
Rebroadcasts: Repeater for KAWZ (FM)
P.O. Box 391, Twin Falls, ID 83303 US
(800) 357-4226
License: Toledo, Lucas County, OH held by CSN International
Group Owner: CSN International; (acq. March 2010)
Arbitron Metro Market: Toledo, OH; *Format:* Religious

WVKS
10-14-1957; 92.5 MHz FM; *Hrs Open:* 24; 50 kw; 479 ft.; N41 31 55 W83 35 37
125 South Superior Street, Toledo, OH 43604 US
(419) 244-8321; *Fax:* (419) 244-7631
www.925kissfm.com
License: Toledo, Lucas County, OH held by Citicasters Licenses Inc.
Group Owner: iHeartMedia; (acq 5-15-99; grpsl).
Nat'l Reps: Clear Channel; *Wire Services:* AP
Arbitron Metro Market: Toledo, OH; *Format:* Contemporary Hits/Top 40; *Hrs. of News Programming:* news progmg one hr wkly; *No. News Employees:* 1; *Target Audience:* 18-49; educated, employed adults, mostly females *Adv. Rates:* 125; 110; 125; 75
Kristy Beebe, Local Sales Manager
Jodi Szczublewski, Promotions Director

***WXTS-FM**
02-01-1975; 88.3 MHz FM; *Hrs Open:* 24; 0.105 kw; 125 ft.; N41 40 7 W83 33 15
2400 Collingwood Blvd., Toledo, OH 43620 US
(419) 244-6875; *Fax:* (419) 249-8248
License: Toledo, Lucas County, OH held by Toledo Board of Education.
Arbitron Metro Market: Toledo, OH; *Format:* Jazz *Special Programming:* Blues 5 hrs wkly; *Target Audience:* 28-55.
John Kuschell, General Manager

***WXUT**
11-04-1990; 88.3 MHz FM; *Hrs Open:* 8 PM-2 AM (M-W); 8 PM-4 AM (Th, F);; 0.1 kw horiz; 190 ft.; N41 39 26 W83 36 57
2801 W. Bancroft Street, Student Union Room 2515, Toledo, OH 43606 US
(419) 530-4172; *Fax:* (419) 530-2210
www.wxut.com
883wxut@gmail.com
License: Toledo, Lucas County, OH held by University of Toledo.
Arbitron Metro Market: Toledo, OH; *Format:* Alternative *Special Programming:* Black 8 hrs, heavy metal 4 hrs, rhythm and blues 2; *Hrs. of News Programming:* News progmg 4 hrs wkly; *Target Audience:* General.
Terrance Teagarden, General Manager
Tyler Mattson, Station Manager
Nathan Carter, Production Director
Jake Warling, Programming Director
Boyce Swift, Promotions Director
Danielle Gamble, News Director
Mike "America" Rogers, PRDirector
Yuning Carter, Chief Engineer
Chad Rankin, Online Content Director
Derrick Lawson, Sports Director
Nate Jones/Tessa Kennedy, Music Directors

Troy

***WYDA**
01-01-1991; 96.9 MHz FM; *Hrs Open:* 24; 6 kw; 312 ft.; N39 56 49 W84 11 29 *Rebroadcasts:* Rebroadcasts KLVR(FM) Santa Rosa 100%
211 South Main Street, Suite 1200, Dayton, OH 45402 US
(916) 251-1600; *Fax:* (916) 251-1650
www.klove.com
klove@klove.com
License: Troy, Miami County, OH held by Educational Media Foundation.
Group Owner: EMF Broadcasting; (acq 7-17-03; $1.2 million).
Nat'l Network: K-Love
Arbitron Metro Market: Dayton, OH; *Format:* Christian; *No. News Employees:* 3; *Target Audience:* 25-44; Judeo Christian, female
Mike Novak, President
David Pierce, Programming Director
Ed Lenane, News Director
Sam Wallington, Engineering Dir
Richard Hunt, News Reporter
Marya Morgan, News Reporter

Uhrichsville

WBTC
12-13-1963; 1540 kHz AM
125 Johnson Drive, Uhrichsville, OH 44683 US
(740) 922-2700; *Fax:* (740) 922-2702
www.wbtclive.com/
wbtc@tusco.net
License: Uhrichsville, OH held by Tuscarawas Broadcasting Co.
Nat'l Network: CBS; *Nat'l Reps:* Rgnl Reps
Arbitron Metro Market: Uhrichsville, OH; *Format:* News, News/Talk, 84, Talk *Special Programming:* Relg 2 hrs wkly; *Target Audience:* 30-55.
James Natoli Jr., President
Kevin Baker, Sales Director
Adam Mackey, News & Sports
Kathy Chaney, Secretary

WTUZ
05-01-1990; 99.9 MHz FM; *Hrs Open:* 24; 5.3 kw; 348 ft.; N40 26 19 W81 26 1
2424 East High Avenue, New Philadelphia, OH 44663 US
(330) 339-2222; *Fax:* (330) 339-5930
www.wtuz.com
info@wtuz.com
License: Uhrichsville, Tuscarawas County, OH held by WTUZ Radio Inc.
Nat'l Network: Fox News Radio; *Wire Services:* AP
Arbitron Metro Market: New Philadelphia, OH; *Format:* Country *Special Programming:* Farm 2 hr, relg 4 hr wkly; *Hrs. of News Programming:* news progmg 7 hrs wkly; *No. News Employees:* 2; *Target Audience:* 25-45;adults; *Adv. Rates:* 50;50;50;30
Brad Shupe, Operations/Sports Director
Melanie Osborn, General Sales Mgr
Pat Smith, Promotions Manager
Jennifer Lourenco, News Director
John Demuth, Chief Engineer

Union City

WTGR
12-31-1994; 97.5 MHz FM; *Hrs Open:* 24; 6 kw; 325 ft.; N40 11 32 W84 47 58
514 Martin St., Greenville, OH 45331 US
(937) 548-5085; *Fax:* (937) 548-5089
www.wtgr.com
License: Union City, Darke County, OH held by Positive Radio Group Inc. of Ohio.
Group Owner: Baker Family Stations
Nat'l Network: CNN Radio; *Regional Network:* Ohio News Network; *Nat'l Reps:* ABN Radio & TV
Arbitron Metro Market: Union City, OH; *Format:* Country; *Hrs. of News Programming:* news progmg one hr wkly; *No. News Employees:* 1; *Target Audience:* 25-54; 25-49 female
Scott Ward, Station Manager/Sales Manager
Alex Mikos, News Director
Jeff Peters, Chief Engineer
Shane Buckingham, Sales/Promotions

University Heights

***WJCU**
05-13-1969; 88.7 MHz FM; *Hrs Open:* 24; 2.5 kw; 341 ft.; N41 29 24 W81 31 54
1 John Carroll Boulevard, University Heights, OH 44118 US
(216) 397-4437; *Fax:* (216) 397-4439
www.wjcu.org
License: University Heights, Cuyahoga County, OH held by John Carroll University.

Arbitron Metro Market: Cleveland, OH; *Format:* Variety/Diverse *Special Programming:* It 2 hrs, Chinese one hr, Pol 2 hrs, Lithuanian 2; *Hrs. of News Programming:* News progmg one hr wkly; *Target Audience:* General.
Mark Krieger, General Manager
Howard Regal, Station Manager
Maddie Baggett, Programming Director
Matt Hribar, Promotions Director
Hailey Meinen, News Director
Eric Sinna, Chief Engineer
Dale Armbruster
Karoline Kramer Gould,Music Director
R.J. Hemme, Webmaster

Upper Arlington

WTOH

05-25-1989; 98.9 MHz FM; *Hrs Open:* 24; 3 kw; 328 ft; N39 58 16 W83 01 40
350 E 1st Ave., Suite 100, Columbus, OH 45237
(614) 487-1444; *Fax:* (614) 487-5862
www.magic989.com
License: Upper Arlington, Franklin County, OH held by Salem Media of Ohio Inc.
Group Owner: Salem Communications Corp.; (acq 2-15-2013; $ 4 million)
Nat'l Reps: Christal
Arbitron Metro Market: Columbus, OH; *No. News Employees:* 1; *Target Audience:* 25-54; upscale, educated, active & responsive
Jeff Wilson, General Manager

Upper Sandusky

*WXML

12-26-1992; 90.1 MHz FM; *Hrs Open:* 24; 15 circular; Ant 500 ft; N40 54 53 W83 07 32
Mailing Address: Box 158, Upper Sandusky, OH 43351
Second Address: 1800 East Wyandot Avenue, Upper Sandusky, OH 43351
(419) 294-2900; *Fax:* (419) 294-1786
www.newvision.fm
contact@newvision.fm
License: Upper Sandusky, Wyandot County, OH held by Kayser Broadcast Ministries Inc.
Nat'l Network: SRN News
Population Served: 695,051 *Hrs. of News Programming:* News progmg 8 hrs wkly; *Target Audience:* General.
Daniel Kayser, President/CEO/General Manager
Carla/Jon Bowlus, Programming Director
Susan Kayser, Secretary/Director
Dick Johnson, Vice President
Joe Perri, Director
Jeff Hall, Director

Urbana

WDHT

08-01-1958; 102.9 MHz FM; *Hrs Open:* 24; 50 kw; 492 ft.; N39 57 11 W83 52 07
717 E. David Rd., Kettering, OH 45429 US
(937) 294-5858; *Fax:* (937) 297-5233
www.hot1029.com
License: Urbana, Champaign County, OH held by Alpha Media Licensee LLC
Group Owner: Alpha Media LLC; (acq 4-17-2014; grpsl).
Nat'l Reps: Katz Radio; *Wire Services:* UPI
Population Served: 81,926; *Arbitron Metro Market:* Dayton, OH; *Format:* Urban Contemporary; *Target Audience:* General.
Brad Waldo, Operations Manager
John King, General Manager

Van Wert

WERT

11-27-1958; 1220 kHz AM; *Hrs Open:* 24; 0.25 kw-D, ND2; 0.029 kw-N, ND2; N40 52 19 W84 33 15
Mailing Address: 9070 Mendon Road, Van Wert, OH 45891 US
Second Address: PO Box 4878, Van Wert, OH 45891
(419) 238-2092; *Fax:* (419) 238-2578
www.vwindependent.com
editor@thevwindependent.com
License: Van Wert, OH held by First Family Broadcasting Inc.
Nat'l Network: ABC; *Nat'l Reps:* Rgnl Reps
Arbitron Metro Market: Van Wert, OH; *Format:* Adult Contemp *Special Programming:* Gospel 3 hrs, Sp one hr wkly; *Hrs. of News Programming:* news progmg 30 hrs wkly; *No. News Employees:* 2; *Target Audience:* 35plus; spendable income
Chris Roberts, President

Wapakoneta

WFGF

07-07-1964; 92.1 MHz FM; *Hrs Open:* 24; 3 kw; 328 ft.; N40 39 20 W84 6 54
57 Town Square, Lima, OH 45801 US
(419) 331-1600; *Fax:* (419) 228-5085
www.921thefrog.com
dave@cmgroup.co
License: Wapakoneta, Allen County, OH held by Childers Media Group, LLC
Group Owner: Childers Media Group, LLC
Arbitron Metro Market: Wapakoneta, OH; *Format:* Country
Special Programming: Nascar Nextel Races; *Target Audience:* 25-54; young, affluent; *Adv. Rates:* 17; 14; 15; 10
Rachel Webster, Sales Manager
Dave Woodward, Programming Director
Garett Searight, Promotions Manager
Deb Klaus, Business Manager

Warren

WHTX

10-02-1954; 1570 kHz AM; *Hrs Open:* 24; 217 kw; N41 46 30 W72 48 2.1
5380 Webb Road, Mineral Ridge, OH 44515 US
(330) 737-1540
www.wanr1570.com
License: Warren, Trumbull County, OH
Group Owner: Sagittarius Communications, LLC.
Nat'l Network: Westwood One
Population Served: 41,358; *Arbitron Metro Market:* Warren, OH; *Hrs. of News Programming:* news progmg 20 hrs wkly; *No. News Employees:* 1; *Target Audience:* 25-49; adult men
Chris Lash, CEO
Tim Phillips, Operations Manager
Jim Davison, Sales Manager
Alan Courtright, News Director
Ben Slagle, Chief Engineer
Bob Church, Sports Director
Nathan Obral, Webmaster

WHKZ

11-11-1941; 1440 kHz AM; 5 kw-D, DA2; 5 kw-N, DA2; N41 9 52 W80 50 47 *Rebroadcasts:* Rebroadcasts WHKW(AM) Cleveland 100%
4 Summit Park Drive, Suite 150, Cleveland, OH 44131 US
(216) 901-0921
www.whkwradio.com
mjaycox@salemcleveland.com
License: Warren, OH held by Salem Media Group LLC
Group Owner: Salem Communications; (acq 5-7-2008; $550,000)
Nat'l Reps: Salem
Arbitron Metro Market: Youngstown-Warren, OH; *Format:* Christian, Talk
Brett Crow, Operations Supervisor
Mark Jaycox, General Manager
Tim Vaughan, General Sales Mgr
Len Howser, Programming Director

Washington Ct House

WCHO

02-01-1952; 1250 kHz AM; 0.5 kw-D, ND1; 0.042 kw-N, ND1; N39 32 59 W83 27 10
1535 N. North Street, Washington Court, OH 43160 US
(740) 335-0941; *Fax:* (740) 335-6869
www.wchoam.com
news@buckeyecountry105.com
License: Washington Ct House, OH held by Citicasters Licenses Inc.
Group Owner: iHeartMedia; (acq 5-4-99; grpsl).
Nat'l Network: ABC; *Nat'l Reps:* Katz Radio
Arbitron Metro Market: Washington Court House, OH; *Format:* Oldies *Special Programming:* Farm 5 hrs wkly; *Hrs. of News Programming:* News progmg 18 hrs wkly; *Adv. Rates:* 10; 10; 10; 10
Dan Latham, Market Manager
Paul Jellison, Engineering Dir

WCHO-FM

12-01-1968; 105.5 MHz FM; 6 kw; 328 ft.; N39 24 1 W83 26 48
1535 N. North Street, Washington Court, OH 43160 US
(740) 335-0941; *Fax:* (740) 335-6869
www.buckeyecountry105.com
news@buckeyecountry105.com
License: Washington Ct House, Fayette County, OH held by Citicasters Licenses Inc.
Group Owner: iHeartMedia
Nat'l Network: ABC
Arbitron Metro Market: Washington Court House, OH; *Format:* Country
Dan Latham, Market President

Wauseon

*WYSA

01-01-1996; 88.5 MHz FM; *Hrs Open:* 24; 10 kw; 292 ft.; N41 33 29 W84 11 8
5105 Glendale Avenue, Suite C, Toledo, OH 43614 US
(419) 389-0893; *Fax:* (419) 381-0731
www.yeshome.com
License: Wauseon, Fulton County, OH held by Side by Side Inc.
Arbitron Metro Market: Wauseon, OH; *Format:* Christian; *Target Audience:* 15-25.
J. Todd Hostetler, General Manager
Jeff Howe, Programming Director

*WNKL

01-01-2003; 96.9 MHz FM; 5 kw; 358 ft.; N41 36 3 W83 54 27
PO Box 2098, Omaha, NE 68103 US
(800) 525-5683; *Fax:* (916) 251-1650
www.klove.com
License: Wauseon, Fulton County, OH held by Educational Media Foundation.
Group Owner: EMF Broadcasting; (acq 4-21-2009; $2,825,000 with WNWT(FM) Rossford)
Nat'l Network: K-Love
Arbitron Metro Market: Omaha, NE; *Format:* Christian; *No. News Employees:* 13
Darrell Chambliss, Chairman
Mlke Novak, President & CEO
Eric Moser, CFO
Alan Mason, COO
D. Kevin Blair, Secretary/General Counsel
David Pierce, Chief Creative Officer

Waverly

WXIC

01-01-1954; 660 kHz AM; *Hrs Open:* Sunrise-sunset; 1 kw-D, NDD; N39 7 50 W83 0 46
P.O. Bx 227, Waverly, OH 45690 US
(740) 947-2166; *Fax:* (740) 947-4600
License: Waverly, OH held by Crystal Communications Corp.
Nat'l Reps: Keystone (unwired net)
Arbitron Metro Market: Waverly, OH; *Format:* Gospel; *Target Audience:* Gospel music lovers; *Adv. Rates:* 11; 9; 11; 9
Gerald Davis, President
Brad Lambert, General Sales Mgr
Tim Hughes, Programming Director/Operations Manager
Roy Belt, News Director

WXIZ

03-01-1971; 100.9 MHz FM; *Hrs Open:* 24; 0.92 kw; 499 ft.; N39 13 17 W82 59 33
P.O. Box 227, Waverly, OH 45690 US
(740) 947-2166
www.wxiz.com
License: Waverly, Pike County, OH held by Crystal Communications Corp.
Arbitron Metro Market: Waverly,ÿOH; *Format:* Country; *Hrs. of News Programming:* news progmg 10 hrs wkly; *No. News Employees:* 1; *Target Audience:* 25-50.
Gerald Davis, President
Brad Lambert, General Sales Mgr
Tim Hughes, Programming Director/Operations Manager
Roy Belt, News Director

Waynesville

*WYNS

01-01-2009; 89.3 MHz FM; 0.1 kw; 49 ft.; N39 29 14 W84 4 29
5114 Princeton-Glendale Road, Hamilton, OH 45011 US
(513) 436-0089
www.classxradio.com
classx@classxradio.com
License: Waynesville, Warren County, OH held by Spyrex Communications, Inc.
Arbitron Metro Market: Waynesville, OH; *Format:* Variety/Diverse
Deborah Ives, Operations Dir

Wellston

WKOV-FM

07-17-1971; 96.7 MHz FM; *Hrs Open:* 24; 16 kw; 129 meters; N39 01 45 W82 35 51
295 E. Main, Jackson, OH 45640
(740) 286-3023; *Fax:* (740) 286-6679
www.jacksonohio.org
License: Wellston, Jackson County, OH held by Jackson County Broadcasting Inc.
Group Owner: Jackson County Broadcasting Inc.
Nat'l Network: Dial Global

Population Served: 585,000 *Format:* Adult Contemp, Contemporary Hits/Top 40; *Hrs. of News Programming:* news progmg 21 hrs wkly; *No. News Employees:* 1; *Target Audience:* 20-55.; *Adv. Rates:* 19; 16; 19; 13
Jerry Mossbarger, General Manager
Ron Speakman, General Sales Mgr
John Pelletier, Programming Director

WYPC
01-01-1953; 1330 kHz AM; *Hrs Open:* 24; 500 w-D, 50 w-N; N39 06 22 W82 34 44
Box 667, 295 E. Main, Jackson, OH 45640
(740) 286-3023; *Fax:* (740) 286-6679
jmossbarger@jcbiradio.com
License: Wellston, Jackson County, OH held by Jackson County Broadcasting Inc.
Group Owner: Jackson County Broadcasting Inc.; acq 9-14-70)
Nat'l Network: Westwood One
Population Served: 42,000 *Format:* Oldies; *Hrs. of News Programming:* news progmg 8 hrs wkly; *No. News Employees:* 1; *Target Audience:* 50 plus.; *Adv. Rates:* 9; 7; 9; 6
Jerry Mossbarger, General Manager
Ron Speakman, General Sales Mgr
John Pelletier, Programming Director

West Carrollton

WROU-FM
11-25-1991; 92.1 MHz FM; *Hrs Open:* 24; 1.05 kw; 535 ft.; N39 43 5 W84 15 21
717 E. David Rd., Kettering, OH 45429 US
(937) 294-5858
www.921wrou.com
License: West Carrollton, Montgomery County, OH held by Alpha Media Licensee LLC
Group Owner: Alpha Media LLC; (acq 4-17-2014; grpsl).
Nat'l Network: ABC; *Nat'l Reps:* Katz Radio
Arbitron Metro Market: Dayton, OH; *Format:* Urban Contemporary; *Target Audience:* 25-54.
John King, General Manager
Keith Wright, Director of Sales

West Chester

***WLHS**
09-03-1976; 89.9 MHz FM; *Hrs Open:* 9 AM-5 PM; 0.1 kw horiz; 341 ft.; N39 19 10 W84 22 4
11700 Vergennes Street, Lowell, MI 49331 US
(616) 987-2547
www.lowellradio.org
License: West Chester, Butler County, OH held by Lakota Local School District.
Wire Services: UPI
Format: Rock/AOR; *Target Audience:* General; div, open minded crowd
R.C. Anderson, Operations Dir
Mark Hattersley, Station Manager
Corey Wyatt, General Sales Mgr
Matt Townsley, Programming Director
Brandon Enright, Assistant Music Director
Danny Hall, Music Director

West Union

***WZWP**
01-01-1990; 89.5 MHz FM; *Hrs Open:* 24; 3.2 kw; 381 ft.; N38 51 26 W83 36 38 *Rebroadcasts:* Simulcasts WZCP(FM) Chillicothe 100%
Mailing Address: PO Box 1423, Somerset, KY 45202 US
Second Address: 93 Rainbow Terrace, Somerset, KY 45201
(606) 679-1342
www.kingofkingsradio.com
License: West Union, Adams County, OH held by One Connection Media Group
Arbitron Metro Market: Peoria, IL; *Format:* Contemporary Hits/Top 40
Eric Faulds, Music Director

Westerville

***WOBN**
10-08-1958; 97.5 MHz FM; 29 w horiz; Ant 66 ft; N40 07 28 W82 56 06
Otterbein College, 33 College view Rd., Westerville, OH 43081
(614) 823-2975; *Fax:* (614) 823-3367
www.wobn.net
License: Westerville, Franklin County, OH held by Otterbein College.
Population Served: 12,530 *Special Programming:* College Alternative University; *Hrs. of News Programming:* News progmg one hr wkly; *Target Audience:* General; Westerville & Otterbein College community
Janice Windborne, Faculty Advisor
Grace Lenaham, General Manager
David Kinder II, Sports Director
Emmy Wells, Music Director
Matt Cole, Programming Director

WVMX
06-21-1991; 107.9 MHz FM; *Hrs Open:* 24; 3 kw; 469 ft.; N40 14 41.5 W82 55 49.1
4401 Carriage Hill Lane, Columbus, OH 43220 US
(614) 451-2191; *Fax:* (614) 451-1831
www.themix1079.com
License: Westerville, Delaware County, OH held by Franklin Communications Inc.
Group Owner: Saga Communications Inc.; (acq 3-27-2003; $9 million)
Nat'l Reps: Christal; *Wire Services:* AP
Arbitron Metro Market: Columbus, OH; *Format:* Adult Contemp; *Hrs. of News Programming:* news progmg 10 hrs wkly; *No. News Employees:* 1; *Target Audience:* 25-44.
Alan Goodman, President
Jimmy Steele, Programming Director
Michelle Hurley, Promotions/Marketing Manager

Whitehouse

***WTPG**
88.9 MHz FM; 12.3 kw; 274 ft.; N41 25 39 W83 36 30
P.O. Box 890820, Temecula, CA 92589 US
(855) 500-3759; *Fax:* (208) 736-1958
wtpg.krtmradio.org
License: Whitehouse, Lucas County, OH held by Penfold Communcations, Inc.
Group Owner: Penfold Communications, Inc.
Arbitron Metro Market: Whitehouse, Ohio; *Format:* Christian

Wilberforce

***WCSU-FM**
12-15-1962; 88.9 MHz FM; 1 kw; 174 ft.; N39 42 57 W83 52 27
1400 Brush Row Rd, Cosby Center, Wilberforce, OH 45384 US
(937) 376-9278; *Fax:* (937) 376-6015
www.wcsufm.org
wcsufm@gmail.com
License: Wilberforce, Greene County, OH held by Central State University.
Arbitron Metro Market: Wilberforce,OH; *Format:* Jazz; *Target Audience:* 12-49; African-Americans
Edwin Clay, Interim General Manager
Tony Chappel, Programming/Operations Director
Stephon Lane, Chief Engineer

Willard

WLRD
01-01-2000; 96.9 MHz FM; 6 kw; 328 ft.; N40 57 36 W82 37 16
3809 Maple Avenue, Castalia, OH 44824 US
(419) 684-5311; *Fax:* (419) 684-5378
www.wlrd.net
License: Willard, Huron County, OH held by Christian Faith Broadcast Inc.
Group Owner: Christian Faith Broadcasting Inc.
Format: Gospel; *Target Audience:* 25-54.
Richard Hawkins, General Manager

Willoughby

WINT
01-25-1965; 1330 kHz AM; *Hrs Open:* 24; 0.5 kw-D, DA2; 0.042 kw-N, DA2; N41 38 57 W81 25 25
Mailing Address: P.O. Box 1330, Willoughby, OH 44094 US
Second Address: 36913 Stevens Boulevard, Willoughby, OH 44094
(440) 946-1330; *Fax:* (440) 953-0320
www.wintradio.com
License: Willoughby, OH held by Spirit Broadcasting Corp.
Nat'l Network: USA; Westwood One; Radio America; Talk Radio Network
Arbitron Metro Market: Cleveland, OH; *Format:* Sports, Talk
Special Programming: Ger one hr; Croation 3 hrs, It one hr; Pol one hr; Spanish contemporary 1 hr; Polka 15 hrs wkly; *Target Audience:* 35 plus; communityadults
Tony Petkovsek, President
Ray Somich, General Manager/General Sales Manager
Ron Somich, Station Manager
Camilla D'Andrea, Programming Director
Allan Parrish, Production Director
Kathy Gee, News Director

Wilmington

WKFI
01-01-1963; 1090 kHz AM; 1 kw-D, DAD; N39 26 12 W83 51 21
Rebroadcasts: Rebroadcasts WBZI(AM) Xenia 80%
23 East 2nd Street, Xenia, OH 45385 US
(937) 372-5804
www.myclassiccountry.com
cds@myclassiccountry.com
License: Wilmington, OH held by Town and Country Broadcasting Inc.
Group Owner: Town and Country Broadcasting Inc.; (acq 12-16-2004; $300,000).
Nat'l Network: Fox News Radio; *Regional Network:* Agrinet; *Nat'l Reps:* Rgnl Reps; *Wire Services:* AP
Format: Country *Special Programming:* Big band 5 hrs wkly; *Hrs. of News Programming:* news progmg 3 hrs wkly; *No. News Employees:* 1; *Target Audience:* General.; *Adv. Rates:* 18; 18; 18; 0
Joe Mullins, General Manager
Roy Hatfield, Programming Director
Megan Brugger, News Director
Bucks Braun, Morning Host
Darrin Johnston, News Commentator

WKLN
01-01-1974; 102.3 MHz FM; 3 kw; 299 ft.; N39 21 54 W83 46 8
200 R Gordon Dr., Wilmington, OH 45177 US
(916) 251-1600; *Fax:* (916) 251-1767
www.klove.com
License: Wilmington, Clinton County, OH held by Vernon R. Baldwin Inc.
Group Owner: Vernon R Baldwin Inc.; (acq 4-22-2003; $1.2 million with co-located AM).
Nat'l Network: K-Love
Format: Christian
Marcella Baldwin, President

Wooster

***WCWS-FM**
04-01-1968; 90.9 MHz FM; *Hrs Open:* 24; 1.05 kw; 223 ft.; N40 49 41 W81 52 14
Lowry Center - 1189 Beall Avenue, Wooster, OH 44691 US
(330) 263-2240; *Fax:* (330) 263-2690
www.woo91.spaces.wooster.edu
License: Wooster, Wayne County, OH held by The College of Wooster.
Arbitron Metro Market: Wooster, Oh; *Format:* Variety/Diverse
Special Programming: Edu 8 hrs wkly; *Hrs. of News Programming:* News progmg 10 hrs wkly; *Target Audience:* General; college students & people of thesurrounding area
Warner Brownfield, General Manager
Emma Gonn, Programming Director
Adrian Rowan/Chelsea Carlson, Promotions Director
Zach Moore, Sports Director
John Finn/Jill Munro, Academic Advisors
Eric Tonian/Sam Corman Penzel, MusicDirectors

***WKRW**
03-29-1993; 89.3 MHz FM; *Hrs Open:* 24; 2.1 kw; 318 ft; N40 46 28 W81 55 05 *Rebroadcasts:* Rebroadcasts WKSU-FM Kent 99%
Mailing Address: Box 5190, Kent, OH 44242
Second Address: 1613 E. Summit St, Kent, OH 44242-0001
(330) 672-3114; *Fax:* (330) 672-4107
www.wksu.org
letters@wksu.org
License: Wooster, Wayne County, OH held by Kent State University.
Nat'l Network: NPR; PRI
Population Served: 91,826 *Special Programming:* Folk 12 hrs wkly; *Hrs. of News Programming:* news progmg 35 hrs wkly; *No. News Employees:* 5; *Target Audience:* 35-65; college grad, professional & upper income
Kandy Neal, Operations Coordinator
Dan Skinner, Executive Director/General Manager
M L Schultze, Web Editor
Ronald Bartlebaugh, Engineering Dir
Kerry Kurchak, Assistant General Manager

WKVX
01-01-1947; 960 kHz AM; *Hrs Open:* 24; 1 kw-D, ND1; 0.032 kw-N, ND1; N40 47 31 W81 54 17
Mailing Address: 186 South Hillcrest Drive, Wooster, OH 44691 US
Second Address: 186 S. Hillcrest Dr., Wooster, OH 44691
(330) 264-5122; *Fax:* (330) 264-3571
www.wkvx.com
wkvx@aol.com
License: Wooster, OH held by WWST Corp. L.L.C.

Group Owner: Wooster Republican Printing Co.
Nat'l Network: Westwood One; CNN Radio *Regional Reps:* Rgnl Reps; *Wire Services:* AP
Format: Oldies
Rich Cornwelll, General Manager
Craig Walton, General Manager
Ron Hamilton, General Sales Mgr
Mike Breckenridge, Programming Director

WQKT
01-01-1947; 104.5 MHz FM; *Hrs Open:* 24; 52 kw; 331 ft.; N40 47 31 W81 54 17
Mailing Address: 186 South Hillcrest Drive, Wooster, OH 44691 US
Second Address: 186 S. Hillcrest Dr., Wooster, OH 44691
(330) 264-5122; *Fax:* (330) 264-3571
www.wqkt.com
wqkt@aol.com
License: Wooster, Wayne County, OH held by WWST Corp. L.L.C.
Group Owner: Wooster Republican Printing Co.
Nat'l Network: Westwood One; CNN Radio *Regional Reps:* Rgnl Reps; *Wire Services:* AP
Format: Country, Sports, 86; *No. News Employees:* 3; *Target Audience:* 35-54.
Craig Walton, General Manager
Ron Hamilton, General Sales Mgr
Mike Breckenridge, Programming Director

Worthington

WJKR
01-01-1998; 103.9 MHz FM; *Hrs Open:* 24; 6 kw; Ant 328 ft; N40 09 33 W82 55 21
1458 Dublin Rd., Columbus, OH 43235 US
(614) 481-7800
1039jackfm.com
License: Worthington, Franklin County, OH held by North American Broadcasting Co. Inc.
Group Owner: North American Broadcasting Co. Inc.
Nat'l Reps: D & R Radio; *Wire Services:* AP
Population Served: 1,200,000; *Arbitron Metro Market:* Columbus, OH

Xenia

WBZI
11-11-1963; 1500 kHz AM; *Hrs Open:* Sunrise-sunset; 0.5 kw-D, NDD; N39 42 48 W83 54 48
23 E. Second St., Xenia, OH 45385 US
(937) 372-5804
www.myclassiccountry.com
cds@myclassiccountry.com
License: Xenia, OH held by Town & Country Broadcasting Inc.
Group Owner: Town and Country Broadcasting Inc.; (acq 10-4-95; $140,000).
Nat'l Network: Fox News Radio; *Regional Network:* Agrinet; *Nat'l Reps:* Rgnl Reps; *Wire Services:* AP
Arbitron Metro Market: Xenia, OH; *Format:* Country *Special Programming:* Gospel 5 hrs, farm 2 hrs wkly; *Hrs. of News Programming:* news progmg 3 hrs wkly; *No. News Employees:* 1; *Target Audience:* 35-64; upperincome, married, homeowners; *Adv. Rates:* 26; 26; 26
Joe Mullins, General Manager
Roy Hatfield, Programming Director
Darrin Johnston, News Director
Bucks Braun, Morning Host
Megan Brugger, Traffic Manager

WZLR
03-03-1967; 95.3 MHz FM; *Hrs Open:* 24; 6 kw; 322 ft.; N39 37 52 W83 53 39
3773 Howard Hughes Pwy, Suite 300n, Las Vegas, NV 89109 US
(937) 259-2111; *Fax:* (937) 259-2168
jennifer.perkins@cmgohio.com
License: Xenia, Greene County, OH held by Cox Radio Inc.
Group Owner: Cox Radio Inc.; (acq 1998; grpsl)
Nat'l Reps: Christal
Arbitron Metro Market: Xenia, OH; *Format:* Contemporary Hits/Top 40, Adult Contemp; *Target Audience:* 25-54.
Rob Rohr, General Manager/Senior Vice President
Kathy Eagle, General Sales Mgr
Nick Roberts, Vice President of Marketing
Jennifer Perkins, Promotions Manager
Chip Beale, General Sales Manager

Yellow Springs

***WYSO**
02-08-1958; 91.3 MHz FM; *Hrs Open:* 24; 50 kw horiz, 45.85 kw vert; 400 ft.; N39 45 46 W83 52 59
150 East South Street, Yellow Springs, OH 45387 US
(937) 767-6420; *Fax:* (937) 769-1382
www.wyso.org
wyso@wyso.org
License: Yellow Springs, Greene County, OH held by Antioch University.
Nat'l Network: PRI; NPR; *Regional Network:* Ohio Educ. Telecommunications
Arbitron Metro Market: Yellow Springs, OH; *Format:* News, Triple A *Special Programming:* Folk 2 hrs, jazz 12 hrs, blues 4 hrs, new age 4 hr; *Hrs. of News Programming:* news progmg 77 hrs wkly; *No. News Employees:* 2 *Target Audience:* 25-54; college educated, professional, mid-upper income; *Adv. Rates:* 45; 30; 35; 20
Peter Hayes, Operations Dir
Neenah Ellis, General Manager
Emily McCord, News Director
Luke Dennis, Development Director
Nikki Dakota, Music Director
Juliet Fromholt, Webmaster

Youngstown

WNCD
06-01-1959; 93.3 MHz FM; 50 kw; 279 ft.; N41 4 50 W80 38 54
7461 South Avenue, Youngstown, OH 44512 US
(330) 965-0057; *Fax:* (330) 729-9991
www.933fmthewolf.com
License: Youngstown, Mahoning County, OH held by Citicasters Licenses Inc.
Group Owner: iHeartMedia
Arbitron Metro Market: Youngstown, OH; *Format:* Classic Rock
Bill Kelly, Regional President
Steve Granato, Senior Vice President of Programming
Bob Hotchkiss, Sales Manager
Jeff Kelly, Programming Director
Thomas John, Digital Content Director
Jim Davis, Regional Senior Vice President ofProgramming

WBBW
02-20-1949; 1240 kHz AM; 1 kw-U, ND1; N41 4 50 W80 38 54
4040 Simon Road, Youngstown, OH 44512 US
(330) 783-1000
License: Youngstown, OH held by Cumulus Licensing Corp.
Group Owner: Cumulus Media Inc.; (acq 3-15-00; grpsl).
Nat'l Network: Westwood One
Arbitron Metro Market: Youngstown-Warren, OH; *Format:* Religious
Brad Marshall, General Sales Mgr
Joe Dobbins, Programming Director
Leah Brenner, Director of Marketing & Promotions
Rick Parrish, Market Manager/Vice President
Bob Greenburg, Sports Director

WHOT-FM
11-01-1959; 101.1 MHz FM; 24 kw; Ant 711 ft; N41 03 28 W80 38 24
4040 Simon Rd., Youngstown, OH 44512 US
(330) 783-1000; *Fax:* (330) 783-0060
www.hot101.com
License: Youngstown, Mahoning County, OH held by Cumulus Media
Arbitron Metro Market: Youngstown-Warren, OH; *Target Audience:* 18-54.
Rick Parrish, Vice President/Market Manager
Brad Marshall, General Sales Mgr
Joe Dobbins, Programming Director
Leah Brenner, Promotions Manager
Kelly Stevens, News Director
Rick Foley, Engineering Dir
Wes Boyd, Chief Engineer

WKBN
01-01-1926; 570 kHz AM; *Hrs Open:* 24
7461 South Avenue, Youngstown, OH 44512 US
(330) 965-0057; *Fax:* (330) 965-8277
www.570wkbn.com
License: Youngstown, OH held by Citicasters Licenses Inc.
Group Owner: iHeartMedia; (acq 1-22-99; $11 million with co-located FM).
Nat'l Network: ABC; CBS
Arbitron Metro Market: Youngstown-Warren, OH; *Format:* News, News/Talk, 84, Talk *Special Programming:* Polka 2 hrs, Croation 2 hrs wkly
Bill Kelly, Market President
Dan Rivers, Senior Vice President of Programming
Robert Hotchkiss, Director of Sales
Thomas John, Digital Content Director
Jeff Kelly, Public Service Coordinator
Jim Davis, Regional Senior VicePresident of Programming

WMXY
08-26-1947; 98.9 MHz FM; 5.9 kw; 1371 ft.; N41 3 24 W80 38 44
7461 South Avenue, Youngstown, OH 44512 US
(330) 965-0057; *Fax:* (330) 965-8277
www.mix989.com
License: Youngstown, Mahoning County, OH held by Citicasters Licenses Inc.
Group Owner: iHeartMedia
Arbitron Metro Market: Youngstown-Warren, OH; *Format:* Adult Contemp
Bill Kelly, Market President
Steve Granato, Senior Vice President of Programming
Karl Brandt, General Sales Mgr
Thomas John, Digital Content Director
Jeff Kelly, Public Service Coordinator
Lindsay Watts, Digital SalesCoordinator
Jim Davis, Regional Senior Vice President of Programming

WNIO
09-07-1939; 1390 kHz AM; *Hrs Open:* 24
7461 South Avenue, Youngstown, OH 44512 US
(330) 965-0057; *Fax:* (330) 965-8277
www.sportsradio1390.com
License: Youngstown, OH held by Citicasters Licenses Inc.
Group Owner: iHeartMedia; (acq 1-15-2004; grpsl).
Arbitron Metro Market: Youngstown-Warr; *Format:* Sports *Special Programming:* lt 3 hrs wkly; *Hrs. of News Programming:* news progmg 3 hrs wkly; *No. News Employees:* 2; *Target Audience:* General.
Bill Kelly, Regional President
Jim Davis, Regional Senior Vice President of Programming
Karl Brandt, General Sales Mgr
Mark French, Programming Director
Thomas John, Digital Content Director

***WYSU**
09-01-1969; 88.5 MHz FM; *Hrs Open:* 24; 50 kw; 376 ft.; N41 3 23.2 W80 38 43.7
410 Wick Avenue, Youngstown, OH 44555 US
(330) 941-3363; *Fax:* (330) 941-1501
www.wysu.org
info@wysu.org
License: Youngstown, Mahoning County, OH held by Youngstown State University.
Nat'l Network: PRI; NPR
Arbitron Metro Market: Youngstown-Warr; *Format:* News *Special Programming:* Folk 3 hrs wkly; *Hrs. of News Programming:* News progmg 48 hrs wkly; *Target Audience:* General.; *Adv. Rates:* 18; 13.75; 18; 8.25
David Luscher, Operations Dir
Gary Sexton, General Manager
Ron Krauss, Chief Engineer

***WYTN**
05-01-1991; 91.7 MHz FM; *Hrs Open:* 24; 0.9 kw; 594 ft.; N41 3 28 W80 38 42
Mailing Address: 4135 Northgate Blvd, Suite 1, Sacramento, CA 95834 US
Second Address: 3930 Sunset Blvd., Youngstown, OH 60435
(815) 725-1331
www.familyradio.com
License: Youngstown, Mahoning County, OH held by Family Stations Inc.
Group Owner: Family Stations Inc.
Arbitron Metro Market: Youngstown-Warr; *Format:* Religious *Special Programming:* Class 2 hrs wkly; *Target Audience:* 25 plus; Christians
Harold Camping, President/General Manager

Zanesville

***WJIC**
01-01-2000; 91.7 MHz FM; *Hrs Open:* 24; 6 kw; 318 ft.; N39 58 2 W82 12 49
Dba Riverside Ministries, 2620 South River Road, Zanesville, OH 43701 US
(414) 935-3000; *Fax:* (414) 935-3015
wjic@vcyamerica.org
License: Zanesville, Muskingum County, OH held by VCY/America Inc.
Group Owner: VCY America Inc.
Nat'l Network: USA
Format: Christian, Religious
Vic Eliason, General Manager
Jim Schneider, Programming Director
Andy Eliason, Chief Engineer

***WOUZ-FM**
11-01-1993; 90.1 MHz FM; *Hrs Open:* 24; 3 kw vert; 279 ft.; N39 48 50 W81 57 21 *Rebroadcasts:* Rebroadcasts WOUB-FM Athens 100%
35 South College Street, Athens, OH 45701 US
(740) 593-1771; *Fax:* (740) 593-0240
www.woub.org
woub@woub.org
License: Zanesville, Muskingum County, OH held by Ohio University.
Format: News, News/Talk, 86; *No. News Employees:* 3
Thomas Hodson, Director/General Manager
Joan Butcher, Programming Director
Tim Sharp, News Director
Ted Ross, Engineering Dir
Mark Breaver, Chief Content Officer
Jeannie Jeffers, Director of Development

Oklahoma

Ada

KADA
09-01-1934; 1230 kHz AM; 1 kw-U, ND1; N34 47 6 W96 40 44
Mailing Address: PO Box 609, Ada, OK 74820 US
Second Address: 1019 N. Broadway, Ada, OK 74820
(580) 332-1212; *Fax:* (580) 332-0128
www.kadaradio.net
kada@cable1.net
License: Ada, OK held by The Chickasaw Nation.
Group Owner: The Chickasaw Nation
Regional Network: Okla. News Net.
Arbitron Metro Market: Ada, OK; *Format:* Sports *Special Programming:* Gospel 5 hrs wkly; *Target Audience:* 25-54.
Roger Harris, General Manager

KADA-FM
01-01-1979; 99.3 MHz FM; 5.5 kw; 276 ft.; N34 42 31 W96 44 24
PO Box 609, Ada, OK 74820 US
(580) 332-1212; *Fax:* (580) 332-0128
www.kadaradio.net
License: Ada, Pontotoc County, OK held by The Chickasaw Nation
Group Owner: The Chickasaw Nation; (acq 7-88)
Arbitron Metro Market: Ada, OK; *Format:* Country; *Adv. Rates:* 15; 15; 15; 15
Roger Harris, General Manager

***KCNP**
01-01-1999; 89.5 MHz FM; *Hrs Open:* 24; 5.8 kw; 581 ft.; N34 41 1 W96 45 44
Route 5, Box 119, Ada, OK 74820 US
(580) 436-2603; *Fax:* (580)272-5267
www.kcnpradio.org/index.htm
License: Ada, Pontotoc County, OK held by The Chickasaw Nation.
Group Owner: The Chickasaw Nation; (acq 9-24-2008; $470,000)
Arbitron Metro Market: Ada, OK
Brian Brashier, General Manager

***KAJT**
01-01-2006; 88.7 MHz FM; *Hrs Open:* 24; 31 kw; 240 ft.; N34 46 32 W96 35 15
Mailing Address: P O Drawer 2440, Tupelo, MS 38803 US
Second Address: 8919 World Ministry Ave., Baton Rouge, LA 70810
(225) 768-3288; *Fax:* (225) 768-3729
www.jsm.org
onair@jsm.org
License: Ada, Pontotoc County, OK held by Family Worship Center Church Inc.
Group Owner: Family Worship Center Church Inc.; (acq 10-7-2005; $500,000 with CP for KSSO(FM) Norman)
Arbitron Metro Market: Ada, OK; *Format:* Gospel
David Whitelaw, COO
Van Michael, President
John Santiago, Programming Director

***KAKO**
01-01-2006; 91.3 MHz FM; 100 kw vert; 442 ft.; N35 13 36 W96 55 42
P.O. Box 3206, Tupelo, MS 38803 US
(662) 844-8888; *Fax:* (662) 842-6791
www.afr.net
faq@afa.net
License: Ada, Pontotoc County, OK held by American Family Association.
Group Owner: American Family Radio
Nat'l Network: American Family Radio
Arbitron Metro Market: Ada, OK; *Format:* Christian
Tim Wildmon, President
Donald Wildmon, Founder
Buddy Smith, Sr VP
Ed Vitagliano, Exec VP
Randy Sharp, Director Of Special Projects
Meeke Addison, Director Of Communications
Abraham Hamilton III, General Sales Mgr

Altus

KEYB
08-08-1988; 107.9 MHz FM; *Hrs Open:* 24; 50 kW; 331 ft.; N34 46 15 W99 32 20
Mailing Address: PO Box 1077, Altus, OK 73522 USA
Second Address: 808 N. Main St., Altus, OK 73521
(580) 482-1555; *Fax:* (580) 482-8353
www.keyb108.net
License: Altus, Jackson County, OK held by Altus FM, Inc.
Group Owner: Altus FM, Inc.
Nat'l Network: Westwood One; AP Network News
Arbitron Metro Market: Altus, OK; *Format:* Country *Special Programming:* Farm 2 hrs wkly; *Hrs. of News Programming:* news progmg 3 hrs wkly; *No. News Employees:* 1; *Target Audience:* 25-54
Gayle Ledbetter, General Manager
Linda Browning, Sales Executive

***KKVO**
01-01-1985; 90.9 MHz FM; *Hrs Open:* 24; 4 kw; 820 ft.; N34 58 39 W99 24 35
P.O. Box 837, Altus, OK 73522 US
(916) 251-1600; *Fax:* (916) 251-1650
www.klove.com
License: Altus, Jackson County, OK held by Educational Media Foundation.
Group Owner: EMF Broadcasting; (acq 6-6-2005; $150,000)
Nat'l Network: K-Love
Format: Christian
Darrell Chambliss, Chairman
Mike Novak, CEO
Mike Novak, President
Alan Mason, Operations Dir
Eric Moser, General Sales Mgr
David Pierce, Programming Director
Ed Lenane, News Director
Sam Wallington, Engineering Dir
ScottSmith, Music Director
Marya Morgan, News Reporter
Scott Smith, News Reporter
Richard Hunt, Regional Manager
Evan Falat, Traffic Manager

KWHW-FM
04-01-1974; 93.5 MHz FM; 45 kw; Ant 528 ft; N34 37 35 W99 20 10
Mailing Address: Box 577, Altus, OK 73522
Second Address: 212 W. Cypress, Altus, OK 73522
(580) 482-1450; *Fax:* (580) 482-3420
mward@kwhw.com
License: Altus, Jackson County, OK
Population Served: 50,000
Lisa Korry Cheek, General Manager

KWHW
04-02-1947; 1450 kHz AM
Mailing Address: P. O. Box 577, Altus, OK 73522 US
Second Address: 212 W. Cypress, Altus, OK 73522
(580) 482-1450; *Fax:* (580) 482-3420
www.kwhw.com
mward@kwhw.com
License: Altus, OK held by Monarch Broadcasting Inc.
Group Owner: Monarch Broadcasting Inc.; (acq 12-31-2003; grpsl)
Regional Network: Okla. News Net.
Arbitron Metro Market: Altus, OK; *Format:* Agriculture, News, 62, Talk, Country *Special Programming:* Sp 16 hrs wkly
Jimmy Young, General Manager

***KOCU**
07-01-2002; 90.1 MHz FM; 5 kw; 85 ft.; N34 40 14 W99 20 13
Rebroadcasts: Rebroadcasts KCCU(FM) Lawton 100%
2800 West Gore, Lawton, OK 73505 US
(580) 581-2472; *Fax:* (580) 581-5571
www.kccu.org
kccu@cameron.edu
License: Altus, Jackson County, OK held by Cameron University.
Nat'l Network: NPR; PRI
Arbitron Metro Market: Lawton, OK; *Format:* Classical, News
Ted Riley, General Manager, Director of Broadcasting
Doug Cole, Station Manager & Operations Director
Clinton Wieden, News Director
Cynthia Sosa, Production Director
Zach McGrew, Development Director

***KTHL**
89.3 MHz FM; 1.5 kw; 253 ft.; N34 38 21 W99 21 19
US
(580) 767-1400; *Fax:* (580) 765-1700
www.thehousefm.com
mail@thehousefm.com
License: Altus, Jackson County, OK held by The Love Station Inc.
Arbitron Metro Market: Altus, OK
Doyle Brewer, CEO/COO
Tony Weir, Music Director
Janelle Keith, Music Director
Darcey Christianson, Chief Engineer
Shaun Michaels, Production Director
Andy Youso, Assistant Program Director
Donna Hollifield, Office Manager

Alva

KALV
10-18-1956; 1430 kHz AM; *Hrs Open:* 24; 0.5 kw-D, DA2; 0.5 kw-N, DA2; N36 49 6 W98 38 38
Rt 1, Box 53, Alva, OK 73117 US
(405) 327-1430; *Fax:* (405) 327-1433
kalvradio@yahoo.com
License: Alva, OK held by MM&K of Alva Inc.
Arbitron Metro Market: Alva, OK; *Format:* Oldies; *Hrs. of News Programming:* news progmg 8 hrs wkly; *No. News Employees:* 1; *Target Audience:* 45-70; loc residents
Randy Mitchel, President

KPAK
97.5 MHz FM; 50 kw; 492 ft.; N37 1 27 W98 41 22
188 South Bellevue#222, Memphis, TN 38104 US
(888) 251-8427; *Fax:* (620) 825-4324
www.kpak.net
License: Alva, Woods County, OK held by George S. Flinn Jr.
Arbitron Metro Market: Kiowa, KS; *Format:* Alternative
George Flinn Jr., President

Anadarko

KVSP
09-01-1981; 103.5 MHz FM; *Hrs Open:* 24; 100 kw; 1969 ft.; N35 15 4 W98 36 53
1457 N.E. 23rd St., Oklahoma City, OK 73111 US
(405) 427-5877
www.kvsp.com
License: Anadarko, Oklahoma County, OK held by Perry Broadcasting of Southwest Oklahoma Inc.
Group Owner: Perry Publishing & Broadcasting Co.; (acq 11-22-2002; grpsl).
Nat'l Network: ABC
Arbitron Metro Market: OK City area, rural areas west of OK; *Format:* Urban Contemporary; *Target Audience:* 18 plus.

Antlers

KDOE
01-01-2006; 102.3 MHz FM; 3.3 kw; 276 ft.; N34 13 35 W95 37 20
Main & High St., Antlers, OK 74560 US
(580) 326-2555; *Fax:* (580) 326-2623
www.kdoe1023.com
License: Antlers, Pushmataha County, OK held by K95.5 Inc.
Group Owner: K95.9 Inc.
Arbitron Metro Market: Antlers, OK; *Format:* Variety/Diverse

Apache

KACO
01-01-1989; 98.5 MHz FM; *Hrs Open:* 24; 18.5 kw; 305 ft.; N34 56 30 W98 22 33
115 W. Broadway, Anadarko, OK 73005 US
(405) 247-6682; *Fax:* (405) 247-1051
www.superstarcountry985.com
License: Apache, Caddo County, OK held by Perry Publishing & Broadcasting
Group Owner: Perry Publishing & Broadcasting Co.; (acq 1-5-98; $475,000).
Nat'l Network: ABC
Arbitron Metro Market: Anadarko, OK; *Format:* Country; *Target Audience:* 25-54.

Ardmore

***KLCU**
06-19-1998; 90.3 MHz FM; 25 kw; 213 ft.; N34 12 10 W97 9 12
Rebroadcasts: Rebroadcasts KCCU(FM) Lawton 98%

2800 W Gore Blvd., Lawton, OK 73505 US
(580) 581-2425; *Fax:* (580) 581-5571
www.kccu.org
kccu@cameron.edu
License: Ardmore, Carter County, OK held by Cameron University.
Nat'l Network: NPR; PRI
Arbitron Metro Market: Lawton, OK; *Format:* Classical
Ted Riley, General Manager
Terry Anderson, General Sales Mgr
Michael Leal, Programming Director

KVSO
09-01-1935; 1240 kHz AM; *Hrs Open:* 24; 1 kw-U, ND1; N34 10 54 W97 8 48
P.O. Box 429, Ardmore, OK 73402 US
(580) 226-0421; *Fax:* (580) 226-0464
www.kvso.com
webmaster@kvso.com
License: Ardmore, OK held by LKCM Radio Group L.P.
Group Owner: LKCM Radio Group L.P.
Nat'l Reps: Christal
Arbitron Metro Market: Ardmore, OK; *Format:* Christian; *Hrs. of News Programming:* news progmg 4 hrs wkly; *No. News Employees:* 1; *Target Audience:* 25 plus.
Michael Baer, General Manager

***KQPD**
01-01-2003; 91.1 MHz FM; 0.25 kw; 167 ft.; N34 11 1 W97 7 23
P.O. Box 3206, Tupelo, MS 38803 US
(662) 844-8888; *Fax:* (662) 842-6791
www.afr.net
faq@afa.net
License: Ardmore, Carter County, OK held by American Family Association.
Group Owner: American Family Radio
Arbitron Metro Market: Tupelo, MS; *Format:* Christian
Tim Wildmon, President
Donald Wildmon, Founder
Buddy Smith, Sr VP
Ed Vitagliano, Exec VP
Randy Sharp, Director Of Special Projects
Meeke Addison, Director Of Communications
Abraham Hamilton III, General Counsel

Atoka

KHKC-FM
06-15-1984; 102.1 MHz FM; 0.75 kw; 449 ft.; N34 25 8 W96 11 24
Mailing Address: 4410 10th Street, Lubbock, TX 79476 US
Second Address: Hwy. 75 N., Atoka, OK 74525
(580) 226-9797; *Fax:* (580) 889-9308
www.khkc1021.com
khkc103@yahoo.com
License: Atoka, Atoka County, OK held by Keystone Broadcasting Corp.
Format: Country; *Target Audience:* Adults; *Adv. Rates:* 5; 5; 5; na
Ricky Chase, General Manager

Bartlesville

KWON
04-01-1942; 1400 kHz AM; *Hrs Open:* 24; 1 kw-U, ND1; N36 45 53 W95 57 35
1200 S.E. Frank Phillips Blvd., Bartlesville, OR 74003 US
(918) 336-1001; *Fax:* (918) 336-6939
www.bartlesvilleradio.com
radio@bartlesvilleradio.com
License: Bartlesville, OK held by KCD Enterprises Inc.
Group Owner: KCD Enterprises Inc.; acq 2-1-97; $625,000 with co-located FM)
Nat'l Network: CBS; *Regional Network:* Okla. News Net.
Regional Reps: Rgnl Reps; *Wire Services:* AP
Arbitron Metro Market: Bartlesville, OK; *Format:* News, News/Talk, 86 *Special Programming:* Relg 5 hrs wkly; *Hrs. of News Programming:* news progmg 25 hrs wkly; *No. News Employees:* 2; *Target Audience:* 25-54;general; *Adv. Rates:* 22; 22; 20; 22

KYFM
11-06-1961; 100.1 MHz FM; *Hrs Open:* 24; 25 kw; Ant 695 ft; N36 37 42 W96 11 26
1200 S.E. Frank Phillips Blvd., Bartlesville, OK 74003
(918) 336-1001; *Fax:* (918) 336-6939
www.bartlesvilleradio.com
radio@bartlesvilleradio.com
License: Bartlesville, Washington County, OK held by KCD Enterprises Inc.
Group Owner: KCD Enterprises Inc.
Nat'l Network: ABC; *Regional Network:* Agri-Net *Regional Reps:* Rgnl Reps; *Wire Services:* AP
Population Served: 720,000 *Special Programming:* Gospel 4 hrs wkly; *Hrs. of News Programming:* News progmg 15 hrs wkly; *Target Audience:* 25-49.; *Adv. Rates:* 22; 22; 22; 22

***KWRI**
01-01-2004; 89.1 MHz FM; *Hrs Open:* 24; 100 kw vert; 627 ft.; N36 42 13 W95 30 57
1425 N. Market Blvd., Suite 9, Sacramento, CA 95834 US
(888) 937-2471; *Fax:* (916) 251-1650
www.air1.com
info@air1.com
License: Bartlesville, Washington County, OK held by Educational Media Foundation.
Group Owner: EMF Broadcasting
Nat'l Network: Air 1
Arbitron Metro Market: Tulsa, OK; *Format:* Alternative, Christian; *No. News Employees:* 3; *Target Audience:* 18-35; Judeo-Christian, female
Darrell Chambliss, Chairman
Alan Mason, COO
Mike Novak, President and CEO
David Pierce, Programming Director
Ed Lenane, News Director
Sam Wallington, Engineering Dir
Marya Morgan, News Reporter
Richard Hunt, News Reporter
Larry Moody, Director
Mitch Barnhart, Director
David R. Ferry, Director
Walter Golembeski, Director

Beaver

***KLDB**
91.9 MHz FM; 0.1 kw horiz; -72 ft.; N36 49 3 W100 31 36 US
(405) 380-3516
www.bpba.us
info@bpba.us
License: Beaver, Beaver County, OK held by Better Public Broadcasting Association.
Arbitron Metro Market: Beaver, OK
Dennis Burton, General Manager

Bennington

KZRC
11-01-1979; 96.1 MHz FM; *Hrs Open:* 5 AM-1 AM; 6 kw; 328 ft.; N33 53 51 W96 8 18
5946 Club Oaks Dr., Dallas, TX 75248 US
(979) 323-7771; *Fax:* (708) 671-1202
License: Bennington, Bryan County, OK held by North Texas Radio Group L.P.
Arbitron Metro Market: Dallas, TX
Richard Witkovski, General Manager

Bethany

KKWD
10-29-1965; 104.9 MHz FM; *Hrs Open:* 24; 6 kw; 328 ft.; N35 29 53 W97 37 10
4045 NW 64th Street, Suite 600, Oklahoma City, OK 73116 US
(405) 848-0100; *Fax:* (405) 843-5288
www.wild1049hd.com
info@wild1049hd.com
License: Bethany, Oklahoma County, OK held by Cumulus Media License Holding
Arbitron Metro Market: Oklahoma City, OK; *Format:* Adult Contemp; *Target Audience:* 35-49 & 25-34; young, professional
Larry Bastida, Market Manager

Bixby

KJMM
11-01-1994; 105.3 MHz FM; *Hrs Open:* 24; 10 kw; 879 ft.; N35 51 41 W95 46 3
7030 S. Yale Ave., Suite 302, Tulsa, OK 74136 US
(918) 494-9886
www.kjmm.com
info@ppbcinc.net
License: Bixby, Tulsa County, OK held by KJMM Inc.
Group Owner: Perry Publishing & Broadcasting Co.; (acq 1-95).
Nat'l Network: ABC; American Urban; Westwood One
Arbitron Metro Market: Tulsa, OK; *Format:* Urban Contemporary; *Hrs. of News Programming:* news progmg 10 hrs wkly; *No. News Employees:* 1; *Target Audience:* 18-35; General
Martha Vaughan, General Manager

Blackwell

KOKB
10-01-1952; 1580 kHz AM; *Hrs Open:* 6 AM-9 PM; 1 kw-D, ND1; 0.049 kw-N, ND1; N36 48 35 W97 15 50 *Rebroadcasts:* Rebroadcasts KOKP(AM) Perry 80%
Mailing Address: P.O. Box 2509, Ponca City, OK 74602 US
Second Address: 122 N. Third St., Ponca City, OK 74602
(580) 765-2485; *Fax:* (580) 767-1103
www.eteamradio.com
kokb@eteamradio.com
License: Blackwell, OK held by Team Radio LLC
Group Owner: Team Radio LLC; acq 10-18-96; $90,000).
Format: Sports, Talk; *Hrs. of News Programming:* News progmg 30 hrs wkly; *Target Audience:* 35-75; adult, upper-middle income
Bill Coleman, President

Blanchard

KKNG-FM
08-18-1977; 97.3 MHz FM; *Hrs Open:* 24; 1 kw; Ant 800 ft; N35 10 38 W97 36 10
5101 S. Shields Blvd., Oklahoma City, OK 73005
(405) 616-5500; *Fax:* (405) 616-5505
www.jackokc.com
License: Blanchard, McClain County, OK held by WPA Radio, LLC
Group Owner: Stanton Nelson; (acq 1-31-2006; $1 million).
Nat'l Reps: D & R Radio
Population Served: 100,000; *Arbitron Metro Market:* Oklahoma City, OK
Skip Stow, CEO
Becca Sharp, Station Manager

Boise City

***KJHL**
01-01-2009; 90.9 MHz FM; 10 kw; 351 ft.; N36 44 5 W102 29 53 US
(620) 873-2991; *Fax:* (620) 873-2755
www.kjil.com
kjil@kjil.com
License: Boise City, Cimarron County, OK held by Great Plains Christian Radio Inc.
Arbitron Metro Market: Boise City, OK; *Format:* Christian, Religious; *No. News Employees:* 1
Robert Hughes, CEO
Michael Luskey, CEO
Glenn Hascall, Station Manager
Bill Lurwick, Music Director
Delvin Kinser, News Director

Bristow

KREK
11-14-1978; 104.9 MHz FM; *Hrs Open:* 24; 5 kw; 351 ft.; N35 47 11 W96 27 35
P.O. Box 1280, Bristow, OK 74010 US
(918) 367-5501; *Fax:* (918) 367-5502
krekfm@yahoo.com
License: Bristow, Creek County, OK held by Big Chief Broadcasting Co. of Bristow Inc.
Arbitron Metro Market: Tulsa, OK; *Format:* Country; *Target Audience:* 0-100.
Clifford Smith, President

Broken Arrow

***KNYD**
08-19-1986; 90.5 MHz FM; *Hrs Open:* 24; 80 kw; 1483 ft.; N35 53 0 W95 46 13
Mailing Address: 11717 S 129th East Ave., Broken Arrow, OK 74011 US
Second Address: 11717 S. 129th East Ave., Broken Arrow, OK 74011
(918) 455-5693; *Fax:* (918) 455-0411
www.oasisnetwork.org
mail@oasisnetwork.org
License: Broken Arrow, Tulsa County, OK held by Creative Educational Media Inc.
Arbitron Metro Market: Tulsa, OK; *Format:* Religious; *Target Audience:* General.
David Ingles, President

KTBT
12-23-1970; 92.1 MHz FM; *Hrs Open:* 24; 27 kw; 656 ft.; N36 6 38 W96 1 57
200 Concord Plaza, Suite 600, San Antonio, TX 78216 US
(918) 388-5100; *Fax:* (918)388-5400
www.921thebeat.com
License: Broken Arrow, Tulsa County, OK held by Clear Channel Broadcasting Licenses Inc.

Group Owner: iHeartMedia
Nat'l Reps: Clear Channel
Arbitron Metro Market: Tulsa, OK; *Format:* Contemporary Hits/Top 40; *Target Audience:* 18-34; women
Don Cristi, Senior Vice President of Programming

Broken Bow

KKBI
01-01-1983; 106.1 MHz FM; *Hrs Open:* 24; 17 kw; 817 ft.; N34 14 45 W94 46 58
103 Hastings Court, Idabel, OK 74745 US
(580) 584-3388; *Fax:* (580) 584-3341
www.kkbifm.com
kkbi@pine-net.com
License: Broken Bow, McCurtain County, OK held by J.D.C. Radio Inc.
Nat'l Network: Jones Radio Networks; *Wire Services:* CNN
Arbitron Metro Market: Texarkana, TX; *Format:* Country *Special Programming:* Farm 5 hrs, gospel 4 hrs wkly; *Hrs. of News Programming:* news progmg 5 hrs wkly; *No. News Employees:* 1; *Target Audience:* 24-55. *Adv. Rates:* 14; 14; 14; 12
David Smulyan, General Manager
Jay Lindley, Programming Director

*KBWW
88.3 MHz FM; 3.4 kw; 689 ft.; N34 12 31 W94 46 58 US
(580) 420-6687
License: Broken Bow, McCurtain County, OK held by Golden Baptist Church.
Arbitron Metro Market: Golden, OK
Ron Carroll, General Manager

Byng

KYKC
09-17-1992; 100.1 MHz FM; *Hrs Open:* 24; 50 kw; 492 ft; N34 43 43 W96 42 45
Mailing Address: Box 609, Ada, OK 74820
Second Address: 1019 N. Broadway, Ada, OK 74820
(580) 436-1616; *Fax:* (580) 436-1617
www.kykc.net
kykc@cableone.net
License: Byng, Pontotoc County, OK held by The Chickasaw Nation.
Group Owner: The Chickasaw Nation; (acq 1-14-2005; $900,000).
Target Audience: 12 plus; across the board; *Adv. Rates:* 12; 10; 12; 6
Roger Harris, General Manager
Pete Roper, General Sales Mgr
Mike Manos, Programming Director

Cache

KJMZ
10-23-1970; 97.9 MHz FM; *Hrs Open:* 24; 6 kw; 318 ft.; N34 35 30.5 W98 32 54.5
1525 S.E. Flowermound Rd., Lawton, OK 73501 US
(580) 355-1050
www.kjmz.com
License: Cache, Comanche County, OK held by Perry Broadcasting of Lawton Inc.
Group Owner: Perry Publishing & Broadcasting Co.
Arbitron Metro Market: Lawton, OK; *Format:* Oldies

*KARU
01-01-2005; 88.9 MHz FM; *Hrs Open:* 24; 0.44 kw vert; 259 ft.; N34 38 10 W98 41 32 US
(888) 937-2471; *Fax:* (916) 251-1650
www.air1.com
info@air1.com
License: Cache, Comanche County, OK held by Educational Media Foundation.
Group Owner: EMF Broadcasting
Nat'l Network: Air 1
Arbitron Metro Market: Cache, OK; *Format:* Alternative, Christian; *No. News Employees:* 3; *Target Audience:* 18-35; Judeo-Christian, female
Darrell Chambliss, Chairman
Alan Mason, COO
Mike Novak, President and CEO
Evan Falat, Operations Dir
Eric Allen, General Sales Mgr
Ed Lenane, News Director
Sam Wallington, Engineering Dir
Paul Goldsmith, Music Director
LarryMoody, Director
Mitch Barnhart, Director
David R. Ferry, Director
Walter Golembeski, Director
David Pierce, Chief Creative Officer

Carnegie

*KJCC
01-01-2005; 89.5 MHz FM; 0.35 kw; 194 ft.; N35 6 59 W98 28 26 *Rebroadcasts:* Rebroadcasts KAWZ (FM)
Mailing Address: P.O. Box 391, Twin Falls, ID 83303 US
Second Address: 300 Towakkonie Rd., Box 87, Fort Cobb, OK 73038
(800) 357-4226; *Fax:* (208) 736-1958
www.csnradio.com
csn@csnradio.com
License: Carnegie, Caddo County, OK held by Calvary Chapel of Twin Falls
Group Owner: CSN International
Arbitron Metro Market: Carnegie, OK; *Format:* Christian, Religious
Mike Kestler, President
Daniel Davidson, Operations Dir
Don Mills, Network Programming Director
Mike Stocklin, Underwriting Director
Kelly Carlson, Engineering Dir

Catoosa

KEOR
01-29-1968; 1120 kHz AM; *Hrs Open:* Sunrise-sunset
P. O. Box 68, Atoka, OK 74525 US
(580) 889-3392; *Fax:* (580) 889-9308
License: Catoosa, OK held by Catholic Diocese of Tulsa
Arbitron Metro Market: Tulsa, OK; *Target Audience:* General.
Edward Slattery, CEO

KZLI
07-03-1950; 1570 kHz AM; *Hrs Open:* Daytime
P.O. Box 1270, Tulsa, OK 74101 US
(918) 496-7700; *Fax:* (918) 746-7615
License: Catoosa, OK held by Reunion Broadcasting L.L.C.
Regional Network: Okla. News Net.
Arbitron Metro Market: Tulsa, OK; *Format:* Adult Contemp; *Hrs. of News Programming:* news progmg 10 hrs wkly; *No. News Employees:* 1; *Target Audience:* 35 plus.; *Adv. Rates:* 30; 30; 30; 30
Stan Tacker, General Manager
Terri Tacker, General Sales Mgr

Chelsea

KTFR
03-01-2001; 100.7 MHz FM; *Hrs Open:* 24; 6 kw; 328 ft.; N36 30 12 W95 26 29 *Rebroadcasts:* Rebroadcasts KXOJ-FM Sapulpa
P.O. Box 1250, Sapulpa, OK 74067 US
(918) 492-2660; *Fax:* (918) 492-8840
www.kxoj.com
kxoj@kxoj.com
License: Chelsea, Rogers County, OK held by Michael P. Stephens.
Group Owner: Adonai Radio Group; (acq 2-17-95;
Arbitron Metro Market: Tulsa, OK; *Format:* Christian
Mike Stephens, President
David Stephens, General Manager
Bob Thornton, Programming Director

Chickasha

KWCO-FM
11-04-1966; 105.5 MHz FM; *Hrs Open:* 24; 3.3 kw; 443 ft; N35 00 38 W97 55 54
627 West Chickasha Ave., Oklahoma City, OK 73129
(405) 224-9105; *Fax:* (405) 224-2890
www.ktuz.com
License: Chickasha, Grady County, OK held by Molmon Communications Inc.
Nat'l Network: Jones Radio Networks
Population Served: 100,000; *Arbitron Metro Market:* Oklahoma City,; *Hrs. of News Programming:* News progmg 10 hrs wkly; *Target Audience:* 18-54; Spanish persons; *Adv. Rates:* 18; 15; 14.50; 10
Matthew Mollman, General Manager
Bruce McGreen, Programming Director
George Plummer, News Director
Patrick Roberts, Chief Engineer

*KFXU
01-01-2008; 90.5 MHz FM; 10 kw; 322 ft.; N34 54 33 W97 57 29
1101 81 Highway North, Marlow, OK 73055 US
(580) 658-9292
License: Chickasha, Grady County, OK held by Sister Sherry Lynn Foundation Inc.
Arbitron Metro Market: Tulsa, OK; *Format:* Classic Rock
Ken Austin, General Manager
Sherry Lynn, General Sales Mgr
Jennifer James, Programming Director
James Wilson, Engineering Dir
Steve Michaels, Music Director

Claremore

*KRSC-FM
08-04-1980; 91.3 MHz FM; *Hrs Open:* 7 AM-11 PM; 2.2 kw; 364 ft.; N36 19 6 W95 38 18
1701 W.Will Rogers Blvd., Claremore, OK 74017 US
(918) 343-7777(918) 343-7669; *Fax:* (918) 343-7952
www.rsu.edu
License: Claremore, Rogers County, OK held by Board of Regents of the University of Oklahoma.
Regional Network: Okla. News Net.
Arbitron Metro Market: Claremore, OK *TV Affiliate:* *KRSC-TV affil.; *Format:* Alternative *Special Programming:* Folk 5 hrs, jazz 5 hrs, progsv 12 hrs, country 5 hrs wkly; *Target Audience:* General; college &community, young & older adults
Steve Doyle, Operations Dir
Cathy Coomer, General Manager

KRVT
01-17-1958; 1270 kHz AM; *Hrs Open:* 24
P.O. Box 1270, Tulsa, OK 74101 US
(918) 496-7700; *Fax:* (918) 746-7615
www.krvt.com
krvt@krvt.com
License: Claremore, OK held by Reunion Broadcasting L.L.C.
Nat'l Network: CBS Radio
Arbitron Metro Market: Tulsa, OK; *Format:* Oldies *Special Programming:* St. Louis Cardinal Baseball; *Hrs. of News Programming:* News progmg 4 hrs wkly; *Target Audience:* 35 plus; upscale adults *Adv. Rates:* 30; 30; 30; 20
D. Stanley Tacker, President

Cleveland

*KJOG
91.1 MHz FM; 25 kw vert; 276 ft.; N36 18 47 W96 46 20 US
(864) 297-0216; *Fax:* (864) 297-0344
networkofglory.com
info@networkofglory.org
License: Cleveland, Pawnee County, OK held by Network of Glory Inc.
Arbitron Metro Market: Cleveland, OK
Lola Richey, President

Clinton

KCLI
04-15-1949; 1320 kHz AM
5105 South Shields Blvd, Oklahoma City, OK 73129 US
(580) 323-0617; *Fax:* (580) 323-0717
www.newstalkkcli.com
sales@wrightradio.com
License: Clinton, OK held by Wright Broadcasting Systems Inc.
Group Owner: Wright Broadcasting Systems; (acq 9-13-2000; $25,000).
Regional Network: Okla. News Net.
Arbitron Metro Market: Oklahoma city, OK; *Format:* News, Talk; *Target Audience:* General.
Harold Wright, President and CEO
Todd Brunner, Operations Dir
Harold Wright, General Manager
Heston Wright, Station and Sales Manager
Ray Bagby, Technical Director
Dianna Scott, Office Manager
Amanda Benton, Area SalesManager
Brianna Reherman, Area Sales Manager
John Liddle, Sports Director/Account Executive
Kelli Haan, Account Executive, Websites and Graphics

KWEY-FM
04-09-1978; 95.5 MHz FM; *Hrs Open:* 24; 18.5 kw; 828 ft.; N35 26 43 W98 59 19
P.O. Box 587, Weatherford, OK 73096 US
(580) 772-5939; *Fax:* (580) 772-1590
www.kwey.com
sales@wrightradio.com
License: Clinton, Custer County, OK held by Wright Broadcasting Systems Inc.
Group Owner: Wright Broadcasting Systems; (acq 1996; $300,000)
Nat'l Network: ABC; *Wire Services:* AP
Format: Country; *Hrs. of News Programming:* News progmg 8 hrs wkly; *Target Audience:* 18-54; upwardly mobile adults
Harold Wright, CEO
Todd Brunner, Operations Dir

Heston Wright, General Manager
Heston Wright, General Sales Mgr
Vanessa Valli, Programming Director
Mike Smith, News Director
Ray Bagby, Engineering Dir

***KYCU**
09-01-2002; 89.1 MHz FM; 40 kw; 633 ft.; N35 26 40 W98 59 22
Rebroadcasts: Rebroadcasts KCCU(FM) Lawton 100%
US
(888) 454-7800; *Fax:* (580) 581-5571
www.kccu.org
kccu@cameron.edu
License: Clinton, Custer County, OK held by Cameron University.
Nat'l Network: NPR; PRI
Arbitron Metro Market: Lawton, OK; *Format:* Classical, News
Ted Riley, General Manager, Director of Broadcasting
Doug Cole, Station Manager
Clinton Wieden, News Director
Cynthia Sosa, Production Director
Zach McGrew, Development Director

Coalgate

KXFC
12-07-2001; 105.5 MHz FM; *Hrs Open:* 24; 20 kw; 364 ft.; N34 41 43 W96 23 17
P. O. Box 1016, Broken Bow, OK 74728 US
(580) 332-1212; *Fax:* (580) 332-0128
www.kxfcradio.com
score@cableone.net
License: Coalgate, Coal County, OK held by The Chickasaw Nation.
Group Owner: The Chickasaw Nation; (acq 10-1-2008; $1.5 million with KTLS-FM Holdenville)
Nat'l Network: AP Radio; Jones Radio Networks
Arbitron Metro Market: Coalgate, OK; *Format:* Contemporary Hits/Top 40; *Target Audience:* 25+.; *Adv. Rates:* 20; 20; 20
Howard Stone, Operations Dir
Rick Woodward, General Manager
Craig Stone, Programming Director
Renae Woodward, News Director

Collinsville

KIZS
06-25-1996; 101.5 MHz FM; 6.2 kw; 656 ft.; N36 20 2 W95 47 8
2625 South Memorial Drive, Tulsa, OK 74129 US
(918) 388-5100; *Fax:* (918) 388-5400
www.1015elpatron.com
License: Collinsville, Tulsa County, OK held by Clear Channel Broadcasting Licenses Inc.
Group Owner: iHeartMedia; (acq 10-6-97; $1.9 million).
Arbitron Metro Market: Tulsa, OK; *Format:* Spanish; *Target Audience:* 25-54; general
Don Cristi, Senior Vice President/Programming

Comanche

KDDQ
04-01-1982; 105.3 MHz FM; *Hrs Open:* 24; 6 kw; 299 ft.; N34 26 12 W97 54 47
1701 West Pine, Duncan, OK 73533 US
(580) 255-1350; *Fax:* (580) 470-9993
www.perrybroadcasting.net/KDDQ/index.html
License: Comanche, Stephens County, OK held by Perry Broadcasting of Southwest Oklahoma Inc.
Group Owner: Perry Publishing & Broadcasting Co.; (acq 1-9-2003; grpsl).
Nat'l Network: ABC
Arbitron Metro Market: Duncan, OK; *Format:* Classic Rock
Special Programming: Gospel 2 hrs wkly; *Hrs. of News Programming:* news progmg 4 hrs wkly; *No. News Employees:* 1; *Target Audience:* 25-54; females withmid-level income

Cordell

KCLI-FM
09-01-1988; 99.3 MHz FM; *Hrs Open:* 24; 10.5 kw; 505 ft; N35 26 49 W98 59 17
700 Frisco Ave., Clinton, OK 73401
(580) 772-5939; *Fax:* (580) 323-0717
kcdl.com
sales@wrightradio.com
License: Cordell, Washita County, OK held by Wright Broadcasting Systems Inc.
Group Owner: Wright Broadcasting Systems; (acq 8-30-99; $350,000)
Nat'l Network: ABC; CNN Radio; *Regional Network:* Agrinet
Target Audience: General.; *Adv. Rates:* 15; 10; 15; 7.50
Harold Wright, CEO
Todd Brunner, Operations Dir
Rob Grogan, Programming Director

Coweta

***KDIM**
02-01-2005; 88.1 MHz FM; *Hrs Open:* 24; 0.05 kw horiz, 100 kw vert; 551 ft.; N35 42 24 W96 5 39
Mailing Address: P.O. Box 1924, Tulsa, OK 74101 US
Second Address: 11717 S. 129th E. Ave., Broken Arrow, OK 74011
(918) 455-5693; *Fax:* (918) 455-0411
www.oasisnetwork.org
mail@oasisnetwork.org
License: Coweta, Wagoner County, OK held by Creative Educational Media Corp. Inc.
Arbitron Metro Market: Coweta, OK; *Format:* Religious; *Target Audience:* General.
Becca Sharp, Station Manager

Cushing

KUSH
01-01-1953; 1600 kHz AM; 1 kw-D, ND1; 0.07 kw-N, ND1; N35 59 11.3 W96 42 37
P.O. Box 791, Cushing, OK 74023 US
(918) 225-0922; *Fax:* (918) 225-0925
www.1600kush.com
kush@yahoo.com
License: Cushing, OK held by Cimarron Valley Broadcasters Inc.
Arbitron Metro Market: Cushing, OK; *Format:* News, News/Talk, 84, Talk
Evert Rossiter, Chairman
Sean Kelly, General Manager
Joe Manning, Jr, Vice Chairman
Brent Thompson, Executive Director

Davis

KKAJ-FM
06-24-1974; 95.7 MHz FM; *Hrs Open:* 24; 100 kw; 449 ft.; N34 5 53 W97 10 54
P.O. Box 429, 1205 Northglen, Ardmore, OK 73402 US
(580) 226-0421; *Fax:* (580) 226-0464
www.kkaj.com
License: Davis, Carter County, OK held by LKCM Radio Group L.P.
Group Owner: LKCM Radio Group L.P.; (acq 2-26-2007; grpsl)
Format: Country; *Hrs. of News Programming:* news progmg 25 hrs wkly; *No. News Employees:* 1; *Target Audience:* 18-54.; *Adv. Rates:* 36; 34; 36; 32
Dave Hilton, Operations Dir
Michael Baer, General Manager

Del City

KEBC
11-01-1969; 1560 kHz AM; *Hrs Open:* 24; 1 kw-D, 250 w-N, DA-2; N35 26 26 W97 29 24 (D), N35 26 27 W97 29 24 (N)
5101 S. Shields, Oklahoma City, OK 73023
(405) 616-5500; *Fax:* (405) 616-5551
License: Del City, Oklahoma County, OK held by Tyler Media LLC
Group Owner: Tyler Media Broadcasting Corp.; (acq 12-15-2003; $250,000).
Population Served: 45,000; *Arbitron Metro Market:* Oklahoma City, OK; *Format:* Sports, Talk; *Hrs. of News Programming:* news progmg 8 hrs wkly; *No. News Employees:* 1; *Target Audience:* 18 plus.; *Adv. Rates:* 20; 20; 20; 5.
Ty Tyler, President

Dickson

KTRX
06-01-2001; 92.7 MHz FM; *Hrs Open:* 24; 5.5 kw; 341 ft.; N34 6 56 W97 0 6
P O Box 429, Ardmore, OK 73407 US
(580) 226-0421; *Fax:* (580) 226-0464
www.texomarocks.com
License: Dickson, Carter County, OK held by LKCM Radio Group L.P.
Group Owner: LKCM Radio Group L.P.; (acq 2-26-2007; grpsl)
Nat'l Network: Jones Radio Networks; *Nat'l Reps:* Christal
Arbitron Metro Market: Ardmore, OK; *Format:* Classic Rock; *Hrs. of News Programming:* news progmg 25 hrs wkly; *No. News Employees:* 1; *Target Audience:* 25-54; men
Gerry Schlegel, Operations Dir
Michael Baer, General Manager
Dave Hilton, Operations Manager

Duncan

KPNS
10-31-1947; 1350 kHz AM; *Hrs Open:* 6 AM-midnight; 0.18 kw-D, ND1; 0.07 kw-N, ND1; N34 30 43 W97 58 5
1701 West Pine, Duncan, OK 73533 US
(580) 255-1350; *Fax:* (580) 355-1050
www.perrybroadcasting.net/KPNS
License: Duncan, OK held by Perry Broadcasting of Southwest Oklahoma Inc.
Group Owner: Perry Publishing & Broadcasting Co.; (acq 11-22-02; grpsl).
Arbitron Metro Market: Lawton, OK; *Format:* Sports, Talk; *Hrs. of News Programming:* news progmg 20 hrs wkly; *No. News Employees:* 1; *Target Audience:* General.

KKEN
12-31-1975; 97.1 MHz FM; 6 kw; 328 ft.; N34 30 43 W97 58 4
115 W. Broadway, Anadarko, OK 73005 US
(580) 255-1350; *Fax:* (580) 470-9993
www.kickincountry971.com
License: Duncan, Stephens County, OK
Arbitron Metro Market: Lawton, OK; *Format:* Country; *Target Audience:* 25-54.; *Adv. Rates:* 15; 9; 12; 8
Joy Chapman, General Manager
Pam Peck, General Sales Mgr
Terry Monday, Programming Director
Mark Edwards, News Director

Durant

***KAYC**
01-01-2000; 91.1 MHz FM; 0.403 kw; 210 ft.; N34 1 17 W96 28 18
P.O. Box 3206, Tupelo, MS 38803 US
(662) 844-8888; *Fax:* (662) 842-6791
www.afr.net
faq@afa.net
License: Durant, Bryan County, OK held by American Family Association.
Group Owner: American Family Radio
Arbitron Metro Market: Tupelo, MS; *Format:* Christian, Religious
Tim Wildmon, President
Donald Wildmon, Founder
Buddy Smith, Sr VP
Ed Vitagliano, Exec VP
Randy Sharp, Director Of Special Projects
Meeke Addison, Director Of Communications
Abraham Hamilton III, General Counsel & Public PolicyAnalyst

KLBC
11-01-1958; 106.3 MHz FM; *Hrs Open:* 24; 16.5 kw; 404 ft.; N34 2 12 W96 25 37
401 West Evergreen, Durant, OK 74701 US
(580) 924-3100; *Fax:* (580) 920-1426
www.klbcfm.com
scott@klbcfm.com
License: Durant, Bryan County, OK held by Texoma Broadcasting Inc.
Group Owner: Texoma Broadcasting Inc.
Nat'l Network: ABC
Arbitron Metro Market: Lawton, OK; *Format:* Country; *Hrs. of News Programming:* news progmg 20 hrs wkly; *No. News Employees:* 1; *Target Audience:* General.; *Adv. Rates:* 18; 18; 18; 9
Todd Tidwell, General Manager
Bob McKinzie, Promotions Manager

KSEO
05-01-1947; 750 kHz AM; *Hrs Open:* 6 AM-7 PM
401 West Evergreen, Durant, OK 74701 US
(580) 924-3100; *Fax:* (580) 920-1426
www.klbcfm.com
License: Durant, OK held by Texoma Broadcasting Inc.
Group Owner: Texoma Broadcasting Inc.; (acq 5-28-99; with co-located FM)
Arbitron Metro Market: Durant, OK; *Format:* Christian; *Hrs. of News Programming:* news progmg 3 hrs wkly; *No. News Employees:* 1; *Target Audience:* Adults; 18-54; *Adv. Rates:* 10; 10; 10; na
Todd Tidwell, President
Bob McKenzie, Operations Dir
Bob McKinzie, Programming Director
Scott Corbin, News Director
Jim Reagan, Public Affairs Director

***KSSU**
02-01-1972; 91.9 MHz FM; *Hrs Open:* 24; 1.5 kw; 341 ft; N34 00 45 W96 19 45
1405 N. 4th St., PMB 4226, Durant, OK 74701
(580) 745-7483; *Fax:* (580) 745-7475

License: Durant, Bryan County, OK held by Southeastern Oklahoma State University.
Population Served: 35,000 *Target Audience:* 18-25; college, high school students & area residents
Prof. Dell McLain, Chairman

Edmond

***KCSC**
04-01-1966; 90.1 MHz FM; *Hrs Open:* 24; 100 kw; 840 ft.; N35 34 24 W97 29 8
100 N. University Drive, Edmond, OK 73034 US
(405) 974-3333; *Fax:* (405) 974-3844
kcscfm@uco.edu
License: Edmond, Oklahoma County, OK held by University of Central Oklahoma.
Nat'l Network: PRI
Arbitron Metro Market: Edmond, OK; *Format:* Talk; *Hrs. of News Programming:* One; *Target Audience:* 35 plus; educated, affluent
Zachary Dumas, Operations Dir
Brad Ferguson, General Manager
Susan Clark, General Sales Mgr
Hal Smith, Chief Engineer

***KOKF**
09-01-1977; 90.9 MHz FM; *Hrs Open:* 24; 100 kw; 436 ft.; N35 33 59 W97 28 28
P.O. Box 22000, Oklahoma City, OK 73132 US
(916) 251-1600; *Fax:* (916) 251-1650
www.air1.com
info@air1.com
License: Edmond, Oklahoma County, OK held by Educational Media Foundation.
Group Owner: EMF Broadcasting; (acq 5-25-2006; $4 million).
Nat'l Network: Air 1
Arbitron Metro Market: Oklahoma City, OK; *Format:* Alternative, Christian
Mike Novak, Operations Dir
David Pierce, Programming Director
Ed Lenane, News Director
Sam Wallington, Engineering Dir
Marya Morgan, News Reporter
Richard Hunt, News Reporter
Evan Falat, Regional Manager

El Reno

KZUE
09-09-1962; 1460 kHz AM; *Hrs Open:* Daytime only; 0.5 kw-D, NDD; N35 30 30 W97 54 0
2715 S. Radio Road, El Reno, OK 73036 US
(405) 262-1460; *Fax:* (405) 262-1886
www.latremendaok.com
kzue@aol.com
License: El Reno, OK held by La Tremenda Inc.
Nat'l Reps: Keystone (unwired net)
Arbitron Metro Market: El Reno, OK.
Nancy Galvan, General Manager

Elk City

KADS
10-01-1932; 1240 kHz FM; *Hrs Open:* 24; 1 kw-U, ND1; N35 22 51 W99 24 25
, Tulsa, OK US
www.thesportsanimal.com
License: Elk City, OK held by Paragon Communications Inc.
Group Owner: Paragon Communications Inc.; acq 6-15-01; $15,000).
Nat'l Network: ESPN Radio; *Wire Services:* AP
Arbitron Metro Market: Elk City, OK; *Format:* Sports; *No. News Employees:* 1; *Adv. Rates:* 12; 9; 12; 6
Jay Davis, General Sales Mgr

KECO
07-20-1982; 96.5 MHz FM; *Hrs Open:* 24; 100 kw; 689 ft.; N35 24 22 W99 29 54
220 S. Pioneer Rd., Elk City, OK 73644 US
(580) 225-9696
www.kecofm.com
License: Elk City, Beckham County, OK held by Paragon Communications Inc.
Group Owner: Paragon Communications Inc.; acq 4-22-98; $100,000 for 72% with KXOO(FM) Elk City).
Arbitron Metro Market: Elk City, OK; *Format:* Country; *Hrs. of News Programming:* news progmg 2.5 hrs wkly; *No. News Employees:* 1; *Target Audience:* General.; *Adv. Rates:* 23; 16; 23; 10

KTIJ
07-15-2000; 106.9 MHz FM; 100 kw; 981 ft.; N34 58 39 W99 24 35
PO Box 349, Dover, NH 03825 US
(580) 726-5656; *Fax:* (580) 726-2222
thezone@itlnet.net
License: Elk City, Beckham County, OK held by Fuchs Radio LLC.
Group Owner: Fuchs Radio L.L.C.
Format: Contemporary Hits/Top 40
Shelly Fox, Operations Dir
Chad Fox, General Manager

KXOO
04-01-1995; 94.3 MHz FM; *Hrs Open:* 24; 12 kw; 469 ft.; N35 24 22 W99 29 54
220 S. Pioneer Rd., Elk City, OK 73644 US
(580) 225-5966
www.kecofm.com
License: Elk City, Beckham County, OK held by Paragon Communications Inc.
Group Owner: Paragon Communications Inc.; acq 4-22-98; $100,000 for 72% with KECO(FM) Elk City).
Arbitron Metro Market: Elk City, OK; *Format:* Adult Contemp, Christian; *Hrs. of News Programming:* news progmg 2 hrs wkly; *No. News Employees:* 1; *Adv. Rates:* 12; 9; 12; 6

Enid

KZLS
01-01-2004; 1640 kHz AM; *Hrs Open:* 24
Mailing Address: 316 E. Willow, Enid, OK 73701 US
Second Address: 316 E. Willow, Enid, OK 73701
(580) 237-1390; *Fax:* (580) 242-1390
www.knid.com
hchamplin@knid.com
License: Enid, OK held by Chisholm Trail Broadcasting Co.
Group Owner: Chisholm Trail Broadcasting Co.
Arbitron Metro Market: Enid, OK; *Format:* Sports; *Target Audience:* 18-54
Ricky Roggow, Operations Dir
Hiram Champlin, General Manager
Sandy Daniels, General Sales Mgr
Chad McKee, Programming Director
Suzi Lakin, Promotions Manager

***KKRD**
10-01-1986; 91.1 MHz FM; *Hrs Open:* 24; 0.41 kw; 312 ft.; N36 23 48 W97 52 38
901 South Cleveland Road, Enid, OK 73703 US
(916) 251-1600; *Fax:* (916) 251-1650
www.air1.com
info@air1.com
License: Enid, Garfield County, OK held by Educational Media Foundation.
Group Owner: EMF Broadcasting; (acq 10-15-2004; $102,500)
Nat'l Network: Air 1
Arbitron Metro Market: Rocklin, CA; *Format:* Alternative, Christian
Mike Novak, President
Evan Falat, General Sales Mgr
David Pierce, Programming Director
Ed Lenane, News Director
Sam Wallington, Engineering Dir
Marya Morgan, News Reporter
Richard Hunt, News Reporter
Tracy Butler, TrafficManager

KCRC
01-01-1926; 1390 kHz AM; *Hrs Open:* 24; 1 kw-U, DA1; N36 25 11 W97 52 28
Mailing Address: 316 East Willow, Enid, OK 73701 US
Second Address: 316 E. Willow, Enid, OK 73701
(580) 237-1390; *Fax:* (580) 242-1390
www.knid.com
ctbradio@yahoo.com
License: Enid, OK held by Chisholm Trail Broadcasting Co.
Group Owner: Chisholm Trail Broadcasting Co.; (acq 6-1-83; $1.38 million;
Nat'l Network: Jones Radio Networks; ESPN Radio; *Regional Network:* Okla. News Net.
Format: News; *Hrs. of News Programming:* news progmg 2 hrs wkly; *No. News Employees:* 1; *Target Audience:* General.
Hiram Champlin, President
Ricky Roggow, Operations Dir
Sandy Daniels, General Sales Mgr
Chad McKee, Programming Director
Suzi Lakin, Promotions Manager
Rob Houston, News Director
G.B. Bonham, Chief Engineer

KGWA
01-01-1950; 960 kHz AM; *Hrs Open:* 24; 1 kw-U, DA1; N36 26 13 W97 55 16
Mailing Address: 300 North Van Buren, P.O.Box 3128, Enid, OK 73703 US
Second Address: 1710 W. Willow Rd., Suite 300, Enid, OK 73703
(580) 234-4230; *Fax:* (580) 234-2971
www.kgwanews.com
radio@kofm.com
License: Enid, OK held by Williams Broadcasting LLC.
Nat'l Network: Fox News Radio; *Regional Network:* Okla. News Net.
Format: News, News/Talk, 86 *Special Programming:* Farm 3 hrs wkly, finance 20 hrs wkly, lifestyle 4 hrs wkly; *Hrs. of News Programming:* news progmg 60 hours wkly; *No. News Employees:* 4; *Target Audience:* P25-54 *Adv. Rates:* 35,35,35,20
Daniel J. Smith, General Manager
Cheryl Myatt, General Sales Mgr
J. Curtis Huckleberry, Programming Director

KQOB
05-01-1967; 96.9 MHz FM; 98 kw; 1480 ft.; N35 58 50 W97 41 42
Mailing Address: 316 East Willow, Enid, OK 73702 US
Second Address: 316 E. Willow, Enid, OK 73701
(580) 237-1390; *Fax:* (580) 242-1390
License: Enid, Garfield County, OK held by Champlin Broadcasting Inc.
Regional Network: Okla. News Net.
Format: Variety/Diverse; *Target Audience:* 18-54.
Michael Presnell, President

KOFM
03-01-1982; 103.1 MHz FM; *Hrs Open:* 24; 25 kw; 299 ft.; N36 26 13 W97 55 16
Mailing Address: 300 North Van Buren, P.O.Box 3128, Enid, OK 73703 US
Second Address: 1710 W. Willow Rd., Suite 300, Enid, OK 73703
(580) 234-6371; *Fax:* (580) 234-2971
www.kofm.com
License: Enid, Garfield County, OK held by Williams Broadcasting LLC.
Nat'l Network: Fox News Radio
Format: Country; *Hrs. of News Programming:* 1 hour weekly; *No. News Employees:* 3; *Target Audience:* P25-54; *Adv. Rates:* 35,35,35,20
Daniel J. Smith, General Manager
Cheryl Myatt, General Sales Mgr
Alan Clepper, Programming Director

Eufaula

KTNT
06-15-1967; 102.5 MHz FM; *Hrs Open:* 24; 10.5 kw; 505 ft.; N35 6 9 W95 36 53
P.O. Box 956, Eufaula, OK 74432 US
(918) 689-3663; *Fax:* (918) 689-5451
www.blakefm1025.com
mike@payneradiogroup.com
License: Eufaula, McIntosh County, OK held by K95.5 Inc.
Group Owner: K95.5 Inc.; acq 9-24-98; $400,000)
Regional Network: Okla. News Net.
Arbitron Metro Market: Eufaula, Ok; *Format:* Country *Special Programming:* Gospel 3 hrs wkly
Mike Rogers, General Manager

Fairview

***KHEV**
01-01-2009; 90.3 MHz FM; 0.49 kw; 607 ft.; N36 13 25 W98 36 7
US
(620) 873-2991; *Fax:* (620) 873-2755
www.khym.org
License: Fairview, Major County, OK held by Great Plains Christian Radio Inc.
Arbitron Metro Market: Fairview, OK; *Format:* Religious
Don Hughes, General Manager

Frederick

***KSYE**
07-01-1992; 91.5 MHz FM; *Hrs Open:* 24; 100 kw; 509 ft.; N34 21 52 W98 50 4
411 Ryan Plaza Drive, Arlington, TX 76011 US
(866) 355-5793(580) 335-5500; *Fax:* (580) 335-5900
License: Frederick, Tillman County, OK held by Criswell College.
Group Owner: Criswell Communications
Nat'l Network: ABC
Arbitron Metro Market: Oklahoma City, OK; *Format:* Christian, Religious; *Target Audience:* General.
Dr. Royce Laycock, Chairman
Dr. Jerry Johnson, President

Mike Tyrone, General Manager
Keith Mayo, Station Manager
Sharon Geiger, Programming Director

KTAT
01-01-1948; 1570 kHz AM; 0.25 kw-D, ND2; 0.006 kw-N, ND2; N34 23 30 W99 1 51
Mailing Address: P.O. Box 1088, Frederick, OK 73542 US
Second Address: 207 W. Grand Ave., Frederick, OK 73542
(580) 335-3874; *Fax:* (580) 335-7659
License: Frederick, OK held by Morey Broadcasting LLC
Arbitron Metro Market: Frederick, OK; *Format:* Easy Listening
Brent Morey, General Manager

KYBE
08-15-1982; 95.7 MHz FM; 6 kw; 249 ft.; N34 23 30 W99 1 51
P.O. Box 1088, Frederick, OK 73542 US
(580) 335-5923; *Fax:* (580) 335-7659
www.coyotenews.com
kybe959@pldi.net
License: Frederick, Tillman County, OK held by Fort Worth Media Group G.P. LLC.
Group Owner: LKCM Radio Group L.P.; (acq 9-9-2005; $325,000)
Arbitron Metro Market: Frederick, OK; *Format:* Country
Scott Maguire, Operations Dir
Don Jacobs, General Manager
Dan Rahman, Programming Director

Glenpool

KTSO
05-24-1976; 94.1 MHz FM; *Hrs Open:* 24; 100 kw; 691 ft.; N36 7 52 W96 4 13
5810 East Skelly Drive, Suite 801, Tulsa, OK 74135 US
(918) 665-3131; *Fax:* (918) 663-6622
www.941THESOUND.com
production@shamrocktuosa.com
License: Glenpool, Tulsa County, OK held by Shamrock Communications Inc.
Group Owner: Shamrock Communications Inc.; acq 1996; $1.8 million)
Nat'l Reps: McGavren Guild
Arbitron Metro Market: Tulsa, OK; *Format:* Contemporary Hits/Top 40, Adult Contemp; *Hrs. of News Programming:* news progmg 35 hrs wkly; *No. News Employees:* 1; *Target Audience:* 35-54.; *Adv. Rates:* 65; 60; 60;40
George Lynett, Jr., CEO
Chuck Browning, General Manager
Ruben Hurtado, General Sales Mgr
Paul Kay, Programming Director
Terry Jenner, Traffic Manager

Goltry

***KGVV**
90.5 MHz FM; 35 kw; Ant 397 ft; N36 40 47 W98 10 43
Box 697, Waukomis, OK
(580) 758-3045
License: Goltry, Alfalfa County, OK held by Waukomis Baptist Church Inc.

Danny Marney, President

Goodwell

***KPSU**
09-01-1977; 91.7 MHz FM; *Hrs Open:* 10 AM to midnight; 0.38 kw; 121 ft.; N36 35 41 W101 38 10
P.O. Box 430, Goodwell, OK 73939 US
(580) 349-2611; *Fax:* (580) 349-2302
www.opsu.edu
License: Goodwell, Texas County, OK held by Oklahoma Panhandle State University.
Target Audience: College age.
Dr. David Bryant, President
Russell Guthrie, General Manager

Grandfield

***KWKL**
09-19-2003; 89.9 MHz FM; *Hrs Open:* 24; 45 kw vert; 499 ft.; N34 16 19 W98 25 30
US
(800) 525-5683; *Fax:* (916) 251-1650
www.klove.com
klove@klove.com
License: Grandfield, Tillman County, OK held by Educational Media Foundation.
Group Owner: EMF Broadcasting
Nat'l Network: K-Love
Arbitron Metro Market: Grandfield, OK; *Format:* Christian; *No. News Employees:* 3; *Target Audience:* 25-44; Judeo Christian, female
Darrell Chambliss, Chairman
Mike Novak, President and CEO
David Pierce, Programming Director
Ed Lenane, News Director
Sam Wallington, Engineering Dir
Marya Morgan, News Reporter
Richard Hunt, News Reporter
Laura Daniels, NewsReporter
Tim Luttrell, News Reporter
Kenny Noble Cortes, News Reporter
Darren Vinson, News Reporter

Granite

KZBS
01-01-2008; 104.3 MHz FM; 1.7 kw; 909 ft.; N34 58 39 W99 24 35
US
(580) 332-0902; *Fax:* (580) 332-0922
www.thegospelstation.com
email@thegospelstation.com
License: Granite, Greer County, OK held by Bcvision.
Arbitron Metro Market: Granite, OK; *Format:* Gospel
Randall Christy, President
Rick Cody, Vice President
Sharla Frederick, Treasurer and CFO

***KHEB**
91.9 MHz FM; 0.1 kw; 774 ft.; N34 58 39 W99 24 35
US
(580) 332-0902
www.thegospelstation.com
email@thegospelstation.com
License: Granite, Greer County, OK held by South Central Oklahoma Christian Broadcasting Inc.
Arbitron Metro Market: Granite, OK
Randall Christy, President
Rick Cody, General Manager
Rick Cody, Vice President
Sharla Frederick, Treasurer / CFO

Grove

KGVE
12-12-1980; 99.3 MHz FM; *Hrs Open:* 24; 14.5 kw; 430 ft.; N36 41 3 W94 53 11
P.O. Box 451749, Grove, OK 74345 US
(918) 786-2211; *Fax:* (918) 786-2284
License: Grove, Delaware County, OK held by Caleb Corp.
Nat'l Network: ABC; *Regional Network:* Okla. News Net.
Format: Country; *No. News Employees:* 1; *Target Audience:* General.
Larry Hestand, President
Janell Hestand, Operations Dir

***KWXC**
01-01-2008; 88.9 MHz FM; 6 kw vert; 240 ft.; N36 35 42 W94 38 5
Route 4 Box 481-4, Grove, OK 74344 US
(918) 854-3523
License: Grove, Delaware County, OK held by Grove Broadcasting Inc.
Format: Talk; *Target Audience:* 30-45.
Darral Martin, President
Travis Martin, Programming Director
Margaret Van Dyke, Promotions Manager

Guthrie

KMFS
11-16-1955; 1490 kHz AM; *Hrs Open:* 24; 1 kw-U, ND1; N35 52 56 W97 23 34
Mailing Address: 1515 East Tropicana, Suite 240, Las Vegas, NV 89119 US
Second Address: 8919 World Ministry Ave., Baton Rouge, LA 70810
(225) 768-3688/8300; *Fax:* (225) 768-3729
www.jsm.org
kawikfish@yahoo.com
License: Guthrie, OK held by Family Worship Center Church Inc.
Group Owner: Family Worship Center Church Inc.; acq 9-27-2002; $150,000).
Nat'l Network: ABC; AP Radio
Arbitron Metro Market: Oklahoma City, OK; *Format:* Religious
David Whitelaw, COO
Jimmy Swaggart, President
John Santiago, Programming Director

Guymon

KGYN
12-12-1948; 1210 kHz AM; *Hrs Open:* 24; 10 kw-D, DAN; 10 kw-N, DAN; N36 40 34 W101 22 58
P. O. Box 130, Guymon, OK 73942 US
(580) 338-1210; *Fax:* (580) 338-8255
www.kgynradio.com
kgyn@kgynradio.com
License: Guymon, OK held by Steckline Communications
Nat'l Network: Jones Radio Networks; AP Network News
Format: Country *Special Programming:* Relg 8 hrs, Sp 8 hrs wkly; *Hrs. of News Programming:* news progmg 12 hrs wkly; *No. News Employees:* 1; *Target Audience:* 25-65; broad based listenership
Todd Thrasher, General Manager
Debbie Browning, Programming Director
Bobby Gee, News Director
Chane Deming, Engineering Dir
Richard Ryther, Chief Engineer
Lisa Bryce, Traffic Manager

KKBS
12-25-1983; 92.7 MHz FM; *Hrs Open:* 24; 11.5 kw; 486 ft.; N36 40 13 W101 28 48
P.O. Box 1756, Guymon, OK 73942 US
(580) 338-5493; *Fax:* (580) 338-0717
www.kkbs.com
kkbs@kkbs.com
License: Guymon, Texas County, OK held by MLS Communications Inc.
Arbitron Metro Market: Lawton, OK; *Format:* Rock/AOR *Special Programming:* Financial markets 5 hrs wkly; *Hrs. of News Programming:* news progmg 17 hrs wkly; *No. News Employees:* 2; *Target Audience:* 25-54+;working people, 2 income families, farmers
Ramey Cozart, Operations Dir
Marsha Strong, General Manager
Amy Ford, General Sales Mgr
Ramey Cozart, Programming Director
Frank Riviera, Music Director
JJ Micheals, Webmaster

***KBIJ**
01-01-2008; 99.5 MHz FM; 100 kw; 269 ft.; N36 50 42 W101 12 15
US
(800) 687-9112; *Fax:* (806) 353-1542
radiobygrace.com
License: Guymon, Texas County, OK held by Grace Community Church of Amarillo
Arbitron Metro Market: Guymon, OK; *Format:* Christian
William Gehm, President

***KNGM**
88.9 MHz FM; 25 kw; Ant 321 ft; N36 40 27 W101 28 09
Box 14, Abilene, KS
(877) 813-5366; *Fax:* (785) 263-3876
www.kjil.com
kjil@kjil.com
License: Guymon, Texas County, OK held by Great Plains Christian Radio Inc.
Population Served: 24,971; *Arbitron Metro Market:* Emporia, KS; *No. News Employees:* 1
Michael Luskey, CEO
Linda Emig, Music Director
Mark Hinca, Station Manager
Delvin Kinser, News Director
Steve Larson, Chief Engineer
Jennifer Pooler, Production Director
Deb Hustus, Director of Underwriting / Development
JerryMann, Business Manager

***KJDR**
04-01-1994; 88.1 MHz FM; 100 kw horiz; 289 ft.; N35 11 57 W101 48 43 *Rebroadcasts:* Rebroadcasts KJRT-FM Amarillo 100%
PO Box 8088, Amarillo, TX 79114 US
(806) 359-8855; *Fax:* (806) 354-2039
License: Guymon, OK held by Top O'Texas Educational Broadcasting Foundation
Group Owner: Top O'Texas Educational Broadcasting Foundation
Arbitron Metro Market: Guymon, OK; *Format:* Religious

Haileyville

KQIK
105.9 MHz FM; 6 kw; 250 ft.
5686 S. Muskegee Ave., Tahlequah, OK 74464 USA
(918) 456-2511; *Fax:* (918) 456-3231
www.k955.com

License: Haileyville, OK held by K95.5 Inc.
Group Owner: K95.5 Inc.

Hammon

*KTHF
89.9 MHz FM; 26.5 kw; 295 ft.; N35 37 16 W99 22 32
US
(580) 767-1400; *Fax:* (580) 765-1700
www.thehousefm.com
mail@thehousefm.com
License: Hammon, Roger Mills County, OK held by The Love Station Inc.
Arbitron Metro Market: Hammon, OK
Doyle Brewer, CEO/COO
Tony Weir, Music Director
Janelle Keith, Music Director
Darcey Christianson, Chief Engineer
Shaun Michaels, Production Director
Andy Youso, Assistant Program Director
Donna Hollifield, Office Manager

Healdton

KICM
10-01-1978; 97.7 MHz FM; 50 kw; 492 ft.; N34 20 57 W97 27 24
5946 Club Oaks Drive, Dallas, TX 75248 US
(580) 226-9797; *Fax:* (580) 226-5113
www.kicm.com
License: Healdton, Carter County, OK held by Keystone Broadcasting Corp.
Format: Country *Special Programming:* Relg 6 hrs wkly; *Target Audience:* 21-49.
Bill Countrymen, General Manager

*KAZC
89.3 MHz FM; 0.3 kw; 56 ft.; N34 13 9 W97 28 27
US
(580) 332-0902; *Fax:* (580) 332-0922
www.thegospelstation.com/dyn/index.php
email@thegospelstation.com
License: Healdton, Carter County, OK held by First Free Will Baptist Church of Healdton.
Arbitron Metro Market: Healdton, OK
Sharla Frederick, Treasurer / CFO
Randall Christy, Founder and President
David Lomineck, General Manager
Rick Cody, Vice President/ Program Director

Heavener

KPRV-FM
10-01-1989; 92.5 MHz FM; *Hrs Open:* 24; 1.55 kw; 640 ft.; N34 53 54 W94 34 30
P.O. Box 368, Poteau, OK 74953 US
(918) 647-3221; *Fax:* (918) 647-5092
www.kprvradio.com
kprv@windstream.net
License: Heavener, Le Flore County, OK held by LeRoy Billy.
Nat'l Network: ABC; *Regional Network:* Okla. News Net.
Arbitron Metro Market: Fort Smith, AR; *Format:* Country, Gospel *Special Programming:* Gospel 24 hrs Sun only; *Hrs. of News Programming:* News progmg 24 hrs wkly; *Target Audience:* 24-54.
LeRoy Billy, President
LeRoy Billy, Operations Dir
David Billy, Programming Director
Allen Riley, Chief Engineer

Henryetta

KXBL
12-20-1966; 99.5 MHz FM; *Hrs Open:* 24; 100 kw; 981 ft.; N35 50 2 W96 7 28
4590 East 29th Street, Tulsa, OK 74114 US
(918) 743-7814; *Fax:* (918) 743-7613
bigcountry995.com
psutterfield@journalbroadcastgroup.com
License: Henryetta, Okmulgee County, OK held by Journal Broadcast Corp.
Group Owner: Journal Communications Inc.; (acq 6-11-99; grpsl).
Arbitron Metro Market: Tulsa, OK; *Format:* Country; *Target Audience:* 18-34.
Randy Bush, Vice President/General Manager
Brian Gann, Operations Manager

*KVAZ
12-26-1985; 91.5 MHz FM; *Hrs Open:* 24; 7.8 kw vert; 564 ft.; N35 32 53 W95 58 14
R#1 Box 65 A, Weleetka, OK 74880 US
(580) 332-0902; *Fax:* (580) 332-0922
www.thegospelstation.com
email@thegospelstation.com
License: Henryetta, Okmulgee County, OK held by South Central Oklahoma Broadcasting Inc.
Arbitron Metro Market: Henryetta, OK; *Format:* Gospel
Sharla Frederick, CFO
Randall Christy, Founder and President
Rick Cody, General Manager
Rick Cody, Vice President/ Program Director

Hobart

KQTZ
05-28-1979; 105.9 MHz FM; *Hrs Open:* 24; 100 kw; 1020 ft.; N34 52 15 W99 17 36
Mailing Address: P.O. Box 577, Altus, OK 73522 US
Second Address: 212 W. Cypress, Altus, OK 73521
(580) 482-1450; *Fax:* (580) 482-3420
www.kwhw.com
mward@kwhw.com
License: Hobart, Kiowa County, OK held by Monarch Broadcasting Inc.
Group Owner: Monarch Broadcasting Inc.; (acq 12-31-2003; grpsl)
Arbitron Metro Market: Lawton, OK; *Format:* Adult Contemp; *Target Audience:* General; contemp adults during the day, rockers at night
Matthew Ward, President
Michael Barnes, Operations Dir

KTJS
06-21-1947; 1420 kHz AM; *Hrs Open:* 24; 1 kw-D, ND1; 0.36 kw-N, ND1; N35 2 57 W99 5 48
1515 N. Broadway, Hobart, OK 73651 US
(580) 726-5656; *Fax:* (580) 726-2222
www.ktjs.com
License: Hobart, OK held by Fuchs Radio LLC.
Group Owner: Fuchs Radio L.L.C.; (acq 11-24-98; $182,000)
Arbitron Metro Market: Hobart, OK; *Format:* Country, News, 62, Talk *Special Programming:* Relg 12 hrs wkly; *Hrs. of News Programming:* News progmg 19 hrs wkly; *Target Audience:* 30 plus; agri-related businessmen *Adv. Rates:* 10; 10; 8; 4
Chad Fox, President
Lance Perritt, Programming Director
Paul Shields, News Director
Shelley Fox, Business Manager

Holdenville

KTLS-FM
11-30-1991; 106.5 MHz FM; *Hrs Open:* 24; 25 kw; 328 ft.; N34 54 50 W96 31 20
5105 S Shields Boulevard, Oklahoma City, OK 73129 US
(580) 332-2211; *Fax:* (580) 436-1629
www.ktlsradio.com
License: Holdenville, Hughes County, OK held by The Chickasaw Nation.
Group Owner: The Chickasaw Nation; (acq 10-1-2008; $1.5 million with KXFC(FM) Coalgate)
Nat'l Network: Jones Radio Networks
Arbitron Metro Market: Ada, OK; *Format:* Classic Rock; *No. News Employees:* 1; *Target Audience:* 25-54.; *Adv. Rates:* 26; 26; 26; 26
Roger Harris, General Manager
Craig Stone, Programming Director
Renae Woodward, News Director

Hollis

KKRE
03-11-2005; 92.5 MHz FM; 6 kW; 219 ft.; N34 36 34 W99 50 57
Mailing Address: PO Box 1077, Altus, OK 73522 USA
Second Address: 808 N. Main St., Altus, OK 73521
(580) 482-1555; *Fax:* (580) 482-8353
www.keyb108.net
License: Hollis, Harmon County, OK held by Altus FM, Inc.
Group Owner: Altus FM, Inc.
Arbitron Metro Market: Hollis, OK; *Format:* Oldies; *Target Audience:* 45-75
Gayle Ledbetter, General Manager

KJOK
07-19-2012; 102.7 MHz FM; 50 kW; 272 ft.; N34 36 34 W99 50 57
PO Box 1077, Altus, OK 73522 USA
(580) 482-1555; *Fax:* (580) 482-8353
www.keyb108.net
License: Hollis, Harmon County, OK held by Altus FM, Inc.
Group Owner: Altus FM, Inc.
Format: Classic Rock

Hugo

KITX
06-01-1983; 95.5 MHz FM; 50 kw; 492 ft.; N33 54 56 W95 28 4
1600 W. Jackson, Hugo, OK 74743 US
(580) 326-2555
www.k955.com
License: Hugo, Choctaw County, OK held by K95.5 Inc.
Group Owner: K95.5 Inc.; (acq 10-95; $400,000)
Arbitron Metro Market: Hugo, OK; *Format:* Country; *Target Audience:* General.

Idabel

KBEL-FM
10-01-1973; 96.7 MHz FM; *Hrs Open:* 24; 25 kw; 299 ft.; N33 52 54 W94 49 10
Mailing Address: Box 67, Gordonville, TX 76245 US
Second Address: 813 Lincoln Rd., Idabel, OK 74745
(580) 286-6642; *Fax:* (580) 286-6643
www.kbelradio.com
kbel967@yahoo.com
License: Idabel, McCurtain County, OK held by Box Broadcasting Corp.
Nat'l Network: Salem Radio Network; *Regional Network:* Agrinet
Arbitron Metro Market: Idabel, OK; *Format:* Country; *Hrs. of News Programming:* news progmg 6 hrs wkly; *No. News Employees:* 1; *Target Audience:* 18 plus; country audience; *Adv. Rates:* 14; 12; 14; 10
Paul W. Box, CEO

KQIB
08-01-1999; 102.9 MHz FM; *Hrs Open:* 24; 6 kw; 318 ft.; N33 59 57 W94 47 29
103 Hastings Court, Idabel, OK 74745 US
(580) 584-3388; *Fax:* (580) 584-3341
www.theq102.com (Under Construction)
kkbi@pine-net.com
License: Idabel, McCurtain County, OK held by JDC Radio Inc.
Nat'l Network: ABC
Arbitron Metro Market: Paris, TX; *Format:* Adult Contemp; *Hrs. of News Programming:* news progmg 5 hrs wkly; *No. News Employees:* 1; *Target Audience:* 25-44.; *Adv. Rates:* 9; 9; 9; 8
David Smulyan, General Manager
Shellye Copeland, Programming Director

*KXRT
01-01-2003; 90.9 MHz FM; 0.5 kw; 210 ft.; N33 53 33 W94 49 26
P.O. Box 3206, Tupelo, MS 38803 US
(662) 844-8888; *Fax:* (662) 842-6791
www.afr.net
faq@afa.net
License: Idabel, McCurtain County, OK held by American Family Association.
Group Owner: American Family Radio; (acq 1-31-2001).
Arbitron Metro Market: Tupelo, MS; *Format:* Christian
Tim Wildmon, President
Donald Wildmon, Founder
Buddy Smith, Sr VP
Ed Vitagliano, Exec VP
Randy Sharp, Director Of Special Projects
Meeke Addison, Director Of Communications
Abraham Hamilton III, General Counsel

Ketchum

*KOSN
05-26-1989; 107.5 MHz FM; *Hrs Open:* 24; 100 kw; 981 ft.; N36 46 13 W95 27 7 *Rebroadcasts:* Simulcast with KOSU-FM Stillwater 100%
1 West Third Street, P O Box 451750, Grove, OK 74345 US
(405) 744-6352; *Fax:* (405) 744-9970
www.kosu.org
info@kosu.org
License: Ketchum, Craig County, OK held by PRC Tulsa I-LLC
Nat'l Network: NPR
Arbitron Metro Market: Tulsa, OK; *Format:* News, News/Talk, 86 *Special Programming:* Classical 30 hrs wkly; *Hrs. of News Programming:* news progmg 130 hrs wkly; *No. News Employees:* 2 *Target Audience:* General.
Rachel Hubbard, General Manager
Don Crider, Development Specialist
Ken Boyd, Engineering Dir
Kelly Burley, Executive Director
Joanna Self, Administrative Assistant

Kingfisher

KINB
01-01-2000; 105.3 MHz FM; 0.93 kw; 833 ft.; N35 43 38 W97 52 30

8225 NW 29, Bethany, OK 73008 US
(405) 848-0100; *Fax:* (405) 843-5288
License: Kingfisher, OK held by The Last Bastion Station Trust LLC.
Group Owner: The Last Bastion Station Trust, LLC.
Arbitron Metro Market: Oklahoma City, OK; *Format:* Sports

Lahoma

KXLS
11-01-1995; 95.7 MHz FM; 14 kw; 449 ft.; N36 32 13 W98 0 39
Mailing Address: 205 W Maple, Suite 900, Enid, OK 73701 US
Second Address: 316 E. Willow Rd., Enid, OK 73701
(580) 237-1390; *Fax:* (580) 242-1390
hchamplin@knid.com
License: Lahoma, Garfield County, OK held by Chisholm Trail Broadcasting Co.
Group Owner: Chisholm Trail Broadcasting Co.; (acq 11-1-99; $525,000).
Nat'l Network: ABC
Format: Adult Contemp; *Hrs. of News Programming:* news progmg 2 hrs wkly; *No. News Employees:* 1; *Target Audience:* 30-60; female
Ricky Roggow, Operations/Programming Director
Sandy Daniels, General Manager
Amy Kelly, Promotions Manager
John Herrick, News Director
Cindy McNaughton, Traffic Manager
Matt Howell, Sports Director

Langston

*KALU
03-03-1975; 89.3 MHz FM; *Hrs Open:* 24; 0.15 kw; 200 ft.; N35 56 36 W97 15 32
P.O. Box 837, Langston, OK 73050 US
(405) 466-2924; *Fax:* (405) 466-2921
www.langston.edu
bishop@yahoo.com
License: Langston, Logan County, OK held by Langston University.
Arbitron Metro Market: Langston, OK; *Format:* Jazz, Religious
Bishop Kendrick, General Manager

Lawton

KBZQ
05-01-1992; 99.5 MHz FM; *Hrs Open:* 24; 25kw; 330 ft; N34 35 31 W98 32 55
Mailing Address: 2331 SW Lee Blvd, Lawton, OK 73506
Second Address: 1006 N.W. 47th St., Suite B, Lawton, OK 73505
(580) 357-9950; *Fax:* (580) 357-9995
www.hitsandfavorites.com
kbzq@sbcglobal.net
License: Lawton, Comanche County, OK held by William R. Fritsch Jr.
Nat'l Network: ABC
Population Served: 113,000; *Arbitron Metro Market:* Lawton, OK
Special Programming: Jazz 2 hrs, Hits of the 80s5 hrs, Sp 4 hrs wkly; *Hrs. of News Programming:* news progmg one hr wkly; *No. News Employees:* 3 *Target Audience:* 25-54; baby boomers, upscale white collar workers; *Adv. Rates:* 10; 15; 10; 5
Chuck Pettigrew, Operations Dir
Rick Fritsch, General Manager
Lino Roldan, Spanish Director

*KCCU
89.3 MHz FM; *Hrs Open:* 24; 5kW; 463 ft.; N34 37 26 W98 16 15
2800 West Gore Blvd, Lawton, OK 73505 US
(888) 454-7800; *Fax:* 580-581-5571
www.kccu.org
kccu@cameron.edu
License: Lawton, Comanche County, OK held by Cameron University.
Nat'l Network: NPR; APM
Arbitron Metro Market: Lawton, OK; *Format:* Classical, News; *Hrs. of News Programming:* 8 hr/Day M-F, 3 hr/day Weekends, 46hr ttl; *No. News Employees:* 5; *Target Audience:* Adult 35+
Marlin Glass, Jr., Chairman
John McArthur, President
Doug Cole, Operations Dir
Doug Cole, General Manager
Doug Cole, Station Manager
Zach McGrew, General Sales Mgr
Doug Cole, Programming Director
Cynthia Sosa, PromotionsManager
Clinton Wieden, News Director
Charles Thurston, Engineering Dir

KLAW
01-01-1965; 101.3 MHz FM; *Hrs Open:* 24; 100 kw; 584 ft.; N34 32 59 W98 32 21
62 SW D Avenue, Lawton, OK 73501 US
(580) 581-3600; *Fax:* (580) 357-2880
www.klaw.com
klaw@gapbroadcasting.com
License: Lawton, Comanche County, OK held by Townsquare Media Lawton License LLC
Group Owner: Townsquare Media; (acq 8-3-2007; grpsl)
Nat'l Reps: Katz Radio
Arbitron Metro Market: Lawton, OK; *Format:* Country; *Hrs. of News Programming:* news progmg 4 hrs wkly; *No. News Employees:* 1; *Target Audience:* 25-54; adults; *Adv. Rates:* 38; 38; 38; 17
Kim Dodds, General Manager
JoAnne Taylor, General Sales Mgr
Frank Seres, Programming Director
Sasha Spielman, Digital Managing Editor

KMGZ
11-01-1982; 95.3 MHz FM; *Hrs Open:* 24; 14 kw; 312 ft.; N34 34 36 W98 28 30
P.O. Box 7953, Lawton, OK 73506 US
(580) 536-9530; *Fax:* (580) 536-3299
www.kmgz.com
gm@kmgz.com
License: Lawton, Comanche County, OK held by Broadco of Texas Inc.
Arbitron Metro Market: Lawton, OK; *Format:* Adult Contemp; *Hrs. of News Programming:* News progmg one hr wkly; *Target Audience:* 18-49.
Chuck Morgan, President
Albert Young, Programming Director

*KVRS
12-01-1989; 90.3 MHz FM; *Hrs Open:* 24; 9.8 kw vert; 262 ft.; N34 31 51 W98 33 10
11 N.W. Winding Creek Rd., Lawton, OK 73505 US
(580) 536-8886; *Fax:* (580) 536-8891
www.afr.net
License: Lawton, Comanche County, OK held by American Family Association.
Group Owner: American Family Radio; (acq 4-29-2004; $10).
Nat'l Network: American Family Radio
Arbitron Metro Market: Lake Charles, LA; *Format:* Christian, Religious; *Hrs. of News Programming:* News progmg 14 hrs wkly; *Target Audience:* General.
Tim Wildmon, President
Donald Wildmon, Founder
Buddy Smith, Senior VP
Ed Vitagliano, Executive VP
Randy Sharp, Director Of Special Projects
Meeke Addison, Director Of Communications
Abraham Hamilton III, General Sounsel & PublicPolicy Analyst
Daniel Allen, Manager

KVRW
03-13-1992; 107.3 MHz FM; *Hrs Open:* 24; 26 kw; 584 ft.; N34 32 59 W98 32 21
626 SW D Avenue, Lawton, OK 73501 US
(580) 581-3600; *Fax:* (580) 357-2880
www.my1073fm.com
psa@my1073fm.com
License: Lawton, Comanche County, OK held by Townsquare Media Lawton License LLC
Group Owner: Townsquare Media; (acq 10-1-2007; grpsl)
Nat'l Reps: Katz Radio
Arbitron Metro Market: Lawton, OK; *Format:* Adult Contemp; *Hrs. of News Programming:* News progmg 2 hrs wkly; *Target Audience:* 25-54.
Kim Dodds, General Manager
Joanne Taylor, General Sales Mgr
Steve Kelly, Programming Director
Sasha Spielman, Digital Managing Editor

KXCA
05-01-1941; 1380 kHz AM; *Hrs Open:* 24; 1 kw-D, DA2; 1 kw-N, DA2; N34 35 24 W98 21 44
1457 N.E. 23rd St., Oklahoma City, OK 73111 US
(405) 425-4100
License: Lawton, OK held by Perry Broadcasting of Southwest Oklahoma Inc.
Group Owner: Perry Publishing & Broadcasting Co.; (acq 11-22-2002; grpsl).
Nat'l Reps: Roslin
Arbitron Metro Market: Lawton, OK; *Format:* Sports, Talk; *Target Audience:* 35 plus.

KZCD
06-08-1987; 94.1 MHz FM; *Hrs Open:* 24; 35 kw; 584 ft.; N34 32 59 W98 32 21
626 SW D Avenue, Lawton, OK 73501 US
(580) 581-3600; *Fax:* (580) 357-2880
www.z94.com
z94@gapbroadcasting.com
License: Lawton, Comanche County, OK held by Townsquare Media Lawton License LLC
Group Owner: Townsquare Media; (acq 8-3-2007; grpsl)
Nat'l Reps: Katz Radio
Arbitron Metro Market: Lawton, OK; *Hrs. of News Programming:* news progmg 2 hrs wkly; *No. News Employees:* 1; *Target Audience:* 18-49; males; *Adv. Rates:* 17; 17; 17; 10
Chris Knight, General Manager
JoAnne Taylor, General Sales Mgr
Don "Critter" Brown, Programming Director

*KJRF
01-01-2001; 91.1 MHz FM; *Hrs Open:* 24; 100 kw; 413 ft.; N34 41 22 W98 7 34
2405 Sw Lee Blvd., Lawton, OK 73505 US
(580) 357-4498; *Fax:* (580) 357-1818
www.thechristian-center.org
covenant@lawtonchristiancenter.org
License: Lawton, Comanche County, OK held by The Christian Center Inc.
Arbitron Metro Market: Lawton, OK; *Format:* Christian
Paul Craig, President
Alan Hampton, Operations Dir
Randy Muirhead, Station Manager
Allan Hampton, Engineering Dir

Lindsay

KBLP
10-01-1988; 105.1 MHz FM; *Hrs Open:* 24; 2 kw; 564 ft.; N34 54 1 W97 33 56
204 South Main Street, Lindsay, OK 73052 US
(405) 756-4438; *Fax:* (405) 756-2040
License: Lindsay, Garvin County, OK held by South Central Oklahoma Broadcasting & Advertising Corp.
Regional Network: Okla. News Net.
Arbitron Metro Market: Lindsay, OK; *Format:* Country; *Hrs. of News Programming:* news progmg 10.5 hrs wkly; *No. News Employees:* 2; *Target Audience:* 21-65; working consumers
Charlie Jones, President

Locust Grove

KEMX
02-14-1991; 94.5 MHz FM; *Hrs Open:* 24; 2.3 kw; 367 ft.; N36 15 5 W95 13 21 *Rebroadcasts:* Rebroadcasts KXOJ-FM Sapulpa 100%
P.O. Box 1250, Sapulpa, OK 74067 US
(918) 492-2660; *Fax:* (918) 492-8840
www.kxoj.com
kxoj@kxoj.com
License: Locust Grove, Mayes County, OK held by KXOJ Inc.
Group Owner: Adonai Radio Group; (acq 4-29-92; grpsl)
Arbitron Metro Market: Tulsa, OK; *Format:* Christian; *Target Audience:* 18-35; young married or single Christians
Mike Stephens, President
David Stephens, General Manager
Bob Thornton, Programming Director

Lone Grove

KYNZ
05-25-1988; 107.1 MHz FM; *Hrs Open:* 24; 24.5 kw; 335 ft.; N34 17 52 W97 9 12
P.O Box 1609, Ardmore, OK 73402 US
(580) 226-0421; *Fax:* (580) 226-0464
www.kynz.com
License: Lone Grove, Carter County, OK held by LKCM Radio Group L.P.
Group Owner: LKCM Radio Group L.P.; (acq 2-26-2007;. grpsl)
Nat'l Reps: Christal
Arbitron Metro Market: Lone Grove, OK.; *Format:* Oldies; *Hrs. of News Programming:* news progmg 25 hrs wkly; *No. News Employees:* 1; *Target Audience:* 18-54.
Michael Baer, General Manager
Terry Bell, Programming Director
Dave Hilton, Operations Director

Madill

KMAD
05-20-1962; 1550 kHz AM; *Hrs Open:* Sunrise-sunset; 0.25 kw-D, ND2; 0.09 kw-N, ND2; N34 6 24 W96 46 30
P.O. Box 576, Madill, OK 73446 US

(580) 795-2345; *Fax:* (580) 795-5623
www.kmad1550.com
kmad1550@yahoo.com
License: Madill, OK held by Robert S. Sullins
Nat'l Network: Jones Radio Networks; *Regional Network:* Okla. News Net.
Format: Country *Special Programming:* Farm 2 hrs wkly; *Hrs. of News Programming:* News progmg 12 hrs wkly; *Target Audience:* General.; *Adv. Rates:* 5.25; 5; 5; 4.60
Jim Fischer, General Manager

Mangum

KHIM
01-01-1998; 97.7 MHz FM; 0.54 kw; 1079 ft.; N34 58 39 W99 24 35
Mailing Address: P.O. Box 837, Altus, OK 73522 US
Second Address: 1515 N. Broadway, Hobart, OK 73651
(580) 726-5656; *Fax:* (580) 726-2222
thezone@itlnet.net
License: Mangum, Greer County, OK held by Fuchs Radio L.L.C.
Group Owner: Fuchs Radio L.L.C.; (acq 4-4-2006; $250,000 with KJCM(FM) Snyder)
Format: Rock/AOR
Chad Fox, General Manager

Marlow

KFXI
08-01-1987; 92.1 MHz FM; *Hrs Open:* 24; 100 kw; 545 ft.; N34 40 50 W98 1 2
1101 Highway 81 North, Marlow, OK 73055 US
(580) 658-9292; *Fax:* (580) 658-2561
kfxi@cableone.net
License: Marlow, Stephens County, OK held by DFWU Inc.
Arbitron Metro Market: Marlow, OK; *Format:* Country *Special Programming:* Gospel 8 hrs wkly; *Target Audience:* 25-55.
Amy Helton, Operations Dir
K.D. Austin, General Manager
Sherry Lynn, General Sales Mgr
Jennifer James, Programming Director

*KFXH
88.7 MHz FM; 2.15 kw; 364 ft.; N34 40 3 W97 56 49.1 US
(580) 658-9292; *Fax:* (580) 658-2561
License: Marlow, Stephens County, OK held by The Sister Sherry Lynn Foundation.
Arbitron Metro Market: Marlow, OK
Sherry Austin, President

McAlester

*KBCW-FM
01-01-1999; 91.9 MHz FM; *Hrs Open:* 24; 0.7 kw; 446 ft.; N34 59 13 W95 42 10 *Rebroadcasts:* Rebroadcasts KCSC(FM) Edmond 100%
100 N. University Drive, Edmond, OK 73003 US
(405) 974-3333; *Fax:* (405) 974-3844
www.kcscfm.com
kcscfm@uco.edu
License: McAlester, Pittsburg County, OK held by The University of Central Oklahoma.
Nat'l Network: PRI
Arbitron Metro Market: Edmond, OK; *Format:* Talk; *Hrs. of News Programming:* One; *Target Audience:* 35 plus; educ, affluent
Barbara Hendrickson, Operations Dir
Bradford Ferguson, General Manager

KNED
03-14-1950; 1150 kHz AM; *Hrs Open:* 24; 1 kw-D, DAN; 0.5 kw-N, DAN; N34 56 12 W95 43 59
Mailing Address: P. O. Box 1068, McAlester, OK 74501 US
Second Address: 1801 E. Electric Ave., McAlester, OK 74501
(918) 423-1460; *Fax:* (918) 423-7119
mcalesterradio.com
kmcokned@mcalesterradio.com
License: McAlester, OK held by Southeastern Oklahoma Radio LLC.
Group Owner: Southeastern Oklahoma Radio LLC; (acq 1-18-2005; $222,223).
Wire Services: AP
Format: Country; *Hrs. of News Programming:* News progmg 10 hrs wkly; *Target Audience:* 45 plus.
Lee Anderson, General Manager
Sheila Turnbow, General Sales Mgr
Megan Waters, Programming Director
John Yates, News Director

KTMC
03-03-1946; 1400 kHz AM; *Hrs Open:* 24
Mailing Address: 209 E. Wyandotte, Suite 200, McAlester, OK 74501 US
Second Address: 1801 E. Electric Ave., McAlester, OK 74502
(918) 426-1050; *Fax:* (918) 423-7119
mcalesterradio.com
License: McAlester, OK held by Southeastern Oklahoma Radio LLC.
Group Owner: Southeastern Oklahoma Radio LLC; (acq 1-18-2005; $444,445 with co-located FM)
Nat'l Network: ABC
Arbitron Metro Market: McAlester, OK; *Format:* Classic Rock *Special Programming:* Gospel 5 hrs wkly; *Hrs. of News Programming:* News progmg 2 hrs wkly; *Target Audience:* 50 plus; older, middle-aged, mature & retiredadults
Lee Anderson, General Manager
Bob Turnbow, General Sales Mgr
John Yates, News Director
Tom Dolph-Production Manager

KTMC-FM
06-24-1987; 105.1 MHz FM; *Hrs Open:* 24; 1.6 kw; 505 ft.; N34 59 13 W95 42 10
Mailing Address: P.O. Box 1068, McAlester, OK 74502 US
Second Address: 1801 E. Electric Ave., McAlester, OK 74502
(918) 426-1050; *Fax:* (918) 423-7119
www.mcalesterradio.com
License: McAlester, Pittsburg County, OK
Group Owner: Southeastern Oklahoma Radio LLC
Arbitron Metro Market: McAlester, OK; *Format:* Classic Rock; *Target Audience:* 34-50.
Lee Anderson, General Manager
Bob Turnbow, General Sales Mgr
Tom Dolph-Production Manager

Miami

KGLC
12-01-1975; 100.9 MHz FM; 6 kw; 276 ft.; N36 53 24 W94 47 8
P.O. Box 1555, Miami, OK 74355 US
(918) 786-2211; *Fax:* (918) 542-1819
www.okradiostation.com
larry@okradiostation.com
License: Miami, Ottawa County, OK held by Northeast Oklahoma Broadcast Network Inc.
Group Owner: Northeast Oklahoma Broadcast Network Inc.; (acq 4-3-2006; $800,000 with KVIS(AM) Miami)
Nat'l Network: USA
Format: Contemporary Hits/Top 40; *Target Audience:* 25-44.; *Adv. Rates:* 8; 8; 8; 8
Christy Benton, General Manager
Larry Hestand, Station Manager
Meg Davis, General Sales Mgr
Whitney Thomas, Programming Director
Nicole Arnzen, Promotions Manager
Mike Cossey, Chief Engineer

KVIS
02-01-1948; 910 kHz AM; *Hrs Open:* 24; 1 kw-U, DA1; N36 53 27 W94 47 0
P.O. Box 1555, Miami, OK 74355 US
(918) 542-1818; *Fax:* (918) 542-1819
www.okradiostation.com/kvis.html
License: Miami, OK held by Northeast Oklahoma Broadcast Network Inc.
Group Owner: Northeast Oklahoma Broadcast Network Inc.; (acq 4-3-2006; $800,000 with KGLC(FM) Miami)
Arbitron Metro Market: Miami, OK; *Format:* Gospel; *Hrs. of News Programming:* news progmg 9 hrs wkly; *No. News Employees:* 1; *Target Audience:* Christian/family.; *Adv. Rates:* 8; 8; 8; 8
Robert Suman, General Manager
Larry Hestand, Station Manager
Shanda Daugherty, Promotions Manager
Kimberley Barnes, News Director
Rusty Wynn, Chief Engineer

Midwest City

KGHM
01-01-1922; 1340 kHz AM; *Hrs Open:* 24; 1 kw-U; N35 29 58 W97 30 33
1900 N.W. Expressway, Suite 1000, Oklahoma City, OK 73118 US
(405) 840-5271; *Fax:* (405) 840-5808
www.1340thegame.com
License: Midwest City, Oklahoma County, OK held by Clear Channel Broadcasting Licenses Inc.
Group Owner: iHeartMedia; (acq 6-10-2002)
Nat'l Network: Fox Sports; *Nat'l Reps:* Katz
Population Served: 800,400; *Arbitron Metro Market:* Oklahoma City, OK; *Format:* Sports
Bill Hurley, Market Manager
Derrick Nance, Senior Vice President of Sales
Tom Travis, Programming Director

KTLV
04-01-1973; 1220 kHz AM; *Hrs Open:* 6 am-7 pm; 0.25 kw-D, DA2; 0.005 kw-N, DA2; N35 23 50 W97 27 4
1325 S.W. 107th Pl., Oklahoma City, OK 73170 US
(405) 672-1220(405) 672-3886; *Fax:* (405) 672-5858
www.ktlv1220.com
ktlv1220@aol.com
License: Midwest City, OK held by First Choice Broadcasting Inc.
Arbitron Metro Market: Oklahoma City, OK; *Format:* Christian, Gospel; *Target Audience:* 24 plus.
Howard Williams, President
Dale Williams, General Manager

Moore

*KMSI
03-26-1991; 88.1 MHz FM; *Hrs Open:* 24; 50 kw vert; 581 ft.; N35 12 7 W97 35 18
Mailing Address: 11717 S. 129 East Ave, Broken Arrow, OK 74011 US
Second Address: 120 S.W. 4th St., Moore, OK 73160
(405) 794-5674; *Fax:* (405) 794-5112
www.oasisnetwork.org
mail@oasisnetwork.org
License: Moore, Cleveland County, OK held by Creative Educational Media Corp. Inc.
Arbitron Metro Market: Oklahoma City, OK; *Format:* Religious; *Target Audience:* General.
David Ingles, President
Cherri Willis, General Manager
David Warren, Programming Director
Hal Smith, Chief Engineer

KWPN
09-26-1922; 640 kHz AM; 5 kw-D, 1 kw-N; N35 17 21 W97 30 8
3280 Peachtree Rd. NW, Suite 2300, Atlanta, GA 30305 US
(404) 949-0700
License: Moore, Cleveland County, OK held by Radio License Holding CBC, LLC
Group Owner: Cumulus Media Inc.
Population Served: 591,967; *Arbitron Metro Market:* Oklahoma City, OK; *Format:* Sports, Talk
Larry Bastida, Marketing Manager
Tricia York, General Sales Mgr
Dax Davis, Programming Director

Muldrow

KXMX
05-18-1959; 105.1 MHz FM; *Hrs Open:* 24; 6 kw; 322 ft.; N35 30 49.1 W94 35 18.1
333 S. Kerr Blvd., Sallisaw, OK 74955 US
(918) 790-4444; *Fax:* (918) 790-1052
www.kxmx.com
License: Muldrow, Sequoyah County, OK held by G2 Media Group LLC
Group Owner: G2 Media Group LLC
Arbitron Metro Market: Muldrow, OK; *Format:* Variety/Diverse
Delanna Nutter, Director of Sales
Marilyn Eckstein, Sales Consultant

Muskogee

KBIX
05-01-1936; 1490 kHz AM; *Hrs Open:* 24
215 N. State Street, Suite 910, Muskogee, OK 74401 US
(918) 682-9700; *Fax:* (918) 682-6775
www.sportsanimaltulsa.com
License: Muskogee, OK held by KMMY Inc.
Group Owner: Adonai Radio Group; (acq 12-11-2002; $1 million with KCXR(FM) Taft).
Arbitron Metro Market: Wagoner, OK; *Format:* Sports
Mark James, General Sales Manager
David Stephens, General Manager

KHTT
02-01-1972; 106.9 MHz FM; *Hrs Open:* 24; 94 kw; 1010 ft.; N35 51 43 W95 46 1
4590 East 29th Street, Tulsa, OK 74114 US
(918) 743-7814; *Fax:* (918) 496-1937
www.khits.com
License: Muskogee, Muskogee County, OK held by Renda Broadcasting Corp.
Group Owner: Renda Broadcasting Corp.; (acq 4-15-93; $1.6 million;

Arbitron Metro Market: Tulsa, OK; *Format:* Contemporary Hits/Top 40; *Target Audience:* 18-34; young adults; *Adv. Rates:* 110; 110; 110; 50
Tony Renda, President
Brian Gann, Operations Dir
Phillip Sutterfield, General Sales Mgr
Bill Sexauer, Promotions Manager
David Thompson, Interactive Manager
Jet Black, Program Director

KYAL-FM
01-19-1984; 97.1 MHz FM; *Hrs Open:* 24; 100 kw; 1969 ft.; N35 24 48 W95 21 55
P.O. Box 1250, Sapulpa, OK 74067 US
(918) 492-2660; *Fax:* (918) 492-8840
www.thesportsanimal.com
kxoj@kxoj.com
License: Muskogee, Muskogee County, OK held by KMMY Inc.
Group Owner: Adonai Radio Group; (acq 9-15-93; $500,000;
Arbitron Metro Market: Tulsa, OK; *Format:* Sports *Special Programming:* Farm 5 hrs wkly; *Target Audience:* 21-49; middle, upper-middle class; *Adv. Rates:* 28; 26; 26; 22
David Stephens, General Manager

Mustang

KNAH
02-01-1981; 99.7 MHz FM; *Hrs Open:* 24; 47 kw; 509 ft.; N35 35 30 W97 51 58
Mailing Address: 316 East Willow, Enid, OK 73701 US
Second Address: 316 E. Willow Rd., Enid, OK 73701
(580) 237-1390; *Fax:* (580) 242-1390
License: Mustang, Canadian County, OK held by Champlin Broadcasting Inc.
Group Owner: Champlin Broadcasting Inc.
Nat'l Network: ABC; *Regional Network:* Mid-America Ag
Arbitron Metro Market: Oklahoma City, OK; *Format:* Country; *Hrs. of News Programming:* news progmg 2 hrs wkly; *No. News Employees:* 1; *Target Audience:* 25-49.
Hiram Champlin, President
Ricky Roggow, Operations Dir
Sandy Daniels, General Manager
Suzi Lakin, Promotions Manager
G.B. Bonham, Chief Engineer

Newcastle

KJKE
03-15-2010; 93.3 MHz FM; 100 kw; 797 ft; N35 11 28 W97 35 49
400 E. Britton Rd., Oklahoma City, OK 73114 US
(405) 478-5104
www.jakefm.com
License: Newcastle, McClain County, OK held by Tyler Broadcasting Corp.
Group Owner: Tyler Media Broadcasting Corp.; (acq 10-95; $441,000).
Nat'l Network: AP Radio; *Nat'l Reps:* D & R Radio
Population Served: 19,300 *Format:* Country; *Target Audience:* 25-54.; *Adv. Rates:* 14; 10; 12; 6
Ty Tyler, President

Norman

***KGOU**
09-25-1970; 106.3 MHz FM; *Hrs Open:* 24; kw
780 Van Vleet Oval, Norman, OK 73019 US
(405) 325-3388; *Fax:* (405) 325-7129
www.kgou.org
manager@kgou.org
License: Norman, Cleveland County, OK held by University of Oklahoma.
Nat'l Network: NPR
Arbitron Metro Market: Oklahoma City, OK; *Format:* News, News/Talk, 86 *Special Programming:* Blues 8 hrs, jazz 15 hrs, automotive 2 hrs wkly; *Hrs. of News Programming:* news progmg 82 hrs wkly *No. News Employees:* 1; *Target Audience:* 25-54; general
Brian Hardzinski, Operations Dir
Karen Holp, General Manager
Jolly Brown, Development Director
Kurt Gwartney, News Director
Patrick Roberts, Chief Engineer
Susan Shannon, Office Manager
Kathy Hawkins, Business Manager

KREF
11-01-1949; 1400 kHz AM; *Hrs Open:* 24; 1 kw-U, ND1; N35 13 4 W97 24 37
2020 Alameda Street, Norman, OK 73072 US
(405) 321-1400; *Fax:* (405) 321-6820
www.kref.com
production@kref.com
License: Norman, OK held by Metro Radio Group
Regional Network: Okla. News Net.
Arbitron Metro Market: Oklahoma City, OK; *Format:* Sports; *No. News Employees:* 1; *Target Audience:* 25-54; middle, upper class adults
John Fox, President
Mike Holt, General Manager
T.J. Perry, Programming Director

***KSSO**
01-01-2007; 89.3 MHz FM; 5.6 kw; 173 ft.; N35 13 22 W97 26 21
Mailing Address: 1101 North 81 Highway, Marlow, OK 73055 US
Second Address: 8919 World Ministry Ave., Baton Rouge, LA 70810
(225) 768-3688; *Fax:* (225) 768-3729
www.jsm.org
kawikfish@yahoo.com
License: Norman, Cleveland County, OK held by Family Worship Center Church Inc.
Group Owner: Family Worship Center Church Inc.; (acq 10-7-2005; $500,000 for CP with KQUJ(FM) Ada)
David Whitelaw, COO
Jimmy Swaggart, President
John Santiago, Programming Director

North Enid

KNID
01-01-2008; 107.1 MHz FM; *Hrs Open:* 24; 14 kw; 449 ft.; N36 32 13 W98 0 39
US
(580) 237-1390; *Fax:* (580) 242-1390
www.todaysbestcountryonline.com
License: North Enid, Garfield County, OK held by Chisholm Trail Broadcasting Inc.
Group Owner: Chisholm Trail Broadcasting Co.
Arbitron Metro Market: North Enid, OK; *Format:* Country; *Target Audience:* 18-54; men and women
Hiram Champlin, President

Nowata

KRIG-FM
01-01-1965; 104.9 MHz FM; *Hrs Open:* 24/7; 8.3 kw; 564 ft.; N36 43 37 W95 46 18
1200 S.E. Frank Phillips Blvd., Bartlesville, OK 74003 US
(918) 336-1001; *Fax:* (918) 336-6939
www.bartlesvilleradio.com
radio@bartlesvilleradio.com
License: Nowata, Nowata County, OK held by KCD Enterprises Inc.
Group Owner: KCD Enterprises Inc.; acq 6-26-98; $775,000)
Nat'l Network: ABC; *Regional Network:* Okla. News Net.; Agri-Net; *Nat'l Reps:* Rgnl Reps *Regional Reps:* Rgnl Reps; *Wire Services:* AP
Format: Country *Special Programming:* Gospel 4 hrs wkly; *Hrs. of News Programming:* News progmg 20 hrs wkly; *No. News Employees:* 2; *Target Audience:* 35-65; mature buyers; *Adv. Rates:* 22; 22; 20; 22

Okarche

KTUZ-FM
09-01-1968; 106.7 MHz FM; *Hrs Open:* 24; 13 kw; 958 ft.; N35 36 49 W97 52 19
5105 S. Shields Blvd, Oklahoma City, OK 73129 US
(405) 616-5500; *Fax:* (405) 616-0328
www.unidosok.com
blanca.s@tylermedia.com
License: Okarche, Kingfisher County, OK held by Tyler Broadcasting Corp.
Group Owner: Tyler Media Broadcasting Corp.; (acq 1-27-98; $100,000 with co-located AM).
Nat'l Reps: Univision Radio National Sales
Arbitron Metro Market: Oklahoma City, OK; *Format:* Sports; *Hrs. of News Programming:* News progmg 16 hrs wkly; *Target Audience:* 18-65.; *Adv. Rates:* 30; 30; 30; 15
Ty Tyler, General Manager
Chris Fusselman, General Sales Mgr

Okemah

***KYLK**
11-01-2002; 103.7 MHz FM; *Hrs Open:* 24; 100 kw; Ant 607 ft; N34 59 13 W95 42 10
3738 W. Charleston Street, Broken Arrow, OK 74502
918-805-0099; *Fax:* 918-517-3317
Rick@rcparrish.com
License: Okemah, Okfuskee County, OK held by KESC Enterprises LLC
Arbitron Metro Market: Tulsa, OK; *Target Audience:* 25-54.
Rick Parrish, Operations Dir

Oklahoma City

KATT
09-16-1976; 100.5 MHz FM; 28.87 kw; 1542 ft.; N35 33 37 W97 29 7
4045 NW 64th St., Suite 600, Oklahoma City, OK 73116 US
(405) 460-5288
www.katt.com
License: Oklahoma City, OK held by Radio License Holding CBC, LLC
Group Owner: Cumulus Media Inc.; (acq 10-28-99; grpsl).
Arbitron Metro Market: Oklahoma City, OK; *Format:* Rock/AOR; *Target Audience:* 18-34; Men
Jake Daniels, Programming Director

KTLR
01-01-1946; 890 kHz AM; *Hrs Open:* 24; 1 kw-D, NDD; N35 33 59 W97 28 28
5105 S. Shields Blvd., Oklahoma City, OK 73129 US
(405) 616-5500; *Fax:* (405) 616-5505
www.ktlr.com
License: Oklahoma City, OK
Nat'l Reps: D & R Radio
Arbitron Metro Market: OK City, OK; *Format:* Talk *Special Programming:* Sp 3 hrs wkly; *Target Audience:* 10-80.
Skip Stow, CEO
Mike Miller, Station Manager

KJYO
04-09-1961; 102.7 MHz FM; *Hrs Open:* 24; 94.1 kw; 1220 ft.; N35 35 52 W97 29 22
1900 NW Expressway, Suite 1000, Oklahoma City, OK 73118 US
(405) 840-5271; *Fax:* (405) 858-5333
www.kj103fm.com
License: Oklahoma City, Oklahoma County, OK held by Clear Channel Broadcasting Licenses, Inc.
Group Owner: iHeartMedia
Arbitron Metro Market: Oklahoma City, OK; *Format:* Contemporary Hits/Top 40
Bill Hurley, Vice President/Market Manager
Derrick Nance, Senior Vice President of Sales
Tom Travis, Programming Director

KMGL
11-25-1965; 104.1 MHz FM; *Hrs Open:* 24; 92 kw; 1549 ft.; N35 33 36 W97 29 7
400 E. Britton Rd., Oklahoma City, OK 73114 US
(405) 478-5104
www.magic104.com
steve.o@tylermedia.com
License: Oklahoma City, Oklahoma County, OK held by Tyler Media, LLC
Group Owner: Tyler Media
Arbitron Metro Market: Oklahoma City, OK; *Format:* Adult Contemp *Special Programming:* Christmas Music (Nov-Dec); *Target Audience:* 25-54;
Steve O'Brien, Programming Director
Jennifer Leigh, Promotions Director

KOKC
12-24-1922; 1520 kHz AM; *Hrs Open:* 24; 50 kw-D, DAN; 50 kw-N, DAN; N35 20 0 W97 30 16
400 E. Britton Rd., Oklahoma City, OK 73113 US
(405) 478-5104; *Fax:* (405) 478-0448
www.kokcradio.com
License: Oklahoma City, OK held by Tyler Broadcasting Corp.
Group Owner: Tyler Media; (acq 6-30-98; grpsl).
Nat'l Network: ABC; *Nat'l Reps:* ABC Radio Sales
Arbitron Metro Market: Oklahoma City, OK; *Format:* News/Talk; *Target Audience:* 25-54.
Ty Tyler, President
Jack Taylor, Programming Director

KOMA
06-22-1992; 92.5 MHz FM; *Hrs Open:* 24; 94 kw; 1549 ft.; N35 33 36 W97 29 7
400 E. Britton Rd., Oklahoma City, OK 73114 US
(405) 478-5104
www.komaradio.com
License: Oklahoma City, Oklahoma County, OK held by Tyler Media, LLC
Group Owner: Tyler Media; (acq 6-30-98; grpsl).
Arbitron Metro Market: Oklahoma City, OK; *Format:* Adult Contemp, Oldies; *Target Audience:* 25-54.

RADIO - U.S.

Kent Jones, Programming Director
Lisa Sykes, Promotions Manager

KQCV
01-01-1948; 800 kHz AM; *Hrs Open:* 24; 2.5 kw-D, DA2; 1 kw-N, DA2; N35 24 45 W97 40 26
1919 N. Broadway Ave., Oklahoma City, OK 73103 US
(405) 521-0800; *Fax:* (405) 521-1391
www.bottradionetwork.com
comments@bottradionetwork.com
License: Oklahoma City, Oklahoma County, OK held by Bott Broadcasting Co.
Group Owner: Bott Radio Network; (acq 1-76)
Arbitron Metro Market: Oklahoma City, OK; *Format:* Christian, Talk; *Target Audience:* 25-54; family oriented
Richard Bott Sr., President & CEO
Eben Fowler, Operations Dir
Paul Sublett, Area Manager
Joseph Palmer, Sales Manager
Candy Green, Program Services Manager
Rachel Launius, Marketing Manager
Jason Potocnik, Director of TrafficOperations

KBRU
06-06-1967; 94.7 MHz FM; *Hrs Open:* 24; 98 kw; 1,387 ft; N35 32 58 W97 29 50
1900 NW Expressway, Suite 1000, Oklahoma City, OK 73118 US
(405) 840-5271; *Fax:* (405) 842-1315
www.947thebrew.com
License: Oklahoma City, Oklahoma County, OK held by Clear Channel Broadcasting Licenses, Inc.
Group Owner: iHeartMedia; (acq 1-94; $7.5 million).
Population Served: 850,000; *Arbitron Metro Market:* Oklahoma City, OK; *Format:* Rock/AOR; *No. News Employees:* 1; *Target Audience:* 25-54.
Bill Hurley, Vice President/Market Manager
Derrick Nance, Sales
Tom Travis, Programming Director

KRXO-FM
01-01-1976; 107.7 MHz FM; *Hrs Open:* 24; 92 kw; 1542 ft.; N35 33 37 W97 29 6
400 E. Britton Rd., Oklahoma City, OK 73113 US
(405) 478-5104; *Fax:* (405) 478-0448
www.krxo.com
bwiley@krxo.com
License: Oklahoma City, Oklahoma County, OK held by Tyler Media, LLC
Group Owner: Tyler Media
Arbitron Metro Market: Oklahoma City, OK; *Format:* Sports
Gene Vidler, General Sales Mgr
Buddy Wiley, Programming Director
Cara Rice, Promotions Manager

KTOK
01-29-1927; 1000 kHz AM; *Hrs Open:* 24; 5 kw-D, DA2; 5 kw-N, DA2; N35 21 29 W97 27 48
Mailing Address: 3305 W. Mountain Rd, #60, Las Vegas, NV 89102 US
Second Address: 1900 Northwest Expressway, Ste 1000, Oklahoma City, OK 73118
(405) 840-5271; *Fax:* (405) 858-5333
www.ktok.com
License: Oklahoma City, OK held by Clear Channel Broadcasting Licences, Inc.
Group Owner: iHeartMedia; acq 8-5-92)
Regional Network: Okla. News Net; *Nat'l Reps:* Clear Channel
Arbitron Metro Market: Oklahoma City, OK; *Format:* News, News/Talk, 86
Bill Hurley, Vice President/Market Manager
Derrick Nance, General Sales Mgr
Tom Travis, Programming Director

KTST
03-16-1962; 101.9 MHz FM; *Hrs Open:* 24; 94.4 kw; 1220 ft.; N35 35 52 W97 29 22
1900 NW Expressway, Suite 1000, Oklahoma City, OK 73118 US
(405) 840-5271; *Fax:* (405) 848-1106
www.thetwister.com
License: Oklahoma City, Oklahoma County, OK held by Clear Channel Broadcasting Licenses, Inc.
Group Owner: iHeartMedia; acq 1996; grpsl)
Arbitron Metro Market: Oklahoma City, OK; *Format:* Country; *No. News Employees:* 1; *Target Audience:* 18-49.
Bill Hurley, Vice President/Market Manager
Derrick Nance, Sales Manager
Tom Travis, Programming Director

KXXY-FM
10-01-1964; 96.1 MHz FM; *Hrs Open:* 24; 94.9 kw; 1220 ft.; N35 35 52 W97 29 22
1900 NW Expressway, Suite 1000, Oklahoma City, OK 73118 US
(405) 840-5271; *Fax:* (405) 842-1315
www.kxy.com
License: Oklahoma City, Oklahoma County, OK held by Clear Channel Broadcasting Licenses Inc.
Group Owner: iHeartMedia; (acq 1996; grpsl).
Arbitron Metro Market: Oklahoma City, OK; *Format:* Country
Bill Hurley, Vice President/Market Manager
Derrick Nance, Sales Manager
Tom Travis, Programming Director

KYIS
06-01-1969; 98.9 MHz FM; *Hrs Open:* 24; 100 kw; 1542 ft.; N35 33 37 W97 29 7
4045 NW 64th St., Suite 600, Oklahoma City, OK 73116 US
(405) 848-0100
www.kyis.com
License: Oklahoma City, OK held by Radio License Holding CBC, LLC
Group Owner: Cumulus Media Inc.; (acq 10-28-99; grpsl).
Nat'l Network: AP Radio
Arbitron Metro Market: Oklahoma City, OK; *Format:* Adult Contemp; *No. News Employees:* 1; *Target Audience:* 25-54; female
Cisco Kidd, Programming Director

***KYLV**
11-03-1980; 88.9 MHz FM; *Hrs Open:* 24; 5.9 kw; 1522 ft.; N35 33 37 W97 29 6 *Rebroadcasts:* Rebroadcasts KLVR(FM) Middletown, CA 100%
2501 E. Memorial Rd., Oklahoma City, OK 73136 US
(800) 525-5683; *Fax:* (916) 251-1650
www.klove.com
info@klove.com
License: Oklahoma City, Oklahoma County, OK held by Educational Media Foundation.
Group Owner: EMF Broadcasting; (acq 11-9-98; $1.2 million)
Nat'l Network: K-Love
Arbitron Metro Market: Oklahoma City, OK; *Format:* Christian *Special Programming:* Black 3 hrs, relg 2 hrs, gospel 4 hrs, pub affrs 4 hrs wkly; *No. News Employees:* 3; *Target Audience:* 25-44; Judeo-Christian female
Darrell Chambliss, Chairman
Mike Novak, CEO/COO
Mike Novak, President
Evan Falat, Operations Dir
David Pierce, Programming Director
Ed Lenane, News Director
Sam Wallington, Engineering Dir
David Pierce, Chief CreativeOfficer
Alan Mason, Chief Operating Officer
Dan Antonelli, Chief Business Development Officer
Eric Moser, Chief Financial Officer
Mitch Barnhart, Director
Larry Moody, Director

WKY
01-01-1922; 930 kHz AM; *Hrs Open:* 24; 5 kw; N35 33 43 W97 30 27
4045 NW 64th St, Suite 600, Oklahoma City, OK 73116 US
(405) 607-2309
www.laindomable.com
cindy.thompson@cumulus.com
License: Oklahoma City, OK held by Radio License Holding CBC, LLC
Group Owner: Cumulus Media Inc.; (acq 1-31-2003; $7.7 million)
Arbitron Metro Market: OK City, OK; *Format:* Tejano; *Target Audience:* 25-54; Men
Dan Davis, Programming Director

K225BN
06-22-1992; 92.9 MHz FM; *Hrs Open:* 24; 0.2 kw; 1549 ft.; N35 32 51 W97 29 30 *Rebroadcasts:* Simulcasting KOMA
400 E. Britton Rd., Oklahoma City, OK 73114 US
(405) 478-5104
License: Oklahoma City, Oklahoma County, OK held by Tyler Media, LLC
Group Owner: Tyler Media; (acq 6-30-98; grpsl).
Arbitron Metro Market: Oklahoma City, OK; *Format:* Contemporary Hits/Top 40; *Target Audience:* 25-54.
Gene Vidler, General Sales Mgr
Tod Tucker, Programming Director

K243BJ
01-01-1976; 107.7 MHz FM; *Hrs Open:* 24; 0.12 kw; 1542 ft.; N35 32 51 W97 29 30 *Rebroadcasts:* Simulcasting KRXO-FM
5101 S. Shields Blvd., Oklahoma City, OK 73129 US
(405) 478-5104; *Fax:* (405) 478-0448
License: Oklahoma City, Oklahoma County, OK held by Tyler Media, LLC
Group Owner: Tyler Media
Arbitron Metro Market: Oklahoma City, OK; *Format:* Spanish, Oldies
Gene Vidler, General Sales Mgr
Buddy Wiley, Programming Director
Cara Rice, Promotions Manager

Okmulgee

KOKL
10-01-1937; 1240 kHz AM; *Hrs Open:* 24; 1 kw-U, ND1; N35 36 31 W95 58 19
Box 756, Okmulgee, OK 74447 US
(918) 756-3646; *Fax:* (918) 756-1800
koklradio@aol.com
License: Okmulgee, OK held by Regency Radio Inc.
Nat'l Network: ABC
Arbitron Metro Market: Tulsa, OK; *Format:* Country, News, 62, Sports, Talk *Special Programming:* Tulsa Univ. sports 10 hrs; *Hrs. of News Programming:* news progmg 16 hrs wkly; *No. News Employees:* 1 *TargetAudience:* 25 plus; mid to upper income; *Adv. Rates:* 18.95; 15.95; 18.95; 11.25
James Brewer, President
Paul Brown, General Manager

Owasso

KTGX
10-01-1981; 106.1 MHz FM; *Hrs Open:* 24; 100 kw; Ant 1,315 ft; N36 31 36 W95 39 12
2625 South Memorial, Tulsa, OK 78216
(918) 388-5100; *Fax:* (918) 388-5400
www.1061thetwister.com
License: Owasso, Tulsa County, OK held by Clear Channel Broadcasting Licenses Inc.
Group Owner: iHeartMedia; (acq 1997; grpsl)
Arbitron Metro Market: Tulsa, OK; *Format:* Contemporary Hits/Top 40; *Target Audience:* Adults 35-54.
Don Cristi, Senior Vice President of Programming

Pawhuska

KOSG
01-01-1997; 103.9 MHz FM; 6 kw; 328 ft.; N36 44 56 W96 17 51
609 Kihekah, Pawhuska, OK 74056 US
(580) 332-0902; *Fax:* (580) 332-0922
www.thegospelstation.com
License: Pawhuska, Osage County, OK held by Tallgrass Broadcasting LLC
Group Owner: Tallgrass Broadcasting LLC; (acq 10-25-2006; $294,000)
Arbitron Metro Market: Ada, OK; *Format:* Gospel

KPGM
10-19-1963; 1500 kHz AM; *Hrs Open:* 6 AM-6 PM; 0.5 kw-D, NDD; N36 45 42 W96 11 58
1200 S.E. Frank Phillips Blvd., Bartlesville, OK 74003 US
(918) 336-1500
www.bartlesvilleradio.com
tami@bartlesvilleradio.com
License: Pawhuska, OK held by Potter Radio LLC.
Group Owner: KCD Enterprises Inc.; (acq 7-1-2005; $100,000).
Nat'l Network: Salem Radio Network
Arbitron Metro Market: Tulsa, OK; *Format:* Christian, News, 86; *Hrs. of News Programming:* news progmg 20 hrs wkly; *No. News Employees:* 1; *Adv. Rates:* 12; 12; 12; 12

Perry

KOKP
07-06-1986; 1020 kHz AM; *Hrs Open:* 24; 0.4 kw-D, DA2; 0.25 kw-N, DA2; N36 15 35 W97 13 1
3130 South Utica, Tulsa, OK 74105 US
(580) 765-2485; *Fax:* (580) 767-1103
www.eteamradio.com
bill@eteamradio.com
License: Perry, OK held by Team Radio L.L.C.
Group Owner: Team Radio LLC; (acq 7-14-98; $308,000 with co-located FM).
Format: Sports; *Target Audience:* 24 plus; agriculture-related country
Bill Coleman, President/General Manager
Chris Johnson, Programming Director

KOSB
11-24-1988; 105.1 MHz FM; *Hrs Open:* 24; 6 kw; 328 ft.; N36 14 15 W97 21 59
3130 South Utica, Tulsa, OK 74105 US

(580) 765-2485; *Fax:* (580) 767-1103
www.eteamradio.com
bill@eteamradio.com
License: Perry, Noble County, OK held by Team Radio, LLC
Group Owner: Team Radio LLC
Nat'l Network: Westwood One
Format: Sports; *No. News Employees:* 1; *Target Audience:* 25-55.
Bill Coleman, President/General Manager
Chris Johnson, Programming Director

Piedmont

***KZTH**
04-01-2008; 88.5 MHz FM; 50 kw; 597 ft.; N35 31 17 W98 9 33
Rebroadcasts: Rebroadcasts KJTH(FM) Ponca City 100%
P.O. Box 14, Ponca City, OK 74602 US
(580) 767-1400; *Fax:* (580) 765-1700
www.thehousefm.com
mail@thehousefm.com
License: Piedmont, Canadian County, OK held by The Love Station Inc.
Arbitron Metro Market: Piedmont, OK; *Format:* Christian
Doyle Brewer, CEO and Founder
Tony Weir, Music Director
Janelle Keith, Music Director
Darcey Christianson, Chief Engineer
Shaun Michaels, Production Director
Andy Youso, Assistant Program Director
Donna Hollifield, OfficeManager
Jennifer Vaughan, Promotions Assistant

Pocola

***KKRI**
06-11-2002; 88.1 MHz FM; *Hrs Open:* 24; 0.001 kw horiz, 17 kw vert; 374 ft.; N35 13 30 W94 18 4
1425 North Market Blvd, Suite 9, Sacramento, CA 95834 US
(888) 937-2471; *Fax:* (916) 251-1650
www.air1.com
info@air1.com
License: Pocola, Le Flore County, OK held by Educational Media Foundation.
Group Owner: EMF Broadcasting
Nat'l Network: Air 1
Arbitron Metro Market: Fort Smith, AR; *Format:* Alternative, Christian; *No. News Employees:* 3; *Target Audience:* 18-35; Judeo-Christian, female
Darrell Chambliss, Chairman
Alan Mason, COO
Mike Novak, President and CEO
Evan Falat, Operations Dir
David Pierce, Programming Director
Tracy Butler, News Director
Sam Wallington, Engineering Dir
Marya Morgan, News Reporter
Richard Hunt, News Reporter
Larry Moody, Director
Mitch Barnhart, Director
David R. Ferry, Director
Walter Golembeski, Director

Ponca City

KQSN
06-01-1984; 104.7 MHz FM; *Hrs Open:* 24; 25 kw; 292 ft.; N36 47 21 W97 2 53
Mailing Address: Post Office Box 2631, Ponca City, OK 74602 US
Second Address: 3924 Santa Fe Rd., Ponca City, OK 74602
(580) 765-5491; *Fax:* (580) 762-8329
www.kixr.com
kixr@kixr.com
License: Ponca City, Kay County, OK held by Mur-Thom Broadcasting Inc.
Nat'l Network: Westwood One
Format: Talk *Special Programming:* Native American 3 hrs wkly; *Hrs. of News Programming:* news progmg 4 hrs wkly; *No. News Employees:* 5; *Target Audience:* 24-55; core audience of females between the ages of 24-45 *Adv. Rates:* 13; 12; 13; 11
Carol Murphy, President
Gordon Thompson, General Manager
Dave Foster, Chief Engineer

KLOR-FM
12-01-1965; 99.3 MHz FM; *Hrs Open:* 24; 3 kw; 289 ft.; N36 46 59 W97 4 15
3130 S. Utica Ave., Tulsa, OK 74105 US
(580) 762-9930; *Fax:* (580) 767-1103
www.eteamradio.com
billc@eteamradio.com
License: Ponca City, Kay County, OK held by Team Radio L.L.C.
Group Owner: Team Radio LLC; acq 3-18-99).
Regional Network: Okla. News Net.
Arbitron Metro Market: Tulsa, OK; *Format:* Classic Rock, Oldies; *Hrs. of News Programming:* news progmg 75 hrs wkly; *No. News Employees:* 1; *Target Audience:* 18-55.
Bill Coleman, President
Darrel Dye, General Sales Mgr
Sean Anderson, Programming Director

***KLVV**
12-01-1992; 88.7 MHz FM; *Hrs Open:* 24; 11.5 kw; 479 ft.; N36 41 25 W97 10 20
Mailing Address: P O Box 14, Ponca City, OK 74602 US
Second Address: 6600 W. Hwy. 60, Ponca City, OK 74601
(580) 767-1400; *Fax:* (580) 765-1700
www.klvv.com
mail@mypraisefm.com
License: Ponca City, Kay County, OK held by The Love Station Inc.
Format: Christian, Religious; *Target Audience:* 25-45; young Christian adults
Doyle Brewer, CEO
Tony Weir, Programming Director
Janelle Keith, Promotions Manager
Darcy Christianson, Chief Engineer

KPNC
06-05-1979; 100.7 MHz FM; *Hrs Open:* 24; 25 kw; 253 ft.; N36 46 59 W97 4 15
Mailing Address: PO Box 2509, Ponca City, OK 74602 US
Second Address: 122 N. 3rd St., Ponca City, OK 74601
(580) 765-2485; *Fax:* (580) 767-1103
www.eteamradio.com
billc@eteamradio.com
License: Ponca City, Kay County, OK held by Team Radio L.L.C.
Group Owner: Team Radio LLC; (acq 7-20-90)
Format: Country *Special Programming:* Farm 5 hrs wkly; *Hrs. of News Programming:* News progmg 20 hrs wkly; *Target Audience:* 25-54; working middle class
Bill Coleman, Chairman
Darrel Dye, General Sales Mgr
Ryan Diamond, Programming Director

WBBZ
01-01-1927; 1230 kHz AM; *Hrs Open:* 24; 1 kw-U, ND1; N36 41 46 W97 3 7
Box 191, Ponca City, OK 74602 US
(800) 877-5600; *Fax:* (916) 251-1650
www.air1.com
info@air1.com
License: Ponca City, OK held by Ponca City Publishing Co.
Nat'l Network: AP Radio
Arbitron Metro Market: Sioux Falls SD; *Format:* Alternative, Christian
Mike Novak, President

***KJTH**
01-01-2004; 89.7 MHz FM; *Hrs Open:* 24; 100 kw; 1007 ft.; N36 35 42 W97 34 38
Mailing Address: P.O. Box 14, Ponca City, OK 74602 US
Second Address: 6600 W. Hwy. 60, Ponca City, OK 74601
(580) 767-1400; *Fax:* (580) 765-1700
www.thehousefm.com
mail@thehousefm.com
License: Ponca City, Kay County, OK held by The Love Station Inc.
Arbitron Metro Market: Ponca City, OK; *Format:* Christian; *Target Audience:* 25-45; young Christian adults
Doyle Brewer, CEO and Founder
Tony Weir, Program/Music Director
Janelle Keith, Program/Music Director
Darcey Christianson, Chief Engineer
Shaun Michaels, Production Director
Janelle Keith, Promotions Director
Andy Youso,Assistant Program Director
Donna Hollifield, Office Manager
Jennifer Vaughan, Promotions Assistant
Stacey Husted, Office Assistant

Poteau

***KARG**
06-01-1998; 91.7 MHz FM; 2.5 kw; 1867 ft.; N35 4 17 W94 40 47
P.O. Box 3206, Tupelo, MS 38803 US
(662) 844-8888; *Fax:* (662) 842-6791
www.afr.net
faq@afa.net
License: Poteau, Le Flore County, OK held by American Family Association.
Group Owner: American Family Radio
Arbitron Metro Market: Tupelo, MO; *Format:* Christian, Religious
Tim Wildmon, President
Donald Wildmon, Founder
Buddy Smith, Sr. VP
Ed Vitagliano, Executive VP
Randy Sharp, Director Of Special Projects
Meeke Addison, Director Of Communications
Abraham Hamilton III, General Counsel & PublicPolicy

KOMS
10-18-1969; 107.3 MHz FM; *Hrs Open:* 24; 100 kw; 1893 ft.; N34 57 47.3 W94 22 30.7
3101 Free Ferry Road, Suite E, Fort Smith, AR 72903 US
(479) 474-3422; *Fax:* (479) 474-2649
www.bigcountry1073.com
License: Poteau, Le Flore County, OK held by Cumulus Licensing Corp.
Group Owner: Cumulus Media Inc.; (acq 5-17-99; $950,000)
Nat'l Network: CNN Radio; *Wire Services:* AP
Arbitron Metro Market: Fort Smith, AR; *Format:* Country; *Hrs. of News Programming:* News progmg 60 hrs wkly; *Target Audience:* 25-54.
Dan Hentschel, Programming Director
Smitty O'Loughlin, Promotions Manager
Don Jones, Engineering Dir
J.P. Morgan, Disc Jockey
Dale Daniel, Market Manager

KPRV
11-25-1953; 1280 kHz AM; *Hrs Open:* 24
PO Box 368, Poteau, OK 74953 US
(918) 647-3221; *Fax:* (918) 647-5092
www.kprvradio.com
kprv@windstream.net
License: Poteau, OK held by LeRoy Billy.
Nat'l Network: ABC; *Regional Network:* Okla. News Net.
Arbitron Metro Market: Fort Smith, AR; *Format:* Country, Gospel; *Hrs. of News Programming:* News progmg 24 hrs wkly; *Target Audience:* 24-54.
LeRoy Billy, President
Joann Billy, General Manager
LeRoy Billy, General Sales Mgr

KZBB
01-01-1967; 97.9 MHz FM; *Hrs Open:* 24; 100 kw; 2001 ft.; N35 4 19 W94 40 46
311 Lexington Avenue, Fort Smith, AR 72901 US
(479) 782-8888; *Fax:* (479) 782-0366
www.kzbb.com
License: Poteau, Le Flore County, OK held by Capstar TX LLC
Group Owner: iHeartMedia; (acq 8-30-00; grpsl)
Arbitron Metro Market: Poteau, OK; *Format:* Adult Contemp
Special Programming: Black 2 hrs, jazz 2 hrs, relg one hr wkly; *Hrs. of News Programming:* News progmg one hr wkly; *Target Audience:* 18-49; upscale
Dave Ashcraft, Senior Vice President of Programming
Clyde Bass, Regional Market President

Pryor

KMYZ-FM
07-03-1969; 104.5 MHz FM; *Hrs Open:* 24; 70 kw; 1129 ft.; N36 1 10 W95 39 24
149 Penn Ave., Scranton, PA 18501 US
(918) 665-3131; *Fax:* (918) 663-6622
www.edgetulsa.com
License: Pryor, Mayes County, OK held by Shamrock Communications Inc.
Group Owner: Shamrock Communications Inc.; acq 4-14-84)
Arbitron Metro Market: Tulsa, OK; *Format:* Alternative
William Lynett, CEO
Chuck Browning, General Manager

Rattan

***KDBQ**
89.7 MHz FM; kw
US
(940) 668-7971
License: Rattan, Pushmataha County, OK held by 1 A Chord Inc.
Arbitron Metro Market: Santa Cruz, CA
Mary Fay Jackson, General Manager

Roland

KREU
12-29-1995; 92.3 MHz FM; 0.74 kw horiz, 0.73 kw vert; 932 ft.; N35 31 22 W94 23 32
2201 1/2 N. 58th Street, Fort Smith, AR 72904 US
(479) 785-2527; *Fax:* (501) 782-9127
License: Roland, Sequoyah County, OK held by Star 92 Co.
Arbitron Metro Market: Fort Smith, AR; *Format:* Spanish

Fred Baker Jr., Operations Dir
Gary Keifer, General Manager
Carol Patterson, General Sales Mgr
Martin Miranda, Programming Director
Dale Davenport, Chief Engineer

Sallisaw

KKBD
05-18-1972; 95.9 MHz FM; *Hrs Open:* 24; 30 kw; 623 ft.; N35 24 26 W94 41 25
311 Lexington Ave., Fort Smith, AR 72901 US
(479) 782-8888
www.bigdog959.com
info@bigdog959.com
License: Sallisaw, Sequoyah County, OK held by Capstar TX LLC
Group Owner: iHeartMedia; (acq 8-30-00; grpsl).
Arbitron Metro Market: Fort Smith, AR; *Format:* Classic Rock; *Target Audience:* 25-49; adults
Mike Burgess, Director of Sales
Corey Winfield, Programming Director

Sand Springs

KRMG-FM
06-01-1989; 102.3 MHz FM; *Hrs Open:* 24; 50 kw; 492 ft.; N36 12 39 W96 6 3 *Rebroadcasts:* Simulcast with KRMG(AM) Tulsa 100%
7136 South Yale Ave., Suite 500, Tulsa, OK 74136 US
(918) 493-7400; *Fax:* (918) 493-2376
www.krmg.com
info@krmg.com
License: Sand Springs, Tulsa County, OK held by Cox Radio Inc.
Group Owner: Cox Radio Inc.; (acq 3-16-99; $3.5 million)
Arbitron Metro Market: Tulsa, OK; *Format:* News/Talk, News/Talk, 86; *Target Audience:* 25-44.
Dan Lawrie, Vice President / Market Manager
Tracie Poe, General Sales Manager
Randy Smith, Director Of Sales
Mary Garciar, Digital Sales Specialist
Kim Dallow, Marketing / Promotions Director
Jack Conway, IT Manager
April Hill,News Director

KJMU
07-22-1961; 1340 kHz AM; *Hrs Open:* 24; 0.5 kw-D, ND2; 1 kw-N, ND2; N36 8 9 W96 5 32
8107 East Admiral Pl., Tulsa, OK 74115 US
(248) 557-3500; *Fax:* (248) 557-2950
www.birach.com
sima@birach.com
License: Sand Springs, Osage County, OK held by Birach Broadcasting Corp.
Group Owner: Birach Broadcasting Corp.; (acq 1-31-2008; $1.5 million with KTUV(AM) Little Rock, AR)
Arbitron Metro Market: Sand Springs, OK; *Format:* Spanish
Sima Birach, President

KWEN
01-01-1961; 95.5Hz FM; *Hrs Open:* 24; 50 kw; 492 ft.; N36 11 46 W96 5 53
7136 South Yale Ave., Suite 500, Tulsa, OK 74136 US
(918) 494-9500; *Fax:* (918) 493-2889
www.krmg.com
License: Sand Springs, Tulsa County, OK held by Cox Radio Inc.
Group Owner: Cox Radio Inc.; (acq 3-16-99; $3.5 million)
Arbitron Metro Market: Tulsa, OK; *Format:* News, News/Talk, 86; *Target Audience:* 25-64
Dan Lawrie, Vice President / Market Manager
Tracie Poe, General Sales Manager
Randy Smith, Director Of Sales
Mary Garciar, Digital Sales Specialist
Kim Dallow, Marketing / Promotions Director
Jack Conway, IT Manager
April Hill,News Director

KJSR
01-01-1961; 103.3Hz FM; *Hrs Open:* 24; 50 kw; 1280 ft.; N36 11 46 W96 5 53
7136 South Yale Ave., Suite 500, Tulsa, OK 74136 US
(918) 493-3434; *Fax:* (918) 493-2376
www.1033theeagle.com
License: Sand Springs, Tulsa County, OK held by Cox Radio Inc.
Group Owner: Cox Radio Inc.; (acq 3-16-99; $3.5 million)
Arbitron Metro Market: Tulsa, OK; *Format:* News, News/Talk, 86; *Target Audience:* 25-64
Dan Lawrie, Vice President / Market Manager
Tracie Poe, General Sales Manager
Randy Smith, Director Of Sales
Mary Garciar, Digital Sales Specialist
Kim Dallow, Marketing / Promotions Director
Jack Conway, IT Manager
April Hill,News Director

Sapulpa

KYAL
06-15-1962; 1550 kHz AM; *Hrs Open:* 24; 2.5 kw-D, DA2; 0.04 kw-N, DA2; N36 1 8 W96 5 55
P. O. Box 1250, Sapulpa, OK 74067 US
(918) 492-2660; *Fax:* (918) 492-8840
www.sportsanimaltulsa.com
studio@sportsanimaltulsa.com
License: Sapulpa, OK held by KXOJ Inc.
Group Owner: Adonai Radio Group; (acq 5-2-73)
Arbitron Metro Market: Tulsa, OK; *Format:* Sports; *Target Audience:* 35 plus.
David Stephens, General Manager

KXOJ-FM
02-22-1977; 100.9 MHz FM; *Hrs Open:* 24; 5 kw; 361 ft.; N36 3 38 W96 6 3
P. O. Box 1250, Sapulpa, OK 74067 US
(918) 492-2660; *Fax:* (918) 492-8840
www.kxoj.com
kxoj@kxoj.com
License: Sapulpa, Creek County, OK held by KXOJ, Inc.
Group Owner: Adonai Radio Group
Arbitron Metro Market: Tulsa, OK; *Format:* Christian
Bob Thornton, General Manager
Mark James, General Sales Mgr
Rick Collier, National Sales Manager

Seminole

KIRC
01-01-1986; 105.9 MHz FM; *Hrs Open:* 24; 4.4 kw; 384 ft.; N35 18 28 W96 45 18
2 E. Main St., Shawnee, OK 74801 US
(405) 878-1803
www.kirc1059.com
License: Seminole, Seminole County, OK held by One Ten Broadcast Group Inc.
Group Owner: One Ten Broadcast Group Inc.; (acq 4-16-2008)
Arbitron Metro Market: Oklahoma City, OK; *Format:* Country
Special Programming: Area tribes one hr wkly; *Hrs. of News Programming:* news progmg 2 hrs wkly; *No. News Employees:* 9; *Target Audience:* 12-55;general; *Adv. Rates:* 22; 20; 22; 18
Linda Jones, President

*KXTH
10-01-2003; 89.1 MHz FM; *Hrs Open:* 24; 2.6 kw; 377 ft.; N35 12 53 W96 44 26
Mailing Address: P O Drawer 2440, Tupelo, MS 38803 US
Second Address: 6600 W. Hwy. 60, Ponca City, OK 74601
(580) 767-1400; *Fax:* (580) 765-1700
www.thehousefm.com
mail@thehousefm.com
License: Seminole, Seminole County, OK held by The Love Station Inc.
Arbitron Metro Market: Ponca City, OK; *Format:* Adult Contemp, Christian; *Target Audience:* 25-45; young Christian adults
Doyle Brewer, CEO and Founder
Tony Weir, Program/Music Director
Janelle Keith, Program/Music Director
Darcey Christianson, Chief Engineer
Shaun Michaels, Production Director
Andy Youso, Assistant Program Director
DonnaHollifield, Office Manager
Jennifer Vaughan, Promotions Assistant
Stacey Husted, Office Assistant

Shawnee

KGFF
12-10-1930; 1450 kHz AM; *Hrs Open:* 24; 1 kw-U; N35 21 39 W96 53 41
Mailing Address: Box 9, Shawnee, OK 74801
Second Address: 1570 S. Gordon Cooper Drive, Shawnee, OK 74801
(405) 273-4390; *Fax:* (405) 273-4530
www.kgff.com
mike@kgff.com
License: Shawnee, Pottawatomie County, OK held by Citizen Band Potawatomi Indian Tribe of Oklahoma I
Nat'l Network: Dial Global; St. Louis Cardinals (sports); *Regional Network:* Okla. News Net.; Learfield Sports
Population Served: 45,000; *Arbitron Metro Market:* Oklahoma City, *Special Programming:* school, University of Oklahoma, Oklahoma Baptist U; *Hrs. of News Programming:* news progmg 20 hrs wkly; *No. News Employees:* 1 *Target Audience:* General
Michael Askins, General Manager
Michael Askins, Station Manager
Carrie Kieffer, General Sales Mgr
Michael Askins, Programming Director
Carrie Kieffer, Promotions Manager
Michael Askins, News Director
Michael Askins, EngineeringDir

KQCV-FM
04-13-1998; 95.1 MHz FM; 100 kw; 1,004 ft.; N35 15 47 W96 22 43
24 E. Main St., Shawnee, OK 74801 US
(405) 521-0800
www.bottradionetwork.com
comments@bottradionetwork.com
License: Shawnee, Pottawatomie County, OK held by Community Broadcasting Inc.
Group Owner: Bott Radio Network
Arbitron Metro Market: Oklahoma City, OK; *Format:* Christian, Talk
Eben Fowler, Operations Dir
Paul Sublett, Area Manager
Joseph Palmer, Sales Manager
Candy Green, Program Services Manager
Rachel Launius, Marketing Manager

Snyder

KJCM
01-01-2000; 100.3 MHz FM; 18 kw; 384 ft.; N34 38 42 W99 5 3
Mailing Address: Post Office Box 837, Altus, OK 73522 US
Second Address: 1515 N. Broadway, Hobart, OK 73651
(580) 726-5656; *Fax:* (580) 726-2222
thezone@itlnet.net
License: Snyder, Kiowa County, OK held by Fuchs Radio L.L.C.
Group Owner: Fuchs Radio L.L.C.; (acq 4-4-2006; $250,000 with KHIM(FM) Mangum)
Format: Adult Contemp
Chad Fox, General Manager
Lance Perritt, Programming Director

Soper

KMMY
01-01-2008; 96.5 MHz FM; *Hrs Open:* 24; 3.4 kw; 443 ft.; N33 59 25 W95 46 48
Main & High St., Antlers, OK 74560 US
(580) 326-2555; *Fax:* (580) 326-2623
www.myrock965.com
License: Soper, Choctaw County, OK held by k95.5 inc.
Group Owner: k95.5 inc.
Arbitron Metro Market: Soper, OK; *Format:* Rock/AOR

Spencer

*KROU
01-28-1993; 105.7 MHz FM; *Hrs Open:* 24 hrs; 1.6 kw; 638 ft.; N35 34 6.8 W97 29 19.9 *Rebroadcasts:* Rebroadcasts KGOU(FM) Norman 100%
Mailing Address: 780 Van Vleet Oval, Norman, OK 73019 US
Second Address: The University of Oklahoma, Spencer, OK
(405) 325-3388; *Fax:* (405) 325-7129
www.kgou.org
manager@kgou.org
License: Spencer, Oklahoma County, OK held by University of Oklahoma.
Nat'l Network: NPR
Arbitron Metro Market: OK City, OK; *Format:* Blues, Jazz *Special Programming:* Blues 8 hrs; *Hrs. of News Programming:* news progmg 82 hrs wkly; *No. News Employees:* 1; *Target Audience:* 25-54; general
Brian Hardzinski, Operations Dir
Karen Holp, General Manager
Jim Johnson, Programming Director
Kurt Gwartney, News Director
Patrick Roberts, Chief Engineer

Sperry

KMUS
01-01-2004; 1380 kHz AM; *Hrs Open:* 24
P.O. Box 52311, 320 S. Boston, Suite 920, Tulsa, OK 74152 US
(918) 250-8484; *Fax:* (918) 250-6464
www.radiodisney.com/tulsa
License: Sperry, OK held by Radio Disney Group LLC.
Arbitron Metro Market: Tulsa, OK; *Format:* Children; *Adv. Rates:* 14; 14; 14; 14
Barbara Jacaby, General Manager
Mark Gould, General Sales Mgr
Amanda Lucie, Promotions Manager

Stigler

*KTKL
01-01-2003; 88.5 MHz FM; *Hrs Open:* 24; 0.001 kw horiz, 22 kw vert; 643 ft.; N35 8 30 W95 21 20
US
(800) 525-5683; *Fax:* (916) 251-1650
www.klove.com
klove@klove.com
License: Stigler, Haskell County, OK held by Educational Media Foundation.
Group Owner: EMF Broadcasting
Nat'l Network: K-Love
Arbitron Metro Market: Stigler, OK; *Format:* Christian; *No. News Employees:* 3; *Target Audience:* 25-44; Judeo Christian, female
Darrell Chambliss, Chairman
Mike Novak, President and CEO
Evan Falat, Operations Dir
David Pierce, Programming Director
Ed Lenane, News Director
Sam Wallington, Engineering Dir
Marya Morgan, News Reporter
Richard Hunt, NewsReporter
Laura Daniels, News Reporter
Tim Luttrell, News Reporter
Kenny Noble Cortes, News Reporter
Darren Vinson, News Reporter

Stillwater

KGFY
04-28-1967; 105.5 MHz FM; *Hrs Open:* 24; 4.2 kW; 364 ft.; N36 10 47 W97 0 38
408 E Thomas Ave, Stillwater, OK 74075 USA
(405) 372-7800; *Fax:* (405) 372-6969
stillwaterradio.net
License: Stillwater, Payne County, OK held by Stillwater Broadcasting
Group Owner: Stillwater Broadcasting
Arbitron Metro Market: Stillwater, OK; *Format:* Country *Special Programming:* Sports News 10 hrs wkly; *Hrs. of News Programming:* news progmg 5 hrs wkly; *No. News Employees:* 1; *Target Audience:* 18-54; young,college community & upscale educated people; *Adv. Rates:* 30; 20; 30; 10

*KOSU
12-29-1955; 91.7 MHz FM; *Hrs Open:* 24; 100 kw; 1010 ft.; N35 46 50 W97 31 29
Rm 302 Paul Miller Bldg., Stillwater, OK 74078 US
(405) 744-6352; *Fax:* (405) 744-9970
www.kosu.org
License: Stillwater, Payne County, OK held by Oklahoma State University.
Nat'l Network: NPR
Format: News *Special Programming:* American Indian one hr wkly; *Hrs. of News Programming:* news progmg 48 hrs wkly; *No. News Employees:* 2; *Target Audience:* General.
Craig Beeby, General Manager
Don Crider, General Sales Mgr
Rachel Hubbard, News Director
Dan Schroeder, Engineering Dir

KSPI AM
06-01-1947; 780 kHz AM; 37 kW; N38 8 8 W91 24 0
408 E Thomas Ave, Stillwater, OK 74075 USA
(405) 372-7800; *Fax:* (405) 372-6969
stillwaterradio.net
License: Stillwater, Payne County, OK held by Stillwater Broadcasting
Group Owner: Stillwater Broadcasting
Arbitron Metro Market: Stillwater, OK; *Format:* Adult Contemp; *No. News Employees:* 1; *Target Audience:* 30 plus.; *Adv. Rates:* 25; 25; 25; 20

KSPI FM
11-01-1947; 93.7 MHz FM; *Hrs Open:* 24; 16 kW; 863 ft.; N36 6 30 W97 11 47
408 E Thomas Ave, Stillwater, OK 74075 USA
(405) 372-7800; *Fax:* (405) 372-6969
stillwaterradio.net
License: Stillwater, Payne County, OK held by Stillwater Broadcasting
Group Owner: Stillwater Broadcasting
Arbitron Metro Market: Stillwater, OK; *Format:* Adult Contemp; *Hrs. of News Programming:* news progmg 11 hrs wkly; *No. News Employees:* 2; *Target Audience:* 18 plus.; *Adv. Rates:* 30; 25; 30; 10

KVRO
04-12-1997; 101.1 MHz FM; *Hrs Open:* 24; 6 kW; 246 ft.; N36 13 6 W97 9 43
408 E Thomas Ave, Stillwater, OK 74075 USA
(405) 372-7800; *Fax:* (405) 372-6969
stillwaterradio.net
License: Stillwater, Payne County, OK held by Stillwater Broadcasting
Group Owner: Stillwater Broadcasting
Arbitron Metro Market: Stillwater, OK; *Format:* Classic Rock; *Hrs. of News Programming:* 24 hrs news progmg wkly; *No. News Employees:* 2; *Target Audience:* 25-54.

Stuart

*KLRB
01-01-2003; 89.9 MHz FM; *Hrs Open:* 24; 31 kw vert; 308 ft.; N34 54 57 W96 8 10
Rt 6 Box 158, McAlester, OK 74501 US
(918) 697-4019; *Fax:* (580) 892-3941
whitehouseradio@hotmail.com
License: Stuart, Hughes County, OK held by Lighthouse of Prayer Inc.
Arbitron Metro Market: Tulsa, OK; *Format:* Christian, Country, 44
Walter Kuhlman, President
Stephen Burke, General Manager

Sulphur

*KFXT
01-01-2000; 90.7 MHz FM; *Hrs Open:* 24; 7 kw; 299 ft.; N34 32 57 W96 58 34
1101 North 81 Highway, Marlow, OK 73055 US
(580) 658-9292, *Fax:* (580) 658-2561
License: Sulphur, Murray County, OK held by Sister Sherry Lynn Foundation Inc.
Arbitron Metro Market: Marlow, OK; *Format:* Gospel; *Target Audience:* 18-54
Ken Austin, General Manager
Sherry Lynn, General Sales Mgr
Jennifer James, Programming Director
James Wilson, Engineering Dir

KIXO
11-11-1979; 106.1 MHz FM; *Hrs Open:* 24; 2.65 kw; 499 ft.; N34 39 3 W96 59 24
1101 North 81 Highway, Marlow, OK 73055 US
(580) 658-9292
License: Sulphur, Murray County, OK held by DFWU Inc.
Format: Country; *Target Audience:* 25-52.
Ken Austin, General Manager
Sherry Lynn, General Sales Mgr
Jennifer James, Programming Director
Amy Helton, News Director

Taft

KCXR
03-20-1990; 100.3 MHz FM; *Hrs Open:* 24; 3.9 kw; 410 ft.; N35 48 42 W95 34 12
215 N. State Street #910, PO Box 2418, Muskogee, OK 74401 US
(918) 492-2660; *Fax:* (918) 492-8840
www.thekross.fm
kxoj@kxoj.com
License: Taft, Muskogee County, OK held by KXOJ Inc.
Group Owner: Adonai Radio Group; (acq 12-11-2002; $1 million with KBIX(AM) Mukogee).
Arbitron Metro Market: Tulsa, OK; *Format:* Christian; *Target Audience:* Christian 18-49
Michael Stephens, President
David Stevens, General Manager

Tahlequah

KEOK
08-20-1966; 102.1 MHz FM; 6 kw; 285 ft.; N35 53 42.67 W94 57 12.16
5686 S. Muskegee Ave., Tahlequah, OK 74464 US
(918) 456-2511; *Fax:* (918) 456-3231
www.lakescountry1021.com
travis@payneradiogroup.com
License: Tahlequah, Cherokee County, OK held by K95.5 Inc.
Group Owner: K95.5 Inc.
Arbitron Metro Market: Tahlequah, OK; *Format:* Country; *Target Audience:* 25-60.
Lou Kelly, Operations Manager & Program Director
Travis Reeves, General Manager
Mick Reed, News Director
Stevie Morgan, Production Director

KTLQ
08-01-1957; 1350 kHz AM; *Hrs Open:* 24; 1 kw-D, ND1; 0.061 kw-N, ND1; N35 53 43 W94 57 12
5686 S. Muskogee Ave., Tahlequah, OK 74464 US
(918) 456-2511; *Fax:* (918) 456-3231
www.lakescountry1021.com
travis@payneradiogroup.com
License: Tahlequah, OK held by K95.5 Inc.
Group Owner: K95.5 Inc.; (acq 11-24-2003; $1.15 million with co-located FM).
Nat'l Network: Westwood One
Arbitron Metro Market: Tahlequah, OK; *Format:* Country, Sports; *Hrs. of News Programming:* news progmg 6 hrs wkly; *No. News Employees:* 1; *Target Audience:* 25-54.
Lou Kelly, Operations Manager/Program Director
Travis Reeves, General Manager
Stevie Morgan, Production Director

Tishomingo

*KTGS
09-29-1998; 88.3 MHz FM; 5.5 kw; 922 ft.; N34 21 34 W96 33 34
Route 5, Box 119, Ada, OK 74820 US
(580) 332-0902; *Fax:* (580) 332-0922
www.thegospelstation.com
email@thegospelstation.com
License: Tishomingo, Johnston County, OK held by South Central Oklahoma Christian Broadcasting Inc.
Arbitron Metro Market: Ada, OK; *Format:* Gospel
Randall Christy, President
Rick Cody, General Manager

KBBC
99.7 MHz FM; 15.5 kw; 128 meters; N34 11 36 W96 32 11
1418 North 1st Avenue, Durant, OK
(580) 924-3100
License: Tishomingo, OK held by Texoma Broadcasting Inc
Group Owner: Texoma Broadcasting Inc.

Gerald Todd Tidwell, President

Tonkawa

*KAYE-FM
06-01-1976; 90.7 MHz FM; *Hrs Open:* 7 AM-midnight (M-F); 1.2 kw; 66 ft.; N36 40 42 W97 17 50
1220 E. Grand, PO Box 310, Tonkawa, OK 74653 US
(580) 628-6446; *Fax:* (580) 628-6209
License: Tonkawa, Kay County, OK held by Northern Oklahoma College.
Arbitron Metro Market: Tonkawa, OK; *Format:* Contemporary Hits/Top 40; *Hrs. of News Programming:* News progmg 6 hrs wkly; *Target Audience:* 13-25.
Dr. Joe Kinzer, President

Tulsa

KAKC
07-15-1938; 1300 kHz AM; *Hrs Open:* 24; 5 kw-D, DA2; 1 kw-N, DA2; N35 59 40 W95 51 27
2625 S. Memorial Dr., Tulsa, OK 74129 US
(918) 388-5100; *Fax:* (918) 388-5400
www.buzztulsa.com
License: Tulsa, Tulsa County, OK held by Clear Channel Broadcasting Licenses Inc.
Group Owner: iHeartMedia; (acq 8-5-92)
Nat'l Network: ESPN Radio; Fox Sports; *Nat'l Reps:* Clear Channel
Arbitron Metro Market: Tulsa, OK; *Format:* Sports; *Target Audience:* 25-54; men
Serene Rogers, Sales
Chris Plank, Programming Director
Brady Johnson, Promotions Manager
Brett Gilbert, Chief Engineer

KBEZ
03-01-1964; 92.9 MHz FM; *Hrs Open:* 24; 100 kw; 1319 ft.; N36 11 26 W96 5 50
4590 East 29th Stret, Tulsa, OK 74114 US
(918) 743-7814; *Fax:* (918) 496-1937
www.929bobfm.com
bgann@jrn.com
License: Tulsa, Tulsa County, OK held by Journal Broadcast Group
Group Owner: Journal Broadcast Group; acq 6-8-90; grpsl;
Arbitron Metro Market: Tulsa, OK; *Format:* Adult Contemp; *Target Audience:* 25-54.
Brian Gann, Operations Dir
Bill Berry, Vice President/General Manager
Phillip Sutterfield, Sales Manager
Paul Kriegler, Programming Director
Alexis Trotter, Digital Branch Manager

KCFO
01-01-1946; 970 kHz AM; *Hrs Open:* 24; 2.5 kw-D, DA2; 1 kw-N, DA2; N36 11 46 W96 2 22
3737 S. 37 W. Avenue, Tulsa, OK 74107 US
(918) 622-0970; *Fax:* (918) 622-0985
www.kcfo.com
info@kcfo.com
License: Tulsa, OK held by Friendship Broadcasting L.P.
Nat'l Network: USA
Arbitron Metro Market: Tulsa, OK; *Format:* Sports, Talk, 74; *Hrs. of News Programming:* News progmg 3 hrs wkly; *Target Audience:* 25-54; Men & women
Ray Clatworthy, President
Kenneth Staley, General Manager

KGTO
01-01-1998; 1050 kHz AM
7030 S. Yale Ave., Tulsa, OK 74136 US
(918) 494-9886; *Fax:* (918) 494-9683
tulsaheartandsoul.com
mvaughan@kjmm.com
License: Tulsa, OK held by KJMM Inc.
Group Owner: Perry Publishing & Broadcasting Co.; (acq 3-30-01; $455,000).
Nat'l Network: Westwood One
Arbitron Metro Market: Tulsa, OK; *Format:* Adult Contemp; *Target Audience:* 35-54.
Martha Vaughan, General Manager

KJSR
11-01-1966; 103.3 MHz FM; *Hrs Open:* 24; 100 kw; 1296 ft.; N36 1 10 W95 39 24
7136 South Yale Avenue, Suite 500, Tulsa, OK 74136 US
(918) 493-3434; *Fax:* (918) 493-2397
License: Tulsa, Tulsa County, OK held by Cox Media Group
Group Owner: Cox Media Group; (acq 3-28-97; grpsl)
Arbitron Metro Market: Tulsa, OK; *Format:* Classic Rock *Special Programming:* Pub affrs 2 hrs wkly; *No. News Employees:* 1; *Target Audience:* 25-44.
Gene Vidler, Vice President/Market Manager
Steve Hunter, Operations Dir
Tracie Poe, General Sales Mgr
Dena Fletcher, Programming Director
Kim Dallow, Promotions Manager
Jack Conway, Web Master
Luke Hively, Digital SalesManager

KMOD-FM
10-10-1959; 97.5 MHz FM; 100 kw; 1486 ft.; N36 11 46 W96 5 53
2625 S. Memorial Drive, Tulsa, OK 74129 US
(918) 388-5100; *Fax:* (918) 388-5400
www.kmod.com
License: Tulsa, Tulsa County, OK held by Clear Channel Broadcasting Licenses Inc.
Group Owner: iHeartMedia
Arbitron Metro Market: Tulsa, OK; *Format:* Rock/AOR; *Target Audience:* 25-49; men
Don Cristi, Senior Vice President/Programming

KTBZ
01-22-1934; 1430 kHz AM
2625 S. Memorial, Tulsa, OK 74129 US
(918) 388-5100; *Fax:* (918) 388-5400
www.buzztulsa.com
License: Tulsa, OK held by Clear Channel Broadcasting Licenses Inc.
Group Owner: iHeartMedia; (acq 1997; grpsl)
Arbitron Metro Market: Tulsa, OK; *Format:* Sports; *Target Audience:* 25-49; men
Serene Rogers, General Sales Mgr
Chris Plank, Programming Director
Brady Johnson, Promotions Manager
Brett Gilbert, Engineering Dir
Terah Williams, Webmaster

KRAV-FM
11-21-1962; 96.5 MHz FM; 100 kw; 1486 ft.; N36 11 46 W96 5 53
7136 South Yale Avenue, Suite 500, Tulsa, OK 74136 US
(918) 491-9696; *Fax:* (918) 493-5385
www.mix96tulsa.com
License: Tulsa, Tulsa County, OK held by Cox Media Group
Group Owner: Cox Radio Inc.; (acq 11-21-96; $5.5 million with co-located AM)
Arbitron Metro Market: Tulsa, OK; *Format:* Adult Contemp; *Target Audience:* 25-54; 30% men, 70% women
Dan Lawrie, Vice President / Market Manager
Tracie Poe, General Sales Manager
Randy Smith, Director Of Sales
Mary Garcia, Digital Sales Specialist
Kim Dallow, Marketing / Promotions Director

KRMG
12-31-1949; 740 kHz AM; *Hrs Open:* 24; 50 kw-D, DA2; 25 kw-N, DA2; N36 4 50 W96 17 9
7136 South Yale Avenue, Suite 500, Tulsa, OK 74136 US
(918) 493-7400; *Fax:* (918) 493-2376
www.krmg.com
info@krmg.com
License: Tulsa, OK held by Cox Media Group
Group Owner: Cox Media Group; (acq 3-28-97; grpsl)
Arbitron Metro Market: Tulsa, OK; *Format:* News, News/Talk, 86; *No. News Employees:* 7; *Target Audience:* 25-54; those interested in news, info & issue oriented talk
Steve Hunter, Operations Dir
Tracie Poe, General Sales Mgr
Levi May, Programming Director
Kim Dallow, Promotions Director
April Hill, News Director
Gene Vidler, Market Manager
Luke Hively, Digital Sales Manager

KFAQ
01-23-1925; 1170 kHz AM; *Hrs Open:* 24
4590 East 29th Street, Tulsa, OK 74114 US
(918) 743-7814; *Fax:* (918) 743-6461
www.1170kfaq.com
bgann@journalbroadcastgroup.com
License: Tulsa, OK held by Journal Broadcast Corp.
Group Owner: Journal Communications Inc.; (acq 6-11-99; grpsl)
Nat'l Network: Fox News Radio; *Nat'l Reps:* Clear Channel
Arbitron Metro Market: Tulsa, OK; *Format:* Talk *Special Programming:* Farm 5 hrs, gospel 2 hrs wkly; *Hrs. of News Programming:* news progmg 24 hrs wkly; *No. News Employees:* 3; *Target Audience:* 35 plus.
Brian Gann, Operations Dir
Bill Berry, Vice President/General Manager
Ray Klotz, Engineering Dir
Phillip Sutterfield, Advertising/Sales Manager
Pat Campbell, Host
Elvis Polo, Host
Eddie Huff, Host

KVOO-FM
11-16-1973; 98.5 MHz FM; *Hrs Open:* 24; 99 kw; 1227 ft.; N36 11 26 W96 5 50
4590 East 29th Street, Tulsa, OK 74114 US
(918) 743-7814; *Fax:* (918) 743-7613
www.kvoo.com
ljensen@journalbroadcastgroup.com
License: Tulsa, Tulsa County, OK held by Journal Broadcast Corp.
Group Owner: Journal Communications Inc.
Arbitron Metro Market: Tulsa, OK; *Format:* Country; *Target Audience:* 25-54.
Brian Gann, Operations Dir
Bill Berry, Vice President/General Manager
Crash Poteet, Programming Director
Ray Klotz, Engineering Dir
Phillip Sutterfield, Advertising Sales Manager
David Thompson, Interactive Manager
AlexisTrotter, Digital Brand Manager

KWEN
01-01-1961; 95.5 MHz FM; *Hrs Open:* 24; 100 kw; 1486 ft.; N36 11 46 W96 5 53
US
(918) 493-9500; *Fax:* (918) 493-2889
info@kwen.com
License: Tulsa, Tulsa County, OK held by Cox Radio, Inc
Group Owner: Cox Media Group
Wire Services: NWS (National Weather Service)
Arbitron Metro Market: Tulsa, OK; *Format:* Country; *No. News Employees:* 1; *Target Audience:* 25-54; country life group
Gene Vidler, Vice President/General Manager
Lisa Guerin, General Sales Mgr
Karla Cantrell, Program Director
Kim Dallow, Marketing/Promotions Director
Pogie Freeman, Internet Content Manager
Jack Conway, Web Master
Matt Bradley,Afternoon Personality/ Asst. Program Director

***KWGS**
10-19-1947; 89.5 MHz FM; *Hrs Open:* 24; 50 kw; 1066 ft.; N36 1 15 W95 40 32
600 S. College, Tulsa, OK 74104 US
(918) 631-2577; *Fax:* (918) 631-3695
www.kwgs.org
public@publicradiotulsa.org
License: Tulsa, Tulsa County, OK held by The University of Tulsa.
Nat'l Network: NPR; PRI *Regional Reps:* Wayne Blackmon
Arbitron Metro Market: Tulsa, OK; *Format:* News; *Hrs. of News Programming:* News progmg 84 hrs wkly; *No. News Employees:* 1; *Target Audience:* General.; *Adv. Rates:* 30; 20; 30; 20
Steve Clem, Operations Dir
Rich Fisher, General Manager
Frank Christel, Programming Director
John Durkee, News Director & Morning Edition Anchor
Brad Newman, Chief Engineer
Frank Christel, Director of Broadcast Services
MarshallStewart, Reporter and All Things Considered Anchor
P.Casey Morgan, Development Director
Scott Gregory, Production Director and host of All This is Jazz

***KWTU**
10-15-2004; 88.7 MHz FM; *Hrs Open:* 24; 5 kw; 1066 ft.; N36 1 15 W95 40 32
Mailing Address: 600 S. College, Tulsa, OK 20036 US
Second Address: OK
(918) 631-2577; *Fax:* (918) 631-3695
www.publicradiotulsa.org
public@publicradiotulsa.org
License: Tulsa, Tulsa County, OK held by The University of Tulsa.
Regional Reps: Wayne Blackmon
Arbitron Metro Market: Tulsa, OK; *Format:* Classical; *Target Audience:* 50+.
Steve Clem, Operations Dir
Rich Fisher, General Manager
Frank Christel, Programming Director
John Durkee, News Director
Brad Newman, Chief Engineer
Frank Christel, Director of Broadcast Services
P. Casey Morgan, DevelopmentDirector
Scott Gregory, Production Director

Valliant

KYHD
94.7 MHz FM; *Hrs Open:* 24; 230 ft.
1600 W. Jackson, Hugo, OK 74743 USA
(580) 326-2555; *Fax:* (580) 326-2623
www.hd947.com
travis@payneradiogroup.com
License: Valliant, OK held by K95.5 Inc.
Group Owner: K95.5 Inc.
Arbitron Metro Market: Valliant, OK

Vinita

KGND
12-07-1954; 1470 kHz AM; *Hrs Open:* 24; 0.5 kw-D, ND1; 0.088 kw-N, ND1; N36 38 34 W95 7 35
Mailing Address: 402 North Wilson, P. O. Box 961, Vinita, OK 74301 US
Second Address: 402 N. Wilson St., Vinita, OK 74301
(918) 256-2255; *Fax:* (918) 256-2633
don@kitofm.com
License: Vinita, OK held by KXOJ Inc.
Group Owner: Stephens Media Group; 7-Sep
Nat'l Network: Fox Sports
Arbitron Metro Market: Tulsa, OK; *Format:* Sports *Special Programming:* Oklahoma State University Sports; *No. News Employees:* 4; *Target Audience:* 30-50.
Bob Thornton, General Manager
Don Wilson, Station Manager
Mark James, General Sales Mgr
Rick Collier, National Sales Manager

KITO-FM
04-09-1981; 96.1 MHz FM; *Hrs Open:* 24; 50 kw; 492 ft.; N36 34 56 W95 1 35
Mailing Address: 402 N.Wilson, P.O. Box 961, Vinita, OK 74301 US
Second Address: 402 N. Wilson St., Vinita, OK 74301
(918) 256-2255; *Fax:* (918) 256-2633
License: Vinita, Craig County, OK held by KXOJ Inc.
Group Owner: Stephens Media Group; (acq 8-1-2007; $1.8 million with co-located AM)
Nat'l Network: Jones Radio Networks; *Regional Network:* Okla. News Net.
Arbitron Metro Market: Tulsa, OK; *Format:* Country *Special Programming:* Oklahoma University Sports; *Hrs. of News Programming:* News progmg 28 hrs wkly; *No. News Employees:* 4; *Target Audience:* General;traditional country music fans
Bob Thornton, General Manager
Mark James, General Sales Mgr
Rick Collier, National Sales Manager

Wagoner

KXTD
03-01-1966; 1530 kHz AM; *Hrs Open:* Daytime; 5 kw-D, DAD; N35 58 30 W95 29 30
2715 S. Radio Rd., El Reno, OK 73036 US
(918) 254-7556; *Fax:* (918) 252-0036
www.quebuenatulsa.com
License: Wagoner, OK held by Gaytan-Galvan Limited Liability Co.
Nat'l Reps: Rgnl Reps
Arbitron Metro Market: Tulsa, OK; *Format:* Tejano *Special Programming:* LiverPulga; *Hrs. of News Programming:* Top of the hour; *Target Audience:* 18-49 A; *Adv. Rates:* 18;20;20;10
Maria DeLeon, CEO

Warner

KTFX-FM
03-01-1995; 101.7 MHz FM; *Hrs Open:* 24; 25 kw; 276 ft.; N35 34 39 W95 12 36
501 N. Main St., Suite 4, Muskogee, OK 74401 US
(918) 684-1022; *Fax:* (918) 686-6159
www.okiecountry1017.com
katey@okiecountry1017.com
License: Warner, Muskogee County, OK held by K95.5 Inc.
Group Owner: K95.5 Inc.
Arbitron Metro Market: Muskogee, OK; *Format:* Country; *Hrs. of News Programming:* news progmg 2 hrs wkly; *No. News Employees:* 1; *Target Audience:* 25-54; Adults
Cliff Casteel, Operations Dir
Katey Sherrick, General Manager
Chris McConnell, Advertising Account Executive
Margaret Chapman, Traffic Manager

Watonga

KIMY
12-12-1987; 93.9 MHz FM; *Hrs Open:* 24; 4.2 kw; 394 ft.; N35 50 27 W98 19 9
502 Santa Fe, Anthony, KS 67003 US
(580) 332-0902
www.thegospelstation.com
email@thegospelstation.com
License: Watonga, Blaine County, OK held by South Central Oklahoma Broadcasting Inc.
Format: Gospel; *Target Audience:* 25-54; general; *Adv. Rates:* 12; 11; 12; 11
Randall Christy, President
Rick Cody, General Manager

Weatherford

***KAYM**
01-01-2000; 90.5 MHz FM; 2.7 kw; 282 ft.; N35 29 47 W98 44 10
P.O. Box 3206, Tupelo, MS 38803 US
(662) 844-8888; *Fax:* (662) 842-6791
www.afr.net
faq@afa.net
License: Weatherford, Custer County, OK held by American Family Association.
Group Owner: American Family Radio
Arbitron Metro Market: Tupelo, MS; *Format:* Christian, Religious
Tim Wildmon, President
Donald Wildmon, Founder
Buddy Smith, Sr VP
Ed Vitaligano, Exec VP
Randy Sharp, Director Of Special Projects
Meeke Addison, Director Of Communications
Abraham Hamilton III, General Counsel & Public Policy

KWEY
06-01-1970; 1590 kHz AM; 1 kw-D, DA2; 0.032 kw-N, DA2; N35 33 33 W98 43 11
P.O. Box 587, Weatherford, OK 73096 US
(580) 772-5939; *Fax:* (580) 772-1590
info@kwey.com
License: Weatherford, OK held by Wright Broadcasting Systems Inc.
Group Owner: Wright Broadcasting Systems; (acq 7-17-91; $407,435 with co-located FM;
Nat'l Network: ABC; *Regional Network:* Agrinet; Okla. News Net.
Arbitron Metro Market: Weatherford, OK; *Format:* Country; *Hrs. of News Programming:* news progmg 14 hrs wkly; *No. News Employees:* 1; *Target Audience:* 25 plus; full service station; *Adv. Rates:* 25; 16; 20; 15.
G. Harold Wright, CEO
Todd Brunner, Operations Dir
Heston Wright, General Manager
Vanessa Valli, Programming Director
Mike Smith, News Director
Ray Bagby', Technical Director
Amanda Benton, Area Sales Manager
Brianna Arherman,Area Sales Manager
John Liddle, Sports Director/ Account Executive
Kelli Haan, Account Executive, Websites and Graphics

Wewoka

KWSH
07-01-1951; 1260 kHz AM; 1 kw-D, DAN; 1 kw-N, DAN; N35 10 10 W96 32 30
2 E. Main St., Shawnee, OK 74801 US
(405) 878-0077
License: Wewoka, OK held by One Ten Broadcast Group Inc.
Group Owner: One Ten Broadcast Group Inc.; (acq 4-16-2008)
Regional Network: Okla. News Net.
Format: Country *Special Programming:* American Indian one hr wkly; *Target Audience:* 21-61.
Linda Jones, President

KSLE
10-01-1997; 104.7 MHz FM; *Hrs Open:* 24; 1.7 kw; 505 ft.; N35 5 31 W96 32 29
2 E. Main Street, Shawnee, OK 74801 US
(405) 878-0077
License: Wewoka, Seminole County, OK held by One Ten Broadcast Group Inc.
Group Owner: One Ten Broadcast Group Inc.; (acq 4-16-2008)
Format: Oldies
Linda Jones, President

Wilburton

KMCO
11-01-1965; 101.3 MHz FM; *Hrs Open:* 24; 100 kw; 617 ft.; N34 59 13 W95 42 10
Mailing Address: P.O. Box 1068, McAlester, OK 74502 US
Second Address: 1801 E. Electric Ave., McAlester, OK 74502
(918) 426-1050; *Fax:* (918) 423-7119
www.mcalesterradio.com
info@mcalesterradio.com
License: Wilburton, Latimer County, OK
Group Owner: Southeastern Oklahoma Radio LLC; (Acq 1-18-2005; $766,666).
Format: Country; *Hrs. of News Programming:* News progmg 5 hrs wkly; *Target Audience:* 18-45.
Lee Anderson, General Manager
Leanne Massensale, Traffic Manager
Bob Turnbow, Sales Manager

Woodward

***KJOV**
01-01-1998; 90.7 MHz FM; 25 kw; 397 ft.; N36 24 8 W99 25 47
Mailing Address: 922 Webster, P.O Box 1888, Woodward, OK 73802 US
Second Address: 922 Webster, Woodward, OK 73802
(620) 873-2991; *Fax:* (620) 873-2755
License: Woodward, Woodward County, OK held by Christian Community Radio.
Format: Christian
Michael Luskey, CEO
Blake Carter, Programming Director
Delvin Kinser, News Director
Steve Larson, Chief Engineer
Polly Hughes, Traffic Manager

KZCU
01-01-2001; 95.9 MHz FM; 6 kw; 328 ft.; N36 24 40 W99 21 5
Third Coast Jt Venture, 3050 Post Oak Blvd #1700, Houston, TX 77056 US
(580) 581-2425; *Fax:* (580) 581-5571
www.kccu.org
kccu@cameron.edu
License: Woodward, Woodward County, OK held by Cameron University

Ted Riley, General Manager

KMZE
10-15-1989; 92.1 MHz FM; *Hrs Open:* 24; 2.15 kw; 1099 ft.; N36 16 6 W99 26 56
101 Centre: 2728 Williams Avenue, Woodward, OK 73801 US
(580) 256-4101
www.z92online.com
License: Woodward, Woodward County, OK held by FM 92 Broadcasters Inc.
Nat'l Network: Jones Radio Networks
Arbitron Metro Market: Oklahoma City, OK; *Format:* Adult Contemp; *No. News Employees:* 1; *Target Audience:* 25-54.
Dou Williams, General Manager
Shawn Miller, Business Manager
Tiffany Phillips, Media/Sales Manager
Sean Kelly, Programming Director
Jessi Prince, Traffic/Billing Manager

KSIW
09-01-1947; 1450 kHz AM; *Hrs Open:* 24; 1 kw-U, ND1; N36 25 42 W99 24 10
Mailing Address: PO Box 1600, Woodward, OK 73651 US
Second Address: 1922 22nd St., Woodward, OK 73801
(580) 256-0935; *Fax:* (580) 254-9102
www.woodwardradio.com
License: Woodward, OK held by Classic Communications Inc.
Group Owner: Classic Communications Inc.; (acq 6-20-2005).
Nat'l Network: ESPN Radio
Arbitron Metro Market: Woodward, OK; *Format:* Sports, Talk; *Target Audience:* Male 18-49.
Sherre House, President
Bret Brewer, Programming Director
Sam Piel, Programming Director

KWDQ
01-09-1990; 102.3 MHz FM; 100 kw; 868 ft.; N36 22 31 W99 28 31
P.O. Box 1600, Woodward, OK 73802 US
(580) 254-9102; *Fax:* (580) 254-9103
cciradio@sbcglobal.net
License: Woodward, Woodward County, OK held by Classic Communications Inc.
Group Owner: Classic Communications Inc.; (acq 3-20-92)
Regional Network: Okla. News Net.
Arbitron Metro Market: Woodward, OK; *Format:* Rock/AOR; *Target Audience:* 18-49.
Sherre House, President
Bret Brewer, Programming Director

KWFX
11-01-1974; 100.1 MHz FM; *Hrs Open:* 24; 100 kw; 868 ft.; N36 22 31 W99 28 31
P O Box 1600, Woodward, OK 73802 US
(580) 256-0935
License: Woodward, Woodward County, OK held by Classic Communications Inc.
Group Owner: Classic Communications Inc.; (acq 4-30-96)
Regional Network: Okla. News Net.
Arbitron Metro Market: Woodward, OK; *Format:* Country; *Target Audience:* 25-65; affluent, males & females
Sherre House, President
Bret Brewer, Operations Dir
LaDonna Herber, General Sales Mgr
Mikel Frederickson, Account Executive
Kendra Wyatt, Account Executive

KWOX
12-16-1983; 101.1 MHz FM; *Hrs Open:* 24; 100 kw; 1,204 ft; N36 16 06 W99 26 56
101 Centre, 2728 Williams Ave., Woodward, OK 73801
(580) 256-4101; *Fax:* (580) 256-3825
k101@k101online.com
License: Woodward, Woodward County, OK held by Omni Communications Corp.
Nat'l Network: Westwood One; ABC; *Regional Network:* Radio Oklahoma Net *Regional Reps:* Regional Reps
Population Served: 150,000; *Arbitron Metro Market:* Oklahoma City, OK *TV Affiliate:* KOMI-TV affil. *Special Programming:* Morning Show; *No. News Employees:* 2; *Target Audience:* General.
J. Douglas Williams, President/CEO
Shawn Miller, Business Manager
Kevin Grice, General Manager/Vice President of Operations
J Douglas Williams, General Sales Mgr
Patrick Ley, Programming Director
Jessi Prince, PromotionsManager
Kevin Grice, Engineering Dir
Shirley Webb, CFO
Matt Storm, Morning Show Host

Oregon

Albany

KEJO
08-01-1955; 1240 kHz AM; 1 kw-U; N44 35 44 W123 14 54
2840 Marion St. S.E., Albany, OR 97322
(541) 926-8628; *Fax:* (541) 928-1261
www.kejoam.com
License: Albany, OR held by Bicoastal Willamette Valley LLC.
Group Owner: Bicoastal Media L.L.C.; (acq 7-2-2007; grpsl)
Population Served: 76,600 *Target Audience:* ages 25-54 men
Jason Hensen, Station Manager
Jon Warren, Programming Director

Kimberly Reznicsek, Promotions Manager
Larry Rogers, Market Manager

KHPE
01-12-1969; 107.9 MHz FM; *Hrs Open:* 24; 100 kw; 1161 ft.; N44 38 46 W123 16 11
P. O. Box 278, 34545 Hwy 20, Albany, OR 97321 US
(541) 926-2233; *Fax:* (541) 926-3925
www.hope1079.com
paul@hope1079.com
License: Albany, Linn County, OR held by Extra Mile Media Inc.
Format: Christian *Special Programming:* Talk 30 hrs wkly; *Target Audience:* 25-54; female
Bill Zipp, President
Jeff McMahon, Operations Dir
Randy Davison, General Manager
Vicki Webber, News Director
John Kenneke, Chief Engineer

KLOO
08-23-1947; 1340 kHz AM; *Hrs Open:* 24
2840 Marion St. S.E., Albany, OR 97322 US
(541) 926-5115
www.klooam.com
jonwarren@bicoastal.media
License: Albany, OR held by Bicoastal Willamette Valley LLC.
Group Owner: Bicoastal Media L.L.C.; (acq 7-2-2007; grpsl)
Arbitron Metro Market: Eugene, OR; *Format:* News, News/Talk, 84, Talk; *Hrs. of News Programming:* news progmg 83 hrs wkly; *No. News Employees:* 1; *Target Audience:* 35-54.
Jason Henson, Station Manager
Larry Rogers, Market Manager
Jon Warren, Programming Director
Kimberly Reznicsek, Promotions Manager

KLOO-FM
01-01-1973; 106.3 MHz FM; *Hrs Open:* 24; 100 kw; 1138 ft.; N44 38 47 W123 16 10
2840 Marion St. S.E., Albany, OR 97322 US
(541) 926-8628; *Fax:* (541) 928-1261
www.kloo.com
jasonhenson@bicoastal.media
License: Albany, OR
Group Owner: Bicoastal Media L.L.C.
Arbitron Metro Market: Albany, OR; *Format:* Classic Rock; *Hrs. of News Programming:* News progmg 15 hrs wkly; *Target Audience:* 18-54.
Jason Henson, Sales Manager
Debi Starr, Programming Director
Kimberly Reznicsek, Promotions Director
Larry Rogers, Market Manager

KTHH
01-01-1959; 990 kHz AM; *Hrs Open:* 24; 0.25 kw-D, ND1; 0.009 kw-N, ND1; N44 35 43 W123 7 34
2840 Marion St. S.E., Albany, OR 97322 US
(541) 926-8628; *Fax:* (541) 928-1261
www.comedy990.com
jasonhenson@bicoastal.media
License: Albany, OR held by Bicoastal Willamette Valley LLC.
Group Owner: Bicoastal Media L.L.C.; (acq 7-2-2007; grpsl)
Nat'l Reps: Tacher
Format: Comedy; *Hrs. of News Programming:* news progmg 10 hrs wkly; *No. News Employees:* 1; *Target Audience:* 25-54.
Jason Henson, General Sales Mgr
Angie Foster, Programming Director
Kimberly Reznicsek, Promotions Manager
Larry Rogers, Market Manager

KRKT-FM
06-01-1978; 99.9 MHz FM; 100 kw; 1070 ft.; N44 38 46 W123 16 11
2840 Marion St. S.E., Albany, OR 97322 US
(541) 926-8628; *Fax:* (541) 928-1261
www.krkt.com
jasonhenson@bicoastal.media
License: Albany, OR
Group Owner: Bicoastal Media L.L.C.
Format: Country
Jason Hensen, Station Manager
Scott Schuler, Programming Director
Kimberly Reznicsek, Promotions Manager
Larry Rogers, Market Manager

KWIL
01-14-1941; 790 kHz AM; *Hrs Open:* 24; 1 kw-D, DA2; 1 kw-N, DA2; N44 37 54 W123 0 57
P. O. Box 278, 34545 Hwy 20, Albany, OR 97321 US
(541) 926-2233; *Fax:* (541) 926-3925
www.kwil790.com
pauldelury@kwil790.com
License: Albany, OR held by Extra Mile Media Inc.
Arbitron Metro Market: Albany, OR; *Format:* Christian
Tim Murphy, General Manager
Jodie Bates, General Sales Mgr
Neal Larson, News Director
Rhett Downing, Chief Engineer

Aloha

KLVP
12-26-1958; 97.9 MHz FM; 10 kw; 470 meters; N45 31 21 W122 44 45
5700 West Oaks Boulevard, Rocklin, CA 95765 US
(916) 251-1600; *Fax:* (916) 251-1650
www.klove.com
License: Aloha, Lane County, OR held by Educational Media Foundation
Group Owner: EMF Broadcasting
Arbitron Metro Market: Eugene, OR; *Format:* Alternative
Mike Novak, President

Altamont

KRAT(FM)
01-01-1991; 97.7 MHz FM; 22 kw; Ant 1,712 ft; N42 10 06 W122 09 06
Box 235, Klamath Falls, OR 97601
(541) 884-8167; *Fax:* (541) 884-8226
License: Altamont, Klamath County, OR held by George J. Wade.
Format: Oldies; *Adv. Rates:* 4; 4; 4; 4
Richard Towne, General Manager

Ashland

KCMX-FM
07-20-1978; 101.9 MHz FM; *Hrs Open:* 24; 42 kw; 1470 ft.; N42 17 55 W122 44 53
1438 Rossanley Dr., Medford, OR 97501 US
(541) 779-1550
www.litefm1019.com
danhanvey@radiomedford.com
License: Ashland, Jackson County, OR held by Mapleton License of Medford LLC.
Group Owner: Mapleton Communications LLC
Nat'l Network: ABC
Arbitron Metro Market: Ashland, OR; *Format:* Adult Contemp; *No. News Employees:* 1; *Target Audience:* 25-54.
Dan Hanvey, Programming Director

***KSMF**
11-07-1987; 89.1 MHz FM; *Hrs Open:* 5 AM-2 AM; 2.3 kw; 1352 ft.; N42 17 54 W122 44 59
P. O. Box 3175, Eugene, OR 97403 US
(541) 552-6301; *Fax:* 9541) 552-8565
www.ijpr.org
jprinfo@sou.edu
License: Ashland, Jackson County, OR held by The State of Oregon, acting by and through the State Board of Higher Education.
Nat'l Network: NPR; PRI; *Wire Services:* AP
Arbitron Metro Market: Ashland, OR; *Format:* Jazz, News, 90 *Special Programming:* Blues 6 hrs, folk 3 hrs, pub affrs 7 hrs wkly; *Hrs. of News Programming:* news progmg 45 hrs wkly; *No. News Employees:* 1 *TargetAudience:* General.
Paul Westhelle, Executive Director
Mitchell Christian, Operations Dir
Eric Teel, Programming Director
Geoffrey Riley, News Director
Darin Ransom, Engineering Dir
Mitchell Christian, CFO
Don Matthews, Music Director

***KSOR**
04-01-1969; 90.1 MHz FM; *Hrs Open:* 5 AM-2 AM; 38 kw; 2657 ft.; N42 41 30 W123 13 44
P.O. Box 3175, Eugene, OR 97403 US
(541) 552-6301; *Fax:* (541) 552-8565
www.ijpr.org
info@ijpr.org
License: Ashland, Jackson County, OR held by The State of Oregon, acting by and through the State Board of Higher Education.
Nat'l Network: PRI; NPR; *Wire Services:* AP
Arbitron Metro Market: Medford-Ashland, OR; *Format:* News *Special Programming:* Pub affrs 7 hrs wkly; *Hrs. of News Programming:* news progmg 35 hrs wkly; *No. News Employees:* 1; *Target Audience:* General.
Paul Westhelle, Executive Director
Mitchell Christian, Operations Manager
Eric Teel, Programming Director
Geoffrey Riley, News Director
Darin Ransom, Engineering Dir
Don Matthews, Music Director

***KSRG**
01-01-1995; 88.3 MHz FM; *Hrs Open:* 5 AM- 2 AM; 0.23 kw; 1345 ft.; N42 17 52 W122 44 58
P.O. Box 3175, Eugene, OR 97403 US
(541) 552-6301; *Fax:* (541) 552-8565
www.ijpr.org
info@ijpr.org
License: Ashland, Jackson County, OR held by The State of Oregon, acting by and through the State Board of Higher Education, for the benefit of Southern Oregon State University.
Nat'l Network: NPR; PRI; *Wire Services:* AP
Arbitron Metro Market: Ashland, OR; *Format:* Classical, Variety/Diverse; *Hrs. of News Programming:* news progmg 35 hrs wkly; *No. News Employees:* 1; *Target Audience:* General.
Paul Westhelle, Executive Director
Mitchell Christian, Operations Manager
Eric Teel, Programming Director
Geoffrey Riley, News Director
Darin Ransom, Engineering Dir
Don Matthews, Music Director

Astoria

KAST
01-01-1922; 1370 kHz AM; *Hrs Open:* 5 AM-midnight
285 SW Main Court, Suite 200, Warrenton, OR 97146 US
(503) 861-6620; *Fax:* (503) 325-5570
www.kast1370.com
License: Astoria, OR held by Ohana Media Group
Group Owner: Ohana Media Group; (acq 10-26-99; grpsl)
Arbitron Metro Market: Warrenton, OR; *Format:* News, News/Talk, 84, Talk; *Hrs. of News Programming:* News progmg 50 hrs wkly; *Target Audience:* 35 plus.
Trila Bumstead, President/CEO
Kris Edwards, Operations Manager

***KMUN**
02-02-1982; 91.9 MHz FM; *Hrs Open:* 5 AM-1 AM; 7.2 kw; 1089 ft.; N46 15 46 W123 53 9
Mailing Address: P.O. Box 269, 1445 Exchange St., Astoria, OR 97103 US
Second Address: 1445 Exchange St., Astoria, OR 97103
(503) 325-0010; *Fax:* (503) 325-3956
www.kmun.org
kmun@kmun.org
License: Astoria, Clatsop County, OR held by Tillicum Foundation.
Nat'l Network: NPR
Format: Easy Listening *Special Programming:* Folk 18 hrs, children's 6 hrs, Sp 3 hrs, American; *Hrs. of News Programming:* news progmg 12 hrs wkly; *No. News Employees:* 1; *Target Audience:* General.
David Hall, President
Joe Patenaude, Operations Dir
Joanne Rideout, General Manager
Elizabeth Menetry, Programming Director
Kathleen Morgain, News Director
Terry Wilson, Engineering Dir
David Paul, Membership Coordinator

***KGIO**
01-01-2006; 90.5 MHz FM; 0 kw horiz, 0.048 kw vert; 469 ft.; N46 10 56 W123 48 9 *Rebroadcasts:* Rebroadcasts KRUC(FM) Las Cruces, NM 100%.
Box 3333, McAllen, TX 78502 US
(956) 787-9788; *Fax:* (956) 787-9783
www.worldradionetwork.org
License: Astoria, Clatsop County, OR held by Carlos Arana Ministries
Arbitron Metro Market: Astoria, OR; *Format:* Spanish, Religious
Glenn Lafitte, CEO
Dr. William Haney, General Manager
Kitty Stinson, Chief Operations Officer
James Gamblin, Director of Broadcast Operations
Jamie Sepulveda, Director of Finance and Administration
Dwight Lind, Western RegionalCoordinator
David Soper, Vice Chairman
Glenn Lafitte, Secretary

***KLOY**
01-01-2006; 88.7 MHz FM; 0.25 kw; 1053 ft.; N46 15 46 W123 53 9 *Rebroadcasts:* Rebroadcasts KLVR(FM) Santa Rosa, CA 100%
P.O. Box 269, Astoria, OR 97103 US
(800) 525-5683; *Fax:* (916) 251-1650
www.klove.com
klove@klove.com
License: Astoria, Clatsop County, OR held by Educational Media Foundation.

Group Owner: EMF Broadcasting; (acq 2-2-2004).
Nat'l Network: K-Love
Arbitron Metro Market: Astoria, OR; *Format:* Christian; *No. News Employees:* 13
Darrell Chambliss, Chairman
Mike Novak, President and CEO
Eric Allen, General Sales Mgr
David Pierce, Programming Director
Ed Lenane, News Director
Sam Wallington, Engineering Dir
Scott Smith, Music Director
Marya Morgan, NewsReporter
Richard Hunt, News Reporter
Mike Lee, Regional Manager
Tracy Butler, Traffic Manager

Athena

KHSS
11-05-1986; 100.7 MHz FM; *Hrs Open:* 24; 6.3 kw; 1322 ft.; N45 59 23 W118 10 31
1230 Colonial Drive, College Place, WA 99324 US
(509) 525-7878; *Fax:* (509) 522-2046
comments@khssradio.com
License: Athena, Walla Walla County, OR held by Two Hearts Communications L.L.C.
Nat'l Reps: Katz Radio
Format: Talk, Christian *Special Programming:* Relg 3 hrs wkly; *Target Audience:* 18-34.
Rodney Fazzari, General Manager
Todd Brandenburg, Chief Engineer

Baker

KBKR
01-01-1939; 1490 kHz AM; *Hrs Open:* 24; 1 kw-U, ND1; N44 47 18 W117 48 35 *Rebroadcasts:* Rebroadcasts KLBM(AM) La Grande 100%
2510 Cove Ave., La Grande, OR 97850 US
(541) 523-4431
www.supertalknews.com
License: Baker, Baker County, OR held by Pacific Empire Radio Corp.
Group Owner: Pacific Empire Radio Corp.; (acq 7-19-2004; grpsl).
Nat'l Network: Westwood One; *Nat'l Reps:* McGavren Guild
Arbitron Metro Market: La Grande, OR; *Format:* News, News/Talk, 86 *Special Programming:* Farm 2 hrs wkly; *Hrs. of News Programming:* news progmg 25 hrs wkly; *No. News Employees:* 1; *Target Audience:* 25-54. *Adv. Rates:* 22; 20; 22; 16
Ben Bonfield, General Manager

KKBC-FM
02-01-1981; 95.3 MHz FM; *Hrs Open:* 24; 6 kw; -200 ft.; N44 47 18 W117 48 35
P.O. Box 907, La Grande, OR 97850 US
(541) 523-4431
www.yourboomerradio.com
License: Baker, Baker County, OR held by Pacific Empire Radio Corp.
Group Owner: Pacific Empire Radio Corp.
Nat'l Reps: McGavren Guild
Arbitron Metro Market: Baker City, OR; *Format:* Oldies; *Hrs. of News Programming:* news progmg 6 hrs wkly; *No. News Employees:* 1; *Target Audience:* 25-54.; *Adv. Rates:* 24; 24; 24; 18
Evan Yeoman, Operations Manager
Ben Bonfield, General Manager

***KANL**
01-01-2005; 90.7 MHz FM; 0.25 kw; 653 ft.; N44 45 58 W117 52 54
P.O. Box 3206, Tupelo, MS 38803 US
(662) 844-8888; *Fax:* (662) 842-6791
www.afr.net
faq@afa.net
License: Baker, Baker County, OR held by American Family Association.
Group Owner: American Family Radio
Arbitron Metro Market: Baker, OR; *Format:* Christian
Tim Wildmon, President
Donald Wildmon, Founder
Buddy Smith, Sr VP
Ed Vitagliano, Exec VP
Randy Sharp, Director Of Special Projects
Meeke Addison, Director Of Communications
Abraham Hamilton III, General Counsel

***KDJC**
01-01-2005; 88.1 MHz FM; 0.775 kw; 1810 ft.; N45 7 26 W117 46 48
P.O. Box 391, Twin Falls, ID 83303 US
(800) 357-4226; *Fax:* (208) 736-1958
www.csnradio.com
csn@csnradio.com
License: Baker, Baker County, OR held by Calvary Chapel of Twin Falls
Group Owner: CSN International
Arbitron Metro Market: Baker City-La Grande, OR; *Format:* Christian, Religious
Mike Kestler, President
Daniel Davidson, Operations Dir
Don Mills, Network Programming Director
Mike Stocklin, Underwriting Director
Kelly Carlson, Engineering Dir

***KANC**
89.9 MHz FM; kw
US
(662) 844-5036; *Fax:* (662) 842-7798
www.afr.net
contact@afa.net
License: Baker, Baker County, OR held by Abundant Life Broadcasting.
Arbitron Metro Market: Tupelo, MS; *Format:* Christian
Tim Wildmon, President
Tamara Durham, Operations Dir
Jennifer Hagman, Programming Director

Baker City

KCMB
04-28-1986; 104.7 MHz FM; 100 kw; 1,747 ft; N45 07 26 W117 46 48
1009-C Adams Ave., La Grande, OR 97850 US
(541) 963-3405; *Fax:* (541) 963-5090
www.myeasternoregon.com
randy@elkhornmediagroup.com
License: Baker City, OR held by KCMB, LLC.
Group Owner: Elkhorn Media Group
Nat'l Network: ABC; *Nat'l Reps:* Tacher
Format: Country; *Target Audience:* 25-54.
Randy McKone, President
Kelly Workman, Operations Mgr
Tori Brock Gandy, General Sales Mgr

***KESY**
01-01-2005; 91.9 MHz FM; 0.32 kw; 1132 ft.; N44 44 22 W117 44 42
US
(314) 921-9330
License: Baker City, Crawford County, OR held by Idaho Conference of Seventh Day Adventists Inc.
Arbitron Metro Market: Baker City, OR; *Format:* Country
David Prest Jr., President

***KOBK**
01-01-2007; 88.9 MHz FM; *Hrs Open:* 24; 0.6 kw; 1834 ft.; N44 35 57 W117 46 58 *Rebroadcasts:* Rebroadcasts KOPB-FM Portland 100%
7140 Sw Macadam Ave., Portland, OR 97219 US
(503) 244-9900; *Fax:* (503) 293-4877
www.opb.org
License: Baker City, Baker County, OR held by Oregon Public Broadcasting.
Nat'l Network: NPR; *Regional Network:* Ore. Pub. Bcstg Radio Net.
Arbitron Metro Market: Baker City, OR; *Format:* News, News/Talk, 86
Steve Bass, President/CEO
Raoul van Hall, Operations Manager
Lynne Clendenin, Vice President of Programming
Steven Kray, Chief Engineer
Dan Metziga, Senior Vice President, Development & Marketing

Bandon

KBDN
10-01-1996; 96.5 MHz FM; 1.5 kw; 1296 ft.; N42 57 27 W124 16 13
320 Central Ave., Suite 519, Coos Bay, OR 97420 US
(541) 267-2121; *Fax:* (541) 267-5229
www.kbdn.com
License: Bandon, Coos County, OR held by Bicoastal Media Licenses III LLC.
Group Owner: Bicoastal Media L.L.C.; (acq 10-16-2003; grpsl)
Nat'l Reps: Tacher
Arbitron Metro Market: Bandon, OR; *Format:* Country; *Target Audience:* 25-54.
Mike Wilson, President & COO

Banks

KXJM
06-01-1990; 107.5 MHz FM; *Hrs Open:* 24; 68 kw; 1,646 ft.; N45 30 58.4 W122 43 58.8
1333 S.W. 68th Pkwy., Suite 310, Tigard, OR 97223 US
(503) 323-6400; *Fax:* (503) 323-6660
www.jamn1075.com
License: Banks, Washington County, OR held by Citicasters Licenses Inc.
Group Owner: iHeartMedia; (acq 4-1-2009; grpsl)
Nat'l Network: Westwood One
Arbitron Metro Market: Portland, OR; *Format:* Urban Contemporary; *Target Audience:* 25-49; adult
Marshal Burgess, General Sales Mgr
Diana Hryciw, Promotions and Digital Coordinator
Dave Hill, Vice President of Programming

Bay City

KTIL-FM
10-01-1998; 95.9 MHz FM; *Hrs Open:* 24; 0.45 kw; 1181 ft.; N45 27 59 W123 55 11
US
(503) 842-4422; *Fax:* (503) 842-2755
License: Bay City, Tillamook County, OR held by Oregon Eagle Inc.
Arbitron Metro Market: Tillamook, OR; *Format:* Adult Contemp; *Target Audience:* General.
Van Moe, President

KTIL-FM
01-01-2005; 95.9 MHz FM; 450 w; Ant 1,181 ft; N45 27 59 W123 55 11
1600 Gray Lynn Dr., Walla Walla, WA 99362
(509) 527-1000; *Fax:* (509) 529-5534
www.kix106online.com
License: Bay City, Tillamook County, OR held by Alexandra Communications Inc.
Group Owner: Alexandra Communications Inc.; (acq 8-2-2005; $150,000 for CP)
Population Served: 13,767; *Arbitron Metro Market:* Hewitt, TX
Tom Hodgins, President

Beaverton

KKCW
02-01-1984; 103.3 MHz FM; *Hrs Open:* 24; 95 kw; 1542 ft.; N45 31 21 W122 44 45
13333 SW 68th Parkway, Tigard, OR 97223 US
(503) 323-6400; *Fax:* (503) 241-1033
www.k103.com
License: Beaverton, Washington County, OR held by Citicasters Licenses Inc.
Group Owner: iHeartMedia; (acq 5-4-99; grpsl).
Nat'l Reps: D & R Radio
Arbitron Metro Market: Portland, OR; *Format:* Adult Contemp; *No. News Employees:* 3; *Target Audience:* 25-54.
Marshal Burgess, Vice President of Sales
Diana Hryciw, Promotions and Digital Coordinator
Dave Hill, Vice President of Programming

Bend

KBND
12-19-1938; 1110 kHz AM; *Hrs Open:* 24; 10 kw-D, DAN; 5 kw-N, DAN; N44 6 25 W121 14 39
63088 NE 18th St., Bend, OR 97701 USA
(541) 382-5263; *Fax:* (541) 388-0456
www.kbnd.com
License: Bend, OR held by Combined Communications.
Group Owner: Combined Communications.; (acq 4-27-90).
Nat'l Network: Fox News Radio; *Nat'l Reps:* McGavren Guild
Format: News, Talk; *No. News Employees:* 2; *Target Audience:* 35-64; upscale, professionals
Frank Bonacquisti, Programming Director

KMGX
07-04-1973; 100.7 MHz FM; 50 kw; 518 ft.; N44 4 40 W121 19 49
345 Cyber Dr., Suite 1, Bend, OR 97702 US
(541) 388-3300; *Fax:* (541) 388-3303
www.themix1007.com
ahilmes@bendradiogroup.com
License: Bend, OR held by GCC Bend, LLC
Group Owner: GCC Bend, LLC
Arbitron Metro Market: Bend, OR; *Format:* Adult Contemp
Andy Hilmes, General Sales Mgr
Mike Flanagan, Programming Director
Bart Platt, Dir of Promotions
RL Garrigus, News Director
Tracee Tuesday, Music Director

KNLR
12-31-1984; 97.5 MHz FM; *Hrs Open:* 24; 97 kw horiz, 42 kw vert; 535 ft.; N44 4 38 W121 19 49
P.O. Box 7408, Bend, OR 97708 US
(541) 389-8873; *Fax:* (541) 389-5291
www.knlr.com
License: Bend, Deschutes County, OR held by Cowan Broadcasting LLC.
Nat'l Network: USA; *Wire Services:* AP
Arbitron Metro Market: Bend, OR; *Format:* Adult Contemp, Christian
Terry Cowan, General Manager

***KOAB-FM**
01-01-1994; 91.3 MHz FM; 75 kw; 653 ft.; N44 4 41 W121 19 57
7140 S.W. Macadam Ave., Portland, OR 97219 US
(503) 293-1905; *Fax:* (503) 293-1919
www.opb.org
info@opb.org
License: Bend, Deschutes County, OR held by Oregon Public Broadcasting.
Nat'l Network: NPR
TV Affiliate: *KOAB-TV affil.; *Format:* News; *Hrs. of News Programming:* news progmg 146 hrs wkly; *No. News Employees:* 5
Steve Bass, President/CEO
Raoul van Hall, Operations Manager
Lynne Clendenin, Vice President of Programming
Steven Kray, Chief Engineer
Dan Metziga, Senior Vice President, Development & Marketing

KQAK
09-05-1986; 105.7 MHz FM; *Hrs Open:* 24; 40 kw; 591 ft.; N44 4 40 W121 19 49
854 NE 4th St., Bend, OR 97701 US
(541) 383-3825; *Fax:* (541) 383-3403
www.kqak.com
License: Bend, Deschutes County, OR held by Horizon Broadcasting Group, LLC.
Group Owner: Horizon Broadcasting Group, LLC; acq 2000; $3.45 million).
Nat'l Reps: Christal
Arbitron Metro Market: Bend, OR; *Format:* Adult Contemp
Special Programming: Inside Central Oregon (Public Affairs); *No. News Employees:* 1; *Target Audience:* 25-54.
Dave Clemens, Programming Director

KTWS
12-21-1990; 98.3 MHz FM; *Hrs Open:* 24; 5.2 kw; 732 ft.; N44 4 39 W121 19 57
63088 NE 18th St., Bend, OR 97701 USA
(541) 382-5263; *Fax:* (541) 388-0456
www.thetwins.com
License: Bend, Deschutes County, OR held by Combined Communications, Inc.
Group Owner: Combined Communications; (acq 9-1-96)
Nat'l Reps: McGavren Guild
Arbitron Metro Market: Bend, OR; *Format:* Classic Rock; *Target Audience:* 25-54.; *Adv. Rates:* 36; 32; 34; 24

KICE
02-04-1960; 940 kHz AM; *Hrs Open:* 24; 10 kw-D, 60 w-N
345 SW Cyber Dr., Suite 101, Bend, OR 97702-1134 US
(541) 388-3300; *Fax:* (541) 388-3303
www.espn940am.com
ahilmes@bendradiogroup.com
License: Bend, OR held by GCC Bend, LLC
Group Owner: GCC Bend, LLC; (acq 1999)
Arbitron Metro Market: Bend, OR; *Format:* Sports
Andy Hilmes, General Sales Mgr
Mike Flanagan, Programming Director
Bart Platt, Dir. of Promotions
RL Garrigus, News Director

KMTK
01-01-2000; 99.7 MHz FM; *Hrs Open:* 24; 26 kw; 682 ft.; N44 4 39 W121 19 57
63088 NE 18th St., Suite 200, Bend, OR 97701 USA
(541) 382-5263; *Fax:* (541) 585-0456
www.997thebull.com
License: Bend, Deschutes County, OR held by Combined Communications Inc.
Group Owner: Combined Communications
Arbitron Metro Market: StreetBend, OR; *Format:* Country

***KVLB**
01-01-2003; 90.5 MHz FM; *Hrs Open:* 24; 1.4 kw vert; 633 ft.; N44 4 40 W121 19 48
P O Drawer 2440, Tupelo, MS 38803 US
(800) 525-5683; *Fax:* (916) 251-1650
www.klove.com
klove@klove.com
License: Bend, Deschutes County, OR held by Educational Media Foundation.
Group Owner: EMF Broadcasting; (acq 3-11-03; grpsl).
Nat'l Network: K-Love
Arbitron Metro Market: Bend, OR; *Format:* Christian; *No. News Employees:* 3; *Target Audience:* 25-44; Judeo Christian, female
Darrell Chambliss, Chairman
Mike Novak, President and CEO
Marya Morgan, News Reporter
Mike Lee, General Sales Mgr
David Pierce, Programming Director
Ed Lenane, News Director
Sam Wallington, Engineering Dir
Richard Hunt, NewsReporter
Laura Daniels, News Reporter
Tim Luttrell, News Reporter
Kenny Noble Cortes, News Reporter
Darren Vinson, News Reporter

***KLBR**
88.1 MHz FM; 5 kw; Ant 850 ft; N44 02 49 W121 31 50
Rebroadcasts: Rebroadcasts KLCC(FM) Eugene 100%
136 W. 8th Ave., Eugene, OR 97405
(541) 463-6000; *Fax:* (541) 463-6046
www.klcc.org
klcc@klcc.org
License: Bend, Deschutes County, OR held by Lane Community College.

Steve Barton, General Manager
Cheryl Crumbley, General Sales Mgr
Don Hein, Programming Director

KRXF
01-01-2006; 92.9 MHz FM; 86 kw; 994 ft.; N44 2 49 W121 31 50
P. O. Box 5068, 1500 NEButler Market Rd, Bend, OR 97708 US
(541)388-3300; *Fax:* (541) 388-3303
www.929online.com
mflanagan@bendradiogroup.com
License: Bend, Deschutes County, OR held by GCC Bend, LLC
Nat'l Reps: Katz Radio
Arbitron Metro Market: Bend, OR; *Format:* Rock/AOR
Jim Gross, Vice President/General Manager
Andy Hilmes, General Sales Mgr
Mike Flanagan, Programming Director
Bart Platt, Promotions Manager
Pam Hudspeth, Traffic Manager

KBNW
08-25-2008; 1340 kHz AM; *Hrs Open:* 24 *Rebroadcasts:* Simulcast with KWLZ-FM Warm Springs 100%
854 NE 4th Street, Bend, OR 97701 US
(541) 383-3825; *Fax:* (541) 383-3403
www.newsradiocentraloregon.com
License: Bend, OR held by Summit Broadcasting Group LLC
Nat'l Network: ABC Information & Entertainment; Premiere Radio Networks; Westwood One; Jones Radio Networks; Talk Radio Network; *Nat'l Reps:* Christal; *Wire Services:* AP
Arbitron Metro Market: Bend, OR; *Format:* News, News/Talk, 86; *Hrs. of News Programming:* 17.5 weekly (local); *No. News Employees:* 3; *Target Audience:* Adults 25-54
Regan Brick, Operations Dir
Keith Shipman, General Manager
Kenn Brown, General Sales Mgr
Glenn Vaagen, Programming/News Director
Heather Roberts, Promotions Director
Jean Morgan, Traffic Manager

Bonanza

***KYSF**
01-01-1999; 102.9 MHz FM; 460 w; Ant 2,106 ft; N42 05 48 W121 37 57
5700 W. Oaks Blvd., Rocklin, CA 98006
(916) 251-1600; *Fax:* (916) 251-1650
www.klove.com
License: Bonanza, Klamath County, OR held by Educational Media Founation
Group Owner: New Northwest Broadcasters LLC; (acq 1-4-2012).

Mike Novak, President/CEO
Rob Siems, General Manager

Brightwood

***KZME**
91.1 MHz FM; 0.125 kw; 1430 ft.; N45 19 44 W121 42 35 US
(503) 618-1071; *Fax:* (503) 667-7710
www.kzme.fm
License: Brightwood, Clackamas County, OR held by MetroEast Community Media.
Arbitron Metro Market: Portland, OR; *Format:* Contemporary Hits/Top 40, Public Affairs
Rob Brading, CEO
Dennise M. Kowalczyk, Director of Organizational Advancement
Taaj Middleton, Director of Volunteer Services

Brookings

KURY
05-02-1958; 910 kHz AM; *Hrs Open:* 24; 1 kw-D, ND1; 0.037 kw-N, ND1; N42 2 34 W124 14 37
605 Railroad St., P.O. Box 1029, Brookings, OR 97415 US
(541) 469-2111; *Fax:* (541) 469-6397
www.kury910.com
License: Brookings, Curry County, OR held by Eureka Broadcasting Co. Inc.
Group Owner: Eureka Broadcasting Co. Inc.; (acq 4-19-2005; $775,000 with co-located FM).
Nat'l Network: Jones Radio Networks; *Nat'l Reps:* Tacher
Arbitron Metro Market: Brookings, OR; *Format:* Oldies; *No. News Employees:* 4; *Target Audience:* General.; *Adv. Rates:* contact for rate card
Hugo Papstein, President
Brian Papstein, General Manager
Debby Phillips, General Sales Mgr
Kevin Bane, Programming Director
Tina Williams, News Director

KURY-FM
05-01-1977; 95.3 MHz FM; *Hrs Open:* 24; 8.7 kw; 1,165 ft.; N42 7 23 W124 17 56
605 Railroad St., P.O. Box 1029, Brookings, OR 97415 US
(541) 469-2111; *Fax:* (541) 469-6397
www.kury953.com
License: Brookings, Curry County, OR held by Eureka Broadcasting Co. Inc.
Group Owner: Eureka Broadcasting Co. Inc.; (acq 5-5-2005).
Nat'l Reps: Tacher; *Wire Services:* AP
Arbitron Metro Market: Brookings, OR; *Format:* Oldies; *Hrs. of News Programming:* news progmg 11 hrs wkly; *No. News Employees:* 4; *Adv. Rates:* Contact for rate card
Hugo Papstein, President
Brian Papstein, General Manager
Debby Phillips, General Sales Mgr
Kevin Bane, Programming Director
Tina Williams, News Director
Steve Braun, Disc Jockey
Robert Brown, Disc Jockey
Kevin Bane, DiscJockey

***KMWR**
10-31-2002; 90.7 MHz FM; *Hrs Open:* 24; 100 w; Ant 1,233 ft; N42 07 23 W124 17 56 *Rebroadcasts:* Rebroadcasts KVIP-FM Redding, CA 100%
1139 Hartnell Ave., Redding, CA 96002 US
(530) 222-4455; *Fax:* (530) 222-4484
www.kvip.org
info@kvip.org
License: Brookings, Curry County, OR held by Pacific Cascade Communications Corp.
Group Owner: Pacific Cascade Communications Corp.
Population Served: 15,000 *Format:* Christian; *No. News Employees:* 2
Phil Morrow, General Manager

Brownsville

KEHK
04-01-1991; 102.3 MHz FM; *Hrs Open:* 24; 100 kw horiz, 43 kw vert; 919 ft.; N44 0 8 W123 6 50
1200 Executive Parkway, Suite 440, Eugene, OR 97401 US
(541) 284-8500; *Fax:* (541) 485-0969
www.starfm1023.com
License: Brownsville, Linn County, OR held by Cumulus Licensing Corp.
Group Owner: Cumulus Media Inc.; (acq 8-24-00; grpsl)
Nat'l Network: Jones Radio Networks; *Nat'l Reps:* McGavren Guild
Arbitron Metro Market: Eugene-Springfield, OR; *Format:* Adult Contemp; *Hrs. of News Programming:* news progmg 2 hrs wkly; *No. News Employees:* 1; *Target Audience:* 25-54.
Bill Bradley, President
BJ O'Brien, Market Manager
Samantha Rumm, Sales Manager
Maverick, Programming Director

Burns

KORC(FM)
09-01-1997; 92.7 MHz FM; *Hrs Open:* 24; 750 w; 905 ft; N43 34 22 W119 07 50
69470 S. Egan Rd., PO Box 877, Burns, OR 97720
(541) 573-2055; *Fax:* (541) 573-5223
License: Burns, Harney County, OR
Nat'l Network: Jones Radio Networks; *Nat'l Reps:* Tacher
Population Served: 10,000 *Format:* Adult Contemp; *Adv. Rates:* Same as AM
Joan Reed-Nickerson, President
Linc Reed-Nickerson, General Manager
Ryan Steineckert, Programming/Sports Director

***KOBN**
90.1 MHz FM; 0.6 kw; 899 ft.; N43 34 23 W119 7 49
7140 SW Macadan Avenue, Portland, OR 97219 US
(503) 293-1905; *Fax:* (503) 293-1919
www.opb.org
opb.org/contactus
License: Burns, Harney County, OR held by Oregon Public Broadcasting.
Arbitron Metro Market: Burns, OR
Steven M. Bass, CEO
Dan Metziga, Senior Vice President, Development and Marketing
Lynne Clendenin, Vice President, Programming
Morgan Holm, Vice President, News and Public Affairs
Steve Amen, Executive Producer

Canyon City

KJDY-FM
12-13-1996; 94.5 MHz FM; *Hrs Open:* 24; 39 kw; 1365 ft.; N44 17 50 W119 2 9
P.O. Box 399, John Day, OR 97845 US
(541) 575-1185; *Fax:* (541) 575-2313
License: Canyon City, Grant County, OR held by Blue Mountain Broadcasting Co. Inc.
Nat'l Network: ABC
Format: Country; *Target Audience:* 25-54.
Phil Gray, General Manager

Canyonville

***KWRZ**
10-22-1990; 92.3 MHz FM; 6 kw; -686 ft.; N42 55 42 W123 17 5
Rebroadcasts: Rebroadcasts KWAX(FM) Eugene 100%
75 Centennial Loop, Eugene, OR 97401 US
(541) 345-0800; *Fax:* (541) 343-2123
www.kwax.com
inquiry@kwax.com
License: Canyonville, Lane County, OR held by Oregon State Board of Higher Education for the University of Oregon
Arbitron Metro Market: Canyonville, OR; *Format:* Contemporary Hits/Top 40; *Target Audience:* General.
Paul C. Bjornstad, Director of Broadcasting

Cave Junction

KCNA
04-30-1985; 102.7 MHz FM; *Hrs Open:* 24; 100 kw; 1975 ft.; N42 15 30 W123 39 38
1257 No. Riverside, Ave, Suite 10, Medford, OR 97501 US
(541) 772-0322; *Fax:* (541) 772-4233
1027TheDrive.com
jim@opusradio.com
License: Cave Junction, Josephine County, OR held by Opus Broadcasting Systems Inc.
Group Owner: Opus Broadcasting Systems Inc.; acq 12-94).
Nat'l Reps: Tacher
Arbitron Metro Market: Cave Junction, OR; *Format:* Contemporary Hits/Top 40, Adult Contemp
Henry Flock, President
Dean Flock, General Manager
Brian Fraser, General Sales Mgr
Oscar Bonilla, Programming Director

Central Point

KFJL
02-14-2012; 1400 kHz AM; 1 kw-U; N42 21 00 W122 54 27
672 Mason Way, Medford, OR
(541) 245-2727; *Fax:* (541) 773-9554
License: Central Point, Jackson County, OR held by Fjarli Broadcasting, a General Partnership.
Arbitron Metro Market: Medford-Ashland
Jo Ann Fjarli, President
Bruce Fjarli, General Manager

Chemult

***KSKX**
89.5 MHz FM; 0.1 kw; 1896 ft.; N43 18 20 W121 42 58 US
(541) 552-6301; *Fax:* (541) 552-8565
www.ijpr.org
License: Chemult, Klamath County, OR held by The State of Oregon Acting By and Through the Oregon State Board of Higher Education for Southern Oregon University.
Arbitron Metro Market: Colorado Springs, CO
Ron Kramer, General Manager

Coburg

KSHL
12-01-1992; 97.7 MHz FM; *Hrs Open:* 24; 7 kw; 850 ft.; N44 45 24 W124 2 53
PO Box 1180, Newport, OR 97365 US
(541) 265-6477; *Fax:* (541) 265-6478
www.kshl.com
info@kshl.com
License: Coburg, Lincoln County, OR held by Stephanie Linn.
Regional Reps: McGavren Guild
Arbitron Metro Market: Newport, OR; *Format:* Country; *Hrs. of News Programming:* News progmg 2 hrs wkly; *Target Audience:* 25-55; general
Stephanie Linn, President
Dick Linn, General Manager

Columbia River

KCGB-FM
12-04-1978; 105.5 MHz FM; 1 kw; 787 ft.; N45 39 45 W121 28 14
1190 22nd St., P.O. Box 360, Hood River, OR 97031 US
(541) 386-1511
www.kcgbfm.com
gary@bicoastalmedia.com
License: Columbia River, OR held by Bicoastal Media Licenses IV LLC.
Group Owner: Bicoastal Media L.L.C.; (acq 12-1-2007; grpsl)
Nat'l Network: ABC
Format: Adult Contemp; *Target Audience:* 18-49.; *Adv. Rates:* 19; 17; 19; 12
Mike Wilson, President & COO
Jeff Skye, Operations Dir
Rick Cavagnaro, General Sales Mgr
Mark Bailey, Programming Director
Matt Green, Engineering Dir
Gary Grossman, Market Manager
Paulette LaRoque, Traffic Manager

Coos Bay

KBBR
12-01-1950; 1340 kHz AM; *Hrs Open:* 24
320 Central Ave., Suite 519, Coos Bay, OR 97420 US
(541) 267-2121; *Fax:* (541) 267-5229
www.1340kbbr.com
License: Coos Bay, OR held by Bicoastal Media Licenses III LLC.
Group Owner: Bicoastal Media L.L.C.
Nat'l Network: CBS Radio; Jones Radio Networks; Westwood One; *Nat'l Reps:* Katz Radio; Tacher
Arbitron Metro Market: Coos Bay, OR; *Format:* News, News/Talk, 86; *Hrs. of News Programming:* News progmg 40 hrs wkly; *Target Audience:* 25-54.; *Adv. Rates:* 13; 11; 13; 7
Mike Wilson, President & COO

KDCQ
05-24-1995; 92.9 MHz FM; *Hrs Open:* 24; 4.5 kw; 524 ft.; N43 21 15 W124 14 34
P.O. Box 478, Coos Bay, OR 97420 US
(541) 269-0929; *Fax:* (541) 267-9376
www.kdcq.com
License: Coos Bay, Coos County, OR held by Bay Cities Building Co. Inc.
Nat'l Network: ABC; *Nat'l Reps:* Tacher; *Wire Services:* AP
Arbitron Metro Market: Coos Bay, OR; *Format:* Contemporary Hits/Top 40, Adult Contemp; *Hrs. of News Programming:* News progmg 5 hrs wkly; *No. News Employees:* 1; *Target Audience:* 35-54; baby boomers
Bruce Latta, President
Mike Chavez, Operations Dir
Stephanie Kilmer, General Manager
Cindi Miller, General Sales Mgr
Evan O, Public Service Director
Julie Cummings, Accounts Executive

KHSN
03-15-1928; 1230 kHz AM; *Hrs Open:* 24
340 Central, Coos Bay, OR 97420 US
(541) 267-2121; *Fax:* (541) 267-5229
www.khsn1230.com
License: Coos Bay, OR held by W7 Broadcasting LLC
Regional Reps: Allied Radio Partners.
TV Affiliate: ESPN; *Format:* Talk; *Hrs. of News Programming:* News progmg 14 hrs wkly; *Target Audience:* 35- plus.; *Adv. Rates:* 13; 11; 13; 7
Mike O'Brien, Operations Dir
Lee Taft, General Manager

KMHS
12-07-1956; 1420 kHz AM
1330 Teakwood, Coos Bay, OR 97420 US
(541) 267-1451; *Fax:* (541) 269-0161
www.marshfield.coos-bay.k12.or.us/kmhs/index.htm
License: Coos Bay, OR held by Coos Bay School District No. 9
Format: Country
Steve Walker, General Manager

KJMX
01-01-1993; 99.5 MHz FM; *Hrs Open:* 24; 11 kw; 400 ft.; N43 40 40 W124 6 36
320 Central Ave., Suite 519, Coos Bay, OR 97420 US
(541) 267-2121; *Fax:* (541) 267-5229
www.kjmx.rocks
License: Coos Bay, Coos County, OR held by Bicoastal Media Licenses III LLC.
Group Owner: Bicoastal Media L.L.C.; (acq 10-16-2003; grpsl)
Format: Classic Rock; *Hrs. of News Programming:* news progmg 2 hrs wkly; *No. News Employees:* 1
DeeDee Dupre, Market Manager

***KSBA**
11-04-1988; 88.5 MHz FM; *Hrs Open:* 5 AM-2 AM; 2.2 kw; 531 ft.; N43 23 26 W124 7 46
PO Box 3175, Eugene, OR 97403 US
(541) 552-6301; *Fax:* (541) 552-8565
www.ijpr.org
jprinfo@sou.edu
License: Coos Bay, Coos County, OR held by The State of Oregon, acting by and through the State Board of Higher Education.
Nat'l Network: NPR; PRI; *Wire Services:* AP
Arbitron Metro Market: Ashland, OR; *Format:* Jazz, News, 90
Special Programming: Blues 6 hrs, folk 3 hrs, pub affrs 7 hrs wkly; *Hrs. of News Programming:* news progmg 45 hrs wkly; *No. News Employees:* 1 *TargetAudience:* General.
Geoffrey Riley, News Director
Darin Ransom, Engineering Dir
Betsy Byers, Administrative Assistant
Paul Westhelle, Executive Director

KYSJ
11-01-1979; 105.9 MHz FM; 15 kw; 902 ft.; N43 27 49 W124 5 44
580 Kingwood Avenue, Coos Bay, OR 97420 US
(800) 447-7664; *Fax:* (541) 267-0114
www.lighthouseradio.com
License: Coos Bay, Coos County, OR held by Lighthouse Radio Group.
Wire Services: AP
Arbitron Metro Market: Coos Bay, OR; *Format:* Jazz, Smooth Jazz
Rick Stevens, General Manager
David DeAndrea, Programming Director

KYTT-FM
11-01-1978; 98.7 MHz FM; *Hrs Open:* 24; 12.55 kw; 961 ft.; N43 27 49 W124 5 44
580 Kingwood Avenue, Coos Bay, OR 97420 US
(800) 447-7664; *Fax:* (541) 267-0114
www.lighthouseradio.com
License: Coos Bay, Coos County, OR held by Lighthouse Radio Group.
Nat'l Network: Salem Radio Network; *Wire Services:* AP
Arbitron Metro Market: Coos Bay, OR; *Format:* Christian; *Hrs. of News Programming:* News progmg 8 hrs wkly
Dave DeAndrea, Operations Dir
Rick Stevens, General Manager
Steve Ramberg, General Sales Mgr
David DeAndrea, Programming Director

***KJCH**
04-01-2005; 90.9 MHz FM; *Hrs Open:* 24; 3.5 kw; 1463 ft.; N42 57 32 W124 16 23 *Rebroadcasts:* Rebroadcasts KAWZ (FM)
Mailing Address: P.O. Box 391, Twin Falls, ID 83303 US
Second Address: CSN International, 4002 N 3300 E, Twin Falls, ID 83301

(800) 357-4226; *Fax:* (208) 736-1958
www.csnradio.com
csn@csnradio.com
License: Coos Bay, Coos County, OR held by Calvary Chapel of Twin Falls, Inc.
Group Owner: CSN International
Arbitron Metro Market: Coos Bay, OR; *Format:* Christian, Religious
Mike Kestler, President
Daniel Davidson, Operations Dir
Don Mills, Network Programming Director
Mike Stocklin, Underwriting Director
Kelly Carlson, Engineering Dir

***KMHS-FM**
01-01-2008; 91.3 MHz FM; 10 kw horiz; -33 ft.; N43 22 7 W124 12 11
1330 Teakwood, Coos Bay, OR 97420 US
(541) 267-3104
www.kmhsradio.cbd9.net
License: Coos Bay, Coos County, OR held by Coos Bay School District No. 9.
Arbitron Metro Market: Coos Bay, OR; *Format:* Contemporary Hits/Top 40
Steve Walker, General Manager

Coquille

KSHR-FM
11-01-1981; 97.3 MHz FM; 25 kw horiz, 5.9 kw vert; 856 ft.; N43 14 51 W124 6 46
320 Central Ave., Suite 519, Coos Bay, OR 97420 US
(541) 267-2121; *Fax:* (541) 267-5229
www.kshr.com
License: Coquille, Coos County, OR held by Bicoastal Media Licenses III LLC.
Group Owner: Bicoastal Media L.L.C.
Arbitron Metro Market: Coos Bay, OR; *Format:* Country
Mike Wilson, President & COO

KWRO
02-01-1949; 630 kHz AM; 5 kw-D, ND2; 0.046 kw-N, ND2; N43 10 17 W124 11 54
320 Central Ave., Suite 519, Coos Bay, OR 97420 US
(541) 267-2121; *Fax:* (541) 267-5229
www.kwro.com
License: Coquille, Coos County, OR held by Bicoastal Media Licenses III LLC.
Group Owner: Bicoastal Media L.L.C.; (acq 10-16-2003; grpsl)
Arbitron Metro Market: Coos Bay, OR; *Format:* News, News/Talk, 86
Mike Wilson, President & COO

Corvallis

***KBVR**
10-26-1965; 88.7 MHz FM; *Hrs Open:* 24; 0.34 kw; -82 ft.; N44 33 50 W123 16 30
Mu East 218, Corvallis, OR 97331 US
(541) 737-2008; *Fax:* (541) 737-4545
www.oregonstate.edu/dept/kbvr/fmradio
License: Corvallis, Benton County, OR held by State Board of Higher Education.
Arbitron Metro Market: Corvallis, OR; *Format:* Alternative, Jazz *Special Programming:* Class 4 hrs, Sp 4 hrs, folk 4 hrs wkly; *Target Audience:* 15-45; general
Ian Rose, Station Manager

***KOAC**
12-07-1922; 550 kHz AM; *Hrs Open:* 5 AM-midnight; 5 kw-D, DA2; 5 kw-N, DA2; N44 38 12 W123 11 33
7140 S.W. Macadam Avenue, Portland, OR 97219 US
(503) 293-1905,(541) 737-5332; *Fax:* (503) 293-1919
License: Corvallis, OR held by Oregon Public Broadcasting.
Nat'l Network: PRI; NPR
TV Affiliate: *KOAC-TV affil; *Format:* News, News/Talk, 86
Special Programming: Jazz 12 hrs wkly; *Hrs. of News Programming:* news progmg 40 hrs wkly; *No. News Employees:* 5; *Target Audience:* 25-54; collegeeducated with an interest in news & mus
Steven Bass, President/CEO
Lynne Clendenin, Vice President of Operations
Matt Fleeger, Programming Director
Mike Foti, Vice President of Engineering
Dan Metziga, SVP, Development & Marketing

Cottage Grove

KMME(FM)
03-21-1994; 100.5 MHz FM; *Hrs Open:* 24; 6 kw; Ant 115 ft; N43 44 41 W123 05 29
4222 Commerce St., Suite E, Box 10, Eugene, OR 97402
(541) 683-3392; *Fax:* (541) 338-7067
License: Cottage Grove, Lane County, OR held by Diamond Peak Investments LLC
Nat'l Reps: Tacher
Arbitron Metro Market: Eugene-Springfield, OR; *Format:* Contemporary Hits/Top 40; *Hrs. of News Programming:* News progmg 6 hrs wkly; *Target Audience:* 25-49.; *Adv. Rates:* 12; 12; 12; na
Steve Master, General Manager

KNND
08-01-1953; 1400 kHz AM; *Hrs Open:* 24
321 Main Street, Cottage Grove, OR 97424 US
(541) 942-2468; *Fax:* (541) 942-5797
paul@knnd.com
License: Cottage Grove, OR held by Schwartzberg Communications Inc.
Nat'l Network: AP Radio
Arbitron Metro Market: Eugene, OR; *Format:* Country, News, 62, Talk *Special Programming:* Relg 3 hrs wkly; *Hrs. of News Programming:* news progmg 40 hrs wkly; *No. News Employees:* 1; *Target Audience:* General. *Adv. Rates:* 14; 12; 12; 10
Paul Schwartzberg, President

Creswell

KUJZ
09-01-1983; 95.3 MHz FM; 0.63 kw; 1207 ft.; N44 0 4 W123 6 45
1200 Executive Parkway, Suite 440, Eugene, AL 97401 US
(541) 484-8500; *Fax:* (541) 485-0969
License: Creswell, Lane County, OR held by Cumulus Licensing Corp.
Group Owner: Cumulus Media Inc.; (acq 2-29-00;; grpsl).
Nat'l Network: ESPN Radio; *Nat'l Reps:* Christal
Arbitron Metro Market: Eugene, OR; *Format:* Sports; *Target Audience:* 18-34.
B.J. O'Brien, Market Manager
Samantha Kumm, Sales Manager
Al Scott, Programming Director

Dallas

KWIP
04-15-1955; 880 kHz AM; 5 kw-D, ND1; 1 kw-N, ND1; N44 55 45 W123 17 22
1405 Ellendale Avenue, Dallas, OR 97338 US
(503) 623-0224; *Fax:* (503) 623-6733
www.kwip.com
info@kwip.com
License: Dallas, OR held by Valley Broadcasting Association
Arbitron Metro Market: Dallas, OR *Special Programming:* Talk 5 hrs wkly; *Target Audience:* 18-54; families & blue collar workers
Ayesh Shanah, General Manager

Depoe Bay

KPPT-FM
12-01-1980; 100.7 MHz FM; 17.5 kw; 837 ft.; N44 45 23 W124 3 1
Mailing Address: P.O. Box 456, 304 S. Coast Highway, Newport, OR 97365 US
Second Address: 145 N. Coast Hwy., Newport, OR 97365
(541) 265-5000; *Fax:* (541) 265-9576
www.bossfmradio.net
info@bossradio.net
License: Depoe Bay, Lincoln County, OR held by Agpal Broadcasting Inc.
Arbitron Metro Market: Central OR Coast; *Format:* Talk
Cheryl Harle, Operations Dir

Elgin

KRJT
01-01-2005; 105.9 MHz FM; *Hrs Open:* 24; 0.115 kw; 1,916 ft.; N45 26 26 W117 53 31
P.O. Box 907, La Grande, OR 97850 US
(541) 963-4121
www.yourboomerradio.com
License: Elgin, Union County, OR held by Pacific Empire Radio Corp.
Group Owner: Pacific Empire Radio Corp.
Nat'l Reps: Interep; McGavren Guild
Arbitron Metro Market: La Grande, OR; *Format:* Oldies; *Target Audience:* 25-54.; *Adv. Rates:* 24; 24; 24; 24
Evan Yeoman, Operations Manager
Ben Bonfield, General Manager
Leslie Gatherer, Traffic Manager

Enterprise

KWVR
06-01-1960; 1340 kHz AM; *Hrs Open:* 24; 1 kw-U, ND1; N45 26 14 W117 17 30
220 West Main Street, Enterprise, OR 97828 US
(541) 426-4577; *Fax:* (541) 426-4578
kwvrradio.net
kwvrradio@gmail.com
License: Enterprise, OR held by Wallowa Valley Radio LLC
Nat'l Network: ABC
Arbitron Metro Market: Enterprise, OR; *Format:* News, News/Talk, 86 *Special Programming:* Farm 4 hrs wkly; *Hrs. of News Programming:* news progmg 11 hrs wkly; *No. News Employees:* 2; *Target Audience:* General.
Lee Perkins, President
Alyssa Werst, Operations Dir
David Frasch, General Manager
Patrick Channing, II, General Sales Mgr
Alyssa Werst, News Director

KWVR-FM
01-01-1986; 92.1 MHz FM; *Hrs Open:* 24; 6 kw; -689 ft.; N45 19 19 W117 13 18
220 West Main Street, Enterprise, OR 97828 US
(541) 426-4577; *Fax:* (541) 426-4578
kwvrradio.net
kwvrradio@gmail.com
License: Enterprise, Wallowa County, OR held by Wallowa Valley Radio LLC
Nat'l Network: ABC; Jones Radio Networks
Arbitron Metro Market: Enterprise, OR; *Format:* Country
Alyssa Werst, Operations Dir
David Frasch, General Manager

***KETP**
88.7 MHz FM; 0.1 kw; 1755 ft.; N45 23 58 W117 23 16
7140 SW Macadam Avenue, Portland, OR 97219 US
(503) 293-1905; *Fax:* (503) 293-1919
www.opb.org
License: Enterprise, Wallowa County, OR held by Oregon Public Broadcasting.
Arbitron Metro Market: Enterprise, OR
Steven M. Bass, CEO
Dan Metziga, Senior Vice President, Development and Marketing
Lynne Clendenin, Vice President, Programming/Operations
Morgan Holm, Vice President, News and Public Affairs
Steve Amen, Executive Producer

Eugene

KDUK-FM
11-21-1983; 104.7 MHz FM; *Hrs Open:* 24; 66 kw; 2320 ft.; N44 17 28 W123 32 18
1500 Valley River Dr., Suite 350, Eugene, OR 97401 US
(541) 284-3600
www.kduk.com
License: Eugene, OR held by Bicoastal Willamette Valley LLC.
Group Owner: Bicoastal Media L.L.C.; (acq 7-2-2007; grpsl)
Arbitron Metro Market: Eugene-Springfield, OR; *Format:* Contemporary Hits/Top 40
Mike Wilson, President & COO
Larry Rogers, Market Manager

KOPB
09-19-1947; 1600 kHz AM
3545 Highway 20, PO Box 278, Albany, OR 97321 US
(503) 293-9900; *Fax:* (503) 293-1919
www.opb.org
License: Eugene, OR held by Oregon Public Broadcasting
Nat'l Network: NPR; *Regional Network:* Ore. Pub. Bcstg Radio Net.
Arbitron Metro Market: Eugene-Springfield, OR; *Format:* News, News/Talk, 86
Steven Bass, President
Cheryl Ikemiya, Director
Julie Arnzen, Associate Director
Jordan Anderson, Associate Director

KFLY
10-01-1966; 101.5 MHz FM; 27.5 kw; 2320 ft.; N44 17 28 W123 32 18
1500 Valley River Dr., Suite 350, Eugene, OR 97401 US
(541) 485-1120
www.us101country.com
us101country@gmail.com
License: Eugene, OR held by Bicoastal Willamette Valley LLC.
Group Owner: Bicoastal Media L.L.C.
Arbitron Metro Market: Eugene, OR; *Format:* Rock/AOR *Special Programming:* Country Music; *Target Audience:* 25-49; general

Val Steele, Operations Dir
Jeff Gaulton, General Sales Mgr
Pat Garrett, Programming Director
Larry Rogers, Market Manager

KKNX
01-01-1992; 840 kHz AM; *Hrs Open:* 24; 1 kw-D, ND2; 0.17 kw-N, ND2; N44 4 54 W123 6 34
945 Garfield Street, Eugene, OR 97402 US
(541) 342-1012; *Fax:* (541) 342-6201
www.radio84.com
john@radio84.com
License: Eugene, OR held by John S. Mielke, Susan J. Mielke.
Nat'l Network: AP Radio *Regional Reps:* Tacher & Co.; *Wire Services:* AP
Arbitron Metro Market: Eugene, OR; *Format:* Oldies *Special Programming:* Black 3 hrs wkly; *Hrs. of News Programming:* news progmg 7 hrs wkly; *No. News Employees:* 1; *Target Audience:* 25-64; general *Adv.Rates:* 18; 16; 18; 10
John Mielke, President

KLZS
09-07-1954; 1450 kHz AM; *Hrs Open:* 24; 1 kw-U, ND1; N44 4 54 W123 6 34
925 County Club Road, Eugene, OR 97401 US
(541) 343-4100; *Fax:* (541) 343-0448
www.radio84.com
License: Eugene, OR held by Churchill Communications LLC
Group Owner: Churchill Communications LLC; (acq 11-3-2004; $87,500).
Nat'l Network: CNN Radio
Arbitron Metro Market: Eugene, OR; *Format:* Oldies; *Hrs. of News Programming:* news progmg 30 hrs wky; *No. News Employees:* 2; *Target Audience:* 25-54.
Mike Triem, General Manager

***KLCC**
02-17-1967; 89.7 MHz FM; *Hrs Open:* 24; 81 kw horiz, 54 kw vert; Ant 1,161 ft; N44 00 05 W123 06 48
136 W. 8th Ave., Eugene, OR 97405
(541) 463-6000; *Fax:* (541) 463-6046
www.klcc.org
klcc@klcc.org
License: Eugene, Lane County, OR held by Lane Community College.
Nat'l Network: NPR
Population Served: 750,000; *Arbitron Metro Market:* Eugene-Springfield, OR *Special Programming:* Sp 5 hrs, folk 12 hrs, Black 3 hrs, blues 4 hrs, world 3 hrs, electronic 6 hrs wkly; *Hrs. of News Programming:* news progmg60 hrs wkly; *No. News Employees:* 1; *Target Audience:* 25-54.
Steve Barton, General Manager
Cheryl Crumbley, General Sales Mgr
Don Hein, Programming Director
Tripp Sommer, News Director

KMGE
10-10-1965; 94.5 MHz FM; 49 kw horiz, 21 kw vert; 1299 ft.; N44 0 4 W123 6 45
Koteen & Naftalin, L.L.P, 1150 Conn. Ave., N.W., Washington, DC 20036 US
(541) 484-9400; *Fax:* (541) 344-9424
www.kmge.com
License: Eugene, OR held by McKenzie River Broadcasting Co. Inc.
Group Owner: McKenzie River Broadcasting Company, Inc.; (acq 3-87; $950,000;
Arbitron Metro Market: Eugene, OR; *Format:* Adult Contemp; *Target Audience:* 18-49.
John Tilson, President
Jeff Baird, Programming Director

KSCR
06-12-1962; 1320 kHz AM; 1 kw-D, ND1; 0.048 kw-N, ND1; N44 5 25 W123 6 43
1200 Executive Parkway, Suite 440, Eugene, OR 97401 US
(541) 485-5846; *Fax:* (541) 485-0969
License: Eugene, OR held by Cumulus Licensing Corp.
Group Owner: Cumulus Media Inc.; (acq 2-29-00; grpsl).
Nat'l Network: ESPN Radio; *Nat'l Reps:* Christal
Arbitron Metro Market: Eugene, OR; *Format:* Sports; *Target Audience:* 18-44; general
Marilyn Lee, Account Executive

KODZ
11-01-1968; 99.1 MHz FM; 100 kw; 1631 ft.; N44 6 57 W122 59 57
Mailing Address: 1500 Valley River Dr., Suite 350, Eugene, OR 97401 US
Second Address: OR
(541) 284-3600; *Fax:* (541) 484-5769
kool991.com
kool991eugene@gmail.com
License: Eugene, OR
Group Owner: Bicoastal Media L.L.C.
Arbitron Metro Market: Eugene-Springfield, OR; *Format:* Adult Contemp; *Target Audience:* 25-54; working women
Larry Rogers, Market Manager

KPNW
07-22-1968; 1120 kHz AM; *Hrs Open:* 24; 50 kw-U, DA1; N43 57 24 W123 2 10
1500 Valley River Dr., Suite 350, Eugene, OR 97401 US
(541) 284-3600
www.kpnw.com
1120kpnw@gmail.com
License: Eugene, OR held by Bicoastal Willamette Valley LLC.
Group Owner: Bicoastal Media L.L.C.; (acq 7-2-2007; grpsl)
Arbitron Metro Market: Eugene-Springfield, OR; *Format:* News, News/Talk, 86 *Special Programming:* Portland Trail Blazers; *No. News Employees:* 2; *Target Audience:* 35 plus; upper income, conservative
Bill Lundun, Programming Director
Larry Rogers, Market Manager

***KRVM**
11-09-1949; 1280 kHz AM; *Hrs Open:* 24; 5 kw-D, 1.5 kw-N, DA-N; N44 06 03 W123 03 06
P.M.B. 237, 1574 Cobug Rd., Eugene, OR 97402
(541) 790-6680; *Fax:* (541) 790-6688
www.krvm.org
info@krvm.org
License: Eugene, Lane County, OR held by Lane County School District 4J.
Nat'l Network: NPR; *Nat'l Reps:* McGavren Guild
Arbitron Metro Market: Eugene-Springfield, OR
Randy Larson, Operations Dir
Randy Larson, General Manager

***KRVM-FM**
12-08-1947; 91.9 MHz FM; *Hrs Open:* 24; 1.1 kw; Ant 745 ft; N44 00 08 W123 06 50
P.M.B. 237, 1574 Cobug Rd., Eugene, OR 97402
(541) 790-6680; *Fax:* (541) 790-6688
www.krvm.org
info@krvm.org
License: Eugene, Lane County, OR held by Lane County School District No. 4J.
Nat'l Network: NPR
Population Served: 200,000; *Arbitron Metro Market:* Eugene-Springfield, OR *Special Programming:* Black 2 hrs, country one hr, folk 3 hrs, Native American 2 hrs wkly; *Target Audience:* General.
Marti Ashcraft, Operations Dir
Jana Smith, General Manager
Gordon Ames, General Sales Mgr
Glenn Taylor, Programming Director
Diane Philips, News Director
Monica Smith, Sales

KUGN
07-04-1946; 590 kHz AM; *Hrs Open:* 24; 5 kw-D, DAN; 5 kw-N, DAN; N44 6 3 W123 3 6
1200 Executive Parkway, Suite 440, Eugene, OR 97401 US
(541) 284-8500; *Fax:* (541) 485-0969
www.kugn.com
kugnpsa@gmail.com
License: Eugene, OR held by Cumulus Licensing Corp.
Group Owner: Cumulus Media Inc.; (acq 6-15-00; grpsl).
Nat'l Network: CBS; *Wire Services:* NWS (National Weather Service)
Arbitron Metro Market: Eugene, OR; *Format:* News, News/Talk, 86; *Hrs. of News Programming:* news progmg 28 hrs wkly; *No. News Employees:* 6; *Target Audience:* 30-65; general
Samantha Kumm, General Sales Mgr
Mark Raney, Programming Director
B.J. O'Brien, Market Manager

***KWAX**
04-04-1951; 91.1 MHz FM; *Hrs Open:* 24; 21.5 kw horiz, 12.5 kw vert; 1214 ft.; N44 0 4 W123 6 45
139 Susan Campbell Hall, University of Oregon, Eugene, OR 97403 US
(541) 345-0800; *Fax:* (541) 343-2123
www.kwax.com
inquiry@kwax.com
License: Eugene, Lane County, OR held by State Board of Higher Education.
Arbitron Metro Market: Eugene-Springfield, OR; *Format:* Talk; *Hrs. of News Programming:* News progmg 7 hrs wkly; *Target Audience:* 35 plus.
Paul Bjornstad, General Manager

***KWVA**
05-27-1993; 88.1 MHz FM; *Hrs Open:* 24; 1 kw; 177 ft.; N44 4 55 W123 6 34
Mailing Address: Erb Memorial Union Ste.4, Univ. of Oregon, Eugene, OR 97403 US
Second Address: Univ. of Oregon, EMU, Suite M-112, Eugene, OR 97403
(541) 346-4091; *Fax:* (541) 346-0648
gladstone.uoregon.edu/~kwva
kwva@gladstone.uoregon.edu
License: Eugene, Lane County, OR held by Associated Students of University of Oregon.
Arbitron Metro Market: Eugene-Springfield, OR; *Format:* Variety/Diverse *Special Programming:* Asian 4 hrs, Black 4 hrs, jazz 6 hrs, country 3 hrs, Japanese 2 hrs, Sp 6 hrs wkly; *Hrs. of News Programming:* News progmg 12hrs wkly; *Target Audience:* 3-30; college, alternative, underrepresented, varying educ levels & music lover
Charlotte Nisser, General Manager
Steven Murschel, Programming Director
Michael Zarkesh, Promotions Manager
Sarah Mollner, News Director
Hiring, Assistant General Manager
Lyzi Diamond, Music Department
Brandon O Rourke, SportsDepartmeent
Lex Chase, Marketing Department

KZEL-FM
04-22-1962; 96.1 MHz FM; 100 kw horiz, 43 kw vert; 1093 ft.; N44 0 5 W123 6 48
1200 Executive Parkway, Suite 440, Eugene, OR 97401 US
(541) 284-8500; *Fax:* (541) 485-4070
www.96kzel.com/main
License: Eugene, Lane County, OR held by Cumulus Licensing Corp.
Group Owner: Cumulus Media Inc.; (acq 2-29-00; grpsl)
Nat'l Network: Westwood One; *Nat'l Reps:* Christal
Arbitron Metro Market: Eugene, OR; *Format:* Classic Rock; *Target Audience:* 18-44.
All Scott, Operations Dir
Mark Raney, Programming Director
B.J. O'Brien, Market Manager

Florence

KCFM(AM)
05-05-1985; 1250 kHz AM; *Hrs Open:* 24; 1 kw-D, 68 w-N; N44 00 38 W124 05 37
Mailing Address: Box 20000, Florence, OR 97439
Second Address: Radio Center Bldg., 4480 Hwy. 101 N., Florence, OR 97439
(541) 997-9136; *Fax:* (541) 997-9165
www.kcst.com
radiowaves@kcst.comÿ
License: Florence, Lane County, OR held by Coast Broadcasting Co. Inc.
Population Served: 370,000; *Arbitron Metro Market:* Florence, OR; *Format:* Contemporary Hits/Top 40; *Target Audience:* 55+.; *Adv. Rates:* 13; 13; 13; 13
John Thompson, General Manager

KCST-FM
10-01-1992; 106.9 MHz FM; *Hrs Open:* 24; 2.3 kw; 509 ft.; N43 57 19 W124 4 26
Mailing Address: P.O. Box 20000, Florence, OR 97439 US
Second Address: 4480 Hwy 101 N., Radio Centre Bldg., Florence, OR 97439
(541) 997-9136; *Fax:* (541) 997-9165
www.kcst.com
radiowaves@kcst.comÿ
License: Florence, Lane County, OR held by Coast Broadcasting Co. Inc.
Nat'l Network: ABC *Regional Reps:* Tacher Company; *Wire Services:* AP
Arbitron Metro Market: Florence, OR; *Format:* Adult Contemp, Country, 64; *Target Audience:* 35+.; *Adv. Rates:* 15; 15; 15; 15
Greg Jacquay, General Manager

***KLFO**
08-16-1999; 88.1 MHz FM; *Hrs Open:* 24; 250 w; Ant 548 ft; N43 57 26 W124 04 26 *Rebroadcasts:* Rebroadcasts KLCC(FM) Eugene 100%
136 W. 8th Ave., 4000 E. 30th Ave., Eugene, OR 97405
(541) 463-6000; *Fax:* (541) 463-6046
www.klcc.org
klcc@klcc.org
License: Florence, Lane County, OR held by Lane Community College.

Steve Barton, General Manager
Cheryl Crumbley, General Sales Mgr

Don Hein, Programming Director
Chris Heck, Chief Engineer

***KWVZ**
01-01-2001; 91.5 MHz FM; 0.15 kw; 548 ft.; N43 57 26 W124 4 26 *Rebroadcasts:* Rebroadcasts KWAX(FM) Eugene 100%
139 Susan Campbell Hall, University of Oregon, Eugene, OR 97403 US
(541) 345-0800
License: Florence, Lane County, OR held by Oregon State Board of Higher Education.
Format: Classical
Rocky Lamanna, Operations Dir
Paul Bjornstad, General Manager
Jack Flemming, Programming Director
Catriona Bolster, Music Director

Garibaldi

KDEP
01-01-2001; 105.5 MHz FM; 0.32 kw; 1181 ft.; N45 27 59 W123 55 11
Mailing Address: 415 Cliff Street, P O Box 516, Depoe Bay, OR 97341 US
Second Address: 1550 N. Main, Tillamook, OR 97141
(503) 842-3888; *Fax:* (503) 842-5640
License: Garibaldi, Tillamook County, OR held by Alexandra Communications Inc.
Group Owner: Alexandra Communications Inc.; (acq 9-21-2005; $250,000).
Format: Classic Rock
Chris Gilbreth, General Manager

Gladstone

KRYP
05-10-1981; 93.1 MHz FM; 1.55 kw; 1270 ft.; N45 29 20 W122 41 40
1006 W Marine Drive, Astoria, OR 97103 US
(503) 786-0600; *Fax:* (503) 786-1551
www.931elrey.com
License: Gladstone, Clackamas County, OR held by Salem Media of Oregon Inc.
Group Owner: Salem Communications Corp.; (acq 1-19-2005)
Arbitron Metro Market: Portland, OR
Chris Kelly, Operations Manager
Dennis Hayes, General Manager

Gleneden Beach

***KOGL**
01-01-2008; 89.3 MHz FM; 0.21 kw; 73 ft.; N44 53 8 W124 0 51
Rebroadcasts: Rebroadcasts KOPB-FM Portland 100%
7140 Sw Macadam Ave, Portland, OR 97219 US
(503) 293-1905; *Fax:* (503) 293-1919
www.opb.org
opb.org/contactus
License: Gleneden Beach, Lincoln County, OR held by Oregon Public Broadcasting.
Regional Network: Ore. Pub. Bcstg Radio Net.
Arbitron Metro Market: Portland, OR; *Format:* News
Steven M. Bass, CEO and General Manager
Dan Metziga, Senior Vice President, Development and Marketing
Lynne Clendenin, Vice President, Programming
Morgan Holm, Vice President, News and Public Affairs
Steve Amen, Executive Producer

***KQOC**
06-01-2008; 88.1 MHz FM; 8.8 kw; 928 ft.; N44 45 23 W124 2 52 *Rebroadcasts:* Rebroadcasts KQAC(FM) Portland 100%
515 N E 15 Th Ave, Portland, OR 97232 US
(503) 943-5828; *Fax:* (503) 802-9456
www.allclassical.org
License: Gleneden Beach, Lincoln County, OR held by KBPS Public Radio Foundation.
Arbitron Metro Market: Portland, OR; *Format:* Classical
Jack Allen, CEO/President
Deborah Rochford, Director of Member Services
John Pitman, Music Director
Kelly Palin, CFO
Andrea Rennie, Executive Assistant
Jenn Woodward, HR & Office Coordinator
John Burk, Vice President ofProgramming

Gold Beach

KGBR
12-01-1984; 92.7 MHz FM; *Hrs Open:* 24; 265 w; 2700 ft; N42 23 50 W124 21 50
Box 787, Gold Beach, OR 97444
(541) 247-7211,(541) 247-7418; *Fax:* (541) 247-4155
www.kgbr.com
info@kgbr.com
License: Gold Beach, Curry County, OR held by St. Marie Communications Inc.
Nat'l Reps: Tacher
Population Served: 20,000 *Hrs. of News Programming:* news progmg 4 hrs wkly; *No. News Employees:* 2; *Target Audience:* 25-54.; *Adv. Rates:* 18; 18; 18; 18
Dale St Marie, Chairman
Dale St Marie, President
Diana St Marie, Operations Dir
Dale St Marie, General Manager
Diana St Marie, Station Manager
Lucie Labonte, General Sales Mgr
Bill Bailey, Programming Director
Diana St Marie,Promotions Manager
Bill Bailey, News Director
Dale St Marie, Engineering Dir

Gold Hill

KRWQ
08-11-1980; 100.3 MHz FM; *Hrs Open:* 24; 30 kw; 1004 ft.; N42 27 11 W123 3 22
3624 Avion Dr., Medford, OR 97504 US
(541) 772-4170; *Fax:* (541) 858-5416
www.q1003.com
ashleymain@bicoastal.media
License: Gold Hill, Jackson County, OR held by Bicoastal Rogue Valley LLC.
Group Owner: Bicoastal Media L.L.C.; (acq 7-2-2007; grpsl)
Nat'l Reps: Tacher
Arbitron Metro Market: Medford-Ashland, OR; *Format:* Country; *No. News Employees:* 1; *Target Audience:* 18-54.
Ashley Main, Programming Director

Grants Pass

***KAGI**
12-16-1939; 930 kHz AM; *Hrs Open:* 24 hrs; 5 kw-D, ND1; 0.123 kw-N, ND1; N42 26 16 W123 21 27
P. O. Box 3175, Eugene, OR 97403 US
(541) 552-6301; *Fax:* (541) 552-8565
www.ijpr.org
jprinfo@sou.edu
License: Grants Pass, OR held by The State of Oregon, acting by and through the State Board of Higher Education, for the benefit of Southern Oregon University.
Nat'l Network: PRI; NPR
Arbitron Metro Market: Ashland, OR; *Format:* News *Special Programming:* Sp 6 hrs wkly
Paoul van Hall, Operations Dir
Paul Westhelle, General Sales Mgr
Eric Teel, Programming Director
Darin Ransom, Engineering Dir
Mitchell Christian, CFO
Don Matthews, Music Director

KAJO
08-15-1957; 1270 kHz AM; *Hrs Open:* 24
Box 230, Grants Pass, OR 97526 US
(541) 476-6608; *Fax:* (541) 476-4018
www.kajo.com
kajo@kajo.com
License: Grants Pass, OR held by Grants Pass Broadcasting Corp.
Nat'l Network: AP Radio; *Nat'l Reps:* Tacher *Regional Reps:* Tacher; *Wire Services:* AP
Arbitron Metro Market: Grants Pass, OR; *Format:* News, News/Talk, 86, Adult Contemp *Special Programming:* Gospel one hr, relg 8 hrs wkly; *Hrs. of News Programming:* news progmg 22 hrs wkly; *No. News Employees:* 2 *Target Audience:* 35 plus.
Carl Wilson, CEO
Brian Diatte, General Sales Mgr
Jeanette Stark, Programming Director
Jill Hamm, Promotions Manager
Chuck Benson, News Director
Joe Torsistano, Chief Engineer
Carl Wilson, CFO

KROG
10-02-1981; 96.9 MHz FM; *Hrs Open:* 24; 25 kw; 2228 ft.; N42 22 56 W123 16 29
511 Rossanley Drive, Medford, OR 97501 US
(541) 772-0322; *Fax:* (541) 772-4233
www.969therogue.com
License: Grants Pass, Josephine County, OR held by Opus Broadcasting Systems Inc.
Group Owner: Opus Broadcasting Systems Inc.; acq 3-6-91; $63,634 with KRTA(AM) Medford;
Nat'l Reps: Tacher
Arbitron Metro Market: Medford, OR, Ashland; *Format:* Rock/AOR; *No. News Employees:* 1; *Target Audience:* 25-54; affluent middle America
Dean Flock, General Manager
Brian Fraser, General Sales Mgr

KCMD
10-18-1925; 99.3 MHz FM; *Hrs Open:* 24; 0.25 kw; 1535 ft.; N42 29 22 W123 18 16
820 NE 7th Street, Suite 1, Grants Pass, OR 97526 US
(541) 476-2137; *Fax:* (503) 497-2314
www.kcmd993.com
License: Grants Pass, Multnomah County, OR
Arbitron Metro Market: Grants Pass, OR; *Format:* Country; *Target Audience:* 35 plus.
Don Monette, President/CEO

Gresham

***KMHD**
01-01-1984; 89.1 MHz FM; *Hrs Open:* 24; 7.9 kw; 1434 ft.; N45 30 58 W122 43 59
26000 S. E. Stark Street, Gresham, OR 97030 US
(503) 661-8900; *Fax:* (503) 491-6999
www.kmhd.org
station-manager@knhd.fm
License: Gresham, Multnomah County, OR held by Mt. Hood Community College.
Nat'l Network: NPR
Arbitron Metro Market: Portland, OR; *Format:* Blues, Jazz *Special Programming:* Blues 15 hrs, news 5 hrs wkly; *Hrs. of News Programming:* News progmg 5 hrs wkly; *Target Audience:* 35-65; music lovers
Dan Gurin, Operations Dir
Doug Sweet, General Manager
Calvin Walker, General Sales Mgr
Greg Gomez, Programming Director

KSZN(AM)
09-28-1956; 1230 kHz AM; *Hrs Open:* 24; 1 kw-U; N45 29 35 W122 24 40
5110 S.E. Stark St., Portland, WA 97215
(503) 234-5550; *Fax:* (503) 234-5583
www.bustosmedia.com
rtatum@bustosmedia.com
License: Gresham, Multnomah County, OR held by Bustos Media of Oregon License LLC.
Group Owner: Bustos Media LLC; (acq 7-15-2003; $1.13 million)
Population Served: 300,000; *Arbitron Metro Market:* Portland, OR *Special Programming:* News 3 hrs, relg one hr wkly; *Hrs. of News Programming:* News progmg 3 hrs wkly; *Target Audience:* 12-54; lower to upper middleincome; *Adv. Rates:* 35; 35; 35
Amador Bustos, President/CEO
Rick Tatum, Vice President
Ruben Muniz, General Manager
Tom Oberg, General Sales Mgr
Zach Kellams, Programming Director
James Boyd, Chief Engineer
Chitra Gade, Business Manager

KRYN(AM)
1230 kHz AM; 920 watts; non-directional; 45 29 03N 122 24 40W
Mailing Address: 5110 S.E. Stark Street, Portland, WA 97215 USA
Second Address: Bustos Media Holdings, 5110 SE Stark Street, Portland, OR 87215
(503) 234-5550
License: Gresham, Multnomah County, OR
Group Owner: Bustos Media Holdings L.L.C.

Amandor Bustos, President/CEO
Rick Tatum, Vice President
Ruben Muniz, General Manager
James Boyd, Chief Engineer
Chitra Gade, Business Manager

Harbeck-Fruitdale

KLDR
05-03-1991; 98.3 MHz FM; *Hrs Open:* 24; 1.85 kw; 2093 ft.; N42 22 56 W123 16 29
P.O. Box 230, Grants Pass, OR 97526 US
(541) 474-7292; *Fax:* (541) 474-7300
www.kldr.com
kldr@kldr.com
License: Harbeck-Fruitdale, Josephine County, OR held by Grants Pass Broadcasting Corp.
Nat'l Network: AP Network News; *Nat'l Reps:* Tacher
Arbitron Metro Market: Medford, OR; *Format:* Adult Contemp; *Hrs. of News Programming:* news progmg 10 hrs wkly; *No. News*

Employees: 3; *Target Audience:* 25-54; Middle Age demo- actually a wide range in listeners *Adv. Rates:* 25; 15; 15; 10
Matt Wilson, CEO
Brian Diatte, General Sales Mgr
Marty Sether, Programming Director
Carl Wilson, CFO

Harrisburg

KNRQ
04-08-1974; 103.7 MHz FM; *Hrs Open:* 24; 100 kw; 2047 ft.; N44 34 49 W122 30 7
3280 Peachtree Rd. NW., Suite 2300, Atlanta, GA 30305 US
(404) 949-0700
www.nrq.com
License: Harrisburg, OR held by Cumulus Licensing LLC
Group Owner: Cumulus Media Inc.; (acq 4-11-2001; $4.1 million)
Nat'l Reps: McGavren Guild
Arbitron Metro Market: Portland, OR; *Format:* Rock/AOR; *Target Audience:* 18-54.; *Adv. Rates:* 24; 24; 24; 20

Hermiston

KOHU
02-06-1956; 1360 kHz AM; *Hrs Open:* 24; 4.3 kw-D, DAN; 0.5 kw-N, DAN; N45 51 57 W119 18 45
P.O. Box 886, Baker City, OR 97814 US
(541) 567-6500; *Fax:* (541) 567-6068
kqfm@eotnet.net
License: Hermiston, OR held by Westend Radio L.L.C.
Nat'l Network: ABC; *Nat'l Reps:* Farmakis *Regional Reps:* Target.
Format: Country *Special Programming:* Sp 6 hrs wkly; *Hrs. of News Programming:* news progmg 10 hrs wkly; *No. News Employees:* 1; *Target Audience:* General; two county loc audience; *Adv. Rates:* 20; 16; 20; 14
Ron Hughes, President
Jeff Walker, Operations Dir
Angela Pursel, General Manager
Adam Russell, News Director
Richard Wilson, Engineering Dir

KQFM
09-18-1978; 100.1 MHz FM; *Hrs Open:* 24; 5.3 kw; 308 ft.; N45 51 57 W119 18 42
PO Box 886, Baker City, OR 97814 US
(541) 567-6500; *Fax:* (541) 567-6068
kqfm@eotnet.net
License: Hermiston, Umatilla County, OR
Nat'l Network: ABC
Format: Adult Contemp; *Hrs. of News Programming:* news progmg 5 hrs wkly; *No. News Employees:* 1; *Target Audience:* 25-54.
Angela Pursel, General Sales Mgr
Jeff Walker, Programming Director
Ron Hughes, Promotions Manager
Pam Rebman, News Director

Hillsboro

KUIK
01-01-1954; 1360 kHz AM; *Hrs Open:* 24; 5 kw-D, DAN; 5 kw-N, DAN; N45 29 13 W122 54 31
Mailing Address: P. O. Box 566, Hillsboro, OR 97123 US
Second Address: 3355 N.E. Cornell Rd., Hillsboro, OR 97124
(503) 640-1360; *Fax:* (503) 640-6108
www.kuik.com
amradio@kuik.com
License: Hillsboro, OR held by Dolphin Radio LLC
Regional Network: Agrinet; *Wire Services:* AP
Arbitron Metro Market: Hillsboro, OR; *Format:* News, News/Talk, 84, Talk *Special Programming:* Relg 2 hrs, Sp 21 hrs wkly; *Hrs. of News Programming:* news progmg 24 hrs wkly; *No. News Employees:* 1 *TargetAudience:* 25-54; Seekers of locally produced unique programming; *Adv. Rates:* 44; 38; 44; 32
Don McCoun, President
Donna McCoun, Operations Dir
Paul Warren, Operations Manager

Hines

***KQDL**
01-01-2008; 89.1 MHz FM; 0.3 kw; 875 ft.; N43 34 23 W119 7 50 *Rebroadcasts:* Rebroadcasts KAWZ (FM)
4002 North 3300 East, Twin Falls, ID 83301 US
(208) 734-6633; *Fax:* (208 736-1958
www.csnradio.com
License: Hines, Harney County, OR held by Calvary Chapel of Twin Falls, Inc.
Group Owner: CSN International
Arbitron Metro Market: Hines, OR; *Format:* Christian, Religious

Hood River

KIHR
10-17-1950; 1340 kHz AM; *Hrs Open:* 24
1190 22nd St., P.O. Box 360, Hood River, OR 97031 US
(541) 386-1511
www.kihramfm.com
gary@bicoastalmedia.com
License: Hood River, OR held by Bicoastal Media Licenses IV LLC.
Group Owner: Bicoastal Media L.L.C.; (acq 12-1-2007; grpsl)
Arbitron Metro Market: Hood River, OR; *Format:* Country; *Hrs. of News Programming:* news progmg 12 hrs wkly; *No. News Employees:* 3; *Target Audience:* 25-54.; *Adv. Rates:* 19; 17; 19; 12
Mike Wilson, President/COO
Jeff Skye, Operations Dir
Gary Grossman, Market Manager
Rick Cavagnaro, General Sales Mgr
Mark Bailey, Programming Director
Matt Green, Engineering Dir
Paulette LeRoque, Traffic Manager

***KHRV**
90.1 MHz FM; 0.065 kw; 745 ft.; N45 39 45 W121 28 14
515 N E 15th Ave, Portland, OR 97323 US
(503) 293-1905; *Fax:* (503) 293-1919
www.opb.org
License: Hood River, Hood River County, OR held by Oregon Public Broadcasting.
Regional Network: Ore. Pub. Bcstg Radio Net.
Arbitron Metro Market: Hood River, OR
Jack Allen, President/CEO
Steve Bass, General Manager

Huntington

KHNO
93.5 MHz FM; 44-21-00.0 N 117-17-49.0 W
25 E. 86th St., New York, NY 10028 USA
(917) 535-0419
License: Huntington, OR held by Alex Media Inc.
Group Owner: Alex Media Inc.
Format: Variety/Diverse
Alexander Berger, President

John Day

KJDY
12-13-1963; 1400 kHz AM; *Hrs Open:* 24; 1 kw-U, ND1; N44 25 17 W118 57 9 *Rebroadcasts:* Rebroadcasts KJDY-FM Canyon City 100%
P.O. Box 399, John Day, OR 97845 US
(541) 575-1400; *Fax:* (541) 575-2313
kjdy@centurytel.net
License: John Day, OR held by Blue Mountain Broadcasting Co.
Nat'l Network: ABC *Regional Reps:* Tacher
Format: Country; *No. News Employees:* 1
Phil Gray, General Manager
Patricia Webb, General Sales Mgr
Kelly Workman, Programming Director
J. Kelly Carlson, Chief Engineer

***KOJD**
89.7 MHz FM; 0.9 kw; -128 ft.; N44 26 3 W118 57 28
7140 SW Macadam Avenue, Portland, OR 97219 US
(503) 224-9900
www.opb.org
License: John Day, Grant County, OR held by Oregon Public Broadcasting.
Regional Network: Ore. Pub. Bcstg Radio Net.
Arbitron Metro Market: John Day, OR
Steve Bass, CEO & President
Raoul Van Hall, Operations Dir
Dan Metziga, Senior VP, Development
Lynne Clendenin, VP, Programming
Morgan Holm, Senior VP & Chief Content Officer
Mike Foti, VP, Engineering
Debbie Rotich, VP, HR andAdministration

***KGNR**
91.9 MHz FM; 1.5 kw H; N44 26 3 W118 57 29 *Rebroadcasts:* Rebroadcasts KAWZ(FM)
P.O. Box 391, Twin Falls, ID 83303
(208) 733-3133
www.csnradio.com
License: John Day, Grant County, OR held by Calvary Chapel of Twin Falls Inc
Group Owner: CSN International
Format: Christian, Religious

Jordan Valley

***KGCL**
01-01-2005; 90.9 MHz FM; *Hrs Open:* 24; 21.5 kw vert; 2161 ft.; N43 0 26 W116 42 23
2310 East Ponderosa Drive, Camarillo, CA 93010 US
(800) 260-5676
www.nuevavida.com
License: Jordan Valley, Malheur County, OR held by Educational Media Foundation.
Group Owner: EMF Broadcasting
Arbitron Metro Market: Jordan Valley, OR; *Format:* Christian; *No. News Employees:* 3; *Target Audience:* 18-35; Judeo-Christian, female
Mike Novak, President

Junction City

KXOR
01-01-1998; 660 kHz AM; *Hrs Open:* 24; 10 kw-D, ND1; 0.075 kw-N, ND1; N44 12 36 W123 10 56
10209 Southeast Division, Portland, OR 97266 US
(541) 343-4100; *Fax:* (541) 343-0448
www.radiozion.net
License: Junction City, OR held by Zion Multimedia Oregon Corp.
Group Owner: Churchill Communications LLC; (acq 1-14-2005; $550,000).
Nat'l Reps: Univision Radio National Sales *Regional Reps:* Julie Schneidar & Paul Danitz; *Wire Services:* AP
Arbitron Metro Market: Junction City, OR.; *Hrs. of News Programming:* 6am-6pm on the hour; *No. News Employees:* 1; *Target Audience:* 25-54; 18-49.
Paul Danitz, General Manager
Phil Polter, General Sales Mgr

***KPIJ**
88.5 MHz FM; 0.55 kw; 2314 ft.; N44 16 44 W123 35 38
Rebroadcasts: Rebroadcasts KAWZ(FM) Twin Falls, ID 100%
Mailing Address: P.O. Box 391, Twin Falls, ID 83303 US
Second Address: 4002 N. 3300 E., Twin Falls, ID 83301
(800) 357-4226; *Fax:* (208) 736-1958
www.csnradio.com
License: Junction City, Lane Central County, OR held by CSN International.
Group Owner: CSN International
Arbitron Metro Market: Junction City, OR; *Format:* Christian, Religious
Mike Kestler, President
Daniel Davidson, Operations Dir
Don Mills, Network Programming Director
Mike Stocklin, Underwriting Director
Kelly Carlson, Engineering Dir

Keizer

KYKN
01-01-1951; 1430 kHz AM; *Hrs Open:* 24; 5 kw-U; N44 55 36 W122 57 19
P.O. Box 1430, Salem, OR 97308
(503) 390-3014; *Fax:* (503) 390-3728
www.kykn.com
mfrith@1430kykn.com
License: Keizer, Marion County, OR held by Willamette Broadcasting Co. Inc.
Nat'l Network: TACHER; *Regional Network:* TACHER
Population Served: 2,000,000; *Arbitron Metro Market:* Portland, OR *Special Programming:* RUSH LIMBAUGH, GLENN BECK, LOCAL NEWS, TALK, WEATHER, TRAFFIC; *Hrs. of News Programming:* news progmg 20 hrs wkly *No. NewsEmployees:* 2; *Target Audience:* 25-64; $50-90K income, homeowners; *Adv. Rates:* 15-70
Gator Gaynor, Operaions/Program Director
Michael Frith, General/Station/Sales Director
Tom Woods, Engineering Dir
Jeff Morgan, Sales
Mike Kotek, Sales
Isaac Maiden, Sales

Keno

KHIC
98.5 MHz FM; 1.8 kw; 42-05050.0 N 121-37-59.0
404 Main Street, Suite 4, Klamath Falls, OR 97601 US
License: Keno, OR
Group Owner: Basin Mediactive LLC

Klamath Falls

KAGO
07-19-1923; 1150 kHz AM

5455 Highland Drive, Bellevue, WA 98006 US
(541) 882-8833; *Fax:* (541) 882-8836
www.mybasin.com
License: Klamath Falls, OR
Group Owner: Basin Mediactive LLC; acq 3-16-99; $1.6 million with co-located FM).
Nat'l Network: CBS
Arbitron Metro Market: Klamath Falls, OR; *Format:* News, News/Talk, 86 *Special Programming:* Farm 3 hrs, Sp 5 hrs wkly; *Target Audience:* 35-65; upscale, professional
Brian Mobley, Operations Dir
Rob Siems, General Manager

KAGO-FM

10-15-1973; 99.5 MHz FM; 60 kw; 367 ft.; N42 12 56 W121 47 51
5455 Highland Drive, Bellevue, WA 98006 US
(541) 882-8833; *Fax:* (541) 882-8836
www.mybasin.com
License: Klamath Falls, Klamath County, OR held by New Northwest Broadcasters LLC
Group Owner: Basin Mediactive LLC
Nat'l Network: CBS
Arbitron Metro Market: Klamath Falls, OR; *Format:* Classic Rock
Rob Siems, General Manager

KFLS

01-01-1946; 1450 kHz AM; *Hrs Open:* 24; 1 kw-U, ND1; N42 12 19 W121 46 4
1338 Oregon Avenue, Klamath Falls, OR 97601 US
(541) 882-4656; *Fax:* (541) 884-2845
www.klamathradio.com
License: Klamath Falls, OR held by Wynne Enterprises LLC.
Group Owner: Wynne Enterprises LLC; (acq 1-1-71)
Nat'l Network: ABC *Regional Reps:* Tacher.
Arbitron Metro Market: Klamath Falls, OR; *Format:* News, News/Talk, 84, Talk; *Target Audience:* 35 plus.
Robert Wynne, President/General Manager
Carol Fritch, Traffic Manager
Robbie Rush, Sales Director
Randy Adams, Programming Director
Paul Hanson, News Director

KKRB

04-01-1983; 106.9 MHz FM; 100 kw; Ant 1,200 ft; N42 13 26 W121 49 02
1338 Oregon Avenue, Klamath Falls, OR 97601
(541) 882-4656; *Fax:* (541) 884-2845
www.klamathradio.com/sunny107
webmaster@klamathradio.com
License: Klamath Falls, Klamath County, OR held by Wynne Enterprises LLC.
Group Owner: Wynne Enterprises LLC

Robert Wynne, General Manager
Robbie Rush, General Sales Mgr
Carol Fritch, Traffic Director

KLAD

09-01-1955; 960 kHz AM
Mailing Address: 5455 Highland Drive, Bellevue, WA 98006 US
Second Address: 4509 S. 6th St., Suite 201, Klamath Falls, OR 97601
(541) 882-8833; *Fax:* (541) 882-8836
License: Klamath Falls, OR
Group Owner: Basin Mediactive LLC; (acq 10-20-98; grpsl)
Arbitron Metro Market: Medford, OR; *Format:* Sports; *Target Audience:* 25-54; mature with spendable income; *Adv. Rates:* 40; 40; 40; 40
Rob Siems, General Manager
Aaron Bentson, Programming Director
James Boyd, Chief Engineer

KLAD-FM

07-19-1974; 92.5 MHz FM; 63 kw; 2142 ft.; N42 5 50 W121 37 59
Mailing Address: 5455 Highland Drive, Bellevue, WA 98006 US
Second Address: 4509 S. 6th St., Suite 201, Klamath Falls, OR 97601
(541) 882-8833; *Fax:* (541) 882-8836
License: Klamath Falls, Klamath County, OR
Group Owner: Basin Mediactive LLC
Nat'l Network: ABC *Regional Reps:* Allied Radio Partners.
Arbitron Metro Market: Medford, OR; *Format:* Country
Rob Siems, General Manager

*KSKF

11-10-1989; 90.9 MHz FM; *Hrs Open:* 5 AM-2 AM; 6.5 kw horiz, 2 kw vert; 2254 ft.; N42 5 50 W121 37 59
1250 S. Siskiyou Boulevard, Ashland, OR 97520 US
(541) 552-6301
jprinfo@sou.edu
License: Klamath Falls, Klamath County, OR held by The State of Oregon, acting by and through the State Board of Higher Education, for the University of Oregon
Nat'l Network: NPR; PRI
Arbitron Metro Market: Ashland, OR; *Format:* Jazz, News, 90 *Special Programming:* Blues 6 hrs, folk 3 hrs, pub affrs 7 hrs wkly; *Hrs. of News Programming:* news progmg 45 hrs wkly; *No. News Employees:* 1 *TargetAudience:* General.
Ronald Kramer, CEO
Paul Westhelle, Executive Director
Eric Teel, Programming Director
Mitchell Christian, Director of Finance
Geoffrey Riley, News Director
Betsy Byers, Administrative Assistant

*KTEC

12-19-1950; 89.5 MHz FM; *Hrs Open:* 9 AM-midnight; 0.21 kw; 184 ft.; N42 12 59 W121 47 57
Oregon Institute of Tech, Klamath Falls, OR 97601 US
(541) 885-1840(541) 885-1841; *Fax:* (541) 885-1857
www.oit.edu/-ktec
ktec@oit.edu
License: Klamath Falls, Klamath County, OR held by Oregon State Board of Higher Education.
Arbitron Metro Market: Klamath Falls, OR; *Format:* Variety/Diverse *Special Programming:* American Indian one hr, Black 3 hrs, folk 3 hrs, Sp 3 hrs, world mus 6 hrs, electronic 9 hrs wkly; *Hrs. of News Programming:* newsprogmg 5 hrs wkly; *No. News Employees:* 1; *Target Audience:* 15 plus; eclectic, free thinking, progsv individuals
Dr. Chris Maples, President
Derek McIntyre, General Manager

KFEG

01-01-2002; 104.7 MHz FM; *Hrs Open:* 24; 51 kw; 645 ft.; N42 13 24 W121 49 2
1338 Oregon Avenue, Klamath Falls, OR 97601 US
(541) 882-4656; *Fax:* (541) 884-2845
www.klamathradio.com
bob@klamathradio.com
License: Klamath Falls, Klamath County, OR held by Cove Road Publishing LLC
Arbitron Metro Market: Klamath Falls, OR; *Format:* Classic Rock; *Target Audience:* 25-54.
Robert Wynne, President/General Manager
Robbie Rush, Sales Director
Randy Adams, Programming Director
Paul Hanson, News Director
Carol Fritch, Traffic Manager

*KLMF

01-01-2002; 88.5 MHz FM; 0.095 kw; 2162 ft.; N42 5 50 W121 37 59
Jefferson Public Radio, 1250 Siskiyou Boulevard, Ashland, OR 97520 US
(541) 552-6301; (800)-782-6191
www.ijpr.org
jprinfo@sou.edu
License: Klamath Falls, Klamath County, OR held by The State of Oregon, acting by and through the State Board of Higher Education, for the benefit of Southern Oregon University.
Nat'l Network: NPR; PRI; *Wire Services:* AP
Arbitron Metro Market: Klamath Falls, OR; *Format:* News; *Hrs. of News Programming:* News progmg 35 hrs wkly; *No. News Employees:* 1
Paul Westhelle, Executive Director
Valerie Ing-Miller, Northern CA Program Coordinator
Jill Hernandez, Accountant Technician

*KKLJ

03-14-2003; 88.9 MHz FM; *Hrs Open:* 24; 0.11 kw; 2185 ft.; N42 4 5 W121 58 13 *Rebroadcasts:* Rebroadcasts KLVR(FM) Middletown, CA 100%
PO Box 2098, Omaha, NE 68103-2098 US
(800) 525-5683
www.klove.com
License: Klamath Falls, Klamath County, OR held by Educational Media Foundation.
Group Owner: EMF Broadcasting
Nat'l Network: K-Love
Arbitron Metro Market: Klamath Falls, OR; *Format:* Christian; *No. News Employees:* 13; *Target Audience:* 25-44; Judeo Christian, female
Darrell Chambliss, Chairman
Mike Novak, President and CEO
David Pierce, Chief Creative Officer and Programming Director
Alan Mason, Chief Operating Officer
Eric Moser, Chief Financial Officer
D. Kevin Blair, Secretary and GeneralCounsel

La Grande

*KEOL

10-01-1973; 91.7 MHz FM; *Hrs Open:* 24; 0.31 kw horiz; -748 ft.; N45 19 16 W118 5 26
1410 L Avenue, La Grande, OR 97850 US
(541) 962-3698
www.eou.edu/keol
91.7keol@gmail.com
License: La Grande, Union County, OR held by Oregon State Board of Higher Education, for Eastern Oregon University
Arbitron Metro Market: Le Grande, OR; *Format:* Contemporary Hits/Top 40, Variety/Diverse *Special Programming:* Black 12 hrs, class 4 hrs, jazz 6 hrs, reggae 7 hrs wkly; *Target Audience:* 14-25; college students & locyouth
Courtney Millsap, Station Manager
Dan Meyer, Programming Director
Jeni Kaybee, Music Director
Jeff Dense, Faculty Advisor

KLBM

01-01-1938; 1450 kHz AM; *Hrs Open:* 24; 1 kw-U, ND1; N45 19 45 W118 4 0 *Rebroadcasts:* Rebroadcasts KBKR(AM) Baker City 100%
2510 Cove Ave., La Grande, OR 97850 US
(541) 963-4122
www.supertalknews.com
License: La Grande, Union County, OR held by Pacific Empire Radio Corp.
Group Owner: Pacific Empire Radio Corp.; acq 7-19-2004; grpsl).
Nat'l Network: Westwood One; ABC *Regional Reps:* McGavren Guild
Arbitron Metro Market: La Grande, OR; *Format:* News, News/Talk, 86 *Special Programming:* Farm 2 hrs wkly; *Hrs. of News Programming:* news progmg 25 hrs wkly; *No. News Employees:* 1; *Target Audience:* 25-54. *Adv. Rates:* 22; 20; 22; 16
Evan Yeoman, Operations Manager
Ben Bonfield, General Manager
Leslie Gatherer, Traffic Manager

KUBQ

08-15-1977; 98.7 MHz FM; *Hrs Open:* 24; 2.25 kw; 1,942 ft.; N45 26 26 W117 53 31
2510 Cove Ave., La Grande, OR 97850 US
(541) 963-4121
www.987therock.com
License: La Grande, Union County, OR held by Pacific Empire Radio Corp.
Group Owner: Pacific Empire Radio Corp.
Nat'l Reps: McGavren Guild
Arbitron Metro Market: La Grande, OR; *Format:* Classic Rock, Rock/AOR; *Hrs. of News Programming:* news progmg 6 hrs wkly; *No. News Employees:* 1; *Target Audience:* 25-54.; *Adv. Rates:* 24; 24; 24; 18
Evan Yeoman, Operations Manager
Ben Bonfield, General Manager
Leslie Gatherer, Traffic Manager

KWRL

09-27-1988; 99.9 MHz FM; *Hrs Open:* 24; 25 kw; 1657 ft.; N45 7 21 W117 46 44
1009-C Adams Ave., La Grande, OR 97850 US
(541) 963-3405; *Fax:* (541) 963-5090
www.myeasternoregon.com
randy@elkhornmediagroup.com
License: La Grande, OR held by KWRL, LLC.
Group Owner: Elkhorn Media Group
Nat'l Reps: Tacher *Regional Reps:* Tacher.
Arbitron Metro Market: La Grande, OR; *Format:* Adult Contemp; *Target Audience:* 18-49; general
Randy McKone, President
Kelly Workman, Operations Dir
Tori Brock Gandy, General Sales Mgr

*KTVR-FM

01-01-2004; 90.3 MHz FM; 0.4 kw; 2520 ft.; N45 18 33 W117 43 54
7140 Sw Macadam Ave., Portland, OR 97219 US
(800) 241-8123
www.opb.org
License: La Grande, Union County, OR held by Oregon Public Broadcasting.
Arbitron Metro Market: Portland, OR; *Format:* News; *Hrs. of News Programming:* news progmg 146 hrs wkly; *No. News Employees:* 5
Steven M. Bass, President and CEO
Dan Metziga, Senior VP, Development
Lynne Clendenin, VP, Programming

Morgan Holm, VP, News and Public Affairs
Mike Foti, VP, Engineering

KVBL
09-27-1988; 99.9 MHz FM; *Hrs Open:* 24; 9.5 kw; 1657 ft.; N45 7 21 W117 46 44
1009-C Adams Ave., La Grande, OR 97850 US
(541) 963-3405; *Fax:* (541) 963-5090
www.myeasternoregon.com
randy@elkhornmediagroup.com
License: La Grande, OR held by KWRL, LLC.
Group Owner: Elkhorn Media Group
Nat'l Reps: Tacher *Regional Reps:* Tacher.
Arbitron Metro Market: La Grande, OR; *Format:* News/Talk; *Target Audience:* 18-49; general
Randy McKone, President
Kelly Workman, Operations Dir
Tori Brock Gandy, General Sales Mgr

La Pine

***KKLP**
01-01-2005; 90.1 MHz FM; *Hrs Open:* 24; 2.5 kw vert; 177 ft.; N43 34 50 W121 34 13 *Rebroadcasts:* Rebroadcasts KLVR(FM) Santa Rosa, CA 100%
PO Box 2098, Omaha, NE 68103-2098 US
(800) 525-5683; *Fax:* (916) 251-1650
www.klove.com
License: La Pine, Deschutes County, OR held by Educational Media Foundation.
Group Owner: EMF Broadcasting
Nat'l Network: K-Love
Arbitron Metro Market: La Pine, OR; *Format:* Christian; *No. News Employees:* 3; *Target Audience:* 25-44; Judeo Christian, female
Darrell Chambliss, Chairman
Mike Novak, President and CEO
David Pierce, Chief Creative Officer
Alan Mason, COO
Eric Moser, CFO
D. Kevin Blair, Secretary/General Counsel

Lake Oswego

KDZR
01-01-1996; 1640 kHz AM
77 W 66th St., 16th Fl., New York, NY 10023-6201 USA
(503) 228-4322; *Fax:* (503) 228-4325
www.radiodisney.com
License: Lake Oswego, OR held by Radio Disney Group LLC
Group Owner: Disney Channels Worldwide; Sale to Salem Media Group pending
Nat'l Network: Radio Disney
Arbitron Metro Market: Portland, OR; *Format:* Children
Gary Marsh, President & Chief Creative Officer

KLTH
08-01-1977; 106.7 MHz FM; *Hrs Open:* 24; 96 kw; 1647 ft.; N45 30 58 W122 43 59
13333 SW 68th Parkway, Suite 310, Portland, OR 97223 US
(503) 323-6400; *Fax:* (503) 323-6660
www.1067theeagle.com
License: Lake Oswego, Clackamas County, OR held by Citicasters Licenses Inc.
Group Owner: iHeartMedia; (acq 4-1-2009; grpsl)
Arbitron Metro Market: Portland, OR; *Format:* Oldies; *No. News Employees:* 1; *Target Audience:* 35-54; 55% women, 45% men
Marshal Burgess, Vice President of Sales
Chris Shebel, Programming Director
Diana Hryciw, Promotions Manager

Lakeview

KLCR
01-01-2003; 95.3 MHz FM; *Hrs Open:* 24; 0.78 kw; 1378 ft.; N42 12 18 W120 19 38.40
P.O. Box 723, Lakeview, OR 97630 US
(541) 947-3325
License: Lakeview, Lake County, OR held by Woodrow Matthew Warren
Group Owner: Woodrow Michael Warren Stns
Arbitron Metro Market: Medford, OR; *Format:* Classic Rock
Mike Warren, General Manager

KORV-FM
01-01-1987; 93.5 MHz FM; *Hrs Open:* 24; 1 kw; Ant 951 ft; N42 12 18 W120 19 39
629 Center St., PO Box 189, Lakeview, OR 97630
(541) 947-3351; *Fax:* (541) 947-3375
kqik@tnet.biz
License: Lakeview, Lake County, OR
Nat'l Network: ABC; *Wire Services:* AP
Population Served: 30,000 *Format:* Contemporary Hits/Top 40; *Target Audience:* General.; *Adv. Rates:* Same as AM
Walt Lawton, Programming Director

***KOAP**
01-01-2000; 88.7 MHz FM; 0.17 kw; -591 ft.; N42 10 42 W120 21 19
7140 Sw Macadam Ave, Portland, OR 97219 US
(800) 241-8123
www.opb.org
License: Lakeview, Lake County, OR held by Oregon Public Broadcasting.
Nat'l Network: NPR; *Regional Network:* Ore. Pub. Bcstg Radio Net.
Arbitron Metro Market: Portland, OR; *Format:* News
Steve Bass, CEO
Lynne Clendenin, Programming Director
Mike Foti, Engineering Dir
Morgan Holm, Chief Content Officer
Dan Metziga, Senior Vice President, Development
Jordan Anderson, Associate Director, Foundation Relations

KORV
93.5 MHz FM; 1 kw; 951 ft.; N42 12 18 W120 19 39
P.O. Box 189, Lakeview, OR 97630 US
(541) 482-3999
www.mcaso.org
License: Lakeview, Jackson County, OR held by Multicultural Association of Southern Oregon.
Arbitron Metro Market: Lakeview, OR; *Format:* Adult Contemp
Jim Bauermeister, President

Lebanon

KGAL
08-05-1995; 1580 kHz AM; *Hrs Open:* 24; 1 kw-U, DA1; N44 34 25 W122 55 5
36991 KGAL Drive, Lebanon, OR 97355 US
(541) 451-5425
www.kgal.com
charlie@kgal.com
License: Lebanon, OR held by EADS Broadcasting Corp.
Nat'l Network: CBS; Westwood One; Salem Radio Network; Sporting News Radio Network; *Nat'l Reps:* McGavren Guild; *Wire Services:* AP
Arbitron Metro Market: Portland, OR; *Format:* News, Sports, 86 *Special Programming:* Local interview show 5 hrs wkly; *Hrs. of News Programming:* news progmg 22 hrs wkly; *No. News Employees:* 5; *Target Audience:* 25-54; active listeners
Florence Eads, CFO
Richard "Charlie" Eads, President
Susie Dowding, Traffic Manager
Ted Jenne, Programming Director
Weldon Greig, News Director
Jim Willhight, Operations Manager
Ryan Murphy, Production Director

KSHO
01-01-1950; 920 kHz AM; *Hrs Open:* 24; 1 kw-U, DA1; N44 34 30 W122 55 15
36991 KGAL Drive, PO Box 749, Lebanon, OR 97355 US
(541) 451-5425
www.ksho.net
kgal@kgal.com
License: Lebanon, OR held by Eads Broadcasting Corp.
Nat'l Network: Jones Radio Networks; AP Radio; *Nat'l Reps:* McGavren Guild; *Wire Services:* AP
Arbitron Metro Market: Lebanon, OR; *Format:* Adult Contemp; *Hrs. of News Programming:* news progmg 7 hrs wkly; *No. News Employees:* 5; *Target Audience:* 35 plus; mature adults with money & leisure
Florence Eads, CFO
Richard "Charlie" Eads, President
Susie Dowding, Traffic Manager
Ted Jenne, Programming Director
Weldon Greig, News Director
"Radio" Ray Pietz, Sports Director
Ryan Murphy, Production Director

***KGRI**
01-01-2005; 88.1 MHz FM; *Hrs Open:* 24; 0.001 kw horiz, 0.17 kw vert; 2474 ft.; N44 28 59 W122 34 55 *Rebroadcasts:* Rebroadcasts KLRD(FM) Yucaipa, CA 100%
PO Box 2118, Omaha, NE 68103-2118 US
(888) 937-2471
www.air1.com
License: Lebanon, Linn County, OR held by Educational Media Foundation.
Group Owner: EMF Broadcasting
Nat'l Network: Air 1
Arbitron Metro Market: Lebanon, OR; *Format:* Alternative, Christian; *No. News Employees:* 3; *Target Audience:* 18-35; Judeo-Christian, female
Darrell Chambliss, Chairman
Alan Mason, COO
Mike Novak, President and CEO
David Pierce, Chief Creative Director
Ed Lenane, News Director
Sam Wallington, Engineering Dir
Paul Goldsmith, Music Director
D. Kevin Blair, GeneralCounsel
Eric Moser, Chief Financial Officer

Lincoln City

KBCH
05-27-1955; 1400 kHz AM; 1 kw-U; N44 59 27 W123 58 45
800 SE Hwy. 101, Suite C, Lincoln City, OR 97367 US
(541) 994-2181
www.kbcham.com
info@kbcham.com
License: Lincoln City, Lincoln County, OR held by Pacific West Broadcasting Inc.
Group Owner: Pacific West Broadcasting Inc.
Regional Reps: Tacher
Population Served: 12,000 *Format:* Adult Contemp, News/Talk; *Hrs. of News Programming:* news progmg 4 hrs wkly; *No. News Employees:* 2
David Miller, Owner/General Manager
Larry Blair, Sales Manager
James Boyd, Chief Engineer
Marilyn Dick, Traffic Manager

KCRF-FM
11-01-1981; 96.7 MHz FM; *Hrs Open:* 24; 19.5 kw; Ant 872 ft; N44 45 22 W124 02 57
906 SW. Alder, PO Box 1430, Newport, OR 97365 US
(541) 265-2266; *Fax:* (541) 265-6397
www.kcrffm.com
info@kcrffm.com
License: Lincoln City, Lincoln County, OR held by Pacific West Broadcasting Inc.
Group Owner: Pacific West Broadcasting Inc.; acq 11-15-00; grpsl).
Regional Reps: Tacher
Population Served: 68,000 *Format:* Classic Rock; *Hrs. of News Programming:* news progmg 2 hrs wkly; *No. News Employees:* 2
David Miller, Owner/General Manager
Larry Blair, Sales Manager
James Boyd, Chief Engineer
Marilyn Dick, Traffic Manager

McMinnville

KLYC
06-18-1949; 1260 kHz AM; *Hrs Open:* 24; 1 kw-U, DA-N; N45 13 19 W123 10 21
1975 NE Colvin Court, McMinnville, OR 97128
(503) 472-1260
www.klyc.us
dave@klyc.us
License: McMinnville, Yamhill County, OR held by Celebrate Life Media, LLC
Nat'l Network: NBC News
Population Served: 90,000; *Arbitron Metro Market:* Portland, OR; *No. News Employees:* 1; *Target Audience:* 25-54.
Dave Adams, General Manager
Brian Eriksen, Sports Director

***KSLC**
01-17-1972; 90.3 MHz FM; *Hrs Open:* 6 AM-noon; 0.75 kw; 335 ft.; N45 9 28 W123 17 22
Linfield College, 900 S. Baker, Mc Minnville, OR 97128 US
(800) 883-2000
www.linfield.edu/kslcfm.html
kslc@linfield.edu
License: McMinnville, Yamhill County, OR held by Linfield College.
Arbitron Metro Market: McMinnville, OR; *Format:* Alternative *Special Programming:* Black 2 hrs, heavy metal 7 hrs wkly, relg 2 hrs wkly; *Hrs. of News Programming:* News progmg 3 hrs wkly; *Target Audience:* 12-25;young people looking for new mus
Sam Krier, General Manager
Jeremy Huntsberger, Faculty Advisor
Jeremy Odden, Technical Director
Ben Niesen, Music Director
Kevin Romero, Sports Director
Eric Frank, Information Director
Bryan Oczkus, News Director

Medford

KBOY-FM
02-01-1958; 95.7 MHz FM; *Hrs Open:* 24; 60 kw; 981 ft.; N42 27 11 W123 3 21
1438 Rossanley Dr., Medford, OR 97501 US
(541) 779-1550
www.957kboy.com
jp@radiomedford.com
License: Medford, Jackson County, OR held by Mapleton License of Medford LLC.
Group Owner: Mapleton Communications LLC; (acq 10-26-2001; grpsl)
Arbitron Metro Market: Medford-Ashland, OR; *Format:* Classic Rock; *Hrs. of News Programming:* One
J.P. Pierce, Programming Director
Joe Mussio, Sales Director

*KDOV
08-01-1995; 91.7 MHz FM; *Hrs Open:* 24; 26 kw; -364 ft.; N42 17 44 W122 48 15
2070 Milligan Way, Medford, OR 97504 US
(541) 776-5368; *Fax:* (541) 842-4334
License: Medford, Jackson County, OR held by UCB USA Inc.
Nat'l Network: Salem Radio Network; *Wire Services:* AP
Arbitron Metro Market: Medford-Ashland, OR; *Format:* News, News/Talk, 86, Religious; *Hrs. of News Programming:* news progmg 5 hrs wkly; *No. News Employees:* 1; *Target Audience:* 25-54; women
Perry Atkinson, President
Mark Portrait, Vice President

KIFS
11-25-1996; 107.5 MHz FM; 5.8 kw; 1375 ft.; N42 17 54 W122 44 53
3624 Avion Dr., Medford, OR 97504 US
(541) 772-4170; *Fax:* (541) 858-5416
www.107kiss.com
License: Medford, OR held by Bicoastal Media LLC.
Group Owner: Bicoastal Media L.L.C.; (acq 7-2-2007; grpsl)
Nat'l Reps: Tacher
Arbitron Metro Market: Medford, OR; *Format:* Contemporary Hits/Top 40; *Target Audience:* 18-49.
George Feola, Market Manager

KLDZ
08-19-1991; 103.5 MHz FM; *Hrs Open:* 24; 100 kw; 479 ft.; N42 17 13 W123 0 15
3624 Arion Dr., Medford, OR 97504 US
(541) 772-4170
www.kool1035.com
License: Medford, Jackson County, OR held by Media Licenses VI, LLC
Group Owner: Bicoastal Media L.L.C.; (acq 7-2-2007; grpsl)
Nat'l Reps: Tacher
Arbitron Metro Market: Medford, OR; *Format:* Contemporary Hits/Top 40; *Target Audience:* 25 plus.
George Feola, Market Manager

*KEZX
05-31-1954; 730 kHz AM; *Hrs Open:* 24; 1 kw-D, ND1; 0.074 kw-N, ND1; N42 18 36 W122 48 41
511 Rossanley Drive, Medford, OR 97501 US
(541) 772-0322
sportsradio730.com
License: Medford, OR held by Opus Broadcasting Systems Inc.
Group Owner: Opus Broadcasting Systems Inc.; (acq 12-17-2003; $70,000)
Nat'l Network: Fox Sports; *Nat'l Reps:* Tacher
Arbitron Metro Market: Medford, OR; *Format:* Sports; *No. News Employees:* 3
Dean Flock, General Manager
Brian Fraser, General Sales Mgr

KMED
01-01-1922; 1440 kHz AM; *Hrs Open:* 24; 5 kw-D, ND2; 1 kw-N, ND2; N42 18 36 W122 48 41
3624 Avion Dr., Medford, OR 97504 US
(541) 772-4170
www.kmed.com
bill@billmeyershow.com
License: Medford, OR held by Media Licenses VI
Group Owner: Bicoastal Media L.L.C.; (acq 7-2-2007; grpsl)
Nat'l Network: Westwood One; CBS
Arbitron Metro Market: Medford, OR; *Format:* News, News/Talk, 86; *Hrs. of News Programming:* news progmg 14 hrs wkly; *No. News Employees:* 1; *Target Audience:* 35 plus.
Bill Ashenden, General Manager

KRTA
10-01-1947; 610 kHz AM; *Hrs Open:* 24; 2.5 kw-D, DA2; 5 kw-N, DA2; N42 23 15 W122 46 11
1257 N. Riverside Ave., #10, Medford, OR 97501 US
(541) 772-0322; *Fax:* (541) 772-4233
brian@opusradio.com
License: Medford, OR held by Opus Broadcasting Systems Inc.
Group Owner: Opus Broadcasting Systems Inc.; acq 7-9-91; $63,634 with KROG(FM) Grants Pass;
Nat'l Network: La Gran D; *Nat'l Reps:* Tacher
Arbitron Metro Market: Medford-Ashland, OR; *Format:* Tejano; *Hrs. of News Programming:* News progmg 9 hrs wkly; *Target Audience:* 12 plus; Hispanic
Dean Flock, General Manager
Brian Fraser, General Sales Mgr
Oscar Bonilla, Programming Director

KTMT-FM
10-15-1970; 93.7 MHz FM; *Hrs Open:* 24; 27 kw; 3215 ft.; N42 4 52 W122 43 9
1438 Rossanley Dr., Medford, OR 97501 US
(541) 779-1550
www.937nowfm.com
danhanvey@radiomedford.com
License: Medford, Jackson County, OR held by Mapleton License of Medford LLC.
Group Owner: Mapleton Communications LLC
Arbitron Metro Market: Medford-Ashland, OR; *Format:* Adult Contemp; *Hrs. of News Programming:* news progmg 3 hrs wkly; *No. News Employees:* 1; *Target Audience:* 18-49.
Dan Hanvey, Programming Director

Merrill

KKKJ
01-01-2008; 105.5 MHz FM; 18 kw; 686 ft.; N42 13 24 W121 49 2
1333 Oregon Avenue, Klamath Falls, OR 97601 US
(541) 882-4656; *Fax:* (541) 884-2845
www.klamathradio.com
webmaster@klamathradio.com
License: Merrill, Klamath County, OR held by Cove Road Publishing
Arbitron Metro Market: Merrill, OR; *Format:* Adult Contemp; *Target Audience:* 18-49.
Robert Wynne, President/General Manager
Randy Adams, Programming Director
Paul Hanson, News Director
Robbie Rush, Director of Sales
Carol Fritch, Traffic Director

Milton-Freewater

*KLRF
01-01-1999; 88.5 MHz FM; *Hrs Open:* 24; 5 kw; Ant 1,302 ft; N45 47 16 W118 10 31
Mailing Address: PO Box 500, Simi Valley, CA 93062
Second Address: 101 Cochran Street, Simi Valley, CA 93065
(800) 775-4673
www.lifetalk.net
office@lifetalk.net
License: Milton-Freewater, Umatilla County, OR held by Stateline Seventh Day Adventist Church
Nat'l Network: Lifetalk Radio Network

Debby Wade, Station Relations Director
Paul Willis, IT Director
John Geli, General Manager
Delonis Trujillo, HR Director

KZTB
09-10-1992; 97.9 MHz FM; *Hrs Open:* 24; 100 kw; 899 ft.; N45 47 41 W118 10 6 *Rebroadcasts:* KMMG-FM
1123 W. Cort St., Pasco, WA 99301 US
(877) 669-0979
License: Milton-Freewater, Umatilla County, OR held by Adelante Media of Eastern Washington License LLC
Group Owner: Adelante Media Group LLC; (acq 2-22-2006; $900,000 plus swap for KUJJ(FM) Weston).
Arbitron Metro Market: Tri-Cities, WA (Richland-Kennewick-Pasco)
Brian Hollenbaugh, General Manager
Gary Shelton, General Sales Mgr
Juan Gonzalez, Programming Director

Milwaukie

KOOR
02-01-1988; 1010 kHz AM; 1.1 kw-C, NDD; 4.5 kw-D, NDD; N45 29 3 W122 24 40
6035 S.E. Milwaukie Ave, Portland, OR 97202 US
(503) 234-5550; *Fax:* (503) 234-5583
www.bustosmedia.com
License: Milwaukie, OR held by Bustos Media of Oregon License LLC.
Group Owner: Bustos Media Holdings L.L.C.; (acq 11-19-2003; $1 million)
Arbitron Metro Market: Portland, OR; *Format:* Adult Contemp; *Adv. Rates:* 25; 20; 25; 15
Chitra Gade, Operations Dir
Ricky Tatum, General Manager

Molalla

KRSK
07-03-1970; 105.1 MHz FM; 21 kw; 1542 ft.; N45 31 21 W122 44 45
700 SW Bancroft St., Portland, OR 97239 US
(503) 223-1441; *Fax:* (503) 223-6909
www.1051thebuzz.com
info@1051thebuzz.com
License: Molalla, Clackamas County, OR held by Entercom License LLC
Group Owner: Entercom Communications Corp.; (acq 4-23-98; grpsl).
Arbitron Metro Market: Portland, OR; *Format:* Adult Contemp
David Field, President
Erin Hubert, General Manager
Dave McDonald, General Sales Mgr
Brian Bridgman, Programming Director

Monmouth

KSND
03-23-1995; 95.1 MHz FM; *Hrs Open:* 24; 1 kw; 1565 ft.; N44 53 19 W123 36 26
PO Box 484, Newport, OR 97365 US
(503) 763-9951; *Fax:* (503) 763-2676
License: Monmouth, Polk County, OR held by Bustos Media Holdings LLC
Wire Services: AP
Arbitron Metro Market: Salem, OR; *Format:* Adult Contemp; *Hrs. of News Programming:* news progmg 5 hrs wkly; *No. News Employees:* 1; *Target Audience:* 25-54.; *Adv. Rates:* 30; 22; 30; 20
Ernie Hopseker, President
Frank Rippey, Operations Dir
Scott Forrest, Programming Director
Lyndi Miles, News Director

Mount Angel

KQRR(AM)
1kHz AM; 25,000 watts; 490 watts; 45 04 35N 122 48 27W
5110 SE Stark Street, Portland, OR 97215 USA
(503) 234-5550
License: Mount Angel, Marion County, OR
Group Owner: Bustos Media Holdings L.L.C.

Terry Tario, General Manager

Myrtle Point

*KOOZ
08-01-1996; 94.1 MHz FM; *Hrs Open:* 5 AM-2 AM; 1 kw; 1457 ft.; N42 57 32 W124 16 23
Mailing Address: 1250 Siskiyou Boulevard, Ashland, OR 97520 US
Second Address: 1721 Market Street, Redding, CA 96001
(541) 552-6301
www.ijpr.org
License: Myrtle Point, Coos County, OR held by JPR Foundation Inc.
Nat'l Network: NPR; PRI; *Wire Services:* AP
Arbitron Metro Market: Ashland, OR; *Format:* News; *Hrs. of News Programming:* news progmg 35 hrs wkly; *No. News Employees:* 1
Ronald Kramer, CEO
Bryon Lambert, Operations Dir
Paul Westhelle, Executive Director
Eric Teel, Programming Director
Darin Ransom, Engineering Dir
Mitchell Christian, Director of Finance
Geoffrey Riley, News Director

Netarts

KTIL(AM)
08-01-1947; 1590 kHz AM; 5 kw-D, 1 kw-N, DA-N; N45 27 24 W123 52 36
Mailing Address: Box 40, Tillamook, OR 97141
Second Address: 170 W. 3rd St., Tillamook, OR 97141
(503) 842-4422; *Fax:* (503) 842-2755
www.ktil-kmbd.com
comments@ktil-kmbd.com
License: Netarts, Tillamook County, OR held by Alexandra Communications Inc.

Group Owner: Alexandra Communications Inc.; (acq 12-29-86; $250,000; grpsl;
Population Served: 4,500 *Format:* News, News/Talk, 84, Talk
Van Moe, President

Newport

KNCU
06-01-2000; 92.7 MHz FM; 3.8 kw; 840 ft; N44 45 22 W124 02 57
Box 1430, 960 SW Alder, Newport, OR 97365 US
(541) 265-2266; *Fax:* (541) 265-6397
www.u92fm.com
info@U92fm.com
License: Newport, Lincoln County, OR held by Pacific West Broadcasting Inc.
Group Owner: Pacific West Broadcasting Inc.; acq 10-27-00; grpsl).
Regional Reps: Tacher.
Population Served: 44,000 *Format:* Country; *Hrs. of News Programming:* news progmg 2 hrs wkly; *No. News Employees:* 1; *Target Audience:* 24-54; adults
David Miller, Owner/General Manager
Larry Blair, Sales Manager
James Boyd, Chief Engineer
Marilyn Dick, Traffic Manager

*KLCO
09-11-1990; 90.5 MHz FM; *Hrs Open:* 24; 3.2 kw; 256 ft; N44 45 22 W124 02 57 *Rebroadcasts:* Rebroadcasts KLCC(FM) Eugene 100%
136 W. 8th Ave., Eugene, OR 92401
(541) 463-6000; *Fax:* (541) 463-6046
www.klcc.org
klcc@klcc.org
License: Newport, Lincoln County, OR held by Lane Community College.
Nat'l Network: NPR
Population Served: 50,000 *Format:* Jazz, News, 94 *Special Programming:* Sp 5 hrs, Black 3 hrs, folk 12 hrs, blues 4 hrs, world 3 hrs, electronic 6 hrs wkly; *Hrs. of News Programming:* news progmg 60 hrs wkly *No. NewsEmployees:* 1; *Target Audience:* 25-54.
John Stark, General Manager
Cheryl Crumbley, Development Director
Don Hein, Programming Director
Gayle Chisholm, Marketing Director
Tripp Sommer, News Director
Chris Heck, Chief Engineer
Kris Fox, Membership Director

KNPT
06-28-1948; 1310 kHz AM; *Hrs Open:* 24; 5 kw-D, 1 kw-N, DA-N; N44 37 40 W123 59 15
Box 1430, 906 S.W. Alder St., Newport, OR 97365
(541) 265-2266; *Fax:* (541) 265-6397
knptam.com
info@knptam.com
License: Newport, Lincoln County, OR held by Yaquina Bay Communications Inc.
Regional Reps: Tacher.
Population Served: 18,000 *Special Programming:* 1 hour religious programming; *Hrs. of News Programming:* news progmg 21 hrs wkly; *No. News Employees:* 2; *Target Audience:* 34 plus.; *Adv. Rates:* 18.40; 13.60;18.40; 6.40
David Miller, President
Larry Blair, General Sales Mgr
Johnny Randolph, Programming Director

KYTE
10-25-1976; 102.7 MHz FM; *Hrs Open:* 24; 66 kw; Ant 881 ft; N44 45 22 W124 02 57
Box 1430, 906 S.W. Alder St., Newport, OR 97365
(541) 265-2266; *Fax:* (541) 265-6397
www.kytefm.com
info@kytefm.com
License: Newport, Lincoln County, OR held by Yaquina Bay Communications Inc.
Regional Reps: Tacher.
Population Served: 120,000 *Hrs. of News Programming:* news progmg 4 hrs wkly; *No. News Employees:* 2; *Target Audience:* 24-49.
David Miller, President
Johnny Randolph, Program Director/Announcer
Howard Wright, Announcer
Heather Hollingsworth, Announcer
Howard Wright, Music Director
Larry Blair, Music Director

*KYOR
01-01-2006; 88.9 MHz FM; 0.035 kw; 899 ft.; N44 45 23 W124 2 59 *Rebroadcasts:* Rebroadcasts KUFR(FM) Salt Lake City, UT 100%
290 Hegenberger Road, Oakland, CA 94621 US
(800) 543-1495
www.familyradio.com
License: Newport, Lincoln County, OR held by Family Stations Inc.
Group Owner: Family Stations Inc.
Arbitron Metro Market: Newport, OR; *Format:* Christian, Religious
Harold Camping, General Manager

North Bend

KOOS
10-01-1990; 107.3 MHz FM; *Hrs Open:* 24; 51 kw; 692 ft.; N43 12 18 W124 18 7
320 Central Ave., Suite 519, Coos Bay, OR 97420 US
(541) 267-2121; *Fax:* (541) 267-5229
www.koosfm.com
License: North Bend, Coos County, OR held by Bicoastal Media Licenses III LLC.
Group Owner: Bicoastal Media L.L.C.; (acq 10-16-2003; grpsl)
Nat'l Network: Jones Radio Networks *Regional Reps:* Tacher
Arbitron Metro Market: Coos Bay, OR; *Format:* Contemporary Hits/Top 40; *Hrs. of News Programming:* News progmg 14 hrs wkly; *Target Audience:* 18-44.; *Adv. Rates:* 18; 14; 18; 7
Mike Wilson, President & COO
DeeDee Dupre, Market Manager

KTEE
12-10-1979; 94.9 MHz FM; 89 kw; 627 ft.; N43 12 18 W124 18 7
320 Central Ave., Suite 519, Coos Bay, OR 97420 US
(541) 267-2121; *Fax:* (541) 267-5529
www.ktee.com
License: North Bend, Coos County, OR held by Bicoastal Media Licenses III LLC.
Group Owner: Bicoastal Media L.L.C.; (acq 10-16-2003; grpsl)
Nat'l Reps: Tacher
Format: Triple A, Christian; *Hrs. of News Programming:* News progmg 8 hrs wkly; *Target Audience:* 25-54.; *Adv. Rates:* 14; 12; 14; 10
Mike Wilson, President

North Powder

*KEFS
89.5 MHz FM; 0.165 kw; 1787 ft.; N45 7 26 W117 46 48
Mailing Address: P.O.Box 271, Twin Falls, ID 83303 US
Second Address: 4002 North 3300 East, Twin Falls, ID 83301
(208) 734-2049; *Fax:* (208) 736-1958
www.effectradio.com
License: North Powder, Union County, OR held by Calvary Chapel of Twin Falls, Inc.
Group Owner: Effect Radio
Format: Christian, Rock/AOR
Jon Gibson, Programming Director

Nyssa

*KARO
01-01-1997; 98.7 MHz FM; *Hrs Open:* 24; 82 kw; 1001 ft.; N43 24 9 W116 54 9 *Rebroadcasts:* Rebroadcasts KLRD(FM) Yucaipa, CA 100%
PO Box 2118, Omaha, NE 68103-2118 US
(888) 937-2471
www.air1.com
License: Nyssa, Malheur County, OR held by Educational Media Foundation
Group Owner: EMF Broadcasting; (acq 2-25-03; $1 million).
Nat'l Network: Air 1
Arbitron Metro Market: Boise, ID; *Format:* Alternative, Christian;
Target Audience: 18-54
Darrell Chambliss, Chairman
Mike Novak, President
Eric Moser, CFO
Alan Mason, COO
David Pierce, Chief Creative Officer

Oakridge

*KAVE
01-01-2006; 88.5 MHz FM; *Hrs Open:* 24; 400 w; Ant -1,286 ft; N43 44 27 W122 26 50
Mailing Address: 2455 Willakenzie Road, Eugene, OR 97401
Second Address: 1574 Coburg Road, Eugene, OR 97401
(541) 790-6686; *Fax:* (541) 790-6688
www.krvm.org
webmaster@krvm.org
License: Oakridge, Lane County, OR held by Lane County School District 4J.
Target Audience: 18-35.
Cambra Ward, Station Manager
Ken Martin, Programming Director
Bobbie Cirel, Development Director

Ontario

KSRV
11-23-1946; 1380 kHz AM; *Hrs Open:* 24
1725 North Orgeon Street, Ontario, OR 97914 US
(541) 889-8651; *Fax:* (541) 889-8733
License: Ontario, OR held by Armstrong Radio Group Inc.
Nat'l Network: ABC; *Wire Services:* AP
Arbitron Metro Market: Ontario, OR; *Format:* Country, News
Special Programming: Farm 15 hrs wkly; *Hrs. of News Programming:* news progmg 15 hrs wkly; *No. News Employees:* 1; *Target Audience:* 25-54 plus.
Jack Armstrong, General Manager

KSRV-FM
07-04-1977; 96.1 MHz FM; *Hrs Open:* 24; 47 kw; 2674 ft.; N43 45 18 W116 5 51
5660 Franklin Road, Suite 200, Nampa, ID 83687 US
(208) 465-9966; *Fax:* (208) 465-2922
www.961bobfm.com
License: Ontario, Malheur County, OR held by FM Idaho Co., LLC
Group Owner: FM Idaho Co. LLC dba Impact Radio Group
Arbitron Metro Market: Nampa, ID; *Format:* Adult Contemp; *Hrs. of News Programming:* News progmg 40 hrs wkly
Mikey Fuentes, Operations Dir
Darrell Calton, General Manager
Mark Broz, General Sales Mgr

Oregon City

KGDD
07-04-1947; 1520 kHz AM; *Hrs Open:* 24; 50 kw-D, DA2; 15 kw-N, DA2; N45 24 44 W122 34 37
401 City Ave., Suite 409, Bala Cynwyd, PA 19004 US
(503) 234-5550; *Fax:* (503) 234-5583
License: Oregon City, OR held by Bustos Media of Oregon License LLC.
Group Owner: Bustos Media L.L.C.; (acq 11-17-2003; $2.8 million).
Nat'l Reps: D & R Radio
Arbitron Metro Market: Portland, OR; *No. News Employees:* 1;
Adv. Rates: 70; 70; 70; 50
Amador Bustos, President
Ricky Tatum, General Manager
Tom Oberg, General Sales Mgr
Henry Cualio, Promotions Manager
Chitra Gade, News Director
James Boyd, Chief Engineer

Pendleton

*KRBM
04-18-1970; 90.9 MHz FM; 24.5 kw horiz, 10.5 kw vert; 591 ft.; N45 35 21 W118 59 53
7140 S.W. Macadam Avenue, Portland, OR 97219 US
(503) 244-9900
www.opb.org
License: Pendleton, Umatilla County, OR held by Oregon Public Broadcasting.
Nat'l Network: PRI; NPR; *Regional Network:* Ore. Pub. Bcstg Radio Net.
Format: News, News/Talk, 86; *Hrs. of News Programming:* news progmg 146 hrs wkly; *No. News Employees:* 5; *Target Audience:* Teens to adults.

KTIX
01-01-1941; 1240 kHz AM; *Hrs Open:* 24
2003 NW 5th Drive, Pendleton, OR 97801 US
(541) 276-1511; *Fax:* (541) 276-1480
www.1240ktix.com
License: Pendleton, OR held by KSRV Inc.
Group Owner: Capps Broadcast Group; (acq 5-14-98; $1.2 million with co-located FM).
Nat'l Network: ESPN Radio; *Nat'l Reps:* Tacher
Arbitron Metro Market: Pendleton, OR; *Format:* Sports; *No. News Employees:* 1; *Target Audience:* 25-54; upscale adults; *Adv. Rates:* 23; 19; 21; 17
Randy McKone, President
J.J. Ford, Operations Dir
John Thomas, Programming Director

KUMA
08-25-1955; 1290 kHz AM; *Hrs Open:* 24; 5 kw-D, DAN; 5 kw-N, DAN; N45 40 25 W118 44 48
2003 NW 56th Drive, Pendleton, OR 97801 US

(541) 276-1511; *Fax:* (541) 276-1480
www.1290kuma.com
jthompson@cappsbroadcastgroup.com
License: Pendleton, OR held by Round-Up Radio Inc.
Group Owner: Capps Broadcast Group; (acq 7-1-93; $340,000 with co-located FM;
Regional Reps: Tacher.
Arbitron Metro Market: Pendleton, OR; *Format:* News, Talk
Special Programming: Farm 10 hrs wkly; *Hrs. of News Programming:* news progmg 20 hrs wkly; *No. News Employees:* 1; *Target Audience:* 25 plus; adults
Dave Capps, President
Randy McKone, Operations Dir
Julie Thompson, Sales Manager
Butch Thurman, News and Sports Director
J.J. Ford, Operations Manager
Stacie Cummings, Traffic Director

KWHT
05-01-1984; 103.5 MHz FM; *Hrs Open:* 24; 100 kw; 719 ft.; N45 48 2 W118 22 36
2003 NW 56th Street, Pendleton, OR 97801 US
(541) 276-1511
www.1035kwheat.com
License: Pendleton, Umatilla County, OR held by KSRV, Inc.
Group Owner: Capps Broadcast Group
Nat'l Network: ABC
Arbitron Metro Market: Pendleton, OR; *Format:* Country; *Hrs. of News Programming:* News progmg 2 hrs wkly; *Target Audience:* 25-54; adults
Randy McKone, General Manager
Julie Thompson, General Sales Mgr
Emily Jaceks, News Director
J.J. Ford, Engineering Dir
Connie Shurtleff, Engineer
Joe Oertel, Sports Director

Phoenix

KAKT
01-01-1991; 105.1 MHz FM; *Hrs Open:* 24; 52 kw; 545 ft.; N42 25 41 W123 0 4
1438 Rossanley Dr., Medford, OR 97501 US
(541) 779-1550
www.thewolf1051.com
bbishop@radiomedford.com
License: Phoenix, Jackson County, OR held by Mapleton License of Medford LLC.
Group Owner: Mapleton Communications LLC; (acq 10-26-2001; grpsl)
Arbitron Metro Market: Medford, OR; *Format:* Country; *No. News Employees:* 1; *Target Audience:* 25-49; female
Joe Mussio, General Sales Mgr
Brian Bishop, Programming Director

***KAPL**
01-02-1977; 1300 kHz AM; 20 kw-D, DAN; 5 kw-N, DAN; N42 17 44 W122 48 15
P.O. Box 1090, Jacksonville, OR 97530 US
(541) 899-5275
www.kaplradio.org
staff@kaplradio.com
License: Phoenix, OR held by Applegate Media Inc.
Arbitron Metro Market: Jacksonville, OR; *Format:* Christian, News, 62, Talk; *Target Audience:* 25-54.
Chris Thompson, General Manager

KCMX
04-07-1962; 880 kHz AM; *Hrs Open:* 24; 1 kw-U, ND1; N42 18 36 W122 48 41
1438 Rossanley Dr., Medford, OR 97501 US
(541) 779-1550
www.kcmxam.com
License: Phoenix, OR held by Mapleton License of Medford LLC.
Group Owner: Mapleton Communications LLC; (acq 10-26-2001; grpsl)
Regional Reps: Art Moore.
Arbitron Metro Market: Medford, OR; *Format:* News, Talk; *No. News Employees:* 1; *Target Audience:* 18 plus.

Pilot Rock

KUMA-FM
10-01-1978; 92.1 MHz FM; 6.9 kw; 633 ft.; N45 35 21 W118 59 54
2003 NW 56th Drive, Pendleton, OR 97801 US
(541) 276-1511
www.mycolumbiabasin.com
License: Pilot Rock, Umatilla County, OR held by UMA, LLC
Group Owner: Capps Broadcast Group
Nat'l Network: ABC
Arbitron Metro Market: Pilot Rock, OR; *Format:* Adult Contemp; *Target Audience:* 18 plus.; *Adv. Rates:* 26; 20; 24; 15
Julie Thompson, Sales Manager
J.J. Ford, Programming Director
Butch Thurman, News and Sports Director
Stacie Cummings, Traffic Director

Pine Grove

***KPFR**
06-22-2005; 89.5 MHz FM; *Hrs Open:* 24; 7 kw vert; 1673 ft.; N45 19 58 W121 42 48
Mailing Address: 1425 N Market Blvd, Suite 9, Sacramento, CA 95834 US
Second Address: 290 Hegenberger Rd., Oakland, CA 94621
(800) 543-1495; *Fax:* (916) 641-8238
www.familyradio.com
info@familyradio.com
License: Pine Grove, Hood River County, OR held by Family Stations Inc.
Group Owner: Family Stations Inc.; (acq 9-9-2002).
Arbitron Metro Market: Portland, OR; *Format:* Christian, Religious
Harold Camping, President

Portland

KBNP
01-01-1949; 1410 kHz AM; *Hrs Open:* 24; 5 kw-D, ND1; 0.009 kw-N, ND1; N45 28 24 W122 39 36
278 S.W. Arthur Street, Portland, OR 97201 US
(503) 223-6769; *Fax:* (503) 223-4305
www.kbnp.com
kbnp@kbnp.com
License: Portland, OR held by 2nd Amendment Foundation.
Arbitron Metro Market: Portland, OR; *Format:* News *Special Programming:* People w/disabilities, computer shows, home improv; *Hrs. of News Programming:* news progmg 163 hrs wkly; *No. News Employees:* 2 *TargetAudience:* General; corporations & individuals concerned with how-to's of making & keeping money; *Adv. Rates:* 75; 65; 75; 35
Keith Lyons, General Manager

***KBOO**
06-01-1968; 90.7 MHz FM; *Hrs Open:* 24; 25.5 kw; 1266 ft.; N45 29 20 W122 41 40
20 S.E. 8th Ave, Portland, OR 97214 US
(503) 231-8032; *Fax:* (503) 231-7145
kboo.fm
program@kboo.org
License: Portland, Multnomah County, OR held by KBOO Foundation.
Arbitron Metro Market: Portland, OR; *Format:* Variety/Diverse *Special Programming:* Sp 10 hrs, Indian one hr, ethnic 4 hrs, African/r; *Hrs. of News Programming:* news progmg 5 hrs wkly; *No. News Employees:* 2 *Target Audience:* General.
Arthur Davis, General Manager
Justin Miller, General Sales Mgr
Chris Merrick, Programming Director
John Mackey, Chief Engineer
Denise Kowalczyk, General Manager

***KBPS**
03-23-1923; 1450 kHz AM; *Hrs Open:* 18; 1 kw-D, ND2; 1 kw-N, ND2; N45 31 38 W122 39 3
515 N.E. 15th Avenue, Portland, OR 97232 US
(503) 916-5830; *Fax:* (503) 916-2642
www.allclassical.org
music.info@allclassical.org
License: Portland, OR held by School District No. 1 Multnomah County, OR.
Arbitron Metro Market: Portland, OR; *Format:* Children *Special Programming:* Sp one hr wkly; *Hrs. of News Programming:* News progmg one hr wkly
Sally Lewis, General Sales Mgr

***KQAC**
08-01-1983; 89.9 MHz FM; *Hrs Open:* 24; 5.9 kw; 1444 ft.; N45 30 58 W122 43 59
515 N.E. 15th Avenue, Portland, OR 97232 US
(503) 943-5828; *Fax:* (503) 802-9456
www.allclassical.org
License: Portland, Multnomah County, OR held by KBPS Public Radio Foundation
Nat'l Network: PRI
Arbitron Metro Market: Portland, OR; *Format:* Classical; *Hrs. of News Programming:* News progmg 5 hrs wkly
Jack Allen, CEO/COO
John Burk, Programming Director
Larry Holtz, Chief Engineer
Kelly Palin, Chief Financial Officer
Deborah Rochord, Director, Member Services

***KBVM**
88.3 MHz FM; *Hrs Open:* 24; 3.5 kw; 1434 ft.; N45 30 58 W122 43 59
Mailing Address: P. O. Box 5888, Portland, OR 97228 US
Second Address: 5000 N. Willamette, msc 160, Portland, OR 97203
(503) 285-5200; *Fax:* (503) 285-3322
www.kbvm.fm
info@kbvm.fm
License: Portland, Multnomah County, OR held by Catholic Broadcasting NW Inc.
Arbitron Metro Market: Portland, OR; *Format:* Religious *Special Programming:* Sp 14 hrs wkly; *Target Audience:* General; anyone desiring Christian music, inspiration, Catholic prayer & evangelism
Tony Galati, Executive Director
David Endres, Development Director
Dina Marie Hale, Programming Director
James Boyd, Chief Engineer

KPOJ
03-25-1922; 620 kHz AM; *Hrs Open:* 24; 25 kw-D, DA2; 10 kw-N, DA2; N45 25 20 W122 33 57
13333 S.W. 68th Pkwy., Suite 310, Tigard, OR 97223 US
(503) 323-6400
www.ripcityradio.com
License: Portland, Multnomah County, OR held by Citicasters Licenses Inc.
Group Owner: iHeartMedia; (acq 1999; grpsl).
Nat'l Network: ABC
Arbitron Metro Market: Portland, OR; *Format:* Sports; *Target Audience:* 25-54.
David Hill, Programming Director
Diana Hryciw, Promotions Manager

KEX
12-24-1926; 1190 kHz AM; *Hrs Open:* 24; 50 kw-D, DAN; 50 kw-N, DAN; N45 25 20 W122 33 57
1333 S.W. 68th Pkwy., Suite 310, Tigard, OR 97223 US
(503) 323-6400
www.1190kex.com
License: Portland, Multnomah County, OR held by Citicasters Licenses Inc.
Group Owner: iHeartMedia
Arbitron Metro Market: Portland, OR; *Format:* News, News/Talk, 86 *Special Programming:* Portland Trailblazers basketball; *Hrs. of News Programming:* News progmg 25 hrs wkly; *Target Audience:* 25-54; general
David Hill, Programming Director
Diana Hryciw, Promotions Manager

KGON
12-01-1967; 92.3 MHz FM; *Hrs Open:* 24; 97 kw; 1266 ft.; N45 29 20 W122 41 40
700 SW Bancroft St., Portland, OR 97239 US
(503) 223-1441; *Fax:* (503) 223-6909
www.kgon.com
jhutchison@entercom.com
License: Portland, Multnomah County, OR held by Entercom Portland License LLC.
Group Owner: Entercom Communications Corp.; (acq 8-1-95; grpsl)
Nat'l Reps: D & R Radio
Arbitron Metro Market: Portland, OR; *Format:* Classic Rock; *Hrs. of News Programming:* news progmg one hr wkly; *No. News Employees:* 3
Ryan Cooley, General Sales Mgr
Bob Harlow, Programming Director
Tim McNamara, Marketing Manager
Bonnie Knox, Music Director

KINK
12-24-1968; 101.9 MHz FM; *Hrs Open:* 24; 99 kw; 1,646 ft.; N45 30 58.4 W122 43 58.8
1211 S.W. 5th Ave., 6th Fl., Portland, OR 97204 US
(503) 517-6000; *Fax:* (503) 517-6401
www.kink.fm
License: Portland, Multnomah County, OR held by Alpha Media Licensee LLC
Group Owner: Alpha Media LLC
Nat'l Network: AP Radio
Arbitron Metro Market: Portland, OR; *Format:* Triple A; *Hrs. of News Programming:* news progmg 3 hrs wkly; *No. News Employees:* 2; *Target Audience:* 25-54; primary, secondary
Milt McConnell, General Manager
Jerome LaChance, Director of Sales
Scott Mahalick, Programming Director
Derek House, Marketing/Promotions Director
Sheila Hamilton, News Director
Torden Wall, National Digital Sales Manager
JaleneBrooks, Sales Account Executive

Cathy Hanauska, Sales Account Executive
Tom Mittelstaedt, Sales Account Executive
Shannon Rodriguez, Sales Account Executive

KKPZ
11-12-1923; 1330 kHz AM; *Hrs Open:* 5 am-12 am (M-F); 6 am-12 am (S, Su; 5 kw-U, DA1; N45 27 13 W122 32 45
9700 SE Eastview Drive, Happy Valley, OR 97086 US
(503) 242-1330; *Fax:* (503) 242-1950
www.kkpz.com
License: Portland, OR held by KPHP Radio Inc.
Group Owner: Crawford Broadcasting Co.; (acq 1995; $2 million)
Arbitron Metro Market: Portland, OR; *Format:* Christian, Talk
Special Programming: Hispanic Christian talk, Hispanic Christian music; *Target Audience:* 34-54.
Donald Crawford Sr., President
Sunny Hudson, General Manager
James Autry, Station Manager
John White, Chief Engineer

KKRZ
05-01-1946; 100.3 MHz FM; 95 kw; 1542 ft.; N45 31 21 W122 44 45
13333 SW 68th Parkway, Tigard, OR 97223 US
(503) 226-0100; *Fax:* (503) 295-9281
www.z100portland.com
License: Portland, Multnomah County, OR held by Citicasters Licenses Inc.
Group Owner: iHeartMedia
Arbitron Metro Market: Portland, OR; *Format:* Contemporary Hits/Top 40; *Target Audience:* 18-49.
Marshal Burgess, Vice President of Sales
Justin Riley, Programming Director
Geoff Owens, Promotions Director

KYCH-FM
04-01-1980; 97.1 MHz FM; 97 kw; 1266 ft.; N45 29 20 W122 41 40
401 City Avenue, Suite 409, Bala Cynwyd, PA 10004 US
(503) 223-1441; *Fax:* (503) 223-6909
www.charliefm.com
cryan@entercom.com
License: Portland, Multnomah County, OR held by Entercom Portland License L.L.C.
Group Owner: Entercom Communications Corp.; (acq 4-23-98; grpsl)
Nat'l Reps: Christal
Arbitron Metro Market: Portland, OR; *Format:* Adult Contemp; *Target Audience:* 25-54.
Eric Simantel, General Sales Mgr
Mark Hamilton, Programming Director
Katy Moore, Promotions Manager
Gary Hilliard, Chief Engineer
Tim McNamara, Marketing Manager

***KOPB-FM**
01-01-1962; 91.5 MHz FM; 70 kw; 1542 ft.; N45 31 21 W122 44 45
7140 S.W. Macadam Ave., Portland, OR 97219 US
(503) 293-1905; *Fax:* (503) 293-1919
www.opb.org
opbnews@opb.org
License: Portland, Multnomah County, OR held by Oregon Public Broadcasting.
Nat'l Network: NPR; PRI
Arbitron Metro Market: Portland, OR *TV Affiliate:* *KOPB-TV affil.; *Format:* News; *Hrs. of News Programming:* news progmg 146 hrs wkly; *No. News Employees:* 5; *Target Audience:* 34-54.
Jack Galmiche, COO
Virginia Breen, Operations Dir

KFXX
01-17-1925; 1080 kHz AM
700 SW Bancroft St., Portland, OR 97239 US
(503) 223-1441; *Fax:* (503) 223-6909
www.1080thefan.com
License: Portland, OR held by Entercom Portland License LLC.
Group Owner: Entercom Communications Corp.; (acq 12-18-2003; $44 million with co-located FM)
Arbitron Metro Market: Portland, OR; *Format:* Sports; *Target Audience:* 25-54.
Ryan Cooley, General Sales Mgr
Jeff Austin, Programming Director
Alicia Shroyer, Promotions Manager
Tim McNamara, Marketing Manager

KPDQ
07-30-1947; 800 kHz AM; *Hrs Open:* 24
6400 SE Lake Rd., Suite 350, Portland, OR 97222 US
(503) 786-0600; *Fax:* (503) 786-1551
www.kpdq.am
License: Portland, OR held by Salem Media of Oregon Inc.
Group Owner: Salem Communications Corp.
Arbitron Metro Market: Portland, OR; *Format:* Christian, Talk; *Target Audience:* 18-54; listeners of talk
Dennis Hayes, General Manager
Segar Kannan, General Sales Mgr
Justin Mansfield, Programming Director
Laura Ahumada, Promotions Manager

KPDQ-FM
01-01-1961; 93.9 MHz FM; *Hrs Open:* 24; 50 kw; 1270 ft.; N45 29 20 W122 41 40
4880 Santa Rosa Rd, #300, Camarillo, CA 93012 US
(503) 786-0600; *Fax:* (503) 786-1551
www.kpdq.com
License: Portland, Multnomah County, OR held by Salem Media of Oregon Inc.
Group Owner: Salem Communications Corp.; (acq 8-86; grpsl;
Arbitron Metro Market: Portland, OR; *Format:* Christian, Talk; *Target Audience:* 25-54; listeners of Christian talk progmg
Dennis Hayes, General Manager
Segar Kannan, General Sales Mgr
Justin Mansfield, Programming Director
Laura Ahumada, Promotions Manager
Georgene Rice, News Director
Don Perkins, Chief Engineer

***KXRY**
05-01-1958; 91.1 MHz FM; 0.0082 kw; 13 ft.; N45 28 51 W122 37 50
3203 Se Woodstock Blvd., Portland, OR 97202 US
(773) 332-6534; *Fax:* (503) 777-7769
License: Portland, Multnomah County, OR held by Common Frequency Inc.
Group Owner: Common Frequency Inc.; (acq 1959)
Arbitron Metro Market: Southest Portland *Special Programming:* Black 10 hrs, class 4 hrs, country 2 hrs, Fr 2 hrs; *Target Audience:* 17-21; Reed College student body
Kristin Holmberg, Operations Dir
Nicholas Wright, General Manager

KUPL
01-01-1948; 98.7 MHz FM; *Hrs Open:* 24; 24 kw; 1,647 ft.; N45 30 58.4 W122 43 58.7
1211 S.W. 5th Ave., Portland, OR 97204 US
(503) 517-6000; *Fax:* (503) 517-6401
www.987thebull.com
License: Portland, Multnomah County, OR held by Alpha Media Licensee LLC
Group Owner: Alpha Media LLC; (acq 8-7-2009; grpsl).
Nat'l Network: AP Radio
Arbitron Metro Market: Portland, OR; *Format:* Country; *No. News Employees:* 1; *Target Audience:* 25-54.
Milt McConnell, General Manager
Cressy Walton, General Sales Mgr
Scott Mahalick, Programming Director
Danny Dwyer, Promotions Manager
Amy Leimbach, Director of Sales
Randi P'Pool, Marketing Director
Karli Dirksen, PromotionsCoordinator

KWJJ-FM
01-01-1968; 99.5 MHz FM; 50 kw; 1266 ft.; N45 29 20 W122 41 40
700 SW Bancroft St., Portland, OR 97239 US
(503) 223-1441; *Fax:* (503) 223-6909
www.thewolfonline.com
info@thewolfonline.com
License: Portland, Multnomah County, OR held by Entercom Portland License LLC.
Group Owner: Entercom Communications Corp.
Arbitron Metro Market: Portland, OR; *Format:* Country; *Target Audience:* 25-54.
David Field, President
Erin Hubert, General Manager
Jerome Lachance, General Sales Mgr
Mike Moore, Programming Director

KXTG
06-18-1965; 750 kHz AM; *Hrs Open:* 24; 50 kw-D, DA2; 20 kw-N, DA2; 990 ft.; N45 24 5 W122 26 47
1211 S.W. 5th Ave., 6th Fl., Portland, OR 97204 US
(503) 517-6000; *Fax:* (503) 517-6401
www.750thegame.com
License: Portland, Multnomah County, OR held by Alpha Media Licensee LLC
Group Owner: Alpha Media LLC
Nat'l Network: CBS Sports Radio
Arbitron Metro Market: Portland, OR; *Format:* Sports
Joel Krebs, Sales Manager
Joe Olson, Digital Content Manager

KXET(AM)
1150 kHz AM; 5000 watts; non-directional; 45 38 34N 122 36 50W
15240 SE 82nd Drive, Clackamas, OR 97015 USA
(503) 234-5550; *Fax:* (503) 234-5583
License: Portland, Multnomah County, OR
Group Owner: Bustos Media Holdings L.L.C.

Terry Tario, General Manager

KBFF
09-25-1960; 95.5 MHz FM; 97 kw; 1,266 ft.; N45 29 20 W122 41 40
1211 S.W. 5th Ave., Suite 600, Portland, OR 97204 US
(503) 517-6000; *Fax:* (503) 517-6401
www.live955.com
License: Portland, Multnomah County, OR held by Alpha Media Licensee LLC
Group Owner: Alpha Media LLC
Arbitron Metro Market: Portland, OR; *Format:* Contemporary Hits/Top 40
Milt McConnell, General Manager
Cressy Walton, General Sales Mgr
Phil Becker, Programming Director
Kelsey McDaniel, Promotions Director
Amy Leimbach, Director of Sales
Joe Olson, Digital Content

KXL-FM
09-12-1948; 101.1 MHz FM; 97 kw; 1,647 ft.; N45 30 58 W122 43 59
1211 S.W. 5th Ave., 6th Fl., Portland, OR 97204 US
(503) 517-6000; *Fax:* (503) 517-6401
www.kxl.com
License: Portland, Multnomah County, OR held by Alpha Media Licensee LLC
Group Owner: Alpha Media LLC
Arbitron Metro Market: Portland, OR; *Format:* News, News/Talk, 86
Milt McConnell, General Manager
Joel Krebs, General Sales Mgr
Scott Mahalick, Programming Director
Derek House, Marketing and Promotions Director
Rebecca Marshall, News Director
Amy Leimbach, Director of Sales
Joe Olson, DigitalContent Manager
Chris Brown, Morning News Producer
Jim Ferretti, Afternoon News Producer

KUFO
03-01-1941; 970 kHz AM; 5 kw-D, DAN; 5 kw-N, DAN; N45 30 56 W122 43 56
1211 S.W. 5th Ave., Suite 600, Portland, OR 97204 US
(503) 517-6000; *Fax:* (503) 517-6401
www.freedom970.com
License: Portland, Multnomah County, OR held by Alpha Media Licensee LLC
Group Owner: Alpha Media LLC
Arbitron Metro Market: Portland, OR; *Format:* Talk
Milt McConnell, General Manager
Joel Krebs, General Sales Mgr
Amy Leimbach, Director of Sales

Prineville

KLTW-FM
04-08-1981; 95.7 MHz FM; *Hrs Open:* 24; 100 kw; 182 meters; N44 04 40 W121 19 49 *Rebroadcasts:* Translators: 104.5 mhz Bend, OR and 104.5 mhz Madras, OR
854 NE 4th St., Bend, OR 97754 97701
(541) 383-3825; *Fax:* (541) 383-3403
www.957myfm.com
License: Prineville, Crook County, OR held by Horizon Broadcasting Group LLC.
Group Owner: Horizon Broadcasting Group, LLC; (acq 2000)
Nat'l Reps: Christal
Population Served: 200,000; *Arbitron Metro Market:* Bend, OR; *Format:* Adult Contemp *Special Programming:* Inside Central Oregon (Public Affairs); *No. News Employees:* 3; *Target Audience:* 25-54.
Robin Fox, Programming Director

KRCO
02-01-1950; 690 kHz AM; *Hrs Open:* 24 *Rebroadcasts:* Translator: 96.9 mhz Prineville, OR
854 NE 4th St., Bend, OR 97701 US
(541) 447-6770; *Fax:* (541) 383-3403
www.krcoam.com
dclemens@horizonbroadcastinggroup.com
License: Prineville, OR held by Horizon Broadcasting Group LLC

Group Owner: Horizon Broadcasting Group, LLC; (acq 3-2-2000; grpsl)
Nat'l Network: ABC; *Nat'l Reps:* Christal
Arbitron Metro Market: Bend, OR; *Format:* Country; *No. News Employees:* 3; *Target Audience:* 35-64.
Keith Shipman, General Manager
Kenn Brown, General Sales Mgr
Dave Clemens, Promotions Manager

KNLX
01-01-2008; 104.9 MHz FM; 0.86 kW; 2215 ft.; N44 26 13 W120 57 11
PO Box 7408, Bend, OR 97708 USA
(541) 389-8873; *Fax:* (541) 389-5291
www.knlr.com
info@knlr.com
License: Prineville, Crook County, OR held by Cowan Broadcasting LLC
Arbitron Metro Market: Prineville, OR; *Format:* Christian
Terry Cowan, General Manager

Redmond

KLRR
06-17-1985; 101.7 MHz FM; 23 kw; 732 ft.; N44 4 39 W121 19 57
63088 NE 18th St., Bend, OR 97701 USA
(541) 382-5263; *Fax:* (541) 388-0456
License: Redmond, OR held by Combined Communications.
Group Owner: Combined Communications
Format: Triple A *Special Programming:* Jazz 5 hrs wkly; *Target Audience:* 25-54; upscale, professional women & men
Chuck Chackel, CEO/COO
Mike Cheney, General Manager
Christine Limburg, General Sales Mgr
Lori Raab, News Director

KSJJ
02-04-1981; 102.9 MHz FM; *Hrs Open:* 24; 100 kw; 886 ft.; N44 2 49 W121 31 50
345 SW Cyber Dr., Suite 101, Bend, OR 97702-1134 US
(541) 388-3300; *Fax:* (541) 388-3303
www.ksjj1029.com
ahilmes@bendradiogroup.com
License: Redmond, OR held by GCC Bend, LLC.
Group Owner: GCC Bend, LLC; (acq 1999; grpsl).
Arbitron Metro Market: Bend, OR; *Format:* Country
Andy Hilmes, General Sales Mgr
Mike Flanagan, Programming Director
Dir. of Promotions, Promotions Manager

*KWRX
01-01-2002; 88.5 MHz FM; 0.95 kw; 2198 ft.; N44 26 14 W120 57 12
139 Susan Campell Hall, Un of Oregon, Eugene, OR 97403 US
(541) 345-0800
www.kwax.com
inquiry@kwax.com
License: Redmond, Deschutes County, OR held by State Board of Higher Education for the University of Oregon.
Arbitron Metro Market: Eugene, OR; *Format:* Classical
Paul Bjornstad, General Manager

KRDM
06-01-2004; 1240 kHz AM; *Hrs Open:* 24
Mailing Address: US
Second Address: 416 S.W. Black Bute Blvd., Redmond, OR 97756
(541) 548-7621; *Fax:* (541) 504-8145
www.radiolabronca.com
License: Redmond, OR held by Red Mountain Broadcasting LLC
Arbitron Metro Market: Redmond, OR; *Format:* Tejano; *Adv. Rates:* 18; 14; 18; 8
Juan Zendejas, President
Selene Zendejas, News Director

*KKJA
07-18-2008; 89.9 MHz FM; 1.5 kw; 2208 ft.; N44 26 17 W120 57 14 *Rebroadcasts:* Rebroadcasts KAWZ(FM) Twin Falls, ID 100%
Mailing Address: P.O. Box 391, Twin Falls, ID 83303 US
Second Address: 4002 North 3300 East, Twin Falls, ID 83301
(208) 734-6633; *Fax:* (208) 736-1958
www.csnradio.com
License: Redmond, Deschutes County, OR held by Calvary Chapel of Twin Falls, Inc.
Group Owner: CSN International
Arbitron Metro Market: San Antonio, TX; *Format:* Christian, Religious
Mike Kestler, President
Daniel Davidson, Operations Dir
Joe Jennings, Station Manager & Program Director
Mike Stocklin, Underwriting Director
Kelly Carlson, Engineering Dir

Reedsport

*KLFR
01-01-1999; 89.1 MHz FM; *Hrs Open:* 24; 1 kw; 400 ft; N43 43 21 W124 05 40
136 W. 8th Ave., Eugene, OR 38803
(541) 463-6000; *Fax:* (541) 463-6046
www.klcc.org
klcc@klcc.org
License: Reedsport, Douglas County, OR held by Lane Community College
Steve Barton, General Manager
Cheryl Crumbley, General Sales Mgr
Don Heim, Programming Director
Gayle Chisholm, Promotions Manager

KDUN
06-02-1961; 1030 kHz AM; *Hrs Open:* 24
1159 Fair Oaks Avenue, Arroyo Grande, CA 93420 US
(541) 271-1030; *Fax:* (541) 271-2598
traffic.kdun@gmail.com
License: Reedsport, OR held by Sand & Sea Broadcasting LLC
Nat'l Network: CBS Radio *Regional Reps:* McGavren-Guild
Arbitron Metro Market: Eugene, OR; *Format:* News, Talk; *Target Audience:* 25 plus.; *Adv. Rates:* 30; 25; 20; 10
Joe Zelinski, Operations Dir
Bill Schweitzer, General Manager
Michael Nadeau, Business Manager

*KSYD
03-01-1990; 92.1 MHz FM; *Hrs Open:* 24; 0.3 kw; 358 ft.; N43 39 26 W124 11 10 *Rebroadcasts:* KRVM FM 92.1
200 North Monroe, Eugene, OR 97402 US
(541) 790-6686; *Fax:* (541) 790-5786
www.krvm.org
info@krvm.org
License: Reedsport, Douglas County, OR held by School District 4J Lane County.
Arbitron Metro Market: Eugene, OR; *Format:* Triple A; *Target Audience:* 12-40.
Carl Sundberg, General Manager
Randy Larson, Station Manager
Bobbie Cirel, General Sales Mgr
Ken Martin, Programming Director
Randy Larson, Chief Engineer

Rockaway Beach

*KLON
01-01-2005; 90.3 MHz FM; *Hrs Open:* 24; 1.8 kw vert; 342 ft.; N45 36 18 W123 55 30 *Rebroadcasts:* Rebroadcasts KLVR(FM) Santa Rosa, CA 100%
1425 N Market Blvd., Suite 9, Sacramento, CA 95834 US
(800) 525-5683; *Fax:* (916) 251-1650
www.klove.com
klove@klove.com
License: Rockaway Beach, Tillamook County, OR held by Educational Media Foundation.
Group Owner: EMF Broadcasting
Nat'l Network: K-Love
Arbitron Metro Market: Rockaway Beach, OR; *Format:* Christian; *No. News Employees:* 13; *Target Audience:* 25-44; Judeo Christian, female
Darrell Chambliss, Chairman
Mike Novak, President and CEO
Mike Lee, General Sales Mgr
David Pierce, Programming Director
Ed Lenane, News Director
Sam Wallington, Engineering Dir
Marya Morgan, News Reporter
Richard Hunt, NewsReporter
Dan Antonelli, Chief Business Development Officer
Eric Moser, Chief Financial Officer
Brian Burger, Vice President of Human Resources
D. Kevin Blair, Secretary and General Counsel

Rogue River

KRRM
10-01-1994; 94.7 MHz FM; *Hrs Open:* 24; 130 w; 2,043 ft; N42 26 44 W123 12 56
225 Rogue River Hwy., Grants Pass, OR 97527
(541) 479-6497; *Fax:* (541) 479-5726
www.krrm.com
krrm@krrm.com
License: Rogue River, Jackson County, OR held by Shirley M. Bell.
Population Served: 99,100; *Arbitron Metro Market:* Medford-Ashland, OR; *Target Audience:* 35 plus.
Herb Bell, General Manager
Shirley Bell, General Sales Mgr

Roseburg

KQEN
09-19-1950; 1240 kHz AM; *Hrs Open:* 24; 1 kw-U, ND1; N43 11 35 W123 21 39
1445 W. Harvard Ave., Roseburg, OR 97471 US
(541) 673-4464; *Fax:* (541) 673-7598
www.541radio.com
License: Roseburg, OR held by Brooke Communications Inc.
Group Owner: Brooke Communications Inc.; acq 5-1-86; $173,000)
Nat'l Network: ESPN Radio; *Nat'l Reps:* Tacher
Format: News/Talk; *Hrs. of News Programming:* news progmg 4 hrs wkly; *No. News Employees:* 2; *Target Audience:* 35 plus; general; *Adv. Rates:* 17; 17; 17; 17
Kyle Bailey, Programming Director
Ashley Smith, Promotions Manager
Kyle Bailey, News Director

KSKR
06-01-1935; 1490 kHz AM; *Hrs Open:* 24; 1 kw; N43 11 35 W123 21 39
1445 W. Harvard Ave., Roseburg, OR 97471 US
(541) 440-0101; *Fax:* (541) 673-7598
www.541radio.com
License: Roseburg, OR held by Brooke Communications Inc.
Group Owner: Brooke Communications Inc.; (acq 1-14-2005)
Nat'l Network: ESPN Radio; *Nat'l Reps:* Tacher
Format: Sports; *No. News Employees:* 2; *Target Audience:* 25 plus.
Ashley Smith, Promotions Manager
Kyle Bailey, News Director

KRSB-FM
10-01-1970; 103.1 MHz FM; *Hrs Open:* 24; 2.75 kw; 308 ft.; N43 12 24 W123 21 47
1445 W. Harvard Ave., Roseburg, OR 97471 US
(541) 440-9103; *Fax:* (541) 673-7598
www.541radio.com
License: Roseburg, Douglas County, OR held by Brooke Communications Inc.
Group Owner: Brooke Communications Inc.; acq 4-30-89)
Nat'l Network: ABC; *Nat'l Reps:* Tacher
Arbitron Metro Market: Roseburg, OR; *Format:* Country; *Hrs. of News Programming:* news progmg 15 hrs wkly; *No. News Employees:* 2; *Target Audience:* 25-54.; *Adv. Rates:* 19; 19; 19; 19
Ashley Smith, Promotions Manager
Kyle Bailey, News Director

*KSRS
12-01-1990; 91.5 MHz FM; *Hrs Open:* 5 AM-2 AM; 2 kw; 305 ft.; N43 12 22 W123 21 48
P.O. Box 3175, Eugene, OR 97403 US
(541) 552-6301; *Fax:* (541) 552-8565
www.ijpr.org
info@ijpr.org
License: Roseburg, Douglas County, OR held by The State of Oregon, Acting By and Through the State Board of Higher Education, for the benefit of Southern Oregon University.
Nat'l Network: NPR; PRI; *Wire Services:* AP
Arbitron Metro Market: Ashland, OR; *Format:* News; *Hrs. of News Programming:* news progmg 35 hrs wkly; *No. News Employees:* 1; *Target Audience:* General.
Ronald Kramer, CEO
Bryon Lambert, Operations Dir
Paul Westhelle, General Sales Mgr
Ransom,Darin, Engineering Dir

*KTBR
11-01-1955; 950 kHz AM; *Hrs Open:* 24 hrs
P.O. Box 1760, Roseburg, OR 97470 US
(541) 552-6301
www.ijpr.org
info@ijpr.org
License: Roseburg, OR held by JPR Foundation Inc.
Nat'l Network: NPR; PRI
Arbitron Metro Market: Ashland, OR; *Format:* News; *No. News Employees:* 1; *Target Audience:* General.
Ronald Kramer, CEO
Bryon Lambert, Operations Dir
Paul Westhelle, General Sales Mgr
Ransom,Darin, Engineering Dir
Mitchell Christian, CFO

***KMPQ**
11-24-2004; 88.1 MHz FM; 950 w; Ant 351 ft; N43 12 22 W123 21 50
136 W. 8th Ave., Eugene, OR 97405
(541) 463-6000; *Fax:* (541) 463-6046
www.klcc.org
klcc@klcc.org
License: Roseburg, Douglas County, OR held by Lane Community College.
Nat'l Network: NPR

Steve Barton, General Manager
Cheryl Crumbley, General Sales Mgr
Don Hein, Programming Director

Salem

KBZY
05-01-1957; 1490 kHz AM; *Hrs Open:* 24; 1 kw-U, ND1; N44 57 3 W123 2 43
2659 Commercial St. SE, Suite 204, Salem, OR 97302 US
(503) 362-1490; *Fax:* (503) 362-6545
www.kbzy.com
kbzy@com.net
License: Salem, OR held by Capital Broadcasting Inc.
Regional Reps: Tacher
Arbitron Metro Market: Salem, OR; *Format:* Oldies; *Target Audience:* 25-54.; *Adv. Rates:* 22; 16; 18; 16
Roy Dittman, President
Roy Dittman, General Manager
Terry Sol, Programming Director

KPJC
12-12-1961; 1220 kHz AM; *Hrs Open:* 24
4303 Market St., N.E., Salem, OR 97301 US
(503) 316-1220; *Fax:* (503) 364-1022
info@thejcmediagroup.com
License: Salem, OR held by KCCS LLC
Nat'l Network: USA; *Nat'l Reps:* Broadcast Reps Canada
Arbitron Metro Market: Salem, OR; *Format:* Christian; *Hrs. of News Programming:* News progmg 14 hrs wkly; *Target Audience:* 25-54; family
Phil Swearingin, Operations Dir
Christina Evans, General Manager

***KWBX**
04-01-2002; 90.3 MHz FM; *Hrs Open:* 24; 0.135 kw vert; 46 ft.; N44 52 57 W122 57 34
5000 Deer Park Drive Se, Salem, OR 97301 US
(503) 589-8197; *Fax:* (503) 585-4316
kwbx@corban.edu
License: Salem, Marion County, OR held by Corban College
Nat'l Network: Air 1
Arbitron Metro Market: Portland, OR; *Format:* Christian; *Hrs. of News Programming:* news progmg one hr wkly; *No. News Employees:* 1; *Target Audience:* 25-44; young adults
Josh Bartlett, COO
Reno Hoff, President
Steve Hunt, General Manager
Josh Bartlett, Station Manager
Steve Hunt, Vice President for Marketing

***KAJC**
01-01-2006; 90.1 MHz FM; *Hrs Open:* 24; 0.56 kw; 128 ft.; N44 45 33 W123 13 34
1475 Monmouth St, Independence, OR 97351 US
(503) 837-1000; *Fax:* (503) 838-2476
www.kajcfm.org
kajc@kajcfm.org
License: Salem, Marion County, OR held by Calvary Chapel Monmouth Independence
Arbitron Metro Market: Salem, OR; *Format:* Christian, Religious

Sandy

***KZRI**
01-01-1997; 88.7 MHz FM; *Hrs Open:* 24; 3.7 kw; 1742 ft.; N45 20 1 W121 42 45 *Rebroadcasts:* Rebroadcasts KLVR(FM) Middletown, CA 100%
1425 N Market Blvd, Suite 9, Sacramento, CA 95834 US
(707) 528-9236; *Fax:* (707) 528-9246
www.klove.com
klove@klove.com
License: Sandy, Clackamas County, OR held by Educational Media Foundation.
Group Owner: EMF Broadcasting
Nat'l Network: K-Love
Arbitron Metro Market: Portland, OR; *Format:* Christian; *No. News Employees:* 3; *Target Audience:* 25-44; Judeo-Christian, female
Darell Chambliss, Chairman
Mike Novak, President

Scappoose

KFIS
05-01-1986; 104.1 MHz FM; 6.9 kw; 1266 ft.; N45 29 20 W122 41 40
190 Queen Anne Avenue North, Suite 100, Seattle, WA 98109 US
(503) 786-0600; *Fax:* (503) 786-1551
www.1041thefish.com
License: Scappoose, Columbia County, OR held by Caron Broadcasting Inc.
Group Owner: Salem Communications Corp.; (acq 9-20-2001; $35.8 million).
Format: Christian; *Target Audience:* 25-54; women
Dennis Hayes, General Manager
Segar Kannan, General Sales Mgr
Chris Kelly, Programming Director
Laura Ahumada, Promotions Manager
Beckii Schiffer, Webmaster

Seaside

KCYS
11-26-1996; 96.5 MHz FM; *Hrs Open:* 24; 6 kw; 328 ft; N45 57 11 W123 56 14
Mailing Address: Box 1258, Astoria, OR 97103
Second Address: 1324 N. Holladay Dr., Seaside, OR 97138
(503) 717-9643; *Fax:* (503) 717-9578
License: Seaside, Clatsop County, OR held by Dave's Broadcasting Corp
Regional Reps: Tacher.
Population Served: 40,000 *Target Audience:* 35-44; working moms with kids, some college; *Adv. Rates:* 12; 12; 12; na
Dave Heick, General Manager

KSWB
07-12-1968; 840 kHz AM; 1 kw-D, ND1; 0.5 kw-N, ND1; N45 58 55 W123 55 2
P.O. Box 566, Hillsboro, OR 97138 US
(503) 738-8668; *Fax:* (503) 738-8778
License: Seaside, OR held by Cannon Beach Radio
Arbitron Metro Market: Seaside, OR; *Format:* Oldies
John Chapman, General Manager

KCRX-FM
01-01-1998; 102.3 MHz FM; 25 kw; 328 ft.; N45 57 8 W123 56 14
P.O. Bpx 566, Hillsboro, OR 97138 US
(503) 325-2911; *Fax:* (503) 325-5570
www.kcrx1023.com
kcrx@nnbradio.com
License: Seaside, Clatsop County, OR
Group Owner: Ohana Media Group LLC; acq 8-24-99; grpsl).
Arbitron Metro Market: Astoria, OR; *Format:* Classic Rock
Tom Freel, Operations Dir
Paul Mitchell, General Manager
Bob Castle, Programming Director

Selma

***KJKL**
01-01-2003; 88.7 MHz FM; 30 kw vert; 1916 ft.; N42 15 29 W123 39 32
1425 N Market Blvd, Suite 9, Sacrmento, CA 95834 US
(800) 525-5683; *Fax:* (916) 251-1650
www.klove.com
klove@klove.com
License: Selma, Josephine County, OR held by Educational Media Foundation.
Group Owner: EMF Broadcasting
Nat'l Network: K-Love
Arbitron Metro Market: Medford, OR; *Format:* Christian; *No. News Employees:* 3; *Target Audience:* 25-44; Judeo Christian, female
Darrell Chambliss, Chairman
Mike Novak, President and CEO
Mike Lee, Operations Dir
David Pierce, Programming Director
Ed Lenane, News Director
Sam Wallington, Engineering Dir
Marya Morgan, News Reporter
Richard Hunt, NewsReporter
Laura Daniels, News Reporter
Tim Luttrell, News Reporter
Kenny Noble Cortes, News Reporter
Darren Vinson, News Reporter

Shaniko

***KHJJ**
90.9 MHz FM; kw
US
(541) 815-1480
License: Shaniko, Wasco County, OR held by Educational Broadcast Service.
Arbitron Metro Market: Shaniko, OR
Dena Crane, President

Sisters

KWPK-FM
06-01-2001; 104.1 MHz FM; *Hrs Open:* 24; 34 kw; 591 ft.; N44 4 40 W121 19 49
854 NE 4th St., Bend, OR 97701 US
(541) 383-3825; *Fax:* (541) 383-3403
www.thepeak1041.com
License: Sisters, Deschutes County, OR held by Horizon Broadcasting Group LLC.
Group Owner: Horizon Broadcasting Group, LLC; (acq 3-31-2005; $475,000).
Nat'l Reps: Christal
Arbitron Metro Market: Bend, OR; *Format:* Adult Contemp
Special Programming: Inside Central Oregon (Public Affairs); *No. News Employees:* 3; *Target Audience:* 18-49.
Robin Fox, Programming Director

***KVRA**
01-01-2006; 89.3 MHz FM; 1.4 kw vert; 633 ft.; N44 4 40 W121 19 48 *Rebroadcasts:* Rebroadcasts KLRD(FM) Yucaipa, CA 100%
1425 N Market Blvd, Suite 9, Sacramento, CA 95834 US
(888) 937-2471; *Fax:* (916) 251-1650
www.air1.com
info@air1.com
License: Sisters, Deschutes County, OR held by Educational Media Foundation.
Group Owner: EMF Broadcasting
Nat'l Network: Air 1
Arbitron Metro Market: Sisters, OR; *Format:* Alternative, Christian
Darrell Chambliss, Chairman
Alan Mason, CEO/COO
Mike Novak, CEO
Mike Lee, Operations Dir
Ed Lenane, News Director
Sam Wallington, Engineering Dir
Marya Morgan, News Reporter
Richard Hunt, News Reporter
David Pierce, ChiefCreative Officer
Dan Antonelli, Chief Business Development Officer
Eric Moser, Chief Financial Officer
Brian Burger, Vice President of Human Resources

Springfield

***KQFE**
03-07-1989; 88.9 MHz FM; *Hrs Open:* 24; 1.25 kw; 951 ft.; N44 0 11 W123 6 48
Mailing Address: 4135 Northgate Blvd., Suite 1, Sacramento, CA 95834 US
Second Address: 290 Hegenberger Rd., Oakland, CA 94621
(916) 641-8191; *Fax:* (916) 641-8238
www.familyradio.com
info@familyradio.com
License: Springfield, Lane County, OR held by Family Stations Inc.
Group Owner: Family Stations Inc.
Nat'l Network: Family Radio
Arbitron Metro Market: Eugene-Springfi; *Format:* Christian; *Target Audience:* 30 plus; older relg
Jim Abrahamson, Operations Dir
Harold Camping, General Manager

Springfield-Eugene

KKNU
12-18-1958; 93.3 MHz FM; *Hrs Open:* 24; 100 kw horiz, 43 kw vert; 1296 ft.; N44 0 4 W123 6 45
925 Country Club Road, Eugene, OR 97401 US
(541) 484-9400; *Fax:* (541) 344-9424
www.kknu.com
License: Springfield-Eugene, Lane County, OR held by McKenzie River Broadcasting Co. Inc.
Group Owner: McKenzie River Broadcasting Company, Inc.; (acq 11-17-92; $1.01 million with KEED(AM) Eugene;
Nat'l Reps: D & R Radio
Arbitron Metro Market: Eugene, OR; *Format:* Country; *Target Audience:* 25-49; country life group

John Tilson, President
Dave Wiles, General Sales Mgr
Jim Davis, Programming Director

KORE
09-01-1927; 1050 kHz AM; *Hrs Open:* 24; 5 kw-D, ND1; 0.149 kw-N, ND1; N44 4 7 W123 1 45
2080 Laura Street, Springfield, OR 97477 US
(541) 747-5673
kore@kore1050am.com
License: Springfield-Eugene, OR held by Support Christian Broadcasting Inc.
Nat'l Network: USA
Arbitron Metro Market: Eugene-Springfield, OR; *Format:* Christian; *Target Audience:* 18 plus.
Larry Knight, General Manager
Sonny Starr, Programming Director
Linda Hill, Business Manager

St. Helens

KOHI
03-02-1960; 1600 kHz AM; *Hrs Open:* 24; 1 kw-D, ND1; 0.012 kw-N, ND1; N45 51 15 W122 49 11 *Rebroadcasts:* Talkstar Radio Network
P.O. Box 398, St. Helens, OR 97051 US
(503) 397-1600; *Fax:* (503) 397-1601
www.am1600kohi.com
kohiradio@gmail.com
License: St. Helens, OR held by Mountain Broadcasting LLC
Nat'l Reps: Keystone (unwired net)
Format: News, Sports, 86 *Special Programming:* Sports Talk, Religion; *Hrs. of News Programming:* news progmg 12 hrs wkly; *No. News Employees:* 1; *Target Audience:* Adults 25-65.; *Adv. Rates:* 25; 25; 25; 25
Marty Rowe, President
Alex Rowe, Programming Director

Stanfield

KLKY
01-01-2005; 96.1 MHz FM; 8.5 kw; 1178 ft.; N45 29 12 W119 25 52
US
(509) 527-1000; *Fax:* (509) 529-5534
www.urockfm.com
License: Stanfield, Umatilla County, OR held by Alexandra Communications Inc.
Group Owner: Alexandra Communications Inc.
Arbitron Metro Market: Stanfield, OR; *Format:* Contemporary Hits/Top 40
Tom Hodgins, General Manager

Stayton

KCKX
06-01-1987; 1460 kHz AM; *Hrs Open:* 24; 1 kw-D, ND1; 0.015 kw-N, ND1; N44 48 10 W122 44 3
17579 S.W. Deemar Way, Lake Oswego, OR 97035 US
(503) 981-9400; *Fax:* (503) 981-3561
License: Stayton, OR held by Sanlee Broadcasting Corp.
Nat'l Network: ABC *Regional Reps:* Allied Radio Partners.
Arbitron Metro Market: Portland, OR; *Format:* Country *Special Programming:* Portland Trailblazers basketball, Forest Dragons arena football, high school sports, farm 15 hrs wkly; *Hrs. of News Programming:* News progmg 3hrs wkly; *Target Audience:* 25 plus; stable, mature adults with above average income; *Adv. Rates:* 24; 23; 24; 15
Donald Coss, President
Chris McCartney, General Manager
Andy McGarrett, General Sales Mgr
Dorecia Luse, Corporate Administrator

Sunriver

KXIX
12-01-1974; 94.1 MHz FM; 18.5 kw; 814 ft.; N44 2 49 W121 31 50
345 SW Cyber Dr., Suite 101, Bend, OR 97702-1134 US
(541) 388-3300; *Fax:* (541) 388-3303
www.power94.fm
ahilmes@bendradiogroup.com
License: Sunriver, OR held by GCC Bend, LLC
Group Owner: GCC Bend, LLC; (acq 2000)
Format: Contemporary Hits/Top 40; *Target Audience:* 18-49.
Andy Hilmes, General Sales Mgr
Mike Flanagan, Programming Director
Bart Platt, Dir. of Promotions
RL Garrigus, News Director

Sutherlin

KSKR-FM
01-01-1998; 101.1 MHz FM; *Hrs Open:* 24; 3.6 kw; 859 ft.; N43 22 19 W123 21 15
1445 W. Harvard Ave, Roseburg, OR 97471 US
(541) 440-0101; *Fax:* (541) 673-7598
www.541radio.com
License: Sutherlin, Douglas County, OR held by Brooke Communications Inc.
Group Owner: Brooke Communications Inc.; (acq 12-16-2002)
Nat'l Network: ESPN Radio *Regional Reps:* Tacher
Arbitron Metro Market: Roseburg, OR; *Format:* Contemporary Hits/Top 40
Rob Thomas, Station Manager
Ashley Smith, Promotions Manager
Kyle Bailey, News Director

Sweet Home

KFIR
08-07-1968; 720 kHz AM
P.O. Box 720, Sweet Home, OR 97386 US
(541) 367-5115
www.kfir720am.com
info@kfir720am.com
License: Sweet Home, OR held by Radio Fiesta Network LLC
Regional Reps: Allied Broadcast Partners.
Arbitron Metro Market: Sweet Home, OR; *Format:* Talk *Special Programming:* Law 3 hrs wkly, country store 7 hrs wkly, Sunday Lutheran 1 hr wkly; *Hrs. of News Programming:* news progmg 100 hrs wkly *Target Audience:* 25-54 plus.
Michael Astalis, General Manager

***KLVU**
09-20-1989; 107.1 MHz FM; *Hrs Open:* 24; 9.3 kw; 2431 ft.; N44 28 59 W122 34 55
1425 N. Market Boulevard, Suite 9, Sacramento, CA 95834 US
(707) 528-9236; *Fax:* (707) 528-9236
www.klove.com
klove@klove.com
License: Sweet Home, Linn County, OR held by Educational Media Foundation.
Group Owner: EMF Broadcasting; (acq 3-12-97; $4 million).
Nat'l Network: K-Love
Format: Christian; *No. News Employees:* 3; *Target Audience:* 25-44; Judeo-Christian female
Darell Chambliss, Chairman
Mike Novak, President
Mike Lee, Operations Dir
David Pierce, Programming Director
Ed Lenane, News Director
Sam Wallington, Engineering Dir
Marya Morgan, News Reporter
Richard Hunt, Marya Morgan

Talent

***KSJK**
10-01-1960; 1230 kHz AM; *Hrs Open:* 24 hrs; 1 kw-U, ND1; N42 13 37 W122 44 33
P.O. Box 3175, Eugene, OR 97403 US
(541) 552-6301; *Fax:* (541) 552-8565
www.ijpr.org
info@ijpr.org
License: Talent, OR held by The State of Oregon, acting by and through the State Board of Higher Education. for the benefit of Southern Oregon University.
Nat'l Network: PRI; NPR
Arbitron Metro Market: Ashland, OR; *Format:* News *Special Programming:* Talk 6 hrs wkly; *Target Audience:* General.
Ronald Kramer, CEO
Bryon Lambert, Operations Dir
Paul Westhelle, General Sales Mgr
Ransom,Darin, Engineering Dir
Mitchell Christian, CFO

The Dalles

KACI
06-01-1955; 1300 kHz AM; *Hrs Open:* 24; 1 kw-D, ND2; 0.013 kw-N, ND2; N45 34 54 W121 7 53
719 E 2nd St., The Dalles, OR 97058 US
(541) 296-2211; *Fax:* (541) 296-2213
www.newsradiokaci.com
gary@bicoastalmedia.com
License: The Dalles, OR held by Bicoastal Media Licenses IV LLC.
Group Owner: Bicoastal Media L.L.C.; (acq 12-1-2007; grpsl)
Nat'l Network: Jones Radio Networks
Arbitron Metro Market: The Dalles, OR; *Format:* News, News/Talk, 86 *Special Programming:* Relg one hr, home improvement 3 hrs, financial tal; *Hrs. of News Programming:* news progmg 14 hrs wkly *No. News Employees:* 1; *Target Audience:* 25-54.
Michael Wilson, President
Randy Haines, Operations Dir
Rick Cavagnaro, General Sales Mgr
Mark Bailey, Programming Director
Matt Green, Engineering Dir
Gary Grossman, Marketing Manager
Paulette LaRoque, Traffic Manager

KACI-FM
02-01-1985; 97.7 MHz FM; *Hrs Open:* 24; 5.1 kw; 889 ft.; N45 38 58 W121 16 25
1190 22nd St., Hood River, OR 97031 US
(541) 386-1511
www.935kaci.com
gary@bicoastalmedia.com
License: The Dalles, Wasco County, OR held by Bicoastal Media Licenses IV LLC.
Group Owner: Bicoastal Media L.L.C.; (acq 12-1-2007; grpsl)
Arbitron Metro Market: The Dalles, OR; *Format:* Oldies; *Adv. Rates:* Same as AM
Jeff Skye, Operations Dir
Rick Cavagnaro, General Sales Mgr
Mark Bailey, Programming Director
Paulette LaRoque, News Director
Matt Green, Engineering Dir
Gary Grossman, Market Manager

KODL
10-12-1940; 1440 kHz AM; 5 kw-D, DAN; 1 kw-N, DAN; N45 35 31 W121 11 57
Mailing Address: 1709 Cherry Heights Road, The Dalles, OR 97058 US
Second Address: 404 E. 2nd St., The Dalles, OR 97058
(541) 296-2101; *Fax:* (541) 296-3766
www.kodl.com
License: The Dalles, OR held by Larson-Wynn Inc.
Format: Adult Contemp *Special Programming:* Farm 4 hrs, Sp 2 hrs wkly
Al Wynn, President
Marcia Wynn, Operations Dir

KMSW
10-01-2002; 92.7 MHz FM; 3.4 kw; 889 ft.; N45 38 58 W121 16 25
719 E. 2nd, The Dalles, OR 97058 US
(541) 296-2211
www.gorgeradio.com
gary@bicoastalmedia.com
License: The Dalles, Wasco County, OR held by Bicoastal Media Licenses IV LLC.
Group Owner: Bicoastal Media L.L.C.; (acq 12-1-2007; grpsl)
Regional Reps: Tacher
Arbitron Metro Market: The Dalles, OR; *Format:* Classic Rock; *Target Audience:* 25-54.
Mike Wilson, President & COO
Jeff Skye, Operations Dir
Bill Nielsen, General Sales Mgr
Mark Bailey, Programming Director
Gary Grossman, Market Manager
Randy Haines, Hood River Operations Director
Gwen Troutner, TrafficManager
Tammy Dirks, Account Executive

***KQHR**
01-01-2002; 88.1 MHz FM; *Hrs Open:* 24; 4 kw; 1115 ft.; N45 43 19 W121 26 14 *Rebroadcasts:* Rebroadcasts KBPS-FM Portland 100%
US
(503) 943-5828; *Fax:* (503) 802-9456
www.allclassical.org
musicinfo@allclassical.org
License: The Dalles, Hood River County, OR held by KBPS Public Radio Foundation.
Arbitron Metro Market: Portland, OR; *Format:* Classical; *Hrs. of News Programming:* News progmg 5 hrs wkly
Jack Allen, President & CEO
Jordan Lewis, Operations Dir
John Burk, Programming Director
Larry Holtz, Chief Engineer
Kelly Palin, CFO
Andrea Rennie, Executive Assistant
Jenn Woodward, HR & Office Coordinator
Deborah Rochford,Director of Member Services
Katherine Lefever, Assistant Director of Member Services
John Pitman, Music Director

***KOTD**
01-01-2008; 89.7 MHz FM; 0.012 kw; 1932 ft.; N45 42 43 W121 6 58 *Rebroadcasts:* Rebroadcasts KOPB-FM Portland 100%

US
(503) 293-1905; *Fax:* (503) 293-1919
www.opb.org/radio/
License: The Dalles, Wasco County, OR held by Oregon Public Broadcasting.
Nat'l Network: NPR; *Regional Network:* Ore. Pub. Bcstg Radio Net.
Arbitron Metro Market: The Dalles, OR
Raoul van Hall, Operations Dir
Steve Bass, General Manager
Lynne Clendenin, Vice President
Beth Hyams, News Director
Steven Kray, Chief Engineer
Morgan Holm, Vice President of News and Public Affairs
Eve Epstein, ManagingEditor

Tigard

***KXPD**
06-28-1993; 1040 kHz AM; *Hrs Open:* 24
1425 N Market Blvd #9, Sacramento, CA 95834 US
(541) 344-5500; *Fax:* (541) 485-2550
License: Tigard, OR held by Churchill Communications LLC.
Group Owner: Churchill Communications LLC; (acq 7-31-2006; $1.8 million).
Arbitron Metro Market: Portland, OR
Suzanne Arlie, General Manager

Tillamook

***KTMK**
01-01-2005; 91.1 MHz FM; 0.14 kw; 1168 ft.; N45 27 59 W123 55 11
1445 Exchange, P O B 269, Astoria, OR 97103 US
(800) 241-8123; *Fax:* (503) 293-1919
www.opb.org
hr@opb.org
License: Tillamook, Tillamook County, OR held by Oregon Public Broadcasting
Arbitron Metro Market: Tillamook, OR; *Format:* News, News/Talk, 86
Steve Bass, General Manager

***KAIK**
01-01-2006; 88.5 MHz FM; 0.06 kw vert; 1276 ft.; N45 27 59 W123 55 11 *Rebroadcasts:* Rebroadcasts KLRD(FM) Yucaipa, CA 100%
US
(888) 937-2471; *Fax:* (916) 251-1650
www.air1.com
info@air1.com
License: Tillamook, Tillamook County, OR held by Educational Media Foundation.
Group Owner: EMF Broadcasting
Nat'l Network: Air 1
Arbitron Metro Market: Tillamook, OR; *Format:* Alternative, Christian; *No. News Employees:* 3; *Target Audience:* 18-35; Judeo Christian female
Darrell Chambliss, Chairman
Alan Mason, COO
Mike Novak, President and CEO
Mike Lee, Operations Dir
David Pierce, Programming Director
Ed Lenane, News Director
Sam Wallington, Engineering Dir
Marya Morgan, News Reporter
Richard Hunt, News Reporter
Eric Moser, Chief Financial Officer
Brian Burger, Vice President of Human Resources
D. Kevin Blair, Secretary and General Counsel
Larry Moody, Director

***KTCB**
08-25-2004; 89.5 MHz FM; *Hrs Open:* 24; 0.38 kw; 1152 ft.; N45 27 59 W123 55 11
7140 Sw Macadam Avenue, Portland, OR 97219 US
(503) 325-0010; *Fax:* (503) 325-3956
www.kmun.org
License: Tillamook, Tillamook County, OR held by Tillicum Foundation
Nat'l Network: NPR; *Wire Services:* AP
Arbitron Metro Market: Cheriton, VA; *Format:* Public Affairs, Variety/Diverse; *Hrs. of News Programming:* News progmg 35 hrs wkly
David Hall, President
Joe Patenaude, Operations Dir
Joanne Rideout, General Manager
Elizabeth Menetry, Programming Director
Kathleen Morgain, News Director
Terry Wilson, Engineering Dir

Tom Hartland, Development Director
DavidPaul, Membership Coordinator

Toledo

KCUP
09-26-1960; 1230 kHz AM; 1 kw-U, ND1; N44 37 47 W123 56 35
P.O. Box 456, Newport, OR 97365 US
(541) 265-5000; *Fax:* (541) 265-9576
www.kcup.net
bobk@kcup.net
License: Toledo, OR held by Agpal Broadcasting Inc.
Nat'l Reps: McGavren Guild
Format: News, Talk; *Target Audience:* 25-54.; *Adv. Rates:* 16; 14; 16; 12
Cheryl Harle, General Manager
Ed Kowas, General Sales Mgr

Tri City

KKMX
06-01-1993; 104.3 MHz FM; *Hrs Open:* 24; 5.6 kw; 1385 ft.; N43 0 13 W123 21 26
1445 W. Harvard Ave., Roseburg, OR 97471 US
(541) 677-0104; *Fax:* (541) 673-7598
www.541radio.com
License: Tri City, Douglas County, OR held by Brooke Communications Inc.
Group Owner: Brooke Communications Inc.; acq 11-21-96)
Nat'l Reps: Tacher
Arbitron Metro Market: Medford, OR; *Format:* Adult Contemp; *Hrs. of News Programming:* news progmg 2 hrs wkly; *No. News Employees:* 2; *Target Audience:* 25-54; general
Rob Thomas, Station Manager
Ashley Smith, Promotions Manager
Kyle Bailey, News Director

Troutdale

KPAM
01-01-1997; 860 kHz AM; *Hrs Open:* 24
6605 S.E. Lake Rd., Portland, OR 97222 US
(503) 223-4321; *Fax:* (503) 294-0074
kpam.com
mgarber@commnewspapers.com
License: Troutdale, OR held by Pamplin Broadcasting-Oregon Inc.
Group Owner: Pamplin Broadcasting; (acq 12-29-97; $652,500 for 87% of stock)
Nat'l Network: ABC; *Nat'l Reps:* Tacher *Regional Reps:* The Tacher Co.; Inc.; *Wire Services:* AP
Arbitron Metro Market: Portland, OR; *Format:* News, News/Talk, 86 *Special Programming:* Wall St. Journal; *Hrs. of News Programming:* news progmg 35.4 hrs wkly; *No. News Employees:* 11; *Target Audience:* 35-54;adults.
Margaret Evans, General Sales Mgr
Misty Osko, Promotions Manager
Jeanne Winters, National Sales Manager
Paul Blaviding, Traffic Manager

Turner

***KMUZ**
88.5 MHz FM; 0.032 kw; 794 ft.; N44 47 0 W122 59 44
US
(503) 990-6101
www.kmuz.org
info@kmuz.org
License: Turner, Marion County, OR held by Salem Folklore Community.
Arbitron Metro Market: Turner, OR
Tim Crosby, President
Karen Holman, General Manager

Umatilla

KLWJ(AM)
06-01-1980; 1090 kHz AM; *Hrs Open:* 6 AM-sunset; 2.5 kw-D; N45 52 46 W119 20 37
80898 Powerline Rd., Umatilla, OR 97882
(541) 567-2102; *Fax:* (541) 567-2103
klwjradio@hotmail.com
License: Umatilla, Umatilla County, OR held by Umatilla Broadcasting Inc.
Nat'l Network: USA
Population Served: 250,000 *Format:* Christian, News, 62, Talk, Religious *Special Programming:* Farm one hr, Sp one hr wkly; *No. News Employees:* 1; *Target Audience:* General.; *Adv. Rates:* 8; 8; 8; 8
Darrell Marlow, President
John Marlow, Operations Dir

Veneta

KEUG
01-01-1998; 105.5 MHz FM; *Hrs Open:* 24; 2.8 kw; 994 ft.; N44 0 11 W123 6 48
P. O. Box 3088, Portland, OR 97228 US
(541) 484-9400; *Fax:* (541) 344-9424
License: Veneta, Lane County, OR held by McKenzie River Broadcasting Co. Inc.
Group Owner: McKenzie River Broadcasting Company, Inc.; (acq 1-28-2004; $1.02 million).
Nat'l Reps: D & R Radio
Arbitron Metro Market: Eugene-Springfield, OR; *Format:* Adult Contemp; *Target Audience:* 25-54; adults
John Tilson, President
Dave Wiles, General Sales Mgr
Jeff Baird, Programming Director

Warm Springs

***KWSO**
09-22-1986; 91.9 MHz FM; *Hrs Open:* 18; 4.3 kw; 1096 ft.; N44 50 24 W121 13 56
Mailing Address: PO Box C, Warm Springs, OR 97761 US
Second Address: 97761 Kahneeta Hamlet Rd., Warm Springs, OR 97761
(541) 553-1968; *Fax:* (541) 553-3348
www.kwso.org
smatters@wstribes.org
License: Warm Springs, Jefferson County, OR held by Confederated Tribes of Warm Springs.
Arbitron Metro Market: Warm Springs, OR; *Format:* Adult Contemp, Native American; *Target Audience:* General.
Sue Matters, General Manager

Warrenton

***KCPB-FM**
04-17-2006; 90.9 MHz FM; 0.24 kw; 1119 ft.; N46 15 46 W123 53 9
121st and Park, Tacoma, WA 98447 US
(503) 325-0010; *Fax:* (503) 325-3956
www.kmun.org
kmun@kmun.org
License: Warrenton, Clatsop County, OR held by Tillicum Foundation
Nat'l Network: NPR
Arbitron Metro Market: Spokane, WA
David Hall, President
Joe Patenaude, Operations Dir
Joanne Rideout, General Manager
Elizabeth Menetry, Programming Director
Terry Wilson, Engineering Dir
Tom Hartland, Development Director
David Paul, Membership Coordinator

Welches

***KXPC**
05-10-2001; 90.3 MHz FM; *Hrs Open:* 24; 0.235 kw; 1742 ft.; N45 20 1 W121 42 45
1425 N Market Blvd., Suite 9, Sacramento, CA 95834 US
(888) 937-2471; *Fax:* (916) 251-1650
www.air1.com
info@air1.com
License: Welches, Clackamas County, OR held by Educational Media Foundation.
Group Owner: EMF Broadcasting
Nat'l Network: Air 1
Arbitron Metro Market: Omaha, NE; *Format:* Alternative, Christian; *No. News Employees:* 3; *Target Audience:* 18-35; Judeo-Christian, female
Darrell Chambliss, Chairman
Mike Novak, President & CEO
Mike Lee, Operations Dir
David Pierce, Programming Director
Ed Lenane, News Director
Sam Wallington, Engineering Dir
Marya Morgan, News Reporter
Richard Hunt, NewsReporter
Tracy Butler, Traffic Manager
Walter Golembeski, Director
David Pierce, Chief Creative Officer
Alan Mason, Chief Operating Officer

West Linn

KWLZ-FM
01-18-1986; 96.3 MHz FM; *Hrs Open:* 24; 100 kw; 1089 ft.; N44 50 24 W121 13 56
P.O. Box 5985, Bend, OR 97708 US

(541) 383-3825; *Fax:* (541) 383-3403
www.newsradiocentraloregon.com
License: West Linn, Jefferson County, OR
Group Owner: C; (acq 3-2-2000; grpsl)
Nat'l Network: ABC Information & Entertainment; Premiere Radio Networks; Westwood One; Jones Radio Networks; Talk Radio Network; *Nat'l Reps:* Christal
Arbitron Metro Market: Bend, OR; *Format:* News, News/Talk, 86 *Special Programming:* Inside Central Oregon (public affairs); *Hrs. of News Programming:* 17.5 weekly (local); *No. News Employees:* 3; *Target Audience:* 25-64.
Dave Clemens, Operations Dir
Keith Shipman, General Manager
Kenn Brown, General Sales Mgr
Annette Weston, Programming Director
Heather Roberts, Promotions Manager
Bill Baker, News Director
Regan Brick, Business Manager

Weston

KZIU-FM
01-01-1997; 101.9 MHz FM; *Hrs Open:* 24; 13.5 kw; Ant 958 ft; N45 47 41 W118 10 06
45 Campbell Rd., Walla Walla, WA 99362
(509) 527-1000; *Fax:* (509) 529-5534
License: Weston, Umatilla County, OR held by Alexandra Communications Inc.
Group Owner: Alexandra Communications Inc.; (acq 4-10-2006; swap for KMMG(FM) Milton-Freewater)
Format: Jazz, Smooth Jazz
Tom Hodgins, General Manager

Winchester

*KLOV
08-01-1997; 89.3 MHz FM; *Hrs Open:* 24; 3.5 kw; 696 ft.; N43 14 8 W123 19 18
1425 N Market Blvd, Suite 9, Sacramento, CA 95834 US
(916) 251-1600; *Fax:* (916) 251-1650
www.klove.com
klove@klove.com
License: Winchester, Douglas County, OR held by Educational Media Foundation.
Group Owner: EMF Broadcasting
Nat'l Network: K-Love
Format: Christian; *No. News Employees:* 3; *Target Audience:* 25-44; Judeo-Christian, female
Mike Novak, President
Mike Lee, Operations Dir
David Pierce, Programming Director
Ed Lenane, News Director
Sam Wallington, Engineering Dir
Marya Morgan, News Reporter
Richard Hunt, Marya Morgan
Tracy Butler, Traffic Manager

Winston

KGRV
02-12-1984; 700 kHz AM; *Hrs Open:* 24
196 SE Main St., PO Box 1598, Winston, OR 97496 US
www.kgrv700.net
info@kgrv700.net
License: Winston, OR held by Pacific Cascade Communications Corp.
Group Owner: Pacific Cascade Communications Corp.; (acq 4-15-85)
Nat'l Network: Moody
Format: Christian *Special Programming:* Southern gospel 3 hrs wkly, Family 20 hrs wkly; *Hrs. of News Programming:* News progmg 10 hrs wkly; *Target Audience:* Christian Adults; *Adv. Rates:* 8.50; 8.50; 8.50; 8.50
Phil Morrow, General Manager

Woodburn

KWBY
07-10-1964; 940 kHz AM; *Hrs Open:* 24; 0.25 kw-D, ND1; 0.2 kw-N, ND1; N45 10 37 W122 50 58
P. O. Box 158, Woodburn, OR 97071 US
(503) 981-9400; *Fax:* (503) 981-3561
www.lapantera940.com
sam@lapantera940.com
License: Woodburn, OR held by Edward C. Distell
Nat'l Network: CNN Radio; *Nat'l Reps:* Lotus Entravision Reps LLC
Arbitron Metro Market: Woodburn, OR; *Format:* Tejano *Special Programming:* Relg 5 hrs, gospel 3 hrs wkly; *Hrs. of News Programming:* news progmg 35 hrs wkly; *No. News Employees:* 1; *Target Audience:* 18-49;younger-larger-than-gen mkt average Hispanic families; *Adv. Rates:* 35; 30; 35; 25

Donald Coss, President
Dorecia Luse, General Manager
Gilberto Galvan, Programming Director
Natasha Holstein, Promotions Manager

Pennsylvania

CMS Station Brokerage, Inc.
1439 Denniston St., Pittsburgh, PA 15217 USA
(412) 421-2600; *Fax:* (412) 421-6001
www.cmsstationbrokerage.com
roger.rafson@genmediapartners.com

Roger Rafson, President
Shirley Brown, Office Manager

Allentown

WAEB
01-01-1949; 790 kHz AM; 3.6 kw-D, DA2; 1.5 kw-N, DA2; N40 39 37 W75 30 50
1541 Alta Drive, 4th Floor, Whitehall, PA 18052 US
(610) 434-1742; *Fax:* (610) 434-6288
www.790waeb.com
License: Allentown, PA held by Capstar TX LLC
Group Owner: iHeartMedia; (acq 8-30-00; grpsl).
Nat'l Network: CBS
Arbitron Metro Market: Durango CO; *Format:* News, News/Talk, 86 *Special Programming:* Czech one hr, farm 10 hrs, relg 3 hrs wkly; *Hrs. of News Programming:* news progmg 15 hrs wkly; *No. News Employees:* 1 *TargetAudience:* 25-54.
Bill Palmeri, Market President
Adrienne Tunke, General Sales Mgr
Craig Stevens, Senior Vice President of Programming
Mandy Schnell, Promotions Director
Pat Gremling, Director of Sales

WAEB-FM
06-30-1961; 104.1 MHz FM; 50 kw; 499 ft.; N40 43 13 W75 35 44
1541 Alta Drive, 4th Floor, Whitehall, PA 18052 US
(610) 434-1742; *Fax:* (610 434-6288
www.b104.com
License: Allentown, Lehigh County, PA held by Capstar TX LLC
Group Owner: iHeartMedia
Arbitron Metro Market: Allentown, PA; *Format:* Contemporary Hits/Top 40
Bill Palmeri, Market President
Craig Stevens, Senior Vice President of Programming
Adrienne Tunke, General Sales Mgr
Mandy Schnell, Promotions Director
Pat Gremling, Director of Sales

*WDIY
01-08-1995; 88.1 MHz FM; *Hrs Open:* 24hrs/day; 0.1 kw vert; 843 ft.; N40 33 54 W75 26 26 *Rebroadcasts:* 93.7 & 93.9MHz translators
301 Broadway, Bethlehem, PA 18015 US
(610) 694-8100; *Fax:* (610) 954-9474
www.wdiy.org
info@wdiy.org
License: Allentown, Lehigh County, PA held by Lehigh Valley Community Broadcasters Association Inc.
Nat'l Network: NPR
Arbitron Metro Market: Lehigh Valley, PA; *Format:* News, Variety/Diverse *Special Programming:* AAA 49hrs, Classical 17 hrs, Folk 13 hrs, Jazz 14 hrs, Ethnic 3hrs (Asian-Indian 1 hr, Arabic 1 hr, Jewish 1 hr), Local publicaffairs 3hrs weekly.; *Hrs. of News Programming:* News progmg 41 hrs wkly; *Target Audience:* General.
Mike Kraynak, President
Neil Hever, Operations Dir
Wagner Previato, Executive Director
Keely Collins, Vice President

WHOL
09-12-1948; 1600 kHz AM; *Hrs Open:* 24; 0.5 kw-D, DA2; 0.056 kw-N, DA2; N40 35 33 W75 28 42
1125 Colorado Street, Allentown, PA 18103 US
(610) 434-4801; *Fax:* (484) 223-0088
www.whol1600.com
info@whol1600.com
License: Allentown, PA held by Matthew P. Braccili
Nat'l Network: USA; Radio Unica; *Nat'l Reps:* Salem
Arbitron Metro Market: Allentown-Bethlehem, PA; *Format:* Contemporary Hits/Top 40, Spanish; *Target Audience:* 18-65.; *Adv. Rates:* 23; 21; 23; 30
Matthew Braccili, President
Jeffrey Maddox, Operations Dir
Matthew Braccili, Station Manager

Olga Negron, General Sales Mgr
Tony Rodriguez, Programming Director

*WJCS
02-29-1996; 89.3 MHz FM; *Hrs Open:* 24; 0.0001 kw horiz, 0.12 kw vert; 915 ft.; N40 33 52 W75 26 25
Mailing Address: PO Box 8900, Allentown, PA 18105 US
Second Address: 300 E. Rock Rd., Suite 205, Allentown, PA 18103
(610) 791-7262; *Fax:* (610) 797-6922
www.wjcs.org
License: Allentown, Lehigh County, PA held by Beacon Broadcasting Corp.
Nat'l Network: Moody
Arbitron Metro Market: Allentown-Bethlehem, PA; *Format:* Christian, News, 62, Talk, Religious; *Target Audience:* General.
Frank Ginther, Station Manager

WSAN
05-24-1923; 1470 kHz AM; 5 kw-D, DAN; 5 kw-N, DAN; N40 38 10 W75 29 6
1541 Alta Drive, Suite 400, Whitehall, PA 18052 US
(610) 434-1742; *Fax:* (610) 434-6288
www.fox1470.com
License: Allentown, PA held by Capstar TX LLC
Group Owner: iHeartMedia; (acq 8-30-2000; grpsl)
Nat'l Reps: D & R Radio
Arbitron Metro Market: Allentown-Bethlehem, PA; *Format:* Sports
Craig Stevens, Senior Vice President of Programming

WLEV
07-01-1947; 100.7 MHz FM; 11 kw; 1073 ft.; N40 33 54 W75 26 26
2158 Avenue C, Suite 100, Bethlehem, PA 18017 US
(610) 266-7600
www.wlevradio.com
License: Allentown, PA held by Radio License Holding CBC, LLC
Group Owner: Cumulus Media Inc.; (acq 9-5-97; $23 million).
Nat'l Reps: Christal; Katz Radio
Arbitron Metro Market: Allentown-Bethlehem, PA; *Format:* Adult Contemp
Laura St. James, Programming Director
Barry Dawson, Promotions Manager

*WMUH
02-06-1966; 91.7 MHz FM; *Hrs Open:* 24; 0.44 kw; -3 ft.; N40 35 52 W75 30 38
2400 Chew Street, Allentown, PA 18104 US
(484) 664-3239; *Fax:* (484) 664-3539
www.muhlenberg.edu/wmuh
wmuh@muhlenberg.edu
License: Allentown, Lehigh County, PA held by Muhlenberg College.
Nat'l Network: NPR
Arbitron Metro Market: Allentown, PA; *Format:* Variety/Diverse *Special Programming:* Sp 4 hrs, Arabic 2 hrs, Ger 2 hrs, It 2 hrs, Pol; *Target Audience:* General.
Joe Swanson, General Manager
Mike Calcagno, Station Manager
Rich Gensiak, Programming Director

WTKZ
09-01-1948; 1320 kHz AM; 0.75 kw-D, DAN; 0.195 kw-N, DAN; N40 35 33 W75 28 42 *Rebroadcasts:* WEEX-AM Simulcast
961 Marcon Blvd., Ste 400, Allentown, PA 18105 US
(610) 258-6155; *Fax:* (610) 253-3384
www.espnlv.com
License: Allentown, PA held by Connoisseur Media Licenses LLC
Group Owner: Connoisseur Media LLC
Nat'l Network: ESPN Radio; *Nat'l Reps:* Katz Radio *Regional Reps:* Glenn Jones
Arbitron Metro Market: Allentown, PA; *Format:* Sports; *Target Audience:* 18-49; Men
Pat Lincoln, General Manager
Tom Fallon, Programming Director
Sarah Weidner, Sales Coordinator

Altoona

WFBG
10-30-1924; 1290 kHz AM; *Hrs Open:* 24; 5 kw-D, DAN; 1 kw-N, DAN; N40 27 20 W78 23 50
1 Forever Dr., Hollidaysburg, PA 16648 US
(814) 941-9800; *Fax:* (814) 943-2754
www.wfbg.com
webmaster@forevermediainc.com
License: Altoona, Blair County, PA held by FM Radio Licenses LLC
Group Owner: Forever Broadcasting; (acq 12-24-90; $2.1 million with co-located FM;
Nat'l Reps: Christal

Arbitron Metro Market: Altoona, PA; *Format:* News, News/Talk, 86; *Hrs. of News Programming:* news progmg 2 hrs wkly; *No. News Employees:* 2; *Target Audience:* 25-54.
Dave Davies, General Manager/Market Manager
Bob Castellucci, General Sales Mgr
Troy Barnhart, Chief Engineer
Leah Elbert, Traffic Manager
P.J. Mitchell, Business Manager
Andy Berkowitz, Production Director

WFGY
10-17-1960; 98.1 MHz FM; *Hrs Open:* 24; 30 kw; 942 ft.; N40 34 1 W78 26 32
1 Forever Dr., Hollidaysburg, PA 16648 US
(814) 941-9800; *Fax:* (814) 943-2754
www.froggyradio.com
webmaster@forevermediainc.com
License: Altoona, Blair County, PA held by FM Radio Licenses LLC
Group Owner: Forever Broadcasting
Nat'l Network: CBS
Arbitron Metro Market: Altoona, PA; *Format:* Country; *No. News Employees:* 1; *Target Audience:* 25-64.
Dave Davies, General Manager/Market Manager
Bobbi Castellucci, General Sales Mgr
Jim Wisor, Programming Director
Troy Barnhart, Chief Engineer
Leah Elbert, Traffic Manager
P.J. Mitchell, Business Manager
Andy Berkowitz,Production Director
Bethany McMamany, EEO Officer

WWOT
07-01-1976; 100.1 MHz FM; 3 kw; 955 ft.; N40 34 11 W78 26 25
1 Forever Dr., Hollidaysburg, PA 16648 US
(814) 941-9800; *Fax:* (814) 943-2754
www.hot100pa.com
webmaster@forevermediainc.com
License: Altoona, Blair County, PA held by FM Radio Licenses LLC
Group Owner: Forever Broadcasting
Arbitron Metro Market: Altoona, PA; *Format:* Contemporary Hits/Top 40; *Target Audience:* 12-34; male & female
Dave Davies, General Manager/Market Manager
Bobbi Castellucci, General Sales Mgr
Troy Barnhart, Chief Engineer
P.J. Mitchell, Business Manager
Leah Elbert, Traffic Manager
Andy Berkowitz, Production Director
Bethany McMamany, EEOOfficer

WRTA
06-12-1946; 1240 kHz AM; *Hrs Open:* 19; 1 kw-U, ND1; N40 30 26 W78 25 15
2513 6th Avenue, Altoona, PA 16602 US
(814) 943-6112; *Fax:* (814) 944-9782
www.wrta.com
contactus@wrta.com
License: Altoona, PA held by Handsome Brothers Inc.
Nat'l Network: Westwood One *Regional Reps:* Marv Roslin
Arbitron Metro Market: Altoona, PA; *Format:* News, News/Talk, 86 *Special Programming:* Sports play-by-play/loc college & high schools; *Hrs. of News Programming:* news progmg 15 hrs wkly; *No. News Employees:* 2 *Target Audience:* 25 plus; middle/upper income, college educated, professional; *Adv. Rates:* 32; 30; 28; 14
David Barger, President
David Wolf, General Manager
Ken Maguda, Station Manager
Dave Weaver, News Director
Bob Taylor, Chief Engineer

WVAM
07-01-1948; 1430 kHz AM; 5 kw-D, DAN; 1 kw-N, DAN; N40 29 42 W78 24 6
1 Forever Dr., Hollidaysburg, PA 16648 US
(814) 941-9800; *Fax:* (814) 943-2754
www.wvamam.com
webmaster@forevermediainc.com
License: Altoona, Blair County, PA held by FM Radio Licenses LLC
Group Owner: Forever Broadcasting; (acq 12-12-2003; $2.1 million with co-located FM).
Nat'l Network: ESPN Radio
Arbitron Metro Market: Altoona, PA; *Format:* Sports *Special Programming:* Pol one hr wkly; *Target Audience:* 25 plus; white collar professionals
Dave Davies, General Manager/Market Manager
Bobbi Castellucci, General Sales Mgr
Troy Barnhart, Chief Engineer
P.J. Mitchell, Business Manager
Leah Elbert, Traffic
Andy Berkowitz, Production Director
Bethany McManamy, EEOOfficer

Ambridge

WMBA
05-01-1957; 1460 kHz AM; *Hrs Open:* 24; 0.5 kw-D, DA2; 0.5 kw-N, DA2; N40 35 8 W80 12 11
Mailing Address: 1316 7th Avenue, Beaver Falls, PA 15010 US
Second Address: PO Box 719, Beaver Falls, PA 15010
(724) 846-4100; *Fax:* (724) 843-7771
www.wbvp-wmba.com
License: Ambridge, PA held by Sound Ideas Media, LLC
Group Owner: Iorio Broadcasting Inc.; (acq 5-23-2000; $325,000)
Nat'l Network: Talk Radio Network; *Wire Services:* AP
Arbitron Metro Market: Pittsburgh, PA; *Format:* Sports, Talk
Special Programming: Polka review 2 hrs, oldies 3 hrs, Polish 2 hrs wkl; *Hrs. of News Programming:* news progmg 10 hrs wkly; *No. News Employees:* 1 *Target Audience:* 35+.
Frank Iorio, President
Mark Peterson, General Manager
John Nuzzo, Programming Director
Pat Septak, News Director
Bob Barrickman, Sports Commentator

Annville-Cleona

WWSM
08-04-1968; 1510 kHz AM; 5 kw-D, DAD; N40 17 44 W76 27 46
277 Gravel Hill Road, Palmyra, PA 17078 US
(717) 272-1510; *Fax:* (717) 832-0209
www.wwsm.us
wwsm2@evenlink.com
License: Annville-Cleona, PA held by Patrick H. Sickafus.
Nat'l Network: Westwood One; USA
Arbitron Metro Market: Lebanon, PA; *Format:* Country *Special Programming:* Polka 2 hrs, bluegrass 3 hrs, gospel music 3 hrs w; *No. News Employees:* 2; *Target Audience:* 34 plus.; *Adv. Rates:* 20; 15; 15; na
Patrick Sickafus, President
Gary Gruver, General Manager
Bob Waters, Production Assistant
Tim Michaels, Director of Sales/Marketing
Jack Weinlein, General Sales Manager

Apollo

WAVL
12-13-1947; 910 kHz AM; 5 kw-D, DAD; 0.069 kw-N, DA2; N40 35 1 W79 31 34
Mailing Address: Radio Station Lane, Apollo, PA 15613 US
Second Address: 1145 S. Jefferson Street, Kittanning, PA 16201
(724) 548-8000; *Fax:* (724) 543-5572
License: Apollo, PA held by Evangel Heights Assembly of God
Nat'l Network: USA
Arbitron Metro Market: Tumon GU; *Format:* Oldies; *Adv. Rates:* 10; 10; 10; 10
Yasunori Kawauchi, President
Kevin Yamazaki, Operations Dir

Avis

WQBR
08-11-1989; 99.9 MHz FM; *Hrs Open:* 24; 570 w; Ant 1,053 ft; N41 13 45 W77 22 02
330 McElhattan Drive, McElhattan, PA 17748
(570) 769-2327
www.bear999.com
bear@kcnet.org
License: Avis, Clinton County, PA held by Maximum Impact Communications Inc.
Nat'l Network: Jones Radio Networks; *Nat'l Reps:* Dome
Population Served: 300,000; *Arbitron Metro Market:* Williamsport, PA; *Hrs. of News Programming:* news progmg 2 hrs wkly; *No. News Employees:* 1; *Target Audience:* 25-54.; *Adv. Rates:* 12; 12; 12; 12
Karyn O'Brien Stratton, General Manager
Jonathan Schwab, Sports Director
Dave Stratton, General Sales Mgr
Michael Ferriola, Engineering Dir
Patti Knepp, Office Manager

Avoca

WILK-FM
04-02-1976; 103.1 MHz FM; *Hrs Open:* 24; 6 kw; 72 ft.; N41 18 20 W75 45 38 *Rebroadcasts:* Simulcast with WILK(AM) Wilkes-Barre 100%
305 Highway 315, Pittston, PA 18640 US
(570) 883-9800
www.wilknetwork.com
License: Avoca, Luzerne County, PA held by Entercom Wilkes-Barre Scranton LLC.
Group Owner: Entercom Communications Corp.; (acq 12-13-99; grpsl)
Arbitron Metro Market: Avoca, PA *TV Affiliate:* WILK-TV; *Format:* News, News/Talk, 86; *Target Audience:* 18-54; general
Ryan Flynn, General Manager
Larry Serafin, Local Sales Manager
Tony Bartocci, Director of Strategic Sales &ÿMarketing

Barnesboro

WNCC
10-15-1950; 950 kHz AM; *Hrs Open:* 24; 0.5 kw-D, ND2; 0.029 kw-N, ND2; N40 40 47 W78 44 26
P.O. Box 371, Kittanning, PA 16201 US
(814) 472-4060; *Fax:* (814) 948-0950
whpa@verizon.net
License: Barnesboro, PA held by Vernal Enterprises Inc.
Group Owner: Vernal Enterprises Inc.; (acq 3-19-97; $20,000 with WRDD(AM) Ebensburg).
Arbitron Metro Market: Northern Cambria, PA; *Format:* Adult Contemp, Oldies; *Hrs. of News Programming:* news progmg 6 hrs wkly; *No. News Employees:* 1; *Target Audience:* 35 plus; females & males in the 35 plus agerange
Larry Schrengost, General Manager

Beaver Falls

WAOB-FM
01-01-1960; 106.7 MHz FM; *Hrs Open:* 24; 37 kw; Ant 554 ft; N40 37 11 W80 05 36
21 Yost Boulevard, Suite 505, Forest Hills, PA 15221
(412) 829-1000
www.wamo100.com
License: Beaver Falls, Beaver County, PA held by Saint Joseph Missions
Group Owner: St. Joseph Missions of Latrobe
Nat'l Network: American Urban; *Nat'l Reps:* McGavren Guild
Population Served: 307,484; *Arbitron Metro Market:* Pittsburgh, PA; *Format:* Religious *Special Programming:* Catholic Programming
Lisha Logan, Director of Promotions
DJ Boogie, Programming Director
Stephanie Baker, Director of Sales

WBVP
05-25-1948; 1230 kHz AM; *Hrs Open:* 24; 1 kw-U, ND1; N40 44 16 W80 17 47
PO Box 719, Beaver Falls, PA 15010 US
(724) 846-4100; *Fax:* (724) 843-7771
www.wbvp-wmba.com
1230@wbvp-wmba.com
License: Beaver Falls, PA held by Sound Ideas Media, LLC
Group Owner: Iorio Broadcasting Inc.; (acq 1996)
Nat'l Network: Talk Radio Network; *Wire Services:* AP
Arbitron Metro Market: Beaver Falls, Pa; *Format:* News, Sports, 86 *Special Programming:* Polka music 2 hrs, relg 2 hrs, gospel 2 hsr wkly; *No. News Employees:* 2; *Target Audience:* 35 plus.
Frank Iorio, President
John Nuzzo, Operations Dir
Mark Peterson, Station Manager
Diane Powers, Business Manager

Beaver Springs

WLZS
02-21-1993; 106.1 MHz FM; *Hrs Open:* 24; 0.175 kw; 1312 ft.; N40 42 4 W77 12 50
PO Box 146, Beaver Springs, PA 17812 US
(717) 436-5504; *Fax:* (800) 654-1061
License: Beaver Springs, Snyder County, PA held by Starview Media Inc.
Regional Network: Radio Pa.
Arbitron Metro Market: Beaver Springs, PA; *Format:* Oldies; *Hrs. of News Programming:* news progmg 2 hrs wkly; *No. News Employees:* 1; *Target Audience:* 25-54.
Curt Dreibelbis, General Manager
Shane Nelson, Programming Director

Bedford

WAYC
12-22-1966; 100.9 MHz FM; *Hrs Open:* 24; 0.19 kw; 1280 ft.; N40 00 46 W78 33 12
Mailing Address: Box 1, Bedford, PA 15522 US
Second Address: 134 E. Pitt St., Bedford, PA 15522
(814) 623-1000
www.bedfordcountyradio.com
info@bedfordcountyradio.com

License: Bedford, Bedford County, PA held by Cessna Communications Inc.
Group Owner: Cessna Communications Inc.
Nat'l Network: Fox News Radio; *Regional Network:* Radio Pa.
Regional Reps: Commercial Media Sales.
Arbitron Metro Market: Arcadia MO; *Format:* Adult Contemp; *Adv. Rates:* 16; 16; 16; 16
Jay Cessna, President
John H. Cessna, Operations Dir

WAYC
08-05-1974; 1600 kHz AM; *Hrs Open:* 24; 2.7 kw-D, 18 w-N; N40 02 35 W78 30 13
Mailing Address: Box 1, Bedford, PA 15522 US
Second Address: 134 E. Pitt St., Bedford, PA 15522
(814) 623-1000
www.bedfordcountyradio.com
info@bedfordcountyradio.com
License: Bedford, Bedford County, PA held by Cessna Communications Inc.
Group Owner: Cessna Communications Inc.
Nat'l Network: Fox News Radio *Regional Reps:* Commercial Media Sales
Population Served: 35,000 *Format:* Adult Contemp; *No. News Employees:* 1; *Target Audience:* 35 plus.; *Adv. Rates:* 16; 16; 16; 16
Jay Cessna, President
John H. Cessna, Operations Dir

WBFD
07-02-1955; 1310 kHz AM; 2.5 kw-D, ND1; 0.085 kw-N, ND1; N40 02 36 W78 30 11
Mailing Address: Box 1, Bedford, PA 15522 US
Second Address: 134 E. Pitt St., Bedford, PA 15522
(814) 623-1000
www.bedfordcountyradio.com
info@bedfordcountyradio.com
License: Bedford, PA held by Cessna Communications Inc.
Group Owner: Cessna Communications Inc.
Nat'l Network: Salem Radio Network; Talk Radio Network; Premiere Radio Networks; *Regional Network:* Radio Pa.
Regional Reps: Commercial Media Sales.
TV Affiliate: News/talk; *Format:* Sports, News/Talk; *Hrs. of News Programming:* 1; *No. News Employees:* 30 plus; general; *Adv. Rates:* 16; 16; 16; 16
Jay Cessna, President
John H. Cessna, Operations Dir

WBVE
08-15-1988; 107.5 MHz FM; *Hrs Open:* 24; 0.37 kw; 1309 ft.; N40 00 46 W78 33 12
Mailing Address: Box 1, Bedford, PA 15522 US
Second Address: 134 E. Pitt St., Bedford, PA 15522
(814) 623-1000; *Fax:* (814) 623-9692
www.bedfordcountyradio.com
info@bedfordcountyradio.com
License: Bedford, Bedford County, PA held by Cessna Communications Inc.
Group Owner: Cessna Communications Inc.
Nat'l Network: Fox News Radio *Regional Reps:* Commerical Media Sales
Arbitron Metro Market: Bedford, PA; *Format:* Classic Rock; *No. News Employees:* 1; *Target Audience:* 25-54.; *Adv. Rates:* 16; 16; 16; 16
Jay Cessna, President
John H. Cessna, Operations Dir

***WUFR**
01-01-2008; 91.1 MHz FM; 2.5 kw vert; 1220 ft.; N40 17 40 W78 34 25 *Rebroadcasts:* Rebroadcasts WFSI(FM) Annapolis, MD 100%
290 Hergenberger Road, Oakland, CA 94621 US
(410) 268-6200
www.familyradio.com
License: Bedford, Bedford County, PA held by Family Stations Inc.
Group Owner: Family Stations Inc.
Nat'l Network: Family Radio
Arbitron Metro Market: Tahlequah, OK; *Format:* Religious
Harold Camping, President
W.A. Sadlier, Station Manager

Bellefonte

WBLF
08-01-1958; 970 kHz AM; 1 kw-D, NDD; 0.07 kw-N, ND1; N40 54 12 W77 46 6
315 S. Atherton Street, State College, PA 16801 US
(814) 272-1320; *Fax:* (814) 272-3291
jerryfisher3@yahoo.com
License: Bellefonte, PA held by Magnum Broadcasting Inc.
Group Owner: Magnum Broadcasting Inc.; (acq 8-31-2005; $150,000) .
Nat'l Network: Fox News Radio; Fox Sports; *Regional Network:* Agrinet; *Nat'l Reps:* Interep
Arbitron Metro Market: State College, PA; *Format:* News, News/Talk, 86; *Target Audience:* Adults 25+.
Michael Stapleford, President
Diana Stapleford, General Manager
Michael Brennen, General Sales Mgr

WZWW
09-15-1986; 95.3 MHz FM; *Hrs Open:* 24; 790 w; Ant 636 ft; N40 53 35 W77 51 48
863 Benner Pike, State College, PA 16801
(814) 231-0953; *Fax:* (814) 231-0950
www.3wz.com
License: Bellefonte, Centre County, PA held by First Media Radio LLC.
Group Owner: First Media Radio LLC; (acq 11-2-2000)
Nat'l Network: CBS Radio *Regional Reps:* Commercial Media Sales.
Population Served: 124,000; *Arbitron Metro Market:* State College, *Special Programming:* Sports 3 hrs wkly; *Hrs. of News Programming:* news progmg 7 hrs wkly; *No. News Employees:* 2; *Target Audience:* 25-54;upscale families
Alex Kolobielski, President
Katie Baney, General Sales Mgr

Bellwood

WALY
03-28-1970; 103.9 MHz FM; *Hrs Open:* 18; 0.38 kw; 919 ft.; N40 34 1 W78 26 32
1 Forever Dr., Hollidaysburg, PA 16648 US
(814) 941-9800; *Fax:* (814) 943-2754
www.waly1039.com
License: Bellwood, Blair County, PA held by FM Radio Licenses LLC
Group Owner: Forever Broadcasting; (acq 7-16-97; grpsl).
Nat'l Network: AP Radio; *Nat'l Reps:* Katz Radio *Regional Reps:* Dome.
Arbitron Metro Market: Altoona, PA; *Format:* Adult Contemp; *Target Audience:* 35-64; earlier boomers, socially & financially active
K.C. O'Day, Programming Director
Jay Parks, News Director

Benton

WGGI
10-04-1985; 95.9 MHz FM; 4.2 kw; 384 ft.; N41 9 32 W76 24 6
305 Highway 315, Pittston, PA 18640 US
(570) 883-1111
www.froggy101.com
License: Benton, Columbia County, PA held by Entercom Scranton Wilkes-Barre License LLC.
Group Owner: Entercom Communications Corp.; (acq 12-13-99; grpsl).
Arbitron Metro Market: Wilkes Barre-Scranton, PA; *Format:* Country; *Target Audience:* 25-54.
John Burkavage, Operations Dir
Ryan Flynn, General Sales Mgr

Berwick

WHLM-FM
02-14-1992; 103.5 MHz FM; 4.1 kw; 387 ft.; N41 5 11 W76 16 41
124 E. Main Street, Bloomsburg, PA 17815 US
(570) 784-1200; *Fax:* (570) 784-6060
www.whlmfm.com
License: Berwick, Columbia County, PA held by Columbia FM Inc.
Arbitron Metro Market: Wilkes Barre-Scranton, PA; *Format:* Contemporary Hits/Top 40, Adult Contemp; *Target Audience:* 25-54; females at work, 18-39 men on weekends; *Adv. Rates:* 18; 18; 18; 15
Joseph Reilly, General Manager
Nancy Reilly, Business Manager
Larry Hopper, VP Sales/Marketing

WBWX(AM)
08-01-1957; 1280 kHz AM; 1 kw-D, 175 w-N; N41 04 36 W76 15 32
124 East Main Street, Bloomsburg, PA 17815
(570) 784-1200; *Fax:* (570) 784-6060
www.whlmam.com
way750am@aol.com
License: Berwick, Columbia County, PA held by Columbia Broadcasting Company
Group Owner: Bold Gold Media Group LP; (acq 1-11-2007; $10,000 plus assumption of debt)
Population Served: 50,000; *Arbitron Metro Market:* Wilkes Barre-Scranton, PA; *Format:* Oldies
Joe Reilly, General Manager
Larry Hopper, VP Sales/Marketing
Nancy Reilly, Business Manager

Bethlehem

WGPA
02-14-1946; 1100 kHz AM; *Hrs Open:* Sunrise-sunset; 0.25 kw-D, NDD; N40 37 27 W75 21 19
528 North New Street, Bethlehem, PA 18018 US
(610) 866-8074
www.wgpasunny1100.com
joetimmer@jollyjoetimmer.com
License: Bethlehem, PA held by Joseph Timmer dba Timmer Broadcasting Co.
Nat'l Network: USA
Arbitron Metro Market: Allentown-Bethlehem, PA; *Format:* News, News/Talk, 86 *Special Programming:* Ger 2 hrs, polka 12 hrs, Sp 4 hrs wkly; *Hrs. of News Programming:* news progmg 2 hrs wkly; *No. News Employees:* 1 *Target Audience:* General.; *Adv. Rates:* 50; 20; 20; 20
Joe Timmer, President
Mark Staller, Operations Dir

***WLVR-FM**
05-03-1973; 91.3 MHz FM; *Hrs Open:* 7 AM-4 AM; 0.013 kw; 558 ft.; N40 36 4 W75 21 34
39 University Drive, Bethlehem, PA 18015 US
(610) 758-4187
www.wlvr.org
inwlvr@lehigh.edu
License: Bethlehem, Northampton County, PA held by Lehigh University.
Arbitron Metro Market: Bethlehem, PA; *Format:* Variety/Diverse *Special Programming:* Black 12 hrs, class 8 hrs, reggae 6 hrs, jazz 12 h; *Hrs. of News Programming:* News progmg 10 hrs wkly; *Target Audience:* General.
Dave Brewster, Music Director
Steve Beckett, General Manager
David Scanlan, Sports Director
A. Fritzinger, Station Manager
Arthur Hedderly-Smith, Programming Director

WZZO
02-14-1946; 95.1 MHz FM; 30 kw; 630 ft.; N40 37 13 W75 17 37
1541 Alta Drive, 4th Floor, Whitehall, PA 18052 US
(610) 434-1742; *Fax:* (610) 434-6288
studio@wzzo.com
License: Bethlehem, Northampton County, PA held by Capstar TX LLC
Group Owner: iHeartMedia; (acq 8-30-00; grpsl).
Nat'l Reps: Katz Radio
Arbitron Metro Market: Whitehall, PA; *Format:* Rock/AOR
Bill Palmeri, Market President
Craig Stevens, Senior Vice President of Programming
Adrienne Tunke, General Sales Mgr
Kyle Anthony, Programming Director
Mandy Schnell, Promotions Director
Pat Gremling, Director of Sales

Blairsville

WLCY
04-15-1985; 106.3 MHz FM; *Hrs Open:* 24; 2.4 kw; 364 ft.; N40 31 10 W79 13 26
840 Philadelphia Street, Indiana, PA 15701 US
(724) 465-4700; *Fax:* (724) 349-6842
License: Blairsville, Indiana County, PA held by The St. Pier Group LLC.
Group Owner: Renda Broadcasting Corp.; (acq 8-1-2004; $900,000).
Nat'l Network: Jones Radio Networks *Regional Reps:* Dome.
Format: Country; *Hrs. of News Programming:* news progmg 2 hrs wkly; *No. News Employees:* 2; *Target Audience:* 25-54.; *Adv. Rates:* 20; 20; 20; 20
Mark Bertig, General Manager
Jim DeCesare, Operations Manager
Mark Hilliard, General Sales Manager
Jack Benedict, Sports Director

Bloomsburg

***WBUQ**
09-16-1986; 91.1 MHz FM; *Hrs Open:* 16; 0.6 kw; -72 ft.; N41 0 29 W76 26 51
400 East Second Street, Bloomsburg, PA 17815 US
(570) 389-4686
www.wbuq.weebly.com
wbuq@huskies.bloomu.edu

License: Bloomsburg, Columbia County, PA held by Bloomsburg University of Pennsylvania.
Arbitron Metro Market: Bloomsburg, Pa; *Format:* Alternative, Rock/AOR *Special Programming:* Talk 10 hrs, urban 10 hrs, metal 15 hrs, indie 10 hrs wkly; *Hrs. of News Programming:* news progmg 2 hrs wkly *No. NewsEmployees:* 1; *Target Audience:* General; college & area high school students; *Adv. Rates:* 8; 7; 8; 7
Daniel J. Rendine, Music Director
Elizabeth Smith/Stephanie Cabral, Promotions Directors
Jake Wilcox, General Manager
Katelyn E. Carralle, Studio Director
Erin Armstrong, News Director

WHLM
09-26-1947; 930 kHz AM; *Hrs Open:* 24
124 East Main Street, Bloomsburg, PA 17815-1807 US
(570) 784-1200; *Fax:* (570) 784-6060
www.whlmam.com
License: Bloomsburg, PA held by Columbia Broadcasting Co.
Nat'l Network: CBS Radio; *Regional Network:* Radio Pa.
Arbitron Metro Market: St.Bloomsburg,PA; *Format:* News, Oldies *Special Programming:* Farm one hr, relg 2 hrs wkly; *Hrs. of News Programming:* news progmg 15 hrs wkly; *No. News Employees:* 1 *Target Audience:* 25-54.; *Adv. Rates:* 15; 10; 15; 8
Joseph Reilly, General Manager
Nancy Reilly, Business Manager
Larry Hopper, VP Sales/Marketing

WFYY
09-01-1956; 106.5 MHz FM; 10.5 kw; 1,027 ft.; N40 56 18 W76 25 38
450 Route 204, Selinsgrove, PA 17870 US
(570) 374-8819; *Fax:* (570) 374-7444
License: Bloomsburg, Columbia County, PA held by MMP License LLC.
Group Owner: MAX Media L.L.C.; (acq 10-17-03; grpsl).
Nat'l Network: Westwood One *Regional Reps:* Dome.
Arbitron Metro Market: Wilkes Barre-Scranton, PA; *Format:* Adult Contemp; *Target Audience:* 18-49.
John Trinder, President
Tom Morgan, Operations Manager
Carol Pierson, General Manager
Greg Adair, Station Manager/Director of Sales
Kyle Alexander, Chief Engineer
Chad Evans, Digital Media Manager
Trevor Polly, Digital MediaManager
Elisa Beaver, Office Manager

Boalsburg

WBUS
04-13-1998; 93.7 MHz FM; 0.33 kw; 1362 ft.; N40 45 8 W77 45 16
2551 Park Center Blvd., State College, PA 16801 US
(814) 237-9800
www.thebus.net
License: Boalsburg, Centre County, PA held by FM Radio Licenses LLC
Group Owner: Forever Broadcasting; (acq 5-1-2005; $2.65 million with WRSC(AM) State College)
Arbitron Metro Market: State College, PA; *Format:* Classic Rock; *Target Audience:* 25-54.
Scott Cohagan, General Manager
Wendy Lynch, General Sales Mgr
Tony Riccardi, Programming Director
Robert Taylor, Chief Engineer
Bobbi Jo Clifford, Business Manager
Linda McCutcheon, Traffic Director
Lucas Bubb, ProductionCoordinator

Boyertown

WBYN-FM
10-31-1960; 107.5 MHz FM; *Hrs Open:* 24; 30 kw; 610 ft.; N40 24 15 W75 39 9
280 Mill Street, Boyertown, PA 19512 US
(610) 369-7777; *Fax:* (610) 369-7780
www.1075alive.com
info@wbynfm.com
License: Boyertown, Berks County, PA held by WDAC Radio Co.
Nat'l Reps: Katz Radio
Arbitron Metro Market: Boyertown, PA; *Format:* Contemporary Hits/Top 40, Adult Contemp; *Target Audience:* 25-54; families
Richard Crawford, President
John White, General Manager

Braddock

WRRK
06-01-1959; 96.9 MHz FM; *Hrs Open:* 24; 45 kw; 531 ft.; N40 24 42 W79 55 53
650 Smithfield Street, Suite 2200, Pittsburgh, PA 15222 US
(412) 316-3342
www.bobfm969.com
info@wrrk.com
License: Braddock, Allegheny County, PA held by Media Subsidiary, LLC
Nat'l Network: ABC
Arbitron Metro Market: Pittsburgh, PA; *Format:* Adult Contemp
Greg Frischling, General Manager
Chris Kohan, General Sales Mgr
John Robertson, Programming Director
Vicki Wolfe, Promotions Director
Amy Crago, News Director
Paul Carroll, Chief Engineer

WZUM
1550 kHz AM; 500 w-D, 900 w-N, DA-2; N42 01 47 W80 07 06
4736 Penn. Ave, Pittsburgh, PA 15224
(412) 301-9986
License: Braddock, Erie County, PA held by AM Guys LLC
Population Served: 53,515; *Arbitron Metro Market:* Pittsburgh
Ed Dehart, Owner
Clarke Ingram, Owner

Bradford

WBRR
12-01-1987; 100.1 MHz FM; *Hrs Open:* 24; 1.65 kw; 525 ft; N41 58 12 W78 42 03
1490 St. Francis Drive, PO Box 545, Bradford, PA 16701
(814) 368-4141; *Fax:* (814) 368-3180
www.100.1thehero.com
License: Bradford, McKean County, PA held by Radio Station WESB Inc.
Arbitron Metro Market: Olean, NY; *Target Audience:* 25-54.; *Adv. Rates:* Same as AM
Donald J Fredeen, President/General Manager
Dan Griffin, Programming/Music Director
Anne Holliday, News Director
Scott Douglas, Promotions Director
Frank Williams, Sports Director

WESB
04-01-1947; 1490 kHz AM; *Hrs Open:* 24; 1 kw-U; N41 27 54 W78 37 01
Box 545, 1490 St. Francis Dr., Bradford, PA 16701
(814) 368-4141; *Fax:* (814) 368-3180
www.wesb.com
1490@wesb.com
License: Bradford, McKean County, PA held by Radio Station WESB Inc.
Nat'l Network: CNN Radio; *Regional Network:* Radio Pa; *Nat'l Reps:* Dome
Population Served: 25,000; *Arbitron Metro Market:* Olean, NY; *No. News Employees:* 1; *Target Audience:* 25-54.; *Adv. Rates:* 15; 15; 15; 15
Donald Fredeen, President/General Manager
Frank Williams, Operations Dir
Peggy Austin, General Sales Mgr
Scott Douglas, Promotions Manager
Anne Holliday, News Director

*WTWT
90.5 MHz FM; 2.5 kw; 568 ft.; N42 3 18 W78 27 28
PO Box 579, 8160 Market Street, Russell, PA 16345 US
(814) 757-8744; *Fax:* (814) 757-8745
www.wtwtfm.org
info@dovefm.org
License: Bradford, McKean County, PA held by Calvary Chapel of Russell.
Arbitron Metro Market: Bradford, PA; *Format:* Christian
Jeffrey York, General Manager

Bristol

*WLBS
04-01-1998; 91.7 MHz FM; *Hrs Open:* 24; 0.1 kw vert; 69 ft.; N40 9 33 W74 51 24 *Rebroadcasts:* Rebroadcasts WRDV(FM) Warminster 100%
P. O. Box 2012, Warminster, PA 18974 US
(215) 674-8002
www.wrdv.org
info@wrdv.org
License: Bristol, Bucks County, PA held by Bux-Mont Educational Radio Association.
Wire Services: AP
Format: Variety/Diverse
Charles Loughary, Chairman
Todd Allen, General Manager

Brookville

WKQL
01-17-2000; 103.3 MHz FM; *Hrs Open:* 24; 10.5 kw; 495 ft.; N41 4 4 W79 4 59
904 North Main St., Punxsutawney, PA 15767 US
(814) 938-6000; *Fax:* (814) 938-4237
www.kool1033fm.com/
License: Brookville, Jefferson County, PA held by Renda Radio Inc.
Group Owner: Renda Broadcasting Corp.
Nat'l Network: ABC
Arbitron Metro Market: Punxsutawney, PA; *Format:* Oldies; *Hrs. of News Programming:* news progmg 2 hrs wkly; *No. News Employees:* 1; *Target Audience:* 35-54; adults; *Adv. Rates:* 24; 20; 24; 16
Jason Hill, General Manager/Sales Manager
John Smathers, Interactive Sales Manager
John Smathers, Web Content Manager

WMKX
08-22-1981; 105.5 MHz FM; *Hrs Open:* 24; 16 kw; 413 ft.; N41 7 21 W79 3 51
51 Pickering Street, Brookville, PA 15825 US
(814) 849-8100; *Fax:* (814) 849-4585
www.megarock.fm
License: Brookville, Jefferson County, PA held by Strattan Broadcasting Inc.
Arbitron Metro Market: Brookville, PA; *Format:* Light Rock *Special Programming:* Jazz 3 hrs, rock classics 6 hrs, oldies 8 hrs wkly; *Hrs. of News Programming:* news progmg 5 hrs wkly; *No. News Employees:* 1 *Target Audience:* 25-54; general
Jim Farley, Chairman
Nathan Sharp, General Manager
Kevin Heinrich, Programming Director

Burgettstown

WOGH
05-01-1947; 103.5 MHz FM; *Hrs Open:* 24; 19.5 kw; Ant 810 ft; N40 20 33 W80 37 14
320 Market Street, Steubenville, PA 43952
(740) 283-4747
www.froggyland.com
License: Burgettstown, Washington County, PA held by Key market license
Nat'l Reps: Katz *Regional Reps:* Regional Reps
Target Audience: 25-54
Lynn Deppen, President
Paul Rothfuss, General Manager/Operations Director
Scott Feist, Programming Director
Stu Schroeder, Promotions Manager
Greg Harper, Engineering Dir
Don Bangor, General Sales Manager

Burnham

WVNW
08-01-1994; 96.7 MHz FM; *Hrs Open:* 24; 0.45 kw; 850 ft.; N40 35 10 W77 41 40
114 N. Logan Blvd., Burnham, PA 17009 US
(717) 248-7827
www.star967.com
wvnw@star967.com
License: Burnham, Mifflin County, PA held by WVNW Inc.
Nat'l Network: ABC; Fox News Radio; *Regional Network:* Radio Pa.
Arbitron Metro Market: Burnham, PA; *Format:* Country; *Target Audience:* 25-54.
Jed Donahue, Operations Dir
Jed Donahue, General Manager
Tom Sheeder, Programming Director
Erik Lane, News Director
Dave Busman, Sports Commentator

Butler

WBUT
03-14-1949; 1050 kHz AM; *Hrs Open:* 24; 0.5 kw-D, ND2; 0.062 kw-N, ND2; N40 53 51 W79 53 22
252 Pillow St., Butler, PA 16001 US
(724) 283-1500; *Fax:* (724) 282-9188
www.wbut.com
frontdesk@bcrnetwork.com
License: Butler, PA held by Butler County Radio Network Inc.
Group Owner: Butler Media Group; (acq 5-19-98; grpsl).
Nat'l Network: CNN Radio
Arbitron Metro Market: Butler, PA; *Format:* Country, News/Talk; *No. News Employees:* 2; *Target Audience:* General.
Victoria Hinterberger, General Manager
Bob Cupp, Programming Director
Kayla Molczan, News Director

WISR
09-26-1941; 680 kHz AM; *Hrs Open:* 24; 0.25 kw-D, ND1; 0.05 kw-N, ND1; N40 52 39 W79 54 9
252 Pillow St., Butler, PA 16001 US
(724) 283-1500; *Fax:* (724) 293-3005
www.wisr680.com
frontdesk@bcrnetwork.com
License: Butler, PA held by Butler County Radio Network Inc.
Group Owner: Butler County Radio Network Inc.; acq 5-19-98; grpsl)
Nat'l Network: CBS; *Regional Network:* Radio Pa.
Arbitron Metro Market: Pittsburgh, PA; *Format:* Sports, News/Talk *Special Programming:* Relg 6 hrs wlky; *Hrs. of News Programming:* news progmg 28 hrs wkly; *No. News Employees:* 2; *Target Audience:* 45 plus.
Victoria Hinterberger, General Manager
Bob Cupp, Programming Director
Kayla Molczan, News Director

WLER-FM
03-14-1949; 97.7 MHz FM; *Hrs Open:* 24; 4.6 kw; 374 ft.; N40 53 51 W79 53 22
252 Pillow St., Butler, PA 16001 US
(724) 283-1500; *Fax:* (724) 283-3005
www.977rocks.com
frontdesk@bcrnetwork.com
License: Butler, Butler County, PA held by Butler County Radio Network Inc.
Group Owner: Butler County Radio Network Inc.
Nat'l Network: Westwood One; CNN Radio
Arbitron Metro Market: Pittsburgh, PA; *Format:* Rock/AOR; *No. News Employees:* 2
Victoria Hinterberger, General Manager
Bob Cupp, Programming Director
Kayla Molczan, News Director

California

***WCAL**
09-01-1973; 91.9 MHz FM; *Hrs Open:* 24; 3 kw; 161 ft.; N40 2 57 W79 54 1
428 Hickory Street, California, PA 15419 US
(724) 938-3000; *Fax:* (724) 938-5959
sal.calu.edu/wcal
License: California, Washington County, PA held by The Student Association Inc.
Nat'l Network: Westwood One
Arbitron Metro Market: California, PA; *Format:* Rock/AOR *Special Programming:* Contemp Christian 6 hrs, urban contemp 12 hrs, rap; *Hrs. of News Programming:* News progmg 5 hrs wkly; *Target Audience:* 18-25; studentsat California Univ
Nick Smith, Operations Dir
Ian Hatfield, Business Director
Kaitlyn O'Toole, Station Manager
Steve Maggin, Programming Director
Steve Dentel, Imaging Director

Cambridge Springs

WXMJ
07-14-1997; 104.5 MHz FM; *Hrs Open:* 24; 2.55 kw; 512 ft.; N41 42 10 W80 9 54
Mailing Address: 900 Water St., Downtown Mall, Meadville, PA 16335 US
Second Address: 1243 Liberty St., Suite 501, Franklin, PA 16323
(814) 724-1111; *Fax:* (814) 333-9628
www.mymajicspace.com
License: Cambridge Springs, Crawford County, PA held by FM Radio Licenses LLC
Group Owner: Forever Broadcasting; (acq 7-21-2000; grpsl)
Arbitron Metro Market: Meadville-Franklin, PA; *Format:* Adult Contemp; *Target Audience:* 21-54; females
Jim Shields, General Manager
Helen Powers, Sales Manager
Scott Woloszyn, Programming Director
Mark Himmler, Chief Engineer
Jill Hamilton, Business Manager

***WCGF**
01-01-2005; 89.9 MHz FM; 25 kw; 531 ft.; N41 49 25 W80 10 23.90 *Rebroadcasts:* Rebroadcasts WCIK(FM) Bath, NY 100%
Mailing Address: PO Box 506, Bath, NY 14810 US
Second Address: 7634 Campbell Creek Rd., Bath, NY 14810
(607) 776-4151
www.fln.org
License: Cambridge Springs, PA held by Family Life Ministries Inc.
Group Owner: Family Life Network
Nat'l Network: Salem Radio Network; *Wire Services:* Metro Weather Service Inc.

Arbitron Metro Market: Dallas, PA; *Format:* Christian; *Hrs. of News Programming:* news progmg 14 hrs wkly; *No. News Employees:* 3; *Target Audience:* 30-54.
Dave Margalotti, Operations Dir
Terese Main, Programming Director
Bob Price, News Director

Canonsburg

WWCS
11-28-1957; 540 kHz AM; *Hrs Open:* 24; 5 kw-D, DA2; 0.5 kw-N, DA2; N40 17 22 W80 11 7
38 Angerer Rd., Canonsburg, PA 15317 US
(724) 745-5400
www.birach.com
sima@birach.com
License: Canonsburg, Washington County, PA held by Birach Broadcasting Corp.
Group Owner: Birach Broadcasting Corp.; (acq 5-28-92; $475,000;
Arbitron Metro Market: Pittsburgh, PA; *Format:* Sports, Talk; *Target Audience:* Educated adults, ethnic groups, open minded.
Sima Birach, Operations Manager

Canton

WHGL-FM
08-30-1978; 100.3 MHz FM; *Hrs Open:* 24; 3.9 kw; 846 ft.; N41 44 32 W76 50 8
PO Box 100, Troy, PA 16947 US
(570) 297-0100
www.wiggle100.com
License: Canton, Bradford County, PA held by Cantroair Communications Inc.
Nat'l Network: ABC
Format: Country; *No. News Employees:* 1; *Target Audience:* 25-54.
Mike Powers, President
Bob Gisler, Operations Dir
Shane Wilber, Programming Director
David Rockwell, Promotions Manager

Carbondale

WTRW(FM)
01-01-1965; 94.3 MHz FM; *Hrs Open:* 24; 1.1 kw; Ant 770 ft; N41 32 37 W75 27 44
1049 N. Sekol Rd., Scranton, PA 18504
(570) 344-1221 ext. 28; *Fax:* (570) 344-0996
boldgoldradionepa.com
bspinelli@boldgoldmedia.com
License: Carbondale, Lackawanna County, PA held by Bold Gold Media Group LP
Group Owner: Bold Gold Media Group LP
Population Served: 821,623; *Arbitron Metro Market:* Lehigh Valley, PA; *Format:* Adult Contemp
Brian Spinelli, General Manager

WCDL
01-01-1950; 1440 kHz AM; 5 kw-D, ND2; 0.037 kw-N, ND2; N41 33 28 W75 29 11
1049 N. Sekol Rd., Scranton, PA 18504 US
(570) 344-1221; *Fax:* (570) 344-0996
boldgoldradionepa.com
License: Carbondale, PA held by Bold Gold Media Group LP
Group Owner: Bold Gold Media Group LP
Arbitron Metro Market: Wilkes Barre-Scranton, PA

Carlisle

***WDCV-FM**
01-01-1972; 88.3 MHz FM; *Hrs Open:* 7 AM-2 AM; 0.45 kw horiz; -43 ft.; N40 12 9 W77 11 46
Dickinson College, College & Louther Street, Carlisle, PA 17013 US
(717) 245-1444
wdcvfm@gmail.com
License: Carlisle, Cumberland County, PA held by Board of Trustees Dickinson College.
Arbitron Metro Market: Carlisle, PA; *Format:* Variety/Diverse *Special Programming:* Jazz 6 hrs, Ger one hr, Sp one hr, funk/rap 15 hrs, Russian one hr, politics one hr, blues 6 hrs wkly; *Hrs. of News Programming:* newsprogmg 5 hrs wkly; *No. News Employees:* 5
Nick Stamos, General Manager
Ben, Programming Director

WHYL
01-01-1948; 960 kHz AM; *Hrs Open:* 24; 5 kw-D, DA2; 0.022 kw-N, DA2; N40 11 34 W77 10 28
1703 Walnut Bottom Road, Carlisle, PA 17015 US
(717) 249-1717; *Fax:* (717) 258-4638
www.whylradio.com
License: Carlisle, PA held by Trustworthy Radio LLC
Nat'l Reps: McGavren Guild
Arbitron Metro Market: Harrisburg-Lebanon-Carlisle, PA; *Format:* News, News/Talk, 86 *Special Programming:* Polka 2 hrs; *No. News Employees:* 1; *Target Audience:* 45 plus; older, mature adults
Kevin Kremer, Operations Dir
Bruce Collier, General Manager
Karen Peiffer, News Director

WCAT-FM
01-01-1959; 102.3 MHz FM; *Hrs Open:* 24; 3 kw horiz, 2.75 kw vert; 328 ft.; N40 17 23 W77 8 10
Mailing Address: 728 North Hanover St., Carlisle, PA 17013 US
Second Address: 1703 Walnut Bottom Rd., Carlisle, PA 17013
(717) 243-1200
www.red1023.com
rickonred@red1023.com
License: Carlisle, Cumberland County, PA held by Radio Carlisle Inc.
Group Owner: Radio Carlisle, Inc.
Nat'l Network: CNN Radio
Arbitron Metro Market: Harrisburg-Lebanon-Carlisle, PA; *Format:* Country; *Target Audience:* 25-54.
David Shadle, General Sales Mgr
Rick Stern, Programming/Music Director
Sam Krepps, Promotions Manager

WIOO
07-08-1965; 1000 kHz AM; *Hrs Open:* Sunrise-sunset/AM, 24/7/FM; 1 kw-D, NDD; Non-Directional; N40 9 30 W77 11 49
180 York Rd, Carlisle, PA 17013 US
(717) 243-1200; *Fax:* (717) 243-1277
www.wioo.com
wioo@pa.net
License: Carlisle, PA held by WIOO, Inc.
Nat'l Network: Motor Racing Net; ABC Information & Entertainment; Westwood One; *Regional Network:* Radio Pa.
Arbitron Metro Market: Harrisburg-Lebanon-Carlisle, PA; *Format:* Country *Special Programming:* Relg 5 hrs wkly; *Hrs. of News Programming:* news progmg 5 hrs wkly; *No. News Employees:* 1; *Target Audience:* 21plus.; *Adv. Rates:* 20; 20; 20; 15
Harold Swidler, President
Florence Fisher, General Manager
Sandy Loy, General Sales Mgr
Ray Thomas, Programming Director
Randy Freed, Senior Account Executive
Ed Swidler, Operations Manager

Cashtown

***WFKJ**
12-07-1988; 890 kHz AM; *Hrs Open:* 7 AM-6 PM; 0.89 kw-D, NDD; N39 52 59 W77 20 43
Mailing Address: P. O. Box 115, Cashtown, PA 17310 US
Second Address: 3425 Chambersburg Rd., Biglerville, PA 17307
(800) 555-4575; *Fax:* (717) 334-8914
djy@wordbroadcast.org
License: Cashtown, PA held by Jesus is Lord Ministries International.
Nat'l Network: Moody
Arbitron Metro Market: York, PA *TV Affiliate:* livestream TV; *Format:* Religious *Special Programming:* Country 4 hrs, children 12 hrs wkly; *Target Audience:* General.
Rev. Michael Yeager, President
Fred Bream, Promotions Manager
Larry Angle, Chief Engineer

Central City

WCCL
10-19-1972; 101.7 MHz FM; *Hrs Open:* 24; 0.72 kw; 643 ft.; N40 6 42 W78 51 33
109 Plaza Dr., Johnstown, PA 15905 US
(814) 255-4186; *Fax:* (814) 255-6145
www.cool101online.com
License: Central City, Somerset County, PA held by FM Radio Licenses LLC
Group Owner: Forever Broadcasting; (acq 2-16-2005; grpsl).
Arbitron Metro Market: Johnstown, PA; *Format:* Oldies *Special Programming:* Relg 4 hrs wkly; *No. News Employees:* 4; *Target Audience:* 25-54.
Mike Stevens, Operations Manager
Terry Deitz, General Manager
Tina Perry, Sales Manager
Rick Shepard, Programming Director
Sean Glenn, Chief Engineer
Shelly Lovenduski, Business Manager
Al Steele, Production Director

GeorgeLucas, Copywriter
Theresa Jarosick, Traffic
Beth Thomas, Traffic/EEO Officer

Centre Hall

WMAJ-FM

05-24-1989; 99.5 MHz FM; *Hrs Open:* 24; 0.85 kw; 1368 ft.; N40 45 9 W77 45 16
2551 Park Center Blvd., State College, PA 16801 US
(814) 237-9800; *Fax:* (814) 237-2477
www.majic99.com
License: Centre Hall, Centre County, PA held by FM Radio Licenses LLC
Group Owner: Forever Broadcasting; (acq 4-29-2002; $875,000 with WHUN(AM) Huntingdon)
Arbitron Metro Market: State College, PA; *Format:* Variety/Diverse; *Target Audience:* 21-54; females
Scott Cohagan, General Manager
Wendy Lynch, General Sales Mgr
Jerry Valeri, Programming Director
Robert Taylor, Chief Engineer
Linda McCutcheon, Traffic Manager
Bobbi Jo Clifford, Business Manager
Lucas Bubb, ProductionCoordinator

Chambersburg

WCHA

08-11-1946; 800 kHz AM; 1 kw-D, ND1; 0.196 kw-N, ND1; N39 55 41 W77 41 44
25 Penncraft Ave., Chambersburg, PA 17201 US
(717) 264-7121; *Fax:* (717) 263-9649
www.thenewfm963.com
feedback@thenewfm963.com
License: Chambersburg, Franklin County, PA held by Alpha Media Licensee LLC
Group Owner: Alpha Media LLC; (acq 4-17-2014; grpsl).
Nat'l Network: ABC
Arbitron Metro Market: Hagerstown-Chambersburg-Waynesboro, MD-PA; *Format:* Oldies, 86 *Special Programming:* Relg 8 hrs, gospel 2 hrs wkly; *No. News Employees:* 1; *Target Audience:* 25-54.
Rich Bateman, General Manager
Ed Dorsey, Sales Manager

WIKZ

04-15-1948; 95.1 MHz FM; 50 kw; 449 ft.; N39 55 41 W77 41 44
25 Penncraft Ave., Chambersburg, PA 17201 US
(717) 263-0813; *Fax:* (717) 263-9649
www.mix95.com
License: Chambersburg, Franklin County, PA held by Alpha Media Licensee LLC
Group Owner: Alpha Media LLC; (acq 4-17-2014; grpsl).
Arbitron Metro Market: Hagerstown-Chambersburg-Waynesboro, MD-PA; *Format:* Adult Contemp; *No. News Employees:* 1; *Target Audience:* 25-44.
Rich Bateman, General Manager
Rick Alexander, Programming Director
Tammy Heckman, Promotions Director
Lisa Kline, News Director
Artie Shultz, Imaging Director
Jeff Wine, Creative Services Director

*WZXQ

01-01-2005; 88.3 MHz FM; 110 w vert; Ant 1,155 ft; N39 57 40 W77 28 32 *Rebroadcasts:* Rebroadcasts WBYO(FM) Sellersville 100%
Box 186, Sellersville, PA 18960
(215) 721-2141; *Fax:* (215) 721-9811
www.wordfm.org
wordfm@wordfm.org
License: Chambersburg, Franklin County, PA held by Four Rivers Community Broadcasting Corp.
Group Owner: Four Rivers Community Broadcasting Corp.
Arbitron Metro Market: Hagerstown-Chambersburg-Waynesboro, MD-PA
Charles Loughery, President
Meg Sabulsky, Operations Dir
David Baker, General Manager
Meg Sabulsky, Programming Director
William Dunn, Promotions Manager
Charles Loughery, Engineering Dir

Chester

*WDNR

04-22-1977; 89.5 MHz FM; *Hrs Open:* 9; 0.008 kw; 85 ft.; N39 51 42 W75 21 20
Box 1000 Widender Univ, Chester, PA 19013 US
(610) 499-4439
www.wdnrfm.org
License: Chester, Delaware County, PA held by Widener University.
Arbitron Metro Market: Philadelphia, PA; *Format:* Variety/Diverse *Special Programming:* Jazz 2 hrs, blues 2 hrs, oldies 2 hrs, children 2 hrs wkly; *Target Audience:* 16-30; high school & college age population
Erik Bjorken, General Manager
Bella Schnoenng, Programming Director
Michael Booth, Production Manager
Dwight DeWerth-Pallmeyer, Faculty Advisor

WPWA

10-01-1947; 1590 kHz AM; *Hrs Open:* 24
12 Kent Road, Aston, PA 19014-1406 US
(610) 358-1400; *Fax:* (610) 358-1845
www.wpwa.net
License: Chester, PA held by Mount Ocean Media L.L.C.
Group Owner: Mountain Broadcasting Corp.; (acq 8-20-2001; $675,000).
Arbitron Metro Market: Philadelphia; *Format:* Christian, Gospel, 74; *Hrs. of News Programming:* News progmg 20 hrs wkly; *Target Audience:* 25-64; affluent, mature adults
Amanly Cora, Operations Director
Ruth Salmeron Shelton, General Manager
Raul Guadalupe, Production Director

WVCH

04-04-1948; 740 kHz AM; *Hrs Open:* 6 AM-6 PM; 1 kw-D, ND1; 0.006 kw-N, ND1; N39 52 38 W75 24 24
Mailing Address: Box 102, Springhouse, PA 19477 US
Second Address: 308 Dutton Mill Rd., Brookhaven, PA 19015
(610) 279-9000; *Fax:* (610) 279-9002
www.wvch.com
License: Chester, PA held by WVCH Communications Inc.
Nat'l Network: Moody; USA
Arbitron Metro Market: Philadelphia, PA; *Format:* Christian, Religious; *Target Audience:* General.
Charlotte Cosden, Advertising Contact

Clarendon

WKNB

08-31-1995; 104.3 MHz FM; *Hrs Open:* 24; 4.7 kw; 371 ft.; N41 48 50 W79 10 4
310 Second Ave, PO Box 824, Warren, PA 16365 US
(814) 723-1310; *Fax:* (814) 723-3356
www.kibcoradio.com
info@kibcoradio.com
License: Clarendon, Warren County, PA held by Radio Partners LLC.
Group Owner: Radio Partners LLC; (acq 9-30-2005; grpsl)
Nat'l Network: AP Radio *Regional Reps:* Commercial Media Sales; *Wire Services:* AP
Format: Country; *No. News Employees:* 1; *Target Audience:* 18-45.
Dale Bliss, General Manager
Samantha Williams, Production Director
Mark Silvis, Programming Director
Jennifer Bliss, Promotions Manager
Karen White, Business Manager

Clarion

WCCR

06-28-1985; 92.7 MHz FM; *Hrs Open:* 24; 3 kw; 279 ft.; N41 14 41 W79 15 42
Mailing Address: 725 Wood St P.O. Box 688, Clarion, PA 16214 US
Second Address: 1168 Greenville Pike, Clarion, PA 16214
(814) 226-4500; *Fax:* (814) 226-5898
clarionradio@comcast.net
License: Clarion, Clarion County, PA
Group Owner: Clarion County Broadcasting Corp.
Regional Reps: Dome & Associates
Arbitron Metro Market: Clarion, PA; *Format:* Adult Contemp; *Hrs. of News Programming:* news progmg 8 hrs wkly; *No. News Employees:* 1; *Target Audience:* 25-54.; *Adv. Rates:* 13; 13; 13; 13

*WCUC-FM

04-01-1977; 91.7 MHz FM; *Hrs Open:* 25.?Â ?; 3.2 kw; 318 ft.; N41 12 35 W79 22 39
G55 Becker Hall, Clarion, PA 16214 US
(814) 393-2330(814) 393-2514; *Fax:* (814) 393-2065
www.wcuc.org
bexley@clarion.edu
License: Clarion, Clarion County, PA held by State College
Wire Services: AP
Arbitron Metro Market: Clarion, PA; *Format:* Contemporary Hits/Top 40 *Special Programming:* Urban 6 hrs, country 6 hrs, jazz 3 hrs, community 12 hrs wkly
Bruce Exley, Operations Dir
Bill Adams, General Manager

WWCH

06-12-1960; 1300 kHz AM; *Hrs Open:* 24
Mailing Address: P.O. Box 688, 1300 Greenville Ave Ext., Clarion, PA 16214 US
Second Address: 1168 Greenville Pike, Clarion, PA 16214
(814) 226-4500; *Fax:* (814) 226-5898
www.clarioncountydailynews.com
clarionradio@comcast.net
License: Clarion, PA held by Clarion County Broadcasting Corp.
Group Owner: Clarion County Broadcasting Corp.
Nat'l Network: CBS Radio; *Regional Network:* Radio Pa; *Nat'l Reps:* Dome
Arbitron Metro Market: Clarion, PA; *Format:* Country, News, 62, Talk *Special Programming:* Pub affrs, relg 8 hrs wkly; *Hrs. of News Programming:* news progmg 8 hrs wkly; *No. News Employees:* 1; *Target Audience:* 25-54.; *Adv. Rates:* 12.50; 12.50; 12.50; 10
William Hearst, President

Clearfield

WCPA

01-01-1947; 900 kHz AM; 2.5 kw-D, DA2; 0.5 kw-N, DA2; N41 2 32 W78 26 54
306 Port St., Easton, MD 21601 US
(410) 822-3301; *Fax:* (410) 822-0576
www.firstmediaradio.com
License: Clearfield, PA held by First Media Radio LLC.
Group Owner: First Media Radio LLC; (acq 1-23-2007; $750,000 with co-located FM)
Nat'l Reps: Dome
Arbitron Metro Market: Clearfield- DuBois,PA; *Format:* Oldies; *Target Audience:* 35 plus.
Alex Kolobielski, President/CEO

WQYX

07-12-1967; 93.1 MHz FM; *Hrs Open:* 24; 1.7 kw; 942 ft.; N41 4 5 W78 31 7
801 E. Dubois Ave., DuBois, PA 15801 US
(814) 371-6100; *Fax:* (814) 765-6333
License: Clearfield, Clearfield County, PA held by First Media Radio, LLC
Group Owner: First Media Radio LLC
Format: Adult Contemp; *Target Audience:* 18-44.
Alex Kolobielski, President/CEO

Coatesville

*WCOJ

11-29-1949; 1420 kHz AM; *Hrs Open:* 24
PO Box 798, Doylestown, PA 18901 US
(215) 345-1570; *Fax:* (215) 345-1946
www.holyspiritradio.org
1570am@holyspiritradio.org
License: Coatesville, PA held by Holy Spirit Radio Foundation Inc.
Nat'l Network: EWTN Radio
Arbitron Metro Market: Chester County, PA; *Format:* Christian
Dale Meier, President

*WRTI

89.3 MHz FM; 0.001 kw horiz, 0.46 kw vert; 287 ft.; N40 1 26 W75 48 48
1509 Cecil B. Moore Avenue, 3rd Floor, Philadelphia, PA 19121 US
(215) 204-8405; *Fax:* (215) 204-7027
www.wrti.org
comments@wrti.org
License: Coatesville, Chester County, PA held by Temple University of The Commonwealth System of Higher Education.
Arbitron Metro Market: Coatesville, PA; *Format:* Classical, Jazz
David Conant, General Manager
Joe Patti, Production Manager
Jane Kelly, Director of Development
Jeffrey De Polo, Director of Engineering
William Johnson, Station Manager
Tobias Poole, Operating Director

Columbia

WVZN

01-01-1957; 1580 kHz AM; *Hrs Open:* 24
1927 Columbia Ave., Lancaster, PA 17603 US
(717) 823-9300; *Fax:* (717) 290-1698
License: Columbia, PA held by Esfuerzo de Union Cristiana
Arbitron Metro Market: Lancaster, PA
Wilson Cortez, General Manager

Conway

***WMTP**
08-08-2012; 96.1 MHz FM; 90 w; 866 feet; N44 03 30 W71 05 31
P.O. Box 398, New Durham, NH 03855 US
(603) 859-9170; *Fax:* (603) 859-8172
www.wsew.org
info@kissfm961.com
License: Conway, Allegheny County, NH held by Word Radio Educational Foundation
Group Owner: Word Radio Educational Foundation
Arbitron Metro Market: Conway, NH; *Format:* Christian
Ronald R. Malone, President
Sharon Malone, Operations Manager

Cooperstown

WUUZ
01-01-2002; 107.7 MHz FM; *Hrs Open:* 24; 4.5 kw; 377 ft.; N41 29 23 W79 44 7
Mailing Address: 900 Water St., Downtown Mall, Meadville, PA 16335 US
Second Address: 1243 Liberty St., Suite 501, Franklin, PA 16323
(814) 724-1111; *Fax:* (814) 333-9628
www.mywuzz.com
License: Cooperstown, Venango County, PA held by FM Radio Licenses LLC
Group Owner: Forever Broadcasting; (acq 7-5-01; $342,000 for CP).
Arbitron Metro Market: Meadville-Franklin, PA; *Format:* Classic Rock, Adult Contemp
Jim Shields, General Manager
Helen Powers, Sales Manager
Rich Anton, Programming Director
Mark Himmler, Chief Engineer
Jill Hamilton, Business Manager

Corry

WWCB(AM)
04-02-1955; 1370 kHz AM; *Hrs Open:* 6 AM-11 PM (M-F); 7 AM-11 PM (S);; 1 kw-D, 500 w-N, DA-N; N41 56 10 W79 39 20
Mailing Address: Box 4, Corry, PA 16407
Second Address: 418 N. Center, Corry, PA 16407
(814) 664-8694; *Fax:* (814) 664-8695
License: Corry, Erie County, PA held by Corry Communications Corp.
Nat'l Network: Motor Racing Net; Westwood One; CBS
Population Served: 101,807; *Arbitron Metro Market:* Erie, PA; *Format:* Classic Rock, Oldies, 84; *Target Audience:* General.; *Adv. Rates:* 10.25; 10.25; 10.25; 10.25
William Hammond III, President

Coudersport

WFRM
05-01-1953; 600 kHz AM; 1 kw-D, ND1; 0.046 kw-N, ND1; N41 45 11 W78 0 3
9 South Main St., Coudersport, PA 16915 US
(814) 274-8600; *Fax:* (814) 274-0760
License: Coudersport, Potter County, PA held by L-COM, Inc.
Group Owner: Allegheny Mountain Network Stations
Nat'l Network: ABC; *Nat'l Reps:* Dome
Format: Adult Contemp *Special Programming:* Farm 2 hrs wkly; *Target Audience:* General.
Cary H. Simpson, President

Covington

WDKC
01-01-1994; 101.5 MHz FM; 1.9 kw; 594 ft.; N41 43 25 W77 2 46
Mailing Address: 83 Jacobs Road, Marlboro, MA 01752 US
Second Address: 8767 Rt. 414, Liberty, PA 16930
(570) 662-9000; *Fax:* (570) 324-1015
kc101@sosbbs.com
License: Covington, Tioga County, PA held by Mid-Atlantic Broadcasting Inc.
Arbitron Metro Market: Elmira, NY; *Format:* Country; *Hrs. of News Programming:* news progmg 3 hrs wkly; *No. News Employees:* 1; *Target Audience:* 25-54; 70% female; *Adv. Rates:* 12; 8; 9; 5
Thomas Gluszczak, Chairman
Kevin Thomas, CEO
Kevin Gluszczak, General Manager

Cresson

WBRX
11-01-1981; 94.7 MHz FM; *Hrs Open:* 24; 0.97 kw; 794 ft.; N40 24 11 W78 31 35
2513 6th Avenue, Altoona, PA 16602 US
(814) 943-6112; *Fax:* (814) 944-9782
www.mymix947.com
License: Cresson, Cambria County, PA held by Sounds Good Inc.
Nat'l Network: Westwood One
Arbitron Metro Market: Altoona, PA; *Format:* Adult Contemp; *Hrs. of News Programming:* news progmg 7 hrs wkly; *No. News Employees:* 1; *Target Audience:* 18-54; males
Diane Boslet, Operations Dir
David Barger, General Manager
Ken Maguda, Programming Director
Jody Gardner, Traffic Manager

Curwensville

WOKW
08-01-1989; 102.9 MHz FM; 0.35 kw; 945 ft.; N41 4 29 W78 31 58
P.O. Box 589, Clearfield, PA 16830 US
(814) 765-4955; *Fax:* (814) 765-7038
www.wokw.com
news@wokw.com
License: Curwensville, Clearfield County, PA held by Raymark Broadcasting Co. Inc.
TV Affiliate: Adult contemp; *Format:* Oldies *Special Programming:* news progmg 14 hrs wkly; *Hrs. of News Programming:* 1; *No. News Employees:* 21-54.
Mark Harley, President

Dallas

WSJR
01-01-1988; 93.7 MHz FM; *Hrs Open:* 24; 1.45 kw; 679 ft.; N41 15 43 W75 58 4
600 Baltimore Dr., Wilkes-Barre, PA 18702 US
(570) 824-9000; *Fax:* (570) 820-0520
www.nashfm937.com
License: Dallas, PA held by Radio License Holding CBC, LLC
Group Owner: Cumulus Media Inc.; (acq 2-4-98; grpsl).
Nat'l Network: CBS; *Nat'l Reps:* Roslin
Arbitron Metro Market: Wilkes Barre-Scranton, PA; *Format:* Country; *No. News Employees:* 1
Shannon Spak, General Sales Mgr
Mike Vincent, Programming Director
Erin Evans, Promotions Director
Joe Rae, IT Manager
Gerald Getz, Market Manager

***WCIG**
01-01-2005; 107.7 MHz FM; 2.35 kw; 531 ft.; N41 18 54 W75 53 19.00 *Rebroadcasts:* Rebroadcasts WCIK(FM) Bath, NY 100%
Mailing Address: PO Box 506, Bath, NY 14810 US
Second Address: 7634 Campbell Creek Rd., Bath, NY 14810
(607) 776-4151
www.fln.org
License: Dallas, Lackawanna County, PA held by Family Life Ministries Inc.
Group Owner: Family Life Network
Nat'l Network: Salem Radio Network; *Wire Services:* Metro Weather Service Inc.
Arbitron Metro Market: Dallas, PA; *Format:* Christian; *Hrs. of News Programming:* news progmg 14 hrs wkly; *No. News Employees:* 3; *Target Audience:* 30-54.
Dave Margalotti, Operations Dir
Terese Main, Programming Director
Bob Price, News Director

Danville

***WPGM**
09-06-1968; 96.7 MHz FM; 0.57 kW; 764 ft.; N40 59 16 W76 32 51
28 E Market St, Danville, PA 17821 USA
(570) 275-1570; *Fax:* (570) 275-4071
wpgmfm.org
License: Danville, PA held by Montrose Broadcasting Corp.
Group Owner: Montrose Broadcasting Corp.
Arbitron Metro Market: Sunbury-Selinsgrove-Lewisburg, PA; *Format:* Religious

Doylestown

WISP
01-01-1948; 1570 kHz AM; *Hrs Open:* 24
PO Box 798, Doylestown, PA 18901 US
(215) 345-1570; *Fax:* (215) 345-1946
www.holyspiritradio.org
1570am@holyspiritradio.org
License: Doylestown, PA held by Holy Spirit Radio Foundation Inc.
Arbitron Metro Market: Philadelphia; *Format:* Religious; *Hrs. of News Programming:* News progmg 14 hrs wkly; *Target Audience:* General.
Dale Meier, CEO

Du Bois

WCED
02-01-1941; 1420 kHz AM; *Hrs Open:* 24
12 West Long Ave., DuBois, PA 15801 US
(814) 375-5260
www.1420wced.com
License: Du Bois, PA held by WCED Radio LLC.
Group Owner: Priority Communications; acq 11-28-2003; $150,000).
Nat'l Network: ABC; ESPN Radio
Arbitron Metro Market: DuBois, PA; *Format:* News/Talk, Sports; *Hrs. of News Programming:* news progmg 20 hrs wkly; *No. News Employees:* 1
Jay Philippone, General Manager
Lori Lewis, Station Manager

***WCOH-FM**
11-12-1975; 107.3 MHz FM; *Hrs Open:* 24; 25 kw; 499 ft.; N41 25 08 W78 39 38
PO Box 506, Bath, NY 14810 US
(607) 776-4151
www.fln.org
License: Du Bois, Clearfield County, PA held by Family Life Ministries Inc.
Group Owner: Family Life Network; (acq 10-6-93; $360,000;
Nat'l Reps: Salem; *Wire Services:* AP
Arbitron Metro Market: DuBois, PA; *Format:* Christian; *Target Audience:* 25-54
Dave Margalotti, Operations Dir
Terese Main, Programming Director
Bob Price, News Director

WOWQ
01-01-1948; 102.1 MHz FM; *Hrs Open:* 24; 28 kw; 663 ft.; N41 2 43 W78 42 11
801 E Dubois Ave., DuBois, PA 15801 US
(814) 371-6100
www.q102radio.fm
License: Du Bois, Clearfield County, PA held by First Media Radio LLC.
Group Owner: First Media Radio LLC; (acq 4-10-2002; $4.2 million with WCED(AM) DuBois)
Format: Country; *Hrs. of News Programming:* news progmg 10 hrs wkly; *No. News Employees:* 1; *Target Audience:* 18 plus.
Alex Kolobielski, CEO

Dushore

WDYS
08-01-1998; 103.9 MHz FM; *Hrs Open:* 24; 4.3 kw; 202 ft.; N41 26 6 W76 28 28
54 Wilmar Dr, P.O. Box 701, Tunkhannock, PA 18657 US
(570) 265-7600; *Fax:* (570) 265-7603
www.iloveyesfm.com
comments@iloveyesfm.com
License: Dushore, Sullivan County, PA held by Geos Communications.
Group Owner: Geos Communications; (acq 8-1-2008)
Arbitron Metro Market: Williamsport, PA; *Format:* Adult Contemp; *Hrs. of News Programming:* News progmg 4 hrs wkly; *Target Audience:* 25-54; adults; *Adv. Rates:* 12; 10; 12; 8

East Nottingham

***WZXE**
88.3 MHz FM; 1 w horiz, 540 w vert; Ant 453 ft; N39 44 00 W75 57 56
Box 186, Sellersville, PA
(215) 721-2141; *Fax:* (215) 721-9811
www.wordfm.org
License: East Nottingham, Chester County, PA held by Four Rivers Community Broadcasting Corp.
Group Owner: Four Rivers Community Broadcasting Corp.

Charles Loughery, President
Meg Sabulsky, Operations Dir
David Baker, General Manager
Meg Sabulsky, Programming Director
William Dunn, Promotions Manager
Charles Loughery, Engineering Dir

East Stroudsburg

***WESS**
03-10-1971; 90.3 MHz FM; 1 kw; -121 ft.; N40 59 50 W75 10 22
Communications Center, East Stroudsburg, PA 18301 US
(570) 422-3512
wess@esu.edu
License: East Stroudsburg, Monroe County, PA held by East Stroudsburg University Board of Trustees/Student Activities Association.
Arbitron Metro Market: East Stroudsburg, PA; *Format:* Alternative, Sports, 94 *Special Programming:* Class 4 hrs, educ 7 hrs, jazz 6 hrs, news/talk 6 hrs,oldies 8 hrs wkly
Cory Nidoh, Station Manager
Amanda Woods, Programming Director
LaShondra Cherry, Promotions Manager
Brianna Strunk, News Director
Shane Adamson, Sports Director
Chris Symonds, Music Director
Greg Curtis, Training Director
Brandon Borgella, Production Manager
Jordan McCoonse, Business Director
Sara Solares, Education Director

Easton

WCTO
01-01-1947; 96.1 MHz FM; *Hrs Open:* 24; 50 kw; 499 ft.; N40 35 55 W75 25 12
2158 Avenue C, Suite 100, Bethlehem, PA 18017 US
(610) 266-7600
www.catcountry96.com
studio@catcountry96.com
License: Easton, Northampton County, PA held by Radio License Holding CBC, LLC
Group Owner: Cumulus Media Inc.
Nat'l Reps: Christal; Katz Radio
Arbitron Metro Market: Allentown-Bethlehem, PA; *Format:* Country
Elizabeth Penbleton, Sales
Jerry Padden, Programming Director
Barry Dawson, Promotions Manager

WEEX
05-01-1956; 1230 kHz AM; 0.84 kw-D, DAD; 1 kw-N, DAD; N40 42 30 W75 13 0
107 Paxionose Rd. W, Easton, PA 18040 US
(610) 258-6155; *Fax:* (610) 258-6292
www.espnlv.com
tomf@espnlv.com
License: Easton, PA held by Connoisseur Media Licenses LLC
Group Owner: Connoisseur Media LLC
Nat'l Network: ESPN Radio; *Nat'l Reps:* Katz Radio *Regional Reps:* Glenn Jones
Arbitron Metro Market: Easton, PA; *Format:* Sports; *Target Audience:* 18-49; men
Rick Musselman, General Manager
Michael Anthony, General Sales Mgr
Tom Fallon, Programming Director
K.J. Zabala, Promotions Manager

WEST
04-01-2006; 1400 kHz AM; *Hrs Open:* 24; 1 kw-U, ND1; N40 40 23 W75 12 30 *Rebroadcasts:* WHOL-AM 100% Simulcast
1125 Colorado Street, Allentown, PA 18103 US
(610) 434-4801; *Fax:* (484) 223-0088
www.laolaradio.com
matthew@laolaradio.com
License: Easton, PA held by WHOL Radio Inc.
Arbitron Metro Market: Allentown, PA; *Format:* Spanish; *Hrs. of News Programming:* 5 hrs per week; *No. News Employees:* 8; *Target Audience:* Hispanic - 25 - 54; *Adv. Rates:* $38 - $52 Gross
Matthew J. Braccili, Owner/President
Jeffrey Maddox, Operations
Olga Negron, Sales
Tony Rodriguez, Programming Director

***WJRH**
03-01-1953; 104.9 MHz FM; *Hrs Open:* 15; 0.008 kw; 23 ft.; N40 41 53 W75 12 30
Farinon Center Box 9473, 111 Quad Drive, Easton, PA 18042-1784 US
(610) 330-5316; *Fax:* (610) 250-5318
www.wjrh.org
wjrh@lafayette.edu
License: Easton, Northampton County, PA held by Lafayette College.
Arbitron Metro Market: Allentown-Bethlehem, PA; *Format:* Variety/Diverse *Special Programming:* Jazz 9 hrs, reggae 6 hrs, metal 6 hrs, Sp 6 hrs, c; *Hrs. of News Programming:* news progmg 6 hrs wkly; *No. News Employees:* 3; *Target Audience:* General; college students & community
Candace Beach, President/General Manager
Jordan Blake, Treasurer
Joe Cericola, Programming Director
Alex Hytha, Chief Engineer
Kathleen Nolan, PR Director
Karina Goodman, Secretary
Marci Weinstein, Community Outreach/EventDirector
Mike Fogarty, Music Director
Jeff Pfaffmann, Faculty Advisor

WODE-FM
06-01-1950; 99.9 MHz FM; 50 kw; 449 ft.; N40 42 30 W75 13 0
200 Concord Plaza, Suite 600, San Antonio, TX 78216 US
(610) 258-6155; *Fax:* (610) 253-3384
License: Easton, Northampton County, PA held by Connoisseur Media Licenses LLC
Group Owner: Connoisseur Media LLC
Nat'l Reps: Katz Radio *Regional Reps:* Glenn Jones
Arbitron Metro Market: Allentown-Bethl *TV Affiliate:* Classic hits
Rick Musselman, General Manager
Michael Anthony, General Sales Mgr
Bill Sheridan, Programming Director
K.J. Zabala, Promotions Manager
Brian Keith, Traffic Manager

Ebensburg

WRKW
07-15-1962; 99.1 MHz FM; 50 kw; 499 ft.; N40 24 41 W78 46 29
109 Plaza Dr., Johnstown, PA 15905 US
(814) 255-4186; *Fax:* (814) 255-6145
www.rocky99.com
License: Ebensburg, Cambria County, PA held by FM Radio Licenses LLC
Group Owner: Forever Broadcasting; (acq 5-1-2005; $2.73 million with WJHT(FM) Johnstown).
Arbitron Metro Market: Johnstown, PA; *Format:* Classic Rock
Terry Deitz, General Manager
Tina Perry, Sales Manager
Mike Stevens, Programming Director
Rick Shepard, News Director
Sean Glenn, Chief Engineer
Shelly Lovenduski, Business Manager
Al Steele, Production Director
George Lucas,Copywriter
Theresa Jarosick, Traffic
Beth Thomas, Traffic/EEO Officer

Edinboro

***WFSE**
04-03-1979; 88.9 MHz FM; *Hrs Open:* 24; 3 kw; 299 ft.; N41 52 38 W80 10 39
Faculty Annex, 110 Edinboro University, Edinboro, PA 16444 US
(814) 732-2641; *Fax:* (814) 732-2270
License: Edinboro, Erie County, PA held by Edinboro University.
Arbitron Metro Market: Erie, PA; *Format:* Alternative *Special Programming:* Football & basketball, Black 15 hrs, relg 4 hrs, l; *Hrs. of News Programming:* News progmg 18 hrs wkly; *Target Audience:* 18-25; collegestudents with community interest
Terrence Warburton, Chairman
Dr. Frank Pogue, CEO
Matthew Benson, General Manager
Richard Smith, General Sales Mgr
Brian Hagberg, Programming Director
Andy Alm, News Director
Steve Caldwell, Music Director
Mike Frank,Production Director
Tad Wissel, Konstantinos Fekos
Public Relations Director

WXTA
01-01-1989; 97.9 MHz FM; *Hrs Open:* 24; 10 kw; 505 ft.; N41 57 59 W80 06 40
471 Robison Rd., Erie, PA 16509 US
(814) 868-5355
www.979nashfm.com
jim.riley@cumulus.com
License: Edinboro, PA held by Radio License Holding CBC, LLC
Group Owner: Cumulus Media Inc.; (acq 5-12-2004; grpsl).
Arbitron Metro Market: Erie, PA; *Format:* Country
Chuck Stevens, Operations Manager
Jim Riley, General Manager

Eldred

WBYB(FM)
09-17-1984; 103.9 MHz FM; *Hrs Open:* 24; 1.2 kw; Ant 733 ft HAAT; N41 37 03 W78 48 13 *Rebroadcasts:* Simulcast With WVTT(FM) Portville, NY 100%
Mailing Address: 29 Fraley St., Kane, PA 16735
Second Address: One Blue Bird Square, Olean, NY 16740
(814) 837-9564; *Fax:* (814) 975-1098
www.twintiernews.blogspot.com
License: Eldred, McKean County, PA held by Colonial Radio Group Inc.
Population Served: 125,000; *Arbitron Metro Market:* Olean, NY; *Format:* Country *Special Programming:* Polka one hr; *Hrs. of News Programming:* news progmg 12 hrs wkly; *No. News Employees:* 1; *Target Audience:* 18-49; female-skewing; *Adv. Rates:* 21; 15; 18; 12
Jeffrey Andrulonis, President
JJ Michaels, Operations Dir
Quentin Shutters, Station Manager
Christy Andrulonis, General Sales Mgr

Elizabethtown

WPDC
05-01-1958; 1600 kHz AM; *Hrs Open:* 24
939 Radio Road, Elizabethtown, PA 17022 US
(717) 367-1600
License: Elizabethtown, PA held by JVJ Communications Inc.
Nat'l Network: ESPN Radio
Arbitron Metro Market: Lancaster, PA; *Format:* Sports; *Hrs. of News Programming:* News progmg 10 hrs wkly; *Target Audience:* 25-54; men; *Adv. Rates:* 25; 25; 25; 18

Elizabethville

WYGL-FM
12-07-1989; 100.5 MHz FM; *Hrs Open:* 24; 1.2 kw; 515 ft.; N40 37 24 W76 49 54
450 Route 204, Selinsgrove, PA 17870 US
(570) 374-8819; *Fax:* (570) 374-9856
License: Elizabethville, Dauphin County, PA held by MMP License LLC.
Group Owner: MAX Media L.L.C.; (acq 10-17-03; grpsl).
Nat'l Network: USA
Arbitron Metro Market: Elizabethville, PA; *Format:* Country; *Hrs. of News Programming:* news progmg 8 hrs wkly; *No. News Employees:* 1; *Target Audience:* 25-54.
John Trinder, President
Tom Morgan, Operations Manager
Carol Pierson, General Manager
Greg Adair, Station Manager/Director of Sales
Shelly Marx, Programming Director
Chad Evans, Digital Media Manager
Trevor Polly, Digital MediaManager

Ellwood City

WKPL
07-04-1968; 92.1 MHz FM; 2.5 kw; 512 ft.; N40 46 9 W80 16 56
123 Blaine Rd., Brownsville, PA 15417 US
(814) 941-9800
www.picklefm.com
License: Ellwood City, Lawrence County, PA held by FM Radio Licenses, LLC.
Group Owner: Keymarket Communications LLC; (acq 6-30-2004; grpsl).
Format: Adult Contemp
Michael Vennare, Market Manager
Dave Anthony, Programming Director
Donnie Fast, Promotions Manager

Emporium

WLEM
03-02-1958; 1250 kHz AM; *Hrs Open:* 16; 2.5 kw-D, ND1; 0.03 kw-N, ND1; N41 30 22 W78 13 26
East 4th Street, Emporium, PA 15834 US
(814) 486-3712; *Fax:* (814) 486-1772
www.theriver989.com
wlemwqky@yahoo.com
License: Emporium, PA held by Salter Communications Inc.
Nat'l Network: Westwood One; *Nat'l Reps:* Commercial Media Sales
Format: Country; *Hrs. of News Programming:* news progmg 3 hrs wkly; *No. News Employees:* 1; *Target Audience:* 25-65.
John Salter, President
Gary Mitchell, Operations Dir
J. Philippone, General Manager

WQKY
05-20-1985; 98.9 MHz FM; 2 kw; 548 ft.; N41 29 32 W78 15 19

6 Franklin Center, St. Marys, PA 15857 US
(814) 834-0070; *Fax:* (877) 987-4837
www.theriver989.com
theriver989@yahoo.com
License: Emporium, Cameron County, PA
Format: Adult Contemp
Roger Haddon, Jr, CEO
Tricia Cease, General Sales Mgr
Drew Kelly, Programming Director
Matt Farrand, News Director
Rob Senter, Music Director

Ephrata

WIOV
11-09-1962; 105.1 MHz FM; 25 kw; 702 ft.; N40 10 30 W76 9 31
Mailing Address: 1060 S. State St., Suite B, Ephrata, PA 17522 US
Second Address: 5989 Susquehanna Plaza Dr., York, PA 17406
(717) 764-1155; *Fax:* (717) 738-1661
www.wiov.com
carol.pierson@cumulus.com
License: Ephrata, PA held by Radio License Holding CBC, LLC
Group Owner: Cumulus Media Inc.; (acq 5-12-2004; grpsl).
Nat'l Reps: McGavren Guild
Arbitron Metro Market: Lancaster, PA; *Format:* Country
Brian Shaffer, Director of Sales
Rich Creeger, Programming Director
Lee Jacoby, Promotions Manager
Carol Pierson, Market Manager

*WRTI
01-01-2000; 90.7 MHz FM; *Hrs Open:* 24; 0.001 kw horiz, 0.65 kw vert; 869 ft.; N40 19 22 W76 11 52 *Rebroadcasts:* Rebroadcasts WRTI(FM) Philadelphia 100%.
1509 Cecil B. Moore Avenue, 3rd Floor, Philadelphia, PA 19121 US
(215) 204-8405; *Fax:* (215) 204-7027
www.wrti.org
comments@wrti.org
License: Ephrata, Lancaster County, PA held by Temple University of The Commonwealth System of Higher Education.
Nat'l Network: NPR
Arbitron Metro Market: Ephrata, PA; *Format:* Classical, Jazz
Dave Conant, General Manager
Jane Kelly, Director of Development
Jeffrey DePolo, Director of Engineering
William Johnson, Station Manager
Tobias Poole, Operating Director

Erie

*WEFR
03-01-1992; 88.1 MHz FM; *Hrs Open:* 24; 0.63 kw; 430 ft.; N41 57 59 W80 6 40
290 Hegenberger Road, Oakland, CA 94621 US
(800) 543-1495
www.familyradio.com
License: Erie, Erie County, PA held by Family Stations Inc.
Group Owner: Family Stations Inc.
Arbitron Metro Market: Erie, PA; *Format:* Christian, Religious; *Target Audience:* General.
Harold Camping, President
John Rorvik, Operations Dir

*WERG
12-01-1972; 90.5 MHz FM; *Hrs Open:* 24; 2.75 kw; 374 ft.; N42 2 34 W80 3 57
109 University Square, Erie, PA 16541 US
(814) 459-9374
www.wergfm.com
johnson126@gannon.edu
License: Erie, Erie County, PA held by Gannon University
Arbitron Metro Market: Erie, PA; *Format:* Alternative *Special Programming:* Sp 3 hrs, Polka 4 hrs wkly; *Hrs. of News Programming:* News progmg 3 hrs wkly; *Target Audience:* 18-plus
Cristianne Johnson, General Manager
Vanessa Johnson, Programming Director
Erika Krenn, News Director
Ted Hallowell, Music Director
Zack Borland, Sports Director
Abby Coppock, Production Director
Becca Dambach, PromotionsDirector
Chet LaPrice, Operations Manager

WXBB
09-01-1993; 94.7 MHz FM; *Hrs Open:* 24; 1.7 kw; 614 ft.; N42 2 26 W80 4 5
1 Boston Store Place, Erie, PA 16501 US
(814) 461-1000; *Fax:* (814) 874-0011
www.947bobfm.com
License: Erie, Erie County, PA held by Connoisseur Media Licenses LLC
Group Owner: Connoisseur Media LLC; (acq 3-30-2006; grpsl)
Arbitron Metro Market: Erie, PA; *Format:* Adult Contemp
Nancy Dymond, General Manager
Joe Lang, Programming Director
Dennis O'Brien, Promotions Manager

WFNN
01-01-1947; 1330 kHz AM
One Broadcast Park, Erie, PA 16428 US
(814) 461-1000; *Fax:* (814) 874-0011
www.sportsradio1330.com
License: Erie, PA held by Connoisseur Media Licenses LLC
Group Owner: Connoisseur Media LLC; (acq 3-31-2006; grpsl)
Nat'l Network: Fox Sports; *Nat'l Reps:* Katz Radio
Arbitron Metro Market: Erie, PA; *Format:* Sports
Joe Lang, Programming Director
Dennis O'Brien, Promotions Manager
Nancy Dymond, Marketing Manager

WQHZ
01-01-1971; 102.3 MHz FM; *Hrs Open:* 24; 1.7 kw; 614 ft.; N42 02 25 W80 04 08
471 Robison Rd., Erie, PA 16509 US
(814) 868-5355
www.z1023online.com
jim.riley@cumulus.com
License: Erie, PA held by Radio License Holding CBC, LLC
Group Owner: Cumulus Media Inc.; (acq 5-12-2004; grpsl).
Nat'l Reps: Katz Radio
Arbitron Metro Market: Erie, PA; *Format:* Classic Rock; *Target Audience:* 25-54; Adults; *Adv. Rates:* 50; 45; 45; 20
Chuck Stevens, Operations Manager
Jim Riley, General Manager

WJET
01-01-1951; 1400 kHz AM; *Hrs Open:* 24; 1 kw-U, ND1; N42 7 28 W80 3 54
1 Boston Store Pl., Erie, PA 16428 US
(814) 461-1000; *Fax:* (814) 874-0011
www.jetradio1400.com
License: Erie, PA held by Connoisseur Media Licenses LLC
Group Owner: Connoisseur Media LLC; (acq 3-31-2006; grpsl).
Regional Network: Radio Pa.
Arbitron Metro Market: Erie, PA; *Format:* News, News/Talk, 86; *No. News Employees:* 1; *Target Audience:* 35 plus; middle to upper middle income, business owners, upscale
Nancy Dymond, General Manager
Joe Lang, Programming Director
Dennis O'Brien, Promotions Manager

*WMCE
02-02-1989; 88.5 MHz FM; *Hrs Open:* 24; 750 w; Ant 499 ft; N42 05 25 W79 56 37
501 E. 38th St., Erie, PA 16546
(814) 824-2260,(814) 824-2261; *Fax:* (814) 824-2590
www.mercyhurst.edu
wshannon@mercyhurst.edu
License: Erie, Erie County, PA held by Mercyhurst College.
Nat'l Network: AP Radio
Population Served: 280,000; *Arbitron Metro Market:* Erie, PA
Special Programming: Pol 3 hrs, Ger 4 hrs, Sp 3 hrs, jazz 4 hrs wkly; *Hrs. of News Programming:* News progmg 6 hrs wkly; *Target Audience:* General;Adults 45+; *Adv. Rates:* 5; 5; 5; 3
Greg Granger, President
William Shannon, General Manager

WPSE
04-21-1935; 1450 kHz AM; *Hrs Open:* 24; 1 kw-U, ND1; N42 8 11 W80 2 25
4071 College Road, Erie, PA 16563-1450 US
(814) 898-6495
www.psbehrend.psu.edu/news-events/wpse-radio
License: Erie, PA held by Board of Trustees, Pennsylvania State University.
Nat'l Network: CBS; Westwood One
Arbitron Metro Market: Erie, PA; *Format:* News, Sports; *Target Audience:* General.
Ron Slomski, Director/General Manager
Vjosa Loshaj, Assistant Station Manager
Val Engelleiter, Programming Specialist

*WQLN-FM
01-07-1973; 91.3 MHz FM; *Hrs Open:* 24; 35 kw; 499 ft.; N42 2 31 W80 3 57
8425 Peach St, Erie, PA 16509 US
(814) 864-3001; *Fax:* (814) 864-4077
www.wqln.org
License: Erie, Erie County, PA held by Public Broadcasting of Northwest Pennsylvania Inc.
Nat'l Network: NPR; PRI
Arbitron Metro Market: Erie, PA *TV Affiliate:* *WQLN(TV) affil.; *Format:* Classical, Jazz, 60 *Special Programming:* Sp one hr, pub affrs 5 hrs, new age 2 hrs, call-in show 3 hrs wkly; *Hrs. of News Programming:* newsprogmg 24 hrs wkly; *No. News Employees:* 1; *Target Audience:* General.
Tom New, President/CEO
Cindy Spizarny, VP/General Manager
Lisa Counasse, Director of Development
Tom Pysz, Director of Corporate Support
Aaron Coseo, Chief Engineer
DaWayne Cleckley, Marketing/Multimedia Manager
Sue Allen, RadioManager
Kathy Carducci, Educational Outreach Services Manager

WRIE
01-01-1941; 1260 kHz AM; *Hrs Open:* 24; 5 kw-D, DA2; 5 kw-N, DA2; N42 3 18 W80 2 24
471 Robison Rd., Erie, PA 16509 US
(814) 868-5355
www.am1260thescore.com
jim.riley@cumulus.com
License: Erie, PA held by Radio License Holding CBC, LLC
Group Owner: Cumulus Media Inc.; (acq 5-12-2004; grpsl)
Nat'l Network: ESPN Radio; *Nat'l Reps:* Katz Radio
Arbitron Metro Market: Erie, PA; *Format:* Sports
Jim Riley, General Manager
Chuck Stevens, Programming Director

WRTS
05-01-1969; 103.7 MHz FM; *Hrs Open:* 24; 50 kw; 499 ft.; N42 5 25 W79 56 37
1 Boston Store Pl., Erie, PA 16510 US
(814) 461-1000; *Fax:* (814) 455-6000
www.star104.com
License: Erie, Erie County, PA held by Connoisseur Media Licenses LLC
Group Owner: Connoisseur Media LLC; (acq 3-30-2006; grpsl).
Arbitron Metro Market: Erie, PA; *Format:* Contemporary Hits/Top 40 *Special Programming:* PSA one hr wkly; *Hrs. of News Programming:* news progmg one hr wkly; *No. News Employees:* 1; *Target Audience:* 25-54.
Michael Malpiedi, Programming Director
Dennis O'Brien, Promotions Manager
Nancy Dymond, Marketing Manager

WXKC
01-01-1949; 99.9 MHz FM; *Hrs Open:* 24; 50 kw; 492 ft.; N42 05 24 W79 57 12
471 Robison Rd., Erie, PA 16509 US
(814) 868-5355
www.classy100.com
jim.riley@cumulus.com
License: Erie, PA held by Radio License Holding CBC, LLC
Group Owner: Cumulus Media Inc.
Arbitron Metro Market: Erie, PA; *Format:* Adult Contemp
Jim Riley, General Manager
Chuck Stevens, Programming Director

Everett

WZSK
03-15-1963; 1040 kHz AM; *Hrs Open:* 0600 - 1815; 4 kw-C, NDD; 10 kw-D, NDD; Non-Directional; N40 0 26 W78 21 44
P. O. Box 187, Everett, PA 15537 US
(814) 652-2600; *Fax:* (814) 652-9347
License: Everett, PA held by New Millennium Communications Group Inc.
Nat'l Network: ABC Information & Entertainment; Jones Radio Networks; Premiere Radio Networks; Radio America; *Regional Network:* Radio Pa. *Regional Reps:* Dome & Associates
Arbitron Metro Market: Johnstown, PA; *Format:* News, News/Talk, 86; *Hrs. of News Programming:* news progmg 10 hrs wkly; *No. News Employees:* 1; *Target Audience:* 25-54
Shane Imler, President
John Imler, General Manager

WSKE
03-15-1988; 104.3 MHz FM; *Hrs Open:* 24; 0.82 kw; 886 ft.; N40 0 11 W78 23 58
Mailing Address: P.O. Box 187, Everett, PA 15537 US
Second Address: 151 E 1st Ave, Everett, PA 15537-1351
(814) 652-2600; *Fax:* (814) 652-9347
wske@penn.com
License: Everett, Bedford County, PA held by New Millennium Communications Group Inc.
Nat'l Network: ABC Information & Entertainment; Jones Radio Networks; *Regional Network:* Radio Pa. *Regional Reps:* Dome & Associates
Format: Country *Special Programming:* Bluegrass, Classic Country, Southern Gospel; *Hrs. of News Programming:* news

progmg 7 hrs wkly; *No. News Employees:* 1; *Target Audience:* 25-54.
Shane Imler, President
John Imler, General Manager

Fairview

WTWF
10-01-2001; 93.9 MHz FM; 6 kw; 299 ft.; N42 1 36 W80 7 18
1 Boston Store Place, Erie, PA 16501 US
(814) 461-1000; *Fax:* (814) 874-0011
www.939thewolf.com
us939@us939.com
License: Fairview, Erie County, PA held by Connoisseur Media Licenses LLC
Group Owner: Connoisseur Media LLC; (acq 3-30-2006; grpsl).
Arbitron Metro Market: Erie, PA; *Format:* Country
Nancy Dymond, General Manager
Chuck Rambaldo, Programming Director
Dennis O'Brien, Promotions Manager

Fallon Station

KZTI(FM)
105.3 MHz FM; 100 kw horiz; 600 meters; N39 54 46 W118 55 18
149 Penn Avenue, Scranton, PA 18503
(570) 349-9103; *Fax:* (570) 348-9109
www.1053martiniradio.com
License: Fallon Station, Churchill County, NV held by Shamrock Communications Inc

William R Lynett, President

Farmington Township

***WCOP**
106.1 MHz FM; 3.2 kw; 443 ft.; N41 26 31 W79 26 40
Box 506, Bath, NY 14810 US
(607) 776-4151
www.fln.org
License: Farmington Township, Clarion County, PA held by Family Life Ministries
Group Owner: Family Life Ministries
Arbitron Metro Market: Farmington, PA; *Format:* Christian
Dave Margalotti, Operations Dir
Terese Main, Programming Director
Bob Price, News Director

Farrell

WLOA
10-03-1954; 1470 kHz AM
444 McCracken Road, Greenville, PA 16125 US
(724) 301-4154
www.940wgrp.com
940wgrp@gmail.com
License: Farrell, PA held by Beacon Broadcasting Inc.
Group Owner: Beacon Broadcasting Inc.; (acq 10-4-2005; $295,000)
Arbitron Metro Market: Youngstown-Warren, OH; *Format:* Country
Estuardo Rodriguez, General Manager

Folsom

***WRSD**
01-05-1983; 94.9 MHz FM; 0.014 kw; 20 ft.; N39 53 12 W75 20 1
1001 Morton Ave., Folsom, PA 19033 US
(610) 534-1900; *Fax:* (610) 461-7083
www.angelfire.com/pa/wrsd
wrsd@lycos.com
License: Folsom, Delaware County, PA held by Ridley School District.
Format: Adult Contemp, Variety/Diverse
Kevin Hitchens, General Manager

Forest City

WEJL-FM
10-31-1973; 100.1 MHz FM; *Hrs Open:* 24; 0.75 kw; 935 ft.; N41 35 35 W75 25 56
149 Penn Avenue, Scranton, PA 18503 US
(570) 346-6555; *Fax:* (570) 346-6038
License: Forest City, Luzerne County, PA held by The Scranton Times L.P.
Group Owner: The Scranton Times L.P.; (acq 8-10-94).
Nat'l Reps: Roslin
Arbitron Metro Market: Wilkes Barre-Scranton, PA; *Format:* Adult Contemp *Special Programming:* Pol 3 hrs wkly; *Hrs. of News Programming:* news progmg 5 hrs wkly; *No. News Employees:* 1; *Target Audience:* 25-54.
William Lynett, CEO
Jim Loftus, General Manager

Franklin

***WAWN**
01-01-1998; 89.5 MHz FM; 2 kw; 315 ft.; N41 23 39 W79 46 20
149 Summit Dr., Franklin, PA 16323 US
(814) 437-5355
www.afr.net
License: Franklin, Venango County, PA held by American Family Association.
Group Owner: American Family Radio
Arbitron Metro Market: Cody WY; *Format:* Religious
Tim Wildmon, President
Donald Wildmon, Founder
Buddy Smith, Sr VP
Ed Vitagliano, Exec VP
Randy Sharp, Director Of Special Projects
Meeke Addison, Director Of Communications
Abraham Hamilton III, General Counsel

WFRA
04-13-1958; 1450 kHz AM; *Hrs Open:* 6 AM-midnight; 0.99 kw-U, ND1; N41 23 30 W79 48 41
1243 Liberty St., Suite 501, Franklin, PA 16323 US
(814) 432-2188; *Fax:* (814) 437-9372
www.myantsnetwork.com
License: Franklin, Venango County, PA held by FM Radio Licenses LLC
Group Owner: Forever Broadcasting; (acq 7-20-2000; grpsl)
Format: News, News/Talk, 84, Talk; *Hrs. of News Programming:* news progmg 12 hrs wkly; *No. News Employees:* 1; *Target Audience:* 30 plus.
Jim Shields, General Manager
Helen Powers, Sales Manager
Andy Alm, Programming Director
Mark Himmler, Chief Engineer
Jill Hamilton, Business Manager

WHMJ
03-05-1971; 99.3 MHz FM; *Hrs Open:* 6 AM-midnight; 7.3 kw; 600 ft.; N41 26 16 W79 55 29
1243 Liberty St., Suite 501, Franklin, PA 16323 US
(814) 432-2188; *Fax:* (814) 427-9372
www.mymajicspace.com
License: Franklin, Venango County, PA held by FM Radio Licenses LLC
Group Owner: Forever Broadcasting
Format: Adult Contemp; *Hrs. of News Programming:* News progmg 4 hrs wkly; *Target Audience:* 18-44.
Jim Shields, General Manager
Helen Powers, Sales Manager
Scott Woloszyn, Programming Director
Mark Himmler, Chief Engineer
Jill Hamilton, Business Manager

Freeland

WKRZ
01-01-1947; 98.5 MHz FM; 8.7 kw; 1171 ft.; N41 11 56 W75 49 6 *Rebroadcasts:* Rebroadcasts WKRZ(FM) Tobyhanna 100%
305 Highway 315, Pittston, PA 18640 US
(570) 883-9800
www.985krz.com
License: Freeland, Luzerne County, PA held by Entercom Scranton Wilkes-Barre License LLC.
Group Owner: Entercom Communications Corp.; (acq 12-13-99; grpsl).
Arbitron Metro Market: Wilkes Barre-Scranton, PA; *Format:* Contemporary Hits/Top 40; *Target Audience:* 19-54; women
Jim Rising, Operations Dir
John Burkavage, General Manager
Ryan Flynn, General Sales Mgr
Tias Schuster, Programming Director
Lamar Smith, Chief Engineer
Elizabeth Masich, Music Director

Galeton

***WCOG-FM**
01-01-1996; 100.7 MHz FM; 7.7 kw; 492 ft.; N41 39 36 W77 38 2 *Rebroadcasts:* Rebroadcasts WCIK(FM) Bath, NY 100%
PO Box 506, Bath, NY 14810 US
(607) 776-4151
www.fln.org
License: Galeton, Potter County, PA held by Family Life Ministries Inc.
Group Owner: Family Life Network; (acq 10-1-96; $20,130).
Nat'l Network: Salem Radio Network; *Wire Services:* Metro Weather Service Inc.
Arbitron Metro Market: Bath,NY; *Format:* Christian; *Hrs. of News Programming:* news progmg 14 hrs wkly; *No. News Employees:* 3; *Target Audience:* 30-54; general
Dave Margalotti, Operations Dir
Terese Main, Programming Director
Bob Price, News Director

Gettysburg

WGET
08-27-1950; 1320 kHz AM; *Hrs Open:* 24; 1 kw-D, DA2; 0.5 kw-N, DA2; N39 50 30 W77 13 25
P.O. Box 3179, 1560 Fairfield Road, Gettysburg, PA 17325 US
(717) 334-3101; *Fax:* (717) 334-5822
www.espnradio1320.com
License: Gettysburg, PA held by Times and News Publishing Co.
Nat'l Network: CBS; *Regional Network:* Radio Pa.; *Wire Services:* AP
Arbitron Metro Market: York, PA; *Format:* Adult Contemp, News, 84; *Hrs. of News Programming:* news progmg 40 hrs wkly; *No. News Employees:* 3; *Target Audience:* 35-64; mainstream mature adults
Cindy Ford, President
Dave Jackson, Operations Dir
John Martin, General Sales Mgr
Kim Alexander, News Director
Daryl Hancock, Engineering Dir
Larry Rhoten, Special Events Coordinator
Shannon Weishaar, Traffic Manager

WGTY
07-05-1962; 107.7 MHz FM; *Hrs Open:* 24; 16 kw horiz, 15.5 kw vert; 850 ft.; N39 51 23 W76 56 57
1560 Fairfield Road, Gettysburg, PA 17325 US
9489) 334-3101; *Fax:* (717) 334-5822
License: Gettysburg, Adams County, PA held by Times and News Publishing Co.
Wire Services: AP
Arbitron Metro Market: York, PA; *Format:* Country; *Hrs. of News Programming:* News progmg 2 hrs wkly; *Target Audience:* 25-54.
Cindy Ford, General Manager
Scott Donato, Operations Director
Stacy Winemiller, Business Manager
Rick Kennis, Promotions Manager
Kim Alexander, News Director

***WZBT**
10-23-1976; 91.1 MHz FM; *Hrs Open:* 8 AM-2 AM; 0.35 kw; 116 ft.; N39 50 29 W77 13 26
300 N. Washington Street, PO Box 435, Gettysburg, PA 17325 US
(717) 337-6315
www.wzbt.org
License: Gettysburg, Adams County, PA held by Gettysburg College.
Arbitron Metro Market: Gettysburg, PA; *Format:* Alternative
Special Programming: Class 3 hrs, folk 6 hrs, jazz 4 hrs, Sp 4 hrs, gos; *Target Audience:* General.
Ryan Gottschall, Station Manager
Laura Benincasa, Programming Director

Glen Mills

***WZZE**
05-20-1975; 97.3 MHz FM; 0.018 kw; 184 ft.; N39 55 15 W75 29 58
Mailing Address: PO Box 1, Concordville, PA 19331 US
Second Address: Glen Mills Schools, Glen Mills Rd., Glen Mills, PA 19342
(610) 459-8100
License: Glen Mills, Delaware County, PA held by Glen Mills Schools.
Nat'l Network: ABC
Arbitron Metro Market: Concordville, PA; *Format:* Contemporary Hits/Top 40
C.D. Ferrainola, President
Mark Smith, Operations Dir

Grantham

***WVMM**
09-29-1989; 90.7 MHz FM; *Hrs Open:* 24/7 beginning 8/27; 0.1 kw; 164 ft.; N40 9 34 W76 59 0
Messiah College, One College Avenue, Mechanicsburg, PA 17055 US
(717) 766-2511
wvmm@messiah.edu
License: Grantham, Cumberland County, PA held by Messiah College.

Nat'l Network: PRI
Arbitron Metro Market: Grantham, PA; *Format:* Christian, Triple A
Special Programming: Praise and worship—7hrs, Gospel—5 hrs, Big Band-; *Hrs. of News Programming:* 25; *Target Audience:* 13-25.
Edward Arke, General Manager
Sheryl Ezbiansky, Promotions Manager

Greencastle

WQCM
05-06-1967; 94.3 MHz FM; *Hrs Open:* 24; 3.5 kw; 430 ft.; N39 47 29 W77 40 30
25 Penncraft Ave., Chambersburg, PA 17201 US
(717) 263-0813; *Fax:* (717) 263-9649
www.wqcmfm.com
License: Greencastle, Franklin County, PA held by Alpha Media Licensee LLC
Group Owner: Alpha Media LLC; (acq 4-17-2014; grpsl).
Arbitron Metro Market: Chambersburg, PA; *Format:* Rock/AOR; *No. News Employees:* 1; *Target Audience:* 25-44.
Rich Bateman, General Manager
Mike Holder, Programming Director
Tammy Heckman, Promotions Director
Jeff Baker, Chief Engineer
Stan Schafer, Chief Engineer
Tina Bressler, Sales
Thomas Blachek, Sales
Stephanie Wilson, Sales

Greenville

WLVX(FM)
07-01-1965; 107.1 MHz FM; *Hrs Open:* 24; 3 kw; Ant 328 ft; N41 22 50 W80 24 48
PO Box 2098, Omaha, NE 68103
(800) 525-5683
www.klove.com
License: Greenville, Mercer County, PA held by Educational Media Foundation
Group Owner: Educational Media Foundation; (acq 9-14-2005; grpsl)
Population Served: 66,571; *Arbitron Metro Market:* Youngstown, OH; *Format:* Christian; *No. News Employees:* 1; *Target Audience:* 14-34.; *Adv. Rates:* 15; 15; 15; 15
Darrell Chambliss, Chairman
Alan Mason, COO
Mike Novak, President/CEO
Eric Moser, CFO
David Pierce, Chief Creative Officer
D. Kevin Blair, Secretary/General Counsel

WGRP
09-19-1959; 940 kHz AM; *Hrs Open:* 24
444 McCracken Rd., Greenville, PA 16125 US
(724) 301-4154
www.940wgrp.com
940wgrp@gmail.com
License: Greenville, PA held by VCI Radio, Inc.
Group Owner: Vilkie Communications; (acq 9-14-2005; grpsl)
Format: Country
Rich Esbenshade, General Manager

***WXTC**
05-14-1930; 88.1 MHz FM; *Hrs Open:* 24; kw
US
(814) 255-4186; *Fax:* (814) 255-6145
License: Greenville, Charleston County, PA
Nat'l Reps: McGavren Guild
Arbitron Metro Market: Charleston, SC; *Format:* Black, Gospel; *No. News Employees:* 1; *Target Audience:* 35-54; women
Chris Johnson, General Manager

Grove City

WWGY
09-10-1962; 95.1 MHz FM; *Hrs Open:* 24; 19 kw horiz, 17 kw vert; 804 ft.; N41 15 8 W80 21 28
219 Savannah Gardner Rd., New Castle, PA 16101 US
(724) 654-5502; *Fax:* (724) 856-4975
www.froggy95pa.com
License: Grove City, Mercer County, PA held by FM Radio Licenses LLC
Group Owner: Forever Broadcasting; (acq 2-23-2004; $2.28 million).
Arbitron Metro Market: New Castle, PA; *Format:* Country; *Hrs. of News Programming:* news progmg 2 hrs wkly; *No. News Employees:* 1; *Target Audience:* 18-34.
Jim Shields, General Manager
Jon Jacubec, Sales Manager
John Thomas, Programming Director
Mike Heim, Chief Engineer
Jill Hamilton, Business Manager
Karen Nies, Traffic Director

***WSAJ-FM**
09-01-1968; 91.1 MHz FM; *Hrs Open:* 24; 2.7 kw; 502 ft.; N41 14 48 W79 54 1
Box 3146, 100 Campus Drive, Grove City, PA 16127 US
(724) 458-2077; *Fax:* (724) 458-2329
wsaj.com/
wsaj@gcc.edu
License: Grove City, Mercer County, PA held by Grove City College.
Format: Talk; *No. News Employees:* 1; *Target Audience:* General; listeners who are generally unfamiliar with class mus & arts
Brittany Morales, General Manager
Darren Morton, Station Director
Lauren Fairley, Programming Director
Claire McCray, Music Director
Cristina Totten, Marketing Director
Victoria O'Brien, News Director

Hanover

WHVR
01-09-1949; 1280 kHz AM; 5 kw-D, DA2; 0.5 kw-N, DA2; N39 49 11 W77 0 25
Mailing Address: PO Box 234, Hanover, PA 17331 US
Second Address: 275 Radio Rd., Hanover, PA
(717) 637-3831; *Fax:* (717) 637-9006
www.realcountry1280whvr.com
License: Hanover, PA held by Radio Hanover Inc.
Arbitron Metro Market: York, PA; *Format:* Country
Joan McAnall, General Manager
Rick McCauslin, General Sales Mgr
Deanna Forney, News Director
Daryll Harcock, Chief Engineer

Harrisburg

WHP
01-01-1924; 580 kHz AM; *Hrs Open:* 24; 5 kw-D, DAN; 5 kw-N, DAN; N40 18 11 W76 57 7
600 Corporate Circle, Harrisburg, PA 17110 US
(717) 540-8800; *Fax:* (717) 671-9973
www.whp580.com
news@whp580.com
License: Harrisburg, PA held by Clear Channel Broadcasting Licenses Inc.
Group Owner: iHeartMedia; (acq 8-5-98; grpsl)
Nat'l Network: Westwood One
Arbitron Metro Market: Harrisburg-Lebanon-Carlisle, PA; *Format:* News, News/Talk, 86; *No. News Employees:* 4; *Target Audience:* 35-64.
Dan Lankford, Regional Market President
R.J. Harris, Operations Dir
Michael Parks, Creative Director

***WITF-FM**
04-01-1971; 89.5 MHz FM; *Hrs Open:* 24; 5.9 kw; 1362 ft.; N40 20 44 W76 52 7
4801 Lindle Road, Harrisburg, PA 17111 US
(717) 704-3000
www.witf.org
customerservice@witf.org
License: Harrisburg, Dauphin County, PA held by WITF Inc.
Nat'l Network: NPR; PRI
Arbitron Metro Market: Harrisburg-Lebanon-Carlisle, PA *TV Affiliate:* *WITF-TV affil.; *Format:* News, News/Talk, 86; *Hrs. of News Programming:* news progmg 43 hrs wkly; *No. News Employees:* 3
Kathleen Pavelko, President/CEO
Justin Weber, Chairman
Gregory Poland, Senior VP/CFO
Ronald Kain, CTO
Darren Smith, Senior VP, Sales

WKBO
01-01-1922; 1230 kHz AM; *Hrs Open:* 24; 0.48 kw-U, ND1; N40 16 52 W76 52 6
25 East Main St., Mechanicsburg, PA 17055 US
(717) 796-9526; *Fax:* (717) 540-8814
www.oneheartministries.com
fortress1230am@oneheartministries.com
License: Harrisburg, PA held by One Heart Ministries Inc.
Group Owner: One Heart Ministries; (acq 8-5-98; grpsl).
Nat'l Reps: Salem
Arbitron Metro Market: Harrisburg-Lebanon-Carlisle, PA; *Format:* Christian *Special Programming:* Pop standards, Music of Your Life; *Hrs. of News Programming:* news progmg 168 hrs wkly; *No. News Employees:* 6 *Target Audience:* 35-54; well educated, upscale professionals
Pete Hamel, General Manager

WNNK
01-01-1962; 104.1 MHz FM; *Hrs Open:* 24; 22.5 kw; 725 ft.; N40 18 59 W76 57 4
2300 Vartan Way, Suite 130, Harrisburg, PA 17110 US
(717) 238-1041; *Fax:* (717) 234-7780
www.wink104.com
john.odea@cumulus.com
License: Harrisburg, PA held by Cumulus Licensing LLC
Group Owner: Cumulus Media Inc.
Arbitron Metro Market: Harrisburg, PA; *Format:* Adult Contemp
John O'Dea, Operations Dir
Janelle Kopchick, Promotions Manager

WRBT
09-30-1962; 94.9 MHz FM; *Hrs Open:* 24; 25 kw horiz, 24.5 kw vert; 699 ft.; N40 18 58 W76 57 1
600 Corporate Circle, Harrisburg, PA 17110 US
(717) 540-8800
www.bob949.com
License: Harrisburg, Dauphin County, PA held by Clear Channel Broadcasting Licenses Inc.
Group Owner: iHeartMedia; (acq 8-5-98; grpsl)
Nat'l Reps: Christal
Arbitron Metro Market: Harrisburg-Lebanon-Carlisle, PA *TV Affiliate:* WHP-TV.; *Format:* Country; *No. News Employees:* 1; *Target Audience:* 25-54.
Jeff Hurley, Regional Program Manager

WRVV
01-01-1946; 97.3 MHz FM; *Hrs Open:* 24; 15 kw; 853 ft.; N40 20 43 W76 52 9
600 Corporate Circle, Harrisburg, PA 17110 US
(717) 540-8800
www.theriver973.com
wrvv@river973.com
License: Harrisburg, Dauphin County, PA held by Clear Channel Broadcasting Licenses Inc.
Group Owner: iHeartMedia
Arbitron Metro Market: Harrisburg-Leba; *Format:* Classic Rock; *Target Audience:* 25-54.
Dan Lankford, Regional Market President
Jeff Hurley, Regional Program Manager

WHGB
05-28-1945; 1400 kHz AM; *Hrs Open:* 24; 1 kw-U, ND1; N40 14 58 W76 52 3
2300 Vartan Way, Harrisburg, PA 17110 US
(717) 238-1041; *Fax:* (717) 234-4842
www.espnradio1400.com
chris.james@cumulus.com
License: Harrisburg, PA held by Cumulus Licensing Corp.
Group Owner: Cumulus Media Inc.; (acq 11-28-2000; grpsl)
Nat'l Network: ESPN Radio
Arbitron Metro Market: Harrisburg, PA; *Format:* Sports; *Target Audience:* 25-54; men
John O'Dea, Operations Dir
Matt Roback, General Sales Mgr
Chris James, Programming Director
Marissa Allen, Promotions Manager

WTKT
02-01-1948; 1460 kHz AM; *Hrs Open:* 24
600 Corporate Circle, Harrisburg, PA 17110 US
(717) 540-8800; *Fax:* (717) 540-8814
www.foxsports1460.com
License: Harrisburg, PA held by Clear Channel Broadcasting Licenses Inc.
Group Owner: iHeartMedia; (acq 8-5-98; grpsl).
Nat'l Reps: Clear Channel
Arbitron Metro Market: Harrisburg, PA; *Format:* Sports, Talk
Special Programming: Gospel 2 hrs, pub service 2 hrs wkly; *Hrs. of News Programming:* news progmg 30 hrs wkly; *No. News Employees:* 4; *Target Audience:* General.
Dan Lankford, Regional Market President
Jeff Hurley, Regional Program Manager

WHKF
07-01-1965; 99.3 MHz FM; 1.35 kw; 679 ft.; N40 11 30 W76 52 5
600 Corporate Circle, Harrisburg, PA 17110 US
(717) 540-8800; *Fax:* (717) 540-8814
www.993kissfm.com
License: Harrisburg, Dauphin County, PA held by Clear Channel Broadcasting Licenses Inc.
Group Owner: iHeartMedia
Arbitron Metro Market: Harrisburg, PA; *Format:* Contemporary Hits/Top 40; *Target Audience:* 18-34.women
Dan Lankford, Regional Market President

***WZXM**
01-01-1995; 88.1 MHz FM; *Hrs Open:* 24; 540 w; Ant 105 ft; N40 15 44 W76 53 11
Box 186, Sellersville, PA 19104
(215) 721-2141; *Fax:* (215) 721-9811
www.wordfm.org
wordfm@wordfm.org
License: Harrisburg, Dauphin County, PA held by Four Rivers Community Broadcasting Corp.
Group Owner: Four Rivers Community Broadcasting Corp.; (acq 10-30-2007; exchange for WXPH)
Population Served: 400,000; *Arbitron Metro Market:* Harrisburg-Leba
Charles Loughery, President
Meg Sabulsky, Operations Dir
David Baker, General Manager
Meg Sabulsky, Programming Director
William Dunn, Promotions Manager
Charles Loughery, Engineering Dir

Havertown

***WHHS**
12-06-1949; 99.9 MHz FM; *Hrs Open:* 2 PM-10 PM (M-F); 0.0095 kw; 161 ft.; N39 58 59 W75 18 10
1801 Darby Road, Havertown, PA 19083 US
(610) 446-7111; *Fax:* (610) 853-5952
www.whhs.org
whhsnewsdirector@yahoo.com
License: Havertown, Delaware County, PA held by School District of Haverford Township.
Format: Variety/Diverse; *Target Audience:* General.
Kevin Moran, General Manager

Hawley

WYCY
09-13-1993; 105.3 MHz FM; *Hrs Open:* 24; 2.9 kw; 479 ft; N41 35 01 W75 10 30
575 Grove St., Honesdale, PA 18431
(570) 253-1616; *Fax:* (570) 253-6297
www.boldgoldlakeregion.com
mstanton@boldgoldmedia.com
License: Hawley, Wayne County, PA held by Bold Gold Media Group L.P.
Group Owner: Bold Gold Media Group LP; (acq 5-23-2005; grpsl).
Nat'l Network: ABC
Hrs. of News Programming: news progmg 5 hrs wkly; *No. News Employees:* 1; *Target Audience:* 25-55.

***WBYH**
12-01-2000; 89.1 MHz FM; *Hrs Open:* 24; 200 w; 525 ft; N41 24 43 W75 09 51 *Rebroadcasts:* Rebroadcasts WBYO(fM) Sellersville 100%
Box 186, Sellersville, PA 18960
(215) 721-2141; *Fax:* (215) 721-9811
www.wordfm.com
wordfm@wordfm.org
License: Hawley, Wayne County, PA held by Four Rivers Community Broadcasting Corp.
Group Owner: Four Rivers Community Broadcasting Corp.
Population Served: 50,000
Charles Loughery, President
Meg Sabulsky, Operations Dir
David Baker, General Manager
Meg Sabulsky, Programming Director
William Dunn, Promotions Manager
Charles Loughery, Engineering Dir

Hazleton

WAZL
12-19-1932; 1490 kHz AM; *Hrs Open:* 24; 1 kw-U, ND1; N40 56 24 W75 58 4
Box 701, Tunkhannock, PA 18657 US
(570) 836-4200; *Fax:* (570) 836-7035
License: Hazleton, PA held by Geos Communications
Group Owner: Geos Communications; (acq 7-14-2008; grpsl)
Nat'l Network: Fox News Radio; *Wire Services:* Metro Weather Service Inc.
Arbitron Metro Market: Halifax NS; *Format:* News, News/Talk, 86; *Adv. Rates:* 15; 10; 15; 10

WBSX
01-01-1949; 97.9 MHz FM; *Hrs Open:* 24; 6.3 kw; 1335 ft.; N41 10 56 W75 52 22
600 Baltimore Dr., Wilkes-Barre, PA 18702 US
(570) 824-9000; *Fax:* (570) 820-0520
www.979x.com
License: Hazleton, PA held by Radio License Holding CBC, LLC
Group Owner: Cumulus Media Inc.; (acq 5-29-97; grpsl).
Arbitron Metro Market: Wilkes Barre, PA; *Format:* Rock/AOR; *Target Audience:* 18-34.
Shannon Spak, General Sales Mgr
Tori Thomas, Programming Director
Erin Evans, Promotions Manager
Gerald Getz, Market Manager

Hershey

WZCY
04-30-1964; 106.7 MHz FM; *Hrs Open:* 24; 14 kw; Ant 928 ft; N40 10 16 W76 35 50
2300 Vartan Way, Suite 130, Harrisburg, PA 17110 US
(717) 238-1041; *Fax:* (717) 234-7780
www.nashfm1067.com
charles.angelo@cumulus.com
License: Hershey, PA held by Radio License Holding CBC, LLC
Group Owner: Cumulus Media Inc.; (acq 5-29-97; grpsl).
Population Served: 1,500,000; *Arbitron Metro Market:* Harrisburg-Lebanon-Carlisle, PA; *Format:* Country
Karen Richards, General Sales Mgr
Janelle Kopchick, Promotions Manager
Event Coordinator, Tommy Reeves

Hollidaysburg

WRKY-FM
12-01-1978; 104.9 MHz FM; 0.73 kw; 906 ft.; N40 34 1 W78 26 32
1 Forever Dr., Hollidaysburg, PA 16648 US
(814) 941-9800; *Fax:* (814) 943-2754
www.rocky1049.com
webmaster@forevermediainc.com
License: Hollidaysburg, Blair County, PA held by FM Radio Licenses LLC
Group Owner: Forever Broadcasting; (acq 2-18-97; $2 million with WKMC(AM) Roaring Spring).
Nat'l Reps: Roslin
Arbitron Metro Market: Altoona, PA; *Format:* Rock/AOR; *Target Audience:* 25-54; adults with significant income
Dave Davies, General Manager/Market Manager
Bobbi Castellucci, General Sales Mgr
Tommy Edwards, Programming Director
Danice Bell, News Director
Troy Barnhart, Chief Engineer
Leah Elbert, Traffic Manager
P.J. Mitchell, BusinessManager
Andy Berkowitz, Production Director
Bethany McManamy, EEO Officer

***WHHN**
01-01-2008; 88.1 MHz FM; 0.85 kw horiz, 0.67 kw vert; 1352 ft.; N40 29 19 W78 21 20
601 Washington Street, Alexandria, LA 71301 US
(888) 408-0201; *Fax:* (318) 449-9954
www.radiomaria.us
License: Hollidaysburg, Blair County, PA held by Radio Maria, Inc.
Arbitron Metro Market: Hollidaysburg, PA; *Format:* Christian, Talk, 74
Shane Connor, Operations Dir
Chip Thomas, General Manager
Phil Hickerson, General Sales Mgr
Jim Smith, Chief Engineer

Homer City

WCCS
10-25-1983; 1160 kHz AM; *Hrs Open:* 24; 10 kw-D, DA2; 1 kw-N, DA2; N40 34 18 W79 10 12
840 Philadelphia Street, Indiana, PA 15701 US
(724) 465-4700; *Fax:* (724) 471-1040
www.1160wccs.com
mbertig@rendabroadcasting.com
License: Homer City, PA held by The St. Pier Group LLC.
Group Owner: Renda Broadcasting Corp.; (acq 10-4-2002; $650,000)
Nat'l Network: ABC *Regional Reps:* Dome & Associates; *Wire Services:* AP
Arbitron Metro Market: Indiana,PA; *Format:* Adult Contemp
Special Programming: Pol 3 hrs, oldies 9 hrs wkly; *Hrs. of News Programming:* news progmg 14 hrs wkly; *No. News Employees:* 2; *Target Audience:* 25-49. *Adv. Rates:* 15; 15; 15; 15
Tony Renda Sr., CEO
Jim DeCesare, Operations Dir
Mark Bertig, General Manager
Jack Benedict, Sports Director
Jon Smathers, Sales Director

Honesdale

WDNH-FM
10-12-1981; 95.3 MHz FM; *Hrs Open:* 24; 1.65 kw; 456 ft.; N41 34 45 W75 10 42
575 Grove St., Honesdale, PA 18431 US
(570) 253-1616; *Fax:* (570) 253-6297
www.boldgoldlakeregion.com
mstanton@boldgoldmedia.com
License: Honesdale, Wayne County, PA held by Bold Gold Media Group L.P.
Group Owner: Bold Gold Media Group LP
Nat'l Network: USA
Arbitron Metro Market: Honesdale, PA; *Format:* Adult Contemp; *Hrs. of News Programming:* news progmg 6 hrs wkly; *No. News Employees:* 1; *Target Audience:* 25-54.

WPSN
09-01-1972; 1590 kHz AM; 2.5 kw-D, ND2; 0.015 kw-N, ND2; N41 33 13 W75 15 18
575 Grove St., Honesdale, PA 18411 US
(570) 253-1616
www.waynepikenews.com
news@boldgoldmedia.com
License: Honesdale, PA held by Bold Gold Media Group L.P.
Group Owner: Bold Gold Media Group LP; (acq 5-23-2005; grpsl)
Nat'l Reps: Dome
Arbitron Metro Market: Honesdale, PA; *Format:* Sports; *Target Audience:* General.

***WZZH**
01-01-2008; 90.9 MHz FM; 200 w; Ant 912 ft; N41 35 35 W75 25 56 *Rebroadcasts:* Rebroadcasts WBYO(FM) Sellersville 100%
Box 186, Sellersville, PA 18960
(215) 721-2141; *Fax:* (215) 721-9811
www.wordfm.org
wordfm@wordfm.org
License: Honesdale, Wayne County, PA held by Four Rivers Community Broadcasting Corp.
Group Owner: Four Rivers Community Broadcasting Corp.

Charles Loughery, President
Meg Sabulsky, Operations Dir
David Baker, General Manager
Meg Sabulsky, Programming Director
William Dunn, Promotions Manager
Charles Loughery, Engineering Dir

Hughesville

WRKK
08-04-1985; 1200 kHz AM; *Hrs Open:* 24; 10 kw-D, DA2; 0.25 kw-N, DA2; N41 12 43 W76 44 55 *Rebroadcasts:* Rebroadcasts WRAK(AM) Williamsport 100%
600 Corporate Circle, Harrisburg, PA 17110 US
(570) 327-1400; *Fax:* (570) 327-8156
www.rock949fm.com
License: Hughesville, PA held by Clear Channel Broadcasting Licenses Inc.
Group Owner: iHeartMedia; (acq 8-5-98; grpsl)
Nat'l Network: ABC; Westwood One
Arbitron Metro Market: Williamsport, PA; *Format:* Rock/AOR; *No. News Employees:* 1; *Target Audience:* 35 plus.
Dan Lankford, Regional Market President

Huntingdon

WHUN
07-05-1972; 1150 kHz AM; 5 kw-D, ND1; 0.036 kw-N, ND1; N40 27 18 W77 58 50
1 Forever Drive, Hollidaysburg, PA 16648 US
(731) 941-9800
License: Huntingdon, PA held by Forever Broadcasting LLC
Group Owner: Forever Communications Inc.; (acq 7-31-2006; grpsl)
Format: Country
Dave Davies, General Manager
Bobbi Castellucci, General Sales Mgr

WHUN
03-02-1947; 1150 kHz AM; *Hrs Open:* 24; 5 kw-D, ND1; 0.036 kw-N, ND1; N40 27 18 W77 58 50 *Rebroadcasts:* Simulcast with WRSC(AM) State College
1 Forever Dr., Hollidaysburg, PA 16648
(814) 941-9800; *Fax:* (814) 943-2754
License: Huntingdon, Huntingdon County, PA held by Southern Belle LLC
Group Owner: Forever Broadcasting; (acq 4-29-2002; $875,000 with WLTS(FM) Mount Union)
Regional Reps: Commercial Media Sales Inc.
Population Served: 56,000; *Arbitron Metro Market:* Altoona, PA; *Format:* Sports *Special Programming:* Relg 2 hrs wkly; *Hrs. of*

News Programming: news progmg 15 hrs wkly; *No. News Employees:* 1 *TargetAudience:* 25 plus; general; *Adv. Rates:* 14; 14; 14; 13
Dave Davies, General Manager/Market Manager
Bobbi Castellucci, General Sales Mgr
Troy Barnhart, Chief Engineer
P.J. Mitchell, Business Manager
Leah Elbert, Traffic
Andy Berkowitz, Production Director
Bethany McManamy, EEOOfficer

***WKVR-FM**
03-01-1978; 92.3 MHz FM; *Hrs Open:* 22; 0.013 kw; -266 ft.; N40 30 0 W78 0 52
1700 Moore Street, Huntingdon, PA 16652 US
(814) 643-5031; *Fax:* (814) 643-4477
License: Huntingdon, Huntingdon County, PA held by Juniata College Board of Trustees.
Format: Classic Rock, Rock/AOR *Special Programming:* CHR 15 hrs, jazz 3 hrs, Black 10 hrs, contemp Chr; *Hrs. of News Programming:* News progmg 8 hrs wkly; *Target Audience:* 18-25; college students
Chad Herzog, General Manager
J. Andrew Scott, Promotions Manager

WMRF
09-12-1967; 103.5 MHz FM; *Hrs Open:* 24; 0.16 kw; 1427 ft.; N40 29 51 W78 8 0 *Rebroadcasts:* Rebroadcasts WMRF-FM Lewistown 95.7%
Mailing Address: 12 1/2 East Market St, Lewiston, PA 17044 US
Second Address: 12 East Market St., 2nd Floor, Lewistown, PA 17044
(717) 248-6757; *Fax:* (717) 248-6759
www.merfradio.com
pete@merfradio.com
License: Huntingdon, Huntingdon County, PA held by First Media Radio LLC.
Group Owner: First Media Radio LLC; (acq 3-28-2001; grpsl)
Format: Adult Contemp; *Target Audience:* 18-44.
Jeff Stevens, Operations Dir
Pete Herman, General Manager
Ron Patterson, Production Director
Rocco Pallotto, Sports/Music Director
Mary Lee Sheaffer, News Director
Tom Laub, Traffic Manager

Indiana

WDAD
11-04-1945; 1450 kHz AM; *Hrs Open:* 24; 1 kw-U, ND1; N40 38 17 W79 8 47
840 Philadelphia St, Indiana, PA 15701 US
(724) 465-4700; *Fax:* (724) 471-1040
www.wdadradio.com
License: Indiana, PA held by The St. Pier Group.
Group Owner: Renda Broadcasting Corp.; (acq 2-13-2004; $3.25 million).
Nat'l Network: CBS; *Nat'l Reps:* Dome
Arbitron Metro Market: Indiana/Johnstown, PA; *Format:* Oldies
Special Programming: Relg 2 hrs wkly; *No. News Employees:* 1; *Target Audience:* 35 plus.; *Adv. Rates:* 24; 20; 20; 16
Tony Renda Sr., President
Jim DeCesare, Operations Dir
Mark Hilliard, General Manager
Jason Hill, General Sales Mgr
Travis Williams, Traffic Manager
John Benedict, Sports Director
John Smathers, Web Content Manager

***WIUP-FM**
10-01-1969; 90.1 MHz FM; *Hrs Open:* 7 AM-2 AM; 1.5 kw; 89 ft.; N40 36 32.3 W79 10 0.9
Indiana University of Pennsylvania, Davis Hall, Indiana, PA 15705 US
(724) 357-9487; *Fax:* (724) 357-5503
www.wiupfm.org
wiupfm@gmail.com
License: Indiana, Indiana County, PA held by Indiana University of Pennsylvania.
TV Affiliate: *WIUP-TV affil.; *Format:* Variety/Diverse *Special Programming:* Black 14 hrs, class 15 hrs, folk 4 hrs, gospel one; *Hrs. of News Programming:* News progmg 11 hrs wkly; *Target Audience:* General.
James Rogers, General Manager
Bridget Clark, Station Manager
Ben Cunningham, Programming Director
Quinn Denio, Promotions Manager
Emily Krause, Music Director
Steve Mozes, Assistant Music Director
George Ribbich, TrainingDirector
Matthew Albright, Production Director
John Rockenbach, Traffic Manager
Steve Mozes, Webmaster

WQMU
08-14-1968; 92.5 MHz FM; *Hrs Open:* 24; 3 kw; 328 ft.; N40 38 17 W79 8 47
840 Philadelphia Street, Indiana, PA 15701 US
(724) 465-4700; *Fax:* (724) 349-6842
www.u92radio.com
License: Indiana, Indiana County, PA held by The St. Pier Group
Group Owner: Renda Broadcasting Corp.
Regional Reps: Dome
Format: Adult Contemp; *Target Audience:* 21-41.; *Adv. Rates:* Same as AM
Jack Gillen, President
Kevin Brenahan, Operations Dir
R.J. Shingleton, General Sales Mgr
Corey Duices, Programming Director
Heather Shingleton, News Director
Mark Bertig, General Manager
Jim DeCesare, Operations Director
MarkHilliard, General Sales Manager
Jack Benedict, Sports Director

Irwin

WKHB
10-28-1934; 620 kHz AM; *Hrs Open:* 24
P.O. Box 990, Greensburg, PA 15601 US
(412) 823-7000
www.khbradio.com
License: Irwin, PA held by Broadcast Communications Inc.
Group Owner: Broadcast Communications Inc.; (acq 10-9-96; $300,000)
Arbitron Metro Market: Pittsburgh, PA; *Format:* Variety/Diverse; *Target Audience:* Adults.
Caleb Michaels, Programming Director

Jackson Township

***WRTY**
08-23-1991; 91.1 MHz FM; *Hrs Open:* 24; 3.5 kw; 866 ft.; N41 2 40 W75 22 45 *Rebroadcasts:* Rebroadcasts WRTI(FM) Philadelphia 100%
1509 Cecil B. Moore Avenue, 3rd Floor, Philadelphia, PA 19121 US
(215) 204-8405; *Fax:* (215) 204-7027
www.wrti.org
comments@wrti.org
License: Jackson Township, Monroe County, PA held by Temple University of The Commonwealth System of Higher Education.
Nat'l Network: NPR
Arbitron Metro Market: Wilkes Barre-Sc; *Format:* Jazz; *Hrs. of News Programming:* news progmg 15 hrs wkly; *No. News Employees:* 1; *Target Audience:* 30-65.
Tobias Poole, Operations Dir
Dave Conant, General Manager
William Johnson, Station Manager
Jack Moore, Music Director
Joe Patti, Production Manager
Jane Kelly, Director of Development
Jeffery DePolo, Engineering Dir

Jeannette

WKFB
01-28-1974; 770 kHz AM; *Hrs Open:* Sunrise-sunset
P.O. Box 990, Greensburg, PA 15601 US
(412) 823-7000
License: Jeannette, PA held by Broadcast Communications Inc.
Group Owner: Broadcast Communications Inc.; (acq 4-98)
Arbitron Metro Market: Tucson AZ; *Format:* Talk
Caleb Michaels, Programming Director

Jenkintown

WPPZ-FM
11-01-1960; 103.9 MHz FM; *Hrs Open:* 24; 0.27 kw; 1109 ft.; N40 2 29.6 W75 14 11.4
2 Bala Plaza, Suite 700, Bala Cynwyd, PA 19004 US
(610) 538-1100
www.praisephilly.com
License: Jenkintown, Montgomery County, PA held by Radio One Licenses LLC.
Group Owner: Radio One Inc.; (acq 11-8-2001; grpsl).
Arbitron Metro Market: Philadelphia; *Format:* Gospel; *Target Audience:* 18-34.
Catherine Nye, General Sales Mgr
Darrick Williams, Programming Director

Jersey Shore

WEJS
07-10-1979; 1600 kHz AM; *Hrs Open:* 24; 1 kw-D, ND1; 0.02 kw-N, ND1; N41 13 32 W77 16 1
460 Market Stret, Suite 310, Williamsport, PA 17701 US
(570) 327-1300; *Fax:* (570) 327-5565
www.espnwilliamsport.com
License: Jersey Shore, PA held by Pioneer Sports Productions, LLC
Nat'l Network: Salem Radio Network; Moody; *Nat'l Reps:* Salem
Arbitron Metro Market: Williamsport, PA; *Format:* Religious
Special Programming: Sacred Classics one hr, southern gospel 4 hrs, Chr; *Hrs. of News Programming:* news progmg 14 hrs wkly; *No. News Employees:* 1 *Target Audience:* General.

WJSA-FM
11-01-1984; 96.3 MHz FM; *Hrs Open:* 24; 2.65 kw; 1004 ft.; N41 13 45 W77 22 2
262 Allegheny St., Jersey Shore, PA 17740 US
(570) 398-7200; *Fax:* (570) 398-7201
www.wjsaradio.com
mail@wjsaradio.com
License: Jersey Shore, Lycoming County, PA held by Covenant Broadcasting Co.
Nat'l Network: Moody; Salem Radio Network; *Nat'l Reps:* Salem
Arbitron Metro Market: Williamsport, PA; *Format:* Religious
Special Programming: Sacred classics one hr, southern gospel 3 hrs, Chr; *Hrs. of News Programming:* news progmg 14 hrs wkly; *No. News Employees:* 1
John K. Hogg, General Manager/Chief Engineer
Liz Brady, News Director
Ann L. Hogg, Traffic Manager

Johnsonburg

WJNG
07-01-1998; 100.5 MHz FM; *Hrs Open:* 24; 1.3 kw; 666 ft.; N41 23 11 W78 41 32 *Rebroadcasts:* Rebroadcasts WMKX(FM) Brookville 100%
51 Pickering Street, Brookville, PA 15825 US
(814) 849-8100; *Fax:* (814) 849-4585
www.megarock.fm
License: Johnsonburg, Elk County, PA held by Strattan Broadcasting Inc.
Format: Classic Rock
Jim Farley, Chairman
Kevin Heinrick, Operations Dir
Nathan Sharp, General Manager
Kevin Heinrich, Programming Director
Amanda Baker, Promotions Director

Johnstown

WCRO
09-01-1947; 1230 kHz AM; *Hrs Open:* 24; 1 kw-U, ND1; N40 19 55 W78 54 46
222 Central Avenue, Johnstown, PA 15906 US
(814) 533-5533; *Fax:* (814) 533-5534
License: Johnstown, PA held by Greater Johnstown School District.
Wire Services: AP
Arbitron Metro Market: Johnstown PA; *Format:* Adult Contemp
Special Programming: University of Pittsburgh Football, basketball, NASCAR racing; *Hrs. of News Programming:* News progmg 35 hrs wkly *Target Audience:* 45 - 64; Fastest growing and most financially secure demographically; *Adv. Rates:* 30; 30; 30; 23
Ed Sherlock, President
Ralph O. Smolinski, General Manager
Ed Scherlock, Station Manager

***WFRJ**
06-06-1986; 88.9 MHz FM; *Hrs Open:* 24; 5.5 kw vert; 1214 ft.; N40 22 17 W78 58 56
290 Hegenberger Road, Oakland, CA 94621 US
(800) 543-1495
www.familyradio.com
License: Johnstown, Cambria County, PA held by Family Stations Inc.
Group Owner: Family Stations Inc.
Format: Christian; *Hrs. of News Programming:* News progmg 6 hrs wkly; *Target Audience:* General; every age group
Harold Camping, President
Gary Johnson, Operations Dir

WJHT
09-01-1974; 92.1 MHz FM; *Hrs Open:* 24; 0.58 kw; 1043 ft.; N40 22 15 W78 59 2
109 Plaza Dr., Johnstown, PA 15905 US
(814) 255-4186; *Fax:* (814) 255-6145
www.hot92hits.com

License: Johnstown, Cambria County, PA held by FM Radio Licenses LLC
Group Owner: Forever Broadcasting; (acq 5-1-2005; $2.73 million with WRKW(FM) Ebensburg).
Arbitron Metro Market: Johnstown, PA; *Format:* Contemporary Hits/Top 40
Mike Stevens, Operations Manager
Terry Deitz, General Manager
Tina Perry, Sales Manager
Russ Beckett, Programming Director
Sean Glenn, Chief Engineer
Shelly Lovenduski, Business Manager
Al Steele, Production Director
GeorgeLucas, Copywriter
Theresa Jarosick, Traffic
Beth Thomas, Traffic/EEO Officer

WFGI-FM
08-01-1949; 95.5 MHz FM; 57 kw; 1060 ft.; N40 22 18 W78 58 57
109 Plaza Dr., Johnstown, PA 15905 US
(814) 255-4186; *Fax:* (814) 255-6145
www.myfroggy95.com
License: Johnstown, Cambria County, PA held by FM Radio Licenses LLC
Group Owner: Forever Broadcasting
Arbitron Metro Market: Johnstown, PA; *Format:* Country; *Target Audience:* 25-54.
Mike Stevens, Operations Manager
Terry Deitz, General Manager
Tina Perry, General Sales Mgr
Lara Mosby, Programming Director
Rick Shepard, News Director
Shelly Lovenduski, Business Manager
Al Steele, Production Director
GeorgeLucas, Copywriter
Theresa Jarosick, Traffic
Beth Thomas, Traffic/EEO Officer

WKYE
08-14-1973; 96.5 MHz FM; *Hrs Open:* 24; 50 kw; 489 ft.; N40 19 45 W78 53 54
109 Plaza Dr., Johnstown, PA 15905 US
(814) 255-4186; *Fax:* (814) 255-6145
www.96key.com
License: Johnstown, Cambria County, PA held by FM Radio Licenses LLC
Group Owner: Forever Broadcasting; (acq 1-30-2004; $9.13 million with co-located AM).
Arbitron Metro Market: Johnstown, PA; *Format:* Adult Contemp
Mike Stevens, Operations Manager
Terry Deitz, General Manager
Tina Perry, Sales Manager
Jack Michaels, Programming Director
Rick Shepard, News Director
Shelly Lovenduski, Business Manager
Al Steele, Production Director
GeorgeLucas, Copywriter
Theresa Jarosick, Traffic
Beth Thomas, Traffic/EEO Officer

WNTJ
08-01-1946; 1490 kHz AM; *Hrs Open:* 24; 1 kw-U, ND1; N40 19 25 W78 53 49
109 Plaza Dr., Johnstown, PA 15905 US
(814) 255-4186; *Fax:* (814) 255-6145
License: Johnstown, Cambria County, PA held by FM Radio Licenses LLC
Group Owner: Forever Broadcasting; (acq 5-1-2005; grpsl)
Arbitron Metro Market: Johnstown, PA; *Format:* News, News/Talk, 86; *Target Audience:* 18-54.
Mike Stevens, Operations Manager
Terry Deitz, General Manager
Tina Perry, Sales Manager
Mitch Edwards, Programming Director
Sean Glenn, Chief Engineer
Shelly Lovendusky, Business Manager
Al Steele, Production Director
GeorgeLucas, Copywriter
Theresa Jarosick, Traffic
Beth Thomas, Traffic/EEO Officer

***WQEJ**
10-01-1998; 89.7 MHz FM; *Hrs Open:* 24; 8.4 kw; 1184 ft.; N40 22 17 W78 58 56 *Rebroadcasts:* Rebroadcasts WQED-FM Pittsburgh 100%
4802 Fifth Ave, Pittsburgh, PA 15213 US
(412) 622-1436; *Fax:* (412) 622-7073
www.wqed.org
radio@wqed.org
License: Johnstown, Cambria County, PA held by WQED Multimedia.
Nat'l Network: AP Radio; NPR; PRI
Format: Classical; *Target Audience:* 35-64; educated, influential, professional, community leaders, mid to high income
William R. Caroselli, Chairman
Deborah Acklin, President/CEO
Darryl Ford-Williams, Operations Dir
Bryan Sejvar, VP Content/Programming Director
Lilli Mosco, Vice President, Development & Membership
Carole Bailey, CFO/Treasurer

WKGE
01-01-1922; 850 kHz AM; 10 kw-U, DA1; N40 10 54 W78 53 20
P.O. Box 88, Ebensburg, PA 15931 US
(814) 619-3284
www.edge-radio.com
License: Johnstown, Cambria County, PA held by Birach Broadcasting Corp.
Group Owner: Birach Broadcasting Corp.
Arbitron Metro Market: Johnstown, PA; *Format:* Talk
Sima Birach, President

Kane

***WPSX**
01-01-1995; 90.1 MHz FM; 17 kw; 761 ft; N41 37 04 W78 48 14
Rebroadcasts: Rebroadcasts WPSU(FM) 100%
WPSU-FM, 120 Outreach Bldg, 100 Innovation Boulevard, University Park, PA 16802
(814) 865-3333
www.wpsu.org
wpsu@psu.edu
License: Kane, McKean County, PA held by The Pennsylvania State University.
Nat'l Network: NPR; PRI; *Wire Services:* AP
Special Programming: Folk 10 hrs, jazz 3 hrs, blues 2 hrs wkly; *Hrs. of News Programming:* news progmg 35 hrs wkly; *No. News Employees:* 1; *Target Audience:* Upscale educated adults
Jo Lash, Chairwoman
Craig Johnson, Operations Dir
Ted Krichels, General Manager
Greg Petersen, Station Manager
Tom Yourchak, General Sales Mgr
Emily Reddy, Programming Director
Leslie Dyer, News Director
Russ Rockwell, ChiefEngineer

King of Prussia

WFYL
12-01-1976; 1180 kHz AM
2400 West Main St., Jeffersonville, PA 19403 US
(610) 539-8255; *Fax:* (610) 539-1799
www.1180wfyl.com
info@1180wfyl.com
License: King of Prussia, PA held by Trinity Associates Broadcasting L.L.C.
Group Owner: Trinity Associated Broadcasting L.L.C.
Arbitron Metro Market: Philadelphia, PA; *Format:* Talk
Alan Loch, General Manager

Kittanning

WTYM
01-01-1948; 1380 kHz AM; 1 kw-D, ND1; 0.028 kw-N, ND1; N40 47 19 W79 32 5
P. O. Box 371, Kittanning, PA 16201 US
(724) 543-1380; *Fax:* (724) 543-5572
www.wtymradio.com
License: Kittanning, PA held by Family-Life Media-Com Inc.
Arbitron Metro Market: Kittanning, PA; *Format:* Oldies, Sports
Special Programming: Relg 4 hrs wkly; *Target Audience:* 20-55.
Larry Schrecongost, President
Nancy Schrecongost, Operations Dir
John DeFeo, General Sales Mgr

Kulpmont

***WZRG(FM)**
91.9 MHz FM; 600 w; Ant 535 ft; N40 49 01 W76 27 00
PO Box 186, Sellersville, PA 18960
(570) 523-1190
www.wordfm.org
License: Kulpmont, Northumberland County, PA held by Salt and Light Media Ministries
Population Served: 2,926; *Arbitron Metro Market:* Kulpmont, PA
Charles Loughery, President

Laceyville

***WCOZ**
90.5 MHz FM; 0.1 kw; 71 ft.; N41 40 27 W76 10 3 US
(607) 427-0452
License: Laceyville, Wyoming County, PA held by Telikoja Educational Broadcasting Inc.
Arbitron Metro Market: Laceyville, PA
Kevin Fitzgerald, President

Lancaster

WDAC
12-13-1959; 94.5 MHz FM; 19 kw; 810 ft.; N39 53 46 W76 14 22
P.O. Box 3022, Lancaster, PA 17604 US
(717) 284-4123; *Fax:* (717) 284-2300
www.wdac.com
postmaster@wdac.com
License: Lancaster, Lancaster County, PA held by WDAC Radio Co.
Nat'l Network: Moody; Salem Radio Network
Arbitron Metro Market: Lancaster, PA; *Format:* Christian, Talk
Special Programming: Farm 4 hrs wkly; *Hrs. of News Programming:* news progmg 8 hrs wkly; *No. News Employees:* 1; *Target Audience:* 25-49;Evangelical Christians, families
Doug Myer, COO/General Manager
Mike Stike, Operations Dir
Joe Hartman, General Sales Mgr
John Eby, Music/Programming Director
Greg Barton, News Director
Ralph Haneman, Chief Engineer

***WFNM**
05-01-1973; 89.1 MHz FM; *Hrs Open:* 20; 0.1 kw; 151 ft.; N40 2 43 W76 19 14
630 College Avenue, Lancaster, PA 17604 US
(717) 291-4096
www.wfnm.org
License: Lancaster, Lancaster County, PA held by Franklin and Marshall College.
Arbitron Metro Market: Lancaster, PA; *Format:* Variety/Diverse
Special Programming: Black 6 hrs, sports talk 2 hrs, class 2 hrs, jazz; *Hrs. of News Programming:* News progmg 4 hrs wkly; *Target Audience:* 13-35.
Herbert M. Gillman Bdimovski, General Manager
Anne E. Piccolo, President
Spencer G. Moore, Co-President
Bryce M. Loebel, Treasurer
Elise M. Tookmanian, Social Media Chair

***WJTL**
08-27-1984; 90.3 MHz FM; 4.7 kw; 198 ft; N40 04 13 W76 17 19
1875 Junction Road, Manheim, PA 17545
(717) 392-3690; *Fax:* (717) 459-3710
www.wjtl.com
contact@wjtl.com
License: Lancaster, Lancaster County, PA held by Creative Ministries Inc.
Nat'l Network: USA
Arbitron Metro Market: Lancaster, PA
Fred McNaughton, Station Manager
John Shirk, Programming Director
John Staffieri, Promotions Manager

WLAN
08-09-1946; 1390 kHz AM; *Hrs Open:* 24
1685 Crown Ave., Suite 100, Lancaster, PA 17601 US
(717) 295-9700
www.rumba1390.com
License: Lancaster, PA held by Clear Channel Broadcasting Licenses Inc.
Group Owner: iHeartMedia; (acq 1996; $7 million with co-located FM)
Nat'l Network: ABC; *Nat'l Reps:* Clear Channel; *Wire Services:* AP
Arbitron Metro Market: Lancaster, PA; *Format:* Spanish; *Hrs. of News Programming:* news progmg 9 hrs wkly; *No. News Employees:* 3; *Target Audience:* 35-64.
Jeff Hurley, Operations Manager
Dan Lankford, Market Manager
Stephanie Winseck, Director of Sales

WLAN-FM
01-01-1948; 96.9 MHz FM; *Hrs Open:* 24; 50 kw; 500 ft; N40 02 52 W76 27 25
1685 Crown Ave., Suite 100, Lancaster, PA 17601 US
(717) 295-9700; *Fax:* (717) 295-7329
www.fm97.com
webmaster@fm97.com
License: Lancaster, Lancaster County, PA held by Clear Channel Broadcasting Licenses Inc.

Group Owner: iHeartMedia
Wire Services: AP
Population Served: 420,000; *Arbitron Metro Market:* Lancaster, PA; *Format:* Contemporary Hits/Top 40; *Hrs. of News Programming:* news progmg 9 hrs wkly; *No. News Employees:* 3; *Target Audience:* 18-49.
Jeff Hurley, Operations Manager
Dan Lankford, Market Manager
Stephanie Winseck, Director of Sales
Troy Becker, Chief Engineer
Damian Rhodes, Production Director
Casey Brackbill, Online Content Director

***WLCH**
09-14-1987; 91.3 MHz FM; 0.16 kw; 135 ft.; N40 4 13 W76 17 19
Mailing Address: 545 Pershing Avenue, Lancaster, PA 17602 US
Second Address: 30 North Ann Street, Lancaster, PA 17602
(717) 295-7996
www.sacapa.org
License: Lancaster, Lancaster County, PA held by Spanish American Civic Association for Equality Inc.
Arbitron Metro Market: Lancaster, PA; *Format:* Variety/Diverse; *Target Audience:* General; Hispanics
Enid Vazquez Pererra, COO
Carlos Groupera, COO/Executive Director
Claudia Galdamez, Director of Broadcasting
Rosa Graupera, CFO
Allison Weber, Director of Development
Hector Valdez, Producer

WLPA
01-01-1922; 1490 kHz AM; *Hrs Open:* 24; 0.6 kw-U, ND1; N40 3 38 W76 18 59
1996 Auction Road, Manheim, PA 17545 US
(717) 653-0800
www.wlpa.com
wlpasports@hallradio.com
License: Lancaster, PA held by Hall Communications Inc.
Group Owner: Hall Communications Inc.; (acq 2-13-77)
Nat'l Network: Fox Sports; *Regional Network:* Radio Pa; *Nat'l Reps:* Katz Radio
Arbitron Metro Market: Lancaster, PA; *Format:* Sports; *Hrs. of News Programming:* News progmg 8 hrs wkly; *Target Audience:* 25-54; men
Bonnie Rowbotham, Chairman
Arthur Rowbotham, President
Sue Sensenig, Programming Director
William Baldwin, Executive Vice President

WROZ
01-01-1944; 101.3 MHz FM; *Hrs Open:* 24; 7.4 kw; 1243 ft.; N40 2 4 W76 37 8
1996 Auction Road, Manheim, PA 17545 US
(717) 653-0800; *Fax:* (717) 653-0122
www.roseradio.com
wroz@hallradio.com
License: Lancaster, Lancaster County, PA held by Hall Communications Inc.
Group Owner: Hall Communications Inc.
Nat'l Reps: Katz Radio; *Wire Services:* AP
Arbitron Metro Market: Lancaster, PA; *Format:* Adult Contemp; *No. News Employees:* 1; *Target Audience:* 25-54; women
Bonnie Hall Rowbotham, Chairman
Art Rowbotham, President
Lorna Fraunfetter, Creative Director
Ronnie Ramone, Promotions Director
Michael Anthony, Programming/Music Director
Edd Monskie, Chief Engineer
Tom Richards, ProductionDirector
Bill Baldwin, General Manager
Loren Good, General Sales Manager
Kacey Ober, Director of Events
Linda Weidman, Traffic Director

Lansdale

WNPV
10-17-1960; 1440 kHz AM; *Hrs Open:* 24; 2.5 kw-D, DA2; 0.5 kw-N, DA2; N40 14 18 W75 19 0
1210 Synder Road, Lansdale, PA 19446 US
(215) 855-8211
www.wnpv1440.com
info@wnpv1440.com
License: Lansdale, PA held by WNPV Inc.
Nat'l Network: Fox News Radio; *Regional Network:* Radio Pa.
Arbitron Metro Market: Philadelphia, PA; *Format:* News, News/Talk, 84, Talk *Special Programming:* Big band 3 hrs, relg 5 hrs, sports 6 hrs wkly; *Hrs. of News Programming:* news progmg 20 hrs wkly; *No. News Employees:* 2; *Target Audience:* 30 plus.; *Adv. Rates:* 15; 15; 15; 15
Phillip Hunt, President/General Manager
Darryl Berger, Programming Director
Jeff Nolan, Sports Director
David McCrork, Engineering Dir

Lansford

WLSH
12-24-1952; 1410 kHz AM; *Hrs Open:* 24; 5 kw-D, DAD; N40 50 40 W75 50 37
Mailing Address: 2147 Market Street, Nesquehoning, PA 18240 US
Second Address: 3835 Quarry Drive, Emmanus, PA 18049
(570) 645-3123; *Fax:* (570) 645-2159
www.wmgh.com
wmgh@wmgh.com
License: Lansford, PA held by J-Systems Franchising Corp.
Group Owner: J-Systems Franchising Corp.; acq 1-89; $300,000;
Nat'l Network: Westwood One; USA; *Regional Network:* Radio Pa.
Arbitron Metro Market: Allentown-Bethlehem, PA; *Format:* Adult Contemp *Special Programming:* Big Band 4 hrs, Oldies 18 hrs wkly; *Target Audience:* 35-64; Mature adults
Harold Fulmer III, CEO
Harold Fulmer, III, President
Christopher Fulmer, Operations Dir
Bill Lakatas, General Manager
Doug Betz, Sales Director

Laporte

***WPAL**
09-01-1968; 91.7 MHz FM; *Hrs Open:* 24; 0.27 kw; 161 ft.; N41 26 6 W76 28 28 US
(843) 529-9293; *Fax:* (843) 746-9299
wayx.wayfm.com
License: Laporte, Dorchester County, PA held by Charles W. Cherry, Receiver for Gresham Communications Inc.
Arbitron Metro Market: Charleston, SC; *Format:* Christian
Bret Bremberg, General Manager

***WPAL(FM)**
91.7 MHz FM; 190 w; Ant 161 ft; N41 26 06 W76 28 28
Box 20155, Scranton, PA 18502
(607) 427-0452
License: Laporte, Sullivan County, PA held by Telikoja Educational Broadcasting Inc.
Population Served: 2,932; *Arbitron Metro Market:* Towanda, PA
Kevin Fitzgerald, President

***WCIS**
01-01-1996; 90.9 MHz FM; 0.25 kw; 492 ft.; N41 30 7 W76 23 34 *Rebroadcasts:* Rebroadcasts WCIK(FM) Bath, NY 100%
PO Box 506, Bath, NY 14810 US
(607) 776-4151
www.fln.org
License: Laporte, PA held by Family Life Ministries Inc.
Group Owner: Family Life Network; (acq 10-1-96; $20,130).
Nat'l Network: Salem Radio Network; *Wire Services:* Metro Weather Service Inc.
Arbitron Metro Market: Bath,NY; *Format:* Christian; *Hrs. of News Programming:* news progmg 14 hrs wkly; *No. News Employees:* 3; *Target Audience:* 30-54; general
Dave Margalotti, Operations Dir
Terese Main, Programming Director
Bob Price, News Director

Latrobe

WCNS
08-11-1956; 1480 kHz AM; *Hrs Open:* 24; 0.5 kw-D, DAN; 1 kw-N, DAN; N40 16 12 W79 23 13
400 Unity Street, Suite 200, Latrobe, PA 15650 US
(724) 537-3338; *Fax:* (724) 539-9798
www.1480wcns.com
mailbox@wcnsradio.com
License: Latrobe, PA held by LHTC Media, Inc.
Nat'l Network: Westwood One
Arbitron Metro Market: Latrobe, Pennsylvania / Pittsburgh, PA; *Format:* Variety/Diverse *Special Programming:* Relg 2 hrs wkly; *Hrs. of News Programming:* news progmg 15 hrs wkly; *No. News Employees:* 3 *TargetAudience:* 25 +; general
John Longo, President
Greg Zahornacky, Station Manager
Dow Carnahan, Programming Director

WQTW
01-01-1952; 1570 kHz AM; 1 kw-D, NDD; N40 18 7 W79 21 56
Rebroadcasts: Rebroadcasts WLSW(FM) Scottdale
R. D. #7, Box 56, Greensburg, PA 15601 US
(724) 532-1778; *Fax:* (724) 532-1779
License: Latrobe, PA held by L. Stanley Wall.
Arbitron Metro Market: Pittsburgh, PA; *Format:* Adult Contemp
L. Stanley Wall, President

Lebanon

WADV
07-04-1976; 940 kHz AM; *Hrs Open:* 19; 1 kw-D, ND1; 0.005 kw-N, ND1; N40 22 22 W76 21 53
P Box 3206, Tupelo, MS 38803 US
(662) 844-8888
www.afr.net
comments@afr.net
License: Lebanon, PA held by WADV Radio, Inc.
Group Owner: American Family Association; (acq 12-4-01).
Nat'l Network: Moody
Format: Gospel
Tim Wildman, President

WLBR
11-13-1946; 1270 kHz AM; *Hrs Open:* 5 AM-1 AM; 5 kw-D, DA2; 1 kw-N, DA2; N40 21 35 W76 27 30
PO Box 1270, Lebanon, PA 17042 US
(717) 272-7651; *Fax:* (717) 274-0161
License: Lebanon, PA held by Lebanon Broadcasting Co.
Regional Network: Radio Pa; *Nat'l Reps:* Roslin *Regional Reps:* Dome
Arbitron Metro Market: Harrisburg-Lebanon-Carlisle, PA; *Format:* News, News/Talk, 86; *No. News Employees:* 2; *Target Audience:* 25-64.
Robert Etter, Operations Dir
Mickey Santora, General Sales Mgr
Gordon Weise, News Director
Glenn Waybright, Chief Engineer
Greg Lyons, Music Director
Laura Lebeau, News Reporter
Scott Bradley, Sports Commentator
Gayle Reich,Traffic Manager

WQIC
01-01-1948; 100.1 MHz FM; *Hrs Open:* 5 AM-1 AM; 3 kw; 266 ft.; N40 21 37 W76 27 31
PO Box 1270, Lebanon, PA 17042 US
(717) 272-7651; *Fax:* (717) 274-0161
License: Lebanon, Lebanon County, PA held by Lebanon Broadcasting Co.
Arbitron Metro Market: Harrisburg-Lebanon-Carlisle, PA; *Format:* Adult Contemp; *Target Audience:* 25-54.
Steve Todd, Programming Director
Gayle Reich, News Director
John Tuscano, Disc Jockey
Phil Liles, Disc Jockey
Mike Ebersole, Music Director
Scott Bradley, Sports Commentator

Leesport

***WYBQ**
08-02-2013; 88.3 MHz FM; 0.001 kw horiz, 0.67 kw vert; 276 ft.; N40 28 9 W76 3 46 *Rebroadcasts:* Rebroadcasts WYFQ(AM) Charlotte 100%
P.O. Box 7300, Charlotte, NC 28241
(800) 888-7077
www.bbnradio.org
bbn@bbnmedia.org
License: Leesport, Berks County, PA held by Bible Broadcasting Network Inc.
Group Owner: Bible Broadcasting Network
Population Served: 168,528; *Arbitron Metro Market:* Leesport, PA; *Format:* Christian, Religious
Lowell Davey, President
Jason Padgett, Operations Manager

Lehighton

WBYN
04-12-1962; 1160 kHz AM; *Hrs Open:* 24; 4 kw-D, DA2; 1 kw-N, DA2; N40 49 3 W75 41 31 *Rebroadcasts:* Rebroadcasts WBYN-FM Boyertown 100%
107 Paxinosa Rd. W, Easton, PA 18040 US
(610) 258-6155; *Fax:* (610) 253-3384
License: Lehighton, PA held by Connoisseur Media Licenses LLC
Group Owner: Connoisseur Media LLC; (acq 4-25-2003; $375,000).
Nat'l Reps: Katz Radio *Regional Reps:* Glenn Jones

Arbitron Metro Market: Allentown-Bethl; *Format:* Contemporary Hits/Top 40
Rick Musselman, General Manager
Michael Anthony, General Sales Mgr
Bill Sheridan, Programming Director
K.J. Zabala, Promotions Manager
Brian Keith, Traffic Manager

Lehman Township

WABT(FM)
10-30-1970; 96.7 MHz FM; *Hrs Open:* 24; 3 kw; Ant 300 ft; N41 22 24 W74 43 49
PO Box 920, Port Jervis, NY 12771
(855) 856-5185
www.pocono967.com
regosterhoudt@pocono967.com
License: Lehman Township, Pike County, PA held by Neversink Radio, LLC
Arbitron Metro Market: Newburgh-Middletown, NY (Mid-Hudson Valley); *No. News Employees:* 2
Bud Williamson, Owner
Reg Osterhoudt, Programming Director

Levittown

WBCB
12-08-1957; 1490 kHz AM; *Hrs Open:* 24; 1 kw-U, ND1; N40 10 8 W74 50 8
PO Box 2098, Omaha, NE 68103 US
(800) 877-5600; *Fax:* (916) 251-1650
www.klove.com
License: Levittown, PA held by Progressive Broadcasting Co.
Nat'l Network: USA
Arbitron Metro Market: El Paso TX; *Format:* Christian
Darrell Chambliss, Chairman
Mike Novak, President/CEO
Alan Mason, COO
Eric Moser, CFO
D. Kevin Blair, Secretary/General Counsel

Lewisburg

WCXR
10-18-1990; 103.7 MHz FM; *Hrs Open:* 24; 0.95 kw; 801 ft.; N40 58 38 W77 7 0 *Rebroadcasts:* Rebroadcasts WZXR(FM) South Williamsport 100%
1685 Four Mile Dr, Williamsport, PA 17701 US
(570) 323-8200; *Fax:* (570) 323-5075
www.wzxr.com
tminier@backyardbroadcasting.com
License: Lewisburg, Union County, PA held by Backyard Broadcasting PA, LLC
Group Owner: Backyard Broadcasting LLC
Nat'l Network: ABC
Arbitron Metro Market: Sunbury-Selinsgrove-Lewisburg, PA; *Format:* Rock/AOR; *No. News Employees:* 3; *Target Audience:* 25-54.; *Adv. Rates:* 30; 30; 30; 20
Dan Farr, President & CEO
Gerald Getz, General Sales Mgr
Ted Minier, Programming Director
John Finn, News Director
Kelly Bailey, Production Manager

*WGRC
04-22-1988; 91.3 MHz FM; *Hrs Open:* 24; 3 kw; 322 ft.; N40 56 40 W76 52 45
101 Armory Boulevard, Lewisburg, PA 17837 US
(570) 523-1190
www.wgrc.com
email@wgrc.com
License: Lewisburg, Union County, PA held by Salt and Light Media Ministries Inc.
Nat'l Network: Salem Radio Network; *Wire Services:* AP
Format: Adult Contemp, Christian; *Hrs. of News Programming:* news progmg 16 hrs wkly; *No. News Employees:* 3; *Target Audience:* 25-54; young to middle-aged adult
Sandra Hare, Chairperson
David Moyer, Vice Chair
Scott Hurst, Treasurer
Rob Kime, Programming Director
Chris Miller, Engineering Dir

*WVBU-FM
10-01-1965; 90.5 MHz FM; *Hrs Open:* 8 AM-2 AM; 0.225 kw; -33 ft.; N40 57 18 W76 52 55
Box C-3956, Lewisburg, PA 17837 US
(570) 577-3489; *Fax:* (570) 577-1174
www.orgs.bucknell.edu/wvbu
License: Lewisburg, Union County, PA held by Bucknell University.
Arbitron Metro Market: Lewisburg, PA; *Format:* Rock/AOR *Special Programming:* Jazz 3 hrs, dance/club 6 hrs, prison request 2 hrs; *Hrs. of News Programming:* News progmg 7 hrs wkly; *Target Audience:* 18-23; collegestudents
Joe Duvall, General Manager
Roy Skinner, Programming Director
Sara Rosenberg, Promotions Director
Todd Fogle, Chief Engineer
James Lee, Faculty Advisor
Steve Hladczuk, Music Director
Deanna Byfogle, Business Director
JohnBrunner, News Director

Lewistown

WCHX
07-01-1987; 105.5 MHz FM; *Hrs Open:* 24; 3 kw; 817 ft; N40 39 43 W77 34 28
114 N. Logan Boulevard, Burnham, PA 17009 US
(717) 242-1055
www.chx105.com
wchx@chx105.com
License: Lewistown, Mifflin County, PA held by Mifflin County Communications Inc.
Nat'l Network: Fox News Radio; *Regional Network:* Radio Pa.
Population Served: 125,000 *Hrs. of News Programming:* news progmg 10 hrs wkly; *No. News Employees:* 1; *Target Audience:* 25-54; mature, affluent, middle & upper class adults
Michelle Long, General Manager
Scott Brattan, General Sales Mgr
Steve Buda, Programming Director

WIEZ
06-01-1941; 670 kHz AM; *Hrs Open:* Sunrise-sunset; 5.4 kw-D, NDD; N40 36 30 W77 34 45
Mailing Address: 12 East Market St., Lewistown, PA 17044 US
Second Address: 12 E. Market St. 2nd Floor, Lewistown, PA 17044
(717) 248-6757; *Fax:* (717) 248-6759
pete@merfradio.com
License: Lewistown, PA
Group Owner: First Media Radio LLC; (acq 3-28-2001; grpsl)
Nat'l Reps: Dome
Format: News; *Hrs. of News Programming:* news progmg 12 hrs wkly; *No. News Employees:* 2; *Target Audience:* 45 plus; adults who control the area's disposable income
Jeff Stevens, Operations Dir
Pete Herman, General Manager
Chuck Curry, General Sales Mgr
Mary Lee Schaeffer, News Director
Ron Patterson, Production Director
Tom Laub, Traffic Director
Rocco Pallotto, Music & Sports Director

*WJRC
07-01-1996; 90.9 MHz FM; *Hrs Open:* 24; 0.094 kw; 1293 ft.; N40 34 20 W77 30 51 *Rebroadcasts:* Rebroadcasts WGRC(FM) Lewisburg 100%
101 Armory Boulevard, Lewisburg, PA 17837 US
(570) 523-1190
www.wgrc.com
email@wgrc.com
License: Lewistown, Mifflin County, PA held by Salt and Light Media Ministries Inc.
Nat'l Network: Salem Radio Network; *Wire Services:* AP
Format: Christian; *Hrs. of News Programming:* news progmg 9 hrs wkly; *No. News Employees:* 3; *Target Audience:* 25-54.
Sandra Hare, Chairperson
David Moyer, Vice Chair
Scott Hurst, Treasurer
Rob Kime, General Manager
Chris Miller, Engineering Dir

WKVA
12-04-1949; 920 kHz AM; *Hrs Open:* 5 AM-midnight; 1 kw-D, DAN; 0.5 kw-N, DAN; N40 34 45 W77 34 18
114 North Logan Boulevard, Burnham, PA 17009 US
(717) 242-1493
www.oldies920.com
kvatoday@wkva920.com
License: Lewistown, PA held by Mifflin County Communications Inc.
Nat'l Network: ABC; CBS Radio; *Regional Network:* Radio Pa.
Format: Oldies; *Hrs. of News Programming:* news progmg 31 hrs wkly; *No. News Employees:* 2; *Target Audience:* 25-54; blue collar mix of agricultural & industrial adults
Anna Hain, President
Jed Donahue, Operations Dir
Erik Lane, News Director

WMRF-FM
10-01-1964; 95.7 MHz FM; *Hrs Open:* 24; 3.9 kw; 407 ft.; N40 36 30 W77 34 45
12 E. Market St, 2nd Fl, Lewistown, PA 17044 US
(717) 248-6757
www.merfradio.com
License: Lewistown, Mifflin County, PA held by First Media Radio LLC.
Group Owner: First Media Radio LLC; (acq 5-14-2001; grpsl)
Arbitron Metro Market: Lewistown, PA; *Format:* Adult Contemp; *Hrs. of News Programming:* news progmg 8 hrs wkly; *No. News Employees:* 2; *Target Audience:* 18-44.
Tom Laub, Traffic Director
Rocco Pallotto, Sports/Music Director
Ron Patterson, Production Director
Pete Herman, General Manager
Jeff Stevens, Operations Manager
May Lee Sheaffer, News Director

Lincoln University

*WWLU
08-01-1975; 88.7 MHz FM; 0.003 kw horiz; 141 ft.; N39 48 36 W75 55 35
1570 Baltimore Pike, Box 179, Lincoln University, PA 19352 US
(484) 365-7791
www.lincoln.edu
License: Lincoln University, Chester County, PA held by Lincoln University.
Format: Urban Contemporary
Whitney G. Walton, General Manager

Linesville

WMVL
05-04-1970; 101.7 MHz FM; *Hrs Open:* 24; 1.4 kw; 554 ft.; N41 42 38 W80 16 29
16271 Conneaut Lake Road, Suite 102, Meadville, PA 16335 US
(814) 333-9011
cool1017online.com
License: Linesville, Crawford County, PA held by Vilkie Communications Inc.
Nat'l Network: ABC *Regional Reps:* Regional Reps; CLE; OH
Arbitron Metro Market: Meadville, PA; *Format:* Oldies; *Hrs. of News Programming:* News progmg 8 hrs wkly; *Target Audience:* 29 plus.; *Adv. Rates:* 16; 15; 16; 9
Joseph Vilkie, President
Eugene Vilkie, Operations Dir
Jim Jewell, General Sales Mgr
Chuck Stopp, Programming Director
Dave Hanahan, Sales Manager
Jenna Wagner, Sales

Lock Haven

WBPZ
02-20-1947; 1230 kHz AM; *Hrs Open:* 24; 1 kw-U, ND1; N41 8 3 W77 28 9
21 East Main Street, Lock Haven, PA 17745 US
(570) 748-4038; *Fax:* (570) 748-0092
www.wsqvradio.com
License: Lock Haven, PA held by Schlesinger Communications Inc.
Nat'l Reps: Keystone (unwired net); Dome
Arbitron Metro Market: Lock Haven, PA; *Format:* Oldies *Special Programming:* Loc sports; *Hrs. of News Programming:* news progmg 10 hrs wkly; *No. News Employees:* 1; *Target Audience:* General.
John Lipez, President
John Lupez, General Sales Mgr
Randy Dorey, Programming Director
Mark Sohmer, News Director
Dennis Sherman, Chief Engineer
Bill Daney, Music Director
Michelle Grove, Traffic Manager

WSQV(FM)
09-01-1965; 92.1 MHz FM; *Hrs Open:* 24; 3 kw; 255 ft; N41 08 49 W77 29 16
21 East Main Street, Lock Haven, PA 17745 B7745
(570) 748-4038; *Fax:* (570) 748-0092
www.wsqvradio.com
License: Lock Haven, Clinton County, PA held by Schlesinger Communications Inc.
Population Served: 70,000; *Arbitron Metro Market:* Williamsport, PA; *Format:* Adult Contemp; *Hrs. of News Programming:* news progmg 6 hrs wkly; *No. News Employees:* 1; *Target Audience:* 21-48.
Michelle Grove, News Director

Loretto

WWGE
12-07-1963; 1400 kHz AM; *Hrs Open:* 24; 1 kw-U, ND1; N40 30 12 W78 38 10
PO Box 88, Edensburg, PA 15931 US
(814) 619-3284
www.edge-radio.com/
License: Loretto, PA held by Pennsylvania Radiowerks LLC
Nat'l Network: Jones Radio Networks
Arbitron Metro Market: Loretto, PA; *Format:* News, News/Talk, 84, Talk; *Adv. Rates:* 4; 3; 2; 1
Rev. Michael Yeager, President
Jennifer Strelnik, General Manager

Manchester Township

WGLD
10-22-1950; 1440 kHz AM; 730 w-D, 53 w-N
5989 Susquehanna Plaza Dr., York, PA 17406 US
(717) 764-1155; *Fax:* (717) 252-4708
www.sportsradio1440.com
License: Manchester Township, PA held by Radio License Holding SRC, LLC
Group Owner: Cumulus Media Inc.; (acq 5-11-2005; $280,000)
Arbitron Metro Market: York, PA; *Format:* Sports, Talk
Brian Shaffer, Director of Sales
Chris Tyler, Programming Director
Lee Jacoby, Promotions Manager
Carol Pierson, Market Manager
Brian Dean, Sports Director

Mansfield

WNBQ
06-01-1999; 92.3 MHz FM; *Hrs Open:* 24; 1.6 kw; 643 ft.; N41 53 53 W77 5 38 *Rebroadcasts:* Rebroadcasts WNBT-FM Wellsboro 100%
P.O. Box 98, Wellsboro, PA 16901 US
(570) 724-1490; *Fax:* (570) 724-6971
www.wnbt.net
wnbt@ynt.net
License: Mansfield, Tioga County, PA held by Farm & Home Broadcasting Co.
Group Owner: Allegheny Mountain Network Stations
Nat'l Network: Westwood One *Regional Reps:* Dome & Assoc.
Arbitron Metro Market: Wellsboro, PA; *Format:* Adult Contemp, Contemporary Hits/Top 40; *Adv. Rates:* 223.80; 186; 223.80; 141.60
Cary H. Simpson, President
Al Harer, Station Manager
Ryan Dalton, Music Director

***WNTE**
09-15-1968; 89.5 MHz FM; 0.115 kw; -279 ft.; N41 48 23 W77 4 25
Alumni Hall, Mansfield, PA 16933 US
(908) 581-5153
www.wnte.com
simmersc25@mounties.mansfield.edu
License: Mansfield, Tioga County, PA held by WNTE-FM Mansfield University
Arbitron Metro Market: Mansfield, PA; *Format:* Contemporary Hits/Top 40, Rock/AOR *Special Programming:* Black 5 hrs, jazz 2 hrs wkly; *Target Audience:* 17-25; college students/community
Randolph Bell, President
Chelsea Simmers, General Manager
Wayne DeSylvia, Station Manager
Kenny Ertel, Programming Director

Markleysburg

***WLOG**
01-01-2002; 89.1 MHz FM; 0.1 kw vert; 328 ft.; N39 43 32 W79 28 53
160 Gooding Street W., Twin Falls, ID 83301 US
(208) 733-3551; *Fax:* (208) 734-0674
www.edgewaterbroadcasting.com
connect@freedomradiofm.com
License: Markleysburg, Fayette County, PA held by Edgewater Broadcasting Inc.
Arbitron Metro Market: Twin Falls, ID; *Format:* Christian
Clark Parrish, President
Bob Adams, Head of Programming & Operations
Steve Atkin, Executive Director
Diana Atkin, Vice President
Earl Williamson, Secretary / Treasurer
John Devine, Director
Dennis Clounch, Director
Tom Golding,Technical Director

Martinsburg

WWBJ
02-27-1968; 1110 kHz AM; 1 kw-D, NDD; N40 18 14 W78 15 59
Mailing Address: 55 West Fort Dade Avenue, Brooksville, FL 34601 US
Second Address: PO Box 1507, Brooksville, FL 34605
(352) 796-7569; *Fax:* (352)796-3074
steve@wwjb.com
License: Martinsburg, PA held by Martinsburg Broadcasting Inc.
Arbitron Metro Market: Altoona, PA; *Format:* News, Talk, 74
Special Programming: Farm one hr wkly; *Target Audience:* General.
Barbara Manuel, Owner/Sales
Bill Williamson, Sales Manager

WJSM-FM
04-19-1965; 92.7 MHz FM; 1.9 kw; 591 ft.; N40 20 50 W78 24 57
724 Rebecca Furnace Road, Martinsburg, PA 16662 US
(814) 793-2188; *Fax:* (814) 793-9727
www.wjsm.com
wjsmradio@gmail.com
License: Martinsburg, Blair County, PA held by Martinsburg Broadcasting Inc.
Nat'l Network: USA
Arbitron Metro Market: Altoona, PA; *Format:* Gospel, News, 62, Talk, Religious
Larry Walters, President
Larry Walters, General Manager
Byrle Hap Ritchey, General Sales Manager/Programming & Music Director
Bill Reed, News Director
Terry MacAlarney, Transmitter Engineer
Cheryl Walters, Traffic Manager
Priscilla Ritchey, Sales Bookkeepers
Kenneth Ferry, Founder
Margaret Ferry, Co-Founder

Masontown

***WRIJ**
11-01-1990; 106.9 MHz FM; *Hrs Open:* 19; 0.98 kw; 810 ft.; N39 42 17 W79 46 30 *Rebroadcasts:* Rebroadcasts WAIJ(FM) Grantsville, MD 100%
Mailing Address: 34 Springs Rd, Grantsville, MD 21536 US
Second Address: PO Box 540, Grantsville, MD 21536
(301) 895-3292; *Fax:* (301) 895-3293
www.hesalive.net
info@hesalive.net
License: Masontown, Fayette County, PA held by He's Alive Inc.
Group Owner: He's Alive Inc.
Nat'l Network: USA
Format: Adult Contemp, Christian, 44, Religious; *Target Audience:* 18-35.
Melissa Flores, General Manager

***WYFU**
01-01-2003; 88.5 MHz FM; 16 kw; 328 ft.; N39 47 13 W79 59 23
Mailing Address: P.O. Box 7300, Charlotte, NC 28241 US
Second Address: 11530 Carmel Commons Blvd., Charlotte, NC 28226
(800) 888-7077
www.bbnradio.org
bbn@bbnmedia.org
License: Masontown, Fayette County, PA held by Bible Broadcasting Network Inc.
Group Owner: Bible Broadcasting Network; (acq 2-12-99; $250,000).
Arbitron Metro Market: Masontown, PA; *Format:* Christian
Jason Padgett, Operations Manager

McConnellsburg

WEEO-FM
01-01-1997; 103.7 MHz FM; 0.135 kw; 1555 ft.; N39 55 25 W77 57 20
37 South Main St., Chambersburg, PA 17201 US
(717) 709-0801; *Fax:* (717) 709-0802
www.newstalk1037fm.com
License: McConnellsburg, Fulton County, PA held by Magnum Broadcasting Inc.
Group Owner: Allegheny Mountain Network Stations; (acq 10-95; $18,000)
Regional Reps: Dome
Arbitron Metro Market: McConnellsburg, PA; *Format:* News, News/Talk, 86; *Adv. Rates:* 33; 30; 33; 26
Patrick Ryan, General Manager

***WWCF**
01-01-2005; 88.7 MHz FM; 0.009 kw; 1194 ft.; N39 54 58 W77 57 25
Rural Delivery-1, Box 211-F, McConnelsburg, PA 17233 US
(717) 485-5526
License: McConnellsburg, Fulton County, PA held by Morris Broadcasting & Communications Inc.
Arbitron Metro Market: McConnellsburg, PA; *Format:* Children
Glenn Morris, President

McKeesport

WEDO
01-01-1947; 810 kHz AM; *Hrs Open:* Sunrise-sunset
1985 Lincoln Way, White Oak, PA 15131 US
(412) 664-4431; *Fax:* (412) 664-1236
www.wedo810.com/
wedoradio@comcast.net
License: McKeesport, PA held by 810 Inc.
Arbitron Metro Market: Mckeesport, PA; *Format:* Talk *Special Programming:* Slovenian one hr, Slovak one hr, Greek one hr, Croation one hr, It one hr wkly; *Target Audience:* 35-65, 25-54, 65+.
Judith Baron, President
John James, Operations Dir
Bill Korch, Programming Director

WMNY
04-01-1947; 1360 kHz AM; *Hrs Open:* 24; 5 kw-D, DAN; 1 kw-N, DAN; N40 24 30 W79 55 40; N40 18 41 W79 50 59
560 7th Street, New Kensington, PA 15068 US
(412) 875-9500; *Fax:* (412) 875-9474
www.wmnyradio.com
License: McKeesport, PA held by Pentecostal Temple Development Group
Nat'l Network: ABC; *Nat'l Reps:* McGavren Guild; *Wire Services:* AP; Metro Weather Service Inc.
Arbitron Metro Market: Pittsburgh, PA; *Format:* Talk *Special Programming:* Oldies 9 hrs, polka 2 hrs wkly; *Hrs. of News Programming:* News progmg 15 hrs wkly; *Target Audience:* 25-54.; *Adv. Rates:* 55; 55; 55;30
Reverend Dr. Loran E. Mann, Owner
Tony Renda Sr., CEO
Tony Renda Jr., General Manager

Meadville

***WARC**
02-03-1963; 90.3 MHz FM; 0.4 kw; 66 ft.; N41 38 57 W80 8 38
520 N Main St - Box C, Meadville, PA 16335 US
(814) 332-3376
warc@allegheny.edu
License: Meadville, Crawford County, PA held by Allegheny College.
Arbitron Metro Market: Meadville, PA.; *Format:* Alternative
Special Programming: Black 8 hrs, class 10 hrs, jazz 4 hrs wkly
Parge Slaughter, General Manager
Nick Christensen, Programming Director
Kate Mayo, Music Director

WMGW
01-01-1947; 1490 kHz AM; 1 kw-U, ND1; N41 37 53 W80 10 37
900 Water St., Downtown Mall, Meadville, PA 16335 US
(814) 724-1111; *Fax:* (814) 333-9628
www.myantsnetwork.com
License: Meadville, Crawford County, PA held by FM Radio Licenses LLC
Group Owner: Forever Broadcasting; (acq 7-20-00; grpsl).
Arbitron Metro Market: Meadville-Franklin, PA; *Format:* News, News/Talk, 84, Talk; *Target Audience:* 25-54.
Jim Shields, General Manager
Helen Powers, Sales Manager
Andy Alm, Programming Director
Mark Himmler, Chief Engineer
Jill Hamilton, Business Manager

WGYY
01-01-1947; 100.3 MHz FM; 20 kw; 587 ft.; N41 37 53 W80 10 37
Mailing Address: 900 Water St., Downtown Mall, Meadville, PA 16335 US
Second Address: 1243 Liberty St., Suite 501, Franklin, PA 16323
(814) 724-1111; *Fax:* (814) 333-9628
www.froggyfun.com
License: Meadville, Crawford County, PA held by FM Radio Licenses LLC
Group Owner: Forever Broadcasting
Arbitron Metro Market: Meadville-Franklin, PA; *Format:* Country
Jim Shields, General Manager
Helen Powers, Sales Manager
Wesley Miller, Programming Director
Mark Himmler, Chief Engineer
Jill Hamilton, Business Manager

***WVME**
01-01-2002; 91.9 MHz FM; *Hrs Open:* 24; 4.4 kW; 308 ft.; N41 37 50 W80 10 38 *Rebroadcasts:* Rebroadcasts WCRF(FM) Cleveland, OH 100%
9756 Barr Rd, Cleveland, OH 44141 USA
(440) 526-1111; *Fax:* (440) 526-1319
www.moodyradio.org/stations/cleveland
License: Meadville, Crawford County, PA held by The Moody Bible Institute of Chicago
Group Owner: The Moody Bible Institute of Chicago
Wire Services: AP
Arbitron Metro Market: Meadville, PA; *Format:* Christian; *Target Audience:* 25-55; Adults

Mechanicsburg

WWKL
09-22-1959; 93.5 MHz FM; 1.25 kw; 719 ft.; N40 10 38 W76 52 38 *Rebroadcasts:* Rebroadcasts WTPA(FM) Mechanicsburg 100%
2300 Vartan Way, Harrisburg, PA 17110 US
(717) 238-1041; *Fax:* (717) 234-7780
www.hot935fm.com
john.odea@cumulus.com
License: Mechanicsburg, Lebanon County, PA held by Cumulus Licensing Corp.
Group Owner: Cumulus Media Inc.; (acq 11-28-2000; grpsl)
Regional Network: Radio Pa.
Arbitron Metro Market: Harrisburg, PA; *Format:* Contemporary Hits/Top 40 *Special Programming:* Relg 6 hrs, Sp 14 hrs, Hershey Bears hockey, Hersh; *Target Audience:* 25-54.
John O'Dea, Operations Dir
Karen Richards, General Sales Mgr
John O'Dea, Programming Director
Phil George, Promotions Director
Dave Supplee, Chief Engineer
Amy Warner, Music Director

Media

WRNB
01-01-1946; 100.3 MHz FM; *Hrs Open:* 5:30 AM-midnight; 17 kw; 863 ft.; N40 2 36 W75 14 33
Two Bala Plaza, Suite 700, Bala Cynwyd, PA 19004 US
(610) 538-1100
www.oldschool1003.com
License: Media, Camden County, PA held by Radio One Licenses LLC.
Group Owner: Radio One Inc.; (acq 2-2-2004; $35 million).
Arbitron Metro Market: Philadelphia; *Format:* Oldies
Catherine Nye, General Sales Mgr
Darrick Williams, Programming Director

Mercer

WLLF
01-01-1985; 96.7 MHz FM; *Hrs Open:* 24; 1.4 kw; 486 ft.; N41 18 43 W80 16 39
2030 Pine Hollow Blvd., Hermitage, PA 16148 US
(724) 346-4113; *Fax:* (724) 981-4545
www.sportsradio967.com
bob.greenburg@cumulus.com
License: Mercer, Mercer County, PA held by Cumulus Licensing LLC
Group Owner: Cumulus Media Inc.; (acq 3-15-00; grpsl).
Nat'l Network: Jones Radio Networks
Arbitron Metro Market: Youngstown-Warren, OH; *Format:* Adult Contemp
Bob Greenburg, General Sales Mgr
Christian Aleshire, Programming Director
Wes Boyd, Chief Engineer
Rick Parrish, Marketing Manager

Mercersburg

WNUZ
01-01-1945; 92.1 MHz FM; *Hrs Open:* 5 AM-11 PM; 4 kw; 295 ft.; N39 48 34 W77 48 22
10960 John Wayne Drive, Greencastle, PA 17725 US
(717) 597-9200; *Fax:* (717) 597-9210
www.now921.com
License: Mercersburg, Talladega County, PA held by HJV Limited Partnership
Arbitron Metro Market: Franklin, PA; *Format:* Contemporary Hits/Top 40 *Special Programming:* Talk 5 hrs, Gospel 7 hrs, bluegrass 6 hrs wkly; *No. News Employees:* 1; *Target Audience:* Women 18-49 *Adv. Rates:* 65; 47; 47; 37
L.E. Willis Sr., President
Jonnie Luster, General Manager
Louis Amerson, Programming Director

Mexico

WJUN
09-08-1955; 1220 kHz AM; *Hrs Open:* 24
PO Box 209, Mexico, PA 17056 US
(717) 436-2135
www.wjun925.com
License: Mexico, PA held by Starview Media Inc.
Nat'l Network: ESPN Radio; *Regional Network:* Radio Pa.
Format: Sports *Special Programming:* Relg 2 hrs wkly; *No. News Employees:* 1; *Target Audience:* 25-54.; *Adv. Rates:* available on request
Douglas George, President
Curt Dreibelbis, General Manager
Laurie Hower, News Director
John Hess, Chief Engineer

WJUN-FM
07-04-1989; 92.5 MHz FM; *Hrs Open:* 24; 0.44 kw; 1181 ft.; N40 34 58 W77 29 48
PO Box 209, Mexico, PA 17056 US
(717) 436-2135
www.wjun925.com
License: Mexico, Juniata County, PA held by Starview Media Inc.
Nat'l Network: Motor Racing Net; *Regional Network:* Radio Pa.
Format: Country; *Hrs. of News Programming:* news progmg 5 hrs wkly; *No. News Employees:* 1
Curt Dreibelbis, General Manager
Mel Thomas, Programming Director

Meyersdale

WQZS
01-01-1992; 93.3 MHz FM; 0.63 kw; 965 ft.; N39 47 49 W79 10 5
128 Hunsrick Road, Meyersdale, PA 15552 US
(814) 634-9111; *Fax:* (814) 634-0882
helenwahl27@hotmail.com
License: Meyersdale, Somerset County, PA held by Roger Wahl.
Format: Oldies *Special Programming:* Gospel 5 hrs wkly; *No. News Employees:* 1; *Target Audience:* 25-60; females 60%, males 40%
Roger Wahl, General Manager
Helen Wahl, Station Programming Director
Jessy Chabol, General Sales Mgr

Middletown

***WMSS**
09-07-1978; 91.1 MHz FM; *Hrs Open:* 7 AM-9 PM; 0.45 kw; 73 ft.; N40 12 44 W76 44 47
215 Oberlin Road, Middletown, PA 17057 US
(717) 948-9136
www.wmssfm.com
sales@wmssfm.com
License: Middletown, Dauphin County, PA held by Middletown Area School District.
Regional Network: Va. News Net.
Arbitron Metro Market: Harrisburg, PA; *Format:* Adult Contemp *Special Programming:* Sports 5 hrs, relg 8 hrs wkly; *Hrs. of News Programming:* News progmg one hr wkly; *Target Audience:* General.
Maureen Denis, Operations Dir
John Wilsbach, General Manager
Steve Leedy, Operations Manager

***WXPH**
01-01-2006; 88.7 MHz FM; 0.075 kw horiz, 7 kw vert; 709 ft.; N40 2 7 W76 37 19 *Rebroadcasts:* Rebroadcasts WXPN(FM) Philadelphia 100%
3025 Walnut Street, Philadelphia, PA 19104 US
(215) 898-6677; *Fax:* (215) 898-0707
www.xpn.org
online@xpn.org
License: Middletown, Dauphin County, PA held by The Trustees of the University of Pennsylvania
Arbitron Metro Market: Middletown, PA; *Format:* Alternative
Roger LaMay, General Manager
Tom Interrante, Sales Director
Kim Winnick, Music Director
John Bartol, IT Director
Dan Reed, Music Director

Mifflinburg

WWBE
01-01-1975; 98.3 MHz FM; *Hrs Open:* 24; 1.4 kw; 482 ft.; N40 53 27 W76 59 54 *Rebroadcasts:* Rebroadcasts WUNS(FM) Lewisburg 100%
450 Route 204, Selinsgrove, PA 17870 US
(570) 374-8819; *Fax:* (570) 374-9856
www.983b.com
License: Mifflinburg, Union County, PA held by MMP License LLC.
Group Owner: MAX Media L.L.C.; (acq 10-17-03; grpsl).
Nat'l Network: Westwood One; Jones Radio Networks; *Nat'l Reps:* Dome
Arbitron Metro Market: Selinsgrove, PA; *Format:* Country *Special Programming:* Gospel 2 hrs wkly; *Hrs. of News Programming:* news progmg 2 hrs wkly; *No. News Employees:* 1; *Target Audience:* 25-54.
John Trinder, President
Tom Morgan, Operations Manager
Carol Pierson, General Manager
Greg Adair, Station Manager/Director of Sales
Shelly Marx, Programming Director
Chad Evans, Digital Media Manager
Trevor Polly, Digital MediaManager

Mifflintown

***WQJU**
10-15-1985; 107.1 MHz FM; *Hrs Open:* 24; 0.37 kw; 1302 ft.; N40 34 20 W77 30 51 *Rebroadcasts:* Rebroadcasts WTLR(FM) State College 100%
2020 Cato Street, State College, PA 16801 US
(814) 237-9857
info@wtlr.org
License: Mifflintown, Juniata County, PA held by Central Pennsylvania Christian Institute Inc.
Nat'l Network: Moody; USA; *Wire Services:* AP
Format: Christian; *Hrs. of News Programming:* news progmg 8 hrs wkly; *No. News Employees:* 1; *Target Audience:* 30-55; adults, family oriented
Mark Van Ouse, General Manager

Milford

WYNY(AM)
1450 kHz AM; 1 kw-U; N41 20 10 W74 47 45
PO Box 920, Port Jervis, NY 12771
(845) 856-6000; *Fax:* (845) 856-4757
www.wynyradio.com
news@neversinkmediagroup.com
License: Milford, Pike County, PA held by Digital Radio Broadcasting Inc.
Group Owner: Digital Radio Broadcasting Inc.
Population Served: 1,014; *Arbitron Metro Market:* Milford, PA
Bud Williamson, President

Mill Hall

WVRT
08-20-1979; 97.7 MHz FM; *Hrs Open:* 24; 6 kw; 295 ft.; N41 13 14 W77 16 39
Mailing Address: 309 West Southern Avenue, South Williamsport, PA 17701 US
Second Address: 1559 West 4th Street, Williamsport, PA 17701
(570) 327-1400; *Fax:* (570) 327-8156
www.v97fm.com
License: Mill Hall, Clinton County, PA held by Capstar TX LLC
Group Owner: iHeartMedia; (acq 3-12-01; $1.5 million).
Nat'l Reps: Christal
Arbitron Metro Market: Williamsport, PA; *Format:* Adult Contemp; *Target Audience:* 18-49.; *Adv. Rates:* 17; 17; 17; 12
Jeff Hurley, Regional Program Manager

Millersburg

WQLV
02-24-1992; 98.9 MHz FM; *Hrs Open:* 24; 0.78 kw; 896 ft.; N40 30 18 W77 7 3
234 Union Street, Millersburg, PA 17061 US
(717) 692-9578
www.wqlvfm.com
info@wqlvfm.com
License: Millersburg, Dauphin County, PA held by Richard L. Cooper D.B.A. Cooper Communications
Nat'l Network: ABC
Arbitron Metro Market: Harrisburg-Lebanon-Carlisle, PA; *Format:* Adult Contemp *Special Programming:* seasonal High school sports; *Hrs. of News Programming:* newscast every hour; *Target Audience:* 25 plus *Adv.Rates:* 41.70; 30.70; 35.55; 20.65
Ric Cooper, General Manager
JD Cooper, Operations Manager

Millersville

***WIXQ**
01-01-1978; 91.7 MHz FM; *Hrs Open:* 7 AM-3 AM; 0.096 kw; 21 ft.; N40 0 3.1 W76 21 43.4
Student Memorial Center, Millersville, PA 17551 US

RADIO - U.S.

(717) 872-3518; *Fax:* (717) 872-3383
www.wixq.com
License: Millersville, Lancaster County, PA held by Millersville University.
Format: Black, Variety/Diverse *Special Programming:* Jazz 2 hrs wkly; *Hrs. of News Programming:* News progmg one hr wkly; *Target Audience:* 18-24; college students
Aaron Rodden, Station Manager
Phil Casey, Programming Director
Amanda McFadden, Promotions Director
Curtis Silverwood, Music Director

Milroy

*WRYV

88.7 MHz FM; 2.2 kw; 869 ft.; N40 35 10 W77 41 40
US
(814) 867-3836
www.revfm.net
tim@revfm.net
License: Milroy, Mifflin County, PA held by Invisible Allies Ministries.
Arbitron Metro Market: Milroy, PA; *Format:* Christian
Michael Schomer, General Manager

Milton

WMLP

10-27-1955; 1380 kHz AM; *Hrs Open:* 24; 1 kw-D, ND1; 0.018 kw-N, ND1; N40 59 52 W76 52 17
PO Box 1070, Sunbury, PA 17801 US
(570) 286-5838; *Fax:* (570) 743-7837
www.1380wmlp.com
License: Milton, PA held by Sunbury Broadcasting Corp.
Group Owner: Sunbury Broadcasting Corp.; (acq 2006; $3 million with co-located FM).
Nat'l Network: CNN Radio; Premiere Radio Networks; Salem Radio Network; Fox Sports; *Nat'l Reps:* Dome; Roslin; *Wire Services:* Accu-Weather
Arbitron Metro Market: Sunbury, PA; *Format:* Talk; *Hrs. of News Programming:* news progmg 12 hrs wkly; *No. News Employees:* 4; *Target Audience:* 25-54.; *Adv. Rates:* 24.50; 24.50; 24.50; 14.25
Roger Haddon Jr., President/CEO
Kevin Herr, Operations Dir
Lynn Hall, Production Director
Jayme Dunkelberger, Director of Sales/Finance
Drew Kelly, Senior Programming Director
Avery Walls, Traffic Director
Sara Bartlett, NewsDirector
Harry Bingaman, Chief Engineer

WVLY-FM

10-01-1967; 100.9 MHz FM; *Hrs Open:* 24; 1.3 kw; 715 ft.; N40 57 12 W76 45 5
PO Box 1070, Sunbury, PA 17801 US
(570) 286-5838; *Fax:* (570) 743-7837
www.wkok.com
License: Milton, Northumberland County, PA held by Sunbury Broadcasting Corp.
Group Owner: Sunbury Broadcasting Corp.
Nat'l Network: Premiere Radio Networks; *Nat'l Reps:* Dome; Roslin; *Wire Services:* Accu-Weather
Arbitron Metro Market: Sunbury, PA; *Format:* Adult Contemp *Special Programming:* Smooth jazz 6 hrs wkly; *Hrs. of News Programming:* news progmg 5 hrs wkly; *No. News Employees:* 4; *Target Audience:* 25-54;adults; *Adv. Rates:* 25.50; 24.50; 24.50; 12.25
Roger Haddon Jr., President/CEO
Kevin Herr, Operations/Sports Director
Avery Walls, Traffic Director
Drew Kelly, Programming Director
Sara Bartlett, News Director
Harry Bingaman, Chief Engineer
Jayme Dunkelberger, Director ofSales & Finance
Tina Fry, Business Manager
Lynn Hall, Production Director

Monroeville

WPGR

09-27-1964; 1510 kHz AM; *Hrs Open:* 24
3660 State Route 30, Suite D, Latrobe, PA 15601 US
(724) 537-5172; *Fax:* (412) 391-3559
License: Monroeville, PA held by St. Joseph Missions
Group Owner: St. Joseph Missions; (acq 9-28-2001; $625,000)
Nat'l Reps: McGavren Guild
Arbitron Metro Market: Monroeville, PA; *Format:* Christian; *Target Audience:* 25-54; middle class & higher income households; *Adv. Rates:* 12; 12; 12; 12
Matthew Gorsich, General Manager
Fr. Boniface Hicks, Programming Director

Montrose

WPEL

06-05-1961; 96.5 MHz FM; *Hrs Open:* 24; 57 kW; 459 ft.; N41 51 16 W75 51 50
251 High St, Montrose, PA 18801 USA
(570) 278-2811
wpel.org
mail@wpel.org
License: Montrose, Susquehanna County, PA held by Montrose Broadcasting Corp.
Group Owner: Montrose Broadcasting Corp.
Nat'l Network: Moody; AP Network News; Salem Radio Network; *Regional Network:* Radio Pa.; *Wire Services:* AP
Arbitron Metro Market: Scranton, PA; Binghamton-Elmira, NY; *Format:* Religious; *Hrs. of News Programming:* News progmg 12 hrs wkly; *Target Audience:* General.
Larry Souder, President

Moon Township

WOGI

04-15-1959; 104.3 MHz FM; *Hrs Open:* 24; 50 kw; 330 ft; N40 37 48 W80 36 10
2 Robinson Plaza, Suite 410, Pittsburgh, PA 15205 US
(412) 275-3393; *Fax:* (412) 275-3165
www.froggyland.com
License: Moon Township, Columbiana County, PA held by FM Radio Licenses, LLC.
Group Owner: Keymarket Communications LLC
Population Served: 500,000; *Arbitron Metro Market:* Pittsburgh, PA; *Format:* Country; *Target Audience:* 25-54.
Dave Anthony, Programming Director
Donald Fast, Promotions Diretor
Michael Vennare, Marketing Manager

Mount Carmel

WVRZ

03-01-1993; 99.7 MHz FM; *Hrs Open:* 24; 0.79 kw; 646 ft.; N40 49 9 W76 27 45
1559 W. 4th St., Williamsport, PA 17701 US
(570) 327-1400; *Fax:* (570) 327-8156
www.v97fm.com
License: Mount Carmel, Northumberland County, PA held by Clear Channel Broadcasting Licenses Inc.
Group Owner: iHeartMedia; (acq 5-26-2005; $460,000)
Format: Contemporary Hits/Top 40; *Target Audience:* 25-65.
Richard J. Bressler, President

Mount Cobb

*WFTE

90.3 MHz FM; 3 kw; 38 ft.; N41 23 9 W75 24 10
US
(570) 504-5803
www.wfte.org
License: Mount Cobb, Lackawanna County, PA held by Community Radio Collective, Inc.
Arbitron Metro Market: Mount Cobb, PA; *Format:* Talk
Jacob Rosen, Chairman
Don Noll, President
Tom Borthwick, Operations Dir

Mount Pleasant

WKVE

04-21-1978; 103.1 MHz FM; *Hrs Open:* 24; 4.4 kw; 801 ft.; N39 54 49.6 W79 37 57.4
PO Box 990, Greensburg, PA 15601 US
(412) 823-7000; *Fax:* (724) 627-4021
www.kve.fm
radiowanb@gmail.com
License: Mount Pleasant, Westmoreland County, PA held by Broadcast Communications Inc.
Group Owner: Broadcast Communications Inc.; (acq 4-1-2002; with co-located AM)
Nat'l Reps: Dome
Arbitron Metro Market: Mount Pleasant, PA; *Format:* Country; *Target Audience:* 20 plus.; *Adv. Rates:* 17; 17; 17; 17.
Judy Rastoka, General Manager
Doug Wilson, Programming Director
Marcia Mackey, News Director
Rick Williams, Chief Engineer

Mountain Top

WBHT

09-01-1992; 97.1 MHz FM; *Hrs Open:* 24; 0.5 kw; 1102 ft.; N41 10 57 W75 52 19
600 Baltimore Dr., Wilkes-Barre, PA 18702 US
(570) 824-9000; *Fax:* (570) 820-0520
www.97bht.com
License: Mountain Top, PA held by Radio License Holding CBC, LLC
Group Owner: Cumulus Media Inc.; (acq 10-23-98; grpsl).
Arbitron Metro Market: Wilkes Barre, PA; *Format:* Contemporary Hits/Top 40; *Target Audience:* 18-34.; *Adv. Rates:* 40; 30; 40; 25
Shannon Spak, General Sales Mgr
Brent Eckart, Programming Director
Erin Evans, Promotions Director
Gerald Gertz, Market Manager

Muncy

WBZD

08-11-1983; 93.3 MHz FM; *Hrs Open:* 24; 0.42 kw; 1224 ft.; N41 12 42 W76 57 16
1685 Four Mile Dr, Williamsport, PA 17701 US
(570) 323-8200; *Fax:* (570) 323-5075
www.wbzd.com
dfarr@backyardbroadcasting.com
License: Muncy, Lycoming County, PA held by Backyard Broadcasting PA, LLC
Group Owner: Backyard Broadcasting LLC; (acq 12-1-02; grpsl).
Arbitron Metro Market: Williamsport, PA; *Format:* Oldies; *Hrs. of News Programming:* news progmg 3 hrs wkly; *No. News Employees:* 1; *Target Audience:* 18-54
Dan Farr, President & CEO
Georgia Stover, Business Manager
Kelly Bailey, Production Director
Ted Minier, Programming Director
John Finn, News Director

Murrysville

*WRWJ

07-01-1994; 88.1 MHz FM; *Hrs Open:* 19; 0.001 kw horiz, 1 kw vert; 302 ft.; N40 31 12 W79 39 29 *Rebroadcasts:* Rebroadcasts WAIJ(FM) Grantsville, MD 100%
Mailing Address: 34 Springs Road, Grantsville, MD 21536 US
Second Address: PO Box 540, Grantsville, MD 21536
(301) 895-3292; *Fax:* (301) 895-3293
www.hesalive.net
info@hesalive.net
License: Murrysville, Westmoreland County, PA held by He's Alive Inc.
Nat'l Network: USA
Arbitron Metro Market: Pittsburgh, PA; *Format:* Religious; *Target Audience:* 18-35.
Melissa Flores, General Manager

Nanticoke

WZMF(AM)

02-01-1947; 730 kHz AM; 1 kw-D, 38 w-N; N41 13 10 W75 59 28
Box 701, Tunkhannock, PA 18657
(570) 836-4200; *Fax:* (570) 836-7035
www.gem104.com
License: Nanticoke, Luzerne County, PA held by Geos Communications
Group Owner: Geos Communications; (acq 7-14-2008; grpsl)
Population Served: 16,632; *Arbitron Metro Market:* Wilkes Barre, PA; *Format:* Light Rock; *Target Audience:* 35 plus.
Ira Rosenblatt, Station Manager

*WSFX

10-25-1987; 89.1 MHz FM; 0.1 kw; -381 ft.; N41 11 42 W75 59 28
1333 S Prospect St., Nanticoke, PA 18634 US
(570) 740-0633
http://depts.luzerne.edu/wsfx/
wsfx@luzerne.edu
License: Nanticoke, Luzerne County, PA held by Luzerne County Community College.
Format: Variety/Diverse; *Target Audience:* 16-25; college age alternative mus audience
Thomas P. Leary, President
Ron Reino, General Manager

Nanty Glo

*WPAI

01-01-2006; 90.7 MHz FM; 2.1 kw vert; 482 ft.; N40 30 20 W78 48 12
PO Box 2118, Omaha, NE 68103 US
(888) 937-2471
www.air1.com
License: Nanty Glo, Cambria County, PA held by Educational Media Foundation.
Group Owner: EMF Broadcasting; (acq 3-23-2007; grpsl)
Nat'l Network: Air 1

Arbitron Metro Market: Nanty Glo, PA; *Format:* Alternative, Christian
Darrell Chambliss, Chairman
Mike Novak, President/CEO
Alan Mason, COO
Eric Moser, CFO
D. Kevin Blair, Secretary/General Counsel
David Pierce, Chief Creative Officer

New Berlin

***WBGM**
09-01-1996; 88.1 MHz FM; 0.55 kW; 417 ft.; N40 53 27 W76 59 54 *Rebroadcasts:* Rebroadcasts WPGM-FM Danville 100%
28 E Market St, Danville, PA 17821 USA
(570) 275-1570; *Fax:* (570) 275-4071
wpgmfm.org
License: New Berlin, Union County, PA held by Montrose Broadcasting Corp.
Group Owner: Montrose Broadcasting Corp.
Arbitron Metro Market: Danville, PA; *Format:* Christian

New Castle

WJST
10-23-1938; 1280 kHz AM; 4.9 kw-D, DAN; 1 kw-N, DAN; N40 57 14 W80 19 5
219 Savannah Gardner Rd., New Castle, PA 16101 US
(724) 654-5502; *Fax:* (724) 856-4975
www.foreverradio.com
License: New Castle, Lawrence County, PA held by FM Radio Licenses LLC
Group Owner: Forever Broadcasting; (acq 6-30-2004; grpsl).
Nat'l Network: ABC; *Nat'l Reps:* Dome; Rgnl Reps
Arbitron Metro Market: New Castle, PA; *Format:* Sports *Special Programming:* Black one hr, class one hr wkly; *Target Audience:* 30 plus.
Jim Shields, General Manager
Jon Jacubec, Sales Manager
Mike Heim, Chief Engineer
Jill Hamilton, Business Manager
Karen Nies, Traffic Director

***WVMN**
11-22-1995; 90.1 MHz FM; *Hrs Open:* 24; 2 kW; 236 ft.; N41 0 47 W80 17 36 *Rebroadcasts:* Rebroadcasts WCRF(FM) Cleveland, OH 100%
9756 Barr Rd, Cleveland, OH 44141 USA
(440) 526-1111; *Fax:* (440) 526-1319
www.moodyradio.org/stations/cleveland
License: New Castle, Lawrence County, PA held by The Moody Bible Institute of Chicago
Group Owner: The Moody Bible Institute of Chicago
Wire Services: AP
Arbitron Metro Market: New Castle, PA; *Format:* Christian; *Target Audience:* 25-55.

WKST
01-01-1938; 1200 kHz AM; 5 kw-D, DAN; 1 kw-N, DAN; N40 56 22 W80 23 38
219 Savannah Gardner Rd., New Castle, PA 16101 US
(724) 654-5502; *Fax:* (724) 856-4975
www.wkst.com
License: New Castle, Lawrence County, PA held by FM Radio Licenses LLC
Group Owner: Forever Broadcasting
Arbitron Metro Market: New Castle, PA; *Format:* News, News/Talk, 86
Jim Shields, General Manager
Jon Jacubec, Sales Manager
Ken Hlebovy, Programming Director
Mike Heim, Chief Engineer
Jill Hamilton, Business Manager
Karen Nies, Traffic Director

New Kensington

WGBN
10-01-1940; 1150 kHz AM; *Hrs Open:* 24; 1 kw-D, 70 w-N, DA-1; N40 34 24 W79 46 58
560 7th St., New Kensington, PA 15206
(724) 337-3588; *Fax:* (724) 337-1318
License: New Kensington, Westmoreland County, PA held by Pentecostal Temple Development Corp.
Nat'l Network: USA; *Nat'l Reps:* Dome
Population Served: 1,209,000; *Arbitron Metro Market:* Pittsburgh, PA *Special Programming:* Pol 3 hrs, It 2 hrs, Irish 2 hrs, relg 2 hrs wkly; *Hrs. of News Programming:* news progmg 19 hrs wkly *No. News Employees:* 1; *Target Audience:* 30 plus; older, upscale

Lauren Mann, General Manager
Calvin Penny, Programming Director
Del King, Chief Engineer

WBZZ
01-19-2011; 100.7 MHz FM; *Hrs Open:* 24; 14.5 kW; 758 ft.; N40 28 20 W79 59 41
651 Holiday Dr., Foster Plaza 5, Pittsburgh, PA 15220 USA
(412) 920-9400
www.starpittsburgh.com
License: New Kensington, Westmoreland County, PA held by CBS Radio Stations Inc.
Group Owner: CBS Radio; (acq 6-8-98; grpsl).
Population Served: 307,484; *Arbitron Metro Market:* Pittsburgh, PA; *Format:* Adult Contemp; *Target Audience:* 18-49
Christine Fallon, General Sales Mgr
Mark Anderson, Programming Director
John D'Amico, Promotions Director

New Wilmington

***WWNW**
01-31-1968; 88.9 MHz FM; *Hrs Open:* 24; 4 kw vert; Ant 128 ft; N41 06 41 W80 20 21
Box 89, Westminster College, New Wilmington, PA 16172
(724) 946-7242; *Fax:* (724) 946-7070
www.westminster.edu
barnerdl@westminster.edu
License: New Wilmington, Lawrence County, PA held by Westminster College Board of Trustees.
Nat'l Network: NBC News Radio; *Wire Services:* AP
Population Served: 60,000 *Special Programming:* Relg 3 hrs wkly; *Hrs. of News Programming:* News progmg 3 hrs wkly; *Target Audience:* 18-49; college students & staff
Richard Dorman, President
David L. Barner, General Manager
Andrew Borts, Chief Engineer

Norristown

WNAP
08-06-1946; 1110 kHz AM
2311 Old Arch Road, Norristown, PA 19401 US
(610) 272-7600; *Fax:* (610) 272-5793
www.mygospelhighway11.com
gospel@wnap1110am.com
License: Norristown, PA held by WNAP, Inc.
Group Owner: GHB Radio Group; (acq 12-15-87; $725,000;
Arbitron Metro Market: Philadelphia, PA; *Format:* Black, Gospel; *Target Audience:* General.
Fred Blain, General Manager
Orey Ferrell, General Sales Mgr
Dave McCrork, Chief Engineer
Robyn McCollum, Music Direcor
David C. McCrork, Chief Operator

North East

WMCE
11-24-1966; 1530 kHz AM; *Hrs Open:* Sunrise-set; 0.25 kw-C, NDD; 1 kw-D, NDD; N42 12 5 W79 51 43
501 East 38th Street, Erie, PA 16546 US
(814) 824-2000
www.wmce.fm
License: North East, PA held by Mercyhurst College
Arbitron Metro Market: North East, PA; *Format:* Oldies; *Target Audience:* 35-64; men & women

WRKT
03-29-1970; 100.9 MHz FM; *Hrs Open:* 24; 4.2 kw; 797 ft.; N42 11 51 W79 45 10
1 Boston Store Pl., Erie, PA 16501 US
(814) 461-1000; *Fax:* (814) 461-1500
rocket101@rocket101.com
License: North East, Erie County, PA held by Connoisseur Media Licenses LLC
Group Owner: Connoisseur Media LLC; (acq 3-30-2006; grpsl).
Arbitron Metro Market: Erie, PA; *Format:* Classic Rock *Special Programming:* Loc bands one hr wkly; *Hrs. of News Programming:* news progmg one hr wkly; *No. News Employees:* 1; *Target Audience:* 25-54.
Richard Rambaldo, General Manager
Michael Malpiedi, General Sales Mgr

Northern Cambria

***WPCL**
09-30-1991; 97.3 MHz FM; *Hrs Open:* 19; 1.75 kw horiz, 1.7 kw vert; 610 ft.; N40 30 27 W78 48 14 *Rebroadcasts:* Rebroadcasts WAIJ (FM) Grantsville, MD 100%
P.O. Box 540, Grantsville, MD 21536 US
(301) 895-3292; *Fax:* (301) 895-3293
www.hesalive.com
hesalive@hesalive.net
License: Northern Cambria, Cambria County, PA held by Central Penn. Christian Institute, Inc.
Group Owner: He's Alive Inc.; acq 3-18-97; $105,000)
Nat'l Network: USA; *Nat'l Reps:* Commercial Media Sales
Format: Adult Contemp, Christian, 44, Religious; *Target Audience:* 18-35.
Melissa Flores, General Manager

Northumberland

WEGH
08-22-1994; 107.3 MHz FM; *Hrs Open:* 24; 0.9 kw; 843 ft.; N40 47 10 W76 41 49
Post Office Box 1070, Sunbury, PA 17801 US
(570) 286-5838; *Fax:* (570) 743-7837
www.wvly.com
License: Northumberland, Northumberland County, PA held by Sunbury Broadcasting Corp.
Group Owner: Sunbury Broadcasting Corp.
Nat'l Reps: Roslin *Regional Reps:* Dome.; *Wire Services:* Accu-Weather
Arbitron Metro Market: Northumberland, PA; *Format:* Contemporary Hits/Top 40, Adult Contemp; *Hrs. of News Programming:* news progmg one hr wkly; *No. News Employees:* 4; *Target Audience:* 25-54.
Roger Haddon Jr., CEO
Roger S. Haddon, Jr., President
Kevin Herr, Operations/Sports Director
Drew Kelly, Programming Director
Lynn Hall, Production Director
Avery Watts, Traffic Director
Tina Fry, Business Manager
HarryBingaman, Chief Engineer
Jayme Dunkelberger, Director of Sales/Finance

Oil City

WKQW
12-01-1986; 1120 kHz AM; 1 kw-D, NDD; N41 23 45 W79 39 53
Mailing Address: 44143 109th Street, Urbandale, IA 50322 US
Second Address: www.venangocountydailynews.com
(515) 331-9200
www.983thetorch.com
License: Oil City, PA held by Clarion County Broadcasting Corp.
Group Owner: Clarion County Broadcasting Corp.; (acq 4-8-2005; $540,000 with co-located FM)
Nat'l Network: CBS Radio; *Nat'l Reps:* Dome
Format: Oldies; *Hrs. of News Programming:* news progmg 4 hrs wkly; *No. News Employees:* 1; *Target Audience:* 25-54.
Sean Elliot, Operations Manager
Bob Jenkins, Sales Manager
Robert Rees, Programming Director
Dianna Kelly, News Director

WKQW-FM
09-01-1992; 96.3 MHz FM; *Hrs Open:* 24; 6 kw; 328 ft.; N41 23 45 W79 39 53
806-C Grandview Road, Oil City, PA 16301 US
(814) 676-8254; *Fax:* (814) 677-4272
www.venangocountydailynews.com
kqwtraffic@usachoice.net
License: Oil City, Venango County, PA held by Clarion County Broadcasting Corp.
Group Owner: Clarion County Broadcasting Corp.
Nat'l Network: CBS Radio *Regional Reps:* Dome & Assoc.
Format: Adult Contemp; *Hrs. of News Programming:* news progmg 4 hrs wkly; *No. News Employees:* 1
William Hearst, President
Steve Truitt, Operations Dir
Sammy Gordon, General Sales Mgr
Mark Heim, Programming Director
Tim Shaw, Program Manager
Joe Lodanowsky, Sports Director

WGYI
05-01-1957; 98.5 MHz FM; 20 kw; 299 ft.; N41 25 4 W79 42 53
Mailing Address: 900 Water St., Downtown Mall, Meadville, PA 16335 US
Second Address: 1243 Liberty St., Suite 501, Franklin, PA 16323
(814) 724-1111; *Fax:* (814) 333-9628
www.froggyfun.com
License: Oil City, Venango County, PA held by FM Radio Licenses LLC
Group Owner: Forever Broadcasting
Arbitron Metro Market: Meadville-Franklin, PA; *Format:* Country
Jim Shields, General Manager
Helen Powers, Sales Manager

RADIO - U.S.

Wesley Miller, Programming Director
Mark Himmler, Chief Engineer
Jill Hamilton, Business Manager

Oliver

WOGG
06-11-1993; 94.9 MHz FM; *Hrs Open:* 24; 1.65 kw; 1234 ft.; N39 52 11 W79 38 22
123 Blaine Rd., Brownsville, PA 15417 US
(866) 878-0949; *Fax:* (724) 938-7824
www.froggyland.com
License: Oliver, Fayette County, PA held by FM Radio Licenses, LLC.
Group Owner: Keymarket Communications LLC; (acq 8-31-99; $2.875 million with WASP(AM) Brownsville).
Arbitron Metro Market: Pittsburgh, PA; *Format:* Country; *No. News Employees:* 1; *Target Audience:* 25-54.
David Pavlic, General Sales Mgr
Liz Kieta, Promotions Manager

Olyphant

WQOR
07-20-1987; 750 kHz AM; *Hrs Open:* Sunrise-sunset; 1.6 kw-D, NDD; N41 28 34 W75 29 41
321 Spruce Street; 3rdfl, Scranton, PA 18503 US
(802) 626-9800; *Fax:* (802) 626-8500
www.jmj750.com
wjpk@gmail.com
License: Olyphant, PA held by JMJ Radio, Inc.
Group Owner: Holy Family Communications; acq 3-24-2003; $170,000).
Arbitron Metro Market: Palm Springs CA; *Format:* Country
Bruce James, General Manager

WBHD
01-01-1991; 95.7 MHz FM; *Hrs Open:* 24; 0.6 kw; 1010 ft.; N41 26 9 W75 43 45 *Rebroadcasts:* Simulcast with WBHT-FM Mountain Top
600 Baltimore Dr., Wilkes-Barre, PA 18702 US
(570) 824-9000; *Fax:* (570) 820-0520
www.97bht.com
License: Olyphant, PA held by Radio License Holding CBC, LLC
Group Owner: Cumulus Media Inc.; (acq 1999; $950,000).
Arbitron Metro Market: Wilkes Barre, PA; *Format:* Contemporary Hits/Top 40
Shannon Spak, General Sales Mgr
Brent Eckart, Programming Director
Erin Evans, Promotions Manager
Gerald Getz, Market Manager

Palmyra

WTPA
11-01-1978; 92.1 MHz FM; 1.5 kw; 601 ft.; N40 23 28 W76 43 31
27 S. 34th St., Camp Hill, PA 17011 US
(717) 901-4908; *Fax:* (717) 695-2408
www.935WTPA.com; www.wtparock.com
License: Palmyra, Cumberland County, PA held by Patrick H. Sickafus
Arbitron Metro Market: Harrisburg, VA; *Format:* Rock/AOR; *Target Audience:* 18-49.
Pat Garrett, President
Tim Michaels, VP/General Manager
Jack Weintein, General Sales Mgr

Patton

WBXQ
01-01-1991; 94.3 MHz FM; 2.1 kw; 548 ft.; N40 39 17 W78 40 34
2513 6th Avenue, Altoona, PA 16602 US
(814) 943-6112; *Fax:* (814) 944-9782
License: Patton, Cambria County, PA held by Sherlock Broadcasting Inc.
Arbitron Metro Market: Altoona, PA; *Format:* Country; *Target Audience:* 35-65.
Ken Maguda, Operations Dir
David Barger, General Manager
Diane Boslet, Sales Manager
Doug Herendeen, Public Service Director

Pen Argyl

***WWPJ**
01-01-2001; 89.5 MHz FM; *Hrs Open:* 24; 0.003 kw horiz, 0.1 kw vert; 1093 ft.; N40 53 1 W75 15 43 *Rebroadcasts:* Rebroadcasts WWFM(FM) Trenton, NJ 100%
1200 Old Trenton Rd, West Windsor, NJ 08550 US
(609) 587-8989; *Fax:* (609) 570-3863
www.wwfm.org
info@wwfm.org
License: Pen Argyl, Northampton County, PA held by Mercer County Community College.
Arbitron Metro Market: Trenton, NJ; *Format:* Classical
Peter Fretwell, General Manager
Alice Weiss, Programming Director
Diane Guvenis, Development Producer
David Osenberg, Music Director
Marcia Galambos, Membership Coordinator
Rachel Katz, Production Manager/Public Affairs Host
Winifred Howard, JazzOn2 Program Manager

Philadelphia

KYW
01-01-1921; 1060 kHz AM; *Hrs Open:* 24; 50 kW; N40 6 12 W75 14 56
1555 Hamilton St., 6th Fl., Philadelphia, PA 19130 USA
(215) 238-1060; *Fax:* (215) 238-4657
www.kyw1060.com
License: Philadelphia, Philadelphia County, PA held by CBS Radio East Inc.
Group Owner: CBS Radio
Nat'l Network: ABC; CBS; CNN Radio; *Nat'l Reps:* CBS Radio; *Wire Services:* AP
Arbitron Metro Market: Philadelphia, PA *TV Affiliate:* KYW-TV affil.; *Format:* News; *Hrs. of News Programming:* news progmg 168 hrs wkly; *No. News Employees:* 34; *Target Audience:* 25-54; adults

WBEB
05-13-1963; 101.1 MHz FM; *Hrs Open:* 24; 14 kw; 942 ft.; N40 2 19 W75 14 14
136 W. 8h Avenue, Eugene, OR 97401 US
(541) 463-6000; *Fax:* (541) 463-6046
www.klcc.org
klcc@klcc.org
License: Philadelphia, Philadelphia County, PA held by Jenny Lee Broadcasting, LLC
Nat'l Reps: McGavren Guild
Arbitron Metro Market: Odessa-Midland TX
Steve Barton, General Manager
Tripp Sommer, News Director
Cheryl Crumbley, Development Director
Chris Heck, Chief Engineer
John Stark, General Manager
Gayle Chisholm, Marketing Director

WDAS-FM
01-01-1959; 105.3 MHz FM; 16.5 kw; 873 ft.; N40 2 30 W75 14 24
111 Presidential Blvd., Suite 100, Bala Cynwyd, PA 19004 US
(610) 784-3333; *Fax:* (610) 784-2098
www.wdasfm.com
License: Philadelphia, Philadelphia County, PA held by AMFM Radio Licenses, LLC
Group Owner: iHeartMedia
Arbitron Metro Market: Philadelphia, PA; *Format:* Adult Contemp, Urban Contemporary; *Target Audience:* 25-54.
Richard Lewis, Market President
Wes Franks, Senior Vice President of Sales
Derrick Corbett, Programming Director

WURD
07-23-1958; 900 kHz AM
1341 N. Delaware Avenue, Suite 300, Philadelphia, PA 19125 US
(215) 425-7875; *Fax:* (215) 634-6003
www,900amwurd.com/
License: Philadelphia, PA held by WURD Radio, LLC
Nat'l Network: CNN Radio; *Nat'l Reps:* McGavren Guild
Arbitron Metro Market: Philadelphia, PA; *Format:* Talk *Special Programming:* Gospel 9 hrs, lt 3 hrs wkly; *Adv. Rates:* 100; 100; 100; 50
Sara Lomax Reese, President/General Manager
Monica Lewis, Sales/Business Development Director
Stephanie Renee, Programming Director
Kia Long, News Director
Lin Ron Anderson-Bell, Director of Marketing

WFIL
01-01-1922; 560 kHz AM; *Hrs Open:* 24; 5 kw-U, DA-2; N40 05 42 W75 16 38
117 Ridge Pike, Lafayette Hill, PA 19444
(610) 941-9560 x10
www.wfil.com
License: Philadelphia, Philadelphia County, PA held by Pennsylvania Media Associates Inc.
Group Owner: Salem Communications Corp.; (acq 11-1-93; $4 million)
Nat'l Network: Salem Radio Network; *Nat'l Reps:* Salem
Population Served: 11,792,380; *Arbitron Metro Market:* Philadelphia; *Hrs. of News Programming:* News progmg 2 hrs wkly; *Target Audience:* 35-64; parents & grandparents
Russ Whitnah, Operations Dir
Carol Healey, General Sales Mgr
Ann Krill, Promotions Manager
Rene Tetro, Chief Engineer
Mark Daniels, Programming
David Handler, New Business Sales Manager
Kevin Manna, Operations Director

WHAT
01-01-1925; 1340 kHz AM; 1 kw-U, ND1; N40 0 6 W75 12 35
109 N. Eagle Road, Suite 6, Haverton, PA 19083 US
(267) 285-5161; *Fax:* (267) 285-5185
www.martiniloungeradio.com
License: Philadelphia, PA held by Azte Capital Partners Inc.
Arbitron Metro Market: Philadelphia; *Format:* Classic Rock
Tom Kelly, President
David Direnzo, General Sales Mgr

***WHYY-FM**
01-01-1954; 90.9 MHz FM; *Hrs Open:* 24; 13.5 kw; 920 ft; N40 02 30 W75 14 24
150 N. 6th St., Independence Mall West, Philadelphia, PA 19083
(215) 351-1200; *Fax:* (215) 351-0398
www.whyy.org
talkback@whyy.org
License: Philadelphia, Philadelphia County, PA held by WHYY Inc.
Nat'l Network: NPR; PRI
Population Served: 3,987,600; *Arbitron Metro Market:* Philadelphia *Special Programming:* Opera 4 hrs, folk 4 hrs, jazz 4 hrs wkly; *Hrs. of News Programming:* news progmg 35 hrs wkly; *No. News Employees:* 7 *TargetAudience:* 35-49.
Gerard Sweeney, Chairman
William Marrazzo, President/CEO
Kyra McGrath, EVP/CCO
Christine Dempsey, Station Manager
Roseann Oleyn, General Sales Mgr
Chris Satullo, VP/News
William Weber, VP/Chief Technical Officer
Jeffrey Bundy,Member Relations Director

WIOQ
01-01-1941; 102.1 MHz FM; *Hrs Open:* 24; 27 kw; 669 ft.; N40 2 37 W75 14 32
111 Presidential Blvd., Suite 100, Bala Cynwyd, PA 19004 US
(610) 784-3333; *Fax:* (610) 784-2075
www.q102.com
License: Philadelphia, Philadelphia County, PA held by AMFM Radio Licenses LLC.
Group Owner: iHeartMedia; (acq 8-30-00; grpsl).
Arbitron Metro Market: Philadelphia; *Format:* Contemporary Hits/Top 40 *Special Programming:* Pub affrs; *Target Audience:* 18-34; females & teens
Richard Lewis, Market President
Wes Franks, Senior Vice President of Sales

WIP
09-02-2011; 94.1 MHz FM; 9.6 kW; 1030 ft.; N40 2 29.6 W75 14 11.5
400 Market St., 9th Fl., Philadelphia, PA 19106 USA
(215) 625-9460
www.cbsphillysports.com
License: Philadelphia, Philadelphia County, PA held by CBS Radio East Inc.
Group Owner: CBS Radio; (acq 8-12-93;
Nat'l Network: Westwood One; *Nat'l Reps:* CBS Radio
Arbitron Metro Market: Philadelphia; *Format:* Sports
Suby Ross, General Sales Mgr
Spike Eskin, Programming Director

WISX
11-11-1959; 106.1 MHz FM; 22.5 kw; 741 ft.; N40 4 58 W75 10 54
111 Presidential Blvd., Suite 100, Bala Cynwyd, PA 19004 US
(610) 784-3333; *Fax:* (610) 784-2083
www.mixphiladelphia.com
License: Philadelphia, Philadelphia County, PA held by AMFM Radio Licenses LLC.
Group Owner: iHeartMedia; (acq 8-30-2000; grpsl).
Nat'l Reps: Christal
Arbitron Metro Market: Philadelphia; *Format:* Adult Contemp; *Target Audience:* 25-54.
Richard Lewis, Market President
Wes Franks, Senior Vice President of Sales

***WKDU**
01-01-1970; 91.7 MHz FM; *Hrs Open:* 24; 0.8 kw; 154 ft.; N39 57 36 W75 11 27

3210 Chestnut Streets, Philadelphia, PA 19104 US
(215) 895-2082
www.wkdu.org
License: Philadelphia, Philadelphia County, PA held by Drexel University.
Arbitron Metro Market: Philadelphia; *Format:* Alternative *Special Programming:* International 12 hrs, rhythm & blues 3 hrs, gospel; *Target Audience:* General.
Ryan McIntyre, Operations Dir
Evan Caposerri, General Manager
Casey Ross, Programming Director
Jim Cavanaugh, Chief Engineer

WMGK
01-01-1942; 102.9 MHz FM; *Hrs Open:* 24; 8.9 kw; Ant 1,148 ft; N40 02 21 W75 14 13
One Bala Plaza, Suite 339, Bala Cynwyd, PA 69004
(610) 667-8500; *Fax:* (610) 664-9610
www.wmgk.com
ckirchner@wmgk.com
License: Philadelphia, Philadelphia County, PA held by Greater Philadelphia Radio Inc.
Group Owner: Greater Media Inc
Population Served: 1,800,000; *Arbitron Metro Market:* Philadelphia
Peter Smyth, President
John Fullam, General Manager
Chris Kirchner, General Sales Mgr
Charley Lake, Programming Director
Dan Fein, Promotions Manager
Larry Paulausky, Engineering Dir

WMMR
04-20-1942; 93.3 MHz FM; *Hrs Open:* 24; 16.5 kw; 866 ft.; N39 57 9 W75 10 5
1 Bala Plaza, Suite 424, Bala Cynwyd, PA 19004 US
(610) 771-0933; *Fax:* (610) 771-9667
www.wmmr.com
License: Philadelphia, Philadelphia County, PA held by Boston Radio Inc.
Group Owner: Beasley Broadcast Group; (acq 7-23-97; grpsl)
Nat'l Network: Westwood One; *Nat'l Reps:* McGavren Guild
Arbitron Metro Market: Philadelphia, PA; *Format:* Rock/AOR; *Hrs. of News Programming:* news progmg 5 hrs wkly; *No. News Employees:* 1; *Target Audience:* 25-54; suburban rockers
Bill Weston, Programming Director
Sean Tyszler, Music Director
Eric Simon, Promotions Director

WNWR
07-11-1947; 1540 kHz AM
2131 Crimmins Lane, Falls Church, VA 22043 US
(610) 664-6780; *Fax:* (610) 664-8529
License: Philadelphia, PA held by Global Radio L.L.C.
Nat'l Reps: Roslin
Arbitron Metro Market: Philadelphia *TV Affiliate:* Var/div, ethnic multicultural; *No. News Employees:* 25-54.

WOGL
07-03-2003; 98.1 MHz FM; 9.6 kW; 1030 ft.; N40 2 29.6 W75 14 11.4
400 Market St., 10th Fl., Philadelphia, PA 19106 USA
(215) 238-2000
www.wogl.com
License: Philadelphia, Philadelphia County, PA held by CBS Radio East Inc.
Group Owner: CBS Radio
Arbitron Metro Market: Philadelphia; *Format:* Oldies *Special Programming:* news progmg 1.25 hrs wkly; *Hrs. of News Programming:* 1; *No. News Employees:* 25-54
Ashley McLaughlin, General Sales Mgr
Anne Gress, Programming Director
Samantha Simon, Promotions Director
Tommy McCarthy, Music Director
Cindy Webster, Marketing Director

***WPEB**
05-15-1981; 88.1 MHz FM; 0.001 kw vert; 69 ft.; N39 56 57 W75 13 9
541B South 52nd St., Philadelphia, PA 19143 US
(215) 472-0881
License: Philadelphia, Philadelphia County, PA held by Scribe Video Center Inc.
Arbitron Metro Market: Philadelphia; *Format:* Variety/Diverse; *Target Audience:* General.
Charles Clarke, Operations Dir
Renee McBride Williams, Station Manager

WKDN
04-01-1929; 950 kHz AM; *Hrs Open:* 24
2 Kennedy Blvd, P.O. Box 1059, East Brunswick, NJ 08816 US
(610) 667-8500; *Fax:* (610) 771-9692
sr950.com
bdeblois@950espn.com
License: Philadelphia, PA held by Family Stations Inc.
Group Owner: Family Stations Inc.; (acq 1-6-75)
Nat'l Network: ESPN Radio
Arbitron Metro Market: Philadelphia; *Format:* Sports
John Fullam, General Manager
Bob DeBlois, Station Manager
Paul Blake, General Sales Mgr
Matt Nahigian, Programming Director
Mike McMonagle, Promotions Manager
Ralph Nieves, General Sales Manager

WPHT
09-17-1996; 1210 kHz AM; 50 kW; N39 58 46 W74 59 13
400 Market St., 10th Fl., Philadelphia, PA 19106 USA
(215) 351-3700
philadelphia.cbslocal.com/station/wpht
License: Philadelphia, Philadelphia County, PA held by CBS Radio East Inc.
Group Owner: CBS Radio; (acq 8-58).
Nat'l Network: CBS; Westwood One; *Nat'l Reps:* CBS Radio
Arbitron Metro Market: Philadelphia; *Format:* Talk; *Hrs. of News Programming:* 2; *Target Audience:* 25-64; adults
Jared Hart, Programming Director

***WRTI**
07-09-1953; 90.1 MHz FM; *Hrs Open:* 24; 7.7 kw; 1217 ft.; N40 2 29.6 W75 14 11.5
1509 Cecil B. Moore Avenue, 3rd Floor, Philadelphia, PA 19122 US
(215) 204-8405; *Fax:* (215) 204-7027
www.wrti.org
comments@wrti.org
License: Philadelphia, Philadelphia County, PA held by Temple University of The Commonwealth System of Higher Education.
Nat'l Network: NPR; PRI; *Wire Services:* AP
Arbitron Metro Market: Philadelphia; *Format:* Jazz; *Hrs. of News Programming:* news progmg 15 hrs wkly; *No. News Employees:* 1; *Target Audience:* 30-65.
David Conant, CEO
Tobias Poole, Operations Dir
David Conant, General Manager
William Johnson, Station Manager
Patricia Prevost, General Sales Mgr
Jack Moore, Programming Director
Porsche Blakey, Promotions Manager
WindsorJohnston, News Director
Jeffrey DePolo, Engineering Dir
Vic Scarpato, CFO
Rick Torpey, National Sales Manager

WTEL
06-15-1970; 610 kHz AM; *Hrs Open:* 17; 5 kw-U; N39 51 55 W75 6 34
555 City Ave., Suite 330, Bala Cynwyd, PA 19004 US
(610) 822-1321
www.610amsports.com
info@610amsports.com
License: Philadelphia, PA held by WXTU License Limited Partnership
Group Owner: Beasley Broadcast Group Inc.; (acq 6-12-97; $1.2 million with WUKS(FM) Saint Pauls).
Regional Network: Southern Farm
Arbitron Metro Market: Philadelphia, PA; *Format:* Sports, Talk *Special Programming:* Farm 5 hrs wkly; *No. News Employees:* 2; *Target Audience:* 24-54.
Bruce Beasley, President

WUSL
01-01-1961; 98.9 MHz FM; *Hrs Open:* 24; 27 kw; 669 ft.; N40 2 37 W75 14 32
111 Presidential Boulevard, Suite 100, Bala Cynwyd, PA 19004 US
(610) 784-3333; *Fax:* (610) 784-2075
www.power99.com
License: Philadelphia, Philadelphia County, PA held by AMFM Radio Licenses LLC
Group Owner: iHeartMedia; (acq 8-30-00; grpsl).
Arbitron Metro Market: Bala Cynwyd, PA *TV Affiliate:* webphilly@clearchannel.com; *Format:* Urban Contemporary *Special Programming:* Gospel 4 hrs wkly; *Hrs. of News Programming:* news progmg 4 hrs wkly *No. NewsEmployees:* 2; *Target Audience:* 18-49.
Richard Lewis, Market President
Wes Franks, Senior Vice President of Sales

WWDB
01-01-1925; 860 kHz AM; *Hrs Open:* Daytime; 10 kw-D; N40 9 16 W75 22 9
555 City Ave., Suite 300, Bala Cynwyd, PA 19004 US
(610) 668-4400; *Fax:* (610) 668-4429
www.wwdbam.com
License: Philadelphia, PA held by Beasley Media Group LLC
Group Owner: Beasley Broadcast Group Inc.; (acq 9-9-86; $2.4 million;
Arbitron Metro Market: Philadelphia, PA; *Format:* Talk; *Target Audience:* 18-49.
Tim Halloran, Operations Manager
Sam Speiser, General Manager

***WXPN**
04-01-1957; 88.5 MHz FM; *Hrs Open:* 24; 5 kw; 919 ft.; N40 2 36 W75 14 33
3025 Walnut Street, Philadelphia, PA 19104 US
(215) 898-6677; *Fax:* (215) 898-0707
www.xpn.org
wxpndesk@xpn.org
License: Philadelphia, Philadelphia County, PA held by Trustees of the University of Pennsylvania.
Nat'l Network: PRI; NPR
Arbitron Metro Market: Philadelphia, PA; *Format:* Alternative *Special Programming:* Children 5 hrs, folk 5 hrs wkly; *Hrs. of News Programming:* News progmg 3 hrs wkly; *Target Audience:* 25-54; educated
Roger LaMay, General Manager
Quyen Shanahan, Development Manager
Bruce Warren, Programming Director
Kim Winnick, Marketing Director
Jay Goldman, Engineering Dir
Tom Interrante, Sales Director
Dan Reed, Music Director

WXTU
09-16-1983; 92.5 MHz FM; *Hrs Open:* 24; 15 kW; 876 ft.; N40 2 19 W75 14 14
555 E City Ave., Suite 330, Bala Cynwyd, PA 19004-1137 USA
(610) 667-9000
www.925xtu.com
License: Philadelphia, Philadelphia County, PA held by CBS Radio Stations Inc.
Group Owner: CBS Radio
Nat'l Reps: D & R Radio
Arbitron Metro Market: Philadelphia, PA; *Format:* Country *Special Programming:* Sundays 6am-6:30am-Philadelphia Focus; *Adv. Rates:* 400;400;400;200
Laura Lombardi, General Sales Mgr
Shelly Easton, Programming Director
Carrie Miller, Promotion Director

WBEN-FM
03-01-1949; 95.7 MHz FM; *Hrs Open:* 24; 8.9 kw; 1148 ft.; N40 2 21 W75 14 13
1 Bala Plaza, Suite 424, Bala Cynwyd, PA 19004 US
(610) 771-0957; *Fax:* (610) 771-9690
questions@ilikebenfm.com
License: Philadelphia, Philadelphia County, PA held by Greater Philadelphia Radio Group.
Group Owner: Beasley Broadcast Group; (acq 5-29-97; $41.8 million)
Arbitron Metro Market: Philadelphia, PA; *Format:* Adult Contemp; *Hrs. of News Programming:* News progmg 3 hrs wkly; *Target Audience:* 25-54; professional, upscale executives
Jim Brown, General Sales Mgr
Chuck Damico, Programming Director
Mark Vizza, Promotions Director
Rich DeSisto, Programming/Music Director

WRFF
02-01-1965; 104.5 MHz FM; *Hrs Open:* 24; 11.5 kw; 1010 ft.; N40 2 30 W75 14 24
111 Presidential Boulevard, Suite 100, Bala Cynwyd, PA 19004 US
(610) 784-3333
www.radio1045.com
License: Philadelphia, Philadelphia County, PA held by AMFM Radio Licenses LLC.
Group Owner: iHeartMedia; (acq 8-30-2000; grpsl)
Arbitron Metro Market: Philadelphia; *Format:* Rock/AOR; *No. News Employees:* 1
Richard Lewis, Market President
Wes Franks, Senior Vice President of Sales

WNTP
01-01-1923; 990 kHz AM; *Hrs Open:* 24; 50 kw-D, 10 kw-N, DA-2; N40 05 43 W75 16 37
117 Ridge Pike, Lafayette Hill, PA 19444
(610) 940-0990; *Fax:* (610) 828-8879
www.wntp.com
contactus@wntp.com
License: Philadelphia, Philadelphia County, PA held by Pennsylvania Media Associates Inc.

RADIO - U.S.

Group Owner: Salem Communications Corp.; (acq 1994; $3.5 million grpsl).
Nat'l Network: Salem Radio Network
Population Served: 7,927,724; *Arbitron Metro Market:* Philadelphia *Special Programming:* Sports, Sp; *Hrs. of News Programming:* 4 times per hr; *Target Audience:* 35-64; Adults
Russ Whitnah, Operations Dir
Carol Healey, General Sales Mgr
Ann Krill, Promotions Manager
Rene Tetro, Chief Engineer
Mark Daniels, Marketing Manager
David Handler, New Business Sales Manager
Kevin Manna, Operations Manager

WZMP
04-20-2015; 96.5 MHz FM; 9.6 kW; 1030 ft.; N40 2 30 W75 14 11
555 E City Ave., Suite 330, Bala Cynwyd, PA 19004-1137 USA
965ampradio.com
License: Philadelphia, Philadelphia County, PA held by CBS Radio Stations Inc.
Group Owner: CBS Radio
Arbitron Metro Market: Philadelphia, PA; *Format:* Contemporary Hits/Top 40
Kenny Paul, General Sales Mgr
Bobby Smith, Programming Director

Philipsburg

WPHB
06-01-1956; 1260 kHz AM; *Hrs Open:* 24; 5 kw-D, ND1; 0.034 kw-N, ND1; N40 53 39 W78 11 51
38 Radio Park, Philipsburg, PA 16866 US
(814) 342-2300
www.wphbradio.com
wphb1260@gmail.com
License: Philipsburg, PA held by Magnum Broadcasting Inc.
Group Owner: Magnum Broadcasting Inc.; (acq 11-24-2004; $2,022,527 with co-located FM)
Nat'l Network: CNN Radio; *Regional Network:* Radio Pa.
Regional Reps: Dome & Assoc
Arbitron Metro Market: State College, PA; *Format:* Country, News, 62, Sports, Talk *Special Programming:* Bluegrass 4 hrs, polka 6 hrs, Gospel 6 hrs, big band 5 hrs wkly; *Target Audience:* Men & women; generally 25+ *Adv. Rates:* 18; 15; 15; 13
Michael Stapleford, President
Cliff Mack, Operations Dir
Laura Shore Mack, General Manager
Marian Kovach, General Sales Mgr
C.J. Daniels, Programming Director
Jason Torrance, Promotions Manager
Mary Beth Thompson, NewsDirector
Joe Portelli, Chief Engineer
Tor Michaels, News Reporter
Sherry Flick, Public Affairs Director

WQCK(FM)
03-01-1989; 105.9 MHz FM; *Hrs Open:* 24; 710 w; Ant 951 ft; N40 47 34 W78 10 29
315 S. Atherton Street, State College, PA 16801
(814) 272-1320
www.1059qwikrock.com
License: Philipsburg, Centre County, PA held by Magnum Broadcasting Inc.
Group Owner: Magnum Broadcasting Inc.
Population Served: 42,499; *Arbitron Metro Market:* State College, PA; *Format:* Alternative; *Hrs. of News Programming:* News progmg 2.5 hrs wkly; *Target Audience:* 18-49; men & women; *Adv. Rates:* 26.50; 21;24.50; 19
Diana Stapleford, General Manager

Phoenixville

WPHE
08-23-1978; 690 kHz AM; 1 kw-D, DAD; N40 8 8 W75 33 37
Mailing Address: P.O. Box 46327, Philadelphia, PA 19160 US
Second Address: 321 W. Sedgley Ave., Philadelphia, PA 19140
(201) 969-3123
www.radiosalvacion.com
License: Phoenixville, PA held by Salvation Broadcasting Co.
Arbitron Metro Market: Philadelphia; *Format:* Variety/Diverse, Religious *Special Programming:* Por 3 hrs wkly
Sarrial Salva, President
Isabel Salva, General Sales Mgr
Juan Izquierdo, Programming Director
Juan Pydeck, Chief Engineer

Pittsburgh

KDKA
02-15-2010; 1020 kHz AM; *Hrs Open:* 24; 41 kW; N40 26 28 W80 1 32
651 Holiday Dr., Foster Plaza Bldg. 5, Pittsburgh, PA 15220 USA
(412) 920-9400
www.kdkaradio.com
License: Pittsburgh, Allegheny County, PA held by CBS Radio Stations Inc.
Group Owner: CBS Radio
Nat'l Network: CBS; CNN Radio; AP Network News; Premiere Radio Networks; Westwood One; *Nat'l Reps:* CBS Radio; *Wire Services:* AP; Accu-Weather
Arbitron Metro Market: Pittsburgh, PA; *Format:* News/Talk, News, 86; *Hrs. of News Programming:* news progmg 75 hrs wkly; *No. News Employees:* 35; *Target Audience:* P25-54

KQV
11-19-1919; 1410 kHz AM; *Hrs Open:* 24; 5 kw-D, DA2; 5 kw-N, DA2; N40 31 24 W80 0 40
Center City Tower, 650 Smithfield Street, Suite 620, Pittsburgh, PA 15222 US
(412) 562-5900; *Fax:* (412) 562-5936
www.kqv.com
kqvnews@kqv.com
License: Pittsburgh, PA held by Calvary Inc.
Nat'l Network: Wall Street; AP Radio; *Regional Network:* Radio Pa.; *Wire Services:* AP
Arbitron Metro Market: Pittsburgh metro area; *Format:* News *Special Programming:* NFL football (regular season, playoffs & Superbowl; *Hrs. of News Programming:* news progmg 168 hrs wkly; *No. News Employees:* 15 *Target Audience:* 35 plus; affluent, info-oriented adults
Robert W. Dickey Sr., President
Cheryl Scott, Operations Dir
Judith Ross, General Sales Mgr
Frank Gottlieb, News Director
Steve Conti, Chief Engineer
Susan Selby, Traffic Director

KDKA-FM
02-15-2010; 93.7 MHz FM; 41 kW; 430 ft.; N40 26 28 W80 1 32
651 Holiday Dr., Foster Plaza Bldg. 5, Pittsburgh, PA 15220 USA
(412) 920-9400
www.937thefan.com
License: Pittsburgh, Allegheny County, PA held by CBS Radio Stations Inc.
Group Owner: CBS Radio; (acq 11-13-98; grpsl)
Population Served: 64,294; *Arbitron Metro Market:* Pittsburgh, PA; *Format:* Sports
Michael Young, General Manager
Michael Spacc, Director of Sales
Jim Graci, Programming Director
Kayla Seybert, Promotions Manager

WDSY
04-21-1992; 107.9 MHz FM; 17.5 kW; 676 ft.; N40 28 20 W79 59 41
651 Holiday Dr., Foster Plaza 5, Pittsburgh, PA 15220 USA
(412) 920-9400
www.y108.com
License: Pittsburgh, Allegheny County, PA held by CBS Radio Stations Inc.
Group Owner: CBS Radio; (acq 12-14-00; grpsl).
Nat'l Network: Westwood One; *Nat'l Reps:* Katz Radio
Arbitron Metro Market: Pittsburgh, PA; *Format:* Country; *Target Audience:* 25-54; general; *Adv. Rates:* 275; 225; 250; 100
Christine Fallon, General Sales Mgr
Mark Anderson, Programming Director
John D'Amico, Promotions Director

***WESA**
12-15-1949; 90.5 MHz FM; *Hrs Open:* 24; 25 kw; 480 ft; N40 25 52 W80 00 26
67 Bedford Square, Pittsburgh, PA 15203
(412) 381-9131
www.wesa.fm
comments@wesa.fm
License: Pittsburgh, Allegheny County, PA held by Pittsburgh EPM, Inc.
Nat'l Network: NPR; PRI; APM; PRX; *Nat'l Reps:* Interep
Arbitron Metro Market: Pittsburgh, PA; *Hrs. of News Programming:* news progmg 47 hrs wkly; *No. News Employees:* 5; *Target Audience:* Educated, moderately affluent
DeAnne Hamilton, General Manager
Tammy Terwelp, Programming Director
Kimberly Datz, Director of Development
Mark Nootbaar, News Director
Carly McCoy, Membership Director

WDVE
05-10-1962; 102.5 MHz FM; 55 kw; 820 ft.; N40 29 38 W80 1 9
200 Fleet St., 4th Floor, Pittsburgh, PA 15220 US
(412) 937-1441; *Fax:* (412) 937-0323
www.dve.com
mosh@wxdx.com
License: Pittsburgh, Allegheny County, PA held by Capstar TX LLC
Group Owner: iHeartMedia; (acq 8-00; grpsl).
Nat'l Reps: Christal
Arbitron Metro Market: Pittsburgh, PA; *Format:* Classic Rock; *No. News Employees:* 1; *Target Audience:* 25-54.
David Edgar, Vice President of Programming

WJAS
10-19-1921; 1320 kHz AM
Broadcast Plaza li, 3rd Floor, 900 Parish St, Pittsburgh, PA 15220 US
(412) 875-9500; *Fax:* (412) 875-9970
www.1320wjas.com
rantill@1320wjas.com
License: Pittsburgh, PA held by Renda Broadcasting Corp.
Group Owner: Renda Broadcasting Corp.; (acq 7-16-85; $700,000;
Arbitron Metro Market: Pittsburgh, PA; *Format:* Adult Contemp, Big Band, 64 *Special Programming:* Big band jump, Frank Sinatra 2 hrs wkly; *Target Audience:* 35 plus; older, upscale; *Adv. Rates:* 90; 90; 90; 50
Anthony Renda, President
Lawrence Weiss, General Manager
David Pavlic, General Sales Mgr
Ron Antill, Programming Director
Chris Shovlin, Promotions Manager
Jason Horvath, Chief Engineer
Chris Shovlin, Director of Marketing
Maureen Brady, NTR Director

WPGB
02-04-1963; 104.7 MHz FM; *Hrs Open:* 24; 13 kw; 827 ft.; N40 28 20 W79 59 41
200 Fleet St., 4th Floor, Pittsburgh, PA 15220 US
(412) 937-1441; *Fax:* (412) 937-0323
www.big1047.com
License: Pittsburgh, Allegheny County, PA held by Capstar TX LLC
Group Owner: iHeartMedia; (acq 8-30-00; grpsl).
Nat'l Network: Fox News Radio; *Wire Services:* AP
Arbitron Metro Market: Pittsburgh, PA; *Format:* Country; *Hrs. of News Programming:* news progmg 5 hrs wkly; *Target Audience:* 25-54; white collar workers
David Edgar, Vice President of Programming
Drew Salamon, Senior Vice President of Sales

WDDZ
02-12-1950; 1250 kHz AM; *Hrs Open:* 24 hrs; 5 kw-D, DAN; 5 kw-N, DAN; N40 23 50 W79 57 43
77 West 66th Street, 16th Floor, New York, NY 10023 US
(401) 722-0839; *Fax:* (401) 722-1459
radio.disney.com
License: Pittsburgh, PA held by Radio Disney Group LLC.
Group Owner: ABC Inc.; (acq 5-29-2001; $2.05 million).
Nat'l Network: Radio Disney
Arbitron Metro Market: Providence-Warwick-Pawtucket, RI; *Format:* Children; *Target Audience:* Children & Teens 3-14, Parents 25-54, esp. moms.
Michael Kellogg, General Manager
Jaccalen Grillo, Promotions Manager
Adria Paquin, Marketing Account Executive
Scott Henderson, Senior Account Manager

WLTJ
04-04-1942; 92.9 MHz FM; *Hrs Open:* 24; 43 kw; 853 ft.; N40 29 43 W80 0 17
650 Smithfield St., Suite 2200, Pittsburgh, PA 15222 US
(412) 316-3342
www.q929fm.com
License: Pittsburgh, Allegheny County, PA held by Media Subsidiary LLC
Nat'l Reps: McGavren Guild
Arbitron Metro Market: Pittsburgh, PA; *Format:* Adult Contemp; *Target Audience:* 25-54; affluent, professional, working public
Saul Frischling, President
Greg Frischling, General Manager
Chris Kohan, General Sales Mgr
Zak Szabo, Programming Director
Paul Carroll, Chief Engineer
Vicki Wolfe, Promotions Director

WORD-FM
01-01-1948; 101.5 MHz FM; 43 kw; 528 ft.; N40 29 2 W79 59 34
7 Parkway Center, Suite 625, Pittsburgh, PA 15220 US
(412) 937-1500; *Fax:* (412) 937-1567
www.wordfm.com
word2@wordfm.com

License: Pittsburgh, Allegheny County, PA held by Pennsylvania Media Associates Inc.
Group Owner: Salem Communications Corp.
Arbitron Metro Market: Pittsburgh, PA *TV Affiliate:* Relg; *No. News Employees:* 25-49.
Tom Lemmon, General Sales Mgr
Gary Dickson, Programming Director

WWNL
01-01-1947; 1080 kHz AM; *Hrs Open:* Sunrise-sunset; 25 kw-C, DAD; 50 kw-D, DAD; N40 36 17 W79 57 37
2652 Library Rd., Pittsburgh, PA 15234 US
(412) 892-8349
www.wilkinsradio.com
denise@wilkinsradio.com
License: Pittsburgh, PA held by Steel City Radio Inc.
Group Owner: Wilkins Communications Network Inc.; (acq 6-14-2001).
Arbitron Metro Market: Pittsburgh, PA; *Format:* Christian, Talk; *Target Audience:* 35 plus.; *Adv. Rates:* 60; 60; 60; 60
Jamie Frey, Station Manager

WPIT
01-01-1947; 730 kHz AM; 5 kw-D, ND1; 0.024 kw-N, ND1; N40 29 2 W79 59 34
7 Parkway Center, Suite 625, Pittsburgh, PA 15220 US
(412) 937-1500; *Fax:* (412) 937-1576
www.wpitam.com
word2@wordfm.com
License: Pittsburgh, PA held by Pennsylvania Media Associates Inc.
Group Owner: Salem Communications Corp.; (Acq 12-2-92; $6.5 million;
Arbitron Metro Market: Pittsburgh, PA; *Format:* Christian
Jeff Baity, Operations Dir
Ron Baity, General Manager
Tom Lemmon, Sales Manager

***WPTS-FM**
08-26-1984; 92.1 MHz FM; *Hrs Open:* 24; 0.016 kw; 463 ft.; N40 26 39 W79 57 12
411 William Pitt Union, 3959 5th Avenue, Pittsburgh, PA 15260 US
(412) 648-7990; *Fax:* (412) 648-7988
www.wptsradio.org
wpts@pitt.edu
License: Pittsburgh, Allegheny County, PA held by University of Pittsburgh.
Arbitron Metro Market: Pittsburgh, PA; *Format:* Variety/Diverse; *Hrs. of News Programming:* news progmg 10 hrs wkly; *No. News Employees:* 3; *Target Audience:* General.
Kevin Wheeler, Sports Director
Zach Luettgen, News Director
Matt Patton, Programming Director
Ali L'Esperance, Promotions Director
Stephen Wuchira, Music Director
Evan Scott, Engineering Director

***WQED-FM**
01-25-1973; 89.3 MHz FM; *Hrs Open:* 24; 28 kw; 653 ft.; N40 26 46 W79 57 51
4802 Fifth Avenue, Pittsburgh, PA 15213 US
(412) 622-1300; *Fax:* (412) 622-1488
www.wqed.org
License: Pittsburgh, Allegheny County, PA held by WQED Multimedia.
Nat'l Network: NPR; PRI
Arbitron Metro Market: Pittsburgh, PA *TV Affiliate:* *WQED(TV) affil.; *Format:* Talk; *Hrs. of News Programming:* News progmg 5 hrs wkly; *Target Audience:* 35-64; educated, influential, professional, communityleaders, mid to high income
William R. Caroselli, Chairman
Deborah L. Acklin, President/CEO
Darryl Ford Williams, VP Content
Lilli Mosco, VP Development
Carole Bailey, CFO

***WRCT**
04-01-1974; 88.3 MHz FM; *Hrs Open:* 24; 1.75 kw; 72 ft.; N40 26 39 W79 56 37
5000 Forbes Avenue, 1 WRCT Plaza, Pittsburgh, PA 15213 US
(412) 621-0728
www.wrct.org
License: Pittsburgh, PA held by WRCT Radio, Inc.
Arbitron Metro Market: Pittsburgh, PA; *Format:* Variety/Diverse *Special Programming:* Black 12 hrs, class 3 hrs, country 3 hrs, folk 3 hrs, experimental 12 hrs, jazz 18 hrs wkly; *Hrs. of News Programming:* News progmg 10hrs wkly; *Target Audience:* General.
Matt Siko, General Manager
Pauline Law, Programming Director
Kathy Lee, PR Director

Joe Riley, Chief Engineer
Josephine Sullivan, General Manager
Bryn Scharenberg, Production Director
Salem Hilal, Programming Director

WSHH
03-08-1948; 99.7 MHz FM; 15.5 kw; 899 ft.; N40 27 48 W80 0 16
900 Parish Street, Pittsburgh, PA 15220 US
(412) 875-9500; *Fax:* (412) 875-9970
www.wshh.com
License: Pittsburgh, Allegheny County, PA held by Renda Broadcasting Corp. of Nevada
Group Owner: Renda Broadcasting Corp.; (acq 11-83; $2.7 million;
Arbitron Metro Market: Pittsburgh, PA; *Format:* Adult Contemp *Special Programming:* Pub affrs one hr wkly; *No. News Employees:* 1; *Target Audience:* 25-54; white collar, upscale office workers, professionals,managers; *Adv. Rates:* 130; 130; 125; 50
Allan Freed, Operations Dir
Chris Shovlin, Director of Marketing/Promotions
Susan Kelly, General Sales Mgr
Ron Antill, Programming Director
Jason Horvath, Chief Engineer

WBGG
01-01-1932; 970 kHz AM; *Hrs Open:* 24; 5 kw-D, DA2; 5 kw-N, DA2; N40 30 30 W80 0 30
200 Fleet St., 4th Floor, Pittsburgh, PA 15220 US
(412) 937-1441; *Fax:* (412) 937-0323
www.espnpgh.com
davidedgar@iheartmedia.com
License: Pittsburgh, PA held by AMFM Radio Licenses L.L.C.
Group Owner: iHeartMedia; (acq 8-30-2000; grpsl)
Nat'l Network: Fox Sports
Arbitron Metro Market: Pittsburgh, PA; *Format:* Sports
David Edgar, Vice President of Programming

WWSW-FM
01-01-1940; 94.5 MHz FM; 50 kw; 810 ft.; N40 27 48 W80 0 18
200 Fleet Street, 4th Floor, Pittsburgh, PA 15220 US
(412) 937-1441; *Fax:* (412) 937-0323
www.3wsradio.com
davidedgar@iheartmedia.com
License: Pittsburgh, Allegheny County, PA held by AMFM Radio Licenses L.L.C.
Group Owner: iHeartMedia
Arbitron Metro Market: Pittsburgh, PA; *Format:* Contemporary Hits/Top 40, Adult Contemp
David Edgar, Vice President of Programming

WXDX-FM
01-01-1960; 105.9 MHz FM; 15.5 kw; 892 ft.; N40 29 38 W80 1 9
200 Fleet St., 4th Floor, Pittsburgh, PA 15220 US
(412) 937-1441; *Fax:* (412) 937-4706
www.1059thex.com
davidedgar@iheartmedia.com
License: Pittsburgh, Allegheny County, PA held by Capstar TX LLC
Group Owner: iHeartMedia; (acq 8-30-00; grpsl).
Nat'l Reps: Christal
Arbitron Metro Market: Pittsburgh, PA; *Format:* Alternative; *Target Audience:* 18-34.
David Edgar, Vice President of Programming

***WYEP-FM**
04-30-1974; 91.3 MHz FM; *Hrs Open:* 24; 18 kw; 381 ft.; N40 24 42 W79 55 53
2313 E. Carson Street, Pittsburgh, PA 15203 US
(412) 381-9900; *Fax:* (412) 381-9126
www.wyep.org
info@wyep.org
License: Pittsburgh, Allegheny County, PA held by Pittsburgh Community Broadcasting Corp.
Nat'l Network: PRI; NPR
Arbitron Metro Market: Pittsburgh, PA; *Format:* Triple A *Special Programming:* Folk 9 hrs, blues 7 hrs, bluegrass 4 hrs, soul 3 h; *Target Audience:* 25-49; socially, politically & culturally aware & active; well-educated
Abby Goldstein, President
Tony Pirollo, General Sales Mgr
Michael Sauter, Programming Director
Kyle Smith, Director of Music
Elizabeth Baisley, Director of Marketing
Kimberly Datz, Director of Development
Brian Siewiorek,Production Director
Sarah Wemple, Director of Finance

***WRCT(FM)**
04-01-1974; 88.3 MHz FM; *Hrs Open:* 24; 1.75 kw; 53 ft; N40 26 39 W79 56 37
One WRCT Plaza, 5000 Forbes Ave., Pittsburgh, PA 15213
(412) 621-0728,(412) 621-9728; *Fax:* (412) 268-6549
www.wrct.org
info@wrct.org
License: Pittsburgh, Allegheny County, PA held by Carnegie Mellon Student Government Corp.
Population Served: 1,500,000; *Arbitron Metro Market:* Pittsburgh, PA *Special Programming:* Black 12 hrs, class 3 hrs, country 3 hrs, folk 3 hrs, experimental 12 hrs, jazz 18 hrs wkly; *Hrs. of News Programming:* Newsprogmg 10 hrs wkly; *Target Audience:* General.
Matt Siko, General Manager
Pauline Law, Programming Director

WKST-FM
08-08-1960; 96.1 MHz FM; 44 kw; 521 ft.; N40 23 49 W79 57 43
200 Fleet St., 4th Floor, Pittsburgh, PA 15220 US
(412) 937-1441; *Fax:* (412) 937-0323
www.961kiss.com
License: Pittsburgh, PA held by Capstar TX LLC
Group Owner: iHeartMedia
Arbitron Metro Market: Pittsburgh, PA; *Format:* Contemporary Hits/Top 40
David Edgar, Vice President of Programming

Pittston

WITK
06-21-1953; 1550 kHz AM; 10 kw-D, DA2; 0.5 kw-N, DA2; N41 20 45 W75 47 8
944 Exeter Ave., Exeter, PA 18643 US
(570) 883-9693
www.wilkinsradio.com
denise@wilkinsradio.com
License: Pittston, PA held by Steel City Radio Inc.
Group Owner: Wilkins Communications Network Inc.; (acq 10-10-2007; $400,000)
Arbitron Metro Market: Wilkes Barre-Scranton, PA; *Format:* Christian
Jim Rising, Station Manager

WHBS
11-01-1983; 102.3 MHz FM; 5.8 kw; 72 ft.; N41 18 20 W75 45 38
10706 Beaver Dam Road, Cockeysville, MD 21030 US
(570) 883-1111; *Fax:* (570) 883-9851
www.102themountain.com
info@102themountain.com
License: Pittston, Luzerne County, PA held by Entercom Wilkes-Barre Scranton LLC.
Group Owner: Entercom Communications Corp.; (acq 12-13-99; grpsl).
Nat'l Network: Jones Radio Networks; *Nat'l Reps:* D & R Radio
Arbitron Metro Market: Wilkes Barre-Sc; *Format:* Triple A *Special Programming:* Philadelphia Eagles, Penn State football; *Target Audience:* 35-64; female
John Burkavage, General Manager
Jim Rising, Station Manager
Andy Zapotek, General Sales Mgr
Jerry Padden, Programming Director
Michael Ignatz, Promotions Manager
Lamar Smith, Chief Engineer
Elizabeth Masich, Music Director

Plains

WYCK
01-01-1923; 1340 kHz AM; *Hrs Open:* 24; 0.81 kw-U, ND1; N41 15 1 W75 49 32 *Rebroadcasts:* Rebroadcasts WICK(AM) Scranton 98%
575 Grove St., Honesdale, PA 18431 US
(570) 253-1616; *Fax:* (570) 253-6297
www.boldgoldlakeregion.com
License: Plains, PA held by Bold Gold Media WBS L.P.
Group Owner: Bold Gold Media Group LP; (acq 3-13-2006; grpsl).
Nat'l Network: Fox Sports; *Wire Services:* Metro Weather Service Inc.
Arbitron Metro Market: Scranton, PA; *Format:* Sports *Special Programming:* Relg 3 hrs wkly, Polish 3 hrs wkly; *Hrs. of News Programming:* 8 hrs progmg wkly; *No. News Employees:* 1; *Target Audience:* Adults35-64; adults who love original hits of top 40 era

Pleasant Gap

WEMR
06-13-1986; 98.7 MHz FM; *Hrs Open:* 18; 2.2 kw; 551 ft.; N40 55 58 W77 45 40

160 Clearview Avenue, State College, PA 16803 US
(814) 238-5085; *Fax:* (814) 238-7932
www.eagle987.com
License: Pleasant Gap, Wyoming County, PA held by 2510 Licenses LLC
Group Owner: 2510 Licenses LLC; (acq 1-30-2004; $515,000 with co-located FM)
Arbitron Metro Market: Wilkes Barre. PA; *Format:* News, News/Talk, 86

Pocono Pines

WPZX
01-01-2000; 105.9 MHz FM; 6 kw; 328 ft.; N41 5 6 W75 38 9
Rebroadcasts: Simulcast with WEZX(FM) Scranton
8280 Greensboro Drive, 7th Floor, McLean, VA 22102 US
(570) 346-6555; *Fax:* (570) 346-6038
www.rock107.com
License: Pocono Pines, Monroe County, PA held by The Scranton Times L.P.
Group Owner: The Scranton Times L.P.; (acq 9-8-00).
Arbitron Metro Market: Scranton, PA; *Format:* Classic Rock
William Lynett, CEO
Sean O'Mealy, General Manager
Dave Mehall, Sales Manager
Scott Laudani, Operations Manger / Program Director
Mark Hoover, Operations Manger / Program Director
Ruth Miller, News Director
Kevin Fitzgerald, ChiefEngineer
Jim Loftus, COO
Jim Morris, National Sales Manager
Krista Saar, Traffic Manager
Mari Olshefski, Traffic & Continuity Director
Donna Ryan, Traffic
Judy Haudenschield, Account Executive

Port Allegany

WHKS
01-01-1990; 94.9 MHz FM; *Hrs Open:* 24; 1.15 kw; 758 ft.; N41 48 36 W78 23 10
Mailing Address: 59 Lent Hollow Rd, Coudersport, PA 16915 US
Second Address: 59 Lent Hollow Rd., Coudersport, PA 16915
(814) 642-7004; *Fax:* (814) 642-9491
License: Port Allegany, McKean County, PA held by L-Com Inc.
Nat'l Network: Jones Radio Networks; AP Radio; *Regional Network:* Radio Pa; *Nat'l Reps:* Dome *Regional Reps:* Commercial Media Sales.
Format: Adult Contemp *Special Programming:* Relg 2 hrs wkly; *Hrs. of News Programming:* News progmg 2 hrs wkly; *Target Audience:* 25-54; general
David Lent, President
Joe Taylor, General Sales Mgr

Port Matilda

*WKVB
10-17-1994; 107.9 MHz FM; *Hrs Open:* 24; 0.45 kw; 1175 ft.; N40 55 11 W77 58 28
P.O. Box 2098, Omaha, NE 68103-2098 US
(800) 525-5683
www.klove.com
License: Port Matilda, Centre County, PA held by Educational Media Foundation
Group Owner: Medica Foundation; (acq 2-16-2005; grpsl).
Nat'l Network: K-Love
Arbitron Metro Market: Port Matilda, PA; *Format:* Talk
Darrel Chambliss, Chairman
Mike Novak, President/CEO
Alan Mason, COO
Eric Moser, CFO
D. Kevin Blair, Secretary/General Counsel
David Pierce, Chief Creative Officer

Portage

*WLKJ
11-15-1990; 105.7 MHz FM; *Hrs Open:* 24; 3 kw; 322 ft.; N40 22 59 W78 39 31
PO Box 2098, Omaha, NE 68103 US
(800) 525-5683
www.klove.com
License: Portage, Cambria County, PA held by Educational Media Foundation
Nat'l Network: K-Love
Format: Christian; *Target Audience:* 18-54; middle to upper income
Darrell Chambliss, Chairman
Alan Mason, COO
Mike Novak, President/CEO
Eric Moser, CFO
David Pierce, Chief Creative Officer
D. Kevin Blair, Secretary/General Counsel

Pottstown

WPAZ
10-01-1951; 1370 kHz AM; *Hrs Open:* 6 AM-7 PM; kw
US
(610) 326-4000,(610) 326-6832; *Fax:* (610) 326-7984
www.1370wpaz.com
License: Pottstown, Montgomery County, PA held by Four Rivers Community Broadcasting Corp.
Group Owner: Four Rivers Community Broadcasting Corp.
Arbitron Metro Market: Philadelphia; *Format:* News, News/Talk, 86 *Special Programming:* Pol one hr, relg 12 hrs wkly; *Hrs. of News Programming:* news progmg 8 hrs wkly; *No. News Employees:* 2 *Target Audience:* 25 plus; most affluent people;
Adv. Rates: 20; 18; 20; 10
Faye Scott, President
Mike LiCata, General Manager
Jay Warren, Programming Director
Paul Fanelli, News Director
Terry Dalton, Chief Engineer

Pottsville

WAVT-FM
11-20-1948; 101.9 MHz FM; *Hrs Open:* 24; 29 kw; 561 ft.; N40 49 50 W76 12 32
212 Centre Street, Pottsville, PA 17901 US
(507) 622-1360
www.t102radio.com
rc@pbcradio.com
License: Pottsville, Schuylkill County, PA held by Pottsville Broadcasting Co. Inc.
Format: Rock/AOR; *No. News Employees:* 1
Larry LeBlanc, Operations Dir
Dave Sturgeon, General Manager
Jim Bowman, Station Manager
Jen Jones, General Sales Mgr
Jeff Spence, Programming Director
Mike Schoen, Promotions Manager
Randall Harder, News Director
Jill Mason,Business Manager
Al Clennon, Local Sales Manager

WPAM
01-01-1946; 1450 kHz AM; *Hrs Open:* 24; 1 kw-U, ND1; N40 41 27 W76 11 39
Mailing Address: 101 N. Centre Street, Pottsville, PA 17901 US
Second Address: PO Box 732, Pottsville, PA 17901-0732
(570) 622-1450; *Fax:* (570) 622-4690
License: Pottsville, PA held by Curran Communications Inc.
Nat'l Network: Jones Radio Networks
Format: Classic Rock *Special Programming:* Gospel, Talk 6 hrs wkly; *Target Audience:* 25-54; active, upwardly mobile adults;
Adv. Rates: 10; 10; 10; 10
Robert Murray, General Manager

WPPA
05-09-1946; 1360 kHz AM; *Hrs Open:* 24; 5 kw-D, DA2; 0.5 kw-N, DA2; N40 41 56 W76 11 43
212 S. Centre Street, Pottsville, PA 17901 US
(570) 622-1360
www.wpparadio.com
License: Pottsville, PA held by Pottsville Broadcasting Co. Inc.
Nat'l Network: CBS
Format: Adult Contemp; *Hrs. of News Programming:* news progmg 14 hrs wkly; *No. News Employees:* 2; *Target Audience:* 25-54.
Argie Tidmore, President
Les Blankenhorn, Operations Dir
William Tidmore, General Sales Mgr
Al Kovy, Programming Director
Jay Levan, News Director
Deb Daugherty, Public Affairs Director

Punxsutawney

WECZ
03-18-1953; 1540 kHz AM; *Hrs Open:* 12; 1 kw-C, NDD; 5 kw-D, NDD; N40 57 36 W79 0 8
904 N. Main St., Punxsutawney, PA 15767 US
(814) 938-6000; *Fax:* (814) 938-4237
www.weczam1540.com/
License: Punxsutawney, PA held by Renda Radio Inc.
Group Owner: Renda Broadcasting Corp.; acq 6-1-81; $512,000;
Nat'l Network: Westwood One
Arbitron Metro Market: Punxsutawney, PA; *Format:* News, Talk *Special Programming:* Pol 3 hrs wkly; *Hrs. of News Programming:* news progmg 10 hrs wkly; *No. News Employees:* 2; *Target Audience:* 45 plus. *Adv.Rates:* 12; 8; 6; na
Anthony Renda, President
Mike Carroll, General Manager
John Smathers, Web Content Manager
Renee Pollippo, Traffic Manager

WPXZ-FM
12-12-1973; 104.1 MHz FM; *Hrs Open:* 24; 3 kw; 295 ft.; N40 57 36 W79 0 8
P.O. Box 458, Route 36 North, Punxsutawney, PA 15767 US
(814) 938-6000; *Fax:* (814) 938-4237
License: Punxsutawney, Jefferson County, PA
Nat'l Network: ABC
Format: Adult Contemp; *Target Audience:* 35-64.; *Adv. Rates:* 20; 16; 20; 12
Larry McGuire, Programming Director

Radnor Township

*WYBF
08-01-1991; 89.1 MHz FM; *Hrs Open:* 7 AM-2 AM (M, W, F); noon-2 AM (Su); 0.7 kw vert; 223 ft.; N40 3 22 W75 22 30
Rebroadcasts: Rebroadcasts WXVU(FM) Villanova
610 King of Prussia Rd., Radnor, PA 19087 US
610-902-8453
www.wybf.com
License: Radnor Township, Chester County, PA held by Cabrini College.
Arbitron Metro Market: Philadelphia; *Format:* News, News/Talk, 86, Variety/Diverse
Justin Sillner, Operations Dir
Alyssa Mentzer, Promotions Manager
ÿLiz Scopelliti, News Director
Megan Sokolowski, Sports Director

Reading

WEEU
01-01-1931; 830 kHz AM; *Hrs Open:* 24
34 North Fourth Street, Reading, PA 19601 US
(610) 376-7335; *Fax:* (610) 376-7756
www.weeu.com
weeu@weeu.com
License: Reading, PA held by WEEU Broadcasting Co.
Nat'l Reps: McGavren Guild
Arbitron Metro Market: Reading, PA; *Format:* News, News/Talk, 84, Talk *Special Programming:* Folk 3 hrs, Ger 2 hrs wkly; *Hrs. of News Programming:* news progmg 6 hrs wkly; *No. News Employees:* 2; *Target Audience:* 30 plus; mature
Dave Kline, Station Manager

WIOV
09-01-1946; 1240 kHz AM; 1 kw-U, ND1; N40 19 28 W75 56 31
5989 Susquehanna Plaza Dr., York, PA 17406 US
(717) 764-1155; *Fax:* (717) 738-1661
www.wiov985.com
License: Reading, PA held by Radio License Holding CBC, LLC
Group Owner: Cumulus Media Inc.; (acq 5-12-2004; grpsl).
Nat'l Network: ESPN Radio
Arbitron Metro Market: Reading, PA; *Format:* Sports, Talk; *Target Audience:* 35-54; Male
Brian Shaffer, General Sales Mgr
Rich Creeger, Programming Director
Lee Jacoby, Promotions Manager
Carol Pierson, Market Manager

WRAW
09-01-1922; 1340 kHz AM; *Hrs Open:* 24; 1 kw-U, ND1; N40 19 27 W75 55 10
1265 Perkiomen Avenue, Reading, PA 19602 US
(610) 376-6671; *Fax:* (610) 376-1270
www.rumba1340.com
License: Reading, PA held by Clear Channel Broadcasting Licenses Inc.
Group Owner: iHeartMedia; (acq 1996; grpsl)
Arbitron Metro Market: Reading, PA; *Format:* Spanish
Jeff Hurley, Operations Manager
Dan Lankford, Market Manager
Mike Jarvie, Director of Sales
Craig Stevens, Programming Director
Troy Becker, Chief Engineer

WRFY-FM
09-23-1962; 102.5 MHz FM; 10 kw; 807 ft.; N40 19 19 W75 53 35
1265 Perkiomen Ave., Suite 600, Reading, PA 19602 US
(610) 376-6671; *Fax:* (610) 376-1270
www.y102reading.com
License: Reading, Berks County, PA held by Clear Channel Broadcasting Licenses Inc.
Group Owner: iHeartMedia
Arbitron Metro Market: Reading, PA; *Format:* Variety/Diverse; *Target Audience:* 18-49.

Jeff Hurley, Operations Manager
Dan Lankford, Market Manager
Mike Jarvie, Director of Sales
Craig Stevens, Programming Director
Troy Becker, Chief Engineer
Leah Tyler, Production/Imaging Director

***WXAC**
01-01-1967; 91.3 MHz FM; 0.22 kw horiz; -23 ft.; N40 21 39 W75 54 37
P. O. Box 15234, 13th & Bern St., Reading, PA 19612 US
(610) 921-7545; *Fax:* (610) 921-7685
www.wxac.squarespace.com
music@albright.edu
License: Reading, Berks County, PA held by Albright College.
Arbitron Metro Market: Reading, PA; *Format:* Jazz, Rock/AOR; *Target Audience:* General; Albright college community & Reading area
Mindy Cohen, Station Manager
Kyrstyn, Program Director & Webmasterÿ
Cassandra, Program Director & Webmasterÿ
Jennifer, Treasurer/News Directorÿ
Yuliza, Music Librarian/Office Managerÿ
Sam, Music Director/Productions Directorÿ
Anthony, Assistantÿ
Peter, Assistantÿ

Red Lion

WSOX
10-01-1960; 96.1 MHz FM; 13.5 kw; 951 ft.; N39 54 16 W76 34 48
5989 Susquehanna Plaza Dr., York, PA 17406 US
(717) 764-1155; *Fax:* (717) 252-4708
www.961wsox.com
bobby.d@cumulus.com
License: Red Lion, PA held by Radio License Holding SRC, LLC
Group Owner: Cumulus Media Inc.; (acq 8-1-2003; $23 million).
Arbitron Metro Market: York, PA; *Format:* Adult Contemp
Brian Shaffer, General Sales Mgr
Bobby D., Programming Director
Lee Jacoby, Promotions Manager
Carol Pierson, Market Manager

Renovo

WQKK(FM)
09-19-1996; 106.9 MHz FM; 800 w; Ant 876 ft; N41 14 15 W77 45 02
240 11th Street, Renovo, PA 17764
(570) 923-9106; *Fax:* (570) 923-9106
morninghive@yahoo.com
License: Renovo, Clinton County, PA held by Magnum Broadcasting Inc.
Group Owner: Magnum Broadcasting Inc.; (acq 7-21-2004; $200,000).
Population Served: 1,235; *Arbitron Metro Market:* Renovo, PA; *Format:* Classic Rock
Michael Stapleford, President
Diana Stapleford, General Manager
Glenn Brooks, Station Manager
Michael Brennen, General Sales Mgr

Reynoldsville

WDSN
02-14-1990; 106.5 MHz FM; *Hrs Open:* 24; 6 kw; 328 ft.; N41 8 41 W78 52 41
12 West Long Ave., DuBois, PA 15801 US
(814) 375-5260; *Fax:* (814) 375-5262
www.sunny106.fm
sunny106@penn.com
License: Reynoldsville, Jefferson County, PA held by Priority Communications.
Group Owner: Priority Communications; (acq 11-6-90; $275,000; *Nat'l Network:* Jones Radio Networks; Fox News Radio *Regional Reps:* Commerical Media Sales; *Wire Services:* AP
Arbitron Metro Market: Reynoldsville, PA; *Format:* Adult Contemp; *Hrs. of News Programming:* news progmg 18 hrs wkly; *No. News Employees:* 1; *Target Audience:* 25-54.
Jay Philippone, General Manager
Lori Lewis, Station Manager

Ridgebury

WVYS
01-01-1991; 96.9 MHz FM; *Hrs Open:* 24; 3.6 kw; 430 ft; N41 55 43 W76 46 58
54 Wilmar Dr., P.O. Box 701, Tunkhannock, PA 18657 US
(570) 265-7600; *Fax:* (570) 265-7603
www.iloveyesfm.com
comments@iloveyesfm.com
License: Ridgebury, Bradford County, PA held by Geos Communications
Group Owner: Geos Communications
Arbitron Metro Market: Elmira-Corning, NY; *Format:* Adult Contemp; *Target Audience:* 25-44

Riverside

WVSL-FM
92.3 MHz FM; 0.93 kw; 833 ft.; N40 57 30 W76 42 53
450 Route 204, Selinsgrove, PA 17870 US
(570) 374-8819; *Fax:* (570) 374-7444
www.923espn.com
License: Riverside, Northumberland County, PA held by MMP License LLC.
Group Owner: MAX Media L.L.C.
Nat'l Network: ESPN Radio
Arbitron Metro Market: Selinsgrove, PA; *Format:* Sports
Tom Morgan, Operations Manager
Carol Pierson, General Manager
Mark Roberts, Programming Director
Kyle Blessing, Production Manager
Chad Evans, Digital Media Manager
Trevor Polly, Digital Media Manager
Elisa Beaver, OfficeManager

Roaring Spring

WKMC
05-01-1955; 1370 kHz AM; 5 kw-D, DA2; 0.038 kw-N, DA2; N40 19 26 W78 23 40
1345 S. Main St., Roaring Spring, PA 16673 US
(814) 224-7501; *Fax:* (814) 224-7504
License: Roaring Spring, PA held by Handsome Brothers Inc.
Arbitron Metro Market: Altoona, PA; *Format:* Adult Contemp; *Target Audience:* 45 plus; mature, loyal listeners
David Barger, President
Mike Martin, General Manager
Robert Lynn, Chief Engineer

Russell

WQFX-FM
11-11-1984; 103.1 MHz FM; 2.5 kw; 351 ft.; N41 57 48 W79 9 42
2 Orchard Rd., Jamestown, NY 14701 US
(716) 664-2313; *Fax:* (716) 488-1471
License: Russell, Warren County, PA held by Media One Group II LLC.
Group Owner: Media One Group; (acq 5-31-2005; grpsl).
Nat'l Reps: Dome
Format: Classic Rock; *Target Audience:* 25-54.
Jeff Storey, General Manager
Jim Yezzi, General Sales Mgr
Andrew Hill, Programming Director

Saegertown

WUZZ
01-19-1979; 94.3 MHz FM; 2.15 kw; 551 ft.; N41 37 53 W80 10 37
Mailing Address: 900 Water St., Downtown Mall, Meadville, PA 16335 US
Second Address: 1243 Liberty St., Suite 501, Franklin, PA 16323
(814) 724-1111; *Fax:* (814) 333-9628
www.mywuzz.com
License: Saegertown, Crawford County, PA held by FM Radio Licenses LLC
Group Owner: Forever Broadcasting; (acq 7-20-2000; grpsl)
Arbitron Metro Market: Meadville-Franklin, PA; *Format:* Classic Rock
Jim Shields, General Manager
Helen Powers, Sales Manager
Rich Anton, Programming Director
Mike Himmler, Chief Engineer
Jill Hamilton, Business Manager

Salladasburg

WBYL
01-01-1989; 95.5 MHz FM; 3.9 kw; 240 ft.; N41 14 0 W77 12 10
1559 W. 4th St., Williamsport, PA 17701 US
(570) 327-1400; *Fax:* (570) 327-8156
www.bill95.com
bill@billcountry.com
License: Salladasburg, Lycoming County, PA held by Clear Channel Broadcasting Licenses Inc.
Group Owner: iHeartMedia; (acq 8-5-98; grpsl)
Arbitron Metro Market: Williamsport, PA; *Format:* Country; *Hrs. of News Programming:* news progmg 4 hrs wkly; *No. News Employees:* 1; *Target Audience:* 35 plus.

Jeff Hurley, Regional Program Manager

Sayre

WATS
06-01-1950; 960 kHz AM; 5 kw-D, ND1; 0.05 kw-N, ND1; N41 59 48 W76 30 3 *Rebroadcasts:* Rebroadcasts WAVR-FM Waverly, NY 100%
204 Desmond Street, Sayre, PA 18840 US
(570) 888-7745; *Fax:* (570) 888-9005
wats.wavr@cqservices.com
License: Sayre, PA held by WATS Broadcasting Inc.
Arbitron Metro Market: Sayre, PA.; *Format:* Adult Contemp
Special Programming: Farm one hr wkly; *Target Audience:* 25-54.; *Adv. Rates:* 21; 16; 20; 12
Charles Carver Jr., President

Schnecksville

***WLHI**
09-23-1983; 90.3 MHz FM; *Hrs Open:* 24; 0.42 kw; 230 ft.; N40 39 43 W75 36 41
4525 Education Park Dr, Schnecksville, PA 18078 US
(610) 799-4141; *Fax:* (610) 799-1571
www.wordfm.org
License: Schnecksville, Lehigh County, PA held by Four Rivers Community Broadcasting Corp.
Group Owner: Four Rivers Community Broadcasting Corp.
Arbitron Metro Market: Schnecksville, PA; *Format:* Triple A
Special Programming: Country, Bluegrass, Rock; *Target Audience:* General.; *Adv. Rates:* 25; 20; 15
Burr Beard, Programming Director
Chris Andrew, Contact Person

Scottdale

WLSW
12-21-1971; 103.9 MHz FM; *Hrs Open:* 24; 0.32 kw; 781 ft.; N40 0 51 W79 31 1
R.D.#7, Box 56, Greensburg, PA 15601 US
(724) 628-2800; *Fax:* (724) 628-7380
www.musicpower104.com/
License: Scottdale, Westmoreland County, PA held by Wall Broadcasting.
Nat'l Network: Westwood One
Arbitron Metro Market: Pittsburgh, PA; *Format:* Adult Contemp, Oldies; *Target Audience:* 25-54; general
L. Stanley Wall, President
Chris Molton, General Manager
Debbie Larson, Programming Director
Connie LaPorte, News Director
Jerry Braveman, Disc Jockey
Charlie Apple, Disc Jockey
Jeff Allen, Disc Jockey
Jamie Allen, DiscJockey

Scranton

WARM
01-01-1940; 590 kHz AM; *Hrs Open:* 24; 5 kw-D, DA2; 5 kw-N, DA2; N41 28 44 W75 52 51
600 Baltimore Dr., Wilkes-Barre, PA 18702 US
(570) 824-9000; *Fax:* (570) 820-0520
www.sportsradio590am.com
License: Scranton, PA held by Radio License Holding CBC, LLC
Group Owner: Cumulus Media Inc.; (acq 7-1-97; grpsl).
Nat'l Network: ABC
Arbitron Metro Market: Scranton, PA; *Format:* Sports *Special Programming:* Sinatra, 2 hrs wkly; *Hrs. of News Programming:* news progmg 1 hrs wkly; *No. News Employees:* 1; *Target Audience:* 35 plus. *Adv.Rates:* 15; 15; 15; 15
Shannon Spak, General Sales Mgr
Stan Phillips, Programming Director
Erin Evans, Promotions Manager
Gerald Getz, Market Mgr

WEJL
11-29-1922; 630 kHz AM *Rebroadcasts:* Rebroadcasts WBAX(AM) Wilkes Barre 100%
149 Penn. Avenue, Scranton, PA 18503 US
(570) 207-8599; *Fax:* (570) 346-6038
www.wejl-wbax.com
License: Scranton, PA held by The Scranton Times LP.
Group Owner: The Scranton Times L.P.; (acq 1922).
Arbitron Metro Market: Scranton, PA; *Format:* Sports
William Lynett, CEO
Tim Durkin, General Sales Mgr
Michael Neff, Programming Director
Mark Hoover, Promotions Manager
Ruth Miller, News Director
Kevin Fitzgerald, Chief Engineer

Jim Loftus, COO
Jenny Arndt, National SalesManager
Krista Saar, Traffic Manager

WEZX
11-01-1967; 106.9 MHz FM; 1.45 kw; 617 ft; N41 20 52 W75 39 03
149 Penn Ave., Scranton, PA 18503
(570) 346-6555; *Fax:* (570) 346-6038
License: Scranton, Lackawanna County, PA
Group Owner: The Scranton Times L.P.; (Acq 1967).
Population Served: 103,564; *Arbitron Metro Market:* Wilkes Barre-Scranton, PA
Sean O'Mealy, General Manager
Scott Laudani, Station Manager
Dave Mehall, General Sales Mgr
Scott Laudani, Programming Director
Mark Hoover, Promotions Manager
Kevin Fritzgerald, Engineering Dir

WBZU
01-12-1925; 910 kHz AM; *Hrs Open:* 24 *Rebroadcasts:* Rebroadcasts WILK(AM) Wilkes Barre 100%
305 Highway 315, Pittston, PA 18640 US
(570) 883-9850; *Fax:* (570) 883-0832
www.wilknewsradio.com
info@wilknewsradio.com
License: Scranton, PA held by Entercom Scranton Wilkes-Barre License LLC.
Group Owner: Entercom Communications Corp.; (acq 12-16-99; grpsl).
Nat'l Reps: D & R Radio; *Wire Services:* ABC; AP; Metro Weather Service Inc.
Arbitron Metro Market: Wilkes Barre-Scranton, PA; *Format:* News, News/Talk, 86 *Special Programming:* Relg one hr wkly; *Hrs. of News Programming:* news progmg 25 hrs wkly; *No. News Employees:* 6; *Target Audience:* 25-54; affluent, educated
Mike O'Donnell, Operations Dir
Ryan Adcock, General Sales Mgr
Nancy Kman, Programming Director
Sara Baggerman, Promotions Manager
Joe Thomas, News Director
Lamar Smith, Chief Engineer
Shannon Ball, Traffic Manager

WGGY
12-25-1948; 101.3 MHz FM; 7 kw; 1198 ft.; N41 25 38 W75 44 53
305 Highway 315, Pittston, PA 18640 US
(570) 883-1111; *Fax:* (570) 883-1360
www.froggy101.com
License: Scranton, Lackawanna County, PA
Group Owner: Entercom Communications Corp.
Nat'l Network: CBS; *Nat'l Reps:* Interep
Arbitron Metro Market: Wilkes Barre-Scranton, PA; *Format:* Country
Mike O'Donnell, Operations Dir
Ryan Adcock, General Sales Mgr
Sara Baggerman, Promotions Manager

WICK
04-17-1954; 1400 kHz AM; *Hrs Open:* 24; 1 kw-U, ND1; N41 25 5 W75 39 43
1049 N. Sekol Rd., Scranton, PA 18504 US
(570) 344-1221; *Fax:* (570) 344-0996
boldgoldradionepa.com
License: Scranton, PA held by Bold Gold Media WBS L.P.
Group Owner: Bold Gold Media Group LP; (acq 3-13-2006; grpsl)
Nat'l Network: Fox Sports
Arbitron Metro Market: Wilkes Barre-Scranton, PA; *Format:* Sports *Special Programming:* Relg 3 hrs, Pol 3 hrs wkly; *Hrs. of News Programming:* news progmg 8 hrs wkly; *No. News Employees:* 2 *Target Audience:* 35-64; adults who love original hits of Top 40 Era
Michael G. Stanton, General Manager

***WUSR**
02-27-1993; 99.5 MHz FM; *Hrs Open:* 11 AM-2 AM; 0.3 kw; 1014 ft.; N41 26 9 W75 43 33
St. Thomas Hall, Scranton, PA 18510 US
(570) 941-7648; *Fax:* (570) 941-4628
www.scranton.edu/wusr
License: Scranton, Lackawanna County, PA held by University of Scranton.
Wire Services: Metro Weather Service Inc.
Arbitron Metro Market: Scranton, PA; *Format:* Alternative, Blues, 52, Rock/AOR *Special Programming:* Class 5 hrs, relg 4 hrs, loud rock 8 hrs, urban co; *No. News Employees:* 1; *Target Audience:* General.
Ken Sandrowicz, General Manager
Gina Staller, Station Manager
John Niemiec, News Director

Katie Goodwin, Alternative Directorÿ
Matt Tarantino, Technology Directorÿ

***WVIA-FM**
04-23-1973; 89.9 MHz FM; *Hrs Open:* 24; 7.4 kw; 1250 ft.; N41 10 55 W75 52 17
70 Old Boston Rd., Pittston, PA 18640 US
(570) 826-6144; *Fax:* (570) 655-1180
www.wvia.org
License: Scranton, Lackawanna County, PA held by N.E. Pa. Educational TV Association.
Nat'l Network: NPR; PRI; *Regional Network:* Pennsylvania Public Television Network
Arbitron Metro Market: Scranton, PA *TV Affiliate:* *WVIA-TV affil.; *Format:* Jazz, News; *Hrs. of News Programming:* News progmg 31 hrs wkly; *Target Audience:* General.
A. William Kelly, CEO
Chris Norton, VP
George Graham, Programming Director
Joseph Glynn, Engineering Dir
Joe Glynn, Engineering Dir
Tom Curra, Executive Vice President & Executive Producer
Andrea O'Neill, Director of Education

***WVMW-FM**
09-01-1974; 91.7 MHz FM; *Hrs Open:* 14; 2 kw; -285 ft.; N41 25 57 W75 38 6
2300 Adams Avenue, Scranton, PA 18509 US
(570) 348-6202; *Fax:* (570) 961-4769
www.vmfm917.com
staff@vmfm917.org
License: Scranton, Lackawanna County, PA held by Marywood College.
Arbitron Metro Market: Scranton, PA; *Format:* Alternative *Special Programming:* Black 2 hrs, class 7 hrs, jazz 10 hrs wkly; *Hrs. of News Programming:* news progmg 7 hrs wkly; *No. News Employees:* 2 *TargetAudience:* 15-25; young adults
Earnest Mengoni, Station Manager
George D. Graham, Chief Engineer

WWRR
11-26-1964; 104.9 MHz FM; *Hrs Open:* 24; 0.27 kw; 1093 ft.; N41 26 6 W75 43 35
1049 N. Sekol Rd., Scranton, PA 18504 US
(570) 344-1221; *Fax:* (570) 344-0996
www.boldgoldradionepa.com
License: Scranton, Lackawanna County, PA held by Bold Gold Media WBS L.P.
Group Owner: Bold Gold Media Group LP
Arbitron Metro Market: Wilkes Barre, PA; *Format:* Contemporary Hits/Top 40, Adult Contemp; *Hrs. of News Programming:* news progmg 8 hrs wkly; *No. News Employees:* 1; *Target Audience:* 25-54; men & women

Selinsgrove

***WQSU**
09-01-1967; 88.9 MHz FM; *Hrs Open:* 24; 12 kw; 620 ft.; N40 57 6 W76 45 3
514 University Ave, Selinsgrove, PA 17870 US
(570) 372-4030; *Fax:* (570) 372-2757
www.wqsu.com
augustin@susqu.edu
License: Selinsgrove, Snyder County, PA held by Susquehanna University.
Nat'l Network: AP Radio; *Wire Services:* AP
Arbitron Metro Market: Sunbury-Selinsgrove-Lewisburg, PA; *Format:* Rock/AOR *Special Programming:* Classic country 6 hrs, sports 4 hrs, bluegrass 7 hrs wkly; *Hrs. of News Programming:* News progmg 7 hrs wkly *TargetAudience:* 18-34.
Larry Augustine, General Manager
Patricia Wendt, News Director
Harry Bingaman, Chief Engineer

Sellersville

***WBYO**
03-01-1991; 88.9 MHz FM; *Hrs Open:* 24; 900 w; Ant 436 ft; N40 23 02 W75 21 02
Box 186, Sellersville, PA 18960
(215) 721-2141; *Fax:* (215) 721-9811
www.wordfm.org
wordfm@wordfm.org
License: Sellersville, Bucks County, PA held by Four Rivers Community Broadcasting Corp.
Group Owner: Four Rivers Community Broadcasting Corp.
Population Served: 300,000 *Special Programming:* Country gospel 2 hrs, gospel bluegrass 2 hrs wkly; *Hrs. of News Programming:* news progmg 10 hrs wkly; *No. News Employees:* 1; *Target Audience:* General.
Charles Loughery, President
Meg Sabulsky, Operations Dir

David Baker, General Manager
Meg Sabulsky, Programming Director
William Dunn, Promotions Manager
Charles Loughery, Engineering Dir

Shamokin

WBLJ-FM
01-01-1968; 95.3 MHz FM; 1.25 kw; 505 ft.; N40 45 36 W76 32 19 *Rebroadcasts:* Rebroadcasts WBYL(FM) Salladasburg 100%
1559 West 4th St., Williamsport, PA 17701 US
(570) 327-1400; *Fax:* (570) 327-8156
www.billcountry.com
bill@billcountry.com
License: Shamokin, Northumberland County, PA held by Clear Channel Broadcasting Licenses Inc.
Group Owner: iHeartMedia; (acq 10-4-01; $800,000 with co-located AM).
Format: Country
Richard J. Bressler, President

Sharon

WPIC
10-25-1938; 790 kHz AM; *Hrs Open:* 24
2030 Pine Hollow Blvd., Hermitage, PA 16148 US
(724) 346-4113; *Fax:* (724) 981-4545
License: Sharon, PA held by Cumulus Licensing Corp.
Group Owner: Cumulus Media Inc.; (acq 3-15-00; grpsl).
Nat'l Network: ABC; Jones Radio Networks; Talk Radio Network; Westwood One
Arbitron Metro Market: Youngstown-Warren, OH; *Format:* News, News/Talk, 86 *Special Programming:* Pol 3 hrs, lt 2 hrs, relg 2 hrs, infomercials 12 hrs wkly; *No. News Employees:* 1; *Target Audience:* 35 plus.
Bob Greenburg, General Sales Mgr
Wes Boyd, Chief Engineer

WYFM
10-25-1947; 102.9 MHz FM; 33 kw; 604 ft.; N41 03 26 W80 38 22
4040 Simon Rd., Youngstown, OH 44515 US
(330) 783-1000; *Fax:* (330) 783-0060
www.y-103.com
Win@y-103.com
License: Sharon, PA held by Cumulus Licensing LLC
Group Owner: Cumulus Media Inc.
Arbitron Metro Market: Sharon, PA; *Format:* Classic Rock; *Target Audience:* 25-54.
Matt Spatz, Programming Director

Sharpsville

WAKZ
12-28-1976; 95.9 MHz FM; 6 kw; 328 ft.; N41 13 5 W80 33 43
7461 South Avenue, Youngstown, OH 44512 US
(330) 965-0057; *Fax:* (330) 729-9991
www.959kiss.com
License: Sharpsville, Mercer County, PA held by Citicasters Licenses Inc.
Group Owner: iHeartMedia; (acq 1-15-2004; grpsl).
Arbitron Metro Market: Youngstown, OH; *Format:* Contemporary Hits/Top 40
Bill Kelly, Regional President
Steve Granato, Senior Vice President of Programming
Bob Hotchkiss, Sales Manager
Thomas John, Digital Content Director
Lindsay Watts, Digital Sales Coordinator
Jim Davis, Regional Senior VicePresident of Programming

Shenandoah

***WCIM**
01-01-2008; 91.5 MHz FM; 1.2 kw; 719 ft.; N40 50 58 W76 6 55 *Rebroadcasts:* Rebroadcasts WCIK(FM) Bath, NY 100%
Box 506, Bath, NY 14810 US
(607) 776-4151
www.fln.org
License: Shenandoah, Schuylkill County, PA held by Family Life Ministries Inc.
Group Owner: Family Life Network; (acq 7-24-2007; $800,000 for CP)
Arbitron Metro Market: Texarkana, TX-AR; *Format:* Christian
Dave Margalotti, Operations Dir
Terese Main, Programming Director
Bob Price, News Director

Shippensburg

WEEO
12-05-1961; 1480 kHz AM; *Hrs Open:* 6 AM-10 PM; 0.46 kw-D, ND1; 0.009 kw-N, ND1; N40 4 30 W77 32 9

601 Fifth Street, Tyrone, PA 16686 US
(717) 697-4297; *Fax:* (717) 243-1277
wioo.com
License: Shippensburg, PA held by Shippensburg Broadcasting Inc.
Regional Network: Radio Pa.
Arbitron Metro Market: Harrisburg-Leba; *Format:* Country; *Target Audience:* 30 plus.; *Adv. Rates:* 10; 10; 10; 10
Eric Swidler, President
Eric Swidler, Operations Dir
Sandy Loy, General Manager
Sandy Loy, Station Manager
Ray Thomas, Programming Director
Matthew Becker, Promotions Manager

***WSYC-FM**
02-01-1975; 88.7 MHz FM; *Hrs Open:* 24; 0.13 kw; -154 ft.; N40 4 30 W77 31 15
Prince Street, Shippensburg, PA 17257 US
(717) 532-6006; *Fax:* (717) 477-4024
www.wsyc.org
License: Shippensburg, Cumberland County, PA held by Shippensburg University.
Nat'l Network: Westwood One
Format: Variety/Diverse *Special Programming:* Black 9 hrs, class 2 hrs, jazz 3 hrs, blues 2 hrs, wkly; *Hrs. of News Programming:* news progmg 3 hrs wkly; *No. News Employees:* 7; *Target Audience:* 16-25; college &area high school students
Travis Hunt, Operations Dir
Sage Ober, General Manager
Jospeh Borreu, General Sales Mgr
Jim Shaffer, Programming Director
Jeff Hollinshead, Chief Engineer
Michael Gardner, Broadcasting Director

Shiremanstown

WHYF(AM)
06-01-1987; 720 kHz AM; *Hrs Open:* 6 AM-sunset; 2 kw-D; N40 11 28 W76 57 09
8 W. Main St., Shiremanstown, PA 17011
(717) 525-8110; *Fax:* (717) 731-4002
License: Shiremanstown, Cumberland County, PA held by Hensley Broadcasting.
Population Served: 49,673; *Arbitron Metro Market:* Harrisburg, PA; *Format:* Christian *Special Programming:* Gospel 2 hrs, polka 7 hrs, Indian one hr, blues 4; *Hrs. of News Programming:* News progmg 2 hrs wkly *Target Audience:* 25 plus; Christian
Joe Green, General Manager
Tom Sullivan, Programming Director

Slippery Rock

***WSRU**
09-20-1991; 88.1 MHz FM; *Hrs Open:* 14; 0.1 kw; 79 ft.; N41 3 43 W80 2 35
211 University Union Bld, Slippery Rock, PA 16057 US
(724) 738-2655,(724) 738-2931; *Fax:* (724) 738-2754
rockradio@hotmail.com
License: Slippery Rock, Butler County, PA held by Slippery Rock University.
Nat'l Network: ABC
Format: Classic Rock, Variety/Diverse *Special Programming:* Relg one hr, campus info one hr, sports one hr wkly; *Hrs. of News Programming:* news progmg 14 hrs wkly; *No. News Employees:* 1; *Target Audience:* 18-24;on & off campus students
Sean Lohrer, General Manager
Paul Joseph, Programming Director
Jami LoAlbo, Promotions Manager
Jason Fialkovich, News Director
Werner Ullrich, Chief Engineer
Sara Faletti, Music Director
Matt Miller, Sports Commentator

Smethport

WXMT
01-01-1990; 106.3 MHz FM; *Hrs Open:* 24; 1.03 kw; 788 ft.; N41 48 36 W78 23 10
211 W. Main St., Smethport, PA 16749 US
(814) 837-9564; *Fax:* (814) 975-1098
www.colonial.cc/rockwithoutthehardedge/
License: Smethport, McKean County, PA held by Colonial Radio Group Inc.
Format: Classic Rock; *Target Audience:* Men.
Jeffrey Andrulonis, President

Somerset

WLKH
06-15-1966; 97.7 MHz FM; *Hrs Open:* 24; 3.5 kw; 430 ft.; N40 1 32 W79 5 44
One Forever Drive, Hollidaysburg, PA 16648 US
(814) 534-8975; *Fax:* (814) 534-8979
www.klove.com
info@klove.com
License: Somerset, Somerset County, PA held by 2510 Licenses LLC.
Group Owner: 2510 Licenses LLC; (acq 5-1-2005; grpsl)
Nat'l Network: K-Love
Format: Religious
Darrell Chambliss, Chairman
Alan Mason, COO
Mike Novak, President
Nick Ferrara, Operations Dir

WLLI
990 kHz AM; 10 kw-D, DA2; 0.1 kw-N, DA2; N40 1 31 W79 5 42
109 Plaza Dr., Johnstown, PA 15905 US
(814) 255-4186; *Fax:* (814) 255-6145
License: Somerset, Somerset County, PA held by FM Radio Licenses LLC
Group Owner: Forever Broadcasting
Arbitron Metro Market: Johnstown, PA; *Format:* Sports
Mike Stevens, Operations Dir
Terry Deitz, General Manager
Tina Perry, Sales Manager
Mitch Edwards, Programming Director
Sean Glenn, Chief Engineer
Shelly Lovenduski, Business Manager
Al Steele, Production Director
George Lucas,Copywriter
Theresa Jarosick, Traffic
Beth Thomas, Traffic/EEO Officer

South Waverly

WPHD
01-01-2003; 96.1 MHz FM; *Hrs Open:* 24; 1.8 kw; 613 ft.; N42 1 54.7 W76 47 2.2
Mailing Address: 583 Long Creek Road, Apalachin, NY 13732 US
Second Address: 495 Court St., 2nd Fl., Binghamton, PA 13904
(607) 795-0795; *Fax:* (607) 795-1095
www.cool96.coolesthits.com
themetrocks@aol.com
License: South Waverly, Bradford County, PA held by Fitzgerald and Hawras Partnership
Nat'l Reps: Katz Radio
Arbitron Metro Market: Elmira-Corning, NY; *Format:* Oldies; *Target Audience:* 35-64; adults; *Adv. Rates:* 15; 15; 15; 10
Kevin Fitzgerald, Operations Dir
George Hawras, General Manager
Bob Smith, Station Manager
April Emerson, General Sales Mgr
Dave Paltrowitz, Promotions Manager
Steve Shimer, Operations Manager
Mina Smallacombe, BusinessManager
Trisha Philip, Office Manager
Kyle Mills, Assistant Promotions Director
Josh Evans, Sales

South Williamsport

WZXR
06-01-1968; 99.3 MHz FM; 0.41 kw; 1237 ft.; N41 12 42 W76 57 16
1685 Four Mile Dr, Williamsport, PA 17701 US
(570) 323-8200; *Fax:* (570) 323-5075
www.wzxr.com
License: South Williamsport, Lycoming County, PA held by Backyard Broadcasting PA, LLC
Group Owner: Backyard Broadcasting LLC; (acq 12-1-02; grpsl).
Nat'l Network: ABC
Population Served: 40,000; *Arbitron Metro Market:* Williamsport, PA; *Format:* Classic Rock, Rock/AOR; *Hrs. of News Programming:* news progmg 7 hrs wkly; *No. News Employees:* 3; *Target Audience:* 25-54. *Adv.Rates:* 30; 30; 30; 20
Dan Farr, President & CEO
Gerald Getz, General Sales Mgr
Ted Minier, Programming Director
John Finn, News Director
Kelly Bailey, Production Director

St. Marys

WKBI
07-23-1950; 1400 kHz AM; *Hrs Open:* 24; 1 kw-U, ND1; N41 24 56 W78 33 56
14902 Boot Jack Rd., P.O. Box O, Ridgway, PA 15853 US
(814) 772-9700; *Fax:* (814) 772-9750
www.wkbiradio.com
License: St. Marys, Elk County, PA held by Laurel Media Inc.
Group Owner: Laurel Media Inc.
Nat'l Network: Westwood One; *Regional Network:* Allegheny Mtn. Net; *Nat'l Reps:* Dome
Format: Adult Contemp; *Hrs. of News Programming:* news progmg 10 hrs wkly; *No. News Employees:* 1; *Target Audience:* 35-55.
Dennis Heindl, President

WKBI-FM
08-01-1966; 93.9 MHz FM; *Hrs Open:* 24; 2.35 kw; 801 ft.; N41 23 11 W78 41 32
14902 Boot Jack Rd., P.O. Box O, Ridgway, PA 15853 US
(814) 772-9700; *Fax:* (814) 772-9750
www.wkbiradio.com
License: St. Marys, Elk County, PA held by Laurel Media Inc.
Group Owner: Laurel Media Inc.
Nat'l Network: Westwood One; Jones Radio Networks
Format: Adult Contemp *Special Programming:* Relg 2 hrs wkly; *Target Audience:* General; young adults
Dennis Heindl, President

WDDH
04-22-1986; 97.5 MHz FM; *Hrs Open:* 24; 19.5 kw; 801 ft.; N41 37 4 W78 48 14
P.O. Box 623, Ridgway, PA 15853 US
(814) 772-9700; *Fax:* (814) 772-9750
www.houndcountry.com
License: St. Marys, Elk County, PA held by Laurel Media Inc.
Group Owner: Laurel Media Inc.; (acq 5-2008)
Nat'l Network: Jones Radio Networks; *Nat'l Reps:* Rgnl Reps
Regional Reps: Dome & AssociatesCommercial Media S
Arbitron Metro Market: State College, PA; *Format:* Country; *Target Audience:* 25-54.; *Adv. Rates:* 16; 14; 16; 13
Dennis Heindl, President
Becky Towne, Station Manager

State College

WBHV-FM
10-23-1991; 94.5 MHz FM; 1.9 kw; 587 ft.; N40 54 4 W77 50 20
One Forever Drive, Hollidaysburg, PA 16648 US
(814) 238-5085; *Fax:* (814) 238-7932
www.b945live.com
B945LIVE@gmail.com
License: State College, Centre County, PA held by 2510 Licenses LLC.
Group Owner: 2510 Licenses LLC; (acq 2-1-2006; $1.2 million)
Nat'l Reps: Christal
Arbitron Metro Market: State College, PA; *Format:* Christian
Nick Ferrara, General Manager
PJ Mullen, Programming Director
Chris Bickel, Assistant Program Director

WFGE
08-15-1961; 101.1 MHz FM; *Hrs Open:* 24; 8.5 kw; 1171 ft.; N40 55 10 W77 58 28
2551 Park Center Blvd., State College, PA 16801 US
(814) 237-9800; *Fax:* (814) 237-2477
www.bigfroggy101.com
License: State College, Centre County, PA held by FM Radio Licenses LLC
Group Owner: Forever Broadcasting; (acq 7-2-2008; $2.5 million)
Arbitron Metro Market: State College, PA; *Format:* Country; *Target Audience:* 25-54; adults
Scott Cohagan, General Manager
Wendy Lynch, General Sales Mgr
Chris Prospero, Programming Director
Robert Taylor, Chief Engineer
Bobbi Jo Clifford, Business Manager
Linda McCutcheon, Traffic Director
Lucas Bubb, ProductionCoordinator

***WKPS**
01-01-1995; 90.7 MHz FM; *Hrs Open:* 24; 0.1 kw; 85 ft.; N40 47 58 W77 52 11
202 Wagner Building, University Park, PA 16802 US
(814) 865-7983; *Fax:* (814) 865-2751
www.thelion.fm
License: State College, Centre County, PA held by Board of Trustees of Pennsylvania State University.
Arbitron Metro Market: State College, PA; *Format:* Variety/Diverse *Special Programming:* Jazz 11 hrs, Sp 8 hrs wkly; *Hrs. of News Programming:* News progmg 4 hrs wkly; *Target Audience:* University students.
Tom Shakely, Operations Dir
Brandon Peach, General Manager
Tristan Vaughan, Operations Director

WQWK
01-01-1945; 1450 kHz AM; *Hrs Open:* 24; 1 kw-U, ND1; N40 48 32 W77 50 28
2551 Park Center Blvd., State College, PA 16801

(814) 237-9800; *Fax:* (814) 237-2477
www.1450espnradio.com
License: State College, Centre County, PA held by FM Radio Licenses LLC
Group Owner: Forever Broadcasting; (acq 3-10-98; $2.9 million with co-located FM).
Nat'l Network: ESPN Radio; *Regional Network:* Radio Pa; *Nat'l Reps:* Christal; *Wire Services:* The Sports Network
Population Served: 110,000; *Arbitron Metro Market:* State College, PA; *Format:* Sports; *Target Audience:* 30 plus; college educated, upscale

Scott Cohagan, General Manager
Wendy Lynch, General Sales Mgr
Robert Taylor, Programming Director
Robert Taylor, Chief Engineer
Bobbi Jo Clifford, Business Manager
Linda McCutcheon, Traffic Director
Lucas Bubb, ProductionCoordinator

***WPSU**
12-06-1953; 91.5 MHz FM; *Hrs Open:* 24; 1.7 kw; Ant 1,197 ft; N40 48 32 W77 50 28
174 Outreach Bldg, University Park, PA 16802
(814) 865-1877; *Fax:* (814) 865-4043
www.wpsu.org
wpsu@psu.edu
License: State College, Centre County, PA held by Pennsylvania State University.
Nat'l Network: PRI; NPR; *Wire Services:* AP
Population Served: 100,000; *Arbitron Metro Market:* State College, PA *Special Programming:* Folk 10, jazz 3 hrs, blues 2 hrs wkly; *Hrs. of News Programming:* news progmg 35 hrs wkly; *No. News Employees:* 1 *TargetAudience:* General; upscale, educated adults

Craig Johnsoqn, Operations Dir
Ted Krichels, General Manager
Greg Petersen, Station Manager
Tom Yourchak, General Sales Mgr
Kristine Allen, Programming Director
Emily Ready, News Director
Russ Rockwell, Chief Engineer
BillHiergeist, Regional Sales Manager
Sam Komlenic, Regional Sales Manager

WRSC
05-29-1961; 1390 kHz AM; 2 kw-D, DAN; 1 kw-N, DAN; N40 48 30 W77 56 32
2551 Park Center Blvd., State College, PA 16801 US
(814) 237-9800; *Fax:* (814) 237-2477
www.wrscfm.com
License: State College, Centre County, PA held by FM Radio Licenses LLC
Group Owner: Forever Broadcasting; (acq 5-1-2005; $2.65 million with WBUS(FM) Boalsburg)
Arbitron Metro Market: State College, PA; *Format:* News, News/Talk, 86

Scott Cohagan, General Manager
Wendy Lynch, General Sales Mgr
Robert Taylor, Chief Engineer
Bobbi Jo Clifford, Business Manager
Linda McCutcheon, Traffic Director
Lucas Bubb, Production Coordinator

***WTLR**
01-01-1978; 89.9 MHz FM; *Hrs Open:* 24; 25 kw; 584 ft.; N40 53 32 W77 51 49
2020 Cato Avenue, State College, PA 16801 US
(814) 237-9857
www.cpci.org
info@wtlr.org
License: State College, Centre County, PA held by Central Pennsylvania Christian Institute Inc.
Wire Services: AP
Arbitron Metro Market: State College, PA; *Format:* Christian; *Hrs. of News Programming:* news progmg 9 hrs wkly; *No. News Employees:* 1; *Target Audience:* 30-55; Adults, family oriented

Mark Van Ouse, General Manager
Dean Christian, Station Manager
Tom Betz, Production Coordinator
Chryss Griffin, Business Manager

***WRXV**
06-18-2004; 89.1 MHz FM; *Hrs Open:* 24; 0.001 kw horiz, 4.4 kw vert; 1099 ft.; N40 43 56 W78 19 33
1313 Valley View Road, Bellefonte, PA 16823 US
(814) 867-3836; *Fax:* (814) 867-1922
www.revfm.net
info@revfm.net
License: State College, Centre County, PA held by Invisible Allies Ministries.
Arbitron Metro Market: State College, PA; *Format:* Christian

Michael Schomer, General Manager
Erik Lane, Station Manager
Jim Schomer, Chief Engineer

***WKDN-FM**
01-01-2008; 88.3 MHz FM; *Hrs Open:* 24; 10 w horiz, 1.8 kw vert; Ant 686 ft; N40 53 35 W77 51 48 *Rebroadcasts:* Rebroadcasts WFSI(FM) Annapolis, MD 100%
918 Chesapeake Ave., Annapolis, MD 21403
(410) 268-6200; *Fax:* (410) 268-0931
www.familyradio.com
info@familyradio.org
License: State College, Centre County, PA held by Family Stations Inc.
Group Owner: Family Stations Inc.
Nat'l Network: Family Radio
Population Served: 10,706; *Arbitron Metro Market:* Vermillion, SD; *Format:* Religious

Harold Camping, President
W.A. Sadlier, Station Manager

WRSC-FM
103.1 MHz FM; 0.37 kw; N40 45 9 W77 45 15
2551 Park Center Blvd., State College, PA 16801 US
(814) 237-9800; *Fax:* (814) 237-2477
License: State College, Centre County, PA held by FM Radio Licenses LLC
Group Owner: Forever Broadcasting
Arbitron Metro Market: State College, PA; *Format:* Contemporary Hits/Top 40

Scott Cohagan, General Manager
Wendy Lynch, General Sales Mgr
Robert Taylor, Chief Engineer
Bobbi Jo Clifford, Business Manager
Linda McCutcheon, Traffic Director
Lucas Bubb, Production Coordinator

Stroudsburg

***WBYX**
10-01-1999; 88.7 MHz FM; *Hrs Open:* 24; 1 w horiz, 4 kw vert; Ant 794 ft; N41 02 40 W75 22 45 *Rebroadcasts:* Rebroadcasts WBYO(FM) Sellersville 100%
Box 186, Sellersville, PA 18960
(215) 721-2141; *Fax:* (215) 721-9811
www.wordfm.org
wordfm@wordfm.org
License: Stroudsburg, Monroe County, PA held by Four Rivers Community Broadcasting Corp.
Group Owner: Four Rivers Community Broadcasting Corp.
Nat'l Network: ABC
Special Programming: Bluegrass Gospel;; *Target Audience:* 25-45.

Charles Loughery, President
Meg Sabulsky, Operations Dir
David Baker, General Manager
Meg Sabulsky, Programming Director
William Dunn, Promotions Manager
Charles Loughery, Engineering Dir

WSBG
10-01-1964; 93.5 MHz FM; 0.55 kw; 764 ft.; N40 56 56 W75 9 29
22 South 6th St., Stroudsburg, PA 18360 US
(570) 421-2100; *Fax:* (570) 421-2040
info@lite935.com
License: Stroudsburg, Monroe County, PA held by Connoisseur Media Licenses LLC
Group Owner: Connoisseur Media LLC
Arbitron Metro Market: Wilkes Barre-Sc; *Format:* Easy Listening
Special Programming: Modern rock 3 hrs wkly; *Target Audience:* 20 plus.

David Meszaros, General Manager
Patrick Lincoln, General Sales Mgr
Rod Bauman, Programming Director

WVPO
01-01-1947; 840 kHz AM; 0.25 kw-D, NDD; N40 58 26 W75 11 43
22 South 6th St., Stroudsburg, PA 18630 US
(570) 421-2100; *Fax:* (570) 421-2040
info@lite935.com
License: Stroudsburg, PA held by Connoisseur Media Licenses LLC
Group Owner: Connoisseur Media LLC; (acq 2-15-02; grpsl).
Arbitron Metro Market: Stroudsburg, PA; *Format:* Talk; *Target Audience:* 35 plus.

Pat Lincoln, General Manager
Rod Bauman, Programming Director
Kyleen Waters, Promotions Manager
Mick Rapear, Engineering Dir
Becky Shevlin, Traffic Manager

Summerdale

***WJAZ**
01-10-1991; 91.7 MHz FM; *Hrs Open:* 24; 1 kw; 702 ft.; N40 18 20 W77 0 27 *Rebroadcasts:* Rebroadcasts WRTI(FM) Philadelphia 100%
Anneberg Hall (011-00), Philadelphia, PA 19122 US
(215) 204-8405; *Fax:* (215) 204-7027
www.wrti.org
comments@wrti.org
License: Summerdale, Cumberland County, PA held by Temple University of the Commonwealth System of Higher Education
Nat'l Network: NPR; *Wire Services:* AP
Format: Classical, Jazz; *Hrs. of News Programming:* news progmg 15 hrs wkly; *No. News Employees:* 1; *Target Audience:* 30-65.

Dave Conant, CEO
Tobias Poole, Operations Dir
Rick Torpey, General Sales Mgr
Jack Moore, Programming Director
Patty Prevost, Promotions Manager
Windsor Johnson, News Director
Jeff DePolo, Chief Engineer
Vic Scarpato, CFO
Porsche Blakey, Promotions Director

Sunbury

WKOK
01-01-1933; 1070 kHz AM; *Hrs Open:* 24
Mailing Address: P.O. Box 1070, Sunbury, PA 17801 US
Second Address: 1227 County Line Rd., Selinsgrove, PA 17870
(570) 286-5838; *Fax:* (570) 743-1605
www.wkok.com
License: Sunbury, PA held by Sunbury Broadcasting Corp.
Group Owner: Sunbury Broadcasting Corp.; (acq 5-33).
Nat'l Network: CBS; CNN Radio; Fox Sports; Wall Street; Westwood One; *Nat'l Reps:* Roslin *Regional Reps:* Dome.; *Wire Services:* AP; Accu-Weather
Format: News, News/Talk, 84, Talk; *Hrs. of News Programming:* news progmg 168 hrs wkly; *No. News Employees:* 4; *Target Audience:* 35-64.

Roger Haddon Jr., CEO
Kevin Herr, Operations Dir
Nicole Shelley, General Sales Mgr
Mark Lawrence, Programming Director
Sara Bartlett, News Director

WQKX
09-15-1948; 94.1 MHz FM; *Hrs Open:* 24; 16 kw; 879 ft.; N40 47 10 W76 41 49
Mailing Address: P.O. Box 1070, Sunbury, PA 17801 US
Second Address: 1227 County Line Rd., Selinsgrove, PA 17870
(570) 286-5838,(570) 743-1841; *Fax:* (570) 743-7837
www.wqkx.com
equest@wqkx.com
License: Sunbury, Northumberland County, PA
Group Owner: Sunbury Broadcasting Corp.
Nat'l Reps: Roslin *Regional Reps:* Dome; *Wire Services:* Accu-Weather; AP
Format: Adult Contemp; *Hrs. of News Programming:* news progmg 7 hrs wkly; *No. News Employees:* 4; *Target Audience:* 25-54.

Roger Haddon, Jr, CEO
Nicole Shelley, General Sales Mgr
Drew Kelly, Programming Director
Sara Bartlett, News Director
Rob Senter, Music Director

Susquehanna

WDRE
03-01-1995; 100.5 MHz FM; *Hrs Open:* 24; 1.6 kw; 643 ft.; N42 3 10 W75 42 7
1907 Darby Road, Havertown, PA 19083 US
(607) 772-1005; *Fax:* (607) 772-2945
cool100oldies@aol.com
License: Susquehanna, Susquehanna County, PA held by Equinox Broadcasting Corp.
Group Owner: Equinox Broadcasting Corp.
Nat'l Reps: Katz Radio
Arbitron Metro Market: Binghamton, NY; *Format:* Oldies *Special Programming:* Polish 5 hrs wkly; *Target Audience:* 35-64.; *Adv. Rates:* 23; 30; 22; 15

George Hawras, President

Swarthmore

***WSRN-FM**
12-31-1939; 91.5 MHz FM; 0.11 kw; 141 ft.; N39 54 18 W75 21 16
500 College Avenue, Swarthmore, PA 19081 US

(610) 328-8336,(610) 328-8335,(610) 328-8000
www.wsrnfm.org
License: Swarthmore, Delaware County, PA held by Swarthmore College.
Format: Variety/Diverse
Roger Shaw, General Manager

Sweet Valley

***WRGN**
10-15-1984; 88.1 MHz FM; *Hrs Open:* 24; 0.5 kw; 302 ft.; N41 17 54 W76 7 28
Rr #3, Hunlock Creek, PA 18621 US
(570) 477-3688; *Fax:* (570) 477-2310
www.wrgn.com
wrgn@epix.net
License: Sweet Valley, Luzerne County, PA held by Gospel Media Institute Inc.
Format: Religious
Burl Updyke, President
Shirley Updyke, Promotions Manager

Sykesville

WZDB
05-05-2009; 95.9 MHz FM; 1.5 kw; 643 ft.; N41 2 44.1 W78 42 11.8
801 E. Dubois Ave., DuBois, PA 15801 US
(814) 371-6100; *Fax:* (410) 822-0576
www.959zdb.com
License: Sykesville, Jefferson County, PA held by First Media Radio LLC.
Group Owner: First Media Radio LLC
Arbitron Metro Market: Sykesville, PA; *Format:* Classic Rock
Alex Kolobielski, CEO/President

Tafton

***WLKA**
01-01-2002; 88.3 MHz FM; 1.1 kw; 823 ft.; N41 32 37 W75 27 44
The Classical Network, 1200 Old Trenton Road, Trenton, NJ 08690 US
(800) 525-5683; *Fax:* (916) 251-1650
www.klove.com
klove@klove.com
License: Tafton, Pike County, PA held by Educational Media Foundation.
Group Owner: EMF Broadcasting; (acq 11-17-2006; $675,000)
Nat'l Network: K-Love
Arbitron Metro Market: Omaha, NE; *Format:* Christian; *No. News Employees:* 13
Darrell Chambliss, Chairman
Mlke Novak, President & CEO
Glenn Goodwin, Operations Dir
Laura Daniels, News Reporter
Tim Luttrell, News Reporter
Kenny Noble Cortes, News Reporter
Darren Vinson, News Reporter

Tamaqua

WMGH-FM
06-14-1965; 105.5 MHz FM; *Hrs Open:* 24; 1.4 kw; 486 ft.; N40 47 14 W76 1 59
Mailing Address: 1444 Hamilton St #606, Allentown, PA 18102 US
Second Address: P.O. Box D, Lansford, PA 18232
(570) 668-2992; *Fax:* (570) 645-2159
www.wmgh.com
wmgh@ptdprolog.net
License: Tamaqua, Schuylkill County, PA held by J-Systems Franchising Corp.
Group Owner: J-Systems Franchising Corp.; acq 2-28-87; $300,000;
Nat'l Network: Westwood One; ABC; USA; *Regional Network:* Radio Pa.
Arbitron Metro Market: Tamaqua, PA; *Format:* Adult Contemp
Special Programming: Oldies 7 hrs, polka 3 hrs wkly; *Target Audience:* 25-54; primary women, secondary adults; *Adv. Rates:* 45; 40; 45; 15
Harold Fulmer III, President
Christopher Fulmer, Operations Dir
Bill Lakatas, General Manager
Mark Marek, News Director
Joe Manjack, Chief Engineer
Kim Noel, Disc Jockey
Nicky Vee, Disc Jockey
Cheryl Lee, Disc Jockey

Tioga

WMTT
05-23-1991; 94.7 MHz FM; *Hrs Open:* 24; 12 kw; 482 ft.; N42 3 43 W77 21 38
Mailing Address: 53 Bridge Street, Suite 2, Corning, NY 14830 US
Second Address: 495 Court St., 2nd Fl, Binghamton, NY 13904
(607) 795-0795,(607) 772-1005; *Fax:* (607) 795-1095,(607) 772-2945
themetrocks@aol.com
License: Tioga, Tioga County, PA held by Europa Communications Inc.
Nat'l Reps: Katz Radio
Arbitron Metro Market: Elmira-Corning, NY; *Format:* Classic Rock, Rock/AOR; *Hrs. of News Programming:* News progmg 2 hrs wkly; *Target Audience:* 25-49.; *Adv. Rates:* 40; 55; 45; 35
Kevin Fitzgerald, Operations Dir
George Harris, General Manager
Robert Smith, Station Manager
Justin McGregor, Promotions Manager
Stephen Shimer, Operations Manager

Titusville

WTIV
11-27-1955; 1230 kHz AM; *Hrs Open:* 6 AM-midnight; 1 kw-D, ND2; 1 kw-N, ND2; N41 37 0 W79 41 32
Mailing Address: 900 Water St., Downtown Mall, Meadville, PA 16335 US
Second Address: 1243 Liberty St., Suite 501, Franklin, PA 16323
(814) 724-1111; *Fax:* (814) 333-9628
www.myantsnetwork.com
License: Titusville, Crawford County, PA held by FM Radio Licenses LLC
Group Owner: Forever Broadcasting; (acq 7-20-00; grpsl).
Regional Network: Radio Pa.
Arbitron Metro Market: Meadville-Franklin, PA; *Format:* News, News/Talk, 86; *Hrs. of News Programming:* News progmg 13 hrs wkly; *Target Audience:* 22-54; mixed; *Adv. Rates:* 18; 13; 18; 11
Jim Shields, General Manager
Helen Powers, Sales Manager
Andy Alm, Programming Director
Mark Himmler, Chief Engineer
Jill Hamilton, Business Manager

Tobyhanna

WKRF
01-15-1993; 107.9 MHz FM; *Hrs Open:* 24; 0.84 kw; 876 ft.; N41 2 37 W75 22 38 *Rebroadcasts:* Rebroadcasts WKRZ(FM) Wilkes-Barre 100%
305 Highway 315, Pittston, PA 18640 US
(570) 883-9858; *Fax:* (570) 883-9851
www.985krz.com
studio@985krz.com
License: Tobyhanna, Monroe County, PA held by Entercom Wilkes-Barre Scranton LLC.
Group Owner: Entercom Communications Corp.; (acq 5-11-00).
Nat'l Network: Jones Radio Networks
Arbitron Metro Market: Wilkes Barre-Scranton, PA; *Format:* Contemporary Hits/Top 40; *Hrs. of News Programming:* news progmg one hr wkly; *No. News Employees:* 1; *Target Audience:* 25-54.
Peter Rothfuss, General Sales Mgr
Mike O'Donnell, Programming Director
Joe Thomas, News Director
Jay Waggoner, Chief Engineer
Elizabeth Masich, Music Director
Bob Demono, National Sales Manager

Towanda

WTTC
01-01-1959; 1550 kHz AM; 0.5 kw-D, ND2; 0.004 kw-N, ND2; N41 45 55 W76 29 10
204 Desmond St., Sayre, PA 18840 US
(570) 888-7745; *Fax:* (570) 888-9005
License: Towanda, PA held by WATS Broadcasting Inc.
Nat'l Network: Motor Racing Net
Arbitron Metro Market: Sayre, PA; *Format:* Oldies; *Target Audience:* General.; *Adv. Rates:* 16; 12; 13; 11
Charles Carver Jr., President
Meade Murtland, Station Manager

WTTC-FM
11-01-1959; 95.3 MHz FM; *Hrs Open:* 6 AM-11 PM; 5.4 kw; 125 ft.; N41 45 55 W76 29 10
204 Desmond St., Sayre, PA 18840 US
(570) 265-9530
www.953thebridge.com
whgl100@gmail.com
License: Towanda, Bradford County, PA
Arbitron Metro Market: Towanda, PA; *Format:* Contemporary Hits/Top 40, Adult Contemp
Joel Clawson, General Sales Mgr

WVYS-FM2
01-01-1991; 96.9 MHz FM; *Hrs Open:* 24; 1.2 kw; N41 47 33 W76 26 3.60 *Rebroadcasts:* Repeater for WVYS (FM)
54 Wilmar Dr., P.O. Box 701, Tunkhannock, PA 18657 US
(570) 265-7600; *Fax:* (570) 265-7603
www.iloveyesfm.com
comments@iloveyesfm.com
License: Towanda, PA held by Geos Communications
Group Owner: Geos Communications
Arbitron Metro Market: Elmira-Corning, NY; *Format:* Adult Contemp; *Target Audience:* 25-44

Trout Run

***WCIT-FM**
01-01-2001; 90.1 MHz FM; 0.35 kw; 295 ft.; N41 27 26 W77 6 55 *Rebroadcasts:* Rebroadcasts WCIK(FM) Bath, NY 100%
Mailing Address: PO Box 506, Bath, NY 14810 US
Second Address: 7634 Campbell Creek Rd., Bath, NY 14810
(607) 776-4151
www.fln.org
License: Trout Run, Lycoming County, PA held by Family Life Ministries Inc.
Group Owner: Family Life Network
Nat'l Network: Salem Radio Network; *Wire Services:* Metro Weather Service Inc.
Arbitron Metro Market: Bath, NY; *Format:* Christian; *Hrs. of News Programming:* news progmg 14 hrs wkly; *No. News Employees:* 3; *Target Audience:* 30-54.
Dave Margalotti, Operations Dir
Terese Main, Programming Director
Bob Price, News Director
Jim Travis, Chief Engineer
Dave Best, Business Manager
Trudi Cook, Radio Receptionist
Gary Farnham, IT Director
Debbie Fero, EventsCoordinator
Jeff Harmon, Chief Operating Officer

Troy

WTZN
03-03-1982; 1310 kHz AM
Mailing Address: 170 Redington Ave, Troy, PA 16947 US
Second Address: 170 Redington Ave., Troy, PA 16947
(570) 297-0100; *Fax:* (570) 297-3193
www.wtzn.com
whgl100@ptd.net
License: Troy, PA held by Cantroair Communications Inc.
Format: Sports; *Target Audience:* 25-54.
Mike Powers, President
Bob Gisler, Operations Dir
Kevin Smith, Chief Engineer

Tunkhannock

WGMF
06-13-1986; 1460 kHz AM; 5 kw-D, 1 kw-N, DA-2; N41 33 46 W75 58 11
Box 701, Tunkhannock, PA 18657 US
(570) 836-4200; *Fax:* (570) 836-7035
www.gem104.com
License: Tunkhannock, Wyoming County, PA held by Geos Communications
Group Owner: Geos Communications

***WCIN-FM**
01-01-2001; 91.3 MHz FM; 0.25 kw; 295 ft.; N41 31 28 W76 04 19 *Rebroadcasts:* Rebroadcasts WCIK(FM) Bath, NY 100%
Mailing Address: PO Box 506, Bath, NY 14810 US
Second Address: 7634 Campbell Creek Rd., Bath, NY 14810
(607) 776-4151
www.fln.org
License: Tunkhannock, PA held by Family Life Ministries Inc.
Group Owner: Family Life Network
Nat'l Network: Salem Radio Network; *Wire Services:* Metro Weather Service Inc.
Arbitron Metro Market: Bath, NY; *Format:* Christian; *Hrs. of News Programming:* news progmg 14 hrs wkly; *No. News Employees:* 3; *Target Audience:* 30-54.
Dave Margalotti, Operations Dir
Terese Main, Programming Director
Bob Price, News Director

Tyrone

WTRN

01-12-1955; 1340 kHz AM; *Hrs Open:* 24; 1 kw; N40 39 48 W78 15 24
P.O. Box 247, Tyrone, PA 16686 US
(814) 684-3200; *Fax:* (814) 684-1220
License: Tyrone, Blair County, PA held by Allegheny Mountain Network
Group Owner: Allegheny Mountain Network Stations
Nat'l Network: Jones Radio Networks; *Regional Network:* Allegheny Mtn. Net; *Nat'l Reps:* Dome
Arbitron Metro Market: Tyrone, PA; *Format:* Adult Contemp
Special Programming: Relg 4 hrs wkly; *Hrs. of News Programming:* News progmg 16 hrs wkly; *Target Audience:* General; total community targeted; *Adv. Rates:* 7; 7; 7; 7
Cary H. Simpson, President

Union City

WCTL

04-23-1967; 106.3 MHz FM; 3.4 kw; 430 ft.; N42 0 3 W79 52 33
10912 Route 19 North, Waterford, PA 16441 US
(814) 796-6000; *Fax:* (814) 796-3200
www.wctl.org
wctl@wctl.org
License: Union City, Erie County, PA held by Inspiration Time Inc.
Nat'l Network: USA; *Nat'l Reps:* Salem
Arbitron Metro Market: Erie, PA; *Format:* Adult Contemp, Christian *Special Programming:* Children one hr wkly; *Hrs. of News Programming:* news progmg 2.5 hrs wkly; *No. News Employees:* 1 *Target Audience:* 25-54; Christian families; *Adv. Rates:* 25; 20; 20; 20
Ed Mattson, President
Ronald Raymond, General Manager
Adam Frase, Programming Director

Uniontown

WMBS

07-15-1937; 590 kHz AM; *Hrs Open:* 24; 1 kw-D, DAN; 1 kw-N, DAN; N39 51 35 W79 44 44
82 W. Fayette Street, Uniontown, PA 15401 US
(724) 438-3900; *Fax:* (724) 438-2406
www.wmbs590.com
sales590@wmbs590.com
License: Uniontown, PA held by Fayette Broadcasting Corp.
Nat'l Network: CBS Radio; Westwood One; *Nat'l Reps:* Commercial Media Sales *Regional Reps:* West Media Group;
Wire Services: AP; Metro Weather Service Inc.
Arbitron Metro Market: Pittsburgh, PA; *Format:* Adult Contemp
Special Programming: Talk shows, polka 3 hrs wkly, Pittsburgh Pirates,; *Hrs. of News Programming:* news progmg 24 hrs wkly; *No. News Employees:* 1 *Target Audience:* 25 plus; General; *Adv. Rates:* 12; 12; 12; 10
Bob Pritts, President
Doreen Minafee, Operations Dir
Brian Mroziak, General Manager
Sandy Tracy, General Sales Mgr
Jim Morgan, News Director
Larry Campbell, Chief Engineer
Michael Pasqua, General Sales Manager
Timothy Schwer,Public Affairs Director

WPKL

12-20-1968; 99.3 MHz FM; *Hrs Open:* 24; 3 kw; 295 ft.; N39 53 9 W79 46 29
123 Blaine Rd., Brownsville, PA 15417 US
(724) 938-2000; *Fax:* (724) 938-7842
www.picklefm.com
License: Uniontown, Fayette County, PA held by FM Radio Licenses, LLC
Group Owner: Keymarket Communications LLC; (acq 1-17-2001; $475,000 with WYJK(AM) Connellsville)
Nat'l Reps: Dome
Arbitron Metro Market: Pittsburgh, PA; *Format:* Oldies; *Target Audience:* 25 plus.; *Adv. Rates:* 25; 25; 25; 25
David Pavlic, General Sales Mgr
Elizabeth Layhew, Production

University Park

WOWY

04-01-1965; 97.1 MHz FM; 2 kw; 404 ft.; N40 48 27 W77 56 29
160 Clearview Ave., State College, PA 16803 US
(814) 238-5085; *Fax:* (814) 238-7932
www.wowyonline.com
License: University Park, Centre County, PA held by 2510 Licenses LLC.
Group Owner: 2510 Licenses LLC; (acq 2-16-2005; grpsl)
Arbitron Metro Market: State College, PA; *Format:* Oldies
Terry Highman, Marketing Manager

Villanova

*WXVU

08-01-1991; 89.1 MHz FM; 0.1 kw vert; 279 ft.; N40 1 58 W75 20 15
800 Lancaster Avenue, 210 Dougherty Hall, Villanova, PA 19085 US
(610) 519-7200; *Fax:* (610) 519-7956
www1.villanova.edu
info@wxvufm.com
License: Villanova, Delaware County, PA held by Villanova University.
Arbitron Metro Market: Villanova, PA; *Format:* Sports, Talk
Special Programming: Black 10 hrs, relg 2 hrs wkly; *Target Audience:* 15-25; youngsters
Kaitlin Santana, Operations Dir
Jarred Cannon, General Manager
Matilda Swartz, Programming Director
Nick Monzo, Promotions Manager
Suzanne Lee, Music Director
Chris Haring, Sports Director
Joe Orkwiszewski, Production Director

Warminster

*WRDV

09-06-1976; 89.3 MHz FM; *Hrs Open:* 24; 0.1 kw horiz, 1 kw vert; 118 ft.; N40 12 19 W75 6 27
Mailing Address: P. O. Box 2012, Warminster, PA 18974 US
Second Address: 126 S. York Rd., Hatboro, PA 19040
(215) 674-8002; *Fax:* (215) 674-4586
wrdv.org
License: Warminster, Bucks County, PA held by Bux-Mont Educational Radio Associates.
Arbitron Metro Market: Philadelphia; *Format:* Variety/Diverse
Special Programming: C&W 4 hrs, blues 3 hrs, folk 4 hrs, new age 3 hrs, jazz 3 hrs wkly; *Hrs. of News Programming:* News progmg 2 hrs wkly *TargetAudience:* General.
Charles Loughery, President
Todd Allen, General Manager

Warren

WNAE

12-31-1946; 1310 kHz AM; *Hrs Open:* 24 hours; 5 kw-D, ND1; 0.094 kw-N, ND1; N41 48 50 W79 10 4
Mailing Address: 310 Second Avenue, Warren, PA 16365 US
Second Address: 310 2nd Ave., Warren, PA 16365
(814) 723-1310; *Fax:* (814) 723-3356
www.kibcoradio.com
info@kibcoradio.com
License: Warren, PA held by Radio Partners LLC.
Group Owner: Radio Partners LLC; (acq 9-30-2005; grpsl)
Nat'l Network: AP Network News; *Wire Services:* AP
Arbitron Metro Market: Warren, PA; *Format:* Talk; *Hrs. of News Programming:* news progmg 11 hrs wkly; *No. News Employees:* 1; *Target Audience:* General.
Frank Iorio, CEO
Karen White, General Manager
David Whipple, Station Manager
David Whipple, General Sales Mgr
Mark Silvis, Programming Director
Dale Bliss, Promotions Manager
Dana Simmons, Traffic Manager

WRRN

03-01-1948; 92.3 MHz FM; *Hrs Open:* 24; 50 kw; 410 ft.; N41 48 50 W79 10 4
310 Second Avenue, Warren, PA 16365 US
(814) 723-1310; *Fax:* (814) 723-3356
www.kibcoradio.com
info@kibcoradio.com
License: Warren, Warren County, PA held by Radio Partners LLC
Group Owner: Radio Partners LLC
Format: Oldies
Frank Iorio, CEO
Dave Whipple, Station Manager

Warwick

*WZZD

12-01-2000; 88.1 MHz FM; *Hrs Open:* 24; 180 w vert; 587 ft; N40 07 45 W75 52 43 *Rebroadcasts:* Rebroadcasts WBYO(FM) Sellersville 90%
Box 186, Sellersville, PA 18960
(215) 721-2141; *Fax:* (215) 721-9811
www.wordfm.org
wordfm@wordfm.org
License: Warwick, Chester County, PA held by Four Rivers Community Broadcasting Corp.
Group Owner: Four Rivers Community Broadcasting Corp.
Population Served: 75,000 *Special Programming:* Bluegrass/gospel 3 hrs wkly
Charles Loughery, President
Meg Sabulsky, Operations Dir
David Baker, General Manager
Meg Sabulsky, Programming Director
William Dunn, Promotions Manager
Charles Loughery, Engineering Dir

Washington

WJPA

02-01-1941; 1450 kHz AM; *Hrs Open:* 24; 1 kw-U, ND1; N40 11 23 W80 14 2
98 South Main Street, Washington, PA 15301 US
(724) 222-2110; *Fax:* (724) 228-2299
www.wjpa.com
email@wjpa.com
License: Washington, PA held by Washington Broadcasting Co.
Regional Network: Radio Pa.
Arbitron Metro Market: Pittsburgh, PA; *Format:* Oldies; *Hrs. of News Programming:* news progmg 6 hrs wkly; *No. News Employees:* 2
Michael Siegel, President
Bob Gregg, Operations Dir
Pete Povich, Programming Director
Dale Allen, Promotions Manager
Jim Jefferson, News Director
Margie Konstantinou, Music Director

WJPA-FM

09-26-1964; 95.3 MHz FM; *Hrs Open:* 24; 2.15 kw; 390 ft.; N40 11 23 W80 14 2
98 South Main Street, Washington, PA 15301 US
(724) 222-2110; *Fax:* (724) 228-2299
www.wjpa.com
email@wjpa.com
License: Washington, Washington County, PA held by Washington Broadcasting Co.
Arbitron Metro Market: Pittsburgh, PA; *Format:* Oldies
Austin Davis, Programming Director
Sherry Flick, News Director
Jill Gleeson, Disc Jockey
Kenny Marks, Disc Jockey
Laura Mack, Disc Jockey
Tor Michaels, News Reporter

*WNJR

11-26-1972; 91.7 MHz FM; *Hrs Open:* 24; 0.95 kw; 112 ft.; N40 10 13 W80 14 43
1 South Lincoln Street, Washington, PA 15301 US
(724) 503-1001
www.wnjr.org
wnjr@washjeff.edu
License: Washington, Washington County, PA held by Washington and Jefferson College.
Wire Services: AP
Arbitron Metro Market: Washington, PA; *Format:* Variety/Diverse; *Hrs. of News Programming:* News progmg 4 hrs wkly; *Target Audience:* All ages; college students, staff, community, alumni; *Adv. Rates:* 150; 150; 150;150
Liz, Station Manager
Anthony Fleury, General Sales Mgr
Khyati, Programming Director
Allyse, Promotions Manager
Dana, Sponsorship Director
Sara, Music Director
Jake, Production Director

Wattsburg

*WCGM

01-01-2001; 102.7 MHz FM; 3.5 kw; 295 ft.; N41 59 57 W79 41 59 *Rebroadcasts:* Rebroadcasts WCIK(FM) Bath, NY 100%
Mailing Address: PO Box 506, Bath, NY 14810 US
Second Address: 7634 Campbell Creek Rd., Bath, NY 14810
(607) 776-4151
www.fln.org
License: Wattsburg, PA held by Family Life Ministries Inc.
Group Owner: Family Life Network
Nat'l Network: Salem Radio Network; *Wire Services:* Metro Weather Service Inc.
Arbitron Metro Market: Bath, NY; *Format:* Christian; *Hrs. of News Programming:* news progmg 14 hrs wkly; *No. News Employees:* 3; *Target Audience:* 30-54.
Dave Margalotti, Operations Dir
Terese Main, Programming Director
Bob Price, News Director

Waynesboro

WBHB-FM

02-03-1959; 101.5 MHz FM; 50 kw horiz, 48 kw vert; 230 ft.; N39 49 44 W77 33 10
Mailing Address: 4850 Conn. Ave NW Ste103, Washington, DC 20008 US
Second Address: 10960 John Wayne Dr., Waynesboro, PA 17225
(406) 755-8700; *Fax:* (406) 755-8770
www.1051cool.com
info@1051cool.com
License: Waynesboro, Franklin County, PA held by HJV L.P.
Group Owner: VerStandig Broadcasting
Arbitron Metro Market: Whitefish MT; *Format:* Oldies
Cassie Bee, General Manager

WCBG

08-19-1953; 1380 kHz AM; 1 kw-D, ND2; 0.02 kw-N, ND2; N39 44 20 W77 36 10
Mailing Address: 4850 Ct Ave., N.W., #103, Washington, DC 20008 US
Second Address: 10960 John Wayne Dr., Greencastle, PA 17225
(717) 597-9200; *Fax:* (717) 597-9210
wcbg@wagner.edu
License: Waynesboro, PA held by HJV L.P.
Group Owner: VerStandig Broadcasting; (acq 1-6-97; $1,068,699 with co-located FM).
Arbitron Metro Market: Hagerstown-Chambersburg-Waynesboro, MD-PA; *Format:* Country; *Target Audience:* 25-54.
Marge Martin, General Manager
Don Brake, Programming Director

Waynesburg

WANB

09-27-1956; 1210 kHz AM; *Hrs Open:* Sunrise-sunset
R.D #3, Gordon Hill, Waynesburg, PA 15370 US
(724) 627-5555; *Fax:* (724) 627-4021
wanbradio@gmail.com
License: Waynesburg, PA held by Broadcast Communications Inc.
Group Owner: Broadcast Communications Inc.
Arbitron Metro Market: Waynesburg, PA
Marcia Mackay, News Director

*WCYJ-FM

07-06-1979; 99.5 MHz FM; *Hrs Open:* 24; 0.007 kw; -3 ft.; N39 53 59 W80 11 7
51 West College St., Waynesburg, PA 15370 US
(724) 852-3310(724) 852-3297; *Fax:* (724) 627-4757
www.waynesburg.edu
License: Waynesburg, Greene County, PA held by Waynesburg College.
Arbitron Metro Market: Waynesburg, PA; *Format:* Adult Contemp *Special Programming:* Oldies 3 hrs, country 3 hrs, Christian 3 hrs, R&B 3 hrs, classic rock 3 hrs wkly; *No. News Employees:* 1; *Target Audience:* 18-25;college & high school students
Travis Gongaware, Operations Dir
Ariel Dugan, General Manager
Mark Perry, Station Manager

Wellsboro

WNBT

05-13-1955; 1490 kHz AM; *Hrs Open:* 24; 1 kw-U, ND1; N41 44 41 W77 17 35
P.O. Box 98, Wellsboro, PA 16901 US
(570) 724-1490; *Fax:* (570) 724-6971
www.wnbt.net
wnbt@ynt.net
License: Wellsboro, Tioga County, PA held by Farm & Home Broadcasting Co.
Group Owner: Allegheny Mountain Network Stations
Nat'l Network: Westwood One; *Regional Network:* Radio Pa;
Nat'l Reps: Dome
Arbitron Metro Market: Wellsboro, PA; *Format:* Adult Contemp;
Hrs. of News Programming: news progmg 10 hrs wkly; *No. News Employees:* 1; *Target Audience:* 45+.; *Adv. Rates:* 12; 12; 12; 12
Cary H. Simpson, President
Al Harer, Station Manager

WNBT-FM

07-02-1969; 104.5 MHz FM; *Hrs Open:* 24; 50 kw; 381 ft.; N41 44 17 W77 21 50
P.O. Box 98, Wellsboro, PA 16901 US
(570) 724-1490; *Fax:* (570) 724-6971
www.wnbt.net
wnbt@ynt.net
License: Wellsboro, Tioga County, PA held by Farm & Home Broadcasting Co.
Group Owner: Allegheny Mountain Network Stations
Nat'l Network: Westwood One
Arbitron Metro Market: Wellsboro, PA; *Format:* Adult Contemp, Contemporary Hits/Top 40; *Hrs. of News Programming:* news progmg 2 hrs wkly; *No. News Employees:* 1; *Target Audience:* 18-55.
Cary H. Simpson, President
Al Harer, Station Manager

West Chester

WCHE

10-04-1963; 1520 kHz AM; *Hrs Open:* Sunrise-sunset
119 West Market Street, West Chester, PA 19382 US
(610) 692-3131; *Fax:* (610) 692-3133
www.wche1520.com
wche@wche1520.com
License: West Chester, PA held by Chester County Radio Inc.
Nat'l Network: USA; Westwood One
Arbitron Metro Market: West Chester,PA; *Format:* Alternative, Talk *Special Programming:* Relg 8 hrs, country 2 hrs wkly; *Hrs. of News Programming:* news progmg 20 hrs wkly; *No. News Employees:* 1; *Target Audience:* 24-64; upscale
David Shur, President
Bill Mason, General Manager

*WCUR

01-01-1999; 91.7 MHz FM; 0.1 kw vert; 112 ft.; N39 57 2 W75 35 58
211 Sykes Union Building, West Chester, PA 19383 US
(610) 436-2478; *Fax:* (610) 436-2477
www.wcur.org
License: West Chester, Chester County, PA held by Student Services Inc.
Arbitron Metro Market: West Chester, PA; *Format:* Variety/Diverse
Matt Toal, General Manager
Jacki Marinich, General Sales Mgr
Brynn Pezzuti, Programming Director

West Hazleton

WKZN

01-01-1982; 1300 kHz AM; *Hrs Open:* 24; 5 kw-D, DA2; 0.5 kw-N, DA2; N40 56 26 W76 0 7 *Rebroadcasts:* Rebroadcasts WILK(AM) Wilks-Barre 100%.
305 Highway 315, Pittston, PA 18640 US
(570) 883-9850; *Fax:* (570) 883-0832
www.wilknewsradio.com
info@wilknewsradio.com
License: West Hazleton, PA held by Entercom Scranton Wilkes-Barre License LLC.
Group Owner: Entercom Communications Corp.; (acq 12-13-99; grpsl).
Nat'l Reps: D & R Radio; *Wire Services:* ABC; AP
Arbitron Metro Market: Wilkes Barre-Scranton, PA; *Format:* News, News/Talk, 86 *Special Programming:* Relg one hr wkly; *Hrs. of News Programming:* news progmg 25 hrs wkly; *No. News Employees:* 6; *Target Audience:* General; affluent, educated; *Adv. Rates:* 35; 45; 35; 25
Jim Rising, Operations Dir
Ryan Flynn, General Manager
Mike Rockwell, General Sales Mgr
Nancy Kman, Programming Director
Casey Consagra, Promotions Manager
Joe Thomas, News Director
Jay Waggoner, Chief Engineer

West Middlesex

WWIZ

10-01-1972; 103.9 MHz FM; 6 kw; 89.7 meters; N41 12 16 W80 21 49
4040 Simon Rd., Youngstown, OH 44512 US
(330) 783-1000; *Fax:* (330) 783-0060
www.realrock104.com
License: West Middlesex, Mercer County, PA held by Cumulus Licensing Corp.
Group Owner: Cumulus Media Inc.; (acq 3-15-00; grpsl).
Arbitron Metro Market: Youngstown, OH; *Format:* Rock/AOR; *Target Audience:* 25-54.
Matt Spatz, Programming Director

Whitneyville

WLIH

03-15-1987; 107.1 MHz FM; *Hrs Open:* 6 AM-Midnight; 3.3 kw; 299 ft.; N41 46 13 W77 12 8
Mailing Address: P. O. Box 97, Wellsboro, PA 16901 US
Second Address: 2352 Charleston Rd, Wellsboro, PA 16901
(570) 724-4272; *Fax:* (570) 724-2302
www.wlih.com
wlih107@quik.com
License: Whitneyville, Tioga County, PA held by Good Christian Radio Broadcasting Inc.
Nat'l Network: USA
Format: Christian, News, 74; *Hrs. of News Programming:* News progmg 28 hrs wkly; *Target Audience:* General; serving the Christian community of the county; *Adv. Rates:* 6; 5; 6; na
Robert Makin, President
Carol Makin, General Manager
George Buickus, Programming Director

Wilkes-Barre

WBAX

05-01-1922; 1240 kHz AM; *Hrs Open:* 24; 1 kw-U, ND1; N41 15 13 W75 54 25 *Rebroadcasts:* Simulcasts with WEJL (AM) Scranton.
149 Penn Avenue, Scranton, PA 18503 US
(208) 263-2179; *Fax:* (208) 265-5440
www.1067thepoint.com
carolynp@953kpnd.com
License: Wilkes-Barre, PA held by The Scranton Times L.P.
Group Owner: The Scranton Times L.P.
Arbitron Metro Market: Kootenai ID; *Format:* Classic Rock
Dylan Benefield, General Manager
Mike Brown, News Director
John Goes, Chief Engineer

*WCLH

02-06-1972; 90.7 MHz FM; *Hrs Open:* 24; 0.205 kw; 971 ft.; N41 11 11 W75 51 33
187 South Franklin St, Wilkes-Barre, PA 18766 US
(570) 408-5907; *Fax:* (570) 408-5908
www.wclh.org
License: Wilkes-Barre, Luzerne County, PA held by Wilkes University.
Nat'l Network: AP Network News
Arbitron Metro Market: Wilkes Barre-Scranton, PA; *Format:* Alternative *Special Programming:* Ger 3 hrs, Sp 3 hrs wkly; *Hrs. of News Programming:* News progmg 7 hrs wkly; *Target Audience:* 12-44.
Renee Loftus, General Manager
Corey M and Joe P, Programming Director

WILK

02-13-1947; 980 kHz AM; *Hrs Open:* 24; 5 kw-D, DAN; 1 kw-N, DAN; N41 13 42 W75 56 53
10706 Beaver Dam Road, Cockeysville, MD 21030 US
(570) 883-9800; *Fax:* (570) 883-9851
www.wilknetwork.com
License: Wilkes-Barre, PA held by Entercom Scranton Wilkes-Barre License LLC.
Group Owner: Entercom Communications Corp.; (acq 12-13-99; grpsl)
Arbitron Metro Market: Wilkes Barre-Scranton, PA; *Format:* News, News/Talk, 86 *Special Programming:* Relg one hr wkly; *Target Audience:* 15-54.
Joseph Fields, President
John Burkavage, General Manager

WMGS

01-01-1946; 92.9 MHz FM; *Hrs Open:* 24; 5.3 kw; 1385 ft.; N41 10 56 W75 52 22
600 Baltimore Dr., Wilkes-Barre, PA 18702 US
(570) 824-9000; *Fax:* (570) 820-0520
www.magic93fm.com
License: Wilkes-Barre, PA held by Radio License Holding CBC, LLC
Group Owner: Cumulus Media Inc.; (acq 7-1-97; grpsl).
Arbitron Metro Market: Wilkes Barre, PA; *Format:* Adult Contemp
Shannon Spak, General Sales Mgr
Stan Phillips, Programming Director
Erin Evans, Promotions Manager
Gerald Getz, Market Manager

*WRKC

09-18-1968; 88.5 MHz FM; *Hrs Open:* 7 AM-2 AM; 1.5 kw; -459 ft.; N41 14 56 W75 52 45
133 North River Street, Wilkes-Barre, PA 18702 US
(570) 208-5931; *Fax:* (570) 825-9049
www.kings.edu/~wrke/
wrkc@kings.edu
License: Wilkes-Barre, Luzerne County, PA held by King's College.
Arbitron Metro Market: Wilkes Barre-Scranton, PA; *Format:* Rock/AOR; *Target Audience:* General; people who need wide-ranging svcs
Sue Henry, General Manager
Pat Barton, Station Manager
Katie Moore, Programming Director

Bob Decker, Metal
Michael Wasenda, Music Director

Wilkinsburg

WAMO
08-01-1948; 660 kHz AM; *Hrs Open:* 24
One Forever Drive, Hollidaysburg, PA 16648 US
(412) 829-1000; *Fax:* (412) 391-3559
www.wamo100.com
info@wamo100.com
License: Wilkinsburg, PA held by McL/McM Pennsylvania LLC.
Group Owner: Sheridan Broadcasting Corp.; (acq 3-1-73)
Nat'l Network: American Urban; *Nat'l Reps:* McGavren Guild
Arbitron Metro Market: Pittsburgh, PA; *Format:* Black, Blues
Ronald Davenport Sr., Chairman
Ronald Davenport Jr., President
Kathy Gersha, Operations Dir
Michael Davenport, General Manager
Mickey Baker, General Sales Mgr
Ron Atkins, Programming Director
Laura Varner-Norman, PromotionsManager
George Cook, Programming Director
Tammy Sadler, Promotions Director
Jon Plesser, Regional Sales Manager

WAMO
660 kHz AM; 1.4 kW; 485 ft.; N40 24 47 W79 51 14
21 Yost Blvd, Suite 505, Forest Hills, PA 15221 USA
(412) 829-0100
www.wamo100.com
License: Wilkinsburg, PA held by Radio Power Inc.
Group Owner: Martz Communications Group
Arbitron Metro Market: Pittsburgh, PA; *Format:* Urban Contemporary
Louis Wingfield, Operations Dir
Jamal Woodson, General Manager
Vanessa Doss, General Sales Mgr
DJ Boogie, Programming Director

Williamsport

WILQ
07-31-1949; 105.1 MHz FM; *Hrs Open:* 24; 9.2 kw; 1135 ft.; N41 11 43 W76 58 18
1685 Four Mile Dr, Williamsport, PA 17701 US
(570) 323-8200; *Fax:* (570) 327-9138
www.wilq.com
dfarr@backyardbroadcasting.com
License: Williamsport, Lycoming County, PA held by Backyard Broadcasting PA, LLC
Group Owner: Backyard Broadcasting LLC; (acq 12-1-02; grpsl).
Arbitron Metro Market: Williamsport, PA; *Format:* Country; *Hrs. of News Programming:* news progmg 7 hrs wkly; *No. News Employees:* 4; *Target Audience:* 25+; *Adv. Rates:* 45; 45; 45; 25
Dan Farr, President & CEO
Ted Minier, Programming Director
John Finn, News Director
Kelly Bailey, Production Director

WKSB
04-01-1948; 102.7 MHz FM; *Hrs Open:* 24; 53 kw; 1270 ft.; N41 11 21 W76 58 53
1559 West 4th St., Williamsport, PA 17701 US
(570) 327-1400; *Fax:* (570) 327-8156
www.kiss1027fm.com
License: Williamsport, Lycoming County, PA held by Clear Channel Broadcasting Licenses Inc.
Group Owner: iHeartMedia
Arbitron Metro Market: Williamsport, PA; *Format:* Adult Contemp; *No. News Employees:* 1; *Target Audience:* 25-54.
Jeff Hurley, Regional Program Manager

WLYC
06-01-1951; 1050 kHz AM; *Hrs Open:* 24; 1 kw-D, ND1; 0.03 kw-N, ND1; N41 15 44 W77 1 59
P.O. Box 545, Williamsport, PA 17703 US
(570) 327-1300; *Fax:* (570) 327-5565
www.espnwilliamsport.com
wlyc1050@yahoo.com
License: Williamsport, PA held by Sentry Communications License LLC
Nat'l Network: ESPN Radio; Westwood One; *Regional Network:* Radio Pa. *Regional Reps:* .
Arbitron Metro Market: Williamsport, PA; *Format:* Sports; *Hrs. of News Programming:* Sports news only; *Target Audience:* 25-54; male; *Adv. Rates:* 25; 15; 20; 7.50
Jeffrey Andruionis, Operations Dir
James McKowne, General Manager
Christy Andruionis, General Sales Mgr

*WPTC
09-03-1980; 88.1 MHz FM; *Hrs Open:* 24; 494 w; -101 ft; N41 14 11 W77 01 26
460 Market Street, Suite 310, Williamsport, PA 17701
(301) 908-4165
License: Williamsport, Lycoming County, PA held by Williamsport Lycoming Broadcast Foundation
Wire Services: AP
Population Served: 99,000; *Arbitron Metro Market:* Williamsport, P *Special Programming:* Jazz inspired with Judy Carmichael, The Jazz Scene; *Hrs. of News Programming:* 1 hour weekly; *Target Audience:* 18-24; collegestudents; *Adv. Rates:* Underwriting $150 per semester
Todd Bartley, President
Brad Nason, General Manager
Skip Smith, Chief Engineer

WRAK
04-10-1930; 1400 kHz AM; *Hrs Open:* 24; 1 kw-U, ND1; N41 14 22 W77 2 27 *Rebroadcasts:* Rebroadcasts WRKK(AM) Hughesville 100%
1559 West 4th St., Williamsport, PA 17701 US
(570) 327-1400; *Fax:* (570) 327-8156
www.wrak.com
wrak@wrak.com
License: Williamsport, PA held by Clear Channel Broadcasting Licenses Inc.
Group Owner: iHeartMedia; (acq 8-5-98; grpsl)
Nat'l Network: Westwood One
Arbitron Metro Market: Williamsport, PA; *Format:* News, News/Talk, 84, Talk; *Hrs. of News Programming:* news progmg 3 hrs wkly; *No. News Employees:* 1; *Target Audience:* 35 plus.
Jeff Hurley, Regional Program Manager

*WRLC
04-05-1976; 91.7 MHz FM; *Hrs Open:* 24; 0.74 kw horiz; -299 ft.; N41 14 42 W76 59 50
College Place, Williamsport, PA 17701 US
(570) 321-4060; *Fax:* (570) 321-4372
wrlc@lycoming.edu
License: Williamsport, Lycoming County, PA held by Lycoming College.
Arbitron Metro Market: Williamsport, PA; *Format:* Alternative, Oldies *Special Programming:* Class one hr, gospel 6 hrs, pub affrs 2 hrs, Christian rock 3 hrs, jazz 8 hrs, blues 3 hrs wkly; *Hrs. of News Programming:* Newsprogmg 15 hrs wkly; *Target Audience:* General; Lycoming College & its surrounding communities
Alan Jackson, Station Manager
Skip Smith, Chief Engineer

WWPA
05-22-1949; 1340 kHz AM; *Hrs Open:* 24; 1 kw-U, ND1; N41 13 45 W77 0 45 *Rebroadcasts:* 1 Translator - W267BJ (FM) 101.3
1585 Four Mile Dr, Williamsport, PA 17701 US
(570) 323-8200; *Fax:* (570) 327-9138
www.wwpa1340amtalkradiowilliamsportpa.com
License: Williamsport, Lycoming County, PA held by Backyard Broadcasting PA, LLC
Group Owner: Backyard Broadcasting LLC; (acq 12-1-02; grpsl).
Nat'l Network: CSN
Arbitron Metro Market: Williamsport, PA; *Format:* Adult Contemp, News/Talk, 86 *Special Programming:* Sports; *Hrs. of News Programming:* news progmg 168 hrs wkly; *No. News Employees:* 1; *Target Audience:* 35plus.; *Adv. Rates:* 15; 15; 15; 8
Dan Farr, General Manager
Ted Minier, Programming Director
Brian Hill, Chief Engineer
Shannon Kriner, Traffic Manager

*WVYA
01-01-2003; 89.7 MHz FM; *Hrs Open:* 24; 3.3 kw; -16 ft.; N41 14 54 W77 1 52 *Rebroadcasts:* Rebroadcasts WVIA-FM Scranton
Old Boston Rd, Pittston, PA 18640 US
(570) 826-6144; *Fax:* (570) 655-1180
www.wvia.org
License: Williamsport, Lycoming County, PA held by Northeastern Pennsylvania Educational TV Association.
Nat'l Network: NPR; *Wire Services:* AP
Arbitron Metro Market: Pittston, PA; *Format:* Jazz, News; *Hrs. of News Programming:* news progmg 30 hrs wkly; *No. News Employees:* 1; *Target Audience:* Upscale, mature audience.
Harmar Brereton, M.D., Chairman
A. William Kelly, President & CEO
Chris Norton, Operations Dir
Larry Vojtko, Programming Director
Tom Curr , Executive Vice President & Executive Producer
Lynn Volk, Senior Vice President ofFinance
Chris Norton, Vice President of Radio
Joe Glynn, Vice President of Engineering
Doug Cook, Vice President of Marketing & Special Events
George Thomas, Vice President of Membership

*WCRG
02-20-2002; 90.7 MHz FM; *Hrs Open:* 24; 3 kw; Ant -216 ft; N41 13 50 W77 08 59 *Rebroadcasts:* Rebroadcasts WGRC(FM) Lewisburg 100%
101 Armory Blvd., Lewisburg, PA 17837
(570) 523-1190; *Fax:* (570) 523-1114
www.wgrc.com
email@wgrc.com
License: Williamsport, Lycoming County, PA held by Salt & Light Media Ministries Inc.
Wire Services: AP
Population Served: 150,000; *Arbitron Metro Market:* Williamsport, PA; *Hrs. of News Programming:* news progmg 12 hrs wkly; *No. News Employees:* 3; *Target Audience:* 25-54.
Larry Weidman, General Manager
Don Casteline, Programming Director
Jim Diehl, News Director
Chris Miller, Chief Engineer
Jim Diehl, News Reporter
John Callahan, News Reporter

WLMY
12-01-2002; 107.9 MHz FM; 0.36 kw; 1,289 feet; N41 12 39 W76 57 17
1685 Four Mile Dr, Williamsport, PA 17701 US
(570) 323-8200; *Fax:* (570) 327-9138
License: Williamsport, PA held by Backyard Broadcasting PA, LLC
Group Owner: Backyard Broadcasting LLC
Format: Adult Contemp, Contemporary Hits/Top 40, 60; *No. News Employees:* 1; *Target Audience:* 25-44
Dan Farr, President & CEO
John Finn, News Director

Wyomissing

*WYTL
01-01-2005; 91.7 MHz FM; 10 w horiz, 320 w vert; Ant 840 ft; W40 19 22 W76 11 52 *Rebroadcasts:* Rebroadcasts WBYO (FM) Sellersville 100%
Box 186, Sellersville, PA 18960
(215) 721-2141; *Fax:* (215) 721-9811
www.wordfm.org
wordfm@wordfm.org
License: Wyomissing, Berks County, PA held by Four Rivers Community Broadcasting Corp.
Group Owner: Four Rivers Community Broadcasting Corp.

Charles Loughery, President
Meg Sabulsky, Operations Dir
David Baker, General Manager
Meg Sabulsky, Programming Director
William Dunn, Promotions Manager
Charles Loughery, Engineering Dir

York

WARM
03-28-1983; 103.3 MHz FM; *Hrs Open:* 24; 6.4 kw; 1306 ft.; N40 1 38 W76 36 0
5989 Susquehanna Plaza Dr., York, PA 17406 US
(717) 764-1155; *Fax:* (717) 252-4708
www.warm1033.com
carol.pierson@cumulus.com
License: York, PA held by Radio License Holding SRC, LLC
Group Owner: Cumulus Media Inc.
Arbitron Metro Market: York, PA; *Format:* Adult Contemp
Brian Shaffer, General Sales Mgr
Dave Russell, Programming Director

WOYK
03-01-1932; 1350 kHz AM; *Hrs Open:* 24; 5 kw-D, DAN; 1 kw-N, DAN; N39 56 0 W76 49 6
Mailing Address: 1360 Copenhaffer Road, York, PA 17404 US
Second Address: 1051 Dairy Ln., Elizabethtown, PA 17022
(717) 840-0355; *Fax:* (717) 840-0355
sportsradioespn1350.com
woyk1350@att.net
License: York, PA held by WOYK Inc.
Nat'l Network: Sporting News Radio Network; *Regional Network:* Radio Pa.
Arbitron Metro Market: York, PA; *Format:* Sports; *Target Audience:* 25-64; men; *Adv. Rates:* 40; 40; 40; 32
Douglas George, President
SAM CONRAD, Operations Dir
Vincent Grande, General Manager

WYYC
01-01-1948; 1250 kHz AM; *Hrs Open:* 24; 1 kw-D, ND1; 0.033 kw-N, ND1; N39 59 56 W76 41 43
1545 North Queen St., York, PA 17404 US
(717) 848-4418
www.wilkinsradio.com
denise@wilkinsradio.com
License: York, PA held by Steel City Radio Inc.
Group Owner: Wilkins Communications Network Inc.; (acq 10-11-2005; $250,000)
Arbitron Metro Market: York, PA; *Format:* Christian, Talk; *Target Audience:* 35 plus.
Reese Crane, Station Manager

WQXA
01-01-1948; 105.7 MHz FM; 25 kw; 705 ft.; N39 59 56 W76 41 41
2300 Vartan Way, Suite 130, Harrisburg, PA 17110 US
(717) 238-1041; *Fax:* (717) 234-7780
www.1057thex.com
chris.james@cumulus.com
License: York, PA held by Radio License Holding CBC, LLC
Group Owner: Cumulus Media Inc.; (acq 5-29-97; grpsl)
Arbitron Metro Market: York, PA; *Format:* Rock/AOR; *Target Audience:* 18-49.
Chris James, Programming Director
Janelle Kopchick, Promotions Manager

WSBA
09-01-1942; 910 kHz AM; *Hrs Open:* 24; 5 kw-D, 1 kw-N
5989 Susquehanna Plaza Dr., York, PA 17406 US
(717) 764-1155; *Fax:* (717) 252-4708
www.wsba910.com
carol.pierson@cumulus.com
License: York, PA held by Radio License Holding SRC, LLC
Group Owner: Cumulus Media Inc.
Arbitron Metro Market: York, PA; *Format:* News/Talk
Brian Shaffer, Director of Sales
Chris Tyler, Programming Director
Lee Jacoby, Promotions Manager
Carol Pierson, Market Manager
Brian Dean, Sports Director

***WVYC**
11-18-1976; 88.1 MHz FM; *Hrs Open:* 18; 0.036 kw horiz; -70 ft.; N39 56 49 W76 43 47
339 Country Club Rd., York, PA 17405 US
(717) 815-1932
www.wvyc.org
tgibson@ycp.edu
License: York, York County, PA held by York College of Pennsylvania.
Arbitron Metro Market: York, PA; *Format:* Variety/Diverse *Special Programming:* Class 8 hrs, jazz 8 hrs, Sp one hr wkly; *Hrs. of News Programming:* news progmg 3 hrs wkly; *No. News Employees:* 1; *Target Audience:* 14-24; new mus lovers
Dr.Brian Furio, Chairman
Michelle Gorecki, General Manager
Thomas.K.Gibson, Faculty Advisor

York-Hanover

WYCR
12-22-1962; 98.5 MHz FM; 10.5 kw; 928 ft.; N39 51 26 W76 56 54
Mailing Address: P. O. Box 234, Hanover, PA 17331 US
Second Address: 275 Radio Rd., Hanover, PA 17331
(717) 792-0098; *Fax:* (717) 637-9006
www.thepeak985.com
License: York-Hanover, York County, PA held by Radio Hanover Inc.
Arbitron Metro Market: York, PA; *Format:* Contemporary Hits/Top 40, Adult Contemp
Tom Jackson, Programming Director
Beth Mowren, News Director
Jim Cooke, Disc Jockey
Paul Scott, Disc Jockey
Lee Sheldon, Disc Jockey
Davy Crockett, Disc Jockey
Jeff Brown, Disc Jockey

Youngsville

***WYVL(FM)**
01-19-1999; 88.5 MHz FM; *Hrs Open:* 24; 100 w; -335 ft; N41 51 01 W79 18 41
409 E. Main St., Youngsville, PA 16371
(814) 563-4903; *Fax:* (814) 563-4903
www.wtmv.com
wtmv@verizon.net
License: Youngsville, Warren County, PA held by Living Word of Faith Christian Outreach.
Nat'l Network: American Family Radio; Moody
Population Served: 1,714; *Arbitron Metro Market:* Youngsville, PA; *Format:* Christian *Special Programming:* Children 10 hrs, class 2.5 hrs wkly; *Hrs. of News Programming:* 12.?AY?; *No. News Employees:* 5 *Target Audience:* 21 plus; Christians of all ages
Rev. William Baker, President
Rev. Patricia Baker, Operations Dir
Khlare Bracken, Music Critic
Kathy Joy, Public Affairs Director

Puerto Rico

Adjuntas

WOQI
01-01-1997; 1020 kHz AM
Box 1507 Cuepo No. 80, Utuado, PR 0761 US
(787) 829-1453; *Fax:* (787) 840-7077
administracion@wpabradio.com
License: Adjuntas, PR held by WPAB Inc.
Arbitron Metro Market: Puerto Rico; *Format:* Variety/Diverse; *Hrs. of News Programming:* news progmg 3 hrs wkly; *No. News Employees:* 1; *Target Audience:* General; General Public; *Adv. Rates:* 10; 10; 10; 8
Alfonso Gimenez-Lucchetti, General Manager

Aguada

WFDT
01-01-1975; 105.5 MHz FM; *Hrs Open:* 24; 3 kw; 997 ft.; N18 18 57 W67 10 54
Mailing Address: P.O. Box 363222, San Juan, PR 00936-3222 US
Second Address: Calle Ponce de Leon, URB El Cerezal #1581, Rio Piedras, PR 926
(787) 294-0050; *Fax:* (787) 767-9343
www.fidelitypr.com
License: Aguada, PR held by Arso Radio Corp.
Group Owner: Uno Radio Group; (acq 4-19-01; $3.2 million).
Nat'l Reps: McGavren Guild
Arbitron Metro Market: Puerto Rico; *Format:* Adult Contemp, Easy Listening; *Target Audience:* 25-49; middle class
Luis Soto, President

Aguadilla

WABA
11-15-1951; 850 kHz AM
P. O. Box 188, Aguadilla, PR 0603 US
(641) 752-4122; *Fax:* (641) 752-5121
ktdvradio.com
info@ktdvradio.com
License: Aguadilla, PR held by Aquadilla Radio & TV Corp. Inc.
Format: Adult Contemp, Christian
Mark Osmundson, General Manager

WIVA-FM
04-16-1964; 100.3 MHz FM; *Hrs Open:* 24; 22 kw; 2014 ft.; N18 9 7 W66 59 15
Ave. Luis Munoz Martin, Esquina Calle 24, Caguas, PR 0726 US
(787) 744-3131; *Fax:* (787) 743-0252
www.salsoul.com
License: Aguadilla, PR held by Arso Radio Corp.
Group Owner: Uno Radio Group; (acq 3-85).
Arbitron Metro Market: Puerto Rico; *Format:* Spanish; *Hrs. of News Programming:* news progmg 5 hrs wkly; *No. News Employees:* 1; *Target Audience:* 12 plus.
Luis Soto, President

WWNA
01-01-1956; 1340 kHz AM
Mailing Address: Box 5734, Puerta De Tierra, San Juan, PR 0906 US
Second Address: Rd. 111, Aquadilla, PR 605
(787) 252-1730; *Fax:* (787) 868-1340
www.radiouna1340.com
License: Aguadilla, PR held by Dominga Barreto Santiago
Arbitron Metro Market: Puerto Rico; *Format:* Spanish *Special Programming:* Jazz 3 hrs wkly; *Target Audience:* 20-55.
Aureo Matos, General Manager
Ron Cushing, Chief Engineer
Felix Gonzalez, Disc Jockey

WTPM
05-27-1971; 92.9 MHz FM; *Hrs Open:* 18; 50 kw; 1207 ft.; N18 18 47 W67 11 6
Sector Cuba #1060, Mayaguez, PR 0680 US
(787) 831-9200; *Fax:* (787) 831-9292
www.wtpm.org
info@wtpm.org
License: Aguadilla, PR held by Corp. of the 7th Day Adventists of West Puerto Rico
Arbitron Metro Market: Mayaguez, PR; *Format:* Adult Contemp *Special Programming:* English one hr, class 7 hrs wkly; *Hrs. of News Programming:* News progmg 11 hrs wkly; *Target Audience:* General; traditionalChristian groups
Pastor James Whiteÿ, General Manager

Arecibo

WCMN
06-24-1947; 1280 kHz AM; *Hrs Open:* 24; 5 kw-D, ND1; 1 kw-N, ND1; N18 28 52 W66 41 16
Mailing Address: P.O. Box 363222, San Juan, PR 00936-3222 US
Second Address: #1581 Ponce de Leon St., Rio Piedras, PR
(787) 474-0630
www.notiuno.com
License: Arecibo, PR held by Caribbean Broadcasting Corp.
Group Owner: Uno Radio Group; (acq 4-7-2004; $5.75 million for stock with co-located FM).
Arbitron Metro Market: Puerto Rico, PR; *Format:* News; *Hrs. of News Programming:* news progmg 50 hrs wkly; *No. News Employees:* 3; *Target Audience:* 30 plus.
Luis Soto, President

WCMN-FM
01-01-1967; 107.3 MHz FM; *Hrs Open:* 24; 50 kw; 1027 ft.; N18 14 52 W66 48 43
P.O. Box 363222, San Juan, PR 00936-3222 US
(787) 474-0630
www.hot102pr.com
License: Arecibo, PR held by Caribbean Broadcasting Corp.
Group Owner: Uno Radio Group
Arbitron Metro Market: Puerto Rico, PR; *Format:* Contemporary Hits/Top 40; *Target Audience:* 18-42; young adults
Hector Matos, Programming Director

WMIA
02-21-1957; 1070 kHz AM; *Hrs Open:* 19; 0.5 kw-D, ND1; 2.5 kw-N, ND1; N18 27 33 W66 45 20
Mailing Address: P. O. Box 1055, Arecibo, PR 0613 US
Second Address: 1168 Miramar Ave., Arecibo, PR 612
(787) 878-2727; *Fax:* 787-878-1275
www.wmia1070.com
epifanioro@gmail.com
License: Arecibo, PR held by Abacoa Radio Corp.
Arbitron Metro Market: Puerto Rico; *Format:* Oldies; *Target Audience:* 25 plus; the buying power in the area
Epifanio Rodriguez-Velez, General Manager

WNIK
01-01-1957; 1230 kHz AM; 1 kw-U, ND1; N18 27 20 W66 44 24
PO Box 0556, Arecibo, PR 0612 US
(787) 880-2461; *Fax:* (787) 880-2461
www.unicaradio1230.com
mss64radio@gmail.comÿ
License: Arecibo, PR held by Unik Broadcasting System Corp.
Arbitron Metro Market: Puerto Rico; *Format:* Variety/Diverse; *Target Audience:* General.
Manuel Santiago, General Manager

WNIK-FM
07-17-1965; 106.5 MHz FM; 25 kw; 20 ft.; N18 27 20 W66 44 24
PO Box 0556, Arecibo, PR 0613 US
(787) 880-2613; *Fax:* (787) 879-1011
License: Arecibo, PR held by Kelly Broadcasting System Inc.
Arbitron Metro Market: Puerto Rico; *Format:* Spanish, Christian
Raul Santiago, General Manager

Barceloneta-Manati

WBQN
03-01-1975; 1160 kHz AM; 5 kw-D, DAD; 2.5 kw-N, DAD; N18 26 23 W66 33 7
P.O.Box 993, Manati, PR 0701 US
(787) 854-2450; *Fax:* (787) 854-3738
www.wbqn1160.com/
riveraolmo@hotmail.com
License: Barceloneta-Manati, PR held by Radio Borinquen Inc.
Arbitron Metro Market: Manati, PR; *Format:* Contemporary Hits/Top 40, Spanish, 86; *Target Audience:* General.
Angel Rivera, President
Luis Rivera Jr., General Manager

Barranquitas

WOLA
03-01-1986; 1380 kHz AM; 1 kw-U, ND1; N18 11 1 W66 18 24

Carr 719 Km1 Bo Helechal, Baranquitas, PR 0618 US
(787) 857-1380; *Fax:* (787) 857-1381
License: Barranquitas, PR held by Torrecillas Broadcasting Corp.
Arbitron Metro Market: Puerto Rico *TV Affiliate:* Sp; *Format:* Jazz; *No. News Employees:* General.
CEO, CEO/COO

Bayamon

WODA
12-03-1959; 94.7 MHz FM; *Hrs Open:* 24; 31 kw; 1837 ft.; N18 16 44 W65 51 12
Mailing Address: P.O. Box 949, Guaynbo, PR 0970 US
Second Address: Amelia Industrial Park, Calle Frances 42, Guaynabo, PR 968
(787) 622-9700; *Fax:* (787) 622-9481
www.lanueva94.com
rogie@sbspuertorico.com
License: Bayamon, PR held by WLDI Inc.
Group Owner: Spanish Broadcasting System Inc.; (acq 11-29-99; grpsl)
Arbitron Metro Market: Guayanbo,PR; *Format:* Contemporary Hits/Top 40; *Target Audience:* 12-24; males & females, middle/upper socio-economic
Raul Alarcon, President
Ismael Nieves, General Manager
Marie Martinez, General Sales Mgr
Rogie Gallart, Programming Director
Luis Rivera, Promotions Manager
Demare Ramirez, News Director
Alejandro Luciano, Chief Engineer

WCMA(AM)
01-01-1966; 1600 kHz AM; *Hrs Open:* 18; 5 kw-U; N18 21 38 W66 09 30
Mailing Address: Box 9394, San Juan, PR 00908-0394
Second Address: 403 Del Parque, 15 th Fl., Santurce, PR 00912-3709
(787) 785-1600,(787) 729-1600; *Fax:* (787) 785-2094,(787) 723-8685
ttrelles@yahoo.com
License: Bayamon, Bayamon County, PR held by Marketing Promotion Network Inc.
Population Served: 2,000,000; *Arbitron Metro Market:* Puerto Rico
Tony Trelles, President
Martha Villanueva, Operations Dir

WRSJ
01-01-1947; 1560 kHz AM; 5 kw-D, ND1; 0.75 kw-N, ND1; N18 24 5 W66 7 14
Box 3986 Valle Arriba Hgts Station, Carolina, PR 0984 US
(787) 274-1800; *Fax:* (787) 281-9758
License: Bayamon, PR held by International Broadcasting Corp.
Group Owner: International Broadcasting Corp.; (acq 7-6-2004; $1.45 million with WCHQ(AM) Quebradillas).
Arbitron Metro Market: Puerto Rico
Pedro Collazo, President
Margarita Nazario, General Manager

WXYX
02-01-1979; 100.7 MHz FM; *Hrs Open:* 24; 50 kw; 1093 ft.; N18 17 29 W66 11 03
Mailing Address: HC 71 Box, Bayamon, PR 00956 US
Second Address: Rd 174, KM 5.0 Bo. Guaraguao, Bayamon, PR 00956-9535
(787) 269-1000
www.lax.fm
License: Bayamon, PR held by RAAD Broadcasting Corp
Group Owner: RAAD Broadcasting Corp
Arbitron Metro Market: Bayamon, PR; *Format:* Contemporary Hits/Top 40; *Target Audience:* 12-34; young teens, adults
Roberto Davila, President
Carlos Alvarez, General Sales Mgr
Herman Davila, Programming Director
Wendy Miranda, Promotions Director

Cabo Rojo

WYAC
01-09-1970; 930 kHz AM; *Hrs Open:* 21; 2.5 kw-U, ND1; N18 6 5 W67 9 17
Mailing Address: Post Office Box 9023916, San Juan, PR 0902 US
Second Address: Radio Centre, Post & Bosgue Sts., Mayaguez, PR 684
(787) 620-9898
www.radiopr740.com
info@wyac.com
License: Cabo Rojo, PR held by Bestov Broadcasting Inc.
Arbitron Metro Market: Mayagueez, PR; *Format:* News, News/Talk, 86; *Target Audience:* General; Mayaguez county residents
Luis Majia, President
Francisco Acosta, General Manager

WMIO
01-10-1988; 102.3 MHz FM; *Hrs Open:* 6 AM-midnight; 3 kw; 781 ft.; N17 59 37 W67 10 27
P.O. Box 363222, San Juan, PR 00936-3222 US
(787) 474-0630; *Fax:* (787) 758-1410
www.hot102pr.com
License: Cabo Rojo, PR held by Arso Radio Corp.
Group Owner: Uno Radio Group; (acq 3-26-2007; $3.25 million)
Arbitron Metro Market: Puerto Rico; *Format:* Contemporary Hits/Top 40; *Target Audience:* 18-45; general
Luis Soto, President

Caguas

WNEL
07-21-1947; 1430 kHz AM; *Hrs Open:* 24; 5 kw-D, ND1; 5 kw-N, ND1; N18 14 53 W66 1 25
P.O. Box 487, Caguas, PR 00726 US
(787) 744-3131; *Fax:* (787) 743-0252
License: Caguas, PR held by Turabo Radio Corp.
Group Owner: Uno Radio Group; (acq 4-1-73).
Arbitron Metro Market: Puerto Rico; *Format:* Oldies; *Hrs. of News Programming:* 15; *Target Audience:* 24 plus.
Luis Soto, President

WVJP
11-24-1947; 1110 kHz AM; *Hrs Open:* 24; 2.5 kw-D, ND1; 0.5 kw-N, ND1; N18 13 25 W66 1 11
Mailing Address: P. O. Box 207, Caguas, PR 0726 US
Second Address: Tomas de Castro #2, Caguas, PR 626
(787) 743-5790; *Fax:* (787) 746-6996
dimension103.com
License: Caguas, PR held by Borinquen Broadcasting Co. Inc.
Arbitron Metro Market: Caguas, PR; *Format:* Adult Contemp
Jancel Pereira, CEO
Bienvenido Rodriguez, General Manager
Norma Rodriquez-Trinidad, Programming Director
Jesus Gomez, Chief Engineer

WVJP-FM
10-01-1968; 103.3 MHz FM; 28 kw; 1906 ft.; N18 16 41 W65 51 9
Mailing Address: P.O. Box 207, Caguas, PR 0726 US
Second Address: Tomas de Castro #2, Caguas, PR 626
(787) 743-5790; *Fax:* (787) 746-6996
dimension103.com
License: Caguas, PR
Arbitron Metro Market: Caguas, PR; *Format:* Classic Rock, Tejano
Ranny Parks, General Manager
Debra Toler, General Sales Mgr
Jeff Halsey, Programming Director

Camuy

WDIN
08-15-1968; 102.9 MHz FM; 50 kw; 1053 ft.; N18 17 27 W66 39 39
Box 780, Camuy, PR 0627 US
(787) 743-5790; *Fax:* (787) 746-6996
www.dimension.fm
License: Camuy, PR held by HQ 103 Inc.
Arbitron Metro Market: Puerto Rico; *Format:* Urban Contemporary
Bienvenido Rodriguez, General Manager
Maggie Lopez, Programming Director

Canovanas

WGIT
01-01-2001; 1660 kHz AM
2001 Penn. Ave., NW, Ste 400 Frm, Washington, DC 20006 US
(787) 776-1616; *Fax:* (787) 281-9758
License: Canovanas, PR held by International Broadcasting Corp.
Group Owner: International Broadcasting Corp.; acq 5-29-03; $1.3 million).
Format: Sports
Pedro Roman-Collazo, General Manager
Margarita Nazario, Station Manager

Carolina

WIDA
03-16-1964; 1400 kHz AM; 1 kw-U, ND1; N18 23 49 W65 56 6
Mailing Address: P.O. Box 188, Carolina, PR 0928 US
Second Address: Ignacio Arzuaga 203-7, Carolina, PR 987
(787) 757-1414; *Fax:* (787) 769-4103
www.cadenaradiovida.com
radiovida@cadenaradiovida.com
License: Carolina, PR held by Radio Vida Inc.
Arbitron Metro Market: Puerto Rico
Yexica Rosario, President
Wanda Pagan, Operations Dir
Hilda Dumont, General Sales Mgr
Alberto Periera, Chief Engineer

*WIDA-FM
08-01-1983; 90.5 MHz FM; 25 kw; 1900 ft.; N18 6 48 W66 3 7
Mailing Address: Calle Arzuaga Number 203, Apartado 188, Carolina, PR 0630 US
Second Address: Ignacio Arzuaga 203-7, Carolina, PR 987
(787) 757-1414; *Fax:* (787) 769-4103
www.cadenaradiovida.com
License: Carolina, PR held by Radio Vida Inc.
Arbitron Metro Market: Puerto Rico
Yexika Rosario, President
Wanda Pagan, Operations Dir
Alberto Pereira, Engineering Dir
Hilda Dumont, Tesorera Junta

WVOZ-FM
03-03-1967; 107.7 MHz FM; 12 kw; 2759 ft.; N18 18 36 W65 47 41
#1554 Bori Street, Antonsanti Development, Rio Pedras, PR 0928 US
(787) 274-1800; *Fax:* (787) 281-9758
www.mix107.fm
License: Carolina, PR held by International Broadcasting Corp.
Group Owner: International Broadcasting Corp.
Arbitron Metro Market: Puerto Rico; *Format:* Adult Contemp
Pedro Roman-Collazo, President
Margarita Nazario, General Manager

Cayey

WLEY
12-03-1965; 1080 kHz AM; *Hrs Open:* 19; 0.25 kw-U, ND1; N18 6 55 W66 8 28 *Rebroadcasts:* WSKN 1320 Radio Isla
G.P.O. Box 7213, Ponce, PR 0731 US
(787) 292-1700; *Fax:* (787) 292-1717
www.laley1079.com
noticias@radioisla1320.com
License: Cayey, PR held by Media Power Group Inc.
Group Owner: Media Power Group Inc.; (acq 9-30-2003; grpsl).
Nat'l Network: CNN Radio
Arbitron Metro Market: Puerto Rico; *Format:* News, Talk; *Hrs. of News Programming:* 24 hrs wkly; *No. News Employees:* 40; *Target Audience:* 35 plus.
Eduardo Rivero, President
Ismael Nieves, Operations Dir
Nora Plaza, General Sales Mgr
Luis Penchi, Programming Director
Fernando Vazquez, Promotions Manager
Orlando Morales, Operations Manager

Ceiba

WFAB
01-01-1993; 890 kHz AM; 0.25 kw-U, ND1; N18 12 16 W65 42 40
Apartado 318, Rio Blanco, PR 0744 US
(787) 874-0890; *Fax:* (787) 874-0190
www.radiounidadcristiana.com
wfab@osnetpr.com
License: Ceiba, PR held by Daniel Rosario Diaz.
Arbitron Metro Market: Ceiba, PR; *Format:* Religious
Daniel Diaz, President
Jose Garcia, Administrative Officer

WQML
12-01-1996; 101.7 MHz FM; *Hrs Open:* 24; 6 kw; 70 meters; N18 17 37.3 W65 38 40.3
P.O. Box 847, Mayaguez, PR 0681 US
(787) 860-1065; *Fax:* (787) 860-1055
License: Ceiba, PR held by Western New Life Inc
Arbitron Metro Market: Culebra, PR; *Format:* Christian; *No. News Employees:* 4; *Target Audience:* 25-54.; *Adv. Rates:* 20; 17; 20; 14
Aureo Matos, General Manager

Cidra

WNVM
03-01-1972; 97.7 MHz FM; *Hrs Open:* 24; 3 kw; 1093 ft.; N18 16 49.27 W66 6 35.3
P.O. Box 364701, San Juan, PR 0936 US

(787) 745-9700(787) 745-9770; *Fax:* (787) 745-9777
License: Cidra, PR held by New Life Broadcasting Inc.
Arbitron Metro Market: Caguas, PR; *Format:* Christian; *Hrs. of News Programming:* news progmg one hr wkly; *No. News Employees:* 1; *Target Audience:* 25-54; women
Juan Matos, President
Orlando Mercado, General Manager

Coamo

WCPR

01-01-1967; 1450 kHz AM; *Hrs Open:* 16; 1 kw-U, ND1; N18 5 29 W66 22 15
P. O. Box 316, Coamo, PR 0640 US
(787) 825-7061; *Fax:* (787) 825-1905
License: Coamo, PR held by Coamo Broadcasting Corp.
Arbitron Metro Market: Puerto Rico PR; *Format:* Adult Contemp; *Hrs. of News Programming:* News progmg 9 hrs wkly; *Target Audience:* General.
Jose David Soler, President

Corozal

WORO

07-01-1968; 92.5 MHz FM; 50 kw; 1198 ft.; N18 15 9 W66 19 58
Mailing Address: P.O. Box 9021967, San Juan, PR 0902 US
Second Address: Box 9021967, San Juan, PR 902
(787) 751-1380; *Fax:* (787) 758-9967
License: Corozal, PR held by Catholic Apostolic & Roman Church San Juan Archdiocese.
Arbitron Metro Market: Puerto Rico *TV Affiliate:* Sp
Chief of Engineering

Culebra

*WJVP

01-01-1998; 89.3 MHz FM; 50 kw vert; 571 ft.; N18 19 37 W65 18 21
Mailing Address: P.O. Box 40,000, Bayamon, PR 0958 US
Second Address: An 167 Calle Granada AM Alahambra, Bayamon, PR 956
(787) 288-4336; *Fax:* (787) 740-7104
www.clamorpr.org
License: Culebra, Culebra County, PR held by Clamor Broadcasting Network Inc.
Arbitron Metro Market: Puerto Rico; *Format:* Religious
Jorde Raschke, General Manager

Fajardo

WRXD

02-15-1969; 96.5 MHz FM; *Hrs Open:* 24; 11.5 kw; 2795 ft.; N18 18 36 W65 47 41
Mailing Address: 3191 Coral Way, Suite 805, Miami, FL 33145 US
Second Address: Amelia Industrial Park, Calle Frances #42, Guaynabo, PR 968
(787) 622-9700; *Fax:* (787) 622-9478
www.spanishbroadcastingsystem.com
License: Fajardo, PR held by WCMA Licensing Inc.
Group Owner: Spanish Broadcasting System Inc.; (acq 8-4-98; $8.25 million)
Arbitron Metro Market: Fajardo, PR; *Format:* News
Falex Bonnet, General Manager

WMDD

05-31-1947; 1480 kHz AM; *Hrs Open:* 24; 5 kw-U, ND1; N18 21 46 W65 38 24
Puerta-Tierra, 306 Ponce Delon Avenue, San Juan, PR 0906 US
(787) 863-0202; *Fax:* (787) 863-0166
License: Fajardo, PR held by Pan Caribbean Broadcasting de P.R. Inc.
Arbitron Metro Market: Puerto Rico; *Format:* Talk; *Target Audience:* 25-49.
Rita Friedman, President

Guayama

*WCRP

01-01-1991; 88.1 MHz FM; 27 kw; 1890 ft.; N18 6 47 W66 3 8
P.O. Box 344, Guayama, PR 0655 US
(787) 653-0880; *Fax:* (787) 653-1988
www.revelacion.fm
License: Guayama, PR held by Ministerio Radial Cristo Viene Pronto Inc.
Arbitron Metro Market: Puerto Rico; *Format:* Religious
Carmita Rodriguez, President

WIBS

03-01-1981; 1540 kHz AM; 1 kw-D, NDD; N17 59 44 W66 4 39
Box 1540, Guayama, PR 0655 US
(787) 274-1800; *Fax:* (787) 281-9758
License: Guayama, PR held by International Broadcasting Corp.
Group Owner: International Broadcasting Corp.; acq 12-3-01; $300,000).
Arbitron Metro Market: Puerto Rico
Pedro Roman-Collazo, CEO
Margarita Nazario, General Manager

WMEG

11-01-1966; 106.9 MHz FM; 24.5 kw; 1949 ft.; N18 6 48 W66 3 7
Mailing Address: 3191 Coral Way, Suite 805, Miami, FL 33145 US
Second Address: Amelia Industrial Park, Calle Frances 42, Guaynabo, PR 968
(787) 622-9700; *Fax:* (787) 622-9478
www.lamega.fm
License: Guayama, PR held by WMEG Licensing Inc.
Group Owner: Spanish Broadcasting System Inc.; (acq 3-15-99; $16 million with WZET(FM) Hormigueros).
Arbitron Metro Market: Puerto Rico; *Format:* Christian
Falex Bonnet, General Manager
Edgardo Aubray, General Sales Mgr

WXRF

07-01-1948; 1590 kHz AM; 1 kw-U, ND1; N17 57 40 W66 8 20
1554 Bori St. Antonsanti Dev., San Juan, PR 0928 US
(787) 274-1800; *Fax:* (787) 281-9758
License: Guayama, PR held by International Broadcasting Corp.
Group Owner: International Broadcasting Corp.; (acq 10-7-2004; $1,382,961 with WVEO(TV) Aguadilla).
Arbitron Metro Market: Guayama, PR; *Format:* Spanish
Pedro Roman-Collazo, President
Margarita Nazario, General Manager

Guayanilla

WOIZ

10-01-1986; 1130 kHz AM; 0.2 kw-D, ND1; 0.7 kw-N, ND1; N18 1 3 W66 46 22
Mailing Address: Box 3800, Guayanilla, PR 0656 US
Second Address: 383 Road klmo.4, Bo Magas Arriba, Guayanilla, PR 656
787-835-3130; *Fax:* (787) 835-3130
radioantillas@yahoo.com
License: Guayanilla, PR held by Radio Antillas of Harriet Broadcasters.
Arbitron Metro Market: Puerto Rico *TV Affiliate:* Sp; *No. News Employees:* 35 plus.; *Adv. Rates:* 12; 12; 12; 12

Hatillo

WMSW

01-01-1980; 1120 kHz AM; 2.6 kw-D, DAN; 5 kw-N, DAN; N18 28 15 W66 50 24
Box 1652, Arecibo, PR 0613 US
(787) 879-4094; *Fax:* (787) 880-0441
www.radioonce.com
mss64radio@gmail.comÿ
License: Hatillo, PR held by Aurora Broadcasting Corp.
Arbitron Metro Market: Puerto Rico; *Format:* News, News/Talk, 86
Manuel Santos, President
Hector Santos, Operations Dir
Lloyd Santos, General Sales Mgr
Ronald Cushing, Chief Engineer

Hormigueros

WZET

10-12-1980; 92.1 MHz FM; 2.95 kw; 1106 ft.; N18 19 6 W67 10 42
Mailing Address: 3191 Coral Way, Suite 805, Miami, FL 33145 US
Second Address: Amelia Industrial Park, Calle Frances 42, Guaynabo, PR 968
(787) 622-9700; *Fax:* (787) 622-9478
www.spanishbroadcastingsystem.com
info@spanishbroadcastingsystem.com
License: Hormigueros, PR held by WSMA Licensing Inc.
Group Owner: Spanish Broadcasting System Inc.; (acq 3-15-99; $16 million with WMEG(FM) Guayama).
Arbitron Metro Market: Hormigueros, PR
Falex Bonnet, General Manager

WRRH

01-01-1998; 106.1 MHz FM; 0.8 kw horiz, 0.71 kw vert; 1932 ft.; N18 8 33 W66 58 56
P. O. Box 174, Lajas, PR 0667 US
(787) 849-1061; *Fax:* (787) 849-6106
www.renacer1061.com
renacer1061@yahoo.com
License: Hormigueros, PR held by Renacer Broadcasters Corp.
Arbitron Metro Market: Puerto Rico; *Format:* Christian
Larry Ramos, General Manager
Kehmuel Ramos, Programming Director

Humacao

WALO

02-11-1958; 1240 kHz AM; *Hrs Open:* 19; 1 kw-U, ND1; N18 8 49 W65 48 49
Call Box 1240, Humacao, PR 0792 US
(787) 725-8265; *Fax:* (787) 852-1280
www.waloradio.com
wlo@prtc.net
License: Humacao, PR held by Ochoa Broadcasting Corp.
Wire Services: CNN
Arbitron Metro Market: Humacao, PR; *Format:* Adult Contemp, News, 62, Sports, Talk *Special Programming:* Relg 2 hrs wkly; *Hrs. of News Programming:* news progmg 60 hrs wkly; *No. News Employees:* 2 *TargetAudience:* 18-54; general; *Adv. Rates:* 42; 42; 42; 45
Efrain Archilla-Roig, CEO
Maribel Ortiz-Del Valle, Operations Dir
Beatriz Archilla, General Manager
Ken Allen, General Sales Mgr

Isabela

WISA

10-19-1961; 1390 kHz AM; 1 kw-U, ND1; N18 30 6 W67 2 1
P.O. Box 9023916, San Juan, PR 0902 US
(787) 872-0100; *Fax:* (787) 872-0802
www.wisa1390.com
License: Isabela, PR held by Isabela Broadcasting Inc.
Arbitron Metro Market: Puerto Rico; *Format:* Adult Contemp
David Marda, General Manager
Edwin Nieves, Programming Director

WELX

01-01-1987; 101.5 MHz FM; 42 kw; Ant -26 ft; N18 26 36 W67 08 50
Box 9023916, San Juan, PR 0902
(787) 620-9898
www.sistema102.com
License: Isabela, PR held by Isabela Broadcasting Inc.
Arbitron Metro Market: Puerto Rico
Luis Mejia, CEO

Island of Vieques

WIVV

12-08-1956; 1370 kHz AM; *Hrs Open:* 24; 5 kw-D, ND1; 1 kw-N, ND1; N18 6 7 W65 28 21 *Rebroadcasts:* Rebroadcasting WBMJ(AM) San Juan 100%
P.O. Box 367000, San Juan, PR 0936 US
(787) 724-1190; *Fax:* (787) 722-5395
License: Island of Vieques, PR held by Calvary Evangelistic Mission Inc.
Group Owner: Calvary Evangelistic Mission Inc.
Nat'l Network: Salem Radio Network
Arbitron Metro Market: Puerto Rico; *Format:* Adult Contemp, Talk, 74 *Special Programming:* News 7 hrs wkly; *Hrs. of News Programming:* News progmg 7 hrs wkly; *Target Audience:* General; eastern Puerto Rico & theLeeward Islands
Janet Luttrell, CEO

Juana Diaz

WCGB

11-23-1967; 1060 kHz AM; *Hrs Open:* 5 AM-midnight
Mailing Address: P. O. Box 9405, Grand Rapids, MN 49509 US
Second Address: Carretera Hwy. 1, KM 112.0, Juana Diaz, PR 795
(787) 837-1060; *Fax:* (787) 260-1060
www.therockradio.org
wcgb@therockradio.org
License: Juana Diaz, PR held by Calvary Evangelistic Mission Inc.
Group Owner: Calvary Evangelistic Mission Inc.; (acq 12-3-2004; $500,000)
Arbitron Metro Market: Juana Diaz,PR; *Format:* Variety/Diverse, Religious; *Hrs. of News Programming:* News progmg 10 hrs wkly; *Target Audience:* Adult.; *Adv. Rates:* 264; 192; 264; 120
Lawrence Trumbower, General Manager

Juncos

WRRE
01-01-1971; 1460 kHz AM; *Hrs Open:* 24
P.O. Box 827, Carolina, PR 0986 US
(787) 561-1460,(888) 561-1460; *Fax:* (787) 716-0808
www.sonidosantidad.com
sonidosantidad@hotmail.com
License: Juncos, PR held by Hacienda San Eladio Inc.
Arbitron Metro Market: Puerto Rico; *Format:* Religious; *Target Audience:* All.
Miguel A. Medina, General Manager

Lajas

WBSG
01-01-1986; 1510 kHz AM; *Hrs Open:* 16; 1 kw-U, DA1; N18 2 11 W67 4 58
Las Torres Sur Ste 10e, Bayamon, PR 0619 US
License: Lajas, PR held by Perry Broadcasting Systems

WXLX
01-05-1994; 103.7 MHz FM; *Hrs Open:* 24; 50 kw; 456 ft; N17 59 37 W67 11 09 *Rebroadcasts:* Rebroadcasts WXYX(FM) Bayamon 100%
HC 71 Box, Bayamon, PR 00956 US
(787) 269-1000
www.lax.fm
License: Lajas, PR held by RAAD Broadcasting Corp
Group Owner: RAAD Broadcasting Corp; (acq 1-20-98; $3 million)
Population Served: 600,000; *Arbitron Metro Market:* Puerto Rico
Roberto Davila, President
Roberto Davila Rios, Operations Dir
Carlos Alvarez, General Sales Mgr
Herman Davila, Programming Director
Wendy Armando, Promotions Manager
Alfredo Gomez, Chief Engineer

Lares

WGDL
02-01-1983; 1200 kHz AM; *Hrs Open:* 12; 0.25 kw-D, NDD; N18 17 40 W66 53 50
P.O. Box 872, Lares, PR 0669 US
(787) 897-1200; *Fax:* (787) 897-7821
wgdl1200@yahoo.com
License: Lares, PR held by Lares Broadcasting Corp.
Arbitron Metro Market: Puerto Rico; *Hrs. of News Programming:* news progmg 20 hrs wkly; *No. News Employees:* 1; *Target Audience:* General.
Pedro Hernandez, President
Julia Bello, General Manager
Angel Perez, Programming Director

Las Piedras

WZOL
11-04-1978; 98.3 MHz FM; 50 kw; Ant 751 ft; N18 19 39 W65 18 05
Box 1047, Fajardo, PR 0929
(787) 860-1065; *Fax:* (787) 860-1055
License: Las Piedras, PR held by La Mas Z Radio Inc.
Arbitron Metro Market: Puerto Rico
Gary King Sr., CEO
James Brown, Operations Dir

Levittown

*WLUZ
10-01-1986; 88.5 MHz FM; 100 w vert; Ant 69 ft; N18 26 55 W66 10 26
Box 371177, Cayey, PR 0958
(787) 798-8850; *Fax:* (787) 798-8851
www.plenitudfm.com
License: Levittown, PR held by La Gigante Siembra Inc.
Arbitron Metro Market: Puerto Rico
Shay Garcya, Station Manager

Luquillo

WYAS
01-01-1976; 92.1 MHz FM; *Hrs Open:* 24; 6.9 kw; Ant 915 ft; N18 19 54 W65 41 11
Box 29027, Rio Piedras, PR 0929
(787) 767-1005; *Fax:* (787) 758-1055
www.radiosol.org
wzol@radiosol.org
License: Luquillo, Luquillo County, PR held by Radio Sol 92, WZOL Inc.
Arbitron Metro Market: Puerto Rico
Pedro Canales, President
William Irizarry, General Manager
Maria Navarro, Programming Director
Raymond Hernandez, Chief Engineer

Manati

WMNT
12-01-1959; 1500 kHz AM; *Hrs Open:* 16; 1 kw-D, ND1; 0.25 kw-N, ND1; N18 26 6 W66 29 54
Mailing Address: Calle Delta #1305, Caparra Terrace, San Juan, PR 0920 US
Second Address: Delta St. #1305 Caparra Terr., San Juan, PR 920
(787) 854-2223; *Fax:* (787) 781-7647
www.radioatenas.com
info@radioatenas.com
License: Manati, PR held by Manati Radio Corp.
Arbitron Metro Market: Manati, PR; *Format:* News, News/Talk, 84, Talk *Special Programming:* NBA, World Series in Sp; *Hrs. of News Programming:* news progmg 25 hrs wkly; *No. News Employees:* 2 *Target Audience:* 25 plus; men & women; *Adv. Rates:* 20; 20; 20; 10
Jose Dominicci, CEO
Jose Ribas-Dominicci, President
Freddy Ribas, Operations Dir
Maria Rodriguez, Station Manager

WNRT
01-01-1973; 96.9 MHz FM; *Hrs Open:* 24 hours; 50 kw; 1125 ft.; N18 15 34 W66 32 15
PO Box 13324, Santurce, PR 0908 US
(787) 999-0360; *Fax:* (787) 999-1560
www.triunfofm.net
License: Manati, PR held by La Voz Evangelica de Puerto Rico Inc.
Arbitron Metro Market: Puerto Rico; *Format:* Christian
Luis Barajas, President
Moises Flores, Operations Dir
Mosses Flores, General Manager
Carlos Flecha, Programming Director
Jorge Figueroa, Engineering Dir
Virgen Perez, Sales VP

Maricao

WAEL-FM
07-01-1970; 96.1 MHz FM; *Hrs Open:* 24; 24 kw; 2011 ft.; N18 9 7 W66 59 15
Mailing Address: P.O. Box 1370, Mayaguez, PR 0681 US
Second Address: 600 Ramirez Pabon St., Guanajibo Homes, Mayaguez, PR 681
(787) 832-4560/ 832-0600; *Fax:* (787) 792-3140
License: Maricao, PR held by WAEL Inc.
Arbitron Metro Market: Puerto Rico; *Format:* Spanish, Christian; *Target Audience:* 12-24.
Maria del Pilar-Pirallo, President
Luis Pirallo, Operations Dir
Lydia Vargas, News Director
Ivan Feliu, Chief Engineer

Mayaguez

WYEL
01-01-1949; 600 kHz AM; *Hrs Open:* 4:30 AM-midnight; 5 kw-D, DA1; 5 kw-N, DA1; N18 10 39 W67 10 15
P.O. Box 1370, Mayaguez, PR 00681 US
(787) 758-5800; *Fax:* (787) 763-1854
www.univision.com
License: Mayaguez, PR held by WLII/WSUR License Partnership G.P.
Group Owner: Univision Radio; (acq 11-17-2006; $2 million)
Arbitron Metro Market: Mayaguez, PR; *Format:* Spanish, Talk
Jaime Bauza, General Manager

WIOB
10-12-1947; 97.5 MHz FM; 50 kw; 991 ft.; N18 19 33 W67 10 13
Rebroadcasts: Rebroadcasts WIOA(FM) San Juan 80%
Mailing Address: P.O. Box 101, San Juan, PR 0970 US
Second Address: Amelia Industrial Park, Calle Frances 42, Guaynabo, PR 968
(787) 622-9700; *Fax:* (787) 622-9478
info@spanishbroadcastingsystem.com
License: Mayaguez, PR held by Cadena Estereotempo Inc.
Group Owner: Spanish Broadcasting System Inc.; (acq 11-29-99; grpsl)
Arbitron Metro Market: Puerto Rico; *Format:* Spanish; *Target Audience:* 30-50; women; *Adv. Rates:* 25; 20; 25; 18
Falex Bonnet, General Manager

WKJB
12-06-1946; 710 kHz AM; 10 kw-D, ND1; 0.75 kw-N, ND1; N18 10 8 W67 9 3
P. O. Box 1293, Mayaguez, PR 0681 US
(787) 834-6666; *Fax:* (787) 831-6925
License: Mayaguez, PR held by WKJB-AM Inc.
Arbitron Metro Market: Puerto Rico; *Format:* News, News/Talk, 86 *Special Programming:* Sp 1 hr wkly
Dennis Bechara, President
Ada Ramos, General Sales Mgr
Eric Graniela, Programming Director
Rafy Aviles, News Director
Pedro Velez Jr., Chief Engineer
Jose Bechara Jr., Executive Vice President
Johhny Flores, SportsCommentators

WORA
05-12-1947; 760 kHz AM; 5 kw-U, DA1; N18 11 30 W67 9 28
Mailing Address: P.O. Box 363222, San Juan, PR 00936-3222 US
Second Address: Calle Ponce de Leon, URB El Cerezal #1581, Rio Piedras, PR
(787) 773-7444; *Fax:* (787) 474-0630
www.notiuno.com
License: Mayaguez, PR held by Arso Radio Corp.
Group Owner: Uno Radio Group; (acq 5-10-01; grpsl).
Arbitron Metro Market: Puerto Rico *TV Affiliate:* News; *Format:* News, News/Talk, 86
Luis Soto, President

WNOD
01-01-1960; 94.1 MHz FM; *Hrs Open:* 24; 25 kw; 1959 ft.; N18 9 5 W66 59 20 *Rebroadcasts:* Rebroadcasts WCOM(FM) San Juan 80%
Post Office Box 1718, Mayaguez, PR 0681 US
(787) 265-9494; *Fax:* (787) 622-9481
www.lamega.fm
License: Mayaguez, PR held by WOYE Inc.
Group Owner: Spanish Broadcasting System Inc.; (acq 11-29-99; grpsl).
Arbitron Metro Market: Puerto Rico; *Format:* Contemporary Hits/Top 40; *Hrs. of News Programming:* news progmg 10 hrs wkly; *No. News Employees:* 1; *Target Audience:* 18-49; young adults; *Adv. Rates:* 30; 25; 30;20
Raul Alarcon, Chairman
Ismael Nieves, General Manager
Marie Martinez, General Sales Mgr
Pedro Arroyo, Programming Director
Luis Rivera, Promotions Manager
Demare Ramirez, News Director
Alejandro Luciano, Chief Engineer

WPRA
10-16-1937; 990 kHz AM; *Hrs Open:* 18; 0.91 kw-U, ND1; N18 10 8 W67 9 3
P.O. Box 1293, Mayaguez, PR 0681 US
(787) 834-6666; *Fax:* (787) 831-6925
License: Mayaguez, PR held by WPRA Inc.
Nat'l Network: AP Radio
Arbitron Metro Market: Puerto Rico; *Format:* Contemporary Hits/Top 40, Talk; *Target Audience:* General.; *Adv. Rates:* 16; 16; 16; 16
Dennis Bechara, President
Jose Bechara, Operations Dir

*WRUO
12-01-1998; 88.3 MHz FM; 2 kw; 1004 ft.; N18 19 31 W67 10 13
P O Box 21305 Upr, San Juan, PR 0931 US
(787) 763-4699; *Fax:* (787) 764-1290
www.wrtu.PR
lluna@wrtu.pr
License: Mayaguez, PR held by University of Puerto Rico.
Arbitron Metro Market: Puerto Rico
Ezequiel Rodr¡guez, Operations Dir
Yolanda Zabala, General Manager
Carlos Camu¤as, Programming Director

WTIL
11-01-1950; 1300 kHz AM; 1 kw-U, ND1; N18 11 0 W67 10 4
Mailing Address: Calle Post Esquina Bosqu, Mayaguez, PR 0681 US
Second Address: Post & Bosque Sts., Mayaguez, PR 680
(787) 832-1300; *Fax:* (787) 265-1300
radioutil@gmail.comÿmatos1040@gmail.com
License: Mayaguez, PR held by International Broadcasting Corp.
Group Owner: International Broadcasting Corp.; acq 5-12-2004; $700,000).
Arbitron Metro Market: Mayaguez, PR; *Format:* Adult Contemp, Oldies, 86; *Target Audience:* 35 plus.
Lynette Matos, Dept.ÿSales and Programming
Jason Matos, ÿDept.ÿAccounting

WUKQ-FM
01-15-1963; 98.7 MHz FM; 25 kw; 1,972 ft.; N18 9 5 W66 59 19
P.O. Box 364668, San Juan, PR 00936 US
(787) 758-5800; *Fax:* (787) 763-1854
www.univision.com
License: Mayaguez, PR held by WLII/WSUR License Partnership G.P.
Group Owner: Univision Radio; (acq 8-1-2003; grpsl).
Arbitron Metro Market: Mayaguez, PR; *Format:* Contemporary Hits/Top 40 *Special Programming:* Jazz 6 hrs wkly
Jaime Bauza, General Manager
Carlos Pagan, General Sales Mgr
Aracelis Cruz, Promotions Manager
Reynaldo Quinones, Director of Sales

Moca

WZNA
12-01-1983; 1040 kHz AM
P.O. Box 7, Moca, PR 0676 US
(787) 745-9770; *Fax:* (787) 745-9777
www.nuevavidafm.com
License: Moca, PR held by Western New Life Inc.
Arbitron Metro Market: Moca, PR; *Format:* Christian
Juan Carlos Barreto, President
Orlando Mercede, General Manager

Morovis

WEKO
12-01-1981; 1580 kHz AM; 5 kw-D, DAD; 2.5 kw-N, DAD; N18 20 32 W66 25 8
1554 Bori St. Caribe Dev., San Juan, PR 0927 US
(787) 864-2460; *Fax:* (787) 281-9758
License: Morovis, PR held by International Broadcasting Corp.
Group Owner: International Broadcasting Corp.; acq 9-29-98; $315,000).
Arbitron Metro Market: Puerto Rico; *Format:* News; *Target Audience:* 30 plus.
Pedro Roman-Collazo, President
Margarita Nazario, General Manager

Naguabo

WYQE
12-01-1994; 92.9 MHz FM; *Hrs Open:* 24; 3.9 kw; 751 ft.; N18 16 50 W65 40 13
Mailing Address: Box 9300, Naguabo, PR 0718 US
Second Address: Apt. 2-A, Naguabo, PR 718
(809) 847-9300; *Fax:* (809) 874-9290
www.yunque93.com
wyqe@yunque93.com
License: Naguabo, Humacao County, PR held by Fajardo Broadcasting Co. Inc.
Arbitron Metro Market: Puerto Rico; *Format:* Spanish; *Hrs. of News Programming:* news progmg 20 hrs wkly; *No. News Employees:* 2; *Target Audience:* 18 plus; general; *Adv. Rates:* 44; 44; 44; 44
Efrain Archilla-Diez, President
Raul Rivera, Operations Dir
Edwin Glass, General Sales Mgr
Vanessa Jimenez, National Sales Manager

Pastillo

***WJDZ**
01-01-2006; 90.1 MHz FM; 0.9 kw; -181 ft.; N17 59 57 W66 27 29
P.O. Box 8072, Ponce, PR 0732 US
License: Pastillo, Santa Isabel County, PR held by Siembra Fertil P.R. Inc.
Arbitron Metro Market: Pastillo, PR; *Format:* Christian, Spanish
Susanne Meyers, General Manager
Bill Phipps, Programming Director

Patillas

WEXS
01-01-1991; 610 kHz AM; *Hrs Open:* 5:30 AM-10 PM; 0.25 kw-D, ND2; 1 kw-N, ND2; N18 0 36 W66 1 28
P.O. Box 640, Patillas, PR 0723 US
(787) 839-0610; *Fax:* (787) 839-0960
License: Patillas, PR held by Community Broadcasting Inc.
Arbitron Metro Market: Patillas, PR; *Format:* Adult Contemp, News *Special Programming:* Relg 2 hrs, sports 6 hrs wkly; *Target Audience:* 18-55.
Enrique Garcia, General Manager

Penuelas

WPPC
05-25-1976; 1570 kHz AM; *Hrs Open:* 12; 1 kw-D, ND1; 0.126 kw-N, ND1; N18 3 47 W66 43 4
P. O. Box 9064, Ponce, PR 0732 US
(809) 836-1570,(809) 848-4670; *Fax:* (787) 848-4670
radiofelicidad@yahoo.com
License: Penuelas, PR held by Radio Felicidad Inc.
Arbitron Metro Market: Puerto Rico; *Format:* Adult Contemp, Religious; *Target Audience:* General.; *Adv. Rates:* 4; 4; 4; N/A
Julio Valazquez, President
Rafael Acosta, Chief Engineer

Ponce

WUKQ
05-01-1957; 1420 kHz AM; *Hrs Open:* 24; 1 kw-U, ND1; N17 59 23 W66 37 21 *Rebroadcasts:* Rebroadcasts WKAQ(AM) San Juan 99%
2250 Las Americas Ave., Suite 529, Ponce, PR 00731 US
(787) 758-5800; *Fax:* (787) 763-1854
www.univision.com
License: Ponce, PR held by WLII/WSUR License Partnership G.P.
Group Owner: Univision Radio; (acq 8-1-2003; grpsl).
Arbitron Metro Market: Ponce, PR; *Format:* News, News/Talk, 86; *Target Audience:* 25-55; young professionals, retirees, middle & upper income
Jaime Bauza, General Manager

***WPUC-FM**
05-17-1984; 88.9 MHz FM; *Hrs Open:* 4 AM-midnight; 11 kw; 2913 ft.; N18 10 27 W66 35 32
2250 Las Americas Avenue, Ste 529, Ponce, PR 0731 US
(787) 844-8809; *Fax:* (787) 651-2022
www.catolicaradiopr.com
info@catolicaradiopr.com
License: Ponce, Ponce County, PR held by Pontifical Catholic University of Puerto Rico Service Association Inc.
Arbitron Metro Market: Ponce, PR; *Format:* Adult Contemp; *Hrs. of News Programming:* news progmg 30 hrs wkly; *No. News Employees:* 2; *Target Audience:* 25-39/40-45; professional young adults, retirees-middle & upperclass
Julio Ramirez, General Manager
Jose Leon, Station Manager
Ediel Montalvo, Programming Director
Rolando Mendez, Promotions Manager
King Moreira, Chief Engineer
Jose ""Jossie"" Tizol, Shift Control Supervisor
Orsini Texeira Betzy,Administrative Officer
Marisel Salazar, Production
Jose ""Pep,n"" Fern ndez, Reporter
Luis R. Varela, Reporter - Sports

WIOC
01-01-1970; 105.1 MHz FM; *Hrs Open:* 24; 47 kw; -200 ft.; N17 59 27 W66 37 45 *Rebroadcasts:* Rebroadcasts WIOA(FM) San Juan 80%
Mailing Address: P.O. Box 1718, Mayaguez, PR 0681 US
Second Address: Amelia Industrial Park, Calle Frances 42, Guaynabo, PR 978
(787) 622-9700; *Fax:* (787) 622-9478
www.lamega.fm
info@lamega.fm
License: Ponce, PR held by Cadena Estereotempo Inc.
Group Owner: Spanish Broadcasting System Inc.; (acq 11-29-99; grpsl)
Arbitron Metro Market: Puerto Rico; *Format:* Adult Contemp; *Hrs. of News Programming:* news progmg one hr wkly; *No. News Employees:* 1; *Target Audience:* 30-50; women; *Adv. Rates:* 25; 20; 25; 18
Raul Alarcon, President
Ismael Nieves, General Manager
Marie Martinez, General Sales Mgr
Pedro Arroyo, Programming Director
Luis Rivera, Promotions Manager
Demare Ramirez, News Director
Alejandro Luciano, Chief Engineer

WISO
09-15-1953; 1260 kHz AM; *Hrs Open:* 16
155 San Antonio St., Floral Park, Hato Rey, PR 0917 US
(787) 763-1066; *Fax:* (787) 763-4195
jblanco25@hotmail.com
License: Ponce, PR held by Wilfredo G. Blanco Pi.
Arbitron Metro Market: Puerto Rico; *Format:* News, News/Talk, 86; *Hrs. of News Programming:* News progmg 26 hrs wkly; *Target Audience:* Adults.
Wilfredo Blanco, President
Jorge Blanco, Operations Dir
Carmen Blanco, General Sales Mgr

WDEP
02-01-1973; 1490 kHz AM; *Hrs Open:* 24; 5 kw-D, ND2; 1 kw-N, ND2; N17 58 52 W66 36 51
Post Office Box 7213, Ponce, PR 0732 US
(787) 292-1700; *Fax:* (787) 292-1717
www.wdepradio.com
noticias@radioisla1320.com
License: Ponce, PR held by Media Power Group Inc.
Group Owner: Media Power Group Inc.; (acq 9-30-2003; grpsl).
Nat'l Network: CNN Radio
Arbitron Metro Market: Puerto Rico; *Format:* News, News/Talk, 86; *Hrs. of News Programming:* News progmg 24 hrs wkly; *Target Audience:* 35 plus.
Eduardo Rivero, President
Ismaez Nieves, Operations Dir
Nora Plaza, General Sales Mgr
Luis Penchi, Programming Director
Fernando Vazquez, Promotions Manager
Orlado Moraless, Operations Manager

WPAB
08-14-1940; 550 kHz AM; *Hrs Open:* 24
Mailing Address: P.O. Box 7243, Playa Ponce, PR 0732 US
Second Address: 1643 Ave. Eduardo Ruberte, Ponce, PR 716
(787) 840-5550; *Fax:* (787) 840-7077
License: Ponce, PR held by WPAB Inc.
Nat'l Network: CNN Radio *Regional Reps:* Sayda Ortiz; *Wire Services:* AP
Arbitron Metro Market: Puerto Rico; *Format:* News, News/Talk, 86; *Hrs. of News Programming:* news progmg 15 hrs wkly; *No. News Employees:* 4; *Target Audience:* 25 plus; concerned adults; *Adv. Rates:* 25; 25;20; 10
Alfonso Gimenez-Porrata, CEO
Alfonso Gimenez-Lucchetti, Operations Dir
Sayda Ortiz, General Sales Mgr
Maria Luisa Gimenez-Lucchetti, Vice President, Operations

WPRP
01-01-1936; 910 kHz AM; 4.4 kw-D, ND2; 4.4 kw-N, ND2; N17 59 27 W66 37 48
Mailing Address: P.O. Box 363222, San Juan, PR 00936-3222 US
Second Address: Calle Ponce de Leon, URB El Cerezal #1581, Rio Piedras, PR
(787) 758-7230
www.notiuno.com
License: Ponce, PR held by Arso Radio Corp.
Group Owner: Uno Radio Group; (acq 5-8-01; grpsl).
Arbitron Metro Market: Puerto Rico; *Format:* News, News/Talk, 86; *Target Audience:* 35 plus.; *Adv. Rates:* 24; 18; 18; 10
Luis Soto, President

WRIO
01-01-1986; 101.1 MHz FM; *Hrs Open:* 24; 50 kw; -46 ft.; N18 1 40 W66 39 14
Ave. Luis Munoz Martin, Esquina Calle 24, Caguas, PR US
(787) 744-3131; *Fax:* (787) 743-0252
www.salsoul.com
License: Ponce, PR held by Arso Radio Corp.
Group Owner: Uno Radio Group
Arbitron Metro Market: Puerto Rico; *Format:* Spanish; *Adv. Rates:* 40; 25; 25; 20
Luis Soto, President

WZAR
03-17-1966; 101.9 MHz FM; *Hrs Open:* 24; 14 kw; 2589 ft.; N18 9 15 W66 33 15
Mailing Address: Box 7213, Ponce, PR 0732 US
Second Address: 46 Sector Purto Viejo, Playa De Ponce, Ponce, PR 732
(787) 842-0048; *Fax:* (787) 840-0049
License: Ponce, PR
Arbitron Metro Market: Puerto Rico; *Format:* Adult Contemp *Special Programming:* Talk show 15 hrs wkly; *Hrs. of News Programming:* News progmg 12 hrs wkly; *Target Audience:* 18-49; blue & white collar, adults,professionals
Jose Juan Santiago, Operations Dir
Pedro Gonzales, Programming Director
Carmen Reyes, News Director
Rafael Acosta, Engineering Dir

WZMT
05-01-1969; 93.3 MHz FM; *Hrs Open:* 20; 14.5 kw; -226 ft.; N17 59 26 W66 37 43 *Rebroadcasts:* Rebroadcasts WZNT(FM) San Juan 100%
Mailing Address: P.O. Box 7243, Ponce, PR 0732 US
Second Address: Amelia Industrial Park, Calle Frances 42, Guaynabo, PR 968

(787) 622-9700; *Fax:* (787) 622-9478
www.lamega.fm
rogie@sbspuertorico.com
License: Ponce, PR held by Potorican American Broadcasting Inc.
Group Owner: Spanish Broadcasting System Inc.; (acq 2000; grpsl)
Arbitron Metro Market: Ponce, PR; *Format:* Spanish; *Hrs. of News Programming:* news progmg 6 hrs wkly; *No. News Employees:* 1; *Target Audience:* 18-49; affluent young adults
Raul Alarcon, President
Ismael Nieves, General Manager
Maria Martinez, General Sales Mgr
Rogie Gallart, Programming Director
Luis Rivera, Promotions Manager
Demare Ramirez, News Director
Alejandro Luciano, Chief Engineer
JoeMackay, National Sales Manager
Edgardo Aubray, Sales
Omar Rodriguez, Internet Web Manager

WLEO
11-03-1956; 1170 kHz AM; *Hrs Open:* 24; 0.2 kw; N17 58 52 W66 36 49
P.O. Box 363222, San Juan, PR 00936-3222 US
(787) 474-0630; *Fax:* (787) 758-1410
www.unoradio.com
ventasurg@unoradio.com
License: Ponce, PR held by Uno Radio of Ponce Inc.
Group Owner: Uno Radio Group; (acq 2-18-00; grpsl).
Arbitron Metro Market: San Juan, PR; *Format:* Oldies *Special Programming:* Sports; *Hrs. of News Programming:* news progmg 50 hrs wkly; *No. News Employees:* 2; *Target Audience:* 25 plus; mature, blue-collar &professionals
Luis Soto, President

Quebradillas

WDNO
02-01-1998; 960 kHz AM; 1 kw-D, 1.7 kw-N, DA-2; N18 26 38 W66 57 43 *Rebroadcasts:* Rebroadcasts WZNA(AM) Moca 100%
Box 4039, Carolina, PR 0676
(787) 750-4090; *Fax:* (787) 750-6440
License: Quebradillas, PR held by International Broadcasting Corp.
Group Owner: International Broadcasting Corp.; (acq 7-6-2004; $1.45 million with WRSJ(AM) Bayamon).
Arbitron Metro Market: Puerto Rico
Luis Rosado, President
Josue Salgado, Programming Director

WIDI
11-17-1974; 99.5 MHz FM; *Hrs Open:* 24; 3 kw; 1001 ft.; N18 23 33 W66 59 46
Box 980, Quebradillas, PR 0742 US
(787) 895-2725,(787) 895-0000; *Fax:* (787) 895-4198
www.magic973.com
magic973@prtc.net
License: Quebradillas, PR held by Jose J. Arzuaga.
Arbitron Metro Market: Puerto Rico; *Format:* Oldies; *Hrs. of News Programming:* News progmg 2 hrs wkly; *Target Audience:* General.
Jose Arzuaga, President
Idalia Arzuaga, Operations Dir
Joshua Arzuaga, General Manager
Idalia Arrieta, Vice President, Operations

***WZCA**
91.7 MHz FM; 720 watts; -8 meters; 18 29 N16 66 56 W37
PO Box 980, Querbradillas, PR 0678
www.sacrafm.com
License: Quebradillas, PR

Rio Grande

WOYE
01-01-2003; 97.3 MHz FM; 0.8 kw; 1906 ft.; N18 16 46 W65 51 12
Avenue Ponce De Leon 760, Miramar, PR 0907 US
(787) 895-0000; *Fax:* (787) 895-4198
www.magic973.com
magic973@prtc.net
License: Rio Grande, Rio Grande County, PR held by Jose J. Arzuaga
Arbitron Metro Market: Quebradillas, PR; *Format:* Oldies
Idalia Arzuaga, Operations Dir
Tommy Carrasquillo, General Manager
Eva Cordero, General Sales Mgr
Joshua Arzuaga, Programming Director
Rafael Brito, News Director

Jose Arzuaga, Engineering Dir
Arlene Perez, AdvertisingDirector
Nitza Mercado, Public Affairs Director
Roberto Toledo, Sales Director

Rio Piedras

WFID
11-17-1958; 95.7 MHz FM; 50 kw; 942 ft.; N18 16 0 W66 5 5
Mailing Address: P.O. Box 363222, San Juan, PR 00936-3222 US
Second Address: Calle Ponce de Leon, URB El Cerezal #1581, Rio Piedras, PR 926
(787) 294-0050; *Fax:* (787) 767-9343
www.fidelitypr.com
License: Rio Piedras, PR held by Madifide Inc.
Group Owner: Uno Radio Group; (acq 3-26-98; $11,537,500).
Nat'l Reps: McGavren Guild
Arbitron Metro Market: Rio Piedras, PR; *Format:* Adult Contemp, Easy Listening; *Target Audience:* 25-49; middle & upper income
Luis Soto, President

Sabana

WJIT
03-31-2000; 1250 kHz AM; *Hrs Open:* 16
Mailing Address: P.O. Box 316, Coamo, PR 0769 US
Second Address: Road #2 km 30.5, Vega Alta, PR 769
(787) 449-9304; *Fax:* (787) 825-1905
License: Sabana, PR held by WJIT Broadcasting Corp.
Arbitron Metro Market: Puerto Rico; *Format:* Variety/Diverse
Olga Fernandez, President
Jose Soler, Programming Director
Carlos Ortiz, News Director

Sabana Grande

WYKO
01-01-1990; 880 kHz AM; 1 kw-D, ND1; 0.5 kw-N, ND1; N18 4 21 W66 57 6
34 Doctor Felix Tio St., Sabana Grande, PR 0637 US
Fax: (787) 873-5795
License: Sabana Grande, PR held by Juan Galiano Rivera
Arbitron Metro Market: Sabana Grande, PR
Juan Rivera, President

Salinas

WHOY
04-06-1967; 1210 kHz AM; 5 kw-D, DA2; 5 kw-N, DA2; N17 58 38 W66 18 14
Road 712 Km. 1.6, Salinas, PR 0751 US
(787) 824-3420; *Fax:* (787) 824-8054
whoyam@coquinet.com
License: Salinas, PR held by Colon Radio Corp.
Arbitron Metro Market: Puerto Rico
Martin Colon, General Manager
Rafael Pagan, Chief Engineer

San German

WEGM
02-01-1969; 95.1 MHz FM; *Hrs Open:* 24; 25 kw; 1969 ft.; N18 8 55 W66 58 54
Mailing Address: P.O. Box 1718, Mayaguez, PR 0681 US
Second Address: Amelia Industrial Park, Calle Frances 42, Guaynabo, PR 968
(787) 622-9700; *Fax:* (787) 622-9478
www.lamega.fm
rogie@sbspuertorico.com
License: San German, PR held by WRPC Inc.
Group Owner: Spanish Broadcasting System Inc.; (acq 11-29-99; grpsl)
Arbitron Metro Market: Puerto Rico PR; *Format:* Contemporary Hits/Top 40; *Target Audience:* 18-49; men
Raul Alarcon, President
Ismael Nieves, General Manager
Marie Martinez, General Sales Mgr
Pedro Arroyo, Programming Director
Luis Rivera, Promotions Manager
Demare Ramirez, News Director
Alejandro Luciano, Chief Engineer
RoqueGallart, Programming Director

WSOL
01-01-1955; 1090 kHz AM; 0.25 kw-D, ND1; 0.73 kw-N, ND1; N18 4 44 W67 1 18
Box 5000, Suite 442, San German, PR 0683 US
(787) 892-2216,(787) 892-2975; *Fax:* (787) 264-1090
w1090sol@yahoo.com
License: San German, PR held by San German Broadcasters Group.

Arbitron Metro Market: Puerto Rico; *Format:* News *Special Programming:* Farm 2 hrs wkly; *Target Audience:* Adults.
Alfredo Cardona, President
Lucy Rivera, Operations Dir
Luz Maria Rivera, General Manager
Gloria Silva, Station Manager

***WNNV**
11-14-1996; 91.7 MHz FM; *Hrs Open:* 24; 5 kw vert; 364 ft.; N18 4 8 W67 2 54
P.O. Box 847, Mayaguez, PR 0681 US
(787) 883-7100; *Fax:* (787) 833-7940
License: San German, San German County, PR held by Siembra Fertil P.R. Inc.
Arbitron Metro Market: Puerto Rico; *Format:* Christian; *Target Audience:* 25-49.
Miguel Marquez, Programming Director

San Juan

WAPA
01-15-1947; 680 kHz AM
134 Domenech Ave, Hato Ray, PR 0918 US
(787) 759-9122; *Fax:* (787) 759-9122
www.waparadio.net
jblanco25@hotmail.com
License: San Juan, PR held by Wifredo G. Blanco Pi
Group Owner: Hemisphere Media Group Inc.; (acq 2-25-91).
Arbitron Metro Market: San Juan, PR; *Format:* News, News/Talk, 86
Jorge Blanco, Operations Dir
Wilfredo Blanco, General Manager

WBMJ
07-19-1968; 1190 kHz AM; *Hrs Open:* 24; 10 kw-D, DA2; 5 kw-N, DA2; N18 21 0 W66 6 50
P.O. Box 367000, San Juan, PR 0936 US
(787) 724-1190; *Fax:* (787) 722-5395(787) 723-9633
www.therockradio.org/
radio@therockradio.org
License: San Juan, PR held by Calvary Evangelistic Mission Inc.
Group Owner: Calvary Evangelistic Mission Inc.; (acq 11-85).
Nat'l Network: Moody; USA; Salem Radio Network
Arbitron Metro Market: San Juan, PR; *Format:* Adult Contemp, Talk, 74; *Hrs. of News Programming:* News progmg 7 hrs wkly; *Target Audience:* General; relg community of central Puerto Rico
Janet Luttrell, CEO
Janet Luttrell, President
Madeline Burgos, Operations Dir
Lawrence Trumbower, Chief Engineer
Nita Luttrell, VP
Judith P,rez, Music Director

WCAD
03-05-1968; 105.7 MHz FM; 50 kw; 1099 ft.; N18 16 54 W66 6 46
Mailing Address: P.O. Box 9024188, San Juan, PR 0902 US
Second Address: 1667 Fernandez Juncos Ave., San Turce, PR 910
(787) 728-7280; *Fax:* (787) 268-3313
www.alfarock.com
alfa@alfarock.com
License: San Juan, PR held by Broadcasting & Programming Systems of Puerto Rico Inc.
Arbitron Metro Market: San Juan, PR; *Format:* Rock/AOR
Ada Cox, Operations Dir
Ralph Perez, General Manager
Pedro Davila, Programming Director
T. Morales, Engineering Dir
Felipe Diaz, Sales Director

WIAC
01-01-1947; 740 kHz AM; *Hrs Open:* 24; 10 kw-U, DA1; N18 21 24 W66 14 5
PO Box 9023916, San Juan, PR 0902 US
(787) 620-9898; *Fax:* (787) 620-0730
License: San Juan, PR held by Bestov Broadcasting Inc.
Arbitron Metro Market: Puerto Rico; *Format:* News; *Target Audience:* General.
Luis Mejia, President
Valerie Majia, Operations Dir
Luis Penchi, News Director
Rey Moraira, Chief Engineer
Johnny Men, Traffic Manager

WTOK-FM
03-01-1961; 102.5 MHz FM; 50 kw; Ant 1,139 ft; N18 25 25 W66 08 20
Box 9023916, San Juan, PR 0902
(787) 620-9898; *Fax:* (787) 620-0730
www.sistema102.com
License: San Juan, PR held by MSG Radio Inc.

Arbitron Metro Market: Puerto Rico
Danny Gonzalez, Operations Dir
Glenn Valares, General Sales Mgr
Valerie Mejia, Programming Director

WIOA
03-01-1961; 99.9 MHz FM; 31 kw; 1837 ft.; N18 16 44 W65 51 12
Mailing Address: P.O. Box 949, Guaynabo, PR 0970 US
Second Address: Amelia Industrial Park, Calle Frances 42, Guaynabo, PR 968
(787) 622-9700; *Fax:* (787) 622-9478
www.lamega.fm
info@lamega.fm
License: San Juan, PR held by Cadena Estereotempo Inc.
Group Owner: Spanish Broadcasting System Inc.; (acq 11-29-99; grpsl)
Arbitron Metro Market: Puerto Rico; *Format:* Adult Contemp; *Target Audience:* 18-49; predominantly women
Raul Alarcon, President
Ismael Nieves, General Manager
Maria Elena Martinez, General Sales Mgr
Fernando de Hostas, Programming Director
Luis Rivera, Promotions Manager
Demare Ramirez, News Director
Alejandro Luciano, ChiefEngineer

***WIPR**
01-26-1948; 940 kHz AM; *Hrs Open:* 24
P. O. Box 190909, San Juan, PR 0919 US
(787) 766-0505; *Fax:* (787) 250-7694
www.prnet.pr
License: San Juan, PR held by Puerto Rico Corp. for Public Broadcasting.
Nat'l Network: NPR
Arbitron Metro Market: Puerto Rico; *Format:* News; *Hrs. of News Programming:* news progmg 7 hrs wkly; *No. News Employees:* 7
Luis Agrait, Chairman
Linda Hernandez, President
Susan Marte, Operations Dir
Raul Carbonell, General Manager
Vilma Reyes, Station Manager
Ileana Rivera, General Sales Mgr
Yolanda Zavala, Executive Vice President
Luis Santiago,Sales Director

***WIPR-FM**
06-03-1960; 91.3 MHz FM; *Hrs Open:* 24; 105 kw; 2707 ft.; N18 6 42 W66 3 5
P. O. Box 190909, San Juan, PR 0919 US
(787) 766-0505; *Fax:* (787) 250-7694
www.prnet.pr
License: San Juan, PR held by Puerto Rico Corp. for Public Broadcasting.
Arbitron Metro Market: Puerto Rico; *Format:* Talk
Sinta Seiber, Operations Dir
Bill Wheelhouse, General Manager
Lisa Clemmons-Stott, General Sales Mgr
Rick Bradley, News Director
Greg Manfroi, Chief Engineer

WKAQ
12-03-1922; 580 kHz AM; *Hrs Open:* 24; 10 kw-U, DA1; N18 25 56 W66 8 9
P.O. Box 364668, San Juan, PR 00936 US
(787) 758-5800; *Fax:* (787) 763-1854
www.univision.com
License: San Juan, PR held by WLII/WSUR License Partnership G.P.
Group Owner: Univision Radio; (acq 8-1-2003; grpsl).
Arbitron Metro Market: San Juan, PR; *Format:* News, News/Talk, 86; *No. News Employees:* 22; *Target Audience:* General.
Jaime Bauza, General Manager
Aracelis Cruz, Promotions Manager
Javier Cosme, Director of News and Content
Nestor Perez, Chief Engineer

WKAQ-FM
10-08-1958; 104.7 MHz FM; 50 kw; 1,220 ft.; N18 16 51 W66 6 38
P.O. Box 364668, San Juan, PR 00936 US
(787) 758-5800; *Fax:* (787) 763-1854
www.univision.com
License: San Juan, PR held by WLII/WSUR License Partnership G.P.
Group Owner: Univision Radio
Arbitron Metro Market: Puerto Rico; *Format:* Contemporary Hits/Top 40
Jaime Bauza, General Manager
Aracelis Cruz, Promotions Manager
Javier Cosme, Director of News and Content

WKVM
01-01-1951; 810 kHz AM; 50 kw-U, DA1; N18 21 47 W66 8 13
Mailing Address: P.O. Box 9021967, San Juan, PR 0902 US
Second Address: c/o Arquidiocesis de San Juan, Apartado 1967, San Juan, PR 00901-1967
(787) 751-1018; *Fax:* (787) 758-9967
License: San Juan, PR held by Catholic, Apostolic & Roman Church, San Juan Archdiocese.
Arbitron Metro Market: Puerto Rico; *Format:* Oldies, Religious
Roberto Gonzalez, President
Allan Corales, Station Manager
Elsa Fernandez, General Sales Mgr
Jose Antonio Cruz, Programming Director
Placido Padilla, News Director
Jose Gomez, Chief Engineer
Judith Rivera, Local News Editor
Efrain Rodriguez, Religion Ed
Enrigue Liboy, Sports Commentator

WOSO
11-21-1977; 1030 kHz AM; *Hrs Open:* 24; 10 kw-U, DA-1; N18 22 07 W66 15 17
Box 11487, San Juan, PR 0902
(787) 724-4242; *Fax:* (787) 723-9676
www.woso.com
License: San Juan, PR held by Sherman Broadcasting Corp.
Nat'l Network: Wall Street; CBS; ABC
Arbitron Metro Market: Puerto Rico; *Hrs. of News Programming:* news progmg 6 hrs wkly; *No. News Employees:* 2; *Target Audience:* 25-49.; *Adv. Rates:* 48; 24; 38; 20
Sherman Wildman, President
Mariano Calderon, Operations Dir
Sergio Fernandez, General Manager
Sherman Wildmon, Programming Director
Gary Tuominen, News Director
Rodolfo Rivas, Chief Engineer
Danette Hudoba, Traffic Manager

WPRM-FM
04-01-1959; 99.1 MHz FM; *Hrs Open:* 24; 25 kw; 1905 ft.; N18 6 47 W66 3 6
Ave. Luis Munoz Martin, Esquina Calle 24, Caguas, PR US
(787) 744-3131; *Fax:* (787) 743-0252
www.salsoul.com
License: San Juan, PR held by Arso Radio Corp.
Group Owner: Uno Radio Group; (acq 4-1-73).
Arbitron Metro Market: Puerto Rico; *Format:* Spanish; *Hrs. of News Programming:* news progmg 3 hrs wkly; *No. News Employees:* 1; *Target Audience:* 18-49.
Luis Soto, President

WQBS
11-01-1954; 870 kHz AM
129 Ave De Diego, San Juan, PR 0927 US
(787) 758-8700; *Fax:* (787) 765-2965
License: San Juan, PR held by Aerco Broadcasting Corp.
Arbitron Metro Market: Puerto Rico *TV Affiliate:* WSJU-TV; *Format:* Variety/Diverse
Luz Alvarez, General Manager

WQII
01-01-1947; 1140 kHz AM; 10 kw-U, DA1; N18 21 30 W66 8 5
Mailing Address: P.O. Box 193779, San Juan, PR 0919 US
Second Address: Box 906 6590, San Juan, PR 00906-6590
(787) 723-4848; *Fax:* (787) 723-4035
License: San Juan, PR held by Communications Council Group Inc.
Arbitron Metro Market: Puerto Rico; *Format:* Talk
Nieves Gonzalez Avreu, President
Jorge Marquina, General Manager
William Padilla, General Sales Mgr
Danny Gonzalez, Programming Director
Raymond Hernandez, Chief Engineer

***WRTU**
02-08-1980; 89.7 MHz FM; *Hrs Open:* 24; 50 kw; 801 ft.; N18 16 0 W66 5 5
Mailing Address: P.O. Box 21305, San Juan, PR 0931 US
Second Address: Mariana Bracetti St., Ponce de Leon Ave., San Juan, PR 931
(787) 763-4699; *Fax:* (787) 764-1290
www.wrtu.pr
lluna@wrtu.pr
License: San Juan, PR held by University of Puerto Rico.
Arbitron Metro Market: Puerto Rico; *No. News Employees:* 8; *Target Audience:* General.
Ezequiel Rodr¡guez, Operations Dir
Yolanda Zabala, General Manager

WUNO
01-11-1960; 630 kHz AM; *Hrs Open:* 24; 5 kw-U, DA1; N18 26 59 W66 16 22
Mailing Address: P.O. Box 363222, San Juan, PR 00936-3222 US
Second Address: Calle Ponce de Leon, URB El Cerezal #1581, Rio Peidras, PR
(787) 758-7230
www.notiuno.com
License: San Juan, PR held by Arso Radio Corp.
Group Owner: Uno Radio Group; (acq 5-8-01; grpsl).
Nat'l Reps: McGavren Guild
Arbitron Metro Market: Puerto Rico; *Format:* News, News/Talk, 86; *No. News Employees:* 22; *Target Audience:* 25 plus.
Luis Soto, President

WSKN
10-15-1949; 1320 kHz AM; *Hrs Open:* 24
Box 363222, San Juan, PR 0936 US
(787) 292-1700; *Fax:* (787) 292-1717
www.radioisla1320.com
License: San Juan, PR held by Media Power Group Inc.
Group Owner: Media Power Group Inc.; (acq 9-30-2003; grpsl).
Nat'l Network: CNN Radio
Arbitron Metro Market: San Juan, PR; *Format:* News, News/Talk, 86; *Hrs. of News Programming:* news progmg 24 hrs wkly; *No. News Employees:* 40; *Target Audience:* 35 plus.
Eduardo Rivero, President
Ismael Nieves, Operations Dir
Nora Plaza, General Sales Mgr
Luis Penchi, Programming Director
Fernando Vazquez, Promotions Manager
Orlando Morales, Operations Manager

WVOZ
07-04-1949; 1520 kHz AM; *Hrs Open:* 16
1554 Bori Street, Caribe Development, Rio Piedras, PR 0928 US
(787) 764-1077; *Fax:* (787) 281-9758
www.mix107.fm
License: San Juan, PR held by Pedro Roman Collazo.
Arbitron Metro Market: Puerto Rico; *Format:* Sports *Special Programming:* Puerto Rican & Latin hits 15 hrs wkly; *Target Audience:* 35 plus; medium & low income individuals
Pedro Roman-Collazo, President
Margarita Nazario, General Manager

WZNT
01-01-1959; 93.7 MHz FM; *Hrs Open:* 24; 28 kw; 1837 ft.; N18 16 44 W65 51 12
Mailing Address: PO Box 949, Guaynabo, PR 0970 US
Second Address: Amelia Industrial Park, Calle Frances 42, Guaynabo, PR 968
(787) 622-9700; *Fax:* (787) 622-9478
www.lamega.fm
rogie@sbspuertorico.com
License: San Juan, PR held by WZNT Inc.
Group Owner: Spanish Broadcasting System Inc.; (acq 2000; grpsl)
Arbitron Metro Market: Guaynabo, PR; *Target Audience:* 18-49; male
Raul Alarcon, President
Ismael Nieves, General Manager
Marie Martinez, General Sales Mgr
Rogie Gallart, Programming Director
Luis Rivera, Promotions Manager
Demare Ramirez, News Director
Alejandro Luciano, Chief Engineer
PedroArroyo, Programming Director
Nestor Rodriguez, Programming Director
Omar Rodriguez, Internet Web Manager
Joe Mackay, National Sales Manager SBS
Edgardo Aubray, National Sales Manager SBS
Andrew Polsky

San Sebastian

WLRP
02-15-1965; 1460 kHz AM; *Hrs Open:* 19; 0.5 kw-U, ND1; N18 20 50 W66 59 56
PO Box 1670, San Sebastian, PR 0755 US
(787) 896-1460; *Fax:* (787) 896-8100
radioraices@prtc.net
License: San Sebastian, PR held by Las Raices Pepinianas Inc.
Arbitron Metro Market: Puerto Rico; *Format:* Adult Contemp; *No. News Employees:* 1
Ramon Colon Pratts, President
Carlos M. Aquino, General Manager
Alfredo Perez, General Sales Mgr
Jose Chaparro, Programming Director

Ramon Pratts, Promotions Manager
Juan Felin, Chief Engineer

WRSS
04-01-1984; 1410 kHz AM; 1 kw-U, DA1; N18 19 14 W66 58 45
Mailing Address: P.O. Box 1410, San Sebastian, PR 0685 US
Second Address: Segundo Ruez # 52 St., San Sebastian, PR 685
(787) 896-2121; *Fax:* (787) 896-5753
tunuevafamilia@hotmail.com
License: San Sebastian, PR held by Angel Vera-Maury
Arbitron Metro Market: Puerto Rico; *Format:* Oldies, Talk; *Hrs. of News Programming:* news progmg 30 hrs wkly; *No. News Employees:* 6; *Target Audience:* 30 plus.
Angel Vera, President
Cesar Vera, General Manager
Arturo Soto, General Sales Mgr
Nestor Gonzalez, Programming Director

Utuado

WUPR
04-18-1964; 1530 kHz AM; *Hrs Open:* 17; 1 kw-D, ND1; 0.25 kw-N, ND1; N18 16 4 W66 42 35
P. O. Box 868, Utuado, PR 0641 US
(787) 894-2460; *Fax:* (787) 894-4955
www.coqui.net
info@coqui.net
License: Utuado, PR held by Central Broadcasting Corp.
Arbitron Metro Market: Utuado, PR; *Format:* News, News/Talk, 86; *Hrs. of News Programming:* news progmg 11 hrs wkly; *No. News Employees:* 2; *Target Audience:* 18-49; middle income adults
Jose Martinez, President
Manuel Martinez, News Director
Epifanio Rodriguez Velez, Chief Engineer
Manuel Andujar, Music Director

Vega Alta

WERR
02-01-1970; 104.1 MHz FM; *Hrs Open:* 24; 50 kw; 988 ft.; N18 17 29 W66 39 39
Mailing Address: P.O. Box 29404, San Juan, PR 0929 US
Second Address: San Felipe # 205, Arecibo, PR 612
(787) 751-1310; *Fax:* (787) 751-6854
www.redentor104fm.com
hernanpantoja@gmail.com
License: Vega Alta, PR held by Radio Redentor Inc.
Arbitron Metro Market: Vega Alta, PR; *Format:* Adult Contemp, Christian; *Hrs. of News Programming:* news progmg one hr wkly; *No. News Employees:* 4; *Target Audience:* General.
Luis Qui¤ones, COO
Rev. Miguel Cintron, President
Omayra Martinez, Operations Dir
Jesus M. Velez Rivera, General Manager
Pantoja Hern n, Programming Director
Brenda Lis Gines, Promotions Manager
Elizabeth Bosques, NewsDirector
Ramon Rivera, Engineering Dir
Omayra Martinez, Administrative Manager
Nydia Guzman, Accounting

Vega Baja

WEGA
10-01-1971; 1350 kHz AM; 2.5 kw-D, DA2; 2.5 kw-N, DA2; N18 28 38 W66 23 43
Box 1488, Vega Baja, PR 0693 US
(787) 855-1350; *Fax:* (787) 855-0916
License: Vega Baja, PR held by A Radio Company Inc.
Arbitron Metro Market: Puerto Rico; *Format:* Variety/Diverse
Gerardo Angulo, President
Carmelo Santiago, General Manager
Hector Santiago, General Sales Mgr
Lloyd Santiago, Promotions Manager
Ronald Cushing, Chief Engineer

Vieques

WVIS
06-10-1973; 106.1 MHz FM; 50 kw; 558 ft.; N18 19 37 W65 18 21
P.O. Box 6556, Loiza Station, San Juan, PR 0914 US
(787) 355-0090; *Fax:* (787) 355-0079
www.radiojoe106.com
License: Vieques, PR held by V.I. Stereo Communications Corporation (PR)
Arbitron Metro Market: Vieques, PR; *Format:* Adult Contemp, Oldies, 72
Michael Bahr, President

Yabucoa

WXEW
01-01-1978; 840 kHz AM; *Hrs Open:* 19; 5 kw-D, DAN; 1 kw-N, DAN; N18 2 58 W65 52 7
Mailing Address: P.O. Box 100, Yabucoa, PR 0767 US
Second Address: Box 100, Yabucoa, PR 767
(787) 893-3065; *Fax:* (787) 850-4055
www.victoria840.com
victor@victoria840.com
License: Yabucoa, PR held by Radio Victoria Inc.
Arbitron Metro Market: Yabucoa, PR; *Format:* Adult Contemp, Talk
Victoria Vargas, President
Victor Calderon, Operations Dir
Caly Burmudez, General Sales Mgr
Luis Calderon, Programming Director
Brenda Calderon, Promotions Manager
Angel Bena, News Director
Alberto Pereira, Chief Engineer
JoseCalderon, Promotions Manager

Yauco

WENA
11-11-1978; 1330 kHz AM; *Hrs Open:* 24
P.O. Box 1338, Yauco, PR 0698 US
(787) 267-1330(787) 856-1330; *Fax:* (787) 267-1340
License: Yauco, PR held by Southern Broadcasting Corp.
Arbitron Metro Market: Yauco, PR; *Format:* Adult Contemp, News, 62, Talk; *Hrs. of News Programming:* news progmg 28 hrs wkly; *No. News Employees:* 5; *Target Audience:* 25 plus; young adults & women *Adv. Rates:* 216; 216; 200; 168
Nephtali Rodriguez, President
Israel Rodriguez, Operations Dir
Ramon Ramos, General Sales Mgr
Guillermo Valls, Programming Director
Isaac Pagan, Engineering Dir
Juan Diaz, Advertising Manager
Ronald Cushing, EngineeringManager
Pedro Gregory, Sales Director

WKFE
11-03-1961; 1550 kHz AM; *Hrs Open:* 24; 0.25 kw-U, ND1; N18 1 24 W66 52 2 *Rebroadcasts:* Rebroadcasts WSKN(AM) San Juan 70%
Box 7213, Ponce, PR 0732 US
(787) 292-1700; *Fax:* (787) 292-1717
noticias@radioisla1320.com
License: Yauco, PR held by Media Power Group Inc.
Group Owner: Media Power Group Inc.; (acq 9-30-2003; grpsl).
Arbitron Metro Market: Puerto Rico; *Format:* News, News/Talk, 86; *Hrs. of News Programming:* news progmg 40 hrs wkly; *No. News Employees:* 2; *Target Audience:* P35-64 P35+.
Eduardo Rivero, President
Jose Pagan, General Manager
Nora Plaza, General Sales Mgr
Orlando Morales, Programming Director

Quebec

Jacksonville

WOKV(AM)
11-01-1925; 690 kHz AM; 50 kw-D, 25 kw-N, DA-N; N30 07 56 W81 42 00
8000 Belford Parkway, Suite 100, Jacksonville, FL 32256
(904) 245-8500; *Fax:* (904) 245-8501
www.wokv.com
aaron.schachter@coxinc.com
License: Jacksonville, FL held by Cox Radio Inc.
Group Owner: Cox Radio Inc.; (acq 2-28-2000; grpsl).
Nat'l Network: Fox News Radio; *Nat'l Reps:* Katz Radio; *Wire Services:* AP
Arbitron Metro Market: Jacksonville, FL; *Format:* News/Talk
Special Programming: 24hrs; *Hrs. of News Programming:* 10
Aaron Schachter, Director Of Branding & Programming
Bob DeBlois, Director Of Sales
Jodi Rainey, National Sales Manager
Ashley Testa, Digital Sales Manager
David Ratz, Promotions & Events Director
Rich Jones, News Director

Rhode Island

Block Island

WKSP(AM)
06-13-1994; 95.9 MHz FM; *Hrs Open:* 24; 6 kw; 249 ft.; N41 10 28 W71 34 20
400 South County Trail, Suite A105, Exeter, RI 02822 US
(401) 294-9274; *Fax:* (401) 294-4034
www.classical959.com
License: Block Island, Washington County, RI held by Judson Group Inc.
Arbitron Metro Market: Rhode Island; *Format:* Talk *Special Programming:* New age 4 hrs, folk 4 hrs, big band 4 hrs, relg 2 hrs wkly; *Target Audience:* General.
Christopher Jones, President
Jamie Jones, General Manager
Matthew Macolini, Station Manager

WMNP
10-03-1988; 99.3 MHz FM; *Hrs Open:* 24; 6 kw; 256 ft.; N41 10 28 W71 34 20
85 Beach Street, Westerly, RI 02891 US
(401) 846-1540; *Fax:* (401) 846-1598
www.wadk.com
License: Block Island, Washington County, RI held by 3G Broadcasting Inc.
Arbitron Metro Market: Newport, RI; *Format:* Adult Contemp; *Target Audience:* 30-50; total community
Bobb Angel, Operations Dir
Bob Melfi, General Manager
Lisa Lancaster, News Director
Maurice Polayes, Chief Engineer
Lisa Lancaster, Traffic Director, Office Manager
Larry Beavers, Engineer

Bristol

***WQRI**
04-01-1989; 88.3 MHz FM; 0.2 kw horiz, 0.8 kw vert; 79 ft.; N41 38 54 W71 15 34
US
(401) 254-3282
generalmanager_wqri@g.rwu.edu
License: Bristol, Bristol County, RI held by Roger Williams University.
Format: Rock/AOR
Henry Lindner, General Manager
Allie Conn, Promotions Director
Tucker Silva, Programming Director/DJ Manager
Mason Fields, Productions Director
Corey Konnick, Live Director
Paul Pettini, Music Director
Marissa Delorey, StationAdministrator
Own Kauppila, Underwriting Director

Coventry

***WCVY**
10-19-1978; 91.5 MHz FM; *Hrs Open:* 2pm - 10pm; 0.2 kw; 36 ft.; N41 41 10 W71 35 37
40 Reservoir Road, Coventry, RI 02816 US
(401) 822-9499; *Fax:* (401) 822-9492
www.coventryschools.net/wcvy
wcvy@gmail.com
License: Coventry, Kent County, RI held by Coventry Rhode Island Public Schools.
Arbitron Metro Market: Coventry, RI; *Format:* Contemporary Hits/Top 40 *Special Programming:* Sports 2 hrs wkly; *Target Audience:* 12-30.
Scott P., Station Manager
Chris Lopes, Treasurer
Rebecca S., Programming
Mariah H., Outreach
Emily F., Assistant Station Manager

East Providence

WPMZ
04-15-1947; 1110 kHz AM; 5 kw-D, DAD; N41 49 40 W71 22 9
1270 Mineral Spring Ave., North Providence, RI 02904-4637 US
(401) 726-8413; *Fax:* (401) 726-8649
www.poder1110.com
License: East Providence, RI held by Videomundo Broadcasting Co. L.L.C.
Arbitron Metro Market: Providence-Warwick-Pawtucket, RI; *Target Audience:* General.
Tony Mendez, Sales

Greenville

WALE
01-01-1948; 990 kHz AM; *Hrs Open:* 6 AM-midnight; 50 kw-D, DA2; 5 kw-N, DA2; N41 57 18 W71 35 39
1185 North Main Street, Providence, RI 02904 US
(401) 521-0990; *Fax:* (401) 521-5077
License: Greenville, RI held by Cumbre Communications Corp., debtor in possession
Arbitron Metro Market: Providence, RI; *Target Audience:* .
Manolo Pazos, General Manager

Hope Valley

WKSP
10-07-1985; 1180 kHz AM; 1.8 kw-D; N41 31 36 W71 44 35
26 Woody Hill Road, Hope Valley, RI 02832
(860) 464-1066
License: Hope Valley, Washington County, RI held by Judson Group Inc.
Nat'l Network: USA
Population Served: 750,000; *Arbitron Metro Market:* Providence-Warwick-Pawtucket, RI; *Format:* News; *Adv. Rates:* 29; 20; 25; na

Kingston

*WRIU
02-16-1964; 90.3 MHz FM; *Hrs Open:* 24; 3.4 kw; 420 ft.; N41 29 52 W71 31 43
326 Memorial Union, Kingston, RI 02881 US
(401) 874-4949
www.wriu.org
comments@wriu.org
License: Kingston, Washington County, RI held by University of Rhode Island.
Format: Variety/Diverse *Special Programming:* Folk 15 hrs, gospel 5 hrs, heavy metal 6 hrs, blues 3 hrs, reggae 7 hrs, Sp 3 hrs wkly; *Target Audience:* Diverse.
Madison Moreau, General Manager
Brianna McNally, News Director
Steve Callahan, Chief Engineer
Cassie Jacob, Business Manager
Matt Dzikiewicz, Production/Recording Studio Manager
Maureen McDermott, Faculty Advisor
Bill Parker,Director of Information
Duffy Egan, Broadcast Engineer/Chief Operator

Middletown

WKKB
10-06-1978; 100.3 MHz FM; *Hrs Open:* 24; 1.55 kw; 656 ft.; N41 35 48 W71 11 24
US
(401) 781-1535
www.latina1003fm.com
License: Middletown, Newport County, RI held by Davidson Media Rhode Island Stations LLC.
Group Owner: Davidson Media Group LLC; (acq 1-31-2005; $7.5 million with WAKX(FM) Narragansett Pier)
Arbitron Metro Market: Providence-Warwick-Pawtucket, RI; *Format:* Spanish; *Hrs. of News Programming:* news progmg 7 hrs wkly; *No. News Employees:* 1; *Target Audience:* 12+; Latino Americans 1st & 2nd generation
Cesar Salas, General Manager
Quilzio Perdon, Programming Director
Carlos Morrero, Traffic Manager

Narragansett Pier

*WRNI-FM
07-15-1990; 102.7 MHz FM; *Hrs Open:* 19; 1.95 kw; 226 ft.; N41 25 27 W71 28 38
1 Union Station, Providence, RI 02903 US
(401) 351-2800; *Fax:* (401) 351-0246
www.ripr.org
info@ripr.org
License: Narragansett Pier, Washington County, RI held by Rhode Island Public Radio
Nat'l Network: NPR
Arbitron Metro Market: Rhode Island; *Format:* News, News/Talk, 86
Susan Greenhalgh, COO
James Baumgartner, Operations/Production Director
Joe O'Connor, General Manager
Catherine Welch, News Director
Tim Monroe, Development Director
Aaron Read, Director, IT/Engineering
Danielle Blasczak,Membership Manager
Donna Bannon, Manager, Corporate Underwriting
Jeff Falewicz, Finance
Jim Moses, Producer

Newport

WADK
11-06-1948; 1540 kHz AM; *Hrs Open:* 6am-6pm; 1 kw-D, NDD; N41 30 13 W71 18 43
11 Marcus Wheatland Blvd., Newport, RI 02840 US
(315) 258-0937; *Fax:* (315) 258-9248
www.fingerlakes1.com
tbaker@flradiogroup.com
License: Newport, RI held by 3G Broadcasting Inc.
Group Owner: 3G Broadcasting Inc.; (acq 8-24-99).
Nat'l Network: ABC; Talk Radio Network
Arbitron Metro Market: Fargo-Moorhead ND-MN; *Format:* Talk; *Target Audience:* General.
Bill Askew, General Sales Mgr
Mike Smith, Programming Director
Ted Baker, News Director

Portsmouth

*WJHD
04-03-1972; 90.7 MHz FM; 0.36 kw horiz; 79 ft.; N41 36 6 W71 16 20
285 Cory's Lane, Portsmouth, RI 02871 US
(401) 683-2000; *Fax:* (401) 683-5888
License: Portsmouth, Newport County, RI held by Portsmouth Abbey School
Format: Variety/Diverse
Edmund Adams, General Manager

Providence

WBRU
02-21-1966; 95.5 MHz FM; *Hrs Open:* 24; 18.5 kw; 456 ft.; N41 49 40 W71 22 9
88 Benevolent Street, Providence, RI 02906 US
(401) 272-9550; *Fax:* (401) 272-9278
www.wbru.com
promotions@wbru.com
License: Providence, Providence County, RI held by Brown Broadcasting Service Inc.
Arbitron Metro Market: Providence, RI; *Format:* Alternative
Special Programming: Black 20 hrs, jazz 18 hrs wkly; *Hrs. of News Programming:* News progmg 3 hrs wkly; *Target Audience:* 18-34; highly educatedprofessionals

*WDOM
03-15-1966; 91.3 MHz FM; *Hrs Open:* 18; 0.125 kw; 131 ft.; N41 50 39 W71 26 14
River Ave., & Eaton St., Providence, RI 02918 US
(401) 865-2091; *Fax:* (401) 865-2822
www.wdom913.com
License: Providence, Providence County, RI held by Providence College.
Arbitron Metro Market: Providence, RI; *Format:* Alternative
Special Programming: Urban contemp 16 hrs, metal 6 hrs, country 2 hrs, classic rock 3 hrs, sports 2 hrs wkly; *Hrs. of News Programming:* News progmg one hrwkly; *Target Audience:* General; college students & professionals
Brian Wall, Operations Dir
Scott Seseske, General Manager
Jaclyn Schede, Assistant Music Director
Dan Devine, Music Director
Carlin Corrigan, Promotions Director
Sott Seseske, Special Events Coordinator

*WELH
09-01-1994; 88.1 MHz FM; *Hrs Open:* 24; 4 kw; 135 ft.; N41 51 26.7 W71 19 5.6
1 Union Station, Providence, RI 02903 US
(401) 351-2800; *Fax:* (401) 351-0246
www.ripr.org/
info@ripr.org
License: Providence, Providence County, RI held by The Wheeler School.
Arbitron Metro Market: Providence, RI; *Format:* Jazz, Variety/Diverse; *Target Audience:* General.
Susan Greenhalgh, COO
James Baumgartner, Operations/Production Manager
Joe O'Connor, General Manager
Jeff Falewicz, Finance
Jim Moses, Producer
Catherine Welch, News Director
Tim Monroe, Development Director
Aaron Read,Director, IT/Engineering
Danielle Blasczak, Membership Manager
Donna Bannon, Manager, Corporate Underwriting

WHJJ
09-06-1922; 920 kHz AM; *Hrs Open:* 24; 5 kw-D, DAN; 5 kw-N, DAN; N41 46 53 W71 19 55
75 Oxford St., Suite #302, Providence, RI 02905 US
(401) 781-9979; *Fax:* (401) 781-9329
www.920whjj.com
billgeorge@clearchannel.com
License: Providence, RI held by Capstar TX LLC
Group Owner: iHeartMedia; (acq 8-30-2000; grpsl)
Nat'l Network: CBS; *Nat'l Reps:* Clear Channel
Arbitron Metro Market: Providence-Warwick-Pawtucket, RI;
Format: News, News/Talk, 86; *Target Audience:* 35-64.
Rhonda Lapham, Market Manager
Bill George, Programming Director

WHJY
03-14-1966; 94.1 MHz FM; 50 kw; 456 ft.; N41 49 40 W71 22 9
75 Oxford St., Suite 302, Providence, RI 02905 US
(401) 781-9979; *Fax:* (401) 781-9329
www.94hjy.com
License: Providence, Providence County, RI held by Capstar TX LLC
Group Owner: iHeartMedia
Arbitron Metro Market: Providence-Warwick-Pawtucket, RI;
Format: Rock/AOR; *Target Audience:* 18-34; adults
Rhonda Lapham, Market Manager

WPRO
10-16-1931; 630 kHz AM; 5 kw-D, DAN; 5 kw-N, DAN; N41 46 28 W71 19 23 *Rebroadcasts:* Simulcast with WEAN-FM Wakefield-Peacedale 100%
1502 Wampanoag Trail, East Providence, RI 02914 US
(401) 433-4200
www.630wpro.com
tony.mascaro@cumulus.com
License: Providence, RI held by Radio License Holding CBC, LLC
Group Owner: Cumulus Media Inc.; (acq 5-29-97; grpsl)
Nat'l Reps: McGavren Guild
Arbitron Metro Market: Providence-Warwick-Pawtucket, RI;
Format: News/Talk
Tony Mascaro, Programming Director
Shelby Rae, Marketing/Events

WPRO
04-17-1948; 92.3 MHz FM; 39 kw; 551 ft.; N41 48 18 W71 28 24
1502 Wampanoag Trail, East Providence, RI 02914 US
(401) 433-4200
www.92profm.com
davey.morris@cumulus.com
License: Providence, RI held by Radio License Holding CBC, LLC
Group Owner: Cumulus Media, Inc.
Arbitron Metro Market: Providence-Warwick-Pawtucket, RI;
Format: Contemporary Hits/Top 40
Davey Morris, Programming
Barbijo Dimaria, Prizes/Events
Holly Paras, Advertising

WSTL
06-16-1946; 1220 kHz AM; *Hrs Open:* 24; 1 kw-D, ND1; 0.166 kw-N, ND1; N41 49 15 W71 23 7
95 Sagamore Road, Seekonk, MA 02771 US
(401) 434-9785; *Fax:* (508) 343-2159
www.wstl.us
info@wstl.us
License: Providence, RI held by New England Christian Media Inc.
Arbitron Metro Market: Providence-Warwick-Pawtucket, RI;
Format: Christian
Patricia Varner, General Manager

WRNI
04-01-1948; 1290 kHz AM; *Hrs Open:* 24
1 Union Station, Providence, RI 02903 US
(401) 351-2800; *Fax:* (401) 351-0246
www.wrni.org
info@wrni.org
License: Providence, RI held by WRNI Foundation
Nat'l Network: NPR; PRI; *Nat'l Reps:* Rgnl Reps
Arbitron Metro Market: Providence-Warwick-Pawtucket, RI;
Format: News, News/Talk, 86; *Hrs. of News Programming:* news progmg 80 hrs wkly; *No. News Employees:* 8; *Target Audience:* 25-54; intelligent adultsinterested in news & politics
Susan Greenhalgh, COO
James Baumgartner, Operations/Production Manager
Jeff Falewicz, Finance
Jim Moses, Producer
Joe O'Connor, General Manager
Tim Monroe, Development Director
Catherine Welch, News Director
Aaron Read,Director, IT/Engineering
Danielle Blasczak, Membership Manager
Donna Bannon, Manager of Corporate Underwriting
Karen Knisely, Development Services Coordinator
Kate Anderson, Deputy Development Director

WPRV
06-14-1922; 790 kHz AM; 5 kw-D, DAN; 5 kw-N, DAN; N41 50 3 W71 21 56
1502 Wampanoag Trail, East Providence, RI 02914 US
(401) 433-4200
www.790business.com
tony.mascaro@cumulus.com
License: Providence, RI held by Radio License Holding CBC, LLC

Group Owner: Cumulus Media Inc.; (acq 5-29-97; grpsl)
Nat'l Reps: McGavren Guild
Arbitron Metro Market: Providence-Warw; *Format:* News/Talk; *Target Audience:* 25-64; upper class, affluent, college educated
Tony Mascaro, Programming Director

WWBB
06-07-1968; 101.5 MHz FM; *Hrs Open:* 24; 13.5 kw; 951 ft.; N41 52 13 W71 17 47
75 Oxford St., Suite 302, Providence, RI 02905 US
(401) 781-9979; *Fax:* (401) 781-9329
www.b101.com
feedback@b101.com
License: Providence, Providence County, RI held by Clear Channel Broadcasting Licenses Inc.
Group Owner: iHeartMedia
Nat'l Network: AP Radio; Premiere Radio Networks; *Nat'l Reps:* Clear Channel
Arbitron Metro Market: Providence, RI; *Format:* Contemporary Hits/Top 40, Adult Contemp; *Target Audience:* 35-54; indispensable & powerful adults
Rhonda Lapham, Market Manager
Bill George, Community Engagement Director

WWLI
07-11-1948; 105.1 MHz FM; 50 kw; 499 ft.; N41 48 24 W71 28 13
1502 Wampanoag Trail, East Providence, RI 02914 US
(401) 433-4200
www.literock105fm.com
brian.demay@cumulus.com
License: Providence, RI held by Radio License Holding CBC, LLC
Group Owner: Cumulus Media Inc.
Arbitron Metro Market: Providence, RI; *Format:* Adult Contemp
Brian Demay, Programming
Holly Paras, Advertising

Smithfield

***WJMF**
08-01-1974; 88.7 MHz FM; *Hrs Open:* 7 AM-2 AM; 1.2 kw; 535 ft.; N41 48 12 W71 33 27
1150 Douglas Pike, Smithfield, RI 02917 US
(401) 232-6150
www.wjmfradio.com
wjmf@bryant.edu
License: Smithfield, Providence County, RI held by Bryant College of Business Administration.
Format: Alternative *Special Programming:* Folk 4 hrs, gospel 2 hrs, relg 2 hrs wkly; *Hrs. of News Programming:* news progmg 12 hrs wkly; *No. News Employees:* 1; *Target Audience:* 16-30; from teenagers to youngexecutives
Kelly DeRoche, Station Manager
Kofo Adebiyi, Programming Director
Greg Swarthout, Sports Director
Dominic Ferrara, Sports Director
Matthew DeVito, Business Director
Alli Yennaco, Office Manager
Jarred DiFazio, Events Director
Dan Anderson, Music Director
Bryant Shapiro, Production Director
Dave Chokski, Marketing Director

Wakefield-Peacedale

WEAN
06-01-1995; 99.7 MHz FM; *Hrs Open:* 24; 2.3 kw; 535 ft.; N41 34 22 W71 37 55 *Rebroadcasts:* Simulcast with WPRO-AM Providence 100%
1502 Wampanoag Trail, East Providence, RI 09214 US
(401) 433-4200
www.630wpro.com
License: Wakefield-Peacedale, RI held by Radio License Holding CBC, LLC
Group Owner: Cumulus Media Inc.
Arbitron Metro Market: Providence, RI; *Format:* News/Talk
Tony Mascaro, Programming Director
Shelby Rae, Marketing/Events
Joe Lembo, Advertising

Warwick

WARV
08-12-1959; 1590 kHz AM; *Hrs Open:* 24; 8 kw-D, DA2; 5 kw-N, DA2; N41 43 40 W71 27 46
19 Luther Ave., Warwick, RI 02886 US
(401) 737-0700; *Fax:* (401) 737-1604
www.lifechangingradio.com
License: Warwick, Kent County, RI held by Blount Communications Inc.
Group Owner: Blount Communications Group; (acq 7-7-78)
Nat'l Network: Salem Radio Network
Arbitron Metro Market: Providence, RI; *Format:* Religious *Special Programming:* Black 2 hrs wkly; *Target Audience:* 25-54; Adults
William Blount, President

West Warwick

WLKW
08-12-1986; 1450 kHz AM; *Hrs Open:* 24
75 Oxford St., Suite 402, Providence, RI 02905 US
(401) 467-4366; *Fax:* (401) 941-2795
www.wlkwradio.com/
License: West Warwick, RI held by Hall Communications Inc.
Group Owner: Hall Communications Inc.; acq 6-4-01; $410,000).
Nat'l Network: ESPN Radio; *Nat'l Reps:* Eastman Radio
Arbitron Metro Market: West Warwick, RI; *Format:* Sports *Special Programming:* Pol 2 hrs wkly; *No. News Employees:* 1; *Target Audience:* 35-64.; *Adv. Rates:* 30; 20; 20; 10
Bonnie Rowbotham, CEO
Arthur Rowbotham, President
Tom Wall, General Manager

Westerly

***WKIV**
12-08-1997; 88.1 MHz FM; 0.001 kw horiz, 1.2 kw vert; 105 ft.; N41 26 13 W71 52 55 *Rebroadcasts:* Rebroadcasts KLVR(FM) Middletown, CA 100%
PO Box 2098, Omaha, NE 68103-2098 US
(800) 877-5600
www.klove.com
License: Westerly, Washington County, RI held by Educational Media Foundation.
Group Owner: EMF Broadcasting; (acq 3-21-2008; $100,000)
Nat'l Network: K-Love
Arbitron Metro Market: Omaha, NE; *Format:* Christian
Darrell Chambliss, Chairman
Mike Novak, President/CEO
David Pierce, Chief Creative Officer
Alan Mason, Chief Operating Officer
D. Kevin Blair, Secretary/General Counsel
Eric Moser, Chief Financial Officer

WBLQ(AM)
07-01-1949; 1230 kHz AM; 1 kw-U; N41 21 57 W71 50 11
Rebroadcasts: Rebroadcasts WRNI(AM) Providence 100%
Mailing Address: 58 High Street, Westerly, RI 02891
Second Address: PO Box 2175, Westerly, RI 02891
(401) 322-1743; *Fax:* (401) 322-1645
www.wblq.net
chris@wblq.net
License: Westerly, Washington County, RI held by WRNI Foundation
Nat'l Network: NPR; PRI
Population Served: 178,053; *Arbitron Metro Market:* Providence, RI; *Format:* News, Talk; *Hrs. of News Programming:* News progmg 80 hrs wkly; *No. News Employees:* 3; *Target Audience:* 25-54; intelligent adultsinterested in news & politics
Chris DiPaola, Owner
Lorren Kleinkauf, Office Manager

Woonsocket

WNRI
11-28-1954; 1380 kHz AM; 2.5 kw-D, ND1; 0.018 kw-N, ND1; N42 0 58 W71 29 30
786 Diamond Hill Road, Woonsocket, RI 02895-1476 US
(401) 769-6925; *Fax:* (401) 762-0442
www.wnri.com
wnriroger@yahoo.com
License: Woonsocket, RI held by Bouchard Broadcasting Inc.
Nat'l Network: USA
Arbitron Metro Market: Providence. RI; *Format:* News, News/Talk, 86 *Special Programming:* Fr 4 hrs, Pol 2 hrs, Por 2 hrs wkly; *Target Audience:* 35 plus.
Roger Bouchard, General Manager
Jeff Gamache, Programming Director
Jerry Sweeton, Webmaster

WOON
11-11-1946; 1240 kHz AM
985 Park Avenue, Woonsocket, RI 02895-6332 US
(401) 762-1240; *Fax:* (401) 769-8232
www.onworldwide.com
us@onworldwide.com
License: Woonsocket, RI held by O-N Radio Inc.
Arbitron Metro Market: Providence-Warw *TV Affiliate:* easy lstng; *Format:* Black, Gospel; *No. News Employees:* 35 plus.
Dave Richards, General Manager
Joe Callahan, General Sales Mgr

WWKX
06-26-1949; 106.3 MHz FM; 1.15 kw; 518 ft.; N41 59 43 W71 26 54
1502 Wampanoag Trail, Suite 302, East Providence, RI 02914 US
(401) 433-4200
www.hot1063.com
davey.morris@cumulus.com
License: Woonsocket, RI held by Radio License Holding CBC, LLC
Group Owner: Cumulus Media Inc.
Arbitron Metro Market: Providence, RI; *Format:* Adult Contemp; *Target Audience:* 18-49.
Davey Morris, Programming Director
Rebekah Berger, Promotions Manager
Holly Paras, Advertising

South Carolina

Abbeville

WABV
03-01-1956; 1590 kHz AM; 1 kw-D, ND1; 0.027 kw-N, ND1; N34 9 3 W82 23 34
P.O. Box 280, Jasper, GA 30143 US
(706) 692-4100
License: Abbeville, SC held by Hellinger Broadcasting Inc.
Arbitron Metro Market: Waterloo-Cedar Falls IA
Gabrielle Jordan, Operations Dir
Bill Wolfenbarger, General Manager
Sally Miller, General Sales Mgr

WZLA-FM
01-01-1990; 92.9 MHz FM; *Hrs Open:* 24; 6 kw; 243 ft.; N34 11 13 W82 19 28
112 North Main Street, P.O. Box 548, Abbeville, SC 29620 US
(864) 366-5785; *Fax:* (864) 366-9391
z93oldies.com
z93@wctel.net
License: Abbeville, Abbeville County, SC held by Shelley Reid.
Nat'l Network: Motor Racing Net; Salem Radio Network
Arbitron Metro Market: Abbeville, SC; *Format:* Oldies *Special Programming:* Gospel 8 hrs wkly; *Target Audience:* 25-65.

Aiken

WKXC-FM
08-01-1966; 99.5 MHz FM; 24 kw; 712 ft.; N33 38 44 W81 55 45
4051 Jimmie Dyess Pkwy., Augusta, GA 30909 US
(706) 396-7000
www.kicks99.com
License: Aiken, Aiken County, SC held by Beasley Media Group LLC
Group Owner: Beasley Broadcast Group Inc.; (acq 4-2-2001; $12 million with WHHD(FM) Clearwater).
Arbitron Metro Market: Augusta, GA; *Format:* Country
Chris O'Kelley, Operations Manager/Program Director
Mark Haddon, VP/Market Manager
Georgia Beasley, General Sales Mgr

***WLJK**
01-01-1990; 89.1 MHz FM; *Hrs Open:* 24; 10 kw; 1,374 ft; N33 24 18 W81 50 15 *Rebroadcasts:* Rebroadcasta WRJA-FM Sumter 100%
1041 George Rogers Blvd., Columbia, SC 29201
(803) 737-3200
www.etvradio.org
csr@scetv.org
License: Aiken, Aiken County, SC held by South Carolina Educational Television Commission
Group Owner: South Carolina Educational Television Commission
Nat'l Network: NPR; PRI; APM
Hrs. of News Programming: News progrmg 120 hrs wkly
John Gasque, Operations Manager/Programming Director
Shari Hutchinson, General Manager
Alfred Turner, Producer/Webmaster

WKSP
09-17-1966; 96.3 MHz FM; 17.5 kw; 846 ft.; N33 41 6 W81 55 36
2743 Perimeter Parkway, Bldg 100, Suite 300, Augusta, GA 30909 US
(706) 396-6000
License: Aiken, Aiken County, SC held by Capstar TX LLC
Group Owner: iHeartMedia; (acq 12-19-00; grpsl).
Arbitron Metro Market: Augusta, GA; *Format:* Blues, Oldies, 92
Ivy Elam, Market President
Sabrena Martin, General Sales Mgr
Minnesota Fattz, Programming Director
Cher Best, Promotions/Marketing Director

Cliff Bennett, Digital Content Director
Cynthia Robinson, Business Manager

Allendale

WDOG-FM
08-29-1983; 93.5 MHz FM; 6 kw; 299 ft.; N33 1 22 W81 19 58
P. O. Box 442, 2447 Augusta Highway, Allendale, SC 29810 US
(803) 584-3500; *Fax:* (240) 358-7473; (803) 584-0202
www.bigdogradio.com
wdog935@aol.com
License: Allendale, Allendale County, SC
Arbitron Metro Market: Allendale, SC

Anderson

WAIM
04-01-1935; 1230 kHz AM; 1 kw-U, ND1; N34 31 52 W82 36 50
2203 Old Williamston Rd, Anderson, SC 29621 US
(864) 226-1511; (864) 225-1230; *Fax:* (864) 226-1513
www.waim.us
info@waim.us
License: Anderson, SC held by Palmetto Broadcasting Corp
Arbitron Metro Market: Anderson, SC; *Format:* News, News/Talk, 86; *Target Audience:* 25-64.
Rick Driver, General Manager

WANS
06-01-1949; 1280 kHz AM; *Hrs Open:* 24; 5 kw-D, DAN; 1 kw-N, DAN; N34 32 17 W82 41 28
141 Powell Road, Anderson, SC 29625 US
(864) 224-9267; *Fax:* (864) 224-9744
License: Anderson, SC held by FM 103 Inc.
Arbitron Metro Market: Anderson, SC; *Format:* Sports
Ray Morris, General Manager

WJMZ-FM
08-01-1963; 107.3 MHz FM; *Hrs Open:* 24; 100 kw; 1010 ft.; N34 42 7 W82 36 19
220 N. Main St., Suite 402, Greenville, SC 29601 US
(864) 235-1073; *Fax:* (864) 370-3403
www.1073jamz.com
karolyn.mulvaney@summitmediacorp.com
License: Anderson, Anderson County, SC held by SM-WJMZ-LLC
Group Owner: SummitMedia LLC; (acq 2-1-2001; grpsl)
Arbitron Metro Market: Greenville-Spartanburg, SC; *Format:* Urban Contemporary
Karolyn Mulvaney, VP and General Manager
Bob Grossmall, General Sales Mgr
Mark Shands, Programming Director
Rhonda Rawlings, News/Community Service Director
Kevin Jenko, Political Manager
Bethan Wimmer, Webmaster
Sara Polk,Traffic Director

WROQ
01-01-1947; 101.1 MHz FM; 100 kw; 971 ft.; N34 38 51 W82 16 13
25 Garlington Rd., Greenville, SC 29615 US
(864) 271-9200; *Fax:* (864) 242-1567
www.wroq.com
mailbag2@thebigshow.com
License: Anderson, Anderson County, SC held by Entercom Greenville License LLC.
Group Owner: Entercom Communications Corp.; (acq 10-7-2005; grpsl).
Arbitron Metro Market: Greenville-Spartanburg, SC; *Format:* Classic Rock; *Target Audience:* 25-54; baby boomers
Randy Cable, Sales
Mark Hendrix, Programming Director
Roy Hummers, Promotions Manager

Andrews

WGTN-FM
08-19-1985; 100.7 MHz FM; *Hrs Open:* 24; 3.1 kw; 446 ft.; N33 24 3 W79 27 30
1416 High Market Street, Georgetown, SC 29440 US
(843) 903-9962; *Fax:* (843) 903-1797
www.wgtnradio.com
License: Andrews, Georgetown County, SC held by Coastline Communications of Carolina Inc.
Arbitron Metro Market: Myrtle Beach, SC; *Format:* Adult Contemp; *Target Audience:* 25-54; Adults
Will Isaacs, General Manager
Jerome Bresson, News Director

Atlantic Beach

WMIR
10-01-1997; 1200 kHz AM; *Hrs Open:* Sunrise-sunset
C/O Purbrese Hunsaker &, Post Office 217, Sterling, VA 20167 US
(843) 399-2653; *Fax:* (843) 399-2659
www.rejoice1200.com
License: Atlantic Beach, SC held by Atlantic Beach Radio Inc.
Arbitron Metro Market: Atlantic Beach, SC; *Format:* Religious; *Target Audience:* 25-65; Urban Black gospel
Dr. Gardner Altman, President
Reggie Dyson, General Manager

WSEA
01-01-1998; 100.3 MHz FM; 12 kw; 476 ft.; N33 47 4 W78 52 44
11640 Highway 17 Bypass South, Murrells Inlet, SC 29576 US
(843) 651-7869; *Fax:* (843) 651-9123
www.teammyrtlebeach.com
License: Atlantic Beach, Horry County, SC held by Cumulus Licensing Corp.
Group Owner: Cumulus Media Inc.; (acq 7-16-98; $1.3 million).
Arbitron Metro Market: Myrtle Beach, S; *Format:* Contemporary Hits/Top 40
David Lewis, Market Manager

Bamberg-Denmark

WVCD
06-23-1957; 790 kHz AM; 1 kw-D, ND1; 0.1 kw-N, ND1; N33 18 50 W81 4 43
Voorhees College, P.O. Box 678, Denmark, SC 29042 US
(803) 780-1790
http://teesajohnson.wix.com/wvcd790am
wvcd@voorhees.edu
License: Bamberg-Denmark, SC held by Voorhees College
Regional Network: S.C. News Net.
Format: Religious *Special Programming:* Farm one hr wkly
Annette Gantt, General Manager

Barnwell

WDOG
01-01-1966; 1460 kHz AM
P.O. Box 442, 2447 Augusta Highway, Allendale, SC 28910 US
(803) 584-3500; *Fax:* (240) 358-7473; (803) 584-0202
www.bigdogradio.com
wdog935@aol.com
License: Barnwell, SC held by Good Radio Broadcasting Inc.
Regional Network: S.C. News Net.
Arbitron Metro Market: Allendale, SC; *Format:* Black, Country

Batesburg

WBLR
05-10-1956; 1430 kHz AM; *Hrs Open:* 24
P.O. Box 510, Appling, GA 30802 US
(800) 926-4669
www.gnnradio.org
brian@gnnradio.org
License: Batesburg, SC held by Barinowski Investment Company
Arbitron Metro Market: Grovetown,GA; *Target Audience:* General.
Clarence Barinowski, President

WZMJ
08-05-1965; 93.1 MHz FM; 2.1 kw; 561 ft.; N33 54 2 W81 24 25
Rebroadcasts: Simulcast with WOIC(AM) Columbia 100%
109R Old Chapin Rd., Lexington, SC 29072 US
(803) 785-9596
www.lakemurrayradio.com
mike@lakemurrayradio.com
License: Batesburg, Lexington County, SC held by Urban Radio II L.L.C.
Group Owner: Inner City Broadcasting; (acq 5-30-2003; $11.1 million with WHXT(FM) Orangeburg).
Nat'l Network: ESPN Radio; Jones Radio Networks
Arbitron Metro Market: Batesburg, SC; *Format:* Christian, News, 86
Michael Willis, President/CEO
Mike Anderson, Operations Manager
Renee Lowder, Sales Manager

Beaufort

*WJWJ-FM
08-01-1980; 89.9 MHz FM; *Hrs Open:* 24; 47 kw; Ant 1,096 ft; N32 42 42 W80 40 54 *Rebroadcasts:* Rebroadcasts WRJA(FM) Sumter 100%
1041 George Rogers Boulevard, Columbia, SC 29201
(803) 737-3200
www.etvradio.org
csr@scetv.org
License: Beaufort, Beaufort County, SC held by South Carolina Educational TV Commission.
Nat'l Network: NPR; PRI; APM
Hrs. of News Programming: News progmg 120 hrs wkly; *Target Audience:* General.
Linda O'Bryon, President/CEO
Shari Hutchinson, General Manager
John Crockett, Chief Engineer
Dena Byrd, Director, Education
Kerry Feduk, Vice President, Content

WVGB
01-01-1959; 1490 kHz AM; 0.5 kw-D, ND1; 1 kw-N, ND1; N32 26 8 W80 41 54
25A Market, Habersham Marketplace, Beaufort, SC 29906 US
(843) 466-1122
www.945thecoast.com
License: Beaufort, SC held by Vivian Broadcasting Inc.
Nat'l Network: American Urban
Arbitron Metro Market: Beaufort, SC; *Format:* Classic Rock
Special Programming: Community progmg, sports; *Target Audience:* 18-65; African American

WYKZ
08-08-1962; 98.7 MHz FM; *Hrs Open:* 24; 99 kw; 715 ft.; N32 19 43 W80 56 17
245 Alfred St., Savannah, GA 31408 US
(912) 964-7794
www.987theriver.com
info@987theriver.com
License: Beaufort, Beaufort County, SC held by Capstar TX LLC
Group Owner: iHeartMedia
Arbitron Metro Market: Beaufort, SC; *Format:* Adult Contemp
Special Programming: Oldies 5 hrs wkly; *Hrs. of News Programming:* news progmg 3 hrs wkly; *No. News Employees:* 1; *Target Audience:* 25-54; female
Wesley Peper, Vice President of Sales
Mark Robertson, Promotions Manager

Belton

*WEPC
05-01-1994; 88.5 MHz FM; *Hrs Open:* 24; 50 kw; 299 ft.; N34 23 43 W82 29 49 *Rebroadcasts:* Rebroadcasts WRAF-FM Toccoa Falls, GA 100%
Mailing Address: PO Box 780, Toccoa Falls, GA 30598 US
Second Address: 292 Old Clarkesville Road, Toccoa, GA 30577
(800) 251-8326; *Fax:* (706) 282-6090
www.myfavoritestation.net
License: Belton, Anderson County, SC held by Toccoa Falls College.
Arbitron Metro Market: Belton, SC; *Format:* Adult Contemp, Christian
Marty Lee, Operations Manager
Bryan Race, Station Manager
Mike Shelley, Assistant Manager
Kevin Klump, Program Coordinator
Mike Shelley, Music Director
Debbie Faubion, Children's Programming
Cathy Klump, Social NetworkingCoordinator
Peggy Leff, Donor Relations Coordinator

WABB
10-01-1956; 1390 kHz AM
490 South Main St, Belton, SC 29627 US
(713) 479-5358
www.wevg1470.com
License: Belton, SC held by Big Fish Broadcasting LLC
Arbitron Metro Market: Greenville-Spartanburg, SC; *Format:* Sports, Talk; *Target Audience:* General.
David Gow, CEO
Jeffrey Roper, General Manager
Craig Larson, Programming Director
Christopher Morales, Assistant Porgram Director
Josh Vexler, Affiliate Relations
Gina Messick, Digital Sales Manager

Belvedere

*WAFJ
08-01-1994; 88.3 MHz FM; *Hrs Open:* 24; 4.5 kw; 1388 ft.; N33 24 29 W81 50 36
102 Le Compte Avenue, North Augusta, SC 29841 US
(803) 819-3125; *Fax:* (803) 819-3129
www.wafj.com
info@wafj.com
License: Belvedere, Aiken County, SC held by Radio Training Network Inc.
Nat'l Network: Fox News Radio
Arbitron Metro Market: Augusta, GA; *Format:* Christian; *No. News Employees:* 1; *Target Audience:* 25-54; women
Steve Swanson, Station Manager/Programming Director
Jill Kauffman, Promotions Director
Joanne Spires, Office Manager

Johanna Antes, Director of Support
John Bryant, Webmaster

Bennettsville

WBSC

06-01-1947; 1550 kHz AM; 10 kw-D, DAN; 5 kw-N, DAN; N34 40 52 W79 42 4
501 Sewanee Street, Bennettsville, SC 29512 US
(803) 479-7121; *Fax:* (803) 479- 4474
wbsc@aol.com
License: Bennettsville, SC held by D. Mitch Broadcasting Inc.
Nat'l Network: ABC; *Nat'l Reps:* Dora-Clayton
Format: Gospel, Oldies *Special Programming:* Black 15 hrs wkly
Dwight Johnson, CEO
Richard Gehm, Chief of Operations

Bishopville

WAGS

02-24-1954; 1380 kHz AM; *Hrs Open:* 6:30 AM-6 PM; 1 kw-D; N34 12 35 W80 13 34
142 Wags Dr., Bishopville, SC 29010
(803) 484-5415; (803) 484-3400
www.wagsradio.com
jim@wagsradio.com
License: Bishopville, Lee County, SC held by Beaver Communications
Group Owner: James D. Jenkins; (acq 11-01-99; $27,500).
Population Served: 22,000 *Special Programming:* Live remotes-parades, civic events, festivals 2 hrs, relg 7 hrs wkly; *Hrs. of News Programming:* News progmg 6 hrs wkly; *Target Audience:* 25-55 plus. *Adv. Rates:* 8; 8; 8; 8
James D. Jenkins, Owner/General Manager
Delores E. Jenkins, Co-Owner

Blackville

WIIZ

04-01-1996; 97.9 MHz FM; 50 kw; 433 ft.; N33 6 52 W81 23 13
Mailing Address: P.O. Box 814, Barnwell, SC 29812 US
Second Address: 8968 Marlboro Avenue, Barnwell, SC 29812
(803) 259-9797; *Fax:* (803) 541-9700
www.wiizfm.com
thewiz@wiiz979.com
License: Blackville, Barnwell County, SC held by NicWild Communications Inc.
Arbitron Metro Market: Augusta, GA; *Format:* Urban Contemporary
Bobby Nichols, CEO
Bobby Nichols, General Manager
Cissie Nichols, Entertainment News Director
Cocoa, Music/Marketing Director

Bluffon

WTYB

10-01-1977; 103.9 MHz FM; 50 kw; Ant 344 ft; N32 03 33 W81 00 57
214 Television Cir., Savannah, GA 31406
(912) 961-9000; *Fax:* (912) 961-7070
www.magic1039fm.com
gil.jones@cumulus.com
License: Bluffon, Chatham County, GA held by Volt Radio LLC
Group Owner: Cumulus Media Inc.; (acq 3-26-98; grpsl).
Arbitron Metro Market: Savannah, GA
Eric Mastel, General Manager
Julie Lee, Advertising Contact

Bluffton

WUBB

06-22-1988; 106.9 MHz FM; *Hrs Open:* 24; 100 kw; 801 ft.; N32 13 36 W80 50 53
401 Mall Blvd., Suite 101-D, Savannah, GA 31406 US
(912) 351-9830; *Fax:* (912) 352-4821
www.bob1069.com
License: Bluffton, Beaufort County, SC held by Alpha Media Licensee LLC
Group Owner: Alpha Media LLC
Nat'l Reps: Christal
Population Served: 500,000; *Arbitron Metro Market:* Savannah, GA; *Format:* Country; *No. News Employees:* 1; *Target Audience:* 18-54; *Adv. Rates:* 60; 60; 60; 60
Rob Walker, Operations Manager
Gigi South, Vice President and Market Manager
Kathryn Wake, Director of Sales
John Marshall, Promotions Director
Claire Beverly, News and Public Affairs Director
Carissa Lozinski-Doig, DigitalMarketing Director

Blythewood

WBAJ

01-01-1999; 890 kHz AM
243-A Riverchase Way, Lexington, SC 29072 US
(803) 794-9673
www.wbaj.net
wbaj_890am@yahoo.com
License: Blythewood, SC held by Family First
Arbitron Metro Market: Cowen WV; *Format:* Classic Rock; *Target Audience:* 18-49.
Al Sergi, President

Bowman

WSPX

10-01-1997; 94.5 MHz FM; *Hrs Open:* 24; 3.5 kw; 434 ft.; N33 19 13 W80 43 52
Mailing Address: P.O. Box 1445, Orangeburg, SC 29116 US
Second Address: 200 Regional Parkway, Building C, Suite 200, Orangeburg, SC 29118
(803) 536-1710; *Fax:* (803) 539-9458
License: Bowman, Orangeburg County, SC held by Community Broadcasters, LLC
Group Owner: Community Broadcasters LLC; (acq. from Glory Communications)
Format: Gospel, Religious
Jack Swart, Station Manager

Branchville

WGFG

105.3 MHz FM; *Hrs Open:* 24; 12.5 kw; 463 ft.; N33 26 35 W80 48 16
51 Commerce St, Orangeburg, SC 29118 US
(803) 536-1710; *Fax:* (803) 531-1089
cborangeburg.com/wgfg
jack_swart@commbroadcasters.com
License: Branchville, Orangeburg County, SC held by Community Broadcasters, LLC
Group Owner: Community Broadcasters LLC; (acq 4-30-2003; $1.25 million with WQKI-FM Orangeburg).
Nat'l Network: ABC
Format: Country; *Target Audience:* 25-64
Jack Swart, Station Manager

Briarcliff Acres

WRXZ

04-05-1975; 107.1 MHz FM; *Hrs Open:* 18; 50 kw; 492 ft.; N33 56 14 W78 57 53
4841 Highway 17 Bypass S., Myrtle Beach, SC 29577 US
(843) 293-0107; *Fax:* (843) 293-1717
www.rock107mb.com
License: Briarcliff Acres, Horry County, SC held by AMFM Radio Licenses LLC.
Group Owner: iHeartMedia; (acq 2014)
Arbitron Metro Market: Myrtle Beach, SC; *Format:* Rock/AOR
Jimmy Feuger, Market President
Ron Roberts, Senior Vice President of Programming
Denise Atkins, Senior Vice President of Sales
Jennifer Habib, Business Manager

Bucksport

WGTR

06-01-1993; 107.9 MHz FM; 20 kw; 784 ft.; N33 35 45 W79 3 11
4841 Highway 17 Bypass S., Myrtle Beach, SC 29577 US
(843) 293-0107; *Fax:* (843) 293-1717
www.gator1079.com
License: Bucksport, Horry County, SC held by AMFM Radio Licenses LLC.
Group Owner: iHeartMedia; (acq 2014)
Arbitron Metro Market: Myrtle Beach, SC; *Format:* Country
Special Programming: Motor racing 8 hrs wkly
Jimmy Feuger, Market President
Ron Roberts, Senior Vice President of Programming
Denise Atkins, Senior Vice President of Sales
Jennifer Habib, Business Manager

Camden

WCAM

07-23-1948; 1590 kHz AM; *Hrs Open:* 6 AM-11 PM
Mailing Address: P.O. Box 753, Camden, SC 29021 US
Second Address: 5 The Commons Ward Rd., Lugoff, SC 29078
(803) 438-9002; *Fax:* (803) 408-2288
www.kool1027.com
wpubradio@bellsouth.net
License: Camden, SC held by Kershaw Radio Corp.
Regional Network: S.C. News Net.
Arbitron Metro Market: Camden, SC; *Format:* Oldies; *Target Audience:* 45 plus.
Chris Johnson, General Manager
Bill Rogers, Programming Director

WPUB-FM

12-01-1974; 102.7 MHz FM; 6 kw; 299 ft.; N34 13 31 W80 40 44
Mailing Address: P.O. Box 753, Lugoff, SC 29020 US
Second Address: 5 The Commons, Camden, SC 29020
(803) 438-9002; *Fax:* (803) 408-2288
wpubradio@bellsouth.net
License: Camden, Kershaw County, SC
Format: Oldies; *Target Audience:* 25-55.; *Adv. Rates:* 13; 13; 13; 13
Gregory Weston, General Manager

Cameron

WTQS

01-01-2008; 1470 kHz AM *Rebroadcasts:* Simulcasts WQXL (AM) 1490 100%
PO Box 951, Columbia, SC 29202 US
(803) 939-9530; *Fax:* (803) 939-9469
www.makethepointradio.com
kev@makethepointradio.com
License: Cameron, SC held by Community Broadcasters, LLC
Group Owner: Community Broadcasters LLC; (acq. from Glory Communications Inc.)
Arbitron Metro Market: Cameron, SC; *Format:* News, News/Talk, 86

Cayce

WLTY

07-11-1974; 96.7 MHz FM; 9 kw; 433 ft.; N34 0 18 W81 0 44
316 Greystone Blvd., Columbia, SC 29210 US
(803) 343-1100; *Fax:* (803) 748-9267
www.967stevefm.com
kelleyroyster@iheartmedia.com
License: Cayce, Lexington County, SC held by Capstar TX LLC
Group Owner: iHeartMedia; (acq 8-30-00; grpsl).
Nat'l Reps: Clear Channel
Arbitron Metro Market: Columbia, SC; *Format:* Variety/Diverse; *Hrs. of News Programming:* News progmg 6 hrs wkly; *Target Audience:* 25-44; professionals & young adults
Ron Hill, Vice President/Market Manager
Todd Shuster, Senior Vice President of Sales

WGCV

08-22-1958; 620 kHz AM; *Hrs Open:* 24
PO Box 951, Columbia, SC 29202 US
(803) 939-9530; *Fax:* (803) 799-1620
www.wgcv.net
gstrange@wfmv.com
License: Cayce, SC held by Glory Communications Inc.
Group Owner: Glory Communications Inc.; acq 10-8-99).
Nat'l Network: American Urban
Arbitron Metro Market: Columbia, SC; *Format:* Gospel; *No. News Employees:* 1; *Target Audience:* 34-65; Black adults
Gil Strange, General Sales Mgr
Tony Jamison, Programming Director

*WYFV

10-10-1990; 88.5 MHz FM; *Hrs Open:* 24; 50 kw; 171 ft.; N33 54 32 W81 5 57
1801 Charleston Hwy., Suite B, Cayce, SC 29033-2019 US
(803) 739-1294
www.bbnradio.org
bbn@bbnmedia.org
License: Cayce, Lexington County, SC held by Bible Broadcasting Network Inc.
Group Owner: Bible Broadcasting Network; acq 6-26-90;
Arbitron Metro Market: Columbia, SC; *Format:* Christian, Religious; *Hrs. of News Programming:* News progmg 10 hrs wkly; *Target Audience:* General.
Lowell Davey, President
Jason Padgett, Operations Manager
Don Leauge, Manager

Charleston

*WALC

04-04-1990; 100.5 MHz FM; *Hrs Open:* 24; 13.5 kw; 448 ft.; N32 49 0.4 W79 50 9.7
50 E. Rivercenter Blvd, Suite 1200, Covington, KY 14011 US
(843) 884-2534; *Fax:* (843) 884-6096
License: Charleston, Charleston County, SC held by Radio Training Network Inc.
Nat'l Reps: Katz Radio
Arbitron Metro Market: Charleston, SC; *Format:* Christian
Allen Henderson, General Manager
Terri Hegel, General Sales Mgr

Willie Bennett, Chief Engineer
Alene Grevey, VP/Market Manager

WEZL
10-03-1970; 103.5 MHz FM; *Hrs Open:* 24; 100 kw; 659 ft.; N32 49 4 W79 50 9
950 Houston Northcutt Blvd., 2nd Floor, Mt. Pleasant, SC 29464 US
(843) 884-2534; *Fax:* (843) 884-6096
www.wezl.com
License: Charleston, Charleston County, SC held by Citicasters Licenses Inc.
Group Owner: iHeartMedia; (acq 5-4-99; grpsl).
Arbitron Metro Market: Charleston, SC; *Format:* Country; *Hrs. of News Programming:* news progmg 3 to 4 hrs wkly; *No. News Employees:* 1
Alene Grevey, Market President
Travis Dylan, Operations Manager
Rhetta Cloyd, Senior Vice President Sales and Marketing
Tyler Reese, Programming Director
Willie Bennett, Chief Engineer
Lisa Cooper, Business Manager
Wesley Sharp,Digital Content Director

***WFCH**
12-01-1986; 88.5 MHz FM; 29.5 kw; 305 ft.; N32 49 4 W79 50 8
290 Hegenberger Road, Oakland, CA 94621 US
(800) 543-1495
www.familyradio.com
License: Charleston, Charleston County, SC held by Family Stations Inc.
Group Owner: Family Stations Inc.
Nat'l Network: Family Radio
Arbitron Metro Market: Charleston, SC; *Format:* Religious
Harold Camping, General Manager
Joe Papp, Chief Engineer

WQNT
01-01-1948; 1450 kHz AM; 1 kw-U; N32 48 15 W79 57 43
60 Markfield Dr., Suite 4, Charleston, SC 29407
(843) 763-6631
License: Charleston, Charleston County, SC held by Kirkman Broadcasting Inc.
Group Owner: Kirkman Broadcasting Inc.; (acq 1995)
Nat'l Network: Fox Sports
Population Served: 460,000; *Arbitron Metro Market:* Charleston, SC; *Format:* Sports, Talk *Special Programming:* Relg one hr wkly; *Target Audience:* 25-54; Men; *Adv. Rates:* 20; 20; 20; 10
Rick Howze, General Sales Mgr

WQSC
01-01-1946; 1340 kHz AM; *Hrs Open:* 24; 1 kw-U; N32 49 07 W79 57 43
60 Markfield Dr., Charleston, SC 29418 US
(843) 763-6631
License: Charleston, Charleston County, SC held by Kirkman Broadcasting Inc.
Group Owner: Kirkman Broadcasting Inc.; acq 11-1-94).
Population Served: 66,945; *Arbitron Metro Market:* Charleston, SC; *Format:* News/Talk; *Target Audience:* 25-54; Adults; *Adv. Rates:* 20; 20; 20; 20
Rick Howze, General Sales Mgr

WLTQ
01-01-1947; 730 kHz AM; *Hrs Open:* 24
US
(866) 263-1700
catholicradioinsc.com
License: Charleston, SC held by Mediatrix SC, Inc.
Arbitron Metro Market: Charleston, SC; *Format:* Religious
Sherria Brooks, General Manager

***WSCI**
01-01-1973; 89.3 MHz FM; *Hrs Open:* 24; 97 kw; 540 ft; N32 47 44 W79 50 27 *Rebroadcasts:* Rebroadcasts WLTR(FM) Columbia 95%
1041 George Rogers Blvd., Columbia, SC 29201
(803) 737-3200
www.etvradio.org
csr@scetv.org
License: Charleston, Charleston County, SC held by South Carolina Educational TV Commission.
Nat'l Network: NPR; PRI; APM
Population Served: 66,945; *Arbitron Metro Market:* Charleston, SC; *Hrs. of News Programming:* News progmg 70 hrs wkly
Linda O'Bryon, President
John Gasque, Operations/Programming Director
Shari Hutchinson, Station Manager/General Manager
Melanie Boyer, General Sales Mgr

WSSX
01-01-1945; 95.1 MHz FM; *Hrs Open:* 24; 100 kw; 1001 ft.; N32 47 44 W79 50 27
4230 Faber Place Dr., Suite 100, North Charleston, SC 29405 US
(843) 277-1200
www.95sx.com
License: Charleston, SC held by Radio License Holding CBC, LLC
Group Owner: Cumulus Media Inc.; (acq 6-9-99; grpsl).
Nat'l Network: Westwood One
Arbitron Metro Market: Charleston, SC; *Format:* Contemporary Hits/Top 40
Lindsay Wine, General Sales Mgr
Yonni Rude, Programming Director

WIWF
04-01-1948; 96.9 MHz FM; 100 kw; 1768 ft.; N32 55 28 W79 41 58
4230 Farber Place Dr., Suite 100, North Charleston, SC 29405 US
(843) 277-1200
www.nashfm969.com
License: Charleston, SC held by Radio License Holding CBC, LLC
Group Owner: Cumulus Media Inc.
Arbitron Metro Market: Charleston, SC; *Format:* Country
Lindsay Wine, General Sales Mgr

WTMA
06-01-1939; 1250 kHz AM; *Hrs Open:* 24; 5 kw-D, 1 kw-N, DA-N; N32 49 27 W80 00 10
4230 Faber Place Dr., Suite 100, N. Charleston, SC 29405 US
(843) 277-1200
www.wtma.com
License: Charleston, SC held by Radio License Holding CBC, LLC
Group Owner: Cumulus Media Inc.; (acq 6-9-99; grpsl).
Population Served: 15,000; *Arbitron Metro Market:* Charleston, SC; *Format:* News/Talk
Lindsay Wine, Sales Manager
John Quincy, Programming Director

WSPO
05-01-1967; 1390 kHz AM; 5 kw-D, DAN; 5 kw-N, DAN; Ant 340 ft; N32 49 28 W80 0 10
140 S. Ash Ave., Tempe, AZ 85281 US
(843) 972-1100; *Fax:* (843) 972-1200
www.wsposports.com
License: Charleston, SC
Arbitron Metro Market: Charleston, SC; *Format:* Sports, Talk
G. Dean Pearce, President

Cheraw

WCRE
07-01-1953; 1420 kHz AM; *Hrs Open:* 24; 1 kw-D, 97 w-N / 250 24 hrs.; N34 40 48 W79 53 58
PO Box 631, Cheraw, SC 29520
(843) 537-7887; *Fax:* (843) 537-7307
www.myfm939.com
janepigg@gmail.com
License: Cheraw, Chesterfield County, SC held by Pee Dee Broadcasting LLC
Population Served: 63,000 *Special Programming:* Black 5 hrs wkly; *Hrs. of News Programming:* news progmg 12 hrs wkly; *No. News Employees:* 1; *Target Audience:* 25 plus; Adults; *Adv. Rates:* 20; 20; 20; 20
Jane Elizabeth Davis-Pigg, President

WJMX-FM
07-17-1979; 103.3 MHz FM; 50 kw; 492 ft.; N34 30 18 W79 54 18
181 East Evans St., Suite 311, Florence, SC 29506 US
(843) 667-9569; *Fax:* (843) 673-7390
www.103xonline.com
License: Cheraw, Chesterfield County, SC held by AMFM Radio Licenses LLC.
Group Owner: iHeartMedia
Regional Network: S.C. News Net; *Nat'l Reps:* McGavren Guild
Arbitron Metro Market: Florence, SC; *Format:* Contemporary Hits/Top 40; *Target Audience:* 18-34.
Denis Davis, Senior Vice President of Programming

Chester

WBT-FM
08-30-1969; 99.3 MHz FM; *Hrs Open:* 24; 7.7 kw; 598 ft.; N34 47 30 W81 16 6 *Rebroadcasts:* Rebroadcasts WBT(AM) Charlotte 100%
One Julian Price Place, Charlotte, NC 28208 US
(704) 374-3500
www.wbt.com
jfurst@wbt.com
License: Chester, Chester County, SC held by Greater Media of Charlotte Inc.
Group Owner: Beasley Broadcast Group; (acq 1-31-2008; grpsl)
Arbitron Metro Market: Charlotte, NC; *Format:* News, News/Talk, 86 *Special Programming:* Gospel 6 hrs wkly; *Hrs. of News Programming:* news progmg 6 hrs wkly; *No. News Employees:* 7; *Target Audience:* 25-54;information, sports seekers
Jason Furst, Programming Director
Matt DuBois, Marketing Director
Rachel Ferebee, Contesting Coordinator
Amelia Davis, Website Coordinator

WGCD
07-19-1948; 1490 kHz AM; 1 kw-U, ND1; N34 41 54 W81 12 6
P. O. Box 117, Chester, SC 29706 US
(803) 329-2760; *Fax:* (803) 329-8652
License: Chester, SC held by Wisdom LLC.
Group Owner: Wisdom LLC; (acq 2-2-2009; grpsl)
Format: Gospel
Frank Neeley, Owner
Frankie Hemphill, Station Manager

Chesterfield

WVSZ
01-01-1993; 107.3 MHz FM; 4.5 kw; 328 ft.; N34 43 12 W80 05 45
Mailing Address: Box 307, Rock Hill, SC 29731 US
Second Address: 142 N. Confederate Ave., Rock Hill, SC 29730
(840) 324-1071
www.wrhi.com/wrhm
License: Chesterfield, Chesterfield County, SC held by Our Three Sons Broadcasting LLP.
Group Owner: Our Three Sons Broadcasting LLP.
Nat'l Network: ABC; *Regional Network:* S.C. News Net.
Arbitron Metro Market: Chesterfield, SC; *Format:* Country; *No. News Employees:* 2
Steven Stone, Operations Dir
Chris Miller, Dir. of Sales
Mike Crowder, News Director

***WRFE**
01-01-2007; 89.3 MHz FM; 1.5 kw; 197 ft.; N34 43 15 W80 5 18
PO Box 25775, Winston-Salem, NC 27114 US
(336) 788-1155; *Fax:* (336) 788-7199
www.joyfm.org
office@joyfm.org
License: Chesterfield, Chesterfield County, SC held by Positive Alternative Radio Inc.
Group Owner: Positive Alternative Radio Inc.; (acq 1-16-2008; $500,000)
Arbitron Metro Market: Chesterfield, SC; *Format:* Gospel
Edward Baker, President
Brian Sanders, General Manager

Clearwater

WHHD
04-01-1987; 98.3 MHz FM; *Hrs Open:* 24; 11.5 kw; 486 ft.; N33 30 44 W82 4 48
4051 Jimmie Dyess Pkwy., Augusta, GA 30909 US
(706) 396-7000
www.hd983.com
License: Clearwater, Aiken County, SC held by Beasley Media Group LLC
Group Owner: Beasley Broadcast Group Inc.; (acq 4-2-2001; $12 million with WKXC-FM Aiken).
Arbitron Metro Market: Augusta, GA; *Format:* Contemporary Hits/Top 40 *Special Programming:* Kidd Kraddick in the Morning; *Target Audience:* 18-49 females; *Adv. Rates:* Inquiries only
Chris O'Kelley, Operations Manager
Kent Murphy, General Sales Mgr
Kris Fisher, Programming Director
Mark Haddon, Vice President/Market Manager
Georgia Beasley, Digital Sales Manager
Joe Coad, Music Director

Clemson

WAHT
07-27-1969; 1560 kHz AM; *Hrs Open:* 6 AM-8 PM; 0.5 kw-C, NDD; 1 kw-D, NDD; N34 42 4 W82 49 30
202 Lawrence Rd., P.O. Box 1560, Clemson, SC 29631 US
(864) 654-4004; *Fax:* (864) 654-3300
License: Clemson, SC held by Byrne Acquisition Group LLC
Regional Network: S.C. News Net.; *Wire Services:* CBS
Arbitron Metro Market: Clemson, SC; *Format:* Oldies; *Hrs. of News Programming:* news progmg 35 hrs wkly; *No. News Employees:* 1; *Target Audience:* 35-58; older yuppies

John B. Byrne, President
Faye Clement, Operations Dir
Jeff Bright, Station Manager

WCCP-FM
04-08-1993; 104.9 MHz FM; *Hrs Open:* 24; 4.6 kw; 371 ft.; N34 38 13 W82 42 30
202 Lawrence Rd., Clemson, SC 29631 US
(864) 654-4004; *Fax:* (864) 654-3300
www.wccpfm.com
info@wccpfm.com
License: Clemson, Pickens County, SC held by Byrne Acquisition Group LLC
Nat'l Network: CBS; Sporting News Radio Network
Arbitron Metro Market: Clemson, SC; *Format:* Sports; *Target Audience:* 91% of the WCCP audience is between the ages of 18-54 & 96% of the WCCP audience is male; *Adv. Rates:* 30; 25; 21; 18
John B. Byrne, President
Barry Clement, Operations Dir
Aly Darby, Station Manager
Chris Downey, General Sales Mgr

***WSBF-FM**
03-16-1961; 88.1 MHz FM; 3 kw; 200 ft.; N34 40 42 W82 49 15
315 Hendrix Center, Clemson, SC 29634 US
(864) 656-9723
wsbf.clemson.edu/
wsbf@clemson.edu
License: Clemson, Pickens County, SC held by Clemson University Board of Trustees.
Nat'l Network: Westwood One
Format: Alternative; *Target Audience:* 16-25.
Garrett Burke, General Manager
Hallie Shafer, Promotions Director
Matt Rana, Chief Engineer
Cole Monroe, Production Director
Briah Doherty, Music Director
Max Franks, Webmaster

Clinton

WPCC
09-11-1957; 1410 kHz AM; *Hrs Open:* 24; 1 kw-D, ND1; 0.1 kw-N, ND1; N34 26 42 W81 53 24
Mailing Address: Hwy 72, S. Greenwood Hwy, Clinton, SC 29325 US
Second Address: 1766 Hwy 72 West, West Clinton, SC 29325
(864) 833-1410; *Fax:* (864) 833-2467
www.sportsradio1410wpcc.com
License: Clinton, SC held by Laurens County Communications Inc.
Nat'l Network: ESPN Radio
Format: Sports *Special Programming:* Moring Show- The Doghouse, Local and Regional Sports; *Hrs. of News Programming:* news progmg one hr wkly; *No. News Employees:* 1; *Target Audience:* General.
A. Cruickshanks, President
Rhonda Cruickshanks, General Manager
Chris Burgin, Programming Director

Cokesbury

***WKRI**
91.9 MHz FM; 20.5 kw; 354 ft.; N34 21 26 W82 9 14
PO Box 78, Cokesbury, SC 47701 US
(812) 425-4226; *Fax:* (812) 421-0005
License: Cokesbury, Greenwood County, SC held by Radio Training Network, Inc.
Group Owner: Radio Training Network, Inc.
Arbitron Metro Market: Cokesbury, SC

Columbia

WARQ
02-06-1971; 93.5 MHz FM; *Hrs Open:* 24; 2.8 kw; 443 ft.; N34 0 4 W81 2 5
1900 Pineview Rd., Columbia, SC 29209 US
(803) 695-8600; *Fax:* (803) 695-8605
www.q935online.com
License: Columbia, Richland County, SC held by Alpha Media Licensee LLC
Group Owner: Alpha Media LLC; (acq 9-16-2013; grpsl).
Nat'l Network: Westwood One; *Wire Services:* Accu-Weather
Arbitron Metro Market: Columbia, SC; *Format:* Adult Contemp; *Hrs. of News Programming:* news progmg 5 hrs wkly; *No. News Employees:* 1; *Target Audience:* 18-49.
Mike Hartel, General Manager
Bryan Hendry, General Sales Mgr
Greg Pitt, Programming Director
Michelle Alston, Promotions Director
Maggie Hanisch, Business Manager

WCOS
01-01-1939; 1400 kHz AM; *Hrs Open:* 24; 1 kw-U, ND1; N34 0 18 W81 0 43
316 Greystone Boulevard, Columbia, SC 29210 US
(803) 343-1100
www.foxsportsradio1400.com
License: Columbia, SC held by Capstar TX LLC
Group Owner: iHeartMedia; (acq 9-1-00; grpsl)
Nat'l Reps: Clear Channel
Arbitron Metro Market: Columbia, SC; *Format:* Sports; *Target Audience:* Men 25-54.
Ron Hill, Market President
Kelley Royster, Business Manager

WCOS-FM
03-01-1951; 97.5 MHz FM; *Hrs Open:* 24; 100 kw; 981 ft.; N34 8 23 W81 3 22
316 Greystone Boulevard, Columbia, SC 29210 US
(803) 343-1100
www.975wcos.com
kelleyroyster@clearchannel.com
License: Columbia, Richland County, SC
Arbitron Metro Market: Columbia, SC; *Format:* Country; *No. News Employees:* 1; *Target Audience:* 25-54.

WCEO
01-01-1994; 840 kHz AM; *Hrs Open:* Sunrise-sunset; 50 kw-D, DAD; N34 12 42 W80 50 5
4801 East Independence Boulevard, Suite 800, Charlotte, NC 28212 US
(704) 579-1828
www.larazalaraza.com
License: Columbia, SC held by Norsan Broadcasting WCEO LLC.
Group Owner: Norsan Consulting and Management Inc.; (acq 10-1-2006; $1.6 million)
Arbitron Metro Market: Columbia, SC; *Adv. Rates:* 40; 35; 40; na
Ronnie Coates, Regional Sales Manager

WISW
01-01-1945; 1320 kHz AM; *Hrs Open:* 24; 5 kw-D, DAN; 2.5 kw-N, DAN; N34 0 16 W81 4 15
1301 Gervais St., Suite 700, Columbia, SC 29201 US
(803) 796-7600
www.1320thefan.com
rick.prusator@cumulus.com
License: Columbia, SC held by Radio License Holding CBC, LLC
Group Owner: Cumulus Media Inc.
Arbitron Metro Market: Columbia, SC; *Format:* Talk, Sports
Rick Prusator, VP/Market Manager

***WLTR**
07-01-1976; 91.3 MHz FM; *Hrs Open:* 24; 96 kw; 761 ft; N34 07 07 W80 56 12
1041 George Rogers Blvd., Columbia, SC 29201
(803) 737-3200
www.etvradio.org
csr@scetv.org
License: Columbia, Richland County, SC held by South Carolina Educ. TV Commission.
Nat'l Network: NPR; PRI; APM
Population Served: 450,000; *Arbitron Metro Market:* Columbia, SC
Linda O'Bryon, President
John Gasque, Operations/Programming Director
Shari Hutchinson, General Manager/Station Manager
Shari Hutchinson, Station Manager
John Crockett, Engineering Dir

***WMHK**
08-30-1976; 89.7 MHz FM; 100 kw; 1398 ft.; N34 5 49 W80 45 51
PO Box 3122, Columbia, SC 29230 US
(803) 754-5400; *Fax:* (803) 714-0849
License: Columbia, Richland County, SC held by Columbia Bible College Broadcasting Co.
Arbitron Metro Market: Columbia, SC; *Format:* Christian; *Target Audience:* 25-44; women
Joe, Director of Broadcasting
John, Operations Manager
Jeff, Programming Director
Kelly, Office Manager
David, Manager of Broadcast Technology

WNOK
07-15-1959; 104.7 MHz FM; *Hrs Open:* 24; 90 kw; 1033 ft.; N34 9 3 W80 54 36
316 Greystone Blvd., Columbia, SC 29210 US
(803) 343-1100; *Fax:* (803) 748-9267
www.wnok.com
License: Columbia, Richland County, SC held by Capstar TX LLC
Group Owner: iHeartMedia; (acq 8-30-00; grpsl).
Arbitron Metro Market: Columbia, SC; *Format:* Contemporary Hits/Top 40; *Target Audience:* 18-34; landed gentry
Ron Hill, Market President
Todd Shuster, Senior Vice President of Sales

WOIC
01-01-1947; 1230 kHz AM; 1 kw-U, ND1; N33 59 34 W81 02 45
1900 Pineview Rd., Columbia, SC 29209 US
(803) 695-8600; *Fax:* (803) 695-8605
www.espncolumbia.com
License: Columbia, Richland County, SC held by Alpha Media Licensee LLC
Group Owner: Alpha Media LLC; (acq 9-16-2013; grpsl).
Nat'l Network: USA; *Nat'l Reps:* Eastman
Population Served: 461,000; *Arbitron Metro Market:* Columbia, SC; *Format:* Sports; *Hrs. of News Programming:* News progmg 3 hrs wkly; *Target Audience:* 25-54; Male
Mike Hartel, Senior Vice President and Market Manager

WLXC
01-01-1982; 103.1 MHz FM; 6 kw; 308 ft.; N34 03 05 W81 00 07
1301 Gervais St., Suite 700, Columbia, SC 29201 US
(803) 796-7600; *Fax:* (803) 739-1072
www.kiss-1031.com
doug.williams@cumulus.com
License: Columbia, SC held by Radio License Holding CBC, LLC
Group Owner: Cumulus Media Inc.
Arbitron Metro Market: Columbia, SC; *Format:* Urban Contemporary
Doug Williams, Programming Director

WQXL
06-15-1945; 1470 kHz AM; *Hrs Open:* 6 AM-8:30 PM
PO Box 50433, Columbia, SC 29250 US
(803) 779-8255; *Fax:* (803) 563-8558
www.makethepointradio.com
kev@makethepointradio.com
License: Columbia, SC held by Capital City Media, LLC
Group Owner: Capital City Media, LLC; (acq 5-11-2007; $200,000)
Nat'l Network: USA
Arbitron Metro Market: Columbia, SC; *Format:* Religious; *Target Audience:* 25-49.

WVOC
08-05-1975; 560 kHz AM; *Hrs Open:* 24; 5 kw-D, DAN; 5 kw-N, DAN; 331 ft; N34 2 0 W81 8 32
316 Greystone Blvd., Columbia, SC 29210-8007 US
(803) 343-1100; *Fax:* (803) 748-6297
www.wvoc.com
License: Columbia, SC held by Capstar TX LLC
Group Owner: iHeartMedia; (acq 8-30-00; grpsl).
Nat'l Network: CBS
Arbitron Metro Market: Columbia, SC; *Format:* News, News/Talk, 84, Talk; *Hrs. of News Programming:* news progmg 17 hrs wkly; *No. News Employees:* 1; *Target Audience:* 35 plus; mature adults
Todd Shuster, Senior Vice President of Sales
Kelley Royster, Market Controller

***WUSC-FM**
01-17-1977; 90.5 MHz FM; *Hrs Open:* 24; 2.5 kw; 253 ft.; N34 0 2 W81 1 19
RHUU Room 343, 1400 Greene Street, Columbia, SC 29208 US
(803) 777-5468
wusc.sc.edu
wuscsm@sc.edu
License: Columbia, Richland County, SC held by University of South Carolina.
Arbitron Metro Market: Columbia, SC; *Format:* Variety/Diverse; *Hrs. of News Programming:* news progmg 3 hrs wkly; *No. News Employees:* 1; *Target Audience:* General; alternative generation
Savannah Walker, Station Manager
Ari Robbins, Programming Director
Keylyn Middeton, Music Director
Mason Youngblood, Music Director
Sean Taylor, Director, Public Affairs
Samuel Forst, Secretary

WCOS-FM
03-01-1951; 97.5 MHz FM; 100 kw; N34 8 23 W81 3 22
316 Greystone Boulevard, Columbia, SC 29210 US
(803) 343-1100
www.975wcos.com
License: Columbia, SC held by Capstar TX LLC
Group Owner: iHeartMedia
Nat'l Reps: Clear Channel
Arbitron Metro Market: Columbia, SC; *Format:* Country

Ron Hill, Market President
Todd Shuster, Senior Vice President of Sales
Kelley Royster, Business Manager

Conway

***WHMC-FM**
09-15-1985; 90.1 MHz FM; *Hrs Open:* 24; 30 kw; 706 ft; N33 57 05 W79 06 31 *Rebroadcasts:* Rebroadcasts WRJA-FM Sumter 100%
1041 George Rogers Blvd., Columbia, SC 29201
(803) 737-3200
www.etvradio.org
csr@scetv.org
License: Conway, Horry County, SC held by South Carolina Educational Television Commission.
Nat'l Network: NPR; PRI; APM
Arbitron Metro Market: Myrtle Beach, S; *Hrs. of News Programming:* New progrmg 120 hrs wkly
Linda O'Bryon, President
John Gassque, Operations/Programming Director
Shari Hutchinson, General Manager/Station Manager
John Crockett, Engineering Dir

WIQB
02-23-1977; 1050 kHz AM; *Hrs Open:* 24; 5 kw-D, 473 w-N, DA-2; N33 50 56 W79 05 03
11640 Hwy. 17 Bypass, Murrells Inlet, SC 29576
(843) 651-7869
License: Conway, Horry County, SC held by Cumulus Licensing Corp.
Group Owner: Cumulus Media Inc.; (acq 12-29-97; grpsl)
Regional Network: S.C. News Net.
Population Served: 256,000; *Arbitron Metro Market:* Myrtle Beach, SC; *Format:* Sports; *No. News Employees:* 1; *Target Audience:* 50 plus; affluent retirees; *Adv. Rates:* 10; 10; 10; 10
Ron Raybourne, General Manager
Dave Solomon, Programming Director
Robert Kesler, News Director
Buddy Womack, Chief Engineer

WJXY-FM
10-01-1990; 93.9 MHz FM; *Hrs Open:* 24; 3.7 kw; Ant 420 ft; N33 50 07 W78 52 06
111 East Kilbourn Avenue, Suite 2700, Milwaukee, WI 53202
(843) 651-7869; *Fax:* (843) 397-3197
License: Conway, Horry County, SC held by Joule Broadcasting LLC
Group Owner: Joule Broadcasting LLC
Nat'l Network: ABC
Arbitron Metro Market: Myrtle Beach, SC; *Hrs. of News Programming:* News progmg 2 hrs wkly; *Target Audience:* 18-34.
Lou Dickey, President
Lisa Van Horn, Operations Dir
Dave Solomon, General Sales Mgr

WPJS
08-01-1945; 1330 kHz AM
1720 Highway 501 West, Conway, SC 29526 US
(843) 248-9040; *Fax:* (843) 248-6365
License: Conway, SC held by WPJS Broadcasters Inc.
Arbitron Metro Market: Myrtle Beach, SC; *Format:* Black, Gospel; *Target Audience:* 12 plus.
P.J. Parrish, General Manager

Coward

WPDT
07-26-1991; 105.1 MHz FM; 18 kw; 384 ft.; N33 54 54 W79 50 19
Mailing Address: P.O. Box 13525, Florence, SC 29504 US
Second Address: 2423 Walker Swinton Rd, Timmonsville, SC 29161
(843) 678-9393
License: Coward, Florence County, SC held by Community Broadcasters, LLC
Group Owner: Community Broadcasters LLC; (acq from Glory Communications)
Arbitron Metro Market: Florence, SC; *Format:* Gospel, Religious
Suzy Rafail, Station Manager

Darlington

WDAR-FM
12-01-1965; 105.5 MHz FM; *Hrs Open:* 24hrs; 17 kw; 400 ft.; N34 18 58 W79 53 17
181 E. Evans St., Florence, SC 29506 US
(843) 432-1055
www.sunny1055online.com
License: Darlington, Darlington County, SC held by AMFM Radio Licenses LLC.
Group Owner: iHeartMedia
Arbitron Metro Market: Florence, SC; *Format:* Christian
Denis Davis, Senior Vice President of Programming

WJMX
01-01-1955; 1400 kHz AM
Mailing Address: Two Bala Plaza, Suite 801, Bala-Cynwyd, PA 19004 US
Second Address: 181 E. Evans St., Suite 311, Florence, SC 29506
(843) 667-4600; *Fax:* (843) 673-7390
www.newstalk1400online.com
License: Darlington, SC held by AMFM Radio Licenses LLC.
Group Owner: iHeartMedia
Arbitron Metro Market: Florence, SC; *Format:* News/Talk; *Target Audience:* 25 plus.
Denis Davis, Senior Vice President of Programming

Dillon

WDSC
05-22-1946; 800 kHz AM; *Hrs Open:* 24
181 E. Evans St., Suite 311, Florence, SC 29501 US
(843) 667-4600; *Fax:* (843) 673-7390
www.sportsconnection800.com
License: Dillon, SC held by AMFM Radio Licenses LLC.
Group Owner: iHeartMedia
Format: Sports; *Target Audience:* General.
Denis Davis, Senior Vice President of Programming

WEGX
02-16-1954; 92.9 MHz FM; *Hrs Open:* 24; 100 kw; 1617 ft.; N34 22 4 W79 19 21
181 E. Evans St., Suite 311, Florence, SC 29506 US
(843) 667-4600; *Fax:* (843) 673-7390
www.eagle929online.com
License: Dillon, Dillon County, SC held by AMFM Radio Licenses LLC.
Group Owner: iHeartMedia
Arbitron Metro Market: Dillon, SC; *Format:* Country *Special Programming:* Jazz one hr wkly
Denis Davis, Senior Vice President of Programming

***WDLL**
01-01-2007; 90.5 MHz FM; 25 kw vert; 276 ft.; N34 19 53 W79 33 37 *Rebroadcasts:* Rebroadcasts WAFR(FM) Tupelo, MS 100%
P.O. Box 3206, Tupelo, MS 38803 US
(662) 844-8888; *Fax:* (662) 842-6791
www.afr.net
faq@afa.net
License: Dillon, Dillon County, SC held by American Family Association.
Group Owner: American Family Radio
Arbitron Metro Market: Dillon, SC; *Format:* Christian
Tim Wildmon, President
Donald Wildmon, Founder
Buddy Smith, Sr VP
Ed Vitagliano, Exec VP
Randy Sharp, Director Of Special Projects
Meeke Addison, Director Of Communications
Abraham Hamilton III, Gerneral Counsel

Dorchester Terrace-Brentwood

WTMZ
11-17-1960; 910 kHz AM; *Hrs Open:* 24; 500 w-U, DA-N; N34 09 03 W82 23 34
60 Markfield Dr., Charleston, SC 29403 US
(843) 763-6631
www.charlestonsportsradio.com
License: Dorchester Terrace-Brentwood, Dorchester County, SC held by Kirkman Broadcasting Inc.
Group Owner: Kirkman Broadcasting Inc.; (acq 1-5-2005; $500,000).
Nat'l Network: ESPN Radio
Population Served: 122,689; *Arbitron Metro Market:* Charleston, SC; *Format:* Sports, Talk
Rick Howze, Sales Manager

Easley

WELP
03-04-1951; 1360 kHz AM; *Hrs Open:* 24; 5 kw-D, ND1; 0.036 kw-N, ND1; N34 50 23 W82 38 22
100 Cross Hill Rd., Easley, SC 29640 US
(864) 855-9300
www.wilkinsradio.com
denise@wilkinsradio.com
License: Easley, SC held by Upstate Radio Inc.
Group Owner: Wilkins Communications Network Inc.; (acq 1999; $150,000).
Arbitron Metro Market: Easley, SC; *Format:* Christian, Talk; *Hrs. of News Programming:* news progmg 22 hrs wkly; *No. News Employees:* 2; *Target Audience:* 35 plus.; *Adv. Rates:* 30; 30; 30; 30
Jerry Rogers, Station Manager

WOLI-FM
01-01-1964; 103.9 MHz FM; 6 kw; 328 ft.; N34 50 21 W82 31 37 US
(864) 751-0113
License: Easley, Pickens County, SC held by Davidson Media Station WOLI Licensee LLC.
Group Owner: Davidson Media Group LLC; (acq 10-6-2005; grpsl).
Arbitron Metro Market: Greenville-Spar *TV Affiliate:* Sp
Chris E. Jeanes, Sales
Angela Lynch, Sales
Mayra Martinez, Billing/Traffic
Patrick Gentry, Operations/Programming
Craig Debolt, Operations/Programming

Eastover

WNKT
01-05-1971; 107.5 MHz FM; *Hrs Open:* 24; 40 kw; 548 ft.; N33 45 46 W80 49 23
1301 Gervais St., Suite 700, Columbia, SC 29201 US
(803) 796-7600
www.1075thegame.com
License: Eastover, SC held by Radio License Holding CBC, LLC
Group Owner: Cumulus Media Inc.; (acq 6-9-99; grpsl)
Nat'l Reps: McGavren Guild
Arbitron Metro Market: Columbia, SC; *Format:* Sports, Talk
Rick Prusator, VP/Market Manager

Elloree

WORG
05-01-1988; 100.3 MHz FM; 25 kw; 328 ft.; N33 21 42 W80 41 5
1675 Chestnut NE, Orangeburg, SC 29118 US
(803) 516-8400; *Fax:* (803) 516-0704
www.worg.com
License: Elloree, Orangeburg County, SC held by Garris Communications Inc.
TV Affiliate: Adult contemp; *Format:* News/Talk *Special Programming:* 6am, 7am, 8am; *No. News Employees:* 25-54.; *Adv. Rates:* 22; 22; 22; 12
Marion Garris, President
Jody Garris, Secretary/Treasurer
Mike Thomas, Chief Engineer

Enoree

***WUBK(FM)**
88.1 MHz FM; 175 w; Ant 253 ft; N34 38 06 W81 58 47
(803) 581-9030
License: Enoree, Spartanburg County, SC held by Richburg Educational Broadcasters
Population Served: 665; *Arbitron Metro Market:* Enoree, SC

Florence

WWRK
07-13-1947; 970 kHz AM; *Hrs Open:* 24; 5 kw-D, 3 kw-N, DA-N; N34 13 47 W79 48 07
Mailing Address: Box 103000, Florence, SC 19004 US
Second Address: 181 E. Evans St., Florence, SC 29506
(843) 667-4600; *Fax:* (843) 673-7390
www.swagga941.com
License: Florence, Florence County, SC held by AMFM Radio Licenses LLC.
Group Owner: iHeartMedia
Nat'l Network: CBS; AP Radio; *Regional Network:* S.C. News Net; *Nat'l Reps:* McGavren Guild
Population Served: 300,000; *Arbitron Metro Market:* Florence, SC; *Format:* Urban Contemporary *Special Programming:* Big band 3 hrs wkly; *Hrs. of News Programming:* news progmg 49 hrs wkly; *No. News Employees:* 1 *Target Audience:* 25-54.
Denis Davis, Senior Vice President of Programming

***WLPG**
05-15-1993; 91.7 MHz FM; *Hrs Open:* 24; 20 kw; 482 ft.; N34 4 10.1 W79 40 42.3
P.O. Box 510, Appling, GA 30802 US
(706) 309-9610
www.gnnradio.org
License: Florence, Florence County, SC held by Augusta Radio Fellowship Institute Inc.
Arbitron Metro Market: Florence, SC; *Format:* Christian; *Hrs. of News Programming:* News progmg 12 hrs wkly

RADIO - U.S.

WOLH
11-18-1937; 1230 kHz AM; 1 kw-U, ND1; N34 13 48 W79 44 49
2423 Walker Swinton Rd, P.O. Box 1269, Timmonsville, SC 29161 US
(843) 678-9393
cbpeedee.com/wolh/
License: Florence, Florence County, SC held by Community Broadcasters, LLC
Group Owner: Commuity Broadcasters LLC; (acq 01-07-2016 from Miller Communications for $2.5 M)
Nat'l Network: ESPN Radio
Arbitron Metro Market: Florence, SC; *Format:* Sports
Suzy Rufail, Station Manager

WYNN
11-05-1958; 540 kHz AM; *Hrs Open:* 24; 0.25 kw-D, ND1; 0.166 kw-N, ND1; N34 13 5 W79 48 30
2014 North Irby St., Florence, SC 29501 US
(843) 661-5000; *Fax:* (843) 661-0888
www.glory985.com
reid.reker@cumulus.com
License: Florence, SC held by Cumulus Licensing Corp.
Group Owner: Cumulus Media Inc.; (acq 12-17-98; with co-located FM)
Nat'l Network: American Urban
Arbitron Metro Market: Florence, SC; *Format:* Black, Blues, 44
Special Programming: Jazz; *Hrs. of News Programming:* news progmg 12 hrs wkly; *No. News Employees:* 1; *Target Audience:* 35 plus; Black
Matt Scurry, Operations Manager
Reid Reker, Market Manager
David Williams, Programming Director
Christy Mitchell, Business Manager

WYNN-FM
10-01-1964; 106.3 MHz FM; *Hrs Open:* 24; 6 kw; 328 ft.; N34 13 5 W79 48 30
2014 North Irby St., Florence, SC 29501 US
(843) 661-5000; *Fax:* (843) 661-0888
www.wynn1063.com
License: Florence, Florence County, SC held by Cumulus Licensing Corp.
Arbitron Metro Market: Florence, SC; *Format:* Urban Contemporary; *Hrs. of News Programming:* news progmg one hr wkly; *No. News Employees:* 1; *Target Audience:* 12-34.
Matt Scurry, Operations Manager
Reid Reker, Market Manager
Gerald McSwain, Programming Director
Christy Mitchell, Business Manager

Folly Beach

WYBB
07-04-1988; 98.1 MHz FM; *Hrs Open:* 24; 50 kw; 479 ft.; N32 39 57 W80 3 11
59 Windermere Blvd., Charleston, SC 29407 US
(843) 769-4799
www.my98rock.com
info@radioofcharleston.com
License: Folly Beach, Charleston County, SC held by L.M. Communications of South Carolina Inc.
Group Owner: L M Communications Inc.; (acq 5-17-88)
Nat'l Network: ABC
Arbitron Metro Market: Charleston, SC; *Format:* Rock/AOR; *Hrs. of News Programming:* News progmg 28 hrs wkly; *Target Audience:* 25-49; men; *Adv. Rates:* 75; 60; 70; 30
Paul Smith, General Sales Mgr
Matthew Potter, Programming Director
Kate Sampson, Promotions Manager

Forest Acres

WWNQ
01-01-2005; 94.3 MHz FM; 2.55 kw; 446 ft.; N34 0 4 W81 2 5
1010 Gervais St., Suite 100, Columbia, SC 29201 US
(803) 753-6800; *Fax:* (803) 753-6806
License: Forest Acres, Richland County, SC held by Hometown Columbia LLC
Group Owner: Davis Media LLC; (acq 9-10-2004; $4.73 million for CP)
Arbitron Metro Market: Columbia, SC; *Format:* Contemporary Hits/Top 40, Adult Contemp; *Target Audience:* 25-50.
Kirk Litton, President/Owner
Tim Miller, General Manager
Marty Hall, Operations Mgr/Program Director
Karen Starnes, Business Manager

Forestbrook

WKZQ-FM
03-11-1985; 96.1 MHz FM; *Hrs Open:* 24; 8.5 kw; 871 ft.; N33 35 27 W79 2 55
1016 Ocala St., Myrtle Beach, SC 29577 US
(843) 448-1041; *Fax:* (843) 626-2508
www.wkzq.net
License: Forestbrook, Horry County, SC held by NM Licensing LLC.
Group Owner: NextMedia Group Inc.; (acq 10-28-2008; swap for WAVF(FM) Hanahan)
Arbitron Metro Market: Ada OK; *Format:* Christian

Fort Mill

***WFBK**
91.5 MHz FM; 0.14 kw horiz, 0.11 kw vert; 118 ft.; N35 0 17 W80 58 54
US
(803) 548-9325
www.wfbk.org
License: Fort Mill, York County, SC held by Fort Mill Community Radio Foundation
Arbitron Metro Market: Fort Mill, SC; *Format:* Triple A

Fountain Inn

WTZQ
10-01-1956; 1600 kHz AM; *Hrs Open:* 24; 1 kw-D, ND1; 0.025 kw-N, ND1; N34 42 28 W82 13 40
Mailing Address: 418 Duncan Road, Flat Rock, NC 28731 US
Second Address: PO Box 462, Hendersonville, NC 28793
(828) 692-1600; *Fax:* (828) 697-1416
www.wtzq.com
License: Fountain Inn, SC
Nat'l Network: Westwood One; Jones Radio Networks; ABC;
Regional Network: S.C. News Net; *Nat'l Reps:* Rgnl Reps
Arbitron Metro Market: Fountain Inn, SC; *Format:* Sports, Talk
Special Programming: Gospel 4, Black 4 hrs, Christian 3 hrs wkly; *Hrs. of News Programming:* news progmg 3 hrs wkly; *No. News Employees:* 1 *TargetAudience:* 25-49; working adults
George Henry, Operations Manager/Programming
Mark Warwick, General Manager/Sales
Tom Brown, Chief Engineer
Paige Posey, Traffic Coordinator

Gaffney

WOSF
01-01-1959; 105.3 MHz FM; *Hrs Open:* 24; 51 kw; 1296 ft.; N35 21 51 W81 11 13
8809 Lenox Pointe Dr., Suite A, Charlotte, NC 28273 US
(704) 548-7800; *Fax:* (704) 548-7810
www.oldschool1053.com
License: Gaffney, Cherokee County, SC held by Gaffney Broadcasting Inc.
Group Owner: Radio One; (acq 10-18-2007; $22 million with co-located AM)
Nat'l Network: CNN Radio; *Wire Services:* AP
Arbitron Metro Market: Charlotte, NC; *Format:* Oldies; *No. News Employees:* 1; *Target Audience:* 18-54.; *Adv. Rates:* 22; 15:55; 15:55; 15:55
Alfred Liggins, President/CEO

WZZQ(AM)
09-28-1962; 1500 kHz AM; 1 kw-D, 500 w-N; N35 05 18 W81 38 40
Mailing Address: Box 1210, Gaffney, SC 29342
Second Address: 340 Providence Rd., Gaffney, SC 29341
(864) 489-9066; *Fax:* (864) 489-9069
www.wzzqradio.com
feedback@wagifm.com
License: Gaffney, Cherokee County, SC held by Gaffney Broadcasting Inc.
Group Owner: Fowler Broadcast Communications, Inc.
Regional Network: S.C. News Net.; *Wire Services:* AP
Population Served: 12,456; *Arbitron Metro Market:* Gaffney, SC; *Format:* Country; *Hrs. of News Programming:* news progmg 2 hrs wkly; *No. News Employees:* 1; *Target Audience:* 18-54.; *Adv. Rates:* 22; 15; 15;12
Laura Haemker, Station Manager
Amy Garelick, Promotions Manager

WFGN
01-01-1948; 1180 kHz AM; *Hrs Open:* 6 AM-8 PM; 2.5 kw-D, NDD; N35 2 59 W81 38 42
470 Leadmine Road, PO Box 1388, Gaffney, SC 29340 US
(864) 489-9430; *Fax:* (864) 489-9440
License: Gaffney, SC held by Hope Broadcasting Inc.
Arbitron Metro Market: Gaffney, SC; *Format:* Religious

***WYFG**
10-12-1982; 91.1 MHz FM; *Hrs Open:* 24; 100 kw; 669 ft.; N35 6 57 W81 46 42
P.O. Box 7300, Charlotte, NC 28241 US
(800) 888-7077
www.bbnradio.org
bbn@bbnmedia.org
License: Gaffney, Cherokee County, SC held by Bible Broadcasting Network Inc.
Group Owner: Bible Broadcasting Network
Nat'l Network: USA
Arbitron Metro Market: Gaffney, SC; *Format:* Christian, Religious; *No. News Employees:* 1; *Target Audience:* General.
Lowell Davey, President
Jason Padgett, Operations Manager

Garden City

WWXM
09-25-1971; 97.7 MHz FM; *Hrs Open:* 24; 100 kw; 719 ft.; N33 35 45 W79 3 11
4841 Highway 17 Bypass S., Myrtle Beach, SC 29577 US
(843) 293-0107; *Fax:* (843) 293-1717
www.mix977.com
License: Garden City, Horry County, SC held by AMFM Radio Licenses LLC.
Group Owner: iHeartMedia; (acq 2014)
Arbitron Metro Market: Garden City, SC; *Format:* Contemporary Hits/Top 40; *Hrs. of News Programming:* news progmg 2 hrs wkly; *No. News Employees:* 1; *Target Audience:* 18-49.
Jimmy Feuger, Market President
Ron Roberts, Senior Vice President of Programming
Denise Atkins, Senior Vice President of Sales
Jennifer Habib, Business Manager

Georgetown

WGTN
07-01-1949; 1400 kHz AM; *Hrs Open:* 24
3926 Wesley Street, #301, Myrtle Beach, SC 29579 US
(843) 903-9962
www.wezv.com
License: Georgetown, SC held by R.J. Stalvey
Group Owner: Coastline Communications of Carolina; (acq 1-24-2001)
Nat'l Network: Fox News Radio
Arbitron Metro Market: Myrtle Beach, SC; *Format:* News, News/Talk, 86; *Hrs. of News Programming:* news progmg 12 hrs wkly; *No. News Employees:* 1; *Target Audience:* 25-54; upscale adult; bus, professional andtechnical
Rod Stalvey, General Manager

WLMC
03-01-1962; 1470 kHz AM; 1 kw-D, ND2; 0.147 kw-N, ND2; N33 22 15 W79 16 39
2508 Highmarket Street, Georgetown, SC 29440 US
(843) 546-1400
www.wlmcradio.com
License: Georgetown, SC held by Cumberland A & A Corp.
Nat'l Network: ABC
Format: Christian, Gospel, 74 *Special Programming:* Talk 4 hrs wkly; *Target Audience:* 25 plus; African-Americans

WLFF
05-01-1973; 106.5 MHz FM; *Hrs Open:* 24; 50 kw; 492 ft.; N33 26 20 W79 8 11
11640 Highway 17 Bypass S., Murrells Inlet, SC 29576 US
(843) 651-7869; *Fax:* (843) 651-9123
www.nashfm1065.com
david.lewis@cumulus.com
License: Georgetown, Georgetown County, SC held by Cumulus Licensing Corp.
Group Owner: Cumulus Media Inc.; (acq 1-27-98)
Arbitron Metro Market: Myrtle Beach, SC; *Format:* Oldies
David Lewis, Marketing Manager

WXJY
09-01-1990; 93.7 MHz FM; *Hrs Open:* 24; 6 kw; 315 ft.; N33 16 5 W79 17 49
330 East Kilbourn Avenue, Suite 250, Milwaukee, WI 53202 US
(404) 949-0700; *Fax:* (404) 949-0740
www.teammyrtlebeach.com
License: Georgetown, Georgetown County, SC held by Cumulus Licensing Corp.
Group Owner: Cumulus Media Inc.; (acq 12-29-97; grpsl)
Arbitron Metro Market: Myrtle Beach, SC; *Format:* Sports; *Hrs. of News Programming:* News progmg 4 hrs wkly; *Target Audience:* 25-49; career-oriented, college-educated adults
Roderick Smith, Operations Dir
Lyne Ryan, General Manager
Kellly Broderick, Programming Director
David Lewis, Market Manager
Todd Cartner, Advertising

Goose Creek

WSCC-FM

05-19-1983; 94.3 MHz FM; 25 kw; 328 ft.; N32 49 4 W79 50 8
950 Houston Northcutt Boulevard, 2nd Floor, Mt. Pleasant, SC 29464 US
(843) 884-2534; *Fax:* (843) 884-6096
www.943wsc.com
License: Goose Creek, Berkeley County, SC held by Clear Channel Broadcasting Licenses Inc.
Group Owner: iHeartMedia; (acq 7-29-2003).
Nat'l Network: Fox News Radio; *Nat'l Reps:* McGavren Guild
Arbitron Metro Market: Charleston, SC; *Format:* News, News/Talk, 86; *No. News Employees:* 3; *Target Audience:* 25-54.
Alene Grevey, Market President
Travis Dylan, Senior Vice President of Programming
Rhetta Cloyd, Senior Vice President of Sales and Marketing
Travis Dylan, Programming Director
Willie Bennett, Chief Engineer
Lisa Cooper, BusinessManager
Wesley Sharp, Digital Content Director

Gray Court

WSSL-FM

11-01-1960; 100.5 MHz FM; *Hrs Open:* 24; 100 kw; 1250 ft.; N34 34 18 W82 6 44
Mailing Address: P.O. Box 100, Greenville, SC 29602 US
Second Address: 101 N. Main St., Suite 1000, Greenville, SC 29601
(864) 242-1005
www.wsslfm.com
License: Gray Court, Laurens County, SC held by Capstar TX LLC
Group Owner: iHeartMedia
Regional Network: S.C. News Net.
Arbitron Metro Market: Greenville-Spartanburg, SC; *Format:* Country
Chris Leavitt, Senior Vice President of Sales
Kix Layton, Programming Director
Joshua Hipp, Promotions Director
Carole Sloan, Market Controller
Aaron Michael, Website Management

Greenville

*WEPR

09-03-1972; 90.1 MHz FM; *Hrs Open:* 24; 85 kw; 1,184 ft; N34 56 26 W82 24 38 *Rebroadcasts:* Rebroadcasts WLTR(FM) Columbia 100%
1041 George Rogers Blvd., Columbia, SC 29201
(803) 737-3200
www.etvradio.org
csr@scetv.org
License: Greenville, Greenville County, SC held by South Carolina Educ. TV Commission.
Nat'l Network: NPR; PRI; APM
Arbitron Metro Market: Greenville-Spar; *Hrs. of News Programming:* New progrmg 70 hrs wkly
Linda O'Bryon, President
John Gasque, Operations/Programming Director
Shari Hutchinson, General Manager/Station Manager
John Crockett, Engineering Dir

WLFJ

03-01-1947; 660 kHz AM; 50 kw-D, 10 kw-CH; N34 53 10 W82 28 03
2420 Wade Hampton Blvd., Greenville, SC 29615
(864) 292-6040; *Fax:* (864) 292-8428
www.christiantalk660.com
License: Greenville, Greenville County, SC held by Clear Channel Broadcasting Licenses Inc.
Group Owner: iHeartMedia; (acq 1998; grpsl).
Nat'l Network: Fox News Radio
Population Served: 61,208; *Arbitron Metro Market:* Greenville-Spartanburg, SC; *Format:* Christian; *Target Audience:* 25-54.
Gary Miller, Operations Manager
Allen Henderson, General Manager
Ted McCall, Chief Engineer
Jerry Michelson, Traffic Manager
Nell Henderson, Office Manager
Sally Leonard, Marketing Consultant
Denise Beam, Business OfficeAdministrative Assistant

WESC-FM

03-01-1948; 92.5 MHz FM; *Hrs Open:* 24; 95 kw; 2001 ft.; N35 8 16 W82 36 31
Mailing Address: 101 North Main St., Suite 100, Greenville, SC 29601 US
Second Address: PO Box 100, Greenville, SC 29602
(864) 242-4660
www.wescfm.com
License: Greenville, Greenville County, SC held by Clear Channel Broadcasting Licenses Inc.
Group Owner: iHeartMedia; (acq 1998; grpsl).
Arbitron Metro Market: Greenville, SC; *Format:* Country
Chris Leavitt, Senior Vice President of Sales
John Landrum, Programming Director
Joshua Hipp, Promotions Director
Carole Sloan, Market Controller
Aaron Michael, Website Management

WFBC-FM

03-01-1947; 93.7 MHz FM; *Hrs Open:* 24; 100 kw; 1811 ft.; N35 6 43 W82 36 24
25 Garlington Road, Greenville, SC 29615 US
(864) 271-9200; *Fax:* (864) 242-1567
www.b937online.com
rhummers@entercom.com
License: Greenville, Greenville County, SC held by Entercom Greenville License LLC
Arbitron Metro Market: Greenville, SC; *Format:* Adult Contemp
Special Programming: Alternative 2 hrs wkly; *Hrs. of News Programming:* news progmg one hr wkly; *No. News Employees:* 4; *Target Audience:* 35-64.
Roy Hummers, Promotions Director

WGVL

01-01-1950; 1440 kHz AM; *Hrs Open:* 24; 5 kw-D, DAN; 5 kw-N, DAN; N34 52 6 W82 28 4
101 North Main Street, Suite 100, Greenville, SC 29601 US
(864) 242-1005; *Fax:* (864) 271-3830
www.foxsports1440.com
License: Greenville, SC held by Capstar TX LLC
Group Owner: iHeartMedia; (acq 8-30-00; grpsl)
Arbitron Metro Market: Greenville-Spartanburg, SC; *Format:* Spanish; *No. News Employees:* 2; *Target Audience:* 25-54.
Chris Leavitt, Senior Vice President of Sales
Brian Hall, Programming Director
Joshua Hipp, Promotions Director
Carole Sloan, Market Controller

*WLFJ-FM

05-01-1983; 89.3 MHz FM; *Hrs Open:* 24; 41 kw; 1,100 ft; N34 56 26 W82 24 44
2420 Wade Hampton Blvd., Greenville, SC 29615
(864) 292-6040; *Fax:* (864) 292-8428
www.hisradio.com
comments@hisradio.com
License: Greenville, Greenville County, SC held by Radio Training Network Inc.
Population Served: 850,000; *Arbitron Metro Market:* Greenville-Spartanburg, SC
Allen Henderson, General Manager
Brian Sumner, Programming Director
Ted McCall, Chief Engineer

WPJF

09-15-1949; 1260 kHz AM; 5 kw-D, ND1; 0.015 kw-N, ND1; N34 54 30 W82 20 41
920 Wade Hampton Blvd., Greenville, SC 29609 US
(864) 241-5355; *Fax:* (864) 241-5353
License: Greenville, SC held by WMUU Inc.
Arbitron Metro Market: Greenville, SC; *Format:* Religious; *Target Audience:* 35 plus.
Ed Dos Santos, General Manager
Joe Norris, Chief Engineer

WGTK-FM

08-15-1960; 94.5 MHz FM; *Hrs Open:* 24; 100 kw; 1490 ft.; N34 56 29 W82 24 41
920 Wade Hamilton Blvd., Greenville, SC 29614 US
(864) 242-6240; *Fax:* (864) 370-3829
www.wmuu.com
License: Greenville, Greenville County, SC held by Caron Broadcasting Inc.
Arbitron Metro Market: Greenville, SC; *Format:* Easy Listening
Special Programming: Class 14 hrs, relg 20 hrs wkly; *Target Audience:* 35 plus.
Paul Wright, General Manager
Brigette Barrett, Programming Director
Jeff Gainous, Promotions Manager
Joe Norris, Engineering Dir

WPCI

02-08-1954; 1490 kHz AM; 1 kw-U, ND1; N34 51 7 W82 24 54
840 North Highway, 25 Bypass, Greenville, SC 29617 US
(864) 834-3193; *Fax:* (864) 834-3551
License: Greenville, SC held by Hunter Broadcast Group.
Group Owner: Paper Cutters, Inc.; (acq 12-88; $15,000;
Arbitron Metro Market: Greenville-Spartanburg, SC; *Format:* Oldies
Randy Mathena, President

*WTBI-FM

06-01-1991; 91.5 MHz FM; *Hrs Open:* 24; 22.5 kw; 420 ft.; N34 49 51 W82 26 55
3931 White Horse Road, Greenville, SC 29611 US
(864) 295-2145; *Fax:* (864) 295-6313
www.wtbi.org
jwatts@tabernacleministries.org
License: Greenville, Greenville County, SC held by Tabernacle Baptist Bible College
Arbitron Metro Market: Greenville-Spartanburg, SC; *Format:* Gospel, Religious; *Target Audience:* General.
Dr. W. Melvin Aiken, CEO
Carolyn Headrick, Operations Dir
Charles R. Garrett Sr., Programming Director
James H. Simpson, Promotions Manager
John H. Watts, COO

WYRD

05-01-1933; 1330 kHz AM; *Hrs Open:* 24; 5 kw-D, DAN; 5 kw-N, DAN; N34 51 18 W82 25 24 *Rebroadcasts:* Rebroadcasts WORD(AM) Spartanburg
25 Garlington Rd., Greenville, SC 29615 US
(864) 271-9200; *Fax:* (864) 242-1567
www.espnupstate.com
mhendrix@entercom.com
License: Greenville, SC held by Entercom Greenville License LLC.
Group Owner: Entercom Communications Corp.; (acq 12-13-99; grpsl).
Nat'l Network: ABC; Salem Radio Network
Arbitron Metro Market: Greenville-Spar; *Format:* News, News/Talk, 86; *Target Audience:* 30-64.
Bob McLain, Operations Manager
Randy Cable, Sales
Mark Hendrix, Programming Director
Roy Hummers, Promotions Manager
Gerald Writesel, Producer

Greenwood

WCRS

09-01-1941; 1450 kHz AM; *Hrs Open:* 24; 1 kw-U, ND1; N34 12 34 W82 9 5
US
(864) 229-7984; *Fax:* (864) 229-5896
www.wlmawcrsradio.com
License: Greenwood, SC held by Peregon Broadcasting LLC
Nat'l Network: CBS; *Regional Network:* S.C. News Net.
Arbitron Metro Market: Greenville SC; *Format:* News, News/Talk, 86, Adult Contemp; *Hrs. of News Programming:* news progmg 20 hrs wkly; *No. News Employees:* 2; *Target Audience:* 25 plus; middle & upper income adults *Adv. Rates:* 12; 10; 10; 8

WCZZ

06-20-1973; 1090 kHz AM; *Hrs Open:* Sunrise-sunset; 2.25 kw-C, NDD; 5 kw-D, NDD; N34 9 46 W82 11 41
210 Montague Avenue, Greenwood, SC 29649 US
(864) 223-4300; *Fax:* (864) 223-4096
www.sunny103-5.com
dave@sunny103-5.com
License: Greenwood, SC held by Broomfield Broadcasting LLC
Nat'l Network: Westwood One
Arbitron Metro Market: Greenwood, SC; *Format:* Gospel; *Hrs. of News Programming:* News progmg 12 hrs wkly; *Target Audience:* 25-65.; *Adv. Rates:* 12; 12; 12; 12
Dave Fezler, General Manager
Austin Landers, Traffic Manager
Aimee Powell, Office Manager
Pam Still, Account Executive, Sales

WZSN

03-01-1989; 103.5 MHz FM; *Hrs Open:* 24; 25 kw; 328 ft.; N34 9 46 W82 11 41
210 Montague Avenue, Greenwood, SC 29649 US
(864) 223-4300; *Fax:* (864) 223-4096
www.sunny103-5.com
dave@sunny103-5.com
License: Greenwood, Greenwood County, SC
Nat'l Network: Westwood One
Arbitron Metro Market: Greenwood, SC; *Format:* Adult Contemp; *Hrs. of News Programming:* News progmg 3 hrs wkly; *Target Audience:* 25-54.; *Adv. Rates:* 30; 30; 30; 30
Dave Fezler, General Manager
Austin Landers, Traffic Manager
Aimee Powell, Office Manager
Pam Still, Account Executive, Sales

Greer

WCKI
03-03-1955; 1300 kHz AM; *Hrs Open:* 6 AM-6 PM; 1 kw-D; N34 55 39 W82 15 42
P.O. Box 905, Greer, SC 29652
(864) 877-8458
www.catholicradioinsc.com
License: Greer, Greenville County, SC held by Mediatrix SC Inc.
Population Served: 10,642; *Arbitron Metro Market:* Greenville-Spartanburg, SC; *Hrs. of News Programming:* News progmg one hr wkly; *Target Audience:* 25-54; working people who spend money

WPJM
06-15-1949; 800 kHz AM; 1 kw-D, ND1; 0.438 kw-N, ND1; N34 56 59 W82 14 43
305 North Tryon St., Greer, SC 29651 US
(864) 877-1112; *Fax:* (864) 877-0342
www.800wpjm.com
License: Greer, Greenville County, SC held by Full Gospel WPJM 800 AM Radio Inc.
Regional Network: S.C. News Net.
Arbitron Metro Market: Greenville-Spartanburg, SC; *Format:* Gospel; *Target Audience:* General.
Elder Bobby Cohen, Owner/Manager
Jimmy Booker, Programming Director
Takeisha Jackson, Office Manager

Hampton

WHGS
09-01-1957; 1270 kHz AM; *Hrs Open:* 24
P. O. Box 666, Hampton, SC 29924 US
(803) 943-2831
License: Hampton, SC held by Bocock Communications LLC
Nat'l Network: CNN Radio; *Regional Network:* S.C. News Net;
Nat'l Reps: Salem *Regional Reps:* Interep
Format: News, Talk; *No. News Employees:* 1
John Bocock, President

WBHC-FM
09-01-1970; 92.1 MHz FM; *Hrs Open:* 24/7; 6 kw; Ant 328 ft; N32 50 38 W81 07 31
(803) 943-2831; *Fax:* (803) 943-5450
http://allhits921.blogspot.com
License: Hampton, Hampton County, SC held by Bocock Communications LLC
Nat'l Network: NBC Radio; *Regional Network:* S.C. News Net.
Regional Reps: Interep
Special Programming: Relg 11 hrs wkly; *No. News Employees:* 1; *Target Audience:* Adults.
John Bocock, President

Hanahan

WAVF
07-03-1969; 101.7 MHz FM; *Hrs Open:* 24; 100 kw; 782 ft.; N32 49 4 W79 50 8
2294 Clements Ferry Rd., Charleston, SC 29492 US
(843) 972-1100; *Fax:* (843) 972-1200
www.1017chuckfm.com
david@apexbroadcasting.com
License: Hanahan, Berkeley County, SC held by Apex Broadcasting Inc.
Group Owner: Apex Broadcasting Inc.; (acq 10-28-2008; swap for WKZQ-FM Forestbrook)
Nat'l Reps: Christal
Arbitron Metro Market: Charleston, SC; *Format:* Adult Contemp
David Abel, General Manager
LaDonna Andrews, General Sales Mgr
Bryan Taylor, Programming Director

Hardeeville

WLVH
08-30-1992; 101.1 MHz FM; *Hrs Open:* 24; 50 kw; 476 ft.; N32 5 48 W81 19 17
245 Alfred Street, Savannah, GA 31408 US
(912) 231-1011; *Fax:* (912) 964-9414
www.love1011.com
tutu@iheartmedia.com
License: Hardeeville, Jasper County, SC held by Capstar TX LLC
Group Owner: iHeartMedia; (acq 8-30-00; grpsl)
Nat'l Network: ABC
Arbitron Metro Market: Savannah, GA; *Format:* Urban Contemporary; *Hrs. of News Programming:* News progmg one hr wkly; *Target Audience:* 25-54; affluent Black adults
Sheryl Collison, Market President
Wesley Peper, Senior Vice President of Sales

Hartsville

WBZF
11-19-1992; 98.5 MHz FM; 6 kw; 328 ft.; N34 27 54 W80 5 45
2014 North Irby Street, Florence, SC 29501 US
(843) 661-5000; *Fax:* (843) 661-0888
www.glory985.com
reid.reker@cumulus.com
License: Hartsville, Darlington County, SC held by Cumulus Licensing Corp.
Group Owner: Cumulus Media Inc.
Arbitron Metro Market: Florence, SC; *Format:* Black, Religious
Matt Scurry, Operations Manager
David Williams, Programming Director
Reid Reker, Marketing Manager
Christy Mitchell, Business Manager

WTOD
10-01-1946; 1450 kHz AM; 1 kw-U; N34 21 16 W80 04 06
2014 N. Irby St., Florence, SC 29501 US
(843) 661-5000; *Fax:* (843) 661-0888
www.thefanfm.com
matt.scurry@cumulus.com
License: Hartsville, SC held by Cumulus Licensing LLC
Group Owner: Cumulus Media Inc.
Format: Sports
Matt Scurry, Operations Manager

Hemingway

***WLGI**
07-01-1984; 90.9 MHz FM; *Hrs Open:* 15; 50 kw; 505 ft.; N33 43 9 W79 19 50
1272 Williams Hill Road, Hemingway, SC 29554 US
(843) 558-9544; *Fax:* (866) 610-8659
www.wlgi.org
info@wlgi.org
License: Hemingway, Williamsburg County, SC held by Regional Baha'i Council of the Southern States.
Wire Services: Weather Wire
Format: Black, Gospel *Special Programming:* Jazz; *Target Audience:* General.
Bhakti Larry Hough, Operations Manager
Greg Kintz, General Manager
Ernest Hilton, Production Manager

Hilton Head Island

WHHW
02-14-1983; 1130 kHz AM; *Hrs Open:* 24; 1 kw-D, DAN; 0.5 kw-N, DAN; N32 12 01 W80 43 27
One Saint Augustine Pl., Hilton Head Island, SC 29928 US
(843) 785-9569; *Fax:* (843) 842-3369
www.am1130theisland.com
License: Hilton Head Island, Beaufort County, SC held by Alpha Media Licensee LLC
Group Owner: Alpha Media LLC; (acq 7-18-2000; grpsl).
Population Served: 50,000; *Arbitron Metro Market:* Hilton Head Island, SC; *Format:* Alternative; *Hrs. of News Programming:* news progmg 5 hrs wkly; *No. News Employees:* 1; *Target Audience:* 35 plus.
Rob Walker, Operations Manager
Gigi South, Vice President and Market Manager
Kathryn Wake, Director of Sales
John Marshall, On Site Promotions Director
Claire Beverly, News and Public Affairs Director
Carissa Lozinski-Doig, DigitalMarketing Director

WFXH-FM
07-14-1973; 106.1 MHz FM; 25 kw; 594 ft.; N32 13 36 W80 50 53
One St. Augustine Pl., Hilton Head Island, SC 29928 US
(843) 785-9569; *Fax:* (843) 842-3369
www.rock1061.com
License: Hilton Head Island, Beaufort County, SC held by Alpha Media Licensee LLC
Group Owner: Alpha Media LLC
Nat'l Reps: Christal
Population Served: 100,000; *Arbitron Metro Market:* Savannah-Hilton Head Island, GA-SC; *Format:* Rock/AOR; *No. News Employees:* 2; *Target Audience:* 18-49; more male than female
Rob Walker, Operations Manager
Gigi South, Vice President and Market Manager
Kathryn Wake, Director of Sales
Gabe Reynolds, Programming Director
John Marshall, On Site Promotions Director
Claire Beverly, News and Public AffairsDirector
Carissa Lozinski-Doig, Digital Marketing Director

Holly Hill

WJBS
12-01-1972; 1440 kHz AM; 1 kw-D, NDD; N33 20 23 W80 26 18
760 Bunch Ford Road, PO Box 1087, Holly Hilly, SC 29059 US
(803) 496-5352
License: Holly Hill, SC held by Harry J. Govan
Format: Gospel *Special Programming:* Black 17 hrs, fishing/hunting 2 hrs, farm 2 hrs wk
Harry J. Govan, Owner

Hollywood

WXST
07-15-1988; 99.7 MHz FM; *Hrs Open:* 24; 70 kw; 781 ft.; N32 49 4 W79 50 8
2294 Clements Ferry Rd., Charleston, SC 29492 US
(843) 972-1100; *Fax:* (843) 972-1200
www.star997.com
david@apexbroadcasting.com
License: Hollywood, Charleston County, SC held by Apex Broadcasting Inc.
Group Owner: Apex Broadcasting Inc.; acq 11-20-01).
Nat'l Network: Jones Radio Networks
Arbitron Metro Market: Charleston, SC; *Format:* Urban Contemporary; *Target Audience:* 25-54; urban professional; *Adv. Rates:* 25; 25; 25; na
David Abel, General Manager
LaDonna Andrews, Sales Manager
Michael Tee, Programming Director

WCKN
01-01-1986; 92.5 MHz FM; *Hrs Open:* 24; 100 kw; N32 49 4 W79 50 8
2294 Clements Ferry Rd., Charleston, SC 29492 US
(843) 972-1100; *Fax:* (843) 972-1200
www.kickin925.com
david@apexbroadcasting.com
License: Hollywood, Charleston County, SC held by Apex Broadcasting Inc.
Group Owner: Apex Broadcasting Inc.
Arbitron Metro Market: Charleston, SC; *Format:* Country; *Target Audience:* 25-54; urban professional; *Adv. Rates:* 25; 25; 25; na
David Abel, General Manager
LaDonna Andrews, Sales Manager
Garret Doll, Programming Director

Homeland Park

WRIX
09-01-1986; 1020 kHz AM; 3 kw-C, NDD; 10 kw-D, NDD; N34 28 14 W82 38 3
102 East Shockley Ferry Road, Watson Village, Anderson, SC 29625 US
(864) 224-6733
License: Homeland Park, SC held by AM 1020 Inc.
Regional Network: S.C. News Net.
Arbitron Metro Market: Greenville-Spartanburg, SC; *Format:* Religious *Special Programming:* Black 7 hrs wkly
Tom Ervin, Owner
Joel Kay, Traffic Director

Honea Path

WRIX-FM
06-10-1977; 103.1 MHz FM; *Hrs Open:* 24; 6 kw; 328 ft.; N34 25 31 W82 32 26
102 East Shockley Ferry Road, Watson Village, Anderson, SC 29624 US
(864) 224-9749
License: Honea Path, Anderson County, SC held by FM 103 Inc.
Nat'l Network: ABC; *Regional Network:* S.C. News Net.
Arbitron Metro Market: Greenville-Spartanburg, SC; *Format:* News, News/Talk, 86 *Special Programming:* Talk 20 hrs wkly
Tom Ervin, Owner
Joel Kay, Traffic Director

Indianapolis

WOLT
01-01-1993; 103.3 MHz FM; 2.7 kw; 495 ft.; N34 59 54 W82 8 17
6161 Fall Creek Road, Indianapolis, IN 46220 US
(317) 257-7565
www.alt1033.com
License: Indianapolis, Marion County, IN held by Capstar TX LLC
Group Owner: iHeartMedia; (acq 10-6-2005; grpsl).
Arbitron Metro Market: Indianapolis; *Format:* Alternative
Rick Green, Market President
Rob Cressman, Senior Vice President of Programming
Michele Kiefer, Senior Vice President of Sales

Kristi Adams, Promotions Director
Melissa Laird, Digital Content Coordinator

Irmo

WWNU
05-23-1987; 92.1 MHz FM; *Hrs Open:* 24; 15 kw; 427 ft.; N34 4 55 W81 7 36
P.O Drawer I, Johnston, SC 29832 US
(803) 753-6800; *Fax:* (803) 753-6806
www.new92.com
kirk@hometowncolumbia.com
License: Irmo, Lexington County, SC held by Hometown Columbia LLC
Group Owner: Davis Media LLC; (acq 11-1-2004; $4.7 million)
Arbitron Metro Market: Columbia, SC; *Format:* Country; *Hrs. of News Programming:* News progmg 7 hrs wkly; *Adv. Rates:* 24; 20; 24; 16
Kirk Litton, President
Tyler Ryan, Operations Dir
Chuck McKay, General Manager

Isle of Palms

WMXZ
11-01-1974; 95.9 MHz FM; *Hrs Open:* 24; 50 kw; 352 ft.; N32 49 27 W80 0 10
2294 Clements Ferry Rd., Charleston, SC 29492 US
(843) 972-1100; *Fax:* (843) 972-1200
www.mix96live.com
david@apexbroadcasting.com
License: Isle of Palms, Walton County, SC held by Apex Broadcasting, Inc.
Group Owner: Apex Broadcasting, Inc.
Nat'l Reps: Katz Radio
Arbitron Metro Market: Fort Walton Beach, FL; *Format:* Adult Contemp; *Hrs. of News Programming:* news progmg 20 hrs wkly; *No. News Employees:* 1; *Target Audience:* 25-54; general
David Abel, General Manager
Chris Saglian, Sales Manager
Mike Edwards, Programming Director

Johnsonville

WALD
08-01-1947; 1080 kHz AM; *Hrs Open:* sunup-sundown
P.O. Box 2355, West Columbia, SC 29121 US
(803) 939-9530
License: Johnsonville, SC held by Glory Communications, Inc.
Format: Gospel

Johnston

WKSX-FM
08-26-1985; 92.7 MHz FM; 1.8 kw; 577 ft.; N33 45 19 W81 50 44
Mailing Address: P.O. Drawer I, Johnston, SC 29832 US
Second Address: 102 Slide Hill Rd., Johnston, SC 29832
(803) 275-4444; *Fax:* (803) 275-3185
License: Johnston, Edgefield County, SC held by Edgefield Saluda Radio Co. Inc.
Nat'l Network: CNN Radio; *Regional Network:* S.C. News Net;
Nat'l Reps: Keystone (unwired net)
Arbitron Metro Market: Augusta, GA; *Format:* Oldies; *Target Audience:* men & women age 25-54; *Adv. Rates:* quoted upon request

Kershaw

WKSC
12-21-1961; 1300 kHz AM; *Hrs Open:* 24; 0.5 kw-D, ND2; 0.088 kw-N, ND2; N34 33 30 W80 33 34
502 West Church Street, Kershaw, SC 29067 US
(803) 475-8585; *Fax:* (805) 966-3530
License: Kershaw, SC held by Kershaw Broadcasting Corp.
Nat'l Network: ABC
Format: Oldies; *Target Audience:* 35-64.
John Griffin, President
Johnny Knight, General Manager

Kiawah Island

WCOO
12-07-1969; 105.5 MHz FM; *Hrs Open:* 24; 50 kw; 436 ft.; N32 39 57 W80 3 11
59 Windermere Blvd, Charleston, SC 29407 US
(843) 769-4799
www.1055thebridge.com
info@radioofcharleston.com
License: Kiawah Island, Charleston County, SC held by L.M. Communications II of South Carolina Inc.
Group Owner: L M Communications Inc.; (acq 3-30-95;
Nat'l Network: ABC
Arbitron Metro Market: Charleston, SC; *Format:* Oldies; *Target Audience:* 25-54; general; *Adv. Rates:* 50; 50; 45; 20
Paul Smith, General Sales Mgr
Laura Lee, Programming Director
Kate Sampson, Promotions Manager

Kingstree

WDKD
1310 kHz AM; *Hrs Open:* 24; 5 kw-D 0/06 kw-N, ND2; N33 42 12 W79 48 58 *Rebroadcasts:* Simulcasts W246BX - FRANK (FM) 97.1
300 First Ave, Suite 204, Needham, MA 02494 US
(781) 247-0730; *Fax:* (617) 247-0730
License: Kingstree, Williamsburg County, SC held by Community Broadcasters, LLC
Group Owner: Community Broadcasters LLC; (acq 12-18-2001; $1,415,456 assumption of debt with co-located FM).
Nat'l Network: ESPN
Arbitron Metro Market: Florence, SC; *Format:* Adult Contemp

WRZE
01-01-1998; 94.1 MHz FM; *Hrs Open:* 24; 6 kw; 328 ft.; N33 43 32 W79 58 19
181 Evans St., Suite 311, Florence, SC 29506 US
(843) 667-4600; *Fax:* (843) 673-7390
www.swagga941.com
License: Kingstree, Williamsburg County, SC held by AMFM Radio Licenses LLC.
Group Owner: iHeartMedia
Format: Urban Contemporary; *Target Audience:* 25-54; urban & caucasian
Richard J. Bressler, President

WWKT-FM
05-28-1966; 99.3 MHz FM; 11 kw; 492 ft.; N33 54 7 W79 59 52
2423 Walker Swinton Rd, Timmonsville, SC 29161 US
(843) 678-9393
License: Kingstree, Williamsburg County, SC held by Community Broadcasters, LLC
Group Owner: Community Broadcasters LLC
Arbitron Metro Market: Florence, SC; *Format:* Country; *Hrs. of News Programming:* news progmg 14 hrs wkly; *No. News Employees:* 1
Suzy Rufail, Station Manager

Ladson

WJNI
06-15-1998; 106.3 MHz FM; *Hrs Open:* 24; 6 kw; 328 ft.; N32 55 42 W80 6 13
5081 Rivers Ave., North Charleston, SC 29418 US
(843) 763-6631; *Fax:* (843) 763-5636
www.wjnifm.com
License: Ladson, Berkeley County, SC held by Thomas B. Daniels.
Group Owner: Kirkman Broadcasting
Nat'l Reps: Interep
Format: Gospel; *Target Audience:* 25 plus.; *Adv. Rates:* 360; 360; 360; 360.
Rick Howze, Sales Manager

***WKCL**
01-11-1982; 91.5 MHz FM; *Hrs Open:* 24; 100 kw; 305 ft.; N33 0 24 W80 5 17
P. O. Box 809, 528 College Park Road, Ladson, SC 29456 US
843) 553-1525; *Fax:* (843) 553-0636
www.915wkcl.com
License: Ladson, Berkeley County, SC held by Chapel of the Holy Spirit and Holy Spirit Bible College.
Format: Adult Contemp, Gospel; *Target Audience:* General; baby boomers
Carl Wiggins Sr., President

Lake City

WHYM
1260 kHz AM; *Hrs Open:* 6 AM-6 PM; 5 kw-D, ND1; 0.055 kw-N, ND1; N33 51 42 W79 44 15 *Rebroadcasts:* Simulcasts WOLS(AM) Florence 75%.
2423 Walker Swinton Rd, Timmonsville, SC 29161 US
(843) 678-9393
License: Lake City, Florence County, SC held by Community Broadcasters, LLC
Group Owner: Community Broadcasters LLC; (acq 7-01-2016; $2.5 M from Miller Communications)
Nat'l Network: ABC; FOX News; *Regional Network:* S.C. News Network *Regional Reps:* Jim D.Jones
Arbitron Metro Market: Florence, SC; *Format:* News, News/Talk, 86; *No. News Employees:* 1; *Target Audience:* 35 plus.

WWFN-FM
05-11-1977; 100.1 MHz FM; 3.3 kw; 433 ft.; N33 58 36 W79 48 32
2014 N. Irby Street, Florence, SC 29501 US
(843) 661-5000; *Fax:* (843) 661-0888
www.thefanfm.com
reid.reker@cumulus.com
License: Lake City, Florence County, SC held by Cumulus Licensing Corp.
Group Owner: Cumulus Media Inc.; (acq 3-12-2001; $850,000).
Arbitron Metro Market: Florence, SC; *Format:* Sports; *Target Audience:* 25-54.
Matt Scurry, Operations Dir
Reid Reker, Marketing Manager
Christy Mitchell, Business/HRÿManager

Lamar

WSIM
10-01-1992; 93.7 MHz FM; *Hrs Open:* 24; 2.8 kw; 485 ft.; N34 12 12 W79 51 52
2423 Walker Swinton Road, Timmonsville, SC 29161 US
(843) 678-9393
www.cbpeedee.com/wsim
License: Lamar, Darlington County, SC held by Community Broadcasters, LLC
Group Owner: Community Broadcasters, LLC; (acq from Miller Communications)
Nat'l Network: ABC
Arbitron Metro Market: Florence, SC; *Format:* Adult Contemp; *No. News Employees:* 1; *Target Audience:* 35-64
Suzy Rufail, Station Manager

Lancaster

WAGL
08-07-1962; 1560 kHz AM; 50 kw-C, DAD; 50 kw-D, DAD; N34 49 53 W80 52 8
P.O. Box 28, Lancaster, SC 29721 US
(803) 283-8431; *Fax:* (803) 286-4702
waglradio@comporium.net
License: Lancaster, SC held by Palmetto Broadcasting System Inc.
Arbitron Metro Market: Charlotte, NC; *Format:* Gospel, Oldies; *No. News Employees:* 6; *Adv. Rates:* 25; 25; 25; 25
Susan Pridgen, Office Manager

WRHM
07-27-1964; 107.1 MHz FM; 2.4 kw; 524 ft.; N34 51 34 W80 47 59
Mailing Address: P.O. Box 307, Rock Hill, SC 29731 US
Second Address: 142 N. Confederate Ave., Rock Hill, SC 29730
(803) 286-1071
www.fm107.com
contact@interstate107.com
License: Lancaster, Lancaster County, SC held by Our Three Sons Broadcasting L.L.P.
Nat'l Network: ABC; *Regional Network:* S.C. News Net.
Arbitron Metro Market: Charlotte-Gastonia-Rock Hill, NC-SC; *Format:* Country, News, 84; *Target Audience:* 25-54.
Steven Stone, Operations Dir
Allan Miller, General Manager
Mike Crowder, News Director

Latta

WCMG
09-18-1970; 94.3 MHz FM; *Hrs Open:* 24; 10.5 kw; 502 ft.; N34 26 20 W79 29 44
2014 North Irby St., Florence, SC 29501 US
(843) 661-5000; *Fax:* (843) 661-0888
www.943thedam.com
reid.reker@cumulus.com
License: Latta, Dillon County, SC held by Cumulus Licensing Corp.
Group Owner: Cumulus Media Inc.; (acq 6-99; $525,000)
Nat'l Network: USA
Arbitron Metro Market: Florence, SC; *Format:* Urban Contemporary; *Hrs. of News Programming:* news progmg 8 hrs wkly; *No. News Employees:* 1; *Target Audience:* 21-54; African-American
Matt Scurry, Operations Dir
Reid Reker, Marketing Manager
Christy Mitchell, Business Manager

Laurens

WLBG
03-01-1947; 860 kHz AM; *Hrs Open:* 24; 1 kw-D, ND1; 0.012 kw-N, ND1; N34 30 13 W82 1 6
Mailing Address: P.O. Box 1289, Laurens, SC 29360 US
Second Address: 315 Hillcrest Drive, Laurens, SC 29360

(864) 984-3544; *Fax:* (864) 984-3545
www.wlbg.com
info@wlbg.com
License: Laurens, SC held by Southeastern Broadcast Associates Inc.
Nat'l Network: Fox News Radio; Fox Sports
Format: Variety/Diverse; *Hrs. of News Programming:* News progmg 4 hrs wkly; *Target Audience:* 30 plus; Black

Lexington

WDEK(AM)
01-01-1983; 1170 kHz AM; *Hrs Open:* Sunrise-sunset; 10 kw-D; N33 58 17 W81 16 43
109 Q Old Chapin Road, Lexington, SC 29072
(803) 785-9335; *Fax:* (803) 785-2257
License: Lexington, Lexington County, SC held by Peregon Communications Inc.
Arbitron Metro Market: Columbia, SC
John Broomfield, CEO
Mary O'Donnell, Sales/Marketing
Ryan Wiley, Programming/Production
Dan Shumpert, Sales
Lindsey Addy, Sales
Dave Fezler, Technical Coordinator
Austin Landers, Traffic
Lisa Currier, Billings

WOMG
08-31-1994; 98.5 MHz FM; *Hrs Open:* 24; 6 kw; 325 ft.; N34 03 05 W81 00 07
1301 Gervais St., Suite 700, Columbia, SC 29201 US
(803) 796-7600
www.985nashicon.com
rick.prusator@cumulus.com
License: Lexington, SC held by Radio License Holding CBC, LLC
Group Owner: Cumulus Media Inc.; (acq 5-30-2000; grpsl)
Arbitron Metro Market: Columbia, SC; *Format:* Country
Rick Prusator, VP/Market Manager

Loris

WLSC
08-01-1958; 1240 kHz AM; *Hrs Open:* 6 AM-midnight
Mailing Address: P. O. Box 578, Loris, SC 29569 US
Second Address: 4242 Main Street, Loris, SC 29569
(843) 808-4437; *Fax:* (801) 838-3262
www.tigerradio.com
info@wlscradio.com
License: Loris, SC held by JARC Broadcasting Inc.
Regional Network: S.C. News Net; *Nat'l Reps:* Keystone (unwired net)
Arbitron Metro Market: Myrtle Beach, SC; *Format:* Variety/Diverse; *Target Audience:* 21-54.
Jerry Jenrette, General Manager

WVCO
11-19-1993; 94.9 MHz FM; *Hrs Open:* 24; 11 kw; 489 ft.; N33 59 39 W78 46 16
Mailing Address: 98 North Ocean Boulevard, North Myrtle Beach, SC 29582 US
Second Address: PO Box 4487, North Myrtle Beach, SC 29582
(843) 663-9492
www.949thesurf.com
License: Loris, Horry County, SC held by Carolina Beach Music Broadcasting Corp.
Arbitron Metro Market: Myrtle Beach, SC; *Format:* Oldies; *Hrs. of News Programming:* News progmg 2 hrs wkly; *Target Audience:* 25-45.
Harvey Graham, CEO
Selene Graham, Operations Dir

Manning

WYMB
07-15-1957; 920 kHz AM; 2.3 kw-D, DAN; 1 kw-N, DAN; N33 41 24 W80 16 23
2014 North Irby Street, Florence, SC 29501 US
(843) 661-5000; *Fax:* (843) 661-0888
www.thefanfm.com
reid.reker@cumulus.com
License: Manning, SC held by Cumulus Licensing Corp.
Group Owner: Cumulus Media Inc.; (acq 3-24-99; with co-located FM).
Nat'l Network: AP Radio; *Nat'l Reps:* Katz Radio
Arbitron Metro Market: Manning, SC; *Format:* Contemporary Hits/Top 40; *Target Audience:* General.
Matt Scurry, Operations Manager
Reid Reker, Marketing Manager
Christy Mitchell, Business Manager

Marion

WHLZ
08-01-1991; 100.5 MHz FM; 25 kw; 328 ft.; N34 23 26 W79 35 25
2014 North Irby Street, Florence, SC 29501 US
(843) 661-5000; *Fax:* (843) 661-0888
www.whlz1005.com
reid.reker@cumulus.com
License: Marion, Marion County, SC held by Cumulus Licensing Corp.
Group Owner: Cumulus Media Inc.; (acq 3-24-99; $3.8 million with WMXT(FM) Pamplico).
Arbitron Metro Market: Florence, SC; *Format:* Country
Matt Scurry, Operations Manager
Reid Reker, Marketing Manager
Christy Mitchell, Business Manager

McClellanville

WWIK
12-01-1994; 98.9 MHz FM; *Hrs Open:* 24; 50 kw; Ant 492 ft; N33 11 20 W79 33 25
60 Markfield Dr., Charleston, SC 29403 US
(843) 763-6631
www.charlestonsportsradio.com
License: McClellanville, Charleston County, SC held by 98.9 Inc.
Group Owner: Kirkman Broadcasting Inc.; (acq 1-5-2001)
Population Served: 44,783; *Arbitron Metro Market:* Summerville, SC; *Format:* Sports, Talk; *Target Audience:* 18-25; adults
Rick Howze, General Sales Mgr

Moncks Corner

WJKB
12-01-1963; 950 kHz AM; *Hrs Open:* 24
60 Markfield Dr., Charleston, SC 29407 US
(843) 763-6631
www.charlestonsportsradio.com/
License: Moncks Corner, SC held by Kirkman Broadcasting Inc.
Group Owner: Kirkman Broadcasting Inc.; (acq 11-29-2000; $150,000).
Nat'l Network: Jones Radio Networks; Motor Racing Net
Arbitron Metro Market: Charleston, SC; *Format:* Talk *Special Programming:* Nascar; *Target Audience:* 25-54; male; *Adv. Rates:* 20; 20; 40; 15
Rick Howze, Sales Manager

Mount Pleasant

WRFQ
06-01-1985; 104.5 MHz FM; *Hrs Open:* 24; 100 kw; 659 ft.; N32 49 4 W79 50 9
950 Houston Northcutt Boulevard, 2nd Floor, Mt. Pleasant, SC 29464 US
(843) 884-2534; *Fax:* (843) 884-6096
www.q1045.com
License: Mount Pleasant, Charleston County, SC held by Citicasters Licenses Inc.
Group Owner: iHeartMedia; (acq 5-4-99; grpsl).
Arbitron Metro Market: Charleston, SC; *Format:* Classic Rock; *Target Audience:* 25-54; adults, men
Alene Grevey, Market President
Travis Dylan, Senior Vice President of Programming
Rhetta Cloyd, Senior Vice President of Sales and Marketing
Willie Bennett, Chief Engineer
Lisa Cooper, Business Manager
Wesley Sharp, Digital ContentDirector

WZJY
05-21-1982; 1480 kHz AM; *Hrs Open:* 24; 0.88 kw-D, ND1; 0.044 kw-N, ND1; N32 49 30 W79 49 53 *Rebroadcasts:* simulcast w/ WAZS-AM
5081 Rivers Avenue, North Charleston, SC 29406 US
(843) 554-1063
License: Mount Pleasant, SC held by Thomas B. Daniels
Group Owner: Jabar Communications Inc.; (acq 6-24-2007; $375,000)
Nat'l Reps: Interep
Arbitron Metro Market: Charleston, SC; *Format:* Spanish; *Hrs. of News Programming:* news progmg 24 hrs wkly; *No. News Employees:* 5; *Target Audience:* 18-35; *Adv. Rates:* 240; 240; 240; 240.
Michael Baynard, General Manager

Mullins

WJAY
06-01-1949; 1280 kHz AM; *Hrs Open:* 18; 4.2 kw-D, ND1; 0.27 kw-N, ND1; N34 11 30 W79 18 55
PO Box 1020, Marion, SC 29571 US
(843) 423-1140; *Fax:* (843) 423-2829
License: Mullins, SC held by The Greater Highway Church of Christ.
Nat'l Network: ABC; *Regional Network:* S.C. News Net.
Format: Gospel *Special Programming:* Farm 10 hrs wkly; *Hrs. of News Programming:* News progmg 8 hrs wkly; *Target Audience:* General.
Curtis Campbell, President

Murrells Inlet

***WMBJ**
01-01-1997; 88.3 MHz FM; *Hrs Open:* 24; 0 kw horiz, 1.8 kw vert; 331 ft.; N33 26 35 W79 8 21 *Rebroadcasts:* His Radio Network
2420 Wade Hampton Boulevard, Greenville, SC 29615 US
(864) 292-6040; *Fax:* (864) 292-8428
www.hisradio.com
License: Murrells Inlet, Georgetown County, SC held by Radio Training Network Inc.
Format: Christian
Allen Henderson, General Manager

WYEZ
04-07-1991; 94.5 MHz FM; *Hrs Open:* 24; 12 kw; 476 ft.; N33 33 13 W79 13 14
3926 Wesley Street, Myrtle Beach, SC 29579 US
(843) 903-9962; *Fax:* (843) 903-1797
License: Murrells Inlet, Georgetown County, SC held by Fidelity Broadcasting Corp.
Arbitron Metro Market: Myrtle Beach, SC; *Format:* Oldies; *Hrs. of News Programming:* news progmg 40 hrs wkly; *No. News Employees:* 1; *Target Audience:* Adults 25-54
Wally B., On-Air Personality
Bill Howard, On-Air Personality

Myrtle Beach

WMYB
01-11-1965; 92.1 MHz FM; *Hrs Open:* 24; 94 kw; 863 ft.; N33 35 27 W79 2 55
1016 Ocala Street, Myrtle Beach, SC 29577 US
(843) 448-1041; *Fax:* (843) 626-2508
www.star921.net
License: Myrtle Beach, Horry County, SC held by NM Licensing LLC.
Group Owner: NextMedia Group Inc.; (acq 11-26-01; grpsl).
Arbitron Metro Market: Myrtle Beach, SC; *Format:* Adult Contemp; *Target Audience:* Women: 25-54.
Carl Hirsch, Chairman
Steven Dinetz, CEO
Skip Weller, President
Barry Brown, General Manager
Art Greene, General Sales Mgr
Bill Catcher, Programming Director
Liza Van Horne, Promotions Manager
Ginny Batchelder, NewsDirector
Paul Matthews, Chief Engineer
Jeff Dinetz, COO

WRNN
04-24-1965; 1450 kHz AM; 1 kw-U, ND1; N33 42 20 W78 53 23
1016 Ocala Street, Myrtle Beach, SC 29577 US
(843) 448-1041; *Fax:* (843) 626-2508
www.wrnn.net
License: Myrtle Beach, SC held by NM Licensing LLC.
Group Owner: NextMedia Group Inc.; (acq 11-26-2001; grpsl)
Arbitron Metro Market: Myrtle Beach, SC; *Format:* Sports; *Target Audience:* 25-60.
Carl Hirsch, Chairman
Steven Dinetz, CEO
Skip Weller, President
Barry Brown, General Manager
Dave Priest, Programming Director

WYAV
07-01-1964; 104.1 MHz FM; 100 kw; 981 ft.; N33 35 27 W79 2 55
1016 Ocala Street, Myrtle Beach, SC 29577 US
(843) 448-1041; *Fax:* (843) 626-2508
www.wave104.net
License: Myrtle Beach, Horry County, SC held by NM Licensing LLC.
Group Owner: NextMedia Group Inc.; (acq 11-26-01; grpsl).
Arbitron Metro Market: Myrtle Beach, SC; *Format:* Classic Rock; *Target Audience:* 18-49.
Carl Hirsch, Chairman
Steven Dinetz, CEO
Skip Weller, President
Barry Brown, General Manager
Art Greene, General Sales Mgr
Mark McKinney, Programming Director
Liza Van Horne, Promotions Manager
Paul Matthews, Chief Engineer

Jeff Dinetz, COO
Scott Mann, Music Director

***DWKEL**
01-01-2008; 1450 kHz AM; Ant 764 ft
310 Sproul Street, McKees Rocks, PA 15136 US
(916) 251-1600; *Fax:* (916) 251-1650
www.klove.com
klove@klove.com
License: Myrtle Beach, SC held by Educational Media Foundation.
Group Owner: EMF Broadcasting
Nat'l Network: K-Love
Arbitron Metro Market: Omaha, NE; *Format:* Christian
Darrell Chambliss, Chairman
Alan Mason, CEO/COO
Mike Novak, CEO
David Pierce, Chief Creative Officer
Dan Antonelli, Chief Business Development Officer
Eric Moser, Chief Financial Officer
Brian Burger, Vice President of HumanResources
D. Kevin Blair, Secretary and General Counsel

New Ellenton

WGUS-FM
12-01-1989; 102.7 MHz FM; *Hrs Open:* 24; 4.3 kw; 387 ft.; N33 30 49 W81 38 3
4051 Jimmie Dyess Pkwy., Augusta, GA 30909 US
(706) 396-7000
www.1027wgus.com
License: New Ellenton, Aiken County, SC held by Beasley Media Group LLC
Group Owner: Beasley Broadcast Group Inc.; (acq 12-22-94; $700,000;
Arbitron Metro Market: Augusta, GA; *Format:* Gospel, Religious; *Hrs. of News Programming:* News progmg 7 hrs wkly; *Target Audience:* 35-64; affluent audience loyal fan base
Chris O'Kelley, Operations Manager
Chris O'Kelley, Programming Director
Mark Haddon, Vice President/Marketing Manager
Georgia Beasley, Digital Sales Manager
Richard Chambers, Music Director

Newberry

WKDK
10-01-1946; 1240 kHz AM; *Hrs Open:* 24 hrs; 1 kw-U, ND1; N34 17 30 W81 37 15
3000 Hazel Street, Newberry, SC 29108 US
(803) 276-2957; *Fax:* (803) 276-3337
www.wkdk.com
contactus@wkdk.com
License: Newberry, SC held by Newberry Broadcasting Co.
Nat'l Network: ABC; *Regional Network:* S.C. News Net.
Format: Adult Contemp, Oldies; *Target Audience:* General.; *Adv. Rates:* 10; 8; 10; 8
James Coggins, Operations Dir
Brice Zimmerman, News Director
Heather Hawkins, Operations Manager

WKMG
05-22-1968; 1520 kHz AM; *Hrs Open:* Sunrise-sunset; 1 kw-D, NDD; N34 15 12 W81 35 44
115-A West Church St, Batesburg, SC 29006 US
(803) 321-0073; *Fax:* (803) 276-2507
License: Newberry, SC held by Cornell Blakely
Format: Spanish *Special Programming:* Relg 2 hrs, gospel 3 hrs, Sp 10 hrs wkly
Cornell Blakely, Owner

North Augusta

WNRR
07-30-1958; 1380 kHz AM; *Hrs Open:* 24; 4 kw-D, 70 w-N; N33 29 17 W81 56 46
445 Carolina Springs Rd., North Augusta, SC 29841
(706) 396-6000; *Fax:* (706) 396-6010
License: North Augusta, Aiken County, SC held by Medici Media, Inc.
Group Owner: Medici Media, Inc.; (acq 12-19-2000; grpsl)
Population Served: 72,000; *Arbitron Metro Market:* Augusta, GA; *Hrs. of News Programming:* news progmg 7 hrs wkly; *No. News Employees:* 1
Tony de Medici, President
Renee de Medici, General Manager

WKZK
05-09-1962; 1600 kHz AM; *Hrs Open:* 6 AM-sunset
US
(706) 738-9191
www.wkzk.net
License: North Augusta, SC held by Gospel Radio Inc.
Nat'l Network: American Urban; *Nat'l Reps:* Dora-Clayton
Arbitron Metro Market: Augusta, GA; *Format:* Black, Gospel, 74; *Target Audience:* Black adults.
Garfield Turner, General Manager

North Charleston

***WYFH**
07-07-1984; 90.7 MHz FM; 50 kw; 492 ft.; N32 58 25 W80 13 46
Mailing Address: P.O. Box 7300, Charlotte, NC 28241 US
Second Address: 11530 Carmel Commons Blvd., Charlotte, NC 28226
(800) 888-7077
www.bbnradio.org
bbn@bbnmedia.org
License: North Charleston, Charleston County, SC held by Bible Broadcasting Network Inc.
Group Owner: Bible Broadcasting Network
Nat'l Network: Bible Bcstg Net
Arbitron Metro Market: Charleston, SC; *Format:* Christian, Religious
Lowell Davey, President
Jason Padgett, Operations Manager

North Myrtle Beach

WNMB
04-01-1983; 900 kHz AM; 0.5 kw-D, DA2; 0.5 kw-N, DA2; N33 49 26 W78 45 59
429 Pine Avenue, N. Myrtle Beach, SC 29582 US
(843) 249-6662
www.wnmb900.com
mattsmith@wnmb900.com
License: North Myrtle Beach, SC held by Norman Communications NMB Inc.
Arbitron Metro Market: Myrtle Beach, SC; *Format:* Religious
Matt Smith, Programming Director
Michael Chapman, Advertising

***WKVC**
09-09-1997; 88.9 MHz FM; *Hrs Open:* 24; 100 kw vert; 581 ft.; N34 5 41 W78 28 27
2630 Mirror Lake Dr, Fayetteville, NC 28303 US
(707) 528-9649; *Fax:* (707) 528-9246
www.klove.com
License: North Myrtle Beach, Horry County, SC held by Educational Media Foundation.
Group Owner: EMF Broadcasting; (acq 5-11-00; $1.2 million).
Nat'l Network: K-Love
Arbitron Metro Market: Little River, SC; *Format:* Religious; *Target Audience:* 25-65; contemp Christian
Richard Jenkins, CEO
Kurt Reeder, General Manager

WEZV
08-15-1972; 105.9 MHz FM; *Hrs Open:* 24; 17 kw; 361 ft.; N33 51 16 W78 43 0
3926 Wesley Street, #301, Myrtle Beach, SC 29579 US
(843) 903-9962
www.wezv.com
License: North Myrtle Beach, Horry County, SC held by Fidelity Broadcasting Corp.
Arbitron Metro Market: Myrtle Beach, SC; *Format:* Easy Listening; *Target Audience:* 35 plus.
Matt Sedota, General Manager

Orangeburg

WHXT
09-01-1973; 103.9 MHz FM; 9.2 kw; 531 ft.; N33 40 13 W80 52 25
1900 Pineview Rd., Columbia, SC 29209 US
(803) 695-8600; *Fax:* (803) 695-8605
www.hot1039fm.com
License: Orangeburg, Orangeburg County, SC held by Alpha Media Licensee LLC
Group Owner: Alpha Media LLC; (acq 9-16-2013; grpsl).
Arbitron Metro Market: Columbia, SC; *Format:* Urban Contemporary
Mike Hartel, Senior Vice President and Market Manager
Bryan Hendry, Sales Director
Chris Connors, Programming Director
Michelle Alston, Promotions Director
Maggie Hanisch, Business Manager

WQKI-FM
10-10-1987; 102.9 MHz FM; *Hrs Open:* 24; 3.1 kw; 457 ft.; N33 26 35 W80 48 16
200 Regional Parkway, Building C, Suite 200, Orangeburg, SC 29118 US
(803) 536-1710; *Fax:* (803) 531-1089
License: Orangeburg, Orangeburg County, SC held by Community Broadcasters, LLC
Group Owner: Community Broadcasters LLC; (acq 07-01-2016 from Miller Communications for $2.5 M)
Format: Reggae; *Target Audience:* 25-54.
Jack Swart, Station Manager

WPJK
11-03-1958; 1580 kHz AM; *Hrs Open:* Sunrise-sunset; 1 kw-D, NDD; N33 28 43 W80 52 46
2358 Amsterdam Dr., Augusta, GA 30906 US
(803) 534-4848; *Fax:* (803) 534-0888
License: Orangeburg, SC held by Radio Orangeburg Partnership.
Nat'l Network: USA
Format: Gospel, Religious
Bose Gowdy, Owner

***WSSB-FM**
03-15-1985; 90.3 MHz FM; *Hrs Open:* 24; 80 kw horiz, 72 kw vert; 217 ft.; N33 29 55 W80 50 30
Mailing Address: P.O. Box 7619, Orangeburg, SC 29117 US
Second Address: 300 College Street, B-114 Nance Hall Building, Orangeburg, SC 29117
(803) 536-8585; *Fax:* (803) 516-4700
www.wssb903fm.org
License: Orangeburg, Orangeburg County, SC held by South Carolina State University.
Nat'l Network: American Urban; NPR
Format: Gospel, Jazz *Special Programming:* Jazz 10 hrs, reggae 4 hrs, blues 2 hrs, rap 4 hrs wkly; *Hrs. of News Programming:* news progmg 7 hrs wkly; *No. News Employees:* 1; *Target Audience:* 8-65.

WTCB
07-06-1967; 106.7 MHz FM; 100 kw; 787 ft.; N33 46 52 W80 55 14
1301 Gervais St., Suite 700, Columbia, SC 29201 US
(803) 796-7600
www.b106fm.com
License: Orangeburg, SC held by Radio License Holding CBC, LLC
Group Owner: Cumulus Media Inc.; (acq 5-30-00; grpsl).
Arbitron Metro Market: Columbia, SC; *Format:* Adult Contemp
William McElveen, President

Pageland

WGSP-FM
02-22-1975; 102.3 MHz FM; 2.55 kw; 512 ft.; N34 53 57 W80 25 46
P.O. Box 5, Pageland, SC 29728 US
(843) 672-7839
www.latina1023.com
License: Pageland, Chesterfield County, SC held by Norsan Media Group of South Carolina LLC.
Group Owner: Norsan Consulting and Management Inc.; (acq 7-13-2006; $975,000)
Nat'l Network: Salem Radio Network
Format: Tejano
Norberto Sanchez, President

Pamplico

WMXT
11-01-1990; 102.1 MHz FM; *Hrs Open:* 24; 50 kw horiz, 49.4 kw vert; 479 ft.; N33 58 36 W79 48 32
2014 North Irby Street, Florence, SC 29501 US
(843) 661-5000; *Fax:* (843) 661-0888
www.1021thefox.com
rick.prusator@cumulus.com
License: Pamplico, Florence County, SC held by Cumulus Licensing Corp.
Group Owner: Cumulus Media Inc.; (acq 3-24-99; $3.8 million with WHLZ(FM) Marion).
Arbitron Metro Market: Florence, SC; *Format:* Light Rock *Special Programming:* Beach music 5 hrs wkly; *Hrs. of News Programming:* news progmg 3 hrs wkly; *No. News Employees:* 2; *Target Audience:* 25-54.
Matt Scurry, Operations Manager
Rick Prusator, Market Manager
Christy Mitchell, Business Manager

Pawleys Island

WDAI
10-02-1993; 98.5 MHz FM; *Hrs Open:* 24; 6.1 kw; 666 ft.; N33 35 27 W79 2 55
11640 Highway 17, Bypass South, Murrells Inlet, SC 29576 US
(843) 651-7869; *Fax:* (843) 651-9123
www.985kissfm.net
david.lewis@cumulus.com

License: Pawleys Island, Georgetown County, SC held by Cumulus Licensing Corp.
Group Owner: Cumulus Media Inc.; (acq 1-27-98)
Nat'l Network: Westwood One
Arbitron Metro Market: Myrtle Beach, SC; *Format:* Urban Contemporary; *Hrs. of News Programming:* news progmg 6 hrs wkly; *No. News Employees:* 1; *Target Audience:* 25-54.
David Lewis, Market Manager

Pickens

WTBI

01-21-1984; 1540 kHz AM; *Hrs Open:* Sunrise-sunset; 1 kw-C, NDD; 10 kw-D, NDD; N34 51 37 W82 43 25 *Rebroadcasts:* Rebroadcasts WTBI-FM Greenville
US
www.wtbi.org
License: Pickens, SC held by Tabernacle Christian Schools
Nat'l Network: USA
Arbitron Metro Market: Greenville-Spartanburg, SC; *Format:* Christian; *Target Audience:* All ages.

Pinopolis

WTUA

05-01-1990; 105.9 MHz FM; 6 kw; 328 ft.; N33 29 36 W79 53 21
PO Box 1240, St. Stephen, SC 29479 US
(843) 567-2091; *Fax:* (843) 567-3088
www.wtuaradio.com
daisynwtua@tds.net
License: Pinopolis, Berkeley County, SC held by Praise Communications Inc.
Group Owner: Glory Communications Inc.; (acq 1-27-2005).
Arbitron Metro Market: Charleston, SC; *Format:* Gospel; *Hrs. of News Programming:* news progmg 5 hrs wkly; *No. News Employees:* 1; *Target Audience:* 20-65; African American; *Adv. Rates:* 8; 8; 8; 6
Alex Snipe, President
Tony Jamison, Network Operations
Alexis Campbell, General Sales Mgr
Lula Greene, Programming Director
Demetrius Seawright, Traffic

Plainfield

WUBG

08-16-1964; 98.3 MHz FM
6161 Fall Creek Road, Indianapolis, IN 46220 US
(317) 257-7565
www.big983indy.com
License: Plainfield, IN held by Capstar TX LLC
Group Owner: iHeartMedia
Arbitron Metro Market: Indianapolis; *Format:* Country
Rick Green, Market President
Rob Cressman, Senior Vice President of Programming
Michele Kiefer, Senior Vice President of Sales
Kristi Adams, Promotions Director
Melissa Laird, Digital Content Coordinator

Port Royal

WVSC

07-01-1985; 103.1 MHz FM; *Hrs Open:* 24; 6.6 kw; 490 ft.; N32 13 25 W80 51 0
10 Westbury Park, Suite 10, Bluffton, SC 29910 US
(843) 363-9956; *Fax:* (843) 363-9957
www.sc103radio.com
mike.buxser@apexbroadcasting.com
License: Port Royal, Beaufort County, SC held by Apex Broadcasting Inc.
Group Owner: Apex Broadcasting Inc.; (acq 11-11-2013).
Nat'l Reps: Christal
Population Served: 500,000; *Arbitron Metro Market:* Savannah-Parris Island-Hilton Head, GA-SC; *Format:* Adult Contemp; *No. News Employees:* 1; *Target Audience:* 25-54; *Adv. Rates:* 25; 25; 25
Mike Buxser, General Manager
Christine Manzione, Sales Manager
Pat Garrett, Programming Director

WRWN

02-01-1988; 107.9 MHz FM; *Hrs Open:* 24; 24 kw; 725 ft.; N32 13 36 W80 50 53
401 Mall Blvd., Suite 101-D, Savannah, GA 31406 US
(912) 351-9830; *Fax:* (912) 352-4821
www.rewind1079.com
License: Port Royal, Beaufort County, SC held by Alpha Media Licensee LLC
Group Owner: Alpha Media LLC; (acq 7-18-2000; grpsl).
Nat'l Reps: Christal
Population Served: 500,000; *Arbitron Metro Market:* Savannah, GA; *Format:* Oldies; *Target Audience:* 45 plus; active, affluent, older
Rob Walker, Operations Manager and Program Director
Gigi South, Vice President and Market Manager
Kathryn Wake, Director of Sales
John Marshall, On Site Promotions Director
Claire Beverly, News and Public Affairs Director
CarissaLozinski-Doig, Digital Marketing Director

Ravenel

WMGL

02-01-1986; 107.3 MHz FM; *Hrs Open:* 24; 16.5 kw; 410 ft.; N32 54 18 W79 55 19
4230 Faver Place Dr., Suite 100, North Charleston, SC 29405 US
(843) 277-1200
www.magic1073fm.com
License: Ravenel, SC held by Radio License Holding CBC LLC
Group Owner: Cumulus Media Inc.; (acq 6-12-2007; grpsl)
Arbitron Metro Market: Charleston, SC; *Format:* Adult Contemp; *Hrs. of News Programming:* news progmg 6 hrs wkly; *No. News Employees:* 2; *Target Audience:* 25-54; upscale adults
Chris Hoffmanÿ, Operations Dir
Paul O'Malley, General Manager
Jerold Jackson, Programming Director
Charles Pack, Promotions Manager

Richburg

*WRBK

01-01-1998; 90.3 MHz FM; *Hrs Open:* 24; 7.5 kw horiz, 7.3 kw vert; 538 ft.; N34 41 46 W81 1 23
P O Box 15, Chester, SC 29706 US
(803) 581-9030; *Fax:* (803) 581-9932
License: Richburg, Chester County, SC held by Richburg Educational Broadcasters Inc.
Format: Oldies; *Target Audience:* 30-60; middle aged adults who like beach flavored oldies
Jeff Sigmon, President

Ridgeland

WLHH

07-15-1986; 104.9 MHz FM; *Hrs Open:* 24; 16 kw; Ant 410 ft; N32 26 10 W80 55 23
10 Westbury Park, Suite 10, Bluffton, SC 29910 US
(843) 363-9956; *Fax:* (843) 363-9957
www.1049thesurf.com
tex@apexbroadcasting.com
License: Ridgeland, Beaufort County, SC held by Apex Broadcasting Inc.
Group Owner: Apex Broadcasting Inc.; (acq 11-2-2006; $800,000)
Population Served: 500,000; *Arbitron Metro Market:* Savannah, GA; *Format:* Oldies; *No. News Employees:* 2; *Target Audience:* 18-49; general; *Adv. Rates:* 50; 50; 50; 50
Mike Buxser, General Manager
Jeff Taylor, Programming Director

Ridgeville

WAYA-FM

10-01-1989; 100.9 MHz FM; *Hrs Open:* 24; 13 kw; 299 ft.; N33 4 25.7 W80 11 54.2
US
(866) 457-9293
www.wayfm.com
supportservices@wayfm.com
License: Ridgeville, Meigs County, SC held by East Tennessee Radio Group III L.P.
Group Owner: East Tennessee Radio Group III L.P.; (acq 5-30-2008; grpsl)
Nat'l Reps: D & R Radio
Format: Christian
Bob Augsburg, Founder/President

Rock Hill

WAVO

05-18-1948; 1150 kHz AM; *Hrs Open:* 24
1150 WAVO, Rock Hill, SC 29731 US
(704) 596-4900
www.1150wavo.com
tomgentry@bellsouth.net
License: Rock Hill, SC held by WHVN Inc.
Group Owner: GHB Radio Group; (acq 2-4-92; $115,000;
Arbitron Metro Market: Stanfield OR; *Format:* Contemporary Hits/Top 40
Brant Hart, Operations Dir
Tom Gentry, General Manager
Rob Caskey, Chief Engineer
Sandra Hendricks, Administrative Assistant

*WNSC-FM

01-03-1978; 88.9 MHz FM; *Hrs Open:* 24; 100 kw; Ant 600 ft; N34 50 24 W81 01 07
1041 George Rogers Blvd., Columbia, SC 29201
(803) 737-3200
www.etvradio.org
csr@scetv.org
License: Rock Hill, York County, SC held by South Carolina Educational Television Commission.
Nat'l Network: NPR; PRI; APM
Arbitron Metro Market: Charlotte-Gasto
Linda O'Bryon, President
John Gasque, Operations/Programming Director
Shari Hutchinson, General Manager/Station Manager
Melanie Boyer, General Sales Mgr
John Crockett, Engineering Dir

WRHI

12-14-1944; 1340 kHz AM; *Hrs Open:* 24 hours; 1 kw-U, ND1; N34 58 59 W81 01 11
Mailing Address: Box 307, Rock Hill, SC 29731 US
Second Address: 142 N. Confederate Ave., Rock Hill, SC 29730
(803) 324-1340; *Fax:* (803) 324-2860
www.wrhi.com
License: Rock Hill, SC held by Our Three Sons Broadcasting LLP.
Group Owner: Our Three Sons Broadcasting LLP.
Nat'l Network: ABC; *Regional Network:* S.C. News Net.
Arbitron Metro Market: Charlotte-Gastonia-Rock Hill, NC-SC; *Format:* News/Talk; *Hrs. of News Programming:* news progmg 14 hrs wkly; *No. News Employees:* 2; *Target Audience:* 30 plus.
Steven Stone, Operations Dir
Chris Miller, Dir. of Sales
Mike Crowder, News Director

Saint Stephen

WEAF

12-10-1970; 1120 kHz AM; 390 w-D; N34 15 32 W80 34 47
Box 1165, Camden, SC 70116
(803) 432-8717; *Fax:* (803) 939-9469
License: Saint Stephen, Kershaw County, SC held by Glory Communications Inc.
Group Owner: Glory Communications Inc.; (acq 7-13-2006; $222,500)
Population Served: 6,902; *Arbitron Metro Market:* Camden, SC
Alex Snipe, General Manager

Sans Souci

WCSZ

05-26-1966; 1070 kHz AM; *Hrs Open:* 24; 50 kw-D, DA2; 1.5 kw-N, DA2; N34 55 5 W82 27 21
200 N. 25 Bypass, Greenville, NC 29617 US
(864) 330-2944
www.lajefa949.com
License: Sans Souci, SC held by WHYZ Radio L.P.
Nat'l Network: Westwood One; American Urban
Arbitron Metro Market: Greenville-Spartanburg, SC; *Format:* Gospel, Religious; *Target Audience:* 25-54; $50,000 plus houshold income, college educated, 60% male, 40% female
Dr. Glenn Cherry, CEO
Linda Fructuoso, Operations Manager
Junior Polames, General Manager

Scranton

WZTF

01-01-1991; 102.9 MHz FM; 2.9 kw; 466 ft.; N34 0 39 W79 45 24
181 E. Evans St., Suite 311, Florence, SC 29506 US
(843) 432-1029
www.theflo1029.com
License: Scranton, Florence County, SC held by AMFM Radio Licenses LLC.
Group Owner: iHeartMedia
Arbitron Metro Market: Florence, SC; *Format:* Urban Contemporary; *Adv. Rates:* 25; 25; 25; 15
Denis Davis, Senior Vice President of Programming

Seneca

WSNW

06-01-1949; 1150 kHz AM; *Hrs Open:* 24; 5.0 kw-D, 0.058 kw-N, ND2 *Rebroadcasts:* W277BX FM Translator 94.1
Mailing Address: P.O. Box 1251, Seneca, SC 29679 US
Second Address: 103 Ram Cat Alley, Seneca, SC 29679
(864) 882-9769; *Fax:* (864) 886-0082
www.wsnwradio.com

License: Seneca, SC held by Tugart Properties LLC.
Group Owner: Georgia-Carolina Radiocasting Companies; (acq 9-28-2001)
Nat'l Network: CBS Radio; *Regional Network:* S.C. News Net.; *Wire Services:* AP
Format: Adult Contemp, News, 56, Talk *Special Programming:* Local Sports; *Hrs. of News Programming:* news progmg 12 hrs wkly; *No. News Employees:* 1; *Target Audience:* 35+
Ian Lundin, Operations Dir
Brandon Kessler, VP/General Manager
Chad Dorsett, News/Sports Director

Simpsonville

WYRD-FM

07-10-1989; 106.3 MHz FM; *Hrs Open:* 24; 25 kw; 328 ft.; N34 50 33 W82 9 59
25 Garlington Road, Greenville, SC 29615 US
(864) 271-9200
www.word1063.com
twest@entercom.com
License: Simpsonville, Greenville County, SC held by Entercom Greenville License LLC.
Group Owner: Entercom Communications Corp.; (acq 10-7-2005; grpsl)
Arbitron Metro Market: Simpsonville, SC; *Format:* News, News/Talk, 86; *Target Audience:* 25-54; adults
Bob McLain, Programming Director
Roy Hummers, Promotions Manager

Socastee

WRNN-FM

01-01-1997; 99.5 MHz FM; 21.5 kw; 354 ft.; N33 43 16 W78 53 45
1016 Ocala Street, Myrtle Beach, SC 29577 US
(843) 448-1041; *Fax:* (843) 626-2508
www.wrnn.net
License: Socastee, Horry County, SC held by NM Licensing LLC.
Group Owner: NextMedia Group Inc.; (acq 11-26-2001; grpsl)
Arbitron Metro Market: Myrtle Beach, SCC; *Format:* Talk
Carl Hirsch, Chairman
Steven Dinetz, CEO
Skip Weller, President
Barry Brown, General Manager
Art Greene, General Sales Mgr
Dave Priest, Programming Director
Liza Van Horne, Promotions Manager
Ginny Batchelder, News Director
Paul Matthews, Chief Engineer
Jeff Dinetz, COO

Society Hill

*WEBK

91.1 MHz FM; 0.43 kw; 127 ft.; N34 32 13 W79 54 29
US
(803) 581-9030; *Fax:* (803) 581-9932
License: Society Hill, Darlington County, SC held by Richburg Educational Broadcasters Inc.
Arbitron Metro Market: Society Hill, SC
Jeff Sigmon, General Manager

South Congaree

WFMV

01-01-1993; 95.3 MHz FM; *Hrs Open:* 24; 6 kw; 328 ft.; N33 53 58 W81 13 29
Mailing Address: PO Box 951, Columbia, SC 29202 US
Second Address: 2440 Milwood Ave., Columbia, SC 29205
(803) 939-9530; *Fax:* (803) 939-9469
www.columbiainspiration.com
acampbell@wfmv.com
License: South Congaree, Lexington County, SC held by Glory Communications.
Group Owner: Glory Communications Inc.
Arbitron Metro Market: Columbia, SC; *Format:* Urban Contemporary; *Target Audience:* Primary : adult 25-54; secondary: Women 25-54
Tony Jamison, Network Operations
Alexis Campbell, General Sales Mgr
Tony Gee, Music Director

Spartanburg

WASC

01-15-1968; 1530 kHz AM; 0.25 kw-C, NDD; 1 kw-D, NDD; N34 56 58 W81 57 33
PO Box 5686, Spartanburg, SC 29301 US
(864) 585-1530; *Fax:* (864) 573-7790
License: Spartanburg, SC held by New South Broadcasting Corp.
Arbitron Metro Market: Spartanburg, SC; *Format:* Black
Sam Floyd, President
K. Joseph Sessoms, Operations Dir
K. Sessmos, General Manager
Ed Waddell, General Sales Mgr

WSPG

09-01-1952; 1400 kHz AM; 1 kw-U, ND1; N34 58 26 W81 55 37
Mailing Address: P.O. Box 5416, Spartanburg, SC 29304 US
Second Address: 340 Garner Rd., Spartanburg, SC 29303
(864) 573-1400; *Fax:* (864) 573-8699
www.espnspartanburg.com
info@espn1400am.com
License: Spartanburg, SC held by Fulmer Broadcasting Inc.
Regional Network: S.C. News Net.; *Wire Services:* AP
Arbitron Metro Market: Greenville-Spartanburg, SC; *Format:* News, News/Talk, 84, Talk; *Target Audience:* Adult male 25-54.
Matthew Fulmer, President
J. Dwayne Corn, General Manager
Jan Scruggs, Programming Director

WOLI

09-01-1940; 910 kHz AM; 3.6 kw-D, DA2; 0.89 kw-N, DA2; N35 1 10 W82 0 36 *Rebroadcasts:* Rebroadcasts WYRD(AM) Greenville 100%
US
(864) 751-0113
www.woli-am.com
cdebolt@davidsonmedia.com
License: Spartanburg, SC held by Davidson Media Station WSPA Licensee LLC.
Group Owner: Davidson Media Group LLC; (acq 10-6-2005; grpsl).
Nat'l Network: CBS; ABC
Arbitron Metro Market: Greenville-Spar *TV Affiliate:* Sports; *Format:* Sports *Special Programming:* news progmg 50 hrs wkly; *Hrs. of News Programming:* 4; *No. News Employees:* 35-64.
Craig Debolt, Operations Manager
Mayra Martinez, Trafic/Office Manager
Patrick Gentry, Assistant Operations Manager/Sports Coordinator
Angela Lynch, Account Executive
Chris E. Jeanes, Account Executive

WORD

02-17-1930; 950 kHz AM; *Hrs Open:* 24
25 Garlington Road, Greenville, SC 29615 US
(864) 271-9200; *Fax:* (864) 242-1567
www.espnupstate.com
bmclain@entercom.com
License: Spartanburg, SC held by Entercom Greenville License L.L.C.
Group Owner: Entercom Communications Corp.; (acq 12-13-99; grpsl).
Nat'l Network: CBS; Motor Racing Net; *Regional Network:* S.C. News Net.
Arbitron Metro Market: Greenville-Spartanburg, SC; *Format:* News, News/Talk, 86; *Hrs. of News Programming:* news progmg 45 hrs wkly; *No. News Employees:* 4; *Target Audience:* 35-64.
Bob McLain, Operations Dir
Randy Cable, Sales
Mark Hendrix, Programming Director
Roy Hummers, Promotions
Tracy West, Website

WSPA-FM

08-29-1946; 98.9 MHz FM; *Hrs Open:* 24; 100 kw; 1903 ft.; N35 10 11 W82 17 28
25 Garlington Road, Greenville, SC 29615 US
(864) 271-9200; *Fax:* (864) 242-1567
www.magic989online.com
rhummers@entercom.com
License: Spartanburg, Spartanburg County, SC held by Entercom Greenville License LLC.
Group Owner: Entercom Communications Corp.; (acq 12-13-99; grpsl)
Arbitron Metro Market: Greenville-Spartanburg, SC; *Format:* Adult Contemp *Special Programming:* Relg 3 hrs, jazz 6 hrs, 70s oldies 10 hrs wkly; *Hrs. of News Programming:* News progmg one hr wkly
Roy Hummers, Promotions Director
John Tesh, Disc Jockey

St. Andrews

WMFX

01-23-1985; 102.3 MHz FM; *Hrs Open:* 24; 6 kw; 328 ft.; N34 5 55 W81 4 48
1900 Pineview Rd., Columbia, SC 29209 US
(803) 695-8600; *Fax:* (803) 695-8605
www.fox1023.com
License: St. Andrews, Richland County, SC held by Alpha Media Licensee LLC
Group Owner: Alpha Media LLC; (acq 9-16-2013; grpsl).
Arbitron Metro Market: Columbia, SC; *Format:* Classic Rock, Rock/AOR; *Hrs. of News Programming:* news progmg one hr wkly; *No. News Employees:* 1; *Target Audience:* 18-49.
Mike Hartel, General Manager
Bryan Hendry, General Sales Mgr
Michelle Alston, Promotions Director
Maggie Hanisch, Business Manager

St. George

WQIZ

08-23-1962; 810 kHz AM
US
(866) 263-1700
www.catholicradioinsc.com/about/maps/wqiz
License: St. George, SC held by Mediatrix SC Inc.
Arbitron Metro Market: Charleston, SC; *Format:* Christian

St. Matthews

WPOG

08-15-1975; 710 kHz AM; *Hrs Open:* 6 AM-6 PM
4305 Columbia Road, Orangeburg, SC 29118 US
(803) 536-4300
www.wwosradio.net
manager@wwosradio.net
License: St. Matthews, SC held by Grace Baptist Church of Orangeburg
Arbitron Metro Market: Columbia, SC; *Format:* Gospel
Darrell Wilkins, Pastor
Blake Lindsey, Station Manager

Summerton

WLJI

03-24-1997; 98.3 MHz FM; *Hrs Open:* 24; 16 kw; 384 ft.; N33 42 58 W80 20 44 *Rebroadcasts:* Simulcast of WFMV(FM) South Congaree 100%
Mailing Address: P.O. Box 1348, Sumter, SC 29151 US
Second Address: 51 Commerce St, Sumter, SC 29151
(803) 775-2321
License: Summerton, Clarendon County, SC held by Community Broadcasters, LLC
Group Owner: Community Broadcasters LLC
Format: Religious, Urban Contemporary, 44; *Target Audience:* Adults 25-54.

Summerville

WAZS

06-07-1963; 980 kHz AM; *Hrs Open:* 24 *Rebroadcasts:* simulcast w/ WZJY-AM
5081 Rivers Ave., North Charleston, SC 29406 US
(843) 554-1063
www.elsol980.com
License: Summerville, SC held by Thomas B. Daniels.
Group Owner: Jabar Communications Inc.; (acq 9-1-2000).
Nat'l Reps: Interep
Arbitron Metro Market: Mertzon TX; *Format:* Christian; *Adv. Rates:* 240; 240; 240; 240.
Thomas B. Daniels, President

WWWZ

05-10-1974; 93.3 MHz FM; 50 kw; 492 ft.; N32 54 18 W79 55 19
4230 Faber Place Dr., Suite 100, North Charleston, SC 29405 US
(843) 277-1200
www.z93jamz.com
License: Summerville, SC held by Radio License Holding CBC, LLC
Group Owner: Cumulus Media Inc.; (acq 6-9-99; grpsl)
Arbitron Metro Market: Charleston, SC; *Format:* Urban Contemporary
Paul O'Malley, General Manager
Terry Base, Programming Director
Judy Herold, News Director

Sumter

WDXY

1240 kHz AM; *Hrs Open:* 24; 1 kw-U, ND1; N33 54 16 W80 19 25
51 Commerce St, P.O. Box 1269, Sumter, SC 29501 US
(803) 775-2321; *Fax:* (803) 773-4856
License: Sumter, SC held by Community Broadcasters, LLC
Group Owner: Community Broadcasters LLC
Arbitron Metro Market: Sumter, SC; *Format:* News, News/Talk, 86; *No. News Employees:* 1
Jim Leven, General Partner, President & CEO

WWBD
06-21-1995; 94.7 MHz FM; *Hrs Open:* 24; 8.1 kw; 571 ft.; N34 2 56 W80 12 51
51 Commerce St, P.O. Box 1269, Sumter, SC 29501 US
(803) 775-2321 ext. 222; *Fax:* (803) 773-4856
cbsumter.com
License: Sumter, Sumter County, SC held by Community Broadcasters, LLC
Group Owner: Community Broadcasters LLC
Nat'l Network: American Urban
Format: Rock/AOR; *No. News Employees:* 1; *Target Audience:* 25-49.
Jack Swart, Station Manager

WWHM
03-16-1940; 1290 kHz AM; 1 kw-D 0.012 kw-N, ND2; N33 55 26 W80 17 12
51 Commerce St, P.O. Box 1269, Sumter, SC 29151 US
(803) 775-2321; *Fax:* (803) 773-4856
License: Sumter, Sumter County, SC held by Community Broadcasters, LLC
Group Owner: Community Broadcasters LLC
Format: Adult Contemp, Blues, 92
Jack Swart, Station Manager

***WRJA-FM**
08-25-1975; 88.1 MHz FM; *Hrs Open:* 24; 98 kw; 1001 ft.; N33 52 52 W80 16 14
1041 George Rogers Blvd, PO Box 11000, Columbia, SC 29201 US
(803) 737-3200
www.etvradio.org
csr@scetv.org
License: Sumter, Sumter County, SC held by South Carolina Educational TV Commission.
Nat'l Network: NPR; PRI
Format: News; *Hrs. of News Programming:* News progrmg 120 hrs wkly
Linda O'Bryon, President/CEO
John Gasque, Operations/Programming Director

WSSC
04-27-1953; 1340 kHz AM; *Hrs Open:* 6 AM-midnight
2295 Harper Street, Sumter, SC 29153 US
(803) 469-0288; *Fax:* (803) 469-0297
License: Sumter, SC held by Sumpter Baptist Temple Inc.
Regional Network: S.C. News Net.
Format: Christian; *Target Audience:* 25-54.
Eddie Richardson, President

WWDM
01-01-1961; 101.3 MHz FM; *Hrs Open:* 24; 100 kw horiz, 82 kw vert; 1,322 ft.; N34 3 4 W80 40 55
1900 Pineview Rd., Columbia, SC 29209 US
(803) 695-8600; *Fax:* (803) 695-8605
www.thebigdm.com
License: Sumter, Sumter County, SC held by Alpha Media Licensee LLC
Group Owner: Alpha Media LLC; (acq 8-7-2000; grpsl).
Nat'l Network: ABC; Westwood One; *Nat'l Reps:* D & R Radio
Arbitron Metro Market: Columbia, SC; *Format:* Urban Contemporary; *Hrs. of News Programming:* news progmg 6 hrs wkly; *No. News Employees:* 1; *Target Audience:* 25-49.
Bryan Hendry, General Sales Mgr
Chris Connors, Programming Director
Michelle Alston, Promotions Director

Sun City-Hilton Head

WNFO
01-01-1964; 1430 kHz AM; *Hrs Open:* Sunrise-sunset; 0.213 kw-D, NDD; N32 21 24 W80 55 23
9-B Wanderer Ln, Hilton Head Island, SC 29928 US
(843) 785-5769; *Fax:* (843) 785-8139
License: Sun City-Hilton Head, SC held by Walter M. Czura
Arbitron Metro Market: Hilton Head Island, SC; *Format:* Spanish
Special Programming: Spanish; *Target Audience:* General; incoming visitors to South Carolina & Spanish speaking people
Walter Czura, President

Surfside Beach

WSYN
04-04-1977; 103.1 MHz FM; *Hrs Open:* 24; 8 kw; 528 ft.; N33 47 4 W78 52 44 *Rebroadcasts:* Rebroadcasts WVCO(FM) Loris 100%
11640 Highway 17, Bypass South, Murrells Inley, SC 29576 US
(843) 651-7869; *Fax:* (843) 651-9123
www.sunny1031.com
License: Surfside Beach, Horry County, SC held by Cumulus Licensing Corp.
Group Owner: Cumulus Media Inc.; (acq 4-30-2001; swap of WSYN(FM) for WQSL(FM) & WXQR(FM) Jacksonville, NC)
Nat'l Network: Westwood One
Arbitron Metro Market: Myrtle Beach, SC; *Format:* Country; *Hrs. of News Programming:* news progmg 4 hrs wkly; *No. News Employees:* 1; *Target Audience:* 25-54; adults & families of loc towns & tourists
David Lewis, Market Manager

Union

WBCU
08-27-1949; 1460 kHz AM; *Hrs Open:* 24; 1 kw-D, DAN; 1 kw-N, DAN; N34 43 10 W81 39 44
210 East Main Street, Union, SC 29379 US
(864) 427-2411; *Fax:* (864) 429-2975
www.wbcuradio.com
chris@wbcuradio.com
License: Union, SC held by Union-Carolina Broadcasting Co. Inc.
Nat'l Network: ABC; *Regional Network:* S.C. News Net.
Arbitron Metro Market: San Antonio TX; *Adv. Rates:* 134; 120; 126; 91
Chad Parrish, General Manager

Walhalla

WGOG
04-19-1991; 101.7 MHz FM; *Hrs Open:* 24; 6 kw; 302 ft.; N34 51 33 W83 3 31
Mailing Address: P.O. Box 10, Walhalla, SC 29691 US
Second Address: 2058 Westminster Hwy., Walhalla, SC 29691
(864) 638-3616; *Fax:* (864) 638-6810
www.wgog.com
License: Walhalla, Oconee County, SC held by Appalachian Broadcasting Co. Inc.
Group Owner: Georgia-Carolina Radiocasting Companies; (acq 10-16-2001; with co-located AM).
Nat'l Network: ABC
Format: Country, News *Special Programming:* Sunday Morning Gospel; *Hrs. of News Programming:* news progmg 15 hrs wkly; *No. News Employees:* 1; *Target Audience:* 25-54.
Kris Butts, Operations Manager
Gary Bryant, VP/General Manager
Gary Butts, Sales & Operations Manager
Dick Mangrum, News Director

Walterboro

WALI
12-13-1991; 93.7 MHz FM; *Hrs Open:* 24; 6 kw; 328 ft.; N32 50 58 W80 33 31
215 N Stonebedge Dr, Columbia, SC 29210 US
(843) 549-1543; *Fax:* (843) 549-2711
License: Walterboro, Colleton County, SC held by Hess Communications L.L.C.
Nat'l Network: ABC Information & Entertainment; *Regional Network:* S.C. News Net. *Regional Reps:* Rgnl Reps.
Arbitron Metro Market: Columbia, SC; *Format:* Country, Sports
Special Programming: 3 HOURS WEEKLY; *Hrs. of News Programming:* News progmg 3 hrs wkly; *Target Audience:* General.
Karl Hess, President

Wedgefield

WIBZ
02-05-1985; 95.5 MHz FM; *Hrs Open:* 24; 4.4 kw; 387 ft.; N33 56 56 W80 23 34
51 Commerce St, P.O. Box 1269, Sumter, SC 29501 US
(803) 775-2321
jack_swart@commbroadcasters.com
License: Wedgefield, Sumter County, SC held by Community Broadcasters, LLC
Group Owner: Community Broadcasters LLC
Nat'l Network: ABC
Format: Adult Contemp, Contemporary Hits/Top 40; *No. News Employees:* 1; *Target Audience:* 18-49.
Jack Swart, Station Manager

West Columbia

WXBT
08-05-1975; 100.1 MHz FM; *Hrs Open:* 24; 5. kw; 328 ft.; N34 4 7 W81 4 17
316 Greystone Blvd., Columbia, SC 29210-8007 US
(803) 343-1100; *Fax:* (803) 748-6297
www.thebeatcolumbia.com
License: West Columbia, SC held by Capstar TX LLC
Group Owner: iHeartMedia
Arbitron Metro Market: Columbia, SC; *Format:* Urban Contemporary
Todd Shuster, Senior Vice President of Sales
Kelley Royster, Market Controller

Whitmire

***WNBK**
01-01-2009; 90.9 MHz FM; *Hrs Open:* 24; 1.8 kw horiz, 1.61 kw vert; 335 ft.; N34 29 52 W81 32 55 *Rebroadcasts:* WRBK 90.3 FM
US
(803) 581-9030
License: Whitmire, Newberry County, SC held by Richburg Educational Broadcasters Inc.
Arbitron Metro Market: Whitmire, SC; *Format:* Oldies; *Target Audience:* 35-75+
Jeff Sigmon, General Manager

Williamston

WHZT
06-06-1953; 98.1 MHz FM; *Hrs Open:* 24; 100 kw; 1,004 ft; N34 41 14 W82 59 12
220 N. Main St., Suite 402, Greenville, SC 29601
(864) 232-9810; *Fax:* (864) 370-3403
www.hot981.com
License: Williamston, Oconee County, SC held by SM-WHZT LLC
Group Owner: SummitMedia LLC; (acq 2-1-2001; grpsl)
Nat'l Network: Westwood One; CBS
Population Served: 800,000; *Arbitron Metro Market:* Greenville-Spartanburg, SC; *Hrs. of News Programming:* news progmg 18 hrs wkly; *No. News Employees:* 2; *Target Audience:* 25-54; affluent adults
Steve Sinicropi, Operations Dir
Rob Grossman, General Sales Mgr
Murph Dawg, Programming Director
Laurie Madden, Promotions Manager
Lemont Bryant, Chief Engineer
Cathy Tabor, National Sales Manager

Williston

WAAW
08-12-1994; 94.7 MHz FM; *Hrs Open:* 24; 2.55 kw; 509 ft.; N33 30 31 W81 37 27
2155 Park Avenue, SE, Aiken, SC 29801 US
(803) 649-6405; *Fax:* (803) 641-8844
www.shout947.com
License: Williston, Barnwell County, SC held by Wisdom LLC.
Group Owner: Wisdom LLC; (acq 2-2-2009; grpsl)
Arbitron Metro Market: Phoenix AZ
Lester A. Smalls, General Manager/Program Director
Izora G. Gunter, Senior Sales Consultant
Arlean J. Edwards, Assistant General Manager/Music Director

Winnsboro

WSCZ
01-01-1990; 93.9 MHz FM; *Hrs Open:* 24; 8.9 kw; 536 ft; N34 21 47 W80 54 40 *Rebroadcasts:* Simulcasts WHXT (FM) 103.9
1900 Pineview Drive, Columbia, SC 29206 US
(803) 695-8600; *Fax:* (803) 695-8605
www.hot1039fm.com
License: Winnsboro, Fairfield County, SC held by Alpha Media License, LLC
Group Owner: Alpha Media LLC; (acq 11-30-2015 from Miller Communications for $900,000 with co-located AM)
Arbitron Metro Market: Columbia, SC; *Format:* Adult Contemp, Urban Contemporary, 14
Mike Hartel, General Manager
Bryan Hendry, General Sales Mgr
Chris Connors, Programming Director
Michelle Alston, Promotions Director

Woodruff

WQUL
03-14-1972; 1510 kHz AM; *Hrs Open:* 6 AM-10 PM; 0.25 kw-C, NDD; 1 kw-D, NDD; 433 ft; N34 45 22 W82 3 18
360 Sloan Road, Post Office Box 340, Woodruff, SC 29388 US
(618) 997-8123,(618) 932-8121; *Fax:* (618) 993-2319
License: Woodruff, SC held by Withers Broadcasting of Southern Illinois LLC.
Group Owner: Withers Broadcasting Co.; (acq 3-17-2008; grpsl)
Arbitron Metro Market: Marion-Carbondale (Southern Illinois);
Format: Classic Rock; *Hrs. of News Programming:* News progmg 2 hrs wkly; *Target Audience:* 25-54; adult
Matt Mellen, Programming Director

WQUL(AM)
07-07-1967; 1510 kHz AM; 1 kw-D, 250 w-CH; N34 45 22 W82 03 18

360 Sloan Road, PO Box 340, Woodruff, SC 29388
www.coolq959.com
License: Woodruff, Spartanburg County, SC held by B&B Media Inc.
Population Served: 18,546; *Arbitron Metro Market:* Elko, NV; *Format:* Religious
T.C. Lewis, General Manager

York

WULR
04-19-1956; 980 kHz AM; *Hrs Open:* 24; 3 kw-D, DA2; 0.167 kw-N, DA2; N34 54 11 W81 5 33
US
(336) 759-0363; *Fax:* (336) 759-0366
info@truthnetwork.com
License: York, SC held by 980 AM Inc.
Nat'l Network: ABC
Arbitron Metro Market: Winston-Salem, NC; *Format:* Christian, Spanish *Special Programming:* Chinese 10 hrs, Greek 10 hrs wkly; *Hrs. of News Programming:* News progmg 6 hrs wkly; *Target Audience:* 22-54.
Michael Glinter, President
Robert Freeze, Operations Dir
Russ Jones, General Manager
Humberto Martinez, Programming Director
Winston Hawkins, Chief Engineer

South Dakota

Aberdeen

KBFO
02-20-1999; 106.7 MHz FM; *Hrs Open:* 24; 100 kw; 446 ft.; N45 27 57 W98 20 8
3304 South Highway 281, PO Box 1930, Aberdeen, SD 57401
US
(605) 229-3632; *Fax:* (605) 229-4849
www.hubcityradio.com
info@hubcityradio.com
License: Aberdeen, Brown County, SD held by Armada Media - Aberdeen Inc.
Group Owner: Armada Media Corp.; (acq 10-31-2006; grpsl)
Regional Reps: Jones Satellite Audio.
Arbitron Metro Market: Aberdeen, SD; *Format:* Adult Contemp; *Target Audience:* 18-35.; *Adv. Rates:* 10; 10; 9; 7
Brian Lundquist, General Manager
Daline Gellhaus, Sales Manager
Doc Sebastian, Program/Operations Manager
Ben Root, Sports Director
Bri Matthews, News Director
Brent Nathaniel, Content Director
Lisa Gauer, OfficeManager/Traffic
Tammie Bader, Sales Manager

KGIM
09-01-1933; 1420 kHz AM
3304 South Highway 281, PO Box 281, Aberdeen, SD 57401
US
(605) 229-3632; *Fax:* (605) 229-4849
www.hubcityradio.com
info@hubcityradio.com
License: Aberdeen, SD held by Armada Media - Aberdeen Inc.
Group Owner: Armada Media Corp.; (acq 10-31-2006; grpsl)
TV Affiliate: ESPN; *Format:* Sports; *Target Audience:* 25 plus; general
Brian Lundquist, Owner/General Manager
Daline Gellhaus, Sales Manager
Doc Sebastian, Programming/Operations Manager
Ben Root, Sports Director
Bri Matthews, News Director
Brent Nathaniel, Content Director
Tammie Bader, SalesManager
Lisa Gauer, Office Manager/Traffic

***KKAA**
09-12-1974; 1560 kHz AM; *Hrs Open:* 24
290 Hegenberger Road, Oakland, CA 94621 US
(800) 543-1495
www.familyradio.com
License: Aberdeen, SD held by Family Stations Inc.
Group Owner: Family Stations Inc.; (acq 11-30-2004; $75,000 with KQKD(AM) Redfield).
Format: Christian, Religious
Harold Camping, President

***KLRJ**
09-01-1979; 94.9 MHz FM; *Hrs Open:* 5 AM-1 AM; 100 kw; 446 ft.; N45 27 57 W98 20 8 *Rebroadcasts:* Rebroadcasts KLVR(FM) Santa Rosa, CA
Mailing Address: 427 Bedford Road, Suite 330, Pleasantville, NY 10570 US
Second Address: K-LOVE, PO Box 2098, Omaha, NE 68103-2098
(800) 525-5683; *Fax:* (916) 251-1650
www.klove.com
klove@klove.com
License: Aberdeen, Brown County, SD held by Educational Media Foundation.
Group Owner: EMF Broadcasting; (acq 11-30-2004; $200,000).
Nat'l Network: K-Love
Format: Christian
Darrell Chambliss, Chairman
Mike Novak, CEO/COO
Mike Novak, President
Alan Mason, Operations Dir
David Pierce, Programming Director
Richard Hunt, News Director
Sam Wallington, Engineering Dir
Marya Morgan, News Reporter

KSDN
04-16-1947; 930 kHz AM; 5 kw-D, DA2; 1 kw-N, DA2; N45 25 29 W98 31 3
3304 South Highway 281, PO Box 1930, Aberdeen, SD 57401
US
(605) 229-3632; *Fax:* (605) 229-4849
www.hubcityradio.com
info@hubcityradio.com
License: Aberdeen, SD held by Armada Media - Aberdeen Inc.
Group Owner: Armada Media Corp.; (acq 10-31-2006; grpsl)
Nat'l Network: ABC
Arbitron Metro Market: Aberdeen, SD; *Format:* Talk *Special Programming:* Farm 15 hrs wkly; *Hrs. of News Programming:* news progmg 15 hrs wkly; *No. News Employees:* 1; *Target Audience:* 25-54. *Adv. Rates:* 10; 10; 10; 9
Brian Lundquist, Owner/General Manager
Daline Gellhaus, Sales Manager
Doc Sebastian, Program/Operations Manager
Ben Root, Sports Director
Bri Matthews, News Director
Tammie Bader, Sales Manager
Brent Nathaniel, ContentDirector
Lisa Gauer, Office Manager/Traffic

KSDN-FM
11-18-1979; 94.1 MHz FM; 100 kw; 440 ft.; N45 25 26 W98 31 1
3304 So. Highway 281, Aberdeen, SD 57401 US
(605) 229-3632; *Fax:* (605) 229-4849
www.hubcityradio.com
info@hubcityradio.com
License: Aberdeen, Brown County, SD
Group Owner: Armada Media Corp.
Arbitron Metro Market: Aberdeen, SD; *Format:* Classic Rock
Brian Lundquist, Owner/General Manager
Saline Gellhaus, Sales Manager
Doc Sebastian, Programming/Operations Manager
Bri Matthews, News Director
Brent Nathaniel, Content Director
Ben Root, Sports Director

***KEEA**
90.1 MHz FM; 1 kw; 98 ft.; N45 28 22 W98 30 16
P.O. Box 3206, Tupelo, MS 38803 US
(662) 844-8888; *Fax:* (662) 842-6791
www.afr.net
faq@afa.net
License: Aberdeen, Brown County, SD held by American Family Association.
Group Owner: American Family Radio; (acq 4-7-2008)
Nat'l Network: American Family Radio
Arbitron Metro Market: Aberdeen, SD; *Format:* Christian
Tim Wildmon, President
Donald Wildmon, Founder
Buddy Smith, Sr VP
Ed Vitagliano, Exec VP
Randy Sharp, Director Of Special Projects
Meeke Addison, Director Of Communications
Abraham Hamilton III, General Counsel

Belle Fourche

KBFS
1450 kHz AM; *Hrs Open:* 24; 1 kw-U, ND1; N44 40 2 W103 51 22 *Rebroadcasts:* Rebroadcasts KYDT(FM) Sundance, WY 99%
Mailing Address: Box 787, 707 Harding Street, Belle Fourche, SD 57717 US
Second Address: 707 Harding St.
(605) 892-2573; *Fax:* (605) 892-2573
www.kbfs.com
karl@kbfs.com
License: Belle Fourche, SD held by Ultimate Caps Inc.
Nat'l Network: Jones Radio Networks; Premiere Radio; Motor Racing Net; Cumulus; Westwood One; *Wire Services:* AP
Arbitron Metro Market: Belle Fourche, SD; *Format:* Country, News, 84, Talk *Special Programming:* Farm 20 hrs, relg 2 hrs wkly; *Hrs. of News Programming:* News progmg 20 hrs wkly; *Target Audience:* 25-54; farmers,ranchers, sports fans
Karl Grimmelmann, President
Karl Grimmelmann, General Manager

KZZI
09-22-1995; 95.9 MHz FM; *Hrs Open:* 24; 100 kw; 1788 ft.; N44 19 35 W103 50 6
Mailing Address: 2827 East Colorado Boulevard, Spearfish, SD 57783 US
Second Address: PO Box 1760, Rapid City, SD 57709
(605) 642-8800; *Fax:* (605) 642-5747
www.myeaglecountry.com/
ted@dberadio.com
License: Belle Fourche, Butte County, SD held by Western South Dakota Broadcasting L.L.C.
Nat'l Reps: Katz Radio
Arbitron Metro Market: Rapid City, SD; *Format:* Country; *Target Audience:* 18-54.; *Adv. Rates:* 21; 19; 20; 19
Ted Peiffer, General Manager
Lil Anderson, General Sales Mgr
Jim Kallas, Programming Director
Paul James, Programming

KFMH
101.9 MHz FM; 100 kw horiz, 0 kw vert; 1490 ft.; N44 19 40 W103 50 6
1711 W. Main St., Rapid City, SD 57701 US
(605) 721-9005
www.oldiesradio1019.com
License: Belle Fourche, Butte County, SD held by Bad Lands Broadcasting Co. Inc.
Group Owner: Oregon Trail Broadcasting, LLC
Arbitron Metro Market: Rapid City, SD; *Format:* Oldies
Steven Silberberg, President
Mark Norby, Account Exectutive

Box Elder

KXMZ
01-01-2008; 102.7 MHz FM; 50 kw; 449 ft.; N44 5 33 W103 14 53
822 Main St., Gambrill Bldg., Rapid City, SD 57701 US
(203) 227-1978; *Fax:* (203) 227-2373
www.hits1027.com
hits1027@hits1027.com
License: Box Elder, Pennington County, SD held by Connoisseur Media Licenses LLC
Group Owner: Connoisseur Media LLC
Arbitron Metro Market: Box Elder, SD; *Format:* Contemporary Hits/Top 40

Brandon

KDEZ
01-01-2007; 100.1 MHz FM; 2.15 kw; 558 ft.; N43 31 7 W96 32 5
US
(605) 361-0300; *Fax:* (605) 361-5410
www.easy1001.com
scott.maguire@results-radio.com
License: Brandon, Minnehaha County, SD held by Townsquare Media Sioux Falls License LLC
Group Owner: Townsquare Media
Arbitron Metro Market: Brandon, SD; *Format:* Easy Listening
Lew Dickey, President
Don Jacobs, General Manager
Barry Roberts, Programming Director
Scott Maguire, Brand Manager
Rick Fink, Director of Sales

Brookings

KBRK
07-28-1955; 1430 kHz AM; 1 kw-D, ND1; 0.1 kw-N, ND1; N44 18 12 W96 46 1
227 22nd Ave. S., Brookings, SD 57006 US
(605) 692-1430; *Fax:* (605) 692-6434
www.brookingsradio.com
info@brookingsradio.com
License: Brookings, SD held by Digity 3E License, LLC
Group Owner: Digity, LLC
Format: Oldies

Cami Powers, General Manager
Kelli Hanson, General Sales Mgr
Bob Wayne, Programming Director

KBRK-FM
08-10-1968; 93.7 MHz FM; *Hrs Open:* 24; 100 kw; 571 ft.; N44 20 22 W97 9 16
227 22nd Ave. S., Brookings, SD 57006 US
(605) 692-1430; *Fax:* (605) 692-6434
www.brookingsradio.com
info@brookingsradio.com
License: Brookings, Brookings County, SD held by Digity 3E License, LLC.
Group Owner: Digity, LLC
Nat'l Network: Westwood One
Format: Adult Contemp; *Target Audience:* 20-45.
Cami Powers, General Manager
Kelli Hanson, General Sales Mgr

***KESD**
07-01-1967; 88.3 MHz FM; 50 kw; 623 ft.; N44 20 10 W97 13 41
555 N. Dakota Street, PO Box 5000, Vermillion, SD 57069 US
(800) 456-0766; *Fax:* (605) 677-5010
www.sdpb.org
fritz.miller@state.sd.us
License: Brookings, Brookings County, SD held by South Dakota Board of Directors for Educational Telecommunications.
Nat'l Network: NPR; PRI
Arbitron Metro Market: Vermillion, SD *TV Affiliate:* *KESD-TV affil.; *Format:* News; *Target Audience:* 35-65; upscale, higher educated & arts-oriented
Fritz Miller, Director, Marketing

***KSDJ**
01-01-1993; 90.7 MHz FM; *Hrs Open:* 24; 1 kw; 125 ft.; N44 19 1 W96 47 2
SDSU Union, Basement, Brookings, SD 57007 US
(605) 688-5559
www.ksdjradio.com
License: Brookings, Brookings County, SD held by South Dakota State University.
Arbitron Metro Market: Brookings, SD; *Format:* Alternative
Special Programming: Black 8 hrs, jazz 2 hrs wkly; *Hrs. of News Programming:* news progmg 5 hrs wkly; *No. News Employees:* 1; *Target Audience:* 17-22;college students
Christina Boerger, Station Manager
Michael Moges, Programming Director
Shaheed Shihan, News Director
Susan Smith, Stadion Advisor
Aiden Bunkers, Music Director
Douglas Geyer, Creative Director

Canton

KYBB
01-01-1996; 102.7 MHz FM; 50 kw; 486 ft.; N43 28 48 W96 41 5
5100 S. Tennis Lane, Sioux Falls, SD 57108 US
(605) 339-0300; *Fax:* (605) 339-2735
www.81027.com
License: Canton, Lincoln County, SD held by Townsquare Media Sioux Falls License LLC
Group Owner: Townsquare Media; (acq 3-29-2004; grpsl)
Nat'l Reps: Christal
Arbitron Metro Market: Sioux Falls; *Format:* Classic Rock; *Target Audience:* 25-49; men
Scott Maguire, Operations Dir
Don Jacobs, General Manager
Rick Fink, Director Of Sales
Dan Rahman, Programming Director

Clear Lake

KDBX
01-01-1968; 107.1 MHz FM; 9.8 kw; 531 ft.; N44 36 44 W96 40 41
227 22nd Ave S., Brookings, SD 57006 US
(605) 692-1430; *Fax:* (605) 692-6434
www.brookingsradio.com
info@brookingsradio.com
License: Clear Lake, Deuel County, SD held by Digity 3E License, LLC
Group Owner: Digity, LLC
Format: Adult Contemp
Cami Powers, General Manager
Kelli Hanson, General Sales Mgr

Custer

KAWK
11-01-1996; 105.1 MHz FM; 7 kw; 1312 ft.; N43 44 41 W103 28 52
145 Mount Rushmore Road, P.O. Box 804, Custer, SD 57730 US
(605) 673-5327; *Fax:* (605) 673-3079
License: Custer, Custer County, SD held by Mt. Rushmore Broadcasting Inc.
Group Owner: Mt. Rushmore Broadcasting Inc.
Format: Oldies
Dwyan Calvert, Chairman
Al Ross, Station Manager

KFCR
05-01-1988; 1490 kHz AM; 0.83 kw-U, ND1; N43 43 3 W103 35 0
145 Mt Rushmore Rd, P.O. Box 804, Custer, SD 57730 US
License: Custer, SD held by Mount Rushmore Broadcasting Inc.
Group Owner: Mt. Rushmore Broadcasting Inc.; (acq 5-6-92;
Arbitron Metro Market: Hot Springs, SD; *Format:* Adult Contemp
Gary Baker, General Manager

Deadwood

KDSJ
07-02-1947; 980 kHz AM; *Hrs Open:* 6:00 a.m.-10:00 p.m. Daily; 5 kw-D, DAN; 1 kw-N, DAN; N44 22 57 W103 39 44
745 Main P.O. Box 567, Deadwood, SD 57732 US
(605) 578-1826; *Fax:* (605) 578-1827
www.kdsj980.com
License: Deadwood, SD held by Goldrush Broadcasting
Nat'l Network: ABC; *Regional Network:* S.D. News Net.
Arbitron Metro Market: Deadwood, SD; *Format:* News, Oldies, 84; *Target Audience:* 25-50
Al Decker, President
Cody Oliver, Programming Director

KSQY
09-04-1982; 95.1 MHz FM; *Hrs Open:* 24; 100 kw; 1709 ft.; N44 19 49 W103 50 10
3601 Canyon Lake Dr., Suite 1, Rapid City, SD 57702 US
(605) 343-0888; *Fax:* (605) 342-3075
www.951ksky.com
studio@951ksky.com
License: Deadwood, Lawrence County, SD held by Haugo Broadcasting Inc.
Group Owner: Haugo Broadcasting Inc.
Nat'l Reps: Midwest Radio *Regional Reps:* Midwest Radio.
Arbitron Metro Market: Rapid City, SD; *Format:* Rock/AOR; *Hrs. of News Programming:* News progmg 2 hrs wkly; *Target Audience:* 18-49; young, active adults within a 5 state region
Houston Haugo, CEO/COO
Christian Haugo, General Manager

Dell Rapids

KQSF
10-02-1998; 95.7 MHz FM; *Hrs Open:* 24; 25 kW; 328 ft.; N43 45 48 W96 48 27
500 S Phillips Ave, Sioux Falls, SD 57104 USA
(605) 331-5350; *Fax:* (605) 336-0415
q957.com
License: Dell Rapids, Minnehaha County, SD held by Midwest Communications Inc.
Group Owner: Midwest Communications Inc.; (acq 8-1-2006; grpsl).
Nat'l Reps: Rgnl Reps; *Wire Services:* AP
Arbitron Metro Market: Sioux Falls, SD; *Format:* Classic Rock, Adult Contemp; *Target Audience:* 20-40; young, active adults with spending ability; *Adv. Rates:* 20; 18; 20; 18
Mark Nelson, Brand Manager

Ethan

KUQL
01-01-1999; 98.3 MHz FM; 100 kw; 896 ft.; N43 45 33 W98 24 44
501 South Ohlman Street, Mitchell, SD 57301 US
(605) 996-9667
www.kool98.com
timsmith@kmit.com
License: Ethan, Jerauld County, SD held by Saga Communications of South Dakota LLC.
Group Owner: Saga Communications Inc.; (acq 5-1-2001; $4.05 million with KMIT(FM) Mitchell)
Format: Oldies *Special Programming:* Theme weekends
Tim Smith, General Manager
Chris Johnson, Brand Manager
Mike Kelly, Production Director

Faith

***KPSD-FM**
06-01-1989; 97.1 MHz FM; 100 kw; 1526 ft.; N45 3 14 W102 15 47 *Rebroadcasts:* Rebroadcasts KUSD(FM) Vermillion.
555 N. Dakota Street, PO Box 5000, Vermillion, SD 57069 US
(888) 456-0766; *Fax:* (605) 677-5010
www.sdpb.org
fritz.miller@state.sd.us
License: Faith, Meade County, SD held by South Dakota Board of Directors for Educational Telecommunications.
Nat'l Network: NPR
Format: Jazz, News
Fritz Miller, Marketing Manager

Fort Pierre

KJBI
12-01-2007; 100.1 MHz FM; *Hrs Open:* 24; 51 kw; 530 ft.; N44 18 30 W100 20 49
Mailing Address: 214 W. Pleasant Drive, Pierre, SD 57501 US
Second Address: 115 W. Lawler, PO Box 317, Chamberlain, SD 57325
(605) 224-8686; *Fax:* (605) 224-8984
www.drgnews.com
License: Fort Pierre, Stanley County, SD held by James River Broadcasting Inc.
Group Owner: Robert Ingstad Broadcast Properties; (acq 7-31-2007; $450,000 for CP)
Arbitron Metro Market: Fort Pierre, SD; *Format:* Contemporary Hits/Top 40, Adult Contemp
Mark Swendsen, General Manager

Frankfort

***KTUT**
89.5 MHz FM; kw
US
(940) 668-7971
License: Frankfort, Spink County, SD held by 1 A Chord Inc.
Group Owner: Agnus Dei Communications, Inc.
Arbitron Metro Market: Frankfort, SD
Dorothy Fay Jones, General Manager

Freeman

***KVCF**
01-01-2002; 90.5 MHz FM; 9 kw; 807 ft.; N43 29 22 W97 26 33
3434 W. Kilbourn Ave., Milwaukee, WI 53208 US
(800) 729-9829
www.vcyamerica.org
vcy@vcyamerica.org
License: Freeman, Hutchinson County, SD held by VCY America Inc.
Group Owner: VCY America Inc.
Arbitron Metro Market: Freeman, SD; *Format:* Christian, Religious
Vic Eliason, General Manager
Jim Schneider, Programming Director
Andy Eliason, Chief Engineer

Gregory

***KVCX**
05-08-1982; 101.5 MHz FM; 100 kw; 640 ft.; N43 7 41 W99 26 1
3434 West Kilbourn Ave, Milwaukee, WI 53208 US
(800) 729-9829
www.vcyamerica.org
vcy@vcyamerica.org
License: Gregory, Gregory County, SD held by VCY/America Inc.
Group Owner: VCY America Inc.; acq 4-87)
Nat'l Network: USA; Moody
Arbitron Metro Market: Milwaukee, WI *TV Affiliate:* KVCX-TV
Dr. Randall Melchert, President
Vic Eliason, Operations Dir
Jim Schneider, Programming Director
Gordon Morris, News Director
Andrew Eliason, Chief Engineer
Tom Schlueter, Music Director

Hermosa

***KWRC**
90.9 MHz FM; 0.4 kw; 1269 ft.; N43 44 40 W103 28 52
Rebroadcasts: Rebroadcasts KAWZ(FM) Twin Falls, ID 100%
Mailing Address: P.O. Box 391, Twin Falls, ID 83303 US
Second Address: 4002 North 3300 East, Twin Falls, ID 83301
(800) 357-4226; *Fax:* (208) 736-1958
www.csnradio.com
License: Hermosa, Custer County, SD held by Calvary Chapel of Twin Falls Inc.
Group Owner: CSN International
Arbitron Metro Market: Rapid City-Southwest South Dakota, SD; *Format:* Christian, Religious
Mike Kestler, President
Daniel Davidson, Operations Dir
Don Mills, Network Programming Director

Mike Stocklin, Underwriting Director
Kelly Carlson, Engineering Dir

Hot Springs

KZMX
07-04-1958; 580 kHz AM; 2.3 kw-D, ND1; 0.31 kw-N, ND1; N43 27 24 W103 28 34
Mailing Address: 437 Montgomery Street, Custer, SD 57730 US
Second Address: North Wind Cave Rd., Hot Springs, SD 57747
(605) 745-3637; *Fax:* (605) 745-3517
info@kzmx.com
themorningshow@email.com
License: Hot Springs, SD held by Mount Rushmore Broadcasting Inc.
Group Owner: Mt. Rushmore Broadcasting Inc.; (acq 5-20-93; $45,000 with co-located FM;
Arbitron Metro Market: Hot Springs, SD; *Format:* Country *Special Programming:* Farm 6 hrs wkly
Gary Baker, General Manager

KZMX-FM
02-10-1981; 96.7 MHz FM; 1.4 kw horiz; 443 ft.; N43 26 34 W103 27 27
Mailing Address: Box 611, Hot Springs, SD 57747 US
Second Address: North Wind Cave Rd., Hot Springs, SD 57747
(605) 745-3637; *Fax:* (605) 745-3517
License: Hot Springs, Fall River County, SD
Group Owner: Mt. Rushmore Broadcasting Inc.
Arbitron Metro Market: Hot Springs, SD; *Format:* Country
Lisa Cheek, General Manager
Sam Scholl, Programming Director

Huron

KIJV
07-01-1947; 1340 kHz AM; *Hrs Open:* 24
1726 Dakota Avenue South, Huron, SD 57350 US
(605) 352-1933; *Fax:* (605) 352-0911
www.performance-radio.com
smartin@kokk.com
License: Huron, SD held by Dakota Communications Ltd.
Group Owner: Performance Radio; (acq 3-11-2004; $400,000 with co-located FM)
Arbitron Metro Market: Huron, SD; *Format:* Oldies, Sports, 86; *No. News Employees:* 1; *Target Audience:* 35 plus.; *Adv. Rates:* 15; 12; 15; 9.
Shawn Martin, General Manager
Kelly Sharp, Sales
Zach Nelson, News Director
Jan Eickhoff, Office Manager
Jeff, Shawn, Matt, Production
Jeff Duffy, Sports Director
Keith Osier, Sales
Mike Lyon, Sales
Shawn Martin, Sales

KOKK
01-13-1976; 1210 kHz AM
1726 Dakota Avenue S., Huron, SD 57350 US
(605) 352-1933; *Fax:* (605) 352-0911
www.kokk.com
smartin@kokk.com
License: Huron, SD held by Dakota Communications Ltd.
Group Owner: Dakota Communications Ltd.
Format: Country
Shawn Martin, General Manager
Zach Nelson, News Director
Jan Eickhoff, Office Manager
Jeff, Shawn, Matt, Production
Jeff Duffy, Sports Director

KZKK
01-01-1993; 105.1 MHz FM; *Hrs Open:* 5:30 AM-midnight; 6 kw; 154 ft.; N44 21 44 W98 9 9
1726 Dakota Avenue S., Huron, SD 57350 US
(605) 352-1933; *Fax:* (605) 352-0911
www.kokk.com
smartin@kokk.com
License: Huron, Beadle County, SD
Group Owner: Dakota Communications Ltd.
Arbitron Metro Market: Huron, SD; *Format:* Adult Contemp; *No. News Employees:* 1
Shawn Martin, General Manager
Jan Eickhoff, Office Manager
Jeff Duffy, Sports Manager
Zach Nelson, News Director
Jeff, Shawn, Matt, Production

***KVCH**
88.7 MHz FM; 60 kw; 528 ft.; N44 11 39 W98 19 5
3434 West Kilbourn Avenue, Milwaukee, WI 53208 US
(800) 729-9829
www.vcyamerica.org
vcy@vcyamerica.org
License: Huron, Beadle County, SD held by VCY America Inc.
Group Owner: VCY America Inc.
Arbitron Metro Market: Huron, SD
Jeff Fitzgerald, Operations Dir
Andrew Kalb, Programming Director

Ipswich

KABD
12-21-2007; 107.7 MHz FM; 51 kw; Ant 354 ft; N45 27 13 W98 48 10
426 N. Hwy. 281, Suite 4, Aberdeen, SD 57401
(605) 725-5551; *Fax:* (605) 725-5553
www.dakotabroadcasting.com
License: Ipswich, Edmunds County, SD held by Dakota Broadcasting LLC
Population Served: 90,000 *Hrs. of News Programming:* 6a-5p; *No. News Employees:* 9
Neil & Terry Lipetzky, Managing Partners
Joel Swanson, General Manager
Kate Von Brook, Office Manager

***KSJP(FM)**
88.9 MHz FM; 20 kw vert; Ant 34 ft; N45 26 56.2 W99 15 08.8
6300 S Old Village Place, Suite 203, Sioux Falls, SD 57108
(605) 275-4659
www.sacredheartaberdeen.net/KSJP-88-9-FM-The-Lamb-Catholic-Radio
License: Ipswich, Edmunds County, SD held by Agnes DEI Communications Inc
Population Served: 951; *Arbitron Metro Market:* Ipswich, SD
Kevin Culhane, Media Contact

Keystone

KRKI
01-01-2003; 99.5 MHz FM; 100 kw horiz, 0 kw vert; N43 51 24 W103 45 50
Mailing Address: 7901 Stoneridge Drive, Cheyenne, WY 82009 US
Second Address: 1711 W. Main St., Rapid City, WY 57702
(877) 996-6369; *Fax:* (605) 721-9007
www.995thefan.com
jameskelley@clearchannel.com
License: Keystone, Weston County, SD held by Bad Lands Broadcasting Company, Inc.
Group Owner: Oregon Trail Broadcasting, LLC
Nat'l Network: ESPN Radio
Arbitron Metro Market: Newcastle, WY; *Format:* Sports
Scott McCormick, Operations Dir
Lonnie Glasford, General Manager
James Kelly, Online Program Director / Webmaster
Craig Hawkesworth, VP of Interactive Sales
Dan Metter, SVP/Director of Talk Radio Sales

Lemmon

KBJM
04-01-1966; 1400 kHz AM; *Hrs Open:* 24; 1 kw-U, ND1; N45 55 5 W102 11 55
PO Box 540, Lemmon, SD 57638 US
(605) 374-5747; *Fax:* (605) 374-5332
www.kbjm.com
kbjm1400@sdplains.com
License: Lemmon, SD held by Media Associates Inc.
Nat'l Reps: Keystone (unwired net)
Arbitron Metro Market: Lemmon, SD; *Format:* Oldies, Country; *Hrs. of News Programming:* News progmg 30 hrs wkly; *Target Audience:* General.
Mike Schweitzer, President
James Schwab, Programming Director

Lennox

KSOO-FM
01-01-2008; 99.1 MHz FM; 25 kw; 328 ft.; N43 22 36 W96 48 19
5100 Tennis Lane, Sioux Fals, SD 57108 US
(605) 361-0300; *Fax:* (605) 361-5410
www.ksoo.com
dave@ksoo.com
License: Lennox, Lincoln County, SD held by Townsquare Media Sioux Falls License LLC
Group Owner: Townsquare Media
Arbitron Metro Market: Sioux Falls, SD; *Format:* News, News/Talk, 84, Talk
Don Jacobs, General Manager
Dave Roberts, Brand Manager
Rick Fink, Director of Sales

Little Eagle

***KLND**
06-25-1997; 89.5 MHz FM; *Hrs Open:* 6 AM-midnight; 100 kw; 679 ft.; N45 44 54 W100 48 30
Mailing Address: Native Voice One, 3600 San Jeronimo Drive, Suite 480, Anchorage, AK 99508 US
Second Address: The Annenberg National Native Voice Studios, 4401 Lomas Boulevard NE, Suite C, Albuquerque, NM 87110
(907) 793-3521; *Fax:* (907) 793-3536
sbeatty@knba.org
License: Little Eagle, Corson County, SD held by Seventh Generation Media Services Inc.
Nat'l Network: PRI
Arbitron Metro Market: Rapid City, SD; *Format:* Variety/Diverse *Special Programming:* Gospel 3 hrs, children 4 hrs, Sp one hr, elders 2; *Hrs. of News Programming:* news progmg 5 hrs wkly; *No. News Employees:* 1 *Target Audience:* General; tribal people on the Standing Rock & Cheyenne River Nations
Shyanna Beatty, Network Manager
Nola Daves Moses, Station Relations Representative
Larry Cleland, Director of Corporate Support
Cindy Hector, NV1 Billing
David House, Webmaster

Lowry

KMLO
01-01-1996; 100.7 MHz FM; 100 kw; 587 ft.; N45 16 26 W99 58 21 *Rebroadcasts:* Rebroadcasts KPLO-FM Reliance 100%
214 W. Plesant Drive, PO Box 1197, Pierre, SD 55501 US
(605) 224-8686; *Fax:* (605) 224-8984
www.drgnews.com
License: Lowry, Walworth County, SD held by James River Broadcasting Inc.
Group Owner: Robert Ingstad Broadcast Properties
Format: Country
Mark Swendsen, General Manager

***KQSD-FM**
01-01-1994; 91.9 MHz FM; 100 kw; 725 ft.; N45 16 34 W99 59 3
555 N. Dakota Street, PO Box 5000, Vermillion, SD 57069 US
(800) 456-0766; *Fax:* (605) 677-5010
www.sdpb.org
License: Lowry, Walworth County, SD held by South Dakota Board of Directors for Educational Telecommunications.
Arbitron Metro Market: Vermillion, SD; *Format:* Classical, Jazz, 60
Owen DeJong, Programming Director

Madison

KJAM
12-03-1959; 1390 kHz AM; *Hrs Open:* 18; 0.5 kw-D, ND1; 0.062 kw-N, ND1; N44 0 37 W97 10 18
101 S. Egan Ave., Madison, SD 57042 US
(605) 256-4514; *Fax:* (605) 256-6477
www.amazingmadison.com
kjamonair@digity.me
License: Madison, SD held by Digity 3E License, LLC
Group Owner: Digity, LLC; (acq 12-8-99; $1.2 million with co-located FM)
Format: Oldies; *No. News Employees:* 13; *Target Audience:* 21 plus.; *Adv. Rates:* 35; 32; 32; 28.
Peg Nordling, General Manager
Matt Groce, Programming Director
Sue Bergheim, News Director
Karen Hagel, Business Manager
Joyce Hyland, Sales Manager

KJAM-FM
12-17-1967; 103.1 MHz FM; *Hrs Open:* 24; 33 kw; 305 ft.; N43 59 8 W97 7 42
101 S. Egan Ave., Madison, SD 57042 US
(605) 256-4514; *Fax:* (605) 256-6477
www.amazingmadison.com
kjamonair@digity.me
License: Madison, Lake County, SD held by Digity 3E License, LLC
Group Owner: Digity, LLC
Format: Country; *Hrs. of News Programming:* news progmg 20 hrs wkly; *No. News Employees:* 2; *Target Audience:* 21 plus.
Peg Nordling, General Manager
Matt Groce, Programming Director
Sue Bergheim, News Director
Karen Hagel, Business Manager
Joyce Hyland, Sales Manager

Martin

*KZSD-FM
07-03-1991; 102.5 MHz FM; 100 kw; 755 ft.; N43 26 6 W101 33 14
555 N. Dakota Street, PO Box 5000, Vermillion, SD 57069 US
(800) 456-0766; *Fax:* (605) 677-5010
www.sdpb.org
License: Martin, Bennett County, SD held by South Dakota Board of Directors for Educational Telecommunications.
Arbitron Metro Market: Martin, SD; *Format:* Classical, Jazz, 60; *No. News Employees:* 10
Owen DeJong, Programming Director
Joe Tlustos, Radio Director

Mibank

KMSD
03-20-1975; 1510 kHz AM
PO Box 1005, Milbank, SD 57252 US
(605) 432-5516; *Fax:* (605) 432-4231
kmsd@bigstoneradio.com
License: Mibank, SD held by Armada Media-Watertown Inc.
Group Owner: Armada Media Corp.; (acq 8-3-2007; grpsl)
Regional Network: S.D. News Net.; *Wire Services:* UPI
Format: News, News/Talk, 64, Talk *Special Programming:* Farm 6 hrs wkly; *Target Audience:* General.
Jeff Kurtz, General Manager

Milbank

KKSD
02-04-1991; 104.3 MHz FM; *Hrs Open:* 24; 97 kw; 981 ft.; N45 10 31 W96 59 15
921 9th Ave. SE., Watertown, SD 57201 US
(605) 886-8444; *Fax:* (605) 886-9306
www.gowatertown.net
License: Milbank, Grant County, SD held by Digity 3E License, LLC
Group Owner: Digity, LLC
Arbitron Metro Market: Sioux City, IA; *Format:* Oldies; *Target Audience:* 25-54.
Brenda Rorvick, General Manager

KXLG
11-01-1972; 99.1 MHz FM; 37 kw; 548 ft.; N45 1 10 W96 56 43
26 S. Broadway, Suite 200, PO Box 850, Watertown, SD 57201 US
(605) 753-9910; *Fax:* (605) 753-9914
www.kxlgradio.com/
carol.zillgitt@kxlgradio.com
License: Milbank, Grant County, SD held by Dakota Communications Ltd.
Group Owner: Dakota Communications Ltd.
Arbitron Metro Market: Milbank, SD; *Format:* Country; *Target Audience:* 25-54.
Carol Zillgitt
David J. Law
Mary Wheeler
Bob Faehn
Jim Aesoph
Dean Johnson

Mitchell

KMIT
03-10-1975; 105.9 MHz FM; *Hrs Open:* 24; 100 kw; 653 ft.; N43 44 16 W98 14 39
501 South Ohlman Street, Mitchell, SD 57301 US
(605) 996-9667; *Fax:* (605) 996-0013
www.kmit.com
kmit@kmit.com
License: Mitchell, Davison County, SD held by Saga Communications of South Dakota LLC.
Group Owner: Saga Communications Inc.; (acq 5-1-2001; $4.05 million with KUQL(FM) Wessington Springs).
Format: Country *Special Programming:* Farm 18 hrs wkly; *No. News Employees:* 2; *Target Audience:* 18-54.
Tim Smith, General Manager
Renee Robbins, Program/Operations Manager
Billy Lurken, News Director
Doug Cunningam, Farm Director

KORN
01-01-1947; 1490 kHz AM; *Hrs Open:* 24; 1 kw-U, ND1; N43 42 14 W97 59 57
Mailing Address: PO Box 921, Mitchell, SD 57301 US
Second Address: 319 N. Main, Mitchell, SD 57301
(605) 996-1490; *Fax:* (605) 996-6680
www.1490korn.com
jkoons@kornq107.com
License: Mitchell, SD held by Sorenson Broadcasting Corp.
Group Owner: Sorenson Broadcasting Corp.; (acq 7-1-97; $1.2 million with co-located FM)
Nat'l Network: Westwood One; ABC; *Wire Services:* AP
Format: News, News/Talk, 84, Talk *Special Programming:* Farm 10 hrs wkly; *Hrs. of News Programming:* news progmg 15 hrs wkly; *No. News Employees:* 1; *Target Audience:* 35 plus; mature adults; *Adv. Rates:* 12;10; 10; 8
Steve Morgan, Operations Manager
John Koons, General Manager
Clint Greenway, Programming Director
J.P. Skelly, News Director

KQRN
08-17-1980; 107.3 MHz FM; *Hrs Open:* 24; 100 kw; 361 ft.; N43 42 14 W97 59 57
Mailing Address: PO Box 921, Mitchell, SD 57301 US
Second Address: 319 N. Main, Mitchell, SD 57301
(605) 996-1073; *Fax:* (605) 996-6680
q107radio.com
jkoons@kornq107.com
License: Mitchell, Davison County, SD
Group Owner: Sorenson Broadcasting Corp.
Wire Services: AP
Arbitron Metro Market: Mitchell, SD; *Format:* Adult Contemp; *Hrs. of News Programming:* news progmg 4 hrs wkly; *No. News Employees:* 1; *Target Audience:* 10-49; adult female; *Adv. Rates:* 20; 15; 20; 12
Steve Morgan, Operations Dir
John Koons, General Manager
Clint Greenway, PSA Director
JP Skelly, News Director

Mobridge

KOLY
08-10-1956; 1300 kHz AM; *Hrs Open:* 24; 5 kw-D, 111 w-N; N45 32 07 W100 20 45
PO Box 400, 118 3rd Street East, Mobridge, SD 57601
(605) 845-3654; *Fax:* (605) 845-5094
www.drgnews.com
License: Mobridge, Walworth County, SD held by James River Broadcasting Co.
Group Owner: Robert Ingstad Broadcast Properties; (acq 7-8-97; $890,742 with co-locat
Population Served: 50,000 *Special Programming:* Farm, American Indian; *Hrs. of News Programming:* news progmg 21 hrs wkly; *No. News Employees:* 1; *Target Audience:* General.
Mark Swendsen, General Manager
Dawn Konold, General Sales Mgr
John Schreier, Programming Director
Mel Hanson, Promotions Manager
Aaron Kurth, News Director
Don Britnall, Chief Engineer
Andy Shumacher, Disc Jockey
Pat Morrison,Sports Commentator

KOLY-FM
10-01-1973; 99.5 MHz FM; 56 kw; 560 ft; N45 31 50 W100 20 30
PO Box 400, 118 3rd Street East, Mobridge, SD 57601
(605) 845-3654; *Fax:* (605) 845-5094
www.drgnews.com
License: Mobridge, Walworth County, SD

Cindy Dafnis, Operations Dir
Dawn Konold, Station Manager
John Schreier, Programming Director
Mel Hanson, Promotions Manager
Aaron Kurth, News Director
Don Britnal, Chief Engineer
John Schreier, Production Manager

Newell

KXZT
107.9 MHz FM; 4.8 kw horiz, 0 kw vert; 1493 ft.; N44 19 40 W103 50 6
US
(859) 879-0818
License: Newell, Butte County, SD held by JER Licenses LLC.
Group Owner: JER Licenses LLC
Arbitron Metro Market: Newell, SD
Jon Robinson, General Manager

Pierpont

*KDSD-FM
04-01-1984; 90.9 MHz FM; 70 kw; 1060 ft.; N45 29 55 W97 40 35 *Rebroadcasts:* Rebroadcasts KUSD(FM) Vermillion.
555 N. Dakota Street, PO Box 5000, Vermillion, SD 57069 US
(800) 456-0766; *Fax:* (605) 677-5010
www.sdpb.org
License: Pierpont, Day County, SD held by South Dakota Board of Directors for Educational Telecommunications.
Nat'l Network: PRI; NPR; *Regional Network:* S.D. Pub
Arbitron Metro Market: Vermillion, SD; *Format:* Jazz, News; *No. News Employees:* 8
Terry Spencer, General Sales Mgr
Owen DeJong, Programming Director
Joe Tlustos, Radio Director

Pierre

KCCR
02-04-1959; 1240 kHz AM; *Hrs Open:* 5:30 AM-midnight; 1 kw-U, ND1; N44 21 2 W100 19 8
106 W. Capitol Avenue, Pierre, SD 57501 US
(605) 224-1240; *Fax:* (605) 945-4270
www.todayskccr.com
steve@todayskccr.com
License: Pierre, SD held by Sorenson Broadcasting Corp.
Group Owner: Sorenson Broadcasting Corp.; (acq 3-1-72)
Nat'l Network: CBS
Arbitron Metro Market: Pierre, SD; *Format:* News, News/Talk, 64, Talk; *Hrs. of News Programming:* news progmg 24 hrs wkly; *No. News Employees:* 2; *Target Audience:* 35 plus; well-educated, upper income, politicallyaware business people, retirees, housewives
Steve White, General Manager
Tara Steiner, Sales

KGFX
01-01-1927; 1060 kHz AM; *Hrs Open:* 24; 10 kw-D, DA2; 1 kw-N, DA2; N44 17 12 W100 20 18
214 W. Pleasant Drive, Pierre, SD 57501 US
(800) 658-5439
www.drgnews.com
License: Pierre, SD held by James River Broadcasting.
Group Owner: Robert Ingstad Broadcast Properties; (acq 11-15-68)
Nat'l Network: ABC Information & Entertainment; *Regional Network:* S.D. News Net.; *Wire Services:* AP
Format: Country; *Hrs. of News Programming:* news progmg 20 hrs wkly; *No. News Employees:* 1; *Target Audience:* 25-54.
Janice Ingstad, President
Mark Swendsen, General Manager
Dawn Marso, General Sales Mgr
Paul Rollie, Programming Director
Chuck Hanson, Promotions Manager
Jeri Thomas, News Director
Dorene Foster, Farm Director

KGFX-FM
01-04-1982; 92.7 MHz FM; *Hrs Open:* 24; 50 kw; 488 ft.; N44 18 30 W100 20 49
214 W. Pleasant Drive, Pierre, SD 57501 US
(800) 658-5439
www.drgnews.com
License: Pierre, Hughes County, SD held by Robert E. Ingstad Properties.
Group Owner: Robert Ingstad Broadcast Properties
Format: Adult Contemp; *Target Audience:* 25-49.
Mark Swendsen, General Manager
Dawn Marso, General Sales Mgr
Chuck Hanson, Promotions Manager
Patrick Callahan, News Director

KLXS-FM
04-15-1981; 95.3 MHz FM; 49 kw; 495 ft.; N44 18 42 W100 21 10
106 W. Capitol Avenue, Pierre, SD 57501 US
(605) 224-0095; *Fax:* (605) 945-4270
www.pierrecountry.com
news@todayskccr.com
License: Pierre, Hughes County, SD held by Sorenson Broadcasting Corp.
Group Owner: Sorenson Broadcasting Corp.
Nat'l Network: Westwood One
Arbitron Metro Market: Rapid City, SD; *Format:* Adult Contemp; *Target Audience:* 18-34; 55% female, 45% male
Steve, Sales
Cindy, Business

*KVFL
01-01-2006; 89.1 MHz FM; *Hrs Open:* 24; 0.4 kw vert; 371 ft.; N44 25 33 W100 21 28
3434 West Kilbourn Ave, Milwaukee, WI 53208 US
(800) 729-9829
www.vcyamerica.org/kvfl
kvfl@vcyamerica.org
License: Pierre, Hughes County, SD held by VCY America Inc.
Group Owner: VCY America Inc.
Arbitron Metro Market: Colorado Springs, CO; *Format:* Christian, Religious

Vic Eliason, Operations Dir
Jim Schneider, Programming Director

Pine Ridge

*KVAR
07-01-2008; 93.7 MHz FM; 12 kw; 479 ft.; N42 49 47 W102 39 8 US
License: Pine Ridge, Shannon County, SD held by Alleycat Communications.
Arbitron Metro Market: Mesquite, TX; *Format:* Variety/Diverse, Rock/AOR; *Target Audience:* 18-54.
Richard Dabney, General Manager

*KVKR
88.3 MHz FM; 10 kw; 436 ft.; N42 49 47 W102 39 8
US
(256) 497-4502
License: Pine Ridge, Shannon County, SD held by Southern Cultural Foundation.
Arbitron Metro Market: Pine Ridge, SD
Richard Dabney, General Manager

Porcupine

*KILI
01-01-1984; 90.1 MHz FM; 100 kw; 509 ft.; N43 10 48 W102 19 25
P.O. Box 150, Porcupine, SD 57772 US
(605) 867-5002; *Fax:* (605) 867-5634
www.kiliradio.org
License: Porcupine, Shannon County, SD held by Lakota Communications Inc.
Arbitron Metro Market: Porcupine, SD; *Format:* Native American
Tom Casey, Manager
Melanie Janis, Volunteer Coordinator

Rapid City

*KBHE-FM
01-01-1984; 89.3 MHz FM; 9.8 kw; 410 ft.; N44 3 9 W103 14 38
555 N. Dakota Street, PO Box 5000, Vermillion, SD 57069 US
(800) 456-0766; *Fax:* (605) 677-5010
www.sdpb.org
fritz.miller@state.sd.us
License: Rapid City, Pennington County, SD held by South Dakota Board of Educational Telecommunications.
Nat'l Network: PRI; NPR; *Regional Network:* S.D. Pub
Arbitron Metro Market: Vermillion, SD; *Format:* Classical, Jazz, 60
Fritz Miller, Director, Marketing

KFXS
04-11-1977; 100.3 MHz FM; *Hrs Open:* 24; 100 kw; 463 ft.; N44 4 13 W103 15 1
Mailing Address: 660 Flormann Street, Suite 100, Rapid City, MN 57709-2480 US
Second Address: PO Box 2480, Rapid City, SD 57709-2480
(605) 348-6161; *Fax:* (605) 348-9012
www.foxradio.com
liagreen@newrushmoreradio.com
License: Rapid City, Pennington County, SD held by New Rushmore Radio Inc.
Group Owner: Schurz Communications Inc.; (acq 10-23-2006; grpsl)
Nat'l Reps: Christal
Arbitron Metro Market: Rapid City, SD; *Format:* Classic Rock; *Hrs. of News Programming:* news progmg 3 hrs wkly; *No. News Employees:* 1; *Target Audience:* 25-54.
Lia Green, General Manager
Micheal Goodroad, Director, Sales
Adrian "Gunner" Ludens, Programming Director

KIMM
03-16-1962; 1150 kHz AM
US
(605) 342-1150
www.kimmradio.net
License: Rapid City, SD held by Aasen Publishing Inc.
Nat'l Reps: Christal
Arbitron Metro Market: Rapid City, SD; *Format:* Talk *Special Programming:* Colorado Rockies baseball, farm one hr wkly; *Target Audience:* 35-64.; *Adv. Rates:* 20; 20; 20; 10

KIQK
01-07-1992; 104.1 MHz FM; *Hrs Open:* 24; 100 kw; 538 ft.; N44 1 19 W103 15 33
3601 Canyon Lake Dr., Suite 1, Rapid City, SD 57702 US
(605) 343-0888; *Fax:* (605) 342-3075
www.kick104.com
studio@kick104.com
License: Rapid City, Pennington County, SD held by Haugo Broadcasting, Inc.
Group Owner: Haugo Broadcasting, Inc.
Arbitron Metro Market: Rapid City, SD; *Format:* Country; *Hrs. of News Programming:* news progmg 3 hrs wkly; *No. News Employees:* 1; *Target Audience:* 25-54.
Houston Haugo, CEO/COO
Christian Haugo, General Manager

KKLS
06-07-1959; 920 kHz AM; *Hrs Open:* 24; 5 kw-D, DA2; 0.111 kw-N, DA2; N44 3 43 W103 10 32
1612 Junction Avenue, Sturgis, SD 57785 US
(605) 347-4455; *Fax:* (605) 347-5120
www.kkls.net
License: Rapid City, SD held by New Rushmore Radio Inc.
Group Owner: Homeslice Media Group, L.L.C.; (acq 10-23-2006; grpsl)
Nat'l Network: Westwood One; *Nat'l Reps:* Christal; *Wire Services:* AP
Arbitron Metro Market: Rapid City, SD; *Format:* Oldies; *Target Audience:* 35-64.
Dean Kinney, General Manager

KKMK
01-01-1971; 93.9 MHz FM; *Hrs Open:* 24; 100 kw; 686 ft.; N44 2 49 W103 14 45
660 Flormann Street, Suite 100, PO Box 2480, Rapid City, SD 57709-2480 US
(609) 343-6161; *Fax:* (605) 343-9012
www.939themix.com
liagreen@newrushmoreradio.com
License: Rapid City, Pennington County, SD
Group Owner: New Rushmore Radio, Inc.
Nat'l Reps: Christal; *Wire Services:* AP
Arbitron Metro Market: Rapid City, SD; *Format:* Adult Contemp; *Target Audience:* 25-54.
Lia Green, General Manager
Micheal Goodroad, Director, Sales
Kurt Summers, Program/Music Director

KTPT
10-01-1968; 97.9 MHz FM; *Hrs Open:* 24; 100 kw; 1900 ft.; N44 19 42 W103 50 3
1853 Fountain Plaza Drive, Rapid City, SD 57702 US
(605) 342-6822; *Fax:* (605) 342-0854
www.979thepoint.com
License: Rapid City, Pennington County, SD held by Bethesda Christian Broadcasting Inc.
Group Owner: Bethesda Christian Broadcasting; (acq 6-25-96; $350,000)
Arbitron Metro Market: Rapid City, SD; *Format:* Christian
Tom Schoenstadt, General Manager
Joe Savery, Producer
John Derrek, Sales Manager
Joseph Standish, Chief Engineer

KOTA
11-01-1936; 1380 kHz AM; *Hrs Open:* 24
518 St. Joseph Street, Rapid City, SD 57701 US
(605) 342-2000; *Fax:* (605) 721-5732
www.kotaradio.com
License: Rapid City, SD held by Duhamel Broadcasting Enterprises.
Group Owner: Duhamel Broadcasting Enterprises; acq 5-54)
Nat'l Network: CBS; *Nat'l Reps:* Katz Radio; *Wire Services:* AP
Arbitron Metro Market: Rapid City, SD *TV Affiliate:* KOTA-TV affil; *Format:* News, News/Talk, 86; *Hrs. of News Programming:* news progmg 10 hrs wkly; *No. News Employees:* 2; *Target Audience:* 35 plus. *Adv.Rates:* 25; 28; 21; 17
William Duhamel, President
Les Tuttle, Station Manager

KOUT
01-01-1993; 98.7 MHz FM; *Hrs Open:* 24; 100 kw; 463 ft.; N44 4 13 W103 15 1
660 Flormann Street, Suite 100, PO Box 2480, Rapid City, SD 57709-2480 US
(605) 343-6161; *Fax:* (605) 343-9012
www.katradio.com
liagreen@newrushmoreradio.com
License: Rapid City, Pennington County, SD held by New Rushmore Radio Inc.
Group Owner: Rushmore Media Company, Inc.; (acq 10-23-2006; grpsl)
Nat'l Reps: Christal
Arbitron Metro Market: Rapid City, SD; *Format:* Country; *Target Audience:* Adults 25-54.
Lia Green, General Manager
Micheal Goodroad, Director, Sales
Mark Houston, Programming Director

KTOQ
09-26-1953; 1340 kHz AM; *Hrs Open:* 24; 1 kw-U, ND1; N44 4 6 W103 10 11
3601 Canyon Lake Dr., Rapid City, SD 57702 US
(605) 343-0888
www.espnrapidcity.com
License: Rapid City, SD held by Haugo Braodcasting Inc.
Group Owner: Haugo Broadcasting Inc.; acq 11-20-98; $1.97 million with co-located FM)
Nat'l Reps: McGavren Guild
Arbitron Metro Market: Rapid City, SD; *Format:* Sports *Special Programming:* Farm 2 hrs wkly; *Hrs. of News Programming:* news progmg 3 hrs wkly; *No. News Employees:* 2; *Target Audience:* 35 plus; upscale
Houston Haugo, CEO/COO
Christian Haugo, General Manager

KZLK
01-01-2001; 106.3 MHz FM; *Hrs Open:* 24; 92 kw; 696 ft.; N44 4 7 W103 15 2
US
(605) 721-1063
www.she1063.com
she1063@dberadio.com
License: Rapid City, Pennington County, SD held by Steven E. Duffy.
Nat'l Reps: Katz Radio; *Wire Services:* AP
Arbitron Metro Market: Rapid City, SD; *Target Audience:* Adult 25-54.; *Adv. Rates:* 25; 22; 23; 18
Les Tuttle, General Manager

KQRQ
10-01-2002; 92.3 MHz FM; *Hrs Open:* 24; 86 kw; 581 ft.; N44 4 7 W103 15 2
518 St. Joseph Street, Rapid City, SD 57701 US
(605) 342-2000; *Fax:* (605) 721-5732
www.q923radio.com
ted@dberadio.com
License: Rapid City, Pennington County, SD held by Duhamel Broadcasting Enterprises
Group Owner: Duhamel Broadcasting Enterprises
Nat'l Reps: Katz Radio; *Wire Services:* AP
Arbitron Metro Market: Rapid City, SD; *Format:* Contemporary Hits/Top 40, Adult Contemp; *Target Audience:* Adults 25-44.; *Adv. Rates:* 24; 23; 24; 18
Ted Peiffer, General Manager
Lil Anderson, General Sales Mgr
Rick Allen, Programming Director

*KQFR
08-05-2005; 89.9 MHz FM; *Hrs Open:* 24; 2.3 kw; 1844 ft.; N44 19 42 W103 50 3
290 Hegenberger Road, Oakland, CA 94621 US
(800) 543-1495
www.familyradio.com
License: Rapid City, Pennington County, SD held by Family Stations Inc.
Group Owner: Family Stations Inc.
Arbitron Metro Market: Rapid City, SD; *Format:* Christian, Religious
Harold Camping, President
Don Horton, Operations Dir

*KLMP
02-17-2005; 88.3 MHz FM; 63 kw; Ant 1,712 ft; N44 19 42 W103 50 03
1853 Fountain Plaza Dr., Rapid City, SD 57702
(605) 342-6822; *Fax:* (605) 342-0854
www.klmp.com
License: Rapid City, Pennington County, SD held by Bethesda Christian Broadcasting Inc.
Group Owner: Bethesda Christian Broadcasting
Nat'l Network: Fox News Radio
Arbitron Metro Market: Rapid City, SD; *Target Audience:* 35 plus; general
Tom Schoenstedt, General Manager
John Derrek, Sales Manager
Dave Masters, Programming Director
Joe Standish, Chief Engineer

*KASD
01-01-2006; 90.3 MHz FM; 1 kw; 407 ft.; N44 4 13 W103 15 1
Rebroadcasts: Rebroadcasts WAFR(FM) Tupelo, MS 100%
P.O. Box 3206, Tupelo, MS 38803 US
(662) 844-8888; *Fax:* (662) 842-6791
www.afr.net
faq@afa.net
License: Rapid City, Pennington County, SD held by American Family Association.
Group Owner: American Family Radio
Nat'l Network: American Family Radio

RADIO - U.S.

Arbitron Metro Market: Rapid City, SD; *Format:* Christian
Tim Wildmon, President
Donald Wildmon, Founder
Buddy Smith, Sr VP
Ed Vitagliano, Exec VP
Randy Sharp, Director Of Special Projects
Meeke Addison, Director Of Communications
Abraham Hamilton III, General Counsel

Redfield

KGIM-FM
04-07-1991; 103.7 MHz FM; *Hrs Open:* 5:30 AM-midnight; 100 kw; 554 ft.; N45 12 30 W98 40 20
3304 South Highway 281, PO Box 1930, Aberdeen, SD 57401 US
(605) 229-3632; *Fax:* (605) 229-4849
www.hubcityradio.com
info@hubcityradio.com
License: Redfield, Spink County, SD held by Armada Media - Aberdeen Inc.
Group Owner: Armada Media Corp.; (acq 10-31-2006; grpsl)
Format: Country *Special Programming:* Farm 12 hrs wkly, Religious 2 hrs wkly; *Hrs. of News Programming:* 10 hrs wkly; *No. News Employees:* 1; *Target Audience:* 25-49.
Brian Lundquist, Owner/General Manager
Daline Gellhaus, Sales Manager
Doc Sebastian, Programming/Operations Manager
Ben Root, Sports Director
Bri Matthews, News Director
Tammie Bader, Sales Manager
Brent Nathaniel, ContentDirector
Lisa Gauer, Office Manager/Traffic

KNBZ
01-01-1999; 97.7 MHz FM; 100 kw; 561 ft.; N45 12 30 W98 40 20
Mailing Address: 3304 S. Highway 281, Aberdeen, SD 57401 US
Second Address: 13541 386th Ave., Aberdeen, SD 57401
(605) 229-3632; *Fax:* (605) 229-4849
www.hubcityradio.com
info@hubcityradio.com
License: Redfield, Spink County, SD held by Prairie Winds Broadcasting, Inc.
Group Owner: Prairie Winds Broadcasting, Inc.; (acq 10-31-2006; grpsl)
Format: Adult Contemp
Brian Lundquist, Owner/General Manager
Daline Gellhaus, Sales
Doc Sebastian, Programming/Operations Manager
Ben Root, Sports Director
Bri Matthews, News Director
Brent Nathaniel, Content Director
Lisa Gauer, Office/TrafficManager

*KQKD
12-01-1962; 1380 kHz AM; *Hrs Open:* 24
290 Hegenberger Road, Oakland, CA 94621 US
(800) 543-1495
www.familyradio.com
License: Redfield, SD held by Family Stations Inc.
Group Owner: Family Stations Inc.; (acq 11-30-2004; $75,000 with KKAA(AM) Aberdeen).
Format: Christian, Religious
Harold Camping, President

Reliance

KPLO-FM
01-01-1986; 94.5 MHz FM; *Hrs Open:* 24; 95 kw; 988 ft.; N43 57 57 W99 36 11
214 W. Pleasant Drive, PO Box 1197, Pierre, SD 57501 US
(605) 224-8686; *Fax:* (605) 224-8984
www.drgnews.com
License: Reliance, Lyman County, SD held by James River Broadcasting Co.
Group Owner: Robert Ingstad Broadcast Properties; (acq 8-21-98; $98,000)
Arbitron Metro Market: Pierre, SD; *Format:* Country *Special Programming:* Farm 5 hrs wkly; *Target Audience:* 25-54.
Mark Swendsen, General Manager

*KTSD-FM
01-01-1984; 91.1 MHz FM; 100 kw; 1480 ft.; N43 57 55 W99 35 56 *Rebroadcasts:* Rebroadcasts KUSD-FM, Vermillion,SD 89.7%.
555 N. Dakota Street, PO Box 5000, Vermillion, SD 57069 US
(800) 456-0766; *Fax:* (605) 677-5010
www.sdpb.org
fritz.miller@state.sd.us
License: Reliance, Lyman County, SD held by S.D. Board of Educational Telecommunications.
Nat'l Network: PRI; NPR
Arbitron Metro Market: Reliance, SD; *Format:* Classical, Jazz, 60 *Special Programming:* Sioux one hr wkly
Fritz Miller, Director, Marketing

Roscoe

KMOM
12-11-2007; 105.5 MHz FM; *Hrs Open:* 24; 100 kw; 456 ft.; N45 27 13 W98 48 10
426 N. Highway 281, Suite 4, Aberdeen, SD 57401 US
(605) 725-5551; *Fax:* (605) 725-5553
www.dakotabroadcasting.com
joel@dakotabroadcasting.com
License: Roscoe, Edmunds County, SD held by Dakota Broadcasting LLC
Arbitron Metro Market: Roscoe, SD; *Format:* Country; *No. News Employees:* 9; *Target Audience:* 18-34, 25-54.
Neil & Terry Lipetzky, Managing Partners
Joel Swanson, General Manager
Kate Von Brook, Office Manager

Rosebud

*KOYA
88.1 MHz FM; 51 kw vert; 640 ft.; N43 13 1 W100 47 28
PO Box 430, 11 Legion Avenue, Rosebud, SD 57570 US
(605) 747-2381
www.koyaradio.wordpress.com
koyaradio@yahoo.com
License: Rosebud, Todd County, SD held by Rosebud Sioux Tribe.
Arbitron Metro Market: Rosebud, SD
Ronald Neiss, General Manager

Salem

KIKN-FM
11-04-1993; 100.5 MHz FM; *Hrs Open:* 24; 100 kw; 940 ft.; N43 29 22 W97 26 33
5100 S. Tennis Lane, Sioux Falls, SD 57108 US
(605) 361-0300; *Fax:* (605) 361-5410
www.kikn.com
don.jacobs@townsquaremedia.co³
License: Salem, McCook County, SD held by Townsquare Media Sioux Falls License LLC
Group Owner: Townsquare Media; (acq 4-1-2004; grpsl)
Nat'l Reps: Christal
Format: Country; *No. News Employees:* 1; *Target Audience:* 18-49.
Don Jacobs, General Manager
JD Collins, Brand Manager
Roger Currier, Director Of Sales
Anthony Wright, Digital Managing Editor

Sioux Falls

*KAUR
10-09-1972; 89.1 MHz FM; *Hrs Open:* 10 AM-3 AM; 0.68 kw; 184 ft.; N43 31 37 W96 44 18
1450 College Way, Worthington, MN 56187 US
(888) 363-7702
http://minnesota.publicradio.org/radio/stations/kaur
msteil@mpr.org
License: Sioux Falls, Minnehaha County, SD held by Augustana College Association.
Nat'l Network: ABC
Format: Alternative, Jazz *Special Programming:* Folk 2 hrs, world mus 6 hrs, blues 12 hrs wkly; *Target Audience:* General.
Mark Steil, Bureau Chief/Reporter
Chris Cross, Regional Network Manager
Gary Osberg, Account Executive/Site Manager
Julie LeGore, Traffic Associate

*KCFS
07-01-1985; 94.5 MHz FM; 2 kw; 197 ft.; N43 31 56 W96 44 20 US
www.usiouxfalls.edu/index.php?option=com_content&task=view&id=892&Itemid=156
kcfs@usiouxfalls.edu
License: Sioux Falls, Minnehaha County, SD held by University of Sioux Falls.
Format: Variety/Diverse *Special Programming:* Urban 6 hrs wkly

*KCSD
07-01-1985; 90.9 MHz FM; *Hrs Open:* 24; 6 kw; 262 ft.; N43 34 28 W96 39 19
555 N. Dakota Street, PO Box 5000, Vermillion, SD 57069 US
(800) 456-0766; *Fax:* (605) 677-5010
www.sdpb.org
fritz.miller@state.sd.us
License: Sioux Falls, Minnehaha County, SD held by South Dakota Board of Directors for Educational Telecommunications
Group Owner: South Dakota Public Broadcasting
Nat'l Network: NPR; *Regional Network:* S.D. Pub
Arbitron Metro Market: Sioux Falls, SD; *Format:* Talk *Special Programming:* Folk 5 hrs, jazz 10 hrs wkly; *Hrs. of News Programming:* news progmg 44 hrs wkly; *No. News Employees:* 1; *Target Audience:* 25 plus;educated males & females
Fritz Miller, Director, Marketing

KTWB
07-11-1965; 92.5 MHz FM; *Hrs Open:* 24; 100 kW; 1821 ft.; N43 31 7 W96 32 5
500 S Phillips Ave, Sioux Falls, SD 57104 USA
(605) 331-5350; *Fax:* (605) 336-0415
ktwb.com
License: Sioux Falls, Minnehaha County, SD held by Midwest Communications Inc.
Group Owner: Midwest Communications Inc.; (acq 4-2005; grpsl).
Nat'l Reps: Katz Radio
Arbitron Metro Market: Sioux Falls, SD; *Format:* Country
Tom Mitchell, Brand Manager

KKLS-FM
03-01-1975; 104.7 MHz FM; 100 kw; 981 ft.; N43 43 46 W97 5 14
5100 S. Tennis Lane, Sioux Falls, SD 57108 US
(605) 361-0300; *Fax:* (605) 361-5410
www.hot1047.com
don.jacobs@townsquaremedia.com
License: Sioux Falls, Minnehaha County, SD held by Townsquare Media Sioux Falls License LLC
Group Owner: Townsquare Media
Arbitron Metro Market: Sioux City, IA; *Format:* Contemporary Hits/Top 40; *Target Audience:* 18-49.
Don Jacobs, General Manager
Andy Erickson, Brand Manager
Roger Currier, Director Of Sales
Anthony Wright, Digital Managing Editor

KMXC
10-01-1973; 97.3 MHz FM; 100 kw; 840 ft.; N43 43 46 W97 5 10
122 S.W. Fourth Street, Rochester, MN 55901 US
(605) 339-1140; *Fax:* (605) 339-2735
www.mix97-3.com
License: Sioux Falls, Minnehaha County, SD held by Townsquare Media Sioux Falls License LLC
Group Owner: Townsquare Media
Format: Adult Contemp; *Target Audience:* 25-44; females
Lew Dickey, President
Don Jacobs, Station Manager
Scott Maguire, Programming Director

*KNWC
03-01-1961; 1270 kHz AM; *Hrs Open:* 24
3003 Snelling Ave. North, St. Paul, MN 55113 US
(877) 933-2484
www.myfaithradio.com
License: Sioux Falls, Minnehaha County, SD held by Northwestern College.
Group Owner: Northwestern College & Radio; (acq 1961).
Format: News, Religious; *Hrs. of News Programming:* news progmg 24 hrs wkly; *No. News Employees:* 1; *Target Audience:* 35-54.
David Martin, Operations Dir
Jeff Rupp, General Manager

*KNWC-FM
03-28-1969; 96.5 MHz FM; *Hrs Open:* 24; 100 kw; 1601 ft.; N43 31 7 W96 32 5
3003 Snelling Ave. North, Roseville, MN 55113 US
(877) 933-2484
www.myfaithradio.com
License: Sioux Falls, Minnehaha County, SD
Group Owner: University of Northwestern - St Paul
Format: Christian; *Hrs. of News Programming:* news progmg 24 hrs wkly; *No. News Employees:* 1; *Target Audience:* 20-54.
Tim Unsinn, Promotions Manager

KRRO
05-06-1969; 103.7 MHz FM; *Hrs Open:* 24; 38 kW; 394 ft.; N43 27 28 W96 40 14
500 S Phillips Ave, Sioux Falls, SD 57104 USA
(605) 331-5350; *Fax:* (605) 336-0415
krro.com
License: Sioux Falls, Minnehaha County, SD held by Midwest Communications Inc.

Group Owner: Midwest Communications Inc.; (acq 4-2005; grpsl).
Nat'l Reps: Katz Radio; *Wire Services:* AP
Arbitron Metro Market: Sioux Falls, SD; *Format:* Rock/AOR; *Target Audience:* 25-49; young adults, family-rearing age with disposable income
Tom Mitchell, Brand Manager

***KRSD**
05-11-1985; 88.1 MHz FM; *Hrs Open:* 24; 2 kw; 184 ft.; N43 31 37 W96 44 18
480 Cedar Street, Saint Paul, MN 55101 US
(651) 290-1500
www.mpr.org
License: Sioux Falls, Minnehaha County, SD held by Minnesota Public Radio.
Nat'l Network: NPR; PRI
Arbitron Metro Market: Sioux Falls, SD; *Format:* News; *No. News Employees:* 1; *Target Audience:* General.
David Kansas, COO
Sylvia Strobel, EVP/General Counsel

KZOY(AM)
06-13-1970; 1520 kHz AM; 500 w-D; N43 33 28 W96 47 46
3205 S Meadow Avenue, Sioux Falls, SD 57104
(605) 335-6896; *Fax:* (605) 330-0047
www.q957.com
License: Sioux Falls, Minnehaha County, SD held by Cup o' Dirt LLC
Nat'l Network: Jones Radio Networks; *Nat'l Reps:* Rgnl Reps; *Wire Services:* AP
Format: Oldies; *Target Audience:* 35-65.; *Adv. Rates:* 15; 13; 15; 13
Mark Nelson, Programming Director

KSOO
01-01-1926; 1140 kHz AM
122 S.W. Fourth Street, Rochester, MN 55901 US
(605) 339-1140; *Fax:* (605) 339-2735
www.ksoo.com
License: Sioux Falls, SD held by Townsquare Media Sioux Falls License LLC
Group Owner: Townsquare Media; (acq 3-29-2004; grpsl)
Nat'l Reps: Christal
Arbitron Metro Market: Sioux Falls, SD; *Format:* News, News/Talk, 84, Talk; *Target Audience:* 35-54.
Lew Dickey, President
Don Jacobs, Station Manager
Dave Roberts, Programming Director
Gene Hetland, News Director
Mike Langford, Chief Engineer

KELO-FM
05-05-1990; 101.9 MHz FM; *Hrs Open:* 24; 34 kW; 581 ft.; N43 45 5 W96 53 22
500 S Phillips Ave, Sioux Falls, SD 57104 USA
(605) 331-5350; *Fax:* (605) 336-0415
kelofm.com
License: Sioux Falls, Minnehaha County, SD held by Midwest Communications Inc.
Group Owner: Midwest Communications Inc.; (acq 4-2005; grpsl).
Nat'l Reps: Katz Radio; *Wire Services:* AP
Arbitron Metro Market: Sioux Falls, SD; *Format:* Adult Contemp; *Hrs. of News Programming:* news progmg 10 hrs wkly; *No. News Employees:* 1; *Target Audience:* 25-54; adult
Rob Poulin, Brand Manager

KWSN
05-06-1948; 1230 kHz AM; *Hrs Open:* 24; 0.44 kW; N43 27 28 W96 40 14
500 S Phillips Ave, Sioux Falls, SD 57104 USA
(605) 271-5873; *Fax:* (605) 336-0415
kwsn.com
License: Sioux Falls, SD held by Midwest Communications Inc.
Group Owner: Midwest Communications Inc.; .
Nat'l Network: ESPN Radio; *Nat'l Reps:* Katz Radio; *Wire Services:* AP
Arbitron Metro Market: Sioux Falls, SD; *Format:* Sports; *Hrs. of News Programming:* news progmg 27 hrs wkly; *No. News Employees:* 2; *Target Audience:* 25-54; adults with disposable income, business leaders
Craig Mattick, Brand Manager

KXRB
02-01-1969; 1000 kHz AM; *Hrs Open:* 24
122 S.W. Fourth Street, Rochester, MN 55901 US
(605) 361-0300; *Fax:* (605) 361-5410
www.kxrb.com
don.jacobs@townsquaremedia.com
License: Sioux Falls, SD held by Townsquare Media Sioux Falls License LLC
Group Owner: Townsquare Media; (acq 3-29-2004; grpsl)
Nat'l Network: CNN Radio; *Nat'l Reps:* Christal; *Wire Services:* UPI
Arbitron Metro Market: Sioux Falls, SD; *Format:* Country; *Hrs. of News Programming:* news progmg 5 hrs wkly; *No. News Employees:* 1; *Target Audience:* 25-54.
Lew Dickey, President
Don Jacobs, General Manager
Randy McDaniel, Programming Director
Jerry Dohmen, News Director
Mike Langford, Chief Engineer
Rick Flink, Director of Sales
Randy McDaniel, Brand Manager

***KSFS**
01-01-2006; 90.1 MHz FM; 18 kw; 112 ft.; N43 32 41 W96 45 45
P O Drawer 2440, Tupelo, MS 38803 US
(800) 877-5600; *Fax:* (916) 251-1650
www.klove.com
License: Sioux Falls, Minnehaha County, SD held by Educational Media Foundation.
Group Owner: EMF Broadcasting; (acq 1-30-2009; $650,000)
Nat'l Network: K-Love
Arbitron Metro Market: Odessa-Midland, TX; *Format:* Christian
Mike Novak, President

KELO-AM
1320 kHz AM; *Hrs Open:* 24; 5 kW-D, 5 kW-N; N43 29 17 W96 38 14
500 S Phillips Ave, Sioux Falls, SD 57104 USA
(605) 331-5350; *Fax:* (605) 336-0415
kelo.com
License: Sioux Falls, Minnehaha County, SD held by Midwest Communications Inc.
Group Owner: Midwest Communications Inc.; (acq 4-2005; grpsl).
Arbitron Metro Market: Sioux Falls, SD; *Format:* News/Talk
Greg Belfrage, Brand Manager

Sisseton

KBWS-FM
12-28-1983; 102.9 MHz FM; 100 kw; 459 ft.; N45 36 52 W97 24 51
Box 1005, Milbank, SD 57252 US
(605) 432-5516
kbwsstudio@venturecomm.net
License: Sisseton, Roberts County, SD held by Armada Media-Watertown Inc.
Group Owner: Armada Media Corp.; (acq 8-3-2007; grpsl)
Arbitron Metro Market: Milbank, SD; *Format:* Country; *Target Audience:* General.
Jeff Kurtz, General Manager
Joan Lien, Sales Manager
Mike Rikker, Program/Sports Director

Spearfish

***KBHU-FM**
10-18-1974; 89.1 MHz FM; *Hrs Open:* 24; 0.1 kw horiz; -348 ft.; N44 29 48 W103 52 13 *Rebroadcasts:* KJKT-FM
US
(605) 642-6389; *Fax:* (605) 642-6265
www.bhsumedia.com
thebuzzfm@gmail.com
License: Spearfish, Lawrence County, SD held by Black Hills State University.
Arbitron Metro Market: Spearfish, SD *TV Affiliate:* KBHU-TV; *Format:* Alternative; *Hrs. of News Programming:* News progmg 3 hrs wkly; *Target Audience:* 12-35.
Dr. Scott Clark, Faculty Advisor
Hannah Kloiber, Station Manager
Scott Lemon, Music Director
Sam Torok, Production Director
Evan Bruce, Webmaster
Andy Black, Public Relations

KDDX
07-19-1985; 101.1 MHz FM; *Hrs Open:* 24; 100 kw; 1788 ft.; N44 19 35 W103 50 6
Mailing Address: 2827 East Colorado Boulevard, Spearfish, SD 57783 US
Second Address: Box 1760, Rapid City, SD 57709
(605) 642-5747; *Fax:* (605) 642-7849
www.xrock.fm
ted@dberadio.com
License: Spearfish, Lawrence County, SD held by Duhamel Broadcasting Enterprises.
Group Owner: Duhamel Broadcasting Enterprises; acq 3-16-92; $525,000;
Arbitron Metro Market: Rapid City, SD; *Format:* Rock/AOR; *Hrs. of News Programming:* news progmg 3 hrs wkly; *No. News Employees:* 1; *Target Audience:* 18-49.; *Adv. Rates:* 25; 23; 25; 19
Ted Peiffer, General Manager
Lil Anderson, Sales Manager
Jim Kallas, Programming Director

KSLT
02-17-1984; 107.1 MHz FM; *Hrs Open:* 24; 100 kw; 1,702 ft; N44 19 36 W103 50 12
1853 Fountain Plaza Dr., Rapid City, SD 57702
(605) 342-6822; *Fax:* (605) 342-0854
www.kslt.com
License: Spearfish, Lawrence County, SD held by Bethesda Christian Broadcasting Inc.
Group Owner: Bethesda Christian Broadcasting
Nat'l Network: Fox News Radio
Arbitron Metro Market: Rapid City, SD; *Target Audience:* 25-49; affluent, educated, 60% female, 40% male
Tom Schoenstadt, General Manager
John Derrek, Sales Manager
Dave Masters, Program/Music Director
Joe Standish, Chief Engineer
Tracy Kaltvedt, Office Manager
Jamie Knapp, Music Director

***KJKT**
04-11-2009; 90.7 MHz FM; 0.7 kw; 1644 ft.; N44 19 42 W103 50 3 *Rebroadcasts:* Simulcasts KBHU(FM) Spearfish 100%
US
(605) 642-6389; *Fax:* (605) 642-6265
www.bhsumedia.com
thebuzzfm@gmail.com
License: Spearfish, Lawrence County, SD held by Black Hills State University
Arbitron Metro Market: Spearfish, SD
Dr. Scott Clark, Faculty Advisor
Hannah Kloiber, Station Manager
Scott Lemon, Music Director
Sam Torok, Production Director
Evan Bruce, Webmaster
Andy Black, Public Relations

Sturgis

KBHB
09-27-1962; 810 kHz AM; *Hrs Open:* Sunrise-sunset
1612 Junction Avenue, Suite 1, Sturgis, SD 57785 US
(605) 347-4455
www.kbhbradio.com
info@kbhbradio.com
License: Sturgis, SD held by New Rushmore Radio Inc.
Group Owner: Schurz Communications Inc.; (acq 10-23-2006; grpsl)
Nat'l Network: ABC; *Regional Network:* Agrinet
Arbitron Metro Market: Sturgis, SD; *Format:* Agriculture *Special Programming:* American Indian one hr, gospel 3 hrs wkly; *Hrs. of News Programming:* news progmg 17 hrs wkly; *No. News Employees:* 1 *TargetAudience:* 35 plus.; *Adv. Rates:* 16; 16; 16; na
Toni Kinney, Operations Dir
Dean Kinney, General Manager
Gary Matthews, Programming Director
Gary Maki, News Director
Gary Peterson, Chief Engineer

KRCS
12-05-1972; 93.1 MHz FM; 97.8 kw; 1060 ft.; N44 19 58 W103 32 20
660 Flormann Street, Suite 100, PO Box 2480, Rapid City, SD 57709-2480 US
(605) 343-6161; *Fax:* (605) 343-9012
www.hot931.com
License: Sturgis, Meade County, SD held by New Rushmore Radio Inc.
Group Owner: Schurz Communications Inc.
Arbitron Metro Market: Rapid City, SD; *Format:* Contemporary Hits/Top 40
Lia Green, General Manager
Micheal Goodroad, Director, Sales
Jay Davis, Programming Director
Gary Peterson, Chief Engineer

Tulare

***KAMF**
91.7 MHz FM; kw
US
(605) 868-0525
License: Tulare, Spink County, SD held by Church Planters of America.
Arbitron Metro Market: Tulare, SD
Danny Hawkins, President

Vermillion

***KAOR**
09-01-1986; 91.1 MHz FM; *Hrs Open:* 18; 120 w; 107 ft; N42 47 01 W96 55 26
555 Dakota Street, Vermillion, SD 57069
(605) 677-5477; *Fax:* (605) 677-4250
www.usd.edu
License: Vermillion, Clay County, SD held by The University of South Dakota.
Population Served: 35,000 *Special Programming:* American Indian 2 hrs wkly; *Hrs. of News Programming:* News progmg 2 hrs wkly; *Target Audience:* 16-30; college age students & the Vermillion Community

KVTK
11-16-1967; 1570 kHz AM; *Hrs Open:* 24; 0.5 kw-D, ND1; 0.071 kw-N, ND1; N42 47 32 W97 0 3
210 West 3rd Street, Yankton, SD 57078 US
(605) 665-2600; *Fax:* (605) 664-4487
www.kvtk.com
john@kvht.com
License: Vermillion, SD held by 5 Star Communications
Nat'l Network: ESPN Radio; Westwood One
Format: Sports; *Hrs. of News Programming:* news progmg 20 hrs wkly; *No. News Employees:* 1; *Target Audience:* 25-54; general; *Adv. Rates:* 21.50; 19.50; 15.25; 12
John Thayer, Programming/Sports

***KUSD**
10-01-1967; 89.7 MHz FM; 32 kw; 663 ft.; N43 3 0 W96 47 12
555 N. Dakota Street, PO Box 5000, Vermillion, SD 57069 US
(800) 456-0766; *Fax:* (605) 677-5010
www.sdpb.org
fritz.miller@state.sd.us
License: Vermillion, Clay County, SD held by South Dakota Board of Directors/Educational Telecommunications.
Nat'l Network: NPR; PRI; *Regional Network:* S.D. Pub
Arbitron Metro Market: Vermillion, SD *TV Affiliate:* *KUSD-TV affil.; *Format:* Classical, Jazz, 60 *Special Programming:* Sioux one hr wkly
Fritz Miller, Director, Marketing

KVHT
11-16-1967; 106.3 MHz FM; *Hrs Open:* 24; 50 kw; 390 ft.; N42 59 45 W96 49 25
210 W. Third Street, Yankton, SD 57078 US
(605) 665-2600; *Fax:* (605) 665-8875
www.kvht.com
License: Vermillion, Clay County, SD held by 5 Star Communications
Nat'l Network: ABC; *Wire Services:* AP
Format: Oldies; *Hrs. of News Programming:* news progmg 42 hrs wkly; *No. News Employees:* 1; *Target Audience:* 25-64.; *Adv. Rates:* 19.50; 19.50; 19.50; 15.25
Jeff Fuller, President, 5 Star Communications
Simon Fuller, Co-Owner/Sales Manager
Karlee Fuller, Office Manager
Randy Hammer, Sales
Dave Gullikson, Sales
Suzann Wiest, Sales

Volga

KJJQ
05-06-1981; 910 kHz AM; *Hrs Open:* 24; 0.5 kw-D, DA2; 0.5 kw-N, DA2; N44 15 1 W96 57 22
227 22nd Ave. S., Brookings, SD 57006 US
(605) 692-1430; *Fax:* (605) 692-6434
info@brookingsradio.com
License: Volga, SD held by Digity 3E License, LLC
Group Owner: Digity, LLC
Nat'l Network: ESPN Radio
Format: Agriculture; *Target Audience:* 25-54
Cami Powers, General Manager
Kelli Hanson, General Sales Mgr

KKQQ
04-15-1984; 102.3 MHz FM; 25 kw; 243 ft.; N44 15 1 W96 57 22
227 22nd Ave. S., Studio 1B, Brookings, SD 57006 US
(605) 692-9125; *Fax:* (605) 692-6434
www.kcountry102.com
License: Volga, Brookings County, SD held by Digity 3E License, LLC
Group Owner: Digity, LLC; (acq 7-1-2004; grpsl)
Arbitron Metro Market: Sioux City, IA; *Format:* Country; *Target Audience:* 18-54.
Cami Powers, General Manager
Kelli Hanson, General Sales Mgr

Wall

KXZS
107.5 MHz FM; 8.4 kw horiz; 246 ft.; N43 56 9 W102 8 29 US
(859) 879-0818
License: Wall, Pennington County, SD held by JER Licenses LLC.
Group Owner: JER Licenses LLC
Arbitron Metro Market: Wall, SD
Jon Robinson, General Manager

Watertown

KDLO-FM
03-01-1968; 96.9 MHz FM; *Hrs Open:* 24; 100 kw; 1572 ft.; N44 57 57 W97 35 22
PO Box 950, Watertown, SD 57201 US
(605) 886-8444; *Fax:* (605) 886-9306
www.kdlocountry.com
john@kdlocountry.com
License: Watertown, Codington County, SD held by Digity 3E License, LLC
Group Owner: Digity, LLC
Nat'l Network: USA
Arbitron Metro Market: Watertown, SD; *Format:* Country; *No. News Employees:* 1; *Target Audience:* 25-54.
Bruce Erlandson, Operations Dir
Dean Johnson, General Manager

KIXX
09-29-1968; 96.1 MHz FM; *Hrs Open:* 6 AM-1 AM; 97 kw; 978 ft.; N45 10 31 W96 59 15
921 9th Ave. SE., Watertown, SD 57201 US
(605) 886-8444; *Fax:* (605) 886-9306
www.gowatertown.net
License: Watertown, Codington County, SD held by Digity 3E License, LLC
Group Owner: Digity, LLC
Format: Adult Contemp; *Target Audience:* 25-54.
Brenda Rorvick, General Manager

KSDR
01-01-1976; 1480 kHz AM; 1 kw-D, ND2; 0.05 kw-N, ND2; N44 55 58 W97 6 19
921 9th Ave. SE, Watertown, SD 57201 US
(605) 886-8444; *Fax:* (605) 886-9306
www.gowatertown.net
brorvick@digity.me
License: Watertown, SD held by Digity 3E License, LLC
Group Owner: Digity, LLC
Arbitron Metro Market: Watertown, SD; *Format:* Talk; *Hrs. of News Programming:* news progmg 15 hrs wkly; *No. News Employees:* 3; *Target Audience:* 25-54.
Brenda Rorvick, General Manager

KSDR-FM
03-10-1992; 92.9 MHz FM; *Hrs Open:* 24; 97 kw; 978 ft.; N45 10 31 W96 59 15
921 9th Ave. SE., Watertown, SD 57201 US
(605) 886-8444; *Fax:* (605) 886-9306
www.gowatertown.net
brorvick@digity.me
License: Watertown, Codington County, SD held by Digity 3E License, LLC
Group Owner: Digity, LLC
Regional Network: Tribune Radio Networks
Arbitron Metro Market: Watertown, SD; *Format:* Country; *No. News Employees:* 1; *Target Audience:* General; rgnl country stn with wide var of ages
Brenda Rorvick, General Manager

KWAT
03-08-1940; 950 kHz AM; 1 kw-D, DAN; 1 kw-N, DAN; N44 52 12 W97 6 49
921 9th Ave. SE., Watertown, SD 57201 US
(605) 886-8444; *Fax:* (605) 886-9306
www.gowatertown.net
brorvick@digity.me
License: Watertown, SD held by Digity 3E License, LLC
Group Owner: Digity, LLC
Nat'l Network: CBS
Arbitron Metro Market: Watertown, SD; *Format:* News/Talk
Brenda Rorvick, General Manager

***KPGT**
08-01-2000; 89.1 MHz FM; *Hrs Open:* 24; 200 w vert; Ant 20 ft; N44 53 57 W97 06 18
PO Box 83, Watertown, SD 57201
(605) 753-8910
www.thetruthfm.com
License: Watertown, Codington County, SD held by Church Planters of America
Population Served: 4,523; *Arbitron Metro Market:* Germantown, NC
Sheila Hawkins, Operations Dir
Danny Hawkins, General Manager

Wessington Springs

KJRV
01-01-2005; 93.3 MHz FM; 65 kw; 623 ft.; N44 11 39 W98 19 5
1726 Dakota Ave. South, Huron, SD 57305 US
(605) 352-8623; *Fax:* (605) 352-0911
www.bigjimrocks.com
mlyon@kokk.com
License: Wessington Springs, Jerauld County, SD held by Alpena Broadcasting Co.
Group Owner: Dakota Communications Ltd.
Format: Classic Rock
D.K. Osier, Sales/Promotions
Shawn Martin, Sales/Promotions
Kelly Sharp, Sales/Promotions
Mike Lyon, Sales/Promotions

Winner

KWYR
09-27-1957; 1260 kHz AM; *Hrs Open:* 24; 5 kw-D, ND1; 0.146 kw-N, ND1; N43 22 57 W99 54 38
PO Box 491, Winner, SD 57580 US
www.kwyr.com
kwyroffice@gwtc.net
License: Winner, SD held by Midwest Radio Corp.
Wire Services: AP
Arbitron Metro Market: Winner, SD; *Format:* Country; *Hrs. of News Programming:* news progmg 14 hrs wkly; *No. News Employees:* 1; *Target Audience:* 25-60.; *Adv. Rates:* 12; 8; 8; 8
Scott Schramm, General Manager
John Driscoll, Sales Manager
Darnell Novotny, Office Manager and Accounting

KWYR-FM
11-25-1971; 93.7 MHz FM; *Hrs Open:* 24; 100 kw; 561 ft.; N43 17 46 W99 52 2
PO Box 491, Winner, SD 57580 US
www.kwyr.com
kwyroffice@gwtc.net
License: Winner, Tripp County, SD held by Midwest Radio Corp.
Nat'l Network: Jones Radio Networks; *Wire Services:* AP
Arbitron Metro Market: Winner, SD; *Format:* Adult Contemp; *Target Audience:* 18-45.
Scott Schramm, General Manager
John Driscoll, Sales Manager
Darnell Novotny, Office Manager and Accounting

Yankton

WNAX-FM
08-09-1973; 104.1 MHz FM; *Hrs Open:* 24; 97 kw; 981 ft.; N42 38 24 W97 3 21
1609 Easy Highway 50, Yankton, SD 57078 US
(605) 665-7442; *Fax:* (605) 665-8788
www.wnax.com
bholst@wnax.com
License: Yankton, Yankton County, SD held by Saga Communications Inc.
Wire Services: NOAA Weather
Arbitron Metro Market: Sioux City, IA; *Format:* Country; *Hrs. of News Programming:* news progmg 3 hrs wkly; *No. News Employees:* 1; *Target Audience:* 25-54.
Steve Crawford, Operations Manager
Bill Holst, General Manager
Steve Imming, Sports Director
Dee Davis, Community Relations
Lee Kurtz, Sales
Jerry Oster, News Director
Michelle Rook, Farm Director
Lou Kastler, ProductionManager
Eric Roozen, FM Brand Manager

KKYA
05-25-1982; 93.1 MHz FM; *Hrs Open:* 24; 100 kw; 469 ft.; N42 43 49 W97 24 13
202 West 2nd Street, Yankton, SD 57078 US
(605) 665-7892; *Fax:* (605) 665-0818
www.kk93.com
License: Yankton, Yankton County, SD
Group Owner: Sorenson Broadcasting Corp.
Regional Network: Waitt Farm Net.
Arbitron Metro Market: Sioux City, IA; *Format:* Country; *Hrs. of News Programming:* news progmg 1.5 hrs wkly; *No. News Employees:* 2; *Adv. Rates:* 15; 15; 15; 10

Dave Lesher, Operations Dir
Curt Dykstra, General Manager
Cynthia Miller, General Sales Mgr
David Leonard, News Director
Tammy Hauger, Traffic Manager
Doyle Becker, Co-Owner
Carolyn Becker, Co-Owner

KYNT
03-15-1955; 1450 kHz AM; *Hrs Open:* 24; 1 kw-U, ND1; N42 53 30 W97 25 10
202 W. 2nd Street, Yankton, SD 57078 US
(605) 665-7892; *Fax:* (605) 665-0818
www.kynt1450.com
License: Yankton, SD held by Sorenson Broadcasting Corp.
Group Owner: Sorenson Broadcasting Corp.; (acq 7-1-73)
Nat'l Network: ABC; *Regional Network:* Waitt Farm Net.
Arbitron Metro Market: Yankton, SD; *Format:* Adult Contemp *Special Programming:* Farm 5 hrs, polka one hr, Pol one hr wkly; *Hrs. of News Programming:* news progmg 25 hrs wkly; *No. News Employees:* 2 *TargetAudience:* General.; *Adv. Rates:* 12; 12; 12; 8
Dave Lesher, Operations Dir
Curt Dykstra, General Manager
Cynthia Miller, General Sales Mgr
Dave Leonard, News Director

WNAX
11-01-1922; 570 kHz AM; *Hrs Open:* 24; 5 kw-D, DAN; 5 kw-N, DAN; N42 54 47 W97 18 58
1609 Easy Highway 50, Yankton, SD 57078 US
(605) 665-7442; *Fax:* (605) 665-8788
www.wnax.com
bholst@wnax.com
License: Yankton, SD held by Saga Communications Inc.
Nat'l Network: CBS; *Regional Network:* MNN; *Nat'l Reps:* Katz Radio; *Wire Services:* NOAA Weather; Knight-Ridder/Tribune Information S
Arbitron Metro Market: Sioux City, IA; *Format:* News, News/Talk, 86 *Special Programming:* Relg 16 hrs, sports 10 hrs, weather 15 hrs, farm n; *Hrs. of News Programming:* news progmg 23 hrs wkly *No. News Employees:* 4; *Target Audience:* 35 plus; farmers & agri-businesses
Steve Crawford, Operations Dir
Bill Holst, General Manager
Jim Reimler, AM Brand Manager
Lou Kastler, Production Manager
Jerry Oster, News Director
Michelle Rook, Farm Director
Steve Imming, Sports Director
Dee Davis, CommunityRelations

Tennessee

Alamo

WWGM
08-10-1989; 93.1 MHz FM; *Hrs Open:* 24; 14 kw; 443 ft.; N35 43 28 W89 3 35
Mailing Address: 319 Vann Drive, Suite E #32, Jackson, TN 38305 US
Second Address: 7713 Highway 412 South, Bells, TN 38006
(731) 663-2327; *Fax:* (731) 663-2427
www.gracebroadcasting.com
lennis@gracebroadcasting.com
License: Alamo, Crockett County, TN held by Grace Broadcasting Services Inc.
Group Owner: Grace Broadcasting Services Inc.; (acq 8-18-97; $800,000).
Arbitron Metro Market: Jackson, TN; *Format:* Christian, Gospel; *Hrs. of News Programming:* news progmg 3 hrs wkly; *No. News Employees:* 1; *Target Audience:* 24-54; upscale women; *Adv. Rates:* 16; 16; 16; 8
Lacy Ennis, President & CEO
John Blankenship, Operations/Production Manager
Rodney Minyard Sr., General Manager
Geraldine Minyard, Secretary/Programming
Phillip Chambers, Sales Representative
Ivan Hodge, Sales Representative

Alcoa

WBCR
08-25-1957; 1470 kHz AM; 0.956 kw-D, ND1; 0.082 kw-N, ND1; N35 45 8 W83 55 4
P.O. Box 130, Alcoa, TN 37701 US
(865) 984-1470; *Fax:* (865) 983-0890
www.truthradio.tv
License: Alcoa, TN held by Blount County Broadcasting Co.
Arbitron Metro Market: Farmington NM

Carl Auel, CEO
Fred Hodges, General Manager

Algood

WATX
10-05-1981; 1600 kHz AM; *Hrs Open:* 6 AM-9 PM
259 S. Willow Avenue, Cookeville, TN 38501 US
(931) 528-6064; *Fax:* (931)520-1590
www.cookevillesnewstalk.com
License: Algood, TN held by JWC Broadcasting
Group Owner: JWC Broadcasting; acq 8-3-01).
Nat'l Network: Salem Radio Network; *Nat'l Reps:* Rgnl Reps
Arbitron Metro Market: Cookeville, TN; *Format:* Christian *Special Programming:* Gospel; *Hrs. of News Programming:* news progmg 34 hrs wkly; *No. News Employees:* 2; *Target Audience:* General. *Adv. Rates:* 12;10;10;8
Jim Stapleton, General Manager

Arlington

WEGR
03-01-1967; 102.7 MHz FM; *Hrs Open:* 24; 100 kw; 942 ft.; N35 16 33 W89 46 38
2650 Thousand Oaks Blvd., Suite 4100, Memphis, TN 38118 US
(901) 259-1300; *Fax:* (901) 259-6456
www.rock103.com
License: Arlington, Shelby County, TN held by CC Licenses LLC
Group Owner: iHeartMedia
Nat'l Reps: Clear Channel
Arbitron Metro Market: Memphis, TN *TV Affiliate:* WPTY-TV, WLMT(TV) affils; *Format:* Classic Rock *Special Programming:* Rockline, flashback, blues show; *Hrs. of News Programming:* news progmg 15 hrs wkly *No. NewsEmployees:* 1; *Target Audience:* 25-54; 25-34 core audience-70% male, 30% female
Morgan Bohannon, Regional Market President

Ashland City

WJNA
07-14-1982; 790 kHz AM
6600 North Andrews Avenue, Suite 160, Fort Lauderdale, FL 33309 US
(954) 315-1515
License: Ashland City, TN held by Sycamore Valley Broadcasting Inc.
Nat'l Network: ABC; *Regional Network:* Tenn. Radio Net.
Arbitron Metro Market: Nashville, TN; *Format:* Variety/Diverse; *No. News Employees:* 4; *Target Audience:* General.; *Adv. Rates:* 7; 7; 7; 7

Athens

WJSQ
12-01-1979; 101.7 MHz FM; *Hrs Open:* 24; 7.5 kw; 528 ft.; N35 31 19 W84 27 29
2110 Oxnard Road, PO Box 986, Athens, TN 37371-0986 US
(423) 745-1000; *Fax:* (423) 745-2000
www.wjsqwlar.com
License: Athens, McMinn County, TN
Format: Country
Kenneth Morris, Promotions Director
Mary Coffman, Office Manager
Bill Hughes, Production/Sales
Karen Webb, Account Executive

WLAR
05-15-1946; 1450 kHz AM; *Hrs Open:* 24; 1 kw-U, ND1; N35 26 44 W84 36 43
2110 Oxnard Road, PO Box 986, Athens, TN 37371-0986 US
(423) 745-1000; *Fax:* (423) 745-2000
www.wjsqwlar.com
License: Athens, TN held by James C. Sliger.
Format: Country *Special Programming:* Farm 2 hrs wkly
Kenneth Morris, Promotions Director
Mary Coffman, Office Manager
Bill Hughes, Production/Sales
Karen Webb, Account Executive

WYXI
10-05-1966; 1390 kHz AM; *Hrs Open:* 6 AM-7 PM; 2.5 kw-D, ND2; 0.062 kw-N, ND2; N35 26 48 W84 34 19
104 Cherry Street, Athens, TN 37303 US
wyxi.com
wyxi@bellsouth.net
License: Athens, TN held by Cornerstone Broadcasting Inc.
Nat'l Network: ABC *Regional Reps:* Rgnl Reps
Arbitron Metro Market: Athens, TN; *Format:* Talk *Special Programming:* Black one hr, relg 8 hrs wkly; *Hrs. of News Programming:* news progmg 10 hrs wkly; *No. News Employees:* 1; *Target Audience:* 25-64; maturemiddle class; *Adv. Rates:* 8.82; 8.82; 8.82; na

Mark Lefler, President
Bob Ketchersid, Operations Dir

Atwood

WTKB-FM
01-01-1992; 93.7 MHz FM; *Hrs Open:* 24; 15 kw; 325 ft.; N35 57 25 W88 41 44
P.O. Box 565, Milan, TN 38358 US
(731) 633-2327; *Fax:* (731) 633-2427
www.gracebroadcasting.com
lennis931@aol.com
License: Atwood, Carroll County, TN held by Solid Rock Broadcasting LLC
Arbitron Metro Market: Atwood, TN; *Format:* Christian, Gospel
John Blankenship, Operations Dir
Rodney Minyard Sr., General Manager
Geraldine Minyard, Programming Director
Phillip Chambers, Sales Representative
Ivan Hodge, Sales Representative

Bartlett

WMPS
08-19-1986; 1210 kHz AM; *Hrs Open:* 24; 10 kw-D, DA2; 0.25 kw-N, DA2; N35 15 40 W89 49 50
6080 Mt. Moriah Road Extended, Memphis, TN 38115 US
(901) 375-9324; *Fax:* (901) 375-5889
www.sunny1210.com
License: Bartlett, TN held by Arlington Broadcasting Co. Inc.
Regional Network: Tenn. Radio Net.
Arbitron Metro Market: Memphis, TN; *Format:* Contemporary Hits/Top 40 *Special Programming:* Relg progmg 7 hrs wkly; *Target Audience:* 25 plus.
Fred Flinn, President
Shea Flinn, General Manager

WMFS-FM
05-01-1994; 92.9 MHz FM; *Hrs Open:* 24; 6 kw; 328 ft; N35 10 20 W89 56 40
1835 Moriah Woods Blvd., Bldg. 1, Memphis, TN 38117
(901) 384-5900; *Fax:* (901) 767-6076
www.espn929.com
License: Bartlett, Shelby County, TN held by Entercom Memphis License LLC.
Group Owner: Entercom Communications Corp.; (acq 11-30-2007; grpsl)
Nat'l Reps: Interep; *Wire Services:* Metro Weather Servic
Population Served: 1,000,000; *Arbitron Metro Market:* Memphis, TN; *Format:* Sports; *Hrs. of News Programming:* News progmg one hr wkly; *Target Audience:* 18-49; adults

***WKVF**
11-01-1994; 94.9 MHz FM; *Hrs Open:* 24; 1.6 kw; 948 ft.; N35 9 16 W89 49 20
5141 Fire Tower Road, Franklin, TN 37064 US
(916) 251-1600; *Fax:* (916) 251-1650
www.klove.com
klove@klove.com
License: Bartlett, Marshall County, TN held by Educational Media Foundation.
Group Owner: EMF Broadcasting; (acq 2-1-00; $1.4 million).
Nat'l Network: K-Love
Arbitron Metro Market: Bartlett, TN; *Format:* Christian; *No. News Employees:* 3; *Target Audience:* 25-44; Judeo Christian, female
Mike Novak, President
Chip Bailey, Operations Dir
Eric Allen, General Sales Mgr
David Pierce, Programming Director
Tracy Butler, News Director
Sam Wallington, Engineering Dir
Scott Smith, Music Director
Richard Hunt, NewsReporter
Marya Morgan, News Reporter

Baxter

WBXE
10-01-1995; 93.7 MHz FM; *Hrs Open:* 24; 6.1 kw; 659 ft.; N36 11 3 W85 24 40
259 S. Willow Avenue, Cookeville, TN 38501 US
(931) 528-6064; *Fax:* (931) 520-1590
www.rock937online.com
License: Baxter, Putnam County, TN held by JWC Broadcasting
Group Owner: JWC Broadcasting; acq 8-29-01).
Nat'l Network: Westwood One; *Nat'l Reps:* Rgnl Reps
Arbitron Metro Market: Cookeville, TN; *No. News Employees:* 1; *Target Audience:* 18-45; Men 25 plus; *Adv. Rates:* 32; 30; 28; 24
Jim Stapleton, General Manager

Belle Meade

WLVU
01-01-2008; 97.1 MHz FM; 44.37 kw; 517 ft.; N36 17 50 W86 45 11 *Rebroadcasts:* Rebroadcasts KLVR(FM) Middletown, CA 100%
5700 West Oaks Boulevard, Rocklin, CA 95765 US
(916) 251-1600; *Fax:* (916) 251-1650
www.klove.com
License: Belle Meade, Dauphin County, TN held by Educational Media Foundation.
Group Owner: EMF Broadcasting; (acq 4-16-2013; exchange for WABD(FM) Mobile, AL)
Nat'l Network: K-Love
Arbitron Metro Market: Torrington, WY; *Format:* Christian
Mike Novak, President

Bellevue

WHPY-FM
10-01-1974; 94.5 MHz FM; *Hrs Open:* 24; 22 kw; Ant 715 ft; N35 45 56 W87 49 50
49 Music Square West, Suite 300, Nashville, TN 37203
(877) 393-1555
www.hippieradio945.com
License: Bellevue, Dickson County, TN held by Kensington Digital Media L.L.C.
Population Served: 590,807; *Arbitron Metro Market:* Nashville, TN; *Format:* Christian; *Hrs. of News Programming:* news progmg 14 hrs wkly; *No. News Employees:* 1; *Target Audience:* 18-54; mid to upper incomeadults with purchasing power; *Adv. Rates:* 132; 132; 132; 132
Barb Deniston, General Manager

Benton

WBIN
05-18-1977; 1540 kHz AM; *Hrs Open:* Sunrise-sunset
108 Lifestyle Way, Benton, TN 37307 US
(423) 338-2864; *Fax:* (423) 338-9180
License: Benton, TN held by John A. Sines and L. Jane Sines, JTWROS
Regional Network: ABN Radio
Arbitron Metro Market: Collegedale, TN; *Format:* Religious; *Target Audience:* All ages; Includes baby boomers and seniors
John A. Sines, Owner
L. Jane Sines, Owner

WSAA
11-01-1996; 93.1 MHz FM; 3.5 kw; 437 ft.; N35 9 54 W84 51 13
PO Box 2118, Omaha, NE 68103-2118 US
(888) 937-2471
http://www.air1.com/
License: Benton, Polk County, TN held by LB Radio of Chattanooga, LLC
TV Affiliate: Relg; *Format:* Sports, Talk; *No. News Employees:* 25-54.; *Target Audience:* Darrell Chambliss; *Adv. Rates:* 35; 20; 25; 15
Darrell Chambliss, Chairman
Mike Novak, President/CEO
David Pierce, CCO
Alan Mason, COO
Eric Moser, CFO
D. Kevin Blair, General Counsel/Secretary

***WTSE**
01-01-2005; 91.1 MHz FM; 8.5 kw vert; 466 ft.; N35 19 25 W84 17 54
P.O. Box J, Twin Falls, ID 83303 US
(888) 533-3551
www.freedomradiofm.com
connect@freedomradiofm.com
License: Benton, Polk County, TN held by Radio Assist Ministry Inc.
Arbitron Metro Market: Benton, TN

Berry Hill

WVOL
12-01-1951; 1470 kHz AM; *Hrs Open:* 24; 5 kw-D, DA2; 1 kw-N, DA2; N36 12 1 W86 46 47
1320 Brick Church Pike, Nashville, TN 37207 US
(615) 226-9510; *Fax:* (615) 226-0709
www.wvol1470.com
License: Berry Hill, TN held by Heidelberg Broadcasting LLC.
Arbitron Metro Market: Nashville, TN; *Format:* Blues, Oldies
Special Programming: Gospel 6 hrs wkly; *Target Audience:* 25-54; relg
John Heidelberg, Chairman
Roderick Heidelberg, Operations Dir
Betty Fykes, News Director
Watt Harriston, Chief Engineer

Blountville

WXSM
09-20-1967; 640 kHz AM; *Hrs Open:* 24; 10 kw-D, DAN; 0.81 kw-N, DAN; N36 31 19 W82 25 25
Mailing Address: 162 Free Hill Rd., Gray, TN 37615 US
Second Address: , Gray, TN 37615
(423) 477-1000
www.640wxsm.com
bill.meade@cumulus.com
License: Blountville, TN held by Radio License Holding CBC, LLC
Group Owner: Cumulus Media Inc.; (acq 5-30-2000; grpsl)
Nat'l Network: ESPN Radio; *Nat'l Reps:* Dora-Clayton
Arbitron Metro Market: Johnson City-Kingsport-Bristol, TN-VA; *Format:* Sports
Paul Overbay, General Sales Mgr
Bill Meade, Programming Director

Bluff City

WFHG-FM
12-10-1966; 92.9 MHz FM; *Hrs Open:* 24; 7.6 kw; 1240 ft.; N36 16 10 W82 20 17
Mailing Address: P.O. Box 1389, Bristol, VA 24203 US
Second Address: 901 East Valley Drive, Bristol, VA 24201
(276) 669-8112
www.supertalkwfhg.com
comments@supertalkwfhg.com
License: Bluff City, Washington County, TN held by Bristol Broadcasting Co. Inc.
Group Owner: Bristol Broadcasting Co. Inc.; acq 11-30-99; with co-located AM).
Arbitron Metro Market: Excelsior Springs MO; *Format:* Christian
Mike MacIntosh, President

Bolivar

WBOL
10-19-1962; 1560 kHz AM; 0.25 kw-D, NDD; N35 15 30 W88 58 50
123 West Market Street, Bolivar, TN 38008 US
(731) 658-3690; *Fax:* (731) 658-3408
License: Bolivar, TN held by Shaw's Broadcasting Co.
Format: Blues, Jazz, 64
Johnny Shaw, General Manager
Dewayne Dickerson, General Sales Mgr
Opal Shaw, Programming Director

WMOD
01-27-1975; 96.7 MHz FM; *Hrs Open:* 24; 3 kw; 299 ft.; N35 15 0 W88 53 28
200 East Market Street, Bolivar, TN 38008 US
(731) 658-7328
http://www.wmodradio.com/wmod
License: Bolivar, Hardeman County, TN held by WMOD Inc.
Nat'l Network: ABC; *Regional Network:* Tenn. Radio Net.
Regional Reps: Midsouth.
Arbitron Metro Market: Bolivar, TN; *Format:* Country; *Hrs. of News Programming:* News progmg 7 hrs wkly; *Target Audience:* 25-55; males & females; *Adv. Rates:* 10; 9; 10; 7
D. Richard Teubner, President
Gail Teubner, Operations Dir

WOJG
06-01-1992; 94.7 MHz FM; 6 kw; 328 ft.; N35 16 39 W88 55 41
123 West Market Street, Bolivar, TN 38008 US
ÿ731-658-3690; *Fax:* (731) 658-3408
http://www.wojg.com/
License: Bolivar, Hardeman County, TN held by Johnny W. Shaw & Opal J. Shaw.
TV Affiliate: Black
Opal Shaw, Owner
Johnny Shaw, CEO
Tracy Shaw, General Manager
DeWayne Dickerson, Operations Manager
Cher Bond, Administrator

Brentwood

WNSR
09-04-1985; 560 kHz AM
810 Dominican Dr., Nashville, TN 37228 US
(615) 844-1039; *Fax:* (615) 777-2284
www.nashvillesportsoriginal.com
License: Brentwood, TN held by Southern Wabash Communications Middle Tennessee Inc.
Group Owner: Southern Wabash Communications Corp.; (acq 11-25-97; $245,000).
Arbitron Metro Market: Nashville, TN; *Format:* Sports; *Target Audience:* 18-54; men
Ted Johnson, General Manager

Bristol

WIGN
08-18-1962; 1550 kHz AM; *Hrs Open:* 24 hours; omnidirectional
Mailing Address: P.O. Box 68, Bristol, TN 37621 US
Second Address: 2042 Euclid Avenue, Bristol, VA 24201
(276) 591-5800
www.wignam.com
manager@wignam.com
License: Bristol, TN held by Sunshine Broadcasters Inc.
Nat'l Network: CBS Radio; ABC
Arbitron Metro Market: Tucson AZ; *Format:* Christian; *Adv. Rates:* 16.00; 25:00;
David Whitelaw, COO

***WHCB**
08-10-1984; 91.5 MHz FM; *Hrs Open:* 24; 1.5 kw; 2346 ft.; N36 26 3 W82 8 3
Mailing Address: P.O. Box 2061, Bristol, TN 37621-2061 US
Second Address: 340 Edgemont Ave., Suite 100, Bristol, TN 37621-2061
(423) 878-6279
www.whcbradio.org
whcbradio@gmail.com
License: Bristol, Sullivan County, TN held by Appalachian Educational Communication Corp.
Nat'l Network: Moody; Salem Radio Network
Arbitron Metro Market: Johnson City-Kingsport-Bristol, TN-VA; *Format:* Christian, Talk *Special Programming:* Class one hr, Appalachian culture 2 hrs, farm one; *Hrs. of News Programming:* news progmg 14 hrs wkly *No.News Employees:* 1; *Target Audience:* General.
Dr. Kenneth C. Hill, President
Frank Waldo, VP
Sandra Gonce, Secretary

WOPI
06-15-1929; 1490 kHz AM; *Hrs Open:* 24; 1 kw-U; N36 35 45 W82 09 42 *Rebroadcasts:* WKPT(AM) 85%
Mailing Address: 222 Commerce St., Kingsport, TN 37660
Second Address: 288 Delaney St., Bristol, TN 37620
(423) 246-9578; *Fax:* (423) 247-9836
www.wopi.com
davidw@wtfm.com
License: Bristol, Sullivan County, TN held by Holston Valley Broadcasting Corp.
Group Owner: Glenwood Communications Corp.; (acq 5-16-96; $140,000;
Nat'l Network: ABC; *Nat'l Reps:* Eastman Radio; *Wire Services:* AP
Population Served: 200,000; *Arbitron Metro Market:* Johnson City-Kingsport-Bristol, TN-VA; *Format:* Classic Rock *Special Programming:* Weekend Blugrass/Classic Country; *No. News Employees:* 2 *Target Audience:* 35 plus.
George DeVault, President
David Widener, General Manager
Charlie Aesque, Sales Manager/Webmaster
Scott Gray, Sports Marketing Director/Advertising Sales

Brownsville

WNWS
10-14-1963; 1520 kHz AM; 0.25 kw-D, NDD; N35 36 30 W89 14 40
PO Box 198, Brownsville, TN 38012 US
(731) 772-3700
License: Brownsville, TN held by The Wireless Group Inc.
Group Owner: The Wireless Group Inc.; acq 4-80; $320,000 with co-located FM;
Nat'l Network: ABC
TV Affiliate: Sp

WTBG
11-09-1965; 95.3 MHz FM; *Hrs Open:* 24; 5 kw; 151 ft.; N35 36 30 W89 14 40 *Rebroadcasts:* Rebroadcasts WNWS-FM Jackson 30%
42 South Washington St, Brownsville, TN 38012 US
(901) 772-3700
www.brownsvilleradio.com
cv@brownsvilleradio.com
License: Brownsville, Haywood County, TN held by The Wireless Group Inc.
Format: Country, News, 62, Talk; *No. News Employees:* 1; *Target Audience:* 25-54.
Carlton Veirs, General Manager
Mary Ann Zaleski, Administrative Assistant
Leigh Turnage, Sales Manager
Joyce Moore, Sales Account Executive
Drew Magruder, Program Manager
Ivory T. Ellison, Gospel Programming Manager

Bulls Gap

WBGQ

01-01-2001; 100.7 MHz FM; *Hrs Open:* 24; 0.33 kw; 1260 ft.; N36 22 48 W83 10 47
Mailing Address: 448 Highway 25E, Bean Station, TN 37708 US
Second Address: PO Box 519, Morristown, TN 37815
(423) 235-4640
www.wbgqfm.com/
radiomanone@hotmail.com
License: Bulls Gap, Hawkins County, TN held by Cherokee Broadcasting
Nat'l Network: CNN Radio
Arbitron Metro Market: Morristown, TN; *Format:* Adult Contemp; *Target Audience:* 18-54; female 65% & male 35%
Clark Quillen, CEO
David Quillen, Operations Dir

Calhoun

WCLE-FM

08-01-1993; 104.1 MHz FM; *Hrs Open:* 24; 2.3 kw; 522 ft.; N35 15 59 W84 50 23
1860 Executive Park Drive, Suite E, Cleveland, TN 37312 US
(423) 472-6700; *Fax:* (423) 476-4686
www.mix104.info
info@mymix1041.com
License: Calhoun, McMinn County, TN held by Hartline LLC
Arbitron Metro Market: Cleveland, TN; *Format:* Adult Contemp; *No. News Employees:* 1; *Target Audience:* 25-54.
Steve Hartline, General Manager
Erin Evors, Publications Editor/Special Events Coordinator
Ashley Rue, Account Executive

Camden

WFWL

09-18-1956; 1220 kHz AM; *Hrs Open:* 24; 0.25 kw-D, ND1; 0.14 kw-N, ND1; N36 3 10 W88 5 15
117 Vicksburg Avenue, Camden, TN 38320 US
(731) 584-4444; *Fax:* (731) 584-7553
www.thecatfishradio.com
jrlane@aeneas.net
License: Camden, TN held by Community Broadcasting Services Inc.
Regional Network: Tenn. Radio Net; *Nat'l Reps:* Keystone (unwired net) *Regional Reps:* Midsouth.
Format: Country *Special Programming:* Gospel 8 hrs wkly; *Target Audience:* 25-49; adult; *Adv. Rates:* 6.95, 6:95, 6:95, 6:65
Ron Lane, General Manager
Jim Hart, Programming Director
Vicky Dotson, Office Manager

WRJB

06-20-1976; 95.9 MHz FM; *Hrs Open:* 24; 6 kw; 285 ft.; N36 3 26 W88 6 14
117 Vicksburg Avenue, Camden, TN 38320 US
(731) 584-4444; *Fax:* (731) 584-7553
www.thecatfishradio.com
jrlane@aeneas.net
License: Camden, Benton County, TN held by Community Broadcasting Services Inc.
Format: Adult Contemp; *Hrs. of News Programming:* News progmg 4 hrs wkly; *Target Audience:* 20-50.
Ron Lane, General Manager
Jim Hart, Programming Director
Vickie Dotson, Office Manager

Carthage

WRKM

06-20-1959; 1350 kHz AM; *Hrs Open:* 12; 1 kw-D, ND1; 0.09 kw-N, ND1; N36 14 42 W85 56 44
104 Z Country Lane, Carthage, TN 37030 US
(615) 735-1350; *Fax:* (615) 735-1351
www.1041theranch.net
dennis@1041theranch.net
License: Carthage, TN held by Wood Broadcasting Inc.
Nat'l Network: Sporting News Radio Network
Format: Sports; *Hrs. of News Programming:* news progmg 2 hrs wkly; *No. News Employees:* 1; *Target Audience:* 35 plus.; *Adv. Rates:* 8; 6:50; 6:50; na
Dennis Banka, President
John Wood, General Manager
Tracy Banka, News Director
Carl Campbell, Chief Engineer

WUCZ

07-18-1975; 104.1 MHz FM; *Hrs Open:* 24; 4.9 kw; 361 ft.; N36 18 43 W85 57 8
104 Z Country Lane, Carthage, TN 37030 US
(615) 735-1350; *Fax:* (615) 735-1351
www.1041theranch.net
dennis@1041theranch.net
License: Carthage, Smith County, TN
Nat'l Network: Westwood One
Arbitron Metro Market: Carthage, TN; *Format:* Country; *Hrs. of News Programming:* news progmg 2 hrs wkly; *No. News Employees:* 1; *Target Audience:* 18-35.; *Adv. Rates:* 14.75; 14.75; 14.75; 14.75
John Wood, Station Manager
Tracy Banka, News Director
Dennis Banka, Radio Jockey
Jim West, Sports/Sales

Celina

WVFB

08-01-1994; 101.5 MHz FM; *Hrs Open:* 6AM - 11PM; 6 kw; 328 ft.; N36 33 28 W85 36 15
352 Radio Station Road, Celina, TN 42167 US
(931) 258-4047; *Fax:* (502) 487-8462
License: Celina, Clay County, TN held by Carol Burrow Administratrix
Nat'l Network: USA; *Nat'l Reps:* Rgnl Reps
Arbitron Metro Market: Celina, TN; *Format:* Country; *Hrs. of News Programming:* news progmg 2 hrs wkly; *No. News Employees:* 2; *Target Audience:* Male 18-55.; *Adv. Rates:* 35; 28; 32; 28

Centerville

WNKX-FM

05-01-1974; 96.7 MHz FM; *Hrs Open:* 24; 6 kw; 299 ft.; N35 49 39 W87 34 2
150 Highway 50, Centerville, TN 37033 US
(931) 729-5191
www.countrykix96.com
tommy@countrykix96.com
License: Centerville, Hickman County, TN held by Hickman County Broadcasting Co. Inc.
Regional Network: Tenn. Radio Net; *Nat'l Reps:* Dora-Clayton
Regional Reps: Midsouth
Arbitron Metro Market: Nashville, TN; *Format:* Country; *Hrs. of News Programming:* news progmg 30 hrs wkly; *No. News Employees:* 3; *Target Audience:* 6-80.; *Adv. Rates:* Same as AM
Steve & Wana Turner, Owners/General Manager
Mickey Bunn, Station Manager/Programming Director
Tommy Vest, Sales Manager
Sheila Atkinson, Administrative Assistant

Chattanooga

WDEF

12-31-1940; 1370 kHz AM; *Hrs Open:* 24; 5 kw-D, 5 kw-N; N35 02 26 W85 20 22
3300 Broad St., Chattanooga, TN 37408 US
(423) 321-6200; *Fax:* (423) 321-6209
www.foxsportschattanooga.com
brad@wdodradio.com
License: Chattanooga, Hamilton County, TN held by Jackson Telecasters Inc.
Group Owner: Bahakel Communications Ltd.
Nat'l Network: Fox Sports
Arbitron Metro Market: Chattanooga, TN; *Format:* Sports; *No. News Employees:* 1; *Target Audience:* 25-64; males
Bernie Barker, General Manager
Danny Howard, Station Manager

WDEF-FM

09-15-1964; 92.3 MHz FM; *Hrs Open:* 24; 97 kw; 1181 ft.; N35 8 6 W85 19 25
2615 Broad St., Chattanooga, TN 37408 US
(423) 321-6200
www.sunny923.com
License: Chattanooga, Hamilton County, TN held by Jackson Telecasters Inc.
Group Owner: Bahakel Communications Ltd.; (acq 1996; grpsl)
Arbitron Metro Market: Chattanooga, TN; *Format:* Adult Contemp; *Hrs. of News Programming:* news progmg 5 hrs wkly; *No. News Employees:* 1; *Target Audience:* 25-54; upscale adults; *Adv. Rates:* 150; 100; 115; 85
Bernie Barker, VP/General Manager
Danny Howard, Station Manager
Cheryl Brown, Local Sales Manager
Kevin Hayes, Promotions Coordinator
Chris Adams, Production Director

WDOD-FM

02-01-1960; 96.5 MHz FM; 100 kw horiz, 88 kw vert; 1102 ft.; N35 9 41 W85 19 5
2615 S. Broad St., Chattanooga, TN 37408 US
(423) 321-6200
www.hits96.com
License: Chattanooga, Hamilton County, TN held by WDOD of Chattanooga Inc.
Group Owner: Bahakel Communications Ltd.
Arbitron Metro Market: Chattanooga, TN; *Format:* Contemporary Hits/Top 40; *Target Audience:* 18-54; upscale, contemp adults
Bernie Barker, General Manager
Cheryl Brown, Sales Manager
Danny Howard, Programming Director
Chris Adams, Traffic Director

*WYBK

11-18-2010; 89.7 MHz FM; *Hrs Open:* 24; 100 kw; 820 ft; N35 10 18 W85 18 59
1815 Union Ave., Charlotte, NC 37404
(704) 523-5555
www.bbnradio.org
bbn@bbnmedia.org
License: Chattanooga, Hamilton County, TN held by Bible Broadcasting Network Inc.
Group Owner: Bible Broadcasting Network
Nat'l Network: USA
Population Served: 170,136; *Arbitron Metro Market:* Chattanooga, TN; *Format:* Religious; *Hrs. of News Programming:* News progmg 2 hrs wkly; *No. News Employees:* 1; *Target Audience:* General; conservativeChristians
Lowell Davey, President
Jason Padgett, Operations Manager

WGOW

01-01-1936; 1150 kHz AM; 5 kw-D, DAN; 1 kw-N, DAN; N35 04 5 W85 20 4
821 Pineville Rd., Chattanooga, TN 37405 US
(423) 756-6141
www.wgowam.com
License: Chattanooga, TN held by Radio License Holding CBC, LLC
Group Owner: Cumulus Media Inc.; (acq 5-30-00; grpsl).
Nat'l Reps: Christal
Arbitron Metro Market: Chattanooga, TN; *Format:* News/Talk
Bill Lockhart, Programming Director

WJOC

07-04-1948; 1490 kHz AM; 1 kw-U, ND1; N35 3 7 W85 16 24
722 South Germantown Rd, Chattanooga, TN 37412 US
(706) 861-0800
www.am1490.net
WJOC1490@aol.com
License: Chattanooga, TN held by Sara Margarett Fryar.
Nat'l Network: USA
Arbitron Metro Market: Chattanooga, TN; *Format:* Christian, Gospel
Trey Searcy, General Manager

WLMR

01-01-1961; 1450 kHz AM; *Hrs Open:* 24; 1 kw-U, ND1; N35 2 54 W85 16 26
3809 Ringgold Rd., Chattanooga, TN 37412 US
(423) 624-4200
www.wilkinsradio.com
denise@wilkinsradio.com
License: Chattanooga, TN held by Grace Media Inc.
Group Owner: Wilkins Communications Network Inc.
Nat'l Network: USA
Arbitron Metro Market: Chattanooga, TN; *Format:* Christian, Talk; *Target Audience:* 35 plus.; *Adv. Rates:* 30; 30; 30; 30
Nolan Hall, Station Manager

*WMBW

08-01-1969; 88.9 MHz FM; *Hrs Open:* 24; 98 kW; 1509 ft.; N34 57 43 W85 22 40 *Rebroadcasts:* WMKW 89.3FM;
1920 E 24th St Place, Chattanooga, TN 37404 USA
(423) 629-8900; *Fax:* (423) 629-0021
www.moodyradio.org/stations/chattanooga
License: Chattanooga, Hamilton County, TN held by The Moody Bible Institute of Chicago
Group Owner: The Moody Bible Institute of Chicago; acq 5-18-73)
Nat'l Network: Moody
Arbitron Metro Market: Chattanooga, TN; *Format:* Christian
Special Programming: Black one hr wkly; *Hrs. of News Programming:* News progmg 12 hrs wkly; *Target Audience:* 25-54.

WNOO

06-01-1951; 1260 kHz AM; *Hrs Open:* 24
Box 5156, 1108 Hendricks, Chattanooga, TN 37406 US
(423) 698-8617; *Fax:* (423) 698-8796
www.wnooradio.com
wnoo@epbinternet.com
License: Chattanooga, TN held by Clear Media LLC

Nat'l Network: American Urban
Arbitron Metro Market: Chattanooga, TN; *Format:* Gospel, Talk; *No. News Employees:* 8; *Target Audience:* 25-54; mature Black adults & children; *Adv. Rates:* 25; 15; 20; 10
Lee Clear, President

WSKZ
11-01-1960; 106.5 MHz FM; 100 kw; 1079 ft.; N35 9 42 W85 19 6
Mailing Address: P.O. Box 8, Bloomington, IL 61702 US
Second Address: 821 Pineville Rd., Chattanooga, TN 37405
(423) 756-6141; *Fax:* (423) 266-3629
www.wskz.com
License: Chattanooga, Hamilton County, TN
Arbitron Metro Market: Chattanooga, TN; *Format:* Triple A

***WUTC**
03-01-1980; 88.1 MHz FM; *Hrs Open:* 24; 30 kw; 889 ft; N35 12 28 W85 16 46
Mailing Address: 104 Cadek Hall/Dept. 1151, 615 McCallie Avenue, Chattanooga, TN 37403
Second Address: 725 Oak Street, Chattanooga, TN 37403
(423) 425-4756; *Fax:* (423) 425-2379
www.wutc.org
dawn-mcfadden@utc.edu
License: Chattanooga, Hamilton County, TN held by Board of Trustees of University of Tennessee.
Nat'l Network: NPR; PRI; AP Radio
Population Served: 460,000; *Arbitron Metro Market:* Chattanooga, TN; *Target Audience:* General.
Dr. John McCormack, General Manager
Ken Dryden, Underwriting Services
Mark Colbert, Programming Director
Dawn McFadden, Member Services

Church Hill

WMCH
05-08-1954; 1260 kHz AM; *Hrs Open:* 24 hours; 1 kw-D, ND2; 0.021 kw-N, ND2; N36 31 15 W82 44 54
PO Box 128, Church Hill, TN 37642 US
(423) 357-5601; *Fax:* (423) 343-5173
www.wmchradio.com
wmchradio@yahoo.com
License: Church Hill, TN held by Media Link, Incorporated
Nat'l Network: USA
Arbitron Metro Market: Johnson City, TN; *Format:* Religious, Talk; *No. News Employees:* 5; *Target Audience:* 25-54; adult audience
Ron W Gordon, General Manager
Bettye Russell, Office Manager

Clarksville

***WAPX-FM**
10-01-1984; 91.9 MHz FM; *Hrs Open:* 24; 6 kw; 194 ft.; N36 32 13 W87 21 26
601 College Street, PO Box 4446, Clarksville, TN 37044 US
(931) 221-7378; *Fax:* (931) 221-7265
www.apsu.edu/communications/media
License: Clarksville, Montgomery County, TN held by Austin Peay State University.
Arbitron Metro Market: Clarksville, TN; *Format:* Variety/Diverse *Special Programming:* Black 6 hrs, jazz 6 hrs wkly; *Hrs. of News Programming:* News progmg 8 hrs wkly; *Target Audience:* 18-34; college students &young professionals
David von Palko, General Manager

WKFN
11-12-1954; 540 kHz AM; *Hrs Open:* 24
P.O. Box 2249, Clarksville, TN 37042 US
(865) 675-4105; *Fax:* (865) 675-4859
License: Clarksville, TN held by Saga Communications of Tuckessee L.L.C.
Group Owner: Saga Communications Inc.; (acq 2-1-2001; grpsl)
Arbitron Metro Market: Clarksville, TN; *Format:* Sports, Talk; *Hrs. of News Programming:* news progmg 36 hrs wkly; *No. News Employees:* 2; *Target Audience:* 25-54.
Scott Chase, Operations Dir
Katie Gambill, General Manager

WJZM
10-19-1941; 1400 kHz AM; *Hrs Open:* 24; 1 kw-U, ND1; N36 30 57 W87 20 57
Mailing Address: PO Box 648, Clarksville, TN 37041 US
Second Address: 925 Martin St., Clarksville, TN 37040
(931) 645-6414
www.wjzm.com
14jzm@wjzm.com
License: Clarksville, TN held by Cumberland Radio Partners Inc.
Format: News, News/Talk, 84, Talk *Special Programming:* Relg; *Hrs. of News Programming:* News progmg 8 hrs wkly; *Target Audience:* 25-60; blue collar, working women, businessmen
John Bastin, Operations Dir
Hank Bonecutter, General Manager
Angie Brown, Programming Director
Ivan Davis, Chief Engineer
Ken Baxter, Disc Jockey
Sharon Fewless, Disc Jockey
Jimmy Baird, Disc Jockey
Jeff Lyon, Disc Jockey

***WAYQ**
10-22-2003; 88.3 MHz FM; *Hrs Open:* 24; 14 kw; 745 ft.; N36 17 36 W87 18 20
2277 C. Wilma Rudolph Boulevard, Box 103, Clarksville, TN 37040 US
(888) 339-2936
www.waym.wayfm.com
supportservices@wayfm.com
License: Clarksville, Montgomery County, TN held by WAY-FM Media Group Inc.
Group Owner: WAY-FM Media Group Inc.
Arbitron Metro Market: Franklin, TN; *Format:* Christian
Teresa White, General Sales Mgr
Jeff Brown, Programming Director
Bob Augsburg, Founder

Cleveland

WBAC
06-18-1945; 1340 kHz AM; *Hrs Open:* 24; 1 kw-U, ND1; N35 9 54 W84 51 13
409 Chestnut Street, Suite A 154, Chattanooga, TN 37402 US
(423) 472-4053; *Fax:* (423) 472-5290
License: Cleveland, TN held by East Tennessee Radio Group III L.P.
Group Owner: East Tennessee Radio Group III L.P.; (acq 5-30-2008; grpsl)
Nat'l Network: ABC; *Regional Network:* Tenn. Radio Net; *Nat'l Reps:* D & R Radio
Arbitron Metro Market: Brewster MA; *Format:* News, News/Talk, 86; *Adv. Rates:* 16; 14; 14; 7
John Voci, Station Manager

WCLE
05-02-1957; 1570 kHz AM; 5 kw-D, ND1; 0.084 kw-N, ND1; N35 10 55 W84 50 55
1860 Executive Park Drive, Suite E, Cleveland, TN 37312 US
(423) 472-6700; *Fax:* (423) 476-4686
www.mix104.info
info@mymix1041.com
License: Cleveland, TN held by Hartline LLC
Arbitron Metro Market: Cleveland, TN; *Format:* News, News/Talk, 86; *Target Audience:* 25-54.; *Adv. Rates:* 14; 12; 12; 8.50
Steve Hartline Jr., President
Steve Hartline, General Manager

WUSY
08-01-1961; 100.7 MHz FM; *Hrs Open:* 24; 100 kw; 1191 ft.; N35 12 26 W85 17 10
7413 Old Lee Highway, Chattanooga, TN 37421 US
(423) 892-3333
www.us101country.com
License: Cleveland, Bradley County, TN held by Capstar TX LLC
Group Owner: iHeartMedia; (acq 8-7-2000; grpsl)
Arbitron Metro Market: Chattanooga, TN; *Format:* Country
Gator Harrison, Operations Manager
Jared Stehney, Market Manager

Clifton

WLVS-FM
01-01-2002; 106.5 MHz FM; 3.8 kw; 416 ft.; N35 28 41 W88 6 36 *Rebroadcasts:* Rebroadcasts WXFL(FM) Florence 100%
C/O Fletcher, Heald Plc, 1300 N. 17th St, 11th Fl, Arlington, VA 22209 US
License: Clifton, Wayne County, TN held by Gold Coast Broadcasting Co.
Arbitron Metro Market: Florence, AL; *Format:* Country

Clinton

***WDVX**
11-01-1997; 89.9 MHz FM; 0.2 kw vert; 1962 ft.; N36 11 53 W84 13 51
Mailing Address: 301 S. Gay Street, Knoxville, TN 37902 US
Second Address: PO Box 27568, Knoxville, TN 37927
(865) 544-1029 ext. 221; *Fax:* (865) 566-0150
www.wdvx.com
info@wdvx.com
License: Clinton, Anderson County, TN held by Cumberland Communities Communications Corp.
Arbitron Metro Market: Clinton, TN; *Format:* Triple A
Tony Lawson, General Manager

***WYFC**
07-04-1966; 95.3 MHz FM; *Hrs Open:* 24; 1.45 kw; 669 ft.; N36 4 18 W84 1 19
P.O. Box 7300, Charlotte, NC 28241 US
(800) 888-7077
www.bbnradio.com
bbn@bbnmedia.org
License: Clinton, Anderson County, TN held by Bible Broadcasting Network Inc.
Group Owner: Bible Broadcasting Network; acq 8-18-89; $450,000;
Arbitron Metro Market: Clinton, TN; *Format:* Christian
Lowell Davey, President
Jason Padgett, Operations Manager

WYSH
11-01-1960; 1380 kHz AM; *Hrs Open:* 24; 1 kw-D, DAN; 0.08 kw-N, DAN; N36 6 48 W84 8 30
Mailing Address: PO Box 329, Clinton, TN 37717 US
Second Address: 119 Pine Road, Clinton, TN 37716
(865) 457-1380; *Fax:* (865) 457-4440
www.wyshradio.com
wysh@wyshradio.com
License: Clinton, TN held by Clinton Broadcasters Inc.
Nat'l Network: AP Radio; *Regional Network:* Tenn. Radio Net; *Nat'l Reps:* Keystone (unwired net)
Arbitron Metro Market: Knoxville, TN; *Format:* Country *Special Programming:* Relg 15 hrs wkly; *Hrs. of News Programming:* news progmg 15 hrs wkly; *No. News Employees:* 1; *Target Audience:* 25-54; families, bluecollar to upper income; *Adv. Rates:* 12; 10; 12; 8
Ronald Meredith Jr., President
Jim Harris, News/Sports Director

Coalmont

WSGM
06-21-1994; 104.7 MHz FM; *Hrs Open:* 6 AM-10 PM; 1 kw; 548 ft.; N35 16 44 W85 44 2
Hcr 77, Box 123, Coalmont, TN 37313 US
(931) 592-7777; *Fax:* (931) 592-7778
License: Coalmont, Grundy County, TN held by Cumberland Communication Corp.
Format: Religious; *Hrs. of News Programming:* News progmg 30 hrs wkly; *Target Audience:* General; interested in community affrs

Collegedale

***WSMC-FM**
11-01-1961; 90.5 MHz FM; 100 kw; 1030 ft.; N35 15 20 W85 13 34
Mailing Address: P. O. Box 370, Collegedale, TN 37315 US
Second Address: 5077 Industrial Drive, Collegedale, TN 37315
(423) 236-2905; *Fax:* (423) 236-1905
www.southern.edu/wsmc
wsmc@southern.edu
License: Collegedale, Hamilton County, TN held by Southern Adventist University.
Nat'l Network: PRI; NPR
Format: News; *Target Audience:* 25-54.
Brenden Dodd, Producer
Joshua Farnsworth, Announcer/Producer
Jonathan Freese, Head of Productions
Mariah Hilsmann, Promotions Coordinator
Tyler Rand, Music Director
Robby Raney IV, Head Announcer

Collierville

WCRV
10-01-1966; 640 kHz AM; *Hrs Open:* 24; 50 kw-D, DAN; 0.48 kw-N, DAN; N34 59 35 W89 53 58
6401 Poplar Ave., Memphis, TN 38119 US
(901) 763-4640
www.bottradionetwork.com
comments@bottradionetwork.com
License: Collierville, Shelby County, TN held by Bott Broadcasting Co./Tennessee
Group Owner: Bott Radio Network
Nat'l Network: USA; *Nat'l Reps:* Salem
Arbitron Metro Market: Memphis, TN; *Format:* Christian, Talk; *Target Audience:* 25-54; family oriented
Eben Fowler, Operations Dir
Todd Payne, General Manager
Pat Rulon, Director of National Sales

Candy Green, Program Services Manager
Rachel Launius, Marketing Manager

Collinwood

WMSR-FM
07-01-1991; 94.9 MHz FM; *Hrs Open:* 24; 7.7 kw; 594 ft.; N35 1 46 W87 47 7
509 N. Main Street, Tuscumbia, AL 35674 US
(256) 383-2525
www.star94fm.net
License: Collinwood, Wayne County, TN held by Urban Radio Licenses LLC
Nat'l Network: Fox News Radio; *Nat'l Reps:* Katz Radio
Arbitron Metro Market: Florence, AL; *Format:* Contemporary Hits/Top 40; *Hrs. of News Programming:* News progmg 8 hrs wkly; *Target Audience:* 18-49; primary women, secondary adults; *Adv. Rates:* 35; 30; 35; 30
Brian Rickman, Program/Music Director

Colonial Heights

WPWT
12-31-1984; 870 kHz AM; *Hrs Open:* Sunrise-sunset; 10 kw-D, NDD; N36 27 40 W82 27 12
Mailing Address: P.O. Box 2061, Bristol, TN 37621 US
Second Address: 340 Edgemont Ave., Suite 100, Bristol, TN 3720
(423) 878-6279; *Fax:* (423) 878-6520
www.powertalk870.com
License: Colonial Heights, TN held by Information Communications Corp.
Group Owner: Information Communications Corp.; (acq 6-29-2001).
Nat'l Network: Fox News Radio; Salem Radio Network; Talk Radio Network; Premiere Radio Networks
Arbitron Metro Market: Johnson City-Kingsport-Bristol, TN-VA; *Format:* Talk *Special Programming:* Health Education one hr wkly; *Hrs. of News Programming:* news progmg 5 hrs wkly; *No. News Employees:* 1 *TargetAudience:* Adults 25-54.
Kenneth Hill, General Manager
Rusty Cury, General Sales Mgr
Mathew Hill, Programming Director
Jerome Jackson III, Promotions Manager
Art Countiss, News Director

WRZK
04-04-1997; 95.9 MHz FM; *Hrs Open:* 24; 7.4 kw; Ant 1,253 ft; N36 31 36 W82 35 13
222 Commerce St., Kingsport, TN 37660
(423) 246-9578
www.wrzk.com
charlie@wrzk.com
License: Colonial Heights, Sullivan County, TN held by Holston Valley Broadcasting Corp.
Group Owner: Glenwood Communications Corp.; (acq 8-14-2008; $3.65 million)
Nat'l Network: ABC; *Nat'l Reps:* Eastman
Population Served: 396,400; *Arbitron Metro Market:* Johnson City-Kingsport-Bristol, TN-VA *TV Affiliate:* WKPT-TV; *Format:* Rock/AOR; *No. News Employees:* 2; *Target Audience:* 18-44; Men
Scott Onks, Programming Director

Columbia

WKOM
01-01-1967; 101.7 MHz FM; *Hrs Open:* 24; 4.1 kw; 387 ft.; N35 37 5 W87 2 33
315 West 7th Street, Columbia, TN 38401 US
(931) 388-3636; *Fax:* (931) 381-1017
License: Columbia, Maury County, TN held by Middle Tennessee Broadcasting Co.
Nat'l Network: Motor Racing Net; ABC
Format: Classic Rock; *Hrs. of News Programming:* news progmg 8 hrs wkly; *No. News Employees:* 1; *Target Audience:* 30-50.
Robert McKay III, CEO

WKRM
11-25-1946; 1340 kHz AM; *Hrs Open:* 24; 1 kw-U, ND1; N35 36 38 W87 3 22
P. O. Box 1377, Columbia, TN 38401 US
(931) 388-3636; *Fax:* (931) 381-1017
License: Columbia, TN held by Robert M. McKay III.
Nat'l Network: ABC; Motor Racing Net; Premiere Radio Networks
Format: Adult Contemp *Special Programming:* Relg 4 hrs wkly; *Hrs. of News Programming:* news progmg 8 hrs wkly; *No. News Employees:* 1; *Target Audience:* 25-54.
Robert McKay III, President

WMCP
11-12-1956; 1280 kHz AM; *Hrs Open:* 24; 5 kw-D, DA2; 0.5 kw-N, DA2; N35 37 8 W86 58 52
816 South Garden, Columbia, TN 38401 US
(931) 388-3241; *Fax:* (931) 381-2510
License: Columbia, TN held by Maury County Boosters Corp.
Regional Network: Tenn. Radio Net.
Arbitron Metro Market: Columbia, TN; *Format:* Country *Special Programming:* Farm 4 hrs weekly; *Hrs. of News Programming:* news progmg 13 hrs wkly; *No. News Employees:* 1; *Target Audience:* 18 plus. *Adv.Rates:* 9.45; 9.45; 9.45; 9.45.
Edna Williford, President
Mack Shaw, Operations Dir

WMRB
08-14-1982; 910 kHz AM; 0.5 kw-D, ND1; 0.101 kw-N, ND1; N35 36 24 W87 1 30
609 West 7th Street, Columbia, TN 38401 US
(931) 381-7100; *Fax:* (931) 381-0088
www.maurywebpages.com/wmrb.htm
License: Columbia, TN held by Ogilvie Family Ministries Inc.
Nat'l Reps: Dora-Clayton
Arbitron Metro Market: Columbia, TN; *Format:* Sports; *Target Audience:* General; Christian families

Cookeville

WKSW
03-26-1964; 98.5 MHz FM; *Hrs Open:* 20; 50 kw; 492 ft.; N36 8 34 W85 28 2
200 Concord Plaza, Suite 600, San Antonio, TX 78216 US
(931) 526-7144; *Fax:* (931) 528-8400
www.magic985.com
License: Cookeville, Putnam County, TN held by Cookeville Communications LLC.
Group Owner: Great Plains Media Inc.; (acq 5-30-2008; grpsl)
Nat'l Network: ABC; *Nat'l Reps:* Clear Channel
Arbitron Metro Market: Cookeville, TN; *Format:* Adult Contemp; *Hrs. of News Programming:* news progmg 8 hrs wkly; *No. News Employees:* 1
Scott Straube, General Sales Mgr
Marty McFly, Programming Director
Helen Daniels, News Director
Jerri-Lynn Zimmer, Public Service Announcement Manager

WGSQ
03-08-1963; 94.7 MHz FM; *Hrs Open:* 24; 100 kw; 1319 ft.; N36 10 26 W85 20 37
698 South Willow Avenue, Cookeville, TN 38501 US
(931) 526-7144
www.countrygiant.com
billym@gpmnow.com
License: Cookeville, Putnam County, TN held by Cookeville Communications LLC.
Group Owner: Great Plains Media Inc.; (acq 5-30-2008; grpsl)
Arbitron Metro Market: Cookeville, TN; *Format:* Country; *Hrs. of News Programming:* news progmg 28 hrs wkly; *No. News Employees:* 2
Rhamey Ihmeidan, Director of Sales
Billy Mac, Program/Music Director
Kayla Smith, Promotions Director

***WHRS**
10-01-1996; 91.7 MHz FM; 0.5 kw; 384 ft.; N36 8 34 W85 28 2
Rebroadcasts: Rebroadcasts WPLN(FM) 90.3, Nashville; 100%
630 Mainstream Drive, Nashville, TN 37228-1204 US
(615) 760-2903; *Fax:* (615) 760-2904
www.nashvillepublicradio.org
License: Cookeville, Putnam County, TN held by Nashville Public Radio.
Format: News *Special Programming:* Bluegrass one hr, song writers one hr wkly
Robert Gordon, President/CEO
Donna Robinson, VP, Development
Zea Miller, Membership Manager
Molly Nicholas, Membership Coordinator

WHUB
07-20-1940; 1400 kHz AM; *Hrs Open:* 24; 1 kw-U, ND1; N36 10 25 W85 30 40
698 S. Willow Avenue, Cookeville, TN 38501 US
(931) 526-7144
www.1400thehub.com
License: Cookeville, TN held by Cookeville Communications LLC.
Group Owner: Great Plains Media Inc.; (acq 5-30-2008; grpsl)
Nat'l Network: CBS; *Regional Network:* Tenn. Radio Net.
Arbitron Metro Market: Cookeville, TN; *Format:* Country, Gospel *Special Programming:* Sports 10 hrs, gospel 11 hrs wkly; *Hrs. of News Programming:* news progmg 18 hrs wkly; *No. News Employees:* 1; *Target Audience:* General.
Marty McFly, Operations Dir
Dave Thomas, General Manager
Jim Stapleton, General Sales Mgr
Mike Dinger, Programming Director
Lehra Heidel, Promotions Manager
Jim Herrin, News Director
Jennifer Henson, Traffic Manager

WPTN
07-10-1962; 780 kHz AM; 1 kw-D, NDD; N36 9 30 W85 31 15
200 Concord Plaza, Suite 600, San Antonio, TX 78216 US
(931) 526-7144; *Fax:* (931) 528-8400
License: Cookeville, TN held by Cookeville Communications LLC.
Group Owner: Great Plains Media Inc.; (acq 5-30-2008; grpsl)
Nat'l Reps: Clear Channel
Arbitron Metro Market: Cookeville, TN; *Format:* News, News/Talk, 86; *Target Audience:* General.
Dave Johnson, Operations Dir
David Roederer, General Manager
Bruce Welker, General Sales Mgr
Marty Selby, Programming Director
Lehra Mayfield, Promotions Manager
Jim Herrin, News Director

***WTTU**
05-22-1972; 88.5 MHz FM; *Hrs Open:* 25.?Â ?; 2 kw horiz; 164 ft.; N36 10 36 W85 30 20
P.O. Box 5113, Cookeville, TN 38505 US
(931) 372-3688
www.tntech.edu/wttu
License: Cookeville, Putnam County, TN held by Tennessee Technological University.
Arbitron Metro Market: Cookeville, TN; *Format:* Alternative *Special Programming:* Jazz, Metal, American, Folk, Rap represented with; *Hrs. of News Programming:* news progmg 5 hrs wkly; *No. News Employees:* 1 *Target Audience:* 14-25.

***WWOG**
01-01-1994; 90.9 MHz FM; *Hrs Open:* 24; 40 kw; 682 ft.; N36 11 5 W85 22 30 *Rebroadcasts:* Rebroadcasts WSGP(FM) Glasgow, KY and WTHL(FM) Somerset, KY 100%
Mailing Address: PO Box 1423, Somerset, KY 42502 US
Second Address: 93 Rainbow Terr., Somerset, TN 42501
(606) 679-1342
www.kingofkingsradio.net
License: Cookeville, Putnam County, TN held by Somerset Educational Broadcasting Foundation.
Arbitron Metro Market: Somerset, KY; *Format:* Gospel, Religious
David Carr, General Manager
Carolyn Jones, Programming Director
Marvin Whittaker, Chief Engineer

Copper Hill

WLYY
12-02-1958; 1400 kHz AM; *Hrs Open:* 6 AM-10 PM; 1 kw-U, ND1; N34 58 4 W84 19 39
PO Box 430, Copperhill, TN 37317 US
(423) 496-3311; *Fax:* (423) 496-2635
www.joychristianradio.com
License: Copper Hill, TN held by Joy Christian Communications Inc.
Group Owner: Joy Christian Communications Inc.; (acq 9-26-2002)
Format: Country
Rebecca St. John, Station Manager

Covington

WKBL
08-16-1954; 1250 kHz AM; *Hrs Open:* 24; 800 w-D, 106 w-N; N35 35 10 W89 38 35
101 WKBL Dr., Covington, TN 38019
(901) 476-7129; *Fax:* (901) 476-7120
www.us51country.com
billy.thomas@us51country.com
License: Covington, Tipton County, TN held by Covington Broadcasting Inc., LMA in 2007 by 51 Ra
Nat'l Network: Dial Global; *Regional Network:* Tenn. Radio Net.
Regional Reps: N/A
Population Served: 100,000; *Arbitron Metro Market:* Memphis, TN *Special Programming:* Black 4 hrs wkly; *Hrs. of News Programming:* news progmg 14 hrs wkly; *No. News Employees:* 1; *Target Audience:* 35 - 64. *Adv. Rates:* 15; 15; 15; 15
Gloria Thomas, Operations Dir
Bill Thomas, General Manager
David Lane, General Sales Mgr
Ron Grayson, Programming Director

WKBQ
08-31-1965; 93.5 MHz FM; *Hrs Open:* 24; 6 kw; Ant 328 ft; N35 35 12 W89 38 21
101 WKBL Dr., Covington, TN 38019
(901) 476-7129; *Fax:* (901) 476-7120
www.us51country.com
david.lane@us51country.com
License: Covington, Tipton County, TN held by Covington Broadcasting Inc.
Nat'l Network: AP Radio; Jones Radio Networks; *Regional Network:* Tenn. Radio Net. *Regional Reps:* N/A
Population Served: 170,000; *Arbitron Metro Market:* Memphis, TN *Special Programming:* University of Tennessee Football, University of M; *Hrs. of News Programming:* news progmg 6.5 hrs wkly; *No. News Employees:* 1 *Target Audience:* 18 - 54; Adults; *Adv. Rates:* 30 (MF6a-7p) Sat 10a-3p
Bill Thomas, General Manager
Rob Grayson, Programming Director
Gloria Thomas, Business Manager
David Lane, Partner/EVP

Cowan

WZYX
03-10-1957; 1440 kHz AM; *Hrs Open:* 24; 5 kw-D, ND1; 0.066 kw-N, ND1; N35 9 39 W86 1 51
Mailing Address: 540 West Cumberland St., Cowan, TN 37318 US
Second Address: PO Box 398, Cowan, TN 37318
(931) 967-7471; *Fax:* (931) 962-1440
www.wzyxradio.net
License: Cowan, TN held by Tims Ford Broadcasting Co. Inc.
Nat'l Network: CNN Radio; *Wire Services:* NOAA Weather
Arbitron Metro Market: Cowan, TN; *Format:* Country, Oldies, 86
Special Programming: Talk, gospel 10 hrs, farm 2 hrs, relg 12 hrs wkly; *Hrs. of News Programming:* news progmg 15 hrs wkly; *No. News Employees:* 1 *Target Audience:* 35-55; middle-of-the-road working people
Mary Lou Gamer, CEO
Jeff Pennington, Operations Dir

Crossville

WAEW
01-01-1952; 1330 kHz AM; *Hrs Open:* 24; 1 kw-D, ND1; 0.035 kw-N, ND1; N35 57 1 W85 2 9
961 Miller Ave., Crossville, TN 38555 US
(931) 707-1102; *Fax:* (931) 707-1220
www.waewradio.com
License: Crossville, TN held by Peg Broadcasting Crossville LLC
Group Owner: Peg Broadcasting Crossville LLC; acq 10-1-2003; grpsl).
Nat'l Network: ABC
Arbitron Metro Market: Cookeville, TN; *Format:* Talk; *Hrs. of News Programming:* news progmg 13 hrs wkly; *No. News Employees:* 2; *Target Audience:* 35-64; adult; *Adv. Rates:* 12; 12; 10; 6
Jeff Shaw, General Manager
Steve Sweeney, Director, Sales
Kendra Williams, Office Manager

WCSV
06-15-1968; 1490 kHz AM; *Hrs Open:* 24; 1 kw-U, ND1; N35 57 1 W85 2 9
961 Miller Ave., Crossville, TN 38555 US
www.1490wcsv.com
License: Crossville, TN held by Peg Broadcasting Crossville LLC
Group Owner: Peg Broadcasting Crossville LLC; acq 10-1-2003; grpsl).
Nat'l Network: ABC
Arbitron Metro Market: Crossville, TN; *Format:* Sports; *Hrs. of News Programming:* news progmg 13 hrs wkly; *No. News Employees:* 2; *Target Audience:* 25-54; men

***WMKW**
11-01-1996; 89.3 MHz FM; *Hrs Open:* 24; 0.5 kW; 1394 ft.; N35 46 38 W84 58 34 *Rebroadcasts:* Rebroadcasts WMBW(FM) Chattanooga 100%
1920 E 24th St Place, Chattanooga, TN 37404 USA
423-629-8900; *Fax:* (423) 629-0021
www.moodyradio.org/stations/chattanooga
License: Crossville, Cumberland County, TN held by The Moody Bible Institute of Chicago
Group Owner: The Moody Bible Institute of Chicago
Arbitron Metro Market: Crossville, TN; *Format:* Christian; *Target Audience:* General.

WOWF
06-15-1990; 102.5 MHz FM; *Hrs Open:* 24; 9 kw; 542 ft.; N36 1 18 W84 58 18
961 Miller Ave, Crossville, TN 38555 US
(931) 707-1102; *Fax:* (931) 707-1220
www.1025wowcountry.com
gordon.stack@pegbroadcasting.com
License: Crossville, Cumberland County, TN held by Peg Broadcasting Crossville LLC
Group Owner: Peg Broadcasting Crossville LLC; acq 1-3-01; $2.5 million).
Nat'l Network: Jones Radio Networks; Fox News Radio *Regional Reps:* Rgnl Reps.; *Wire Services:* AP
Format: Country; *Hrs. of News Programming:* news progmg 10 hrs wkly; *No. News Employees:* 2; *Target Audience:* 25 -54; adults; *Adv. Rates:* 40; 36; 40; 24
Gordon Stack, Operations Dir
Steve Sweeney, Sales

WPBX
05-12-1967; 99.3 MHz FM; *Hrs Open:* 24; 1.4 kw; 572 ft.; N36 1 18 W84 58 18
961 Miller Avenue, Crossville, TN 38555 US
(931) 707-1102; *Fax:* (931) 707-1220
mix993.net
gordon.stack@pegbroadcasting.com
License: Crossville, Cumberland County, TN held by Peg Broadcasting Crossville LLC
Group Owner: Peg Broadcasting Crossville LLC; acq 10-1-2003: grpsl).
Nat'l Network: ABC; *Nat'l Reps:* Clear Channel
Arbitron Metro Market: Knoxville, TN; *Format:* Adult Contemp; *Hrs. of News Programming:* news progmg 10 hrs wkly; *No. News Employees:* 2; *Target Audience:* 25-54; women; *Adv. Rates:* 18; 14; 18; 9
Gordon Stack, Operations Dir
Steve Sweeney, Sales

Dayton

WDNT
12-06-1957; 1280 kHz AM *Rebroadcasts:* Rebroadcasts WBAC(AM) Cleveland 100%
P.O. Box 1235, Dayton, TN 37321 US
(423) 285-6411; *Fax:* b423) 472-5290
comments@rheacountyradio.com
License: Dayton, TN held by East Tennessee Radio Group III L.P.
Group Owner: East Tennessee Radio Group III L.P.; (acq 5-30-2008; grpsl)
Nat'l Network: ABC; *Regional Network:* Tenn. Radio Net; *Nat'l Reps:* D & R Radio
Arbitron Metro Market: Rhea County, TN; *Format:* Adult Contemp; *Hrs. of News Programming:* news progmg 26 hrs wkly; *No. News Employees:* 1; *Target Audience:* 45 plus.; *Adv. Rates:* 16; 14; 14; 7
Mike Powers, Operations Dir
Charles Sells, General Manager
John Holland, General Sales Mgr
Corky Whitlock, Programming Director

Dibrell

***WRCC**
88.3 MHz FM; 0.085 kw; 344 ft.; N35 50 20 W85 47 2
PO Box 1343, Ada, OK 74821 US
(580) 332-0902; *Fax:* (580) 332-0922
www.thegospelstation.com
email@thegospelstation.com
License: Dibrell, Warren County, TN held by Pearl Communications Group.
Arbitron Metro Market: Dibrell, TN
Randall Christy, Founder/President
Rick Cody, Vice President/Programming Director
Sharla Frederick, Treasurer/CFO

Dickson

WDKN
01-01-1955; 1260 kHz AM; *Hrs Open:* 6 AM-6:30 PM; 5 kw-D, ND2; 0.018 kw-N, ND2; N36 6 31 W87 22 14
106a E. College Street, Dickson, TN 37055 US
(615) 446-4000
www.wdkn.com
License: Dickson, TN held by Edmission & Eubank Communications Inc.
Arbitron Metro Market: Nashville, TN; *Target Audience:* General.
Tommy Edmisson, President
Oscar Eubank, Operations Dir
Kenneth Forte, General Manager
Big Zak, Programming Director
Chris Norman, Operations/News

***WNRZ**
04-07-1997; 91.5 MHz FM; *Hrs Open:* 24; 8 kw; 262 ft.; N36 0 36 W87 30 47 *Rebroadcasts:* Rebroadcasts WNAZ-FM Nashville 100%
333 Murfreesboro Road, Nashville, TN 37210 US
(913) 642-7770; *Fax:* (913) 642-1319
www.bottradionetwork.com
comments@bottradionetwork.com
License: Dickson, Dickson County, TN held by Trevecca Nazarene University Inc.
Arbitron Metro Market: Dickson, TS; *Format:* Christian; *Target Audience:* 14-28; Christians
Mark Myers, CFO
Dr. Dan Boone, President
Dave Queen, Operations Dir
David Deese, General Manager
Paul Eby, Station Manager

Donelson

WCRT
04-12-1971; 1160 kHz AM; *Hrs Open:* 24; 50 kw-D, DAN; 1 kw-N, DAN; N36 9 49 W86 42 56
15 Century Blvd., Nashville, TN 37214 US
(615) 871-1160
www.bottradionetwork.com
comments@bottradionetwork.com
License: Donelson, Davidson County, TN held by Bott Communications Inc.
Group Owner: Bott Radio Network; (acq 1-11-2006; $5 million)
Arbitron Metro Market: Nashville, TN; *Format:* Christian, Talk
Eben Fowler, Operations Dir
Todd Payne, Regional Manager
Pat Rulon, Director of National Sales
Candy Green, Program Services Manager
Rachel Launius, Marketing Manager

Dresden

WCDZ
11-18-1991; 95.1 MHz FM; *Hrs Open:* 24; 21.5 kw; 276 ft.; N36 15 50 W88 40 3
Mailing Address: 1410 N. Lindell St., Martin, TN 38237 US
Second Address: 223 Westgate Dr., Union City, TV 38260
(731) 587-9526; *Fax:* (731) 587-5079
www.thunderboltradio.com/star-95-1
License: Dresden, TN held by Thunderbolt Broadcasting Co.
Group Owner: Thunderbolt Broadcasting Co.; (acq 1-28-94; $320,000;)
Format: Adult Contemp, Oldies; *No. News Employees:* 1; *Adv. Rates:* 40; 30; 40; 25
Paul Tinkle, President

Dunlap

WSDQ
11-01-1980; 1190 kHz AM; 1 kw-C, NDD; 5 kw-D, NDD; N35 21 41 W85 22 33
712 Old York Hwy North, Ste B, Dunlap, TN 37327 US
(423) 949-4114; *Fax:* (423) 949-5143
wsdq1190@gmail.com
License: Dunlap, TN held by Rodgson Inc.
Regional Network: Tenn. Radio Net.
Arbitron Metro Market: Chattanooga, TN; *Format:* Country
Special Programming: Gospel 7 hrs wkly
Charles Rodgers, President
Howard Staten, Station Manager

Dyer

WTJJ
02-01-1995; 94.3 MHz FM; *Hrs Open:* 24; 6 kw; 328 ft.; N36 6 12 W89 7 45
US
(731) 427-3316
www.wtjs.com/
vprice@forevercomm.com
License: Dyer, Gibson County, TN held by Forever South Licenses LLC.
Group Owner: Forever Communications Inc.; (acq 7-31-2006; grpsl)
Arbitron Metro Market: Dyer, TN; *Format:* News, News/Talk, 86; *Target Audience:* 18-49
Verla Price, General Manager
Buzz, Programming Director
Tim Forrest, Production Director

Dyersburg

WASL
07-01-1968; 100.1 MHz FM; *Hrs Open:* 24; 26 kw; 676 ft.; N36 6 0 W89 29 12

2555 Burks Place, Dyersburg, TN 38024 US
(731) 285-1339; *Fax:* (731) 287-0100
www.sl100rocks.com
roger@burksb.com
License: Dyersburg, Dyer County, TN
Group Owner: Dr. Pepper Pepsi-Cola Bottling Co. of Dyersburg
Nat'l Network: ABC; *Nat'l Reps:* Rgnl Reps; *Wire Services:* AP
Special Programming: John Boy and Billy, Tenn Titans; *No. News Employees:* 1; *Target Audience:* 18-54.
Jeff Cohen, Operations Manager
Roger Vestal, General Manager
Kaylin Dortch, Traffic/Multimedia Director
Tom Hunt, Partyline/News Director
Natalie Patterson, Director of Sales/Marketing

***WZKV**
10-30-1992; 90.7 MHz FM; *Hrs Open:* 24; 9.9 kw horiz, 100 kw vert; 561 ft.; N36 6 0 W89 29 12
P.O. Box 241880, Memphis, TN 38124 US
www.klove.com
License: Dyersburg, Dyer County, TN held by Educational Media Foundation.
Group Owner: EMF Broadcasting; (acq 3-29-2007; $825,000)
Nat'l Network: K-Love
Format: Christian
Mike Novak, President

WTRO
07-13-1946; 1450 kHz AM; *Hrs Open:* 24; 1 kw-U, ND1; N36 3 2 W89 22 7 *Rebroadcasts:* FM Translator 101.7
2555 Burks Place, Dyersburg, TN 38024 US
(731) 285-1450; *Fax:* (731) 287-0100
wtroradio.net
roger@burksb.com
License: Dyersburg, TN held by Dr. Pepper/Pepsi Cola Bottling Co. of Dyersburg Inc.
Group Owner: Dr. Pepper Pepsi-Cola Bottling Co. of Dyersburg; (acq 1991)
Nat'l Network: ABC; *Wire Services:* AP
Arbitron Metro Market: Dyersburg, TN; *Format:* Oldies *Special Programming:* St. Louis Cardinals, Tenn Vols; *Hrs. of News Programming:* news prgmg 5 hrs/week; *No. News Employees:* 1; *Target Audience:* 35 plus.
Jeff Cohen, Operations Manager
Roger Vestal, General Manager
Natalie Patterson, Director of Sales
Kaylin Dortch, Traffic/Multimedia Director
Tom Hunt, Partyline/News Director
Tom Hunt, Partyline Host

East Ridge

WOGT
11-09-1990; 107.9 MHz FM; 25 kw; 328 ft.; N35 07 33 W85 17 25
821 Pineville Rd., Chattanooga, TN 37405 US
(423) 756-6141
www.1079nashicon.com
License: East Ridge, TN held by Radio License Holding CBC, LLC
Group Owner: Cumulus Media Inc.; (acq 5-30-00; grpsl).
Arbitron Metro Market: Chattanooga, TN; *Format:* Country

Elizabethton

WTZR
05-17-1968; 99.3 MHz FM; 3.6 kw; 810 ft.; N36 24 7 W82 12 12
901 East Valley Drive, Bristol, VA 24201 US
(276) 669-8112; *Fax:* (276) 669-0541
www.zrock993.com
jay@zrock993.com
License: Elizabethton, Carter County, TN held by Bristol Broadcasting Co.
Group Owner: Bristol Broadcasting Co. Inc.; (acq 2-13-97; $3 million).
Nat'l Reps: Christal
Arbitron Metro Market: Johnson City-Kingsport-Bristol, TN-VA; *Format:* Alternative; *Target Audience:* 18-49.
Winnie Quaintance, Sales Manager
Jay Patrix, Programming Director

WBEJ
07-01-1946; 1240 kHz AM; *Hrs Open:* 24; 1 kw-U, ND1; N36 20 7 W82 13 3
510 Broad Street, Elizabethton, TN 37643 US
(423) 542-2184; *Fax:* (423) 542-3192
www.wbej.com
License: Elizabethton, TN held by CB Radio Inc.
Nat'l Network: Westwood One
Arbitron Metro Market: Kerville TX; *Format:* Gospel, Religious; *Target Audience:* 35-55.; *Adv. Rates:* 17; 15; 17; 15
Don Crisp, President
Cleo Reed, Station Manager
Barton Edens, Sales Manager
Shannon Crisp, Products/Sports Board Operator

***WUMC**
01-01-1999; 90.5 MHz FM; 0.5 kw; -285 ft.; N36 17 58 W82 17 28
1 Blowers Boulevard, Milligan College, TN 37682 US
www.milliganradio.com
wumc@milligan.edu
License: Elizabethton, Carter County, TN held by Milligan College.
Arbitron Metro Market: Milligan College, TN; *Format:* Contemporary Hits/Top 40, Christian
Dr. Carrie Swanay, General Manager
Hobie Vannoy, Station Manager
Caleb Perhne, Station Manager

Englewood

WENR
04-21-1967; 1090 kHz AM; 1 kw-D, NDD; N35 25 35 W84 30 57
136 County Road 611, Athens, TN 37303 US
(423) 337-5025; *Fax:* (423) 337-5026
wenrradio@yahoo.com
License: Englewood, TN held by Paul Wilson dba 1090 Radio, a Tennessee sole proprietorship
Arbitron Metro Market: Englewood, TN; *Format:* Gospel
Carolyne Wilson, General Manager

Erwin

WEMB
05-17-1956; 1420 kHz AM; 5 kw-D, ND1; 0.02 kw-N, ND1; N36 6 58 W82 26 49
P.O. Box 280, Erwin, TN 37650 US
(423) 743-6123(423) 743-6124; *Fax:* (423) 743-6122
www.wemb.com/
License: Erwin, TN held by WEMB Inc.
Regional Network: Tenn. Radio Net.
Arbitron Metro Market: Erwin, TN; *Format:* Country, Gospel, 84 *Special Programming:* Bluegrass 2 hrs, gospel 10 hrs wkly
Jim Crawford, President
Charles Ray, Operations Dir
Kathy Thornberry, News Director
Fred Lance, Edit Director

Etowah

WCPH
01-01-1955; 1220 kHz AM; 1 kw-D, ND1; 0.109 kw-N, ND1; N35 19 15 W84 30 34
P. O. Box 676, Etowah, TN 37331 US
(423) 263-5555
www.homegrownradio1220.com
c.hudson@homegrownradio1220.com
License: Etowah, TN held by Starr Mountain Broadcasting Co.
Arbitron Metro Market: Chattanooga, TN; *Format:* Easy Listening, News, 62, Sports, Talk
Andy Bell, Operations Manager
Cliff Hudson, Chief Engineer
Erika Collins, Web Developer

WLLJ
01-01-1977; 103.1 MHz FM; *Hrs Open:* 24; 50 kw; 492 ft.; N35 27 24 W84 40 43 *Rebroadcasts:* Rebroadcasts WBDX(FM) Trenton, GA 100%
Mailing Address: PO Box 9396, Chattanooga, TN 37412 US
Second Address: 5512 Ringgold Road, Suite 214, Chattanooga, TN 37412
(423) 892-1200
www.j103.com
info@j103.com
License: Etowah, McMinn County, TN held by Friendship Broadcasting LLC.
Nat'l Network: Salem Radio Network
Arbitron Metro Market: Etowah, TN; *Format:* Adult Contemp, Christian; *Hrs. of News Programming:* news progmg 2 hrs wkly; *No. News Employees:* 1; *Target Audience:* 18-49; female
Bob Lubell, CEO
Steve Green, Station Manager
Debbie Lubell, Promotions Manager
Freda Thornton, News Director
Dave Skinner, CFO
Kendall Payne, Local News Editor

Farragut

WMTY
11-10-1988; 670 kHz AM; 2.5 kw-D, NDD; N35 53 12 W84 14 48
P.O. Box 330, Sweetwater, TN 37874 US
(423) 337-5025; *Fax:* (423) 337-5026
License: Farragut, TN held by Horne Radio L.L.C.
Group Owner: Horne Radio Group; (acq 1999; $275,000).
Nat'l Network: USA
Arbitron Metro Market: Knoxville, TN; *Format:* Talk; *Target Audience:* 25-54; upscale adults

Fayetteville

WEKR
10-01-1948; 1240 kHz AM; *Hrs Open:* 4:30 AM-10 PM; 1 kw-U, ND1; N35 9 28 W86 35 25
P.O. Box 656, Fayetteville, TN 37334 US
(931) 433-3545; *Fax:* (931) 438-0620
License: Fayetteville, TN held by Elk River Broadcasting, Inc.
Nat'l Network: CNN Radio; *Regional Network:* Tenn. Radio Net.
Arbitron Metro Market: Fayetteville, TN; *Format:* Country, Gospel, 84 *Special Programming:* Farm one hr wkly; *Hrs. of News Programming:* news progmg 5 hrs wkly; *No. News Employees:* 1; *Target Audience:* 25plus; general; *Adv. Rates:* 14.12; 14.12; 14.12; na
Joseph Young, CEO
Jim Young, Station Manager
Jennifer Denise, Programming Director
Wayne Thomas, News Director
Charles Hicks, Disc Jockey
Jack Atchley, Sports Commentator

WYTM-FM
03-27-1970; 105.5 MHz FM; *Hrs Open:* 5 AM-10 PM; 6 kw; 295 ft.; N35 7 39 W86 34 49
P. O. Box 717, Fayetteville, TN 37334 US
(931) 433-1531
www.wytmfm.co
License: Fayetteville, Lincoln County, TN held by Time Broadcasters Inc.
Nat'l Network: ABC
Arbitron Metro Market: Fayetteville, TN; *Format:* Country
Joseph Young, President

Franklin

WAKM
03-18-1953; 950 kHz AM; *Hrs Open:* 24
US
(615) 794-1950; *Fax:* (615) 794-1595
wakm950@comcast.net
License: Franklin, TN held by Franklin Radio Associates Inc.
Nat'l Network: CNN Radio; *Regional Network:* Tenn. Radio Net.
Arbitron Metro Market: Nashville, TN; *Format:* Country, News, 62, Talk *Special Programming:* Relg 6 hrs, NASCAR racing 6 hrs wkly; *Hrs. of News Programming:* news progmg 14 hrs wkly; *No. News Employees:* 2 *TargetAudience:* 24 plus; community interested adults; *Adv. Rates:* 20; 18; 20; 18

WRLT
11-16-1961; 100.1 MHz FM; *Hrs Open:* 24; 0.2 kw; 1181 ft.; N36 2 6 W86 50 54
1310 Clinton Street, Suite 215, Nashville, TN 37203 US
(615) 242-5600; *Fax:* (615) 296-9039
www.lightning100.com
kraen@lightning100.com
License: Franklin, Williamson County, TN held by Tuned In Broadcasting Inc.
Nat'l Network: Westwood One; *Nat'l Reps:* Roslin
Arbitron Metro Market: Nashville, TN; *Format:* Triple A *Special Programming:* Retro Rock 4 hrs, Local Music 3 hrs, Music Business Talk 2 hrs, Indie Rock 1 hr, Blues 1 hr weekly; *Target Audience:* Adults 18+
Gary Kraen, Operations/Programming Director
Lt. Dan Buckley, Assistant Program Director/Production Director
Rev. Keith Coes, Music Director
Tom Hansen, General Sales/Marketing Manager
Jayson Challant, Promotion Director/AccountExecutive
Tom Hansen, Chief Engineer

WHEW
02-01-1969; 1380 kHz AM; 2.8 kw-D; N35 54 22 W86 54 21
1811 Carters Creek Pike, Franklin, TN 37064-6823 US
(615) 599-1384
License: Franklin, TN held by SG Communications Inc.

Salvador Guzman, General Manager

Friendsville

WNML
01-05-1989; 99.1 MHz FM; *Hrs Open:* 24; 6 kw; 328 ft.; N35 47 10 W84 17 24 *Rebroadcasts:* Simulcast with WNML-AM
4711 Old Kingston Pike, Knoxville, TN 37919 US

(865) 656-9900
www.sportsradiownml.com
License: Friendsville, TN held by Radio License Holding CBC, LLC
Group Owner: Cumulus Media Inc.
Arbitron Metro Market: Knoxville, TN; *Format:* Sports, Talk
Mickey Dearstone, Programming Director

Gallatin

WGFX
12-01-1960; 104.5 MHz FM; *Hrs Open:* 24; 58 kw; 1207 ft.; N36 16 5 W86 47 45
10 Music Circle E., Nashville, TN 37203 US
(615) 321-1067
www.1045thezone.com
dave.elliott@cumulus.com
License: Gallatin, TN held by Radio License Holding CBC, LLC
Group Owner: Cumulus Media Inc.; (acq 4-26-01; grpsl).
Nat'l Reps: Katz Radio
Arbitron Metro Market: Nashville, TN; *Format:* Sports, Talk; *Target Audience:* 18-49.
Allison Warren, General Manager
Dave Elliott, General Sales Mgr
Brad Willis, Programming Director
Marie Miscia, Promotions Manager

WHIN
08-02-1948; 1010 kHz AM; *Hrs Open:* 24; 5 kw-D, ND1; 0.047 kw-N, ND1; N36 26 0 W86 28 0
1625 Highway 109 North, P.O. Box 1685, Gallatin, TN 37066 US
(615) 451-0450; *Fax:* (615) 452-9446
www.whinradio.com
whinam@comcast.net
License: Gallatin, TN held by WHIN Inc.
Arbitron Metro Market: Nashville, TN; *Format:* Country *Special Programming:* Black 2 hrs, farm 5 hrs wkly; *Hrs. of News Programming:* news progmg 14 hrs wkly; *No. News Employees:* 1; *Target Audience:* 25-54;upper middle to lower middle income
Jack Williams, President

WMRO
02-19-1994; 1560 kHz AM; *Hrs Open:* Daytime
PO Box 1445, Gallatin, TN 37066 US
(615) 451-2131
www.magic1560.com
wmroam@comcast.net
License: Gallatin, TN held by Classic Broadcasting Inc.
Nat'l Network: ABC Music Radio *Regional Reps:* .
Arbitron Metro Market: Gallatin, TN; *Format:* Adult Contemp *Special Programming:* Relg 11 hrs. wkly; *Hrs. of News Programming:* news progmg 4 hrs wkly; *No. News Employees:* 2; *Target Audience:* 25-54; middle toupper class adults; *Adv. Rates:* 7; 6; 7; 2
Scott Bailey, Owner/Operator/General Manager

*WVCP
01-04-1979; 88.5 MHz FM; *Hrs Open:* 24; 1 kw; 390 ft; N36 22 36.1 W86 28 20.9
1480 Nashville Pike, Ramer Bldg., Ste. 101, Gallatin, TN 37066
(615) 230-3618; *Fax:* (615) 230-4803
www.wvcp.net
howard.espravnik@volstate.edu
License: Gallatin, Sumner County, TN held by Volunteer State Community College.
Wire Services: AP
Arbitron Metro Market: Nashville, TN *Special Programming:* Christian Rock 4 hrs wkly, Classic country 2 hrs w; *Hrs. of News Programming:* News progmg 5 hrs wkly; *Target Audience:* General.
Howard Espravnik, G
James L. Miliner, Chief Engineer
Justin Fernandes, Operations Assistant

WYXE
11-01-1966; 1130 kHz AM; 0.94 kw-C, NDD; 2.3 kw-D, NDD; N36 24 38 W86 27 16
1079 East Trinity Lane, Nashville, TN 37216 US
(866) 650-8432
www.radiovida1130.com
License: Gallatin, TN held by Jon Gary Enterprises Inc.
Arbitron Metro Market: Nashville, TN; *Format:* Religious
Richard Deck Jr., General Manager

Gatlinburg

WSEV-FM
01-01-1983; 105.5 MHz FM; *Hrs Open:* 24; 0.53 kw; 1056 ft.; N35 42 13 W83 33 57
196 West Dumplin Valley Rd., Kodak, TN 37764 US
(865) 932-6002
www.mixx1055.com
License: Gatlinburg, Sevier County, TN held by East Tennessee Radio Group L.P.
Group Owner: East Tennessee Radio Group L.P.; (acq 3-22-2000; $1.45 million with WSEV(AM) Sevierville).
Nat'l Network: Fox News Radio; *Regional Network:* Tenn. Radio Net.
Arbitron Metro Market: Knoxville, TN; *Format:* Adult Contemp; *No. News Employees:* 1; *Target Audience:* 25-54; loc adults, tourists
Steve Hartford, Operations Dir
Bill Burkett, Station Manager

Germantown

WHBQ-FM
06-01-1994; 107.5 MHz FM; *Hrs Open:* 24; 3.9 kw; 407 ft.; N35 10 30 W89 44 26
188 South Bellevue, Suite 222, Memphis, TN 38104 US
(901) 375-9324; *Fax:* (901) 375-0041
www.q1075.com
License: Germantown, Shelby County, TN held by Flinn Broadcasting Corp.
Arbitron Metro Market: Memphis, TN; *Format:* Contemporary Hits/Top 40
Donald Biggs, General Manager

WKQK
04-15-1977; 94.1 MHz FM; 50 kw; 472 ft.; N34 59 22 W89 51 45
1835 Moriah Woods Blvd., Suite #1, Memphis, TN 38117 US
(901) 384-5900
www.941thewolf.com
License: Germantown, Shelby County, TN held by Entercom Memphis License LLC.
Group Owner: Entercom Communications Corp.; (acq 12-13-99; grpsl)
Arbitron Metro Market: Memphis, TN *TV Affiliate:* Classic hits *Special Programming:* news progmg 2 hrs wkly; *Hrs. of News Programming:* 1; *No. News Employees:* 18-49; adults with discre

WOWW
10-01-1955; 1430 kHz AM
230-2 Goodman Road East, Suite 202, Southaven, MS 38671 US
(901) 272-9953
www.lovetherebel.com
License: Germantown, TN held by Flinn Broadcasting Corp.
Arbitron Metro Market: Memphis, TN; *Format:* Children; *Target Audience:* 25-54.

Goodlettsville

WQZQ
01-24-1980; 830 kHz AM; *Hrs Open:* 24
Mailing Address: P.O. Box 150846, Nashville, TN 37215 US
Second Address: 1824 Murfreesboro Pike, Nashville, TN 37217
(615) 399-1029; *Fax:* (615) 361-9873
www.wqzq.com
jhampton@cromwellradio.com
License: Goodlettsville, Davidson County, TN held by Winston Communications Inc.
Group Owner: The Cromwell Group Inc.; (acq 10-17-91)
Arbitron Metro Market: Nashville, TN; *Format:* Classic Rock, Easy Listening, 64; *Target Audience:* 24-56; talk radio audience
Jana Hampton, Market Manager
Jana Hampton, Station Manager
Jeff Kolb, Station Manager
Dennis Swartz, Operations Director
Andrea Kamer, Business Manager
Elizabeth Koch, Traffic Manager

WQQK
10-16-1970; 92.1 MHz FM; *Hrs Open:* 24; 3.1 kw; 461 ft.; N36 17 50 W86 45 11
10 Music Circle East, Nashville, TN 37203 US
(615) 321-1067; *Fax:* (615) 321-5771
www.92qnashville.com
License: Goodlettsville, Sumner County, TN held by Cumulus Licensing LLC.
Group Owner: Cumulus Media Inc.; (acq 3-28-2002; grpsl).
Nat'l Network: ABC
Arbitron Metro Market: Nashville, TN; *Format:* Urban Contemporary *Special Programming:* Gospel 6 hrs wkly; *Target Audience:* 18-49; relg; *Adv. Rates:* 170; 170; 180; 150
Rhonda Rollins, Sales
Cori Vallentine, Promotions
Kenny Smoov, Programming
Ernie Allen, News/PSA Announcements

WQZQ-FM
01-24-1980; 93.3 kHz FM; *Hrs Open:* 24
Mailing Address: P.O. Box 150846, Nashville, TN 37215 US
Second Address: 1824 Murfreesboro Pike, Nashville, TN 37217
(615) 399-1029; *Fax:* (615) 361-9873
www.wqzq.com
jhampton@cromwellradio.com
License: Goodlettsville, Davidson County, TN held by Winston Communications Inc.
Group Owner: The Cromwell Group Inc.; (acq 10-17-91)
Arbitron Metro Market: Nashville, TN; *Format:* Classic Rock, Easy Listening, 64; *Target Audience:* 24-56; talk radio audience
Jana Hampton, Market Manager
Jana Hampton, Station Manager
Jeff Kolb, Station Manager
Dennis Swartz, Operations Director
Andrea Kamer, Business Manager
Elizabeth Koch, Traffic Manager

Graysville

*WAYB-FM
01-01-1994; 95.7 MHz FM; 6 kw; 328 ft.; N35 24 39 W85 7 54
1860 Executive Park Drive NW, Graysville, TN 37312 US
(423) 775-2331; *Fax:* (423) 775-9368
License: Graysville, Rhea County, TN held by Family Worship Center Church Inc.
Group Owner: Family Worship Center Church Inc.; acq 5-20-02).
Arbitron Metro Market: Rock River WY; *Format:* Contemporary Hits/Top 40
Andy Hoefer, General Manager
Eric Henderson, General Sales Mgr

Greeneville

WGRV
01-01-1946; 1340 kHz AM; *Hrs Open:* 24; 1 kw-U, ND1; N36 10 10 W82 50 52
Box 278, 1004 Arnold Rd., Greeneville, TN 37744 US
(423) 638-4147; *Fax:* (423) 638-1979
www.greeneville.com/wgrv
wgrv@greeneville.com
License: Greeneville, TN held by Radio Greeneville Inc.
Group Owner: Radio Greeneville Inc.
Regional Network: Tenn. Radio Net.
Format: News/Talk; *No. News Employees:* 3
Ron P. Metcalfe, Operations Dir
Paul R. Metcalfe, General Manager
Brian Stayton, Programming/Promotions Director
Jim Miller, News Director
Ray C. Elliot, Chief Engineer

WAEZ
01-01-1956; 94.9 MHz FM; *Hrs Open:* 24; 100 kw horiz, 87 kw vert; 1089 ft.; N36 4 34 W82 41 28
Mailing Address: P. O. Box 1389, Bristol, VA 24203 US
Second Address: 901 East Valley Drive, Bristol, VA 24201
(276) 669-8112; *Fax:* (276) 669-0541
www.electric949.com
License: Greeneville, Greene County, TN held by Bristol Broadcasting Co. Inc.
Group Owner: Bristol Broadcasting Co. Inc.; acq 6-22-00)
Nat'l Reps: Rgnl Reps
Arbitron Metro Market: Johnson City-Kingsport-Bristol, TN-VA; *Format:* Contemporary Hits/Top 40 *Special Programming:* Univ. of Tennessee football & basketball; *No. News Employees:* 2; *Target Audience:* 25-49.
Pete Nininger, President
Bill Hickey, Operations Dir

WSMG
12-01-1961; 1450 kHz AM; *Hrs Open:* 24
Box 278, 1004 Arnold Rd, Greeneville, TN 37744 US
(423) 638-4147; *Fax:* (423) 638-1979
www.greeneville.com/wsmg
wsmg@greeneville.com
License: Greeneville, TN held by Radio Greeneville Inc.
Group Owner: Radio Greeneville Inc.; acq 6-22-00; $1.8 million with WIKQ(FM) Tusculum)
Wire Services: AP
Format: Oldies; *Target Audience:* General.; *Adv. Rates:* 12; 12; 12; 8.
Ron P. Metcalfe, Operations Dir
Paul R. Metcalfe, General Manager
Brian Stayton, Programming Director

Halls Crossroads

WMYL
08-15-1991; 96.7 MHz FM; 2.8 kw; 489 ft.; N36 4 21 W84 1 18
119 Pine Road, P.O. Box 329, Clinton, TN 37717 US
(865) 896-1380; *Fax:* (865) 457-4440
www.merlefm.com
License: Halls Crossroads, Knox County, TN held by M & M Broadcasting
Nat'l Network: ABC; CNN Radio; *Nat'l Reps:* Rgnl Reps

Arbitron Metro Market: Knoxville, TN; *Format:* Country *Special Programming:* Farm 2 hrs, gospel 2 hrs, relg 2 hrs wkly; *Target Audience:* 25-54; community-oriented adults
Ron Meredith, Owner
Jack Ryan, Owner/Partner
Jennifer Clabo, Account Executive/Promotions
Jim Harris, News/Sports Director
Kelly Harris, Traffic/Billing Director
Will Housley, Digital, Web & Communication Media Director

Harriman

WIJV
01-21-1981; 92.7 MHz FM; 2.65 kw; 502 ft.; N35 52 4 W84 25 56
P.O. Box 387, Rockwood, TN 37854 US
License: Harriman, Roane County, TN held by Progressive Media Inc.
Arbitron Metro Market: Knoxville, TN; *Format:* Christian
Kirk Tollett, General Manager
Scott Humphrey, News Director
Jennifer Tollett, Traffic Manager

Harrison

WMPZ
01-01-1995; 93.5 MHz FM; *Hrs Open:* 24; 6 kw horiz, 5.88 kw vert; 315 ft.; N35 7 33 W85 17 25
1305 Carter St., Chattanooga, TN 37402 US
(423) 265-9494; *Fax:* (423) 266-2335
www.groove93.com
License: Harrison, Hamilton County, TN held by J.L. Brewer Broadcasting LLC.
Group Owner: Brewer Broadcasting Corp.; (acq 11-96).
Nat'l Network: ABC; *Nat'l Reps:* D & R Radio
Arbitron Metro Market: Chattanooga, TN; *Format:* Adult Contemp, Urban Contemporary; *Target Audience:* 25-54; adults
Jim Brewer II, President
Keith Landecker, Operations Manager
Mike Baskin, Director of Sales
Jay Holloway, Production Director

Harrogate

***WLMU**
08-05-1987; 91.3 MHz FM; *Hrs Open:* 24; 0.19 kw; 285 ft.; N36 35 10 W83 39 54
Highway 25E, Harrogate, TN 37752 US
(423) 869-6335; *Fax:* (423) 869-6435
www.913thegap.com
License: Harrogate, Claiborne County, TN held by Lincoln Memorial University.
Format: Country; *Target Audience:* 25-54.
Dr. Nancy Moody, President
Dustin McCoy, Operations Dir
Travis Moody, General Manager
Larry Carter, General Sales Mgr

WCXZ
11-10-1980; 740 kHz AM; *Hrs Open:* 24
6965 Cumberland Gap Parkway, Box 2025, Harrogate, TN 37752 US
(423) 869-7400; *Fax:* (423) 869-6435
www.74wcxz.com
License: Harrogate, TN held by Pine Hills of Tenn. Inc.
Wire Services: AP
Arbitron Metro Market: Knoxville, TN; *Format:* Talk; *Hrs. of News Programming:* news progmg 150 hrs wkly; *No. News Employees:* 4; *Target Audience:* 34-65.; *Adv. Rates:* 19; 17; 19; 13
Tom Amis, General Manager
Dustin McCoy, Programming Director

Hartsville

WTNK
09-01-1966; 1090 kHz AM; *Hrs Open:* 24; 1 kw-D, 2 w-N; N36 23 17 W86 09 55
165 Marlene St., Hartsville, TN 37074
(615) 374-2111; *Fax:* (615) 374-3544
www.wtnk.com
License: Hartsville, Trousdale County, TN held by G & L Aircasters Inc.
Nat'l Reps: Keystone (unwired net)
Population Served: 500,000 *Special Programming:* Gospel 4 hrs wkly; *Hrs. of News Programming:* News progmg 5 hrs wkly; *Target Audience:* 35 plus.; *Adv. Rates:* 7; 7; 7; na
Bryce Foster, Operations Manager
Lisa Frank, General Manager
Jerry Richmond, Sports Director

Henderson

***WFHU**
05-22-1967; 91.5 MHz FM; *Hrs Open:* 24; 10.5 kw; 308 ft.; N35 27 40 W88 40 51
Gardner Center 303, Henderson, TN 38340 US
(731) 989-6749
www.fhu.edu/fm91
License: Henderson, Chester County, TN held by Freed-Hardeman University.
Arbitron Metro Market: Henderson, TN; *Format:* Classic Rock, Classical, 52 *Special Programming:* Class 10 hrs, gospel 9 hrs, jazz 45 hrs wkly; *Hrs. of News Programming:* news progmg 5 hrs wkly *No. News Employees:* 1; *Target Audience:* General; young adults to senior citizens
Milton Sewell, President
Ron Means, General Manager

WFKX
02-01-1984; 95.7 MHz FM; *Hrs Open:* 24; 4.4 kw; 383 ft.; N35 29 52 W88 42 29
111 W. Main St., Jackson, TN 38301 US
(901) 427-9616
www.96kix.net
License: Henderson, Chester County, TN held by Thomas Radio LLC
Group Owner: Thomas Media Group
Nat'l Network: ABC
Arbitron Metro Market: Jackson, TN; *Format:* Black *Special Programming:* Gospel 3 hrs wkly; *Hrs. of News Programming:* news progmg 5 hrs wkly; *Target Audience:* 18-54; the general Black population & contemp women *Adv. Rates:* 36; 34; 38; 24

WHHM-FM
11-19-1990; 107.7 MHz FM; *Hrs Open:* 24; 50 kw horiz, 49.07 kw vert; 459 ft.; N35 27 23 W88 37 36
111 W. Main St., Jackson, TN 38301 US
(731) 427-9616
www.mystar1077.com
License: Henderson, Chester County, TN held by Thomas Radio LLC
Group Owner: Thomas Media LLC
Regional Network: Tenn. Agri-Net; *Wire Services:* AP
Arbitron Metro Market: Jackson, TN; *Format:* Adult Contemp *Special Programming:* Gospel 10 hrs wkly; *Hrs. of News Programming:* news progmg 5 hrs wkly; *No. News Employees:* 1; *Target Audience:* 25-54; adults *Adv. Rates:* 24; 26; 24; 17

Hendersonville

WWTN
06-20-1962; 99.7 MHz FM; 100 kw; 1296 ft.; N35 49 3 W86 31 24
10 Music Circle E., Nashville, TN 37203 US
(615) 321-1067
www.997wtn.com
ralph@997wtn.com
License: Hendersonville, Coffee County, TN held by Cumulus Licensing Corp.
Group Owner: Cumulus Media Inc.; (acq 7-21-2003; $65 million with WSM-FM Nashville).
Nat'l Network: ABC; CBS Radio; *Wire Services:* UPI
Arbitron Metro Market: Nashville, TN; *Format:* News, News/Talk, 84, Talk; *Target Audience:* 25-54; general
Dave Elliot, Sales
Dan Mandis, Programming Director
Cori Vallentine, Promotions

Henry

WMUF
04-12-1999; 104.7 MHz FM; *Hrs Open:* 24; 2.9 kw; 476 ft.; N36 8 19 W88 15 52 *Rebroadcasts:* Rebroadcasts WMUF(AM) Paris 100%
110 India Road, Paris, TN 38242 US
(731) 644-9455; *Fax:* (731) 644-9421
www.wmufradio.com
License: Henry, Henry County, TN held by Benton-Weatherford Broadcasting Inc. of Tennessee
Group Owner: Benton-Weatherford Broadcasting Inc. of Tennessee
Nat'l Network: ABC
Arbitron Metro Market: Paris, TN; *Format:* Country; *Target Audience:* 25-54.
Tim Alsobrooks, News Director
Lane Pierce, Sports Director

Hohenwald

***WAUO**
01-01-1998; 90.7 MHz FM; 0.5 kw; 233 ft.; N35 33 56 W87 33 27
P.O. Box 3206, Tupelo, MS 38803 US
(662) 844-8888; *Fax:* (662) 842-6791
www.afr.net
faq@afa.net
License: Hohenwald, Lewis County, TN held by American Family Association.
Group Owner: American Family Radio
Arbitron Metro Market: Phoenix, AZ; *Format:* Christian, Religious, 86
Tim Wildmon, President
Donald Wildmon, Founder
Buddy Smith, Sr VP
Ed Vitagliano, Exec VP
Randy Sharp, Director Of Special Projects
Meeke Addison, Director Of Communications
Abraham Hamilton, General Counsel

WMLR
07-04-1970; 1230 kHz AM; *Hrs Open:* 24; 1 kw-U, ND1; N35 31 22 W87 32 40
184 Switzerland Road, Hohenwald, TN 38462 US
(931) 796-5966
wmlr1230am@bellsouth.net
License: Hohenwald, TN held by Two Brothers Broadcasting
Nat'l Network: ABC
Arbitron Metro Market: Hohenwald, TN; *Format:* Country *Special Programming:* Gospel; *Adv. Rates:* 6; 4; 6; 4
Ronnie/Robert Brewer, Owners

Humboldt

WIRJ
01-20-1949; 740 kHz AM; 0.25 kw-D, ND1; 0.016 kw-N, ND1; N35 48 52 W88 54 51
Mailing Address: P.O. Box 740, Humbolt, TN 38343 US
Second Address: 2606 East End Dr., Humboldt, TN 38343
(731) 784-5000; *Fax:* (731) 784-2533
BRANDY@CLICK1.NET
License: Humboldt, TN held by John F. Warmath.
Format: Oldies, Talk
John Warmath, General Manager

WDVW(FM)
01-19-1989; 105.3 MHz FM; *Hrs Open:* 24; 3 kw; Ant 328 ft; N35 50 41 W88 54 08
Mailing Address: 319 Vann Drive, Suite 3 #32, Jackson, TN 38305
Second Address: 7713 Highway 412 South, Bells, TN
(731) 663-2327; *Fax:* (731) 663-2427
www.gracebroadcasting.com
License: Humboldt, Gibson County, TN held by Grace Broadcasting Services Inc.
Group Owner: Grace Broadcasting Services Inc.
Arbitron Metro Market: Jackson, TN; *Target Audience:* 18-49.
Dave Hacker, Engineering Dir

WZDQ
09-01-1964; 102.3 MHz FM; *Hrs Open:* 24; 6 kw; 299 ft.; N35 45 45 W88 51 42
111 W. Main St., Jackson, TN 38302 US
(731) 427-9616
therocketjackson.com
License: Humboldt, Gibson County, TN held by Thomas Radio LLC.
Group Owner: Thomas Media LLC
Nat'l Network: ABC; CBS
Arbitron Metro Market: Jackson, TN; *Target Audience:* 25-49; middle to upper class; *Adv. Rates:* 28; 26; 28; 20

Huntingdon

WWDX
10-21-1975; 1530 kHz AM; *Hrs Open:* 7 AM-5 PM; 0.25 kw-C, NDD; 1 kw-D, NDD; N36 0 4 W88 26 2
215 Baker Road, Huntington, TN 38201 US
Fax: (731) 986-8557
www.thefarmradio.com
License: Huntingdon, TN held by Jim W. Freeland.
Group Owner: Freeland Broadcasting Stations; (acq 3-13-2007; $110,000)
Arbitron Metro Market: Huntingdon, TN; *Format:* Country; *No. News Employees:* 2; *Target Audience:* General.
Mark Johnson, General Manager
Sarah Dunning, General Sales Mgr
Jay Jackson, News Director

WEIO(FM)
11-01-1979; 100.9 MHz FM; *Hrs Open:* 24; 6 kw; 300 ft; N35 57 05 W88 27 47
215 Baker Rd., Huntingdon, TN 38344
Fax: (731) 986-8557
thefarmradio.com

License: Huntingdon, Carroll County, TN held by Jim W. Freeland.
Group Owner: Freeland Broadcasting Stations; (acq 9-16-2005; $650,000)
Regional Network: Tenn. Radio Net.
Population Served: 3,976; *Arbitron Metro Market:* Huntingdon, TN; *Format:* Country
Michael Ray, Operations Dir
Jerry Vandiver, General Manager
Dave Hacker, Chief Engineer

Jackson

***WAMP**
01-01-1995; 88.1 MHz FM; 0.75 kw; 135 ft.; N35 39 38 W88 51 30
P.O. Box 11597, Jackson, TN 38308 US
(731) 664-3882
www.afr.net
License: Jackson, Madison County, TN held by American Family Association.
Group Owner: American Family Radio
Arbitron Metro Market: Jackson, TN; *Format:* Christian
Tim Wildom, President
Donald Wildmon, Founder
Buddy Smith, Sr VP
Ed Vitagliano, Executive VP
Randy Sharp, Director Of Social Projects
Meeke Addison, Director Of Communications
Abraham Hamilton III, General Counsel & Public PolicyAnalyst

WDXI
10-31-1948; 1310 kHz AM; *Hrs Open:* 24; 5 kw-D, DAN; 1 kw-N, DAN; N35 39 50 W88 49 20
One Radio Park, Jackson, TN 38301 US
(731) 424-1310; *Fax:* (731) 424-1321
www.wdxi.com/
wdxi1310@yahoo.com
License: Jackson, TN held by Gerald W. Hunt
Nat'l Reps: D & R Radio
Arbitron Metro Market: Jackson, TN; *Format:* News *Special Programming:* Farm 12 hrs, gospel 16 hrs, sports 16 hrs wkly; *Hrs. of News Programming:* news progmg 10 hrs wkly; *No. News Employees:* 1; *Target Audience:* 25 plus.
Gerald Hunt, General Manager

***WIGH**
09-30-1995; 88.7 MHz FM; *Hrs Open:* 24; 14 kw; 538 ft.; N35 43 19 W88 36 7
1970-D N. Highland Ave., Jackson, TN 38305 US
(901) 427-8000; *Fax:* (901) 427-0730
www.afr.net
License: Jackson, Madison County, TN held by American Family Association.
Group Owner: American Family Radio; (acq 5-22-03; $20,000).
Nat'l Network: American Family Radio
Format: Christian; *Target Audience:* Visually & physically impaired.
Tim Wildmon, President
Donald Wildmon, Founder
Buddy Smith, Sr VP
Ed Vitagliano, Exec VP
Randy Sharp, Director Of Special Projects
Meeke Addison, Director Of Communications
Abraham Hamilton, General Counsel

***WKNP**
12-17-1990; 90.1 MHz FM; *Hrs Open:* 24; 18 kw; 512 ft.; N35 38 49 W88 50 0 *Rebroadcasts:* Rebroadcasts WKNO-FM Memphis 100%
Mailing Address: 7151 Cherry Farms Road, Cordova, TN 38016 US
Second Address: TN
(800) 766-9566; *Fax:* (901) 729-8176
www.wknofm.org
radio@wkno.org
License: Jackson, Madison County, TN held by Mid-South Public Communications Foundation.
Nat'l Network: NPR; PRI
TV Affiliate: *WKNO-TV affil; *Format:* Classical, News; *Hrs. of News Programming:* news progmg 51 hrs wkly; *No. News Employees:* 2; *Target Audience:* 35 plus.
Christopher Blank, News Director

WMXX-FM
05-09-1979; 103.1 MHz FM; 42 kw; 538 ft.; N35 32 39 W88 47 18
PO Box 3845, Jackson, TN 38303 US
(731) 424-1310; *Fax:* (731) 424-1321
www.kool103.com
License: Jackson, Madison County, TN
Arbitron Metro Market: Jackson, TN; *Format:* Oldies; *Target Audience:* 25-54.
Dave Lozzi, Programming Director

WNWS-FM
08-01-1993; 101.5 MHz FM; 2.2 kw; 381 ft.; N35 38 59 W88 46 11
207 West Lafayette Street, Jackson, TN 38301 US
(731) 423-8316
www.point5digital.com
carlton@wnws.com
License: Jackson, Madison County, TN held by Radiocorp of Jackson Inc.
Group Owner: The Wireless Group Inc.; (acq 12-6-00; $925,000).
Nat'l Network: CBS
TV Affiliate: Talk *Special Programming:* news progmg 25 hrs wkly; *Hrs. of News Programming:* 2; *No. News Employees:* 25 plus; upscale adults
Carlton Veirs, President
Greg Wood, Operations Manager
Larry Wood, General Manager
Keith Sherley, News Director/Online Editor
Joe Sills, Digital Media/Projects

WTJS
01-01-1931; 1390 kHz AM; *Hrs Open:* 24; 5 kw-D, 1 kw-N, DA-N; N35 38 50 W88 50 00
122 Radio Rd., Jackson, TN 78701
(731) 427-3316
www.wtjs.com
License: Jackson, Madison County, TN held by Forever South Licenses LLC.
Group Owner: Forever Communications Inc.; (acq 5-12-2006; grpsl).
Regional Network: Tenn. Radio Net.
Population Served: 290,120; *Arbitron Metro Market:* Jackson, TN; *Hrs. of News Programming:* news progmg 30 hrs wkly; *No. News Employees:* 3; *Target Audience:* 35 plus; general
Verla Price, General Manager
Buzz, Programming Director
Tim Forrest, Production Director
Dave Hacker, Chief Engineer
Connie Cain, Traffic Manager

WOGY
01-01-1947; 104.1 MHz FM; 100 kw; 682 ft.; N35 38 49 W88 50 0
122 Radio Road, Jackson, TN 38301 US
(731) 427-3316
www.froggy1041.com
studio@froggy1041.com
License: Jackson, Madison County, TN
Group Owner: Forever Communications Inc.
Arbitron Metro Market: Jackson, TN; *Format:* Country; *Target Audience:* 18-54.
Deb Smith, Promotions Manager
Rusty Mac, News Director

Jamestown

WCLC
10-28-1957; 1260 kHz AM; 1 kw-D, NDD; N36 26 10 W84 55 42
224 West Central Avenue, PO Box 1509, Jamestown, TN 38556 US
(931) 879-8188; *Fax:* (931) 879-1733
www.newlife105.com
info@newlife105.com
License: Jamestown, TN held by Bible Believers Network Inc.
Arbitron Metro Market: Jamestown, TN; *Format:* Religious *Special Programming:* Farm 2 hrs, bluegrass 3 hrs wkly
Connie Cody, Station Manager
Cheryl Wright, Music/Programming Director
Steve Boutelle, News Director
Sheliah Hughes, Traffic/Promotions Director

WCLC-FM
01-01-1985; 105.1 MHz FM; 6 kw; 328 ft.; N36 18 45 W84 56 13
224 West Central Avenue, PO Box 1509, Jamestown, TN 38556 US
(931) 879-8188; *Fax:* (931) 879-1733
www.newlife105.com
info@newlife105.com
License: Jamestown, Fentress County, TN
Arbitron Metro Market: Jamestown, TN; *Format:* Religious
Connie Cody, Station Manager
Cheryl Wright, Music/Programming Director
Steve Boutelle, News Director
Sheliah Hughes, Traffic/Promotions Director

WDEB
01-12-1968; 1500 kHz AM; *Hrs Open:* Sunrise-sunset; 0.5 kw-C, NDD; 1 kw-D, NDD; N36 25 31 W84 56 32
403 Livingston Avenue, Jamestown, TN 38556 US
(931) 879-8164
License: Jamestown, TN held by BAZ Broadcasting Inc.
Regional Network: Tenn. Radio Net.
Arbitron Metro Market: Cookeville, TN; *Format:* Country, Religious *Special Programming:* Farm 3 hrs wkly; *Hrs. of News Programming:* news progmg 10 hrs wkly; *No. News Employees:* 7; *Target Audience:* 18-54;household members who spend money in the marketplace
N.A. Baz, President
Jean Baz, Operations Dir
Gary Crocket, Programming Director
Gunther Muhsemann, Chief Engineer
Turk Baz, Local News Editor
Kevin Baz, Music Director

WDEB-FM
10-10-1972; 103.9 MHz FM; *Hrs Open:* 5 AM-10:15 PM; 3.4 kw; 443 ft.; N36 25 31 W84 56 32
403 Livingston Avenue, Jamestown, TN 38556 US
(931) 879-8164
License: Jamestown, Fentress County, TN
Wire Services: NOAA Weather
Arbitron Metro Market: Cookeville, TN; *Format:* Country, Gospel
Jean Baz, General Sales Mgr
Cindy Mitchell, Programming Director
John Mullinix, Disc Jockey
Kevin Baz, Disc Jockey
Turk Baz, Disc Jockey
N. Baz, Regional Sales Manager

Jefferson City

WNRX
01-01-1977; 99.3 MHz FM; *Hrs Open:* 24; 0.2 w; 653 ft.; N36 4 28 W83 34 56
PO Box 430, Jefferson City, TN 37760 US
(865) 475-3135
License: Jefferson City, TN held by Lakeway Broadcasting LLC
Group Owner: Lakeway Broadcasting LLC; (acq 7-20-2004; $1.65 million).
Arbitron Metro Market: Jefferson City, TN; *Format:* Classic Rock; *No. News Employees:* 1

WJFC
11-01-1961; 1480 kHz AM; 0.5 kw-D, ND2; 0.034 kw-N, ND2; N36 6 15 W83 29 10
1227 N. Hwy. 92, Jefferson City, TN 37760 USA
(865) 475-3135
www.wjfcradio.com
stiners2@k12tn.net
License: Jefferson City, TN held by Lakeway Broadcasting LLC
Group Owner: Lakeway Broadcasting, LLC
Format: Country

Jellico

WEKX
01-01-1993; 102.7 MHz FM; *Hrs Open:* 24; 0.63 kw; 1007 ft.; N36 41 28 W84 12 31
522 Main Street, Williamsburg, KY 40769 US
(606) 549-2285; *Fax:* (606) 549-5565
www.werock1027.com
License: Jellico, Campbell County, TN held by Whitley Broadcasting Co. Inc.
Regional Reps: Rgnl Reps.
Arbitron Metro Market: Jellico, TN; *Format:* Classic Rock; *Hrs. of News Programming:* News progmg 5 hrs wkly
David Estes, General Manager
Rick Campbell, Programming Director
Frank Folsom, Chief Engineer

WJJT
02-01-1972; 1540 kHz AM; *Hrs Open:* Sunup to Sundown
Mailing Address: 230 N. Florence Avenue, Jellico, TN 37762 US
Second Address: PO Box 88, Jellico, TN 37762
(423) 494-1582; *Fax:* (423) 784-5991
www.wjjtradio.com
info@wjjtradio.com
License: Jellico, TN held by Southeast Broadcasting Corp.
Nat'l Network: Salem Radio Network
Format: Gospel; *Hrs. of News Programming:* news progmg 4 hrs wkly; *No. News Employees:* 3
James Kilgore, President
Glenda Kilgore, Executive Vice President

Johnson City

WETB
10-01-1947; 790 kHz AM; *Hrs Open:* 6 AM-11 PM; 5 kw-D, ND1; 0.072 kw-N, ND1; N36 19 43 W82 24 39
231 Brandonwood Drive, Johnson City, TN 37604 US

(423) 928-7131; *Fax:* (423) 928-8392
www.wetb790am.wix.com/wetb
wetb790am@yahoo.com
License: Johnson City, TN held by Mountain Signals Inc.
Nat'l Network: USA
Arbitron Metro Market: Johnson City, TN; *Format:* Gospel; *Hrs. of News Programming:* news progmg 3 hrs wkly; *No. News Employees:* 1; *Target Audience:* General.; *Adv. Rates:* 216; 216; 216; 216
Teresa Gobble, Office Staff
Nola Peterson, Office Staff
Dick McClellan, Announcer
Mark Hatcher, Announcer
James Allen, Announcer

***WETS-FM**
02-26-1974; 89.5 MHz FM; *Hrs Open:* 24; 66 kw; 2270 ft.; N36 26 2 W82 8 8
Mailing Address: 1125 Centennial Drive, Johnson City, TN 37614 US
Second Address: PO Box 70630, Johnson City, TN 37614
(423) 439-6440
www.wets.org
wets@etsu.edu
License: Johnson City, Washington County, TN held by East Tennessee State University.
Nat'l Network: NPR; PRI
Arbitron Metro Market: Johnson City, TN; *Format:* News, News/Talk, 86 *Special Programming:* Blues 12 hrs, Sp one hr wkly; *Hrs. of News Programming:* News progmg 22 hrs wkly; *Target Audience:* General.
Nick Roosa, Operations Manager
Wayne Winkler, Station Manager
Jim Blalock, Programming Director
Fred Sauceman, News Director
Mitch Sandidge, Chief Engineer
Dave Edwards, Engineer
Tina Pasquale, Development Associate
Tony Coker,Membership Coordinator

WJCW
12-13-1938; 910 kHz AM; *Hrs Open:* 24; 5 kw-D, DAN; 1 kw-N, DAN; N36 24 37 W82 27 13
162 Free Hill Rd., Gray, TN 37615 US
(423) 467-2616
www.wjcw.com
patti.johnson@cumulus.com
License: Johnson City, TN held by Radio License Holding CBC, LLC
Group Owner: Cumulus Media Inc.; (acq 5-30-2000; grpsl)
Nat'l Network: CBS; ABC
Arbitron Metro Market: Johnson City-Kingsport-Bristol, TN-VA; *Format:* News/Talk
Paul Overbay, General Sales Mgr
Bill Meade, Programming Director

WQUT
03-01-1948; 101.5 MHz FM; *Hrs Open:* 24; 99 kw; 1499 ft.; N36 16 7 W82 20 21
162 Free Hill Rd., Gray, TN 37615 US
(423) 467-2608
www.wqut.com
john.patrick@cumulus.com
License: Johnson City, TN held by Radio License Holding CBC, LLC
Group Owner: Cumulus Media Inc.
Arbitron Metro Market: Johnson City-Kingsport-Bristol, TN-VA; *Format:* Classic Rock
John Patrick, Programming Director
Steve Haas, Promotions Manager

Jonesborough

WKTP
10-01-1958; 1590 kHz AM; *Hrs Open:* 24; 5 kw-U, DA-2; N36 19 54 W82 28 27 *Rebroadcasts:* Rebroadcasts WKPT(AM) Kingsport 95%
222 Commerce St., Kingsport, TN 37660
(423) 246-9578; *Fax:* (423) 247-9836
www.espntricities.com
charlie@espntricities.com
License: Jonesborough, Washington County, TN held by Holston Valley Broadcasting Corp.
Group Owner: Glenwood Communications Corp.; (acq 1-25-90; $90,000;
Nat'l Network: ABC; *Nat'l Reps:* Eastman; *Wire Services:* AP
Population Served: 200,000; *Arbitron Metro Market:* Johnson City-Kingsport-Bristol, TN-VA *TV Affiliate:* WKPT-TV; *Format:* Sports; *Hrs. of News Programming:* news progmg 24 hrs wkly; *No. News Employees:* 2 *Target Audience:* 35 plus.
George Devault, President
David Widener, General Manager
Charlie Aesque, VP/Sales Manager
Melanie Lisenby, Advertising Sales/Marketing
Scott Gray, Sports Marketing Director/Advertising Sales
David Dowell, Advertising Sales/VikingsPlay by Play Announcer

Karns

WNOX
01-08-1989; 93.1 MHz FM; 2.4 kw; 512 ft.; N35 57 46 W84 1 23
P.O. Box 693, 720 East Capitol Drive, Milwaukee, WI 53212 US
(865) 824-1021; *Fax:* (865) 693-8493
info@wmyu.com
License: Karns, Knox County, TN held by Journal Broadcast Corp.
Group Owner: Journal Communications Inc.; (acq 5-19-97)
Arbitron Metro Market: Knoxville, TN; *Format:* Country
Andy Laird, Operations Dir
Chris Protzman, General Manager
Dan McKee, General Sales Mgr
Mike Hammond, Programming Director
Rich Bailey, Operations Manager

Kingsport

***WCQR-FM**
12-01-1996; 88.3 MHz FM; 1.2 kw; 2133 ft.; N36 25 53 W82 8 16
2312 Oak Street, Gray, TN 37615 US
(423) 477-5676; *Fax:* (423) 477-7060
www.wcqr.org
office@wcqr.org
License: Kingsport, Sullivan County, TN held by Positive Alternative Radio Inc.
Group Owner: Positive Alternative Radio Inc.
Nat'l Network: Salem Radio Network
Arbitron Metro Market: Johnson City-Kingsport-Bristol, TN-VA; *Format:* Christian; *Target Audience:* 25-54.
Mike Perry, General Manager

***WCSK**
11-05-1984; 90.3 MHz FM; 195 w; 23 ft; N36 31 37 W82 35 12
Kingsport City Schools, Administrative Support Center, 400 Clinchfield Street, Kingsport, TN 37660
(423) 378-2111
http://kingsport.schoolfusion.us
jhall@k12k.com
License: Kingsport, Sullivan County, TN held by Kingsport Board of Education.
Population Served: 70,000; *Arbitron Metro Market:* Johnson City-Ki
Jeff Hall, Station Manager

WHGG
06-01-1967; 1090 kHz AM; *Hrs Open:* 12
P.O. Box 2061, Bristol, TN 37621 US
License: Kingsport, TN held by Information Communication Corp.
Group Owner: Information Communications Corp.; (acq 1-1-2006; $250,000 with WABN(AM) Abingdon, VA).
Arbitron Metro Market: Johnson City-Kingsport-Bristol, TN-VA; *Format:* Oldies; *Hrs. of News Programming:* news progmg 10 hrs wkly; *No. News Employees:* 1; *Target Audience:* 24-55.

WGOC
10-01-1951; 1320 kHz AM; *Hrs Open:* 24; 5 kw-D, DAN; 0.5 kw-N, DAN; N36 33 12 W82 28 58
Mailing Address: 162 Free Hill Rd., Gray, TN 37615 US
Second Address: PO Box 8, Bloomington, IL 61702
(423) 477-1000; *Fax:* (423) 477-4747
License: Kingsport, TN held by Radio License Holding CBC, LLC
Group Owner: Cumulus Media Inc.; (acq 5-30-2000; grpsl)
Nat'l Network: ESPN Radio; CBS Radio; *Nat'l Reps:* Katz Radio; *Wire Services:* AP
Arbitron Metro Market: Johnson City-Kingsport-Bristol, TN-VA; *Format:* News

WKOS
02-21-1979; 104.9 MHz FM; 2.75 kw; 492 ft.; N36 33 14 W82 27 0
Mailing Address: 162 Free Hill Rd., Gray, TN 37615 US
Second Address: PO Box 8668, Gray, TN 37615
(423) 477-1000
www.1049nashicon.com
paul.overbay@cumulus.com
License: Kingsport, TN held by Radio License Holding CBC, LLC
Group Owner: Cumulus Media Inc.
Nat'l Network: Westwood One
Arbitron Metro Market: Johnson City-Kingsport-Bristol, TN-VA; *Format:* Country; *Target Audience:* 25-54.
Paul Overbay, General Sales Mgr
Debbie Caso, Market Manager

WKPT
07-14-1940; 1400 kHz AM; *Hrs Open:* 24; 1 kw-U; N36 32 37 W82 31 21
222 Commerce St., Kingsport, TN 37660
(423) 246-9578; *Fax:* (423) 247-9836
www.espntricities.com
charlie@espntricities.com
License: Kingsport, Sullivan County, TN held by Holston Valley Broadcasting Corp.
Group Owner: Glenwood Communications Corp.; (acq 6-1-66)
Nat'l Network: ABC; *Regional Network:* U T Vol Network; *Nat'l Reps:* Eastman; *Wire Services:* AP
Population Served: 650,000; *Arbitron Metro Market:* Johnson City-Kingsport-Bristol, TN-VA *TV Affiliate:* WKPT-TV; *Format:* Sports; *No. News Employees:* 2; *Target Audience:* 35 plus.
George Devault, President
David Widener, General Manager
Charlie Aesque, General Sales Mgr
Melanie Lisenby, Advertising Sales/Marketing
Scott Gray, Sports Marketing Director
N. David Widener, Executive Vice President
RogerEpperson, News Reporter
Emily Pridemore, Traffic Manager
David Light, Women's Int Ed

WTFM
02-01-1948; 98.5 MHz FM; *Hrs Open:* 24; 74 kw; Ant 2,241 ft; N36 25 54 W82 08 15
222 Commerce St., Kingsport, TN 37660
(423) 246-9578; *Fax:* (423) 247-9836
www.wtfm.com
bob@wtfm.com
License: Kingsport, Sullivan County, TN held by Holsten Valley Broadcasting
Group Owner: Glenwood Communications Corp.; 06-01-1966
Nat'l Network: ABC; *Nat'l Reps:* Eastman; *Wire Services:* AP
Population Served: 1,000,000; *Arbitron Metro Market:* Johnson City-Kingsport-Bristol, TN-VA *TV Affiliate:* WKPT-TV affil; *Format:* Adult Contemp; *No. News Employees:* 2; *Target Audience:* 25-54 Women
George Devault, President
David Widener, General Manager

Kingston

WBBX
07-01-1978; 1410 kHz AM; *Hrs Open:* 8 AM-6 PM; 0.5 kw-D, NDD; N35 52 49 W84 30 56
705 Greenwood, Box 389, Kingston, TN 37763 US
(615) 376-6954
License: Kingston, TN held by Pilgrim Pathway Inc.
Arbitron Metro Market: North Platte NE
Mike Kestler, President

***WKTS**
09-11-2006; 90.1 MHz FM; *Hrs Open:* 24; 0.055 kw vert; 633 ft.; N35 45 57 W84 34 33
331 Skyline View Lane, Kingston, TN 37763 US
License: Kingston, Roane County, TN held by Foothills Broadcasting, Inc.
Arbitron Metro Market: Kingston, TN; *Format:* Christian *Special Programming:* 2 church services, 2hrs; *Hrs. of News Programming:* news progmg 3 hrs wkly; *No. News Employees:* 1
Lee Brandel, Manager

Kingston Springs

WFFI
01-15-1993; 93.7 MHz FM; *Hrs Open:* 24; 1.15 kw; 755 ft.; N36 8 10 W86 59 4 *Rebroadcasts:* Simulcasts with WFFH(FM) Smyrna US
www.94fmthefish.net
License: Kingston Springs, Cheatham County, TN held by Caron Broadcasting Inc.
Group Owner: Salem Communications Corp.; (acq 12-18-2002; $5.6 million with WFFH(FM) Smyrna).
Nat'l Network: Salem Radio Network; *Nat'l Reps:* Salem
Arbitron Metro Market: Nashville, TN; *Format:* Christian; *Target Audience:* 25-54; adults

Knoxville

WNPZ
05-21-1961; 1580 kHz AM; 1 kw-C, NDD; 5 kw-D, NDD; N35 54 42 W83 53 33
1515 Magnolia Avenue, Knoxville, TN 37917 US
License: Knoxville, TN held by Metropolitan Management Corp. of Tennessee
Arbitron Metro Market: Knoxville, TN

RADIO - U.S.

Randal Mangham, President
Rev. Maurice Gaines, Programming Director

WVLZ
06-01-1988; 1180 kHz AM; 2.6 kw-C, NDD; 10 kw-D, NDD; N35 58 48 W83 49 9
US
www.oldies1180.com
License: Knoxville, TN held by Kirkland Wireless Broadcasters Inc.
Arbitron Metro Market: Knoxville, TN; *Format:* Sports; *Target Audience:* 30 plus; young, married with small children
John Hodge, Station Manager

WIFA
01-21-1941; 1240 kHz AM; *Hrs Open:* 24; 1 kw-U, ND1; N35 57 17 W83 57 4
P.O. Box 3848, Evansvill, IN 47736 US
License: Knoxville, TN held by Progressive Media Inc.
Arbitron Metro Market: Knoxville, TN; *Format:* Adult Contemp, Christian
Barry Culberson, President
Brian Brooks, General Manager

WIMZ
10-01-1949; 103.5 MHz FM; 79 kW; 1722 ft.; N36 8 6 W83 43 29
1100 Sharps Ridge Memorial Park Dr, Knoxville, TN 37917 USA
(865) 525-6000; *Fax:* (865) 525-2000
wimz.com
License: Knoxville, Knox County, TN held by Midwest Communications Inc.
Group Owner: Midwest Communications Inc.
Arbitron Metro Market: Knoxville, TN; *Format:* Classic Rock
Randy Chambers, Brand Manager

WITA
09-01-1960; 1490 kHz AM; *Hrs Open:* 24 hrs; 1 kw-U, ND1; N35 58 11 W83 57 56
1300 WWCR Avenue, Nashville, LA 37218 US
(865) 240-4084; *Fax:* (615) 255-1311
www.1490wita.com
License: Knoxville, TN held by RR Broadcast Group Inc.
Arbitron Metro Market: Knoxville, TN; *Format:* Christian, Talk *Special Programming:* Black 8 hrs wkly; *Target Audience:* General.
Brad Murray, Station Manager
Chris Buchanan, Programming Director/Sales
Phil Patton, Chief Engineer

WIVK
12-16-1965; 107.7 MHz FM; *Hrs Open:* 24; 91 kw; 2077 ft.; N35 48 41 W83 40 10
4711 Old Kingston Pike, Knoxville, TN 37919 US
(865) 588-6511; *Fax:* (865) 588-3725
www.wivk.com
License: Knoxville, TN held by Radio License Holding CBC, LLC
Group Owner: Cumulus Media Inc.
Arbitron Metro Market: Knoxville, TN; *Format:* Country
John Crooks, Programming Director

WKVL
01-16-1989; 850 kHz AM; 50 kw-D, DAD; N36 4 12 W83 58 19
261 Hannum Street, Alcoa, TN 37701 US
(865) 724-1100
www.wkvl.com
info@wkvl.com
License: Knoxville, TN held by Blount Broadcasting Corporation
Group Owner: Blount Broadcasting Corporation; (acq 10-15-99; grpsl).
Arbitron Metro Market: Knoxville, TN; *Format:* Talk; *Target Audience:* 25 plus; educated, informed adults

WJXB
04-10-1967; 97.5 MHz FM; *Hrs Open:* 24; 96 kW; 1,296 ft; N36 00 36 W83 55 57
1100 Sharps Ridge Memorial Park Dr, Knoxville, TN 37917
(865) 525-6000; *Fax:* (865) 656-3292
b975.com
License: Knoxville, Knox County, TN held by Midwest Communications Inc.
Group Owner: Midwest Communications Inc.
Population Served: 174,589; *Arbitron Metro Market:* Knoxville, TN; *Format:* Adult Contemp
Shane Cox, Brand Manager

***WKCS**
12-01-1952; 91.1 MHz FM; *Hrs Open:* 8 AM-3:30 PM; 0.31 kw horiz; 72 ft.; N35 59 36 W83 55 24
2509 Broadway Street Northeast, Knoxville, TN 37917 US
(865) 594-1259
www.wkcsradio.org
wkcs@knoxschools.org
License: Knoxville, Knox County, TN held by Fulton High School.
Arbitron Metro Market: Knoxville, TN; *Format:* Oldies; *Hrs. of News Programming:* News progmg 3 hrs wkly; *Target Audience:* 18 plus; University of Tennessee
Russell Mayes, General Manager

WKGN
09-28-1947; 1340 kHz AM; 1 kw-U, ND1; N35 57 20 W83 58 14
4801 East Independence Boulevard, Charlotte, NC 28212 US
(800) 975-0760
rcoates@norsanmedia.com
License: Knoxville, TN held by Norsan Consulting and Management Inc.
Group Owner: Norsan Consulting and Management Inc.; (acq 3-8-2006; $500,000).
Nat'l Network: Westwood One; *Nat'l Reps:* Roslin
Arbitron Metro Market: Knoxville, TN; *Format:* Gospel *Special Programming:* Relg 5 hrs, medicine/health one hr wkly; *Target Audience:* 18-34; young, mobile adults
Ronnie Coates, National/Regional Sales

WKXV
02-01-1953; 900 kHz AM; *Hrs Open:* 24 hours; 1 kw-D, ND1; 0.258 kw-N, ND1; N35 58 52 W83 59 15
5106 Middlebrook Pike, Knoxville, TN 37921 US
(865) 558-0900
www.wkxvradio.com
wkxv@bellsouth.net
License: Knoxville, TN held by Ratel Broadcasting Co. Inc.
Arbitron Metro Market: Knoxville, TN; *Format:* Gospel, Religious; *Target Audience:* 18+; *Adv. Rates:* 12;20
Ted Lowe
Brandon Lewis
Eva Ruffin

WETR
07-05-1995; 760 kHz AM; *Hrs Open:* Day-time; 2.4 kw-D, NDD; N35 59 18 W83 50 35
1621 E. Magnolia Ave., Knoxville, TN 37917 US
(865) 525-0620
www.talkradio760.com
info@talkradio760.com
License: Knoxville, TN held by Thomas H. Moffit Jr.
Nat'l Network: Salem Radio Network; Talk Radio Network
Arbitron Metro Market: Knoxville, TN; *Format:* News, News/Talk, 86; *Target Audience:* 25-54; blue collar men & women
Bob Bell, Sales Manager
Doug Elkins, Account Executive

WNML
01-01-1921; 990 kHz AM; *Hrs Open:* 24; 10 kw *Rebroadcasts:* Simulcast with WNML-FM
4711 Old Kingston Pike, Knoxville, TN 37919 US
(865) 656-9900
www.sportsradiownml.com
License: Knoxville, TN held by Radio License Holding CBC, LLC
Group Owner: Cumulus Media Inc.
Arbitron Metro Market: Knoxville, TN; *Format:* Sports, Talk
Mickey Dearstone, Programming Director

WKHT
11-01-1991; 104.5 MHz FM; 2.3 kw; 528 ft.; N36 0 8 W83 56 41
1533 Amherst Road, Knoxville, TN 37909 US
(865) 824-1021
www.hot1045.net
jtack@jrn.com
License: Knoxville, Knox County, TN held by Journal Broadcast Corp.
Group Owner: Journal Communications Inc.; (acq 3-4-98; $5.745 million with WQBB(AM) Powell).
Nat'l Reps: Roslin
Arbitron Metro Market: Knoxville, TN; *Format:* Classic Rock *Special Programming:* Pub affrs 2 hrs wkly; *Target Audience:* 35 plus; female
Rich Bailey, Operations Manager
Dan McKee, General Sales Mgr
Joey Tack, Programming Director

WRJZ
02-12-1927; 620 kHz AM; *Hrs Open:* 24; 5 kw-D, DAN; 5 kw-N, DAN; N35 59 24 W83 50 15
1621 E. Magnolia Ave, Knoxville, TN 37917 US
(865) 525-0620
www.wrjz.com
bbell@wrjz.com
License: Knoxville, TN held by Tennessee Media Associates.
Nat'l Network: Salem Radio Network; *Nat'l Reps:* Salem
Arbitron Metro Market: Knoxville, TN; *Format:* Christian, Talk; *Hrs. of News Programming:* News progmg 5 hrs wkly; *Target Audience:* 25-54; white collar men & woman
Dave Clabo, Operator/Producer
Bob Bell, Manager
Sam Truan, Operator/Producer
Doug Elkins, Sales Executive
Lee Brandel, Business Coordinator

***WUOT**
10-01-1949; 91.9 MHz FM; *Hrs Open:* 24; 64 kw; 1752 ft.; N35 59 44 W83 57 23
209 Communications Bldg., Knoxville, TN 37996-0322 US
(865) 974-5375; *Fax:* (865) 974-3941
www.wuot.org
wuot@utk.edu
License: Knoxville, Knox County, TN held by University of Tennessee.
Nat'l Network: PRI; NPR; *Wire Services:* AP
Arbitron Metro Market: Knoxville, TN; *Format:* Classical, Jazz, 60; *Hrs. of News Programming:* news progmg 37 hrs wkly; *No. News Employees:* 3; *Target Audience:* 35-54.
Regina Dean, General Manager
Tammy Berry, Office Manager
Matt Shafer Powell, Director of News Content/Executive Producer
Mike Murrell, Chief Engineer
Cindy Hassil, Corporate/Community Relations Director
Dawn Goodall, UnderwritingCoordinator
Denise Carpenter, Webmaster/Traffic Coordinator/Operations Assistant
Elizabeth Hall, Business Manager
Greg Hill, Director of Programming/Operations
Jennie Caissie, Membership Coordinator

***WUTK-FM**
01-04-1982; 90.3 MHz FM; *Hrs Open:* 24; 0.8 kw vert; 69 ft.; N35 57 9 W83 55 34
P103 Andy Holt Tower, Knoxville, TN 37996-0333 US
(865) 974-5242; *Fax:* (865) 974-2814
www.wutkradio.com
wutk@utk.edu
License: Knoxville, Knox County, TN held by University of Tennessee.
Arbitron Metro Market: Knoxville, TN; *Format:* Rock/AOR; *Target Audience:* 18-45; male/female
Dr. Peter Gross, Faculty Advisor
Benny Smith, General Manager/Programming & Promotions Director
Todd Roberts, Production Director
Graham Smith, Production Assistant Director
Damian Messer, News Director
Tony Farina,Underwriting/Digital Media Sales Director
Ben Smith, Music Department Co-Director
Kevin Summitt, Music Department Co-Director
Kyle Tasman, Sports Co-Director
Riley Duncan, Sports Digital Media Director

La Follette

WQLA
09-01-1983; 960 kHz AM; *Hrs Open:* 24 HRS; 1 kw-D, ND2; 0.033 kw-N, ND2; N36 22 2 W84 8 50
Box 1530, Lafollette, TN 37766 US
(423) 566-1000; *Fax:* (423) 566-7070
wqla@bellsouth.net
License: La Follette, TN held by Beverly Broadcasting Co., LLC
Nat'l Reps: Roslin
Format: Classic Rock *Special Programming:* LET IT RIP; *Hrs. of News Programming:* TOP OF HOUR; *No. News Employees:* 3; *Target Audience:* General.
Cliff Jennings, President
BARBARA NULF, General Manager

WLAF
05-17-1953; 1450 kHz AM; *Hrs Open:* 24; 1 kw-U, ND1; N36 22 52 W84 7 32
210 North 5th Street, Lafollette, TN 37766 US
(423) 562-1450
www.1450wlaf.com
License: La Follette, TN held by Stair Co. Inc.
Nat'l Network: USA; *Regional Network:* Tenn. Radio Net.
Format: Gospel *Special Programming:* Bluegrass 7 hrs wkly; *Hrs. of News Programming:* news progmg 7 hrs wkly; *No. News Employees:* 1; *Target Audience:* 12+ or 25+.; *Adv. Rates:* 10; 10; 10; 10
Jim Stair, President
Bill Waddell, Operations Dir

WTNQ
09-01-1982; 104.9 MHz FM; *Hrs Open:* 24; 2.3 kw; 499 ft.; N36 21 8 W84 5 20

305 East Central Avenue, Lafollette, TN 37766 US
(423) 562-0550; *Fax:* (423) 562-0105
www.wtnqfm.com
License: La Follette, Campbell County, TN
Format: Sports, Country; *Target Audience:* 18 plus.; *Adv. Rates:* 15; 15; 15; 15
Barbara Nuls, General Sales Mgr

La Vergne

WBUZ
05-01-1962; 102.9 MHz FM; *Hrs Open:* 24; 100 kw; 955 ft.; N35 48 1 W86 37 17
Mailing Address: 1824 Murfreesboro Pike, Nashville, TN 37217 US
Second Address: PO Box 290099, Nashville, TN 37217
(615) 399-1029; *Fax:* (615) 361-9873
www.1029thebuzz.com
jhamtpon@cromwellradio.com
License: La Vergne, Rutherford County, TN held by WYCQ Inc.
Group Owner: The Cromwell Group Inc.; (acq 11-28-89).
Arbitron Metro Market: Nashville, TN; *Format:* Rock/AOR *Special Programming:* Farm one hr wkly; *Target Audience:* 18-34; residents in middle TN
Tincy Crouse, General Manager
Jana Hampton, Station Manager
Zigz, Programming Director
Chad Fournier, Promotions Director/Digital Manager

Lafayette

WEEN
11-03-1958; 1460 kHz AM; *Hrs Open:* Daytime; 0.86 kw-D, ND1; 0.119 kw-N, ND1; N36 32 6 W86 0 27
P.O. Box 160, Lafayette, TN 37083 US
(615) 666-2169; *Fax:* (615) 666-8056
www.wlct.com/
License: Lafayette, TN held by Lafayette Broadcasting Co. Inc.
Nat'l Network: Salem Radio Network; *Regional Network:* Tenn. Radio Net.
Arbitron Metro Market: Lafayette, TN; *Format:* Gospel *Special Programming:* Farm 5 hrs wkly; *Target Audience:* General; 25-54 year olds; *Adv. Rates:* 8.95; 8.95; 8.95; n/a
Ivan Davis, CEO
Randall Swaffer, General Manager
Randy Swaffer, Station Manager

WLCT
07-01-1995; 102.1 MHz FM; *Hrs Open:* 5 AM-11 PM; 6 kw; 325 ft.; N36 32 6 W86 0 27
P.O. Box 160, Lafayette, TN 37083 US
(615) 666-2169; *Fax:* (615) 666-8056
www.wlct.com
License: Lafayette, Macon County, TN held by Lafayette Broadcasting Co. Inc.
Format: Country; *Target Audience:* 20-60.; *Adv. Rates:* 8.95; 8.95; 8.95; 8.95
Randy Swaffer, General Manager
Jamie Dallas, General Sales Mgr
Melinda White, News Director
Jamie DAllas, Promotions Director

Lakeland

WMQM
04-27-1955; 1600 kHz AM; *Hrs Open:* 24
3704 Whitter Road, Memphis, TN 38108 US
(901) 327-2500; *Fax:* (901) 327-2777
www.1600wmqm.com
License: Lakeland, TN held by WMQM Inc.
Group Owner: F W Robbert Broadcasting Co. Inc.
Arbitron Metro Market: Memphis, TN; *Format:* Religious; *Target Audience:* General.
David Brown, Station Manager
Shane Poole, Programming/Sales Director
Phil Patton, Chief Engineer

Lakesite

WALV-FM
07-01-1976; 105.1 MHz FM; *Hrs Open:* 24; 0.85 kw; 879 ft.; N35 15 20 W85 13 34
1305 Carter St., Chattanooga, TN 37402 US
(423) 265-9494; *Fax:* (423) 266-2335
www.espnchattanooga.com
License: Lakesite, Hamilton County, TN held by J.L. Brewer Broadcasting of Cleveland LLC.
Group Owner: Brewer Broadcasting Corp.; 1-May
Nat'l Network: ESPN Radio; *Nat'l Reps:* Katz Radio
Population Served: 450,000; *Arbitron Metro Market:* Chattanooga, TN; *Format:* Sports; *Target Audience:* A18+; *Adv. Rates:* 30; 25; 30; 20

Keith Landecker, Operations Manager
Mike Baskin, Director of Sales
Wells Guthrie, Programming Director

Lawrenceburg

***WAWI**
01-01-1999; 89.7 MHz FM; 6 kw; 148 ft.; N35 16 4 W87 19 25
105 Helton Dr., Lawrenceburg, TN 38464 US
(931) 766-9741
www.afr.net
faq@afa.net
License: Lawrenceburg, Lawrence County, TN held by American Family Association.
Group Owner: American Family Radio
Arbitron Metro Market: Mills WY; *Format:* Religious
Tim Wildmon, President
Donald Wildmon, Founder
Buddy Smith, Sr VP
Ed Vitagliano, Exec VP
Randy Sharp, Director Of Special Projects
Meeke Addison, Director Of Communications
Abraham Hamilton III, General Counsel

WDXE
07-21-1951; 1370 kHz AM; 1 kw-D, ND1; 0.044 kw-N, ND1; N35 15 25 W87 18 24
29 Public Square, Lawrenceburg, TN 38464 US
(931) 762-4411; *Fax:* (931) 762-4789
www.wdxe.com
License: Lawrenceburg, TN held by Lakewood Communications LLC
Regional Network: Tenn. Radio Net.
Arbitron Metro Market: Lawrenceburg, TN; *Format:* Country
Brad Brown, General Manager
Heidi Osterheld, Sales
Ron Fisher, Sales
Kim Lovelace, Receptionist
Phillip Kemper, Chief Engineer
Ronnie Allen, Disc Jockey
Sunny Cull, Disc Jockey
Paula Walker, Women's Int Ed

WDXE-FM
08-28-1964; 98.3 MHz FM; 6 kw; 292 ft.; N35 15 25 W87 18 24
29 Public Square, Lawrenceburg, TN 38464 US
(931) 762-4411
www.wdxe.com
License: Lawrenceburg, Lawrence County, TN held by Pulaski Broadcasting
Arbitron Metro Market: Lawrenceburg, TN; *Format:* Adult Contemp
Jack Cheatwood, General Manager

WLLX
05-01-1991; 97.5 MHz FM; *Hrs Open:* 24; 42 kw; 528 ft.; N35 16 56 W87 6 18
Mailing Address: PO Box 156, Lawrenceburg, TN 38464 US
Second Address: 1212 N. Locust Ave., Lawrenceburg, TN 38464
(931) 762-6200; *Fax:* (931) 762-6200
www.wlxonline.com
proscomm@bellsouth.net
License: Lawrenceburg, Lawrence County, TN held by Roger W. Wright dba Prospect Communications
Format: Country; *No. News Employees:* 1; *Target Audience:* 25-54.
Roger Wright, Owner/Station Manager
Janet Wright, Sales Manager
Jenifer Cull, News Director
Ben Luna, Public Relations/Weather

WWLX
06-21-1987; 590 kHz AM; *Hrs Open:* 24
Mailing Address: PO Box 156, Lawrenceburg, TN 38464 US
Second Address: 1212 N. Locust Ave., Lawrenceburg, TN 38464
(931) 762-6200; *Fax:* (931) 762-6200
www.wlxonline.com
proscomm@bellsouth.net
License: Lawrenceburg, TN held by Roger W. Wright dba Prospect Communications.
Arbitron Metro Market: Lawrenceburg, TN; *Format:* Country *Special Programming:* Oldies R&R 8 hrs, old country 8 hrs wkly; *Hrs. of News Programming:* news progmg 10 hrs wkly; *No. News Employees:* 1 *TargetAudience:* General.
Roger Wright, Owner/Station Manager
Janet Wright, Sales Manager
Jenifer Cull, News Director
Ben Luna, Public Relations/Weather

***WZXX**
01-01-2005; 88.5 MHz FM; 0.076 kw; 545 ft.; N35 12 12 W87 19 39
P O Box 887, Brentwood, TN 37024 US
(208) 733-3551; *Fax:* (208) 733-3548
www.edgewaterbroadcasting.com
License: Lawrenceburg, Lawrence County, TN held by Radio Assist Ministry Inc.
Arbitron Metro Market: Florence, AL; *Format:* Christian
Ben Mccarron, Chief Operating Engineer
Clark Parrish, President & Technical Director
Robert L. Jackson, Head of Programming & Operations
Jim Long, General Manager
Steve Atkin, Promotions Manager
Diana Atkin, Vice President
EarlWilliamson, Secretary / Treasurer
John Devine, Director
Dennis Clounch, Director

Lebanon

WANT
10-01-1993; 98.9 MHz FM; *Hrs Open:* 24; 5 kw; 318 ft.; N36 12 24 W86 16 2
P.O. Box 399, Lebanon, TN 37088 US
(615) 449-3699; *Fax:* (615) 443-4235
www.wantfm.com
info@WANTFM.com
License: Lebanon, Wilson County, TN held by Bay-Pointe Broadcasting Co. Inc.
Arbitron Metro Market: Lebanon, TN,; *Format:* Country; *No. News Employees:* 1; *Target Audience:* General.
Susie James, Account Executive
Jo Smith, Account Executive

WKDA
10-05-1949; 900 kHz AM; *Hrs Open:* 24
1617 Lebanon Pike, Lebanon, TN 37210 US
(615) 889-1962
License: Lebanon, TN held by Wilson County Broadcasting, Inc.
Arbitron Metro Market: Nashville, TN; *Format:* Spanish; *No. News Employees:* 1; *Target Audience:* General.

***WFMQ**
12-15-1966; 91.5 MHz FM; *Hrs Open:* 24; 0.5 kw horiz; 82 ft.; N36 12 13 W86 18 1
P.O. Box 609, Lebanon, TN 37087 US
(615) 444-2562; *Fax:* (615) 444-2569
License: Lebanon, Wilson County, TN held by Cumberland University.
Format: Jazz *Special Programming:* Class 6 hrs wkly
Dr. Harvill Eaton, President

WRVW
08-31-1962; 107.5 MHz FM; *Hrs Open:* 24; 46 kw; 1342 ft.; N36 15 50 W86 47 39
55 Music Square West, Nashville, TN 37203 US
(615) 664-2400
www.1075theriver.com
License: Lebanon, Wilson County, TN held by Capstar TX LLC
Group Owner: iHeartMedia; (acq 8-30-00; grpsl).
Arbitron Metro Market: Nashville, TN; *Format:* Contemporary Hits/Top 40; *Hrs. of News Programming:* news progmg 4 hrs wkly; *No. News Employees:* 1; *Target Audience:* 18-49.
Melissa Kent, General Sales Mgr
Jonathan Shuford, Programming Director
Emma Applebome, Promotions Manager
Karlie Powell, Digital Program Director

WCOR
12-07-2005; 1490 kHz AM; *Hrs Open:* 24
PO Box 399, Lebanon, TN 37088 US
(615) 449-3699; *Fax:* (615) 443-4235
www.wantfm.com
info@WANTFM.com
License: Lebanon, TN held by Finbar Broadcasting Company Inc.
Nat'l Network: ABC
Arbitron Metro Market: Lebanon, TN; *Format:* News, News/Talk, 84, Talk
Jo Smith, Account Executive
Susie James, Account Executive

***WRSN**
88.1 MHz FM; 0.185 kw; 303 ft.; N36 17 36.3 W86 15 27 US
(919) 874-1500; *Fax:* (919_ 876-8578
License: Lebanon, Wilson County, TN held by St. John Vianney Roman Catholic School.
Nat'l Network: EWTN Radio
Arbitron Metro Market: Lebanon, TN; *Format:* Christian
John Sappenfield, General Manager

Lenoir City

WBLC

06-15-1965; 1360 kHz AM; *Hrs Open:* 24; 1 kw-D, ND1; 0.024 kw-N, ND1; N35 47 32 W84 17 45
Mailing Address: 412 Executive Tower Drive, Suite 205, Knoxville, TN 37922 US
Second Address: 4787 Browder Hollow Rd., Lenoir City, TN 37771
(618)627-4651; *Fax:* (618)627-2726
www.3abn.org/
wblc3abn@bellsouth.net
License: Lenoir City, TN held by Three Angels Broadcasting Network Inc.
Arbitron Metro Market: West Frankfort,IL; *Format:* Christian, Religious; *Target Audience:* 35 plus.; *Adv. Rates:* 6; 6; 6; 4
Jim Morris, General Manager

WLIL

05-30-1950; 730 kHz AM; *Hrs Open:* 24; 1 kw-D, ND1; 0.214 kw-N, ND1; N35 46 12 W84 16 47
Mailing Address: 14542 El Camino Lane, Lenoir City, TN 37772 US
Second Address: PO Box 520, Lenoir City, TN 37771
(865) 986-7536
www.wlilcountry.com
wlilcountry@aol.com
License: Lenoir City, TN held by B.P. Broadcasters L.L.C.
Nat'l Network: CNN Radio; *Nat'l Reps:* Keystone (unwired net)
Regional Reps: Rgnl Reps.
Arbitron Metro Market: Knoxville, TN; *Format:* Country *Special Programming:* Black one hr, farm one hr, gospel 18 hrs, American; *Hrs. of News Programming:* news progmg 20 hrs wkly; *No. News Employees:* 1 *TargetAudience:* General; adults; *Adv. Rates:* 50; 50; 50; 40
Norman Rhyne, Operations/Advertising Executive
Glenn McNish, General Manager/General Sales Manager

WKZX-FM

09-19-1967; 93.5 MHz FM; 2 kw; 577 ft.; N35 42 38 W84 10 46
406 East Broadway, Lenoir City, TN 37771 US
(865) 455-2267; *Fax:* (865) 986-9850
www.lalider.wix.com/935fm
laliderwkzx@gmail.com
License: Lenoir City, Loudon County, TN held by B.P. Broadcasters L.L.C.
Arbitron Metro Market: Knoxville, TN; *Hrs. of News Programming:* news progmg 20 hrs wkly; *No. News Employees:* 1; *Target Audience:* General; Adults

Lewisburg

WAXO

09-01-1980; 1220 kHz AM; 1 kw-D, ND2; 0.144 kw-N, ND2; N35 25 42 W86 46 22
217 W. Commerce St., Lewisburg, TN 37091 US
(931) 359-6641
License: Lewisburg, TN held by Marshall County Radio Corp.
Nat'l Network: AP Network News
Arbitron Metro Market: Grand Island NE; *Format:* Christian, Religious; *Adv. Rates:* Call for Rates (Radio and TV P
Greg Bradley, Operations Manager
Sharrin Smartt, General Manager
Scoop Troop, Video
Troy Cashion, Sports Director

WJJM

05-15-1947; 1490 kHz AM; 1 kw-U; N35 27 03 W86 46 57
Mailing Address: Box 2025, Lewisburg, TN 37091
Second Address: 344 E. Church St., Lewisburg, TN 37091
(931) 359-4511; *Fax:* (931) 270-9556
www.wjjm.com
wjjm@wjjm.com
License: Lewisburg, Marshall County, TN held by WJJM Inc.
Regional Network: Tenn. Radio Net.; Fox Network News; *Nat'l Reps:* Keystone (unwired net)
Population Served: 7,207 *Hrs. of News Programming:* news progmg one hr wkly; *No. News Employees:* 1; *Target Audience:* 25-65; manufacturing, business, family programming; *Adv. Rates:* 5.50; 5.50; 5.50; 5.50
Missie Haislip, General Manager/Sales
Jeff Haislip, Production & News Manager/Sports Director
Don Roden, Chief Engineer
Doug Hazelwood, Music Director

WJJM-FM

02-20-1969; 94.3 MHz FM; *Hrs Open:* 17; 6 kw; 115 ft.; N35 27 3 W86 46 57
Mailing Address: P. O. Box 2025, Lewisburg, TN 37091 US
Second Address: 344 E. Church St., Lewisburg, TN 37091
(931) 359-4511; *Fax:* (931) 270-9556
www.wjjm.com
wjjm@wjjm.com
License: Lewisburg, Marshall County, TN held by WJJM Inc.
Format: Country
Missie Haislip, General Manager/Sales
Jeff Haislip, News & Production Manager/Sports Director
Tommy Allen, Disc Jockey
Jennifer St. John, Disc Jockey
Linda Dugan, Disc Jockey
Chris Bates, Disc Jockey

Lexington

WDXL

07-01-1954; 1490 kHz AM; *Hrs Open:* 24; 1 kw-U, ND1; N35 38 5 W88 23 34
Mailing Address: P. O. Box 170, Lexington, TN 38351 US
Second Address: 584 Smith Ave., Lexington, TN 38351
(731) 968-3500(731) 968-9990; *Fax:* (731) 968-0380
License: Lexington, TN held by Lexington Broadcast Service Inc.
Nat'l Network: Jones Radio Networks
Arbitron Metro Market: Lexington, TN; *Format:* Gospel *Special Programming:* Black 4 hrs, gospel 10 hrs wkly; *Hrs. of News Programming:* news progmg 10 hrs wkly; *No. News Employees:* 1; *Target Audience:* 30plus.
Dan Hughes, General Manager
Terry Rhodes, Programming Director

WZLT

09-01-1964; 99.3 MHz FM; *Hrs Open:* 24; 5 kw; 151 ft.; N35 38 5 W88 23 34
P. O. Box 279, 584 Smith Street, Lexington, TN 38351 US
(731) 968-9990; *Fax:* (731) 968-0380
www.wzlt993.com
ramonawzlt@yahoo.com
License: Lexington, Henderson County, TN held by Lexington Broadcast Service Inc.
Arbitron Metro Market: Lexington, TN; *Format:* Adult Contemp; *Target Audience:* General.
Don Enochs, Owner
Ramona Moore, Office Manager
Kerry Mallard, Sports Director

Linden

WOPC

101.3 MHz FM; 2.35 kw; 105.2 meters; N35 37 36.4 W87 51 28.9
129 Holmes Avenue, Covington, TN 38019
(731) 663-2327; *Fax:* (731) 663-2427
License: Linden, TN held by Grace Broadcasting Services Inc.
Group Owner: Grace Broadcasting Services Inc.

Livingston

WLIV

11-26-1956; 920 kHz AM; *Hrs Open:* 24; 1 kw-D, ND1; 0.038 kw-N, ND1; N36 22 28 W85 18 20
1130 West Main Street, Livingston, TN 38570 US
(931) 823-1226; *Fax:* (931) 823-6005
License: Livingston, TN held by Sunny Broadcasting G.P.
Nat'l Network: CNN Radio; *Regional Network:* Tenn. Radio Net; *Nat'l Reps:* Keystone (unwired net)
Format: News, Sports *Special Programming:* Farm 2 hrs, relg 15 hrs, gospel 18 hrs wkly; *Hrs. of News Programming:* news progmg 7 hrs wkly; *No. News Employees:* 2; *Target Audience:* General.; *Adv. Rates:* 9; 9;9; 9.
Millard Oakley, President
Craig Cantrell, Operations Dir
Joel Upton, General Manager
Carolyn Peterman, Station Manager
Shirley Burnette, News Director
Austin Stinnett, Chief Engineer
Mark Young, Public Service Director
RogerEaley, Sports Director

WLQK

12-01-1966; 95.9 MHz FM; 27 kw; 669 ft.; N36 11 3 W85 24 40
259 S. Willow, Cookeville, TN 38501 US
(931) 526-6064; *Fax:* (931) 520-1590
www.literock959.com
License: Livingston, Overton County, TN held by JWC Broadcasting
Group Owner: JWC Broadcasting; acq 12-18-98).
Nat'l Reps: Rgnl Reps
Arbitron Metro Market: Cookeville, TN; *Format:* Classic Rock; *Target Audience:* General.; *Adv. Rates:* 30; 28; 30; 24
Scott Stevens, Operations Dir
Jim Stapleton, General Manager

Lobelville

WMAK

11-16-1955; 1570 kHz AM; *Hrs Open:* 24
US
(731) 663-2327; *Fax:* (731) 663-2427
www.gracebroadcasting.com
License: Lobelville, TN held by Grace Broadcasting Services Inc.
Group Owner: Grace Broadcasting Services Inc.; (acq 11-1-2008; $75,000)
Arbitron Metro Market: Nashville, TN
Lacy Ennis, CEO/COO
Charles Ennis, President
John Blackenship, Operations Dir
Rodney Minyard, General Manager
Geraldine Minyard, Programming Director

Lookout Mountain

WFLI

02-20-1961; 1070 kHz AM; *Hrs Open:* 24; 50 kw-D, DA2; 2.5 kw-N, DA2; N35 2 42 W85 21 44
621 O'Grady Dr., Chattanooga, TN 37409 US
(423) 821-3555; *Fax:* (423) 821-3557
License: Lookout Mountain, TN held by WFLI Inc.
Nat'l Network: USA
Arbitron Metro Market: Chattanooga, TN; *Format:* Gospel, Religious *Special Programming:* College football; *Target Audience:* 18-54.; *Adv. Rates:* 18; 18; 18; 10
Ying Hua Benns, President
Paul White, Station Manager

Loretto

WKSR-FM

01-12-1970; 98.3 MHz FM; 18 kw; 377 ft.; N35 9 0 W87 17 45
104 S. Second Street, Pulaski, TN 38478 US
(931) 363-2505; *Fax:* (931) 424-3157
www.wksr.com
License: Loretto, Lawrence County, TN held by Pulaski Broadcasting Inc.
Nat'l Network: ABC
Format: Country; *No. News Employees:* 2; *Adv. Rates:* 18; 14; 16; 12
Scott Stewart, General Manager/Sales Manager/Sports Director
Tiffany Hagood, Sales Representative
Taren Eastep, News Director

Loudon

WFIV-FM

05-20-1991; 105.3 MHz FM; *Hrs Open:* 24; 6 kw; 328 ft.; N35 48 40 W84 16 2
517 Watt Rd., Knoxville, TN 37934 US
(865) 675-4105
www.myi105.com
License: Loudon, Loudon County, TN held by Horne Radio L.L.C.
Group Owner: Horne Radio Group; (acq 8-29-2001; grpsl).
Nat'l Network: CBS
Arbitron Metro Market: Loudon, TN; *Format:* Triple A; *Hrs. of News Programming:* News progmg 3 hrs wkly; *Target Audience:* 25-50; baby boomers; *Adv. Rates:* 40; 40; 40; 20
Tony Cox, General Manager
Joe Stutler, Programming Director

WLOD

01-01-1983; 1140 kHz AM; *Hrs Open:* Sunrise-sunset; 1 kw-D, NDD; N35 43 35 W84 20 49
261 Hannum St., Alcoa, TN 37701 US
(865) 724-1100
wkvl.com
info@wkvl.com
License: Loudon, TN held by Blount Broadcasting Corporation
Group Owner: Blount Broadcasting Corporation
Arbitron Metro Market: Knoxville, TN; *Format:* News, News/Talk, 86; *No. News Employees:* 1; *Target Audience:* 35 plus.; *Adv. Rates:* 8; 8; 8; 6

Lynchburg

*WGBQ

91.9 MHz FM; 0.9 kw; 351 ft.; N35 16 32 W86 21 37
926 Tanyard Hill Rd., Lynchburg, TN 37352 US
(931) 759-5669
www.afr.net
License: Lynchburg, Moore County, TN held by American Family Association.
Group Owner: American Family Radio
Arbitron Metro Market: Lynchburg, TN; *Format:* Christian, Religious

Tim Wildmon, President
Donald Wildmon, Founder
Buddy Smith, Sr VP
Ed Vitagliano, Exec VP
Randy Sharp, Director Of Special Projects
Meeke Addison, Director Of Communications
Abraham Hamilton III, General Counsel

Madison

WPLN
09-14-1958; 1430 kHz AM; *Hrs Open:* 24
630 Mainstream Drive, Nashville, TN 37228-1204 US
(615) 760-2903; *Fax:* (615) 760-2904
www.nashvillepublicradio.org
rgordon@wpln.org
License: Madison, TN held by Nashville Public Radio
Arbitron Metro Market: Nashville, TN; *Format:* News, News/Talk, 86; *Target Audience:* General.
Rob Gordon, President/CEO
Scott Smith, Operations/Production Manager
Donna Robinson, VP of Development
Zea Miller, Membership Manager
Henry Fennell, VP of Programming
Anita Bugg, News Director
Tom Knox, Chief Engineer
MollyNicholas, Membership Coordinator
Carl Pedersen, VP of Finance/Technology
Evelyn Roberts, Accounting Mangaer
Mack Linebaugh, Director of Digital Services

Madisonville

WRKQ
07-12-1967; 1250 kHz AM; *Hrs Open:* 6 AM-6 PM; 0.5 kw-D, ND2; 0.084 kw-N, ND2; N35 30 29 W84 22 45 US
(423) 442-1446
www.wrkq.net
monroe.radio@live.com
License: Madisonville, TN held by Beverly Broadcasting Co. LLC
Nat'l Network: CBS Radio
Format: News, News/Talk, 86; *No. News Employees:* 1; *Target Audience:* General.
Mike Beverly, President

WYGO
11-15-1992; 99.5 MHz FM; *Hrs Open:* 24; 2.7 kw; 489 ft.; N35 31 19 W84 27 29
PO Box 933, 2110 Oxnard Road, Athens, TN 37371-0933 US
(423) 337-0995; *Fax:* (423) 745-2000
www.wygofm.com
License: Madisonville, Monroe County, TN held by Major Broadcasting Corp.
Arbitron Metro Market: Madisonville, TN; *Format:* Oldies, Adult Contemp; *Target Audience:* 18-54.
Randy Sliger, General Manager

Manchester

WFTZ
11-16-1992; 101.5 MHz FM; *Hrs Open:* 24; 3 kw; 328 ft.; N35 23 51 W86 8 39
Mailing Address: PO Box 1015, Manchester, TN 37349 US
Second Address: 1025 Hillsboro Highway, Manchester, TN 37355
(931) 728-3458
www.fantasyradio.com
avdotson@fantasyradio.com
License: Manchester, Coffee County, TN held by Phase Two Communications Inc.
Nat'l Network: ABC; *Wire Services:* AP
Arbitron Metro Market: Nashville, TN; *Format:* Adult Contemp; *Hrs. of News Programming:* news progmg 4 hrs wkly; *No. News Employees:* 1; *Target Audience:* 25-45; white collar, educated
Amber Dotson, General Manager
Ryan French, Assistant General Manager
Josh Kuhn, District Sales Manager
Ivy Petty, District Sales Manager
Ali Reynolds, Marketing Specialist
Wayne Hudgens, News Director

WMSR
04-07-1957; 1320 kHz AM; *Hrs Open:* 24; 5 kw-D, ND1; 0.079 kw-N, ND1; N35 28 3 W86 5 42
1030 Oakdale Street, Manchester, TN 37355 US
(931) 728-1320; *Fax:* (931) 728-3527
www.thunder1320.com
wmsr@thunder1320.com
License: Manchester, TN held by Coffee County Broadcasting Inc.
Wire Services: AP
Arbitron Metro Market: Manchester, TN; *Format:* Oldies, Sports, 86 *Special Programming:* High school sports, farm; *Hrs. of News Programming:* news progmg 21 hrs wkly; *No. News Employees:* 1 *Target Audience:* General.
Rob Clutter, General Manager
Brian Marcrom, Programming Director
Lucky Knott, News/Sports Director
Tiffany Clutter, Business Manager
Samantha Terrell-Watters, On-Air Host/Sales Associate

Martin

WCMT
06-08-1957; 1410 kHz AM; *Hrs Open:* 24; 0.7 kw-D, ND1; 0.058 kw-N, ND1; N36 21 45 W88 50 57
Mailing Address: 1410 N. Lindell St., Martin, TN 38237 US
Second Address: 223 Westgate Dr., Union City, TN 38260
(731) 587-9526; *Fax:* (731) 587-5079
www.thunderboltradio.com/wcmt
License: Martin, TN held by Thunderbolt Broadcasting Co.
Group Owner: Thunderbolt Broadcasting Co.
Arbitron Metro Market: Jackson, TN; *Format:* News/Talk
Paul Tinkle, President

WCMT
09-26-1967; 101.3 MHz FM; *Hrs Open:* 24; 22 kw; 308 ft.; N36 29 0 W88 57 10
Mailing Address: 1410 N. Lindell St., Martin, TN 38237 US
Second Address: 223 Westgate Dr., Union City, TN 38260
(731) 587-9526; *Fax:* (731) 587-5079
www.thunderboltradio.com/wcmt
License: Martin, TN held by Thunderbolt Broadcasting Co.
Group Owner: Thunderbolt Broadcasting Co.
Arbitron Metro Market: Jackson, TN; *Format:* Adult Contemp
Paul Tinkle, President

***WUTM**
09-01-1971; 90.3 MHz FM; *Hrs Open:* 6 AM-midnight; 0.175 kw; 282 ft.; N36 20 23 W88 51 35
The University of Tennessee at Martin, 538 University Street, 305 Gooch Hall, Martin, TN 38238 US
(731) 881-7095; *Fax:* (731) 881-7551
www.utm.edu/organizations/wutm
wutm@utm.edu
License: Martin, Weakley County, TN held by University of Tennessee.
Regional Network: Tenn. Radio Net.
Arbitron Metro Market: Martin, TN; *Format:* Contemporary Hits/Top 40; *Target Audience:* General; Univ
Matt Borden, Programming Director
Aimee Bilger, News Director
MaryLynn Williams, Sports Director
Katelyn Long, Digital Content Director

Maryville

WGAP
08-13-1947; 1400 kHz AM; *Hrs Open:* 24; 1 kw-U, ND1; N35 45 41 W83 58 57
261 Hannum St., Alcoa, TN 37701 US
(865) 724-1100
wkvl.com
info@wkvl.com
License: Maryville, TN held by Blount Broadcasting Corporation
Group Owner: Blount Broadcasting Corporation
Nat'l Reps: Rgnl Reps
Arbitron Metro Market: Knoxville, TN; *Format:* Country; *Hrs. of News Programming:* news progmg 18 hrs wkly; *No. News Employees:* 1; *Target Audience:* 25 plus; general; *Adv. Rates:* 24; 20; 24; 14

WKCE
01-01-1989; 1120 kHz AM
802 S. Central Ave., Knoxville, TN 37902 US
(865) 673-8570; *Fax:* (865) 637-7133
License: Maryville, TN held by Kirkland Wireless Broadcasters Inc.
Nat'l Network: ESPN Deportes
Arbitron Metro Market: Knoxville, TN; *Format:* Sports
Rob Robinson, Operations Dir

WVRX
02-02-1990; 95.7 MHz FM; *Hrs Open:* 24; 6 kw; 322 ft.; N35 49 53 W84 1 25
P.O. Box 3848, Evansville, IN 47720 US
(865) 525-6000; *Fax:* (865) 656-4386
www.jackfmknoxville.com
rchambers@sccradio.com
License: Maryville, Blount County, TN held by South Central Communications Corp.
Group Owner: South Central Communications Corp.
Arbitron Metro Market: Knoxville, TN; *Target Audience:* 35-59; adults
J.P. Engelbrecht, CEO
Craig Jacobus, President
Terry Gillingham, Operations Dir
Randy Chambers, Programming Director
Judy Dyke, News Director
Randy Ross, Sales Director

WDKW
95.7 MHz FM; 6 kW; 322 ft; N35 49 52 W84 01 26
1100 Sharps Ridge Memorial Park Dr, Knoxville, TN 37917 USA
(865) 525-6000; *Fax:* (865) 525-2000
theduke.fm
License: Maryville, TN held by Midwest Communications Inc.
Group Owner: Midwest Communications Inc.
Arbitron Metro Market: Knoxville, TN; *Format:* Country
Randy Chambers, Brand Manager

Maynardville

***WYLV(FM)**
01-01-2001; 88.3 MHz FM; 2.85 kw horiz; Ant 1,489 ft; N36 00 13 W83 56 34
PO Box 2098, Omaha, NE 68103-2098
(800) 525-5683
www.klove.com
License: Maynardville, Union County, TN held by Foothills Broadcasting Inc.
Population Served: 2,423; *Arbitron Metro Market:* Maynardville, TN; *Format:* Christian

***WYLV**
02-14-1993; 88.3 MHz FM; *Hrs Open:* 24; 2.85 kw horiz; N36 0 13 W83 56 34
304 Crane Cove, Longwood, FL 32750 US
(865) 521-8910; *Fax:* (865) 521-8923
www.love89.org
info@love89.org
License: Maynardville, Blount County, TN held by Foothills Broadcasting Inc.
Arbitron Metro Market: Maynardville, TN; *Format:* Christian
David Wells, General Manager
Jonathan Unthank, Programming Director
Marisa Lykins, Promotions Manager

McKenzie

WHDM
01-29-1954; 1440 kHz AM; 500 w-D, 91 w-N; N36 07 20 W88 31 31
PO Box 878, Marion, IL 62959
www.whdmradio.com
webmaster@wmufradio.com
License: McKenzie, Carroll County, TN held by WHDM Broadcasting Inc.
Group Owner: Benton-Weatherford Broadcasting Inc. of Tennessee; (acq 1-4-2002; $69,000).
Nat'l Network: ABC
Population Served: 5,651 *Hrs. of News Programming:* news progmg 4 hrs wkly; *No. News Employees:* 1; *Adv. Rates:* 7;30;9.
Gary Benton, President
Janice Benton, Operations Dir

WWYN
02-11-1963; 106.9 MHz FM; *Hrs Open:* 24; 100 kw; 886 ft.; N35 54 5 W88 46 51
111 W. Main St., Jackson, TN 38301 US
(731) 427-9616
www.wwyn1069.com
License: McKenzie, Carroll County, TN held by Thomas Media
Group Owner: Thomas Media, LLC
Arbitron Metro Market: McKenzie, TN; *Format:* Country; *Hrs. of News Programming:* news progmg 4 hrs wkly; *No. News Employees:* 1; *Target Audience:* 25-54; adults; *Adv. Rates:* 28; 26; 27; 20

***WAJJ**
01-01-2002; 89.3 MHz FM; *Hrs Open:* 24; 1 kw; 328 ft.; N36 6 55 W88 30 38
P. O. Box 964, McKenzie, YN 38201 US
(731) 352-6034
www.wajjradio.org
comments@wajjradio.org
License: McKenzie, Carroll County, TN held by Temple Broadcasting Co.
Arbitron Metro Market: McKenzie, TN; *Format:* Christian
Gary L. Hall, Pastor/Director
Bro. Steve Vincent, Programming Director
Ruth Back, Secretary

McKinnon

WTPR-FM

01-01-1992; 101.7 MHz FM; *Hrs Open:* 24; 1.8 kw; 607 ft.; N36 24 39 W87 58 6 *Rebroadcasts:* Rebroadcasts WTPR(AM) Paris 100%
Mailing Address: 1729 Nailling Drive, Union City, TN 38261 US
Second Address: 206 N. Brewer Street, Paris, TN 38242
(731) 885-1240; *Fax:* (731) 885-3405
www.wenkwtpr.com
thailey@wenkwtpr.com
License: McKinnon, Houston County, TN held by WENK of Union City Inc.
Group Owner: WENK of Union City Inc.; (acq 1996; $200,000)
Regional Reps: Rgnl Reps.
Arbitron Metro Market: Paris, TN; *Format:* Oldies; *Hrs. of News Programming:* news progmg 12 hrs wkly; *No. News Employees:* 1; *Target Audience:* 35-54.
Terry L. Hailey, President and General Manager
Lorrie Matlock, Sales Representative

McMinnville

WAKI

01-01-1947; 1230 kHz AM; *Hrs Open:* 5 AM-midnight
US
www.1230waki.com
License: McMinnville, TN held by Peg Broadcasting Crossville LLC.
Group Owner: Peg Broadcasting Crossville LLC; (acq 6-30-2008; grpsl)
Arbitron Metro Market: McMinnville, TN; *Format:* News, News/Talk, 86 *Special Programming:* Farm 2 hrs wkly; *Hrs. of News Programming:* news progmg 24 hrs wkly; *No. News Employees:* 1; *Target Audience:* 25-54;general
David Roederer, General Manager

WBMC

05-01-1955; 960 kHz AM; *Hrs Open:* 5 AM-8 PM
230 West Colville Street, McMinnville, TN 37111 US
(931) 473-9253; *Fax:* (931) 473-4149
www.960wbmc.com/
License: McMinnville, TN held by Peg Broadcasting Crossville LLC.
Group Owner: Peg Broadcasting Crossville LLC; (acq 6-30-2008; grpsl)
Nat'l Network: ABC
Arbitron Metro Market: McMinnville, TN; *Format:* Contemporary Hits/Top 40, Country, 44 *Special Programming:* Farm 5 hrs wkly; *Hrs. of News Programming:* news progmg 10 hrs wkly; *No. News Employees:* 1 *TargetAudience:* General.

*WCPI

02-01-1997; 91.3 MHz FM; *Hrs Open:* 24; 1.6 kw; 157 ft.; N35 39 41 W85 45 6
PO Box 728, McMinnville, TN 37110 US
(931) 506-9274
wcpi@blomand.net
License: McMinnville, Warren County, TN held by Warren County Education Foundation.
Wire Services: AP
Arbitron Metro Market: Cookeville, TN; *Target Audience:* 6 plus.
Jeff Golden, Owner
Gloria Grissom, Owner
Dr. Norman Rone, Owner/General Manager
Jeff Lytle, Chief Operator

Memphis

WUMY

07-19-1947; 830 kHz AM; *Hrs Open:* Sunrise-sunset; 10 kw-D; N36 13 29 W90 04 31
Mailing Address: Box 271, Kennett, MO 63967
Second Address: 700 N. Bypass, Kennett, MO 63857
(573) 686-3700; *Fax:* (573) 686-6116
www.foxradionetwork.com
kotc@sheltonbbs.com
License: Memphis, Shelby County, TN held by Eagle Bluff Enterprises
Population Served: 20,000; *No. News Employees:* 1; *Target Audience:* 28-55.; *Adv. Rates:* 10; 10; 10; na
Steven Fuchs, President
Charles Isabell, News Director
P.J. Johnson, Chief Engineer

KWAM

01-01-1946; 990 kHz AM
5495 Murray Rd., Memphis, TN 38119 US
(901) 261-4200; *Fax:* (901) 261-4210
www.kwam990.com/
info@kwam990.com
License: Memphis, TN held by Legacy Media Memphis, LLC
Arbitron Metro Market: Memphis, TN; *Format:* News, Talk; *Target Audience:* 25 plus; general
George Bryant, President/General Manager

WBBP

04-11-1964; 1480 kHz AM; *Hrs Open:* 24; 5 kw-D, ND2; 0.041 kw-N, ND2; N35 3 18 W90 5 15
369 G. E. Patterson Avenue, Memphis, TN 38126 US
(901) 278-7878; *Fax:* (901) 332-1707
www.bbless.org/wbbp.htm
License: Memphis, TN held by Bountiful Blessings Inc.
Format: Alternative, Christian; *Adv. Rates:* 40; 30; 40; 30

WDIA

06-07-1947; 1070 kHz AM; *Hrs Open:* 24; 50 kw-D, DA2; 5 kw-N, DA2; N35 16 5 W90 1 3
2560 Thousand Oaks Blvd., Suite 4100, Memphis, TN 38118 US
(901) 259-1300; *Fax:* (901) 259-6456
www.mywdia.com
License: Memphis, TN held by CC Licenses LLC.
Group Owner: iHeartMedia; (acq 1996; grpsl)
Nat'l Network: ABC; *Nat'l Reps:* Clear Channel
Arbitron Metro Market: Memphis, TN; *Format:* Urban Contemporary *Special Programming:* Gospel; *Target Audience:* 25-54; Black adults
Morgan Bohannon, Regional Market President
Bobby O'Jay, Programming Director

*WEVL

05-01-1976; 89.9 MHz FM; *Hrs Open:* 20; 4.8 kw; 381 ft.; N35 8 37 W89 48 22
P.O. Box 40952, Memphis, TN 38174 US
(901) 528-0560
www.wevl.org
stnmgr@wevl.org
License: Memphis, Shelby County, TN held by Southern Communication Volunteers Inc.
Arbitron Metro Market: Memphis, TN; *Format:* Blues *Special Programming:* Jazz 15 hrs, C&W 15 hrs, Fr one hr, Irish 4 hrs, Indian subcontinent one hr wkly; *Hrs. of News Programming:* News progmg 2 hrs wkly *TargetAudience:* General.
Judy Dorsey, Station Manager
Brian Craig, Programming Director

WGKX

01-10-1968; 105.9 MHz FM; *Hrs Open:* 24; 100 kw; 993 ft.; N35 9 16 W89 49 20
5629 Murray Rd., Memphis, TN 38119 US
(901) 682-1106
www.kix106.com
License: Memphis, Shelby County, TN held by Radio License Holding CBC, LLC
Group Owner: Cumulus Media Inc.; (acq 3-23-2004; grpsl).
Nat'l Reps: Katz Radio
Arbitron Metro Market: Memphis, TN; *Format:* Country; *Target Audience:* 25-54.; *Adv. Rates:* 300; 250; 250; 100
Krista Freeman, Advertising

WHBQ

03-18-1925; 560 kHz AM; *Hrs Open:* 24; 5 kw-D, DA2; 1 kw-N, DA2; N35 15 12 W90 2 51
6080 Mt. Moriah Ext., Memphis, TN 38115 US
(901) 375-9324
www.sports56whbq.com
License: Memphis, TN held by Flinn Broadcasting Corp.
Nat'l Network: CBS
Arbitron Metro Market: Memphis, TN; *Format:* Sports; *Hrs. of News Programming:* News progmg 2 hrs wkly; *Target Audience:* 18-54.
George Flinn, President
Chris Coates, General Manager
Eli Savoie, Programming Director

WHRK

01-01-1961; 97.1 MHz FM; *Hrs Open:* 24; 100 kw; 531 ft.; N35 13 23 W90 2 33
2650 Thousand Oaks Blvd., Suite 4100, Memphis, TN 38118 US
(901) 259-1300; *Fax:* (901) 259-6456
www.k97fm.com
License: Memphis, Shelby County, TN held by CC Licenses LLC
Group Owner: iHeartMedia
Arbitron Metro Market: Memphis, TN; *Format:* Urban Contemporary; *Target Audience:* 18-49.
Morgan Bohannon, Regional Market President
Devin Steel, Operations Dir

*WKNO-FM

03-01-1972; 91.1 MHz FM; *Hrs Open:* 24; 100 kw; 574 ft.; N35 9 14 W89 49 19
Mailing Address: 751 Cherry Farms Road, Cordova, TN 38016 US
Second Address: TN
(800) 766-9566; *Fax:* (901) 729-8176
www.wknofm.org
radio@wkno.org
License: Memphis, Shelby County, TN held by Mid-South Public Communications Foundation.
Nat'l Network: NPR; PRI
Arbitron Metro Market: Memphis, TN *TV Affiliate:* *WKNO-TV affil; *Format:* Classical, News; *Hrs. of News Programming:* 51 hrs news progmg wkly; *No. News Employees:* 2; *Target Audience:* 35 plus.
Christopher Blank, News Director

WLOK

03-01-1956; 1340 kHz AM; *Hrs Open:* 24; 1 kw-U; N35 07 01 W90 00 59
363 S. Second Street, Memphis, TN 38103
(901) 527-9565; *Fax:* (901) 528-0335
www.wlok.com
wlokradio@aol.com
License: Memphis, Shelby County, TN held by Gilliam Communications Inc.
Nat'l Reps: Local Focus
Population Served: 1,000,000; *Arbitron Metro Market:* Memphis, TN; *No. News Employees:* 1; *Target Audience:* 25-54.
Art Gilliam, President/CEO
Michael Anderson, General Sales Mgr
Walter Hunter, Local Sales Manager
Delsa Fleming, Music Director
Delsa Fleming, Music Director
Falesha Stafford, Public Affairs Director

WMC

01-21-1923; 790 kHz AM; *Hrs Open:* 24
1835 Moriah Woods Boulevard, Building #1, Memphis, TN 38117 US
(901) 384-5900; *Fax:* (901) 767-6076
www.fm100memphis.com
License: Memphis, TN held by Entercom Memphis License Inc.
Group Owner: Entercom Communications Corp.; (acq 11-30-2007; grpsl)
Nat'l Reps: CBS Radio; *Wire Services:* Metro Weather Service Inc.
Arbitron Metro Market: Memphis, TN; *Format:* Sports; *No. News Employees:* 1
Terry Wood, Operations Dir

WMC-FM

05-22-1947; 99.7 MHz FM; *Hrs Open:* 24; 290 kw horiz, 96 kw vert; 909 ft.; N35 10 9 W89 53 10
1835 Moriah Woods Blvd., Building #1, Memphis, TN 38117 US
(901) 384-5900; *Fax:* (901) 767-6076
www.fm100memphis.com
License: Memphis, Shelby County, TN held by Entercom Memphis License Inc
Group Owner: Entercom Communications Corp.
Arbitron Metro Market: Memphis, TN; *Format:* Adult Contemp; *Target Audience:* 25-54; adults
William Shannon, General Manager

*WQOX

04-08-1974; 88.5 MHz FM; *Hrs Open:* 24; 30 kw; 430 ft.; N35 9 17 W89 49 20
2485 Union Avenue, Memphis, TN 38112 US
(901) 320-3460; *Fax:* (901) 454-7673
www.scsk12.org/uf/tcc/885.php
License: Memphis, Shelby County, TN held by Board of Education Memphis City Schools.
Arbitron Metro Market: Memphis, TN; *Format:* Adult Contemp; *No. News Employees:* 1; *Target Audience:* 12-54; Students, teachers, parents & admin staff
Derek Wagner, General Manager
Paul Gubala, Programming Director
Derick McMillan, Chief Engineer
Chris Malone, Assistant Music Director
Sherman Austin, Public Affairs Director

WREC

09-01-1922; 600 kHz AM; *Hrs Open:* 24
2650 Thousand Oaks Blvd., Suite 4100, Memphis, TN 38118 US
(901) 259-1300; *Fax:* (901) 259-6456
www.600wrec.com
news@600wrec.com
License: Memphis, TN held by CC Licenses LLC.
Group Owner: iHeartMedia; (acq 1996; grpsl).
Nat'l Network: Westwood One; ABC; *Regional Network:* Tenn. Radio Net; *Nat'l Reps:* Clear Channel; *Wire Services:* NWS (National Weather Service)
Arbitron Metro Market: Memphis, TN; *Format:* News, News/Talk, 84, Talk *Special Programming:* Farm 3 hrs, relg 4 hrs wkly; *Hrs. of News Programming:* news progmg 5 hrs wkly; *No. News Employees:* 2; *Target Audience:* 35 plus; upscale, professional, males 70%

Morgan Bohannon, Regional Market President
Frank Gilbert, Promotions Manager
Alonzo Pendleton, Chief Engineer

WRVR
09-15-1968; 104.5 MHz FM; 100 kw; 751 ft.; N35 9 16 W89 49 20
1835 Moriah Woods Blvd., Building #1, Memphis, TN 38117 US
(901) 384-5900; *Fax:* (901) 767-6076
www.1045theriver.com
License: Memphis, Shelby County, TN
Group Owner: Entercom Communications Corp.
Arbitron Metro Market: Memphis, TN; *Format:* Adult Contemp; *Hrs. of News Programming:* news progmg 2 hrs wkly; *No. News Employees:* 1
Dan Barron, Operations Dir
Rondi Atkinson, General Sales Mgr
Jerry Dean, Programming Director
Mike Schwartz, Chief Engineer
Rachel Dewitt, General Sales Manager

WGSF
02-01-1984; 1030 kHz AM; *Hrs Open:* 24; 10 kw-C, DAN; 50 kw-D, DAN; DAN; 1 kw-N; N35 10 59 W89 56 17
3654 Park Avenue, Memphis, TN 38111 US
(901) 454-9948; *Fax:* (901) 454-1027
www.miradioambiente.com
License: Memphis, TN held by Arlington Broadcasting Co. Inc.
Nat'l Network: Westwood One; CBS
Arbitron Metro Market: Memphis, TN; *Adv. Rates:* 40; 40; 60; 30
Norma Gonzalez, Promotions Director

***WUMR**
08-01-1979; 91.7 MHz FM; *Hrs Open:* 6 AM-midnight; 25 kw horiz, 24 kw vert; 394 ft.; N35 9 17 W89 51 28
Dept of Communications, 3745 Central Ave, Memphis, TN 38152 US
(901) 678-2560
www.memphis.edu/wumr/
wumr@memphis.edu
License: Memphis, Shelby County, TN held by The University of Memphis.
Arbitron Metro Market: Memphis, TN; *Format:* Jazz, Sports; *Hrs. of News Programming:* news progmg 2 hrs wkly; *No. News Employees:* 1; *Target Audience:* 18-49; upscale, college-educated; *Adv. Rates:* 50; 50; 50;50
Malvin Massey, General Manager
Chris Davis, Programming Director
Michael Rhodes, Chief Engineer
Rika Hudson, Administrative
John Hardin, Production Director
Jacob Woloshin, Sports Director
Dylan Ellison, Underwriting Director
Chris Freitas, Webmaster

***WYPL**
04-17-1991; 89.3 MHz FM; *Hrs Open:* 24; 100 kw; 1253 ft.; N35 28 3 W90 11 27
1850 Peabody Avenue, Memphis, TN 38104 US
(901) 415-2752; *Fax:* (901) 323-7902
www.memphislibrary.org/wypl
info@memphislibrary.org
License: Memphis, Shelby County, TN held by Memphis Public Library & Information Center.
Arbitron Metro Market: Memphis, TN; *Format:* News *Special Programming:* Sp one hr wkly; *Hrs. of News Programming:* News progmg 110 hrs wkly; *Target Audience:* General.
Tommy Warren, General Manager

Middleton

WYDL
01-01-2001; 100.3 MHz FM; 25 kw; 328 ft.; N35 0 13 W88 39 39
102 North Cass Street, Suite D, Corinth, MS 38834 US
(662) 284-4611; *Fax:* (662) 284-9609
www.wydl.com
mike@wydl.com
License: Middleton, Hardeman County, TN held by Flinn Broadcasting Corp.
Arbitron Metro Market: Tahlequah OK; *Format:* Religious
Mike Brandt, General Manager
Heather Simmons, Sales Manager
Dave Smith, Production

Milan

WYNU
12-12-1964; 92.3 MHz FM; *Hrs Open:* 24; 100 kw; 991 ft.; N35 54 6 W88 46 55
US
(731) 427-3316
www.fmu92.com
License: Milan, Gibson County, TN held by Forever South Licenses LLC.
Group Owner: Forever Communications Inc.; (acq 5-12-2006; grpsl).
Arbitron Metro Market: Jackson, TN; *Format:* Classic Rock; *Hrs. of News Programming:* news progmg 5 hrs wkly; *No. News Employees:* 1; *Target Audience:* 18-54; middle/upper income adults with disposable income &buying power; *Adv. Rates:* 50; 48; 52; 38
Dave Hacker, Operations Dir
Roger Vestal, General Manager
Gina Langley, General Sales Mgr
Steve Burke, Programming Director

Millersville

WNFN
01-01-1998; 106.7 MHz FM; 2.95 kW; 966 ft.; N36 15 50 W86 47 39
504 Rosedale Ave, Nashville, TN 37211 USA
(615) 259-4567
i1067.com
License: Millersville, Sumner County, TN held by Midwest Communications Inc.
Group Owner: Midwest Communications Inc.
Arbitron Metro Market: Nashville, TN; *Format:* Contemporary Hits/Top 40
Joe Breezy, Brand Manager

Millington

WLRM
06-22-1962; 1380 kHz AM; 2.5 kw-D, DA2; 1 kw-N, DA2; N35 18 56 W89 55 23
6960 Bucknell Road, Millington, TN 38053 US
(901) 872-8861; *Fax:* (901) 872-8863
www.1380wlrm.com/
License: Millington, TN held by CPT & T Radio Station Inc.
Arbitron Metro Market: Memphis, TN *TV Affiliate:* Relg
David Brown, Station Manager
Andre Money, Programming Director
Phil Patton, Chief Engineer

WXMX
04-12-1960; 98.1 MHz FM; 100 kw; 869 ft.; N35 09 16 W89 49 20
5629 Murray Rd., Memphis, TN 38119 US
(901) 682-1106
www.981themax.com
License: Millington, TN held by Radio License Holding CBC, LLC
Group Owner: Cumulus Media Inc.; (acq 3-23-2004; grpsl).
Arbitron Metro Market: Memphis, TN; *Format:* Rock/AOR
Krista Freeman, Advertising

Minor Hill

WEUZ
09-02-1983; 92.1 MHz FM; 2.6 kw; 479 ft.; N35 7 18 W87 11 17
Rebroadcasts: Simulcast with WEUP-FM Moulton, AL; 100%
2609 Jordan Lane NW, Huntsville, AL 35816 US
(256) 837-9387; *Fax:* (256) 837-9404
www.103weup.com
hundley@103weup.com
License: Minor Hill, Giles County, TN held by Broadcast One Inc.
Arbitron Metro Market: Minor Hill, TN; *Format:* Blues
Hundley Batts, President

Monterey

WKXD-FM
03-03-1986; 106.9 MHz FM; *Hrs Open:* 24; 23 kw; 735 ft.; N36 7 13 W85 14 44
259 South Willow Avenue, Cookville, TN 38501 US
(931) 528-6064; *Fax:* (931) 520-1590
www.1069kicksfm.com
License: Monterey, Putnam County, TN held by JWC Broadcasting
Group Owner: JWC Broadcasting; acq 8-3-01).
Nat'l Network: ABC; *Nat'l Reps:* Rgnl Reps
Arbitron Metro Market: Cookeville, TN; *Hrs. of News Programming:* news progmg one hr wkly; *No. News Employees:* 1; *Target Audience:* 18-49; young, adult & affluent audiences; *Adv. Rates:* 28; 24; 26; 20
Jim Stapleton, General Manager

WLIV-FM
01-08-1997; 104.7 MHz FM; *Hrs Open:* 24; 1.25 kw; 712 ft.; N36 15 42 W85 16 35
P.O. Box 520, 1024 West Main Street, Livingston, TN 38570 US
(931) 823-1226; *Fax:* (931) 823-6005
License: Monterey, Putnam County, TN held by Sunny Broadcasting G.P.
Nat'l Network: Westwood One; Fox News Radio; *Wire Services:* AP
Format: Country, Sports; *Hrs. of News Programming:* news progmg 4 hrs wkly; *No. News Employees:* 1; *Target Audience:* General.; *Adv. Rates:* 9; 9; 9; 9
Millard Oakley, President
Craig Cantrell, Operations Dir
Joel Upton, General Manager
Carolyn Peterman, Station Manager
Mark Young, General Sales Mgr
Shirley Burnette, News Director
Austin Stinnett, Chief Engineer
Roger Ealey,News & Sports Director

Morrison

WOWC
08-02-1964; 105.3 MHz FM; *Hrs Open:* 24; 6 kw; 243 ft.; N35 37 27 W85 53 37
230 W. Colville St., McMinnville, TN 37111 US
(931) 836-1055,(931) 836-2824; *Fax:* (931) 836-2320
License: Morrison, Warren County, TN held by Peg Broadcasting Crossville LLC.
Group Owner: Peg Broadcasting Crossville LLC; (acq 6-30-2008; grpsl)
Format: Classic Rock; *No. News Employees:* 1; *Target Audience:* 18-34.
Don Howard, Operations Dir

Morristown

WCRK
10-01-1947; 1150 kHz AM; *Hrs Open:* 24; 5 kw-D, DAN; 0.5 kw-N, DAN; N36 14 11 W83 18 33
PO Box 220, 510 West Economy Road, Morristown, TN 37815 US
(423) 586-9101; *Fax:* (423) 587-2866
www.wcrk.com
ed@wcrk.com
License: Morristown, TN held by Radio Acquisition Corp.
Nat'l Network: ABC; *Nat'l Reps:* Rgnl Reps
Arbitron Metro Market: Morristown, TN; *Format:* Contemporary Hits/Top 40; *Hrs. of News Programming:* news progmg 45 hrs wkly; *No. News Employees:* 1; *Target Audience:* 25-54; slighty more female, average income$50,000 yearly
Edwin Arnold, General Manager
Mike Rypel, Sports Director
Stephanie Christian, Office/Traffic Manager

WMTN
10-19-1957; 1300 kHz AM; 5 kw-D, ND1; 0.096 kw-N, ND1; N36 12 15 W83 19 57
PO Box 220, 510 West Economy Rd, Morristown, TN 37815 US
(423) 586-9101; *Fax:* (423) 587-2866
www.wmtnradio.com
ed@wcrk.com
License: Morristown, TN held by Radio Acquisition Corp.
Nat'l Network: USA; *Regional Network:* Tenn. Radio Net.
Arbitron Metro Market: Morristown, TN; *Format:* Country
Ed Arnold, General Manager
Mike Rypel, Sports Director
Stephanie Christian, Office/Traffic Manager

***WMXK**
05-31-1964; 94.1 MHz FM; 1 kw; 810 ft.; N36 13 42 W83 19 56
P.O. Box 70, 510 West Economy Rd, Morristown, TN 37815 US
(916) 251-1600; *Fax:* (916) 251-1650
www.klove.com
License: Morristown, Hamblen County, TN held by Educational Media Foundation.
Group Owner: EMF Broadcasting; (acq 6-17-2008; $640,000)
Nat'l Network: K-Love
Arbitron Metro Market: Rocklin, CA; *Format:* Christian
Mike Novak, President

Mount Pleasant

WXRQ
12-15-1981; 1460 kHz AM; *Hrs Open:* 6 AM-8 PM; 1 kw-D, ND1; 0.169 kw-N, ND1; N35 31 21 W87 11 34
P.O. Box 31, 209 Bond Street, Mt. Pleasant, TN 38474 US
(931) 379-3119; *Fax:* (931) 379-3129
License: Mount Pleasant, TN held by New Life Broadcasting Inc.
Nat'l Network: USA
Arbitron Metro Market: Mount Pleasant, TN; *Format:* Gospel *Special Programming:* Black 4 hrs wkly; *Hrs. of News Programming:* news progmg 7 hrs wkly; *No. News Employees:* 1; *Target Audience:* General. *Adv.Rates:* 5.50; 5.50; 5.50; na.

Mountain City

WMCT
12-08-1967; 1390 kHz AM; *Hrs Open:* 6 AM-6 PM; 1 kw-D, ND2; 0.058 kw-N, ND2; N36 29 23 W81 47 12
B7683 US
www.wmctradio.net
License: Mountain City, TN held by Johnson County Broadcasting Co.
Nat'l Network: ABC; *Regional Network:* Tenn. Radio Net; *Nat'l Reps:* Rgnl Reps *Regional Reps:* Linley Grande
Arbitron Metro Market: Mountain City, TN; *Format:* Country; *No. News Employees:* 1; *Target Audience:* 25-50.; *Adv. Rates:* 10; 10; 10; 10
Janice Russell, Owner/Operator/Programming Director
Jim Gilley, Sales Manager
Billy Gambill, Production Manager
Jody Simpson, Music Director

Munford

WKIM
01-01-1958; 98.9 MHz FM; 100 kw horiz, 98.1 kw vert; 614 ft.; N35 9 16 W89 49 20
5629 Murray Rd., Memphis, TN 38119 US
(901) 682-1106
www.989thevibe.com
License: Munford, TN held by Radio License Holding CBC, LLC
Group Owner: Cumulus Media Inc.; (acq 3-23-2004; grpsl).
Nat'l Reps: Katz Radio
Arbitron Metro Market: Memphis, TN; *Format:* Urban Contemporary
Krista Freeman, Market Manager

Murfreesboro

*WFCM-FM
09-01-1997; 91.7 MHz FM; *Hrs Open:* 24; 2.48 kW; 758 ft.; N35 48 1 W86 37 17
615 Potomac Place, Smyrna, TN 37167 USA
(615) 534-1850
www.moodyradio.org/stations/nashville
License: Murfreesboro, Rutherford County, TN held by The Moody Bible Institute of Chicago
Group Owner: The Moody Bible Institute of Chicago
Nat'l Network: Moody
Arbitron Metro Market: Murfreesboro-Nashville; *Format:* Christian; *Target Audience:* 25-54.

WGNS
12-31-1946; 1450 kHz AM; *Hrs Open:* 24; 1 kw-U, ND1; AM, TV and 2 FM translato; N35 50 26 W86 23 27 *Rebroadcasts:* 100% on FM 100.5; FM 101.9...FM translators rebroadcasting WGNS (AM)
306 South Church Street, Murfreesboro, TN 37130 US
(615) 893-5373
www.wgnsradio.com
License: Murfreesboro, TN held by The Rutherford Group Inc.
Nat'l Network: ABC; Premiere Radio Networks; Radio America; *Regional Network:* Tenn. Radio Net.
Arbitron Metro Market: Nashville, TN *TV Affiliate:* WETV-class A (ch. 11); *Format:* News, News/Talk, 84, Talk *Special Programming:* Black 8 hrs, farm 3 hrs, relg 6 hrs wkly; *Hrs. of News Programming:* News progmg80 hrs wkly; *No. News Employees:* 4; *Target Audience:* 25 plus; active adults, movers & shakers in economic & educ groupings
Bart Walker, President
Lee Ann Walker, Operations Dir
Scott Walker, General Sales Mgr
Jeff Jordan, Programming Director
Zach Troutman, Promotions Manager
Gary Brown, Chief Engineer
Kristin Walker, Community Relations
BobbieHayes, Director, Religious Programming
Bryan Barrett, Operations Director
Melissa McCullough, Traffic Director

WMGC
11-01-1953; 810 kHz AM; 5 kw-D, NDD; 0.006 kw-N, ND1; N35 50 14 W86 25 0 *Rebroadcasts:* Rebroadcasts WNSR(AM) Brentwood 55%
2514 Eugenia Avenue, Nashville, TN 37211 US
(615) 251-1222; *Fax:* (615) 313-9933
www.eljefe967fm.com
info@eljefe967fm.com
License: Murfreesboro, TN held by Radio 810 Nashville Ltd.
Group Owner: Southern Wabash Communications Corp.; (acq 7-10-01).
Nat'l Network: ABC
Arbitron Metro Market: Nashville, TN *Special Programming:* Relg 4 hrs wkly; *Target Audience:* 18-54; adults
Ted Johnson, General Manager

*WMOT
04-09-1969; 89.5 MHz FM; *Hrs Open:* 24; 100 kw; 676 ft.; N36 5 7 W86 26 22
MTSU Box 3, Murfreesboro, TN 37132 US
(615) 898-2800; *Fax:* (615) 898-2774
www.wmot.org
greg.hunt@mtsu.edu
License: Murfreesboro, Rutherford County, TN held by Middle Tennessee State University.
Nat'l Network: NPR; AP Radio
Arbitron Metro Market: Nashville, TN; *Format:* Jazz; *Hrs. of News Programming:* news progmg 10 hrs wkly; *No. News Employees:* 2; *Target Audience:* 24 plus; general
Greg Lee Hunt, Programming Director
Mike Osborne, Director of News/Public Affairs
Gary Brown, Chief Engineer
Keith Palmer, Development Director

*WMTS-FM
01-01-1996; 88.3 MHz FM; *Hrs Open:* 24; 0.68 kw; 138 ft.; N35 50 56 W86 21 11
MTSU Box 3, Murfreesboro, TN 37132 US
(615) 898-5051
www.wmts.org
manager@wmts.org
License: Murfreesboro, Rutherford County, TN held by Middle Tennessee State University.
Arbitron Metro Market: Murfreesboro, TN; *Format:* Variety/Diverse *Special Programming:* Polka 2 hrs, electronic 10 hrs, jazz 4 hrs, funk 2; *Target Audience:* 18-26; College age, diverse
Ethan Frana, General Manager
Eryka Hammond, Programming Director
Patty Greer, Promotions Director
David Lannom, Music Director
Camisha Tapscott, Business Director
Klint Kashenider, Technical Director
Beth Casey, Drive TimeProducer

WCJK
08-10-1963; 96.3 MHz FM; *Hrs Open:* 24; 39 kW; 1417 ft.; N36 15 50 W86 47 39
504 Rosedale Ave, Nashville, TN 37211 USA
(615) 259-4567; *Fax:* (615) 259-4594
963jackfm.com
License: Murfreesboro, Rutherford County, TN held by Midwest Communications Inc.
Group Owner: Midwest Communications Inc.
Arbitron Metro Market: Nashville, TN; *Format:* Adult Contemp; *No. News Employees:* 1; *Target Audience:* A 25-54
Ron Allen, Brand Manager

Nashville

WENO
05-23-1988; 760 kHz AM; *Hrs Open:* Sunrise-sunset; 1 kw-D, NDD; N36 8 28 W86 45 23
545 Mainstream Drive, Nashville, TN 37228 US
(615) 742-6506 x. 22
www.760thegospel.com
info@760TheGospel.com
License: Nashville, TN held by WENO Inc.
Nat'l Network: AP Radio
Arbitron Metro Market: Nashville, TN; *Format:* Christian, Religious; *Hrs. of News Programming:* News progmg 6 hrs wkly; *Target Audience:* 25-54.
Mark Myers, CFO
Dan Boone, President
David Deese, General Manager
Dave Queen, Station Manager
Jennifer Houchin, News Director
Dan Klimkowski, Chief Engineer

*WFCN
02-20-2002; 1200 kHz AM; 10 kW; N36 12 30 W86 52 22
615 Potomac Place, Smyrna, TN 37617 USA
(615) 534-1850
www.moodyradio.org/stations/nashville
License: Nashville, TN held by The Moody Bible Institute of Chicago
Group Owner: The Moody Bible Institute of Chicago
Arbitron Metro Market: Nashville; *Format:* Christian

*WFSK-FM
04-14-1973; 88.1 MHz FM; *Hrs Open:* 24; 0.7 kw horiz; 7 ft.; N36 10 0 W86 48 17
1000 17th Avenue North, Nashville, TN 37208 US
(615) 329-8574; *Fax:* (615) 329-8711
www.wfskfm.org
License: Nashville, Davidson County, TN held by Fisk University.
Nat'l Network: PRI
Arbitron Metro Market: Nashville, TN; *Format:* Jazz, Smooth Jazz, 86
Sharon Kay, General Manager
Xuam Lawson, Programming Director
Clinton Hooper, Chief Engineer

WJXA
04-03-1976; 92.9 MHz FM; *Hrs Open:* 24; 97 kW; 1053 ft.; N36 7 14 W86 58 7
504 Rosedale Ave, Nashville, TN 37211 USA
(615) 259-0929; *Fax:* (615) 259-4594
mix929.com
License: Nashville, Davidson County, TN held by Midwest Communications Inc.
Group Owner: Midwest Communications Inc.
Arbitron Metro Market: Nashville, TN; *Format:* Adult Contemp; *Target Audience:* A 25-54
Barbara Bridges, Brand Manager

WAMB
12-21-2001; 1200 kHz AM; *Hrs Open:* 24
Mailing Address: 1617 Lebanon Road, Nashville, TN 37210 US
Second Address: 2514 Eugenia Avenue, Nashville, TN 37211
(615) 889-1960; *Fax:* (615) 902-9108
wamb@bellsouth.net
License: Nashville, TN held by Great Southern Broadcasting Co. Inc.
Nat'l Network: CNN Radio
Arbitron Metro Market: Nashville, TN; *Format:* Adult Contemp
Santo Gonzalez, Radio Advertising Sales & Marketing
Gary Brown, Chief Engineer

WKDF
01-01-1967; 103.3 MHz FM; 100 kw; 1234 ft.; N36 02 8 W86 50 56
10 Music Cir. E, Nashville, TN 37203 US
(615) 321-1067
www.nashfm1033.com
allison.warren@cumulus.com
License: Nashville, TN held by Radio License Holding CBC, LLC
Group Owner: Cumulus Media Inc.; (acq 4-26-01; grpsl).
Arbitron Metro Market: Nashville, TN; *Format:* Country; *Target Audience:* 18-34; general
Allison Warren, General Manager/Sales Manager
Charlie Cook, Programming Director
Marie Miscia, Promotions Director

WLAC
11-24-1926; 1510 kHz AM; *Hrs Open:* 24
55 Music Square West, Nashville, TN 37203 US
(615) 664-2400
www.wlac.com
scooter@iheartmedia.com
License: Nashville, TN held by Capstar TX LLC
Group Owner: iHeartMedia; (acq 8-30-00; grpsl)
Nat'l Network: Wall Street; ABC
Arbitron Metro Market: Nashville, TN; *Format:* News, News/Talk, 86, Religious *Special Programming:* Black 20 hrs wkly; *Hrs. of News Programming:* news progmg 18 hrs wly; *No. News Employees:* 3; *Target Audience:* 35-64; professionals, business owners & managers
Lisa Ballance, General Sales Mgr
Scooter, Programming Director
Emma Applebome, Promotions Manager
Karlie Powell, Digital Program Director

WMDB
08-15-1983; 880 kHz AM
3051 Stokers Lane, Nashville, TN 37218 US
(615) 742-6506 x 22; *Fax:* (615) 242-8223
www.760thegospel.com
License: Nashville, TN held by Davidson Media Station WMDB Licensee LLC.
Group Owner: Davidson Media Group LLC; (acq 9-1-2005; $1.6 million)
Arbitron Metro Market: Nashville, TN; *Format:* Gospel; *Target Audience:* 18 plus; Black relg
Armando Quintero, General Manager

WNAH
12-24-1949; 1360 kHz AM; *Hrs Open:* 24; 1 kw-D, ND1; 0.027 kw-N, ND1; N36 11 30 W86 46 26
44 Music Square East, Nashville, IN 37203 US
(615) 254-7611
www.wnah.com
License: Nashville, TN held by Hermitage Broadcasting Corp.
Arbitron Metro Market: Nashville, TN; *Format:* Gospel; *Hrs. of News Programming:* News progmg 5 hrs wkly; *Target Audience:* 21-50.
Tony Cappuccilli, General Sales Mgr

***WECV-FM**
05-23-1967; 89.1 MHz FM; *Hrs Open:* 24; 1.4 kw; Ant 200 ft; N36 08 28 W86 45 23
10550 Barkley, Overland Park, KS 66212
(615) 871-1160; *Fax:* (615) 871-9355
www.bottradionetwork.com/station/wcrt-103-9-fm/
dboyd@bottradionetwork.com
License: Nashville, Davidson County, TN held by Trevecca Nazarene University Inc.
Population Served: 447,877; *Arbitron Metro Market:* Nashville, TN; *Format:* Christian; *Hrs. of News Programming:* News progmg 3 hrs wkly; *Target Audience:* 18-30; college & young professionals
Don Boyd, Nashvill Regional Manager

WNQM
07-01-1948; 1300 kHz AM; *Hrs Open:* 24
1300 WWCR Avenue, Nashville, TN 37218 US
(615) 255-1300; *Fax:* (615) 255-1311
www.1300wnqm.com
License: Nashville, TN held by WNQM Inc.
Group Owner: F W Robbert Broadcasting Co. Inc.; (acq 1-83; $700,000;
Nat'l Network: USA
Arbitron Metro Market: Nashville, TN; *Format:* Religious *Special Programming:* Sp; *Hrs. of News Programming:* News progmg 2 hrs wkly; *Target Audience:* General.
Brady Murray, Operations Manager
Eric Westenberger, Station Manager
Rick Shelton, Sales
Cathy Soares, Programming Director
Phil Patton, Chief Engineer
Chris Buchanan, Production Director

WNRQ
01-01-1953; 105.9 MHz FM; *Hrs Open:* 24; 98 kw; 1234 ft.; N36 2 8 W86 50 56
55 Music Square W, Nashville, TN 37203 US
(615) 664-2400
www.1059therock.com
License: Nashville, Davidson County, TN held by Capstar TX LLC
Group Owner: iHeartMedia
Arbitron Metro Market: Nashville, TN; *Format:* Adult Contemp *Special Programming:* Christian 6 hrs wkly; *Hrs. of News Programming:* news progmg 3 hrs wkly; *No. News Employees:* 1; *Target Audience:* 25-54;upwardly mobile adults
Lisa Ballance, General Sales Mgr
David Rossi, Programming Director
Emma Applebome, Promotions Manager
Karlie Powell, Digital Program Director

WNVL
01-01-1948; 1240 kHz AM; *Hrs Open:* 24; 1 kw-U, ND1; N36 9 23 W86 46 16
US
(615) 242-1411
www.activa1240.com
License: Nashville, TN held by Davidson Media Station WNSG Licensee LLC.
Group Owner: Davidson Media Group LLC; (acq 8-1-2005; $2.7 million).
Arbitron Metro Market: Nashville, TN; *Target Audience:* 25-54.
Peter Davidson, President
Orlaindo Rosa, Operations Dir
Armando Quintero, General Manager
Alberto Pena, Programming Director
Jay Shoemaker, Chief Engineer

***WPLN-FM**
12-17-1962; 90.3 MHz FM; 80 kw; 1132 ft.; N36 2 8 W86 50 56
630 Mainstream Drive, Nashville, TN 37228-1204 US
(615) 760-2903; *Fax:* (615) 760-2904
www.nashvillepublicradio.org
License: Nashville, Davidson County, TN held by Nashville Public Radio.
Nat'l Network: NPR; PRI
Arbitron Metro Market: Nashville, TN; *Format:* News; *Target Audience:* General.
Rob Gordon, President/CEO
Donna Robinson, VP, Development
Zea Miller, Membership Manager
Molly Nicholas, Membership Coordinator

***WCFL(FM)**
12-03-1971; 91.1 MHz FM; *Hrs Open:* 24; 14.5 kw; 457 ft; N36 08 27 W86 51 56
Box 9100-B, Vanderbilt Univ., Nashville, TN 37235
(615) 322-3691; *Fax:* (615) 343-2582
www.wrvu.org
wrvugm@gmail.com
License: Nashville, Davidson County, TN held by Vanderbilt Student Communications.
Nat'l Network: ABC
Population Served: 447,877; *Arbitron Metro Market:* Nashville, TN; *Format:* Variety/Diverse; *Target Audience:* General; div, adventurous individuals
Robert Ackley, General Manager
Scott Cardone, Programming Director
Kate Koschewa, Promotions Manager

WSIX-FM
01-01-1948; 97.9 MHz FM; *Hrs Open:* 24; 100 kw; 1145 ft.; N36 2 50 W86 49 48
55 Music Square W., Nashville, TN 37203 US
(615) 664-2400
www.thebig98.com
License: Nashville, Davidson County, TN held by Capstar TX LLC
Group Owner: iHeartMedia; (acq 8-30-00; grpsl).
Arbitron Metro Market: Nashville, TN; *Format:* Country; *Hrs. of News Programming:* news progmg one hr wkly; *No. News Employees:* 2; *Target Audience:* 25-54.
Melissa Kent, General Sales Mgr
Michael Bryan, Programming Director
Kimsey Kerr, Promotions Manager
Karlie Powell, Digital Program Director

WSM
10-05-1925; 650 kHz AM; *Hrs Open:* 24; 50 kw-U, ND1; N35 59 50 W86 47 32
US
(615) 458-4650
www.wsmonline.com
randy@wsmonline.com
License: Nashville, TN held by Grand Ole Opry LLC
Nat'l Network: ABC; *Nat'l Reps:* Christal
Arbitron Metro Market: Nashville, TN; *Format:* Country *Special Programming:* Farm 6 hrs, Grand Ole Opry 12 hrs wkly; *Hrs. of News Programming:* news progmg 11 hrs wkly; *No. News Employees:* 12; *Target Audience:* 35 plus; high school graduates, married homeowners, income $25,000 plus
Randy Bush, General Manager
Dean Warfield, Programming Director
Nicole Judd, Promotions Manager
Jason Cooper, Chief Engineer
Jonathan Shaffer, Production Manager
Eric Marcum, Traffic Manager

WSM-FM
11-01-1962; 95.5 MHz FM; 100 kw; 1230 ft.; N36 8 27 W86 51 56
10 Music Circle E., Nashville, TN 37203 US
(615) 321-1067; *Fax:* (615) 321-5771
www.955thewolf.com
charlie.cook@cumulus.com
License: Nashville, Davidson County, TN held by Cumulus Licensing LLC.
Group Owner: Cumulus Media Inc.; (acq 7-21-2003; $65 million with WWTN(FM) Manchester).
Arbitron Metro Market: Nashville, TN; *Format:* Country; *Target Audience:* 25-54.
Rhonda Rollins, General Sales Mgr
Charlie Cook, Programming Director
Cori Vallentine, Promotions Manager

***WYFN**
01-07-1927; 980 kHz AM; 5 kw-D, DAN; 5 kw-N, DAN; N36 12 25 W86 40 25
P.O. Box 7300, Charlotte, NC 28241 US
(800) 888-7077
www.bbnradio.org
bbn@bbnmedia.org
License: Nashville, TN held by Bible Broadcasting Network Inc.
Group Owner: Bible Broadcasting Network; acq 1-31-91; $600,000;
Nat'l Reps: McGavren Guild
Arbitron Metro Market: Nashville, TN; *Format:* Religious
Jason Padgett, Operations Manager

New Johnsonville

***WAY**
01-01-2001; 89.9 MHz FM; *Hrs Open:* 24; 3.1 kw; 466 ft.; N35 56 17 W87 53 39
1095 W. McEwen Dr., Franklin, TN 37067 US
(615) 261-9293
www.wayfm.com
waym@wayfm.com
License: New Johnsonville, Humphreys County, TN held by WAY-FM Media Group Inc.
Group Owner: WAY-FM Media Group Inc.; acq 2-1-01).
Arbitron Metro Market: Colorado Springs, CO; *Format:* Christian
Bob Augsburg, President/Founder

Newport

WLIK
04-09-1954; 1270 kHz AM; *Hrs Open:* 24; 5 kw-D, DAN; 0.5 kw-N, DAN; N35 57 49 W83 12 31
640 West Highway 25/70, Newport, TN 37821 US
(423) 623-3095; *Fax:* (423) 623-3096
wlik.net
wlik@wlik.net
License: Newport, TN held by WLIK Inc.
Nat'l Network: CNN Radio; *Regional Network:* Tenn. Radio Net.
Regional Reps: Regional Reps
Format: Oldies *Special Programming:* Relg 18 hrs wkly; *Hrs. of News Programming:* news progmg 7 hrs wkly; *No. News Employees:* 1; *Target Audience:* General.; *Adv. Rates:* 10; 10; 10; 6
Dwight Wilkerson, President
Angela Wilkerson, Operations Manager/Sales Associate
Johnnie Swann, VP/Secretary
Rick Brooks, News Director
Johnnie Swann, Chief of Operations

WLNQ-FM
02-01-1993; 92.9 MHz FM; *Hrs Open:* 24; 3.1 kw; 459 ft; N35 57 27 W83 05 03 *Rebroadcasts:* Rebroadcasts WNPC(AM) Newport 100%
377 Graham St., Newport, TN 37821
(423) 623-8743; *Fax:* (423) 623-8744
www.thundercountry1047.com/
License: Newport, Cocke County, TN
Group Owner: Bristol Broadcasting Co. Inc.
Arbitron Metro Market: White Pine, TN
Jim Phillips, Programming Director

***WGSN**
01-01-2008; 90.7 MHz FM; 1 kw vert; Ant 2,296 ft; N35 54 20 W83 17 48
224 West Central Avenue, PO Box 1509, Jamestown, TN 38556
(931) 879-2364; *Fax:* (931) 879-1733
www.wgsnradio.com
License: Newport, Cocke County, TN held by Bible Believers Network Inc.

Andy Lowe, Station Manager
Cheryl Wright, Music/Programming Director
Steve Boutelle, Assistant Manager
Wayne Cook, East Tennessee Director
Sheliah Hughes, Promotions/Reception/Traffic Director
Connie Cody, Business Manager

Norris

WFGW(FM)
04-01-2001; 106.7 MHz FM; *Hrs Open:* 24; 1.1 kw; Ant 751 ft; N36 07 12 W83 55 30 *Rebroadcasts:* Rebroadcasts WTXM(FM) Maryville 100%
6808 Hanna Lake S.E., Caledonia, MI 49316
(616) 698-1831
License: Norris, Anderson County, TN held by Blue Ridge Broadcasting Corp.
Group Owner: Blue Ridge Broadcasting Corp.
Wire Services: AP
Population Served: 4,524; *Arbitron Metro Market:* Polson MT; *Adv. Rates:* 20; 20; 20; 10
P.R. Frank, Operations Dir
Ken Kreitzer, General Manager
Christopher Hartley, Programming Director
Tom Nornhold, Chief Engineer
Jennifer Bryant, Assistant Music Director

Oak Ridge

WCYQ
04-20-1974; 100.3 MHz FM; 100 kw; 2001 ft.; N36 11 53 W84 13 51
Mailing Address: 15233 Amherst Rd., Knoxville, TN 37909 US
Second Address: 4711 Old Kingston Pike, Knoxville, TN 37919
(865) 588-6511; *Fax:* (865) 588-3725
www.wnoxnewstalk.com
License: Oak Ridge, Anderson County, TN held by Journal Broadcast Corp.
Group Owner: Journal Communications Inc.
Nat'l Reps: Katz Radio; *Wire Services:* AP
Arbitron Metro Market: Knoxville, TN *TV Affiliate:* News/talk
Operations Manager

Olive Hill

*WDNX

01-10-1975; 89.1 MHz FM; *Hrs Open:* 24; 52 kw; 591 ft.; N35 12 23 W88 3 32
3575 Lonesome Pine Road, Savannah, TN 38372 US
(731) 925-9236; *Fax:* (731) 925-4238
www.harberthills.org/wdnx-radio-station/
sheriwdnx@yahoo.com
License: Olive Hill, Hardin County, TN held by Rural Life Foundation.
Arbitron Metro Market: Savannah, TN; *Format:* Christian, Religious *Special Programming:* Class 5 hrs, farm one hr wkly; *Hrs. of News Programming:* news progmg 5 hrs wkly; *No. News Employees:* 1; *Target Audience:* General; families

Oliver Springs

WOKI

09-15-1989; 98.7 MHz FM; *Hrs Open:* 24; 8 kw; 571 ft.; N36 06 48 W84 03 44
4711 Old Kingston Pike, PO Box 11167, Knoxville, TN 37919 US
(865) 588-6511; *Fax:* (865) 588-3725
www.newstalk987.com
License: Oliver Springs, TN held by Radio License Holding CBC, LLC
Group Owner: Cumulus Media Inc.; (acq 4-26-2001; grpsl)
Arbitron Metro Market: Knoxville, TN; *Format:* News/Talk; *Target Audience:* 18 plus.
Tammy Browning, General Sales Mgr
Joe Stutler, Programming Director

WJRV(FM)

106.1 MHz FM; 190 w; Ant 1,746 ft; N36 06 29 W84 20 08
408 N. Cedar Bluff Rd., Knoxville, TN 37923
(865) 246-3848; *Fax:* (865) 246-7979
www.river106.com
s.miller@wtnqfm.com
License: Oliver Springs, Roane County, TN held by Momentum Broadcasting LLC.
Population Served: 253; *Arbitron Metro Market:* Louisville, KY
Norman Alpert, President

Oneida

WBNT-FM

06-10-1965; 105.5 MHz FM; *Hrs Open:* 18; 3 kw horiz; 285 ft.; N36 30 3 W84 29 24
PO Box 4370, Oneida, TN 37841-4370 US
(423) 569-8598; *Fax:* (423) 569-5572
www.hive105.com
wbnt@highland.net
License: Oneida, Scott County, TN held by Oneida Broadcasters Inc.
Nat'l Network: ABC
Arbitron Metro Market: Oneida, TN; *Format:* Adult Contemp, Country; *Target Audience:* 16-56; male/female working class-retirees
Paul C. Strunk, Operations/HR/Sales Manager
Hillard Mattie, General Manager/General Sales Manager

WOCV

08-01-1959; 1310 kHz AM; 1 kw-D, NDD; N36 30 3 W84 29 24
Rebroadcasts: Rebroadcasts WBNT-FM Oneida 100%
P.O. Box 4370, Oneida, TN 37841-4370 US
(423) 569-8598; *Fax:* (423) 569-5572
www.hive105.com
wbnt@highland.net
License: Oneida, TN held by Oneida Broadcasters Inc.
Nat'l Network: ABC
TV Affiliate: Adult contemp *Special Programming:* news progmg 15 hrs wkly; *Hrs. of News Programming:* 4; *No. News Employees:* 22-55; male & female; *Adv. Rates:* 6.50; 6.50; 6.50; 6.50
Paul C. Strunk, Operations/HR/Sales Manager
Hillard Mattie, General Manager/General Sales Manager

Ooltewah

WPLZ

02-27-1980; 95.3 MHz FM; *Hrs Open:* 24; 3.4 kw; 902 ft.; N35 7 45 W85 20 2
1305 Carter St., Chattanooga, TN 37402 US
(423) 265-9494; *Fax:* (423) 266-2335
www.big953.com
License: Ooltewah, Hamilton County, TN held by J.L. Brewer Broadcasting of Cleveland LLC.
Group Owner: Brewer Broadcasting Corp.; May-98
Nat'l Reps: Katz Radio *Regional Reps:* Eastman
Population Served: 500,000; *Arbitron Metro Market:* Chattanooga, TN; *Format:* Contemporary Hits/Top 40; *Target Audience:* A25-54; *Adv. Rates:* 30; 25; 30; 20
Janice Colby, Operations Manager
Mike Baskin, Sales Manager

Paris

WAKQ

09-01-1967; 105.5 MHz FM; 3.7 kw; 420 ft.; N36 16 45 W88 20 31 *Rebroadcasts:* Rebroadcasts WWKF(FM) Union City 100%
Mailing Address: 1729 Nailling Drive, Union City, TN 38261 US
Second Address: 206 N. Brewer Street, Paris, TN 38242
(731) 885-1240; *Fax:* (731) 885-3405
www.kf99kq105.com
thailey@wenkwtpr.com
License: Paris, Henry County, TN
Group Owner: WENK of Union City Inc.
Arbitron Metro Market: Clarksville TN; *Format:* Contemporary Hits/Top 40; *Hrs. of News Programming:* news progmg one hr wkly; *No. News Employees:* 1; *Target Audience:* adults 18-34; *Adv. Rates:* Same as AM
Terry L. Hailey, President/General Manager
Wilma Payne, Traffic/Bookkeeping

WLZK

11-01-1991; 94.1 MHz FM; *Hrs Open:* 24; 10.5 kw; 328 ft.; N36 18 50 W88 17 33
US
(731) 644-9455
License: Paris, Henry County, TN held by Benton-Weatherford Broadcasting Inc. of Texas
Group Owner: Benton-Weatherford Broadcasting Inc. of Tennessee; (Acq 3-15-91;
Nat'l Network: Jones Radio Networks
Arbitron Metro Market: Paris, TN; *Format:* Adult Contemp; *Hrs. of News Programming:* news progmg 7 hrs wkly; *No. News Employees:* 1; *Adv. Rates:* Same as AM
Tim Alsobrooks, News Director
Lance Pierce, Sports Director

WRQR(AM)

05-09-1980; 1000 kHz AM; 5 kw-D, DA; N36 18 50 W88 17 33
(731) 644-9455; *Fax:* (731) 644-9421
www.wmufradio.com/indexwrqr.html
License: Paris, Henry County, TN held by Benton-Weatherford Broadcasting Inc.of Tennessee
Group Owner: Benton-Weatherford Broadcasting Inc. of Tennessee; acq 4-1-85).
Nat'l Network: ABC
Population Served: 50,000; *Arbitron Metro Market:* Paris, TN; *Format:* Country *Special Programming:* Farm 2 hrs wkly; *Hrs. of News Programming:* news progmg 3 hrs wkly; *No. News Employees:* 1; *Target Audience:* 25-54; people with disposable income
Tim Alsobrooks, News Director
Lance Pierce, Sports Director

WTPR

05-07-1947; 710 kHz AM; *Hrs Open:* Sunrise-sunset; 0.75 kw-D, NDD; N36 16 47 W88 20 32 *Rebroadcasts:* Reboadcasts WTPR-FM Paris 100%
Mailing Address: 1729 Nailing Drive, Union City, TN 38261 US
Second Address: 206 N. Brewer Street, Paris, TN 38242
(731) 885-1240; *Fax:* (731) 885-3405
www.wenkwtpr.com
thailey@wenkwtpr.com
License: Paris, TN held by WENK of Uniion City Inc.
Group Owner: WENK of Union City Inc.; acq 10-28-89;
Nat'l Network: ABC *Regional Reps:* Rgnl Reps
Arbitron Metro Market: Paris, TN; *Format:* Oldies; *Hrs. of News Programming:* news progmg 12 hrs wkly; *No. News Employees:* 1; *Target Audience:* 35-54.; *Adv. Rates:* 11.75; 17.75; 17.75; 8.80
Terry L. Hailey, President/General Manager
Terry Hailey, Sales Representative
Lorie Matlock, Sales Representative

*WPRH

90.9 MHz FM; 5.4 kw vert; 315 ft.; N36 15 29 W88 11 11
88 Casey Jones Blvd., Jackson, TN 38305 US
(662) 844-8888; *Fax:* (662) 842-6791
www.afr.net
faq@afa.net
License: Paris, Henry County, TN held by American Family Association.
Group Owner: American Family Radio; (acq 1-16-2007)
Nat'l Network: American Family Radio
Arbitron Metro Market: Paris, TN; *Format:* Christian
Tim Wildmon, President
Donald Wildmon, Founder
Buddy Smith, Sr VP
Ed Vitagliano, Executive VP
Randy Sharp, Director Of Special Project
Meeke Addison, Director Of Communications
Abraham Hamilton III, General Counsel

Parker's Crossroads

WBFG

01-01-1999; 96.5 MHz FM; 6 kw; 328 ft.; N35 45 33 W88 23 15
Mailing Address: P.O. Box 279, Lexington, TN 38351 US
Second Address: 584 Smith Ave., Lexington, TN 38351
(731) 968-9990; *Fax:* (731) 968-0380
www.wbfg965.com
wbfg965@yahoo.com
License: Parker's Crossroads, Henderson County, TN held by Crossroads Broadcasting LLC.
Nat'l Network: ESPN Radio
Format: Sports
Lori Becker, Operations Dir
Dan Hughes, General Manager

Parsons

WKJQ-FM

06-04-1990; 97.3 MHz FM; *Hrs Open:* 24; 6 kw; 256 ft.; N35 39 39 W88 7 5
PO Box 576, 109 Iron Hill Road, Parsons, TN 38363 US
(731) 847-3011; *Fax:* (731) 847-4600
www.q973fm.com
License: Parsons, Decatur County, TN held by Clenney Broadcasting Corp.
Format: Country; *Target Audience:* 25-54.; *Adv. Rates:* 10; 10; 10; na
Ralph Clenny
Steve Clenney
Bill Murphy
JoAnn Clenney

Pegram

WPRT

04-27-1964; 102.5 MHz AM; *Hrs Open:* 24; 100 kw; 974 ft.; N36 17 36 W87 18 20
Mailing Address: 1824 Murfreesboro Pike, Nashville, TN 37217 US
Second Address: PO Box 290099, Nashville, TN 37229-0099
(615) 399-1029; *Fax:* (615) 399-1023
www.thegamenashville.com
tcrouse@cromwellradio.com
License: Pegram, Cheatham County, TN held by Montgomery Broadcasting.
Group Owner: The Cromwell Group Inc.; (acq 1990)
Nat'l Reps: McGavren Guild
Arbitron Metro Market: Nashville, TN; *Format:* Adult Contemp; *Target Audience:* 18-34; S. KY residents
Tincy Crouse, General Manager
Jeff Kolb, Sales Manager
Jeremy Bennefield, Programming Director
Brian Jones, Promotions Director/Digital Strategy Coordinator

WPRT-FM

04-27-1964; 94.9 MHz FM; *Hrs Open:* 24; 100 kw; 974 ft.; N36 17 36 W87 18 20
Mailing Address: 1824 Murfreesboro Pike, Nashville, TN 37217 US
Second Address: PO Box 290099, Nashville, TN 37229-0099
(615) 399-1029; *Fax:* (615) 399-1023
www.thegamenashville.com
tcrouse@cromwellradio.com
License: Pegram, Cheatham County, TN held by Montgomery Broadcasting.
Group Owner: The Cromwell Group Inc.; (acq 1990)
Nat'l Reps: McGavren Guild
Arbitron Metro Market: Nashville, TN; *Format:* Adult Contemp; *Target Audience:* 18-34; S. KY residents
Tincy Crouse, General Manager
Jeff Kolb, Sales Manager
Jeremy Bennefield, Programming Director
Brian Jones, Promotions Director/Digital Strategy Coordinator

Pigeon Forge

WPFT

01-01-2007; 106.3 MHz FM; 0.5 kw; 1117 ft.; N35 42 13 W83 33 57
196 W. Dumplin Valley Rd., Kodak, TN 37764 US
(865) 932-6002
www.mountain1063.com
feedback@mountain1063.com
License: Pigeon Forge, Sevier County, TN held by East Tennessee Radio Group L.P.
Group Owner: East Tennessee Radio Group L.P.

Arbitron Metro Market: Pigeon Forge, TN; *Format:* Sports, Talk
Paul Fink, General Manager

Pikeville

WUAT
12-19-1972; 1110 kHz AM; 0.25 kw-D, NDD; N35 36 18 W85 11 14
P.O. Box 128, Pikeville, TN 37367 US
(423) 447-2906
www.wuatradio.com
License: Pikeville, TN held by Joyce V. Bownds.
Arbitron Metro Market: Pikeville, TN; *Format:* Country, Gospel
Special Programming: Farm 5 hrs, relg 15 hrs wkly
Joyce Bownds, Manager

Portland

WQKR
07-15-1980; 1270 kHz AM; *Hrs Open:* 24
100 Main Street, Suite 210, Portland, TN 37148 US
(615) 325-3250
www.wqkr.com
License: Portland, TN held by Venture Broadcasting LLC
Nat'l Network: ABC; *Regional Network:* Tenn. Radio Net.
Arbitron Metro Market: Nashville, TN; *Format:* Oldies; *No. News Employees:* 1; *Target Audience:* 25-54.
Lee Dorman, General Manager
Wanda Rogers, Sales Representative
Brandon Roberts, Technical, Website
Dutch Maris, Board Op/News/Creative Services

Powell

WNFZ
02-01-1967; 94.3 MHz FM; 2.95 kw; 472 ft.; N35 57 58 W84 4 6
8081 Kingston Pike, Suite 100, Knoxville, TN 37919 US
(865) 531-2000; *Fax:* (865) 474-7486
www.knoxtalkradio.com
License: Powell, Anderson County, TN held by John A. Pirkle.
Arbitron Metro Market: Knoxville, TN; *Format:* Alternative; *Target Audience:* General.
John Pirkle, President/CEO
Terry Gillingham, Operations Dir
Jeff Cutshaw, General Sales Mgr
Shane Cox, Programming Director

WJBE
08-15-1984; 1040 kHz AM; 3 kw-C, NDD; 10 kw-D, NDD; N36 2 34 W84 2 51
Mailing Address: 3355 S. Valley View Blvd., Las Vegas, NV 09102 US
Second Address: Box 50158, Knoxville, TN 37950
(865) 824-1021; *Fax:* (865) 824-1880
bpatrick@journalbroadcastgroup.com
License: Powell, TN held by Arm and Rage LLC
Nat'l Network: AP Radio; Jones Radio Networks
Arbitron Metro Market: Knoxville, TN; *Format:* Classic Rock
Dan McKee, General Sales Mgr
Bruce Patrick, Programming Director

Pulaski

WKSR
05-06-1947; 1420 kHz AM
104 South Second Street, Pulaski, TN 38478 US
(931) 363-2505; *Fax:* (931) 424-3157
www.wksr.com
scott@wksr.com
License: Pulaski, TN held by Pulaski Broadcasting Inc.
Nat'l Network: ABC
Format: Oldies; *Hrs. of News Programming:* one.; *Target Audience:* 25-54.
Scott Stewart, General Manager/Station Manager/Sports Director
Tiffany Hagood, Sales Representative
Taren Eastep, News Director

Red Bank

***WJBP**
09-12-1980; 91.5 MHz FM; *Hrs Open:* 24; 11 kw horiz, 10 kw vert; 328 ft.; N34 56 37 W85 18 1
Mailing Address: PO Box 35300, Tucson, AZ 85740 US
Second Address: 7355 N. Oracle Road, Tucson, AZ 85704
(800) 776-1070
www.myflr.org
License: Red Bank, Hamilton County, TN held by Family Life Broadcasting Inc.
Group Owner: Family Life Communications Inc.; (acq 12-10-2008; $1.5 million)
Arbitron Metro Market: Dripping Springs TX; *Format:* Christian, Religious

WJTT
11-01-1972; 94.3 MHz FM; *Hrs Open:* 24; 4.7 kw; 371 ft.; N35 7 33 W85 17 25
1305 Carter St., Chattanooga, TN 37402 US
(423) 265-9494; *Fax:* (423) 266-2335
www.power94.com
License: Red Bank, Hamilton County, TN held by Brewer Broadcasting of Chattanooga Inc.
Group Owner: Brewer Broadcasting Corp.; (acq 12-26-93; $1.68 million).
Nat'l Reps: D & R Radio
Arbitron Metro Market: Chattanooga, TN; *Format:* Urban Contemporary *Special Programming:* Relg 4 hrs wkly; *Target Audience:* 18-49.
Jim Brewer II, President
Keith Landecker, Operations Manager
Mike Baskin, Director of Sales
Jay Holloway, Production Director

Ripley

***WAUV**
01-01-2000; 89.7 MHz FM; 6.4 kw; 394 ft.; N35 46 31 W89 28 18
P.O. Box 3206, Tupelo, MS 38803 US
(662) 844-8888; *Fax:* (662) 842-6791
www.afr.net
faq@afa.net
License: Ripley, Lauderdale County, TN held by American Family Association.
Group Owner: American Family Radio
Arbitron Metro Market: Ripley, TN; *Format:* Religious
Tim Wildmon, President
Donald Wildmon, Founder
Buddy Smith, Sr VP
Ed Vitagliano, Exec VP
Randy Sharp, Director Of Special Projects
Meeke Addison, Director Of Communications
Abraham Hamilton III, General Counsel

WTRB
12-11-1954; 1570 kHz AM; *Hrs Open:* 17; 1 kw-D, ND1; 0.053 kw-N, ND1; N35 43 46 W89 32 33
PO Box 410, 372 S. Jefferson Street, Ripley, TN 38063 US
(731) 635-1570; *Fax:* (731) 635-9722
www.1570wtrb.com
License: Ripley, TN held by West Tennessee Regional Broadcasting Inc.
Regional Network: Tenn. Radio Net; *Nat'l Reps:* Keystone (unwired net)
Arbitron Metro Market: Ripley, TN; *Format:* Country *Special Programming:* Gospel 6 hrs wkly
Palmer Johnson, General Manager
Mickey Hamlin, Sales
Randy Byrd, Sports Director

Rockwood

WYHM
05-12-1957; 580 kHz AM; 1 kw-D, 49 w-N; N35 49 40 W84 39 19
319 W. Rockwood St., Rockwood, TN 37854
(865) 354-0200
www.radio580.com
License: Rockwood, Roane County, TN held by The Holler Inc.
Population Served: 607,315 *Hrs. of News Programming:* news progrmg 3 hrs wkly; *No. News Employees:* 3; *Target Audience:* 35 plus; adults; *Adv. Rates:* 24; 18; 24; 12
Nick Barrett, General Manager

WIHG
07-09-1991; 105.7 MHz FM; 2.4 kw; 1014 ft.; N35 53 27 W84 52 1
37 South Drive, Crossville, TN 38555 US
(931) 484-1057; *Fax:* (931) 707-0580
www.1057thehog.com
License: Rockwood, Roane County, TN held by Southern Media Group Inc.
Nat'l Network: CNN Radio *Regional Reps:* Rgnl Reps; *Wire Services:* AP
Arbitron Metro Market: Knoxville, TN *TV Affiliate:* classic hits
Special Programming: News progmg 4 hrs wkly; *No. News Employees:* 25-54.; *Adv. Rates:* 42; 36; 42; 24

Rogersville

WJDT
12-01-1990; 106.5 MHz FM; *Hrs Open:* 24; 0.3 kw; 1378 ft.; N36 22 51 W83 10 47
Mailing Address: 448 Highway 25E, Bean Station, TN 37708 US
Second Address: PO Box 519, Morristown, TN 37815
(423) 235-4640
www.wjdtfm.com
wjdt106.5@gmail.com
License: Rogersville, Hawkins County, TN held by C & S Broadcasting.
Nat'l Network: CNN Radio
Arbitron Metro Market: Johnson City-Kingsport-Bristol, TN-VA; *Format:* Country; *Hrs. of News Programming:* News progmg 6 hrs wkly; *Target Audience:* 18-59; female 65%, male 35%
David Quillen, Operations Dir
Clark Quillen, General Manager
John Donovan, Programming Director

WRGS
08-20-1954; 1370 kHz AM; *Hrs Open:* 24; 1 kw-D, 40 w-N; N36 24 58 W82 59 04
211 Burem Rd., Rogersville, TN 37857
(423) 272-2628; *Fax:* (423) 272-0328
www.wrgsradio.com
stationmanager@wrgsradio.com
License: Rogersville, Hawkins County, TN held by WRGS Inc.
Nat'l Network: USA; *Nat'l Reps:* Rgnl Reps
Population Served: 50,000; *Arbitron Metro Market:* Johnson City-Kingsport-Bristol, TN-VA; *Target Audience:* General.
Debbie Beal, General Manager
Philip Beal, Radio Advertising
Jay Phillips, Sports

Savannah

***WAZD**
01-01-2001; 88.1 MHz FM; 0.38 kw; 128 ft.; N35 12 58 W88 14 30
P.O. Box 3206, Tupelo, MS 38803 US
(662) 844-8888; *Fax:* (662) 842-6791
www.afr.net
faq@afa.net
License: Savannah, Hardin County, TN held by American Family Association.
Group Owner: American Family Radio
Arbitron Metro Market: Centreville MS; *Format:* Christian, Religious
Tim Wildmon, President
Donald Wildmon, Founder
Buddy Smith, Sr VP
Ed Vitagliano, Exec VP
Randy Sharp, Director Of Special Projects
Meeke Addison, Director Of Communications
Abraham Hamilton III, General Counsel

WKWX
93.5 MHz FM; 25 kw; 299 ft.; N35 17 8 W88 10 3
P. O. Box 40, Savannah, TN 38372 US
(731) 925-9600; *Fax:* (731) 925-8828
www.wkwxfm.com
wkwx@bellsouth.net
License: Savannah, Hardin County, TN held by Melco Inc.
Nat'l Network: AP Radio; *Regional Network:* Tenn. Radio Net.
Format: Country
Steve Carnal, President
Jane Haggard, General Manager
Jim Jerrolds, General Sales Mgr
Dennis Brown, Programming Director
Tom Treadway, Chief Engineer

WORM
06-29-1956; 1010 kHz AM; 0.25 kw-D, ND1; 0.027 kw-N, ND1; N35 14 24 W88 14 29
P.O. Box 550, Savannah, TN 38372 US
(731) 925-4981; *Fax:* (731) 925-4981
thewormq105@yahoo.com
License: Savannah, TN held by Gerald W. Hunt.
Regional Network: Tenn. Radio Net.
TV Affiliate: Pure Gold
Music Director

WORM-FM
08-25-1966; 101.7 MHz FM; 3 kw horiz; 174 ft.; N35 14 24 W88 14 29
P. O. Box 550, Savannah, TN 38372 US
(731) 925-4981
License: Savannah, Hardin County, TN held by Gerald W. Hunt
TV Affiliate: Country
T.J. Michaels, General Sales Mgr

Selmer

WDTM
10-31-1967; 1150 kHz AM; 1 kw-D, NDD; N35 11 27 W88 35 21
P.O. Box 388, Selmer, TN 38375 US

(731) 663-3931; *Fax:* (731) 663-9804
www.gracebroadcasting.com
License: Selmer, TN held by Grace Broadcasting Services Inc.
Group Owner: Grace Broadcasting Services Inc.; (acq 7-25-2005; $200,000 with co-located FM)
Arbitron Metro Market: Selmer, TN; *Format:* Christian
Lacy Ennis, President

WSIB
01-01-1990; 93.9 MHz FM; *Hrs Open:* 24; 6 kw; 328 ft.; N35 11 27 W88 35 21
430 Wayne Road, Savannah, TN 38372 US
(731) 925-6464; *Fax:* (731) 925-0217
License: Selmer, McNairy County, TN
Group Owner: Grace Broadcasting Services Inc.
Format: Religious; *Target Audience:* 20-45.
Dennis Lavon Brown, Owner

WXOQ
06-15-1986; 105.5 MHz FM; *Hrs Open:* 24; 6 kw; 299 ft.; N35 13 11 W88 40 23
302 E. Poplar, Selmer, TN 38375 US
(731) 645-9880
License: Selmer, McNairy County, TN held by Gerald W. Hunt.
Nat'l Network: Westwood One
Arbitron Metro Market: Selmer, TN; *Format:* Country; *No. News Employees:* 2; *Target Audience:* General.
Gerald W. Hunt, Owner

***WXKV**
01-01-2008; 90.5 MHz FM; 20 kw; 413 ft.; N35 10 44 W88 33 45
Rebroadcasts: Rebroadcasts KLVR(FM) Middletown, CA 100%
PO Box 2098, Omaha, NE 68103-2098 US
(800) 525-5683
www.klove.com
License: Selmer, McNairy County, TN held by Educational Media Foundation.
Group Owner: EMF Broadcasting; (acq 11-1-2006; grpsl)
Nat'l Network: K-Love
Arbitron Metro Market: Selmer, TN; *Format:* Christian
Darrell Chambliss, Chairman
Mike Novak, President
Crystal Wojteczko, Operations Dir

Sevierville

WWST
02-03-1961; 102.1 MHz FM; *Hrs Open:* 24; 15 kw; 1978 ft.; N35 48 41 W83 40 8
1533 Amherst Rd., Knoxville, TN 37909 US
(865) 824-1021
www.star1021fm.com
dmckee@journalbroadcastgroup.com
License: Sevierville, Sevier County, TN held by Journal Broadcast Corp.
Group Owner: Journal Communications Inc.; (acq 5-19-97)
Nat'l Network: ABC
Arbitron Metro Market: Knoxville, TN; *Format:* Contemporary Hits/Top 40; *Hrs. of News Programming:* News progmg 4 hrs wkly; *Target Audience:* 25-54.; *Adv. Rates:* 115; 105; 95; 25
Dan McKee, General Sales Mgr
Rich Bailey, Programming Director
Brad Allen, Disc Jockey
Randy Chambers, Disc Jockey
Jerry Agar, Disc Jockey
Scott Bohannon, Music Director
Dan McKee, Regional Sales Manager

WSEV
04-23-1955; 930 kHz AM; *Hrs Open:* 24; 5 kw-D, ND1; 0.148 kw-N, ND1; N35 52 42 W83 33 18
196 West Dumplin Valley Road, Kodak, TN 37764 US
(865) 932-6002
www.easttennesseeradio.com
License: Sevierville, TN held by Grand Crowne Resorts of Pigeon Forge LLC
Nat'l Network: CBS; *Regional Network:* Tenn. Radio Net; *Nat'l Reps:* Rgnl Reps
Arbitron Metro Market: Knoxville, TN; *Format:* Adult Contemp; *Hrs. of News Programming:* news progmg 6 hrs wkly; *No. News Employees:* 1; *Target Audience:* 25 plus.
Bill Burkett, Operations Dir

Sewanee

***WUTS**
05-01-1972; 91.3 MHz FM; 0.014 kw horiz; 656 ft.; N35 12 23 W85 55 4
735 University Ave, Sewanee, TN 37383-1000 US
(931) 598-1112
wuts@sewanee.edu
License: Sewanee, Franklin County, TN held by University of the South.
Arbitron Metro Market: Sewanee, TN; *Format:* Variety/Diverse
Special Programming: Black 2 hrs, class 4 hrs, country 2 hrs, jazz 4 hr; *Target Audience:* General; college students

Seymour

WJBZ-FM
03-31-1991; 96.3 MHz FM; *Hrs Open:* 24; 2.9 kw; 479 ft.; N35 56 17 W83 42 11
Mailing Address: 7101 Chapman Highway, Knoxville, TN 37920 US
Second Address: PO Box 2526, Knoxville, TN 37901
(865) 577-4885
www.praise963.com
info@praise963.com
License: Seymour, Sevier County, TN held by Seymour Communications.
Arbitron Metro Market: Knoxville, TN; *Format:* Gospel
Charlotte Mull, CEO
Doug Hutchison, President
Mike Clark, Operations Dir
Jamie Lewis, General Sales Mgr
Tim Guinn, Programming Director
Staci Beal, News Director
Tim Berry, Chief Engineer

Shelbyville

***WBIA**
01-01-1999; 88.3 MHz FM; 0.25 kw; 46 ft.; N35 28 54 W86 27 28
P.O. Box 3206, Tupelo, MS 38803 US
(662) 844-8888; *Fax:* (662) 842-6791
www.afr.net
faq@afa.net
License: Shelbyville, Bedford County, TN held by American Family Association.
Group Owner: American Family Radio
Arbitron Metro Market: Shelbyville, TN; *Format:* Christian
Tim Wildmon, President
Donald Wildmon, Founder
Buddy Smith, Sr VP
Ed Vitagliano, Exec VP
Randy Sharp, Director Of Special Projects
Meeke Addison, Director Of Communications
Abraham Hamilton III, General Counsel

WLIJ
12-02-1959; 1580 kHz AM; *Hrs Open:* 24; 5 kw-D, ND1; 0.012 kw-N, ND1; N35 27 19 W86 27 7
PO Box 7, Shelbyville, TN 37162 US
(931) 680-1214
www.thisisjaxradio.com
jaxradio1@gmail.com
License: Shelbyville, TN held by Jax Broadcasting, LLC
Format: Country, Gospel *Special Programming:* Black one hr, farm 3 hrs, relg 11 hrs wkly; *Hrs. of News Programming:* news progmg 14 hrs wkly; *No. News Employees:* 1; *Target Audience:* General.
Rusty Reed, President
Keith Cook, General Sales Mgr

WZNG
12-01-1946; 1400 kHz AM; *Hrs Open:* 24; 1 kw-U, ND1; N35 28 26 W86 26 45
PO Box 7, Shelbyville, TN 37162 US
(931) 680-1214
jaxradio1@gmail.com
License: Shelbyville, TN held by Jax Broadcasting, LLC
Arbitron Metro Market: Shelbyville, TN; *Format:* Talk *Special Programming:* Relg 5 hrs wkly; *Target Audience:* General; residents of the loc area
Rusty Reed, President

Signal Mountain

WLND
08-29-1994; 98.1 MHz FM; *Hrs Open:* 24; 1 kw; 794 ft.; N35 5 16 W85 21 47
7413 Old Lee Highway, Chattanooga, TN 37421 US
(423) 892-3333
www.981thelake.com
License: Signal Mountain, Hamilton County, TN held by Capstar TX LLC
Group Owner: iHeartMedia; (acq 8-15-2000; grpsl)
Arbitron Metro Market: Chattanooga, TN; *Format:* Adult Contemp; *Hrs. of News Programming:* news progmg 4 hrs wkly; *No. News Employees:* 1; *Target Audience:* 35-54.
John Bouwhuis, Director of Sales

Smithville

WJLE
04-11-1964; 1480 kHz AM; *Hrs Open:* 16; 1 kw-D, ND1; 0.034 kw-N, ND1; N35 55 31 W85 49 14
2606 McMinnville Highway, Smithville, TN 37166 US
(615) 597-4265; *Fax:* (615) 597-6025
www.wjle.com
wjle@dtccom.net
License: Smithville, TN held by Center Hill Broadcasting Corp.
Format: Country *Special Programming:* Gospel 15 hrs wkly; *Hrs. of News Programming:* news progmg 14 hrs wkly; *No. News Employees:* 1; *Target Audience:* General.

WJLE-FM
01-01-1970; 101.7 MHz FM; *Hrs Open:* 16; 4.4 kw; 194 ft.; N35 55 31 W85 49 14
2606 McMinnville Hwy, Smithville, TN 37166 US
(615) 597-4265; *Fax:* (615) 597-6025
www.wjle.com
wjle@dtccom.net
License: Smithville, De Kalb County, TN held by Center Hill Broadcasting Corp.
Format: Country

Smyrna

WFFH
10-07-1993; 94.1 MHz FM; *Hrs Open:* 24; 3.2 kw; 453 ft.; N36 1 14 W86 38 18 *Rebroadcasts:* Simulcasts with WFFI(FM) Kingston Springs
US
www.94fmthefish.net
License: Smyrna, Rutherford County, TN held by Caron Broadcasting Inc.
Group Owner: Salem Communications Corp.; (acq 12-18-02; $5.6 million with WFFI(FM) Kingston Springs).
Nat'l Network: Salem Radio Network; *Nat'l Reps:* Salem
Arbitron Metro Market: Nashville, TN; *Format:* Christian; *Target Audience:* 25-54; adults
Michael Miller, General Manager
Kevin Anderson, General Sales Mgr
Vance Dillard, Programming Director
Dick Marsh, Promotions Manager
Kim Bindel, News Director
Carl Campbell, Chief Engineer
Ed Evenson, Traffic Manager
CarolynFelco, Traffic/Billing Manager

Soddy-Daisy

WGOW
07-14-1977; 102.3 MHz FM; 6 kw; 285 ft.; N35 11 45 W85 13 45
821 Pineville Rd., Chattanooga, TN 37405 US
(423) 756-6141
www.wgow.com
License: Soddy-Daisy, Hamilton County, TN held by Radio License Holding CBC, LLC
Group Owner: Cumulus Media Inc.; (acq 5-30-00; grpsl).
Arbitron Metro Market: Chattanooga, TN; *Format:* News/Talk
Dan Brown, General Manager
Kennard Yamada, General Sales Mgr
Bill Lockhart, Programming Director
Kevin West, News Director

WSDT
02-27-1970; 1240 kHz AM; *Hrs Open:* 24; 1 kw-U, ND1; N35 16 16 W85 10 28
4706 Hixson Pike, Suite 104 D, Chattanooga, TN 37343 US
(423) 800-8949
www.hotnewstalkradio.com
License: Soddy-Daisy, TN held by Serendipity Ventures II LLC
Nat'l Network: USA
Arbitron Metro Market: Chattanooga, TN; *Format:* Oldies; *Hrs. of News Programming:* TOH-Daytime
Steve Vogt, General Manager

South Pittsburg

WEPG
07-09-1954; 910 kHz AM; 5 kw-D, 95 w-N; N35 00 57 W85 42 00
212 West 5th Street, Jasper, TN 37347
(423) 837-0747; *Fax:* (423) 837-2974
wepgwebmaster@gmail.com
License: South Pittsburg, Marion County, TN held by Stone/Collins Communications Inc.
Population Served: 80,000; *Arbitron Metro Market:* Chattanooga, TN *Special Programming:* Gospel 10 hrs wkly; *Target Audience:* 18-50; females; *Adv. Rates:* 7.25; 5.37; 6.25; 4.20
Charles Rodgers, Owner/Manager

WUUQ
11-05-1990; 97.3 MHz FM; *Hrs Open:* 24; 16 kw; 856 ft.; N34 58 22 W85 37 58
2615 Broad St., Chattanooga, TN 37408 US
(423) 321-6200
www.wuuqradio.com
License: South Pittsburg, Marion County, TN held by Jackson Telecasters Inc.
Group Owner: Bahakel Communications Ltd.; (acq 6-22-2007; grpsl)
Arbitron Metro Market: Chattanooga, TN; *Format:* Country, Adult Contemp; *Hrs. of News Programming:* news progmg 20 hrs wkly; *No. News Employees:* 2; *Target Audience:* 18-54.
Bernie Barker, VP/General Manager
Danny Howard, Station Manager
Cheryl Brown, Local Sales Manager
Chris Adams, Production Director

Sparta

WSMT
04-26-1953; 1050 kHz AM; *Hrs Open:* 24
PO Box 1505, Glasgow, KY 42142 US
(931) 836-1055; *Fax:* (931) 836-2320
www.1050wsmt.com
License: Sparta, TN held by Peg Broadcasting Crossville LLC.
Group Owner: Peg Broadcasting Crossville LLC; (acq 7-1-2008; grpsl)
Format: Gospel *Special Programming:* Relg 10 hrs wkly; *Hrs. of News Programming:* news progmg 10 hrs wkly; *No. News Employees:* 1; *Target Audience:* General.
Duke Rice, Operations Dir
Bryan Kell, General Manager
Anthony Griffen, Engineering Dir

WTZX
11-26-1971; 860 kHz AM; *Hrs Open:* 24; 1 kw-D, ND1; 0.01 kw-N, ND1; N35 55 20 W85 26 50
PO Box 1505, Glasgow, KY 42142 US
(931) 836-1055; *Fax:* (931) 836-2320
License: Sparta, TN held by Peg Broadcasting Crossville LLC.
Group Owner: Peg Broadcasting Crossville LLC; (acq 7-1-2008)
Arbitron Metro Market: Cookeville, TN; *Format:* Country; *No. News Employees:* 1; *Target Audience:* General.
Duke Rice, Operations Dir
Bryan Kell, General Manager
Anthony Griffen, Engineering Dir

Spencer

WTRZ
08-01-1993; 107.3 MHz FM; 2 kw; 509 ft.; N35 39 55 W85 31 19
230 W. Colville Street, McMinnville, TN 37111 US
(931) 473-9253
www.star107fm.net
bryan.kell@pegbroadcasting.com
License: Spencer, Van Buren County, TN held by Peg Broadcasting Crossville LLC.
Group Owner: Peg Broadcasting Crossville LLC; (acq 6-30-2008; grpsl)
Arbitron Metro Market: Spencer, TN; *Format:* Contemporary Hits/Top 40
Bryan Kell, Sales
Jay Walker, News
Duke Rice, Production

***WZYZ**
01-01-2003; 90.1 MHz FM; *Hrs Open:* 24; 0.03 kw; 591 ft.; N35 44 3 W85 27 33
P.O. Box 1452, Washington, DC 20013 US
License: Spencer, Van Buren County, TN held by Church Faith Trinity Assemblies
Format: Religious
Daniel Lawson, General Manager

Spring City

WRHA(AM)
07-12-1979; 970 kHz AM; *Hrs Open:* 6 AM-6 PM; 500 w-D; N35 39 59 W84 52 44 *Rebroadcasts:* Rebroadcasts WBAC(AM) Cleveland 100%
P.O. Box 1235, Dayton, TN 37321
(423) 285-6441
www.rheacountyradio.com
comments@rheacountyradio.com
License: Spring City, Rhea County, TN held by Beverly Broadcasting Co. LLC
Group Owner: Beverly Broadcasting Co. LLC; (acq 5-30-2008; grpsl)
Nat'l Network: ABC; *Regional Network:* Tenn. Radio Net; *Nat'l Reps:* D & R Radio
Population Served: 41,723; *Arbitron Metro Market:* Cleveland, TN; *Format:* News, News/Talk, 86; *Hrs. of News Programming:* news progmg 16 hrs wkly; *No. News Employees:* 1; *Target Audience:* 35-64.; *Adv. Rates:* 16; 14; 14; 7
Mike Powers, Operations Dir
Charles Sells, General Manager
John Holland, General Sales Mgr
Corky Whitlock, Programming Director

Spring Hill

***WAYM**
01-01-1992; 88.7 MHz FM; *Hrs Open:* 24; 5 kw; 1083 ft.; N36 2 49.7 W86 49 48.9
1095 West McEwan Drive, Franklin, TN 37067 US
(888) 339-2936
www.wayfm.com
supportservices@wayfm.com
License: Spring Hill, Maury County, TN held by WAY-FM Media Group Inc.
Group Owner: WAY-FM Media Group Inc.; acq 3-13-91;
Arbitron Metro Market: Stevensville MT; *Format:* Adult Contemp; *No. News Employees:* 1; *Target Audience:* Adults 18-49.
Bob Augsburg, Founder

Springfield

WDBL
07-24-1950; 1590 kHz AM; *Hrs Open:* 19; 0.71 kw-D, ND1; 0.03 kw-N, ND1; N36 29 42 W86 54 22
101 Broadway, Nashville, TN 37201 US
(615) 384-5541; *Fax:* (615) 384-9325
www.wsgi1100.com
License: Springfield, TN held by Lightning Broadcasting LLC
Regional Network: Tenn. Radio Net.
Arbitron Metro Market: Springfield, TN; *Format:* Christian *Special Programming:* Farm 10 hrs, gospel 10 hrs wkly; *Hrs. of News Programming:* news progmg 16 hrs wkly; *No. News Employees:* 1; *Target Audience:* 18plus.
Lee Logan, Operations Dir
Susan Quesenberry, General Manager
J.C. Morrow, Chief Engineer

WSGI
12-15-1982; 1100 kHz AM; *Hrs Open:* 6 AM-sunset; 1 kw-D, NDD; N36 31 0 W86 53 30
101 Broadway, Nashville, TN 37201 US
(615) 384-5541; *Fax:* (615) 384-9325
www.wsgi1100.com
License: Springfield, TN held by Lightning Broadcasting LLC
Regional Network: Tenn. Radio Net.
Arbitron Metro Market: Nashville, TN; *Format:* Variety/Diverse
Special Programming: Relg, farm 5 hrs, gospel 16 hrs wkly;
Target Audience: General.; *Adv. Rates:* 7; 5.50; 4; na
Neil Petersen, President
Jo Petersen, Operations Dir
Billy Gray, General Sales Mgr

St. Joseph

WMXV
01-01-1991; 101.5 MHz FM; 2.85 kw; 484 ft.; N34 55 47 W87 31 44
509 N. Main St., Tuscumbia, AL 35674 US
(256) 383-2525; *Fax:* (256) 383-4450
www.wmxv1015.com
License: St. Joseph, Lawrence County, TN held by Urban Radio Licenses LLC.
Group Owner: Urban Radio Licenses LLC; (acq 5-13-2005; grpsl).
Arbitron Metro Market: Florence-Muscle Shoals, AL; *Format:* Adult Contemp, Urban Contemporary
Randy Paul, Operations Dir
Rick Brown, General Manager
Lance Knoll, General Sales Mgr
Lonnie Box, Programming Director
Tony Fowler, Promotions Manager
Sandi Summers, News Director
Craig Westbrook, Chief Engineer
Jane Hoslan,Advertising Manager

Static

WSBI
04-07-1986; 1210 kHz AM; *Hrs Open:* Sunrise-sunset
Route 4, Box 893, Albany, KY 42602 US
(606) 387-6625; *Fax:* (606) 387-8126
License: Static, TN held by Donnie S. Cox.
Nat'l Network: USA
Format: Country *Special Programming:* Gospel 10 hrs, bluegrass one hr wkly; *Hrs. of News Programming:* news progmg 15 hrs wkly; *No. News Employees:* 1; *Target Audience:* 25 plus.

Surgoinsville

WEYE
11-01-1990; 104.3 MHz FM; *Hrs Open:* 24; 4.1 kw; 397 ft.; N36 32 5 W82 47 52
Mailing Address: Route 6, Box 1, Rogersville, TN 37857 US
Second Address: 439 Richmond St.., Church Hill, TN 37642
(800) 450-1043; *Fax:* (423) 357-3635
dsandz@yahoo.com
License: Surgoinsville, Hawkins County, TN held by ASRadio LLC
Nat'l Network: USA; *Nat'l Reps:* Rgnl Reps
Arbitron Metro Market: Surgoinsville, TN; *Format:* Country
David DeFranzo, Station Manager
Daryl Smith, Chief Engineer

Sweetwater

WDEH
01-01-1955; 800 kHz AM; *Hrs Open:* 24; 1 kw-D, ND1; 0.379 kw-N, ND1; N35 36 49 W84 27 33
P.O. Box 330, 124 Old Hwy 11 N, Sweetwater, TN 37874 US
(423) 337-5025; *Fax:* (423) 337-5026
www.wdeh.weebly.com
License: Sweetwater, TN held by Horne Radio L.L.C.
Group Owner: Horne Radio Group; (acq 1999; $425,000 with co-located FM).
Arbitron Metro Market: Sweetwater, TN; *Format:* Gospel; *Adv. Rates:* 12; 12; 12; 8
Bryan Burchfield, Station Manager

WMTY-FM
09-01-1967; 98.3 MHz FM; *Hrs Open:* 24; 6 kw; Ant 135 ft; N35 36 49 W84 27 33
P.O. Box 330, Sweetwater, TN 37874 USA
(423) 337-5025; *Fax:* (423) 337-5026
www.mytrueoldies.com
License: Sweetwater, Monroe County, TN held by Horne Radio L.L.C.
Group Owner: Horne Radio Group
Population Served: 250,000
Tony Cox, General Manager

Tazewell

WNTT
07-01-1960; 1250 kHz AM; *Hrs Open:* 6AM-sunset
Mailing Address: PO Box 95, Tazewell, TN 37879 US
Second Address: TN
(423) 626-4203; *Fax:* (423) 626-3040
www.wntt1250am.com
aileen@centurylink.net
License: Tazewell, TN held by WNTT Inc.
Group Owner: ABC Inc.; (acq 9-1-94; $90,000)
Nat'l Network: ABC
Arbitron Metro Market: Tazewell, TN; *Format:* Country, News, 64
Special Programming: gospel,bluegrass; *Hrs. of News Programming:* 12 hrs wkly; *Target Audience:* 18-65; general.
Aileen Craft, General Manager/Station Owner
Susan Stearns, Webmaster

Tiptonville

WTNV
07-01-2007; 97.3 MHz FM; 1.9 kw; 591 ft.; N36 16 11 W89 19 25
2555 Burks Pl., Dyersburg, TN 38024 US
(731) 285-1339; *Fax:* (731) 287-0100
eagle973.net
roger@burksb.com
License: Tiptonville, Lake County, TN held by Dr. Pepper Pepsi-Cola Bottling Co. of Dyersburg.
Group Owner: Dr. Pepper Pepsi-Cola Bottling Co. of Dyersburg
Nat'l Network: Fox News Radio; *Regional Network:* Tenn. Agri-Net; Tenn. Radio Net; *Nat'l Reps:* Rgnl Reps
Arbitron Metro Market: Tiptonville, TN; *Format:* Country; *Target Audience:* 18-54.
Jeff Cohen, Operations Manager
Roger Vestal, General Manager
Natalie Patterson, Director of Sales
Tom Hunt, Partyline/News Director
Kaylin Dortch, Traffic/Multimedia Director

Trenton

WTNE
12-09-1966; 1500 kHz AM; *Hrs Open:* 24
Mailing Address: 319 Vann Drive, Suite E #32, Jackson, TN 38305 US
Second Address: 7713 Highway 412 South, Bells, TN
(731) 663-2327; *Fax:* (731) 663-2427
www.gracebroadcasting.com

RADIO - U.S.

License: Trenton, TN held by Grace Broadcasting Services Inc.
Group Owner: Grace Broadcasting Services Inc.
Regional Reps: Midsouth.
Arbitron Metro Market: Jackson, TN; *Format:* Adult Contemp
Special Programming: Sports; *Target Audience:* General; Gibson county, news oriented people
Lacy Ennis, CEO/President
John Blankenship, Operations Dir
Rodney minyard Sr., General Manager
Geraldine Minyard, Programming Director
Phillip Chambers, Sales Rep
Glendell Fullerton, Sales Rep

WYJJ
08-01-1980; 97.7 MHz FM; 50 kw; 123 meters; N35 44 35 W88 59 19
122 Radio Road, Jackson, TN 38301
(731) 427-3316
www.jamminjackson.com
License: Trenton, TN held by Forever South Licensen LLC
Group Owner: Forever Communications Inc.

Tullahoma

***WLYJ(FM)**
01-01-1998; 88.5 MHz FM; 1.9 kw; 177 ft; N35 20 30 W86 11 05
Box 3, Tullahoma, TN 37388
(931) 222-1633
www.joychristianradio.com
License: Tullahoma, Coffee County, TN held by Joy Christian Communications Inc.
Group Owner: Joy Christian Communications Inc.
Population Served: 90,000; *Arbitron Metro Market:* Devil's Lake, ND; *Format:* Religious
Ed Smith, President
Jim Stanley, Operations Dir
Ron Shank, Programming Director

WHMT(AM)
08-01-1947; 740 kHz AM; *Hrs Open:* 24; 250 w-D, 67 w-N; N35 20 36 W86 12 00
PO Box 1686, Tullahoma, TN 37388
(931) 454-1005
License: Tullahoma, Coffee County, TN held by NRS Enterprises Inc.
Nat'l Network: Salem Radio Network; *Regional Network:* Tenn. Radio Net.
Population Served: 18,000 *Format:* Christian; *Target Audience:* 35 plus.; *Adv. Rates:* 12; 12; 12; 12
Roy Woods, President
Joyce Woods, General Manager
Heath Laws, Programming Director
Mark Tavernier, Disc Jockey

***WTML**
01-01-2001; 91.5 MHz FM; 1.55 kw; 269 ft.; N35 23 53 W86 8 40 *Rebroadcasts:* Rebroadcasts WPLN-FM Nashville 100%
630 Mainstream Drive, Nashville, TN 37228 US
(615) 760-2903; *Fax:* (615) 760-2904
License: Tullahoma, Coffee County, TN held by Nashville Public Radio.
Arbitron Metro Market: Nashville, TN; *Format:* Classical, News
Rob Gordon, President and General Manager

Tusculum

WIKQ
02-01-1996; 103.1 MHz FM; *Hrs Open:* 24; 6 kw; -223 ft.; N36 7 40 W82 37 57
Box 278, 1004 Arnold Rd., Greeneville, TN 37744 US
(423) 638-4147; *Fax:* (423) 638-1979
www.greeneville.com
wsmg@greeneville.com
License: Tusculum, Greene County, TN held by Radio Greeneville Inc.
Group Owner: Radio Greeneville Inc.; (acq 6-22-2000; $1.8 million with WSMG(AM) Greeneville)
Format: Country; *No. News Employees:* 1; *Target Audience:* 25-55; middle to upper middle income; *Adv. Rates:* 14; 12; 12; 12
Ron P. Metcalfe, Operations Dir
Paul R. Metcalfe, General Manager
Brian Stayton, Programming Director

***WZTH**
91.1 MHz FM; 0 kw horiz, 17 kw vert; 285 ft.; N36 5 53 W82 56 37
401 West Main Street, Suite B, Greeneville, TN 37743 US
(877) 746-7913
www.truthfm.net
info@truthfm.net
License: Tusculum, Greene County, TN held by Solid Foundation Broadcasting Corp.
Arbitron Metro Market: Greeneville, TN; *Format:* Religious
James Smith, President

Union City

WENK
10-26-1946; 1240 kHz AM; *Hrs Open:* 24; 1 kw-U, ND1; N36 25 28 W89 2 17 *Rebroadcasts:* Rebroadcasts WTPR-FM McKinnon 100%
Mailing Address: 1729 Nailling Drive, Union City, TN 38261 US
Second Address: 206 N. Brewer Street, Paris, TN 38242
(731) 885-1240; *Fax:* (731) 885-3405
www.wenkwtpr.com/
thailey@forevercom.com
License: Union City, TN held by WENK of Union City Inc.
Group Owner: WENK of Union City Inc.; (acq 1-74)
Nat'l Reps: Rgnl Reps
Arbitron Metro Market: Union City, TN; *Format:* Oldies; *Hrs. of News Programming:* news progmg 15 hrs wkly; *No. News Employees:* 1; *Target Audience:* 35-54.
Terry Hailey, President/General Manager
Jim Adcock, Sales Representative
Lorie Matlock, Sales Representative
Wilma Payne, Traffic/Bookkeeping
Jerry McCann, Traffic/Bookkeeping

WQAK
03-01-1994; 105.7 MHz FM; 6 kw; 308 ft.; N36 31 7 W89 5 41
Mailing Address: 1410 N. Lindell St., Martin, TN 38237 US
Second Address: 233 Westgate Dr., Union City, TN 38260
(731) 587-9526; *Fax:* (731) 587-5079
www.thunderboltradio.com
License: Union City, TN held by Thunderbolt Broadcasting Co.
Group Owner: Thunderbolt Broadcasting Co.
Format: Alternative
Paul Tinkle, President

KYTN
09-20-1974; 104.9 MHz FM; *Hrs Open:* 24; 6 kw; Ant 328 ft; N36 28 25 W88 56 41
Mailing Address: 1410 N. Lindell St., Martin, TN 38237 US
Second Address: 223 Westgate Dr., Union City, TN 38260
(731) 587-9526; *Fax:* (731) 587-5079
www.thunderboltradio.com/kytn
License: Union City, TN held by Thunderbolt Broadcasting Co.
Group Owner: Thunderbolt Broadcasting Co.
Population Served: 301,843 *Format:* Country; *Adv. Rates:* 40; 35; 40; 30.
Paul Tinkle, President

***WTAI**
01-01-2005; 88.9 MHz FM; 0.86 kw vert; 623 ft.; N36 24 48 W89 8 59
188 South Bellevue, Suite 222, Memphis, TN 38104 US
(888) 937-2471; *Fax:* (916) 251-1650
www.air1.com
info@air1.com
License: Union City, Obion County, TN held by Educational Media Foundation.
Group Owner: EMF Broadcasting; (acq 6-21-2005; $25,000 for CP)
Nat'l Network: Air 1
Arbitron Metro Market: Union City, TN; *Format:* Alternative, Christian
Darrell Chambliss, Chairman
Alan Mason, COO
Mike Novak, President and CEO
Ed Lenane, News Director
Sam Wallington, Engineering Dir
Dan Antonelli, Chief Business Development Officer
Eric Moser, Chief Financial Officer
BrianBurger, Vice President of Human Resources
D. Kevin Blair, Secretary and General Counsel
Larry Moody, Director
Mitch Barnhart, Director

Wartburg

WECO
08-31-1970; 940 kHz AM; 5 kw-D, ND2; 0.016 kw-N, ND2; N36 5 48 W84 35 31
US
(423) 346-3900; *Fax:* (423) 346-7686
www.wecoradio.com/
wecoradio@highland.net
License: Wartburg, TN held by Morgan County Broadcasting Co. Inc.
Regional Network: Tenn. Radio Net.
Arbitron Metro Market: Wartburg, TN; *Format:* Gospel
Gary Stone, Operations Dir
Ed Knight, General Manager/Sales Manager
Aaron Harvey, News Director
Susan Knight, Office Manager

WECO-FM
08-01-1988; 101.3 MHz FM; 3.5 kw; 771 ft.; N36 11 25 W84 37 24
US
(423) 346-3900; *Fax:* (423) 346-7686
www.wecoradio.com/
wecoradio@highland.net
License: Wartburg, Morgan County, TN
Arbitron Metro Market: Wartburg, TN; *Format:* Country; *Target Audience:* 25-49.
Gary Stone, Operations Manager
Ed Knight, General Manager/Sales Manager
Aaron Harvey, News Director
Susan Knight, Office Manager

***WWQW(FM)**
90.3 MHz FM; 550 w vert; Ant -47 ft; N36 05 48 W84 35 31
PO Box 52, Greenville, SC 29602
(877) 700-8047
www.thelifefm.com/wwqw
License: Wartburg, Morgan County, TN held by Corporation for Radio Education Inc.
Population Served: 13,557; *Arbitron Metro Market:* Warsaw, IN
Richard Lynn, President

Waverly

WQMV
09-25-1963; 1060 kHz AM; *Hrs Open:* 24
PO Box 610, Waverly, TN 37175 US
(931) 296-9768; *Fax:* (931) 296-9892
www.wqmv1060.com
wqmv@comcast.net
License: Waverly, TN held by C & L Broadcasting Corp.
Nat'l Network: ABC; *Regional Network:* Tenn. Radio Net.
Format: Oldies; *Target Audience:* Adults 35-65.; *Adv. Rates:* 10.35; 10.35; 10.35; 10.35
Richard Albright, President

WVRY
09-26-1972; 105.1 MHz FM; *Hrs Open:* 24; 50 kw; Ant 492 ft; N36 05 16 W87 51 19
2263 N. Highland Ave., 25 Stonebrook Pl., Suite #322, Jackson, TN 37228
(731) 855-9394; *Fax:* (731) 855-1600
www.gracebroadcasting.com
info@salemmusicnetwork.com
License: Waverly, Humphreys County, TN held by JWL Communications LLC
Nat'l Network: Salem Radio Network; *Regional Network:* Tenn. Radio Net; *Nat'l Reps:* Salem
Population Served: 1,500,000; *Arbitron Metro Market:* Nashville, TN; *Target Audience:* 25-54.
Jim Cumbee, CEO
Rodney Minyard, General Manager

Waynesboro

WWON
01-31-1970; 930 kHz AM; *Hrs Open:* 24; 0.47 kw-D, ND2; 0.091 kw-N, ND2; N35 18 30 W87 44 42
US
BIGOldies930@yahoo.com
License: Waynesboro, TN held by Small Potatoes Broadcasting Co. LLC
Arbitron Metro Market: Waynesboro, TN; *Format:* Oldies; *Hrs. of News Programming:* News progmg 13 hrs wkly; *Target Audience:* 18-54; listeners interested in rgnl & natl issues
Chris Lash, General Manager

White Bluff

WQSE
07-18-1982; 1030 kHz AM; 1 kw-D, DAN; 0.25 kw-N, DAN; N36 8 3 W87 12 58
201 Hall Place, White Bluff, TN 37187 US
(615) 797-9785; *Fax:* (615) 797-9788
License: White Bluff, TN held by JWL Communications LLC
Arbitron Metro Market: Nashville, TN; *Format:* Gospel
Duane Jeffrey, President
Kerry Lampley, General Sales Mgr
Mary Jeffrey, Programming Director
Shery Swaw, News Director

White Pine

WLNQ
104.7 MHz FM; 2.8 kw; 492 ft.; N36 13 0 W83 11 38 US
www.thundercountry1047.com
License: White Pine, Rhea County, TN held by Bristol Broadcasting Company, Inc.
Arbitron Metro Market: White Pine, TN; *Format:* Country
Richard Lynn, President

Winchester

WCDT
03-08-1948; 1340 kHz AM; *Hrs Open:* 24; 1 kw-U; N35 10 51 W86 05 34
1201 S. College St., Winchester, TN 37398
(931) 967-2201; *Fax:* (931) 967-2201
www.wcdt1340.com
wcdt@bellsouth.net
License: Winchester, Franklin County, TN held by Franklin County Radio & Broadcasting Co. Inc.
Nat'l Network: ABC; *Regional Network:* Tenn. Radio Net.
Population Served: 65,000 *Special Programming:* Farm 15 hrs, Relg 6 hrs wkly; *Hrs. of News Programming:* news progmg 15 hrs wkly; *No. News Employees:* 1; *Target Audience:* General.
Betty Yarbrough, Owner/General Manager
Al Tipps, Programming Director
Jan Tavalin, News Director
Karen Shetters, Office/Traffic Manager

Woodbury

WBOZ
10-05-1994; 104.9 MHz FM; *Hrs Open:* 24; 6 kw; 328 ft.; N35 49 33 W86 9 28 US
(615) 367-2210; *Fax:* (615) 890-3233
www.salem.cc/radio-stations/wboz-fm-104-9/
License: Woodbury, Cannon County, TN held by Reach Satellite Network Inc.
Group Owner: Salem Communications Corp.; (acq 4-1-00; $3.1 million for stock with WVRY(FM) Waverly).
Nat'l Network: Salem Radio Network; *Nat'l Reps:* Salem
Arbitron Metro Market: Woodbury, TN; *Format:* Christian, Country, 44 *Special Programming:* Sports 5 hrs wkly; *Hrs. of News Programming:* News progmg 14 hrs wkly; *Target Audience:* 35+; adults
Mike Miller, General Manager

Texas

Abilene

***KACU**
06-02-1986; 89.7 MHz FM; *Hrs Open:* 24; 33 kw; 217 ft.; N32 28 34 W99 42 22
Mailing Address: 1925 Campus Court, Office 100, Abileen, TX 79601 US
Second Address: ACU Box 27820, Abilene, TX 79699
(325) 674-2441; *Fax:* (325) 674-2417
www.kacu.org
info@kacu.org
License: Abilene, Taylor County, TX held by Abilene Christian University.
Nat'l Network: NPR
Arbitron Metro Market: Abilene, TX; *Format:* Adult Contemp, News *Special Programming:* Jazz 3 hrs wkly; *Hrs. of News Programming:* News progmg 42 hrs wkly; *Target Audience:* 35 plus; middle-to-upper incomeprofessionals
Nathan Gibbs, General Manager
Meagan Freeman, News/Operations Director
Caleb Robinson, Business Manager
Cara Lee Cranford, Media Sales Manager
James Thompson, Senior Broadcast Engineer

***KAQD**
01-01-1998; 91.3 MHz FM; 2.8 kw; 325 ft.; N32 29 58 W99 58 19
P.O. Box 3206, Tupelo, MS 38803 US
(662) 844-8888; *Fax:* (662) 842-6791
www.afr.net
faq@afa.net
License: Abilene, Taylor County, TX held by American Family Association.
Group Owner: American Family Radio
Arbitron Metro Market: Tupelo, MO; *Format:* Gospel
Tim Wildmon, President
Donald Wildmon, Founder
Buddy Smith, Senior VP
Ed Vitaglio, Executive VP
Randy Sharp, Director Of Special Projects
Meeke Addison, Director Of Communications
Abraham Hamilton III, General Counsel & PublicPolicy

KABW
09-09-1999; 95.1 MHz FM; *Hrs Open:* 24; 100 kw; Ant 872 ft; N32 17 06 W99 38 39
1500 Industrial Boulevard, Suite 200, Abilene, TX 79602
(325) 437-9596; *Fax:* (325) 673-1819
www.wolfabilene.com
dklement@abileneradio.com
License: Abilene, Callahan County, TX held by Doud Media Group LLC
Nat'l Network: Fox News Radio; *Nat'l Reps:* Rgnl Reps
Population Served: 500,000; *Arbitron Metro Market:* Abilene, TX; *Hrs. of News Programming:* news prgmg 10 hrs wkly; *No. News Employees:* 1; *Target Audience:* 18-49; women & teens
D. Klement, General Manager

KYYW
10-01-1936; 1470 kHz AM
3911 South 1st Street, Abilene, TX 79605 US
(325) 676-7711
www.1470kyyw.com
karenhines@townsquaremedia.com
License: Abilene, TX held by Townsquare Media Abilene License LLC
Group Owner: Townsquare Media; (acq 8-3-2007; grpsl)
Nat'l Network: CBS
Arbitron Metro Market: Abilene, TX; *Format:* Talk
Jess Hanson, General Manager
Jess Hanson, Director Of Sales
Robert Snyder, Brand Manager

KEAN-FM
07-01-1969; 105.1 MHz FM; *Hrs Open:* 24; 100 kw; 886 ft.; N32 16 35 W99 35 38
3911 S. First St., Abilene, TX 79605 US
(325) 676-5326; *Fax:* (325) 676-3851
www.keanradio.com
License: Abilene, Taylor County, TX held by Townsquare Media Abilene License LLC
Group Owner: Townsquare Media
Nat'l Network: ABC
Arbitron Metro Market: Abilene, TX; *Format:* Country
Jess Hanson, General Manager
Rudy Fernandez, Brand Manager
Jess Hanson, Director Of Sales
Frank Pain, Digital Managing Editor

KEYJ-FM
04-30-1961; 107.9 MHz FM; 100 kw; 886 ft.; N32 16 35 W99 35 38
3911 South First St, Abilene, TX 79605 US
(325) 677-7225(325) 676-7711; *Fax:* (325) 676-3851
www.keyj.com
info@keyj.com
License: Abilene, Taylor County, TX held by Townsquare Media Abilene License LLC
Group Owner: Townsquare Media; (acq 8-3-2007; grpsl)
Arbitron Metro Market: Abilene, TX; *Format:* Alternative; *Target Audience:* 18-49; men
James Cameron, Operations Dir
Karen Hines, General Manager
Renee Gonzalez, General Sales Mgr
Frank Pain, Programming Director

KSLI
06-15-1957; 1280 kHz AM; *Hrs Open:* 24; 0.5 kw-D, ND1; 0.226 kw-N, ND1; N32 26 30 W99 43 8
Mailing Address: 1350 One Galleria Tower, Dallas, TX 75240 US
Second Address: 3911 S. First St., Abilene, TX 79605
(325) 676-7711; *Fax:* (325) 676-3851
www.1280ksli.com
License: Abilene, TX held by Townsquare Media Abilene License LLC
Group Owner: Townsquare Media; (acq 8-3-2007; grpsl)
Nat'l Network: Jones Radio Networks
Arbitron Metro Market: Abilene, TX; *Format:* Country; *Hrs. of News Programming:* News progmg 4 hrs wkly; *Target Audience:* 18-49; Hispanic; *Adv. Rates:* 20; 20; 20; 20
Jess Hanson, General Manager
Rudy Fernandez, Brand Manager
Jess Hanson, Director Of Sales
Frank Pain, Digital Managin Editor

***KGNZ**
03-07-1981; 88.1 MHz FM; *Hrs Open:* 24; 91 kw; 827 ft.; N32 13 47 W99 37 42
542 Butternut, Abilene, TX 79602-1329 US
(325) 673-8801; *Fax:* (325) 672-7938
www.kgnz.com
gary@kgnz.com
License: Abilene, Taylor County, TX held by Christian Broadcasting Co.
Nat'l Network: USA
Arbitron Metro Market: Abilene, TX; *Format:* Adult Contemp, Christian *Special Programming:* Black 2 hrs, gospel 2 hrs wkly
Gary Hill, General Manager/Programming Director
Glenn Arnold, Chief Engineer
Holley Hill, Office Manager/Director, Donor Relations
James Graham, Underwriting Director
James Lester, IT Manager

KKHR
06-01-1988; 106.3 MHz FM; *Hrs Open:* 24; 50 kw; Ant 184 ft; N32 28 34 W99 42 22
radioabilene.com
License: Abilene, Taylor County, TX held by Canfin Enterprises Inc.
Group Owner: Canfin Enterprises Inc.; (acq 3-25-2005; $684,000).
Nat'l Reps: Lotus Entravision Reps LLC
Arbitron Metro Market: Abilene, TX; *Hrs. of News Programming:* News progmg 3 hrs wkly; *Target Audience:* 18-49.
Parker Cannon, General Manager
Ben Gonzalez, Programming Director
James Thompson, Chief Engineer

KZQQ
08-29-1962; 1560 kHz AM; *Hrs Open:* 24 US
www.radioabilene.com
License: Abilene, TX held by Canfin Enterprises Inc.
Group Owner: Canfin Enterprises Inc.
Nat'l Network: ESPN Radio; *Regional Network:* Texas State Networks
Arbitron Metro Market: Abilene, TX; *Format:* Sports, Talk; *No. News Employees:* 1; *Target Audience:* 18 plus.
Parker Cannan, General Manager

KULL
09-01-1974; 100.7 MHz FM; 100 kw; 1,260 ft; N32 24 48 W100 06 25
3911 South 1st, Abilene, TX 79605
(325) 676-5100
www.koolfmabilene.com
karenhines@townsquaremedia.com
License: Abilene, Taylor County, TX held by Townsquare Media Abilene License LLC
Group Owner: Townsquare Media; (acq 8-3-2007; grpsl)
Population Served: 200,000; *Arbitron Metro Market:* Abilene, TX *Special Programming:* Oldies 2 hrs wkly; *Target Audience:* 18-34; women
Jess Hanson, General Manager
Frank Pain, Brand Manager
Jess Hanson, Director Of Sales
Frank Pain, Digital Managing Editor

KMWX
04-01-1998; 92.5 MHz FM; 27.5 kw; Ant 663 ft; N32 16 35 W99 35 38
3911 S. 1st St., Abilene, TX 75240
(325) 677-7225; *Fax:* (325) 677-3851
www.mix925abilene.com
info@kull.com
License: Abilene, Taylor County, TX held by Townsquare Media Abilene License LLC
Group Owner: Townsquare Media; (acq 8-3-2007; grpsl)
Nat'l Network: ABC
Population Served: 250,000; *Arbitron Metro Market:* Abilene, TX
Jess Hanson, General Manager
Frank Pain, Brand Manager
Jess Hanson, Director Of Sales
Frank Pain, Digital Managing Editor

KWKC
06-19-1948; 1340 kHz AM; *Hrs Open:* 24; 1 kw-U, ND1; N32 25 14 W99 43 54 US
www.radioabilene.com
License: Abilene, TX held by Canfin Enterprises Inc.
Group Owner: Canfin Enterprises Inc.
Nat'l Network: CBS Radio; *Regional Network:* Texas State Networks
Arbitron Metro Market: Abilene, TX; *Format:* News, News/Talk, 86; *No. News Employees:* 2; *Target Audience:* 25 plus.
Parker Cannan, President

***KAGT**
11-05-2002; 90.5 MHz FM; *Hrs Open:* 24; 100 kw; 315 ft.; N32 30 37 W99 44 28

PO Box 2118, Omaha, NE 68103-2118 US
(888) 937-2471
www.air1.com
License: Abilene, Taylor County, TX held by Educational Media Foundation.
Group Owner: EMF Broadcasting; (acq 12-31-2006; $450,000)
Nat'l Network: Air 1
Arbitron Metro Market: Abilene, TX; *Format:* Alternative, Christian
Darrell Chambliss, Chairman
Alan Mason, COO
Mike Novak, President and CEO
Mark Voltmann, Director
Dan Antonelli, Director
Dr. David R. Ferry, Director
Mitch Barnhart, Director
Larry Moody, Director
Walter Golembeski,Director
Eric Moser, Chief Financial Officer
D. Kevin Blair, Secretary and General Counsel

Alamo

KJAV
08-17-1980; 104.9 MHz FM; 6 kw; 324 ft.; N26 13 0 W98 5 23
1201 N. Jackson Road, Suite 900, McAllen, TX 78501 US
(956) 992-8895
www.valleyjack.com
License: Alamo, Hidalgo County, TX held by R Communications
Arbitron Metro Market: McAllen-Brownsville-Harlingen, TX; *Format:* Adult Contemp
Thomas Castro, President
Jeff Koch, Operations Dir
Jose Munoz, General Manager

Alamo Heights

KDRY
11-08-1963; 1100 kHz AM; *Hrs Open:* 24
16414 San Pedro Avenue, Suite 575, San Antonio, TX 78232 US
(210) 545-1100
www.kdry.com
License: Alamo Heights, TX held by KDRY Radio Inc.
Arbitron Metro Market: San Antonio, TX; *Format:* Religious; *Target Audience:* General.
Diane Rainey, General Manager

Alice

KNDA
01-01-1974; 102.9 MHz FM; 50 kw; 492 ft.; N27 42 26 W97 46 54
2001 Saratoga Boulevard, Corpus Christi, TX 78417 US
(361) 814-1030; *Fax:* (361) 814-1036
www.1029dabomb.com
License: Alice, Jim Wells County, TX held by Encarnacion A. Guerra
Arbitron Metro Market: Corpus Christi, TX; *Format:* Urban Contemporary, Blues
Jesse Rodriguez, General Manager

KOPY
01-01-1947; 1070 kHz AM; *Hrs Open:* 24; 1 kw-D, DAN; 1 kw-N, DAN; N27 46 39 W98 4 53
US
www.alicecoyote.com/kopy
kopysports@hotmail.com
License: Alice, TX held by Claro Communications Ltd.
Group Owner: Claro Communications Ltd.; (acq 8-31-2007; $300,000 with KOPY-FM Alice)
Format: Country; *Hrs. of News Programming:* news progmg 2 hrs wkly; *No. News Employees:* 12; *Target Audience:* 18-59.; *Adv. Rates:* 13; 10; 13; 7
Bobby Pena, Station Manager
Jackie Hinojosa, General Sales Mgr

KOPY-FM
01-20-1976; 92.1 MHz FM; *Hrs Open:* 24; 6 kw; 308 ft.; N27 46 39 W98 4 52
US
www.alicecoyote.com/kopy
License: Alice, Jim Wells County, TX held by Claro Communications Ltd.
Group Owner: Claro Communications Ltd.; (acq 8-31-2007; $300,000 with KOPY(AM) Alice)
Format: Tejano; *Hrs. of News Programming:* News progmg 8 hrs wkly; *Target Audience:* General.; *Adv. Rates:* 13; 10; 13; 6
Bobby Pena, Programming Director

*KIFR
88.3 MHz FM; 23 kw vert; 292 ft.; N27 45 8 W98 7 55
5700 West Oaks Boulevard, Rocklin, CA 95765 US
(916) 251-1600; *Fax:* (916) 251-1650
www.air1.com
License: Alice, Jim Wells County, TX held by Educational Media Foundation
Group Owner: EMF Broadcasting
Arbitron Metro Market: Alice, TX
Mike Novak, President

Allen

KESN
12-01-1981; 103.3 MHz FM; 98 kw; 1988 ft.; N33 32 8 W96 49 54
77 W 66th St., 16th Fl., New York, NY 10023 USA
(214) 526-2400; *Fax:* (214) 525-2525
www.kesn1033.com
License: Allen, Collin County, TX held by KESN Assets LLC
Group Owner: ESPN Inc.
Nat'l Network: ESPN Radio
Arbitron Metro Market: Allen, TX; *Format:* Sports; *Target Audience:* 25-54; males and females

Alpine

KALP
09-01-1986; 92.7 MHz FM; *Hrs Open:* 6 AM-10 PM; 2.35 kw; 328 ft.; N30 19 9 W103 37 4
P. O. Box 9650, Alpine, TX 79831 US
(432) 837-2144; *Fax:* (915) 837-3984
License: Alpine, Brewster County, TX held by Rio Grande Broadcasting Co.
Arbitron Metro Market: Alpine, TX; *Format:* Country
Gene Ray Hendryx, President/General Manager

KVLF
02-27-1947; 1240 kHz AM; *Hrs Open:* 6 AM-10 PM; 1 kw-U, ND1; N30 22 25 W103 39 44
PO Box 779, Alpine, TX 79831 US
(432) 837-2144; *Fax:* (432) 837-3984
www.bigbendradio.com
License: Alpine, TX held by Big Bend Broadcasters.
Nat'l Network: ABC
Arbitron Metro Market: Alpine, TX; *Format:* Variety/Diverse *Special Programming:* Sp 10 hrs wkly; *Hrs. of News Programming:* News progmg 21 hrs wkly
Gene Ray Hendryx Jr., President/General Manager

Alvin

*KACC
11-01-1993; 89.7 MHz FM; *Hrs Open:* 24; 5.6 kw; 331 ft.; N29 24 1 W95 12 13
3110 Mustang Road, Alvin, TX 77511 US
(281) 756-3766
www.kaccradio.com
mossman@kaccradio.com
License: Alvin, Brazoria County, TX held by Alvin Community College.
Wire Services: AP
Arbitron Metro Market: Alvin, TX; *Format:* Rock/AOR; *Hrs. of News Programming:* news progmg 3 hrs wkly; *No. News Employees:* 1; *Target Audience:* General.
A. Rodney Allbright, President
Mark Moss, Operations Dir

KTEK
11-01-1981; 1110 kHz AM; *Hrs Open:* Sunrise-sunset; 2.5 kw-C, DAD; 2.5 kw-D, DAD; N29 22 51 W95 14 15
6161 Savoy, #1200, Houston, TX 77036 US
(713) 260-6113; *Fax:* (713) 266-3614
www.business1110ktek.com
comments@business1110ktek.com
License: Alvin, TX held by BusinessRadio Houston Licensee LLC
Nat'l Network: USA
Arbitron Metro Market: Houston, TX; *Format:* Talk; *Target Audience:* 25-54; upscale families, 60% women, 40% male
Chuck Tiller, Operations Manager
Chuck Jewell, General Manager
Ron Samuels, Programming Director
Amy Quinn, Promotions/Marketing/Events
Marsha Lambeth, Production Director
Scott VanPelt, Business Manager

Amarillo

*KACV-FM
03-15-1976; 89.9 MHz FM; *Hrs Open:* 6 AM-midnight; 100 kw; 1155 ft.; N35 20 33 W101 49 21
P. O. Box 447, Amarillo, TX 79178 US
(806) 371-5228
www.kacvfm.org
License: Amarillo, Potter County, TX held by Amarillo Junior College District.
Nat'l Network: ABC
Arbitron Metro Market: Amarillo, TX *TV Affiliate:* *KACV-TV affil.; *Format:* Alternative *Special Programming:* Jazz 12 hrs, Texas 6 hrs wkly

*KJJP
12-06-1991; 105.7 MHz FM; *Hrs Open:* 24; 43 kw; 525 ft.; N35 17 33 W101 50 48
104 SW 6th Avenue, Suite B-4, Amarillo, TX 79101 US
(806) 367-9088
www.hppr.org
License: Amarillo, Potter County, TX held by Kanza Society Inc.
Arbitron Metro Market: Garden City, KS; *Format:* Christian; *Target Audience:* General.
Deb Oyler, Executive Director
Adam Vos, Operations Coordinator
Dave Bolton, Director, Programming/Operations
Chuck Springer, Chief Engineer
Barb Blevins, Director, Business Support
Ben Brandow, Membership Services Manager
JessicaWikoff, Business Manager

KATP
03-11-1976; 101.9 MHz FM; *Hrs Open:* 24; 100 kw; 935 ft.; N35 20 33 W101 49 21
6214 W. 34th Street, Amarillo, TX 79109 US
(806) 320-1019
www.blakefm.com
bricesheets@townsquaremedia.com
License: Amarillo, Potter County, TX held by Townsquare Media Amarillo License LLC
Group Owner: Townsquare Media; (acq 10-1-2007; grpsl)
Arbitron Metro Market: Amarillo, TX; *Format:* Country; *Hrs. of News Programming:* News progmg 2 hrs wkly; *Target Audience:* 18-49.; *Adv. Rates:* 14; 12; 12; 10
Brice Sheets, General Manager
Gary Boyett, Director Of Sales

*KAVW
07-01-1998; 90.7 MHz FM; 1 kw; 213 ft.; N35 11 57 W101 48 43
P.O. Box 3206, Tupelo, MS 38803 US
(662) 844-8888; *Fax:* (662) 842-6791
www.afr.net
faq@afa.net
License: Amarillo, Potter County, TX held by American Family Association.
Group Owner: American Family Radio
Arbitron Metro Market: Tupelo, MS; *Format:* Christian, Religious
Tim Wildmon, President
Donald Wildmon, Founder
Buddy Smith, Sr VP
Ed Vitagliano, Exec VP
Randy Sharp, Director Of Special Projects
Meeke Addison, Director Of Communications
Abraham Hamilton III, General Counsel & Public Policy

KMXJ-FM
03-01-1946; 94.1 MHz FM; *Hrs Open:* 24; 100 kw; 1083 ft.; N35 20 33 W101 49 21
600 Congress Avenue, Suite 1400, Austin, TX 78701 US
(806) 355-9777; *Fax:* (806) 355-5832
www.mix941kmxj.com
rickandrews@townsquaremedia.com
License: Amarillo, Potter County, TX held by Townsquare Media Amarillo License LLC
Group Owner: Townsquare Media; (acq 10-1-2007; grpsl)
Nat'l Network: ABC
Arbitron Metro Market: Amarillo, TX; *Format:* Adult Contemp; *Hrs. of News Programming:* news progmg 2 hrs wkly; *No. News Employees:* 1; *Target Audience:* General.
Brice Sheets, General Manager
Lori Crofford, Brand Manager
Gary Boyett, Director Of Sales

KBZD
03-01-1994; 99.7 MHz FM; 21.5 kw; 351 ft.; N35 6 50 W101 49 16
3639 Wolflin Ave., Amarillo, TX 79102 US
(806) 355-1044; *Fax:* (806) 457-0642
License: Amarillo, Potter County, TX held by Tejas Broadcasting Ltd. LLP
Group Owner: Tejas Broadcasting Ltd. LLP; (acq 11-15-2004; grpsl)
Arbitron Metro Market: Amarillo, TX; *Format:* Tejano
Mac Douglas, General Manager
Brad Gonzalez, General Sales Mgr
Israel Salazar, Programming Director
Emelia Chacon, News Director
Charlie Singleton, Chief Engineer

KDJW
09-15-1955; 1360 kHz AM
701 S. Pierce St., Suite 101, Amarillo, TX 79101 US
(806) 350-1360; *Fax:* (806) 350-1360
www.kdjw.com
stval@kdjw.org
License: Amarillo, TX held by Avondale Operating Inc.
Arbitron Metro Market: Amarillo, TX; *Format:* Country; *Target Audience:* 45 plus; adults with money
Ron Slover, President

KGNC
05-19-1922; 710 kHz AM; *Hrs Open:* 24; 10 kw-D, DA2; 10 kw-N, DA2; N35 25 12 W101 33 20
3505 Olsen Blvd., Suite 117, Amarillo, TX 79109 US
(806) 355-9801; *Fax:* (806) 354-8779
www.kgncnewsnow.com
License: Amarillo, Potter County, TX held by Alpha Media Licensee LLC
Group Owner: Alpha Media LLC; (acq 9-2-2015; grpsl).
Nat'l Network: ABC; *Regional Network:* Texas State Networks; *Nat'l Reps:* Katz Radio; *Wire Services:* Reuters
Population Served: 400,000; *Arbitron Metro Market:* Amarillo, TX; *Format:* News, News/Talk, 86; *Target Audience:* General; upscale adults & agricultural business listeners
Tim Butler, Operations Manager
Greg Ball, Director of Sales
Mike Hill, News Director
James Hunt, Agri-Business Director
Mike Roden, Sports Director

KGNC-FM
12-24-1958; 97.9 MHz FM; *Hrs Open:* 24; 100 kw; 1,306 ft.; N35 18 53 W101 50 47
3505 Olsen Blvd., Suite 117, Amarillo, TX 79109 US
(806) 355-9801; *Fax:* (806) 354-8779
www.kgncfm.com
kgnc@kgnc.com
License: Amarillo, Potter County, TX held by Alpha Media Licensee LLC
Group Owner: Alpha Media LLC
Wire Services: Reuters
Arbitron Metro Market: Amarillo, TX; *Format:* Country; *Target Audience:* General; upscale adults & agricultural business listeners
Tim Butler, Operations Manager
Greg Ball, Director of Sales

KIXZ
06-01-1947; 940 kHz AM; *Hrs Open:* 24
6214 W. 34th St., Amarillo, TX 79109 US
(806) 355-9777
bricesheets@townsquaremedia.com
License: Amarillo, TX held by Townsquare Media Amarillo License LLC
Group Owner: Townsquare Media; (acq 10-1-2007; grpsl)
Arbitron Metro Market: Amarillo, TX; *Format:* News, News/Talk, 86 *Special Programming:* Talk 2 hrs, gospel 6 hrs wkly; *Hrs. of News Programming:* news progmg 8 hrs wkly; *No. News Employees:* 1; *Target Audience:* General.
Brice Sheets, General Manager
James G., Brand Manager
Gary Boyett, Director Of Sales

***KJRT**
04-01-1994; 88.3 MHz FM; 20 kw horiz, 6 kw vert; 289 ft.; N35 11 57 W101 48 43
PO Box 8088, Amarillo, TX 79114 US
(806) 359-8855; *Fax:* (806) 354-2039
License: Amarillo, Potter County, TX held by Top O'Texas Educational Broadcasting Foundation
Group Owner: Top O'Texas Educational Broadcasting Foundation
Arbitron Metro Market: Amarillo, TX; *Format:* Religious

***KXLV**
08-01-1989; 89.1 MHz FM; *Hrs Open:* 24; 27.5 kw; 401 ft.; N35 15 41 W101 52 52
7355 North Oracle Rd., Tucson, AZ 85704 US
(916) 251-1600; *Fax:* (916) 251-1650
www.klove.com
klove@klove.com
License: Amarillo, Potter County, TX held by Educational Media Foundation.
Group Owner: EMF Broadcasting; (acq 11-4-99; $450,000).
Nat'l Network: K-Love
Arbitron Metro Market: Amarillo, TX; *Format:* Christian; *No. News Employees:* 3; *Target Audience:* 25-44; Judeo Christian, female
Mike Novak, President
Eric Allen, General Sales Mgr
David Pierce, Programming Director
Ed Lenane, News Director
Sam Wallington, Engineering Dir
Scott Smith, Music Director
Marya Morgan, Richard Hunt
News Reporter

KXSS-FM
03-01-1985; 96.9 MHz FM; *Hrs Open:* 24; 100 kw; 614 ft.; N35 17 33 W101 50 48
6214 W. 34th St., Amarillo, TX 79109 US
(806) 355-9777
www.kissfm969.com
bricesheets@townsquaremedia.com
License: Amarillo, Potter County, TX held by Townsquare Media Amarillo License LLC
Group Owner: Townsquare Media; (acq 10-1-2007; grpsl)
Nat'l Network: ABC
Arbitron Metro Market: Amarillo, TX; *Format:* Contemporary Hits/Top 40; *Hrs. of News Programming:* news progmg 2 hrs wkly; *No. News Employees:* 1; *Target Audience:* General.
Brice Sheets, General Manager
Gary Boyett, Director Of Sales

KPRF
10-01-1979; 98.7 MHz FM; *Hrs Open:* 24; 100 kw; 469 ft.; N35 11 2 W101 58 11
600 Congress Avenue, Suite 1400, Austin, TX 78701 US
(806) 355-9777; *Fax:* (806) 355-5832
www.987jackfm.com
info@987jackfm.com
License: Amarillo, Potter County, TX held by Townsquare Media Amarillo License LLC
Group Owner: Townsquare Media; (acq 10-1-2007; grpsl)
Nat'l Network: ABC
Arbitron Metro Market: Amarillo, TX; *Format:* Adult Contemp; *Hrs. of News Programming:* news progmg 2 hrs wkly; *No. News Employees:* 1; *Target Audience:* General.
Adam West, Brand Manager
Jeff Lyon, Director Of Sales

KXGL
11-01-1997; 100.9 MHz FM; *Hrs Open:* 24; 100 kw; 1,306 ft.; N35 18 53 W101 50 47
3505 Olsen Blvd., Suite 120, Amarillo, TX 79109 US
(806) 355-9801; *Fax:* (806) 354-8779
www.1009theeagle.com
License: Amarillo, Potter County, TX held by Alpha Media Licensee LLC
Group Owner: Alpha Media LLC; (acq 9-2-2015).
Nat'l Reps: Katz Radio; *Wire Services:* AP
Arbitron Metro Market: Amarillo, TX; *Format:* Contemporary Hits/Top 40; *Hrs. of News Programming:* news progmg 5 hrs wkly; *No. News Employees:* 1; *Target Audience:* 25-54.
Greg Ball, Director of Sales

KPUR
08-01-1949; 1440 kHz AM; *Hrs Open:* 24; 5 kw-D, DAN; 1 kw-N, DAN; N35 7 20 W101 48 9
111 East Kilbourn Ave., Suite 2700, Milwaukee, WI 53202 US
(806) 342-5200; *Fax:* (806) 342-5202
www.cumulus.com
License: Amarillo, TX held by Cumulus Licensing Corp.
Group Owner: Cumulus Media Inc.; (acq 3-12-98; $820,000 with KPUR-FM Canyon)
Arbitron Metro Market: Amarillo, TX; *Format:* Oldies; *Target Audience:* 25-54.; *Adv. Rates:* 14; 14; 14; 10
Lewis W Dickey, Jr., Chairman
Chairman/CEO/President, CEO/COO
Jim Worthington, General Manager
Matt Darby, Programming Director
Craig Vaughn, Promotions Manager
J.P. Wolf, Chief Engineer

KQIZ-FM
11-01-1976; 93.1 MHz FM; *Hrs Open:* 24; 100 kw; 699 ft.; N35 17 33 W101 50 48
US
www.931thebeat.com
jim.faires@cumulus.com
License: Amarillo, Potter County, TX held by Cumulus Licensing Corp.
Group Owner: Cumulus Media Inc.; (acq 3-5-98; $3.057 million)
Arbitron Metro Market: Amarillo, TX; *Format:* Contemporary Hits/Top 40 *Special Programming:* Relg 2 hrs wkly; *Target Audience:* 18-44; young families
Jim Faires, General Manager
Element, Programming Director
Charlie Fuller, Chief Engineer
Carol Titus, Traffic Director
Susan Reams, Business Manager

***KEYU-FM**
10-06-1986; 102.9 MHz FM; *Hrs Open:* 24; 100 kw; 292 ft.; N35 15 40 W101 52 52
7355 North Oracle Rd., Tucson, AZ 85704 US
License: Amarillo, Potter County, TX held by Midessa Broadcasting Limited Partnership
Nat'l Network: USA
Arbitron Metro Market: Amarillo, TX; *Format:* Religious; *Hrs. of News Programming:* News progmg 4 hrs wkly; *Target Audience:* 28 plus; mature Christian, mainstream evangelical
Steve Wright, Station Manager
Steve Johnson, News Director

KTNZ
01-01-1946; 1010 kHz AM; 5 kw-D, DA2; 0.5 kw-N, DA2; N35 11 3 W101 41 28
3639-B Wolflin Ave., Amarillo, TX 79102 US
(806) 372-6543; *Fax:* (806) 379-8973
License: Amarillo, TX held by Tejas Broadcasting Ltd. LLP
Group Owner: Tejas Broadcasting Ltd. LLP
Arbitron Metro Market: Amarillo, TX; *Format:* Christian
Israel Salazar, Programming Director

***KXRI**
11-01-1993; 91.9 MHz FM; *Hrs Open:* 24; 4 kw; 459 ft.; N35 14 31 W101 48 43
PO Box 2118, Omaha, NE 68103-2118 US
(888) 937-2471
www.air1.com
License: Amarillo, Potter County, TX held by Educational Media Foundation.
Group Owner: EMF Broadcasting; (acq 5-1-2000; $750,000 with KKLU(FM) Lubbock).
Nat'l Network: Air 1
Arbitron Metro Market: Amarillo, TX; *Format:* Alternative, Christian; *No. News Employees:* 3; *Target Audience:* 18-35; Judeo Christian female
Darrell Chambliss, Chairman
Mike Novak, President/General Manager
David Pierce, Chief Creative Officer
Alan Mason, Chief Operating Officer
Eric Moser, Chief Financial Officer
D. Kevin Blair, Secretary/General Counsel
DanAntonelli, Director
Mark Voltmann, Director
Dr. David R. Ferry, Director
Mitch Barnhart, Director
Larry Moody, Director
Walter Golembeski, Director

KZIP
09-15-1955; 1310 kHz AM; *Hrs Open:* 6 AM-10 PM; 1 kw-D, ND2; 0.088 kw-N, ND2; N35 11 2 W101 58 11
US
License: Amarillo, TX held by Del Norte Communications Inc.
Arbitron Metro Market: Amarillo, TX; *Format:* Talk; *Hrs. of News Programming:* news progmg one hr wkly; *No. News Employees:* 1; *Target Audience:* General.; *Adv. Rates:* 12; 12; 12; 12
Mac Douglas, General Manager

Andrews

KACT
01-12-1955; 1360 kHz AM; 1 kw-D, ND1; 0.24 kw-N, ND1; N32 20 50 W102 33 23
2125 N. Highway 385, PO Box 524, Clovis, NM 79714 US
(432) 523-2845; *Fax:* (432) 523-5671
www.kactradio.com
kact1055@windstream.net
License: Andrews, TX held by Zia Broadcasting Co.
Group Owner: Zia Broadcasting Co.; (acq 5-26-76)
Nat'l Network: CBS Radio; Radio America; Talk Radio Network; Westwood One
Arbitron Metro Market: Andrews, TX; *Format:* News, Sports, 86; *Hrs. of News Programming:* CBS News hourly; *No. News Employees:* 1; *Adv. Rates:* 5.25, 5.25, 5.25, 5.25
Gerald Reid, Station Manager

KACT-FM
01-01-1980; 105.5 MHz FM; 3 kw; 210 ft.; N32 20 50 W102 33 23
2125 N. Highway 385, PO Box 524, Clovis, NM 79714 US
(432) 523-2845; *Fax:* (432) 523-5671
www.kactradio.com
kact1055@windstream.net
License: Andrews, Andrews County, TX held by Zia Broadcasting Co.
Group Owner: Zia Broadcasting Co.
Arbitron Metro Market: Andrews, TX; *Format:* Country
Geral Reid, Station Manager

Anson

KTLT
06-01-1988; 98.1 MHz FM; *Hrs Open:* 24; 50 kw; 305 ft.; N32 39 49 W99 51 18
2525 South Danville, Abilene, TX 79605 US
(940) 793-9700; *Fax:* (325) 692-1576
www.the98x.com
License: Anson, Jones County, TX held by Cumulus Licensing Corp.
Group Owner: Cumulus Media Inc.; (acq 1999)
Arbitron Metro Market: Anson, TX; *Format:* Alternative
Ronnie L. Baird, General Manager
Chris Andrews, Chief Engineer
Lori Morris, Business Manager
Jennifer Jerez, Webmaster

Aransas Pass

*KKWV
01-01-2008; 88.1 MHz FM; 28 kw vert; 367 ft.; N27 52 2 W97 13 7 *Rebroadcasts:* Rebroadcasts KLRD(FM) Yucaipa, CA 100%
PO Box 2118, Omaha, NE 68103-2118 US
(800) 937-2471
www.air1.com
License: Aransas Pass, San Patricio County, TX held by Educational Media Foundation.
Group Owner: EMF Broadcasting; (acq 7-23-2007; grpsl)
Nat'l Network: Air 1
Arbitron Metro Market: Belcourt, ND; *Format:* Alternative, Christian
Darrell Chambliss, Chairman
Mike Novak, President/General Manager
David Pierce, Chief Creative Officer
Alan Mason, COO
Eric Moser, CFO
D. Kevin Blair, Secretary/General Counsel

Arlington

KLTY
04-01-1949; 94.9 MHz FM; *Hrs Open:* 24; 99 kw; 1667 ft.; N32 35 19 W96 58 5
6400 N. Belt Line Road, Suite 120, Irving, TX 75063 US
(972) 870-9949; *Fax:* (214) 561-2155
www.klty.com
webmaster@klty.com
License: Arlington, Tarrant County, TX held by Inspiration Media of Texas LLC.
Group Owner: Salem Communications Corp.; 2000
Nat'l Reps: Katz Radio
Arbitron Metro Market: Irving, TX; *Format:* Adult Contemp; *Hrs. of News Programming:* News progmg 2 hrs wkly; *No. News Employees:* 1; *Target Audience:* 25-54; female dominant, family oriented, upscale, conservative *Adv. Rates:* 70; 50; 70; 40
John L. Peroyea, General Manager/Regional VP, Operations
Mike Krejci, National Sales Manager
Mike Prendergast, Director of Programming/Music
Nick "Nyce" Reeder, Director of Promotions
Andy Pickard, Chief Engineer
Kelly Trentham,Office Manager/Regional VP, Operations
Gary McColley, Business Manager/HR
Jeff Mitchell, Director of Sales

Athens

KLVQ
05-17-1948; 1410 kHz AM; 1 kw-D, ND1; 0.139 kw-N, ND1; N32 9 22 W95 50 31
11125 Highway 31 E, PO Box 489, Malakoff, TX 75148 US
(903) 489-1238; *Fax:* (903) 489-2671
www.kcklfm.com/klvq
cquinn@kcklfm.com
License: Athens, TX held by Lake Country Radio L.P.
Nat'l Network: Salem Radio Network; *Wire Services:* NOAA Weather; UPI
Arbitron Metro Market: Tyler, TX; *Hrs. of News Programming:* Southern gospel; *No. News Employees:* Black one hr, relg 8 hrs; *Target Audience:* news progmg 7 hrs wkly; *Adv. Rates:* 16; 14;14;12
David Gates, Owner
Jim Stansell, Owner
Tim Howard, Programming/News/Sports Director
Robin Smetak, Trafic/Promotions Manager
Tasha Crum, Promotions Coordinator

Atlanta

KPYN
10-18-1950; 900 kHz AM; *Hrs Open:* 24; 1 kw-D, ND1; 0.033 kw-N, ND1; N33 4 58 W94 10 58
PO Box 900, Atlanta, TX 75551 US
(903) 796-2817
www.casscountytoday.com/kpyn
License: Atlanta, TX held by Freed AM Corp.
Arbitron Metro Market: Atlanta, TX; *Format:* Christian; *Target Audience:* .
Bob DelGiorno, CEO
Robert Delgiorno Jr., President
Randy Smith, Operations Dir
Don Peace, General Sales Mgr
Jeff Akin, Programming Director

*KNRB
12-22-1978; 100.1 MHz FM; *Hrs Open:* 24; 50 kw; 492 ft.; N33 15 18 W94 5 16
Mailing Address: 8919 World Ministries Avenue, Baton Rouge, LA 70810 US
Second Address: PO Box 262550, Baton Rouge, LA 70826
(225) 768-8300
www.jsm.org
License: Atlanta, Cass County, TX held by Family Worship Center Church Inc.
Group Owner: Family Worship Center Church Inc.; (acq 3-7-2002; grpsl)
Regional Reps: Riley.
Arbitron Metro Market: Texarkana, TX-AR; *Format:* Christian; *Hrs. of News Programming:* News progmg 15 hrs wkly; *Target Audience:* General.; *Adv. Rates:* 24; 18; 18; 18
David Whitelaw, COO
Jimmy Swaggart, President
John Santiago, Programming Director

Austin

KASE-FM
03-30-1969; 100.7 MHz FM; *Hrs Open:* 24; 100 kw; 1,191 ft.; N30 19 10 W97 48 6
3601 S. Congress Ave., Building F, Austin, TX 78704 US
(512) 684-7300
www.kase101.com
jtbosch@iheartmedia.com
License: Austin, Travis County, TX held by Capstar TX LLC
Group Owner: iHeartMedia; (acq 8-30-00; grpsl).
Arbitron Metro Market: Austin, TX; *Format:* Country; *Target Audience:* 18-44.
Steve Sherrill, General Sales Mgr
JT Bosch, Programming Director
Travis Hill, Promotions and Marketing Director
Bob Worden, Website/Digital

*KAZI
08-29-1982; 88.7 MHz FM; *Hrs Open:* 24; 1.6 kw; 351 ft.; N30 16 37 W97 49 34
8906 Wall Street, Suite 203, Austin, TX 78754-4541 US
(512) 836-9544; *Fax:* (512) 836-9563
www.kazifm.org
License: Austin, Travis County, TX held by Austin Community Radio.
Arbitron Metro Market: Austin, TX; *Format:* Gospel *Special Programming:* Reggae 6 hrs, blues 6 hrs, gospel 18 hrs, talk 10; *Hrs. of News Programming:* news progmg 12 hrs wkly; *No. News Employees:* 1 *TargetAudience:* General; all ages, all ethnic groups
Steve Savage, Station Manager
Marion Nickerson, Programming Director
Sharon J, Music Director

KLGO
01-01-1922; 1490 kHz AM; *Hrs Open:* 24; 1 kw-U; N30 15 13 W97 42 25
6633 Highway 290 E., Suite 302, Austin, TX 78723
(512) 637-9300; *Fax:* (512) 416-8205
License: Austin, Travis County, TX held by BMP Austin License Company L.P.
Group Owner: Border Media Partners LLC; (acq 2-10-2005; grpsl).
Population Served: 500,000; *Arbitron Metro Market:* Austin, TX; *Target Audience:* 18 plus; men
Pedro Gasc, General Manager

KKMJ-FM
01-05-1968; 95.5 MHz FM; *Hrs Open:* 24; 49 kw; 1306 ft.; N30 19 23 W97 47 58
4301 Westbank Dr., Escalade B 3rd Fl., Austin, TX 78746 US
(512) 327-9595
www.majic.com
catthomas@entercom.com
License: Austin, Travis County, TX held by Entercom Austin License LLC
Group Owner: Entercom Communications Corp.; (acq 11-30-2007; grpsl)
Nat'l Reps: Katz Radio
Arbitron Metro Market: Austin, TX; *Format:* Adult Contemp; *Target Audience:* 25-54.
Alan Kirshbom, General Manager
Heather Baumli, Sales/Advertising Manager
Cat Thomas, Programming Director
Aaron Hurd, Promotions Director

KLBJ
01-01-1939; 590 kHz AM; *Hrs Open:* 24; 5 kw-D, DAN; 1 kw-N, DAN; N30 14 16 W97 37 47
8309 North IH 35, Austin, TX 78753 USA
(877) 590-5525
www.newsradioklbj.com
License: Austin, TX held by Emmis Austin Radio Broadcasting Company LP
Group Owner: Emmis Communications Corp.
Nat'l Reps: McGavren Guild; *Wire Services:* NWS (National Weather Service)
Arbitron Metro Market: Austin, TX; *Format:* News/Talk; *Hrs. of News Programming:* news progmg 14 hrs wkly; *No. News Employees:* 6
Mark Caesar, Programming Director
John Laird, Promotions Director
Todd Jeffries, News Director

KLBJ-FM
01-01-1960; 93.7 MHz FM; 97 kw; 1050 ft.; N30 18 36 W97 47 33
8309 N IH 35, Austin, TX 78753 USA
(512) 832-4000; *Fax:* (512) 832-4081
www.klbjfm.com
License: Austin, Travis County, TX held by Emmis Austin Radio Broadcasting Company LP
Group Owner: Emmis Communications Corp.
Arbitron Metro Market: Austin, TX; *Format:* Rock/AOR
Bruce Walden, General Manager
James White, General Sales Mgr
LA Lloyd, Programming Director
John Laird, Promotions Director

*KMFA
01-01-1967; 89.5 MHz FM; *Hrs Open:* 24; 40 kw; 1306 ft.; N30 19 23 W97 47 58
3001 N Lamar, Suite 100, Austin, TX 78705 US
(512) 476-5632; *Fax:* (512) 474-7463
www.kmfa.org
info@kmfa.org
License: Austin, Travis County, TX held by Capitol Broadcasting Association Inc.
Arbitron Metro Market: Austin, TX; *Format:* Talk *Special Programming:* Educ 2 hrs wkly; *Target Audience:* General.
Ann Hume Wilson, President/General Manager
Sarah Addison, Traffic/Operations Coordinator
Emma Schneider, Public Relations Manager
Tom Morris, Chief Engineer
David Hammond, Director of Development
Cara Kannen, Constituent RelationsManager
John Clare, Content Director
Chris Johnson, Music Director
Jeffrey Blair, Production Manager
Phil Pollack, Technical Operations Manager

KPEZ
08-13-1976; 102.3 MHz FM; *Hrs Open:* 24; 26 kw; 686 ft.; N30 13 24 W97 49 39
3601 S. Congress Ave., Building F, Austin, TX 78704 US
(512) 684-7300
www.thebeatatx.com
License: Austin, Travis County, TX held by CC Licenses LLC
Group Owner: iHeartMedia; (acq 7-24-92).
Nat'l Reps: Clear Channel
Arbitron Metro Market: Austin, TX; *Format:* Contemporary Hits/Top 40; *Hrs. of News Programming:* news progmg 3 hrs wkly; *No. News Employees:* 1; *Target Audience:* 25-54; young adults with families, above averageincome, education
Melody Caldwell, General Sales Mgr
Ryan Kramer, Programming Director
Travis Hill, Promotions and Marketing Director
Bob Worden, Website/Digital

*KUT
11-10-1958; 90.5 MHz FM; 100 kw; 679 ft.; N30 18 51 W97 51 58
300 W. Dean Keeton (A0704), Austin, TX 78712-1061 US
(512) 471-1631; *Fax:* (512) 471-3700
www.kut.org
kut@kut.org
License: Austin, Travis County, TX held by University of Texas at Austin.
Nat'l Network: NPR; PRI
Arbitron Metro Market: Austin, TX; *Format:* News *Special Programming:* Folk 4 hrs, blues 6 hrs wkly; *Hrs. of News*

Programming: news progmg 25 hrs wkly; *No. News Employees:* 5; *Target Audience:* 25-54;educated; influential decision makers & arts community
Stewart Vanderwilt, General Manager, KUT Public Media

KVET
01-01-1946; 1300 kHz AM; *Hrs Open:* 24
3601 S. Congress Ave., Building F, Austin, TX 78704 US
(512) 684-7300
www.am1300thezone.com
License: Austin, TX held by Capstar TX LLC
Group Owner: iHeartMedia
Arbitron Metro Market: Austin, TX; *Format:* Sports, Talk; *Hrs. of News Programming:* news progmg 25 hrs wkly; *No. News Employees:* 6; *Target Audience:* 25-64.
Greg McKitrick, General Sales Mgr
Ryan Kramer, Programming Director
Travis Hill, Promotions and Marketing Director
Bob Worden, Website/Digital

KVET-FM
01-01-1950; 98.1 MHz FM; *Hrs Open:* 24; 49.8 kw; 1302 ft.; N30 19 23 W97 47 58
3601 S. Congress Avenue, Building F, Austin, TX 78704 US
(512) 684-7300
www.981kvet.com
License: Austin, Travis County, TX held by Capstar TX LLC
Group Owner: iHeartMedia; (acq 8-30-00; grpsl).
Nat'l Network: Westwood One
Arbitron Metro Market: Austin, TX; *Format:* Country; *No. News Employees:* 4; *Target Audience:* 35-64.
Mike McDonald, General Sales Mgr
JT Bosch, Programming Director
Travis Hill, Promotions and Marketing Director
Bob Worden, Website/Digital

***KVRX**
11-01-1994; 91.7 MHz FM; 3 kw; 85 ft.; N30 16 0 W97 40 27
Mailing Address: PO Box D, Austin, TX 78713 US
Second Address: Hearst Student Media Building (HSM), 2500 Whitis Avenue, Room 4.II2, Austin, TX 78713
(512) 495-5879
www.kvrx.org
cartergoss@austin.utexas.edu
License: Austin, Travis County, TX held by University of Texas at Austin.
Arbitron Metro Market: Austin, TX; *Format:* Alternative *Special Programming:* Share frequency with KOOP-FM; *Target Audience:* 18-34; general; *Adv. Rates:* 25; 25; 25; 25
Rodrigo Leal, Station Manager
Joey Oaxaca, Production Department
Will Kurzner, Production Department
Carter Goss, Underwriting/Advertising
Matt Page, Music Department
Liz Garcia, Music Department
Blake Gentry, TrafficDirector
Jeff Boer, Digital Databse Manager
Victoria Montalvo, Volunteer Director

Azle

***KYDA**
06-29-1967; 101.7 MHz FM; *Hrs Open:* 24; 92 kw; 2034 ft.; N33 26 13 W97 29 5 *Rebroadcasts:* Rebroadcasts KLRD(FM) Yucaipa, CA 100%
5700 West Oaks Boulevard, Rocklin, CA 95765 US
(916) 251-1600; *Fax:* (916) 251-1650
www.air1.com
License: Azle, Tarrant County, TX held by Educational Media Foundation
Group Owner: EMF Broadcasting; (acq 11-2-2006; grpsl)
Arbitron Metro Market: Azle, TX; *Format:* Spanish
Mike Novak, President

Balch Springs

KSKY
09-30-1941; 660 kHz AM; *Hrs Open:* 24
6400 N. Belt Line Rd., #110, Irving, TX 75063 US
(972) 870-9949
www.ksky.com
mike.krejci@klty.com
License: Balch Springs, TX held by Townsquare Media Group
Group Owner: Townsquare Media Group; (acq 4-24-2000; $7.5 million plus seller gets KMOM(FM) Fountain, CO).
Arbitron Metro Market: Irving, TX; *Format:* News, Talk *Special Programming:* High school, college sports; *Target Audience:* 35-59; middle income white female
David Darling, Operations Manager
John L Peroyea, VP, Operations/General Manager
Jeff Mitchell, Director of Sales, Salem-Dallas
Mike Krejci, General Sales Manager

Nick "Nyce" Reeder, Promotions Director
Andy Pickard, ChiefEngineer
Bob Johnson, General Sales Manager

Ballinger

KKCN
04-01-2012; 103.1 MHz FM; *Hrs Open:* 24; 100 kw; Ant 456 ft; N31 39 37 W100 05 23
1301 South Abe Street, San Angelo, TX 79762
(325) 655-7161; *Fax:* (325) 658-7377
www.103kkcn.com
john.flint@townsquaremedia.com
License: Ballinger, Runnels County, TX held by Townsquare Media San Angelo License LLC
Group Owner: Townsquare Media; (acq 3-15-2006; grpsl).
Population Served: 150,000; *Arbitron Metro Market:* San Angelo, TX
John Flint, General Manager
Chris Austin, Brand Manager
Shannon Lewis, Digital Managing Editor

KRUN
08-01-1947; 1400 kHz AM; *Hrs Open:* 24 hrs; 1 kw-U, ND1; N31 43 31 W99 57 42
Mailing Address: PO Box 230, Ballinger, TX 76821 US
Second Address: 1920 Hutchings Avenue, Ballinger, TX 76821
(325) 365-5500; *Fax:* (325) 365-3407
www.krunam.com
krun1400@hotmail.com
License: Ballinger, TX held by Graham Brothers Communications L.L.C.
Nat'l Network: ABC; *Regional Network:* Texas State Networks; Voice of Southwest Agriculture Radio
Arbitron Metro Market: Ballinger, TX; *Format:* Country, Sports
Special Programming: Christian 4 hrs wkly; *Hrs. of News Programming:* news progmg 2 hrs wkly; *No. News Employees:* 1; *Target Audience:* 25-54. *Adv. Rates:* 15; 15; 15; 12.50
Toby Virden, Station Manager
Jeri Smith, Music Director/Account Executive

Bandera

KEEP
07-11-1981; 103.1 MHz FM; *Hrs Open:* 24; 3.5 kw; 430 ft.; N29 51 21 W99 5 26 *Rebroadcasts:* Rebroadcasts KFAN-FM Johnson City 100%
P.O. Box 311, Fredericksburg, TX 78624 US
(830) 997-2197; *Fax:* (830) 997-2198
www.texasrebelradio.com
txradio@ktc.com
License: Bandera, Bandera County, TX held by J. & J. Fritz Media Ltd.
Group Owner: J. & J. Fritz Media Ltd.; acq 7-99; $108,000).
Format: Triple A; *No. News Employees:* 1; *Target Audience:* 25-49.; *Adv. Rates:* 28; 28; 28; 28
Jayson Fritz, President
Jan Fritz, Operations Dir
Mac McClennahan, Programming Director
Rick Star, Music Director
Gloria Ottmers, Operations Manager
Ariana Fritz, Promotions Manager

Bastrop

***KHIB**
01-01-1998; 88.5 MHz FM; 4 kw vert; 308 ft.; N30 12 57 W97 8 31
2424 South Blvd., Houston, TX 77098 US
(713) 520-5200
www.khcb.org
email@khcb.org
License: Bastrop, Bastrop County, TX held by Houston Christian Broadcasters Inc.
Group Owner: Houston Christian Broadcasters Inc.; (acq 1-19-2005; $112,000).
Nat'l Network: Moody
Arbitron Metro Market: Huston, TX; *Format:* Christian
Bruce E. Munsterman, President

KLZT
107.1 MHz FM; 49 kW
8309 N IH-35, Austin, TX 78753 USA
(512) 832-4000
www.1071laz.com
License: Bastrop, TX held by Emmis Austin Radio Broadcasting Company LP
Group Owner: Emmis Communications Corp.
Format: Spanish
Bruce Walden, General Sales Mgr
Jose Gadea, Programming Director

Batesville

***KRZU**
90.7 MHz FM; 100 kw; 149 meters; N28 47 54 W99 35 37
5005 East Belmont Avenue, Fresno, CA
(559) 455-5777; *Fax:* (559) 455-5778
www.radiobilingue.org
License: Batesville, TX held by Radio Bilingue Inc
Hugo Morales, Executive Director
Ethel Meyer, Operations Dir
Walter Ramirez, News Director

Bay City

KMKS
07-27-1984; 102.5 MHz FM; *Hrs Open:* 24; 100 kw; 466 ft.; N28 47 49 W96 9 20
Mailing Address: P.O.Box 789, Bay City, TX 77404-0789 US
Second Address: 2309 5th St., Bay City, TX 77414
(979) 244-4242; *Fax:* (979) 245-0107
www.kmks.com
kmks@kmks.com
License: Bay City, Matagorda County, TX held by Sandlin Broadcasting Co. Inc.
Format: Country; *Target Audience:* 24-54.
CW, Operations Manager/Music Director
Larry Sandlin, General Manager/Technical Director
Margaret Kay Sandlin, Station Manager
Judith Gardiner, Sales Manager
Ryan Stone, Promotions Manager

KNTE
02-12-1996; 101.7 MHz FM; 35 kw; 1476 ft; N28 43 53 W96 05 26 *Rebroadcasts:* Simulcast Of KEYH Houston
3000 Bering Dr., Houston, TX 77057
(713) 315-3400; *Fax:* (713) 315-3565
laranchera1017.estrellatv.com
License: Bay City, Matagorda County, TX held by Liberman Broadcasting of Houston License LLC.
Group Owner: Liberman Broadcasting Inc.; (acq 10-11-2002; $3.15 million with KNTE-FM El Campo)
Nat'l Network: ABC
Population Served: 670,000 *Format:* Spanish; *Adv. Rates:* 22; 22; 22; 14
Leonard Liberman, CEO
Winter Horton, Chief Operating Officer
Ezequiel Gonzalez, Programming Director
Meliza Posada, News Director
Mike Todd, Engineering Dir

***KZBJ**
01-01-2005; 89.5 MHz FM; 35 kw; Ant 479 ft; N29 08 58 W95 59 14 *Rebroadcasts:* Rebroadcasts KSBJ(FM) Humble 100%
1722 Treble Dr., Humble, TX 33487
(281) 446-5725; *Fax:* (281) 540-2198
www.ksbj.org
webmaster@ksbj.org
License: Bay City, Matagorda County, TX held by KSBJ Educational Foundation
Population Served: 17,663; *Arbitron Metro Market:* Bay City, TX
Tim McDermott, President and General Manager
Tim McDermott, General Manager
Carlos Aguiar, Programming Director
Brittany Whatley, Promotions Manager
Don Chapman, Chief Engineer
Bill Hartman, Broadcast Engineer
Tim Dimas,Facilities Supervisor
Pam Kelly, Assistant Program Director
Rhonda Hall, Community Relations Director
Richard Silva, Special Events Manager
Stephanie Meeks, Director of Donor Relations

***KEDR**
01-01-2007; 88.1 MHz FM; 3.6 kw; 1434 ft.; N28 48 3 W96 7 32
Rebroadcasts: Rebroadcasts WBFR(FM) Birmingham, AL 100%
4135 Northgate Blvd., Suite 1, Sacramento, CA 95834 US
(205) 942-3530; *Fax:* (510) 568-6190
www.familyradio.com
License: Bay City, Matagorda County, TX held by Family Stations Inc.
Group Owner: Family Stations Inc.
Arbitron Metro Market: Bay City, TX; *Format:* Religious
Stanley Jackson, General Manager

Baytown

KWWJ
10-01-1947; 1360 kHz AM; *Hrs Open:* 24; 5 kw-D, DA2; 1 kw-N, DA2; N29 46 28 W95 0 55
4638 Decker Drive, Baytown, TX 77520 US

(281) 837-8777; *Fax:* (281) 424-7588
www.kwwj.org
kwwj1360@yahoo.com
License: Baytown, TX held by Salt of the Earth Broadcasting Inc.
Nat'l Network: American Urban
Arbitron Metro Market: Baytown, TX; *Format:* Gospel; *No. News Employees:* 1; *Target Audience:* General.
Darrell Martin, Owner

Beaumont

KIKR
01-01-1938; 1450 kHz AM; 1 kw-D, ND2; 1 kw-N, ND2; N30 3 52 W94 7 12
755 S. 11th St., Suite 102, Beaumont, TX 77701 US
(409) 833-9421; *Fax:* (409) 833-9296
www.lagrand1450.com
License: Beaumont, TX held by Cumulus Licensing Corp.
Group Owner: Cumulus Media Inc.; (acq 3-9-98; grpsl).
Nat'l Reps: McGavren Guild
Arbitron Metro Market: Beaumont-Port A; *Format:* Sports; *Target Audience:* 25-54.
B Shaw, Programming Director
Ashlie Christie, Promotions Manager
Greg Davis, Chief Engineer
Patrick Sanders, Assistant Program Director
Ashlie Christie, Program Director

KLVI
01-01-1924; 560 kHz AM; *Hrs Open:* 24
2885 I-10 E, Beaumont, TX 77702 US
(409) 896-5555; *Fax:* (409) 896-5500
www.klvi.com
License: Beaumont, TX held by Capstar TX LLC
Group Owner: iHeartMedia; (acq 8-30-00; grpsl).
Arbitron Metro Market: Beaumont-Port Arthur-Orange, TX; *Format:* News, News/Talk, 86; *Hrs. of News Programming:* news progmg 5 hrs wkly; *No. News Employees:* 4; *Target Audience:* 25-54; informed professionals *Adv.Rates:* 78; 78; 78; 78
Trey Poston, Operations Manager
Tim Thomas, Market Manager
Jim Love, Programming Director
Kevin Born, Production Director
Susan Labure, Business Manager

KQXY-FM
09-01-1966; 94.1 MHz FM; *Hrs Open:* 24; 100 kw; 600 ft.; N30 6 56 W94 0 0
755 S. 11th St., Suite 102, Beaumont, TX 77701 US
(409) 833-9421
www.kqxy.com
License: Beaumont, Jefferson County, TX held by Cumulus Licensing Corp.
Group Owner: Cumulus Media Inc.; (acq 3-9-98; grpsl)
Arbitron Metro Market: Beaumont-Port Arthur, TX; *Format:* Contemporary Hits/Top 40; *Hrs. of News Programming:* news progmg 5 hrs wkly; *No. News Employees:* 1; *Target Audience:* 18-49; skewed female
Rick Prusator, General Manager
Mike Simpson, General Sales Mgr
Greg Davis, Chief Engineer

KTCX
01-01-1996; 102.5 MHz FM; 50 kw; 492 ft.; N29 59 20 W94 14 42
755 South 11th Street, Suite 102, Beaumont, TX 77701 US
www.ktcx.com
License: Beaumont, Jefferson County, TX held by Cumulus Licensing Corp.
Group Owner: Cumulus Media Inc.; (acq 3-26-98; $3.6 million)
Arbitron Metro Market: Beaumont-Port Arthur, TX; *Format:* Urban Contemporary
Jim West, Operations Dir
Zanetta Kelley, General Manager
Ed Turner, Station Manager
Walter Brickhouse, General Sales Mgr
Douglas Harris, Programming Director
Mark Guzman, Promotions Manager
Greg Davis, Chief Engineer
AdrianScott, Assistant Music Director
Marco Camacho, Regional Sales Manager
Wes Matejka, Sales Director

*KTXB
01-23-1990; 89.7 MHz FM; *Hrs Open:* 24; 9 kw vert; 568 ft.; N30 9 27 W93 48 6
290 Hegenberger Road, Oakland, CA 94621 US
(800) 543-1495
www.familyradio.com
License: Beaumont, Jefferson County, TX held by Family Stations Inc.
Group Owner: Family Stations Inc.
Arbitron Metro Market: Beaumont, TX; *Format:* Christian
Harold Camping, President
Martha Tallent, Station Manager

*KVLU
01-01-1974; 91.3 MHz FM; *Hrs Open:* 24; 40 kw; 449 ft.; N30 6 40 W94 3 10
Lamar University, PO Box 10064, Beaumont, TX 77710 US
(409) 880-8164
www.kvlu.org
License: Beaumont, Jefferson County, TX held by Lamar University.
Nat'l Network: NPR
Arbitron Metro Market: Beaumont-Port Arthur, TX; *Format:* Jazz, News *Special Programming:* Sp 5 hrs wkly; *Target Audience:* 35 plus.
Byron Balentine, Station Manager/Operations
Ken Wilson, Chief Engineer
Melanie Dishman, Station Manager/Advancement
Joe Elwell, Music Director
Stacey Haynes, Webmaster
Jason Miller, Production Director
Alicia Hargreaves,Membership Coordinator

KQQK
07-10-1967; 107.9 MHz FM; *Hrs Open:* 24; 90 kw; 1955 ft.; N30 1 1 W94 32 47 *Rebroadcasts:* Simulcasts KNTE(FM) El Campo
3000 Bering Dr, Houston, TX 77057 US
(731) 315-3400; *Fax:* (713) 315-3565
houstoninfo@lbimedia.com
License: Beaumont, Jefferson North County, TX held by Liberman Broadcasting of Houston License LLC.
Group Owner: Liberman Broadcasting Inc.; (acq 10-11-2002; $24 million)
Arbitron Metro Market: Houston, TX; *Format:* Spanish
Lenard Liberman, President
Eduardo Leon, Vice President, Programming

KYKR
02-01-1966; 95.1 MHz FM; *Hrs Open:* 24; 100 kw; 430 ft.; N30 3 43 W93 58 50
2885 Interstate 10 E, Beaumont, TX 77702 US
(409) 896-5555; *Fax:* (409) 896-5599
www.kykr.com
License: Beaumont, Jefferson County, TX held by Capstar TX LLC
Group Owner: iHeartMedia; (acq 8-30-2000; grpsl).
Nat'l Reps: Clear Channel; *Wire Services:* AP
Arbitron Metro Market: Beaumont-Port Arthur, TX; *Format:* Country; *Hrs. of News Programming:* news progmg 2 hrs wkly; *No. News Employees:* 3; *Target Audience:* 18-54.; *Adv. Rates:* 63; 63; 63; 63
Evan Armstrong, Regional Market President
Susan LaBure, Business Manager

KZZB
05-01-1947; 990 kHz AM; *Hrs Open:* 24; 1 kW; N30 8 57 W94 7 59
2531 Calder Ave, Beaumont, TX 77702 USA
(409) 833-0990
www.kzzbradio.org
License: Beaumont, TX held by Martin Broadcasting Inc.
Group Owner: Martin Broadcasting Inc.; (acq 7-28-92;
Nat'l Reps: Christal
Arbitron Metro Market: Beaumont-Port Arthur; *Format:* Gospel; *No. News Employees:* 1; *Target Audience:* 18-49.

*KLBT
08-17-2006; 88.1 MHz FM; 0 kw horiz, 7 kw vert; 476 ft.; N29 54 52 W94 17 6
1872 Calder Avenue, Beaumont, TX 77701 US
(409) 833-0045
www.myklbt.org
License: Beaumont, Jefferson County, TX held by The King's Musician Educational Foundation Inc
Arbitron Metro Market: Beaumont, TX; *Format:* Christian
Jeanette Harvey, Partnership Coordinator

*KGHY
88.5 MHz FM; 13.5 kw vert; 344 ft.; N30 16 23 W93 57 23
PO Box 22602, Beaumont, TX 77720 US
(409) 299-3339
www.kghy.org
License: Beaumont, Jefferson County, TX held by CCS Radio Inc.
Arbitron Metro Market: Beaumont, TX; *Format:* Contemporary Hits/Top 40, Gospel
Otis Dyson, President

Bee Cave

KTXX-FM
01-01-1984; 104.9 MHz FM; *Hrs Open:* 24; 2.35 kw; Ant 531 ft; N30 11 54 W98 00 46
912 S. Capital of Texas Hwy., Suite 400, Austin, TX 78746
(512) 416-1100
www.hornfm.com
lancealdridge@austinradionetwork.com
License: Bee Cave, Hays County, TX held by Total Austin Sports Radio LLC
Arbitron Metro Market: Austin, TX; *Target Audience:* 25-54; upscale, retired, affluent
Lance Aldridge, General Manager

Beeville

KIBL
10-20-1949; 1490 kHz AM; *Hrs Open:* 5 AM-10 PM; 1 kw-U, ND1; N28 23 8 W97 43 42
P.O. Box 252, McAllen, TX 78502 US
(512) 358-1490; *Fax:* (956) 358-7814
License: Beeville, TX held by David Martin Phillip
Arbitron Metro Market: Beeville, TX; *Format:* Christian
Eloy Bernal, General Manager
John Ross, Chief Engineer

KTKO
12-12-1976; 105.7 MHz FM; *Hrs Open:* 24hours; 25 kw; 328 ft.; N28 28 16 W97 48 39
2300 S. Washington, Beeville, TX 78102 US
(361) 358-1490
kicker106@yahoo.com
License: Beeville, Bee County, TX held by Texas Gulfwest Broadcasting Inc.
Wire Services: NOAA Weather
Arbitron Metro Market: Corpus Christi, TX; *Format:* Country; *Hrs. of News Programming:* news progmg 13 hrs wkly; *No. News Employees:* 1; *Target Audience:* 18-64.; *Adv. Rates:* 18: 16: 18: 16
Bebe Adamez, General Manager

*KVFM
01-01-2000; 91.3 MHz FM; 1 kw vert; 302 ft.; N28 26 42 W97 45 50
P.O. Box 252, McAllen, TX 78505 US
License: Beeville, Bee County, TX held by Paulino Bernal Evangelism.
Arbitron Metro Market: McAllen, TX
Vic Eliason, Operations Dir
Jim Schneider, Programming Director

KRXB
12-02-1988; 107.1 MHz FM; *Hrs Open:* 24; 1.5 kw; 337 ft.; N28 27 45 W97 46 50
Mailing Address: 8584 Katy Fwy., Ste 300, Houston, TX 77024 US
Second Address: TX
License: Beeville, Bee County, TX held by Shaffer Communications Group Inc.
Nat'l Network: Jones Radio Networks
Arbitron Metro Market: Beeville, TX; *Format:* Classic Rock; *No. News Employees:* 4; *Target Audience:* 25 plus.
Joe Shaffer, President
Marlene Rivera, General Manager
Joy Burkhardt, News Director

Bellaire

KGOW
06-07-1961; 1560 kHz AM; *Hrs Open:* 6 AM-sunset
5353 W. Alabama, Suite 415, Houston, TX 77056 US
(713) 479-5300; *Fax:* (713) 479-5333
www.ysr1560.com
david.gow@gowmedia.com
License: Bellaire, TX held by Gow Communications L.L.C.
Arbitron Metro Market: Houston-Galvest; *Format:* Sports
David Gow, CEO
Chris Hall, VP/General Manager
David Tepper, Programming Director
Michelle MacDonald, Promotions Director
Brandon Strange, VP, New Media/Digital Products

Bellmead

KWBT
08-29-1983; 104.9 MHz FM; 2.85 kw; Ant 482 ft; N31 38 39 W96 36 51
Box 1590, Mexia, TX 76667
(254) 562-5328; *Fax:* (254) 562-6729
License: Bellmead, Limestone County, TX held by M&M Broadcasters Ltd.

Group Owner: M&M Broadcasters Ltd.
Nat'l Network: CBS
Population Served: 30,000 *Adv. Rates:* 13; 10; 10; 9.
Bill Ferris, Operations Dir
Susan Cholopisa, Station Manager
Brandi Garza, News Director
Dave Campbell, Sports Commentator

Bells

KMKT
09-01-1997; 93.1 MHz FM; 6.8 kw; 627 ft.; N33 41 31 W96 26 36
One Grand Center, 1800 Teague Drive, Suite 300, Sherman, TX 75090 US
(903) 463-6800; *Fax:* (903) 463-9816
www.931kmkt.com
License: Bells, Grayson County, TX held by NM Licensing LLC.
Group Owner: NextMedia Group Inc.; (acq 11-26-01; grpsl).
Format: Country
Jason Taylor, Operations Dir
David Smith, General Manager

Bellville

KULF
08-08-1974; 1090 kHz AM; 250 w-D; N29 56 50 W96 15 54
Rebroadcasts: Rebroadcasts KLTR(FM) Caldwell 100%
PO Box 948, Houston, TX 77001
www.kulfradio.com
License: Bellville, Austin County, TX held by JLF Communications, LLC

Roy Henderson, President

Belton

KOOC(FM)
04-25-1970; 106.3 MHz FM; *Hrs Open:* 24; 11.5 kw; Ant 489 ft; N31 03 46 W97 31 54
608 Moody Ln., Temple, TX 76504
(254) 773-5252; *Fax:* (254) 773-0115
www.myb106.com
License: Belton, Bell County, TX held by Townsquare Media Killeen-Temple License LLC
Group Owner: Townsquare Media; (acq 2-2-2000; grpsl).
Population Served: 162,000; *Arbitron Metro Market:* Killeen-Temple, TX; *Format:* Adult Contemp; *No. News Employees:* 1; *Target Audience:* 25-54.
Scott Smith, General Manager
Johnny Thrash, Brand Manager
Stacy Gellner, Digital Sales Manager
Aaron Galloway, Digital Managing Editor

Benbrook

KESS
01-01-1990; 107.1 MHz FM; *Hrs Open:* 24; 74 kw; 1,050 ft.; N32 35 10 W97 49 52
7700 John W. Carpenter Fwy., Dallas, TX 75247 US
(214) 525-0400; *Fax:* (214) 206-9022
www.univision.com
License: Benbrook, Tarrant County, TX held by KCYT-FM License Corp.
Group Owner: Univision Radio; (acq 9-22-2003; grpsl).
Population Served: 3,000,000; *Arbitron Metro Market:* Dallas-Fort Worth, TX; *Format:* Spanish
Mark Masepohl, Vice President and General Manager
Patrick Parks, Chief Engineer
Karem Hocking, National Sales Manager
Myrna Vera, Research Director

KFLC
01-01-1922; 1270 kHz AM; *Hrs Open:* 24; 50 kw-D, DA2; 5 kw-N, DA2; N32 43 36 W97 11 30
7700 John W. Carpenter Fwy., Dallas, TX 75247 US
(214) 525-0429; *Fax:* (214) 206-9022
www.univision.com
License: Benbrook, Tarrant County, TX held by KESS-AM License Corp.
Group Owner: Univision Radio; (acq 9-22-2003; grpsl)
Arbitron Metro Market: Dallas-Fort Worth, TX; *Format:* News, News/Talk, 84, Talk; *Hrs. of News Programming:* news progmg 11 hrs wkly; *No. News Employees:* 2; *Target Audience:* 25-54.
Mark Masepohl, Vice President and General Manager
Patrick Parks, Chief Engineer
Karem Hocking, National Sales Manager
Myrna Vera, Research Director

Big Sandy

***KTAA**
11-06-1995; 90.7 MHz FM; *Hrs Open:* 24; 42 kw; 545 ft.; N32 37 49 W94 53 43
10550 Barkley St., Suite 100, Overland Park, KS 66212 US
(913) 642-7770; *Fax:* (913) 642-1319
www.bottradionetwork.com
comments@bottradionetwork.com
License: Big Sandy, Upshur County, TX held by Community Broadcasting Inc.
Group Owner: Bott Radio Network; (acq 9-6-2006; $450,000)
Nat'l Network: USA
Arbitron Metro Market: Longview-Tyler, TX; *Format:* Christian, Talk; *Target Audience:* 25-54; adults
Eben Fowler, Operations Dir
Pat Rulon, Regional Manager
Candy Green, Program Services Manager
Rachel Launius, Marketing Manager

Big Spring

***KBCX**
01-01-2001; 91.5 MHz FM; 1 kw; 305 ft.; N32 11 6 W101 27 56
P.O. Box 3206, Tupelo, MS 38803 US
(662) 844-8888; *Fax:* (662) 842-6791
www.afr.net
faq@afa.net
License: Big Spring, Howard County, TX held by American Family Association.
Group Owner: American Family Radio
Arbitron Metro Market: Tupelo, MS; *Format:* Christian, Religious
Tim Wildmon, President
Donald Wildmon, Founder
Buddy Smith, Senior VP
Ed Vitagliano, Executive VP
Randy Dharp, Director Of Special Projects
Meeke Addison, Director Of Communications
Abraham Hamilton III, General Counsel & PublicPolicy Analyst

KBST
12-23-1936; 1490 kHz AM; 1 kw-U; N32 15 44 W101 27 37
608 Johnson Street, Big Spring, TX 79720
(432) 267-6391; *Fax:* (432) 267-1579
www.kbestmedia.com
License: Big Spring, Howard County, TX held by Rhattigan Broadcasting (Texas) LP
Group Owner: Rhattigan Broadcasting (Texas) LP; (acq 8-19-2004; grpsl)
Nat'l Network: Fox Sports; *Regional Network:* Texas State Networks; *Nat'l Reps:* Riley
Population Served: 28,735 *Target Audience:* 25 plus.
Guy Gill, CEO
Charles Sagona, Operations Dir
Malinda Flenniken, General Manager
Bill Norris, News Director

KBST-FM
01-01-1961; 95.7 MHz FM; 33 kw; 459 ft.; N32 13 13 W101 26 25
608 Johnson Street, Big Spring, TX 79720 US
(432) 267-6391; *Fax:* (432) 267-1579
www.kbestmedia.com
License: Big Spring, Howard County, TX held by Rhattigan Broadcasting (Texas) LP.
Group Owner: Rhattigan Broadcasting (Texas) LP; (acq 8-19-2004; grpsl)
Format: Country, News, 62, Talk
Michael Rhattigan, General Manager

KBTS
08-14-1995; 94.3 MHz FM; 8.3 kw; 561 ft.; N32 13 13 W101 26 25
608 Johnson Street, Big Spring, TX 79720 US
(432) 267-6391; *Fax:* (432) 267-1579
License: Big Spring, Howard County, TX held by Rhattigan Broadcasting (Texas) LP
Group Owner: Rhattigan Broadcasting (Texas) LP; (acq 6-3-2004; grpsl).
Arbitron Metro Market: Big Spring, TX; *Format:* Adult Contemp
Malinda Ellison Flenniken, General Manager
Tim Knox, Programming Director
Bill Norris, News Director

KBYG
01-01-1948; 1400 kHz AM; *Hrs Open:* 24; 1 kw-U, ND1; N32 13 22 W101 28 35
2801 Wasson Road, Big Spring, TX 79720 US
(432) 263-6351; *Fax:* (432) 263-8223
www.kbygradio.com
License: Big Spring, TX held by Ballard Drew.
Regional Network: Southwest Agri-Radio
Arbitron Metro Market: Big Spring, TX; *Format:* Oldies, Talk; *No. News Employees:* 1; *Target Audience:* 25-54; Anglo-Hispanic
John Weeks, President/General Manager
Joe Murphy, Operations Manager
David Pappajohn, Sales Manager
Vents Allyn Solis, Programming Director
Chad Coleman, IT/Traffic Director

KBQX
730 kHz AM
US
(432) 352-9110
License: Big Spring, TX held by Trade Media Corp.
Arbitron Metro Market: Big Spring, TX; *Format:* Christian
Mark Nolte, Operations Dir

Bishop

KMZZ
06-15-1980; 106.9 MHz FM; *Hrs Open:* 24; 25 kw; 246 ft.; N27 40 16 W97 44 17
P.O. Box 5206, Corpus Christi, TX 78465 US
License: Bishop, Nueces County, TX held by Claro Communications Ltd.
Group Owner: Claro Communications Ltd.; (acq 11-4-2004; $550,000)
Arbitron Metro Market: Bishop, TX; *Format:* Religious; *No. News Employees:* 1; *Target Audience:* 18-49; people with buying power
Lionel Davila, General Manager
Mike Aradillias, General Sales Mgr
Jeremy Lopez, Programming Director
George Sanders, Chief Engineer

Bloomington

KLUB
12-01-1992; 106.9 MHz FM; *Hrs Open:* 24; 18.5 kw; 381 ft.; N28 42 24 W96 50 6
Mailing Address: 107 N. Star Drive, Victoria, TX 78701 US
Second Address: Box 3325, Victoria, TX 77904
(361) 573-0777; *Fax:* (361) 578-0059
www.1069therock.com
kixs@gapbroadcasting.com
License: Bloomington, Victoria County, TX held by Townsquare Media Victoria License LLC
Group Owner: Townsquare Media; (acq 10-1-2007; grpsl)
Format: Classic Rock *Special Programming:* Blues; *Hrs. of News Programming:* news progmg 4 hrs wkly; *No. News Employees:* 1; *Target Audience:* 25-59; listeners in a growth & acquisition mode; *Adv. Rates:* 15;13; 15; 13
Adam West, Brand Manager
Jeff Lyon, Director Of Sales
Becky Snell, Traffic Manager

***KHVT**
01-01-2006; 91.5 MHz FM; 46 kw; 482 ft.; N29 0 4 W97 0 5
Rebroadcasts: Rebroadcasts KHCB-FM Houston 95%
2424 South Blvd., Houston, TX 77098 US
(713) 520-5200
www.khcb.org
email@khcb.org
License: Bloomington, Victoria County, TX held by Houston Christian Broadcasters Inc.
Group Owner: Houston Christian Broadcasters Inc.
Arbitron Metro Market: Bloomington, TX; *Format:* Christian
Special Programming: Sp Christian 6 hrs wkly
Bruce E. Munsterman, President

Boerne

KBRN
05-10-1982; 1500 kHz AM; 0.25 kw-D, NDD; N29 48 44 W98 43 41
US
(210) 829-5557; *Fax:* (210) 829-5155
License: Boerne, TX held by Claro Communications Ltd.
Group Owner: Claro Communications Ltd.; (acq 6-25-2004; $200,000)

Gerry Benavides, General Manager

Bonham

KFYN
05-01-1948; 1420 kHz AM; *Hrs Open:* 5 AM-1 AM; 250 w-D, 148 w-N; N33 34 40 W96 09 55
506 N. Main Street, Bonham, TX 75248
(903) 583-3151
www.kfyn1420.com
alex@vmgradio.com

License: Bonham, Fannin County, TX held by Vision Media Group Inc.
Nat'l Network: ABC; *Regional Network:* Texas State Networks
Population Served: 238,000 *Special Programming:* Farm 6 hrs, relg 6 hrs, oldies rock 6 hrs wkly; *Adv. Rates:* 14; 12; 14; 12
Alex Green
Wanda Neal

Borger

***KASV**
01-01-1998; 88.7 MHz FM; *Hrs Open:* 24; 10 kw horiz, 3 kw vert; 203 ft.; N35 40 42 W101 23 18 *Rebroadcasts:* Rebroadcasts KJRT(FM) Amarillo 100%
P.O. Box 469, Wheeler, TX 79096 US
(806) 359-8855; *Fax:* (806) 354-2039
www.kingdomkeysradio.org
License: Borger, Hutchinson County, TX held by Top O' Texas Ed. Broadcasting.
Arbitron Metro Market: Amarillo, TX; *Format:* Religious
Jeremy Pfeil, Operations Dir
Ricky Pfeil, General Manager

KQFX
03-01-1975; 104.3 MHz FM; 100 kw; 574 ft.; N35 25 34 W101 36 47
3639 Wolflin Ave., Amarillo, TX 79102 US
(806) 355-1044
License: Borger, Hutchinson County, TX held by Tejas Broadcasting Ltd. LLP.
Group Owner: Tejas Broadcasting Ltd. LLP; (acq 11-15-2004; grpsl).
Arbitron Metro Market: Amarillo area; *Format:* Tejano
Chris Harper, Regional/National Sales
Roberto Solorio, Programming Director
Vanesa Jacobo, Promotions Manager
Paco Jacobo, Marketing Manager
Johnny Mata, Producer

KQTY
01-10-1947; 1490 kHz AM; *Hrs Open:* 24; 1 kw-U; N35 41 05 W101 23 20
113 Union Street, PO Box 165, Borger, TX 79007
(806) 273-7533,(806) 273-5889; *Fax:* (806) 273-3727
kqtyradio.com
kqtyradio@yahoo.com
License: Borger, Hutchinson County, TX held by Zia Broadcasting.
Group Owner: Zia Broadcasting Co.; (acq 12-1-79)
Population Served: 26,800 *Target Audience:* 25-54; blue collar workers with traditional values & beliefs; *Adv. Rates:* 12; 12; 12; 12
Lonnie Ausups, CEO
Rick Keefer, General Manager
George Grover, Station Manager

KQTY-FM
01-01-1999; 106.7 MHz FM; *Hrs Open:* 24; 6 kw; Ant 259 ft; N35 41 05 W101 23 12
113 Union Street, PO Box 165, Borger, TX 79007
(806) 273-7533; (806) 273-5889; *Fax:* (806) 273-3727
www.kqtyradio.com
kqtyradio@yahoo.com
License: Borger, Hutchinson County, TX held by Zia Broadcasting Co.
Group Owner: Zia Broadcasting Co.
Nat'l Network: ABC
Population Served: 26,800 *Special Programming:* Religious, 1hr; southern gospel, 3hrs; christian country, 5hrs; Texas country, 10hrs; *Hrs. of News Programming:* News progmg 15 hrs wkly; *Target Audience:* 25-54; Bluecollar workers w/traditional values & beliefs; *Adv. Rates:* 12; 12; 12; 12
Lonnie Allsups, CEO
Rick Keefer, General Manager
George Grover, Station Manager

***KWAS**
04-01-1994; 88.7 MHz FM; 10 kw horiz, 3 kw vert; 289 ft.
PO Box 8088, Amarillo, TX 79114 US
(806) 359-8855; *Fax:* (806) 354-2039
License: Borger, TX held by Top O'Texas Educational Broadcasting Foundation
Group Owner: Top O'Texas Educational Broadcasting Foundation
Arbitron Metro Market: Vernon, TX; *Format:* Religious

Bovina

KKNM
01-01-2008; 96.5 MHz FM; 50 kw; 459 ft.; N34 41 17 W102 56 53
US
License: Bovina, Parmer County, TX held by Tejas Broadcasting Ltd. LLP.
Group Owner: Tejas Broadcasting Ltd. LLP
Arbitron Metro Market: Bovina, TX
Charles Brooks, President

***KOVA**
90.9 MHz FM; kw
US
(214) 525-7700; *Fax:* (214) 525-7750
License: Bovina, Parmer County, TX held by Ron Elmore Ministries Inc.
Arbitron Metro Market: Houston, TX
Ron Elmore, President

Bowie

KNTX
05-29-1959; 1410 kHz AM; *Hrs Open:* 24 hrs; 500 w-D, DA; N33 35 10 W97 48 23
PO Box 1080, Bowie, TX 76230
(940) 872-2288; *Fax:* (940) 872-1228
kntxradio.com
onair@kntxradio.com
License: Bowie, Montague County, TX held by Henderson Broadcasting Co. L.P.
CBS Radio; *Regional Network:* Texas State Networks
Population Served: 30,000; *Arbitron Metro Market:* Wichita Falls, *Special Programming:* Gospel 4 hrs wkly; *Hrs. of News Programming:* news progmg 15 hrs wkly; *No. News Employees:* 1; *Target Audience:* 25-54. *Adv. Rates:* 13; 10; 13; 7
Wendy Hill, Operations Director
Chad Henderson, Programming Director

Brady

KNEL
12-01-1935; 1490 kHz AM; 1 kw-U, ND1; N31 7 48 W99 19 21
Mailing Address: 117 S. Blackburn, Brady, TX 76825 US
Second Address: PO Box 630, Brady, TX 76825
(325) 597-2119; *Fax:* (325) 597-1925
www.knelradio.com
knel@airmail.net
License: Brady, TX held by Farris Broadcasting Inc.
Nat'l Network: ABC; *Regional Network:* Texas State Networks
Format: Oldies; *Target Audience:* General.
Lynn Farris, President
Stan Cooper, Chief Engineer

KNEL-FM
08-21-1979; 95.3 MHz FM; 6 kw; 299 ft.; N31 7 27 W99 21 34
Mailing Address: 117 S. Blackburn Street, Brady, TX 76825 US
Second Address: PO Box 630, Brady, TX 76825
(325) 597-2119; *Fax:* (325) 597-1925
www.knelradio.com
knel@airmail.net
License: Brady, McCulloch County, TX
Regional Network: Texas State Networks
Format: Country; *Target Audience:* General.
Lynn Farris, General Manager

Breckenridge

KLXK
08-01-1982; 93.5 MHz FM; 12.5 kw; 459 ft.; N32 47 32 W98 56 24
415 W. Williams, Breckenridge, TX 76424 US
(254) 559-3311
www.lakecountyradio.net/klakes
gm@kwkq-kswa.com
License: Breckenridge, Stephens County, TX
Group Owner: Graham Newspapers Inc.
Nat'l Network: ABC
Arbitron Metro Market: Abilene, TX; *Format:* Country *Special Programming:* Agricultural programming 5 hrs wkly; *Hrs. of News Programming:* news progmg 1.5 hrs wkly; *No. News Employees:* 1 *Target Audience:* 25-54; general; *Adv. Rates:* 15; 15; 15; 15
Greg Tiller, Operations Dir
Joe Graham, General Manager
Cindy Lewis, Sales Manager

KROO
09-01-1947; 1430 kHz AM; *Hrs Open:* 24
Mailing Address: 101 East Walker Street, PO Box 951, Breckenridge, TX 76424 US
Second Address: 100 S. Main Street, PO Box 2019, Albany, TX 76430
(254) 559-6543; *Fax:* (254) 559-6545
www.lakecountyradio.net/kroo
License: Breckenridge, TX held by Graham Newspapers Inc.
Group Owner: Graham Newspapers Inc.; (acq 4-12-2001; with co-located FM)
Nat'l Network: ABC
Arbitron Metro Market: Abilene, TX; *Format:* Adult Contemp; *Hrs. of News Programming:* news progmg 2.5 hrs wkly; *No. News Employees:* 1; *Target Audience:* Adults 25-54; adults; *Adv. Rates:* 15; 15; 15; 15
Greg Tiller, Operations Dir
Joe Graham, General Manager
Cindy Lewis, Sales Manager

***KQXB**
89.9 MHz FM; 17.9 kw; Ant 325 ft; N32 35 48 W98 44 26
Box 497933, Garland, TX
(469) 245-3604
License: Breckenridge, Stephens County, TX held by Gospel American Network.

William Wright, General Manager

Brenham

KTTX
09-15-1964; 106.1 MHz FM; 50 kw; 492 ft.; N30 21 48 W96 34 33
Mailing Address: 223 East Main Street, Brenham, TX 77833 US
Second Address: PO Box 1280, Brenham, TX 77834
(979) 836-3655; *Fax:* (979) 830-8141
tom@ktex.com
License: Brenham, Washington County, TX held by Tom S. Whitehead, Inc.
Nat'l Reps: Rgnl Reps
Arbitron Metro Market: Brenham, TX; *Format:* Country; *Hrs. of News Programming:* news progmg 1.5 hrs wkly; *No. News Employees:* 1; *Target Audience:* 18-49.; *Adv. Rates:* 20; 15; 18; 11
Tom D Whitehead, President/General Manager
Ken Murray, Operations Manager
Carolyn Warmke, Sales Manager
Troy Arndt, Production Director
Hollye Simpson, Promotions Director
Frank Wagner, News Director
Mark Whitehead, ChiefEngineer
Ed Pothul, Sports Director
Michele Daniels, Traffic Director

KLTR
08-01-1988; 94.1 MHz FM; *Hrs Open:* 24; 6.4 kw; 328 ft.; N30 8 31 W96 25 0
530 W. Main St., Brenham, TX 77833 US
(979) 836-9411
www.litefm941.com
License: Brenham, Washington County, TX held by Roy E. Henderson.
Group Owner: Fort Bend Broadcasting Co.; (acq 5-31-2001; $1.5 million)
Arbitron Metro Market: Brenham, TX; *Format:* Adult Contemp *Special Programming:* Gospel 10 hrs wkly; *Hrs. of News Programming:* news progmg 18 hrs wkly; *No. News Employees:* 1; *Target Audience:* 18-49.
Roy Henderson, President

KWHI
04-15-1947; 1280 kHz AM; 1 kw-D, ND1; 0.072 kw-N, ND1; N30 10 5 W96 25 20
Mailing Address: P. O. Box 1280, Brenham, TX 77833 US
Second Address: 223 E. Main St., Brenham, TX 77834
(979) 836-3655; *Fax:* (979) 830-8141
www.kwhi.com
mail@kwhi.com
License: Brenham, TX held by Tom S. Whitehead Inc.
Nat'l Network: ABC; *Nat'l Reps:* Rgnl Reps
Arbitron Metro Market: Brenham, TX; *Format:* Country, News, 62, Talk *Special Programming:* Polka 2 hrs, relg 3 hrs, farm 3 hrs wkly; *Hrs. of News Programming:* news progmg 14 hrs wkly; *No. News Employees:* 2 *Target Audience:* 25-54.; *Adv. Rates:* 24; 19; 22; 10
Tom D. Whitehead, President and General Manager
Carolyn Wamke, Sales Manager
Craig Montana, Programming Director
Hollye Hatfield, Promotions Director
Mary-Janet, News Director
Mark Whitehead, Chief Engineer
Ed Pothul, SportsDirector
Michele Daniels, Office Manager

***KUBJ**
01-01-2008; 89.7 MHz FM; 17.5 kw; 407 ft.; N30 3 17 W96 30 26
P.O. Drawer 2440, Tupelo, MS 38803 US
(281) 446-5725; *Fax:* (281 540-2198
www.ksbj.org

License: Brenham, Washington County, TX held by KSBJ Educational Foundation.
Arbitron Metro Market: Benton, AR; *Format:* Christian
Tim McDermott, General Manager

Bridgeport

KBOC
08-02-1982; 98.3 MHz FM; *Hrs Open:* 24; 93 kw; 2034 ft.; N33 26 13 W97 29 5
2410 Gateway Dr, Irving, TX 75063 US
(972) 652-2900; *Fax:* (972) 652-2144
lunadallas.estrellatv.com
License: Bridgeport, Wise County, TX held by Liberman Broadcasting of Dallas License LLC.
Group Owner: Liberman Broadcasting Inc.; (acq 11-2-2006; grpsl)
Arbitron Metro Market: Dallas-Fort Worth, TX; *Format:* Adult Contemp
Alex Sanchez, General Manager

Brookshire

KCHN
01-01-2001; 1050 kHz AM
27 William St., 11th Floor, New York, NY 10005 US
(212) 966-1059; *Fax:* (212) 625-2894
www.kchnradio.com
License: Brookshire, TX held by Multicultural Radio Broadcasting Licensee, LLC
Group Owner: Multicultural Radio Broadcasting Inc.
Arbitron Metro Market: Greater Houston, TX; *Format:* Ethnic
Arthur Liu, CEO/COO

Brownfield

KKUB
08-01-1949; 1300 kHz AM
1277 Brownfield Radio, Inc., Brownfield, TX 79316 US
(806) 637-4531; *Fax:* (806) 637-4610
License: Brownfield, TX held by Dios Llega Al Hombre Ministries
Arbitron Metro Market: Lubbock, TX; *Format:* Country; *Target Audience:* 24 and up.
Adolph Hernandez, General Manager

KTTU
01-01-2004; 104.3 MHz FM; *Hrs Open:* 24; 50 kw; Ant 466 ft; N33 25 03 W102 08 51
9800 University Ave., Lubbock, TX 79423 USA
(806) 745-3434
www.doublet1043.com
License: Brownfield, TX held by Ramar Communications, Ltd.
Group Owner: Ramar Communications, Ltd.
Arbitron Metro Market: Lubbock, TX; *Format:* Sports
Brad Moran, President
Gary Reed, General Sales Mgr

Brownsville

*KBNR
04-10-1984; 88.3 MHz FM; *Hrs Open:* 24; 5.5 kw; 289 ft.; N25 55 10 W97 31 44
Mailing Address: P.O. Box 5480, Brownsville, TX 78523-5480 US
Second Address: 901 Mexico Blvd., Brownsville, TX 78520
(956) 542-6933; *Fax:* (956) 542-0523
www.radiokbnr.org
License: Brownsville, Cameron County, TX held by World Radio Network Inc.
Group Owner: World Radio Network Inc.
Arbitron Metro Market: McAllen-Brownsville-Harlingen, TX; *Format:* Religious; *Hrs. of News Programming:* News progmg 3 hrs wkly; *Target Audience:* 20-45; Hispanic, middle & upper income
Ted Haney, President
Abelardo Limon, Operations Dir
Moises Flores, Station Manager

KKPS
01-17-1978; 99.5 MHz FM; *Hrs Open:* 24; 100 kw; 1037 ft.; N26 4 53 W97 49 44
801 N. Jackson Rd., McAllen, TX 78501 US
(956) 687-4848; *Fax:* (956) 687-7784
www.995lanueva.com
License: Brownsville, Cameron County, TX held by Entravision Holdings L.L.C.
Group Owner: Entravision Communications Corp.; (acq 7-20-00; grpsl)
Arbitron Metro Market: McAllen, TX; *Format:* Tejano; *No. News Employees:* 1; *Target Audience:* 18-49; Hispanic females, young adults

Debby Flores, Senior VP
Scott Savage, General Manager

KVNS
01-01-1999; 1700 kHz AM; *Hrs Open:* 24; 8.8 kw-D, ND1; 0.88 kw-N, ND1; N25 56 57 W97 33 15
901 E. Pike Blvd., Walasco, TX 78596 US
(956) 973-2115
www.foxsports1700.com
License: Brownsville, TX held by Clear Channel Broadcasting Licenses Inc.
Group Owner: iHeartMedia; (acq 12-9-2003; grpsl).
Arbitron Metro Market: McAllen-Brownsville-Harlingen; *Format:* Sports
Chris Aldrich, Sales Manager
Jojo Cerda, Programming Director
Jay Cantu, Webmaster

Brownwood

*KBUB
03-12-1987; 90.3 MHz FM; 5.5 kw; 289 ft.; N31 43 10 W99 0 57
Mailing Address: P.O. Box 1549, Brownwood, TX 76804 US
Second Address: 910 Main Street, Brownwood, TX 76801
(325) 646-5993; *Fax:* (325) 643-9772
www.kpsm.net/kbub
License: Brownwood, Brown County, TX held by Living Word Church of Brownwood Inc.
Format: Christian
Angelia Schum, General Manager

KBWD
08-17-1941; 1380 kHz AM; 1 kw-D, ND1; 0.5 kw-N, ND1; N31 42 36 W98 57 36
Mailing Address: P. O. Box 280, Brownwood, TX 76801 US
Second Address: 300 Carnegie St., Brownwood, TX 76804
(325) 646-3505; *Fax:* (325) 646-2220
www.koxe.com
upfront@koxe.com
License: Brownwood, TX held by Brown County Broadcasting Co.
Arbitron Metro Market: Brownwood, TX; *Format:* Adult Contemp
Don Dillard, Operations Dir
Barbara McAnally, General Manager

*KHBW
09-01-1998; 91.7 MHz FM; *Hrs Open:* 24; 420 w; Ant 571 ft; N31 43 32 W99 00 48
2424 South Blvd., Houston, TX 77098 US
(713) 520-5200
www.khcb.org
email@khcb.org
License: Brownwood, Brown County, TX held by Houston Christian Broadcasters Inc.
Group Owner: Houston Christian Broadcasters Inc.; (acq 2-27-2009; $40,000)
Population Served: 25,000 *Format:* Christian
Bruce E. Munsterman, President

KOXE
05-17-1975; 101.3 MHz FM; 100 kw; 577 ft.; N31 43 45 W99 1 12
Mailing Address: 300 Carnegie Blvd, Brownwood, TX 76801 US
Second Address: PO Box 280, Brownwood, TX 76804
(325) 646-3505; *Fax:* (325) 646-2220
www.koxe.com
upfront@koxe.com
License: Brownwood, Brown County, TX held by Brown County Broadcasting Co.
Format: Country
Barbara McAnally, General Manager

KPSM
04-11-1981; 99.3 MHz FM; 100 kw; 446 ft.; N31 43 10 W99 0 57
Mailing Address: P.O. Box 1549, Brownwood, TX 76804 US
Second Address: 10 Main Street, Brownwood, TX 76801
(325) 646-5993; *Fax:* (325) 643-9772
www.kpsm.net
License: Brownwood, Brown County, TX held by Living Word Church of Brownwood Inc.
Nat'l Network: Salem Radio Network
Format: Christian *Special Programming:* Children 3 hrs, Christian hip hop 5 hrs, Southern
Jack Ruth, CEO
Angelia Schum, General Manager
Brigitte Rittenour, Station Manager
Erich Schnitz, Programming Director
Tom Zintgraff, Chief Engineer
Kevin Koontz, Promotions Manager

KQBZ
01-01-1953; 1240 kHz AM; *Hrs Open:* 24; 1 kw-U; N31 42 21 W98 59 45
600 Fisk Ave., Brownwood, TX 76801
(325) 646-3535; *Fax:* (325) 646-5347
www.wendleebroadcasting.com
License: Brownwood, Brown County, TX held by Wendlee Broadcasting
Group Owner: Wendlee Broadcasting
Regional Network: Texas State Networks; *Nat'l Reps:* Roslin
Population Served: 35,000 *Special Programming:* Christian Sp 36 hrs wkly; *Hrs. of News Programming:* news progmg 8 hrs wkly; *No. News Employees:* 2; *Target Audience:* 18+; Spanish; *Adv. Rates:* Same as AM
Chema Martinez, Programming Director
Helen Lehman, News Director

KQBZ
09-15-1982; 96.9 MHz FM; *Hrs Open:* 24; 331 ft.; N31 42 16 W99 05 00
600 Fisk St., Brownwood, TX 76801 USA
(325) 646-3535; *Fax:* (325) 646-5347
www.wendleebroadcasting.com
License: Brownwood, TX held by Tackett-Boazman Broadcasting LP
Group Owner: Tackett-Boazman Broadcasting LP; (acq 4-28-2006; grpsl)
Nat'l Network: ABC
Arbitron Metro Market: Brownwood, TX; *Target Audience:* 18+

Bryan

KAGC
12-27-1977; 1510 kHz AM; 0.5 kw-D, NDD; N30 39 6 W96 23 6
2700 Earl Rudder Fwy., Suite 5000, College Station, TX 77845 US
(979) 695-9595; *Fax:* (979) 695-1933
www.kagc1510.com
License: Bryan, Brazos County, TX held by Bryan Broadcasting License Corp.
Group Owner: Bryan Broadcasting Corp.; (acq 3-87)
Nat'l Network: Salem Radio Network
Arbitron Metro Market: College Station, TX; *Format:* Christian, Talk *Special Programming:* Black 2 hrs, Czech music 2 hrs wkly; *Hrs. of News Programming:* News progmg 6 hrs wkly; *Target Audience:* 25-54; upscale,higher income & conservative; *Adv. Rates:* 12.50; 11; 12;50; na
William R. Hicks, President
Tucker Young, Operations Manager
Ben Downs, Vice President and General Manager
Sam Jones, Sales Manager
Katy Dempsey, Promotions Director
Chris Dusterhoff, Chief Engineer
Alisa Dusterhoff, OfficerManager

KNFX-FM
10-07-1991; 99.5 MHz FM; *Hrs Open:* 24; 6 kw; 187 ft.; N30 39 9 W96 20 16
1716 Briarcrest Dr., Suite 150, Bryan, TX 77802 US
(979) 846-5597; *Fax:* (979) 268-9090
www.995thefox.com
License: Bryan, Brazos County, TX held by CC Licenses LLC
Group Owner: iHeartMedia; (acq 7-20-01; $2.5 million).
Arbitron Metro Market: Bryan-College Station, TX; *Format:* Classic Rock; *Target Audience:* General.; *Adv. Rates:* 18; 18; 18; 18
Zack Owens, Regional Operations Manager
Evan Armstrong, Market Manager
Jim Harrington, General Sales Mgr
K.C. Wheeler, Programming Director

KKYS
07-28-1984; 104.7 MHz FM; *Hrs Open:* 24; 50 kw; 285 ft.; N30 42 59 W96 22 20
1716 Briarcrest Drive, Suite 150, Bryan, TX 77802 US
(979) 846-5597; *Fax:* (979) 268-9090
www.mix1047.com
License: Bryan, Brazos County, TX held by CC Licenses LLC
Group Owner: iHeartMedia; (acq 10-10-00; grpsl).
Arbitron Metro Market: Bryan, TX; *Format:* Adult Contemp; *Hrs. of News Programming:* News progmg 15 hrs wkly; *Target Audience:* 18-49; heavy office lstng; *Adv. Rates:* 30; 40; 30; 25
Zack Owens, Regional Operations Manager
Evan Armstrong, Market Manager
Jim Harrington, General Sales Mgr
Ashlee Young, Programming Director

KORA-FM
04-01-1966; 98.3 MHz FM; 0.9 kw; 528 ft.; N30 39 0.985 W96 20 57.34

RADIO - U.S.

Mailing Address: 2402 Broadmoor, Bldg, D-2, Suite 101, Bryan, TX 77802 US
Second Address: 1240 Villa Maria Rd, Bryan, TX 77802
(979) 776-1240; *Fax:* (979) 776-0123
License: Bryan, Brazos County, TX held by Brazos Valley Communications Ltd.
Group Owner: Brazos Valley Communications Ltd.
Nat'l Reps: Katz Radio
Arbitron Metro Market: Bryan-College Station, TX; *Format:* Country *Special Programming:* ABC News; *Target Audience:* P18-49, P25-54
Dan Ginzel, Operations Dir
Chris Kiske, General Manager
Nathan Peacock, General Sales Mgr
Roger Garrett, Programming Director
Lance Parr, Chief Engineer

KTAM
09-10-1947; 1240 kHz AM
Mailing Address: 2402 Broadmoor, Bldg, D-2, Suite 101, Bryan, TX 77802 US
Second Address: 1240 Villa Maria Rd, Bryan, TX 77802
(979) 776-1240; *Fax:* (979) 776-0123
License: Bryan, TX held by Brazos Valley Communications Ltd.
Group Owner: Brazos Valley Communications Ltd.; (acq 8-31-2006; grpsl)
Nat'l Reps: Univision Radio National Sales
Arbitron Metro Market: Bryan-College Station, TX; *Format:* Tejano *Special Programming:* GLR News, ESPN Deportes; *Target Audience:* 18-34, 18-49
Dan Ginzel, Operations Dir
Chris Kiske, General Manager
Nathan Peacock, General Sales Mgr
Carolyn Benavides, Programming Director
Lance Parr, Chief Engineer

Buda

KROX-FM
09-01-1984; 101.5 MHz FM; *Hrs Open:* 24; 12.5 kw; 847 ft.; N30 19 20 W97 48 3
8309 North IH 35, Austin, TX 78753 USA
(512) 832-4000; *Fax:* (512) 832-4071
www.101x.com
lawless@krox.com
License: Buda, Hays County, TX held by Emmis Austin Radio Broadcasting Company LP
Group Owner: Emmis Communications Corp.
Nat'l Reps: McGavren Guild
Arbitron Metro Market: Austin-Round Rock metro area; *Format:* Alternative; *Target Audience:* 18-34; young adults; *Adv. Rates:* 140; 150; 160; 70
James White, Sales Manager
Lynn Barstow, Programming Director
Frankie Ruiz, Promotions Manager
Toby Ryan, Music Director

Buffalo

WTAW-FM
103.5 MHz FM; 6 kw; 285 ft.; N31 21 42 W95 58 15
Mailing Address: P.O. Box 3248, Bryan, TX 77805 US
Second Address: 2700 Earl Rudder Fwy., Suite 5000, College Station, TX 77845
(979) 695-9595
www.wtaw.com
news@wtaw.com
License: Buffalo, Leon County, TX held by Bryan Broadcasting License Corp.
Group Owner: Bryan Broadcasting Corp.
Arbitron Metro Market: Bryan, TX; *Format:* News, News/Talk, 86
Tucker Young, Operations Manager
Ben Downs, Vice President and General Manager
Sam Jones, Sales Manager
Katy Dempsey, Promotions Director
Bill Oliver, News Director
Chris Dusterhoff, Chief Engineer
Alisa Dusterhoff, OfficeManager

Burkburnett

KYYI
06-01-1989; 104.7 MHz FM; *Hrs Open:* 24; 92 kw; 1017 ft.; N34 5 35 W98 52 44
4302 Call Field Rd., Wichita Falls, TX 76308 US
(940) 691-2311; *Fax:* (940) 696-2255
www.bear104.com
License: Burkburnett, Wichita County, TX held by Cumulus Licensing Corp.
Group Owner: Cumulus Media Inc.; (acq 10-3-97; grpsl)
Arbitron Metro Market: Burkburnett, TX; *Format:* Classic Rock
Keith Vaughn, Operations Dir
Lindy Parr, General Manager
John Tidwell, Sales Manager
Keith Vaughn, Programming Director
Dana Jameson, News Director
Jeff Chancey, Chief Engineer

Burleson

KCLE
07-22-1922; 1460 kHz AM; *Hrs Open:* 24
P.O. Box 1629, Cleburne, TX 76033 US
(817) 645-6643; *Fax:* (817) 645-6644
www.countrygoldradio.com
License: Burleson, TX held by M&M Broadcasters Ltd.
Group Owner: M&M Broadcasters Ltd.; (acq 4-26-99; $450,000)
Arbitron Metro Market: Dallas, TX; *Format:* Country
Gary Moss, General Manager

Burnet

KBEY
04-01-1993; 103.9 MHz FM; 1.8 kw; Ant 604 ft; N30 44 29 W98 19 05
1007 Avenue K, Marble Falls, TX 78654
(830) 693-7152
www.kbeyfm.com
License: Burnet, Burnet County, TX held by Victory Publishing Company Ltd.

Connie Swinney, News Director
Ben Shields, Traffic Manager

Bushland

***KTXP**
01-01-2004; 91.5 MHz FM; *Hrs Open:* 24; 1 kw; 262 ft.; N35 8 51 W102 5 56 *Rebroadcasts:* Rebroadcasts KANZ(FM) Garden City 100%
Mailing Address: 210 North 7th Street, Garden City, KS 67846 US
Second Address: 104 SW 6th Avenue, Suite B-4, Amarillo, TX 79101
(620) 275-7444
www.hppr.org
License: Bushland, Potter County, TX held by Kanza Society Inc.
Nat'l Network: NPR; AP Radio; PRI
Arbitron Metro Market: Bushland, Texas; *Format:* News, Variety/Diverse
Adam Vos, Operations Coordinator
Cindee Talley, Regional Programming Director
Mike Fuller, Music Director
Skip Mancini, Producer

Byrne

***KLRW**
01-01-2004; 88.5 MHz FM; 2.5 kw; 689 ft.; N31 25 16 W100 32 36
P. O. Box 2098, Omaha, NE 68103-2098 US
(800) 525-5683
www.klove.com
License: Byrne, Tom Green County, TX held by Educational Media Foundation.
Group Owner: EMF Broadcasting; (acq 5-8-2003; $75,000 for CP).
Nat'l Network: K-Love
Arbitron Metro Market: San Angelo, TX; *Format:* Christian; *No. News Employees:* 13
Darrell Chambliss, Chairman
Mike Novak, President and CEO
David Pierce, Chief Creative Officer
Alan Mason, Chief Operating Officer
Eric Moser, Chief Financial Officer

Caldwell

KAPN
01-01-2002; 107.3 MHz FM; *Hrs Open:* 24; 6 kw; 328 ft.; N30 33 31 W96 34 50
1240 East Villa Maria, Bryan, TX 77802 US
(979) 776-1240; *Fax:* (979) 776-0123
License: Caldwell, Burleson County, TX held by Brazos Valley Communications Ltd.
Group Owner: Brazos Valley Communications Ltd.; (acq 11-18-2008; $875,000)
Nat'l Reps: Katz Radio
Arbitron Metro Market: Bryan-College S; *Format:* Adult Contemp *Special Programming:* Kidd Kraddick AM Show; *Target Audience:* p18-34, p18-49
Dan Ginzel, Operations Dir
Chris Kiske, General Manager
Nathan Peacock, General Sales Mgr
Raquel Pena, Programming Director
Lance Parr, Chief Engineer

Callisburg

***KPFC**
04-01-1998; 91.9 MHz FM; *Hrs Open:* 24; 0.3 kw; 66 ft.; N33 40 11 W97 0 50
P O Box 918, Gainesville, TX 76241 US
www.kpfc.org
kpfcradio@gmail.com
License: Callisburg, Cooke County, TX held by Camp Sweeney.
Format: Contemporary Hits/Top 40
Chad Henderson, Programming Director

Cameron

KMIL
01-01-2002; 105.1 MHz FM; 15 kw; 328 ft.; N30 51 30 W97 1 47
901 East First Street, PO Box 832, Cameron, TX 76520 US
(254) 697-6633; *Fax:* (254) 697-6330
www.kmil.com
kmil@kmil.com
License: Cameron, Milam County, TX held by Cameron Broadcasting Co.
Nat'l Network: CBS Radio
Format: Country *Special Programming:* Farm 5 hrs wkly; *Hrs. of News Programming:* news progmg 5 hrs wkly
Rob Reed, Operations Manager
Bret Eberhart, Traffic Manager

KTON
09-01-1955; 1330 kHz AM; 0.5 kw-D, ND1; 0.097 kw-N, ND1; N30 50 48 W96 57 55
Mailing Address: P. O. Box 832, Cameron, TX 76520 US
Second Address: 901 E. First, Cameron, TX 76520
(254) 697-6633; *Fax:* (254) 697-6330
www.kmil.com
kmil@tlab.net
License: Cameron, TX held by M&M Broadcasters Ltd.
Group Owner: M&M Broadcasters Ltd.; (acq 12-31-97)
Nat'l Reps: Keystone (unwired net)
Format: Country *Special Programming:* Gospel 6 hrs, Czech 8 hrs wkly; *Target Audience:* General.
Joe Smitherman, General Manager
Eric Haussecker, Programming Director
A.T. Sheffield, Disc Jockey
Nonito Martinez, A.T. Sheffield
Sarah Haussecker, Traffic Manager

Campbell

KRVA-FM
08-01-1969; 107.1 MHz FM; 3.6 kw; 423 ft.; N33 7 30 W95 44 32
1436 Auburn Boulevard, Sacramento, CA 95815 US
(817) 332-0959; *Fax:* (817) 348-8373
www.kfwr.com/#1
ContactUs@TheRanchRadio.com
License: Campbell, Hunt County, TX held by LKCM Radio Group L.P.
Group Owner: LKCM Radio Group L.P.; (acq 5-21-2004; $1 million with KRVF(FM) Kerens).
Arbitron Metro Market: Campbell, TX; *Format:* Oldies; *No. News Employees:* 2
Gerry Schlegel, President
Joel Gough, General Sales Mgr
Chuck Taylor, Programming Director
Molly Prince, Promotions Manager
Jane Wasson, News Director
Michael Margrave, Chief Engineer

Canton

KWJB
09-12-1963; 1510 kHz AM; *Hrs Open:* Sunrise-suset; 500 w-D; N32 41 02 W95 29 44
Fax: (903) 740-5952
www.kwjb.com
jb@kwjb.com
License: Canton, Van Zandt County, TX held by RDH Land & Cattle Co. Inc.
Population Served: 50,000 *Hrs. of News Programming:* News progmg 6 hrs wkly; *Target Audience:* General.; *Adv. Rates:* 15; 10; 10; na
Mike Newby
John Butler

Canyon

KPUR-FM
01-12-1981; 107.1 MHz FM; *Hrs Open:* 24; 6 kw; 315 ft.; N35 5 9 W101 54 48
US
www.kpur107.com
jim.faires@cumulus.com
License: Canyon, Randall County, TX held by Cumulus Licensing Corp.
Group Owner: Cumulus Media Inc.; (acq 5-98; $820,000 with KPUR(AM) Amarillo)
Arbitron Metro Market: Amarillo, TX; *Format:* Country; *Hrs. of News Programming:* news progmg 5 hrs wkly; *No. News Employees:* 1; *Target Audience:* 35-55; boomers
Jim Faires, General Manager
Craig Vaughn, Programming Director
Charlie Fuller, Chief Engineer
Carol Titus, Traffic Director
Susan Reams, Business Manager

***KWTS**
01-01-1971; 91.1 MHz FM; *Hrs Open:* 24; 6 kw; 141 ft.; N34 59 22 W101 54 45
West Texas A&M University, PO Box 60747, Canyon, TX 79016 US
(806) 651-2797; *Fax:* (806) 651-2818
www.wtamu.edu/kwts
kwtsgm@gmail.com
License: Canyon, Randall County, TX held by West Texas A & M University.
Arbitron Metro Market: Canyon, TX *Special Programming:* Class 4 hrs, jazz 3 hrs, Black 3 hrs, techo 5 hrs, acoustic 3 hrs, Britsh rock 3 hrs, Sp 3 hrs wkly; *Hrs. of News Programming:* news progmg 3 hrs wkly *No. NewsEmployees:* 2; *Target Audience:* 16-25.
Allison Myers, Operations Dir
Bri Leeper, Programming Director
Kase Willbanks, News Director
Randy Ray, Chief Engineer
Patrick Shaw, Music Director
Anthony Miller, Sports Manager
Johnny Story, Brodcast Engineer

KNSH
05-08-1962; 1550 kHz AM; *Hrs Open:* 6 AM-6 PM; 1 kw-D, ND1; 0.219 kw-N, ND1; N34 58 54 W101 57 18
111 East Kilbourn Ave., Suite 2700, Milwaukee, WI 53202 US
License: Canyon, TX held by Cumulus Licensing Corp.
Group Owner: Cumulus Media Inc.
Arbitron Metro Market: Amarillo, TX; *Format:* Sports, Talk; *Adv. Rates:* 10; 10; 10; 8

KZRK-FM
09-30-1985; 107.9 MHz FM; *Hrs Open:* 24; 100 kw; 476 ft.; N35 13 36 W102 0 24
US
amarillosrockstation.com/
jim.faires@cumulus.com
License: Canyon, Randall County, TX held by Cumulus Licensing Corp.
Group Owner: Cumulus Media Inc.; (acq 3-3-98; $1 million with co-located AM).
Nat'l Network: Westwood One; *Nat'l Reps:* Roslin
Arbitron Metro Market: Amarillo, TX; *Format:* Rock/AOR; *Hrs. of News Programming:* news progmg 3 hrs wkly; *No. News Employees:* 1; *Target Audience:* 18-34; general; *Adv. Rates:* 35; 32; 35; 24
Jim Faires, General Manager
Chase Elder, Music Director
Charlie Fuller, Engineer
Carol Titus, Traffic Director
Susan Reams, Business Manager

Carrizo Springs

KBEN
08-09-1955; 1450 kHz AM; 1 kw-U, ND1; N28 31 15 W99 51 30
Route 1, Box 168, Heritage Farms, Eagle Pass, TX 78852 US
(210) 876-2210; *Fax:* (210) 876-5489
License: Carrizo Springs, TX held by Sylvia Mijares
Arbitron Metro Market: Carrizo Springs, TX; *Format:* Religious; *Target Audience:* English & Sp listeners.
Gordon Baehre, General Manager

***KCZO**
01-01-1991; 92.1 MHz FM; 25 kw; 302 ft.; N28 33 24 W99 53 49
307 East Jackson, McAllen, TX 78501 US
(956) 781-5528; *Fax:* (956) 686-2999
License: Carrizo Springs, Dimmit County, TX held by Paulino Bernal Evangelism.
Format: Christian
Eloy Bernal, General Manager

KAJP
01-01-2008; 93.5 MHz FM; 6 kw; 253 ft.; N28 30 32.3 W99 52 37
US
License: Carrizo Springs, Dimmit County, TX held by Hispanic Target Media Inc.
Group Owner: Hispanic Target Media Inc.
Arbitron Metro Market: Carrizo Springs, TX; *Format:* Tejano
Francisco San Millan, President
Meredith Senter, General Manager

Carrollton

KJON
12-17-1970; 850 kHz AM
8828 N. Stemmons Freeway, Suite 106, Dallas, TX 75247 US
(214) 951-0132; *Fax:* (214) 951-8622
www.grnonline.com
davepalmer@grnonline.com
License: Carrollton, TX held by Chatham Hill Foundation Inc.
Arbitron Metro Market: Dallas, TX; *Format:* Spanish, Christian

Carthage

KGAS
10-01-1955; 1590 kHz AM; 2.5 kw-D, ND1; 0.128 kw-N, ND1; N32 9 12 W94 18 52
215 S. Market, Carthage, TX 75633 US
(903) 693-6668; *Fax:* (903) 693-7188
www.easttexastoday.com
info@kgasradio.com
License: Carthage, TX held by Jerry T. Hanszen
Regional Network: Texas State Networks; *Wire Services:* NOAA Weather
Arbitron Metro Market: Carthage, TX; *Format:* Sports; *Hrs. of News Programming:* News 20 hrs wkly; *Target Audience:* General.
Jerry & Wana Hanszen, Owners
Melissa Ruffner, Office Manager
Judy McNatt, Sales Manager
Mark Bownds, News/Sports Manager

KGAS-FM
08-01-1992; 104.3 MHz FM; 6 kw; 328 ft.; N32 8 33 W94 25 39
215 S. Market, Carthage, TX 75633 US
(903) 693-6668; *Fax:* (903) 693-7188
www.easttexastoday.com
info@kgasradio.com
License: Carthage, Panola County, TX held by Jerry T. Hanszen.
Nat'l Network: ABC; Westwood One
Arbitron Metro Market: Carthage, TX; *Format:* Country; *Target Audience:* General.
Jerry & Wanda Hanszen, Owners
Melissa Ruffner, Office Manager
Judy McNatt, Sales Manager
Mark Bownds, News/Sprots Manager

KTUX
04-01-1985; 98.9 MHz FM; *Hrs Open:* 24; 100 kw; 719 ft.; N32 23 19 W94 1 10
5005 W. Monkhouse, Shreveport, LA 71109 US
(318) 688-1130; *Fax:* (318) 688-9839
www.therockstation99x.com
License: Carthage, Panola County, TX held by Townsquare Media Shreveport License LLC
Group Owner: Townsquare Media; (acq 8-3-2007; grpsl)
Arbitron Metro Market: Shreveport, LA; *Format:* Rock/AOR; *Target Audience:* 18-49; super-active adults
Lisa Janes, General Manager
Casey Ryan, Director of Sales
Paul Cannell, Brand Manager

Cedar Park

KGSR
08-01-1961; 93.3 MHz FM; 100 kw; Ant 1,948 ft; N30 43 34 W97 59 23
8309 N IH 35, Austin, TX 78753 USA
(512) 832-4000; *Fax:* (512) 832-4071
www.kgsr.com
License: Cedar Park, Williamson County, TX held by Emmis Austin Radio Broadcasting Company LP
Group Owner: Emmis Communications Corp.
Population Served: 2,000,000; *Arbitron Metro Market:* Austin, TX; *Format:* Alternative, Adult Contemp *Special Programming:* Pub service 2 hrs, Sp one hr, Latino one hr wkly; *Target Audience:* 18-34; women & men wholike current music
Chase, Operations Manager
Bruce Walden, General Manager
Tatjana Deegan, Sales Manager
Haley Jones, Programming Director
John Laird, Promotions Director
Emily McIntosh, Music Director

Center

KDET
02-22-1949; 930 kHz AM; 1 kw-D, 36 w-N; N31 50 03 W94 12 53
307 San Augustine St., Center, TX 75935
(936) 598-3304; *Fax:* (936) 598-9537
www.cbc-radio.com
License: Center, Shelby County, TX held by Center Broadcasting Co. Inc.
Group Owner: Center Broadcasting Co. Inc.; (acq 3-26-98; grpsl)
Regional Network: Texas State Networks; *Nat'l Reps:* Riley
Population Served: 29,000 *Format:* News, News/Talk, 86
Lori Alvis, Sales
Jessie Jacobs, Programming Director
Joey Monk, News Director
Jessica Quigley, Traffic Manager

KQBB
07-05-1978; 100.5 MHz FM; 8.7 kw; Ant 567 ft; N31 43 34 W94 15 27
307 San Augustine St., Center, TX 75935
(936) 598-3304; *Fax:* (936) 598-9537
www.cbc-radio.com
License: Center, Shelby County, TX held by Center Broadcasting Co. Inc.
Group Owner: Center Broadcasting Co. Inc.
Format: Country; *Target Audience:* Shelby County
Lori Alvis, Sales
Jessie Jacobs, Programming Director
Joey Monk, News Director
Jessica Quigley, Traffic Manager

Centerville

***KUZN**
01-01-2001; 105.9 MHz FM; *Hrs Open:* 24; 25 kw; 328 ft.; N31 16 56 W95 53 42
1600 Pasadena Blvd., Pasadena, TX 77502 US
(713) 920-1840
www.radioaleluya.org
License: Centerville, Leon County, TX held by Aleluya Broadcasting Network
Arbitron Metro Market: Spokane, WA; *Format:* Religious
Ruben Villarreul, General Manager

Charlotte

KSAQ
102.3 MHz FM; 6 kw; 148 ft.; N28 45 47 W98 42 0
US
License: Charlotte, Atascosa County, TX held by Peter J Salazar d/b/a/ Salazar Consulting
Arbitron Metro Market: Charlotte, TX
Gary Hess, General Manager

Childress

KCTX
05-08-1947; 1510 kHz AM; *Hrs Open:* 6:30 AM-6 PM; 0.25 kw-D, NDD; N34 25 41 W100 13 47
1111 16th Street NW, Childress, TX 79201 US
(940) 937-6316; *Fax:* (940) 937-6551
www.kctxradio.net
kctxradio@gmail.com
License: Childress, TX held by James G. Boles
Format: Oldies
James Boles, General Manager
Chao Ware, General Sales Mgr
J. Scott, Programming Director
Mona Boles, News Director

KCTX-FM
07-01-1984; 96.1 MHz FM; 50 kw; 476 ft.; N34 26 20 W100 13 10
1111 16th Street NW, Childress, TX 79201 US
(940) 937-6316; *Fax:* (940) 937-6551
www.kctx.com
kctxradio@gmail.com
License: Childress, Childress County, TX held by James G. Boles
Nat'l Reps: Riley
Arbitron Metro Market: Childress, TX; *Format:* Country *Special Programming:* Relg 5 hrs wkly; *Target Audience:* General.
James Boles, General Manager
Chad Ware, General Sales Mgr
J. Scott, Programming Director

Clarendon

KEFH
09-01-2000; 99.3 MHz FM; *Hrs Open:* 24; 44 kw; 522 ft.; N35 4 36 W100 53 33
US
(806) 874-9930; *Fax:* (806) 874-4411
www.kool993.net
License: Clarendon, Donley County, TX held by RoHo Broadcasting Co.
Arbitron Metro Market: Claredon, TX; *Format:* Oldies
Ken Meinhart, General Manager
Jodie Lockeby, Sales Associate
Britton Hall, Production Director

Clarksville

KCAR
04-27-1956; 1350 kHz AM; *Hrs Open:* 24; 0.41 kw-D, ND1; 0.065 kw-N, ND1; N33 36 47 W95 1 3
P.O. Box 609, Clarksville, TX 75426 US
(903) 793-1109; *Fax:* (903) 794-4717
License: Clarksville, TX held by American Media Investments Inc.
Group Owner: American Media Investments Inc.; (acq 2-17-2009; grpsl)
Nat'l Network: Jones Radio Networks; *Regional Network:* Texas State Networks
Arbitron Metro Market: Paris, TX; *Format:* Country *Special Programming:* Gospel 6 hrs, sports 10 hrs, farm 2 hrs wkly; *Hrs. of News Programming:* News progmg 10 hrs wkly; *Target Audience:* General; rural,agricultural, middle-aged; *Adv. Rates:* 25; 25; 25; 10
Tex Phillips, General Manager
Mike Monday, Programming Director
Dale Gorsuch, Chief Engineer

KGAP
12-11-1990; 98.5 MHz FM; *Hrs Open:* 24; 50 kw; 308 ft.; N33 36 47 W95 1 3
1323 College Drive, Texarkana, TX 75503 US
(903) 793-1109
www.alwayskool.com
kool@ami-texarkana.com
License: Clarksville, Red River County, TX held by American Media Investments Inc.
Group Owner: American Media Investments Inc.; (acq 2-17-2009; grpsl)
Nat'l Network: ABC
Arbitron Metro Market: Clarksville, TX; *Format:* Oldies; *Hrs. of News Programming:* News progmg one hr wkly; *Target Audience:* 25-64.

Claude

KARX
04-12-1992; 95.7 MHz FM; *Hrs Open:* 24; 100 kw; 390 ft.; N35 6 16 W101 39 28
US
www.957thekar.com
jim.faires@cumulus.com
License: Claude, Armstrong County, TX held by Cumulus Licensing Corp.
Group Owner: Cumulus Media Inc.; (acq 2-2-98; $675,000).
Arbitron Metro Market: Amarillo, TX; *Format:* Classic Rock; *Hrs. of News Programming:* news progmg 10 hrs wkly; *No. News Employees:* 1; *Target Audience:* 25-54; male; *Adv. Rates:* 45; 50; 48; 34
Jim Faires, General Manager
Charlie Fuller, Chief Engineer
Dale Miller, Music Director
Carol Titus, Traffic Director
Susan Reams, Business Manager

Cleburne

KHFX
04-01-1947; 1140 kHz AM; *Hrs Open:* 24
PO Box 1629, Cleburne, TX 76033 US
License: Cleburne, TX held by Siga Broadcasting Corp.
Group Owner: SIGA Broadcasting Corp.; (acq 9-24-2008; $1.4 million)
Arbitron Metro Market: Dallas-Fort Worth, TX; *Format:* Country
Gabriel Arango, President

Cleveland

KTHT
01-05-1991; 97.1 MHz FM; 100 kw; 1847 ft.; N30 32 6 W95 1 4
1990 Post Oak Blvd., #2300, Houston, TX 77056 US
(713) 963-1200; *Fax:* (713) 622-5457
www.countrylegends971.com
mark.krieschen@coxinc.com
License: Cleveland, Liberty County, TX held by Cox Radio Inc.
Group Owner: Cox Radio Inc.; (acq 8-15-2000; grpsl)
Arbitron Metro Market: Houston, TX; *Format:* Country
Bill Tatar, Chief Engineer
Mark Krieschen, VP/Market Manager
Judy Lakin, Director of Sales
Johnny Chiang, Operations Manager
Christi Brooks, Music Director
Lisa Searcy, Marketing Director
Candy Mendex, Promotions Manager

Clifton

KWOW
01-01-1989; 104.1 MHz FM; *Hrs Open:* 24; 21 kw; 470 ft.; N31 44 11 W97 19 27
6401 Cobbs Dr., Waco, TX 76710 US
(254) 772-6104
www.laley104.com
License: Clifton, Bosque County, TX held by Waco Entertainment Group LLC
Group Owner: Prophecy Media Group LLC; (acq 11-9-2004; grpsl).
Nat'l Reps: Lotus Entravision Reps LLC
Arbitron Metro Market: Waco, TX; *Format:* Tejano; *Target Audience:* 18-54; adults; *Adv. Rates:* 50 40; 50; 20
Cynthia Lopez, Operations Manager
Jaime Martinez, Programming Director

Coahoma

KXCS(FM)
01-01-2006; 105.5 MHz FM; 5.1 kw; Ant 358 ft; N32 21 52 W101 19 35 *Rebroadcasts:* Rebroadcasts KSRD(FM) Saint Joseph, MO 100%
c/o KSRD(FM), 1212 Faraon St., Coahoma, TX 64501
(816) 233-5773; *Fax:* (816) 233-5777
License: Coahoma, Howard County, TX held by Weeks Broadcasting Inc
Population Served: 820; *Arbitron Metro Market:* Coahoma, TX; *Format:* Christian
Mike MacIntosh, President
Brian Jones, General Manager

Cockrell Hill

KRVA
09-29-1947; 1600 kHz AM; *Hrs Open:* 24
10935 Estate Lane, Suite 180, Dallas, TX 75238 US
(214) 389-2563; *Fax:* (855) 503-7687
www.saigondallasradio.com
sg1600am@yahoo.com
License: Cockrell Hill, TX held by Mortenson Broadcasting Co. of Texas Inc.
Group Owner: Mortenson Broadcasting Co.; (acq 8-30-2004; $3.5 million)
Arbitron Metro Market: Dallas-Fort Worth; *Format:* Ethnic
Thu Nga, General Manager/Programming Director
Quan Hung, Station Manager
Thu Huong, Business Manager

Coleman

KSTA
11-01-1947; 1000 kHz AM; 0.25 kw-D, NDD; N31 51 16 W99 25 36
600 Fisk St., Brownwood, TX 76801 US
(325) 646-3535; *Fax:* (325) 646-5347
www.wendleebroadcasting.com/ksta-country-1000-the-voice-of-colemann-county/
License: Coleman, TX held by Tackett-Boazman Broadcasting LP.
Group Owner: Tackett-Boazman Broadcasting LP; (acq 4-11-2006; grpsl).
Nat'l Network: Jones Radio Networks; *Regional Network:* Texas State Networks
Arbitron Metro Market: Brownwood, TX; *Format:* Country *Special Programming:* Farm 14 hrs, Sp 5 hrs, gospel 7 hrs wkly; *Target Audience:* General.

KXYL-FM
09-01-1965; 102.3 MHz FM; *Hrs Open:* 24; 12 kw; 689 ft.; N31 44 54 W99 19 57
600 Fisk St., Brownwood, TX 76801 US
(325) 646-3535; *Fax:* (325) 646-5347
www.wendleebroadcasting.com
License: Coleman, Brown County, TX held by Tackett-Boazman Broadcasting LP
Group Owner: Tackett-Boazman Broadcasting LP; (acq 4-11-2006; grpsl).
Nat'l Network: ABC
Arbitron Metro Market: Brownwood, TX; *Format:* News, News/Talk, 86; *No. News Employees:* 3; *Target Audience:* 18+.; *Adv. Rates:* 15; 12; 15; 10

College Station

***KAMU-FM**
03-30-1977; 90.9 MHz FM; *Hrs Open:* 6 AM-midnight; 2.4 kw horiz, 32 kw vert; 341 ft.; N30 37 47 W96 20 33
Mailing Address: Texas A&M University, 4244 TAMU, College Station, TX 77843-4244 US
Second Address: Moore Communications Center, Houston St. at John David Crow Dr., College Station, TX 77843-4244
(979) 845-5611; *Fax:* (979) 845-1643
www.kamu.tamu.edu
penny@kamu.tamu.edu
License: College Station, Brazos County, TX held by Texas A&M University.
Nat'l Network: NPR; PRI
Arbitron Metro Market: College Station, TX; *Format:* Jazz, News *Special Programming:* Folk 3 hrs, new age 5 hrs, international 5 hrs wkl; *Hrs. of News Programming:* News progmg 35 hrs wkly *Target Audience:* General.
Penny Zent, Station Manager
Wayne Pecena, Chief Engineer
Vicki Holloway, Manager, Marketing/Fund Raising
B. Howard Johnson, Web Administrator

WTAW
10-01-1922; 1620 kHz AM; 10 kw-D, ND2; 1 kw-N, ND2; N30 37 15 W96 15 16
Mailing Address: P.O. Box 3248, Bryan, TX 77805 US
Second Address: 2700 Earl Rudder Fwy., Suite 5000, College Station, TX 77845
(979) 695-9595
www.wtaw.com
news@wtaw.com
License: College Station, Brazos County, TX held by Bryan Broadcasting License Corp.
Group Owner: Bryan Broadcasting Corp.
Arbitron Metro Market: Bryan, TX; *Format:* News, News/Talk, 86
Tucker Young, Operations Manager
Ben Downs, Vice President and General Manager
Sam Jones, Sales Manager
Katy Dempsey, Promotions Director
Bill Oliver, News Director
Chris Dusterhoff, Chief Engineer
Alisa Dusterhoff, OfficeManager

***KEOS**
03-25-1995; 89.1 MHz FM; *Hrs Open:* 24; 100 w vert; 254 ft; N30 38 54 W96 23 23
Mailing Address: PO Box 78, College Station, TX 77841
Second Address: 202 E. Carson St., Bryan, TX 77801
(979) 779-5367; *Fax:* (979) 779-7259
www.keos.org
keos@keos.org
License: College Station, Brazos County, TX held by Brazos Educational Radio.
Nat'l Network: PRI
Population Served: 130,000; *Arbitron Metro Market:* Bryan-College Station, TX *Special Programming:* Folk 10 hrs, gospel 3 hrs, jazz 3 hrs, Jewish & Israeli 2 hrs wkly; *Hrs. of News Programming:* News progmg 25 hrs wkly *Target Audience:* General.

KNDE
08-08-1964; 95.1 MHz FM; 38 kw; 561 ft.; N30 41 15 W96 25 32
2700 Earl Rudder Fwy., Suite 5000, College Station, TX 77845
US
(979) 764-9595; *Fax:* (979) 695-1933
www.candy95.com
License: College Station, Brazos County, TX held by Bryan Broadcasting License Corp.
Group Owner: Bryan Broadcasting Corp.
Arbitron Metro Market: College Station, TX; *Format:* Contemporary Hits/Top 40
Tucker Young, Operations Manager
Ben Downs, Vice President and General Manager
Sam Jones, Sales Manager
Katy Dempsey, Promotions Director
Chris Dusterhoff, Chief Engineer
Alisa Dusterhoff, Office Manager

KWBC
09-21-1960; 1550 kHz AM; 1.5 kw-D, DA2; 0.045 kw-N, DA2; N30 37 54 W96 21 28
303 E. Washington, Suite A, Navasota, TX 77868 US

(936) 825-9007; *Fax:* (936) 825-1019
www.navasotanews.com
news@navasotanews.com
License: College Station, Brazos County, TX held by Bryan Broadcasting License Corp.
Group Owner: Bryan Broadcasting Corp.; (acq 7-31-2007; $275,000)
Arbitron Metro Market: Navasota, TX; *Format:* News, News/Talk, 86
Tucker Young, Operations Manager
Ben Downs, Vice President and General Manager
Michele McNew, General Sales Mgr
Katy Dempsey, Promotions Director
Tom Turner, News Director
Chris Dusterhoff, Chief Engineer
Alisa Dusterhoff, OfficeManager

KZNE
10-02-1922; 1150 kHz AM; *Hrs Open:* 24; 1 kw-D, DAN; 0.5 kw-N, DAN; N30 37 54 W96 21 27
2700 Earl Rudder Fwy., Suite 5000, College Station, TX 77845 US
(979) 695-9595
www.kzne.com
questions@bryanbroadcasting.com
License: College Station, Brazos County, TX held by Bryan Broadcasting License Corp.
Group Owner: Bryan Broadcasting Corp.; (acq 8-7-97; with co-located FM).
Arbitron Metro Market: Bryan-College Station, TX; *Format:* Sports, Talk *Special Programming:* Farm 10 hrs wkly; *Hrs. of News Programming:* news progmg 58 hrs wkly; *No. News Employees:* 3 *Target Audience:* 25-54.
Ben Downs, General Manager
Sam Jones, Sales Manager
Louie Belina, Programming Director
Bill Oliver, News Director
Kevin O'Connor, Sports Director

***KLGS**
01-01-2007; 89.9 MHz FM; 8.4 kw vert; 358 ft.; N30 28 35 W96 25 57 *Rebroadcasts:* Rebroadcasts WAFR(FM) Tupelo, MS 100%
P.O. Box 3206, Tupelo, MS 38803 US
(662) 844-8888; *Fax:* (662) 842-6791
www.afr.net
faq@afa.net
License: College Station, Brazos County, TX held by American Family Association.
Group Owner: American Family Radio; (acq 1-3-2006; $10 for CP)
Arbitron Metro Market: College Station, TX; *Format:* Christian
Tim Wildmon, President
Donald Wildmon, Founder
Buddy Smith, Sr VP
Ed Vitagliano, Exec VP
Randy Sharp, Director Of Special Projects
Meeke Addison, Director Of Communications
Abraham Hamilton III, General Counsel

Colorado City

KAUM
03-29-1983; 107.1 MHz FM; 3 kw; 157 ft.; N32 23 15 W100 53 33
P. O. Box 990, Colorado City, TX 79512 US
(325) 728-5224
www.kvmckaum.blogspot.com
kvmckaum@sbcglobal.net
License: Colorado City, Mitchell County, TX
Arbitron Metro Market: CO City, TX; *Format:* Country
Jim & Linda Baum, Owners

KVMC
06-16-1950; 1320 kHz AM; 1 kw-D, NDD; N32 23 15 W100 53 33
PO Box 990, Colorado City, TX 79512 US
(325) 728-5224
www.kvmckaum.blogspot.com
kvmckaum@sbcglobal.net
License: Colorado City, TX held by James G. Baum
Regional Network: Texas State Networks
Arbitron Metro Market: Colorado City, TX; *Format:* Country
Jim & Linda Baum, Owners

Columbus

KULM-FM
09-03-1973; 98.3 MHz FM; *Hrs Open:* 24; 6 kw; 253 ft.; N29 42 3 W96 34 24
P.O. Box 111, Columbus, TX 78934 US
(979) 732-5766
kulmradio.com
kulmradio@yahoo.com
License: Columbus, Colorado County, TX held by Roy E. Henderson.
Group Owner: Fort Bend Broadcasting Co.; (acq 5-16-2000; grpsl)
Nat'l Network: ABC; *Regional Network:* Texas State Networks
Arbitron Metro Market: Columbus, TX; *Format:* Country *Special Programming:* Polka 12 hrs wkly; *Hrs. of News Programming:* News progmg 12 hrs wkly; *Target Audience:* General.; *Adv. Rates:* 12.50; 12.50; 12.50;12.50

Comanche

KCOM
04-01-1962; 1550 kHz AM; *Hrs Open:* 24; 0.25 kw-D, ND1; 0.054 kw-N, ND1; N31 53 54 W98 35 14
105 North Sand St., Comanche, TX 76442 US
(325) 356-2558; *Fax:* (325) 356-3120
License: Comanche, TX held by CCR-Stephenville III LLC.
Group Owner: Cherry Creek Radio LLC; (acq 8-2-2005; $164,000).
Regional Network: Texas State Networks
Arbitron Metro Market: Comanche, TX; *Format:* Country, Gospel *Special Programming:* Gospel 5 hrs wkly; *Target Audience:* 35-64; Men & Women; *Adv. Rates:* 8; 8; 8; 8
Joseph Schwartz, President
Marcus Nettleton, General Manager
John Barnes, General Sales Mgr
Peggy Vineyard, Programming Director
Stan Cooper, Chief Engineer
Bill Cole, Disc Jockey

KYOX
03-01-1999; 94.3 MHz FM; 32 kw; 620 ft.; N31 54 51 W98 41 48
P.O. Box 289, Stephenville, TX 76401 US
(325) 356-3090; *Fax:* (325) 356-3120
www.kyoxfm.com
943theox@gmail.com
License: Comanche, Comanche County, TX held by CCR-Stephenville III LLC.
Group Owner: Cherry Creek Radio LLC; (acq 6-10-2004; grpsl).
Arbitron Metro Market: Comanche, TX; *Format:* Country; *Target Audience:* 35-64; men & women
Richard Niblett, General Manager
Pam Niblett, Programming Director
Justin McClure, Chief Engineer
Jerri Lynn Robinson, Music Director

Comfort

KMYO
02-26-1994; 95.1 MHz FM; *Hrs Open:* 24; 100 kw; 659 ft.; N29 38 3 W98 47 57.8
12451 Network Blvd., Suite 140, San Antonio, TX 78249 US
(210) 610-4300
www.univision.com
License: Comfort, Kendall County, TX held by Univision Radio License Corp.
Group Owner: Univision Radio; (acq 9-22-2003; grpsl)
Arbitron Metro Market: San Antonio, TX; *Format:* Urban Contemporary; *Hrs. of News Programming:* news progmg 4 hrs wkly; *No. News Employees:* 1; *Target Audience:* 25-54; average, middle income with small town & rurallifestyle
Chris Morris, General Manager
Barbara Carreon, Sales Manager
Homie Marco, Programming Director
Jennifer Gomez, Promotions Manager
Brett Huggins, Engineering Dir
Raul Faz, Digital Content Manager
Robert Morris, Digital ContentManager
Colleen Carnahan, Research Director
Sonia Trevenio, Business Manager

Commerce

***KETR**
04-07-1975; 88.9 MHz FM; *Hrs Open:* 24; 100 kw; 381 ft.; N33 14 17 W95 55 27
2600 S. Neal, P.O. Box 4504, Commerce, TX 75429 US
(903) 886-5848; *Fax:* (903) 886-5850
ketr.org
ketr@ketr.org
License: Commerce, Hunt County, TX held by Board of Regents Texas A&M University-Commerce.
Nat'l Network: NPR
Arbitron Metro Market: Commerce, TX; *Format:* Adult Contemp, Jazz, 60 *Special Programming:* Bluegrass 3 hrs wkly; *Hrs. of News Programming:* news progmg 7 hrs wkly; *No. News Employees:* 1 *Target Audience:* 21-66; general; *Adv. Rates:* 11; 10; 11; 10
Jerrod Knight, General Manager
Beverly Nanos, General Sales Mgr
Kevin Jeffries, News Director
Robert Goodwin, Chief Engineer
Deborah Smith, Administrative Assistant
Brad Kellar, News Reporter
Deborah Smith, Traffic Manager

***KYJC**
91.3 MHz FM; 0.35 kw horiz; 175 ft.; N33 15 37 W95 52 59
5617 Diamond Oaks South, Suite 200, Fort Worth, TX 76117 US
(817) 831-9130; *Fax:* (888) 781-6007
www.kdkr.org
License: Commerce, Hunt County, TX held by Penfold Communications, Inc.
Group Owner: Penfold Communications, Inc.
Arbitron Metro Market: Kasilof, AK; *Format:* Christian, Gospel, 86

Conroe

***KAFR**
10-01-1998; 88.3 MHz FM; 100 kw vert; 443 ft.; N30 27 52 W95 30 20
P.O. Box 3206, Tupelo, MS 38803 US
(662) 844-8888; *Fax:* (662) 842-6791
www.afr.net
faq@afa.net
License: Conroe, Montgomery County, TX held by American Family Association.
Group Owner: American Family Radio
Arbitron Metro Market: Tupelo, MS; *Format:* Christian, Religious
Tim Wildmon, President
Donald Wildmon, Founder
Buddy Smith, Sr VP
Ed Vitagliano, Exec VP
Randy Sharp, Director Of Special Projects
Meeke Addison, Director Of Communications
Abraham Hamilton III, General Counsel & Public Policy

KYOK
04-13-1981; 1140 kHz AM; 5 kW; N30 20 40 W95 27 32
15307 Falcon Ridge Dr, Humble, TX 77396 USA
(281) 441-3665
License: Conroe, TX held by Martin Broadcasting Inc.
Group Owner: Martin Broadcasting Inc.; (acq 2-10-92; $175,000;
Arbitron Metro Market: Houston, TX; *Format:* Gospel; *Target Audience:* 24-55.

KJOZ
04-16-1951; 880 kHz AM; 10 kw-D, 1 kw-N, DA-2; N30 17 38 W95 25 55
3000 Bering Dr., Houston, TX 77057
(713) 271-7888; *Fax:* (713) 271-9333
www.littlesaigonradio.com
License: Conroe, Montgomery County, TX held by Daij Media LLC
Group Owner: Daij Media LLC; (acq 4-26-2012; $1 million)
Arbitron Metro Market: Houston-Galveston
Winter Horton, CEO/COO
Wynette Ortiz, General Sales Mgr

Converse

KTMR
07-28-1980; 1130 kHz AM
Good News Brdct. of Tx, 2702 Pine Street, Laredo, TX 78046 US
(713) 868-5559; *Fax:* (713) 868-9631
www.bizradio.com
docarango@houston.rr.com
License: Converse, TX held by SIGA Broadcasting Corp.
Group Owner: SIGA Broadcasting Corp.; (acq 5-4-99; $333,750)
Arbitron Metro Market: San Antonio, TX; *Format:* Talk
Gabriel Arango, General Manager

Copperas Cove

KSSM
11-21-1977; 103.1 MHz FM; *Hrs Open:* 24; 8.6 kw; 558 ft.; N31 5 5 W97 57 7
Post Office Box 607, Copperas Cove, TX 76522 US
(254) 773-5252; *Fax:* (254) 773-0115
www.1031kissfm.com
License: Copperas Cove, Coryell County, TX held by Townsquare Media Killeen-Temple License LLC
Group Owner: Townsquare Media; (acq 2-2-00)
Nat'l Reps: Interep
Arbitron Metro Market: Killeen-Temple, TX; *Format:* Adult Contemp *Special Programming:* Gospel; *Hrs. of News Programming:* News progmg 3 hrs wkly; *Target Audience:* 25-54.
Trey The Choklit, Brand Manager
Laura Wiederhold, Director Of Sales

Kelsey Kilter, Digital Sales Manager
Jason Eisengerg, Digital Managing Editor

Corpus Christi

***KBNJ**
01-01-1985; 91.7 MHz FM; *Hrs Open:* 24; 6.1 kw; 554 ft.; N27 45 23 W97 36 25
Box 3765, McAllen, TX 78502 US
(361) 855-0975; *Fax:* (361) 855-0977
www.kbnj.org
kbnj@lwrn.org
License: Corpus Christi, Nueces County, TX held by World Radio Network Inc.
Group Owner: World Radio Network Inc.; acq 6-5-84; $36,000;
Nat'l Network: Moody; USA
Arbitron Metro Market: Corpus Christi, TX; *Format:* Religious; *Hrs. of News Programming:* News progmg 7 hrs wkly; *Target Audience:* General.
Joe Fahl, General Manager
Jimmy Stinson, Chief Engineer

KBSO
01-01-1992; 94.7 MHz FM; 25 kw; 285 ft.; N27 49 50 W97 32 34
107 Lost Creek, Portland, TX 78374 US
(361) 289-0999
davilabroadcasti@bizstx.rr.com
License: Corpus Christi, Nueces County, TX held by Reina Broadcasting Inc.
Arbitron Metro Market: Corpus Christi, TX; *Format:* Tejano
Manuel Davila Jr., General Manager

KCCT
06-01-1954; 1150 kHz AM; *Hrs Open:* 24; 1 kw-D, DA2; 0.5 kw-N, DA2; N27 48 1 W97 28 44
P.O. Box 5278, Corpus Christi, TX 78465 US
(361) 289-0999; *Fax:* (361) 289-0810
License: Corpus Christi, TX held by Radio KCCT Inc.
Arbitron Metro Market: Corpus Christi, TX; *Format:* Talk
Manuel Davila Jr., President
George Sanders, Chief Engineer

KCTA
10-24-1959; 1030 kHz AM; *Hrs Open:* Sunrise-sunset
1602 S. Brownlee, Corpus Christi, TX 78403 US
(361) 882-7711; *Fax:* (361) 882-3038
www.kctaradio.com
kcta@usawide.net
License: Corpus Christi, TX held by Broadcasting Corp. of the Southwest.
Nat'l Network: USA
Arbitron Metro Market: Corpus Christi, TX; *Format:* Religious
Special Programming: Sp 6 hrs wkly; *Target Audience:* 35 plus.; *Adv. Rates:* 12; 12; 12; 12
Bill York, President
David Freymiller, Operations Dir
Russell Vaughan, Chief Engineer

***KEDT-FM**
03-02-1982; 90.3 MHz FM; *Hrs Open:* 24; 100 kw; 801 ft.; N27 39 12 W97 33 55
4455 S Padre Island #38, Corpus Christi, TX 78411 US
(361) 855-2213; *Fax:* (361) 855-3877
www.kedt.org
License: Corpus Christi, Nueces County, TX held by South Texas Public Broadcasting System Inc.
Nat'l Network: NPR
Arbitron Metro Market: Corpus Christi, TX; *Format:* Jazz, News
Special Programming: Sp 4 hrs wkly; *Hrs. of News Programming:* news progmg 37 hrs wkly; *No. News Employees:* 1; *Target Audience:* General.
Don Dunlap, President
Don Dunlap, General Manager
Bob Scott, Programming Director
Shane Barker, News Director
Bob Scott, Engineering Dir
Myra Lombardo, Vice President

KEYS
03-01-1941; 1440 kHz AM; *Hrs Open:* 24; 1 kW; N27 47 2 W97 27 29
2117 Leopard St, Corpus Christi, TX 78408 USA
(361) 883-3516; *Fax:* (361) 882-9767
keys1440.com
License: Corpus Christi, TX held by Malkan Interactive Communications
Group Owner: Malkan Interactive Communications; (acq 1965)
Nat'l Network: ESPN Radio; *Regional Network:* Texas State Networks; *Nat'l Reps:* Katz Radio; *Wire Services:* Accu-Weather
Arbitron Metro Market: Corpus Christi, TX; *Format:* News, News/Talk, 84, Talk; *No. News Employees:* 2; *Target Audience:* 25+; *Adv. Rates:* $35

Rodney Brown, General Manager

***KKLM**
03-11-1991; 88.7 MHz FM; *Hrs Open:* 24; 8 kw; 866 ft.; N27 44 29 W97 36 9 *Rebroadcasts:* Rebroadcasts KLVR(FM) Middletown, CA 100%
P.O. Box 1177, Corpus Christi, TX 78403 US
(916) 251-1600 (860) 434-8400; *Fax:* (916) 251-1650
www.klove.com
info@klove.com
License: Corpus Christi, Nueces County, TX held by Educational Media Foundation.
Group Owner: EMF Broadcasting; (acq 6-5-2002; $500,000)
Nat'l Network: K-Love
Arbitron Metro Market: Corpus Christi, TX; *Format:* Christian; *Hrs. of News Programming:* News progmg 10 hrs wkly; *Target Audience:* 35 plus.
Darrell Chambliss, Chairman
Mike Novak, CEO/COO
Mike Novak, President

KLTG
09-01-1967; 96.5 MHz FM; 97 kw; 955 ft.; N27 44 28 W97 36 8
1733 S. Brownlee Blvd., Corpus Christi, TX 78404 US
(361) 883-1600; *Fax:* (361) 888-5685
www.thebeach965fm.com
License: Corpus Christi, Nueces County, TX held by Tejas Broadcasting Ltd. LLP.
Group Owner: Tejas Broadcasting Ltd. LLP; (acq 11-15-2004; grpsl).
Arbitron Metro Market: Corpus Christi, TX; *Format:* Adult Contemp; *Target Audience:* 25-54.
Gloria Apolinario, Programming Director

KMXR
01-01-1970; 93.9 MHz FM; *Hrs Open:* 24; 100 kw; 932 ft.; N27 45 7 W97 38 17
501 Tupper Lane, Corpus Christi, TX 78417 US
(361) 289-0111; *Fax:* (361) 289-5035
www.big939.com
License: Corpus Christi, Nueces County, TX held by Capstar TX LLC
Group Owner: iHeartMedia; (acq 8-30-00; grpsl).
Nat'l Network: AP Radio
Arbitron Metro Market: Corpus Christi, TX; *Format:* Oldies; *Hrs. of News Programming:* news progmg 5 hrs wkly; *No. News Employees:* 1; *Target Audience:* 25-54.
John Richards, General Manager
Chris Aldrich, General Sales Mgr
Jeffery DeWitt, Programming Director

KKTX
01-01-2002; 1360 kHz AM; *Hrs Open:* 24; 1 kw-U, ND1; N27 48 1 W97 27 41
501 Tupper Lane, Corpus Christi, TX 78417 US
(361) 289-0111; *Fax:* (361) 289-5024
www.1360kktx.com
License: Corpus Christi, TX held by Capstar TX LLC
Group Owner: iHeartMedia
Nat'l Network: ABC
Arbitron Metro Market: Corpus Christi, TX; *Format:* News, News/Talk, 86; *Target Audience:* 2-18; children
Chris Aldrich, Director of Sales
Frank Edwards, Programming Director

KRYS-FM
12-05-1982; 99.1 MHz FM; *Hrs Open:* 24; 100 kw; 932 ft.; N27 45 7 W97 38 17
501 Tupper Lane, Corpus Christi, TX 78418 US
(361) 289-0111; *Fax:* (361) 289-5024
www.k99country.com
k99@clearchannel.com
License: Corpus Christi, Nueces County, TX held by Capstar TX LLC
Group Owner: iHeartMedia; (acq 8-30-00; grpsl).
Nat'l Network: ABC
Arbitron Metro Market: Corpus Christi, TX; *Format:* Country; *No. News Employees:* 1; *Target Audience:* 25-54.
Chris Aldrich, Director of Sales
Frank Edwards, Programming Director

KSIX
09-01-1947; 1230 kHz AM; *Hrs Open:* 24
PO Box Tv-10, 301 Artesian, Corpus Christi, TX 78403 US
(361) 882-5749; *Fax:* (361) 884-1240
www.espn1230ksix.com
License: Corpus Christi, TX held by Withers Family Texas Holding LP
Nat'l Network: ESPN Radio
Arbitron Metro Market: Corpus Christi, TX; *Format:* Sports
Jim Withers, General Manager
Scott Howe, General Sales Mgr

Bill Doerner, Programming Director
Valerie Smith, News Director

KUNO
05-01-1950; 1400 kHz AM; *Hrs Open:* 24; 1 kw-D, ND1; 1 kw-N, ND1; N27 45 36 W97 26 14
501 Tupper Lane, Corpus Christi, TX 78417 US
(361) 289-0111; *Fax:* (361) 289-5035
www.1400kuno.com
License: Corpus Christi, TX held by Capstar TX LLC
Group Owner: iHeartMedia; (acq 8-30-00; grpsl)
Arbitron Metro Market: Corpus Christi, TX; *Format:* Spanish; *Hrs. of News Programming:* News progmg 17 hrs wkly; *Target Audience:* 25-64.
John Richards Fritz, President
Chris Aldrich, Senior Vice President of Sales

KZFM
12-07-1964; 95.5 MHz FM; *Hrs Open:* 24; 100 kW; 882 ft.; N27 39 33 W97 34 12
2117 Leopard St, Corpus Christi, TX 78408 USA
(361) 883-3516; *Fax:* (361) 882-9767
hotz95.com
License: Corpus Christi, Nueces County, TX held by Malkan Interactive Communications
Group Owner: Malkan Interactive Communications; (acq 1976).
Nat'l Reps: Katz Radio
Arbitron Metro Market: Corpus Christi, TX; *Format:* Contemporary Hits/Top 40, Urban Contemporary; *Target Audience:* 18-34; *Adv. Rates:* 68; 68; 68; 68
Gino Flores, Operations Manager
Rodney Brown, General Manager
Gino Flores, Programming Director
Daniel Luna, Promotions Director
Erika Navarijo, Music Director

Corrigan

KYTM
99.3 MHz FM; kw
US
License: Corrigan, Polk County, TX held by Tammy L. Pearce.
Arbitron Metro Market: Corrigan, TX
Tammy Pearce, General Manager

Corsicana

KAND
05-17-1937; 1340 kHz AM; *Hrs Open:* 24; 1 kw-U, ND1; N32 6 53 W96 27 47
701 South Main Street, Suite 1340, Corsicana, TX 75110 US
(903) 874-7421; *Fax:* (903) 874-0789
www.kandradio.com
mail@kandradio.com
License: Corsicana, TX held by Yates Communications LLC
Regional Network: Texas State Networks
Arbitron Metro Market: Corsicana, TX; *Format:* Talk; *Hrs. of News Programming:* news progmg 25 hrs wkly; *No. News Employees:* 1; *Target Audience:* General.
Kevin Ward, Sales
Rusty Hitt, Sports
Brett Eberhart, Traffic/Billing

Crane

KMMZ
01-01-1995; 101.3 MHz FM; *Hrs Open:* 24; 100 kw; 486 ft.; N31 41 2 W102 19 13
Mailing Address: 620 N. Grant, Ste 1013, Odessa, TX 79761 US
Second Address: 12200 W. I-20 E., Crane, TX 79711
(432) 563-2266; *Fax:* (432) 563-2288
License: Crane, Crane County, TX held by Don L. Cook.
Arbitron Metro Market: Odessa, TX; *Format:* Contemporary Hits/Top 40; *Target Audience:* 25-54.; *Adv. Rates:* 15; 15; 15; 9
Don Cook, General Manager

KXOI
12-01-1959; 810 kHz AM; *Hrs Open:* 6 AM-midnight; 1 kw-D, DA1; 0.5 kw-N, DA1; N31 28 39 W102 20 24
P.O. Box 2344, Odessa, TX 79760 US
(432) 333-5061; *Fax:* (432) 333-6067
License: Crane, TX held by Hispanic Outreach Ministries Inc.
Target Audience: General.
Rev. Pedro Emiliano, President
Eli Emiliano, General Manager
Don Cook, Chief Engineer

Crockett

KBPC
11-15-1982; 93.5 MHz FM; *Hrs Open:* 24; 50 kw; 479 ft.; N31 20 3 W95 47 13

US
(800) 460-5877
www.kbpcfm.com
news@kbpcfm.com
License: Crockett, Houston County, TX held by KBPC LLC
Group Owner: Weston Entertainment L.P.; (acq 10-4-2005; $1.43 million)
Arbitron Metro Market: Crockett, TX; *Format:* Country *Special Programming:* Gospel 6 hrs wkly; *No. News Employees:* 7; *Target Audience:* 25-54.
Lori Shannon, Account Executive

KIVY
11-11-1949; 1290 kHz AM; *Hrs Open:* 24; 2.5 kw-D, ND1; 0.175 kw-N, ND1; N31 18 20 W95 27 6
102 S. Fifth St., Crockett, TX 75835 US
(936) 544-2171; *Fax:* (936) 544-4891
www.kivy.com
kivy@kivy.com
License: Crockett, TX held by Leon Hunt
Group Owner: Star Radio Network; (acq 9-19-2002; $1.1 million with co-located FM)
Nat'l Network: ABC; *Regional Network:* Texas State Networks
Format: Oldies; *Target Audience:* General.; *Adv. Rates:* 18; 16; 16; 12
Leon Hunt, President
Vince Astramovich, Programming Director

KIVY-FM
01-01-1982; 92.7 MHz FM; *Hrs Open:* 24; 50 kw; 492 ft.; N31 18 20 W95 27 6
102 S. Fifth St., Crockett, TX 75835 US
(936) 544-2171; *Fax:* (936) 544-4891
www.kivy.com
kivy@kivy.com
License: Crockett, Houston County, TX held by Leon Hunt.
Group Owner: Star Radio Network
Nat'l Network: ABC; *Regional Network:* Texas State Networks
Format: Country
Leon Hunt, President

*KCKT
02-01-2003; 88.5 MHz FM; 0.25 kw; 161 ft.; N31 19 37 W95 28 26
P.O. Box 3206, Tupelo, MS 38803 US
(662) 844-8888; *Fax:* (662) 842-6791
www.afr.net
faq@afa.net
License: Crockett, Houston County, TX held by American Family Association.
Group Owner: American Family Radio; (acq 1-17-01).
Arbitron Metro Market: Tupelo, MS; *Format:* Christian
Tim Wildmon, President
Donald Wildmon, Founder
Buddy Smith, Sr VP
Ed Vitagliano, Exec VP
Randy Sharp, Director Of Special Projects
Meeke Addison, Director Of Communications
Abraham Hamilton III, General Counsel

Crystal Beach

KSTB
01-01-1996; 101.5 MHz FM; *Hrs Open:* 24; 6 kw; 184 ft.; N29 30 7 W94 31 15
8229 Maryland Avenue, St. Louis, MO 63105 US
(409) 833-9421; *Fax:* (409) 833-9296
www.kayd.com
License: Crystal Beach, Galveston County, TX held by Cumulus Licensing Corp.
Group Owner: Cumulus Media Inc.; (acq 5-20-02; $2.5 million).
Nat'l Reps: Roslin
Arbitron Metro Market: Beaumont, TX; *Format:* Country; *Hrs. of News Programming:* news progmg 12 hrs wkly; *No. News Employees:* 2; *Target Audience:* 18-49.
Jim West, Operations Dir
Rick Prusater, General Manager
Liz Ferguson, News Director
Greg Davis, Chief Engineer

Crystal City

KHER
09-05-1985; 94.3 MHz FM; 3 kw; 135 ft.; N28 39 57 W99 48 58
Rt. 1 Box 168, Heritage Farms, Eagle Pass, TX 78852 US
(210) 374-2803
kherfm@yahoo.com
License: Crystal City, Zavala County, TX held by Sylvia Mijares.
Regional Network: Texas State Networks
Format: News, News/Talk, 86 *Special Programming:* Relg 2 hrs wkly; *Target Audience:* 18-54; 90% Hispanic, 10% non-minority
Sylvia Mijares, President
Rudy Gomez, General Sales Mgr
Marie Martinez, News Director
Charlie Schmele, Chief Engineer
Becky Reyes, Traffic Manager

Cuero

*KTLZ
01-01-2003; 89.9 MHz FM; *Hrs Open:* 24; 5 kw; 243 ft.; N29 2 23 W97 19 24
2702 Pine St., Laredo, TX 78046 US
(208) 733-3551; *Fax:* (208) 734-0674
www.edgewaterbroadcasting.com
License: Cuero, DeWitt County, TX held by Radio Assist Ministry Inc.
Arbitron Metro Market: Cuero, TX; *Format:* Christian, Spanish
Ben Mccarron, Chief Operating Engineer
Clark Parrish, President & Technical Director
Robert L. Jackson, Head of Programming & Operations
Jim Long, General Manager
Steve Atkin, Promotions Manager
Diana Atkin, Vice President
EarlWilliamson, Secretary / Treasurer
John Devine, Director
Dennis Clounch, Director

Cypress

KYND
12-01-1991; 1520 kHz AM; 2.6 kw-C, DAD; 3 kw-D, DAD; N30 0 37 W95 41 40 *Rebroadcasts:* Rebroadcasts KJOJ(AM) Conroe 100%
740 Voss Road, Houston, TX 77024 US
(281) 373-1520; *Fax:* (713) 271-9333
www.littlesaigonradio.com
radio@littlesaigonradio.com
License: Cypress, TX held by Matthew Provenzano.
Arbitron Metro Market: Houston TX; *Format:* Ethnic, Vietnamese; *Target Audience:* General.
Matt Provenzano, CEO

Daingerfield

KNGR
08-01-1966; 1560 kHz AM; *Hrs Open:* 24
Box 497931, Garland, TX 75049 US
(903) 645-4325; *Fax:* (903) 645-4357
www.kingcountry.org
License: Daingerfield, TX held by Network Communications Co.
Arbitron Metro Market: Tyler-Longview, TX; *Format:* Country; *Hrs. of News Programming:* News progmg 3 hrs wkly; *Adv. Rates:* 10; 10; 10; 10
Bob Wilson, General Manager
Glory Wilson, Programming Director

Dalhart

KXIT
01-01-1948; 1240 kHz AM; *Hrs Open:* 24; 1 kw-U, ND1; N36 5 45 W102 30 38
P. O. Box 1350, Dalhart, TX 79022 US
(806) 249-4747
www.kxit.com
License: Dalhart, TX held by Dalhart Radio Inc.
Regional Network: Texas State Networks
Format: Country *Special Programming:* Farm 7 hrs wkly
George Chambers, President
Jusin Bliss, Programming Director

KBEX
01-01-1962; 96.3 MHz FM; *Hrs Open:* 24; 100 kw; Ant 472 ft; N35 53 46 W102 23 03
Box 1359, Hwy. 385 N., Dalhart, TX 79022
(806) 249-4747
License: Dalhart, Dallam County, TX held by Radio Dalhart
Population Served: 12,500
George Chambers, General Manager

*KTDA
01-01-2009; 91.7 MHz FM; 0.83 kw; 128 ft.; N36 3 20 W102 30 34 *Rebroadcasts:* Rebroadcasts WAFR(FM) Tupelo, MS 100%
P.O. Box 3206, Tupelo, MS 38803 US
(662) 844-8888; *Fax:* (662) 842-6791
www.afr.net
faq@afa.net
License: Dalhart, Dallam County, TX held by American Family Association.
Group Owner: American Family Radio; (acq 6-9-2006)
Nat'l Network: American Family Radio
Arbitron Metro Market: Dalhart, TX; *Format:* Christian
Tim Wildmon, President
Donald Wildmon, Founder
Buddy Smith, Senior VP
Ed Vitagliano, Exec VP
Randy Sharp, Director Of Special Projects
Meeke Addison, Director Of Communications
Abraham Hamilton III, General Counsel

Dallas

KBFB
01-01-1965; 97.9 MHz FM; 99 kw; 1883 ft.; N32 35 2 W96 57 48
13760 Noel Rd., Suite 1100, Dallas, TX 75240 US
(972) 331-5400; *Fax:* (972) 331-5560
www.thebeatdfw.com
License: Dallas, Dallas County, TX held by Radio One Licenses LLC.
Group Owner: Radio One Inc.; (acq 2000; grpsl)..
Nat'l Reps: CBS Radio
Arbitron Metro Market: Dallas, TX; *Format:* Urban Contemporary; *Target Audience:* 25-50.
Mark McCray, Operations Mgr/Program Dir.

*KCBI
05-19-1976; 90.9 MHz FM; *Hrs Open:* 24; 98 kw; 1509 ft.; N32 35 22 W96 58 10
Mailing Address: 750 N. St. Paul Street, Suite 1050, Dallas, TX 75201 US
Second Address: PO Box 130870, Dallas, TX 75313
(469) 801-7000
www.kcbi.org
License: Dallas, Dallas County, TX held by Criswell College.
Group Owner: Criswell Communications
Nat'l Network: AP Radio
Arbitron Metro Market: Dallas, TX; *Format:* Christian, Religious; *Hrs. of News Programming:* news progmg 4 hrs wkly; *No. News Employees:* 4; *Target Audience:* 35-54; Christian families
Matt Austin, General Manager
Joel Burke, Programming Director
Sharon Geiger, Assistant GM/Outreach Director

KDMX
01-01-1965; 102.9 MHz FM; *Hrs Open:* 24; 100 kw; 1,591 ft.; N32 34 54 W96 58 32
14001 N. Dallas Pkwy., Suite 300, Dallas, TX 75240 US
(214) 866-8000
www.1029now.com
jayshannon@iheartmedia.com
License: Dallas, Dallas County, TX held by Citicasters Licenses Inc.
Group Owner: iHeartMedia; (acq 5-4-99; grpsl)
Arbitron Metro Market: Dallas-Fort Worth, TX; *Format:* Adult Contemp; *Hrs. of News Programming:* News progmg 3 hrs wkly; *Target Audience:* 25-49; upper income females
Jay Shannon, Programming Director
Anna De Haro, Public Affairs Director

KBXD
01-01-1952; 1480 kHz AM; *Hrs Open:* 24; 5 kw-D, 1.9 kw-N, DA-2; N32 39 42 W96 39 20
2221 E. Lamar Blvd., Suite 300, Arlington, TX 75219
(817) 695-0878; *Fax:* (817) 695-3505
License: Dallas, Dallas County, TX held by ACM JCE IV B LLC.
Group Owner: ACM JCE IV B LLC.
Arbitron Metro Market: Dallas-Fort Worth; *Format:* Gospel
Mark Jorgenson, President

*KERA
07-11-1974; 90.1 MHz FM; 100 kw; 1273 ft.; N32 34 43 W96 57 12
3000 Harry Hines Blvd., Dallas, TX 75201 US
(214) 871-1390; *Fax:* (214) 740-9369
www.kera.org
kerafm@kera.org
License: Dallas, Dallas County, TX held by North Texas Public Broadcasting.
Nat'l Network: NPR; PRI; *Wire Services:* AP
Arbitron Metro Market: Dallas-Fort Worth; *Format:* News, News/Talk, 86; *Hrs. of News Programming:* news progmg 80 hrs wkly; *No. News Employees:* 5; *Target Audience:* 35-54; general
Barger Tygart, Chairman
Kevin Martin, COO
Jeff Luchsinger, Station Manager
Patricia Lyons, General Sales Mgr

KGGR
06-08-1947; 1040 kHz AM
3270 Blazer Pkwy, Suite 101, Lexington, KY 40509 US
(972) 572-5447; *Fax:* (214) 330-6133
www.kggram.com
License: Dallas, TX held by MBC of Texas-KGGR Inc.

Group Owner: Mortenson Broadcasting Co.; (acq 5-1-96; $1.15 million)
Nat'l Network: American Urban
Arbitron Metro Market: Dallas-Fort Worth; *Format:* Black, Talk, 74 *Special Programming:* Scripture 5 hrs wkly; *Target Audience:* 18 plus.
Ann Arnold, General Manager
Christie Wafer, General Sales Mgr

KKDA
06-08-1947; 104.5 MHz FM; *Hrs Open:* 24; 99 kw; 1667 ft.; N32 35 19 W96 58 05
621 NW 6th St., Grand Prairie, TX 59703 USA
(972) 647-5000
www.myk104.com
License: Dallas, TX held by Service Broadcasting Group LLC.
Group Owner: Service Broadcasting Group, LLC
Arbitron Metro Market: Dallas, TX; *Format:* Urban Contemporary
Frances Davis, Dir. of Promotions

KLIF
06-21-1922; 570 kHz AM; *Hrs Open:* 24; 5 kw-D, 5 kw-N.; N32 56 40 W96 59 25
3090 Olive Street, West Victory Plaza #400, Dallas, TX 75219 US
(214) 526-2400; *Fax:* (214) 520-4343
www.klif.com
klif@klif.com
License: Dallas, TX held by KLIF LICO, Inc.
Group Owner: Cumulus Media Inc.; (acq 12-15-89).
Nat'l Network: Fox News Radio
Arbitron Metro Market: Dallas, TX; *Format:* News; *No. News Employees:* 1
Tyler Cox, Programming Director
Victoria Albrecht, Promotions Manager
Dan Bennett, VP/Market Manager

KFXR
01-01-1947; 1190 kHz AM; *Hrs Open:* 24; 50 kw-D, DA2; 5 kw-N, DA2; N32 47 10 W96 57 0; N32 53 57 W96 24 47
14001 North Dallas Pkwy., Suite 300, Dallas, TX 75240 US
(214) 866-8000
www.1190talkradio.com
License: Dallas, TX held by Capstar TX LLC
Group Owner: iHeartMedia; (acq 3-27-2001; $16 million)
Nat'l Network: CNN Radio
Arbitron Metro Market: Dallas, TX; *Format:* News, News/Talk, 86; *Target Audience:* 25-54; general
Charlie Wilkinson, Market President

KLUV
06-07-2006; 98.7 MHz FM; *Hrs Open:* 24; 99 kW; 1486 ft.; N32 35 19 W96 58 5
TX USA
(214) 525-7000
www.kluv.com
License: Dallas, Dallas County, TX held by CBS Radio Texas Inc.
Group Owner: CBS Radio; (acq 9-17-94; $51 million)
Arbitron Metro Market: Dallas-Fort Worth Metroplex; *Format:* Oldies; *No. News Employees:* 2; *Target Audience:* 35-54

***KNON**
08-03-1983; 89.3 MHz FM; *Hrs Open:* 24; 55 kw; 850 ft.; N32 35 24 W96 58 21
5353 Maple Avenue, Suite 200, Dallas, TX 75235 US
(214) 828-9500
www.knon.org
keving@knon.org
License: Dallas, Dallas County, TX held by Agape Broadcasting Foundation Inc.
Arbitron Metro Market: Dallas, TX; *Format:* Variety/Diverse; *Target Audience:* General.
Kevin Gilhooly, President
Dave Chaos, S
Joe Ellison, Production/Traffic Manager
Christian Lee, Music Tracking/Pledge Coordinator

KJKK
06-30-2004; 100.3 MHz FM; 97 kW; 1689 ft.; N32 35 2 W96 57 48
4131 N Central Expwy, Suite 1000, Dallas, TX 75204 USA
(214) 525-7000
www.jackontheweb.com
License: Dallas, Dallas County, TX held by CBS Radio Texas Inc.
Group Owner: CBS Radio; (acq 11-13-98; grpsl)
Nat'l Network: ABC; *Nat'l Reps:* CBS Radio
Arbitron Metro Market: Dallas-Fort Worth Metroplex; *Format:* Adult Contemp; *Target Audience:* 18-49

Kevin Cassidy, General Sales Mgr
Jay Michaels, Programming Director
Jacob Springer, Brand Advocate
John Lindner, Digital Sales Manager
Mark Sanders, National Sales Manager
Jana Schunck, HR Director

KRLD
10-01-1926; 1080 kHz AM; *Hrs Open:* 24; 50 kW; N32 53 25 W96 38 44
TX USA
www.krld.com
License: Dallas, TX held by CBS Radio Texas Inc.
Group Owner: CBS Radio
Regional Network: Texas State Networks; *Nat'l Reps:* CBS Radio
Arbitron Metro Market: Dallas-Fort Worth Metroplex; *Format:* News *Special Programming:* Texas Rangers baseball; *Hrs. of News Programming:* news progmg 119 hrs wkly; *No. News Employees:* 35 *Target Audience:* 25-54

KTCK
01-01-1920; 1310 kHz AM; *Hrs Open:* 24; 25 kw-D, 5 kw-N
3090 Olive St., West Victory Plaza #400, Dallas, TX 75219 US
(214) 526-2400; *Fax:* (214) 525-2525
www.theticket.com
dan.bennett@cumulus.com
License: Dallas, TX held by Radio License Holding SRC, LLC
Group Owner: Cumulus Media Inc.; (acq 1996; $14 million)
Arbitron Metro Market: Dallas-Fort Worth; *Format:* Sports, Talk; *Target Audience:* 25-54; men & sport enthusiasts
Jeff Catlin, Operations Dir/Program Dir
Dan Bennett, Market Manager
Alec Drake, General Sales Mgr
Kristi Crisp, Promotions Director
Tom Dailey, Business Manager
James Roman, Local Sales Manager
Janet DuPree, Digital SalesManager
Allen Free, Digital Director
Kimberly Jolly, Traffic Manager

KRLD-FM
12-12-2008; 105.3 MHz FM; *Hrs Open:* 24; 97 kW; 1689 ft.; N32 35 2 W96 57 48
4131 North Central Expressway, Suite 100, Dallas, TX 75204 USA
(214) 525-7000
www.1053thefan.com
License: Dallas, Dallas County, TX held by CBS Radio Texas Inc.
Group Owner: CBS Radio; (acq 11-13-98; grpsl)
Nat'l Network: FOX Sports; *Nat'l Reps:* CBS Radio
Arbitron Metro Market: Dallas, TX; *Format:* Sports; *Target Audience:* 18-49; general

KZPS
04-01-1948; 92.5 MHz FM; *Hrs Open:* 24; 99 kw; 1667 ft.; N32 35 19 W96 58 5
14001 N. Dallas Pkwy, Suite 300, Dallas, TX 75240 US
(214) 866-8000
www.lonestar925.com
dondavis@iheartmedia.com
License: Dallas, Dallas County, TX held by AMFM Texas Licenses LLC
Group Owner: iHeartMedia; (acq 8-30-2000; grpsl)
Arbitron Metro Market: Dallas, TX; *Format:* Classic Rock; *No. News Employees:* 1; *Target Audience:* 25-44; upscale young adults
Don Davis, Programming Director
Anna De Haro, Public Affairs Director

WRR
01-01-1948; 101.1 MHz FM; *Hrs Open:* 24; 98 kw; 1667 ft.; N32 35 19 W96 58 5
Mailing Address: 1516 First Avenue, Dallas, TX 75210 US
Second Address: PO Box 159001, Dallas, TX 75315-9001
(214) 670-8888; *Fax:* (214) 670-8394
www.wrr101.com
info@wrr101.com
License: Dallas, Dallas County, TX held by City of Dallas.
Nat'l Network: AP Network News; *Nat'l Reps:* McGavren Guild
Arbitron Metro Market: Dallas-Fort Worth; *Format:* Classical
Special Programming: Children 2 hrs wkly; *No. News Employees:* 22; *Target Audience:* 25-54; all ages
D. Fisher, Station Manager

Decatur

***KDKR**
01-01-1998; 91.3 MHz FM; *Hrs Open:* 24; 40 kw horiz, 100 kw vert; 1785 ft.; N33 23 12 W97 33 57
Mailing Address: P.O. Box 890820, Temecula, CA 99258 US
Second Address: 5617 Diamond Oaks Dr South, Suite 200, Forth Worth, TX 76117
(817) 831-9130; *Fax:* (888) 781-6007
www.kdkr.org
jerry@kdkr.org
License: Decatur, Wise County, TX held by Penfold Communications, Inc.
Group Owner: Penfold Communications, Inc.; acq 7-12-2000).
Arbitron Metro Market: Dallas-Fort Worth; *Format:* Christian, Religious

KRNB
01-01-1996; 105.7 MHz FM; *Hrs Open:* 24; 93 kw; 492 ft; N32 11 11 W98 17 26
621 NW 6th St., Grand Prairie, TX 59703 USA
(972) 647-5000
www.krnb.com
License: Decatur, TX held by Service Broadcasting Group LLC.
Group Owner: Service Broadcasting Group, LLC
Population Served: 75,000; *Arbitron Metro Market:* Dallas-Fort Wor; *Format:* Urban Contemporary
Frances Davis, Dir. of Promotions

Deer Park

KAMA-FM
08-08-1968; 104.9 MHz FM; 10.5 kw; 984 ft.; N29 45 26 W95 20 19
5100 S.W. Fwy., Houston, TX 77056 US
(713) 965-2400; *Fax:* (713) 965-2401
www.univision.com
License: Deer Park, Harris County, TX held by Tichenor License Corp.
Group Owner: Univision Radio; (acq 9-22-2003; grpsl)
Arbitron Metro Market: Houston-Galveston, TX; *Format:* Spanish
David Loving, General Manager
Nestor Enriquez, Client Services Director

Del Mar Hills

KVOZ
04-15-1952; 890 kHz AM; 10 kw-D, DAN; 1 kw-N, DAN; N27 32 57 W99 22 21
P.O. Box 252, McAllen, TX 78502 US
(956) 781-5528(956) 686-6382; *Fax:* (956) 686-2999
License: Del Mar Hills, TX held by Consolidated Radio Inc.
Arbitron Metro Market: McAllen, TX; *Format:* Gospel; *Target Audience:* 18 plus.
Pete Guzman, Operations Dir
Paulino Bernal, General Manager
Eloy Bernal, Station Manager

Del Rio

KDLK-FM
08-15-1966; 94.1 MHz FM; *Hrs Open:* 24; 18 kw; Ant 310 ft; N29 25 45 W100 54 17
Box 1489, Del Rio, TX 78840
(830) 775-9583; *Fax:* (830) 774-4009
www.kdlk.com
License: Del Rio, Val Verde County, TX
Nat'l Network: Westwood One
Target Audience: 18 plus.
Larry Mariner, President
Jay Gonzalez, Operations Dir
Travis Mariner, VP Sales
Jay Gonzalez, Programming Director

KTDR
03-31-1986; 96.3 MHz FM; *Hrs Open:* 24; 100 kw; 505 ft.; N29 32 25 W101 7 21
P.O.Box 420848, Del Rio, TX 78842 US
(830) 775-6291(830) 775-6291(830) 774-6436; *Fax:* (830) 775-6545
License: Del Rio, Val Verde County, TX held by Grande Broadcasting of Del Rio Inc.
Arbitron Metro Market: Del Rio, TX; *Format:* Adult Contemp
Special Programming: Relg 3 hrs wkly; *Hrs. of News Programming:* News progmg 1 hr wkly; *Target Audience:* 25-54; male; *Adv. Rates:* 35; 25; 30; 25
Frank Mendoza, President
Chris Russell, General Sales Mgr
Rodney Lyman, Programming Director
Margaritta Martinez, Research Director
Charlene Duncan, Traffic Manager

KLTO
01-01-1947; 1230 kHz AM; *Hrs Open:* 24; 860 w-U; N29 25 45 W100 54 17
Box 1489, Del Rio, TX 78840
(830) 775-9583; *Fax:* (830) 774-4009

License: Del Rio, Val Verde County, TX held by Forum Broadcasting Inc.
Population Served: 50,000 *Target Audience:* 25-54.
Larry Mariner, President
Rudy Briones, Operations Dir
Jay Gonzalez, Programming Director
Christina Rangel, News Director

KWMC
08-20-1967; 1490 kHz AM; *Hrs Open:* 24; 1 kw-U, ND1; N29 22 17 W100 51 55
903 E. Cortinas Street, Del Rio, TX 78840 US
(830) 775-3544; *Fax:* (830) 775-3546
www.kwmc1490.com/
kwmc1490@wcsonline.net
License: Del Rio, TX held by Minerva Garza Valdez.
Regional Network: Texas State Networks; *Wire Services:* NOAA Weather
Arbitron Metro Market: Del Rio, TX; *Format:* Oldies *Special Programming:* Relg 5 hrs wkly; *No. News Employees:* 2
Alfredo Garza, President
Minerva Garza-Valdez, Operations Dir
Guillermo Garza, Station Manager
Javier Martinez, General Sales Mgr
Guillermo Garza, Engineer
Javier Martinez Jr, Manager
Angelina Rivera, Business Manager
ErnestMesta, Angelina Rivera
Angel Torres, Production Director

***KDLI**
01-01-2007; 89.9 MHz FM; 1 kw; 171 ft.; N29 25 24 W100 54 21
Rebroadcasts: Rebroadcasts WAFR(FM) Tupelo, MS 100%
P.O. Box 3206, Tupelo, MS 38803 US
(662) 844-8888; *Fax:* (662) 842-6791
www.afr.net
faq@afa.net
License: Del Rio, Val Verde County, TX held by American Family Association.
Group Owner: American Family Radio
Arbitron Metro Market: Tupelo, MS; *Format:* Christian
Tim Wildmon, President
Donald Wildmon, Founder
Buddy Smith, Sr VP
Ed Vitagliano, Exec VP
Randy Sharp, Director Of Special Projects
Meeke Addison, Director Of Communications
Abraham Hamilton III, General Counsel

Del Valle

KIXL
08-08-1959; 970 kHz AM; *Hrs Open:* 24
11615 Angus Road, Suite 120 B, Austin, TX 78704 US
(512) 390-5495; *Fax:* (512) 241-0510
www.relevantradio.com
KIXL@relevantradio.com
License: Del Valle, TX held by Starboard Media Foundation Inc.
Group Owner: Relevant Radio; (acq 1-20-2006; $3.58 million)
Arbitron Metro Market: Austin, TX; *Format:* Talk, Christian
Ted Wrenn, General Manager
Ruben Villarreal, Station Manager

Denison

***KYFB**
01-19-2007; 91.5 MHz FM; 4.5 kw; 220 ft.; N33 42 10 W96 34 5
P.O. Box 7300, Charlotte, NC 28241 US
(800) 888-7077
www.bbnradio.org
bbn@bbnmedia.org
License: Denison, Grayson County, TX held by Bible Broadcasting Network Inc.
Group Owner: Bible Broadcasting Network
Arbitron Metro Market: Denison, TX; *Format:* Christian
Lowell Davey, President
Jason Padgett, Operations Manager

Denton

KDXX
09-01-1988; 99.1 MHz FM; *Hrs Open:* 24; 100 kw; 1,168 ft.; N33 23 22 W97 33 53
7700 John W. Carpenter Fwy., Dallas, TX 75247 US
(214) 525-0400; *Fax:* (214) 206-9022
www.univision.com
License: Denton, Denton County, TX held by KHCK-FM License Corp.
Group Owner: Univision Radio; (acq 9-22-2003; grpsl).
Arbitron Metro Market: Dallas-Fort Worth, TX; *Format:* Spanish; *Hrs. of News Programming:* news progmg one hr wkly; *No. News Employees:* 1; *Target Audience:* 25-54; affluent/educated adults
Mark Masepohl, Vice President and General Manager
Patrick Parks, Chief Engineer
Karem Hocking, National Sales Manager
Myrna Vera, Research Director

KHKS
01-01-1947; 106.1 MHz FM; *Hrs Open:* 24; 99 kw; 1,667 ft.; N32 35 19 W96 58 5
14001 N. Dallas Pkwy., Suite 300, Dallas, TX 75240 US
(866) 464-4749; *Fax:* (214) 866-8501
www.1061kissfm.com
License: Denton, Denton County, TX held by AMFM Texas Licenses LLC
Group Owner: iHeartMedia; (acq 8-30-00; grpsl).
Arbitron Metro Market: Dallas-Fort Worth, TX; *Format:* Contemporary Hits/Top 40; *No. News Employees:* 1; *Target Audience:* 18-49.
Anna De Haro, Public Affairs Director
Priscilla Kinkaid, Music Director

Devine

KRPT
11-17-1982; 92.5 MHz FM; *Hrs Open:* 24; 50 kw; 492 ft.; N28 55 32 W99 2 53
6222 Interstate 10 Frontage Rd., San Antonio, TX 78201 US
(210) 736-9700; *Fax:* (210) 735-8811
www.thebullcountry.com
License: Devine, Medina County, TX held by CC Licenses LLC
Group Owner: iHeartMedia; (acq 10-2-98; $1.5 million).
Arbitron Metro Market: San Antonio, TX; *Format:* Country
Marlene Trevino, Market President
Julie Miller, Vice President of Sales
Bree Wagner, Programming Director
Vanessa Garcia, Promotions Director
Michelle Lopez, Media Integration Coordinator
Linda Lynn, PSA Director
Sochy Ortiz,Press Release Manager

Diboll

KAFX-FM
06-29-1960; 95.5 MHz FM; *Hrs Open:* 24; 100 kw; 568 ft.; N31 24 28 W94 45 53
1216 S. 1st Street, Lufkin, TX 75901 US
(936) 639-5595
kfox95.com
johnnylathrop@townsquaremedia.com
License: Diboll, Angelina County, TX held by Townsquare Media Lufkin License LLC
Group Owner: Townsquare Media; (acq 8-3-2007; grpsl)
Arbitron Metro Market: Lufkin, TX; *Format:* Adult Contemp; *Hrs. of News Programming:* news progmg 2 hrs wkly; *No. News Employees:* 1; *Target Audience:* 25-44; female
Johnny Lathrop, General Manager
Dan Patrick, Brand Manager
Paula Divello, Director Of Sales
James Sitllwell, Digital Managing Editor

KSML
06-02-1957; 1260 kHz AM; *Hrs Open:* 24
P.O. Box 1345, Lufkin, TX 75902 US
(409) 634-6661; *Fax:* (409) 632-5722
info@ksml.com
License: Diboll, TX held by Stephen W. & Karla Yates.
Hrs. of News Programming: news progmg 14 hrs wkly; *No. News Employees:* 1
Stephen Yates, President
Oscar Chavez, Programming Director
Steve Comer, Chief Engineer

Dilley

KVWG-FM
03-01-1984; 95.3 MHz FM; 0.1 kw; 121 ft.; N28 40 23 W99 10 8
8203vantage Dr., Suite 840, San Antonio, TX 78230 US
License: Dilley, Frio County, TX held by Pearsall Radio Works Ltd.
Arbitron Metro Market: Dilley, TX
Trace Taul, Operations Dir
Doug Downs, General Manager
Ron Allen, Programming Director

KLMO-FM
01-01-2001; 98.9 MHz FM; 92 kw; 722 ft.; N28 56 34 W99 16 47
115 West Avenue D, Robstown, TX 78320 US
(210) 532-9858; *Fax:* (361) 289-7722
License: Dilley, Frio County, TX held by Dilley Broadcasters.
Arbitron Metro Market: Robstown, TX; *Format:* Spanish
Jose Guzman, General Manager
Salvador Prieto, Programming Director

KKDL
93.7 MHz FM; 2.5 kw; 266 ft.; N28 38 53 W99 10 50
US
(956) 726-4738
License: Dilley, Frio County, TX held by La Nueva Cadena Radio Luz Inc.
Arbitron Metro Market: Dilley, TX
Israel Tellez, President

Dimmitt

KDHN
12-22-1963; 1470 kHz AM; 0.5 kw-D, ND1; 0.149 kw-N, DA2; N34 35 11 W102 18 35
704 W. Cleveland St, Dimmitt, TX 79027 US
(806) 647-4161; *Fax:* (806) 647-4715
License: Dimmitt, TX held by Collins Communications Co.
Format: Religious, Country *Special Programming:* Sp 17 hrs wkly; *Hrs. of News Programming:* News progmg 8 hrs wkly; *Target Audience:* General.
Wayne Collins, President

KNNK
06-13-1998; 100.5 MHz FM; *Hrs Open:* 24; 43 kw; Ant 489 ft; N34 44 49 W102 29 37
Box 1635, 207 S. 25-Mile Ave., Hereford, TX 79045
(806) 363-1005; *Fax:* (806) 364-0226
www.knnk.net
knnk@wtrt.net
License: Dimmitt, Castro-Deaf Smith County, TX held by James D. Peeler.
Nat'l Network: Moody
Population Served: 253,002; *Arbitron Metro Market:* Amarillo, TX *Special Programming:* Soft instrumentals 35 hrs wkly; *Target Audience:* General; mature adults
Terry Smothermon, Operations Dir
Alva Lee Peeler, General Manager

Doss

***KGLF**
88.1 MHz FM; 6 kw; 328 ft.; N30 22 22 W99 5 2
P.O. Box 26142, Austin, TX 78755 US
(800) 525-5683
www.klove.com
klove@klove.com
License: Doss, Gillespie County, TX held by Legacy Austin Broadcasting Foundation Inc.
Arbitron Metro Market: Omaha, NE; *Format:* Christian; *No. News Employees:* 13
Darrell Chambliss, Chairman
Mlke Novak, President and CEO
Pam Patrick-Thompson, Operations Dir
Eric Allen, General Manager
David Pierce, Programming Director
Ed Lenane, News Director
Sam Wallington, Engineering Dir
MaryaMorgan, News Reporter
Richard Hunt, News Reporter
Laura Daniels, News Reporter
Tim Luttrell, News Reporter
Kenny Noble Cortes, News Reporter
Darren Vinson, News Reporter

Dripping Springs

***KLLR**
01-01-2007; 91.9 MHz FM; 1.1 kw; 472 ft.; N30 11 53 W98 0 45
Rebroadcasts: Rebroadcasts KLVR(FM) Santa Rosa, CA 100%
8103 Brodie Lane, Suite #3, Austin, TX 78745 US
(800) 877-5600; *Fax:* (916) 251-1650
www.klove.com
License: Dripping Springs, Hays County, TX held by Educational Media Foundation.
Group Owner: EMF Broadcasting
Nat'l Network: K-Love
Arbitron Metro Market: Dripping Springs, TX; *Format:* Christian
Mike Novak, President
Eric Allen, General Sales Mgr
David Pierce, Programming Director
Ed Lenane, News Director
Sam Wallington, Engineering Dir
Scott Smith, Music Director
Marya Morgan, News Reporter
Richard Hunt, NewsReporter
Tracy Butler, Traffic Manager

Dublin

KSTV-FM
08-15-1968; 93.1 MHz FM; *Hrs Open:* 24; 7 kw; 584 ft.; N32 10 59 W98 17 12
3209 West Washington St, Stephensville, TX 76401 US
(254) 968-2141; *Fax:* (254) 968-6221
www.377net.com
License: Dublin, Erath County, TX held by CCR-Stephenville III LLC.
Group Owner: Cherry Creek Radio LLC; (acq 6-24-2004; grpsl).
Arbitron Metro Market: Stephenville, TX; *Format:* Country
Robert Elliot, General Manager
Robert Haschke, General Sales Mgr
Tony Hart, Programming Director
Nyki Wyatt, News Director
Justin McClure, Chief Engineer
Troy Stark, Traffic Manager

Dumas

KDDD
05-01-1948; 800 kHz AM; *Hrs Open:* 6 AM-sunset; 0.25 kw-D, ND2; 0.008 kw-N, ND2; N35 51 42 W101 55 50
Mailing Address: P. O. Box 555, Dumas, TX 79029 US
Second Address: 408 N. Dumas Ave., Dumas, TX 79029
(806) 935-4141; *Fax:* (806) 935-3836
kddd@amaonline.com
License: Dumas, TX held by PBI LLC
Format: Country; *Target Audience:* General.
Candy Bray, News Director

KDDD-FM
06-29-1960; 95.3 MHz FM; *Hrs Open:* 24; 6.6 kw; 259 ft.; N35 51 51 W101 55 44
Mailing Address: P. O. Box 555, Dumas, TX 79029 US
Second Address: 408 N. Dumas Ave., Dumas, TX 79029
(806) 935-4141; *Fax:* (806) 935-3836
License: Dumas, Moore County, TX held by PBI LLC
Nat'l Network: ABC
Format: Oldies *Special Programming:* Farm 5 hrs, gospel 5 hrs wkly; *Hrs. of News Programming:* news progmg 13 hrs wkly; *No. News Employees:* 1; *Target Audience:* 25-65; farmers, community, factory; *Adv. Rates:* 20; 20; 20; 20
Steve Bayless, Operations Dir
Kandi Bray, General Manager
Ali Allison, News Director
Stephen White, Chief Engineer

Eagle Pass

***KEPI**
05-13-1995; 88.7 MHz FM; *Hrs Open:* 24; 1 kw; 180 ft.; N28 39 26 W100 25 0
Box 3333, McAllen, TX 78502 US
(830) 757-0895; *Fax:* (830) 757-8950
License: Eagle Pass, Maverick County, TX held by World Radio Network Inc.
Arbitron Metro Market: Eagle Pass, TX; *Format:* Christian
James Gamblin, General Manager

KEPS
08-01-1957; 1270 kHz AM
Mailing Address: 2402 Broadmoor, Bldg, D-2, Suite 101, Bryan, TX 77802 US
Second Address: 127 Kilowatt Dr., Eagle Pass, TX 78852
(830) 773-9247; *Fax:* (830) 773-9500
kinlkepsrg@bizzstx.rr.com
License: Eagle Pass, TX held by Rhattigan Broadcasting (Texas) LP
Group Owner: Rhattigan Broadcasting (Texas) LP; (acq 8-19-2004; grpsl)
Arbitron Metro Market: Eagle Pass, TX; *Format:* Tejano; *Target Audience:* 18-49; middle income, Texas-born Hispanics
Rosa De La Garza, General Manager
Rosa De La Garza, General Sales Mgr
Jose Perez, Programming Director
Mario Martinez, News Director
Gary Graham, Chief Engineer

***KEPX**
09-09-1994; 89.5 MHz FM; *Hrs Open:* 24; 52 kw; 256 ft.; N28 39 26 W100 25 0
P.O. Box 3333, McAllen, TX 78502 US
(830) 757-0895; *Fax:* (830) 757-8950
License: Eagle Pass, Maverick County, TX held by World Radio Network Inc.
Arbitron Metro Market: Eagle Pass, TX; *Format:* Christian; *Hrs. of News Programming:* News progmg 3 hrs wkly; *Target Audience:* Hispanic; Mexican
Arturo Lazano, General Manager

KINL
11-02-1971; 92.7 MHz FM; 20 kw; 184 ft.; N28 43 57 W100 29 34
Mailing Address: 2402 Broadmoor, Bldg, D-2, Suite 101, Bryan, TX 77802 US
Second Address: 127 Kilowatt Dr., Eagle Pass, TX 78852
(830) 773-9247; *Fax:* (830) 773-9500
License: Eagle Pass, Maverick County, TX held by Rhattigan Broadcasting (Texas) LP.
Group Owner: Rhattigan Broadcasting (Texas) LP
Format: Oldies
Cesar Galindo, Programming Director

Eastland

KATX
09-01-1986; 97.7 MHz FM; *Hrs Open:* 24; 3 kw; 203 ft.; N32 23 47 W98 46 26
306 S. Seaman, Box 590, Eastland, TX 76448 US
(254) 629-2621; *Fax:* (254) 629-8520
silverspursbroadcasting@gmail.com
License: Eastland, Eastland County, TX held by Partnership Broadcasting Inc.
Arbitron Metro Market: Abilene, TX; *Format:* Classic Rock, Oldies; *Hrs. of News Programming:* news progmg 8 hrs wkly; *No. News Employees:* 3; *Target Audience:* 25-54; adults; *Adv. Rates:* 7.00/14.00
Chuck Statler, President

***KQXE**
01-01-2008; 91.1 MHz FM; 14.5 kw; 436 ft.; N32 28 37.5 W98 48 34
206 Wiggs Lane, Weatherford, TX 76086 US
(817) 341-2337; *Fax:* (817) 596-9842
www.qxfm.com
License: Eastland, Eastland County, TX held by CSSI Non-Profit Educational Broadcasting Corp.
Arbitron Metro Market: Eastland, TX
John Peterson, General Manager

Edinburg

KBFM
02-01-1972; 104.1 MHz FM; *Hrs Open:* 24; 100 kw; 1,224 ft.; N26 6 2 W97 50 21
901 E. Pike Blvd., Welasco, TX 78596 US
(956) 973-9202; *Fax:* (956) 973-9355
www.wild104.net
License: Edinburg, Hidalgo County, TX held by Capstar TX LLC
Group Owner: iHeartMedia; (acq 8-15-00; grpsl).
Nat'l Reps: Christal
Arbitron Metro Market: Weslaco, TX; *Format:* Contemporary Hits/Top 40 *Special Programming:* Community affrs; *No. News Employees:* 1; *Target Audience:* 18-34; females; *Adv. Rates:* 100; 75; 100; 50
Billy Santiago, Senior Vice President of Programming

***KOIR**
02-05-1983; 88.5 MHz FM; *Hrs Open:* 24; 3 kw; 285 ft.; N26 7 49 W98 10 51
4300 S. Business 281, Edinburg, TX 78539 US
(956) 380-8100,(956) 380-3435; *Fax:* (956) 380-8156
License: Edinburg, Hidalgo County, TX held by Rio Grande Bible Institute Inc.
Wire Services: UPI
Arbitron Metro Market: McAllen-Brownsville-Harlingen, TX; *Format:* Religious; *Target Audience:* General.
Gerardo Lorenzo, General Manager
Jerry Jeske, Chief Engineer

KURV
10-01-1947; 710 kHz AM; *Hrs Open:* 24; 1 kw-D, DA2; 0.91 kw-N, DA2; N26 19 43 W98 9 35; N26 19 42 W98 9 36
2921 N. Closner, Edinburg, TX 78539 US
(956) 992-8895; *Fax:* (956) 992-8897
www.kurv.com
License: Edinburg, TX held by BMP RGV License Co. L.P.
Group Owner: Border Media Partners LLC; (acq 2-6-2004; $7.5 million with KSOX(AM) Raymondville)
Nat'l Network: CBS; *Regional Network:* Texas State Networks
Arbitron Metro Market: Edinburg, TX; *Format:* News, News/Talk, 84, Talk; *Hrs. of News Programming:* news progmg 30 hrs wkly; *No. News Employees:* 2; *Target Audience:* 35-64.
Jose Munoz, General Manager

KVLY
01-01-1974; 107.9 MHz FM; 100 kw; 843 ft.; N26 5 18 W98 3 44
801 N. Jackson Rd., McAllen, TX 78501 US
(956) 687-4848; *Fax:* (956) 687-7784
www.mix1079.net
License: Edinburg, Hidalgo County, TX held by Entravision Holdings LLC.
Group Owner: Entravision Communications Corp.; (acq 7-20-00; grpsl)
Arbitron Metro Market: McAllen-Brownsville-Harlingen, TX; *Format:* Contemporary Hits/Top 40; *Target Audience:* 25-54.
Willie Rosales, General Manager
Alex Duran, Programming Director
Shirley Kennedy, News Director

Edna

KIOX-FM
09-20-1998; 96.1 MHz FM; 13 kw; 456 ft.; N29 6 5 W96 27 19
111 N. Main, Hallettsville, TX 77964 US
(974) 543-8282
License: Edna, Jackson County, TX held by Buckalew Media Inc.
Format: Country
Ryan Henderson, General Manager

El Campo

***KXBJ**
09-01-1968; 96.9 MHz FM; *Hrs Open:* 24; 100 kw; 981 ft; N29 05 44 W96 27 25 *Rebroadcasts:* Rebroadcasts KSBJ(FM) 89.3
1722 Treble Dr., Humble, TX 77338
(281) 446-5725; *Fax:* (281) 540-2198
www.ksbj.org
License: El Campo, Wharton County, TX held by KSBJ Educational Foundation
Group Owner: KSBJ Educational Foundation; (acq 13-04-2012 from Liberman Broadcasting)
Format: Adult Contemp, Christian
Tim McDermott, President & General Manager

KULP
01-01-1948; 1390 kHz AM; *Hrs Open:* 6 AM-10 PM; 0.5 kw-D, ND1; 0.18 kw-N, ND1; N29 12 34 W96 15 50
Mailing Address: P.O. Box 390, El Campo, TX 77437 US
Second Address: 515 E. Jackson St., El Campo, TX 77437
(979) 543-3303; *Fax:* (979) 543-1546
www.kulpradio.com
contact@kulpradio.com
License: El Campo, TX held by Wharton County Radio Inc.
Regional Network: Texas State Networks
Arbitron Metro Market: El Campo, TX; *Format:* Country, News, 62, Sports, Talk *Special Programming:* Sp 14 hrs, Czech 5 hrs wkly; *Hrs. of News Programming:* news progmg 5 hrs wkly; *No. News Employees:* 2 *TargetAudience:* 25 plus.; *Adv. Rates:* 276; 228; 228; 228
Bob Buckalew, President
Clint Robinson, Operations Dir
Stephen Zetsche, General Manager
Jerry Aulds, Station Manager
Bob Nason, News Director
Mike Wenglar, Engineering Dir
Kate Manrriquez, Traffic Manager

El Paso

KAMA
07-13-1972; 750 kHz AM; *Hrs Open:* 24; 10 kw-D, DA2; 1 kw-N, DA2; N31 46 30 W106 16 48
2211 E. Missouri Ave., El Paso, TX 79903 US
(915) 544-9797
www.univision.com
License: El Paso, El Paso County, TX held by Tichenor License Corp.
Group Owner: Univision Radio; (acq 9-22-2003; grpsl).
Arbitron Metro Market: El Paso, TX; *Format:* News, News/Talk, 82, Talk; *Hrs. of News Programming:* news progmg 8 hrs wkly; *No. News Employees:* 1; *Target Audience:* 25-54; women
Angela Navarrete, General Manager and Director of Sales

KYSE
11-29-1958; 94.7 MHz FM; *Hrs Open:* 24; 97 kw horiz, 65 kw vert; 1191 ft.; N31 47 34 W106 28 47
5426 N. Mesa, El Paso, TX 79912 US
(915) 581-1126
www.tricolor947.com
License: El Paso, El Paso County, TX held by Entravision Holdings L.L.C.
Group Owner: Entravision Communications Corp.; (acq 10-19-99).
Nat'l Reps: Lotus Entravision Reps LLC
Arbitron Metro Market: El Paso, TX; *Format:* Tejano
Diana Zamudio, Senior VP
Mark Garcia, National Sales Mgr

KSVE
03-18-1994; 1650 kHz AM; 100 kw *Rebroadcasts:* Simulcast KINT-FM El Paso
5426 N. Mesa, El Paso, TX 79912 US

(915) 581-1126; *Fax:* (915) 532-4970
www.jose939.com
License: El Paso, TX held by Entravision Holdings LLC.
Group Owner: Entravision Communications Corp.
Arbitron Metro Market: El Paso, TX; *Format:* Adult Contemp, Spanish
Mark Garcia, General Sales Mgr

KQBU
06-01-1947; 920 kHz AM; 1 kw-D, DAN; 0.36 kw-N, DAN; N31 44 9 W106 22 24
2211 E. Missouri Ave., El Paso, TX 79903 US
(915) 544-9797
www.univision.com
License: El Paso, El Paso County, TX held by Tichenor License Corp.
Group Owner: Univision Radio; (acq 9-22-2003; grpsl)
Arbitron Metro Market: El Paso, TX; *Format:* Spanish
Angela Navarrete, General Manager and Director of Sales

KBNA-FM
08-15-1969; 97.5 MHz FM; 100 kw horiz, 48 kw vert; 1,089 ft.; N31 47 34 W106 28 47
2211 E. Missouri Ave., El Paso, TX 79903 US
(915) 544-9797
www.univision.com
License: El Paso, El Paso County, TX held by Tichenor License Corp.
Group Owner: Univision Radio
Arbitron Metro Market: El Paso, TX; *Format:* News, News/Talk, 82, Talk
Angela Navarrete, General Manager and Director of Sales

KELP
04-10-1959; 1590 kHz AM; *Hrs Open:* 24; 5 kw-D, DA2; 0.8 kw-N, DA2; N31 44 38 W106 23 45
6900 Commerce, El Paso, TX 79915 US
(915) 779-0016; *Fax:* (915) 779-6641
www.kelpradio.com
tina@kelpradio.com
License: El Paso, TX held by McClatchey Broadcasting.
Nat'l Network: Salem Radio Network
Arbitron Metro Market: El Paso, TX; *Format:* Christian, Talk
Special Programming: Spanish 12 hrs wklly; *Target Audience:* 25-54; Christian community of El Paso, Las Cruces, Northern Mexico
Jay Gilliland, Operations Dir
Arnie McClatchey, General Manager
Jay Gilliland, Programming Director
Tina Casano, Office Manager

KXPL
09-16-1985; 1060 kHz AM; 10 kw-D, NDD; N31 48 41 W106 31 53
2211 E. Missouri E-237, El Paso, TX 79903 US
(915) 587-8822; *Fax:* (915) 587-8602
newsroomlavoz@yahoo.com
License: El Paso, TX held by New Radio System Inc.
Arbitron Metro Market: El Paso, TX; *Format:* News
Maria Lazo, General Manager
Jose Camacho, Programming Director
Paul Gregg, Chief Engineer

KTSM
01-01-1947; 690 kHz AM; *Hrs Open:* 24; 10 kw-D, DA2; 10 kw-N, DA2; N31 58 11 W106 21 15
4045 N. Mesa Rd., El Paso, TX 79902 US
(915) 351-5400
www.ktsmradio.com
License: El Paso, El Paso County, TX held by CC Licenses LLC
Group Owner: iHeartMedia; (acq 5-16-96; grpsl).
Nat'l Reps: Clear Channel
Arbitron Metro Market: El Paso, TX; *Format:* News, News/Talk, 86 *Special Programming:* Relg 3 hrs, radio health journal one hr, El Paso p; *Hrs. of News Programming:* News 100 hrs wkly; *Target Audience:* 25-54; men
Bill Tole, Operations Manager/Program Director
Mike Ryan, Market Manager
Walter Alvarez, Sales Manager

KHEY-FM
08-01-1974; 96.3 MHz FM; *Hrs Open:* 24; 88 kw; 1391 ft.; N31 47 47 W106 28 55
200 Concord Plaza, Suite 600, San Antonio, TX 78216 US
(915) 351-5400; *Fax:* (915) 351-3102
www.khey.com
info@khey.com
License: El Paso, El Paso County, TX held by CC Licenses LLC
Group Owner: iHeartMedia
Nat'l Network: ABC
Arbitron Metro Market: El Paso, TX; *Format:* Country; *Target Audience:* 25-54.
Bill Tole, Operations Manager
Mike Ryan, Market Manager
Walter Alvarez, Sales Manager
Bobcat Brown, Programming Director

KINT-FM
03-18-1994; 93.9 MHz FM; 100 kw; 1421 ft.; N31 47 46 W106 28 57 *Rebroadcasts:* Simulcast KSVE El Paso
5426 N. Mesa St., El Paso, TX 79912 US
(915) 581-1126
www.jose939.com
License: El Paso, El Paso County, TX held by Entravision Holdings, LLC.
Group Owner: Entravision Communications Corp.; (acq 6-4-97; grpsl)
Nat'l Reps: Lotus Entravision Reps LLC
Arbitron Metro Market: El Paso, TX; *Format:* Adult Contemp, Spanish; *Hrs. of News Programming:* News progmg 4 hrs wkly; *Target Audience:* 25-54.
Mark Garcia, General Sales Mgr

KLAQ
10-01-1978; 95.5 MHz FM; 88 kw; 1391 ft.; N31 47 47 W106 28 55
4150 Pinnacle, El Paso, TX 79902 US
(915) 544-9550; *Fax:* (915) 532-6342
www.klaq.com
info@klaq.com
License: El Paso, El Paso County, TX held by Townsquare Media of El Paso Inc.
Group Owner: Townsquare Media
Arbitron Metro Market: El Paso, TX; *Format:* Rock/AOR; *Target Audience:* 18-49; adults who grew up on FM rock and roll
Johnny Lathrop, General Manager
Dan Patrick, Brand Manager
Paula Divello, Director Of Sales
James Sitllwell, Digital Sales Manager

KOFX
06-06-1978; 92.3 MHz FM; *Hrs Open:* 24; 100 kw; 1860 ft.; N31 48 55 W106 29 20
5426 N. Mesa, El Paso, TX 79912 US
(915) 581-1126
www.923thefox.com
License: El Paso, El Paso County, TX held by Entravision Holdings LLC.
Group Owner: Entravision Communications Corp.; (acq 10-19-99)
Arbitron Metro Market: El Paso, TX; *Format:* Oldies; *No. News Employees:* 2; *Target Audience:* 25-54; upscale
Diana Zamudio, Senior VP
Mark Garcia, General Sales Mgr

KPRR
12-05-1969; 102.1 MHz FM; *Hrs Open:* 24; 100 kw horiz, 66 kw vert; 1191 ft.; N31 47 34 W106 28 47
4045 N. Mesa St., El Paso, TX 79912 US
(915) 351-5400; *Fax:* (915) 351-3102
www.kprr.com
info@kprr.com
License: El Paso, El Paso County, TX held by CC Licenses LLC
Group Owner: iHeartMedia; (acq 5-16-96; grpsl).
Nat'l Reps: Clear Channel
Arbitron Metro Market: El Paso, TX; *Format:* Contemporary Hits/Top 40; *Target Audience:* 18-34.
Bill Tole, Operations Manager
Mike Ryan, Market Manager
Walter Alvarez, Sales Manager
Patti Diaz, Programming Director
Raul Figueroa, Website/Digital

KROD
06-01-1940; 600 kHz AM; *Hrs Open:* 24
4180 N. Mesa St., El Paso, TX 79912 US
(915) 544-9550; *Fax:* (915) 532-6342
www.krod.com
License: El Paso, TX
Group Owner: Townsquare Media; (acq 12-1-99; grpsl).
Regional Network: Texas State Networks; *Nat'l Reps:* D & R Radio
Arbitron Metro Market: El Paso, TX; *Format:* Sports; *Hrs. of News Programming:* news progmg 3 hrs wkly; *No. News Employees:* 1; *Target Audience:* 25-54; adult listeners who grew up on the roots of rock and roll
Brad Dubow, General Manager
Kevin Vargas, Brand Manager
JT Chapman, Director Of Sales
Jed Knapp, Digital Sales Manager
Scott Lewis, Digital Managing Editor
Ron Haney, Chief Engineer

KSII
12-30-1975; 93.1 MHz FM; *Hrs Open:* 24; 98 kw; 1421 ft.; N31 47 46 W106 28 57
4180 N. Mesa St., El Paso, TX 79912 US
(915) 544-9300; *Fax:* (915) 544-9536
License: El Paso, El Paso County, TX
Group Owner: Townsquare Media; (acq 12-1-99; grpsl).
Arbitron Metro Market: El Paso, TX; *Format:* Adult Contemp; *Hrs. of News Programming:* news progmg 2 hrs wkly; *No. News Employees:* 1; *Target Audience:* 25-54; 60% male, 40% female
Johnny Lathrop, President/Chief Revenue Officer
John Roberts, Operations Manager
Michelle Hiltzman, Director Of Sales
Abel Sanchez, Digital Sales Manager
Lucky Larry, Program Director

KHRO
06-01-1958; 1150 kHz AM; *Hrs Open:* 24; 5 kw-D, 0.38 kw-N
5426 N. Mesa St., El Paso, TX 79912 US
(915) 581-1126
www.fox1150.com
License: El Paso, TX held by Entravision Holdings, LLC
Group Owner: Entravision Communications Corp.
Nat'l Reps: Lotus Entravision Reps LLC
Arbitron Metro Market: El Paso, TX; *Format:* Oldies; *Target Audience:* 18-54.
Mark Garcia, General Sales Mgr

*KTEP
09-14-1950; 88.5 MHz FM; *Hrs Open:* 24; 94 kw; 732 ft.; N31 47 17 W106 28 46
500 W. University Ave, El Paso, TX 79968 US
(915) 747-5152(915) 880-5837; *Fax:* (915) 747-5641
www.ktep.org
ktep@utep.edu
License: El Paso, El Paso County, TX held by University of Texas at El Paso.
Nat'l Network: PRI; NPR
Arbitron Metro Market: El Paso, TX; *Format:* Jazz, News *Special Programming:* Gospel 4 hrs, folk 3 hrs wkly; *Hrs. of News Programming:* news progmg 39 wkly; *No. News Employees:* 1; *Target Audience:* 35 plus;college educated, upper-income
Dennis Woo, Operations Dir
Patrick Piotrowaski, General Manager
Joe Torres, General Sales Mgr
Louie Saenz, News Director
Norbert Miles, Chief Engineer
Norma Martinez, Traffic Manager

KHEY
08-22-1929; 1380 kHz AM; *Hrs Open:* 24; 5 kw-D, ND1; 0.5 kw-N, ND1; N31 45 26 W106 22 33
4045 N. Mesa St., El Paso, TX 79912 US
(915) 351-5400; *Fax:* (915) 351-3102
www.khey1380.com
License: El Paso, TX held by CC Licenses LLC
Group Owner: iHeartMedia; (acq 5-29-98; $10.5 million with co-located FM)
Nat'l Reps: Clear Channel
Arbitron Metro Market: El Paso, TX; *Format:* Sports; *Target Audience:* General.
Bill Tole, Operations Manager
Mike Ryan, Market Manager
Walter Alvarez, Sales Manager
Raul Figueroa, Website/Digital

KTSM-FM
06-11-1962; 99.9 MHz FM; 87 kw; 1821 ft.; N31 48 19 W106 28 57
4045 N. Mesa St., El Paso, TX 79912 US
(915) 351-5400; *Fax:* (915) 351-3102
www.sunny999fm.com
License: El Paso, El Paso County, TX held by CC Licenses LLC
Group Owner: iHeartMedia
Nat'l Network: CBS
Arbitron Metro Market: El Paso, TX; *Format:* Adult Contemp
Bill Tole, Operations Manager/Program Director
Mike Ryan, Market Manager
Walter Alvarez, Sales Manager
Raul Figueroa, Website/Digital

*KVER
01-01-1993; 91.1 MHz FM; *Hrs Open:* 24; 0.51 kw; 1115 ft.; N31 47 34 W106 28 47
4126 N. Mesa St., El Paso, TX 79912 US
(915) 544-9190
www.kver.org
License: El Paso, El Paso County, TX held by World Network Radio Inc.
Group Owner: World Radio Network Inc.

Arbitron Metro Market: El Paso, TX; *Format:* Religious; *Target Audience:* Hispanic
Marcos Barraza, Station Manager
Gracel Calleros, Programming Director

KVIV
12-03-1949; 1340 kHz AM
4900 Montana Ave, El Paso, TX 79903 US
(915) 565-2999; *Fax:* (915) 880-5848
www.kviv1340.com
radiovictoria@mail.com
License: El Paso, TX held by El Paso y Juarez Companerismo-Cristiano
Arbitron Metro Market: El Paso, TX; *Format:* Religious; *Target Audience:* Mexican-American.
Alfonso Cabrera, President
Jesus Cruz, Programming Director

***KKLY**
05-01-1985; 89.5 MHz FM; *Hrs Open:* 24; 3.5 kw; 1211 ft.; N31 47 42 W106 28 51
2023 Myrtle Avenue, El Paso, TX 79901 US
(916) 251-1600; *Fax:* (916) 251-1650
www.klove.com
klove@klove.com
License: El Paso, El Paso County, TX held by Educational Media Foundation.
Group Owner: EMF Broadcasting; (acq 11-18-2002; $1 million).
Nat'l Network: K-Love
Arbitron Metro Market: El Paso, TX; *Format:* Christian; *No. News Employees:* 3; *Target Audience:* 25-44.
Mike Novak, President
David Pierce, Programming Director
Ed Lenane, News Director
Sam Wallington, Engineering Dir
Marya Morgan, News Reporter
Richard Hunt, News Reporter

Eldorado

KLDE
01-01-2007; 104.9 MHz FM; 50 kw; 279 ft.; N30 51 55 W100 35 36
US
(325) 853-1049
www.klderadio.com
License: Eldorado, Schleicher County, TX held by Tenn-Vol Corp.
Arbitron Metro Market: Eldorado, TX; *Format:* Oldies
Danny Ray Boyer, General Manager

Electra

KOLI
01-01-1998; 94.9 MHz FM; 50 kw; 492 ft.; N34 5 1 W98 59 29
4302 Call Field, Wichita Falls, TX 76308 US
(940) 691-2311; *Fax:* (940) 696-2255
info@cumulus.com
License: Electra, Wichita County, TX held by Cumulus Licensing Corp.
Group Owner: Cumulus Media Inc.; (acq 8-10-99; $238,400)
Arbitron Metro Market: Wichita Falls, TX; *Format:* Country
Brent Warner, Operations Dir
Lindy Parr, General Manager
Andrea Lewis, General Sales Mgr
Jim Russell, News Director
Jeff Chan, Chief Engineer
Dana Jameson, Traffic Manager

Elgin

KWNX
04-01-1948; 1260 kHz AM; *Hrs Open:* 24
P.O. Box 484, Austin, TX 78767 US
(512) 346-8255; *Fax:* (512) 346-8262
License: Elgin, TX held by Total Austin Sports Radio LLC
Nat'l Network: ESPN Deportes
Arbitron Metro Market: Austin, TX; *Format:* Sports
Steve Wilder, General Manager
Neil Parker, Promotions Manager
Flavia Chen, News Director
J. Cole McClellan, Chief Engineer

KVLR
92.5 MHz FM
5700 West Oaks Boulevard, Rocklin, CA 95765 US
(916) 251-1600; *Fax:* (916) 252-1650
www.klove.com
License: Elgin, TX held by Educational Media Foundation
Group Owner: EMF Broadcasting
Nat'l Network: K-Love
Mike Novak, President

Elkhart

***KATG**
01-01-2006; 88.1 MHz FM; 80 kw vert; Ant 544 ft; N32 02 41 W95 40 37
P.O. Box 3206, Tupelo, MS 38803
(662) 844-8888; *Fax:* (662) 842-6791
www.afr.net
faq@afa.net
License: Elkhart, Anderson County, TX held by American Family Association.
Group Owner: American Family Radio
Arbitron Metro Market: Tyler-Longview, TX; *Format:* Christian
Tim Wildmon, President
Donald Wildmon, Founder
Buddy Smith, Sr VP
Ed Vitagliano, Exec VP
Randy Sharp, Director Of Special Projects
Meeke Addison, Director Of Communications
Abraham Hamilton, General Counsel

Fabens

KPAS
03-24-1979; 103.1 MHz FM; *Hrs Open:* 18; 3 kw; 299 ft.; N31 35 42 W106 11 58
8564 North Loop Road, El Paso, TX 79907 US
(915) 851-3382; *Fax:* (915) 851-4360
License: Fabens, El Paso County, TX held by Algie A. Felder.
Nat'l Network: USA
Arbitron Metro Market: El Paso, TX; *Format:* Religious; *Hrs. of News Programming:* News progmg 6 hrs wkly; *Adv. Rates:* 25.50; 25.50; 25.50
Algie Felder, General Manager

Fairfield

KNES
12-01-1983; 99.1 MHz FM; *Hrs Open:* 24; 11.5 kw; 482 ft.; N31 40 55 W96 1 22
P.O. Box 347, Fairfield, TX 75840 US
(903) 389-5637; *Fax:* (903) 389-7172
www.texas99.com
texas99@texas99.com
License: Fairfield, Freestone County, TX held by J & J Communications Inc.
Nat'l Network: Jones Radio Networks; *Regional Network:* Texas State Networks; *Nat'l Reps:* Riley
Format: Country *Special Programming:* Farm 3 hrs, talk 15 hrs, Black 3 hrs, gospel 3 hrs; *Hrs. of News Programming:* news progmg 6 hrs wkly; *No. News Employees:* 1; *Target Audience:* General.
Joe Reid, General Manager
Buzz Russell, Programming Director

Falfurrias

KDFM
103.3 MHz FM; 3 kw; 328 ft.; N27 15 29 W98 7 8
P O Box 252, McAllen, TX 78505 US
(956) 686-6382(956) 686-2992; *Fax:* (956) 686-2999
www.kdfc.com
License: Falfurrias, Brooks County, TX held by La Radio Cristiana Network Inc.
Arbitron Metro Market: Falfurrias, TX
Bill Lueth, Operations Dir
Dwight Walker, General Manager
Joe Schembri, General Sales Mgr

KLDS
01-01-1953; 1260 kHz AM; *Hrs Open:* 6 AM-midnight; 0.5 kw-D, ND1; 0.33 kw-N, ND1; N27 14 11 W98 10 22
Mailing Address: 304 E Rice, Falfurrias, TX 78355 US
Second Address: 215 W. Adam St., Falfurrias, TX 78355
(361) 325-1212; *Fax:* (361) 325-5003
License: Falfurrias, TX held by The Evangelistic Worship Center
Arbitron Metro Market: Corpus Christi, TX; *Format:* Christian; *Target Audience:* General.
Timothy Trevino, General Manager
Steve Cantu, Chief Engineer

KPSO-FM
11-01-1983; 106.3 MHz FM; *Hrs Open:* 6 AM-10 PM; 6 kw; 184 ft.; N27 14 11 W98 10 22
304 E Rice, Falfurrias, TX 78355 US
(361) 325-2112; *Fax:* (361) 325-2112
kpso@awesomenet.net
License: Falfurrias, Brooks County, TX held by Brooks Broadcasting Corp.
Regional Network: Texas State Networks
Arbitron Metro Market: Corpus Christi, TX; *Format:* Tejano; *Hrs. of News Programming:* News progmg 10 hrs wkly; *Target Audience:* All groups.; *Adv. Rates:* 11
Raymond Creely, General Manager
Steve Cantu, General Sales Mgr

Fannett

***KZFT**
10-31-2003; 90.5 MHz FM; 40 kw vert; 361 ft.; N29 53 33 W94 8 6
6895 Fannett Rd., Beaumont, TX 77705-7116 US
(409) 838-6677
www.afr.net
License: Fannett, Jefferson County, TX held by American Family Association.
Group Owner: American Family Radio
Arbitron Metro Market: Fannett, TX; *Format:* Christian
Tim Wildmon, President
Donald Wildmon, Founder
Buddy Smith, Sr VP
Ed Vitagliano, Exec VP
Randy Sharp, Director Of Special Projects
Meeke Addison, Director Of Communications
Abraham Hamilton III, General Counsel

Farmersville

KFCD
11-01-1947; 990 kHz AM; *Hrs Open:* 24
P.O. Box 12345, Dallas, TX 75225 US
(972) 354-1990; *Fax:* (972) 354-0820
www.radioexitosfm.com
dagoberto@radioexitosfm.net
License: Farmersville, TX held by Bernard Dallas LLC
Group Owner: Bernard Radio LLC; (acq 1-31-2007; $9 million with KHSE(AM) Wylie)
Nat'l Network: CNN Radio
Arbitron Metro Market: Farmersville, TX; *Format:* Talk; *Target Audience:* 35 plus; men; *Adv. Rates:* 100; 100; 100; 20.
Dagoberto Rodriguez, CEO/COO
Dave Marcum, Operations Dir
Jerry Overton, General Manager
Jesus Dominguez, Sales Manager
Leslie Cooke, News Director
Jose Sanchez ', Tech Support
Dave Schum, Chief Engineer

KXEZ
09-01-1998; 92.1 MHz FM; 1.95 kw; 584 ft.; N33 16 31 W96 22 2
P.O. Box 94094, Plano, TX 75094 US
(972) 633-0953; *Fax:* (972) 396-1643
www.kxez.com
info@kxez.com
License: Farmersville, Collin County, TX held by Metro Broadcasters-Texas Inc.
Nat'l Network: Jones Radio Networks
Arbitron Metro Market: Dallas, TX; *Format:* Country
Ken Jones, CEO
Jack Bishop, Operations Dir
Joshua Jones, General Sales Mgr
Glenda Jones, CFO
Lou Rogers, Technical Support

Farwell

KICA-FM
09-15-1984; 98.3 MHz FM; *Hrs Open:* 24; 51 kw; 174 ft.; N34 24 31 W103 11 15
1000 Sycamore Street, Clovis, NM 88101 US
(505) 762-6200; *Fax:* (505) 762-8800
License: Farwell, Parmer County, TX held by Tallgrass Broadcasting LLC.
Group Owner: Tallgrass Broadcasting LLC; (acq 4-2-2007; grpsl)
Format: Classic Rock; *Hrs. of News Programming:* news progmg 3 hrs wkly; *No. News Employees:* 1; *Target Audience:* 18-49.
Dana Taylor, Programming Director
Shannon Phillips, News Director

KIJN
04-17-1958; 1060 kHz AM; 10 kw-D, DAD; N34 23 14 W103 1 51
Mailing Address: 2909 N. Prince, Suite C, Clovis, NM 88101 US
Second Address: PO Box 458, Farwell, TX 79325-0458
(575) 693-3693
www.angelfire.com/biz/KIJN
License: Farwell, TX held by Unidos Para Cristo, Inc.
Group Owner: Unidos Para Cristo, Inc.; (acq 9-97; with co-located FM)
Format: Christian, Religious; *Target Audience:* General.; *Adv. Rates:* 15; 15; 15; na

Mike Rodriquez, General Manager
David Pollard, Programming Director

KIJN-FM
08-01-1985; 92.3 MHz FM; *Hrs Open:* 24; 100 kw; 354 ft.; N34 32 26 W102 47 56
PO Box 8088, Amarillo, TX 79114 US
(806) 359-8855; *Fax:* (806) 354-2039
www.kingdomkeysradio.org
License: Farwell, Parmer County, TX held by Top O' Texas Educational Broadcasting Foundation, Inc.
Group Owner: Top O' Texas Educational Broadcasting Foundation, Inc.
Format: Christian, Religious; *Adv. Rates:* 18; 18; 18; 15
Ricky Pfeil, President

KMUL
07-06-1956; 830 kHz AM
1000 Sycamore Street, Clovis, NM 88101 US
(806) 272-4273; *Fax:* (806) 272-5067
License: Farwell, TX held by Tallgrass Broadcasting LLC.
Group Owner: Tallgrass Broadcasting LLC; (acq 4-2-2007; grpsl)
Special Programming: Farm 3 hrs wkly
Noe Anzaldua, General Manager
Martha Alvarado, Programming Director
Rick Keefer, Chief Engineer

Ferris

KDFT
07-13-1988; 540 kHz AM; *Hrs Open:* 24
5801 Marvin D Love Freeway, Suite 409, Dallas, TX 75237 US
(972) 572-1540; *Fax:* (972) 572-1263
www.kdft540.com
yaryu@mrbi.net
License: Ferris, TX held by Way Broadcasting Licensee, LLC
Group Owner: Multicultural Radio Broadcasting Inc.; (acq 4-19-2000; grpsl).
Regional Reps: In Language Radio; San Francisco
Arbitron Metro Market: Dallas-Fort Worth; *Format:* Christian, Spanish; *Target Audience:* 25-59; Sp
Arthur Liu, CEO

Floresville

KTFM
06-15-1977; 94.1 MHz FM; *Hrs Open:* 24; 40 kw; 548 ft.; N29 11 3 W98 30 49
4050 Eisenhauer Rd., San Antonio, TX 78218 US
(210) 654-5100; *Fax:* (210) 855-5076
www.ktfm.com
License: Floresville, Wilson County, TX held by Alpha Media Licensee LLC
Group Owner: Alpha Media LLC; (acq 1-31-2014; grpsl).
Arbitron Metro Market: San Antonio, TX; *Format:* Contemporary Hits/Top 40; *Target Audience:* 18-49.
Greg Martin, General Manager
Janie Lees, Sales Manager
Pat Cerullo, Programming Director

***KJMA**
01-01-1993; 89.7 MHz FM; 100 kw; 564 ft.; N28 57 40 W98 15 31
1905 Tenth Street, Floresville, TX 78114 US
(210) 821-5050; *Fax:* (210) 821-5052
www.gmonline.com
License: Floresville, Wilson County, TX held by La Promesa Foundation.
Group Owner: La Promesa Foundation; (acq 6-25-2007; $130,000)
Nat'l Network: EWTN Radio
Arbitron Metro Market: Floresville, TX; *Format:* Christian
Leonard Oswald, President
Cissy Gonzalez, General Manager

Flower Mound

KTCK
01-01-1967; 96.7 MHz FM; *Hrs Open:* 24; 90 kw; Ant 2,034 ft; N33 15 41 W97 17 42
3090 Olive St., West Victory Plaza #400, Dallas, TX 75219 US
(214) 526-2400; *Fax:* (214) 525-2525
www.theticket.com
License: Flower Mound, TX held by Radio License Holdings LLC
Group Owner: Cumulus Media Inc.; (acq 6-12-2007; grpsl).
Population Served: 132,000; *Arbitron Metro Market:* Dallas-Fort Worth; *Format:* Sports, Talk; *Target Audience:* 35-54 Adults
Jeff Catlin, Operations Dir
Dan Bennett, General Manager
Alec Drake, General Sales Mgr

Jeff Catlin, Programming Director
Kristi Crisp, Promotion Director

Floydada

KFLP-FM
04-01-1985; 106.1 MHz FM; *Hrs Open:* 24; 25 kw; 233 ft.; N33 58 7 W101 21 15
Rt. 2, Box 60, Floydada, TX 79235 US
(806) 983-5704
www.kflp.net
License: Floydada, Floyd County, TX held by Anthony L. Ricketts.
Nat'l Reps: Interep
Arbitron Metro Market: Floydada, TX; *Format:* Agriculture, News; *Target Audience:* Farmers
A.T. Moore, President
Dan Perkins, Operations Dir
Donna Cole, General Manager
Joe Miot, Programming Director

KFLP
01-01-1951; 900 kHz AM
Rt. 2, Box 60, Floydada, TX 79235 US
(806) 983-5704
www.kflp.net
kflp@kflp.net
License: Floydada, TX held by Anthony L. Ricketts.
Nat'l Network: USA; *Regional Network:* American Ag; *Nat'l Reps:* Interep
Arbitron Metro Market: Floydada, TX; *Format:* Country; *Hrs. of News Programming:* news progmg 12 hrs wkly; *No. News Employees:* 1; *Target Audience:* 18-64
Tony St. James, General Manager

Fort Stockton

KFST
05-08-1954; 860 kHz AM; *Hrs Open:* 24; 0.25 kw-D, ND1; 0.25 kw-N, ND1; N30 52 37 W102 53 30
Rt. 1, Box 165, Fort Stockton, TX 79735 US
(432) 336-2228; *Fax:* (432) 336-5834
www.kfstradio.com
kfst@sbcglobal.net
License: Fort Stockton, TX held by Fort Stockton Radio Co Inc.
Regional Network: Texas State Networks; *Wire Services:* NOAA Weather
Arbitron Metro Market: Fort Stockton, TX; *Format:* Adult Contemp, Religious *Special Programming:* School and seniors 1 hr wkly; *Hrs. of News Programming:* news progmg 6 hrs wkly; *No. News Employees:* 2 *TargetAudience:* General.
Ken Ripley, General Manager

KFST-FM
11-01-1974; 94.3 MHz FM; 3 kw; 236 ft.; N30 52 37 W102 53 30
Rt. 1, Box 165, Fort Stockton, TX 79735 US
(432) 336-2228; *Fax:* (432) 336-5834
www.kfstradio.com
kfst@sbcglobal.net
License: Fort Stockton, Pecos County, TX held by Fort Stockton Radio Co. Inc.
Wire Services: NOAA Weather
Arbitron Metro Market: Fort Stockton, TX; *Format:* Country *Special Programming:* School and seniors 1 hr wkly; *Hrs. of News Programming:* news progmg 6 hrs wkly; *Target Audience:* Families
Matthew Boan, Operations Dir
Don Priest, General Manager
Joe Moore, Station Manager
Frank Delgado, Programming Director
Matt Garcia, Music Director

Fort Worth

KEGL
04-01-1959; 97.1 MHz FM; *Hrs Open:* 24; 97 kw; 1,667 ft.; N32 35 19 W96 58 5
14001 N. Dallas Pkwy., Suite 300, Dallas, TX 75240 US
(214) 866-8000
www.kegl.com
License: Fort Worth, Tarrant County, TX held by Citicasters Licenses Inc.
Group Owner: iHeartMedia; (acq 5-4-99; grpsl)
Arbitron Metro Market: Dallas-Fort Worth, TX; *Format:* Rock/AOR
Don Davis, Programming Director

KFJZ
02-15-1947; 870 kHz AM
2214 East 4th Street, Fort Worth, TX 76102 US
(817) 429-1630; *Fax:* 817-338-1205
License: Fort Worth, TX held by SIGA Broadcasting Corp.
Group Owner: SIGA Broadcasting Corp.; (acq 1-10-2008; $1.8 million)
Arbitron Metro Market: Fort Worth, TX
Gabriel Arango, President

KHVN
12-06-1946; 970 kHz AM; *Hrs Open:* 24; 1 kW; N32 47 56 W97 17 43
5787 S Hampton, Suite 285, Dallas, TX 75232 USA
(214) 331-5486; *Fax:* (214) 331-1908
www.khvnam.com
License: Fort Worth, TX held by Mortenson Broadcasting Co. of Texas, Inv.
Group Owner: Mortenson Broadcasting Co.; (acq 5-31-2002; $4.5 million with KNAX(AM) Fort Worth).
Nat'l Reps: Interep
Arbitron Metro Market: Dallas-Fort Worth; *Format:* Gospel; *Hrs. of News Programming:* news progmg 10 hrs wkly; *No. News Employees:* 1; *Target Audience:* Adults 24-64+

KLNO
12-24-1964; 94.1 MHz FM; *Hrs Open:* 24; 98 kw; 1,591 ft.; N32 35 22 W96 58 10
7700 John W. Carpenter Fwy., Dallas, TX 75247 US
(214) 525-0400; *Fax:* (214) 206-9022
www.univision.com
License: Fort Worth, Tarrant County, TX held by Univision Radio License Corp.
Group Owner: Univision Radio; (acq 9-22-2003; grpsl).
Nat'l Network: ABC
Arbitron Metro Market: Dallas, TX; *Format:* Tejano
Mark Masepohl, Vice President and General Manager
Patrick Parks, Chief Engineer
Karem Hocking, National Sales Manager
Myrna Vera, Research Director

KMVK
10-09-2006; 107.5 MHz FM; *Hrs Open:* 24; 16.5 kW; 1689 ft.; N32 35 2 W96 57 48
4131 N Central Expressway, Suite 1000, Dallas, TX 75204 USA
(214) 525-7000; *Fax:* (214) 905-5052
www.lagrande1075.com
lagrande@cbsradio.com
License: Fort Worth, Tarrant County, TX held by CBS Radio Texas Inc.
Group Owner: CBS Radio; (acq 6-26-96; grpsl)
Arbitron Metro Market: Dallas-Fort Worth Metroplex; *Format:* Spanish; *Target Audience:* 25-54
Nora Sandoval, General Sales Mgr
Jimmy Gonzalez, Programming Director
Mark Sanders, National Sales Manager

KKGM
01-01-2002; 1630 kHz AM; *Hrs Open:* 24 hrs
5787 S. Hampton Rd., Dallas, TX 75232 US
(214) 337-5700; *Fax:* (214) 337-5707
www.kkgmam.com
License: Fort Worth, TX held by Mortenson Broadcasting Co. of Texas Inc.
Group Owner: Mortenson Broadcasting Co.; (acq 5-31-2002; with KHVN(AM) Fort Worth).
Arbitron Metro Market: Dallas-Fort Worth; *Format:* Gospel, Sports; *Target Audience:* 30-64.; *Adv. Rates:* 50; 40; 50; 30
Paul Hughes, Operations Dir
Lon Sosh, General Manager
Jack Davis, Programming Director
Mike Price, Chief Engineer
Beverly Black, Office Manager
Nancy Burns, Public Service Director

KPLX
12-15-1962; 99.5 MHz FM; *Hrs Open:* 24; 100 kw; 1677 ft.; N32 34 54 W96 58 32
3090 Olive St., West Victory Plaza #400, Dallas, TX 75219 US
(214) 526-2400; *Fax:* (214) 525-2525
www.995thewolf.com
License: Fort Worth, TX held by KPLX LICO Inc.
Group Owner: Cumulus Media Inc.; (acq 1974)
Nat'l Network: AP Network News
Arbitron Metro Market: Dallas-Fort Worth; *Format:* Country; *No. News Employees:* 1; *Target Audience:* 25-54; loyal listeners throughout the day
Jeff Catlin, Operations Dir
Richard Frish, General Sales Mgr
Mark Phillips, Programming Director

KSCS
03-08-1949; 96.3 MHz FM; *Hrs Open:* 24; 99 kw; 1611 ft.; N32 35 15 W96 57 59
3090 Olive St., West Victory Plaza #400, Dallas, TX 75219 US
(214) 526-2400; *Fax:* (214) 525-2525
www.kscs.com

License: Fort Worth, TX held by Radio License Holdings LLC
Group Owner: Cumulus Media Inc.
Nat'l Reps: ABC Radio Sales
Arbitron Metro Market: Dallas-Fort Worth; *Format:* Country
Jeff Catlin, Operations Dir
James A. Roman, General Sales Mgr
JR Schumann, Programming Director
Rebecca Kaplan, Promotions Manager

***KTCU**
01-01-1965; 88.7 MHz FM; *Hrs Open:* 6 AM-1 AM; 10 kw; 320 ft; N32 42 40 W97 22 58
Box 298020, Fort Worth, TX 76129 US
(817) 257-7631
www.ktcu.tcu.edu
ktcu@ktcu.tcu.edu
License: Fort Worth, TX held by Texas Christian University
Group Owner: Texas Christian University
Population Served: 1,000,000; *Arbitron Metro Market:* Dallas-Fort Worth; *Format:* Variety/Diverse
Russell Scott, General Manager

WBAP
05-02-1922; 820 kHz AM; *Hrs Open:* 24; 50 kw-U, ND1; N32 36 38 W97 10 0
3090 Olive St., West Victory Plaza Suite 400, Dallas, TX 75219 US
(214) 526-2400
www.wbap.com
License: Fort Worth, TX held by Radio License Holdings LLC
Group Owner: Cumulus Media Inc.; (acq 6-12-2007; grpsl)
Nat'l Reps: ABC Radio Sales
Arbitron Metro Market: Las Vegas NV; *Format:* News/Talk
Tyler Cox, Operations Manager
RJ Lane, General Sales Mgr
Victoria Albrecht, Promotions Manager

Fort Worth-Dallas

KDGE
04-10-1962; 102.1 MHz FM; *Hrs Open:* 24; 100 kw; 1591 ft.; N32 34 54 W96 58 32
14001 N. Dallas Pkwy, Suite 300, Dallas, TX 75240 US
(214) 866-8000
www.kdge.com
jayshannon@iheartmedia.com
License: Fort Worth-Dallas, Tarrant County, TX held by Capstar TX LLC
Group Owner: iHeartMedia; (acq 8-30-2000; grpsl).
Nat'l Reps: CBS Radio
Arbitron Metro Market: Fort Worth, TX; *Format:* Alternative; *Hrs. of News Programming:* news progmg 5 hrs wkly; *No. News Employees:* 1; *Target Audience:* 20-44.
Jay Shannon, Programming Director
Anna De Haro, Public Affairs Director

Franklin

KJXJ
04-08-1985; 103.9 MHz FM; *Hrs Open:* 24; 8.7 kw; 197.5 feet; 30-53-05.7 N 096-32-29.6 W
Mailing Address: Box 3069, Bryan, TX 77802
Second Address: 1240 E. Villa Maria Rd., Bryan, TX 77802
(979) 776-1240; *Fax:* (979) 776-0123
License: Franklin, Robertson County, TX held by Brazos Valley Communications Ltd.
Group Owner: Brazos Valley Communications Ltd.; (acq 8-31-2006; grpsl)
Nat'l Reps: Katz Radio
Population Served: 150,000; *Arbitron Metro Market:* Bryan-College Station, TX *Special Programming:* Letterman, SNL; *Target Audience:* 18-49; 25-54.
Dan Ginzel, Operations Dir
Chris Kiske, General Manager
Nathan Peacock, General Sales Mgr
Lance Parr, Chief Engineer

Frankston

KOYE
06-15-1970; 96.7 MHz FM; *Hrs Open:* 24; 50 kw; 492 ft.; N32 2 22 W95 24 39
210 S. Broadway, Suite 100, Tyler, TX 75702 US
(903) 581-9966; *Fax:* (903) 534-5300
www.lainvasora.fm
License: Frankston, Anderson County, TX held by Alpha Media Licensee LLC
Group Owner: Alpha Media LLC; (acq 4-14-2015; grpsl).
Nat'l Reps: McGavren Guild
Arbitron Metro Market: Tyler, TX; *Format:* Tejano; *Target Audience:* 18-49.; *Adv. Rates:* 45; 45; 45; 45

Dru Laborde, Operations Manager
Ginger Dockery, General Manager
Corinna Ruiz, Sales Manager
Juan Ovalle, Programming Director
Harlen Lobley, Director of Sales

Fredericksburg

KNAF
11-01-1947; 910 kHz AM; 1 kw-D, ND1; 0.174 kw-N, ND1; N30 17 12 W98 52 58
Mailing Address: 210 Woodcrest, Fredericksburg, TX 78624 US
Second Address: 210 Woodcrest, Fredericksburg, TX 78624
(830) 997-2197; *Fax:* (830) 997-2198
License: Fredericksburg, TX held by J. & J. Fritz Media Ltd.
Group Owner: J. & J. Fritz Media Ltd.; (acq 1-23-91;
Format: Country, Talk *Special Programming:* Farm 5 hrs, Polka 4.5 hrs wkly; *Adv. Rates:* 14; 14; 14; 14
Jayson Fritz, President
Jan Fritz, Operations Dir
Rick Star, Programming Director
Arziana Carruth, Promotions Manager
Holley Day, Music Director

KNAF-FM
01-01-2005; 105.7 MHz FM; 9.1 kw; 538 ft.; N30 21 49 W98 54 47
Mailing Address: P.O. Box 311, Fredericksburg, TX 78624 US
Second Address: 210 Woodcrest, Fredericksburg, TX 78624
(830) 997-2197; *Fax:* (830) 997-2198
www.knafam.com
txradio@ktc.com
License: Fredericksburg, Gillespie County, TX
Group Owner: J. & J. Fritz Media Ltd.
Arbitron Metro Market: Fredericksburg, TX; *Format:* Country; *Target Audience:* 18-54.; *Adv. Rates:* 18; 18; 18; 18
Jayson Fritz, Engineering Dir

***KBLC**
08-01-2008; 91.5 MHz FM; 3.1 kw; 394 ft.; N30 11 49 W98 38 19
2424 South Blvd., Houston, TX 77098 US
(713) 520-5200
www.khcb.org
email@khcb.org
License: Fredericksburg, Gillespie County, TX held by Houston Christian Broadcasters Inc.
Group Owner: Houston Christian Broadcasters Inc.
Arbitron Metro Market: Fredericksburg, TX; *Format:* Christian; *Hrs. of News Programming:* News progmg 6 hrs wkly
Bruce E. Munsterman, President

Freeport

KJOJ-FM
01-01-1987; 103.3 MHz FM; 100 kw; 994 ft.; N28 48 57 W95 36 3 *Rebroadcasts:* Simulcasts La Raza alongside KTJM(FM)
3000 Bering Dr, Houston, TX 77057 US
(713) 315-3400; *Fax:* (713) 315-3565
larazahouston.estrellatv.com
houstoninfo@lbimedia.com
License: Freeport, Brazoria County, TX held by Liberman Broadcasting of Houston License LLC.
Group Owner: Liberman Broadcasting Inc.; (acq 3-20-2001; grpsl)
Arbitron Metro Market: Houston-Galveston, TX; *Format:* Spanish; *Target Audience:* 18-49.
Lenard Liberman, CEO
Winter Horton, Operations Dir
Gerardo Reyes, General Sales Mgr
Cheque Gonzalez, Programming Director
Meliza Posada, News Director

Fremont

***KLBD(FM)**
88.1 MHz FM; 100 w vert; Ant 220 ft; N27 17 20 W98 07 23
PO Box 260715, Corpus Christi, TX 78426-0715
(361) 299-1960
License: Fremont, Brooks County, TX held by The Worship Center of Knoxville
Population Served: 307,953; *Arbitron Metro Market:* Corpus Christi, TX
Rutino Sendenjo, President/General Manager
Veronica Gaytan, Programming Director
AJ Soliz, Operations Manager/Chief Engineer

Friona

KGRW
11-01-1994; 94.7 MHz FM; 48 kw; 500 ft.; N34 41 17 W102 56 53 *Rebroadcasts:* Rebroadcasts KQFX(FM) Borger 100%
2402 Broadmoor, Bldg D-2, Suite 101, Bryan, TX 77802 US
(806) 355-1044; *Fax:* (806) 457-0642
www.gruvworks.com
gruvworks@aol.com
License: Friona, Parmer County, TX held by Tejas Broadcasting Ltd. LLP.
Group Owner: Tejas Broadcasting Ltd. LLP; (acq 11-15-2004; grpsl).
Format: Variety/Diverse; *Target Audience:* 25-54; working class Texas born Hispanic audience
Daniel, Marketing/Sales

Frisco

KATH
10-01-1936; 910 kHz AM
8828 N. Stemmons Freeway, Suite 106, Dallas, TX 75247 US
(214) 951-0132; *Fax:* (214) 951-8622
davepalmer@grnonline.com
License: Frisco, TX held by Chatham Hill Foundation Inc.
Arbitron Metro Market: Dallas-Fort Worth; *Format:* Sports; *Target Audience:* Ages 18-44; Hispanic sports & music fans; *Adv. Rates:* 60; 40; 80; 20
Dave Palmer, General Manager

Gainesville

KSOC
01-01-1958; 94.5 MHz FM; *Hrs Open:* 24; kw
13760 Noel Rd., Suite 1100, Dallas, TX 75240 US
(972) 331-5400; *Fax:* (972) 331-5560
License: Gainesville, Cooke County, TX held by Radio One Licenses LLC.
Group Owner: Radio One Inc.; (acq 11-8-01; grpsl).
Arbitron Metro Market: Dallas-Fort Worth; *Format:* Urban Contemporary; *Hrs. of News Programming:* news progmg one hr wkly; *No. News Employees:* 1; *Target Audience:* 18-44; affluent generation X'ers
Alfred Liggins, President/CEO

KGAF
01-01-1947; 1580 kHz AM; 0.25 kw-D, DAN; 0.25 kw-N, DAN; N33 37 42 W97 6 25
PO Box 368, Gainesville, TX 76241 US
(940) 665-5546; *Fax:* (940) 665-1580
www.1580kgaf.com
License: Gainesville, TX held by First IV Media Inc.
Regional Network: Texas State Networks
Arbitron Metro Market: Gainesville, TX; *Format:* Adult Contemp, News, 62, Oldies, Talk *Special Programming:* Farm 3 hrs, sports 3 hrs wkly, community 3 hrs wkly; *No. News Employees:* 1; *Target Audience:* 25-54; m/f
Steve Eberhart, Manager
John Hambrecht, General Sales Mgr
Dee Blanton, Programming Director
Darren Allred, Sports

Galveston

KGBC
05-01-1947; 1540 kHz AM; *Hrs Open:* 24
1302 North Shepherd, Houston, TX 77008 US
(713) 868-5559; *Fax:* (713) 868-9631
www.kgbc1540.com
sigabroadcasting@gmail.com
License: Galveston, TX held by SIGA Broadcasting Corp.
Group Owner: SIGA Broadcasting Corp.; acq 5-9-2002; $900,000).
Arbitron Metro Market: Galveston, TX; *Format:* Chinese; *Target Audience:* Chinese Adults
Gabriel Arango, President
Julian Arango, Operations
Dade Moore, Chief Engineer

KOVE-FM
07-01-2001; 106.5 MHz FM; *Hrs Open:* 24; 98 kw; 1,962 ft.; N29 18 0 W95 6 40
5100 S.W. Fwy., Houston, TX 77056 US
(713) 965-2400; *Fax:* (713) 965-2401
www.univision.com
License: Galveston, Galveston County, TX held by Univision Radio License Corp.
Group Owner: Univision Radio; (acq 9-22-2003; grpsl)
Arbitron Metro Market: Houston, TX; *Format:* Spanish; *Hrs. of News Programming:* news progmg 3 hrs wkly; *No. News Employees:* 1; *Target Audience:* 18-49; assimilated Hispanics
David Loving, General Manager
Nestor Enriquez, Client Services Director
Marty Scruggs, Chief Engineer
Kim Mercier, National Sales Manager

Ganado

KHTZ
11-26-1997; 104.7 MHz FM; *Hrs Open:* 24; 50 kw; 459 ft.; N28 55 37 W96 46 54
102 Jason Plaza, Victoria, TX 77901 US
(979) 836-9411; *Fax:* (361) 579-4105
www.lonestarfm.com
License: Ganado, Jackson County, TX held by Roy E. Henderson.
Group Owner: Fort Bend Broadcasting Co.; (acq 5-10-2001; $1.5 million)
Regional Network: Texas State Networks
Arbitron Metro Market: Ganado, TX; *Format:* Country; *Target Audience:* 25-64; skews males
Ryan Henderson, General Manager

Gardendale

KFZX
01-09-1984; 102.1 MHz FM; *Hrs Open:* 24; 100 kw; 984 ft.; N31 57 55 W102 46 10
600 Congress Avenue, Suite 1400, Austin, TX 78701 US
(432) 563-9102; *Fax:* (432) 580-9102
www.classicrock102.net
License: Gardendale, Ector County, TX
Group Owner: ICA Radio Ltd.; (acq 10-1-2007; grpsl)
Nat'l Reps: Eastman Radio
Arbitron Metro Market: Odessa, TX; *Format:* Classic Rock; *Target Audience:* 25-54.
Mike Gatons, General Manager
Robert Hallmark, Programming Director
Rodney Norris, Chief Engineer

Garland

KAAM
01-01-1973; 770 kHz AM; *Hrs Open:* 24; 10 kw-D, 1 kw-N, DA-2; N33 01 58 W96 34 31
3201 Royalty Row, Irving, TX 75062
(972) 445-1700; *Fax:* (972) 438-6574
www.kaamradio.com
sarahfb.djr@gmail.com
License: Garland, Dallas County, TX held by DJRD Broadcasting
Group Owner: Crawford Broadcasting Co.; (acq 1979).
Population Served: 6,000,000; *Arbitron Metro Market:* Dallas-Fort Worth; *Format:* Christian, Religious; *Target Audience:* 35 plus; Christian
Donald B. Crafword, President
Sarah Lee, Finance Diretor/Station Manager
Emmi McMinn, Traffic Manager
Casey Lightford, Writer/Producer

Gatesville

***KVLW**
01-01-2005; 88.1 MHz FM; 16.5 kw vert; Ant 1,096 ft; N31 18 53 W97 19 36
Mailing Address: American Educational Broadcasting Inc., 3185 S. Highland Dr., Las Vegas, NV 33406
Second Address: 3411 Market Loop, Studio, Suite 108, Temple, TX 76502
(254) 791-5251; *Fax:* (254) 791-0200
License: Gatesville, McLennan County, TX held by American Educational Broadcasting Inc.
Nat'l Network: K-Love
Arbitron Metro Market: Waco, TX
Carl Auel, President
James Auel, General Manager

George West

KGWT
01-01-2008; 93.5 MHz FM; 22.5 kw; 344 ft.; N28 17 37 W98 13 16
US
(361) 449-1315
License: George West, Live Oak County, TX held by Hispanic Target Media Inc.
Group Owner: Hispanic Target Media Inc.
Arbitron Metro Market: George West, TX; *Format:* Country
Francisco San Millan, President

Georgetown

KLJA
10-31-1991; 107.7 MHz FM; *Hrs Open:* 24; 10.5 kw; 508 ft.; N30 37 22 W97 38 33
2233 W. North Loop Blvd., Austin, TX 78756 US
(512) 533-2840
www.univision.com
License: Georgetown, Williamson County, TX held by Univision Radio License Corp.
Group Owner: Univision Radio; (acq 9-22-2003; grpsl)
Arbitron Metro Market: Austin, TX; *Format:* Adult Contemp, Spanish; *Target Audience:* 18-34; male; *Adv. Rates:* 85; 85; 90; 20
Jeff Zimmerman, General Manager

KHFI-FM
03-01-1972; 96.7 MHz FM; *Hrs Open:* 24; 100 kw; 951 ft.; N30 19 20 W97 48 3
3601 S. Congress Ave., Building F, Austin, TX 78704 US
(512) 684-7300
www.967kissfm.com
License: Georgetown, Williamson County, TX held by CC Licenses LLC
Group Owner: iHeartMedia; (acq 3-9-93; $3.5 million;
Nat'l Reps: Clear Channel
Arbitron Metro Market: Austin, TX; *Format:* Contemporary Hits/Top 40; *Hrs. of News Programming:* news progmg one hr wkly; *No. News Employees:* 1; *Target Audience:* 18-49; adult women
Melody Caldwell, General Sales Mgr
Zach Dillon, Programming Director
Travis Hill, Promotions and Marketing Director

Giddings

***KANJ**
10-28-1999; 91.1 MHz FM; *Hrs Open:* 24; 0.45 kw; 335 ft.; N30 9 56 W96 52 15 *Rebroadcasts:* Rebroadcasts KHCB-FM Houston 100%
2424 South Blvd., Houston, TX 77098 US
(713) 520-5200
www.khcb.org
email@khcb.org
License: Giddings, Lee County, TX held by Houston Christian Broadcasters Inc.
Group Owner: Houston Christian Broadcasters Inc.
Nat'l Network: Moody
Arbitron Metro Market: Houston, TX; *Format:* Christian
Bruce E. Munsterman, President

Gilmer

KFRO-FM
07-24-1980; 95.3 MHz FM; *Hrs Open:* 24; 5.9 kw; 666 ft.; N32 37 50 W94 53 44
3400 West Marshall Avenue, Suite 307, Longview, TX 75608 US
(903) 663-2477; *Fax:* (903) 663-9492
www.mybreezefm.com
License: Gilmer, Upshur County, TX held by Walller Media LLC.
Group Owner: Waller Broadcasting; (acq 6-15-98; $1.425 million with KFRO(AM) Longview).
Nat'l Reps: Roslin
Arbitron Metro Market: Gilmer, TX; *Format:* Spanish; *Target Audience:* 25-49.
Bill Walter, President of Operations
Christin Chifwepa, Business Manager

Glen Rose

KTFW-FM
01-01-1989; 92.1 MHz FM; 25 kw; 1417 ft.; N32 16 31 W98 1 22
201 Main, Fort Worth, TX 76102 US
(817) 332-0959; *Fax:* (817) 348-8373
www.921hankfm.com
License: Glen Rose, Somervell County, TX held by LKCM Radio Group L.P.
Group Owner: LKCM Radio Group L.P.; (acq 1-13-2006; $10,142,816).
Regional Network: Texas State Networks
Arbitron Metro Market: Fort Worth, TX; *Format:* Country; *Target Audience:* 40 plus.
Gerry Schlegel, President
George Marti, Operations Dir
Mike Crow, Programming Director

Goldsmith

KTXO
94.7 MHz FM; 6 kw; 318 ft.; N31 52 2 W102 39 18
US
(512) 467-0643
License: Goldsmith, Ector County, TX held by Matinee Radio LLC.
Group Owner: Matinee Radio LLC
Arbitron Metro Market: Monterey-Salinas-Santa Cruz, CA
Robert Walker, President

Goliad

KHMC
01-01-1995; 95.9 MHz FM; *Hrs Open:* 24; 25 kw; 322 ft.; N28 40 57 W97 18 50
115 West Avenue D, Robstown, TX 78380 US
(361) 575-9533; *Fax:* (361) 575-9502
www.majic95fm.com
majictejano@yahoo.com
License: Goliad, Goliad County, TX held by Cinco de Mayo Broadcasting.
Format: Tejano; *Target Audience:* Spanish Adults
Homer Lopez, General Manager
Ralph Salezar, General Sales Mgr
Lilo Arguellez, Program Director

Gonzales

KCTI
12-17-1947; 1450 kHz AM; 1 kw-U, ND1; N29 30 35 W97 24 51
615 Saint Paul Street, Gonzales, TX 78629 US
(830) 672-3631; *Fax:* (830) 672-9603
egon@kcti1450.com
License: Gonzales, TX held by Gonzales Communications, a Texas L.P.
Regional Network: Texas State Networks
Arbitron Metro Market: Gonzales, TX; *Format:* Country; *Target Audience:* General.
Colton Filip, Program/Music/Promotions/Production Director
Bill Woleben, Chief Engineer
Rafael Gallegos, Advertising Sales
Dian Dowman-Myers, Traffic

***KMLR**
03-01-1986; 106.3 MHz FM; 15 kw; 423 ft.; N29 41 17 W97 40 39
PO Box 2098, Omaha, NE 68103-2098 US
(916) 251-1600; *Fax:* (916) 251-1650
www.klove.com
License: Gonzales, Gonzales County, TX held by Educational Media Foundation.
Group Owner: EMF Broadcasting; (acq 3-31-2006; $6 million with KYLR(FM) Hutto).
Nat'l Network: K-Love
Arbitron Metro Market: Rocklin, CA; *Format:* Christian
Darrell Chambliss, Chairman
Mike Novak, President/CEO
David Pierce, Chief Creative Officer
Alan Mason, COO
Eric Moser, CFO
D. Kevin Blair, Secretary/General Counsel

***KRNZ**
01-01-2008; 88.1 MHz FM; 1.3 kw; Ant 384 ft; N29 29 09 W97 29 17 *Rebroadcasts:* Rebroadcasts KLRD(FM) Yucaipa, CA 100%
2351 Sunset Blvd., Suite 170-218, Rocklin, CA 78046
(916) 251-1600; *Fax:* (916) 251-1650
www.air1.com
info@air1.com
License: Gonzales, Gonzales County, TX held by Educational Media Foundation.
Group Owner: EMF Broadcasting; (acq 2-28-2006; $36,000 for CP)
Nat'l Network: Air 1

Mike Novak, President
David Pierce, Programming Director
Ed Lenane, News Director
Sam Wallington, Engineering Dir
Marya Morgan, News Reporter
Richard Hunt, News Reporter

Graham

KSWA
01-01-1948; 1330 kHz AM; *Hrs Open:* 24; 0.5 kw-D, NDD; 0.051 kw-N, ND1; N33 7 37 W98 35 35
620 Oak Street, Graham, TX 76046 US
(940) 549-7800
www.lakecountryradio.net/kswa
License: Graham, TX held by Graham Newspapers Inc.
Group Owner: Graham Newspapers Inc.; (acq 1996)
Regional Network: Texas State Networks
Arbitron Metro Market: Graham, TX; *Format:* Country *Special Programming:* Bluegrass 2 hrs, gospel 2 hrs, Texas mus 2 hrs wkly; *Hrs. of News Programming:* news progmg 10 hrs wkly; *No. News Employees:* 1 *TargetAudience:* Adults 35 plus.; *Adv. Rates:* 15; 15; 15; 15
Roy Robinson, Operations Dir
Joe Graham, General Manager
Cindy Lewis, General Sales Mgr

Greg Tiller, Programming Director
James Jones, News Director
Christy Garcia, Traffic Manager

KWKQ
08-01-1975; 94.7 MHz FM; *Hrs Open:* 24; 10.5 kw; 486 ft.; N33 2 30 W98 46 44
620 Oak Street, Graham, TX 76450 US
(940) 549-7800
www.lakecountryradio.net/kwkq
License: Graham, Young County, TX
Group Owner: Graham Newspapers Inc.
Regional Network: Texas State Networks
Arbitron Metro Market: Graham, TX; *Format:* Classic Rock
Special Programming: Alternative 6 hrs wkly; *Hrs. of News Programming:* news progmg 5 hrs wkly; *No. News Employees:* 1; *Target Audience:* Adults 25-54. *Adv. Rates:* 15; 15; 15; 15
Roy Robinson, Operations Dir
Joe Graham, General Manager
Jim Jones, News Director

Granbury

KPIR
03-13-1980; 1420 kHz AM; *Hrs Open:* 24; 0.5 kw-D, DA2; 0.5 kw-N, DA2; N32 27 43 W97 47 19
1620 Weatherford Highway, Granbury, TX 76048 US
(817) 736-0360; *Fax:* (817) 736-0344
www.kpir.com
License: Granbury, TX held by Pirate Broadcasters Inc.
Arbitron Metro Market: Dallas-Fort Worth; *Format:* Country
Special Programming: Farm one hr wkly; *Hrs. of News Programming:* news progmg 21 hrs wkly; *No. News Employees:* 1; *Target Audience:* 25-55; general
Bob Haschke, General Manager
Shayne Hollinger, Programming Director
Sue Haschke, News Director
Justin McClure, Chief Engineer

Grand Prairie

KKDA
08-01-1957; 730 kHz AM; 0.5 kw-D, DAN; 0.5 kw-N, DAN; N32 45 51 W96 57 38
2356 Glenda Ln., Dallas, TX 75229 USA
(972) 620-6296
License: Grand Prairie, TX held by SKR Partners, LLC
Group Owner: Service Broadcasting Group, LLC
Arbitron Metro Market: Dallas, TX; *Format:* Korean
Scott Kim, President

Greenville

KGVL
03-26-1946; 1400 kHz AM; 1 kw-U; N33 10 02 W96 05 55
1517 Wolfe City Dr., Greenville, TX 75401
(214) 693-4289
License: Greenville, TX held by Hunt Country Radio LLC
Group Owner: Hunt County Radio LLC; (acq 1-11-2005; $500,000).
Nat'l Network: Fox News Radio; *Regional Network:* Texas State Networks
Population Served: 70,000 *Format:* Country; *No. News Employees:* 2; *Target Audience:* 25 plus.
Jim Patrick, Programming Director

KIKT
09-15-1978; 93.5 MHz FM; *Hrs Open:* 24; 12.5 kw; Ant 328 ft; N33 13 16 W95 41 20
1517 Wolfe City Dr., Greenville, TX 75401
(214) 693-4289
License: Greenville, Hunt County, TX held by Hunt County Radio LLC
Group Owner: Hunt County Radio LLC; (acq 9-2-99; with co-located AM).
Regional Network: Fox News Radio
Format: Country; *Hrs. of News Programming:* News progmg 15 hrs wkly; *Target Audience:* General.
Mike Horne, General Manager

***KTXG**
01-01-2006; 90.5 MHz FM; 38 kw; 722 ft.; N33 19 0 W96 24 27
Rebroadcasts: Rebroadcasts WAFR(FM) Tupelo, MS 100%
P.O. Box 3206, Tupelo, MS 38803 US
(662) 844-8888; *Fax:* (662) 842-6791
www.afr.net
faq@afa.net
License: Greenville, Hunt County, TX held by American Family Association.
Group Owner: American Family Radio
Arbitron Metro Market: Greenville, TX; *Format:* Christian
Tim Wildmon, President
Donald Wildmon, Founder
Buddy Smith, Sr VP
Ed Vitagliano, Exec VP
Randy Sharp, Director Of Special Projects
Meeke Addison, Director Of Communications
Abraham Hamilton III, General Counsel

Gregory

KPUS
01-01-1999; 104.5 MHz FM; *Hrs Open:* 24; 14 kw; 446 ft.; N27 52 2 W97 13 7
615 N. Upperbroadway, Corpus Christi, TX 78405 US
(361) 814-3800; *Fax:* (361) 855-3770
classicrock1045.com
License: Gregory, San Patricio County, TX held by Convergent Broadcasting Corpus Christi LP.
Group Owner: Convergent Broadcasting LP; (acq 1-12-2004; grpsl).
Arbitron Metro Market: Corpus Christi, TX; *Format:* Classic Rock; *Target Audience:* Adults; 25-54
Rene Saenz, Programming Director

Groves

KCOL-FM
09-17-1983; 92.5 MHz FM; *Hrs Open:* 24; 31 kw; 430 ft.; N30 3 43 W93 58 50
2885 IH 10 East., Beaumont, TX 77702 US
(409) 896-5555; *Fax:* (409) 896-5566
www.cool925.com
info@cool925.com
License: Groves, Jefferson County, TX held by Clear Channel Broadcasting Licenses Inc.
Group Owner: iHeartMedia; (acq 1-29-2004; $4.5 million).
Arbitron Metro Market: Beaumont-Port Arthur, TX; *Format:* Oldies; *Target Audience:* 35 plus.; *Adv. Rates:* 63; 63; 63; 63
Evan Armstrong, Regional Market President
Jim Love, Programming Director
Harold Mann, News Director

Hallettsville

KTXM
10-29-1997; 99.9 MHz FM; 3.4 kw; 348 ft.; N29 27 45 W96 56 4
Rebroadcasts: Rebroadcasts KYKM(FM) Yoakum 100%
701 North Avenue East, Shiner, TX 77984 US
(361) 594-8433
www.texasthunderradio.com
texasthunderradio@yahoo.com
License: Hallettsville, Lavaca County, TX held by Kremling Enterprises Inc.
Arbitron Metro Market: Hallettsville, TX; *Format:* Country
Laura Kremling, Station Manager
Travis Kremling, Programming Director

Haltom City

KLIF
01-01-1996; 93.3 MHz FM; 50 kw; 276 ft; N32 46 44 W96 55 22
3090 Olive St., Suite 400, Dallas, TX 75219 US
(214) 526-7400; *Fax:* (214) 525-2525
www.hot933hits.com
License: Haltom City, TX held by Radio License Holding SRC, LLC
Group Owner: Cumulus Media Inc.; (acq 1-28-97).
Arbitron Metro Market: Dallas-Fort Worth; *Format:* Contemporary Hits/Top 40
Louie Diaz, Operations Dir
Alec Drake, General Sales Mgr
Kristi Crisp, Promotions Director

Hamilton

KCLW
05-22-1948; 900 kHz AM; *Hrs Open:* 24; 0.25 kw-D, ND1; 0.01 kw-N, ND1; N31 43 8 W98 8 39
Mailing Address: P.O. Box 552, Hamilton, TX 76531 US
Second Address: 115 A N. Rice, Hamilton, TX 76531
(254) 221-4802; *Fax:* (254) 386-8804
www.kclwradio.com
tim@kclwradio.com
License: Hamilton, TX held by Lasting Value Broadcasting Group Inc.
Nat'l Network: CBS; Jones Radio Networks
Arbitron Metro Market: Killeen,ÿTX; *Format:* Country *Special Programming:* Relg 6 hrs, Sp 12 hrs wkly; *Hrs. of News Programming:* news progmg 6 hrs wkly; *No. News Employees:* 1; *Target Audience:* 18-65. *Adv.Rates:* 27; 22; 27; 10
Meredith Beal, President
Ronald Beal, Operations Dir
Sammie Casey, General Manager

Hamlin

KCDD
01-30-1987; 103.7 MHz FM; 98 kw; 984 ft.; N32 43 31 W100 4 19
2525 S. Danville, Abilene, TX 79605 US
(325) 793-9700; *Fax:* (325) 692-1576
www.power103.com
License: Hamlin, Jones County, TX held by Cumulus Licensing Corp.
Group Owner: Cumulus Media Inc.; (acq 2-13-98; grpsl)
Arbitron Metro Market: Abilene, TX; *Format:* Contemporary Hits/Top 40
Ronnie L. Baird, General Manager
Lori Morris, Business Manager
Chris Andrews, Engineer
Terri Knight, Promotional Consideration
Jennifer Jerez, Webmaster

Harker Heights

KUSJ
06-01-1987; 105.5 MHz FM; 33 kw; 600 ft.; N30 59 9 W97 37 51
608 Moody Lane, Temple, TX 76504 US
(254) 773-5252; *Fax:* (254) 773-0015
www.myus105.com
bourdon.wooten@townsquaremedia.com
License: Harker Heights, Bell County, TX held by Townsquare Media Killeen-Temple License LLC
Group Owner: Townsquare Media; (acq 2-2-00; grpsl).
Arbitron Metro Market: Harker Heights, TX; *Format:* Country; *Target Audience:* 25-54.
Was Adams, Brand Manager
Laura Wiederhold, Director Of Sales
Kelsey Kilter, Digital Sales Manager
Jason Eisenberg, Digital Managing Editor

Harlingen

KFRQ
01-01-1960; 94.5 MHz FM; *Hrs Open:* 24; 100 kw; 1158 ft.; N26 8 55 W97 49 17
801 N. Jackson Rd., McAllen, TX 78501 US
(956) 687-4848; *Fax:* (956) 687-7784
www.q945therock.com
aduran@entravision.com
License: Harlingen, Cameron County, TX held by Entravision Holdings LLC.
Group Owner: Entravision Communications Corp.
Arbitron Metro Market: Harlington TX; *Format:* Rock/AOR; *No. News Employees:* 1; *Target Audience:* 25-54.
Alex Duran, Programming Director
Monica Quintanilla, Promotions Manager

KGBT
01-01-1941; 1530 kHz AM; *Hrs Open:* 24; 50 kw-D, DA2; 10 kw-N, DA2; N26 22 33 W97 53 43
200 S. 10th St., Suite 600, McAllen, TX 78501 US
(956) 631-5499
www.univision.com
License: Harlingen, Cameron County, TX held by Tichenor License Corp.
Group Owner: Univision Radio; (acq 9-22-2003; grpsl)
Arbitron Metro Market: McAllen, TX; *Format:* Spanish; *No. News Employees:* 2; *Target Audience:* 18 plus.
Victoria Guerrero, Vice President and General Manager
Hugo De La Cruz, Programming Director
Jorge Garza, Chief Engineer

KBTQ
07-01-1975; 96.1 MHz FM; 100 kw; 988 ft.; N26 8 56 W97 49 18
200 S. 10th St., Suite 600, McAllen, TX 78501 US
(956) 631-5499
www.univision.com
License: Harlingen, Cameron County, TX held by Tichenor License Corp.
Group Owner: Univision Radio
Population Served: 101,500; *Arbitron Metro Market:* McAllen-Brownsville-Harlingen, TX; *Format:* Spanish
Victoria Guerrero, Vice President and General Manager
Cesar Chapa, Promotions Director
Kim Mercier, National Sales Manager

***KMBH-FM**
04-30-1991; 88.9 MHz FM; *Hrs Open:* 24; 3 kw; 299 ft.; N26 10 46 W97 30 6
(956) 421-4111; *Fax:* (956) 421-4150
www.kmbh.org

License: Harlingen, Cameron County, TX held by RGV Educational Broadcasting Inc.
Nat'l Network: NPR
Arbitron Metro Market: McAllen, TX TV Affiliate: *KMBH(TV) affil; Format: Jazz, News Special Programming: Sp 3 hrs wkly; Hrs. of News Programming: News progmg 34 hrs wkly; Target Audience: General.
Bishop Daniel E. Flores, Chairman
Andy Hagan, Vice Chair
Richard Walker, Treasurer
Monsignor Gustavo Barrera, Secretary

Hart

*KKFC
89.3 MHz FM; 0.2 kw; 36 ft.; N34 23 23 W102 7 14
US
(940) 668-7971
www.kkfcradio.com
License: Hart, Castro County, TX held by 1 A Chord Inc.
Arbitron Metro Market: Gainesville, TX
Mary Fay Jackson, General Manager

Harts Bluff

*KPKP
89.1 MHz FM; kw
US
(903) 466-6791
License: Harts Bluff, Red River County, TX held by Millennium Broadcasting Corp.
Arbitron Metro Market: Harts Bluff, TX
James Furlow Jr., President

Haskell

KVRP-FM
04-08-1981; 97.1 MHz FM; Hrs Open: 24; 100 kw; 531 ft; N33 09 40 W99 48 57
PO Box 1118, Haskell, TX 79521
(940) 864-8505; Fax: (940) 864-8001
www.kvrp.com
news@kvrp.com
License: Haskell, Haskell County, TX held by 1 Chronicles 14 L.P.
Group Owner: Weston Entertainment L.P.; (acq 8-4-2004; $700,000 with KVRP(A
Regional Network: Texas State Networks; Nat'l Reps: Katz Radio
Population Served: 45,000; Arbitron Metro Market: Abilene, TX
Special Programming: Farm 5 hrs, relg 6 hrs wkly; Hrs. of News Programming: News progmg 5 hrs wkly; Target Audience: 25 plus.
Gary Barrett, Senior Account Executive
Keith Daniels, Programming/Production Director
Sarah Kalen, Chief Operator

Hearne

KVJM
05-15-1985; 103.1 MHz FM; 5 kw horiz, 4.9 kw vert; 361 ft.; N30 45 35 W96 28 0
1716 Briarcrest Drive, Suite 150, Bryan, TX 77802 US
(979) 846-5597; Fax: (979) 268-9090
www.kissfm1031.com
License: Hearne, Robertson County, TX held by Clear Channel Broadcasting Licenses Inc.
Group Owner: iHeartMedia
Arbitron Metro Market: Bryan, TX; Format: Contemporary Hits/Top 40; Target Audience: 18-54.
Evan Armstrong, Market Manager
Zack Owens, Regional Operations Manager
Jim Harrington, Director of Sales
Ashlee Young, Programming Director

*KEDC
88.5 MHz FM; 2.5 kw; 184 ft.; N30 46 12.6 W96 32 33
603 Church Avenue, College Station, TX 77840 US
(979) 255-2633
www.redcradio.org
License: Hearne, Robertson County, TX held by Brazos Valley Coalition for Life.
Nat'l Network: EWTN Radio
Arbitron Metro Market: Hearne, TX; Format: Christian
Dennis Macha, General Manager

Hebbronville

*KEKO
01-01-2003; 101.7 MHz FM; 3 kw; 328 ft.; N27 18 46 W98 39 51
2702 Pine St, Laredo, TX 78043 US
License: Hebbronville, Jim Hogg County, TX held by La Nueva Cadena Radio Luz Inc.
Format: Christian

Helotes

KONO-FM
02-18-1971; 101.1 MHz FM; Hrs Open: 24; 96 kw; 991 ft.; N29 31 25 W98 43 25
8122 Datapoint Drive, Suite 600, San Antonio, TX 78229 US
(210) 615-5400; Fax: (210) 615-5300
ben.reed@coxinc.com
License: Helotes, Bexar County, TX held by Cox Radio Inc.
Group Owner: Cox Radio Inc.; (acq 2-12-98; $23 million with KONO(AM) San Antonio)
Nat'l Reps: Katz Radio; Wire Services: AP
Arbitron Metro Market: San Antonio, TX; Format: Oldies; Hrs. of News Programming: news progmg one hr wkly; No. News Employees: 1; Target Audience: 25-54; total audience appeal
Ben Reed, Vice President / Market Manager
Tori Finch, Promotions Manager
Jim Dyer, General Sales Manager
Jeff Garrison, Operations Manager

Hemphill

KTHP
11-01-2000; 103.9 MHz FM; Hrs Open: 24 hours; 4.5 kw; 377 ft.; N31 25 24 W93 50 30
Mailing Address: 595 San Antonio Ave, Many, LA 71449 US
Second Address: 174 East Main Street, Hemphill, TX 75948
(318) 256-5924; Fax: (318) 256-0950
License: Hemphill, Sabine County, TX held by Baldridge-Dumas Communications Inc.
Group Owner: Baldridge-Dumas Communications Inc.
Arbitron Metro Market: Shreveport, LA; Format: Country
Michael Parker, Operations Dir
Rhonda Benson, VP/General Manager
Cindy Ezernack, Station Manager
Jenny Hodge, General Sales Mgr
Tedd Dumas, Owner
Ed Baldridge, Co-Owner

Hempstead

KTWL
01-01-1999; 105.3 MHz FM; 9.2 kw; 545 ft.; N30 18 19 W96 1 40 Rebroadcasts: Simulcasts KLTR(FM) Caldwell 100%
530 W. Main Street, Brenham, TX 77833 US
(979) 836-0214; Fax: (979) 836-9435
www.texasmix1053.com
License: Hempstead, Waller County, TX held by Farmers Communications.
Arbitron Metro Market: Brenham, TX; Format: Adult Contemp
Roy Henderson, CEO
Steve Britewell, Engineering Dir

Henderson

KWRD
03-01-1956; 1470 kHz AM; Hrs Open: 24; 5 kw-D, NDD; N32 10 55 W94 47 49
1101 Kilgore Drive, Henderson, TX 75652 US
(903) 655-1800; Fax: (903) 655-1808
info@kwrdonline.com
License: Henderson, TX held by Jerry Hanszen dba Hanszen Broadcasting Company
Nat'l Network: ESPN Radio; Regional Network: Texas State Networks; Wire Services: ABC
Arbitron Metro Market: Henderson, TX; Format: Sports; No. News Employees: 1; Target Audience: General.
David Jacobs, Operations Manager
Judy Guthrie, General Manager
Julie Nichols, Sales Executive
Dennis Rivers, Sports Color Analyst
Jason Wade, Sports Director
Miles Toler, Sportscaster

Hereford

KJNZ
12-12-2000; 103.5 MHz FM; 50 kw; 279 ft.; N34 45 0 W102 22 54
C/O Fisher Wayland, 2001 Pennsylvania Ave NW, Washington, DC 20006 US
License: Hereford, Deaf Smith County, TX held by Hereford Broadcasting LLC

Jose Aguillon, CEO
Joel Gallegos, General Manager

KPAN
08-01-1948; 860 kHz AM; Hrs Open: 24; 250 w-D, 231 w-N; N34 47 33 W102 25 45
218 East Fifth Street, Hereford, TX 79045
(806) 364-1860; Fax: (806) 364-5814
www.kpanradio.com
kpan@kpanradio.com
License: Hereford, Deaf Smith County, TX held by KPAN Broadcasters.
Nat'l Network: CBS; Regional Network: Texas State Networks; Wire Services: AP
Population Served: 350,000 Special Programming: Tejano 15 hrs, farm 12 hrs wkly; Hrs. of News Programming: news progmg 20 hrs wkly; No. News Employees: 1; Target Audience: General.
Josie Nava, Office Manager
Brad Land, Sales Manager

KPAN-FM
09-01-1965; 106.3 MHz FM; Hrs Open: 24; 30 kw; 259 ft; N34 47 33 W102 25 45 Rebroadcasts: Rebroadcasts KPAN(AM) Hereford.
Box 1757, 218 E. 5th St., Hereford, TX 79045
(806) 364-1860; Fax: (806) 364-5814
www.kpanradio.com
License: Hereford, Deaf Smith County, TX
Nat'l Network: CBS Radio; Regional Network: Texas State Networks; Wire Services: AP
Target Audience: General.
Brad Land, Sales Manager
Josie Nava, Office Manager

*KRLH
01-01-2009; 90.9 MHz FM; 0.13 kw; 269 ft.; N34 51 2 W102 23 38 Rebroadcasts: Rebroadcasts KLVR(FM) Middletown, CA 100%
PO Box 2098, Omaha, NE 68103-2098 US
(916) 251-1600
www.klove.com
License: Hereford, Deaf Smith County, TX held by Educational Media Foundation.
Group Owner: EMF Broadcasting; (acq 3-23-2007; grpsl)
Nat'l Network: K-Love
Arbitron Metro Market: Hereford, TX; Format: Christian
Darrell Chambliss, Chairman
Mike Novak, President/CEO
David Pierce, Chief Creative Officer
Alan Mason, Chief Operating Officer
Eric Moser, Chief Financial Officer
D. Kevin Blair, Secretary and General Counsel

Hico

KTAE
107.7 MHz FM
PO Box 1629, Cleburne, TX
(817) 645-6643
License: Hico, TX held by M&M Broadcasters LTD
Group Owner: M&M Broadcasters Ltd.

Highland Park

KVCE
03-01-1960; 1160 kHz AM; Hrs Open: 24
6400 W. Belt Line Road, Irving, TX 75063 US
(972) 870-9949
www.kvceradio.com
robin@kvceradio.com
License: Highland Park, TX held by Dallas Broadcasting LLC
Arbitron Metro Market: Dallas-Fort Worth; Format: Talk
John Peroyea, President
Melinda Kettler, Office Manager
David Darling, Operations Manager
Robin Valetutto, General Manager/Sports Director

Highland Park-Dallas

KVIL
04-21-2006; 103.7 MHz FM; Hrs Open: 24; 99 kW; 1486 ft.; N32 35 19 W96 58 5
TX USA
(214) 525-7000
www.kvil.com
License: Highland Park-Dallas, Dallas County, TX held by CBS Radio Texas Inc.
Group Owner: CBS Radio; (acq 7-2-87)
Nat'l Network: CBS
Arbitron Metro Market: Dallas, TX; Format: Adult Contemp

Highland Village

KWRD-FM
11-15-1988; 100.7 MHz FM; Hrs Open: 18; 98 kw; 1988 ft.; N33 32 8 W96 49 54
6400 N. Belt Line Road, Suite 110, Irving, TX 75063 US

(972) 870-9949
www.thewordfm.com
michael.krejci@klty.com
License: Highland Village, Denton County, TX held by Inspiration Media of Texas LLC.
Group Owner: Salem Communications Corp.; (acq 1-17-2001; grpsl).
Arbitron Metro Market: Dallas-Fort Worth Metroplex/Sherman/Denison/Gaines; *Format:* Christian, Talk
David Darling, Operations Manager
John L. Peoryea, Vice President/General Manager
Mike Krejci, General Sales Mgr
Nick Reeder, Promotions Director
Andy Pickard, Chief Engineer

Hillsboro

KBRQ
10-20-1959; 102.5 MHz FM; *Hrs Open:* 24; 100 kw; 449 ft.; N31 49 23 W97 9 35
314 West State Highway 6, Waco, TX 76712 US
(254) 776-3900
www.1025thebear.com
thebear@clearchannel.com
License: Hillsboro, Hill County, TX held by Aloha Station Trust LLC, as Trustee
Arbitron Metro Market: Waco, TX; *Format:* Classic Rock; *Target Audience:* 25-49; men
Evan Armstrong, General Manager
Kahilla Hakimzadeh, Sales Director
Dana McKenzie, Programming Director

KHBR
05-21-1948; 1560 kHz AM; *Hrs Open:* 12; 0.25 kw-D, NDD; N32 1 0 W97 6 32
335 Country Club Road, Hillsboro, TX 76645 US
(254) 582-3431
www.hillsbororeporter.com
info@khbrhillsboro.com
License: Hillsboro, TX held by KHBR Radio Inc.
Regional Network: Texas State Networks; *Wire Services:* NOAA Weather
Format: Country *Special Programming:* Czech 1.5 hrs, gospel 6 hrs wkly; *Hrs. of News Programming:* News progmg 18 hrs wkly; *Target Audience:* General.; *Adv. Rates:* 15;15; 15; na
Roger Galle, President
Rick Bailey, General Manager
Roger Creech, Programming Director

Holliday

KWFB
09-01-1982; 100.9 MHz FM; *Hrs Open:* 24; 18.5 kw; 299 ft.; N33 49 42 W98 40 13
4245 Kemp Boulevard, Suite 1009, Wichita Falls, TX 76308 US
(940) 322-1009; *Fax:* (940) 767-3299
www.bobradio.fm
sales@bobradio.fm
License: Holliday, Hardeman County, TX held by KIXC-FM L.L.C.
Format: Variety/Diverse *Special Programming:* Farm 3 hrs, relg 2 hrs wkly; *Hrs. of News Programming:* News progmg 10 hrs wkly; *Target Audience:* General.
Glen Ingram, President
John White, Operations Dir
Michael Reeves, General Manager

*KGVB
90.9 MHz FM; 7.5 kw; 351 ft.; N33 44 18 W98 54 28 US
(580) 332-0902; *Fax:* (580) 332-0922
www.thegospelstation.com
License: Holliday, Archer County, TX held by South Central Oklahoma Christian Broadcasting Inc.
Arbitron Metro Market: Holliday, TX
Randall Christy, Founder/President
Rick Cody, Vice President/Programming Director
Sharla Frederick, Treasurer / CFO

Hondo

KCWM
02-13-1970; 1460 kHz AM; *Hrs Open:* 6 AM-10 PM; 500 w-D, 226 w-N; N29 21 42 W99 07 42
www.kcwm.net
kcwm@aol.com
License: Hondo, Medina County, TX held by Hondo Communications Inc.
Regional Network: Texas State Networks; *Nat'l Reps:* Keystone (unwired net)
Population Served: 35,000 *Hrs. of News Programming:* news progmg 20 hrs wkly; *No. News Employees:* 1; *Target Audience:* General.
Tom Fusselmen, Traffic Director

KAHL-FM
01-01-1993; 105.9 MHz FM; 6 kw; Ant 328 ft; N29 18 48 W99 16 03
8023 Vantage Dr., Suite 840, San Antonio, TX 78230
(210) 341-1310; *Fax:* (210) 341-1777
www.call1310.com
info@call1310.com
License: Hondo, Medina County, TX held by Hondo RadioWorks Ltd.

John Barger, Sales Representative

Hooks

KPWW
12-22-1985; 95.9 MHz FM; *Hrs Open:* 24; 11.5 kw; 486 ft.; N33 27 25 W94 10 59
600 Congress Avenue, Suite 1400, Austin, TX 78701 US
(870) 772-3771; *Fax:* (870) 772-0364
www.power959.com
License: Hooks, Bowie County, TX held by Townsquare Media Texarkana License LLC
Group Owner: Townsquare Media; (acq 8-3-2007; grpsl)
Nat'l Reps: McGavren Guild
Arbitron Metro Market: Texarkana; *Format:* Contemporary Hits/Top 40; *No. News Employees:* 1; *Target Audience:* 18-49; contemp adults, upscale middle America
Johnny Lathrop, General Manager
Dan Patrick, Brand Manager
Paula Divello, Director Of Sales
James Stillwell, Digital Managing Editor

Hornsby

*KOOP
11-01-1994; 91.7 MHz FM; *Hrs Open:* 9 AM-7 PM (M-F); 9 AM-10 PM (S, Su); 3 kw; 85 ft.; N30 16 0 W97 40 27
Mailing Address: 3823 Airport Boulevard, Suite 13, Austin, TX 78722-1347 US
Second Address: PO Box 2116, Austin, TX 78768-2116
(512) 472-1369,(512) 472-5667; *Fax:* (512) 472-6149
www.koop.org
info@koop.org
License: Hornsby, Travis County, TX held by Texas Educational Broadcasting Inc.
Format: Variety/Diverse *Special Programming:* American Indian one hr, Black 2 hrs, folk 7 hrs, Ger 5 hrs, Pol 5 hrs, Sp 10 hrs wkly; *Hrs. of News Programming:* News progmg 14 hrs wkly
Thomas Durnin, President
Mark Boyden, Vice President
Rod Moag, Secretary
Kim McCarson, Executive Director
Leah Manners, Development Director

Houston

KBME
10-16-1944; 790 kHz AM; *Hrs Open:* 24; 5 kw-D, DA2; 5 kw-N, DA2; N29 54 54 W95 27 42
2000 W. Loop S., Suite 300, Houston, TX 77027 US
(713) 212-8000
www.sports790.com
License: Houston, Harris County, TX held by AMFM Texas Licenses LLC
Group Owner: iHeartMedia; (acq 8-30-2000; grpsl).
Nat'l Network: ESPN Radio; *Nat'l Reps:* Christal
Arbitron Metro Market: Houston-Galveston, TX; *Format:* Sports
Bryan Erickson, Operations Manager
Kelly Scott, Sales Manager
Christopher Gordy, Programming Director
Melissa Brezner, Promotion Director

KBXX
01-01-1958; 97.9 MHz FM; 95 kw; 1919 ft.; N29 34 34 W95 30 36
1010 Wayne Ave., Silver Spring, MD 20910 US
(713) 623-2108; *Fax:* (713) 390-5979
www.theboxhouston.com
License: Houston, Harris County, TX held by Radio One Licenses LLC.
Group Owner: Radio One Inc.; (acq 2000).
Nat'l Reps: Clear Channel
Arbitron Metro Market: Houston, TX; *Format:* Urban Contemporary; *Target Audience:* 18-29; females
Terri Thomas, Operations/Programming Director
Gary Spurgeon, General Manager
Mark Schecterle, General Sales Mgr

KSHJ
01-01-1952; 1430 kHz AM; *Hrs Open:* 24
5011 Alameda, Houston, TX 77004 US
(713) 522-1001; *Fax:* (713) 521-0769
www.kcohradio.com
License: Houston, TX held by KCOH Inc.
Nat'l Network: Westwood One; *Nat'l Reps:* Roslin
Arbitron Metro Market: Houston, TX; *Format:* Black, Talk *Special Programming:* Sports; *Hrs. of News Programming:* news progmg 15 hrs wkly; *No. News Employees:* 2; *Target Audience:* 25-54; upbeat, knowledgeable,civic & politically minded adults
Mike Petrizzo, President
Travis Gardner, Operations Dir
Michael Harris, News Director
Don Samuel, Assistant Music Director

KNTH
01-17-1968; 1070 kHz AM; 10 kw-D, DA2; 5 kw-N, DA2; N29 59 33 W95 28 23
6161 Savoy Drive, Suite 1200, Houston, TX 77036 US
(713) 260-3600
www.am1070theanswer.com
webmanager@salem.cc
License: Houston, TX held by South Texas Broadcasting Inc.
Group Owner: Salem Communications Corp.; (acq 1-6-95; $2.5 million;
Nat'l Reps: Salem
Arbitron Metro Market: Houston-Galveston; *Format:* News, News/Talk, 86
Paul Baker, Operations Dir
Chuck Jewell, General Manager
Dan Doster, General Sales Mgr
Kent McDonald, News Director
Sidney Jones, Chief Engineer
Ken Garza, Public Affairs Director

KEYH
11-01-1974; 850 kHz AM; 10 kw-D, DA1; 0.185 kw-N, DA1; N29 39 19 W95 40 19
3000 Bering Dr, Houston, TX 77057 US
(713) 315-3400; *Fax:* (713) 315-3506
larancherahouston.estrellatv.com
houstoninfo@lbimedia.com
License: Houston, Harris Inner County, TX held by Liberman Broadcasting of Houston License LLC.
Group Owner: Liberman Broadcasting Inc.; (acq 4-22-2003; $5.70 million)
Arbitron Metro Market: Houston-Galveston, TX; *Format:* Spanish, Variety/Diverse; *Target Audience:* 24-65; Hispanic Adults
Lenard Liberman, CEO
Winter Horton, Chief Operating Officer
Gerardo Reyes, General Sales Mgr
Ezequiel Gonzalez, Programming Director
Meliza Posada, News Director
Mike Todd, Engineering Dir

*KHCB-FM
03-09-1962; 105.7 MHz FM; *Hrs Open:* 24; 100 kw; 1614 ft.; N29 34 6 W95 29 57
2424 South Blvd., Houston, TX 77098 US
(713) 520-5200
www.khcb.org
email@khcb.org
License: Houston, Harris County, TX held by Houston Christian Broadcasters Inc.
Group Owner: Houston Christian Broadcasters Inc.
Nat'l Network: Moody
Arbitron Metro Market: Houston-Galveston; *Format:* Christian
Bruce E. Munsterman, President

KHMX
07-19-1990; 96.5 MHz FM; 97 kW; 1906 ft.; N29 34 34 W95 30 36
24 Greenway Plaza, Suite 1900, Houston, TX 77046 USA
(713) 881-5100
www.mix965houston.com
License: Houston, Harris County, TX held by CBS Radio Stations Inc.
Group Owner: CBS Radio; (acq 4-1-2009; grpsl)
Arbitron Metro Market: Houston-Galveston *TV Affiliate:* CBS; *Format:* Adult Contemp; *Target Audience:* 25-40
Charese Fruge, Programming Director
Tracy Wilkinson, Promotions Manager

KKHH
04-01-2008; 95.7 MHz FM; *Hrs Open:* 24; 95 kW; 1906 ft.; N29 34 34 W95 30 36
24 Greenway Plaza, Suite 1900, Houston, TX 77046 USA
(713) 881-5100
www.hothits957.com
License: Houston, Harris County, TX held by CBS Radio Texas Inc.
Group Owner: CBS Radio; (acq 11-13-98; grpsl)
Nat'l Network: CBS; *Nat'l Reps:* CBS Radio

Arbitron Metro Market: Houston-Galveston; *Format:* Contemporary Hits/Top 40; *Target Audience:* 25-54
Charese Fruge, Programming Director
Tracy Wilkinson, Promotions Manager

KILT
01-01-1948; 610 kHz AM; 5 kW; N29 55 4 W95 25 33
24 Greenway Plaza, Suite 1900, Houston, TX 77046 USA
(713) 881-5100
www.sportsradio610.com
houstonpsa@cbsradio.com
License: Houston, TX held by CBS Radio Texas Inc.
Group Owner: CBS Radio; (acq 12-89)
Nat'l Reps: CBS Radio
Arbitron Metro Market: Houston-Galveston; *Format:* Sports
Matt Ledbetter, Sales Manager

KILT-FM
02-01-1985; 100.3 MHz FM; *Hrs Open:* 24; 95 kW; 1906 ft.; N29 34 34 W95 30 36
24 Greenway Plaza, Suite 1900, Houston, TX 77046 USA
(713) 881-5100
www.1003thebull.com
License: Houston, Harris County, TX held by CBS Radio Texas Inc.
Group Owner: CBS Radio
Arbitron Metro Market: Houston-Galveston; *Format:* Country
Bruce Logan, Programming Director
Tracy Wilkinson, Promotions Manager

KQBT
01-01-1964; 93.7 MHz FM; 100 kw; 1719 ft.; N29 34 27 W95 29 37
2000 West Loop S., Suite 300, Houston, TX 77027 US
(713) 212-8000; *Fax:* (713) 830-8099
www.937thebeathouston.com
License: Houston, Harris County, TX held by Capstar TX LLC
Group Owner: iHeartMedia; (acq 8-30-00; grpsl).
Arbitron Metro Market: Houston, TX; *Format:* Urban Contemporary; *Target Audience:* 25-54.
Kelly Scott, Sales Manager
Rob Skinner, Promotion Director
Rod Windham, Political Coordinator

KLAT
07-31-1961; 1010 kHz AM; 5 kw-D, DA2; 3.6 kw-N, DA2; N29 53 47 W95 17 25; N29 51 44 W95 30 42
5100 S.W. Fwy., Houston, TX 77056 US
(713) 965-2400; *Fax:* (713) 965-2401
www.univision.com
License: Houston, Harris County, TX held by Tichenor License Corp.
Group Owner: Univision Radio; (acq 9-22-2003; grpsl)
Arbitron Metro Market: Houston, TX; *Format:* News, News/Talk, 82, Talk; *Target Audience:* 25-54; Hispanic
David Loving, General Manager
Glenn Coleman, General Sales Mgr
Aracely Rivera, Programming Director
Marty Scruggs, Chief Engineer

KTBZ-FM
11-01-1964; 94.5 MHz FM; 97 kw; 1919 ft.; N29 34 34 W95 30 36
2000 West Loop S., Suite 300, Houston, TX 77027 US
(713) 212-8000
www.thebuzz.com
License: Houston, Harris County, TX held by AMFM Texas Licenses LLC
Group Owner: iHeartMedia; (acq 8-30-00; grpsl).
Nat'l Reps: D & R Radio
Arbitron Metro Market: Houston, TX; *Format:* Oldies *Special Programming:* Talk 2 hrs, relg one hr, pub affrs one hr wkly; *Target Audience:* 25-54; baby boomers
Kelly Scott, Sales Manager
Elliott Wood, Programming Director
Rob Skinner, Promotion Director
Rod Windham, Political Coordinator

KLOL
01-01-1947; 101.1 MHz FM; 96 kW; 1906 ft.; N29 34 34 W95 30 36
24 Greenway Plaza, Suite 1900, Houston, TX 77046 USA
(713) 881-5100
www.mega101fm.com
License: Houston, Harris County, TX held by CBS Radio Stations Inc.
Group Owner: CBS Radio; (acq 4-1-2009; grpsl)
Nat'l Reps: CBS Radio
Arbitron Metro Market: Houston, TX; *Format:* Spanish; *Target Audience:* 18-54
Andrea Parra, Promotions Manager

KLTN
10-04-1960; 102.9 MHz FM; *Hrs Open:* 24; 99.5 kw; 984 ft.; N29 45 26 W95 20 19
5100 S.W. Fwy., Houston, TX 77056 US
(713) 965-2400; *Fax:* (713) 965-2401
www.univision.com
License: Houston, Harris County, TX held by Univision Radio Houston License Corp.
Group Owner: Univision Radio; (acq 9-22-2003; grpsl)
Arbitron Metro Market: Houston, TX; *Format:* Tejano; *No. News Employees:* 1; *Target Audience:* 18-49; Hispanics
David Loving, General Manager
Raul Brindis, Programming Director
Nestor Enriquez, Client Services Director
Marty Scruggs, Chief Engineer
Anna Munoz, National Sales Manager
Kim Mercier, National Sales Manager

KMJQ
02-01-1964; 102.1 MHz FM; *Hrs Open:* 24; 100 kw; 1719 ft.; N29 34 27 W95 29 37
Suite 900, 24 Greenway Plaza, Houston, TX 77046 US
(713) 623-2108; *Fax:* (713) 300-5764
www.myhoustonmajic.com
License: Houston, Harris County, TX held by Radio One Licenses LLC.
Group Owner: Radio One Inc.; (acq 11-8-01; grpsl).
Nat'l Network: ABC; *Nat'l Reps:* Clear Channel
Arbitron Metro Market: Houston, TX; *Format:* Urban Contemporary *Special Programming:* Talk 3 hrs wkly; *No. News Employees:* 2; *Target Audience:* 25-54; African-Americans
Terri Thomas, Operations Mgr/Program Dir

KODA
11-09-1958; 99.1 MHz FM; *Hrs Open:* 24; 96 kw; 1919 ft.; N29 34 34 W95 30 36
2000 West Loop S., Suite 3000, Houston, TX 77027 US
(713) 212-8000; *Fax:* (713) 830-8099
www.sunny99.com
License: Houston, Harris County, TX held by AMFM Texas Licenses LLC
Group Owner: iHeartMedia; (acq 8-30-00; grpsl).
Arbitron Metro Market: Houston-Galveston, TX; *Format:* Adult Contemp *Special Programming:* Jazz 4 hrs wkly; *Hrs. of News Programming:* news progmg 22 hrs wkly; *No. News Employees:* 1; *Target Audience:* 25-54.
Kelly Scott, Sales Manager
Marc Sherman, Programming Director
Raylynne Perez, Promotions Director
Rod Windham, Political Coordinator

***KPFT**
03-01-1970; 90.1 MHz FM; *Hrs Open:* 24; 100 kw; 673 ft.; N29 53 15 W95 31 22
419 Lovett Blvd., Houston, TX 77006 US
(713) 526-4000; *Fax:* (713) 526-5750
www.kpft.org
License: Houston, Harris County, TX held by Pacifica Foundation Inc.
Group Owner: Pacifica Foundation Inc.
Nat'l Network: PRI
Arbitron Metro Market: Houston-Galveston; *Format:* News, Variety/Diverse *Special Programming:* Black 15 hrs; *Target Audience:* General.
Dwande Bradley, General Manager
Donna Platt, General Sales Mgr
Otis Maclay, Programming Director
Ernesto Aguilar, News Director
Steve Brightwell, Engineering Dir
Phil Edwards, Music Director
Renee Feltz, News Director

KPRC
05-09-1925; 950 kHz AM; *Hrs Open:* 24
2000 West Loop S., Suite 3000, Houston, TX 77027 US
(713) 212-8000; *Fax:* (713) 212-8950
www.kprcradio.com
License: Houston, TX held by CCB Texas Licenses LLC
Group Owner: iHeartMedia; (acq 3-14-95;
Nat'l Network: CBS; Fox News Radio; Westwood One; *Regional Network:* Texas State Networks; *Nat'l Reps:* Clear Channel
Arbitron Metro Market: Greater Houston; *Format:* News, News/Talk, 86 *Special Programming:* Gardening 7 hrs, home handyman 6 hrs, automotive 3; *Hrs. of News Programming:* news progmg 32 hrs wkly *No. News Employees:* 15; *Target Audience:* 25-54.
Bryan Erickson, Operations Manager
Kelly Scott, Sales Manager
Ramon Robles, Programming Director
Rob Skinner, Promotions Director
Rod Windham, Political Coordinator

***KSHJ**
02-18-1948; 1430 kHz AM; *Hrs Open:* 24; 5 kw-D, DA2; 1 kw-N, DA2; N29 45 21 W95 16 37
11511 Katy Fwy, #301, Houston, TX 77079 US
(832) 786-4500
grnonline.com/stations/1430-am-kshj-houston
License: Houston, TX held by La Promesa Foundation
Group Owner: La Promesa Foundation; (acq 2-28-2013 from LBI media; $2.141 million)
Nat'l Network: Guadalupe Radio Network; EWTN
Arbitron Metro Market: Houston-Galveston, TX; *Format:* Christian, Religious
Joe McClane, General Manager

KRBE
11-08-1959; 104.1 MHz FM; 92.18 kw; 1919 ft.; N29 34 34 W95 30 36
9801 Westheimer, Suite 700, Houston, TX 77042 US
(713) 266-1000
www.krbe.com
License: Houston, TX held by Radio License Holding SRC LLC
Group Owner: Cumulus Media Inc.; (acq 11-86; $25 million with co-located AM;)
Arbitron Metro Market: Greater Houston; *Format:* Contemporary Hits/Top 40; *Target Audience:* 18-34; general
Tim Gratzer, General Sales Mgr
Leslie Whittle, Programming Director
Summer O'Hare, Promotions Manager

KTRH
03-29-1930; 740 kHz AM; 50 kw-D, DA2; 50 kw-N, DA2; N29 57 57 W94 56 32
510 Lovett Blvd, Houston, TX 77006 US
(713) 526-5874; *Fax:* (713) 212-8000
www.ktrh.com
info@ktrh.com
License: Houston, TX held by AMFM Texas Licenses LLC
Group Owner: iHeartMedia; (acq 8-30-2000; grpsl).
Nat'l Network: ABC; *Nat'l Reps:* Christal
Arbitron Metro Market: Houston-Galveston; *Format:* News, News/Talk, 86; *Target Audience:* 25-54.
Bryan Erickson, Operations Manager
Kelly Scott, Sales Manager
Melissa Brezner, Promotions Director
Rod Windham, Political Coordinator

***KTRU(FM)**
05-20-1971; 90.1 MHz FM; *Hrs Open:* 24; 30 kw; 492 ft; N29 53 15 W95 31 22
Mailing Address: Rice University, 6100 S. Main, Houston, TX 77005
Second Address: P.O. Box 1892, Houston, TX 77251-1892
(713) 348-4098; *Fax:* n/a
www.ktru.org
ktru@ktru.org
License: Houston, Harris County, TX held by Rice University.
Population Served: 6,000,000; *Arbitron Metro Market:* Houston-Galveston *Special Programming:* Eclectic 104 hrs, jazz 9 hrs, world 2 hrs, Americana 1 hr, experimental 3 hrs, post-punk 1 hr, local 2 hrs, hip hop 3 hrs, reggae 2hrs, blues 2 hrs; *Target Audience:* General.
Will Robedee, General Manager
Nick Ryder, Station Manager
Ross Cooper, Chief Engineer

***KTSU**
10-01-1973; 90.9 MHz FM; *Hrs Open:* 24; 18.5 kw; 266 ft.; N29 43 25 W95 21 52
3100 Cleburne, Houston, TX 77004 US
(713) 313-7591; *Fax:* (713) 313-7479
www.ktsu.info
License: Houston, Harris County, TX held by Board of Regents Texas Southern University.
Arbitron Metro Market: Houston, TX; *Format:* Jazz, Variety/Diverse *Special Programming:* Reggae 8 hrs wkly; *Hrs. of News Programming:* news progmg 10 hrs wkly; *No. News Employees:* 1; *Target Audience:* 25-54.
John Rudley, President
Charles Hudson, Operations Dir
George Thomas, General Manager
Larry Johson, General Sales Mgr
Charles Hudson, Operations Manager/Gospel Program Director
Maurice Hopethompson, News Director
Dave Biondi,Chief Engineer
Donna Franklin, Interim Assistant General Manager/Programming
Larry Johnson, Development Director
Deborah Chambers, Development Manager
Deborah Adams, Membership Coordinator

Sheldon T. Nunn, Music Director
Rick Lauderdale,Production Manager

***KUHF**
11-06-1950; 88.7 MHz FM; *Hrs Open:* 24; 100 kw; 1719 ft.; N29 34 27 W95 29 37
4800 Calhoun Road, Houston, TX 77004 US
(713) 743-0887; *Fax:* (713) 743-0868
www.kuhf.org
communications@kuhf.org
License: Houston, Harris County, TX held by University of Houston.
Nat'l Network: NPR; PRI
Arbitron Metro Market: Houston, TX; *Format:* News; *Hrs. of News Programming:* news progmg 25 hrs wkly; *No. News Employees:* 7; *Target Audience:* 25 plus.
Debra Fraser, Director of Operations & Stations Manager
Lisa Trapani Shumate, Executive Director & General Manager
Victor Kendall, General Sales Mgr
St. John Flynn, Programming Director
Jack Williams, News Director
Alex Schneider,Engineering Dir
Sidney Knight, Engineering Dir
Catherine Lu, Associate Producer
Ed Mayberry, News Reporter
Rod Rice, News Reporter
Jim Bell, News Reporter
Robert Stevenson, Producer, The Front Row
Troy Schulze, Production Assistant

KXYZ
08-08-1930; 1320 kHz AM; 5 kw-D, DAN; 5 kw-N, DAN; N29 42 39 W95 10 30
27 William St., 11th Floor, Houston, TX 77056 US
(713) 490-2538; *Fax:* (713) 984-1721
License: Houston, TX held by Multicultural Radio Broadcasting Licensee LLC.
Group Owner: Multicultural Radio Broadcasting Inc.; (acq 12-1-2003; grpsl).
Arbitron Metro Market: Huston, TX; *Format:* Talk
Arthur Liu, CEO/COO

KMIC
01-01-1955; 1590 kHz AM; *Hrs Open:* 24
3050 Post Oak Blvd., Suite 220, Houston, TX 77056 US
(713) 552-1590; *Fax:* (713) 552-1588
www.radio.disney.com
License: Houston, TX held by Radio Disney Group LLC.
Group Owner: ABC Inc.; (acq. 1999).
Nat'l Network: Radio Disney
Arbitron Metro Market: Houston, TX.; *Format:* Children; *Target Audience:* 6-14; 25-49; kids, parents; *Adv. Rates:* 275.00; 275.00; 275.00; 50
Chris Martin, General Manager
Laura Pena, Promotions Manager
Johanna Anderson, News Director
A. Rigmaiden, Chief Engineer

Howe

KHYI
04-01-1949; 95.3 MHz FM; *Hrs Open:* 24; 15 kw; 889 ft.; N33 28 12 W96 47 19
Mailing Address: 103-B West Main Street, Allen, TX 75013 US
Second Address: 12225 Greenville Ave. Ste.356, Suite 120, Dallas, TN 75074
(972) 633-0955; *Fax:* (972) 633-0957
www.khyi.com
License: Howe, Grayson County, TX held by Metro Broadcasters-Texas Inc.
Nat'l Network: Jones Radio Networks
Arbitron Metro Market: Dallas-Fort Worth; *Format:* Country
Special Programming: Gospel 4 hrs wkly, Agriculture 5 hrs wkly; *Hrs. of News Programming:* news progmg 3 hrs wkly; *No. News Employees:* 1 *TargetAudience:* 25-54; affluent, white collar, middle to upper income listeners
Ken Jones, CEO
Lisa Hooks, Operations Dir
Joshua Jones, General Manager
Glenda Jones, CFO

Hudson

KZXL
01-01-2002; 96.3 MHz FM; 13.5 kw; 491 ft.; N31 20 5 W94 40 10
Old Us Highway 35 North, Linvingston, TX 77351 US
(877) 963-9696
License: Hudson, Angelina County, TX held by The Turning Leaf LLC
Arbitron Metro Market: Lufkin-Nacogdoches, NY
Vance Barbee, General Manager

Humble

KGOL
09-12-1983; 1180 kHz AM; 50 kw-D, 3 kw-N
5353 W. Alabama, Suite 450, Houston, TX 77056 US
(713) 349-9880; *Fax:* (713) 349-9365
License: Humble, TX held by Entravision Holdings LLC.
Group Owner: Entravision Communications Corp.; (acq 7-28-00; grpsl).
Arbitron Metro Market: Houston-Galvest, TX; *Format:* Spanish, Sports, 86; *No. News Employees:* 1; *Target Audience:* General; Ethnic & Asian
Kent Tank, General Manager

***KSBJ**
07-06-1982; 89.3 MHz FM; *Hrs Open:* 24; 100 kw; 837 ft.; N30 12 26 W95 5 28
Mailing Address: P.O. Box 187, Humble, TX 77347 US
Second Address: 1722 Treble Dr., Humble, TX 77338
(281) 446-5725; *Fax:* (281) 540-2198
www.ksbj.org
info@ksbj.org
License: Humble, Harris County, TX held by KSBJ Educational Foundation.
Arbitron Metro Market: Humble, TX; *Format:* Christian; *Hrs. of News Programming:* news progmg 4 hrs wkly; *No. News Employees:* 31; *Target Audience:* 25-49; Christian adults
J.R. Hernandez, Operations Dir
Tim McDermott, General Manager
John Hull, Programming Director
Jason Ray, Promotions Manager
Amanda Carroll, News Director
George Schank, Chief Engineer
Jon Hull, Disc Jockey
Jim Beeler, MusicDirector
Tom Carter, Promotions Manager

Hunt

***KLKV**
99.9 MHz FM; 11 kw; 129 meters; N30 08 51 W99 13 14
5700 West Oaks Boulevard, Rocklin, CA 97565 US
(916) 251-1600; *Fax:* (916) 251-1650
www.klove.com
License: Hunt, Kerr County, TX held by Educational Media Foundation
Group Owner: EMF Broadcasting
Arbitron Metro Market: Hunt, TX; *Format:* Variety/Diverse
Mike Novak, President

KYRT
97.9 MHz FM; 6 kw; Ant 279 ft; N30 44 48 W99 14 58
381 Casa Linda Plaza, Suite 347, Dallas, TX
(972) 241-2110; *Fax:* (830) 693-5107
License: Hunt, Mason County, TX held by Munbilla Broadcasting Properties Ltd.
Group Owner: Munbilla Broadcasting Properties Ltd.

B. Shane Fox, General Manager

Huntington

KSML-FM
03-01-1994; 101.9 MHz FM; *Hrs Open:* 24; 15 kw; Ant 827 ft; N31 20 05 W94 40 10
Yates Broadcasting, 121 Cotton Sq., Lufkin, TX 77505
(936) 634-4584; *Fax:* (936) 632-5722
License: Huntington, Angelina County, TX held by Yates Broadcasting Corp.

Keith Sims, Operations Dir
Steven Yates, General Manager

Huntsville

***KHCH**
10-04-1982; 1410 kHz AM; *Hrs Open:* 24; 250 w-D, 87 w-N
2424 South Blvd., Houston, TX 77098 US
(713) 520-5200
www.khcb.org
email@khcb.org
License: Huntsville, TX held by Houston Christian Broadcasters, Inc.
Group Owner: Houston Christian Broadcasters Inc.; (acq 10-97; $145,000)
Format: Christian
Bruce E. Munsterman, President

KHVL
11-03-1938; 1490 kHz AM; *Hrs Open:* 24; 1 kw-U, ND1; N30 41 48 W95 33 8
Mailing Address: P.O. Box 330, Huntsville, TX 77340 US
Second Address: 622 Interstate 45 S., Huntsville, TX 77340
(936) 295-2651; *Fax:* (936) 295-8201
www.khvl.com
License: Huntsville, TX held by HEH Communications LLC
Nat'l Network: ABC
Arbitron Metro Market: Huntsville, TX; *Format:* Oldies *Special Programming:* Black 5 hrs wkly; *Hrs. of News Programming:* 5 local news casts per day; *No. News Employees:* 1; *Target Audience:* 30 plus.
Brooke Addams, Operations Dir
Steve Everett, General Manager
Larry Crippen, News Director
Stacy Selman, Traffic Manager

KSAM-FM
08-01-1965; 101.7 MHz FM; *Hrs Open:* 24; 3.7 kw; 420 ft.; N30 41 48 W95 33 8
Mailing Address: P.O. Box 330, Huntsville, TX 77342 US
Second Address: 622 Interstate 45 S., Huntsville, TX 77340
(936) 295-2651; *Fax:* (936) 295-8201
www.ksam1017.com
ksammail@yahoo.com
License: Huntsville, Walker County, TX held by HEH Communications LLC
Arbitron Metro Market: Huntsville, TX; *Format:* Country; *Hrs. of News Programming:* 6 local news casts per day; *No. News Employees:* 1; *Target Audience:* 25-54; women
Brooke Addams, Operations Dir
Kooter Roberson, Sports Director

***KSHU**
10-01-1973; 90.5 MHz FM; *Hrs Open:* 24; 3 kw; 255 ft; N30 42 50 W95 32 58
Box 2207, 1804 Avenue J, Huntsville, TX 77341-2207
(936) 294-3939
www.kshu.org
thekatshu@gmail.com
License: Huntsville, Walker County, TX held by Sam Houston State University.
Population Served: 40,000 *Special Programming:* Sp 4 hrs wkly; *Hrs. of News Programming:* News progmg 25 hrs wkly; *Target Audience:* General; rural
Le Ann Muns, Operations Dir
Steve Sandlin, Chief Engineer

Hurst

KMNY
04-01-1947; 1360 kHz AM; *Hrs Open:* 24
5801 Marvin D Love Freeway, Suite 409, Dallasrk, TX 75237 US
(972) 572-1540
lavoz1360dallas.com/lavoz
License: Hurst, TX held by Multicultural Radio Broadcasting Licensee LLC.
Group Owner: Multicultural Radio Broadcasting Inc.; (acq 2-4-2004; grpsl)
Nat'l Network: Air America; USA
Arbitron Metro Market: Dallas, TX; *Format:* Spanish
Sidney Yary, General Manager

Hutto

***KYLR**
02-01-1980; 92.1 MHz FM; 2.5 kw; 449 ft.; N30 32 4 W97 34 52
1707 N. Mays Street, Round Rock, TX 78664 US
(800) 525-5683; *Fax:* (916) 251-1650
www.klove.com
klove@klove.com
License: Hutto, Williamson County, TX held by Educational Media Foundation.
Group Owner: EMF Broadcasting; (acq 3-31-2006; $6 million with KMLR(FM) Gonzales).
Format: Christian
Mike Novak, President
David Pierce, Programming Director
Ed Lenane, News Director
Sam Wallington, Engineering Dir
Marya Morgan, News Reporter
Richard Hunt, News Reporter

Idalou

KRBL
09-18-1995; 105.7 MHz FM; 5.5 kw; 328 ft.; N33 39 47 W101 35 52
6257 Brisa Del Mar, El Paso, TX 79925 US
(806) 749-1057; *Fax:* (806) 749-1177
License: Idalou, Lubbock County, TX held by Triumph Communications Inc.
Arbitron Metro Market: Lubbock, TX; *Format:* Religious; *Target Audience:* 24-64.

Paul Beane, General Manager
Steve Ritchie, General Sales Mgr
Anthony Garza, Programming Director
Wanda Byers, Traffic Manager

Ingram

*KTXI

11-01-1998; 90.1 MHz FM; *Hrs Open:* 24; 50 kw; 453 ft.; N30 6 14 W99 4 36 *Rebroadcasts:* Rebroadcasts KPAC(FM) San Antonio 75% , KSTX(FM) San Antonio 25%
8401 Datapoint Drive, Suite 800, San Antonio, TX 78229-5903 US
(210) 614-8977; *Fax:* (210) 614-8983
news@tpr.org
License: Ingram, Kerr County, TX held by Texas Public Radio.
Nat'l Network: NPR; PRI
Arbitron Metro Market: Ingram, TX; *Format:* News; *Target Audience:* 25 plus.
Joyce Slocum, President/CEO
Wayne Coble, VP, Operations
Paul Flahive, Program Manager
Doug Demore, Chief Engineer
Annette Ewer, Traffic Director
Janet Grojean, VP, Development
Connie Leyva, VP, Finance
Steve Short, NewsDirector

KKGN

01-01-2007; 96.5 MHz FM; 8.4 kw; 430 ft.; N30 7 4 W99 11 40 US
(830) 896-4990
License: Ingram, Kerr County, TX held by Radio Ranch Ltd.
Group Owner: Radio Ranch Ltd.
Arbitron Metro Market: Ingram, TX; *Format:* Adult Contemp
Benjamin Homel, President
Alyson Foster, General Sales Mgr
Ed Chandler, Programming Director
Mike Taylor, Assistant Program Director

Iowa Park

KXXN

06-01-2009; 96.3 MHz FM; *Hrs Open:* 24 7; 6 kw; 256 ft.; N33 58 20 W98 45 35
813 8th Street, Suite 550, Wichita Falls, TX 76301 US
www.grownfolkjamz.com
k96@grownfolkjamz.com
License: Iowa Park, Wichita County, TX held by Tower Investment Trust Inc.
Group Owner: Tower Investment Trust Inc.
Arbitron Metro Market: Iowa Park, TX; *Format:* Christian
Denise Sherman, Sales Director
T-O Double, Programming Director
Don Sherman, Operations Director

Jacksboro

KFWR

03-01-1970; 95.9 MHz FM; *Hrs Open:* 24; 80 kw; 1079 ft.; N32 39 50 W98 9 47
201 Main Street, Fort Worth, TX 76102 US
(817) 332-0959; *Fax:* (817) 348-8373
959theranch.com
ContactUs@TheRanchRadio.com
License: Jacksboro, Palo Pinto County, TX held by LKCM Radio Group L.P.
Group Owner: LKCM Radio Group L.P.; acq 9-30-02; $6 million).
Arbitron Metro Market: Mineral Wells, TX; *Format:* Country; *Target Audience:* 25-54; local, Texas country
Gerry Schlegel, President
Joel Gough, General Sales Mgr
Chuck Taylor, Programming Director
Molly Prince, Promotions Manager
Jane Wasson, News Director
Michael Margrave, Chief Engineer

Jacksonville

*KBJS

05-16-1987; 90.3 MHz FM; 16 kw; 1286 ft.; N32 3 40 W95 18 50
P.O. Box 193, 406 Nacogdoches St, Jacksonville, TX 75766 US
(903) 586-5257; *Fax:* (903) 586-4986
www.kbjs.org
License: Jacksonville, Cherokee County, TX held by East Texas Media Association Inc.
Nat'l Network: Moody
Arbitron Metro Market: Jacksonville, TX; *Format:* Christian, Religious *Special Programming:* Black one hr, Sp one hr wkly
Bob Shivery, President
Randy Featherston, Station Manager
John Paul Little, Operations Director

KEBE

01-12-1947; 1400 kHz AM; *Hrs Open:* 24; 1 kw-U, ND1; N31 58 11 W95 15 52
Mailing Address: P.O. Box 1648, Jacksonvillle, TX 75766 US
Second Address: Radio Ctr., 402 S. Ragsdale, Jacksonville, TX 75766
(903) 586-2527; *Fax:* (903) 586-1394
info@wallerbroadcasting.com
License: Jacksonville, TX held by Waller Broadcasting Inc.
Group Owner: Waller Broadcasting; (acq 11-58; $75,000).
Nat'l Reps: McGavren Guild
Arbitron Metro Market: Tyler-Longview, TX; *Format:* Country
Special Programming: Farm 9 hrs wkly; *Hrs. of News Programming:* news progmg 6 hrs wkly; *No. News Employees:* 2; *Target Audience:* 25-54. *Adv.Rates:* 10; 8; 6; 8
Dudley Waller, CEO
Alan Mather, Operations Dir
Tina Harper, CFO

KLJT

01-01-1993; 102.3 MHz FM; *Hrs Open:* 24; 50 kw; 492 ft.; N31 52 18 W95 10 0
Mailing Address: 3400 West Marshall Avenue, Suite 307, Longview, TX 75608 US
Second Address: 402 S. Ragsdale, Jacksonville, TX 75766
(903) 663-2477; *Fax:* (903) 663-9492
License: Jacksonville, Cherokee County, TX held by Waller Media LLC.
Group Owner: Waller Broadcasting; (acq 12-9-02).
Nat'l Network: ABC; *Nat'l Reps:* McGavren Guild; *Wire Services:* AP
Arbitron Metro Market: Tyler, TX; *Format:* Adult Contemp; *Hrs. of News Programming:* news progmg 6 hrs wkly; *No. News Employees:* 1; *Adv. Rates:* 30; 24; 20; 16
Bill Waller, President of Operations
Chrispin Chifwepa, Business Manager

KOOI

09-09-1967; 106.5 MHz FM; *Hrs Open:* 24; 100 kw; 1,480 ft.; N32 3 40 W95 18 50
210 S. Broadway, Suite 100, Tyler, TX 75702 US
(903) 581-9966; *Fax:* (903) 534-5300
www.kooi.com
License: Jacksonville, Cherokee County, TX held by Alpha Media Licensee LLC
Group Owner: Alpha Media LLC; (acq 4-14-2015; grpsl).
Nat'l Network: Fox News Radio; *Regional Network:* Texas State Networks; *Nat'l Reps:* McGavren Guild
Arbitron Metro Market: Tyler-Longview, TX; *Format:* Adult Contemp; *Target Audience:* 25-54.; *Adv. Rates:* 60; 60; 60; 60
Dru Laborde, Operations Manager
Ginger Dockery, General Manager
Corinna Ruiz, Sales Manager
AJ Redd, Programming Director
Harlen Lobley, Director of Sales

Jasper

KJAS

01-01-1996; 107.3 MHz FM; *Hrs Open:* 24; 8 kw; 328 ft.; N30 58 31 W93 59 24
765 Hemphill St., Jasper, TX 75951 US
(409) 384-2626; *Fax:* (409) 383-1979
www.kjas.com
License: Jasper, Jasper County, TX held by DBA Rayburn Broadcasting Co.
Arbitron Metro Market: Beaumont-Port Arthur, TX; *Format:* Adult Contemp *Special Programming:* Oldies 4 hrs wkly; *Hrs. of News Programming:* news progmg 4 hrs wkly; *No. News Employees:* 1 *Target Audience:* 24-54; females/buying group; *Adv. Rates:* 14; 12; 9; 6.50
James M. Lout, Owner/General Manager
Steve Stewart, News
Garrett Foster, Production
Dianne Cansler, Office/Traffic Manager
Debbie Foster, Sales Manager

KCOX

08-06-1948; 1350 kHz AM; *Hrs Open:* 24; 5 kw-D, ND1; 0.037 kw-N, ND1; N30 55 11 W93 58 13
1408 East Gibson Street, Jasper, TX 79951 US
(409) 384-4500
www.1027ktxj.com
License: Jasper, TX held by Cross Texas Media Inc.
Nat'l Network: Salem Radio Network
Arbitron Metro Market: Jasper, TX; *Format:* Christian; *Target Audience:* 18-35.
T.J. Bordelon, Operations Dir
Rick Tallent, General Manager
Dale Cucancic, General Sales Mgr
Barbara Bordelon, News Director
Carol Tallent, Business Manager

KTXJ-FM

11-01-1964; 102.7 MHz FM; *Hrs Open:* 24; 46 kw; 513 ft.; N31 3 36 W93 57 42
1408 East Gibson Street, Jasper, TX 75951 US
(409) 384-4500; *Fax:* (409) 384-4525
www.1027ktxj.com
License: Jasper, Jasper County, TX held by Cross Texas Media Inc.
Nat'l Network: Salem Radio Network
Arbitron Metro Market: Jasper, TX; *Format:* Gospel; *Target Audience:* Very broad receptive demographic
Dan Skinner, President
Laverne Dittx, General Sales Mgr
Nathan Cone, Programming Director
Dave Davies, News Director
Wayne Coble, Engineering Dir
Randy Anderson, Music Director
Janet Grojean, Sales

Jefferson

KJTX

10-01-1990; 104.5 MHz FM; *Hrs Open:* 24; 4.4 kw; 384 ft.; N32 49 23 W94 28 32
707 Valentine Lane, Longview, TX 75604 US
(903) 759-1243; *Fax:* (903) 759-1243
www.kjtx1045fm.com
License: Jefferson, Marion County, TX held by Wisdom Ministries Inc.
Format: Christian, Gospel; *Hrs. of News Programming:* News progmg 2 hrs wkly; *Target Audience:* 16 plus.
Leroy Richardson, President
Annie Thompson, Operations Dir
Brenda Richardson, General Sales Mgr
Sharon Herbert, News Director
Jocelyn Jordan, Music Director

*KHCJ

01-01-2003; 91.9 MHz FM; *Hrs Open:* 24; 3.2 kw; 459 ft.; N32 50 7 W94 28 53 *Rebroadcasts:* Rebroadcasts KHCB-FM Houston 95%
2424 South Blvd., Houston, TX 77098 US
(713) 520-5200
www.khcb.org
email@khcb.org
License: Jefferson, Marion County, TX held by Houston Christian Broadcasters Inc.
Group Owner: Houston Christian Broadcasters Inc.
Nat'l Network: Moody
Arbitron Metro Market: Texarkana, TX; *Format:* Christian
Bruce E. Munsterman, President

Johnson City

KFAN-FM

01-01-1991; 107.9 MHz FM; *Hrs Open:* 24; 8.7 kw; 551 ft.; N30 11 49 W98 38 19
210 Woodcrest, Fredrickburg, TX 78624 US
(952) 417-3000; *Fax:* (612) 417-3001
www.kfan.com
info@k102.com
License: Johnson City, Blanco County, TX held by J. & J. Fritz Media Ltd.
Group Owner: J. & J. Fritz Media Ltd.
Arbitron Metro Market: Minneapolis-St. Paul, MN; *Format:* Triple A *Special Programming:* Jazz 5 hrs wkly; *No. News Employees:* 1; *Target Audience:* 25-49.; *Adv. Rates:* 28; 28; 28; 28
Jayson Fritz, President
Jan Fritz, Operations Dir
Rick Star, Programming Director
Robbie Fish, News Director
Ariana Carruth, Promotions Manager
Kyle Province, Public Affairs Director

Jourdanton

KLEY-FM

01-01-2001; 95.7 MHz FM; 11 kw; 1,037 ft.; N28 54 57.4 W98 39 39
4050 Eisenhauer Rd., San Antonio, TX 78218 US
(210) 654-5100; *Fax:* (210) 855-5076
www.laleysa.com
License: Jourdanton, Atascosa County, TX held by Alpha Media Licensee LLC
Group Owner: Alpha Media LLC; (acq 1-31-2014; grpsl).
Arbitron Metro Market: San Antonio, TX; *Format:* Tejano

Greg Martin, General Manager
Coreena Hazelett, General Sales Mgr
Alfonso Flores, Programming Director

Junction

KMBL
01-01-1953; 1450 kHz AM; *Hrs Open:* 24; 1 kw-U, ND1; N30 29 34 W99 45 41
Mailing Address: 5550 Friendship Blvd, Chevy Chase, MD 20815 US
Second Address: 214 Pecan St., Junction, TX 76899
(830) 896-1230; *Fax:* (830) 792-4142
generalmanager@krvl.com
License: Junction, TX held by Foster Charitable Foundation Inc.
Group Owner: Revolution Broadcast Company of the West; (acq 5-31-2007)
Nat'l Network: Westwood One; *Regional Network:* Texas State Networks
Format: Country *Special Programming:* Farm 6 hrs wkly; *Hrs. of News Programming:* news progmg 6 hrs wkly; *No. News Employees:* 1; *Target Audience:* General.; *Adv. Rates:* 8; 7; 8; 4.20
David Greenwald, President
Harley Belew, Operations Dir
Monte Spearman, General Manager
Steve Alex, Station Manager
A.J. Hernandez, Programming Director
Monte Speaman, Advertising Director
Glen Taylor

KOOK
01-01-1997; 93.5 MHz FM; *Hrs Open:* 24; 50 kw; 492 ft.; N30 29 31 W100 2 3
5550 Friendship Blvd., Suite 260, Chevy Chase, MD 20815 US
(830) 896-1230; *Fax:* (830) 792-4142
License: Junction, Kimble County, TX held by Foster Charitable Foundation Inc.
Group Owner: Revolution Broadcast Company of the West; (acq 5-31-2007)
Nat'l Network: ABC; *Regional Network:* Texas State Networks
Format: Country *Special Programming:* Gospel 2 hrs wkly; *Adv. Rates:* 7.90; 6.30; 7.90; 6.30
Donna Keese, Operations Dir
Monte Spearman, General Manager

Karnes City

KHHL
03-01-2005; 103.1 MHz FM; 34 kw; 592 ft.; N29 00 46 W97 40 02
4050 Eisenhauer Rd., San Antonio, TX 78218 US
(210) 654-5100; *Fax:* (210) 855-5016
License: Karnes City, Karnes County, TX held by Alpha Media Licensee LLC
Group Owner: Alpha Media LLC
Arbitron Metro Market: San Antonio, TX; *Format:* Spanish, Sports
Lance Hawkins, General Manager
Pat Cerullo, Programming Director

Keene

*KJRN
06-13-1974; 88.3 MHz FM; *Hrs Open:* 24; 23 kw; 180 ft; N32 24 19 W97 19 55
PO Box 567, Keene, TX 76059
(817) 202-6788; *Fax:* (817) 202-6790
License: Keene, Johnson County, TX held by Southwestern Adventist University.
Population Served: 1,500,000; *Arbitron Metro Market:* Dallas-Fort Wor; *Hrs. of News Programming:* News progmg 2 hrs wkly; *Target Audience:* 25-54
Eric Anderson, President
Michael Agee, General Manager
Karen Knaubert, General Sales Mgr
Ron Macomber, Chief Engineer

Kempner

KOOV
12-15-1978; 106.9 MHz FM; 2.3 kw; 538 ft.; N31 6 1 W97 55 39
2402 Broadmoor, Bldg, D-2, Suite 101, Bryan, TX 77802 US
(254) 772-0330; *Fax:* (254) 833-8844
http://www.1660espn.com/
smoaky@1660espn.com
License: Kempner, Lampasas County, TX held by M&M Broadcasters Ltd.
Group Owner: M&M Broadcasters Ltd.
Nat'l Network: ABC
TV Affiliate: ESPN; *Format:* Sports; *Hrs. of News Programming:* news progmg 3 hrs wkly; *No. News Employees:* 2; *Target Audience:* 25-54.; *Adv. Rates:* 20; 18; 18; 15.
Laura Uvalle, General Manager
Ben Shields, Programming Director
Bill Woleban, Chief Engineer
David Smoak, Program Director
Bill LeGrand, Marketing Director
Terry Taker, Sports Marketing Consultant

Kenedy

*KTNR
09-01-1982; 92.1 MHz FM; 6 kw; 262 ft.; N28 45 35 W97 51 45
Post Office Box 1614, Laredo, TX 78044 US
(214) 879-0081; *Fax:* (214) 879-0083
License: Kenedy, Karnes County, TX held by Hispanic Christian Community Network Inc.
Arbitron Metro Market: Dallas, TX
Antonio Cesar Guel, President

Kenedy-Karnes City

KAML
11-01-1954; 990 kHz AM; *Hrs Open:* 24; 0.25 kw-D, ND1; 0.07 kw-N, ND1; N28 51 2 W97 52 48
Rt. 1, Box 990, Kenedy, TX 78119 US
(830) 583-2990; *Fax:* (830) 583-3994
License: Kenedy-Karnes City, TX held by SIGA Broadcasting Corp.
Group Owner: SIGA Broadcasting Corp.; acq 1-17-2002).
Nat'l Reps: Dome; *Wire Services:* U.S. Weather Service
Arbitron Metro Market: Kenedy, TX; *Format:* Country, News, 84; *Hrs. of News Programming:* news progmg 8 hrs wkly; *No. News Employees:* 2; *Target Audience:* 24-54; male-female; *Adv. Rates:* 12; 12; 12; 10
Gabriel Arango, President
Clyde Eckols, General Manager
Steve Eckols, Programming Director

Kerens

KRVF
05-23-1979; 106.9 MHz FM; 21.5 kw; 365 ft.; N32 6 12 W96 22 33
1436 Auburn Boulevard, Sacramento, CA 96815 US
(903) 874-8884; *Fax:* (903) 885-9107
www.1069theranch.com/
License: Kerens, Navarro County, TX held by LKCM Radio Group L.P.
Group Owner: LKCM Radio Group L.P.; (acq 5-21-2004; $1 million with KRVA-FM Campbell).
Arbitron Metro Market: Kerens, TX; *Format:* Oldies
Bert Goldman, President
Chris McMurray, General Manager

Kermit

KERB-FM
01-01-1983; 106.3 MHz FM; 3 kw; 276 ft.; N31 50 5 W103 8 10
P.O. Box 252, McAllen, TX 78502 US
(956) 781-5528; *Fax:* (956) 686-2999
www.laradiocristiana.com
License: Kermit, Winkler County, TX held by La Radio Cristiana Network Inc.
Arbitron Metro Market: Odessa-Midland, TX
Barger Tygart, Chairman
Kevin Martin, COO
Jeff Luchsinger, Station Manager
Patricia Lyons, General Sales Mgr

Kerrville

*KKER
12-08-2000; 88.7 MHz FM; *Hrs Open:* 24; 100 kw; 1614 ft.; N29 34 05 W95 29 57
2424 South Blvd., Houston, TX 77098 US
(713) 520-5200
www.khcb.org
email@khcb.org
License: Kerrville, Kerr County, TX held by Houston Christian Broadcasters Inc.
Group Owner: Houston Christian Broadcasters Inc.
Nat'l Network: Moody
Arbitron Metro Market: Houston, TX; *Format:* Christian *Special Programming:* Sp 6 hrs, Chinese one hr wkly
Bruce E. Munsterman, President

KERV
11-05-1948; 1230 kHz AM; *Hrs Open:* 24; 0.99 kw-U, ND1; N30 4 14 W99 11 7
Suite 200, 1021 E. Main St., Kerrville, TX 78028 US
(830) 896-1230; *Fax:* (830) 792-4142
www.revfmradio.com
info@kerv.com
License: Kerrville, TX held by Foster Charitable Foundation Inc.
Group Owner: Revolution Broadcast Company of the West; (acq 5-31-2007)
Nat'l Network: ABC
Arbitron Metro Market: Kerville, TX; *Format:* Jazz, Smooth Jazz, 86; *Hrs. of News Programming:* news progmg 3 hrs wkly; *No. News Employees:* 1; *Target Audience:* 45 plus; educated professionals; *Adv. Rates:* 14;12; 14; 12.
Dennis Anderson, President

KRNH
06-01-1994; 92.3 MHz FM; *Hrs Open:* 24; 20 kw; 666 ft.; N30 3 42 W99 3 43
P.O. Drawer 2037, Canyon Lake, TX 78130 US
(830) 896-4990; *Fax:* (830) 896-4991
www.923theranch.com
License: Kerrville, Kerr County, TX held by Radio Ranch Ltd.
Group Owner: Radio Ranch Ltd.; (acq 9-6-00; $245,000)
Format: Country; *Target Audience:* 18-64.
JD Rose, Operations Dir
Mark Grubbs, General Manager
Kelli McLaughlin, General Sales Mgr

*KHKV
01-01-1998; 91.1 MHz FM; *Hrs Open:* 24; 0.3 kw; 207 ft.; N30 02 37 W99 07 17
2424 South Blvd., Houston, TX 77098 US
(713) 520-5200
www.khcb.org
email@khcb.org
License: Kerrville, Kerr County, TX held by Houston Christian Broadcasters Inc.
Group Owner: Houston Christian Broadcasters Inc.
Arbitron Metro Market: San Antonio, TX; *Format:* Christian
Bruce E. Munsterman, President

KRVL
09-12-1975; 94.3 MHz FM; *Hrs Open:* 24; 33 kw; 400 ft.; N30 15 8 W99 8 1
301 Junction Hwy, Suite 320, Kerrville, TX 78028 US
(830) 896-1230; *Fax:* (830) 792-4142
www.revfmradio.com
info@revfmradio.com
License: Kerrville, Kerr County, TX held by Foster Charitable Foundation Inc.
Group Owner: Revolution Broadcast Company of the West; (acq 5-31-2007)
Nat'l Network: ABC
Format: Triple A *Special Programming:* Gospel one hr, local church service one hr wkly; *Target Audience:* 25-49.; *Adv. Rates:* 25; 20; 25; 18.
Marti Ashcraft, Operations Dir
Jana Smith, General Manager
Gordon Ames, General Sales Mgr
Glenn Taylor, Programming Director
Diane Philips, News Director
Monica Smith, Sales

KKVR
09-01-2007; 106.1 MHz FM; *Hrs Open:* 24; 6 kw; 328 ft.; N30 2 27 W99 10 19
US
(830) 896-4990; *Fax:* (830) 896-4991
www.theriver1061.com
License: Kerrville, Kerr County, TX held by Radio Ranch Ltd.
Group Owner: Radio Ranch Ltd.
Arbitron Metro Market: Kerrville, TX; *Format:* Contemporary Hits/Top 40, Adult Contemp
Bret Huggins, General Manager
Alyson Foster, General Sales Mgr
Ed Chandler, Programming Director
Mike Taylor, Assistant Program Director

Kilgore

KKTX-FM
12-23-1976; 96.1 MHz FM; 50 kw; 492 ft.; N32 22 14 W94 56 20
3810 Brrokside Dr., Tyler, TX 75701 US
(903) 581-0606; *Fax:* (903) 581-2011
www.kktx.com
License: Kilgore, Gregg County, TX held by GAP Broadcasting Tyler License LLC
Group Owner: Townsquare Media; (acq 8-3-2007; grpsl)
Arbitron Metro Market: Tyler, TX; *Format:* Classic Rock; *Target Audience:* 25-54.
Johnny Lathrop, President/Chief Revenue Officer
John Roberts, Operations Manager

Michelle Hiltzman, Director Of Sales
Abel Sanchez, Digital Sales Manager

***KZLO**
02-04-1991; 88.7 MHz FM; *Hrs Open:* 19; 63 kw horiz, 79 kw vert; 551 ft.; N32 20 14 W95 2 41
904 Houston Street, Kilgore, TX 75662 US
(916) 251-1600; *Fax:* (916) 251-1650
www.klove.com
License: Kilgore, Gregg County, TX held by Educational Media Foundation.
Group Owner: EMF Broadcasting; (acq 2-15-2007; $2 million)
Nat'l Network: K-Love
Arbitron Metro Market: Tyler-Longview, TX; *Format:* Christian
Mike Novak, CEO/COO
Mike Novak, President
Darrell Chambliss-Chairman

Killeen

KIIZ-FM
12-10-1990; 92.3 MHz FM; *Hrs Open:* 24; 6 kw; 240 ft.; N31 6 29 W97 39 50
100 W. Center Expressway, Harker Heights, TX 76348 US
(254) 699-5000
www.kiiz.com
License: Killeen, Bell County, TX held by Capstar TX LLC
Group Owner: iHeartMedia; (acq 8-30-2000; grpsl)
Arbitron Metro Market: Killeen-Temple, TX; *Format:* Urban Contemporary; *Hrs. of News Programming:* News progmg 2 hrs wkly; *Target Audience:* 18-49.
Evan Armstrong, General Manager
Jerry Ferch, General Sales Mgr

***KNCT-FM**
11-23-1970; 91.3 MHz FM; *Hrs Open:* 24; 50 kw; 1171 ft.; N30 59 12 W97 37 47
6200 W. Central Texas, Expressway, Killeen, TX 76542 US
(254) 526-1176; *Fax:* (254) 526-1850
www.knct.org
License: Killeen, Bell County, TX held by Central Texas College.
Nat'l Network: AP Network News
Arbitron Metro Market: Killeen-Temple, *TV Affiliate:* *KNCT(TV) affil; *Format:* News *Special Programming:* Jazz 15 hrs wkly, big band 6 hrs wkly; *Target Audience:* 45 plus.
Max Rudolph, General Manager
Dan Hull, Programming Director
Steve Sulzer, Chief Engineer

KRMY
07-04-1955; 1050 kHz AM; 0.25 kW; N31 6 53 W97 42 0
15307 Falcon Ridge Dr, Humble, TX 77396 USA
(281) 441-3665
License: Killeen, TX held by Martin Broadcasting Inc.
Group Owner: Martin Broadcasting Inc.; acq 11-89; grpsl;
Arbitron Metro Market: Killeen, TX; *Format:* Gospel; *Target Audience:* 18-44.

Kingsville

KFTX
05-02-1970; 97.5 MHz FM; *Hrs Open:* 24; 97 kw; 955 ft.; N27 44 28 W97 36 8
1520 South Port Avenue, Corpus Christi, TX 78405 US
(361) 883-5987; *Fax:* (361) 883-3648
www.kftx.com
License: Kingsville, Kleberg County, TX held by Quality Broadcasting Corp.
Arbitron Metro Market: Corpus Christi, TX; *Format:* Country *Special Programming:* Religious 10 hrs wkly; *Hrs. of News Programming:* news progmg 2 hrs wkly; *No. News Employees:* 1; *Target Audience:* 25-49;educated, affluent young adults
Cyndi Rowden, General Manager
Cyndi Rowden, General Sales Mgr
Chuck Abel, Programming Director
Wendy Hatley, News Director
Mark Earle, Chief Engineer
Austin Daniels, Music Director

KINE
11-01-1948; 1330 kHz AM; *Hrs Open:* 24; 1 kw-D, ND1; 0.28 kw-N, ND1; N27 36 36 W97 47 42
115 West Avenue D, Robstown, TX 78380 US
(361) 855-1330; *Fax:* (361) 289-7722
License: Kingsville, TX held by Cotton Broadcasting.
Arbitron Metro Market: Corpus Christi, TX; *Format:* Religious; *Target Audience:* 25-54.
Humberto Lopez, CEO
Carlos Lopez, General Manager
Minerva Lopez, General Sales Mgr
Homer Lopez, Programming Director
Manuel Lopez, Promotions Manager

Tommy Greg, Chief Engineer
Ernest Lopez, Sales VP

KKBA
11-01-1981; 92.7 MHz FM; *Hrs Open:* 24; 13 kW; 803 ft.; N27 39 33 W97 34 12
2117 Leopard St, Corpus Christi, TX 78408 USA
(361) 883-3516; *Fax:* (361) 882-9767
rock927.com
License: Kingsville, Kleberg County, TX held by Malkan Interactive Communications
Group Owner: Malkan Interactive Communications; (acq 9-13-95;
Nat'l Reps: Katz Radio
Arbitron Metro Market: Kingsville-Corpus Christi-Alice, TX; *Format:* Rock/AOR

***KTAI**
02-23-1970; 91.1 MHz FM; *Hrs Open:* Noon-12:30 AM (M-F); 4 PM-10 PM (Su; 0.1 kw horiz, 0 kw vert; N27 31 24 W97 52 42
MSC 178, 700 University Boulevard, Kingsville, TX 78363 US
(361) 593-2137
www.ktai.com
ktaifm@hotmail.com
License: Kingsville, Kleberg County, TX held by Texas A&M University-Kingsville.
Arbitron Metro Market: Kingsville, TX *Special Programming:* Black 8 hrs, gospel 6 hrs, mus from India 3 hrs, mus from Mexico 3 hrs wkly; *Target Audience:* 16-25; high school & college ages
Rumaldo Juarez, President

Krum

KNOR
11-11-1984; 93.7 MHz FM; *Hrs Open:* 24; 43 kw; 1969 ft.; N33 29 5 W97 24 44
2410 Gateway Dr, Irving, TX 75063 US
(972) 652-2900
www.larazadallas.estrellatv.com
dallasinfo@lbimedia.com
License: Krum, Denton County, TX held by Liberman Broadcasting of Dallas License LLC.
Group Owner: Liberman Broadcasting Inc.; (acq 5-13-2004; $15.5 million)
Nat'l Reps: Roslin
Arbitron Metro Market: Dallas-Fort Worth, TX; *Format:* Spanish; *Hrs. of News Programming:* news 20 hrs wkly; *Target Audience:* Hispanic; *Adv. Rates:* 15; 13; 15; 13

Kurten

KPWJ
107.7 MHz FM; 3.5 kw; 328 ft.; N30 37 12 W96 15 13
2700 Earl Rudder Fwy., Suite 5000, College Station, TX 77845 US
(979) 695-9595; *Fax:* (979) 695-1933
www.peace107.com
contact@peace107.com
License: Kurten, Brazos County, TX held by Bryan Broadcasting License Corp.
Group Owner: Bryan Broadcasting Corp.
Arbitron Metro Market: Bryan-College Station, TX; *Format:* Christian
Tucker Young, Operations Dir
Ben Downs, General Manager
Brian Christopher, Programming Director
Lauren Rouse, Creative Director

La Grange

KBUK
12-21-1970; 104.9 MHz FM; 1.75 kw; 527 ft.; N29 52 32 W96 52 39
US
(979) 968-3173
www.kvlgkbuk.com
License: La Grange, Fayette County, TX
Arbitron Metro Market: La Grange, TX
John Haworth, Co-Owner
Dan Mueller, Co-Owner
Mike Anders, Programming/Business/Traffic Manager & Engineer
Sylvia Bookout, Webmaster

KVLG
06-27-1959; 1570 kHz AM; 0.25 kw-D, DA2; 0.011 kw-N, DA2; N29 52 58 W96 51 57
(979) 968-3173; *Fax:* (409) 968 6196
www.kvlgkbuk.com
License: La Grange, TX held by Fayette Broadcasting Corp.
Regional Network: Texas State Networks

Arbitron Metro Market: La Grange; *Format:* Country *Special Programming:* Ger one hr, Black one hr, farm 4 hrs, Pol/Czech 12 hrs, relg 5 hrs wkly; *Target Audience:* General.
John Haworth, Co-Owner
Dan Mueller, Co-Owner
Mike Anders, Programming/Business/Traffic Manager & Engineer
Sylvia Bookout, Webmaster

La Porte

KHJK
01-01-1992; 103.7 MHz FM; 94.86 kw; Ant 1,935 ft; N29 56 09 W94 30 38
5700 West Oaks Blvd., Rocklin, CA 95765 US
(916) 251-1600
www.klove.com
License: La Porte, TX held by Educational Media Foundation
Group Owner: Educational Media Foundation
Arbitron Metro Market: Houston-Galveston; *Format:* Christian, Rock/AOR
Mike Novak, President

Lake Jackson

KGLK
11-10-1980; 107.5 MHz FM; 91.6 kw; 1965 ft.; N30 13 53 W95 7 26
1990 Post Oak Blvd., Suite 2300, Houston, TX 77056 US
(713) 963-1200; *Fax:* (713) 622-5457
www.houstoneagle.com
mark.krieschen@coxinc.com
License: Lake Jackson, Brazoria County, TX held by Cox Radio Inc.
Group Owner: Cox Radio Inc.; (acq 8-24-2000; grpsl)
Arbitron Metro Market: Houston, TX; *Format:* Oldies
Mark Krieschen, Vice President / Market Manager
Judy Lakin, Director Of Sales
Alana Lujan, General Sales Manager
Johnny Chiang, Operations Manager
Lisa Searcy, Marketing Director
Candy Graham, Promotions Manager
Bill Tatar,Digital Content Manager
Chris Fair, Promotions Manager

KGLK
04-01-1963; 107.5 MHz FM; *Hrs Open:* 24; 100 kw; Ant 2,000 ft; N29 17 16 W95 13 53
1990 Post Oak Blvd., Suite 2300, Houston, TX 77056
(713) 963-1200; *Fax:* (713) 622-5457
www.houstonseagle.com
johnny.chiang@coxinc.com
License: Lake Jackson, Brazoria County, TX held by Cox Radio Inc.
Group Owner: Cox Radio Inc.; (acq 8-30-2000; grpsl)
Population Served: 47,743; *Arbitron Metro Market:* Houston-Galveston; *Format:* Oldies; *Hrs. of News Programming:* news progmg 5 hrs wkly; *No. News Employees:* 2; *Target Audience:* 25-54; college grads from the60s, 70s & 80s
Bill Tatar, Digital Content Manager
Candy Mendez, Digital Content Manager
Mark Krieschen, VP/Marketing Manager
Judy Lakin, Director of Sales
Alan Thomas, General Sales Manager
Johnny Chiang, Operations Manager
Scott Sparks, MusicDirector
Lisa Searcy, Marketing Director

***KYBJ**
07-02-2012; 91.1 MHz FM; 5 kw; 459 ft; N29 02 37 W95 20 11
Rebroadcasts: Rebroadcasts KSBJ(FM) Humble 100%
1722 Treble Drive, Humble, TX 77338
(281) 446-5725; *Fax:* (281) 540-2198
www.ngenradio.com
dj@ngenradio.com
License: Lake Jackson, Brazoria County, TX held by KSJB Educational Foundation Inc.
Target Audience: 12-35
Tim McDermott, General Manager
Carlos Agular, Programming Director
Tamara Brubaker, Assistant General Manager
Mark Wanner, Sr. Dir. Planning & Technology Director
Nikki Sparks, Sr. Dir. Creative Services
Jon Hull, Sr. Dir.Outreach

Lamesa

***KBKN**
91.3 MHz FM; 0.25 kw; 157 ft.; N32 45 34 W101 57 9
PO Box 10571, Midland, TX 79702 US

(432) 638-1150; *Fax:* (432) 682-5230
www.grnonline.com
faustino@grnonline.com
License: Lamesa, Dawson County, TX held by La Promesa Foundation.
Group Owner: La Promesa Foundation; (acq 5-4-2004; $108,000 including six translator stns).
Arbitron Metro Market: Lamesa, TX; *Format:* Christian
Leonard J. Oswald, President
Mary M. Diaz, Vice President
Toya E. Hall, Vice President
Janice Gist, Secretary

KPET
05-21-1947; 690 kHz AM; *Hrs Open:* 24; 0.25 kw-U, ND1; N32 42 27 W101 56 11
Mailing Address: P. O. Box 1188, Lamesa, TX 79331 US
Second Address: 1 Radio Road, Lamesa, TX 79331
(806) 872-6511; *Fax:* (806) 872-6514
kpet.radio@gmail.com
License: Lamesa, TX held by DCB License Sub LLC
Group Owner: Dawson County Broadcasting LLC; (acq 10-5-2007; $290,000)
Nat'l Network: ABC; *Regional Network:* Texas State Networks
Format: Country; *Hrs. of News Programming:* news progmg 2 hrs wkly; *No. News Employees:* 1; *Target Audience:* 18-65.; *Adv. Rates:* 10.50; 10.50; 10.50; 10.50
Fernando Armendariz, Office/Traffice/Sales Manager

KTXC
05-01-1988; 104.7 MHz FM; *Hrs Open:* 24; 100 kw; 801 ft.; N32 23 47 W101 57 24
Mailing Address: 1130 West Country Road 127, Midland, TX 79711 US
Second Address: PO Box 60150, Midland, TX 79711
(432) 567-9991; *Fax:* (432) 567-9999
www.newswest9.com
dmarino@kwes.com
License: Lamesa, Dawson County, TX held by Graham Brothers Comm. L.L.C.
Arbitron Metro Market: Lamesa, TX; *Target Audience:* 25-54; college-educated, upper-income families
Jackie Rutledge, General Manager
Christine Couldridge, Sales Manager
Laura Hernandez, Traffic Manager
Ronnie Marley, Content Director

***KRJA**
88.9 MHz FM; 250 watts; 22 meters; N32 44 06.2 W101 57 35
(432) 683-0972
License: Lamesa, TX held by Templo Piedra Angular

Lampasas

KCYL
01-01-1948; 1450 kHz AM; *Hrs Open:* 5 AM-11 PM; 0.8 kw-U, ND1; N31 2 57 W98 10 10
505 N. Key Ave., Lampasas, TX 76550 US
(512) 556-6193; *Fax:* (512) 556-2197
www.lampasasradio.com
License: Lampasas, TX held by Ronald K. Witcher.
Regional Network: Texas State Networks
Arbitron Metro Market: Lampasas, TX; *Format:* Country *Special Programming:* Farm 5 hrs, loc news & community service 14 hrs, sports 8 hrs, relg 10 hrs wkly; *Hrs. of News Programming:* news progmg 15 hrs wkly *No. NewsEmployees:* 3; *Target Audience:* 30 plus; agriculture, farm & ranch
Ronnie Witcher, President
Joe Lombardi, Promotions Manager
Lela Cooper, News Director

Laredo

***KBNL**
07-27-1985; 89.9 MHz FM; *Hrs Open:* 24; 100 kw; 604 ft.; N27 39 27 W99 35 10
PO Box 2325, Laredo, TX 78043 US
www.kbnl.org
kbnl@lwrn.org
License: Laredo, Webb County, TX held by World Radio Network Inc.
Group Owner: World Radio Network Inc.; (acq 10-24-85)
Arbitron Metro Market: Laredo, TX; *Format:* Spanish; *Hrs. of News Programming:* News progmg 2 hrs wkly; *Target Audience:* Male-Females 18-54.
Arturo Lozano, Manager
Rose Rabell, Programming Director

***KHOY**
11-01-1985; 88.1 MHz FM; 1.8 kw; 348 ft.; N27 31 14 W99 31 19
1901 Corpus Christi St., Laredo, TX 78043 US
(956) 722-4167; *Fax:* (956) 722-4464
www.khoy.org
khoy@khoy.org
License: Laredo, Webb County, TX held by Laredo Catholic Communications Inc.
Format: Religious, Spanish; *Hrs. of News Programming:* news progmg 8 hrs wkly; *Target Audience:* Christian Families
Bennett McBride, General Manager
Jose Angel Jimenez, Programming Director

KJBZ
12-29-1982; 92.7 MHz FM; *Hrs Open:* 24; 3 kw; 289 ft.; N27 31 4 W99 31 20
6402 N. Bartlett Avenue, Laredo, TX 78401 US
(956) 726-9393; *Fax:* (956) 724-9915
License: Laredo, Webb County, TX held by Encarnacion A. Guerra.
Arbitron Metro Market: Laredo, TX; *Format:* Tejano; *Target Audience:* General; all ages
Belinda Guerra-Muerer, CEO
Roberto Estrada, Station Manager
Randy Cruz, Music Programmer
Arturo Trevino, Chief Engineer
Dave Gonzalez, Production Director
Fernando Rodriguez, Traffic Manager

KLAR
01-01-1956; 1300 kHz AM; *Hrs Open:* 24
(210) 724-7898; *Fax:* (210) 723-9539
License: Laredo, TX held by Faith and Power Communications Inc.
Arbitron Metro Market: Laredo, TX; *Format:* Christian; *Hrs. of News Programming:* news progmg 18 hrs wkly; *No. News Employees:* 2; *Target Audience:* 18-54; Hispanic & Anglo middle to upper-middle class
Hector Patino, President

KLNT
04-20-1990; 1490 kHz AM; *Hrs Open:* 24
505 Houston St/ Po 814, Laredo, TX 78040 US
(956) 725-1491; *Fax:* (956) 725-3424
License: Laredo, TX held by BMP 100.5 FM L.P.
Group Owner: Border Media Partners LLC; (acq 11-9-2004; grpsl).
Arbitron Metro Market: Laredo, TX
Thomas Castro, President
Ruben Villareal, Operations Dir
Raul Rodriguez, General Manager
Joe Flores, General Sales Mgr

KNEX
01-01-1992; 106.1 MHz FM; 6 kw; 177 ft.; N27 31 12 W99 31 19
P. O. Box 814, Laredo, TX 78042 US
(956) 725-1000; *Fax:* (956) 794-9155
www.hot1061.net
License: Laredo, Webb County, TX held by BMP 100.5 FM L.P.
Group Owner: Border Media Partners LLC; (acq 11-9-2004; grpsl).
Arbitron Metro Market: Laredo, TX; *Format:* Contemporary Hits/Top 40, Spanish
Miguel Villarreal, General Manager

KQUR
02-02-1972; 94.9 MHz FM; 100 kw; 810 ft.; N27 31 14 W99 31 19
107 Calle Del Norte Drive, #212, Laredo, TX 78041 US
(956) 725-1000
www.hot1061.com
License: Laredo, Webb County, TX held by Border Broadcasters Inc.
Nat'l Reps: Roslin
Arbitron Metro Market: Laredo, TX; *Format:* Adult Contemp; *Target Audience:* 25-54; general
Miguel Villarreal, General Manager

KRRG
10-01-1982; 98.1 MHz FM; 96 kw; 699 ft.; N27 31 14 W99 31 19
6402 N. Bartlett, Suite 1, Laredo, TX 78041 US
(956) 724-9800; *Fax:* (956) 724-9915
www.bigbuck98.com
restrada@krrg.com
License: Laredo, Webb County, TX held by Guerra Enterprises
Nat'l Reps: D & R Radio
Arbitron Metro Market: Laredo, TX; *Format:* Country
Roberto Estrada, General Manager
David Gonzalez, Programming Director

Laughlin Afb

KDRX
106.9 MHz FM; 6 kw; 328 ft.; N29 24 21 W100 39 41 US
(772) 286-5586
License: Laughlin Afb, Edwards County, TX held by MBM Radio Del Rio, LLC
Arbitron Metro Market: Del Rio, TX; *Format:* Country

League City

***KHCB**
04-27-1927; 1400 kHz AM; *Hrs Open:* 24; 1 kw-D, 1 kw-N; N29 17 24 W94 50 12
2424 South Blvd., Houston, TX 77098 US
(713) 520-5200
www.khcb.org
email@khcb.org
License: League City, Galveston County, TX held by Houston Christian Broadcasters Inc.
Group Owner: Houston Christian Broadcasters Inc.; (acq 12-4-90; $150,000)
Population Served: 1,500,000; *Arbitron Metro Market:* Houston-Galveston; *Format:* Christian; *No. News Employees:* 1; *Target Audience:* General.
Bruce E. Munsterman, President

Leakey

KXQK
06-10-1997; 104.3 MHz FM; 1 kw; 594 ft.; N29 41 34 W99 48 56
Mailing Address: 8620 N. New Braunfels, San Antonio, TX 78217 US
Second Address: 935 East Main, Uvalde, TX 78801
(830) 278-3693; *Fax:* (830) 278-2329
www.kbnu.fm
kbradioranch@hotmail.com
License: Leakey, Real County, TX held by Radio Cactus Ltd.
Arbitron Metro Market: Leakey, TX; *Format:* Christian; *Target Audience:* General.
John Furr, President
Regenia Tumbarello, General Manager

Leander

***KUTX**
05-16-1976; 98.9 MHz FM; *Hrs Open:* 24; 29 kw; Ant 515 ft; N30 23 26 W97 50 13
912 Capital of Texas Hwy, Suite 400, Austin, TX 18503
(512) 416-1100; *Fax:* (512) 416-8205
License: Leander, Williamson County, TX held by BMP Austin License Company L.P.
Group Owner: Border Media Partners LLC; (acq 11-9-2004; grpsl)
Nat'l Network: ABC; Westwood One; *Nat'l Reps:* D & R Radio
Population Served: 926,300; *Arbitron Metro Market:* Austin, TX; *Target Audience:* 25-54; adults; *Adv. Rates:* 38; 38; 38; 38
Ian Hernandez, Operations Dir
Paul Danitz, General Manager
Daniel Martinez, Programming Director

Levelland

KLVT
08-01-1949; 1230 kHz AM; 1 kw-U, ND1; N33 35 54 W102 23 8
611 N. West Avenue, Levelland, TX 79336 US
(806) 894-3134; *Fax:* (806) 894-3135
www.klvtradio.com
License: Levelland, TX held by Profit Programming of Northern Texas
Regional Network: Texas State Networks
Format: Country
Tania Moody, Owner
Michael West, Station Manager/Sports Director
Jody Rose, News/Programming/Operations Director
Halie Rodriguez, Traffic
Anthony Garza, Chief Engineer

KJDL-FM
11-08-1983; 105.3 MHz FM; 23.5 kw; 712 ft.; N33 25 24 W102 7 41
132 Liveoak, Hereford, TX 79045 US
(806) 744-6864; *Fax:* (806) 744-8018
License: Levelland, Hockley County, TX held by Walker FM Holdings LLC
Format: Country
Dennis Leverett, General Manager
Jess Walker, Station Manager

Lewisville

KFZO
04-10-1999; 107.9 MHz FM; *Hrs Open:* 24; 100 kw; 981 ft.; N33 19 42 W97 3 56
7700 John W. Carpenter Fwy., Dallas, TX 75247 US
(214) 525-0400; *Fax:* (214) 206-9022
www.univision.com
License: Lewisville, Denton County, TX held by KECS-FM License Corp.
Group Owner: Univision Radio; (acq 9-22-2003; grpsl).
Arbitron Metro Market: Dallas-Fort Worth, TX; *Format:* Tejano
Mark Masepohl, Vice President and General Manager
Patrick Parks, Chief Engineer
Karem Hocking, National Sales Manager
Myrna Vera, Research Director

Liberty

KSHN
08-29-1991; 99.9 MHz FM; *Hrs Open:* 24; 26 kw; 679 ft; N30 03 05 W94 31 37
2099 Sam Houston St., Liberty, TX 77575
(936) 336-5793; *Fax:* (936) 336-5250
www.kshn.com
kshn@kshn.com
License: Liberty, Liberty County, TX held by Trinity River Valley Broadcasting Co.
Regional Network: Texas State Networks
Population Served: 700,000; *Arbitron Metro Market:* Houston-Galvest *Special Programming:* Black 4 hrs, bluegrass 2 hrs, relg 5 hrs wkly; *Hrs. of News Programming:* news progmg 36 hrs wkly; *No. News Employees:* 2 *Target Audience:* 34 plus; Adults; *Adv. Rates:* 15; 15; 15; 15
Bill Buchanan, General Manager
Tiffany York, News Director
Barbara Moss, Office Manager

Littlefield

KZZN
01-01-1947; 1490 kHz AM; 1 kw-U, ND1; N33 56 17 W102 20 38
PO Box 288, Littlefield, TX 79339 US
(806) 385-1490
www.kzznradio.com
KZZN@HPRNetwork.com
License: Littlefield, TX held by Juan Alejandro Ibarra
Nat'l Network: USA; *Regional Network:* Texas State Networks
Arbitron Metro Market: Littlefield, TX; *Format:* Country, Gospel
Special Programming: Farm 7 hrs, relg 5 hrs wkly; *Target Audience:* General; try to reach all ages
Cody West, Owner/General Manager
Anthony Garza, Chief Engineer

Livingston

KETX
06-28-1957; 1440 kHz AM; *Hrs Open:* 6 AM-midnight; 5 kw-D, ND1; 0.091 kw-N, ND1; N30 44 23 W94 55 30
P. O. Box 1236, Livingston, TX 77351 US
(409) 327-8916; *Fax:* (409) 327-8477
License: Livingston, TX held by Telcom Supply Inc.
Format: Country
Curtis Walzel, President

KETX-FM
09-01-1970; 92.3 MHz FM; 32 kw; 607 ft.; N30 44 18 W94 55 26
P. O. Drawer 1236, Livingston, TX 77351 US
(936) 327-8916; *Fax:* (936) 327-8477
License: Livingston, Polk County, TX held by Telcom Supply Inc.
Format: Country; *Target Audience:* General.
Curtis Walzel, President

Llano

KAJZ
01-01-2000; 106.5 MHz FM; 7 kw; 573 ft.; N30 40 36 W98 33 59
7700 John W. Carpenter Fwy., Dallas, TX 75247 US
(325) 247-4539
www.kajzradio.com
info@kajzradio.com
License: Llano, Llano County, TX held by Rawhide Radio LLC.
Group Owner: Univision Radio; (acq 9-22-2003; grpsl).
Arbitron Metro Market: Llano, TX; *Format:* Smooth Jazz
Dan Wilson, General Manager

KITY
01-01-2004; 102.9 MHz FM; 2 kw; 495 ft.; N30 40 37 W98 33 59
719 Ford Street, Suite 200, Llano, TX 78643 US
(325) 247-4539
www.kityradio.com
info@kityradio.com
License: Llano, Llano County, TX held by Bryan A. King
Nat'l Network: CNN Radio; Westwood One
Arbitron Metro Market: Llano, TX; *Format:* Oldies
Bryan King, General Manager

Lockhart

KFIT
02-01-1967; 1060 kHz AM; *Hrs Open:* 6 AM-8 PM; 2 kw-D, DAD; N30 19 13 W97 38 59
(512) 328-8400
www.gospel1060.com
License: Lockhart, TX held by KFIT Inc.
Nat'l Network: Westwood One
Arbitron Metro Market: Austin, TX; *Format:* Gospel; *No. News Employees:* 2; *Target Audience:* 18-65.
Darrell Marshi, CEO
Terri Lewis, General Manager

Lometa

KACQ
01-01-1996; 101.9 MHz FM; 6 kw; 328 ft.; N31 14 33 W98 19 19
505 N. Key Avenue, Lampasas, TX 76550 US
(512) 556-6193; *Fax:* (512) 556-2197
lampasasradio.com
License: Lometa, Lampasas County, TX held by Debra L. Witcher.
Arbitron Metro Market: Lampasas, TX; *Format:* Country
Ronnie Witcher, General Manager
Norma Spinner, General Sales Mgr
Joe Lombardi, Programming Director
Lela Cooper, News Director

Longview

KFRO
02-06-1935; 1370 kHz AM; *Hrs Open:* 24; 1 kw-D, DAN; 1 kw-N, DAN; N32 30 7 W94 42 12
13355 Noel Road, 1350 One Galleria Tower, Dallas, TX 75240 US
(903) 663-9800; *Fax:* (903) 663-9458
License: Longview, TX held by RCA Broadcasting, LLC.
Group Owner: RCA Broadcasting LLC; (acq 1-7-2005; grpsl).
Nat'l Network: ABC; Westwood One
Arbitron Metro Market: Tyler, TX; *Format:* Christian, Talk *Special Programming:* Black 3 hrs wkly; *Hrs. of News Programming:* news progmg 30 hrs wkly; *No. News Employees:* 1; *Target Audience:* 25-54; general
Sydney Small, CEO
Chesley Maddox-Dorsey, President
Richard Guest, General Manager
Robert Taylor, General Sales Mgr
Dru Laborde, Programming Director
Shelley Miller, News Director
Sans Hawkins, Engineering Dir
Debbie Tilley,CFO

KYKX
07-01-1974; 105.7 MHz FM; *Hrs Open:* 24; 100 kw; 1,155 ft.; N32 35 37 W94 49 10
Mailing Address: 4408 US Hwy. 259 N., Longview, TX 75605 US
Second Address: 210 S. Broadway Ave., Tyler, TX 75702
(903) 663-9800; *Fax:* (903) 663-1022
www.kykx.com
License: Longview, Gregg County, TX held by Alpha Media Licensee LLC
Group Owner: Alpha Media LLC; (acq 4-14-2015; grpsl).
Nat'l Reps: McGavren Guild
Arbitron Metro Market: Tyler-Longview, TX; *Format:* Country; *Hrs. of News Programming:* news progmg 6 hrs wkly; *No. News Employees:* 1; *Target Audience:* General.
Dru Laborde, Operations Manager
Ginger Dockery, General Manager
Robert Taylor, Sales Manager
Harlen Lobley, Director of Sales

Lorena

*KYAR
04-06-1976; 98.3 MHz FM; *Hrs Open:* 24; 4.1 kw; 397 ft.; N31 24 45 W97 12 40
PO Box 2118, Omaha, NE 68103-2118 US
(916) 251-1600; *Fax:* (916) 251-1650
www.air1.com
License: Lorena, Coryell County, TX held by Educational Media Foundation.
Group Owner: EMF Broadcasting; (acq 3-21-2003; $100,000).
Nat'l Network: Air 1
Arbitron Metro Market: Rocklin, CA; *Format:* Alternative, Christian; *No. News Employees:* 3; *Target Audience:* 25-44; Judeo Christian, female
Darrell Chambliss, Chairman
Mike Novak, President/CEO
David Pierce, Chief Creative Officer
Alan Mason, COO
Eric Moser, CFO
D. Kevin Blair, Secretary/General Counsel

Lorenzo

KKCL
01-01-1989; 98.1 MHz FM; *Hrs Open:* 24; 36 kw; 574 ft.; N33 31 3 W101 51 24
600 Congress Avenue, Suite 1400, Austin, TX 78701 US
(806) 798-7078
www.98kool.com
License: Lorenzo, Crosby County, TX held by Townsquare Media Lubbock License LLC
Group Owner: Townsquare Media
Nat'l Network: ABC
Arbitron Metro Market: Lubbock, TX; *Format:* Oldies *Special Programming:* Talk 17 hrs wkly; *Hrs. of News Programming:* news progmg 14 hrs wkly; *No. News Employees:* 8; *Target Audience:* 25-54; upscale 55% male,45% female; *Adv. Rates:* 35; 45; 25; 10
Dale Harris, General Manager
Renee Gonzalez, General Sales Mgr
Ladon King, Programming Director

Los Ybanez

KJJT
12-01-1990; 98.5 MHz FM; *Hrs Open:* 24; 50 kw; 459 ft.; N32 43 22 W102 1 50
P.O Box 1143 (#15), Los Ybanez, TX 79331 US
License: Los Ybanez, Dawson County, TX held by KYMI License Sub LLC
Arbitron Metro Market: Los Ybanez, TX
David Stewart, General Manager

Louise

*KABA
12-25-1986; 90.3 MHz FM; kw
1600 Pasadena Boulvard, Pasadena, TX 77502 US
(713) 920-1840
info@radioaleluya.org
License: Louise, Anchorage County, TX held by Tati Broadcasting LLC
Arbitron Metro Market: Anchorage, AK; *Format:* Talk
Mike Robbins, General Manager

Lubbock

*KAMY
10-01-1990; 90.1 MHz FM; *Hrs Open:* 24; 63 kw; 482 ft.; N33 30 8 W101 52 20
7355 North Oracle Rd., Tucson, AZ 85704 US
(806) 794-1766; *Fax:* (806) 798-3251
www.myflr.org
License: Lubbock, Lubbock County, TX held by Family Life Broadcasting Inc.
Group Owner: Family Life Communications Inc.; (acq 6-24-98; grpsl).
Arbitron Metro Market: Lubbock, TX; *Format:* Christian, Religious; *Target Audience:* 28 plus; 35-54 female; Christian community of Lubbock
Don Webster, General Manager
Dave Borowsky, Promotions Manager

KBZO
04-01-1953; 1460 kHz AM; *Hrs Open:* 24; 1 kw-D, 0.243 kw-N
1220 Broadway, Suite 600, Lubbock, TX 79401 US
(806) 763-6051; *Fax:* (806) 744-8363
www.espn1460am.com
License: Lubbock, TX held by Entravision Holdings LLC.
Group Owner: Entravision Communications Corp.; (acq 10-7-99).
Nat'l Reps: Lotus Entravision Reps LLC
Arbitron Metro Market: Lubbock, TX; *Format:* Spanish, Adult Contemp; *Target Audience:* Hispanic.
Leticia Flores, General Manager
Erick Segura, Promotions Manager

KQBR
07-15-1964; 99.5 MHz FM; 100 kw; 817 ft.; N33 31 5 W101 51 25
4443 82nd St., #300, Lubbock, TX 79424 US
(806) 798-7078; *Fax:* (806) 798-7052
www.kqbr.com
info@kqbr.com

License: Lubbock, Lubbock County, TX held by Townsquare Media Lubbock License LLC
Group Owner: Townsquare Media; (acq 8-3-2007; grpsl)
Arbitron Metro Market: Lubbock, TX; *Format:* Country
Brice Sheets, General Manager
Lori Crofford, Brand Manager
Gary Boyett, President

KDAV
05-14-1947; 1590 kHz AM
1714 Buddy Holly Avenue, Lubbock, TX 79401 US
(806) 744-5859
www.kdav.com
License: Lubbock, TX held by Renaissance Broadcasting Inc.
Wire Services: ESSA Weather Service
Arbitron Metro Market: Lubbock, TX; *Format:* Oldies; *Hrs. of News Programming:* 5 hrs. news progmg wkly; *No. News Employees:* 1; *Target Audience:* 50 plus.
Bill Clement, President
Bud Andrews, General Manager
Jan Reeves, General Sales Mgr

KEJS
01-01-1993; 106.5 MHz FM; 34 kw; 587 ft.; N33 30 8 W101 52 20
1607 13th Street, Lubbock, TX 79401 US
(806) 747-5951; *Fax:* (806) 747-3524
License: Lubbock, Lubbock County, TX held by Barton Broadcasting Co.
Arbitron Metro Market: Lubbock, TX; *Format:* Tejano
Gilbert Esparza, Programming Director

KFMX-FM
08-01-1966; 94.5 MHz FM; 100 kw; 817 ft.; N33 31 5 W101 51 25
600 Congress Avenue, Suite 1400, Austin, TX 78701 US
(806) 798-7078; *Fax:* (806) 798-7052
www.kfmx.com
License: Lubbock, Lubbock County, TX held by Townsquare Media Lubbock License LLC
Group Owner: Townsquare Media
Arbitron Metro Market: Lubbock, TX; *Format:* Rock/AOR; *Target Audience:* 18-64
Philip Hand, General Manager
Wes Nessman, Brand Manager
Jeff Brown, Director Of Sales
Jeff Brown, Director Of Sales
Justin Massoud, Digital Managing Editor

KFYO
09-06-1927; 790 kHz AM; *Hrs Open:* 24; 5 kw-D, DA2; 1 kw-N, DA2; N33 27 50 W101 55 30
4443 82nd St., 300, Lubbock, TX 79424 US
(801) 394-8833; *Fax:* (806) 798-7052
www.bbnradio.org
bbn@bbnmedia.org
License: Lubbock, TX held by Townsquare Media Lubbock License LLC
Group Owner: Townsquare Media; (acq 8-3-2007; grpsl)
Nat'l Network: CBS; *Regional Network:* Texas State Networks
Arbitron Metro Market: Ogden, UT; *Format:* News, News/Talk, 86; *Hrs. of News Programming:* news progmg 12 hrs wkly; *No. News Employees:* 2; *Target Audience:* Christian Adults
Philip Hand, General Manager
Rob Snyder, Brand Manager
Jeff Brown, Director Of Sales
Jeff Brown, Digital Sales Manager
Justin Massoud, Digital Managing Editor

KKAM
01-01-1955; 1340 kHz AM; 1 kw-U, ND1; N33 33 24 W101 51 46
4413 82nd St., #300, Lubbock, TX 79424 US
(806) 798-7078; *Fax:* (806) 798-7052
www.kfmx.com
info@kfmx.com
License: Lubbock, TX held by Townsquare Media Lubbock License LLC
Group Owner: Townsquare Media; (acq 8-3-2007; grpsl)
Nat'l Network: ABC; CBS
Arbitron Metro Market: Lubbock, TX; *Format:* Rock/AOR
Philip Hand, General Manager
Rob Snyder, Brand Manager
Jeff Brown, Director Of Sales
Jeff Brown, Digital Sales Manager
Justin Massoud, Digital Managing Editor

KJDL
11-15-1966; 1420 kHz AM; *Hrs Open:* 18
1603 13th Street, Suite 210, Lubbock, TX 79401 US
(806) 741-1420
www.thereddirtrebel.com
License: Lubbock, TX held by Walker Broadcasting & Communications Ltd.
Regional Network: Texas State Networks
Arbitron Metro Market: Lubbock, TX; *Format:* News, News/Talk, 86
David Walker, President
Helen Castro, Promotions Manager
Bill Enloe, Chief Engineer

KLLL-FM
03-01-1958; 96.3 MHz FM; *Hrs Open:* 24; 100 kw; 817 ft.; N33 31 4 W101 51 23
#33 Briercroft Park Office Park, Lubbock, TX 79423 US
(806) 762-3000
www.klll.com
License: Lubbock, Lubbock County, TX held by Alpha Media Licensee LLC
Group Owner: Alpha Media LLC; (acq 5-15-2015; grpsl).
Nat'l Network: ABC
Arbitron Metro Market: Lubbock, TX; *Format:* Country; *Target Audience:* 25-54.
Jeff Scott, Operations Manager
Jay Richardson, General Manager
Randy Gattis, Sales Manager

***KTTZ-FM**
01-01-1973; 89.1 MHz FM; *Hrs Open:* 24; 70 kw; Ant 567 ft; N33 34 55 W101 53 25
Mailing Address: 1901 University Ave., Suite 603-B, Lubbock, TX 79409
Second Address: Box 45891, Lubbock, TX 79409
(806) 742-3100; *Fax:* (806) 742-3716
www.kohm.org
kohm@ttu.edu
License: Lubbock, Lubbock County, TX held by Texas Tech University.
Nat'l Network: NPR; PRI
Population Served: 250,000; *Arbitron Metro Market:* Lubbock, TX
TV Affiliate: *KTXT-TV affil.
Derrick Ginter, General Manager
Sherril Skibell, General Sales Mgr
Clinton Barrick, Programming Director

KONE
01-01-1975; 101.1 MHz FM; *Hrs Open:* 24; 100 kw; 883 ft.; N33 26 31 W101 52 40
#33 Briercroft Park Office Park, Lubbock, TX 79423 US
(806) 762-3000; *Fax:* (806) 762-8419
www.rock101.fm
License: Lubbock, Lubbock County, TX held by Alpha Media Licensee LLC
Group Owner: Alpha Media LLC; (acq 5-15-2015; grpsl).
Nat'l Network: ABC
Arbitron Metro Market: Lubbock, TX; *Format:* Classic Rock; *Target Audience:* 25-54.
Jeff Scott, Operations Manager
Jay Richardson, General Manager
Randy Gattis, Sales Manager

KRFE
09-19-1953; 580 kHz AM; *Hrs Open:* 24; 0.5 kw-D, DA2; 0.29 kw-N, DA2; N33 32 0 W101 49 14
6602 Martin L. King Blvd, Lubbock, TX 79404 US
(806) 745-1197; *Fax:* (806) 745-1088
www.am580lubbock.com
wade@wadewilkes.com
License: Lubbock, TX held by KRFE Radio Inc.
Nat'l Network: ABC
Arbitron Metro Market: Lubbock, TX; *Format:* News, News/Talk, 86 *Special Programming:* News/talk 15 hrs wkly; *Hrs. of News Programming:* news progmg 5 hrs wkly; *No. News Employees:* 1; *Target Audience:* 40plus.
Wade Wilkes, OWN

***KTXT-FM**
04-01-1961; 88.1 MHz FM; *Hrs Open:* 24; 35 kw; 423 ft.; N33 34 55 W101 53 25
P.O. Box 43082, Lubbock, TX 79409 US
(806) 742-3388; *Fax:* (806) 742-2434
www.ktxt.net
License: Lubbock, Lubbock County, TX held by Texas Tech University.
Arbitron Metro Market: Lubbock, TX; *Format:* Variety/Diverse
Nick Carissimi, Station Manager
Sheri Lewis, General Sales Mgr
Ali Rana, Programming Director

KJTV
01-01-1947; 950 kHz AM; *Hrs Open:* 24; 5 kw-D, DA2; 0.5 kw-N, DA2; N33 34 53 W101 49 38
9800 University Ave., Lubbock, TX 79423 USA
(806) 745-3434
www.am9501007fm.com
License: Lubbock, TX held by Ramar Communications II Ltd.
Group Owner: Ramar Communications, Ltd.
Arbitron Metro Market: Lubbock, TX; *Format:* Talk, Sports
Brad Moran, General Manager
Gary Reed, General Sales Mgr
Jeff Klotzman, News Director
Christopher Adams, Weather Anchor

KXTQ
11-01-1963; 93.7 MHz FM; *Hrs Open:* 24; 100 kw; 743 ft.; N33 30 8 W101 52 20
9800 University Ave., Lubbock, TX 79423 US
(806) 745-3434
www.magic937.fm
License: Lubbock, TX held by Ramar Communications, Inc.
Group Owner: Ramar Communications, Ltd.
Arbitron Metro Market: Lubbock, TX; *Format:* Tejano
Brad Moran, President
Gary Reed, General Sales Mgr

***KKLU**
10-24-1993; 90.9 MHz FM; *Hrs Open:* 24; 21 kw; 597 ft.; N33 31 33 W101 52 7
8030 Arrowridge Blvd., Charlotte, NC 28273 US
(916) 251-1600; *Fax:* (916) 251-1650
www.klove.com
License: Lubbock, Lubbock County, TX held by Educational Media Foundation.
Group Owner: EMF Broadcasting; (acq 5-1-2000; $750,000 with KXRI(FM) Amarillo).
Nat'l Network: K-Love
Arbitron Metro Market: Lubbock, TX; *Format:* Christian; *Target Audience:* All ages.
Richard Jenkins, President
Mike Novak, Programming Director

KZII-FM
03-10-1982; 102.5 MHz FM; *Hrs Open:* 24; 100 kw; 817 ft.; N33 31 5 W101 51 25
600 Congress Avenue, Suite 1400, Austin, TX 78701 US
(806) 798-7078
www.1025kiss.com
phillip.hand@townsquaremedia.com
License: Lubbock, Lubbock County, TX held by Townsquare Media Lubbock License LLC
Group Owner: Townsquare Media
Arbitron Metro Market: Lubbock, TX; *Format:* Contemporary Hits/Top 40; *Target Audience:* 18-49.
Philip Hand, General Manager
Jeff Brown, Director Of Sales
Jeff Brown, Digital Sales Manager
Justin Massoud, Digital Managing Editor

Lufkin

***KAVX**
12-25-1998; 91.9 MHz FM; *Hrs Open:* 24; 23 kw; 728 ft.; N31 22 8 W94 38 45
Mailing Address: PO Box 151340, Lufkin, TX 75915-1340 US
Second Address: 151 Holmes Road, Lufkin, TX 75904
(936) 639-5673; *Fax:* (936) 639-5677
www.kavx.org
919kavx@kavx.org
License: Lufkin, Angelina County, TX held by Lufkin Educational Broadcasting Foundation.
Nat'l Network: USA
Arbitron Metro Market: Lufkin, TX; *Format:* Talk *Special Programming:* Praise & Worship - Weekends; *Target Audience:* Persons 30 Plus; *Adv. Rates:* 10, 20
Dwyan Calvert, President
Al Ross, General Manager
Michelle Ross, Programming Director
Tim Swanson, Production Director
Drew Wilson, Promotions Director

***KLDN**
05-02-1991; 88.9 MHz FM; *Hrs Open:* 24; 50 kw; 650 ft.; N31 24 28 W94 45 53 *Rebroadcasts:* Rebroadcasts KDAQ(FM) Shreveport, LA 100%
One University Place, Shreveport, LA 71115 US
(318) 797-5150; *Fax:* (318) 797-5265
www.redriverradio.org
listenermail@redriverradio.org
License: Lufkin, Angelina County, TX held by Board of Supervisors of Louisiana State University.
Nat'l Network: NPR; PRI
Format: Classical, Jazz, 60; *Target Audience:* 25+.
Rick Shelton, Operations Dir
Kermit Poling, General Manager

KRBA
05-03-1938; 1340 kHz AM; *Hrs Open:* 24; 1 kw-U, ND1; N31 21 53 W94 43 8
Mailing Address: P.O. Box 1345, Lufkin, TX 75902 US
Second Address: 121 Cotton Sq., Lufkin, TX 75901
(936) 634-6661; *Fax:* (936) 632-5722
License: Lufkin, TX held by Stephen W. Yates.
Format: Country; *Hrs. of News Programming:* news progmg 7 hrs wkly; *No. News Employees:* 1; *Target Audience:* General.
Stephen Yates, General Manager
Kevin Sims, Programming Director
Jeremy Chance, News Director

***KSWP**
08-31-1985; 90.9 MHz FM; *Hrs Open:* 24; 100 kw; 807 ft.; N31 22 8 W94 38 45
Mailing Address: Rt. 17, Box 6395, Lufkin, TX 75904 US
Second Address: , Nacogdoches, TX
(936) 639-6400; *Fax:* (936) 639-5677
www.kswp.org
alross@kswp.org
License: Lufkin, Angelina County, TX held by Lufkin Educational Broadcasting Foundation.
Nat'l Network: USA
Arbitron Metro Market: Lufkin, TX; *Format:* Christian *Special Programming:* Pub affrs talk show 2 hrs wkly; *Target Audience:* Woman 25-54, Persons 25-54; *Adv. Rates:* 10, 20
Dwyan Calvert, President
Al Ross, General Manager
Michelle Ross, Programming Director
Tim Swanson, Production Director
Drew Wilson, Promotions Director

KYBI
05-01-1978; 100.1 MHz FM; *Hrs Open:* 24; 20 kw; 787 ft.; N31 20 5 W94 40 10
Mailing Address: 3 Deerwood, Lufkin, TX 75901 US
Second Address: 121 Cotton Sq., Lufkin, TX 75902
(936) 634-4584; *Fax:* (936) 632-5722
www.kybiradio.com
traffic@yatesmedia.com
License: Lufkin, Angelina County, TX
Arbitron Metro Market: Lufkin, TX; *Format:* Adult Contemp; *Target Audience:* 25-54.
Stephen Yates, General Manager

KYKS
07-09-1976; 105.1 MHz FM; *Hrs Open:* 24; 100 kw; 1066 ft.; N31 22 8 W94 38 45
Mailing Address: 1216 South First St., Lufkin, TX 75901 US
Second Address: 1216 S. First St., Lufkin, TX 75901
(936) 639-4455; *Fax:* (936) 632-5957
www.kicks105.com
License: Lufkin, Angelina County, TX held by Townsquare Media Lufkin License LLC
Group Owner: Townsquare Media; (acq 8-3-2007; grpsl)
Arbitron Metro Market: Lufkin, TX; *Format:* Country; *No. News Employees:* 1; *Target Audience:* 25-54.
Johnny Lathrop, President/Chief Revenue Officer
Danny Merrell, Brand Manager
Paula Divello, Director Of Sales
James Sitllwell, Digital Managing Editor

KAGZ(FM)
01-01-2008; 93.9 MHz FM; 1.7 kw; Ant 610 ft; N31 21 55 W94 45 59
24018 Middle Fork, San Antonio, TX 78258
(830) 980-7111
License: Lufkin, Angelina County, TX held by E-String Wireless Ltd.
Population Served: 35,425; *Arbitron Metro Market:* Lufkin, TX
Bret Huggins, General Manager

Luling

KAMX
03-22-1987; 94.7 MHz FM; *Hrs Open:* 24; 99 kw; 1306 ft.; N30 19 23 W97 47 58
4301 Westbank Drive, Escalade Building B 3rd Floor, Austin, TX 78746 US
(512) 327-9595
mix947.com
catthomas@entercom.com
License: Luling, Caldwell County, TX held by Entercom Austin License LLC.
Group Owner: Entercom Communications Corp.; (acq 11-30-2007; grpsl)
Nat'l Reps: Katz Radio
Arbitron Metro Market: Austin, TX; *Format:* Adult Contemp
Special Programming: Pub affrs 2 hrs wkly; *Target Audience:* 18-49; upscale adults
Alan Kirshbom, General Manager
Cat Thomas, Programming Director
Heather Baumli, Mix Sales & Advertising
Aaron Hurd, Mix Promotions Director
Dave Munoz, Webmaster

Lumberton

KSET
10-13-1959; 1300 kHz AM; *Hrs Open:* 24
103 Entrance Drive, Suite 1, Livingston, TX 77351 US
(409) 385-2883; *Fax:* (409) 386-1001
kset@kset1300.com
License: Lumberton, TX held by Proctor-Williams Inc.
Regional Network: Texas State Networks
Arbitron Metro Market: Beaumont, TX; *Format:* Sports; *Target Audience:* General.
Dave Collier, CEO

KKHT-FM
12-01-1987; 100.7 MHz FM; *Hrs Open:* 24; 100 kw; 1952 ft.; N30 3 5 W94 31 37
6161 Savoy, Suite 1200, Houston, TX 77036 US
(713) 260-3600; *Fax:* (713) 260-3628
www.kkht.com
comments@kkht.com
License: Lumberton, Chambers County, TX held by Salem Media of Illinois LLC.
Group Owner: Salem Communications Corp.; (acq 1-7-2005; with WIND(AM) Chicago, IL and KNIT(AM) Dallas in exchange for WPPN(FM) Des Plaines, IL).
Nat'l Reps: Salem
Arbitron Metro Market: Houston, TX; *Format:* Christian, Talk
Paul Baker, Operations Dir
Chuck Jewell, General Manager
Dan Doster, General Sales Mgr
Kent McDonald, News Director
Sidney Jones, Chief Engineer
Marsha Lambeth, Music Director
Ken Garza, Public Affairs Director

Lytle

***KZLV**
01-20-1990; 91.3 MHz FM; *Hrs Open:* 24; 50 kw; 492 ft.; N29 14 39 W98 44 27
1425 North Market Boulevard, Suite 9, Sacramento, CA 95839 US
(210) 824-9100; *Fax:* (210) 824-8870
www.klove.com
info@kzlv.com
License: Lytle, Atascosa County, TX held by Educational Media Foundation.
Group Owner: EMF Broadcasting; (acq 4-28-99).
Nat'l Network: K-Love
Format: Adult Contemp, Christian; *Target Audience:* 25-49; professional adult & parents
Dick Jenkins, President
Ed Lenane, Operations Dir
Lloyd Parker, General Manager

Mabank

KTXV
01-01-2007; 890 kHz AM; 20 kw-D, DA; N32 17 13 W95 58 39
10613 Bellaire Blvd., Suite 900, Houston, TX
(713) 917-0050; *Fax:* (713) 917-0213
www.radiosaigonhouston.com
License: Mabank, Kaufman County, TX held by Bustos Media Holdings L.L.C.
Group Owner: Bustos Media Holdings L.L.C.; (acq 9-5-2007; $1 million)

Thuy Vu, General Manager

Madisonville

KAGG
12-05-1989; 96.1 MHz FM; *Hrs Open:* 24; 40 kw; 538 ft.; N30 48 2 W96 7 0
1716 Briarcrest Dr., Suite 150, Bryan, TX 77802 US
(979) 846-5597; *Fax:* (979) 268-9090
www.aggie96.com
License: Madisonville, Madison County, TX held by CC Licenses LLC
Group Owner: iHeartMedia; (acq 10-10-00; grpsl).
Arbitron Metro Market: Bryan, TX; *Format:* Country
Evan Armstrong, Market Manager
Jim Harrington, Sales Manager

KMVL
10-01-1989; 1220 kHz AM; *Hrs Open:* 24; 0.5 kw-D, ND1; 0.011 kw-N, ND1; N30 57 56 W95 53 52
102 W. Main St., Madisonville, TX 77864 US
(936) 348-9200; *Fax:* (936) 348-9201
www.kmvl.net
kmvl@kmvl.net
License: Madisonville, TX held by Leon Hunt
Group Owner: Star Radio Network
Regional Network: Texas State Networks
Format: Oldies; *Hrs. of News Programming:* news progmg 15 hrs wkly; *No. News Employees:* 1; *Target Audience:* General.
Leon Hunt, President
Becky Neal, General Sales Mgr

KMVL-FM
04-01-1997; 100.5 MHz FM; *Hrs Open:* 24; 13 kw; 449 ft; N31 06 40 W95 57 09
102 W. Main St., Madisonville, TX 77864 US
(936) 348-9200; *Fax:* (936) 348-9201
www.kmvl.net
kmvl@kmvl.net
License: Madisonville, Madison County, TX held by Leon Hunt
Group Owner: Star Radio Network
Nat'l Network: ABC
Format: Country; *Target Audience:* 25-49.
Leon Hunt, President
Becky Neal, General Sales Mgr

***KHML**
01-01-2006; 91.5 MHz FM; *Hrs Open:* 24; 95 kw; 341 ft.; N31 6 39.6 W95 57 8.6 *Rebroadcasts:* Rebroadcasts KHCB-FM Houston 95%
2424 South Blvd., Houston, TX 77098 US
(713) 520-5200
www.khcb.org
email@khcb.org
License: Madisonville, Madison County, TX held by Houston Christian Broadcasters Inc.
Group Owner: Houston Christian Broadcasters Inc.
Nat'l Network: Moody
Arbitron Metro Market: Austin, TX; *Format:* Christian *Special Programming:* Sp Christian 6 hrs wkly
Bruce E. Munsterman, President

Malakoff

KCKL
08-08-1983; 95.9 MHz FM; *Hrs Open:* 24; 6 kw; 295 ft.; N32 8 48 W95 58 25
11125 Highway 31 East, P.O. Box 489, Malakoff, TX 75148 US
(903) 489-1238; *Fax:* (903) 489-2671
www.kcklfm.com
cquinn@kcklfm.com
License: Malakoff, Henderson County, TX held by Lake Country Radio L.P.
Nat'l Network: ABC
Arbitron Metro Market: Tyler-Longview, TX; *Format:* Country
Special Programming: Relg 7 hrs wkly; *Hrs. of News Programming:* news progmg 10 hrs wkly; *No. News Employees:* 1; *Target Audience:* 25-54;country/city folk, weekenders & visitors to Cedar Creek Lake; *Adv. Rates:* 22.50; 18.50; 22.50; 16.50
Chris Quinn, Station Manager
Robin Smetak, Business Manager/Traffic Director
Tim Howard, Programming/News/Sports Director
Tasha Crum, Promotions Coordinator
Nancy Morish, Business Manager
Tasha Crum, Promotions Coordinator

Manor

KTXW
1120 kHz AM
US
License: Manor, TX held by JNE Investments Inc.
Group Owner: Bustos Media Holdings L.L.C.
Arbitron Metro Market: Manor, TX

KELG
04-22-1981; 1440 kHz AM; 0.8 kw-D, 0.5 kw-N, DA-2; N30 19 36 W97 32 35
9434 Parkfield Drive, Austin, TX 78758 US
(512) 453-1491; *Fax:* (512) 453-6809
License: Manor, TX held by Encino Broadcasting LLC
Group Owner: Encino Broadcasting LLC

Jose J. Garcia Jr., General Manager

Marble Falls

***KBMD**
01-01-2002; 88.5 MHz FM; *Hrs Open:* 24; 6 kw vert; 89 ft.; N30 33 12 W98 15 30 *Rebroadcasts:* EWTN
P.O. Box 10571, Midland, TX 79702 US
(888) 784-3476
www.gmonline.com
richard@gmonline.com
License: Marble Falls, Burnet County, TX held by La Promesa Foundation.
Group Owner: La Promesa Foundation; (acq 2-24-2005; $130,000).
Arbitron Metro Market: Marble Falls, TX; *Format:* Religious, Christian; *No. News Employees:* 2; *Adv. Rates:* 10; 10; 10; 10
Leonard J. Oswald, President
Mary M. Diaz, Vice President
Toya E. Hall, Vice President
Janice Gist, Secretary

Marfa

***KRTS**
01-01-2007; 93.5 MHz FM; 33 kw; 1463 ft.; N30 33 50.2 W104 9 44.8
Mailing Address: US
Second Address: 111 S. Highland Ave., Marfa, TX 79843
(432) 729-4578
www.marfapublicradio.org
info@marfapublicradio.org
License: Marfa, Presidio County, TX held by Matinee Radio LLC.
Group Owner: Matinee Radio LLC
Arbitron Metro Market: Marfa, TX; *Format:* Triple A
Tom Michael, General Manager
Rachel Osier Lindley, Production Director
Anne Adkins, Office Manager & Volunteer Coordinator
Nicolas Miller, Operations & Traffic Manager

Marion

***KBIB**
09-21-1989; 1000 kHz AM; 0.25 kw-D, DAD; N29 34 9 W98 9 47
290 N. Santa Clara Road, Marion, TX 78124 US
www.kbib.org
License: Marion, TX held by Hispanic Community College.
Arbitron Metro Market: San Antonio, TX; *Format:* Religious; *Target Audience:* General.
Pastor Ken Hutchinson, General Manager

Markham

KKHA
08-01-2000; 92.5 MHz FM; *Hrs Open:* 24; 6 kw; 328 ft.; N28 52 26 W96 8 22
1713 Seventh St., Bay City, TX 77414 US
(979) 323-7771
yoursoutheasttexas.com
License: Markham, TX held by Edwards Broadcasting Co.
Group Owner: Tomlinson-Leis Communications LP
Format: Contemporary Hits/Top 40, Adult Contemp; *No. News Employees:* 1; *Target Audience:* 25-54; White equally mixed gender
Lee Parkinson, General Manager

Marlin

KRMX(FM)
04-02-1977; 92.9 MHz FM; *Hrs Open:* 24; 3 kw; 500 ft; N31 19 31 W96 54 36
5501 Bagby Ave., Waco, TX 76711
(254) 772-0930; *Fax:* (254) 753-0499
License: Marlin, Falls County, TX held by M&M Broadcasters Ltd.
Group Owner: M&M Broadcasters Ltd.; (acq 6-3-2010; grpsl)
Nat'l Reps: Roslin
Population Served: 109,000; *Arbitron Metro Market:* Waco, TX; *No. News Employees:* 1; *Target Audience:* 25-49.; *Adv. Rates:* 40; 40; 40; NA
Rob Reed, Operations Dir
Daryl O'Neal, General Manager
Bill LeGrande, General Sales Mgr
Dustin Drew, Programming Director
Flavia Chen, News Director
Cole McClellan, Chief Engineer

KRMX
01-01-1958; 92.9 MHz FM; *Hrs Open:* 24; 50 kw; 492 ft.; N31 24 45 W97 12 40 *Rebroadcasts:* KNKN Sunday mass 10:15 am
1018 N. Valley Mills Dr., Waco, TX 76710 US
(719) 545-2883; *Fax:* (719) 547-9301
knfoffice@qwestoffice.net
License: Marlin, Pueblo County, TX held by United States CP LLC.
Group Owner: United States CP LLC; (acq 3-10-2008; $1.75 million with KNKN(FM) Pueblo)
Arbitron Metro Market: Waco, TX; *Format:* Country; *Target Audience:* General; Hispanic families; *Adv. Rates:* 26; 26; 26; 26
Lupe Brown, General Manager

Marshall

***KBWC**
03-01-1977; 91.1 MHz FM; *Hrs Open:* 24; 0.135 kw; 112 ft.; N32 32 12 W94 22 29
711 Wiley Avenue, Marshall, TX 75670 US
(903) 927-3266; *Fax:* (903) 935-0153
www.wileyc.edu
License: Marshall, Harrison County, TX held by Wiley College.
Nat'l Network: American Urban
Arbitron Metro Market: Marshall, TX; *Format:* Adult Contemp; *Target Audience:* 18-34.
Shanon Levingston, General Manager

KCUL
10-07-1957; 1410 kHz AM; *Hrs Open:* 5:30 AM-11 PM; 0.5 kw-D, DA2; 0.09 kw-N, DA2; N32 29 30 W94 21 52
210 S. Broadway Ave., Suite 100, Tyler, TX 75702 US
(903) 581-9966
www.theranch.fm
studio@theranch.fm
License: Marshall, TX held by Alpha Media Licensee LLC
Group Owner: Alpha Media LLC; (acq 5-9-2000; grpsl)
Nat'l Network: Fox News Radio; *Regional Network:* Texas State Networks
Format: Country, News *Special Programming:* Farm 3 hrs wkly; *Hrs. of News Programming:* news progmg 15 hrs wkly; *No. News Employees:* 1; *Target Audience:* General.
Cary Camp, General Manager
Harlen Lobley, General Sales Mgr
Charlie O'Douglas, Programming Director

KCUL-FM
01-01-1992; 92.3 MHz FM; *Hrs Open:* 24; 5.8 kw; 328 ft.; N32 32 26 W94 24 3
210 S. Broadway Ave., Suite 100, Tyler, TX 75702 US
(903) 581-9966
www.lainvasora.fm
License: Marshall, Harrison County, TX held by Alpha Media Licensee LLC.
Group Owner: Alpha Media LLC
Regional Network: Texas State Networks
Format: Tejano; *Target Audience:* 25 plus.
Cary Camp, General Manager
Harlen Lobley, General Sales Mgr
Juan Ovalle, Programming Director

KMHT
01-01-1947; 1450 kHz AM; 0.65 kw-U, ND1; N32 33 50 W94 21 4
2323 Jefferson Avenue, Marshall, TX 75670 US
(903) 923-8000; *Fax:* (903) 935-2481
License: Marshall, TX held by Hanszen Broadcast Group Inc.
Format: Sports
Chris Paddie, General Manager

KMHT-FM
09-04-1977; 103.9 MHz FM; 1.85 kw; 423 ft.; N32 33 50 W94 21 4
2323 Jefferson Avenue, Marshall, TX 75670 US
(903) 923-8000; *Fax:* (903) 935-2481
www.kgasradio.com/
info@kmhtradio.com
License: Marshall, Harrison County, TX
Arbitron Metro Market: Marshall, TX; *Format:* Country
Chris Paddie, General Manager

Mason

KOTY
01-01-2004; 95.7 MHz FM; 50 kw; 436 ft.; N30 33 53 W99 27 13
1809 Lightsey Rd., Austin, TX 78704 US
(512) 444-9268
www.kityradio.com
kity@tstar.net
License: Mason, Mason County, TX held by Bryan A. King
Arbitron Metro Market: Mason, TX; *Format:* Oldies
Bryan King, General Manager

KHLB
01-01-2005; 102.5 MHz FM; 26 kw; 630 ft.; N30 42 3 W99 13 59
1818 N Street NW, Suite 700, Washington, DC 20036 US
(830) 693-5551; *Fax:* (830) 593-5107
License: Mason, Mason County, TX held by Munbilla Broadcasting Properties Ltd.
Group Owner: Munbilla Broadcasting Properties Ltd.
Arbitron Metro Market: Killeen, TX; *Format:* Country
Cindi Ashford, General Manager
Ben Shields, Programming Director
Bill Woleban, Chief Engineer

Mc Allen

***KVMV**
03-01-1972; 96.9 MHz FM; *Hrs Open:* 24; 100 kw; 1148 ft.; N26 4 53 W97 49 44
Mailing Address: P.O. Box 3333, McAllen, TX 78502 US
Second Address: 715 E. Thomas Dr., Pharr, TX 78502
(956) 787-9700; *Fax:* (956) 787-9783
www.kvmv.org
info@kvmv.com
License: Mc Allen, Hidalgo County, TX held by World Radio Network Inc.
Group Owner: World Radio Network Inc.; acq 8-27-84)
Nat'l Network: Moody
Arbitron Metro Market: Pharr, TX; *Format:* Christian; *Hrs. of News Programming:* News progmg 4 hrs wkly; *Target Audience:* 30-65; general
James Gamblin, General Manager
Bob Malone, Music Director

McAllen

KGBT-FM
01-01-1964; 98.5 MHz FM; 100 kw; 997 ft.; N26 7 14 W97 49 18
200 S. 10th Ave., Suite 600, McAllen, TX 78501 US
(956) 631-5499
www.univision.com
License: McAllen, Hidalgo County, TX held by Tichenor License Corp.
Group Owner: Univision Radio; (acq 9-22-2003; grpsl).
Arbitron Metro Market: McAllen, TX; *Format:* Tejano; *Target Audience:* 18 plus
Victoria Guerrero, Vice President and General Manager
Hugo De La Cruz, Programming Director
Jorge Garza, Chief Engineer

***KHID**
07-16-1992; 88.1 MHz FM; *Hrs Open:* 24; 2.1 kw; 253 ft.; N26 21 44 W98 19 26 *Rebroadcasts:* Rebroadcasts KMBH-FM Harlingen
Mailing Address: P.O. Box 2147, Harlingen, TX 78551 US
Second Address: 1701 E. Tennessee Ave., Harlingen, TX 78550
(956) 421-4111; *Fax:* (956) 421-4150
www.kmbh.org
License: McAllen, Hidalgo County, TX held by RGV Educational Broadcasting Inc.
Arbitron Metro Market: McAllen-Brownsv; *Format:* Jazz, News; *Hrs. of News Programming:* News progmg 34 hrs wkly; *Target Audience:* General.
Pedro Briseno, General Manager
Chris Malley, News Director

KRIO
01-01-1947; 910 kHz AM; *Hrs Open:* 24
4300 S. Business 281, Edinburg, TX 78539 US
(956) 380-3435; *Fax:* (956) 380-8156
www.radioesperanza.com
correo@radioesperanza.com
License: McAllen, TX held by Rio Grande Bible Institute Inc.
Wire Services: UPI
Arbitron Metro Market: McAllen-Brownsville-Harlingen; *Format:* Christian; *Hrs. of News Programming:* News progmg 5 hrs wkly; *Target Audience:* General.
Larry Windle, President
Gerardo Lorenzo, General Manager
Jerry Joske, Chief Engineer

McCook

***KCAS**
01-01-2001; 91.5 MHz FM; *Hrs Open:* 24; 2.5 kw; 358 ft.; N26 28 51 W98 23 45
Mailing Address: 4301 N Shary Rd., Mission, TX 78572 US
Second Address: PO Box 8106, Mission, TX 78572
(956) 424-9098; *Fax:* (956) 581-7786
www.kcasradio.org
kcas@kcasradio.org
License: McCook, Hidalgo County, TX held by Faith Baptist Church Inc.
Nat'l Network: USA
Arbitron Metro Market: Mission, TX; *Format:* Religious; *Hrs. of News Programming:* News progmg 20 hrs wkly; *Target Audience:* 30-85; male & female
David Harris, President
Don Prentice, General Manager
Don Prentice, Station Manager
Jerry Jeske, Chief Engineer

McKinney

*KNTU

11-01-1969; 88.1 MHz FM; *Hrs Open:* 24; 100 kw; 443 ft.; N33 17 24 W97 8 10
Mailing Address: P.O. Box 13585, Denton, TX 76203 US
Second Address: 1179 Union Cir. #262, Denton, TX 76201
(940) 565-3688; *Fax:* (940) 565-2518
www.kntu.com
kntu@unt.edu
License: McKinney, Collin County, TX held by University of North Texas.
Nat'l Network: AP Radio; *Wire Services:* AP
Arbitron Metro Market: Dallas, TX; *Format:* Jazz *Special Programming:* Class 6 hrs, Sp 6 hrs, new mus 2 hrs, pub affrs 2; *Hrs. of News Programming:* News progmg 12.5 hrs wkly; *No. News Employees:* 6 *TargetAudience:* 18 +.
Russ Campbell, General Manager
Mark Lambert, Programming Director

McQueeney

KZAR

07-01-1989; 97.7 MHz FM; *Hrs Open:* 24; 100 kw; 981 ft.; N29 22 11 W97 39 44
P.O. Box 2118, Omaha, NE 68103-2118 US
(888) 937-2471
www.air1.com
License: McQueeney, Guadalupe County, TX held by Educational Media Foundation
Group Owner: EMF Broadcasting
Population Served: 1,206,495; *Arbitron Metro Market:* San Antonio, TX; *Format:* Christian, Rock/AOR; *Target Audience:* 12-17, 18-34.
Mike Novak, President
Ed Lehane, General Manager

Memphis

KLSR-FM

01-01-1982; 105.3 MHz FM; *Hrs Open:* 24; 100 kw; 486 ft.; N34 51 52 W100 36 55
114 N. 17th, P.O. Box 400, Memphis, TX 79245 US
(806) 259-3511; *Fax:* (806) 259-2397
klsr105fm@arn.net
License: Memphis, Hall County, TX held by Davis Broadcast Company Inc.
Arbitron Metro Market: Amarillo, TX; *Format:* Variety/Diverse, Country *Special Programming:* Sp 6 hrs, good time oldies 60s & 70s 10 hrs, relg
Donna Davis, President
Brandi Davis-Tatum, Operations Dir
Joe Davis, General Manager

Mercedes

KTEX

01-01-1975; 100.3 MHz FM; *Hrs Open:* 24; 100 kw; 1224 ft.; N26 6 1 W97 50 21
901 E. Pike Blvd., Weslaco, TX 78596 US
(956) 973-9202; *Fax:* (956) 975-2101
www.ktex.net
License: Mercedes, Hidalgo County, TX held by Capstar TX LLC
Group Owner: iHeartMedia; (acq 8-15-2000; grpsl)
Arbitron Metro Market: Weslaco, TX; *Format:* Country; *No. News Employees:* 1; *Target Audience:* 25-54; male & female; *Adv. Rates:* 50; 40; 50; 30
Billy Santiago, Senior Vice President of Programming
Evan Armstrong, Regional Market President
Chris Aldrich, Senior Vice President of Sales

Meridian

KOME-FM

95.3 MHz FM; 6 kw horiz; 226 ft.; N31 54 17 W97 40 49 US
(817) 332-0959
License: Meridian, Bosque County, TX held by LKCM Radio Group LP.
Group Owner: LKCM Radio Group L.P.
Arbitron Metro Market: Meridian, TX
Gerry Schlegel, President

Merkel

KHXS

11-04-1983; 102.7 MHz FM; *Hrs Open:* 24; 99.2 kw; 745 ft.; N32 24 39 W100 6 26
2525 South Danville, Abilene, TX 79605 US
(325) 793-9700; *Fax:* (325) 692-1576
www.102thebear.com
License: Merkel, Taylor County, TX held by Cumulus Licensing Corp.
Group Owner: Cumulus Media Inc.; (acq 6-15-98; $1.6 million)
Arbitron Metro Market: Abilene, TX; *Format:* Classic Rock
John Scott, Operations Dir
Jim Christoferson, General Manager
Lori Barrett, News Director
Chris Andrews, Chief Engineer

KMXO

06-01-1963; 1500 kHz AM; 0.25 kw-D, NDD; N32 28 17 W100 0 19
5234 North 3 Street, Abilene, TX 79603 US
(325) 928-3060; *Fax:* (325) 928-4683
www.kmxoradiofe.com
License: Merkel, TX held by Ray R. Silva.
Arbitron Metro Market: Merkel, TX; *Format:* Christian
Zacarias Serrato, General Manager

Mertzon

*KMEO

01-01-2006; 91.9 MHz FM; 6.5 kw vert; 522 ft.; N31 25 16 W100 32 36
P.O. Box 3206, Tupelo, MS 38803 US
(662) 844-8888; *Fax:* (662) 842-6791
www.afr.net
faq@afa.net
License: Mertzon, Irion County, TX held by American Family Association.
Group Owner: American Family Radio; (acq 8-9-2005)
Arbitron Metro Market: Mertzon, TX; *Format:* Christian
Tim Wildmon, President
Donald Wildmon, Founder
Buddy Smith, Sr VP
Ed Vitagliano, Exec VP
Randy Sharp, Director Of Special Projects
Meeke Addison, Director Of Communications
Abraham Hamilton III, General Counsel

Mesquite

*KEOM

09-04-1984; 88.5 MHz FM; *Hrs Open:* 24; 61 kw; 574 ft.; N32 45 46 W96 38 4
405 East Davis Street, Mesquite, TX 75149 US
(972) 888-7560
www.keom.fm
pbrooks@mesquiteisd.org
License: Mesquite, Dallas County, TX held by Mesquite Independent School District.
Regional Network: Texas State Networks
Arbitron Metro Market: Mesquite, TX; *Format:* Variety/Diverse; *Target Audience:* General; citizens of Mesquite & surrounding area
Peggy Brooks, Station Manager

Mexia

KLRK

05-21-1956; 1590 kHz AM; *Hrs Open:* 24; 500 w-D, 128 w-N; N31 41 10 W96 27 18
Mailing Address: Box 1590, Mexia, TX 76667
Second Address: 1006-B Milam St., Mexia, TX 76667
(254) 562-5328; *Fax:* (254) 562-6729
radio@kycxfm.com
License: Mexia, Limestone County, TX held by M&M Broadcasters Ltd.
Group Owner: M*M Broadcasters Ltd.; (acq 6-3-2010; grpsl)
Nat'l Network: ABC; *Regional Network:* Texas State Networks
Population Served: 30,000 *Special Programming:* Farm 12 hrs, Gospel 3 hrs wkly; *Target Audience:* General; 20-59; *Adv. Rates:* 13; 10; 10; 9
Bill Ferris, Operations Dir
Susan Cholopisa, General Manager
Jan Phillips, News Director
Dave Campbell, Sports Commentator
Brandi Garza, Traffic Manager

Midland

KZBT

01-01-1974; 93.3 MHz FM; *Hrs Open:* 24; 100 kw; 440 ft.; N31 57 30 W102 3 59
11300 Highway 191, #2, Midland, TX 79707 US
(432) 563-9300
www.b93.net
shalayna.valencia@townsquaremedia.com
License: Midland, Midland County, TX held by Townsquare Media Odeassa-Midland II License LLC
Group Owner: Townsquare Media; (acq 12-17-98; grpsl)
Arbitron Metro Market: Odessa, TX; *Format:* Contemporary Hits/Top 40; *Hrs. of News Programming:* news progmg 2 hrs wkly; *No. News Employees:* 1; *Target Audience:* 18-44.
Shalayna Valencia, General Manager
Leo Caro, Brand Manager
Shalayna Valencia, Director Of Sales
Cary Hinterlong, Digital Managing Editor

KCHX

08-15-1988; 106.7 MHz FM; *Hrs Open:* 24; 100 kw; 679 ft.; N31 54 53 W101 57 49
1330 E. 8th St., Suite 207, Odessa, TX 79761 US
(432) 563-9102; *Fax:* (432) 580-9102
License: Midland, Midland County, TX
Group Owner: ICA Radio Ltd.; (acq 10-1-2007; grpsl)
Arbitron Metro Market: Odessa-Midland, TX; *Format:* Adult Contemp; *Hrs. of News Programming:* News progmg 2 hrs wkly; *Target Audience:* 25-54; general; *Adv. Rates:* 60; 60; 50; 24
Gloria Apolinario, General Manager
Laura Florez, General Sales Mgr
Rob Norris, Engineering Dir

KCRS

12-20-1935; 550 kHz AM; *Hrs Open:* 24; 5 kw-D, DA2; 1 kw-N, DA2; N32 4 10 W102 1 46
1001 South Midkiff, Midland, TX 79701 US
(432) 563-9102; *Fax:* (432) 580-9102
www.newstalkkcrs.com
License: Midland, TX
Group Owner: ICA Radio Ltd.; (acq 8-3-2007; grpsl)
Regional Network: Texas State Networks
Arbitron Metro Market: Odessa-Midland, TX; *Format:* News, News/Talk, 86; *Hrs. of News Programming:* news progmg 30 hrs wkly; *No. News Employees:* 2; *Target Audience:* 25-54.
Steve Driscoll, Operations Dir
Gloria Apolinario, General Manager
Jesse Grimes, News Director
Rod Norris, Engineering Dir
Robert Hallmark, Operations Manager
Shelly Todd, Traffic Manager

KCRS-FM

05-25-1976; 103.3 MHz FM; *Hrs Open:* 24; 95 kw; 919 ft.; N32 5 11 W102 17 10
1001 South Midkiff, Midland, TX 79701 US
(432) 563-9102; *Fax:* (432) 580-9102
www.1033kissfm.net
License: Midland, Midland County, TX
Group Owner: ICA Radio Ltd.
Arbitron Metro Market: Odessa-Midland, TX; *Format:* Adult Contemp
Jesse Grimes, Operations Dir
Ric Elliott, Programming Director
Shelly Todd, News Director
Robert Hallmark, Special Events Coordinator

KLPF

08-06-1950; 1150 kHz AM; *Hrs Open:* 24 *Rebroadcasts:* EWTN
1903 S. Lames Sa Road, Midland, TX 79701 US
(432) 638-1150; *Fax:* (432) 682-5230
www.grnonline.com
robertd@grnonline.com
License: Midland, TX held by La Promesa Foundation.
Group Owner: La Promesa Foundation; (acq 2-11-2002; $85,000)
Arbitron Metro Market: Odessa-Midland, TX; *Format:* Christian; *No. News Employees:* 3; *Adv. Rates:* 10; 10; 10; 10
Robert Dominguez, General Manager
Toya Hall, Programming Director

KMND

11-27-1963; 1510 kHz AM; 2.4 kw-D, NDD; N31 57 49 W102 4 53
111 East Kilbourn Avenue, Suite 2700, Milwaukee, WI 53202 US
(432) 563-5636; *Fax:* (432) 563-3823
www.kmnd.com
gary.hinterlong@townsquaremedia.com
License: Midland, TX held by Townsquare Media Odessa-Midland II License LLC
Group Owner: Townsquare Media; (acq 12-17-98; grpsl).
Nat'l Network: ESPN Radio
Arbitron Metro Market: Odessa, TX; *Format:* Sports *Special Programming:* Jazz one hr wkly
Shalayna Valencia, General Manager
Gary Hinterlong, Station Contact

KNFM

11-02-1959; 92.3 MHz FM; 100 kw; 984 ft.; N32 5 51 W102 17 21
1300 Highway 191, #2, Midland, TX 79707 US

(432) 563-5636; *Fax:* (432) 563-3823
www.lonestar92.com
License: Midland, Midland County, TX
Arbitron Metro Market: Odessa, TX; *Format:* Country
Leo Caro, Operations Dir
Gwen McCown, Programming Director
Tonya Calloway, Promotions Manager
Rodney Norris, Engineering Dir

KQRX
10-20-1995; 95.1 MHz FM; *Hrs Open:* 24; 10.5 kw; 505 ft.; N32 3 9 W102 17 39
P.O. Box 14895, Odessa, TX 79768 US
(432) 520-9912; *Fax:* (432) 520-0112
www.boblivesintexas.com
ooradio01@aol.com
License: Midland, Midland County, TX
Group Owner: Brazos Communications West LLC; (acq 2006; grpsl)
Nat'l Reps: Katz Radio
Arbitron Metro Market: Midland-Odessa; *Format:* Adult Contemp
Kelly Peterson, Operations Dir
John Moesch, General Manager
Michael Todd, Programming Director

KWEL
04-01-1957; 1070 kHz AM; *Hrs Open:* 6 AM-9 PM; 2.5 kw-D, NDD; N31 57 44 W102 4 7
Mailing Address: 1110 E. Scharbauer Drive, Midland, TX 79705 US
Second Address: 310 W. Wall, Ste 104, Midland, TX 79701
(915) 685-1950; *Fax:* (915) 687-0586
www.kwel.com
craiganderson@kwel.com
License: Midland, TX held by Faustino Quiroz.
Nat'l Network: ABC
Arbitron Metro Market: Odessa, TX; *Format:* News, Talk; *Hrs. of News Programming:* News progmg 60 hrs wkly; *Target Audience:* 35 plus; adults; *Adv. Rates:* 20
Craig Anderson, CEO
Doris Anderson, News Director
Jason Moore, Engineering Dir
Garry Vaughn, Engineer

***KVDG**
09-01-2006; 90.9 MHz FM; 1.5 kw; 430 ft.; N31 54 32 W102 4 1
6910 NW 2nd Terrace, Boca Raton, FL 33487 US
(432) 682-1485; *Fax:* (432) 682-5230
License: Midland, Midland County, TX held by La Promesa Foundation.
Group Owner: La Promesa Foundation; (acq 11-6-2007; $175,000)
Nat'l Network: EWTN Radio
Arbitron Metro Market: Midland, TX
Leonard Oswald, President

Mineola

KMOO-FM
09-01-1977; 99.9 MHz FM; *Hrs Open:* 24; 6 kw; 295 ft.; N32 45 4 W95 33 18
Mailing Address: P. O. Box 628, Mineola, TX 75773 US
Second Address: Hwy. 69 N., Mineola, TX 75773
(903) 569-3823; *Fax:* (903) 569-6641
www.kmoo.com
License: Mineola, Wood County, TX held by Hightower Radio Inc.
Regional Network: Texas State Networks
Arbitron Metro Market: Tyler, TX; *Format:* Country; *Hrs. of News Programming:* news progmg 3 hrs wkly; *No. News Employees:* 1; *Target Audience:* 25-64.; *Adv. Rates:* 18;18;18;15
Jason Hightower, President
Amy Castleberry, Operations Dir
Marlene Keahey, Public Affairs Director

Mineral Wells

KVTT
12-01-1946; 1120 kHz AM; *Hrs Open:* 6 AM-sunset; 250 w-D; N32 47 12 W98 05 53
305 Millsap Hwy., Mineral Wells, TX 76067
(940) 325-1140; *Fax:* (940) 325-1164
www.bizradio.com
License: Mineral Wells, Palo Pinto County, TX held by Texoma Broadcasting Inc.
Population Served: 75,000; *Arbitron Metro Market:* Dallas-Fort Worth
Gary Moss, General Manager

Mirando City

KBDR
04-01-1993; 100.5 MHz FM; *Hrs Open:* 24; 42 kw; 535 ft.; N27 21 17 W99 13 52
1919 Victoria Street, Laredo, TX 78040 US
(956) 725-1000; *Fax:* (956) 718-1000
www.laley1005.com
License: Mirando City, Webb County, TX held by BMP 100.5 FM LP.
Group Owner: Border Media Partners LLC; (acq 5-30-2003; $8 million with KBUC(FM) Raymondville).
Arbitron Metro Market: Laredo, TX; *Format:* Tejano; *Target Audience:* 18-45; upper-income bracket
Tom Castro, CEO
Steve Stephenson, Operations Dir
Nestor Cobos, Station Manager
Joe Flores, General Sales Mgr
Rogelio Botello Rios, Programming Director
Robert Garcia, Promotions Manager
Joe Espinoza, Chief Engineer
Hugo DelPozzo, CFO
Issac Carrillo, Operations Manager

Mission

KIRT
02-23-1958; 1580 kHz AM; 1 kw-D, ND1; 0.302 kw-N, ND1; N26 17 36 W98 19 50
608 S. 10th St., McAllen, TX 78501 US
(956) 519-9999; *Fax:* (956) 581-0546
kirtradio@aol.com
License: Mission, TX held by Bravo Broadcasting Co. Inc.
Regional Network: Texas State Networks
Arbitron Metro Market: McAllen-Brownsville-Harlingen, TX
Walter Gomez, General Manager
Rosie Pedraza, General Sales Mgr
Armando Pedraza, Programming Director
John Pankratz, Chief Engineer

KQXX-FM
01-01-1989; 105.5 MHz FM; *Hrs Open:* 24; 3 kw; 285 ft.; N26 13 50 W98 20 18 *Rebroadcasts:* Rebroadcasts KTJN(FM) Brownsville 100%
1050 McIntosh, Brownsville, TX 78521 US
(956) 973-9202; *Fax:* (956) 544-0311
www.1055thex.com
License: Mission, Hidalgo County, TX held by Clear Channel Broadcasting Licenses Inc.
Group Owner: iHeartMedia; (acq 12-9-2003; grpsl).
Arbitron Metro Market: McAllen-Brownsville-Harlingen, TX; *Format:* Oldies; *No. News Employees:* 3
Billy Santiago, Senior Vice President of Programming
Chris Aldrich, Sales Manager
Jeff DeWitt, Programming Director

Missouri City

KBRZ
10-01-1952; 1460 kHz AM
1914 North Hwy 523, Freeport, TX 77541 US
(713) 589-1336; *Fax:* (713) 589-1335
License: Missouri City, TX held by Daij Media LLC
Group Owner: Daij Media LLC; (acq 12-16-2011)
Arbitron Metro Market: Houston-Galveston; *Format:* Christian
Ruben Villarreal, General Manager

Monahans

KBAT
11-01-1983; 99.9 MHz FM; *Hrs Open:* 24; 100 kw; 574 ft.; N31 45 40 W102 31 28
11300 Highway 191, Bldg. 2, Midland, TX 79707 US
(432) 563-5499; *Fax:* (432) 563-5530
www.kbat.com
License: Monahans, Ward County, TX held by Townsquare Media Odessa-Midland II License LLC
Group Owner: Townsquare Media; (acq 12-17-98; grpsl).
Arbitron Metro Market: Odessa, TX; *Target Audience:* 25-54; general
Shalayna Valencia, General Manager
Chris Stevens, Brand Manager
Shalayna Valencia, Director Of Sales
Gary Hinterlong, Digital Managing Editor

KCKM
03-12-1947; 1330 kHz AM; *Hrs Open:* 24
Box 270, Monahans, TX 79756 US
(432) 943-2588; *Fax:* (432) 943-7314
License: Monahans, TX held by Sandhills Communication Inc.
Nat'l Network: CBS; *Regional Network:* Texas State Networks; *Nat'l Reps:* Riley
Format: Oldies *Special Programming:* Gospel 3 hrs wkly; *No. News Employees:* 1; *Target Audience:* 25-54; general
Rick Anderson, General Manager
David McCaffity, Programming Director
Allen Martin, News Director
Dexter Nichols, Sports Commentator

Mont Belvieu

KFNC
01-01-1948; 97.5 MHz FM; *Hrs Open:* 24; 100 kw; Ant 1,955 ft; N29 41 52 W94 24 09
5353 W. Alabama, Suite 415, Houston, TX 77056
(713) 479-5300; *Fax:* (713) 479-5333
www.espn975.com
License: Mont Belvieu, Jefferson County, TX held by GOW Communications
Group Owner: GOW Communications; (acq 5-3-2006; grpsl)
Nat'l Network: ESPN Radio
Arbitron Metro Market: Houston-Galveston
David Gow, CEO
Chris Hall, VP/General Manager
David Tepper, Programming Director
Michelle MacDonald, Promotions Manager
Brandon Strange, VP, Digital Projects

Morton

***KPGA**
01-16-2009; 91.9 MHz FM; 100 kw; 522 ft.; N33 33 1 W102 13 7
Rebroadcasts: Rebroadcasts KLRD(FM) Yucaipa, CA 100%
P O Box 187, Humble, TX 77347 US
(888) 937-2471; *Fax:* (916) 251-1650
www.air1.com
info@air1.com
License: Morton, Cochran County, TX held by Educational Media Foundation.
Group Owner: EMF Broadcasting
Nat'l Network: Air 1
Arbitron Metro Market: Morton, TX; *Format:* Alternative, Christian
Darrell Chambliss, Chairman
Alan Mason, CEO/COO
Mike Novak, CEO
David Pierce, Chief Creative Officer
Dan Antonelli, Chief Business Development Officer
Eric Moser, Chief Financial Officer
Brian Burger, Vice President of HumanResources
D. Kevin Blair, Secretary and General Counsel

Mount Pleasant

KIMP
10-08-1948; 960 kHz AM; 1 kw-D, ND2; 0.075 kw-N, ND2; N33 9 54 W95 0 27
1798 US Hwy. 67 W., PO Box 990, Mt. Pleasant, TX 75456 US
(903) 572-8726; *Fax:* (903) 572-7232
www.easttexasradio.com
License: Mount Pleasant, TX held by East Texas Broadcasting Inc.
Group Owner: East Texas Broadcasting Inc.; (acq 11-21-91; $850,000 with co-located FM;
Format: News/Talk; *Hrs. of News Programming:* news progmg 10 hrs wkly; *No. News Employees:* 10; *Target Audience:* General.; *Adv. Rates:* 17; 15; 17
Bud Kitchens, President/General Maanger

***KYZQ**
88.3 MHz FM; 3 kw vert; Ant 149 ft; N33 10 10.4 W95 05 59.3
1039 CR 2920, Pittsburg, TX
(903) 466-6791
License: Mount Pleasant, Titus County, TX held by Millennium Broadcasting Corp.

James Furlow Jr., President

Mountain Home

KAXA
102.1 MHz FM; 6 kw; Ant 272 ft; N30 10 34 W99 23 02
Box 717, Pickerington, OH
(239) 877-4605
License: Mountain Home, Kerr County, TX held by In Phase Broadcasting Inc.

Peter Cea, President

Muenster

KZZA
12-23-1991; 106.7 MHz FM; *Hrs Open:* 24; 75 kw; 2034 ft.; N33 26 13 W97 29 5
2410 Gateway Dr, Irving, TX 75063 US

(972) 652-2900
labonita1067.estrellatv.com
dallasinfo@lbimedia.com
License: Muenster, Cooke County, TX held by Liberman Broadcasting of Dallas License LLC.
Group Owner: Liberman Broadcasting Inc.; (acq 11-2-2006; grpsl)
Nat'l Reps: Eastman Radio
Arbitron Metro Market: Dallas-Fort Wort, TX; *Format:* Spanish
Alex Sanchez, General Manager

***KTMU**
88.7 MHz FM; 0.5 kw; 69 ft.; N33 43 32 W97 28 26
US
(940) 668-7971
License: Muenster, Cooke County, TX held by 1 A Chord Inc.
Arbitron Metro Market: Gainesville, TX
Mary Fay Jackson, President

Muleshoe

KMUL-FM
02-06-1966; 103.1 MHz FM; 6 kw; 75 ft.; N34 13 39 W102 44 10
1000 Sycamore Street, Clovis, NM 88101 US
(505) 762-6200; *Fax:* (505) 762-8800
License: Muleshoe, Bailey County, TX held by Tallgrass Broadcasting LLC.
Group Owner: Tallgrass Broadcasting LLC; (acq 4-2-2007; grpsl)
Format: Country
David Lippe, General Sales Mgr
Michael Jacinto, Programming Director

Nacogdoches

KJCS
05-01-1967; 103.3 MHz FM; 22.5 kw; 735 ft.; N31 25 59 W94 49 3
111 W. Pillar, Nacogdoches, TX 75961 US
(936) 559-8800; *Fax:* (936) 559-8801
License: Nacogdoches, Nacogdoches County, TX held by Radio Licensing Inc.
Nat'l Network: ABC
Format: Country *Special Programming:* Gospel 3 hrs wkly
Bill Vance Jr., General Manager
Carolyn Gage, Station Manager
Della Huse, General Sales Mgr
Lou Bennett, Programming Director
Gwen Jordan, News Director

***KSAU**
07-05-1975; 90.1 MHz FM; *Hrs Open:* 10 AM-2 AM; 3.5 kw; 449 ft.; N31 37 45 W94 40 44
Mailing Address: P. O. Box 13048, Nacogdoches, TX 75962 US
Second Address: 1936 North St., Boynton Building, Nacogdoches, TX 75961
(936) 468-4000; *Fax:* (936) 468-1331
www.sfasu.edu/ksau
ksau@sfasu.edu
License: Nacogdoches, Nacogdoches County, TX held by Stephen F. Austin State University.
Nat'l Network: ABC; *Wire Services:* AP
Arbitron Metro Market: Nacogdoches, TX; *Format:* Jazz; *Hrs. of News Programming:* News progmg 3 hrs wkly; *Target Audience:* 18-54.
Sherry Williford, General Manager
John Chapman, Engineering Dir

KSFA
06-02-1947; 860 kHz AM
600 Congress Avenue, Suite 1400, Austin, TX 78701 US
(936) 639-4455; *Fax:* (936) 639-4440
www.ksfa860.com
License: Nacogdoches, TX held by Townsquare Media Lufkin License LLC
Group Owner: Townsquare Media; (acq 8-3-2007; grpsl)
Arbitron Metro Market: Lufkin, TX; *Format:* News, News/Talk, 86
Special Programming: Houston Astros baseball, farm 7 hrs wkly;
Target Audience: 25 plus; upscale, upper income level men
Johny Lathrop, General Manager
Dan Patrick, Brand Manager
Paula Divello, Director Of Sales
James Stillwell, Digital Managing Editor

KTBQ
07-15-1967; 107.7 MHz FM; *Hrs Open:* 24; 13 kw; 400 ft.; N31 34 58 W94 39 59
600 Congress Avenue, Suite 1400, Austin, TX 78701 US
(936) 639-4455; *Fax:* (936) 639-4440
www.q1077.com
License: Nacogdoches, Nacogdoches County, TX held by Townsquare Media Lufkin License LLC
Group Owner: Townsquare Media
Arbitron Metro Market: Lufkin, TX; *Format:* Classic Rock; *No. News Employees:* 1; *Target Audience:* 18-49; upscale women
Johnny Lathrop, General Manager
Dan Patrick, Brand Manager
Paula Divello, Director Of Sales
James Stillwell, Digital Managing Editor

Natalia

***KYRQ**
90.3 MHz FM; 3 kw; 135 ft.; N29 9 20 W98 53 6
P O Box 7337, Mayaguez, TX 0681 US
(210) 440-9894
License: Natalia, Medina County, TX held by Community Public Radio Inc.
Arbitron Metro Market: Natalia, TX; *Format:* Christian, Spanish
Penny Jackson, President

Navasota

***KWUP**
03-01-1989; 92.5 MHz FM; *Hrs Open:* 24; 3.3 kw; 446 ft.; N30 27 58 W96 2 57
304 East Houston, Crockett, TX 75835 US
(281) 446-5725; *Fax:* (281) 540-2198
License: Navasota, Grimes County, TX held by KSBJ Educational Foundation
Arbitron Metro Market: Bryan-College S
Tim McDermott, General Manager

Nederland

KBED
01-11-1969; 1510 kHz AM; *Hrs Open:* Sunrise-sunset; 5 kw-D, DAD; N30 3 40 W93 58 48
75 South 11th St., #102, Beaumont, TX 77707 US
(409) 951-2500; *Fax:* (409) 833-9296
www.lagrand1450.com
info@cumulus.com
License: Nederland, TX held by Cumulus Licensing Corp.
Group Owner: Cumulus Media Inc.; (acq 3-9-98; grpsl).
Nat'l Network: ESPN Radio
Arbitron Metro Market: Beaumont-Port Arthur area; *Format:* Tejano *Special Programming:* Relg 4 hrs wkly; *Hrs. of News Programming:* news progmg 5 hrs wkly; *No. News Employees:* 1; *Target Audience:* 18-49; males
Zanetta Kelley, General Manager
Wes Matejka, General Sales Mgr
Jim West, Programming Director
Mark Guzman, Promotions Manager
Richard Core, News Director
Greg Davis, Chief Engineer
Liz Ferguson, Traffic Manager

New Boston

KEWL-FM
07-01-1995; 95.1 MHz FM; *Hrs Open:* 24; 25 kw; Ant 325 ft; N33 26 15 W94 25 11
1323 College Dr., Texarkana, TX 75503
(903) 793-1100
www.alwayskool.com
kool@ami-texarkana.com
License: New Boston, Bowie County, TX held by American Media Investments Inc.
Group Owner: American Media Investments Inc.; (acq 2-17-2009; grpsl)
Arbitron Metro Market: Texarkana, TX-A; *Target Audience:* 35-64.
Mike Basso, General Manager

KLBW
11-16-1969; 1530 kHz AM; *Hrs Open:* 6 AM-6 PM; 2.5 kw-D, NDD; N33 28 56 W94 25 25
P.O. Box 848, New Boston, TX 75570 US
(903) 628-2561
License: New Boston, TX held by Chapel of Light
Arbitron Metro Market: Texarkana, TX; *Format:* Adult Contemp, Christian; *Target Audience:* General.
Carmen Johnson, General Manager

KZRB
11-16-1997; 103.5 MHz FM; *Hrs Open:* 24; 50 kw; 492 ft.; N33 24 54 W94 38 10
3720 County Avenue, Texarkana, AR 75502 US
(903) 547-3223; *Fax:* (903) 547-3095
realcowboyassociation.com/kzrb.html
License: New Boston, Bowie County, TX held by B & H Broadcasting System Inc.
Nat'l Network: American Urban; *Nat'l Reps:* Christal
Arbitron Metro Market: New Boston, TX; *Format:* Adult Contemp, Oldies; *Hrs. of News Programming:* news progmg 9 hrs wkly; *No. News Employees:* 1; *Target Audience:* 25-54; all age buyers
Ray Bursey Jr., CEO
Sandy Hunter, Operations Dir
Brigette Talbert, Programming Director
Gray Graham, Engineering Dir

KTTY
06-01-2009; 105.1 MHz FM; 4.3 kw; 387 ft.; N33 28 0 W94 27 48
Mailing Address: US
Second Address: 1305 S Glenburnie Road, New Bern, NC 2526363333
bill@bigfishfm.com
License: New Boston, Bowie County, TX held by Tower Investment Trust Inc.
Group Owner: Tower Investment Trust Inc.
Nat'l Reps: Salem
Arbitron Metro Market: New Boston, TX; *Format:* Christian; *Target Audience:* W 25 - 54
William Brothers, President

New Braunfels

KGNB
04-01-1950; 1420 kHz AM; *Hrs Open:* 24; 1 kw-D, ND1; 0.196 kw-N, ND1; N29 39 45 W98 10 29
1540 Loop 337 North, New Braunfels, TX 78130 US
(830) 625-7311; *Fax:* (830) 625-7336
www.kgnb.am
License: New Braunfels, TX held by New Braunfels Communications Inc.
Nat'l Network: CNN Radio; Westwood One
Arbitron Metro Market: San Antonio, TX; *Format:* Country, News; *Hrs. of News Programming:* news progmg 26 hrs wkly; *No. News Employees:* 3; *Target Audience:* 25-54; men
Bill Rainer, CEO
Mattson Rainer, Operations Dir
Stuart Wolfe, Advertising Sales Manager

KNBT
11-22-1968; 92.1 MHz FM; *Hrs Open:* 24; 6 kw; 312 ft.; N29 43 50 W98 7 12
1540 Loop 337 North, New Braunfels, TX 78130 US
(830) 625-7311; *Fax:* (830) 625-7336
www.knbtfm.com
License: New Braunfels, Comal County, TX held by New Braunfels Communications Inc.
Arbitron Metro Market: San Antonio, TX; *Format:* Triple A *Special Programming:* Relg 3 hrs wkly; *Target Audience:* 25-54.
Mattson Rainer, General Manager

New Deal

KLZK
09-01-1961; 97.3 MHz FM; *Hrs Open:* 24; 30.5 kw; 614 ft.; N33 30 8 W101 52 20
9800 University Ave., Lubbock, TX 79423 US
(806) 745-3434
License: New Deal, Lubbock County, TX held by Ramar Communications, Inc.
Group Owner: Ramar Communications, Inc.
Arbitron Metro Market: Lubbock, TX; *Format:* Adult Contemp
Brad Moran, President

New Ulm

KNRG
01-01-1999; 92.3 MHz FM; 6 kw; 328 ft.; N29 53 30 W96 38 22
P.O.Box 948, Houston, TX 77001 US
(979) 732-5766; *Fax:* (979) 732-6377
License: New Ulm, Austin County, TX held by New Ulm Broadcasting Co.
Format: Contemporary Hits/Top 40, Adult Contemp; *Adv. Rates:* 12.50; 12.50; 12.50; 12.50
Carl Geisler, General Manager

Nolanville

KLFX
01-01-1994; 107.3 MHz FM; 1.35 kw; 548 ft.; N31 5 38 W97 34 51
100 West Center Expressway, Harker Heights, TX 76348 US
(254) 699-5000; *Fax:* (254) 680-4212
www.1073rocks.com
License: Nolanville, Bell County, TX held by Clear Channel Broadcasting Licenses Inc.
Group Owner: iHeartMedia; (acq 1-15-2004; $2.6 million).
Arbitron Metro Market: Killeen, TX; *Format:* Rock/AOR

Evan Armstrong, General Manager
Jerry Ferch, Director of Sales
Dana McKenzie, Programming Director

Odem

KMJR
02-18-1985; 98.3 MHz FM; *Hrs Open:* 24; 50 kw; Ant 433 ft; N27 47 26 W97 27 02
1300 Antelope, Corpus Christi, TX 78467
(361) 883-1600; *Fax:* (361) 883-9303
club983.com
johnnyo@johnnyoradio.com
License: Odem, San Patricio County, TX held by Tejas Broadcasting Ltd. LLP.
Group Owner: Tejas Broadcasting Ltd. LLP; (acq 11-15-2004; grpsl).
Population Served: 400,000; *Arbitron Metro Market:* Corpus Christi, TX; *Target Audience:* 18-49; progsv, affluent, middle class Hispanics; *Adv. Rates:* 85; 75; 85; 50
Bert Clark, Operations Dir
Paul Danitz, General Manager

Odessa

*KBMM
01-01-2004; 89.5 MHz FM; 25 kw; 535 ft.; N31 40 35 W102 21 32
P.O. Box 3206, Tupelo, MS 38803 US
(662) 844-8888; *Fax:* (662) 842-6791
www.afr.net
faq@afa.net
License: Odessa, Ector County, TX held by American Family Association.
Group Owner: American Family Radio
Arbitron Metro Market: Odessa-Midland, TX; *Format:* Christian
Tim Wildmon, President
Donald Wildmon, Founder
Buddy Smith, Sr VP
Ed Vitagliano, Exec VP
Randy Sahrp, Director Of Special Projects
Meeke Addison, Director Of Communications
Abraham Hamilton III, General Counsel &ÆPublic PolicyAnalyst

*KFLB
01-29-1947; 920 kHz AM; *Hrs Open:* 24
7355 N. Oracle Rd., Tucson, AZ 85704 US
(520) 742-6976; *Fax:* (520) 469-7312
www.myflr.org
License: Odessa, TX held by Family Life Broadcasting System.
Group Owner: Family Life Communications Inc.; (acq 6-24-98; grpsl)
Arbitron Metro Market: Odessa-Midland, TX; *Format:* Christian, Religious; *Target Audience:* 34-59; females
Warren J. Bolthouse, Chairman
Randy L. Carlson, President
Dawn Bumstead, General Manager
Adam Biddell, Programming Director

KHKX
07-01-1977; 99.1 MHz FM; *Hrs Open:* 24; 100 kw; 407 ft.; N32 3 9 W102 17 39
3303 N. Midkiff, Suite 115, Midland, TX 79405 US
(432) 520-9912; *Fax:* (432) 520-0112
www.kicks99.net
morningkicks@aol.com
License: Odessa, Ector County, TX
Group Owner: Brazos Communications West LLC; (acq 2006; grpsl).
Nat'l Network: USA
Arbitron Metro Market: Odessa, TX; *Format:* Country; *Hrs. of News Programming:* News progmg one hr wkly; *Target Audience:* 25-54; general
Terry Bond, CEO
Dana Carole, General Sales Mgr
Mike Lawrence, Programming Director

KMCM
01-01-1961; 96.9 MHz FM; 100 kw; 452 ft.; N32 5 8 W102 17 11
4101 East 42nd, Suite J2, Odessa, TX 79762 US
(432) 520-9912; *Fax:* (432) 520-0112
www.97gold.com
License: Odessa, Ector County, TX
Group Owner: Brazos Communications West LLC; (acq 2006; grpsl).
Nat'l Reps: Katz Radio
Arbitron Metro Market: Midland, TX; *Format:* Contemporary Hits/Top 40, Adult Contemp; *Hrs. of News Programming:* News progmg 2 hrs wkly; *Target Audience:* 25-54; men; *Adv. Rates:* 30; 25; 30; 15
Terry Bond, CEO

KMRK-FM
08-23-1991; 96.1 MHz FM; *Hrs Open:* 24; 27.5 kw; 948 ft.; N32 5 11 W102 17 10
600 Congress Avenue, Suite 1400, Austin, TX 78701 US
(432) 563-9102; *Fax:* (432) 580-9102,
www.mycountry961.com
License: Odessa, Ector County, TX
Group Owner: ICA Radio Ltd.; (acq 10-1-2007; grpsl)
Nat'l Network: American Urban; *Wire Services:* AP
Arbitron Metro Market: Odessa, TX; *Format:* Country; *Hrs. of News Programming:* news progmg 2 hrs wkly; *No. News Employees:* 1; *Target Audience:* 18-34.; *Adv. Rates:* 48; 40; 40; 18
Steve Driscoll, Operations Dir
Gloria Apolinario, General Manager

*KXWT
01-06-1964; 91.3 MHz FM; *Hrs Open:* 6 AM-midnight; 5 kw; 300 ft; N31 51 30 W102 23 00
Odessa College, 201 W. University Blvd., Odessa, TX 79764
(432) 580-9130; *Fax:* (915) 337-0529
www.odessa.edu
License: Odessa, Ector County, TX held by Odessa College.
Nat'l Network: NPR
Population Served: 78,380; *Arbitron Metro Market:* Odessa-Midland, TX *Special Programming:* Jazz 4 hrs, opera 4 hrs, folk 4 hrs, blues 4 hrs, bluegrass 2 hrs, Celtic 4 hrs wkly; *Hrs. of News Programming:* news progmg 33hrs wkly; *No. News Employees:* 1; *Target Audience:* 35 plus; educated, affluent adults
Carl Evans, Operations Dir

KODM
01-01-1965; 97.9 MHz FM; *Hrs Open:* 24; 100 kw; 361 ft.; N31 47 39 W102 10 42
111 East Kilbourn Avenue, Suite 2700, Milwaukee, WI 53202 US
432) 563-5499; *Fax:* (432) 563-5330
www.kodm.com
License: Odessa, Ector County, TX held by Townsquare Media Odessa-Midland II License LLC
Group Owner: Townsquare Media; (acq 12-17-98; grpsl)
Nat'l Network: ABC
Arbitron Metro Market: Odessa-Midland, TX; *Format:* Adult Contemp; *Target Audience:* 25-54; women
Shalayna Valencia, General Manager
Leo Caro, Brand Manager
Shalayna Valencia, Director Of Sales
Gary Hinterlong, Digital Managing Editor

KOZA
01-20-1947; 1230 kHz AM; *Hrs Open:* 24
1100 South Grant, Odessa, TX 79763 US
(432) 332-1230; *Fax:* (432) 335-0064
License: Odessa, TX held by Stellar Media Inc.
Arbitron Metro Market: Odessa-Midland, TX; *Target Audience:* 18-54.
Benjamin Velasquez, General Manager

KQLM
03-11-1996; 107.9 MHz FM; *Hrs Open:* 24; 100 kw; 846 ft.; N32 5 51 W102 17 21
4350 North Fairfax Drive, Suite 900, Arlington, VA 22203 US
(432) 333-1227; *Fax:* (432) 335-0064
www.q108fm.com
benjaminv@kqlm.com
License: Odessa, Ector County, TX held by Stellar Media Inc.
Arbitron Metro Market: Odessa-Midland, TX; *Format:* Spanish; *Hrs. of News Programming:* News progmg 10 hrs wkly; *Target Audience:* General; Hispanics/Latinos; *Adv. Rates:* 27; 27; 27; na
Benjamin Velasquez, CEO
Belinda Carrasco, General Sales Mgr

KRIL
06-01-1946; 1410 kHz AM *Rebroadcasts:* Rebroadcasts KMND(AM) Midland 100%
P. O. Box 4312, Odessa, TX 79760 US
(432) 563-5636; *Fax:* (432) 563-3823
www.1410kril.com
jmesher@aol.com
License: Odessa, TX held by Townsquare Media Odessa-Midland II License LLC
Group Owner: Townsquare Media; (acq 8-10-99; $110,000)
Nat'l Network: ESPN Radio
Arbitron Metro Market: Odessa-Midland,; *Format:* Country; *Target Audience:* 25 plus; higher educ level, higher income level
George Demarco, General Manager
Robie Burns, Programming Director
Gary Vaugn, Chief Engineer

*KLVW
01-01-2001; 90.5 MHz FM; *Hrs Open:* 24; 86 kw; 614 ft.; N32 5 51 W102 17 21
7355 North Oracle Rd., Tucson, AZ 85704 US
(800) 525-5683; *Fax:* (916) 251-1650
www.klove.com
klove@klove.com
License: Odessa, Ector County, TX held by Educational Media Foundation.
Group Owner: EMF Broadcasting
Nat'l Network: K-Love
Arbitron Metro Market: Omaha, NE; *Format:* Christian; *No. News Employees:* 13; *Target Audience:* 25-44; Judeo Christian, female
Darrell Chambliss, Chairman
MIke Novak, President & CEO
David Pierce, Programming Director
Ed Lenane, News Director
Sam Wallington, Engineering Dir
Richard Hunt, News Reporter
Marya Morgan, News Reporter
Laura Daniels, NewsReporter
Tim Luttrell, News Reporter
Kenny Noble Cortes, News Reporter
Darren Vinson, News Reporter

Orange

KIOC
02-28-1977; 106.1 MHz FM; *Hrs Open:* 24; 100 kw; 1,070 ft.; N30 9 20 W93 59 10
2885 I-10 Frontage Rd., Beaumont, TX 77702 US
(409) 896-5555
www.bigdog106.com
License: Orange, Orange County, TX held by Capstar TX LLC
Group Owner: iHeartMedia; (acq 8-30-00; grpsl).
Arbitron Metro Market: Beaumont-Port Arthur, TX; *Format:* Rock/AOR; *Target Audience:* 18-49; adults who have discretionary income; *Adv. Rates:* 63; 63; 63; 63
Richard J. Bressler, President

KKMY
01-01-1972; 104.5 MHz FM; 100 kw; 764 ft.; N30 9 20 W93 59 10
600 Congress Avenue, Suite 1400, Austin, TX 78701 US
(409) 896-5555; *Fax:* (409) 896-5500
www.kiss1045fm.com
License: Orange, Orange County, TX held by Capstar TX LLC
Group Owner: iHeartMedia; (acq 8-30-00; grpsl).
Arbitron Metro Market: Beaumont, TX; *Format:* Adult Contemp; *Target Audience:* 25-54; at-work lstng audience; *Adv. Rates:* 63; 63; 63; 63
Richard J. Bressler, President

KOGT
01-01-1948; 1600 kHz AM; 1 kw-D, DAN; 1 kw-N, DAN; N30 8 25 W93 45 11
Mailing Address: P.O. Box 1667, Orange, TX 77630 US
Second Address: 5304 Meeks Dr., Orange, TX 77632
(409) 883-4381; *Fax:* (409) 883-7996
www.kogt.com
news@kogt.com
License: Orange, TX held by G-CAP Communications Inc.
Regional Network: Texas State Networks
Arbitron Metro Market: Beaumont-Port Arthur, TX; *Format:* News, Sports, 30; *Target Audience:* 25 plus.
Gary Stelly, President
Richard Corder, General Sales Mgr
Glenn Earle, News Director
Russ Ingram, Engineering Dir
Reg Russell, Disc Jockey
Clay Williams, Disc Jockey
Terry Lyons, Disc Jockey
Iva Odom, Traffic Manager

Ore City

KAZE
05-01-1991; 106.9 MHz FM; 8.2 kw; 502 ft.; N32 41 54 W94 37 4
212 Old Grande Blvd., Suite B100, Tyler, TX 75703 US
(903) 581-5259
www.theblaze.fm
License: Ore City, Upshur County, TX held by Reynolds Radio Inc.
Group Owner: Reynolds Radio Inc.; acq 1-9-97)
Arbitron Metro Market: Tyler, TX; *Format:* Urban Contemporary

Overland

*KKVI
01-01-2008; 89.9 MHz FM; 0.12 kw vert; 98 ft.; N33 4 0 W95 46 10

US
(469) 245-3604; *Fax:* (972) 414-8149
License: Overland, Hopkins County, TX held by Gospel American Network.
Arbitron Metro Market: Overland, TX; *Format:* Christian
Bill Wright, General Manager

Overton

KPXI
10-08-1961; 100.7 MHz FM; *Hrs Open:* 24; 8.1 kw; 571 ft.; N32 9 7 W95 3 27
1350 One Galleria Tower, 13355 Noel Rd, Dallas, TX 75240 US
(903) 655-1800; *Fax:* (903) 655-1808
www.mykpxi.com
info@mykpxi.com
License: Overton, Rusk County, TX held by Inspiration Media of Texas LLC.
Group Owner: Salem Communications Corp.; (acq 11-6-2000; with KWRD-FM Highland Village).
Arbitron Metro Market: Tyler-Longview; *Format:* Country
Jerry Hanszen, President
David Jacobs, Operations Dir
David Chenault, General Manager
John McMillian, Programming Director

Ozona

KYXX
11-25-1976; 94.3 MHz FM; 3 kw; 394 ft.; N30 42 42.6 W101 7 28.7
Hc 65, Box 50, Sonora, TX 76950 US
(830) 896-1230; *Fax:* (830) 792-4142
www.revfmradio.com/
khoskyxx@verizon.net
License: Ozona, Crockett County, TX held by Foster Charitable Foundation Inc.
Group Owner: Revolution Broadcast Company of the West; (acq 5-31-2007)
Nat'l Network: ABC; *Regional Network:* Texas State Networks
Arbitron Metro Market: Ozona, TX; *Format:* Country; *Target Audience:* 12-50 plus.
Marti Ashcraft, Operations Dir
Eddy Smith, Engineering Dir

Palestine

KNET
07-01-1987; 1450 kHz AM; *Hrs Open:* 24; 630 watts
Box 3649, 800 W. Palestine Ave., Palestine, TX 75802 US
(903) 729-6077
www.youreasttexas.com
License: Palestine, TX held by Tomlinson-Leis Communications LP
Group Owner: Tomlinson-Leis Communications LP
Format: News/Talk; *Hrs. of News Programming:* news progmg 6 hrs wkly; *No. News Employees:* 1; *Target Audience:* 35 plus.; *Adv. Rates:* 10; 10; 10; 10
Lee Parkinson, General Manager
Michael McCulloch, Programming Director
Gary Richards, News Director

*KYFP
05-15-2000; 89.1 MHz FM; *Hrs Open:* 24; 100 kw; 486 ft.; N32 0 12 W95 43 6
P.O. Box 7300, Charlotte, NC 28241 US
(800) 888-7077
www.bbnradio.org
bbn@bbnmedia.org
License: Palestine, Anderson County, TX held by Bible Broadcasting Network Inc.
Group Owner: Bible Broadcasting Network
Arbitron Metro Market: Charlotte, NC; *Format:* Religious
Lowell Davey, President
Jason Padgett, Operations Manager
Ron Muffley, Chief Engineer

KYYK
11-18-1981; 98.3 MHz FM; *Hrs Open:* 24; 5 kw; Ant 728 ft; N31 55 33 W95 38 48
Box 3649, 800 W. Palestine Ave., Palestine, TX 75802 US
(903) 729-6077
www.youreasttexas.com
License: Palestine, TX held by Tomlinson-Leis Communications LP
Group Owner: Tomlinson-Leis Communications LP
Population Served: 115,000 *Hrs. of News Programming:* news progmg 1 hr wkly; *No. News Employees:* 3; *Target Audience:* 18-54.; *Adv. Rates:* 20; 20; 20; 20
Lee Parkinson, General Manager
Michael McCulloch, Programming Director
Gary Richards, News Director

Pampa

*KAVO
07-01-1998; 90.9 MHz FM; 17 kw; 364 ft.; N35 33 8 W101 2 42
Rebroadcasts: Rebroadcasts WAFR(FM) Tupelo, MS 100%
P.O. Box 3206, Tupelo, MS 38803 US
(662) 844-8888; *Fax:* (662) 842-6791
www.afr.net
faq@afa.net
License: Pampa, Gray County, TX held by American Family Association.
Group Owner: American Family Radio
Nat'l Network: American Family Radio
Arbitron Metro Market: Tupelo, MS; *Format:* Christian, Religious
Tim Wildmon, President
Donald Wildmon, Founder
Buddy Smith, Sr VP
Ed Vitagliano, Exec VP
Randy Sharp, Director Of Special Projects
Meeme Addison, Director Of Communications
Abraham Hamilton III, General Counsel & Public Policy

KGRO
01-01-1947; 1230 kHz AM; 1 kw-U, ND1; N35 34 39 W100 57 8
P.O. Box 3121, Carlsbad, NM 88220 US
(806) 669-6809; *Fax:* (806) 669-0662
www.kgrokomxradio.com
production@kgrokomxradio.com
License: Pampa, TX held by Pampa Broadcasters Inc.
Nat'l Network: Jones Radio Networks; ABC
Format: Adult Contemp; *Target Audience:* 18-45.
James Hughes, President
Darrell Sehorn, General Manager
Donny Hooper, News Director
Greg Campbell, Chief Engineer
Jimmy Story, Disc Jockey
Linda Sehorn, Traffic Manager

KOMX
05-18-1981; 100.3 MHz FM; 32 kw; Ant 300 ft; N35 34 39 W100 57 08
Box 1779, Pampa, TX 88220
(806) 669-6809; *Fax:* (806) 669-0662
License: Pampa, Gray County, TX held by Pampa Broadcasters Inc.
Nat'l Network: ABC; Jones Radio Networks; *Regional Network:* Texas State Networks
Population Served: 125,000 *Target Audience:* 20 plus.
James Hughes, President
Darrell Sahara, Operations Dir
Darrell Sahara, General Manager
Darrell Sahara, Station Manager
Jimmy Story, Programming Director
Linda Sehorn, News Director
Greg Campbell, Chief Engineer
Donny Hooper,Sports Commentator

Paris

*KHCP
01-10-2001; 89.3 MHz FM; *Hrs Open:* 24; 52 kw; 354 ft.; N33 49 36 W95 27 49
2424 South Blvd., Houston, TX 77098 US
(713) 520-5200
www.khcb.org
email@khcb.org
License: Paris, Lamar County, TX held by Houston Christian Broadcasters Inc.
Group Owner: Houston Christian Broadcasters Inc.
Nat'l Network: Moody
Arbitron Metro Market: Houston, TX; *Format:* Christian
Bruce E. Munsterman, President

KBUS
06-03-1985; 101.9 MHz FM; *Hrs Open:* 24; 50 kw; 492 ft.; N33 44 54 W95 24 52
2810 Pine Mill Rd., Paris, TX 75460 US
(903) 784-1293; *Fax:* (903) 785-7176
www.easttexasradio.com
jyoung@easttexasradio.com
License: Paris, Lamar County, TX held by East Texas Broadcasting Inc.
Group Owner: East Texas Broadcasting Inc.; acq 5-11-01; grpsl).
Format: Classic Rock *Special Programming:* Farm 6 hrs wkly; *Hrs. of News Programming:* news progmg 20 hrs wkly; *No. News Employees:* 1; *Target Audience:* 25-54.
Bob Haschke, General Manager

KZHN
09-11-1950; 1250 kHz AM; *Hrs Open:* 24; 0.5 kw-D, ND1; 0.095 kw-N, ND1; N33 43 21 W95 32 50
Mailing Address: 2400 Clarksville Street, Paris, TX 75460 US
Second Address: 402 Munson Ave. Suite 111, Rockwall, TX 75087
(214) 499-1158; *Fax:* (972) 771-1775
www.txn1250.com
txn1250@gmail.com
License: Paris, TX held by Eiffel Tower Broadcasting
Nat'l Network: USA; *Regional Network:* Agrinet *Regional Reps:* Eiffel Tower Broadcasting; *Wire Services:* AP
Arbitron Metro Market: Dallas-Fort Worth; *Format:* Country
Special Programming: Variety/diversified.; *Hrs. of News Programming:* news progmg 24 hrs wkly; *No. News Employees:* 4; *Target Audience:* 24-54+. *Adv. Rates:* 45; 45; 45; 45
Larry Ryan, CEO
Samantha Nicole, Operations Dir
B.J. Clayton, General Manager
MaryAnn Ryan, General Sales Mgr
Crystal Jewel, Programming Director
B.J.Clayton, Promotions Manager
Andy Jackson, News Director
Norm Laramie, ChiefEngineer
Dawn Mitchell, Local Sales Manager
Robert Ryan, Production Director

KOYN
10-06-1988; 93.9 MHz FM; *Hrs Open:* 24; 50 kw; 492 ft.; N33 49 36 W95 27 49
2810 Pine Mill Rd., Paris, TX 75460 US
(903) 785-1068; *Fax:* (903) 785-7176
www.easttexasradio.com
jyoung@easttexasradio.com
License: Paris, Lamar County, TX held by East Texas Broadcasting Inc.
Group Owner: East Texas Broadcasting Inc.; acq 5-11-01; grpsl).
Nat'l Network: USA
Format: Country; *Hrs. of News Programming:* news progmg 3 hrs wkly; *No. News Employees:* 2; *Target Audience:* 12 plus.
Bob Haschke, General Manager

KPLT
11-19-1936; 1490 kHz AM; *Hrs Open:* 24; 1 kw-U; N33 38 07 W95 33 14
2810 Pine Mill Rd., Paris, TX 75460 US
(903) 785-1068; *Fax:* (903) 785-7176
www.easttexasradio.com
License: Paris, Lamar County, TX held by East Texas Broadcasting Inc.
Group Owner: East Texas Broadcasting Inc.; acq 5-11-01; grpsl).
Nat'l Network: FOX News
Population Served: 55,000 *Format:* Country *Special Programming:* Gospel 15 hrs wkly; *Target Audience:* General.
Bob Haschke, General Manager

KPLT-FM
08-14-1966; 107.7 MHz FM; 50 kw; 492 ft.; N33 44 55 W95 24 53
2810 Pine Mill Rd., Paris, TX 75460 US
(903) 785-1068; *Fax:* (903) 785-7176
www.easttexasradio.com
bobh@easttexasradio.com
License: Paris, Lamar County, TX held by East Texas Broadcasting, Inc.
Group Owner: East Texas Broadcasting, Inc.
Nat'l Network: ABC
Arbitron Metro Market: Paris, TX; *Format:* Adult Contemp; *Target Audience:* 18-35; heavy female/listen at work
Bob Haschke, General Manager

Pasadena

*KFTG
02-01-1981; 88.1 MHz FM; *Hrs Open:* 24; 0.7 kw horiz, 0.658 kw vert; 187 ft.; N29 41 18 W95 12 7
8315 Cr 198, Alvin, TX 77511 US
(281) 393-3116; *Fax:* (281) 393-1652
License: Pasadena, Harris County, TX held by Aleluya Broadcasting Network
Arbitron Metro Market: Pasadena, TX; *Format:* Religious, Spanish; *Target Audience:* Christians
Roberto Villarreal, General Manager

KIKK
10-01-1957; 650 kHz AM; 0.25 kW; N29 41 18 W95 10 29
24 Greenway Plaza, Suite 1900, Houston, TX 77046 USA
(713) 881-5100
www.cbssportsradio650.com
License: Pasadena, TX held by CBS Radio Texas Inc.
Group Owner: CBS Radio; (acq 10-20-93;
Nat'l Network: CBS; *Nat'l Reps:* CBS Radio
Arbitron Metro Market: Houston-Galveston; *Format:* Sports
Special Programming: Health 2 hrs wkly; *Hrs. of News Programming:* news 60 hrs wkly; *Target Audience:* 25-44.

KKBQ-FM
08-01-1962; 93.7 MHz FM; *Hrs Open:* 24; 93.7 kw; 1906 ft.; N29 34 34 W95 30 36
1990 Post Oak Boulevard, Suite 2300, Houston, TX 77056 US
(713) 963-1200; *Fax:* (713) 622-5457
www.KKBQ.com
mark.krieschen@coxinc.com
License: Pasadena, Harris County, TX held by Cox Radio Inc.
Group Owner: Cox Radio Inc.; (acq 8-7-2000; grpsl)
Arbitron Metro Market: Houston, TX; *Format:* Country; *Target Audience:* 25-54
Mark Kreischen, Vice President / Market Manager
Johnny Lakin, Operations Manager
Judy Lakin, Director Of Sales
Lisa Searcy, Marketing Director
Candy Graham, Promotions Manager

KLVL
05-05-1950; 1480 kHz AM
1302 N. Shepherd, Houston, TX 77008 US
(713) 868-5559; *Fax:* (713) 868-9631
www.klvl1480.com
License: Pasadena, TX held by SIGA Broadcasting Corp.
Group Owner: SIGA Broadcasting Corp.; acq 5-16-97; $1.25 million)
Arbitron Metro Market: Houston, TX; *Format:* Christian, Sports, 86 *Special Programming:* Black 4 hrs wkly
Julian Arango, Operations Dir
Hector Guevara, General Manager
Dade Moore, Engineering Dir

Pearsall

KMFR
11-03-1962; 1280 kHz AM; 500 w-D; N28 53 13 W99 06 40
Mailing Address: Box K, Pearsall, TX 78230
Second Address: 205 S. Walnut St., Pearsall, TX 78061
(830) 334-8900; *Fax:* (830) 334-3448
License: Pearsall, Frio County, TX held by Pearsall Radio Works Ltd.
Population Served: 47,000
John Barger, President

KSAH-FM
08-04-2002; 104.1 MHz FM; *Hrs Open:* 24; 100 kw; 981 ft; N28 43 16 W98 45 43
4050 Eisenhauer Rd., San Antonio, TX 78218 US
(210) 654-5100; *Fax:* (210) 855-5076
www.nortenosa.com
License: Pearsall, Frio County, TX held by Alpha Media Licensee LLC
Group Owner: Alpha Media LLC; (acq 1-31-2014; grpsl).
Arbitron Metro Market: San Antonio, TX; *Format:* Tejano
Greg Martin, General Manager
Coreena Hazelett, General Sales Mgr
Alfonso Flores, Programming Director

KSAG
103.3 MHz FM; 6 kw; 328 ft.; N29 1 4 W99 9 25
US
(956) 489-1013
License: Pearsall, Frio County, TX held by Gary S. Hess
Arbitron Metro Market: Pearsall, TX
Gary Hess, General Manager

Pecan Grove

KREH
01-01-1952; 900 kHz AM; *Hrs Open:* Sunrise-sunset
P.O Box 60991, Palo Alto, CA 94306 US
(713) 917-0050; *Fax:* (713) 917-0213
www.radiosaigonhouston.com
info@daisaigon.com
License: Pecan Grove, TX held by Bustos Media Holdings L.L.C.
Group Owner: Bustos Media Holdings L.L.C.; (acq 6-11-2002)
Arbitron Metro Market: Greater Houston; *Format:* Japanese, Korean, 18
Thuy Vu, General Manager
Duong Phuc & Vu Thanh Thuy / FOUNDERS

Pecos

KIUN
10-23-1935; 1400 kHz AM; *Hrs Open:* 24; 1 kw-U, ND1; N31 26 9 W103 30 14
316 South Cedar St., Pecos, TX 79772 US
(432) 445-2497; *Fax:* (432) 445-4092
www.98xfm.com
kiun@valornet.com
License: Pecos, TX held by Pecos Radio Co.
Regional Network: Texas State Networks
Format: Country; *Target Audience:* General.
Bill Cole, General Manager

KGEE
01-01-1999; 97.3 MHz FM; 0.3 kw; 70 ft.; N31 25 7 W103 30 58
Rebroadcasts: Simulcast with KZBT(FM) Midland 100%
Box 2537, Bay City, TX 77414 US
(432) 563-9300; *Fax:* (432) 563-3823
www.b93.net
License: Pecos, Reeves County, TX held by Townsquare Media Odessa-Midland II License LLC
Group Owner: Townsquare Media; (acq 6-11-2002; $1 million)
Arbitron Metro Market: Odessa, TX; *Format:* Blues
Jeff Stone, General Manager
Leo Caro, Programming Director

KPTX
08-03-1981; 98.3 MHz FM; *Hrs Open:* 6 AM-10 PM; 9.5 kw; 423 ft.; N31 29 56 W103 19 50
P. O. Box 469, Pecos, TX 79772 US
(432) 445-2497; *Fax:* (432) 445-4092
www.98xfm.com
info@98xfm.com
License: Pecos, Reeves County, TX held by Parday Inc.
Nat'l Network: ABC
Arbitron Metro Market: Odessa-Midland; *Format:* Adult Contemp; *Target Audience:* 25 plus; adult
Bill Randall, General Manager
Joe Bevilacqua, Programming Director

***KPKO**
91.3 MHz FM; 0.9 kw; 62 ft.; N31 25 6 W103 30 55
P.O. Box 3206, Tupelo, MS 38803 US
(662) 844-8888; *Fax:* (662) 842-6791
www.afr.net
faq@afa.net
License: Pecos, Reeves County, TX held by American Family Association.
Group Owner: American Family Radio
Nat'l Network: American Family Radio
Arbitron Metro Market: Pecos, TX; *Format:* Christian
Tim Wildmon, President
Donald Wildmon, Founder
Buddy Smith, Sr VP
Ed Vitagliano, Exec VP
Randy Sharp, Director Of Special Projects
Meeke Addison, Director Of Communications
Abraham Hamilton III, General Counsel

Perryton

KEYE
11-19-1948; 93.7 kHz AM; 1 kw-U; N36 23 20 W100 49 37
Box 630, Perryton, TX 79070
(806) 435-5458; *Fax:* (806) 435-5393
www.keye.net
License: Perryton, Ochiltree County, TX held by Perryton Radio Inc.
Regional Network: Texas State Networks
Population Served: 40,000 *Special Programming:* Farm 2 hrs, relg 3 hrs wkly
Chris Samples, General Manager
Lynlee Mullins, News Director

KEYE-FM
01-01-1978; 93.7 MHz FM; 8.5 kw; 402 ft.; N36 21 54 W100 46 45
7430 Colshire #4, McLean, VA 22102 US
(806) 435-5458; *Fax:* (806) 435-5393
www.keye.net
keye@keye.net
License: Perryton, Ochiltree County, TX held by Perryton Radio Inc.
Arbitron Metro Market: Perryton, TX; *Format:* Oldies
Darin Clark, General Manager
David Schwalk, News Director

Pflugerville

KOKE
01-01-2011; 1600 kHz AM; 5 kw-D, 0.7 kw-D, DA-2; N30 20 44 W97 32 46
9434 Parkfield Drive, Austin, TX 78758 US
(512) 453-1491; *Fax:* (512) 834-1491
License: Pflugerville, TX held by Encino Broadcasting LLC
Group Owner: Encino Broadcasting LLC

Jose J. Garcia Jr., General Manager

Pharr

KVJY
02-01-1985; 840 kHz AM; 5 kw-D, DA2; 1 kw-N, DA2; N26 19 0 W98 6 16
P.O. Box 484, Austin, TX 78767 US
(956) 668-8585; *Fax:* (956) 668-9996
License: Pharr, TX held by BMP RGV License Co. L.P.
Group Owner: Border Media Partners LLC; (acq 3-31-2005; grpsl).
Arbitron Metro Market: McAllen-Brownsville-Harlingen, TX; *Format:* Country
Thomas Castro, President
Jeff Koch, Operations Dir
Jose Luis Munoz, General Manager

Pilot Point

KZMP-FM
10-17-1983; 104.9 MHz FM; 20.15 kw; 67 ft.; N33 33 37 W96 57 34
2410 Gateway Dr., Irving, TX 75063 US
(972) 652-2900
www.funasia.net/index.php
dallasinfo@lbimedia.com
License: Pilot Point, Denton County, TX held by Liberman Broadcasting of Dallas License LLC.
Group Owner: Liberman Broadcasting Inc.; (acq 11-2-2006; grpsl)
Arbitron Metro Market: Dallas-Fort Worth, TX; *Format:* Ethnic

Pittsburg

KSCN
03-01-1999; 95.9 MHz FM; *Hrs Open:* 24; 14 kw; 390 ft; N33 00 31 W95 04 14
930 Gilmer St., Sulphur Spings, TX 75482 US
(903) 885-1546; *Fax:* (903) 885-1101
www.easttexasradio.com
bud@easttexasradio.com
License: Pittsburg, Camp County, TX held by East Texas Broadcasting Inc.
Group Owner: East Texas Broadcasting Inc.
Population Served: 68,000 *Format:* Country; *Hrs. of News Programming:* news progmg 3 hrs wkly; *No. News Employees:* 2; *Target Audience:* 25-54; general; *Adv. Rates:* 26; 23; 26; 21
Bud Kitchens, General Manager

KMPA
12-15-1986; 103.1 MHz FM; *Hrs Open:* 24; 10 kw; Ant 672 ft; N32 52 50 W94 58 13
Mailing Address: Box 1648, Jacksonville, TX 75644
Second Address: 402 S. Ragsdale, Jacksonville, TX 75766
(903) 586-2527; *Fax:* (903) 589-0677
License: Pittsburg, Camp County, TX held by Waller Media LLC.
Group Owner: Waller Broadcasting; (acq 8-24-2005; $975,000 with KXAL-FM Tatum).
Population Served: 280,000 *Hrs. of News Programming:* news progmg 6 hrs wkly; *No. News Employees:* 1; *Adv. Rates:* 30; 24; 20; 10
Dudley Waller, General Manager

***KGWP**
01-01-2003; 91.1 MHz FM; *Hrs Open:* 24; 1.1 kw vert; 194 ft.; N32 57 49.5 W94 55 10
US
(951) 737-1717; *Fax:* (903) 575-1984
www.radioimpacto.org
License: Pittsburg, Camp County, TX held by Andres Serranos Ministries Inc.
Arbitron Metro Market: Pittsburg, TX; *Format:* Christian; *Hrs. of News Programming:* news progmg 10 hrs wkly; *No. News Employees:* 1; *Target Audience:* 30-55 plus.; *Adv. Rates:* 10; 10; 10; 5
Rafael Garcia, President

***KPIT**
01-01-2008; 91.7 MHz FM; 0.45 kw vert; 131 ft.; N33 2 45.5 W95 3 23.2
US
(903) 466-6791
www.kpitradio.com
License: Pittsburg, Camp County, TX held by Millennium Broadcasting Corp.
Arbitron Metro Market: Pittsburg, TX; *Format:* Tejano
James Furlow, President

Plains

***KPHS**
11-14-1977; 90.3 MHz FM; *Hrs Open:* 8:30 AM-3:15 PM; 0.22 kw horiz; 135 ft.; N33 11 16 W102 49 20

P.O. Box 479, Plains, TX 79355 US
(806) 456-7445; *Fax:* (806) 456-4325
License: Plains, Yoakum County, TX held by Plains Independent School District.
Target Audience: High School Radio
Rennetta O'Quinn, General Manager

Plainview

*KBAH

03-18-2004; 90.5 MHz FM; 75 kw; 427 ft.; N34 3 58 W101 42 16
P.O. Box 3206, Tupelo, MS 38803 US
(662) 844-8888; *Fax:* (662) 842-6791
www.afr.net
faq@afa.net
License: Plainview, Hale County, TX held by American Family Association.
Group Owner: American Family Radio
Arbitron Metro Market: Tupelo, MS; *Format:* Christian
Tim Wildmon, President
Donald Wildmon, Founder
Buddy Smith, Sr VP
Ed Vitagliano, Exec VP
Randy Sharp, Director Of Special Projects
Meeke Addison, Director Of Communications
Abraham Hamilton III, General Counsel & Public PolicyAnalysist

KVOP

10-01-1974; 1090 kHz AM; *Hrs Open:* 24; 5 kw-D, DA2; 0.5 kw-N, DA2; N34 5 32 W101 38 26
Mailing Address: 3218 N. Quincy, Plainview, TX 79072 US
Second Address: Box 147, Plainview, TX 79073
(806) 296-2771; *Fax:* (806) 293-5732
License: Plainview, TX held by Rhattigan Broadcasting (Texas) LP
Group Owner: Rhattigan Broadcasting (Texas) LP; (acq 8-19-2004; grpsl)
Nat'l Reps: Katz Radio
Arbitron Metro Market: Lubbock, TX; *Format:* Sports, Talk
Special Programming: Farm 12 hrs wkly; *Hrs. of News Programming:* News progmg 10 hrs wkly; *Target Audience:* Adults; 25-54; *Adv. Rates:* 20; 14; 18; 12
Tom Hall, Operations Dir
Dana Huggins, General Manager
Ben Cately, Programming Director
Michelle Johnson, Traffic Director

KKYN-FM

01-01-1987; 106.9 MHz FM; *Hrs Open:* 24; 50 kw; 469 ft.; N34 15 47 W101 40 30
Mailing Address: 2402 Broadmoor, Building D-2, Suite #101, Bryan, TX 77802 US
Second Address: Box 147, Plainview, TX 79073
(806) 296-2771; *Fax:* (806) 293-5732
www.kkyn.net
License: Plainview, Hale County, TX held by Rhattigan Broadcasting (Texas) LP
Group Owner: Rhattigan Broadcasting (Texas) LP
Arbitron Metro Market: Lubbock, TX; *Format:* Country; *Hrs. of News Programming:* news progmg 5 hrs wkly; *No. News Employees:* 1; *Target Audience:* 35 plus.; *Adv. Rates:* 20; 14; 16; 12
Tom Hall, Operations Dir
Dana Huggins, General Manager
Jerry Larsen, Station Manager
Dimas Garcia, Programming Director

KREW

08-14-1944; 1400 kHz AM; *Hrs Open:* 24; 1 kw-U, ND1; N34 12 55 W101 43 25
Mailing Address: 2402 Broadmoor, Bldg, D-2, Suite 101, Bryan, TX 77802 US
Second Address: Box 1420, Plainview, TX 79072
(806) 293-2661; *Fax:* (806) 293-5732
License: Plainview, TX held by Rhattigan Broadcasting (Texas) LP
Group Owner: Rhattigan Broadcasting (Texas) LP; (acq 8-19-2004; grpsl)
Regional Network: Texas State Networks; *Wire Services:* AP
Arbitron Metro Market: Plainview, TX; *Format:* Oldies; *Hrs. of News Programming:* News progmg 7 hrs wkly; *Target Audience:* Adults 35+; baby boomers; *Adv. Rates:* 14; 10; 12; 8
Michael Rhattigan, General Manager
Tom Hall, Station Manager
Brandy Haines, Programming Director
Dana Huggins, Traffic Manager

KRIA

01-01-1999; 103.9 MHz FM; 25 kw; 367 ft.; N34 15 47 W101 40 30
Mailing Address: 2402 Broadmoor, Bodg D-2, Suite 101, Bryan, TX 77802 US
Second Address: Box 1420, Plainview, TX 79073
(806) 293-2661; *Fax:* (806) 293-5732
License: Plainview, Hale County, TX held by Rhattigan Broadcasting (Texas) LP
Group Owner: Rhattigan Broadcasting (Texas) LP
Nat'l Network: CSN
Arbitron Metro Market: Plainview, TX; *Format:* Classic Rock; *Hrs. of News Programming:* News progmg 10 hrs wkly; *Target Audience:* Hispanic; 18-49; *Adv. Rates:* 18; 14; 16; 10.
Tom Hall, Operations Dir
Michael Rhattigan, General Manager
Brandy Haines, Programming Director
Dana Huggins, Traffic Director

*KWLD

01-01-1952; 91.5 MHz FM; *Hrs Open:* 24; 0.37 kw; 105 ft.; N34 11 14 W101 43 32
1900 W. 7th St., Plainview, TX 79072 US
(806) 291-1091; *Fax:* (806) 291-1963
www.wbu.edu
kwld@wbu.edu
License: Plainview, Hale County, TX held by Wayland Baptist University.
Nat'l Network: USA
Arbitron Metro Market: Plainview, TX; *Format:* Contemporary Hits/Top 40, Jazz, 20; *Hrs. of News Programming:* News progmg 14 hrs wkly; *Target Audience:* 15-30; high school through college, young adult, afternoon & evening
Jim Smith, CFO
Paul Armes, President
Claude Lusk, Operations Dir
Steve Long, General Manager
Paul Sutton, Programming Director
David Carr, Chief Engineer
Bill Hardage, Executive Vice President
Betty Donaldson, Vice President

*KPMB

88.5 MHz FM; 3 kw; 282 ft.; N34 13 14 W101 42 52
P.O. Box 252, McAllen, TX 78505 US
(956) 686-6382; *Fax:* (956) 686-2999
License: Plainview, Hale County, TX held by Paulino Bernal Evangelism.
Arbitron Metro Market: McAllen, TX; *Format:* Religious
Larry Roberts, General Manager
Bryce Philippy, General Sales Mgr
Kent Phillips, Programming Director
Jennifer Pirak, Promotions Manager
Lindsey Fields, News Director
John Barrett, Chief Engineer
Gary Greenberg, National SalesManager

Plano

KMKI

07-15-1999; 620 kHz AM; *Hrs Open:* 24; 5 kw-D, DA2; 4.5 kw-N, DA2; N33 14 34 W96 32 29
13725 Montfort Dr., Dallas, TX 75240 US
(817) 695-1333; *Fax:* (817) 695-3556
www.radiodisney.com
License: Plano, TX held by Radio Disney Dallas LLC.
Group Owner: ABC Inc.; (acq 9-4-98; $12.1 million).
Nat'l Network: Radio Disney; *Nat'l Reps:* Interep
Arbitron Metro Market: Dallas, TX; *Format:* Contemporary Hits/Top 40; *Target Audience:* 6-12; 25-49; women adults; *Adv. Rates:* Varies by inventory
Jamie Ramsey, Station Manager
Molly Bunker, Promotions Manager

Pleasant Valley

KZAM

01-01-2008; 98.7 MHz FM; 6 kw; 318 ft.; N34 2 54 W98 39 38 US
(956) 487-8015
License: Pleasant Valley, Wichita County, TX held by South Texas FM Investments LLC.
Group Owner: South Texas FM Investments LLC; (acq 9-16-2008; grpsl)
Arbitron Metro Market: Pleasant Valley, TX; *Format:* Variety/Diverse
Eloy Vera, General Manager

Pleasanton

*KWMF

02-08-1951; 1380 kHz AM; *Hrs Open:* 24 hrs
Mailing Address: 127 Mamanasco Road, Ridgefield, CT 06876 US
Second Address: 3308 Broadway, San Antonio, TX 78209
(432)682-5476; *Fax:* (432) 684-5588
www.grnonline.com
License: Pleasanton, TX held by La Promesa Foundation.
Group Owner: La Promesa Foundation; (acq 12-13-2006; grpsl)
Nat'l Network: EWTN Radio
Arbitron Metro Market: Pleasanton, TX; *Format:* Christian *Special Programming:* Vatican Radio 1 hr wkly; *Target Audience:* Christian Families
Robert Dominguez, General Manager

Port Arthur

*KDEI

08-01-1934; 1250 kHz AM; *Hrs Open:* 24
601 Washington Street, Alexandria, LA 71301 US
(888) 408-0201; *Fax:* (318) 449-9954
www.radiomaria.us
License: Port Arthur, TX held by Radio Maria Inc.
Group Owner: Radio Maria Inc.; acq 9-20-99).
Nat'l Network: American Urban
Arbitron Metro Market: Alexandria, LA; *Format:* Christian, Talk, 74; *Hrs. of News Programming:* News progmg 10.5 hrs wkly; *Target Audience:* General; isolated and under-represented groups in society, sick, elderly etc
Father Robert Young, Director

KOLE

01-01-1947; 1340 kHz AM; *Hrs Open:* 24; 1 kw-U, ND1; N29 54 15 W93 56 10
Mailing Address: P.O. Box 22257, Beaumont, TX 77720-2257 US
Second Address: 303 Katherine St., Orange, TX 77630
(248) 557-3500
www.birach.com
sima@birach.com
License: Port Arthur, Jefferson County, TX held by Birach Broadcasting Corp.
Group Owner: Birach Broadcasting Corp.; (acq 3-20-2008; $450,000)
Nat'l Network: USA; Fox News Radio; Talk Radio Network;
Regional Network: Texas State Networks
Arbitron Metro Market: Beaumont-Port Arthur, TX; *Format:* News, News/Talk, 86; *Hrs. of News Programming:* news progmg 40 hrs wkly; *No. News Employees:* 2; *Target Audience:* 25 plus.; *Adv. Rates:* 24; 20; 22; 18
Sima Birach, President
Clayton Hanna, General Manager

KQBU-FM

07-04-1969; 93.3 MHz FM; *Hrs Open:* 24; 97 kw; 1,952 ft.; N30 3 5 W94 31 37
5100 S.W. Fwy., Houston, TX 77056 US
(713) 965-2400; *Fax:* (713) 965-2401
www.univision.com
License: Port Arthur, Jefferson County, TX held by Tichenor License Corp.
Group Owner: Univision Radio
Arbitron Metro Market: Houston-Galveston, TX; *Format:* Tejano; *Target Audience:* 18-34; urban/Latin audience
David Loving, General Manager

KTJM

04-15-1963; 98.5 MHz FM; *Hrs Open:* 24; 100 kw; 1955 ft.; N30 1 1 W94 32 47
3000 Bering Dr, Houston, TX 77057 US
(713) 315-3400; *Fax:* (713) 315-3565
www.laraza.fm
houstoninfo@lbimedia.com
License: Port Arthur, Jefferson County, TX held by Liberman Broadcasting of Houston License LLC.
Group Owner: Liberman Broadcasting Inc.
Nat'l Reps: SMRT
Arbitron Metro Market: Beaumont-Port Arthur, TX *TV Affiliate:* Estrella TV; *Format:* Spanish
Lenard Liberman, CEO

Port Isabel

KNVO-FM

01-01-1989; 101.1 MHz FM; *Hrs Open:* 24; 50 kw; 486 ft.; N26 19 30 W97 25 25
801 N. Jackson Rd., McAllen, TX 78501 US
(956) 687-4848; *Fax:* (956) 687-7784
www.995lanueva.com
License: Port Isabel, Cameron County, TX held by Entravision Holdings LLC.
Group Owner: Entravision Communications Corp.; (acq 7-20-2000; grpsl)
Nat'l Network: Westwood One
Arbitron Metro Market: McAllen, TX; *Format:* Spanish, Adult Contemp; *Hrs. of News Programming:* news progmg one hr wkly; *No. News Employees:* 1; *Target Audience:* 25-55.

Willie Rosales, General Manager
Mando Sanroman, Programming Director
Dora Borjas, News Director

Port Lavaca

KITE

08-01-1976; 93.3 MHz FM; 100 kw; 318 ft.; N28 42 22 W96 48 3
Mailing Address: 8023 Vantage Dr., Suite 840, San Antonio, TX 78230 US
Second Address: 3613 N. Main St., Victoria, TX 77903
(361) 576-6111; *Fax:* (361) 572-0014
License: Port Lavaca, Calhoun County, TX held by Victoria RadioWorks Ltd.
Group Owner: Victoria RadioWorks Ltd.; (acq 10-29-98; $500,000).
Nat'l Reps: McGavren Guild
Format: Oldies *Special Programming:* Farm one hr wkly
Cindy Cox, General Manager

Port Neches

KBPO

06-13-1959; 1150 kHz AM
419 Stadium Road, Port Arthur, TX 77642 US
(409) 985-2323; *Fax:* (409) 983-5858
www.radiovida1150.com
License: Port Neches, TX held by Vision Latina Broadcasting Inc.
Nat'l Network: Fox Sports
Arbitron Metro Market: Port Neches, TX; *Format:* Sports
Eloy Castro, President
Marco Mata, General Sales Mgr
Patricia Montenegro, Programming Director
Richard Ryele, Chief Engineer
Lauri Grantham, Disc Jockey
Jeremy Ryan, Disc Jockey
Don Hebert, Disc Jockey

Port O'Connor

*KHPO

01-01-2007; 91.9 MHz FM; 4 kw; 308 ft.; N28 25 44 W96 26 54
Rebroadcasts: Rebroadcasts KHCB-FM Houston 95%
2424 South Blvd., Houston, TX 77098 US
(713) 520-5200
www.khcb.org
email@khcb.org
License: Port O'Connor, Calhoun County, TX held by Houston Christian Broadcasters Inc.
Group Owner: Houston Christian Broadcasters Inc.
Nat'l Network: Moody
Arbitron Metro Market: Port O'Connor, TX; *Format:* Christian; *Hrs. of News Programming:* News progmg 6 hrs wkly
Bruce E. Munsterman, President

Portland

KLHB

12-15-1979; 105.5 MHz FM; *Hrs Open:* 24; 1.9 kw; 354 ft; N27 47 48 W97 23 51
1300 Antelope, Corpus Christi, TX 78729
(361) 883-1600; *Fax:* (361) 888-5685
License: Portland, San Patricio County, TX held by Tejas Broadcasting Ltd. LLP.
Group Owner: Tejas Broadcasting Ltd. LLP; (acq 11-15-2004; grpsl).
Arbitron Metro Market: Corpus Christi, TX; *Target Audience:* 18-49; general
Eddie Alonzo, General Manager
Julie Garza, Programming Director
Lon Gonzalez, News Director
Henry Turner, Chief Engineer
Debbie Reid, Traffic Manager

*KSGR

10-01-2000; 91.1 MHz FM; 5.4 kw horiz, 25 kw vert; 328 ft.; N27 59 49 W97 14 46
3001 Roddfield Rd, Corpus Christi, TX 78414 US
(361) 814-7775; *Fax:* (361) 814-7779
www.ksgr.org
info@ksgr.org
License: Portland, San Patricio County, TX held by Calvary Chapel of Coastlands, Inc.
Format: Religious
Mike Kestler, President
Daniel Davidson, Operations Dir
Kelly Carlson, Engineering Dir

Post

KSSL

05-01-1991; 107.3 MHz FM; *Hrs Open:* 24; 22 kw; Ant 748 ft; N33 13 23 W101 26 26 *Rebroadcasts:* Rebroadcasts KLRD(FM) Yucaipa, CA 100%
2351 Sunset Blvd., Suite 170-218, Rocklin, CA 74067
(916) 251-1600, (800) 464-5817; *Fax:* (916) 251-1650
www.godscountryradionetwork.com
License: Post, Garza County, TX held by Educational Media Foundation.
Group Owner: EMF Broadcasting; (acq 5-21-2004; $550,000)
Population Served: 200,000
Mike Novak, President

Prairie View

*KPVU

11-26-1981; 91.3 MHz FM; *Hrs Open:* 24; 31 kw; 421 ft.; N30 5 21 W95 59 46
P. O. Box 156, Prairie View, TX 77446 US
(936) 261-3750; *Fax:* (936) 261-3769
www.pvamu.edu/kpvu
kpvu_fm@pvamu.edu
License: Prairie View, Waller County, TX held by Prairie View A&M University.
Nat'l Network: NPR
Arbitron Metro Market: Houston-Galveston; *Format:* Urban Contemporary, Variety/Diverse; *Hrs. of News Programming:* News progmg 24 hrs daily; *Target Audience:* 18 plus.
George LaBlanche, Operations Dir
Cheryl Granger Brooks, General Manager
Danielle Arriola, General Sales Mgr
Jeffrey Kelley, Programming Director
Leonard Moon, News Director
Dave Cassels, Chief Engineer

Ranchitos Las Lomas

*KLIT

01-01-2001; 93.3 MHz FM; 25 kw; 328 ft.; N27 0 22 W99 22 53
2702 Pine At Louisiana, Laredo, TX 78043 US
(956) 726-4738
radiooluz@border.net
License: Ranchitos Las Lomas, Zapata County, TX held by La Nueva Cadena Radio Luz Inc.
Arbitron Metro Market: Laredo, TX; *Format:* Christian
Isreal Tellez, Station Manager

Ranger

KWBY-FM

07-01-1990; 98.5 MHz FM; *Hrs Open:* 24; 5.8 kw; Ant 335 ft; N32 20 48 W98 42 50
471 N. Harbin Dr., Suite 102, Stephenville, TX 59911
(254) 968-7459; *Fax:* (254) 968-6258
www.mandatoryfm.com
john@mandatoryfm.com
License: Ranger, Eastland County, TX held by Mandatory Broadcasting Inc.
Nat'l Network: Jones Radio Networks; *Regional Network:* Texas State Networks
Target Audience: 20-65; all-important age group of today's buying public; *Adv. Rates:* 22; 18; 18; 15
John Hollinger, General Manager
Jon Gibson, General Sales Mgr
Jim Rhodes, Chief Engineer

Raymondville

*KBIC

01-01-1997; 105.7 MHz FM; *Hrs Open:* 24; 1.8 kw; 427 ft.; N26 26 37 W97 42 8
Box 1290, Weslaco, TX 78596 US
(956) 968-7777; *Fax:* (956) 968-5143
www.radiovida.com
License: Raymondville, TX held by Christian Ministries of the Valley Inc.
Group Owner: Christian Ministries of the Valley Inc.; (acq 2-4-93;).
Arbitron Metro Market: Weslaco, TX; *Format:* Religious
Eduardo Luevano, General Manager

KBUC

01-01-1979; 102.1 MHz FM; *Hrs Open:* 6 AM-midnight; 18 kw; 758 ft.; N26 38 9 W97 50 10
1 Paseo Del Prado, Bldg. 102, Edinburg, TX 78539 US
(956) 992-8895; *Fax:* (956) 992-8897
www.supertejano1021.com
License: Raymondville, Willacy County, TX held by BMP RGV License Company L.P.
Group Owner: Border Media Partners LLC; (acq 5-30-2003; $8 million with KBDR(FM) Mirando City).
Arbitron Metro Market: McAllen-Brownsv
Rogelio Rios, Operations Dir
Jose Munoz, General Manager
Maria Alvarez, General Sales Mgr
Angela Pina, News Director
Joe Espinoza, Chief Engineer

KSOX

06-01-1957; 1240 kHz AM; *Hrs Open:* 6 AM-midnight
1 Paseo Del Prado, Bldg. 102, Edinburg, TX 78539 US
(956) 383-2777; *Fax:* (956) 383-2570
License: Raymondville, TX held by BMP RGV License Co. L.P.
Group Owner: Border Media Partners LLC; (acq 2-6-2004; $7.5 million with KURV(AM) Edinburg)
Arbitron Metro Market: McAllen-Brownsville-Harlingen, TX; *Format:* Sports; *Target Audience:* 25-55.
Angela Pina, News Director

Refugio

KXAI

05-20-1968; 103.7 MHz FM; 100 kw; 952 ft.; N28 2 7 W97 26 11
5700 West Oaks Boulevard, Rocklin, CA 78401 US
(916) 251-1600; *Fax:* (916) 251-1650
www.air1.com
License: Refugio, San Patricio County, TX held by Educational Media Foundation
Group Owner: EMF Broadcasting; (acq 8-29-2013; $1.25 million).
Arbitron Metro Market: Corpus Christi, TX; *Format:* Country; *Target Audience:* 25-49; general
Mike Novak, President

KYRK

10-05-1979; 106.1 MHz FM; 25 kw; Ant 328 ft; N28 08 15 W97 12 45
710 Buffalo St., Suite 608, Corpus Christi, TX 74876
(314) 345-1030,(361) 882-5749; *Fax:* (361) 884-1240
jim@koplar.com
License: Refugio, Refugio County, TX held by Pacific Broadcasting of Missouri L.L.C.
Population Served: 400,000; *Arbitron Metro Market:* Corpus Christi, TX
James Withers, General Manager

Reno

KLOW

06-01-2009; 98.9 MHz FM; 5.9 kw; 331 ft.; N33 38 54 W95 36 12
US
2526363333
License: Reno, Lamar County, TX held by Tower Investment Trust Inc.
Group Owner: Tower Investment Trust Inc.
Nat'l Reps: Salem
Arbitron Metro Market: Reno, TX; *Format:* Christian; *Target Audience:* Contempary Christian
William Brothers, President

Richardson

KKLF

01-01-1999; 1700 kHz AM; 10 kw-D, 1 kw-N; N33 25 23 W96 39 45 *Rebroadcasts:* Rebroadcasts KTCK(AM) Dallas 100%
3500 Maple Ave., Suite 1310, Dallas, TX 17401
(214) 526-7400; *Fax:* (214) 525-2525
www.theticket.com
License: Richardson, Dallas County, TX held by Volt Radio LLC
Arbitron Metro Market: Dallas-Fort Worth
Gordon Johnson, President

Rio Grande City

KQBO

04-01-1985; 107.5 MHz FM; *Hrs Open:* 5 AM-midnight; 12 kw; 994 ft.; N26 31 1 W98 39 7
Rt 5, Box 103 Fm, Rio Grande City, TX 78582 US
(956) 487-8224; *Fax:* (815) 361-6185
License: Rio Grande City, Starr County, TX held by Gustavo Valadez Jr.
Arbitron Metro Market: McAllen-Brownsville-Harlingen, TX; *Format:* Ethnic; *Hrs. of News Programming:* News progmg 5 hrs wkly; *Target Audience:* 18-45.
Gustavo Valadez Jr., President

KRGX

95.1 MHz FM; 6 kw; 328 ft.; N26 26 4.9 W98 55 45.3
US

(956) 487-5621
www.exafm.com
exa95.1@gmail.com
License: Rio Grande City, Starr County, TX held by James Falcon.
Arbitron Metro Market: Rio Grande City, TX
James Falcon, General Manager

Robinson

KWPW
11-01-1972; 107.9 MHz FM; *Hrs Open:* 24; 6 kw; 328 ft.; N31 30 33 W97 10 03
6401 Cobbs Dr., Waco, TX 76710 US
(254) 772-6104
www.power108fm.com
License: Robinson, McLennan County, TX held by Waco Entertainment Group LLC
Group Owner: Prophecy Media Group LLC
Population Served: 35,000; *Arbitron Metro Market:* Waco, TX; *Format:* Contemporary Hits/Top 40; *Target Audience:* 18-54.
Carter Bentley, General Manager
Joey Butler, Programming Director
Jaime Martinez, Chief Engineer

Robstown

KROB
02-22-1963; 1510 kHz AM
N. 9th Street, Robstown, TX 78380 US
(302) 566-5762; *Fax:* (361) 299-6002
www.krobradio.com
krobam1510@sbcglobal.net
License: Robstown, TX held by B Communications Joint Venture.
Group Owner: Claro Communications Ltd.; (acq 1-4-2002)
Arbitron Metro Market: Corpus-Christi, TX; *Format:* Oldies, Spanish; *Target Audience:* 25-54.
Jerry Benavides, President
Jerry Benevides, General Manager
Ben Benavides, General Sales Mgr
Bob Pena, Programming Director
Peter Hemphill, News Director
Gary Graham, Chief Engineer

*KLUX
03-17-1985; 89.5 MHz FM; *Hrs Open:* 24; 60 kw; Ant 954 ft; N27 46 50 W97 38 03
1200 Lantana, Corpus Christi, TX 78407
(361) 289-2487; *Fax:* (361) 289-1420
www.klux.org
klux@goccn.org
License: Robstown, Nueces County, TX held by Diocesan Telecommunications Corp.
Nat'l Network: USA; IRN/USA
Population Served: 500,000; *Arbitron Metro Market:* Corpus Christi *Special Programming:* Sp 3 hrs wkly; *Hrs. of News Programming:* news progmg 13 hrs wkly; *No. News Employees:* 1; *Target Audience:* 35 plus;total persons
Rev. Msgr. Michael Howell, Chairman
Marty Wind, CEO/COO
Marty Wind, President
Russ Martin, Operations Dir
Marty Wind, General Manager
Marty Wind, Station Manager
Russ Martin, Programming Director
Russ Martin, PromotionsManager
Russ Martin, News Director
Marty Wind, Engineering Dir
Marty Wind, Chief Engineer
Russ Martin, Underwriting Director

KMIQ
07-23-1989; 104.9 MHz FM; 31 kw; 482 ft.; N27 46 35 W97 55 10
115 West Avenue D, Robstown, TX 78380 US
(361) 289-8877; *Fax:* (361) 289-7722
License: Robstown, Nueces County, TX held by Cotton Broadcasting.
Arbitron Metro Market: Corpus Christi, TX; *Format:* Tejano
Special Programming: Relg 6 hrs wkly; *Target Audience:* 18 plus.
Carlo Lopez, General Manager
Santos Leal, Programming Director

KSAB
10-13-1966; 99.9 MHz FM; 100 kw; 932 ft.; N27 45 7 W97 38 17
501 Tupper Lane, Corpus Christi, TX 78417 US
(361) 289-0111; *Fax:* (361) 289-5035
www.ksabfm.com
ksab@clearchannel.com
License: Robstown, Nueces County, TX held by Capstar TX LLC
Group Owner: iHeartMedia; (acq 8-30-00; grpsl)
Arbitron Metro Market: Corpus Christi, TX; *Format:* Tejano
Billy Santiago, Operations Manager
John Richards, General Manager
Chris Aldrich, General Sales Mgr
Dan Pena, Programming Director

Rockdale

KRXT
02-27-1989; 98.5 MHz FM; *Hrs Open:* 24 hrs; 6 kw; 328 ft.; N30 38 32 W97 2 13
P. O. Box 1560, Rockdale, TX 76567 US
(512) 446-6985; *Fax:* (512) 446-6987
www.krxt985.com
License: Rockdale, Milam County, TX held by KRXT Inc.
Regional Network: Texas State Networks
Arbitron Metro Market: Rockdale, TX; *Format:* Country; *Hrs. of News Programming:* news progmg 20 hrs wkly; *No. News Employees:* 1; *Target Audience:* General.; *Adv. Rates:* 11.50;11.50;11.50;11.50
Charles McGregor, President
Dave Gonnella, General Sales Mgr

Rockport

KKPN
10-01-1986; 102.3 MHz FM; *Hrs Open:* 24; 50 kw; 446 ft.; N27 52 2 W97 13 7
7755 Carondelet Avenue, Clayton, MO 63105 US
(361) 814-3800; *Fax:* (361) 855-3770
www.planet1023.com
License: Rockport, Aransas County, TX held by Convergent Broadcasting Corpus Christi LP.
Group Owner: Convergent Broadcasting LP; (acq 1-12-2004; grpsl).
Arbitron Metro Market: Corpus Christi, TX; *Format:* Contemporary Hits/Top 40; *Target Audience:* Adult; 18-49
Mark White, General Manager
Dallas Garcia, General Sales Mgr
Scott Holt, Programming Director
William Hooper, Chief Engineer

Rollingwood

KJCE
08-12-1958; 1370 kHz AM
4301 Westbrook Drive, Building B 3rd Floor, Austin, TX 78746 US
(512) 327-9595; *Fax:* (512) 329-6255
License: Rollingwood, TX held by Entercom Austin License LLC
Group Owner: Entercom Communications Corp.; .
Nat'l Network: Westwood One; ABC; Salem Radio Network;
Regional Network: Texas State Networks
Arbitron Metro Market: Austin, TX; *Format:* Talk; *Hrs. of News Programming:* news progmg 10 hrs wkly; *No. News Employees:* 1; *Target Audience:* Males 18-54.
Jenelle Schargios, General Manager

Roma

*KRIO-FM
04-30-1983; 97.7 MHz FM; *Hrs Open:* 18; 3 kw; 298 ft; N26 24 22 W99 00 37
4300 S US Highway 281, Edinburg, TX 78539
(956) 380-3435; *Fax:* (956) 380-8156
www.radioesperanza.com
correo@radioesperanza.com
License: Roma, Starr County, TX held by Rio Grande Bible Institute
Nat'l Network: CNN Radio
Population Served: 50,000 *Target Audience:* General; Sp speaking audience
Arturo Gonzalez, General Manager

Rosenberg-Richmond

KQUE
11-15-1948; 980 kHz AM; *Hrs Open:* 24
5100 S.W. Fwy., Houston, TX 77056 US
(713) 589-1336; *Fax:* (713) 589-1335
www.radioaleluya.org
License: Rosenberg-Richmond, Fort Bend County, TX held by Daij Media LLC
Group Owner: Daij Media LLC; (acq 12-16-2011)
Arbitron Metro Market: Pasadena, TX; *Format:* Religious
Ruben Villarreal, General Manager

Round Rock

KFMK
10-01-1998; 105.9 MHz FM; 4.5 kw; 1302 ft.; N30 19 23 W97 47 58
3600 N. Capital of Texas Hwy., Suite A200, Austin, TX 78746 US
(512) 329-4400; *Fax:* (512) 329-4380
www.spirit1059.com
comments@spirit1059.com
License: Round Rock, Williamson County, TX held by CRISTA Ministries
Group Owner: CRISTA Broadcasting; (acq 7-30-2008; grpsl)
Arbitron Metro Market: Austin, TX; *Format:* Christian
Mel Jones, General Sales Mgr
Channah Hanberg, Digital Sales Manager
Ann Marie E. Mulholland, Director of Sales
Rick Hart, Regional Sales Executive

*KNLE-FM
08-17-1981; 88.1 MHz FM; *Hrs Open:* 24; 3 kw; 233 ft.; N30 26 58 W97 39 44
Mailing Address: 12703 Research Blvd, Suite 222, Austin, TX 78759 US
Second Address: 12703 Research Dr., Suite 222, Austin, TX 78759
(512) 257-8881; *Fax:* (512) 257-8880
www.candle88.com
License: Round Rock, Williamson County, TX held by Ixoye Productions Inc.
Arbitron Metro Market: Austin, TX; *Format:* Adult Contemp
Special Programming: Children 4 hrs wkly; *Hrs. of News Programming:* News progmg 6 hrs wkly; *Target Audience:* 18-49; primarily female
Sherland Priest, General Manager

Rudolph

*KTER
90.7 MHz FM; *Hrs Open:* 24; 2.4 kw; 282 ft.; N26 41 13 W97 45 52
4501 West Expressway 83, Harlingen, TX 78552 US
(956) 412-5600; *Fax:* (956) 428-7556
License: Rudolph, Kenedy County, TX held by Faith Pleases God Church Corp.
Format: Christian *Special Programming:* Children 4 hrs wkly; *Target Audience:* General.
Aracelis Ortiz, CEO
Clark Ortiz, President
Tonya Porter, Operations Dir
Ricardo Mejia, General Manager

Rusk

KTLU
01-01-1955; 1580 kHz AM; *Hrs Open:* 24; 0.84 kw-D, ND1; 0.165 kw-N, ND1; N31 49 12 W95 10 19
Mailing Address: P. O. Box 475, Rusk, TX 75785 US
Second Address: 618 N. Main St., Rusk, TX 75785
(903) 586-7771(903) 683-2257; *Fax:* (903) 683-5104
kwrw@mediactr.com
License: Rusk, TX held by E.H. Whitehead.
Nat'l Network: ABC; *Regional Network:* Texas State Networks
Arbitron Metro Market: Tyler-Longview, TX; *Format:* Oldies
Special Programming: Sp 10 hrs wkly; *Hrs. of News Programming:* news progmg 3 hrs wkly; *No. News Employees:* 1; *Target Audience:* 35-65.
Marie Whitehead, President
Robert Gonzalez, General Manager

KWRW
07-01-1981; 97.7 MHz FM; *Hrs Open:* 24; 14.5 kw; 407 ft.; N31 49 12 W95 10 19
Mailing Address: Box 475, Rusk, TX 75785 US
Second Address: 618 N. Main St., Rusk, TX 75785
(903) 586-7771; *Fax:* (903) 683-5104
License: Rusk, Cherokee County, TX held by Marie Whitehead
Arbitron Metro Market: Rusk, TX *Special Programming:* Sp 10 hrs wkly; *Target Audience:* 25-54.; *Adv. Rates:* 9; 8; 9; 7.50
William Kling, President

San Angelo

KCRN
01-01-1947; 1340 kHz AM; *Hrs Open:* 24; 1 kw-U; N31 28 43 W100 27 50
Mailing Address: 750 Staint Paul St., Suite 1050, Dallas, TX 75201 US
Second Address: 17 S. Chadbourne, Suite 500, San Angelo, TX 76903
(325) 655-6917
www.kcrn.org
License: San Angelo, Tom Green County, TX held by First Dallas Media Inc
Group Owner: Criswell Communications

Population Served: 100,000; *Arbitron Metro Market:* San Angelo, TX; *Hrs. of News Programming:* News progmg 2 hrs wkly; *Target Audience:* 35-54; adults with children in the home
John Grabie, President
Sharon Geiger, Operations Dir
Mark Mohr, General Manager
Mark Mohr, Programming Director
Keith Mayo, Chief Engineer

***KCRN-FM**
02-01-1965; 93.9 MHz FM; *Hrs Open:* 24; 100 kw; 650 ft.; N31 42 11 W100 19 20
750 staint paul st., Suite 1050, Dallas, TX 75261 US
(325) 655-6917
www.kcrn.org
License: San Angelo, Tom Green County, TX held by Criswell College
Group Owner: Criswell Communications; (acq 6-18-91; $350,000 with co-located AM;
Population Served: 100,000; *Arbitron Metro Market:* San Angelo, TX; *Format:* Christian, Religious; *Hrs. of News Programming:* News progmg 2 hrs wkly; *Target Audience:* 25 plus.
Mark Mohr, Station Manager
Rachel Mohr, Administrative Assistant
Roland Nadeau, Business Underwriter
Steve Hayes, Production Director

KDCD
06-01-1980; 92.9 MHz FM; 100 kw; 600 ft.; N31 26 8 W100 34 8
3298 Sherwood Way, San Angelo, TX 76901 US
(325) 947-0899; *Fax:* (325) 947-0996
terry.radio@lonestarmix.com
License: San Angelo, Tom Green County, TX held by Four R Broadcasting Inc.
Arbitron Metro Market: San Angelo, TX; *Format:* Country *Special Programming:* Relg 2 hrs wkly; *Target Audience:* 18-49.
Frank De Francesco, President
Chris Ling, General Manager
Paul Gibson, Programming Director

KELI
11-01-1986; 98.7 MHz FM; *Hrs Open:* 24; 93 kw; 1289 ft.; N31 22 1 W100 2 48
P.O. Box 3834, 910 W. 14th, San Angelo, TX 76902 US
(325) 655-7161; *Fax:* (325) 658-7377
www.bob987.com
License: San Angelo, Tom Green County, TX held by Townsquare Media San Angelo License LLC
Group Owner: Townsquare Media; (acq 3-15-2006; grpsl)
Arbitron Metro Market: San Angelo, TX; *Format:* Adult Contemp *Special Programming:* Relg 6 hrs wkly; *Hrs. of News Programming:* news progmg 6 hrs wkly; *No. News Employees:* 1; *Target Audience:* 25-54.
John Flint, General Manager
Boomer Kingston, Brand Manager
Shannon Lewis, Digital Managin Editor

KGKL
12-04-1928; 960 kHz AM
Mailing Address: P. O. Box 1878, San Angelo, TX 76902 US
Second Address: 1301 S. Abe, San Angelo, TX 76903
(325) 655-7161; *Fax:* (325) 658-7377
960kgkl.com
boomerkingston@townsquaremedia.com;
dewey.weaver@townsquaremedia.com;
ashley.haney@townsquaremedia.c
License: San Angelo, TX held by Townsquare Media San Angelo License LLC
Group Owner: Townsquare Media; (acq 3-15-2006; grpsl)
Nat'l Reps: Katz Radio
Arbitron Metro Market: San Angelo, TX; *Format:* News, Sports, 86 *Special Programming:* Farm 6 hrs wkly; *Hrs. of News Programming:* News progmg 10 hrs wkly; *Target Audience:* 35 plus.
John Flint, General Manager
Boomer Kingston, Brand Manager
Shannon Lewis, Digital Managing Editor

KGKL-FM
12-24-1965; 97.5 MHz FM; *Hrs Open:* 24; 100 kw; 410 ft.; N31 29 46 W100 24 50
Mailing Address: P. O. Box 1878, San Angelo, TX 76902 US
Second Address: 1301 S. Abe, San Angelo, TX 76903
(325) 655-7161; *Fax:* (325) 658-7377
www.975kgkl.com
License: San Angelo, Tom Green County, TX held by Townsquare Media San Angelo License LLC
Group Owner: Townsquare Media
Nat'l Network: ABC
Arbitron Metro Market: San Angelo, TX; *Format:* Country; *Hrs. of News Programming:* News progmg 3 hrs wkly; *Target Audience:* 25-54.
John Flint, General Manager
Boomer Kingston, Brand Manager
Shannon Lewis, Digital Managing Editor

KIXY-FM
10-01-1966; 94.7 MHz FM; *Hrs Open:* 24; 100 kw; 358 ft.; N31 29 14 W100 26 57
2824 Sherwood Way, San Angelo, TX 76901 US
(325) 949-3333
www.kixyfm.com
kixy@kixyfm.com
License: San Angelo, Tom Green County, TX
Group Owner: Foster Communications Co. Inc.
Nat'l Network: CNN Radio; *Nat'l Reps:* McGavren Guild
Arbitron Metro Market: San Angelo, TX; *Format:* Adult Contemp, Contemporary Hits/Top 40; *No. News Employees:* 1; *Target Audience:* 18-49.
Shannon Roach, CFO
David Carr, Programming Director

KKSA
1260 kHz AM; *Hrs Open:* 24; 0.54 kw-D, ND2; 0.071 kw-N, ND2; N31 29 14 W100 26 57
Mailing Address: P.O. Box 2191, San Angelo, TX 76902 US
Second Address: 2824 Sherwood Way, San Angelo, TX 76901
(325) 944-0851; *Fax:* (325) 944-0851
www.kksa-am.com
kixy@kixyfm.com
License: San Angelo, TX held by Foster Communications Company Inc.
Group Owner: Foster Communications Co. Inc.; (acq 4-9-84).
Nat'l Network: Westwood One; Fox News; Fox Sports; Dial Global; Premiere Radio; *Regional Network:* Texas State Networks; *Nat'l Reps:* McGavren Guild; *Wire Services:* UPI
Arbitron Metro Market: San Angelo, TX; *Format:* News, News/Talk, 84, Talk; *Hrs. of News Programming:* news progmg 20 hrs wkly; *No. News Employees:* 1; *Target Audience:* 25-54.
Fred Key, President/CEO
Rick Mantooth, VP/GM
John Flint, General Sales Mgr
David Carr, Programming Director
Jeff Rottman, News Director
Gary Smith, Chief Engineer

KMDX
12-05-1998; 106.1 MHz FM; 50 kw; 456 ft.; N31 26 8 W100 34 8
3298 Sherwood Way, San Angelo, TX 76901 US
(325) 947-0899; *Fax:* (325) 947-0996
License: San Angelo, Tom Green County, TX held by Four R Broadcasting Inc.
Nat'l Network: Jones Radio Networks; *Nat'l Reps:* Interep
Arbitron Metro Market: San Angelo, TX; *Format:* Adult Contemp; *No. News Employees:* 1; *Target Audience:* 25-54.
Frank De Francesco, President
Aaron Harris, Operations Dir
Terry Hucks, General Manager
Biss Casey, News Director
Len Martinez, Engineering Dir
Debbie Smith, Traffic Manager

KSJT-FM
10-07-1985; 107.5 MHz FM; *Hrs Open:* 24; 100 kw; 604 ft.; N31 26 19 W100 34 18
207 W Bearegard, San Angelo, TX 76903 US
(325) 655-1717; *Fax:* (325) 6557-0601
www.k107.net/K107-Guestbook.php
License: San Angelo, Tom Green County, TX held by La Unica Broadcasting Co.
Arbitron Metro Market: San Angelo, TX; *Target Audience:* 18-55.
Louis Perez, President
Armando Martinez, Station Manager
Cody Austin, General Sales Mgr
Arturo Madrid, News Director
Dania Salas, Traffic Manager

***KNCH(FM)**
04-01-1996; 90.1 MHz FM; 5 kw; 909 ft; N31 35 21 W100 31 00
Rebroadcasts: Rebroadcasts KUT(FM) Austin 100%
1 University Station A 0704, Univ. of Texas, Austin, TX 78712-1090
(512) 471-1631
kut@kut.org
License: San Angelo, Tom Green County, TX held by University of Texas at Austin.
Nat'l Network: NPR; PRI
Population Served: 100,000; *Arbitron Metro Market:* San Angelo, TX *Special Programming:* Folk 4 hrs, blues 6 hrs wkly; *Target Audience:* 25-54; educated opinions, leaders and arts community
Stewart Vanderwilt, General Manager

KWFR
11-01-1995; 101.9 MHz FM; *Hrs Open:* 24; 100 kw; 341 ft.; N31 29 29 W100 26 3
Mailing Address: 2824 Sherwood Way, San Angelo, TX 76901 US
Second Address: KIXY Complex, 2824 Sherwood Way, San Angelo, TX 76901
(325) 949-3333; *Fax:* (325) 944-0851
www.kwfrfm.com
License: San Angelo, Tom Green County, TX held by Foster Communications Co. Inc.
Group Owner: Foster Communications Co. Inc.; acq 12-1-94; $219,000 with KFXJ(FM) Abilene;
Nat'l Reps: McGavren Guild
Arbitron Metro Market: San Angelo, TX; *Format:* Classic Rock; *No. News Employees:* 1
Fred Key, President
Jay Michaels, Operations Dir
Doug Smith, General Sales Mgr
Chase O'Reily, Programming Director
Jeff Rottman, News Director
Adolph Ganza, Chief Engineer

KCLL
08-17-1995; 100.1 MHz FM; *Hrs Open:* 24; 50 kw; 385 ft.; N31 31 49 W100 29 5
422 N. Van Buren St., San Angelo, TX 76901 US
(325) 949-3333; *Fax:* (325) 944-0851
www.kcll-fm.com
License: San Angelo, Tom Green County, TX held by Foster Communications Co. Inc.
Group Owner: Foster Communications Co. Inc.; (acq 5-19-2004; $450,000).
Arbitron Metro Market: San Angelo, TX; *Format:* Tejano; *Target Audience:* 18-49; Hispanics, demographics
Fred M. Key, CEO/COO
Fred Key, President
Jay Michaels, General Manager
John Flynt, General Sales Mgr
Juan Vela, Programming Director
Freddy Maskill, Promotions Manager
Jeff Rottman, News Director

***KNAR**
01-01-2006; 89.3 MHz FM; 1 kw; 801 ft.; N31 41 59 W100 26 30
Rebroadcasts: Rebroadcasts KLRD(FM) Yucaipa, CA 100%
188 South Bellevue, Suite 222, Memphis, TN 38104 US
(888) 937-2471; *Fax:* (916) 251-1650
www.air1.com
info@air1.com
License: San Angelo, Tom Green County, TX held by Educational Media Foundation.
Group Owner: EMF Broadcasting; (acq 9-22-2005; $40,000 for CP).
Nat'l Network: Air 1
Arbitron Metro Market: San Angelo, TX; *Format:* Alternative, Christian
Darrell Chambliss, Chairman
Alan Mason, COO
Mike Novak, President and CEO
David Pierce, Programming Director
Ed Lenane, News Director
Sam Wallington, Engineering Dir
Marya Morgan, News Reporter
Richard Hunt, News Reporter
Eric Moser, Chief Financial Officer
Brian Burger, Vice President of Human Resources
D. Kevin Blair, Secretary and General Counsel
Larry Moody, Director

***KLTP**
01-01-2008; 90.9 MHz FM; 2.915 kw; 627 ft.; N31 25 16 W100 32 36
US
(325) 673-3045; *Fax:* (325) 672-7938
www.kgnz.com
studio@kgnz.com
License: San Angelo, Tom Green County, TX held by Christian Broadcasting Co. Inc.
Arbitron Metro Market: San Angelo, TX; *Format:* Christian
Gary Hill, General Manager

San Antonio

KAJA
01-01-1951; 97.3 MHz FM; *Hrs Open:* 24; 98 kw; 984 ft.; N29 31 25 W98 43 25
6222 Interstate 10 Frontage Rd., San Antonio, TX 78201 US
(210) 736-9700; *Fax:* (210) 735-8811
www.kj97.com

License: San Antonio, Bexar County, TX held by CC Licenses LLC
Group Owner: iHeartMedia
Nat'l Reps: Clear Channel
Arbitron Metro Market: San Antonio, TX; *Format:* Country; *Hrs. of News Programming:* News progmg 2 hrs wkly; *Target Audience:* 18-54.
Marlene Trevino, Market President
Julie Miller, Vice President of Sales
Lance Tidwell, Programming Director
Vanessa Garcia, Promotions Director

KCHL

06-01-1960; 1480 kHz AM; *Hrs Open:* 15; 2.5 kW; N29 24 45 W98 24 52
1211 W Hein Rd, San Antonio, TX 78220 USA
(210) 333-0050; *Fax:* (210) 333-0081
www.kchl.org
kchlradio@yahoo.com
License: San Antonio, TX held by Martin Broadcasting Inc.
Group Owner: Martin Broadcasting Inc.; acq 6-4-92;
Nat'l Reps: McGavren Guild
Arbitron Metro Market: San Antonio, TX; *Format:* Gospel; *No. News Employees:* 1; *Target Audience:* 25-54.

KCOR

02-01-1946; 1350 kHz AM; 5 kw-D, DAN; 5 kw-N, DAN; N29 31 27 W98 37 5
12451 Network Blvd., San Antonio, TX 78249 US
(210) 610-4300
www.univision.com
License: San Antonio, Bexar County, TX held by Tichenor License Corp.
Group Owner: Univision Radio; (acq 9-22-2003; grpsl)
Arbitron Metro Market: San Antonio, TX; *Format:* News, News/Talk, 82, Talk; *Target Audience:* 25-54; adults
Chris Morris, Vice President and General Manager

KCYY

06-25-1966; 100.3 MHz FM; *Hrs Open:* 24; 98 kw; 984 ft.; N29 31 25 W98 43 25
8122 Datapoint Dr., Suite 600, San Antonio, TX 78229 US
(210) 615-5400; *Fax:* (210) 615-5300
www.y100fm.com
yvonne.gutierrez@coxinc.com
License: San Antonio, Bexar County, TX
Group Owner: Cox Radio Inc.
Arbitron Metro Market: San Antonio, TX; *Format:* Country; *No. News Employees:* 1; *Target Audience:* 25-54.
Jeff Garrison, Operations/Programming Director
Mary Rogers, Director of Sales
Jim Dyer, General Sales Manager
Lena Rodriguez, Sales Operations Manager
Yvnne Gutierrez, Promotions Director
Alfonso Monteamyor, Digital SalesManager
Dan Lawrie, VP/Market Manager

KEDA

03-17-1966; 1540 kHz AM; 5 kw-D, DA2; 1 kw-N, DA2; N29 21 30 W98 21 5
1246 W. Laurel Street, San Antonio, TX 78201 US
(210) 226-5254
www.kedaradio.com
License: San Antonio, TX held by D & E Broadcasting Co.
Regional Network: Texas State Networks
Arbitron Metro Market: San Antonio, TX; *Format:* Tejano *Special Programming:* Salsa 4 hrs wkly; *Target Audience:* 25-54.
Belinda Aguilar, Secretary/Traffic

KRDY

11-13-1961; 1160 kHz AM; *Hrs Open:* 24; 10 kw-D, DA2; 1 kw-N, DA2; N29 32 11 W98 41 11
5400 Fredericksburg Rd., San Antonio, TX 78229 US
(210) 530-5360; *Fax:* (210) 530-5304
www.radio.disney.com
License: San Antonio, TX held by Radio Disney Group LLC.
Group Owner: ABC Inc.; (acq 5-30-2003; $3.2 million).
Nat'l Network: Radio Disney
Arbitron Metro Market: San Antonio, TX; *Format:* Children
Fred Stockwell, General Manager

KFIT EXP S

01-01-1989; 1060 kHz AM; *Hrs Open:* 6 AM-8 PM; 1 kw-D, DA; N29 17 32 W98 31 57 *Rebroadcasts:* Rebroadcasts KFIT(AM) Lockhart
Mailing Address: 110 Wild Basin Rd., Box 160158, Lockhart, TX 78746
Second Address: 110 Wild Basin Rd., Suite 375, Austin, TX 78716
(512) 328-8400; *Fax:* (512) 328-8437
License: San Antonio, Bexar County, TX held by KFIT Inc.

Population Served: 500,000; *Arbitron Metro Market:* San Antonio, TX; *Format:* Gospel
Rev. Darrell Martin, General Manager
Terri Lewis, Programming Director

KISS-FM

12-01-1946; 99.5 MHz FM; *Hrs Open:* 24; 97.7 kw; 1486 ft.; N29 16 29 W98 15 52
3773 Howard Hughes Pwy, Suite 300, Las Vegas, NV 89109 US
(210) 615-4500; *Fax:* (210) 615-5331
www.kissrocks.com
ben.reed@coxinc.com
License: San Antonio, Bexar County, TX held by Cox Radio Inc.
Group Owner: Cox Radio Inc.; (acq 8-4-97; grpsl)
Nat'l Reps: Christal
Arbitron Metro Market: San Antonio, TX; *Format:* Classic Rock; *Target Audience:* 18-44; men
Keith Hastings, Program Director
Ben Reid, Vice President / Marketing Manager
Jeff Garrison, Operations Manager
Mary Rogers, Director Of Sales

KKYX

01-01-1926; 680 kHz AM; *Hrs Open:* 24
8122 Datapoint Drive, Suite 600, San Antonio, TX 78229 US
(210) 615-5400; *Fax:* (210) 615-5300
www.kkyx.com
ben.reed@coxinc.com
License: San Antonio, TX held by Cox Radio Inc.
Group Owner: Cox Radio Inc.; (acq 3-28-97; grpsl)
Arbitron Metro Market: San Antonio, TX; *Format:* Country *Special Programming:* Pub affrs 2 hrs wkly; *Hrs. of News Programming:* news progmg 3 hrs wkly; *No. News Employees:* 1; *Target Audience:* 35-64
Roger Allen, Program Director
Ben Reed, Vice President / Market Manager
Jeff Garrison, Operations Manager
Mary Rogers, Director Of Sales
Jim Dyer, General Sales Manager

KONO

01-17-1927; 860 Hz AM; *Hrs Open:* 24; 5 kw-D, 1 kw-N, DA-N; N29 26 14 W98 25 19
8122 Datapoint Dr., Suite 600, San Antonio, TX 78229 US
(210) 646-0105; *Fax:* (210) 615-5300
www.kono1011.com
ben.reed@coxinc.com
License: San Antonio, Bexar County, TX held by Cox Radio Inc.
Group Owner: Cox Radio Inc.; (acq 2-12-98; $23 million with KONO
Population Served: 1,300,000; *Arbitron Metro Market:* San Antonio, TX; *Format:* Contemporary Hits/Top 40; *Hrs. of News Programming:* news progmg one hr wkly; *No. News Employees:* 1; *Target Audience:* 25-64; totalaudience appeal
Ben Reed, Vice President / Market Manager
Jeff Garrison, Operations Manager
Mary Rogers, Director Of Sales
Jim Dyer, General Sales Manager

*KPAC

11-07-1982; 88.3 MHz FM; *Hrs Open:* 24; kw
8401 Datapoint Dr. #1050, San Antonio, TX 78229 US
(210) 614-8977; *Fax:* (210) 614-8983
www.tpr.org
info@tpr.org
License: San Antonio, Bexar County, TX held by Texas Public Radio.
Nat'l Network: PRI
Arbitron Metro Market: San Antonio, TX; *Format:* Talk; *Hrs. of News Programming:* News progmg 3 hrs wkly; *Target Audience:* 25 plus; educated, upscale financially, mature, influential opinion leaders
Dan Skinner, President
Laverne Ditts, General Sales Mgr
Nathan Cone, Programming Director
Wayne Coble, Engineering Dir
Randy Anderson, Music Director
Janet Grojean, Sales

KQXT-FM

11-19-1967; 101.9 MHz FM; *Hrs Open:* 24; 100 kw; 663 ft.; N29 25 6 W98 29 1
6222 Interstate 10 Frontage Rd., San Antonio, TX 78201 US
(210) 736-9700; *Fax:* (210) 735-8811
www.q1019.com
License: San Antonio, Bexar County, TX held by CC Licenses LLC
Group Owner: iHeartMedia; (acq 1-27-93; $8 million;
Regional Reps: Clear Channel.
Arbitron Metro Market: San Antonio, TX; *Format:* Adult Contemp *Special Programming:* Contemp jazz 4 hrs, relg 2 hrs, pub affrs one hr w; *Hrs. of News Programming:* news progmg 2 hrs wkly;

No. News Employees: 1 *Target Audience:* 25-54; core target is women 30-44
Marlene Trevino, Market President
Julie Miller, Vice President of Sales
Chase Murphy, Programming Director
Raven Riojas, Promotions Director
Sochy Ortiz, Media Integration Coordinator
Linda Lynn, PSA Director

KROM

06-01-1947; 92.9 MHz FM; 45 kw; 1,352 ft.; N29 16 29 W98 15 52
12451 Network Blvd., Suite 140, San Antonio, TX 78249 US
(210) 610-4300
www.univision.com
License: San Antonio, Bexar County, TX held by Tichenor License Corp.
Group Owner: Univision Radio
Arbitron Metro Market: San Antonio, TX; *Format:* Tejano; *Target Audience:* 19-49; male
Chris Morris, Vice President and General Manager

*KRTU-FM

01-22-1976; 91.7 MHz FM; *Hrs Open:* 24; 8.9 kw; 118 ft.; N29 27 51 W98 28 56
715 Stadium Drive, San Antonio, TX 78284 US
(210) 999-8917; *Fax:* (210) 999-8355
www.krtu.org
krtu@trinity.edu
License: San Antonio, Bexar County, TX held by Trinity University
Arbitron Metro Market: San Antonio, TX; *Format:* Jazz *Special Programming:* student alt-rock overnight; *Target Audience:* well-connected, community-oriented opinion leaders; broad spectrum of ages, skewing 35-64;innovator; *Adv. Rates:* 210-999-8337 - Kate Rawley-War
Rob Huesca, Operations Dir
William Christ, General Manager
Chris Karcher, General Sales Mgr
Ron Nirenberg, Programming Director
Kate Rawley-Warters, Director of Development
Alfredo Cruz, Music Director

KSLR

12-26-1926; 630 kHz AM; *Hrs Open:* 24; 5 kw-D, DA2; 4.3 kw-N, DA2; N29 23 29 W98 21 0; N29 31 50 W98 7 13
4880 Santa Rosa Rd #300, Camarillo, CA 93012 US
(210) 344-8481; *Fax:* (210) 340-1213
www.kslr.com
kslr@kslr.com
License: San Antonio, TX held by Salem Media of Texas Inc.
Group Owner: Salem Communications Corp.; (acq 8-6-94)
Nat'l Network: Salem Radio Network
Arbitron Metro Market: San Antonio, TX; *Format:* Christian, Talk *Special Programming:* Sp 18 hrs wkly; *No. News Employees:* 1; *Target Audience:* 18-54; women & families
Baron Wiley, Operations Dir
David Ziebell, General Manager
James Herring, General Sales Mgr

KSMG

09-09-1970; 105.3 MHz FM; *Hrs Open:* 24; 97.5 kw; 1486 ft.; N29 16 29 W98 15 52
8122 Datapoint Drive, Suite 600, San Antonio, TX 78229 US
(210) 615-5400; *Fax:* (210) 615-5331
www.magic1053.com
jeff.garrison@coxinc.com
License: San Antonio, Brazia County, TX held by Cox Radio Inc.
Group Owner: Cox Radio Inc.; (acq 8-4-97; grpsl)
Nat'l Reps: Christal
Arbitron Metro Market: San Antonio, TX; *Format:* Adult Contemp; *Hrs. of News Programming:* news progmg 5 hrs wkly; *No. News Employees:* 1; *Target Audience:* 25-49; females
Jeff Garrison, Operations Manager / Program Director
Ben Reed, Vice President / Market Manager
Mary Rogers, Director Of Sales
Jim Dyer, General Sales Manager
Tori Finch, Promotions Manager

*KSTX

10-01-1988; 89.1 MHz FM; *Hrs Open:* 24; kw
8401 Datapoint Drive, San Antonio, TX 78229 US
(210) 614-8977; *Fax:* (210) 614-8983
www.tpr.org
info@tpr.org
License: San Antonio, Bexar County, TX held by Texas Public Radio.
Nat'l Network: NPR; PRI; *Wire Services:* AP
Arbitron Metro Market: San Antonio, TX; *Format:* News *Special Programming:* Jazz 6 hrs, var talk 6 hrs, folk 5 hrs, blues 6 hrs wkly; *Hrs. of News Programming:* news progmg 67 hrs wkly; *No.*

News Employees: 5 *Target Audience:* 25 plus; educated, upscale financially, influential opinion leaders
Pat MacGowan, Chairman
Dan Skinner, CEO/COO
Dan Skinner, President
Laverne Pitts, General Sales Mgr
Nathan Cone, Programming Director
Dave Davies, News Director
Wayne Coble, Engineering Dir
Janet Grojean, Sales

***KSYM-FM**
09-15-1966; 90.1 MHz FM; *Hrs Open:* 24; 5.7 kw; 128 ft.; N29 26 50 W98 29 55
1300 San Pedro Avenue, San Antonio, TX 78212 US
(210) 733-2787; *Fax:* (210) 486-1373
www.ksym.org
License: San Antonio, Bexar County, TX held by San Antonio College.
Arbitron Metro Market: San Antonio, TX; *Format:* Alternative, Triple A; *Target Audience:* 12-54; depending on block format;
Adv. Rates: 15; 15; 20; 15
John Onderdonk, General Manager
Marlene Romo, General Sales Mgr
Charlie Castleman, Programming Director
Victor Pfau, Chief Engineer
Chelsea Owen-Music Director, Music Director

KJXK
01-01-1969; 102.7 MHz FM; 100 kw; 663 ft.; N29 25 6 W98 29 1
4050 Eisenhauer Rd., San Antonio, TX 78218 US
(210) 654-5100; *Fax:* (210) 855-5056
www.hellojack.com
License: San Antonio, Bexar County, TX held by Alpha Media Licensee LLC
Group Owner: Alpha Media LLC
Arbitron Metro Market: San Antonio, TX; *Format:* Contemporary Hits/Top 40; *Target Audience:* 12 plus.
Greg Martin, General Manager
Janie Lees, Sales Manager
Pat Cerullo, Programming Director

KTKR
05-10-1984; 760 kHz AM; *Hrs Open:* 24
3305 W. Mountain Rd, #60, Las Vegas, NV 89102 US
(210) 736-9700; *Fax:* (210) 735-8811
www.ticket760.com
License: San Antonio, TX held by CC Licenses LLC
Group Owner: iHeartMedia; (acq 6-16-93; $800,000;
Nat'l Network: Westwood One; *Nat'l Reps:* Clear Channel
Arbitron Metro Market: San Antonio, TX; *Format:* Sports; *Target Audience:* 25-49; male
Marlene Trevino, Market President
Julie Miller, Vice President of Sales

KTSA
05-09-1922; 550 kHz AM; *Hrs Open:* 24; 5 kw-D, DAN; 5 kw-N; N29 29 46 W98 24 54
4050 Eisenhauer Rd., San Antonio, TX 78218 US
(210) 654-5100; *Fax:* (210) 855-5016
www.ktsa.com
License: San Antonio, Bexar County, TX held by Alpha Media Licensee LLC
Group Owner: Alpha Media LLC; (acq 1-31-2014; grpsl).
Arbitron Metro Market: San Antonio, TX; *Format:* News, News/Talk, 86; *Hrs. of News Programming:* news progmg 35 hrs wkly; *No. News Employees:* 11; *Target Audience:* 25-54.
Greg Martin, General Manager and Program Director
Coreena Hazelett, Sales Manager
Bill O'Neil, News Director

KAHL
01-01-1948; 1310 kHz AM; *Hrs Open:* 24; 5 kw-D, DA2; 0.28 kw-N, DA2; N29 24 53 W98 20 36
3102 Oak Lawn Ave., Suite 215, Dallas, TX 75219 US
(210) 341-1310; *Fax:* (210) 341-1777
www.call1310.com
info@call1310.com
License: San Antonio, TX held by Pearsall RadioWorks Ltd.
Nat'l Reps: McGavren Guild
Arbitron Metro Market: San Antonio, TX; *Format:* Adult Contemp
John Barger, President
John Barger, Sales Representative

KXTN-FM
12-31-1967; 107.5 MHz FM; 95.1 kw; 1,486 ft.; N29 16 29 W98 15 52
12451 Network Blvd., Suite 140, San Antonio, TX 78249 US
(210) 610-4300
www.kxtn.com
License: San Antonio, Bexar County, TX held by Tichenor License Corp.
Group Owner: Univision Radio
Arbitron Metro Market: San Antonio, TX; *Format:* Tejano; *Target Audience:* 25-49; contemp Sp, affluent, upscale
Chris Morris, Manager
Barbara Carreon, Sales Manager
Jon Ramirez, Program Director and Music Director
Jennifer Gomez, Promotions Manager
Bret Huggins, Chief Engineer
Raul Faz, Digital Content Manager
Robert Morris, DigitalContent Manager
Veronica Ynclan, Research Director
Sonia Trevino, Business Manager

KXXM
05-05-1964; 96.1 MHz FM; *Hrs Open:* 24; 99 kw; 597 ft.; N29 38 1 W98 37 54
6222 Interstate 10 Frontage Rd., San Antonio, TX 78201 US
(210) 736-9700; *Fax:* (210) 736-8811
www.mix961.com
License: San Antonio, Bexar County, TX held by CC Licenses LLC
Group Owner: iHeartMedia; (acq 6-19-98; $15 million).
Arbitron Metro Market: San Antonio, TX; *Format:* Contemporary Hits/Top 40; *Hrs. of News Programming:* news progmg 3 hrs wkly; *No. News Employees:* 1; *Target Audience:* 18-34; females
Marlene Trevino, Market President
Stacy Beigel, Vice President of Sales
Chase Murphy, Programming Director
Raven Riojas, Promotions Director

***KYFS**
11-07-1982; 90.9 MHz FM; *Hrs Open:* 24; 100 kw; 476 ft.; N29 40 21 W98 14 49
9330 Corporate Dr., Schertz, TX 78154 US
(210) 651-9093
www.bbnradio.org
bbn@bbnmedia.org
License: San Antonio, Bexar County, TX held by Bible Broadcasting Network Inc.
Group Owner: Bible Broadcasting Network; acq 11-20-91; $75,000;
Arbitron Metro Market: Charlotte, NC; *Format:* Christian; *Target Audience:* 2 plus.
Jason Padgett, Operations Manager

KZDC
01-01-1953; 1250 kHz AM; *Hrs Open:* 24; 25 kw-D, DA2; 0.92 kw-N, DAN; N29 17 1 W98 28 28
4050 Eisenhauer Rd., San Antonio, TX 78218 US
(210) 654-5100; *Fax:* (210) 855-5076
www.espnsa.com
License: San Antonio, Bexar County, TX held by Alpha Media Licensee LLC
Group Owner: Alpha Media LLC; (acq 1-31-2014; grpsl).
Nat'l Network: ESPN Radio
Arbitron Metro Market: San Antonio, TX; *Format:* Sports
Greg Martin, General Manager and Program Director
Janie Lees, Sales Manager

KZEP-FM
10-01-1966; 104.5 MHz FM; *Hrs Open:* 24; 100 kw; 663 ft.; N29 25 6 W98 29 1
6222 Interstate 10 Frontage Rd., San Antonio, TX 78201 US
(210) 736-9700; *Fax:* (210) 735-8811
www.hot1045.com
License: San Antonio, Bexar County, TX held by Citicasters Licenses Inc.
Group Owner: iHeartMedia; (acq 7-29-2008; exchange for KVMX(FM) Bakersfield, CA and KWID(FM) Las Vegas, NV)
Nat'l Reps: D & R Radio
Arbitron Metro Market: San Antonio, TX; *Format:* Classic Rock; *Hrs. of News Programming:* news progmg 3 hrs wkly; *No. News Employees:* 1; *Target Audience:* 25-54; males
Marlene Trevino, Market President
Julie Miller, Vice President of Sales
Lance Tidwell, Senior Vice President of Programming

WOAI
09-29-1922; 1200 kHz AM; 50 kw-U, ND1; N29 30 7 W98 7 43
6222 Interstate 10 Frontage Rd., San Antonio, TX 78201 US
(210) 736-9700
www.woai.com
License: San Antonio, Bexar County, TX held by CC Licenses LLC
Group Owner: iHeartMedia; (acq 1975).
Nat'l Network: Fox News Radio; *Regional Network:* Texas State Networks; *Nat'l Reps:* Clear Channel; *Wire Services:* AP
Arbitron Metro Market: San Antonio, TX *TV Affiliate:* Talk; *Format:* News, News/Talk, 86 *Special Programming:* news progmg 20 hrs wkly; *Hrs. of News Programming:* 13; *No. News Employees:* 35-64; general
Brian Gann, Programming Director
Robbie Cantu, Promotions Director
Jim Forsyth, News Director
Marlene Trevino, Market President
Julie Miller, VP of Sales
Callie Hoch, Director of Marketing and Digital

KISS-FM
12-01-1946; 99.5 MHz FM; *Hrs Open:* 24; 97.7 kw; 1486 ft.; N29 16 29 W98 15 52
3773 Howard Hughes Pwy, Suite 300n, Las Vegas, NV 89109 US
(210) 646-0105; *Fax:* (210) 646-9711
www.kissrocks.com
License: San Antonio, Bexar County, TX held by Cox Radio Inc.
Group Owner: Cox Radio Inc.; (acq 8-4-97; grpsl)
Nat'l Reps: Christal
Arbitron Metro Market: San Antonio, TX; *Format:* Rock/AOR; *Target Audience:* 18-44; men
Ben Reid, Vice President / Market Manager
Keith Hastings, Program Director
Jeff Garrison, Operations Manager
Jim Dyer, General Sales Manager
Ric Gonzalez, Creative Services Director / Production

San Augustine

KXXE-FM
12-29-1993; 92.5 MHz FM; *Hrs Open:* 24; 2.55 kw; Ant 220 ft; N31 32 48 W94 05 47.2 *Rebroadcasts:* Rebroadcasts KDET(AM) Center 100%
307 San Augustine St., Center, TX 75935
(936) 598-3304; *Fax:* (936) 598-9537
www.cbc-radio.com
License: San Augustine, San Augustine County, TX held by Center Broadcasting Co. Inc.
Group Owner: Center Broadcasting Co. Inc.; acq 3-26-98; grpsl)
Nat'l Network: ABC; *Regional Network:* Texas State Networks
Population Served: 25,000 *Format:* Country; *No. News Employees:* 1; *Target Audience:* 35-65.
Lori Alvis, Sales
Jessie Jacobs, Programming Director
Joey Monk, News Director
Jessica Quigley, Traffic Manager

San Benito

KHKZ
09-10-1982; 106.3 MHz FM; *Hrs Open:* 24; 6.3 kw; 653 ft.; N26 8 33.3 W97 49 59.2
901 East Park Boulevard, Weslaco, TX 78596 US
(866) 973-1063
www.kiss1063.net
License: San Benito, Hidalgo County, TX held by Clear Channel Broadcasting Licenses Inc.
Group Owner: iHeartMedia; (acq 12-9-2003; grpsl).
Nat'l Network: USA
Arbitron Metro Market: McAllen-Brownsville-Harlingen, TX; *Format:* Adult Contemp *Special Programming:* Black 3 hrs, southern gospel 2 hrs, Christian rock 3 hrs wkly; *No. News Employees:* 3 *Target Audience:* General.
Billy Santiago, Senior Vice President of Programming
Evan Armstrong, Regional Market President

San Diego

KUKA
07-14-1993; 105.9 MHz FM; *Hrs Open:* 24; 10 kw; 413 ft.; N27 38 59 W98 7 44
P.O. Box 589, Alice, TX 78333 US
(361) 668-6666; *Fax:* (361) 668-6661
info@kuka.com
License: San Diego, Duval County, TX held by Claro Communications Ltd.
Group Owner: Claro Communications Ltd.; (acq 11-30-2007; $250,000)
Arbitron Metro Market: San Diego, TX; *Hrs. of News Programming:* news progmg one hr wkly; *No. News Employees:* 1; *Target Audience:* 18-34; middle to upper class; *Adv. Rates:* 15; 10; 15; 10
Estela Nava, Operations Dir
Teo Pena, General Manager
Zulema Marroquin, General Sales Mgr
Pedro Vasquez, Programming Director
Tio Pena, Promotions Manager
Peter Vasquez, News Director
Armando Marroquin Jr., Marketing Manager
Javier Villanueva, Regional Sales Manager

San Juan

KUBR
01-01-1991; 1210 kHz AM; *Hrs Open:* 24; 10 kw-D, DA2; 5 kw-N, DA2; N26 14 41 W98 5 25; N26 14 38 W98 5 25
PO Box 252, McAllen, TX 78505 US
(956) 686-6382; *Fax:* (956) 686-2999
www.laradiocristiana.com
paulinobernal@hotmail.com
License: San Juan, TX held by Paulino Bernal
Arbitron Metro Market: San Juan, TX; *Format:* Christian
Paulino Bernal, Owner

San Marcos

KBPA
01-01-1971; 103.5 MHz FM; *Hrs Open:* 24; 100 kw; 1257 ft.; N30 2 42 W97 52 50
8309 N. IH 35, Austin, TX 78753 USA
(512) 832-4000; *Fax:* (512) 832-4081
www.1035bobfm.com
bob@1035bobfm.com
License: San Marcos, Hays County, TX held by Emmis Austin Radio Broadcasting Company LP
Group Owner: Emmis Communications Corp.
Nat'l Reps: Clear Channel
Arbitron Metro Market: Austin, TX; *Format:* Adult Contemp; *Hrs. of News Programming:* news progmg 4 hrs wkly; *No. News Employees:* 1; *Target Audience:* 25-64.
Jeff Smulyan, Chairman & CEO

***KTSW**
04-15-1992; 89.9 MHz FM; *Hrs Open:* 24; 10.5 kw; 213 ft.; N29 39 20 W98 7 59
US
(512) 245-3490
www.ktsw.txstate.edu
ds46@txstate.edu
License: San Marcos, Hays County, TX held by Texas State University-San Marcos.
Arbitron Metro Market: Austin, TX; *Format:* Alternative, News, 62, Sports, Talk; *Hrs. of News Programming:* News progmg 9 hrs wkly; *Target Audience:* 18-24; college students & young adults
Dan Schumacher, General Manager
Melissa Bond, Station Manager
Conor Yarbrough, Programming Director
Will Sarver, Promotions Director
Reynaldo Leanos Jr., News Director
Andrea Windmeyer, Chief Engineer
Erin Cantu, OfficeManager
Juliana Jankowski, Production Director
Allison Johnson, Music Director
Warren Schorr, Sports Director
Jordan Gas-Poore, Web Content Manager
Ethan Vogt, Webmaster

San Saba

KNUZ
01-01-1996; 106.1 MHz FM; *Hrs Open:* 24; 3 kw; Ant 20 ft; N31 11 26 W98 42 55
PO Box 126, 705 South Live Oak, San Saba, TX 77802
(325) 372-5225; *Fax:* (325) 372-3817
www.sansabaradio.com
knuz@sansabaradio.com
License: San Saba, San Saba County, TX held by Roy E. Henderson
Regional Network: Texas State Networks
Target Audience: General.

KNVR
01-01-1954; 1410 kHz AM; *Hrs Open:* 24; 0.8 kw-D, ND1; 0.203 kw-N, ND1; N31 11 26 W98 42 55
US
(325) 372-5225; *Fax:* (325) 372-3817
www.sansabaradio.com
knuz@sansabaradio.com
License: San Saba, TX held by Roy E. Henderson
Regional Network: Texas State Networks
Arbitron Metro Market: San Saba, TX; *Format:* Adult Contemp

Sanger

***KVRK**
07-08-1999; 89.7 MHz FM; *Hrs Open:* 24; 14 kw; 1,699 ft; N33 33 36 W96 57 35
11601 Shady Tr., Dallas, TX 75229
(214) 353-8970
www.kvrk.com
chris@kvrk.com
License: Sanger, Denton County, TX held by Research Educational Foundation Inc.
Stanley Thomas, General Manager
Eddie Alcaraz, Station Manager
David Thomas, Operations Director
Chris Goodwin, Music Director
Dawn Henderson, Promotions Manager
Kent Loney, Chief Engineer

Savoy

KQDR
01-01-2009; 107.3 MHz FM; 3.7 kw; 421 ft.; N33 42 31 W96 24 9
900 East Pecan Grove Road, Sherman, TX 75090 US
(903) 893-5625
www.1073docfm.com
License: Savoy, Fannin County, TX held by Prophecy Radio Group LLC.
Group Owner: William W. McCutchen III Stns
Arbitron Metro Market: Savoy, TX; *Format:* Contemporary Hits/Top 40
Rob Endsley, Market Manager
Joey, Programming Director

Schertz

KBBT
02-01-1976; 98.5 MHz FM; *Hrs Open:* 24; 97 kw; 991 ft.; N29 31 25 W98 43 25
12451 Network Blvd., Suite 140, San Antonio, TX 78249 US
(210) 610-4300
www.thebeatsa.com
License: Schertz, Guadalupe County, TX held by Univision Radio License Corp.
Group Owner: Univision Radio; (acq 9-22-2003; grpsl).
Arbitron Metro Market: San Antonio, TX; *Format:* Urban Contemporary
Chris Morris, Vice President and General Manager
Barbara Carreon, Sales Manager
Homie Marco, Programming Director
Alex Gairo, Promotions Manager
Bret Huggins, Chief Engineer
Raul Faz, Digital Content Manager
Robert Morris,Digital Content Manager
Hamm, Music Director
Colleen Carnahan, Research Director
Sonia Trevenio, Business Manager

Scotland

KXPN-FM
10-06-1996; 95.5 MHz FM; *Hrs Open:* 24; 6 kw; 328 ft.; N33 19 43 W98 16 46
1776 East Tufts Avenue, Englewood, CO 80110 US
(940) 567-6600; *Fax:* (940) 567-6602
License: Scotland, Jack County, TX held by LKCM Radio Group L.P.
Format: Classic Rock
Janice Hunt, CEO
Jim Hunt, President
Debbie Watts, Station Manager
Jerrod Knight, Programming Director

Seabrook

KROI
04-23-1984; 92.1 MHz FM; *Hrs Open:* 24; 21.36 kw; 1726 ft.; N29 17 56 W95 14 11
24 Greenway Plaza, Suite 900, Houston, TX 77046 US
(713) 623-2108; *Fax:* (713) 300-5795
www.boom92houston.com
License: Seabrook, Harris County, TX held by Radio One Licenses LLC.
Group Owner: Radio One Inc.; (acq 7-20-2004; $72.5 million).
Arbitron Metro Market: Houston, TX; *Format:* Urban Contemporary; *Target Audience:* General.
Terri Thomas, Operations Mgr/Program Dir.
Jonathan Cook, Promotions Manager

Seadrift

KMAT
05-01-1999; 105.1 MHz FM; *Hrs Open:* 24; 38.5 kw; Ant 456 ft; N28 26 17.1 W96 26 54.6
License: Seadrift, Calhoun County, TX held by Cordell Communications Inc.
Population Served: 89,470 *Hrs. of News Programming:* News progmg 2 hrs wkly; *Target Audience:* 30-50.
Bill Cordell, President
Dolly Martin, Programming Director

Seguin

KWED
09-09-1948; 1580 kHz AM; *Hrs Open:* 24; 1 kw-D, ND1; 0.253 kw-N, ND1; N29 34 48 W97 59 5
609 East Court Street, Seguin, TX 78155 US
(830) 379-2234; *Fax:* (830) 379-2238
www.seguintoday.com
darren@kwed1580.com
License: Seguin, TX held by Guadalupe Media, Ltd.
Nat'l Network: Westwood One; CNN Radio; Premiere Radio Networks; *Nat'l Reps:* Rgnl Reps; *Wire Services:* AP
Arbitron Metro Market: Seguin, TX; *Format:* Country, News, 62, Talk *Special Programming:* Farm 6 hrs wkly; *Hrs. of News Programming:* news progmg 30 hrs wkly; *No. News Employees:* 5; *Target Audience:* 35-64.
Darren Dunn, General Manager
Cindy Aguirre-Herrera, News Director

Seminole

KIKZ
04-15-1954; 1250 kHz AM; *Hrs Open:* 24; 1 kw-D, ND1; 0.25 kw-N, ND1; N32 41 58 W102 38 12
105 N.W. 11th Street, Seminol, TX 79360 US
(432) 758-5878; *Fax:* (432) 758-5474
www.kikzksem.com
kikz-ksem@bajabb.com
License: Seminole, TX held by Gaines County Broadcasting LLC
Regional Network: Texas State Networks
Format: Country; *Target Audience:* General.
Dave Fisher, News/Sports Director
Angie Rodriguez, Office Manager/Sales

KSEM
03-15-1985; 106.3 MHz FM; *Hrs Open:* 24; 3 kw; Ant 174 ft; N32 41 58 W102 38 12
105 N.W. 11th St., Seminole, TX 79360
(432) 758-5878; *Fax:* (432) 758-5474
kikz-ksem@bajabb.com
License: Seminole, Gaines County, TX held by Gaines County Broadcasting LLC.

Dave Fisher, News/Sports Director
Angie Rodriguez, Office Manager/Sales

Seymour

KSEY
10-26-1950; 1230 kHz AM; 1 kw-U, ND1; N33 35 49 W99 16 42
1 Radio Lane, Seymour, TX 76380 US
(940) 889-2637
www.radioksey.com
License: Seymour, TX held by Mark Aulabaugh.
Wire Services: NWS (National Weather Service)
Arbitron Metro Market: Seymour, TX; *Adv. Rates:* 18; 18; 18; 18
Mark Aulabaugh, Owner/Sales Manager
Sue Harney, Sales/Billing

KSEY-FM
06-26-1981; 94.3 MHz FM; 3 kw; 112 ft.; N33 35 49 W99 16 42
1 Radio Lane, Seymour, TX 76380 US
(940) 889-2637
www.radioksey.com
License: Seymour, Baylor County, TX
Arbitron Metro Market: Seymour, TX; *Format:* Variety/Diverse
Mark Aulabaugh, Owner/Sales Manager
Sue Harney, Sales/Billing

Shanandoah

KRCM
07-01-1947; 1380 kHz AM; *Hrs Open:* 6 AM-6 PM; 1 kw-D, 127 w-N; N30 02 09 W94 08 31 *Rebroadcasts:* Rebroadcasts KOLE(AM) Port Arthur 50%
27 Sawyer St., Beaumont, TX 77070
(409) 835-1340,(409) 835-1340; *Fax:* (409) 832-5686
manager@newsradiofox.com
License: Shanandoah, Jefferson County, TX held by Daij Media LLC
Group Owner: Daij Media LLC; (acq 1-29-03).
Nat'l Network: Fox News Radio; Talk Radio Network; USA;
Regional Network: Texas State Networks
Population Served: 115,917; *Arbitron Metro Market:* Beaumont-Port Arthur, TX; *Hrs. of News Programming:* news progmg 40 hrs wkly; *No. News Employees:* 2
Ralph McBride, President
Jeff Roberts, Operations Dir
Brent Bobbitt, General Sales Mgr
Dominick Brascia, Programming Director
Jeanette Harvey, News Director
Russ Ingram, Engineering Dir

Sherman

KJIM

12-19-1947; 1500 kHz AM; 1 kw-D, DAD; N33 41 30 W96 33 29
Route 3 Box 176-K, Denison, TX 75020 US
(903) 893-1197
License: Sherman, TX held by Bob Mark Allen Productions Inc.
Nat'l Network: Westwood One; CBS
Format: News, Sports; *Target Audience:* 40-65.
Bob Mark Allen, President

Silsbee

KAYD-FM

06-21-1980; 101.7 MHz FM; 10.5 kw; 503 ft.; N30 6 54 W93 59 56
755 South 11th Street, Suite 102, Beaumont, TX 77704 US
(409) 951-2500
www.nashfm1017.com
j.bernard@cumulus.com
License: Silsbee, Hardin County, TX held by Cumulus Licensing LLC.
Group Owner: Cumulus Media Inc.; (acq 11-8-2004; $2.1 million).
Arbitron Metro Market: Beaumont-Port Arthur, TX; *Format:* Country; *Hrs. of News Programming:* News progmg 20 hrs wkly; *Target Audience:* 25-54; persons; *Adv. Rates:* 55; 50; 55; 40.
Jay Bernard, Programming/Music Director

Sinton

KDAE

01-01-1954; 1590 kHz AM; *Hrs Open:* 24; 1 kw-D, DA2; 0.5 kw-N, DA2; N28 1 16 W97 28 14
P.O. Box 260715, Corpus Christi, TX 78426-0715 US
(361) 299-1960
www.radiolibertad.net
License: Sinton, TX held by The Worship Center of Kingsville.
Nat'l Network: ABC; *Nat'l Reps:* McGavren Guild
Arbitron Metro Market: Corpus Christi, TX; *Format:* Adult Contemp, Christian, 82 *Special Programming:* Farm 6 hrs wkly; *Hrs. of News Programming:* news progmg 2 hrs wkly; *No. News Employees:* 1; *Target Audience:* 35-64.
Rufino Sendejo, President/General Manager
A.J. Solis, Operations Manager/Chief of Engineering
Veronica Gaytan, Programming Director
George Sanders, Chief Engineer

KNCN

07-01-1972; 101.3 MHz FM; *Hrs Open:* 24; 100 kw; 361 ft.; N27 55 24 W97 25 26
501 Tupper Lane, Corpus Christi, TX 78417 US
(361) 289-0111
www.c101.com
monte@c101.com
License: Sinton, San Patricio County, TX held by Capstar TX LLC
Group Owner: iHeartMedia; (acq 8-30-00; grpsl).
Arbitron Metro Market: Corpus Christi, TX; *Format:* Rock/AOR *Special Programming:* Coastal Bend Forum one hr, In Concert 2 hrs, In th; *Hrs. of News Programming:* News progmg one hr wkly; *Target Audience:* 18-49;active
Billy Santiago, Operations Manager
John Richards, General Manager
Chris Aldrich, General Sales Mgr
Monte Montana, Programming Director
Steve Freeman, Chief Engineer

Slaton

KJAK

02-12-1978; 92.7 MHz FM; *Hrs Open:* 24; 100 kw; 584 ft.; N33 32 32 W101 50 14
6504 East Slaton Highway 84, Lubbock, TX 79404 US
(806) 745-6677; *Fax:* (806) 745-8140
www.kjak.com
License: Slaton, Lubbock County, TX held by G.O. Williams Oil Co. Inc. dba Williams Broadcasting Group
Arbitron Metro Market: Lubbock, TX; *Format:* Christian *Special Programming:* Sports 5 hrs wkly; *Target Audience:* General; Christians & those looking for answers to everyday problems

Snyder

KSNY

12-22-1949; 1450 kHz AM; *Hrs Open:* 24; 1 kw-U; N32 43 33 W100 56 30
2301 Avenue R., Snyder, TX 79549
(325) 573-9322
www.ksnyradio.com
License: Snyder, Scurry County, TX held by Snyder Broadcasting Co.
Nat'l Network: ABC
Population Served: 11,171 *Target Audience:* General.
Lydia Foree, Operations Dir
Dink Foree, General Manager
Alice Swiney, Programming Director

KSNY-FM

09-02-1980; 101.5 MHz FM; *Hrs Open:* 24; 35 kw; 500 ft; N32 53 29 W101 06 29
2301 Avenue R., Snyder, TX 79549
(325) 573-9322
www.ksnyradio.com
License: Snyder, Scurry County, TX held by Snyder Broadcasting Company
Nat'l Network: ABC
Hrs. of News Programming: news progmg 5 hrs wkly; *No. News Employees:* 1; *Target Audience:* 25-54.
Lydia Foree, Operations Dir
Dink Foree, General Manager
Alice Swiney, Programming Director

KLYD

01-01-2003; 98.9 MHz FM; *Hrs Open:* 24; 5.6 kw; 341 ft.; N32 45 23 W100 54 9
2800 34th Street, Snyder, TX 79549 US
License: Snyder, Scurry County, TX held by Delbert Foree.
Arbitron Metro Market: San Francisco, CA; *Format:* Rock/AOR
Dink Foree, General Manager
Anne Hudson, General Sales Mgr
Tony Ng, Promotions Manager
JayPlus, Assistant Promotion Director

*KGWB

08-04-2008; 91.1 MHz FM; 0.24 kw; 36 ft.; N32 40 46 W100 54 51
6200 College Avenue, Snyder, TX 79549 US
(325) 574-7626; *Fax:* (325) 573-9321
wtc.edu/kgwb/
info@wtc.edu
License: Snyder, Scurry County, TX held by Scurry County Junior College District.
Arbitron Metro Market: Snyder, TX; *Format:* Variety/Diverse

Somerset

KYTY

03-01-1988; 810 kHz AM; *Hrs Open:* 24; 250 w-U, DA-2; N29 18 48 W98 30 29
www.star810.com
staram810@yahoo.com
License: Somerset, Bexar County, TX held by Maranatha Broadcasting Inc.
Population Served: 1,200,000; *Arbitron Metro Market:* San Antonio, TX; *Target Audience:* 35-45; female
Mary Kaye, Operations Dir
Myron Wade, General Manager
Reuben Garcia, Programming Director

Sonora

KHOS-FM

05-01-1979; 92.1 MHz FM; *Hrs Open:* 24; 3 kw; 299 ft.; N30 33 33 W100 37 54
14609 South Main Street, Sonora, TX US
(866) 559-2705
License: Sonora, Sutton County, TX held by Foster Charitable Foundation Inc.
Group Owner: Revolution Broadcast Company of the West; (acq 5-31-2007)
Nat'l Network: ABC; *Regional Network:* Texas State Networks; Voice of Southwest Agriculture Radio
Format: Country; *Target Audience:* 12-50 plus.
Marti Ashcraft, Operations Dir
Eddy Smith, Engineering Dir

South Padre Island

KESO

08-27-1996; 92.7 MHz FM; *Hrs Open:* 24; 38 kw; 461 ft.; N26 3 12.8 W97 12 46.4
1201 N. Jackson Road, McAllen, TX 78501 US
(956) 992-8895
License: South Padre Island, Cameron County, TX held by BMP RGV License Company L.P.
Group Owner: Border Media Partners LLC; (acq 1-28-2005; $6.6 million with KZSP(FM) South Padre Island)
Arbitron Metro Market: McAllen-Brownsville-Harlingen, TX; *Format:* Tejano
Terry Kimball, Station Manager
Jim Wilson, Programming Director

KZSP

07-27-1990; 95.3 MHz FM; *Hrs Open:* 24; 2.9 kw; 421 ft.; N26 3 12.8 W97 12 46.4 *Rebroadcasts:* Simulcast with KURV(AM) Edinburg 100%
Mailing Address: 5009 Padre Blvd, Suite 16, South Padre Island, TX 78597 US
Second Address: 1201 N. Jackson Road, #900, McAllen, TX 78501
License: South Padre Island, Cameron County, TX held by BMP RGV License Company L.P.
Group Owner: Border Media Partners LLC; (acq 1-28-2005; $6.6 million with KESO(FM) South Padre Island)
Arbitron Metro Market: South Padre Island, TX; *Format:* News, News/Talk, 86
Jose Munoz, General Manager

Spearman

KXDJ

12-16-1963; 98.3 MHz FM; *Hrs Open:* 24; 17.5 kw; 837 ft.; N36 3 44 W101 1 56
US
(806) 648-2650
www.kxdjradio.com
License: Spearman, Hansford County, TX held by Chris Samples Broadcasting
Nat'l Network: CBS Radio; AP Radio
Arbitron Metro Market: Amarillo, TX; *Format:* Country; *Hrs. of News Programming:* News progmg 25 hrs wkly; *Adv. Rates:* 12; 12; 12; 12
Chris Samples, President/General Manager

*KTOT

01-01-2003; 89.5 MHz FM; *Hrs Open:* 24; 100 kw; 1066 ft.; N36 3 44 W101 1 56
207 N. 7th Street, Garden City, KS 67846 US
(620) 275-7444
www.hppr.org
hppr@hppr.org
License: Spearman, Hansford County, TX held by Kanza Society Inc.
Nat'l Network: AP Radio; NPR; PRI
Arbitron Metro Market: Spearman, Texas; *Format:* News; *Target Audience:* 25-80; educated
Mike Fuller, Music Director
Cindee Talley, Regional Programming Director
Adam Vos, Operations Coordinator

Springtown

*KSQX

08-01-1985; 89.1 MHz FM; *Hrs Open:* 24; 3 kw; 184 ft.; N32 58 53 W97 42 18
1612 S. Main Street, Weatherford, TX 76086 US
(817) 341-2337; *Fax:* (817) 613-0230
shilo@qxfm.com
License: Springtown, Parker County, TX held by CSSI Non-Profit Educational Broadcasting Corp.
Format: Big Band, News, 64, Talk; *Hrs. of News Programming:* news progmg 5 hrs wkly; *No. News Employees:* 3
Brent Baker, News/Sports
Shilo Treille, Underwriting Specialist

Stamford

KLGD

02-22-1999; 106.9 MHz FM; 40 kw; 548 ft.; N32 56 16 W99 57 20
US
www.klgd.com
License: Stamford, Jones County, TX held by Texas Gulfwest Communications Corp.
Arbitron Metro Market: Abilene, TX; *Format:* Country; *Target Audience:* 35 plus; adults; *Adv. Rates:* 25; 20; 25;15

KVRP

07-01-1947; 1400 kHz AM; *Hrs Open:* 24; 1 kw-U; N32 55 52 W99 47 00
Box 1118, Haskell, TX 79521
(940) 864-8505; *Fax:* (940) 864-8001
www.kvrp.com
news@kvrp.com
License: Stamford, Jones County, TX held by 1 Chronicles 14 L.P.
Group Owner: Weston Entertainment L.P.; (acq 8-4-2004; $700,000 with KVRP-F
Nat'l Network: Salem; *Nat'l Reps:* Salem
Population Served: 50,000; *Arbitron Metro Market:* Abilene, TX; *Target Audience:* 35+.
Gary Barrett, Senior Account Executive
Keith Daniels, Programming/Production Director
Sarah Kalen, Chief Operator

Stanton

*KFLB-FM
09-01-1989; 88.1 MHz FM; *Hrs Open:* 24; 100 kw; 457 ft.; N32 5 44 W101 48 47
Mailing Address: PO Box 3300, Tucson, AZ 85740 US
Second Address: 7355 N. Oracle Road, Tucson, AZ 85704
(520) 742-6976; *Fax:* (520) 469-7312
www.myflr.org
License: Stanton, Ector County, TX held by Family Life Broadcasting Inc.
Group Owner: Family Life Communications Inc.
Arbitron Metro Market: Odessa-Midland, TX; *Format:* Christian, Religious
Dr. Randy L. Carlson, President
Evan Carlson, VP, Ministry
Alonzo Williams, VP, Operations
Rod Robinson, VP, Development
Marc Piotrowski, Controller

Stephenville

KSTV
01-01-1947; 1510 kHz AM; 0.5 kw-D, NDD; N32 12 8 W98 14 54
3209 W. Washington, Stephenville, TX 76401 US
(254) 968-2141; *Fax:* (254) 968-6221
www.kstvfm.com
kstv@htcomp.net
License: Stephenville, TX held by CCR-Stephenville III LLC.
Group Owner: Cherry Creek Radio LLC; (acq 6-24-2004; grpsl).
Arbitron Metro Market: Stephenville, TX; *Format:* Tejano *Special Programming:* Farm 5 hrs, relg 6 hrs wkly; *Target Audience:* 54 plus; general
Robert Elliott, Market Manager
John Kirby, Sales Manager
Erin McAvoy, Business Manager
Justin McClure, Chief Engineer
Troy Stark, Traffic Manager

*KQXS
01-01-2004; 89.1 MHz FM; 1.2 kw vert; 424 ft.; N32 16 9 W98 18 51
206 Wiggs Lane, Weatherford, TX 76086 US
(817) 341-8950; *Fax:* (817) 596-9842
qxfmnews@yahoo.com
License: Stephenville, Erath County, TX held by CSSI Non-Profit Educational Broadcasting Corp.
Arbitron Metro Market: Abilene, TX; *Format:* Big Band, News, 64; *No. News Employees:* 3
Jean Hudgens, General Manager

*KEQX
89.7 MHz FM; *Hrs Open:* 24; 6 kw vert; 492 ft.; N32 7 24 W97 58 48
3780 W. State Highway 6, Dublin, TX 76446 US
(254) 445-2473; *Fax:* (254) 445-2765
www.keqx897.com
License: Stephenville, Erath County, TX held by CSSI Non-Profit Educational Broadcasting Corp.
Arbitron Metro Market: Stephenville, TX; *Format:* Country
Sam Upshaw, Operator
Robert Webb, Engineer

Sterling City

KNRX
12-01-1998; 96.5 MHz FM; *Hrs Open:* 24; 40 kw; 545 ft.; N31 35 56 W100 50 42
6999 East Highway 80, Odessa, TX 79762 US
(325) 655-7161; *Fax:* (325) 658-7377
965therock.com
License: Sterling City, Sterling County, TX held by Townsquare Media San Angelo License LLC
Group Owner: Townsquare Media; (acq 3-15-2006; grpsl)
Arbitron Metro Market: San Angelo, TX; *Format:* Classic Rock; *Target Audience:* 25-64.; *Adv. Rates:* 10; 10; 10; 10
John Flint, General Manager
Boomer Kingston, Brand Manager
Shannon Lewis, Digital Managing Editor

Stockdale

KQQB
09-05-1979; 1520 kHz AM; *Hrs Open:* Sunrise-sunset; 2.5 kw-D; N29 26 38 W96 57 22
111 N. Main St., Hallettsville, TX 77965
(361) 798-4333; *Fax:* (361) 798-3798
texasthunderradio@yahoo.com
License: Stockdale, Lavaca County, TX held by Matthew Provenzano
Regional Network: Texas State Networks; *Wire Services:* NWS (National Weather Service)
Special Programming: Farm 5 hrs, Czech 5 hrs, Ger 5 hrs wkly; *Hrs. of News Programming:* news progmg 13 hrs wkly; *No. News Employees:* 1; *Target Audience:* General.
Laura Kremling, General Manager
Travis Kremling, Programming Director

Stratford

*KOGW
91.1 MHz FM; 100 w horiz; Ant 118 ft; N36 19 31 W102 03 11
116 Hillcrest Dr., Seminole, OK
(405) 380-3516
www.bpba.us
info@bpba.us
License: Stratford, Sherman County, TX held by Better Public Broadcasting Association.

Dennis Burton, General Manager

Sulphur Bluff

KETE
99.7 MHz FM; 6 kw; Ant 318 ft; N33 27 29 W95 19 35
License: Sulphur Bluff, Hopkins County, TX held by The Way Radio Group LLC

Leo Ashcraft, General Manager

Sulphur Springs

KSCH
08-30-1982; 96.9 MHz FM; *Hrs Open:* 24; 6 kw; 285 ft.; N33 9 7 W95 36 12 *Rebroadcasts:* Rebroadcasts KSCN(FM) Pittsburg 90%
1798 US Hwy. 67 W., PO Box 990, Mount Pleasant, TX 75456 US
(903) 572-8726; *Fax:* (903) 572-7232
www.easttexasradio.com
License: Sulphur Springs, Hopkins County, TX held by East Texas Broadcasting Inc.
Group Owner: East Texas Broadcasting Inc.; acq 9-30-99).
Arbitron Metro Market: Sulphur Springs, TX; *Format:* Country; *Hrs. of News Programming:* news progmg 13 hrs wkly; *No. News Employees:* 3; *Target Audience:* 18-60.; *Adv. Rates:* 22.50; 21; 22.50; 17
Bud Kitchens, General Manager

KSST
03-01-1947; 1230 kHz AM; *Hrs Open:* 24; 1 kw-U, ND1; N33 7 0 W95 35 5
www.ksstradio.com
License: Sulphur Springs, TX held by Hopkins County Broadcasting Co.
Nat'l Network: ABC; *Regional Network:* Texas State Networks
Arbitron Metro Market: Sulphur Spring, tx; *Format:* Variety/Diverse, Adult Contemp; *Hrs. of News Programming:* news progmg 30 hrs wkly; *No. News Employees:* 2; *Target Audience:* 25-54.
William Bradford, CEO
Dwayne Grimes, Operations Dir
Enola Gay, Promotions Manager
Don Julian, News Director
Patsy Bradford, Advertising Director

Sweetwater

KXOX
11-01-1939; 1240 kHz AM; *Hrs Open:* 24; 1 kw-U, ND1; N32 29 16 W100 23 31
P. O. Box 570, Sweetwater, TX 79556 US
(325) 236-6655; *Fax:* (325) 235-4391
License: Sweetwater, TX held by Stein Broadcasting Co.
Regional Network: Texas State Networks; *Wire Services:* AP
Arbitron Metro Market: Sweetwater, TX; *Format:* Country *Special Programming:* Farm 5 hrs, Sp 8 hrs, gospel 4 hrs wkly; *Hrs. of News Programming:* News progmg 2 plus hrs wkly; *Target Audience:* 25-54.
Jack Stein, President/General Manager

KXOX-FM
04-07-1976; 96.7 MHz FM; *Hrs Open:* 18; 2.9 kw; Ant 154 ft; N32 29 16 W100 23 31
Box 570, Sweetwater, TX 79556
(325) 236-6655; *Fax:* (325) 235-4391
License: Sweetwater, Nolan County, TX held by Stein Broadcasting Co.
Wire Services: AP
No. News Employees: 1
Jeff Stein, President/General Manager

Tahoka

KAMZ
01-01-2001; 103.5 MHz FM; *Hrs Open:* 24; 20 kw; 328 ft.; N33 19 26 W101 48 15
4821 73rd Street, Lubbock, TX 79424 US
(806) 741-0701; *Fax:* (806) 741-0705
License: Tahoka, Lynn County, TX held by Albert Benavides.
Arbitron Metro Market: Lubbock, TX; *Format:* Tejano
Rick Benavides, General Manager
Bob Benavides, Programming Director
Lou Gum, News Director
Bill Enloe, Chief Engineer

KMMX
08-13-1987; 100.3 MHz FM; *Hrs Open:* 24; 100 kw; 883 ft.; N33 26 31 W101 52 40
#33 Briercroft Park Office Park, Lubbock, TX 79412 US
(806) 762-3000; *Fax:* (806) 770-5363
www.mix100lubbock.com
License: Tahoka, Lynn County, TX held by Alpha Media Licensee LLC
Group Owner: Alpha Media LLC; (acq 5-15-2015; grpsl).
Nat'l Network: ABC
Arbitron Metro Market: Lubbock, TX; *Format:* Contemporary Hits/Top 40; *Hrs. of News Programming:* news progmg 5 hrs wkly; *No. News Employees:* 1; *Target Audience:* 25-54; females
Jeff Scott, Operations Manager
Jay Richardson, General Manager
Randy Gattis, Sales Manager
Damon Scott, Programming Director

Tatum

KZQX
08-01-1965; 100.3 MHz FM; *Hrs Open:* 24; 2.45 kw; Ant 518 ft; N32 22 37 W94 34 18
Mailing Address: Box 1008, Kilgore, TX 75663
Second Address: 402 Ragsdale, Jacksonville, TX 75766
(903) 643-7711; *Fax:* (903) 643-8272
License: Tatum, Rusk County, TX held by Waller Media LLC.
Group Owner: Waller Broadcasting; (acq 8-24-2005; $975,000 with KDVE(FM) Pittsburg).
Population Served: 250,000; *Arbitron Metro Market:* Tyler-Longview, TX; *Target Audience:* 25-54.
Chuck Conrad, Owner/GM

Taylor

KLQB
04-04-1975; 104.3 MHz FM; *Hrs Open:* 24; 48 kw; 492 ft.; N30 26 4 W97 21 53
10801 N. Mopac Expressway, Austin, TX 78759 US
(512) 340-7100
www.univision.com
License: Taylor, Williamson County, TX held by Univision Radio License Corp.
Group Owner: Univision Radio; (acq 11-30-2007; grpsl)
Nat'l Reps: Katz Radio
Arbitron Metro Market: Austin, TX; *Format:* Tejano
Angela Navarrete, General Manager

Temple

*KBDE
01-01-2001; 89.9 MHz FM; 11.5 kw vert; 489 ft.; N31 16 5 W97 21 34
P.O. Box 3206, Tupelo, MS 38803 US
(662) 844-8888; *Fax:* (662) 842-6791
www.afr.net
faq@afa.net
License: Temple, Bell County, TX held by American Family Association.
Group Owner: American Family Radio
Arbitron Metro Market: Temple, TX; *Format:* Christian
Tim Wildmon, President
Donald Wildmon, Founder
Buddy Smith, Senior VP
Ed Vitagliano, Executive VP
Randy Sharp, Director Of Special Projects
Meeke Addison, Director Of Communications
Abraham Hamilton III, General Counsel & PublicPolicy Analyst

KLTD
01-01-1995; 101.7 MHz FM; 16.5 kw; 410 ft.; N31 16 24 W97 23 31
P. O. Box 1110, Temple, TX 76503 US
(254) 773-5252; *Fax:* (254) 547-2394
www.1017theticket.com
License: Temple, Bell County, TX held by Townsquare Media Killeen-Temple License LLC
Group Owner: Townsquare Media

Arbitron Metro Market: Killeen, TX; *Format:* Sports
Johnny Lathrop, General Manager
Dan Patrick, Brand Manager
Paula Divello, Director Of Sales
James Sitllwell, Digital Managing Editor

KTEM
11-25-1936; 1400 kHz AM; *Hrs Open:* 24
608 Moody Lane, Temple, TX 76504 US
(254) 773-5252; *Fax:* (254) 773-0115
www.myktem.com
jamie.garrett@cumulus.com
License: Temple, TX held by Townsquare Media Killeen-Tem,Ple License LLC
Group Owner: Townsquare Media; (acq 3-12-01; $425,000).
Nat'l Network: CBS
Arbitron Metro Market: Temple, TX; *Format:* News, News/Talk, 84, Talk *Special Programming:* Czech 3 hrs wkly; *Hrs. of News Programming:* news progmg 30 hrs wkly; *No. News Employees:* 1; *Target Audience:* 35-64;affluent, educated, politically active
Bourdon Wooten, General Manager
Bourdon Wooten, General Sales Mgr
Jamie Garrett, Programming Director
Brian Brown, Promotions Manager
Doug Bernhardt, Chief Engineer
Romeo Medina-Brand Manager

***KVLT**
05-01-2003; 88.5 MHz FM; *Hrs Open:* 24; 5 kw vert; 617 ft.; N30 59 8 W97 37 56
PO Box 2098, Omaha, NE 68103-2098 US
(800) 525-5683
www.klove.com
License: Temple, Bell County, TX held by American Educational Broadcasting Inc.
Nat'l Network: K-Love
Arbitron Metro Market: Temple, TX; *Format:* Christian; *No. News Employees:* 13
Darrell Chambliss, Chairman
Mike Novak, President and CEO
David Pierce, Chief Creative Officer and Programming Director
Alan Mason, Chief Operating Officer
Eric Moser, Chief Financial Officer
D. Kevin Blair, Secretary and GeneralCounsel

Terrell

KPYK
10-01-1947; 1570 kHz AM; *Hrs Open:* 24
(972) 524-5795; *Fax:* (972) 524-5795
www.kpyk.com
License: Terrell, TX held by Mohnkern Electronics Inc.
Nat'l Network: USA
Arbitron Metro Market: Dallas-Fort Worth; *Format:* Big Band; *Hrs. of News Programming:* news progmg 15 hrs wkly; *No. News Employees:* 1; *Target Audience:* 40 plus; mature adults; *Adv. Rates:* 15; 12.50; 15; na
Chuck Mohnkern, Engineer
Susan Pinson, Traffic/Public Affairs Manager

Terrell Hills

KTKX
12-31-1967; 106.7 MHz FM; *Hrs Open:* 24; 100 kw; 310 m; N29 11 03 W98 30 49
8122 Datapoint Dr., Suite 600, San Antonio, TX 78229
(210) 615-5400; *Fax:* (210) 615-5300
www.eaglesanantonio.com
keith.hastings@coxinc.com
License: Terrell Hills, Bexar County, TX held by Cox Radio Inc.
Group Owner: Cox Radio Inc.; (acq 3-28-97; grpsl)
Wire Services: AP
Population Served: 1,300,000; *Arbitron Metro Market:* San Antonio, TX; *Format:* Classic Rock; *No. News Employees:* 1; *Target Audience:* 18-34.
Jeff Garrison, Operations Manager
Jim Dyer, General Sales Manager
Mary Rogers, Director of Sales
Keith Hastings, Programming Director
Jennifer Schultz, Promotions Manager
Lena Rodriguez, Sales Operations Manager
AlfonsoMontemayor, Digital Sales Manager
Dan Lawrie, Vice President/Market Manager
Ric Gonzalez, Creative Services/Production Director

KLUP
10-17-1947; 930 kHz AM; *Hrs Open:* 24; 5 kw-D, DAN; 1 kw-N, DAN; N29 31 6 W98 24 25
9601 McAllister Freeway, Suite 1200, San Antonoi, TX 78216 US
(210) 344-8481
www.klup.com
michael.payne@salemcommunications.com
License: Terrell Hills, TX held by South Texas Broadcasting Inc.
Group Owner: Salem Communications Corp.; (acq 7-27-00; grpsl).
Nat'l Network: Salem Radio Network
Arbitron Metro Market: San Antonio, TX; *Format:* News, News/Talk, 86; *Target Audience:* 35-64; upper & middle income, empty nesters
Michael Payne, General Manager
Jan Johnson, Business/HR Manager
Julie Taylor, Traffic Director
Barry Besse, Operations/Programming Manager
Baron Wiley, General Sales Manager

Texarkana

KCMC
02-26-1932; 740 kHz AM; *Hrs Open:* 24; 1 kw-U, DA1; N33 26 17 W94 8 33
615 Olive Street, Texarkana, TX 75501 US
(903) 793-4671; *Fax:* (903) 792-4261
scott@texarkanaradio.com
License: Texarkana, TX held by ArkLaTex LLC.
Group Owner: Arklatex LLC; (acq 1-3-2007; grpsl)
Nat'l Network: ESPN Radio; *Nat'l Reps:* Interep
Arbitron Metro Market: Texarkana, TX; *Format:* Sports; *Target Audience:* 18 plus; sports fans
John McCoy, Operations Manager
Scott Gray, General Manager
Roy Roane, General Sales Mgr
Scott Gray, CFO

KKTK
01-01-1946; 1400 kHz AM; *Hrs Open:* 24; 1 kw-U, ND1; N33 26 28 W94 3 16
3446 Summerhill Road, Texarkana, TX 75503 US
(903) 255-7935
www.casscountytoday.com/ktkt
License: Texarkana, TX held by American Media Investments Inc.
Group Owner: American Media Investments Inc.; (acq 2-17-2009; grpsl)
Nat'l Network: Fox News Radio
Arbitron Metro Market: Texarkana, TX-AR; *Format:* Talk; *Target Audience:* 35 plus.
Mike Basso, General Manager

KKYR-FM
07-15-1965; 102.5 MHz FM; 100 kw; 459 ft.; N33 25 48 W94 5 8
2324 Arkansas Blvd., Texarkana, AR 71854 US
(870) 772-3771; *Fax:* (870) 772-0364
www.kkyr.com
wesspicher@gapbroadcasting.com
License: Texarkana, Bowie County, TX held by Townsquare Media Texarkana License LLC
Group Owner: Townsquare Media; (acq 8-3-2007; grpsl)
Arbitron Metro Market: Texarkana, TX; *Format:* Country; *Target Audience:* General.
Philip Hand, General Manager
Jeff Brown, Director Of Sales
Jeff Brown, Digital Sales Manager
Justin Massoud, Digital Managing Editor

KTAL-FM
01-01-1945; 98.1 MHz FM; *Hrs Open:* 24; 100 kw; 1,362 ft.; N32 54 11 W94 0 20
208 N. Thomas Dr., Shreveport, LA 71137 US
(318) 222-3122
www.98rocks.fm
License: Texarkana, Bowie County, TX held by Alpha Media Licensee LLC
Group Owner: Alpha Media LLC; (acq 4-14-2015; grpsl).
Arbitron Metro Market: Shreveport, LA; *Format:* Classic Rock; *No. News Employees:* 1; *Target Audience:* 25-54.
Cary Camp, Market Manager
Johnette Robinson, General Market Sales Manager
Greg Hanson, Programming Director

KTFS
10-23-1961; 940 kHz AM; *Hrs Open:* 24; 2.5 kw-D, ND1; 0.011 kw-N, ND1; N33 24 28 W94 2 45
615 Olive Street, Texarkana, TX 75501 US
(903) 793-4671; *Fax:* (903) 792-4261
www.texarkanaradio.com
info@texarkanaradio.com
License: Texarkana, TX held by ArkLaTex LLC.
Group Owner: Arklatex LLC; (acq 1-3-2007; grpsl)
Nat'l Network: Premiere Radio Networks; Radio America; Fox News Radio; Talk Radio Network; *Nat'l Reps:* Interep
Arbitron Metro Market: Texarkana, TX; *Format:* News, News/Talk, 86; *Hrs. of News Programming:* news progmg 25 hrs wkly; *No. News Employees:* 1; *Target Audience:* 35 plus.
Harold Sudbury, CEO
Scott Gray, CFO/Vice President

***KTXK**
02-01-1984; 91.5 MHz FM; *Hrs Open:* 24; 100 kw; 305 ft.; N33 23 33 W94 14 44
2500 N. Robinson Road, Texarkana, TX 75599 US
(903) 823-3269; *Fax:* (903) 823-3451
www.ktxk.org
steve@ktxk.org
License: Texarkana, Bowie County, TX held by Texarkana College.
Nat'l Network: PRI; NPR
Arbitron Metro Market: Texarkana, TX; *Format:* News *Special Programming:* Jazz 15 hrs wkly; *Hrs. of News Programming:* news progmg 35 hrs wkly; *No. News Employees:* 1; *Target Audience:* 35 plus.
Steve Mitchell, General Manager
Sabrina McCormick Norton, News Director
Scott Williams, Chief Engineer
Frank Miller, Music Director
Alton Pettigrew, Classical Director

Texas City

KYST
11-01-1947; 920 kHz AM; 5 kw-D, DA2; 1 kw-N, DA2; N29 25 3 W94 56 12
7322 S.W. Freeway, Suite 500, Houston, TX 77074 US
(713) 779-9292
sales@kyst920am.com
License: Texas City, TX held by Hispanic Broadcasting Inc.
Arbitron Metro Market: Texas City, TX
Cruz Velasquez, General Manager

Thorndale

KOKE-FM
09-30-2005; 99.3 MHz FM; *Hrs Open:* 24; 6 kw; Ant 328 ft; N30 29 23 W97 17 56
912 S. Capital of Texas Highway, Suite 400, Austin, TX 78746
(512) 416-1100
www.kokefm.com
info@kokefm.com
License: Thorndale, Milam County, TX held by Jackson Lake Broadcasting Co.
Nat'l Network: Moody; Salem Radio Network
Special Programming: Black 6 hrs wkly; *Hrs. of News Programming:* News progmg 10 hrs wkly
Kelly Nassour, Operations Dir
Lance Aldridge, General Manager
Dick Ellis, News Director

Three Rivers

KEMA
01-01-2003; 94.5 MHz FM; 48 kw; 492 ft.; N28 43 10 W98 2 34
404 Woodbury Lane, Hiawatha, KS 66434 US
(512) 383-1112
License: Three Rivers, Live Oak County, TX held by Roy E. Henderson

Roy Henderson, General Manager

Tom Bean

KLAK
01-06-1984; 97.5 MHz FM; *Hrs Open:* 24; 32 kw; 617 ft.; N33 28 30 W96 26 45
1700 Redbud Boulevard, Suite 185, McKinney, TX 75069-3270 US
(972) 542-9755; *Fax:* (972) 838-1330
www.975klak.com
david.smith@digity.me
License: Tom Bean, Grayson County, TX held by NM Licensing LLC.
Group Owner: NextMedia Group Inc.; (acq 11-26-2001; grpsl).
Nat'l Network: ABC
Arbitron Metro Market: Dallas, TX; *Format:* Adult Contemp; *Hrs. of News Programming:* news progmg 7 hrs wkly; *No. News Employees:* 1; *Target Audience:* 25-54; women
David Smith, General Manager
Leslee Hunter, Sales Manager
Johnny B, Programming Director
Laura Villa, Promotions Director
Alan Freemont, Production Director

Tomball

KSEV
12-01-1986; 700 kHz AM; 15 kw-D, DA2; 1 kw-N, DA2; N30 11 34 W95 35 40
11451 Katy Freeway, Suite 215, Houston, TX 77079 US
(281) 588-4800
www.ksevradio.com
info@ksevradio.com
License: Tomball, Harris Outer County, TX held by Patrick Broadcasting LP
Group Owner: Patrick Broadcasting LP
Nat'l Network: The Blaze Radio Network
Arbitron Metro Market: Houston-Galveston, TX; *Format:* News, News/Talk, 86
Dan Patrick, General Manager

Troup

KTBB
01-01-1981; 97.5 MHz FM; *Hrs Open:* 24; 13 kw; 443 ft.; N32 22 28 W95 16 24
1001 ESE Loop 323, Suite 455, Tyler, TX 75701 US
(903) 593-2519; *Fax:* (903) 597-8378
www.ktbb.com
License: Troup, Smith County, TX held by ATW Media, LLC
Group Owner: Gleiser Communications, LLC; (acq 11-21-2003; grpsl)
Arbitron Metro Market: Tyler-Longview, TX; *Format:* News/Talk; *Hrs. of News Programming:* news progmg 2 hrs wkly; *No. News Employees:* 1; *Target Audience:* 35 plus.; *Adv. Rates:* 30; 25; 30; 15
Paul Berry, Operations Dir
Mike Edwards, News Director

Tulia

KBTE
04-01-1991; 104.9 MHz FM; *Hrs Open:* 24; 96.6 kw; 978 ft.; N33 57 35 W101 35 20
#33 Briercroft Park Office Park, Lubbock, TX 79423 US
(806) 762-3000; *Fax:* (806) 770-5363
www.1049thebeat.com
License: Tulia, Swisher County, TX held by Alpha Media Licensee LLC
Group Owner: Alpha Media LLC; (acq 5-15-2015; grpsl).
Nat'l Network: ABC
Arbitron Metro Market: Lubbock, TX; *Format:* Urban Contemporary; *Target Audience:* 18-34.
Jeff Scott, Operations Manager
Jay Richardson, General Manager
Randy Gattis, Sales Manager
Damon Scott, Programming Director

Tye

KBCY
10-01-1983; 99.7 MHz FM; *Hrs Open:* 24; 100 kw; 745 ft.; N32 24 39 W100 6 26
2525 South Danville, Abilene, TX 79605 US
(325) 793-9700; *Fax:* (325) 692-1576
www.kbcy.com
License: Tye, Taylor County, TX held by Cumulus Licensing Corp.
Group Owner: Cumulus Media Inc.; (acq 2-13-98; grpsl)
Arbitron Metro Market: Abilene, TX; *Format:* Country *Special Programming:* Relg 5 hrs wkly; *Hrs. of News Programming:* News progmg 21 hrs wkly; *Target Audience:* 25-49; upscale adults
Ronnie L. Baird, General Manager
Kelly Jay, Programming Director
Lori Morris, Business Manager
Chetenne Turner, Texs Music

KWFA
1030 kHz AM; 5 kw-D, 370 w-N, DA-2; N32 27 37 W99 50 03
6720 Lakeview Dr., Carmichael, CA 95608
License: Tye, Taylor County, TX held by Marlene V. Borman.
Population Served: 61,762; *Arbitron Metro Market:* Carmichael, CA
Marlene Borman, General Manager

Tyler

KGLD
07-05-2004; 1330 kHz AM; *Hrs Open:* 24; 1 kw-D, ND1; 0.077 kw-N, ND1; N32 22 35 W95 15 55
2737 S. Broadway, Tyler, TX 75701 US
(903) 526-1330
www.kgld.org
kgldradio@yahoo.com
License: Tyler, TX held by Salt of the Earth Broadcasting Inc.
Format: Gospel *Special Programming:* Urban 3 hrs wkly; *No. News Employees:* 2; *Target Audience:* African American
Darrell Martin, General Manager

***KGLY**
06-01-1988; 91.3 MHz FM; *Hrs Open:* 24; 12 kw; 463 ft.; N32 21 6 W95 16 0
Mailing Address: 2721 E. Erwin, Tyler, TX 75708 US
Second Address: PO Box 8525, Tyler, TX 75711
(903) 593-5863; *Fax:* (903) 593-2663
www.kgly.com
License: Tyler, Smith County, TX held by Educational Radio Foundation of East Texas Inc.
Nat'l Network: Moody; USA
Format: Religious; *Hrs. of News Programming:* News progmg 3 hrs wkly; *Target Audience:* 35 plus.
Troy Kriechbaum, President/CEO
Gary Lesniewski, VP Broadcasting/Station Manager
Chad Stanley, Director of Development
Jill Smith, Director of Community Connections
Leah Coombs, Director of Community Outreach/Donor Relations

KKUS
01-01-1990; 104.1 MHz FM; *Hrs Open:* 24; 50 kw; 492 ft.; N32 29 32 W95 28 51
210 S. Broadway, Suite 100, Tyler, TX 75702 US
(903) 581-9966; *Fax:* (903) 534-5300
www.theranch.fm
License: Tyler, Smith County, TX held by Alpha Media Licensee LLC
Group Owner: Alpha Media LLC; (acq 4-14-2015; grpsl).
Nat'l Network: Fox News Radio; *Nat'l Reps:* McGavren Guild
Arbitron Metro Market: Tyler, TX; *Format:* Country; *Target Audience:* 35+.; *Adv. Rates:* 50; 50; 50; 50
Dru Laborde, Operations Manager
Ginger Dockery, General Manager
Corinna Ruiz, Sales Manager
Gary Walker, Programming Director
Harlen Lobley, Director of Sales

KNUE
12-31-1964; 101.5 MHz FM; *Hrs Open:* 24; 98 kw; 1073 ft.; N32 15 35 W94 57 2
3810 Brookside Drive, Tyler, TX 75701 US
(903) 581-0606; *Fax:* (903) 581-2011
www.knue.com
License: Tyler, Smith County, TX held by Townsquare Media Tyler License LLC
Group Owner: Townsquare Media; (acq 8-3-2007; grpsl)
Arbitron Metro Market: Tyler, TX; *Format:* Country; *Target Audience:* General.
Johnny Lathrop, President/Chief Revenue Officer
John Roberts, Operations Manager
Michelle Hiltzman, Director Of Sales
Abel Sanchez, Digital Sales Manager

KTBB
08-28-1947; 600 kHz AM; *Hrs Open:* 24; 5 kw-D, 2.5 kw-N; N32 16 18 W95 12 23
1001 ESE Loop 323, Suite 455, Tyler, TX 75701 US
(903) 593-2519; *Fax:* (903) 597-4141
www.ktbb.com
License: Tyler, TX held by Gleiser Communications LLC
Group Owner: Gleiser Communications LLC; acq 11-21-2003; grpsl).
Regional Network: Texas State Networks
Arbitron Metro Market: Tyler-Longview, TX; *Format:* News, Talk, 84; *Hrs. of News Programming:* news progmg 70 hrs wkly; *No. News Employees:* 7; *Target Audience:* 35 plus.
Paul Berry, Operations Dir
Mike Edwards, News Director

KTYL-FM
02-01-1966; 93.1 MHz FM; *Hrs Open:* 24; 82 kw; 938 ft.; N32 15 35 W94 57 2
3810 Brookside Drive, Tyler, TX 75701 US
(903) 581-0606; *Fax:* (413) 734-4434
www.mix931.com
danielle@mix931.com
License: Tyler, Smith County, TX held by Townsquare Media Tyler License LLC
Group Owner: Townsquare Media; (acq 8-3-2007; grpsl)
Arbitron Metro Market: Tyler, TX; *Format:* Adult Contemp; *Target Audience:* 18-54.
Johnny Lathrop, President/Chief Revenue Officer
John Roberts, Operations Manager
Michelle Hiltzman, Director Of Sales
Abel Sanchez, Digital Sales Manager
Lucky Larry, Program Director

***KVNE**
10-15-1983; 89.5 MHz FM; *Hrs Open:* 24; 90 kw; 912 ft.; N32 32 21 W95 13 16
PO Box 8525, Tyler, TX 75711 US
(903) 593-5863; *Fax:* (903) 593-2663
www.kvne.com
License: Tyler, Smith County, TX held by Educational Radio Foundation of East Texas Inc.
Arbitron Metro Market: Tyler-Longview, TX; *Format:* Religious *Special Programming:* Gospel 4 hrs, children 4 hrs, Sp 2 hrs wkly; *Hrs. of News Programming:* News progmg 6 hrs wkly; *Target Audience:* 20-45; families
Jeff Strout, Chairman
Mike Harper, Station Manager
Dean Waskowiak, Vice Chairman
Lynn Roseman, Secretary/ Treasurer

KYZS
01-01-1930; 1490 kHz AM; *Hrs Open:* 24; 1 kw-U, ND1; N32 22 28 W95 16 24
1001 ESE Loop 323, Suite 455, Tyler, TX 75701 US
(903) 593-2519; *Fax:* (903) 597-4141
www.ktbb.com
License: Tyler, TX held by Gleiser Communications LLC
Group Owner: Gleiser Communications LLC; acq 11-21-2003; grpsl).
Arbitron Metro Market: Tyler, TX; *Format:* Sports
Paul Berry, Operations Dir
Mike Edwards, News Director

KRWR
01-01-1975; 92.1 MHz FM; *Hrs Open:* 24; 9.6 kw; N32 22 28 W95 16 24
1001 ESE Loop 323, Suite 455, Tyler, TX 75701 US
(903) 593-2519; *Fax:* (903) 597-4141
www.ktbb.com
License: Tyler, TX held by Gleiser Communications LLC
Group Owner: Gleiser Communications LLC
Arbitron Metro Market: Tyler, TX; *Format:* Sports
Paul Berry, Operations Dir
Mike Edwards, News Director

Umbarger

***KRBG**
01-01-2008; 88.7 MHz FM; 9.5 kw; Ant 374 ft; N34 53 50 W102 14 08
5331 Mt. Alifan Dr., San Diego, CA 95834
(858) 277-4991; *Fax:* (858) 277-1365
www.radiobygrace.com
contact@radiobygrace.com
License: Umbarger, Deaf Smith County, TX held by Grace Community Church of Amarillo

Mike MacIntosh, President

Universal City

KSAH
11-01-1986; 720 kHz AM; *Hrs Open:* 24; 10 kw-D, DA2; 0.89 kw-N, DA2; N29 31 51 W98 10 39
4050 Eisenhauer Rd., San Antonio, TX 78218 US
(210) 654-5100; *Fax:* (210) 855-5016
License: Universal City, Bexar County, TX held by Alpha Media Licensee LLC
Group Owner: Alpha Media LLC; (acq 1-31-2014; grpsl).
Arbitron Metro Market: San Antonio, TX; *Format:* Tejano; *Hrs. of News Programming:* news progmg 2 hrs wkly; *No. News Employees:* 1; *Target Audience:* 18-49.
Lance Hawkins, General Manager
Juan Mendez, General Sales Mgr
Pat Cerullo, Programming Director
Jeff Caudell, Chief Engineer

University Park

KTNO
01-01-1938; 1440 kHz AM; *Hrs Open:* 24
6400 N. Belt Line Road, Irving, TX 75063 US
(214) 574-5866; *Fax:* (214) 561-9662
www.ktnoam.com
License: University Park, TX held by Salem Communications Corp.
Group Owner: Salem Communications Corp.; (acq 8-8-97; $650,000).
Nat'l Network: ABC
Arbitron Metro Market: Dallas-Fort Worth; *Format:* Christian, Talk; *Hrs. of News Programming:* news progmg 40 hrs wkly; *No. News Employees:* 2; *Target Audience:* 25 plus.
Jose Castillo, General Manager
Erica Garcia, News Director
Mike Benhauser, Chief Engineer

KZMP
09-04-2016; 1540 kHz AM; *Hrs Open:* 24; 32 kw-D, DA2; 0.75 kw, DA2; N32 48 45 W97 0 30 *Rebroadcasts:* Simulcasts KZZA(FM)
2410 Gateway Dr, Irving, TX 75063 US
(972) 652-2900
dallasinfo@lbimedia.com
License: University Park, Dallas County, TX held by Liberman Broadcasting of Dallas License LLC.
Group Owner: Liberman Broadcasting Inc.; (acq 11-2-2006; grpsl)
Arbitron Metro Market: University Park, TX; *Format:* Spanish
Lenard Liberman, President
Eduardo Leon, Vice President, Programming

Uvalde

KBNU
01-01-1996; 93.9 MHz FM; *Hrs Open:* 24; 25 kw horiz, 14.3 kw vert; 292 ft.; N29 16 34 W99 41 44 *Rebroadcasts:* Rebroadcast KBLT(FM) Leakey 100%
8620 North New Braunfels, Suite 305, San Antonio, TX 78217 US
(830) 278-3693; *Fax:* (830) 278-2329
License: Uvalde, Uvalde County, TX held by Radio Cactus Ltd.
Format: Country; *Target Audience:* General; 18-49; *Adv. Rates:* 8; 8; 8; 5
John Furr, CEO
Regenia Tumbarello, General Manager
Paula Furr, CFO

KUVA
08-20-1984; 102.3 MHz FM; *Hrs Open:* 24; 4 kw; 217 ft.; N29 11 16 W99 46 36
1400 Batesville Road, Uvalde, TX 78801 US
(806) 853-9147; *Fax:* (815) 346-2084
License: Uvalde, Uvalde County, TX held by Rhattigan Broadcasting (Texas) LP
Group Owner: Rhattigan Broadcasting (Texas) LP; acq 6-3-2004; grpsl).
Nat'l Network: ABC; *Regional Network:* Texas State Networks
Arbitron Metro Market: Uvalde, TX; *Format:* Tejano; *Hrs. of News Programming:* 6 hrs wkly; *No. News Employees:* 1; *Target Audience:* 16-60; Hispanic
Glenn Tryon, General Manager
Jose Rodriguez, Station Manager
Hank Dicke, Sales
Elizabeth Zarate, Sales
Erica Uriegas, Office

KGWU
04-04-1947; 1400 kHz AM; *Hrs Open:* 24; 1 kw-U; N29 11 16 W99 46 36
Mailing Address: Box 758, Uvalde, TX 77802
Second Address: 1400 Batesville Rd., Uvalde, TX 78801
(830) 278-2555; *Fax:* (830) 278-9461
www.uvalderadio.com
production@uvalderadio.com
License: Uvalde, Uvalde County, TX held by Rhattigan Broadcasting (Texas) LP
Group Owner: Rhattigan Broadcasting (Texas) LP; (acq 8-19-2004; grpsl)
Regional Network: Texas State Networks
Population Served: 85,800 *Special Programming:* Farm 12 hrs wkly; *Hrs. of News Programming:* news progmg 15 hrs wkly; *No. News Employees:* 1; *Target Audience:* 25-54; general
Glenn Tryon, General Manager

KVOU-FM
09-09-1976; 104.9 MHz FM; *Hrs Open:* 24; 25 kw; 272 ft.; N29 11 16 W99 46 37
Mailing Address: 2402 Broadmoor, Bldg, D-2, Suite 101, Bryan, TX 77802 US
Second Address: 1400 Batesville Rd., Uvalde, TX 78801
(806) 853-9147; *Fax:* (815) 346-2084
www.uvalderadio.com
production@uvalderadio.com
License: Uvalde, Uvalde County, TX held by Rhattigan Broadcasting (Texas) LP
Group Owner: Rhattigan Broadcasting (Texas) LP; (acq 8-19-2004; grpsl)
Regional Network: Texas State Networks
Arbitron Metro Market: Uvalde, TX; *Format:* Country *Special Programming:* High school play-by-play sports; *Hrs. of News Programming:* 15+ hrs wkly; *No. News Employees:* 1; *Target Audience:* 18-49.
Glenn Tryon, General Manager

Van Horn

***KVHR**
91.5 MHz FM; 0.1 kw; -95 ft.; N31 2 2 W104 51 19
P.O. Box 3206, Tupelo, MS 38803 US
(662) 844-8888; *Fax:* (662) 842-6791
www.afr.net
faq@afa.net
License: Van Horn, Culberson County, TX held by American Family Association.
Group Owner: American Family Radio
Arbitron Metro Market: Van Horn, TX; *Format:* Christian
Tim Wildmon, President
Donald Wildmon, Founder
Buddy Smith, Sr VP
Ed Vitagliano, Exec VP
Randy Sharp, Director Of Special Projects
Meeke Addison, Director Of Communications
Abraham Hamilton III, General Counsel

Vernon

KVWC
07-01-1939; 1490 kHz AM; *Hrs Open:* 6 AM-10 PM; 1 kw-U; N34 09 12 W99 16 09
Mailing Address: Box 1419, Vernon, TX 76385
Second Address: 302 E. Wilbarger St., Vernon, TX 76384
(940) 552-6221; *Fax:* (940) 553-4222
www.kvwc.com
kvwc@kvwc.com
License: Vernon, Wilbarger County, TX held by KVWC Inc.
Nat'l Reps: Riley
Population Served: 25,000 *Special Programming:* Gospel 16 hrs wkly; *Hrs. of News Programming:* news progmg 10 hrs wkly; *No. News Employees:* 1; *Target Audience:* General; Wilbarger & surrounding counties
Mike Klappenbach, General Manager
Shirley Yoakum, Traffic Manager

KVWC-FM
04-10-1972; 103.1 MHz FM; *Hrs Open:* 6 AM-10 PM; 6 kw; Ant 141 ft; N34 09 12 W99 16 09
Mailing Address: Box 1419, Vernon, TX 76384
Second Address: 302 E. Wilbarger St., Vernon, TX 76384
(940) 552-6221; *Fax:* (940) 553-4222
www.kvwc.com
License: Vernon, Wilbarger County, TX
Population Served: 100,000
Mike Klappenbach, General Manager
Shirley Yoakum, Traffic Director

***KVED**
04-01-1994; 88.5 MHz FM; 3 kw vert; 289 ft.
PO Box 8088, Amarillo, TX 79114 US
(806) 359-8855; *Fax:* (806) 354-2039
License: Vernon, TX held by Top O'Texas Educational Broadcasting Foundation
Group Owner: Top O'Texas Educational Broadcasting Foundation
Arbitron Metro Market: Vernon, TX; *Format:* Religious

Victoria

KVNN
01-01-1940; 1340 kHz AM; *Hrs Open:* 24; 1 kw-U, ND1; N28 49 49 W97 0 33
8023 Vantage Dr., Suite 840, San Antonio, TX 78230 US
License: Victoria, TX held by Victoria RadioWorks Ltd.
Group Owner: Victoria RadioWorks Ltd.; (acq 10-26-98; $2.1 million with co-located FM).
Regional Network: Texas State Networks; *Nat'l Reps:* McGavren Guild
Arbitron Metro Market: Victoria, TX; *Format:* Country; *Target Audience:* 25-54; adults
Cindy Cox, General Manager

***KAYK**
10-01-2003; 88.5 MHz FM; 50 kw vert; 282 ft.; N28 46 43 W97 2 51
P.O. Box 3206, Tupelo, MS 38803 US
(662) 844-8888; *Fax:* (662) 842-6791
www.afr.net
faq@afa.net
License: Victoria, Victoria County, TX held by American Family Association.
Group Owner: American Family Radio
Arbitron Metro Market: Tupelo, MS; *Format:* Christian
Tim Wildmon, President
Donald Wildmon, Founder
Buddy Smith, Sr VP
Ed Vitagliano, Exec VP
Randy Sharp, Director Of Special Projects
Meeke Addison, Director Of Communications
Abraham Hamilton III, General Counsel & Public Policy

KBAR-FM
02-02-1989; 100.9 MHz FM; 15 kw; 427 ft.; N28 46 55 W96 56 29
8023 Vantage Dr., Suite 840, San Antonio, TX 78230 US
License: Victoria, Victoria County, TX held by Victoria RadioWorks Ltd.
Group Owner: Victoria RadioWorks Ltd.; (acq 1999; $27,500)
Arbitron Metro Market: San Antonio, TX; *Format:* Rock/AOR
Cindy Cox, General Manager

KIXS
12-04-1980; 107.9 MHz FM; 100 kw; 505 ft.; N28 42 24 W96 50 6
Mailing Address: 600 Congress Avenue, Suite 1400, Austin, TX 78701 US
Second Address: 107 North Star Dr., Victoria, TX 77904
(361) 573-0777; *Fax:* (361) 578-0059
www.kixs.com
kixs@gapbroadcasting.com
License: Victoria, Victoria County, TX held by Townsquare Media Victoria License LLC
Group Owner: Townsquare Media; (acq 10-1-2007; grpsl)
Arbitron Metro Market: San Antonio, TX; *Format:* Country; *Target Audience:* 25-49; listeners in a growth & acquisition mode
Joe Bob Burris, Brand Manager
Jeff Lyon, Director Of Sales

KTXN-FM
12-01-1994; 98.7 MHz FM; *Hrs Open:* 24; 100 kw; 253 ft.; N28 48 46 W97 3 45
107 North Star, Victoria, TX 77904 US
(361) 573-0777
www.987jack.com
AdamWest@townsquaremedia.com
License: Victoria, Victoria County, TX held by Broadcast Equities Texas Inc.
Arbitron Metro Market: Victoria, TX; *Format:* Adult Contemp; *Target Audience:* 18-54; general
Jeff Lyon, Director of Sales
Adam West, Brand Manager

KVIC
04-08-1976; 104.7 MHz FM; *Hrs Open:* 24; 12.7 kw; 459 ft.; N28 46 55 W96 56 29
Mailing Address: 8023 Vantage Dr., Suite 840, San Antonio, TX 78230 US
Second Address: 3613 N. Main St., Victoria, TX 77901
(361) 576-6111; *Fax:* (361) 572-0014)
License: Victoria, Victoria County, TX
Group Owner: Victoria RadioWorks Ltd.
Arbitron Metro Market: Victoria, TX; *Format:* Adult Contemp; *Target Audience:* 18-49.
Michael Cutchall, President
Jose Rodilles, General Manager
Ellen Cavanaugh, General Sales Mgr
Jaque Bosque Diaz, National Sales Manager

KQVT
12-01-1990; 92.3 MHz FM; *Hrs Open:* 24; 6 kw; 299 ft.; N28 46 7 W96 59 10
107 North Star, Victoria, TX 77904 US
(940) 763-1290; *Fax:* (361) 578-0059
www.newstalk1290.com
AdamWest@townsquaremedia.com
License: Victoria, Victoria County, TX held by Townsquare Media Victoria License LLC
Group Owner: Townsquare Media; (acq 10-1-2007; grpsl)
Arbitron Metro Market: Victoria, TX; *Format:* Adult Contemp
Scott Smith, General Manager
Mike Hendren, Brand Manager
Stacy Gellner, Digital Sales Manager
Aaron Galloway, Digital Managing Editor

***KVRT**
01-01-1995; 90.7 MHz FM; 30 kw; 328 ft.; N28 46 55 W96 56 30
Rebroadcasts: Rebroadcasts KEDT-FM Corpus Christi 100%
4455 S.Padre Isl.Dr.#38, Corpus Christi, TX 78411 US
(361) 855-2213; *Fax:* (361) 855-3877
www.kedt.org
bobscott@kedt.org
License: Victoria, Victoria County, TX held by South Texas Public Broadcasting System Inc.
Nat'l Network: NPR
Format: Jazz, News
Don Dunlap, President/General Manager
Bob Scott, Engineering Director
Ted Nelson, News Director
Myra A. Lombardo, VP
Mary Ann Buchanan, Director, Membership

Leanne Winkler, Director, Corporate Support
Stewart Jacoby, Director,Radio Programming
Pam Stakes, Music Director

***KXGJ**
09-01-1994; 89.3 MHz FM; 9.5 kw; 115 meters; N28 46 20 W96 57 17 *Rebroadcasts:* Rebroadcasts KSBJ(FM) Humble 100%
1600 Pasadena Blvd, Pasadena, TX 77347
(713) 589-1336; *Fax:* (713) 589-1335
www.radioaleluya.org
License: Victoria, Victoria County, TX held by Aleluya Broadcasting Network
Washington Law Firm: Dan J Alpert
Nat'l Network: USA
Population Served: 72,596 *Target Audience:* 25-54.
Roberto Villarreal, President

KNAL
04-16-1948; 1410 kHz AM; *Hrs Open:* 24
Mailing Address: 8030 Arrowridge Boulevard, Charlotte, NC 28273 US
Second Address: 3613 N. Main St., Victoria, TX 77901
(361) 510-3600
License: Victoria, TX held by Victoria RadioWorks Ltd.
Group Owner: Victoria RadioWorks Ltd.; (acq 2-1-2002; $100,000).
Arbitron Metro Market: San Antonio, TX; *Format:* Adult Contemp
Cindy Cox, General Manager

Waco

KRZI
01-01-2001; 1660 kHz AM
US
(254) 388-5000
www.1660espn.com
License: Waco, TX held by M&M Broadcasters Ltd.
Group Owner: M&M Broadcasters Ltd.; (acq 6-3-2010; grpsl)
Nat'l Network: ESPN Radio
Arbitron Metro Market: Waco, TX; *Format:* Sports
Tom Barfield, Operations Dir
Daryl O'Neal, General Manager
Bill Le Grand, General Sales Mgr

KBBW
04-01-1953; 1010 kHz AM
1019 Washington Avenue, Waco, TX 76701 US
(800) 460-1010
www.kbbw.com
info@kbbw.com
License: Waco, TX held by Steve Williams dba American Broadcasting of Texas.
Arbitron Metro Market: Waco, TX; *Format:* Christian; *Target Audience:* 25-54.
Steve Williams, President
Ryan Williams, Operations Dir
Elizabeth Layne, Station Manager
Dave Fricker, Chief Engineer

KBCT
08-01-1996; 94.5 MHz FM; *Hrs Open:* 24; 3.2 kw; 453 ft.; N31 30 31 W97 10 3
4701 West Waco Drive, Waco, TX 76710 US
(254) 313-1450; *Fax:* (254) 313-1420
www.centraltexasbeat.com
License: Waco, McLennan County, TX held by Kennelwood Broadcasting Co. Inc.
Arbitron Metro Market: Waco, TX; *Format:* News, News/Talk, 86; *Adv. Rates:* 18; 18; 18; 10
Jerry Lenamon, President

KBGO
09-06-1959; 95.7 MHz FM; *Hrs Open:* 24; 24 kw; 505 ft.; N31 30 51 W97 11 43
314 W. State Hwy. 6, Waco, TX 76712 US
(254) 776-3900
www.kbgo.com
License: Waco, McLennan County, TX held by Capstar TX LLC
Group Owner: iHeartMedia; (acq 8-30-00; grpsl).
Arbitron Metro Market: Waco, TX; *Format:* Oldies; *Target Audience:* 35-64.
Evan Armstrong, General Manager
Jerry Ferch, Director of Sales
DeWayne Wells, Programming Director

***KWBU-FM**
03-15-1966; 103.3 MHz FM; *Hrs Open:* 7-1 am; 2.75 kw; 492 ft.; N31 26 27 W97 10 41
Mailing Address: One Bear Place, #97296, Waco, TX 76798-7296 US
Second Address: 2100 River Street, Waco, TX 76707
(254) 710-3695; *Fax:* (254) 710-3874
www.kwbu.org
License: Waco, McLennan County, TX held by Baylor University.
Nat'l Network: NPR; PRI
Arbitron Metro Market: Waco, TX; *Format:* Variety/Diverse
Special Programming: Jazz 10 hrs wkly; *Hrs. of News Programming:* news progmg 10 hrs wkly; *No. News Employees:* 1; *Target Audience:* under 45; collegeage
Joe Riley, President/CEO
Brodie Bashaw, Station Manager
Carla Hervey, Business Affairs Manager
Dave Ulman, Director of Development
Loretta Howard, Membership Manager

KWTX
05-01-1946; 1230 kHz AM; *Hrs Open:* 24; 1 kw-U, ND1; N31 31 42 W97 7 14
314 West State Highway 6, Waco, TX 76712 US
(254) 776-3900
www.newstalk1230.com
License: Waco, TX held by Capstar TX LLC
Group Owner: iHeartMedia; (acq 8-30-2000; grpsl)
Nat'l Network: ABC; *Nat'l Reps:* Clear Channel
Arbitron Metro Market: Waco, TX; *Format:* News, News/Talk, 86; *Target Audience:* 35-64; adults
Evan Armstrong, General Manager
Jerry Ferch, Director of Sales
DeWayne Wells, Programming Director

KWTX-FM
12-01-1970; 97.5 MHz FM; *Hrs Open:* 24; 100 kw; 1480 ft.; N31 20 15 W97 18 37
314 West State Highway 6, Waco, TX 76712 US
(254) 776-3900
www.975online.com
License: Waco, McLennan County, TX held by Capstar TX LLC
Group Owner: iHeartMedia
Arbitron Metro Market: Waco, TX; *Format:* Contemporary Hits/Top 40; *Target Audience:* 25-49; women
Evan Armstrong, General Manager
Jerry Ferch, Director of Sales
Tamme Taylor, PSA Director

WACO-FM
06-01-1960; 99.9 MHz FM; 90 kw; 1660 ft.; N31 20 15 W97 18 37
314 West State HI 6, Waco, TX 76712 US
(254) 776-3900
www.waco100.com
License: Waco, McLennan County, TX held by Capstar TX LLC
Group Owner: iHeartMedia; (acq 8-30-00; grpsl).
Arbitron Metro Market: Waco, TX; *Format:* Country; *No. News Employees:* 2; *Target Audience:* 25-54.
Evan Armstrong, General Manager
Jerry Ferch, Director of Sales
Zack Owen, Programming Director

Wake Village

***KHTA**
09-22-2000; 92.5 MHz FM; *Hrs Open:* 24; 25 kw; 328 ft.; N33 24 53 W93 58 12
2424 South Blvd., Houston, TX 77098 US
(713) 520-5200
www.khcb.org
email@khcb.org
License: Wake Village, Bowie County, TX held by Houston Christian Broadcasters Inc.
Group Owner: Houston Christian Broadcasters Inc.
Nat'l Network: Moody
Arbitron Metro Market: Houston, TX; *Format:* Christian; *Target Audience:* General; all ages, families
Bruce E. Munsterman, President

Waskom

KQHN
01-01-1968; 97.3 MHz FM; *Hrs Open:* 24; 42 kw; 533 ft.; N32 29 36 W93 45 55
270 Plaza Loop, Bossier City, LA 71111 US
(318) 549-8500; *Fax:* (318) 549-8545
i973hits@gmail.com
License: Waskom, Harrison County, TX held by Cumulus Licensing LLC.
Group Owner: Cumulus Media Inc.; (acq 11-1-2002; $1.75 million).
Arbitron Metro Market: Bossier City, LA; *Format:* Adult Contemp
Phil Robkin, General Manager
Gary Robinson, Promotions Manager
Dani Coate, News Director
Jasen Bragg, Engineering Dir
Danielle Kaiser, Regional Sales Manager

Waxahachie

KBEC
06-01-1955; 1390 kHz AM; *Hrs Open:* 24; 0.48 kw-D, DA2; 0.26 kw-N, DA2; N32 26 45 W96 48 15
711 Ferris Ave., Waxahachie, TX 75165 US
(972) 923-1390; *Fax:* (972) 935-0871
www.kbec.com
License: Waxahachie, TX held by Faye and Richard Tuck Inc.
Regional Network: Texas State Networks
Arbitron Metro Market: Waxahachie, TX; *Format:* Country *Special Programming:* Farm 5 hrs; *Hrs. of News Programming:* news progmg 15 hrs wkly; *No. News Employees:* 1; *Target Audience:* 25-54.
Ken Roberts, General Manager
Nancy Speelman, Office Manager

Weatherford

***KYQX**
01-05-1986; 89.5 MHz FM; *Hrs Open:* 24; 4.5 kw; 518 ft.; N32 51 5 W98 6 31
1612 S. Main Street, Weatherford, TX 76086 US
(817) 341-2337; *Fax:* (817) 598-1661
www.qxfm.com
brent@qxfm.com
License: Weatherford, Parker County, TX held by CSSI Non Profit Educational Broadcasting Corp.
Arbitron Metro Market: Weatherford, TX; *Format:* Classic Rock; *Hrs. of News Programming:* news progmg 7 hrs wkly; *No. News Employees:* 3
Brent Baker, News/Sports
Shilo Treille, Underwriting Representative

KZEE
08-12-1956; 1220 kHz AM
(817) 577-1220
www.radio1220am.com
info@radiohotpepper.com
License: Weatherford, TX held by Tarrant Radio Broadcasting Inc.
Arbitron Metro Market: Weatherford, TX; *Format:* Christian, Gospel
Parvez Malik, President

***KMQX**
01-01-1995; 88.5 MHz FM; *Hrs Open:* 24; 3.5 kw; 518 ft.; N32 51 5 W98 6 31
1612 S. Main, Weatherford, TX 76086 US
(817) 341-2337; *Fax:* (817) 613-0230
www.qxfm.com
brent@qxfm.com
License: Weatherford, Parker County, TX held by CSSI Non-Profit Educational Broadcast Inc.
Arbitron Metro Market: Weatherford, TX; *Format:* News, Oldies, 84; *No. News Employees:* 3
Brent Baker, News/Sports
Shilo Treille, Underwriting Representative

Wells

KVLL-FM
01-01-1993; 94.7 MHz FM; *Hrs Open:* 24; 50 kw; 384 ft.; N31 6 47 W94 48 32
Mailing Address: 1470 Ben Sawyer Blvd, Suite 16, Mount Pleasant, SC 29464 US
Second Address: 1216 S. 1st St., Lufkin, TX 75901-4716
(936) 639-4455; *Fax:* (936) 632-5957
www.my947.com
johnny.lathrop@townsquaremedia.com
License: Wells, Cherokee County, TX held by Townsquare Media Lufkin License LLC
Group Owner: Townsquare Media; (acq 10-2-2007; $750,000)
Arbitron Metro Market: Lufkin, TX; *Format:* Oldies
Johnny Lathrop, General Manager
Dan Patrick, Brand Manager
Paula Divello, Director Of Sales
James Stillwell, Digital Managing Editor

Weslaco

KRGE
01-01-1926; 1290 kHz AM; *Hrs Open:* 24; 5 kw-D, DAN; 5 kw-N, DAN; N26 12 36 W97 54 33
P.O. Box 1290, Weslaco, TX 78596 US
(956) 968-7777
www.radiovida.com
License: Weslaco, TX held by Christian Ministries of the Valley.
Arbitron Metro Market: McAllen-Brownsv; *Format:* Christian; *Hrs. of News Programming:* News progmg 3 hrs wkly; *Target Audience:* 18-34.

Enrique Garza, General Manager
Candy Garza
Eduardo Lueuano

West Lake Hills

KTXZ

06-09-1982; 1560 kHz AM; 2.5 kw-U, DA-2
9434 Parkfield Drive, Austin, TX 78758 US
(512) 789-3265
License: West Lake Hills, TX held by Encino Broadcasting LLC
Group Owner: Encino Broadcasting LLC

Jose J. Garcia Jr., General Manager

West Odessa

*KFRI

01-01-2005; 88.7 MHz FM; *Hrs Open:* 24; 100 kw; 427 ft.; N31 50 53 W102 27 4 *Rebroadcasts:* Rebroadcasts KLRD(FM) Yucaipa, CA 100%
1425 North Market Blvd, Suite 9, Sacramento, CA 95834 US
(888) 937-2471; *Fax:* (916) 251-1650
www.air1.com
License: West Odessa, Ector County, TX held by Educational Media Foundation.
Group Owner: EMF Broadcasting
Nat'l Network: Air 1
Arbitron Metro Market: West Odessa, TX; *Format:* Alternative, Christian; *No. News Employees:* 3; *Target Audience:* 18-35.
Darrell Chambliss, Chairman
Alan Mason, COO
Mike Novak, President and CEO
David Pierce, Chief Creative Officer
Eric Moser, Chief Financial Officer
D. Kevin Blair, Secretary and General Counsel

Wharton

KANI

06-17-1962; 1500 kHz AM; 0.5 kW; N29 19 22 W96 3 32
15307 Falcon Ridge Dr, Humble, TX 77396 USA
(281) 441-3665
License: Wharton, TX held by Martin Broadcasting Inc.
Group Owner: Martin Broadcasting Inc.
Regional Network: Texas State Networks
Arbitron Metro Market: Houston, TX; *Format:* Gospel, Christian, 74 *Special Programming:* Sp 3 hrs, Pol 6 hrs wkly

Wheeler

*KPDR

08-31-1986; 90.3 MHz FM; *Hrs Open:* 24; 100 kw horiz; 594 ft.; N35 31 6 W100 32 43
PO Box 8088, Amarillo, TX 79114 US
(806) 359-8855; *Fax:* (806) 354-2039
www.kingdomkeysradio.org
License: Wheeler, Wheeler County, TX held by Top O' Texas Educational Broadcasting Foundation
Group Owner: Top O' Texas Educational Broadcasting Foundation
Nat'l Network: USA
Format: Religious *Special Programming:* Sp 5 hrs wkly; *Target Audience:* General.
Ricky Pfeil, President
Jeremy Pfeil, Promotions Manager

*KBDW

91.5 MHz FM; 3 kw horiz; 348 ft.; N35 31 6 W100 32 43 US
(806) 826-5202
License: Wheeler, Wheeler County, TX held by Solid Rock Foundation.
Arbitron Metro Market: Wheeler, TX
Gary Ware, President

Wheelock

KKEE

01-01-1950; 100.9 MHz FM; *Hrs Open:* 24; kw
US
(503) 861-6620; *Fax:* (503) 861-6630
License: Wheelock, Clatsop County, TX held by New Northwest Broadcasters LLC
Group Owner: New Northwest Broadcasters LLC; acq 8-24-99; grpsl)
Arbitron Metro Market: Wheelock, TX; *Format:* Talk; *Hrs. of News Programming:* news progmg 7 hrs wkly; *No. News Employees:* 1; *Target Audience:* 25-54; diverse
Kris Edwards, Operations Dir
Tom Freel, General Manager

White Oak

KAPW

05-17-2002; 99.3 MHz FM; *Hrs Open:* 24; 34 kw; 541 ft.; N32 35 17 W94 58 53
212 Old Grande Blvd., Suite B100, Tyler, TX 75703 US
(903) 581-5259
mega993.com
License: White Oak, Gregg County, TX held by Reynolds Radio Inc.
Group Owner: Reynolds Radio Inc.
Arbitron Metro Market: Tyler-Longview, TX; *Format:* Adult Contemp

Whitehouse

KISX

08-15-1982; 107.3 MHz FM; *Hrs Open:* 24; 50 kw; 486 ft.; N32 17 19 W95 11 56
3810 Brookside Dr., Tyler, TX 75701 US
(903) 581-0606; *Fax:* (903) 581-2011
craigreininger@gapbroadcasting.com
License: Whitehouse, Smith County, TX held by Townsquare Media Tyler License LLC
Group Owner: Townsquare Media; (acq 8-3-2007; grpsl)
Arbitron Metro Market: Tyler-Longview, TX; *Format:* Contemporary Hits/Top 40; *Target Audience:* 18-44.
President, Johnny Lathrop
John Roberts, Operations Manager
Michelle Hiltzman, Director Of Sales
Abel Sanchez, Digital Sales Manager
Shani Scott, Program Director

Whitesboro

KMAD-FM

06-01-1985; 102.5 MHz FM; *Hrs Open:* 24; 18 kw; 673 ft.; N33 41 31 W96 26 36
1800 Teague Drive, Suite 300, Sherman, TX 75090 US
(903) 463-6800; *Fax:* (903) 463-9816
www.theclassicrockexperience.com
License: Whitesboro, Grayson County, TX held by NM Licensing LLC.
Group Owner: NextMedia Group Inc.; (acq 11-26-2001; grpsl).
Format: Classic Rock
David Smith, General Manager
David Macmullen, General Sales Mgr
Jason Taylor, Programming Director
Jennifer Isbell, Promotions Manager

Wichita Falls

KLUR

04-14-1963; 99.9 MHz FM; 100 kw; 808 ft.; N33 54 4 W98 32 21
4302 Call Field Rd., Wichita Falls, TX 76308 US
(940) 691-2311; *Fax:* (940) 696-2255
www.klur.com
License: Wichita Falls, Wichita County, TX held by Cumulus Licensing Corp.
Group Owner: Cumulus Media Inc.; (acq 10-3-97; grpsl)
Arbitron Metro Market: Wichita Falls,; *Format:* Country
Jim Marks, General Manager
Lindy Parr, General Sales Mgr
Zach Morton, Programming Director
Jeff Chancey, Chief Engineer
Andrea Lewis, Regional Sales Manager

*KMOC

07-09-1987; 89.5 MHz FM; *Hrs Open:* 24 hours a day; 3 kw; 656 ft.; N33 53 23 W98 33 30
Mailing Address: P.O. Box 41, Wichita Falls, TX 76307 US
Second Address: 1040 W. Wenonah St., Wichita Falls, TX 76309
(940) 767-3303; *Fax:* (940) 723-5807
www.kmocfm.com
kmocfm@wf.net
License: Wichita Falls, Wichita County, TX held by Christian Service Foundation Inc.
Arbitron Metro Market: Wichita, TX; *Format:* Christian; *Target Audience:* 25-54.
Liz Sanderson, General Manager
Keith Sanderson, Station Manager
Daniel Boyd, Programming Director
Delvin Kinser, News Director

KNIN-FM

05-12-1975; 92.9 MHz FM; *Hrs Open:* 24; 100 kw; 808 ft.; N33 54 4 W98 32 21
6 Whitefield Drive, Lafayette Hill, PA 19444 US
(940) 763-1111; *Fax:* (940) 322-3166
www.929nin.com
info@929nin.com
License: Wichita Falls, Wichita County, TX held by Townsquare Media Wichita Falls License LLC
Group Owner: Townsquare Media; (acq 8-3-2007; grpsl)
Nat'l Reps: McGavren Guild
Arbitron Metro Market: Wichita Falls,; *Format:* Contemporary Hits/Top 40; *Target Audience:* 18-49.; *Adv. Rates:* 35; 25; 25; 20
Scott Smith, General Manager
Drew Bartlett, Brand Manager
Stacy Gellner, Digital Sales Manager
Aaron Galloway, Digital Managing Editor

KQXC-FM

01-07-1994; 103.9 MHz FM; *Hrs Open:* 24; 19 kw; 807 ft.; N33 54 4 W98 32 21
111 East Kilbourn Ave., Suite 2700, Milwaukee, WI 53202 US
(940) 691-2311; *Fax:* (940) 696-2255
www.thehot1039.com
License: Wichita Falls, Wichita County, TX held by Cumulus Licensing Corp.
Group Owner: Cumulus Media Inc.; (acq 10-3-97; grpsl).
Nat'l Network: ABC
Arbitron Metro Market: Wichita Falls metro area; *Format:* Contemporary Hits/Top 40; *Target Audience:* 18-45; males
Jim Marks, General Manager
Zach Morton, Programming Director
Susan Adkins, Promotions Manager
Jeff Chancey, Chief Engineer
Belda Holt, Regional Sales Manager

*KZKL

09-01-1993; 90.5 MHz FM; *Hrs Open:* 24; 7 kw; 430 ft.; N33 53 50 W98 32 33
3700 Onaway Tr., Wichita Falls, TX 76309 US
(916) 251-1600; *Fax:* (916) 251-1650
www.klove.com
License: Wichita Falls, Wichita County, TX held by Educational Media Foundation.
Group Owner: EMF Broadcasting; (acq 10-20-2005; $600,000)
Nat'l Network: K-Love
Arbitron Metro Market: Rocklin, CA; *Format:* Christian
Darrell Chambliss, Chairman
Mike Novak, CEO/COO
Mike Novak, President
David Pierce, Programming Director
Ed Lenane, News Director
Sam Wallington, Engineering Dir
Marya Morgan, News Reporter
Richard Hunt, News Reporter

KBZS

11-15-1984; 106.3 MHz FM; *Hrs Open:* 24; 50 kw; 423 ft.; N33 53 18 W98 34 8
2525 Kell Blvd., Suite 200, Wichita Falls, TX 76308 US
(940) 763-1111; *Fax:* (940) 322-3166
www.1063thebuzz.com
scottsmith@townsquaremedia.com
License: Wichita Falls, Wichita County, TX held by Townsquare Media Wichita Falls License LLC
Group Owner: Townsquare Media; (acq 8-3-2007; grpsl)
Nat'l Network: Westwood One; *Nat'l Reps:* McGavren Guild
Arbitron Metro Market: Wichita Falls, TX; *Format:* Adult Contemp, Rock/AOR; *Target Audience:* 18-49.; *Adv. Rates:* 30; 25; 25; 20
Scott Smith, General Manager
Johnny Thrash, Brand Manager
Stacy Gellner, Digital Sales Manager
Aaron Galloway, Digital Managing Editor

KWFS

01-01-1948; 1290 kHz AM; *Hrs Open:* 24; 5 kw-D, DAN; 0.073 kw-N, ND1; N33 57 38 W98 33 42
6 Whitefield Drive, Lafayette Hill, PA 19444 US
(940) 763-1111; *Fax:* (940) 322-3166
www.newstalk1290.com
License: Wichita Falls, TX held by Townsquare Media Wichita Falls License LLC
Group Owner: Townsquare Media; (acq 8-3-2007; grpsl)
Regional Network: Texas State Networks; *Nat'l Reps:* Clear Channel
Arbitron Metro Market: Wichita Falls, TX; *Format:* News, News/Talk, 86 *Special Programming:* Sp 4 hrs wkly; *Hrs. of News Programming:* news progmg 12 hrs wkly; *No. News Employees:* 1; *Target Audience:* 25 plus. *Adv. Rates:* 15; 8; 8; 8;
Scott Smith, General Manager
Mike Hendren, Brand Manager
Stacy Gellner, Digital Sales Manager
Aaron Galloway, Digital Managing Editor

KWFS-FM

01-01-1961; 102.3 MHz FM; *Hrs Open:* 24; 100 kw; 449 ft.; N33 53 51 W98 32 32
6 Whitefield Drive, Lafayette Hill, PA 19444 US

(940) 763-1111; *Fax:* (940) 322-3166
www.1023blakefm.com
License: Wichita Falls, Wichita County, TX held by Townsquare Media Wichita Falls License LLC
Group Owner: Townsquare Media
Arbitron Metro Market: Wichita Falls, TX; *Format:* Country; *Hrs. of News Programming:* News progmg one hr wkly; *Target Audience:* 18-49.; *Adv. Rates:* 30; 25; 25; 20
Scott Smith, General Manager
Drew Bartlett, Brand Manager
Stacy Gellner, Digital Sales Manager
Aaron Galloway, Digital Managing Editor

***KMCU**
88.7 MHz FM; *Hrs Open:* 24; 0.005 kw horiz, 3 kw vert; 253 ft.; N33 56 30 W98 34 6 *Rebroadcasts:* KCCU,KLW,KOCU,KYCU Lawton,Clinton,Ardmore,Altus, Oaklahoma, 90%
2800 West Gore Blvd, Lawton, OK 73505 US
(888) 454-7800; *Fax:* (580) 581-5571
www.kccu.org
kccu@cameron.edu
License: Wichita Falls, Wichita County, TX held by Cameron University.
Nat'l Network: NPR; PRI
Arbitron Metro Market: Wichita Falls, TX; *Format:* Classical, Jazz, 60; *Hrs. of News Programming:* news progmg 36 hrs wkly; *No. News Employees:* 2; *Target Audience:* 35 plus.
Ted Riley, General Manager, Director of Broadcasting
Doug Cole, Station Manager
Clinton Wieden, News Director
Cynthia Sosa, Production Director
Zach McGrew, Development Director

Willis

KVST
01-01-1998; 99.7 MHz FM; 2.9 kw; 482 ft.; N30 26 55 W95 31 48
1212 South Frazier, Conroe, TX 77301 US
(936) 788-1035; *Fax:* (936) 788-2525
www.kvst.com
dave@kstarcountry.com
License: Willis, Montgomery County, TX held by New Wavo Communication Group Inc.
Arbitron Metro Market: Willis, TX; *Format:* Country
Ben Amato, President
William Boggs, General Sales Mgr
Larry Galla, Programming Director
Mike Shilo, News Director
Dade Moore, Engineering Dir
Linda Lott, Traffic Manager
John Erle, Traffic Manager
Christine Amato, AccountManager
Sherry Ingram, Account Manager
Karen White, Account Manager
Barbara Farr, Account Manager

Winfield

KALK
09-27-1987; 97.7 MHz FM; *Hrs Open:* 24; 22.5 kw; 328 ft.; N33 11 1 W95 12 32
1798 US Hwy. 67 W., PO Box 990, Mount Pleasant, TX 75456 US
(903) 577-9775; *Fax:* (903) 572-7232
www.easttexasradio.com
bud@easttexasradio.com
License: Winfield, Titus County, TX held by East Texas Broadcasting Inc.
Group Owner: East Texas Broadcasting Inc.; acq 1999; $600,000).
Arbitron Metro Market: Mount Pleasant, TX; *Format:* Adult Contemp *Special Programming:* Gospel one hr wkly; *Hrs. of News Programming:* news progmg one hr wkly; *No. News Employees:* 1; *Target Audience:* 18-54;younger, upwardly mobile, white collar; *Adv. Rates:* 26; 23; 26; 21
Bud Kitchens, President/General Manager
Bryan Friesth, General Sales Mgr
Clint Cooper, News Director

Winnsboro

KWNS
09-01-1983; 104.7 MHz FM; *Hrs Open:* 24; 2.75 kw; 492 ft.; N33 4 17 W95 17 22
PO Box 54, 215 Market St., Winnsboro, TX 75494 US
(903) 342-3501
License: Winnsboro, Wood County, TX held by Lottie L. Foster, executor of estate of Richard E. Foster.
Arbitron Metro Market: Winnsboro, TX; *Format:* Gospel; *No. News Employees:* 1; *Target Audience:* 35-70.; *Adv. Rates:* 18; 18; 18; 18
Lottie Foster, President

Winona

KBLZ
102.7 MHz FM; 9.3 kw; 531 ft.; N32 23 9 W95 6 43
212 Old Grande Blvd., Suite B100, Tyler, TX 75703 US
(903) 581-5259
www.theblaze.fm
License: Winona, Smith County, TX held by S.O. 2,000 LLC.
Group Owner: Reynolds Radio Inc.; (acq 8-26-99)
Arbitron Metro Market: Tyler, TX; *Format:* Urban Contemporary

Winters

KORQ
11-01-1981; 96.1 MHz FM; *Hrs Open:* 24; 50 kw; Ant 492 ft; N32 12 52 W99 53 22
1500 Industrial Boulevard, Suite 200, Abilene, TX 79602
(325) 437-9596; *Fax:* (325) 673-1819
www.qabilene.com
dklement@abileneradio.com
License: Winters, Runnels County, TX held by Doud Media Group LLC
Nat'l Network: Fox News Radio; *Nat'l Reps:* Local Focus
Population Served: 425,000; *Arbitron Metro Market:* Abilene, TX; *Hrs. of News Programming:* news prgmg 10 hrs/week; *No. News Employees:* 1; *Target Audience:* 25-54; 18-49.

Wixon Valley

KBXT
11-07-1994; 101.9 MHz FM; *Hrs Open:* 24; 2.5 kw; 156.2 meters; 30 48 05N 96 27 58W
Mailing Address: Box 3069, Bryan, TX 78729
Second Address: 1240 E Villa Maria Rd, Bryan, TX 77802
(979) 776-1240; *Fax:* (979) 776-0123
License: Wixon Valley, Brazos County, TX held by Brazos Valley Communications Ltd.
Group Owner: Brazos Valley Communications Ltd.; (acq 8-31-2006; grpsl)
Nat'l Network: American Urban; *Nat'l Reps:* Katz Radio
Population Served: 150,000; *Arbitron Metro Market:* Bryan-College Station, TX *Special Programming:* Russ Parr AM Show
Dan Ginzel, Operations Dir
Chris Kiske, General Manager
Nathan Peacock, General Sales Mgr
Joseph Sanchez, Programming Director
Lance Parr, Chief Engineer

Wolfforth

KAIQ
01-01-2000; 95.5 MHz FM; *Hrs Open:* 24; 100 kw; 676 ft.; N33 31 3 W101 51 24
6502 Caprock Dr., Lubbocke, TX 79412 US
(806) 763-6051; *Fax:* (806) 744-8363
www.tricolor955.com
lflores@entravision.com
License: Wolfforth, Lubbock County, TX held by Entravision Holdings LLC.
Group Owner: Entravision Communications Corp.; (acq 2-10-2005; $1.5 million).
Nat'l Reps: Lotus Entravision Reps LLC
Arbitron Metro Market: Lubbock, TX; *Format:* Tejano; *Target Audience:* Hispanic.
Leticia Flores, General Manager
Isla Islas, Promotions Manager

Woodville

KWUD
01-04-1968; 1490 kHz AM; *Hrs Open:* 24; 1 kw-U, ND1; N30 44 52 W94 25 56
Mailing Address: 532 Magnolia Bend, League City, TX 77573 US
Second Address: 105 E Wheat, Woodville, TX 75979
(409) 283-8500; *Fax:* (409) 283-8500
License: Woodville, TX held by KWUD Inc.
Nat'l Network: ABC; Jones Radio Networks; *Regional Network:* Texas State Networks
Arbitron Metro Market: Woodville, TX; *Format:* Country *Special Programming:* Farm 2 hrs, gospel 6 hrs, relg 3 hrs wkly; *Hrs. of News Programming:* news progmg 12 hrs wkly; *No. News Employees:* 1; *Target Audience:* 18-55.; *Adv. Rates:* 10; 10; 10; 6
Jim Carroll, General Manager
Richard McCullough, Programming Director
Carol Carroll, News Director
Chester Leediker, Chief Engineer

Wylie

KHSE
01-01-2004; 700 kHz AM; *Hrs Open:* 24; directional US
(972) 354-1990
www.funasia.net
License: Wylie, TX held by Bernard Dallas LLC
Group Owner: Bernard Radio LLC; (acq 1-31-2007; $9 million with KFCD(AM) Farmersville)
Arbitron Metro Market: Wylie, TX; *Format:* Ethnic
Otter Miller, General Manager

Yoakum

KYKM
01-01-1982; 92.5 MHz FM; *Hrs Open:* 24; 3 kw; 299 ft.; N29 21 3 W97 11 32
111 North Main, Hallettsville, TX 77964 US
(361) 798-4333; *Fax:* (361) 798-3798
www.texasthunderradio.com
texasthunderradio@yahoo.com
License: Yoakum, Lavaca County, TX held by Kremling Enterprises Inc.
Arbitron Metro Market: Hallettsville, TX; *Format:* Country *Special Programming:* Polka 9 hrs wkly; *Hrs. of News Programming:* news progmg 12 hrs wkly; *No. News Employees:* 1; *Target Audience:* General.
Laura Kremling, General Manager
Travis Kremling, Programming Director

Yorktown

KGGB
01-01-2009; 96.3 MHz FM; 6 kw; 328 ft.; N29 2 43 W97 24 23 US
License: Yorktown, De Witt County, TX held by Gerald Benavides.
Group Owner: Claro Communications Ltd.
Arbitron Metro Market: Yorktown, TX
Gerald Benavides, Owner/General Manager

Zapata

KJJS
103.9 MHz FM; 4.5 kw; 377 ft.; N26 55 3 W99 15 0 US
License: Zapata, Zapata County, TX held by Hispanic Target Media Inc.
Group Owner: Hispanic Target Media Inc.
Arbitron Metro Market: Zapata, TX
Francisco San Millan, President
Meredith Senter, General Manager

Utah

Ballard

KFMR
95.5 MHz FM; 0.89 kw; 1660 ft.; N40 32 16 W109 41 57 US
(520) 797-4434
License: Ballard, Sublette County, UT held by SkyWest Media L.L.C.
Group Owner: SkyWest Media L.L.C.
Arbitron Metro Market: Houston-Galveston
Ted Tucker, General Manager

Beaver

***KEZB**
90.7 MHz FM; 0.1 kw; -509 ft.; N38 17 13.2 W112 38 18.5
220 East Center Street, PO Box 2132, Beaver, UT 84713 US
(435) 438-2342
www.fbcbeaver.wordpress.com
License: Beaver, Beaver County, UT held by Christian Vision Inc.
Arbitron Metro Market: Beaver, UT; *Format:* Religious
Lois McLario, President

Blanding

KBDX
92.7 MHz FM; *Hrs Open:* 8am-5pm; 0.594 kw horiz, 0.255 kw vert; 3406 ft.; N37 50 24 W109 27 41
2423 East Main Street, Cortez, CO 81321 US
(970) 564-7170; *Fax:* (888) 429-7722
www.redrock92.com
License: Blanding, San Juan County, UT held by KBDX Blanding L.L.C.
Arbitron Metro Market: Kailua-Kona, HI; *Format:* Oldies; *Adv. Rates:* 10; 10; 10; 10

Bountiful

KJMY
03-15-1988; 99.5 MHz FM; *Hrs Open:* 24; 39 kw; 2953 ft.; N40 36 29 W112 9 33
280 S. Decker Lake Dr., Salt Lake City, UT 84119 US
(801) 908-1300
www.my995fm.com
License: Bountiful, Davis County, UT held by Citicasters Licenses Inc.
Group Owner: iHeartMedia; (acq 1999; grpsl).
Nat'l Reps: Clear Channel; Katz Radio
Arbitron Metro Market: Bountiful, UT; *Format:* Adult Contemp; *Target Audience:* 18-49; adults
Stu Stanek, Regional President
Judy Copier, Senior Vice President of Sales

Brian Head

KREC
11-14-1988; 98.1 MHz FM; *Hrs Open:* 24; 54 kw; 2526 ft.; N37 32 32 W113 4 5
750 W. Ridge View Drive, St. George, UT 84770 US
(435) 673-3579; *Fax:* (435) 673-8900
www.star98online.com
License: Brian Head, Iron County, UT held by CCR-St. George IV LLC.
Group Owner: Cherry Creek Radio LLC; (acq 8-10-2006; grpsl)
Arbitron Metro Market: St. George; *Format:* Adult Contemp; *Target Audience:* 25-54.; *Adv. Rates:* 25; 18; 18; 16
Chris McCarthy, General Sales Mgr
Rick Parrish, Promotions Manager
Dave Cory, Chief Engineer

Brigham City

KEGH
10-20-1972; 106.9 MHz FM; 5.2 kw; 2165 ft.; N41 47 3 W112 13 55
50 W. Broadway, Suite 200, Salt Lake City, UT 84101 US
(801) 524-2600
www.1015theeagle.com
jdanielson@bwaymedia.com
License: Brigham City, Box Elder County, UT held by Broadway Media LS, LLC
Group Owner: Broadway Media Group; (acq 4-19-2004; $3.95 million)
Arbitron Metro Market: Salt Lake City, UT; *Format:* Country
Brandon Francis, General Sales Mgr
Jared Danielson, Programming Director

KXOL
07-01-1998; 1660 kHz AM; *Hrs Open:* 24
80 S. Redwood Rd., North Salt Lake, UT 84054 US
(801) 936-0706; *Fax:* (801) 936-0670
info@kxol.com
License: Brigham City, UT held by Inca Communications
Arbitron Metro Market: Salt Lake City-Ogden-Provo, UT; *Format:* Tejano
Jennifer Rodriguez, General Manager
Daniel Advincule, General Sales Mgr
Valentin Alvarez, Programming Director

Cedar City

KCIN
05-10-1974; 94.9 MHz FM; 55 kw; -121 ft.; N37 45 51 W113 6 15
5 North Main Street, Suite 209, Cedar City, UT 84720 US
(435) 867-8156; *Fax:* (435) 673-8900
www.bigkickincountry.com
License: Cedar City, Iron County, UT held by CCR-St. George IV LLC.
Group Owner: Cherry Creek Radio LLC; (acq 5-3-2006; grpsl)
Format: Contemporary Hits/Top 40
Chris McCarthy, General Sales Mgr
Rick Parrish, Promotions Manager

KXBN
10-15-1976; 92.1 MHz FM; *Hrs Open:* 24; 95 kw; 1745 ft.; N37 38 43 W113 22 22
750 W. Ridge View Drive, St. George, UT 84770 US
(435) 673-3579; *Fax:* (435) 673-8900
www.b92fmonline.com
License: Cedar City, Iron County, UT
Group Owner: Cherry Creek Radio LLC
Nat'l Network: Jones Radio Networks
Arbitron Metro Market: Cedar City, UT; *Format:* Oldies; *Hrs. of News Programming:* News progmg 5 hrs wkly

KSUB
07-04-1937; 590 kHz AM; *Hrs Open:* 24
5 N. Main Street, Cedar City, UT 84720 US
(435) 867-8156; *Fax:* (435) 586-4444
www.ksub590.com
License: Cedar City, UT held by CCR-St. George IV LLC.
Group Owner: Cherry Creek Radio LLC; (acq 5-3-2006; grpsl).
Nat'l Network: CBS *Regional Reps:* Target Radio.
Arbitron Metro Market: Saint George, UT; *Format:* News, News/Talk, 86 *Special Programming:* Relg, loc talk, farm 6 hrs wkly; *Hrs. of News Programming:* news progmg 15 hrs wkly; *No. News Employees:* 1 *TargetAudience:* 35-65; adults
Brent Miner, General Manager
Steve Miner, Programming Director
Dan Hobson, Chief Engineer

***KSUU**
10-01-1966; 91.1 MHz FM; *Hrs Open:* 6 AM-midnight (winter); 10 AM-10 PM; 10 kw; -463 ft.; N37 38 55 W113 5 32
351 West University Blvd., Student Center 176C, Cedar City, UT 84720 US
(435) 704-4733
www.power91radio.com
License: Cedar City, Iron County, UT held by Southern Utah University.
Arbitron Metro Market: Cedar City, UT; *Format:* Contemporary Hits/Top 40 *Special Programming:* News, class 3 hrs, rhythm and blues 4 hrs, rock 4 hrs wkly; *Hrs. of News Programming:* News progmg 2 hrs wkly *TargetAudience:* 12-34; children, university students
John Gholdston, Overseer
Chris Holmes, News/Sports Director
Cal Rollins, Station Manager

***KCHG**
88.9 MHz FM; 6.7 kw; 2605 ft.; N37 32 29 W113 4 4
101 East Nichols Canyon Road, Unit A-5, Cedar City, UT 84721 US
(435) 263-0300; *Fax:* (435) 586-2700
www.crossoverfm.org
info@crossoverfm.org
License: Cedar City, Iron County, UT held by Calvary Chapel Cedar City Inc.
Arbitron Metro Market: Cedar City, UT
Cathy Horton, Operations Manager
Joe Carroll, General Manager
Georgene Flegle, Program Manager

Centerville

KTUB
12-01-1957; 1600 kHz AM; *Hrs Open:* 24; 5 kw-D, DAN; 1 kw-N, DAN; N40 54 8 W111 55 40
2722 S. Redwood Rd., Suite 1, Salt Lake City, UT 84119 US
(801) 908-8777; *Fax:* (801) 908-8782
License: Centerville, Davis County, UT held by Alpha Media Licensee LLC
Group Owner: Alpha Media LLC; (acq 7-16-2015; grpsl).
Nat'l Network: Ke-Buena
Arbitron Metro Market: Salt Lake City-Ogden-Provo, UT; *Format:* Tejano
Mary Lee Robinson, Market Manager

Coalville

KSQN
01-01-2004; 103.1 MHz FM; 89 kw horiz; Ant 2,122 ft; N40 52 16 W110 59 43
257 E. 200 S., Suite 400, Salt Lake City, UT 84111
(801) 364-9836; *Fax:* (801) 364-8086
www.sunny103fm.com
comments@sunny103fm.com
License: Coalville, Summit County, UT

Matt Webb, General Manager
Jody Adams, Sales Manager
Rob Riesen, Program/Operations Director
Gary Stanger, Promotions/Marketing
Sherri Jensen, Office Manager

KZNSFM)
09-06-2005; 97.5 MHz FM; 89 kw horiz; Ant 2,122 ft; N40 52 16 W110 59 43
301 West South Temple, Salt Lake City, UT 84101
(855) 340-9663
www.1280thezone.com
sgarrard@kjzz.com
License: Coalville, Summit County, UT held by 3 Point Media - Franklin L.L.C., debtor-in-possession
Group Owner: 3 Point Media; (acq 7-17-2007)
Arbitron Metro Market: Salt Lake City-Ogden-Provo, UT
Randy Rodgers, General Manager

Delta

KYAH
02-25-1974; 540 kHz AM; *Hrs Open:* 24; 1 kw-U; N39 20 12 W112 33 21
PO Box 574, Portsmouth, RI 02871
www.yahradio540.com
License: Delta, Millard County, UT held by DCO Holding LC
Population Served: 50,000 *Special Programming:* Farm 5 hrs wkly; *Hrs. of News Programming:* News progmg 15 hrs wkly; *Target Audience:* 20-50.

KMGR
09-05-1989; 95.9 MHz FM; *Hrs Open:* 24; 100 kw horiz; 961 ft.; N39 43 58 W111 56 34
Mailing Address: P.O. Box 40, 1600 West 500 North, Manti, UT 84642 US
Second Address: 390 East Annabella Road, Richfield, UT 84701
(435) 835-7301; *Fax:* (435) 835-2250
www.midutahradio.com/kmgr
License: Delta, Millard County, UT held by 3 Point Media - Delta LLC.
Group Owner: 3 Point Media; (acq 8-1-2003; $1.25 million).
Arbitron Metro Market: Delta, UT
Douglas L. Barton, Owner/CEO
JD Fox, Program/Promotions Director
Darcie Dickinson, Community Events/Sales
Mike Traina, Sports/Sales Representative
Brad James, Webmaster/News/Sports

***KEYD**
91.9 MHz FM; kw
307 South 1600 West, Provo, UT 84601-3932 US
(801) 374-5210
www.keyradio.org
mail@keyradio.org
License: Delta, Millard County, UT held by Biblical Ministries Worldwide.
Arbitron Metro Market: Delta, UT; *Format:* Religious
Mike Zander, General Manager
Karisa Clark, Public Relation Director

Elsinore

KWUT(FM)
01-01-1978; 97.7 MHz FM; 43 kw; Ant 2,883 ft; N38 32 30 W112 03 31
Mailing Address: PO Box 40, 1600 West 500 North, Manti, UT 84642
Second Address: 390 East Annabella Road, Richfield, UT 84701
(435) 896-4456; *Fax:* (435) 896-9333
License: Elsinore, Sevier County, UT held by Mid-Utah Radio Inc.
Arbitron Metro Market: Central UT; *Format:* Country
Douglas Barton, Owner/CEO

Ephraim

***KAGJ**
88.9 MHz FM; 0.38 kw; 2323 ft.; N39 19 18 W111 46 11
150 E. College Ave., Ephraim, UT 84627 US
(435) 283-7000
License: Ephraim, Sanpete County, UT held by Snow College.
Arbitron Metro Market: Ephraim, UT; *Format:* Classic Rock
Gary Chidester, General Manager

Kanab

KPLD
01-01-1986; 105.1 MHz FM; *Hrs Open:* 24; 100 kw; 600 meters; N36 43 18 W112 12 57
204 Playa Della Rosita, Washington, UT 60611
(435) 628-3643; *Fax:* (435) 673-1210
License: Kanab, Kane County, UT held by Canyon Media Group LLC
Group Owner: Canyon Media Group LLC; (acq 1999; $1.75 million with KUNF(AM) Washington).
Adv. Rates: 40; 40; 40; 40
Carl Lamar, Operations Dir

Kaysville

KKLV
11-15-1978; 107.5 MHz FM; *Hrs Open:* 24; 45 kw; Ant 2,850 ft; N40 16 48 W111 56 05
Box 2098, Omaha, NE 2098 US
(800) 525-5683
www.klove.com
License: Kaysville, UT held by Educational Media Foundation
Group Owner: Educational Media Foundation; (acq 12-18-96).
Arbitron Metro Market: Salt Lake City-Ogden-Provo, UT; *Format:* Christian; *Target Audience:* 25-54.

Leeds

KCLS
11-01-1986; 101.5 MHz FM; *Hrs Open:* 24; 40 kw; Ant 804 ft; N39 14 46 W114 55 39
College Creek Media LLC, 980 N. Michigan Ave., Chicago, IL 89301
(312) 204-9900
License: Leeds, Washington County, UT held by Canyon Media Group LLC
Group Owner: Canyon Media Group LLC; (acq 10-25-2005; exchange for KOYT(FM) Elko)
Adv. Rates: 21; 18; 15; 13
Neal Robinson, President

Levan

KQMB
01-01-2001; 96.7 MHz FM; 67 kw horiz; 1919 ft.; N39 20 12 W111 27 6
P.O. Box 828, Orem, UT 84059 US
(801) 524-2600; *Fax:* (801) 521-9234
License: Levan, Juab County, UT held by Zeta Holdings LLC.
Arbitron Metro Market: Orem, UT; *Format:* Adult Contemp
Robert Morey, General Manager

Logan

KBLQ-FM
08-01-1977; 92.9 MHz FM; 100 kw; 207 ft.; N41 52 18 W111 48 31
810 West 200 North, Logan, UT 84321-3726 US
(435) 752-1390; *Fax:* (435) 752-1392
www.q92.fm
License: Logan, Cache County, UT
Arbitron Metro Market: Logan, UT; *Format:* Adult Contemp
Special Programming: Gospel 8 hrs, jazz 4 hrs wkly; *Target Audience:* 25-54; general
Bill Walter, Programming Director
Laurie Gill, News Director

KLGN
03-01-1968; 1390 kHz AM; 5 kw-D, DAN; 0.5 kw-N, DAN; N41 44 4 W111 51 13
810 W. 200 N., Logan, UT 84321 US
(435) 752-1390
www.1390klgn.com
webmaster@cvdaily.com
License: Logan, UT held by Sun Valley Radio Inc.
Group Owner: Sun Valley Radio Inc.; acq 12-27-91; $572,279 with co-located FM).
Nat'l Network: Westwood One; CBS
Arbitron Metro Market: Salt Lake City, UT; *Format:* Adult Contemp *Special Programming:* Talk; *Target Audience:* 45 plus.
Kent Frandsen, President
Michael Carver, Operations Dir
Jay Eubanks, General Manager
Dan Baker, Chief Engineer

*KUSR
03-01-1999; 89.5 MHz FM; *Hrs Open:* 24 hours; 0.82 kw; -571 ft.; N41 44 43 W111 48 16
8505 Old Main Hill, Logan, UT 84322 US
(435) 797-3138
www.upr.org
License: Logan, Cache County, UT held by Utah State University of Agricultural and Applied Science.
Nat'l Network: NPR
Arbitron Metro Market: Logan, UT; *Format:* Classical, News, 62, Talk

*KUSU-FM
04-01-1953; 91.5 MHz FM; *Hrs Open:* 24; 90 kw; 1138 ft.; N41 53 11 W112 4 17
Mailing Address: Utah Public Radio, 8505 Old Main Hill, Logan, UT 84322-8505 US
Second Address: 745 North 1200 East, Logan, UT 84322
(435) 797-3138
www.upr.org
License: Logan, Cache County, UT held by Utah State University.
Nat'l Network: NPR; PRI
Arbitron Metro Market: Logan, UT; *Format:* News, News/Talk, 86; *No. News Employees:* 2; *Target Audience:* General.
Peg Arnold, Station Manager
Kerry Bringhurst, News
Teri Guy, Underwriting
Bryan Earl, Membership
Tom Williams, Programming

KVFX
11-11-1974; 94.5 MHz FM; *Hrs Open:* 24; 94 kw; 1148 ft.; N41 53 50 W111 57 39
810 West 200 North, Logan, UT 84321 US
(435) 752-1390; *Fax:* (435) 752-1392
www.utahsvfx.com
License: Logan, Cache County, UT
Arbitron Metro Market: Logan, UT; *Format:* Contemporary Hits/Top 40; *Hrs. of News Programming:* News progmg 2 hrs wkly; *Target Audience:* 18-35.; *Adv. Rates:* 32; 32; 32; 25
Blair Carter, Programming Director
Kenton Frat Boy, Disc Jockey

KVNU
11-20-1938; 610 kHz AM; *Hrs Open:* 24
810 West 200 North, Logan, UT 84321 US
(435) 752-5141; *Fax:* (435) 753-5555
www.610kvnu.com
License: Logan, UT held by Sun Valley Radio Inc.
Group Owner: Sun Valley Radio Inc.; acq 1996; $900,000 with co-located FM).
Nat'l Network: ABC
Arbitron Metro Market: Logan, UT; *Format:* News, News/Talk, 86
Special Programming: Farm 2 hrs, relg 2 hrs wkly; *Hrs. of News Programming:* news progmg 15 hrs wkly; *No. News Employees:* 2 *Target Audience:* General.; *Adv. Rates:* 36; 36; 36; 28
Al Lewis, General Manager
James Murdock, General Sales Mgr
Jennie Christensen, News Director
Bill Walter, Chief Engineer
Eric Frandsen, News Reporter
Heather Bailey, Reporter

*KUEU
01-01-2008; 90.5 MHz FM; 1 kw; Ant 367 ft; N41 36 41 W111 57 05
101 South Wasatch Drive #240, Salt Lake City, UT 84112
(801) 581-6625; *Fax:* (801) 581-6758
www.kuer.org
License: Logan, Cache County, UT held by Listeners Community Radio of Utah Inc.

Donna Maldonado, General Manager

Manti

KMTI
06-07-1976; 650 kHz AM; *Hrs Open:* 24; 10 kw-D, DA2; 0.9 kw-N, DA2; N39 17 39 W111 38 13
Mailing Address: PO Box 40, 500 North 1600 West, Manti, UT 84642 US
Second Address: 390 East Annabella Road, Richfield, UT 847-1
(435) 835-7301; *Fax:* (435) 835-2250
www.midutahradio.com/kmti
License: Manti, UT held by Sanpete County Broadcasting Co.
Group Owner: Sanpete County Broadcasting Co.
Nat'l Network: ABC; *Wire Services:* AP
Format: Country, News *Special Programming:* Farm 5 hrs wkly; *Hrs. of News Programming:* news progmg 20 hrs wkly; *No. News Employees:* 1; *Target Audience:* 25-60.
Douglas L. Barton, Owner/CEO
J.D. Fox, Program/Promotions Director
Larry J. Masco, Program Director
Darcie Dickinson, Community Events/Sales
Mike Traina, Sports

KAUU
12-01-1978; 105.1 MHz FM; *Hrs Open:* 24 hours; 48 kw horiz; 2244 ft.; N39 45 37 W111 34 38
50 W. Broadway, Suite 200, Salt Lake City, UT 84101 US
(801) 524-2600
www.1015theeagle.com
License: Manti, Sanpete County, UT held by Millcreek Broadcasting L.L.C.
Group Owner: Millcreek Broadcasting L.L.C.; (acq 4-17-2001)

Randy Rodgers, General Manager

Midvale

KSL-FM
01-01-1995; 102.7 MHz FM; *Hrs Open:* 24; 25 kw; 3,740 ft.; N40 39 34 W112 12 5 *Rebroadcasts:* Rebroadcasts KSL(AM) Salt Lake City 100%
5 Triad Center, 55 N. 3rd W., Salt Lake City, UT 84180-1109 US
(801) 575-5555; *Fax:* (801) 575-5560
www.ksl.com
support@ksl.com
License: Midvale, Salt Lake County, UT held by Bonneville International Corporation
Group Owner: Bonneville International Corporation; (acq 12-5-2003; grpsl).
Arbitron Metro Market: Salt Lake City-Ogden-Provo, UT; *Format:* News, News/Talk, 84, Talk
Ike Yospe, Promotions Manager
John Dehnel, Chief Engineer
Stephanie Palmer, Advertising

Moab

KCYN
09-20-1998; 97.1 MHz FM; *Hrs Open:* 24; 29 kw; 1293 ft.; N38 31 37 W109 18 21
1030 South Bowling Alley Lane, Suite 3, Moab, UT 84532 US
(435) 259-1035
License: Moab, Grand County, UT held by Moab Communications LLC.
Group Owner: Carlson Communications International; (acq 8-15-97).
Nat'l Network: Fox News Radio; Jones Radio Networks; *Nat'l Reps:* Rgnl Reps; *Wire Services:* Metro Weather Service Inc.
Arbitron Metro Market: Moab, UT; *Format:* Country; *Hrs. of News Programming:* news progmg 12 hrs wkly; *No. News Employees:* 1; *Target Audience:* 18-54.
Ralph J. Carlson, President
Phillip Mueller, General Manager
Holly Wilson, News Director
Kenneth Meyer, Chief Engineer
Holly Wilson, Traffic Manager

*KZMU
04-01-1992; 90.1 MHz FM; *Hrs Open:* 24; 0.4 kw; 1280 ft.; N38 31 37 W109 18 21
P. O. Box 1076, Moab, UT 84532 US
(435) 259-8824; *Fax:* (435) 259-8763
www.kzmu.org
info@kzmu.org
License: Moab, Grand County, UT held by Moab Public Radio.
Arbitron Metro Market: Moab, UT; *Format:* Variety/Diverse
Special Programming: Asian one hr, American Indian 5 hrs, Black 3 hrs, Sp one hr, folk 6 hrs, blues 19 hrs wkly; *Hrs. of News Programming:* news progmg 8 hrswkly; *No. News Employees:* 1; *Target Audience:* General.
Jeff Flanders, Station Manager
Christy Williams, Programming Director
Bob Owen, Chief Engineer
Glen Peart, Music Director
Marlene Moody, Administrative Assistant

Mona

KPUT
92.9 MHz FM; 0.1 kw; 138 meters; 39-43-58.0 N 111-56-35.0 W
25 E. 86th St., New York, NY 10028 USA
(917) 535-0419
License: Mona, UT held by Alex Media Inc.
Group Owner: Alex Media Inc.
Format: Variety/Diverse
Alexander Berger, President

Monroe

KMXD
08-01-2007; 100.5 MHz FM; *Hrs Open:* 24; 33 kw; Ant 3,257 ft; N38 23 08 W112 19 57
License: Monroe, Sevier County, UT held by Sanpete County Broadcasting Co.
Group Owner: Sanpete County Broadcasting Co.
Nat'l Network: ABC
Population Served: 3,297; *Arbitron Metro Market:* Monroe, UT; *Target Audience:* 30-65.

Mount Pleasant

KUTC
01-01-2000; 93.7 MHz FM; *Hrs Open:* 24; 66 kw; 2356 ft.; N39 19 17 W111 46 11
P.O. Box 40, Manti, UT 84642 US
(435) 835-7301; *Fax:* (435) 835-2250
www.klgl.com
License: Mount Pleasant, Sevier County, UT held by Sanpete County Broadcasting Co.
Group Owner: Sanpete County Broadcasting Co.; (acq 3-1-2006; swap for KCYQ(FM) Elsinore).
Arbitron Metro Market: Manti, UT; *Format:* Contemporary Hits/Top 40; *Hrs. of News Programming:* news progmg 11 hrs wkly; *No. News Employees:* 1; *Target Audience:* General.
J.D. Fox, Programming Director

Murray

KJQS
11-08-1948; 1230 kHz AM; *Hrs Open:* 24; 1 kw-U, ND1; N40 39 57 W111 54 26
3280 Peachtree Rd. NW, Suite 2300, Atlanta, GA 30305 US
(404) 949-0700
License: Murray, UT held by Radio License Holding CBC, LLC
Group Owner: Cumulus Media Inc.; (acq 2-29-00; $104,202).
Nat'l Network: ESPN Radio
Arbitron Metro Market: Salt Lake City-Ogden-Provo, UT; *Format:* Sports
Eric Hauenstein, General Manager
Terry Mathis, General Sales Mgr
Scott Gerard, Programming Director
Liz Mills, News Director
Richard Bauer, Chief Engineer

Naples

KCUA
01-01-1993; 92.5 MHz FM; 0.84 kw; 1660 ft.; N40 32 16 W109 41 57
Box 1372, Park City, UT 84060 US
(801) 649-9004; *Fax:* (435) 645-0963
License: Naples, Uintah County, UT held by 3 Point Media - Coalville LLC.
Group Owner: 3 Point Media; (acq 5-28-2004; $1.7 million).
Format: Classic Rock
Joe Evans, Station Manager

Nephi

KUDE
05-09-1990; 103.9 MHz FM; *Hrs Open:* 24; 74 kw horiz; 2244 ft.; N39 45 37 W111 34 38 *Rebroadcasts:* Rebroadcasts KUDD(FM) Roy 100%.
50 West Broadway, Suite 200, Salt Lake City, UT 84101 US
(855) 649-1079
www.mix1079fm.com
License: Nephi, Juab County, UT held by Millcreek Broadcasting L.L.C.
Group Owner: Millcreek Broadcasting L.L.C.; (acq 4-17-2001).
Arbitron Metro Market: Salt Lake City, UT; *Format:* Adult Contemp; *Target Audience:* 18-45.
Brian Michel, Operations Dir
Randy Rodgers, General Manager
Lutisha Merrill, General Sales Mgr
Scott St. John, Promotions Manager
Kevin Terry, Engineering Dir

***KBJF**
90.5 MHz FM; 75 kw; 2157 ft.; N39 45 37 W111 34 38
PO Box 391, Twin Falls, ID 83303 US
(800) 357-4226; *Fax:* (208) 736-1958
License: Nephi, Juab County, UT held by First Baptist Church of Nephi, Utah.
Arbitron Metro Market: Nephi, UT
Joe Jennings, Operations Dir
Don Mills, Programming Director/Music Director
Kelly Carlson, Engineering Dir

North Ogden

***KNKL**
01-29-2004; 88.7 MHz FM; *Hrs Open:* 24; 73 kw vert; 976 ft.; N41 35 30 W112 14 57
PO Box 2098, Omaha, NE 68103-2098 US
(916) 251-1600
www.klove.com
License: North Ogden, Weber County, UT held by Educational Media Foundation.
Group Owner: Educational Media Foundation.
Nat'l Network: K-Love
Arbitron Metro Market: North Ogden, UT; *Format:* Christian; *No. News Employees:* 3; *Target Audience:* 25-44; female-Judeo Christian
Mike Novak, President/CEO

North Salt Lake City

KALL
09-22-1981; 700 kHz AM; *Hrs Open:* 24
50 W. Broadway, Suite 200, Salt Lake City, UT 84101 US
(877) 353-0700, (801) 524-2600
www.espn700sports.com
bill@espn700sports.com
License: North Salt Lake City, UT held by Broadway Media LS, LLC
Group Owner: Broadway Media Group
Arbitron Metro Market: Salt Lake City, UT; *Format:* Sports, Talk; *Hrs. of News Programming:* news progmg 20 hrs wkly; *No. News Employees:* 1; *Target Audience:* 18-49; men
Tally Lloyd, General Sales Mgr
Bill Riley, Programming Director

Oakley

KEGA
01-01-2003; 101.5 MHz FM; 89 kw horiz; 2123 ft.; N40 52 16 W110 59 43
50 W. Broadway, Salt Lake City, UT 84101 US
(801) 524-2600
www.1015theeagle.com
License: Oakley, Summit County, UT held by Broadway Media
Group Owner: Broadway Media; (acq 4-4-2001; grpsl)
Arbitron Metro Market: Salt Lake City, UT; *Format:* Country
Craig Hanson, President
Stephen Johnson, General Manager
Erika Hernandez, Promotions

Ogden

KBER
07-13-1975; 101.1 MHz FM; *Hrs Open:* 24; 25 kw; 3740 ft.; N40 39 34 W112 12 5
434 Bearcat Dr., Salt Lake City, UT 84115 US
(801) 485-6700
www.kber.com
License: Ogden, UT held by Radio License Holding CBC, LLC
Group Owner: Cumulus Media Inc.; (acq 1996; $7.7 million).
Nat'l Reps: Katz Radio
Arbitron Metro Market: Salt Lake City, UT; *Format:* Rock/AOR; *No. News Employees:* 1; *Target Audience:* 18-49; men
Eric Hauenstein, General Manager
Zandi Wilcox, General Sales Mgr
Kelly Hamer, Programming Director
Joel Smith, Promotions Manager
Richie Bauer, Engineering Dir
Diane Curtis, National Sales Manager

KBZN
01-01-1978; 97.9 MHz FM; 26 kw; 3770 ft.; N40 39 35 W112 12 5
257 E 2nd S. Suite 400, Salt Lake City, UT 84111 US
(801) 364-9836; *Fax:* (801) 364-8068
www.kbzn.com
comments@now979.com
License: Ogden, Weber County, UT held by Capitol Broadcasting Inc.
Arbitron Metro Market: Salt Lake City, UT; *Format:* Adult Contemp; *Adv. Rates:* 50; 60; 60; 25
Matt Webb, General Manager
Jody Adams, General Sales Mgr
Rob Reisen, Programming/Operations Director
Gary Stanger, Promotions/Marketing
Sheri Jensen, Office Manager

KLO
01-01-1924; 1430 kHz AM
257 E. 200 S., Suite 400, Salt Lake City, UT 84111 US
(801) 364-9836; *Fax:* (801) 364-8086
www.kloradio.com
comments@kloradio.com
License: Ogden, UT held by KLO Broadcasting Co.
Arbitron Metro Market: Salt Lake City, UT; *Format:* News, Sports, 86
Matt Webb, General Manager
Rob Riesen, Program/Operations Director
Gary Stanger, Promotions/Marketing
Jody Adams, Sales Manager
Sheri Jensen, Office Manager

KSVN
01-01-1946; 730 kHz AM; *Hrs Open:* 24; 1 kw-D, ND1; 0.066 kw-N, ND1; N41 11 17 W112 4 52
323 E. San Joaquin St., Tulare, CA 93274 US
(801) 292-1799
License: Ogden, UT held by Azteca Broadcasting Corp.
Group Owner: Azteca Broadcasting Corp.; acq 2-1-86)
Arbitron Metro Market: West Haven, UT; *Format:* Tejano

***KWCR-FM**
05-21-1966; 88.1 MHz FM; *Hrs Open:* 24; 2 kw; -315 ft.; N41 11 17 W111 56 43
2188 University Circle, Ogden, UT 84408 US
(801) 626-8800
www.881weberfm.org
License: Ogden, Weber County, UT held by Weber State University Board of Trustees.
Wire Services: UPI
Arbitron Metro Market: Ogden, UT; *Format:* Contemporary Hits/Top 40, Classic Rock *Special Programming:* Relg 3 hrs, gospel 3 hrs, Sp 16 hrs wkly; *Hrs. of News Programming:* News progmg 4 hrs wkly *Target Audience:* 18-26; college students, male & female; *Adv. Rates:* 25; 25; 25; 25
J.P. Orquiz, General Manager
Austin Hatch, Programming Director
Felix Baca, Promotions Manager
Nathan Clark, News Director
Taylor Byrd, Chief Engineer
Nick Bailey, Sports Director
Daniel Martinez, Sponsorship Director
SpencerHart, Production Director
Erik Bremer, Content Director
Rachel Hernandez, Music Director
Manny Gonzalez-Reyna, Spanish Programming/IT Director

KOGN
04-01-1948; 1490 kHz AM; *Hrs Open:* 24
314 South Redwood, Salt Lake City, UT 84104 US
(801) 390-4119
License: Ogden, UT held by Familia Broadcasting LLC
Arbitron Metro Market: Salt Lake City-Ogden-Provo, UT; *Format:* News, Adult Contemp
Danette Acosta, President

***KYFO-FM**
06-01-1983; 95.5 MHz FM; *Hrs Open:* 24; 100 kw; 719 ft.; N41 14 59 W112 14 11
1506 Gibson Ave., Ogden, UT 84404 US
(801) 394-8833; *Fax:* (801) 394-8833
www.bbnradio.org
bbn@bbnmedia.org
License: Ogden, Weber County, UT held by Bible Broadcasting Network Inc.
Group Owner: Bible Broadcasting Network; (acq 1994).
Arbitron Metro Market: Charlotte, NC; *Format:* Christian
Jason Padgett, Operations Manager

Orem

***KKLV**
09-01-1999; 107.5 MHz FM; 43 kw; 2851 ft.; N40 16 48 W111 56 5
PO Box 2098, Omaha, NE 68103-2098 US
(800) 525-5683
www.klove.com
License: Orem, Crittenden County, UT held by Educational Media Foundation.
Group Owner: Educational Media Foundation.; (acq 10-20-2000; grpsl).
Nat'l Network: K-Love
Arbitron Metro Market: Memphis, TN; *Format:* Christian
Mike Novak, President/CEO

***KOHS**
10-01-1994; 91.7 MHz FM; 1.75 kw; -869 ft.; N40 17 32 W111 40 58
175 South 400 East, Orem, UT 84097 US
(801) 610-8165; *Fax:* (801) 227-8774
License: Orem, Utah County, UT held by Alpine School District
Format: Alternative

Paragonah

***KRRA**
91.3 MHz FM; kw
US
(580) 653-2777
License: Paragonah, Iron County, UT held by Ron Elmore Ministries Inc.
Arbitron Metro Market: Springer, OK; *Format:* Religious
Ron Elmore, President

Park City

***KPCW**
07-02-1980; 91.9 MHz FM; 105 w; Ant -23 ft; N40 40 59 W111 31 22
Mailing Address: 460 Swede Alley, Suite 200, Park City, UT 84060
Second Address: PO Bow 1372, Park City, UT 84060
(435) 649-9004; *Fax:* (435) 645-9063
www.kpcw.org
info@kpcw.org
License: Park City, Summit County, UT held by Community Wireless of Park City.
Population Served: 13,000 *Special Programming:* Class 17 hrs, C&W 18 hrs, jazz 12 hrs wkly
Larry Warren, President/General Manager
Emily Elliott, Underwriting Director
Monika Guendner, Marketing Director

Andy Martin, Program/Production/Music Director & Chief Operator
Ethel Preston, Office Manager
Leslie Thatcher, NewsDirector

Parowan

KENT
10-06-2006; 1400 kHz AM; 1 kw-U; N37 48 22 W112 56 40
2975 Valmont Road, #230, Boulder, CO
(435) 477-2000; *Fax:* (435) 477-1400
legacy1@infowest.com
License: Parowan, Iron County, UT held by Canyon Media Group LLC
Group Owner: Canyon Media Group LLC; (acq 4-25-2011)
Population Served: 38,311
Lee Weinstein Esq., President

Payson

KTCE
11-01-1993; 92.1 MHz FM; 0.125 kw; 2156 ft.; N40 5 21 W111 49 15
P.O. Box 10, Provo, UT 84603 US
(801) 370-9999; *Fax:* (801) 370-0999
www.ktce921.com
License: Payson, Utah County, UT held by Moenkopi Communications Inc.
Arbitron Metro Market: Salt Lake City-Ogden-Provo, UT; *Format:* Adult Contemp; *Adv. Rates:* 60; 30; 15; 7.50
Corey Sorenson, Station Manager
Kevin Cruise, Programming Director

Pleasant Grove

*KPGR
05-01-1976; 88.1 MHz FM; *Hrs Open:* 6:30 AM-10 PM; 0.115 kw; -1129 ft.; N40 21 48 W111 43 30
700 East 200 South, Pleasant Grove, UT 84062 US
(801) 785-8700
www.kpgr.tripod.com
pleasantgroveradio@hotmail.com
License: Pleasant Grove, Utah County, UT held by Alpine School District.
Format: Variety/Diverse *Special Programming:* All Pleasant Grove High football, basketball, base; *Target Audience:* 12-18; students
Mike Basso, General Manager

Price

KARB
07-01-1977; 98.3 MHz FM; 7 kw; -105 ft.; N39 36 33 W110 48 50
US
(435) 637-1167; *Fax:* (435) 637-1177
www.castlecountryradio.com
paul@koal.net
License: Price, Carbon County, UT held by Eastern Utah Broadcasting Co.
Arbitron Metro Market: Price, UT; *Format:* Country
Paul Anderson, General Manager
Andy Urbanik, Sales Manager
Kara Maynes, Sales
Ann Anderson, Office/Traffic Manager
Jordan Buscarini, Sports Director
Rick Sherman, News Director

KOAL
10-01-1936; 750 kHz AM; 10 kw-D, DAN; 6.8 kw-N, DAN; N39 34 2 W110 47 53
US
(435) 637-1167; *Fax:* (435) 637-1177
www.castlecountryradio.com
License: Price, UT held by Eastern Utah Broadcasting Co.
Format: News, News/Talk, 84, Talk *Special Programming:* Farm 5 hrs wkly
Paul Anderson, General Manager
Andy Urbanik, Sales Manager
Kara Maynes, Sales
Ann Anderson, Office/Traffic
Rick Sherman, News Director
Jordan Buscarini, Sports Director

KWSA
12-01-1985; 100.1 MHz FM; *Hrs Open:* 24; 3 kw; 135 ft.; N39 32 42 W110 48 57
Mailing Address: 163 East 100 North, Price, UT 84501 US
Second Address: 163 E. 100 N., Price, UT 84501
(435) 637-1080; *Fax:* (435) 637-8191
License: Price, Carbon County, UT
Format: Classic Rock
Paul Bjornstad, General Manager

KSLL
09-06-1980; 1080 kHz AM; 5 kw-C, NDD; 10 kw-D, NDD; N39 33 43 W110 46 36
6 East Main Street, Price, UT 84501 US
(435) 637-1080
www.gofm100.com
kusabuzz@gmail.com
License: Price, UT held by AJB Broadcasting
Arbitron Metro Market: Central UT; *Format:* Country; *Target Audience:* General.
Bobby Sherman, Programming Director
Taylor Nielsen, Office Manager/Traffic Director

*KCEU
89.7 MHz FM; 0.44 kw; -164 ft.; N39 36 41 W110 48 36
US
License: Price, Carbon County, UT held by Utah State University - College of Eastern Utah (USU Eastern)
Arbitron Metro Market: Price, UT
Ryan Thomas, President
Troy Hunt, General Manager

*KEYP
91.9 MHz FM; 0.1 kw; -423 ft.; N39 36 7.13 W110 48 15.43
307 South 1600 West, Provo, UT 84601-3932 US
(801) 374-5210
www.keyradio.org
mail@keyradio.org
License: Price, Carbon County, UT held by Biblical Ministries Worldwide.
Arbitron Metro Market: Price, UT; *Format:* Religious
Mike Zander, General Manager
Karisa Clark, Public Relation Director

Provo

*KBYU-FM
11-01-1960; 89.1 MHz FM; *Hrs Open:* 24; 30 kw; 2976 ft.; N40 36 28 W112 9 33
Brigham Young University, Provo, UT 84602 US
(800) 298-5298
www.classical89.org
License: Provo, Utah County, UT held by Brigham Young University.
Nat'l Network: PRI; AP Radio; NPR
Arbitron Metro Market: Salt Lake City-Ogden-Provo, UT *TV Affiliate:* *KBYU-TV affil.; *Format:* News, News/Talk, 86; *Hrs. of News Programming:* news progmg 5 hrs wkly; *No. News Employees:* 2; *Target Audience:* 35plus.

*KEYY
12-01-1949; 1450 kHz AM; *Hrs Open:* 24; 1 kw-U; N40 13 49 W111 41 12
307 South 1600 West, Provo, UT 84601-3932
(801) 374-5210
www.keyradio.org
mail@keyradio.org
License: Provo, Utah County, UT held by Biblical Ministries Worldwide.
Nat'l Network: Moody; Salem Radio Network
Population Served: 450,000; *Arbitron Metro Market:* Salt Lake City; *Hrs. of News Programming:* news progmg 8 hrs wkly; *Target Audience:* General.
Mike Zander, General Manager

KENZ
01-01-1981; 94.9 MHz FM; *Hrs Open:* 24; 48 kw; 3740 ft.; N40 39 34 W112 12 5
434 Bearcat Dr., Salt Lake City, UT 84115 US
(801) 485-6700
www.949thevibe.com
License: Provo, UT held by Radio License Holding CBC, LLC
Group Owner: Cumulus Media Inc.; (acq 7-30-2004; $16 million).
Nat'l Network: ABC
Arbitron Metro Market: Salt Lake City, UT; *Format:* Urban Contemporary; *No. News Employees:* 1; *Target Audience:* 25-54.
Randy Rodgers, General Manager
Biff Raff, Programming Director

KOVO
09-12-1939; 960 kHz AM; *Hrs Open:* 24; 5 kw-D, DAN; 1 kw-N, DAN; N40 12 44 W111 40 13 *Rebroadcasts:* Rebroadcasts KZNS (AM) Salt Lake City 100%
50 W. Broadway, Suite 200, Salt Lake City, UT 84101 US
(801) 524-2600
espn960sports.com
bill@espn700sports.com
License: Provo, UT held by Broadway Media LS, LLC
Group Owner: Broadway Media Group
Arbitron Metro Market: Salt Lake City-Ogden-Provo, UT; *Format:* Sports, Talk; *Target Audience:* 35 plus; upper income affluent males & females 35-65
Tally Lloyd, General Sales Mgr
Bill Riley, Programming Director

KSRR
11-24-1947; 1400 kHz AM; *Hrs Open:* 24; 1 kw-U, ND1; N40 15 29 W111 42 24
1454 West Business Park Drive, Orem, UT 84097 US
(801) 224-1400
www.kstarradio.wordpress.com
kstar1400@gmail.com
License: Provo, UT held by Zeta Holdings LLC
Format: Adult Contemp; *Hrs. of News Programming:* News progmg one hr wkly; *Target Audience:* 18-54.
Robert Morey, General Manager

KXRK
02-14-1968; 96.3 MHz FM; *Hrs Open:* 24; 25 kw; 3740 ft.; N40 39 34 W112 12 5
50 W. Broadway, Suite 200, Salt Lake City, UT 84101 US
(801) 359-9696
www.x96.com
todd@bwaymedia.com
License: Provo, Utah County, UT held by Broadway Media IS, LLC
Group Owner: Broadway Media Group; (acq 4-4-2001; grpsl)
Arbitron Metro Market: Salt Lake City-Ogden-Provo, UT; *Format:* Alternative; *Target Audience:* 18-34; young, affluent executives; *Adv. Rates:* 120; 120; 120; 100
Mike Lund, General Sales Mgr
Todd Nukem, Programming Director

KENZ
01-01-1981; 94.9 MHz FM; *Hrs Open:* 24; 48 kw; 2799 ft.; N40 16 58 W111 56 11
434 Bearcat Dr., Salt Lake City, UT 84115 US
(801) 485-6700
www.949thevibe.com
License: Provo, UT held by Radio License Holding CBC, LLC
Group Owner: Cumulus Media Inc.; (acq 8-13-2008)
Arbitron Metro Market: Provo, UT; *Format:* Urban Contemporary
Judith Ellis, COO

Randolph

KDUT
01-01-2001; 102.3 MHz FM; *Hrs Open:* 24; 89 kw horiz; 2,123 ft.; N40 52 16 W110 59 43
2722 S. Redwood Rd., Suite 1, Salt Lake City, UT 84119 US
(801) 908-8777; *Fax:* (801) 908-8782
License: Randolph, Rich County, UT held by Alpha Media Licensee LLC
Group Owner: Alpha Media LLC; (acq 7-16-2015; grpsl).
Arbitron Metro Market: Salt Lake City, UT; *Format:* Tejano
Mary Lee Robinson, Market Manager

Richfield

KSVC
09-01-1947; 980 kHz AM; *Hrs Open:* 24
Mailing Address: P.O. Box 40, 1600 West 500 North, Manti, UT 84642 US
Second Address: 390 East Annabella Road, Richfield, UT 84701
(435) 896-4456; *Fax:* (435) 896-9333
www.midutahradio.com/ksvc
dougb@midutahradio.com
License: Richfield, UT held by Mid-Utah Radio Inc.
Arbitron Metro Market: Richfield, UT; *Format:* News, News/Talk, 84, Talk *Special Programming:* Farm one hr wkly; *Hrs. of News Programming:* News progmg 18 hrs wkly; *Target Audience:* 18-54.
Douglas L. Barton, Owner/CEO
J.D. Fox, Programming/Promotions Director
Darcie Dickinson, Community Events/Sales
Mike Traina, Sports
Kirk Williams, Chief Engineer

*KUSL
89.3 MHz FM; 2 kw; 3192 ft.; N38 23 8 W112 19 57
8505 Old Main Hill, Logan, UT 84322-8505 US
(435) 797-3138
www.upr.org
peg.arnold@usu.edu
License: Richfield, Sevier County, UT held by Utah State University of Agriculture and Applied Science.
Arbitron Metro Market: Richfield, UT
Peg Arnold, Station Manager
Tom Williams, Programming Director
Kerry Bringhurst, News Director

Teri Guy, Underwriting
Bryan Earl, Membership

***KEYR**
91.7 MHz FM; 0.85 kw; 3136 ft.; N38 23 8 W112 19 56
307 South 1600 West, Provo, UT 84601-3932 US
(801) 374-5210
www.keyradio.org
mail@keyradio.org
License: Richfield, Sevier County, UT held by Biblical Ministries Worldwide.
Arbitron Metro Market: Richfield, UT; *Format:* Religious
Mike Zander, General Manager
Karisa Clark, Public Relation Director

Roosevelt

KIFX
12-14-1987; 98.5 MHz FM; *Hrs Open:* 24; 3.2 kw; 1690 ft.; N40 32 16 W109 41 57
Rt.2, P.O. Box 2384, Roosevelt, UT 84066 US
(435) 722-5011
www.stormpc.com/fox/foxlink.htm
radio@ubtanet.com
License: Roosevelt, Duchesne County, UT held by Evans Broadcasting Inc.
Regional Reps: Art Moore.
Format: Adult Contemp; *Hrs. of News Programming:* news progmg 5 hrs wkly; *No. News Employees:* 1; *Target Audience:* 21-45.
Joseph Evans, President
Vickie Reary, Operations Dir
Teena Christopherson, General Sales Mgr
Earl Hawkins, Programming Director
Jean Liddell, News Director
Steve Sprouce, Chief Engineer

KNEU
01-06-1978; 1250 kHz AM; *Hrs Open:* 5 AM-11 PM; 5 kw-D, ND1; 0.129 kw-N, ND1; N40 17 13 W109 57 32
Route 2 Box 2384, Roosevelt, UT 84066 US
(435) 722-5011
License: Roosevelt, UT held by Country Gold Broadcasting.
Format: Country; *Hrs. of News Programming:* news progmg 10 hrs wkly; *No. News Employees:* 1; *Target Audience:* 25-54.
Joseph Evans, President
Teddie Evans, Operations Dir
Teena Christopherson, General Sales Mgr
Earl Hawkins, Programming Director
Jean Liddell, News Director
Jonathan Hawkins, Chief Engineer

KXRQ
12-18-1998; 94.3 MHz FM; 17.5 kw; 1864 ft.; N40 31 15 W109 42 25
29 S. Vernal Avenue, Suite #2, Vernal, UT 84078 US
(435) 781-1100
www.channelx94.com
License: Roosevelt, Duchesne County, UT held by Uinta Broadcasting L.C.
Wire Services: Metro Weather Service Inc.
Arbitron Metro Market: Vernal, UT; *Format:* Adult Contemp, Contemporary Hits/Top 40 *Special Programming:* Relg 8 hrs wkly; *Target Audience:* 25-54.; *Adv. Rates:* 22; 15; 22; 15
Charlie Hall, General Manager
Natasha Huber, News Director

Roy

***KANN**
09-01-1961; 1120 kHz AM; *Hrs Open:* 24
Mailing Address: PO Box 3880, Ogden, UT 84409 US
Second Address: 2201 S. 6th Street, Las Vegas, NV 89104
(801) 776-0249; *Fax:* (702) 731-1992
www.sosradio.net
info@sosradio.net
License: Roy, UT held by Faith Communications Corp.
Group Owner: Faith Communications Corp.
Arbitron Metro Market: Las Vegas, NV; *Format:* Adult Contemp, Christian; *Hrs. of News Programming:* News progmg 6 hrs wkly; *Target Audience:* 25-44; young families
Brad Staley, President/General Manager
Bob Alzugarat, Station Manager
Scott Herrold, Programming Director
Robert Forbes, Promotions Director
Tim Hunt, Director, Network Engineering
Marney Domeraski, Donor Services
Dan Young,Music Director
Chris Staley, VP, Programming/Administration

KUDD
09-01-1986; 107.9 MHz FM; *Hrs Open:* 24; 75 kw horiz; 2283 ft.; N41 15 27 W112 26 24 *Rebroadcasts:* Rebroadcasts KUDD(FM) Nephi.
50 W. Broadway, Suite 200, N. Salt Lake, UT 84101 US
(855) 649-1079
www.mix1079fm.com/
License: Roy, Weber County, UT held by Millcreek Broadcasting L.L.C.
Group Owner: Millcreek Broadcasting L.L.C.; (acq 4-17-2001; grpsl).
Nat'l Reps: Interep
Arbitron Metro Market: Salt Lake City-Ogden-Provo, UT; *Format:* Adult Contemp; *Target Audience:* General.
Randy Rodgers, General Manager
Lutisha Merrill, General Sales Mgr
Brian Michel, Programming Director
Scott St. John, Promotions Manager
Kevin Terry, Chief Engineer

Saint George

KIYK
06-15-1973; 107.3 MHz FM; 3 kw; -125 ft; N37 06 54 W113 34 23
750 W. Ridgeview Dr., Suite 204, Saint George, UT 84101
(435) 673-3579; *Fax:* (435) 673-8900
License: Saint George, Washington County, UT held by CCR-St. George IV LLC.
Group Owner: Cherry Creek Radio LLC
Target Audience: 12-49.
Chris McCarthy, General Sales Mgr
Rick Parrish, Promotions Manager

***KSGU**
01-01-2005; 90.3 MHz FM; 2 kw; Ant 1,820 ft; N36 50 49 W113 29 28 *Rebroadcasts:* Rebroadcasts KNPR(FM) Las Vegas, NV 100%
1289 S. Torrey Pines Dr., Las Vegas, NV 89146
(702) 258-9895; *Fax:* (702) 258-5646
www.knpr.org
flo@knpr.org
License: Saint George, Washington County, UT held by Nevada Public Radio
Population Served: 120,000
Florence Rogers, President/CEo
Dave Becker, Programming Director
Melanie Cannon, Director of Development
Phil Burger, Director of Broadcast Operations
Adam Burke, News Director

Salt Lake City

KWDZ
01-01-1945; 910 kHz AM; *Hrs Open:* 24; 5 kw-D, 1 kw-N, DA-2; N40 30 48 W112 00 23
2801 S. Decker Lake Dr., Suite 100, Salt Lake City, UT 84119 US
(801) 908-5152
License: Salt Lake City, Salt Lake County, UT held by Radio Disney Group LLC.
Group Owner: ABC Inc.; (acq 4-30-03; $3.7 million).
Nat'l Network: Radio Disney
Population Served: 1,361,800; *Arbitron Metro Market:* Salt Lake City-Ogden-Provo, UT
Pamela Ketel, Radio Disney West Region Director

KKAT
01-01-1956; 860 kHz AM; 10 kw-D, 195.8 w-N, 3 kw-CH; N40 42 47 W111 55 53
434 Bearcat Dr., Salt Lake City, UT 84115 US
(801) 485-6700
www.860utahsbigtalker.com
License: Salt Lake City, UT held by Radio License Holding CBC, LLC
Group Owner: Cumulus Media Inc.
Nat'l Reps: Christal
Arbitron Metro Market: Salt Lake City, UT; *Format:* Country; *Target Audience:* 25-54.
Eric Hauenstein, General Manager

KBEE
06-15-1979; 98.7 MHz FM; 40 kw; 2933 ft.; N40 36 30 W112 9 34
434 Bearcat Dr., Salt Lake City, UT 84115 US
(801) 485-6700
www.b987.com
License: Salt Lake City, UT held by Radio License Holding CBC, LLC
Group Owner: Cumulus Media Inc.; (acq 7-18-97; $2,873,027 with co-located AM).
Arbitron Metro Market: Salt Lake City, UT; *Format:* Adult Contemp; *Target Audience:* General.
Eric Hauenstein, General Manager

***KCPW-FM**
01-01-1992; 88.3 MHz FM; *Hrs Open:* 24; 2.35 kw; -200 ft.; N40 45 48 W111 53 23
Mailing Address: P.O. Box 510730, Salt Lake City, UT 84151-0730 US
Second Address: 210 East 400 South, Suite 7, Salt Lake City, UT 84111
(801) 359-5279; *Fax:* (801) 355-1582
www.kcpw.org
License: Salt Lake City, Salt Lake County, UT held by Community Wireless of Park City Inc.
Nat'l Network: NPR; PRI
Arbitron Metro Market: Salt Lake City-Ogden-Provo, UT; *Format:* News, News/Talk, 86; *Target Audience:* 25 plus.
Jesse Ellis, Operations Dir
Tyler Ford, General Manager
Lauren Colucci, Interim Station Manager
Roger McDonough, News Director
Ross Chambless, Producer/Host

KZNS
02-01-1945; 1280 kHz AM
301 W.S. Temple, Salt Lake City, UT 84101 US
(855) 340-9663
www.1280thezone.com
john.kimball@utahjazz.com
License: Salt Lake City, UT held by Larry H. Miller Communications Corp.
Group Owner: Larry H. Miller Communications Corp.
Arbitron Metro Market: Salt Lake City-Ogden-Provo, UT; *Format:* Sports, Talk; *Target Audience:* 35 plus; retired, affluent, responsible & loyal
John Kimball, Promotions Manager

KFNZ
01-01-1923; 1320 kHz AM; 5 kw-U, DA1; N40 38 36 W111 55 24
434 Bearcat Dr., Salt Lake City, UT 84115 US
(801) 485-6700; *Fax:* (801) 485-6611
www.1320kfan.com
License: Salt Lake City, UT held by Radio License Holding CBC, LLC
Group Owner: Cumulus Media Inc.
Arbitron Metro Market: Salt Lake City, UT; *Format:* Sports

KZHT
02-01-1961; 97.1 MHz FM; *Hrs Open:* 24; 25 kw; 3,740 ft.; N40 39 34 W112 12 5
2801 S. Decker Lake Dr., Salt Lake City, UT 84119 US
(801) 908-1300
www.971zht.com
License: Salt Lake City, Salt Lake County, UT held by CC Licenses LLC.
Group Owner: iHeartMedia; (acq 7-10-2000).
Nat'l Reps: Katz Radio
Arbitron Metro Market: Salt Lake City-Ogden-Provo, UT; *Format:* Contemporary Hits/Top 40; *Target Audience:* 18-49.
Judy Copier, Senior Vice President of Sales
Jeff McCartney, Programming Director
Stacy Sappenfield, Account Executive

KNRS
08-01-1938; 570 kHz AM; *Hrs Open:* 24; 5 kw-U, DA1; N40 49 9 W111 55 56
2801 South Decker Lake Drive, Salt Lake City, UT 84119 US
(801) 908-1300
www.knrs.com
License: Salt Lake City, UT held by Citicasters Licenses Inc.
Group Owner: iHeartMedia; (acq 1999; grpsl).
Nat'l Reps: Clear Channel
Arbitron Metro Market: Salt Lake City, UT *TV Affiliate:* KTVX(TV); *Format:* News, News/Talk, 86; *Hrs. of News Programming:* news progmg 2 hrs wkly; *No. News Employees:* 1; *Target Audience:* 25-54; adults
Jeff Cochran, Senior Vice President of Programming
Stu Stanek, Regional President
Judy Copier, Senior Vice President of Sales

KODJ
12-01-1968; 94.1 MHz FM; *Hrs Open:* 24; 21.5 kw; 3999 ft.; N40 39 35 W112 12 5
2801 South Decker Lake Drive, Salt Lake City, UT 84119 US
(801) 908-1300
www.941kodj.com
License: Salt Lake City, Salt Lake County, UT held by Citicasters Licenses Inc.
Group Owner: iHeartMedia; (acq 5-4-99; grpsl).
Nat'l Reps: Clear Channel; Katz Radio

Arbitron Metro Market: Salt Lake City-Ogden-Provo, UT *TV Affiliate:* KUTV(TV) affil; *Format:* Oldies; *Hrs. of News Programming:* News progmg 2 hrs wkly; *Target Audience:* 25-54; adults
Stu Stanek, Regional President

***KRCL**
12-03-1979; 90.9 MHz FM; *Hrs Open:* 24; 25 kw; 3740 ft.; N40 39 34 W112 12 5 *Rebroadcasts:* Rebroadcasts KZMU(FM) Moab 50%
1971 West North Temple, Salt Lake City, UT 84116 US
(801) 363-1818; *Fax:* (801) 533-9136
www.krcl.org
comments@krcl.org
License: Salt Lake City, Salt Lake County, UT held by Listeners Community Radio of Utah Inc.
Arbitron Metro Market: Salt Lake City-Ogden-Provo, UT; *Format:* Talk *Special Programming:* Black 20 hrs, Sp 9 hrs, American Indian 4 hrs, A; *Hrs. of News Programming:* news progmg 3 hrs wkly *No. News Employees:* 1; *Target Audience:* General.
Daela Taeoalii, Chairman
Tino Arana, Operations Dir
Vicki Mann, General Manager
Felix Gonzalez, Chief Engineer
Amy Dwyer, Development Director
Ebay Jamil Hamilton, Music Director
John K. Johnson, Legal Counsel
Sue Gerber,Membership

KRSP-FM
08-21-1968; 103.5 MHz FM; 25 kw; 3,740 ft.; N40 39 34 W112 12 5
55 N. 300 W., Salt Lake City, UT 84180 US
(801) 575-5555
www.1035thearrow.com
License: Salt Lake City, Salt Lake County, UT held by Bonneville International Corporation
Group Owner: Bonneville International Corporation; (acq 12-5-2003; grpsl).
Arbitron Metro Market: Salt Lake City-Ogden-Provo, UT; *Format:* Classic Rock; *Target Audience:* 18-34.
Tanya Vea, Vice President and General Manager
Emily Hunt, Local Sales Manager

KSFI
12-26-1946; 100.3 MHz FM; 25 kw; 3,740 ft.; N40 39 34 W112 12 5
55 N. 300 W., Salt Lake City, UT 84180 US
(801) 575-5555
www.fm100.com
License: Salt Lake City, Salt Lake County, UT held by Bonneville International Corporation
Group Owner: Bonneville International Corporation; (acq 12-5-2003; grpsl).
Arbitron Metro Market: Salt Lake City-Ogden-Provo, UT; *Format:* Adult Contemp; *Target Audience:* 25-54; general
Tanya Vea, Vice President and General Manager

KSL
05-06-1922; 1160 kHz AM; *Hrs Open:* 24; 50 kw-U, ND1; N40 46 46 W112 5 56
5 Triad Center, 55 N. 3rd W., Salt Lake City, UT 84180-1109 US
(801) 575-7601; *Fax:* (801) 575-5560
www.ksl.com
support@ksl.com
License: Salt Lake City, Salt Lake County, UT held by Bonneville International Corporation
Group Owner: Bonneville International Corporation
Nat'l Network: CBS; *Wire Services:* Reuters; UPI
Arbitron Metro Market: Salt Lake City-Ogden-Provo, UT *TV Affiliate:* KSL-TV affil.; *Format:* News, News/Talk, 84, Talk; *No. News Employees:* 12; *Target Audience:* 25-54.
Ike Yospe, Promotions Manager
John Dehnel, Chief Engineer
Stephanie Palmer, Advertising

KSOP-FM
12-10-1964; 104.3 MHz FM; *Hrs Open:* 24; 25 kw; 3740 ft.; N40 39 34 W112 12 5
1285 W 2320 S, West Valley City, UT 84119 US
(801) 972-1043; *Fax:* (801) 974-0868
www.ksopcountry.com
License: Salt Lake City, Salt Lake County, UT held by KSOP Inc.
Nat'l Reps: McGavren Guild
Arbitron Metro Market: Salt Lake City-Ogden-Provo, UT; *Format:* Country; *No. News Employees:* 1; *Target Audience:* 18 plus.
Greg Hilton, General Manager
Phil Pond, Programming Director

KUBL-FM
07-31-1965; 93.3 MHz FM; 25 kw; 3740 ft.; N40 39 34 W112 12 5
424 Bearcat Drive, Salt Lake City, UT 84115 US
(801) 485-6700
www.kbull93.com
License: Salt Lake City, Salt Lake County, UT held by Citadel Broadcasting Co.
Arbitron Metro Market: Salt Lake City, UT; *Format:* Country
Terry Mathis, General Sales Mgr
Ed Hill, Programming Director
Randi P' Poll, Promotions Manager
Julie Johnson, News Director
Richie Bauer, Chief Engineer

***KUER-FM**
06-04-1960; 90.1 MHz FM; 38 kw; 2995 ft.; N40 36 30 W112 9 34
101 South Waswatch Drve, #240, Salt Lake City, UT 84112 US
(801) 581-6625; *Fax:* (801) 581-6758
www.kuer.org
news@kuer.org
License: Salt Lake City, Salt Lake County, UT held by University of Utah.
Nat'l Network: NPR; PRI
Arbitron Metro Market: Salt Lake City, UT; *Format:* Jazz, News
John Greene, General Manager
Susan Kropf, Director, Development/Marketing
Terry Gildea, News Director
Lewis Downey, Chief Engineer
Amy Fowler, Accountant

***KUFR**
12-14-1989; 91.7 MHz FM; *Hrs Open:* 24; 0.22 kw; -318 ft.; N40 46 9 W111 53 12
290 Hegenberger Road, Oakland, CA 94621 US
(800) 543-1495
www.familyradio.com
License: Salt Lake City, Salt Lake County, UT held by Family Stations Inc.
Group Owner: Family Stations Inc.
Arbitron Metro Market: Salt Lake City, UT; *Format:* Christian, Religious
Harold Camping, President
James Abrahamson, Operations Dir
Roger Crawford, Station Manager
Thad McKinney, General Sales Mgr

Sandy

KBJA
06-01-2001; 1640 kHz AM; *Hrs Open:* 24
US
(801) 808-5056
info@kbja1640.com
License: Sandy, UT held by United Broadcasting Co. Inc.
Arbitron Metro Market: Salt Lake City-Ogden-Provo, UT; *Format:* Spanish; *Hrs. of News Programming:* news progmg 41.5 hrs wkly; *No. News Employees:* 5; *Target Audience:* Hispanic adults; adult Hispanic market
Jose Rivera, General Manager
Karla Hernandez, General Sales Mgr
Daniel Rivera, Programming Director
Patricia Rivera, Promotions Manager
Carmen Vargas, News Director
Dennis Silver, Chief Engineer
Christian Rivera, PromotionsDirector

KTKK
05-13-1960; 630 kHz AM; *Hrs Open:* 24; 1 kw-D, DA2; 0.5 kw-N, DA2; N40 41 30 W111 55 30
10348 South Redwood Rd, South Jordan, UT 84095-9339 US
(801) 253-4883; *Fax:* (801) 253-9085
www.k-talk.com
License: Sandy, UT held by United Broadcasting Co.
Arbitron Metro Market: Salt Lake City-Ogden-Provo, UT; *Format:* Talk; *Target Audience:* 35 plus.
Dennis Silver, Chief Engineer

Santa Clara

KRQX-FM
01-01-2002; 98.9 MHz FM; 14.5 kw; Ant 2,034 ft; N36 50 49 W113 29 28
License: Santa Clara, Washington County, UT held by CBL Investments LLC

G. Craig Hanson, General Manager

***KXDS**
91.3 MHz FM; 0.38 kw; 1854 ft.; N36 50 49 W113 29 28
Jennings Building, Room 103, 225 S. 700 E., St. George, UT 84770 US
(435) 319-0910
913TheStorm@Gmail.com
License: Santa Clara, Washington County, UT held by Dixie College.
Arbitron Metro Market: Saint George, UT; *Format:* Alternative, Contemporary Hits/Top 40

Smithfield

KGNT
02-01-1983; 99.1 MHz FM; 3 kw; -131 ft.; N41 48 44 W111 47 31
810 West 200 North, Logan, UT 84231 US
(435) 752-1390; *Fax:* (435) 752-1392
www.kool.fm
License: Smithfield, Cache County, UT held by Frandsen Media Co. LLC.
Group Owner: Sun Valley Radio Inc.; (acq 2-4-02; $775,000).
Nat'l Network: CBS; Westwood One
Arbitron Metro Market: Logan, UT; *Format:* Oldies; *Target Audience:* 18-49; 55% female, 45% male middle class; *Adv. Rates:* 21; 18; 20; 14.50
Jay Eubanks, Station Manager
Lori Gill, General Sales Mgr
Paul Anderson, Chief Engineer
David Denton, Program Director

South Jordan

KUUU
09-01-1979; 92.5 MHz FM; *Hrs Open:* 24; 0.5 kw; 3930 ft.; N40 39 35 W112 12 4
50 W. Broadway, Suite 200, Salt Lake City, UT 84101 US
(801) 258-0925, (844) 420-9250
u92slc.com
djerockalypze@bwaymedia.com
License: South Jordan, Salt Lake County, UT held by Broadway Media LS, LLC
Group Owner: Broadway Media Group
Arbitron Metro Market: South Jordan, UT; *Format:* Urban Contemporary, Blues; *Hrs. of News Programming:* news progmg 15 hrs wkly; *No. News Employees:* 1; *Target Audience:* General.; *Adv. Rates:* 125; 125; 125;125
Josu, Ramirez, General Sales Mgr
DJ Erockalypze, Programming Director

South Salt Lake

KDYL
09-02-1967; 1060 kHz AM; *Hrs Open:* 24
Mailing Address: P.O. Box 57760, Salt Lake City, UT 84157 US
Second Address: 3606 South 500 West, Salt Lake City, UT 84115
(801) 262-5624; *Fax:* (801) 266-1510
www.kdylam.com
kdyl@kdylam.com
License: South Salt Lake, UT held by Holiday Broadcasting Co.
Group Owner: Carlson Communications International
Wire Services: CNN
Arbitron Metro Market: Salt Lake City, UT; *Format:* Oldies; *Hrs. of News Programming:* News progmg 13 hrs wkly; *Target Audience:* 35-64; general; *Adv. Rates:* 40; 40; 40; 40
Brent J. Carlson, Operations Dir
Ralph J. Carlson, General Manager
R. Steve Carlson, Vice President, Operations

KSOP
02-01-1955; 1370 kHz AM; *Hrs Open:* 24; 5 kw-D, DAN; 0.5 kw-N, DAN; N40 43 12 W111 55 42; N40 43 12 W111 55 41
1285 West 2320 South, West Valley City, UT 84119 US
(801) 972-1370
www.cc1370.com
License: South Salt Lake, UT held by KSOP Inc.
Group Owner: 3 Daughters Media Inc.
Nat'l Reps: McGavren Guild
Arbitron Metro Market: Salt Lake City-Ogden-Provo, UT; *Format:* Country; *No. News Employees:* 1; *Target Audience:* 25-54+.
Greg Hilton, President
Don Hilton, Programming Director
Dick Jacobson, News Director
Bill Traue, Chief Engineer

Spanish Fork

KHQN
07-24-1960; 1480 kHz AM; 1 kw-D, NDD; 0.133 kw-N, ND1; N40 4 30 W111 39 42
Mailing Address: 2250 North University Parkway, Space 4890, Provo, UT 84604 US
Second Address: 8628 S. State Road, Spanish Fork, UT 84660
(800) 776-1913; *Fax:* (801) 501-9949
License: Spanish Fork, UT held by Robyn Howell

Arbitron Metro Market: Salt Lake City, UT; *Format:* News, News/Talk, 84, Talk *Special Programming:* Sunday Accents 24 hrs wkly; *Target Audience:* 25-54
Sam Bushman, General Manager

KAAZ-FM
11-01-1967; 106.7 MHz FM; *Hrs Open:* 24; 25 kw; 3740 ft.; N40 39 34 W112 12 5
2801 S. Decker Lake Dr., Salt Lake City, UT 84119 US
(801) 908-1300; *Fax:* (801) 908-1459
www.1067rocks.com
License: Spanish Fork, Utah County, UT held by Citicasters Licenses Inc.
Group Owner: iHeartMedia; (acq 5-3-2004; $22 million with KXRV(FM) Centerville)
Nat'l Reps: Clear Channel; Katz Radio
Arbitron Metro Market: Salt Lake City-Ogden-Provo, UT; *Format:* Adult Contemp; *Target Audience:* 25-44; women
Stu Stanek, Regional President

Spanish Valley

KCPX
06-15-2009; 1490 kHz AM; *Hrs Open:* 24
1030 S. Bowling Alley Lane, Moab, UT 84532 US
(435) 259-1035; *Fax:* (435) 259-1037
License: Spanish Valley, UT held by Moab Communications LLC.
Group Owner: Carlson Communications International
Nat'l Network: Fox News Radio; Premiere Radio Networks; *Nat'l Reps:* Rgnl Reps; *Wire Services:* Metro Weather Service Inc.
Arbitron Metro Market: Spanish Valley, UT; *Format:* Talk; *Hrs. of News Programming:* 15; *No. News Employees:* 1
Ralph Carlson, President
Phillip Mueller, General Manager

St. George

KDXU
07-03-1957; 890 kHz AM
750 W. Ridgeview Drive, St. George, UT 84770-2665 US
(435) 673-3579; *Fax:* (435) 673-8900
www.newstalk890.com
License: St. George, UT held by CCR-St. George IV LLC.
Group Owner: Cherry Creek Radio LLC; (acq 8-10-2006; grpsl)
Arbitron Metro Market: Saint George, UT; *Format:* News, News/Talk, 86 *Special Programming:* Relg 4 hrs wkly; *Target Audience:* 25-54.
Joseph Schwartz, CEO
Debbie Calobeer, Operations Dir
Chris McCarthy, General Sales Mgr
Peter Gardner, Programming Director
Rick Parrish, Promotions Manager
Dave Cory, Chief Engineer

KONY
11-12-1994; 99.9 MHz FM; *Hrs Open:* 24; 89 kw; 2034 ft.; N36 50 49 W113 29 28
619 S. Bluff St., Tower 1, Suite 300, St. George, UT 84770 US
(435) 628-3643
www.999konycountry.com
License: St. George, Washington County, UT held by Canyon Media Corp.
Nat'l Network: Fox News Radio; *Nat'l Reps:* Katz Radio *Regional Reps:* Kathy Bingham
Arbitron Metro Market: Saint George, UT; *Format:* Country; *Target Audience:* 25-64; male & female; *Adv. Rates:* 62; 55; 58; 47
M. Kent Frandsen, President
Marty Lane, Operations Dir
Carl Lamar, General Manager
Ben Lindquist, General Sales Mgr

KZNU
10-09-1957; 1450 kHz AM; *Hrs Open:* 24
619 S. Bluff Street, Tower 1, Suite 300, St. George, UT 84770 US
(435) 628-3643
www.foxnews1450.com
License: St. George, UT held by Canyon Media Corp..
Nat'l Network: Fox News Radio; *Nat'l Reps:* Katz Radio *Regional Reps:* Kathy Bingham
Arbitron Metro Market: Saint George, UT; *Format:* News, News/Talk, 86
Carl Lamar, General Manager
Ben Lindquist, General Sales Mgr

KZHK
01-01-1997; 95.9 MHz FM; 100 kw; 1952 ft.; N36 50 49 W113 29 28
619 S. Bluff Street, Tower 1, Suite 300, St. George, UT 84770 US
(435) 628-3643
www.959thehawk.com
License: St. George, Washington County, UT held by Marvin Kent Frandsen.
Group Owner: Sun Valley Radio Inc.
Arbitron Metro Market: St. George, UT; *Format:* Classic Rock; *Adv. Rates:* 40; 40; 40; 40
M.K. Frandsen, President
Carl Lamar, General Manager
Marty Lane, Station Manager
Ben Lindquist, General Sales Mgr
Jon Smith, Programming Director
Aaronee Allen, Promotions Manager
Kelton Lloyd, Chief Engineer

Taylorsville

KUTR
05-09-2005; 820 kHz AM
3701 Harrison Boulevard, Ogden, UT 84403 US
(801) 393-4882; *Fax:* (336) 759-0366
www.truthnetwork.com/stations/am-820-kutr.html
kutrstudio@gmail.com
License: Taylorsville, UT held by Julie Epperson
Arbitron Metro Market: Taylorsville, UT; *Format:* Christian
Russ East, Station Manager

Vernal

KLCY
05-01-1975; 105.5 MHz FM; *Hrs Open:* 24; 3.3 kw; 1699 ft.; N40 32 16 W109 41 57
Mailing Address: 2425 North Vernal Avenue, Vernal, UT 84078 US
Second Address: PO Box 307, Vernal, UT 84078
(435) 789-1059; *Fax:* (435) 789-6977
www.klcy.com
productions@klcy.com
License: Vernal, Uintah County, UT held by Ashley Communications Inc.
Nat'l Network: ABC; Jones Radio Networks
Arbitron Metro Market: Grand Junction, CO; *Format:* Country; *Hrs. of News Programming:* News progmg 2 hrs wkly; *Target Audience:* 18-54; active
Steve Evans, Owner/Manager
Janet Crinklaw, Office Manager
Michael Evans, Marketing Consultant

KRAM
12-01-1987; 1400 kHz AM; *Hrs Open:* Sunrise-sunset
US
(541) 884-8074; *Fax:* (541) 884-8226
License: Vernal, UT held by Scott D. MacArthur, Personal Rep., estate of Sandra A. Falk

Scott MacArthur, General Manager

KVEL
01-19-1947; 920 kHz AM; *Hrs Open:* 24; 5 kw-D, DAN; 1 kw-N, DAN; N40 29 30 W109 31 45
Mailing Address: 2425 North Vernal Avenue, Vernal, UT 84078 US
Second Address: PO Box 307, Vernal, UT 84078
(435) 789-0920; *Fax:* (435) 789-6977
www.920kvel.com
production@kvel.com
License: Vernal, UT held by Ashley Communications Inc.
Arbitron Metro Market: Vernal, UT; *Format:* News, News/Talk, 84, Talk *Special Programming:* Farm 2 hrs, relg, Sp, pub affrs one hr wkly; *Hrs. of News Programming:* news progmg 20 hrs wkly; *No. News Employees:* 1 *Target Audience:* 35-64; affluent, upscale
Steve Evans, Owner/Manager
Janet Crinklaw, Office Manager
Michael Evans, Marketing Consultant
Brian Baldwin, Production

***KEYV**
91.7 MHz FM; 910 w; Ant 1,637 ft; N40 32 16 W109 41 57
307 South 1600 West, Provo, UT 84601-3932
(801) 374-5210
www.keyradio.org
mail@keyradio.org
License: Vernal, Uintah County, UT held by Biblical Ministries Worldwide.
Nat'l Network: Moody Broadcasting Network

Mike Zandler, General Manager

Washington

KHKR
06-06-1982; 1210 kHz AM; *Hrs Open:* 24; 10 kw-D, ND1; 0.25 kw-N, ND1; N37 8 38 W113 30 3
980 North Michigan Avenue, Suite 1880, Chicago, IL 60611 US
(435) 673-3579; *Fax:* (435) 673-8900
License: Washington, UT held by CCR-St. George IV LLC.
Group Owner: Cherry Creek Radio LLC; (acq 8-10-2006; grpsl)
Nat'l Network: ESPN Radio
Format: Sports, Talk; *Target Audience:* 18-64.; *Adv. Rates:* 22; 22; 22; 16
Debbie Calobeer, Operations Dir
Chris McCarthy, General Sales Mgr
Mike McGary, Programming Director
Rick Parrish, Promotions Manager
Michelle Matthews, News Director
Dave Cory, Chief Engineer

Wellington

KRPX
01-01-2006; 95.3 MHz FM; 6 kw; -138 ft.; N39 36 33 W110 48 50
US
(435) 637-1167; *Fax:* (435) 637-1177
License: Wellington, Carson County, UT held by Eastern Utah Broadcasting Co.
Arbitron Metro Market: San Antonio, TX; *Format:* Light Rock
Neal Robinson, President
Tom Anderson, General Manager

West Jordan

KLLB
01-01-1982; 1510 kHz AM; 1 kw-C, NDD; 10 kw-D, NDD; N40 33 6 W111 58 17
US
www.kllbam.com
License: West Jordan, UT held by United Security Financial Inc.
Arbitron Metro Market: Salt Lake City, UT; *Format:* Gospel
Lois Johnson, General Manager
Joel Cosby, General Sales Mgr
D.J. Stone, Programming Director
Darrell Cosby, Chief Engineer

West Valley City

KMRI
11-16-1956; 1550 kHz AM; *Hrs Open:* 24; 10 kw-D, ND2; 0.34 kw-N, ND2; N40 43 16 W112 2 29
US
(801) 886-1550
License: West Valley City, UT held by Alpha & Omega Communications LLC
Arbitron Metro Market: Salt Lake City, UT; *Format:* Christian; *Hrs. of News Programming:* news progmg 40 hrs wkly; *No. News Employees:* 2; *Target Audience:* 16-50.; *Adv. Rates:* 40; 40; 40; 40
Andy Acosta, General Manager

Woodruff

KYMV
06-01-2002; 100.7 MHz FM; 88 kw horiz; N40 52 16 W110 59 43
50 W. Broadway, Suite 200, Salt Lake City, UT 84101 US
(801) 524-2600, (877) 807-1007
www.rewind1007.com
jtaylor@bwaymedia.com
License: Woodruff, Rich County, UT held by Broadway Media LS, LLC
Group Owner: Broadway Media Group; (acq 4-4-2001; grpsl)
Arbitron Metro Market: Salt Lake City, UT; *Format:* Adult Contemp
Brandon Francis, General Sales Mgr
Justin Taylor, Programming Director

Vermont

Addison

WIFY
01-01-1999; 93.7 MHz FM; 21 kw; Ant 354 ft; N44 13 15 W73 24 37
169 River Street, Montpelier, VT 05602
(802) 223-2396
www.pointfm.com
License: Addison, Addison County, VT held by Radio Broadcasting Services Inc.

Group Owner: Northeast Broadcasting Company Inc.; (acq 12-19-2000; $434,000)
Nat'l Network: Jones Radio Networks

Rich Delancy, General Manager
Rich Delancey, General Sales Mgr
J.J. Prieve, Programming Director
Chris Fells, News Director
Mike Raymond, Chief Engineer

Barre

*WCMD-FM
08-01-1998; 89.9 MHz FM; *Hrs Open:* 24; 0.94 kw; 591 ft.; N44 7 32 W72 28 36 *Rebroadcasts:* Rebroadcasts WCMK(FM) Bolton 99%
140 Main Street, Essex Junction, VT 05452 US
(866) 878-8885
thelightradio.net
License: Barre, Washington County, VT held by Christian Ministries Inc.
Nat'l Network: Moody
Arbitron Metro Market: Essex,VT; *Format:* Christian, Religious; *Hrs. of News Programming:* News progmg 15 hrs wkly; *Target Audience:* General; Christian, middle income
Ric McClary, General Manager

WRFK
08-05-1974; 107.1 MHz FM; 3.9 kw; 410 ft.; N44 9 30 W72 28 46
2150 Washington Street, Suite 250, Newton, MA 02462 US
(802) 476-4168; *Fax:* (802) 479-5893
License: Barre, Washington County, VT
Group Owner: Great Eastern Radio LLC
TV Affiliate: Classic hits

WSNO
10-13-1959; 1450 kHz AM; *Hrs Open:* 24; 1 kw-U, ND1; N44 11 40 W72 30 52
2150 Washington Street, Suite 250, Newton, MA 02462 US
(802) 476-4168; *Fax:* (802) 479-5893
License: Barre, VT held by Great Eastern Radio LLC
Group Owner: Great Eastern Radio LLC; (acq 8-2-2004; grpsl).
Nat'l Network: CBS
Format: News, News/Talk, 84, Talk
Ken Barlow, General Manager
Jim Severance, Programming Director

Barton

WQJQ
01-01-2008; 100.3 MHz FM; 100 w; Ant 525 ft; N44 45 57 W72 09 10
39 Church Street, Lyndonville, VT 05851
(802) 626-9800; *Fax:* (802) 626-8500
www.magic977.com
magic977@gmail.com
License: Barton, Orleans County, VT held by Vermont Broadcast Associates Inc.
Group Owner: Vermont Broadcast Associates Inc.

Bruce James, General Manager

Bellows Falls

WZLF
11-01-1981; 107.1 MHz FM; *Hrs Open:* 24; 1.15 kw; 531 ft.; N43 12 33 W72 19 58 *Rebroadcasts:* Rebroadcasts WSSH(FM) Marlboro 100%
Post Office Box 1230, Route 12 and 103, Claremont, NH 03743 US
(603) 298-0332; *Fax:* (603) 727-0134
www.953thewolf.com
mtrombly@nassaubroadcasting.com
License: Bellows Falls, Windham County, VT held by WBIN Media Co. Inc.
Group Owner: WBIN Media Co. Inc.; (acq 8-2-2004; grpsl).
Nat'l Reps: Roslin
Arbitron Metro Market: West Lebanon, NH; *Format:* Country
Special Programming: Farm one hr wkly; *Hrs. of News Programming:* news progmg 5 hrs wkly; *No. News Employees:* 1; *Target Audience:* 25-54; general
Mike Trombly, General Manager
Matt Houseman, Programming Director
Brett Franklin, Public Service Director

Bennington

WBTN
09-23-1953; 1370 kHz AM; *Hrs Open:* 24/7; 1 kw-D, ND1; 0.085 kw-N, ND1; N42 54 19 W73 12 32
407 Hardwood Hill, Bennington, VT 05201 US
(802) 442-6321; *Fax:* (802) 442-3112
www.wbtnam.org
info@wbtnam.org
License: Bennington, VT held by Shires Media Partnership Inc (not-for-profit)
Nat'l Network: Westwood One; *Wire Services:* AP
Arbitron Metro Market: Bennington, VT; *Format:* News, News/Talk, 86 *Special Programming:* Red Sox/N.E. Patriots; *Hrs. of News Programming:* 7-8 a.m.; 12-12:30 p.m.; *Target Audience:* 24-54.; *Adv. Rates:* Openrate: $15/30 second spot
Spencer Sweet, General Manager
Ted Hollo, Sales Manager
Aaron Sawyer, Production Manager

*WBTN-FM
11-04-1978; 94.3 MHz FM; *Hrs Open:* 5:30 AM-midnight; 3 kw; 112 ft.; N42 56 52.9 W73 10 33.9
365 Troy Avenue, Colchester, VT 05446 US
(802) 655-9451; *Fax:* (802) 655-2799
www.vpr.net
news@vpr.net
License: Bennington, Bennington County, VT held by Vermont Public Radio.
Arbitron Metro Market: Colchester, VT; *Format:* Classical; *Hrs. of News Programming:* news progmg 4 hrs wkly; *No. News Employees:* 1; *Target Audience:* 18-45.
Brian Tagliaferro, Manager of Special Giving
Brian Marshall, Manager of Special Giving
Aaron Kimball, Board Operator
Amy Kolb Noyes, Public Post Reporter
Angela Evancie, Digital Producer
Betty Smith-Mastaler, Producer
BrendanKinney, VP, Development/Marketing
Brian Donahue, VP, Finance/Operations & CFO

Berlin

WWFY
04-02-1975; 100.9 MHz FM; *Hrs Open:* 24; 4.5 kw; 778 ft.; N44 7 30.4 W72 28 27.9
3043 Lake Road West, Ashtabula, OH 44004 US
(802) 476-4168; *Fax:* (802) 479-5893
www.froggy1009.com
License: Berlin, Washington County, VT held by Great Eastern Radio LLC
Group Owner: Great Eastern Radio LLC; (acq 8-2-2004; grpsl).
Arbitron Metro Market: Middlebury, VT; *Format:* Country; *Target Audience:* 18-49; young professionals
John Gales, General Manager
Jim Severance, Programming Director

Bolton

*WGLY-FM
01-01-1996; 91.5 MHz FM; *Hrs Open:* 24; 1 kw; 935 ft.; N44 21 53 W72 55 52 *Rebroadcasts:* Rebroadcasts WCMD(FM) Barre 100%
140 Main Street, Essex Jct., VT 05452 US
(802) 878-8885
thelightradio.net
License: Bolton, Chittenden County, VT held by Christian Ministries Inc.
Nat'l Network: Moody
Arbitron Metro Market: Burlington, VT; *Format:* Religious
Ric McClary, General Manager

Brandon

WEXP
05-01-2000; 101.5 MHz FM; *Hrs Open:* 24; 0.35 kw; 1306 ft.; N43 39 31 W73 6 26
9 Stowe St., P.O. Box 550, Waterbury, VT 05676 US
(802) 244-1764
101theone.com
101theone@radiovermont.com
License: Brandon, Rutland County, VT held by Woodchuck Radio LLC
Group Owner: Radio Vermont Group Inc.; (acq 1-21-2005; $2.5 million with WTHK(FM) Wilmington)
Nat'l Network: Westwood One
Arbitron Metro Market: Brandon, VT; *Format:* Classic Rock, Rock/AOR; *Target Audience:* 25-54; male
Steve Cormier, General Manager
Frankie Allen, Programming Director

Brattleboro

WKVT
11-29-1959; 1490 kHz AM; *Hrs Open:* 24; 1 kw-U, ND1; N42 50 51 W72 34 56
458 Williams Street, Brattleboro, VT 05301 US
(802) 254-2343; *Fax:* (802) 254-6683
www.1490wkvt.com
pc@wkvt.com
License: Brattleboro, VT held by Saga Communications of New England LLC.
Group Owner: Saga Communications Inc.; (acq 5-1-2002; grpsl)
Nat'l Network: CBS; *Wire Services:* AP
Format: News, News/Talk, 86; *Hrs. of News Programming:* news progmg 30 hrs wkly; *No. News Employees:* 1; *Target Audience:* 35-64; news & info oriented adults; *Adv. Rates:* 144; 120; 144; 120
Peter Case, Operations Dir

WKVT-FM
01-01-1980; 92.7 MHz FM; *Hrs Open:* 24; 1.8 kw; 610 ft.; N42 53 45 W72 39 49
458 Williams Street, Brattleboro, NH 05301 US
(802) 254-2343; *Fax:* (802) 254-6683
www.1490wkvt.com
pc@wkvt.com
License: Brattleboro, Windham County, VT
Group Owner: Saga Communications Inc.
Nat'l Network: AP Radio; *Wire Services:* AP
Format: Contemporary Hits/Top 40, Adult Contemp; *Hrs. of News Programming:* news progmg 8 hrs wkly; *No. News Employees:* 1; *Target Audience:* 18-44.
Peter Case, Operations Dir

WTSA
04-19-1950; 1450 kHz AM; *Hrs Open:* 24; 1 kw-U, ND1; N42 52 13 W72 33 35
PO Box 819, 464 Putney Road, Brattleboro, VT 05302 US
(802) 254-4577; *Fax:* (802) 257-4644
www.wtsa.net
news@wtsa.net
License: Brattleboro, VT held by Tri-State Broadcasters Inc.
Nat'l Reps: D & R Radio
Arbitron Metro Market: Brattleboro, VT; *Format:* Sports; *No. News Employees:* 1; *Target Audience:* General.
Kelli Corbell, General Manager
Steve Cormier, Station Manager
Stephanie Larson, Promotions Coordinator
Tim Johnson, News Director
Lillian Fowler, Business Manager
Dan Taylor, Traffic Manager

WTSA-FM
12-15-1975; 96.7 MHz FM; 5.2 kw; 135 ft.; N42 53 21 W72 36 47
P.O. Box 819, 464 Putney Road, Brattleboro, VT 05302 US
(802) 254-4577; *Fax:* (802) 257-4644
www.wtsa.net
news@wtsa.net
License: Brattleboro, Windham County, VT held by Tri-State Broadcasters Inc.
Arbitron Metro Market: Brattleboro, VT; *Format:* Adult Contemp
Special Programming: Oldies 16 hrs wkly; *Target Audience:* 12 plus.
Kelli Corbell, General Manager
Steve Cormier, Station Manager
Stephanie Larson, Promotions Coordinator
Tim Johnson, News Director
Dan Taylor, Traffic Manager
Lillian Fowler, Business Manager

Brighton

*WVTI
106.9 MHz FM; 1.42 kw; 694 ft.; N44 47 2 W71 53 13
365 Troy Avenue, Colchester, VT 05446 US
(802) 655-9451; *Fax:* (802) 655-2799
www.vpr.net
news@vpr.net
License: Brighton, Essex County, VT held by Vermont Public Radio.
Arbitron Metro Market: Brighton, VT; *Format:* Classical
Charlie Kireker, Chairman
Brian Marshall, Chief Engineer
Aaron Kimball, Board Operator
Angela Evancie, Digital Producer
Betty Smith-Mastaler, Producer
Brendan Kinney, VP, Development/Marketing
Brian Donahue, CFO/VP, Finance &Operations
Brian Tagliaferro, Manager of Special Giving

Bristol

WTNN
01-01-2007; 97.5 MHz FM; 8.7 kw; 518 ft.; N44 24 23.1 W73 8 12.8
4049 Williston Road, Suite 7, South Burlington, VT 05403 US

(802) 864-9750; *Fax:* (802) 864-9777
www.eaglecountry975.com
License: Bristol, Addison County, VT held by Impact Radio Inc.
Arbitron Metro Market: Bristol, VT; *Format:* Country
John J. Fuller, General Manager
Brian Ram, Vice President, Programming
Debbie Frenier, Traffic Manager
Rebecca Morse Whitten, Promotions Manager

***WXLQ**
01-01-2009; 90.5 MHz FM; 0.16 kw; 594 ft.; N44 13 24 W73 7 27 *Rebroadcasts:* Rebroadcasts WSLU(FM) Canton, NY 100%
Mailing Address: North Country Public Radio, St. Lawrence University, Canton, NY 13617 US
Second Address: EJ Noble Medical Building, Room 201, 80 East Main Street, Canton, NY 13617
(315) 229-5356; *Fax:* (315) 229-5373
www.northcountrypublicradio.org
martha@ncpr.org
License: Bristol, Addison County, VT held by St. Lawrence University
Nat'l Network: NPR
Arbitron Metro Market: Bristol, VT; *Format:* News
Shelly Pike, Operations Manager
Ellen Rocco, Station Manager
Jackie Sauter, Programming Director
Bob Sauter, Chief Engineer
Sandy Demarest, Development Director
Martha Foley, News Director
Bill Haenel, New Media Developer
DaleHobson, Web Manager
Joel Hurd, Production Manager
June Peoples, Membership Director

Burlington

WEZF
07-19-1968; 92.9 MHz FM; *Hrs Open:* 24; 46 kw; 2703 ft.; N44 31 40 W72 48 58
265 Hegeman Avenue, Colchester, VT 05446 US
(802) 655-0093; *Fax:* (802) 655-0478
www.star929.com
License: Burlington, Chittenden County, VT held by Vox AM/FM LLC.
Group Owner: Vox AM/FM LLC; (acq 7-25-2008; grpsl)
Nat'l Reps: Clear Channel
Arbitron Metro Market: Burlington, VT; *Format:* Adult Contemp; *Hrs. of News Programming:* news progmg 7 hrs wkly; *No. News Employees:* 1; *Target Audience:* 25-54.
Slater, Operations Manager
Jamie Dennis, Chief Engineer

WJOY
09-14-1946; 1230 kHz AM; *Hrs Open:* 24; 1 kw-U, ND1; N44 27 3 W73 11 51
70 Joy Drive, South Burlington, VT 05403 US
(802) 658-1230; *Fax:* (802) 862-0786
www.wjoy.com
wjoy@hallradio.com
License: Burlington, VT held by Hall Communications Inc.
Group Owner: Hall Communications Inc.; (acq 12-1-83;
Nat'l Network: Westwood One; *Nat'l Reps:* D & R Radio
Arbitron Metro Market: Burlington-Plattsburgh, VT-NY; *Format:* News; *Hrs. of News Programming:* news progmg 4 hrs wkly; *No. News Employees:* 1; *Target Audience:* General; affluent, empty nesters, well educated
Bonnie Rowbotham, Chairman
Arthur Rowbotham, President
Bill Baldwin, Operations Dir
Dan Dubonnet, General Manager
Lee Bodette, General Sales Mgr
Wendy Naylor, Promotions Manager
Ginny McGehee, News Director
Richard Reed,Executive Vice President
Steve Pelkey, Operations Director

WCAT
04-19-1954; 1390 kHz AM; *Hrs Open:* 24; 5 kw-D, DAN; 5 kw-N, DAN; N44 29 47 W73 12 49
9 Stowe Street, Waterbery, VT 05676 US
(802) 655-6753; *Fax:* (802) 544-6977
www.wcat1390.com
License: Burlington, VT held by Radio Broadcasting Services Inc.
Group Owner: Northeast Broadcasting Company Inc.; (acq 8-3-2006; $400,000).
Nat'l Network: ESPN Radio; *Nat'l Reps:* McGavren Guild; *Wire Services:* AP
Arbitron Metro Market: Burlington-Plattsburgh, VT-NY; *Format:* Sports; *Adv. Rates:* 25; 20; 22; 15
Steven Silberberg, President
Richard DeLancey Sr., General Manager
J.J. Prieve, Programming Director
Chris Fells, News Director

WOKO
06-26-1962; 98.9 MHz FM; 100 kw; 308 ft.; N44 27 3 W73 11 51
70 Joy Drive, South Burlington, VT 05403 US
(802) 658-1230; *Fax:* (802) 862-0786
www.woko.com
License: Burlington, Chittenden County, VT held by Hall Communications Inc.
Group Owner: Hall Communications Inc.
Arbitron Metro Market: Burlington-Plat *TV Affiliate:* Country
Disc Jockey, Thom Richards
Disc Jockey, Cal Daniels
Disc Jockey, C.K. Coin
Disc Jockey, Ginny McGehee
Local News Editor

***WRUV**
10-03-1965; 90.1 MHz FM; *Hrs Open:* 24; 0.46 kw; 131 ft.; N44 28 49 W73 12 7
Davis Student Center, UVM, Burlington, VT 05405 US
(802) 656-0796
www.wruv.org
wruv@wruv.org
License: Burlington, Chittenden County, VT held by University of Vermont & State Agricultural College.
Arbitron Metro Market: Burlington-Plat; *Format:* Jazz, Variety/Diverse *Special Programming:* Non-commercial free format, progmg varies
Karla Noboa, Station Manager
Cristina MacKinnon, Programming Director
Julia Moreno, Chief Engineer
Joe Palchak, Music Director
Cam Kostrya, Business Director
Dina Goodhue, Fundraising
Ruby LaBrusciano-Carris, Public Relations
Brendan Auth, Chief Operator
Claire Macon, Events

WVMT
05-20-1922; 620 kHz AM; *Hrs Open:* 24; 5 kw-D, DA2; 5 kw-N, DA2; N44 32 4 W73 13 15
US
(802) 655-1620; *Fax:* (802) 655-1329
www.newstalk620wvmt.com
paulg@95triplex.com
License: Burlington, VT held by Sison Broadcasting Inc.
Nat'l Network: ABC Information & Entertainment; *Nat'l Reps:* McGavren Guild
Arbitron Metro Market: Burlington, VT; *Format:* News, News/Talk, 84, Talk; *Hrs. of News Programming:* news progmg 14 hrs wkly; *No. News Employees:* 2; *Target Audience:* 35-65.
Paul Goldman, Sales Manager

***WVPS**
10-15-1980; 107.9 MHz FM; *Hrs Open:* 24; 48.8 kw; 2717 ft.; N44 31 32 W72 48 58
365 Troy Avenue, Colchester, VT 05446 US
(802) 655-9451; *Fax:* (802) 655-2799
www.vpr.net
new@vpr.net
License: Burlington, Chittenden County, VT held by Vermont Public Radio.
Nat'l Network: NPR; PRI
Arbitron Metro Market: Burlington, VT; *Format:* Jazz, News
Special Programming: Switchboard call-in progmg 3 hrs, opera 5 hrs, fol; *Hrs. of News Programming:* news progmg 43 hrs wkly; *No. News Employees:* 9 *Target Audience:* General.
Brian Marshall, Chief Engineer
Aaron Kimball, Board Operator
Angela Evancie, Digital Producer
Brendan Kinney, VP for Development & Marketing
Betty Smith-Mastaler, Producer
Brian Donahue, CFO/VP, Finance & Operations
BrianTagliaferro, Manager of Special Giving

Castleton

***WIUV**
10-01-1976; 91.3 MHz FM; 0.23 kw horiz; -236 ft.; N43 36 29 W73 10 54
Castleton College, Castleton, VT 05735 US
(800) 639-8521
www.castleton.edu/campus-life/clubs-activities/clubs/wiuv/
info@castleton.edu
License: Castleton, Rutland County, VT held by Board of Trustees.
Format: Alternative *Special Programming:* Jazz 10 hrs, reggae 6 hrs, rap-urban 5 hrs, folk 4; *Target Audience:* General; smart people
Robert Gershon, General Manager

Colchester

***WWPV-FM**
08-10-1973; 88.7 MHz FM; *Hrs Open:* 8 AM-2 PM; 0.1 kw; 82 ft.; N44 29 38 W73 9 51
Saint Michael's College, One Winooski Park, Colchester, VT 05439 US
(802) 654-2334
wwpv@mail.smcvt.edu
License: Colchester, Chittenden County, VT held by Board of Trustees, St. Michaels College.
Arbitron Metro Market: Colchester, VT; *Format:* Variety/Diverse; *Target Audience:* 14-65; varies by time of day & progmg
Katie Petrozzo, Station Manager
Xander Shaw, Programming Director
Nate Goyette, Technology Director
Tony Terracciano, Public Relations Director
Conor Disher, Music Director
Dan Kuhn, Music Director
Reilly Dillon, PSA/NewsDirector
Maggie Farrington, Business Manager

Danville

WDOT
01-01-1996; 95.7 MHz FM; 3.8 kw; 246 ft.; N44 24 58 W72 3 32
Rebroadcasts: Rebroadcasts WNCS(FM) Montpelier 90%
169 River Street, Montpelier, VT 05602 US
(802) 223-2396; *Fax:* (802) 748-6939
www.pointfm.com
License: Danville, Caledonia County, VT held by Montpelier Broadcasting Inc.
Group Owner: Northeast Broadcasting Company Inc.; (acq 1996; $152,500 for CP)
Format: Variety/Diverse
Terry Lieberman, General Manager
Kim Buckminster, General Sales Mgr
Jamie Canfield, Programming Director
John Hosford, Chief Engineer

Derby Center

WMOO
04-01-1991; 92.1 MHz FM; *Hrs Open:* 24; 2.25 kw horiz, 2.15 kw vert; 620 ft.; N44 58 23 W72 4 30
P.O. Box 92, Derby, VT 05829 US
(802) 766-9236; *Fax:* (802) 766-8067
http://www.moo92.com
License: Derby Center, Orleans County, VT held by Vermont Broadcast Associates Inc.
Group Owner: Vermont Braodcast Associates Inc.; (acq 12-22-2004; $2.35 million with WIKE(AM) Newport).
Wire Services: AP
Arbitron Metro Market: Derby Center, VT; *Format:* Adult Contemp
Special Programming: Community events 8 hrs wkly; *Hrs. of News Programming:* news progmg 16 hrs wkly; *No. News Employees:* 1 *Target Audience:* General.; *Adv. Rates:* 16; 14; 15; 12
Dawn Prudhomme, Operations Dir
Doug Weldon, Programming Director

Grand Isle

WIXM
04-01-1970; 102.3 MHz FM; *Hrs Open:* 24; 20 w; Ant 364 ft; N44 45 53 W73 35 16
372 Dorset Street, South Burlington, VT 05403
(802) 863-1010
www.themix1023.com
License: Grand Isle, Franklin County, VT held by Radio Broadcasting Services Inc.
Population Served: 270,000; *Arbitron Metro Market:* Burlington-Plattsburgh, VT-NY; *Hrs. of News Programming:* news progmg 5 hrs wkly; *No. News Employees:* 1; *Target Audience:* 18-49; men
Bob Rowe, General Manager
Carolyn Seifert, General Sales Mgr
J.J. Prieve, Programming Director

Hartford

WMYV
03-15-1992; 104.3 MHz FM; *Hrs Open:* 24; 5.6 kw; 495 ft.; N43 39 15 W72 21 32
PO Box 8260, Essex, VT 05451 US
(603) 298-0332; *Fax:* (603) 727-0134
www.bestoldies104.com
License: Hartford, Windsor County, VT held by Electromegnetic Company LLC
Nat'l Network: USA

Format: Oldies *Special Programming:* Children 3 hrs, country gospel 2 hrs wkly; *No. News Employees:* 1; *Target Audience:* 25 plus.
Mike Trombly, General Manager
Matt Houseman, Programming Director
Brett Franklin, Public Service Director

WXLF
02-01-1969; 95.3 MHz FM; 6 kw; 285 ft.; N43 39 14 W72 17 44
8 Glen Road, West Lebanon, NH 03784 US
(603) 298-0123; *Fax:* (603) 298-0150
www.953thewolf.com
License: Hartford, Windsor County, VT held by Nassau Broadcasting III LLC
Group Owner: Nassau Broadcasting Partners L.P.
Nat'l Network: Jones Radio Networks; Westwood One
Arbitron Metro Market: Hartford, VT; *Format:* Country; *Hrs. of News Programming:* News progmg one hr wkly; *Target Audience:* 35-54.
Mike Trombly, General Manager
Matt Houseman, Programming Director
Brett Franklin, Public Service Directorÿÿÿ

Irasberg

WJJZ
94.5 MHz FM; 6 kw; 30.14 meters; N44 53.7 W72 14 13.2
License: Irasberg, VT held by Vermont Broadcast Associates Inc
Group Owner: Vermont Broadcast Associates Inc.

Bruce A James, President

Johnson

***WJSC-FM**
07-16-1972; 90.7 MHz FM; 0.2 kw; -489 ft.; N44 38 29 W72 40 20
337 College Hill, Johnson, VT 05656 US
(800) 635-2356
www.jsc.edu/student-life/arts-recreation/arts-culture/wjsc-90.7-radio-johnson/
License: Johnson, Lamoille County, VT held by Board of Trustees, Vermont State College.
Format: Alternative, Variety/Diverse *Special Programming:* Class 3 hrs, C&W 3 hrs wkly
Andrew Frappier, General Manager

Killington

WJEN
08-04-1993; 105.3 MHz FM; *Hrs Open:* 24; 1.25 kw; 2241 ft.; N43 38 22 W72 50 12
Mailing Address: 67 Merchants Row, Rutland, VT 05701 US
Second Address: PO Box 30, Rutland, VT 05702
(802) 775-7500; *Fax:* (802) 775-7555
www.catcountryvermont.com
ghawley@catamountradio.com
License: Killington, Rutland County, VT held by 6 Johnson Road Licenses Inc.
Group Owner: Pamal Broadcasting Ltd.; (acq 10-19-2001; grpsl).
Arbitron Metro Market: Killington, VT; *Format:* Country; *Target Audience:* 18-49; adult, income $35,000 plus, homeowners
Terry Jaye, Operations Manager
Glenda Hawley, General Manager
Brian Collamore, General Sales Mgr
Willie Clark, Programming Director
Judy Anderson, Promotions Director

Lunenburg

WOTX
05-05-2008; 93.7 MHz FM; 0.46 kw; 915 ft.; N44 23 39 W71 39 20
US
www.outlawfm.com
License: Lunenburg, Essex County, VT held by Alexxon Corp.
Arbitron Metro Market: Lunenburg, VT; *Format:* Classic Rock
Barry Lunderville, President

Lyndon

WGMT
05-19-1990; 97.7 MHz FM; *Hrs Open:* 24; 0.6 kw; 1883 ft.; N44 34 15 W71 53 40
39 Church Street, Lyndonville, VT 05851 US
(802) 626-9800; *Fax:* (802) 626-8500
www.magic977.com
magic977@gmail.com
License: Lyndon, Caledonia County, VT held by Vermont Broadcast Associates Inc.
Group Owner: Vermont Broadcast Associates Inc.
Nat'l Network: CNN Radio; *Nat'l Reps:* Roslin
Format: Adult Contemp; *Hrs. of News Programming:* news progmg 5 hrs wkly; *No. News Employees:* 2; *Target Audience:* 22-54; families, more female, disposable income, mobile
Bruce James, President
Steve Nichols, General Sales Mgr
Mike Barrett, Programming Director
Don Smith, Chief Engineer

Lyndonville

***WWLR**
02-04-1977; 91.5 MHz FM; *Hrs Open:* 24 hrs; 2.75 kw; -75 ft.; N44 32 2 W72 1 45
Lyndon State College, PO Box 919, 1001 College Road, Lyndonville, VT 05851 US
www.lyndonstate.edu/offices-services/wwlr-radio-station/
License: Lyndonville, Caledonia County, VT held by Board of Trustees, Vermont State Colleges.
Arbitron Metro Market: Lyndonville, VT; *Format:* Rock/AOR
Special Programming: Class 2 hrs, jazz 3 hrs wkly; *Target Audience:* Everyone.

Manchester

WEQX
11-01-1984; 102.7 MHz FM; *Hrs Open:* 24; 1.25 kw; 2490 ft.; N43 9 58 W73 6 59
P.O. Box 1027, Manchester, VT 95254 US
(802) 362-4800; *Fax:* (802) 362-5555
www.weqx.com
eqx@weqx.com
License: Manchester, Bennington County, VT held by Northshire Communications Inc.
Nat'l Network: AP Radio
Arbitron Metro Market: Manchester, VT; *Format:* Alternative
Special Programming: Jazz 4 hrs, AAA 4 hrs, locl 2 hrs, new music 3 hrs wkly; *Hrs. of News Programming:* News progmg 5 hrs wkly; *Target Audience:* 25-44.
A. Brooks Brown, President
Melinda Brown, Operations Dir
Tim Bronson, Programming Director

***WVNK**
91.1 MHz FM; 0.115 kw; 317 ft.; N43 14 12 W73 1 44
365 Troy Avenue, Colchester, VT 05446 US
(802) 655-9451; *Fax:* (802) 655-2799
www.vpr.net
news@vpr.net
License: Manchester, Bennington County, VT held by Vermont Public Radio.
Regional Network: Vermont Public Radio
Arbitron Metro Market: Manchester, VT; *Format:* Classical; *No. News Employees:* 6
Brian Marshall, Chief Engineer
Brian Tagliaferro, Manager of Special Giving
Brian Donahue, Vice President for Finance & Operations/CFO
Brendan Kinney, Vice President for Development and Marketing
Angela Evancie, Digital Producer
Betty Smith-Mastaler, Producer

Marlboro

WRSY
07-01-1996; 101.5 MHz FM; 0.12 kw; 745 ft.; N42 50 46 W72 41 16 *Rebroadcasts:* Rebroadcasts WRSI(FM) Turners Falls, MA 100%
15 Hampton Avenue, Northampton, MA 01060 US
(413) 586-7400; *Fax:* (413) 585-0927
www.wrsi.com
dmus@whmp.com
License: Marlboro, Windham County, VT held by Saga Communications of New England LLC.
Group Owner: Saga Communications Inc.; (acq 2-13-2004; grpsl).
Format: Triple A; *Target Audience:* 35 plus; women
Dave Musante, Sales/General Manager
Joan Holliday, Website
Michael Sokol, Production

Middlebury

WFAD
12-24-1965; 1490 kHz AM; *Hrs Open:* 24; 1 kw-U, ND1; N43 59 57 W73 9 35
14 Lakeside Court, Plattsburgh, NY 12901 US
(802) 388-9000; *Fax:* (802) 388-3000
License: Middlebury, VT held by Addison Broadcasting Co. Inc.
Group Owner: Northeast Broadcasting Company Inc.; (acq 6-22-2001).
Nat'l Network: ESPN Radio
Arbitron Metro Market: Middlebury, VT; *Format:* Sports
Bob Rowe, Operations Dir
Richard DeLancey Sr., General Manager
J.J. Prieve, Programming Director

***WRMC-FM**
05-01-1949; 91.1 MHz FM; *Hrs Open:* 24; 2.9 kw; -30 ft.; N44 0 25 W73 10 40
Middlebury College, Middlebury, VT 05753 US
(802) 443-6324; *Fax:* (802) 443-5108
wrmc.middlebury.edu
wrmc911@gmail.com
License: Middlebury, Addison County, VT held by President and Fellows of Middlebury College.
Nat'l Network: AP Radio
Format: Variety/Diverse *Special Programming:* Urban contemp 12 hrs, class 15 hrs, folk 15 hrs, relg one hr, blues 10 hrs, jazz 10 hrs, Sp one hr wkly; *Hrs. of News Programming:* News progmg 8 hrs wkly *Target Audience:* General.
Halley Lamberson, General Manager
Julia Welsh, Programming Director
Eric Haas, Technical Director
Kate Leib, Creative Director/Social Media Manager
Chad Clemens, Music Director
Dyland Otterbein, Music Director
Aashna Aggarwal,Business Director

***WOXM**
90.1 MHz FM; 1.2 kw; 313 ft.; N44 1 34 W73 9 44
365 Troy Avenue, Colchester, VT 05446 US
(802) 655-9451; *Fax:* (802) 655-2799
www.vpr.net
news@vpr.net
License: Middlebury, Addison County, VT held by Vermont Public Radio.
Arbitron Metro Market: Middlebury, VT; *Format:* Classical; *No. News Employees:* 6
Brian Marshall, Chief Engineer
Aaron Kimball, Board Operator
Brian Donahue, Vice President for Finance & Operations/CFO
Brendan Kinney, Vice President for Development and Marketing
Angela Evancie, Digital Producer
BettySmith-Mastaler, Producer
Brian Tagliaferro, Manager of Special Giving

Montpelier

WNCS
06-13-1977; 104.7 MHz FM; *Hrs Open:* 24; 1.9 kw; 2080 ft.; N44 25 14 W72 49 42
169 River Street, Montpelier, VT 05602 US
(802) 223-2396
www.pointfm.com
License: Montpelier, Washington County, VT held by Montpelier Broadcasting Co. Inc.
Group Owner: Northeast Broadcasting Company Inc.; (acq 2-12-87).
Arbitron Metro Market: Montpelier, VT; *Format:* Triple A *Special Programming:* Folk 4 hrs, jazz 5 hrs wkly; *Target Audience:* 25-40; above-average income & educated, baby boomers
Steven Silberberg, President
Terry Lieberman, General Manager
Caroline Scribner, General Sales Mgr
Jamie Canfield, Programming Director
John Hosford, Chief Engineer

WSKI
12-07-1947; 1240 kHz AM; 1 kw-U, ND1; N44 14 40 W72 32 47
288 South River Road, Bedford, NH 03110 US
(802) 223-5275; *Fax:* (802) 223-1520
www.pointfm.com
License: Montpelier, VT held by Galloway Communications Inc.
Group Owner: Northeast Broadcasting Company Inc.; (acq 5-2-00; grpsl).
Format: Oldies; *Target Audience:* 35-64; 60% female, 40% male; *Adv. Rates:* 17.50; 12; 13.75; 10

Morrisville

WLVB
08-01-1993; 93.9 MHz FM; 5.4 kw; 121 ft.; N44 34 42 W72 38 9
303 VT Route 15 W, P.O. Box 94, Morrisville, VT 05661 US
(802) 888-4294; *Fax:* (802) 888-8523
www.wlvbradio.com
wlvb@radiovermont.com
License: Morrisville, Lamoille County, VT held by Radio Vermont Inc.
Group Owner: Radio Vermont Group Inc.
Arbitron Metro Market: Morrisville, VT; *Format:* Country

Newport

WIKE
10-12-1952; 1490 kHz AM; *Hrs Open:* 24; 1 kw-U, ND1; N44 56 28 W72 13 35
Mailing Address: P.O. Box 92, Derby Center, VT 05829 US
Second Address: Derby Newport Rd., Derby, VT 5829
(802) 766-9236; *Fax:* (802) 766-8067
www.moo92.com
License: Newport, VT held by Vermont Broadcast Associates Inc
Group Owner: Vermont Broadcast Associates Inc.; (acq 12-22-2004; $2.35 million with WMOO(FM) Derby Center).
Format: Country *Special Programming:* Loc info/entertainment 5 hrs wkly; *Hrs. of News Programming:* news progmg 4 hrs wkly; *No. News Employees:* 1; *Target Audience:* 18 plus.; *Adv. Rates:* 14; 12; 13; 11
Dawn Prudhomme, Operations Dir
William Macek, General Manager

Northfield

*WNUB-FM
12-08-1967; 88.3 MHz FM; *Hrs Open:* 24; 0.285 kw; -387 ft.; N44 8 32 W72 39 31
158 Harmon Drive, Northfield, VT 05663 US
(802) 485-2000
License: Northfield, Washington County, VT held by The Trustees of Norwich University.
Arbitron Metro Market: Northfield, VT; *Format:* Rock/AOR, Triple A; *Target Audience:* 15-40.

Norwich

*WNCH
01-01-2004; 88.1 MHz FM; *Hrs Open:* 24; 1.55 kw; 2251 ft.; N43 26 15 W72 27 8
365 Troy Avenue, Colchester, VT 05446 US
(802) 655-9451; *Fax:* (802) 655-2799
www.vpr.net
news@vpr.net
License: Norwich, Windsor County, VT held by Vermont Public Radio.
Nat'l Network: NPR; *Regional Network:* Vermont Public Radio
Arbitron Metro Market: Norwich, VT; *Format:* Ethnic
Brian Marshall, Chief Engineer
Betty Smith-Mastaler, Producer
Brian Donahue, Vice President for Finance & Operations/CFO
Brendan Kinney, Vice President for Development and Marketing
Angela Evancie, Digital Producer
BrianTagliaferro, Manager of Special Giving

Plainfield

*WGDR
05-11-1973; 91.1 MHz FM; 1.7 kw; -348 ft.; N44 17 4 W72 26 28
123 Pitkin Road, Plainfield, VT 05667 US
(802) 454-7367
www.wgdr.org
david.ferland@goddard.edu
License: Plainfield, Washington County, VT held by Goddard College Corp.
Format: Talk, Variety/Diverse; *Target Audience:* Multiple.
Kris Gruen, Director
Dave Ferland, Operations Manager

Poultney

WVNR
08-01-1981; 1340 kHz AM; *Hrs Open:* 5:30 AM-midnight; 1 kw-U, ND1; N43 30 16 W73 12 11
P.O. Box 568, East Poultney, VT 05741 US
(802) 287-9031
License: Poultney, VT held by Pine Tree Broadcasting Co.
Arbitron Metro Market: Poultney, VT; *Format:* Adult Contemp, Country, 64 *Special Programming:* Big band 3 hrs, loc sports 6 hrs, swap shop one h; *Hrs. of News Programming:* news progmg 3 hrs wkly; *No. News Employees:* 1; *Target Audience:* 25-54; active, community oriented, working and professional, and families; *Adv. Rates:* 10.25; 10.25; 10.25; 10.25

Putney

*WCMK
01-01-2003; 91.9 MHz FM; 0.08 kw; 758 ft.; N42 58 28 W72 36 12
140 Main Street, Essex Jct, VT 05452 US
(866) 878-8885
www.thelightradio.net
License: Putney, Windham County, VT held by Christian Ministries Inc.
Arbitron Metro Market: Essex, VT; *Format:* Christian
Ric McClary, General Manager

Randolph

WVXR
10-25-1982; 102.1 MHz FM; *Hrs Open:* 24; 11 kw; Ant 436 ft; N43 57 20 W72 36 10
365 Troy Avenue, Colchester, VT 05446
(802) 655-9451; *Fax:* (802) 655-2799
www.vpr.net
news@vpr.net
License: Randolph, Orange County, VT held by Vox AM/FM LLC.
Group Owner: Vox AM/FM LLC; (acq 7-25-2008; grpsl)
Population Served: 315,000 *Hrs. of News Programming:* News progmg 6 hrs wkly; *Target Audience:* 25-54; 50% men & 50 % women; *Adv. Rates:* 24; 18; 24; 16
Brian Marshall, Chief Engineer
Aaron Kimball, Board Operator
Angela Evancie, Digital Producer
Bett Smith-Mastaler, Producer
Brendan Kinney, VP, Development/Marketing
Brian Donahue, CFO/VP, Finance & Operations
Brian Tagliaferro,Manager of Special Giving

WCVR(AM)
11-26-1968; 1320 kHz AM; 1 kw-D, 66 w-N; N43 56 21 W72 38 13
62 Radio Dr., Randolph, VT 05060-9138
(802) 728-4411
www.realcountry1320.com
ray@listenvermont.com
License: Randolph, Orange County, VT held by Vox AM/FM LLC.
Group Owner: Vox AM/FM LLC; (acq 7-25-2008; grpsl)
Population Served: 4,853; *Arbitron Metro Market:* Randolph, VT; *Format:* News, News/Talk, 86; *Target Audience:* 18-49.; *Adv. Rates:* 20; 10; 20; 12
Tom Barney, General Manager

Randolph Center

*WVTC
08-29-1983; 90.7 MHz FM; *Hrs Open:* 24; 0.3 kw; 210 ft.; N43 56 7 W72 36 10
Vermont Technical College, 1 Main Street, Randolph Center, VT 05061 US
(802) 728-1515
www.wvtc.net
License: Randolph Center, Orange County, VT held by Vermont State Colleges Vermont Technical College.
Arbitron Metro Market: Randolph Center, VT; *Format:* Alternative; *Target Audience:* General.
Steve Wichmann, President
T.J. Manton, Vice President
Patrick Schlott, Chief Engineer
David Hamilton, Jr., Music Director

Royalton

WRJT
01-01-1996; 103.1 MHz FM; 1.35 kw; 682 ft.; N43 46 28 W72 23 55 *Rebroadcasts:* Rebroadcasts WNCS(FM) Montpelier 90%
169 River Street, Montpelier, VT 05602 US
(802) 223-2396
www.pointfm.com
License: Royalton, Windsor County, VT held by Lisbon Communications Inc.
Group Owner: Northeast Broadcasting Company Inc.; (acq 11-30-01).
Format: Triple A
Ed Flanagan, General Manager
Mark Miller, Programming Director
Tanya Stepasiuk, Promotions Manager
Jon Hosford, Chief Engineer

Rupert

WMNV
04-10-1990; 104.1 MHz FM; *Hrs Open:* 24; 4.3 kw horiz; 200 ft.; N43 16 1 W73 15 21 *Rebroadcasts:* Rebroadcasts WHAZ(AM) Troy, NY 100%
30 Park Ave, Cohoes, NY 12047-3330 US
(518) 237-1330; *Fax:* (518) 235-4468
www.aliveradionetwork.com
events@aliveradionetwork.com
License: Rupert, Bennington County, VT held by Capital Media Corp.
Group Owner: Capital Media Corp.; (acq 4-15-97)
Arbitron Metro Market: Cohoes, NY; *Format:* Christian, Religious; *Target Audience:* 25-75.
Paul Lotters, President/General Manager
Steve Klob, Operations Dir

Rutland

*WFTF
01-10-1987; 90.5 MHz FM; *Hrs Open:* 24; 0.72 kw; -561 ft.; N43 37 9 W72 59 4
140 Main Street, Essex Junction, VT 05452 US
(866) 878-8885
thelightradio.net
License: Rutland, Rutland County, VT held by Christian Ministries, Inc.
Nat'l Network: Moody
Format: Christian, Religious
Ronald Systo, President

WDVT
10-01-1988; 94.5 MHz FM; *Hrs Open:* 24; 6 kw; 322 ft.; N43 34 4 W73 0 32
Mailing Address: 67 Merchants Row, Rutland, VT 05701 US
Second Address: PO Box 30, Rutland, VT 05701
(802) 775-7500; *Fax:* (802) 775-7555
www.945thedrive.com
ghawley@catamountradio.com
License: Rutland, Rutland County, VT held by 6 Johnson Road Licenses Inc.
Group Owner: Pamal Broadcasting Ltd.; (acq 10-19-2001; grpsl)
Format: Contemporary Hits/Top 40, Adult Contemp
Terry Jaye, Operations Manager
Glenda Hawley, General Manager
Brian Collamore, General Sales Mgr
Ed Kelly, Programming Director
Dave Tibbs, Promotions Director
Carrie Allen, National Sales Manager

WJJR
03-25-1971; 98.1 MHz FM; *Hrs Open:* 24; 1.15 kw; 2592 ft.; N43 36 17 W72 49 14
Mailing Address: PO Box 30, Rutland, VT 05702 US
Second Address: 67 Merchants Row, Ruthland, VT 05702
(802) 775-7500; *Fax:* (802) 775-7555
www.wjjr.net
wjjr@catamountradio.com
License: Rutland, Rutland County, VT held by 6 Johnson Road Licenses Inc.
Group Owner: Pamal Broadcasting Ltd.; (acq 10-19-2001; grpsl).
Format: Adult Contemp *Special Programming:* News, pub affrs one hr wkly; *Hrs. of News Programming:* news progmg one hr wkly; *No. News Employees:* 1; *Target Audience:* 25-54; in-office managerial, professional
Terry Jaye, Promotions/Programming/Operations Manager
Glenda Hawley, General Manager
Brian Collamore, General Sales Mgr

*WRVT
01-10-1989; 88.7 MHz FM; 4 kw horiz, 4.8 kw vert; 1352 ft.; N43 39 31 W73 6 25 *Rebroadcasts:* Rebroadcasts WVPS(FM) Burlington 100%
365 Troy Avenue, Colchester, VT 05546 US
(802) 655-9451; *Fax:* (802) 655-2799
www.vpr.net
news@vpr.net
License: Rutland, Rutland County, VT held by Vermont Public Radio.
Nat'l Network: NPR; PRI; *Regional Network:* Vermont Public Radio
Format: Jazz *Special Programming:* Switchboard call-in 3 hrs, folk 4 hrs wkly; *Target Audience:* General.
Brian Marshall, Chief Engineer
Aaron Kimball, Board Operator
Angela Evancie, Digital Producer
Betty Smith-Mastaler, Producer
Brendan Kinney, VP, Development and Marketing
Brian Donohue, CFO/VP, Finance & Operations
BrianTagliaferro, Manager of Special Giving

WSYB
12-10-1930; 1380 kHz AM; 5 kw-D, DAN; 1 kw-N, DAN; N43 35 35 W72 59 25
Mailing Address: 67 Merchants Row, Rutland, VT 05701 US
Second Address: B50 Dorr Dr.
(802) 773-9792
www.wsyb1380am.com
ghawley@catamountradio.com
License: Rutland, VT held by 6 Johnson Road Licenses Inc.
Group Owner: Pamal Broadcasting Ltd.; (acq 4-1-2007; grpsl)
Nat'l Reps: McGavren Guild
Format: News, News/Talk, 86; *Target Audience:* 35-64.
Glenda Hawley, General Manager
Brian Collamore, General Sales Mgr
Charlie Meeks, Programming Director
Tim Philbin, Promotions Director

WZRT
01-01-1974; 97.1 MHz FM; *Hrs Open:* 24; 1.15 kw; 2592 ft.; N43 36 17 W72 49 14
Mailing Address: PO Box 30, Rutland, VT 05702 US
Second Address: 67 Merchants Row, Rutland, VT 05701
(802) 775-7500; *Fax:* (802) 775-7555
www.z971.com
ghawley@catamountradio.com
License: Rutland, Rutland County, VT
Group Owner: Pamal Broadcasting Ltd.
Arbitron Metro Market: Rutland, VT; *Format:* Adult Contemp; *Hrs. of News Programming:* news progmg 5 hrs wkly; *No. News Employees:* 2; *Target Audience:* 18-49.
Terry Jaye, Operations Manager
Glenda Hawley, General Manager
Brian Collamore, General Sales Mgr
Kawme Dankwa, Programming Director
Amber Huyghe, Promotions/Community Affairs Director

South Burlington

WXXX
11-16-1984; 95.5 MHz FM; *Hrs Open:* 24; 25 kw; 236 ft.; N44 30 34 W73 10 59
Mailing Address: 95 Triple X, PO Box 620, Colchester, VT 05446 US
Second Address: , Colchester, VT 5446
(802) 655-9550; *Fax:* (802) 655-1329
www.95triplex.com
paulg@95triplex.com
License: South Burlington, Chittenden County, VT held by Sison Broadcasting Inc.
Nat'l Reps: McGavren Guild
Arbitron Metro Market: Burlington, VT; *Format:* Contemporary Hits/Top 40; *Hrs. of News Programming:* news progmg one hr wkly; *No. News Employees:* 1; *Target Audience:* 18-49.
Paul Goldman, General Manager

Springfield

WCFR
05-26-1954; 1480 kHz AM; *Hrs Open:* 24; 5 kw-D, NDD; N43 16 54 W72 29 21
10 Clinton St., Springfield, VT 05156 US
www.wcfram1480.com
ray@springfieldsvariety.com
License: Springfield, VT held by KOOR Communications Inc.
Group Owner: KOOR Communications Inc.; (acq 12-19-2001; $75,000).
Arbitron Metro Market: Springfield, VT; *Format:* Contemporary Hits/Top 40, Adult Contemp; *Hrs. of News Programming:* news progmg 7 hrs wkly; *No. News Employees:* 1; *Target Audience:* 45 plus; 35-54
Ray Lemire, General Manager

St. Albans

WRSA
01-01-1930; 1420 kHz AM; *Hrs Open:* 24; 1 kw-D, ND1; 0.107 kw-N, ND1; N44 49 52 W73 5 25
288 S. River Rd., Bedford, NH 03110 US
License: St. Albans, VT
Group Owner: Northeast Broadcasting Company Inc.; (acq 9-18-98; $500,000 with co-located FM).
Arbitron Metro Market: Saint Albans, VT; *Format:* Sports, Talk; *Hrs. of News Programming:* news progmg 20 hrs wkly; *No. News Employees:* 1; *Target Audience:* General.

St. Johnsbury

***WCKJ**
08-01-1998; 90.5 MHz FM; 1 kw; 738 ft.; N44 24 40 W71 58 13
Rebroadcasts: Rebroadcasts WGLY(FM) Bolton 100%
140 Main Street, Essex Junction, VT 05452 US
(866) 878-8885
www.thelightradio.net
License: St. Johnsbury, Caledonia County, VT held by Christian Ministries Inc.
Nat'l Network: Moody
Arbitron Metro Market: Essex,VT; *Format:* Christian
Ric McClary, General Manager

WKXH
08-01-1985; 105.5 MHz FM; *Hrs Open:* 24; 1.25 kw; 712 ft.; N44 24 38 W71 58 13
1303 Concord Avenue, St. Johnsbury, VT 05819 US
(802) 748-2345; *Fax:* (802) 748-2361
www.kix1055.com
kix105@kix1055.com
License: St. Johnsbury, Caledonia County, VT held by Vermont Broadcast Associates Inc.
Group Owner: Vermont Broadcast Associates Inc.
Nat'l Network: ABC; Westwood One
Format: Country; *No. News Employees:* 2; *Target Audience:* 24-55; families
Jim Stapleton, General Manager

WSTJ
07-10-1949; 1340 kHz AM; *Hrs Open:* 24; 1 kw-U, ND1; N44 25 6 W71 59 45
US
www.wstj1340.com
License: St. Johnsbury, VT held by Vermont Broadcast Associates Inc.
Group Owner: Vermont Broadcast Associates Inc.; (acq 4-3-98; $630,000 with co-located FM)
Nat'l Network: ABC; Jones Radio Networks
Format: Adult Contemp; *Hrs. of News Programming:* news progmg 20 hrs wkly; *No. News Employees:* 1; *Target Audience:* 35-75; adults and work places
Bruce James, President
Candis Leopold, Operations Dir
Dave Labounty, Programming Director
Don Smith, Chief Engineer

***WVPA**
01-01-1999; 88.5 MHz FM; 0.85 kw; 1867 ft.; N44 34 15 W71 53 38
365 Troy Ave, Colchester, VT 05446 US
(802) 655-9451; *Fax:* (802) 655-2799
www.vpr.net
news@vpr.net
License: St. Johnsbury, Caledonia County, VT held by Vermont Public Radio.
Nat'l Network: NPR; *Regional Network:* Vermont Public Radio
Arbitron Metro Market: St. Johnsbury, VT; *Format:* Jazz, News
Brian Marshall, Chief Engineer
Aaron Kimball, Board Operator
Brian Donahue, VP For Finance & Operations/CFO
Angela Evancie, Digital Producer
Brendan Kinney, VP for Development & Marketing
Betty Smith-Mastaler, Producer
BrianTagliaferro, Manager of Special Giving

Stowe

WCVT
02-28-1977; 101.7 MHz FM; *Hrs Open:* 24; 1 kw; 2661 ft.; N44 31 32 W72 48 54
9 Stowe St., Waterbury, VT 05676 US
(802) 244-1764
101theone.com
101theone.com
License: Stowe, Lamoille County, VT held by Radio Vermont Group/Ken Squier
Group Owner: Radio Vermont Group Inc.; (acq 6-19-97; $450,000)
Nat'l Reps: McGavren Guild
Arbitron Metro Market: Burlington-Plattsburgh, VT-NY; *Format:* Classical *Special Programming:* Children one hr wkly; *Target Audience:* 25-54; educated, upscale adults & families with active lifestyles *Adv. Rates:* 23; 21; 24; 19
Steve Cormier, General Manager
Frankie Allen, Programming Director

Sunderland

***WVTQ**
05-01-1991; 95.1 MHz FM; *Hrs Open:* 24; 0.096 kw; 2398 ft.; N43 9 58 W73 7 2 *Rebroadcasts:* Rebroadcasts WNCH(FM) Norwich 100%
365 Troy Avenue, Colchester, VT 05446 US
(802) 655-9451; *Fax:* (802) 655-2799
www.vpr.net
news@vpr.net
License: Sunderland, Bennington County, VT held by Vermont Public Radio
Nat'l Network: NPR; *Regional Network:* Vermont Public Radio
Format: Classical; *Target Audience:* 18-49.
Brian Marshall, Chief Engineer
Aaron Kimball, Board Operator
Angela Evancie, Digital Producer
Betty Smith-Mastaler, Producer
Brendan Kinney, VP, Development/Marketing
Brian Donahue, CFO/VP, Finance & Operations
Brian Tagliaferro,Manager of Special Giving

Swanton

***WNGF**
89.9 MHz FM; 0.225 kw; -16 ft.; N44 55 2 W73 7 27
US
(518) 686-0975; *Fax:* (518) 686-0975
License: Swanton, Franklin County, VT held by Northeast Gospel Broadcasting Inc.
Arbitron Metro Market: Swanton, VT; *Format:* Christian, Gospel
Bill Dagle, Vice President

Vergennes

WIZN
11-15-1983; 106.7 MHz FM; *Hrs Open:* 24; 50 kw; 374 ft.; N44 18 40 W73 14 33
450 Weaver Street, Winooski, VT 05404 US
(802) 860-2440; *Fax:* (802) 860-1818
www.wizn.com
cleopold@hallradio.com
License: Vergennes, Addison County, VT held by Hall Communications Inc.
Group Owner: Hall Communications Inc.; (acq 10-31-2005; $17 million)
Nat'l Reps: Katz Radio
Arbitron Metro Market: Burlington-Plattsburgh, VT-NY; *Format:* Rock/AOR *Special Programming:* Oldies 3 hrs, reggae one hr, progsv one hr, blues; *Target Audience:* 18-49.
Candis Leopold, Sales Manager

Warren

WDEV-FM
08-11-1989; 96.1 MHz FM; *Hrs Open:* 24; 0.4 kw; 2277 ft.; N44 7 37 W72 55 43 *Rebroadcasts:* Rebroadcasts WDEV(AM) Waterbury 100%
9 Stowe St., P.O. Box 550, Waterbury, VT 05676 US
(802) 244-7321; *Fax:* (802) 244-1771
www.wdevradio.com
ksquier@radiovermont.com
License: Warren, Washington County, VT held by Radio Vermont Inc.
Group Owner: Radio Vermont Group Inc.; (acq 10-15-92; $643,000 with WKDR(AM) Burlington;
Nat'l Network: ABC
Arbitron Metro Market: Burlington-Plattsburgh, VT-NY; *Format:* News, News/Talk, 84, Talk; *Hrs. of News Programming:* news progmg 2 hrs wkly; *No. News Employees:* 1; *Target Audience:* 25-54; affluent, upscale babyboomer generation
Kee Kittell, Programming Director

Waterbury

WDEV
07-16-1931; 550 kHz AM
9 Stowe St., P.O. Box 550, Waterbury, VT 05676 US
(802) 244-7321; *Fax:* (802) 244-1771
www.wdevradio.com
ksquier@radiovermont.com
License: Waterbury, VT held by Radio Vermont Inc.
Group Owner: Radio Vermont Group Inc.; (acq 1969)
Arbitron Metro Market: Waterbury, VT; *Format:* News, Sports, 94 *Special Programming:* Class one hr wkly
Steve Cormier, General Manager
Kee Kittell, Programming Director

WWMP
02-14-1985; 103.3 MHz FM; *Hrs Open:* 24; 2.85 kw; 932 ft.; N44 21 52 W72 55 53
372 Dorset Street, South Burlington, VT 05403 US
(802) 863-1010
www.mp103.com
License: Waterbury, Washington County, VT held by Radio Broadcasting Services Inc.
Group Owner: Northeast Broadcasting Company Inc.; (acq 5-4-2000).
Nat'l Network: USA
Arbitron Metro Market: Burlington-Plattsburgh, VT-NY; *Format:* Variety/Diverse *Special Programming:* Children 3 hrs wkly; *Hrs. of News Programming:* news progmg 16 hrs wkly; *No. News Employees:* 1 *TargetAudience:* 25-54.
Rich Delancey, General Manager
J.J. Prieve, Programming Director
Mike Raymond, Chief Engineer

Wells River

WTWN
10-03-1976; 1100 kHz AM; *Hrs Open:* Sunrise-sunset; 2 kw-C, NDD; 5 kw-D, NDD; N44 8 55 W72 4 2
P.O. Box 1100, Wells River, VT 53865 US
(802) 757-3311; *Fax:* (802) 757-2774
www.wtwnradio.com
info@wtwnradio.com
License: Wells River, VT held by Puffer Broadcasting Inc.
Nat'l Network: Moody; *Nat'l Reps:* Roslin
Arbitron Metro Market: Wells River, VT; *Format:* Religious *Special Programming:* Children, gospel; *Hrs. of News*

Programming: News progmg 9 hrs wkly; *Target Audience:* 25 plus.
Stephen Puffer, President
Teresa Puffer, Operations Dir
Glenn Hatch, Station Manager

Westminster

WKKN
01-01-1971; 101.9 MHz FM; *Hrs Open:* 24; 1.05 kw; 774 ft.; N43 2 0 W72 22 3.7
106 North Main Street, West Lebanon, NH 03784 US
(603) 298-0332
www.kixx.com
nromano@greateasternradio.com
License: Westminster, Windham County, VT held by Great Eastern Radio LLC.
Group Owner: Great Eastern Radio LLC; (acq 10-30-2007; grpsl)
Nat'l Network: Westwood One
Arbitron Metro Market: Westminster, VT; *No. News Employees:* 1; *Target Audience:* 25-54.
Nichole Romano, General Manager
Justin Tyler, VP/Programming

Wilmington

WTHK
06-01-1989; 100.7 MHz FM; *Hrs Open:* 24; 0.13 kw; 1483 ft.; N42 57 33 W72 55 22 *Rebroadcasts:* Simulcast with WEXP(FM) Brandon 100%
Mailing Address: P.O. Box 1230, Claremont, NH 03743 US
Second Address: Box 850, West Dover, VT 5356
(802) 464-1350; *Fax:* (802) 747-0553
www.101thefox.com
License: Wilmington, Windham County, VT held by Great Eastern Radio LLC
Group Owner: Great Eastern Radio LLC; (acq 1-21-2005; $2.5 million with WEXP(FM) Brandon).
Nat'l Reps: McGavren Guild
Arbitron Metro Market: Wilmington, VT; *Format:* Light Rock; *Target Audience:* 25-54; residents, tourists, upscale Mt
John Gales, General Manager
Kelly Kowalski, Programming Director

Windsor

***WVPR**
08-13-1977; 89.5 MHz FM; 1.7 kw; 2277 ft.; N43 26 15 W72 27 8 *Rebroadcasts:* Rebroadcasts WVPS(FM) Burlington 100%
365 Troy Avenue, Colchester, VT 05446 US
(802) 655-9451; *Fax:* (802) 655-2799
www.vpr.net
news@vpr.net
License: Windsor, Windsor County, VT held by Vermont Public Radio.
Nat'l Network: NPR; PRI
Arbitron Metro Market: Windsor, VT; *Format:* Jazz, News *Special Programming:* Switchboard call-in 3 hrs, folk 6 hrs wkly; *Target Audience:* General.
Brian Marshall, Chief Engineer
Brian Donahue, VP For Finance & Operations/CFO
Aaron Kimball, Board Operator
Brendan Kinney, VP for Development & Marketing
Angela Evancie, Digital Producer
Betty Smith-Mastaler, Producer
BrianTagliaferro, Manager of Special Giving

Woodstock

***WGLV**
01-01-2003; 91.7 MHz FM; 0.1 kw; 2277 ft.; N43 38 22 W72 50 12 *Rebroadcasts:* Rebroadcasts WGLY-FM Bolton 100%
140 Main Street, Essex Junction, VT 05452 US
(866) 878-8885
www.thelightradio.net
License: Woodstock, Windsor County, VT held by Christian Ministries Inc.
Nat'l Network: Salem Radio Network; Moody
Arbitron Metro Market: Essex, VT; *Format:* Christian
Ric McClary, General Manager

WWOD
04-18-1989; 93.9 MHz FM; *Hrs Open:* 24; 3.1 kw horiz, 2.98 kw vert; 456 ft.; N43 38 49 W72 21 49
52 Main Street, West Lebanon, NH 03784 US
(603) 448-1400; *Fax:* (603) 448-1755
www.maxx939.com
License: Woodstock, Windsor County, VT held by Great Eastern Radio LLC.
Group Owner: Great Eastern Radio LLC; (acq 10-30-2007; grpsl)
Arbitron Metro Market: Lebanon, NH; *Format:* Contemporary Hits/Top 40
Tim Plante, General Manager
Chris Olsen, General Sales Mgr
Steven Smith, Programming Director

Virgin Islands

Charlotte Amalie

WUVI(AM)
01-01-1992; 1090 kHz AM; 250 w-D; N18 18 57 W64 53 02
Penha House, 3rd Floor University of the Virgin Islands, #2 John Brewer's Bay, St. Thomas, VI 00802
(340) 643-1099
www.wuvi.am
wuviradio@gmail.com
License: Charlotte Amalie, VI held by Three Angels Broadcasting Corp. Inc.

April Rose Falke-Knight, Station Manager

WGOD-FM
09-01-1980; 97.9 MHz FM; 50 kw; 1558 ft.; N18 21 25 W64 58 0
22 A Estate Dorothea, PO Box 305012, St. Thomas, VI 00803 US
(340) 774-4498; *Fax:* (340) 777-9978
www.wgodvi.org
License: Charlotte Amalie, VI
Format: Religious
Reynald Charles, President
Veeda Charles, Business Manager
Marie Rhymer-Martin, General Manager
Ulric Ferrari, Programming Director
Creg Cyntje, Chief Engineer

***WIUJ**
10-05-1979; 102.9 MHz FM; 1.5 kw; 1427 ft.; N18 21 26 W64 56 50
PO Box 2477, St. Thomas, VI 00803 US
information@wiuj.com
License: Charlotte Amalie, VI held by Virgin Islands Youth Development Radio.
Format: Adult Contemp, Big Band *Special Programming:* Class 5 hrs, jazz 6 hrs, Fr 4 hrs, Sp 4 hrs wkly; *No. News Employees:* 1; *Target Audience:* General.
Leo Morone, General Manager

WIVI
04-26-1992; 96.1 MHz FM; *Hrs Open:* 24; 2.4 kw horiz; 1499 ft.; N18 21 33 W64 58 18
P.O. Box 302179, St. Thomas, VI 00803 US
(340) 776-1000; *Fax:* (340) 776-5357
www.amg.vi
lljisd@gmail.com
License: Charlotte Amalie, VI held by Rox Radio Enterprises Inc.
Format: Classic Rock, Triple A; *Hrs. of News Programming:* News progmg one hr wkly; *Target Audience:* 25-54; general;
Adv. Rates: 15; 10; 15; 10
Lou Lambert, General Manager
Dorene Carle, General Sales Mgr

WSTA
08-01-1950; 1340 kHz AM; *Hrs Open:* 24; 1 kw-D, ND1; 1 kw-N, ND1; N18 20 10 W64 57 17
121 Sub Base, St. Thomas, VI 00802 US
(340) 774-1340
www.lucky13wsta.com
info@lucky13wsta.com
License: Charlotte Amalie, VI held by Ottley Communications Corp.
Nat'l Network: ABC; CNN Radio
Format: Oldies, Variety/Diverse; *Hrs. of News Programming:* news progmg 20 hrs wkly; *No. News Employees:* 3; *Target Audience:* General.
Peter Ottley, Operations Dir

WVGN
01-01-2002; 107.3 MHz FM; 1.65 kw; 1440 ft.; N18 21 24 W64 57 59
8000 Nisky Center, Suite 714, St. Thomas, VI 00802 US
(800) 275-6437
info@wvgn.org
License: Charlotte Amalie, VI held by LKK Group Corp.
Nat'l Network: NPR
Arbitron Metro Market: Charlotte Amalie, VI; *Format:* News, News/Talk, 86
Patricia Bourne, Operations Dir
Victoria Squires, General Sales Mgr

WVJZ
03-15-1986; 105.3 MHz FM; *Hrs Open:* 24; 30.2 kw; 1585 ft.; N18 21 33 W64 58 18
P.O. Box 302179, St. Thomas, VI 00803 USA
(340) 776-1000; *Fax:* (340) 776-5357
www.amg.vi
License: Charlotte Amalie, St. Thomas County, VI held by Ackley Media Group
Group Owner: Ackley Media Group; (acq 6-4-98)
Arbitron Metro Market: Charlotte Amalie, VI; *Format:* Reggae; *No. News Employees:* 2; *Target Audience:* 18-49; young adults, business professionals & college students

WZIN
11-02-1976; 104.3 MHz FM; 44 kw; 1617 ft.; N18 21 35 W64 58 19
Post Office Box 4084, Christiansted, VI 0822 US
(340) 776-1043; *Fax:* (340) 775-3446
www.buzzrocks.com
License: Charlotte Amalie, VI held by Pan Caribbean Broadcasting de P.R. Inc.
Arbitron Metro Market: Charlotte Amalie, VI; *Format:* Alternative; *Target Audience:* 18-34.
Alan Friedman, Operations Dir

WVWI
11-19-1962; 1000 kHz AM; *Hrs Open:* 24; 5 kw-D, ND1; 1 kw-N, ND1; N18 20 11 W64 56 41
P.O. Box 302179, St Thomas, VI 00803 US
(340) 776-1000; *Fax:* (340) 776-5357
www.amg.vi
License: Charlotte Amalie, St. Thomas County, VI held by Ackley Media Group
Group Owner: Ackley Media Group; (acq 1996; $250,000)
Nat'l Network: CBS; Westwood One
Arbitron Metro Market: Charlotte Amalie, VI; *Format:* News, News/Talk, 84, Talk *Special Programming:* Relg 6 hrs, West Indian one hr, East Indian one hr; *Hrs. of News Programming:* news progmg 25 hrs wkly *No. NewsEmployees:* 2; *Target Audience:* 25-54; middle/upper income professionals

Christiansted

***WIVH**
07-01-1993; 89.9 MHz FM; *Hrs Open:* 24; 1.4 kw; 997 ft.; N17 45 21 W64 47 56
2457 State Route 118, Hunlock Creek, PA 18621 US
(570) 477-3688
www.wrgn.com/wivh.php
License: Christiansted, VI held by Gospel Media Institute Inc.
Format: Religious; *Target Audience:* General.
Burl Updyke, President
Shirley Updyke, Programming Director

WJKC
10-29-1983; 95.1 MHz FM; 50 kw; 791 ft.; N17 44 7 W64 40 46
5020 Anchor Way, St. Croix, VI 00824 US
(340) 773-0995; *Fax:* (340) 773-9093
www.isle95.com
jkc@viradio.com
License: Christiansted, VI held by Radio 95 Inc.
Format: Reggae; *Target Audience:* General.
Jonathan Keyes, Programming/Music/Marketing

WMNG
01-01-1997; 104.9 MHz FM; 15 kw; 755 ft.; N17 44 8 W64 40 47
P.O. Box 4084, Christiansted, VI 00822 US
License: Christiansted, VI held by Clara Communications Corp.
Arbitron Metro Market: Christianstead, VI; *Format:* Contemporary Hits/Top 40
Jonathan Cohen, General Manager
Amanda Cohen, General Sales Mgr
Tom Yarbaugh, Programming Director
Celia Jean, News Director
Herb Schoenbahm, Chief Engineer

WVIQ
05-17-1965; 99.5 MHz FM; 32 kw; 738 ft.; N17 44 7 W64 40 46 US
www.viradio.com
tom@visitstcroix.com
License: Christiansted, VI held by JKC Communications of the Virgin Islands Inc.
Arbitron Metro Market: St. Croix, VI; *Format:* Adult Contemp;
Adv. Rates: 17; 10; 17; 10
Jonathan Cohen, General Manager
Tom Yarborough, Programming Director
Alvin Gee, News Director

WVVI-FM
02-26-1989; 93.5 MHz FM; *Hrs Open:* 24; 9.6 kw; 807 ft.; N17 43 53 W64 41 17
Mailing Address: Carr. 167, Marginal #5, Bayamon, PR 0956 US
Second Address: 5027 Anchor Way, Christiansted, VI 820

(340) 773-3693; *Fax:* (340) 719-1800
paradise935fm@yahoo.com
License: Christiansted, VI held by The Rain Broadcasting Inc.
Arbitron Metro Market: Christiansted, VI; *Format:* Country *Special Programming:* Relg 3 hrs wkly; *Hrs. of News Programming:* News progmg one hr wkly; *Target Audience:* General; affluent young adult permanentresidents
Roger Morgan, President
Herb Schoenbohm, Chief Engineer

WSTX
01-01-1952; 970 kHz AM; 5 kw-D, ND1; 1 kw-N, ND1; N17 45 23 W64 41 38
US
www.wstxradio.com
License: Christiansted, VI held by Family Broadcasting Inc.
Arbitron Metro Market: Christiansted, VI; *Format:* Ethnic
Barbara James-Petersen, General Manager
Al Clarke, Programming Director
Arthur Bird, News Director
Herb Schoenbohm, Chief Engineer

WSTX-FM
09-01-1984; 100.3 MHz FM; 50 kw; Ant 1,030 ft; N17 45 20 W64 47 55
www.wstxradio.com
License: Christiansted, VI
Format: Reggae
Brian Sands, General Manager

***WVSE**
91.9 MHz FM; 7400 watts; 274 meters; 17 44 N51 64 50 W11
Suite 101, Barren Village Mall, Christiansted, VI 00823 USA
(340) 226-0913
www.radiopapilove.com
License: Christiansted, VI
Group Owner: Crucial Educational Non-Profit

Cruz Bay

WWKS
02-03-1997; 101.3 MHz FM; *Hrs Open:* 24; 50 kw; 1227 ft.; N18 20 30 W64 43 59
P.O. Box 302179, St Thomas, VI 00803 US
(340) 776-1000; *Fax:* (340) 776-5357
www.amg.vi
License: Cruz Bay, VI held by Ackley Media Group
Group Owner: Gordon Ackley Stns; (acq 1996; $225,000)
Nat'l Network: ABC
Arbitron Metro Market: Cruz Bay, VI; *Format:* Urban Contemporary *Special Programming:* West Indian/calypso 25 hrs wkly; *Hrs. of News Programming:* news progmg 2 hrs wkly; *No. News Employees:* 2; *Target Audience:* 25-54; middle/upper income professionals

WIVI
08-24-1988;; 1228 ft.; N18 20 30 W64 43 59
P.O. Box 302179, St Thomas, VI 00803 USA
(340) 776-1000; *Fax:* (340) 776-5357
www.amg.vi
License: Cruz Bay, VI held by Ackley Media Group
Group Owner: Ackley Media Group; (aqc 04-2006)

Frederiksted

WAXJ
01-01-1999; 103.5 MHz FM; *Hrs Open:* 24; 6 kw; -33 ft.; N17 43 28 W64 53 3 *Rebroadcasts:* Rebroadcasts WDHP (AM) Frederiksted 50%
79A Castle Coakley, Christiansted, VI 00820 US
(703) 719-1620; *Fax:* (340) 778-1686
www.reefbroadcasting.com
reefbroadcasting@yahoo.com
License: Frederiksted, VI held by Reef Broadcasting Inc.

David Wilson, General Manager

WDHP
05-01-1999; 1620 kHz AM
79-A Castle Coakley, Christiansted St. Cx, VI 0820 US
(340) 719-1620; *Fax:* (340) 778-1686
www.reefbroadcasting.com
License: Frederiksted, VI held by Reef Broadcasting Inc.
Arbitron Metro Market: St. Croix, U.S. Virgin Islands; *Format:* Variety/Diverse
Hugh Pemberton, General Manager
Beverley Meyers, General Sales Mgr

WMYP
01-01-2002; 98.3 MHz FM; *Hrs Open:* 24; 1.9 kw; 915 ft.; N17 44 51 W64 50 11
Dba Sky Broadcasting Co, P O Box 154, San German, PR 00683 US
License: Frederiksted, VI held by Amanda Friedman
Format: Tejano; *Target Audience:* 18-49.
Jose Martinez, General Manager

WEVI
01-01-2003; 102.1 MHz FM; 3.5 kw; 294 meters; N17 44 51 W64 50 11
Box 26313, St. Croix, VI 00824 US
(340) 514-2525; *Fax:* (340) 719-8783
License: Frederiksted, VI held by Lifeline LLC
Format: Christian

Methuen

WCCM
12-22-1963; 1570 kHz AM; 31,000 watts; N42 40 26.72 W71 11.25 82
90 Madison St., Suite 302, Worcester, MA 01608 USA
(774) 420-7773
turadio.wixsite.com/galaxia
galaxia1570am@gmail.com
License: Methuen, MA held by Costa-Eagle Radio Ventures L.P.
Group Owner: Costa-Eagle Radio Ventures L.P.

Virginia

Abingdon

WABN
12-10-1956; 1230 kHz AM; *Hrs Open:* 6 AM-midnight
P.O. Box 1067, Abingdon, VA 24210 US
(434) 220-2300; *Fax:* (434) 220-2304
www.wvax.com
License: Abingdon, VA held by Information Communication Corp.
Group Owner: Information Communications Corp.; (acq 1-1-2006; $250,000 with WHGG(AM) Kingsport, TN).
Arbitron Metro Market: Grand Junction CO; *Format:* Talk; *No. News Employees:* 4; *Target Audience:* 25-54; adult
John Kappes, General Sales Mgr
Jay James, Programming Director
Rob Graham, News Director

Accomac

WVES
08-13-1990; 99.3 MHz FM; *Hrs Open:* 24; 22 kw; 344 ft.; N37 47 5 W75 36 16
27214 Muttonhunk Road, Parksley, VA 23421 US
(757) 665-6500
License: Accomac, Accomack County, VA held by Chincoteague Broadcasting Corp.
Nat'l Network: USA; Westwood One
Arbitron Metro Market: Parksley, VA; *Format:* Country; *Hrs. of News Programming:* News progmg 3 hrs wkly; *Target Audience:* 25 plus.
Stephen Marks, President
Mark Dodds, General Manager
Dave Bralley, News Director
Tom Reynolds, Chief Engineer
Kelli Spragg, Public Affairs Director

Alberta

WWDW
01-01-2001; 107.7 MHz FM; 2.2 kw; 535 ft.; N36 52 2 W77 53 31 *Rebroadcasts:* Rebroadcasts WSMY(AM) Weldon, NC 100%
PO Box 539, C/O Putrese & Hunsaker, McLean, VA 22101 US
(252) 536-0209; *Fax:* (252) 538-0378
www.3wdfm.com/
Greg@Bestradioaround.com
License: Alberta, Brunswick County, VA held by First Media Radio LLC.
Group Owner: First Media Radio LLC; (acq 12-3-2003; grpsl)
Arbitron Metro Market: Alberta, VA; *Format:* Adult Contemp
Alex Kolobielski, President/CEO

Alexandria

WTNT
12-10-1945; 730 kHz AM; *Hrs Open:* 24; 8 kw-D, 25 w-N; N38 44 43 W77 05 58
(703) 659-0406; *Fax:* (703) 865-6316
www.730wtnt.com
info@somoslacapital.com
License: Alexandria, Alexandria City County, VA held by Red Zebra Broadcasting Licensee LLC.
Group Owner: Red Zebra Holdings LLC; (acq 5-9-2006; grpsl)
Nat'l Network: ESPN Deportes
Population Served: 55,500; *Arbitron Metro Market:* Washington, DC

Altavista

WKDE
04-29-1962; 1000 kHz AM; *Hrs Open:* Sunrise-sunset; 1 kw-D; N37 07 20 W79 17 20
200 Frazier Road, Altavista, VA 24517
(434) 369-5588
www.kdcountry.com
info@kdcountry.com
License: Altavista, Campbell County, VA held by DJ Broadcasting Inc.
Population Served: 250,000; *Arbitron Metro Market:* Roanoke-Lynchbu *Special Programming:* Southern gospel 1 hr wkly; *Hrs. of News Programming:* Top of the hour news; *Target Audience:* 25-54 yrs of age; *Adv. Rates:* 12; 8; 12; na
Elizabeth Hoehne, President
Dave Hoehne, General Manager
Elizabeth Hoehne, News Director

WKDE-FM
06-30-1969; 105.5 MHz FM; *Hrs Open:* 24; 6000 kw; 328 ft; N37 09 37 W79 13 28
200 Frazier Road, Altavista, VA 24517
(434) 369-5588
www.kdcountry.com
info@kdcountry.com
License: Altavista, Campbell County, VA held by DJ Broadcasting Corp.
Nat'l Network: Westwood
Population Served: 322,000; *Arbitron Metro Market:* Roanoke-Lynchburg *Special Programming:* Black gospel 5 hrs, bluegrass 4 hrs wkly; *No. News Employees:* 1; *Target Audience:* 25-54.; *Adv. Rates:* 20; 15; 20;12
Elizabeth Hoehne, President
David Hoehne, General Manager
Kyle Hoehne, Programming Director
John Hart, Chief Engineer
Eleanor Hoehne, Traffic Manager

Amherst

WAMV
10-01-1976; 1420 kHz AM; 2.2 kw-D, ND1; 0.047 kw-N, ND1; N37 32 23 W79 3 10; N37 32 23 W79 5 30
Mailing Address: P.O. Box 1420, Amherst, VA 24521 US
Second Address: 132 School Rd., Amherst, VA 24521
www.wamvradio1420.com
License: Amherst, VA held by Community First Broadcasters Inc.
Nat'l Network: USA
Arbitron Metro Market: Amherst, VA; *Format:* Gospel; *Target Audience:* 50+.
Bob Langstaff, President/General Manager
Justin Bishop, Sales Manager/Sports Director
Alexis Hamlin, Webmaster/Administrator

WYYD
01-27-1981; 107.9 MHz FM; *Hrs Open:* 24; 19 kw; 1801 ft.; N37 28 19 W79 22 28
3807 Brandon Avenue, Suite 2350, Roanoke, VA 24018 US
(434) 725-1220; *Fax:* (434) 725-1245
www.newcountry1079.com
License: Amherst, Amherst County, VA held by Capstar TX LLC
Group Owner: iHeartMedia; (acq 8-30-00; grpsl)
Nat'l Network: ABC; *Nat'l Reps:* McGavren Guild
Arbitron Metro Market: Roanoke-Lynchbu; *Format:* Country; *No. News Employees:* 1; *Target Audience:* 25-54; those with moderate high expendable income
Sarah Leftwich, Market Manager
Tammy Cazad, General Sales Mgr
Scott Stevens, Programming Director

Appomattox

WJJX
05-17-1989; 102.7 MHz FM; 22 kw; 745 ft.; N37 28 7 W79 0 27
Mailing Address: 3807 Brandon Avenue, Suite 2350, Roanoake, VA 24018 US
Second Address: 3305 Old Forest Road, Lynchburg, VA 24501
(540) 725-1220
www.wjjs.com
sarahleftwich@iheartmedia.com
License: Appomattox, Appomattox County, VA held by Capstar TX LLC
Group Owner: iHeartMedia; (acq 8-30-2000; grpsl)

Arbitron Metro Market: Roanoke-Lynchburg, VA; *Format:* Contemporary Hits/Top 40; *Target Audience:* 35-54.
Sarah Leftwich, Market Manager
Tammy Cazad, General Sales Mgr

***WTTX-FM**
09-01-1976; 107.1 MHz FM; 1.7 kw; 427 ft.; N37 22 19 W78 50 6
P.O. Box 25775, Winston-Salem, NC 27114 US
(336) 788-1155; *Fax:* (336) 788-7199
www.joyfm.org
office@joyfm.org
License: Appomattox, Appomattox County, VA held by Positive Alternative Radio Inc.
Group Owner: Positive Alternative Radio Inc.; (acq 1-11-2006; $1.8 million)
Arbitron Metro Market: Appomattox, VA; *Format:* Gospel
Daniel Brit, Operations Dir
Adam McCain, Promotions Manager
Shelley Hicks, Office Manager
Candi Chandler, Music Director
Sam Stutts, Market Manager

WOWZ
06-01-1974; 1280 kHz AM; *Hrs Open:* 6 AM-8 PM; 1 kw-D, NDD; N37 22 19 W78 50 6
P.O. Box 637, Appomattox, VA 24522 US
(540) 343-7109; *Fax:* (540) 343-2306
License: Appomattox, VA held by Perception Media Inc.
Arbitron Metro Market: Roanoke, VA; *Format:* News
Ben Peyton, President

Arlington

WAVA
11-07-1946; 780 kHz AM; *Hrs Open:* 6AM-6PM-or daylight hours
1901 North Moore Street, Suite 200, Arlington, VA 22209 US
(703) 807-2266
www.wava.com
comment@wava.com
License: Arlington, VA held by Salem Media of Virginia Inc.
Group Owner: Salem Communications Corp.; (acq 1-10-2000)
Nat'l Network: Salem Radio Network; *Nat'l Reps:* Salem
Arbitron Metro Market: Glen Elder KS; *Adv. Rates:* 50; 30; 40; na

WAVA-FM
08-01-1948; 105.1 MHz FM; 33 kw; 604 ft.; N38 53 30 W77 7 55
1901 North Moore Street, Suite 200, Arlington, VA 22209 US
(703) 807-2266
www.wava.com
comment@wava.com
License: Arlington, Arlington County, VA held by Salem Media of Virginia Inc.
Group Owner: Salem Communications Corp.; (acq 2-13-92; $20 million;
Nat'l Network: Salem Radio Network; *Nat'l Reps:* Salem
Arbitron Metro Market: Alliance OH; *Format:* Adult Contemp; *Hrs. of News Programming:* news progmg 4 hrs wkly; *No. News Employees:* 2; *Target Audience:* 25-54.; *Adv. Rates:* 250; 180; 200; 125

WZHF
04-07-1947; 1390 kHz AM; 5 kw-D, DA2; 5 kw-N, DA2; N38 54 15 W77 9 54
27 William St., 11th Floor, New York, NY 10005 US
(212) 966-1059; *Fax:* (212) 625-2894
www.mrbi.net
License: Arlington, VA held by Way Broadcasting Licensee LLC.
Group Owner: Multicultural Radio Broadcasting Inc.; (acq 5-30-00; grpsl).
Arbitron Metro Market: Washington, DC; *Format:* Russian, News
Arthur Liu, CEO/COO

Ashland

WHAN
05-01-1962; 650 kHz AM; *Hrs Open:* Sunrise-sunset; 1 kw-D, ND1; 0.031 kw-N, ND1; N37 44 46 W77 29 44
Mailing Address: P.O. Box 148, Ashland, VA 23005 US
Second Address: 11337 Ashcake Rd, Ashland, VA 23005
(804) 798-1010; *Fax:* (804) 798-7933
www.whan1430.com
Bill@whan1430.com
License: Ashland, VA held by Fifth Estate Communications LLC
Nat'l Network: USA; Moody
Arbitron Metro Market: Richmond, VA; *Format:* Talk; *Hrs. of News Programming:* News progmg 7 hrs wkly; *Target Audience:* 18-35; general; *Adv. Rates:* 11.50; 10.50; 11.50; na
William Roberts, President
Skip Andrews, Programming Director
Arnold Meyer, News Director
Jim Grainger, Chief Engineer

***WYFJ**
12-07-1967; 99.9 MHz FM; *Hrs Open:* 24; 6 kw; 328 ft.; N37 33 50 W77 27 29
P.O. Box 7300, Charlotte, NC 28241
(800) 888-7077
www.bbnradio.org
bbn@bbnmedia.org
License: Ashland, Hanover County, VA held by Bible Broadcasting Network Inc.
Group Owner: Bible Broadcasting Network; acq 2-1-80)
Nat'l Network: Bible Bcstg Net
Format: Christian, Religious; *Hrs. of News Programming:* News progmg 9 hrs wkly
Lowell Davey, President
Jason Padgett, Operations Manager

Bassett

WCBX
10-01-1960; 900 kHz AM; *Hrs Open:* 24; 1.1 kw-D, ND1; 0.18 kw-N, ND1; N36 42 36 W79 57 58
Mailing Address: P.O. Box 929, Blacksburg, VA 24063 US
Second Address: PO Box 25775, Winston-Salem, NC 27114
(336) 788-1155; *Fax:* (336) 788-7199
wcbxwodyfic@yahoo.com
License: Bassett, VA held by Base Communications Inc.
Nat'l Network: Fox Sports
Arbitron Metro Market: Blacksburg, VA; *Format:* Sports; *Hrs. of News Programming:* news progmg 12 hrs wkly; *No. News Employees:* 1; *Target Audience:* 35-55.

Bayside

WBVA
05-01-1999; 1450 kHz AM; 1 kw-D, ND2; 1 kw-N, ND2
P.O. Box 55387, Bayside, VA 23471 US
(757) 478-2891; *Fax:* (603) 299-8921
www.birach.com
sima@birach.com
License: Bayside, VA held by Birach Broadcasting Corp.
Group Owner: Birach Broadcasting Corp.
Arbitron Metro Market: Norfolk-Virginia Beach-Newport News, VA; *Format:* News, News/Talk, 86
Sima Birach, President

Bedford

WZZI(FM)
10-20-1992; 106.9 MHz FM; *Hrs Open:* 24; 290 w; Ant 1,276 ft; N37 19 14 W79 37 59
Mailing Address: Box 11798, Lynchburg, VA 24506
Second Address: 19-C Wadsworth St., Lynchburg, VA 24501
(434) 845-3698,(866) 431-5253; *Fax:* (434) 845-2063
www.rocktheplanet.fm
License: Bedford, Bedford County, VA held by WVJT LLC
Group Owner: WVJT LLC; (acq 8-11-2005; $1.9 million)
Nat'l Network: ABC; Jones Radio Networks; *Nat'l Reps:* McGavren Guild; *Wire Services:* AP
Arbitron Metro Market: Roanoke-Lynchburg, VA; *Hrs. of News Programming:* news progmg 14 hrs wkly; *No. News Employees:* 3
Bob Abbott, Operations Dir
Ron Gaylor, General Sales Mgr
Kara Butterworth, News Director
Michael Williams, Business Manager
Sandi Conner, Production Director

WBLT
02-09-1950; 1350 kHz AM
PO Box 348, Forest, VA 24551 US
(434) 534-6100; *Fax:* (434) 534-6101
www.espninva.com/espn-bedford
License: Bedford, VA held by 3 Daughters Media Inc.
Group Owner: 3 Daughters Media Inc.; (acq 11-1-2005; $240,000)
Nat'l Network: ESPN Radio
Arbitron Metro Market: Eugene-Springfield, OR; *Format:* Sports
Gary Burns, CEO
Randy Thompson, Vice President
Melinda Schamerhorn, Business/Traffic Director
Ashley Schamerhorn, Operations Director

Berryville

WXBN
05-19-1980; 105.5 MHz FM; 3 kw; Ant 300 ft; N39 07 03 W77 58 22 *Rebroadcasts:* Simulcast with WWRT(FM) Strasburg 100%
Mailing Address: Box 3300, Winchester, VA 22604
Second Address: 520 N. Pleasant Valley Rd., Winchester, VA 22601
(540) 667-2224; *Fax:* (540) 722-3295
www.everythingthatrocks.fm
License: Berryville, Clarke County, VA held by Centennial Licensing II LLC
Group Owner: Centennial Broadcasting II LLC; (acq 5-28-97; $850,000 with WWRT(FM) Strasburg).
Population Served: 280,000; *Arbitron Metro Market:* Winchester, VA; *Target Audience:* 18 plus.
Allen Shaw, President
Jeff Adams, Operations Dir
Kathy Flerx, General Manager
Ron Baker, Programming Director
Robert Allen, News Director
Archie McKay, Chief Engineer

Big Island

WHTU
11-20-1982; 103.9 MHz FM; 150 w; Ant 1,909 ft; N37 54 12 W79 52 15
Box 710 1047 Ingalls st., Clifton Forge, VA 24422
License: Big Island, Alleghany County, VA held by WVJT LLC
Group Owner: WVJT LLC
Population Served: 29,000; *No. News Employees:* 1; *Target Audience:* 18-54; Targeting mostly women 25-54; *Adv. Rates:* 108; 108; 108; 90
Dennis Royer Jr., Programming Director

Big Stone Gap

WAXM
04-08-1975; 93.5 MHz FM; *Hrs Open:* 24; 2.45 kw; 1883 ft.; N36 54 50 W82 53 40
724 Park Avenue NW, Norton, VA 24273 US
(276) 679-1901; *Fax:* (276) 679-1198
www.waxm.com
93@waxm.com
License: Big Stone Gap, Wise County, VA held by Valley Broadcasting Inc.
Nat'l Network: CBS
Arbitron Metro Market: Winchendon MA; *Format:* Christian

WLSD
08-20-1953; 1220 kHz AM; 1 kw-D, ND1; 0.045 kw-N, ND1; N36 50 26 W82 44 14
US
(276) 523-1700; *Fax:* (276) 679-1198
www.wlsdradio.com
93.5@waxm.com
License: Big Stone Gap, VA held by Valley Broadcasting and Communications Inc.
Nat'l Network: CBS
Format: Religious; *Target Audience:* 19-60.
Willie Stanley, General Manager
Rick Phillips, Programming Director
Adam Sturgill, Staff Engineer

Blacksburg

WBRW
12-01-1964; 105.3 MHz FM; *Hrs Open:* 24; 12 kw; 479 ft.; N37 11 12 W80 28 54
7080 Lee Highway, Radford, VA 24141 US
(540) 731-6000; *Fax:* (540) 731-6074
www.1053thebear.com
License: Blacksburg, Montgomery County, VA held by Cumulus Licensing LLC.
Group Owner: Cumulus Media Inc.; (acq 3-31-2004; grpsl).
Arbitron Metro Market: Radford, VA; *Format:* Rock/AOR; *Hrs. of News Programming:* News progmg 10 hrs wkly; *Target Audience:* 18-49.
Scott Stevens, Operations Dir
Scott Claytons, General Sales Mgr
Courtney Quinn, Programming Director
Marty Gordon, News Director
Dave Dalesky, Chief Engineer

WFNR
01-01-1973; 710 kHz AM
7080 Lee Highway, Radford, VA 24141 US
(540) 731-6000; *Fax:* (540) 731-6074
www.710wfnr.com
License: Blacksburg, VA held by Cumulus Licensing LLC.
Group Owner: Cumulus Media Inc.; (acq 3-31-2004; grpsl).
Regional Network: Va. News Net.
Format: News, News/Talk, 86 *Special Programming:* financial advise; *Target Audience:* 25 plus; general
Scott Stevens, Operations Dir
Sarah Leftwich, General Manager

WKEX
07-10-1969; 1430 kHz AM; *Hrs Open:* 24; 1 kw-D, ND2; 0.062 kw-N, ND2; N37 13 57 W80 26 40
P.O. Box 889, Blacksburg, VA 24063 US

(540) 951-9791; *Fax:* (540) 961-2021
www.espnblacksburg.com
License: Blacksburg, Montgomery County, VA held by Base Communications Inc.
Group Owner: Baker Family Stations; (acq 6-30-98; $60,000)
Nat'l Network: ESPN Radio
Format: Sports, Talk *Special Programming:* High School Sports, Redskins, MLB; *Target Audience:* 35 plus; mature adults, all income levels
Edward A. Baker, President

***WUVT-FM**
10-23-1969; 90.7 MHz FM; *Hrs Open:* 24; 6.5 kw; 429 ft.; N37 11 12 W80 28 53.8
350 Squires Student Center, Blacksburg, VA 24060 US
(540) 231-9880; *Fax:* (208) 692-5239
www.wuvt.vt.edu
wuvtamfm@vt.edu
License: Blacksburg, Montgomery County, VA held by Educational Media Corporation at Virginia Tech.
Arbitron Metro Market: Blacksburg, VA; *Format:* Variety/Diverse *Special Programming:* American Indian 2 hrs, Greek 2 hrs, Chinese 2 hrs,; *No. News Employees:* 1; *Target Audience:* general; college students
Ian Clemons, Promotions Director
Jessica Snead, Production Director
Matt Hazinski, IT Director
Shaun Zirges, Chief Engineer
Pierce Sprague, General Manager
Ben Conlon, Business Manager
Courtney Wilson, Office Manager
CozetteComer, Sales Manager
Steve Ibanez, Music Director
Ben Jaques, FM Programming Director

Blackstone

WBBC-FM
11-17-1975; 93.5 MHz FM; *Hrs Open:* 24; 17.5 kw; 394 ft.; N37 3 14 W78 1 15
P.O. Box 300, Blackstone, VA 23824 US
(434) 292-4146; *Fax:* (416) 292-4574
www.bobcatcountryradio.com
wbbc@bobcatcountryradio.com
License: Blackstone, Nottoway County, VA
Nat'l Network: Westwood One
Arbitron Metro Market: Tyler-Longview TX; *Format:* Ethnic; *Adv. Rates:* 22; 22; 22; 22

WKLV
01-01-1947; 1440 kHz AM; *Hrs Open:* Sunrise-sunset; 5 kw-D, ND1; 0.072 kw-N, ND1; N37 3 14 W78 1 15 US
(800) 849-4146
License: Blackstone, VA held by Denbar Communications Inc.
Nat'l Network: ESPN Radio
Format: Sports; *Target Audience:* 25-54.; *Adv. Rates:* 15; 15; 15; 15
Dennis Royer, General Manager
Shelby Thompson, Sales Marketing

Bluefield

WHKX
12-01-1970; 106.3 MHz FM; *Hrs Open:* 24; 0.33 kw; 1,378 ft.; N37 15 5 W81 11 20
900 Bluefield Ave., Bluefield, WV 24701 US
(304) 327-7114; *Fax:* (304) 325-7850
www.kickscountry.com
License: Bluefield, Tazewell County, VA held by Alpha Media Licensee LLC
Group Owner: Alpha Media LLC; (acq 12-3-2012).
Nat'l Network: Westwood One
Arbitron Metro Market: Bluefield, WV; *Format:* Country; *Hrs. of News Programming:* News progmg 17 hrs wkly
Danny Clemons, Vice President

Bon Air

WLES
09-01-1959; 590 kHz AM; *Hrs Open:* 24 *Rebroadcasts:* Rebroadcasts WTRU(AM) Kernersville, NC 95%
4405 Providence Lane, Suite D, Winston-Salem, NC 27106 US
(336) 759-0363; *Fax:* (336) 759-0366
www.truthnetwork.com
License: Bon Air, VA held by Chesapeake-Portsmouth Broadcasting Corp.
Group Owner: Chesapeake-Portsmouth Broadcasting Corp.; (acq 7-19-2000)
Regional Network: Va. News Net.
Arbitron Metro Market: Richmond, VA; *Format:* Christian
Stu Epperson, President
Mike Carbone, COO
Mandel Owens, Chief Engineer
Anita Dean, Sales/Marketing
Richard Beattie, Director, Syndicaton

Bowling Green

WWUZ
01-01-1998; 96.9 MHz FM; *Hrs Open:* 24; 2.95 kw; 472 ft.; N37 57 56 W77 22 19
616 Amelia St., Fredericksburg, VA 22401 US
(540) 373-1500; *Fax:* (540) 374-5525
www.969therock.com
License: Bowling Green, Caroline County, VA held by Alpha Media Licensee LLC
Group Owner: Alpha Media LLC; (acq 5-1-2015; grpsl).
Nat'l Network: AP Radio *Regional Reps:* RMR; *Wire Services:* AP
Arbitron Metro Market: Fredericksburg, VA; *Format:* Classic Rock; *Hrs. of News Programming:* news progmg 2.5 hours wkly; *No. News Employees:* 1; *Target Audience:* 35 plus; male
Ralph Saliemo, General Manager and Director of Sales
Jeff Beck, Programming Director
Sharon DeSouza, Promotions Director
Bob Clinton, Chief Engineer
Sandy Ridgeway, Business and Traffic Manager
Shelly Bynum, ProductionDirector
Marion Edward Weatherington II, Promotions Coordinator
Bonnie Miller, Programming Coordinator

Brandy Station

***WPRZ-FM**
01-01-2008; 88.1 MHz FM; 10 kw; 449 ft.; N38 30 41.55 W78 3 22 *Rebroadcasts:* Rebroadcasts KLVR(FM) Middletown, CA 100%
219 East Davis Street, Suite 220, Culpepper, VA 22701 US
(540) 727-9779
www.praisecommunications.org
info@wprz.org
License: Brandy Station, Caldwell County, VA held by Educational Media Foundation.
Group Owner: EMF Broadcasting; (acq 5-22-2008; $299,600 for CP)
Nat'l Network: K-Love
Arbitron Metro Market: Brandy Station, VA; *Format:* Christian

Bridgewater

WTGD
03-03-1989; 105.1 MHz FM; *Hrs Open:* 24; 6 kw; 328 ft.; N38 27 8 W78 54 32
1820 Heritage Center Way, Harrisonburg, VA 22801 US
(540) 434-0331
License: Bridgewater, Rockingham County, VA held by M. Belmont VerStandig Inc.
Group Owner: VerStandig Broadcasting; (acq 1993; $10,000 with WHBG(AM) Harrisonburg;
Nat'l Network: La Gran D
Arbitron Metro Market: Harrisonburg, VA; *No. News Employees:* 2; *Target Audience:* 24-54.
Susanne Myers, General Manager
Kim Mitchell, Sales Manager
Dave Thomas, Programming Director

Bristol

WFHG
01-01-1947; 980 kHz AM; *Hrs Open:* 24; 5 kw-D, DAN; 1 kw-N, DAN; N36 36 30 W82 9 36
Mailing Address: P.O. Box 1389, Bristol, VA 24203 US
Second Address: 901 E. Valley Dr., Bristol, VA 24201
(276) 669-8112
www.supertalkwfhg.com
comments@supertalkwfhg.comÿ
License: Bristol, VA held by Bristol Broadcasting Inc.
Group Owner: Bristol Broadcasting Co. Inc.; (acq 1972).
Nat'l Network: Fox Sports; *Nat'l Reps:* McGavren Guild
Arbitron Metro Market: Bristol, VA; *Format:* Sports
Lisa Hale, President
Bill Hagy, General Manager
Winnie Quaintance, General Sales Mgr
Roger Bouldin, Promotions Manager
Anna Honaker, News Director
Rick Perry, Chief Engineer
George Grant, Sports Commentator

WXBQ-FM
01-01-1945; 96.9 MHz FM; 75 kw; 2241 ft.; N36 25 59 W82 8 11
Mailing Address: 901 East Valley Drive, Bristol, VA 24201 US
Second Address: PO Box 1389, Bristol, VA 24203
(276) 669-8112; *Fax:* (276) 669-0541
www.wxbq.com
info@wxbq.com
License: Bristol, Sullivan County, VA held by Bristol Broadcasting Inc.
Group Owner: Bristol Broadcasting Co. Inc.
Nat'l Reps: McGavren Guild
Arbitron Metro Market: Bristol, VA; *Format:* Country; *Target Audience:* 25-54.
Bill Hagy, Programming Director

WZAP
01-01-1946; 690 kHz AM; *Hrs Open:* 6 AM-midnight; 10 kw-D, 14 w-N; N36 37 51 W82 09 53
Box 369, Bristol, VA 24203
(276) 669-6950
www.wzapradio.com
wzapradio@aol.com
License: Bristol, Bristol County, VA held by RAM Communications Inc.
Nat'l Network: USA
Population Served: 502,000; *Arbitron Metro Market:* Johnson City-Ki; *Hrs. of News Programming:* News progmg 8 hrs wkly; *Target Audience:* General.; *Adv. Rates:* 12; 10; 10; 9
Glenn Harlow, General Manager/Programming Director
Chuck Lawson, Chief Engineer

Broadway

WJDV
12-18-1989; 96.1 MHz FM; *Hrs Open:* 24; 2.6 kw; 1010 ft.; N38 33 50 W78 57 0
Mailing Address: 1820 Heritage Center Way, Harrisonbur, VA 22801 US
Second Address: VA
(540) 434-0331
smyers@valleyradio.com
License: Broadway, Rockingham County, VA held by HJV L.P.
Group Owner: VerStandig Broadcasting; (acq 3-12-2001; swap with WLTK(FM) New Market).
Arbitron Metro Market: Harrisonburg, VAA; *Format:* Adult Contemp; *Target Audience:* 25-44.
Susanne Meyers, General Manager
Kim Mitchell, Sales Manager
Dave Thomas, Programming Director

Broadway-Timberville

WBTX
05-18-1972; 1470 kHz AM; *Hrs Open:* 6 AM-sunset; 5 kw-D, ND2; 0.036 kw-N, ND2; N38 37 24 W78 48 52
P.O. Box 337, Broadway, VA 22815 US
(540) 896-8933
www.wbtxradio.com
License: Broadway-Timberville, VA held by Massanutten Broadcasting Co. Inc.
Nat'l Network: USA; *Nat'l Reps:* Salem
Arbitron Metro Market: Harrisonburg, VA; *Format:* Gospel *Special Programming:* Farm one hr wkly; *Hrs. of News Programming:* News progmg 8 hrs wkly; *Target Audience:* 35 plus.; *Adv. Rates:* 16, 14 : 16, 14
Karen Kenney, Traffic Manager
Jim Snavely, Programming Director
Greg Crabtree, Production Director
Christine Pompeo, Station Manager
Chistine Crider, Financial Manager

Brookneal

WODI
02-01-1997; 1230 kHz AM; 1 kw-U, ND1; Rohn Guided; N37 2 17 W78 56 30
License: Brookneal, VA held by D & M Communications Inc.
Nat'l Network: CBS; *Regional Network:* Va. News Net.
Arbitron Metro Market: Roanoke-Lynchbu *TV Affiliate:* Oldies *Special Programming:* news progmg 6 hrs wkly; *Hrs. of News Programming:* 3; *No. News Employees:* 25-54; general; *Adv. Rates:* 12

Buena Vista

WWZW
01-01-1981; 96.7 MHz FM; 2 kw; 1135 ft.; N37 43 37 W79 18 24
392 E. Midland Trail, Lexington, VA 24450 US
(540) 463-2161; *Fax:* (540) 463-9524
www.3wzfm.com
License: Buena Vista, Buena Vista County, VA held by First Media Radio LLC.
Group Owner: First Media Radio LLC; (acq 6-21-2004; $1.33 million with WREL(AM) Lexington)
Nat'l Network: NBC Radio

Format: Adult Contemp; *Target Audience:* 25-54.; *Adv. Rates:* 30; 20; 25; 15
Kevan Kavanaugh, General Sales Mgr
Jim Bresnahan, News/Sports Director

Buffalo Gap

WBOP

01-01-1988; 95.5 MHz FM; *Hrs Open:* 24; 6 kw; 308 ft.; N38 10 55 W79 13 34
1971 University Blvd., Lynchburg, VA 24515 USA
(434) 582-3688
www.liberty.edu
License: Buffalo Gap, Augusta County, VA held by Liberty University Inc.
Group Owner: Liberty University Inc.
Arbitron Metro Market: Harrisonburg, VA; *Format:* Christian
Chris Wygal, Operations Dir
Barry Armstrong, General Manager
Mike Weston, Programming Director
Pattie Silverthorn, Promotions Manager

Cedar Bluff

WYRV

03-01-1985; 770 kHz AM; *Hrs Open:* Sunrise-sunset; 5 kw-D; N37 05 05 W81 46 07
www.youradio.net
License: Cedar Bluff, Tazewell County, VA held by Faith Christian Music Broadcasting Ministries Inc.
Population Served: 285,000; *Arbitron Metro Market:* Bluefield, WV; *Hrs. of News Programming:* news progmg 3 hrs wkly; *No. News Employees:* 1; *Target Audience:* 30 plus.

Charles City

*WAUQ

01-01-2000; 89.7 MHz FM; 10 kw vert; 351 ft.; N37 25 58 W77 11 38
P.O. Box 2098, Omaha, NE 68103-2098 US
(800) 525-5683
www.klove.com
License: Charles City, Charles City County, VA held by Educational Media Foundation
Group Owner: EMF Broadcasting
Arbitron Metro Market: Visalia-Tulare-Hanford, CA; *Format:* Christian, Religious
Mike Novak, President

Charlottesville

WCHV

01-01-1930; 1260 kHz AM; *Hrs Open:* 24; 5 kw-D, DA2; 2.5 kw-N, DA2; N38 6 52 W78 27 18
US
(434) 978-4408
www.wchv.com
joe@wchv.com
License: Charlottesville, VA held by Monticello Media LLC.
Group Owner: Monticello Media LLC; (acq 10-4-2007; grpsl)
Nat'l Network: Fox News Radio; Wall Street; *Nat'l Reps:* Christal
Arbitron Metro Market: Charlottesville, VA; *Format:* News, News/Talk, 86; *Hrs. of News Programming:* 20 hrs wkly; *No. News Employees:* 4; *Target Audience:* Adults 35+.; *Adv. Rates:* 20; 20; 20; 10
Mike Schneider, Sales Manager
Joe Thomas, Programming Director
Joe Thomas, PD

WINA

09-01-1949; 1070 kHz AM; *Hrs Open:* 24; 5 kw-D, DAN; 5 kw-N, DAN; N38 5 22 W78 30 14
1140 Rose Hill Drive, Charlottesville, VA 22903 US
(434) 220-2300; *Fax:* (434) 220-2304
www.wina.com
rick@wina.com
License: Charlottesville, VA held by Saga Communications of Charlottesville LLC.
Group Owner: Saga Communications Inc.; (acq 1-6-2005; grpsl)
Nat'l Network: CBS; *Nat'l Reps:* Katz Radio
Arbitron Metro Market: Charlottesville, VA; *Format:* News, News/Talk, 84, Talk; *Hrs. of News Programming:* news progmg 20 hrs wkly; *No. News Employees:* 4; *Target Audience:* General.; *Adv. Rates:* 55; 25; 35; 15
Rick Daniels, Brand/Operations Manager
Jim Principi, VP/General Manager
Rob Graham, News Director
Jay James, Sports Director

WKAV

10-01-1957; 1400 kHz AM; *Hrs Open:* 24; 1 kw-U, ND1; N38 1 49 W78 29 22
1150 Pepsi Place, #300, Charlottesville, VA 22901 US
(434) 978-4408; *Fax:* (434) 978-0723
www.wkav.com
vkice@cvillestations.com
License: Charlottesville, VA held by Monticello Media LLC.
Group Owner: Monticello Media LLC; (acq 10-4-2007; grpsl)
Nat'l Network: Fox Sports; *Nat'l Reps:* Christal
Arbitron Metro Market: Charlottesville, VA; *Format:* Sports; *Target Audience:* 18 - 54; Men; *Adv. Rates:* 10; 10; 10; 7
Steve Gaines, General Manager

*WNRN

09-01-1996; 91.9 MHz FM; *Hrs Open:* 24; 0.32 kw; 1066 ft.; N37 58 55 W78 29 3 *Rebroadcasts:* Rebroadcasts WNRS-FM Sweetbriar 85%
2250 Old Ivy Road, Suite 2, Charlottesville, VA 22903 US
(434) 971-4096; *Fax:* (434) 971-6562
www.wnrn.org
info@wnrn.org
License: Charlottesville, Charlottesville City County, VA held by Stu-Comm Inc.
Arbitron Metro Market: Charlottesville, VA; *Format:* Alternative, Triple A *Special Programming:* Folk 19 hrs, techno 6 hrs, industrial 2 hrs, punk; *Target Audience:* 18-49; educated, upscale young professionals andstudents; *Adv. Rates:* 28; 22; 27; 19
Paul Wright, President
Halsey Blake-Scott, Vice President
Shawn Brydge, Treasurer
Ashley Carroll, Secretary

WQMZ

10-01-1954; 95.1 MHz FM; 6 kw; 325 ft.; N38 2 54 W78 28 12
1140 Rose Hill Drive, Charlottesville, VA 22903 US
(434) 220-2300; *Fax:* (434) 220-2304
www.literockz951.com
License: Charlottesville, Charlottesville City County, VA held by Saga Communications of Charlottesville LLC.
Group Owner: Saga Communications Inc.
Arbitron Metro Market: Charlottesville, VA; *Format:* Adult Contemp; *Adv. Rates:* 50; 50; 50; 20
Jim Principi, General Manager
Rick Daniels, Operations Manager
Les Sinclair, Brand Manager

*WTJU

05-10-1957; 91.1 MHz FM; *Hrs Open:* 24; 0.6 kw; 1066 ft.; N37 58 55 W78 29 3
Mailing Address: PO Box 400811, University of VA, Charlottesville, VA 22904-4811 US
Second Address: 64 Lambeth Commons, 2nd Floor, University of VA, Charlottesville, VA 22904
(434) 924-0885; *Fax:* (434) 924-8996
www.wtju.net
wtju@virginia.edu
License: Charlottesville, Charlottesville City County, VA held by Rector & Board of Visitors, University of Virginia
Nat'l Network: PRI
Arbitron Metro Market: Charlottesville, VA; *Format:* Variety/Diverse *Special Programming:* Black 8 hrs, children 2 hrs, folk 20 hrs,gospel on; *Hrs. of News Programming:* News progmg 6 hrs wkly *No. News Employees:* 1; *Target Audience:* General; from rural population to college educated; *Adv. Rates:* underwriting (call)
Nathan Moore, General Manager
Robert Nowicki, Underwriting Manager
Jane McDonald, Business Manager
Lewis Reining, Producer/Content Director
Gayle Poirier, Office Administrator

WCHV-FM

01-01-1995; 107.5 MHz FM; 210 w; Ant 1,109 ft; N37 59 05 W78 28 49
(434) 978-4408
www.wchv.com
joe@wchv.com
License: Charlottesville, Charlottesville City County, VA held by Monticello Media LLC.
Group Owner: Monticello Media LLC; (acq 10-4-2007; grpsl)
Arbitron Metro Market: Charlottesville, VA
Mike Schneider, Sales Manager
Joe Thomas, Programming Director
Kishore Persaud, Chief Engineer

WUVA

06-22-1979; 92.7 MHz FM; *Hrs Open:* 24; 0.75 kw; 899 ft.; N37 59 8 W78 28 47
US
(434) 817-6880; *Fax:* (434) 817-6884
License: Charlottesville, Charlottesville City County, VA held by WUVA Inc.
Nat'l Reps: Katz Radio
Arbitron Metro Market: Charlottesville, VA; *Format:* Urban Contemporary; *Hrs. of News Programming:* news progmg 20 hrs wkly; *No. News Employees:* 20; *Target Audience:* 18-54.; *Adv. Rates:* 40; 40; 40; 40
Tanisha Thompson, Operations Dir

*WVTU

01-08-1991; 89.3 MHz FM; 0.195 kw horiz, 0.16 kw vert; 1696 ft.; N38 3 58 W78 47 54 *Rebroadcasts:* Rebroadcasts WVTF(FM) Roanoke 100%
3520 Kingsbury Lane, Roanoke, VA 24014 US
(540) 989-8900
www.wvtf.org
mfranchi@vt.edu
License: Charlottesville, Charlottesville City County, VA held by Virginia Tech. Foundation Inc.
Nat'l Network: NPR; PRI; *Regional Network:* Va. News Net.
Arbitron Metro Market: Charlottesville, VA; *Format:* Jazz
Glenn Gleixner, General Manager
Mary Grace Franchi, Business Manager

*WVTW

01-01-1997; 88.5 MHz FM; 1 kw; 1040 ft.; N37 58 55 W78 29 3 *Rebroadcasts:* Rebroadcasts WVTF(FM) Roanoke 100%
3520 Kingsbury Lane, Roanoke, VA 24014 US
(540) 989-8900
www.wvtf.org
mfranchi@vt.edu
License: Charlottesville, Charlottesville City County, VA held by Virginia Tech Foundation Inc.
Nat'l Network: NPR
Arbitron Metro Market: Charlottesville, VA; *Format:* Jazz
Glenn Gleixner, General Manager
Mary Grace Franchi, Business Manager

WWWV

01-01-1959; 97.5 MHz FM; 8.9 kw; 1132 ft.; N37 59 5 W78 28 49
1140 Rose Hill Drive, Charlottsville, VA 22903 US
(434) 220-2300; *Fax:* (434) 220-2304
www.3wv.com
pstone@3wv.com
License: Charlottesville, Charlottesville City County, VA held by Saga Communications of Charlottesville LLC.
Group Owner: Saga Communications Inc.; (acq 1-6-2005; grpsl)
Nat'l Reps: Katz Radio
Arbitron Metro Market: Charlottesville, VA; *Target Audience:* 18-49.; *Adv. Rates:* 50; 45; 45; 20
Perry Stone, Brand Manager
John Spangler, Music Director

WVAX

04-01-2006; 1450 kHz AM; *Hrs Open:* 24
1140 Rose Hill Drive, Charlottesville, VA 22903 US
(434) 220-2300; *Fax:* (434) 220-2304
www.wvax.com
jjames@wvax.com
License: Charlottesville, VA held by Saga Communications of Charlottesville LLC.
Group Owner: Saga Communications Inc.; (acq 11-22-2005; $150,000 for CP)
Nat'l Network: CNN Radio; *Nat'l Reps:* Katz Radio
Arbitron Metro Market: Grand Junction, CO; *Format:* Talk; *No. News Employees:* 4; *Target Audience:* 25-54; adult; *Adv. Rates:* 25; 20; 25; 10
Rick Daniels, Operations Manager
Jim Principi, General Manager
Jay James, Brand Manager

Chase City

*WMVE

10-10-2007; 90.1 MHz FM; *Hrs Open:* 24; 8 kw; 371 ft.; N36 46 29 W78 20 41 *Rebroadcasts:* Rebroadcasts WCVE(FM) Richmond 100%
23 Sesame Street, Richmond, VA 23235 US
(804) 320-1301
www.ideastations.org
License: Chase City, Mecklenburg County, VA held by Commonwealth Public Broadcasting Corp.
Nat'l Network: NPR; PRI; *Wire Services:* AP
Arbitron Metro Market: Chase City, VA; *Format:* Classical, News, 62, Talk
Bill Miller, General Manager

WJYK

01-18-1959; 980 kHz AM; 0.5 kw-D, NDD; N36 48 22 W78 26 22
1612 Milo Road, Richmond, VA 23225 US
(804) 896-6565
www.joyam980.com
License: Chase City, VA held by Stephen C. Battaglia Sr. & Janis G. Battaglia

Arbitron Metro Market: Chase City, VA; *Format:* Christian, Religious; *Adv. Rates:* 5; 5; 5; na
Stephen Battaglia Sr., General Manager

Chatham

WKBY
06-08-1966; 1080 kHz AM; 1 kw-D, NDD; N36 46 54 W79 23 29
2341 East Seven Mile Road, Detroit, MI 48234 US
(434) 432-8108; *Fax:* (434) 432-1523
License: Chatham, VA held by William L. Bonner.
Format: Gospel; *No. News Employees:* 1
William Bonner, President

Cheriton

***WWIP**
01-01-2005; 89.1 MHz FM; 20 kw; Ant 449 ft; N37 10 53 W75 57 47
2202 Jolliff Rd., Chesapeake, VA 23321
(757) 465-1603; *Fax:* (757) 488-7761
www.thewordinpraise.org
info@wwip.org
License: Cheriton, Northampton County, VA held by Delmarva Educational Association.

Colleen Dick, Station Manager

Chesapeake

WCPK
01-01-1967; 1600 kHz AM; *Hrs Open:* 24; 4.2 kw-D, ND1; 0.023 kw-N, ND1; N36 48 10 W76 16 58
3780 Will Scarlet Road, Winston-Salem, NC 27104 US
(757) 488-1010
License: Chesapeake, VA held by Christian Broadcasting of Chesapeake Inc.
Group Owner: Willis Broadcasting Corp.; (acq 10-17-97; $200,000)
Arbitron Metro Market: Norfolk, VA; *Format:* Gospel; *No. News Employees:* 1; *Target Audience:* 45+; working class listeneres; *Adv. Rates:* 40; 30; 40; 15
L. E. Willis, II, CEO
Hortense Willis, President
Walter Allen Brickhouse, General Manager
Julian Joyner, Programming Director
Terry Love, Chief Engineer
Ernestine Willis, Corporate Officer
Christine Willis, Corporate Officer
Celestine Willis, Corporate Officer
Lonnie Perry, Program Director

***WFOS**
09-14-1977; 88.7 MHz FM; 15.5 kw; 157 ft.; N36 43 18 W76 18 3
1617 Cedar Road, Chesapeake, VA 23320 US
(757) 547-1036; *Fax:* (757) 547-0160
richard.babb@cpschools.com
License: Chesapeake, Chesapeake City County, VA held by Chesapeake School Board.
Arbitron Metro Market: Norfolk-Virginia Beach-Newport News, VA; *Format:* Big Band, Blues, 64; *Target Audience:* High school.
Richard Babb, Director

WNOB
11-30-1973; 93.7 MHz FM; *Hrs Open:* 24; 100 kw; 997 ft; N36 32 57 W76 11 21
Suite 500, 999 Waterside Dr., Norfolk, VA 23510
(757) 640-8500; *Fax:* (757) 640-8552
www.937bobfm.com
License: Chesapeake, Chesapeake City County, VA held by Commonwealth Radio L.L.C.
Group Owner: Sinclair Communications Inc.; (acq 1996; $8.1 million with WTAR(AM) Norfolk).
Nat'l Reps: McGavren Guild; Interep
Population Served: 1,400,000; *Arbitron Metro Market:* Norfolk-Virginia Beach-Newport News, VA; *Hrs. of News Programming:* news progmg 2 hrs wkly; *No. News Employees:* 1; *Target Audience:* 25-54.
Jay West, Programming Director
Donna Agresto-Seavey, Promotions Manager

WWIP
01-01-2007; 89.1 MHz FM; *Hrs Open:* 24; 2 kw; N37 10 53 W75 57 47
2202 Joliff Rd., Chesapeake, VA 23321 US
(757) 465-1603; *Fax:* (757) 488-7761
www.thewordinpraise.org
License: Chesapeake, VA held by Delmarva Educational Association
Group Owner: Delmarva Educational Association
Format: Religious, Adult Contemp
Colleen Dick, Station Manager
Christina Bruno, Promotions Manager
Courtney Banks, Producer

Chester

WNTW
09-01-1964; 820 kHz AM; *Hrs Open:* 24; 10 kw-D, 1 kw-N, DA-2; N37 22 54 W77 25 40
4301 W. Hundred Rd., Chester, VA 23831 US
(804) 717-2000; *Fax:* (804) 717-2209
www.820theanswer.com
colleen@cpbroadcasting.com
License: Chester, VA held by Delmarva Educational Association
Group Owner: Delmarva Educational Association
Wire Services: Metro Weather Servic
Population Served: 900,000; *Arbitron Metro Market:* Richmond, VA; *Format:* Talk; *Target Audience:* 25-49.; *Adv. Rates:* 20; 20; 20; 15
Christina Bruno, Promotions Manager
Courtney Banks, Producer

Chincoteague

WCTG
01-01-2004; 96.5 MHz FM; *Hrs Open:* 24; 5.3 kw; 344 ft.; N37 55 14 W75 23 7
Mailing Address: 6455 Maddox Boulevard, Suite 3, Chincoteague Island, VA 23336 US
Second Address: PO Box 65, Chincoteague Island, VA 23336
(757) 336-1118; *Fax:* (757) 336-1805
www.965ctg.com
staff@wctg.fm
License: Chincoteague, Accomack County, VA held by Sebago Broadcasting Co. L.L.C.
Arbitron Metro Market: Chincoteague, VA; *Format:* Triple A
A. Wray Fitch III, President

Christiansburg

WNMX
01-01-1990; 100.7 MHz FM; *Hrs Open:* 17; 3 kw; 328 ft; N37 08 01 W80 21 17
7080 Lee Hwy., Radford, VA 24141
(540) 731-6000; *Fax:* (540) 731-6074
www.mix100fm.com
License: Christiansburg, Montgomery County, VA held by Cumulus Licensing LLC.
Group Owner: Cumulus Media Inc.; (acq 3-31-2004; grpsl).
Regional Network: Va. News Net.
Population Served: 561,000 *Hrs. of News Programming:* News progmg 7 hrs wkly; *Target Audience:* 25 plus.
Scott Stevens, Operations Dir
Sarah Leftwich, General Manager
Don Walker, Programming Director
Sam Parks, Chief Engineer

***WWVT**
10-01-1954; 1260 kHz AM; *Hrs Open:* 6am-sunset
Rebroadcasts: Rebroadcasts WWFC (FM) Ferrum 100%
US
(540) 989-8900
www.wvtf.org
mfranchi@vt.edu
License: Christiansburg, VA held by Virginia Tech Foundation Inc.
Nat'l Network: NPR; PRI
Arbitron Metro Market: Christiansburg, VA; *Format:* Talk; *Hrs. of News Programming:* News progmg 60 hrs wkly; *No. News Employees:* 8; *Target Audience:* 30-54; business professionals
Glenn Gleixner, General Manager
Mary Grace Franchi, Business Manager

Churchville

WNLR
03-09-1962; 1150 kHz AM; 2.5 kw-D, ND1; 0.035 kw-N, ND1; N38 12 39 W79 7 53
35 Eagle Rock Lane, Staunton, VA 24401 US
(540) 885-1150; *Fax:* (540) 886-8624
www.nlministries.org
License: Churchville, VA held by New Life Ministries Inc.
Nat'l Network: Moody; USA
Arbitron Metro Market: Churchville, VA; *Format:* Adult Contemp, Religious; *Target Audience:* 22-55; females with family size above average; *Adv. Rates:* 9; 8; 9; 8
Russ Whitesell, Programming Director
Lindon Kiser, Music Director

Claremont

WRJR
08-19-1997; 670 kHz AM; *Hrs Open:* Sunrise-sunset; 20 kw-D, 3 w-N, DA-2; N37 10 29 W76 53 49
2202 Jolliff Rd., Chesapeake, VA 23321
(757) 488-1010; *Fax:* (757) 488-7761
License: Claremont, Surry County, VA held by Iglesia Nuevavida of High Point
Group Owner: Iglesia Nuevavida of High Point; (acq 3-2-2001; $950,000)

Henry Hoot, General Manager

Clarksville

WLUS-FM
01-01-1984; 98.3 MHz FM; *Hrs Open:* 24; 17.5 kw; 390 ft.; N36 29 45 W78 33 16
109 Hillsboro Street, Oxford, NC 27565 US
(919) 693-7900; *Fax:* (919) 693-9585
www.us983.com
License: Clarksville, Mecklenburg County, VA held by Lakes Media Holding Company LLC.
Group Owner: Birch Broadcasting Corp.; (acq 2-1-2005; grpsl).
Nat'l Network: ABC
Format: Country; *Hrs. of News Programming:* news progmg 2 hrs wkly; *No. News Employees:* 3; *Target Audience:* 25-54; male & female; *Adv. Rates:* 20; 18; 23; 15
Mark Reid, Regional Manager
Melissa Wilkerson, Local Sales Manager
Chris Michaels, Operations Manager

Clifton Forge

WXCF
10-19-1950; 1230 kHz AM; *Hrs Open:* 24; 1 kw-U, ND1; N37 49 18 W79 48 50
4 Professional Drive, Suite 145, Gaithersburg, MD 20877 US
(540) 862-5751; *Fax:* (540) 862-2120
wkeywigo@aol.com
License: Clifton Forge, VA held by Quorum Radio Partners of Virginia Inc.
Group Owner: WVJT LLC; (acq 5-03; with co-located FM).
Arbitron Metro Market: Clifton Forge, VA; *Format:* Gospel; *Hrs. of News Programming:* News progmg one hr wkly; *Target Audience:* 40 & up.; *Adv. Rates:* 84; 84; 84; 60
Michael Stone, President
Marcia Smith, General Sales Mgr
Lawrence Mason, Chief Engineer

***WVRI**
90.9 MHz FM; 1 kw; 1840 ft.; N37 54 2 W79 18 00
Rebroadcasts: Rebroadcasts WVRL (FM)
1971 University Boulevard, Lynchburg, VA 24502
(434) 582-3688
www.myjourneyfm.com
License: Clifton Forge, Alleghany County, VA held by Liberty University, Inc.
Group Owner: Liberty University, Inc.; (acq. 2009)
Format: Adult Contemp, Christian, 74
Chris Wygal, Operations Manager
Barry Armstrong, General Manager
Mike Weston, Programming Director

Clinchco

WDIC
05-01-1961; 1430 kHz AM; *Hrs Open:* 24; 5 kw-D, ND2; N37 8 42 W82 23 22
2298 Rose Ridge, Clintwood, VA 24228 US
(276) 835-8626; *Fax:* (276) 835-8627
www.wdicradio.com/
wdic@wdicradio.com
License: Clinchco, VA held by Dickenson County Broadcasting Corp.
Nat'l Network: ABC; *Regional Network:* Va. News Net; *Nat'l Reps:* Rgnl Reps *Regional Reps:* Rgnl Reps.
Arbitron Metro Market: Clinchco-Clintwood-Grundy, Virginia; *Format:* Country *Special Programming:* Trading Post - M-F 10:35 am; *Hrs. of News Programming:* news progmg 8 hrs wkly; *No. News Employees:* 3 *TargetAudience:* General.; *Adv. Rates:* 8; 8; 8; 8
Betty Fleming, Operations Dir

WDIC-FM
07-02-1989; 92.1 MHz FM; *Hrs Open:* 24; 2.5 kw; 505 ft.; N37 8 42 W82 23 22
2298 Rose Ridge, Clintwood, VA 24228 US

(276) 835-8626; *Fax:* (276) 835_8627
www.wdicradio.com
wdic@wdicradio.com
License: Clinchco, Dickenson County, VA held by Dickenson County Broadcasting
Nat'l Network: ABC; *Regional Network:* Va. News Net; *Nat'l Reps:* Rgnl Reps *Regional Reps:* Regnl Reps
Arbitron Metro Market: Clinchco-Clintwood-Grundy, Virginia; *Format:* News, Oldies, 84 *Special Programming:* On House Sunday 9 - 10:00 am; *Hrs. of News Programming:* News progmg 3 hrs wkly; *No. News Employees:* 3 *Target Audience:* 25-55; baby boomers; *Adv. Rates:* 10 - 10 - 10 - 10
Betty N. FLeming, Operations Dir

Coeburn

WGCK-FM
04-15-1991; 99.7 MHz FM; 1.95 kw; 1168 ft.; N37 3 15 W82 38 34
P. O. Box 2098, Omaha, NE 68103-2098 US
(800) 525-5683
www.klove.com
License: Coeburn, Wise County, VA held by Letcher County Broadcasting Inc.
Nat'l Network: K-Love
Arbitron Metro Market: Omaha, NE; *Format:* Adult Contemp
Darrell Chambliss, Chairman
Mike Novak, President & CEO
D. Kevin Blair, Secretary/General Counsel
Alan Mason, COO
Eric Moser, CFO
David Pierce, Chief Creative Officer

Collinsville

WFIC
03-01-1970; 1530 kHz AM; 0.25 kw-C, NDD; 1 kw-D, NDD; N36 42 56 W79 55 15
520 Roberts Rd., Newport, NC 28570 US
(252) 223-4600
www.fbnradio.com
License: Collinsville, Henry County, VA held by Grace Missionary Baptist Church dba Grace Christian School
Group Owner: Fundamental Broadcasting Network; (acq 9-3-97; $60,000).
Nat'l Network: USA
Arbitron Metro Market: Collinsville, VA; *Format:* Gospel, Religious; *Target Audience:* 35 plus; general; *Adv. Rates:* 5; 5; 5; na
Kristi Gernoske, Marketing Director

Colonial Heights

WDZY
01-01-1955; 1290 kHz AM; *Hrs Open:* 24; 25 kw-D, ND1; 0.041 kw-N, ND1; N37 15 30 W77 23 40
2602 Whitehouse Rd., Suite E, South Chesterfield, VA 23834 US
(804) 898-3160
www.wilkinsradio.com
denise@wilkinsradio.com
License: Colonial Heights, VA held by Richmond Christian Radio Corp.
Group Owner: Wilkins Communications Network Inc.; (acq 8-22-00; grpsl).
Arbitron Metro Market: Richmond, VA; *Format:* Christian, Talk; *Hrs. of News Programming:* News progmg 7 hrs wkly; *Target Audience:* 2-12, 25-54; children & women
Herb Pollard, Station Manager

WKHK
11-17-1972; 95.3 MHz FM; *Hrs Open:* 24; 47 kw; 512 ft.; N37 26 22 W77 26 1
812 Moorefield Park Dr., #300, Richmond, VA 23236 US
(804) 330-5700; *Fax:* (804) 330-4079
www.k95country.com
info@k95country.com
License: Colonial Heights, Chesterfield County, VA held by SM-WKHK LLC
Group Owner: SummitMedia LLC; (acq 8-31-00; grpsl)
Arbitron Metro Market: Richmond, VA; *Format:* Country; *Hrs. of News Programming:* news progmg 8 hrs wkly; *No. News Employees:* 1; *Target Audience:* 25-54.
Bob Willoughby, General Manager
Buddy VanArsdale, Programming Director
Laura Kibler, Promotions Manager
Becky Wentworth, News Director
Gary Harrison, Chief Engineer

*WKYV
90.1 MHz FM; 0.56 kw; 282 ft.; N37 15 2 W77 18 23 US
(916) 251-1600
www.klove.com
License: Colonial Heights, Chesterfield County, VA held by Educational Media Foundation
Group Owner: EMF Broadcasting
Arbitron Metro Market: Colonial Heights, VA; *Format:* Christian, Gospel
Darrell Chambliss, Chairman
Mike Novak, President/CEO
Alan Mason, COO
Eric Moser, CFO
D. Kevin Blair, Secretary/General Counsel
David Pierce, Chief Creative Officer

WDZY
103.3 MHz FM; *Hrs Open:* 24
2602 Whitehouse Rd., Suite E, South Chesterfield, VA 23834 US
(804) 898-3160
www.wilkinsradio.com
denise@wilkinsradio.com
License: Colonial Heights, VA held by Richmond Christian Radio Corp.
Group Owner: Wilkins Communications Network Inc.
Arbitron Metro Market: Richmond, VA; *Format:* Christian, Talk; *Hrs. of News Programming:* News progmg 7 hrs wkly; *Target Audience:* 2-12, 25-54; children & women
Herb Pollard, Station Manager

Columbia City

WHPP
10-13-1968; 106.3 MHz FM; 5.6 kw; 103.5 meters; N37 18 30 W80 9 46
9604 Coldwater Road, Suite 201, Fort Wayne, IN 46825 US
(260) 482-9288; *Fax:* (260) 482-8655
License: Columbia City, Whitley County, IN held by Oasis Radio 2 Corp.
Arbitron Metro Market: Fort Wayne, IN; *Format:* Adult Contemp; *Adv. Rates:* 30; 20; 25; 10
Phil Becker, General Manager

Covington

WKEY
05-23-1941; 1340 kHz AM; *Hrs Open:* 24; 1 kw-U, ND1; N37 46 3 W79 59 6
Post Office Box 710, Covington, VA 24426 US
(540) 962-1133
www.big country101.com
License: Covington, VA held by WVJT LLC
Group Owner: WVJT LLC; (acq 4-20-2005; with co-located FM).
Format: Oldies *Special Programming:* Black one hr, gospel 2 hrs wkly; *Hrs. of News Programming:* news progmg 12 hrs wkly; *No. News Employees:* 1; *Target Audience:* 25 plus; younger country listeners; *Adv. Rates:* 6; 6; 6; 6
Michael Stone, President
Marcia Smith, General Sales Mgr
Dwight Rohr, News Director
Lawrence Mason, Chief Engineer

Crewe

WPZZ
06-09-1949; 104.7 MHz FM; 100 kw; 981 ft.; N37 10 15 W77 57 16
2809 Emerywood Pkwy., Suite 300, Richmond, VA 23294 US
(804) 672-9299
www.praiserichmond.com
License: Crewe, Nottoway County, VA held by Radio One Licenses LLC.
Group Owner: Radio One Inc.; (acq 11-8-2001; grpsl).
Nat'l Reps: Eastman Radio
Arbitron Metro Market: Richmond, VA; *Format:* Gospel; *Target Audience:* 25-54; adults
Reggie Baker, Operations Mgr/Program Dir.
Marsha Landess, General Manager
Clovia Lawrence, News Director

WSVS
04-07-1947; 800 kHz AM; *Hrs Open:* 24
PO Box 47, 1032 Melody Lane, Crewe, VA 23930 US
(434) 645-7734; *Fax:* (434) 645-1701
License: Crewe, VA held by Colonial Broadcasting of Crewe Inc.
Nat'l Network: Family Radio
Format: Country; *Hrs. of News Programming:* news progmg 7 hrs wkly; *No. News Employees:* 1; *Target Audience:* 35 plus.; *Adv. Rates:* 10; 10; 10; na
Hope Epperson, CFO
Steve Winn, Programming Director
John Hart, Chief Engineer

Crozet

*WMRY
05-01-1995; 103.5 MHz FM; *Hrs Open:* 24; 0.28 kw; 1463 ft.; N37 57 2 W78 43 46 *Rebroadcasts:* Rebroadcasts WMRA(FM) Harrisonburg 100%
983 Reservoir Street, Harrisonburg, VA 22801 US
(540) 568-6221
www.wmra.org
wmra@jmu.edu
License: Crozet, Albemarle County, VA held by James Madison University Board of Visitors.
Nat'l Network: NPR; PRI
Arbitron Metro Market: Charlottesville, VA; *Format:* News, Talk *Special Programming:* Folk 8 hrs, blues 5 hrs wkly; *Hrs. of News Programming:* news progmg 80 hrs wkly; *No. News Employees:* 2 *Target Audience:* 35-64; well educated; *Adv. Rates:* 33; 17; 33; 15
Al Bartholet, Executive Director
Meghan McCoy, Business Manager
Ivette Churney, Director of Corporate Support
Vicki Joslyn, Underwriting Executive
Dan Easley, Operations/Website Coordinator

WZGN
09-01-1980; 102.3 MHz FM; 4.9 kw; 354 ft.; N38 4 47 W78 44 22
1150 Pepsi Place, Suite 300, Charlottesville, VA 22903 US
(434) 978-4408
www.generations1023.com
mschneider@cvillestations.com
License: Crozet, Albemarle County, VA held by Monticello Media LLC.
Group Owner: Monticello Media LLC; (acq 10-4-2007; grpsl)
Nat'l Reps: Christal
Arbitron Metro Market: Charlottesville, VA; *Format:* Contemporary Hits/Top 40, Adult Contemp; *No. News Employees:* 1; *Target Audience:* 25 - 54/35 - 54; general; *Adv. Rates:* 25; 22; 25; 10
Vinnie Kice, Operations Dir
Mike Schneider, Sales Manager
Ja Lopez, Programming Director

Culpeper

*WARN
01-01-1997; 91.5 MHz FM; 0.93 kw; 121 ft.; N38 27 15 W77 59 10
P.O. Box 3206, Tupelo, MS 38803 US
(662) 844-8888; *Fax:* (662) 842-6791
www.afr.net
faq@afa.net
License: Culpeper, Culpeper County, VA held by American Family Association.
Group Owner: American Family Radio
Arbitron Metro Market: Culpeper, VA; *Format:* Christian, Religious
Tim Wildmon, President
Donald Wildmon, Founder
Buddy Smith, Sr VP
Ed Vitagliano, Exec VP
Randy Sharp, Director Of Special Projects
Meeke Addison, Director Of Communications
Abraham Hamilton III, General Counsel

WJMA
12-04-1971; 103.1 MHz FM; 600 w; Ant 1,027 ft; N38 18 38 W78 00 12
207 Spicers Mill Road, PO Box 271, Orange, VA 22960
(540) 672-1000
www.wjmafm.com
License: Culpeper, Culpeper County, VA held by Piedmont Communications Inc.
Group Owner: Piedmont Communications Inc.; 1993
Wire Services: AP
Population Served: 118,000; *No. News Employees:* 1; *Target Audience:* 25-54; male & female
John Schick, President
Phil Goodwin, News
Frank Wells, Programming Director
Gary Harrison, Operations/Engineering

WCVA
02-01-1949; 1490 kHz AM; *Hrs Open:* 24; 0.68 kw-U, ND1; N38 29 4 W77 59 22
207 Spicers Mill Road, PO Box 271, Orange, VA 22960 US
(540) 672-1000
www.1055samfm.com
License: Culpeper, VA held by Piedmont Communications Inc.

Group Owner: Piedmont Communications Inc.; acq 11-21-2003; grpsl).
Nat'l Network: Westwood One; ABC
Arbitron Metro Market: Culpeper, VA; *Format:* Adult Contemp; *Hrs. of News Programming:* news progmg 10 hrs wkly; *No. News Employees:* 1; *Target Audience:* 45 plus.
Gary Harrison, Operations/Engineering

***WPER**
01-01-1999; 89.9 MHz FM; 41 kw; 417 ft.; N38 40 42 W77 47 18
P. O. Box 929, Blacksburg, VA 24063 US
(540) 347-4825; *Fax:* (540) 347-3562
www.yourper.com
info@positivehits.org
License: Culpeper, Culpeper County, VA held by Positive Alternative Radio Inc.
Group Owner: Positive Alternative Radio Inc.
Format: Christian
Frankie Morea, General Manager/VP Programming

Danville

WAKG
06-03-1968; 103.3 MHz FM; *Hrs Open:* 24; 100 kw; 653 ft.; N36 44 28 W79 23 5
PO Box 1629, Danville, VA 24543 US
(434) 797-4290; *Fax:* (434) 797-3918
www.wakg.com
License: Danville, Danville City County, VA
Arbitron Metro Market: Danville, VA; *Format:* Country; *Target Audience:* 18-54.
Sherri Crowder, Programming Director
Carol Metz, Promotions Manager
Ginyah W. Mullins, Social Media Director

WBTM
05-24-1930; 1330 kHz AM; *Hrs Open:* 24; 5 kw-D, 1 kw-N, DA-N; N36 36 36 W79 25 47
710 Grove Street, Danville, VA 24541
(434) 793-4411; *Fax:* (434) 797-3918
www.wbtmdanville.com
License: Danville, Danville City County, VA held by Piedmont Broadcasting Corp.
Population Served: 42,852; *Arbitron Metro Market:* Danville, VA; *Hrs. of News Programming:* news progmg 5 hrs wkly; *No. News Employees:* 2; *Target Audience:* 24 plus; young working adults
Phil Watlington, Public Service Director

WDVA
06-29-1947; 1250 kHz AM; *Hrs Open:* 24; 5 kw-U, DA-N; N36 34 53 W79 26 33
(434) 797-1250; *Fax:* (434) 797-1255
License: Danville, Danville City County, VA held by Mitchell Communications Inc.
Nat'l Network: CBS
Population Served: 1,900,000 *Hrs. of News Programming:* News progmg 12 hrs wkly; *No. News Employees:* 2; *Target Audience:* 18 plus.; *Adv. Rates:* 30; 20; 60; 70
George Hairston, CEO/COO
C.G. Hairston, President
George Hairston, Operations Dir
George Hairston, General Manager
George Hairston, Station Manager
George Hairston, General Sales Mgr
George Hairston, Programming Director
GeorgeHairston, Promotions Manager
George Hairston, News Director

WWDN
08-25-1957; 1580 kHz AM; *Hrs Open:* Sunrise-sunset; 1 kw-D; N36 34 03 W79 22 50
1336 Piney Forest Road, Danville, VA 24540
(434) 799-1010; *Fax:* (800) 536-6194
www.1045thedan.com
tombirch@lakesmediallc.com
License: Danville, Danville City County, VA held by Tol-Tol Communications Inc.
Nat'l Network: American Urban
Population Served: 100,000 *Target Audience:* General; ethnic (Black) and citizens who enjoy div progmg; *Adv. Rates:* 9; 9; 9; 9
Tom Birch, President
Justin Lloyd, Operations Manager
Barbara Seamster, General Sales Mgr

***WOKD-FM**
01-01-1998; 91.1 MHz FM; 18 kw; 466 ft.; N36 44 30 W79 23 7
Rebroadcasts: Rebroadcasts WPAR(FM) Salem 100%
Mailing Address: P O Box 929, Blacksburg, VA 24063 US
Second Address: 22226 Timberlake Road, Lynchburg, VA 24502
434-237-9798; *Fax:* 434-237-1025
www.spiritfm.com
License: Danville, Danville City County, VA held by Positive Alternative Radio Inc.
Group Owner: Positive Alternative Radio Inc.
TV Affiliate: Relg
Jessica Giles, Office Manager
Brock Round, Engineer
Jackie Howard, Director of Operations
Marc Tischart, General Manager

WMPW
970 kHz AM; *Hrs Open:* unlimited; 250 watts; 41 meters; 36 36 N41 79 23 W06
1336 Piney Forest Road, Danville, VA 24541
(434) 799-1010; *Fax:* (800) 536-6194
www.countrylegends1037.com
barbaraseamster@lakesmediallc.com
License: Danville, VA held by Lakes Media LLC

Tom Birch, President
Barbara Seamster, General Manager/Local Sales Manager
Justin Lloyd, Operations Manager

Deltaville

WTYD
01-05-1999; 92.3 MHz FM; *Hrs Open:* 24; 2.4 kw; 525 ft.; N37 29 37 W76 26 30
4732 Longhill Rd., Suite 2201, Williamsburg, VA 23188 US
(757) 565-1079; *Fax:* (757) 565-7094
tideradio.com
contact@tideradio.com
License: Deltaville, Middlesex County, VA held by Local Voice Media Group
Group Owner: Local Voice Media Group; (acq 3-3-2005).
Wire Services: AP
Format: Triple A; *No. News Employees:* 1; *Adv. Rates:* 26; 22; 26; 18

Dillwyn

WBNN-FM
07-01-2000; 105.3 MHz FM; *Hrs Open:* 24; 6 kw; 328 ft.; N37 34 50 W78 37 18
P.O. Box 7111, Charlotttesville, VA 22906 US
(434) 296-3300; *Fax:* (434) 983-6772
www.bigcountryradioonline.com
License: Dillwyn, Buckingham County, VA held by WKGM Inc.
Group Owner: Baker Family Stations
Nat'l Network: CNN Radio; Premiere Radio Networks; *Regional Network:* Va. News Net.
Arbitron Metro Market: Charlottesville, VA; *Format:* Country
Special Programming: Relg; *Target Audience:* 18-49 and 25-54.; *Adv. Rates:* 28; 28; 28; 28.
Greg Breeden, General Manager
Nancy McCaig, General Sales Mgr

Dublin

WPIN
01-01-1995; 810 kHz AM; 4.2 kw-D, NDD; N37 7 55 W80 37 7
P.O. Box 889, Blacksburg, VA 24063 US
(540) 951-9791; *Fax:* (540) 961-2021
810wpin.com
License: Dublin, VA held by Dublin Radio.
Format: News, News/Talk, 86
Amy Burnette, General Manager

***WPIN-FM**
01-01-1994; 91.5 MHz FM; 0.035 kw horiz, 0.085 kw vert; 1243 ft.; N37 1 29 W80 44 46 *Rebroadcasts:* Rebroadcasts WPAR(FM) Salem 100%
22226 Timberlake Road, Lynchburg, VA 24502 US
(434) 237-9798; *Fax:* (434) 237-1025
www.spiritfm.com
License: Dublin, Pulaski County, VA held by Positive Alternative Radio Inc.
Group Owner: Positive Alternative Radio Inc.
Format: Adult Contemp, Christian
Jessica Giles, Office Manager
Brock Round, Engineer
Jackie Howard, Operations Director
Marc Tischart, General Manager

Dumfries-Triangle

WPWC
12-22-1961; 1480 kHz AM
1918 Martin Luther King Avenue SW, Washington, DC 20020 US
www.weactradio.com
freeman@weactradio.com
License: Dumfries-Triangle, VA held by JMK Communications Inc.
Arbitron Metro Market: Washington, DC
Kymone Freeman, Programming
Pete James Callahan, News Director

Earlysville

WKTR
02-17-1991; 840 kHz AM; *Hrs Open:* Daytime; 8.2 kw-D, DAD; N38 15 57 W78 24 53
P.O. Box 711, Charlottesville, VA 22906 US
(434) 296-3300; *Fax:* (434) 983-6772
www.bigcountryradioonline.com
License: Earlysville, Albemarle County, VA held by WKTR Inc.
Group Owner: Baker Family Stations
Arbitron Metro Market: Charlottesville, VA; *Format:* Country
Edward A. Baker, President

Eastville

WHRE
91.9 MHz FM; 4400 watts; 118 meters; 37 21 N32 75 56 W31
5200 Hampton Boulevard, Norfolk, VA 23508
(757) 903-2302
www.whro.org
info@whro.org
License: Eastville, VA

Bert Schmidt, President

Edinburg

***WOTC**
04-01-1994; 88.3 MHz FM; 1 kw; 404 ft.; N38 48 13 W78 41 21
146 Parons Point Lane, Edinburg, VA 22824 US
(540) 984-8998; *Fax:* (540) 984-8477
www.valleybaptistchurch.net
wotcfm@shentel.net
License: Edinburg, Shenandoah County, VA held by Valley Baptist Church-Christian School.
Nat'l Network: USA
Format: News, Religious; *Target Audience:* General; relg, children
Karl DeMay, General Manager

Elkton

WACL
03-06-1989; 98.5 MHz FM; *Hrs Open:* 24; 0.9 kw; 1608 ft.; N38 23 36 W78 46 14
207 University Boulevard, Harrisonburg, VA 22801 US
(540) 434-1777; *Fax:* (540) 432-9968
www.98rockme.com
License: Elkton, Rockingham County, VA held by Capstar TX LLC
Group Owner: iHeartMedia; (acq 3-12-01; grpsl).
Arbitron Metro Market: Harrisonburg, VA; *Format:* Rock/AOR
Steve Knupp, Operations Manager
Bridgett Knupp, Advertising Sales
Mark Ness, Chief Engineer

Elliston-Lafayette

WVBB(FM)
12-06-1983; 97.7 MHz FM; *Hrs Open:* 24; 260 watts; 470 meters; N37 18 30 W80 9 46
3934 Electric Road SW, Roanoke, VA 24018
(540) 989-4591; *Fax:* (540) 744-5667
www.vibe100.com
License: Elliston-Lafayette, Greenbrier County, VA held by Mel Wheeler Inc.
Population Served: 75,000 *Target Audience:* 25-60.; *Adv. Rates:* 8; 8; 8; 4
Leonard Wheeler, President

Emory

***WEHC**
11-15-1994; 90.7 MHz FM; *Hrs Open:* 24; 8.7 kw; 374 ft.; N36 46 1 W81 50 18
Administration Building, Emory, VA 24327 US
(276) 944-6593; *Fax:* (276) 944-6934
www.ehc.edu/student-life/facilities/wehc-radio/
License: Emory, Washington County, VA held by Emory and Henry College.
Arbitron Metro Market: Emory, VA; *Format:* Variety/Diverse; *Hrs. of News Programming:* News progmg 3 hrs wkly; *Target Audience:* College community.

Emporia

WEVA
11-04-1952; 860 kHz AM; *Hrs Open:* 24; 1 kw-D, NDD; N36 41 56 W77 32 55
705 Washington Street, Emporia, VA 23847 US
(434) 634-2133; *Fax:* (434) 634-5050
www.wevaradio.com
info@wevaradio.com
License: Emporia, VA held by Colonial Media Corp.
Nat'l Network: CBS; Westwood One; *Regional Network:* Va. News Net.
Arbitron Metro Market: Emporia, VA; *Format:* Adult Contemp, Talk *Special Programming:* Beach Music; *Hrs. of News Programming:* News progmg 14 hrs wkly; *Target Audience:* 25 plus; Adults 25-64; *Adv. Rates:* 15;15; 15; 7.50
James Vautrot, CEO
Andy Lucy, Station Manager
Jim Wood, General Sales Mgr
Darrius Herring, Programming Director
Joseph Wetherbee, Chief Engineer

*WJYA
01-01-1999; 89.3 MHz FM; *Hrs Open:* 24; 2 kw vert; 443 ft.; N36 46 4 W77 43 39
22226 Timberlake Road, Lynchburg, VA 24502 US
(434) 237-9798; *Fax:* (434) 237-1025
www.spiritfm.com
License: Emporia, Greensville County, VA held by Positive Alternative Radio Inc.
Group Owner: Positive Alternative Radio Inc.; (acq 12-30-2005; grpsl)
Format: Christian
Brock Round, Engineer
Jessica Giles, Office Manager
Jackie Howard, Director of Operations
Marc Tishart, General Manager

WYTT
01-01-2003; 99.5 MHz FM; 1.27 kw; 501 ft.; N36 39 20 W77 34 22
3 E. 1st St., Weldon, NC 27890 US
(252) 536-0209; *Fax:* (252) 538-0378
www.995jamz.com
License: Emporia, Emporia City County, VA held by First Media Radio LLC.
Group Owner: First Media Radio LLC; (acq 12-3-2003; grpsl)
Arbitron Metro Market: Emporia, VA; *Format:* Urban Contemporary
Al Haskins, General Mgr/Sales Mgr
CJ Riddick, Programming Director

Ettrick

WWLB
11-22-1971; 98.9 MHz FM; *Hrs Open:* 5 AM-midnight; 5.2 kw; 348 ft.; N37 16 21 W77 33 59
300 Arboretum Pl., Suite 590, Richmond, VA 23236 US
(804) 327-9902; *Fax:* (804) 327-9911
www.931hankfm.com
License: Ettrick, Chesterfield County, VA held by Alpha Media Licensee LLC
Group Owner: Alpha Media LLC; (acq 4-17-2014; grpsl).
Arbitron Metro Market: Petersburg-Richmond, VA; *Format:* Country
Bill West, Operations Manager
Paul Johnson, Market Manager
James Levy, Director of Sales

Exmore

WROX-FM
01-01-1986; 96.1 MHz FM; *Hrs Open:* 24; 23 kw; 722 ft.; N37 15 45 W76 0 45
999 Waterside Drive, Suite 500, Norfolk, VA 23510 US
(757) 640-8500; *Fax:* (757) 640-8552
www.96x.fm
donna@96x.com
License: Exmore, Northampton County, VA held by Sinclair Telecable Inc.
Group Owner: Sinclair Communications Inc.; (acq 9-28-93; $1.3 million;
Nat'l Reps: McGavren Guild; Interep
Arbitron Metro Market: Norfolk-Virginia Beach-Newport News, VA; *Format:* Rock/AOR; *No. News Employees:* 1; *Target Audience:* 18-34; men
Donna Agresto-Seavey, Promotions Manager
Dave Thompson/Jamie Harlow, Website
Ginger Power, National Sales Manager

Fairfax

WDCT
09-25-1955; 1310 kHz AM; *Hrs Open:* 6 AM-midnight; 5 kw-D, DA2; 0.5 kw-N, DA2; N38 51 8 W77 18 57
Suite 506, 3251 Old Lee Hwy, Fairfax, VA 22030 US
(703) 273-4000; *Fax:* (703) 273-1015
www.familyradio.com
License: Fairfax, VA held by Family Radio Ltd.
Nat'l Network: Moody
Arbitron Metro Market: Washington, DC; *Format:* Korean; *Target Audience:* 25-54; 60% female, 40% male
Kenneth Shin, General Manager
Ronnie Shin, Programming Director

Fairlawn

WKNV
01-01-1998; 890 kHz AM; 10 kw-D, DAD; N37 7 55 W80 37 7
P.O. Box 889, Blacksburg, VA 24063 US
(540) 951-9791; *Fax:* (540) 961-2021
www.joyam.org
License: Fairlawn, Pulaski County, VA held by Base Communications Inc.
Group Owner: Baker Family Stations
Format: Christian, Gospel, 74
Alison Baker, Manager

Fairview Beach

WGRQ
05-03-1986; 95.9 MHz FM; *Hrs Open:* 24; 1.9 kw; 595 ft.; N38 13 44 W77 7 28
4419 Lafayette Boulevard, Suite 100, Fredericksburg, VA 22408 US
(540) 891-9696; *Fax:* (540) 891-1656
www.959wgrq.com
tcooper@959wgrq.com
License: Fairview Beach, Westmoreland County, VA held by Telemedia Broadcasting Inc.
Nat'l Network: ABC; *Nat'l Reps:* Roslin
Format: Oldies; *Hrs. of News Programming:* news progmg 3 hrs wkly; *No. News Employees:* 1; *Target Audience:* 25 plus; baby boomers; *Adv. Rates:* 50; 45; 50; 30.
Cathy Sato, Traffic Director
Thomas Cooper, General Manager
Edwin Pardue, Sales Manager
Paumark Clifford, Programming Director
Paul Hayden, Production Director
Karen Crosby, Local Sales Manager
Sheila Quinn, News Director

Falls Church

WFAX
09-15-1948; 1220 kHz AM; *Hrs Open:* 6 am-midnight; 5 kw-D, ND1; 0.048 kw-N, ND1; N38 52 47 W77 10 18
161-B Hillwood Avenue, Falls Church, VA 22046 US
(703) 532-1220; *Fax:* (703) 533-7572
www.wfax.com
License: Falls Church, VA held by Newcomb Broadcasting Corp.
Arbitron Metro Market: Falls Church, VA; *Format:* Religious *Special Programming:* Black 15 hrs, lt one hr wkly; *Hrs. of News Programming:* News progmg one hr wkly; *Target Audience:* 34-54.
Doris Newcomb, President and General Manager
R. C. Woolfenden, Operations Dir
Roy Martin, Programming Director
Henry Stewart, Chief Engineer
Sandra Swan, Marketing Director

Falmouth

WGRX
05-17-2001; 104.5 MHz FM; 2.7 kw; 492 ft.; N38 16 31 W77 32 34
4414 Lafayette Blvd., Suite 100, Fredericksburg, VA 22408 US
(540) 891-9696; *Fax:* (540) 891-1656
www.thunder1045.com
tcooper@959wgrq.com
License: Falmouth, Stafford County, VA held by Telemedia Broadcasting Inc.
Nat'l Reps: Roslin
Arbitron Metro Market: Falmouth, VA; *Format:* Country; *Hrs. of News Programming:* News progmg 3 hrs wkly; *Target Audience:* 18-49; male audience, working class; *Adv. Rates:* 50; 45; 50; 30.
Cathy Sato, Traffic Manager
Tom Cooper, General Manager
Edwin Pardue, Sales Director
Andi King, Promotions Manager
Sheila Quinn, News Director
Christal Blue, Programming Director
Karen Crosby, Local Sales Manager

Farmville

WFLO
08-01-1947; 870 kHz AM; *Hrs Open:* Sunrise-sunset; 1 kw-D, NDD; N37 19 35 W78 23 9
P. O. Box 367, 1582 Cumberland Road, Farmville, VA 23901 US
(434) 392-4195; *Fax:* (434) 392-1823
www.wflo.net
news@wflo.net
License: Farmville, VA held by Colonial Broadcasting Co. Inc.
Regional Network: Va. News Net; *Nat'l Reps:* Salem; *Wire Services:* AP
Format: News, News/Talk, 86, Country *Special Programming:* Call Flo Radio Show, Relg 10 hrs wkly; *Hrs. of News Programming:* news progmg 4 hrs wkly; *No. News Employees:* 1; *Target Audience:* 25 plus.; *Adv. Rates:* 9; 9; 9; 9
Henry Fulcher, Co-Owner
Francis Wood, General Manager
Polly A. Davis, Sales Manager
Christine C. Wood, Programming Director
Christopher Brochon, Operations Director

WFLO-FM
05-01-1961; 95.7 MHz FM; *Hrs Open:* 24; 50 kw; 492 ft.; N37 19 35 W78 23 9
P.O. Box 367, 1582 Cumberland Road, Farmville, VA 23901 US
(434) 392-4195; *Fax:* (434) 392-1823
www.wflo.net
news@wflo.net
License: Farmville, Prince Edward County, VA
Nat'l Network: Jones Radio Networks; AP Radio; *Regional Network:* Va. News Net.; *Wire Services:* AP
Format: Adult Contemp; *Hrs. of News Programming:* news progmg 4 hrs wkly; *No. News Employees:* 1; *Target Audience:* 25 plus.; *Adv. Rates:* 14; 14; 14; 14
Henry Fulcher, Co-Owner
Francis Wood, General Manager
Polly A. Davis, Sales Manager
Christine C. Wood, Programming Director
Christopher Brochon, Operations Director

*WMLU
01-01-1988; 91.3 MHz FM; *Hrs Open:* 24; 0.001 kw horiz, 0.15 kw vert; 72 ft.; N37 17 50 W78 23 42 *Rebroadcasts:* NPR
201 High Street, Farmville, VA 23901 US
(434) 395-2792
www.wmlu.org
generalmanager@wmlu.org
License: Farmville, Prince Edward County, VA held by Longwood University.
Nat'l Network: NPR
Arbitron Metro Market: Richmond, VA; *Format:* Variety/Diverse; *Target Audience:* 18-23; div college students
Carly Bell, Operations Dir
Keith Baldwin, General Manager
Jason Tsai, Programming Director
Summer Astelford, Chief Engineer
Kyle Kurpa, Business Manager
Kyle Transue, Music Diretor
Wesley Barnhill, News Director
ElizabethStapula, Publicity Director
Derrick Bennington, Sports Director

WPAK
06-15-1978; 1490 kHz AM; 1 kw-U, ND1; N37 18 47 W78 23 41
1005 Richmond Road, Williamsburg, VA 23185 US
(434) 392-8114; *Fax:* (434) 392-8115
License: Farmville, VA held by Great Virginia Venture Inc.
Format: Religious *Special Programming:* Farm one hr, gospel 12 hrs wkly
George Granger, President
Mark Neimand, General Manager

WVHL
09-01-1997; 92.9 MHz FM; *Hrs Open:* 24; 6 kw; 328 ft; N37 17 06 W78 29 39
131 Old Colony Road, Madison Heights, VA 24572
(434) 528-9300
www.wvhl.net
wrmvradio@aol.com
License: Farmville, Prince Edward County, VA held by The Farmville Herald Inc.
Nat'l Network: ABC
Population Served: 100,000 *Target Audience:* General.
Larry Ames, Operations Dir
Steve Wall, General Manager
Doug McClure, General Sales Mgr

Ferrum

***WFFC**
01-01-1989; 89.9 MHz FM; *Hrs Open:* 16; 1.1 kw; 679 ft.; N36 54 50 W79 57 7
US
(540) 989-8900
www.wvff.org
mfranchi@vt.edu
License: Ferrum, Franklin County, VA held by Virginia Tech Foundation Inc.
Nat'l Network: NPR
Arbitron Metro Market: Ferrum, VA; *Format:* Talk
Glenn Gleixner, General Manager
Mary Grace Franchi, Business Manager

Fieldale

WODY
07-01-1993; 1160 kHz AM; 5 kw-D, DAN; 0.25 kw-N, DAN; N36 42 36 W79 57 58
P.O. Box 889, Blacksburg, VA 24063 US
(540) 951-9791; *Fax:* (540) 961-2021
License: Fieldale, Henry County, VA held by Positive Alternative Radio Inc.
Group Owner: Baker Family Stations; (acq 4-17-98)
Nat'l Network: ESPN Radio
Format: Sports; *No. News Employees:* 25-54.
Ed Lane, General Manager

Floyd

WGFC
04-20-1985; 1030 kHz AM; *Hrs Open:* Sunrise-sunset; 1 kw-D, NDD; N36 55 33 W80 16 34
Mailing Address: PO Box 1268, Hillsville, VA 24343 US
Second Address: 401 Shooting Creek Rd. S.E., Floyd, VA 24091
(276) 730-0704; *Fax:* (276) 730-0705
www.nlcm.net
ministry@nlcm.net
License: Floyd, VA held by New Life Christian Communications Inc.
Format: Gospel; *Hrs. of News Programming:* news progmg 10 hrs wkly; *No. News Employees:* 2; *Target Audience:* General; loc community interest
R. Leon Goad, CEO
Jackie Goad, Operations Dir
Leon Goad, Chief Engineer

Forest

WIQO-FM
10-01-1964; 100.9 MHz FM; *Hrs Open:* 24; 210 watts; 511 meters; N37 47 36 W79 55 57
Box 710, Covington, VA 24426
(540) 962-1133
www.bigcountry101.com
wkeywiqo@aol.com
License: Forest, Covington City County, VA held by WVJT LLC
Group Owner: WVJT LLC
Population Served: 85,000 *Hrs. of News Programming:* news progmg 10 hrs wkly; *No. News Employees:* 1; *Target Audience:* 25-54; general
Pat Pleasant, Programming Director

Fort Lee

WKLR
07-29-1963; 96.5 MHz FM; *Hrs Open:* 24; 50 kw; 453 ft.; N37 20 22 W77 24 31
600 Congress Ave., Suite 1400, Austin, TX 78701 US
(804) 330-5700; *Fax:* (320) 330-4079
www.965theplanet.com
fisher@coxradio.com
License: Fort Lee, Prince George County, VA held by SM-WKLR LLC
Group Owner: SummitMedia LLC; (acq 8-31-00; grpsl)
Arbitron Metro Market: Richmond, VA; *Format:* Classic Rock; *Hrs. of News Programming:* news progmg 5 hrs wkly; *No. News Employees:* 1; *Target Audience:* 25-49.
James Kennedy, Chairman
Bob Willoughby, General Manager
Rene Clark, General Sales Mgr
Paul Cannell, Programming Director
Gary Harrison, Engineering Dir
Sam Giles, Disc Jockey
David Koye, National Sales Manager

Franklin

WLQM
10-13-1956; 1250 kHz AM; *Hrs Open:* 24; 1 kw-D, NDD; N36 40 57 W76 55 43
Mailing Address: PO Box 735, Franklin, VA 23851 US
Second Address: 320 N. Franklin St., Franklin, VA 23851
(757) 562-3135; *Fax:* (757) 562-2345
www.wlqmradio.com
wlqm@wlqmradio.com
License: Franklin, VA held by Franklin Broadcasting Corp.
Nat'l Network: American Urban
Format: Gospel; *No. News Employees:* 3; *Target Audience:* 35-64.
Michael Clark, Operations Dir
Louise Morings, Programming Director
Mickel Pruden, Chief Engineer

WLQM-FM
01-01-1988; 101.7 MHz FM; 3 kw; 469 ft.; N36 41 17 W77 0 58
Mailing Address: 320 N. Franklin Street, Franklin, VA 23851 US
Second Address: PO Box 735, Franklin, VA 23851
(757) 562-3135; *Fax:* (757) 562-2345
www.wlqmradio.com
wlqm@wlqmradio.com
License: Franklin, Franklin City County, VA held by Franklin Broadcasting Corp.
Nat'l Network: Westwood One
Format: Country; *No. News Employees:* 9; *Target Audience:* 35 plus; men & women
Michael Clark, Operations Dir
Tim Parsons, News Director
Mickel Pruden, Chief Engineer
Neal Steele, Assistant Vice President

Fredericksburg

WBQB
05-15-1960; 101.5 MHz FM; *Hrs Open:* 24; 50 kw; 492 ft.; N38 19 57 W77 23 41
Mailing Address: P. O. Box 3300, Winchester, VA 22604 US
Second Address: 1914 Mimosa St., Fredericksburg, VA 22405
(540) 373-7721; *Fax:* (540) 899-3879
www.b1015.com
info@b1015.com
License: Fredericksburg, Fredericksburg City County, VA held by Centennial Licensing II LLC
Group Owner: Centennial Broadcasting II LLC
Nat'l Network: Westwood One
Arbitron Metro Market: Fredericksburg, VA; *Format:* Adult Contemp; *Hrs. of News Programming:* news progmg 8 hrs wkly; *No. News Employees:* 3; *Target Audience:* 18-49.
Chuck Archer, Operations Dir
Shawn Sloan, General Manager
Ted Schubel, News Director
Tom Hamilton, Market Manager

WFLS-FM
06-12-1962; 93.3 MHz FM; *Hrs Open:* 24; 50 kw; 492 ft.; N38 18 46 W77 26 20
616 Amelia St., Fredericksburg, VA 22401 US
(540) 373-1500; *Fax:* (540) 374-5525
www.wfls.com
License: Fredericksburg, Fredericksburg City County, VA held by Alpha Media Licensee LLC
Group Owner: Alpha Media LLC; (acq 5-1-2015; grpsl).
Wire Services: AP
Arbitron Metro Market: Fredericksburg, VA; *Format:* Country; *No. News Employees:* 4; *Target Audience:* 25-54; adults
Ralph Saliemo, General Manager and Director of Sales
Jeff Beck, Programming Director
Sharon DeSouza, Promotions Director
Bob Clinton, Chief Engineer
Sandy Ridgeway, Business and Traffic Manager
Shelly Bynum, ProductionDirector
Marion Edward Weatherington II, Promotions Coordinator
Bonnie Miller, Programming Coordinator

WFVA
09-08-1939; 1230 kHz AM; *Hrs Open:* 24; 1 kw-U, ND1; N38 16 50 W77 26 11
Mailing Address: P. O. Box 3300, Winchester, VA 22604 US
Second Address: 1914 Mimosa St., Fredericksburg, VA 22405
(540) 373-7721; *Fax:* (540) 899-3879
www.newstalk1230.net
info@newstalk1230.net
License: Fredericksburg, VA held by Centennial Licensing II LLC
Group Owner: Centennial Broadcasting II LLC
Format: News, News/Talk, 86; *Hrs. of News Programming:* news progmg 15 hrs wkly; *No. News Employees:* 3; *Target Audience:* 35 plus.
John Lewis, President
Chuck Archer, Operations Dir
Shawn Sloan, General Manager
Tom Hamilton, General Sales Mgr
Mark Clifford, Programming Director
Maureen Posillico, Promotions Manager
Ted Schubel, News Director
JohnDiamantis, Chief Engineer
Sean Quinn, Events Director

***WJYJ**
05-06-1983; 90.5 MHz FM; *Hrs Open:* 24; 26 kw; 409 ft.; N37 57 56 W77 22 19 *Rebroadcasts:* Simulcasts WPER(FM) Culpeper 100%
Mailing Address: P.O. Box 43, Warrenton, VA 20188 US
Second Address: 4522 Plank Road, Fredericksburg, VA 22407
(540) 347-4825; *Fax:* (540) 347-3562
www.virginiapositivehits.com
info@positivehits.org
License: Fredericksburg, Fredericksburg City County, VA held by Positive Alternative Radio Inc.
Group Owner: Positive Alternative Radio Inc.; (acq 12-30-2005; grpsl)
Format: Christian
Frankie Morea, General Manager

WNTX
07-15-1960; 1350 kHz AM; *Hrs Open:* 24; 1 kw-D, ND1; 0.037 kw-N, ND1; N38 18 46 W77 26 20
616 Amelia St., Fredericksburg, VA 22401 US
(540) 373-1500; *Fax:* (540) 374-5525
www.wntxradio.com
License: Fredericksburg, Fredericksburg City County, VA held by Alpha Media Licensee LLC
Group Owner: Alpha Media LLC; (acq 5-1-2015; grpsl).
Population Served: 85,000; *Arbitron Metro Market:* Fredericksburg, VA; *Format:* News, News/Talk, 84, Talk; *Hrs. of News Programming:* news progmg 12 hrs wkly; *No. News Employees:* 3; *Target Audience:* General.
Paul Johnson, General Manager
Ralph Salierno, Director of Sales
Frank Hammon, Programming Director
Sharon DeSouza, Promotions Director
Bob Clinton, Chief Engineer
Sandy Ridgeway, Business and Traffic Manager
Shelly Bynum,Production Director
Marion Edward Weatherington II, Promotions Coordinator
Bonnie Miller, Programming Coordinator

Front Royal

WFQX
01-17-1973; 99.3 MHz FM; *Hrs Open:* 24; 6 kw; 328 ft.; N39 3 56 W78 22 58
510 Pegasus Court, Winchester, VA 22602 US
(540) 662-5101
www.993thefox.com
davidmiller@iheartmedia.com
License: Front Royal, Warren County, VA held by Capstar TX LLC
Group Owner: iHeartMedia; (acq 8-30-00; grpsl).
Arbitron Metro Market: Winchester, VA; *Format:* Rock/AOR; *Hrs. of News Programming:* news progmg one hr wkly; *No. News Employees:* 3; *Target Audience:* 25-49; men; *Adv. Rates:* 30; 30; 28; 15
Daniel Martin, General Sales Mgr
David Miller, Programming Director
Scott Bradley, Promotions Manager

WFTR
09-19-1948; 1450 kHz AM; *Hrs Open:* 24; 1 kw-U, ND1; N38 54 31 W78 10 37
Mailing Address: 1106 Elm Street, Front Royal, NY 22630 US
Second Address: 1106 Elm St., Front Royal, VA 22630
(540) 635-4121
License: Front Royal, VA held by Royal Broadcasting Inc.
Nat'l Network: ABC *Regional Reps:* Commercial Media Sales.
Arbitron Metro Market: Winchester, VA; *Format:* Country; *Hrs. of News Programming:* news progmg 20 hrs wkly; *No. News Employees:* 1; *Target Audience:* 25-54.; *Adv. Rates:* 10; 6; 8; 4.
Andrew Shearer, CEO
Lonnie Hill, Operations Dir
Kathy Willis, News Director
Mike O'Dell, COO

WZRV
01-01-1981; 95.3 MHz FM; *Hrs Open:* 24; 6 kw; 299 ft.; N38 58 31 W78 12 6
1106 Elm Street, Front Royal, NY 22630 US

(540) 665-9595; *Fax:* (540) 635-9387
www.theriver953online.com
License: Front Royal, Warren County, VA
Nat'l Network: ABC
Format: Oldies; *No. News Employees:* 1; *Target Audience:* 25-54.; *Adv. Rates:* 24; 16; 20; 12
Mike O'Dell, General Sales Mgr
Randy Woodward, Programming Director
Mario Retrosi, News Director
Kathy Willis, Traffic Manager

Galax

WBRF

12-15-1961; 98.1 MHz FM; *Hrs Open:* 24; 100 kw horiz, 96 kw vert; 1755 ft.; N36 33 34 W80 49 25
Mailing Address: 312 Robin Road, Mount Airy, NC 27030 US
Second Address: 325 Poplar Knob Rd., Galax, VA 24333
(276) 236-9273; *Fax:* (276) 236-7198
www.blueridgecountry98.com
debby@blueridgecountry98.com
License: Galax, Galax City County, VA held by Blue Ridge Radio Inc.
Group Owner: Blue Ridge Radio Inc.; (acq 4-19-85;
Nat'l Network: CBS; Motor Racing Net
Arbitron Metro Market: Galax,VA; *Format:* Country; *Target Audience:* General.
Ray Bass, Operations Dir
Debby Stringer, General Manager
Deborah Epperson, General Sales Mgr
Betty Liddle, Programming Director
John Mullins, Chief Engineer
Jason Blevins, Music Director

WWWJ

02-01-1947; 1360 kHz AM; *Hrs Open:* 6 AM-10 PM; 5 kw-D, ND2; 0.031 kw-N, ND2; N36 39 48 W80 54 52
P. O. Box 270, Galax, VA 24333 US
(276) 236-2921; *Fax:* (276) 236-2922
www.wwwj1360.com
License: Galax, VA held by Twin County Broadcasting Corp.
Group Owner: Blue Ridge Radio Inc.; (acq 4-19-85; $200,000;
Nat'l Network: CBS; *Regional Network:* Va. News Net.
Arbitron Metro Market: Caroll County, VA; *Format:* Gospel
Special Programming: Sp 20 hrs, farm one hr wkly; *Hrs. of News Programming:* News progmg one hr wkly; *Target Audience:* 18 plus.; *Adv. Rates:* 6.45;6.45; 6.45; 6.45
Deborah Stringer, Owner/General Manager
Carole Bonn, Office Manager
Tony Phillips, Promotions Manager
John Mullins, Chief Engineer
Ray Bass, Production Manager
Michelle Lintecum, Marketing Director
Hal Epperson, SportsDirector

*WOKG

01-01-2005; 90.3 MHz FM; 2.7 kw; 538 ft.; N36 39 27 W80 54 22
Post Office Box 889, Blacksburg, VA 24063 US
(434) 237-9798; *Fax:* (434) 237-1025
www.spiritfm.com
License: Galax, Galax City County, VA held by Positive Alternative Radio Inc.
Group Owner: Positive Alternative Radio Inc.
Arbitron Metro Market: Galax, VA; *Format:* Christian
Paul Hunt, General Manager

Gate City

WGAT

07-24-1959; 1050 kHz AM; *Hrs Open:* 24; 1 kw-D, ND1; 0.267 kw-N, ND1; N36 37 59 W82 34 56
117 E. Jackson St., #2, Gate City, VA 24251 US
(276) 386-7025; *Fax:* (276) 386-7025
wgatradio@earthlink.com
License: Gate City, VA held by Tri-Cities Broadcasting Corp.
Nat'l Network: Salem Radio Network; *Regional Network:* Va. News Net.
Arbitron Metro Market: Johnson City-Kingsport-Bristol, TN-VA; *Format:* Gospel, Sports; *Hrs. of News Programming:* news progmg 10 hrs wkly; *No. News Employees:* 1; *Target Audience:* 25 plus.; *Adv. Rates:* 16; 16;16; 16
Alan Giles, President
Mike Long, General Manager

Glade Spring

WFYE

01-01-2008; 100.5 MHz FM; 6 kw; -14 ft.; N36 48 45.38 W81 33 20.38
US
(317) 541-0417
License: Glade Spring, Washington County, VA held by ASRadio LLC.
Arbitron Metro Market: Glade Spring, VA
Alan Sneed, General Manager

Glen Allen

WTOX

01-01-2004; 1480 kHz AM; *Hrs Open:* 24
US
www.lagrand1480.com
License: Glen Allen, VA held by Davidson Media Station WTOX Licensee LLC.
Group Owner: Davidson Media Group LLC; (acq 5-13-2005; grpsl)
Arbitron Metro Market: Glen Allen, VA; *No. News Employees:* 1; *Target Audience:* 25 plus; Hispanic; *Adv. Rates:* 50; 40; 45; 20
Felix Perez, President
Tim Hurley, Operations Dir
Jim Jacobs, General Manager
Carolyn Resendiz, General Sales Mgr
Selvin Paredes, Programming Director

Gloucester

WXGM

01-20-1957; 1420 kHz AM; *Hrs Open:* 24; 0.74 kw-D, ND1; 0.058 kw-N, ND1; N37 24 36 W76 32 52
6267 Professional Drive, Gloucester, VA 23061 US
(804) 693-2105; *Fax:* (804) 693-2182
www.xtra99.com
License: Gloucester, VA held by WXGM Inc.
Nat'l Network: ABC; *Regional Network:* Agrinet; Va. News Net.
Arbitron Metro Market: Gloucester, VA; *Format:* Adult Contemp
Special Programming: Farm 2 hrs, relg 2 hrs wkly; *Hrs. of News Programming:* news progmg 7 hrs wkly; *No. News Employees:* 1
Target Audience: 25-54.; *Adv. Rates:* 23; 21; 23; 17
Thomas Robinson, President
Harvey King, Operations Dir
Iris Lassister, General Sales Mgr
Herman King, News Director
Bill Swartz, Chief Engineer
Pat Clemmer Collins, Advertising

WXGM-FM

07-29-1991; 99.1 MHz FM; *Hrs Open:* 24; 6 kw; 328 ft.; N37 24 36 W76 32 52
6267 Professional Drive, Gloucester, VA 23061 US
(804) 693-2105; *Fax:* (804) 693-2182
www.xtra99.com
License: Gloucester, Gloucester County, VA held by WXGM Inc.
Arbitron Metro Market: Gloucester, VA; *Format:* Adult Contemp
Keith Lawless, Operations Dir
Shane Reeve, General Sales Mgr
Pat Clemmer Collins, Advertising

Gloucester Courthouse

WHRJ

89.9 MHz FM; 750 watts; 83.6 meters; 37 24 N36 76 32 W52
5200 Hampton Boulevard, Norfolk, VA
(757) 889-9400; *Fax:* (757) 489-0007
www.whro.org
info@whro.org
License: Gloucester Courthouse, VA held by Hampton Roads Telecommunications

Bert Schmidt, President

Goochland

WZEZ

04-01-2001; 100.5 MHz FM; *Hrs Open:* 24; 2.6 kw; 509 ft.; N37 47 37 W77 55 57
701 German School Road, Richmond, VA 23225-5357 US
(804) 223-7666; *Fax:* (804) 223-7611
www.espn950am.com
License: Goochland, Goochland County, VA held by Hoffman Communications
Nat'l Network: CNN Radio; *Wire Services:* Metro Weather Service Inc.
Arbitron Metro Market: Chester, VA; *Format:* Oldies; *Adv. Rates:* 30; 30; 30; 10
Buck Albritton, General Manager

Gretna

WMNA

08-11-1956; 730 kHz AM; *Hrs Open:* 6 AM-10 PM; 1 kw-D, DA2; 0.028 kw-N, DA2; N36 55 31 W79 19 50 *Rebroadcasts:* Rebroadcasts WLNI(FM) Lynchburg 80%
PO Box 348, Forest, VA 24551 US
(434) 534-6100; *Fax:* (434) 534-6101
www.espninva.com/espn-Gretna
License: Gretna, VA held by 3 Daughters Media Inc.
Group Owner: 3 Daughters Media Inc.; (acq 11-14-2002; $300,000 with co-located FM).
Regional Network: Agrinet
Arbitron Metro Market: Gretna, VA; *Format:* News, News/Talk, 86
Special Programming: Farm 8 hrs, Black 2 hrs, bluegrass 20 hrs, sports; *Hrs. of News Programming:* news progmg 19 hrs wkly;
No. News Employees: 1 *Target Audience:* 18-55; family groups;
Adv. Rates: 7; 7; 7; 7
Gary Burns, CEO
Randy Thompson, Vice President
Melinda Schamerhorn, Business/Traffic Director
Ashley Schamerhorn, Operations Director

WMNA-FM

02-28-1959; 106.3 MHz FM; *Hrs Open:* 5:30 AM-10 PM; 6 kw; 259 ft.; N36 55 31 W79 19 50 *Rebroadcasts:* Rebroadcasts WLNI(FM) Lynchburg 85%
US
(434) 534-8500
www.wiqoradio.com
rich@wiqoradio.com
License: Gretna, Pittsylvania County, VA held by 3 Daughters Media Inc
Group Owner: 3 Daughters Media Inc.
Regional Network: Agrinet
Arbitron Metro Market: Gretna, VA; *Format:* Sports; *Hrs. of News Programming:* News progmg 10 hrs wkly; *Target Audience:* 24-54; active & mature

Grundy

WMJD

06-21-1965; 100.7 MHz FM; *Hrs Open:* 24; 2.3 kw; 535 ft.; N37 18 8 W82 7 4
1011 Radio Drive, Grundy, VA 24614 US
(276) 935-7227; *Fax:* (276) 935-2587
www.wmjdfm.com
wmjd.fm@gmail.com
License: Grundy, Buchanan County, VA held by Peggy Sue Broadcasting Media Corp.
Group Owner: Peggy Sue Broadcasting Corp.
Nat'l Network: ABC
Arbitron Metro Market: Grundy, VA; *Format:* Country; *No. News Employees:* 5; *Target Audience:* 24-59.
Dirk Hall, Station Manager
Bink Rush, Programming Director

WNRG

11-16-1955; 940 kHz AM; 5 kw-D, ND1; 0.014 kw-N, ND1; N37 18 8 W82 7 4
Mailing Address: P.O. Box 2045, Grundy, VA 24614 US
Second Address: Rt. 460 W., Grundy, VA 24614
(276) 935-2587; *Fax:* (276) 935-2967
License: Grundy, VA held by Peggy Sue Broadcasting Media Corp.
Group Owner: Peggy Sue Broadcasting Corp.; acq 3-29-2004; $200,000 with co-located FM).
Nat'l Network: ABC; Salem Radio Network
Arbitron Metro Market: Grundy, VA; *Format:* Gospel *Special Programming:* Farm 5 hrs wkly; *No. News Employees:* 2
Dirk Hall, General Manager

*WNBV

01-01-2009; 88.1 MHz FM; 0.1 kw vert; 148 ft.; N37 17 18 W82 5 9
US
(740) 432-5605
www.yourradioplace.com
info@yourradioplace.com
License: Grundy, Buchanan County, VA held by New Beginning World Outreach Inc.
Arbitron Metro Market: Grundy, VA

Hampden-Sydney

*WWHS-FM

10-11-1972; 92.1 MHz FM; *Hrs Open:* 6 AM-2 AM; 0.01 kw horiz; 217 ft.; N37 14 23 W78 27 48
P. O. Box 128, Hampden-Sydney, VA 23943 US
(434) 223-6009; *Fax:* (434) 223-6009
License: Hampden-Sydney, Prince Edward County, VA held by President & Board of Trustees of Hampden-Sydney College.
Arbitron Metro Market: Hampden Sydney, VA; *Format:* Variety/Diverse *Special Programming:* Blues 2 hrs, class 2 hrs, jazz 6 hrs, reggae 4 hrs; *Hrs. of News Programming:* News progmg 5 hrs wkly *Target Audience:* 18-25; college community
John Wirges, General Manager
Logan Pryor, Programming Director
Chris Meyers, Technical Director

Hampton

WXTG
07-01-1948; 1490 kHz AM; *Hrs Open:* 24
232 Business Park Drive, Suite 120, Virginia Beach, VA 23462 US
(757) 490-2750; *Fax:* (757) 490-2755
www.1021thegame.com
decandidoj@redskins.com
License: Hampton, VA held by Red Zebra Broadcasting Licensee (Norfolk) LLC.
Group Owner: Red Zebra Holdings LLC; (acq 12-10-2007; $950,000)
Nat'l Network: Fox Sports
Arbitron Metro Market: Virginia Beach, VA; *Format:* Sports

***WHOV**
03-05-1964; 88.1 MHz FM; *Hrs Open:* 17; 2 kw horiz, 8 kw vert; 194 ft.; N37 1 3 W76 20 13
US
www.whov.org
License: Hampton, Hampton City County, VA held by Hampton University.
Format: Variety/Diverse *Special Programming:* Sp 12 hrs, blues 3 hrs, reggae 4 hrs wkly; *Hrs. of News Programming:* News progmg 2 hrs wkly; *Target Audience:* 18-54.

WWDE-FM
06-01-1962; 101.3 MHz FM; 50 kw; 499 ft.; N36 49 41 W76 15 5
236 Clearfield Avenue, Suite 206, Virginia Beach, VA 23462 US
(757) 497-2000
www.2wd.com
License: Hampton, Hampton City County, VA held by Entercom Norfolk License LLC.
Group Owner: Entercom Communications Corp.; (acq 12-13-99; grpsl).
Nat'l Reps: D & R Radio
Arbitron Metro Market: Hampton, VA; *Format:* Adult Contemp; *Hrs. of News Programming:* News progmg one hr wkly
David Field, CEO
Steve Godofsky, Operations Dir
Jeff Brown, General Manager
Sandy Smith, General Sales Mgr
Kym Wollman, News Director
Steve Fisher, CFO
Don London, Operations Manager
Tim Robisch, Advertising

Harrisonburg

***WEMC**
01-01-1955; 91.7 MHz FM; *Hrs Open:* 24; 1.85 kw; 190 ft.; N38 28 20 W78 52 57
1200 Park Rd, Harrisonburg, VA 22802-2462 US
(540) 432-4000; *Fax:* (540) 432-4444
License: Harrisonburg, Harrisonburg City County, VA held by Eastern Mennonite University.
Nat'l Network: NPR
Arbitron Metro Market: Harrisonburg, VA; *Format:* Classical, News; *Hrs. of News Programming:* news progmg 15 hrs wkly; *No. News Employees:* 2; *Target Audience:* General.
Thomas DuVal, General Manager

WHBG
08-01-1956; 1360 kHz AM; *Hrs Open:* 24
Mailing Address: 4850 Connecticut Ave. NW, Suite 103, Washington, DC 20008 US
Second Address: VA
(540) 434-0331; *Fax:* (540) 434-7087
License: Harrisonburg, VA held by M. Belmont VerStandig Inc.
Group Owner: VerStandig Broadcasting
Nat'l Network: ESPN Radio
Arbitron Metro Market: Harrisonburg, VA; *Format:* Sports; *Target Audience:* 24-50.
Susanne Myers, General Manager
Frank Wilt, Programming Director

WKCY
05-11-1967; 1300 kHz AM
207 University Boulevard, Harrisonburg, VA 22801 US
(540) 434-1777; *Fax:* (540) 432-9968
www.wkcyam.com
steveknupp@iheartmedia.com
License: Harrisonburg, VA held by Capstar TX LLC
Group Owner: iHeartMedia; (acq 3-12-01; grpsl).
Nat'l Network: USA
Arbitron Metro Market: Harrisonburg, VA; *Format:* News, News/Talk, 86 *Special Programming:* Relg 2 hrs wkly; *Target Audience:* 55 plus.
Steve Knupp, Operations Manager
Bridgett Knupp, Sales Manager
Mark Ness, Chief Engineer

WKCY-FM
11-01-1980; 104.3 MHz FM; *Hrs Open:* 24; 50 kw; 410 ft.; N38 23 47 W79 8 28
207 University Boulevard, Harrisonburg, VA 22604 US
(540) 434-1777; *Fax:* (540) 462-9968
www.kcycountry.com
steveknupp@iheartmedia.com
License: Harrisonburg, Rockingham County, VA held by Capstar TX LLC
Group Owner: iHeartMedia
Arbitron Metro Market: Harrisonburg, VA; *Format:* Country; *Target Audience:* 25-54.
Steve Knupp, Operations Manager
Bridgett Knupp, Sales Manager
Mark Ness, Chief Engineer

***WMRA**
06-18-1975; 90.7 MHz FM; *Hrs Open:* 24; 10.5 kw; 1043 ft.; N38 33 50 W78 57 0
983 Reservoir Street, Harrisonburg, VA 22801 US
(540) 568-6221; *Fax:* (540) 568-3814
www.wmra.org
wmra@jmu.edu
License: Harrisonburg, Harrisonburg City County, VA held by James Madison University Board of Visitors.
Nat'l Network: NPR; PRI
Arbitron Metro Market: Harrisonburg, VAA; *Format:* News, Talk *Special Programming:* Folk 8 hrs, blues 5 hrs wkly; *Hrs. of News Programming:* news progmg 80 hrs wkly; *No. News Employees:* 2 *Target Audience:* 35-64; well-educated; *Adv. Rates:* 33; 17; 33; 15
Al Bartholey, Executive Director
Meghan McCoy, Business Manager
Ivette Churney, Director of Underwriting/Foundation Grants
William Fawcett, Engineering

WQPO
12-03-1946; 100.7 MHz FM; *Hrs Open:* 24; 50 kw; 492 ft.; N38 27 8 W78 54 32
Mailing Address: 1802 Heritage Center Way, Harrisonburg, VA 22801 US
Second Address: VA
(540) 434-0331
smeyers@valleyradio.com
License: Harrisonburg, Rockingham County, VA
Group Owner: VerStandig Broadcasting
Arbitron Metro Market: Harrisonburg, VA; *Format:* Contemporary Hits/Top 40; *No. News Employees:* 3
Susanne Myers, General Manager
Dave Thomas, Programming Director

WSVA
06-09-1935; 550 kHz AM; *Hrs Open:* 24
1802 Heritage Center Way, Harrisonburg, VA 22801 US
(540) 434-0331
wsvaonline.com
smeyers@valleyradio.com
License: Harrisonburg, VA held by M. Belmont VerStandig Inc.
Group Owner: VerStandig Broadcasting; (acq 4-17-87).
Nat'l Network: ABC; *Regional Network:* Va. News Net.
Arbitron Metro Market: Harrisonburg, VA; *Format:* News, News/Talk, 86 *Special Programming:* Farm 8 hrs wkly; *No. News Employees:* 5; *Target Audience:* 35 plus.
Susanne Myers, General Manager
Kim Mitchell, Sales Manager
Frank Wilt, Operations Manager
Mike Schiteman, Programming/News Director

***WXJM**
09-01-1990; 88.7 MHz FM; *Hrs Open:* 6 AM-2 AM; 0.39 kw; 62 ft.; N38 26 22 W78 52 21
983 Reservoir Street, Harrisonburg, VA 22801 US
(540) 568-6878
www.wxjm.org
wxjm@jmu.eduÿ
License: Harrisonburg, Harrisonburg City County, VA held by James Madison University Board of Visitors.
Arbitron Metro Market: Harrisonburg, VA; *Format:* Alternative *Special Programming:* Jazz 14 hrs, Sp 2 hrs wkly; *Hrs. of News Programming:* News progmg 7 hrs wkly; *Target Audience:* General.
Kelly Carlin, General Manager
Kat Caren, Programming Director
Julia Slattery, Music Director

Heathsville

***WCNV**
01-01-2007; 89.1 MHz FM; 0 kw horiz, 3.8 kw vert; 318 ft.; N37 54 22 W76 29 9
23 Sesame Street, Richmond, VA 23235 US
(804) 320-1301
www.ideastations.org/radio
License: Heathsville, Northumberland County, VA held by Commonwealth Public Broadcasting Corp.
Nat'l Network: NPR; PRI; *Wire Services:* AP
Arbitron Metro Market: Heathsville, VA; *Format:* News, News/Talk, 86
Bill Miller, General Manager

Highland Springs

WCLM
05-18-1959; 1450 kHz AM; *Hrs Open:* 24; 0.96 kw-U, ND1; N37 32 39 W77 20 47
3165 Hull Street, Richmond, VA 23224 US
(804) 231-2186; *Fax:* (804) 231-2186
www.wclmradio.com
mrptbrown@aol.com
License: Highland Springs, VA held by World Media Broadcast Co.
Arbitron Metro Market: Richmond, VA; *Format:* Variety/Diverse *Special Programming:* Gospel, blues 5 hrs wkly, country, Top 40; *Target Audience:* 25-65.
Preston Brown, CEO
George Lacey, General Sales Mgr
Jim Grainger, Chief Engineer
Jay Love, Disc Jockey
Curtis Bowman, Disc Jockey
Kimberly Osacio, General Sales Manager

***WHCE**
09-29-1980; 91.1 MHz FM; 3 kw horiz; 105 ft.; N37 32 18 W77 19 27
100 Tech Drive, Highland Springs, VA 23075 US
License: Highland Springs, Henrico County, VA held by Henrico County Schools.
Arbitron Metro Market: Highland Springs, VA; *Format:* Contemporary Hits/Top 40; *Target Audience:* 12-20; teenagers, young adults
Bob Kaufman, General Manager

Hillsville

WHHV
09-16-1961; 1400 kHz AM; *Hrs Open:* 6 AM-midnight; 1 kw-U, ND1; N36 45 0 W80 43 20
Mailing Address: 234 Virginia Street, Hillsville, VA 24343 US
Second Address: 343 Virginia St., Hillsville, VA 24343
(276) 750-0708; *Fax:* (276) 730-0705
www.whhvradio.com
wnlb@wnlbradio.com
License: Hillsville, VA held by New Life Christian Communications Inc.
Format: Gospel *Special Programming:* Farm one hr wkly; *Hrs. of News Programming:* News progmg 20 hrs wkly; *Target Audience:* General.
Jackie Goad, Operations Dir

Hopewell

WHAP
01-16-1949; 1340 kHz AM; *Hrs Open:* 24; 1 kw-U, ND1; N37 17 46 W77 18 50
306 West Broad Street, Richmond, VA 23220 US
(804) 452-4999
License: Hopewell, VA held by WHAP Radio Network
Arbitron Metro Market: Richmond, VA; *Format:* Gospel, Oldies; *Target Audience:* 25-65.
Preston Brown, CEO
Judy Brown, General Manager

Hot Springs

***WCHG**
09-01-1995; 107.1 MHz FM; *Hrs Open:* 6 AM-10 PM; 0.16 kw; 1407 ft.; N38 1 53 W79 46 52 *Rebroadcasts:* Rebroadcasts WVMR(AM) Frost, WV 50%
US
(540) 839-5400; *Fax:* (540) 839-5403
www.alleghenymountainradio.org
License: Hot Springs, Bath County, VA held by Pocahontas Communications Cooperative Corp.
Regional Network: Va. News Net.
Arbitron Metro Market: Hot Springs,VA; *Format:* Variety/Diverse; *Hrs. of News Programming:* News progmg 15 hrs wkly; *Target Audience:* General.

Jonesville

WJNV
01-01-2000; 99.1 MHz FM; 4 kw; 404 ft.; N36 42 5 W83 10 14
Rt 2 Box 128b, Jonesville, VA 24263 US

RADIO - U.S.

(276) 346-2000; *Fax:* (276) 346-2049
License: Jonesville, Lee County, VA held by Regina Kay Moore.
Format: Country
Regina Moore, General Manager

Keswick

WCNR
03-02-1991; 106.1 MHz FM; 0.6 kw; 1024 ft.; N37 59 6 W78 28 48
1140 Rose Hill Drive, Charlottesville, VA 22903 US
(434) 220-2300; *Fax:* (434) 220-2304
www.1061thecorner.com
brad@1061thecorner.com
License: Keswick, Albemarle County, VA held by Saga Communications of Charlottesville LLC.
Group Owner: Saga Communications Inc.; (acq 11-2-2006; $2.9 million)
Arbitron Metro Market: Charlottesville, VA; *Format:* Triple A; *Adv. Rates:* 30; 25; 30; 15
Brad Savage, Brand Manager

Kilmarnock

WKWI
09-01-1975; 101.7 MHz FM; *Hrs Open:* 24; 2.2 kw; 400 ft.; N37 43 25 W76 23 28.8
101 Radio Road, Kilmarnock, VA 22482 US
(804) 435-1313; *Fax:* (804) 435-0484
www.middleneck.com/bay-fm
onair@1017bayfm.com
License: Kilmarnock, Lancaster County, VA held by Two Rivers Communications Inc.
Nat'l Network: AP Network News; CBS
Format: Adult Contemp; *No. News Employees:* 1; *Target Audience:* 25-64.
Tawne Hayes, Programming Director

Lakeside

WHTI(FM)
12-01-1968; 100.9 MHz FM; 15 kw; Ant 367 ft; N37 26 21 W77 25 57
812 Moorefield Park Dr., Suite 300, Richmond, VA 23236
(804) 330-5700; *Fax:* (804) 330-4079
y101rocks.com
License: Lakeside, Chesterfield County, VA held by SM-WHTI LLC
Group Owner: SummitMedia LLC; (acq 2-1-2001; grpsl)
Wire Services: UPI
Arbitron Metro Market: Richmond, VA; *Target Audience:* 18-34.
Rene Clark, General Sales Mgr
Mike Fisher, Programming Director
Gary Harrison, Chief Engineer

Lawrenceville

WVNC
09-01-1991; 105.5 MHz FM; 6 kw; 154 ft; N36 45 10 W77 51 49
102 East Hicks Street, Suite 200, Lawrenceville, VA 23868
(434) 848-9862
License: Lawrenceville, Brunswick County, VA held by Imperial Broadcasting Company
Group Owner: Imperial Broadcasting Company; acq 4-27-99; $350,000 with co-located AM)

Lebanon

WLRV
10-28-1974; 1380 kHz AM; *Hrs Open:* 24; 1 kw-D, ND1; 0.063 kw-N, ND1; N36 55 18 W82 6 16
P. O. Box 939, Lebanon, VA 24266 US
(276) 889-1380; *Fax:* (276) 889-1388
www.wlrv.com
License: Lebanon, VA held by Gary W. Ward Broadcasting Corp.
Nat'l Network: USA
Format: Country, Gospel; *Target Audience:* 25 plus.
Gary W. Ward, President/General Manager
Mike Lowe, Programming Director

WXLZ-FM
02-01-1993; 107.3 MHz FM; *Hrs Open:* 24; 1 kw; 774 ft.; N36 50 38 W82 11 4
P. O. Box 1299, Lebanon, VA 24266 US
(276) 889-1073; *Fax:* (276) 889-3677
www.wxlz.net
wxlz1073@bvu.net
License: Lebanon, Russell County, VA held by Yeary Broadcasting Inc.
Nat'l Network: CBS
Arbitron Metro Market: Saint Paul, VA; *Format:* Country; *Hrs. of News Programming:* news progmg 3 hrs wkly; *No. News Employees:* 2; *Target Audience:* 18 plus; students, farmers, miners, executives & rural residents
Lannis Yeary, Owner/General Manager
Wilma Kiser, Office Manager

Leesburg

WCRW(AM)
03-06-1958; 1190 kHz AM; *Hrs Open:* 24; 50 kw-D, DA; N39 02 28 W77 26 42 *Rebroadcasts:* (CP: 1190 khz; 50 kw-D, DA. TL: N39 02 28 W77 26 42)
711 Wage Dr. S.W., Leesburg, VA 22075
License: Leesburg, Loudoun County, VA held by New World Radio
Regional Network: Va. News Net.
Population Served: 100,000; *Arbitron Metro Market:* Washington, DC; *Hrs. of News Programming:* news progmg 114 hrs wkly; *No. News Employees:* 1; *Target Audience:* 25 plus; above average income, families, homeowners
Grenville Emmet III, President
Dene Hill, Station Manager
Chris King, Programming Director
Jeremy Huber, News Director
Ron Kitemiller, Sports Commentator

Lexington

*WLUR
02-27-1967; 91.5 MHz FM; *Hrs Open:* 6:30 AM-2 AM; 0.175 kw; -167 ft.; N37 47 42 W79 26 49
204 West Washington Street, Lexington, VA 24450 US
(540) 458-4017
www2.wlu.edu/x37490
wlurais@wlu.edu
License: Lexington, Lexington City County, VA held by Washington & Lee University.
Format: Variety/Diverse; *Hrs. of News Programming:* News progmg 2 hrs wkly; *Target Audience:* General; college students, city and county residents
Jeremy Franklin, General Manager/Programming Director
Will Bartlett/Micah Fleet, Sports
Trevin Ivory, Traffic Director

*WMRL
06-01-1992; 89.9 MHz FM; *Hrs Open:* 24; 0.1 kw; -266 ft.; N37 47 25 W79 26 5 *Rebroadcasts:* Rebroadcasts WMRA(FM) Harrisonburg 100%
983 Reservoir Street, Harrisonburg, VA 22801 US
(540) 568-6221; *Fax:* (540) 568-3814
www.wmra.org
wmra@jmu.edu
License: Lexington, Lexington City County, VA held by James Madison University Board of Visitors.
Nat'l Network: NPR; PRI
Arbitron Metro Market: Harrisonburg, VAA; *Format:* News, Talk
Special Programming: Folk 8 hrs, blues 5 hrs wkly; *Hrs. of News Programming:* news progmg 80 hrs wkly; *No. News Employees:* 2 *Target Audience:* 35-64; well-educated; *Adv. Rates:* 33; 17; 33; 15
Al Bartholet, Executive Director
Meghan McCoy, Business Manager
Ivette Churney, Direction of Underwriting/Foundation Grants
Stan Farthing, Director of Corporate Support
Dan Easley, Operations/Website Coordinator
William Fawcett,Engineering

WREL
11-14-1948; 1450 kHz AM; *Hrs Open:* 24; 1 kw-U, ND1; N37 46 0 W79 25 56
392 E. Midland Trail, Lexington, VA 22450 US
(540) 463-2161; *Fax:* (540) 463-9524
License: Lexington, VA held by First Media Radio LLC.
Group Owner: First Media Radio LLC; (acq 6-21-2004; $1.33 million with WWZW-FM Buena Vista)
Nat'l Reps: Keystone (unwired net)
Format: News/Talk, Sports; *Hrs. of News Programming:* news progmg 6 hrs wkly; *No. News Employees:* 1; *Target Audience:* 35 plus.; *Adv. Rates:* 12; 10; 12; 9
Kevan Kavanaugh, General Sales Mgr
Jim Bresnahan, News/Sports Director

*WRIQ
88.7 MHz FM; 3.9 kw; 259 ft.; N37 53 18 W79 17 50
US
(540) 989-8900
www.wvtf.org
License: Lexington, Lexington City County, VA held by Virginia Tech Foundation Inc.
Arbitron Metro Market: Lexington, VA; *Format:* Classical, Jazz; *No. News Employees:* 8
Glenn Gleixner, General Manager
Mary Grace Franchi, Business Manager

Louisa

WOJL
07-10-1980; 105.5 MHz FM; *Hrs Open:* 24; 6 kw; 325 ft.; N38 1 37 W78 1 5
207 Spicers Mill Road, PO Box 271, Orange, VA 22960 US
(540) 672-1000
www.1055samfm.com
License: Louisa, Louisa County, VA held by Piedmont Communications Inc.
Group Owner: Piedmont Communications Inc.; (acq 5-27-2004)
Nat'l Network: Westwood One
Arbitron Metro Market: Charlottesville, VA; *Format:* Adult Contemp; *Hrs. of News Programming:* news progmg 2 hrs wkly; *No. News Employees:* 1; *Target Audience:* 25-54.
Gary Harrison, Operations/Engineering
Phil Goodwin, News

Luray

WMXH-FM
10-16-1979; 105.7 MHz FM; 0.15 kw; 1972 ft.; N38 35 59 W78 38 1
130 University Boulevard, Suite B, Harrisonburg, VA 22801 US
(540) 801-1057; *Fax:* (540) 743-5168
www.easyradioinc.com
stardust1057@easyradioinc.com
License: Luray, Page County, VA
Regional Network: Va. News Net.
Arbitron Metro Market: Luray, VA; *Format:* Adult Contemp
Special Programming: Relg 5 hrs wkly; *Target Audience:* 18-54; working people with disposable income interested in mus, news & sports

WRAA
10-01-1962; 1330 kHz AM
US
(540) 801-1057; *Fax:* (540) 564-2873
License: Luray, VA held by Easy Radio Inc.
Regional Network: Va. News Net.; Agrinet; *Nat'l Reps:* Keystone (unwired net)
Format: Country *Special Programming:* Relg 7 hrs wkly; *Target Audience:* 18-49; middle to upper income, mobile
Jason Cave, President
Joshua Cave, Operations Dir

*WYFT
10-01-1986; 103.9 MHz FM; 6 kw; 302 ft.; N38 38 17 W78 24 4
598 5th St., Luray, VA 22835 US
(540) 743-7602
www.bbnradio.org
bbn@bbnmedia.org
License: Luray, Page County, VA held by Bible Broadcasting Network Inc.
Group Owner: Bible Broadcasting Network; (acq 12-22-86).
Arbitron Metro Market: Luray, VA; *Format:* Religious; *Hrs. of News Programming:* News progmg 13 hrs wkly; *Target Audience:* General.
Lowell Davey, President
Jason Padgett, Operations Manager

Lynchburg

WBRG
09-06-1956; 1050 kHz AM; *Hrs Open:* 24
P. O. Box 1079, Lynchburg, VA 24572 US
(434) 401-0230
www.wbrgradio.com/
License: Lynchburg, VA held by Tri-County Broadcasting Inc.
Nat'l Network: ABC; Westwood One; Motor Racing Net; *Regional Network:* Va. News Net.
Arbitron Metro Market: Lynchburg, VA; *Format:* News, News/Talk, 84, Talk; *Hrs. of News Programming:* news progmg 12 hrs. wkly; *No. News Employees:* 2; *Target Audience:* 25-54; College educated,professional/management, high household income, married with children; *Adv. Rates:* 28; 18; 28; 16
Brent Epperson, General Manager

WSNZ
08-01-1964; 101.7 MHz FM; 3.4 kw; 289 ft.; N37 25 37 W79 7 26 *Rebroadcasts:* Simulcast with WSNV(FM) Salem 100%
3807 Brandon Avenue, Suite 2350, Roanoke, VA 24018 US
(540) 725-1220
www.1061stevefm.com
steve@stevefm.com
License: Lynchburg, Lynchburg City County, VA held by Aloha Station Trust LLC
Arbitron Metro Market: Roanoke-Lynchburg, VA; *Format:* Adult Contemp; *Target Audience:* 35-54.

Steve Cross, Programming Director

WKPA
07-07-1988; 1390 kHz AM *Rebroadcasts:* Rebroadcasts WKBA (AM) Vinton 100%
301 Hillcrest Heights, Salem, VA 24121 US
(540) 721-4004; *Fax:* (540) 721-4941
License: Lynchburg, VA held by Tinker Creek Broadcasters
Arbitron Metro Market: Roanoke-Lynchburg, VA; *Format:* Religious; *Target Audience:* General.
Dorothy Durrett, General Manager
Zeke Leonard, General Sales Mgr
Sharon Moran, Promotions Manager
Buddy Durrett, Music Director

WLLL
11-01-1963; 930 kHz AM
Mailing Address: PO Box 11305, Lynchburg, VA 24506 US
Second Address: 105 Whitehall Rd., Lynchburg, VA 24501
(434) 385-4564
wllam930@aol.com
License: Lynchburg, VA held by Hubbards Advertising Agency Inc.
Arbitron Metro Market: Roanoke-Lynchburg, VA; *Format:* Gospel
Fletcher Hubbard, President
Savannah Hubbard, News Director

WLNI
02-02-1994; 105.9 MHz FM; *Hrs Open:* 24; 6 kw; 266 ft.; N37 25 37 W79 7 26
P.O. Box 348, Forest, VA 24551 US
www.wlni.com
License: Lynchburg, Lynchburg City County, VA held by Centennial Broadcasting LLC.
Group Owner: Centennial Broadcasting LLC; (acq 1-7-2005; grpsl)
Nat'l Network: ABC; Westwood One; Fox News Radio; Talk Radio Network; *Nat'l Reps:* McGavren Guild; *Wire Services:* AP
Arbitron Metro Market: Roanoke-Lynchburg, VA; *Format:* News, News/Talk, 86; *Hrs. of News Programming:* news progmg 20 hrs wkly; *No. News Employees:* 3; *Target Audience:* 25-54.
Bob Abbott, Operations Dir
Ron Gaylor, General Manager
Mari White, News Director
Michael Williams, Business Manager
Sandi Conner, Production Director
Kara Butterworth, Traffic Manager

WLVA
04-21-1930; 580 kHz AM; *Hrs Open:* 24
4119 Boonsboro, #220, Lynchburg, VA 24503 US
License: Lynchburg, VA held by Chesapeake-Portsmouth Broadcasting Corp.
Group Owner: Chesapeake-Portsmouth Broadcasting Corp.; (acq 1-30-2009; $560,000)
Arbitron Metro Market: Lynchburg, VA; *Format:* Religious; *Target Audience:* 25-54
Vic Bosiger, General Manager

WVBE-FM
01-01-1948; 100.1 MHz FM; *Hrs Open:* 24; 20 kw; 328 ft.; N37 27 0 W79 4 29 *Rebroadcasts:* Rebroadcasts WVBE(AM) Roanoke 90%
US
www.vibe100.com
License: Lynchburg, Lynchburg City County, VA held by Mel Wheeler Inc.
Group Owner: Mel Wheeler Inc.; acq 3-12-97; $7.5 million with WXLK(FM) Roanoke).
Arbitron Metro Market: Lynchburg, VA; *Format:* Urban Contemporary; *Hrs. of News Programming:* News progmg one hr wkly; *Target Audience:* 25-54; skew women, skew black
Tom Joyner, On-Air Personality

***WRVL**
88.3 MHz FM; 50 kw horiz, 42 kw vert; 1083 ft.; N37 11 50 W79 21 7
1971 University Boulevard, Lynchburg, VA 24502 US
(434) 582-3688; *Fax:* (434) 424-9594
www.myjourneyfm.com
License: Lynchburg, Lynchburg City County, VA held by Liberty University, Inc.
Group Owner: Liberty University, Inc.
Format: Adult Contemp, Christian, 74 *Special Programming:* Liberty Univ. football & basketball; *Hrs. of News Programming:* news progmg 8 hrs wkly; *No. News Employees:* 1; *Target Audience:* 25 plus.
Chris Wygal, Operations Manager
Barry Armstrong, General Manager

WZZU
09-01-1970; 97.9 MHz FM; *Hrs Open:* 24; 0.57 kw; 1926 ft.; N37 33 46 W79 11 38 *Rebroadcasts:* Simulcasts WZZI(FM) Vinton 100%
Mailing Address: 210 Fiest Street, Sw, Suite 240, Roanoke, VA 24011 US
Second Address: 19-C Wadsworth St., Lynchburg, VA 24501
(434) 845-3698; *Fax:* (434) 845-2063
www.rocktheplanet.fm
License: Lynchburg, Lynchburg City County, VA held by WVJT LLC
Group Owner: WVJT LLC; (acq 11-23-2004; $4.15 million with WZZI(FM) Vinton)
Nat'l Network: Fox News Radio; *Nat'l Reps:* McGavren Guild; *Wire Services:* AP
Arbitron Metro Market: Roanoke-Lynchbu; *Format:* Rock/AOR
Special Programming: Relg one hr wkly; *No. News Employees:* 3
Bob Abbott, Operations Dir
Mike Williams, General Manager
Bob Abbott, General Sales Mgr
Kara Butterworth, News Director
Michael Williams, Business Manager
Sandi Conner, Production Director

WVGM
02-22-1962; 1320 kHz AM; *Hrs Open:* 24; 1 kw-D, ND1; 0.024 kw-N, ND1; N37 25 37 W79 7 26
Mailing Address: PO Box 348, Forest, VA 24551 US
Second Address: 103 Avalon Drive, Forest, VA 24551
(434) 534-6100; *Fax:* (434) 534-6101
www.espninva.com
gary@espninva.com
License: Lynchburg, VA held by 3 Daughters Media Inc.
Group Owner: 3 Daughters Media Inc.; (acq 6-22-2007; grpsl)
Nat'l Network: ESPN Radio; *Nat'l Reps:* Katz Radio
Arbitron Metro Market: Roanoke, VA; *Format:* Sports, Talk; *Hrs. of News Programming:* News progmg 10 hrs wkly
Gary Burns, CEO
Randy Thompson, Vice President
Ashley Schamerhorn, Operations Dir
Melinda Schamerhorn, Business & Traffic Director
Jonny Fairplay, Account Executive

***WWMC**
02-01-1993; 90.9 MHz FM; *Hrs Open:* 24; 100 w; 604 ft; N37 20 56 W79 10 05
1971 Univ. Blvd., Lynchburg, VA 24502
(434) 582-3691; *Fax:* (434) 582-7461
www.liberty.edu/thelight
wwmcfm@liberty.edu
License: Lynchburg, Lynchburg City County, VA held by Liberty University Inc.
Arbitron Metro Market: Roanoke-Lynchburg, VA; *Hrs. of News Programming:* News progmg 5 hrs wkly; *Target Audience:* 12-45; high school, college & young adult
Jamie Hall, Station Manager
Chris Wygal, Chief Engineer

WKHF(FM)
93.7 MHz FM; 1600 watts; 197 meters; 37 20 56N 79 10 05W
1200 West Cornwalls, Greensboro, NC 27408 USA
(434) 455-4321
www.lynchburgradiogroup.com
License: Lynchburg, Amherst County, VA
Group Owner: United States CP LLC

***WQLU**
90.9 MHz FM; 50 kw H 42 kw V; 1082 ft; N36 18 40 W76 17 34
1971 University Blvd, Lynchburg, VA 24502 US
(434) 582-3691; *Fax:* (434) 582-7461
www.liberty.edu/thelight
wwmcfm@liberty.edu
License: Lynchburg, Lynchburg City County, VA held by Liberty University, Inc.
Group Owner: Liberty University, Inc.
Format: Christian
Chris Wygal, Engineer
Jamie Hall, Station Manager

Manassas

WKDV
10-01-1957; 1460 kHz AM; *Hrs Open:* 24; 5 kw-D, DA2; 5 kw-N, DA2; N38 45 0 W77 30 49
US
(703) 659-0406
www.somoslaley.com
sales@somoslaley.com
License: Manassas, VA held by Metro Radio Inc.
Group Owner: Metro Radio Inc.; (acq 8-1-2005; exchange for WFBR(AM) Glen Burnie, MD)
Arbitron Metro Market: Washington, DC; *Format:* Talk

WWWT-FM
03-28-1966; 107.7 MHz FM; *Hrs Open:* 24; 29 kw; 646 ft.; N38 44 30 W77 50 8 *Rebroadcasts:* Rebroadcasts WTOP-FM Washington, DC 100%
3400 Idaho Ave. N.W., Washington, DC 20016 US
(202) 895-5000
www.wtop.com
License: Manassas, Prince William County, VA held by Washington DC FCC License Sub LLC
Group Owner: Hubbard Broadcasting Inc.; (acq 1-19-2011)
Nat'l Network: CBS; *Regional Network:* Va. News Net; *Nat'l Reps:* Katz Radio
Arbitron Metro Market: Washington, DC; *Format:* News; *No. News Employees:* 2; *Target Audience:* 25-54.
Joel Oxley, General Manager
Matt Mills, Director of Sales
Mike McMearty, Director of News and Programming
Mary Kay LeMay, Director of Marketing
John Meyer, Director of Digital Operations
Skip Quast, Sales Manager
Steve Goldstein,Digital Sales Manager
Jeffrey Wolinsky, Federal Sales

Marion

WUKZ(AM)
12-12-1948; 1010 kHz AM; *Hrs Open:* 24; 1 kw-D, 30 w-N; N36 51 23 W81 30 21
1041 Radio Hill Rd., Marion, VA 24354
(276) 783-3151; *Fax:* (276) 783-3152
www.fm94.com
License: Marion, Smyth County, VA held by Holston Valley Broadcasting Corp.
Group Owner: Glenwood Communications Corp.; (acq 7-1-98; $1.65 million with co-located FM)
Nat'l Network: NBC; Motor Racing Network *Regional Reps:* Rgnl Reps
Population Served: 500,000; *Arbitron Metro Market:* Johnson City-Kingsport-Bristol, TN-VA *TV Affiliate:* WKPT-TV; *Format:* Classic Rock *Special Programming:* Gospel 2 hrs, relg 8 hrs wkly; *Hrs. of News Programming:* News progmg 3 hrs wkly; *Target Audience:* 18-54.
George DeVault Jr., President
Jim Mabe, Operations Dir
N. David Widener, General Manager
Tiffany Hickman, General Sales Mgr
Lynn Rutledge, Programming Director
Duane Nelson, News Director
Henry Thomas, Disc Jockey
Evelyn Payne,Traffic Manager

WMEV-FM
06-21-1961; 93.9 MHz FM; 100 kw; 1,480 ft; N36 54 08 W81 32 33
1041 Radio Hill Rd., Marion, VA 37662
(276) 783-3151; *Fax:* (276) 783-3152
www.fm94.com
kz107@fm94.com
License: Marion, Smyth County, VA held by Holston Valley Broadcasting Corp.
Group Owner: Glenwood Communications Corp.; 1-Jul-98
Nat'l Network: NBC; NASCAR-MRN; *Wire Services:* AP
Arbitron Metro Market: Johnson City-Kingsport-Bristol, TN-VA *TV Affiliate:* WKPT-TV; *Format:* Country *Special Programming:* Nascar; *No. News Employees:* 2; *Target Audience:* Persons 25-54
George Devault, President
Lynn Rutledge, Operations Dir
N. David Widener, General Manager
Tiffany Hickman, General Sales Mgr
Henry Thomas, Programming Director
Duane Nelson, News Director
Jim Mabe, Assistant Station Manager

WITM
04-25-1962; 1330 kHz AM; 5 kw-D, ND2; 0.031 kw-N, ND2; N36 49 11 W81 28 12
P. O. Box 31, Marion, VA 24354 US
(423) 878-6279; *Fax:* (423) 878-6520
License: Marion, VA held by Appalachian Educational Communications Corp.
TV Affiliate: Relg

WOLD-FM
03-14-1968; 102.5 MHz FM; 0.44 kw; 1204 ft.; N36 54 10 W81 32 27
P. O. Box 85, Marion, VA 24354 US

(276) 783-4042
dale@mountainempiremedia.com
License: Marion, Smyth County, VA held by T.E.C. 2 Broadcasting Inc.
Nat'l Network: CNN Radio
TV Affiliate: Classic Rock

***WVTR**
11-22-1991; 91.9 MHz FM; 4.5 kw; 1490 ft.; N36 44 52 W81 18 15 *Rebroadcasts:* Rebroadcasts WVTF(FM) Roanoke 100%
3520 Kingsbury Lane, Roanoke, VA 24014 US
(434) 293-2515
www.wvtf.org
mfranchi@vt.edu
License: Marion, Smyth County, VA held by Virginia Tech Foundation Inc.
Nat'l Network: NPR
Format: Jazz
Glenn Gleixner, General Manager

WZVA
09-02-1996; 103.5 MHz FM; *Hrs Open:* 24; 3.7 kw; 423 ft.; N36 54 10 W81 22 56
US
(276) 783-4042; *Fax:* (276) 783-2120
License: Marion, Smyth County, VA held by T.E.C.O. Broadcasting Inc.
Arbitron Metro Market: Marion, VA; *Format:* Adult Contemp, Contemporary Hits/Top 40; *Target Audience:* 18-49; women & men
Dale Powers, Director of Sales
Kendra, Business Manager/Traffic Director

Martinsville

WHEE
08-04-1954; 1370 kHz AM; 5 kw-D, NDD; N36 41 9 W79 54 14
1129 Chatham Road, Martinsville, VA 24112 US
(276) 632-2152; *Fax:* (888) 478-4506
martinsvillemedia.com
License: Martinsville, VA held by Martinsville Media Inc.
Nat'l Network: CBS
Format: Talk; *Target Audience:* 17-60; agriculture & mfg area audience
Bill Wyatt, President
T.L. Walker, Chief Engineer

***WPIM**
01-01-1997; 90.5 MHz FM; 4 kw; 387 ft.; N36 42 16 W79 50 5
22226 Timberlake Road, Lynchburg, VA 24502 US
(434) 237-9798; *Fax:* (434) 237-1025
www.spiritfm.com
License: Martinsville, Martinsville City County, VA held by Positive Alternative Radio Inc.
Group Owner: Positive Alternative Radio Inc.
Format: Adult Contemp, Christian
March Tischart, General Manager
Jackie Howard, Director of Operations
Jessica Giles, Office Manager
Brock Round, Engineer

WROV-FM
01-01-1950; 96.3 MHz FM; 14 kw; 2077 ft.; N37 7 0 W80 0 58
3807 Brandon Ave., Suite 2350, Roanoke, VA 24018 US
(540) 725-1220; *Fax:* (540) 725-1245
www.rovrocks.com
License: Martinsville, Martinsville City County, VA held by Capstar TX LLC
Group Owner: iHeartMedia; (acq 8-30-00; grpsl).
Nat'l Reps: D & R Radio
Arbitron Metro Market: Roanoke-Lynchburg, VA; *Format:* Rock/AOR; *Target Audience:* 18-49; general
Sarah Leftwich, Market Manager
Tammy Cazad, General Sales Mgr

WMVA
12-01-1941; 1450 kHz AM; 1 kw-U, ND1; N36 42 0 W79 51 7
1129 Chatham Road, Martinsville, VA 24112 US
(276) 632-2152; *Fax:* (888) 478-4506
www.martinsvillemedia.com
93.5@waxm.com
License: Martinsville, VA held by Martinsville Media Inc.
Arbitron Metro Market: Lafayette, LA; *Format:* Talk
Bill Wyatt, President

Mechanicsville

WCDX
10-07-1985; 92.1 MHz FM; 4.5 kw; 771 ft.; N37 36 52 W77 30 56
2809 Emerywood Pkwy., Suite 300, Richmond, VA 23294 US
(804) 672-9299
www.ipowerrichmond.com/
License: Mechanicsville, Hanover County, VA held by Radio One Licenses LLC.
Group Owner: Radio One Inc.; (acq 11-8-2001; grpsl).
Nat'l Reps: Eastman Radio
Arbitron Metro Market: Richmond, VA; *Format:* Urban Contemporary; *Target Audience:* Ages 18-44.
Jeff Anderson, Operations Mgr/Program Dir.
Marsha Landess, General Manager

Midlothian

WLFV
01-01-2001; 98.9 MHz FM; 4.8 kw; 746 ft.; N37 36 52 W77 30 56
300 Arboretum Pl., Suite 590, Richmond, VA 23236 US
(804) 327-9902
License: Midlothian, Chesterfield County, VA held by Alpha Media Licensee LLC
Group Owner: Alpha Media LLC; (acq 4-17-2014; grpsl).
Arbitron Metro Market: Richmond, VA; *Format:* Country
Bill West, Operations Manager
Paul Johnson, Market Manager
James Levy, Director of Sales
Braden Smith, Programming Director

Minooka

01-01-2012; 88.5 MHz FM; 200 w; 32 meters; N41 29 47 W88 17 56
6139 Franklin Park Road, McLean, VA 22101
(703) 761-5013
License: Minooka, Grundy County, IL held by Silver Fish Broadcasting Inc
A Wray Fitch III, President

Moneta

WSLK
11-01-1991; 880 kHz AM; *Hrs Open:* 12; 0.9 kw-D, NDD; N37 10 0 W79 37 50
P.O. Box 880, 1126 Hendricks Store Road, Suite B, Moneta, WA 24121 US
(540) 297-7880; *Fax:* (540) 343-2306
wslk880.com
info@wslk880.com
License: Moneta, VA held by Smile Broadcasting LLC
Arbitron Metro Market: Roanoke, VA; *Format:* Oldies; *Target Audience:* 35 plus; mostly middle aged, affluent, cosmopolitan
Dale Cook, Chief Engineer
Martin Jeffrey, Sales

Monterey

***WVLS**
09-01-1995; 89.7 MHz FM; *Hrs Open:* 6 AM-10 PM; 0.36 kw vert; 1460 ft.; N38 20 39 W79 35 47 *Rebroadcasts:* Rebroadcasts WVMR(AM) Frost, WV 60%
US
(540) 468-1234; *Fax:* (540) 468-123
www.alleghenymountainradio.org
License: Monterey, Highland County, VA held by Pocahontas Communications Cooperative Corp.
Arbitron Metro Market: Dunmore, WV; *Format:* Variety/Diverse; *Target Audience:* General.
Erin Will, Station Coordinator

Mount Jackson

WSIG
10-01-1988; 96.9 MHz FM; *Hrs Open:* 24; 4.3 kw; 558 ft.; N38 36 31 W78 54 7
1820 Heritage Center Way, Harrisonburg, VA 22801 USA
(540) 432-0331
969wsig.com
License: Mount Jackson, Shenandoah County, VA held by Tidewater Communications LLC
Group Owner: Saga Communications
Nat'l Network: ABC Radio News
Arbitron Metro Market: Harrisonburg, V; *Format:* Country *Special Programming:* Bluegrass 6 hrs, gospel 4 hrs wkly
Steve Davis, General Manager

WSVG
04-23-1954; 790 kHz AM; *Hrs Open:* Sunrise-sunset; 1 kw-D, ND1; 0.04 kw-N, ND1; N38 46 15 W78 37 17
P.O. Box 275, Mt. Jackson, VA 22842 US
(540) 477-4443; *Fax:* (540) 477-4407
wsvgradio.com
wsvgam@hotmail.com
License: Mount Jackson, VA held by Hometown Broadcasting of Mt. Jackson LLC
Arbitron Metro Market: Winchester, VA; *Format:* Talk
Alan Arehart, General Manager
Patty Shaffer, General Manager

Narrows

WZFM
01-01-1992; 101.3 MHz FM; 0.21 kw; 1201 ft.; N37 17 54 W80 48 36
P.O. Box 889, Blacksburg, VA 24063 US
(540) 951-9791; *Fax:* (540) 961-2021
License: Narrows, Giles County, VA held by WZFM LLC
Group Owner: Baker Family Stations; (acq 5-19-2006; $600,000).
Nat'l Network: ABC Music Radio
Arbitron Metro Market: Narrows, VA; *Format:* Classic Rock, Oldies; *Target Audience:* 30+
Edward A. Baker, President

Narrows-Pearisburg

WNRV
08-01-1953; 990 kHz AM; *Hrs Open:* 24; 5 kw-D, NDD; 0.01 kw-N, ND1; N37 20 39 W80 46 36 *Rebroadcasts:* Rebroadcast WWWR(AM) Roanoke 90%
P.O. Box 99, 1535 Narrows Road, Narrows, VA 24124 US
(540) 921-0166; *Fax:* (540) 343-2306
www.wnrvbluegrassradio.com
info@wnrvbluegrassradio.com
License: Narrows-Pearisburg, VA held by Perception Media Group Inc.
Arbitron Metro Market: Narrows, VA; *Format:* Blues
Terry Reed, President
Dennis Welch, Operations Dir
Dean Reed, General Manager

Nassawadox

***WHRX**
01-01-2005; 90.3 MHz FM; 450 w vert; Ant 199 ft; N37 33 27 W75 49 44
5200 Hampton Blvd, Norfolk, VA 23508
(757) 889-9400; *Fax:* (757) 489-0007
www.whro.org
info@whro.org
License: Nassawadox, Northampton County, VA held by Hampton Roads Telecommunications Assoc Inc
Group Owner: Positive Alternative Radio Inc.; (acq 12-7-2012)
Bert Schmidt, President
Doug Weiss, Vice President of Operations
Martha Edwards, Program Manager
Mark Burnett, Director of Production and Media

New Market

WLTK
01-01-1997; 102.9 MHz FM; *Hrs Open:* 24; 2.1 kw; 544 ft; N38 36 31 W78 54 07
58 Kenmore Street, Harrisonburg, VA 22801
(540) 896-8933; *Fax:* (540) 896-1448
License: New Market, Shenandoah County, VA held by Massanutten Broadcasting Co.
Nat'l Network: USA; *Nat'l Reps:* Salem
Population Served: 150,000; *Arbitron Metro Market:* Harrisonburg, VA; *Hrs. of News Programming:* News progmg 9 hrs wkly; *Target Audience:* 25-44.; *Adv. Rates:* 20; 17; 20; 17
David Eshelman, President
David Eshleman, General Manager
Christine Pompeo, General Sales Mgr
Greg Crabtree, Programming Director
Judy Shafer, News Director
Dave Wyant, Disc Jockey
Karen Kenney, Disc Jockey

Newport News

WGH
10-01-1928; 1310 kHz AM; *Hrs Open:* 24; 20 kw-D, DA2; 5 kw-N, DA2; N37 2 43 W76 26 54
5589 Greenwich Rd., Suite 200, Virginia Beach, VA 23462 US
(757) 671-1000; *Fax:* (757) 490-8973
www.star1310.com
theboss@star1310.com
License: Newport News, VA held by MHR License LLC
Group Owner: MAX Media L.L.C.
Arbitron Metro Market: Norfolk-Virginia Beach-Newport News, VA; *Format:* Gospel; *Target Audience:* General.
John Shomby, Operations Manager
Dave Paulus, General Manager

Carol Bryant, General Sales Mgr
Joe Britton, Promotions Director
Paul Campbell, Chief Engineer
Keith Barton, Director of Sales
Jackie Bales, Business Manager
ErinGalant, Director of Interactive Sales
Jeff Schmidt, Production Director

WGH-FM
11-01-1948; 97.3 MHz FM; 74 kw; 394 ft.; N36 57 47 W76 24 42
5589 Greenwood Rd., Suite 200, Virginia Beach, VA 23462 US
(757) 671-1000; *Fax:* (757) 671-1010
www.eagle97.com
theboss@eagle97.com
License: Newport News, VA held by MHR License LLC
Group Owner: MAX Media L.L.C.; (acq 3-24-2005; grpsl).
Arbitron Metro Market: Norfolk-Virginia Beach-Newport News, VA; *Format:* Country; *Target Audience:* Adults 25-54
John Shomby, Operations Manager
Dave Paulus, General Manager
Carol Bryant, General Sales Mgr
Joe Britton, Promotions Director
Paul Campbell, Chief Engineer
Keith Barton, Director of Sales
Jackie Bales, Business Manager
ErinGalant, Director of Interactive Sales
Jeff Schmidt, Production Director

WTJZ
11-01-1947; 1270 kHz AM; *Hrs Open:* 24
3780 Will Scarlet Road, Winston-Salem, NC 27104 US
(757) 722-2584; *Fax:* (757) 723-0820
www.lifestream.tv
wtjz1270@gmail.com
License: Newport News, VA held by Chesapeake-Portsmouth Broadcasting Corp.
Group Owner: Chesapeake-Portsmouth Broadcasting Corp.; (acq 1999; $380,000)
Arbitron Metro Market: Hampton, VA; *Format:* Gospel *Special Programming:* 5 hrs wkly; *Target Audience:* African American
Martin Culpepper, General Manager

Norfolk

WYRM
04-06-1976; 1110 kHz AM; *Hrs Open:* day; 50 kw-D, DAD; N36 56 34 W76 31 56
700 Monticello Avenue, Suite 305, Norfolk, VA 23510 US
(757) 622-9256; (888) 249-9151; *Fax:* (757) 622-9253
wyrm1110@hotmail.com
License: Norfolk, VA held by Word Broadcasting Network Inc.
Group Owner: Word Broadcasting Network Inc.; acq 7-29-2003; $1.25 million with WYMM(AM) Jacksonville, FL).
Arbitron Metro Market: Norfolk-Virginia Beach-Newport News, VA; *Format:* Religious
Larry Cobb, General Manager
Paula Cobb, Office Manager

WVXX
07-01-1954; 1050 kHz AM; 5 kw-D, DA2; 0.358 kw-N, DA2; N36 49 44 W76 12 26
700 Monticello Avenue, Suite 301, Norfolk, VA 23510 US
(757) 627-9899; *Fax:* (757) 627-0123
www.selecta1050.com
License: Norfolk, VA held by Davidson Media Station WVXX Licensee LLC.
Group Owner: Davidson Media Group LLC; (acq 2-10-2005; $975,000).
Arbitron Metro Market: Hampton Roads, VA; *Format:* Spanish; *Target Audience:* 18-54; Hispanic adults
Andy Hindlin, President

WVHT
04-29-2009; 100.5 MHz FM; *Hrs Open:* 24; 50 kw; 499 ft.; N36 49 44 W76 12 26
5589 Greenwich Rd., Suite 200, Virginia Beach, VA 23462 US
(757) 671-1000; *Fax:* (757) 671-1212
www.hot1005.com
theboss@hot1005.com
License: Norfolk, VA held by MHR License LLC.
Group Owner: MAX Media L.L.C.; (acq 3-24-2005; grpsl)
Nat'l Reps: Christal
Arbitron Metro Market: Hampton Roads, VA; *Format:* Contemporary Hits/Top 40; *Target Audience:* Adults 18-49
John Shomby, Operations Manager
Dave Paulus, General Manager
Carol Bryant, General Sales Mgr
Joe Britton, Promotions Director
Paul Campbell, Chief Engineer
Jackie Bales, Business Manager
Erin Galant, Director of InteractiveSales
Keith Barton, Director of Sales
Jeff Schmidt, Production Director

***WHRO-FM**
01-01-1990; 90.3 MHz FM; *Hrs Open:* 20; kw
5200 Hampton Boulevard, Norfolk, VA 23508 US
(757) 889-9400; *Fax:* (757) 489-0007
www.whro.org
info@whro.org
License: Norfolk, Norfolk City County, VA held by Hampton Roads Educational Telecommunications Association Inc.
Nat'l Network: NPR; PRI; *Wire Services:* AP
Arbitron Metro Market: Norfolk-Virginia Beach-Newport News, VA
TV Affiliate: *WHRO-TV affil.; *Format:* News; *Target Audience:* 35 plus; well-educated, exec leaders class
Bert Schmidt, President
Philip Perdue, Development
Sherby Wilks, Human Resources

***WHRV**
01-01-1974; 89.5 MHz FM; *Hrs Open:* 24; 34 kw; 596 ft.; N36 48 32 W76 30 13
5200 Hampton Boulevard, Norfolk, VA 23508 US
(757) 889-9400; *Fax:* (757) 489-0007
www.whro.org
info@whro.org
License: Norfolk, Norfolk City County, VA held by Hampton Roads Educational Telecommunications Association, Inc.
Nat'l Network: NPR; PRI; *Wire Services:* AP
Arbitron Metro Market: Norfolk-Virginia Beach-Newport News, VA
TV Affiliate: *WHRO-TV affil.; *Format:* Alternative, Jazz, 60, News/Talk, Talk *Special Programming:* Progsv 14 hrs, folk 7 hrs wkly *Hrs. of NewsProgramming:* news progmg 105 hrs wkly; *No. News Employees:* 1; *Target Audience:* 35 plus.
Bert Schmidt, CEO
Doug Weiss, Vice President of Operations
Virginia Thumm, General Sales Mgr
Heather Mazzon, Programming Director
Colleen Ingraham, CFO

WJOI
01-01-1949; 1230 kHz AM
870 Greenbrier Circle, Suite 399, Chesapeake, VA 23320 US
(757) 366-9900; *Fax:* (757) 366-0022
www.1230wjoi.com
License: Norfolk, VA held by Tidewater Communications LLC.
Group Owner: Saga Communications Inc.; (acq 9-15-86)
Nat'l Reps: McGavren Guild
Arbitron Metro Market: Norfolk-Virginia Beach-Newport News, VA; *Format:* Adult Contemp
Dave Paulus, President
Mike Beck, Operations Dir
Wayne Leland, General Manager
Dave Taylor, Promotions Manager
Don Crowder, Chief Engineer
Sonja Morrell, Marketing Director
Chuck Cooney, Production Manager
Laurie Bodner,Business Manager
Keri Credle, Traffic Manager

WNIS
09-21-1923; 790 kHz AM; *Hrs Open:* 24; 5 kw-U, DA1; N37 4 25 W76 17 31
500 Dominion Tower, 999 Waterside Drive, Norfolk, VA 23510 US
(757) 640-8500; (888) 756-7979; *Fax:* (757) 622-6397
www.wnis.com
jaywest@sinclairstations.com
License: Norfolk, VA held by Sinclair Communications Inc.
Group Owner: Sinclair Communications Inc.
Nat'l Network: ABC; Westwood One; *Regional Network:* Va. News Net; *Nat'l Reps:* McGavren Guild; Interep; *Wire Services:* AP
Arbitron Metro Market: Norfolk, VA; *Format:* News, News/Talk, 86; *Target Audience:* 25-54.
Bob Sinclair, CEO
Dave Morgan, Operations Dir
Lisa Sinclair, Station Manager
Juli Zobel, General Sales Mgr
Jay West, Programming Director
Donna Agresto, Promotions Manager
Ginger Power, National Sales Manager

WNOR
01-01-1961; 98.7 MHz FM; 46 kw; 518 ft.; N36 50 4 W76 16 11
870 Greenbrier Circle, Suite 399, Chesapeake, VA 23320 US
(757) 366-9900; *Fax:* (757) 366-0022
www.fm99.com
info@fm99.com
License: Norfolk, Norfolk City County, VA held by Tidewater Communications LLC.
Group Owner: Saga Communications Inc.
Arbitron Metro Market: Norfolk, VA; *Format:* Rock/AOR
Wayne Leland, General Manager
Harvey Najen, Programming Director

***WNSB**
03-22-1980; 91.1 MHz FM; 8.1 kw; 433 ft.; N36 46 32 W76 23 11
700 Park Avenue, Norfolk, VA 23504 US
(757) 823-8600; *Fax:* (757) 823-2385
wnsb@nsu.edu
License: Norfolk, Norfolk City County, VA held by Norfolk State University Board of Visitors.
Nat'l Network: NPR
Arbitron Metro Market: Norfolk, VA; *Format:* Urban Contemporary; *Target Audience:* 18-24.
Wanda Brockington, General Manager
Edward Turner, Station Manager
Douglas Perry, Programming Director

WNVZ
07-01-1967; 104.5 MHz FM; 49 kw; 479 ft.; N37 2 17.6 W76 18 28.7
236 Clearfield Avenue, Suite 206, Virginia Beach, VA 23402 US
(757) 497-2000; *Fax:* (757) 497-7158
www.z104.com
tias@entercom.com
License: Norfolk, Norfolk City County, VA held by Entercom Norfolk License LLC.
Group Owner: Entercom Communications Corp.; (acq 12-13-99; grpsl).
Nat'l Reps: D & R Radio
Arbitron Metro Market: Norfolk-Virgini *TV Affiliate:* Hip hop; *Format:* Adult Contemp *Special Programming:* News progmg one hr wkly; *No. News Employees:* 18-34; females
Dave Field, CEO
Don London, Operations Manager
Cheri Pridgen, General Sales Mgr
Mike Klein, Programming Director
Jade Kozup, Promotions Director
CFO, Cheri Pridgen
National Sales Manager, Don London
Operations Manager, SteveGodofsky
Vice President

WOWI
06-01-1948; 102.9 MHz FM; 50 kw; 472 ft.; N36 45 23 W76 23 6
1003 Norfolk Square, Norfolk, VA 23502 US
(757) 466-0009
www.103jamz.com
License: Norfolk, Norfolk City County, VA held by CC Licenses LLC.
Group Owner: iHeartMedia; (acq 1996; grpsl)
Nat'l Reps: McGavren Guild
Arbitron Metro Market: Norfolk-Virginia Beach-Newport News, VA; *Format:* Urban Contemporary; *Target Audience:* 18-34.
Derrick Martin, Market President
Matt Derrick, Operations Manager
Mike Street, Programming Director
Jay Flanagan, Digital Content Director

WTAR
09-01-1952; 850 kHz AM; *Hrs Open:* 24
999 Waterside Dr., Norfolk, VA 23510 US
(757) 640-8500; *Fax:* (757) 640-8552
License: Norfolk, VA held by Sinclair Communications Inc.
Group Owner: Sinclair Communications Inc.; (acq 9-87; $725,000;
Nat'l Reps: McGavren Guild; Interep
Arbitron Metro Market: Norfolk-Virginia Beach-Newport News, VA; *Format:* Sports; *Target Audience:* 25-54.
Bob Sinclair, CEO
Lisa Sinclair, General Manager
Juli Zobel, General Sales Mgr
Jay West, Programming Director
Donna Agresto, Promotions Manager
Ginger Power, National Sales Manager

WVKL
09-21-1961; 95.7 MHz FM; 40 kw; 879 ft.; N36 48 56 W76 28 0
10706 Beaver Dam Road, Cockeysville, MD 21030 US
(757) 497-2000; *Fax:* (757) 456-5458
www.957mb.com
info@957mb.com
License: Norfolk, Norfolk City County, VA held by Entercom Norfolk License LLC.
Group Owner: Entercom Communications Corp.; (acq 12-13-99; grpsl).
Arbitron Metro Market: Virginia Beach, VA; *Format:* Blues
David Field, CEO
Steve Godofsky, Operations Dir
Jeff Brown, General Manager
Hope Angelone, General Sales Mgr

Karen Parker-Chesson, News Director
Steve Fisher, CFO
Don London, Operations Manager
Hope Angelone, AdvertisingContact

***WYFI**
10-02-1971; 99.7 MHz FM; 50 kw; 456 ft.; N36 49 41 W76 15 5
2420 Phelps Ave., Norfolk, VA 23502 US
(800) 888-7077
www.bbnradio.org
bbn@bbnmedia.org
License: Norfolk, Norfolk City County, VA held by Bible Broadcasting Network Inc.
Group Owner: Bible Broadcasting Network; acq 12-24-70)
Arbitron Metro Market: Virginia-Norfolk-Newport, VA-NC; *Format:* Religious
Lowell Davey, President
Jason Padgett, Operations Manager

WMOV-FM
107.7 MHz FM; 15 kw; N36 48 37 W76 16 58.7
1003 Norfolk Square, Norfolk, VA 23502 US
(757) 466-0009
www.movin1077.com
License: Norfolk, Norfolk City County, VA held by CC Licenses LLC.
Group Owner: iHeartMedia
Arbitron Metro Market: Norfolk-Virginia Beach-Newport News, VA; *Format:* Adult Contemp; *Target Audience:* 18-34.
Derrick Martin, Market President
Matt Derrick, Senior Vice President of Programming
Marlon George, Senior Vice President of Sales
Nathan James, Promotions Manager
Jay Flanagan, Digital Content Director

Norton

WNVA
03-01-1946; 1350 kHz AM; 5 kw-D, ND1; 0.037 kw-N, ND1; N36 57 58 W82 35 17
US
www.markwnva.wix.com/wnvaradio
License: Norton, VA held by Radio-Wise Inc.
Regional Reps: Regnl Reps
TV Affiliate: Adult contemp; *Format:* Gospel, Religious *Special Programming:* News progmg 2 hrs wkly; *No. News Employees:* 25-65; adults & young adu; *Adv. Rates:* 7; 6.50; 7; 6

Onley-Onancock

WESR
01-23-1958; 1330 kHz AM; 5 kw-D, ND1; 0.051 kw-N, ND1; N37 43 2 W75 41 1
PO Box 460, Onley, VA 23418 US
(757) 787-3200; *Fax:* (757) 787-3819
www.shoredailynews.com
charlie@wesr.net
License: Onley-Onancock, VA held by Eastern Shore Radio Inc.
Nat'l Network: ABC; *Nat'l Reps:* Dome
Arbitron Metro Market: Onley, VA; *Format:* Country, Talk
Charles Russell, General Manager and Owner
Will Russell, Programming Director

WESR-FM
01-01-1968; 103.3 MHz FM; 50 kw; 322 ft.; N37 43 2 W75 41 1
PO Box 460, Onley, VA 23418 US
(757) 787-3200; *Fax:* (757) 787- 3819
www.shoredailynews.com
charlie@wesr.net
License: Onley-Onancock, Accomack County, VA
Nat'l Network: ABC
Arbitron Metro Market: Onley, VA; *Format:* Adult Contemp
Charles Russell, General Manager and Owner
Will Russell, Programming Director

Orange

WVCV
09-10-1949; 1340 kHz AM; 1 kw-U, ND1; N38 15 14 W78 7 15
Rebroadcasts: Simulcasts WCVA (AM) Culpeper 100%
Mailing Address: P.O. Box 271, Orange, VA 22960 US
Second Address: 207 Spicers Mill Rd., Orange, VA 22960
(540) 672-1000; *Fax:* (540) 672-0282
www.wjmafm.com
advertising@wjmafm.com
License: Orange, VA held by Piedmont Communications Inc.
Group Owner: Piedmont Communications Inc.; acq 2-18-93; $30,000 with co-located FM;
Nat'l Network: Westwood One; ABC
Arbitron Metro Market: Orange, VA; *Format:* Adult Contemp
Special Programming: Gospel 2 hrs, relg one hr, news 18 hrs wkly; *No. News Employees:* 1; *Target Audience:* 45 plus.

John Schick, President
Frank Wells, Programming Director
Kathy Campbell, Contact Rep
Elizabeth Duncan, Contact Rep

Pamplin City

***WEQP**
90.5 MHz FM; 0.08 kw; 410 ft.; N37 12 7 W78 41 31
742 Leesville Road, Lynchburg, VA 24502 US
(434)455-0306; *Fax:* (434) 239-6368
www.equipfm.org
info@equipfm.org
License: Pamplin City, Appomattox County, VA held by Airwaves for Jesus Inc.
Arbitron Metro Market: Pamplin, VA; *Format:* Religious
Art Ramos, President
Scott Paulette, Station Manager

Pennington Gap

WSWV
06-01-1959; 1570 kHz AM; *Hrs Open:* 24; 2.3 kw-D, ND1; 0.191 kw-N, ND1; N36 44 2 W83 2 34
US
(276) 546-2520; *Fax:* (276) 546-1356
www.wswv.net
sales@wswv.net
License: Pennington Gap, VA held by B C Broadcasting Co. Inc.
Nat'l Network: AP Network News; *Nat'l Reps:* Rgnl Reps
Format: Gospel; *Target Audience:* 24-54; young, working adults

WSWV-FM
01-01-1973; 105.5 MHz FM; *Hrs Open:* 24; 6 kw; 276 ft.; N36 44 2 W83 2 34
US
(276) 546-2520; *Fax:* (276) 546-1356
www.wswv.net
License: Pennington Gap, Lee County, VA
Format: Country

Petersburg

WTPS
05-07-1945; 1240 kHz AM; *Hrs Open:* 24; 1 kw-U, ND1; N37 14 1 W77 22 36
2809 Emerywood Pkwy., Suite 300, Richmond, VA 23294 US
(804) 672-9299
www.urbanpetersburg.com
License: Petersburg, VA held by Radio One Licenses LLC.
Group Owner: Radio One Inc.; (acq 7-26-99; grpsl)
Nat'l Reps: McGavren Guild
Arbitron Metro Market: Richmond, VA; *Format:* News/Talk; *Target Audience:* 25-54.
Jeff Anderson, Operations Mgr/Program Dir.
Marsha Landess, General Manager

WKJM
10-01-1966; 99.3 MHz FM; 6 kw; 328 ft.; N37 14 1 W77 22 36
2809 Emerywood Pkwy., Suite 300, Richmond, VA 23294 US
(804) 672-9299
www.kissrichmond.com
License: Petersburg, Petersburg City County, VA held by Radio One Licenses, LLC
Group Owner: Radio One Inc.
Arbitron Metro Market: Richmond, VA; *Format:* Urban Contemporary; *Target Audience:* 25-54; Black adults; *Adv. Rates:* 14; 14; 14; 14
Jeff Anderson, Operations Mgr/Program Dir.
Marsha Landess, General Manager

WARV-FM
12-01-1992; 100.3 MHz FM; 4.5 kw; 381 ft.; N37 10 55 W77 24 1 *Rebroadcasts:* Simulcast with WBBT-FM Powhatan 100%
300 Arboretum Pl., Suite 590, Richmond, VA 23236 US
(804) 327-9902; *Fax:* (804) 327-9911
www.989wolf.com
License: Petersburg, Petersburg City County, VA held by Alpha Media Licensee LLC
Group Owner: Alpha Media LLC; (acq 4-17-2014; grpsl).
Arbitron Metro Market: Petersburg, VA; *Format:* Country
Bill West, Operations Manager
Paul Johnson, Market Manager
James Levy, Director of Sales
Braden Smith, Programming Director

***WVST-FM**
07-12-1987; 91.3 MHz FM; *Hrs Open:* 19; 2.2 kw vert; 167 ft.; N37 14 15 W77 24 55
P.O. Box 9067, 130 Harris Hall, Petersburg, VA 23806 US
(804) 524-5000
www.vsu.edu/wvst

License: Petersburg, Petersburg City County, VA held by Virginia State University.
Regional Network: Va. News Net.
Arbitron Metro Market: Richmond, VA; *Format:* Jazz, Variety/Diverse *Special Programming:* Gospel 13 hrs wkly; *Target Audience:* 25 plus; general

Pocahontas

WKQB
02-01-1990; 102.9 MHz FM; *Hrs Open:* 24; 0.1 kw; Ant 1,490 ft.; N37 13 12 W81 15 20
18385 Coal Heritage Rd., Welch, WV 24801
(304) 436-2131
www.kissplaysthehits.com
License: Pocahontas, Tazewell County, VA held by West Virginia-Virginia Media LLC
Group Owner: West Virginia-Virginia Holding Co. LLC
Wire Services: AP
Population Served: 50,000 *Format:* Contemporary Hits/Top 40; *No. News Employees:* 2; *Target Audience:* 25-54.; *Adv. Rates:* 6.50; 6.50; 6.50; 6.50.
Bob Spencer, Manager

Poquoson

WUSH
04-01-2001; 106.1 MHz FM; *Hrs Open:* 24; 11 kw; 490 ft.; N36 51 39 W76 21 13
999 Waterside Drive, Suite 500, Norfolk, VA 23510 US
(757) 640-8500; *Fax:* (757) 640-8552
www.us1061.com
License: Poquoson, York County, VA held by Commonwealth Broadcasting L.L.C.
Group Owner: Sinclair Communications Inc.; (acq 8-24-2001; $1.883 million for CP)
Nat'l Reps: McGavren Guild; Interep
Arbitron Metro Market: Norfolk, VA; *Format:* Country
Lisa Sinclair, General Manager
Julie Zobel, General Sales Mgr
Brandon O'Brien, Program & Music Director
Donna Agresto-Seavey, Program & Music Director
Ginger Power, National Sales Manager
Dave Thompson, Website
Jamie Harlow,Website
Jeanette Robinson, Regional Sales Manager

Portsmouth

WGPL
01-01-1942; 1350 kHz AM; *Hrs Open:* 24; 5 kw-D, DA2; 5 kw-N, DA2; N36 53 0 W76 22 22
645 Church Street, Suite 400, Norfolk, VA 23510 US
(757) 622-4600; *Fax:* (757) 624-6515
willisradio@gmail.com
License: Portsmouth, VA held by Christian Broadcasting of Norfolk Inc.
Group Owner: Willis Broadcasting Corp.
Arbitron Metro Market: Norfolk-Virginia Beach-Newport News, VA; *Format:* Gospel; *Hrs. of News Programming:* news progmg 6 hrs wkly; *No. News Employees:* 2; *Target Audience:* W25-54.
L. E. Willis, II, CEO
Hortense Willis, President
Walter Allen Brickhouse, General Manager
Julian Joyner, Programming Director
Terry Love, Chief Engineer
Ernestine Willis, Corporate Officer
Christine Willis, Corporate Officer
Celestine Willis, Corporate Officer

WHKT
01-01-1999; 1650 kHz AM
3780 Will Scarlet Rd, Winston-Salem, NC 27104 US
(757) 488-1010; *Fax:* (757) 488-6161
License: Portsmouth, VA held by Radio Disney Group LLC.
Group Owner: ABC Inc.; (acq 6-5-2002; $1.08 million with WRJR(AM) Portsmouth).
Arbitron Metro Market: Norfolk-Virginia Beach-Newport News, VA; *Format:* Children
Colleen Dick, Assistant Director
Tom Winslow, Chief Engineer

WPCE
01-11-1964; 1400 kHz AM; *Hrs Open:* 24; 1 kw-U, ND1; N36 49 45 W76 19 23
645 Church St., Ste. 400, Norfolk, VA 23510 US
(804) 624-6523; *Fax:* (804) 624-6515
willisbroadcasting@yahoo.com
License: Portsmouth, VA held by Christian Broadcasting of Portsmouth Inc.
Group Owner: Willis Broadcasting Corp.; (acq 3-4-92; grpsl;

Arbitron Metro Market: Norfolk-Virginia Beach-Newport News, VA; *Format:* Gospel *Special Programming:* Block Programming; *Target Audience:* W 35+
L E Willis II, CEO
Hortense Willis, President
Walter Allen Brickhouse, General Manager
Julian Joyner, Programming Director
Terry Love, Chief Engineer
Ernestine Willis, Corporate Officer
Christine Willis, Corporate Officer
Celestine Willis, Corporate Officer
Shaye Southall, Program Director

WPMH
01-09-1972; 1010 kHz AM; 5 kw-D, 449 w-N, DA-2; N36 49 20 W76 26 38
2202 Jolliff Rd., Chesapeake, VA 27104
(757) 488-1010; *Fax:* (757) 488-7761
http://wpmh1010.com
License: Portsmouth, Portsmouth City County, VA held by Radio Disney Group LLC.
Group Owner: ABC Inc.; (acq 6-5-2002; $1.08 million with WHKT(AM) Portsmouth).
Population Served: 75,000; *Arbitron Metro Market:* Norfolk-Virginia Beach-Newport News, VA
Dan Gregory, Operations Manager
Colleen Dick, Assistant Manager
Tim Winslow, Chief Engineer

Pound

WDXC
01-01-1990; 102.3 MHz FM; *Hrs Open:* 24; 0.35 kw; 1316 ft.; N37 9 7 W82 38 41
12552 Orby Cantrell Highway, Pound, VA 24279 US
(276) 796-5411; *Fax:* (276) 796-5412
www.wdxcfm.com
wdxc102fm@windstream.net
License: Pound, Wise County, VA held by WDXC Radio Inc.
Arbitron Metro Market: Pound, VA; *Format:* Country; *Target Audience:* General.
Howard Cornett, President
M.K. Combs, Operations Dir
Jackie Cornett, Executive Vice President

Powhatan

WBBT-FM
01-01-1999; 107.3 MHz FM; 1.4 kw; 679 ft.; N37 30 16 W77 42 14
300 Arboretum Pl., Suite 590, Richmond, VA 23236 US
(804) 327-9902; *Fax:* (804) 327-9911
www.1073bbt.com
License: Powhatan, Powhatan County, VA held by Alpha Media Licensee LLC
Group Owner: Alpha Media LLC; (acq 4-17-2014; grpsl).
Arbitron Metro Market: Richmond, VA; *Format:* Oldies
Bill West, Operations Manager
Paul Johnson, Market Manager
James Levy, Director of Sales
Jim Conlee, Programming Director

Pulaski

WPSK-FM
12-01-1967; 107.1 MHz FM; *Hrs Open:* 24; 1.75 kw; 1207 ft.; N37 1 28 W80 44 47
7080 Lee Highway, Radford, VA 24141 US
(540) 731-6000; *Fax:* (540) 731-6074
www.107countrypsk.com
License: Pulaski, Pulaski County, VA held by Cumulus Licensing LLC.
Group Owner: Cumulus Media Inc.; (acq 3-31-2004; grpsl).
Format: Country; *Hrs. of News Programming:* news progmg 10 hrs wkly; *No. News Employees:* 1; *Target Audience:* 25-54.
Scott Stevens, Operations Dir
Sarah Leftwich, General Manager
Sam Parks, Chief Engineer

Quantico

WURA
920 kHz AM
14416 Jefferson Davis Highway, Suite 11, Woodbridge, VA 22192 US
(703) 490-0920; *Fax:* (202) 728-0354
www.radiounida920.com
License: Quantico, VA held by Prince William Broadcasting L.L.C.
Arbitron Metro Market: Quantico, VA
Matthew McCormick, General Manager
Second Amin, Programming Director

Radford

WWBU
01-01-1965; 101.7 MHz FM; 5.8 kw; 66 ft.; N37 8 33 W80 34 39
7080 Lee Highway, Radford, VA 24141 US
(540) 731-6000; *Fax:* (540) 731-6074
www.supersports1017.com
License: Radford, Montgomery County, VA
Arbitron Metro Market: Radford, VA; *Format:* Talk
Sarah Leftwich, General Manager

WRAD
01-01-1950; 1460 kHz AM; *Hrs Open:* 5 AM-11 PM; 5 kw-D, DAN; 0.5 kw-N, DAN; N37 8 35 W80 34 38
Mailing Address: 7080 Lee Highway, Radford, VA 22141 US
Second Address: 7080 Lee Hwy., Radford, VA 24141
(540) 731-6000; *Fax:* (540) 731-6074
License: Radford, VA held by Cumulus Licensing LLC.
Group Owner: Cumulus Media Inc.; (acq 3-31-2004; grpsl).
Format: Sports, Oldies; *Target Audience:* 25 plus.
Ron Walton, General Manager
Scott Stevens, General Sales Mgr
David Dalesky, Chief Engineer

***WVRU-FM**
10-09-1978; 89.9 MHz FM; *Hrs Open:* 24; 0.5 kw; 16 ft.; N37 8 26 W80 33 11
Mailing Address: P.O. Box 6973, Radford, VA 24142 US
Second Address: 236 Porterfield, Radford, VA 24142
(540) 831-6059; *Fax:* (540) 831-5893
www.wvru.org
wvru@radford.edu
License: Radford, Montgomery County, VA held by Radford University.
Nat'l Network: PRI
Arbitron Metro Market: Radford, VA; *Format:* Jazz, Triple A
Special Programming: Jazz 19 hrs, class 15 hrs, Black 6 hrs, folk one hr; *Hrs. of News Programming:* News progmg 6 hrs wkly; *Target Audience:* General.
Jonathan Benfield, Operations Dir
Ashlee Claud, General Manager
Randy McCallister, Engineering Dir
Sandy Schronce, Office Manager

Richlands

WGTH
10-05-1951; 540 kHz AM; *Hrs Open:* 24; 1 kw-D, 97 w-N; N37 05 01 W81 46 58
Box 370, Richlands, VA 24641
(276) 964-2502; *Fax:* (276) 964-4500
License: Richlands, Tazewell County, VA held by High Knob Broadcasters Inc.
Nat'l Network: Salem Radio Network
Population Served: 50,000; *Arbitron Metro Market:* Bluefield, WV; *Hrs. of News Programming:* News progmg 7 hrs wkly; *Target Audience:* General.; *Adv. Rates:* Same as FM
Ron Brown, General Manager

WGTH-FM
01-03-1977; 105.5 MHz FM; *Hrs Open:* 24; 0.45 kw; 801 ft.; N37 9 20 W81 46 11
P.O. Drawer 370, Richlands, VA 24641 US
(276) 964-2502; *Fax:* (276) 964-4500
www.wgth.net
wgth@wgth.net
License: Richlands, Tazewell County, VA held by High Knob Broadcasters Inc.
Nat'l Network: Salem Radio Network
Arbitron Metro Market: Bluefield, WV; *Format:* Gospel, Religious; *Hrs. of News Programming:* News progmg 6 hrs wkly; *Target Audience:* General.; *Adv. Rates:* 10; 6; 10; 6
Ron Brown, President
Eric Miller, Operations Dir
Charlene Pinkerton, General Sales Mgr
Mike Luttrel, Chief Engineer

WRIC-FM
11-01-1989; 97.7 MHz FM; *Hrs Open:* 24; 3.2 kw; 751 ft.; N37 9 4 W81 53 56
Mailing Address: #1 Radio Lane, Princeton, WV 24740 US
Second Address: 201 Suffolk Ave, Suite 210, Richlands, VA 24641
(304) 425-2151; (855)-782-7959; *Fax:* (304) 487-2016
www.star95.com
wric@netscope.net
License: Richlands, Tazewell County, VA held by Peggy Sue Broadcasting Corp.
Group Owner: Peggy Sue Broadcasting Corp.; acq 12-1-98; $190,000).
Nat'l Network: USA; *Regional Network:* Va. News Net.
Arbitron Metro Market: Bluefield, WV; *Format:* Adult Contemp; *Hrs. of News Programming:* news progmg 2 hrs wkly; *No. News Employees:* 3; *Target Audience:* 24-54; young adult professionals; *Adv. Rates:* 14; 12;12; 8
Dirk Hall, President
Sue Hall, Operations Dir
Matthew Caudill, Chief Engineer
Dave Mann, Chief of Operations

Richmond

***WCVE-FM**
05-06-1988; 88.9 MHz FM; 17.5 kw horiz; 840 ft.; N37 34 0 W77 28 36
23 Sesame Street, North Chesterfield, VA 23235 US
(804) 320-1301; (800)-476-2357; *Fax:* (804) 320-8729
www.ideastations.org/radio
mlloyd@ideastations.org
License: Richmond, Richmond City County, VA held by Commonwealth Public Broadcasting Corp.
Nat'l Network: NPR; PRI; *Wire Services:* AP
Arbitron Metro Market: Richmond, VA *TV Affiliate:* *WCVE-TV affil.; *Format:* Classical, News, 62, Talk *Special Programming:* Folk 6 hrs, blues 3 hrs, jazz 18 hrs wkly; *Hrs. of News Programming:* news progmg 35 hrswkly; *No. News Employees:* 1; *Target Audience:* 35 plus.
Bill Miller, Operations Dir
Lisa Tait, General Sales Mgr
Peter Solomon, Operations Manager

***WDCE**
09-07-1977; 90.1 MHz FM; *Hrs Open:* 24; 0.1 kw; 85 ft.; N37 34 48 W77 32 35
35 North Court Basement, University of Richmond, Richmond, VA 23173 US
(804) 289-8698; *Fax:* (804) 289-8996
www.wdce.org
License: Richmond, Richmond City County, VA held by University of Richmond.
Arbitron Metro Market: Richmond, VA; *Format:* Variety/Diverse
Special Programming: Class 3 hrs, jazz 9 hrs, relg 3 hrs wkly; *Hrs. of News Programming:* News progmg 3 hrs wkly; *Target Audience:* 15-30.
Marielle Jones, General Manager
Will Johnson, Programming Director
Steven Thompson, Promotions Manager

WFTH
06-16-1964; 1590 kHz AM; 5 kw-D, ND1; 0.019 kw-N, ND1; N37 30 2 W77 27 28
P.O. Box 24625, Richmond, VA 23224 US
(804) 233-0765; *Fax:* (804) 233-3725
License: Richmond, VA held by Tri-City Christian Radio Inc.
Arbitron Metro Market: Richmond, VA; *Format:* Gospel
Jack Johnson, President
Mary Johnson, Operations Dir
Shawn Nicholson, General Manager

WKJS
01-01-1996; 105.7 MHz FM; 2.3 kw; 531 ft.; N37 30 52 W77 30 28 *Rebroadcasts:* 100% simulcast 99.3& 105.7(WKJM)
2809 Emerywood Pkwy., Suite 300, Richmond, VA 23294 US
(804) 672-9299
www.kissrichmond.com
License: Richmond, Richmond City County, VA held by Radio One Licenses LLC.
Group Owner: Radio One Inc.; (acq 11-8-2001; grpsl).
Nat'l Network: ABC; *Nat'l Reps:* Eastman Radio
Arbitron Metro Market: Richmond, VA; *Format:* Urban Contemporary; *Target Audience:* 25-54; general
Jeff Anderson, Operations Mgr/Program Dir.
Marsha Landess, General Manager

WVNZ
09-01-1955; 1320 kHz AM; *Hrs Open:* 24; 5 kw-D, DA2; 0.008 kw-N, DA2; N37 28 0 W77 27 8
308 West Broad Street, Richmond, VA 23220 US
(804) 643-0990; *Fax:* (804) 643-4990
www.selecta1320.com
jjacobs@davidsonmediagroup.com
License: Richmond, VA held by Davidson Media Station WVNZ Licensee LLC.
Group Owner: Davidson Media Group LLC; (acq 5-13-2005; grpsl)
Nat'l Network: ABC
Arbitron Metro Market: Richmond, VA; *Hrs. of News Programming:* news progmg 15 hrs wkly; *No. News Employees:* 3; *Target Audience:* 25 plus; Hispanic population; *Adv. Rates:* 55; 45; 50; 20
Felix Perez, President
Tim Hurley, Operations Dir
Jim Jacobs, General Manager

Carolyn Resendiz, General Sales Mgr
Selvin Paredes, Programming Director

WURV(FM)
12-23-1961; 103.7 MHz FM; *Hrs Open:* 24; 18.5 kw; 750 ft; N37 30 31 W77 34 37
812 Moorefield Park Dr., Suite 300, Richmond, VA 23236
(804) 330-5700; *Fax:* (804) 330-4079,(804) 323-1524 sls
License: Richmond, Richmond City County, VA held by SM-WURV LLC
Group Owner: SummitMedia Inc.; (acq 8-00; grpsl).
Nat'l Network: ABC; *Nat'l Reps:* McGavren Guild
Population Served: 766,100; *Arbitron Metro Market:* Richmond, VA; *Hrs. of News Programming:* news progmg 8 hrs wkly; *No. News Employees:* 1; *Target Audience:* 25-54; predominately female
James Kennedy, COO
Bob Willoughby, General Manager
Amy DeVries, General Sales Mgr
Fisher, Programming Director

WBTJ
05-01-1957; 106.5 MHz FM; *Hrs Open:* 24; 14.5 kw; 919 ft.; N37 30 45 W77 36 5.7
3425 Basie Road, Richmond, VA 23228 US
(804) 474-0000; *Fax:* (804) 474-0167
www.1065thebeat.com
License: Richmond, Richmond City County, VA held by Capstar TX LLC
Group Owner: iHeartMedia; (acq 8-30-00; grpsl).
Nat'l Reps: Christal
Arbitron Metro Market: Richmond, VA; *Format:* Blues, Urban Contemporary; *Hrs. of News Programming:* news progmg 5 hrs wkly; *No. News Employees:* 1; *Target Audience:* 18-44.; *Adv. Rates:* 85; 100; 75; 75
Dave Carwile, Market President
Brett Pomykala, General Sales Mgr
Mike Street, Programming Director
Jasmine Snead, Promotions Director
Kim Hutcheson, Traffic Manager

WREJ
05-08-1964; 1540 kHz AM; *Hrs Open:* 24; 10 kw-D, DA2; 0.007 kw-N, DA2; N37 37 8 W77 25 27
308 West Broad Street, Richmond, VA 23220 US
(804) 643-0990; *Fax:* (804) 474-5070
www.rejoice1540.com
License: Richmond, VA held by Davidson Media Station WREJ Licensee LLC.
Group Owner: Davidson Media Group LLC; (acq 5-13-2005; grpsl)
Nat'l Network: ABC
Arbitron Metro Market: Richmond, VA; *Format:* Religious; *No. News Employees:* 1; *Target Audience:* 35-64; African-American concerned about financial, civic & economic issues; *Adv. Rates:* 40; 30; 30; 15
Felix Perez, President
Tim Hurley, Operations Dir
Jim Jacobs, General Manager
Bryan Hill, General Sales Mgr
B.L. Westbrook, Programming Director

WRNL
11-15-1937; 910 kHz AM; *Hrs Open:* 24; 5 kw-D, DAN; 1.5 kw-N, DAN; N37 36 50 W77 30 53
3425 Basie Road, Richmond, VA 23228 US
(804) 474-0000; *Fax:* (804) 474-0167
www.foxsportsrichmond.com
License: Richmond, VA held by CC Licenses LLC.
Group Owner: iHeartMedia; (acq 8-10-93; $9.75 million with co-located FM;
Regional Network: Va. News Net.
Arbitron Metro Market: Richmond, VA; *Format:* Sports; *Target Audience:* 25-54; men
Dave Carwile, Market President
Brett Pomykala, General Sales Mgr
Aaron Trimmer, Programming Director

WRVA
11-02-1925; 1140 kHz AM; *Hrs Open:* 24; 50 kw-U, DA1; N37 24 13 W77 18 59
3245 Basie Road, Richmond, VA 23228 US
(804) 474-0000; *Fax:* (804) 474-0167
www.1140wrva.com
License: Richmond, VA held by CC Licenses LLC.
Group Owner: iHeartMedia; (acq 6-26-92; grpsl;
Nat'l Network: ABC; *Nat'l Reps:* Clear Channel
Arbitron Metro Market: Richmond, VA; *Format:* News, News/Talk, 86 *Special Programming:* Relg 10 hrs, computers 2 hrs, gardening 3 hrs, hom; *Hrs. of News Programming:* news progmg 24 hrs wkly; *No. News Employees:* 10 *Target Audience:* 35-54.
Dave Carwile, Market President
Stacey Trexler, General Sales Mgr
Aaron Trimmer, Programming Director
Aaron Sutten, Promotions Director

WRVQ
08-04-1948; 94.5 MHz FM; 200 kw; 351 ft.; N37 24 13 W77 18 59
3245 Basie Road, Richmond, VA 23228 US
(804) 474-0000; *Fax:* (804) 474-0090
www.q94radio.com
License: Richmond, Richmond City County, VA held by CC Licenses LLC.
Group Owner: iHeartMedia
Nat'l Network: ABC
Arbitron Metro Market: Richmond, VA; *Format:* Contemporary Hits/Top 40; *Target Audience:* 18-44; women
Dave Carwile, Market President
Stacey Trexler, General Sales Mgr
Jasmine Snead, Promotions Director

WRXL
03-04-1949; 102.1 MHz FM; *Hrs Open:* 24; 20 kw; 791 ft.; N37 36 52 W77 30 56
3245 Basie Road, Richmond, VA 23228 US
(804) 474-0000; *Fax:* (804) 474-0092
www.xl102richmond.com
License: Richmond, Richmond City County, VA held by CC Licenses LLC.
Group Owner: iHeartMedia
Arbitron Metro Market: Richmond, VA; *Format:* Alternative; *Target Audience:* 25-44.
Dave Carwile, Market President
Brett Pomykala, General Sales Mgr
Dustin Fletcher, Programming Director
Nikki Corl, Promotions Director

WBTK
09-01-1926; 1380 kHz AM; *Hrs Open:* 24 hrs/7 days a week; 5 kw-U, DA-2; N37 37 13 W77 26 57
2809 Emerywood Parkway, Suite 540, Richmond, VA 23294 US
(804) 353-8544; *Fax:* (804) 353-8549
www.wbtk.com
License: Richmond, Richmond City County, VA held by Mount Rich Media LLC.
Group Owner: Mountain Broadcasting Corp.; (acq 5-30-2006; $1.5 million).
Nat'l Network: CNN en Espanol
Population Served: 205,533; *Arbitron Metro Market:* Richmond, VA *Special Programming:* CNN en Espanol & local programming; *Target Audience:* Hispanic A25-54
Glen Motto, Operations Dir

WTVR-FM
02-01-1946; 98.1 MHz FM; 50 kw horiz; 840 ft.; N37 34 0 W77 28 36
3245 Basie Rd., Richmond, VA 23228 US
(804) 474-0000; *Fax:* (804) 474-0167
www.lite98.com
License: Richmond, Richmond City County, VA held by CC Licenses LLC.
Group Owner: iHeartMedia; (acq 1996; $18 million with co-located AM).
Nat'l Reps: Clear Channel
Arbitron Metro Market: Richmond, VA; *Format:* Adult Contemp
Dave Carwile, Market President
Stacey Trexler, General Sales Mgr
Nikki Corl, Promotions Director

WLEE
05-04-1951; 990 kHz AM; *Hrs Open:* 24; 1 kw-D, ND1; 0.013 kw-N, ND1; N37 31 40 W77 22 48
308 West Broad Street, Richmond, VA 23220 US
(804) 643-0990; *Fax:* (804) 643-4990
License: Richmond, VA held by Davidson Media Station WLEE Licensee LLC.
Group Owner: Davidson Media Group LLC; (acq 5-13-2005; grpsl)
Nat'l Network: CNN Radio; CBS
Arbitron Metro Market: Richmond, VA; *Format:* News, News/Talk, 86; *Target Audience:* 25-64; white collar, upscale professionals; *Adv. Rates:* 40; 35; 40; 15
Felix Perez, President
Tim Hurley, Operations Dir
Jim Jacobs, General Manager
Bryan Hill, General Sales Mgr

WXGI
10-01-1947; 950 kHz AM; *Hrs Open:* 5:30 AM-midnight; 3.9 kw-D, ND1; 0.045 kw-N, ND1; N37 30 52 W77 30 28
701 German School Rd, Richmond, VA 23225 US
(804) 233-7666; *Fax:* (804) 233-7681
espn950am.com
buck@redskins.com
License: Richmond, VA held by Red Zebra Broadcasting Licensee (Richmond) LLC.
Group Owner: Red Zebra Holdings LLC; (acq 9-27-2006; $1.4 million)
Nat'l Network: ESPN Radio; *Wire Services:* AP
Arbitron Metro Market: Richmond, VA; *Format:* Sports; *Target Audience:* 30 plus.
Buck Albritton, General Manager
Scott Hawthorne, Sales Manager
Mitchell Bradley, Operations/Programming/Production Director

***WRIH**
01-01-2007; 88.1 MHz FM; 5 kw vert; 479 ft.; N37 42 54 W77 21 55 *Rebroadcasts:* Rebroadcasts WAFR(FM) Tupelo, MS 100%
P.O. Box 3206, Tupelo, MS 38803 US
(662) 844-8888; *Fax:* (662) 842-6791
www.afr.net
faq@afa.net
License: Richmond, Henrico County, VA held by American Family Association.
Group Owner: American Family Radio
Nat'l Network: American Family Radio
Arbitron Metro Market: Richmond, VA; *Format:* Christian
Tim Wildmon, President
Donald Wildmon, Founder
Buddy Smith, Sr VP
Ed Vitagliano, Exec VP
Randy Sharp, Director Of Special Projects
Meeke Addison, Director Of Communications
Abraham Hamilton III, General Counsel

Roanoke

WFIR
06-20-1924; 960 kHz AM; *Hrs Open:* 24
Mailing Address: 3934 Electric Road, Roanoke, VA 24018 US
Second Address: Box 92, Roanoke, VA 24022
(540) 345-1511; *Fax:* (504) 342-2270
www.wfir960.com
License: Roanoke, VA held by Mel Wheeler Inc.
Group Owner: Mel Wheeler Inc.; acq 3-31-00; with co-located FM).
Nat'l Network: ABC; Fox News Radio; *Nat'l Reps:* Katz Radio
Arbitron Metro Market: Roanoke, VA; *Format:* News, News/Talk, 86; *No. News Employees:* 4; *Target Audience:* 25-54; adult, skewed male 35-54
Anne Booze, General Sales Mgr
Jim Murphy, Programming Director
Jim Kent, News Director
Velvet Hall, Producer

WGMN
01-01-1946; 1240 kHz AM; 1 kw-U, ND1; N37 16 12 W79 58 14
Mailing Address: P.O. Box 348, Forest, VA 24551 US
Second Address: 1035 Avalon Drive, Forest, VA 24551
(434) 534-6100; *Fax:* (434) 534-6101
www.espninva.com
wblt@inbox.com
License: Roanoke, VA held by 3 Daughters Media Inc.
Group Owner: 3 Daughters Media Inc.; (acq 6-22-2007; grpsl)
Nat'l Network: ESPN Radio; *Regional Network:* Va. News Net;
Nat'l Reps: D & R Radio
Arbitron Metro Market: Roanoke-Lynchburg, VA; *Format:* Sports; *Target Audience:* 25-54.
Gary Burns, CEO
Gary Burns, President
Ashley Schamerhorn, Operations Dir
Randy Thompson, Vice President
Melinda Schamerhorn, Business & Traffic Director
Jonny Fairplay, Account Executive

WSLC-FM
11-01-1948; 94.9 MHz FM; *Hrs Open:* 24; 98 kw; 1982 ft.; N37 11 50 W80 9 11
Mailing Address: 3934 Elecric Road, Roanoke, VA 24002 US
Second Address: Box 92, Roanoke, VA 24022
(540) 774-0102; *Fax:* (540) 774-5667
www.949starcountry.com
License: Roanoke, Roanoke City County, VA
Group Owner: Mel Wheeler Inc.
Nat'l Reps: Katz Radio
Arbitron Metro Market: Roanoke-Lynchburg, VA; *Format:* Country; *Target Audience:* 25-54.
Stan Reynolds, General Sales Mgr
Brett Sharp, Programming Director
Rachel Rodes, Promotions Manager

WJJS
11-01-1993; 104.9 MHz FM; *Hrs Open:* 24; 14.5 kw; 925 ft.; N37 22 23 W79 55 40
3807 Brandon Ave., Suite 2350, Roanoke, VA 24018 US
(434) 385-8298; *Fax:* (434) 385-8991
www.wjjs.com
License: Roanoke, Roanoke City County, VA held by Capstar TX LLC
Group Owner: iHeartMedia; (acq 8-30-2000; grpsl)
Arbitron Metro Market: Roanoke-Lynchburg, VA; *Format:* Contemporary Hits/Top 40; *No. News Employees:* 2
Sarah Leftwich, Market Manager
Tammy Cazad, General Sales Mgr

WRTZ
02-28-1953; 1410 kHz AM; *Hrs Open:* 24; 5 kw-D, ND1; 0.072 kw-N, ND1; N37 16 47 W79 59 29
Mailing Address: 219 Luckett Street, NW, P.O. Box 6099, Roanoke, VA 24017 US
Second Address: 219 Luckett St. N.W., Roanoke, VA 24017
(540) 342-1410,(540) 342-7811; *Fax:* (540) 342-5952
License: Roanoke, VA held by Metromedia Broadcasting LC
Regional Network: Va. News Net.
Arbitron Metro Market: Roanoke-Lynchburg, VA; *Format:* Religious; *No. News Employees:* 1; *Target Audience:* 35-75.
Russ Brown, Operations Dir

***WRXT**
07-31-1994; 90.3 MHz FM; 5.5 kw; 1112 ft.; N37 23 9 W79 40 10
22226 Timberlake Road, Lynchburg, VA 24502 US
(434) 237-9798; *Fax:* (434) 237-1025
www.spiritfm.com
office@spiritfm.com
License: Roanoke, Roanoke City County, VA held by Positive Alternative Radio Inc.
Group Owner: Positive Alternative Radio Inc.; (acq 4-15-2002)
Arbitron Metro Market: Roanoke-Lynchbu; *Format:* Religious
Colleen Larkins, Assistant Manager
Marc Tischart, Programming Director
Jackie Howard, Director of Operations

WVBE
10-01-1940; 610 kHz AM; *Hrs Open:* 24; 5 kw-D, DA2; 1 kw-N, DA2; N37 18 11 W80 2 33 *Rebroadcasts:* Rebroadcasts WVBE Lynchburg 100%
Mailing Address: 5009 South Hulen, Suite 101, Fort Worth, TX 76132 US
Second Address: Box 92, Roanoke, VA 24022
(540) 989-4591; *Fax:* (540) 774-5667
www.vibe100.com
sreynolds@wheelerbroadcasting.com
License: Roanoke, VA held by Mel Wheeler Inc.
Group Owner: Mel Wheeler Inc.; (acq 10-1-76).
Nat'l Reps: Katz Radio
Arbitron Metro Market: Roanoke-Lynchbu; *Format:* Urban Contemporary; *Target Audience:* Adult 25-54; skew female, skew black
Stan Reynolds, General Sales Mgr
Walt Ford, Programming Director

WSLQ
11-01-1947; 99.1 MHz FM; *Hrs Open:* 24; 150 kw; 1991 ft.; N37 11 41 W80 9 22
Mailing Address: 3934 Electric Road Southwest, Roanoke, VA 24018 US
Second Address: Box 92, Roanoke, VA 24018
(540) 387-0234; *Fax:* (540) 389-0837
www.q99fm.com
License: Roanoke, Roanoke City County, VA held by Mel Wheeler Inc.
Group Owner: Mel Wheeler Inc.
Nat'l Reps: Katz Radio
Arbitron Metro Market: Roanoke-Lynchbu; *Format:* Adult Contemp; *Hrs. of News Programming:* News progmg 1 hr wkly; *Target Audience:* 25-54; skew female
Anne Booze, General Sales Mgr
Kevin Scott, Programming Director
Lauren Smith, Promotions Manager

***WVTF**
08-01-1973; 89.1 MHz FM; *Hrs Open:* 24; 100 kw; 1969 ft.; N37 11 56 W80 9 2
3520 Kingsbury Lane, Roanoke, VA 24014 US
(540) 989-8900; *Fax:* (540) 776-2727
www.wvtf.org
info@wvtf.org
License: Roanoke, Roanoke City County, VA held by Virginia Tech Foundation Inc.
Nat'l Network: PRI; NPR; *Regional Network:* Va. News Net.
Arbitron Metro Market: Roanoke, VA; *Format:* Jazz; *Hrs. of News Programming:* news progmg 39 hrs wkly; *No. News Employees:* 8; *Target Audience:* General.
Glenn Gleixner, General Manager
Karen Dillon, General Sales Mgr
Rick Mattoni, Programming Director
Connie Stevens, News Director
Bart Prater, Traffic Director
Cynthia Gray, Development Director
Mary Grace Franchi, BusinessManager
Brian Black, Administrative Assistant
Ben Martin, Operations Assistant & Producer/Radio Reading Serv

WFJX
04-01-1957; 910 kHz AM; *Hrs Open:* 24; 1 kw-D, 84 w-N; N37 16 06 W79 54 46
1848 Clay St. S.E., Roanoke, VA 24013
(540) 343-7109; *Fax:* (540) 343-2306
foxradioroanoke.com
License: Roanoke, Roanoke City County, VA held by Perception Media Group Inc.
Nat'l Network: USA
Arbitron Metro Market: Roanoke-Lynchburg, VA; *Target Audience:* 35-64.
Ben Peyton, President
Sharron Jeffrey, Station Manager
Martin Jeffrey, General Sales Mgr
Howie McKinney, Programming Director
Dale Cook, Chief Engineer

WXLK
12-17-1960; 92.3 MHz FM; 100 kw; 1985 ft.; N37 11 51 W80 9 10
Mailing Address: 5009 South Hulen, Suite 101, Fort Worth, TX 76132 US
Second Address: 3934 Electric Rd. S.W., Roanoke, VA 24018
(540) 774-9200; *Fax:* (540) 774-5667
www.k92radio.com
sreynolds@wheelerbroadcasting.com
License: Roanoke, Roanoke City County, VA held by Mel Wheeler Inc.
Group Owner: Mel Wheeler Inc.; acq 3-12-97; $7.5 million with WVBE-FM Lynchburg).
Arbitron Metro Market: Roanoke, VA; *Format:* Contemporary Hits/Top 40; *Target Audience:* 18-44; women
Stan Wheeler, Sales Manager
Sandra Pratt, Director of Community Affairs

Rocky Mount

WYTI
03-31-1957; 1570 kHz AM; *Hrs Open:* 6 AM-9 PM; 2.5 kw-D, 220 w-N; N36 58 37 W79 53 45
Mailing Address: Box430, Rocky Mount, VA 24151
Second Address: 275 Glenwood Dr, Rocky Mount, VA 24151
(540) 483-9955,(540) 483-2166; *Fax:* (540) 483-7802
www.wytiradio.com
wyti@wytiradio.com
License: Rocky Mount, Franklin County, VA held by WYTI Inc.
Nat'l Network: ABC
Population Served: 37,500 *Special Programming:* NASCAR races, relg 10 hrs wkly; *Target Audience:* 30 plus; general; *Adv. Rates:* 11.29; 11.29; 11.29; 5.64
William Jefferson, President
Susan Mullins, Operations Director/Vice President
Susan Mullins, General Manager
Susan Mullins, Station Manager
Susan Mullins, General Sales Mgr
Bill Jefferson, Programming Director
Susan Mullins,Promotions Manager
Jesse Ramsey, News Director
Carl Castillo, Engineering Dir
Scott Gardener, Chief Engineer
Susan Mullins, Executive Vice President

Ruckersville

WHTE-FM
03-29-1990; 101.9 MHz FM; *Hrs Open:* 24; 6 kw; 223 ft.; N38 18 5 W78 31 57
1150 Pepsi Place, Charlotte, NC 22901 US
(434) 978-4408; *Fax:* (434) 978-0723
www.1019hot.com
License: Ruckersville, Greene County, VA held by Monticello Media LLC.
Group Owner: Monticello Media LLC; (acq 10-4-2007; grpsl)
Nat'l Reps: Christal
Arbitron Metro Market: Charlottesville, VA; *Format:* Contemporary Hits/Top 40; *Hrs. of News Programming:* News progmg 5 hrs wkly; *Target Audience:* 18-24.
Vinnie Kice, Operations Dir
Dennis Mockler, General Manager
Mike Chiumento, General Sales Mgr
P.J. Styles, Programming Director
Steve Gaines, Market Manager
Vinnie Kice, Operations Manager
Mike Chiumento, Sales Manager

Rural Retreat

WLOY
05-15-1985; 660 kHz AM; *Hrs Open:* Daytime; 0.55 kw-D, NDD; 90.2 meters; N36 55 17 W81 14 34
P.O. Box 660, Rural Retreat, VA 24368 US
(410) 617-1620; *Fax:* (276) 228-9261
wloy@loyola.edu
License: Rural Retreat, VA held by Three Rivers Media Corp.
Group Owner: Three Rivers Media Corp.; (acq 10-16-2006; $125,000)
Nat'l Reps: Rgnl Reps
Arbitron Metro Market: Rural Retreat-Wythe County, VA; *Format:* News, Sports, 86; *No. News Employees:* 1; *Target Audience:* 25-54.; *Adv. Rates:* 15; 15; 15; 15
Gary W.Hagerich, President
Christa Constantine, General Manager
Kate Marshall, Programming Director
Molly Dressel, Promotions Manager

WXBX
06-11-1992; 95.3 MHz FM; *Hrs Open:* 24; 6 kw; 190 ft.; N36 55 17 W81 14 34
110 West Spiller Street, Wytheville, PA 24382 US
(276) 228-3185; *Fax:* (276) 228-9261
office@threeriversmedia.net
License: Rural Retreat, Wythe County, VA held by Three Rivers Media Corp.
Group Owner: Three Rivers Media Corp.; (acq 10-01-98; $200,000)
Nat'l Network: AP Network News; Jones Radio Networks
Regional Reps: Rgnl Reps
Arbitron Metro Market: Wytheville, VA; *Format:* Oldies; *Hrs. of News Programming:* news progmg 12 hrs wkly; *No. News Employees:* 1; *Target Audience:* 25 plus.; *Adv. Rates:* 24; 24; 24; 24
Gary Hagerich, CEO
Kristy Wrobel, News Director
Misty Pack, Sales and Office Staff
Deborah Crigger, Sales and Office Staff
Jerry Stone, Sales and Office Staff
Danny Gordon, Sales and Office Staff

Rustburg

***WWEM**
91.7 MHz FM; 1.15 kw; 748 ft.; N37 17 7 W79 5 26
830 Gunnery Hill Road, Spotsylvania, VA 22553 US
(540) 582-9700
www.classicradio.org
License: Rustburg, Campbell County, VA held by Educational Media Corp.
Arbitron Metro Market: Rustburg, VA; *Format:* Variety/Diverse
Peter Stover, President

Salem

WSNV
03-07-1969; 93.5 MHz FM; *Hrs Open:* 24; 5.8 kw; 98 ft.; N37 16 47 W79 59 29
3807 Brandon Avenue, Suite 2350, Roanoke, VA 24018 US
(540) 725-1220; *Fax:* (540) 725-1245
www.mysunnyfm.com
stevencross@clearchannel.com
License: Salem, Salem City County, VA held by Aloha Station Trust LLC
Nat'l Network: Westwood One
Arbitron Metro Market: Roanoke-Lynchburg, VA; *Format:* Adult Contemp; *Hrs. of News Programming:* News progmg one hr wkly; *Target Audience:* 24 plus.
Dave Carwile, General Manager
Tammy Cazad, General Sales Mgr
Steve Cross, Programming Director
Ed Kilbane, News Director

***WPAR**
04-01-1994; 91.3 MHz FM; *Hrs Open:* 24; 3.3 kw; 886 ft.; N37 22 23 W79 55 37
22226 Timberlake Road, Lynchburg, VA 24502 US
(434) 237-9798; *Fax:* (434) 237-1025
www.spiritfm.com
mail@spiritfm.com
License: Salem, Salem City County, VA held by Positive Alternative Radio Inc.

Group Owner: Positive Alternative Radio Inc.; (acq 5-90;
Nat'l Network: USA
Arbitron Metro Market: Roanoke-Lynchburg, VA; *Format:* Adult Contemp, Christian; *Target Audience:* 25-54; adults with families
Mark Tischart, General Manager

WTOY
09-07-1956; 1480 kHz AM; 5 kw-D, ND1; 0.02 kw-N, ND1; N37 16 21 W80 4 52
504 23rd St, N.W., Roanoke, VA 24017 US
(540) 344-9869; *Fax:* (540) 344-0976
License: Salem, VA held by Ward Broadcasting Corp.
Arbitron Metro Market: Roanoke,VA; *Format:* Urban Contemporary
Irving Ward Sr., Owner
Daniel Ellington, Programming Director

Saltville

WXMY
11-05-1981; 1600 kHz AM; *Hrs Open:* 6 AM-sunset; 5 kw-D; N36 51 43 W81 43 29
Route 2 28-B, Clintwood, VA 24228
(540) 496-0016; *Fax:* (540) 496-0005
www.heartofbluegrass.com
1600wxmy@gmail.com
License: Saltville, Smyth County, VA held by Continental Media Group LLC
Target Audience: 25-54.

Smithfield

WKGM
12-18-1974; 940 kHz AM; *Hrs Open:* 24; 10 kw-D, 3.1 kw-N; N37 5 51 W76 40 16
P.O. Box 339, Smithfield, VA 23431 US
(757) 357-9546
yourministrystation.com
License: Smithfield, Isle of Wight County, VA held by WKGM Inc.
Group Owner: Baker Family Stations
Arbitron Metro Market: Norfolk-Virginia Beach-Newport News, VA; *Format:* Religious *Special Programming:* Farm 2 hrs, Ger one hr, Sp one hr, gospel 5 hrs wk; *Hrs. of News Programming:* News progmg one hr wkly *TargetAudience:* 25 plus.
T.R. Bumgardner, Station Manager

South Boston

WHLF
09-01-1992; 95.3 MHz FM; *Hrs Open:* 24; 6 kw; 246 ft.; N36 42 24 W78 55 28
Mailing Address: P.O. Box 526, South Boston, VA 24592 US
Second Address: 1210 Porter Ln, South Boston, VA 24592
(434) 572-2988; *Fax:* (434) 572-4013
www.whlf.com
whlf@whlf.com
License: South Boston, South Boston City County, VA held by JLC Properties Inc.
Nat'l Network: ABC; *Wire Services:* AP
Format: Adult Contemp; *Hrs. of News Programming:* news progmg 8 hrs wkly; *No. News Employees:* 1; *Target Audience:* 25-54; those that have spendable income; *Adv. Rates:* 15; 13; 15; 10
Tom Birch, President
Holly Melton, Operations Manager
Nick Long, General Manager

WSBV
01-01-1980; 1560 kHz AM; 0.25 kw-C, NDD; 2.5 kw-D, NDD; N36 42 35 W78 52 28
P.O. Box 778, South Boston, VA 24592 US
(434) 572-4418; *Fax:* (434) 572-9245
www.wsbvsouthboston.com
License: South Boston, VA held by Linda Waller-Barton
Format: Religious *Special Programming:* Farm one hr wkly; *Target Audience:* 40 plus.

WAJL
05-05-2010; 1400 kHz AM; *Hrs Open:* 24; 1 kw-U; N36 42 35 W78 52 28
License: South Boston, Halifax County, VA held by Linda Waller-Barton.
Special Programming: Southern Gospel
Linda Waller-Barten, Owner

South Hill

WSHV
11-01-1953; 1370 kHz AM; *Hrs Open:* 6 AM-6 PM
26256 Highway 47, South Hill, VA 23970 US
(434) 447-4007; *Fax:* (434) 447-4789
chrismichaels@lakesmediallc.com
License: South Hill, VA held by Lakes Media Holding Company LLC.
Group Owner: Birch Broadcasting Corp.; (acq 2-1-2005; grpsl).
Nat'l Network: ABC
Format: Black; *No. News Employees:* 1; *Target Audience:* General.
Tom Birch, President
Mark Reid, Oxford/South Hill Regional Manager
Chris Michaels, Operations Manager

WKSK-FM
12-23-1966; 101.9 MHz FM; 6 kw horiz, 5.7 kw vert; 315 ft.; N36 44 39 W78 9 42
26256 Highway 47, South Hill, VA 23970 US
(434) 447-4007; *Fax:* (434) 447-4789
www.rewind1019.com
tombirch@lakesmediallc.com
License: South Hill, Mecklenburg County, VA
Group Owner: Birch Broadcasting Corp.
Nat'l Network: ABC
Format: Country; *Hrs. of News Programming:* news progmg 2 hrs wkly; *No. News Employees:* 1; *Target Audience:* General; adults 25-54
Chris Michael, Operations Manager
Mark Reid, Regional Manager
Alison Arrington, Account Manager

Spotsylvania

***WWED**
01-01-2005; 89.5 MHz FM; 8 kw; 495 ft.; N38 11 48 W77 33 45
P.O. Box 905, Spotsylvania, VA 22553 US
(540) 582-9700
License: Spotsylvania, Spotsylvania County, VA held by Educational Media Corp.
Nat'l Network: Moody
Arbitron Metro Market: Saint George, UT; *Format:* Blues
Peter Stover, President

***WQIQ**
88.3 MHz FM; 3500 watts; 120 meters; 38 07 N47 77 42 W55 , Fredericksburg, VA
(540) 989-8900
www.wvtf.org
mfranchi@vt.edu
License: Spotsylvania, VA

Glenn Gleixner, General Manager

WVBX
01-26-1988; 99.3 MHz FM; 3 kw; 328 ft.; N38 8 30 W77 41 34
616 Amelia St., Fredericksburg, VA 22401 US
(540) 373-1500; *Fax:* (540) 374-5525
www.993thevibe.com
License: Spotsylvania, Spotsylvania County, VA held by Alpha Media Licensee LLC
Group Owner: Alpha Media LLC; (acq 5-1-2015; grpsl).
Wire Services: AP
Arbitron Metro Market: Fredericksburg, VA; *Format:* Contemporary Hits/Top 40
Ralph Salierno, General Manager and Director of Sales
Tony Bennett, Programming Director
Sharon DeSouza, Promotions Director
Bob Clinton, Chief Engineer
Sandy Ridgeway, Business and Traffic Manager
Shelly Bynum, ProductionDirector
Marion Edward Weatherington II, Promotions Coordinator
Bonnie Miller, Programming Coordinator

St. Paul

WXLZ
11-03-1981; 1140 kHz AM; *Hrs Open:* Sunrise-sunset; 1.1 kw-C, NDD; 2.5 kw-D, NDD; N36 52 15 W82 18 21 *Rebroadcasts:* Rebroadcasts WXLZ-FM Lebanon 80%
P.O. Box 1299, Lebanon, VA 24266 US
(276) 889-1073; *Fax:* (276) 889-3677
www.wxlz.net
wxlz1073@bvu.net
License: St. Paul, VA held by Yeary Broadcasting Inc.
Nat'l Network: CBS
Arbitron Metro Market: Saint Paul, VA; *Format:* Country, Religious *Special Programming:* Gospel 15 hrs wkly; *Hrs. of News Programming:* news progmg 3 hrs wkly; *No. News Employees:* 3; *Target Audience:* 25 plus;students, farmers, miners & rural area residents
Lannis Yeary, General Manager
Marshall Hendrix, Programming Director
Wilma Kiser, Office Manager

Stanleytown

WZBB
03-01-1989; 99.9 MHz FM; *Hrs Open:* 24; 3.6 kw; 722 ft.; N36 54 50 W79 57 7
10899 Virginia Avenue, Bassett, VA 24055 US
(540) 489-9999; *Fax:* (276) 629-8399
www.supercountryonline.com
License: Stanleytown, Henry County, VA held by WNLB Radio Inc.
Regional Network: Va. News Net.
Arbitron Metro Market: Stanleytown, VA; *Format:* Country; *Target Audience:* 21 plus.
Donny Brook, President
Glenn Lynch, Operations Dir
Kristi Banks, General Manager
Amy Coleman, Station Manager
Craig Richards, Programming Director
Lisa Layne, News Director

Staunton

WCYK-FM
09-01-1984; 99.7 MHz FM; *Hrs Open:* 24; 3.3 kw; 1693 ft.; N38 3 52 W78 48 18
1150 Pepsi Place, Suite 300, Charlottesville, VA 22901 US
(437) 978-4404; *Fax:* (434) 978-0723
www.hitkicker997.com
pmadison@cvillestations.com
License: Staunton, Staunton City County, VA held by Monticello Media LLC.
Group Owner: Monticello Media LLC; (acq 10-4-2007; grpsl)
Nat'l Network: Motor Racing Net; *Nat'l Reps:* Christal
Arbitron Metro Market: Charlottesville, VA; *Format:* Country; *Target Audience:* 25-54.
Vinnie Kice, Operations Manager
Steve Gaines, General Manager
Pauly Madison, Programming Director

WKDW
04-01-1954; 900 kHz AM; *Hrs Open:* 24
207 University Boulevard, Harrisonburg, VA 22801 US
(540) 434-1777; *Fax:* (540) 434-9968
www.wkdwam.com
License: Staunton, VA held by CC Licenses LLC.
Group Owner: iHeartMedia; (acq 11-15-2000; grpsl).
Format: Country *Special Programming:* Farm one hr, blue grass one hr wkly; *Hrs. of News Programming:* news progmg 15 hrs wkly; *No. News Employees:* 1; *Target Audience:* 25-54.; *Adv. Rates:* 30; 30; 30; 10
Steve Knupp, Operations Manager
Bridgett Knupp, Sales Manager
Mark Ness, Chief Engineer

WSVO
05-29-1959; 93.1 MHz FM; 2.8 kw; 338 ft.; N38 10 32 W79 4 12
207 University Blvd., Harrisonburg, VA 22801 US
(540) 434-1777; *Fax:* (540) 432-9968
www.mix931online.com
License: Staunton, Staunton City County, VA held by CC Licenses LLC.
Group Owner: iHeartMedia
Format: Adult Contemp; *Hrs. of News Programming:* news progmg 15 hrs wkly; *No. News Employees:* 1; *Target Audience:* 35-54.
Steve Knupp, Operations Manager
Bridgett Knupp, Sales Manager
Mark Ness, Chief Engineer

WTON
03-09-1946; 1240 kHz AM; *Hrs Open:* 24; 1 kw-U, ND1; N38 8 30 W79 2 33
Mailing Address: Box 1085, Staunton, VA 24402 US
Second Address: 304 W. Beverly St., Staunton, VA 24401
(540) 885-5188; *Fax:* (540) 885-1240
www.star94radio.com
License: Staunton, VA held by High Impact Communications Inc.
Nat'l Network: CBS; ESPN Radio
Arbitron Metro Market: Staunton,VA; *Format:* Sports *Special Programming:* Virginia Tech SPorts; *Hrs. of News Programming:* News progmg one hr wkly; *Target Audience:* 18-49.; *Adv. Rates:* 15; 10; 15; 7
J. Gary Ratcliff, President and Owner
Brenda Ratcliff, General Manager
Cass Johnson, Programming Director

WTON-FM
11-01-1990; 94.3 MHz FM; *Hrs Open:* 24; 0.34 kw; 2231 ft.; N38 9 55 W79 18 51
Mailing Address: 304 W. Beverly St., Staunton, VA 24401 US
Second Address: 304 W. Beverly St., Staunton, VA

(540) 885-5188; *Fax:* (540) 885-1240
www.star94radio.com
License: Staunton, Staunton City County, VA held by High Impact Communications, INc.
Nat'l Network: CBS *Regional Reps:* Rgnl Reps
Arbitron Metro Market: Staunton,VA; *Format:* Contemporary Hits/Top 40, Adult Contemp *Special Programming:* UVA Sports; *Hrs. of News Programming:* News progmg 3 hrs wkly; *Target Audience:* 25-54; 60% women, 40% men *Adv. Rates:* 30; 22; 28; na

J. Gary Ratcliff, President and Owner
Cass Johnson, Operations Dir
Brenda Ratcliff, General Manager

Stephens City

WKSI-FM

08-28-1966; 98.3 MHz FM; *Hrs Open:* 24; 1.75 kw; 617 ft.; N39 10 38 W78 15 53
510 Pegasus Court, Winchester, VA 22602 US
(540) 662-5101; *Fax:* (540) 662-8610
www.kiss983.com
License: Stephens City, Frederick County, VA held by AMFM Radio Licenses LLC.
Group Owner: iHeartMedia
Arbitron Metro Market: Stephens City, VA; *Format:* Contemporary Hits/Top 40; *Target Audience:* 25-54.

Daniel Martin, General Sales Mgr
Ricky Thomas, Programming Director
Scott Bradley, Promotions Director

Strasburg

WZFC

104.9 MHz FM; 4100 w; 57.9 meters; 39 01 06 N 78 25 35 W
P.O. Box 3300, Winchester, VA 22604 US
License: Strasburg, Shenandoah County, VA
Group Owner: Centennial Broadcasting II LLC

Stuart

WHEO

10-12-1959; 1270 kHz AM; *Hrs Open:* 6 AM-sunset; 5 kw-D, NDD; N36 37 25 W80 15 50
3824 Wayside Road, Stuart, VA 24171 US
(276) 694-3114; *Fax:* (276) 694-2241
License: Stuart, VA held by Mountain View Communications Inc.
Nat'l Network: CNN Radio; *Regional Network:* Va. News Net.
Format: News, News/Talk, 86 *Special Programming:* Farm 4 hrs, relg 10 hrs, loc news 10 hrs wkly; *Hrs. of News Programming:* news progmg 25 hrs wkly; *No. News Employees:* 1; *Target Audience:* General.; *Adv. Rates:* 156; 140; 156; na

Dean Goad, President
Jamie Clark, Operations Dir
La Vergne Collins, General Sales Mgr
Richard Rogers, Programming Director

Suffolk

WAFX

12-12-1983; 106.9 MHz FM; 100 kw; 984 ft.; N36 48 9 W76 45 19
Suite 339, 870 Greenbriar Cir., Chesapeake, VA 23320 US
(757) 366-9900; *Fax:* (757) 366-0022
License: Suffolk, Suffolk City County, VA held by Tidewater Communications LLC.
Group Owner: Saga Communications Inc.; (acq 3-15-94; $4 million;
Nat'l Reps: McGavren Guild
Arbitron Metro Market: Norfolk-Virginia Beach-Newport News, VA; *Format:* Classic Rock; *Target Audience:* 18-49.

Wayne Leland, Vice President/General Manager

WVBW

12-01-1965; 92.9 MHz FM; *Hrs Open:* 24; 50 kw; 486 ft.; N36 52 35 W76 23 28
5589 Greenwich Rd., Suite 200, Virginia Beach, VA 23462 US
(757) 671-1000
www.929thewave.com
theboss@929thewave.com
License: Suffolk, VA held by MHR License LLC.
Group Owner: MAX Media L.L.C.; (acq 3-24-2005; grpsl).
Nat'l Reps: Christal
Arbitron Metro Market: Norfolk-Virginia Beach-Newport News, VA; *Format:* Contemporary Hits/Top 40 *Special Programming:* Relg 2 hrs, Sunday Morning Magazine one hr wkly; *Target Audience:* 25-54; women

John Shomby, Operations Manager
Dave Paulus, General Manager
Carol Bryant, General Sales Mgr
Joe Britton, Promotions Director
Paul Campbell, Chief Engineer
Keith Barton, Director of Sales
Jackie Bales, Business Manager
ErinGalant, Director of Interactive Sales
Jeff Schmidt, Production Director

Sweet Briar

*WNRS-FM

01-01-1980; 89.9 MHz FM; *Hrs Open:* 24; 0.03 kw; 1942 ft.; N37 33 50 W79 11 34 *Rebroadcasts:* Rebroadcasts WNRN(FM) Charlottesville
Radio Station Wudz, P.O. Box 143, Sweet Briar, VA 24595 US
(434) 971-4096; *Fax:* (434) 971-6562
info@wnrn.org
License: Sweet Briar, Amherst County, VA held by Sweet Briar College.
Arbitron Metro Market: Roanoke-Lynchbu; *Format:* Rock/AOR; *Target Audience:* General.

Maynard Sipe, President
Victoria Nelson, General Manager
Ashley Carroll, Station Manager
John Jaffe, General Sales Mgr
Allsion Bailey, Programming Director
Lauren Schein, Music Director
Jon Hall, Vice President
Paul Wright,Treasurer
John Jaffe, Secretary

Tappahannock

*WRAR

11-01-1970; 1000 kHz AM
P.O. Box 1023, Tappahannock, VA 22560 US
(804) 443-6572
License: Tappahannock, VA held by A.C.T.I.O.N. Inc.
Regional Reps: Virginia Broadcast SolutionsRegnl R
Format: Talk

Geoffrey Coleman, President
Rich Morgan, News Director

WRAR-FM

07-26-1971; 105.5 MHz FM; *Hrs Open:* 24; 6 kw; 328 ft.; N37 52 27 W76 43 37
Mailing Address: P. O. Box 1023, Tappahannock, VA 22560 US
Second Address: 156 Prince St., Tappahannock, VA 22560
(804) 443-4321; *Fax:* (804) 443-1055
www.realradio804.com
contact@realradio804.com
License: Tappahannock, Essex County, VA held by Real Media Inc.
Nat'l Network: ABC; *Nat'l Reps:* Rgnl Reps; *Wire Services:* AP
Format: Adult Contemp

Billy Flynn, Programming Director
Tom Davis, News Director
Terry Brooks, Traffic Manager

Tazewell

*WKQY

09-01-1968; 100.1 MHz FM; *Hrs Open:* 24; 4.2 kw; 390 ft.; N37 8 1 W81 35 42 *Rebroadcasts:* Rebroadcasts KAWZ(FM) Twin Falls, ID 100%
Box 271, Twin Falls, ID 83303 US
(800) 357-4226; *Fax:* (304) 325-7850
www.csnradio.com
License: Tazewell, Tazewell County, VA held by Calvary Chapel of Twin Falls Inc.
Arbitron Metro Market: Bluefield, WV; *Format:* Oldies; *Target Audience:* 25 plus.

WTZE

04-22-1966; 1470 kHz AM; *Hrs Open:* 6 AM-sunset; 5 kw-D, NDD; N37 7 57 W81 33 21
Mailing Address: Box 271, Twin Falls, ID 83303 US
Second Address: 4002 North 3300 East, Twin Falls, ID 83301
(208) 734-2049; *Fax:* (208) 736-1958
www.effectradio.com
License: Tazewell, VA held by Calvary Church of Twin Falls Inc.
Group Owner: Effect Radio
Arbitron Metro Market: Bluefield, WV; *Format:* Christian, Rock/AOR; *Target Audience:* 21-54.

Jon Gibson, Programming Director

Vinton

WSFF

01-01-1994; 106.1 MHz FM; 6 kw; 95 ft.; N37 17 3 W79 59 14
3807 Brandon Avenue, Suite 2350, Roanoke, VA 24018 US
(540) 725-1220; *Fax:* (540) 725-1245
www.1061stevefm.com/main
steve@1061stevefm.com
License: Vinton, Roanoke County, VA held by Aloha Station Trust LLC
Arbitron Metro Market: Roanoke-Lynchburg, VA; *Format:* Adult Contemp

Chris Clendenen, General Manager
Ron Gaylor, General Sales Mgr
David Lee Michaels, Programming Director
Ed Kilbane, News Director
Jeff Parker, Chief Engineer
Sarah Leftwich, Advertising
Tammy Cazad, Advertizing
Lisa Layne,Advertizing

WKBA

10-09-1961; 1550 kHz AM; 10 kw-D, DAD; N37 17 24 W79 55 22
2043 10th Street N.E., Roanoke, VA 24012 US
(540) 343-5597; *Fax:* (540) 345-4064
www.wkbaradio.com
wkba@cox.net
License: Vinton, VA held by Tinker Creek Broadcasters Inc.
Arbitron Metro Market: Roanoke-Lynchburg, VA; *Format:* Religious *Special Programming:* Black 10 hrs wkly; *Target Audience:* General.

Dorothy Durrett, General Manager
Dale Cook, Chief Engineer

WVMP

12-12-1995; 101.5 MHz FM; *Hrs Open:* 24; 630 w; Ant 705 ft; N37 21 57 W79 52 01
611 South Jefferson Street, Suite 7, Roanoke, VA 24011
(540) 344-2800; *Fax:* (540) 344-4001
www.1015tvmp.com
wvmp@1015tvmp.com
License: Vinton, Roanoke County, VA held by Cityworks Community Broadcasting LLC
Nat'l Network: Fox News Radio; *Nat'l Reps:* McGavren Guild
Arbitron Metro Market: Roanoke-Lynchburg, VA; *Hrs. of News Programming:* news progmg 2 hrs wkly; *No. News Employees:* 1

Edward B. Walker, President
Tom Kennedy, General Manager
Dale Cook, Chief Engineer

Virginia Beach

WXTG-FM

01-01-2002; 102.1 MHz FM; 6 kw; 328 ft.; N36 45 7 W76 8 57
232 Business Park Drive, Suite 120, Virginia Beach, VA 23462 US
(757) 747-1021; *Fax:* (757) 490-2755
www.1021fmthegame.com
buck@redskins.com
License: Virginia Beach, Virginia Beach County, VA held by Red Zebra Broadcasting Licensee (Norfolk) LLC.
Group Owner: Red Zebra Holdings LLC; (acq 12-4-2006; $4.25 million)
Nat'l Network: Fox Sports
Arbitron Metro Market: Virginia Beach, VA; *Format:* Sports, Talk

buck albriton, General Manager
Buck Albritton, Station Manager
John Decandido, Programming Director
Joe Weatherbee, Chief Engineer

*WJLZ

02-12-1989; 88.5 MHz FM; 1.2 kw; 118 ft.; N36 50 30.7 W76 5 37 *Rebroadcasts:* W279AD 103.7,W280CX 103.9, W250AE 97.9
3500 Va Beach Blvd., Suite 207, Virginia Beach, VA 23452 US
(757) 498-9632; *Fax:* (757) 498-8609
www.currentfm.com
info@currentfm.com
License: Virginia Beach, Virginia Beach City County, VA held by Virginia Beach Educational Broadcasting Foundation Inc.
Arbitron Metro Market: Norfolk-Virgini *TV Affiliate:* Relg CHR; *No. News Employees:* General.

Bill Verebely, President
Anne Verebely, General Manager
Kathy Mechem, Sales Executive

WPTE

05-05-1984; 94.9 MHz FM; *Hrs Open:* 24; 50 kw; 499 ft.; N36 48 37 W76 16 59
236 Clearfield Avenue, Suite 206, Virginia Beach, VA 23462 US
(757) 497-2000; *Fax:* (757) 456-5458
www.pointradio.com
info@pointradio.com
License: Virginia Beach, Virginia Beach City County, VA held by Entercom Norfolk License LLC.
Group Owner: Entercom Communications Corp.; (acq 12-13-99; grpsl).
Nat'l Reps: D & R Radio

Arbitron Metro Market: Norfolk-Virginia Beach-Newport News, VA; *Format:* Rock/AOR; *Hrs. of News Programming:* News progmg one hr wkly; *Target Audience:* 18-49.
David Field, CEO
Jeff Brown, General Manager
Hope Angelone, General Sales Mgr
Barry McKay, Programming Director
Jane Kozup, Promotions Manager
Kym Wollman, News Director

WVAB
12-10-1954; 1550 kHz AM; 5 kw-D, ND2; 0.009 kw-N, ND2; N36 51 29 W76 9 28
1428 Franklin Dr., Virginia Beach, VA 23454 US
(757) 522-1797; *Fax:* (603) 299-8921
www.birach.com
sima@birach.com
License: Virginia Beach, VA held by Birach Broadcasting Corp.
Group Owner: Birach Broadcasting Corp.
Arbitron Metro Market: Norfolk Virginia Beach, VA; *Format:* Christian
Sima Birach, President

Warrenton

WKCW
12-07-1957; 1420 kHz AM; *Hrs Open:* 6 AM-sunset
9540 Godwin Drive, Manassas, VA 20110 US
(703) 279-1010; *Fax:* (703) 331-4706
metroradioinc@aol.com
License: Warrenton, VA held by Metro Radio Inc.
Group Owner: Metro Radio Inc.; (acq 1-2-2004; $400,000)
Format: Spanish *Special Programming:* Bluegrass, farm one hr, rel 6 hrs wkly; *Hrs. of News Programming:* news progmg 2 hrs wkly; *No. News Employees:* 1; *Target Audience:* 25-54; mature adults with discretionaryincome of $30,000 plus; *Adv. Rates:* 20; 20; 20; 10
David Houston, CEO
Bruce Houston, President
Kelly Koonce, COO

WWXX
11-02-1978; 94.3 MHz FM; *Hrs Open:* 24; 3 kw; Ant 397 ft; N38 40 42 W77 47 18
(301) 230-0980
www.espn980.com
management@espn980.com
License: Warrenton, Fauquier County, VA held by Red Zebra Broadcasting Licensee LLC.
Group Owner: Red Zebra Holdings LLC; (acq 5-9-2006; grpsl).
Nat'l Network: ESPN Radio
Population Served: 58,000; *Arbitron Metro Market:* Washington, DC
Bruce Gilbert, CEO
Tod Castleberry, General Manager

WKDL
11-21-1957; 1250 kHz AM; *Hrs Open:* 24
P. O. Box 3220, Warrenton, VA 20188 US
(703) 330-8244; *Fax:* (703) 331-4706
www.1260wrc.com
metroradioinc@aol.com
License: Warrenton, VA held by Metro Radio Inc.
Group Owner: Metro Radio Inc.; (acq 10-4-2007; $1.1 million)
Format: Country
David Houston, CEO
Bruce Houston, President
Kelly Koonce, COO

Warsaw

WNNT-FM
03-01-1967; 107.5 MHz FM; 6 kw; 328 ft.; N37 56 39 W76 45 5
Mailing Address: P.O. Box 877, Warsaw, VA 22572 US
Second Address: 156 Prince Street, Tappahannock, VA 22560
(804) 333-4900; *Fax:* (804) 443-1055
www.wnntfm.com
contact@wnntfm.com
License: Warsaw, Richmond County, VA held by Northern Neck & Tidewater Communications Inc.
Arbitron Metro Market: Warsaw, VA; *Format:* Country
Rich Morgan, General Manager
A.C. Walker, Programming Director
Frank Miner, Chief Engineer

Waynesboro

WKCI
03-10-1965; 970 kHz AM; *Hrs Open:* 24; 5 kw-D, DA2; 1 kw-N, DA2; N38 5 12 W78 54 42 *Rebroadcasts:* Rebroadcasts WKCY(AM) Harrisonburg 100%
207 University Blvd., Harrisonburg, VA 22801 US
(540) 434-1777; *Fax:* (540) 432-9968
www.wkcyam.com
License: Waynesboro, VA held by CC Licenses LLC.
Group Owner: iHeartMedia; (acq 11-16-2000; grpsl).
Format: News, News/Talk, 86 *Special Programming:* Black 3 hrs, farm 2 hrs wkly; *Hrs. of News Programming:* news progmg 2 hrs wkly; *No. News Employees:* 1; *Target Audience:* 25-54.
Steve Knupp, Operations Manager
Bridgett Knupp, Sales Manager
Mark Ness, Chief Engineer

***WPVA**
01-01-1999; 90.1 MHz FM; 2.5 kw; 961 ft.; N38 1 16 W78 52 38
22226 Timberlake Road, Lynchburg, VA 24502 US
(434) 237-9798; *Fax:* (434) 237-1025
www.spiritfm.com
office@spiritfm.com
License: Waynesboro, Waynesboro City County, VA held by Positive Alternative Radio Inc.
Group Owner: Positive Alternative Radio Inc.; (acq 12-30-2005; grpsl)
Format: Christian
Jackie Howard, Director of Operations
Marc Tischart, General Manager

Weber City

WVEK-FM
12-01-1994; 102.7 MHz FM; *Hrs Open:* 24; 1.65 kw; Ant 1,233 ft; N36 31 36 W82 35 13
222 Commerce St., Kingsport, TN 37660
(423) 247-7102
www.classichits1027.com
psa@wtfm.com
License: Weber City, Scott County, VA held by Holston Valley Broadcasting Corp.
Group Owner: Glenwood Communications Corp.; (acq 7-16-2008; $270,000)
Nat'l Reps: Eastman
Population Served: 150,000; *Arbitron Metro Market:* Johnson City-Kingsport-Bristol, TN-VA *TV Affiliate:* WKPT-TV
George Devault, President
David Widener, General Manager
Tim Loy, General Sales Mgr
Steve Mann, Programming Director
Brittany Moore, Promotions Manager
Duane Nelson, News Director

West Point

WBQK
07-01-1991; 107.9 MHz FM; *Hrs Open:* 24; 4 kw; 328 ft.; N37 27 0 W76 48 46
4732 Longhill Rd., Suite 2201, Williamsburg, VA 23188 US
(757) 565-1079; *Fax:* (757) 565-7094
wydaily.com/bachfm
music@wbach.net
License: West Point, King William County, VA held by Local Voice Media Group
Group Owner: Local Voice Media Group; (acq 6-17-2005; $1.13 million).
Format: Classical

White Stone

WIGO-FM
09-01-1995; 104.9 MHz FM; 4.1 kw; 400 ft.; N37 43 25 W76 23 28.8
101 Radio Raod, Kilmarnock, VA 22482 US
(804)435-1414
www.middlenecknews.com
License: White Stone, Lancaster County, VA held by Two Rivers Communications Inc.
Nat'l Network: Westwood One; AP Radio; *Wire Services:* AP
Arbitron Metro Market: White Stone, VA; *Format:* Country; *No. News Employees:* 1; *Target Audience:* 25-54.; *Adv. Rates:* 20; 18; 20; 15
Deanna Chadwick, Business Manager
Carter Bonner, Webmaster

Williamsburg

***WCWM**
09-28-1959; 90.9 MHz FM; *Hrs Open:* 24; 13.5 kw; 269 ft.; N37 21 16 W76 59 58
% Kenneth E. Smith, Jr., PO Box 8795, Williamsburg, VA 23185 US
(757) 221-3287
www.wcwm.blogs.wm.edu
tcvanluling@email.wm.edu
License: Williamsburg, James City County, VA held by College of William & Mary.
Nat'l Network: Moody
Arbitron Metro Market: Williamsburg, VA; *Format:* Alternative, Variety/Diverse *Special Programming:* Jazz 13 hrs, class 11 hrs, reggae 6 hrs, blues 3 hrs wkly; *Hrs. of News Programming:* News progmg 3 hrs wkly *TargetAudience:* General.
Arthi Aravind, Vice President
Todd van Luling, Station Manager
David Jordan, Programming Director
TD Crowley, Production Manager

WMBG
01-01-1958; 740 kHz AM; *Hrs Open:* 24
1005 Richmond Road, Williamsburg, VA 23185 US
(757) 229-7400; *Fax:* (757) 220-3074
www.wmbgradio.com
info@wmbgradio.com
License: Williamsburg, VA held by Williamsburg's Radio Station Inc.
Nat'l Network: AP Radio; Jones Radio Networks
Arbitron Metro Market: Norfolk, VA; *Format:* Adult Contemp *Special Programming:* Gospel 5 hrs wkly; *Hrs. of News Programming:* news progmg one hr wkly; *No. News Employees:* 1; *Target Audience:* 45 plus; wealthy& mature in Williamsburg; *Adv. Rates:* 120; 72; 96; 60
Greg Granger, President

Winchester

WINC
06-15-1941; 1400 kHz AM; *Hrs Open:* 24
Mailing Address: P. O. Box 3300, Winchester, VA 22601 US
Second Address: 520 N. Pleasant Valley Rd., Winchester, VA 22601
(540) 667-2224; *Fax:* (540) 722-3295
www.winc.fm
brian@rockthebone.com
License: Winchester, VA held by Centennial Licensing II LLC
Group Owner: Centennial Broadcasting II LLC
Nat'l Network: Westwood One; CBS
Arbitron Metro Market: Winchester, VA; *Format:* News, News/Talk, 84, Talk; *Hrs. of News Programming:* news progmg 128 hrs wkly; *No. News Employees:* 3; *Target Audience:* 25 plus; mid-to-upscale active adults
John Lewis, President
Jeff Adams, Operations Dir
Chris Lewis, General Manager
Brian Beddow, Programming Director
Steve Edwards, News Director
Archie McKay, Chief Engineer
Pam Christian, Traffic Manager

WINC-FM
10-01-1946; 92.5 MHz FM; *Hrs Open:* 24; 22 kw; 1424 ft.; N38 57 21 W78 1 28
Mailing Address: P.O. Box 3300, Winchester, VA 22604 US
Second Address: 520 N. Pleasant Valley Rd., Winchester, VA 22601
(540) 667-2224; *Fax:* (540) 722-3295
www.winc.fm
License: Winchester, Winchester City County, VA held by Centennial Licensing II LLC
Group Owner: Centennial Broadcasting II LLC
Nat'l Network: Westwood One
Arbitron Metro Market: Winchester, VA; *Format:* Adult Contemp; *Hrs. of News Programming:* news progmg 6 hrs wkly; *No. News Employees:* 4; *Target Audience:* 18-49; active, upscale listeners
Chris Roth, Programming Director
Cindy Maguire, Promotions Manager
Robert Allen, News Director

WXVA
01-27-1961; 610 kHz AM; *Hrs Open:* 24; 500 w-U, DA-2; N39 11 53 W78 13 13
Mailing Address: PO Box 367, Haddon Heights, VA 08035
Second Address: 2047 Valley Avenue, Suite 200, Winchester, VA 22601
(540) 409-5220; *Fax:* (540) 409-5221
License: Winchester, Winchester City County, VA held by Capstar TX L.P.
Group Owner: Winchester Radio Broadcasters LLC; (acq 8-30-2000; grpsl)
Population Served: 127,500; *Arbitron Metro Market:* Winchester, VA

***WTRM**
07-01-1986; 91.3 MHz FM; *Hrs Open:* 24; 5.6 kw; 1401 ft.; N39 11 2 W78 23 15
2835 Front Royal Pike, Winchester, VA 22602-4914 US
(540) 869-4997; *Fax:* (540) 869-7173
www.afr.net
faq@afa.net

License: Winchester, Frederick County, VA held by American Family Association Inc.
Group Owner: American Family Radio
Nat'l Network: USA
Arbitron Metro Market: Winchester, VA; *Format:* Religious, Talk; *Target Audience:* General.
Tim Wildmon, President
Donald Wildmon, Founder
Buddy Smith, Sr VP
Ed Vitagliano, Exec VP
Randy Sharp, Director Of Special Projects
Meeke Addison, Director Of Communications
Abraham Hamilton III, General Counsel

WUSQ-FM
12-10-1965; 102.5 MHz FM; *Hrs Open:* 24; 32 kw; 630 ft.; N39 10 38 W78 15 53
510 Pegasus Court, Winchester, VA 22602 US
(540) 662-5101; *Fax:* (540) 662-8610
www.shenandoahcountryq102.com
License: Winchester, Winchester City County, VA held by Capstar TX LLC
Group Owner: iHeartMedia
Arbitron Metro Market: Winchester, VA; *Format:* Country; *Hrs. of News Programming:* News progmg one hr wkly; *Target Audience:* 25-54; males; *Adv. Rates:* 125; 110; 110; 55
Daniel Martin, General Sales Mgr
Brad Collins, Programming Director
Scott Bradley, Promotions Manager

Windsor

WNOH
08-03-1962; 105.3 MHz FM; 50 kw; 499 ft; N36 48 43 W76 27 49
1003 Norfolk Sq., Norfolk, VA 23502-4948 US
(757) 466-0009; *Fax:* (757) 466-4043
www.now105.com
License: Windsor, Norfolk City County, VA held by CC Licenses LLC.
Group Owner: iHeartMedia; (acq 1996; grpsl).
Nat'l Reps: Roslin
Arbitron Metro Market: Norfolk-Virginia Beach-Newport News, VA; *Format:* Contemporary Hits/Top 40; *Target Audience:* 25-54.
Derrick Martin, Market President
Matt Derrick, Senior Vice President of Programming
Marlon George, Senior Vice President of Sales
Nathan James, Marketing and Promotions
Jay Flanagan, Digital Content Director

Wise

***WISE-FM**
08-01-1999; 90.5 MHz FM; *Hrs Open:* 24; 0.22 kw; 669 ft.; N36 57 39 W82 30 56 *Rebroadcasts:* Rebroadcasts WVTF(FM) Roanoke 100%
3520 Kingsbury Lane, Roanoke, VA 24014 US
(540) 989-8900; *Fax:* (540) 776-2727
www.wvtf.org
License: Wise, Wise County, VA held by Clinch Valley College of the University of Virginia.
Nat'l Network: NPR; PRI; *Regional Network:* Va. News Net.
Format: Jazz *Special Programming:* Jazz 9 hrs, Celtic 2 hrs wkly; *Hrs. of News Programming:* News progmg 45 hrs wkly; *Target Audience:* General.
Glenn Gleixner, General Manager

Woodbridge

WMAL
01-01-1962; 105.9 MHz FM; 28 kw; Ant 648 ft; N38 52 28 W77 13 24
4400 Jenifer St. NW, Suite 400, Washington, DC 20015 US
(888) 630-9625
www.wmal.com
bill.hess@cumulus.com
License: Woodbridge, VA held by Radio License Holdings LLC
Group Owner: Cumulus Media Inc.; (acq 6-12-2007; grpsl)
Population Served: 426,800; *Arbitron Metro Market:* Washington, DC; *Format:* Talk
Bill Hess, Programming Director

Woodstock

WAMM
10-09-1981; 1230 kHz AM; *Hrs Open:* 24; 1 kw-D, ND1; 0.25 kw-N, ND2; N38 51 11 W78 31 30
P.O. Box 275, Mount Jackson, VA 22842 US
(540) 477-4443; *Fax:* (540) 477-4407
www.wsvgradio.com
wsvgam@hotmail.com
License: Woodstock, VA held by Jason M. Rodriguez
Arbitron Metro Market: Woodstock, VA; *Format:* Ethnic
Jason Rodriguez, General Manager

WAZR
10-18-1985; 93.7 MHz FM; *Hrs Open:* 24; 8.5 kw; 420 ft.; N38 37 4 W78 42 39
Mailing Address: 123 East Court Street, Woodstock, VA 22664 US
Second Address: 207 University Blvd., Harrisonburg, VA 22801
(540) 459-8810; *Fax:* (540) 459-5834
www.937now.com
License: Woodstock, Shenandoah County, VA held by CC Licenses LLC.
Group Owner: iHeartMedia; (acq 6-3-2002; $1.35 million including five-year noncompete agreement).
Nat'l Network: Jones Radio Networks
Arbitron Metro Market: Tuscaloosa AL; *Format:* Contemporary Hits/Top 40
Steve Knupp, Operations Manager
Bridgett Knupp, Advertising Sales
Mark Ness, Chief Engineer

Wytheville

WYVE
09-21-1949; 1280 kHz AM; *Hrs Open:* 24; 2.5 kw-D, ND1; 0.164 kw-N, ND1; N36 57 54 W81 4 50
110 West Spiller Street, Wytheville, PA 24382 US
(276) 228-3185; *Fax:* (276) 228-9261
office@threeriversmedia.net
License: Wytheville, VA held by Three Rivers Media Corp.
Group Owner: Three Rivers Media Corp.; (acq 10-1-98; $250,000).
Nat'l Network: AP Network News; Jones Radio Networks
Regional Reps: Rgnl Reps
Arbitron Metro Market: Wytheville, VA; *Format:* News, Sports, 30 *Special Programming:* Gospel 4 hrs wkly; *Hrs. of News Programming:* news progmg 10 hrs wkly; *No. News Employees:* 1; *Target Audience:* 25 plus;general; *Adv. Rates:* 20; 20; 20; 20
Gary W. Hagerich, CEO
Gary W. Hagerich, President
Danny Gordon, Operations Dir
Teresa Kingl, News Director

Yorktown

WVSP-FM
07-04-1975; 94.1 MHz FM; *Hrs Open:* 24; 50 kw; 531 ft.; N37 12 33 W76 32 35
5589 Greenwich Rd., Suite 200, Virginia Beach, VA 23462 US
(757) 671-1000; *Fax:* (757) 518-9364
www.espnradio941.com
theboss@espnradio941.com
License: Yorktown, York County, VA held by MHR License LLC.
Group Owner: MAX Media L.L.C.; (acq 3-24-2005; grpsl).
Nat'l Reps: Christal
Arbitron Metro Market: Norfolk-Virginia Beach-Newport News, VA; *Format:* Sports; *No. News Employees:* 8; *Target Audience:* 35-64.
John Shomby, Operations Manager
Dave Paulus, General Manager
Carol Bryant, General Sales Mgr
Joe Britton, Promotions Manager
Paul Campbell, Chief Engineer
Keith Barton, Director of Sales
Jackie Bales, Business Manager
ErinGalant, Director of Interactive Sales
Jeff Schmidt, Production Director

***WYCS**
02-01-1966; 91.5 MHz FM; *Hrs Open:* 24; 1.3 kw horiz, 20 kw vert; 331 ft.; N37 12 17 W76 30 7
US
(757) 886-7490
License: Yorktown, York County, VA held by Creative Educational Media Corp. Inc.
Arbitron Metro Market: Yorktown, VA; *Format:* Religious; *Target Audience:* General.
Greg Roth, General Manager

Washington

Aberdeen

KBKW
1450 kHz AM; *Hrs Open:* 24; 1 kw-U; N46 56 59 W123 49 13
1520 Simpson Ave., Aberdeen, WA 98520 US
(360) 533-3000; *Fax:* (360) 532-1456
www.kbkw.com
bossbill@jodesha.com
License: Aberdeen, Grays Harbor County, WA held by Jodesha Broadcasting Inc.
Group Owner: Jodesha Broadcasting Inc.; acq 2-28-03; $750,000 with KSWW(FM) Montesano).
Nat'l Network: ABC Information & Entertainment; *Wire Services:* AP
Population Served: 52,200 *Format:* News/Talk; *Hrs. of News Programming:* 13; *No. News Employees:* 1; *Target Audience:* 25-54.; *Adv. Rates:* 16; 12; 14; 12
Gabrielle Jordan, General Manager
Bill Wolfenbarger, General Sales Mgr

KWOK
11-16-1961; 1490 kHz AM; *Hrs Open:* 24; 1 kw-D, ND2; 0.76 kw-N, ND2; N46 57 30 W123 48 35
1308 Coolidge Rd., Aberdeen, WA 98520 US
(360) 533-1320; *Fax:* (360) 532-0935
License: Aberdeen, Grays Harbor County, WA held by Alpha Media Licensee LLC
Group Owner: Alpha Media LLC; (acq 9-2-2015; grpsl).
Arbitron Metro Market: Hoquiam, WA; *Format:* Sports, Talk; *Target Audience:* 26-65.
Pat Anderson, Operations Manager
Donna Rosi, General Manager and General Sales Manager
Harvey Brooks, Chief Engineer

KXRO
05-28-1928; 1320 kHz AM; *Hrs Open:* 24; 5 kw-D, DAN; 1 kw-N, DAN; N46 57 27 W123 48 33
1308 Coolidge Rd., Aberdeen, WA 98520 US
(360) 533-1320; *Fax:* (360) 532-0935
www.kxro.com
License: Aberdeen, Grays Harbor County, WA held by Alpha Media Licensee LLC
Group Owner: Alpha Media LLC; (acq 9-2-2015; grpsl).
Nat'l Network: CBS; *Nat'l Reps:* McGavren Guild
Arbitron Metro Market: Aberdeen, WA; *Format:* News, News/Talk, 86; *Hrs. of News Programming:* news progmg 6 hrs wkly; *No. News Employees:* 2; *Target Audience:* 35-64.
Pat Anderson, Operations Manager
Donna Rosi, General Manager
Daniel Hargrove, News Director

***KBSG**
90.3 MHz FM; kw
US
(360) 539-2233
License: Aberdeen, Lewis County, WA held by Samsno Educational Media.
Arbitron Metro Market: Tacoma, WA *Special Programming:* Soul
Jennifer Diane Reitz, President

Airway Heights

KXLX
10-01-1986; 700 kHz AM; 10 kW; N47 36 31 W117 22 25
500 W Boone Ave, Spokane, WA 99201 USA
700espn.com
License: Airway Heights, Spokane County, WA held by QueenB Radio Inc.
Group Owner: Morgan Murphy Media; (acq 9-1-2005; $236,000)
Nat'l Network: ESPN Radio; *Nat'l Reps:* Katz Radio
Format: Sports
Tery Garras, General Sales Mgr
Denise Hombel, National/Regional Sales

Anacortes

KWLE
12-18-1957; 1340 kHz AM; *Hrs Open:* 24; 1 kw-U, ND1; N48 29 44 W122 36 15
26910 92nd Avenue N.W. C5, Starwood, WA 98292 US
(360) 293-3141; *Fax:* (360) 293-9463
License: Anacortes, WA held by San Juan Communications Inc.
Nat'l Network: Westwood One; CBS; ABC
Arbitron Metro Market: Seattle, WA; *Format:* Adult Contemp
Special Programming: Sp 6 hrs, relg one hr wkly; *Hrs. of News Programming:* news progmg 30 hrs wkly; *No. News Employees:* 3; *Target Audience:* 25-60. *Adv. Rates:* 21; 19; 21; 14
Jennifer Uteda, President
Lynn Mc Mullen, Operations Dir
William Berry, General Manager
Glen Harris, Programming Director
Dedrick Allen, Operations Manager

DKORC
07-01-1988; 820 kHz AM
2104 North 30th, Tacoma, WA 98403 US
(541) 563-5100; *Fax:* (541) 563-5116
License: Anacortes, Lincoln County, WA held by Larry D. and Margaret E. Profitt, a General Partnership
Format: Easy Listening

Larry Profitt, General Manager

Asotin

KCLK
03-02-1971; 1430 kHz AM; *Hrs Open:* 24; 5 kw-D, DA2; 1 kw-N, DA2; N46 18 59 W117 2 24
P.O. Box 669, Clarkston, WA 99403 US
(208) 758-3361; *Fax:* (208) 758-4986
License: Asotin, Asotin County, WA held by Pacific Empire Radio Corp.
Group Owner: Pacific Empire Radio Corp.; (acq 9-12-2008; grpsl)
Arbitron Metro Market: Lewiston, ID; *Format:* Sports, Talk; *No. News Employees:* 1; *Target Audience:* 15 plus; sports interested
Evan Yeoman, Operations Manager
Ben Bonfield, General Manager
Leslie Gatherer, Traffic Manager

Auburn

*KGRG-FM
12-01-1974; 89.9 MHz FM; *Hrs Open:* 24; 0.25 kw; 367 ft.; N47 15 23 W122 13 7
12401 S.E. 320th Street, Auburn, WA 98002 US
(206) 833-9111; *Fax:* (206) 939-5135
www.kgrg.com
programming@kgrg.com
License: Auburn, King County, WA held by Green River Community College.
Arbitron Metro Market: Seattle-Tacoma, WA; *Format:* Rock/AOR
Special Programming: Loc music 3 hrs, rap 3 hrs, metal 2 hrs, punk 4 hr; *Hrs. of News Programming:* News progmg 2 hrs wkly; *Target Audience:* 16-34.
Tom Evans Krause, General Manager
Keith Bolender, Programming Director
Jeremy Hopkins, Promotions Manager
Curtis Rogers, News Director
Jon Kasprick, Chief Engineer
Brandon Johnson, Assistant Program Director

Auburn-Federal Way

KMIA
08-06-1958; 1210 kHz AM; *Hrs Open:* 24; 27.5 kw-D, 10 kw-N, DA-2; N47 18 20 W122 14 53
www.kmia.latinosoloexitos.com
License: Auburn-Federal Way, King County, WA
Group Owner: Adelante Media Group LLC; (acq 1-21-2005; $6 million)
Nat'l Network: Ke-Buena
Population Served: 2,500,000; *Arbitron Metro Market:* Seattle-Tacoma, WA

Basin City

KOLW
02-01-1992; 97.5 MHz FM; *Hrs Open:* 24; 50 kw; 620 ft.; N46 17 23 W119 25 28
2621 West A Street, Pasco, WA 99301 US
(509) 547-9791; *Fax:* (509) 547-8509
www.975coolfm.com
License: Basin City, Franklin County, WA held by GAP Broadcasting Tri-Cities License LLC.
Group Owner: GAPWEST Broadcasting; (acq 2-13-2008; grpsl)
Nat'l Network: Jones Radio Networks *Regional Reps:* Wheeler Broadcasting.
Arbitron Metro Market: Basin City, WA; *Format:* Contemporary Hits/Top 40, Adult Contemp; *Target Audience:* 25-49; 60% male, 40% female; *Adv. Rates:* 12; 12; 12; 8
Cheryl Salomone, General Manager
Lee Jamison, Sales Director
Paul Drake, Programming Director

Bellevue

*KASB
03-22-1971; 89.9 MHz FM; 0.06 kw; 33 ft.; N47 36 15 W122 11 50
10416 S.E. Wolverine Way, Bellevue, WA 98004 US
(425) 456-7101; *Fax:* (425) 456-7110
www.kasbfm.com
congerb@kasbfm.com
License: Bellevue, King County, WA held by Bellevue School District No. 405.
Arbitron Metro Market: Bellevue, WA *Special Programming:* Local School News and Events; *Target Audience:* High School; *Adv. Rates:* na
Wes Zujko, General Manager

*KBCS
02-03-1973; 91.3 MHz FM; *Hrs Open:* 24; 8 kw; 213 ft.; N47 35 9 W122 8 41
3000 Landerholm Cir Se, Bellevue, WA 98007 US
(425) 564-2427; *Fax:* (425) 564-5697
kbcs.fm
kbcs@ctc.edu
License: Bellevue, King County, WA held by Bellevue Community College.
Arbitron Metro Market: Bellevue, WA; *Format:* Jazz; *Hrs. of News Programming:* News progmg 4 hrs wkly; *Target Audience:* General.
Bruce Wirth, Operations Dir
Steve Ramsey, General Manager
Sabrina Roach, General Sales Mgr
Bruce Wirth, Programming Director
Sam Roffe, Chief Engineer

KQMV
11-01-1964; 92.5 MHz FM; 56.8 kw; 2290 ft.; N47 30 17.3 W121 58 3.4
Newport Tower, Suite 550, 3650 131st Avenue, Se, Bellevue, WA 98006 US
(425) 653-9462; *Fax:* (425) 653-9464
www.movin925.com
info@movin925.com
License: Bellevue, King County, WA held by Bellevue Radio Inc.
Group Owner: Sandusky Radio
Nat'l Reps: Christal
Arbitron Metro Market: Seattle, WA; *Format:* Adult Contemp; *Hrs. of News Programming:* News progmg one hr wkly; *Target Audience:* 25-49; working women & families; *Adv. Rates:* 400; 300; 300; 100
Norman Rau, President
Marc Kaye, Operations Dir
Lois Mares, General Sales Mgr
Maynard Cohen, Programming Director
Cindy Gilsdorf, Promotions Manager

KXPA
03-01-1958; 1540 kHz AM; 5 kw-D, DAN; 5 kw-N, DAN; N47 35 29 W122 10 56
27 William St., 11th Floor, New York, NY 10005 US
(212) 966-1059; *Fax:* (212) 625-2894
www.kxpa.com
License: Bellevue, WA held by Multicultural Radio Broadcasting Licensee LLC.
Group Owner: Multicultural Radio Broadcasting Inc.; (acq 2-13-98; grpsl).
Arbitron Metro Market: Seattle-Tacoma, WA; *Format:* Ethnic, Variety/Diverse
Arthur Liu, CEO/COO

Bellingham

KAFE
07-02-1965; 104.1 MHz FM; *Hrs Open:* 24; 60 kw; 2300 ft.; N48 40 49.6 W122 50 26.3
73 Kercheval Avenue, Grosse Pointe Farms, MI 48236 US
(360) 734-9790; *Fax:* (360) 733-4551
www.kafe.com
michael@cascaderadiogroup.com
License: Bellingham, Whatcom County, WA
Arbitron Metro Market: Bellingham, WA; *Format:* Adult Contemp
Don Curtis, General Manager
Don Kurtis, General Sales Mgr
Ken Richards, Programming Director
Scotty VanDryver, Promotions Manager
Bill Baker, News Director
Krista Kay, Disc Jockey
Like Caus, Disc Jockey
Lynn Roberts, DiscJockey
Jeff Nelson, Disc Jockey
Steve Sandmeyer, News Reporter
Mikelanne Burk, News Reporter

KGMI
01-01-1927; 790 kHz AM; 5 kw-D, DAN; 1 kw-N, DAN; N48 43 9 W122 26 43
73 Kercheval Ave., Grosse Pointe Farms, MI 48236 US
(360) 734-9790; *Fax:* (360) 733-4551
www.kgmi.com
kgmi@kgmi.com
License: Bellingham, WA held by Saga Broadcasting LLC.
Group Owner: Saga Communications Inc.; (acq 9-24-98; $8 million with co-located FM)
Nat'l Reps: McGavren Guild
Format: News, News/Talk, 86 *Special Programming:* Home Improvement 2 hrs wkly; *Hrs. of News Programming:* News 140 hrs wkly; *Target Audience:* 35-64.
Ed Christian, President
Don Kurtis, General Manager
Brett Bonner, Programming Director
Scotty van Dryver, Promotions Manager
Doug Lange, News Director
Will Vos, Chief Engineer
Steve Ricci, Women's Int Ed

KISM
03-01-1960; 92.9 MHz FM; 50 kw; 2441 ft.; N48 40 48 W122 50 24
2219 Yew Street Road, Bellingham, WA 98229 US
(360) 734-9790; *Fax:* (360) 733-4551
www.kism.com
kism@kism.com
License: Bellingham, Whatcom County, WA held by Saga Broadcasting LLC.
Group Owner: Saga Communications Inc.
Format: Classic Rock; *Target Audience:* 25-44.
Scott Less, Brand Manager
Don Kurtis, Sales Manager
Nancy Tuppeny, Business Manager
Carol Hofacker, Traffic Manager

KBAI
04-04-1958; 930 kHz AM; *Hrs Open:* 24
73 Kercheval Avenue, Grosse Pointe Farms, MI 48236 US
(360) 734-9790; *Fax:* (360) 733-4551
License: Bellingham, WA held by Saga Broadcasting LLC.
Group Owner: Saga Communications Inc.; (acq 3-8-99; $1 million).
Nat'l Reps: Tacher
Format: Alternative, Talk; *Hrs. of News Programming:* news progmg 5 hrs wkly; *No. News Employees:* 1
Ed Christian, President
Don Kurtis, General Manager

KPUG
02-29-1948; 1170 kHz AM; *Hrs Open:* 24
73 Kercheval Avenue, Grosse Pointe Farms, MI 48236 US
(360) 734-9790; *Fax:* (360) 733-4551
www.kpug1170.com
thezone@kpug1170.com
License: Bellingham, WA held by Saga Broadcasting LLC.
Group Owner: Saga Communications Inc.; (acq 10-30-98; $5,825,000 with co-located FM).
Nat'l Reps: McGavren Guild
Arbitron Metro Market: Whatcom County; *Format:* Sports, Talk; *Hrs. of News Programming:* news progmg 24 hrs wkly; *No. News Employees:* 3; *Target Audience:* 25-54.
Ed Chrtistian, President
Michael O'Shea, General Manager
Doug Lange, Programming Director
Will Vos, Chief Engineer

*KUGS
01-29-1974; 89.3 MHz FM; *Hrs Open:* 7 AM-12AM; 0.1 kw; 384 ft.; N48 44 11 W122 28 47
410 Viking Union, Bellingham, WA 98225 US
(360) 650-4771; *Fax:* (360) 650-2696
www.kugs.org
as.productions@wwu.edu
License: Bellingham, Whatcom County, WA held by Western Washington University.
Wire Services: AP
Arbitron Metro Market: Bellingham, WA; *Format:* News, News/Talk, 86 *Special Programming:* Black 10 hrs, Hawaiian 2 hrs wkly; *Hrs. of News Programming:* News progmg 17 hrs wkly; *Target Audience:* 18-34; collegestudents & adults; *Adv. Rates:* 10; 10; 10; 10
Ethan Glemaker, President
Nicholas Keefe, Operations Dir
Jamie Hoover, General Manager
Patrick Stickney, Programming Director
Casey Nolan, Promotions Manager
Jeff Emtman, News & Public Affairs Director
Matthew Eschbach, ChiefEngineer
Nicholas Thacker, Music Director
Kelsey Lorberau, Specialty Music Director
Daley Smith, Productions Director
Tristan Wood, Productions Assistant Director for Marketing & Ass
Cody Olsen, Films Coordinator
Drake Wilcox, Pop MusicCoordinator

*KZAZ
09-01-1991; 91.7 MHz FM; *Hrs Open:* 24; 0.12 kw; 335 ft.; N48 48 4 W122 27 40 *Rebroadcasts:* Rebroadcasts KRFA-FM Pullman 95%
382 Murrow Center, PO Box 642530, Pullman, WA 99164 US

(509) 335-6500; *Fax:* (509) 335-6577
www.nwpr.org
nwpr@wsu.edu
License: Bellingham, Whatcom County, WA held by Washington State University.
Nat'l Network: NPR; PRI
Arbitron Metro Market: Bellingham, WA; *Format:* Jazz, News *Special Programming:* Folk 8 hrs, world music 7 hrs wkly; *Hrs. of News Programming:* News progmg 40 hrs wkly; *Target Audience:* 25-54; general *Adv.Rates:* 160; 60; 160; 140
Kerry Swanson, Station Manager
Gillian Coldsnow, Programming Director
Robin Rilette, Music Director

Benton City

KMMG
08-01-1974; 96.7 MHz FM; *Hrs Open:* 24; 0.82 kw; 889 ft.; N46 14 4 W119 19 13
P.O. Box 2888, Yakima, WA 98907 US
(509) 543-3334; *Fax:* (509) 452-0541
License: Benton City, Benton County, WA
Group Owner: Adelante Media Group LLC; (acq 11-18-2004; grpsl)
Arbitron Metro Market: Benton City, WA.; *Hrs. of News Programming:* news progmg 22 hrs wkly; *No. News Employees:* 1; *Target Audience:* 25 plus.
Bob Berry, General Manager
Bob Berrt, General Sales Mgr
Martin Ortiz, Programming Director
Keith Teske, Chief Engineer

Blaine

KARI
02-12-1960; 550 kHz AM; *Hrs Open:* 24; 5 kw-D, 2.5 kw-N, DA-2; N48 57 15 W122 44 36
4840 Lincoln Rd., Blaine, WA 98230 US
(360) 371-5500
www.kari55.com
License: Blaine, Whatcom County, WA held by Way Broadcasting Licensee LLC
Group Owner: Multicultural Radio Broadcasting, Inc.; (acq 7-20-00; $3 million with KVRI(AM) Blaine).
Population Served: 3,750,000 *Format:* Christian; *Target Audience:* 35 plus.; *Adv. Rates:* 22; 22; 22; na
Arthur Liu, CEO/COO

KVRI
01-01-2001; 1600 kHz AM
12830-80 Ave., Surrey, BC V3W 3A8 US
(604) 592-9393; *Fax:* (604) 592-9091
www.radioindia.ca
License: Blaine, WA held by Way Broadcasting Licensee LLC
Group Owner: Multicultural Radio Broadcasting Inc.; (acq 5-23-00; with KARI(AM) Blaine).
Arbitron Metro Market: Blaine, WA; *Format:* Ethnic
Arthur Liu, CEO/COO

Bremerton

KBRO
05-01-1947; 1490 kHz AM; *Hrs Open:* 6 AM-midnight; 1 kw-U, ND1; N47 33 52 W122 39 26
P.O. Box 348, 2539 North Highway 67, Sedalia, CO 80135 US
(206) 878-6070; (877)-725-9777; *Fax:* (206) 824-2573
www.espndeportesseattle.com
maria.s@espndeportesseattle.com
License: Bremerton, WA held by Seattle Streaming Radio LLC.
Group Owner: Seattle Streaming Radio LLC; (acq 8-26-2005; $900,000 with KNTB(AM) Lakewood)
Nat'l Network: ESPN Deportes
Arbitron Metro Market: Seattle-Tacoma, WA; *Format:* Sports
Maria Sotelo, General Manager

KRWM
08-22-1964; 106.9 MHz FM; *Hrs Open:* 24; 49 kw; 1299 ft.; N47 32 39 W122 6 29
3650 131st Avenue, Suite 550, Bellevue, WA 98006 US
(425) 373-5545; *Fax:* (425) 373-5507
www.warm1069.com
License: Bremerton, Kitsap County, WA held by Seascape Radio Inc.
Group Owner: Sandusky Radio; (acq 9-12-96; $29.25 million)
Nat'l Reps: Christal
Arbitron Metro Market: Bellevue, WA; *Format:* Adult Contemp; *Target Audience:* 35-54; educated, upscale professionals, family oriented, white/blue collar; *Adv. Rates:* 250; 300; 250; 75
Marc Kaye, Operations Dir
Marc Kaye, General Manager
Julie Judge, General Sales Mgr

Laura Dane, Programming Director
Jennifer Taniguchi, Promotions & Marketing Manager

Burbank

KUJ-FM
01-01-1997; 99.1 MHz FM; *Hrs Open:* 16; 52 kw; Ant 1,263 ft; N46 05 58 W119 07 40
830 N. Columbia Center Blvd., Suite B-2, Kennewick, WA 99362
(509) 783-0783; *Fax:* (509) 735-8627
www.power991fm.com
License: Burbank, Walla Walla County, WA held by Instad Radio Washington LLC
Group Owner: Ingstad Radio Washington LLC; (acq 6-22-2004; $1.68 million)
Arbitron Metro Market: Tri-Cities, WA (Richland-Kennewick-Pasco); *Target Audience:* 18-34.

KVAN
01-01-2007; 1560 kHz AM
US
(360) 944-1550; *Fax:* (360) 944-6679
www.laestaciondelafamilia.org
laestaciondelafamilia@gmail.com
License: Burbank, WA held by Compadres LC
Arbitron Metro Market: Burbank, WA; *Format:* News
Angel Castaneda, General Manager

Burien-Seattle

KGNW
10-10-1970; 820 kHz AM; *Hrs Open:* 24; 50 kw-D, DA2; 5 kw-N, DA2; N47 26 0 W122 28 2
2201 6th Avenue, Suite 1500, Seattle, WA 98121 US
(206) 443-8200; *Fax:* (206) 777-1133
www.kgnw.com
webmaster@kgnw.com
License: Burien-Seattle, WA held by Inspiration Media Inc.
Group Owner: Salem Communications Corp.; (acq 1984)
Nat'l Reps: Salem
Arbitron Metro Market: Seattle-Tacoma, WA; *Format:* Christian, Talk, 74 *Special Programming:* Talk, women, loc affrs, health; *Hrs. of News Programming:* News progmg 3 hrs wkly; *Target Audience:* 35 plus.
Stuart Epperson, Chairman
Edward Atsinger III, President
Joshua Main, Operations Dir
Tim Harper, General Manager
Andrew Adams, Programming Director
Rob Allyn, Engineering Dir
Monte Passmore, Chief Engineer
Dave Drui, ProgramDirector

Camas

KNRK
11-01-1992; 94.7 MHz FM; *Hrs Open:* 24; 6.3 kw; 1322 ft.; N45 29 20 W122 41 40
0700 SW Bancroft Street, Portland, OR US
(503) 223-1441
www.947.fm
mhamilton@945.fm
License: Camas, Clark County, WA held by Entercom Portland License L.L.C.
Group Owner: Entercom Communications Corp.
Arbitron Metro Market: Portland, OR; *Format:* Alternative; *No. News Employees:* 1; *Target Audience:* 25-54.
Eric Simantel, Sales Manager
Mark Hamilton, Programming Director

Cashmere

KWWX
01-01-1993; 106.7 MHz FM; 6 kw; -240 ft.; N47 30 21 W120 24 33
North 1212 Washington, Suite 307, Spokane, WA 99201 US
(509) 665-6565; *Fax:* (509) 663-1150
www.lasuperz.com/
License: Cashmere, Chelan County, WA held by CCR-Wenatchee IV LLC.
Group Owner: Cherry Creek Radio LLC; (acq 10-31-2006; grpsl)
Nat'l Reps: McGavren Guild
Arbitron Metro Market: Cashmere, WA; *Format:* Classic Rock; *Target Audience:* 25-54.
Jim Senst, General Manager
Leona Frank, General Sales Mgr
Dave Keefer, Programming Director

Centralia

*KCED
02-17-1975; 91.3 MHz FM; 1 kw; -72 ft.; N46 42 56 W122 57 48
600 W. Locust, Centralia, WA 98531 US
(360) 736-9391 x343; *Fax:* (360) 330-7509
License: Centralia, Lewis County, WA held by Board of Trustees, Centralia College.
Format: Variety/Diverse *Special Programming:* Sports 3 hrs wkly
Wade Fisher, General Manager

KYNW
08-24-1965; 102.9 MHz FM; *Hrs Open:* 24; 70 kw; 2192 ft.; N46 58 31 W123 8 16
50 East Rivercenter Blvd, Suite 1200, Covington, KY 41011 US
(206) 494-2000; *Fax:* (206) 286-2376
www.1029nowhits.com
License: Centralia, Lewis County, WA held by Citicasters Licenses Inc.
Group Owner: iHeartMedia; (acq 5-4-99; grpsl)
Arbitron Metro Market: Seattle, WA; *Format:* Contemporary Hits/Top 40; *Hrs. of News Programming:* news progmg 7 hrs wkly; *No. News Employees:* 2; *Target Audience:* 18 plus.
Robert Russell, Senior Vice President of Sales

Centralia-Chehalis

KELA
11-01-1937; 1470 kHz AM; *Hrs Open:* 24; 5 kw-D, ND1; 1 kw-N, ND1; N46 41 47 W122 57 23
1635 S. Gold St., Centralia, WA 98531 US
(360) 736-3321; *Fax:* (360) 736-0150
www.kelaam.com
larryminer@bicoastalmedia.com
License: Centralia-Chehalis, WA held by Bicoastal Media Licenses IV LLC.
Group Owner: Bicoastal Media L.L.C.; (acq 12-1-2007; $4.175 milllion with KMNT(FM) Chehalis)
Nat'l Network: Fox News Radio; *Nat'l Reps:* Tacher
Arbitron Metro Market: Centralia, WA; *Format:* News, News/Talk, 84, Talk *Special Programming:* Home Improvement; *Hrs. of News Programming:* news progmg 28 hrs wkly; *No. News Employees:* 2; *Target Audience:* 35plus.
Ryan Trotter, Operations/Programming Director
Larry Miner, General Manager/General Sales Manager
Major Logan, Promotions/Public Serivce
Steve George, News Director

Chehalis

KMNT
01-01-2005; 104.3 MHz FM; 2.35 kw; 1056 ft.; N46 33 18 W123 3 27
1635 South Gold St., Centralia, WA 98531 US
(360) 736-3321; *Fax:* (360) 736-0150
www.kmnt.com
larryminer@bicoastalmedia.com
License: Chehalis, Lewis County, WA held by Bicoastal Media Licenses IV LLC.
Group Owner: Bicoastal Media L.L.C.; (acq 12-1-2007; $4.175 million with KELA(AM) Centralia-Chehalis)
Nat'l Reps: Tacher *Regional Reps:* Tacher
Arbitron Metro Market: Chehalis, WA; *Format:* Country *Special Programming:* NFL Football; *Hrs. of News Programming:* 60 minutes weekly; *No. News Employees:* 1
Larry Miner, Market Manager
Ryan Trotter, Programming Director
Major Logan, Promotions Manager
Steve George, News Director

*KSWS
88.9 MHz FM; 1 kw; 1004 ft.; N46 33 16 W123 3 26
PO Box 642530, Pullman, WA 99164 US
(509) 335-6511
www.nwpr.org
nwpr@wsu.edu
License: Chehalis, Lewis County, WA held by Washington State University.
Arbitron Metro Market: Chehalis, WA; *Format:* Classical
Kerry Swanson, Station Manager
Cricket Cordova, Development Coordinator
Gillian Coldsnow, Assistant Manager, Programming and Operations

Chehalis-Centralia

KITI
10-01-1954; 1420 kHz AM; *Hrs Open:* 24; 5 kw-U, DA-2; N46 42 08 W122 55 58
1133 Kresky, Centralia, WA 98531
(360) 736-1355; *Fax:* (360) 736-4761
www.live95.com
live95@live95.com
License: Chehalis-Centralia, Lewis County, WA held by Premier Broadcasters Inc.

Group Owner: Premier Broadcasters; (acq 10-77)
Population Served: 60,000 *Special Programming:* Elvis Only, Goddards Gold; *Hrs. of News Programming:* news progmg 15 hrs wkly; *No. News Employees:* 1; *Target Audience:* 35-64.; *Adv. Rates:* 6am-7pm: $20
Jo-Anne Church, Office/Traffic Manager
Matt Shannon, Station Manager/Programming Director
Derek Shannon, General Manager

Chelan

KOZI
03-01-1957; 1230 kHz AM; *Hrs Open:* 24
Mailing Address: Box 819, Chelan, WA 98816 US
Second Address: 123 E. Johnson, Chelan, WA 98816
(509) 682-4033; *Fax:* (509) 682-4035
www.kozi.com
e.salmon@iciclebroadcasting.com
License: Chelan, WA held by Icicle Broadcasting Co.
Group Owner: Icicle Broadcasting Inc.; (acq 8-26-99; grpsl)
Nat'l Reps: Target Broadcast Sales
Format: Adult Contemp *Special Programming:* Farm 3 hrs, Sp 5 hrs wkly; *Hrs. of News Programming:* news progmg 32 hrs wkly; *No. News Employees:* 3; *Target Audience:* General.
Elliott Salmon, Station Manager
Hayli Libbey-Thompson, News Director

KOZI-FM
08-26-1981; 93.5 MHz FM; 0.6 kw; 1037 ft.; N47 51 2 W119 52 26
Mailing Address: Box 819, Chelan, WA 98816 US
Second Address: 123 E. Johnson, Chelan, WA 98816
(509) 682-4033; *Fax:* (509) 682-4035
www.kozi.com
e.salmon@iciclebroadcasting.com
License: Chelan, Chelan County, WA held by Icicle Broadcasting, Inc.
Group Owner: Icicle Broadcasting Inc.
Format: Adult Contemp
Elliott Salmon, Station Manager
Hayli Libbey-Thompson, News Director

Cheney

*KEWU-FM
04-03-1950; 89.5 MHz FM; *Hrs Open:* 6 AM-12 AM (M-F); 9 AM-12 AM (S, Su; 10 kw; 1407 ft.; N47 34 43 W117 17 50
104 RTU Building, Cheney, WA 99004 US
(509) 359-6390
jazz@mail.ewu.edu
License: Cheney, Spokane County, WA held by Eastern Washington University Board of Trustees.
Arbitron Metro Market: Cheney, WA; *Format:* Jazz *Special Programming:* Latin,World,Ambient
Peter Porter, General Manager
Elizabeth A. Farriss, Programming/Music Director
Tom Alderson, Chief Engineer

KEYF-FM
05-04-1986; 101.1 MHz FM; *Hrs Open:* 24; 100 kw; 1608 ft.; N47 35 35 W117 17 46
1601 E. 57th Ave., Spokane, WA 99223 US
(509) 448-1000; *Fax:* (509) 448-7015
www.key101fm.com
gtillotson@radiospokane.com
License: Cheney, Spokane County, WA held by Mapleton License of Spokane LLC.
Group Owner: Mapleton Communications LLC; (acq 12-3-2007; grpsl)
Arbitron Metro Market: Spokane, WA; *Format:* Oldies; *Hrs. of News Programming:* News progmg 15 hrs wkly; *Target Audience:* 35-64.
Greg Tillotson, Programming Director
Karen Dineen, Promotions Manager

Clarkston

KCLK-FM
01-01-1974; 94.1 MHz FM; *Hrs Open:* 24; 100 kw; 1,234 ft.; N46 27 27 W117 6 3
P.O. Box 669, Clarkston, WA 99403 US
(509) 758-3361; *Fax:* (509) 758-4986
jaymlazgar@pacempire.com
License: Clarkston, Asotin County, WA held by Pacific Empire Radio Corp.
Group Owner: Pacific Empire Radio Corp.; (acq 9-12-2008; grpsl)
Arbitron Metro Market: Lewiston, ID; *Format:* Oldies, Adult Contemp; *Target Audience:* 25 plus.
Evan Yeoman, Operations Manager
Ben Bonfield, General Manager
Leslie Gatherer, Traffic Manager

*KNWV
07-11-1995; 90.5 MHz FM; *Hrs Open:* 24; 0.42 kw; 1056 ft.; N46 27 26 W117 6 0 *Rebroadcasts:* Rebroadcasts KRFA-FM Moscow, ID 100%
PO Box 642530, Pullman, WA 99164 US
(509) 335-6500; *Fax:* (509) 335-3772
www.nwpr.org
nwpr@wsu.edu
License: Clarkston, Asotin County, WA held by Washington State University.
Format: News; *Hrs. of News Programming:* news progmg 37 hrs wkly; *No. News Employees:* 1
Karen Olstad, COO
Scott Weatherly, Operations Dir
Dennis Haarsager, General Manager
Kerry Swanson, Station Manager
Sarah McDaniel, General Sales Mgr
Mary Hawkins, Programming Director
John Paxson, News Director
Ralph Hogan,Engineering Dir
Robin Rilette, Music Director

KVAB
07-15-1997; 102.9 MHz FM; *Hrs Open:* 24; 0.44 kw; 1,171 ft.; N46 27 27 W117 6 3
P.O. Box 669, Clarkston, WA 99403 US
(509) 758-3361; *Fax:* (509) 758-4986
License: Clarkston, Asotin County, WA held by Pacific Empire Radio Corp.
Group Owner: Pacific Empire Radio Corp.; (acq 9-12-2008; grpsl)
Nat'l Network: Westwood One; *Nat'l Reps:* Tacher
Arbitron Metro Market: Clarkston, WA; *Format:* Classic Rock; *Target Audience:* 25-55.
Evan Yeoman, Operations Manager
Ben Bonfield, General Manager
Leslie Gatherer, Traffic Manager

*KUCC
88.1 MHz FM; 0.24 kw; 453 ft.; N46 27 47 W116 54 25
P O Box 19039, Spokane, WA 99219 US
(509) 838-2761; *Fax:* (509) 838-4882
www.uccsda.org/communications
LidiaR@uccsda.org
License: Clarkston, Asotin County, WA held by Upper Columbia Media Association.
Arbitron Metro Market: Clarkston, WA; *Format:* Religious
Bob Folkenberg, Jr., President
Lauren Adams, General Manager
Darin Patzer, Station Manager
Cindy Williams, Programming Director
Jay Wintermeyer, Communications Director/Media Relations
Randall Terry, VP for Finance
Doug Johnson,VP for Administration
Jay Wintermeyer, Director
Jon Dalrymple, Communications Assistant
Kathy Marson, Administrative Assistant

Cle Elum

KXAA
11-01-2002; 100.3 MHz FM; *Hrs Open:* 24; 6 kw; 95 ft.; N47 9 6 W120 47 23
717 NE12th Street, East Wenatchee, WA 98802 US
(509) 662-3842; *Fax:* (509) 662-2482
License: Cle Elum, Kittitas County, WA held by Wheeler Broadcasting Inc.
Group Owner: Wheeler Broadcasting Inc.; acq 5-28-2004; exercise of option).
Nat'l Network: Jones Radio Networks
Arbitron Metro Market: Cle Elum, WA; *Format:* Contemporary Hits/Top 40, Adult Contemp
Jeri Trantham, Operations Dir
Mark Wheeler, General Sales Mgr
Nel Wheeler, National & Political Sales Manager
Bill Hansen, Local Sales

Colfax

KCLX
01-01-1950; 1450 kHz AM
805 Stewart Ave., Lewiston, ID 83501 US
(208) 743-1551
shad@inlandradio.com
License: Colfax, WA held by Inland Northwest Broadcasting LLC
Group Owner: Inland Northwest Broadcasting LLC
Nat'l Reps: Farmakis
Arbitron Metro Market: Spokane, WA; *Format:* Country *Special Programming:* Farm 5 hrs, sports 7 hrs wkly; *Target Audience:* 25 plus; agricultural-urban; *Adv. Rates:* Same as FM
Gary Cummings, General Manager
Robert Hauser, General Sales Mgr
Steve Grubbs, Programming Director

KMAX
01-01-1998; 840 kHz AM; *Hrs Open:* 24; 10 kw-D, ND2; 0.28 kw-N, ND2; N46 54 50 W117 19 28
805 Stewart Ave., Lewiston, ID 83501 US
(208) 743-1551
shad@inlandradio.com
License: Colfax, WA held by Inland Northwest Broadcasting LLC.
Group Owner: Inland Northwest Broadcasting LLC; (acq 6-28-2005; grpsl)
Nat'l Network: Westwood One
Format: Talk; *Hrs. of News Programming:* news progmg 15 hrs wkly; *No. News Employees:* 2; *Target Audience:* 25-60; established professional aged people - young marrieds couples; *Adv. Rates:* 21; 19; 19; 15
Gary Cummings, General Manager
Ben Bonfield, General Sales Mgr
Darin Sievert, Programming Director
Glen Vaagen, News Director
Steve Franko, Chief Engineer

KRAO-FM
10-10-1994; 102.5 MHz FM; *Hrs Open:* 24; 2.2 kw; 1079 ft.; N46 51 44 W117 10 20
805 Stewart Ave., Lewiston, ID 83501 US
(208) 743-1551
shad@inlandradio.com
License: Colfax, Whitman County, WA held by Inland Northwest Broadcasting LLC
Group Owner: Inland Northwest Broadcasting LLC; (acq 6-28-2005; grpsl)
Format: Adult Contemp; *Target Audience:* 18-45.; *Adv. Rates:* 23.80; 23.80; 23.80; 17
Gary Cummings, General Manager
Johnny Mann, Programming Director
Steve Franco, Chief Engineer

College Place

*KGTS
10-05-1963; 91.3 MHz FM; *Hrs Open:* 24; 7 kw; 1250 ft.; N45 59 20 W118 10 29
204 South College, College Place, WA 99324 US
(509) 527-2991; *Fax:* (509) 527-2611
www.plr.org
studio@plr.org
License: College Place, Walla Walla County, WA held by Walla Walla College.
Format: Christian *Special Programming:* Family 30 hrs wkly, church service varies; *Target Audience:* 35-64.
Paul Richardson, General Manager
Sali Miller, Office/Promotions Manager
Ernest Beck, Programming Director
Rick Johnson, Underwriting Market Director

Colville

KCRK-FM
10-13-1981; 92.1 MHz FM; *Hrs Open:* 24; 5.4 kw; 344 ft.; N48 34 30 W117 55 0
www.kclv.com
partyline@kcvl.com
License: Colville, Stevens County, WA held by North Country Broadcasting.
Nat'l Network: Westwood One
Format: Adult Contemp

KCVL
11-15-1955; 1240 kHz AM; *Hrs Open:* 24; 1 kw-U, ND1; N48 31 15 W117 54 28
US
www.kcvl.com
partyline@kcvl.com
License: Colville, WA held by North Country Broadcasting.
Arbitron Metro Market: Colville, WA; *Format:* Country

Cosmopolis

KLSY
01-01-2008; 107.3 MHz FM; 0.79 kw; 906 ft.; N46 41 44 W123 46 17
1520 Simpson Avenue, Aberdeen, WA 98520 US
(360) 533-3000; *Fax:* (360) 532-1456
www.jodesha.com
info@jodesha.com
License: Cosmopolis, Pacific County, WA held by South Sound Broadcasting LLC.
Arbitron Metro Market: Cosmopolis, WA; *Format:* Classic Rock

Bill Wolfenbarger, President/Sales Manager
Gabriel Jordan, General Manager

Covington

KMCQ

11-28-1968; 104.5 MHz FM; *Hrs Open:* 24; 7.1 kw; 1273 ft.; N47 32 35 W122 6 25
P.O. Box 104, The Dalles, OR 97058 US
(541) 298-5116; *Fax:* (541) 298-5119
License: Covington, Wasco County, WA held by First Broadcasting Capital Partners LLC.
Group Owner: First Broadcasting Operating Inc.; (acq 3-22-2007; $5.1 million)
Nat'l Network: CNN Radio; *Nat'l Reps:* McGavren Guild
Format: Adult Contemp *Special Programming:* Blues 4 hrs, teen show 3 hrs wkly; *Hrs. of News Programming:* news progmg 7 hrs wkly; *No. News Employees:* 1; *Target Audience:* Females 25-49; mothers & family friendly *Adv. Rates:* 18; 18; 16
Gary Lawrence, President
John Huffman, Operations Dir
Trila Bumstead, General Manager
Bill Sigmar, General Sales Mgr
Paula Fairclo, Operations Director

Davenport

*KKRS

01-01-1998; 97.3 MHz FM; *Hrs Open:* 24; 5.1 kw; 722 ft.; N47 35 14 W117 53 26
P.O. Box 913, Aledo, TX 76008 US
(855) 500-3759; *Fax:* (509) 244-2232
kkrs.krtmradio.org
License: Davenport, Lincoln County, WA held by Penfold Communications, Inc.
Group Owner: Penfold Communications, Inc.; acq 1999; $111,425).
Format: Christian, Religious

Dayton

KZHR

08-01-1992; 92.5 MHz FM; *Hrs Open:* 24; 54 kw; 1243 ft.; N45 59 19 W118 10 28
Mailing Address: Hc-11 Box N, Prescott, WA 99348 US
Second Address: 2823 W. Lewis St., Pasco, WA 99301
(509) 547-1618; *Fax:* (509) 546-2678
www.kzhr.com
License: Dayton, Columbia County, WA held by CCR-Tri Cities IV LLC.
Group Owner: Cherry Creek Radio LLC; (acq 12-19-2003; grpsl).
Nat'l Reps: Interep; McGavren Guild
Arbitron Metro Market: Dayton, WA; *Format:* Tejano; *Hrs. of News Programming:* news progmg 7 hrs wkly; *No. News Employees:* 1; *Target Audience:* 25-54; adult; *Adv. Rates:* 23; 23; 16; na
Scott Smith, General Manager
Gonzalo Cortez, Station Manager
Daena Medina, News Director
Art Blum, Chief Engineer

Deer Park

KPKL

09-01-1983; 107.1 MHz FM; 25 kw; Ant 328 ft; N48 01 45 W117 35 57
400 S. Jefferson, Suite 304, Spokane, WA 99204
(509) 290-6200
www.kool1071.com
License: Deer Park, Spokane County, WA held by Spokane Broadcasting Co
Arbitron Metro Market: Spokane, WA

Dishman

KEYF

10-03-1984; 1050 kHz AM; *Hrs Open:* 24
1601 E. 57th Ave., Spokane, WA 99223 US
(509) 448-1000; *Fax:* (509) 448-7015
License: Dishman, WA held by Mapleton License of Spokane LLC.
Group Owner: Mapleton Communications LLC; (acq 12-3-2007; grpsl)
Arbitron Metro Market: Spokane, WA; *Format:* Adult Contemp; *Hrs. of News Programming:* News progmg 15 hrs wkly; *Target Audience:* 54 plus.

KSPO

01-01-1996; 106.5 MHz FM; *Hrs Open:* 24; 2.25 kw; 528 ft.; N47 41 39 W117 20 3
P.O. Box 31000, Spokane, WA 99223 US
(509) 443-1000
www.kspo.com
kspo@kspo.com
License: Dishman, Spokane County, WA held by Thomas W. Read dba Classical Broadcasting.
Nat'l Network: USA; Salem Radio Network
Arbitron Metro Market: Spokane, WA; *Format:* Talk, Religious; *Target Audience:* 35 plus.
Thomas Read, President
Melinda Read, Operations Dir

East Wenatchee

KYSN

12-25-1980; 97.7 MHz FM; *Hrs Open:* 24; 6 kw; -98 ft.; N47 22 51 W120 17 15
231 North Wenatchee Avenue, Wenatchee, WA 98801 US
(509) 665-6565; *Fax:* (509) 663-1150
www.kysn.com
License: East Wenatchee, Chelan County, WA held by CCR-Wenatchee IV LLC.
Group Owner: Cherry Creek Radio LLC; (acq 10-31-2006; grpsl)
Arbitron Metro Market: East Wenatchee, WA; *Format:* Country
Special Programming: Farm one hr, relg one hr wkly; *Hrs. of News Programming:* news progmg 20 hrs wkly; *No. News Employees:* 1 *Target Audience:* 25-54.
Todd Allen, Operations Dir
Steven Miller, General Manager
Leona Frank, General Sales Mgr
Jessi Clay, Programming Director
Dave Bernstein, News Director
Manuel Garcia, Chief Engineer
Lisa Rodriguez, Traffic Manager

*KLUW

01-01-2008; 88.1 MHz FM; 0.6 kw; -131 ft.; N47 22 52 W120 17 16 *Rebroadcasts:* Rebroadcasts KLVR(FM) Middletown, CA 100%
P.O. Box 31000, Spokane, WA 99223 US
(800) 877-5600; *Fax:* (916) 251-1650
www.klove.com
License: East Wenatchee, Chelan County, WA held by Educational Media Foundation.
Group Owner: EMF Broadcasting; (acq 2-11-2008; $100,000 for CP)
Nat'l Network: K-Love
Arbitron Metro Market: East Wenatchee, WA; *Format:* Christian
Alan Mason, Chief Operating Officer
Michael Novak, President/Chief Executive Officer

Eatonville

KKBW

01-01-1995; 104.9 MHz FM; *Hrs Open:* 24; 17 kw; Ant 407 ft; N46 50 24 W122 15 27
645 Elliott Ave. W., Suite 400, Seattle, WA 98119
(206) 494-2000; *Fax:* (206) 286-2376
www.funkymonkey1049.fm
doug@thebrew1049.com
License: Eatonville, Pierce County, WA held by Citicasters Licenses Inc.
Group Owner: iHeartMedia; (acq 2-12-2003; $4.5 million).
Population Served: 250,000; *Arbitron Metro Market:* Seattle-Tacoma, WA; *Format:* Alternative
Mark Glynn, Sales Manager
Rich Davis, Programming Director
Paige Gamboa, Promotions Manager
Doug Deuce, Production

Edmonds

KCIS

01-01-1954; 630 kHz AM; *Hrs Open:* 24; 5 kw-D, 2.5 kw-N, DA-N; N47 51 00 W122 09 38
19303 Fremont Ave. N., Seattle, WA 98133
(866) 546-7350; *Fax:* (206) 289-7792
www.kcisradio.com
comments@kcisradio.com
License: Edmonds, Snohomish County, WA held by CRISTA Ministries
Group Owner: CRISTA Broadcasting
Nat'l Network: USA; Moody; AP Radio; *Wire Services:* AP; U.S. Newswire
Population Served: 29,200; *Arbitron Metro Market:* Seattle-Tacoma, WA; *Format:* Christian; *Hrs. of News Programming:* news progmg 40 hrs wkly; *No. News Employees:* 1; *Target Audience:* 45-64. *Adv. Rates:* Call for rates
Stan Mak, Vice President and General Manager
Ann Marie E. Mulholland, Director of Sales
Mark Holland, Programming Director
Camille Birk, Marketing and Promotions Director
Julie Bradford, National Sales Manager

KCMS

03-11-1960; 105.3 MHz FM; *Hrs Open:* 24; 54 kw; Ant 1,263 ft; N47 32 40 W122 06 26
19303 Fremont Ave. N., Seattle, WA 98133
(206) 546-7350; *Fax:* (206) 546-7372
www.spirit1053.com
comments@spirit1053.com
License: Edmonds, Snohomish County, WA held by CRISTA Ministries
Group Owner: CRISTA Broadcasting
Wire Services: AP; U.S. Newswire
Population Served: 300,000; *Arbitron Metro Market:* Seattle-Tacoma, WA; *Format:* Adult Contemp, Christian; *Hrs. of News Programming:* News progmg one hr wkly; *Target Audience:* 25-44.; *Adv. Rates:* 300; 250; 275;150
Stan Mak, Vice President and General Manager
Ann Marie E. Mulholland, Director of Sales
Mark Holland, Programming Director
Camille Birk, Marketing and Promotions Director
Julie Bradford, National Sales Manager

Ellensburg

*KCSH

01-01-1998; 88.9 MHz FM; 0.38 kw; 548 ft.; N47 10 2 W120 45 50
415 W. 14th Avenue, Ellensburg, WA 98926-2425 US
(509) 964-2061; *Fax:* (509) 964-2825
www.ellensburgadventist22.adventistchurchconnect.org
License: Ellensburg, Kittitas County, WA held by Lifetalk Broadcasting Association.
Arbitron Metro Market: Ellensburg, WA; *Format:* Religious

*KCWU

04-30-1999; 88.1 MHz FM; *Hrs Open:* 24; 0.5 kw; -194 ft.; N47 0 21 W120 30 55
400 East University Way, SURC Room 120, Ellensburg, WA 98926 US
(509) 963-2283 2282; *Fax:* (509) 963-1688
www.881theburg.com
kcwu@cwu.edu
License: Ellensburg, Kittitas County, WA held by Trustees of Central Washington University.
Arbitron Metro Market: Ellensburg, WA; *Format:* Alternative, Variety/Diverse; *Hrs. of News Programming:* News progmg 5 hrs wkly; *Target Audience:* 15-49; 18-34 core
Chris Hull, General Manager
John Cerney, Programming Director
Kurt Oberloh, Broadcast Technician

*KNWR

06-01-1992; 90.7 MHz FM; *Hrs Open:* 24; 4.6 kw; 2549 ft.; N47 15 48 W120 23 31 *Rebroadcasts:* Rebroadcasts KRFA-FM Moscow, ID 100%
PO Box 642530, Pullman, WA 99164 US
(509) 335-6500; *Fax:* (509) 335-3772
www.nwpr.org
nwpr@wsu.edu
License: Ellensburg, Kittitas County, WA held by Washington State University.
Nat'l Network: NPR; PRI
Format: News *Special Programming:* Jazz, folk; *Hrs. of News Programming:* news progmg 37 hrs wkly; *No. News Employees:* 1; *Target Audience:* General.
Karen Olstad, COO
Scott Weatherly, Operations Dir
Kerry Swanson, General Manager/Station Manager
Sarah McDaniel, General Sales Mgr
Gillian Coldsnow, Programming Director
John Paxson, News Director
Ralph Hogan, Engineering Dir
Robin Rilette, Music Director

KXLE

01-01-1946; 1240 kHz AM; *Hrs Open:* 24
2111 Sixth Ave N, Ste 200, Seattle, WA 98109 US
(509) 925-1240; *Fax:* (509) 962-7882
License: Ellensburg, WA held by KXLE Inc.
Nat'l Network: CBS; *Nat'l Reps:* Tacher; *Wire Services:* AP
Arbitron Metro Market: Ellensburg, WA; *Format:* News, News/Talk, 84, Talk; *Hrs. of News Programming:* news progmg 40 hrs wkly; *No. News Employees:* 4; *Target Audience:* 25-54; adults; *Adv. Rates:* 240; 240; 240;200
Sol Tacher, President
Brad Tacher, Operations Dir
Steve Scellick, Programming Director
Patti Burke, Promotions & Traffic Manager
Rob Lowery, News Director
Kevin Whitaker, Engineering Dir

Elma

KDDS-FM
01-01-1981; 99.3 MHz FM; 64 kw; 2434 ft.; N47 18 46 W123 22 15
13612 Northwest 37th Place, Bellevue, WA 98005 US
(253) 735-9700; *Fax:* (253) 735-7424
www.radiogrande.com
License: Elma, Grays Harbor County, WA
Group Owner: Adelante Media Group LLC; (acq 9-28-2005; $20 million).
Arbitron Metro Market: Seattle, WA
Amador Bustos, President
Jose Diaz, General Manager
Cesar Valdiosera, Programming Director

Enumclaw

KGRG
03-01-1992; 1330 kHz AM; *Hrs Open:* 24; 0.5 kw-D, ND1; 0.026 kw-N, ND1; N47 12 53 W121 58 19
US
www.kgrg1.com
tkrause@greenriver.edu
License: Enumclaw, WA held by Green River Foundation
Arbitron Metro Market: Auburn, WA; *Format:* Alternative; *Adv. Rates:* 21.25; 18.75; 20; 12
Tom Evans Krause, General Manager
John Kasprick, Engineering Dir

Ephrata

KTAC
01-01-1998; 93.9 MHz FM; *Hrs Open:* 24; 18 kw; 384 ft.; N47 19 13 W119 34 22 *Rebroadcasts:* Simulcast with KTBI(AM) Ephrata
P.O. Box 31000, Spokane, WA 99223 US
(509) 754-2000; *Fax:* (509) 448-3811
www.ktac.com
ktac@ktac.com
License: Ephrata, Grant County, WA held by TRMR Inc.
Arbitron Metro Market: Spokane, WA
Richard Bott II, President
Pat Rulon, General Sales Mgr
Candy Green, Programming Director
Rachel Moser, Promotions Manager
Jason Potocnik, News Director
John Tillman-Production Manager

KTBI
08-17-1950; 810 kHz AM; *Hrs Open:* Sunrise-sunset; 23 kw-C, NDD; 50 kw-D, NDD; N47 21 22 W119 28 56 *Rebroadcasts:* Simulcast with KTAC(FM) Ephrata
P.O. Box 31000, Spokane, WA 99223 US
(509) 443-1000; *Fax:* (509) 448-3811
www.ktbi.com
ktbi@ktbi.com
License: Ephrata, WA held by Tacoma Broadcasters Inc.
Arbitron Metro Market: Spokane, WA; *Format:* Talk, Religious
Special Programming: Farm 15 hrs wkly; *Target Audience:* 35 plus.
Thomas Read, President
Melinda Read, Operations Dir
George Frese, Engineering Dir
John Tillman, Operations Manager

KULE
01-01-1952; 730 kHz AM
Mailing Address: 910 Basin Street, Sw, Ephrata, WA 98823 US
Second Address: 910 Basin S.W., Ephrata, WA 98823
(509) 754-4661; *Fax:* (509) 754-4110
License: Ephrata, WA
Group Owner: Adelante Media Group LLC; (acq 11-18-2004; grpsl).
Nat'l Network: Westwood One; CBS
Arbitron Metro Market: Ephrata, WA; *Format:* News, News/Talk, 84, Talk *Special Programming:* Farm 1 hr wkly; *Hrs. of News Programming:* news progmg 20 hrs wkly; *No. News Employees:* 1; *Target Audience:* 25-54. *Adv. Rates:* 10; 10; 10; 10
Amador Bustos, President
Keith Teske, Operations Dir
Bob Berry, General Manager
Martin Ortiz, Programming Director
Judith McInnis, Promotions Manager

KZUS
12-25-1982; 92.3 MHz FM; 26 kw; 673 ft.; N47 18 18 W119 35 53
Mailing Address: 910 Basin Street, Sw, Ephrata, WA 98823 US
Second Address: 910 Basin S.W., Ephrata, WA 98823
(509) 457-1000; *Fax:* (509) 754-4110
License: Ephrata, Grant County, WA
Group Owner: Adelante Media Group LLC
Nat'l Network: CBS
Arbitron Metro Market: Ephrata, WA; *Format:* Country
Keith Teske, Operations Dir
Bob Berry, General Manager
Tom Vinup, News Director

Everett

KRKO
08-01-1920; 1380 kHz AM; *Hrs Open:* 24; 5 kw-D, DAN; 5 kw-N, DAN; N47 55 32 W122 11 19
Suite 1380, 2707 Colby Avenue, Everett, WA 98201 US
(425) 304-1381; *Fax:* (425) 304-1382
www.krko.com
chuck.maylin@krko.com
License: Everett, WA held by S - R Broadcasting Co., Inc.
Nat'l Network: Westwood One; Fox Sports
Arbitron Metro Market: Seattle Metro area; *Format:* Sports; *Hrs. of News Programming:* news progmg 24 hrs wkly; *No. News Employees:* 1; *Target Audience:* Men 25-54; residents of Northern Puget Sound; *Adv. Rates:* 80; 50; 50; 25
Chuck Maylin, General Manager

*KSER
02-09-1991; 90.7 MHz FM; *Hrs Open:* 24; 5.8 kw; 302 ft.; N48 1 28 W122 6 41
2623 Wetmore Avenue, Everett, WA 98201 US
(425) 303-9070; *Fax:* (425) 303-9075
www.kser.org
info@kser.com
License: Everett, Snohomish County, WA held by KSER Foundation.
Nat'l Network: PRI
Arbitron Metro Market: Everett, WA; *Format:* Variety/Diverse
Special Programming: American Indian 2 hrs, folk 2 hrs, jazz 2 hrs, reggae 2 hrs, blues 6 hrs wkly; *Hrs. of News Programming:* news progmg 17 hrs wkly *No.News Employees:* 1; *Target Audience:* General; public radio; *Adv. Rates:* 25; 25; 25; 25
Brenda Mann Harrison, President
Hayden Bixby, Vice President
Bruce Wirth, General Manager
Tom Clendening, Station Manager
Chris Wartes, Chief Engineer
Maria Hamilton Lucas, Treasurer

KWYZ
07-21-1957; 1230 kHz AM; 1 kw-U, ND1; N47 58 6 W122 10 24
Rebroadcasts: Rebroadcasts KSUH(AM) Puyallup
200 S. 33rd Sttreet, Suite 100, Federal Way, WA 98003 US
(253) 815-1212; *Fax:* (253) 815-1913
www.radiohankook.com
License: Everett, WA held by Jean J. Suh dba Radio Hankook.
Nat'l Reps: Roslin
Arbitron Metro Market: Federal Way, WA; *Format:* Korean
Sung Hong, General Manager

Ferndale

KRPI
05-01-1963; 1550 kHz AM; *Hrs Open:* 24; 50 kw-D, DA2; 10 kw-N, DA2; N48 50 35 W122 36 5
Mailing Address: 5538 Imhof Road, PO Box 3213, Ferndale, CA 98248 US
Second Address: 5538 Imhoff Rd., Ferndale, WA 98248
(360) 384-5117; *Fax:* (360) 380-4202
www.krpiradio.com
License: Ferndale, WA held by BBC Broadcasting Inc.
Arbitron Metro Market: Ferndale, WA; *Format:* Ethnic; *Hrs. of News Programming:* News progmg 14 hrs wkly; *Target Audience:* 35 plus; East Indian adults; *Adv. Rates:* 21; 21; 25; 15
Suki Badh, General Manager
Grace Phelan, Station Manager

Forks

KBDB-FM
01-01-1985; 96.7 MHz FM; 6 kw; -75 ft.; N47 57 14 W124 23 20
PO Box 450, Forks, WA 98331 US
(360) 374-6233; *Fax:* (360) 374-6852
License: Forks, Clallam County, WA held by Forks Broadcasting Inc.
Format: Contemporary Hits/Top 40
Marvin Sanders, General Manager

KFKB
10-01-1967; 1490 kHz AM; *Hrs Open:* 24; 1 kw-U; N47 57 16 W124 23 20
Mailing Address: Box 450, Forks, WA 98331
Second Address: 260 Cedar, Forks, WA 9833331
(360) 374-6233; *Fax:* (360) 374-6852
License: Forks, Clallam County, WA held by Forks Broadcasting Inc.
Regional Reps: Tacher.
Special Programming: NFL, Sonics, college & high school football, Mariners 20 hrs, gospel 6.5 hrs wkly; *Hrs. of News Programming:* news progmg 2 hrs wkly; *No. News Employees:* 2; *Target Audience:* 25-54; general
Gary Lawrence, President
Al Monroe, General Manager
Marcia Nearhoff, General Sales Mgr
Arthur George, Min Affairs Director

*KNWU
91.5 MHz FM; 0.17 kw; -7 ft.; N47 56 0 W124 23 41
PO Box 642530, Pullman, WA 99164 US
(509) 335-6500; *Fax:* (509) 335-6577
www.nwpr.org
nwpr@wsu.edu
License: Forks, Clallam County, WA held by Washington State University.
Arbitron Metro Market: Forks, WA; *Format:* Classical
Tony Wright, General Manager
Kerry Swanson, Station Manager
John Paxson, News Director
Aki Wright, Development Coordinator
Gillian Coldsnow, Assistant Manager of Programming and Operations
Kevin Rinker, Traffic Manager
SarahMcDaniel, Membership Director

Friday Harbor

*KSJU
91.9 MHz FM; 0.1 kw; 82 ft.; N48 31 21 W123 1 36
US
(360) 378-3779
License: Friday Harbor, San Juan County, WA held by San Juan Island Community Radio.
Arbitron Metro Market: Friday Harbor, WA
Michael Calhoun, President

Gig Harbor

*KGHP
08-30-1988; 89.9 MHz FM; *Hrs Open:* 24; 1.35 kw horiz, 0.8 kw vert; 200 ft.; N47 14 27 W122 46 16
14105 Purdy Drive NW, Gig Harbor, WA 98332 US
(253) 857-3589; *Fax:* (253) 853-5841
abersolds@psd401.net
License: Gig Harbor, Pierce County, WA held by Peninsula School District No. 401.
Format: Easy Listening *Special Programming:* jazz 5 hr wkly, reggae 5 hrs wkly, radio horror classics 2 hrs wkly, book club 2 hr wkly; *Hrs. of News Programming:* News progmg 10 hrs wkly; *Target Audience:* General;diverse community audience; *Adv. Rates:* 100; 75; 100; 50
Leland Smith, General Manager
Spencer Abersold, Station Manager
Theresa Evans, Programming Director
Keith Stiles, Chief Engineer

Glenoma

*KGHE
89.1 MHz FM; 225 watts; 94 meters; N46 32 37 W122 03 36
PO Box 1892, Westport, WA 98595-1892
(360) 705-0619
www.kghifm.org
License: Glenoma, Lewis County, WA held by Northwest Indy Radio.

Stephen Lepisto, President

Goldendale

KLCK
09-04-1984; 1400 kHz AM
P. O. Box 305, Goldendale, WA 98620 US
(541) 296-9102; *Fax:* (541) 298-7775
www.klck1400.com
License: Goldendale, WA held by Klickitat Valley Broadcasting Services Inc.
Arbitron Metro Market: Yakima, WA; *Format:* Oldies
Danny Manciu, President
Betsy Hadden, General Sales Mgr
Kevin Malcolm, Programming Director
Hannah Settje, News Director
Cole Malcolm, Chief Engineer

KYYT
01-06-1992; 102.3 MHz FM; 2.1 kw; 1873 ft.; N45 40 53 W120 54 30
620 East 3rd Street, The Dalles, WA 97058 US

(541) 296-9102; *Fax:* (503) 200-1194
www.gorgecountry.com
info@haystackbroadcasting.com
License: Goldendale, Klickitat County, WA held by Haystack Broadcasting Inc.
Arbitron Metro Market: Goldendale, WA; *Format:* Country
Danny Manciu, President
Betsy Hadden, General Sales Mgr
Kevin Malcolm, Programming Director

Grand Coulee

KEYG
01-01-1979; 1490 kHz AM; *Hrs Open:* 24
58053 Spokane Boulevard NE, PO Box K, Grand Coulee, WA 99133 US
(509) 633-2020(509) 633-1490; *Fax:* (509) 633-1014
www.keyg985.com/keygam.html
keygfm@nwi.net
License: Grand Coulee, WA held by Wheeler Broadcasting Inc.
Group Owner: Wheeler Broadcasting Inc.; (acq 12-6-85)
Arbitron Metro Market: Grand Coulee, WA; *Format:* Country
Special Programming: Class 4 hrs, mus to remember 4 hrs, big band 4 hrs wkly; *Hrs. of News Programming:* news progmg 4 hrs wkly; *No. News Employees:* 1 *Target Audience:* 25 plus.
Verl Wheeler, CEO
Mark Wheeler, General Manager
Mark Wheeler, General Sales Mgr
Mike Helgerson, Chief Engineer
Nel Wheeler, National and Political Sales Manager

KEYG-FM
02-10-1984; 98.5 MHz FM; *Hrs Open:* 24; 100 kw horiz, 85 kw vert; 994 ft.; N47 49 18 W118 55 59
58053 Spokane Boulevard NE, PO Box K, Grand Coulee, WA 99133 US
(509) 633-2020(509) 633-1490; *Fax:* (509) 633-1014
www.keyg985.com
keygfm@nwi.net
License: Grand Coulee, Grant County, WA held by Wheeler Broadcasting Inc.
Group Owner: Wheeler Broadcasting Inc.
Arbitron Metro Market: Grand Coulee, WA; *Format:* Contemporary Hits/Top 40, Adult Contemp
Mark Wheeler, General Manager
Tim Cotter, Programming Director
Larry Weir, News Director
Dave Ratener, Chief Engineer
Brenda Anderson, Traffic Manager
National and Political Sales Manager

Grandview

KARY-FM
08-21-1989; 100.9 MHz FM; *Hrs Open:* 24; 7.8 kw; Ant 1,210 ft; N46 29 12 W120 00 05
1200 Chesterly Dr., Suite 160, Yakima, WA 98006
(509) 248-2900; *Fax:* (509) 452-9661
cherryfm.com
License: Grandview, Yakima County, WA held by Ingstad Radio Washington LLC
Group Owner: Ingstad Radio Washington LLC; acq 10-20-98; grpsl).
Population Served: 140,000; *Arbitron Metro Market:* Yakima, WA
Special Programming: Relg 8 hrs wkly; *Target Audience:* 25-54.; *Adv. Rates:* 28; 28; 28; 20
Pete Benedetti, CEO
Joe Benedetti, General Manager
Kevin Miskimins, General Sales Mgr
Dewey Boynton, Programming Director

Hamilton

*KSVU
90.1 MHz FM; 0.33 kw; -522 ft.; N48 33 16 W121 47 40
2405 East College Way, Mount Vernon, WA 98273 US
(360) 416-7711; *Fax:* (360) 416-7822
www.ksvu.org
mail@ksvr.org
License: Hamilton, Skagit County, WA held by Board of Trustees of Skagit Valley College.
Arbitron Metro Market: Hamilton, WA
Rip Robbins, General Manager
Jan Raschko, Station Manager
Joseph C. McGuire, Production Manager

Hoquiam

KXXK
09-03-1965; 95.3 MHz FM; *Hrs Open:* 24; 3.5 kw; 423 ft.; N46 55 55 W123 44 4
1308 Coolidge Rd., Aberdeen, WA 98520 US
(360) 533-1320; *Fax:* (360) 532-0935
www.kix953.com
License: Hoquiam, Grays Harbor County, WA held by Alpha Media Licensee LLC
Group Owner: Alpha Media LLC; (acq 9-2-2015; grpsl).
Arbitron Metro Market: Aberdeen, WA; *Format:* Country; *Target Audience:* 26-54.
Pat Anderson, Operations Manager
Donna Rosi, General Manager
Harvey Brooks, Chief Engineer

KDUX-FM
10-04-1964; 104.7 MHz FM; 31 kw; 361 ft.; N46 56 1 W123 43 49
1308 Coolidge Rd., Aberdeen, WA 98520 US
(360) 533-1320; *Fax:* (360) 532-0935
www.kdux.com
License: Hoquiam, Grays Harbor County, WA held by Alpha Media Licensee LLC
Group Owner: Alpha Media LLC; (acq 9-2-2015; grpsl).
Arbitron Metro Market: Hoquiam, WA; *Format:* Classic Rock
Pat Anderson, Operations Manager
Donna Rosi, General Manager

Ilwaco

KVAS-FM
01-01-2000; 103.9 MHz FM; 10 kw; Ant 171 ft; N46 18 51 W124 03 07
285 SW Main Court, Suite 200, Warrenton, OR 97146
(503) 861-6620; *Fax:* (503) 861-6630
www.eaglecountry1039.com
License: Ilwaco, Pacific County, WA
Group Owner: Ohana Media Group LLC; acq 8-25-99; $250,000 for CP).

Tom Freel, Operations Dir
Paul Mitchell, General Manager
Brian Riffe, General Sales Mgr

Kelso

KLOG
10-08-1949; 1490 kHz AM; *Hrs Open:* 24; 1 kw-U, ND1; N46 7 0 W122 53 7
(360) 636-0110
www.klog.com
License: Kelso, WA held by Washington Interstate Broadcasting Co. Inc.
Arbitron Metro Market: Portland, OR; *Format:* Adult Contemp; *No. News Employees:* 2; *Target Audience:* 25-54.
Joel Hanson, General Manager
Bill Dodd, Programming Director

KLYK
08-07-1991; 94.5 MHz FM; *Hrs Open:* 24; 3 kw; 476 ft.; N46 16 49 W122 52 34
1130 14th Ave., Longview, WA 98632 US
(360) 425-1500; *Fax:* (360) 423-1554
www.klykradio.com
bruce@bicoastalmedia.com
License: Kelso, Cowlitz County, WA held by Bicoastal Media Licenses IV LLC.
Group Owner: Bicoastal Media L.L.C.; (acq 3-31-2005; grpsl)
Nat'l Network: Westwood One
Arbitron Metro Market: Kelso, WA; *Format:* Adult Contemp; *Hrs. of News Programming:* News progmg 2 hrs wkly; *Target Audience:* 18-49.
Bruce Pollock, Market Manager

Kennewick

*KBLD
01-01-1998; 91.7 MHz FM; 1.8 kw; 971 ft.; N46 4 58 W119 9 39
10611 West Clearwater Ave., Kennewick, WA 99336 US
(509) 392-8111; *Fax:* (509) 586-0521
www.kbld.com
kbld91.7@gmail.com
License: Kennewick, Benton County, WA held by Calvary Chapel of Tri-Cities
Group Owner: CSN International; acq 6-12-97; $14,120).
Arbitron Metro Market: Kennewick, WA; *Format:* Christian
Mike Kestler, President
Daniel Davidson, Operations Dir
Don Mills, Network Programming Director
Mike Stocklin, Underwriting Director
Kelly Carlson, Engineering Dir

KONA-FM
08-01-1969; 105.3 MHz FM; *Hrs Open:* 24; 100 kw; 1138 ft.; N46 5 51 W119 11 30
Mailing Address: P.O. Box 2623, Tri-Cities, WA 99302 US
Second Address: Box 2623, Tri Cities, WA 99302
(509) 547-1618; *Fax:* (509) 546-2678
www.mix1053.com
License: Kennewick, Benton County, WA
Group Owner: Cherry Creek Radio LLC
Regional Reps: Allied Radio Partners.
Arbitron Metro Market: Tri-Cities, WA (Richland-Kennewick-Pasco); *Format:* Adult Contemp; *Hrs. of News Programming:* news progmg 3 hrs wkly; *No. News Employees:* 2; *Adv. Rates:* 25; 22; 25; 19
Dennis Goodman, COO
Tami Peterson, General Manager
Bert Thompson, General Sales Mgr
Allison Crawford, Programming Director
Linda Howard, News Director
Dennis Shannon, Local News Editor
Willy Contretas, Spanish Director
MikeMcDonnal, Sports Commentator

KJOX
08-01-1945; 1340 kHz AM; 1 kw-U; N46 13 16 W119 11 20
830 N. Columbia Ctr. Blvd., Suite B-2, Kennewick, WA 92101
(509) 783-0783; *Fax:* (509) 735-8627
License: Kennewick, Benton County, WA held by Ingstad Radio Washington LLC
Group Owner: Ingstad Radio Washington LLC; acq 12-10-99; grpsl).
Nat'l Reps: Christal
Population Served: 125,000; *Arbitron Metro Market:* Tri-Cities, WA (Richland-Kennewick-Pasco); *Target Audience:* 25-64.

*KTCV
12-10-1984; 88.1 MHz FM; *Hrs Open:* 12; 3.5 kw vert; -92 ft.; N46 13 7 W119 12 1
5929 W Metaline, Kennewick, WA 99336 US
(509) 734-3621(509) 734-3622; *Fax:* (509) 734-3609
dailed@ksd.org
License: Kennewick, Benton County, WA held by Kennewick School District No. 17.
Arbitron Metro Market: Kennewick, WA; *Format:* Alternative
Ed Dailey, General Manager

Kennewick-Richland-P

KONA
01-01-1948; 610 kHz AM; *Hrs Open:* 24; 5 kw-D, DA2; 5 kw-N, DA2; N46 10 23 W119 4 7
Mailing Address: P. O. Box 2623, Tri-Cities, WA 99302 US
Second Address: Box 2623, Tri Cities, WA 99302
(509) 547-1618; *Fax:* (509) 546-2678
www.610kona.com
kona@konaradio.com
License: Kennewick-Richland-P, WA held by CCR-Tri Cities IV LLC.
Group Owner: Cherry Creek Radio LLC; (acq 12-19-2003; grpsl).
Arbitron Metro Market: Tri-Cities, WA (Richland-Kennewick-Pasco); *Format:* News, News/Talk, 86
Special Programming: Farm 3 hrs, sports 8 hrs wkly; *Hrs. of News Programming:* news progmg 25 hrs wkly *No. NewsEmployees:* 2; *Target Audience:* 25-54.; *Adv. Rates:* 25; 22; 25; 19
Tami Peterson, General Manager
Phil Jimenez, General Sales Mgr
Michael McDonnal, Programming Director
Jeff Pohjola, News Director
Art Blum, Chief Engineer
Michael McDonnal, Disc Jockey
Bob Martin, Disc Jockey
Rusty Faust, DiscJockey

Kirkland

*KARR
01-01-1964; 1460 kHz AM; *Hrs Open:* 24
Mailing Address: 4135 Northgate Blvd., #1, Sacramento, CA 95834 US
Second Address: 290 Hegenberger Rd., Oakland, CA 94621
(800) 543-1495
www.familyradio.com
info@familyradio.org
License: Kirkland, WA held by Family Stations Inc.
Group Owner: Family Stations Inc.; (acq 10-22-86; $50,000;
Arbitron Metro Market: Oakland, CA; *Format:* Christian, Religious; *Hrs. of News Programming:* News progmg 5 hrs wkly; *Target Audience:* General; conservative Christians & evangelicals
Harold Camping, President
Thad McKinney, General Sales Mgr
Jim Dalke, Chief Engineer

Lacey

KBRD
06-01-1986; 680 kHz AM; *Hrs Open:* 6 AM-6 PM
PO Box 7034, Olympia, WA 98507 US
(360) 491-6800
www.kbrd.org
ad1@kbrd680.com
License: Lacey, WA held by BJ & Skip's for the Music
Nat'l Network: AP Radio
Arbitron Metro Market: Seattle-Tacoma, WA; *Format:* Oldies
Special Programming: Jazz one hr wkly; *Target Audience:* General.
Adrian DeBee, General Manager

KLDY
09-22-1983; 1280 kHz AM; *Hrs Open:* 24; 1 kw-D, ND1; 0.5 kw-N, ND1; N47 3 44 W122 49 49
PO Box 348, 2539 North Highway 67, Sedalia, CO 80135 US
(206) 878-6070; (877) 725-9777; *Fax:* (206) 824-2573
www.espndeportesseattle.com
License: Lacey, WA held by Seattle Streaming Radio LLC.
Group Owner: Seattle Streaming Radio LLC; (acq 4-25-2007; $300,000)
Arbitron Metro Market: Seattle, WA
Maria Sotelo, General Manager

Lakewood

KLAY
01-01-1991; 1180 kHz AM; *Hrs Open:* 24; 5 kw-D, DAN; 1 kw-N, DAN; N47 9 0 W122 24 38
10025 Lakewood Dr.,Sw #B, Tacoma, WA 98499 US
(253) 581-0324; *Fax:* (253) 581-0326
www.klay1180.com
License: Lakewood, WA held by Clay Frank Huntington.
Nat'l Network: Westwood One
Arbitron Metro Market: Seattle, WA; *Format:* Talk; *Hrs. of News Programming:* news progmg 11 hrs wkly; *No. News Employees:* 2; *Target Audience:* 30-65.
Clay Frank Huntington, President
Mike Franco, Operations Dir
Bob McCluskey, General Sales Mgr
Bruce Bond, Programming Director
Anna Winter, News Director
Nick Winter, Engineering Dir

KNTB
09-01-1978; 1480 kHz AM; *Hrs Open:* 6 AM-sunset; 1 kw-D, DAD; 0.111 kw-N, DA2; N47 9 56 W122 34 32
PO Box 348, 2539 North Highway 67, Sedalia, CO 80135 US
(303) 688-5162; (877) 725-9777; *Fax:* (303) 660-4930
License: Lakewood, WA held by Seattle Streaming Radio LLC.
Group Owner: Seattle Streaming Radio LLC; (acq 8-26-2005; $900,000 with KBRO(AM) Bremerton)
Arbitron Metro Market: Seattle, WA
Oscar Ibarra, General Manager

Leavenworth

KOHO
01-01-1998; 101.1 MHz FM; 0.93 kw; 2044 ft.; N47 36 7 W120 30 32
32 N. Mission, Suite A, Wenatchee, WA 98801 US
(509) 667-2400
www.kohoradio.com
License: Leavenworth, Chelan County, WA held by Icicle Broadcasting Inc.
Group Owner: Icicle Broadcasting Inc.; acq 8-26-99; grpsl).
Arbitron Metro Market: Wenatchee-Wash; *Format:* Triple A
Elliot Salmon, General Manager
Clint Strand, News Dir./Program Dir
Dan Langager, News Director

Longview

KBAM
08-15-1955; 1270 kHz AM
1130 14th Ave., Longview, WA 98632 US
(360) 425-1500; *Fax:* (360) 423-1554
www.kbamcountry.com
bruce@bicoastalmedia.com
License: Longview, WA held by Bicoastal Media Licenses IV LLC.
Group Owner: Bicoastal Media L.L.C.; (acq 3-31-2005; grpsl)
Nat'l Network: CBS; *Nat'l Reps:* McGavren Guild
Arbitron Metro Market: Longview, WA; *Format:* Country
Bruce Pollock, Market Manager

KEDO
05-01-1938; 1400 kHz AM; *Hrs Open:* 24
1130 14th Ave., Longview, WA 98632 US
(360) 425-1500; *Fax:* (360) 423-1554
www.kedoam.com
bruce@bicoastalmedia.com
License: Longview, WA held by Bicoastal Media Licenses IV LLC.
Group Owner: Bicoastal Media L.L.C.; (acq 3-31-2005; grpsl)
Regional Reps: Art Moore.
Format: News, Oldies *Special Programming:* Pub affrs 2 hrs wkly; *Hrs. of News Programming:* news progmg 15 hrs wkly; *No. News Employees:* 1; *Target Audience:* 25-54.
Bruce Pollock, Market Manager

*KJVH
01-01-1988; 89.5 MHz FM; 0.1 kw vert; 781 ft.; N46 9 52 W122 51 13
290 Hegenberger Road, Oakland, CA 94621 US
(800) 543-1495
www.familyradio.com
License: Longview, Cowlitz County, WA held by Family Stations Inc.
Group Owner: Family Stations Inc.
Arbitron Metro Market: Salt Lake City, UT; *Format:* Christian, Religious
Harold Camping, President
Roger Crawford, Station Manager

KUKN
07-07-1962; 105.5 MHz FM; *Hrs Open:* 24; 0.7 kw; 860 ft.; N46 9 52 W122 51 13
Mailing Address: PO Box 90, Kelso, WA 98626 US
Second Address: 506 Cowlitz Way W., Longview, WA 98626
(360) 633-0110; *Fax:* (360) 577-6949
www.kukn.com
License: Longview, Cowlitz County, WA
Arbitron Metro Market: Portland, OR; *Format:* Country; *Hrs. of News Programming:* news progmg 2 hrs wkly; *No. News Employees:* 2
Beth Jensen, Operations Dir
Joel Hanson, General Sales Mgr
John Mitchel, Programming Director
Jadd Curtis, Promotions Manager
Ray Byers, News Director
Bill Dodd, Disc Jockey
Ray Bartley, Bill Dodd
Kirc Rolland, SportsCommentator

KRQT
01-01-1994; 107.1 MHz FM; 0.8 kw; 1716 ft.; N46 20 18 W123 5 45
1130 14th Ave., Longview, WA 98632 US
(360) 425-1500; *Fax:* (360) 423-1554
www.rocket107.com
bruce@bicoastalmedia.com
License: Longview, WA held by Bicoastal Media Licenses IV LLC.
Group Owner: Bicoastal Media L.L.C.; (acq 3-31-2005; grpsl)
Nat'l Network: ABC
Format: Light Rock; *Hrs. of News Programming:* One
Bruce Pollock, Marketing Manager

*KLWO
10-22-1987; 90.3 MHz FM; *Hrs Open:* 24; 400 w vert; Ant 892 ft; N46 09 47 W122 51 14
PO Box 2098, Omaha, NE 68103-2098
www.klove.com
License: Longview, Cowlitz County, WA held by Educational Media Foundation
Group Owner: Educational Media Foundation; (acq 8-1-2003; with KWYA(FM) Astoria, OR)
Target Audience: 19-34.
Darrell Chambliss, Chairman
Mike Novak, President/CEO
Alan Mason, COO
David Pierce, Chief Creative Officer
Eric Moser, CFO
D. Kevin Blair, Secretary/General Counsel

Lynden

KWPZ
11-08-1960; 106.5 MHz FM; *Hrs Open:* 24; 63 kw; 2333 ft.; N48 40 46 W122 50 31
1843 Front St., Lynden, WA 98264 US
(360) 354-5596; *Fax:* (360) 354-7517
www.praise1065.com
comment@praise1065.com
License: Lynden, Whatcom County, WA held by CRISTA Ministries
Group Owner: CRISTA Broadcasting; (acq 12-80).
Arbitron Metro Market: Bellingham, WA; *Format:* Christian, Religious; *Target Audience:* 25-54; female; *Adv. Rates:* 45; 40; 42; 28
John Randolph, General Manager
Ann Marie E. Mulholland, Director of Sales
Marvin Mickley, Director of Fundraising
Julie Bradford, National Sales Manager

Mabton

KMNA
01-01-1997; 98.7 MHz FM; 11.5 kw; 874 ft.; N46 28 33 W120 8 37
361 West Monroe Street, Post Office Box 10, Mabton, WA 98935 US
(509) 786-1209; *Fax:* (509) 786-1181
License: Mabton, Yakima County, WA held by MBProsser Licensee LLC.
Group Owner: Moon Broadcasting; (acq 2-6-2004; $1.9 million).
Arbitron Metro Market: Richland, WA; *Format:* Spanish
Carol Crider, General Manager

Manson

KZAL
01-01-2007; 94.7 MHz FM; 10.3 kw; 518 ft.; N47 51 16 W120 9 59
Mailing Address: Box 2675, Wenetchee, WA 98807 US
Second Address: 32 N. Mission, Wenatchee, WA 98807
(509) 667-2400; *Fax:* (509) 663-9497
www.zcountry947.com
znation@zcountry947.com
License: Manson, Chelan County, WA held by Icicle Broadcasting Inc.
Group Owner: Icicle Broadcasting Inc.
Arbitron Metro Market: Commerce, TX; *Format:* Country
Elliot Salmon, General Manager
Randy Roadz, Programming Director

*KHNW
88.3 MHz FM; 380 w; Ant 499 ft; N47 51 16 W120 09 59
12501 Park Avenue S., Tacoma, WA
(253) 535-7758; *Fax:* 253-535-8769
info@kplu.org
License: Manson, Chelan County, WA held by Pacific Lutheran University.

Paul Stankavich, General Manager
Jeff Bauman, Programming Director
Lowell Kiesow, Chief Engineer
Nick Francis, Music Director
Joey Cohn, Program Director

McCleary

KYYO
10-01-1992; 96.9 MHz FM; *Hrs Open:* 24; 11 kw; 1053 ft.; N47 5 9 W123 11 17
1240 Washington St., Ne, Olympia, WA 98501 US
(360) 943-1240; *Fax:* (360) 352-1222
www.southsoundcountry.com
kgysales@kgyradio.com
License: McCleary, Grays Harbor County, WA held by KGY Inc.
Format: Country; *No. News Employees:* 2; *Target Audience:* 35 plus.
Jackson Weaver, General Manager
Heidi Persson, General Sales Mgr
Jeanna Spain, News Director
Tom Trotzer, Chief Engineer

Medical Lake

*KTSL
03-07-1989; 101.9 MHz FM; *Hrs Open:* 24; 28.5 kw; 650 ft.; N47 42 11 W117 44 26
10209 Southeast Division Street, Portland, OR 97266 US
(509) 326-9500; *Fax:* (509) 326-1560
www.air1.com
info@air1.com
License: Medical Lake, Spokane County, WA held by Educational Media Foundation.
Group Owner: EMF Broadcasting; (acq 5-23-2008; $2.15 million)
Arbitron Metro Market: Medical Lake, WA; *Format:* Alternative, Christian
Darrell Chambliss, Chairman
Alan Mason, COO
Mike Novak, President and CEO
Tracy Butler, News Director
Sam Wallington, Engineering Dir
Marya Morgan, News Reporter
Richard Hunt, News Reporter
Larry Moody, Director
MitchBarnhart, Director
David R. Ferry, Director
Walter Golembeski, Director

Mercer Island

*KMIH
02-01-1970; 88.9 MHz FM; *Hrs Open:* 24; 0.03 kw; 226 ft.; N47 34 21 W122 13 5
9100 S.E. 42nd Street, Mercer Island, WA 98040 US
(206) 275-9104; *Fax:* (206) 236-3342
hotjamz.org
pd@hotjamz.org
License: Mercer Island, King County, WA held by Mercer Island School District No. 400.
Arbitron Metro Market: Seattle, WA; *Format:* Contemporary Hits/Top 40; *Target Audience:* 18-34; Female
Charlie Hilen, General Manager
Bob Casserd, General Sales Mgr
Nic Alquist, Programming Director
John Van Oppen, Chief Engineer

Mercer Island/Seattl

KIXI
01-01-1947; 880 kHz AM; *Hrs Open:* 24
3650 131st Avenue SE, Suite 550, Bellevue, WA 98006 US
(425) 562-8964
www.kixi.com
info@kixi.com
License: Mercer Island/Seattl, WA held by Bellevue Radio Inc.
Group Owner: Sandusky Radio; (acq 11-15-91; $3.5 million;
Nat'l Network: Music of Your Life; *Nat'l Reps:* Christal
Arbitron Metro Market: Seattle-Tacoma, WA; *Format:* Adult Contemp; *Target Audience:* 35 plus; mature active adults
Marc Kaye, General Manager
Lois Mares, Sales Manager
Susan Hoffman, Sales Director
Julie Judge, National Sales Manager
Dan Murphy, Operations Manager

Montesano

KANY
01-01-2008; 93.7 MHz FM; 14 kw; 400 ft.; N46 56 0 W123 43 57
1520 Simpson Ave., Aberdeen, WA 98520 US
(360) 533-3000; *Fax:* (360) 532-1456
www.bigfoot1073.com
License: Montesano, Grays Harbor County, WA held by Jodesha Broadcasting, LLC.
Group Owner: Jodesha Broadcasting Inc.; (acq 3-16-2007; $600,000 for CP)
Nat'l Network: Jones Radio Networks
Arbitron Metro Market: Waterloo-Cedar Falls, IA; *Format:* Country
Gabrielle Jordan, General Manager
Bill Wolfenbarger, General Sales Mgr

Moses Lake

KBSN
11-01-1947; 1470 kHz AM; *Hrs Open:* 24; 5 kw-D, DA2; 1 kw-N, DA2; N47 6 16 W119 17 32
1802 136th Place N.E., Bellevue, WA 98005 US
(509) 765-3441; *Fax:* (509) 766-0273
License: Moses Lake, WA held by KSEM Inc.
Nat'l Network: ABC; *Nat'l Reps:* McGavren Guild
Format: News, News/Talk, 84, Talk *Special Programming:* Sp 9 hrs wkly; *No. News Employees:* 3; *Target Audience:* General.
Jim Davis, General Manager
Stacey Lehman, General Sales Mgr
Bill Ecret, Programming Director
Butch Bare, News Director
Will Vos, Chief Engineer
Dennis Clay, Outdoor Ed
Dave Heaverlo, Sports Commentator
Colleen Roth, TrafficManager

KDRM
10-01-1980; 99.3 MHz FM; 3 kw; 275 ft; N47 05 54 W119 17 47
1802 136th Place NE, Bellevue, WA 98005
(509) 765-3441; *Fax:* (509) 766-0273
License: Moses Lake, Grant County, WA held by KSEM Inc.
Nat'l Reps: McGavren Guild
Hrs. of News Programming: 1; *Target Audience:* 18-34.
Bill Ecret, General Manager
Stacey Lehman-Garcia, General Sales Mgr
Bill Ecret, Programming Director
Butch Bare, News Director
Dale Roth, Public Service Director
Colleen Roth, Traffic Manager

*KLWS
04-10-1997; 91.5 MHz FM; *Hrs Open:* 24; 7.2 kw; 686 ft.; N47 18 50 W119 34 55 *Rebroadcasts:* Rebroadcasts KWSU(AM) Pullman 100%
P.O. Box 642530, 382 Murrow Center, Pullman, WA 99165 US
(509) 335-6500; *Fax:* (509) 335-3772
www.nwpr.org
nwpr@wsu.edu
License: Moses Lake, Grant County, WA held by Washington State University.
Arbitron Metro Market: Washington; *Format:* News
Scott Weatherly, Operations Dir
Dennis Haarsager, General Manager
Kerry Swanson, Station Manager
Gillian Coldsnow, Programming Director
John Paxson, News Director
Robin Rilette, Music Director

*KMLW
05-04-1997; 88.3 MHz FM; 4 kW; 679 ft; N46 56 31 W119 25 41
Rebroadcasts: Rebroadcasts KMBI-FM Spokane 100%
5408 S Freya St, Spokane, WA 99223 USA
(509) 448-2555; *Fax:* (509 448-6855
www.moodyradio.org/stations/northwest
License: Moses Lake, Grant County, WA held by The Moody Bible Institute of Chicago
Group Owner: The Moody Bible Institute of Chicago
Arbitron Metro Market: Moses Lake, WA; *Format:* Christian
Special Programming: Class one hr wkly; *Target Audience:* 35-54; Christians

KWIQ-FM
05-22-1968; 100.5 MHz FM; *Hrs Open:* 24; 50 kw; 167 ft.; N47 6 9 W119 14 24
11768 Kittleson Rd. N.E., Moses Lake, WA 98837 US
(509) 765-1761; *Fax:* (509) 765-8901
www.kwiq.com
License: Moses Lake, Grant County, WA held by Alpha Media Licensee LLC
Group Owner: Alpha Media LLC
Nat'l Reps: Katz Radio *Regional Reps:* Allied Radio Partners.
Arbitron Metro Market: Wenatchee, WA; *Format:* Country; *No. News Employees:* 1; *Adv. Rates:* Same as AM
Gary Patrick, General Manager
Jeff Dahlstrom, Sales Manager
Ryan Nelson, Programming Director
Charlie Osgood, Chief Engineer
Kelley Rose, Business Manager
Shari Alexander, Traffic Director
Robin Fazende-Goude, Sales Executive
Carol Arevalo, Sales Executive
Todd Farrar, Sales Executive
Jennifer Heneghen, Sales Executive

Moses Lake North

KWIQ
02-20-1956; 1020 kHz AM; *Hrs Open:* 24; 2 kw-D, DA2; 2 kw-N, DA2; N47 9 48 W119 21 39
1124 N. Miller St., Wenatchee, WA 98801 US
(509) 663-5186; *Fax:* (509) 663-8779
www.kkrt.com
License: Moses Lake North, Grant County, WA held by Alpha Media Licensee LLC
Group Owner: Alpha Media LLC; (acq 9-2-2015; grpsl).
Nat'l Network: ESPN Radio; *Nat'l Reps:* Katz Radio
Arbitron Metro Market: Wenatchee, WA; *Format:* Sports; *Hrs. of News Programming:* news progmg 6 hrs wkly; *No. News Employees:* 1; *Target Audience:* 18-49; men; *Adv. Rates:* 18; 16; 18; 14
Gary Patrick, General Manager
Jeff Dahlstrom, Sales Manager
Charlie Osgood, Chief Engineer
Kelley Rose, Business Manager
Shari Alexander, Traffic Director

Mount Vernon

KAPS
03-17-1963; 660 kHz AM; *Hrs Open:* 24; 10 kw-D, DA2; 1 kw-N, DA2; N48 26 19 W122 20 39
2029 Freeway Drive, Mount Vernon, WA 98273 US
(360) 424-7676; *Fax:* (360) 424-1660
www.kapsradio.com
kapsradio@gmail.com
License: Mount Vernon, WA held by Valley Broadcasters Inc.
Regional Reps: McGaven Guild
Arbitron Metro Market: Mount Vernon, WA; *Format:* Country; *Hrs. of News Programming:* news progmg hourly; *No. News Employees:* 1; *Target Audience:* General.
Jim Keane, President
Jerry Keane, General Sales Mgr
Mike Yeoman, Programming Director

KBRC
12-11-1946; 1430 kHz AM; *Hrs Open:* 24; 5 kw-D, DAN; 1 kw-N, DAN; N48 25 22 W122 21 10
Mailing Address: P.O. Box 250, Mount Vernon, WA 98273 US
Second Address: 2029 Freeway Dr., Mount Vernon, WA 98273
(360) 424-4278; *Fax:* (360) 424-1660
kbrcradio.com
kbrcradio@gmail.com
License: Mount Vernon, WA held by Valley Broadcasting.
Nat'l Network: ABC *Regional Reps:* Tacher.
Format: Oldies *Special Programming:* Sp 3 hrs, farm 5 hrs wkly; *No. News Employees:* 2; *Target Audience:* 25-54.
James Keane, President
Jerry Keane, General Sales Mgr
Mike Yoeman, Programming Director
Kirk Tollifson, News Director
Mike Gilbert, Chief Engineer
Julia Rasmussen, Traffic Manager

*KMWS
05-04-1973; 89.7 MHz FM; *Hrs Open:* 24; 1.5 kw; 118 ft.; N48 32 30 W122 17 43 *Rebroadcasts:* Rebroadcasts KWSU(AM) Pullman 100%
Washington State University, PO Box 642530, Pullman, WA 99164-2530 US
(509) 335-6500
www.nwpr.org
nwpr@wsu.edu
License: Mount Vernon, Skagit County, WA held by Washington State University
Arbitron Metro Market: Pullman. WA; *Format:* News, News/Talk, 86
Bethany Lee, Community Partnerships/Development Coordinator
Brett Charvat, Traffic/Promotions Coordinator
Don Eckis, Broadcast Chief Engineer
John Paxson, News Director
Kerry Swanson, Station Manager

*KSVR
01-01-2002; 91.7 MHz FM; 0.17 kw; 669 ft.; N48 23 49 W122 18 26
2405 East College Way, Mt. Vernon, WA 98273 US
(360) 416-7711
www.ksvr.org
info@ksvr.org
License: Mount Vernon, Skagit County, WA held by Board of Trustees of Skagit Valley College
Arbitron Metro Market: Mount Vernon, WA; *Format:* News, News/Talk, 86
Rip Robbins, KSVR General Manager, Media Instructor
Dave McConnell, Station Manager
Joseph C. McGuire, Production Manager

Naches

KIT-FM
11-01-2000; 99.3 MHz FM; 790 w; Ant 899 ft; N46 36 02 W120 52 06
4010 Summitview Ave., Yakima, WA 98908
(509) 972-3461; *Fax:* (509) 972-3540
www.my993fm.com
License: Naches, Yakima County, WA held by GAP Broadcasting Yakima License LLC.
Group Owner: GAPWEST Broadcasting; (acq 2-13-2008; grpsl)
Dave Ettl, Brand Manager
Jamie Stickel, Director of Sales
John Taylor, Digital Managing Editor

KZTA
10-25-1988; 96.9 MHz FM; *Hrs Open:* 24; 14 kw; 935 ft.; N46 35 59 W120 52 8
Mailing Address: PO Box 2888, Yakima, WA 98907 US
Second Address: 706 Butterfield Rd., Yakima, WA 98901
(509) 457-1000; *Fax:* (509) 452-0541
License: Naches, Yakima County, WA
Group Owner: Adelante Media Group LLC; (acq 11-18-2004; grpsl)
Nat'l Reps: Tacher
Arbitron Metro Market: Naches, WA; *Hrs. of News Programming:* News progmg 3 hrs wkly; *Target Audience:* 18-35; Hispanic; *Adv. Rates:* 31; 28; 25; 21
Ed Krampf, COO
Jay Meyers, CEO
Amador Bustos, President
Keith Teske, Operations Dir
Bob Berry, General Manager

Judith McInnes, Programming Director
Jesus Rosales, News Director

Newport

KGZG-FM
12-01-1989; 104.5 MHz FM; 87 kw hoirz; Ant 1,046 ft; N48 23 09 W117 14 15
(509) 589-1045
www.1045jamz.com
License: Newport, Pend Oreille County, WA held by Radio Station KMJY LLC
Arbitron Metro Market: Spokane, WA; *Target Audience:* 18-34.

***KUBS**
09-10-1973; 91.5 MHz FM; 0.15 kw horiz; 735 ft.; N48 10 42 W117 4 59
US
(509) 447-4931
www.kubsradio.com
License: Newport, Pend Oreille County, WA held by Newport Consolidated School District #56415.
Arbitron Metro Market: Newport, WA; *Format:* Variety/Diverse

KPWL
1370 kHz AM
US
(213) 494-3377
License: Newport, WA held by Scott Powell.
Arbitron Metro Market: Newport, WA
Scott Powell, General Manager

Nile

***KSBC**
01-01-2003; 88.3 MHz FM; *Hrs Open:* 24; 0.2 kw; -1145 ft.; N46 50 2 W120 56 13
402 E Yakima Ave, Suite 1320, Yakima, WA 98901 US
(501) 321-2923; *Fax:* (501) 321-2816
www.klove.com
klove@klove.com
License: Nile, Yakima County, WA held by Educational Media Foundation.
Group Owner: EMF Broadcasting; (acq 10-2-2003; grpsl).
Nat'l Network: K-Love
Format: Christian; *No. News Employees:* 3; *Target Audience:* 25-44; Judeo Christian female
Mike Novak, President
Mike Lee, Operations Dir
David Pierce, Programming Director
Ed Lenane, News Director
Sam Wallington, Engineering Dir
Marya Morgan, News Reporter

Oak Harbor

KRPA
12-14-1984; 1110 kHz AM; *Hrs Open:* 5:30 AM-6 PM; 500 w-D; N48 17 27 W122 42 28
904 32nd Street, Anacortes, WA 98221
(360) 240-1110; *Fax:* (206) 414-4099
License: Oak Harbor, Island County, WA held by Impact Directories of Northwest Washington, LLC
Nat'l Network: Fox News Radio
Population Served: 68,500; *Arbitron Metro Market:* Seattle-Tacoma, WA; *Hrs. of News Programming:* 6 Hours A Week; *No. News Employees:* 1; *Target Audience:* 20-60.; *Adv. Rates:* 20; 15; 20; 15

Oakville

KOMO-FM
10-26-1984; 97.7 MHz FM; *Hrs Open:* 24; 63 kw; Ant 2,388 ft; N47 18 46 W123 22 15
Mailing Address: 13612 NE 37th Place, Bellevue, WA 98005
Second Address: 1803 State Ave. N.E., Olympia, WA 98506
(360) 918-9000; *Fax:* (360) 236-8786
www.977theeagle.com
License: Oakville, Grays Harbor County, WA held by South Sound Broadcasting LLC
Nat'l Reps: McGavren Guild
Population Served: 2,600,000; *Arbitron Metro Market:* Tacoma, OK; *Format:* Christian *Special Programming:* Live performance 10 hrs wkly,; *Hrs. of News Programming:* News progmg 10 hrs wkly *Target Audience:* Christian Families
Bill Bradley, General Manager
Craig Sullivan, Programming Director
Jeff Turnbow, News Director

Ocean Park

***KWAO**
01-01-2006; 88.1 MHz FM; *Hrs Open:* 24; 550 w; Ant 1,044 ft; 46 41 46 W123 46 17 *Rebroadcasts:* Rebroadcasts KLVR(FM) Santa Rosa, CA 100%
2351 Sunset Blvd., Suite 170-218, Rocklin, CA
(916) 251-1600; *Fax:* (916) 251-1650
www.klove.com
klove@klove.com
License: Ocean Park, Pacific County, WA held by Educational Media Foundation.
Group Owner: EMF Broadcasting
Nat'l Network: K-Love
No. News Employees: 3; *Target Audience:* 25-44; Judeo Christian, female
Mike Novak, President
Mike Lee, Operations Dir
Eric Allen, General Sales Mgr
David Pierce, Programming Director
Ed Lenane, News Director
Sam Wallington, Engineering Dir
Scott Smith, Music Director
Marya Morgan, NewsReporter
Richard Hunt, News Reporter
Tracy Butler, Traffic Manager

Ocean Shores

KSWW
01-01-1998; 102.1 MHz FM; *Hrs Open:* 24; 14 kw; 322 ft.; N46 56 00 W123 43 57
1520 Simpson Ave., Aberdeen, WA 95820 US
(360) 533-3000; *Fax:* (360) 532-1456
www.jodesha.com
info@jodesha.com
License: Ocean Shores, Grays Harbor County, WA held by Jodesha Broadcasting Inc.
Group Owner: Jodesha Broadcasting Inc.; acq 2-28-03; $750,000 with KBKW(AM) Aberdeen).
Nat'l Network: ABC *Regional Reps:* Tacher; *Wire Services:* AP
Arbitron Metro Market: Aberdeen, WA; *Format:* Adult Contemp; *Hrs. of News Programming:* 7 hrs wkly; *No. News Employees:* 1; *Target Audience:* 25-54.; *Adv. Rates:* 30; 26; 28; na
Gabrielle Jordan, General Manager
Bill Wolfenbarger, General Sales Mgr

Olympia

***KAOS**
01-01-1973; 89.3 MHz FM; *Hrs Open:* 24; 1.5 kw; -19 ft; N47 04 22 W122 58 51
CAB 301, Olympia, WA 98505
(360) 867-6888
www.kaosradio.org
kaos@evergreen.edu
License: Olympia, Thurston County, WA held by Evergreen State College.
Nat'l Network: Pacifica
Population Served: 100,000 *Special Programming:* Folks 3 hrs, Asian 10 hrs, American Indian 4 hrs,; *Hrs. of News Programming:* News progmg 7.5 hrs wkly; *Target Audience:* 18-35.; *Adv. Rates:* $12.50 per :20underwriting
Ruth Brownstein, Operations Dir
Jerry Drummond, General Manager
John Ford, General Sales Mgr
Rob Rensel, Chief Engineer

KGTK
10-01-1956; 920 kHz AM; *Hrs Open:* 24 *Rebroadcasts:* Rebroadcasts KITZ(AM) Silverdale 90%
Mailing Address: 120 State Ave N.E., Mb 95, Olympia, WA 98501 US
Second Address: 1700 Mile High Dr., Suite 201A, Port Orchard, WA 98366
(360) 876-1400; *Fax:* (360) 876-7920
www.kgtk.com
info@kitz1400.com
License: Olympia, WA held by KITZ Radio Inc.
Nat'l Network: USA; Radio America *Regional Reps:* Tacher
Arbitron Metro Market: Seattle-Tacoma, WA; *Format:* Talk; *Hrs. of News Programming:* News progmg 7 hrs wkly; *Target Audience:* 18-65; diversified adults; *Adv. Rates:* 25; 15; 25; 10
Alan Gottlieb, President
Kevin Corcoran, Operations Dir
Conn Williamson, General Manager
Conn Williamson, General Sales Mgr
Kevin Corcoran, Operations Manager

KGY
04-15-1922; 1240 kHz AM; *Hrs Open:* 24
Mailing Address: 1240 Washington St, Ne, Olympia, WA 98507 US
Second Address: 1700 Marine Dr. N.E., Olympia, WA 98501
(360) 943-1240; *Fax:* (360) 352-1222
www.kgyradio.com
feedback@kgyradio.com
License: Olympia, WA held by KGY Inc.
Nat'l Network: CBS Radio; *Wire Services:* AP
Arbitron Metro Market: Seattle-Tacoma, WA; *Format:* Adult Contemp; *No. News Employees:* 2; *Target Audience:* General.; *Adv. Rates:* 372; 288; 288; 240
Dick Pust, General Manager
Darlene Kemery, General Sales Mgr
Kevin Huffer, Programming Director
Steve George, News Director
Tom Trotzer, Chief Engineer
Jeanna Spain, Traffic Manager

KXXO
01-16-1990; 96.1 MHz FM; *Hrs Open:* 24; 85 kw; Ant 2,099 ft; N46 38 07 W122 28 01
Mailing Address: Box 7937, Olympia, WA 98507
Second Address: Rockway/Leland Bldg., 119 N. Washington Ave., Olympia, WA 98501
(360) 943-9937; *Fax:* (360) 352-3643
www.mixx96.com
admin@mixx96.com
License: Olympia, Thurston County, WA held by 3 Cities Inc.
Population Served: 1,325,000; *Arbitron Metro Market:* Seattle-Tacoma, WA; *Hrs. of News Programming:* news progmg one hr wkly; *No. News Employees:* 1; *Target Audience:* 25-54; general
David Rauh, President
Toni Holm, Operations Dir
Toni Holm, Station Manager
Brian Butler, General Sales Mgr
John Foster, Programming Director
Ann D'Angelo, News Director
Tim Vik, Chief Engineer

***KPLI**
09-01-2006; 90.1 MHz FM; 100 w; Ant -59 ft; N47 02 20 W122 54 00 *Rebroadcasts:* Rebroadcasts KPLU-FM Tacoma 100%
PO Box 25, Olympia, WA 98507
(253) 536-5009; *Fax:* 253-535-8769
License: Olympia, Thurston County, WA held by Pacific Lutheran University Inc.
Nat'l Network: NPR; PRI; *Wire Services:* AP
Population Served: 60,000 *Hrs. of News Programming:* news progmg 54 hrs wkly; *No. News Employees:* 7
Jeff Bauman, Operations Dir
Paul Stankavich, General Manager
Joey Cohn, Programming Director
Brenda Goldstein-Young, Promotions Manager
Erin Hennessey, News Director
Lowell Kiesow, Chief Engineer
Nick Francis, Music Director
Jennifer Strchan, News Media Director

Omak

KNCW
04-10-1978; 92.7 MHz FM; *Hrs Open:* 24; 4.1 kw; 942 ft.; N48 19 12 W119 32 18
P.O. Box 151, 320 Emery Street, Omak, WA 98841 US
(509) 826-0100; (800) 725-5669; *Fax:* (509) 826-3929
www.komw.net
info@komw.net
License: Omak, Okanogan County, WA
Format: Country; *Target Audience:* General.
David Miller, President
John P. Andrist, Station Manager
Rick Duck, Sales Manager
Chris Schmidt, Programming Director

KOMW
09-30-1947; 680 kHz AM; 5 kw-D, NDD; N48 23 40 W119 32 0
Mailing Address: PO Box 151, Omak, WA 98841 US
Second Address: 320 Emery St., Omak, WA 98841
(509) 826-0100; *Fax:* (509) 826-3929
www.komw.net
License: Omak, WA held by North Cascades Broadcasting Inc.
Group Owner: North Cascades Broadcasting Inc.; acq 7-90)
Nat'l Network: ABC
Format: Adult Contemp *Special Programming:* Farm 2 hrs, Sp 2 hrs wkly; *Target Audience:* 18-45.
John Andrist, Station Manager/Owner
Chris Schmidt, Programming Director

***KQWS**
01-06-1999; 90.1 MHz FM; *Hrs Open:* 24; 3 kw; 2457 ft.; N48 44 37 W119 37 16 *Rebroadcasts:* Rebroadcasts KWSU(AM) Pullman 100%
PO Box 642530, 382 Murrow Center, Pullman, WA 99164 US
(509) 335-6500; *Fax:* (509)335-3772
www.nwpr.org
nwpr@wsu.edu
License: Omak, Okanogan County, WA held by Washington State University.
Format: News, News/Talk, 86; *Hrs. of News Programming:* news progmg 60 hrs wkly; *No. News Employees:* 1
Scott Weatherly, Operations Dir
Dennis Haarsager, General Manager
Roger Johnson, Station Manager
Kerry Swanson, General Sales Mgr
Gillian Coldsnow, Assistant Programming Director
John Paxson, News Director
Ralph Hogan, ChiefEngineer

KZBE
06-22-1998; 104.3 MHz FM; *Hrs Open:* 24; 3.5 kw; 981 ft.; N48 19 12 W119 32 18
Mailing Address: PO Box 151, Omak, WA 98841 US
Second Address: 320 Emery St., Omak, WA 98841
(509) 826-0100; *Fax:* (509) 826-3929
www.komw.net
License: Omak, Okanogan County, WA held by North Cascades Broadcasting Inc.
Group Owner: North Cascades Broadcasting Inc.; acq 10-14-97; $47,606)
Nat'l Network: ABC
Arbitron Metro Market: Omak, WA; *Format:* Adult Contemp; *Hrs. of News Programming:* news progmg 3 hrs wkly; *No. News Employees:* 2; *Target Audience:* 18 plus.
John Andrist, CEO/Station Manager
Chris Schmidt, Programming Director

Opportunity

KTRW
11-01-1955; 630 kHz AM; *Hrs Open:* 24; 0.53 kw-D, ND1; 0.053 kw-N, ND1; N47 36 31 W117 22 25
500 West Boone Avenue, PO Box 31000, Spokane, WA 99223 US
(509) 443-1000; *Fax:* (509) 448-3811
www.ktrw.com
ktw@ktw.name
License: Opportunity, WA held by Mutual Broadcasting System LLC
Nat'l Network: Fox News Radio; Salem Radio Network; USA
Arbitron Metro Market: Spokane, WA; *Format:* Big Band, Oldies, 86
Thomas Read, General Manager

KIIX-FM
04-01-1961; 96.1 MHz FM; 64 kw; 2418 ft.; N47 34 14 W117 4 55
600 Congress Avenue, Suite 1400, Austin, TX 78701 US
(509) 242-2400; *Fax:* (509) 242-1160
www.kix961.com
License: Opportunity, Spokane County, WA held by Capstar TX LLC
Group Owner: iHeartMedia; (acq 8-30-00; grpsl).
Arbitron Metro Market: Spokane, WA; *Format:* Country; *Target Audience:* 25-54.
Cal Hall, Market President
Brad Miller, Senior Vice President of Programming
Brent Phillipy, Sales Manager
Matt Auclair, Promotions Director
Andrea Williams, Digital Director

Othello

KRSC
09-01-1957; 1400 kHz AM
180 Main St., Othello, WA 99344 US
(509) 488-2791; *Fax:* (509) 488-7252
License: Othello, WA held by Centro Familiar Cristiano
Arbitron Metro Market: Othello, WA
Betsy Gomez, General Manager

Pacific

KZIZ
01-01-1990; 1560 kHz AM; *Hrs Open:* 24
Mailing Address: 2600 S. Jackson Street, Seattle, WA 98144 US
Second Address: 2600 South Jackson Street, Seattle, WA 98144
(206) 323-3070; *Fax:* (206) 322-6518
www.ztwins.com
ztwins@aol.com
License: Pacific, WA held by KRIS Bennett Broadcasting Inc.
Nat'l Network: American Urban
Arbitron Metro Market: Pacific, WA.; *Format:* Gospel *Special Programming:* Relg 18 hrs wkly; *Target Audience:* 12 plus; African-American
Frank Barrow, Operations Dir
Christopher Bennett, General Manager
Gloria Bennett, Station Manager
Priscilla Hailey, Chief Engineer

Parachute

KDBL
01-01-2008; 101.1 MHz FM; 200 w; Ant -1,397 ft; N39 26 31 W108 01 15
315 Kennedy Ave., Grand Junction, CO 55409
(970) 242-7788; *Fax:* (970) 243-0567
License: Parachute, Garfield County, CO held by Cumulus Licensing LLC.
Group Owner: Cumulus Media Inc.

Mike Shafer, Operations Dir
Kevin Wodlinger, General Manager

Pasco

KEYW
06-30-1986; 98.3 MHz FM; *Hrs Open:* 25; 12.5 kw; 997 ft.; N46 4 58 W119 9 39
2621 West A Street, Pasco, WA 99301 US
(509) 547-9791; *Fax:* (509) 547-8509
www.keyw.com
License: Pasco, Franklin County, WA held by GAP Broadcasting Tri-Cities License LLC.
Group Owner: GAPWEST Broadcasting; (acq 2-13-2008; grpsl)
Arbitron Metro Market: Tri-Cities, WA (Richland-Kennewick-Pasco); *Format:* Adult Contemp; *Target Audience:* 18-49.
Cheryl Salomone, General Manager
Lee Jamison, General Sales Mgr
Jim Florea, Programming Director
Bill Glenn, Chief Engineer

KFLD
07-28-1956; 870 kHz AM; *Hrs Open:* 24; 10 kw-D, ND1; 0.25 kw-N, ND1; N46 13 41 W119 7 32
Mailing Address: City Center West, 7201 W. Lake Mead Blvd, Las Vegas, NV 89128 US
Second Address: 2621 W.A. St., Pasco, WA 99301
(509) 547-9791; *Fax:* (509) 547-8509
www.newstalk870.am
License: Pasco, WA held by GAP Broadcasting Tri-Cities License LLC.
Group Owner: GAPWEST Broadcasting; (acq 2-13-2008; grpsl)
Regional Reps: Art Moore.
Arbitron Metro Market: Pasco, WA; *Format:* News, News/Talk, 86 *Special Programming:* Travel 1 hr wkly, 5 hrs sports wkly; *Hrs. of News Programming:* news progmg 140 hrs wkly; *No. News Employees:* 1 *TargetAudience:* 18-64.
Cheryl Salomone, General Manager
Lee Jamison, General Sales Mgr
John McKay, Programming Director
Chuck Ince, Chief Engineer

KGDN
02-01-1992; 101.3 MHz FM; *Hrs Open:* 24; 2.75 kw; 1001 ft.; N46 5 47 W119 11 36
Mailing Address: P.O. Box 3238, Tri-Cities, WA 99302 US
Second Address: 830 N. Columbia Center Blvd., Suite B3, Pasco, WA 99336
(509) 783-8600; *Fax:* (509) 448-3811
www.kgdn.com
kgdn@kgdn.com
License: Pasco, Franklin County, WA held by West Pasco Fine Arts Radio.
Arbitron Metro Market: Tri-Cities, WA; *Format:* Christian; *Target Audience:* 35 plus.
Thomas Read, General Manager
Bill Glenn, Station Manager
Melinda Read, General Sales Mgr
Joseph Spinelli, Programming Director

KRKG-FM
04-01-1997; 93.7 MHz FM; *Hrs Open:* 24; 600 w; 958 ft; N46 04 59 W119 09 38
Box 2852, Pasco, WA 99301
(509) 547-5196; *Fax:* (509) 547-5203
License: Pasco, Franklin County, WA held by Gospel Music Broadcasting Corp.
Arbitron Metro Market: Tri-Cities, WA (Richland-Kennewick-Pasco)
Martin Gibbson, President
Sharon Harmon, Programming Director
Martin Gibbs, Chief Engineer

***KOLU**
09-01-1971; 90.1 MHz FM; 4.1 kw; 1001 ft.; N46 4 59 W119 9 38
4921 West Wernett Street, Pasco, WA 99301 US
(509) 547-2021; *Fax:* (509) 544-0340
www.riverviewbaptist.org
info@kolu.com
License: Pasco, Franklin County, WA held by Riverview Baptist Christian Schools.
Arbitron Metro Market: Tri-Cities, WA (Richland-Kennewick-Pasco); *Format:* Religious
John Paisley, General Manager

Port Angeles

***KNWP**
03-23-1998; 90.1 MHz FM; *Hrs Open:* 24; 1.6 kw; 197 ft.; N48 9 3 W123 40 9 *Rebroadcasts:* Rebroadcasts KRFA-FM Moscow, ID 100%
PO Box 642530, 382 Murrow Center, Pullman, WA 99165 US
(509) 335-6500; *Fax:* (509) 335-3772
www.nwpr.org
nwpr@wsu.edu
License: Port Angeles, Clallam County, WA held by Washington State University.
Format: Classical, News; *Hrs. of News Programming:* news progmg 37 hrs wkly; *No. News Employees:* 1
Gillian Coldsnow, Operations Dir
Dennis Haarsager, General Manager
Kerry Swanson, Station Manager
Sarah McDaniel, General Sales Mgr
Mary Hawkins, Programming Director
Ralph Hogan, Chief Engineer

KONP
01-01-1945; 1450 kHz AM
P.O. Box 1450, 721 East First Street, Port Angeles, WA 98362 US
(360) 457-1450; *Fax:* (360) 457-9114
www.konp.com
info@konp.com
License: Port Angeles, WA held by Radio Pacific Inc.
Format: News, News/Talk, 86; *Target Audience:* 28-54.
Brown Maloney, Chairman
Todd Ortloff, General Manager
Stan Comeau, General Sales Mgr

***KVIX**
03-22-2005; 89.3 MHz FM; 0.6 kw; 489 ft.; N48 9 3 W123 40 9
Rebroadcasts: Rebroadcasts KPLU-FM Tacoma 100%
12180 Park Avenue South, Tacoma, WA 98447 US
(253) 535-7758; *Fax:* (253) 535-8332
www.kplu.org
info@kplu.org
License: Port Angeles, Clallam County, WA held by Pacific Lutheran University Inc.
Nat'l Network: NPR; PRI; *Wire Services:* AP
Arbitron Metro Market: Port Angeles, WA; *Format:* Blues, Jazz, 60
Jeff Bauman, Operations Dir
Erik Nycklemoe, General Manager
Joey Cohn, Programming Director
Erin Hennessey, News Director
Lowell Kiesow, Chief Engineer
Nick Francis, Music Director
Jennifer Strachan, Assistant GM & Director ofPublic Media
Jeff Bauman, Assistant GM & Director of Support Services
Joey Cohn, Assistant GM & Director of Content

Port Townsend

***KPTZ**
91.9 MHz FM; 0.9 kw; 335 ft.; N48 7 42 W122 49 39
PO Box 2091, Port Townsend, WA 98368 US
(360) 379-8122; *Fax:* (360) 379-6886
www.kptz.org
info@kptz.org
License: Port Townsend, Jefferson County, WA held by Radio Port Townsend.
Arbitron Metro Market: Port Townsend, WA; *Format:* Talk; *No. News Employees:* 1
Sherry Jones, President
Nora Petrich, Station Manager
Larry Stein, Programming Director
David Cunningham, News Director
Bill Putney, Chief Engineer

Prosser

KZXR
12-14-1956; 1310 kHz AM; 5 kw-D, ND1; 0.066 kw-N, ND1; N46 14 3 W119 48 49
1200 West Venice, Los Angeles, CA 90006 US
(509) 786-1209; *Fax:* (509) 786-1181
info@kzxr.com
License: Prosser, WA held by MBProsser Licensee LLC
Group Owner: Moon Broadcasting; (Acq 2-24-2000; $500,000).
Arbitron Metro Market: Prosser, WA; *Format:* Tejano; *Target Audience:* 25-54.
Frank Allec, General Manager

KLES
09-06-1962; 101.7 MHz FM; 3.5 kw; 869 ft.; N46 11 12 W119 45 13
1200 West Venice, Los Angeles, CA 90006 US
(509) 786-1209; *Fax:* (509) 786-1181
License: Prosser, Benton County, WA held by MBProsser Licensee LLC
Group Owner: Moon Broadcasting; (acq 2-15-2000; $750,000).
Nat'l Reps: Target Broadcast Sales
Arbitron Metro Market: Prosser, WA; *Format:* Spanish; *Target Audience:* 18-49.
Carol Crider, General Manager

Pullman

KHTR
01-01-1967; 104.3 MHz FM; 24 kw; 1670 ft.; N46 48 40 W116 54 55
Mailing Address: PO Box 1, Pullman, WA 99163 US
Second Address: 1101 Old Wawawai, Pullman, WA 99163
(509) 332-6551; *Fax:* (509) 332-5151
www.pullmanradio.com
License: Pullman, Whitman County, WA
Format: Contemporary Hits/Top 40; *Hrs. of News Programming:* news progmg 24 hrs wkly; *No. News Employees:* 1; *Target Audience:* General.
Jeremy West, Programming Director

KQQQ
01-01-1938; 1150 kHz AM; *Hrs Open:* 24
Mailing Address: 1101 Old Wawawai Road, Pullman, WA 99163 US
Second Address: Box 1, Pullman, WA 99163
(509) 332-6551; *Fax:* (509) 332-5151
License: Pullman, WA held by Radio Palouse Inc.
Group Owner: Radio Palouse Inc.; acq 12-74).
Regional Reps: Allied Radio Partners.
Arbitron Metro Market: Pullman-Moscow; *Format:* News, News/Talk, 86 *Special Programming:* Farm 3 hrs, loc news 10 hrs wkly; *Hrs. of News Programming:* news progmg 28 hrs wkly; *No. News Employees:* 1 *TargetAudience:* General.
Larry Weir, Operations Dir
Bill Weed, General Manager
Rod Schwartz, General Sales Mgr
Evan Ellis, News Director
Steve Franko, Chief Engineer

*KRLF
07-01-1991; 88.5 MHz FM; *Hrs Open:* 24; 0.4 kw vert; 807 ft.; N46 38 4 W117 5 22
345 Sw Kimball, Pullman, WA 99163 US
(509) 332-3545; *Fax:* (509) 332-5433
www.krlf.org
krlf@krlf.org
License: Pullman, Whitman County, WA held by Living Faith Fellowship Educational Ministries.
Nat'l Network: Salem Radio Network
Arbitron Metro Market: Pullman-Moscow; *Format:* Christian *Special Programming:* Alternative/CHR one hr, children 5 hrs—1 hr/weekd; *Hrs. of News Programming:* News progmg 18 hrs wkly; *Target Audience:* 13-52. *Adv. Rates:* underwriting $6/spot
Phillip Vance, President
Frank Younce, Station Manager
Ruth Younce, Programming Director
Frank Younce, Chief Engineer

*KWSU
06-01-1922; 1250 kHz AM; *Hrs Open:* 24; 5 kw-D, ND2; 5 kw-N, ND2; N46 41 47 W117 14 44
PO Box 642530, Pullman, WA 99164 US
(509) 335-6500; *Fax:* (509) 335-3772
www.nwpr.org
nwpr@wsu.edu
License: Pullman, WA held by Washington State University.
Nat'l Network: NPR
Arbitron Metro Market: Pullman, WA *TV Affiliate:* *KWSU-TV affil.; *Format:* News *Special Programming:* Jazz 14 hrs wkly; *Hrs. of News Programming:* news progmg 60 hrs wkly; *No. News Employees:* 1 *TargetAudience:* General.
Karen Olstad, COO
Scott Weatherly, Operations Dir
Tony Wright, General Manager
Kerry Swanson, Station Manager
Sarah McDaniel, General Sales Mgr
Mary Hawkins, Programming Director
Aki Wright, Development Coordinator
Andi Wilson,Music and Culture
Brett Charvat, Announcer
Courtney Flatt, Multimedia Journalist

*KZUU
09-21-1979; 90.7 MHz FM; *Hrs Open:* 24; 0.42 kw; 100 ft.; N46 43 51 W117 9 42
P.O. Box 642530, 382 Murrow Center, Pullman, WA 99165 US
(509) 335-2208; *Fax:* (509) 335-3772
www.kzuu.wsu.edu/
kzuu@wsu.edu
License: Pullman, Whitman County, WA held by Washington State University Board of Regents.
Arbitron Metro Market: Pullman, WA; *Format:* Jazz, Variety/Diverse *Special Programming:* Jazz 12 hrs, Black 12 hrs, folk 4 hrs, Sp 3 hrs, new mus 10 hrs, environmental protection 2 hrs wkly *Hrs. of News Programming:* news progmg 5 hrs wkly; *No. News Employees:* 1; *Target Audience:* 18-49; college students
Jasmine Albertson, General Manager
Alex Siddons, Programming Director
Stacy Kim, Promotions Manager

KZZL-FM
11-01-1991; 99.5 MHz FM; *Hrs Open:* 24; 77 kw; 1060 ft.; N46 40 52 W116 58 16
805 Stewart Ave., Lewiston, ID 83501 US
(208) 743-1551
shad@inlandradio.com
License: Pullman, Whitman County, WA held by Inland Northwest Broadcasting
Group Owner: Inland Northwest Broadcasting; (acq 6-28-2005; grpsl)
Arbitron Metro Market: Pullman, WA; *Format:* Country; *Hrs. of News Programming:* news progmg 2 hrs wkly; *No. News Employees:* 1; *Target Audience:* 25 plus.
Gary Cummings, General Manager
Ben Bonfield, General Sales Mgr
Ryan Chambers, Programming Director
Steve Franco, Chief Engineer

Puyallup

KSUH
12-01-1951; 1450 kHz AM; *Hrs Open:* 24; 1 kw-U, ND1; N47 10 41 W122 16 24
807 South 336th Street, Federal Way, WA 98003 US
(253) 815-1212; *Fax:* (253) 815-1913
www.radiohankook.com
info@radiohankook.com
License: Puyallup, WA held by Jean J. Suh.
Arbitron Metro Market: Federal Way, WA; *Format:* Korean, Variety/Diverse; *No. News Employees:* 2; *Target Audience:* 25-65; working folks
Sung Hong, General Manager
Nancy Haan, Station Manager

Quincy

KZML
10-01-1998; 95.9 MHz FM; *Hrs Open:* 24; 11 kw; 1050 ft.; N47 19 13 W119 47 59 *Rebroadcasts:* Rebroadcasts KZTA(FM) Naches 100%
Mailing Address: Post Office Box 31000, Spokane, WA 99223 US
Second Address: 706 Butterfield Rd., Yakima, WA 98901
(509) 457-1000; *Fax:* (509) 452-0541
www.radiolagrande.com
zorro@radiozorro.com
License: Quincy, Grant County, WA
Group Owner: Adelante Media Group LLC; (acq 11-18-2004; grpsl).
Regional Reps: Tacher
Format: Tejano; *Hrs. of News Programming:* news progmg 3 hrs wkly; *No. News Employees:* 1; *Target Audience:* 18-35; Hispanic; *Adv. Rates:* 31; 28; 25; 21
Keith Teske, Operations Dir
Bob Berry, General Manager
Martin Ortiz, Programming Director
Judith McInnis, News Director

KWNC
09-10-1957; 1370 kHz AM; 1 kw-D, ND1; 0.039 kw-N, ND1; N47 17 30 W119 51 10
32 North Mission, Wenatchee, WA 98802 US
(509) 787-5121; *Fax:* (509) 664-6799
License: Quincy, WA held by Wescoast Broadcasting Co. Inc.
Arbitron Metro Market: Wenatchee, WA; *Format:* News *Special Programming:* Farm 5 hrs wkly; *Hrs. of News Programming:* news progmg 168 hrs wkly; *No. News Employees:* 3; *Target Audience:* 35 plus; farm-oriented *Adv. Rates:* 10; 10; 10; na
Jim Wallace Jr., President
Debbie Capestrini, Operations Dir
Steve Hair, News Director

KWWW-FM
08-29-1985; 96.7 MHz FM; *Hrs Open:* 24; 0.44 kw; 1033 ft.; N47 19 13 W119 48 0
N. 1212 Washington, Suite 307, Spokane, WA 99201 US
(509) 665-6565; *Fax:* (509) 663-1150
www.kw3.com
License: Quincy, Grant County, WA held by CCR-Wenatchee IV LLC.
Group Owner: Cherry Creek Radio LLC; (acq 10-31-2006; grpsl)
Nat'l Reps: McGavren Guild
Arbitron Metro Market: Wenatchee, WA; *Format:* Christian; *Target Audience:* 18-49.
Lisa Rodriguez, Operations Dir
Jim Senst, General Manager
Leona Frank, General Sales Mgr
Dale Roth, Promotions Manager
Dave Bernstein, News Director
Manuel Garcia, Chief Engineer
Dave Herald, National Sales Manager
JenniferBusboug, Research Director

Rainier

*KACS
08-18-1993; 90.5 MHz FM; *Hrs Open:* 24; 6 kw; 187 ft.; N46 43 52 W123 1 28
2451 NEKresky, Suite A, Chehalis, WA 98532 US
(360) 740-9436; *Fax:* (360) 740-9415
www.kacs.org
kacs@kacs.org
License: Rainier, Lewis County, WA held by Chehalis Valley Educational Foundation.
Arbitron Metro Market: Chehalis, WA; *Format:* Religious; *Hrs. of News Programming:* News progmg 6 hrs wkly; *Target Audience:* 45-54.; *Adv. Rates:* $10 ROS
Kerry O'Connor, Chairman
Cameron Beirle, General Manager

Raymond

KJET
105.7 MHz FM; *Hrs Open:* 24; 58 kw; Ant 518 ft; N46 56 30 W123 47 07
1520 Simpson Ave., Aberdeen, WA 98520-6016 US
(360) 532-1456; *Fax:* (360) 532-1456
www.1057thejet.com
info@jodesha.com
License: Raymond, Pacific County, WA held by Jodesha Broadcasting Inc.
Group Owner: Jodesha Broadcasting Inc.
Nat'l Network: ABC; *Nat'l Reps:* Tacher; *Wire Services:* AP
Population Served: 85,000 *Format:* Adult Contemp; *Hrs. of News Programming:* news progmg 7 hrs wkly; *No. News Employees:* 1; *Target Audience:* 18-49.; *Adv. Rates:* 24; 20; 22; na
Gabrielle Jordan, General Manager
Bill Wolfenbarger, General Sales Mgr

Renton

KRIZ
02-02-1982; 1420 kHz AM; *Hrs Open:* 24; 1 kw-D, DA2; 0.5 kw-N, DA2; N47 26 25 W122 12 9
Mailing Address: 2600 S. Jackson Street, Seattle, WA 98144 US
Second Address: Box 22462, Seattle, WA 98122-0462
(206) 323-3070; *Fax:* (206) 322-6518
www.ztwins.com
License: Renton, WA held by KRIZ Broadcasting Inc.
Nat'l Network: American Urban
Arbitron Metro Market: Seattle; *Format:* Adult Contemp, Blues *Special Programming:* Relg 18 hrs wkly; *Target Audience:* 18 plus.
Christopher Bennett, President
Gloria Bennett, Operations Dir
Frank Barrow, Chief of Operations

KYIZ
01-01-1998; 1620 kHz AM

Mailing Address: 2600 S. Jackson, Seattle, WA 98144 US
Second Address: Box 22462, Seattle, WA 98144
(206) 323-3070; *Fax:* (206) 322-6518
www.ztwins.com
License: Renton, WA held by KRIZ Broadcasting Inc.
Arbitron Metro Market: Seattle-Tacoma, WA; *Format:* Blues
Christopher Bennett, President
Gloria Bennett, Operations Dir
Priscilla Hailey, News Director
Frank Barrow, Chief of Operations

Richland

KALE
04-01-1950; 960 kHz AM; *Hrs Open:* 24; 5 kw-D, 1 kw-N, DA-N; N46 14 34 W119 10 48
830 N. Columbia Center Blvd., Suite B-2, Kennewick, WA 92101
(509) 783-0783; *Fax:* (509) 735-8627
License: Richland, Benton County, WA held by Ingstad Radio Washington LLC
Group Owner: Ingstad Radio Washington LLC; acq 12-10-99; grpsl).
Nat'l Reps: D & R Radio
Population Served: 157,000; *Arbitron Metro Market:* Tri-Cities, WA (Richland-Kennewick-Pasco); *No. News Employees:* 1; *Target Audience:* 25 plus; general
Don Morin, General Manager

KEGX
06-10-1992; 106.5 MHz FM; 100 kw; Ant 1,392 ft; N46 05 58 W119 07 40
830 N. Columbia Ctr. Blvd., Suite B-2, Kennewick, WA 92101
(509) 783-0783; *Fax:* (509) 735-8627
www.kegx.com
info@kegx.com
License: Richland, Benton County, WA held by Ingstad Radio Washington LLC
Group Owner: Ingstad Radio Washington LLC
Population Served: 250,000; *Arbitron Metro Market:* Tri-Cities, WA (Richland-Kennewick-Pasco); *Target Audience:* 25-54.
Pat McMahon, Operations Dir
J.D. Freeman, General Manager

*KFAE-FM
07-01-1982; 89.1 MHz FM; *Hrs Open:* 24; 100 kw horiz, 67 kw vert; 1148 ft.; N46 5 43 W119 11 41 *Rebroadcasts:* Rebroadcasts KRFA-FM Moscow, ID 100%
Mailing Address: PO Box 642530, Pullman, WA 99164 US
Second Address: Washington State Univ. at Tri-Cities, 100 Sprout Rd., Richland, WA 99164-2530
(509) 335-6500; *Fax:* (509) 335-3772
www.nwpr.org
nwpr@wsu.edu
License: Richland, Benton County, WA held by Washington State University.
Nat'l Network: PRI; NPR
Arbitron Metro Market: Tri-Cities, WA (Richland-Kennewick-Pasco) *TV Affiliate:* *KTNW(TV) affil.; *Format:* News *Special Programming:* Folk, jazz 15 hrs wkly; *Hrs. of News Programming:* news progmg 37 hrs wkly *No.News Employees:* 1; *Target Audience:* General.
Scott Weatherly, Operations Dir
Dennis Haarsager, General Manager
Kerry Swanson, Station Manager
Sarah McDaniel, General Sales Mgr
Mary Hawkins, Programming Director
John Paxson, News Director
Gillian Coldsnow, Assistant Managerof Programming & Operations

KIOK
10-03-1978; 94.9 MHz FM; 100 kw; 1,250 ft; N46 05 47 W119 11 36
830 N. Columbia Center Blvd., Suite B-2, Kennewick, WA 92101
(509) 783-0783; *Fax:* (509) 735-8627
www.949thewolfpack.com
License: Richland, Benton County, WA held by Ingstad Radio Washington LLC
Group Owner: Ingstad Radio Washington LLC
Population Served: 250,000; *Arbitron Metro Market:* Tri-Cities, WA (Richland-Kennewick-Pasco)

KORD-FM
10-15-1965; 102.7 MHz FM; 100 kw; 1325 ft.; N46 5 58.4 W119 7 40.2
Mailing Address: City Center West, 7201 W. Lake Mead Blvd, Las Vegas, NV 89128 US
Second Address: 2621 West A. St., Pasco, WA 99301
(509) 547-9791; *Fax:* (509) 547-8509
www.1027kord.com
License: Richland, Benton County, WA held by GAP Broadcasting Tri-Cities License LLC.
Group Owner: GAPWEST Broadcasting; (acq 2-13-2008; grpsl)
Arbitron Metro Market: Tri-Cities, WA (Richland-Kennewick-Pasco); *Format:* Country; *Target Audience:* 25-54.
Cheryl Salomone, General Manager
Lee Jamison, General Sales Mgr
Paul Drake, Programming Director

Rock Island

KAAP
09-19-1990; 99.5 MHz FM; *Hrs Open:* 24; 5.3 kw; -82 ft.; N47 22 52 W120 17 15
231 N. Wenatchee Avenue, Wenatchee, WA 98801 US
(509) 665-6565; *Fax:* (509) 663-1150
www.applefm.com
License: Rock Island, Douglas County, WA held by CCR-Wenatchee IV LLC.
Group Owner: Cherry Creek Radio LLC; (acq 10-31-2006; grpsl)
Nat'l Reps: McGavren Guild
Format: Adult Contemp; *No. News Employees:* 1; *Target Audience:* 25-54.
Jim Senst, General Manager
Leona Frank, General Sales Mgr
Lisa Rodriguez, News Director
Joe Bowers, Engineering Dir
Manuel Garcia, Chief Engineer
Todd Johnson, Promotions Manager
Jennifer Busboug, Research Director
Jose LuisHigh, Spanish Director

Roy

*KWFJ
09-01-1995; 89.7 MHz FM; 1 kw horiz, 0.78 kw vert; 98 ft.; N46 57 59 W122 32 56
P.O. Box 401, Roy, WA 98580 US
(206) 843-1692; *Fax:* (360) 458-6649
www.bbnradio.org
bbn@bbnmedia.org
License: Roy, Pierce County, WA held by Bible Broadcasting Network Inc.
Group Owner: Bible Broadcasting Network
Nat'l Network: Bible Bcstg Net
Arbitron Metro Market: Roy, WA; *Format:* Christian, Religious
Lowell Davey, President
Jason Padgett, Operations Manager

Royal City

KRCW
01-01-1995; 96.3 MHz FM; *Hrs Open:* 24; 19.5 kw; 791 ft.; N46 45 55 W119 16 51
PO Box 62, Keene, CA 93531 US
(928) 782-5995; *Fax:* (928) 782-3874
www.campesina.net
License: Royal City, Grant County, WA held by Farmworker Educational Radio Network, Inc.
Group Owner: Farmworker Educational Radio Network, Inc.
Arbitron Metro Market: Tri-Cities, Washington; *Format:* Tejano; *Target Audience:* 25-54; Hispanic market
Paul Chavez, President

KWDR
93.5 MHz FM; 0.21 kw; 1667 ft.; N46 48 25 W119 33 20 US
(858) 277-4991; *Fax:* (858) 277-1365
License: Royal City, Grant County, WA held by Jacobs Radio Broadcasting LLC
Arbitron Metro Market: Royal City, WA; *Format:* Christian
Mike MacIntosh, President

Seattle

KNTS
03-31-2003; 1680 kHz AM; *Hrs Open:* 24
2201 6th Avenue, Suite 1500, Seattle, WA 98121 US
(206) 443-8200; *Fax:* (206) 777-1133
wilmerh@salemradioseattle.com
License: Seattle, WA held by Inspiration Media Inc.
Group Owner: Salem Communications Corp.
Arbitron Metro Market: Seattle-Tacoma, WA; *Format:* Christian, Talk
Joshua Main, Operations Dir
Tim Harper, General Manager
Wilmer Herrera, General Sales Mgr

*KBLE
01-01-1948; 1050 kHz AM; *Hrs Open:* 6 AM-midnight; 5 kw-D, ND1; 0.44 kw-N, ND1; N47 33 41 W122 21 34
Mailing Address: 114 Lakeside Ave., Seattle, WA 98122 US
Second Address: PO Box 2482, Kirkland, WA 98083
(425) 867-2340; (800) 949-1050
www.sacredheartradio.org
info@sacredheartradio.org
License: Seattle, WA held by Sacred Heart Radio Inc.
Arbitron Metro Market: Kirkland, WA; *Format:* Religious
Ron Belter, General Manager

*KEXP-FM
01-01-1972; 90.3 MHz FM; *Hrs Open:* 24; 4.7 kw; 692 ft.; N47 36 58 W122 18 28
Mailing Address: Box 353750, Ds-50, Seattle, WA 98195 US
Second Address: 113 Dexter Avenue N., Seattle, WA 98109
(206) 520-5800; *Fax:* (206) 520-5899
www.kexp.org
info@kexp.org
License: Seattle, King County, WA held by Regents of University of Washington.
Nat'l Network: NPR
Arbitron Metro Market: Seattle, WA; *Format:* Alternative, Variety/Diverse; *Target Audience:* 18-44; educated, culturally interested, active outdoors, prof/mngr/tech positions
Jack Walters, Operations Dir
Andrew Corey, General Manager
Tom Mara, Station Manager
Mel Trejo, Programming Director
Courtney Miller, Promotions Manager
Jamie Alls, Chief Engineer
Mike McCormick, Public Affairs Director

*KING-FM
01-01-1947; 98.1 MHz FM; *Hrs Open:* 24; 66 kw; 2320 ft.; N47 30 14 W121 58 29
10 Harrison Street, Suite 100, Seattle, WA 98109 US
(206) 691-2981; *Fax:* (206) 691-2982
www.king.org
web@king.org
License: Seattle, King County, WA held by Classic Radio Inc.
Nat'l Reps: Katz Radio
Arbitron Metro Market: Seattle-Tacoma, WA; *Format:* Contemporary Hits/Top 40; *Hrs. of News Programming:* News progmg 2 hrs wkly
Jennifer Ridewood, General Manager
Bob Goldfarb, Programming Director
Shawna Keen, Promotions Manager
Buzz Anderson, Chief Engineer

KIRO
01-01-1927; 710 kHz AM; *Hrs Open:* 24; 50 kw-D, DAN; 50 kw-N, DAN; N47 23 55 W122 26 0
1820 Eastlake Ave. E., Seattle, WA 98102 US
(206) 726-7000
www.mynorthwest.com
License: Seattle, King County, WA held by Bonneville International Corporation
Group Owner: Bonneville International Corporation; (acq 3-14-2008; grpsl)
Nat'l Network: ESPN Radio
Arbitron Metro Market: Seattle-Tacoma, WA; *Format:* Sports; *Target Audience:* 25-54.
David Pridemore, Vice President and General Manager
Cathy Cangiano, General Sales Mgr

KISW
01-01-1950; 99.9 MHz FM; *Hrs Open:* 24; 67 kw; 2320 ft.; N47 30 14 W121 58 29
1101 Olive Way, Suite 1650, Seattle, WA 98101 US
(206) 285-7625; *Fax:* (206) 215-9355
www.kisw.com
rcastle@entercom.com
License: Seattle, King County, WA held by Entercom Seattle License LLC.
Group Owner: Entercom Communications Corp.; (acq 1996).
Nat'l Reps: D & R Radio
Arbitron Metro Market: Seattle-Tacoma, WA; *Format:* Rock/AOR; *Target Audience:* 18-49; men
David Field, President
Amy Griesheimer, Operations Dir
Jennifer Wisbey, General Sales Mgr
Dave Richards, Programming Director
Brian Thorpe, Promotions Director
Joyce Jinka, News Director
Dwight Small, Chief Engineer

KJR
01-01-1921; 950 kHz AM
645 Elliot Avenue West, Suite 400, Seattle, WA 98119 US
(206) 286-9595;(800) 829-0950; *Fax:* (206) 286-2376
www.sportsradiokjr.com
info@kjram.com
License: Seattle, WA held by Citicasters Licenses Inc.
Group Owner: iHeartMedia; (acq 6-14-2002; grpsl)
Nat'l Reps: D & R Radio

Arbitron Metro Market: Seattle, WA; *Format:* Sports; *Target Audience:* 25-54.
Nik Krastins, Sales Manager
Rich Moore, Programming Director
Jenny Gudmundson, Promotions Manager
Jason Puckett, Sports Director
Seth Thompson, Digital

KJR-FM
05-25-1960; 95.7 MHz FM; 98 kw; 1270 ft.; N47 32 40 W122 6 26
645 Elliot Avenue West, Suite 400, Seattle, WA 98119 US
(206) 494-2000; *Fax:* (206) 286-2376
www.957kjrfm.com
info@957kjrfm.com
License: Seattle, King County, WA held by Citicasters Licenses Inc.
Group Owner: iHeartMedia
Arbitron Metro Market: Seattle, WA; *Format:* Contemporary Hits/Top 40, Adult Contemp; *Target Audience:* 30-44.
Mark Glynn, Sales Manager
Chris Sargent, Programming Director
Paige Gamboa, Promotions Manager
Seth Thompson, Digital
Emoree Martin, Traffic Anchor
Kimi Kline, Traffic Anchor
Doug Duin, Imaging

KKDZ
05-15-1993; 1250 kHz AM; *Hrs Open:* 24
200 First Ave. W. # 104, Attn: David Ebers, Seattle, WA 98119 US
(206) 281-5300; *Fax:* (206) 281-8881
www.radiodisney.com
License: Seattle, WA held by WMAL Inc.
Group Owner: The Walt Disney Company
Arbitron Metro Market: Seattle, WA; *Format:* Children; *No. News Employees:* 5; *Target Audience:* 6-14; Kids; *Adv. Rates:* 125; 100; 125; 50
Bob Nordberg, General Manager
Laura Dunham, Promotions Manager

KKOL
01-01-1922; 1300 kHz AM; *Hrs Open:* 24
2201 6th Avenue, Suite 1500, Seattle, WA 98121 US
(206) 443-8200; *Fax:* (206) 777-1133
www.kkol.com
License: Seattle, WA held by Inspiration Media Inc.
Group Owner: Salem Communications Corp.; (acq 4-17-97; $2 million)
Nat'l Reps: Salem
Arbitron Metro Market: Seattle, WA; *Format:* News; *Target Audience:* 35 plus; men & women
Joshua Main, Operations Dir
Andrew Adams, General Manager
Chad Gammage, General Sales Mgr
Dave Drui, Programming Director
Clara Hylarides, Promotions Manager
Monte Passmore, Chief Engineer
Wendy Bergsma-Passmore, BusinessManager

KLFE
09-10-1956; 1590 kHz AM; *Hrs Open:* 24; 5 kw-D, DAN; 5 kw-N, DAN; N47 39 19 W122 31 6
2201 6th Avenue, Suite 1500, Seattle, WA 98121 US
(206) 443-8200; *Fax:* (206) 777-1133
www.freedom1590.com
webmaster@kgnw.com
License: Seattle, WA held by Inspiration Media Inc.
Group Owner: Salem Communications Corp.; (acq 1994; $500,000)
Nat'l Reps: Salem
Arbitron Metro Market: Seattle, WA; *Format:* Christian, Talk
Special Programming: Russian 12 hrs; *Target Audience:* 25-54.
Joshua Main, Operations Dir
Andrew Adams, General Manager
Chad Gammage, General Sales Mgr
Dave Duri, Programming/Production Manager
Monte Passmore, Chief Engineer

KFNQ
11-14-2012; 1090 kHz AM; *Hrs Open:* 24; 50 kW; N47 23 38 W122 25 25
1000 Dexter Ave. N, Suite 100, Seattle, WA 98109 USA
(206) 805-1090; *Fax:* (206) 805-0932
www.1090thefan.com
License: Seattle, King County, WA held by CBS Radio Stations Inc.
Group Owner: CBS Radio; (acq 11-13-98; grpsl).
Arbitron Metro Market: Seattle, WA; *Format:* Sports
Mike Oboy, General Sales Mgr
Ansel Olson, Digital Sales Manager

KMPS
07-31-1978; 94.1 MHz FM; 69 kW; 213 ft.; N47 30 17 W121 58 4
1000 Dexter Ave. N, Seattle, WA 98124 USA
(206) 805-0941; *Fax:* (206) 805-0911
www.kmps.com
License: Seattle, King County, WA held by CBS Radio Stations Inc.
Group Owner: CBS Radio; (acq 11-13-98; grpsl).
Arbitron Metro Market: Seattle, WA; *Format:* Country; *Hrs. of News Programming:* one.; *Target Audience:* General
Cindy Johnson, Sales Manager
Carey Curelop, Programming Director
Alexandria English, Promotions Manager

KNDD
03-09-1985; 107.7 MHz FM; *Hrs Open:* 24; 67 kw; 2320 ft.; N47 30 14 W121 58 29
1100 Olive Way, Suite 1650, Seattle, WA 96101 US
(206) 622-3251; *Fax:* (206) 682-8349
www.1077theend.com
License: Seattle, King County, WA held by Entercom Seattle License L.L.C.
Group Owner: Entercom Communications Corp.; (acq 1996)
Nat'l Reps: D & R Radio
Arbitron Metro Market: Seattle, WA; *Format:* Alternative; *No. News Employees:* 1; *Target Audience:* 18-34; well educated active adults
Amy Griesheimer, Operations Dir
Jennifer Wisbey, General Sales Mgr
Garrett Michaels, Programming Director
Ryan Schroeder, Promotions Directors
Dwight Smalls, Chief Engineer

*KNHC
01-25-1971; 89.5 MHz FM; *Hrs Open:* 24; 8.5 kw; 1220 ft.; N47 32 35 W122 6 25
10750 30th Avenue, N. E., Seattle, WA 98125 US
(206) 252-3800; *Fax:* (206) 252-3805
www.c895worldwide.com
License: Seattle, King County, WA held by Seattle Public Schools.
Wire Services: AP
Arbitron Metro Market: Seattle, WA; *Format:* Contemporary Hits/Top 40 *Special Programming:* Black, gospel 6 hrs, gothic/industrial 6 hrs wkly; *Hrs. of News Programming:* News progmg 9 hrs wkly *Target Audience:* 18-34; male & female
Richard Dalton, Operations Dir
Gregg Neilson, General Manager
Jon McDaniel, Programming Director
Buzz Anderson, Chief Engineer

KTTH
01-01-1925; 770 kHz AM; *Hrs Open:* 24; 50 kw-D, DA2; 5 kw-N, DA2; N47 23 38 W122 25 25
1820 Eastlake Ave. E., Seattle, WA 98102 US
(206) 726-7000
www.mynorthwest.com
License: Seattle, King County, WA held by Bonneville International Corporation
Group Owner: Bonneville International Corporation; (acq 3-14-2008; grpsl)
Arbitron Metro Market: Seattle-Tacoma, WA; *Format:* Talk; *No. News Employees:* 6; *Target Audience:* 25-54; adults
David Pridemore, Vice President and General Manager
Jason Antebi, Programming Director

KOMO
01-01-1926; 1000 kHz AM; *Hrs Open:* 24; 50 kw-D, DAN; 50 kw-N, DAN; N47 27 49 W122 26 27
140 Fourth Avenue, North, Seattle, WA 98109 US
(206) 404-4000; *Fax:* (206) 404-3646
www.KOMO1000news.com
comments@KOMO1000news.com
License: Seattle, WA held by Fisher Broadcasting - Seattle Radio L.L.C.
Group Owner: Fisher Communications Inc.
Nat'l Network: ABC; *Wire Services:* AP
Arbitron Metro Market: Seattle-Tacoma, WA *TV Affiliate:* KOMO-TV affil.; *Format:* News; *Hrs. of News Programming:* news progmg 168 hrs wkly; *No. News Employees:* 50; *Target Audience:* 25-54.
Colleen Brown, CEO
Larry Roberts, General Manager
Joe Heslet, General Sales Mgr
Doreen Kaylor, Programming Director
Jen Pivak, Promotions Manager
Brian Calvert, News Director
Lee Wood, Chief Engineer
Gary Greenberg, NationalSales Manager

Charles Gouge, Regional Sales Manager
Julie Ross, Traffic Manager

KPLZ-FM
09-01-1959; 101.5 MHz FM; *Hrs Open:* 24; 99 kw; 1263 ft.; N47 32 40 W122 6 26
100 - 4th Ave. North, Seattle, WA 98109 US
(206) 404-4000; *Fax:* (206) 404-1015
www.star1015.com
starcomment@fisherradio.com
License: Seattle, King County, WA held by Fisher Broadcasting - Seattle Radio L.L.C.
Group Owner: Fisher Communications Inc.; (acq 5-5-94; with co-located AM)
Nat'l Reps: Eastman Radio; *Wire Services:* AP
Arbitron Metro Market: Seattle-Tacoma; *Format:* Adult Contemp
Special Programming: John Tesh at night; *Hrs. of News Programming:* news progmg one hr wkly; *No. News Employees:* 2; *Target Audience:* 25-54; women
Janine Drafs, General Manager/Vice President
Bryce Phillipy, General Sales Mgr
Kent Phillips, Programming Director
Jennifer Pirak, Promotions Manager
Sheri Blatman, News Director
John Barrett, Chief Engineer
Gary Greenberg,National Sales Manager

KKWF
01-01-1946; 100.7 MHz FM; *Hrs Open:* 24; 67 kw; 2320 ft.; N47 30 14 W121 58 29
1100 Olive Way, Suite 1650, Seattle, WA 98101 US
(206) 285-7625; *Fax:* (206) 381-0997
www.seattlewolf.com
License: Seattle, King County, WA held by Entercom Seattle License LLC.
Group Owner: Entercom Communications Corp.
Arbitron Metro Market: Seattle-Tacoma, WA; *Format:* Country; *Hrs. of News Programming:* News progmg 15 hrs wkly
Steve Oshin, Operations Dir
Ron Steinman, General Sales Mgr
Lance Tidwell, Programming Director
Dwight Small, Chief Engineer
Melissa Forrest, Operations Manager

KKNW
01-01-1926; 1150 kHz AM; *Hrs Open:* 24
3650 131st Street, Se, Ste 550, Newport Tower, Bellevue, WA 98006 US
(425) 373-5536; *Fax:* (425) 373-5507
www.1150kknw.com
ericb@1150kknw.com
License: Seattle, WA held by Orca Radio Inc.
Group Owner: Sandusky Radio
Arbitron Metro Market: Belleuve, WA; *Format:* News, News/Talk, 86 *Special Programming:* Loc sports 15 hrs, Russian 5 hrs wkly; *Hrs. of News Programming:* news progmg 10 hrs wkly; *No. News Employees:* 1 *TargetAudience:* 35-64; active, well educated adults with middle to upper income
Eric Burris, Operations Dir
Erik Krema, Station Manager
Alan Hines, News Director

KUBE
05-06-1964; 93.3 MHz FM; *Hrs Open:* 24; 98 kw; 1270 ft.; N47 32 40 W122 6 26
645 Elliot Avenue West, Suite 400, Seattle, WA 98119 US
(206) 494-2000; *Fax:* (206) 286-2376
www.kube93.com
License: Seattle, King County, WA held by Citicasters Licenses Inc.
Group Owner: iHeartMedia; (acq 6-14-2002; grpsl).
Arbitron Metro Market: Seattle, WA; *Format:* Contemporary Hits/Top 40
Mark Glynn, Sales Manager
Eric Powers, Programming Director
Hannah Kress, Promotions Manager
Luciana Bosio, Community Events and Announcements

*KUOW-FM
01-16-1952; 94.9 MHz FM; *Hrs Open:* 24; 100 kw; 735 ft.; N47 36 58 W122 18 28
Box 353750, Seattle, WA 98195 US
(206) 543-2710; *Fax:* (206) 616-9125
www.kuow.org
letters@kuow.org
License: Seattle, King County, WA held by University of Washington.
Nat'l Network: NPR; PRI
Arbitron Metro Market: Seattle, WA; *Format:* News *Special Programming:* Sp 2 hrs, jazz 5 hrs wkly; *Hrs. of News Programming:* news progmg 60 hrs wkly; *No. News Employees:*

15; *Target Audience:* 25-54; highlyeducated, influential,decision makers
Wayne Roth, President/General Manager
Dane Johnson, Operations Dir
Marcia Scholl, General Sales Mgr
Jeff Hansen, Programming Director
Guy Nelson, News Director
Terry Denbrook, Chief Engineer
Ben Klasky, Treasurer

KVI
01-01-1926; 570 kHz AM; *Hrs Open:* 24; 5 kw-U, ND1; N47 25 19 W122 25 44
570 4th Avenue North, Seattle, WA 98109 US
(206) 404-4000; *Fax:* (206) 404-3648
License: Seattle, WA held by Fisher Broadcasting - Seattle Radio L.L.C.
Group Owner: Fisher Communications Inc.
Nat'l Network: Fox News Radio; *Nat'l Reps:* Eastman Radio; *Wire Services:* AP
Arbitron Metro Market: Seattle, WA; *Format:* Talk; *Hrs. of News Programming:* news progmg 20 hrs wkly; *No. News Employees:* 2; *Target Audience:* 25-54.
Janene Drafs, General Manager
Bryce Phillipy, General Sales Mgr
Paul Duckworth, Programming Director
Jen Pirak, Promotions Manager
Anna Johnson, News Director
Gary Greenberg, National Sales Manager

KLCK-FM
11-01-1954; 98.9 MHz FM; *Hrs Open:* 24; 63.9 kw; 698 meters; N47 32 41 W122 06 28
3650 131st Ave. S.E., Suite 550, Bellevue, WA 98006
(425) 373-5536; *Fax:* (425) 653-1133
www.click989.com
License: Seattle, King County, WA held by Orca Radio Inc.
Group Owner: Sandusky Radio; (acq 1996; $26 million with co-located AM)
Nat'l Network: Westwood One; *Nat'l Reps:* Christal
Population Served: 3,084,700; *Arbitron Metro Market:* Seattle-Tacoma, WA; *Hrs. of News Programming:* news progmg 9 hrs wkly; *No. News Employees:* 2; *Target Audience:* 25-54; younger active, mid to upper income adults *Adv. Rates:* 250; 250; 250; 75
Marc Kaye, General Manager
Susan Hoffman, General Sales Mgr
Lisa Adams, Programming Director
Cindy Gilsdorf, Promotions Manager

KJAQ
04-29-2005; 96.5 MHz FM; *Hrs Open:* 24; 49 kW; 213 ft.; N47 30 17 W121 58 3
1000 Dexter Ave. N, Seattle, WA 98109 USA
(206) 805-0965; *Fax:* (206) 805-0920
www.jackseattle.com
License: Seattle, King County, WA held by CBS Radio Stations Inc.
Group Owner: CBS Radio; (acq 11-13-98; grpsl).
Arbitron Metro Market: Seattle-Tacoma, WA; *Format:* Adult Contemp; *Target Audience:* 25-54
Cindy Johnson, General Sales Mgr
Helene Cohn, Promotion Coordinator

KZOK
03-22-1983; 102.5 MHz FM; *Hrs Open:* 24; 68 kW; 213 ft.; N47 30 17 W121 58 4
1000 Dexter Ave. N, Suite 100, Seattle, WA 98109 USA
(206) 805-1025
www.kzok.com
License: Seattle, King County, WA held by CBS Radio Stations Inc.
Group Owner: CBS Radio; (acq 11-13-98; grpsl).
Arbitron Metro Market: Seattle, WA; *Format:* Classic Rock; *Target Audience:* 25-49; *Adv. Rates:* 300; 300; 275; 85
Carey Curelop, Programming Director
Beth Sylves, Marketing Director

Selah

KTCR
01-01-1955; 980 kHz AM; *Hrs Open:* 24; 5 kw-D, 500 w-N, DA-N; N46 36 46 W120 28 24
1200 Chesterley Dr., #160, Yakima, WA 98006
(509) 248-2900; *Fax:* (509) 452-9661
License: Selah, Yakima County, WA held by Ingstad Radio Washington LLC
Group Owner: Ingstad Radio Washington LLC; acq 12-1-98; grpsl).
Nat'l Network: ABC; USA *Regional Reps:* Allied Radio Partners.
Population Served: 193,000; *Arbitron Metro Market:* Yakima, WA; *No. News Employees:* 1; *Target Audience:* 35-64.
Pete Benedetti, CEO
Brent Phillipy, Operations Dir
Kit Osborne, General Sales Mgr
Jenifer Wilde, Promotions Manager
Trila Bumstead, COO
Ron King, National Sales Manager
Lou Barfelli, Operations Director

***KYKV**
11-24-1983; 103.1 MHz FM; 5.4 kw; 1427 ft.; N46 38 27 W120 23 46 *Rebroadcasts:* Rebroadcasts KLVR(FM) Middletown, CA 100%
103 E. 4th, Ste 209, Ellensburg, WA 98926 US
(800) 525-5683; *Fax:* (916) 251-1650
www.klove.com
klove@klove.com
License: Selah, Kittitas County, WA held by Educational Media Foundation.
Group Owner: EMF Broadcasting; (acq 6-13-2008; $825,000)
Nat'l Network: K-Love
Arbitron Metro Market: Yakima, WA; *Format:* Christian
Mike Novak, President

KBBO
980 kHz AM
1200 Chesterley Drive, #160, Yakima, WA 98902 US
(509) 248-2900; *Fax:* (509) 452-9661
deweyb@yakimaradiogroup.com
License: Selah, Yakima County, WA held by James D. Ingstad
Group Owner: Ingstad Radio Washington LLC

Nancy Odney, COO
Dewey Boynton, Operations Manager
Kelly Gasseling, Market Manager

Sequim

***KSQM**
01-01-2009; 91.5 MHz FM; 0.7 kw; -276 ft.; N48 4 30 W123 11 32
PO Box 723, Sequim, WA 98382 US
(360) 681-0000
www.ksqmfm.com
radio@ksqmfm.com
License: Sequim, Clallam County, WA held by Sequim Community Broadcasting.
Arbitron Metro Market: Sequim, WA
Bob Schilling, General Manager
Dorothy Zapata, Programming Director
Steve Kellmeyer, Music Director
Tama Bankston, Volunteer Coordinator and Underwriting Assistant

Shelton

KMAS
09-21-1962; 1030 kHz AM; *Hrs Open:* 24; 10 kw-D, 1 kw-N; N47 13 17 W123 04 46
Box 760, 210 W. Cota St., Shelton, WA 98584
(360) 426-1030; *Fax:* (360) 427-5268
kmas1030@kmas.com
License: Shelton, Mason County, WA held by Olympic Broadcasting Inc.
Nat'l Network: ARNN *Regional Reps:* Tacher.; *Wire Services:* AP
Population Served: 320,000 *Special Programming:* Relg 1.5 hrs wkly; *Hrs. of News Programming:* news progmg 70 hrs wkly; *No. News Employees:* 3; *Target Audience:* 35-64.; *Adv. Rates:* 30; 30; 30; 30
Dale Hubbard, President/Owner
Jerry Eckenrode, Owner
Jeff Slakey, Programming Director
Carol Gardner, Media Director
Jack Oronchek, Chief Engineer

KRXY
10-01-1998; 94.5 MHz FM; *Hrs Open:* 24; 0.71 kw; 955 ft.; N47 8 18 W123 8 28
2124 Pacific Avenue SE, Olympia, WA 98506-4753 US
(360) 236-1010; *Fax:* (360) 236-1133
www.945roxy.com
krxy@krxy.com
License: Shelton, Mason County, WA held by Premier Broadcasters Inc.
Group Owner: Premier Broadcasters
Arbitron Metro Market: Olympia, WA; *Format:* Contemporary Hits/Top 40; *No. News Employees:* 1; *Adv. Rates:* 64; 47; 52; 29
Derek Shannon, General Manager
Bob Hart, Station Manager
Jerry Farmer, General Sales Mgr
Paul Walker, News Director

Silverdale

KITZ
10-26-1948; 1400 kHz AM; 1 kw-D, ND1; 0.89 kw-N, ND1; N47 37 45 W122 39 52
1700 Mile Hill Drive, Suite 243, Port Orchard, WA 98366 US
(360) 876-1400; *Fax:* (360) 876-7920
kitz1400.com
License: Silverdale, WA held by KITZ Radio Inc.
Nat'l Network: Westwood One
Arbitron Metro Market: Seattle-Tacoma, WA; *Format:* Talk; *Target Audience:* 25 plus; adults; *Adv. Rates:* 20; 16; 18; 10
Alan Gottlieb, Chairman
Kevin Corcoran, Operations Dir
Conn Williamson, General Manager

Spokane

KZBD
11-08-1965; 105.7 MHz FM; 100 kw; 1909 ft.; N47 34 44 W117 17 46
1601 E. 57th Ave., Spokane, WA 99223 US
(509) 448-1000
www.1057nowfm.com
tdelrio@radiomontereybay.com
License: Spokane, Spokane County, WA held by Mapleton License of Spokane LLC.
Group Owner: Mapleton Communications LLC; (acq 12-3-2007; grpsl)
Nat'l Network: ABC
Arbitron Metro Market: Spokane, WA; *Format:* Alternative; *Target Audience:* 18-49.
Karen Dineen, General Sales Mgr
Tommy Del Rio, Programming Director

***KAGU**
03-16-1988; 88.7 MHz FM; 5 kw; 1529 ft.; N47 34 52 W117 17 47
East 502 Boone Avenue, Spokane, WA 99258 US
(509) 328-4220; (800) 986-9585; *Fax:* (509) 324-5718
www.gonzaga.edu/kagu/
License: Spokane, Spokane County, WA held by Gonzaga University Telecommunications Association.
Arbitron Metro Market: Spokane, WA; *Format:* Adult Contemp
Special Programming: Class 2 hrs, jazz 2 hrs, folk 2 hrs, drama 2 hrs w
Fr. Robert Lyons, General Manager
Matt Caputo, Promotions Manager

KQNT
01-01-1922; 590 kHz AM; 5 kw-U, ND1; N47 36 55 W117 14 57
808 E. Sprague Ave., Spokane, WA 99202 US
(509) 242-2400; *Fax:* (509) 242-1160
www.590kqnt.com
License: Spokane, Spokane County, WA held by Capstar TX LLC
Group Owner: iHeartMedia; (acq 8-30-00; grpsl).
Wire Services: Reuters
Arbitron Metro Market: Spokane, WA; *Format:* News, News/Talk, 86; *Target Audience:* 35-64.
Cal Hall, Market President
Brent Phillipy, Sales Manager
Brad Miller, Senior Vice President of Programming
Matt Auclair, Promotions Director
Andrea Williams, Digital Director

KDRK-FM
01-01-1965; 93.7 MHz FM; *Hrs Open:* 24; 60 kw; 2425 ft.; N47 34 14 W117 4 55
1601 E. 57th Ave., Spokane, WA 99223 US
(509) 448-1000; *Fax:* (509) 448-7015
www.937themountain.com
gtillotson@radiospokane.com
License: Spokane, Spokane County, WA held by Mapleton License of Spokane LLC.
Group Owner: Mapleton Communications LLC; (acq 12-3-2007; grpsl)
Arbitron Metro Market: Spokane, WA; *Format:* Country; *Target Audience:* 25-54.
Greg Tillotson, Programming Director
Karen Dineen, Promotions Manager
Jamie Patrick, Music Director

***KEEH**
07-01-1991; 104.9 MHz FM; *Hrs Open:* 24; 10.5 kw; 1549 ft.; N47 34 45 W117 17 51 *Rebroadcasts:* Rebroadcasts KGTS(FM) College Place 100%
3715 S. Grove Road, Spokane, WA 99219 US
(509) 456-4870; *Fax:* (509) 838-4882
www.plr.org
keeh@plr.org

License: Spokane, Spokane County, WA held by Upper Columbia Media Association
Nat'l Network: USA
Arbitron Metro Market: Spokane, WA; *Format:* Christian; *Target Audience:* General.
John Dolrymple, General Manager

KEZE
12-25-1992; 96.9 MHz FM; *Hrs Open:* 24; 8.2 kW; 1198 ft.; N47 43 33 W117 10 06
500 W Boone Ave, Spokane, WA 99201 USA
(509) 324-4000; *Fax:* (509) 324-8992
hot969.com
License: Spokane, Spokane County, WA held by QueenB Radio Inc.
Group Owner: Morgan Murphy Media
Nat'l Network: USA; *Nat'l Reps:* Katz Radio
Arbitron Metro Market: Spokane, WA *TV Affiliate:* KXLY-TV affil; *Format:* Contemporary Hits/Top 40, Urban Contemporary; *Target Audience:* 25 plus; general
Tery Garras, General Sales Mgr
Denise Hombel, National/Regional Sales

KGA
01-01-1926; 1510 kHz AM; *Hrs Open:* 24
11601 E. 57th Ave., Spokane, WA 99223 US
(509) 448-1000; *Fax:* (509) 448-7015
www.1510kga.com
License: Spokane, WA held by Mapleton License of Spokane LLC.
Group Owner: Mapleton Communications LLC; (acq 12-3-2007; grpsl)
Arbitron Metro Market: Spokane, WA; *Format:* Sports, Talk
Special Programming: Farm one hr wkly; *Target Audience:* 18-34.

KISC
05-01-1966; 98.1 MHz FM; 92.1 kw; 2031 ft.; N47 34 52 W117 17 47
808 East Sprague Avenue, Spokane, WA 99202 US
(509) 242-2400; *Fax:* (509) 242-1160
www.kiss981.com
License: Spokane, Spokane County, WA held by Capstar TX LLC
Group Owner: iHeartMedia
Arbitron Metro Market: Spokane, WA; *Format:* Adult Contemp
Cal Hall, Market President
Brad Miller, Senior Vice President of Programming
Brent Phillipy, Sales Manager
Matt Auclair, Promotions Director
Andrea Williams, Digital Director

KJRB
01-01-1947; 790 kHz AM; *Hrs Open:* 24; 5 kw-D, DA2; 3.8 kw-N, DA2; N47 30 8 W117 23 6
1601 E. 57th Ave., Spokane, WA 99223 US
(509) 448-1000; *Fax:* (509) 448-7015
www.790kjrb.com
License: Spokane, WA held by Mapleton License of Spokane LLC.
Group Owner: Mapleton Communications LLC; (acq 12-3-2007; grpsl)
Arbitron Metro Market: Spokane, WA; *Format:* News, Talk; *Target Audience:* 25-54.

KKZX
10-10-1975; 98.9 MHz FM; *Hrs Open:* 24; 100 kw; 1608 ft.; N47 35 35 W117 17 46
808 East Sprague Avenue, Spokane, WA 99202 US
(509) 242-2400; *Fax:* (509) 242-2482
www.989kkzx.com
License: Spokane, Spokane County, WA held by Capstar TX LLC
Group Owner: iHeartMedia
Arbitron Metro Market: Spokane, WA; *Format:* Classic Rock
Special Programming: Blues 2 hrs wkly; *Hrs. of News Programming:* News progmg one hr wkly; *Target Audience:* 25-54.
Cal Hall, Market President
Brent Phillipy, Sales Manager
Brad Miller, Senior Vice President of Programming
Matt Auclair, Promotions Director
Andrea Williams, Digital Director

***KMBI**
07-12-1959; 107.9 MHz FM; *Hrs Open:* 6 AM-sunset; 64 kW; N47 34 15 W117 5 0
5408 S Freya St, Spokane, WA 99223 USA
(509) 448-2555; *Fax:* (509) 448-6855
www.moodyradio.org/stations/northwest
License: Spokane, WA held by The Moody Bible Institute of Chicago
Group Owner: The Moody Bible Institute of Chicago; (Acq 6-74)
Arbitron Metro Market: Spokane, WA; *Format:* Christian; *Hrs. of News Programming:* News progmg 6 hrs wkly; *Target Audience:* 35-54; Christian men & women

***KPBX-FM**
01-01-1970; 91.1 MHz FM; *Hrs Open:* 24; 56 kw; 2379 ft.; N47 34 13 W117 5 0
Mailing Address: 2319 N. Monroe Street, Spokane, WA 99205 US
Second Address: , Coeur d'Alene, ID
(509) 328-5729; (800)-328-5729; *Fax:* (509) 328-5764
www.kpbx.org
kppx@kpbx.org
License: Spokane, Spokane County, WA held by Spokane Public Radio Inc.
Nat'l Network: NPR; PRI
Arbitron Metro Market: Spokane, WA; *Format:* Jazz, News
Special Programming: Jazz, folk, world mus, new age/space, new mus; *Hrs. of News Programming:* news progmg 50 hrs wkly; *No. News Employees:* 3 *TargetAudience:* General; educated
Brian Flick, Operations Dir
Cary Boyce, President/General Manager
Verne Windham, Programming Director
Jerry Olson, Chief Engineer
Patrick Klausen, Production Manager

KSBN
09-01-1921; 1230 kHz AM; *Hrs Open:* 24; 1 kw-U; N47 39 30 W117 25 08
7 South Howard, Suite 430, Spokane, WA 99202
(509) 838-4000; *Fax:* (509) 838-4800
License: Spokane, Spokane County, WA held by KSBN Radio Inc.
Wire Services: Bloomberg Financial
Population Served: 400,000; *Arbitron Metro Market:* Spokane, WA; *Hrs. of News Programming:* news progmg 24 hrs wkly; *No. News Employees:* 1; *Target Audience:* 30-65; upscale; business owners; *Adv. Rates:* 15;15;15;15
Alan Gottlieb, Chairman
Brad Kemmer, General Manager
Patrick Carey, General Sales Mgr
Conrad Agate, Chief Engineer

***KSFC**
03-01-1973; 91.9 MHz FM; *Hrs Open:* 24; 2.2 kw; 1098 ft.; N47 48 48 W117 30 23
2319 N. Monroe Street, Spokane, WA 99205 US
(509) 328-5729; *Fax:* (509) 328-5764
rkunkel@kpbx.org
License: Spokane, Spokane County, WA held by Spokane Public Radio Inc.
Nat'l Network: NPR; PRI
Arbitron Metro Market: Spokane, WA; *Format:* News *Special Programming:* American Indian 5 hrs, black 2 hrs wkly; *Target Audience:* Curious.
Tom Parker, Chairman
Cary Boyce, General Manager
Verne Windham, Programming Director
Jerry Olson, Chief Engineer
Christie P. Anderson, Vice Chair

KTTO
01-01-1947; 970 kHz AM; *Hrs Open:* 24; 5 kw-D, DAN; 1 kw-N, DAN; N47 36 59 W117 21 55
PO Box 2482, Kirkland, WA 98083 US
(425) 867-2340; (800) 949-1050; *Fax:* (509) 327-5171
www.sacredheartradio.org
info@sacredheartradio.org
License: Spokane, WA held by Sacred Heart Radio Inc.
Arbitron Metro Market: Spokane, WA; *Format:* Christian
Sr. Patricia Proctor, General Manager

KZFS
01-01-1965; 1280 kHz AM; *Hrs Open:* 6 AM-9 PM
808 E. Sprague Ave., Spokane, WA 99202 US
(509) 242-2400; *Fax:* (509) 242-1160
www.up993spokane.com
License: Spokane, WA held by Capstar TX LLC
Group Owner: iHeartMedia; (acq 8-30-2000; grpsl).
Nat'l Network: USA; *Nat'l Reps:* D & R Radio *Regional Reps:* Tacher.
Arbitron Metro Market: Spokane, WA; *Format:* Christian; *Hrs. of News Programming:* News progmg one hr wkly; *Target Audience:* General.
Brad Miller, Senior Vice President of Programming
Cal Hall, Market President
Brent Phillipy, Sales Manager
Matt Auclair, Promotions Director
Andrea Williams, Digital Director

KBBD
01-01-1988; 103.9 MHz FM; *Hrs Open:* 24; 39 kw; 1417 ft.; N47 36 4 W117 17 53
1601 E. 57th Ave., Spokane, WA 99223 US
(509) 448-1000; *Fax:* (509) 448-7015
www.1039bobfm.com
License: Spokane, Spokane County, WA held by Mapleton License of Spokane LLC.
Group Owner: Mapleton Communications LLC; (acq 12-3-2007; grpsl)
Nat'l Network: ABC
Arbitron Metro Market: Spokane, WA; *Target Audience:* 25-49.
Karen Dineen, Promotions Manager

KXLY-AM
10-01-1922; 920 kHz AM; *Hrs Open:* 24
Mailing Address: 500 West Boone, Spokane, WA 99201 US
Second Address: 504 Sherman Avenue, Cour d'Alene, ID 83814
(208) 664-9271
www.kxly.com
info@kxly.com
License: Spokane, WA held by QueenB Radio Inc.
Group Owner: Morgan Murphy Media (Evening Telegram Co); (acq 3-21-62)
Nat'l Network: CBS; Wall Street; *Nat'l Reps:* Katz Radio
Arbitron Metro Market: Spokane, WA; *Format:* News, News/Talk, 86 *Special Programming:* Sports talk 5 hrs, sports play-by-play 20 hrs, local talk 15 hrs wkly; *Hrs. of News Programming:* news progmg 30 hrs wkly *No. NewsEmployees:* 25; *Target Audience:* Adults 35 plus; upper end education & income levels
Stephen Herling, Operations Dir
Chris Garras, General Manager
Teddie Gibbon, Station Manager
Roger Nelson, General Sales Mgr
Dennis Patchin, Programming Director
Gina Mauro, Promotions Manager
Dick Brantley, Regional SalesManager

KXLY-FM
09-01-1959; 99.9 MHz FM; *Hrs Open:* 24; 37 kW; 2999 ft.; N47 55 18 W117 06 48
500 W Boone Ave, Spokane, WA 99201 USA
(509) 324-4000; *Fax:* (509) 324-8992
thebig999coyotecountry.com
License: Spokane, Spokane County, WA held by QueenB Radio Inc.
Group Owner: Morgan Murphy Media
Nat'l Network: Westwood One; Jones Radio Networks; *Nat'l Reps:* Katz Radio
Arbitron Metro Market: Spokane, WA; *Format:* Country
Tery Garras, General Manager
Denise Hombel, National/Regional Sales

KZZU
09-01-1955; 92.9 MHz FM; 81 kW; 2080 ft.; N47 35 42 W117 17 53
500 W Boone Ave, Spokane, WA 99201 USA
(509) 324-4000; *Fax:* (509) 324-8992
929zzu.com
kzzu@kzzu.com
License: Spokane, Spokane County, WA held by QueenB Radio Inc.
Group Owner: Morgan Murphy Media; (acq 4-1-96; $1.75 million with co-located AM).
Nat'l Reps: Katz Radio
Arbitron Metro Market: Spokane, WA *TV Affiliate:* KXLY-TV; *Format:* Adult Contemp, Contemporary Hits/Top 40; *Target Audience:* 18-49.
Denise Hombel, National/Regional Sales
Ken Hopkins, Programming Director
Chris Garras, Local Sales Manager

***KPBZ**
90.3 MHz FM; *Hrs Open:* 24; 0.55 kw; 1082 ft.; N47 48 48 W117 30 23
2319 N Monroe Street, Spokane, WA 99205 US
(509) 328-5729; *Fax:* (509) 328-5764
www.kpbx.org
kpbx@kpbx.org
License: Spokane, Spokane County, WA held by Spokane Public Radio Inc.
Arbitron Metro Market: Spokane, WA
Tom Parker, Chairman
Brian Flick, Operations Dir
Cary Boyce, General Manager
Verne Windham, Programming Director
Steve Jackson, News Director
Jerry Olson, Chief Engineer
Christie P. Anderson, Vice Chairman
Patrick Klausen,Production Director
Linda K. Stow, Business & Membership Director

Sunnyside

***KAYB**
01-01-1998; 88.1 MHz FM; 0.25 kw; -190 ft.; N46 19 53 W120 0 51
P.O. Box 3206, Tupelo, MS 38803 US
(662) 844-8888; *Fax:* (662) 842-6791
www.afr.net
faq@afa.net
License: Sunnyside, Yakima County, WA held by American Family Association.
Group Owner: American Family Radio
Arbitron Metro Market: Tupelo, MS; *Format:* Christian, Religious
Tim Wildmon, President
Donald Wildmon, Founder
Buddy Smith, Sr VP
Ed Vitagliano, Executive VP
Randy Sharp, Director Of Special Projects
Meeke Addison, Director Of Communications
Abraham Hamilton III, General Counsel & PublicPolicy

KDYM
09-01-1950; 1230 kHz AM; *Hrs Open:* 24
Mailing Address: P.O. Box 2888, Yakima, WA 98907 US
Second Address: 706 Butterfield Rd., Yakima, WA 98901
(509) 457-1000; *Fax:* (509) 452-0541
www.adelantemediagroup.com
zorro@radiozorro.com
License: Sunnyside, WA held by Bustos Media of Eastern Washington License LLC.
Group Owner: Bustos Media LLC; (acq 11-18-2004; grpsl)
Nat'l Network: La Gran D; *Nat'l Reps:* Tacher
Arbitron Metro Market: Yakima, WA; *Format:* Oldies, Spanish; *No. News Employees:* 1; *Target Audience:* 25-55; Hispanic; *Adv. Rates:* 13; 13; 13; 11
Ed Krampf, COO
Jay Meyers, CEO
Amador Bustos, President
Keith Teske, Operations Dir
Bob Berry, General Manager
Jaun Gonzalez, Programming Director
Lisa Gonzalez, News Director
Kevin Douglass, Chief Engineer

Tacoma

KBKS-FM
05-01-1959; 106.1 MHz FM; 68 kw; 2,290 ft.; N47 30 17 W121 58 4
645 Elliot Ave. W., Suite 400, Seattle, WA 98119 US
(206) 494-2000; *Fax:* (206) 286-2376
www.kissfmseattle.com
License: Tacoma, Pierce County, WA held by AMFM Texas Licenses LLC
Group Owner: iHeartMedia; (acq 4-1-2009; grpsl)
Arbitron Metro Market: Seattle, WA; *Format:* Contemporary Hits/Top 40; *Target Audience:* 25-54.
Mark Glynn, Sales Manager
Valerie Koch, Promotions Manager

KIRO-FM
10-26-1948; 97.3 MHz FM; *Hrs Open:* 24; 52 kw; 2,392 ft.; N47 30 14 W121 58 29
1820 Eastlake Ave. E., Seattle, WA 98102 US
(206) 726-7000
www.mynorthwest.com
newsdesk@973kiro.com
License: Tacoma, Pierce County, WA held by Bonneville International Corporation
Group Owner: Bonneville International Corporation; (acq 3-14-2008; grpsl)
Nat'l Reps: D & R Radio
Arbitron Metro Market: Seattle-Tacoma, WA; *Format:* News, News/Talk, 84, Talk; *Target Audience:* 25-54.
Carl Gardner, Vice President and Market Manager
Tina Sorensen, General Sales Mgr
Pete Gammell, Programming Director
Jenette Warne, Senior Manager of Promotions and Partnerships
Tom Pierson, Engineering Dir

***KXOT**
06-01-1949; 91.7 MHz FM; *Hrs Open:* 24; 23 kw; 732 ft.; N47 18 14 W122 23 43
4518 University Way NE, Suite 310, Seattle, WA 98105 US
(206) 543-2710; *Fax:* (206) 520-5899
www.kuow.org
letter@kuow.org
License: Tacoma, Pierce County, WA held by PRC Tacoma — I LLC
Nat'l Network: NPR
Arbitron Metro Market: Seattle-Tacoma, WA; *Format:* News, News/Talk, 86; *Target Audience:* .
Wayne Roth, President/General Manager
Dane Johnson, Operations Dir
Gary Rubin, General Sales Mgr
Jeff Hansen, Programming Director

KHHO
08-01-1942; 850 kHz AM; *Hrs Open:* 24; 10 kw-D, DA2; 1 kw-N, DA2; N47 13 56 W122 23 22
645 Elliot Ave. W., Suite 400, Seattle, WA 98119 US
(206) 494-2000
www.sportsradiokjr.com
License: Tacoma, Pierce County, WA held by Citicasters Licenses Inc.
Group Owner: iHeartMedia; (acq 6-14-2002; grpsl).
Arbitron Metro Market: Seattle-Tacoma, WA; *Format:* Sports; *Target Audience:* 25-55.
Nik Krastins, Sales Manager
Rich Moore, Programming Director
Jenny Gudmundson, Promotions Manager
Jason Puckett, Sports Director

KKMO
01-01-1922; 1360 kHz AM; *Hrs Open:* 24; 5 kw-U, ND1; N47 18 19 W122 26 33
4880 Santa Rosa Road, Suite 300, Camarillo, CA 93012 US
(206) 436-7851; *Fax:* (206) 443-1561
License: Tacoma, WA held by Inspiration Media Inc.
Group Owner: Salem Communications Corp.; (acq 8-12-98; $500,000)
Arbitron Metro Market: Seattle, WA; *Target Audience:* 35 plus.
Chuck Olmstead, Operations Dir
Tim Harper, General Manager
Doug Rice, General Sales Mgr
Juanita Jasso, Promotions Manager
Monte Passmore, Chief Engineer

KHTP
06-02-1958; 103.7 MHz FM; *Hrs Open:* 24; 67 kw; 2320 ft.; N47 30 14 W121 58 29
Suite 409, 401 City Avenue, Bala Cynwyd, PA 19004 US
(206) 233-1037; *Fax:* (206) 233-8979
www.kmtt.com
studio@kmtt.com
License: Tacoma, Pierce County, WA held by Entercom Seattle License L.L.C.
Group Owner: Entercom Communications Corp.; (acq 6-73; with co-located AM)
Nat'l Reps: D & R Radio
Arbitron Metro Market: Seattle, WA; *Format:* Triple A; *Hrs. of News Programming:* news progmg 3 hrs wkly; *No. News Employees:* 1; *Target Audience:* 25-49.
David Field, President
Steve Oshin, General Manager
Traci Gregory, General Sales Mgr
Shaun Stewart, Programming Director
Jennifer Orr, Promotions Manager
Mike West, News Director
Dwight Smalls, Chief Engineer
Joyce Jinka,Traffic Manager

***KPLU-FM**
11-01-1966; 88.5 MHz FM; *Hrs Open:* 24; 64 kw; 2320 ft.; N47 30 14 W121 58 29
Mailing Address: 121st and Park Avenue, Tacoma, WA 98447 US
Second Address: 2601 4th Ave., Suite 150, Seattle, WA 98121
(253) 535-7758; *Fax:* (253) 535-8332
www.kplu.org
info@kplu.org
License: Tacoma, Pierce County, WA held by Pacific Lutheran University.
Nat'l Network: NPR; PRI; *Wire Services:* AP
Arbitron Metro Market: Seattle-Tacoma, WA; *Format:* Blues, Jazz, 60; *Hrs. of News Programming:* news progmg 54 hrs wkly; *No. News Employees:* 7; *Target Audience:* 25-54; upscale, highly educated professionals
Jeff Bauman, Operations Dir
Erik Nycklemoe, General Manager
Joey Cohn, Programming Director
Brenda Goldstein-Young, Promotions Director
Jennifer Strachen, News Director
Lowell Kiesow, Chief Engineer
Nick Francis, MusicDirector

***KUPS**
02-28-1978; 90.1 MHz FM; *Hrs Open:* 24; 0.1 kw; 230 ft.; N47 15 48 W122 28 37
1500 North Warner St., Tacoma, WA 98416 US
(253) 879-2415
www.kups.net
info@kups.net
License: Tacoma, Pierce County, WA held by University of Puget Sound.
Arbitron Metro Market: Tacoma, WA; *Format:* Alternative *Special Programming:* Black 18 hrs, jazz 12 hrs, reggae 6 hrs, world mus 4 hrs, blues 6 hrs, metal 8 hrs wkly; *Target Audience:* 18-45.
Doug Herstad, Operations Dir
Kim Clancy, General Manager
Daniel Salas, Programming Director
Will Peil, Production Director

***KVTI**
11-15-1955; 90.9 MHz FM; *Hrs Open:* 24; 51 kw; 364 ft; N47 09 39 W122 34 35
Northwest Public Radio
4500 Steilacoom Blvd. S.W., Lakewood, WA 98499
(253) 589-5884; *Fax:* (253) 589-5797
www.nwpr.org
License: Tacoma, Pierce County, WA held by Clover Park Technical College.
Wire Services: AP
Population Served: 2,500,000; *Arbitron Metro Market:* Seattle-Tacoma, WA *Special Programming:* Live mus 3 hrs, talk 4 hrs wkly; *Hrs. of News Programming:* Northwest Public Radio; *Target Audience:* 12-34; youngadults & teens
John Mangan, General Manager
Al Bednarczyk, Chief Engineer
Beth Valiant, Music Director

***KYFQ**
08-25-2015; 91.7 MHz FM; 4.3 kw; 1909 ft.; N47 32 53 W122 48 22
P.O. Box 7300, Charlotte, NC 28241
(800) 888-7077
www.bbnradio.org
bbn@bbnmedia.org
License: Tacoma, Pierce County, WA held by Bible Broadcasting Network Inc.
Group Owner: Bible Broadcasting Network
Population Served: 168,528; *Arbitron Metro Market:* Tacoma, WA; *Format:* Christian, Religious
Lowell Davey, President
Jason Padgett, Operations Manager

Toppenish

KYNR
05-16-1954; 1490 kHz AM; *Hrs Open:* 24; 1 kw-U, ND1; N46 22 33 W120 19 18
Mailing Address: P. O. Box 350, Toppenish, WA 98948 US
Second Address: 711 King Ln., Toppenish, WA 98948
(509) 865-5363; *Fax:* (509) 865-2129
kyn@yakama.com
License: Toppenish, WA held by Confederated Tribes and Bands of the Yakama Nation
Arbitron Metro Market: Yakima, WA; *Format:* Classic Rock, Country, 52, News, Oldies, Sports *Special Programming:* American Indian 20 hrs wkly; *Hrs. of News Programming:* News progmg one hr wkly *Target Audience:* 18-58.
Lenny Abrams, General Manager
Reggie George, Programming Director

KDBL(FM)
10-31-1977; 92.9 MHz FM; *Hrs Open:* 24; 17 kw; 843 ft; N46 30 15 W120 23 33
4010 Summitview Ave., Yakima, WA 98908
(509) 972-3461
www.929thebull.com
cherylsalomone@townsquaremedia.com
License: Toppenish, Yakima County, WA held by Townsquare Media
Group Owner: Townsquare Media
Nat'l Reps: McGavren Guild
Population Served: 190,000; *Arbitron Metro Market:* Yakima, WA; *Format:* Country; *No. News Employees:* 2; *Target Audience:* 18-49.
Gary Donovan, President
Ron Harris, Operations Dir
Aimee Yoerger, General Manager
Aimee Yoerger, General Sales Mgr
Rik Mikals, Programming Director

Tumwater

KUOW
08-01-1987; 1340 kHz AM; *Hrs Open:* 24 *Rebroadcasts:* Rebroadcasts KUOW-FM Seattle 100%
6005 Capitol Blvd. S.E., Tumwater, WA 98501 US

(206) 543-2710; *Fax:* (206) 616-9125
www.kuow.org
letters@kuow.org
License: Tumwater, WA held by KUOW/Puget Sound Public Radio
Nat'l Network: NPR; PRI
Arbitron Metro Market: Seattle-Tacoma, WA; *Format:* News
Wayne Roth, President/General Manager
Dave Johnson, Operations Dir
Jeff Hanson, Programming Director

Twisp

KCSY
06-01-1993; 106.3 MHz FM; 0.22 kw; 1637 ft.; N48 19 6 W120 6 46
P.O. Box 1118, Twisp, WA 98856 US
(509) 977-5857; *Fax:* (509) 997-5859
kcsyfm.com
License: Twisp, Okanogan County, WA held by Resort Radio LLC
Arbitron Metro Market: Wenatchee, WA; *Format:* Oldies
Aaron Griffith, Operations Dir
David Herald, General Manager/ Partner
Debbie Griggs, General Sales Mgr
Lonnie England, Chief Engineer
Teri Moore, Executive Office Manager
Mike Moore, Account Executive

Union Gap

KDYK
09-13-1983; 1020 kHz AM; *Hrs Open:* 24
Mailing Address: 5110 SE Start Street, Yakima, WA 98907 US
Second Address: 706 Butterfield Rd., Union Gap, WA 98907
(509) 457-1000; *Fax:* (509) 452-0541
www.adelantemediagroup.com
zorro@radiozorro.com
License: Union Gap, WA
Group Owner: Adelante Media Group LLC; (acq 11-18-2004; grpsl)
Nat'l Network: La Gran D *Regional Reps:* Tacher.
Arbitron Metro Market: Union Gap, WA; *Target Audience:* 25-49; Hispanic adults; *Adv. Rates:* 25; 20; 25; 15
Ed Krampf, COO
Jay Meyers, CEO
Keith Teske, Operations Dir
Brian Hollenbaugh, General Manager
Martin Ortiz, Programming Director
Kevin Douglas, Chief Engineer

Vancouver

KBMS
01-01-1955; 1480 kHz AM; *Hrs Open:* 24; 1 kw-D, DAN; 2.5 kw-N, DAN; N45 36 6 W122 43 6
601 Main Street, Suite 400, Vancouver, WA 98660 US
(360) 699-1881; *Fax:* (360) 699-5370
avjkbms@aol.com
License: Vancouver, WA held by Christopher H. Bennett Broadcasting Co. of WA Inc.
Nat'l Network: ABC
Arbitron Metro Market: Portland, OR; *Format:* Talk; *Target Audience:* 54; male & female; *Adv. Rates:* 65; 65; 65; 65
Chris Bennett, General Manager
Angela Jenkins, Station Manager

KMTT
09-01-1946; 910 kHz AM; *Hrs Open:* 24; 5 kw-U, DA-2; N45 33 28 W122 30 09
6400 S.E. Lake Rd., Suite 350, Portland, OR 10004
(503) 786-0600; *Fax:* (503) 786-1551
www.sports910.com
License: Vancouver, Clark County, WA held by Entercom Portland License LLC.
Group Owner: Entercom Communications Corp.; (acq 4-23-98; grpsl)
Nat'l Network: ESPN Deportes; *Nat'l Reps:* D & R Radio
Population Served: 230,600; *Arbitron Metro Market:* Portland, OR; *Format:* Sports
Dennis Hayes, General Manager
Justin Mansfield, Programming Director
Jordan Smith, Promotions Manager

KKOV
08-10-1963; 1550 kHz AM; *Hrs Open:* 24; 50 kw-D, 12 kw-N, DA-N; N45 38 47 W122 30 51
6605 S.E. Lake Rd., Portland, OR 97222 USA
(503) 223-4321; *Fax:* (503) 294-0074
www.sunny1550.com
mgarber@commnewspapers.com
License: Vancouver, Clark County, WA held by Pamplin Broadcasting-Washington Inc.
Group Owner: Pamplin Broadcasting; (acq 11-20-98; $1.65 million)
Nat'l Network: AP Network News; *Nat'l Reps:* Tacher *Regional Reps:* The Tacher Co.; INc.; *Wire Services:* AP
Arbitron Metro Market: Portland, OR *Special Programming:* Portland Beaver baseball 18 hrs wkly; *Hrs. of News Programming:* news progmg 5.6 hrs wkly; *No. News Employees:* 2; *Target Audience:* 35-64.
Margaret Evans, General Sales Mgr
Misty Osko, Promotions Manager
Jeanne Winters, National Sales Manager
Paul Blanding, Traffic Manager

Walla Walla

KGDC
12-06-1956; 1320 kHz AM; *Hrs Open:* 24; 1 kw-D, ND1; 0.066 kw-N, ND1; N46 1 25 W118 21 17
P.O. Box 941, Walla Walla, WA 99362 US
(509) 525-0434; *Fax:* (509) 522-2046
comments@kgdcradio.com
License: Walla Walla, WA held by Two Hearts Communications LLC
Format: News, News/Talk, 86; *Hrs. of News Programming:* News progmg 5 hrs wkly; *Target Audience:* General.; *Adv. Rates:* 9; 8; 8; 8
Rod Fazzari, President

KKSR
01-01-1980; 95.7 MHz FM; 100 kw; Ant 1,401 ft; N45 59 04 W118 10 08
830 N. Columbia Center Blvd., Suite B-2, Kennewick, WA 99336
(509) 783-0783; *Fax:* (509) 735-8627
rik.mikals@nnbradio.com
License: Walla Walla, Walla Walla County, WA held by Ingstad Radio Washington LLC
Group Owner: Ingstad Radio Washington LLC; (acq 1999)
Nat'l Reps: Christal
Arbitron Metro Market: Tri-Cities, WA (Richland-Kennewick-Pasco); *Target Audience:* 25-54.
Lisa Perez, News Director

KTEL
10-01-1946; 1490 kHz AM; *Hrs Open:* 24; 1 kw-U, ND1; N46 2 33 W118 20 0
2003 NW 56th Drive, Pendleton, OR 97801 US
(509) 522-1383; *Fax:* (509) 522-0211
www.1490ktel.com
License: Walla Walla, WA held by WW2 L.L.C.
Group Owner: Capps Broadcast Group; (acq 6-2-03)
Nat'l Network: Jones Radio Networks; ABC *Regional Reps:* Tacher
Arbitron Metro Market: Walla Walla, WA; *Format:* Oldies *Special Programming:* Farm 5 hrs wkly; *Target Audience:* 25 plus; general; *Adv. Rates:* 23; 19; 21; 17
Dave Capps, President
Randy McKone, Operations Dir
Liz Halley, General Sales Mgr
Joe Oertel-Sports Director

*KRKL
05-10-1977; 93.3 MHz FM; *Hrs Open:* 24; 42 kw; 1378 ft.; N45 59 19 W118 10 28
112 N. E. 5th Street, Milton-Freewater, OR 97862 US
(800) 525-5683; *Fax:* (916) 251-1650
www.klove.com
klove@klove.com
License: Walla Walla, Walla Walla County, WA held by Educational Media Foundation.
Group Owner: EMF Broadcasting; (acq 4-1-02; $1 million).
Nat'l Network: K-Love
Arbitron Metro Market: Walla Walla, WA; *Format:* Christian; *No. News Employees:* 13; *Target Audience:* 25-44; Judeo Christian, female
Darrell Chambliss, Chairman
Mike Novak, President and CEO
Mike Lee, Operations Dir
David Pierce, Programming Director
David Pierce, Chief Creative Officer
Ed Lenane, News Director
Sam Wallington, Engineering Dir
Marya Morgan,News Reporter
Richard Hunt, News Reporter
Alan Mason, Chief Operating Officer
Dan Antonelli, Chief Business Development Officer
Eric Moser, Chief Financial Officer
Brian Burger, Vice President of Human Resources

KUJ
01-01-1928; 1420 kHz AM; *Hrs Open:* 24
Rt 5, Box 513, Walla Walla, WA 99362 US
(509) 527-1000; *Fax:* (509) 529-5534
www.kujam.com
info@kujam.com
License: Walla Walla, WA held by Alexandra Communications Inc.
Group Owner: Alexandra Communications Inc.; (acq 4-13-2001).
Nat'l Network: Westwood One *Regional Reps:* Tacher.
Arbitron Metro Market: Walla Walla, WA; *Format:* News, News/Talk, 84, Talk; *Hrs. of News Programming:* news progmg 15 hrs wkly; *No. News Employees:* 1; *Target Audience:* 25 plus.; *Adv. Rates:* 16; 12; 16; 10
Tom Hodgins, CEO
Cheryl Hodgins, President

*KWCW
01-01-1971; 90.5 MHz FM; *Hrs Open:* 24; 0.16 kw; -52 ft.; N46 4 11 W118 19 51
200 Boyer Avenue, Walla Walla, WA 99362 US
(509) 527-5285
www.kwcw.net
License: Walla Walla, Walla Walla County, WA held by The Associated Students of Whitman College Radio Committee.
Arbitron Metro Market: Walla Walla, WA; *Format:* Variety/Diverse; *Hrs. of News Programming:* news progmg 2.5 hrs wkly; *No. News Employees:* 1
Nicole Holoboff, General Manager
Henry Carges, Music Director

*KWWS
03-06-1997; 89.7 MHz FM; 3.2 kw; 1345 ft.; N45 59 4 W118 10 8 *Rebroadcasts:* Rebroadcasts KWSU(AM) Pullman 100%
PO Box 642530, Pullman, WA 99164 US
(509) 335-6500; *Fax:* (509) 335-6577
www.nwpr.org
nwpr@wsu.edu
License: Walla Walla, Walla Walla County, WA held by Washington State University.
Arbitron Metro Market: Pullman, WA; *Format:* News, News/Talk, 86
Karen Olstad, COO
Scott Weatherly, Operations Dir
Dennis Haarsager, General Manager
Kerry Swanson, Station Manager
Sarah McDaniel, General Sales Mgr
Mary Hawkins, Programming Director
Aki Wright, Development Coordinator
AndiWilson, Music and Culture

KXRX
08-01-1977; 97.1 MHz FM; *Hrs Open:* 24; 100 kw; 1329 ft.; N45 59 4 W118 10 9
Mailing Address: City Center West, 7201 W. Lake Mead Blvd, Las Vegas, NV 89128 US
Second Address: 2621 West A. St., Pasco, WA 99301
(509) 547-9791; *Fax:* (509) 547-8509
License: Walla Walla, Walla Walla County, WA held by GAP Broadcasting Tri-Cities License LLC.
Group Owner: GAPWEST Broadcasting; (acq 2-13-2008; grpsl)
Arbitron Metro Market: Paso, WA; *Hrs. of News Programming:* news progmg one hr wkly; *No. News Employees:* 1; *Target Audience:* 25 plus; middle to upper income level listeners
CherylSalomone@townsquaremedia.com, General Manager
Cheryl Salomone, General Sales Mgr
Heath AJ Brewster, Programming Director
Adam Lamberd, Brand Manager

Wapato

*KSOH
03-06-1992; 89.5 MHz FM; 9.5 kw; 974 ft.; N46 31 42 W120 31 16
PO Box 500, Simi Valley, CA 93062 US
(800) 775-4673; *Fax:* (615) 216-7266
www.lifetalk.net
ksoh@lifetalk.net
License: Wapato, Yakima County, WA held by Life Talk Broadcasting Association.
Arbitron Metro Market: Wapato, WA; *Format:* Religious; *Target Audience:* 25-50; families, singles needing courage, hope & answers to societal ills
Steve Gallmore, General Manager
John Geli, Programming/Operations Manager
Warren Judd, Director

Wenatchee

KKRT
11-17-1956; 900 kHz AM; *Hrs Open:* 24; 1 kw-D, NDD; 0.072 kw-N, ND1; N47 27 44 W120 21 28
1124 N. Miller St., Wenatchee, WA 98801 US
(509) 663-5186; *Fax:* (509) 663-8779
www.kkrt.com
License: Wenatchee, Chelan County, WA held by Alpha Media Licensee LLC
Group Owner: Alpha Media LLC; (acq 9-2-2015; grpsl).
Nat'l Network: ESPN Radio; *Nat'l Reps:* Katz Radio
Arbitron Metro Market: Wenatchee, WA; *Format:* Sports; *Target Audience:* 18-54; men
Gary Patrick, General Manager
Jeff Dahlstrom, Sales Manager
Charlie Osgood, Chief Engineer
Kelley Rose, Business Manager
Shari Alexander, Traffic Director
Todd Farrar, Sales Executive
Jennifer Heneghen, Sales Executive
BrentRhodes, Sales Executive

KKRV
05-01-1976; 104.7 MHz FM; *Hrs Open:* 24; 6.5 kw; 1,322 ft.; N47 28 44 W120 12 49
1124 N. Miller St., Wenatchee, WA 98801 US
(509) 663-5186; *Fax:* (509) 663-8779
www.kkrv.com
License: Wenatchee, Chelan County, WA held by Alpha Media Licensee LLC
Group Owner: Alpha Media LLC
Arbitron Metro Market: Wenatchee, WA; *Format:* Country; *Target Audience:* 25-54; women
Gary Patrick, General Manager
Jeff Dahlstrom, Sales Manager
Ryan Nelson, Programming Director
Charlie Osgood, Chief Engineer
Kelley Rose, Business Manager
Shari Alexander, Traffic Director
Todd Farrar, Sales Executive
JenniferHeneghen, Sales Executive
Brent Rhodes, Sales Executive

*KPLW
01-01-1996; 89.9 MHz FM; *Hrs Open:* 24; 5 kw; 1391 ft.; N47 19 25 W120 13 56
606 North Western Ave., Wenatchee, WA 98801 US
(509) 665-6641; *Fax:* (509) 665-3126
www.plr.org
kplw@plr.org
License: Wenatchee, Chelan County, WA held by Growing Christian Foundation.
Format: Christian, News, 74; *Hrs. of News Programming:* News progmg 2 hrs wkly; *Target Audience:* 35-54; female
Kevin Krueger, President
Sean Ruud, General Manager

KPQ
12-01-1929; 560 kHz AM; *Hrs Open:* 24; 5 kw-D, DAN; 5 kw-N, DAN; N47 27 12 W120 19 43
Mailing Address: 32 N. Misssion Street, Wenatchee, WA 98801 US
Second Address: 231 North Wenatchee Ave, Wenatchee, WA 98801
(509) 665-6565; *Fax:* (509) 663-1150
www.kpq.com
info@cherrycreekradio.com
License: Wenatchee, WA held by Wescoast Broadcasting Co.
Nat'l Reps: Tacher
Arbitron Metro Market: Wenatchee; *Format:* News, News/Talk, 86 *Special Programming:* Farm 3 hrs wkly; *Hrs. of News Programming:* News progmg 165 hrs wkly; *Target Audience:* 35 plus.
Jim Wallace Jr., President
Debi Campestrini, Operations Dir
Greg McEwen, General Sales Mgr
Steve Hair, News Director
Pete Peterson, Chief Engineer
Tom Cashman, News Reporter
Eric Granstrom, Sports Commentator
Janette Morris,Traffic Manager

KPQ-FM
12-01-1967; 102.1 MHz FM; *Hrs Open:* 24; 35 kw; 2654 ft.; N47 16 28 W120 25 30
Mailing Address: 32 North Mission Street, Wenatchee, WA 98801 US
Second Address: 231 North Wenatchee Ave, Wenatchee, WA 98807
(509) 665-6565
www.thequake1021.com
info@cherrycreekradio.com
License: Wenatchee, Chelan County, WA
Arbitron Metro Market: Wenatchee, Yakima; *Format:* Classic Rock; *Hrs. of News Programming:* News progmg one hr wkly; *Target Audience:* 25 plus.
Janette Morris, News Director
Kelly Hart, Local News Editor
Tom Cashman, News Reporter
Eric Granstrom, Sports Commentator

KZNW
01-01-1948; 1340 kHz AM; *Hrs Open:* 24
N. 1212 Washington, Suite 307, Spokane, WA 99201 US
(509) 665-6565; *Fax:* (509) 663-1150
License: Wenatchee, WA held by CCR-Wenatchee IV LLC.
Group Owner: Cherry Creek Radio LLC; (acq 10-31-2006; grpsl)
Nat'l Reps: McGavren Guild
Arbitron Metro Market: Wenatchee, WA; *Hrs. of News Programming:* news progmg 10 hrs wkly; *No. News Employees:* 1; *Target Audience:* General; Hispanic; *Adv. Rates:* 14; 14; 14; 14
Steve Miller, General Manager
Leona Frank, General Sales Mgr
Elsa Esparza, Programming Director
Manuel Garcia, Chief Engineer

West Clarkston

*KAUC
89.7 MHz FM; 0.5 kw; -607 ft.; N46 26 20 W117 0 31
P.O. Box 19039, Spokane, WA 99219 US
License: West Clarkston, Asotin County, WA held by Upper Columbia Media Corp.
Arbitron Metro Market: Spokane, WA
Tommy Austin, Operations Dir
Dennis Lamme, General Manager
Beth Davis, General Sales Mgr
John Helmkamp, Promotions Manager
Dan Sullivan, General Sales Manager

Westport

*KLWA
101.3 MHz FM; 1.2 kw; -6 meters; N46 53 04 W124 00 44
Rebroadcasts: KLVR(FM) Middletown, Ca
5700 West Oaks Blvd, Rocklin, CA
(916) 251-1600; *Fax:* (916) 251-1650
www.klove.com
License: Westport, Grays Harbor County, WA held by Educational Media Foundation LLC
Group Owner: Educational Media Foundation

Mike Novak, President

*KCFL
91.1 MHz FM; 4 kw horiz; 26 meters; N47 00 35 W124 09 09
717 Lincoln Street, Hoquiam, WA
(360) 580-4001
www.ghinstitute.org
License: Westport, WA held by Grays Harbor Institute

Gary Murrell, President

White Salmon

*KBNO-FM
01-01-2001; 89.3 MHz FM; 0 kw horiz, 0.016 kw vert; 1102 ft.; N45 43 23 W121 26 42
Box 3765, McAllen, TX 78502 US
(956) 787-9788
License: White Salmon, Klickitat County, WA held by World Radio Network Inc.
Arbitron Metro Market: McAllen, TX; *Format:* Religious
Dr. Abelardo Lim¢n, Chairman
Glenn Lafitte, CEO
John Estey, General Manager
Kitty Stinson, Chief Operations Officer
James Gamblin, Director of Broadcast Operations
Jamie Sepulveda, Director of Finance and Administration
DwightLind, Western Regional Coordinator
David Soper, Vice Chairman
Glenn Lafitte, Secretary

Wilson Creek

KWLN
11-01-1994; 103.3 MHz FM; *Hrs Open:* 24; 25 kw; 243 ft.; N47 16 40 W119 0 0
1124 N. Miller St., Wenatchee, WA 98801 US
(509) 663-5186; *Fax:* (509) 663-8779
www.lanuevaradio.com
License: Wilson Creek, Grant County, WA held by Alpha Media Licensee LLC
Group Owner: Alpha Media LLC; (acq 9-2-2015; grpsl).
Nat'l Reps: Katz Radio
Arbitron Metro Market: Wenatchee, WA; *Format:* Spanish; *Target Audience:* 15 plus.
Gary Patrick, General Manager
Jeff Dahlstrom, Sales Manager
Jose Luis High, Programming Director

Winlock

KITI-FM
08-15-1995; 95.1 MHz FM; *Hrs Open:* 24; 380 w; Ant 879 ft; N46 32 35 W123 01 14
1133 Kresky Rd., Centralia, WA 98531
(360) 736-1355; *Fax:* (360) 736-4761
www.live95.com
live95@live95.com
License: Winlock, Lewis County, WA held by Premier Broadcasters Inc.
Group Owner: Premier Broadcasters Inc.
Regional Reps: Allide
Population Served: 76,000; *No. News Employees:* 1; *Target Audience:* 21-49.; *Adv. Rates:* Enquire with station.
Rod Etherton, President
Rod Etherton, General Manager
Matt Shannon, Station Manager
Matt Shannon, General Sales Mgr
Matt Shannon, Programming Director
Miles McKnight, News Director
Rong Gallagher, Engineering Dir
Harvey Brooks,Chief Engineer

Winthrop

KTRT
01-01-2008; 97.5 MHz FM; 0.33 kw; 1650 ft.; N48 19 6 W120 6 47
PO Box 3008, Winthrop, VA 98862 US
(509) 996-8200
www.radioroot.com
License: Winthrop, Okanogan County, WA held by Tin Can Communications LLC.
Arbitron Metro Market: Barling, AR; *Format:* Triple A
Don Ashford, General Manager

Yakima

KATS
12-15-1968; 94.5 MHz FM; *Hrs Open:* 24; 100 kw; 909 ft.; N46 31 59 W120 30 14
4010 Summitview Avenue, Yakima, WA 98908 US
(509) 972-3461; *Fax:* (509) 972-3540
www.katsfm.com
KATSFM@GMail.com
License: Yakima, Yakima County, WA held by GAP Broadcasting Yakima License LLC.
Group Owner: GAPWEST Broadcasting; (acq 2-13-2008; grpsl)
Arbitron Metro Market: Yakima, WA; *Format:* Rock/AOR; *No. News Employees:* 1; *Target Audience:* 20-45.
Aimee Yoerger, General Manager
Aimee Yoerger, General Sales Mgr
Todd Lyons, Programming Director
Lance Tormey, News Director

KTCR
01-01-1947; 1390 kHz AM; *Hrs Open:* 24; 5 kw-D, 500 w-N, DA-2; N46 34 17 W120 27 15
1200 Chesterly Dr., Suite 160, Yakima, WA 98006
(509) 248-2990; *Fax:* (509) 452-9661
License: Yakima, Yakima County, WA held by James D Ingstad
Group Owner: James D. Ingstad Stns; (acq 10-20-98; grpsl)
Nat'l Network: USA
Population Served: 140,000; *Arbitron Metro Market:* Yakima, WA
Special Programming: Black 2 hrs, gospel 2 hrs wkly; *Hrs. of News Programming:* news progmg 12 hrs wkly; *No. News Employees:* 2 *Target Audience:* 35-64; family oriented; *Adv. Rates:* 20; 20; 20; 12
Pete Benedetti, CEO
Brent Phillipy, Operations Dir
Kit Osborne, General Sales Mgr
Lou Bartelli, Programming Director
Jenifer Wilde, Promotions Manager
Trila Houston, CFO
Trila Bumstead, COO
Ron King, National Sales Manager

***KDNA**
12-19-1979; 91.9 MHz FM; *Hrs Open:* 6 AM-midnight; 18.5 kw; 919 ft.; N46 31 42 W120 31 3
P.O. Box 800, 121 Sunnyside Avenue, Granger, WA 98932 US
(509) 854-1900; (509) 854-2222; *Fax:* (509) 854-2223
www.kdna.org
info@kdna.org
License: Yakima, Yakima County, WA held by Northwest Communities Educational Center.
Arbitron Metro Market: Yakima, WA; *Format:* Spanish *Special Programming:* Relg 4 hrs, children 5 hrs, Sp 106 hrs wkly; *Hrs. of News Programming:* news progmg 8 hrs wkly; *No. News Employees:* 1; *Target Audience:* General; Sp speaking farm workers
Irma Jimenez de Prieto, Chairman
Pat McMahon, Operations Dir
J.D. Freeman, General Manager
Gabriel Martinez, Station Manager
Jeff Mitchell, General Sales Mgr
Saida Rodruguez, Programming Director
Steve Lee, Promotions Manager
Francisco Rios, News Director
Louis Sutton, Engineering Dir

KFFM
08-31-1970; 107.3 MHz FM; *Hrs Open:* 24; 100 kw; 1512 ft.; N46 38 26 W120 23 45
P.O. Box 1248, Minnetonka, MN 55345 US
(509) 972-3461; *Fax:* (509) 972-3540
www.kffm.com
jessicastuckel@gapbroadcasting.com
License: Yakima, Yakima County, WA held by GAP Broadcasting Yakima License LLC.
Group Owner: GAPWEST Broadcasting; (acq 2-13-2008; grpsl)
Nat'l Reps: McGavren Guild
Arbitron Metro Market: Yakima, WA; *Format:* Contemporary Hits/Top 40; *Hrs. of News Programming:* news progmg one hr wkly; *No. News Employees:* 1; *Target Audience:* 18-34.
Aimee Yoerger, General Manager
Aimee Yoerger, General Sales Mgr
Rik Mikals, Programming Director
Esther Johnson, News Director

KHHK
12-01-1984; 99.7 MHz FM; *Hrs Open:* 5 AM-midnight; 4.1 kw; 804 ft.; N46 31 20 W120 20 8
1200 Chesterly Drive, Yakima, WA 98902 US
(509) 248-2900; *Fax:* (509) 452-9661
www.newhot997.com
License: Yakima, Yakima County, WA held by Ingstad Radio Washington LLC
Group Owner: Ingstad Radio Washington LLC; acq 12-1-98; grpsl).
Arbitron Metro Market: Yakima, WA; *Format:* Urban Contemporary; *Target Audience:* 18-34.
Pete Benedetti, CEO
Dewey Boynton, Operations Dir
Don Morin, General Manager

KIT
04-08-1929; 1280 kHz AM; *Hrs Open:* 24; 5 kw-D, ND1; 1 kw-N, ND1; N46 34 19 W120 29 41
Post Office Box 1248, Minnetonka, MN 55345 US
(509) 972-3461; *Fax:* (509) 972-3540,(509) 972-3542
www.newstalkkit.com
License: Yakima, WA held by GAP Broadcasting Yakima License LLC.
Group Owner: GAPWEST Broadcasting; (acq 2-13-2008; grpsl)
Nat'l Network: CBS; *Nat'l Reps:* McGavren Guild
Arbitron Metro Market: Yakima, WA; *Format:* News, News/Talk, 86 *Special Programming:* Farm 6 hrs wkly; *No. News Employees:* 2; *Target Audience:* 25-64; professional, mature
Gary Donovan, President
Ron Harris, Operations Dir
Aimee Yoerger, General Manager/General Sales Manager
Connie Johnston, General Sales Mgr
Dave Ettl, Programming Director
Lance Tormey, News Director
John Wilbanks, ChiefEngineer

KUTI
10-19-1944; 1460 kHz AM; *Hrs Open:* 24; 5 kw-D, DAN; 3.7 kw-N, DAN; N46 33 29 W120 27 2
4701 E. Lake Hariet Pywy, Minneapolis, MN 55409 US
(509) 972-3461; *Fax:* (509) 972-3540
www.1460espnyakima.com
AM1460KUTI@yahoo.com
License: Yakima, WA held by GAP Broadcasting Yakima License LLC.
Group Owner: GAPWEST Broadcasting; (acq 2-13-2008; grpsl)
Nat'l Reps: McGavren Guild
Arbitron Metro Market: Yakima, WA; *Format:* Country; *Hrs. of News Programming:* news progmg 2 hrs wkly; *No. News Employees:* 1; *Target Audience:* 35 plus.
Gary Donavan, President
Ron Harris, Operations Dir
Aimee Yoeger, General Manager/General Sales Manager
Mike Bastinelli, Programming Director
Lance Tormey, News Director
John Wilbanks, Chief Engineer
Lueta Bishop, TrafficManager

***KNWY**
02-20-1993; 90.3 MHz FM; *Hrs Open:* 24; 1.9 kw; 843 ft.; N46 31 57 W120 30 37 *Rebroadcasts:* Rebroadcasts KFAE-FM Richland 100%
PO Box 642530, Pullman, WA 99164 US
(509) 335-6500; *Fax:* (509) 335-3772
www.nwpr.org
nwpr@wsu.edu
License: Yakima, Yakima County, WA held by Washington State University.
Arbitron Metro Market: Yakima, WA; *Format:* News; *Hrs. of News Programming:* news progmg 37 hrs wkly; *No. News Employees:* 1
Karen Olstad, COO
Scott Weatherly, Operations Dir
Dennis Haarsager, General Manager
Kerry Swanson, Station Manager
Sarah McDaniel, General Sales Mgr
Mary Hawkins, Programming Director
John Paxson, News Director

KRSE
08-18-1977; 105.7 MHz FM; *Hrs Open:* 24; 100 kw; Ant 584 ft; N46 42 45 W120 37 46
1200 Chesterly Dr., Suite 160, Yakima, WA 98006
(509) 248-2990; *Fax:* (509) 452-9661
k105.com
info@k105.com
License: Yakima, Yakima County, WA held by Ingstad Radio Washington LLC
Group Owner: Ingstad Radio Washington LLC
Arbitron Metro Market: Yakima, WA; *Target Audience:* 25-64; upscale listener, primarily women; *Adv. Rates:* 34; 34; 34; 20
Kendall Weaver, Programming Director
Gail Dahl, News Director

KXDD
07-01-1971; 104.1 MHz FM; *Hrs Open:* 24 hrs; 61 kw; 781 ft; N46 30 48 W120 24 05
1200 Chesterley Dr., #160, Yakima, WA 98006
(509) 248-2900; *Fax:* (509) 452-9661
License: Yakima, Yakima County, WA held by Ingstad Radio Washington LLC
Group Owner: Ingstad Radio Washington LLC; 2012
Nat'l Reps: The Teacher Company
Arbitron Metro Market: Yakima, WA; *Target Audience:* 18-54.
Nancy Odney, COO
James Ingstad, President
Dewey Boynton, Operations Dir
Kelly Gasseling, Station Manager
Kelly Gasseling, General Sales Mgr
Charlie Brooks, Promotions Manager
Lou Bartelli, News Director

KYAK
10-17-1962; 930 kHz AM; *Hrs Open:* 24
P.O. Box 31000, Spokane, WA 99223 US
(509) 452-5925; *Fax:* (509) 448-5811
kyak.com
kyak@kyak.com
License: Yakima, WA held by Thomas W. Read dba Yakima Christian Broadcasting.
Nat'l Network: Salem Radio Network; USA
Arbitron Metro Market: Yakima, WA; *Format:* Christian
Melinda Read, General Manager
Bill Glenn, Station Manager

***KYPL**
10-15-1997; 91.1 MHz FM; *Hrs Open:* 24; 26 kw; 794 ft.; N46 30 48 W120 24 3 *Rebroadcasts:* Rebroadcasts KGTS(FM) College Place 95%
PO Box 9306, Yakima, WA 98909 US
(509) 457-0725; *Fax:* (509) 457-0658
www.plr.org
studio@plr.org
License: Yakima, Yakima County, WA held by Growing Christian Foundation.
Arbitron Metro Market: Yakima, WA; *Format:* Christian; *Hrs. of News Programming:* News progmg 8 hrs wkly; *Target Audience:* 35-64; family-oriented, Christian
Kevin Krueger, General Manager
Harry Watts, General Sales Mgr
Elizabeth Nelson, Programming Director
Walter Cox, Chief Engineer

***KYVT**
09-01-1980; 88.5 MHz FM; *Hrs Open:* 24; 3 kw; -256 ft.; N46 35 6 W120 31 41
1116 South 15th Ave., Yakima, WA 98902 US
(509) 573-5013; *Fax:* (509) 573-5022
www.nwpr.org
License: Yakima, Yakima County, WA held by Yakima School District No. 7.
Arbitron Metro Market: Yakima, WA; *Format:* Alternative *Special Programming:* Urban alternative 3 hrs wkly; *Hrs. of News Programming:* news progmg 2 hrs wkly; *No. News Employees:* 1; *Target Audience:* 18-25;student & working people
John Schieche, President
Randy Beckstead, General Manager
Andy Ward, Promotions Manager

West Virginia

Barrackville

WFGM-FM
07-01-1993; 93.1 MHz FM; *Hrs Open:* 24; 2.6 kw; 495 ft.; N39 26 40 W79 59 10
343 High St, Morgantown, WV 26505 US
(304) 292-2222; *Fax:* (304) 296-3876
License: Barrackville, Marion County, WV held by AJG Corporation
Group Owner: West Virginia Radio Corp.; (acq 10-18-2005; $250,000)
Nat'l Network: ABC; IND *Regional Reps:* Dome.
Arbitron Metro Market: Morgantown, WV; *Format:* Oldies, Classic Rock; *No. News Employees:* 1; *Target Audience:* 25-54.; *Adv. Rates:* 27; 27; 27; 27
Dave Miller, President

Beckley

WCIR-FM
06-01-1971; 103.7 MHz FM; *Hrs Open:* 24; 5 kw; 1483 ft.; N37 56 51 W81 18 32
Mailing Address: P.O. Box 1037, Beaver, WV 25813 US
Second Address: 306 South Kanawna Street, Beckley, WV 25801
(304) 253-7000; *Fax:* (304) 255-1044
www.103cir.com
jayq@radiocitywv.com
License: Beckley, Raleigh County, WV held by Southern Communications Corp.
Group Owner: Southern Communications Corp.
Nat'l Reps: Katz Radio
Arbitron Metro Market: Beckley, WV; *Format:* Contemporary Hits/Top 40; *Hrs. of News Programming:* news progmg 2 hrs wkly; *No. News Employees:* 2; *Target Audience:* 25-54.
Quesenberry, Jay, General Manager
Rhonda Pritt, News Director

WBKW(AM)
11-14-1966; 1070 kHz AM; 10 kw-D; N37 45 18 W81 14 12
306 S. Karawha St., Beckley, WV 25801-5619
(304) 253-7000; *Fax:* (304) 255-1044
License: Beckley, Raleigh County, WV held by Southern Communications Corp.
Group Owner: Southern Communications Corp.; (acq 1976)
Population Served: 70,000; *Arbitron Metro Market:* Beckley, WV; *Target Audience:* 18-54; traveling motorists
Jay Quesenberry, General Manager
Rennolt Madrazo, General Sales Mgr
Rick Pizer, Promotions Manager
Rhonda Pritt, News Director
Randy Kerbawy, Chief Engineer

WJLS
03-05-1939; 560 kHz AM; *Hrs Open:* 24; 4.5 kw-D, DAN; 0.47 kw-N, DAN; N37 45 32 W81 11 12
Mailing Address: P.O. Box 5499, Beckley, WV 25801 US
Second Address: 102 N. Kanawha St, Beckley, WV 25801
(304) 253-7311
www.wjls.com
License: Beckley, Raleigh County, WV held by West Virginia Radio Company of Raleigh, LLC
Group Owner: West Virginia Radio Corp.
Nat'l Network: WWO; NBCSP
Arbitron Metro Market: Beckley, WV; *Format:* Gospel *Special Programming:* Sports 3 hrs wkly; *Hrs. of News Programming:* news progmg 4 hrs wkly; *No. News Employees:* 5; *Target Audience:* 25-54.

Mark Reid, General Manager

WJLS-FM
11-06-1946; 99.5 MHz FM; *Hrs Open:* 24; 34 kw; 1050 ft.; N37 35 23 W81 6 51
Mailing Address: P.O. Box 5499, Beckley, WV 25801 US
Second Address: 102 N. Kanawha St, Beckley, WV 25801
(304) 253-7311
www.wjls.com
License: Beckley, Raleigh County, WV held by West Virginia Radio Company of Raleigh, LLC
Group Owner: West Virginia Radio Corp.; (acq 02-15-2013; $4.5 million; co-located with AM)
Nat'l Network: WWO; CMLS *Regional Reps:* Dome; *Wire Services:* AP
Arbitron Metro Market: Beckley, WV; *Format:* Country; *Hrs. of News Programming:* news progmg 10 hrs wkly; *No. News Employees:* 15; *Target Audience:* 25+
Mark Reid, General Manager
Becky Gilreath, General Sales Mgr

***WVPB**
05-01-1974; 91.7 MHz FM; *Hrs Open:* 24; 10.4 kw; 919 ft.; N37 53 46 W80 59 21
600 Capitol Street, Charleston, WV 25301 US
(304) 556-4900; *Fax:* (304) 556-4981
www.wvpubcast.org
feedback@wvpubcast.org
License: Beckley, Raleigh County, WV held by West Virginia Educational Broadcasting Authority.
Nat'l Network: NPR; PRI
Arbitron Metro Market: Beckley, WV; *Format:* Jazz, News
Rita Ray, General Manager
Marilyn DiVita, General Sales Mgr
Craig Lanham, Programming Director
Beth Vorhees, Director of News and Public Affairs
Dennis Adkins, Executive Director
Bill Acker, Director of Broadcasting &Technology
Marilyn DiVita, Director of Development
Michael L. Meador, Director of Finance
Shawn Patterson, Director of Marketing

WWNR
08-09-1946; 620 kHz AM; *Hrs Open:* 5 AM-midnight
PO Box 757, Daniels, WV 25832 US
(304) 253-7000; *Fax:* (304) 255-1044
http://wwnrnewstalk620.com
wwnr@radiocitywv.com
License: Beckley, WV held by Southern Communications Corp.
Group Owner: Southern Communications Corp.; acq 1-26-2004).
Nat'l Network: CBS Radio
Arbitron Metro Market: Beckley, WV; *Format:* News, Sports, 86; *Hrs. of News Programming:* news progmg 35 hrs wkly; *No. News Employees:* 2; *Target Audience:* 25-54.; *Adv. Rates:* 30; 25; 30; 20
R. Shane Southern, President
Jay Quesenberry, General Manager
Rennold Madrazo, General Sales Mgr
Rick Rizer, Promotions Manager
Warren Ellison, News Director
Randy Kerbawy, Chief Engineer
Shane Sothern, General Sales Manager
Rhonda Pritt, Traffic Manager

***WBKW**
1070 kHz AM; Ant 679 ft
Mailing Address: P.O. Box 1037, Beaver, WV 25813 US
Second Address: 306 South Kanawha Street, Beckley, WV 25801
(203) 268-9667
http://wbkradio.com
License: Beckley, WV held by Monroe Board of Education.
Arbitron Metro Market: Beckley, WV
Jane Stadler, Operations Dir
Kurt Anderson, General Manager

***WJJJ**
10-30-2007; 88.1 MHz FM; 0.84 kw; 1142 ft.; N37 35 24 W81 6 54
Mailing Address: 118 McGovran Road, Charleston, WV 25314 US
Second Address: P.O. Box 883, Mabscott, WV 25871
(412) 937-1441; (888) 382-0881; *Fax:* (412) 937-0323
www.wjjjfm.org
License: Beckley, Raleigh County, WV held by Shofar Broadcasting Corp.
Arbitron Metro Market: Beckley, WV; *Format:* Religious
James Jenkins, General Manager

Berkeley Springs

WCST
09-07-1958; 1010 kHz AM
1010 Radio Station Road, Berkeley Springs, WV 25411 US
(304) 258-1010; *Fax:* (304) 258-1976
License: Berkeley Springs, WV held by Capper Broadcasting Co.
Arbitron Metro Market: Berkeley Springs, WV; *Format:* News, Talk
Laura Haber, General Manager
Shari Leadman, General Sales Mgr
Lee Bohrer, Programming Director
Mike Hurst, Chief Engineer

WDHC
12-01-1965; 92.9 MHz FM; 3.2 kw; 456 ft.; N39 37 0 W78 13 3
440 Radio Station Lane, Berkley Springs, WV 25411 US
(304) 258-1010; *Fax:* (304) 258-1976
www.wdhc.com
stacydrake@yahoo.com
License: Berkeley Springs, Morgan County, WV
Arbitron Metro Market: Berkeley Springs, WV
Stacy Drake, General Manager
Shari Leadman, General Sales Mgr
Lee Bohrer, Programming Director

Bethany

***WYZR**
01-01-1967; 88.1 MHz FM; 1.1 kw; 410 ft.; N40 12 58 W80 33 31
Renner Union, Bethany, WV 26032 US
(304) 829-7853
www.bethanywv.edu
admission@bethanywv.edu
License: Bethany, Brooke County, WV held by Pittsburgh Public Media
Nat'l Network: AP Radio; *Wire Services:* AP
Arbitron Metro Market: Bethany, WV; *Format:* Variety/Diverse
Special Programming: Christian rock 4 hrs, folk 2 hrs, classic rock 8 h; *Hrs. of News Programming:* News progmg one hr wkly; *Target Audience:* 18-34;high school & college students
Patrick Sutherland, General Manager

Bethlehem

WUKL
02-27-2004; 105.5 MHz FM; *Hrs Open:* 6 am-midnight; 13.5 kw; 312 ft.; N40 3 17 W80 42 26
56325 High Ridge Rd., Bellaire, OH 43906 US
(740) 676-5661; *Fax:* (740) 676-2742
www.mykool105.com
kool105@hotmail.com
License: Bethlehem, Ohio County, WV held by FM Radio Licenses, LLC
Group Owner: Keymarket Communications LLC; (acq 2-4-2004; $1.35 million).
Nat'l Network: ABC
Arbitron Metro Market: Dallas, TX; *Format:* Oldies; *No. News Employees:* 1; *Target Audience:* 35-54.
Gerald Getz, President
Jason Pettit, Promotions Director

Blennerhassett

***WPJY**
01-01-2008; 88.7 MHz FM; 10 kw; 341 ft.; N39 14 0 W81 53 26
3027 Lester Lane, Ashland, KY 41102 US
(540) 552-4252; (877) 456-9361; *Fax:* (540) 951-5282
www.walkfm.org
License: Blennerhassett, Wood County, WV held by Positive Alternative Radio Inc.
Group Owner: Positive Alternative Radio Inc.
Arbitron Metro Market: Blennerhassett, WV; *Format:* Christian
Vernon Baker, President
Adam McDowell, Operations Dir
Jeremy Wolfe, Operations Manager
Elisha Dorsey, Production Assistant
Mike Nelson, Underwriting Representative/Sales Dept
Mel Mendoza, Marketing & Creative Manager

Bluefield

WHAJ
04-23-1963; 104.5 MHz FM; 93 kw horiz, 62 kw vert; 1,549 ft.; N37 15 5 W81 11 20
900 Bluefield Ave., Bluefield, WV 24701 US
(304) 327-7114; *Fax:* (304) 325-7850
www.j1045.com
License: Bluefield, Mercer County, WV held by Alpha Media Licensee LLC
Group Owner: Alpha Media LLC; (acq 12-3-2012).
Arbitron Metro Market: Bluefield, WV; *Format:* Adult Contemp; *Target Audience:* 25-54.
Danny Clemons, Vice President
Lee Rappolt, Continuity Director

WHIS
06-27-1929; 1440 kHz AM; 5 kw-D, ND1; 0.5 kw-N, ND1; N37 16 33 W81 15 6
900 Bluefield Ave., Bluefield, WV 24701 US
(304) 327-7114; *Fax:* (304) 325-7850
www.whistalkradio.com
License: Bluefield, Mercer County, WV held by Alpha Media Licensee LLC
Group Owner: Alpha Media LLC; (acq 12-3-2012).
Arbitron Metro Market: Bluefield, WV; *Format:* News, News/Talk, 86, Religious; *Target Audience:* 35 plus; upper income, leaders of the community
Danny Clemons, Vice President
Lee Rappolt, Continuity Director

WKEZ
05-18-1948; 1240 kHz AM; *Hrs Open:* 24; 1 kw-U, ND1; N37 15 57 W81 11 20
900 Bluefield Ave., Bluefield, WV 24701 US
(304) 327-7114; *Fax:* (304) 325-7850
www.roosterclassiccountry.com
License: Bluefield, Mercer County, WV held by Alpha Media Licensee LLC
Group Owner: Alpha Media LLC; (acq 12-3-2012).
Arbitron Metro Market: Bluefield, WV; *Format:* Country *Special Programming:* Relg 5 hrs wkly
Ken Dietz, Operations Manager
Danny Clemons, Vice President
Lee Rappolt, Continuity Director

***WPIB**
09-01-1995; 91.1 MHz FM; 12 kw; 1184 ft.; N37 15 26 W81 10 43
Mailing Address: P. O. Box 889, Blacksburg, VA 24063 US
Second Address: 22226 Timberlake Road, Lynchburg, VA 24502
(434) 237-9798; *Fax:* (434) 237-1025
www.spiritfm.com
office@spiritfm.com
License: Bluefield, Mercer County, WV held by Positive Alternative Radio Inc.
Group Owner: Positive Alternative Radio Inc.; (acq 4-22-92)
Nat'l Network: USA
Format: Adult Contemp, Christian
Edward Baker, President
Jackie Howard, Operations Dir

Bridgeport

WETT
06-29-1991; 104.1 MHz FM; *Hrs Open:* 24; 3 kw; 328 ft.; N39 17 59 W80 17 30
5 Television Drive, Bridgeport, WV 26330
(304) 842-7501
License: Bridgeport, Harrison County, WV held by WDCI Radio Inc.
Nat'l Network: Jones Radio Networks *Regional Reps:* Dome.
Population Served: 125,000; *Arbitron Metro Market:* Morgantown-Clarksburg-Fairmont, WV; *Target Audience:* 25-54.
Bruce Wallace, President
Tom Thompson, General Sales Mgr
Tina Grefak, Programming Director
Hank Vest, Chief Engineer

Buckhannon

WBRB
06-16-1990; 101.3 MHz FM; *Hrs Open:* 24; 50 kw; 490 ft.; N38 56 40 W80 10 46
1065 Radio Park Dr., Mount Clare, WV 26408 US
(304) 623-6546
www.1013thebear.com
License: Buckhannon, Upshur County, WV held by West Virginia Radio Corporation of Buckhannon.
Group Owner: West Virginia Radio Corp.; (acq 10-18-2005; $4,267,900 with WBUC(AM) Buckhannon)
Arbitron Metro Market: Mount Claire, WV; *Format:* Country; *Hrs. of News Programming:* news progmg 4 hrs wkly; *No. News Employees:* 1; *Target Audience:* 25-54; *Adv. Rates:* 27; 27; 27; 27
Dave Miller, President

WBTQ
01-01-1984; 93.5 MHz FM; *Hrs Open:* 24; 16 kw; 417 ft.; N38 58 11 W80 1 58 *Rebroadcasts:* simulcasts Talk Radio 103.3 WAJR
1251 Ear L. Core Rd., Morgantown, WV 26505 US

RADIO - U.S.

(304) 296-0029
www.wajr.com
License: Buckhannon, Upshur County, WV held by West Virginia Radio Corporation of Elkins.
Group Owner: West Virginia Radio Corp.; (acq 5-15-2008; $1.25 million)
Nat'l Network: ABC *Regional Reps:* Dome.
Arbitron Metro Market: Elkins,WV; *Format:* News, Talk, 84; *Hrs. of News Programming:* news progmg 3 hrs wkly; *No. News Employees:* 1; *Target Audience:* 18-49.; *Adv. Rates:* 25; 20; 23; 18
Dave Miller, President

WBUC
12-13-1959; 1460 kHz AM; *Hrs Open:* Sunrise-sunset; 5.5 kw-D, ND1; 0.024 kw-N, ND1; N38 58 28 W80 12 26 *Rebroadcasts:* Simulcasts WAJR Morgantown
1251 Earl L. Core Road, Morgantown, WV 26505 US
(304) 296-0029
www.wajr.com
License: Buckhannon, Upshur County, WV held by West Virginia Radio Corporation of Buckhannon.
Group Owner: West Virginia Radio Corp.; (acq 10-18-2005; $4,267,900 with WBRB(FM) Buckhannon)
Format: Talk, News, 84; *No. News Employees:* 1; *Target Audience:* General.
Dale Miller, President

***WVPW**
09-01-1968; 88.9 MHz FM; *Hrs Open:* 24; 14 kw; 850 ft.; N39 2 4 W80 33 47
600 Capitol Street, Charleston, WV 25301 US
(304) 556-4900; *Fax:* (304) 556-4981
www.wvpubcast.org
feedback@wvpubcast.org
License: Buckhannon, Upshur County, WV held by West Virginia Education Broadcasting Authority.
Nat'l Network: NPR; PRI
Arbitron Metro Market: Buckhannon, WV; *Format:* Jazz, News
Rita Ray, General Manager
Marilyn DiVita, General Sales Mgr
Craig Lanham, Programming Director
Beth Vorhees, Director of News and Public Affairs
Dennis Adkins, Executive Director
Bill Acker, Director of Broadcasting &Technology
Marilyn DiVita, Director of Development
Michael L. Meador, Director of Finance
Shawn Patterson, Director of Marketing

***WVWC**
09-15-1997; 92.1 MHz FM; 0.013 kw horiz; -69 ft.; N38 59 24 W80 13 10
Box 167, Wvwc, Buckhannon, WV 26201 US
(304) 473-8292; *Fax:* (304) 472-2571
www.wvwc.edu/c92
c92@wvwc.edu
License: Buckhannon, Upshur County, WV held by West Virginia Wesleyan College.
Arbitron Metro Market: Buckhannon, WV; *Format:* Classic Rock, Variety/Diverse *Special Programming:* Black 4 hrs, class 2 hrs, jazz 8 hrs, relg 4 hrs,; *Target Audience:* 12-25; high school & college audience
Liz Short, General Manager
Marybeth Yoder, Programming Director
Whitney Law, Promotions Manager
Brian Schooley, Sports Director
Travis Rexroad, Training Director
Amanda Jones, Training Director
Sarah Carr, Music Director
MicahOsborne, Music Director

Charleston

WKAZ
01-01-1946; 680 kHz AM; *Hrs Open:* 24; 10 kw-D, DAN; 0.221 kw-N, DAN; N38 19 7 W81 32 28
1251 Earl Core Rd., Morgantown, WV 26505 US
(304) 296-0029
License: Charleston, WV held by West Virginia Radio Corporation of Charleston
Group Owner: West Virginia Radio Corp.; (acq 7-14-93; $1.1 million with co-located FM)
Nat'l Network: ABC
Arbitron Metro Market: Morgantown, WV; *Format:* Oldies; *No. News Employees:* 1; *Target Audience:* 25-54.
Dave Smith, President

WCHS
09-15-1927; 580 kHz AM; 5 kw-D, DAN; 5 kw-N, DAN; N38 21 51 W81 46 5
1111 Virginia St. E., Charleston, WV 25301 US
(304) 342-8131
License: Charleston, WV held by West Virginia Radio Corporation of Charleston
Group Owner: West Virginia Radio Corp.; (acq 6-1-92; $1.74 million with co-located FM)
Nat'l Network: CBS
Arbitron Metro Market: Charleston, WV; *Format:* News, Talk, 84; *No. News Employees:* 2; *Target Audience:* 25-54.
Dale Miller, President

WKWS
09-16-1969; 96.1 MHz FM; 45 kw; 515 ft.; N38 21 54 W81 46 6
1111 Virginia St. E., Charleston, WV 25301 US
(304) 342-8131
www.961thewolf.com
License: Charleston, Kanawha County, WV held by West Virginia Radio Corporation of Charleston
Group Owner: West Virginia Radio Corp.
Nat'l Network: CMLS
Arbitron Metro Market: Charleston, WV; *Format:* Country; *Target Audience:* 25+
Dave Miller, President

WBES
02-16-1957; 950 kHz AM; 5 kw-D, 1 kw-N, DA-N; N38 23 00 W81 42 52
Box 871, 4250 Washington St. W., Charleston, WV 24203
(304) 744-7020; *Fax:* (304) 744-8562
www.95thesportsfox.com
License: Charleston, Kanawha County, WV held by Bristol Broadcasting Co. Inc.
Group Owner: Bristol Broadcasting Co. Inc.; acq 5-1-64).
Nat'l Reps: McGavren Guild
Population Served: 640,500; *Arbitron Metro Market:* Charleston, WV
Mike Robinson, Sales Manager

WQBE-FM
02-16-1957; 97.5 MHz FM; 50 kw; 499 ft.; N38 24 22 W81 43 26
817 Suncrest Place, Charleston, WV 25303 US
(304) 744-7020; *Fax:* (304) 744-8562
www.wqbe.com
info@wqbe.com
License: Charleston, Kanawha County, WV
Arbitron Metro Market: Charleston, WV
Terri Outlaw, Sales Manager

WSWW
01-01-1939; 1490 kHz AM; *Hrs Open:* 24; 1 kw-U, ND1; N38 21 28 W81 37 0
1111 Virgnia St. E., Charleston, WV 25301 US
(304) 342-8131; *Fax:* (304) 344-4745
www.charlestonespn.com
License: Charleston, Kanawha County, WV held by West Virginia Radio Corp.
Group Owner: West Virginia Radio Corp.; (acq 6-5-97; $2.15 million with WKAZ-FM Miami)
Nat'l Network: ESPN Radio; APNET; *Nat'l Reps:* D & R Radio
Arbitron Metro Market: Charleston, WV; *Format:* Sports; *Target Audience:* Men, 25+
Dale Miller, President

WVAF
02-01-1965; 99.9 MHz FM; 24.5 kw; 705 ft.; N38 16 25 W81 31 27
1111 Virginia St. E., Charleston, WV 25301 US
(304) 342-8131; *Fax:* (304) 344-4745
www.v100.fm
License: Charleston, Kanawha County, WV held by West Virginia Radio Corporation of Charleston.
Group Owner: West Virginia Radio Corp.
Nat'l Network: WWO; CMLS
Arbitron Metro Market: Charleston, WV; *Format:* Adult Contemp; *Target Audience:* Women, 25-54.
Dave Miller, President

***WVPN**
05-08-1979; 88.5 MHz FM; *Hrs Open:* 24; 44 kw; 440 ft.; N38 22 34.3 W81 39 24
600 Capitol Street, Charleston, WV 25301 US
(304) 556-4900
www.wvpubcast.org
feedback@wvpubcast.org
License: Charleston, Kanawha County, WV held by West Virginia Educational Broadcasting Authority.
Nat'l Network: NPR; PRI
Arbitron Metro Market: Charleston, WV; *Format:* Jazz, News
Rita Ray, General Manager
Marilyn DiVita, General Sales Mgr
Craig Lanham, Programming Director
Beth Vorhees, Director of News and Public Affairs
Dennis Adkins, Executive Director
Bill Acker, Director of Broadcasting &Technology
Marilyn DiVita, Director of Development
Michael L. Meador, Director of Finance
Shawn Patterson, Director of Marketing

WVSR-FM
09-01-1964; 102.7 MHz FM; 50 kw; 404 ft.; N38 21 26 W81 40 5
Mailing Address: P.O Box 1389, Bristol, VA 24203 US
Second Address: 4250 Washington St., Charleston, WV 25313
(304) 342-3136; *Fax:* (304) 342-3118
www.electric102.com
info@electric102.com
License: Charleston, Kanawha County, WV
Arbitron Metro Market: Charleston, WV; *Format:* Contemporary Hits/Top 40
Candis Isberner, CEO
Mike Zelten, Operations Dir
Jeff Williams, Station Manager
Renee Dillard, General Sales Mgr
Brandy Thomas-Ray, Local Sales Manager

***WXAF**
01-01-1994; 90.9 MHz FM; 0.8 kw; 623 ft.; N38 16 25 W81 31 27
P. O. Box 7575, Huntington, WV 25777 US
(740) 867-5333
www.wxaffm.org
WJJFM@Suddenlinkmail.com
License: Charleston, Kanawha County, WV held by Maranatha Broadcasting Inc.
Arbitron Metro Market: Charleston, WV; *Format:* Religious
Paul Warren, President

WVTS(AM)
1240 kHz AM; 1000 watts; non-directional; 38 23 08N 81 42 51W
817 Suncrest Place, Charleston, WV 25303 USA
(304) 744-7020; *Fax:* (304) 744-8562
License: Charleston, Kanawha County, WV
Group Owner: Bristol Broadcasting Inc

Charlestown

WMRE
05-28-1962; 1550 kHz AM; *Hrs Open:* Sunrise-sunset; 5 kw-D, ND2; 0.006 kw-N, ND2; N39 16 23 W77 51 56
510 Pegasus Court, Winchester, VA 22602 US
(540) 662-5101; *Fax:* (540) 662-8610
www.foxsports1550.com
davidmiller@iheartmedia.com
License: Charlestown, WV held by AMFM Radio Licenses LLC.
Group Owner: iHeartMedia; (acq 2-16-2001; $1.525 million with co-located FM)
Nat'l Network: Fox Sports; *Nat'l Reps:* Roslin
Arbitron Metro Market: Winchester, VA; *Format:* Sports; *No. News Employees:* 2
David Miller, Regional Programming Manager
Daniel Martin, General Sales Mgr
Scott Bradley, Promotions Manager
Ricky Thomas, Online Digital Director

Clarksburg

WWLW
01-01-1973; 106.5 MHz FM; *Hrs Open:* 24; 28 kw; 653 ft.; N39 15 44 W80 28 1
1065 Radio Park Dr., Mount Clare, WV 26408 US
(304) 623-6546
www.wvmagic.com
License: Clarksburg, Harrison County, WV held by West Virginia Radio Corporation of Clarksburg.
Group Owner: West Virginia Radio Corp.; (acq 3-2-93; $1.2 million)
Nat'l Network: CMLS
Arbitron Metro Market: Clarksburg, WV; *Format:* Adult Contemp; *Hrs. of News Programming:* news progmg 2 hrs wkly; *No. News Employees:* 1; *Target Audience:* 25-55.
Dale Miller, President

WXKX
11-28-1946; 1340 kHz AM; *Hrs Open:* 24; 1 kw-U, ND1; N39 17 27 W80 18 56
P.O. Box 2423, Clarksburg, WV 26302 US
(304) 624-5525; *Fax:* (304) 624-5526
www.espnradio1340.com
License: Clarksburg, Harrison County, WV held by Burbach of DE LLC
Group Owner: Burbach Broadcasting Group; (acq 11-2-00; $435,000 cash with co-located FM).
Nat'l Network: ESPN Radio; *Nat'l Reps:* Roslin; Rgnl Reps
Arbitron Metro Market: Morgantown-Clarksburg-Fairmont, WV; *Format:* Sports *Special Programming:* Pittsburgh Pirates,

Alderson-Broadus College baske; *Hrs. of News Programming:* News progmg 14 hrs wkly; *Target Audience:* 35 plus; office workers, retirees, upper income; *Adv. Rates:* 17.50; 14.50; 17.50; 14.50
Michael Pasqua, Director of Sales
Stacy Schulman, Account Manager

***WKJL**
10-01-1992; 88.1 MHz FM; *Hrs Open:* 19; 19 kw horiz, 32 kw vert; 489 ft.; N39 17 59 W80 17 30 *Rebroadcasts:* Rebroadcasts WAIJ(FM) Grantsville, Md. 100%
34 Springs Road, Grantsville, MD 21536 US
(301) 895-3292; *Fax:* (301) 895-3293
www.hesalive.net
hesalive@hesalive.net
License: Clarksburg, Harrison County, WV held by He's Alive Inc.
Nat'l Network: USA
Arbitron Metro Market: Morgantown-Clarksburg-Fairmont, WV; *Format:* Christian, Gospel; *Target Audience:* 18-35.
Melissa Flores, General Manager

WPDX
08-19-1947; 750 kHz AM; 1 kw-D, NDD; N39 14 40 W80 23 5
7013 Mountains Park Drive, Fairmont, WV 22835 US
(304) 363-3851; *Fax:* (304) 363-3852
www.wpdxcountry.com
License: Clarksburg, WV held by Tschudy Broadcasting Corp.
Nat'l Network: AP Radio *Regional Reps:* Commercial Media Sales
Arbitron Metro Market: Morgantown-Clarksburg-Fairmont, WV; *Format:* Country; *Target Audience:* 35-54; blue collar; *Adv. Rates:* 15; 15; 15; 12
Mike Oberg, President
Lyric Klaske, General Manager
Robert Hoffer, General Sales Mgr
Susann Gamble, Programming Director
Wendy Oberg, Executive Vice President

WPDX-FM
08-19-1974; 104.9 MHz FM; *Hrs Open:* 24; 7.4 kw; Ant 597 ft; N39 15 22 W80 06 46
7013 Mountains Park Dr., Fairmont, WV 22835
(304) 363-3851; *Fax:* (304) 363-3852
www.wpdxcountry.com
License: Clarksburg, Harrison County, WV held by Tschudy Broadcasting Corp.
Nat'l Network: AP Radio *Regional Reps:* Commercial Media Sales
Population Served: 400,000; *Arbitron Metro Market:* Morgantown-Clarksburg-Fairmont, WV; *Hrs. of News Programming:* News progmg 5 hrs wkly; *Target Audience:* 35-54; blue collar; *Adv. Rates:* 15; 15; 15; 12
Tony Gee, Programming Director

WGIE
01-01-1975; 92.7 MHz FM; *Hrs Open:* 24; 0.62 kw; 669 ft.; N39 17 27 W80 18 56 *Rebroadcasts:* Rebroadcasts WGYE(FM) Mannington, WV 100%
1489 Locust Ave., Suite C, Fairmont, WV 26554 US
(304) 363-8838; *Fax:* (304) 367-1885
froggycountry@resultsradiowv.com
License: Clarksburg, Harrison County, WV held by Burbach of DE LLC
Group Owner: Burbach Broadcasting Group
Arbitron Metro Market: Morgantown, WV; *Format:* Country; *Hrs. of News Programming:* News progmg 3 hrs wkly; *Target Audience:* 25-45; young professionals
Michael Pasqua, Director of Sales
Stacy Schulman, Account Manager

***WCKU**
01-01-1993; 90.1 MHz FM; 4 kw; 705 ft.; N39 19 9 W80 23 31
P.O. Box 7575, Huntington, WV 25777 US
(916) 251-1600; *Fax:* (916) 251-1650
www.klove.com
klove@klove.com
License: Clarksburg, Harrison County, WV held by Educational Media Foundation.
Group Owner: EMF Broadcasting; (acq 2-29-2008; $900,000 with WHKU(FM) Proctorville, OH)
Nat'l Network: K-Love
Arbitron Metro Market: Clarksburg, WV; *Format:* Christian
Darrell Chambliss, Chairman
Alan Mason, CEO/COO
Mike Novak, CEO
David Pierce, Chief Creative Officer
Dan Antonelli, Chief Business Development Officer
Eric Moser, Chief Financial Officer
Brian Burger, Vice President of HumanResources
D. Kevin Blair, Secretary and General Counsel

Cowen

WKQV
01-01-2007; 105.5 MHz FM; *Hrs Open:* 24; 3.5 kw; 883 ft.; N38 21 35 W80 38 51
US
(304) 765-7373; *Fax:* (304) 765-7836
www.105kqv.com
info@105kqv.com
License: Cowen, Webster County, WV held by Summit Media Broadcasting LLC.
Group Owner: Summit Media Broadcasting LLC; (acq 3-15-2006; $482,500 for CP)
Nat'l Network: CNN Radio; *Nat'l Reps:* Rgnl Reps
Arbitron Metro Market: Cowen, WV; *Format:* Classic Rock; *Target Audience:* 18-49.; *Adv. Rates:* 20; 16; 20; 13
Al Sergi, President

Craigsville

WSWW-FM
01-01-2008; 95.7 MHz FM; 25 kw; 325 ft; N38 24 56 W80 31 49
Mailing Address: 812 Northside Dr, Suite 1, Summersville, WV 26651 US
Second Address: 1251 Earl L. Core Rd, Morgantown, WV 26505
(304) 872-6403; *Fax:* (304) 872-6816
www.3ws957.com
License: Craigsville, Nicholas County, WV held by West Virginia Radio Corporation of Charleston.
Group Owner: West Virginia Radio Corp.; (acq 9-11-2007)
Nat'l Network: NBCSP; FOXNEW
Format: Variety/Diverse
Dale Miller, President

Danville

WZAC-FM
10-09-1989; 92.5 MHz FM; 0.61 kw; 696 ft.; N38 5 1 W81 48 17
Mailing Address: P. O. Box 87, Danville, WV 25053 US
Second Address: 457 Main St., Madison, WV 25130
(304) 369-5200; *Fax:* (304) 369-5200
License: Danville, Boone County, WV held by Price Broadcasting Co.
Arbitron Metro Market: Danville, WV; *Format:* Country; *Target Audience:* General.
Wayne Price, General Manager

Dunbar

WVTS-FM
10-13-1988; 94.5 MHz FM; *Hrs Open:* 24; 9.6 kw; Ant 525 ft; N38 25 11 W81 43 24
Mailing Address: Box 871, Charleston, WV 24201
Second Address: 4250 Washington St., Charleston, WV 25313
(304) 744-7020; *Fax:* (304) 744-8562
License: Dunbar, Kanawha County, WV held by Bristol Broadcasting Co. Inc.
Group Owner: Bristol Broadcasting Co. Inc.; acq 1996; grpsl).
Nat'l Network: Moody; Westwood One; *Nat'l Reps:* Dome; Rgnl Reps; Katz Radio
Arbitron Metro Market: Charleston, WV *Special Programming:* Class 2 hrs wkly
Mike Robinson, General Manager
Dave Evans, Programming Director
Barrie Hamm, Promotions Manager
Randy Justice, Chief Engineer

WVTS
11-04-1946; 1240 kHz AM; 1 kw-U; N38 23 08 W81 42 51
Mailing Address: Box 871, Charleston, WV 24203
Second Address: 4250 Washington St., Charleston, WV 25313
(304) 744-7020; *Fax:* (304) 744-8562
95thesportsfox.com
MSH@95thesportsfox.com
License: Dunbar, Kanawha County, WV held by Bristol Broadcasting Co. Inc.
Group Owner: Bristol Broadcasting Co. Inc.; acq 8-90; grpsl).
Population Served: 51,177; *Arbitron Metro Market:* Charleston, WV; *Target Audience:* 18-49.
Mike Robinson, General Manager
John Gush, General Sales Mgr
Brandy Thomas-Ray, Local Sales Manager

WLUX
1450 kHz AM; 1 kw-U; N38 20 57 W81 44 53
Mailing Address: P.O. Box 3744, Charleston, WV 25337
Second Address: 1114 Virginia St. E., Charleston, WV 25301
(304) 342-8131
License: Dunbar, Kanawha County, WV held by St. Paul Radio Co.
Group Owner: St. Paul Radio Co.
Arbitron Metro Market: Charleston, WV; *Format:* Religious; *Adv. Rates:* N/A
Mark Sadd, President

Elizabeth

WXIL
09-01-1975; 95.1 MHz FM; *Hrs Open:* 24; 50 kw; 499 ft.; N39 14 47 W81 28 19
5 Rosemar Circle, Parkersburg, WV 26104 US
(304) 485-4565; *Fax:* (304) 424-6955
www.95xil.com
License: Elizabeth, Wirt County, WV held by Burbach of DE LLC
Group Owner: Burbach Broadcasting Group; (acq 9-1-80; $1 million;
Nat'l Reps: Katz Radio
Arbitron Metro Market: Parkersburg, WV; *Format:* Adult Contemp, Contemporary Hits/Top 40; *Hrs. of News Programming:* news progmg 6 hrs wkly; *No. News Employees:* 1; *Target Audience:* 25-54; women
Nicholas Galli, President
Don Staats, General Manager
Chuck Helmick, Local Sales Manager
Charles Roberts, Account Manager
Amy Landis, Account Manager
Rich Rule, Account Manager
Lauren Queen, Account Manager

Elkins

***WBHZ**
01-01-1999; 91.9 MHz FM; 0.275 kw; 1119 ft.; N38 52 18 W79 55 39
P.O. Box 3206, Tupelo, MS 38803 US
(662) 844-8888; *Fax:* (662) 842-6791
www.afr.net
faq@afa.net
License: Elkins, Randolph County, WV held by American Family Association.
Group Owner: American Family Radio
Arbitron Metro Market: Elkins, WV; *Format:* Christian
Tim Wildmon, President
Donald Wildmon, Founder
Buddy Smith, Sr VP
Ed Vitagliano, Exec VP
Randy Sharp, Director Of Special Projects
Meeke Addison, Director Of Communications
Abraham Hamilton III, General Counsel

WDNE
02-01-1948; 1240 kHz AM; *Hrs Open:* 8am-5pm; 1.0 kw-D, ND2; 1.0 kw-N, ND2; N38 55 24 W79 51 45
Washington Ave. & West Davis St., Elkins, WV 26241 US
License: Elkins, WV held by West Virginia Radio Corporation of Elkins
Group Owner: West Virginia Radio Corp.; (acq 6-17-97; $750,000 with co-located FM)
Arbitron Metro Market: Elkins-Randolph County, WV; *Format:* Country; *No. News Employees:* 1; *Target Audience:* 18 plus.; *Adv. Rates:* 18; 18; 18; 18
Dale Miller, President

WDNE-FM
06-15-1985; 98.9 MHz FM; *Hrs Open:* 21; 5.1 kw; 725 ft.; N38 54 36 W79 47 18
101 Washington Ave., Elkins, WV 26241 US
(304) 636-1300
www.wdnefm.com
License: Elkins, Randolph County, WV held by West Virginia Radio Corporation of Elkins
Group Owner: West Virginia Radio Corp.
Nat'l Network: ABC
Arbitron Metro Market: Elkins-Randolph County, WV; *Format:* Country
Dave Miller, President

WELK
10-17-1982; 94.7 MHz FM; *Hrs Open:* 24; 5 kw; 728 ft.; N38 54 43 W79 47 19
101 Washington Ave., Elkins, WV 26241 US
(304) 636-1300
www.947welk.com
License: Elkins, Randolph County, WV held by West Virginia Radio Corporation of Elkins
Group Owner: West Virginia Radio Corp.; (acq 5-15-2008; $1.05 million)
Nat'l Network: CNN Radio
Arbitron Metro Market: Elkins, WV; *Format:* Adult Contemp; *Hrs. of News Programming:* news progmg 3 hrs wkly; *No. News Employees:* 1; *Target Audience:* Women; 25-54.
Dave Miller, President

Fairmont

WKKW
10-01-1975; 97.9 MHz FM; 29 kw; 640 ft.; N39 25 4 W80 3 44
1251 Earl L. Core Rd, Morgantown, WV 26505 US
(304) 554-3925
www.wkkwfm.com
License: Fairmont, Marion County, WV held by AJG Broadcasting Company
Group Owner: West Virginia Radio Corp.; (acq 9-13-00; $1.5 million)
Nat'l Network: CMLS; WWO; PRMIER
Arbitron Metro Market: Morgantown-Clarksburg-Fairmont, WV; *Format:* Country; *Target Audience:* 25-55.
Dave Miller, President

WMMN
12-22-1928; 920 kHz AM; 5 kw-D, ND1; 0.2 kw-N, ND1; N39 28 3 W80 12 20
P.O. Box 1549, Fairmont, WV 26555 US
(304) 366-3700; *Fax:* (304) 366-3706
License: Fairmont, WV held by Spectrum Radio Fairmont LLC
Group Owner: Spectrum Radio Group LLC
Nat'l Network: Fox Sports *Regional Reps:* Commercial Media Sales.
Arbitron Metro Market: Morgantown, WV; *Format:* Sports; *Target Audience:* 18 plus.
Bill Dunn, Operations Dir

WRLF
08-26-1989; 94.3 MHz FM; *Hrs Open:* 24; 3.6 kw; 249 ft.; N39 28 19 W80 8 26
Mailing Address: P.O. Box 1549, Fairmont, WV 26554 US
Second Address: 450 Leonard Ave., Fairmont, WV 26554
(304) 366-3700; *Fax:* (304) 366-3706
www.wrlf.com
License: Fairmont, Marion County, WV held by Spectrum Radio Fairmont LLC
Group Owner: Spectrum Radio Group LLC
Arbitron Metro Market: Morgantown-Clarksburg-Fairmont, WV; *Format:* Classic Rock; *Target Audience:* 25-55; 60% male, 40% female
Bill Dunn, Operations Dir
Nick Fantasia, General Manager

WTCS
01-01-1948; 1490 kHz AM; *Hrs Open:* 24; 1 kw-U, ND1; N39 28 19 W80 8 26
Mailing Address: P. O. Box 1549, Fairmont, WV 26555 US
Second Address: 450 Leonard Ave., Fairmont, WV 26554
(304) 366-3700; *Fax:* (304) 366-3706
www.1490wtcs.com
License: Fairmont, WV held by Spectrum Radio Fairmont LLC
Group Owner: Spectrum Radio Group LLC; (acq 5-1-56)
Nat'l Network: CNN Radio; *Regional Network:* W. Va. MetroNews Network *Regional Reps:* Commercial Media Sales.
Arbitron Metro Market: Morgantown, WV; *Format:* News, News/Talk, 86 *Special Programming:* It 3 hrs wkly; *Target Audience:* 35 plus.
Nick Fantasia, General Manager
Bill Dunn, General Sales Mgr
Bob Ice, Chief Engineer

Fayetteville

WVBD
100.7 MHz FM; 0.48 kw; 1125 ft.; N37 55 40.4 W80 58 11.5
US
(304) 765-7373; *Fax:* (304)765-7836
www.wvbigdaddy.com
License: Fayetteville, Fayette County, WV held by Daniel W. Finch Jr.
Arbitron Metro Market: Fayetteville, WV; *Format:* Country
Daniel Finch Jr., General Manager

Fisher

WELD
08-01-1956; 690 kHz AM; *Hrs Open:* 24
126 Kessel Road, Fisher, WV 26818 US
(304) 538-6062; *Fax:* (304) 538-7032
WELD@hardynet.com
License: Fisher, WV held by Thunder Associates LLC
Nat'l Network: ABC; *Regional Network:* W. Va. MetroNews Network; *Nat'l Reps:* Dome
Arbitron Metro Market: Fisher, WV; *Format:* Contemporary Hits/Top 40, Adult Contemp; *Hrs. of News Programming:* News progmg 3 hrs wkly; *No. News Employees:* 1; *Target Audience:* 25+; 25+; *Adv. Rates:* 14; 14;14; 14
Curtis Durst, President
Alan Yokum, General Manager
Sandra Durst, Executive Vice President

WQWV
07-01-1998; 103.7 MHz FM; *Hrs Open:* 24; 0.31 kw; 1385 ft.; N39 2 16 W79 5 23
Mailing Address: US
Second Address: 2 Alt Ave., Petersburg, WV 26847
(304) 257-4432; *Fax:* (304) 257-9733
License: Fisher, Hardy County, WV held by McGuire Broadcasting L.L.C.
Nat'l Network: CNN Radio
Format: Contemporary Hits/Top 40, Variety/Diverse
Kevin Spencer, Operations Dir
Eric McGuire, General Manager
Angel Blizzard, General Sales Mgr

Fort Gay

*WFGH
06-04-1973; 90.7 MHz FM; *Hrs Open:* 24; 7.8 kw; 203 ft.; N38 7 58 W82 35 37
P.O. Box 410, Fort Gay, WV 25514 US
(304) 648-5752; *Fax:* (304) 648-5447
www.wfghfm.com
License: Fort Gay, Wayne County, WV held by Wayne County Board of Education.
Wire Services: AP
Arbitron Metro Market: Fort Gay, WV; *Format:* Country, Gospel, 64 *Special Programming:* Oldies; *Hrs. of News Programming:* news progmg 15 hrs wkly; *No. News Employees:* 2; *Target Audience:* General.
Vernon Stanfill, General Manager
Hazel Damron, Programming Director

Franklin

*WVPC
91.1 MHz FM; kw
US
(304) 799-6004; *Fax:* (304) 799-7444
www.alleghenymountainradio.org
License: Franklin, Pendleton County, WV held by Pocahontas Communications Cooperative Corp.
Arbitron Metro Market: Franklin, WV
Cheryl Kinderman, General Manager

Frost

*WVMR
08-17-1981; 1370 kHz AM; 5 kw-D, NDD; N38 17 25 W79 55 52
9836 Browns Creek Road, Dunmore, WV 24934 US
(304) 799-6004; *Fax:* (304) 799-7444
www.alleghenymountainradio.org
amrinet@starband.net
License: Frost, WV held by Pocahontas Communications Cooperative Corp.
Arbitron Metro Market: Dunmore, WV; *Format:* Country *Special Programming:* Farm 5 hrs, relg 10 hrs, big band 3 hrs, bluegrass; *Target Audience:* General.
Richard Hise, Managing Director
Sue Fertig, Resource Director

Gary

WHQX
01-01-1989; 107.7 MHz FM; *Hrs Open:* 24; 8.6 kw; 564 ft.; N37 8 1 W81 35 42
900 Bluefield Ave., Bluefield, WV 24701 US
(304) 327-7114; *Fax:* (304) 325-7850
www.kickscountry.com
License: Gary, McDowell County, WV held by Alpha Media Licensee LLC
Group Owner: Alpha Media LLC; (acq 12-3-2012).
Arbitron Metro Market: Bluefield, WV; *Format:* Country; *No. News Employees:* 1
Danny Clemons, Vice President
Lee Rappolt, Continuity Director

Glenville

WVRW
01-01-2008; 107.7 MHz FM; 1.7 kw; Ant 623 ft; N38 54 29 W80 49 48
303 Harrison Ave., Weston, WV 26452
(304) 462-7771; *Fax:* (304) 269-4800
www.wvrwfm.com
info@wvrwfm.com
License: Glenville, Gilmer County, WV held by Della Jane Woofter.
Nat'l Network: Cumlus
Arbitron Metro Market: Metro Clarksbur; *Hrs. of News Programming:* 11:55am 4:50pm; *Target Audience:* 35+; *Adv. Rates:* 8.25; 30; 10.25; 60
Della Jane Woofter, General Manager

Grafton

WVUS
01-01-1948; 1190 kHz AM; *Hrs Open:* 24 hrs
P.O. Box 2, Grafton, WV 26354 US
(304) 598-0026; *Fax:* (304) 265-0972
www.wvlol.org
License: Grafton, WV held by Appalachian Radio LLC
Arbitron Metro Market: Grafton, WV; *Format:* Adult Contemp; *Hrs. of News Programming:* News progmg 15 hrs wkly; *Target Audience:* 18-65.
Melanie Tocco, General Manager

*WDKL
09-10-1979; 95.9 MHz FM; *Hrs Open:* 24; 6 kw; 299 ft.; N39 21 16 W80 1 27
P.O. Box 2, Grafton, WV 26354 US
(916) 251-1600; *Fax:* (916) 251-1650
www.klove.com
klove@klove.com
License: Grafton, Taylor County, WV held by Educational Media Foundation
Group Owner: EMF Broadcasting; (acq 5-28-02).
Nat'l Network: K-Love
Arbitron Metro Market: Grafton, WV; *Format:* Christian; *No. News Employees:* 3; *Target Audience:* 25-44; female-Judeo Christian
Darrell Chambliss, Chairman
Mike Novak, CEO
Mike Novak, President
Pam Patrick-Thompson, Operations Dir
David Pierce, Programming Director
Ed Lenane, News Director
Sam Wallington, Engineering Dir
Marya Morgan, News Reporter
Richard Hunt, News Reporter
Mitch Barnhart, Director
Larry Moody, Director
Dr.David.R.Ferry, Director

Green Valley

WAMN
01-01-1987; 1050 kHz AM; *Hrs Open:* 24; 1.43 kw-D, ND1; 0.2 kw-N, ND1; N37 18 20 W81 7 30
4415 Blue Prince Rd., Bluefield, WV 24701 US
(304) 327-9266; *Fax:* (304) 325-8058
www.mywillie.com
License: Green Valley, Mercer County, WV held by West Virginia-Virginia Media LLC
Group Owner: West Virginia-Virginia Holding Co. LLC
Arbitron Metro Market: Bluefield, WV; *Format:* Country
Bob Spencer, Manager

Hillsboro

*WVMR-FM
91.9 MHz FM; 0.55 kw; -35 ft.; N38 11 30 W80 11 44
9836 Browns Creek Road, Dunmore, WV 24934 US
(304) 799-6004; *Fax:* (304) 799-7444
www.alleghenymountainradio.org
dsamr@frontier.com
License: Hillsboro, Pocahontas County, WV held by Pocahontas Communications Cooperative Corp.
Arbitron Metro Market: Hillsboro, WV; *Format:* Country; *No. News Employees:* 1
Cheryl Kinderman, General Manager
Bonnie Ralston, Station Manager
Heather Niday, Programming Director
Geoff Hamill, News Director
Chuck Niday, Chief Engineer
Gibbs Kinderman, Director of Special Projects

Hinton

WMTD
01-11-1963; 1380 kHz AM; *Hrs Open:* 24 *Rebroadcasts:* Rebroadcasts WAXS(FM) Oak Hill 75%
PO Box 100, Hinton, WV 25951 US
(304) 466-1380; *Fax:* (304) 466-8082
www.radioam1380.com
License: Hinton, WV held by Southern Communications Corp.
Group Owner: Southern Communications Corp.; (acq 4-19-2000; $107,000 with co-located FM).
Nat'l Network: CBS
Arbitron Metro Market: Beckley, WV; *Format:* Contemporary Hits/Top 40; *Hrs. of News Programming:* news progmg 9 hrs wkly; *No. News Employees:* 3; *Target Audience:* General.; *Adv. Rates:* 75; 50; 50; 40
R. Shane Southern, President
Jay Quesenberry, General Manager
Rennold Madrazo, General Sales Mgr
Rick Rizer, Programming Director

Rhonda Pritt, News Director
Randy Kerbawy, Engineering Dir
Steve Coleman, Regional Sales Manager

WMTD-FM
10-01-1985; 102.3 MHz FM; *Hrs Open:* 24; 0.37 kw; 1273 ft.; N37 42 53 W80 57 9
415 2nd Avenue, Hinton, WV 25951 US
(304) 253-7000; *Fax:* (304) 255-1044
www.theticket102.com
License: Hinton, Summers County, WV held by Southern Communications Corp.
Group Owner: Southern Communications Corp.
Arbitron Metro Market: Beckley, WV; *Format:* Sports; *Hrs. of News Programming:* news progmg 1 hr wkly; *No. News Employees:* 1; *Target Audience:* Adults 18-49.; *Adv. Rates:* 70; 50; 60; 40
Shane Boone, Operations Manager
Kate Isner, Production

Huntington

WEMM
09-06-1971; 107.9 MHz FM; *Hrs Open:* 24; 190 kW; 1496 ft; N30 44 49 W89 3 30
703 3rd Avenue, Huntington, WV 25701 USA
(304) 525-5141; *Fax:* (304) 525-0748
wemmfm.com
License: Huntington, Cabell County, WV held by Mortenson Broadcasting Co.
Group Owner: Mortenson Broadcasting Co.
Nat'l Network: USA
Arbitron Metro Market: Huntington, WV; *Format:* Gospel; *Hrs. of News Programming:* News progmg 4 hrs wkly; *Target Audience:* Adults 25-64+
Brian Fowler, General Manager

WVHU
07-01-1947; 800 kHz AM; 5 kw-D, ND1; 0.185 kw-N, ND1; N38 23 35 W82 28 24
134 4th Ave., Huntington, WV 25701 US
(304) 525-7788; *Fax:* (304) 525-6281
www.800wvhu.com
License: Huntington, WV held by Capstar TX LLC
Group Owner: iHeartMedia; (acq 8-30-2000; grpsl)
Arbitron Metro Market: Huntington-Ashland, WV-KY; *Format:* News, News/Talk, 86; *Target Audience:* 25-54; older, professional, higher income
Judy Jennings, Market President
Jim Davis, Regional Senior Vice President of Programming
Mark Wood, Programming Director
Cameron Blevins, Digital News Director

WKEE-FM
11-01-1947; 100.5 MHz FM; 53 kw; 561 ft.; N38 23 35 W82 28 24
134 4th Avenue, Huntington, WV 25701 US
(304) 525-7788; *Fax:* (304) 525-6281
www.kee100.com
License: Huntington, Cabell County, WV held by Capstar TX LLC
Group Owner: iHeartMedia; (acq 8-30-2000; grpsl)
Arbitron Metro Market: Huntington-Ashland, WV-KY; *Format:* Contemporary Hits/Top 40; *Target Audience:* 18-42.
Judy Jennings, Market President
Jim Davis, Regional Senior Vice President of Programming

***WMUL**
11-01-1961; 88.1 MHz FM; *Hrs Open:* 6 AM-3 AM; 1.15 kw; -56 ft.; N38 25 26 W82 25 39
1 John Marshall Drive, Huntington, WV 25755 US
(304) 696-6640; *Fax:* (304) 696-3232
www.marshall.edu/wmul
wmul@marshall.edu
License: Huntington, Cabell County, WV held by Marshall University Board of Governors
Wire Services: AP
Arbitron Metro Market: Huntington, WV; *Format:* Variety/Diverse; *Hrs. of News Programming:* News progmg 7 hrs wkly; *Target Audience:* General.
Dr. Stephen Kopp, President
Michael Stanley, Operations Dir
Dr. Chuck G. Bailey, General Manager
Adam Cavalier, Station Manager
Jessie Kirk, Programming Director
Jason van Meter, Promotions Manager
Leannda Carey, NewsDirector
Chuck Cook, Chief Engineer
Delaney McLemore, Production Director
Ryan Epling, Sports Commentator

WRVC
10-23-1923; 930 kHz AM; *Hrs Open:* 24
555 5th Avenue, Huntington, WV 25701 US
(304) 523-8401; *Fax:* (304) 523-4848
www.supertalk941.com
studio@huntingtonsupertalk.com
License: Huntington, WV held by Fifth Avenue Broadcasting Co. Inc.
Group Owner: Kindred Communications Inc.; (acq 6-1-70)
Nat'l Network: ESPN Radio; ABC; CBS Radio; Motor Racing Net; Westwood One; *Regional Network:* W. Va. MetroNews Network;
Nat'l Reps: McGavren Guild; *Wire Services:* AP; Accu-Weather; ESPN/SportsTicker
Arbitron Metro Market: Huntington-Ashl; *Format:* Sports *Special Programming:* Relg 3 hrs wkly; *Hrs. of News Programming:* news progmg 40 hrs wkly; *No. News Employees:* 1
Tom Wolf, CEO
Mike Kirtner, President
Rae Ann Parsons, General Sales Mgr
Cameron Smith, Engineering Dir
Rich Myhrwold, Regional Sales Manager

WTCR-FM
05-01-1966; 103.3 MHz FM; 50 kw; 492 ft.; N38 25 11 W82 24 6
134 4th Avenue, Huntington, WV 25701 US
(304) 525-7788; *Fax:* (304) 525-6281
www.tcrcountry.com
License: Huntington, Cabell County, WV held by Capstar TX LLC
Group Owner: iHeartMedia; (acq 8-30-00; grpsl)
Nat'l Network: ABC; *Nat'l Reps:* Rgnl Reps; Katz Radio
Arbitron Metro Market: Huntington, WV; *Format:* Country
Judy Jennings, Market President
Jim Davis, Regional Senior Vice President of Programming

***WVWV**
11-28-1977; 89.9 MHz FM; *Hrs Open:* 24; 8.1 kw; 1165 ft.; N38 29 41 W82 12 3
600 Capitol Street, Charleston, WV 25301 US
(304) 556-4900; *Fax:* (304) 556-4981
www.wvpubcast.org
License: Huntington, Cabell County, WV held by West Virginia Educational Broadcasting Authority.
Nat'l Network: NPR; PRI
Arbitron Metro Market: Huntington, WV; *Format:* Jazz, News
Rita Ray, General Manager
Marilyn DiVita, General Sales Mgr
Craig Lanham, Programming Director
Beth Vorhees, Director of News and Public Affairs
Dennis Adkins, Executive Director
Bill Acker, Director of Broadcasting &Technology
Marilyn DiVita, Director of Development
Michael L. Meador, Director of Finance
Shawn Patterson, Director of Marketing

Hurricane

WMUX
07-02-1971; 1110 kHz AM; *Hrs Open:* 10; 1 kw-D; N38 26 41 W82 00 54
Mailing Address: P.O. Box 3744, Charleston, WV 25337
Second Address: 1114 Virginia St. E., Charleston, WV 25301
(304) 342-8131
License: Hurricane, Putnam County, WV held by St. Paul Radio Co.
Group Owner: St. Paul Radio Co.; (acq 1996; $20,000)
Population Served: 800,000; *Arbitron Metro Market:* Hurricane, WV; *Format:* Religious
Mark Sadd, President
Jim Blankenship, Director
Joe Deegan, Director
Paul Howard, Director
Mike Kawash, Director
Tony Marks, Director

***WPJW**
01-01-2009; 91.5 MHz FM; 3 kw; 302 ft.; N38 26 41 W82 0 54
Post Office Box 889, Blacksburg, VA 24063 US
(540) 552-4252
www.walkfm.org
License: Hurricane, Putnam County, WV held by Positive Alternative Radio Inc.
Group Owner: Positive Alternative Radio Inc.
Arbitron Metro Market: Hurricane, WV
Vernon Baker, President
Adam McDowell, Operations Dir
Jeremy Wolfe, Operations Manager
Elisha Dorsey, Production Assistant
Mike Nelson, Underwriting Representative/Sales Dept
Mel Mendoza, Marketing & Creative Manager

Kenova

WTCR
08-01-1954; 1420 kHz AM; 5 kw-D, DAN; 0.5 kw-N, DAN; N38 24 42 W82 36 13
134 4th Avenue, Huntington, WV 25701 US
(304) 525-7788; *Fax:* (304) 525-6281
www.foxsports1420.com
License: Kenova, WV held by Capstar TX LLC
Group Owner: iHeartMedia; (acq 8-30-00; grpsl)
Nat'l Reps: Rgnl Reps; Katz Radio
Arbitron Metro Market: Huntington, WV; *Format:* Sports; *Target Audience:* 35 plus.
Judy Jennings, Market President
Jim Davis, Regional Senior Vice President of Programming
Clint McElroy, Programming Director

WMGA
01-01-2006; 97.9 MHz FM; 3.5 kw; 436 ft.; N38 25 26 W82 32 8
Mailing Address: US
Second Address: 919 Fifth Ave., Suite 210, Huntington, WV 25701
(304) 399-9603; *Fax:* (304) 399-9608
www.magic979.com
License: Kenova, Wayne County, WV held by Fifth Avenue Broadcasting Co. Inc.
Group Owner: Kindred Communications Inc.
Arbitron Metro Market: Oakland, CA; *Format:* Adult Contemp
Newman Adkins, General Manager

Keyser

WCBC-FM
01-01-1990; 107.1 MHz FM; 0.48 kw; 830 ft.; N39 31 30 W78 51 43
P.O. Box 1290, Cumberland, MD 21501 US
(301) 724-5000; (301) 722-8225; *Fax:* (301) 722-8336
www.wcbcradio.com
info@wcbcradio.com
License: Keyser, Mineral County, WV held by Cumberland Broadcasting Company
Arbitron Metro Market: Cumberland, MD; *Format:* Oldies
Mary Clites, General Manager
Andee Thompson, Sales
Roxanne Christiansen, Sales
Becki Mittenberg, Sales
Martin White, Chief Engineer

WKLP
08-31-1965; 1390 kHz AM; *Hrs Open:* 24; 1 kw-D, ND1; 0.074 kw-N, ND1; N39 26 12 W78 57 21
15 E. Industrial Blvd, Cumberland, MD 21502 US
(301) 759-1005
www.1390espn.com
License: Keyser, Mineral County, WV held by Starcast Systems, Inc.
Group Owner: West Virginia Radio Corp.; (acq 12-29-2006; with co-located FM)
Nat'l Network: ESPN; *Regional Network:* -
Arbitron Metro Market: Keyser, WV; *Format:* Sports; *Target Audience:* Men 25+
Pat Sullivan, Programming Director

WQZK-FM
09-15-1973; 94.1 MHz FM; *Hrs Open:* 24; 13 kw; 928 ft.; N39 25 7 W78 57 15
15 E. Industrial Blvd, Cumberland, MD 21502 US
(301) 759-1005
www.941qzk.com
License: Keyser, Mineral County, WV held by Starcast Systems, Inc.
Group Owner: West Virginia Radio Corp.
Nat'l Network: CMLS; WWO; PRMIER
Format: Contemporary Hits/Top 40; *Target Audience:* Teens & Adults 18+
Pat Sullivan, Programming Director

Kingwood

WFSP
08-25-1967; 1560 kHz AM; 0.25 kw-C, NDD; 1 kw-D, NDD; N39 28 50 W79 43 11
P. O. Box 567, Kingwood, WV 26537 US
(304) 329-1780; *Fax:* (304) 329-1781
www.prestoncounty.com/wfsp
wfsp@wvdsl.net
License: Kingwood, WV held by WFSP Inc.
Nat'l Network: CBS; *Nat'l Reps:* Dome
Format: News, Talk; *No. News Employees:* 1; *Target Audience:* 20 plus.; *Adv. Rates:* 12; 12; 12; 12
David Willis, Owner
David Price, Sales

Kathy Casseday, News Director
Donna Nestor, Offie Manager
Chuck Clemence, Chief Engineer
Kathy Casseday, Public Affairs Director
Art George, Radio Announcer
Dave Price, Sales
DonnaNestor, Office Manager

WFSP-FM
06-10-1991; 107.7 MHz FM; *Hrs Open:* 24; 1.6 kw; 449 ft.; N39 28 50 W79 43 11
Post Office Box 567, Kingwood, WV 26537 US
(304) 329-1780; *Fax:* (304) 329-1781
wfsp@wvdsl.net
License: Kingwood, Preston County, WV held by WFSP Radio, LLC
Nat'l Network: Westwood One; *Nat'l Reps:* Dome
Format: Oldies, Religious; *Hrs. of News Programming:* news progmg 25 hrs wkly; *No. News Employees:* 1; *Target Audience:* 18-45.; *Adv. Rates:* 12; 12; 12; 12
David Willis, Owner
Sales, General Sales Mgr
Kathy Cassedy, News Director
Donna Nestor, Office Manager

WKMM
12-01-1986; 96.7 MHz FM; *Hrs Open:* 24; 0.3 kw; 797 ft.; N39 27 29 W79 35 18
106 E Main Street, Kingwood, WV 26537 US
(304) 329-0967; *Fax:* (304) 329-2131
www.wkmmfm.com
wkmmfm@yahoo.com
License: Kingwood, Preston County, WV held by MarPat Corp.
Nat'l Network: Westwood One; CNN Radio
Format: Country; *Target Audience:* 25-55.

Lewisburg

WRON-FM
10-01-1981; 103.1 MHz FM; *Hrs Open:* 24; 3.3 kw; 896 ft.; N37 47 54 W80 30 56
Mailing Address: P.O. Box 610, White Sulphur Spring, WV 24986 US
Second Address: 276 Seneca Trail, Ronceverte, WV 24970
(304) 536-1310; *Fax:* (304) 536-1311
www.wron.com
radio@wron.com
License: Lewisburg, Greenbrier County, WV held by Radio Greenbrier LLC
Group Owner: Radio Greenbrier LLC; (acq 1-7-2008; exchange for WKCJ(FM) Ronceverte)
Nat'l Network: ABC; *Nat'l Reps:* Rgnl Reps
Format: Country *Special Programming:* Gospel 6 hrs, relg 4 hrs, farm 3 hrs wkly; *Hrs. of News Programming:* News progmg 12 hrs wkly; *Target Audience:* 25-55.; *Adv. Rates:* 7.25; 7.25; 7.25; 7.25
Joyce Tucker, General Manager
Marcia Smith, General Sales Mgr
Chuck Harper, Programming Director

Lindside

***WHFI**
09-01-1990; 106.7 MHz FM; *Hrs Open:* 24; 6 kw; 121 ft.; N37 28 56 W80 39 40
P. O. Box 330, Union, WV 24983 US
(304) 753-9971; *Fax:* (304) 753-9792
License: Lindside, Monroe County, WV held by Monroe County Board of Education
Format: Adult Contemp
James Higginbotham, General Manager

Logan

WVOW
05-01-1954; 1290 kHz AM; *Hrs Open:* 24
204 Main Street, Suite 201, Logan, WV 25601 US
(304) 752-5080; (304) 752-5081; *Fax:* (304) 752-5711
www.wvowradio.com
advertise@wvowradio.com
License: Logan, WV held by Logan Broadcasting Corp.
Arbitron Metro Market: Logan, WV; *Format:* Adult Contemp; *No. News Employees:* 2; *Target Audience:* General.
John Pennington, Executive Producer
Larry Bevins, Station Manager
Howard Jemerison, Programming Director

WVOW-FM
08-01-1969; 101.9 MHz FM; *Hrs Open:* 24; 15 kw horiz, 13.5 kw vert; 830 ft.; N37 51 24 W81 58 18
204 Main Street, Suite 201, Logan, WV 25601 US
(304) 752-5080; (304) 752-5081; *Fax:* (304) 752-5711
www.wvowradio.com
advertise@wvowradio.com
License: Logan, Logan County, WV
Arbitron Metro Market: Logan, WV; *Format:* Adult Contemp
John Pennington, Executive Producer
Larry Bevins, Station Manager
Howard Jemerison, Programming Director
Rhonda Bryant, Traffic Manager

Lost Creek

WHAW
02-14-1948; 980 kHz AM; *Hrs Open:* 24; 1 kw-D, 50 w-N; N39 02 25 W80 27 16
300 Harrison Ave., Weston, WV 26452
(304) 269-5555; *Fax:* (304) 269-4800
www.whawradio.com
info@whawradio.com
License: Lost Creek, Lewis County, WV held by Della Jane Woofter
Nat'l Network: CUMULUS
Special Programming: Bluegrass 8 hrs, folk 4 hrs, gospel 18 hrs wkly; *Hrs. of News Programming:* news progmg 2 hrs wkly; *No. News Employees:* 1; *Target Audience:* General.; *Adv. Rates:* 10; 10; 10; 10
Della Jane Woofter, General Manager

WOTR(FM)
12-09-1991; 96.3 MHz FM; *Hrs Open:* 8 AM-10 PM; 6 kw horiz; 302 ft; N39 04 15 w80 31 14
303 Harrison Avenue, Weston, WV 26452
(304) 269-5555; *Fax:* (304) 269-4800
www.wotrfm.com
info@wotrfm.com
License: Lost Creek, Harrison County, WV held by Della Jane Woofter
Population Served: 50,000 *Format:* Gospel, Religious; *Target Audience:* 25-99.
Della Jane Woofter, General Manager

Mannington

WGYE
12-01-1992; 102.7 MHz FM; *Hrs Open:* 24; 3.2 kw; 453 ft.; N39 28 3 W80 12 20
1489 Locust Ave., Suite C, Fairmont, WV 26554 US
(304) 363-8888; *Fax:* (304) 367-1885
www.froggycountry.net
froggycountry@resultsradiowv.com
License: Mannington, Marion County, WV held by Burbach of DE LLC
Group Owner: Burbach Broadcasting Group; (acq 6-20-2000; grpsl).
Arbitron Metro Market: Morgantown, WV; *Format:* Country; *Hrs. of News Programming:* news progmg 4 hrs wkly; *No. News Employees:* 1; *Target Audience:* 25-54.; *Adv. Rates:* 17; 13; 15; 10
Michael Pasqua, Director of Sales
Stacy Schulman, Account Manager

Marlinton

***WVMR**
88.5 MHz FM; 1 kw; -216 ft.; N38 13 40 W80 4 40
9836 Browns Creek Road, Dunmore, WV 24934 US
(304) 799-6004; *Fax:* (304) 799-7444
www.alleghenymountainradio.org
dsamr@frontier.com
License: Marlinton, Pocahontas County, WV held by Pocahontas Communications Cooperative Corp.
Arbitron Metro Market: Marlinton, WV; *No. News Employees:* 1
Richard Hise, Managing Director
Sue Fertig, Resource Director
Erin R. Will, Station Coordinator
James Clay, Operations Manager
Melodie Wilson, Underwriting Manager

Marmet

***WKVW**
06-30-1995; 93.3 MHz FM; *Hrs Open:* 24; 1.7 kw; 620 ft.; N38 16 25 W81 31 27
PO Box 2098, Omaha, NE 68103-2098 US
(800) 525-5683; *Fax:* (916) 251-1650
www.klove.com
License: Marmet, Kanawha County, WV held by Educational Media Foundation
Group Owner: EMF Broadcasting; (acq 7-1-2002; $500,000)
Nat'l Network: K-Love
Arbitron Metro Market: Marmet, WV; *Format:* Christian; *No. News Employees:* 13; *Target Audience:* 25-44; Judeo Christian, female
Darrell Chambliss, Chairman
Mike Novak, President & CEO
David Pierce, Chief Creative Officer
Alan Mason, Chief Operating Officer
Eric Moser, Chief Financial Officer
D. Kevin Blair, Secretary/General Counsel

Martinsburg

WEPM
10-13-1946; 1340 kHz AM; 1 kw-U, ND1; N39 27 48 W77 59 11
1606 W. King St., Martinsburg, WV 25401 US
(304) 263-8868
www.wepm.com
License: Martinsburg, Berkeley County, WV held by West Virginia Radio Corporation of the Alleghenies
Group Owner: West Virginia Radio Corp.; (acq 1-1-87; $2 million)
Nat'l Network: WWO; ESPN; FOXNEW; *Nat'l Reps:* Katz Radio
Arbitron Metro Market: Martinsburg, WV; *Format:* News/Talk, Sports *Special Programming:* Relg 6 hrs wkly; *Target Audience:* 35+
Mike McGough, General Manager

WLTF
01-01-1949; 97.5 MHz FM; *Hrs Open:* 24; 11.4 kw; 1037 ft.; N39 27 33 W78 3 48
1606 W. King St, Martinsburg, WV 25401 US
(304) 263-8868
www.todays975.com
License: Martinsburg, Berkeley County, WV held by West Virginia Radio Corporation of the Alleghenies
Group Owner: West Virginia Radio Corp.
Nat'l Network: WWO; PRMIER
Arbitron Metro Market: Hagerstown-Chambersburg-Waynesboro, MD-PA; *Format:* Adult Contemp; *Target Audience:* 25-55.
Mike McGough, General Manager

WRNR
04-16-1976; 740 kHz AM; *Hrs Open:* 24; 0.5 kw-D, DA2; 0.021 kw-N, DA2; N39 28 25 W77 55 57
P.O. Box 709, Martinsburg, VA 25401 US
(304) 263-6586; *Fax:* (304) 263-3082
License: Martinsburg, WV held by Shenandoah Communications Inc.
Nat'l Network: Westwood One; CBS; CNN Radio; *Nat'l Reps:* Rgnl Reps
Format: News, News/Talk, 84, Talk; *Hrs. of News Programming:* news progmg 28 hrs wkly; *No. News Employees:* 3; *Target Audience:* 35 plus; middle to upper age & income; *Adv. Rates:* 26.05; 25.05; 26.05; 25.05
Richard Wachtel, President
Matt Miller, Operations Dir
Tom Tucker, Promotions Manager
Fran Little, Chief Engineer
Gregg Wachtel, Executive Vice President

***WVEP**
02-11-1987; 88.9 MHz FM; *Hrs Open:* 24; 3.6 kw horiz; 1624 ft.; N39 8 38 W78 26 9
600 Capitol Street, Charleston, WV 25301 US
(304) 556-4900; (888) 596-9729; *Fax:* (304) 556-4981
www.wvpubcast.org
feedback@wvpubcast.org
License: Martinsburg, Berkeley County, WV held by West Virginia Educational Broadcasting Authority.
Nat'l Network: NPR; PRI
Arbitron Metro Market: Charleston, WV; *Format:* Jazz, News
Scott Finn, CEO/Executive Director
Adam Harris, Executive Producer
Suzanne Higgins, Senior Producer
Beth Vorhees, Director of News and Public Affairs
Glynis Board, Reporter/Producer
Clark Davis, Reporter/Producer

Matewan

WHJC
12-02-1951; 1360 kHz AM; 1 kw-D, NDD; N37 37 2 W82 10 4
Mailing Address: 156 Radio Hill, McCarr, KY 41544 US
Second Address: 156 Radio Hill, McCarr, KY 41544
(606) 427-7261; *Fax:* (606) 427-7260
License: Matewan, WV held by Three States Broadcasting Co. Inc.
Format: Gospel
George Warren, President
Evelyn Warren, General Manager
Melissa White, Programming Director
Russell Laferty, Chief Engineer

WVKM
08-30-1989; 106.7 MHz FM; *Hrs Open:* 24; 4.3 kw; 751 ft.; N37 36 49 W82 11 22
Mailing Address: P.O. Box 68, Matewan, WV 25678 US
Second Address: 156 Radio Hill, McCarr, KY 41544
kixx1067@yahoo.com
License: Matewan, Mingo County, WV held by Three States Broadcasting Co. Inc.
Arbitron Metro Market: Matewan, WV; *Format:* Classic Rock; *Adv. Rates:* 25; 12; 12; 12
Melissa White, News Director

Miami

WKAZ-FM
06-06-1983; 107.3 MHz FM; *Hrs Open:* 24; 23.5 kw; 676 ft.; N38 16 25 W81 31 27
1111 Virginia St. E., Charleston, WV 25301 US
(304) 342-8131
www.tailgate1073.com
License: Miami, Kanawha County, WV held by West Virginia Radio Corporation of Charleston
Group Owner: West Virginia Radio Corp.; (acq 6-5-97; $2.15 million with WCZR(AM) Charleston)
Nat'l Network: WWO; CMLS; *Nat'l Reps:* D & R Radio
Arbitron Metro Market: Charleston, WV; *Format:* Adult Contemp; *Target Audience:* 25-55
Dave Miller, President

Middlebourne

***WRSG**
01-01-2001; 91.5 MHz FM; *Hrs Open:* 24; 0.9 kw; 157 ft.; N39 30 59 W80 54 0
P. O. Box 25, Middlebourne, WV 26149 US
(304) 758-9007; *Fax:* (304) 758-9006
wrsgfm@yahoo.com
License: Middlebourne, Tyler County, WV held by Tyler County Board of Education.
Arbitron Metro Market: Sistersville, WV; *Format:* Variety/Diverse
Tom Charity, Operations Dir
John Maloney, General Sales Mgr
Ray Hall, Programming Director
Jerry Barco, News Director

Milton

WAMX
10-01-1980; 106.3 MHz FM; *Hrs Open:* 24; 1.65 kw; 1109 ft.; N38 30 21 W82 12 33
134 4th Avenue, Huntington, WV 25701 US
(304) 525-7788; *Fax:* (304) 525-6281
www.1063thebrew.com
License: Milton, Cabell County, WV held by Capstar TX LLC
Group Owner: iHeartMedia; (acq 8-30-00; grpsl)
Arbitron Metro Market: Milton, WV; *Format:* Rock/AOR; *Hrs. of News Programming:* news progmg 4 hrs wkly; *No. News Employees:* 1; *Target Audience:* 25-49; males in their late teens to late '40s
Jim Davis, Regional Senior Vice President of Programming
Judy Jennings, Market President
Nick Kuhn, Programming Director

WZZW
06-26-1973; 1600 kHz AM; 5 kw-D, ND1; 0.026 kw-N, ND1; N38 25 46 W82 6 21
134 4th Avenue, Huntington, WV 25701 US
(304) 525-7788; *Fax:* (304) 525-6281
www.800wvhu.com
judyjennings@clearchannel.com
License: Milton, WV held by Aloha Station Trust LLC
Arbitron Metro Market: Huntington, WV; *Format:* Christian; *Target Audience:* 25-44; adult, upscale baby boomers
Judy Jennings, General Market Manager
Jim Davis, Operations Manager/Program Director

Montgomery

WMON
07-14-1946; 1340 kHz AM; 1 kw-U, ND1; N38 10 38 W81 18 51
100 Kanawha Terrace, St. Albans, WV 25177 US
(304) 722-3308; *Fax:* (304) 727-1300
www.wklc.com
105spots@wklc.com
License: Montgomery, WV held by L.M. Communications of Kentucky LLC.
Group Owner: L M Communications Inc.; (acq 4-1-03; grpsl).
Nat'l Network: Salem Radio Network
Arbitron Metro Market: Montgomery, WV; *Format:* Rock/AOR; *Target Audience:* 25 plus.
Dotsy Klei, Market Manager
Jill Wheeler, Sales Manager
Chili Walker, Programming Director
Dave Miller, News Director
Anna Graley, Traffic Director
Matt James, Production Director

Moorefield

WELD-FM
02-06-1987; 101.7 MHz FM; *Hrs Open:* 24; 0.285 kw; 1493 ft.; N38 58 58 W78 54 30
126 Kessel Road, Fisher, WV 26818 US
(304) 538-6062; *Fax:* (304) 538-7032
www.weldamfmradio.com
License: Moorefield, Hardy County, WV held by Fisher
Nat'l Network: ABC; *Nat'l Reps:* Dome; Keystone (unwired net)
Arbitron Metro Market: Fisher, WV; *Format:* Country, Religious
Special Programming: Gospel 3 hrs wkly/contemporary christian/talk 6hrs wkly; *Hrs. of News Programming:* news progmg 10 hrs wkly *No. News Employees:* 1; *Target Audience:* 25 plus.; *Adv. Rates:* 14; 14; 14; 12
Curtis Durst, President
Alan Yokum, General Manager
Sandra Durst, Executive Vice President

Morgantown

WAJR
12-07-1940; 1440 kHz AM; *Hrs Open:* 24; 5 kw-D, DA2; 0.5 kw-N, DA2; N39 40 34 W80 0 12
1251 Earl L. Core Rd., Morgantown, WV 26505 US
(304) 296-0029
www.wajr.com
License: Morgantown, WV held by West Virginia Radio Corp.
Group Owner: West Virginia Radio Corp.
Nat'l Network: ABC
Arbitron Metro Market: Morgantown, WV; *Format:* News, Talk, 84; *Hrs. of News Programming:* news progmg 15 hrs wkly; *No. News Employees:* 7; *Target Audience:* 25+.
Dale Miller, President

WCLG
12-01-1954; 1300 kHz AM; 2.5 kw-D, ND1; 0.044 kw-N, ND1; N39 37 40 W79 58 11
Mailing Address: 343 High Street, Morgantown, WV 26505 US
Second Address: 343 High St., Morgantown, WV 26505
(304) 292-2222; *Fax:* (304) 292-2224
www.wclg.com
License: Morgantown, WV held by Bowers Broadcasting Corp.
Nat'l Reps: Dome
Arbitron Metro Market: Morgantown, WV; *Format:* Oldies
Garry Bowers, President
Debbie Lofstead, Sales Manager
Jeffrey Miller, Programming Director
Lucinda Funk, News Director
Ken Tennant, Chief Engineer

WCLG-FM
09-28-1974; 100.1 MHz FM; 6 kw; 299 ft.; N39 37 40 W79 58 11
Po.Box 885, Morgantown, WV 26507 US
(304) 292-2222
www.wclg.com
jmurphy@ajgradio.com
License: Morgantown, Monongalia County, WV held by Bowers Broadcasting Corp.
Arbitron Metro Market: Morgantown, WV; *Format:* Classic Rock
Jack Murphy, Sales Manager

WVAQ
01-01-1948; 101.9 MHz FM; *Hrs Open:* 24; 50 kw; 499 ft.; N39 36 30 W79 59 7
Mailing Address: Rt 7 Greer Building, Morgantown, WV 26505 US
Second Address: 1251 Earl L. Core Rd, Morgantown, WV 26505
(304) 296-0029; *Fax:* (304) 296-3876
www.wvaq.com
License: Morgantown, Monongalia County, WV held by West Virginia Radio Corp.
Group Owner: West Virginia Radio Corp.
Nat'l Network: IND
Arbitron Metro Market: Morgantown, WV; *Format:* Contemporary Hits/Top 40; *Hrs. of News Programming:* news progmg one hr wkly; *No. News Employees:* 2; *Target Audience:* Teens & Adults, 18+
Dave Miller, President

***WVPM**
05-27-1981; 90.9 MHz FM; *Hrs Open:* 24; 5 kw; 1440 ft.; N39 41 45 W79 45 45
600 Capitol Street, Charleston, WV 25301 US
(304) 556-4900; *Fax:* (304) 556-4960
www.wvpubcast.org
feedback@wvpubcast.org
License: Morgantown, Monongalia County, WV held by West Virginia Educational Broadcasting Authority.
Nat'l Network: NPR; PRI
Arbitron Metro Market: Morgantown, WV; *Format:* Jazz, News
Marilyn DiVita, General Manager
Marilyn DiVita, General Sales Mgr
Craig Lanham, Programming Director
Beth Vorhees, Director of News and Public Affairs
Dennis Adkins, Executive Director
Bill Acker, Director of Broadcasting &Technology
Marilyn DiVita, Director of Development
Michael L. Meador, Director of Finance
Shawn Patterson, Director of Marketing

***WWVU-FM**
08-20-1982; 91.7 MHz FM; *Hrs Open:* 24; 2.6 kw; 180 ft.; N39 38 9 W79 56 38
Mountainlair, West Virginia University, PO Box 6446, Morgantown, WV 26506 US
(304) 293-3329; *Fax:* (304) 293-7363
u92.wvu.edu
u92@mail.wvu.edu
License: Morgantown, Monongalia County, WV held by West Virginia University Board of Governors
Arbitron Metro Market: Morgantown, WV; *Format:* Variety/Diverse *Special Programming:* New age 6 hrs, reggae 4 hrs, metal 6 hrs, bluegras; *Hrs. of News Programming:* News progmg 2 hrs wkly; *Target Audience:* 18-35;mostly college & high school students
Jackson Montgomery, Production Director
Sara Cottle, Programming Director
Zach Oser, Sports Director
James Guiliano, Program Director
Jared Peterson, Music Director
Clariss Cottrill, News Director

Moundsville

WVLY
10-01-1950; 1370 kHz AM; *Hrs Open:* 24; 5 kw-D, ND1; 0.02 kw-N, ND1; N39 54 20 W80 46 42
1143 Main Street, Suite 200, Wheeling, WV 26003 US
(304) 233-9859; *Fax:* (304) 214-9859
www.talkradio1370.com
wvlyradio@aol.com
License: Moundsville, WV held by RCK 1 Group LLC
Nat'l Network: CNN Radio; *Regional Network:* W. Va. MetroNews Network
Arbitron Metro Market: Wheeling, WV; *Format:* News, News/Talk, 86; *Hrs. of News Programming:* News progmg 14 hrs wkly; *Target Audience:* 25-54; adults
Howard Monroe, President

WBGI-FM
01-15-1990; 96.5 MHz FM; *Hrs Open:* 24; 2.5 kw; 138 meters; N39 50 51 W80 45 23
56325 High Ridge Road, Bellaire, OH 15301
(740) 676-5661; *Fax:* (740) 676-2742
www.biggie965.com
License: Moundsville, Marshall County, WV held by Keymart Licenses LlCdation.
Group Owner: EMF Broadcasting; (acq 12-15-2011)
Arbitron Metro Market: Wheeling, WV
Scott Miller, Marketing Director

Mount Hope

WTNJ
06-01-1980; 105.9 MHz FM; *Hrs Open:* 24; 4.4 kw; 1532 ft.; N37 56 51 W81 18 29
I
306 S. Kanawha Street, Beckley, WV 25801 USA
(800) 588-1059
www.wtnjfm.com
License: Mount Hope, Fayette County, WV held by Southern Communications
Group Owner: Southern Communications Corp.; (acq 3-12-01; $2.375 million).
Arbitron Metro Market: Beckley, WV; *Format:* Country *Special Programming:* NASCAR races, West Virginia Univ. sports; *Hrs. of News Programming:* news progmg 12 hrs wkly; *No. News Employees:* 1 *Target Audience:* 25-54.
Shane Southern, Owner
Jay Quesenberry, General Manager
Dave Willis, Programming Director

RADIO - U.S.

Mullens

WKQR
09-30-1981; 92.7 MHz FM; 6 kw; 328 ft.; N37 31 7 W81 22 43
18385 Coal Heritage Rd., Welch, WV 24801
(304) 436-2131
www.kissplaysthehits.com
License: Mullens, Wyoming County, WV held by West Virginia-Virginia Media LLC
Group Owner: West Virginia-Virginia Holding Co. LLC; (acq 3-29-2006; $120,000)
Nat'l Network: ABC
Format: Contemporary Hits/Top 40
Bob Spencer, Manager

New Martinsville

WETZ
05-25-1953; 1330 kHz AM; *Hrs Open:* 24; 1 kw-D, ND2; 0.059 kw-N, ND2; N39 39 27 W80 51 34
Mailing Address: PO Box 10, New Martinsville, WV 26155 US
Second Address: 325 N.Main St., New Martinsville, WV 26155
(304) 455-1111; *Fax:* (304) 455-1170
wetz@verizon.net
License: New Martinsville, WV held by Dailey Corp.
Group Owner: Dailey Corp.; (acq 2-1-2001; grpsl).
Nat'l Network: ABC
Arbitron Metro Market: Wheeling, WV; *Format:* Classic Rock; *Hrs. of News Programming:* News progmg 10 hrs wkly; *Target Audience:* 25-64.; *Adv. Rates:* 12; 12; 12; 8.
Calvin Dailey Jr., President
Dennis Gage, General Manager

WETZ(FM)
12-01-1977; 103.9 MHz FM; *Hrs Open:* 24; 2.5 kw; Ant 502 ft; N39 39 10 W80 54 47
Mailing Address: Box 10, New Martinsville, WV 26155
Second Address: 325 N.Main St., New Martinsville, WV 26155
(304) 455-1111; *Fax:* (304) 455-1170
www.powercountry104.com
wetz@verizon.net
License: New Martinsville, Wetzel County, WV
Nat'l Network: ABC
Population Served: 28,355; *Arbitron Metro Market:* Wheeling, WV; *Hrs. of News Programming:* News progmg 10 hrs wkly; *Target Audience:* 25-54; country; *Adv. Rates:* 22; 22; 22; 14
Paul Stanton, President
Wayne Winkler, General Manager
Larry Mayer, Programming Director
Mitch Sandidge, Chief Engineer
Jim Blalock, Music Director
Susan Lachmann, Women's Int Ed

WXCR
01-01-2002; 92.3 MHz FM; *Hrs Open:* 24; 3.2 kw; 453 ft.; N39 40 16 W80 53 4
Mailing Address: P O Box 564, New Martinsville, WV 26155 US
Second Address: Box 374, Saints Marys, WV 26170
(800) 296-2617; *Fax:* (304) 684-9241
www.wxcr.com
License: New Martinsville, Wetzel County, WV held by Seven Ranges Radio Co. Inc.
Arbitron Metro Market: New Martinsville, WV; *Format:* Classic Rock; *Target Audience:* 25-54; 70% men, 30% women; *Adv. Rates:* 6.50; 6; 6; 5
Sam Yoho, President
Lou Petronio, Operations Dir
Lisa Wilson, Sales

WYMJ
12-01-2002; 99.5 MHz FM; *Hrs Open:* 24; 2.7 kw; 482 ft.; N39 39 10 W80 54 47
P O Box 83, Proctor, WV 26055 US
(800) 833-9211; *Fax:* (304) 455-1170
www.oldiesradioonline.com
webmaster@greatestmojo.com
License: New Martinsville, Wetzel County, WV held by Dailey Corp.
Group Owner: Dailey Corp.; acq 2-6-2001; grpsl).
Arbitron Metro Market: Dallas, TX; *Format:* Adult Contemp; *No. News Employees:* 3
Dex Gage, General Manager
Ed Wilhelm, Chief Engineer

Oak Hill

WAXS
01-01-1948; 94.1 MHz FM; *Hrs Open:* 24; 25.5 kw; 650 ft.; N37 57 30 W81 9 3
306 S. Kanawha Street, Beckley, WV 25801 US
(304) 461-9260; *Fax:* (304) 253-7000
www.groovy94.com
softailed@hotmail.com
License: Oak Hill, Fayette County, WV held by Plateau Broadcasting Inc.
Group Owner: Southern Communications Corp.; (acq 3-12-01; $875,000).
Nat'l Network: ABC
Arbitron Metro Market: South Park WY
Ted Tucker, General Manager

WOAY
02-22-1947; 860 kHz AM; 5 kw-C, ND1; 10 kw-D, ND1; ND1; 0.011 kw; N37 57 30 W81 9 3
240 Central Avenue, Oak Hill, WV 25901 US
(304) 465-0534; *Fax:* (304) 465-1486
www.woayradio.com
info@woayradio.com
License: Oak Hill, WV held by Foothills Resource Group, Inc.
Arbitron Metro Market: Beckley, WV *TV Affiliate:* Relg; *No. News Employees:* General.
Vernon Drumheller, Sales Manager/Community Relations
Mike Carter, Operations/Traffic/Production

Parkersburg

WADC
04-09-1954; 1050 kHz AM; *Hrs Open:* 24; 5 kw-D, ND2; 0.144 kw-N, ND2; N39 15 29 W81 33 49
5 Rosemar Circle, Parkersburg, WV 26104 US
(304) 485-4565; *Fax:* (304) 424-6955
www.wadcradio.com
License: Parkersburg, Wood County, WV held by Burbach of DE LLC
Group Owner: Burbach Broadcasting Group; (acq 3-19-98; $1.775 million with co-located FM).
Nat'l Network: CNN Radio
Arbitron Metro Market: Parkersburg, WV; *Format:* Adult Contemp; *Adv. Rates:* 20; 20; 20; 20
Don Staats, General Manager
Chuck Helmick, Sales Manager
Charles Roberts, Account Manager
Amy Landis, Account Manager
Rich Rule, Account Manager
Lauren Queen, Account Manager

WHBR-FM
03-01-1967; 103.1 MHz FM; *Hrs Open:* 24; 2.1 kw; 561 ft.; N39 21 0 W81 33 56
#5 Rosemar Circle, Parkersburg, WV 26104 US
(304) 485-4565; *Fax:* (304) 424-6955
www.1031thebear.net
chelmick@resultsradiowv.com
License: Parkersburg, Wood County, WV held by Burbach of DE LLC
Group Owner: dba Results Radio, Llc
Arbitron Metro Market: Parkersburg-Marietta, WV-OH; *Format:* Rock/AOR; *Hrs. of News Programming:* news progmg 6 hrs wkly; *No. News Employees:* 1; *Target Audience:* 18-49; active/modern rock listeners; *Adv. Rates:* 25; 25; 25; 25
Don Staats, General Manager

WVNT
09-01-1947; 1230 kHz AM; *Hrs Open:* 24; 0.88 kw-D, ND2; 0.88 kw-N, ND2; N35 15 29 W81 33 49
5 Rosemar Circle, Parkersburg, WV 26104 US
(304) 485-4565; *Fax:* (304) 424-6955
www.wvnt.net
License: Parkersburg, Wood County, WV held by Burbach of DE LLC
Group Owner: Burbach Broadcasting Group; (acq 1-1-97; grpsl).
Nat'l Network: CNN Radio; *Nat'l Reps:* McGavren Guild
Arbitron Metro Market: Parkersburg-Marietta, WV-OH; *Format:* News, News/Talk, 86 *Special Programming:* Gospel 4 hrs wkly; *No. News Employees:* 1; *Target Audience:* 30-50.; *Adv. Rates:* 12; 12; 12; 12
Don Staats, General Manager
Chuck Helmick, Local Sales Manager
Charles Roberts, Account Manager
Amy Landis, Account Manager
Rich Rule, Account Manager
Lauren Queen, Account Manager

WHNK
07-12-1935; 1450 kHz AM; *Hrs Open:* 24; 1 kw-U, ND1; N39 17 23 W81 31 36
6006 Grand Central Ave, Vienna, WV 26105 US
(304) 295-6070; *Fax:* (304) 295-4389
License: Parkersburg, WV held by CC Licenses LLC.
Group Owner: iHeartMedia; (acq 4-17-2001).
Nat'l Reps: Clear Channel
Arbitron Metro Market: Parkersburg, WV; *Format:* Country; *Hrs. of News Programming:* news progmg 3 hrs wkly; *No. News Employees:* 1; *Target Audience:* 25-54; middle-aged, middle to upper income; *Adv. Rates:* 12;10; 12; 6
Rodney Ortiz, Market Senior Vice President of Programming

WRZZ
01-01-1986; 106.1 MHz FM; *Hrs Open:* 24; 3.3 kw; 453 ft.; N39 14 47 W81 28 19
5 Rosemar Circle, Parkersburg, WV 26104 US
(304) 485-4565; *Fax:* (304) 424-6955
www.z106.net
License: Parkersburg, Wood County, WV held by Burbach of DE LLC
Group Owner: Burbach Broadcasting Group; (acq 8-8-2005; $750,000)
Nat'l Network: Westwood One
Arbitron Metro Market: Parkersburg, WV; *Format:* Classic Rock; *Target Audience:* 25-54; baby boomer rock listeners
Don Staats, General Manager
Chuck Helmick, Local Sales Manager
Charles Roberts, Account Manager
Amy Landis, Account Manager
Rich Rule, Account Manager
Lauren Queen, Account Manager

*WVPG
04-04-1985; 90.3 MHz FM; *Hrs Open:* 24; 9 kw; 322 ft.; N39 12 44 W81 35 30
600 Capitol Street, Charleston, WV 25301 US
(304) 556-4900; *Fax:* (304) 556-4960
www.wvpubcast.org
feedback@wvpubcast.org
License: Parkersburg, Wood County, WV held by West Virginia Educational Broadcasting Authority.
Nat'l Network: NPR; PRI
Arbitron Metro Market: Parkersburg, WV; *Format:* Jazz, News *Special Programming:* Mountain Stage 2 hrs, children one hr wkly; *No. News Employees:* 2
Scott Finn, Executive Director
Marilyn DiVita, Director, Development/Marketing
Dave McClanahan, Engineering Dir
Tammy Treadway, CFO
Craig Lonham, Director of TV Programming
Kristi George, Director of Radio Programming
ChadMatlicki, Director of Digitial
Chuck Roberts, Director of Video Production
Beth Voorhees, Director of News/Public Affairs

WGGE
09-01-1965; 99.1 MHz FM; 11.5 kw; 486 ft.; N39 17 15 W81 39 25
5 Rosemar Circle, Parkersburg, WV 26104 US
(304) 485-4565; *Fax:* (304) 424-6955
www.froggy99.net
License: Parkersburg, Wood County, WV held by Burbach of DE LLC
Group Owner: Burbach Broadcasting Group
Arbitron Metro Market: Parkersburg, WV; *Format:* Country *Special Programming:* Farm 2 hrs, NASCAR 5 hrs wkly; *Target Audience:* 25-54; loyal modern country listeners
Don Staats, General Manager
Chuck Helmick, Local Sales Manager
Charles Roberts, Account Manager
Amy Landis, Account Manager
Rich Rule, Account Manager
Lauren Queen, Account Manager

Petersburg

*WAUA
12-01-1997; 89.5 MHz FM; *Hrs Open:* 24; 10 kw; 1056 ft.; N39 12 7 W79 16 31
600 Capitol Street, Charleston, WV 25301 US
(304) 556-4900; *Fax:* (304) 556-4981
www.wvpubcast.org
feedback@wvpubcast.org
License: Petersburg, Grant County, WV held by West Virginia Educational Broadcasting Authority.
Nat'l Network: NPR; PRI
Arbitron Metro Market: Petersburg, WV; *Format:* News
Rita Ray, General Manager
Marilyn DeVita, General Sales Mgr
James Muhammad, Programming Director
Greg Collard, News Director
Jack Wells, Chief Engineer
Teresa Wills, Traffic Manager

Philippi

*WQAB
10-01-1975; 91.3 MHz FM; *Hrs Open:* 8 AM-10 PM; 7.2 kw; 180 ft.; N39 9 52 W80 2 57
P.O. Box 1428, Philippi, WV 26416 US

(304) 457-6281,(304) 457-6271; *Fax:* (304) 457-6239
www.ab.edu/performing-arts/wqab-fm
License: Philippi, Barbour County, WV held by Alderson-Broaddus College.
Nat'l Network: AP Radio
Format: Adult Contemp, Variety/Diverse *Special Programming:* Jazz 4 hrs, Black 2 hrs, radio drama 2 hrs, children's 2 hrs wkly; *Hrs. of News Programming:* News progmg 5 hrs wkly; *Target Audience:* 15-40; collegestudents
Dr. Jim Willie, Faculty Advisor
Kiersten Long, Student Station Manager

Pineville

WWYO
01-01-1949; 970 kHz AM; 1 kw-D, ND2; 0.026 kw-N, ND2; N37 35 20 W81 32 25
P. O. Box 647, Bluefield, WV 24701 US
(304) 732-8552; *Fax:* (304) 327-5651
www.am970wwyo.com
wwyo970am@frontier.com
License: Pineville, WV held by MRJ Inc.
Arbitron Metro Market: Pineville, WV; *Format:* Variety/Diverse *Special Programming:* Folk one hr, sports 18 hrs, educ 2 hrs, community; *Target Audience:* 25-65; housewives; *Adv. Rates:* 5.15; 5.15; 5.15; na
Rudolph Jennings, President

Pocatalico

WRVZ
01-01-1995; 98.7 MHz FM; 0.63 kw; 617 ft.; N38 23 53 W81 41 6
1111 Virginia St. E., Charleston, WV 25301 US
(304) 342-8131
www.987thebeat.com
License: Pocatalico, Kanawha County, WV held by West Virginia Radio Corporation of Charleston
Group Owner: West Virginia Radio Corp.; (acq 3-12-2001; $800,000)
Nat'l Network: IND
Arbitron Metro Market: Charleston, WV; *Format:* Contemporary Hits/Top 40; *Target Audience:* 25+
Dave Miller, President

Point Pleasant

WBGS
01-01-1994; 1030 kHz AM; 2.9 kw-C, DAD; 10 kw-D, DAD; N38 48 42 W82 5 59
303 8th St., Point Pleasant, WV 25550 US
(304) 675-2727; *Fax:* (304) 675-2771
License: Point Pleasant, Mason County, WV held by Big River Radio Inc.
Group Owner: Baker Family Stations
Arbitron Metro Market: Point Pleasant, VA; *Format:* Gospel
Randy Parsons, General Manager
Claire Beaver, Manager
Karen Wright, Manager
Rick Towe, Manager
Shari Cochran, Manager

WBYG
01-01-1994; 99.5 MHz FM; 4.7 kw; Ant 328 ft; N38 50 49 W82 07 50
303 8th St., Point Pleasant, WV 25550
(304) 675-2763; *Fax:* (304) 675-2771
www.wbyg.com
wbyg@wbyg.com
License: Point Pleasant, Mason County, WV held by Big River Radio, Inc.

Shari Cochran, Station Manager/General Sales Manager
Tom Payne, News Director
Noah Tyree, Studio Engineer
Nick Stephens, Studio Engineer

*WPCN(FM)
12-21-2000; 88.1 MHz FM; *Hrs Open:* 24; 3 kw; Ant 289 ft; N38 50 49 W82 07 50
303 8th Street, Point Pleasant, WV 25550
(304) 675-2727; *Fax:* (304) 675-2771
joyfm881@yahoo.com
License: Point Pleasant, Mason County, WV held by Positive Alternative Radio Inc.
Group Owner: Positive Alternative Radio Inc.
Format: Gospel
Randy Parson, General Manager

Princeton

WAEY
12-01-1947; 1490 kHz AM; *Hrs Open:* 24; 1 kw-U, ND1; N37 23 23 W81 5 58
Mailing Address: 1345 Mercer Street, Princeton, WV 24740 US
Second Address: Lilly Grove Addition, 1 Radio Ln., Princeton, WV 24740
(304) 425-2151; *Fax:* (304) 487-2016
www.star95.com
License: Princeton, WV held by Princeton Broadcasting Inc.
Arbitron Metro Market: Princeton, WV; *Format:* Gospel; *Hrs. of News Programming:* news progmg 14 hrs wkly; *No. News Employees:* 1; *Target Audience:* 25 plus; blue collar
Linda Witt, President
Pat Tolley, Operations Dir
Bob Spencer, General Manager
Ron Witt, Programming Director
Amy Mills, News Director
Wayne Boone, Chief Engineer
Patricia Tolley, Min Affairs Director
Jason Reed, OperationsManager

WKOY-FM
04-01-1983; 100.9 MHz FM; *Hrs Open:* 24; 0.34 kw; 1,342 ft.; N37 15 5 W81 11 20
900 Bluefield Ave., Bluefield, WV 24701 US
(304) 327-7114; *Fax:* (304) 325-7850
www.theeaglefm.com
License: Princeton, Mercer County, WV held by Alpha Media Licensee LLC
Group Owner: Alpha Media LLC
Nat'l Network: ABC; *Nat'l Reps:* Katz Radio; Rgnl Reps
Arbitron Metro Market: Bluefield, WV; *Format:* Classic Rock; *No. News Employees:* 1; *Target Audience:* 25 plus.
Ken Dietz, Operations Manager
Danny Clemons, Vice President
Lee Rappolt, Continuity Director

WSTG
04-01-1973; 95.9 MHz FM; *Hrs Open:* 24; 0.48 kw; 1142 ft.; N37 15 30 W81 10 37
Mailing Address: 1345 Mercer Street, Princeton, WV 24740 US
Second Address: Lilly Grove Addition, 1Radio Ln, Princeton, WV 24740
(304) 425-2151; *Fax:* (304) 487-2016
www.star95.com
License: Princeton, Mercer County, WV held by L & P Broadcasting Inc.
Arbitron Metro Market: Bluefield, WV; *Format:* Contemporary Hits/Top 40; *No. News Employees:* 1
Linda Witt, General Sales Mgr
Jeff Davis, Programming Director
Amy Mills, News Director
Jason Reed, Disc Jockey
Bob Spencer, Disc Jockey
Charlie Brown, Local News Editor
Jim Nelson, Sports Commentator

*WPWV
09-01-2003; 90.1 MHz FM; 2.5 kw vert; 1040 ft.; N37 30 35 W81 12 55
P.O. Box 3206, Tupelo, MS 38803 US
(662) 844-8888; *Fax:* (662) 842-6791
www.afr.net
faq@afa.net
License: Princeton, Mercer County, WV held by American Family Association.
Group Owner: American Family Radio
Arbitron Metro Market: Princeton, WV; *Format:* Christian
Tim Wildmon, President
Donald Wildmon, Founder
Buddy Smith, Sr VP
Ed Vitagliano, Exec VP
Randy Sharp, Director Of Special Projects
Meeke Addison, Director Of Communications
Abraham Hamilton III, General Counsel

Rainelle

WRLB
02-01-1977; 95.3 MHz FM; *Hrs Open:* 24; 13 kw; 456 ft.; N37 57 28 W80 45 45
P.O. Box 1450, Lewisburg, WV 24901 US
(304) 647-3606
www.wrlb.com
License: Rainelle, Greenbrier County, WV held by Faith Communications Network Inc.
Format: Christian, Religious; *Target Audience:* 25-54.
Norma Mnich, Chairman
Matthew Mnich, CEO
Mark Jividen, Operations Dir
Jim Pontius, General Sales Mgr
Hal Fish, Programming Director
Greg Moebius, Promotions Manager
Eric Feucht, General Sales Manager
Ronni Hunter, MusicDirector

WRRL
01-01-1973; 1130 kHz AM; 1 kw-D, NDD; N37 57 28 W80 45 45
507 Main Street, Rainelle, WV 25962 US
(304) 438-8537 phone/fax
wrrlam@mountain.net
License: Rainelle, WV held by Faith Mountain Communications Inc.
Regional Network: W. Va. MetroNews Network
Format: Christian, Gospel, 60, News/Talk, Talk; *Target Audience:* 35 plus.; *Adv. Rates:* 3; 3; 3; 3
Nancy Whitt, CEO
Allen Whitt, President

Ravenswood

WMOV
01-01-1953; 1360 kHz AM; *Hrs Open:* 24 hours
527 Gibbs Street, Ravenswood, WV 26164 US
(304) 273-2544
http://www.wmov1360.com
webmaster@wmov1360.com
License: Ravenswood, WV held by Vandalia Media Partners LLC
Nat'l Network: CBS Radio; Westwood One; Jones Radio Networks; *Regional Network:* W. Va. MetroNews Network; Radio Sound Net.
Arbitron Metro Market: Charleston, WV; *Format:* News, Talk
Special Programming: Cincinnati Reds baseball; Cincinnati Bengal footba; *Hrs. of News Programming:* news programming 12 hrs weekly; *No. News Employees:* 1 *Target Audience:* 35 plus; *Adv. Rates:* 6.50; 6.50; 6.50; 2.50
Burke Allen, President
Greg Gack, General Manager

Richwood

WVAR
01-01-1956; 600 kHz AM; *Hrs Open:* 6 AM-sunset; 1 kw-D, NDD; 0.055 kw-N, NDD; N38 13 50 W80 32 49 *Rebroadcasts:* Rebroadcasts WSGB(AM) Sutton 100%
180 Main Street, Sutton, WV 26601 US
(304) 765-7373; *Fax:* (304) 765-7836
www.theboss97fm.com
al@summitmediawv.com
License: Richwood, WV held by Summit Media Inc.
Group Owner: Summit Media Broadcasting LLC; (acq 3-8-2007; $1.24 million with WAFD(FM) Webster Springs)
Nat'l Network: ABC; *Regional Network:* W. Va. MetroNews Network; *Nat'l Reps:* Rgnl Reps
Arbitron Metro Market: Sutton, WV; *Format:* Contemporary Hits/Top 40, Adult Contemp; *Hrs. of News Programming:* News progmg 5 hrs wkly; *Target Audience:* 35-64; male and female; *Adv. Rates:* 9; 7; 9; 6
Al Sergi, General Sales Mgr
Lisa Mace Godwin, Programming Director
Danny Finch, Office Manager

Ridgeley

WDYK
01-01-2006; 100.5 MHz FM; 6 kw; 328 ft.; N39 42 49.6 W78 42 56.5
15 E. Industrial Blvd., Cumberland, MD 21502 US
(301) 759-1005; *Fax:* (301) 759-3124
www.cumberlandsmagic.com
License: Ridgeley, Mineral County, WV held by West Virginia Radio Corporation of the Alleghenies
Group Owner: West Virginia Radio Corp.
Nat'l Network: FOXNEW
Arbitron Metro Market: Ridgeley, WV; *Format:* Adult Contemp; *Target Audience:* 25-54.
Dale Miller, President

Ripley

WCEF
02-24-1981; 98.3 MHz FM; *Hrs Open:* 24; 6 kw; 308 ft.; N38 46 4 W81 41 9
P.O. Box 798, Ripley, WV 25271 US
(304) 372-9800; *Fax:* (304) 372-9811
www.c98.com
License: Ripley, Jackson County, WV held by Big River Radio Inc.
Group Owner: Baker Family Stations; (acq 1-31-2003; $762,500).
Nat'l Network: ABC

Arbitron Metro Market: Ripley, WV; *Format:* Country; *Target Audience:* 25-54.
Ric Shannon, Station Manager
Lee Ann Irvin, Account Representative

***WLKV**
03-26-1994; 90.7 MHz FM; 3 kw; 328 ft.; N38 51 44 W81 41 27
P.O. Box 568, Belpre, OH 45714 US
(916) 251-1600; *Fax:* (916) 251-1650
www.klove.com
klove@klove.com
License: Ripley, Jackson County, WV held by Educational Media Foundation.
Group Owner: EMF Broadcasting; (acq 3-31-2005; $700,000 with WLKP(FM) Belpre, OH).
Nat'l Network: K-Love
Arbitron Metro Market: Ripley, WV; *Format:* Christian; *No. News Employees:* 3; *Target Audience:* 25-44; female-Judeo Christian
Darrell Chambliss, Chairman
Mike Novak, President/CEO
Alan Mason, COO
Eric Moser, CFO
D. Kevin Blair, Secretary/General Counsel
Walter Golembeski, Director
David Pierce, Chief Creative Officer
Mitch Barnhart, Director
LarryMoody, Director
Dan Antonelli, Director

Romney

***WVSB**
03-30-1973; 104.1 MHz FM; *Hrs Open:* 24; 0.1 kw; 781 ft.; N39 18 56 W78 43 4
301 East Main Street, Romney, WV 26757 US
(304) 822-4860; *Fax:* (304) 822-4870
wvsdb.state.k12.wv.us/radio_station.htm
License: Romney, Hampshire County, WV held by West Virginia Schools for the Deaf & Blind.
Format: Country; *Target Audience:* General.
Mark Gandolfi, CFO
George Park, General Manager

WVMD
01-01-2008; 100.1 MHz FM; 0.9 kw; 823 ft.; N39 25 20 W78 47 25
15 E. Industrial Blvd, Cumberland, MD 21502 US
(301) 759-1005; *Fax:* (301) 759-3124
www.tristateswolf.com
License: Romney, Hampshire County, WV held by West Virginia Radio Corporation of the Alleghenies
Group Owner: West Virginia Radio Corp.; (acq 1-18-2007; $375,000 for CP)
Nat'l Network: CMLS; PRMIER; FOXNEW
Arbitron Metro Market: Romney, WV; *Format:* Country
Dale Miller, President

Ronceverte

WRON
01-01-1947; 1400 kHz AM; *Hrs Open:* 24; 1 kw-U, ND1; N37 45 36 W80 27 8
276 Seneca Trail North, Ronceverte, WV 24970 US
(304) 645-1400,(304) 645-1327; *Fax:* (304) 647-4802
www.wron.com
radio@wron.net
License: Ronceverte, WV held by Radio Greenbrier LLC.
Group Owner: Radio Greenbrier LLC
Nat'l Network: Premiere Radio Networks; Westwood One; Talk Radio Network; *Nat'l Reps:* Dome; Rgnl Reps; *Wire Services:* AP
Format: News, Talk *Special Programming:* Relg 2 hrs wkly; *Hrs. of News Programming:* News progmg 21 hrs wkly; *Target Audience:* 35; & under; *Adv. Rates:* 6.90; 6.90; 6.90; 3.00
Roy Jarrell, Operations Dir
Michael Kidd, General Manager
Larry Carver, Chief Engineer
Jeff Campbell, Sports Commentator

Rupert

WYKM
12-09-1981; 1250 kHz AM; *Hrs Open:* 6 AM-sunset; 5 kw-D, NDD; N37 59 35 W80 41 3
Mailing Address: Box 627, Rupert, WV 25984 US
Second Address: 714 Nicholas St., Rupert, WV 25984
(304) 392-6003; *Fax:* (304) 392-5352
www.todaysbestcountryonline.com
License: Rupert, WV held by Mountain State Broadcasting Co.
Nat'l Network: CBS
Arbitron Metro Market: Rupert, WV; *Format:* Country, Gospel; *Hrs. of News Programming:* News progmg 7 hrs wkly; *Adv. Rates:* 5.50; 5.50; 5.50; 5.50
Betty Crookshanks, President
Donald Crookshanks, Executive Vice President

Salem

WOBG-FM
11-01-1990; 105.7 MHz FM; 1.95 kw; 581 ft.; N39 19 6 W80 26 18
1489 Locust Ave., Suite C, Fairmont, WV 26554 US
(304) 363-8888; *Fax:* (304) 367-1885
www.rock1057.com
License: Salem, Harrison County, WV held by Burbach of DE LLC
Group Owner: Burbach Broadcasting Group; (acq 5-17-00; grpsl).
Regional Reps: Commercial Media Sales.
Arbitron Metro Market: Clarksburg-Fairmont, WV *TV Affiliate:* Classic rock; *Format:* Rock/AOR; *No. News Employees:* 25-54.
Nicholas Galli, President
Michael Pasqua, Director of Sales
Stacy Schulman, Account Manager

WAJR-FM
01-01-1999; 103.3 MHz FM; 1.8 kw; 590 ft.; N39 15 44 W80 28 1 *Rebroadcasts:* Simulcasts WAJR-AM 90%
Mailing Address: 1065 Radio Park Dr, Mount Claire, WV 26408 US
Second Address: 1251 Earl L. Core Rd, Morgantown, WV 26505
(304) 296-0029; *Fax:* (304) 623-6547
www.wajr.com
License: Salem, Harrison County, WV held by West Virginia Radio Corporation of Salem
Group Owner: West Virginia Radio Corp.
Nat'l Network: CMLS; WWO; YAHSP
Arbitron Metro Market: Salem, WV; *Format:* News/Talk, Sports
Dale Miller, President

Shepherdstown

***WSHC**
01-01-1974; 89.7 MHz FM; *Hrs Open:* 24; 0.95 kw; -10 ft.; N39 25 53 W77 48 18
Knutti Hall Shepard Col., Shepherdstown, WV 25443 US
(304) 876-5134; *Fax:* (304) 876-5405
wshc@shepherd.edu
License: Shepherdstown, Jefferson County, WV held by Shepherd College Board of Governors
Nat'l Network: ABC
Format: Variety/Diverse; *Hrs. of News Programming:* News progmg 7 hrs wkly; *Target Audience:* 18-24; college/young adult
Buck Lam, General Manager

South Charleston

WMXE
07-29-1985; 100.9 MHz FM; *Hrs Open:* 24; 3 kw; 299 ft.; N38 22 34 W81 42 13
100 Kanowha Terrace, St. Albans, WV 25177-2771 US
(304) 722-3308; *Fax:* (304) 727-1300
www.wmxe.net
License: South Charleston, Kanawha County, WV held by L.M. Communications of Kentucky, LLC
Group Owner: L M Communications of Kentucky, LLC
Arbitron Metro Market: Charleston, WV; *Format:* Adult Contemp, Religious; *Target Audience:* 25-54.
Mark Atkinson, Programming Director

WSCW
12-13-1963; 1410 kHz AM
6815 Shallowford Road, Chattanooga, TN 37421 US
(304) 722-3308; *Fax:* (304) 727-1300
License: South Charleston, WV held by L.M. Communications of Kentucky LLC.
Group Owner: L M Communications Inc.; (acq 4-1-03; grpsl).
Arbitron Metro Market: Charleston, WV; *Format:* Country; *Target Audience:* 25-64.
Ron Walton, General Manager
Chris Colagrasso, Programming Director
Emma Allen, News Director
Fred Francis, Chief Engineer

***WWLA**
89.3 MHz FM; 2.3 kw; 207 ft.; N38 23 47 W81 35 28
188 South Belleuve, Suite 222, Memphis, TN 38104 US
(901) 726-8970; *Fax:* (901) 375-0041
mail@flinn.com
License: South Charleston, Kanawha County, WV held by Broadcasting for the Challenged Inc.
Arbitron Metro Market: Charleston, WV
George Flinn Jr., President

Spencer

WVRC
09-12-1961; 1400 kHz AM; 1 kw-U, ND1; N38 48 23 W81 21 40
106 Radio Street, Spencer, WV 25276 US
(304) 927-3760; *Fax:* (304) 927-2877
www.wvrcfm.com
License: Spencer, WV held by Star Communications Inc.
Nat'l Reps: Rgnl Reps
Arbitron Metro Market: Spencer, WV; *Format:* Gospel
Larry Koenig, President
Bob Edwards, Operations Dir
Kim Parrish, News Director

WVRC-FM
10-01-1992; 104.7 MHz FM; 4.8 kw; 367 ft.; N38 47 40 W81 17 36
106 Radio Street, Spencer, WV 25276 US
(304) 927-3760; *Fax:* (304) 927-2877
www.wvrcfm.com
License: Spencer, Roane County, WV
Arbitron Metro Market: Spencer, WV; *Format:* Country
Larry Koening, President

St. Albans

WJYP
01-14-1956; 1300 kHz AM; *Hrs Open:* 24
100 Kanawha Terrace, St. Albans, WV 25177 US
(304) 722-3308; *Fax:* (304) 727-1300
www.wjypam.com
chris@wjypam.com
License: St. Albans, WV held by WKLC Inc.
Group Owner: L M Communications Inc.; (acq 2-23-80).
Arbitron Metro Market: Kanawha County-Putnam County, WV; *Format:* Talk, Religious; *Target Audience:* 18-49.
Ron Walton, General Manager
Chris Colagrosso, Programming Director
Emma Allen, News Director
Fred Francis, Chief Engineer

WKLC-FM
01-01-1966; 105.1 MHz FM; *Hrs Open:* 24; 3.6 kw; 1663 ft.; N38 25 15 W81 55 27
100 Kanawha Terrace, St. Albans, WV 25177 US
(304) 722-3308; *Fax:* (304) 727-1300
www.wklc.com
105spots@wkcl.com
License: St. Albans, Kanawha County, WV
Group Owner: L M Communications Inc.
Nat'l Network: ABC
Arbitron Metro Market: Charleston, WV; *Format:* Rock/AOR
Matt James, Production Director
Dotsy Klei, Marketing Manager
Jill Wheeler, Sales Manager
Anna Graley, Traffic Director
Chili Walker, Programming Director
Dave Miller, News Director

St. Marys

WRRR-FM
11-16-1983; 93.9 MHz FM; 17 kw; 390 ft.; N39 22 49 W81 11 36
PO Box 374, St. Marys, WV 26170 US
(800) 296-2617; *Fax:* (304) 684-9241
www.literock93r.com
srr@sevenrangesradio.com
License: St. Marys, Pleasants County, WV held by Seven Ranges Radio Co. Inc.
Arbitron Metro Market: Parkersburg-Marietta, WV-OH; *Format:* Adult Contemp; *Hrs. of News Programming:* news progmg 9 hrs wkly; *No. News Employees:* 1; *Target Audience:* 25-49.; *Adv. Rates:* 15; 14; 14; 12
Sam Yoho, President

WJAW
10-01-1984; 630 kHz AM; *Hrs Open:* 24; 1 kw-D, ND1; 0.037 kw-N, ND1; N39 23 42 W81 13 49
925 Lancaster Street, Marietta, OH 45750 US
(740) 373-1490; *Fax:* (740) 373-1717
www.wmoa1490.com
kwenzel@wmoa1490.com
License: St. Marys, WV held by JAWCO Inc.
Nat'l Network: ESPN Radio
Arbitron Metro Market: St.Marys, WV; *Format:* Sports; *No. News Employees:* 3
John Wharf III, President
Jamey Styer, Operations Dir
Stephanie Wiles, Station Manager
Andy Rex, Programming Director
Bryon Sunderman, Chief Engineer

Jamey Styer, Chief Operator
Kyle Wenzel, Public Service Director

Star City

***WLOL-FM**
89.7 MHz FM; 0.08 kw; 185 ft.; N39 40 9.3 W80 0 11
Light of Life Community, 132 Carubia Drive, Core, WV 26541 US
(304) 879-5752
www.wvlol.org
info@lolradio.org
License: Star City, Monongalia County, WV held by Light of Life Community Inc.
Nat'l Network: EWTN Radio
Arbitron Metro Market: Star City, WV
Robert Carubia, President

Summersville

WCWV
03-13-1983; 92.9 MHz FM; *Hrs Open:* 24; 11 kw; 899 ft.; N38 21 37 W80 38 49
180 Main Street, Sutton, WV 26601 US
(304) 765-7373; *Fax:* (304) 765-7836
www.nick929.com
License: Summersville, Nicholas County, WV held by Summit Media
Nat'l Network: Westwood One; *Nat'l Reps:* Dome
Arbitron Metro Market: Summersville WV; *Format:* Adult Contemp *Special Programming:* Gospel 15 hrs, relg 18 hrs wkly; *Hrs. of News Programming:* News progmg 23 hrs wkly; *Target Audience:* 18-54. *Adv. Rates:* 15; 15; 15; 10
Al Sergi, GM/Sales Manager
Lis Godwin, Programming Manager
Daniel Finch, Financial Manager

***WMLJ**
01-01-1993; 90.5 MHz FM; *Hrs Open:* 24; 11 kw; 1033 ft.; N38 6 42 W80 35 52 *Rebroadcasts:* Rebroadcasts WOTJ(FM) Morehead City, NC 90%
520 Roberts Road, Newport, NC 28570 US
(252) 223-4600; (800) 245-9685
www.fbnradio.com
License: Summersville, Nicholas County, WV held by Grace Missionary Baptist Church
Arbitron Metro Market: Summersville, WV; *Format:* Children, Gospel *Special Programming:* Sp one hr wkly; *Target Audience:* General.
Clyde Ebron, President
Chris Brown, General Manager
Mike Tyler, Chief Engineer

***WSJE**
91.3 MHz FM; 0.24 kw; 819 ft.; N38 21 38.5 W80 38 50.4
PO Box 388, Summersville, WV 26651 US
wsje91.3fm@frontier.com
License: Summersville, Nicholas County, WV held by Evangelist Communications, Inc.
Arbitron Metro Market: Summersville, WV
Gary Criste, President

Sutton

WDBS
04-25-1987; 97.1 MHz FM; *Hrs Open:* 24; 22 kw; 751 ft.; N38 27 5 W80 27 14
189a Main St., Sutton, WV 26601 US
(304) 765-7373; *Fax:* (304) 765-7836
theboss97fm.com
al@summitmediawv.com
License: Sutton, Braxton County, WV held by Summit Media Broadcasting LLC
Group Owner: Summit Media Broadcasting LLC; (acq 12-30-99)
Nat'l Network: Dial Global Mainstream Country; AP Radio; *Regional Network:* WV MetroNews; *Nat'l Reps:* Rgnl Reps
Arbitron Metro Market: Sutton, WV; *Format:* Country; *Hrs. of News Programming:* News progmg 9 hrs wkly; *Target Audience:* 18-49; young adults females/males; *Adv. Rates:* 25; 20; 25; 15
Al Sergi, General Manager
Al Sergi, General Sales Mgr
Lisa Mace-Godwin, Programming Director
Danny Finch, Office Manager/ Traffic / Billing

WSGB
01-22-1964; 1490 kHz AM; *Hrs Open:* 24
180 a Main Street, Sutton, WV 26601 US
(304) 765-7373; *Fax:* (304) 765-7836
www.theboss97fm.com/wsgb.html
al@summitmediawv.com
License: Sutton, WV held by Summit Media Broadcasting L.L.C.
Group Owner: Summit Media Broadcasting LLC; (acq 12-30-99; $250,000 with co-located FM)
Nat'l Network: ABC; *Regional Network:* W. Va. MetroNews Network; *Nat'l Reps:* Rgnl Reps *Regional Reps:* Dome; Regnl Reps
Format: Contemporary Hits/Top 40, Adult Contemp; *Hrs. of News Programming:* News prgmg 5 hrs per week; *Target Audience:* 35-64; male and female; *Adv. Rates:* 9; 7; 9; 6
Al Sergi, General Manager
Lisa Mace-Godwin, Programming Director
Danny Finch, Office Manager/Traffic/Billing

Vienna

WDMX
05-22-1989; 100.1 MHz FM; *Hrs Open:* 24; 1.65 kw; 440 ft.; N39 20 18 W81 30 1
6006 Grand Central Ave, Parkersburg, WV 26105 US
(304) 295-6070; *Fax:* (304) 295-4389
www.mymix100.com
License: Vienna, Wood County, WV held by CC Licenses LLC.
Group Owner: iHeartMedia; (acq 4-17-2001; grpsl).
Nat'l Network: ABC; *Nat'l Reps:* Clear Channel
Arbitron Metro Market: Parkersburg-Marietta, WV-OH; *Format:* Oldies; *No. News Employees:* 2; *Target Audience:* 25-54.; *Adv. Rates:* 35; 30; 35; 18
Rodney Ortiz, Programming Director

Wardensville

WTCF
08-15-2012; 103.3 MHz FM; 350 w; 410 meters
P.O. Box 2098, Omaha, NE 68103-2098 USA
(800) 525-5683
www.klove.com
License: Wardensville, Hardy County, WV held by Educational Media Foundation
Group Owner: EMF Broadcasting
Format: Christian
Darrell Chambliss, Chairman
Mike Novak, CEO/COO
Mike Novak, President

Webster Springs

WAFD
02-01-1996; 100.3 MHz FM; *Hrs Open:* 24; 26 kw; 682 ft.; N38 27 39 W80 25 13
180 Main Street, Sutton, WV 26601 US
(304) 765-7373; *Fax:* (304) 765-7836
www.theboss97fm.com/wafd.html
al@summitmediawv.com
License: Webster Springs, Webster County, WV held by Summit Media Inc.
Group Owner: Summit Media Broadcasting LLC; (acq 3-8-2007; $1.24 million with WVAR(AM) Richwood)
Nat'l Network: CNN Radio; *Nat'l Reps:* Rgnl Reps
Arbitron Metro Market: Webster Springs, WV; *Format:* Adult Contemp; *Hrs. of News Programming:* News prgmg 3 hrs/week; *Target Audience:* M-F/18-49.; *Adv. Rates:* 20; 16; 20; 13
Al Sergi, General Manager
Lisa Mace-Godwin, Programming Director
Danny Finch, Office Manager/Traffic/Billing

Weirton

WEIR
09-15-1950; 1430 kHz AM; *Hrs Open:* 24; 1 kw-D, DA2; 1 kw-N, DA2; N40 26 42 W80 37 41
2307 Pennsylvania Ave., Weirton, WV 26062 US
(304) 723-1444; *Fax:* (304) 723-1688
www.weirsports.net
License: Weirton, WV held by Priority Communications Ohio LLC.
Group Owner: Priority Communications; (acq 12-4-98; $475,000 with WCDK(FM) Cadiz, OH)
Nat'l Network: Westwood One *Regional Reps:* Dome
Arbitron Metro Market: Weirton, WV; *Format:* Adult Contemp, Talk *Special Programming:* lt 3 hrs, Gr 1 hr wkly; *Hrs. of News Programming:* news progmg 25 hrs wkly; *No. News Employees:* 1 *Target Audience:* General.
Dee Dee Dupre, General Manager

Welch

WELC
08-19-1950; 1150 kHz AM; *Hrs Open:* 6 AM- Sunset; 5 kw-D, NDD; N37 25 1 W81 36 58
Mailing Address: P. O. Box 949, Welch, WV 24801 US
Second Address: U.S. Rt. 52, Welch, WV 24801
(304) 436-2131; *Fax:* (304) 436-2132
www.welcamfm.com
License: Welch, WV held by Pocahontas Broadcasting Co.
Nat'l Network: AP Radio *Regional Reps:* Rgnl Reps.; *Wire Services:* AP
Arbitron Metro Market: Welch, WV; *Format:* Adult Contemp
Special Programming: Relg 15 hrs wkly; *No. News Employees:* 2; *Target Audience:* 21-54.; *Adv. Rates:* 6.50; 6.50; 6.50; 6.50
Laura Green, Operations Dir
Rick Lambert, Station Manager
Rod O'dell, General Sales Mgr
Bob Spencer, Member/Manager

West Liberty

***WGLZ**
09-04-1990; 91.5 MHz FM; 0.15 kw; 213 ft.; N40 9 49 W80 36 6
West Liberty University, 208 University Drive, CU Box 143, West Liberty, WV 26074 US
(304) 336-8508
www.westliberty.edu/wglz
wglz@westliberty.edu
License: West Liberty, Ohio County, WV held by West Liberty State College.
Format: Alternative
Christian Lee, Station Manager
Kali Davis, General Station Manager
Megan Jones, Operations Director
Kevin Powell, On-Air Promotions
Kevin Childers, Off-Air Promotions

West Union

***WVGV**
89.7 MHz FM; 2.35 kw; 395 ft.; N39 17 22 W80 48 16
Mailing Address: 104 Sisterville Pike (Route 18N), West Union, WV 26456 US
Second Address: PO Box 301, West Union, WV 26456
(304) 873-2225
www.wvgvradio.com
License: West Union, Doddridge County, WV held by Araiza Revival Ministries Inc.
Arbitron Metro Market: West Union, WV; *Format:* Gospel
Oliver Araiza, President

Weston

WFBY
08-29-1972; 102.3 MHz FM; *Hrs Open:* 24; 10 kw; 509 ft.; N39 1 27 W80 19 16
1065 Radio Park Dr., Mount Claire, WV 26408 US
(304) 623-6546; *Fax:* (304) 623-6547
www.wfby.com
License: Weston, Lewis County, WV held by AJG Corporation
Group Owner: West Virginia Radio Corp.; (acq 1994; $250,000)
Nat'l Network: WWO; MRN
Arbitron Metro Market: Weston, WV; *Format:* Classic Rock; *Target Audience:* 25-44.
Dale Miller, President

Westover

WZST
01-05-1983; 100.9 MHz FM; 3 kw; 266 ft.; N39 32 44 W79 55 58
15 Campbell Street, Luray, VA 22835 US
(304) 292-1101; *Fax:* (304) 366-3706
License: Westover, Monongalia County, WV held by Spectrum Radio Fairmont LLC
Group Owner: Spectrum Radio Group LLC; (acq 6-27-2008; $750,000)
Arbitron Metro Market: Fairmont, WV; *Format:* Adult Contemp
Special Programming: Relg mus 2 hrs wkly
Dick Yoder, General Manager
Bill Dunn, Sales Manager
Mike Donota, Programming Director

Wheeling

WBBD
05-02-1941; 1400 kHz AM; *Hrs Open:* 24; 1 kw-U, ND1; N40 5 49 W80 42 6
1015 Main St., Wheeling, WV 26003 US
(304) 232-1170; *Fax:* (304) 234-0041
www.foxsports1400wheeling.com
License: Wheeling, WV held by Capstar TX LLC
Group Owner: iHeartMedia; (acq 8-30-00; grpsl).
Arbitron Metro Market: Wheeling, WV; *Format:* Sports
Chuck Poet, Market President
Jim Elliott, Senior Vice President of Programming
Scott Deel, Director of Sales
Ken Andrews, Production Director

WEGW
10-01-1966; 107.5 MHz FM; *Hrs Open:* 24; 16 kw; 883 ft.; N40 3 41 W80 45 9
1015 Main Street, Wheeling, WV 26003 US
(304) 232-1107
www.eagle1075.com
License: Wheeling, Ohio County, WV held by Capstar TX LLC
Group Owner: iHeartMedia; (acq 8-30-00; grpsl).
Arbitron Metro Market: Wheeling, WV; *Format:* Rock/AOR; *Target Audience:* 25-54.
Bill Kelly, Regional President
Jim Davis, Regional Senior Vice President of Programming
Chuck Poet, Market President
Scott Deel, Director of Sales
Jim Elliott, Senior Vice President of Programming
Ken Andrews, ProductionDirector

WKWK-FM
03-17-1948; 97.3 MHz FM; *Hrs Open:* 24; 50 kw; 420 ft.; N40 5 49 W80 42 6
1015 Main Street, Wheeling, WV 26003 US
(304) 232-1170; *Fax:* (304) 234-0041
www.mix973wheeling.com
License: Wheeling, Ohio County, WV held by Capstar TX LLC
Group Owner: iHeartMedia
Arbitron Metro Market: Wheeling, WV; *Format:* Adult Contemp; *Target Audience:* 25-54.
Chuck Poet, Market President
Scott Deel, Director of Sales
Jim Elliott, Senior Vice President of Programming
Ken Andrews, Production Director

WKKX
04-07-1963; 1600 kHz AM; 5 kw-D, ND1; 0.033 kw-N, ND1; N40 5 26 W80 42 11
1201 Main Street, Wheeling, WV 26003 US
(304) 214-1610; *Fax:* 304-214-1610
www.watchdognetwork.com
License: Wheeling, WV held by RCK 1 Group LLC
Nat'l Network: ESPN Radio; *Nat'l Reps:* Christal
Arbitron Metro Market: Wheeling, WV *TV Affiliate:* Sports talk; *No. News Employees:* 25-54; men
Eirc Belancic, Sales Manager

WOVK
09-01-1947; 98.7 MHz FM; 50 kw; 390 ft.; N40 4 58 W80 46 18
1015 Main St., Wheeling, WV 26003 US
(304) 232-1170; *Fax:* (304) 234-0041
www.wovk.com
License: Wheeling, Ohio County, WV held by Capstar TX LLC
Group Owner: iHeartMedia
Arbitron Metro Market: Wheeling, WV; *Format:* Country
Chuck Poet, Market President
Jim Elliott, Senior Vice President of Programming
Scott Deel, Director of Sales
Ken Andrews, Production Director
Bill Kelly, Regional President
Jim Davis, Regional Senior Vice President ofProgramming

***WPHP**
04-04-1977; 91.9 MHz FM; 0.1 kw horiz; 259 ft.; N40 4 7 W80 39 4
1976 Park View Road, Wheeling, WV 26003 US
(304) 243-0400; *Fax:* (304) 243-0449
License: Wheeling, Ohio County, WV held by Ohio County Board of Education.
Arbitron Metro Market: Wheeling, WV; *Format:* Contemporary Hits/Top 40 *Special Programming:* Black 4 hrs, jazz one hr wkly
Carolyn Ihlenfeld, General Manager

***WVNP**
10-07-1981; 89.9 MHz FM; *Hrs Open:* 24; 25 kw; 499 ft.; N40 12 58 W80 33 31
600 Capitol Street, Charleston, WV 25301 US
(304) 556-4900; *Fax:* (888) 596-9729
www.wvpubcast.org
License: Wheeling, Ohio County, WV held by West Virginia Educational Broadcasting Authority.
Nat'l Network: NPR; PRI
Arbitron Metro Market: Wheeling, WV; *Format:* Jazz, News
Scott Finn, Executive Director/CEO
Suzanne Higgins, Sr. Producer
Bob Powell, Operations Dir
Beth Vorhees, Director of News and Public Affairs

WWVA
12-01-1926; 1170 kHz AM; 50 kw-D, DAN; 50 kw-N, DAN; N40 6 7 W80 52 2
1015 Main Street, Wheeling, WV 26003 US
(304) 232-1170; *Fax:* (304) 234-0041
www.newsradio1170.com
License: Wheeling, WV held by Capstar TX LLC
Group Owner: iHeartMedia; (acq 8-30-00; grpsl)
Nat'l Reps: McGavren Guild
Arbitron Metro Market: Wheeling, WV; *Format:* News, News/Talk, 86 *Special Programming:* Farm 2 hrs wkly; *Target Audience:* 25-54.
Chuck Poet, Market President
Jim Elliott, Senior Vice President of Programming
Scott Deel, Director of Sales
Ken Andrews, Production Director
Bill Kelly, Regional President
Jim Davis, Regional Senior Vice President ofProgramming

White Sulphur Spring

WSLW
01-01-1971; 1310 kHz AM; *Hrs Open:* 6 AM-sunset; 5 kw-D, NDD; N37 48 17 W80 21 3
Mailing Address: P.O. Box 610, White Sulphur Spring, WV 24986 US
Second Address: Rt. 60 W. Harts Run, Ronceverte, WV 24986
(304) 536-1310; *Fax:* (304) 536-1311
www.wron.com
License: White Sulphur Spring, WV held by Radio Greenbrier LLC
Group Owner: Radio Greenbrier LLC; (acq 4-20-2005; grpsl).
Nat'l Reps: Rgnl Reps
Format: Sports; *Hrs. of News Programming:* News progmg 8 hrs wkly; *Target Audience:* 16-25 (60 plus).; *Adv. Rates:* 6.50; 6.50; 6.50; na
Joyce Tucker, General Manager
Mike Kidd, Station Manager
Larry Carver, Chief Engineer
Roy Jarrell, Production Manager

Williamson

WBTH
04-19-1939; 1400 kHz AM; 1 kw-U; N37 40 09 W82 16 09
1240 Radio Drive, PO Box 2200, Pikeville, KY 41502 US
(606) 437-4051; *Fax:* (606) 432-2809
www.900wlsi.com
License: Williamson, Mingo County, WV held by East Kentucky Broadcasting.
Group Owner: East Kentucky Broadcasting.; acq 4-4-00; $630,000 with co-located FM).
Population Served: 70,000 *Format:* News/Talk, Sports; *Target Audience:* 25-54.
Cindy May Johnson, General Manager

WXCC
10-27-1978; 96.5 MHz FM; 75 kw; 1112 ft.; N37 30 48 W82 15 20
1240 Radio Drive, PO Box 2200, Pikeville, KY 41502 US
(606) 437-4051; *Fax:* (606) 432-2809
www.wxccfm.com
License: Williamson, Mingo County, WV held by East Kentucky Radio Network, Inc.
Group Owner: East Kentucky Broadcasting Corp.
Regional Network: Ky. News Net
Arbitron Metro Market: Williamson, WV; *Format:* Country
Walter.E.May, Owner & CEO
Cindy May Johnson, President/General Manager
Kim Little, General Sales Mgr

Williamstown

WVVV
01-01-2000; 96.9 MHz FM; 3.5 kw; 423 ft.; N39 20 18 W81 30 1
1627 Rosemar Road, Parkersburg, WV 26105 US
(304) 295-3100; *Fax:* (304) 684-9241
www.v969radio.net
samyoho@v969radio.net
License: Williamstown, Wood County, WV held by Seven Ranges Radio Co., Inc.
Arbitron Metro Market: Parkersburg, WV; *Format:* Variety/Diverse
Sam Yoho, General Manager
Jack Horton, Programming Director
Tom Taggart, Chief Engineer
Scott Northcraft, Operations Manager

Wisconsin

Adams

WDKM
10-08-1993; 106.1 MHz FM; *Hrs Open:* 24; 6 kw; 328 ft.; N43 57 29 W89 49 43
Mailing Address: 408 Hillwood Lane, Friendship, WI 53934 US
Second Address: 1040 W. Center St., Adams, WI 53910
(608) 339-3221; *Fax:* (608) 339-2403
www.wdkmfm.com
License: Adams, Adams County, WI held by Roche-A-Cri Broadcasting.
Arbitron Metro Market: Wisconsin Dells, WI; *Format:* Contemporary Hits/Top 40, Adult Contemp *Special Programming:* Polka 14 hrs wkly
Heidi Roekle, General Manager
Drew Smith, Station Manager

***WHAA**
89.1 MHz FM; 28.5 kw; 581 ft.; N44 1 13 W89 33 31
821 University Avenue, Madison, WI 53706 US
(608) 263-3970; *Fax:* (608) 263-9763
www.wpr.org
listener@wpr.org
License: Adams, Adams County, WI held by State of Wisconsin-Educational Communications Board.
Arbitron Metro Market: Adams, WI; *Format:* Talk
Phil Corriveau, General Manager
Michael Leland, News Director
Allen Rieland, Chief Engineer
Mike Crane, Director of Radio
Michael Arnold, Associate Director of Radio
Mary Kay Dadisman, Director of Development
Steve Johnston,Director of Engineering & Operations
Sheryl Gasser, Ideas Network Director
David Hyland, Director of Online Content

Algoma

WBDK
11-12-1986; 96.7 MHz FM; *Hrs Open:* 24; 8 kW; 538 ft.; N44 42 26 W87 24 26
30 N 18th Ave, Suite 8, Sturgeon Bay, WI 54235 USA
(920) 746-9430; *Fax:* (920) 746-9433
www.doorcountrydailynews.com
wbdk@doorcountrydailynews.com
License: Algoma, Kewaunee County, WI held by Nicolet Broadcasting Inc.
Group Owner: Nicolet Broadcasting Inc.; acq 9-3-93;
Arbitron Metro Market: Green Bay, WI; *Format:* Easy Listening, Country

WRLU
08-01-1999; 104.1 MHz FM; 2.4 kW; 518 ft.; N44 42 26 W87 24 26
30 N 18th Ave, Suite 8, Sturgeon Bay, WI 54235 USA
(920) 746-9430; *Fax:* (920) 746-9433
www.doorcountydailynews.com
wbdk@doorcountydailynews.com
License: Algoma, Kewaunee County, WI held by Nicolet Broadcasting Inc.
Group Owner: Nicolet Broadcasting Inc.
Arbitron Metro Market: Green Bay, WI; *Format:* Country; *Hrs. of News Programming:* News progmg 3 hrs wkly

Allouez

WKRU
01-01-1996; 106.7 MHz FM; *Hrs Open:* 24; 25 kw; Ant 328 ft; N44 29 03 W87 56 12
810 Victoria St., Green Bay, WI 53202
(920) 468-4100; *Fax:* (920) 468-0250
www.wkrufm.com
License: Allouez, Brown County, WI held by Cumulus Licensing LLC
Nat'l Network: Talk Radio Network; *Nat'l Reps:* Katz Radio
Population Served: 832,000; *Arbitron Metro Market:* Green Bay, WI; *Hrs. of News Programming:* news progmg 5 hrs wkly; *No. News Employees:* 1; *Target Audience:* 18-49; educated, 65/35 male skew; *Adv. Rates:* 50;50; 50; 20
Mike Thompson, Market Manager
Candace Straeble, General Sales Manager
Max, Programming Director

Altoona

WISM
11-15-1991; 98.1 MHz FM; *Hrs Open:* 24; 25 kW; 276 ft.; N44 46 38 W91 28 29
944 Harlem St, Altoona, WI 54720 USA
(715) 832-1530
greatesthits981.com
License: Altoona, Eau Claire County, WI held by Mid-West Management, Inc.
Group Owner: Mid-West Family Broadcasting; 2016, $970K
Nat'l Reps: Clear Channel
Arbitron Metro Market: Eau Claire, WI; *Format:* Oldies *Special Programming:* Christmas; *No. News Employees:* 2; *Target Audience:* 25-54.; *Adv. Rates:* 25; 25; 25; 15
Luc Anthony, Promotion Director

Amery

WXCE
01-23-1978; 1260 kHz AM; *Hrs Open:* 5 AM-noon; 5 kw-D, DA2; 5 kw-N, DA2; N45 15 25 W92 22 0
PO Box 9115, Fargo, ND 58106 US
(715) 268-7185; *Fax:* (715) 268-7187
www.radioredzone.com
License: Amery, WI held by Red Rock Radio Corp.
Nat'l Network: ABC; *Regional Network:* Tribune Radio Networks; Wisconsin Radio Net.
Format: News, News/Talk, 86; *Hrs. of News Programming:* news progmg 20 hrs wkly; *No. News Employees:* 1; *Target Audience:* 35 plus.; *Adv. Rates:* 9.50; 9.50; 9.50; na
Kathy Lau, CEO

Antigo

WACD
01-01-1998; 106.1 MHz FM; 10 kw; 276 ft.; N45 6 23 W89 9 9
N 2237 US Highway 45 South, Antigo, WI 54409 US
(715) 623-4124; *Fax:* (715) 627-4497
www.country106.fm
country106@gmail.com
License: Antigo, Langlade County, WI held by Results Broadcasting Inc.
Group Owner: Results Broadcasting; (acq 4-29-2005; $500,000 with WATK(AM) Antigo).
Arbitron Metro Market: Medford-Ashland OR
Bruce Grassman, General Manager

WATK
03-15-1948; 900 kHz AM; *Hrs Open:* 24; 0.25 kw-D, ND1; 0.195 kw-N, ND1; N45 6 23 W89 9 9
N 2237 US Highway 45 South, Antigo, WI 54409 US
(715) 623-4124; *Fax:* (715) 627-4497
www.watkantigo.com/
country106@gmail.com
License: Antigo, WI held by Results Broadcasting Inc.
Group Owner: Results Broadcasting; (acq 4-29-2005; $500,000 with WACD(FM) Antigo).
Nat'l Network: Jones Radio Networks
Arbitron Metro Market: Antigo,WI; *Format:* Adult Contemp
Special Programming: Gospel 2 hrs wkly; *Hrs. of News Programming:* news progmg 12 hrs wkly; *No. News Employees:* 2; *Target Audience:* 25-59; two-incomefamilies
Duff Damos, Operations Dir
Tom Hopfensperger, General Manager
Shaughn Novy, General Sales Mgr
Dave St. Peter, Programming Director
Cliff Groth, Chief Engineer

WRLO-FM
11-11-1973; 105.3 MHz FM; *Hrs Open:* 24; 100 kw; 541 ft.; N45 22 4 W89 8 20
3616 Highway 47 N, Rhinelander, WI 54501 US
(715) 362-1975; *Fax:* (715) 362-1973
www.wrlo.com
License: Antigo, Langlade County, WI held by NRG License Sub. LLC.
Group Owner: NRG Media LLC; (acq 10-31-2005; grpsl)
Format: Classic Rock; *Target Audience:* 25-54; *Adv. Rates:* 33; 30; 32; 11
Duff Damos, Operations Dir
Steve Albertson, General Sales Mgr

Appleton

WAPL
12-24-1965; 105.7 MHz FM; *Hrs Open:* 24; 100 kw; 1175 ft.; N44 21 32 W87 59 7
PO Box 1519, Appleton, WI 54912 US
(920) 281-ROCK
www.wapl.com
waplstudio@wcinet.com
License: Appleton, Outagamie County, WI held by Woodward Communications Inc.
Group Owner: Woodward Communications Inc.; (acq 3-75)
Nat'l Reps: McGavren Guild; *Wire Services:* AP
Arbitron Metro Market: Appleton, WI; *Format:* Rock/AOR; *Hrs. of News Programming:* News progmg 2 hrs wkly; *Target Audience:* 20-plus; professional & semi-professional adults
Greg Bell, General Manager
Elwood, Programming Director
Roxanne Steele, Promotions Director
Borna Velic, Music Director
Kelly Randandt, Sales Manager

***WEMI**
01-01-1994; 91.9 MHz FM; *Hrs Open:* 24; 3.1 kw; Ant 328 ft; N44 15 17 W88 26 13
1909 W. 2nd St., Appleton, WI 54914
(920) 749-9364; *Fax:* (920) 749-0474
License: Appleton, Outagamie County, WI held by Evangel Ministries Inc.
Group Owner: Evangel Ministries Inc.
Nat'l Network: Moody; Salem Radio Network
Population Served: 300,000; *Arbitron Metro Market:* Appleton-Oshkosh, WI; *Hrs. of News Programming:* News progmg 10 hrs wkly; *No. News Employees:* 14; *Target Audience:* 25-54; women; *Adv. Rates:* 240; 204; 240;204
Peggy Ament, Chairman
Paul Cameron, General Manager
Andy Kilgar, General Sales Mgr
Terry Michaels, Programming Director
Bill Moede, Chief Engineer
Andy Kilgas, Sales Director

***WOVM**
03-10-1956; 91.1 MHz FM; *Hrs Open:* 5 AM-midnight; 3.6 kw; 417 ft.; N44 15 37 W88 22 0
2800 Riverside Drive, Green Bay, WI 54301 US
(920) 271-2700
www.avenueradio.com
License: Appleton, Outagamie County, WI held by Music That Matters Inc.
Group Owner: Relevant Radio; (acq 9-20-2005; $300,000)
Arbitron Metro Market: Appleton-Oshkosh, WI; *Format:* Adult Contemp
Rob Moore, President/CEO

WSCO
01-01-1952; 1570 kHz AM; *Hrs Open:* 24 hrs; 1 kw-D, ND1; 0.331 kw-N, ND1; N44 13 4 W88 24 33
Mailing Address: 2800 East College Avenue, Appleton, WI 54915 US
Second Address: 801 Hoffman Road, Suite 114, Green Bay, WI 54301
(920) 734-9226; *Fax:* (920) 739-0494
www.953wsco.com
License: Appleton, WI held by Woodward Communications Inc.
Group Owner: Woodward Communications Inc.; acq 12-3-01; $450,000).
Nat'l Network: Fox Sports; Sporting News Radio Network
Arbitron Metro Market: Appleton-Oshkosh, WI; *Format:* Sports; *Target Audience:* 25-54; Male
Mike Wolf, Corporate Director of Programming
Greg Bell, General Manager
John Wanie, Sales Manager
Skip Hunter, Corporate Director of Engineering
Dan Wheeler, VP/General Manager
Steve Brown, Chief Engineer

Ashland

WATW
05-01-1940; 1400 kHz AM; *Hrs Open:* 24; 0.78 kw-U, ND1; N46 34 25 W90 51 56
2320 Ellis Ave., Ashland, WI 54806 US
(715) 682-2727; *Fax:* (715) 682-9338
www.watwam.com
sjaegergm@chareter.net
License: Ashland, WI held by Heartland Communications License LLC.
Group Owner: Heartland Communications Group LLC; (acq 4-23-2004; grpsl).
Nat'l Network: ABC
Arbitron Metro Market: Ashland, WI; *Format:* News/Talk *Special Programming:* Relg 5 hrs wkly; *Hrs. of News Programming:* news progmg 17 hrs wkly; *No. News Employees:* 1; *Target Audience:* 40 plus; middle toupper income adults
Scott Jaeger, General Manager

WBSZ
07-25-1994; 93.3 MHz FM; *Hrs Open:* 24; 71 kw; 246 ft.; N46 34 25 W90 51 56
2320 Ellis Ave., Ashland, WI 54806 US
(715) 682-2727; *Fax:* (715) 292-2619
www.wbszfm.com
License: Ashland, Ashland County, WI held by Heartland Communications License LLC.
Group Owner: Heartland Communications Group LLC; (acq 4-23-2004; grpsl).
Nat'l Network: ABC; Westwood One
Arbitron Metro Market: Ashland, WI; *Format:* Country; *Target Audience:* 18-49.
Scott Jaeger, General Manager
Skip Hunter, Programming Director

WJJH
08-01-1970; 96.7 MHz FM; *Hrs Open:* 24; 50 kw; 246 ft.; N46 34 25 W90 51 56
2320 Ellis Ave., Ashland, WI 54806 US
(715) 682-2727; *Fax:* (715) 292-2619
www.wjjhfm.com
License: Ashland, Ashland County, WI held by Heartland Communications License LLC
Group Owner: Heartland Communications Group LLC
Nat'l Network: ABC
Format: Classic Rock; *Target Audience:* 25-45.
Scott Jaeger, General Manager
Skip Hunter, Programming Director

***WUWS**
90.9 MHz FM; 24.5 kw; 231 ft.; N46 36 28 W90 50 13
821 University Avenue, Madison, WI 53706 US
(608) 263-3970; *Fax:* (608) 263-9763
www.wpr.org
Listener@wpr.org
License: Ashland, Ashland County, WI held by Board of Regents of the University of Wisconsin System.
Arbitron Metro Market: Ashland, OR
Mary Kay Dadismon, Development Director
Susan Oman, Director, Finance
Lisa Balbandian, Milwaukee Regional Manager
John Gaddo, La Crosse Regional Manager
Rick Reyer, Wausau Regional Manager
Dean Kallenbach, Senior RegionalManager

Auburndale

***WLBL**
01-01-1922; 930 kHz AM; *Hrs Open:* Sunrise-sunset
3319 W. Beltline Hwy., Madison, WI 53713 US
(715) 261-6298; *Fax:* (715) 848-28
www.wpr.org
listener@wpr.org
License: Auburndale, WI held by State of Wisconsin, Education Communications Board.
Nat'l Network: NPR; PRI
Format: Adult Contemp, News, 62, Talk; *No. News Employees:* 4
Phil Corriveau, General Manager
Rick Reyer, Station Manager

Baileys Harbor

WLGE
04-26-2008; 106.9 MHz FM; 6 kw; 184 ft.; N45 3 14 W87 8 37
10331 N Water Street, Ephram, WI 54211 US
(920) 854-3400; *Fax:* (800) 799-7143
www.fm1069thelodge.com
License: Baileys Harbor, Door County, WI held by Michael J. Mesic.
Arbitron Metro Market: Baileys Harbor, WI; *Format:* Triple A
Mike Mesic, President
Michael Mesic, General Manager
Carrie Mesic, Vice President
Martha Scully Beller, Business Development Manager
Jaime Forest, Marketing Advisor and Creative Director
Chrystal Kugle, Marketing Advisor
MeghanHolly, Office Manager/Promotions Manager

Baldwin

WDMO
10-24-1973; 95.7 MHz FM; 4 kw; 407 ft.; N44 56 33 W92 24 59
Box 190, Hwy 63 S, Shell Lake, WI 54871 US
(715) 468-9500
www.thunder959.com
License: Baldwin, Pepin County, WI held by Zoe Communications Inc.
Group Owner: Zoe Communications Inc.; (acq 7-31-2001; with co-located AM).
Format: Country
Bo Landry, Operations Dir

Balsam Lake

WLMX-FM
02-14-1997; 104.9 MHz FM; 22 kw; 348 ft.; N45 29 27 W92 11 32
Mailing Address: PO Box 1260, Amery, WI 54001 US
Second Address: 328 100th St., Amery, WI 54001
(715) 268-7185; *Fax:* (715) 268-7187
www.radio715.com
info@radio715.com
License: Balsam Lake, Polk County, WI held by Red Rock Radio Corp.
Group Owner: Red Rock Radio Corp.; (acq 9-1-2006; grpsl)
Nat'l Network: ABC; *Regional Network:* Wisconsin Radio Net.
Arbitron Metro Market: Balsam Lake, WI; *Format:* Country; *Hrs. of News Programming:* News progmg 5 hrs wkly; *Target Audience:* 18-49; adults
Tom Stocker, General Manager
Marcia Clark, Business/Traffic Manager

Baraboo

WOLX-FM
03-03-1946; 94.9 MHz FM; 37 kw; 1299 ft.; N43 25 40 W89 39 14
7601 Ganser Wy, Madison, WI 53719 US
(608) 826-0077; *Fax:* 608-826-1245
www.wolx.com
info@wolx.com
License: Baraboo, Sauk County, WI held by Entercom Madison Licensee LLP.
Group Owner: Entercom Communications Corp.; (acq 7-10-00; grpsl)
Nat'l Reps: Christal
Arbitron Metro Market: Madison, WI *TV Affiliate:* Oldies; *Format:* Classic Rock *Special Programming:* news progmg 2 hrs wkly; *Hrs. of News Programming:* 2; *No. News Employees:* 25-54.
David Field, President/CEO
Steve Fisher, EVP/CFO
Weezie Kramer, Station Group President
Pat Paxton, President, Programming
Deborah Kane, President, Sales
Michael Doyle, Regional President
Andrew Sutor, Senior VP/GeneralCounsel
Operations Manager

WRPQ
06-01-1967; 740 kHz AM; *Hrs Open:* 24; 0.25 kw-D, ND1; 0.006 kw-N, ND1; N43 27 19 W89 45 13
407 Oak Street, PO Box #456, Baraboo, IL 53913 US
(608) 356-3974; *Fax:* (608) 355-9952
www.wrpq.com
wrpqtv43@wrpq.com
License: Baraboo, WI held by Baraboo Broadcasting Co.
Nat'l Network: CNN Radio; *Regional Network:* Wisconsin Radio Net.
TV Affiliate: W43BR; *Format:* Adult Contemp *Special Programming:* Relg 5 hrs wkly; *Hrs. of News Programming:* news progmg 8 hrs wkly; *No. News Employees:* 1; *Target Audience:* 25-54.; *Adv. Rates:* 8; 8;8; 8
Jeff Smith, President
Brian Sparks, Director, Sales

Barron

WAQE-FM
01-01-1999; 97.7 MHz FM; 15.5 kw; 289 ft.; N45 32 16 W91 45 50
1859 21st Avenue, Rice Lake, WI 54868 US
(715) 234-9059; *Fax:* (715) 234-6942
www.waqe.com
info@waqe.com
License: Barron, Barron County, WI held by TKC Inc.
Hrs. of News Programming: news progmg 5 hrs wkly; *No. News Employees:* 1; *Target Audience:* 25-54; general; *Adv. Rates:* 12; 8; 10; 6
Tom Koser, General Manager
Brian Schultz, Station Manager
Sondra Maanum, News Director

Beaver Dam

WBEV
03-21-1951; 1430 kHz AM; *Hrs Open:* 24; 1 kw-D, DAN; 1 kw-N, DAN; N43 25 43 W88 53 33
100 Bill McCollum Way, Beaver Dam, WI 53916 US
(920) 885-4442; *Fax:* (920) 885-2152
dailydodge.com
License: Beaver Dam, WI held by Good Karma Broadcasting L.L.C.
Group Owner: Good Karma Broadcasting L.L.C.; acq 12-2-97; grpsl).
Wire Services: Wheeler News Service
Arbitron Metro Market: Beaver Dam, WI; *Format:* Adult Contemp, News, 62, Talk *Special Programming:* Farm 8 hrs, sports 18 hrs wkly; *Hrs. of News Programming:* news progmg 20 hrs wkly; *No. News Employees:* 3 *Target Audience:* 30 plus; general

WXRO
07-15-1968; 95.3 MHz FM; *Hrs Open:* 24; 6 kw; 328 ft.; N43 28 9 W88 49 32
100 Bill McCollum Way, Beaver Dam, WI 53916 US
(920) 885-4442; *Fax:* (920) 885-2152
dailydodge.com
License: Beaver Dam, Dodge County, WI held by Good Karma Broadcasting
Group Owner: Good Karma Broadcasting L.L.C.
Wire Services: Wheeler News Service
Arbitron Metro Market: Beaver Dam, WI; *Format:* Country *Special Programming:* Farm 6 hrs wkly; *Hrs. of News Programming:* news progmg 10 hrs wkly; *No. News Employees:* 3; *Target Audience:* 25-54; general

Beloit

***WBCR-FM**
11-30-1965; 90.3 MHz FM; 0.13 kw; 59 ft.; N42 30 13 W89 1 55
700 College St., Beloit, WI 53511 US
(608) 363-2402; *Fax:* (870) 363-2718
www.beloit.edu/wber
wbcrmanager@gmail.com
License: Beloit, Rock County, WI held by Beloit College.
Arbitron Metro Market: Las Vegas NV; *Format:* Adult Contemp
Bradford Caldwell, General Manager
Francesca Alfano, Station Manager
Maureen Johnson, Station Manager
Mac Calvert, Programming Director

WGEZ
09-26-1948; 1490 kHz AM; *Hrs Open:* 24; 1 kw-U, ND1; N42 29 45 W89 1 3
622 Public Avenue, Beloit, WI 53511 US
(608) 365-8865; *Fax:* (608) 365-8867
wgezam@hotmail.com
License: Beloit, WI held by Alliance Communications Inc.
Nat'l Network: ABC Music Radio; AP Network News; *Regional Network:* Brownfield; Wisconsin Radio Net.
Arbitron Metro Market: Rockford, IL; *Format:* Oldies; *No. News Employees:* 1; *Target Audience:* 25-54; baby boomers
Alan Kearns, General Manager
Keith Salerno, General Sales Mgr
Carla Cornell, News Director

Berlin

WBJZ
07-31-1972; 104.7 MHz FM; *Hrs Open:* 24; 5.2 kw; 351 ft.; N43 53 57 W88 53 37
3911 S. Washburn Street, Oshkosh, WI 54904 US
(920) 230-1047; *Fax:* (208)906-8536
www.b104online.com/
License: Berlin, Green Lake County, WI held by Caxambas Corp.
Arbitron Metro Market: Oshkosh, WI; *Format:* Adult Contemp; *Target Audience:* 35-54; upscale, adults; *Adv. Rates:* 15; 15; 15; 12
Marty Schibbelhut, President
Mike Enfelt, General Manager
Alex Mason, Programming Director
Amber Sanders, Marketing Consultant
Lynne Schibbelhut, Vice President
Amber Disterhaft, Director, Engineering

WISS
06-28-1971; 1100 kHz AM; *Hrs Open:* Sunrise-sunset
PO Box 71, 156 Huron Street, Berlin, WI 54923 US
(920) 361-3551; *Fax:* (866) 594-4698
www.wissradio.com
production@hometownbroadcasting.com
License: Berlin, WI held by Hometown Broadcasting LLC
Format: Country, Oldies; *Hrs. of News Programming:* news progmg 10 hrs wkly; *No. News Employees:* 1; *Target Audience:* 25-54; local community
Tom Boyson, Owner
Joann Boyson, Owner
Bernie Phillips, General Manager
Jean Hoffmann, Traffic/Billing

Birnamwood

WYNW
01-01-2003; 92.9 MHz FM; 6 kw; 328 ft.; N44 59 50 W89 22 7
Mailing Address: 1496 Bellevue Street, Suite 202, Green Bay, WI 54311 US
Second Address: PO Box 10707, Green Bay, WI 54307-0707
(920) 884-1460; *Fax:* (920) 465-9986
www.relevantradio.com
info@relevantradio.com
License: Birnamwood, Shawano County, WI held by Starboard Media Foundation Inc.
Group Owner: Relevant Radio; (acq 7-9-2002).
Arbitron Metro Market: Green Bay, WI; *Format:* Christian
Thomas Vorpahl, Chairman
Mike Strub, Station Manager
Rev. Francis J. Hoffman, JCD, Executive Director
Amy Vanden Langenberg, Chief Financial Officer
Nancy Jensen, Chief Marketing Officer
Mike Kendall, Chief Programming Officer
Bob Benes, Chief Sales Officer

Black River Falls

WWIS
08-23-1958; 1260 kHz AM; *Hrs Open:* 6 AM-sunset; 0.58 kw-D, NDD; N44 19 11 W90 53 31
Route 1, Box 279a, Black River Falls, WI 54615 US
(715) 284-4391; *Fax:* (715) 284-9740
www.wwisradio.com
wwis@wwisradio.com
License: Black River Falls, WI held by WWIS Radio Inc.
Nat'l Network: CBS Radio; *Regional Network:* Brownfield; *Wire Services:* Wheeler News Service
Arbitron Metro Market: Black River Falls, WI; *Format:* Oldies; *Hrs. of News Programming:* News progmg 6 hrs wkly; *Target Audience:* General.; *Adv. Rates:* 8.50; 6.50; 6.50, na
Nelson Lent, Director
Bob Gabrielson, Vice President & General Manager
Tony Hart, News Director
Brian B, Sports Director

WWIS-FM
01-21-1991; 99.7 MHz FM; *Hrs Open:* 24; 25 kw; 328 ft.; N44 19 11 W90 53 31
Route 1 Box 279a, Black River Falls, WI 54615 US
(715) 284-4391; *Fax:* (715) 284-9740
www.wwisradio.com
License: Black River Falls, Jackson County, WI held by WWIS Radio Inc.
Nat'l Network: CBS; *Wire Services:* Wheeler News Service
Arbitron Metro Market: Black River Falls, WI; *Format:* Adult Contemp; *Hrs. of News Programming:* News progmg 12 hrs wkly; *Target Audience:* 25-55.; *Adv. Rates:* 13; 13; 13; 12
Nelson Lent, Director
Bob Gabrielson, Vice President & General Manager
Tony Hart, News Director
Brian B, Sports Director

Bloomer

WQRB
01-01-1993; 95.1 MHz FM; *Hrs Open:* 24; 8.9 kw; 545 ft.; N44 55 44 W91 32 31
619 Cameron Street, Eau Claire, WI 54703 US
(715) 832-2951
www.b95radio.com
License: Bloomer, Chippewa County, WI held by Capstar TX LLC
Group Owner: iHeartMedia; (acq 2000; grpsl)
Nat'l Reps: Clear Channel
Arbitron Metro Market: Eau Claire, WI; *Format:* Country; *No. News Employees:* 2; *Target Audience:* 25-54.
Dave Deville, Operations Manager
Rick Hencley, Market Manager
Bill Sparkes, General Sales Mgr
Mike McKay, Programming Director

Brillion

WDUZ-FM
03-01-1993; 107.5 MHz FM; *Hrs Open:* 24; 3.6 kw; 879 ft.; N44 21 32 W87 59 7
810 Victoria Street, Green Bay, WI 54302 US
(920) 468-4100; *Fax:* (920) 468-0250
www.thefan1075.com
thefan@cumulus.comÿ
License: Brillion, Calumet County, WI held by Cumulus Licensing LLC
Group Owner: Cumulus Media Inc.; (acq 2013)
Nat'l Network: ABC; ESPN Radio; Premiere Radio Networks
Arbitron Metro Market: Green Bay, WI; *Format:* Sports, Talk; *Target Audience.:* 18-49; educated, affluent, upper-income; *Adv. Rates:* 70; 70; 70; 10
Mike Thompson, Market Manager/General Sales Manager
Jimmy Clark, Programming Director

Brule

***WHSA**
09-14-1952; 89.9 MHz FM; *Hrs Open:* 24; 38 kw; 551 ft.; N46 27 59 W91 33 56
821 University Avenue, Madison, WI 53706 US
(715) 394-8530; *Fax:* (715) 394-8404
www.wpr.org
listener@wpr.org
License: Brule, Douglas County, WI held by State of Wisconsin Educational Communications Board.
Nat'l Network: NPR; *Regional Network:* Wis. Public Radio
Arbitron Metro Market: Duluth-Superior, MN-WI; *Format:* News, News/Talk, 86 *Special Programming:* Folk 3 hrs, jazz 6 hrs wkly; *Hrs. of News Programming:* news progmg 39 hrs wkly; *No. News Employees:* 1 *TargetAudience:* 34 plus.
David Hyland, Chief Engineer
Phil Corriveau, General Manager
Michael Leland, News Director
Mike Crane, Director of Radio
Michael Arnold, Associate Director of Radio
Mary Kay Dadisman, Director, Development
Sheryl Gasser, IdeasNetwork Director

Burlington

*WBSD
04-07-1975; 89.1 MHz FM; *Hrs Open:* 24; 0.21 kw; 92 ft.; N42 40 14 W88 16 18
225 Robert Street, Burlington, WI 53105 US
(262) 763-0195
www.wbsdfm.com
music@wbsdfm.com
License: Burlington, Racine County, WI held by Burlington Area School District.
Arbitron Metro Market: Burlington,WI; *Format:* Alternative *Special Programming:* Jazz 8 hrs, reggae 3 hrs, ska/punk 2 hrs, metal one hr, blues 4 hrs, folk 5 hrs wkly; *Hrs. of News Programming:* One; *Target Audience:* 25-54.
Kevin Fay, Station Engineer
Thomas Gilding, General Manager
Eric Burling, Station Administrator
Heather Gilding, Music Director
Alex Nazarkewich, Production Director
Nigel Reed, Assistant to the General Manager

Chetek

WATQ
05-17-1997; 106.7 MHz FM; *Hrs Open:* 24; 35 kw; 584 ft.; N45 11 4 W91 43 52
619 Cameron Street, Eau Claire, WI 54703 US
(715) 830-4000
www.moose106.com
License: Chetek, Barron County, WI held by Capstar TX LLC
Group Owner: iHeartMedia; (acq 2000; grpsl)
Nat'l Network: CNN Radio; *Regional Network:* Brownfield; *Nat'l Reps:* Clear Channel
Arbitron Metro Market: Eau Claire, WI; *Format:* Country; *No. News Employees:* 2; *Target Audience:* 35-64.
Rick Hencley, Vice President/Market Manager
Dave Deville, Operations Manager
Bill Sparkes, General Sales Mgr

Chilton

WKZY
92.9 MHz FM; 5.8 kw; 102 meters; N44 04 22.6 W88 15 24.3
Box 1519, Appleton, WI 54912-1519 US
(920) 831-5655; *Fax:* (536) 588-5739
License: Chilton, Calumet County, WI held by Woodward Communications Inc.
Group Owner: Woodward Communications Inc.
Tom Woodward, President

Chippewa Falls

WCFW
10-20-1968; 105.7 MHz FM; *Hrs Open:* 24; 25 kw; 305 ft.; N44 52 18 W91 17 11
P.O. Box 16, Eau Claire, WI 54702 US
(715) 723-2257; *Fax:* (715) 723-8276
wcfwradio@clearwire.net
License: Chippewa Falls, Chippewa County, WI held by Radio Specialties/WCFW
Wire Services: AP
Arbitron Metro Market: Eau Claire, WI; *Format:* Adult Contemp *Special Programming:* Relg 2 hrs wkly; *Hrs. of News Programming:* News progmg 8 hrs wkly; *Target Audience:* 35 plus; upscale; *Adv. Rates:* 15; 15;15; 10
Roland Bushland, General Manager
Patricia Bushland, General Sales Mgr

WEAQ
09-07-1958; 1150 kHz AM; 5 kW; N44 53 5 W91 23 25
944 Harlem St, Altoona, WI 54720 USA
(715) 832-1530
www.facebook.com/959jamz
License: Chippewa Falls, WI held by Mid-West Management, Inc.
Group Owner: Mid-West Family Broadcasting; (acq 6-13-2003; grpsl).
Nat'l Reps: Katz Radio
Arbitron Metro Market: Eau Claire, WI; *Format:* Contemporary Hits/Top 40, Urban Contemporary

Cleveland

WLKN
04-25-1985; 98.1 MHz FM; *Hrs Open:* 24; 5.8 kw; Ant 292 ft; N43 59 03 W87 45 55
PO Box 26, Cleveland, WI 53015
(920) 693-3103
www.wlkn.com
manager@wlkn.com
License: Cleveland, Manitowoc County, WI held by Seehafer Broadcasting Corp
Wire Services: AP
Population Served: 225,000; *Arbitron Metro Market:* Sheboygan, WI; *Hrs. of News Programming:* news progmg 7 hrs wkly; *No. News Employees:* 1; *Target Audience:* 25-54; active, upscale; *Adv. Rates:* 21; 20; 21; 14
Jack Taddeo, CEO
Don Seehafer, President
Mark Seehafer, Vice President
David Jetzer, Station Manager
Sandi Davis, News Director

Clintonville

WOTE
02-28-1983; 1380 kHz AM; *Hrs Open:* 24
1456 E. Green Bay Street, Shawano, WI 54166 US
(715) 524-2194
www.1380thelounge.com
License: Clintonville, WI held by Results Broadcasting Inc.
Group Owner: Results Broadcasting; (acq 1996)
Nat'l Network: ABC; *Regional Network:* Wisconsin Radio Net.
Arbitron Metro Market: Clintonville, WI; *Format:* Oldies *Special Programming:* Farm 8 hrs wkly; *Hrs. of News Programming:* news progmg 12 hrs wkly; *No. News Employees:* 1; *Target Audience:* 35-64; *Adv. Rates:* 23; 23; 23; 23
Eric Voight, General Manager
Walt Baldwin, Chief Engineer

WJMQ
10-27-1986; 92.3 MHz FM; *Hrs Open:* 24; 6 kw; 299 ft.; N44 34 1 W88 44 33
1456 East Green Bay Street, Shawano, WI 54166 US
(715) 524-2194
www.frogcountry923.com
resultsbroadcasting@gmail.com
License: Clintonville, Waupaca County, WI held by Results Broadcasting Inc.
Group Owner: Results Broadcasting
Arbitron Metro Market: Appleton-Oshkosh, WI; *Format:* Country; *Hrs. of News Programming:* news progmg 12 hrs wkly; *No. News Employees:* 1; *Target Audience:* 18-54; *Adv. Rates:* 23; 23; 23; 23
Eric Voight, Station Manager

Columbus

WTTN
04-02-1950; 1510 kHz AM; *Hrs Open:* 24
15 N. Pinckney St., Madison, WI 53703 US
(608) 245-9859; *Fax:* (608)245-1720
www.espn.com/milwaukee
krovak@goodkarmabrands.com
License: Columbus, WI held by Good Karma Broadcasting L.L.C.
Group Owner: Good Karma Broadcasting L.L.C.; acq 8-26-99; $525,000)
Nat'l Network: CNN Radio; *Wire Services:* Wheeler News Service
Arbitron Metro Market: Madison, WI; *Format:* Oldies *Special Programming:* Relg 4 hrs wkly; *Hrs. of News Programming:* news progmg 15 hrs wkly; *No. News Employees:* 2; *Target Audience:* 25-64. *Adv. Rates:* 18; 15; 15; 15
Ken Rovak, General Manager
Jesse Nelson, Station Manager
Eric Davidson, Director of Partnership Development

Cornell

WDRK
01-01-2001; 99.9 MHz FM; 25 kw; 328 ft.; N45 7 22 W91 24 23
944 Harlem Street, Altoona, WI 54720 US
(715) 832-1530; *Fax:* (715) 832-5329
www.bobfm999.com
rickroberts@midwestfamilyec.com
License: Cornell, Chippewa County, WI held by Blugold Radio LLC
Group Owner: Univeristy of Wisconsin-Eau Claire Foundation, Inc.; (acq 6-13-2003; grpsl).
Arbitron Metro Market: Eau Claire, WI; *Hrs. of News Programming:* news progmg one hr wkly; *No. News Employees:* 1
Dan Gainey, Director of Sales
Rick Roberts, Programming Director

Cross Plains

WMAD
09-18-1964; 96.3 MHz FM; *Hrs Open:* 24; 5.1 kw; 699 ft.; N43 12 44 W89 35 59
2651 S. Fish Hatchery Road, Fitchberg, WI 53711 US
(608) 274-5450
www.963starcountry.com
License: Cross Plains, Sauk County, WI held by Capstar TX LLC
Group Owner: iHeartMedia; (acq 8-30-2000; grpsl).
Nat'l Reps: Christal
Arbitron Metro Market: Madison, WI; *Format:* Country; *Hrs. of News Programming:* news progmg one hr wkly; *No. News Employees:* 1; *Target Audience:* 25-49.
Tim Etes, Senior Vice President of Sales
Katie Kruz, Programming Director

De Forest

WJQM
01-01-2003; 93.1 MHz FM; 5.4 kW; 322 ft.; N43 9 34 W89 12 55
730 Rayovac Dr, Madison, WI 53711 USA
(608) 273-1000
www.madtownjamz.com
License: De Forest, Dane County, WI held by Mid-West Management Inc.
Group Owner: Mid-West Family Broadcasting; (acq 8-13-2002)
Arbitron Metro Market: Madison, WI; *Format:* Contemporary Hits/Top 40, Urban Contemporary

De Pere

WKSZ
10-01-1984; 95.9 MHz FM; *Hrs Open:* 24; 4.5 kw; 774 ft.; N44 21 32 W87 59 7
Mailing Address: 2800 East College Avenue, Appleton, WI 54915 US
Second Address: 801 Hoffman Road, Suite 114, Green Bay, WI 54301
(920) 734-9226; *Fax:* (920) 739-0494
www.959kissfm.com
License: De Pere, Brown County, WI held by Woodward Communications Inc.
Group Owner: Woodward Communications Inc.; acq 1995).
Nat'l Reps: McGavren Guild
Arbitron Metro Market: Green Bay, WI; *Format:* Contemporary Hits/Top 40; *Target Audience:* 18-34; females
Greg Bell, General Manager
Mary Anne Drewek, General Sales Mgr
Dayton Kane, Programming Director
Karli Brooks, Chief Engineer

Delafield

*WHAD
05-30-1948; 90.7 MHz FM; *Hrs Open:* 24; 72 kw; 682 ft.; N43 1 42 W88 23 32 *Rebroadcasts:* Rebroadcasts WHA(AM) Madison 60%
310 West Wisconsin Avenue, Suite 750 E, Milwaukee, WI 53203 US
(414) 227-2040; *Fax:* (414) 227-2043
www.wpr.org
whad@wpr.org
License: Delafield, Waukesha County, WI held by State of Wisconsin Educational Communications Board.
Nat'l Network: NPR
Arbitron Metro Market: Milwaukee-Racine, WI; *Format:* News, News/Talk, 86; *Hrs. of News Programming:* news progmg 11 hrs wkly; *No. News Employees:* 1; *Target Audience:* 35-55; general
Phil Corrireau, General Manager
Michael Leland, News Director
Mike Crane, Director, Radio
Mary Kay Dadisman, Director, Development

Denmark

WPCK
09-01-1969; 104.9 MHz FM; *Hrs Open:* 24; 10 kw; 515 ft.; N44 29 17 W87 45 40
810 Victoria Street, Green Bay, WI 54302 US
(920) 468-4100; *Fax:* (920) 468-0250
www.nashfmwisconsin.com
License: Denmark, Brown County, WI held by Cumulus Licensing LLC
Group Owner: Cumulus Media Inc.; (acq 2013)
Nat'l Reps: Katz Radio
Arbitron Metro Market: Green Bay, WI; *Format:* Country; *Target Audience:* 25-54; adults; *Adv. Rates:* 55; 55; 55; 10
Mike Thompson, Market Manager
John Stiloski, Promotions Director

WGBW
10-29-1951; 1590 kHz AM; *Hrs Open:* 24; 10 kw-D, 500 w-N; N44 18 50 W87 47 16.3
722 Green Bay Rad, Denmark, WI 54208
(920) 863-1234
wgbwradio.com
wgbw@lsol.net

License: Denmark, Brown County, WI held by WTRW Inc.
Nat'l Network: ABC Radio Network News; Westwood One
Population Served: 330,000 *Hrs. of News Programming:* news progmg 10 hrs wkly; *No. News Employees:* 1; *Target Audience:* 35-54; baby boomers & professionals; *Adv. Rates:* 24; 24; 24; 24
Mark Heller, President/General Manager

Dickeyville

WVRE
02-01-2003; 101.1 MHz FM; *Hrs Open:* 24; 3.7 kw; 423 ft.; N42 31 44 W90 36 58
Mailing Address: 1055 University Avenue, Dubuque, IA 52001 US
Second Address: PO Box 659, Dubuque, IA 52004
(563) 690-0800; *Fax:* (563) 588-5688
www.1011theriver.com
theriver@1011theriver.com
License: Dickeyville, Grant County, WI held by Radio Dubuque Inc.
Group Owner: Radio Dubuque Inc.; acq 8-1-01).
Nat'l Reps: International Media; Katz Radio
Arbitron Metro Market: Dickeyville, WI; *Format:* Country; *No. News Employees:* 1; *Target Audience:* Adults; 25-54
Josh Crowell, Programming Director

Dodgeville

WDMP
11-01-1968; 810 kHz AM; *Hrs Open:* 24
2163 Highway 151, PO Box 9, Dodgeville, WI 53523 US
(608) 935-2302; *Fax:* (608) 935-3464
www.d99point3.com
wdmp@mhtc.net
License: Dodgeville, WI held by Dodge-Point Broadcasting Co.
Arbitron Metro Market: Madison, WI; *Format:* Country; *Hrs. of News Programming:* news progmg 5 hrs wkly; *No. News Employees:* 1; *Target Audience:* General.
Kurt Reinicke, General Manager
Michael Anthony, Programming Director

WDMP-FM
11-01-1968; 99.3 MHz FM; *Hrs Open:* 24; 1.55 kw; 459 ft.; N42 55 10 W90 8 6
2163 Highway 151, PO Box 9, Dodgeville, WI 53523 US
(608) 935-2302; *Fax:* (608) 935-3464
www.d99point3.com
wdmp@mhtc.net
License: Dodgeville, Iowa County, WI held by Dodge-Point Broadcasting Co. Inc.
Arbitron Metro Market: Madison, WI; *No. News Employees:* 1
Kurt Reinicke, General Manager
Michael Anthony, Programming Director

Durand

WRDN
11-21-1968; 1430 kHz AM; *Hrs Open:* 18; 2 kw-D, 152 w-N; N44 38 28 W91 55 22
114 West Main Street, Durand, WI 54736
(715) 672-8989
www.reelcountry1430.com
License: Durand, Pepin County, WI held by Durand Broadcasting
Population Served: 2,103; *Arbitron Metro Market:* Eau Claire, WI
Karla Winnekins, Owner
Brian Winnekins, Owner

Eagle River

WERL
05-23-1961; 950 kHz AM; *Hrs Open:* 24; 1 kw-D, ND1; 0.051 kw-N, ND1; N45 58 32 W89 14 44
909 N. Railroad, PO Box 309, Eagle River, WI 54521 US
(715) 479-4451; *Fax:* (715) 479-6511
www.werlam.com
craig@wrjo.com
License: Eagle River, WI held by Heartland Communications License LLC.
Group Owner: Heartland Communications Group LLC; (acq 12-7-2004; $2.2 million with co-located FM).
Arbitron Metro Market: Eagle River, WI; *Format:* News/Talk; *Hrs. of News Programming:* news progmg 7 hrs wkly; *No. News Employees:* 1; *Target Audience:* General.; *Adv. Rates:* 11; 11; 11; na
Craig Whetstine, General Manager

WRJO
07-31-1971; 94.5 MHz FM; *Hrs Open:* 24; 50 kw; 492 ft.; N46 9 57 W89 21 57
909 N. Railroad, PO Box 309, Eagle River, WI 54521 US
(715) 479-4451; *Fax:* (715) 479-6511
www.wrjo.com
info@wrjo.com
License: Eagle River, Vilas County, WI held by Hearland Communications License, LLC
Group Owner: Heartland Communications Group LLC
Format: Oldies; *Adv. Rates:* 21; 21; 21; 16
Craig Whetstine, General Manager

Eau Claire

WAXX
02-01-1965; 104.5 MHz FM; *Hrs Open:* 24; 100 kW; 1801 ft.; N44 39 50 W90 57 40
944 Harlem St, Altoona, WI 54720 USA
(715) 832-1530; *Fax:* (715) 832-5329
waxxradio.com
License: Eau Claire, Eau Claire County, WI held by Mid-West Management Inc.
Group Owner: Mid-West Family Broadcasting
Arbitron Metro Market: Eau Claire, WI; *Format:* Country; *Target Audience:* 25-54
Alex Edwards, Programming Director

WAYY
05-01-1937; 790 kHz AM; *Hrs Open:* 24; 5 kW; N44 49 51 W91 26 58
944 Harlem St, Altoona, WI 54720 USA
(715) 832-1530
wayyradio.com
License: Eau Claire, WI held by Mid-West Management, Inc.
Group Owner: Mid-West Family Broadcasting
Regional Network: Wisconsin Radio Net.
Arbitron Metro Market: Eau Claire, WI; *Format:* Sports

WBIZ
11-11-1947; 1400 kHz AM; *Hrs Open:* 24
619 Cameron Street, Eau Claire, WI 54703 US
(715) 830-4000
www.sportsradio1400.com
davedeville@clearchannel.com
License: Eau Claire, WI held by Capstar TX LLC
Group Owner: iHeartMedia; (acq 2000; grpsl)
Nat'l Network: CBS; *Nat'l Reps:* Clear Channel
Arbitron Metro Market: Eau Claire, WI; *Format:* Sports; *Target Audience:* 25-54.
Rick Hencley, Vice President/Market Manager
Dave Deville, Operations Manager
Bill Sparkes, General Sales Mgr

WBIZ-FM
12-01-1967; 100.7 MHz FM; 100 kw; 482 ft.; N44 55 44 W91 32 31
619 Cameron Street, Eau Claire, WI 54703 US
(715) 830-4000
www.z100radio.com
davedeville@clearchannel.com
License: Eau Claire, Eau Claire County, WI held by Capstar TX LLC
Group Owner: iHeartMedia
Nat'l Reps: Clear Channel
Arbitron Metro Market: Eau Claire, WI; *Format:* Contemporary Hits/Top 40; *Hrs. of News Programming:* 2; *Target Audience:* 18 - 49.
Rick Hencley, Vice President/Market Manager
Dave Deville, Operations Manager
Bill Sparkes, General Sales Mgr

*WDVM
04-01-1948; 1050 kHz AM
Mailing Address: 1496 Believue Street, Suite 202, Green Bay, WI 54311 US
Second Address: PO Box 10707, Green Bay, WI 54307-0707
(920) 884-1460; *Fax:* (920) 465-9986
www.relevantradio.com
info@relevantradio.com
License: Eau Claire, WI held by Starboard Media Foundation Inc.
Group Owner: Relevant Radio; (acq 7-6-2001).
Arbitron Metro Market: Eau Claire, WI; *Format:* Talk, Religious; *No. News Employees:* 1; *Target Audience:* 35 plus; mature adults; *Adv. Rates:* 6; 6; 6; 6
Thomas Vorpahl, Chairman
Rev. Francis Hoffman, Executive Director
Linda Ruff, National Development Director
Mike Kendall, Chief Program Officer
Bob Benes, Chief Sales Officer
Amy Vanden Langenberg, CFO
Nancy Jensen, CMO

*WHEM
08-22-1995; 91.3 MHz FM; *Hrs Open:* 24; 0.3 kw; 285 ft.; N44 45 50 W91 31 6
228 E. Lowes Creek Rd, Eau Claire, WI 54701 US
(715) 838-9595
www.whem.com
whem@whem.com
License: Eau Claire, Eau Claire County, WI held by Fourth Dimension Inc.
Arbitron Metro Market: Eau Claire, WI; *Format:* Christian
Harlan Reinders, General Manager/Engineer
Phyllis Reinders, Programming Director

WIAL
01-01-1948; 94.1 MHz FM; *Hrs Open:* 24; 84 kW; 351 ft.; N44 49 48 W91 26 48
944 Harlem St, Altoona, WI 54720 USA
(715) 832-1530; *Fax:* (715) 832-5329
www.i94online.com
License: Eau Claire, Eau Claire County, WI held by Mid-West Management, Inc.
Group Owner: Mid-West Family Broadcasting
Arbitron Metro Market: Eau Claire, WI; *Format:* Adult Contemp; *No. News Employees:* 1; *Target Audience:* Women 25-54

*WUEC
10-27-1975; 89.7 MHz FM; *Hrs Open:* 24; 5.2 kw; 630 ft; N44 47 58 W91 27 59
Wisconsin Public Radio, 1221 W. Clairemont Ave., Eau Claire, WI 54701
(715) 839-3868
www.wpr.org
listener@wpr.org
License: Eau Claire, Eau Claire County, WI held by Board of Regents, University of Wisconsin.
Nat'l Network: NPR; *Regional Network:* Wis. Public Radio
Population Served: 168,000; *Arbitron Metro Market:* Eau Claire, WI *Special Programming:* Folk 3 hrs, blues 3 hrs wkly; *Hrs. of News Programming:* News progmg 24 hrs wkly; *Target Audience:* General.
Dean Kallenbach, Regional Manager
Steve Johnston, Chief Engineer
Jeff Potter, Director, Marketing
Susan Oman, Director, Finance
Sheryl Gasser, Director, Ideas Network
Peter Bryant, NPR News/Classical Programming Director
MichaelLeland, Director, News
Mary Kay Dadisman, Director, Development

*WVCF
01-01-1997; 90.5 MHz FM; *Hrs Open:* 24; 1600 w; 112 m; N44 58 57 W91 25 47
VCY/America Inc., 3434 W. Kilbourn Ave., Milwaukee, WI 53208
(800) 729-9829
www.vcyamerica.org
vcy@vcyamerica.org
License: Eau Claire, Eau Claire County, WI held by VCY America Inc.
Group Owner: VCY America Inc.
Nat'l Network: IRN/USA; Moody
Arbitron Metro Market: Eau Claire, WI; *Target Audience:* All ages
Dr. Randall Melchert, President
Vic Eliason, General Manager
Jim Schneider, Programming Director
Andy Eliason, Chief Engineer
Gordon Morris, Operations Manager

Elk Mound

WECL
03-01-2004; 92.9 MHz FM; *Hrs Open:* 24; 3.3 kw; 446 ft.; N44 53 4 W91 35 4
944 Harlem St, Altoona, WI 54720 USA
(715) 832-1530; *Fax:* (715) 832-5329
www.929thex.com
License: Elk Mound, Dunn County, WI held by Mid-West Management, Inc.
Group Owner: Mid-West Family Broadcasting; (acq 6-13-2003; grpsl).
Arbitron Metro Market: Elk Mound, WI; *Format:* Rock/AOR
Kris Cooper, Programming Director

Elm Grove

WGLB
12-06-1963; 1560 kHz AM; *Hrs Open:* 24
900 E Green Bay Road, Port Washington, WI 53074 US
(414) 527-4365; *Fax:* (414) 527-4367
www.wglbam1560.com
License: Elm Grove, WI held by Joel J. Kinlow
Arbitron Metro Market: Milwaukee-Racine, WI; *Format:* Gospel; *Target Audience:* African American
Joel Kinlow, CEO
Joel Kinlow, President
Willis Payne Jr., Station Manager

Ephraim

WSBW
01-01-2007; 105.1 MHz FM; *Hrs Open:* 24; 3.1 kW; 466 ft.; N45 14 5 W87 5 27
30 N 18th Ave, Suite 8, Sturgeon Bay, WI 54235 USA
(920) 746-9430; *Fax:* (920) 746-9433
www.doorcountrydailynews.com
wbdk@doorcountrydailynews.com
License: Ephraim, WI held by Nicolet Broadcasting Inc.
Group Owner: Nicolet Broadcasting Inc.
Arbitron Metro Market: Ephraim, WI; *Format:* Adult Contemp; *Hrs. of News Programming:* news prgmg 10 hrs wkly; *No. News Employees:* 2

Evansville/Rockten

WWHG
105.9 MHz FM; Evansville/Rockton
1 Parker Place, Suite 485, Janesville, WI 53545 US
(608) 758-9025
1059thehog.com
License: Evansville/Rockten, Rock/Winnebago County, WI held by Good Karma Broadcasting
Group Owner: Good Karma Broadcasting
Arbitron Metro Market: Madison/Rockford; *Target Audience:* 25-54

Fond Du Lac

KFIZ
07-06-1922; 1450 kHz AM; 1 kw-U, ND1; N43 47 28 W88 28 16
254 Winnebago Drive, Fond Du Lac, WI 54935 US
(920) 921-1071; *Fax:* (920) 921-0757
www.kfiz.com
info@kfiz.com
License: Fond Du Lac, WI held by RBH Enterprises Inc.
Group Owner: Mountain Dog Media; (acq 1-23-97; $1 plus assumption of liabilities with co-located FM).
Arbitron Metro Market: Fond du Lac, WI; *Format:* News, News/Talk, 84, Talk *Special Programming:* Farm 10 hrs wkly; *Hrs. of News Programming:* news progmg 10 hrs wkly; *Target Audience:* 35-64; Men & Women
Randy Hopper, CEO/General Manager
Wade Bates, Programming Director
Bob Nelson, News Director

WFON
10-05-1967; 107.1 MHz FM; *Hrs Open:* 24; 6 kw; 299 ft.; N43 50 20 W88 22 8
254 Winnebago Drive, Fond Du Lac, WI 54935 US
(920) 921-1071; *Fax:* (920) 921-0757
www.k107.com
rhopper@mdogmedia.com
License: Fond Du Lac, Fond du Lac County, WI held by RBH Enterprises Inc.
Group Owner: Mountain Dog Media; (acq 1-23-97).
Arbitron Metro Market: Fond du Lac, WI; *Format:* Adult Contemp; *Hrs. of News Programming:* news progmg 1 hr wkly; *No. News Employees:* 1; *Target Audience:* Women 25-54.
Randy Hopper, CEO/General Manager

***WDKV**
01-01-2005; 91.7 MHz FM; 20 kw vert; 357 ft.; N43 39 35 W88 26 26
K-LOVE, PO Box 2098, Omaha, NE 68103-2098 US
(800) 525-5683; *Fax:* (916) 251-1650
www.klove.com
License: Fond Du Lac, Fond du Lac County, WI held by Educational Media Foundation.
Group Owner: EMF Broadcasting; (acq 2-21-2006; $350,000)
Nat'l Network: K-Love
Arbitron Metro Market: Fond du Lac, WI; *Format:* Christian; *No. News Employees:* 13
Darrell Chambliss, Chairman
Mike Novak, President and CEO
David Pierce, Chief Creative Officer
Alan Mason, Chief Operating Officer
Eric Moser, Chief Financial Officer
D. Kevin Blair, Secretary and General Counsel

***WVFL**
01-01-2007; 89.9 MHz FM; 1 kw vert; 384 ft.; N43 48 9 W88 20 18 *Rebroadcasts:* Rebroadcasts WVCY-FM Milwaukee 100%
3434 W Kilbourn Avenue, Milwaukee, WI 53208 US
(800) 729-9829
www.vcyamerica.org
vcy@vcyamerica.org
License: Fond Du Lac, Fond du Lac County, WI held by VCY America Inc.
Group Owner: VCY America Inc.
Nat'l Network: USA
Arbitron Metro Market: Fond Du Lac, WI; *Format:* Christian, Religious
Vic Eliason, Operations Dir
Jim Schneider, Programming Director
Andy Eliason, Chief Engineer

Forestville

WRKU
08-01-1999; 102.1 MHz FM; 2.6 kW; 499 ft.; N44 42 26 W87 24 26
30 N 18th Ave, Suite 8, Sturgeon Bay, WI 54235 USA
(920) 746-9430; *Fax:* (920) 746-9433
www.doorcountydailynews.com
wbdk@doorcountydailynews.com
License: Forestville, Door County, WI held by Nicolet Broadcasting Inc.
Group Owner: Nicolet Broadcasting Inc.
Arbitron Metro Market: Green Bay, WI; *Format:* Oldies; *Hrs. of News Programming:* News progmg 3 hrs wkly

Fort Atkinson

WFAW
01-24-1963; 940 kHz AM; 500 w-D, 550 w-N, DA-2; N42 54 24 W88 45 06
Mailing Address: Box 94, Fort Atkinson, WI 53538
Second Address: W 6355 Eastern Avenue, Fort Atkinson, WI 53538
(920) 563-9329; *Fax:* (920) 563-0315
www.940wfaw.com
License: Fort Atkinson, Jefferson County, WI held by NRG License Sub. LLC.
Group Owner: NRG Media LLC; (acq 10-31-2005; grpsl)
Nat'l Reps: Regional Reps
Population Served: 9,782; *No. News Employees:* 1; *Adv. Rates:* 25; 24; 24; 22
Mary Quass, CEO
Gary Douglas Lundberg, Operations Manager
Jim Vriezen, General Manager
Shane Sparks, General Sales Mgr
Michael Clish, News Director

WSJY
09-04-1959; 107.3 MHz FM; *Hrs Open:* 24; 26 kw; 676 ft.; N42 48 2 W89 3 16
Mailing Address: PO Box 2073, Janesville, WI 53547 US
Second Address: W 6355 Eastern Avenue, Fort Atkinson, WI 53538
(608) 756-0747; *Fax:* (608) 563-0315
www.lite1073.com
jvriezen@nrgmedia.com
License: Fort Atkinson, Jefferson County, WI held by NRG License Sub, LLC
Group Owner: NRG Media LLC
Nat'l Reps: McGavren Guild
Arbitron Metro Market: Madison, WI; *Format:* Adult Contemp; *No. News Employees:* 1; *Target Audience:* 25-54.; *Adv. Rates:* 30; 29; 29; 27
Gary Douglas Lundberg, Operations Dir
James Vriezen, General Manager
Shane Sparks, General Sales Mgr

Goodman

***WMVM**
05-03-1993; 90.7 MHz FM; 7 kw; 285 ft.; N45 46 23 W88 24 38
PO Box 212, Suring, WI 54174-0212 US
(920) 842-2900
www.wrvm.org
wrvm@wrvm.org
License: Goodman, Marinette County, WI held by WRVM Inc.
Format: Christian
Michael Cornell, General Manager
Bryan Hay, Music Director
Dennis Jones, Programming Director
Alan Kilgore, Chief Engineer
Rich Frischkorn, Public Coordinator
Michael Fletcher, Promotions Director

Green Bay

WDUZ
06-19-1947; 1400 kHz AM; *Hrs Open:* 24; 1 kw-U, ND1; N44 29 36 W87 59 13
810 Victoria St., Green Bay, WI 54302 US
(920) 468-4100; *Fax:* (920) 468-0250
www.thefan1075.com
thefan@cumulus.com
License: Green Bay, WI held by Cumulus Licensing LLC
Group Owner: Cumulus Media Inc.; (acq 4-10-2009; grpsl)
Nat'l Network: ESPN Radio; ABC; Premiere Radio Networks;
Nat'l Reps: Katz Radio
Arbitron Metro Market: Green Bay, WI; *Format:* Sports; *Target Audience:* 18-54; high income, male skew; *Adv. Rates:* 70; 70; 70; 15
Mike Thompson, Market Manager/General Sales Manager
Jimmy Clark, Programming Director

***WEMY**
08-26-1974; 91.5 MHz FM; *Hrs Open:* 24; 710 w; 741 ft; N44 21 32 W87 59 07 *Rebroadcasts:* Rebroadcasts WEMI(FM) Appleton 95%
1909 W. 2nd St., Appleton, WI 54914-4630
(920) 499-9957; *Fax:* (920) 749-0474
919.thefamily.net
License: Green Bay, Brown County, WI held by Evangel Ministries Inc.
Group Owner: Evangel Ministries Inc.; acq 3-10-98).
Nat'l Network: Salem Radio Network; USA
Population Served: 200,000; *Arbitron Metro Market:* Green Bay, WI; *Hrs. of News Programming:* News progmg 10 hr wkly; *No. News Employees:* 5; *Target Audience:* 25-54; women; *Adv. Rates:* 21; 21; 21; 21
Andy Kilgar, Director, Business/Ministry Sponsorships
Bill Moede, Chief Engineer
Andy Kilgas, Sales Director

WTAQ-AM
04-06-1925; 1360 kHz AM; 10 kW; N44 25 51 W88 04 51
1420 Bellevue St, Green Bay, WI 54311 USA
(902) 435-3771; *Fax:* (920) 321-2300
wtaq.com
License: Green Bay, WI held by Midwest Communications Inc.
Group Owner: Midwest Communications Inc.; acq 1975).
Nat'l Reps: Christal
Arbitron Metro Market: Green Bay; *Format:* News/Talk, News, 86 *Special Programming:* Farm 5 hrs wkly; *No. News Employees:* 4; *Target Audience:* 30 plus.
Jason Hillery, Brand Manager

***WHID**
04-01-1997; 88.1 MHz FM; *Hrs Open:* 24; 17 kw; 1014 ft.; N44 21 32 W87 59 7
1221 W. Clairemont Avenue, Eau Claire, WI 54701 US
(715) 839-3868; *Fax:* (920) 465-2576
www.wpr.org
listener@wpr.org
License: Green Bay, Brown County, WI held by Board of Regents of University of Wisconsin Systems.
Nat'l Network: NPR; PRI
Arbitron Metro Market: Green Bay, WI; *Format:* Talk *Special Programming:* Hmong Public Radio, 2 hrs wkly; *Hrs. of News Programming:* news progmg 18 hrs wkly; *No. News Employees:* 1; *Target Audience:* 35 plus;socially active, life-long learners; *Adv. Rates:* 45; 30; 40; 25
Mark Kay Dadisman, Chief Engineer
Jeff Potter, Director, Marketing
Susan Oman, Director, Finance
Mike Crane, Director, Radio
Sheryl Gasser, Director, Ideas Network
Michael Leland, Director, News
Steve Johnson, Director,Engineering Operations

WIXX
11-01-1960; 101.1 MHz FM; 96 kW; 1079 ft.; N44 24 35 W88 0 5
1420 Bellevue St, Green Bay, WI 54311 USA
(920) 435-3771; *Fax:* (920) 321-2300
wixx.com
License: Green Bay, Brown County, WI held by Midwest Communications, Inc.
Group Owner: Midwest Communications Inc.
Arbitron Metro Market: Green Bay; *Format:* Contemporary Hits/Top 40
Corey Carter, Brand Manager

WNFL-AM
12-12-1947; 1440 kHz AM; *Hrs Open:* 24; 5 kW; N44 28 40 W88 0 0
1420 Bellevue St, Green Bay, WI 54311 USA
(920) 435-3771; *Fax:* (920) 321-2300
wnflsports.com
License: Green Bay, WI held by Midwest Communications Inc.
Group Owner: Midwest Communications Inc.; acq 12-10-96; grpsl).
Nat'l Network: Fox Sports; Westwood One; *Nat'l Reps:* Christal; *Wire Services:* AP
Arbitron Metro Market: Green Bay; *Format:* Sports; *Hrs. of News Programming:* news progmg 10 hrs wkly; *No. News Employees:* 4; *Target Audience:* 35-64; people in upper-income level with above average education
Jason Hillery, Brand Manager

***WORQ**
02-01-1994; 90.1 MHz FM; 11 kw; 646 ft.; N44 21 32 W87 59 7
1253 Scheunng Road, Building 2B, De Pere, WI 54115 US
(920) 494-9010
www.q90fm.com
nancy@q90fm.com
License: Green Bay, Brown County, WI held by Lakeshore Communications Inc.
Nat'l Network: USA
Arbitron Metro Market: Green Bay, WI *TV Affiliate:* Relg *Special Programming:* News progmg 7 hrs wkly; *No. News Employees:* 30; & under, rock and rol; *Adv. Rates:* 9; 9; 7; 5
Jason Leino, Network Manager/IT
Mike LeMay, General Manager
Matt Metzler, Production Director

***WPNE-FM**
01-15-1973; 89.3 MHz FM; *Hrs Open:* 24; 100 kw; 940 ft; N44 24 35 W88 00 05
1221 W. Clairemont Avenue, Eau Claire, WI 54701
(715) 839-3868; *Fax:* (920) 465-2576
www.wpr.org
listener@wpr.org
License: Green Bay, Brown County, WI held by State of Wisconsin Educational Communications Board.
Nat'l Network: NPR; PRI
Population Served: 300,000; *Arbitron Metro Market:* Green Bay, WI; *Format:* Classical, News *Special Programming:* Jazz 10 hrs, folk 3 hrs, Native American 2 hrs, blues 2 hrs, experimental 2 hrs, wkly *Hrs. of NewsProgramming:* news progmg 29 hrs wkly; *No. News Employees:* 2; *Target Audience:* 35 plus; socially aware, artistically stimulated; *Adv. Rates:* 55; 40; 50; 35
Mary Kay Dadisman, Chief Engineer
Jeff Potter, Director, Marketing
Susan Oman, Director, Finance
Mike Crane, Director, Radio
Sheryl Gasser, Director, Ideas Network
Michael Leland, Director, News
Steve Johnson, Director,Engineering Operations

WQLH
07-01-1967; 98.5 MHz FM; 100 kw; 499 ft.; N44 38 41 W88 8 13
810 Victoria Street, Green Bay, WI 54302 US
(920) 468-4100; *Fax:* (920) 468-0250
www.star98.net
jimmy.clark@cumulus.com
License: Green Bay, Brown County, WI held by Cumulus Licensing LLC
Group Owner: Cumulus Media Inc.; (acq 8-30-2013)
Nat'l Reps: Katz Radio
Arbitron Metro Market: Green Bay, WI; *Format:* Adult Contemp; *Target Audience:* Adults 25-54.; *Adv. Rates:* 110; 110; 110; 25.
Mike Thompson, Market Manager
Candace Straebel, Director of Sales
Jimmy Clark, Programming Director

Greenfield

WZTI
04-27-1947; 1290 kHz AM; *Hrs Open:* 24; 5 kw-D, DA2; 5 kw-N, DA2; N42 55 11 W87 59 17
N72 W12922 Good Hope Rd., Milwaukee, WI 53051-4441 USA
(414) 444-1290; *Fax:* (414) 771-3036
milwaukeestrueoldies.com
steve.kosbau@milwaukeeradio.com
License: Greenfield, WI held by Milwaukee Radio Alliance L.L.C.
Group Owner: Milwaukee Radio Alliance L.L.C.; (acq 9-23-97; grpsl)
Arbitron Metro Market: Milwaukee, WI; *Format:* Talk *Special Programming:* Blues 6 hrs, gospel 5 hrs, Sp 5 hrs, church 3.25 h; *Hrs. of News Programming:* news progmg 7 hrs wkly; *No. News Employees:* 1 *TargetAudience:* 25-54; upwardly mobile Blacks; *Adv. Rates:* 31; 21; 21; 17

Hallie

WOGO
06-01-1985; 680 kHz AM; 2.5 kw-D, DA2; 0.5 kw-N, DA2; N44 53 22 W91 23 3
2396 Hallie Road, Suite 1, Chippewa Falls, WI 54729 US
(715) 723-1037; *Fax:* (715) 723-1348
www.wogo.com
wogo@wogo.com
License: Hallie, WI held by Stewards of Sound Inc.
Nat'l Network: USA
Arbitron Metro Market: Eau Claire, WI *TV Affiliate:* Talk *Special Programming:* news progmg 16 hrs wkly; *Hrs. of News Programming:* 1; *No. News Employees:* 25-54.
Paul Anthony, Creative Director
Greg Steward, Program, Sports & Weather Director
Mark Halvorsen, News Director
Terry Steward, General Manager
Pat Wahl, Chief Engineer

WWIB
12-30-1972; 103.7 MHz FM; *Hrs Open:* 24; 100 kw; 679 ft.; N45 6 7 W91 9 33
2396 Hallie Road, Chippewa Falls, WI 54729 US
(715) 723-1037; *Fax:* (715) 723-1348
www.wwib.com
studio@wwib.com
License: Hallie, Chippewa County, WI held by Stewards of Sound Inc.
Nat'l Network: USA
Arbitron Metro Market: Hallie, WI; *Format:* Christian; *Hrs. of News Programming:* news progmg 16 hrs wkly; *No. News Employees:* 1; *Target Audience:* 25-54.
Terry Steward, General Manager
Greg Steward, Programming Director
Pat Wahlÿ, Chief Engineer
Mark Halvorsen, News Director
Steve Flater, Advertising Sales Manager
Dave Staszcuk, Advertising Sales
Molly Lee, Traffic Manager
SueSteward, Accounting

Hartford

WTKM
01-01-1951; 1540 kHz AM; *Hrs Open:* Sunrise-sunset; 500 w-D; N43 16 48 W88 23 02
Box 270526, Hartford, WI 53027
(262) 673-7500
www.wtkm.com
wtkm@nconnect.com
License: Hartford, Washington County, WI held by Tomsun Media LLC
Regional Network: Agrinet; *Nat'l Reps:* Farmakis
Arbitron Metro Market: Milwaukee-Racin; *Adv. Rates:* same as FM
David M. Stout, General Manager
Connie Stout, General Sales Mgr

WTKM-FM
10-01-1973; 104.9 MHz FM; *Hrs Open:* 24; 5.8 kw; Ant 300 ft; N43 16 48 W88 23 02
Box 270526, Hartford, WI 53207
(262) 673-7800; *Fax:* (262) 673-5472
www.wtkm.com
wtkm@nconnect.net
License: Hartford, Washington County, WI held by Tomsun Media LLC
Wire Services: AP
Population Served: 1,500,000; *Arbitron Metro Market:* Milwaukee-Racin; *Hrs. of News Programming:* news progmg 20 hrs wkly; *No. News Employees:* 2; *Target Audience:* 35 plus.; *Adv. Rates:* 30; 30; 30; 25
David M. Stout, General Manager
Connie Stout, General Sales Mgr

Hayward

WHSM
12-21-1957; 910 kHz AM; *Hrs Open:* 24; 5 kw-D, 75 w-N; N45 59 07 W91 32 21
16880 W. US Hwy. 63, Hayward, WI 54843
(715) 634-4836; *Fax:* (715) 634-8256
www.whsm.com
License: Hayward, Sawyer County, WI held by Red Rock Radio Corp.
Group Owner: Red Rock Radio Corp.; (acq 9-1-2006; grpsl)
Nat'l Network: Dial Global
Population Served: 40,000; *Arbitron Metro Market:* Duluth/Superior; *Format:* Sports; *Hrs. of News Programming:* news progmg 2 hrs wkly; *No. News Employees:* 1; *Target Audience:* 34-70.
Darrin White, General Sales Mgr

WHSM-FM
06-21-1980; 101.1 MHz FM; *Hrs Open:* 24; 1.45 kw; Ant 410 ft; N45 59 07 W91 32 23
16880 W. US Hwy. 63, Hayward, WI 54843
(715) 634-4836; *Fax:* (715) 634-8256
www.whsm.com
License: Hayward, Sawyer County, WI held by Red Rock Radio Corp.
Group Owner: Red Rock Radio Corp.; (acq 9-1-2006; grpsl)
Nat'l Network: Dial Global
Arbitron Metro Market: Duluth/Superior; *No. News Employees:* 1; *Target Audience:* 24-60.
Darrin White, General Sales Mgr

WRLS-FM
04-16-1968; 92.3 MHz FM; *Hrs Open:* 24; 6 kw; 322 ft.; N46 1 14 W91 30 41
P.O. Box 1008, Hayward, WI 54843 US
(715) 634-4871
www.wrlsfm.com
wrls@cheqnet.net
License: Hayward, Sawyer County, WI held by Vacationland Broadcasting Inc.
Nat'l Network: CNN Radio; AP Radio; *Regional Network:* Wisconsin Radio Net.; *Wire Services:* AP
Format: Adult Contemp; *Hrs. of News Programming:* news progrmg 10 hrs wkly; *No. News Employees:* 1; *Target Audience:* 25 plus; general
Tom Koser, President
Robert Koser, Operations Dir
Steve Kaner, General Manager
Grant Turpin, Operations Manager
Dick Bender, Sports Director
Scott Klohn, News Director
Nancy Pieters, Traffic Director

Highland

***WHHI**
09-14-1952; 91.3 MHz FM; *Hrs Open:* 24; 100 kw; 559 ft.; N43 2 55.6 W90 22 7.5 *Rebroadcasts:* Rebroadcasts WHA(AM) Madison 100%
1221 W. Clairemont Avenue, Eau Claire, WI 54701 US
(715) 839-3868
www.wpr.org
listener@wpr.org
License: Highland, Iowa County, WI held by State of Wisconsin Educational Communications Board.
Nat'l Network: NPR; PRI
Format: News, News/Talk, 86; *No. News Employees:* 9; *Target Audience:* 35-54; Skews female: issue oriented talk-variety of perspectives
Phil Corriveau, General Manager
Mary Sherer, General Sales Mgr
Steve Johnston, Engineering Dir
Dean Kallenbach, Regional Manager
Jeff Potter, Marketing Director
Susan Oman, Director of Finance
Mike Crane, Director of Radio
Michael Leland, News Director
Mary Kay Dadisman, Development Director

Holmen

WKBH
07-28-1984; 1570 kHz AM; *Hrs Open:* 24; 1 kw-D, ND1; 0.36 kw-N, ND1; N43 55 32 W91 16 2
Mailing Address: 1496 Bellevue Street, Suite 202, Green Bay, WI 54311 US
Second Address: PO Box 10707, Green Bay, WI 54307-0707
(920) 884-1460; *Fax:* (920) 465-9986
www.relevantradio.com
info@relevantradio.com
License: Holmen, WI held by Starboard Media Foundation Inc.
Group Owner: Relevant Radio; (acq 1-17-2003; $210,000).
Format: Talk, Christian; *Hrs. of News Programming:* news progmg 35 hrs wkly; *No. News Employees:* 1; *Target Audience:* 40 plus; those interested in Catholic news, talk & opinion
Thomas Vorpahl, Chairman
Rev. Francis Hoffman, Executive Director
Linda Ruf, National Development Director
Amy Vanden Langenberg, CFO
Mike Kendall, Chief Programming Officer
Bob Benes, Chief Sales Officer
Nancy Jensen, CMO

Hudson

WDGY
12-14-1983; 740 kHz AM; *Hrs Open:* 6 AM-7 PM
P.O. Box 25130, St. Paul, MN 55125 US
(651) 436-4000; *Fax:* (651) 436-6770
www.wdgyradio.com
License: Hudson, WI held by WRPX Inc.
Arbitron Metro Market: Minneapolis, MN; *Format:* Oldies; *Target Audience:* 25-54.
Gregory Borgen, President
Jeff Borgen, General Sales Mgr
Tom Witschen, Programming Director
Paul Orth, Chief Engineer

Hurley

WHRY
03-01-1985; 1450 kHz AM; 1 kw-U, ND1; N46 24 56 W90 9 34

209 Harrison Street, Ironwood, MI 49938 US
(906) 932-5234
www.wupm-whry.com
License: Hurley, WI held by Big G Little O Inc.
Format: Oldies
Charles Gervasio, President
Norma Rigoni, Operations Dir
Laura Keller, Programming Director

Iron River

WNXR

11-01-1994; 107.3 MHz FM; 21 kw; 361 ft.; N46 32 49 W91 24 50
2320 Ellis Ave., Ashland, WI 54806 US
(715) 682-2727; *Fax:* (715) 682-9338
www.wnxrfm.com
License: Iron River, Bayfield County, WI held by Heartland Communications License LLC.
Group Owner: Heartland Communications Group LLC; (acq 4-23-2004; grpsl).
Nat'l Network: Westwood One
Arbitron Metro Market: Duluth-Superior *TV Affiliate:* Hits of the 50s, 60s & 70s; *Format:* Oldies
Scott Jaeger, General Manager
Skip Hunter, Programming Director

Jackson

WAUK

05-01-1964; 540 kHz AM; *Hrs Open:* 24
310 W. Wisconsin Ave., Suite 100, Milwaukee, WI 53203 US
(414) 273-3776; *Fax:* (414) 291-3776
www.espnmilwaukee.com
feedback@goodkarmabrands.com
License: Jackson, Washington County, WI held by Good Karma Broadcasting LLC.
Group Owner: Good Karma Broadcasting L.L.C.; (acq 3-28-2008; $3.8 million)
Nat'l Network: ESPN Radio
Arbitron Metro Market: Milwaukee-Racin; *Format:* Sports; *Adv. Rates:* 28; 28; 28; 24

Janesville

WCLO

07-01-1930; 1230 kHz AM; *Hrs Open:* 24; 1 kw-U, ND1; N42 39 35 W89 2 32
Mailing Address: PO Box 5001, Janesville, WI 53547 US
Second Address: One S. Parker Dr., Janesville, WI 53547
(608) 752-7895; *Fax:* (608) 752-4438
www.wclo.com
programming@wclo.com
License: Janesville, WI held by Southern Wisconsin Broadcasting L.L.C.
Group Owner: Bliss Communications Inc.
Nat'l Network: CNN Radio; Talk Radio Network; Premiere Radio Networks; Westwood One; *Regional Network:* Brownfield; Wisconsin Radio Net.
Arbitron Metro Market: Janesville, WI; *Format:* Rock/AOR, Country; *Hrs. of News Programming:* news progmg 9 hrs wkly; *No. News Employees:* 3; *Target Audience:* 30+ years
Tim Bremel, Operations Manager
Mike O'Brien, VP/General Manager
Al Fagerli, Sports Director
Jim Thomas, Creative Services
Mel Cushing, Advertising Sales Manager

WJVL

10-01-1947; 99.9 MHz FM; 11 kw; 502 ft.; N42 43 47 W89 10 10
Mailing Address: PO Box 5001, Janesville, WI 53547 US
Second Address: One S. Parker Dr., Janesville, WI 53547
(608) 752-7895; *Fax:* (608) 752-4438
www.wjvl.com
tbremel@wclo.com
License: Janesville, Rock County, WI held by Southern Wisconsin Broadcasting, LLC
Format: Country; *Target Audience:* 25 plus.
Tim Bremel, Operations Manager
Mike O'Brien, General Manager
Rob West, Program Director
Jim Thomas, Creative Services
Al Fagerli, Sports Director
Chet Daniels, Promotions Coordinator
Misty Lantz, Traffic Clerk

WJVL

07-01-1930; 99.9 Hz FM; *Hrs Open:* 24; 1 kw-U, ND1; N42 39 35 W89 2 32
1 South Parker Drive, Janesville, WI 53547 US
(608) 752-5500; *Fax:* (800) 261-0999
www.wjvl.com
programming@wclo.com
License: Janesville, WI held by Southern Wisconsin Broadcasting L.L.C.
Group Owner: Bliss Communications Inc.
Nat'l Network: CNN Radio; Talk Radio Network; Premiere Radio Networks; Westwood One; *Regional Network:* Brownfield; Wisconsin Radio Net.
Arbitron Metro Market: Janesville, WI; *Format:* Country; *Hrs. of News Programming:* news progmg 9 hrs wkly; *No. News Employees:* 3; *Target Audience:* 30+ years
Tim Bremel, Operations Manager
Mike O'Brien, VP/General Manager
Al Fagerli, Sports Director
Jim Thomas, Creative Services
Mel Cushing, Advertising Sales Manager

WRJN

07-01-1930; 1400 Hz AM; *Hrs Open:* 24; 1 kw-U, ND1; N42 39 35 W89 2 32
4201 Victory Avenue, Racine, WI 53405 US
(262) 634-3311; *Fax:* (262) 634-6515
www.wrjn.com
License: Janesville, WI held by Southern Wisconsin Broadcasting L.L.C.
Group Owner: Bliss Communications Inc.
Nat'l Network: CNN Radio; Talk Radio Network; Premiere Radio Networks; Westwood One; *Regional Network:* Brownfield; Wisconsin Radio Net.
Arbitron Metro Market: Janesville, WI; *Format:* News/Talk; *Hrs. of News Programming:* news progmg 9 hrs wkly; *No. News Employees:* 3; *Target Audience:* 30+ years
Tim Bremel, Operations Manager
Mike O'Brien, VP/General Manager
Al Fagerli, Sports Director
Jim Thomas, Creative Services
Mel Cushing, Advertising Sales Manager

WEZY

07-01-1930; 92.1 Hz FM; *Hrs Open:* 24; 1 kw-U, ND1; N42 39 35 W89 2 32
4201 Victory Avenue, Racine, WI 53405 US
(262) 634-3311; *Fax:* (262) 634-6515
www.literock921.com
License: Janesville, WI held by Southern Wisconsin Broadcasting L.L.C.
Group Owner: Bliss Communications Inc.
Nat'l Network: CNN Radio; Talk Radio Network; Premiere Radio Networks; Westwood One; *Regional Network:* Brownfield; Wisconsin Radio Net.
Arbitron Metro Market: Janesville, WI; *Format:* Adult Contemp, Rock/AOR; *Hrs. of News Programming:* news progmg 9 hrs wkly; *No. News Employees:* 3; *Target Audience:* 30+ years
Tim Bremel, Operations Manager
Mike O'Brien, VP/General Manager
Al Fagerli, Sports Director
Jim Thomas, Creative Services
Mel Cushing, Advertising Sales Manager

WIBD

07-01-1930; 101.3 Hz FM; *Hrs Open:* 24; 1 kw-U, ND1; N42 39 35 W89 2 32
2410 South Main Street, West Bend, WI 53095 US
(262) 334-2344
www.wibdwestbend.com
License: Janesville, WI held by Southern Wisconsin Broadcasting L.L.C.
Group Owner: Bliss Communications Inc.
Regional Network: Brownfield; Wisconsin Radio Net.
Arbitron Metro Market: Janesville, WI; *Format:* Sports, Talk; *Hrs. of News Programming:* news progmg 9 hrs wkly; *No. News Employees:* 3; *Target Audience:* 30+ years
Tim Bremel, Operations Manager
Mike O'Brien, VP/General Manager
Al Fagerli, Sports Director
Jim Thomas, Creative Services
Mel Cushing, Advertising Sales Manager

WBWI

07-01-1930; 92.5 Hz FM; *Hrs Open:* 24; 1 kw-U, ND1; N42 39 35 W89 2 32
2410 South Main Street, West Bend, WI 53095 US
(262) 334-2344; *Fax:* (262) 334-1512
www.buzzcountry.com
License: Janesville, WI held by Southern Wisconsin Broadcasting L.L.C.
Group Owner: Bliss Communications Inc.
Regional Network: Brownfield; Wisconsin Radio Net.
Arbitron Metro Market: Janesville, WI; *Format:* Country; *Hrs. of News Programming:* news progmg 9 hrs wkly; *No. News Employees:* 3; *Target Audience:* 30+ years
Tim Bremel, Operations Manager
Mike O'Brien, VP/General Manager
Al Fagerli, Sports Director
Jim Thomas, Creative Services
Mel Cushing, Advertising Sales Manager

Kaukauna

WJOK

09-25-1965; 1050 kHz AM; *Hrs Open:* 24; 1 kw-D, DA2; 0.5 kw-N, DA2; N44 14 51 W88 18 0
Mailing Address: 1496 Bellevue Street, Suite 202, Green Bay, WI 54311 US
Second Address: PO Box 10707, Green Bay, WI 54307-0707
(920) 469-3021; *Fax:* (920) 469-3023
www.relevantradio.com
info@relevantradio.com
License: Kaukauna, WI held by Starboard Media Foundation Inc.
Group Owner: Relevant Radio; (acq 8-28-2001; $500,000).
Nat'l Network: USA; Moody
Arbitron Metro Market: Appleton-Oshkosh, WI; *Format:* Christian
Special Programming: Relg 2 hrs wkly; *Target Audience:* 35-54.; *Adv. Rates:* 11; 11; 11; 11
Thomas Vorpahl, Chairman
Rev. Francis Hoffman, Executive Director
Linda Ruf, National Development Director
Amy Vanden Langenberg, CFO
Nancy Jensen, CMO
Bob Benes, Chief Sales Officer
Mike Kendall, Chief Programming Officer

Kenosha

*WGTD

12-23-1975; 91.1 MHz FM; 3.2 kw; 203 ft.; N42 36 32 W87 50 56
3520 - 30th Avenue, Kenosha, WI 53140 US
(262) 564-3870; *Fax:* (262) 564-3801
wgtd.org
coled@gtc.edu
License: Kenosha, Kenosha County, WI held by Gateway Technical College.
Nat'l Network: NPR; *Regional Network:* Wis. Public Radio; *Wire Services:* AP
Format: Classical, News *Special Programming:* Ger one hr wkly; *No. News Employees:* 2; *Target Audience:* General.
David Cole, General Manager
David McGrath, News Director
Greg Berg, Fine Arts Director
Steven Brown, Feature/Radio Play Producer

WLIP

05-11-1947; 1050 kHz AM; *Hrs Open:* 24; 0.25 kw-D, ND1; 0.25 kw-N, ND1; N42 33 10 W87 53 38
8500 Green Bay Road, Pleasant Prairie, WI 53158 US
(262) 694-7800; *Fax:* (262) 694-7767
www.wlip.com
License: Kenosha, WI held by NM Licensing LLC.
Group Owner: NextMedia Group Inc.; (acq 11-26-00; grpsl).
Regional Network: Wisconsin Radio Net.
Arbitron Metro Market: Chicago, IL; *Format:* Talk; *No. News Employees:* 2; *Target Audience:* 35 plus.
Stu Wattles, Chief Engineer
John Perry, Operations Manager/Programming Director
Karl Wertzler, General Manager
Kare Vernezze, General Sales Manager
Peter Serzant, News Director
Dan Hanni, Production Director
Lori Madison, TrafficDirector

Kewaunee

WAUN

01-01-1973; 92.7 MHz FM; *Hrs Open:* 5 AM-10 PM; 6 kw; 328 ft.; N44 29 50 W87 35 12
1021 N. Superior Ave., Suite 205, Tomah, WI 54660 US
(920) 833-7522; *Fax:* (920) 495-3313
www.lamasgrandegb.com
License: Kewaunee, Kewaunee County, WI held by Magnum Broadcasting Inc.
Group Owner: Magnum Communications, Inc.; (acq 12-2-98).
Arbitron Metro Market: Durango, CO; *Format:* Tejano
David R. Magnum, President

Kiel

*WSTM

91.3 MHz FM; 1.1 kw; 473 ft.; N43 43 23 W88 3 51.7
PO Box 259, Plymouth, WI 53073 US

(920) 893-2661; *Fax:* (920) 892-2706
www.wstmfm.org
wstm@jmiradio.org
License: Kiel, Manitowoc County, WI held by Jubilation Ministries Inc.
Arbitron Metro Market: Kiel, WI; *Format:* Christian
Rachel Knight & Darcie Laack, Operations Coordinators
Bill Horsch, General Manager
Susan Noordyk, Director, FM Operations
Dave Hendrickson, News Director
Christopher Holycross, Account Executive

Kimberly

WHBY
12-01-1925; 1150 kHz AM; *Hrs Open:* 24
Mailing Address: 801 Hoffman Road, Suite 114, Green Bay, WI 54301 US
Second Address: 2800 E. College Ave., Appleton, WI 54915
(920) 733-9226; *Fax:* (920) 739-0494
www.whby.com
License: Kimberly, WI held by Woodward Communications Inc.
Group Owner: Woodward Communications Inc.; (acq 3-75).
Regional Network: Wisconsin Radio Net; *Nat'l Reps:* McGavren Guild; *Wire Services:* AP
Arbitron Metro Market: Appleton-Oshkosh, WI; *Format:* News, News/Talk, 86; *Hrs. of News Programming:* news progmg 25 hrs wkly; *No. News Employees:* 3; *Target Audience:* 35 plus; upper middle class, educated
Greg Bell, General Manager
John Wanie, Sales Manager
Dave Edwards, Programming Director
Mike Kemmeter, News Director

La Crosse

***WHLA**
11-21-1950; 90.3 MHz FM; *Hrs Open:* 24; 97 kw; 1007 ft.; N43 48 17 W91 22 6 *Rebroadcasts:* Rebroadcasts WHA(AM) Madison 95%
1221 W. Clairemont Avenue, Eau Claire, WI 54701 US
(715) 839-3868
www.wpr.org/whla
listener@wpr.org
License: La Crosse, La Crosse County, WI held by State of Wis. Educational Communications Board.
Nat'l Network: NPR; PRI; *Wire Services:* AP
Format: Talk; *No. News Employees:* 3; *Target Audience:* 35-54; skews female: issue oriented talk-var of perspectives
Steve Johnson, Engineering Dir
Dean Kallenbach, Regional Manager
Jeff Potter, Marketing Director
Susan Oman, Director of Finance
Mike Crane, Director of Radio
Michael Leland, News Director
May Kay Dadisman, DevelopmentDirector

WIZM-AM
01-02-1923; 1410 kHz AM; *Hrs Open:* 24; 5 kW; N43 50 49 W91 13 7
201 State St, La Crosse, WI 54601 USA
(608) 782-1230
www.z933.com
License: La Crosse, WI held by Family Radio Inc.
Group Owner: Mid-West Family Broadcasting; (acq 7-12-71; $500,000)
Nat'l Network: Westwood One; CBS; *Nat'l Reps:* Christal; *Wire Services:* AP
Arbitron Metro Market: La Crosse, WI; *Format:* News/Talk
Special Programming: Asian 2 hrs wkly; *Hrs. of News Programming:* news progmg 18 hrs wkly; *No. News Employees:* 5; *Target Audience:* 35 plus. *Adv.Rates:* 49; 44; 45; 32

WIZM-FM
01-01-1966; 93.3 MHz FM; *Hrs Open:* 24; 100 kW; 1020 ft.; N43 48 23 W91 22 4
201 State St, La Crosse, WI 54601 USA
(608) 782-1230
www.z933.com
License: La Crosse, La Crosse County, WI held by Family Radio Inc.
Group Owner: Mid-West Family Broadcasting; (acq 6-15-76)
Wire Services: AP
Arbitron Metro Market: La Crosse, WI; *Format:* Contemporary Hits/Top 40; *Hrs. of News Programming:* news progmg 2 hrs wkly; *No. News Employees:* 5; *Target Audience:* 18-49.; *Adv. Rates:* 102; 92; 94; 78

WKTY
05-01-1948; 580 kHz AM; *Hrs Open:* 24; 5 kw-D, 0.74 kw-N; N43 44 25 W91 12 21
201 State St, La Crosse, WI 54601 USA
(608) 782-1230
www.wktysports.com
License: La Crosse, WI held by Family Radio Inc.
Group Owner: Mid-West Family Broadcasting; (acq 1996; $1.3 million)
Nat'l Network: ABC; *Nat'l Reps:* Christal; *Wire Services:* AP
Format: Sports *Special Programming:* Farm 5 hrs wkly; *Hrs. of News Programming:* news progmg 18 hrs wkly; *No. News Employees:* 5; *Target Audience:* 25-54.; *Adv. Rates:* 45; 43; 44; 37
Howard Gloede, General Manager
Brian Michaels, Station Manager
Theresa Timm, Director of Sales
Scott Robert Shaw, Programming Director
Mitch Reynolds, News Director

WLFN
05-01-1947; 1490 kHz AM; *Hrs Open:* 24; 1 kw-U, ND1; N43 49 42 W91 14 27
1407 2nd Ave. N., Onalaska, WI 54650 US
(608) 782-8335; *Fax:* (608) 782-8340
www.1490wlfn.com
License: La Crosse, La Crosse County, WI held by Mississippi Valley Broadcasters LLC.
Group Owner: La Crosse Radio Group
Arbitron Metro Market: La Crosse, WI; *Format:* Talk; *Hrs. of News Programming:* news progmg 5 hrs wkly; *No. News Employees:* 1; *Target Audience:* 35 plus.
Pat Smith, General Manager
Erik Sjolander, Sales Manager
Debbie Brague, Programming Director
Heidi Hanse, Promotions Director
Caroline Grosvold, Business Manager
JoAnn Steffes, HR Director
Laurie Lane, Traffic Director
LoisLosby, Public Service
Isaac Wenzel, Director of Interactive Media

***WLSU**
01-04-1971; 88.9 MHz FM; *Hrs Open:* 24; 8.2 kw; 928 ft.; N43 48 17 W91 22 6
1221 W. Clairemont Avenue, Eau Claire, WI 54701 US
(715) 839-3868
www.wpr.org/wlsu
Listener@wpr.org
License: La Crosse, La Crosse County, WI held by University of Wisconsin System.
Nat'l Network: NPR; PRI; *Wire Services:* AP
Arbitron Metro Market: La Crosse, WI; *Format:* Jazz, News; *Hrs. of News Programming:* news progmg 40 hrs wkly; *No. News Employees:* 3; *Target Audience:* General.
Michael Leland, News Director
Steve Johnston, Engineering Dir
Dean Kallenbach, Regional Manager
Jeff Potter, Marketing Director
Susan Oman, Director of Finance
Mary Kay Dadisman, Development Director
Mike Crane, Director ofRadio

WLXR-FM
03-01-1975; 104.9 MHz FM; 0.8 kw; 659 ft.; N43 43 17 W91 17 24
1407 2nd Ave. N., Onalaska, WI 54650 US
(608) 782-8335; *Fax:* (608) 782-8340
www.wlxr.com
License: La Crosse, La Crosse County, WI held by Mississippi Valley Broadcasters LLC.
Group Owner: La Crosse Radio Group
Arbitron Metro Market: La Crosse, WI; *Format:* Adult Contemp; *Target Audience:* 18-49.
Pat Smith, General Manager
Erik Sjolander, Sales Manager
Debbie Brague, Programming Director
Heidi Hanse, Promotions Director
Caroline Grosvold, Business Manager
JoAnn Steffes, HR Director
Laurie Lane, Traffic Director
LoisLosby, Public Service
Isaac Wenzel, Director of Interactive Media

WQCC
03-31-1994; 106.3 MHz FM; *Hrs Open:* 24; 18 kw; 387 ft.; N43 51 2 W91 12 8
1407 2nd Ave. N., Onalaska, WI 54650 US
(608) 782-8335; *Fax:* (608) 782-8340
www.kicks1063.com
License: La Crosse, La Crosse County, WI held by Mississippi Valley Broadcasters LLC.
Group Owner: La Crosse Radio Group; (acq 12-31-96).
Format: Country
Pat Smith, General Manager
Erik Sjolander, Sales Manager
John Stevenson, Programming Director
Heidi Hanse, Promotions Director
Caroline Grosvold, Business Manager
JoAnn Steffes, HR Director
Laurie Lane, Traffic Director
LoisLosby, Public Service
Isaac Wenzel, Director of Interactive Media

WRQT
01-01-1972; 95.7 MHz FM; 50 kW; 492 ft.; N43 37 57 W91 17 6
201 State St, La Crosse, WI 54601 USA
(608) 782-1230
License: La Crosse, La Crosse County, WI held by Family Radio Inc.
Group Owner: Mid-West Family Broadcasting; (acq 1996)
Format: Rock/AOR; *Hrs. of News Programming:* News progmg 5 hrs wkly; *Target Audience:* 18-49.; *Adv. Rates:* 50; 45; 48; 41
Howard Gloede, General Manager
Brian Michaels, Station Manager
Theresa Timm, Director of Sales
Scott Robert Shaw, Programming Director
Mitch Reynolds, News Director

Ladysmith

WJBL
10-01-1984; 93.1 MHz FM; *Hrs Open:* 24; 4.9 kw; 358 ft.; N45 27 59 W91 7 23
Mailing Address: P. O. Box 351, Ladysmith, WI 54848 US
Second Address: W8746 Hwy. 8, Ladysmith, WI 54848
(715) 532-5588; *Fax:* (715) 532-7357
wldy@centurytel.net
License: Ladysmith, Rusk County, WI held by Flambeau Broadcasting Co., Inc.
Nat'l Network: ABC
Format: Oldies; *Hrs. of News Programming:* news progmg 10 hrs wkly; *No. News Employees:* 1; *Target Audience:* 25-54.
Randy Hudzinski, Owner
Robert Krejcarek, General Sales Mgr
Sandy Zajec, Programming Director
Tom Costello, News Director

WLDY
09-01-1948; 1340 kHz AM; *Hrs Open:* 24; 1 kw-U, ND1; N45 27 59 W91 7 23
Mailing Address: W 8746 Highway 8, Ladysmith, WI 54848 US
Second Address: W8746 Hwy. 8, Ladysmith, WI 54848
(715) 532-5588; *Fax:* (715) 532-7357
wldy@centurytel.net
License: Ladysmith, WI held by Flambeau Broadcasting Co., Inc.
Nat'l Network: ABC; *Wire Services:* UPI
Format: Country, News, 62, Talk *Special Programming:* Polka 3 hrs wkly; *Hrs. of News Programming:* news progmg 15 hrs wkly; *No. News Employees:* 1; *Target Audience:* 35 plus; mature audience; *Adv. Rates:* 10;10; 10; 2
Randy Hudzinski, Owner
Sandra Roth, President
David Roth, General Sales Mgr
Jocelyn Kilmer, Programming Director
Tom Costello, News Director
Del Dayton, Chief Engineer
Robert Krejcarek, Farm Director
Judi Novak, TrafficManager

Lake Geneva

WLKG
06-06-1994; 96.1 MHz FM; *Hrs Open:* 24; 6 kw; 328 ft.; N42 36 34 W88 26 36
500 Interchange North, Box 9610, Lake Geneva, WI 53147 US
(262) 249-9600; *Fax:* (262) 249-9630
www.wlkg.com
License: Lake Geneva, Walworth County, WI held by CTJ Communications Ltd.
Format: Adult Contemp *Special Programming:* Hits of the 70s 10 hrs, sports 2 hrs wkly; *Hrs. of News Programming:* News progmg 15 hrs wkly; *Target Audience:* 25-54; mainly female
Tom Kwiatkowski, Owner/President
Nancy Douglass, General Manager
David Michaels, Programming Director
Ted Pankau, News Director
Mike Coolidge, Sports Director

Lancaster

WGLR
09-09-1982; 97.7 MHz FM; *Hrs Open:* 24; 11.5 kW; 482 ft.; N42 51 48 W90 42 11
51 Means Dr, Platteville, WI 53818 USA

(608) 349-2000
wglr.com
License: Lancaster, Grant County, WI held by QueenB Radio Wisconsin Inc.
Group Owner: Morgan Murphy Media; (acq 1998)
Nat'l Network: ABC; Premiere Radio Networks; *Regional Network:* Radio Iowa; Wisconsin Radio Net. *Regional Reps:* Local Focus
Arbitron Metro Market: Dubuque, IA; *Format:* Country *Special Programming:* News, Sports and Agriculture; *Hrs. of News Programming:* News prgmg 2 hrs per day; *Target Audience:* 25-64.; *Adv. Rates:* 25; 20; 25;15

*WJTY

03-12-1983; 88.1 MHz FM; *Hrs Open:* 24; 7 kw horiz, 50 kw vert; 476 ft.; N42 57 8 W90 25 47
Mailing Address: Family Life Radio, PO Box 35300, Tucson, AZ 85740 US
Second Address: Family Life Communications Incorporated, 7355 N. Oracle Road, Tucson, AZ 85704
(800) 776-1076
www.myflr.org
License: Lancaster, Grant County, WI held by Family Life Broadcasting Inc.
Group Owner: Family Life Communications Inc.; (acq 5-23-2007; grpsl)
Nat'l Network: Moody; USA
Arbitron Metro Market: Dubuque, IA; *Format:* Christian, Religious; *Hrs. of News Programming:* news progmg 11 hrs wkly; *No. News Employees:* 1; *Target Audience:* 30-90; families

Dr. Randy L. Carlson, President
Evan Carlson, VP, Ministry
Alonzo Williams, VP, Operations
Rod Robison, VP, Development
Warren J. Bolthouse, Board Chairman
Mack Piotrowski, Controller

Lomira

WFDL-FM

04-01-1993; 97.7 MHz FM; *Hrs Open:* 24; 17.5 kw; 400 ft.; N43 39 14 W88 26 25
210 South Main Street, Fond Du Lac, WI 54935 US
(920) 924-9697; *Fax:* (920) 929-8865
www.sunny977.com
License: Lomira, Dodge County, WI held by Radio Plus of Fond du Lac Inc.
Arbitron Metro Market: Fond du Lac, WI; *Format:* Adult Contemp; *No. News Employees:* 1; *Target Audience:* 30-54.; *Adv. Rates:* 25; 20; 22; 15

Chris Bernier, President
Terry Davis, Operations Dir
Keith Heisler, Programming Director
Greg Stensland, News Director
Mike Enfelt, Operations Manager
Kerry Longrie, Traffic Manager
Paul Millard, Assistant Web Master and ProjectManager
Terry Davis, Sales and Advertising
Andrew Schwenn, Promotions/Community Announcements

Madison

*WERN

03-30-1947; 88.7 MHz FM; *Hrs Open:* 24; 20.5 kw; 1263 ft.; N43 3 21 W89 32 6
1221 W. Clairemont Avenue, Eau Claire, WI 54701 US
(715) 839-3868
www.wpr.org
Listener@wpr.org
License: Madison, Dane County, WI held by State of Wisconsin Educational Communications Board.
Nat'l Network: NPR; PRI; *Regional Network:* Wis. Public Radio
Arbitron Metro Market: Madison, WI; *Format:* Classical, News; *Hrs. of News Programming:* news progmg 29 hrs wkly; *No. News Employees:* 9; *Target Audience:* 25-64; persons seeking quality music & intellectualstimulation

Steve Johnston, Director of Engineering & Operations
Michael Leland, News Director
Susan Oman, Chief Engineer
Mike Crane, Director of Radio
Michael Arnold, Associate Director of Radio
Sarah Jacobs, Audience Services Manager
Jeffrey Potter, Marketing Director
Rebecca Dopart, Director, Membership and Corporate Support
Mary Kay Dadisman, Director of Development

*WHA

01-01-1922; 970 kHz AM; *Hrs Open:* 24; 5 kw-D, ND1; 0.051 kw-N, ND1; N43 2 30 W89 24 31
1221 W. Clairemont Avenue, Eau Claire, WI 54701 US
(715) 839-3868
www.wpr.org
listener@wpr.org
License: Madison, WI held by Regents of University of Wisconsin System.
Nat'l Network: NPR; PRI; *Regional Network:* Wis. Public Radio;
Wire Services: NOAA Weather
Arbitron Metro Market: Madison, WI *TV Affiliate:* *WHA-TV affil;
Format: News, Talk; *No. News Employees:* 9; *Target Audience:* 35-54; male/female, educated, skews female: issue oriented talk-variety of perspectives

Mike Crane, Chief Engineer
Jeffrey Potter, Director, Marketing
Rebecca Dopart, Director, Membership
Steve Johnston, Director, Engineering Operations
Susan Oman, Director, Finance
Mary Kay Dadisman, Director, Development
MichaelLeland, Director, News

WHIT

08-14-1964; 1550 kHz AM; *Hrs Open:* 24; 5 kW; N43 0 8 W89 23 13
730 Rayovac Dr, Madison, WI 53711 USA
(608) 273-1000; *Fax:* (608) 274-0100
www.hankonline.net
hank@hankonline.net
License: Madison, WI held by Mid-West Management Inc.
Group Owner: Mid-West Family Broadcasting; (acq 8-12-97; $6.4 million with WWQM-FM Middleton)
Nat'l Network: ABC; *Nat'l Reps:* McGavren Guild
Arbitron Metro Market: Madison, WI; *Format:* Country; *Target Audience:* Adults 45+

WIBA

04-02-1925; 1310 kHz AM; 5 kw-D, DAN; 5 kw-N, DAN; N42 59 58 W89 25 47
2651 S. Fish Hatchey Road, Madison, WI 53711 US
(608) 274-5450
www.wiba.com
License: Madison, WI held by Capstar TX LLC
Group Owner: iHeartMedia; (acq 8-30-2000; grpsl)
Nat'l Network: CBS; Wall Street
Arbitron Metro Market: Madison, WI; *Format:* News, News/Talk, 86; *Target Audience:* 25-64.

Colleen Valkoun, Market President
Tim Etes, General Sales Mgr
Tim Scott, Senior Vice President of Programming
James Kaska, Online Content Director

WMGN

09-01-1948; 98.1 MHz FM; *Hrs Open:* 24; 36 kW; 577 ft.; N42 57 46 W89 22 47
730 Rayovac Dr, Madison, WI 53711 USA
(608) 321-0098
www.magic98.com
dj@magic98.com
License: Madison, Dane County, WI held by Mid-West Management Inc.
Group Owner: Mid-West Family Broadcasting
Nat'l Reps: McGavren Guild
Arbitron Metro Market: Madison, WI; *Format:* Adult Contemp; *Target Audience:* Adults 25-54

*WNWC-FM

04-30-1959; 102.5 MHz FM; 50 kw; 492 ft.; N43 2 8 W89 30 25
5606 Medical Circle, Madison, WI 53719-1232 US
(866) 999-1025; *Fax:* (608) 271-1150
www.life1025.com
License: Madison, Dane County, WI held by University of Northwestern - St. Paul
Group Owner: Northwestern College & Radio; (acq 1-19-73).
Nat'l Network: AP Radio; *Wire Services:* AP
Arbitron Metro Market: Madison, WI *TV Affiliate:* Contemp Christian Music *Special Programming:* news progmg 20 hrs wkly; *Hrs. of News Programming:* 1; *No. News Employees:* 35-45.

*WORT

12-01-1975; 89.9 MHz FM; 2 kw; 938 ft.; N43 3 3 W89 29 13
118 South Bedford Street, Madison, WI 53703 US
(608) 256-2695; *Fax:* (608) 256-3704
www.wortfm.org
License: Madison, Dane County, WI held by Back Porch Radio Broadcasting Inc.
Arbitron Metro Market: Madison, WI *TV Affiliate:* Div, class; *Format:* Jazz, Spanish *Special Programming:* news progmg 20 hrs wkly; *Hrs. of News Programming:* 1; *No. News Employees:* all *Adv. Rates:* non-comm - underwriting

Tessa Wyllie de Echeveria, President
Vickie Eiden, Vice President
Jody McCann, Treasurer
Norman Stockwell, Operations Coordinator
Laura Gutknecht, Chief Engineer
Tim Schneider, Web Director
Sybil Augustine, Music Director
DougHoltz, Business/Event Development Director
Susan Sheldon, Listener Sponsor Development Director

*WSUM

01-01-2003; 91.7 MHz FM; *Hrs Open:* 24; 5.5 kw; 338 ft.; N42 54 16 W89 33 20
333 East Campus Mall, Suite 4100, Madison, WI 53715-1380 US
(608) 262-1864
www.wsum.org
wsum@wsum.wisc.edu
License: Madison, Dane County, WI held by Board of Regents of the University of Wisconsin.
Arbitron Metro Market: Madison, WI

Dave Black, General Manager
Reid Magnum, Sports Director
Laura Gutknecht, Chief Engineer
Evan Boyd, Production Director
Estra Pratl-Kielley, Creative Director
Anna Batz, Promotions Director
Lorenza Zebell, Lead TrafficDirector
Maddie O'Neill, News Director
Rob Chantigian, Assistant Technical Director

WLMV

09-01-1948; 1480 kHz AM; *Hrs Open:* 24; 5 kW; N43 1 30 W89 23 48
730 Rayovac Dr, Madison, WI 53711 USA
(608) 273-1000; *Fax:* (608) 441-0098
www.lamovidaradio.com
License: Madison, WI held by Mid-West Management Inc.
Group Owner: Mid-West Family Broadcasting
Nat'l Reps: Christal Radio
Arbitron Metro Market: Madison, WI; *Format:* Spanish, Variety/Diverse; *Target Audience:* Adults 18+

Luis Montoto, Director de Programaci¢n
Lupita Montoto, Director de Promociones

WOZN

01-01-1998; 1670 kHz AM; *Hrs Open:* 24; 10 kW-D, 1 kW-N
730 Rayovac Dr, Madison, WI 53711 USA
(608) 273-1000
madcitysportszone.com
License: Madison, WI held by Mid-West Management Inc.
Group Owner: Mid-West Family Broadcasting
Nat'l Reps: McGavren Guild
Arbitron Metro Market: Madison, WI; *Format:* Sports, Talk; *Hrs. of News Programming:* news progmg 15 hrs wkly; *No. News Employees:* 6; *Target Audience:* Male Adults 18+

WTSO

01-01-1948; 1070 kHz AM; *Hrs Open:* 24; 10 kw-D, DA2; 5 kw-N, DA2; N42 59 45 W89 18 50
2651 S. Fish Hatchery Road, Madison, WI 53711 US
(608) 274-5450; *Fax:* (608) 274-9422
www.thebig1070.com
License: Madison, WI held by Capstar TX LLC
Group Owner: iHeartMedia; (acq 8-30-2000; grpsl)
Regional Network: Wisconsin Radio Net.
Arbitron Metro Market: Madison, WI; *Format:* Sports *Special Programming:* Farm 20 hrs wkly; *No. News Employees:* 6; *Target Audience:* 25-54.

Tim Scott, Senior Vice President of Programming
Tim Etes, General Sales Mgr
James Kaska, Online Content Director

WZEE

01-01-1948; 104.1 MHz FM; *Hrs Open:* 24; 12 kw; 1004 ft.; N43 3 3 W89 29 13
2651 S. Fish Hatchery Road, Fitchburg, WI 53711 US
(608) 274-5450
www.z104fm.com
info@z104fm.com
License: Madison, Dane County, WI held by Capstar TX LLC
Group Owner: iHeartMedia
Arbitron Metro Market: Madison, WI; *Format:* Adult Contemp; *Hrs. of News Programming:* news progmg one hr wkly; *No. News Employees:* 2

Tim Scott, Senior Vice President of Programming
Tim Etes, General Sales Mgr
James Kaska, Online Content Director

Manitowoc

WLTU

09-01-1966; 92.1 MHz FM; *Hrs Open:* 24; 3.7 kw; 420 ft.; N44 7 31 W87 37 41
Mailing Address: 1915 Mirro Drive, Manitowoc, WI 54220 US
Second Address: 1915 Mirro Dr., Manitowoc, WI 54220

(920) 683-6800; *Fax:* (920) 683-6807
www.cubradio.com
License: Manitowoc, Manitowoc County, WI held by Cub Radio, Inc.
Nat'l Reps: Katz Radio
Arbitron Metro Market: Manitowoc, WI; *Format:* Oldies; *No. News Employees:* 1; *Target Audience:* 25-64.
Lee Davis, General Manager
Dean Lester, Programming Director
Jack Davison, News Director
Greg Bartusiak, Farm Director

WOMT
11-08-1926; 1240 kHz AM; 0.992 kw-U, ND1; N44 7 31 W87 37 41
3730 Mangin Street, PO Box 1385, Manitowoc, WI 54221 US
(920) 682-0351; *Fax:* (920) 682-1008
www.womtradio.com
womt@me.com
License: Manitowoc, WI held by Seehafer Broadcasting Corp.
Group Owner: Seehafer Broadcasting Corp.; (acq 1-1-70).
Nat'l Network: CBS; *Regional Network:* Wisconsin Radio Net.; *Wire Services:* AP
TV Affiliate: Adult Contemp, Sports; *Format:* News *Special Programming:* news progmg 45 hrs wkly; *Hrs. of News Programming:* 2; *No. News Employees:* 25-64; business executive; *Adv. Rates:* 52.75; 52.75; 52.75;40.60
Mark Seehafer, VP/General Manager
Terry Stevenson, Sales Manager

WQTC-FM
11-19-1965; 102.3 MHz FM; *Hrs Open:* 24; 3 kw; 328 ft; N44 07 31 W87 37 41
Box 1385, 3730 Mangin St., Manitowoc, WI 54221-1385
(920) 682-0351; *Fax:* (920) 682-1008
www.wqtcfm.com
License: Manitowoc, Manitowoc County, WI held by Seehafer Broadcasting Corp.
Group Owner: Seehafer Broadcasting Corp.
Nat'l Network: CUMULU; *Regional Network:* Wisconsin Radio Net.; *Wire Services:* AP
Population Served: 150,000 *Hrs. of News Programming:* news progmg 8 hrs wkly; *No. News Employees:* 8; *Target Audience:* 18-49.; *Adv. Rates:* 40; 40; 40; 30.80
Don Seehafer, President
Courtny Hermson, Operations Dir
Russ Matan, General Sales Mgr
Tim Strews, Programming Director
Russ Matan, Promotions Manager
Damon Ryan, News Director
Terry Stevenson, Sales Manager
Joel Nelson, ChiefEngineer
Mark Seehafer, Vice President/General Manager

Marathon

WKQH
01-01-1988; 104.9 MHz FM; 21 kw; 358 ft.; N44 50 13 W89 45 57
500 Division St., Stevens Point, WI 54481 US
(715) 341-9800; *Fax:* (715) 341-0000
www.b1049.com
License: Marathon, Marathon County, WI held by Muzzy Broadcast Group, LLC
Group Owner: Muzzy Broadcasting L.L.C.; (acq 1994; $150,000)
Arbitron Metro Market: Wausau-Stevens Point, WI (Central Wisconsin); *Format:* Country; *No. News Employees:* 3; *Target Audience:* 25-54; adult
T.K. Michaels, Operations Manager
Richard Muzzy, General Manager
Scott Krueger, Sports Director

Marinette

WLST
09-01-1976; 95.1 MHz FM; *Hrs Open:* 24; 100 kw; 436 ft.; N45 3 48 W87 39 26
68 Bay Point Drive, San Rafael, CA 94901 US
(906) 863-5551; *Fax:* (906) 863-5679
www.baycitiesradio.net/whyb/
License: Marinette, Marinette County, WI held by Armada Media - Menominee Inc.
Group Owner: Armada Media Corp.
Wire Services: AP
Format: Country; *No. News Employees:* 1; *Target Audience:* 25-54
Jim Callow, Operations Dir
Chris Bernier, General Manager
Barb VanDeHei, General Sales Mgr
Ken Conners, News Director

WMAM
10-08-1939; 570 kHz AM; *Hrs Open:* 24; 0.25 kw-D, ND1; 0.1 kw-N, ND1; N45 6 2 W87 37 30
68 Bay Point Drive, San Rafael, CA 94901 US
906-863-5551; *Fax:* 906-863-5679
www.espn570.com
jimcallow@baycitiesradio.net
License: Marinette, WI held by Armada Media - Menominee Inc.
Group Owner: Armada Media Corp.; (acq 12-19-2006; grpsl)
Nat'l Network: NBC Radio; ESPN Radio; *Regional Network:* Wisconsin Radio Net; *Nat'l Reps:* Michigan Spot Sales; *Wire Services:* AP
Format: Sports *Special Programming:* Milwaukee Brewers, Green Bay Packers, Wisconsin Ba; *Hrs. of News Programming:* news progmg 4 hrs wkly; *No. News Employees:* 1; *Target Audience:* 18+
Jim Callow, Operations Dir
Chris Bernier, General Manager
Barb VanDeHi, General Sales Mgr
Ken Conners, News Director

Marshall

***WJWD**
01-01-2003; 90.3 MHz FM; 0.051 kw horiz, 9.9 kw vert; 312 ft.; N43 20 40 W89 6 10
150 West Lincolnway, Suite 2001, Valparaiso, IN 46383 US
(219) 548-5800
www.calvaryradionetwork.com
info@calvaryradionetwork.com
License: Marshall, Dane County, WI held by Calvary Radio Network, Inc.
Group Owner: Calvary Radio Network, Inc.
Arbitron Metro Market: Fall River, WI; *Format:* Religious

Marshfield

WDLB
02-02-1947; 1450 kHz AM; *Hrs Open:* 24; 1 kw-U; N44 41 49 W90 09 20
1714 N. Central Ave., Marshfield, WI 54449
(715) 384-2191; *Fax:* (715) 387-3588
www.wdlbam.com
License: Marshfield, Wood County, WI held by Seehafer Broadcasting Corp.
Group Owner: Seehafer Broadcasting Corp.; (acq 6-1-2006; swap with WOSQ(FM) Spencer and WFHR(AM) Wisconsin Rapids for WBCV(FM) Wausau)
Nat'l Network: ABC; Westwood One; *Regional Network:* Brownfield
Population Served: 150,000; *Arbitron Metro Market:* Wausau-Stevens Point, WI (Central Wisconsin); *No. News Employees:* 2; *Target Audience:* 25-54
Don Seehafer, President
Jon Albrecht, Operations Dir
Mike Warren, News Director
Chuck Gennaro, Engineering Dir

WYTE
12-01-1965; 106.5 MHz FM; 100 kw; 801 ft.; N44 38 39 W89 51 12
1301 Plover Road, Plover, WI 54467 US
(715) 341-8838; *Fax:* (715) 341-9744
www.wyte.com
License: Marshfield, Wood County, WI held by NRG License Sub, LLC.
Group Owner: NRG Media LLC; (acq 10-31-2005; grpsl)
Nat'l Reps: McGavren Guild
Arbitron Metro Market: Wausau-Stevens Point, WI (Central Wisconsin); *Format:* Country; *Target Audience:* 25-54.
Mark Skibba, Operations Dir
Benjamin Rosenthal, General Manager
Bob Jung, General Sales Mgr

Mauston

WRJC
01-04-1962; 1270 kHz AM; *Hrs Open:* 24; 0.5 kw-D, ND1; 0.027 kw-N, ND1; N43 49 52 W90 4 51 *Rebroadcasts:* translator FM 92.9 FM
N 5240, Fairway Lane, Mauston, WI 53948 US
(608) 847-6565
www.wrjc.com
info@wrjc.com
License: Mauston, WI held by Murphy's Law Media Group, LLC
Nat'l Network: CBS; *Nat'l Reps:* Rgnl Reps; *Wire Services:* AP
Format: Oldies; *Hrs. of News Programming:* news progmg 8 hrs wkly; *No. News Employees:* 1; *Target Audience:* 35 plus; general; *Adv. Rates:* 25; 25; 25; 25
Rick Charles, President
Greg Lawrence, Promotions Manager
June Gill, News Director
Ken Ebneter, Chief Engineer

WRJC-FM
01-01-1976; 92.1 MHz FM; *Hrs Open:* 24; 2 kw; 571 ft.; N43 47 16 W90 11 52
N 5240, Fairway Lane, Mauston, WI 53948 US
(608) 847-6565
www.wrjc.com
info@wrjc.com
License: Mauston, Juneau County, WI held by Murphy's Law Media Group, LLC
Nat'l Network: CBS Radio; *Nat'l Reps:* Rgnl Reps; *Wire Services:* AP
Format: Adult Contemp; *Hrs. of News Programming:* news progmg 10 hrs wkly; *No. News Employees:* 1; *Target Audience:* 18 plus; adults; *Adv. Rates:* Same as AM
Rick Charles, CEO

Mayville

WMDC
10-31-1998; 98.7 MHz FM; *Hrs Open:* 24; 6 kw; 328 ft.; N43 26 17 W88 31 35
132 N. Main Street, Suite #1, Mayville, WI 53050 US
(920) 387-0000; *Fax:* (920) 387-2222
www.great98.net
bigsky@great98.net
License: Mayville, Dodge County, WI held by Radio Plus Inc.
Arbitron Metro Market: Mayville, WI; *Format:* Contemporary Hits/Top 40; *No. News Employees:* 1; *Target Audience:* 25-54.; *Adv. Rates:* 20; 20; 20; 12
Tom Biolo, General Manager
Norm Grey, General Sales Mgr

Medford

WIGM
10-26-1941; 1490 kHz AM; *Hrs Open:* 24
630 S. 8th Street, Medford, WI 54451 US
(715) 748-2566; *Fax:* (715) 748-2752
www.k99wigm.com
License: Medford, WI held by WIGM Inc.
Nat'l Network: ESPN Radio; *Wire Services:* AP
Format: Sports *Special Programming:* Farm 10 hrs wkly; *Hrs. of News Programming:* news progmg 14 hrs wkly; *No. News Employees:* 1; *Target Audience:* 21 plus.
Brad Dahlvig, President
Karen Dahlvig, General Sales Mgr
Paula Liske, News Director
Del Dayton, Chief Engineer

WKEB
09-01-1967; 99.3 MHz FM; *Hrs Open:* 24; 23 kw; 341 ft.; N45 9 51 W90 20 28
630 S. 8th Street, Medford, WI 54451 US
(715) 748-2566; *Fax:* (715) 748-2752
www.k99wigm.com
License: Medford, Taylor County, WI held by WIGM Inc.
Nat'l Network: ABC; *Wire Services:* AP
Format: Contemporary Hits/Top 40
Brad Dahlvig, CEO
Karen Dahlvig, Operations Dir
Del Dayton, Engineering Dir

Menomonee Falls

WJMR-FM
06-26-1956; 98.3 MHz FM; *Hrs Open:* 24; 4.9 kw; 364 ft.; N43 2 49 W87 58 52
5407 West McKinley Ave, Milwaukee, WI 53208 US
(414) 978-9000; *Fax:* (414) 978-9001
www.jammin983.com
atopel@jammin983.com
License: Menomonee Falls, Waukesha County, WI held by Lakefront Communications LLC.
Group Owner: Saga Communications Inc.; (acq 4-24-97; $5 million with WJZX(FM) Brookfield)
Nat'l Reps: Katz Radio
Arbitron Metro Market: Milwaukee-Racine, WI; *Format:* Urban Contemporary; *Hrs. of News Programming:* news progmg 4 hrs wkly; *No. News Employees:* 1; *Target Audience:* 25 plus.; *Adv. Rates:* 85; 100; 90; 50
Tom Joerres, President
Annmarie Topel, General Manager
Traci Northrop, General Sales Mgr
LaTonya Lucas, Promotions Manager
Tyrene Jackson, Brand Manager

Menomonie

*WHWC
06-28-1950; 88.3 MHz FM; *Hrs Open:* 24; 70 kw; 1050 ft.; N45 2 49 W91 51 47 *Rebroadcasts:* Rebroadcasts WHAD(FM) Delafield 90%
1221 W. Clairemont Avenue, Eau Claire, WI 54701 US
(715) 839-3868
www.wpr.org
info@wpr.org
License: Menomonie, Dunn County, WI held by State of Wisconsin Educational Communications Board.
Nat'l Network: NPR; PRI; *Regional Network:* Wis. Public Radio
Format: Talk *Special Programming:* Folk 7 hrs wkly; *Target Audience:* 35-54.
Mary Kay Dadisman, Director, Development
Susan Oman, Director, Development
Mike Crane, Director, Radio
Michael Arnold, Associate Director, Radio
Michael Leland, Director, News
Jeffrey Potter, Director, Marketing
Rebecca Dopart,Director, Membership
Steve Johnston, Director, Engineering

WMEQ
05-01-1951; 880 kHz AM; *Hrs Open:* 24; 10 kw-D, DAN; 0.21 kw-N, DAN; N44 50 44 W91 50 45
1501 9th Street East, Menomonie, WI 54751 US
(715) 830-4000
www.wmeq.com
License: Menomonie, WI held by Capstar TX LLC
Group Owner: iHeartMedia; (acq 2000; grpsl)
Nat'l Network: CBS Radio; *Nat'l Reps:* Clear Channel
Arbitron Metro Market: Eau Claire, WI; *Format:* News, News/Talk, 84, Talk; *No. News Employees:* 2; *Target Audience:* 25 plus.
Dave Deville, Operations Manager
Rick Hencley, Vice President/Market Manager
Bill Sparkes, General Sales Mgr

WMEQ-FM
07-19-1967; 92.1 MHz FM; *Hrs Open:* 24; 17.5 kw; 719 ft.; N44 54 59 W91 41 55
619 Cameron Street, Eau Claire, WI 54703 US
(715) 830-4000
www.rock921.com
License: Menomonie, Dunn County, WI held by Capstar TX LLC
Group Owner: iHeartMedia
Nat'l Reps: Clear Channel
Arbitron Metro Market: Eau Claire, WI; *Format:* Classic Rock; *No. News Employees:* 2; *Target Audience:* 25-54.
Dave Deville, Operations Manager
Rick Hencley, Vice President/Market Manager
Bill Sparkes, General Sales Mgr

*WVSS
04-22-1969; 90.7 MHz FM; *Hrs Open:* 24; 0.59 kw; 427 ft.; N44 54 56 W92 4 34 *Rebroadcasts:* Rebroadcasts WERN(FM) Madison 90%
1221 West Clairemont Avenue, Eau Claire, WI 54701 US
(715) 839-3868; *Fax:* (715) 839-2939
www.wpr.org
info@wpr.org
License: Menomonie, Dunn County, WI held by Board of Regents, University of Wisconsin Systems.
Regional Network: Wis. Public Radio
Arbitron Metro Market: Menomonie, WI; *Format:* News, News/Talk, 86 *Special Programming:* Folk 6 hrs, jazz 5 hrs wkly; *Target Audience:* 45-64.
Dean Kallenbach, General Manager
Susan Oman, Chief Engineer
Mary Kay Dadismon, Director, Development
Mike Crane, Director, Radio
Michael Arnold, Associate Director, Radio
Mihcael Leland, Director, News
Rebecca Dopart, Director,Membership
Steve Johnson, Director, Engineering

Merrill

WJMT
05-10-1960; 730 kHz AM; *Hrs Open:* 24; 1 kw-D, ND1; 0.127 kw-N, ND1; N45 10 45 W89 38 20
120 S. Mill Street, Merrill, WI 54452 US
(715) 536-6262; *Fax:* (715) 536-6208
www.wjmt.com
License: Merrill, WI held by Quicksilver Broadcasting LLC.
Nat'l Reps: D & R Radio
Format: Adult Contemp, Talk *Special Programming:* Relg 3 hrs, farm 7 hrs, Pol 3 hrs wkly; *No. News Employees:* 1; *Target Audience:* 35-59.
David Winters, President
Steven Resnick, General Manager
Christine Vorpagel, General Sales Mgr
Nick Summers, Programming Director
Joe Weniger, News Director
Chuck Genarro, Chief Engineer

WMZK
08-25-1968; 104.1 MHz FM; *Hrs Open:* 24; 24 kw; 617 ft.; N45 6 14 W89 43 5
1106 W. Main Street, Merrill, WI 54452 US
(715) 536-6262; *Fax:* (715) 536-0583
License: Merrill, Lincoln County, WI held by Quicksilver Broadcasting LLC.
Arbitron Metro Market: Wausau, WI; *Format:* Rock/AOR; *No. News Employees:* 1; *Target Audience:* 18-49.
James Hoge, President

*WHJL
88.1 MHz FM; 63 kw; 620 ft.; N45 21 7.6 W89 39 12.7
PO Box 212, Suring, WI 54174-0212 US
(920) 842-2900
www.wrvm.org
wrvm@wrvm.org
License: Merrill, Lincoln County, WI held by WRVM Inc.
Arbitron Metro Market: Merrill, WI; *Format:* Christian, Religious
Elwood Anderson, President
Michael Cornell, General Manager
Dennis Jones, Programming Director
Alan Kilgore, Chief Engineer
Brian Hay, Music Director
Rich Frischkorn, Public Service Coordinator
Michael Fletcher, PromotionsDirector

Middleton

WWQM-FM
10-20-1970; 106.3 MHz FM; *Hrs Open:* 24; 4.5 kW; 374 ft.; N43 3 3 W89 29 13
730 Rayovac Dr, Madison, WI 53711 USA
(608) 273-1000
www.q106.com
License: Middleton, Dane County, WI held by Mid-West Management Inc.
Group Owner: Mid-West Family Broadcasting; (acq 8-15-97; $6.4 million with WHIT(AM) Madison)
Nat'l Reps: McGavren Guild
Arbitron Metro Market: Madison, WI; *Format:* Country; *Target Audience:* Adults 25-54
Fletcher Keyes, Program Director
Dave Ogden, Promotions Director

Milladore

*WGNV
02-13-1986; 88.5 MHz FM; *Hrs Open:* 24; 50 kw; 584 ft; N44 38 37 W89 50 48 *Rebroadcasts:* 94.1 Antigo
PO Box 88, Milladore, WI 54454-0088
(715) 457-2988; *Fax:* (715) 457-2987
christianfamilyradio.net
wgnv@christianfamilyradio.net
License: Milladore, Wood County, WI held by Evangel Ministries Inc.
Group Owner: Evangel Ministries Inc.
Nat'l Network: Moody; Salem Radio Network
Arbitron Metro Market: Wausau-Stevens Point, WI (Central Wisconsin) *Special Programming:* Children 4 hrs wkly; *Hrs. of News Programming:* News progmg 10 hrs wkly; *Target Audience:* Women; 35-49; *Adv. Rates:* 15.40;15.40; 15.40; 14
Karen Bencke, Operations Dir
Paul Cameron, General Manager
Bill Schumacher, General Sales Mgr
Mark Bystrom, Programming Director
Vicky Hofkens, News Director
Todd Christopher, Music Director

Milwaukee

WSSP
10-14-1935; 105.7 MHz FM; *Hrs Open:* 24
11800 West Grange Avenue, Hales Corners, WI 53130 US
(414) 529-1250; *Fax:* (414) 529-2122
www.1057fmthefan.com
live@1057fmthefan.com
License: Milwaukee, WI held by Entercom Milwaukee License LLC.
Group Owner: Entercom Communications Corp.; (acq 12-13-99; grpsl).
Arbitron Metro Market: Milwaukee, WI; *Format:* Sports *Special Programming:* Relg 3 hrs, Ger 8 hrs, Sp 3 hrs wkly; *Target Audience:* 25-49.
Craig Hodgson, General Manager
Alan Kirshbom, General Sales Mgr
Glenn Redd, Programming Director
Jim Morales, Promotions Manager
Michael Clemens, News Director
Chris Tarr, Chief Engineer
Andrea Biebel, National Sales Manager

WISN
01-01-1922; 1130 kHz AM; *Hrs Open:* 24; 50 kw-D, DA2; 10 kw-N, DA2; N42 45 18 W88 4 53
12100 W. Howard Avenue, Greenfield, WI 53228 US
(414) 545-8900; *Fax:* (414) 944-5484
www.newstalk1130.com
jerrybott@iheartmedia.com
License: Milwaukee, WI held by Capstar TX LLC
Group Owner: iHeartMedia; (acq 8-30-2000; grpsl)
Nat'l Network: Fox News Radio; Premiere Radio Networks
Arbitron Metro Market: Milwaukee-Racine, WI; *Format:* News, News/Talk, 86; *No. News Employees:* 4; *Target Audience:* 25-54.
Colleen Valkoun, Market President
Phil Kurth, Sales Manager
Jerry Bott, Programming Director
Ken Herrera, News/Public Affairs Director

WJYI
01-01-1955; 1340 kHz AM; *Hrs Open:* 24
5407 W. McKinley Ave., Milwaukee, WI 53208 US
(414) 978-9000; *Fax:* (414) 978-9001
www.joy1340.com
ryansalzer@joy1340.com
License: Milwaukee, WI held by Lakefront Communications LLC.
Group Owner: Saga Communications Inc.; (acq 2-23-94; $7 million with co-located FM;
Nat'l Network: CBS
Arbitron Metro Market: Milwaukee-Racine, WI; *Format:* Christian; *Target Audience:* 18-54.
Tom Joerres, President
Ryan Salzer, Sales Manager
Stacey Kolterjahn, News Director
Phil Longenecken, Chief Engineer

WLDB
06-01-1958; 93.3 MHz FM; *Hrs Open:* 24; 16 kw; 886 ft.; N43 5 46 W87 54 15
N72 W12922 Good Hope Rd., Menomonee Falls, WI 53051-4441 US
(414) 778-1933; *Fax:* (414) 771-3036
www.b933fm.com
steve.kosbau@milwaukeeradio.com
License: Milwaukee, Milwaukee County, WI held by Milwaukee Radio Alliance L.L.C.
Group Owner: Milwaukee Radio Alliance L.L.C.; (acq 9-23-97; grpsl)
Arbitron Metro Market: Milwaukee-Racine, WI; *Format:* Classic Rock; *Target Audience:* 25-54; general; *Adv. Rates:* 100; 90; 100; 70
Steve Kosbau, General Manager

WKLH
01-01-1958; 96.5 MHz FM; *Hrs Open:* 24; 20 kw; 810 ft.; N43 5 48 W87 54 19
5407 W. McKinley Ave, Milwaukee, WI 53208 US
(414) 978-9000; *Fax:* (414) 978-9009
www.wklh.com
klhstudio@wklh.com
License: Milwaukee, Milwaukee County, WI held by Lakefront Communications LLC.
Group Owner: Saga Communications Inc.; (acq 7-18-90).
Nat'l Reps: Katz Radio
Arbitron Metro Market: Milwaukee-Racine, WI; *Format:* Contemporary Hits/Top 40, Adult Contemp; *No. News Employees:* 1; *Target Audience:* 35-54; baby boomers
Tom Joerres, President
Annmarie Topel, Programming Director
Scott Schubert, Promotions Manager
Carole Caine, News Director
Phil Longenecker, Chief Engineer
Bob Bellini, Programming Director
Stacey Kolterjahn, Traffic Manager

WLWK-FM
06-01-1959; 94.5 MHz FM; *Hrs Open:* 24; 14 kw; 955 ft.; N43 5 29 W87 54 7
Mailing Address: 720 East Capitol Drive, Milwaukee, WI 53212 US
Second Address: Box 693, Milwaukee, WI 53201

(414) 332-9611; *Fax:* (414) 967-5266
info@wkti.com
License: Milwaukee, Milwaukee County, WI held by Journal Broadcast Corp.
Group Owner: Journal Communications Inc.
Arbitron Metro Market: Milwaukee-Racine, WI *TV Affiliate:* WTMJ-TV affil; *Format:* Adult Contemp; *No. News Employees:* 1; *Target Audience:* 25-54.
Jon Schweitzer, Station Manager
John Roberts, Programming Director
J. Pat Miller, Promotions Director
Jason Bjorson, Marketing Director

WRNW
01-01-1961; 97.3 MHz FM; *Hrs Open:* 24; 15.5 kw; Ant 980 ft; N43 06 41 W87 55 38
12100 W. Howard Ave., Greenfield, WI 53228 US
(414) 545-8900; *Fax:* (414) 327-3200
www.973now.com
License: Milwaukee, Milwaukee County, WI held by Capstar TX LLC
Group Owner: iHeartMedia
Nat'l Network: ABC
Population Served: 717,099; *Arbitron Metro Market:* Milwaukee-Racine, WI; *Format:* Contemporary Hits/Top 40
Colleen Valkoun, Market President
Bekki Yang, General Sales Mgr
Brett Andrews, Programming Director
Hannah Kultgen, Promotions Director

WLUM-FM
09-01-1960; 102.1 MHz FM; 8.8 kw; 843 ft.; N43 6 42 W87 55 50
N72 W12922 Good Hope Rd., Menomonee Falls, WI 53051-4441 USA
(414) 771-1021; *Fax:* (414) 771-3036
www.fm1021milwaukee.com
License: Milwaukee, Milwaukee County, WI held by Milwaukee Radio Alliance LLC
Group Owner: Milwaukee Radio Alliance L.L.C.
Wire Services: CBS
Arbitron Metro Market: Milwaukee, WI; *Format:* Alternative; *Target Audience:* 18-49; teens & adults

WHQG
10-01-1960; 102.9 MHz FM; *Hrs Open:* 24; 50 kw; 427 ft.; N43 2 49 W87 58 52
5407 W. McKinley Ave, Miwaukee, WI 53208 US
(414) 978-9000; *Fax:* (414) 978-9001
www.1029thehog.com
headhog@1029thehog.com
License: Milwaukee, Milwaukee County, WI held by Lakefront Communications, LLC
Group Owner: Saga Communications Inc.
Arbitron Metro Market: Milwaukee, WI; *Format:* Rock/AOR
Tom Joerres, President
Stacey Kolterjahn, Operations Dir
Annmarie Topel, Programming Director
Scott Schubert, Promotions Manager
J. Calgaro, Programming Director

***WMSE**
03-14-1981; 91.7 MHz FM; *Hrs Open:* 24; 3.2 kw; 131 ft.; N43 2 44 W87 54 28
1025 N. Broadway Street, Milwaukee, WI 53202 US
(414) 277-7247; *Fax:* (414) 277-7149
www.wmse.org
wmse@msoe.edu
License: Milwaukee, Milwaukee County, WI held by Milwaukee School of Engineering.
Arbitron Metro Market: Milwaukee, WI; *Format:* Alternative
Special Programming: Black 13 hrs, jazz 15 hrs, lt 3 hrs, Sp 3 hrs, cla; *Target Audience:* 18-35; young adults
Tom Crawford, General Manager
Tom Crawford, Station Manager
Sid McCain, Promotions Director
Julie Cudahy, Chief Engineer
Justin Shoman, Development Director/Member Support
Erin Wolf, Music Director
Matt Schoeffler, UnderwritingDirector

***WMWK**
12-07-1990; 88.1 MHz FM; *Hrs Open:* 24; 1.1 kw; 906 ft.; N43 5 26 W87 53 50
290 Hegenberger Road, Oakland, CA 94621 US
(800) 543-1495
www.familyradio.com
info@familyradio.com
License: Milwaukee, Milwaukee County, WI held by Family Stations Inc.
Group Owner: Family Stations Inc.
Arbitron Metro Market: Milwaukee, CA; *Format:* Christian, Religious
Harold Camping, President
John Rorvik, Operations Dir

WMYX-FM
11-01-1962; 99.1 MHz FM; 50 kw; 449 ft.; N42 56 44 W88 3 39
1108 West Grange Avenue, Hales Corners, WI 53130 US
(414) 529-1250; *Fax:* (414) 529-2122
www.991themix.com
License: Milwaukee, Milwaukee County, WI held by Entercom License, LLC
Group Owner: Entercom Communications Corp.
Nat'l Network: Westwood One; *Nat'l Reps:* D & R Radio
Arbitron Metro Market: Milwaukee, WI; *Format:* Adult Contemp
Special Programming: Relg one hr wkly; *Target Audience:* 25-49; women
Jane Matenaer, Operations Dir
Tom Gjerdrum, Programming Director

WNOV
08-15-1946; 860 kHz AM; 0.25 kw-D, NDD; 0.005 kw-N, ND1; N43 4 20 W87 57 7
2003 W. Capitol Drive, Milwaukee, WI 53206 US
(414) 449-5490
www.wnovmusic.com
License: Milwaukee, WI held by Courier Communications Corp.
Arbitron Metro Market: Milwaukee, WI; *Format:* Urban Contemporary
Jerrel Jones, CEO
Sandra Robinson, General Manager
Douglas Kelley, Sales Manager
Homer Blow, Programming Director
Amari Brown, News Director
Keyon Jackson Malone, Board Operator

WOKY
01-01-1947; 920 kHz AM; 5 kw-D, DA2; 1 kw-N, DA2; N42 58 32 W88 3 56
12100 W. Howard Avenue, Greenfield, WI 53228 US
(414) 545-8900; *Fax:* (414) 327-3200
www.thebig920.com
License: Milwaukee, WI held by Clear Channel Broadcasting Licenses Inc.
Group Owner: iHeartMedia; (acq 3-17-97; $40 million with WMIL(FM) Waukesha)
Nat'l Network: CBS Radio; *Nat'l Reps:* Clear Channel; *Wire Services:* AP
Arbitron Metro Market: Milwaukee-Racin *TV Affiliate:* Classic country; *Format:* Sports *Special Programming:* news progmg 15 hrs wkly; *Hrs. of News Programming:* 3; *No. News Employees:* 35-64.
Colleen Valkoun, Market President
Phil Kurth, Sales Manager
Gregory Jon, Programming Director

WTMJ
07-25-1927; 620 kHz AM; 50 kw-D, DA2; 10 kw-N, DA2; N42 42 28 W88 3 57
Mailing Address: P.O. Box 693, 720 East Capitol Drive, Milwaukee, WI 53212 US
Second Address: Box 693, Milwaukee, WI 53201
(414) 799-1620; *Fax:* (414) 967-5561
www.620wtmj.com
tsheridan@620wtmj.com
License: Milwaukee, WI held by Journal Broadcast Corp.
Group Owner: Journal Communications Inc.
Nat'l Network: ABC; *Nat'l Reps:* Christal
Arbitron Metro Market: Milwaukee-Racin; *Format:* News, News/Talk, 84, Talk *Special Programming:* Relg 2 hrs wkly; *Target Audience:* General.
Eric Brooks, Executive Producer
Jason Bjorson, Sales Manager
J. Pat Miller, Director, Marketing/Innovation
Doug Russel, Executive Producer, Sports
Carl Moll, Director, Network Operations

***WUWM**
09-24-1964; 89.7 MHz FM; *Hrs Open:* 24; 15 kw; 871 ft; N43 05 24 W87 53 47
111 East Wisconsin Avenue, Suite 700, Milwaukee, WI 53202
(414) 227-3355
www.wuwm.com
wuwm@uwm.edu
License: Milwaukee, Milwaukee County, WI held by Board of Regents of University of Wisconsin.
Nat'l Network: PRI; NPR
Arbitron Metro Market: Milwaukee-Racine, WI; *No. News Employees:* 12; *Target Audience:* General.
Laura Gough, Chairperson
Dave Edwards, Director/General Manager
Gina Dragutnovich, Director, Corporate Sponsorship Sales
David Felland, Chief Engineer

***WVCY-FM**
01-01-1961; 107.7 MHz FM; *Hrs Open:* 24; 43 kw; 528 ft.; N42 57 46 W88 4 23
3434 West Kilbourn Ave, Milwaukee, WI 53208 US
(800) 729-9829
www.vcyamerica.org
vcy@vcyamerica.org
License: Milwaukee, Milwaukee County, WI held by VCY/America Inc.
Group Owner: VCY America Inc.; (acq 1-70)
Nat'l Network: USA; Moody
Arbitron Metro Market: Milwaukee, WI; *Format:* Christian, Religious
Dr. Randall Melchert, President
Victor Eliason, Operations Dir
Jim Schneider, Programming Director
Gordon Morris, Operations Manager

***WYMS**
03-05-1973; 88.9 MHz FM; *Hrs Open:* 24; 1.45 kw; 948 ft.; N43 5 26 W87 53 50
88 Nine Radio Milwaukee, 220 Easy Pittsburgh Avenue, Milwaukee, WI 53204 US
(414) 892-8900
www.radiomilwaukee.org
info@radiomilwaukee.org
License: Milwaukee, Milwaukee County, WI held by Milwaukee Board of School Directors.
Wire Services: AP
Arbitron Metro Market: Milwaukee-Racin; *Format:* Triple A; *Target Audience:* 20-40.
Mary Louise Mussoline, Executive Director
Linda Daley, CFO
Francesca Kemper, Development Director
Sandi Anderson, Director of Events
Sean Demery, Programming Director
Tarik Moody, Digital Director
Sarah Fierek, UnderwritingDirector

WRIT-FM
05-10-1961; 95.7 MHz FM; 34 kw; 610 ft.; N43 5 24 W87 54 55
12100 W. Howard Avenue, Greenfield, WI 53228 US
(414) 545-8900; *Fax:* (414) 546-9654
www.957bigfm.com
License: Milwaukee, Milwaukee County, WI held by Clear Channel Broadcasting Licenses Inc.
Group Owner: iHeartMedia; (acq 10-97; $14.5 million)
Nat'l Reps: Clear Channel
Arbitron Metro Market: Greenfield, WI; *Format:* Adult Contemp; *Target Audience:* 25-54; baby boomers
Kerry Wolfe, Operations Manager
Nathan Tonarelli, Senior Vice President of Sales
Brett Andrews, Programming Director
Hannah Kultgen, Promotions Director

Minocqua

WLKD
08-01-1978; 1570 kHz AM; *Hrs Open:* 24; 5 kw-D, ND1; 0.5 kw-N, ND1; N45 49 13 W89 43 27
3616 Highway 47N, Rhinelander, WI 54501 US
(715) 362-1975; *Fax:* (715) 362-1973
www.am1570wlkd.com
License: Minocqua, WI held by Raven License Sub. LLC.
Group Owner: NRG Media LLC; (acq 10-31-2005; grpsl)
Nat'l Network: Fox News Radio; *Nat'l Reps:* Katz Radio; *Wire Services:* Wheeler News Service
Format: Contemporary Hits/Top 40; *No. News Employees:* 1; *Target Audience:* 35 plus.; *Adv. Rates:* 8; 6; 6; 3
Duff Damos, Operations Dir
Steve Albertson, Station Manager

WMQA-FM
04-03-1975; 95.9 MHz FM; *Hrs Open:* 24; 22 kw; 351 ft.; N45 49 19 W89 43 16
7380 Hwy 51 South Box 96, Minocqua, WI 54548 US
(715) 362-1975; *Fax:* (715) 362-1973
www.wmqa.com
License: Minocqua, Oneida County, WI held by Raven License Sub. LLC
Group Owner: NRG Media LLC
Nat'l Network: Fox News Radio; *Nat'l Reps:* Katz Radio
Arbitron Metro Market: Rhinelander, WI; *Format:* Adult Contemp; *No. News Employees:* 1; *Target Audience:* 35-64; *Adv. Rates:* 23; 20; 21; 8
Duff Damos, Operations Dir
Steve Albertson, General Sales Mgr
Dave Imlah, Programming Director

Mishicot

WZOR
12-17-1994; 94.7 MHz FM; *Hrs Open:* 24; 21.5 kw; 354 ft.; N44 20 30 W87 47 10
2800 East College Avenue, Appleton, WI 54915 US
(920) 734-9226; *Fax:* (920) 739-0494
www.razor947.com
License: Mishicot, Manitowoc County, WI held by Woodward Communications Inc.
Group Owner: Woodward Communications Inc.; acq 1-27-00).
Nat'l Reps: McGavren Guild
Arbitron Metro Market: Green Bay, WI; *Format:* Rock/AOR; *Target Audience:* 18-34; men
Greg Bell, General Manager
Kelly Radandt, General Sales Mgr
Elwood, Programming Director
Roxanne Steele, Promotions Manager
Borna Velic, Music Director

Monona

WTLX
07-16-1990; 100.5 MHz FM; *Hrs Open:* 24; 6 kw; 180 ft.; N43 8 4 W89 23 56
7025 Raymond Road, Madison, WI 53719 US
(608) 245-9859; *Fax:* (608) 245-1720
www.espnmadison.com
License: Monona, Columbia County, WI held by Good Karma Broadcasting L.L.C.
Group Owner: Good Karma Broadcasting L.L.C.; (acq 12-2-97; grpsl)
Nat'l Network: ESPN Radio
Arbitron Metro Market: Madison, WI; *Format:* Sports, Talk; *Target Audience:* 25-54; males
Jesse Nelson, Station Manager

Monroe

WEKZ
07-27-1951; 1260 kHz AM; *Hrs Open:* 24; 1 kw-D, ND1; 0.019 kw-N, ND1; N42 35 40 W89 35 34
D/B/A Green Country B/C, 916 17th Avenue, Monroe, WI 53566 US
(608) 325-2161; *Fax:* (608) 325-2164
www.wekz.com
wekz@wekz.com
License: Monroe, WI held by Scott A. Thompson dba Big Radio
Nat'l Network: ABC
Arbitron Metro Market: Monroe, WI; *Format:* Country *Special Programming:* Ger 3 hrs, Swiss 3 hrs wkly; *Hrs. of News Programming:* news progmg 16 hrs wkly; *No. News Employees:* 4; *Target Audience:* 35 plus. *Adv. Rates:* 12; 12; 12; 12
Kent McConnell, Operations Dir
Wyatt Herrmann, Programming Director
Don Jacobson, News Director
Todd Hausser, Chief Engineer
Becky Koester, Traffic Manager

WEKZ-FM
06-01-1959; 93.7 MHz FM; *Hrs Open:* 24; 36 kw; 581 ft.; N42 34 35 W89 41 35
W 4765 Radio Lane, Monroe, WI 53566 US
(608) 325-2161; *Fax:* (608) 325-2164
www.wekz.com
License: Monroe, Green County, WI held by Scott A. Thompson dba Big Radio.
Nat'l Network: ABC
Arbitron Metro Market: Monroe, WI; *Format:* Adult Contemp; *Hrs. of News Programming:* news progmg 10 hrs wkly; *No. News Employees:* 4; *Target Audience:* 25-54.; *Adv. Rates:* 14; 14; 14; 14
Kent McConnell, Operations Dir
Wyatt Herrmann, Programming Director
Don Jacobson, News Director
Todd Hausser, Chief Engineer
Becky Koester, Traffic Manager

Mosinee

WOZZ
10-07-1991; 94.7 MHz FM; *Hrs Open:* 24; 50 kW; 492 ft; N44 59 18 W89 59 42 *Rebroadcasts:* Simulcast with WIZD(FM) Rudolph 100%
557 Scott St, Wausau, WI 54403 USA
(715) 842-1672; *Fax:* (715) 848-3158
rock947.com
License: Mosinee, Marathon County, WI held by WRIG Inc.
Group Owner: Midwest Communications Inc.; (acq 9-24-97; $35,000 for 70%)
Nat'l Reps: Christal
Population Served: 212,000; *Arbitron Metro Market:* Wausau, WI; *Format:* Rock/AOR; *Hrs. of News Programming:* news progmg 2 hrs wkly; *No. News Employees:* 1; *Target Audience:* 25-54; upscale baby boomers
Terry Stevens, Brand Manager

Mount Horeb

WOZN-FM
10-01-2004; 106.7 MHz FM; 2.9 kw; Ant 479 ft; N43 00 19 W89 52 25 *Rebroadcasts:* Simulcast with WWQM-FM Middleton 100%
Box 2058, Madison, WI 54660
(608) 273-1000; *Fax:* (608) 271-8182
www.q106.com
License: Mount Horeb, Dane County, WI held by Mid-West Management Inc.
Group Owner: The Mid-West Family Broadcast Group; (acq 3-20-2003; $2,166,000 for CP)
Nat'l Reps: McGavren Guild
Arbitron Metro Market: Madison, WI; *Target Audience:* 25-54; general
Tom Walker, General Manager
Ted Waldbillig, General Sales Mgr
Brad Austin, Programming Director
John Bauer, Chief Engineer

Mukwonago

***WLVE**
01-01-2002; 105.3 MHz FM; *Hrs Open:* 24; 1.65 kw; Ant 633 ft; N42 58 05 W88 11 20
K-LOVE, PO Box 2098, Omaha, NE 68103-2098
(800) 525-5683
www.klove.com
License: Mukwonago, Waukesha County, WI held by Educational Media Foundation.
Group Owner: EMF Broadcasting; (acq 5-30-2008; $8.05 million)
Nat'l Network: K-Love
Arbitron Metro Market: Milwaukee-Racine, WI
Darrell Chambliss, Chairman
Alan Mason, COO
Eric Moser, CFO
David Pierce, Chief Creative Officer
D. Kevin Blair, Secretary/General Counsel

Neenah-Menasha

WNAM
05-23-1947; 1280 kHz AM; *Hrs Open:* 24; 5 kw-D, DA2; 5 kw-N, DA2; N44 6 1 W88 32 2
1280 WNAM, 491 S. Washburn Street, Suite 400, Oshkosh, WI 54904 US
(920) 426-3239; *Fax:* (920) 231-0145
www.1280wnam.com
License: Neenah-Menasha, WI held by Cumulus Broadcasting L.L.C.
Group Owner: Cumulus Media Inc.; (acq 6-30-97; grpsl)
Arbitron Metro Market: Appleton, WI; *Format:* Adult Contemp; *Hrs. of News Programming:* news progmg 13 hrs wkly; *No. News Employees:* 3; *Target Audience:* 35 plus.
Guy Dark, Programming
Jeffrey Schmidt, General Manager
Jim Hodges, General Sales Mgr
Joe Pitt, Promotions Director

WNCY
09-09-1977; 100.3 MHz FM; *Hrs Open:* 24; 45 kW; 489 ft.; N44 15 27 W88 11 41
1500 N Casaloma Dr, Suite 301, Appleton, WI 54913-8220 USA
(920) 435-3771; *Fax:* (920) 321-2300
wncy.com
License: Neenah-Menasha, Winnebago County, WI held by Midwest Communications Inc.
Group Owner: Midwest Communications Inc.; acq 12-10-96; grpsl)
Arbitron Metro Market: Appleton, WI; *Format:* Country
Dan Stone, Brand Manager

WYDR
11-01-1971; 94.3 MHz FM; 13 kW; 459 ft; N44 09 30 W88 17 03
1500 N Casaloma Dr, Suite 301, Appleton, WI 54913-8220
(920) 435-3771; *Fax:* (920) 321-2300
943jackfm.com
License: Neenah-Menasha, Winnebago County, WI held by Midwest Communications Inc.
Group Owner: Midwest Communications Inc.; acq 12-10-96; grpsl)
Population Served: 27,600; *Arbitron Metro Market:* Appleton-Oshkosh, WI; *Format:* Contemporary Hits/Top 40; *Target Audience:* 25-54.
Jason Hillery, Brand Manager

Neillsville

WCCN
09-22-1957; 1370 kHz AM; *Hrs Open:* 24
1201 E. Division Street, PO Box 387, Neillsville, WI 54456 US
(715) 743-3333; *Fax:* (715) 743-2288
www.cwbradio.com
License: Neillsville, WI held by Central Wisconsin Broadcasting Inc.
Group Owner: Central Wisconsin Broadcasting Inc.; acq 12-87
Nat'l Network: ABC; *Regional Network:* Wisconsin Radio Net.
Arbitron Metro Market: Neillsville,WI; *Format:* Big Band, Oldies
Special Programming: Farm 19 hrs, Polka 2 hrs wkly; *Hrs. of News Programming:* news progmg 20 hrs wkly; *No. News Employees:* 1; *Target Audience:* 45 plus.; *Adv. Rates:* 19; 17; 16; 13
J. Kevin Grap, President

WCCN-FM
07-01-1964; 107.5 MHz FM; *Hrs Open:* 24; 100 kw; 577 ft.; N44 35 30 W90 37 9
1201 E Division Street, PO Box 387, Neillsville, WI 54456 US
(715) 743-3333; *Fax:* (715) 743-2288
www.cwbradio.com
License: Neillsville, Clark County, WI held by Central Wisconsin Broadcasting Inc.
Group Owner: Central Wisconsin Broadcasting Inc.
Arbitron Metro Market: Neillsville,WI; *No. News Employees:* 1; *Target Audience:* 25-40.; *Adv. Rates:* 27; 25; 24; 20

WPKG
02-01-2004; 92.7 MHz FM; *Hrs Open:* 24; 3.4 kw; 440 ft.; N44 35 30 W90 37 9
W4798 Moonlite Road, Neillsville, WI 54456 US
(715) 743-3333; *Fax:* (715) 743-2288
www.todaysbesthits.com
License: Neillsville, Clark County, WI held by Central Wisconsin Broadcasting Inc.
Group Owner: Central Wisconsin Broadcasting Inc.
Nat'l Network: ABC
Arbitron Metro Market: Neillsville, WI; *Format:* Adult Contemp; *Target Audience:* 18+; Females; *Adv. Rates:* 22.50; 18; 17; 15
J. Kevin Grap, General Manager

Nekoosa

WMMA
01-01-2002; 93.9 MHz FM; *Hrs Open:* 24; 18 kw; 367 ft.; N44 13 23 W89 49 46
Mailing Address: 1496 Bellevue Street, Suite 202, Green Bay, WI 54311 US
Second Address: PO Box 10707, Green Bay, WI 54307-0707
(920) 884-1460; *Fax:* (920) 465-9986
www.relevantradio.com
info@relevantradio.com
License: Nekoosa, Wood County, WI held by Starboard Media Foundation Inc.
Group Owner: Relevant Radio; (acq 12-20-2001; $2.3 million with WIBU(AM) Wisconsin Dells).
Arbitron Metro Market: Nekoosa, WI; *Format:* Religious
Thomas Vorpahl, Chairman
Mike Kendall, Chief Programming Officer
Amy Vanden Langenberg, Chief Financial Officer
Linda Ruf, National Development Director
Nancy Jensen, Chief Marketing Officer
Bob Benes, Chief Sales Officer

WLJY
01-01-2003; 105.5 MHz FM; 6 kw; 279 ft.; N44 21 45 W90 3 58
Gammon & Grange Pc, 8280 Greensboro Dr, McLean, VA 22102 US
(715) 424-1300; *Fax:* (715) 424-1347
www.wrcwfm.com
blocked@northwoodstech.com
License: Nekoosa, Wood County, WI held by Seehafer Broadcasting Corp.
Group Owner: Seehafer Broadcasting Corp.; 3/5/2008
Arbitron Metro Market: Nekoosa, WI; *Format:* Oldies
Donald Seehafer, President
Kent Reeves, Operations Dir
Jeff Sigler, General Sales Mgr

New Holstein

WLWB
05-25-1984; 1530 kHz AM; *Hrs Open:* Sunrise-sunset; 250 w-D; N44 01 10 W88 09 32
Mailing Address: Box 1450, Fond du Lac, WI 53014
Second Address: 354 Winnebago Dr., Fond du Lac, WI 54935
(920) 921-1071; *Fax:* (920) 921-0757
License: New Holstein, Calumet County, WI held by Maszka-Pacer Radio Inc.

Nat'l Network: USA
Arbitron Metro Market: Appleton-Oshkosh, WI; *No. News Employees:* 2; *Target Audience:* 18-54; male sports fans; *Adv. Rates:* 36; 36; 36; 36
R.B. Hopper, General Manager
Mark Kastein, General Sales Mgr
Shawn Kiser, Programming Director
Cindy Konen, News Director
Stu Muck, Engineering Dir

New London

WGEE-FM
10-06-1967; 93.5 MHz FM; *Hrs Open:* 24; 50 kW; 492 ft; N44 32 47 W88 32 57
1420 Bellevue St, Green Bay, WI 54311 USA
(920) 435-3771; *Fax:* (920) 321-2300
duke.fm
License: New London, Outagamie County, WI held by Midwest Communications Inc.
Group Owner: Midwest Communications Inc.; (acq 6-30-93; $1.85 million with WZBY(FM) Sturgeon Bay;
Population Served: 837,000; *Arbitron Metro Market:* Green Bay; *Format:* Country; *Hrs. of News Programming:* news progmg 8 hrs wkly; *No. News Employees:* 2; *Target Audience:* 25-44.
Jason Hillery, Brand Manager

New Richmond

WIXK
09-29-1960; 1590 kHz AM; *Hrs Open:* 24
Mailing Address: 125 E. 3rd St., New Richmond, WI 54017 US
Second Address: 125 East 3rd St., New Richmond, WI
(715) 246-2254; *Fax:* (715) 246-7090
License: New Richmond, WI held by WIXK-AM LLC.
Group Owner: Hubbard Broadcasting Inc.; (acq 5-18-2000; with co-located FM)
Nat'l Network: ABC; *Regional Network:* Wisconsin Radio Net.
Arbitron Metro Market: Minneapolis-St. Paul, MN *TV Affiliate:* KSTP; *Format:* Country; *Hrs. of News Programming:* news progmg 9 hrs wkly; *No. News Employees:* 1; *Target Audience:* 25-54.
Stanley Hubbard, CEO
Virginia Morris, President
Todd Fisher, General Manager

Oconto

WOCO
03-11-1966; 1260 kHz AM; 1 kw-D, ND1; 0.029 kw-N, ND1; N44 53 31 W87 57 18
3829 Wisconsin 22, Oconto, WI 54153 US
(920) 834-3540
www.wocoradio.com
License: Oconto, WI held by Lamardo Inc.
TV Affiliate: Country; *No. News Employees:* 29 plus.
Regional Sales Manager

WOCO-FM
08-01-1968; 107.1 MHz FM; 3 kw; 210 ft.; N44 53 31 W87 57 18
3829 Wisconsin 22, Oconto, WI 54153 US
(920) 834-3540
www.wocoradio.com
License: Oconto, Oconto County, WI held by Lamardo Inc.
TV Affiliate: Nostalgia
Sports Commentator

Omro

WPKR
07-12-1990; 99.5 MHz FM; *Hrs Open:* 24; 25 kw; 495 ft.; N43 49 44 W88 40 6
Mailing Address: 491 S. Washburn Street, Suite 400, Osh Kosh, WI 54904 US
Second Address: 810 Victoria Street, Green Bay, WI 54302
(920) 426-3239
www.nashfmwisconsin.com
License: Omro, Winnebago County, WI held by Cumulus Licensing LLC.
Group Owner: Cumulus Media Inc.; (acq 11-10-2003; $8.1 million with WPCK(FM) Denmark).
Arbitron Metro Market: Appleton-Oshkosh, WI; *Format:* Country *Special Programming:* Farm one hr wkly; *Hrs. of News Programming:* news progmg 2 hrs wkly; *No. News Employees:* 1; *Target Audience:* 25-54. *Adv.Rates:* 60; 54; 60; 48
Jeff Schmidt, General Manager
Jim Hodges, Sales
Joe Pitt, Promotions Director
Eddie, Programming Director

Oshkosh

WOSH
12-31-1941; 1490 kHz AM
491 S. Washburn Street, Suite 400, Oshkosh, WI 54904 US
(920) 426-3239; *Fax:* (920) 231-0145
www.1490wosh.com
License: Oshkosh, WI held by Cumulus Licensing LLC
Group Owner: Cumulus Media Inc.; (acq 9-1-97; grpsl)
Nat'l Reps: D & R Radio
Arbitron Metro Market: Appleton-Oshkosh, WI; *Format:* News, News/Talk, 84, Talk; *Target Audience:* 25 plus.
Jim Hodges, Sales
Jonathan Krause, Programming Director
Joe Pitt, Promotions/Web Director
Steve Griesbach, Chief Engineer
Alexandra Marohn, Traffic Manager

*WRST-FM
04-20-1966; 90.3 MHz FM; 960 w; 125 ft; N44 01 45 W88 33 08
926 Woodland Avenue, Oshkosh, WI 54901
(920) 424-3113
www.uwosh.edu/wrst
License: Oshkosh, Winnebago County, WI held by Board of Regents, University of Wisconsin System.
Nat'l Network: NPR; *Regional Network:* Wis. Public Radio; *Wire Services:* Wheeler News Service
Population Served: 60,000; *Arbitron Metro Market:* Appleton-Oshkos; *Target Audience:* General.

*WVCY
07-01-1969; 690 kHz AM; *Hrs Open:* 24; 0.25 kw-D, DA1; 0.077 kw-N, DA1; N44 4 51 W88 33 53
3434 West Kilbourne Ave., Milwaukee, WI 53208 US
(800) 729-9829
www.vcyamerica.org
vcy@vcyamerica.org
License: Oshkosh, WI held by VCY/America Inc.
Group Owner: VCY America Inc.; acq 1-19-95)
Nat'l Network: USA
Arbitron Metro Market: Oshkos, WI; *Format:* Religious

WWWX
01-30-1967; 96.9 MHz FM; 6 kw; 328 ft.; N44 6 1 W88 32 2
111 East Kilbourn Ave., Suite 2700, Milwaukee, WI 53202 US
(920) 426-3239; *Fax:* (920) 231-0145
www.fox969.com
License: Oshkosh, Winnebago County, WI held by WI Radio LLC, as trustee
Nat'l Network: ABC; *Wire Services:* UPI
Arbitron Metro Market: Oshkosh, WI; *Target Audience:* 25-54.
Jeff Schmidt, General Manager
Guy Dark, Programming Director

Owen

*WVCS
90.1 MHz FM; 1.9 kw; 502 ft.; N45 1 11 W90 29 48 US
(414) 935-3000; *Fax:* (414) 935-3015
www.vcyamerica.org
vcy@vcyamerica.org
License: Owen, Clark County, WI held by VCY America Inc.
Group Owner: VCY America Inc.; (acq 12-30-2008; $7,000 for CP)
Arbitron Metro Market: Owen, WI; *Format:* Christian
Vic Eliason, President

Park Falls

WCQM
04-13-1968; 98.3 MHz FM; *Hrs Open:* 24; 100 kw; 440 ft.; N45 52 56 W90 26 15
P.O. Box 339, Luxemburg, WI 54217 US
(715) 762-3221; *Fax:* (715) 762-2358
www.wcqm.com
wcqm@wcqm.com
License: Park Falls, Price County, WI held by Park Falls Community Broadcasting Corporation
Group Owner: Stephen Marks
Nat'l Network: ABC
Arbitron Metro Market: Luxemburg, WI; *Format:* Country; *Hrs. of News Programming:* news progmg 6 hrs wkly; *No. News Employees:* 1; *Target Audience:* 20-70.; *Adv. Rates:* 19.95; 19.95; 19.95; 19.95
Kirk Knoll, News Director

*WHBM
11-11-1988; 90.3 MHz FM; *Hrs Open:* 24; 35 kw; 712 ft.; N45 56 43 W90 16 22 *Rebroadcasts:* Rebroadcasts WHA (AM) Madison 100%
3319 W. Beltline Highway, Madison, WI 53713 US
(715) 261-6298; *Fax:* (715) 848-2890
www.wpr.org
reyer@wpr.org
License: Park Falls, Price County, WI held by State of Wisconsin Educational Communications Board.
Regional Network: Wis. Public Radio
Format: News, News/Talk, 86; *No. News Employees:* 9; *Target Audience:* 35-54; skews female: Issue oriented talk-var of perspectives
Wendy Wink, CEO
Tom Martin-Erickson, Operations Dir
Phil Corriveau, General Manager
Rick Reyer, General Sales Mgr
Allen Rieland, Chief Engineer
Ted Tobie, CFO

WPFP
01-01-1953; 980 kHz AM; *Hrs Open:* 24; 1 kw-D, 105 w-N; N45 55 04 W90 26 58
Mailing Address: Box 309, Park Falls, WI 54217
Second Address: Hwy. 13 S., Park Falls, WI 54552
(715) 762-3221; *Fax:* (715) 762-2358
wnbi@pctcnet.net
License: Park Falls, Price County, WI
Nat'l Network: ABC
Population Served: 18,000 *Special Programming:* Relg one hr, loc community talk 5 hrs wkly; *Hrs. of News Programming:* news progmg 12 hrs wkly; *No. News Employees:* 2; *Target Audience:* 25-54; adults withdisposable income; *Adv. Rates:* 12; 12; 12; 12
Joel Karnick, Operations Dir
James Gregori, General Manager
Darla Isham, General Sales Mgr
Arthur Dunham, Chief Engineer
Kirk Knoll, Traffic Manager

Peshtigo

WSFQ
08-05-1996; 96.3 MHz FM; *Hrs Open:* 24; 49 kw; 482 ft.; N45 7 19 W87 51 7
413 10th Ave., Menominee, MI 49858 US
906-863-5551; *Fax:* 906-863-5679
baycitiesradio.net
License: Peshtigo, Marinette County, WI held by Armada Media - Menominee Inc.
Group Owner: Armada Media Corp.; (acq 12-19-2006; grpsl)
Format: Oldies; *No. News Employees:* 1; *Target Audience:* 35-54
Jim Callow, Operations Dir
Chris Bernier, General Manager
Barb VanDeHei, General Sales Mgr
Ken Conners, News Director

Platteville

WPVL-AM
02-22-1955; 1590 kHz AM; *Hrs Open:* 24; 0.97 kW-D; 0.47 kW-N; N42 45 20 W90 30 20
51 Means Dr, Platteville, WI 53818 USA
am1590wpvl.com
License: Platteville, WI held by QueenB Radio Wisconsin Inc.
Group Owner: Morgan Murphy Media; (acq 3-18-98; $825,000 with co-located FM)
Nat'l Network: ESPN Radio
Arbitron Metro Market: Dubuque, IA; *Format:* Sports *Special Programming:* Farm 12 hrs, sports 15 hrs wkly; *Hrs. of News Programming:* news progmg 10 hrs wkly; *No. News Employees:* 2; *Target Audience:* 35 plus. *Adv. Rates:* 15; 12; 14; 11

WPVL-FM
09-01-1966; 107.1 MHz FM; *Hrs Open:* 24; 4.2 kW; 394 ft; N46 06 11.4 W 119 08 0.6
51 Means Dr, Platteville, WI 53818 USA
(608) 349-2000; *Fax:* (608) 349-2002
x1071.com
xtremehitradio@hotmail.com
License: Platteville, Grant County, WI held by QueenB Radio Wisconsin Inc.
Group Owner: Morgan Murphy Media
Arbitron Metro Market: Dubuque, IA; *Format:* Contemporary Hits/Top 40

*WSUP
02-25-1964; 90.5 MHz FM; *Hrs Open:* 20; 1 kw; 148 ft.; N42 43 57 W90 29 9
1220 Linden Drive, Madison, WI 53706 US
(608) 342-1165,(608) 342-1291; *Fax:* (608) 342-1290
ums.www.uwplatt.edu/~wsup/
wsup@uwplatt.edu
License: Platteville, Grant County, WI held by Board of Regents, University of Wisconsin System.
Arbitron Metro Market: Dubuque, IA; *Format:* Rock/AOR *Special Programming:* Class 4 hrs, jazz 3 hrs, alternative 6 hrs, metal 6

hrs, dance 4 hrs wkly; *Hrs. of News Programming:* News progmg 10 hrs wkly *TargetAudience:* 18-24; college-age
George Smith, General Manager
Laura Lohfink, Station Manager

***WSSW**
02-01-2007; 89.1 MHz FM; 0.06 kw; 561 ft.; N42 45 50.7 W90 24 19.7 *Rebroadcasts:* Rebroadcasts WERN(FM) Madison 100%
3319 W Beltline Highway, Madison, WI 53713 US
(608) 263-3970; *Fax:* (608) 263-9763
www.wpr.org
License: Platteville, Grant County, WI held by State of Wisconsin-Educational Communications Board.
Nat'l Network: NPR; *Regional Network:* Wis. Public Radio
Arbitron Metro Market: Platteville, WI; *Format:* Classical
Tim Allen, Operations Dir
Phil Corniveau, General Manager
Michael Leland, News Director
Mike Crane, Director of Radio
Michael Arnold, Associate Director
Mary Kay Dadisman, Director of Development
Steve Johnston, Director ofEngineering & Operations

Plymouth

WJUB
04-01-1954; 1420 kHz AM; *Hrs Open:* 24; 0.5 kw-D, ND1; 0.062 kw-N, ND1; N43 44 33 W87 56 21
N5569 Sth 57, Plymouth, WI 53073 US
(920) 893-2661; *Fax:* (920) 892-2706
www.1420thebreeze.com
1420amthebreeze@jmiradio.org
License: Plymouth, WI held by Jubilation Ministries Inc.
Nat'l Network: USA
Arbitron Metro Market: Sheboygan, WI; *Format:* Adult Contemp *Special Programming:* Farm 5 hrs wkly; *Hrs. of News Programming:* News progmg 11 hrs wkly; *Target Audience:* 25-54.
Gerry Krebsbach, President
William Horsch, General Manager
David Hendrickson, Programming Director

WXER
10-03-2000; 104.5 MHz FM; *Hrs Open:* 24; 5.1 kW; 354 ft.; N43 43 32 W88 3 7
2100 Washington Ave, Sheboygan Falls, WI 53081 USA
(920) 458-2107; *Fax:* (920) 458-9775
wxerfm.com
License: Plymouth, Sheboygan County, WI held by Midwest Communications Inc.
Group Owner: Midwest Communications Inc.; (acq 11-1-2005; $2.3 million)
Arbitron Metro Market: Sheboygan, WI; *Format:* Contemporary Hits/Top 40 *Special Programming:* Ger 3 hrs wkly; *Target Audience:* 29-54.
Jeff Frieders, Brand Manager

Port Washington

WPJP
10-01-1969; 100.1 MHz FM; *Hrs Open:* 24; 6 kw; 318 ft.; N43 25 14 W87 59 40
900 East Green Bay Road, Port Washington, WI 53074 US
(920) 469-3021; *Fax:* (262) 784-2149
www.live365.com
License: Port Washington, Ozaukee County, WI held by Starboard Media Foundation Inc.
Group Owner: Relevant Radio; (acq 5-15-2003; $900,000).
Arbitron Metro Market: Milwaukee-Racine, WI
Mark Follett, CEO
Neil Robbins, Station Manager

Portage

WBKY
01-01-1999; 95.9 MHz FM; *Hrs Open:* 24; 5.4 kw; 322 ft.; N43 38 17 W89 34 16
Mailing Address: N6912 Highway 51 S., Portage, WI 53901 USA
Second Address: N2349 WIBU Rd., Poynette, WI 53955
(608) 742-1001; *Fax:* (608) 742-1688
www.buckycountry959.com
info@magnumbroadcasting.com
License: Portage, WI held by Magnum Communications, Inc.
Group Owner: Magnum Communications Inc.
Arbitron Metro Market: Portage, WI; *Format:* Country; *No. News Employees:* 2
David R. Magnum, President

WDDC
11-08-1966; 100.1 MHz FM; *Hrs Open:* 24; 3.1 kw; 374 ft.; N43 31 42 W89 26 1
Mailing Address: N6912 Highway 51 S., PO Box 448, Portage, WI 53901 US
Second Address: 201 8th Ave., Baraboo, WI 53913
(608) 742-1001; *Fax:* (608) 742-1688
www.thunder100fm.com
info@magnumbroadcasting.com
License: Portage, WI held by Magnum Communications, Inc
Group Owner: Magnum Communications, Inc
Arbitron Metro Market: Madison, WI; *Format:* Country
David R. Magnum, President

WPDR
07-31-1952; 1350 kHz AM; *Hrs Open:* 24; 1 kw-D, ND1; 0.041 kw-N, ND1; N43 31 42 W89 26 1
Mailing Address: N6912 Highway 51 S., PO Box 448, Portage, WI 53901 US
Second Address: 201 8th Ave., Baraboo, WI 53913
(608) 742-1001; *Fax:* (608) 742-1688
www.wpdr.com
info@magnumbroadcasting.com
License: Portage, WI held by Magnum Communications, Inc.
Group Owner: Magnum Communications, Inc.
Format: Oldies
David R. Magnum, President

Poynette

WHFA
07-01-1925; 1240 kHz AM; *Hrs Open:* 24; 1 kw-U, ND1; N43 21 38 W89 24 8
1021 N. Superior Ave., Suite 5, Tomah, WI 54660 US
(920) 469-3021; *Fax:* (608) 833-7117
www.relevantradio.com
whfa@relevantradio.com
License: Poynette, WI held by Starboard Media Foundation Inc.
Group Owner: Relevant Radio; (acq 6-28-2001; $1 million).
Nat'l Network: ABC; *Regional Network:* Tribune Radio Networks; Wisconsin Radio Net.
Arbitron Metro Market: Madison, WI; *Format:* Christian; *Hrs. of News Programming:* News progmg 3 hrs wkly; *Target Audience:* 35-64.
Martin Jury, Operations Dir

Prairie Du Chien

WPRE
12-11-1952; 980 kHz AM; *Hrs Open:* 24
WI US
(608) 326-2411; *Fax:* (608) 326-2412
www.wpreradio.com
wqpcwpre@mwt.net
License: Prairie Du Chien, WI held by Robinson Corp.
Group Owner: Robinson Corporation; (acq 1-7-98; with co-located FM).
Nat'l Network: Westwood One
Format: Oldies; *No. News Employees:* 1

WQPC
01-01-1968; 94.3 MHz FM; *Hrs Open:* 24; 36 kw; 525 ft.; N43 3 35 W91 6 2
WI US
(608) 326-2411; *Fax:* (608) 326-2412
www.wqpcradio.com
wqpcwpre@mwt.net
License: Prairie Du Chien, Crawford County, WI held by Robinson Corp.
Group Owner: Robinson Corporation
Format: Country

Racine

WVTY
01-01-1961; 92.1 MHz FM; *Hrs Open:* 24; 2.7 kw; 492 ft.; N42 45 36 W87 57 53
4201 Victory Ave., Racine, WI 53405 USA
(262) 634-3311; *Fax:* (262) 634-6515
www.921theshore.com
License: Racine, WI held by Magnum Communications, Inc.
Group Owner: Magnum Communications, Inc.
Arbitron Metro Market: Racine, WI; *Format:* Adult Contemp
David R. Magnum, President

WKKV-FM
08-01-1948; 100.7 MHz FM; *Hrs Open:* 24; 50 kw; 499 ft.; N42 48 18 W88 2 54
12100 W. Howard Ave., Greenfield, WI 53228 US
(414) 321-1007; *Fax:* (414) 546-9654
www.v100.com
info@v100.com
License: Racine, Racine County, WI held by Clear Channel Broadcasting Licenses Inc.
Group Owner: iHeartMedia; (acq 1996; grpsl)
Nat'l Network: Premiere Radio Networks; Superadio; *Nat'l Reps:* Clear Channel
Arbitron Metro Market: Milwaukee-Racine, WI; *Format:* Blues, Urban Contemporary *Special Programming:* Gospel 6 hrs wkly; *Target Audience:* 18-44; general
Colleen Valkoun, Market President
Phil Kurth, Sales Manager
Bailey Coleman, Programming Director

WRJN
12-01-1926; 1400 kHz AM; *Hrs Open:* 24; 1 kw-U, ND1; N42 42 38 W87 49 49
4201 Victory Ave., Racine, WI 53405 USA
(262) 634-3311; *Fax:* (262) 634-6515
www.wrjn.com
wrjn@wi.net
License: Racine, WI held by Magnum Communications, Inc.
Group Owner: Magnum Communications, Inc.
Arbitron Metro Market: Milwaukee-Racine, WI; *Format:* Oldies, Adult Contemp
Dave Magnum, President

Reedsburg

WBDL
01-01-1997; 102.9 MHz FM; 3.6 kw; 423 ft.; N43 35 32 W90 0 42
Mailing Address: E5680A Highway 33, Reedsburg, WI 53959 USA
Second Address: 201 8th Ave., Baraboo, WI 53913
(608) 524-1400; *Fax:* (608) 524-2474
www.wbdlfm.com
info@magnumbroadcasting.com
License: Reedsburg, Sauk County, WI held by Magnum Communications Inc.
Group Owner: Magnum Communications Inc.; (acq 10-18-2007; grpsl)
Nat'l Network: ABC
Arbitron Metro Market: Mesquite TX; *Format:* Adult Contemp
David R. Magnum, President

WNFM
07-16-1967; 104.9 MHz FM; *Hrs Open:* 24; 3.2 kw; 449 ft.; N43 35 32 W90 0 42
E5680A Highway 33, Reedsburg, WI 53913 USA
(608) 524-1049; *Fax:* (608) 524-2474
www.wnfmcountry.com
info@magnumbroadcasting.com
License: Reedsburg, WI held by Magnum Communications, Inc.
Group Owner: Magnum Communications Inc.
Arbitron Metro Market: Reedsburh, WI; *Format:* Country; *No. News Employees:* 1
David R. Magnum, President

WRDB
02-06-1953; 1400 kHz AM; *Hrs Open:* 24; 1 kw-U, ND1; N43 32 30 W90 2 5
Mailing Address: E5680A Highway 33, PO Box 349, Reedsburg, WI 53959 USA
Second Address: 201 8th Ave., Baraboo, WI 53913
(608) 524-1400; *Fax:* (608) 524-2474
www.wrdbam.com
info@magnumbroadcasting.com
License: Reedsburg, WI held by Magnum Communications Inc.
Group Owner: Magnum Communications Inc.
Format: Oldies, Sports
David R. Magnum, President

Reedsville

WOGB
01-01-1996; 103.1 MHz FM; 3.6 kw; 879 ft.; N44 21 32 W87 59 7
810 Victoria St., Green Bay, WI 54302 US
(920) 468-4100; *Fax:* (920) 468-0250
www.wogb.fm
wogb@cumulus.com
License: Reedsville, Outagamie County, WI held by Cumulus Licensing LLC
Group Owner: Cumulus Media Inc.; (acq 8-30-2013)
Nat'l Reps: Katz Radio; *Wire Services:* AP
Arbitron Metro Market: Appleton-Oshkos; *Format:* Oldies; *No. News Employees:* 35-54; affluent baby-boom; *Adv. Rates:* 90; 90; 90; 25
Mike Thompson, Market Manager/General Sales Manager
Dan Markus, Programming Director

Reserve

***WOJB**
04-01-1982; 88.9 MHz FM; 100 kw; 604 ft; N45 52 16 W91 20 56

RADIO - U.S.

13386 W. Trepania Rd., Hayward, WI 54843
(715) 634-4070; *Fax:* (715) 634-4070
www.wojb.org
generalmanager@wojb.org
License: Reserve, WI held by Lac Courte Oreilles Ojibwe Public Broadcasting Corp.
Nat'l Network: NPR; PRI
Special Programming: Indian 15 hrs, country 15 hrs, jazz 10 hrs, bluegrass 2 hrs wkly
Sid Kellar, General Manager

Rhinelander

WHDG
09-01-1994; 97.3 MHz FM; *Hrs Open:* 24; 100 kw; 551 ft.; N45 22 50 W89 11 22
P. O. Box 96, 7380 Hwy 51 South, Minocqua, WI 54548 US
(715) 362-1975; *Fax:* (715) 362-1973
www.whdg.com
whdg@whdg.com
License: Rhinelander, Oneida County, WI held by Raven License Sub. LLC.
Group Owner: NRG Media LLC; (acq 10-31-2005; grpsl)
Wire Services: Wheeler News Service
Format: Country; *Hrs. of News Programming:* news progmg 10 hrs wkly; *No. News Employees:* 1; *Target Audience:* 25-54.; *Adv. Rates:* 45; 42; 44; 15
Duff Damos, Operations Dir
Steve Albertson, General Manager
Bill Mitchell, Programming Director
Mary Spatz, News Director
Al Johnson, Chief Engineer

WOBT
03-09-1947; 1240 kHz AM
980 North Michigan Ave, Ste. 1880, Chicago, IL 60611 US
715-362-6140; *Fax:* 715-362-4200
License: Rhinelander, WI held by NRG License Sub. LLC.
Group Owner: NRG Media LLC; (acq 10-31-2005; grpsl)
TV Affiliate: Sports *Special Programming:* news progmg 10 hrs wkly; *Hrs. of News Programming:* 1; *No. News Employees:* 18+.

WRHN
01-26-1966; 100.1 MHz FM; *Hrs Open:* 24; 100 kw; 292 ft.; N45 37 42 W89 23 38
980 North Michigan Ave, Ste. 1880, Chicago, IL 60611 US
(715) 362-1975; *Fax:* (715) 362-1973
www.wrhn.com
License: Rhinelander, Oneida County, WI held by NRG License Sub. LLC.
Group Owner: NRG Media LLC
Format: Adult Contemp; *Target Audience:* 18-49.; *Adv. Rates:* 30; 27; 29; 9
Duff Damos, Operations Dir
Steve Albertson, General Sales Mgr

***WXPR**
04-24-1983; 91.7 MHz FM; *Hrs Open:* 5 AM-midnight; 100 kw; 420 ft.; N45 46 28 W89 14 54
303 W. Prospect St., Rhinelander, WI 54501 US
(715) 362-6000; *Fax:* (715) 362-6007
www.wxpr.org
wxpr@wxpr.org
License: Rhinelander, Oneida County, WI held by White Pine Community Broadcasting Inc.
Nat'l Network: NPR
Arbitron Metro Market: Rhinelander, WI; *Format:* Variety/Diverse
Special Programming: Jazz 8 hrs wkly
Mick Fiocchi, President
Walt Gander, Operations Dir
Peg Arnold, Station Manager
Ken Krall, News Director
Elmer Goetsch, Chief Engineer
Mick Fiocchi, Executive Advisor
Becky Tegen, Membership Director
Marcia Barkusÿ, MusicDirector
Cara Kulhanek, Database Manager
Jessie Dickÿ, Development Director

***KSPP**
89.1 MHz FM; 8.5 kw vert; 89.9 meters; N45 46 30.5 W89 14 55.1
1980 Moraine Terrace, Suite 9, Green Bay, WI
(262) 349-3254
License: Rhinelander, WI held by Northwoods Catholic Radio

Christopher P. Cichanter, President

WHOH
96.5 MHz FM; 2.45 kw; 318 m; N45 40 03 W89 12 29
1456 East Green Bay Street, Shawano, WI 54166-2258 US
(715) 524-2194; *Fax:* (715) 524-9980
License: Rhinelander, Oneida County, WI held by Results Broadcasting of Rhinelander Inc.
Group Owner: Results Broadcasting

Rice Lake

WAQE
08-06-1979; 1090 kHz AM; 5 kw-D, NDD; N45 32 16 W91 45 50
1859 21st Ave., Rice Lake, WI 54868 US
(715) 234-2131; *Fax:* (715) 234-6942
www.waqe.com
info@wage.com
License: Rice Lake, WI held by TKC Inc.
Group Owner: Koser Radio Group; (acq 1999)
Arbitron Metro Market: Rice Lake, WI; *Format:* Sports, Talk; *Hrs. of News Programming:* news progmg 5 hrs wkly; *No. News Employees:* 1; *Target Audience:* 24-59; traditional country mus listeners *Adv. Rates:* 12; 8; 10; na
Thomas A. Koser, President

WKFX
11-20-1980; 97.7 MHz FM; *Hrs Open:* 24; 44 kw; 522 ft.; N45 22 23 W91 55 22
1859 21st Avenue, Rice Lake, WI 54868 US
(715) 234-9059; *Fax:* (715) 234-6942
www.fox99.com
info@fox99.com
License: Rice Lake, Barron County, WI held by TKC Inc.
Arbitron Metro Market: Rice Lake, WI; *Format:* Contemporary Hits/Top 40, Adult Contemp; *Hrs. of News Programming:* news progmg 3 hrs wkly; *No. News Employees:* 1; *Target Audience:* 18-49; young, upscale adults *Adv. Rates:* 12; 8; 10; 6
Tom Koser, CEO
Peter Neuser, Station Manager

WJMC
01-01-1938; 1240 kHz AM; *Hrs Open:* 24; 1 kw-U, ND1; N45 30 31 W91 46 26
1859 21st Ave., Rice Lake, WI 54868 US
(715) 234-2131
www.wjmcradio.com
info@wjmcradio.com
License: Rice Lake, WI held by TKC Inc.
Group Owner: Koser Radio Group; (acq 1-1-89)
Regional Network: Wisconsin Radio Net.
Format: News/Talk; *Target Audience:* 25-54.
Thomas A. Koser, President

WJMC-FM
01-01-1947; 96.1 MHz FM; *Hrs Open:* 24; 50 kw; 482 ft.; N45 37 14 W91 44 44
Mailing Address: 1859 21st Ave., Rice Lake, WI 54868 US
Second Address: 1859 21st Ave., Rice Lake, WI 54868
(715) 234-2131
www.wjmcradio.com
info@wjmcradio.com
License: Rice Lake, Barron County, WI held by TKC Inc.
Group Owner: Koser Radio Group
Format: Country; *Target Audience:* 25-54.
Thomas A. Koser, President

Richland Center

WRCO
10-18-1949; 1450 kHz AM; *Hrs Open:* 24; 1 kw-U, ND1; N43 18 58 W90 22 31
P.O. Box 529, 2111 Bohmann Drive, Richland Center, WI 53581 US
(608) 647-2111; *Fax:* (608) 647-8025
www.wrco.com
wrconews@wrco.com
License: Richland Center, WI held by Fruit Broadcasting LLC.
Nat'l Network: CBS; Westwood One; *Wire Services:* AP; Wheeler News Service
Format: Adult Contemp *Special Programming:* Farm 2.hrs wkly; *Hrs. of News Programming:* news progmg 20 hrs wkly; *No. News Employees:* 1; *Target Audience:* 25-54; general; *Adv. Rates:* 6; 5; 5; 3
Ron Fruit, President
Alice Schulte, General Sales Mgr
Phil Nee, Programming Director
Aaron Joyce, News Director
Dennis Baldridge, Chief Engineer
Amy Cook, Traffic Manager

WRCO-FM
08-01-1965; 100.9 MHz FM; *Hrs Open:* 24; 8.4 kw; 559 ft.; N43 18 55.5 W90 25 34.6
2111 Bohmann Drive, PO Box 529, Richland Center, WI 53581 US
(608) 647-21111; *Fax:* (608) 647-8025
www.wrco.com
wrconews@wrco.com
License: Richland Center, Richland County, WI
Nat'l Network: CBS Radio; *Regional Network:* Wisconsin Radio Net.; *Wire Services:* AP; Wheeler News Service
Format: Country, News *Special Programming:* Farm 18 hrs, Gospel 6 hrs wkly; *Hrs. of News Programming:* news progmg 45 hrs wkly; *No. News Employees:* 2; *Target Audience:* General; adult; *Adv. Rates:* 12; 10;12; 8
Ron Fruit, Operations Dir
Alice Schulte, General Sales Mgr
Phil Nee, Programming Director
Dennis Baldridge, Chief Engineer
Ray Schroeder, Disc Jockey
Tammy Dotson, Disc Jockey
Adam Hess, Disc Jockey

Ripon

***WRPN-FM**
09-15-1957; 90.1 MHz FM; *Hrs Open:* 24; 0.23 kw horiz; 144 ft.; N43 50 37 W88 50 31
300 Seward Street, Ripon, WI 54971 US
(920) 748-8147,(920) 748-8115 (college); *Fax:* (920) 748-7243
www.homestead.com
wrpnfm@yahoo.com
License: Ripon, WI held by Board of Trustees of Ripon College.
Nat'l Network: CBS; ABC; *Nat'l Reps:* Farmakis; *Wire Services:* Wheeler News Service
Format: Classic Rock, Variety/Diverse *Special Programming:* Pol 2 hrs, sports 15 hrs wkly; *Hrs. of News Programming:* news progmg 25 hrs wkly; *No. News Employees:* 4
Joe Laedtke, Operations Dir
Guy McHendry, General Manager

WTCX
02-01-1965; 96.1 MHz FM; *Hrs Open:* 24; 4 kw; 404 ft.; N43 49 10 W88 43 20
6 Western Avenue, Fond Du Lac, WI 54935 US
(920) 924-9697; *Fax:* (920) 929-8865
www.961tcx.com
License: Ripon, Fond du Lac County, WI
Arbitron Metro Market: Ripon, WI; *Format:* Adult Contemp, Rock/AOR; *Hrs. of News Programming:* news progmg 3 hrs wkly; *No. News Employees:* 1; *Target Audience:* 25-54; women
Terry Davis, Operations Dir
Gregg Owens, Programming Director
Kimberley Kings, Promotions Manager
Greg Stensland, News Director
Mike Enfelt, Operations Manager

WRPN
09-15-1957; 1600 kHz AM; *Hrs Open:* 24; 5 kw-D, DA2; 5 kw-N, DA2; N43 49 1 W88 50 49
6 Western Avenue, Fond Du Lac, WI 54935 US
(920) 748-5111; *Fax:* (920) 748-5530
www.wrpnam.com
wrpn@wrpnam.com
License: Ripon, WI held by Radio Broadcasting L.P.
Nat'l Network: CBS; ABC; *Nat'l Reps:* Farmakis; *Wire Services:* Wheeler News Service
Arbitron Metro Market: Ripon, WI; *Format:* News, News/Talk, 86; *Hrs. of News Programming:* news progmg 25 hrs wkly; *No. News Employees:* 4; *Target Audience:* 25 plus.
Mike Enfelt, President & CEO
Mike Enfelt, General Manager
Jason Marsmith, Programming Director
Sarah Kesich, News and Producer / Traffic & Billing
Jean Hoffmann, Traffic & Billing

River Falls

WEVR
09-14-1969; 1550 kHz AM; *Hrs Open:* 6 AM-sunset; 0.92 kw-D, ND1; 0.004 kw-N, ND1; N44 53 19 W92 39 2
178 Radio Road, River Falls, WI 54022 US
(715) 425-1111(612) 381-1111
License: River Falls, WI held by Hanten Broadcasting Co. Inc.
Nat'l Network: USA; *Wire Services:* Wheeler News Service
Arbitron Metro Market: River Falls, WI; *Format:* Adult Contemp, Sports *Special Programming:* Farm 18 hrs wkly; *Hrs. of News Programming:* News progmg 5 hrs wkly; *Target Audience:* General.
Carol Hanten, President

WEVR-FM
09-30-1970; 106.3 MHz FM; *Hrs Open:* 6 AM-11 PM; 6 kw; 328 ft.; N44 53 19 W92 39 2
178 Radio Road, River Falls, WI 54022 US
(715) 425-1111; *Fax:* (715) 381-1111

License: River Falls, Pierce County, WI held by Hanten Broadcasting Co. Inc.
Wire Services: Wheeler News Service
Arbitron Metro Market: River Falls, WI; *Format:* Adult Contemp, News, 84; *Hrs. of News Programming:* News progmg 18 hrs wkly; *Target Audience:* General.
Carol Hanten, President

***WRFW**
11-02-1968; 88.7 MHz FM; *Hrs Open:* 24; 3 kw; 82 ft.; N44 53 8 W92 39 20
1220 Linden Drive, Madison, WI 53706 US
(715) 425-3886/3887
www.uwrf.edu/wrfw
License: River Falls, Pierce County, WI held by University of Wisconsin System.
Nat'l Network: NPR *Regional Reps:* Wisconsin Public Radio
Arbitron Metro Market: Minneapolis-St. Paul, MN; *Format:* Variety/Diverse *Special Programming:* Farm 10 hrs wkly
Rick Burgsteiner, General Manager
Adam Lee, Programming Director
Nick Hassel, Promotions Manager
Tara Sowle, News Director
Paul Karklus, Music Director

Rothschild

WDTX
100.5 MHz FM; 25 kw; 276 ft.; N44 50 13 W89 45 57 US
(715) 845-8218; *Fax:* (715) 845-6582
www.espn1005.com
License: Rothschild, Marathon County, WI held by JER Licenses LLC.
Group Owner: JER Licenses LLC
Arbitron Metro Market: Rothschild, WI; *Format:* Sports, Talk
Jon Robinson, General Manager

Rudolph

WSAU-FM
09-30-1990; 99.9 MHz FM; *Hrs Open:* 24; 13 kW; 453 ft; N44 20 19 W89 38 55 *Rebroadcasts:* Simulcast with WOFM(FM) Mosinee 100%
557 Scott St, Wausau, WI 54403 USA
(715) 842-1672; *Fax:* (715) 848-3158
wsau.com
License: Rudolph, Wood County, WI held by WRIG Inc.
Group Owner: Midwest Communications Inc.; (acq 1999; $1.4 million)
Nat'l Network: Fox News Radio; *Nat'l Reps:* Christal
Arbitron Metro Market: Wausau, WI; *Format:* News/Talk; *Hrs. of News Programming:* news progmg 3 hrs wkly; *No. News Employees:* 3; *Target Audience:* 35 plus; upper income
Chris Conley, Brand Manager

Sarona

WPLT
01-01-2003; 106.3 MHz FM; *Hrs Open:* 24; 3.4 kw; 440 ft.; N45 40 28 W91 58 52
Box 190, Hwy 63 S, Shell Lake, WI 54871 US
(715) 468-9500; *Fax:* (715) 468-9505
www.zoestations.com
License: Sarona, Washburn County, WI held by Zoe Communications Inc.
Group Owner: Zoe Communications Inc.; acq 12-6-00; $439,000 for CP).
Arbitron Metro Market: Shell Lake, WI; *Format:* Country
Bo Landry, Operations Dir

Sauk City

WIBA-FM
03-01-1947; 101.5 MHz FM; 12 kw; 1014 ft.; N43 3 21 W89 32 6
600 Congress Ave., Suite 1400, Austin, TX 78701 US
(608) 274-5450; *Fax:* (608) 274-5521
www.wibafm.com
info@wibafm.com
License: Sauk City, Dane County, WI held by Capstar TX LLC
Group Owner: iHeartMedia
Arbitron Metro Market: Madison, WI; *Format:* Classic Rock
Colleen Valkoun, Market President
Tim Etes, General Sales Mgr
Tim Scott, Senior Vice President of Programming
James Kaska, Online Content Director

Schofield

WRIG
08-01-1958; 1390 kHz AM; *Hrs Open:* 24; 10 kW-D, 7.2 kW-N; N44 59 18 W89 59 42
557 Scott St, Wausau, WI 54403 USA
(715) 842-1672; *Fax:* (715) 848-3158
foxsportswausau.com
License: Schofield, WI held by WRIG Inc.
Group Owner: Midwest Communications Inc.
Arbitron Metro Market: Wausau, WI; *Format:* Sports; *Hrs. of News Programming:* news progmg 2 hrs wkly; *No. News Employees:* 2
Ken Clark, Brand Manager

Seymour

WKZG
05-01-1998; 104.3 MHz FM; 5.6 kw; Ant 341 ft; N44 31 26 W88 19 56
Box 1519, Appleton, WI 54165
(920) 734-9226; *Fax:* (920) 739-0494
License: Seymour, Outagamie County, WI held by Woodward Communications Inc.
Group Owner: Woodward Communications Inc.; acq 6-23-2003; $1.75 million).
Population Served: 152,069; *Arbitron Metro Market:* Green Bay, WI
Greg Bell, General Manager
Kelly Radandt, General Sales Mgr
Dayton Kane, Programming Director
Steve Brown, Chief Engineer

Shawano

WOWN
12-01-1966; 99.3 MHz FM; *Hrs Open:* 24; 14 kw; 440 ft.; N44 45 14 W88 20 1
1456 East Green Bay St., Shawano, WI 54166 US
(715) 524-2194; *Fax:* (715) 524-9980
License: Shawano, Shawano County, WI
Group Owner: Results Broadcasting
Nat'l Network: ABC
Arbitron Metro Market: Green Bay, WI; *Format:* Contemporary Hits/Top 40, Adult Contemp; *Hrs. of News Programming:* news progmg 13 hrs wkly; *No. News Employees:* 1; *Target Audience:* 20-45.
Bruce Grassman, CEO

WTCH
09-03-1948; 960 kHz AM; *Hrs Open:* 24
1456 East Green Bay St., Shawano, WI 54166 US
(715) 524-2194; *Fax:* (715) 524-9980
www.wtcham960.com
ResultsBroadcasting@gmail.com
License: Shawano, WI held by Results Broadcasting Inc.
Group Owner: Results Broadcasting; (acq 12-23-96; $2,704,670 for 50% of stock with co-located FM).
Nat'l Network: CBS
Arbitron Metro Market: Green Bay, WI; *Format:* Country *Special Programming:* Farm 21 hrs wkly; *Hrs. of News Programming:* news progmg 25 hrs wkly; *No. News Employees:* 1; *Target Audience:* 25-54; northeastWisconsin adults
Bruce Grassman, Chairman
Trisha Peterson, Operations Dir

Sheboygan

WBFM
03-01-1977; 93.7 MHz FM; 6 kW; 253 ft.; N43 43 12 W87 44 4
2100 Washington Ave, Sheboygan, WI 53081 USA
(920) 458-2107; *Fax:* (920) 458-9775
b93radio.com
License: Sheboygan, Sheboygan County, WI held by Midwest Communications Inc.
Group Owner: Midwest Communications Inc.
Nat'l Network: Fox News Radio *Regional Reps:* Rgnl Reps
Arbitron Metro Market: Sheboygan, WI; *Format:* Country; *Hrs. of News Programming:* news progmg 24 hrs wkly; *No. News Employees:* 2; *Target Audience:* 25-54; adults in Sheboygan county/Northern Milwaukee metro area *Adv. Rates:* 50; 50; 50; 20
Jonathan Henseler, Brand Manager

WCLB
01-01-1956; 950 kHz AM; *Hrs Open:* 18; 0.5 kw-D, DA2; 0.011 kw-N, DA2; N43 44 33 W87 49 0
254 Winnebago Drive, Fond du Lac, WI 54937 US
(920) 921-1071; *Fax:* (920) 467-4300
www.950thegame.com
wbates@mdogmedia.com
License: Sheboygan, WI held by RBH Enterprises Inc. dba Yellow Dog Broadcasting.
Group Owner: Mountain Dog Media; (acq 6-23-00; $700,000 with WXER(FM) Plymouth).
Nat'l Network: Westwood One
Arbitron Metro Market: Sheboygan, WI; *Format:* Sports; *Hrs. of News Programming:* news progmg 8 hrs wkly; *No. News Employees:* 2; *Target Audience:* 35-64.; *Adv. Rates:* 22; 20; 22
Randy Hopper, General Manager

WHBL
01-01-1926; 1330 kHz AM; *Hrs Open:* 24; 5 kW-D, 1 kW-N; N43 43 14 W87 44 4
2100 Washington Ave, Sheboygan, WI 53081 USA
(920) 458-2107; *Fax:* (920) 458-9775
whbl.com
License: Sheboygan, WI held by Midwest Communications Inc.
Group Owner: Midwest Communications Inc.; (acq 8-8-2000; grpsl)
Nat'l Network: Fox News Radio; *Regional Network:* Wisconsin Radio Net; *Nat'l Reps:* Rgnl Reps
Arbitron Metro Market: Sheboygan, WI; *Format:* News/Talk *Special Programming:* Farm 10 hrs wkly; *Hrs. of News Programming:* news progmg 24 hrs wkly; *No. News Employees:* 2; *Target Audience:* 35-64 *Adv.Rates:* 50; 50; 50; 20
Kelly Meyer, Brand Manager

***WSHS**
11-19-1971; 91.7 MHz FM; *Hrs Open:* 24; 0.175 kw vert; 85 ft.; N43 46 32 W87 43 4
830 Virginia Avenue, Sheboygan, WI 53081 US
(920) 459-3500; *Fax:* (920) 803-7612
www.sheboygan.k12.wi.us
wshs@sheboygan.k12.wi.us
License: Sheboygan, Sheboygan County, WI held by Sheboygan Area School District.
Nat'l Network: NPR; *Regional Network:* Wis. Public Radio
Regional Reps: Glenn Slatts
Arbitron Metro Market: Sheboygan, WI; *Format:* Adult Contemp, Rock/AOR *Special Programming:* Hmong 3 hrs, Sp 3 hrs wkly; *Target Audience:* 18-45; young adults & teens
Ron Rindfleish, President
Jon Etter, General Manager

Sheboygan Falls

WHBZ
04-01-1997; 106.5 MHz FM; 6 kW; 240 ft.; N43 43 16 W87 44 3
2100 Washington Ave, Sheboygan, WI 53081 USA
(920) 458-2107; *Fax:* (920) 458-9775
1065thebuzz.com
License: Sheboygan Falls, Sheboygan County, WI held by Midwest Communications Inc.
Group Owner: Midwest Communications Inc.; acq 8-8-00; grpsl).
Nat'l Network: Fox News Radio; *Nat'l Reps:* Rgnl Reps
Arbitron Metro Market: Sheboygan, WI; *Hrs. of News Programming:* News progmg 10 hrs wkly; *No. News Employees:* 2; *Target Audience:* Males 18-49; *Adv. Rates:* 65; 65; 65; 65
Jeff Frieders, Brand Manager

Shell Lake

WCSW
12-30-1967; 940 kHz AM; 1 kW-D, NDD; N45 41 36 W91 57 57
Box 190, Hwy 63 S, Shell Lake, WI 54871-0190 US
(253) 887-8464; *Fax:* (253) 887-8661
www.pilgrimcommunicationsinc.com
License: Shell Lake, WI held by Zoe Communications Inc.
Group Owner: Zoe Communications Inc.; acq 1-1-00; with co-located FM)
Nat'l Network: ABC
Arbitron Metro Market: Eau Claire WI; *Format:* News/Talk *Special Programming:* Farm 3 hrs wkly; *Target Audience:* General.
Bo Landry, Operations Dir

Siren

WXCX
01-01-2000; 105.7 MHz FM; *Hrs Open:* 24; 6 kw; 328 ft.; N45 49 43 W92 28 41
15429 Pokegama Lake Rd., Pine City, MN 55063 US
(320) 629-7575
www.redrockonair.com
License: Siren, Burnett County, WI held by Red Rock Radio Corp.
Group Owner: Red Rock Radio Corp.; (acq 9-1-2006; grpsl)
Nat'l Network: Jones Radio Networks; *Nat'l Reps:* Midwest Radio
Regional Reps: MidwestRadio
Arbitron Metro Market: Sebring, FL; *Format:* Adult Contemp; *No. News Employees:* 1; *Target Audience:* 35-64.
Romeo Grignon, CEO/COO
Scott Christensen, General Sales Mgr

Sister Bay

***WHDI**
01-01-2000; 91.9 MHz FM; 3.4 kw; 476 ft.; N45 14 19 W87 5 27

3319 West Beltline Hwy, Madison, WI 53713 US
(608) 264-9600; *Fax:* (608) 264-9664
www.ecb.org
info@ecb.org
License: Sister Bay, Door County, WI held by State of Wisconsin-Educational Communications Board.
Nat'l Network: NPR; *Regional Network:* Wis. Public Radio
Format: Talk
Gene Purcell, General Manager
Phil Corriveau, Station Manager

***WHND**
09-16-1999; 89.7 MHz FM; *Hrs Open:* 24; 3.4 kw; 538 ft.; N45 14 19 W87 5 27
Mailing Address: 3319 West Beltline Hwy, Madison, WI 53713 US
Second Address: 821 University Ave., Madison, WI 53706
(920) 465-2444; *Fax:* (920) 465-2576
www.wpr.org
listener@wpr.org
License: Sister Bay, Door County, WI held by State of Wisconsin Educational Communications Board.
Nat'l Network: NPR; PRI
Format: Classical, News *Special Programming:* Native American 2 hrs, blues 2 hrs, folk 2 hrs, ja; *Hrs. of News Programming:* news progmg 29 hrs wkly; *No. News Employees:* 1; *Target Audience:* 35 plus; sociallyaware, educated & financially secure; *Adv. Rates:* 55; 40; 50; 35
Lisa Nalbandian, General Sales Mgr
Patty Murray, News Director

Soldiers Grove

WKPO
06-03-2009; 105.9 MHz FM; *Hrs Open:* 24; 25 kw; 328 ft.; N43 34 26 W90 48 55
WI USA
(608) 326-2411; *Fax:* (608) 326-2412
www.wqpcradio.com
wqpcwpre@mwt.net
License: Soldiers Grove, Crawford County, WI held by Robinson Corp.
Group Owner: Robinson Corporation; (acq 6-5-2008; $250,000)
Arbitron Metro Market: Soldiers Grove, WI; *Format:* Adult Contemp; *No. News Employees:* 1

Sparta

WCOW-FM
03-01-1960; 97.1 MHz FM; *Hrs Open:* 24; 100 kw; 587 ft.; N43 58 6 W90 51 35
P.O. Box 539, Sparta, WI 54656 US
(608) 269-3100; *Fax:* (608) 269-5170
www.cow97.com
License: Sparta, Monroe County, WI held by Sparta-Tomah Broadcasting Co. Inc.
Group Owner: Sparta-Tomah Broadcasting Co. Inc.
Nat'l Reps: Rgnl Reps; *Wire Services:* CNN
Arbitron Metro Market: La Crosse,WI; *Format:* Country *Special Programming:* Green Bay Packers; *Hrs. of News Programming:* news progmg 15 hrs wkly; *Target Audience:* 25 plus; rural & city residents
Shelly Holen, President
William Hoffman, General Manager
Jake Preston, Programming Director
Clary Harris, News Director
Arnie Andrews, Music Director

WKLJ
06-01-1951; 1290 kHz AM; *Hrs Open:* 6 AM-6 PM; 5 kw-D, ND1; 0.059 kw-N, ND1; N43 58 6 W90 51 35
P.O. Box 539, Sparta, WI 54656 US
(608) 269-3100; *Fax:* (608) 269-5170
www.espnlacrosse.com
info@espnlacrosse.com
License: Sparta, WI held by Sparta-Tomah Broadcasting Co. Inc.
Group Owner: Sparta-Tomah Broadcasting Co. Inc.; (Acq 1-19-89)
Nat'l Network: ESPN Radio; *Nat'l Reps:* Rgnl Reps
Format: Sports
Shelly Holen, President
William Hoffman, General Manager

Spencer

WOSQ
09-20-1984; 92.3 MHz FM; *Hrs Open:* 24; 6 kw; 299 ft.; N44 48 32 W90 21 41
980 North Michigan Avenue, Suite 1880, Chicago, IL 60611 US
(715) 384-2191; *Fax:* (715) 387-3588
www.wdlbwosq.com
License: Spencer, Marathon County, WI held by Seehafer Broadcasting Corp.
Group Owner: Seehafer Broadcasting Corp.; (acq 6-1-2006; swap with WDLB(AM) Marshfield and WFHR(AM) Wisconsin Rapids for WBCV(FM) Wausau)
Nat'l Network: ESPN Radio; *Regional Network:* Brownfield; *Wire Services:* Wheeler News Service
Arbitron Metro Market: Wausau-Stevens Point, WI (Central Wisconsin); *Format:* Sports; *Hrs. of News Programming:* news progmg 7 hrs wkly; *No. News Employees:* 2; *Target Audience:* 25-54.
Don Seehafer, President
Kent Reeves, Operations Dir
Mike Warren, News Director
Chuck Gennaro, Chief Engineer

Spooner

WGMO
12-01-1974; 95.3 MHz FM; *Hrs Open:* 24; 7.1 kw; 499 ft.; N45 40 28 W91 58 52
Mailing Address: P. O. Box 190, Shell Lake, WI 54871 US
Second Address: 345 Hwy. 63 S., Shell Lake, WI 54871
(715) 468-9500; *Fax:* (715) 468-9505
www.95gmo.com
info@95gmo.com
License: Spooner, Washburn County, WI
Nat'l Network: Westwood One
Format: Classic Rock; *No. News Employees:* 1
Donna Nelson, News Director

Stevens Point

WPCN
01-01-1948; 1010 kHz AM; 1 kw-D; N44 32 17 W89 35 43
500 Division St., Stevens Point, WI 54481
(715) 341-9800; *Fax:* (715) 341-0000
License: Stevens Point, Portage County, WI held by Muzzy Broadcast Group, LLC
Group Owner: Muzzy Broadcasting L.L.C.; (acq 1996; $1.2 million with co-located FM)
Population Served: 23,631; *Arbitron Metro Market:* Wausau-Stevens Point, WI (Central Wisconsin); *Format:* News, News/Talk, 84, Talk *Special Programming:* Pol one hr wkly; *Target Audience:* 25-54; upscale,male-orientated
Richard Muzzy, President

WSPT
05-01-1961; 97.9 MHz FM; 100 kw; Ant 338 ft; N44 32 17 W89 35 43
500 Division St., Stevens Point, WI 54481
(715) 341-9800; *Fax:* (715) 341-0000
www.979wspt.com
License: Stevens Point, Portage County, WI held by Muzzy Broadcast Group, LLC
Group Owner: Muzzy Broadcasting L.L.C.
Population Served: 210,600; *Arbitron Metro Market:* Wausau-Stevens Point, WI (Central Wisconsin); *Format:* Oldies; *Target Audience:* 25-54; adult
Richard Muzzy, President

***WWSP**
09-28-1968; 89.9 MHz FM; *Hrs Open:* 6 AM-2 AM; 30 kw; 321 ft.; N44 28 55 W89 40 35
1220 Linden Drive, Madison, WI 53706 US
(715) 346-3755; *Fax:* (715) 346-4012
License: Stevens Point, Portage County, WI held by Board of Regents, University of Wisconsin System.
Wire Services: Wheeler News Service; UPI
Arbitron Metro Market: Stevens Point, WI; *Format:* Jazz *Special Programming:* Hmong one hr, pub affrs 5 hrs, sports 3 hrs, blues; *Target Audience:* College students.
Mark Tolstedt, General Manager
Courtney Sikorski, Station Manager
Cynthia Atchison, General Sales Mgr
Jesse Hinze, Programming Director
Dana Scheffen, News Director
Dan Neckar, Production Director
Taylor Christian, MusicDirector
Andrew Quaschnick, Computer Operations Director
Matthew Pagel, Business Director
Nicole Allee, Underwriting/Sponsorship Director
Megan Turbin, PR Director

Sturgeon Bay

WDOR
09-08-1951; 910 kHz AM; *Hrs Open:* 6 AM-sunset; 1 kw-D; N44 49 38 W87 21 27
Box 549, 800 S. 15th Ave., Sturgeon Bay, WI 54235
(920) 487-2822,(920) 743-4411; *Fax:* (920) 743-2334
wdor.com
email@wdor.com
License: Sturgeon Bay, Door County, WI held by Door County Broadcasting Co. Inc.
Nat'l Network: ABC
Population Served: 50,000 *Hrs. of News Programming:* news progmg 23 hrs wkly; *No. News Employees:* 1; *Target Audience:* 21-50; general; *Adv. Rates:* 12.50; 9.40; 9.40; na
Edward Allen III, President
Edward Allen, General Sales Mgr
Edward Allen IV, Programming Director
Roger Levendusky, News Director
Steve Konopka, Engineering Dir
Dan Allen, Music Director
Peggy Pfister, Traffic Manager

WDOR-FM
12-12-1966; 93.9 MHz FM; *Hrs Open:* 5 AM-midnight; 77 kw; 640 ft; N44 54 23 W87 22 15
Box 549, 800 S. 15th Ave., Sturgeon Bay, WI 54235
(920) 487-2822; *Fax:* (920) 743-4411,(920) 743-2334
wdor.com
email@wdor.com
License: Sturgeon Bay, Door County, WI held by Door County Broadcasting Co. Inc.
Nat'l Network: ABC; Milwaukee Brewers Network; *Wire Services:* Wheeler News Service
Population Served: 100,000 *Special Programming:* Farm 3 hrs wkly; *Hrs. of News Programming:* News progmg 25 hrs wkly; *No. News Employees:* 1.5; *Target Audience:* 20-40; general
Edward Allen, General Manager

***WPFF**
08-01-1991; 90.5 MHz FM; *Hrs Open:* 24; 100 kw; 640 ft.; N44 54 14 W87 22 13
1723 Michigan Street, PO Box 444, Sturgeon Bay, WI 54235 US
(920) 743-7443
www.wpff.com
License: Sturgeon Bay, Door County, WI held by Bethesda Christian Broadcasting.
Group Owner: Bethesda Christian Broadcasting; (acq 12-31-2007; $1.7 million with WNLI(FM) Sturgeon Bay)
Nat'l Network: USA
Format: Christian; *Hrs. of News Programming:* News progmg 12 hrs wkly; *Target Audience:* 25-49; baby boomers
Mark Schwarzbauer, General Manager
Andy King, Station Manager

***WNLI**
07-01-1998; 88.5 MHz FM; *Hrs Open:* 24; 50 kw; 518 ft.; N44 54 14 W87 22 13
Mailing Address: 1723 Michigan Street, Sturgeon Bay, WI 54235 US
Second Address: 1723 Michigan St., Sturgeon Bay, WI 54235
(920) 743-7443; *Fax:* (920) 743-7543
www.wrgx.com
License: Sturgeon Bay, Door County, WI held by Bethesda Christian Broadcasting.
Group Owner: Bethesda Christian Broadcasting; (acq 12-31-2007; $1.7 million with WPFF(FM) Sturgeon Bay)
Format: Christian, Rock/AOR; *Target Audience:* 13-35; teens & generation x listeners
Mark Pluimer, President
Dr. Mark Schwarzbaur, General Manager

WQDC
04-18-1988; 97.7 MHz FM; *Hrs Open:* 24; 1.85 kw; 597 ft.; N44 54 14 W87 22 13
C/O David R. Magnum,#105, 1021 N. Superior Ave, Tomah, WI 54660 US
(920) 743-6677; *Fax:* (920) 743-9183
info@wsrc.com
License: Sturgeon Bay, Door County, WI held by Al Johnson Broadcasting LLC
Nat'l Network: Jones Radio Networks
Format: Adult Contemp; *No. News Employees:* 2; *Target Audience:* 25-54.; *Adv. Rates:* 18; 14; 14; 12
Rick Jensen, Operations Dir
Dave Magnum, General Sales Mgr

Sturtevant

WDDW
06-18-1993; 104.7 MHz FM; *Hrs Open:* 24; 4.2 kw; 338 ft.; N42 51 20 W87 50 41
8800 Route 14, Crystal Lake, IL 60012 US
(262) 694-7800; *Fax:* (262) 694-7767
License: Sturtevant, Racine County, WI

Group Owner: Adelante Media Group LLC; (acq 1-6-2006; $10.2 million).
Arbitron Metro Market: Milwaukee, WI; *Target Audience:* 18-49.
John Perry, Operations Dir
Kira LaFond, General Manager
Jerod Bast, General Sales Mgr
Lisa Tyler, News Director
Mark Anthony, Chief Engineer
Lisa Sladek, Traffic Manager

Sun Prairie

WXXM
04-12-1972; 92.1 MHz FM; 3.7 kw; 410 ft.; N43 10 10 W89 15 38
2651 S. Fish Hatchery Rd., Madison, WI 53711 US
(608) 274-5450; *Fax:* (608) 276-9422
www.themic921.com
info@themic921.com
License: Sun Prairie, Dane County, WI held by Capstar TX LLC
Group Owner: iHeartMedia; (acq 8-30-2000; grpsl)
Nat'l Network: Fox Sports
Arbitron Metro Market: Madison, WI; *Format:* Talk; *Target Audience:* General, progsv people
Colleen Valkoun, Market President
Tim Scott, Senior Vice President of Programming
Tim Etes, General Sales Mgr
James Kaska, Online Content Director

*WNWC
01-12-1982; 1190 kHz AM
3003 Snelling Avenue North, St. Paul, MN 55113 US
651-631-5000; *Fax:* (608) 271-1150
www.faith1190.com
feedback@faithradionet.com
License: Sun Prairie, WI held by Northwestern College.
Group Owner: Northwestern College & Radio; (acq 12-19-96; $250,000).
Arbitron Metro Market: Madison, WI *TV Affiliate:* Relg, talk

Superior

*KUWS
01-31-1966; 91.3 MHz FM; *Hrs Open:* 24; 83 kw; 646 ft.; N46 47 21 W92 6 51
1220 Linden Drive #1866, Madison, WI 53706 US
(715) 394-8530; *Fax:* (715) 394-8404
www.kuws.fm
jmunson@uwsuper.edu
License: Superior, Douglas County, WI held by Board of Regents, University of Wisconsin System.
Nat'l Network: NPR; *Regional Network:* Wis. Public Radio
Arbitron Metro Market: Superior, WI; *Format:* News, News/Talk, 86, Variety/Diverse *Special Programming:* Alternative 16 hrs, jazz 15 hrs,; *Hrs. of News Programming:* news progmg 20 hrs wkly; *No. News Employees:* 1 *Target Audience:* 12 plus; above average income & education
John Munson, Station Manager and WPR Northern Regional Manager
Mike Simonson, News Director and WPR Northern Bureau Corresponden
Rudy Listing, Chief Engineer
Kim Gustafson, Office Manager
Sara Broshofske, Jazz Director
John Munson,Sports Director
Patrick Lilja, Sports Director
Crystal Detlefsen, Deans List Director
Walt Dizzo, Deans List Director

WDSM
10-01-1939; 710 kHz AM; *Hrs Open:* 24; 10 kW; N46 39 13 W92 8 50
11 E Superior St, Suite 380, Duluth, MN 55802 USA
(218) 722-4321; *Fax:* (218) 722-5423
wdsm710.com
License: Superior, WI held by Midwest Communications Inc.
Group Owner: Midwest Communications Inc.; (acq 8-1-2001; grpsl)
Nat'l Network: ABC; Talk Radio Network; Salem Radio Network; Premiere Radio Networks; CNN Radio; *Regional Network:* MNN; Wisconsin Radio Net.; *Wire Services:* AP
Arbitron Metro Market: Duluth, MN - Superior, WI; *Format:* Talk; *Target Audience:* 25-54.
Tom Roubik, Brand Manager

KDKE
09-09-1979; 102.5 MHz FM; *Hrs Open:* 24; 100 kW; 600 ft; N46 47 21 W92 07 09
11 E Superior St, Suite 380, Duluth, MN 55802 USA
(218) 722-4321; *Fax:* (218) 722-5423
dukefmduluth.com
License: Superior, Douglas County, WI held by Midwest Communications Inc.
Group Owner: Midwest Communications Inc.
Arbitron Metro Market: Duluth, MN; *Format:* Country; *Hrs. of News Programming:* News progmg 3 hrs wkly; *Target Audience:* 18-49.

WDUL
970 kHz AM; 1 kW; N46 47 27 W92 06 59
11 E Superior St, Suite 380, Duluth, MN 55802 USA
(218) 722-4321; *Fax:* (218) 722-5423
License: Superior, WI held by Midwest Communications Inc.
Group Owner: Midwest Communications Inc.
Arbitron Metro Market: Duluth, MN - Superior, WI; *Format:* Sports
Tom Roubik, Brand Manager

Suring

*WRVM
09-17-1967; 102.7 MHz FM; *Hrs Open:* 24; 98 kw; 981 ft.; N44 59 50 W88 23 49
Mailing Address: P. O. Box 212, Suring, WI 54174 US
Second Address: Hwy. 32 N., Suring, WI 54174
(920) 842-2900; *Fax:* (920) 842-2704
www.wrvm.org
wrvm@wrvm.org
License: Suring, Oconto County, WI held by WRVM Inc.
Nat'l Network: Moody
Format: Religious; *Target Audience:* General; family stn with children's programs
Michael Cornell, General Manager
Brian Hay, General Sales Mgr
Dennis Jones, Programming Director
Michael Fletcher, Promotions Manager
Alan Kilgore, Chief Engineer
Dave Ogren, Assistant to Engineer

Sussex

WKSH
11-01-2002; 1640 kHz AM; *Hrs Open:* 24
18501 Follett Dr., Brookfield, WI 53045 US
(262) 695-9500; *Fax:* (262) 691-2378
www.radiodisney.com
License: Sussex, WI held by Radio Disney Group LLC.
Group Owner: ABC Inc.; (acq 9-26—02; $2.6 million).
Nat'l Network: Radio Disney; *Nat'l Reps:* McGavren Guild
Arbitron Metro Market: Milwaukee-Racine, WI; *Format:* Children; *Target Audience:* Kids 6-14 & Women 25-49.; *Adv. Rates:* 70; 70; 70; 25
Debra Bratel, Station Manager
Melissa Schumacher, General Sales Mgr
Patricia Schultz, Promotions Manager

Three Lakes

WCYE
08-01-1994; 93.7 MHz FM; *Hrs Open:* 24; 100 kw; 407 ft.; N45 46 30 W89 14 55
980 North Michigan Ave, Ste. 1880, Chicago, IL 60611 US
(715) 369-9575; *Fax:* (715) 369-9475
www.mycoyoteradio.com
wcyeginger@newnorth.net
License: Three Lakes, Oneida County, WI held by Results Broadcasting of Rhinelander Inc.
Group Owner: Results Broadcasting; (acq 3-10-2000; $500,000)
Nat'l Network: Premiere Radio Networks
Format: Country; *Hrs. of News Programming:* news progmg 4 hrs wkly; *No. News Employees:* 1; *Target Audience:* 25-54.
Bruce Grassman, CEO
Ben Rosenthal, General Manager
Ben Merritt, Disc Jockey
Brian Douglas, Disc Jockey
Jeff Young, Disc Jockey

Tomah

WTMB
07-11-1990; 94.5 MHz FM; *Hrs Open:* 24; 8.3 kw; 564 ft.; N43 53 56 W90 29 23
1021 N. Superior Ave., Suite 5, Tomah, WI 54660 US
(608) 372-9600; *Fax:* (608) 372-7566
www.classicrockwtmb.com
info@magnumbroadcasting.com
License: Tomah, WI held by Magnum Radio, Inc.
Group Owner: Magnum Radio Inc.
Arbitron Metro Market: Tomah, WI; *Format:* Classic Rock
David R. Magnum, President

WBOG
04-19-1959; 1460 kHz AM; *Hrs Open:* 24; 1 kw-D, NDD; N43 58 7 W90 30 50
Mailing Address: 1021 N. Superior Ave., Suite 5, Tomah, WI 54660 US
Second Address: 505 King St., La Crosse, WI 54601
(608) 372-9600; *Fax:* (608) 372-7566
www.koolgold1460.com
info@magnumbroadcasting.com
License: Tomah, WI held by Magnum Radio Inc.
Group Owner: Magnum Radio Inc.
Regional Network: Wisconsin Radio Net.
Arbitron Metro Market: Tomah, WI; *Format:* Oldies; *No. News Employees:* 2; *Target Audience:* 35 plus.
David R. Magnum, President
Diane Pergande, General Sales Mgr

WXYM
03-11-1992; 96.1 MHz FM; *Hrs Open:* 24; 44 kw; 525 ft.; N44 1 32 W90 48 58
Mailing Address: 1021 N. Superior Ave., Tomah, WI 54660 US
Second Address: 505 King St., La Crosse, WI 54601
(608) 372-9600; *Fax:* (608) 372-7566
www.mix96wxym.com
info@magnumbroadcasting.com
License: Tomah, WI held by Magnum Radio Inc.
Group Owner: Magnum Radio Inc.
Regional Network: Wisconsin Radio Net.
Arbitron Metro Market: Tomah, WI; *Format:* Adult Contemp; *Target Audience:* 25-54.; *Adv. Rates:* 19; 19; 19; 18
David R. Magnum, President

*WVCX
01-29-1965; 98.9 MHz FM; *Hrs Open:* 24; 100 kw; 984 ft.; N43 51 10 W90 27 36
3434 West Kilbourn Ave., Milwaukee, WI 53208 US
(414) 935-3000; *Fax:* (414) 935-3015
www.vcyamerica.org
wvcx@vcyamerica.org
License: Tomah, Monroe County, WI held by VCY/America Inc.
Group Owner: VCY America Inc.; acq 1984)
Nat'l Network: USA; Moody
Arbitron Metro Market: Milwaukee, WI; *Format:* Christian, Talk, 74
Dr. Randall Melchert, President
Victor Eliason, Operations Dir
Jim Schneider, Programming Director
Gordon Morris, News Director
Andy Eliason, Chief Engineer

Tomahawk

WJJQ
08-01-1968; 810 kHz AM; *Hrs Open:* 24
Mailing Address: D/B/A Albert B/Casting, P.O. Box 10, Tomahawk, WI 54487 US
Second Address: 81 E. Mohawk Dr., Tomahawk, WI 54487
(715) 453-4482; *Fax:* (715) 453-7169
www.wjjq.com
wjjq@wjjq.com
License: Tomahawk, WI held by Albert Broadcasting II LLC
Nat'l Network: CBS; ESPN Radio; Westwood One; *Regional Network:* Wisconsin Radio Net; *Nat'l Reps:* Rgnl Reps; *Wire Services:* AP
Format: Sports; *Hrs. of News Programming:* news progmg 15 hrs wkly; *No. News Employees:* 1; *Target Audience:* 25 plus.; *Adv. Rates:* 7; 7; 5; 5
Gregg Albert, President
Margaruite Albert, Operations Dir
Tim Albert, Programming Director

WJJQ-FM
10-15-1984; 92.5 MHz FM; *Hrs Open:* 24; 25 kw; 259 ft.; N45 29 27 W89 43 36
Mailing Address: D/B/A Albert B/Casting, P.O. Box 10, Tomahawk, WI 54487 US
Second Address: 81 E. Mohawk Dr., Tomahawk, WI 54487
(715) 453-4482; *Fax:* (715) 453-7169
www.wjjq.com
galbert@wjjq.com
License: Tomahawk, Lincoln County, WI held by Albert Broadcasting II LLC.
Nat'l Network: CBS Radio; *Regional Network:* Wisconsin Radio Net; *Nat'l Reps:* Rgnl Reps *Regional Reps:* Regional Reps; *Wire Services:* AP
Format: News, Oldies, 84; *Hrs. of News Programming:* news progmg 30 hrs wkly; *No. News Employees:* 1; *Target Audience:* 25 plus.; *Adv. Rates:* 15; 15; 12; 12
Gregg Albert, President
Mary Lu Voermans, General Sales Mgr
Tim Albert, Programming Director
Mark Everett, Disc Jockey
Michael McGovern, Disc Jockey

Trempealeau

WFBZ
11-24-1984; 105.5 MHz FM; *Hrs Open:* 24; 2.1 kw; 531 ft.; N43 56 33 W91 26 3
1407 2nd Avenue North, Onalaska, WI 54650 US
(608) 269-3100; *Fax:* (608) 269-5170
www.espnlacrosse.com
info@espnlacrosse.com
License: Trempealeau, Trempealeau County, WI held by Sparta-Tomah Broadcasting Co. Inc.
Group Owner: Sparta-Tomah Broadcasting Co. Inc.; (acq 10-19-2006; $850,000)
Nat'l Network: ESPN Radio; *Nat'l Reps:* Rgnl Reps; *Wire Services:* ESPN/SportsTicker
Arbitron Metro Market: Trempealeau, WI; *Format:* Sports
Shelly Holen, President
William Hoffman, General Manager

Two Rivers

WCUB
11-01-1952; 980 kHz AM; *Hrs Open:* 24; 5 kw-D, DA2; 5 kw-N, DA2; N44 3 50 W87 41 49
Mailing Address: P.O. Box 1990, Manitowoc, WI 54221 US
Second Address: 1915 Mirro Dr., Manitowoc, WI 54220
(920) 683-6800; *Fax:* (920)683-6807
www.cubradio.com
License: Two Rivers, WI held by Cub Radio Inc.
Nat'l Reps: Katz Radio
Format: Country; *Hrs. of News Programming:* news progmg 16 hrs wkly; *No. News Employees:* 2; *Target Audience:* 35 plus.
Lee Davis, President
Dean Lester, Programming Director
Bryan Lundberg, News Director

Union Grove

WIIL
01-01-1961; 95.1 MHz FM; 50 kw; 384 ft.; N42 33 10 W87 53 38
8800 Route 14, Crystal Lake, IL 60012 US
(262) 694-7800; *Fax:* (262) 694-7767
www.95wiil.com
License: Union Grove, Kenosha County, WI held by NM Licensing LLC
Arbitron Metro Market: Chicago, IL; *Target Audience:* 18-54.
Chris Allinger, Operations Dir
Susan Johnston, General Manager

Verona

WMMM-FM
07-04-1991; 105.5 MHz FM; 2 kw; 574 ft.; N42 57 32 W89 29 25
7601 Ganser Wy, Madison, WI 53719 US
(608) 826-0077; *Fax:* (608) 826-1244
www.1055triplem.com
demoore@entercom.com
License: Verona, Dane County, WI held by Entercom Madison Licensee LLP.
Group Owner: Entercom Communications Corp.; (acq 7-10-00; grpsl)
Arbitron Metro Market: Madison, WI; *Format:* Triple A; *Target Audience:* 25-44; upscale, college educated adults
Steve Fisher, CFO
David Field, President
David Moore, Operations Dir
Pat Gallagher, Programming Director

Viroqua

WVRQ
02-25-1958; 1360 kHz AM; *Hrs Open:* 24; 1 kw-D, 23 w-N; N43 32 04 W90 52 23
WI USA
(608) 326-2411; *Fax:* (608) 326-2412
www.wqpcradio.com
wqpcwpre@mwt.net
License: Viroqua, Vernon County, WI held by Robinson Corp.
Group Owner: Robinson Corporation
Nat'l Network: ABC; *Regional Network:* Wisconsin Radio Net.; *Wire Services:* AP
Population Served: 43,762 *Special Programming:* Farm one hr, relg 6 hrs, polka 6 hrs wkly; *Hrs. of News Programming:* news progmg 14 hrs wkly; *No. News Employees:* 1; *Target Audience:* 25 plus.

WVRQ-FM
10-06-1967; 102.3 MHz FM; *Hrs Open:* 24; 3.3 kw; 299 ft.; N43 31 27 W90 51 51
WI US
(608) 326-2411; *Fax:* (608) 326-2412
www.wqpcradio.com
wqpcwpre@mwt.net
License: Viroqua, Vernon County, WI held by Robinson Corp.
Group Owner: Robinson Corporation
Wire Services: AP
Arbitron Metro Market: La Crosse, WI; *Format:* Country *Special Programming:* Bluegrass 2 hrs, farm one hr wkly; *Hrs. of News Programming:* News progmg 20 hrs wkly; *No. News Employees:* 1 *Target Audience:* 25-54.

***WDRT**
91.9 MHz FM; 0.48 kw; 435 ft.; N43 36 28 W90 53 24
US
(608) 638-9378
www.wdrt.org
info@wdrt.org
License: Viroqua, Vernon County, WI held by Driftless Community Radio Inc.
Arbitron Metro Market: Viroqua, WI; *Format:* Variety/Diverse
Bob Hill, President
Eddy Nix, Vice President
Jane Even, Secretary
Charlie Knower, Treasurer
John Tully

Washburn

***WEGZ**
10-05-1981; 105.9 MHz FM; *Hrs Open:* 24; 98 kw; 741 ft.; N46 41 31 W90 59 27
115 Candlestick Road, North Andover, MA 01845 US
(715) 373-5151; *Fax:* (715) 373-5805
www.vcyamerica.org
wegz@vcyamerica.org
License: Washburn, Bayfield County, WI held by Keweenaw Bay Broadcasting Inc.
Group Owner: VCY America Inc.; (acq 4-19-2002).
Nat'l Network: USA
Arbitron Metro Market: Washburn, WI; *Format:* Christian, Religious, 86
Dr. Randall Melchert, President
Victor Eliason, Operations Dir
Jim Schneider, Programming Director
Gordon Morris, Operations Director

Watertown

WJJO
08-01-1961; 94.1 MHz FM; *Hrs Open:* 24; 50 kw; 492 ft; N43 3 32 W89 3 45
730 Rayovac Dr, Madison, WI 53711 USA
(608) 273-1000; *Fax:* (608) 271-0400
www.wjjo.com
License: Watertown, Jefferson County, WI held by Mid-West Management Inc.
Group Owner: Mid-West Family Broadcasting; (acq 6-18-93; $1.6 million;
Nat'l Reps: McGavren Guild
Population Served: 450,000; *Arbitron Metro Market:* Madison, WI; *Format:* Rock/AOR, Classic Rock; *Target Audience:* Adults 18-49
Randy Hawke, Programming Director

Waukesha

WRRD
03-27-1947; 1510 kHz AM; *Hrs Open:* 6 AM-8:30 PM
1224 E. Brady St., Milwaukee, WI 53202 US
(844) 967-2789
newstalk1510am.com
License: Waukesha, WI held by New WRRD, LLC
Group Owner: New WRRD, LLC; (acq 6-01-2017; $760,000)
Arbitron Metro Market: Eugene-Springfield, OR; *Format:* Sports
Mike Crute, Operations Dir

***WCCX**
09-01-1978; 104.5 MHz FM; *Hrs Open:* 24; 0.013 kw; 49 ft.; N43 0 16 W88 13 39
221 North East Avenue, Waukesha, WI 53186 US
(262) 524-7355; *Fax:* (262) 650-4950
wccx.carrollu.edu
wccx@carrollu.edu
License: Waukesha, Waukesha County, WI held by Trustees Carroll College.
Arbitron Metro Market: Waukesha, WI; *Format:* Variety/Diverse *Special Programming:* Sp 8 hrs, metal 3 hrs, rap 3 hrs wkly; *Target Audience:* General; high school & college students
Ed Tuten, President
Howard Tuten, General Manager

WMIL-FM
01-01-1982; 106.1 MHz FM; *Hrs Open:* 24; 12 kw; 997 ft.; N43 5 46 W87 54 15
12100 W. Howard Ave., Greenfield, WI 53228 US
(414) 545-8900; *Fax:* (414) 327-3200
www.fm106.com
License: Waukesha, Waukesha County, WI held by Clear Channel Broadcasting Licenses Inc.
Group Owner: iHeartMedia; (acq 3-17-97; $40 million with WOKY(AM) Milwaukee)
Nat'l Reps: Clear Channel
Arbitron Metro Market: Milwaukee, WI; *Format:* Country; *Hrs. of News Programming:* news progmg 1.5 hrs wkly; *No. News Employees:* 4; *Target Audience:* 25-54; middle America; *Adv. Rates:* 210; 200; 200; 55
Colleen Valkoun, Market President
Phil Kurth, Sales Manager
Kerry Wolfe, Programming Director
Hannah Kultgen, Promotions Director

Waunakee

WMHX
04-20-1992; 105.1 MHz FM; 6 kw; 243 ft.; N43 13 20 W89 18 1
7601 Ganser Wy, Madison, WI 53719 US
(608) 826-0077; *Fax:* (608) 826-1244
www.mix1051fm.com
License: Waunakee, Dane County, WI held by Entercom Madison Licensee LLP.
Group Owner: Entercom Communications Corp.; (acq 7-10-2000; grpsl)
Arbitron Metro Market: Madison, WI; *Format:* Classic Rock; *Target Audience:* 18-49.
David Moore, Operations & Programming Director
Ed Schulz, Director of Sales

Waupaca

WDUX
04-29-1956; 800 kHz AM; *Hrs Open:* 24 hours; 5 kw-D, DA2; 0.5 kw-N, DA2; N44 21 15 W89 3 29
Mailing Address: P.O. Box 310, Green Bay, WI 54305 US
Second Address: 200 Tower Rd., Waupaca, WI 54981
(715) 258-5528; *Fax:* (715) 258-7711
www.wdux.net/
mail@wdux.net
License: Waupaca, WI held by Laird Broadcasting Co.
Nat'l Network: Jones Radio Networks; ABC; *Regional Network:* Brownfield; Wisconsin Radio Net; *Nat'l Reps:* Katz Radio; *Wire Services:* AP
Arbitron Metro Market: Waupaca, WI; *Format:* Country *Special Programming:* Farm 1 hr wkly; *Hrs. of News Programming:* news progmg 20 hrs wkly; *No. News Employees:* 1; *Target Audience:* 35 plus.; *Adv. Rates:* 18; 16; 16; 12
William Laird, President
Jack Barry, Operations Dir
Tina Grenlie, Station Manager
Ann Myer, Traffic Manager

WDUX-FM
01-29-1967; 92.7 MHz FM; *Hrs Open:* 24; 6 kw; 243 ft; N44 21 14 W89 03 44
Mailing Address: Box 247, Waupaca, WI 54305
Second Address: 200 Tower Rd., Waupaca, WI 54981
(715) 258-5528; *Fax:* (715) 258-7711
www.wduxradio.com
License: Waupaca, Waupaca County, WI held by Laird Broadcasting Co.
Nat'l Network: ABC; Westwood One; *Regional Network:* Wisconsin Radio Net; *Nat'l Reps:* Katz Radio; *Wire Services:* AP
Arbitron Metro Market: Green Bay, WI *Special Programming:* Sports 15 hrs wkly; *No. News Employees:* 1; *Target Audience:* 25-54.; *Adv. Rates:* 18; 16; 16; 12
Tina Grenlie, General Manager
Tina Grenlie, Station Manager
Larry Stevens, General Sales Mgr
Rick Winters, Programming Director
Jack Barry, News Director
Jack Barry, News Director

Waupun

WFDL
05-26-1966; 1170 kHz AM; *Hrs Open:* Sunrise to sunset; 1 kw-D, NDD; N43 38 30 W88 43 22
609 Home Avenue, Waupun, WI 53963 US
(920) 324-4441; *Fax:* (920) 324-3139
www.am1170.com
nickr@wfdl.com
License: Waupun, WI held by Radio Plus Inc.
Nat'l Network: CBS Radio

Arbitron Metro Market: Waupun, WI; *Format:* Adult Contemp *Special Programming:* Farm 5 hrs wkly; *Target Audience:* 35 plus; mature adults; *Adv. Rates:* 15; 12; 12; n/a
Chris Bernier, President
Mike Enfelt, Operations Dir
Terry Davis, General Manager
Todd Dehring, Programming Director
Greg Stensland, News Director
Kerry Longrie, Traffic Manager

Wausau

*WCLQ
05-23-1988; 89.5 MHz FM; *Hrs Open:* 24; 90 kw; 607 ft.; N44 55 11 W89 40 45
536 Grand Ave., Schofield, WI 54476 US
(715) 355-5151; *Fax:* (715) 359-3128
www.89q.org
coy@89q.org
License: Wausau, Marathon County, WI held by Christian Life Communications Inc.
Nat'l Network: USA
Arbitron Metro Market: Wausau-Stevens Point, WI; *Format:* Contemporary Hits/Top 40; *Hrs. of News Programming:* News progmg 9 hrs wkly; *Target Audience:* 18-35; Christian/young family
Coy Sawyer, CFO
Coy Sawyer, General Manager
Scott Michaels, Programming Director
Frank Zastrow, Chief Engineer

WDEZ
03-27-1964; 101.9 MHz FM; *Hrs Open:* 24; 100 kW; 1079 ft; N44 55 14 W89 41 28
557 Scott St, Wausau, WI 54403 USA
(715) 842-1672; *Fax:* (715) 848-3158
wdez.com
License: Wausau, Marathon County, WI held by WRIG Inc.
Group Owner: Midwest Communications Inc.
Nat'l Reps: Christal; *Wire Services:* Wheeler News Service; UPI
Population Served: 212,000; *Arbitron Metro Market:* Wausau; *Format:* Country *Special Programming:* Farm 4 hrs wkly; *Hrs. of News Programming:* news progmg 4 hrs wkly; *No. News Employees:* 1; *Target Audience:* 25-54.
Derek Moran, Brand Manager

*WHRM
06-10-1949; 90.9 MHz FM; *Hrs Open:* 24; 81 kw; 1079 ft.; N44 55 14 W89 41 28
3319 W. Beltline Hwy., Madison, WI 53713 US
(715) 848-1978; *Fax:* (715) 848-2890
www.wpr.org
listener@wpr.org
License: Wausau, Marathon County, WI held by State of Wisconsin Educational Communications Board.
Nat'l Network: NPR; PRI
Arbitron Metro Market: Wausau-Stevens Point, WI (Central Wisconsin); *Format:* News; *Hrs. of News Programming:* News progmg 29 hrs wkly; *Target Audience:* 25-64; male/female
Wendy Wink, CEO
Maru Nonn, Operations Dir
Phil Corriveau, General Manager
Rick Reyer, Station Manager
Allen Rieland, Chief Engineer
Ted Tobie, CFO
Tom Martin-Erickson, Chief of Operations

WIFC
01-01-1947; 95.5 MHz FM; *Hrs Open:* 24; 95.5 kW; 1079 ft.; N44 55 14 W89 41 28
557 Scott St, Wausau, WI 54403 USA
(715) 842-1672; *Fax:* (715) 848-3158
wifc.com
License: Wausau, Marathon County, WI held by WRIG Inc.
Group Owner: Midwest Communications
Arbitron Metro Market: Wausau, WI; *Format:* Contemporary Hits/Top 40; *No. News Employees:* 2; *Target Audience:* 18-49.
Nikki Montgomery, Brand Manager

*WLBL-FM
11-01-1995; 91.9 MHz FM; *Hrs Open:* 5 AM-midnight (M-F); 6 AM-midnight; 0.054 kw; 837 ft.; N44 55 14 W89 41 28
3319 West Beltline Hwy, Madison, WI 53713 US
(715) 848-1978; *Fax:* (715) 848-2890
www.wpr.org
rick.reyer@wpr.org
License: Wausau, Marathon County, WI held by State of Wisconsin-Educational Communications Board.
Nat'l Network: NPR; *Regional Network:* Wisconsin Radio Net.
Arbitron Metro Market: Wausau-Stevens Point, WI (Central Wisconsin); *Format:* Talk *Special Programming:* Folk 3 hrs wkly
Wendy Wink, CEO
Phil Corriveau, General Manager
Rick Reyer, Station Manager
Allen Rieland, Chief Engineer

WSAU-AM
01-30-1937; 550 kHz AM; *Hrs Open:* 24; 15 kW-D, 20 kW-N
557 Scott St, Wausau, WI 54403 USA
(715) 842-1672; *Fax:* (715) 848-3158
wsau.com
License: Wausau, WI held by WRIG Inc.
Group Owner: Midwest Communications Inc.; (acq 1996; $3.5 million with co-located FM)
Nat'l Reps: Christal
Arbitron Metro Market: Wausau, WI; *Format:* News/Talk *Special Programming:* Farm 5 hrs, Polish 3 hrs, religious 3 hrs wkly; *No. News Employees:* 2; *Target Audience:* 35-64.
Chris Conley, Brand Manager

WXCO
08-01-1953; 1230 kHz AM; *Hrs Open:* 24; 1 kw-U, ND1; N44 58 10 W89 36 25
1110 E. Wausau Avenue, Wausau, WI 54402 US
(715) 845-8218; *Fax:* (715) 845-6582
www.1230wxco.com
License: Wausau, WI held by Seehafer Broadcasting Corp.
Group Owner: Seehafer Broadcasting Corp.; (acq 9-26-73).
Nat'l Network: CBS; Westwood One; ESPN Radio
Arbitron Metro Market: Wausau, WI; *Format:* Sports, Talk; *No. News Employees:* 1; *Target Audience:* 25 plus; professionals/business; *Adv. Rates:* 14; 13; 13; 7
Chad Holmes, Operations Dir
Steve Resnick, General Manager
Ken Rajek, General Sales Mgr
Chad Holmes, Programming Director
Kim Weyers, News Director
Charles Gennaro, Chief Engineer
Roger Bertramÿ, Account Executive
Jamie Potter,Account Executive
Cole Corrigan, Account Executive
Kim Weyers, Traffic Manager

*WXPW
02-01-1996; 91.9 MHz FM; 0.054 kw; 837 ft.; N44 55 14 W89 41 28 *Rebroadcasts:* Rebroadcasts WXPR(FM) Rhinelander
303 W. Prospect Street, Rhinelander, WI 54501 US
(715) 362-6000; *Fax:* (715) 362-6007
www.wxpr.org
License: Wausau, Marathon County, WI held by White Pine Community Broadcasting Inc.
Arbitron Metro Market: Wausau, WI; *Format:* News
Mick Fiocchi, President
Walt Gander, Operations Dir
Jessie Dick, General Sales Mgr
Ken Krall, News Director
Elmer Goetsch, Chief Engineer

WBCV
02-01-1985; 107.9 MHz FM; 100 kw; 1030 ft.; N45 3 33 W89 26 10
1110 E. Wausau Ave, Wausau, WI 54401 US
1-866-967-9983; *Fax:* (715) 341-9744
www.bigcheese1079.net
License: Wausau, Marathon County, WI held by NRG License Sub, LLC.
Group Owner: NRG Media LLC; (acq 5-31-2006; swap for WDLB(AM) Marshfield, WOSQ(FM) Spencer and WFHR(AM) Wisconsin Rapids)
Nat'l Reps: McGavren Guild
Arbitron Metro Market: Wausau, WI; *Format:* Rock/AOR
Ben Rosenthal, General Manager
Jon Albrecht, General Sales Mgr
Panama Jack, Programming Director

Wautoma

WAUH
01-01-2001; 102.3 MHz FM; 5.3 kw; 349 ft.; N44 1 54 W89 9 7
6161 N Santa Monica Blvd, Whitefish Bay, WI 53217 US
(902) 787-7720; *Fax:* (866) 594-4698
www.wauhradio.com
thebug@wauhradio.com
License: Wautoma, Waushara County, WI held by Hometown Broadcasting LLC
Arbitron Metro Market: Wautoma, WI; *Format:* Contemporary Hits/Top 40, Adult Contemp
JoAnn Boyson, CEO
Bernie Phillips, General Manager
Bill Denkert, General Sales Mgr
JoAnn Boyson, Co-Owner
Mark Melby, Account Executive
John Peck, Account Executive
Joshua Werner, IT & Webmaster
Jean Hoffmann, Traffic &Billing

Wauwatosa

WXSS
01-01-1961; 103.7 MHz FM; *Hrs Open:* 24; 19.5 kw; 843 ft.; N43 5 48 W87 54 18
10706 Beaver Dam Road, Cockeysville, MD 21030 US
(414) 529-1250; *Fax:* (414) 529-2122
www.1037kissfm.com
License: Wauwatosa, Milwaukee County, WI held by Entercom Milwaukee License LLC.
Group Owner: Entercom Communications Corp.; (acq 12-13-99; grpsl).
Arbitron Metro Market: Milwaukee, WI; *Format:* Contemporary Hits/Top 40; *No. News Employees:* 1; *Target Audience:* 18-44; women
Alan Kirshbon, General Sales Mgr
Brian Kelly, Programming Director
Jane Matenaer, News Director
Chris Tarr, Chief Engineer
Andrea Biebel, National Sales Manager

West Allis

WJTI
06-04-1950; 1460 kHz AM; *Hrs Open:* 24; 500 w-D, 65 w-N; N42 45 06 W87 49 55
1530 N Cass St., Suite A, Milwaukee, WI 60085
(414) 899-9902
License: West Allis, Racine County, WI held by El Sol Broadcasting LLC
Population Served: 1,300,000; *Arbitron Metro Market:* Milwaukee-Racine, WI; *No. News Employees:* 3; *Target Audience:* Sp all ages; *Adv. Rates:* 50; 50; 50; 50
John Torres, General Manager

West Bend

WBKV
11-01-1950; 1470 kHz AM; *Hrs Open:* 24; 2.5 kw
2410 S. Main St., West Bend, WI 53095 US
(262) 334-2344; *Fax:* (262) 334-1512
www.wbkv.com
License: West Bend, WI held by Magnum Communications, Inc.
Group Owner: Magnum Communications, Inc.
Arbitron Metro Market: West Bend, WI; *Format:* Adult Contemp, Oldies
Rick Jensen, News Director

WMBZ
09-01-1958; 92.5 MHz FM; *Hrs Open:* 24; 17.5 kw; 538 ft.; N43 25 46 W88 18 2
2410 S. Main St., West Bend, WI 53095 US
(262) 334-2344; *Fax:* (262) 334-1512
www.buzzcountry.com
License: West Bend, WI held by Magnum Communications, Inc.
Group Owner: Magnum Communications, Inc.
Arbitron Metro Market: West Bend, WI; *Format:* Country
David R. Magnum, President

West Salem

WKBH-FM
03-15-1982; 100.1 MHz FM; *Hrs Open:* 24; 3.6 kw; 427 ft.; N43 51 2 W91 12 8
1407 2nd Ave. N., Onalaska, WI 54650 US
(608) 782-8335; *Fax:* (608) 782-8340
www.classicrock1001.com
License: West Salem, La Crosse County, WI held by Mississippi Valley Broadcasters LLC.
Group Owner: La Crosse Radio Group; (acq 12-16-2000).
Arbitron Metro Market: La Crosse, WI; *Format:* Classic Rock; *No. News Employees:* 1; *Target Audience:* 25-54.
Pat Smith, General Manager
Erik Sjolander, Sales Manager
Kelly Wilde, Programming Director
Heidi Hanse, Promotions Director
Caroline Grosvold, Business Manager
JoAnn Steffes, HR Director
Laurie Lane, Traffic Director
LoisLosby, Public Service
Isaac Wenzel, Director of Interactive Media

Westby

*WTPN
103.9 MHz FM; 2.75 kw; Ant 477 ft; N43 37 36 W90 41 57
5331 Mount Alifan Dr., San Diego, CA
(858) 277-4991; *Fax:* (858) 277-1365

License: Westby, Vernon County, WI held by The Salvation Poem Foundation Inc.

Michael MacIntosh, President

Whitehall

WHTL-FM

09-10-1981; 102.3 MHz FM; *Hrs Open:* 24; 1.55 kw; 400 ft.; N44 24 45 W91 16 53
Hwy 53 South, P.O. Box 66, Whitehall, WI 54773 US
(715) 538-4341; *Fax:* (715) 538-4360
www.whtlradio.com
License: Whitehall, Trempealeau County, WI held by The WHTL Group L.L.C.
Nat'l Network: Jones Radio Networks; *Regional Network:* Wisconsin Radio Net.
Format: Contemporary Hits/Top 40; *Hrs. of News Programming:* news progmg 24 hrs wkly; *No. News Employees:* 1; *Target Audience:* 25 plus; adult fans who make household buying decisions; *Adv. Rates:* 15; 15; 16; 12

Barb Semb, Operations Dir
Butch Halama, General Manager
Mary Little, Programming Director
Marty Little, News Director

Whitewater

WKCH

01-02-1998; 106.5 MHz FM; 6 kw; 200 ft.; N42 54 20 W88 45 5
980 North Michigan Avenue, Suite 1880, Chicago, IL 60611 US
(920) 563-9329; *Fax:* (920) 563-0315
fortproduction@nrgmedia.com
License: Whitewater, Walworth County, WI held by NRG License Sub. LLC.
Group Owner: NRG Media LLC; (acq 10-31-2005; grpsl)
Format: Oldies

Mary Quass, CEO
Gary Douglas, Operations Dir
James Vriezen, General Manager
Shane Sparks, General Sales Mgr
Michael Clish, News Director
George Nicholas, Chief Engineer
Tami Billmore, CFO
Jaimie Flom, Traffic Manager

WSLD

11-16-1992; 104.5 MHz FM; *Hrs Open:* 24; 6 kw; 328 ft.; N42 43 38 W88 44 54
N6534 State Rd. 89, Whitewater, WI 53190 US
(608) 883-6677; *Fax:* (608) 883-2054
www.1045wsld.com
nora.karbash@prairiecommunications.net
License: Whitewater, Walworth County, WI held by WPW Broadcasting Inc.
Group Owner: Prairie Radio Communications; (acq 8-4-99; $700,000)
Format: Country; *Hrs. of News Programming:* news progmg 10 hrs wkly; *No. News Employees:* 1; *Target Audience:* General.

Nora Karbash, General Manager
Brad Deschner, General Sales Mgr

*WSUW

01-10-1965; 91.7 MHz FM; *Hrs Open:* 6 AM-2 AM; 1.3 kw; 180 ft.; N42 50 10 W88 44 36
1220 Linden Drive, Madison, WI 53706 US
(262) 472-1323,(262) 472-1314; *Fax:* (262) 472-5029
www.wsuw.org
wsuw@uww.edu
License: Whitewater, Walworth County, WI held by Board of Regents University of Wisconsin System.
Format: Alternative *Special Programming:* Heavy metal 14 hrs, jazz/world beat 6 hrs, urban contemp 14 hrs wkly; *Target Audience:* 18-44.

Wilfred Tremblay, General Manager
Kelly O'Brien, Programming Director
Mark Neilsen, Promotions Manager

Winneconne

WVBO

09-01-1966; 103.9 MHz FM; 24.95 kw; 328 ft.; N44 8 23 W88 29 2 *Rebroadcasts:* Rebroadcasts WOGB(FM) Kaukauna 80%
111 East Kilbourn Ave., Suite 2700, Milwaukee, WI 53202 US
(920) 426-3239; *Fax:* (920) 231-1040
www.1039wvbo.com
License: Winneconne, Winnebago County, WI held by Cumulus Broadcasting Inc.
Nat'l Network: Westwood One
Arbitron Metro Market: Oshkosh, WI; *Format:* Oldies; *Target Audience:* 35-54.

Guy Dark, Operations Dir
Jason Davis, General Sales Mgr
Jim Franklin, Program Director/Brand Manager
Steve Edwards, Program Director/Brand Manager
Jonathan Krause, News Director
Steve Griesbach, Chief Engineer
Ellie Jackson,Business Manager

Wisconsin Dells

WDLS

05-01-1969; 900 kHz AM; *Hrs Open:* 24; 1 kw-D, ND1; 0.22 kw-N, ND1; N43 38 23 W89 43 14
Mailing Address: N6912 Highway 51 S., PO Box 448, Portage, WI 53901 USA
Second Address: 201 8th Ave., Baraboo, WI 53913
(608) 742-1001; *Fax:* (608) 742-1688
www.wdlsam.com
info@magnumbroadcasting.com
License: Wisconsin Dells, WI held by Magnum Communications Inc.
Group Owner: Magnum Communications Inc.
Arbitron Metro Market: Wisconsin Dells, WI; *Format:* Country; *No. News Employees:* 1

David R. Magnum, President

WNNO

05-01-1974; 106.9 MHz FM; *Hrs Open:* 24; 6 kw; 322 ft.; N43 38 23 W89 43 14
Mailing Address: N6912 Highway 51 S., PO Box 448, Portage, WI 53901 USA
Second Address: 201 8th Ave., Baraboo, WI 53959
(608) 742-1001; *Fax:* (608) 742-1688
www.mix106wnno.com
info@magnumbroadcasting.com
License: Wisconsin Dells, WI held by Magnum Communications Inc.
Group Owner: Magnum Communications Inc.
Arbitron Metro Market: Columbia, WI; *Format:* Adult Contemp

David R. Magnum, President

Wisconsin Rapids

WFHR

11-05-1940; 1320 kHz AM; 5 kw-D, DAN; 0.5 kw-N, DAN; N44 24 56 W89 50 6
645 25th Avenue, Wisconsin Rapids, WI 54495 US
(715) 424-1300; *Fax:* (715) 424-1347
www.wfhr.com
License: Wisconsin Rapids, WI held by Seehafer Broadcasting Corp.
Group Owner: Seehafer Broadcasting Corp.; (acq 6-1-2006; swap with WDLB(AM) Marshfield and WOSQ(FM) Spencer for WBCV(FM) Wausau)
Nat'l Network: CBS
Arbitron Metro Market: Wisconsin Rapids, WI; *Format:* News, News/Talk, 86

Donald Seehafer, President
Jeff Sigler, Sales Manager
Bob Look, Programming Director
Carl Hilke, News Director
Chuck Gennaro, Chief Engineer
Pam Hilke, Traffic Director

WGLX-FM

08-01-1946; 103.3 MHz FM; 65 kw; 801 ft.; N44 38 39 W89 51 12
2301 Plover Road, Plover, WI 54467 US
(715) 341-8838; *Fax:* (715) 341-9744
www.wglx.com
kluchs@nrgmedia.com
License: Wisconsin Rapids, Wood County, WI held by NRG License Sub, LLC.
Group Owner: NRG Media LLC; (acq 10-31-2005; grpsl)
Arbitron Metro Market: Wausau-Stevens Point, WI (Central Wisconsin); *Format:* Classic Rock; *Target Audience:* 25-49.

RW Smith, Operations Manager
Kurt Luchs, General Manager
Panama Jack, Programming Director

*WRAO

91.9 MHz FM; kw
Mailing Address: US
Second Address: 611 24th St. N., Wisconsin Rapids, WI 54494-5509
(715) 325-3486
License: Wisconsin Rapids, Wood County, WI held by Wisconsin Rapids Seventh-Day Adventist Church.
Arbitron Metro Market: Wisconsin Rapids, WI

Fred Miller, General Manager

Wittenberg

*WVRN

12-27-2007; 88.9 MHz FM; 25 kw; Ant 482 ft; N44 57 54 W89 00 18
3434 W. Kilbourn Ave., Milwaukee, WI 53208
(800) 729-9829
www.vcyamerica.org
vcy@vcyamerica.org
License: Wittenberg, Shawano County, WI held by VCY America Inc.
Group Owner: VCY America Inc.
Population Served: 1,077; *Arbitron Metro Market:* Wittenberg, WI

Vic Eliason, Operations Dir
Jim Schneider, Programming Director
Andy Eliason, Chief Engineer

Wyoming

Afton

KRSV

08-13-1985; 1210 kHz AM; 5 kw-D, ND1; 0.25 kw-N, ND1; N42 43 22 W110 57 39
PO Box 1210, Afton, WY 83110 US
(307) 885-5778
License: Afton, WY held by Western Wyoming Radio Inc.
Group Owner: Western Wyoming Radio Inc.
Arbitron Metro Market: Afton, WY; *Format:* Country, News, 84; *Adv. Rates:* 10; 8; 9; na

Jerry Hansen, President
Jennie Hansen, General Sales Mgr
Dan Dockstader, News Director

KRSV

11-13-1985; 98.7 MHz FM; 3 kw; -289 ft.; N42 51 2 W110 58 46
PO Box 1210, Afton, WY 83110 US
(307) 885-5778
License: Afton, WY held by Western Wyoming Radio Inc.
Group Owner: Western Wyoming Radio Inc.
Arbitron Metro Market: Afton, WY; *Format:* Country

Jerry Hansen, General Manager

*KUWA

07-01-1998; 91.3 MHz FM; *Hrs Open:* 24; 0.4 kw; -312 ft.; N42 51 2 W110 58 46 *Rebroadcasts:* Rebroadcasts KUWR(FM) Laramie 100%
P.O. Box 3984, 1000 East University Avenue, Laramie, WY 82071 US
(307) 766-4240; *Fax:* (307) 766-6184
www.wyomingpublicradio.net
wprhelp@uwyo.edu
License: Afton, Lincoln County, WY held by University of Wyoming.
Nat'l Network: NPR; PRI; *Wire Services:* AP
Arbitron Metro Market: Afton, WY; *Format:* News, News/Talk, 86
Special Programming: Folk 5 hrs, jazz 5 hrs wkly; *Hrs. of News Programming:* News progmg 4 hrs wkly; *Target Audience:* 25-54 plus; demographic, highincome, education

Roger Adams, Operations Dir
Christina Kuzmych, General Manager
Grady Kirkpatrick, Programming Director
Bob Beck, News Director
Reid Fletcher, Chief Engineer
Brenda Bland, Sustainability & Services Director
Micah Schweizer,Cultural Affairs & Production Director
Erin O'Doherty, Membership Director

Albin

KKWY

01-01-2001; 107.3 MHz FM; 9.3 kw; 531 ft.; N41 29 31 W104 5 7 *Rebroadcasts:* Rebroadcasts KZDR(FM) Cheyenne 100%
C/O Brill Media Co., P.O. Box 3353, Evansville, IN 47732 US
(307) 638-8921; *Fax:* (307) 638-8922
License: Albin, Laramie County, WY held by Laramie Mountain Broadcasting LLC
Format: Country

Eric Hauenstein, General Manager
Diane Curtis, General Sales Mgr
Bruce Jones, Programming Director
Kurt Johnson, Promotions Manager

Antelope Valley Crestview

KLED

93.3 MHz FM; 13.5 kw; 136.2 meters; N44 14 35 W105 32 19
2810 Southern Drive, Gillette, WY 82718
(307) 686-2242; *Fax:* (307) 686-7736
www.basinradio.com
reception@basinsradio.com

License: Antelope Valley Crestview, Weston County, WY held by VCY America Inc.
Group Owner: Horizon Christian Fellowship

Don Clonch, General Manager
Mark Warren, Director of Sales
Paul Edwards, Chief Engineer

Bar Nunn

KDAD
01-01-2007; 92.5 MHz FM; 3.1 kw; 521 meters; N42 16 05 W105 26 33
2109 E. 10th St., Cheyenne, WY
(307) 638-8921; *Fax:* (307) 638-8922
License: Bar Nunn, Converse County, WY held by The Casper Radio Group Inc.
Group Owner: Northeast Broadcasting Company Inc.

Steven Silberberg, President
Roger Ingram, General Manager

Basin

KBHM
107.9 MHz FM; 100 kw; 418 meters; N44 34 11 W108 49 07
PO Box 5086, Sheriden, WY 82801
(307) 672-7421; *Fax:* (307) 672-2933
www.sheridanmedia.com
info@sheridanmedia.com
License: Basin, WY held by Lovecom Inc

Kim Love, Owner
Tommy B, Programming Director
Leslie Straetmoen, News Director
Trevor Jackson, Sports Director
Liz Reynolds, Traffic Manager
Steve Sisson, Operations Manager
Bob Grammens, General Manager

Buffalo

KBBS
04-17-1956; 1450 kHz AM; *Hrs Open:* 24; 1 kw-U, ND1; N44 20 33 W106 40 54
1221 Fort St., Buffalo, WY 82834 US
(307) 684-5126; *Fax:* (307) 684-7676
www.bighornmountainradio.com
reception@bighornmountainradio.com
License: Buffalo, WY held by Legend Communications of Wyoming L.L.C.
Group Owner: Legend Communications L.L.C.; (acq 9-1-2000; $1.05 million with KLGT(FM) Buffalo)
Nat'l Reps: McGavren Guild
Arbitron Metro Market: Buffalo, WY; *Format:* News, News/Talk, 64, Sports, Talk; *Hrs. of News Programming:* News progmg 10 hrs wkly; *Target Audience:* 35-64; age group with the most money to spend; *Adv. Rates:* 10.50;10.50; 10.50; 9.50
Don Clonch, General Manager
Jessica Pierce, General Sales Mgr
Bailey Roebling, Director of Digital & Social Media
Jonna Gunsolley, Production Director
Jeff Rickett, Sports Director

*KBUW
01-01-2000; 90.5 MHz FM; 0.43 kw; -197 ft.; N44 20 50 W106 43 25
Dept 3984, 1000 East University Avenue, Laramie, WY 82071 US
(307) 766-4240; *Fax:* (307) 766-6184
wyomingpublicmedia.org
wprhelp@uwyo.edu
License: Buffalo, Johnson County, WY held by University of Wyoming.
Format: News, Triple A
Christina Kuzmych, General Manager
Grady Kirkpatrick, Programming Director
Bob Beck, News Director
Reid Fletcher, Chief Engineer
Micah Schweizer, Cultural Affairs & Production Director
Brenda Bland, Director of Sustainability &Services
Erin O'Doherty, Membership Director

KLGT
03-07-1983; 96.5 MHz FM; *Hrs Open:* 24; 100 kw; 333 ft.; N44 34 31.9 W106 52 21.7
1221 Fort St., Buffalo, WY 82834 US
(307) 684-5126; *Fax:* (307) 684-7676
www.bighornmountainradio.com
reception@bighornmountainradio.com
License: Buffalo, Johnson County, WY held by Legend Communications of Wyoming L.L.C.
Group Owner: Legend Communications L.L.C.; (acq 9-1-2000)
Nat'l Network: Jones Radio Networks; *Nat'l Reps:* McGavren Guild
Arbitron Metro Market: Casper, WY; *Format:* Country *Special Programming:* Relg one hr wkly; *Hrs. of News Programming:* news progmg 9 hrs wkly; *No. News Employees:* 1; *Target Audience:* 24-54; those withspendable income; *Adv. Rates:* 16; 16; 16; 13
Don Clonch, General Manager
Jessica Pierce, General Sales Mgr
Bailey Roebling, Director of Digital & Social Media

Burns

KIGN
09-26-1990; 101.9 MHz FM; *Hrs Open:* 24; 50 kw; 492 ft.; N41 7 1 W104 40 7
1513 Carey Avenue, Cheyenne, WY 82001 US
(307) 632-4400; *Fax:* (307) 632-1818
www.kingfm.com
License: Burns, Laramie County, WY held by Townsquare Media Cheyenne License LLC
Group Owner: Townsquare Media; (acq 2-13-2008; grpsl)
Arbitron Metro Market: Cheyenne, WY; *Format:* Rock/AOR; *Hrs. of News Programming:* news progmg 3 hrs wkly; *No. News Employees:* 1; *Target Audience:* 25-54.
Rick Darcy, Operations Dir
Craig Cochran, General Manager
Geoff Gundy, Programming Director
Amy Richards, News Director
Jim Mross, Chief Engineer

*KIHI
01-01-2008; 88.9 MHz FM; 600 w; Ant 118 ft; N41 09 45 W104 30 16
87 Jasper Lake Rd., Loveland, CO
(970) 669-9200; *Fax:* (970) 669-0800
License: Burns, Laramie County, WY held by Cedar Cove Broadcasting Inc.
Group Owner: Cedar Cove Broadcasting Inc.

Victor Michael Jr., President

Casper

KASS
10-15-1990; 106.9 MHz FM; *Hrs Open:* 24; 100 kw; 1765 ft.; N42 44 37 W106 18 31
218 N. Wolcott, Casper, WY 82602 US
(307) 265-1984; *Fax:* (307) 473-7461
License: Casper, Natrona County, WY held by Mt. Rushmore Broadcasting Inc.
Group Owner: Mt. Rushmore Broadcasting Inc.; (acq 1995; $150,000).
Arbitron Metro Market: Casper, WY; *Format:* Classic Rock
Jan Charles Gray, President

KHOC
01-01-1997; 102.5 MHz FM; *Hrs Open:* 24; 100 kw; 1696 ft.; N42 44 37 W106 18 31
218 N. Wolcott, Casper, WY 82601 US
(307) 265-1984; *Fax:* (307) 266-3295
License: Casper, Natrona County, WY held by Mt. Rushmore Broadcasting Inc.
Group Owner: Mt. Rushmore Broadcasting Inc.; (acq 10-29-98; $300,000).
Arbitron Metro Market: Casper, WY; *Format:* Adult Contemp; *No. News Employees:* 1; *Target Audience:* m/f 18-45
Jan Charles Gray, President

KKTL
01-01-1999; 1400 kHz AM; 1 kw-U, ND1; N42 51 22 W106 21 41
555 13th Street, N.W., Washington, DC 20004 US
(307) 266-5252; *Fax:* (307) 235-9143
www.am1400espn.com
bobprice@townsquaremedia.com
License: Casper, WY held by Townsquare Media Casper License LLC
Group Owner: Townsquare Media; (acq 2-13-2008; grpsl)
Arbitron Metro Market: Casper, WY; *Format:* Sports
Bob Price, General Manager
Donvan Short, Brand Manager
Bob Price, Director Of Sales

KMLD
10-01-1967; 94.5 MHz FM; 65 kw; 1909 ft.; N42 44 3 W106 20 0
218 N. Wolcott St., Casper, WY 82602-1923 US
(307) 265-1984; *Fax:* (307) 473-7461
License: Casper, Natrona County, WY held by Mt. Rushmore Broadcasting Inc.
Group Owner: Mt. Rushmore Broadcasting Inc.; (acq 3-12-2001; grpsl).
Arbitron Metro Market: Casper, WY; *Format:* Oldies; *Target Audience:* 35-64.
Jan Charles Gray, President

KRNK
01-01-1998; 96.7 MHz FM; 2.85 kw; Ant 1,771 ft; N42 44 37 W106 18 26
150 N. Nichols Ave., Casper, WY 82601
(307) 266-5252; *Fax:* (307) 235-9143
www.rock967online.com
bobprice@townsquaremedia.com
License: Casper, Natrona County, WY held by Townsquare Media Casper License LLC
Group Owner: Townsquare Media; (acq 2-13-2008; grpsl)
Arbitron Metro Market: Casper, WY
Bob Price, General Manager
Donovan Short, Brand Manager
Bob Price, Director Of Sales

KQLT
10-07-1983; 103.7 MHz FM; *Hrs Open:* 24; 97 kw; 1860 ft.; N42 44 37 W106 18 31
218 N. Wolcott, Casper, WY 82602 US
(307) 265-1984; *Fax:* (307) 473-7461
License: Casper, Natrona County, WY held by Mt. Rushmore Broadcasting Inc.
Group Owner: Mt. Rushmore Broadcasting Inc.; (acq 8-17-94; $230,000;
Nat'l Reps: McGavren Guild
Arbitron Metro Market: Casper, WY; *Format:* Country; *Target Audience:* General.
Jan Charles Gray, President

KTRS-FM
01-01-1997; 104.7 MHz FM; 18 kw; 1818 ft.; N42 44 37 W106 18 24
6807 Foxglove Drive, Cheyenne, WY 82009 US
(307) 266-5252; *Fax:* (307) 235-9143
kisscasper.com
bobprice@townsquaremedia.com
License: Casper, Natrona County, WY held by Townsquare Media Casper License LLC
Group Owner: Townsquare Media; (acq 2-13-2008; grpsl)
Arbitron Metro Market: Casper, WY; *Format:* Contemporary Hits/Top 40; *Target Audience:* 12-24.
Bob Price, General Manager
Donovan Short, Brand Manager
Bob Price, Director OF Sales

KTWO
01-02-1930; 1030 kHz AM
50 East Rivercenter Blvd., Suite 1200, Covington, KY 41011 US
(307) 266-5252; *Fax:* (307) 235-9143
www.k2radio.com
bobprice@townsquaremedia.com
License: Casper, WY held by Townsquare Media Casper License LLC
Group Owner: Townsquare Media; (acq 2-13-2008; grpsl)
Nat'l Network: CBS
Arbitron Metro Market: Casper, WY; *Format:* Talk; *Target Audience:* 25-54.
Bob Price, General Manager
Donovan Short, Brand Manager
Bob Price, Director Of Sales
Ian Delap, Digital Managing Editor

*KUWC
01-01-2000; 91.3 MHz FM; 0.53 kw; 1785 ft.; N42 44 26 W106 21 34
P O Box 3434, 1000 East University Avenue, Laramie, WY 82071 US
(307) 766-4240; *Fax:* (307) 766-6184
www.wyomingpublicmedia.org
wprhelp@uwyo.edu
License: Casper, Natrona County, WY held by University of Wyoming.
Arbitron Metro Market: Casper, WY; *Format:* News, Triple A
Christina Kuzmych, General Manager
Grady Kirkpatrick, Programming Director
Bob Beck, News Director
Ben Slater, Engineer
Reid Fletcher, Chief Engineer
Brenda Bland, Director of Sustainability & Services
Micah Schweizer, CulturalAffairs & Production Director
Erin O'Doherty, Membership Director

KVOC
09-29-1946; 1230 kHz AM; 1 kw-U, ND1; N42 50 5 W106 17 44
212 N. Wolcott, Casper, WY 82601 US
(307) 265-1984; *Fax:* (307) 473-7461

License: Casper, WY held by Mt. Rushmore Broadcasting Inc.
Group Owner: Mt. Rushmore Broadcasting Inc.; (acq 6-12-97; $105,000).
Arbitron Metro Market: Casper, WY; *Format:* Talk
Jan Charles Gray, President

*KLWC
01-01-2005; 89.1 MHz FM; 2.7 kw vert; 1850 ft.; N42 44 3 W106 20 0 *Rebroadcasts:* Rebroadcasts KLVR(FM) Santa Rosa, CA).
PO Box 2098, Omaha, NE 68103-2098 US
(800) 525-5683; *Fax:* (916) 251-1650
www.klove.com
klove@klove.com
License: Casper, Natrona County, WY held by Educational Media Foundation.
Group Owner: EMF Broadcasting; (acq 1-11-2005; $100,000 for CP with CP for KLRV(FM) Billings, MT).
Nat'l Network: K-Love
Arbitron Metro Market: Casper, WY; *Format:* Christian
Darrell Chambliss, Chairman
Mike Novak, President and CEO
Eric Moser, CFO
Alan Mason, COO
D. Kevin Blair, Secretary/General Counsel
David Pierce, Chief Creative Officer
Ed Lenane, News Director
Sam Wallington, EngineeringDir

KWYX
93.5 MHz FM; 3.8 kw; 1739 ft.; N42 44 28 W106 18 31 US
(703) 812-0482
www.kwyx.com
License: Casper, Natrona County, WY held by Cochise Broadcasting LLC.
Group Owner: Cochise Broadcasting LLC
Arbitron Metro Market: Casper, WY
Ted Tucker, General Manager

*KKRR
01-01-2008; 88.3 MHz FM; 0.5 kw vert; 1726 ft.; N42 44 26 W106 21 34
2232 Dell Range Blvd., Suite 306, Cheyenne, WY 82009 US
(307) 637-7777
License: Casper, Natrona County, WY held by WCN Inc.
Arbitron Metro Market: Casper, WY; *Format:* Oldies
Robert Rule, President

*KCSP
08-25-1999; 90.3 MHz FM; *Hrs Open:* 24; 100 kw; N42 44 24 W106 18 23
PO Box 21888, Carson City, NV 89721 US
(775) 883-5647
www.pilgrimradio.com
info@pilgrimradio.com
License: Casper, WY held by Western Inspirational Broadcasters Inc.
Group Owner: Western Inspirational Broadcasters Inc.
Population Served: 330,000; *Arbitron Metro Market:* Casper, WY; *Format:* Christian; *No. News Employees:* 1; *Target Audience:* General.
Tom Hesse, General Manager

Cheyenne

KFBC
01-01-1940; 1240 kHz AM; *Hrs Open:* 24; 0.7 kw-U, ND1; N41 7 17 W104 50 22
1806 Capitol Avenue, Cheyenne, WY 82009 US
(307) 634-4462
www.kfbcradio.com
License: Cheyenne, WY held by Montgomery Broadcasting L.L.C.
Nat'l Network: ABC
Arbitron Metro Market: Cheyenne, WY; *Format:* News, Sports; *Hrs. of News Programming:* news progmg 25 hrs wkly; *No. News Employees:* 5; *Target Audience:* 35-54.; *Adv. Rates:* 12; 8; 12; 5
Dave Montgomery, Owner/General Manager

KXBG
09-01-1968; 97.9 MHz FM; *Hrs Open:* 24; 100 kw; 541 ft.; N41 6 1 W105 0 23
4270 Byrd Dr., Loveland, CO 80538 US
(970) 461-2560
www.bigcountry979.com
License: Cheyenne, Laramie County, WY held by Citicasters Licenses Inc.
Group Owner: iHeartMedia; (acq 1999; grpsl)
Arbitron Metro Market: Cheyenne, WY; *Format:* Country; *Hrs. of News Programming:* news progmg 2 hrs wkly; *No. News Employees:* 3; *Target Audience:* 25-54.
Garner Goin, Operations Manager/Program Director
Stu Haskell, General Manager
Kathy Arias, General Sales Mgr
Mike Sanchez, Promotions Manager

KJUA
01-01-1952; 1380 kHz AM; *Hrs Open:* 24
110 East 17th Street, Suite 205, Cheyenne, WY 82001 US
(307) 635-8787; *Fax:* (307) 635-8788
License: Cheyenne, WY held by La Familia Broadcasting, LLC
Nat'l Network: CNN Radio
Arbitron Metro Market: Cheyenne, WY; *Format:* Adult Contemp
Special Programming: Gospel one hr wkly; *Hrs. of News Programming:* news progmg 22 hrs wkly; *No. News Employees:* 2; *Target Audience:* 35 plus;mature adults; *Adv. Rates:* 18; 16; 18; 14
Paul Montoya, President

KLEN
09-26-1983; 106.3 MHz FM; *Hrs Open:* 24; 6 kw; 325 ft.; N41 3 9 W104 49 55
50 East Rivercenter Blvd, Suite 1200, Covington, KY 41011 US
(307) 632-4400; *Fax:* (307) 632-1818
cheyenneaudio@clearchannel.com
License: Cheyenne, Laramie County, WY held by Townsquare Media Cheyenne License LLC
Group Owner: Townsquare Media; (acq 2-13-2008; grpsl)
Arbitron Metro Market: Cheyenne, WY; *Format:* Country; *No. News Employees:* 3; *Target Audience:* 25-54.
Rick Darcy, Operations Dir
Craig Cochran, General Manager
Amy Richards, News Director
Jim Mross, Chief Engineer
Lesley Martin, Traffic Manager

KOLZ
08-01-1961; 100.7 MHz FM; 100 kw; 663 ft.; N41 2 55 W104 53 28
4270 Byrd Drive, Loveland, CO 80538 US
(307) 632-4400; *Fax:* (307) 632-1818
www.koltfm.com
License: Cheyenne, Laramie County, WY held by Citicasters Licenses Inc.
Group Owner: iHeartMedia
Arbitron Metro Market: Cheyenne, WY; *Format:* Country
Kathy Arias, General Sales Mgr

KRAE
04-29-1961; 1480 kHz AM
P. O. Box 189, Cheyenne, WY 82001 US
(307) 638-8921; *Fax:* (307) 638-8922
news@1049krrr.com
License: Cheyenne, WY held by Proshop Radio Broadcasting LLC
Nat'l Network: ESPN Radio
Arbitron Metro Market: Cheyenne, WY; *Format:* Sports *Special Programming:* Sp 2 hrs wkly; *Adv. Rates:* 144; 132; 120; 96
Larry Proietti, General Manager
Jessica Cooper, General Sales Mgr
Larry Proeitti, Programming Director
R.J. Fox, News Director
Rob Thomas, Chief Engineer
Sandra Cooper, Traffic Manager

KKPL
01-01-1997; 99.9 MHz FM; 50 kw; Ant 492 ft; N40 59 22 W105 03 47
600 Main St., Windsor, CO 80550
(970) 674-2700
www.999thepoint.com
pat.kelley@townsquaremedia.com
License: Cheyenne, Laramie County, WY held by Townsquare Media of Fort Collins Inc
Group Owner: Townsquare Media; (acq 11-15-2004; $7.75 million with KARS-FM Laramie)
Arbitron Metro Market: Cheyenne, WY
Mark Callaghan, Operations Dir
Pat Kelley, General Manager
Zandi Wilcox, Sales Director

KRRR
01-01-1997; 104.9 MHz FM; 25.5 kw; 115 ft.; N41 8 4 W104 41 32
1600 Van Lennen Avenue, Cheyenne, WY 82001 US
(307) 638-8921; *Fax:* (307) 638-8922
www.1049krrr.com/
sales@radiowyo.com
License: Cheyenne, Laramie County, WY held by Brahmin Broadcasting Corp.
Arbitron Metro Market: Cheyenne, WY; *Format:* Oldies; *Target Audience:* 25-54.
Roger Ingram, General Manager

*KAIX
01-01-2006; 88.1 MHz FM; 1.9 kw; 207 ft.; N41 9 37 W104 42 13 *Rebroadcasts:* Rebroadcasts KLRD(FM) Yucaipa, CA 100%
PO Box 2118, Omaha, NE 68103-2118 US
(888) 937-2471; *Fax:* (916) 251-1650
www.air1.com
info@air1.com
License: Cheyenne, Laramie County, WY held by Educational Media Foundation.
Group Owner: EMF Broadcasting; (acq 3-23-2007; grpsl)
Nat'l Network: Air 1
Arbitron Metro Market: Cheyenne, WY; *Format:* Alternative, Christian
Darrell Chambliss, Chairman
Alan Mason, COO
Mike Novak, President and CEO
Ed Lenane, Chief Creative Officer
Sam Wallington, Engineering Dir
Eric Moser, Chief Financial Officer
D. Kevin Blair, Secretary and General Counsel

KAZY
06-15-2006; 93.7 MHz FM; 25 kw; 115 ft.; N41 8 4 W104 41 32
1600 Van Lennen Avenue, Cheyenne, WY 82001 US
(307) 638-8921; *Fax:* (307) 638-8922
www.937kazy.com
kazyfin@gmail.com
License: Cheyenne, Laramie County, WY held by Friesland Broadcasting Corp.
Group Owner: Northeast Broadcasting Company Inc.
Arbitron Metro Market: Auburn, WA; *Format:* Rock/AOR
Steven Silberberg, President
Roger Ingram, General Manager

Chugwater

*KLWV
01-01-2004; 90.9 MHz FM; *Hrs Open:* 24; 100 kw; 1183 ft.; N41 18 39 W105 27 12
PO Box 2098, Omaha, NE 68103-2098 US
(800) 525-5683
www.klove.com
License: Chugwater, Platte County, WY held by Educational Media Foundation.
Group Owner: EMF Broadcasting; (acq 10-2-03; grpsl).
Nat'l Network: K-Love
Arbitron Metro Market: Cheyenne, WY; *Format:* Christian; *No. News Employees:* 3; *Target Audience:* 25-44; Judeo Christian, female
Darrell Chambliss, Chairman
Mike Novak, President and CEO
David Pierce, Chief Creative Officer
Ed Lenane, News Director
Sam Wallington, Engineering Dir
Alan Mason, COO
D. Kevin Blair, Secretary/General Counsel

Clearmont

KLQQ
01-01-2006; 104.9 MHz FM; 100 kw; 1207 ft.; N44 37 20 W107 6 57
PO Box 5086, Sheridan, WY 82801 US
(307) 672-7421; *Fax:* (307) 672-2933
www.sheridanmedia.com
info@sheridanmedia.com
License: Clearmont, Sheridan County, WY held by Lovcom Inc.
Group Owner: Lovcom Inc.
Arbitron Metro Market: Clearmont, WY; *Format:* Contemporary Hits/Top 40
Kim Love, Owner
Bob Grammens, General Manager
Jim Schellinger, General Sales Mgr
Tommy B., Programming Director
Trevor Jackson, Sports Director
Leslie Streatmoen, News Director
Liz Reynolds, Traffic Manager
Steve Sisson,Operations Manager

KZWY-HD
01-01-2006; 105.9 MHz FM; 100 kw; 1207 ft.; N44 37 20 W107 6 57
PO Box 5086, Sheridan, WY 82801 US
(307) 672-7421; *Fax:* (307) 672-2933
www.sheridanmedia.com
info@sheridanmedia.com
License: Clearmont, Sheridan County, WY held by Lovcom Inc.
Group Owner: Lovcom Inc.
Arbitron Metro Market: Clearmont, WY; *Format:* Oldies
Kim Love, Owner
Bob Grammens, General Manager

Jim Schellinger, General Sales Mgr
Tommy B., Programming Director
Trevor Jackson, Sports Director
Leslie Straetmoen, News Director
Liz Reynolds, Traffic Manager
Steve Sisson,Operations Manager

Cody

KODI
03-01-1947; 1400 kHz AM; *Hrs Open:* 6 AM-midnight
1949 Mountain View Dr., Cody, WY 82414 US
(307) 578-5014
www.mybighornbasin.com
mcrump@bhrnwy.com
License: Cody, WY held by Legend Communications of Wyoming LLC.
Group Owner: Legend Communications L.L.C.; (acq 6-29-99; $890,000 with co-located FM)
Wire Services: NWS (National Weather Service)
Format: News, News/Talk, 84, Talk; *Hrs. of News Programming:* news progmg 20 hrs wkly; *No. News Employees:* 1; *Target Audience:* 35 plus.
Rita Conners, VP of Business Affairs
Mark Crump, General Manager
Jed Burns, General Sales Mgr
Wendy Corr, News Director
Tim Anderson, Sports Director

KTAG
11-30-1981; 97.9 MHz FM; *Hrs Open:* 6 AM-midnight; 100 kw; 1890 ft.; N44 29 42 W109 9 10
1949 Mountain View Dr., Cody, WY 82414 US
(307) 578-5000
www.mybighornbasin.com
mcrump@bhrnwy.com
License: Cody, Park County, WY held by Legend Communications of Wyoming
Group Owner: Legend Communications L.L.C.
Arbitron Metro Market: Cody, WY; *Format:* Adult Contemp; *Hrs. of News Programming:* News progmg 6 hrs wkly; *Target Audience:* 25-39; upper middle class, young families, suburban w/some college, 60% female
Rita Conners, VP of Business Affairs
Mark Crump, General Manager
Jed Burns, General Sales Mgr
Wendy Corr, News Director

KROW
96.7 MHz FM; 2.4 kw; Ant 1,831 ft; N44 29 49 W109 09 19
207 East 1st Street, Powell, WY 82435
(307) 764-3771
www.rocksthebighorns.com
krowfm@gmail.com
License: Cody, Park County, WY held by White Park Broadcasting Inc.
Group Owner: Northeast Broadcasting Company Inc.

Steven Silberberg, President

*KOFG
91.1 MHz FM; 8.7 kw; 1795 ft.; N44 29 46 W109 9 9
US
(903) 503-0304
www.oldfashiongospel.org
License: Cody, Park County, WY held by Tres Hermanas Educational Media Foundation of Texas Inc.
Arbitron Metro Market: Cody, WY; *Format:* Gospel
Lonnie Horton, President

Cowley

KBEN-FM
103.3 MHz FM; 100 kw; 1401 ft.; N44 34 13 W108 49 9
207 East 1st Street, Powell, WY 82435 US
(307) 764-3771
www.bighornsrange.com
License: Cowley, WY held by White Park Broadcasting Inc.
Group Owner: Northeast Broadcasting Company Inc.

Steven Silberberg, President

Daniel

KFZE
104.3 MHz FM; kw
US
(206) 805-0965; *Fax:* (206) 805-0932
License: Daniel, Sweetwater County, WY held by Martin Dirst
Arbitron Metro Market: Daniel, WY
Martin Dirst, General Manager

Dayton

KOWY
102.3 MHz FM; 2100 watts; 343 meters; 44 37 N20 107 06 W57
PO Box 5086, Sheridan, WY 82801
(307) 672-7421; *Fax:* (307) 672-2933
www.sheridanmedia.com
info@sheridanmedia.com
License: Dayton, WY held by Lovcom, Inc.

Kim Love, President/Owner
Steve Sisson, Operations Dir
Bob Grammens, General Manager
Jim Schellinger, General Sales Mgr
Tommy B., Programming Director
Trevor Jackson, Sports Director
Leslie Straetmoen, News Director
LizReynolds, Traffic Manager

Diamondville

KDWY
01-01-2000; 105.3 MHz FM; 16 kw; 886 ft.; N41 50 18 W110 30 11
36 Cross Highway, Redding, CT 06896 US
(307) 877-4422; *Fax:* (307) 877-5537
kmer@onewest.net
License: Diamondville, Lincoln County, WY held by Red Rock Broadcasting-Slc, Ls, LLC
Group Owner: Red Rock Broadcasting
Arbitron Metro Market: Kemmerer, WY; *Format:* Country; *Hrs. of News Programming:* news progmg one hr wkly; *No. News Employees:* 1; *Target Audience:* 25-55.; *Adv. Rates:* 12; 12; 12; 12
Jim Thoeny, Operations Dir
Jim Carroll, General Manager

Douglas

KKTY
06-22-1957; 1470 kHz AM; *Hrs Open:* 24; 1 kw-D, ND2; 0.5 kw-N, ND2; N42 45 48 W105 23 32
247 Russell Avenue, Douglas, WY 82633 US
(307) 358-3636
www.kktyonline.com
License: Douglas, WY held by Douglas Broadcasting Inc.
Nat'l Network: Westwood One; CNN Radio *Regional Reps:* Regnl Reps; *Wire Services:* AP
Arbitron Metro Market: Casper, WY; *Format:* Oldies; *Hrs. of News Programming:* News progmg 28 hrs wkly; *Target Audience:* Adults 18+; *Adv. Rates:* 9.25; 9.25; 9.25; na
Dennis Switzer, General Manager

KKTS-FM
12-06-1982; 99.3 MHz FM; *Hrs Open:* 24; 813 w; 530 ft; N42 43 42 W105 31 46
247 N. Russell Avenue, Douglas, WY 82633
(307) 358-3636
www.kktsonline.com
kkts@kktsonline.com
License: Douglas, Converse County, WY held by Douglas Broadcasting
Nat'l Network: Jones Radio Networks; CNN Radio
Hrs. of News Programming: news progmg 28 hrs wkly; *No. News Employees:* 1; *Target Audience:* General.; *Adv. Rates:* Same as AM
Dennis Switzer, General Manager

*KDUW
01-01-2000; 91.7 MHz FM; 0.45 kw; 312 ft.; N42 43 24 W105 18 21
P.O. Box 3984, 1000 East University Avenue, Laramie, WY 82071 US
(307) 766-4240; *Fax:* (307) 766-6184
www.wyomingpublicmedia.org
wprhelp@uwyo.edu
License: Douglas, Converse County, WY held by University of Wyoming.
Arbitron Metro Market: Laramie, WY; *Format:* News
Christina Kuzmych, General Manager
Grady Kirkpatrick, Programming Director
Bob Beck, News Director
Reid Fletcher, Chief Engineer
Erin O'Doherty, Membership Director
Micah Schweizer, Cultural Affairs/Production Director
BrendaBland, Director of Sustainability & Services

*KKAW
88.7 MHz FM; 7 kw; 240 ft.; N42 51 29 W105 14 3
US
(307) 460-4224
License: Douglas, Converse County, WY held by Wren Communications Inc.
Arbitron Metro Market: Douglas, WY
Tara Parker, President

Esterbrook

*KQCO
89.5 MHz FM; 320 watts; Ant 3,165 ft; N42 16 06 W105 26 31
87 Jasper Lake Rd., Loveland, CO
(970) 669-9200
License: Esterbrook, Converse County, WY held by Cedar Cove Broadcasting Inc.
Group Owner: Cedar Cove Broadcasting Inc.

Victor Michael, President

Ethete

*KWRR
01-01-2000; 89.5 MHz FM; 85 kw; 1821 ft.; N43 27 30 W108 11 39
3600 San Jeronimo Drive, Suite 480, Anchorage, AK 99508 US
(907) 793-3521; *Fax:* (907) 793-3536
www.nv1.org
sbeatty@knba.org
License: Ethete, Fremont County, WY held by Business Council of the Northern Arapaho Tribe.
Arbitron Metro Market: Kinnear, WY; *Format:* Native American
Shyanne Beatty, General Manager
Nola Daves Moses, Distribution Director
Larry Cleland, Director of Corporate Support

Evanston

*KPMD
08-25-1999; 88.1 MHz FM; *Hrs Open:* 24; 92 watts; N41 21 10 W110 54 29
P.O Box 21888, Carson City, NV 89721 US
(775) 883-5647
www.pilgrimradio.com
info@pilgrimradio.com
License: Evanston, WY held by Western Inspirational Broadcasters Inc.
Group Owner: Western Inspirational Broadcasters Inc.
Population Served: 330,000; *Arbitron Metro Market:* Evanston, WY; *Format:* Christian; *No. News Employees:* 1; *Target Audience:* General.
Tom Hesse, General Manager

KEVA
06-27-1953; 1240 kHz AM; *Hrs Open:* 24; 0.88 kw-U, ND1; N41 15 29 W111 0 51
P. O. Box 190, Evanston, WY 82930 US
(307) 789-9101(307) 789-9102; *Fax:* (307) 789-8521
keva@vcn.com
License: Evanston, WY held by Sagebrush Broadcasting Co. Inc.
Group Owner: Carol Carroll Stns; (acq 1-23-2001).
Arbitron Metro Market: Evanston, WY; *Format:* Country; *Target Audience:* 25-54.
Linda Burris, General Manager
Linda Burns, General Sales Mgr
Bill Smith, Programming Director
J.C. Jewett, News Director
Michael Richard, Chief Engineer

KBMG
06-01-1982; 106.3 MHz FM; 89 kw horiz; 2,123 ft.; N40 52 16 W110 59 43
P.O. Box 190, Evanston, WY 82931 US
(801) 908-8777; *Fax:* (801) 908-8782
License: Evanston, Uinta County, WY held by Alpha Media Licensee LLC
Group Owner: Alpha Media LLC; (acq 7-16-2015; grpsl).
Arbitron Metro Market: Salt Lake City, UT; *Format:* Spanish
Mary Lee Robinson, Market Manager

KADQ-FM
01-01-2008; 98.3 MHz FM; 1.2 kw; 1490 ft.; N41 21 10 W110 54 31
1044 Main Street, Evanston, WY 82930 US
(307) 789-8116
knyn@k-9radio.com
License: Evanston, Uinta County, WY held by Frandsen Media Company, LLC
Group Owner: College Creek Media LLC
Arbitron Metro Market: Evanston, WY
Julie Burleigh, Sales Manager
Kaylene Anderson, Office Manager

Evansville

KUYO
08-23-1985; 830 kHz AM; *Hrs Open:* Sunrise-sunset
Box 5067, Casper, WY 82605-0607 US
(307) 577-5896
www.kuyo.com
joy@kuyo.com
License: Evansville, WY held by Wyoming Christian Broadcasting Co.
Arbitron Metro Market: Evansville, WY; *Format:* Christian, Talk; *Target Audience:* 35-65; general
Steve Stumbo, President
Aaron Remington, Operations Dir

KTED
01-01-2008; 100.5 MHz FM; 10 kw; 1434 ft.; N42 45 30 W106 19 23
145 S. Durbin Street, Suite 303, Casper, WY 82601 US
(307) 232-2155
www.kted1005.com
License: Evansville, Converse County, WY held by The Casper Radio Group, Inc.
Group Owner: Northeast Broadcasting Company Inc.
Arbitron Metro Market: Evansville, WY
Steven Silberberg, President
Rood Dogg, Programming Director
Courtney Williams, Sales Representative

Fort Bridger

KNYN
01-01-2001; 103.9 MHz FM; 27.5 kw; 1604 ft.; N41 21 10 W110 54 26
1044 Main Street, Suite B, Evanston, WY 82930 US
(307) 789-8116; *Fax:* (307) 789-8205
www.k-9radio.com
website@k-9radio.com
License: Fort Bridger, Uinta County, WY held by M. Kent Frandsen.
Format: Adult Contemp
Julie Burleigh, Sales Manager
Kaylene Anderson, Office Manager

Fort Washakie

*KRKM
91.7 MHz FM; 6 kw horiz; 1309 ft.; N42 34 42 W108 42 46
PO Box 2098, Omaha, NE 68103-2098 US
(800) 525-5683
www.klove.com
klove@klove.com
License: Fort Washakie, Summit County, WY held by Educational Media Foundation
Arbitron Metro Market: Fort Washakie, WY; *Format:* Christian, Gospel
Darrell Chambliss, Chairman
Mike Novak, President/CEo
Alan Mason, COO
Ed Lenane, News Director
Sam Wallington, Engineering Dir
David Pierce, Chief Creative Officer
Eric Moser, Chief Financial Officer
D. Kevin Blair, Secretaryand General Counsel

*KUWW
90.9 MHz FM; 8 kw; 495 ft.; N42 54 27 W108 44 50 US
(307) 332-5983; *Fax:* (307) 332-7267
License: Fort Washakie, Fremont County, WY held by Fremont County School District #21.
Arbitron Metro Market: Fort Washakie, WY
Gregory Cox, General Manager

Fox Farm

KRND
01-01-1998; 1630 kHz AM; *Hrs Open:* 24
110 E. 17th Street, Ste 205, Cheyenne, WY 82001 US
(307) 635-8787; *Fax:* (307) 635-8788
License: Fox Farm, WY held by La Familia Broadcasting, LLC
Nat'l Network: AP Network News
Arbitron Metro Market: Cheyenne, WY; *Format:* Country; *Hrs. of News Programming:* news progmg 22 hrs wkly; *No. News Employees:* 1; *Target Audience:* 35 plus; mature adults; *Adv. Rates:* 18; 16; 18; 16
Paul Montoya, President

Gillette

KAML-FM
05-01-1976; 97.3 MHz FM; *Hrs Open:* 24; 100 kw; 1098 ft.; N43 59 57 W105 15 15
2810 Southern Dr., Gillette, WY 82718 US
(307) 686-2242; *Fax:* (307) 686-7736
www.basinsradio.com
reception@basinsradio.com
License: Gillette, Campbell County, WY held by Legend Communications of Wyoming LLC.
Group Owner: Legend Communications L.L.C.; (acq 1-16-2007; $300,000 with KIML(AM) Gillette)
Arbitron Metro Market: Gillette, WY; *Format:* Adult Contemp; *Hrs. of News Programming:* news progmg one hr wkly; *Target Audience:* 25-54.; *Adv. Rates:* 18; 16; 17; 14
Don Clonch, General Manager
Jessica Pierce, General Sales Mgr
Paul Wallem, News Director
Bailey Roebling, Director of Digital & Social Media

*KAXG
03-27-2003; 89.7 MHz FM; *Hrs Open:* 24; 0.4 kw vert; 449 ft.; N44 12 34 W105 28 4 *Rebroadcasts:* Rebroadcasts KXEI(FM) Havre, MT 100%
PO Box 2426, 317 1st Street, Havre, MT 59501 US
(800) 442-9222
www.ynop.org
ynop@ynop.org
License: Gillette, Campbell County, WY held by Hi-Line Radio Fellowship Inc.
Nat'l Network: Salem Radio Network; *Wire Services:* AP
Arbitron Metro Market: Havre, MT; *Format:* Christian, Religious; *Target Audience:* General; those looking for inprirational Christian music & progmg
Roger Lonnquist, General Manager
Brenda Boyum, Station Manager
David Brown, Programming Director
Ron Huckeby, Chief Engineer
Nicholas Tobiason, Music/IT Director

KGWY
01-05-1983; 100.7 MHz FM; *Hrs Open:* 24; 98 kw; 620 ft.; N44 14 35 W105 32 19
2810 Soutern Dr., Gillette, WY 82718 US
(307) 686-2242; *Fax:* (307) 686-7736
www.basinsradio.com
reception@basinsradio.com
License: Gillette, Campbell County, WY held by Legend Communications of Wyoming LLC.
Group Owner: Legend Communications L.L.C.; (acq 5-29-2001; $1.9 million)
Format: Country; *No. News Employees:* 1; *Target Audience:* 20-45.
Don Clonch, General Manager
Jessica Pierce, General Sales Mgr
Paul Wallem, News Director
Bailey Roebling, Director of Digital & Social Media

KIML
09-13-1957; 1270 kHz AM; *Hrs Open:* 24; 5 kw-D, DAN; 1 kw-N, DAN; N44 18 12 W105 29 52
2810 Southern Dr., Gillette, WY 82718 US
(307) 686-2242; *Fax:* (307) 686-7736
www.basinsradio.com
reception@basinsradio.com
License: Gillette, WY held by Legend Communications of Wyoming LLC.
Group Owner: Legend Communications L.L.C.; (acq 1-16-2007; $300,000 with KAML-FM Gillette)
Nat'l Network: Fox News Radio; Fox Sports; *Wire Services:* AP
Format: News, News/Talk, 84, Talk; *Hrs. of News Programming:* news progmg 40 hrs wkly; *No. News Employees:* 1; *Target Audience:* 25 plus.; *Adv. Rates:* 16; 15; 16; 12
Don Clonch, General Manager
Jessica Pierce, General Sales Mgr
Paul Wallem, News Director
Bailey Roebling, Director of Digital & Social Media

*KLWD
01-01-2001; 91.9 MHz FM; *Hrs Open:* 24; 1 kw; 318 ft.; N44 13 50 W105 27 45
P.O. Box 391, Twin Falls, ID 83303 US
(800) 658-5923; *Fax:* (307) 682-8509
klwd.vcn.com
calvarycomm@vcn.com
License: Gillette, Campbell County, WY held by Calvary Chapel Of Twin Falls, Inc.
Format: Christian, Religious
Mike Kestler, President
Daniel Davidson, Operations Dir
Kelly Carlson, Engineering Dir

*KUWG
01-01-1997; 90.9 MHz FM; 0.45 kw; 413 ft.; N44 12 34 W105 28 4 *Rebroadcasts:* Rebroadcasts KUWR(FM) Laramie 100%
P.O. Box 3984, 1000 East University Avenue, Laramie, WY 82071 US
(307) 766-4240; *Fax:* (307) 766-6184
www.wyomingpublicmedia.org
wprhelp@uwyo.edu
License: Gillette, Campbell County, WY held by University of Wyoming.
Arbitron Metro Market: Gillette, WY; *Format:* News
Christina Kuzmych, General Manager
Grady Kirkpatrick, Programming Director
Bob Beck, News Director
Reid Fletcher, Chief Engineer
Brenda Bland, Director of Sustainability & Services
Micah Schweizer, Cultural Affairs/ProductionDirector
Erin O'Doherty, Membership Director

KGCC
01-01-2004; 99.9 MHz FM; 51 kw; 114 meters; N44 13 50 W105 27 45
Box 2230, Gillette, WY 60611 US
(307) 687-1003; *Fax:* (307) 687-1006
License: Gillette, Campbell County, WY held by Keyhole Broadcasting LLC
Group Owner: Keyhole Broadcasting LLC
Arbitron Metro Market: Gillette, WY; *Format:* Classic Rock
Debora Semple, General Manager

*KLOF
01-01-2000; 88.9 MHz FM; 0.44 kw; 397 ft.; N44 12 34 W105 28 4
PO Box 2098, Omaha, NE 68103-2098 US
(800) 525-5683
www.klove.com
klove@klove.com
License: Gillette, Campbell County, WY held by Educational Media Foundation.
Group Owner: EMF Broadcasting; (acq 3-29-2007; $55,000)
Nat'l Network: K-Love
Arbitron Metro Market: Gillette, WY; *Format:* Christian
Darrell Chambliss, Chairman
Alan Mason, COO
Mike Novak, President/CEO
Ed Lenane, News Director
Sam Wallington, Engineering Dir
David Pierce, Chief Creative Officer
Eric Moser, Chief Financial Officer
D. Kevin Blair, Secretaryand General Counsel

*KGLL
88.1 MHz FM; 0.2 kw vert; 279 ft.; N44 13 50 W105 27 45
P.O. Box 3206, Tupelo, MS 38803 US
(662) 844-8888; *Fax:* (662) 842-6791
www.afr.net
faq@afa.net
License: Gillette, Campbell County, WY held by American Family Association
Group Owner: American Family Radio
Arbitron Metro Market: Gillette, WY; *Format:* Christian, Talk
Tim Wildmon, President
Donald Wildmon, Founder
Buddy Smith, Sr VP
Ed Vitagliano, Exec VP
Randy Sharp, Director Of Special Projects
Meeke Addison, Director Of Communications
Abraham Hamilton, General Counsel

Glendo

KKTY-FM
07-10-1999; 100.1 MHz FM; *Hrs Open:* 24; 100 kw; Ant 456 ft; N42 46 13 W105 13 21
247 Russell Avenue, Douglas, WY 82633
(307) 358-3636
www.kktyonline.com
License: Glendo, Platte County, WY held by Douglas Broadcasting, Inc.
Nat'l Network: Westwood One; CBS Radio
Population Served: 50,000; *Arbitron Metro Market:* Casper, WY
Special Programming: Religious, 3hrs wkly; *Hrs. of News Programming:* news progmg one hr wkly; *No. News Employees:* 1; *Target Audience:* 25-54. *Adv. Rates:* 9; 7; 9; 5
Darrell Woolsey, General Manager
Mary Woolsey, Station Manager

Glenrock

KGRK
01-01-2007; 98.5 MHz FM; 3.5 kw; 1699 ft.; N42 44 28 W106 18 31
7901 Stonridge Drive, Cheyenne, WY 82009 US
(970) 669-9200
ted@silvercityradio.com
License: Glenrock, Converse County, WY held by Michael Radio Group LLC.
Group Owner: Michael Radio Group
Arbitron Metro Market: Glenrock, WY
Victor Michael Jr., General Manager

Green River

KFRZ
09-23-1999; 92.1 MHz FM; *Hrs Open:* 24; 90 kw; 1138 ft.; N41 29 47 W109 20 44
40 Shoshone Avenue, Green River, WY 82935 US
(800) 254-5847
www.theradionetwork.net
License: Green River, Sweetwater County, WY held by Wagonwheel Communications Corp.
Group Owner: Wagonwheel Communications Corp.
Nat'l Network: Westwood One
Arbitron Metro Market: Green River, WY; *Format:* Country; *Hrs. of News Programming:* news progmg 3 hrs wkly; *No. News Employees:* 1; *Target Audience:* General.; *Adv. Rates:* Same as AM
Al Harris, CEO
Steve Core, General Manager
Jeff Driggs, General Sales Mgr
Dave Arambel, Sales
Ryan Claxton, Sales

KUGR
06-18-1976; 1490 kHz AM; *Hrs Open:* 24; 1 kw-U, ND1; N41 30 56 W109 26 11
40 Shoshone Avenue, Green River, WY 82935 US
(800) 254-5847
www.theradionetwork.net
alankugr@hotmail.com
License: Green River, WY held by Wagon Wheel Communications Corp.
Group Owner: Wagonwheel Communications Corp.; (acq 1-1-79).
Nat'l Network: CBS; Westwood One
Arbitron Metro Market: Green River, WY; *Format:* Adult Contemp
Special Programming: Sp 5 hrs wkly; *Hrs. of News Programming:* news progmg 4 hrs wkly; *No. News Employees:* 1; *Target Audience:* 30 plus. *Adv.Rates:* 13.60; 11.90; 13.60; 10.20
Al Harris, CEO
Steve Core, General Manager
Jeff Driggs, General Sales Mgr
Joyce Cox, Traffic Manager
Faith Harris
Ryan Claxton, Sales

KZWB
01-01-2005; 97.9 MHz FM; *Hrs Open:* 24; 10.5 kw; 1073 ft.; N41 29 47 W109 20 44
40 Shoshone Avenue, Green River, WY 82935 US
(800) 254-5847
theradionetwork.net
License: Green River, Sweetwater County, WY held by Wagonwheel Communications Corp.
Group Owner: Wagonwheel Communications Corp.
Arbitron Metro Market: Green River, WY; *Format:* Contemporary Hits/Top 40, Adult Contemp; *No. News Employees:* 1
Alan Harris, CEO
Steve Core, General Manager
Jeff Driggs, General Sales Mgr
Joyce Cox, Traffic Manager
Dave Arambel, Sales
Ryan Claxton, Sales

Greybull

KZMQ-FM
02-21-1986; 100.3 MHz FM; 53 kw; 2444 ft.; N44 48 41 W107 55 6
1949 Mountain View Dr., Cody, WY 82414 US
(307) 578-5000
www.mybighornbasin.com
mcrump@bhrnwy.com
License: Greybull, Big Horn County, WY held by Legend Comm of Wyoming, LLC
Group Owner: Legend Communications L.L.C.
Arbitron Metro Market: Greybull, WY; *Format:* Country
Mark Crump, General Manager
Jed Burns, General Sales Mgr
Wendy Corr, News Director
Tim Anderson, Sports Director

Guernsey

KANT
01-01-2008; 104.1 MHz FM; 36 kw; 564 ft.; N42 20 46.6 W105 2 3.9
1600 Van Lennen Avenue, Cheyenne, WY 82001 US
(307) 638-8921; *Fax:* (307) 638-8922
1049krrr.com
sales@radiowyo.com
License: Guernsey, Platte County, WY held by Peak Radio LLC
Group Owner: Northeast Broadcasting Company Inc.
Arbitron Metro Market: Guernsey, WY; *Format:* Oldies
Steven Silberberg, President
Roger Ingram, General Manager

Hanna

KBDY
01-01-2009; 102.1 MHz FM; 0.63 kw; 3445 ft.; N41 38 0.9 W106 31 32.1
US
(307) 326-8642
License: Hanna, Carbon County, WY held by Toga Radio LLC
Arbitron Metro Market: Hanna, WY; *Format:* Country
Don Day Jr., General Manager

Hillsdale

KYOY
01-01-1999; 92.3 MHz FM; *Hrs Open:* 24; 12 kw; 144 ft.; N41 14 55 W104 27 46
2232 Dell Range Boulevard, Suite 102, Cheyenne, WY 82009 US
(307) 637-0301; *Fax:* (307) 637-0325
www.kyoy.net
License: Hillsdale, Kimball County, WY held by Proshop Radio Broadcasting, LLC
Group Owner: Michael Radio Group; (acq 4-2-2007; $300,000 with KIMB(AM) Kimball)
Nat'l Network: AP Radio
Arbitron Metro Market: Kimball, NB; *Format:* Oldies; *No. News Employees:* 2
Larry Proleth, General Manager
MJ Reid, Chief Engineer
Sonia Lamone, Sales Director
Brett Henderson, Sports Director

Hudson

KTUG
105.1 MHz FM; 12.5 kw horiz; 262 ft.; N43 2 32 W108 26 28
Mailing Address: PO Box 6036, Riverton, WY 82501 US
Second Address: 612 W. Main Street, Riverton, WY 82501
(307) 855-4002; *Fax:* (307) 855-4005
License: Hudson, Fremont County, WY held by Higher Calling Comm., Inc.
Group Owner: Northeast Broadcasting Company Inc.
Arbitron Metro Market: Hudson, WY; *Format:* Christian
Steven Silberberg, President
Russ Harper, Station Owner/Sales Manager
Shane Haynes, Station Manager
Kevin Tippets, Production/Studio Manager

Jackson

KJAX
01-01-2000; 93.5 MHz FM; 90 kw; 315 meters; N43 27 40 W110 45 9
P. O. Box 291, Jackson, WY 83001 US
(307) 733-2120; *Fax:* (307) 733-4760
www.kjaxfm.com
License: Jackson, Teton County, WY held by RP Broadcasting Idaho LS LLC
Group Owner: Chaparral Communications; (acq 4-1-2013; grpsl)
Arbitron Metro Market: Jackson, WY; *Format:* Country
Scott Anderson, General Manager

KMTN
12-16-1974; 96.9 MHz FM; 50 kw; 1060 ft.; N43 27 42 W110 45 10
Mailing Address: P.O. Box 100, Jackson, WY 83001 US
Second Address: 645 S. Cache St., Jackson, WY 83001
(307) 733-2120; *Fax:* (307) 733-4760
www.jacksonholeradio.com
License: Jackson, Teton County, WY held by RP Broadcasting Idaho LS LLC
Group Owner: Rich Broadcasting
Nat'l Network: ABC
Format: Rock/AOR; *Target Audience:* 18-54.
Mark Fishman, Programming Director
Lynda John, News Director

KSGT
07-20-1962; 1340 kHz AM
Mailing Address: P.O. Box 100, Jackson, WY 83001 US
Second Address: 645 S. Cache St., Jackson, WY 83001
(307) 733-2120; *Fax:* (307) 733-4760
www.jacksonholeradio.com
License: Jackson, WY held by RP Broadcasting Idaho LS LLC
Group Owner: Rich Broadcasting LLC; (acq 4-1-2013; grpsl)
Arbitron Metro Market: Jackson, WY; *Format:* Country; *Target Audience:* 25 plus.
Scott Anderson, General Manager
Del Ray, Programming Director
Tom Ninneman, News Director

*KUWJ
11-01-1992; 90.3 MHz FM; *Hrs Open:* 5 AM-midnight; 3 kw; 1106 ft.; N43 27 40 W110 45 9 *Rebroadcasts:* Rebroadcasts KUWR(FM) Laramie 100%
Dept. 3984, 1000 East University Avenue, Laramie, WY 82071 US
(307) 766-4240; *Fax:* (307) 766-6184
www.wyomingpublicradio.net
wprhelp@uwyo.edu
License: Jackson, Teton County, WY held by University of Wyoming.
Nat'l Network: NPR; PRI
Arbitron Metro Market: Jackson, WY; *Format:* News *Special Programming:* Folk 10 hrs, jazz 6 hrs, state news 3 hrs wkly; *Hrs. of News Programming:* news progmg 42 hrs wkly; *No. News Employees:* 3; *Target Audience:* 25-54; educated, upper-income professionals; *Adv. Rates:* 14; 10; 14; 10
Christina Kuzmych, General Manager
Hank Arnold, General Sales Mgr
Grady Kirkpatrick, Programming Director
Bob Beck, News Director
Paul Montoya, Chief Engineer
Brenda Bland, Director of Sustainability Services
Micah Schweizer,Production Director
Shane Toven, Coordinator Engineer
Erin O'Doherty, Membership Director

KZJH
07-13-1989; 95.3 MHz FM; *Hrs Open:* 24; 100 kw; 1056 ft.; N43 27 40 W110 45 9
P.O. Box 2158, Ketchum, ID 83340 US
(307) 733-1770; *Fax:* (307) 733-4760
www.jacksonholeradio.com
acksonholeradionews@gmail.com
License: Jackson, Teton County, WY held by RP Broadcasting Idaho LS LLC
Group Owner: Rich Broadcasting LLC; (acq 4-11-2013; grpsl).
Nat'l Network: ABC
Arbitron Metro Market: Jackson, WY; *Format:* Classic Rock; *No. News Employees:* 1; *Target Audience:* 18-55.
Scott Anderson, General Manager
Jay Martin, Programming Director
Patricia Karnik, Promotions Manager
Dee Dee Dudley, News Director

*KHOL
04-04-2008; 89.1 MHz FM; 2.2 kw; Ant 1,102 ft; N43 27 40 W110 45 09
Mailing Address: 265 South Cache Street, Jackson, WY 83001
Second Address: PO Box 588, Jackson, WY 83001
(307) 733-4030
www.jhcr.org
info@jhcr.org
License: Jackson, Teton County, WY held by Jackson Hole Community Radio Inc.

Jim Tallichet, General Manager

*KMLT
01-01-2008; 88.3 MHz FM; 0.3 kw; 938 ft.; N43 27 43 W110 45 12 *Rebroadcasts:* Rebroadcasts KLVR(FM) Middletown, CA 100%
PO Box 2098, Omaha, NE 68103-2098 US
(800) 525-5683
www.klove.com
License: Jackson, Teton County, WY held by Educational Media Foundation.
Group Owner: EMF Broadcasting; (acq 7-23-2007; grpsl)
Nat'l Network: K-Love
Arbitron Metro Market: Jackson, WY; *Format:* Christian
Darrell Chambliss, Chairman
Mike Novak, President/CEO
D. Kevin Blair, Secretary/General Counsel
Alan Mason, COO

David Pierce, Chief Creative Officer
Eric Moser, CFO

***KMWY**
91.1 MHz FM; 0.35 kW; 1024 ft.; N43 27 40 W110 45 9
5408 S Freya St, Spokane, WA 99223 USA
(509) 448-2555; *Fax:* (509) 448-6855
www.moodyradio.org/stations/northwest
License: Jackson, Teton County, WY held by The Moody Bible Institute of Chicago
Group Owner: The Moody Bible Institute of Chicago
Arbitron Metro Market: Jackson, WY; *Format:* Christian

***KJCV**
1450 kHz AM; 1 kw-D, ND2; 1 kw-N, ND2; N43 27 45 W110 47 37
10550 Barkley St., Suite 100, Overland Park, KS 64052 US
(913) 642-7770
www.bottradionetwork.com
comments@bottradionetwork.com
License: Jackson, Teton County, WY held by Community Broadcasting Inc.
Group Owner: Bott Radio Network
Arbitron Metro Market: Jackson Hole, WY; *Format:* Christian, Talk
Richard Bott Sr., President & CEO
Eben Fowler, Operations Dir
Pat Rulon, Regional Manager
Candy Green, Program Services Manager
Rachel Launius, Marketing Manager
Jason Potocnik, Director of Traffic Operations

Kemmerer

KAOX
10-01-1999; 107.3 MHz FM; *Hrs Open:* 24; 13.5 kw; 948 ft.; N41 50 18 W110 30 11
Mailing Address: 1510 Canyon Road, Kemmerer, WY 83101 US
Second Address: 436 Fossil Butte, Kemmerer, WY 83101
(307) 877-4422; *Fax:* (307) 877-5527
kmer@onewest.net
License: Kemmerer, Lincoln County, WY held by Broadway Media LS, LLC
Nat'l Network: CBS
Arbitron Metro Market: Kemmerer, WY; *Format:* Adult Contemp; *Hrs. of News Programming:* news progmg 2 hrs wkly; *No. News Employees:* 1; *Target Audience:* 35 plus; male / female; *Adv. Rates:* 12; 12; 12; 12
Jim Thoeny, Operations Dir
Jim Carroll, General Manager

KMER
12-07-1962; 940 kHz AM
Mailing Address: P.O. Box 100, Jackson, WY 83001 US
Second Address: 436 Fossil Butte Dr., Kemmerer, WY 83101
(307) 877-4422; *Fax:* (307) 877-5537
License: Kemmerer, WY held by Simmons-SLC, LS LLC.
Group Owner: Simmons Media Group; (acq 5-20-2004; grpsl)
Format: Oldies *Special Programming:* News/talk 7 hrs, farm 3 hrs wkly; *Hrs. of News Programming:* news progmg one hr wkly; *No. News Employees:* 1; *Target Audience:* 25-54.; *Adv. Rates:* 12; 12; 12; 12
Jim Thoeny, Operations Dir
Jim Carroll, General Manager

Kirby

***KKBY**
90.5 MHz FM; kw
US
License: Kirby, Hot Springs County, WY held by Union Valley Baptist Church Inc.
Arbitron Metro Market: Kirby, WY
Steve Vandegrift, President

La Barge

***KRBR**
88.9 MHz FM; 40 watts; 425 meters; 42 19 N30 110 19 W12
PO Box 1096, Mount Vernon, TX
(888) 732-3599; *Fax:* (214) 231-9325
License: La Barge, WY held by Intermountain Public Radio

Lander

KDLY
01-01-1975; 97.5 MHz FM; *Hrs Open:* 24; 62 kw; -364 ft.; N42 49 15 W108 45 53
1530 Main Street, Lander, WY 82520 US
(307) 332-5683
www.fremontcountyradio.com
License: Lander, Fremont County, WY held by Fremont Broadcasting Inc.
Nat'l Network: Fox News Radio; *Nat'l Reps:* Commercial Media Sales; *Wire Services:* AP
Arbitron Metro Market: Lander, WY; *Format:* Classic Rock; *Hrs. of News Programming:* news progmg 5 hrs wkly; *No. News Employees:* 1; *Target Audience:* 18-49; general; *Adv. Rates:* 24; 11.75; 9.75; 11.75
Joe Kenney, General Manager

KOVE
01-01-1947; 1330 kHz AM
1530 Main Street, Lander, WY 82520 US
(307) 332-5683
www.fremontcountyradio.com
License: Lander, WY held by Fremont Broadcasting Inc.
Nat'l Network: Fox News Radio; *Nat'l Reps:* Commercial Media Sales; *Wire Services:* AP
Format: Country *Special Programming:* Talk 15 hrs wkly; *Hrs. of News Programming:* one.; *Target Audience:* 25 plus.
Joe Kenney, General Manager

Laramie

KCGY
11-07-1983; 95.1 MHz FM; *Hrs Open:* 24; 100 kw; 1070 ft.; N41 18 34 W105 27 11
Mailing Address: 3525 Soldier Springs Rd., Laramie, WY 82070 US
Second Address: 3525 Soldier Springs Rd., Laramie, WY 82070
(307) 745-4888; *Fax:* (307) 742-4576
www.y95country.com
andyhoefer@gapbroadcasting.com
License: Laramie, Albany County, WY held by Townsquare Media Laramie License LLC
Group Owner: Townsquare Media; (acq 2-13-2008; grpsl)
Nat'l Network: Jones Radio Networks; *Nat'l Reps:* Katz Radio; *Wire Services:* AP
Arbitron Metro Market: Cheyenne, WY; *Format:* Country; *Target Audience:* 25-54.; *Adv. Rates:* 22; 22; 22; 22
Andrew Hoefer, General Manager
Eric Henderson, General Sales Mgr
Dave Shannon, Programming Director
Jim Mross, Chief Engineer

KHAT
02-27-1962; 1210 kHz AM; 10 kw-D, DAN; 1 kw-N, DAN; N41 15 19 W105 33 1
36 Cross Hwy, Rd #4, West Redding, CT 06896 US
(307) 232-2155
License: Laramie, WY held by Appaloosa Broadcasting Co.
Group Owner: Northeast Broadcasting Company Inc.; (acq 3-2-2004; $160,000)
Nat'l Network: ESPN Radio
Arbitron Metro Market: Cheyenne, WY; *Format:* Sports *Special Programming:* Farm one hr wkly
Mike Schutta, General Manager

KOWB
02-20-1948; 1290 kHz AM; *Hrs Open:* 24; 5 kw-D, DA2; 1 kw-N, DA2; N41 17 2 W105 34 51
Mailing Address: 3525 Soldier Springs Rd, Laramie, WY 82070 US
Second Address: 3525 Soldier Springs Rd., Laramie, WY 82070
(307) 745-4888; *Fax:* (307) 742-4576
www.kowb1290.com
License: Laramie, WY held by Townsquare Media Laramie License LLC
Group Owner: Townsquare Media; (acq 2-13-2008; grpsl)
Nat'l Network: Fox News Radio; *Nat'l Reps:* Katz Radio; *Wire Services:* AP
Format: News, News/Talk, 84, Talk; *Hrs. of News Programming:* news progmg 7 hrs wkly; *No. News Employees:* 1; *Target Audience:* 25-54.; *Adv. Rates:* 20; 20; 20; 20
David Settle, Operations Dir
Andrew Hoefer, General Manager
Eric Henderson, General Sales Mgr
Jim Mross, Chief Engineer

KARS-FM
09-23-1974; 102.9 MHz FM; 100 kw; Ant 1,220 ft; N41 18 39 W105 27 12
600 Main St., Windsor, CO 80550
(970) 674-2700; *Fax:* (970) 686-7491
www.rock1029.com
jordan.dawson@townsquaremedia.com
License: Laramie, Albany County, WY held by The Fort Collins/Layfayette Devestiture Trust
Group Owner: Townsquare Media; (acq 11-15-2004; $7.75 million with KKPL(FM) Cheyenne).
Wire Services: CBS
Population Served: 80,000; *Arbitron Metro Market:* Cheyenne, WY; *Target Audience:* 18-44.; *Adv. Rates:* 11; 10; 11; 6
Shawn Steinmetz, General Manager

***KUWR**
09-10-1966; 91.9 MHz FM; *Hrs Open:* 5 AM-midnight; 100 kw; 1099 ft.; N41 18 36 W105 27 17
P.O. Box 3984, 1000 E University Avenue, Laramie, WY 82071 US
(307) 766-4240; *Fax:* (307) 766-6184
www.wyomingpublicradio.org
wprhelp@uwyo.edu
License: Laramie, Albany County, WY held by University of Wyoming.
Nat'l Network: NPR; PRI
Arbitron Metro Market: Laramie, WY; *Format:* News *Special Programming:* Folk 10 hrs, jazz 6 hrs, state news 3 hrs wkly; *Hrs. of News Programming:* news progmg 42 hrs wkly; *No. News Employees:* 3; *Target Audience:* 25-54; educated, college graduates, professionals, upper income
Christina Kuzmych, General Manager
Don Woods, General Sales Mgr
Grady Kirkpatrick, Interim Program Director
Bob Beck, News Director
Reid Fletcher, Chief Engineer
Brenda Blond, Director, Sustainability Services
Micah Scweizer,Cultural Affairs/Production Director
Erin O'Doherty, Membership Director

KRQU
01-01-2006; 98.7 MHz FM; 110 w; Ant 1,073 ft; N41 18 39 W105 27 12
302 S. 2nd St., Suite 204, Laramie, WY 82604
(307) 745-5208; *Fax:* (307) 745-8570
License: Laramie, Albany County, WY held by Murray Grey Broadcasting Inc.
Group Owner: Northeast Broadcasting Company Inc.; (acq 12-21-2005; $750,000 with KVUW(FM) Wendover, NV)

Steven Silberberg, President
Jim O'Reilly, General Manager

***KAIW**
01-01-2006; 88.9 MHz FM; 1.15 kw; 645 ft.; N41 17 46 W105 53 30
PO Box 2118, Omaha, NE 68103-2118 US
(888) 937-2471
www.air1.com
License: Laramie, Albany County, WY held by Educational Media Foundation.
Group Owner: EMF Broadcasting
Nat'l Network: Air 1
Arbitron Metro Market: Laramie, WY; *Format:* Alternative, Christian
Darrell Chambliss, Chairman
Mike Novak, President/CEO
Alan Mason, Chief Operating Officer
David Pierce, Chief Creative Officer
Eric Moser, CFO
D. Kevin Blair, Secretary/General Counsel
Marya Morgan, News Reporter
Richard Hunt,News Reporter

***KUWY**
01-01-2008; 88.5 MHz FM; *Hrs Open:* 24; 0.135 kw; 978 ft.; N41 18 36 W105 27 17
Dept 3984, 1000 East University Avenue, Laramie, WY 82071 US
(307) 766-4240; *Fax:* (307) 766-6184
www.wyomingpublicmedia.org
wprhelp@uwyo.edu
License: Laramie, Albany County, WY held by University of Wyoming.
Regional Network: Wyoming Public Radio
Arbitron Metro Market: Laramie, WY; *Format:* Jazz
Christina Kuzmych, General Manager
Grady Kirkpatrick, Programming Director
Bob Beck, News Director
Reid Fletcher, Chief Engineer
Brenda Bland, Director, Sustainability Services
Erin O'Doherty, Membership Director

***KUWL**
01-01-2008; 90.1 MHz FM; *Hrs Open:* 24; 0.11 kw; 968 ft.; N41 18 36 W105 27 17
Dept. 3984, 1000 East University Avenue, Laramie, WY 82071 US
(307) 766-4240; *Fax:* (307) 766-6184
www.wyomingpublicmedia.org
wprhelp@uwyo.edu
License: Laramie, Albany County, WY held by University of Wyoming.

Regional Network: Wyoming Public Radio
Arbitron Metro Market: Laramie, WY; *Format:* Jazz
Christina Kuzmych, General Manager
Grady Kirkpatrick, Programming Director
Bob Beck, News Director
Reid Fletcher, Chief Engineer
Brenda Bland, Director of Sustainability & Services
Erin O'Doherty, Membership Director

***KTDX**
01-01-2008; 89.3 MHz FM; 0.45 kw; 1138 ft.; N41 18 39 W105 27 12 *Rebroadcasts:* Rebroadcasts KTLF(FM) Colorado Springs, CO 100%
1665 Briargate Blvd, Colorado Springs, CO 80920 US
(719) 593-0600
www.lightpraise.org
lightpraise@ktlf.org
License: Laramie, Albany County, WY held by Educational Communications of Colorado Springs Inc.
Arbitron Metro Market: Laramie, WY; *Format:* Christian; *Target Audience:* 45-60; Christian
Ron Johnson, Chairman
Robyn Sedgwick, General Manager
Sharick Wade, Programming Director
Nathan Steele, Chief Engineer
Lauren Johnson, Operations Director
Marge Wallace, Office Manager

Lost Cabin

KWYW
01-01-2001; 99.1 MHz FM; 50 kw; 1896 ft.; N43 26 18 W107 59 37
3565 Standish Avenue, Santa Rosa, CA 95407 US
(307) 864-2119; *Fax:* (307) 864-3937
License: Lost Cabin, Fremont County, WY held by Jimmy Ray Carroll.
Group Owner: Carol Carroll Stns; (acq 6-25-2001; $30,000 for CP).
Arbitron Metro Market: Thermopolis, WY; *Format:* Country
Jimmy Carroll, President
Cheerie Dorris, General Manager
Jeremy James, Programming Director
Amanda Plant, Promotions Manager
Mike St. Clair, News Director

Lovell

KWHO
107.1 MHz FM; 64 kw; Ant 2,375 ft; N44 48 38 W107 55 18
288 S. River Rd., Bedford, NH
(603) 668-6470
License: Lovell, Big Horn County, WY held by White Park Broadcasting Inc.
Group Owner: Northeast Broadcasting Company Inc.

Steven Silberberg, President

Lusk

KQWY
96.3 MHz FM; kw
US
(202) 251-7589
License: Lusk, Niobrara County, WY held by Alma Corp.
Group Owner: Alma Corp.
Arbitron Metro Market: Lusk, WY
Dennis Wallace, President

Lyman

KNIV
07-01-1983; 104.7 MHz FM; *Hrs Open:* 24; 89 kw horiz; Ant 2,122 ft; N40 52 16 W110 59 43
31 North Redwood Road, Suite 1, North Salt, UT 85054
(801) 326-0552; *Fax:* (801) 936-0352
www.mipreferidafm.com
License: Lyman, Uinta County, WY held by 3 Point Media - Utah LLC, debtor-in-possession
Group Owner: 3 Point Media; (acq 11-28-2001; $1.73 million)
Nat'l Network: CBS
Population Served: 300,000; *Arbitron Metro Market:* Salt Lake City-Ogden-Provo, UT; *Target Audience:* 35-54.
Kent Frandsen, President
Jay Eubanks, General Manager
Lori Gill, News Director
Paul Anderson, Chief Engineer

Manderson

KYTS
105.7 MHz FM; 75 kw; 492 ft.; N44 3 34 W107 51 13
US
(307) 578-5000; *Fax:* (307) 527-5045
www.mybighornbasin.com
License: Manderson, Washakie County, WY held by Global News Consultants
Group Owner: Global News Consultants
Arbitron Metro Market: Manderson, WY
Roger Gelder, EVP/General Manager
Rita Conners, VP, Business Affairs
Mike Fell, Sales Director
Tim Anderson, Sports Director

Medicine Bow

KHAN
01-01-2007; 99.7 MHz FM; 9.6 kw; Ant 239 ft; N41 46 04 W104 49 00
2109 E. 10th St., Cheyenne, WY
(307) 638-8921; *Fax:* (307) 638-8922
License: Medicine Bow, Platte County, WY held by Michael Radio Group
Group Owner: Michael Radio Group

Roger Ingram, General Manager

Midwest

KWYY
11-30-1981; 95.5 MHz FM; 100 kw; 1939 ft.; N42 44 37 W106 18 24
251 West First Street, Casper, WY 82601 US
(307) 266-5252; *Fax:* (307) 235-9143
www.mycountry955.com
donovanshort@townsquaremedia.com
License: Midwest, Natrona County, WY held by Twonsquare Media Casper License LLC
Group Owner: Townsquare Media; (acq 2-13-2008; grpsl)
Arbitron Metro Market: Casper, WY; *Format:* Country; *Target Audience:* 25-54.
Bob Price, General Manager
Donovan Short, Brand Manager
Bob Price, Director Of Sales

Mills

KZQL
01-01-2008; 105.5 MHz FM; 5 kw; 1699 ft.; N42 44 30 W106 18 23
US
(603) 668-6470
License: Mills, Natrona County, WY held by The Casper Radio Group, Inc.
Group Owner: Northeast Broadcasting Company Inc.
Arbitron Metro Market: Mills, WY; *Format:* Adult Contemp
Steven Silberberg, President

Moorcroft

KXXL
01-01-2008; 106.1 MHz FM; 100 kw; 392 ft.; N44 13 50 W105 27 45
305 S. Garner Lake Rd., Gillette, WY 82716 US
(307) 687-1006; *Fax:* (307) 687-1006
License: Moorcroft, Crook County, WY held by Keyhole Broadcasting LLC
Group Owner: Keyhole Broadcasting LLC
Arbitron Metro Market: Moorcroft, WY; *Format:* Classic Rock
Debora Semple, General Manager

Moose Wilson Road

KXJN
98.5 MHz FM; 25 watts; 804 meters; N43 35 50 W110 52 12
Box 11060, Jackson, WY
License: Moose Wilson Road, Fremont County, WY held by Cochise Media Licenses LLC

Ted Tucker, General Manager

Newcastle

KASL
07-10-1953; 1240 kHz AM; *Hrs Open:* 24; 1 kw-U, ND1; N43 50 47 W104 12 45
2208 West Main Street, Newcastle, WY 82701 US
(307) 746-4433; *Fax:* (307) 746-4435
website@kaslradio.com
License: Newcastle, WY held by Val Rasmuson Cook
Arbitron Metro Market: Newcastle, WY; *Format:* Country *Special Programming:* Farm 5 hrs, relg 2 hrs wkly; *Hrs. of News Programming:* news progmg 35 hrs wkly; *No. News Employees:* 1; *Target Audience:* General;town & county residents, children through adults; *Adv. Rates:* 7.55; 7.55; 7.55; 6.55
Kevin Senger, General Manager

***KUWN**
01-01-1998; 90.5 MHz FM; 0.4 kw; 203 ft.; N43 49 57 W104 13 8 *Rebroadcasts:* Rebroadcasts KUWR(FM) Laramie 100%
P.O. Box 3984, 1000 East University Avenue, Laramie, WI 82071 US
(307) 766-4240; *Fax:* (307) 766-6184
www.wyomingpublicradio.net
wprhelp@uwyo.edu
License: Newcastle, Weston County, WY held by University of Wyoming.
Arbitron Metro Market: Newcastle, WY; *Format:* News
Christina Kuzmych, General Manager
Grady Kirkpatrick, Interim Program Director
Bob Beck, News Director
Reid Fletcher, Chief Engineer
Micah Schweizer, Cultural Affairs/Production Director
Brenda Bland, Director of Sustainability &Services
Erin O'Doherty, Membership Director

Orchard Valley

KGAB
01-01-1952; 650 kHz AM; *Hrs Open:* 24
50 East Rivercenter Blvd, Suite 1200, Covington, KY 41011 US
(307) 632-4400; *Fax:* (307) 632-1818
www.kgab.com
License: Orchard Valley, WY held by Townsquare Media Cheyenne License LLC
Group Owner: Townsquare Media; (acq 2-13-2008; grpsl)
Arbitron Metro Market: Cheyenne, WY; *Format:* News, News/Talk, 86; *No. News Employees:* 3; *Target Audience:* 25-64.
Dave Chaffin, Operations Dir
Craig Cochran, General Manager
Amy Richards, News Director
Jim Mross, Chief Engineer

Pine Haven

KYDT
11-01-1997; 103.1 MHz FM; *Hrs Open:* 24; 25 kw; 1650 ft.; N44 28 35 W104 26 54 *Rebroadcasts:* Rebroadcasts KBFS(AM) Belle Fourche 99.9%
Mailing Address: P.O. Box 787, Belle Fourche, SD 57717 US
Second Address: PO Box 1128, Sundance, WY 82729
(605) 892-2571; *Fax:* (307) 283-1155
www.kydt.com
karl@kbfs.com
License: Pine Haven, Crook County, WY held by Ultimate Caps Inc.
Nat'l Network: ESPN Radio; Westwood One; AP Network News; Radio America; Jones Radio Networks; *Wire Services:* AP
Arbitron Metro Market: Belle Fourche, SD; *Format:* Country, News, 84, Talk; *Hrs. of News Programming:* News progmg 25 hrs wkly; *Target Audience:* General; rural, suburban, country mus, sports fans
Karl Grimmelmann, Owner/General Manager
Elsie Rounds, Sales

KWAP(FM)
99.1 MHz FM; 100 kw; Ant 308 ft; N44 19 04 W104 46 31
PO Box 36717, Tucson, AZ 85740-6717
(520) 797-1008
License: Pine Haven, Crook County, WY held by Davao LLC.
Population Served: 8,092; *Arbitron Metro Market:* Wasilla, AK
Hursel Adkins Jr., CEO

Pinedale

KPIN
12-01-1997; 101.1 MHz FM; *Hrs Open:* 24 Hours; 4 kw; 476 ft.; N42 50 39 W109 55 23
Rule Communications, 2232 Dell Range Blvd, Cheyenne, WY 82009 US
(307) 367-2000; *Fax:* (307) 367-3300
www.pinedaleonline.com/b-radio.htm
kpin@wyoming.com
License: Pinedale, Sublette County, WY held by Robert R. Rule dba Rule Communications.
Wire Services: AP
Format: Country *Special Programming:* Heavy local events coverage; *Hrs. of News Programming:* Weekday mornings 5 7 9 10 AM; *No. News Employees:* 1; *Target Audience:* Everyone in the county *Adv. Rates:* $11.50/30 Sec $19.95/60 Sec Al
Bob Rule, CEO

***KUWX**
01-01-2000; 90.9 MHz FM; 0.45 kw; 440 ft.; N42 50 40 W109 55 24

P.O. Box 3984, 1000 East University Avenue, Laramie, WI 82071 US
(307) 766-4240; *Fax:* (307) 766-6184
www.wyomingpublicmedia.org
wprhelp@uwyo.edu
License: Pinedale, Sublette County, WY held by University of Wyoming.
Arbitron Metro Market: Laramie, WY; *Format:* News
Christina Kuzmych, General Manager
Grady Kirkpatrick, Programming Director
Bob Beck, News Director
Reid Fletcher, Chief Engineer
Brenda Bland, Director of Sustainability & Services
Micah Schweizer, Cultural Affairs/ProductionDirector

KWCN
89.9 MHz FM; 1.25 kw; 128 meters; N42 50 39.2 W109 55 29.44
970 West Broadway, Suite 371, Jackson Hole, WY
(480) 282-8545
License: Pinedale, WY held by W S Educational Broadcasting

Powell

KPOW
03-30-1941; 1260 kHz AM; *Hrs Open:* 6 AM-1 AM; 5 kw-D, DAN; 1 kw-N, DAN; N44 42 0 W108 46 0
Mailing Address: P.O. Box 100, Jackson, WY 83001 US
Second Address: 912 Ln. 11 1/2, Powell, WY 82435
(307) 754-5183; *Fax:* (307) 754-9667
www.1260kpow.com (COMING SOON)
License: Powell, WY held by MGR Media LLC
Format: Country, News, 86 *Special Programming:* Farm 19 hrs wkly; *Hrs. of News Programming:* News progmg 38 hrs wkly; *Target Audience:* 29-64.; *Adv. Rates:* 13.50; 13.50;13.50; 13.50
Scott Anderson, General Manager
Scott Mangold, General Sales Mgr

***KUWP**
01-01-2000; 90.1 MHz FM; 0.43 kw; 1624 ft.; N44 35 14 W108 51 8
P. O. Box 3984, 1000 East University Avenue, Laramine, WY 82071 US
(307) 766-4240; *Fax:* (307) 766-6184(
www.wyomingpublicmedia.org
wprhelp@uwyo.edu
License: Powell, Park County, WY held by University of Wyoming.
Arbitron Metro Market: Laramie WY; *Format:* News
Christina Kuzmych, General Manager
Grady Kirkpatrick, Programming Director
Bob Beck, News Director
Micah Schweizer, Cultural Affairs/Production Director
Reid Fletcher, Chief Engineer
Brenda Bland, Director of SustainabilityServices
Erin O'Doherty, Membership Director

KCGL
11-26-2001; 104.1 MHz FM; *Hrs Open:* 24; 100 kw; 1795 ft.; N44 29 42 W109 9 10
1949 Mountain View Dr., Cody, WY 82414 US
(307) 578-5011
www.mybighornbasin.com
mcrump@bhrnwy.com
License: Powell, Park County, WY held by Legend Communications of Wyoming LLC.
Group Owner: Legend Communications L.L.C.; (acq 4-3-02; $450,000).
Arbitron Metro Market: Cody, WY; *Format:* Classic Rock
Mark Crump, General Manager
Jed Burns, General Sales Mgr
Wendy Corr, News Director
Tim Anderson, Sports Director
Rita Conners, VP of Business Affairs

Ranchester

KHRW
92.7 MHz FM; 2.3 kw; 1135 ft.; N44 37 20 W107 6 57
US
(307) 672-2690; *Fax:* (307) 672-1722
www.bighornmountainradio.com
License: Ranchester, Campbell County, WY held by Global News Consultants LLC
Arbitron Metro Market: Ranchester, WY; *Format:* Contemporary Hits/Top 40, Adult Contemp
Mike MacIntosh, President
Dave Wooten, General Manager
Brenna Mack, Programming Director
Justin Wolffing, News Director
April Link, Web Design/Administration
Debbie McMahon, Admistrative Assistant

Jeff Rickett, SportsProgramming
Jonna Nimick, Account Executive

Rawlins

KIQZ
11-12-1981; 92.7 MHz FM; 3 kw; 299 ft.; N41 46 16 W107 14 15
218 No Wolcott, Casper, WY 82601 US
(307) 324-3315; *Fax:* (307) 324-3509
www.kiqz-kral.com
License: Rawlins, Carbon County, WY
Group Owner: Mt. Rushmore Broadcasting Inc.

Allen Brill, Chairman
Ward Holmes, Operations Dir
Kristin Dills, Business Manager

KRAL
02-01-1947; 1240 kHz AM; *Hrs Open:* 24; 1 kw-U, ND1; N41 46 55 W107 15 40
218 N. Wolcott, Casper, WY 82601 US
(307) 324-3315; *Fax:* (307) 324-3509
jackmorgan@vcn.com
License: Rawlins, WY held by Mount Rushmore Broadcasting Inc.
Group Owner: Mt. Rushmore Broadcasting Inc.; (acq 8-6-93; $80,000 with co-located FM;
Nat'l Network: ABC; *Wire Services:* UPI
Format: Adult Contemp; *Target Audience:* 14 plus.; *Adv. Rates:* 12.95; 10.95; 12.95; 10.95
Jack Morgan, Programming Director

KLLM(FM)
107.5 MHz FM; 0.53 kw; 1093 ft.; N41 49 0 W105 3 48
US
(307) 638-8921; *Fax:* (307)638-8922
www.1049krrr.com
sales@radiowyo.com
License: Rawlins, Platte County, WY held by Michael Radio Group
Group Owner: Michael Radio Group
Arbitron Metro Market: Rawlins, WY; *Format:* Oldies

***KUWI**
89.9 MHz FM; 2 kw; 986 ft.; N41 40 46 W107 14 8
Box 3984, 1000 East University Avenue, Laramie, WY 82071 US
(307) 766-4240; *Fax:* (307) 766-6184
www.wyomingpublicradio.net
wprhelp@uwyo.edu
License: Rawlins, Carbon County, WY held by University of Wyoming.
Regional Network: Wyoming Public Radio
Arbitron Metro Market: Rawlins, WY
Christina Kuzmych, General Manager
Grady Kirkpatrick, Programming Director
Bob Beck, News Director
Reid Fletcher, Chief Engineer
Micah Schweitzer, Cultural Affairs/Production Director
Brenda Bland, Director, Sustainability &Services
Erin O'Doherty, Membership Director

***KRWY**
89.3 MHz FM; kw
US
(940) 668-7971
License: Rawlins, Carbon County, WY held by 1 A Chord Inc.
Arbitron Metro Market: Gainesville, TX
Mary Fay Jackson, General Manager

Reliance

KWXR
98.7 MHz FM; 0.25 kw; 509 ft.; N41 39 24 W109 9 32
US
License: Reliance, Sweetwater County, WY held by Cochise Broadcasting LLC.
Group Owner: Cochise Broadcasting LLC
Arbitron Metro Market: Reliance, WY; *Format:* Variety/Diverse
Ted Tucker, General Manager

***KZUW**
88.5 MHz FM; 0.26 kw; 1550 ft.; N41 25 39 W109 7 17
Rebroadcasts: Rebroadcasts KUWYFM) Laramie 100%
Box 3894, 1000 East University Avenue, Laramie, WY 82071 US
(307) 766-4240; *Fax:* (307) 766-6184
www.wyomingpublicradio.org
wprhelp@uwyo.edu
License: Reliance, Sweetwater County, WY held by University of Wyoming.

Arbitron Metro Market: Reliance, WY; *Format:* Classical; *No. News Employees:* 4
Christina Kuzmych, General Manager
Grady Kirkpatrick, Programming Director
Bob Beck, News Director
Reid Fletcher, Chief Engineer
Brenda Blair, Director, Sustainability & Services
Erin O'Doherty, Membership Director
MicahSchweizer, Cultural Affairs/Production Directors

***KTME**
09-29-2010; 89.5 MHz FM; *Hrs Open:* 24; 0.35 kw; N41 6 2 W105 1 29.1
PO Box 21888, Carson City, NV 89721 US
(775) 883-5647
www.pilgrimradio.com
info@pilgrimradio.com
License: Reliance, WY held by Western Inspirational Broadcasters Inc.
Group Owner: Western Inspirational Broadcasters Inc.
Format: Religious; *No. News Employees:* 1
Tom Hesse, General Manager

Riverton

***KCWC-FM**
03-01-1974; 88.1 MHz FM; *Hrs Open:* 24; 3 kw; 1450 ft.; N42 34 59 W108 42 36
2660 Peck Avenue, Riverton, WY 82501 US
(307) 855-2000; *Fax:* (800) 735-8418
www.cwc.edu
jgabriel@cwc.edu
License: Riverton, Fremont County, WY held by Central Wyoming College.
Arbitron Metro Market: Riverton, WY; *Format:* Jazz
JoAnne McFarland, President
Dale Smith, Station Manager

KTAK
12-15-1976; 93.9 MHz FM; 50 kw; 951 ft.; N42 43 10 W108 8 45
125 Eagles Nest Dr., Seneca, SC 29678 US
(307) 856-2251; *Fax:* (307) 856-0252
www.wrrnetwork.com
License: Riverton, Fremont County, WY held by Edwards Communications L.C.
Group Owner: Edwards Communications L.C.
Arbitron Metro Market: Riverton, WY; *Format:* Country
Ray Rintamaki, General Manager
Rebecca Pitt, Office Manager
Jim McGilvray, Advertising Manager

KTRZ
12-04-1984; 93.1 MHz FM; *Hrs Open:* 24; 100 kw; 883 ft.; N42 43 10 W108 8 41
Mailing Address: Box 808, 1002 N. 8th West, Riverton, WY 82501 US
Second Address: 1002 N. 8th West, Riverton, WY 82501
(307) 856-2922; *Fax:* (307) 856-7552
www.ktrzfm.com
License: Riverton, Fremont County, WY held by Jimmy Ray Carroll.
Group Owner: Carol Carroll Stns; (acq 4-1-02).
Nat'l Network: AP Network News; *Wire Services:* AP
Arbitron Metro Market: Riverton, WY; *Format:* Adult Contemp; *Hrs. of News Programming:* news progmg 2 hrs wkly; *No. News Employees:* 1; *Target Audience:* 25 plus; rgnl/loc tourists, agribusiness, core population *Adv. Rates:* 11.50; 10.50; 11.50; 10.50
Jim Carroll, CEO
Jim Hockett, General Manager

KVOW
07-02-1948; 1450 kHz AM; 1 kw-U, ND1; N43 1 35 W108 20 45
125 Eagles Nest Dr., Seneca, SC 29678 US
(864) 882-3272; *Fax:* (864) 882-3718
www.rivertonradio.com
License: Riverton, WY held by Edwards Communications L.C.
Group Owner: Edwards Communications L.C.; (acq 6-22-99; $875,000 with co-located FM).
Arbitron Metro Market: Riverton, WY; *Format:* Talk *Special Programming:* Farm 5 hrs wkly
Ray Rintamaki, General Manager
Rebecca Pitt, Office Manager
Jim McGilvray, Advertising Manager

Rock River

KLMI
01-01-2008; 106.1 MHz FM; 25 kw; 171 ft.; N41 29 5 W106 3 6
PO Box 1789, Columbus, IN 47202 US

(812) 372-4448
www.1061theriver.com
riverstudio@1061theriver.com
License: Rock River, Albany County, WY held by Wolf Creek Radio Broadcasting, LLC
Group Owner: Wolf Creek Radio Broadcasting, LLC; (acq 4-18-2008; $250,000 for CP)
Arbitron Metro Market: Rock River, WY; *Format:* Contemporary Hits/Top 40
John Foster, General Manager
Bob Morrison, General Sales Mgr
Rich Anthony, Programming Director
Sam Simmermaker, Sports Director

Rock Springs

KSIT
10-01-1981; 99.7 MHz FM; *Hrs Open:* 24; 99 kw; 1619 ft.; N41 26 0 W109 7 2
Mailing Address: 2727 Yellowstone Road, Rock Springs, WY 82901 US
Second Address: 1800 Yellowstone Rd., Rock Springs, WY 82901
(307) 362-3793; *Fax:* (307) 875-5755
wyoradio@wyoradio.com
License: Rock Springs, Sweetwater County, WY held by Big Thicket Broadcasting Co. of Wyoming Inc.
Group Owner: Communications Corp. of the Americas Inc.; (acq 12-2-2005; grpsl)
Format: Classic Rock; *Hrs. of News Programming:* news progmg 10 hrs wkly; *No. News Employees:* 1; *Target Audience:* 18-45; general
Bill Luzmoor, President
Jon Collins, General Manager
Tom Ellis, General Sales Mgr
John Collins, Programming Director
Doug Randall, News Director
Kim Walker, Traffic Manager

KQSW
01-01-1977; 96.5 MHz FM; 98 kw; 1621 ft.; N41 25 54 W109 7 1
Mailing Address: 3280 Peachtree Road NW, Suite 2300, Atlanta, GA 30305 US
Second Address: 2717 Yellowstone Rd., Rock Springs, WY 82902
(404) 949-0700; *Fax:* (404) 949-0740
www.bestcountryaround.com
License: Rock Springs, Sweetwater County, WY held by Big Thicket Broadcasting Co. of Wyoming Inc.
Group Owner: Cumulus Media Inc.
Format: Country
W. Grant Hafley, President
Dave Kessel, General Manager
Mike Puetz, General Sales Mgr
John Herring, Programming Director

KRKK
01-01-1938; 1360 kHz AM; 5 kw-D, DAN; 1 kw-N, DAN; N41 37 12 W109 14 20
Mailing Address: 1800 Yellowstone Road, Rock Springs, WY 82901 US
Second Address: 2717 Yellowstone Rd., Rock Springs, WY 82901
(307) 362-3793; *Fax:* (307) 875-5755
wyoradio@wyoradio.com
License: Rock Springs, WY held by Big Thicket Broadcasting Co. of Wyoming Inc.
Group Owner: Communications Corp. of the Americas Inc.; (acq 12-2-2005; grpsl)
Arbitron Metro Market: Southwestern WY; *Format:* Talk
Bill Luzmoor, President
Jon Collins, General Manager
Tom Ellis, General Sales Mgr
Doug Randall, News Director
Tim Walker, Traffic Manager

*KUWZ
11-01-1994; 90.5 MHz FM; *Hrs Open:* Sunrise-sunset; 35 kw; 1680 ft.; N41 25 39 W109 7 17 *Rebroadcasts:* Rebroadcasts KUWR(FM) Laramie 100%
P.O. Box 3984, 1000 East University Avenue, Laramie, WY 82071 US
(307) 766-4240; *Fax:* (307) 766-6184
www.wyomingpublicradio.net
wprhelp@uwyo.edu
License: Rock Springs, Sweetwater County, WY held by University of Wyoming.
Nat'l Network: NPR; PRI
Arbitron Metro Market: Rock Springs, WY; *Format:* News *Special Programming:* Folk 10 hrs, jazz 6 hrs, state news 3 hrs wkly; *Hrs. of News Programming:* news progmg 52 hrs wkly; *No. News Employees:* 3 *TargetAudience:* 25-54; college graduates, professionals, mgrs, upper income
Christina Kuzmych, General Manager
Grady Kirkpatrick, Programming Director
Bob Beck, News Director
Reid Fletcher, Chief Engineer
Micah Schweizer, Cultural Affairs/Production Director
Brenda Bland, Director of Sustainability &Services
Erin O'Doherty, Membership Director

KYCS
10-01-1986; 95.1 MHz FM; *Hrs Open:* 24; 94 kw; 1165 ft.; N41 29 50 W109 20 36
40 Shoshone Avenue, Green River, WY 82935 US
www.theradionetwork.net
mail@theradionetwork.net
License: Rock Springs, Sweetwater County, WY held by Wagonwheel Communications Corp.
Group Owner: Wagonwheel Communications Corp.
Arbitron Metro Market: Green River, WY; *Format:* Contemporary Hits/Top 40; *No. News Employees:* 1
Al Harris, Owner
Faith Harris, President
Steve Core, General Manager/Sports Director
Jeff Driggs, General Sales Mgr

Saratoga

KTGA
01-01-2008; 99.3 MHz FM; *Hrs Open:* 24; 18 kw; 1063 ft.; N41 40 46 W107 14 8
Mailing Address: PO Box 990, Saratoga, WY 82331 US
Second Address: 106 N. First St., Saratoga, WY 82331
(307) 326-8642; *Fax:* (307) 326-8340
www.bigfoot99.com
bigfoot@bigfoot99.com
License: Saratoga, Carbon County, WY held by Toga Radio LLC
Arbitron Metro Market: Saratoga, WY; *Format:* Country; *No. News Employees:* 3
Jim O'Reilly, General Manager

Sheridan

KROE
03-18-1961; 930 kHz AM; *Hrs Open:* 24; 5 kw-D, ND1; 0.117 kw-N, ND1; N44 47 54 W106 55 51
Mailing Address: PO Box 5086, Sheridan, WY 82801 US
Second Address: 1716 KROE Ln., Sheridan, WY 82801
(307) 672-7421; *Fax:* (307) 672-2933
www.sheridanmedia.com
info@sheridanmedia.com
License: Sheridan, WY held by Lovcom Inc.
Group Owner: Lovcom Inc.
Nat'l Network: CBS; *Wire Services:* AP
Format: News, News/Talk, 86; *No. News Employees:* 3; *Target Audience:* 25-54; general; *Adv. Rates:* 14.50; 14; 11.75; 10
Kim Love, Owner
Steve Sisson, Operations Manager
Bob Grammens, General Manager
Jim Schellinger, General Sales Mgr
Tommy B., Programming Director
Mary Johnson, News Director
Trevor Jackson, Sports Director
Leslie Straetmoen,News Director
Liz Reynolds, Traffic Director

*KSUW
01-01-1998; 91.3 MHz FM; 0.45 kw; 1132 ft.; N44 36 9 W106 55 51 *Rebroadcasts:* Rebroadcasts KUWR(FM) Laramie 100%
P O Box 3984, 1000 East University Avenue, Laramie, WY 82071 US
(307) 766-4240; *Fax:* (307) 766-6184
www.wyomingpublicradio.net
wprhelp@uwyo.edu
License: Sheridan, Sheridan County, WY held by University of Wyoming.
Arbitron Metro Market: Laramie, WY; *Format:* News
Christina Kuzmych, General Manager
Grady Kirkpatrick, Programming Director
Bob Beck, News Director
Reid Fletcher, Chief Engineer
Erin O'Doherty, Membership Director
Micah Schweizer, Cultural Affairs/Production Director
BrendaBland, Director of Sustainability & Services

KWYO
07-09-1934; 1410 kHz AM; *Hrs Open:* 24
Mailing Address: Box 5086, Sheridan, WY 82801 US
Second Address: 1716 Kroe Ln, Sheridan, WY 82801
(307) 672-7421; *Fax:* (307) 672-2933
www.sheridanmedia.com
info@sheridanmedia.com
License: Sheridan, WY held by Lovcom Inc.
Group Owner: Lovcom Inc.; acq 9-11-03).
Arbitron Metro Market: Sheridan, WY; *Format:* Adult Contemp; *Hrs. of News Programming:* news progmg 20 hrs wkly; *No. News Employees:* 1; *Target Audience:* 25-54.; *Adv. Rates:* 10.75; 10.75; 10.75; 10.75.
Kim Love, Owner
Steve Sisson, Operations Dir
Bob Grammens, General Manager
Jim Schellinger, General Sales Mgr
Tommy B., Programming Director
Leslie Straetmoen, News Director
Trevor Jackson, Sports Director
Liz Reynolds, TrafficDirector

KYTI
09-01-1978; 93.7 MHz FM; *Hrs Open:* 24; 75 kw; 1207 ft.; N44 37 20 W107 6 57
Mailing Address: PO Box 5086, Sheridan, WY 82801 US
Second Address: 1716 KROE Lane, Sheridan, WY 82801
(307) 672-7421; *Fax:* (307) 672-2933
www.sheridanmedia.com
info@sheridanmedia.com
License: Sheridan, Sheridan County, WY held by Lovcom Inc.
Group Owner: Lovcom Inc.; acq 5-15-97).
Nat'l Network: ABC
Arbitron Metro Market: Sheridan, WY; *Format:* Country; *Hrs. of News Programming:* News progmg 4 hrs wkly; *Target Audience:* 25-50.; *Adv. Rates:* 14.50; 14; 11.75; 10
Kim Love, Owner
Steve Sisson, Operations Manager
Bob Grammens, General Manager
Jim Schellinger, General Sales Mgr
Tommy B., Programming Director
Leslie Straetmoen, News Director
Liz Reynolds, Traffic Director
Trevor Jackson,Sports Director

KZWY
12-01-1977; 94.9 MHz FM; *Hrs Open:* 24; 75 kw; 1207 ft.; N44 37 20 W107 6 57
Mailing Address: Box 5086, Sheridan, WY 82801 US
Second Address: 1716 KROE Ln., Sheridan, WY 82801
(307) 672-7421; *Fax:* (307) 672-7421
www.sheridanmedia.com
info@sheridanmedia.com
License: Sheridan, Sheridan County, WY held by Lovcom Inc.
Group Owner: Lovcom Inc.
Arbitron Metro Market: Sheridan, WY; *Format:* Classic Rock; *Target Audience:* 18-49; general; *Adv. Rates:* Same as AM
Kim Love, Owner
Steve Sisson, Operations Manager
Bob Grammens, General Manager
Jim Schellinger, General Sales Mgr
Tommy B., Programming Director
Leslie Straetmoen, News Director
Trevor Jackson, Sports Director

*KOHR
01-01-2004; 88.9 MHz FM; *Hrs Open:* 24; 0.425 kw vert; 72 ft.; N44 47 54 W106 55 51 *Rebroadcasts:* Rebroadcasts KXEI(FM) Havre, MT 100%
P O Drawer 2426, 317 1st Street, Havre, MT 58501 US
(800) 442-9222
www.ynop.org
info@ynop.org
License: Sheridan, Sheridan County, WY held by Hi-Line Radio Fellowship Inc.
Wire Services: AP
Arbitron Metro Market: Sheridan, WY; *Format:* Christian, Religious
Roger Lonnquist, General Manager
Brenda Boyum, Station Manager
David Brown, Programming Director
Nicholas Tobiason, Music/IT Director
Ron Huckeby, Chief Engineer
Beth Jorgensen, Office Manager/Webmaster

*KPRQ
01-01-2006; 88.1 MHz FM; 0.45 kw; 1119 ft.; N44 37 26 W107 7 2
1500 University Drive, Billings, MT 59101 US
(406) 657-2941; *Fax:* (406) 657-2977
www.yellowstonepublicradio.org
mail@ypradio.org
License: Sheridan, Sheridan County, WY held by Montana State University-Billings.
Nat'l Network: NPR

Format: Classical, Jazz, 60
Ken Sieberr, General Manager
Jackie Yamanaka, News Director
Jim Nichols, Chief Engineer

***KVLZ**
01-01-2009; 90.3 MHz FM; 0.15 kw; -138 ft.; N44 47 54 W106 55 51 *Rebroadcasts:* Rebroadcasts KLVR(FM) Middletown, CA 100&
P.O. Box 2098, Omaha, NE 68103-2098 US
(800) 525-5683
www.klove.com
License: Sheridan, Sheridan County, WY held by Educational Media Foundation.
Group Owner: EMF Broadcasting; (acq 3-23-2007; grpsl)
Nat'l Network: K-Love
Arbitron Metro Market: Sheridan, WY; *Format:* Christian
Darrell Chambliss, Chairman
Alan Mason, COO
Mike Novak, President/CEO
David Pierce, Chief Creative Officer
Eric Moser, Chief Financial Officer
D. Kevin Blair, Secretary and General Counsel

Sleepy Hollow

KQOL
01-01-2001; 105.3 MHz FM; *Hrs Open:* Unlimited; 51 kw; 374 ft.; N44 17 33 W105 26 10
305 S. Garner Lake Rd., Gillette, WY 82718 US
(307) 687-1003
License: Sleepy Hollow, Clark County, WY held by Keyhole Broadcasting LLC
Group Owner: Keyhole Broadcasting LLC
Arbitron Metro Market: Portland, OR; *Format:* Oldies
Debora Semple, General Manager

South Greeley

***KDNR**
12-23-2003; 88.7 MHz FM; *Hrs Open:* 24; 0.5 kw; 423 ft.; N41 6 2 W105 1 29.1
PO Box 21888, Carson City, NV 89721 US
(775) 883-5647
www.pilgrimradio.com
info@pilgrimradio.com
License: South Greeley, Laramie County, WY held by Western Inspirational Broadcasters Inc.
Group Owner: Western Inspirational Broadcasters Inc.; (acq 2-21-2006; $200,000)
Arbitron Metro Market: South Greeley, WY; *Format:* Religious; *No. News Employees:* 1
Tom Hesse, General Manager

South Park

KJXN
01-01-2008; 105.1 MHz FM; 0.15 kw; 1076 ft.; N43 29 34 W110 57 19
US
License: South Park, Teton County, WY held by Cochise Media Licenses LLC
Arbitron Metro Market: South Park, WY
Ted Tucker, General Manager

Story

KZZS
11-13-2003; 98.3 MHz FM; *Hrs Open:* 24; 100 kw; 249 ft.; N44 34 31.9 W106 52 21.7
324 Coffeen Ave., Sheridan, WY 82801 US
(307) 684-9505; *Fax:* (307) 672-1722
www.bighornmountainradio.com
shrecep@bighornmountainradio.com
License: Story, Sheridan County, WY held by Legend Communications of Wyoming L.L.C.
Group Owner: Legend Communications L.L.C.; (acq 5-31-00; $200,000 for CP).
Arbitron Metro Market: Santa Rosa, CA; *Format:* Contemporary Hits/Top 40; *Hrs. of News Programming:* news progmg 6 hrs wkly; *No. News Employees:* 1; *Target Audience:* 18-35.; *Adv. Rates:* 15; 15; 15; 12
Bon Clonch, General Manager
Jessica Pierce, General Sales Mgr
Bailey Roebling, Director of Digital & Social Media

Sundance

***KUWD**
01-01-2000; 91.5 MHz FM; 0.43 kw; 1591 ft.; N44 28 35 W104 26 54
P.O. Box 3984, 1000 East University Avenue, Laramie, WY 82071 US
(307) 766-4240; *Fax:* (307) 766-6184
www.wyomingpublicmedia.org
wrphelp@uwyo.edu
License: Sundance, Cibola County, WY held by University of Wyoming.
Arbitron Metro Market: Laramie, WY; *Format:* News
Christina Kuzmych, General Manager
Grady Kirkpatrick, Programming Director
Bob Beck, News Director
Reid Fletcher, Chief Engineer
Micah Schweizer, Cultural Affairs & Production Director
Erin O'Doherty, Membership Director
BrendaBland, Director of Sustainability & Services

Superior

KMRZ-FM
07-15-2008; 106.7 MHz FM; 7 kw; 1581 ft.; N41 25 28 W109 7 54
1800 Yellowstone Road, Rock Springs, WY 02901 US
(307) 362-3793
www.wyoradio.com
License: Superior, Sweetwater County, WY held by Big Thicket Broadcasting Co. of Wyoming Inc.
Group Owner: Communications Corp. of the Americas Inc.; (acq 8-1-2008; $400,000)

Wiliam Luzmoor III, President
Jon Collins, General Manager

Ten Sleep

KZMQ
05-20-1979; 1140 kHz AM; 10 kw-D; N44 06 12 W107 28 50
1949 Mountain View Dr., Cody, WY 82414 USA
(307) 578-5016
www.mybighornbasin.com
mcrump@bhrnwy.com
License: Ten Sleep, Big Horn County, WY held by Legend Communications of Wyoming L.L.C.
Group Owner: Legend Communications L.L.C.; (acq 1-27-98; $1.5 million with co-located FM)
Population Served: 50,000 *Target Audience:* 25-49.
Rita Conners, VP of Business Affairs
Mark Crump, General Manager
Jed Burns, General Sales Mgr
Wendy Corr, News Director

Thayne

***KTYN**
91.9 MHz FM; 0.077 kw; 2329 ft.; N43 6 18 W111 7 17
P. O. Box 156, Thayne, WY 83127 US
(801) 580-4339
License: Thayne, Lincoln County, WY held by Intermountain Public Radio.
Arbitron Metro Market: Thayne, WY
Carolyn Ashauer, President

Thermopolis

KDNO
08-30-2001; 101.7 MHz FM; 16.25 kw; 1902 ft.; N43 26 18 W107 59 37
Mailing Address: P O Box 866, Thermopolis, WY 82443 US
Second Address: 420 Arapahoe, Thermopolis, WY 82443
(307) 864-2119; *Fax:* (307) 864-3937
kthe@directairnet.com
License: Thermopolis, Hot Springs County, WY held by Carjim LLC.
Group Owner: Carol Carroll Stns; (acq 9-13-2001; $20,000 for CP).
Arbitron Metro Market: Thermopolis, WY; *Format:* Country
Jim Carroll, President
Dick Howe, General Manager
Dennis Silver, Chief Engineer

KTHE
04-01-1957; 1240 kHz AM
Mailing Address: P.O. Box 591, Thermopolis, WY 82443 US
Second Address: 420 Arapahoe, Thermopolis, WY 82443
(307) 864-2119; *Fax:* (307) 864-3937
kthe@directairnet.com
License: Thermopolis, WY held by Carjim LLC.
Group Owner: Carol Carroll Stns; (acq 5-7-2002).
Arbitron Metro Market: Thermopolis, WY; *Format:* Adult Contemp, Oldies; *Target Audience:* 25-54; varied
Jim Carroll, President
Dick Howe, General Manager

***KUWT**
01-01-2001; 91.3 MHz FM; 2 kw; 1962 ft.; N43 26 16 W107 59 48 *Rebroadcasts:* Rebroadcasts KUWR(FM) Laramie 100%
P. O. Box 3984, 1000 East University Avenue, Laramie, WY 82071 US
(307) 766-4240; *Fax:* (307) 766-6184
www.wyomingpublicmedia.org
wprhelp@uwyo.edu
License: Thermopolis, Hot Springs County, WY held by University of Wyoming.
Arbitron Metro Market: Laramie, WY; *Format:* News
Christina Kuzmych, General Manager
Bob Beck, News Director
Reid Fletcher, Chief Engineer
Micah Schweizer, Cultural Affairs & Production Director
Erin O'Doherty, Membership Director
Brenda Bland, Director of Sustainability &Services

Torrington

KERM
12-15-1976; 98.3 MHz FM; 3 kw; 299 ft.; N41 59 41 W104 12 5
7060 Radio Road, Torrington, WY 82240 US
(307) 532-2158; *Fax:* (307) 532-2641
www.kgoskerm.com
License: Torrington, Goshen County, WY held by Kath Broadcasting Co., LLC
Group Owner: Mt. Rushmore Broadcasting Inc.
Arbitron Metro Market: Torrington, WY; *Format:* Country
Grant Kath, Owner
Dick Fullmer, Sports Director

KGOS
05-15-1950; 1490 kHz AM; *Hrs Open:* 5:30 AM-10:15 PM; 1 kw-U; N42 04 20 W104 13 40
7060 Radio Rd., Torrington, WY 82240
(307) 532-2158; *Fax:* (307) 532-2641
www.kgoskerm.com
License: Torrington, Goshen County, WY held by Kath Broadcasting Co., LLC
Group Owner: Mt. Rushmore Broadcasting Inc.
Regional Reps: Art Moore.
Population Served: 30,000 *Target Audience:* 20 plus; general
Grant Kath, General Manager
Dick Fullmer, Sports Director

Upton

KHAD
104.5 MHz FM; 28.5 kw; 1572 ft.; N44 28 29 W104 26 27
US
(603) 668-6400; *Fax:* (603) 668-6470
License: Upton, Weston County, WY held by The Casper Radio Group, Inc.
Group Owner: Northeast Broadcasting Company Inc.

Steven Silberberg, President

Vista West

KRVK
01-01-2001; 107.9 MHz FM; 15.5 kw; 1939 ft.; N42 44 37 W106 18 24
33 Hale Street, Pittston, PA 18640 US
(307) 266-5252; *Fax:* (307) 235-9143
theriver1079.com
bobprice@townsquaremedia.com
License: Vista West, Natrona County, WY held by Townsquare Media Casper License LLC
Group Owner: Townsquare Media; (acq 2-13-2008; grpsl)
Arbitron Metro Market: Casper, WY; *Format:* Classic Rock
Bob Price, General Manager
Donovan Short, Brand Manager
Bob Price, Director Of Sales

Wamsutter

KKAR
104.9 MHz FM; 0.12 kw; 52 ft.; N41 39 56 W107 58 11
US
(307) 638-8921; *Fax:* (307) 638-8922
www.1049krrr.com
License: Wamsutter, Sweetwater County, WY held by White Park Broadcasting Inc.
Group Owner: Northeast Broadcasting Company Inc.
Arbitron Metro Market: Wamsutter, WY; *Format:* Oldies
Steven Silberberg, President

Warren Afb

KOLT-FM
08-04-1978; 92.9 MHz FM; *Hrs Open:* 24; 33 kw; 607 ft.; N41 4 35 W105 12 10
1806 Capitol Avenue, Cheyenne, WY 82001 US
(307) 637-7771
License: Warren Afb, Laramie County, WY held by Valley Bank & Trust
Arbitron Metro Market: Cheyenne, WY
David Montgomery, Owner/General Manager
Stephen Van Court, Manager

KRAN
103.3 MHz FM; 37 kw; 256 ft.; N41 9 34 W104 43 19 US
(307) 638-8921
www.1033therange.com
License: Warren Afb, Laramie County, WY held by Friesland Broadcasting Corp.
Group Owner: Northeast Broadcasting Company Inc.
Arbitron Metro Market: Warren AFB, WY; *Format:* Country
Steven Silberberg, President

Wheatland

KYCN
11-16-1960; 1340 kHz AM; *Hrs Open:* 24; 0.25 kw-U, ND1; N42 2 44 W104 56 47
Mailing Address: P. O. Box 248, Wheatland, WY 82201 US
Second Address: 450 E. Cole, Wheatland, WY 82201
(307) 322-5926
www.wheatlandradio.com
kzew@wheatlandradio.com
License: Wheatland, WY held by Smith Broadcasting Inc.
Nat'l Network: ABC; *Nat'l Reps:* Target Broadcast Sales
Format: Country *Special Programming:* Farm 7 hrs wkly; *Hrs. of News Programming:* news progmg 14 hrs wkly; *No. News Employees:* 1; *Target Audience:* General.; *Adv. Rates:* 8.50; 8.50; 8.50; 8
Kent Smith, President
Catherine Smith, General Sales Mgr
Derek Barton, News Director

KZEW
02-01-1985; 101.7 MHz FM; *Hrs Open:* 24; 3 kw; 125 ft.; N42 2 44 W104 56 47
Mailing Address: P. O. Box 248, Wheatland, WY 82201 US
Second Address: 450 E. Cole, Wheatland, WY 82201
(307) 322-5926
www.wheatlandradio.com
kzew@wheatlandradio.com
License: Wheatland, Platte County, WY held by Smith Broadcasting Inc.
Nat'l Network: Jones Radio Networks
Arbitron Metro Market: Wheatland,WY; *Format:* Adult Contemp; *Adv. Rates:* 8.75; 8.75; 8.75; 8
Kent Smith, Operations Dir

KRKU
106.5 MHz FM; 100 watts; 423 feet; N41 56 13 W104 55 50
911 Colonial Dr., Cheyenne, WY
(307) 638-1345
License: Wheatland, Platte County, WY held by Lorenz E. Proietti.

Lorenz Proietti, General Manager

Worland

KKLX
12-01-1980; 96.1 MHz FM; 63 kw; 576 ft.; N44 3 33.6 W107 51 12.7
1949 Mountain View Dr., Cody, WY 82414 US
(307) 347-3231; *Fax:* (307) 347-4880
www.mybighornbasin.com
mcrump@bhrnwy.com
License: Worland, Washakie County, WY held by Legend Comm. of Wyoming, LLC
Group Owner: Legend Communications L.L.C.
Arbitron Metro Market: Casper, WY; *Format:* Oldies
Mark Crump, General Manager
Jed Burns, General Sales Mgr
Wendy Corr, News Director
Rita Conners, VP of Business Affairs

KWOR
03-07-1946; 1340 kHz AM; 1 kw-U, ND1; N44 1 2 W107 58 14
1949 Moutain View Dr., Cody, WY 82414 US
(307) 347-3231; *Fax:* (307) 347-4880
www.mybighornbasin.com
mcrump@bhrnwy.com
License: Worland, WY held by Legend Communications of Wyoming LLC.
Group Owner: Legend Communications L.L.C.; (acq 12-31-2007; $750,000 with co-located FM)
Arbitron Metro Market: Worland, WY; *Format:* Oldies; *Target Audience:* General.
Mark Crump, General Manager
Jed Burns, General Sales Mgr
Wendy Corr, News Director
Rita Conners, VP of Business Affairs

Wright

KDDV-FM
01-01-2008; 101.5 MHz FM; 100 kw; 1098 ft.; N43 59 57 W105 15 15
2810 Southern Dr., Gillette, WY 82718 US
(307) 686-2242; *Fax:* (307) 686-7736
www.basinsradio.com
reception@basinsradio.com
License: Wright, Campbell County, WY held by Legend Communications of Wyoming LLC.
Group Owner: Legend Communications L.L.C.
Format: Contemporary Hits/Top 40, Adult Contemp
Don Clonch, General Manager
Jessica Pierce, General Sales Mgr
Bailey Roebling, Director of Digital & Social Media
Paul Wallem, News Director

U.S.-Based International Radio

Adventist World Radio
12501 Old Columbia Pike, Silver Spring, MD 20904-6600
(301) 680-6304; *Fax:* (301) 680-6303
www.awr.org
info@awr.org
Benjamin D. Schoun, President
AWR has 70 production studios bcstg worldwide in over 75 languages thousands of hours daily via AM/FM, shortwave & internet.

American Forces Radio & Television Service (AFRTS)
Department of Defense, American Forces Info Service, 601 N. Fairfax St., Alexandria, VA 22314
(951) 413-2339; *Fax:* (703) 428-0624
Andreas I. Friedrich, General Manager
AFRTS has radio & TV svc 177 countries & on bd U.S. Navy ships. AFRTS stns operate in 15 countries providing rgnl & loc info to large concentrations of U.S. forces. All of the entertainment progmg, U.S sporting events, & natl. &international news is provided to the outlets either directly via international satellites from the AFRTS Broadcast Center at March Air Reserve Base, CA., or through the AFRTS operated stns which insert their rgnl & loc radio drive-time programs &radio & TV news & spot announcements. A rgnl AFRTS svc in Europe delivers the AFRTS fed progmg & rgnl news & info via EUTELSAT to affils located in seven nations as well as directly to cable head-ends, remote transmitters, homes throughout Europe &the Middle East. The worldwide AFRTS-TV progmg consists of: an entertainment svc time shifted for the various parts of the globe & providing the best of U.S. net TV progmg; a news svc providing natl & international news from CNN, Fox News, MSNB,major U.S. networks; a sports ch providing sports news & sporting events from ESPN, ESPN2 & the major U.S. nets & a fourth svc devoted to alternative entertainment progmg primarily oriented on family-type programs from PBS & from U.S.cable TV chs. Afifth & sixth svc were added in 2005 for family entertainmnet & full-time movies. A seventh svc began in 2006 providing additional sporting events. Finally, the Pentagon Channel is also carried by AFRTS.
AFRTS Broadcast Center
1363 Z St, Bldg. 2730, March Air Reserve Base, CA 92518-2077
(909) 413-2201
Tom Weber, Industry Liaison
Larry Sichter, Mgr Affiliate Rel

Blue Ridge Communications Inc.
Shortwave Radio Station WWRB, c/o Airline Transport Communications, Box 7, Manchester, TN 37349-0007
(931) 841-0492, (931) 728-6087
www.wwrb.org
WWRB Manchester, TN. Worldwide bcstg utilizing 5 shortwave transmitters & 6 major antenna systems (azimuths); more than 10 years of well established global audience.

Broadcasting Board of Governors
330 Independence Ave. S.W., Rm. 3360, Washington, DC 20237
(202) 203-4545; *Fax:* (202) 203-4585
www.bbg.gov
The bd makes & supervises grants to Radio Free Europe, Radio Liberty, & Radio Free Asia, the Middle East Bcstg Networks & assures that funds are applied consistently with the broad foreign policy objectives of the U.S. govt. The BBG servesas the governing body for all non-military U.S. bcstg including VOA, OCB, RFE/RL, RFA, & MBN.

EWTN
90 million U.S. SUbscribers served
Div/DBA: The Global Catholic Network
5817 Old Leeds Rd., Irondale, AL 35210
(205) 271-2900; *Fax:* (205) 271-2925
www.ewtn.com
Satellite: Galaxy 15*Transponder:* 5
America's largest religious cable network offers family and religious programming from a Catholic point of view in English and Spanish. Providing more than 80% original programming, EWTN offers inspiring talk shows, entertaining children'sanimation, exclusive teaching series, live coverage of Church events, and thought-provoking documentaries.

Far East Broadcasting Co. Inc.
Box 1, La Mirada, CA 90637
(562) 947-4651; *Fax:* (310) 943-0160
www.febc.org
febc@febc.org
Dr. Robert S. Fortner, Chairman
Broadcasts 560 hrs of progmg in 150 languages, to a potential audience of more than 2.5 billion people. FEBC's broadcasts are heard in many countries with limited access to Christian ministry, or where there is tremendous political andcultural opposition to the gospel.

Fundamental Broadcasting Network
c/o Grace Missionary Baptist Church, 520 Roberts Rd., Newport, NC 28570
(252) 223-4600; *Fax:* (252) 223-2201
www.fbnradio.com
fbn@fbnradio.com
WBOH Newport, NC, Broadcasts on 5.920 mhz 24 hrs a day.
WTJC Newport, NC, Broadcasts on 9.370 mhz 24 hrs a day.

Good News World Outreach
WRNO Worldwide, Box 895, Fort Worth, TX 76101-0895
(817) 850-9990; *Fax:* (817) 850-9994
www.wrnoworldwide.org
wrnoradio@mailup.net
Dr. Robert E. Mawire, CEO
WRNO New Orleans. 50 kw shortwave transmitter reaching North America, Central America, Europe, & Far East. Format: news, talk (educational, Christian), sports, music.

Hill Radio International
5920 Oak Manor Dr., Milton, FL 32570-7704
CP for New International HF Broadcast Station in MIlton, FL.

International Fellowship of Churches Inc.
Div/DBA: dba IMF World Missions
Radio Station KIMF, 9746 6th St., Rancho Cucamonga, CA 91730
(909) 466-4793
www.tvspotnet.com
earlcant@comcast.net
Earl F. Reilly, President
Bcst rep, representing U.S. TV stns in Canada. Also licensed bcst stn brokers.
Box 1300, Freeland, WA 98249-1300
(206) 331-7223; *Fax:* (206) 331-7223

La Voz de Restauracion Broadcasting Inc.
Box 56320, Los Angeles, CA 90056
(323) 766-2454; *Fax:* (323) 766-2458
www.restauracion.com
info@restauracion.com
Rene F. Molina, General Manager
KVOH Rancho Simi, CAFormat: Sp.

Leap of Faith Inc.
661 Ormond Dr., Nashville, TN 37205
New international HF broadcast stn in Lebanon, TN.

Radio Free Asia
2025 M Street NW, Suite 300, Washington, DC 20036
(202) 530-4900; *Fax:* (202) 530-7797
www.rfa.org
contact@rfa.org
Rohit Mahajan, Media Relations Manager
John A. Estrella, VP of Communications and Government Relations
Provides info, news & commentary about events in the respective countries of Asia & elsewhere. The svc is intended to be a forum for a var of opinions & voices from within Asian nations whose people do not fully enjoy freedom of expression.

Radio Free Europe/Radio Liberty
Div/DBA: (RFE/RL Inc.)
1201 Connecticut Ave. NW., Suite 400, Washington, DC 20036
(202) 457-6900; *Fax:* (202) 457-6992
www.rferl.org
Through bcsts in 28 languages to 20 countries, RFE/RL provides news, info, responsible dicussion of domestic & international issues to countries where free & ind media are not permitted, or not yet fully established.

Radio Miami International
175 Fontainebleau Blvd., Suite 1N4, Miami, FL 33172
(305) 559-9764; *Fax:* (305) 559-8186
www.wrmi.net
info@wrmi.net
Jeff White, General Manager
WRMI Miami. Stn sells block airtime for $1/minute to organizations wanting to reach any part of the Americas in any language. 7,385 & 9,955 & 15,725 khz shortwave, 50 kw power.

Trans World Radio
Box 8700, Cary, NC 27512-8700
(919) 460-3700; *Fax:* (919) 460-3702
www.twr.org
info@twr.org
Thomas Lowell, CEO
KTWR Agana, Guam. Guam E-mail: twrguamk@twr.hafa.net.gu
Four 100-kw shortwave transmitters to bcst to Australia, Bali, China, the eastern & central part of the Commonwealth of Independent States, Far East, India, Indonesia, Japan, Korea,Myanmar, Southeast Asia. Format: Relg (more than 30 languages).

Trinity Broadcasting Network
2442 Michelle Drive, Tustin, CA 92780
(714) 832-2950; *Fax:* (714) 730-0657
www.tbn.org
comments@tbn.org
Ownership: Nonprofit corporation.
Paul Crouch, President
Rod Henke, VP of Sales
Janice Crouch, VP of Programming
Ben Miller, VP of Engineering

Two If By Sea Broadcasting Corp.
1784 W. Northfield Blvd., Suite 305, Murfreesboro, TN 37129-1702
www.sound4film-tv.com
senator@sound4film-tv.com
Mike Michaels, President
Stringers, crew news, sports, features, remote bcsts, engrs, announcers, reporters, equipment for radio, TV, film & video.
8715 Waikiki Stn., Honolulu, HI
(888) 389-7372; *Fax:* (213) 389-3299
www.sound4film-tv.com
senator@sound4film-tv.com

United Nations
Div/DBA: Audio-Visual Promotion & Distribution
405 E. 42nd St., Rm. S-805, HQ-Secretariat Bldg., New York, NY 10017
(212) 963-6982, (212) 963-7318; *Fax:* (212) 963-6869
www.unmultimedia.org
Antonio Carlos Da Silva, Promotions Manager
TV coverage of UN meetings events, the production, promotion & distribution of UN TV radio progmg, photo & footage. All major UN events are also recorded on audio for radio distribution. Offices in 63 countries of 192 member countries.

Voice of America
330 Independence Ave. S.W., Washington, DC 20237
(202) 203-4959; *Fax:* (202) 203-4960
www.voanews.com
publicrelations@voanews.com
Danforth W. Austin, General Manager
Went on the air in 1942, is a multimedia international bcstg svc funded by the U.S govt through Bcstg Bd of Governors. Bcsts more than 1,000 hrs of news, info, educ, & cultural progmg every week to an estimated worldwide audience of morethan 138 million people. Programs are produced in 45 languages. AM/FM & shortwave transmitters are located at over 30 transmitting sites world-wide.

The Voice of the OAS
17th & Constitution N.W., Washington, DC 20006
(202) 458-3000; *Fax:* (202) 458-3930
www.oas.org
informacion-publica@oas.org
Claudio Lessa, Programming Director
Radio programs with news, interviews, info & music from Latin America. Concentrating on the acitivities of the Organization of American States.

WBCQ Radio
274 Britton Rd., Monticello, ME 04760-3110
(207) 538-9180
www.wbcq.com
wbcq@wbcq.com
Allan H. Weiner, General Manager
WBCQ Monticello, Me. International bcst shortwave stn. Lease & program time available. 5.105 mhz, 7.415 mhz, 9.330 mhz & 17.495 mhz. Serves North, Central, South America & the Carribean.

WJIE International Shortwave
Box 197309, Louisville, KY 40259
(502) 968-1220; *Fax:* (502) 964-3304
wjiesw@hotmail.com
Robert W. Rodgers, President
Greg Holt, Operations Dir
Doug Rumsey, General Manager
WJIE Millerstown, Ky. On two sw frequencies operating 24 hours daily. Target areas: Europe & Asia. Also operates WJIE-FM on 88.5 mhz with 24.5 kw horiz, 18.5 kw vert in Okolona, Ky.

WMLK Radio
Assemblies of Yahweh, Box C, Bethel, PA 19507
(717) 933-4518, (800) 523-3827
www.assembliesofyahweh.com
Elder Jacob O. Meyer, President

Branch offices in Metro-Manila, Phillippines; San Juan, Port of Spain, Trinidad & Tobago; Leeds, England. WMLK Bethel, PA. Bcstg to Europe & the Middle East 5 hours, five days a week, Mon-Fri, with relg instruction content.

WNQM Inc.

Div/DBA: Group owner: F.W. Robbert Broadcasting Inc.
1300 WWCR Ave., Nashville, TN 37218
(615) 255-1300, (800) 238-5576; *Fax:* (615) 255-1311
www.wwcr.com
Eric Westenberger, CEO
WWCR Nashville. Frequencies: 3.210 mhz, 5.070 mhz, 5.935 mhz, 7.465 mhz, 9.475 mhz, 12.160 mhz, 15.825 mhz.

World Christian Broadcasting Corp.

Operations Center, 605 Bradley Court, Franklin, TN 37067-8200
(615) 371-8707; *Fax:* (615) 371-8791
www.knls.org
gcrowe@worldchristian.org
Charles Caudill, CEO
KNLS Anchor Point, Alaska (transmission facilities): Relg & secular progmg beamed to Asia, eastern Europe & the Pacific Rim on the international shortwave bands.
KNLS
Box 473, Anchor Point, AK 99556-0473
(907) 235-8262, (907) 235-8462
Kevin Chambers, Chief Eng

World Harvest Radio International

61300 Ironwood Rd., South Bend, IN 46614
(574) 291-8200; *Fax:* (574) 291-9043
www.whr.org
whr@lesea.com
Pete Sumarall, President
Joe Hill, General Sales Mgr
Douglas Garlinger, Chief Engineer
WHRI Indianapolis. Two 100 kw transmitters serving Europe, Russia, North, Central & South America. KWHR Naalehu, Hawaii. Two 100 kw transmitters serving primarily Asia, & also Oceania & Australia/New Zealand. WHRA Greenbush, Me.One 250 kw transmitter serving Africa & the Middle East. Shortwave transmitters are available for lease (time sls).

World International Broadcasters Inc.

Box 88, Red Lion, PA 17356
(717) 246-1681, EXT. 140; *Fax:* (717) 244-9316
www.wgcbtv.com
John H. Norris, President
Patricia Norris-Slaughter, Operations Dir
Fred Wise, General Manager
WINB Red Lion, Pa. Shortwave progmg of programs to Western Europe, the Mediterranean, North Africa, Mexico, Philippines, Guam, Formosa & Australia. Format: Relg.

U.S.-Based Satellite Radio

Sirius Radio (XM), United States

1221 Avenue of the Americas, 49th Street, New York, NY 10020
(888) 539-7474
www.siriusxm.com
care@siriusxm.com
Mel Karmazin, CEO
Scott Greenstein, President/Chief Content Officer
James Meyer, President/Operations/Sales
Dora Altman, EVP
Patrick Donnelly, EVP/General Counsel
David Frear, EVP/CFO
Canada Office
135 Liberty Street, 4th Floor, Toronto, ON M6K 1A7; Tel: (416) 408-6000; www.siriusxm.ca; care@siriusxm.ca.

U.S. AM Radio Stations by Call Letters

DKEZD Windsor, California
DKORC Anacortes, Washington
DWKEL Myrtle Beach, South Carolina
KAAA Kingman, Arizona
KAAB Batesville, Arkansas
KAAM Garland, Texas
KAAN Bethany, Missouri
KAAY Little Rock, Arkansas
KABC Los Angeles, California
KABI Abilene, Kansas
KABQ Albuquerque, New Mexico
KACH Preston, Idaho
KACI The Dalles, Oregon
KACT Andrews, Texas
KADA Ada, Oklahoma
KADI Springfield, Missouri
KADR Elkader, Iowa
KAFF Flagstaff, Arizona
KAFY Bakersfield, California
KAGC Bryan, Texas
KAGE Winona, Minnesota
KAGH Crossett, Arkansas
KAGI Grants Pass, Oregon
KAGO Klamath Falls, Oregon
KAGV Big Lake, Alaska
KAGY Port Sulphur, Louisiana
KAHI Auburn, California
KAHL San Antonio, Texas
KAHS El Dorado, Kansas
KAHZ Pomona, California
KAIR Atchison, Kansas
KAJO Grants Pass, Oregon
KAKC Tulsa, Oklahoma
KAKK Walker, Minnesota
KALE Richland, Washington
KALI West Covina, California
KALL North Salt Lake City, Utah
KALM Thayer, Missouri
KALV Alva, Oklahoma
KAMA El Paso, Texas
KAMI Cozad, Nebraska
KAML Kenedy-Karnes City, Texas
KAMQ Carlsbad, New Mexico
KANA Anaconda, Montana
KAND Corsicana, Texas
KANE New Iberia, Louisiana
KANI Wharton, Texas
KANN Roy, Utah
KAOI Kihei, Hawaii
KAOK Lake Charles, Louisiana
KAOL Carrollton, Missouri
KAPE Cape Girardeau, Missouri
KAPL Phoenix, Oregon
KAPR Douglas, Arizona
KAPS Mount Vernon, Washington
KARI Blaine, Washington
KARN Little Rock, Arkansas
KARR Kirkland, Washington
KARS Belen, New Mexico
KART Jerome, Idaho
KARV Russellville, Arkansas
KASA Phoenix, Arizona
KASI Ames, Iowa
KASL Newcastle, Wyoming
KASM Albany, Minnesota
KASO Minden, Louisiana
KAST Astoria, Oregon
KATA Eureka, California
KATD Pittsburg, California
KATE Albert Lea, Minnesota
KATH Frisco, Texas
KATK Carlsbad, New Mexico
KATL Miles City, Montana
KATO Safford, Arizona
KATQ Plentywood, Montana
KATZ St. Louis, Missouri
KAUS Austin, Minnesota
KAVA Pueblo, Colorado
KAVL Lancaster, California
KAVP Colona, Colorado
KAWC Yuma, Arizona
KAWL York, Nebraska
KAWW Heber Springs, Arkansas
KAYL Storm Lake, Iowa
KAYS Hays, Kansas
KAZA Gilroy, California
KAZG Scottsdale, Arizona
KAZM Sedona, Arizona
KAZN Pasadena, California
KBAD Las Vegas, Nevada
KBAI Bellingham, Washington
KBAM Longview, Washington
KBAR Burley, Idaho
KBBI Homer, Alaska
KBBO Selah, Washington
KBBR Coos Bay, Oregon
KBBS Buffalo, Wyoming
KBBW Waco, Texas
KBCH Lincoln City, Oregon
KBCK Deer Lodge, Montana
KBCL Bossier City, Louisiana
KBCQ Roswell, New Mexico
KBCR Steamboat Springs, Colorado
KBCV Hollister, Missouri
KBEC Waxahachie, Texas
KBED Nederland, Texas
KBEN Carrizo Springs, Texas
KBEW Blue Earth, Minnesota
KBFI Bonners Ferry, Idaho
KBFL-AM Springfield, Missouri
KBFP Bakersfield, California
KBFS Belle Fourche, South Dakota
KBGG Des Moines, Iowa
KBGN Caldwell, Idaho
KBHB Sturgis, South Dakota
KBHC Nashville, Arkansas
KBHS Hot Springs, Arkansas
KBIB Marion, Texas
KBIF Fresno, California
KBIM Roswell, New Mexico
KBIX Muskogee, Oklahoma
KBIZ Ottumwa, Iowa
KBJA Sandy, Utah
KBJD Denver, Colorado
KBJM Lemmon, South Dakota
KBJT Fordyce, Arkansas
KBKB Fort Madison, Iowa
KBKR Baker, Oregon
KBKW Aberdeen, Washington
KBLA Santa Monica, California
KBLE Seattle, Washington
KBLF Red Bluff, California
KBLG Billings, Montana
KBLI Blackfoot, Idaho
KBLJ La Junta, Colorado
KBLL Helena, Montana
KBLU Yuma, Arizona
KBLY Idaho Falls, Idaho
KBMB Black Canyon City, Arizona
KBME Houston, Texas
KBMO Benson, Minnesota
KBMR Bismarck, North Dakota
KBMS Vancouver, Washington
KBMW Breckenridge, Minnesota
KBND Bend, Oregon
KBNN Lebanon, Missouri
KBNO Denver, Colorado
KBNP Portland, Oregon
KBNW Bend, Oregon
KBOA-AM Kennett, Missouri
KBOE Oskaloosa, Iowa
KBOI Boise, Idaho
KBOK Malvern, Arkansas
KBOV Bishop, California
KBOW Butte, Montana
KBOZ Bozeman, Montana
KBPO Port Neches, Texas
KBPS Portland, Oregon
KBQX Big Spring, Texas
KBRB Ainsworth, Nebraska
KBRC Mount Vernon, Washington
KBRD Lacey, Washington
KBRE Merced, California
KBRF Fergus Falls, Minnesota
KBRH Baton Rouge, Louisiana
KBRI Brinkley, Arkansas
KBRK Brookings, South Dakota
KBRL McCook, Nebraska
KBRN Boerne, Texas
KBRO Bremerton, Washington
KBRT Avalon, California
KBRV Soda Springs, Idaho
KBRW Barrow, Alaska
KBRX O'Neill, Nebraska
KBRZ Missouri City, Texas
KBSN Moses Lake, Washington
KBSR Laurel, Montana
KBST Big Spring, Texas
KBSU-FM Boise, Idaho
KBSZ Apache Junction, Arizona
KBTA Batesville, Arkansas
KBTC Houston, Missouri
KBTM Jonesboro, Arkansas
KBTN Neosho, Missouri
KBUF Holcomb, Kansas
KBUL Billings, Montana
KBUN Bemidji, Minnesota
KBUR Burlington, Iowa
KBUY Ruidoso, New Mexico
KBWD Brownwood, Texas
KBXD Dallas, Texas
KBYG Big Spring, Texas
KBYO Tallulah, Louisiana
KBYR Anchorage, Alaska
KBZO Lubbock, Texas
KBZY Salem, Oregon
KBZZ Sparks, Nevada
KCAA Loma Linda, California
KCAB Dardanelle, Arkansas
KCAL(AM) Redlands, California
KCAM Glennallen, Alaska
KCAP Helena, Montana
KCAR Clarksville, Texas
KCAT Pine Bluff, Arkansas
KCBC Manteca, California
KCBF Fairbanks, Alaska
KCBL Fresno, California
KCBQ San Diego, California
KCBR Monument, Colorado
KCBS San Francisco, California
KCCB Corning, Arkansas
KCCC Carlsbad, New Mexico
KCCR Pierre, South Dakota
KCCT Corpus Christi, Texas
KCCV Overland Park, Kansas
KCCY Pueblo, Colorado
KCEE Tucson, Arizona
KCEO Vista, California
KCFC Boulder, Colorado
KCFI(AM) Cedar Falls, Iowa
KCFJ Alturas, California
KCFM(AM) Florence, Oregon
KCFO Tulsa, Oklahoma
KCGS Marshall, Arkansas
KCHA Charles City, Iowa
KCHE Cherokee, Iowa
KCHI Chillicothe, Missouri
KCHJ Delano, California
KCHK New Prague, Minnesota
KCHL San Antonio, Texas
KCHN Brookshire, Texas
KCHR Charleston, Missouri
KCHS Truth or Consequences, New Mexico
KCHU Valdez, Alaska
KCID Caldwell, Idaho
KCII Washington, Iowa
KCIM Carroll, Iowa
KCIS Edmonds, Washington
KCJB Minot, North Dakota
KCJJ Iowa City, Iowa
KCKK Littleton, Colorado
KCKM Monahans, Texas
KCKN Roswell, New Mexico
KCKX Stayton, Oregon
KCKY Coolidge, Arizona
KCLE Burleson, Texas
KCLF New Roads, Louisiana
KCLI Clinton, Oklahoma
KCLK Asotin, Washington
KCLN Clinton, Iowa
KCLU Santa Barbara, California
KCLV Clovis, New Mexico
KCLW Hamilton, Texas
KCLX Colfax, Washington
KCMC Texarkana, Texas
KCMO Kansas City, Missouri
KCMX Phoenix, Oregon
KCMY Carson City, Nevada
KCNI Broken Bow, Nebraska
KCNM Saipan, Guam
KCNR Shasta, California
KCNW Fairway, Kansas
KCNZ Cedar Falls, Iowa
KCOB Newton, Iowa
KCOG Centerville, Iowa
KCOL Wellington, Colorado
KCOM Comanche, Texas
KCOR San Antonio, Texas
KCOW Alliance, Nebraska
KCOX Jasper, Texas
KCPS Burlington, Iowa
KCPX Spanish Valley, Utah
KCQL Aztec, New Mexico
KCRC Enid, Oklahoma
KCRN San Angelo, Texas
KCRO Omaha, Nebraska
KCRS Midland, Texas
KCRT Trinidad, Colorado
KCRV-AM Caruthersville, Missouri
KCSF Colorado Springs, Colorado
KCSJ Pueblo, Colorado
KCSP Kansas City, Missouri
KCSR Chadron, Nebraska
KCTA Corpus Christi, Texas
KCTE Independence, Missouri
KCTI Gonzales, Texas
KCTO Cleveland, Missouri
KCTX Childress, Texas
KCTY Wayne, Nebraska
KCUB Tucson, Arizona
KCUE Red Wing, Minnesota
KCUL Marshall, Texas
KCUP Toledo, Oregon
KCUZ Clifton, Arizona
KCVL Colville, Washington
KCVR Lodi, California
KCWJ Blue Springs, Missouri
KCWM Hondo, Texas
KCXL Liberty, Missouri
KCYK Yuma, Arizona
KCYL Lampasas, Texas
KCZZ Mission, Kansas
KDAE Sinton, Texas
KDAK Carrington, North Dakota
KDAL-AM Duluth, Minnesota
KDAO Marshalltown, Iowa
KDAP Douglas, Arizona
KDAV Lubbock, Texas
KDAZ Albuquerque, New Mexico
KDBM Dillon, Montana
KDBS Alexandria, Louisiana
KDBV Salinas, California
KDCC Dodge City, Kansas
KDCE Espanola, New Mexico
KDDD Dumas, Texas
KDDR Oakes, North Dakota
KDDZ Arvada, Colorado
KDEB(AM) Estes Park, Colorado
KDEC Decorah, Iowa
KDEF Albuquerque, New Mexico
KDEI Port Arthur, Texas
KDET Center, Texas
KDEX Dexter, Missouri
KDFN Doniphan, Missouri
KDFT Ferris, Texas
KDGO Durango, Colorado
KDHL Faribault, Minnesota
KDHN Dimmitt, Texas
KDIA Vallejo, California
KDIL Jerome, Idaho
KDIO Ortonville, Minnesota
KDIS Pasadena, California
KDIX Dickinson, North Dakota
KDIZ Golden Valley, Minnesota
KDJI Holbrook, Arizona
KDJS Willmar, Minnesota
KDJW Amarillo, Texas
KDKA Pittsburgh, Pennsylvania
KDKD Clinton, Missouri
KDKT Beulah, North Dakota
KDLA De Ridder, Louisiana
KDLG Dillingham, Alaska
KDLM Detroit Lakes, Minnesota
KDLR Devils Lake, North Dakota
KDLS Perry, Iowa
KDMA Montevideo, Minnesota
KDMO Carthage, Missouri
KDMS El Dorado, Arkansas
KDOM Windom, Minnesota
KDOW Palo Alto, California
KDQN De Queen, Arkansas
KDRO Sedalia, Missouri
KDRS Paragould, Arkansas
KDRY Alamo Heights, Texas
KDSJ Deadwood, South Dakota
KDSK Los Ranchos De Albuquerque, New Mexico
KDSN Denison, Iowa
KDTA Delta, Colorado
KDTD Kansas City, Kansas

KDTH Dubuque, Iowa
KDUN Reedsport, Oregon
KDUS Tempe, Arizona
KDUZ Hutchinson, Minnesota
KDWA Hastings, Minnesota
KDWN Las Vegas, Nevada
KDXE North Little Rock, Arkansas
KDXU St. George, Utah
KDYA Vallejo, California
KDYK Union Gap, Washington
KDYL South Salt Lake, Utah
KDYM Sunnyside, Washington
KDYN Ozark, Arkansas
KDZR Lake Oswego, Oregon
KEAR San Francisco, California
KEBC Del City, Oklahoma
KEBE Jacksonville, Texas
KEBR Rocklin, California
KECR El Cajon, California
KEDA San Antonio, Texas
KEDO Longview, Washington
KEEL Shreveport, Louisiana
KEIB Los Angeles, California
KEIN Great Falls, Montana
KEJO Albany, Oregon
KEJY Eureka, California
KELA Centralia-Chehalis, Washington
KELD El Dorado, Arkansas
KELE Mountain Grove, Missouri
KELG Manor, Texas
KELK Elko, Nevada
KELO-AM Sioux Falls, South Dakota
KELP El Paso, Texas
KELY Ely, Nevada
KENA Fort Smith, Arkansas
KENI Anchorage, Alaska
KENN Farmington, New Mexico
KENO Las Vegas, Nevada
KENT Parowan, Utah
KEOR Catoosa, Oklahoma
KEPN Lakewood, Colorado
KEPS Eagle Pass, Texas
KERI Bakersfield, California
KERN Wasco-Greenacres, California
KERR Polson, Montana
KERV Kerrville, Texas
KESJ St. Joseph, Missouri
KESM Eldorado Springs, Missouri
KESP Modesto, California
KESQ Indio, California
KEST San Francisco, California
KETX Livingston, Texas
KEUN Eunice, Louisiana
KEVA Evanston, Wyoming
KEVT Sahuarita, Arizona
KEWI Benton, Arkansas
KEX Portland, Oregon
KEXO Grand Junction, Colorado
KEXS Excelsior Springs, Missouri
KEYE Perryton, Texas
KEYF Dishman, Washington
KEYG Grand Coulee, Washington
KEYH Houston, Texas
KEYL Long Prairie, Minnesota
KEYQ Fresno, California
KEYS Corpus Christi, Texas
KEYY Provo, Utah
KEYZ Williston, North Dakota
KEZJ Twin Falls, Idaho
KEZM Sulphur, Louisiana
KEZW Aurora, Colorado
KEZX Medford, Oregon
KEZY San Bernardino, California
KFAB Omaha, Nebraska
KFAL Fulton, Missouri
KFAN Rochester, Minnesota
KFAQ Tulsa, Oklahoma
KFAR Fairbanks, Alaska
KFAX San Francisco, California
KFAY Farmington, Arkansas
KFBC Cheyenne, Wyoming
KFBK Sacramento, California
KFBX Fairbanks, Alaska
KFCD Farmersville, Texas
KFCR Custer, South Dakota
KFEL Pueblo, Colorado
KFEQ St. Joseph, Missouri
KFFA Helena, Arkansas
KFFF(AM) Boone, Iowa
KFFK Rogers, Arkansas
KFFN Tucson, Arizona
KFGO Fargo, North Dakota
KFH Wichita, Kansas
KFI Los Angeles, California
KFIA Carmichael, California
KFIG Fresno, California
KFIL Preston, Minnesota
KFIR Sweet Home, Oregon
KFIT Lockhart, Texas
KFIT EXP S San Antonio, Texas
KFIV Modesto, California
KFIZ Fond Du Lac, Wisconsin
KFJB Marshalltown, Iowa
KFJL Central Point, Oregon
KFJZ Fort Worth, Texas
KFKA Greeley, Colorado
KFKB Forks, Washington
KFLB Odessa, Texas
KFLC Benbrook, Texas
KFLD Pasco, Washington
KFLG Bullhead City, Arizona
KFLN Baker, Montana
KFLP Floydada, Texas
KFLS Klamath Falls, Oregon
KFLT Tucson, Arizona
KFMB San Diego, California
KFMO Park Hills, Missouri
KFMZ Brookfield, Missouri
KFNN Mesa, Arizona
KFNQ Seattle, Washington
KFNS Wood River, Illinois
KFNW West Fargo, North Dakota
KFNX Cave Creek, Arizona
KFNY Riverside, California
KFNZ Salt Lake City, Utah
KFOR Lincoln, Nebraska
KFOX Torrance, California
KFPT Clovis, California
KFPW Fort Smith, Arkansas
KFQD Anchorage, Alaska
KFRA Franklin, Louisiana
KFRM Salina, Kansas
KFRN Long Beach, California
KFRO Longview, Texas
KFRU Columbia, Missouri
KFSA Fort Smith, Arkansas
KFSD Escondido, California
KFSG Roseville, California
KFSP Mankato, Minnesota
KFSQ Thousand Palms, California
KFST Fort Stockton, Texas
KFSW Fort Smith, Arkansas
KFTA Rupert, Idaho
KFTM Fort Morgan, Colorado
KFUN Las Vegas, New Mexico
KFUO Clayton, Missouri
KFVR Crescent City, California
KFXD Boise, Idaho
KFXN Minneapolis, Minnesota
KFXR Dallas, Texas
KFXX Portland, Oregon
KFXZ Lafayette, Louisiana
KFYI Phoenix, Arizona
KFYN Bonham, Texas
KFYO Lubbock, Texas
KFYR Bismarck, North Dakota
KGA Spokane, Washington
KGAB Orchard Valley, Wyoming
KGAF Gainesville, Texas
KGAK Gallup, New Mexico
KGAL Lebanon, Oregon
KGAS Carthage, Texas
KGBA Heber, California
KGBC Galveston, Texas
KGBT Harlingen, Texas
KGDC Walla Walla, Washington
KGDD Oregon City, Oregon
KGED Fresno, California
KGEM Boise, Idaho
KGEN Tulare, California
KGEO Bakersfield, California
KGEZ Kalispell, Montana
KGFF Shawnee, Oklahoma
KGFL Clinton, Arkansas
KGFW Kearney, Nebraska
KGFX Pierre, South Dakota
KGGF AM Coffeyville, Kansas
KGGN Gladstone, Missouri
KGGR Dallas, Texas
KGHL Billings, Montana
KGHM Midwest City, Oklahoma
KGHS International Falls, Minnesota
KGIM Aberdeen, South Dakota
KGIR Cape Girardeau, Missouri
KGIW Alamosa, Colorado
KGKL San Angelo, Texas
KGLA Gretna, Louisiana
KGLB Glencoe, Minnesota
KGLD Tyler, Texas
KGLE Glendive, Montana
KGLN Glenwood Springs, Colorado
KGLO Mason City, Iowa
KGME Phoenix, Arizona
KGMI Bellingham, Washington
KGMS Tucson, Arizona
KGMT Fairbury, Nebraska
KGMY Springfield, Missouri
KGNB New Braunfels, Texas
KGNC Amarillo, Texas
KGND Vinita, Oklahoma
KGNM St. Joseph, Missouri
KGNO Dodge City, Kansas
KGNU Denver, Colorado
KGNW Burien-Seattle, Washington
KGO San Francisco, California
KGOE Eureka, California
KGOL Humble, Texas
KGOS Torrington, Wyoming
KGOW Bellaire, Texas
KGOW(AM) Bellaire, Hawaii
KGRE Greeley, Colorado
KGRG Enumclaw, Washington
KGRN Grinnell, Iowa
KGRO Pampa, Texas
KGRV Winston, Oregon
KGRZ Missoula, Montana
KGSO Wichita, Kansas
KGST Fresno, California
KGTK Olympia, Washington
KGTL Homer, Alaska
KGTL(AM) Homer, Alaska
KGTO Tulsa, Oklahoma
KGU Honolulu, Hawaii
KGUM Hagatna, Guam
KGVL Greenville, Texas
KGVO Missoula, Montana
KGVY Green Valley, Arizona
KGWA Enid, Oklahoma
KGWU Uvalde, Texas
KGY Olympia, Washington
KGYM Cedar Rapids, Iowa
KGYN Guymon, Oklahoma
KHAC Tse Bonito, New Mexico
KHAR Anchorage, Alaska
KHAS Hastings, Nebraska
KHAT Laramie, Wyoming
KHBM Monticello, Arkansas
KHBR Hillsboro, Texas
KHCB League City, Texas
KHCH Huntsville, Texas
KHCM Honolulu, Hawaii
KHDN Hardin, Montana
KHEY El Paso, Texas
KHFX Cleburne, Texas
KHGG Van Buren, Arkansas
KHGZ Glenwood, Arkansas
KHHO Tacoma, Washington
KHIL Willcox, Arizona
KHIT Reno, Nevada
KHJ Los Angeles, California
KHKA(AM) Honolulu, Hawaii
KHKR Washington, Utah
KHLO Hilo, Hawaii
KHMO Hannibal, Missouri
KHNC Johnstown, Colorado
KHND Harvey, North Dakota
KHNR Honolulu, Hawaii
KHNU Hilo, Hawaii
KHNU(AM) Hilo, Hawaii
KHOB Hobbs, New Mexico
KHOJ St. Charles, Missouri
KHOT Madera, California
KHOW Denver, Colorado
KHOZ Harrison, Arkansas
KHPP(AM) Waukon, Iowa
KHPY Moreno Valley, California
KHQN Spanish Fork, Utah
KHRA Honolulu, Hawaii
KHRO El Paso, Texas
KHRT Minot, North Dakota
KHSE Wylie, Texas
KHSN Coos Bay, Oregon
KHTK Sacramento, California
KHTS Canyon Country, California
KHTY Bakersfield, California
KHUB Fremont, Nebraska
KHVH Honolulu, Hawaii
KHVL Huntsville, Texas
KHVN Fort Worth, Texas
KHWG Fallon, Nevada
KIAM Nenana, Alaska
KIBL Beeville, Texas
KICA Clovis, New Mexico
KICD Spencer, Iowa
KICE Bend, Oregon
KICS Hastings, Nebraska
KICY Nome, Alaska
KID Idaho Falls, Idaho
KIDD Monterey, California
KIDO Nampa, Idaho
KIDR Phoenix, Arizona
KIEV Burbank, California
KIFG Iowa Falls, Iowa
KIFM West Sacramento, California
KIFW Sitka, Alaska
KIGO St. Anthony, Idaho
KIGS Hanford, California
KIHC Arroyo Grande, California
KIHH Eureka, California
KIHM Reno, Nevada
KIHP Mesa, Arizona
KIHR Hood River, Oregon
KIID Sacramento, California
KIIK Waynesville, Missouri
KIIX Fort Collins, Colorado
KIJN Farwell, Texas
KIJV Huron, South Dakota
KIKC Forsyth, Montana
KIKI Honolulu, Hawaii
KIKK Pasadena, Texas
KIKR Beaumont, Texas
KIKZ Seminole, Texas
KILJ Mount Pleasant, Iowa
KILR Estherville, Iowa
KILT Houston, Texas
KIMB Kimball, Nebraska
KIML Gillette, Wyoming
KIMM Rapid City, South Dakota
KIMP Mount Pleasant, Texas
KINA Salina, Kansas
KIND Independence, Kansas
KINE Kingsville, Texas
KINN Alamogordo, New Mexico
KINO Winslow, Arizona
KINY Juneau, Alaska
KIOL Iola, Kansas
KION Salinas, California
KIOU Shreveport, Louisiana
KIPA Hilo, Hawaii
KIQI San Francisco, California
KIQQ Barstow, California
KIQS Willows, California
KIRN Simi Valley, California
KIRO Seattle, Washington
KIRT Mission, Texas
KIRV Fresno, California
KIRX Kirksville, Missouri
KIT Yakima, Washington
KITI Chehalis-Centralia, Washington
KITZ Silverdale, Washington
KIUL Garden City, Kansas
KIUN Pecos, Texas
KIUP Durango, Colorado
KIVA Albuquerque, New Mexico
KIVY Crockett, Texas
KIWA Sheldon, Iowa
KIXI Mercer Island/Seattl, Washington
KIXL Del Valle, Texas
KIXW Apple Valley, California
KIXZ Amarillo, Texas
KIYU Galena, Alaska
KJAA Globe, Arizona
KJAL Tafuna, American Samoa
KJAM Madison, South Dakota
KJAN Atlantic, Iowa
KJAY Sacramento, California
KJBN Little Rock, Arkansas
KJCB Lafayette, Louisiana
KJCE Rollingwood, Texas
KJCK Junction City, Kansas
KJCV Jackson, Wyoming
KJDJ San Luis Obispo, California
KJDL Lubbock, Texas
KJDY John Day, Oregon

KJEF Jennings, Louisiana
KJFF Festus, Missouri
KJIM Sherman, Texas
KJIN Houma, Louisiana
KJJD Windsor, Colorado
KJJK Fergus Falls, Minnesota
KJJQ Volga, South Dakota
KJJR Whitefish, Montana
KJLT North Platte, Nebraska
KJME Fountain, Colorado
KJMJ Alexandria, Louisiana
KJMP Pierce, Colorado
KJMU Sand Springs, Oklahoma
KJNO Juneau, Alaska
KJNP North Pole, Alaska
KJOC Davenport, Iowa
KJOL Grand Junction, Colorado
KJON Carrollton, Texas
KJOP Lemoore, California
KJOX Kennewick, Washington
KJOZ Conroe, Texas
KJPG Frazier Park, California
KJPR Shasta Lake City, California
KJPW Waynesville, Missouri
KJQS Murray, Utah
KJR Seattle, Washington
KJRB Spokane, Washington
KJRG Newton, Kansas
KJSK Columbus, Nebraska
KJTV Lubbock, Texas
KJUA Cheyenne, Wyoming
KJUG Tulare, California
KJXX Jackson, Missouri
KKAA Aberdeen, South Dakota
KKAM Lubbock, Texas
KKAN Phillipsburg, Kansas
KKAQ Thief River Falls, Minnesota
KKAT Salt Lake City, Utah
KKAY White Castle, Louisiana
KKBJ Bemidji, Minnesota
KKCQ Fosston, Minnesota
KKDA Grand Prairie, Texas
KKDD San Bernardino, California
KKDZ Seattle, Washington
KKEA Honolulu, Hawaii
KKGM Fort Worth, Texas
KKGR East Helena, Montana
KKIM Albuquerque, New Mexico
KKIN Aitkin, Minnesota
KKJL San Luis Obispo, California
KKLE Winfield, Kansas
KKLF Richardson, Texas
KKLL Webb City, Missouri
KKLO Leavenworth, Kansas
KKLS Rapid City, South Dakota
KKMC Gonzales, California
KKMO Tacoma, Washington
KKMS Richfield, Minnesota
KKNE Waipahu, Hawaii
KKNO Gretna, Louisiana
KKNS Corrales, New Mexico
KKNT Phoenix, Arizona
KKNW Seattle, Washington
KKNX Eugene, Oregon
KKOB Albuquerque, New Mexico
KKOB Exp S Santa Fe, New Mexico
KKOH Reno, Nevada
KKOJ Jackson, Minnesota
KKOL Seattle, Washington
KKON Kealakekua, Hawaii
KKOV Vancouver, Washington
KKOW Pittsburg, Kansas
KKOY Chanute, Kansas
KKOZ Ava, Missouri
KKPC Pueblo, Colorado
KKPZ Portland, Oregon
KKRT Wenatchee, Washington
KKSA San Angelo, Texas
KKSF Oakland, California
KKSM Oceanside, California
KKTK Texarkana, Texas
KKTL Casper, Wyoming
KKTX Corpus Christi, Texas
KKTY Douglas, Wyoming
KKUB Brownfield, Texas
KKVV Las Vegas, Nevada
KKXL Grand Forks, North Dakota
KKXX Paradise, California
KKYX San Antonio, Texas
KKZN Thornton, Colorado
KKZZ Port Hueneme, California
KLAA Orange, California
KLAC Los Angeles, California
KLAD Klamath Falls, Oregon
KLAM Cordova, Alaska
KLAR Laredo, Texas
KLAT Houston, Texas
KLAV Las Vegas, Nevada
KLAY Lakewood, Washington
KLBB Stillwater, Minnesota
KLBJ Austin, Texas
KLBM La Grande, Oregon
KLBS Los Banos, California
KLBW New Boston, Texas
KLCB Libby, Montana
KLCK Goldendale, Washington
KLCL Lake Charles, Louisiana
KLCN Blytheville, Arkansas
KLDC Denver, Colorado
KLDS Falfurrias, Texas
KLDY Lacey, Washington
KLEA Lovington, New Mexico
KLEB Golden Meadow, Louisiana
KLEE Ottumwa, Iowa
KLEM Le Mars, Iowa
KLER Orofino, Idaho
KLEX Lexington, Missouri
KLEY Wellington, Kansas
KLFD Litchfield, Minnesota
KLFE Seattle, Washington
KLFJ Springfield, Missouri
KLGA Algona, Iowa
KLGN Logan, Utah
KLGO Austin, Texas
KLGR Redwood Falls, Minnesota
KLHC Bakersfield, California
KLHT Honolulu, Hawaii
KLIB Roseville, California
KLIC Richwood, Louisiana
KLID Poplar Bluff, Missouri
KLIF Dallas, Texas
KLIK Jefferson City, Missouri
KLIM Black Forest, Colorado
KLIN Lincoln, Nebraska
KLIO Wichita, Kansas
KLIV San Jose, California
KLIX Twin Falls, Idaho
KLIZ Brainerd, Minnesota
KLKC Parsons, Kansas
KLLA Leesville, Louisiana
KLLB West Jordan, Utah
KLLV Breen, Colorado
KLMR Lamar, Colorado
KLMS Lincoln, Nebraska
KLMX Clayton, New Mexico
KLNG Council Bluffs, Iowa
KLNT Laredo, Texas
KLO Ogden, Utah
KLOA Ridgecrest, California
KLOC Turlock, California
KLOE Goodland, Kansas
KLOG Kelso, Washington
KLOH Pipestone, Minnesota
KLOK San Jose, California
KLOO Albany, Oregon
KLPF Midland, Texas
KLPL(AM) Lake Providence, Louisiana
KLPW Union, Missouri
KLPZ Parker, Arizona
KLRK Mexia, Texas
KLSD San Diego, California
KLSQ Whitney, Nevada
KLTC Dickinson, North Dakota
KLTF Little Falls, Minnesota
KLTI Macon, Missouri
KLTK Centerton, Arkansas
KLTO Del Rio, Texas
KLTT Commerce City, Colorado
KLTX Long Beach, California
KLTZ Glasgow, Montana
KLUP Terrell Hills, Texas
KLVI Beaumont, Texas
KLVL Pasadena, Texas
KLVQ Athens, Texas
KLVT Levelland, Texas
KLVZ Brighton, Colorado
KLWJ(AM) Umatilla, Oregon
KLWN Lawrence, Kansas
KLWT Lebanon, Missouri
KLXR Redding, California
KLXX Bismarck-Mandan, North Dakota
KLYC McMinnville, Oregon
KLYQ Hamilton, Montana
KLYR Clarksville, Arkansas
KLZ Denver, Colorado
KLZN Susanville, California
KLZS Eugene, Oregon
KMA Shenandoah, Iowa
KMAD Madill, Oklahoma
KMAJ Topeka, Kansas
KMAL Malden, Missouri
KMAM Butler, Missouri
KMAN Manhattan, Kansas
KMAQ Maquoketa, Iowa
KMAS Shelton, Washington
KMAX Colfax, Washington
KMBL Junction, Texas
KMBS West Monroe, Louisiana
KMBX Soledad, California
KMBZ Kansas City, Missouri
KMCD Fairfield, Iowa
KMCL(AM) Donnelly, Idaho
KMDO Fort Scott, Kansas
KMED Medford, Oregon
KMER Kemmerer, Wyoming
KMET Banning, California
KMFR Pearsall, Texas
KMFS Guthrie, Oklahoma
KMHI Mountain Home, Idaho
KMHL Marshall, Minnesota
KMHR(AM) Boise, Idaho
KMHS Coos Bay, Oregon
KMHT Marshall, Texas
KMIA Auburn-Federal Way, Washington
KMIC Houston, Texas
KMIK Tempe, Arizona
KMIN Grants, New Mexico
KMIS-AM Portageville, Missouri
KMJ Fresno, California
KMJC Mount Shasta, California
KMJM Cedar Rapids, Iowa
KMKI Plano, Texas
KMKY Oakland, California
KMLB Monroe, Louisiana
KMMJ Grand Island, Nebraska
KMMM Pratt, Kansas
KMMO Marshall, Missouri
KMMQ Plattsmouth, Nebraska
KMMS Bozeman, Montana
KMND Midland, Texas
KMNQ Brooklyn Park, Minnesota
KMNS Sioux City, Iowa
KMNV St. Paul, Minnesota
KMNY Hurst, Texas
KMOG Payson, Arizona
KMON Great Falls, Montana
KMOX St. Louis, Missouri
KMOZ Rolla, Missouri
KMPC Los Angeles, California
KMPG Hollister, California
KMPH Modesto, California
KMPT East Missoula, Montana
KMRB San Gabriel, California
KMRC Morgan City, Louisiana
KMRF Marshfield, Missouri
KMRI West Valley City, Utah
KMRN Cameron, Missouri
KMRS Morris, Minnesota
KMRY Cedar Rapids, Iowa
KMSD Mibank, South Dakota
KMSR Mayville, North Dakota
KMTA Miles City, Montana
KMTI Manti, Utah
KMTL Sherwood, Arkansas
KMTT Vancouver, Washington
KMTX Helena, Montana
KMUL Farwell, Texas
KMUS Sperry, Oklahoma
KMVI Kahului, Hawaii
KMVL Madisonville, Texas
KMVP Phoenix, Arizona
KMXA Aurora, Colorado
KMXO Merkel, Texas
KMYC Marysville, California
KMZQ Las Vegas, Nevada
KNAB Burlington, Colorado
KNAF Fredericksburg, Texas
KNAL Victoria, Texas
KNAX McCook, Nebraska
KNBR San Francisco, California
KNBY Newport, Arkansas
KNCB Vivian, Louisiana
KNCK Concordia, Kansas
KNCO Grass Valley, California
KNCR Fortuna, California
KNCY Nebraska City, Nebraska
KNDC Hettinger, North Dakota
KNDI Honolulu, Hawaii
KNDK Langdon, North Dakota
KNDN Farmington, New Mexico
KNDY Marysville, Kansas
KNEA Jonesboro, Arkansas
KNEB Scottsbluff, Nebraska
KNED McAlester, Oklahoma
KNEK Washington, Louisiana
KNEL Brady, Texas
KNEM Nevada, Missouri
KNET Palestine, Texas
KNEU Roosevelt, Utah
KNEW Oakland, California
KNFL Fargo, North Dakota
KNFT Bayard, New Mexico
KNGL McPherson, Kansas
KNGN McCook, Nebraska
KNGR Daingerfield, Texas
KNHD Camden, Arkansas
KNIA Knoxville, Iowa
KNIH Paradise, Nevada
KNIM Maryville, Missouri
KNIR New Iberia, Louisiana
KNLV Ord, Nebraska
KNML Albuquerque, New Mexico
KNMX Las Vegas, New Mexico
KNND Cottage Grove, Oregon
KNNR Sparks, Nevada
KNNS Larned, Kansas
KNOC Natchitoches, Louisiana
KNOM Nome, Alaska
KNOT Prescott, Arizona
KNOX Grand Forks, North Dakota
KNPT Newport, Oregon
KNRO Redding, California
KNRS Salt Lake City, Utah
KNRV Englewood, Colorado
KNRY Monterey Bay, California
KNSA Unalakleet, Alaska
KNSH Canyon, Texas
KNSI St. Cloud, Minnesota
KNSN San Diego, California
KNSP Staples, Minnesota
KNSS Wichita, Kansas
KNST Tucson, Arizona
KNTB Lakewood, Washington
KNTF Oroville, California
KNTH Houston, Texas
KNTR Lake Havasu City, Arizona
KNTS Seattle, Washington
KNTX Bowie, Texas
KNUJ New Ulm, Minnesota
KNUS Denver, Colorado
KNUV Tolleson, Arizona
KNVR San Saba, Texas
KNWA Bellefonte, Arkansas
KNWC Sioux Falls, South Dakota
KNWH Yucca Valley, California
KNWQ Palm Springs, California
KNWS Waterloo, Iowa
KNWZ Coachella, California
KNX Los Angeles, California
KNXN Sierra Vista, Arizona
KNZR Bakersfield, California
KNZZ Grand Junction, Colorado
KOA Denver, Colorado
KOAC Corvallis, Oregon
KOAK Red Oak, Iowa
KOAL Price, Utah
KOAN Anchorage, Alaska
KOAN Anchorage, Alaska
KOAQ Terrytown, Nebraska
KOAZ Isleta, New Mexico
KOBB Bozeman, Montana
KOBE Las Cruces, New Mexico
KOBO Yuba City, California
KODI Cody, Wyoming
KODL The Dalles, Oregon
KODY North Platte, Nebraska
KOEL Oelwein, Iowa
KOFC Fayetteville, Arkansas
KOFE St. Maries, Idaho
KOFI Kalispell, Montana
KOFO Ottawa, Kansas
KOGA Ogallala, Nebraska
KOGN Ogden, Utah
KOGO San Diego, California

KOGT Orange, Texas
KOHI St. Helens, Oregon
KOHU Hermiston, Oregon
KOIL Omaha, Nebraska
KOJM Havre, Montana
KOKA Shreveport, Louisiana
KOKB Blackwell, Oklahoma
KOKC Oklahoma City, Oklahoma
KOKE Pflugerville, Texas
KOKK Huron, South Dakota
KOKL Okmulgee, Oklahoma
KOKO Warrensburg, Missouri
KOKP Perry, Oklahoma
KOKX Keokuk, Iowa
KOLE Port Arthur, Texas
KOLM Rochester, Minnesota
KOLT Scottsbluff, Nebraska
KOLY Mobridge, South Dakota
KOMC Branson, Missouri
KOMJ Omaha, Nebraska
KOMO Seattle, Washington
KOMW Omak, Washington
KOMY La Selva Beach, California
KONA Kennewick-Richland-P, Washington
KONO San Antonio, Texas
KONP Port Angeles, Washington
KOOQ North Platte, Nebraska
KOOR Milwaukie, Oregon
KOPB Eugene, Oregon
KOPY Alice, Texas
KORE Springfield-Eugene, Oregon
KORL Honolulu, Hawaii
KORN Mitchell, South Dakota
KORT Grangeville, Idaho
KOSE Wilson, Arkansas
KOSS Lancaster, California
KOSY Texarkana, Arkansas
KOTA Rapid City, South Dakota
KOTK Omaha, Nebraska
KOTS Deming, New Mexico
KOTZ Kotzebue, Alaska
KOUU Pocatello, Idaho
KOVC Valley City, North Dakota
KOVE Lander, Wyoming
KOVO Provo, Utah
KOWB Laramie, Wyoming
KOWL South Lake Tahoe, California
KOXR Oxnard, California
KOY Phoenix, Arizona
KOZA Odessa, Texas
KOZE Lewiston, Idaho
KOZI Chelan, Washington
KOZN Bellevue, Nebraska
KOZY Grand Rapids, Minnesota
KPAM Troutdale, Oregon
KPAN Hereford, Texas
KPAY Chico, California
KPDQ Portland, Oregon
KPEL Lafayette, Louisiana
KPET Lamesa, Texas
KPGE Page, Arizona
KPGM Pawhuska, Oklahoma
KPHI Honolulu, Hawaii
KPHN Kansas City, Missouri
KPHX Phoenix, Arizona
KPIO Loveland, Colorado
KPIR Granbury, Texas
KPJC Salem, Oregon
KPKE Gunnison, Colorado
KPLT Paris, Texas
KPLY Reno, Nevada
KPMO Mendocino, California
KPNP Watertown, Minnesota
KPNS Duncan, Oklahoma
KPNW Eugene, Oregon
KPOC Pocahontas, Arkansas
KPOD Crescent City, California
KPOF Denver, Colorado
KPOJ Portland, Oregon
KPOK Bowman, North Dakota
KPOW Powell, Wyoming
KPQ Wenatchee, Washington
KPRC Houston, Texas
KPRK Livingston, Montana
KPRL Paso Robles, California
KPRM Park Rapids, Minnesota
KPRO Riverside, California
KPRP Honolulu, Hawaii
KPRT Kansas City, Missouri
KPRV Poteau, Oklahoma
KPRZ San Marcos-Poway, California
KPSI Palm Springs, California
KPSZ Des Moines, Iowa
KPTO Pocatello, Idaho
KPTR Palm Springs, California
KPUA Hilo, Hawaii
KPUG Bellingham, Washington
KPUR Amarillo, Texas
KPWB Piedmont, Missouri
KPWL Newport, Washington
KPXQ Glendale, Arizona
KPYK Terrell, Texas
KPYN Atlanta, Texas
KPZK Little Rock, Arkansas
KQAB(AM) Lake Isabella, California
KQAD Luverne, Minnesota
KQAM Wichita, Kansas
KQAQ Austin, Minnesota
KQBU El Paso, Texas
KQBZ Brownwood, Texas
KQCV Oklahoma City, Oklahoma
KQDI Great Falls, Montana
KQDJ Jamestown, North Dakota
KQEN Roseburg, Oregon
KQEQ Fowler, California
KQKD Redfield, South Dakota
KQLL Henderson, Nevada
KQLX Lisbon, North Dakota
KQMG Independence, Iowa
KQMS Redding, California
KQNA Prescott Valley, Arizona
KQNG Eleele, Hawaii
KQNK Norton, Kansas
KQNM Milan, New Mexico
KQNT Spokane, Washington
KQPN West Memphis, Arkansas
KQQB Stockdale, Texas
KQQQ Pullman, Washington
KQQZ Fairview Heights, Missouri
KQRR(AM) Mount Angel, Oregon
KQSC Santa Barbara, California
KQSP Shakopee, Minnesota
KQTY Borger, Texas
KQUE Rosenberg-Richmond, Texas
KQV Pittsburgh, Pennsylvania
KQWB West Fargo, North Dakota
KQWC Webster City, Iowa
KQYX Galena, Kansas
KRAC Quincy, California
KRAE Cheyenne, Wyoming
KRAI Craig, Colorado
KRAK Hesperia, California
KRAL Rawlins, Wyoming
KRAM Vernal, Utah
KRBA Lufkin, Texas
KRBT Eveleth, Minnesota
KRCM Shanandoah, Texas
KRCN Longmont, Colorado
KRCO Prineville, Oregon
KRDD Roswell, New Mexico
KRDM Redmond, Oregon
KRDO Colorado Springs, Colorado
KRDU Dinuba, California
KRDY San Antonio, Texas
KRDZ Wray, Colorado
KREA Honolulu, Hawaii
KREB Bentonville-Bella, Arkansas
KREF Norman, Oklahoma
KREH Pecan Grove, Texas
KREI Farmington, Missouri
KREL Colorado Springs, Colorado
KREW Plainview, Texas
KRFE Lubbock, Texas
KRFO Owatonna, Minnesota
KRFS Superior, Nebraska
KRGE Weslaco, Texas
KRGI Grand Island, Nebraska
KRGS Rifle, Colorado
KRHW Sikeston, Missouri
KRIB Mason City, Iowa
KRIL Odessa, Texas
KRIO McAllen, Texas
KRIZ Renton, Washington
KRJO Monroe, Louisiana
KRKC King City, California
KRKE Milan, New Mexico
KRKK Rock Springs, Wyoming
KRKO Everett, Washington
KRKS Denver, Colorado
KRKY Granby, Colorado
KRLA Glendale, California
KRLC Lewiston-Clarkston, Idaho
KRLD Dallas, Texas
KRLL California, Missouri
KRLN Canon City, Colorado
KRLV Las Vegas, Nevada
KRLW Walnut Ridge, Arkansas
KRMD Shreveport, Louisiana
KRMG Tulsa, Oklahoma
KRML Carmel, California
KRMO Cassville, Missouri
KRMS Osage Beach, Missouri
KRMY Killeen, Texas
KRND Fox Farm, Wyoming
KRNI Mason City, Iowa
KRNT Des Moines, Iowa
KROB Robstown, Texas
KROC Rochester, Minnesota
KROD El Paso, Texas
KROE Sheridan, Wyoming
KROF Abbeville, Louisiana
KROO Breckenridge, Texas
KROP Brawley, California
KROS Clinton, Iowa
KROX Crookston, Minnesota
KRPA Oak Harbor, Washington
KRPI Ferndale, Washington
KRPL Moscow, Idaho
KRRP Coushatta, Louisiana
KRRS Santa Rosa, California
KRRZ Minot, North Dakota
KRSC Othello, Washington
KRSL Russell, Kansas
KRSN Los Alamos, New Mexico
KRSV Afton, Wyoming
KRSY Alamogordo, New Mexico
KRTA Medford, Oregon
KRTK Chubbuck, Idaho
KRTN Raton, New Mexico
KRUE Waseca, Minnesota
KRUI Ruidoso Downs, New Mexico
KRUN Ballinger, Texas
KRUS Ruston, Louisiana
KRVA Cockrell Hill, Texas
KRVM Eugene, Oregon
KRVN Lexington, Nebraska
KRVT Claremore, Oklahoma
KRVZ Springerville, Arizona
KRWB Roseau, Minnesota
KRWC Buffalo, Minnesota
KRXA Carmel Valley, California
KRXK Rexburg, Idaho
KRXR Gooding, Idaho
KRYN(AM) Gresham, Oregon
KRZI Waco, Texas
KRZR Visalia, California
KRZY Albuquerque, New Mexico
KSAH Universal City, Texas
KSAL Salina, Kansas
KSAM Whitefish, Montana
KSAZ Marana, Arizona
KSBN Spokane, Washington
KSBQ Santa Maria, California
KSCB Liberal, Kansas
KSCJ Sioux City, Iowa
KSCO Santa Cruz, California
KSCR Eugene, Oregon
KSDN Aberdeen, South Dakota
KSDO San Diego, California
KSDP Sand Point, Alaska
KSDR Watertown, South Dakota
KSDT Hemet, California
KSEI Pocatello, Idaho
KSEK Pittsburg, Kansas
KSEL Portales, New Mexico
KSEN Shelby, Montana
KSEO Durant, Oklahoma
KSET Lumberton, Texas
KSEV Tomball, Texas
KSEW Seward, Alaska
KSEY Seymour, Texas
KSFA Nacogdoches, Texas
KSFB San Francisco, California
KSFN Piedmont, California
KSFO San Francisco, California
KSGF Springfield, Missouri
KSGG Reno, Nevada
KSGL Wichita, Kansas
KSGM Chester, Illinois
KSGT Jackson, Wyoming
KSHJ Houston, Texas
KSHJ Houston, Texas
KSHO Lebanon, Oregon
KSHP North Las Vegas, Nevada
KSIB Creston, Iowa
KSID Sidney, Nebraska
KSIG Crowley, Louisiana
KSIM Sikeston, Missouri
KSIR Brush, Colorado
KSIS Sedalia, Missouri
KSIV Clayton, Missouri
KSIW Woodward, Oklahoma
KSIX Corpus Christi, Texas
KSJB Jamestown, North Dakota
KSJK Talent, Oregon
KSJX San Jose, California
KSKE Buena Vista, Colorado
KSKR Roseburg, Oregon
KSKY Balch Springs, Texas
KSL Salt Lake City, Utah
KSLD Soldotna, Alaska
KSLI Abilene, Texas
KSLL Price, Utah
KSLO Opelousas, Louisiana
KSLR San Antonio, Texas
KSLV Monte Vista, Colorado
KSMA Santa Maria, California
KSMH West Sacramento, California
KSML Diboll, Texas
KSMM Liberal, Kansas
KSMO Salem, Missouri
KSMX Santa Maria, California
KSNM Las Cruces, New Mexico
KSNM-FM Georgetown, Delaware
KSNY Snyder, Texas
KSOK Arkansas City, Kansas
KSOO Sioux Falls, South Dakota
KSOP South Salt Lake, Utah
KSOU Sioux Center, Iowa
KSOX Raymondville, Texas
KSPA Ontario, California
KSPD Boise, Idaho
KSPI AM Stillwater, Oklahoma
KSPN Los Angeles, California
KSPT Sandpoint, Idaho
KSPZ Ammon, Idaho
KSRA Salmon, Idaho
KSRM Soldotna, Alaska
KSRO Santa Rosa, California
KSRR Provo, Utah
KSRV Ontario, Oregon
KSSK Honolulu, Hawaii
KSST Sulphur Springs, Texas
KSTA Coleman, Texas
KSTC Sterling, Colorado
KSTE Rancho Cordova, California
KSTL St. Louis, Missouri
KSTN Stockton, California
KSTP St. Paul, Minnesota
KSTV Stephenville, Texas
KSUB Cedar City, Utah
KSUE Susanville, California
KSUH Puyallup, Washington
KSUM Fairmont, Minnesota
KSVA Albuquerque, New Mexico
KSVC Richfield, Utah
KSVE El Paso, Texas
KSVN Ogden, Utah
KSVP Artesia, New Mexico
KSWA Graham, Texas
KSWB Seaside, Oregon
KSWM Aurora, Missouri
KSWV Santa Fe, New Mexico
KSYB Shreveport, Louisiana
KSYC Yreka, California
KSYL Alexandria, Louisiana
KSZL Barstow, California
KSZN(AM) Gresham, Oregon
KTAM Bryan, Texas
KTAN Sierra Vista, Arizona
KTAP Santa Maria, California
KTAR Phoenix, Arizona
KTAT Frederick, Oklahoma
KTBA Tuba City, Arizona
KTBB Tyler, Texas
KTBI Ephrata, Washington
KTBL Los Ranchos, New Mexico
KTBR Roseburg, Oregon
KTBZ Tulsa, Oklahoma
KTCK Dallas, Texas
KTCR Yakima, Washington
KTCR Selah, Washington
KTCS Fort Smith, Arkansas
KTCT San Francisco, California

KTDD San Bernardino, California
KTEK Alvin, Texas
KTEL Walla Walla, Washington
KTEM Temple, Texas
KTFI Wendell, Idaho
KTFJ Dakota City, Nebraska
KTFS Texarkana, Texas
KTGE Salinas, California
KTGG Okemos, Michigan
KTGO Tioga, North Dakota
KTGR Columbia, Missouri
KTHE Thermopolis, Wyoming
KTHH Albany, Oregon
KTHO South Lake Tahoe, California
KTHS Green Forest, Arkansas
KTIB Thibodaux, Louisiana
KTIC West Point, Nebraska
KTIE San Bernardino, California
KTIK Nampa, Idaho
KTIL(AM) Netarts, Oregon
KTIP Porterville, California
KTIS Minneapolis, Minnesota
KTIX Pendleton, Oregon
KTJS Hobart, Oklahoma
KTKC Springhill, Louisiana
KTKK Sandy, Utah
KTKN Ketchikan, Alaska
KTKR San Antonio, Texas
KTKT Tucson, Arizona
KTKZ Sacramento, California
KTLK Minneapolis, Minnesota
KTLO Mountain Home, Arkansas
KTLQ Tahlequah, Oklahoma
KTLR Oklahoma City, Oklahoma
KTLU Rusk, Texas
KTLV Midwest City, Oklahoma
KTMC McAlester, Oklahoma
KTMM Grand Junction, Colorado
KTMR Converse, Texas
KTMS Santa Barbara, California
KTNC Falls City, Nebraska
KTNF St. Louis Park, Minnesota
KTNM Tucumcari, New Mexico
KTNN Window Rock, Arizona
KTNO University Park, Texas
KTNQ Los Angeles, California
KTNS Oakhurst, California
KTNZ Amarillo, Texas
KTOB Petaluma, California
KTOE Mankato, Minnesota
KTOK Oklahoma City, Oklahoma
KTON Cameron, Texas
KTOP Topeka, Kansas
KTOQ Rapid City, South Dakota
KTOX Needles, California
KTPA Prescott, Arkansas
KTPI Mojave, California
KTRB San Francisco, California
KTRC Santa Fe, New Mexico
KTRF Thief River Falls, Minnesota
KTRH Houston, Texas
KTRP Weiser, Idaho
KTRS St. Louis, Missouri
KTRW Opportunity, Washington
KTSA San Antonio, Texas
KTSM El Paso, Texas
KTSN Elko, Nevada
KTTH Seattle, Washington
KTTN Trenton, Missouri
KTTO Spokane, Washington
KTTP Pineville, Louisiana
KTTR AM Rolla, Missouri
KTTT Columbus, Nebraska
KTUB Centerville, Utah
KTUC Tucson, Arizona
KTUI Sullivan, Missouri
KTUV Little Rock, Arkansas
KTWG Agana, Guam
KTWO Casper, Wyoming
KTXV Mabank, Texas
KTXW Manor, Texas
KTXZ West Lake Hills, Texas
KTYM Inglewood, California
KTZN Anchorage, Alaska
KTZR Tucson, Arizona
KUAI Kekaha, Hawaii
KUAM Agana, Guam
KUAU Haiku, Hawaii
KUAZ Tucson, Arizona
KUBA Yuba City, California
KUBC Montrose, Colorado
KUBR San Juan, Texas
KUFO Portland, Oregon
KUGN Eugene, Oregon
KUGR Green River, Wyoming
KUHL Santa Maria, California
KUIK Hillsboro, Oregon
KUJ Walla Walla, Washington
KUKI Ukiah, California
KUKU Willow Springs, Missouri
KULE Ephrata, Washington
KULF Bellville, Texas
KULP El Campo, Texas
KULY Ulysses, Kansas
KUMA Pendleton, Oregon
KUNO Corpus Christi, Texas
KUNX Santa Paula, California
KUOA Siloam Springs, Arkansas
KUOM Minneapolis, Minnesota
KUOW Tumwater, Washington
KUPA Pearl City, Hawaii
KURM Rogers, Arkansas
KURS San Diego, California
KURV Edinburg, Texas
KURY Brookings, Oregon
KUSH Cushing, Oklahoma
KUTI Yakima, Washington
KUTR Taylorsville, Utah
KUTY Palmdale, California
KUVR Holdrege, Nebraska
KUYO Evansville, Wyoming
KUZZ Bakersfield, California
KVAK Valdez, Alaska
KVAN Burbank, Washington
KVBR Brainerd, Minnesota
KVCE Highland Park, Texas
KVCK Wolf Point, Montana
KVCU Boulder, Colorado
KVDW England, Arkansas
KVEC San Luis Obispo, California
KVEL Vernal, Utah
KVEN Ventura, California
KVET Austin, Texas
KVFC Cortez, Colorado
KVFD Fort Dodge, Iowa
KVGB Great Bend, Kansas
KVI Seattle, Washington
KVIN Ceres, California
KVIP Redding, California
KVIS Miami, Oklahoma
KVIV El Paso, Texas
KVJY Pharr, Texas
KVKK Verndale, Minnesota
KVLE Vail, Colorado
KVLF Alpine, Texas
KVLG La Grange, Texas
KVLV Fallon, Nevada
KVMA Magnolia, Arkansas
KVMC Colorado City, Texas
KVML Sonora, California
KVNA Flagstaff, Arizona
KVNI Coeur D'Alene, Idaho
KVNN Victoria, Texas
KVNR Santa Ana, California
KVNS Brownsville, Texas
KVNT Eagle River, Alaska
KVNU Logan, Utah
KVOC Casper, Wyoming
KVOE Emporia, Kansas
KVOG Agana, Guam
KVOI Cortaro, Arizona
KVOK Kodiak, Alaska
KVOL Lafayette, Louisiana
KVOM Morrilton, Arkansas
KVON Napa, California
KVOP Plainview, Texas
KVOQ(AM) Denver, Colorado
KVOR Colorado Springs, Colorado
KVOT Taos, New Mexico
KVOW Riverton, Wyoming
KVOZ Del Mar Hills, Texas
KVPI Ville Platte, Louisiana
KVRC Arkadelphia, Arkansas
KVRH Salida, Colorado
KVRI Blaine, Washington
KVRP Stamford, Texas
KVSA McGehee, Arkansas
KVSF Santa Fe, New Mexico
KVSH Valentine, Nebraska
KVSI Montpelier, Idaho
KVSL Show Low, Arizona
KVSO Ardmore, Oklahoma
KVSV Beloit, Kansas
KVTA Ventura, California
KVTK Vermillion, South Dakota
KVTO Berkeley, California
KVTT Mineral Wells, Texas
KVVN Santa Clara, California
KVWC Vernon, Texas
KVWM Show Low, Arizona
KVXR Moorhead, Minnesota
KWAC Bakersfield, California
KWAD Wadena, Minnesota
KWAI Honolulu, Hawaii
KWAK Stuttgart, Arkansas
KWAL Wallace, Idaho
KWAM Memphis, Tennessee
KWAP Wasilla, Alaska
KWAT Watertown, South Dakota
KWAY Waverly, Iowa
KWBC College Station, Texas
KWBE Beatrice, Nebraska
KWBG Boone, Iowa
KWBW Hutchinson, Kansas
KWBY Woodburn, Oregon
KWCK Searcy, Arkansas
KWDF Ball, Louisiana
KWDJ Ridgecrest, California
KWDZ Salt Lake City, Utah
KWED Seguin, Texas
KWEI Notus, Idaho
KWEI(AM) Payette, Idaho
KWEL Midland, Texas
KWES Ruidoso, New Mexico
KWEY Weatherford, Oklahoma
KWFA Tye, Texas
KWFM(AM) South Tucson, Arizona
KWFS Wichita Falls, Texas
KWG Stockton, California
KWHI Brenham, Texas
KWHN Fort Smith, Arkansas
KWHW Altus, Oklahoma
KWIK Pocatello, Idaho
KWIL Albany, Oregon
KWIP Dallas, Oregon
KWIQ Moses Lake North, Washington
KWIX Moberly, Missouri
KWJB Canton, Texas
KWKA Clovis, New Mexico
KWKC Abilene, Texas
KWKH Shreveport, Louisiana
KWKU Pomona, California
KWKW Los Angeles, California
KWKY Des Moines, Iowa
KWLC Decorah, Iowa
KWLE Anacortes, Washington
KWLM Willmar, Minnesota
KWLO Waterloo, Iowa
KWMC Del Rio, Texas
KWMF Pleasanton, Texas
KWML-AM Georgetown, Delaware
KWMO Washington, Missouri
KWMT Fort Dodge, Iowa
KWNA Winnemucca, Nevada
KWNC Quincy, Washington
KWNO Winona, Minnesota
KWNX Elgin, Texas
KWOA Worthington, Minnesota
KWOC Poplar Bluff, Missouri
KWOK Aberdeen, Washington
KWON Bartlesville, Oklahoma
KWOR Worland, Wyoming
KWOS Jefferson City, Missouri
KWPC Muscatine, Iowa
KWPM West Plains, Missouri
KWPN Moore, Oklahoma
KWRD Henderson, Texas
KWRE Warrenton, Missouri
KWRF Warren, Arkansas
KWRM Corona, California
KWRN Apple Valley, California
KWRO Coquille, Oregon
KWRT Boonville, Missouri
KWRU Fresno, California
KWSH Wewoka, Oklahoma
KWSL Sioux City, Iowa
KWSN Sioux Falls, South Dakota
KWST El Centro, California
KWSU Pullman, Washington
KWSW Eureka, California
KWSX Stockton, California
KWTL Grand Forks, North Dakota
KWTO-AM Springfield, Missouri
KWTX Waco, Texas
KWUD Woodville, Texas
KWUF Pagosa Springs, Colorado
KWVE(AM) Oildale, California
KWVR Enterprise, Oregon
KWWJ Baytown, Texas
KWWN Las Vegas, Nevada
KWXT Dardanelle, Arkansas
KWXY AM Cathedral City, California
KWYN Wynne, Arkansas
KWYO Sheridan, Wyoming
KWYR Winner, South Dakota
KWYS West Yellowstone, Montana
KWYZ Everett, Washington
KXAR Hope, Arkansas
KXBX Ukiah, California
KXCA Lawton, Oklahoma
KXEG Phoenix, Arizona
KXEL Waterloo, Iowa
KXEN St. Louis, Missouri
KXEO Mexico, Missouri
KXEQ Reno, Nevada
KXET(AM) Portland, Oregon
KXEW South Tucson, Arizona
KXEX Fresno, California
KXFN Saint Louis, Missouri
KXGF Great Falls, Montana
KXGN Glendive, Montana
KXIC Iowa City, Iowa
KXIT Dalhart, Texas
KXJK Forrest City, Arkansas
KXKS Albuquerque, New Mexico
KXLE Ellensburg, Washington
KXLO Lewistown, Montana
KXLQ Indianola, Iowa
KXLX Airway Heights, Washington
KXLY-AM Spokane, Washington
KXMR Bismarck, North Dakota
KXNO Des Moines, Iowa
KXNT North Las Vegas, Nevada
KXO El Centro, California
KXOI Crane, Texas
KXOL Brigham City, Utah
KXOR Junction City, Oregon
KXOX Sweetwater, Texas
KXPA Bellevue, Washington
KXPD Tigard, Oregon
KXPL El Paso, Texas
KXPN Kearney, Nebraska
KXPO Grafton, North Dakota
KXPS Thousand Palms, California
KXRA Alexandria, Minnesota
KXRB Sioux Falls, South Dakota
KXRE Manitou Springs, Colorado
KXRO Aberdeen, Washington
KXSP Omaha, Nebraska
KXSS Waite Park, Minnesota
KXST North Las Vegas, Nevada
KXTA Rupert, Idaho
KXTD Wagoner, Oklahoma
KXTG Portland, Oregon
KXTK Arroyo Grande, California
KXTL Butte, Montana
KXTO Reno, Nevada
KXXA(AM) Conway, Arkansas
KXXJ Juneau, Alaska
KXXT Tolleson, Arizona
KXXX Colby, Kansas
KXYZ Houston, Texas
KXZZ Lake Charles, Louisiana
KYAA Soquel, California
KYAH Delta, Utah
KYAK Yakima, Washington
KYAL Sapulpa, Oklahoma
KYBC Cottonwood, Arizona
KYCA Prescott, Arizona
KYCN Wheatland, Wyoming
KYCR Golden Valley, Minnesota
KYES Rockville, Minnesota
KYET Golden Valley, Arizona
KYFI St. Louis, Missouri
KYFR Shenandoah, Iowa
KYIZ Renton, Washington
KYKK Humble City, New Mexico
KYKN Keizer, Oregon
KYLS Fredericktown, Missouri
KYLT Missoula, Montana
KYLW Lockwood, Montana
KYMN-AM Northfield, Minnesota
KYMO East Prairie, Missouri
KYND Cypress, Texas

KYNG Springdale, Arkansas
KYNO Fresno, California
KYNR Toppenish, Washington
KYNS San Luis Obispo, California
KYNT Yankton, South Dakota
KYOK Conroe, Texas
KYOO Bolivar, Missouri
KYOS Merced, California
KYPA Los Angeles, California
KYRO Troy, Missouri
KYST Texas City, Texas
KYTY Somerset, Texas
KYUK Bethel, Alaska
KYUL Scott City, Kansas
KYVA Gallup, New Mexico
KYW Philadelphia, Pennsylvania
KYYA Billings, Montana
KYYS Kansas City, Kansas
KYYW Abilene, Texas
KYZS Tyler, Texas
KZDC San Antonio, Texas
KZDG San Francisco, California
KZEE Weatherford, Texas
KZER Santa Barbara, California
KZFS Spokane, Washington
KZHN Paris, Texas
KZHS Hot Springs, Arkansas
KZIM Cape Girardeau, Missouri
KZIP Amarillo, Texas
KZIZ Pacific, Washington
KZLI Catoosa, Oklahoma
KZLS Enid, Oklahoma
KZMP University Park, Texas
KZMQ Ten Sleep, Wyoming
KZMX Hot Springs, South Dakota
KZNE College Station, Texas
KZNG Hot Springs, Arkansas
KZNS Salt Lake City, Utah
KZNT Colorado Springs, Colorado
KZNU St. George, Utah
KZNW Wenatchee, Washington
KZOO Honolulu, Hawaii
KZOT Bellevue, Nebraska
KZOY(AM) Sioux Falls, South Dakota
KZPA Fort Yukon, Alaska
KZQQ Abilene, Texas
KZQZ St. Louis, Missouri
KZRG Joplin, Missouri
KZSB Santa Barbara, California
KZSF San Jose, California
KZSJ San Martin, California
KZTD Cabot, Arkansas
KZUE El Reno, Oklahoma
KZXR Prosser, Washington
KZYM Joplin, Missouri
KZZB Beaumont, Texas
KZZJ Rugby, North Dakota
KZZN Littlefield, Texas
KZZZ Bullhead City, Arizona
V6AH(AM) Pohnpei, 66
WAAM Ann Arbor, Michigan
WAAV Leland, North Carolina
WAAX Gadsden, Alabama
WABA Aguadilla, Puerto Rico
WABB Belton, South Carolina
WABC New York City, New York
WABF Fairhope, Alabama
WABG Greenwood, Mississippi
WABH Bath, New York
WABJ Adrian, Michigan
WABL Amite, Louisiana
WABN Abingdon, Virginia
WABO Waynesboro, Mississippi
WABQ Painesville, Ohio
WABV Abbeville, South Carolina
WABY Watervliet, New York
WACA Wheaton, Maryland
WACB Taylorsville, North Carolina
WACC Hialeah, Florida
WACE Chicopee, Massachusetts
WACK Newark, New York
WACM West Springfield, Massachusetts
WACQ Tuskegee, Alabama
WACT Tuscaloosa, Alabama
WADB(AM) Asbury Park, New Jersey
WADC Parkersburg, West Virginia
WADE Wadesboro, North Carolina
WADK Newport, Rhode Island
WADO New York, New York
WADS Ansonia, Connecticut
WADV Lebanon, Pennsylvania
WAEB Allentown, Pennsylvania
WAEC Atlanta, Georgia
WAEI Bangor, Maine
WAEW Crossville, Tennessee
WAEY Princeton, West Virginia
WAFC Clewiston, Florida
WAFS Atlanta, Georgia
WAFZ Immokalee, Florida
WAGF Dothan, Alabama
WAGG Birmingham, Alabama
WAGL Lancaster, South Carolina
WAGN Menominee, Michigan
WAGR Lumberton, North Carolina
WAGS Bishopville, South Carolina
WAGY Forest City, North Carolina
WAHT Clemson, South Carolina
WAIK Galesburg, Illinois
WAIM Anderson, South Carolina
WAIN Columbia, Kentucky
WAIS Buchtel, Ohio
WAIT Crystal Lake, Illinois
WAIZ Hickory, North Carolina
WAJD Gainesville, Florida
WAJL South Boston, Virginia
WAJR Morgantown, West Virginia
WAKE Valparaiso, Indiana
WAKE-AM Georgetown, Delaware
WAKI McMinnville, Tennessee
WAKK McComb, Mississippi
WAKM Franklin, Tennessee
WAKO Lawrenceville, Illinois
WAKR Akron, Ohio
WAKV Otsego, Michigan
WAKY Radcliff, Kentucky
WALD Johnsonville, South Carolina
WALE Greenville, Rhode Island
WALG Albany, Georgia
WALK Patchogue, New York
WALL Middletown, New York
WALO Humacao, Puerto Rico
WALT Meridian, Mississippi
WAMA Tampa, Florida
WAMB Nashville, Tennessee
WAMB Brazil, Indiana
WAMC Albany, New York
WAMD Aberdeen, Maryland
WAME Statesville, North Carolina
WAMG Dedham, Massachusetts
WAMI Opp, Alabama
WAML Laurel, Mississippi
WAMM Woodstock, Virginia
WAMN Green Valley, West Virginia
WAMO Wilkinsburg, Pennsylvania
WAMO Wilkinsburg, Pennsylvania
WAMT Pine Castle Sky Lake, Florida
WAMV Amherst, Virginia
WAMW-AM Washington, Indiana
WAMY Amory, Mississippi
WANB Waynesburg, Pennsylvania
WANG Havelock, North Carolina
WANI Opelika, Alabama
WANO Pineville, Kentucky
WANS Anderson, South Carolina
WANY Albany, Kentucky
WAOC Saint Augustine, Florida
WAOK Atlanta, Georgia
WAOS Austell, Georgia
WAOV Vincennes, Indiana
WAPA San Juan, Puerto Rico
WAPF McComb, Mississippi
WAPI Birmingham, Alabama
WAQE Rice Lake, Wisconsin
WAQI Miami, Florida
WARD Petoskey, Michigan
WARE Ware, Massachusetts
WARF Akron, Ohio
WARK Hagerstown, Maryland
WARL Attleboro, Massachusetts
WARM Scranton, Pennsylvania
WARR Warrenton, North Carolina
WARU Peru, Indiana
WARV Warwick, Rhode Island
WASB Brockport, New York
WASC Spartanburg, South Carolina
WASG Daphne, Alabama
WASK Lafayette, Indiana
WASR Wolfeboro, New Hampshire
WATA Boone, North Carolina
WATB Decatur, Georgia
WATH Athens, Ohio
WATK Antigo, Wisconsin
WATN Watertown, New York
WATR Waterbury, Connecticut
WATS Sayre, Pennsylvania
WATT Cadillac, Michigan
WATV Birmingham, Alabama
WATW Ashland, Wisconsin
WATX Algood, Tennessee
WAUB Auburn, New York
WAUC Wauchula, Florida
WAUD Auburn, Alabama
WAUG New Hope, North Carolina
WAUK Jackson, Wisconsin
WAUR Sandwich, Illinois
WAVA Arlington, Virginia
WAVL Apollo, Pennsylvania
WAVN Southaven, Mississippi
WAVO Rock Hill, South Carolina
WAVQ Jacksonville, North Carolina
WAVS Davie, Florida
WAVU Albertville, Alabama
WAVZ New Haven, Connecticut
WAWK Kendallville, Indiana
WAWO Alma, Georgia
WAXB Ridgefield, Connecticut
WAXE Vero Beach, Florida
WAXO Lewisburg, Tennessee
WAXY South Miami, Florida
WAYC Bedford, Pennsylvania
WAYE Birmingham, Alabama
WAYN Rockingham, North Carolina
WAYR Orange Park, Florida
WAYS Macon, Georgia
WAYY Eau Claire, Wisconsin
WAZL Hazleton, Pennsylvania
WAZN Watertown, Massachusetts
WAZS Summerville, South Carolina
WAZX Smyrna, Georgia
WAZZ Fayetteville, North Carolina
WBAA West Lafayette, Indiana
WBAC Cleveland, Tennessee
WBAE Portland, Maine
WBAF Barnesville, Georgia
WBAG Burlington-Graham, North Carolina
WBAJ Blythewood, South Carolina
WBAL Baltimore, Maryland
WBAP Fort Worth, Texas
WBAT Marion, Indiana
WBAX Wilkes-Barre, Pennsylvania
WBBD Wheeling, West Virginia
WBBF Buffalo, New York
WBBM Chicago, Illinois
WBBP Memphis, Tennessee
WBBR New York, New York
WBBT Lyons, Georgia
WBBW Youngstown, Ohio
WBBX Kingston, Tennessee
WBBZ Ponca City, Oklahoma
WBCB Levittown, Pennsylvania
WBCE Wickliffe, Kentucky
WBCF Florence, Alabama
WBCH Hastings, Michigan
WBCK Battle Creek, Michigan
WBCN Charlotte, North Carolina
WBCO Bucyrus, Ohio
WBCP Urbana, Illinois
WBCR Alcoa, Tennessee
WBCU Union, South Carolina
WBEC Pittsfield, Massachusetts
WBEJ Elizabethton, Tennessee
WBEN Buffalo, New York
WBES Charleston, West Virginia
WBET Sturgis, Michigan
WBEV Beaver Dam, Wisconsin
WBEX Chillicothe, Ohio
WBFC Stanton, Kentucky
WBFD Bedford, Pennsylvania
WBFJ Winston-Salem, North Carolina
WBFN Battle Creek, Michigan
WBGA Brunswick, Georgia
WBGC Chipley, Florida
WBGG Pittsburgh, Pennsylvania
WBGN Bowling Green, Kentucky
WBGS Point Pleasant, West Virginia
WBGX Harvey, Illinois
WBGZ Alton, Illinois
WBHA Wabasha, Minnesota
WBHB Fitzgerald, Georgia
WBHF Cartersville, Georgia
WBHN Bryson City, North Carolina
WBHP Huntsville, Alabama
WBHR Sauk Rapids, Minnesota
WBHY Mobile, Alabama
WBIB Centreville, Alabama
WBIG Aurora, Illinois
WBIN Benton, Tennessee
WBIP Booneville, Mississippi
WBIW Bedford, Indiana
WBIZ Eau Claire, Wisconsin
WBKK Wilton, Minnesota
WBKV West Bend, Wisconsin
WBKW Beckley, West Virginia
WBKW(AM) Beckley, West Virginia
WBLA Elizabethtown, North Carolina
WBLC Lenoir City, Tennessee
WBLF Bellefonte, Pennsylvania
WBLJ Dalton, Georgia
WBLL Bellefontaine, Ohio
WBLO Thomasville, North Carolina
WBLQ(AM) Westerly, Rhode Island
WBLR Batesburg, South Carolina
WBLT Bedford, Virginia
WBMC McMinnville, Tennessee
WBMD Baltimore, Maryland
WBMJ San Juan, Puerto Rico
WBML Macon, Georgia
WBMQ Savannah, Georgia
WBNL Boonville, Indiana
WBNM Alexander City, Alabama
WBNR Beacon, New York
WBNS Columbus, Ohio
WBNW Concord, Massachusetts
WBOB(AM) Jacksonville, Florida
WBOG Tomah, Wisconsin
WBOJ Columbus, Georgia
WBOK New Orleans, Louisiana
WBOL Bolivar, Tennessee
WBOW Terre Haute, Indiana
WBOX Bogalusa, Louisiana
WBPZ Lock Haven, Pennsylvania
WBQH Silver Spring, Maryland
WBQN Barceloneta-Manati, Puerto Rico
WBRD Palmetto, Florida
WBRG Lynchburg, Virginia
WBRI Indianapolis, Indiana
WBRK Pittsfield, Massachusetts
WBRM Marion, North Carolina
WBRN Big Rapids, Michigan
WBRT Bardstown, Kentucky
WBRV Boonville, New York
WBSA Boaz, Alabama
WBSC Bennettsville, South Carolina
WBSG Lajas, Puerto Rico
WBSM New Bedford, Massachusetts
WBSR Pensacola, Florida
WBSS Pleasantville, New Jersey
WBSS(AM) Pleasantville, New Jersey
WBT Charlotte, North Carolina
WBTA Batavia, New York
WBTC Uhrichsville, Ohio
WBTE Windsor, North Carolina
WBTG Sheffield, Alabama
WBTH Williamson, West Virginia
WBTK Richmond, Virginia
WBTM Danville, Virginia
WBTN Bennington, Vermont
WBTX Broadway-Timberville, Virginia
WBUC Buckhannon, West Virginia
WBUR West Yarmouth, Massachusetts
WBUT Butler, Pennsylvania
WBVA Bayside, Virginia
WBVP Beaver Falls, Pennsylvania
WBWX(AM) Berwick, Pennsylvania
WBXR Hazel Green, Alabama
WBYN Lehighton, Pennsylvania
WBYS Canton, Illinois
WBZ Boston, Massachusetts
WBZI Xenia, Ohio
WBZQ Huntington, Indiana
WBZT West Palm Beach, Florida
WBZU Scranton, Pennsylvania
WCAB Rutherfordton, North Carolina
WCAM Camden, South Carolina
WCAO Baltimore, Maryland
WCAP Lowell, Massachusetts
WCAR Livonia, Michigan
WCAT Burlington, Vermont
WCAZ Carthage, Illinois
WCBA Corning, New York
WCBC Cumberland, Maryland
WCBG Waynesboro, Pennsylvania
WCBL Benton, Kentucky
WCBM Baltimore, Maryland

WCBQ Oxford, North Carolina
WCBR Richmond, Kentucky
WCBS New York, New York
WCBT Roanoke Rapids, North Carolina
WCBX Bassett, Virginia
WCBY Cheboygan, Michigan
WCCC West Hartford, Connecticut
WCCD Parma, Ohio
WCCF Punta Gorda, Florida
WCCM Methuen, Virgin Islands
WCCN Neillsville, Wisconsin
WCCO Minneapolis, Minnesota
WCCS Homer City, Pennsylvania
WCCW Traverse City, Michigan
WCCY Houghton, Michigan
WCDL Carbondale, Pennsylvania
WCDO Sidney, New York
WCDS Glasgow, Kentucky
WCDT Winchester, Tennessee
WCEC Haverhill, Massachusetts
WCED Du Bois, Pennsylvania
WCEH Hawkinsville, Georgia
WCEM Cambridge, Maryland
WCEO Columbia, South Carolina
WCEV Cicero, Illinois
WCFO East Point, Georgia
WCFR Springfield, Vermont
WCGA Woodbine, Georgia
WCGB Juana Diaz, Puerto Rico
WCGC Belmont, North Carolina
WCGL Jacksonville, Florida
WCGO Evanston, Illinois
WCGR Canandaigua, New York
WCGW Nicholasville, Kentucky
WCHA Chambersburg, Pennsylvania
WCHB Taylor, Michigan
WCHE West Chester, Pennsylvania
WCHI Chillicothe, Ohio
WCHJ Brookhaven, Mississippi
WCHK Canton, Georgia
WCHL Chapel Hill, North Carolina
WCHM Clarkesville, Georgia
WCHN Norwich, New York
WCHO Washington Ct House, Ohio
WCHP Champlain, New York
WCHR Flemington, New Jersey
WCHS Charleston, West Virginia
WCHT Escanaba, Michigan
WCHV Charlottesville, Virginia
WCIL Carbondale, Illinois
WCIS Morganton, North Carolina
WCIT(AM) Lima, Ohio
WCJU Columbia, Mississippi
WCJW Warsaw, New York
WCKA Jacksonville, Alabama
WCKB Dunn, North Carolina
WCKI Greer, South Carolina
WCKL Catskill, New York
WCKW Garyville, Louisiana
WCKY Cincinnati, Ohio
WCLA Claxton, Georgia
WCLB Sheboygan, Wisconsin
WCLC Jamestown, Tennessee
WCLD Cleveland, Mississippi
WCLE Cleveland, Tennessee
WCLG Morgantown, West Virginia
WCLM Highland Springs, Virginia
WCLN Clinton, North Carolina
WCLO Janesville, Wisconsin
WCLT Newark, Ohio
WCLU Glasgow, Kentucky
WCLW Eden, North Carolina
WCLY Raleigh, North Carolina
WCMA(AM) Bayamon, Puerto Rico
WCMC Wildwood, New Jersey
WCMD Cumberland, Maryland
WCME(AM) Brunswick, Maine
WCMI Ashland, Kentucky
WCMN Arecibo, Puerto Rico
WCMP Pine City, Minnesota
WCMR Elkhart, Indiana
WCMT Martin, Tennessee
WCMX Leominster, Massachusetts
WCMY Ottawa, Illinois
WCNC Elizabeth City, North Carolina
WCND Shelbyville, Kentucky
WCNF Dothan, Alabama
WCNL Newport, New Hampshire
WCNN North Atlanta, Georgia
WCNS Latrobe, Pennsylvania
WCNW Fairfield, Ohio
WCNZ Marco Island, Florida
WCOA Pensacola, Florida
WCOC Dora, Alabama
WCOG Greensboro, North Carolina
WCOH Newnan, Georgia
WCOJ Coatesville, Pennsylvania
WCOK Sparta, North Carolina
WCON Cornelia, Georgia
WCOR Lebanon, Tennessee
WCOS Columbia, South Carolina
WCPA Clearfield, Pennsylvania
WCPC Houston, Mississippi
WCPH Etowah, Tennessee
WCPK Chesapeake, Virginia
WCPM Cumberland, Kentucky
WCPR Coamo, Puerto Rico
WCPS Tarboro, North Carolina
WCPT-AM Willow Springs, Illinois
WCRA Effingham, Illinois
WCRA Effingham, Illinois
WCRE Cheraw, South Carolina
WCRK Morristown, Tennessee
WCRL Oneonta, Alabama
WCRM Fort Myers, Florida
WCRN Worcester, Massachusetts
WCRO Johnstown, Pennsylvania
WCRS Greenwood, South Carolina
WCRT Donelson, Tennessee
WCRU Dallas, North Carolina
WCRV Collierville, Tennessee
WCRW(AM) Leesburg, Virginia
WCSA Ripley, Mississippi
WCSI Columbus, Indiana
WCSJ Morris, Illinois
WCSL Cherryville, North Carolina
WCSM Celina, Ohio
WCSR Hillsdale, Michigan
WCSS Amsterdam, New York
WCST Berkeley Springs, West Virginia
WCSV Crossville, Tennessee
WCSW Shell Lake, Wisconsin
WCSZ Sans Souci, South Carolina
WCTC New Brunswick, New Jersey
WCTF Vernon, Connecticut
WCTN Potomac-Cabin John, Maryland
WCTR Chestertown, Maryland
WCTS Maplewood, Minnesota
WCTT Corbin, Kentucky
WCUB Two Rivers, Wisconsin
WCUE Cuyahoga Falls, Ohio
WCUM Bridgeport, Connecticut
WCVA Culpeper, Virginia
WCVC Tallahassee, Florida
WCVG Covington, Kentucky
WCVL Crawfordsville, Indiana
WCVP Murphy, North Carolina
WCVR(AM) Randolph, Vermont
WCVX Florence, Kentucky
WCWA Toledo, Ohio
WCWC Williamsburg, Kentucky
WCXI Fenton, Michigan
WCXN Claremont, North Carolina
WCXZ Harrogate, Tennessee
WCYN Cynthiana, Kentucky
WCZZ Greenwood, South Carolina
WDAD Indiana, Pennsylvania
WDAE St. Petersburg, Florida
WDAK Columbus, Georgia
WDAL Dalton, Georgia
WDAN Danville, Illinois
WDAO Dayton, Ohio
WDAY Fargo, North Dakota
WDBC Escanaba, Michigan
WDBL Springfield, Tennessee
WDBO Orlando, Florida
WDBQ Dubuque, Iowa
WDBZ Cincinnati, Ohio
WDCF Dade City, Florida
WDCT Fairfax, Virginia
WDCX Rochester, New York
WDCY Douglasville, Georgia
WDCZ Buffalo, New York
WDDO Macon, Georgia
WDDV Venice, Florida
WDDY Albany, New York
WDDZ Pittsburgh, Pennsylvania
WDEA Ellsworth, Maine
WDEB Jamestown, Tennessee
WDEF Chattanooga, Tennessee
WDEH Sweetwater, Tennessee
WDEK(AM) Lexington, South Carolina
WDEL Wilmington, Delaware
WDEO Ypsilanti, Michigan
WDEP Ponce, Puerto Rico
WDER Derry, New Hampshire
WDEV Waterbury, Vermont
WDEX Monroe, North Carolina
WDFB Junction City, Kentucky
WDFN Detroit, Michigan
WDGR Dahlonega, Georgia
WDGY Hudson, Wisconsin
WDHP Frederiksted, Virgin Islands
WDIA Memphis, Tennessee
WDIC Clinchco, Virginia
WDIG Steubenville, Ohio
WDIS Norfolk, Massachusetts
WDIZ Panama City, Florida
WDJA Delray Beach, Florida
WDJL Huntsville, Alabama
WDJS Mount Olive, North Carolina
WDJZ Bridgeport, Connecticut
WDKD Kingstree, South Carolina
WDKN Dickson, Tennessee
WDLA Walton, New York
WDLB Marshfield, Wisconsin
WDLC Port Jervis, New York
WDLM-AM East Moline, Illinois
WDLR Delaware, Ohio
WDLS Wisconsin Dells, Wisconsin
WDLW Lorain, Ohio
WDLX Washington, North Carolina
WDMC Melbourne, Florida
WDMG Douglas, Georgia
WDMJ Marquette, Michigan
WDMP Dodgeville, Wisconsin
WDMV Walkersville, Maryland
WDNC Durham, North Carolina
WDND South Bend, Indiana
WDNE Elkins, West Virginia
WDNG Anniston, Alabama
WDNO Quebradillas, Puerto Rico
WDNT Dayton, Tennessee
WDNY Dansville, New York
WDOC Prestonsburg, Kentucky
WDOE Dunkirk, New York
WDOG Barnwell, South Carolina
WDOR Sturgeon Bay, Wisconsin
WDOS Oneonta, New York
WDOV Dover, Delaware
WDPC Dallas, Georgia
WDPN Alliance, Ohio
WDQN Duquoin, Illinois
WDRC Hartford, Connecticut
WDRJ Inkster, Michigan
WDRU Creedmore, North Carolina
WDSC Dillon, South Carolina
WDSL Mocksville, North Carolina
WDSM Superior, Wisconsin
WDSP De Funiak Springs, Florida
WDSR Lake City, Florida
WDTK Detroit, Michigan
WDTM Selmer, Tennessee
WDTW Dearborn, Michigan
WDUL Superior, Wisconsin
WDUN Gainesville, Georgia
WDUR Durham, North Carolina
WDUX Waupaca, Wisconsin
WDUZ Green Bay, Wisconsin
WDVA Danville, Virginia
WDVH Gainesville, Florida
WDVM Eau Claire, Wisconsin
WDWD Atlanta, Georgia
WDWR Pensacola, Florida
WDWS Champaign, Illinois
WDXE Lawrenceburg, Tennessee
WDXI Jackson, Tennessee
WDXL Lexington, Tennessee
WDXQ Cochran, Georgia
WDXR Paducah, Kentucky
WDXY Sumter, South Carolina
WDXZ Robertsdale, Alabama
WDYN Rossville, Georgia
WDYT Kings Mountain, North Carolina
WDYZ Orlando, Florida
WDZ Decatur, Illinois
WDZY Colonial Heights, Virginia
WEAF Saint Stephen, South Carolina
WEAL Greensboro, North Carolina
WEAQ Chippewa Falls, Wisconsin
WEAV Plattsburgh, New York
WEBC Duluth, Minnesota
WEBJ Brewton, Alabama
WEBO Owego, New York
WEBQ Harrisburg, Illinois
WEBS Calhoun, Georgia
WEBY Milton, Florida
WECK Cheektowaga, New York
WECO Wartburg, Tennessee
WECR Newland, North Carolina
WECU Winterville, North Carolina
WECZ Punxsutawney, Pennsylvania
WEDI Eaton, Ohio
WEDM(AM) Fort Walton Beach, Florida
WEDO McKeesport, Pennsylvania
WEEB Southern Pines, North Carolina
WEED Rocky Mount, North Carolina
WEEF Deerfield, Illinois
WEEI Boston, Massachusetts
WEEN Lafayette, Tennessee
WEEO Shippensburg, Pennsylvania
WEEU Reading, Pennsylvania
WEEX Easton, Pennsylvania
WEGA Vega Baja, Puerto Rico
WEGG Rose Hill, North Carolina
WEGO(AM) Winston-Salem, North Carolina
WEGP Presque Isle, Maine
WEHH Elmira Hts-Horsehds, New York
WEIR Weirton, West Virginia
WEIS Centre, Alabama
WEJL Scranton, Pennsylvania
WEJS Jersey Shore, Pennsylvania
WEKB Elkhorn City, Kentucky
WEKC Williamsburg, Kentucky
WEKG Jackson, Kentucky
WEKI Decatur, Alabama
WEKO Morovis, Puerto Rico
WEKR Fayetteville, Tennessee
WEKT Elkton, Kentucky
WEKY Richmond, Kentucky
WEKZ Monroe, Wisconsin
WELB Elba, Alabama
WELC Welch, West Virginia
WELD Fisher, West Virginia
WELE Ormond Beach, Florida
WELI New Haven, Connecticut
WELM Elmira, New York
WELO Tupelo, Mississippi
WELP Easley, South Carolina
WELS Kinston, North Carolina
WELY Ely, Minnesota
WELZ Belzoni, Mississippi
WEMB Erwin, Tennessee
WEMG Camden, New Jersey
WEMJ Laconia, New Hampshire
WENA Yauco, Puerto Rico
WENC Whiteville, North Carolina
WENE Endicott, New York
WENG Englewood, Florida
WENI Corning, New York
WENK Union City, Tennessee
WENN Birmingham, Alabama
WENO Nashville, Tennessee
WENR Englewood, Tennessee
WENT Gloversville, New York
WENU South Glen Falls, New York
WENY Elmira, New York
WEOA Evansville, Indiana
WEOK Poughkeepsie, New York
WEOL Elyria, Ohio
WEPG South Pittsburg, Tennessee
WEPM Martinsburg, West Virginia
WEPN New York, New York
WERC Birmingham, Alabama
WERE Cleveland Heights, Ohio
WERH Hamilton, Alabama
WERL Eagle River, Wisconsin
WERT Van Wert, Ohio
WESB Bradford, Pennsylvania
WESO Southbridge, Massachusetts
WESR Onley-Onancock, Virginia
WEST Easton, Pennsylvania
WESX Nahant, Massachusetts
WESY Leland, Mississippi
WETB Johnson City, Tennessee
WETC Wendell-Zebulon, North Carolina
WETR Knoxville, Tennessee
WETZ New Martinsville, West Virginia
WEUP Huntsville, Alabama
WEUV Moulton, Alabama
WEVA Emporia, Virginia
WEVG Evergreen, Alabama
WEVR River Falls, Wisconsin
WEW St. Louis, Missouri

WEWC Callahan, Florida
WEWO Laurinburg, North Carolina
WEXL Royal Oak, Michigan
WEXS Patillas, Puerto Rico
WEXY Wilton Manors, Florida
WEZE Boston, Massachusetts
WEZO Augusta, Georgia
WEZR Lewiston, Maine
WEZS Laconia, New Hampshire
WEZZ Brantley, Alabama
WFAB Ceiba, Puerto Rico
WFAD Middlebury, Vermont
WFAI Salem, New Jersey
WFAM Augusta, Georgia
WFAN New York, New York
WFAS White Plains, New York
WFAU Gardiner, Maine
WFAW Fort Atkinson, Wisconsin
WFAX Falls Church, Virginia
WFAY Fayetteville, North Carolina
WFBG Altoona, Pennsylvania
WFBL Syracuse, New York
WFBR Glen Burnie, Maryland
WFBX Spring Lake, North Carolina
WFCN Nashville, Tennessee
WFCV Fort Wayne, Indiana
WFDF Farmington Hills, Michigan
WFDL Waupun, Wisconsin
WFDR Manchester, Georgia
WFEA Manchester, New Hampshire
WFEB Sylacauga, Alabama
WFED Washington, District of Columbia
WFER Iron River, Michigan
WFFF Columbia, Mississippi
WFFG Marathon, Florida
WFFX(AM) Hattiesburg, Illinois
WFGL Fitchburg, Massachusetts
WFGN Gaffney, South Carolina
WFHG Bristol, Virginia
WFHK Pell City, Alabama
WFHR Wisconsin Rapids, Wisconsin
WFHT Avon Park, Florida
WFIA Louisville, Kentucky
WFIC Collinsville, Virginia
WFIF Milford, Connecticut
WFIL Philadelphia, Pennsylvania
WFIN Findlay, Ohio
WFIR Roanoke, Virginia
WFIW Fairfield, Illinois
WFJS Trenton, New Jersey
WFJX Roanoke, Virginia
WFKJ Cashtown, Pennsylvania
WFKN Franklin, Kentucky
WFLA Tampa, Florida
WFLE Flemingsburg, Kentucky
WFLF Pine Hills, Florida
WFLI Lookout Mountain, Tennessee
WFLL Fort Lauderdale, Florida
WFLN Arcadia, Florida
WFLO Farmville, Virginia
WFLR Dundee, New York
WFLT Flint, Michigan
WFLW Monticello, Kentucky
WFMB Springfield, Illinois
WFMC Goldsboro, North Carolina
WFMD Frederick, Maryland
WFMH Cullman, Alabama
WFMO Fairmont, North Carolina
WFMW Madisonville, Kentucky
WFNC Fayetteville, North Carolina
WFNF Brazil, Indiana
WFNI Indianapolis, Indiana
WFNL Raleigh, North Carolina
WFNN Erie, Pennsylvania
WFNO Norco, Louisiana
WFNR Blacksburg, Virginia
WFNS Blackshear, Georgia
WFNT Flint, Michigan
WFNW Naugatuck, Connecticut
WFNY Gloversville, New York
WFNZ Charlotte, North Carolina
WFOB Fostoria, Ohio
WFOM Marietta, Georgia
WFOR Hattiesburg, Mississippi
WFOY St. Augustine, Florida
WFPA Fort Payne, Alabama
WFPB Orleans, Massachusetts
WFPR Hammond, Louisiana
WFQY Brandon, Mississippi
WFRA Franklin, Pennsylvania
WFRB Frostburg, Maryland
WFRF Tallahassee, Florida
WFRL Freeport, Illinois
WFRM Coudersport, Pennsylvania
WFRX West Frankfort, Illinois
WFSC Franklin, North Carolina
WFSI Baltimore, Maryland
WFSP Kingwood, West Virginia
WFSR Harlan, Kentucky
WFST Caribou, Maine
WFTD Marietta, Georgia
WFTG London, Kentucky
WFTH Richmond, Virginia
WFTL West Palm Beach, Florida
WFTM Maysville, Kentucky
WFTN Franklin, New Hampshire
WFTR Front Royal, Virginia
WFTU Riverhead, New York
WFTW Fort Walton Beach, Florida
WFUN Ashtabula, Ohio
WFUR Grand Rapids, Michigan
WFVA Fredericksburg, Virginia
WFWL Camden, Tennessee
WFWN Fort Myers, Florida
WFXJ Jacksonville, Florida
WFXN Moline, Illinois
WFXY Middlesboro, Kentucky
WFYC Alma, Michigan
WFYL King of Prussia, Pennsylvania
WFZX Anniston, Alabama
WGAB Newburgh, Indiana
WGAC Augusta, Georgia
WGAD Rainbow City, Alabama
WGAI Elizabeth City, North Carolina
WGAM Manchester, New Hampshire
WGAM(AM) Manchester, New Hampshire
WGAN Portland, Maine
WGAP Maryville, Tennessee
WGAS South Gastonia, North Carolina
WGAT Gate City, Virginia
WGAU Athens, Georgia
WGAW Gardner, Massachusetts
WGBB Freeport, New York
WGBF Evansville, Indiana
WGBN New Kensington, Pennsylvania
WGBR Goldsboro, North Carolina
WGBW Denmark, Wisconsin
WGCD Chester, South Carolina
WGCH Greenwich, Connecticut
WGCL Bloomington, Indiana
WGCM Gulfport, Mississippi
WGCR Pisgah Forest, North Carolina
WGCV Cayce, South Carolina
WGDJ Rensselaer, New York
WGDL Lares, Puerto Rico
WGDN Gladwin, Michigan
WGEA Geneva, Alabama
WGEM Quincy, Illinois
WGES St. Petersburg, Florida
WGET Gettysburg, Pennsylvania
WGEZ Beloit, Wisconsin
WGFA Watseka, Illinois
WGFC Floyd, Virginia
WGFP Webster, Massachusetts
WGFS Covington, Georgia
WGFT Campbell, Ohio
WGFY Charlotte, North Carolina
WGGA Gainesville, Georgia
WGGG Gainesville, Florida
WGGH Marion, Illinois
WGGO Salamanca, New York
WGH Newport News, Virginia
WGHB Farmville, North Carolina
WGHM Nashua, New Hampshire
WGHN Grand Haven, Michigan
WGHQ Kingston, New York
WGHT Pompton Lakes, New Jersey
WGIG Brunswick, Georgia
WGIL Galesburg, Illinois
WGIN Biddeford, Maine
WGIR Manchester, New Hampshire
WGIT Canovanas, Puerto Rico
WGIV Pineville, North Carolina
WGJK Rome, Georgia
WGKA Atlanta, Georgia
WGL Fort Wayne, Indiana
WGLB Elm Grove, Wisconsin
WGLD Manchester Township, Pennsylvania
WGLL Auburn, Indiana
WGLM Greenville, Michigan
WGMA Spindale, North Carolina
WGMF Tunkhannock, Pennsylvania
WGMI Bremen, Georgia
WGML Hinesville, Georgia
WGMN Roanoke, Virginia
WGMP Montgomery, Alabama
WGN(AM) Chicago, Illinois
WGNC Gastonia, North Carolina
WGNR-AM Anderson, Indiana
WGNS Murfreesboro, Tennessee
WGNU Granite City, Illinois
WGNY Newburgh, New York
WGNZ Fairborn, Ohio
WGOC Kingsport, Tennessee
WGOH Grayson, Kentucky
WGOK Mobile, Alabama
WGOL Russellville, Alabama
WGOP Pocomoke City, Maryland
WGOS High Point, North Carolina
WGOW Chattanooga, Tennessee
WGPA Bethlehem, Pennsylvania
WGPC Albany, Georgia
WGPL Portsmouth, Virginia
WGR Buffalo, New York
WGRA Cairo, Georgia
WGRB Chicago, Illinois
WGRI Cincinnati, Ohio
WGRK Jeffersontown, Kentucky
WGRM Greenwood, Mississippi
WGRO Lake City, Florida
WGRP Greenville, Pennsylvania
WGRV Greeneville, Tennessee
WGRY Grayling, Michigan
WGSB Mebane, North Carolina
WGSF Memphis, Tennessee
WGSO New Orleans, Louisiana
WGSP Charlotte, North Carolina
WGST Atlanta, Georgia
WGSV Guntersville, Alabama
WGTA Summerville, Georgia
WGTH Richlands, Virginia
WGTJ Murrayville, Georgia
WGTK Louisville, Kentucky
WGTN Georgetown, South Carolina
WGTO Cassopolis, Michigan
WGUL Dunedin, Florida
WGUN Valdosta, Georgia
WGVA Geneva, New York
WGVL Greenville, South Carolina
WGVM Greenville, Mississippi
WGVS Muskegon, Michigan
WGVU Kentwood, Michigan
WGWM London, Kentucky
WGY Schenectady, New York
WGYM Hammonton, New Jersey
WGYV Greenville, Alabama
WHA Madison, Wisconsin
WHAG Halfway, Maryland
WHAK Rogers City, Michigan
WHAL Phenix City/Columbus, Alabama
WHAM Rochester, New York
WHAN Ashland, Virginia
WHAP Hopewell, Virginia
WHAS Louisville, Kentucky
WHAT Philadelphia, Pennsylvania
WHAW Lost Creek, West Virginia
WHAZ Troy, New York
WHB Kansas City, Missouri
WHBB Selma, Alabama
WHBC Canton, Ohio
WHBE Newburg, Kentucky
WHBG Harrisonburg, Virginia
WHBK Marshall, North Carolina
WHBL Sheboygan, Wisconsin
WHBN Harrodsburg, Kentucky
WHBO Pinellas Park, Florida
WHBQ Memphis, Tennessee
WHBT Tallahassee, Florida
WHBU Anderson, Indiana
WHBY Kimberly, Wisconsin
WHCG Metter, Georgia
WHCO Sparta, Illinois
WHCU Ithaca, New York
WHDD Sharon, Connecticut
WHDL Olean, New York
WHDM McKenzie, Tennessee
WHEE Martinsville, Virginia
WHEN Syracuse, New York
WHEO Stuart, Virginia
WHEP Foley, Alabama
WHEW Franklin, Tennessee
WHFA Poynette, Wisconsin
WHFB Benton Harbor-St. Jo, Michigan
WHFS Seffner, Florida
WHGB Harrisburg, Pennsylvania
WHGG Kingsport, Tennessee
WHGS Hampton, South Carolina
WHGT Maugansville, Maryland
WHHQ Bridgeport, Michigan
WHHV Hillsville, Virginia
WHHW Hilton Head Island, South Carolina
WHIC Rochester, New York
WHIE Griffin, Georgia
WHIM Coral Gables, Florida
WHIM(AM) Coral Gables, Florida
WHIN Gallatin, Tennessee
WHIO Dayton, Ohio
WHIP Mooresville, North Carolina
WHIR Danville, Kentucky
WHIS Bluefield, West Virginia
WHIT Madison, Wisconsin
WHIY Huntsville, Alabama
WHJA Laurel, Mississippi
WHJC Matewan, West Virginia
WHJD Hazlehurst, Georgia
WHJJ Providence, Rhode Island
WHK Cleveland, Ohio
WHKP Hendersonville, North Carolina
WHKT Portsmouth, Virginia
WHKW Cleveland, Ohio
WHKY Hickory, North Carolina
WHKZ Warren, Ohio
WHLD Niagara Falls, New York
WHLI Hempstead, New York
WHLJ(AM) Moultrie, Georgia
WHLL Springfield, Massachusetts
WHLM Bloomsburg, Pennsylvania
WHLN Harlan, Kentucky
WHLO Akron, Ohio
WHLS Port Huron, Michigan
WHLX Marine City, Michigan
WHLY South Bend, Indiana
WHMA Anniston, Alabama
WHMP Northampton, Massachusetts
WHMQ Greenfield, Massachusetts
WHMT(AM) Tullahoma, Tennessee
WHNC Henderson, North Carolina
WHNK Parkersburg, West Virginia
WHNP East Longmeadow, Massachusetts
WHNR Cypress Gardens, Florida
WHNZ Tampa, Florida
WHO Des Moines, Iowa
WHOC Philadelphia, Mississippi
WHOG Hobson City, Alabama
WHOL Allentown, Pennsylvania
WHON Centerville, Indiana
WHOO Kissimmee, Florida
WHOP Hopkinsville, Kentucky
WHOS Decatur, Alabama
WHOW Clinton, Illinois
WHOY Salinas, Puerto Rico
WHP Harrisburg, Pennsylvania
WHPY Clayton, North Carolina
WHRY Hurley, Wisconsin
WHSM Hayward, Wisconsin
WHSR Pompano Beach, Florida
WHSY Hattiesburg, Mississippi
WHTB Fall River, Massachusetts
WHTC Holland, Michigan
WHTG Eatontown, New Jersey
WHTH Heath, Ohio
WHTK Rochester, New York
WHTX Warren, Ohio
WHTY(AM) Riviera Beach, Florida
WHUB Cookeville, Tennessee
WHUC Hudson, New York
WHUN Huntingdon, Pennsylvania
WHUN Huntingdon, Pennsylvania
WHVN Charlotte, North Carolina
WHVO Hopkinsville, Kentucky
WHVR Hanover, Pennsylvania
WHVW Hyde Park, New York
WHWH Princeton, New Jersey
WHYF(AM) Shiremanstown, Pennsylvania
WHYL Carlisle, Pennsylvania
WHYM Lake City, South Carolina
WHYN Springfield, Massachusetts
WIAC San Juan, Puerto Rico
WIAM Williamston, North Carolina
WIAN Ishpeming, Michigan
WIBA Madison, Wisconsin
WIBG Ocean City/Somers Po, New Jersey
WIBH Anna, Illinois
WIBM Jackson, Michigan

WIBQ Terre Haute, Indiana
WIBR Baton Rouge, Louisiana
WIBS Guayama, Puerto Rico
WIBW Topeka, Kansas
WIBX Utica, New York
WICC Bridgeport, Connecticut
WICH Norwich, Connecticut
WICK Scranton, Pennsylvania
WICO Salisbury, Maryland
WICY Malone, New York
WIDA Carolina, Puerto Rico
WIDG St. Ignace, Michigan
WIDS Russell Springs, Kentucky
WIDU Fayetteville, North Carolina
WIEL Elizabethtown, Kentucky
WIEZ Lewistown, Pennsylvania
WIFA Knoxville, Tennessee
WIFI Florence, New Jersey
WIFN Atlanta, Georgia
WIGM Medford, Wisconsin
WIGN Bristol, Tennessee
WIGO Morrow, Georgia
WIHB Macon, Georgia
WIHM Taylorville, Illinois
WIIN Ridgeland, Mississippi
WIJD Prichard, Alabama
WIJK(AM) Ocean City, Maryland
WIJR Highland, Illinois
WIKE Newport, Vermont
WILB Canton, Ohio
WILC Laurel, Maryland
WILD Boston, Massachusetts
WILE Cambridge, Ohio
WILI Willimantic, Connecticut
WILK Wilkes-Barre, Pennsylvania
WILL Urbana, Illinois
WILM Wilmington, Delaware
WILO Frankfort, Indiana
WILS Lansing, Michigan
WILY Centralia, Illinois
WIMA Lima, Ohio
WIMG Ewing, New Jersey
WIMO Winder, Georgia
WIMS Michigan City, Indiana
WINA Charlottesville, Virginia
WINC Winchester, Virginia
WIND Chicago, Illinois
WINE Brookfield, Connecticut
WING Dayton, Ohio
WINI Murphysboro, Illinois
WINR Binghamton, New York
WINS New York, New York
WINT Willoughby, Ohio
WINU Shelbyville, Illinois
WINW Canton, Ohio
WINY Putnam, Connecticut
WINZ Miami, Florida
WIOD Miami, Florida
WIOI New Boston, Ohio
WIOL Columbus, Georgia
WION Ionia, Michigan
WIOO Carlisle, Pennsylvania
WIOS Tawas City-East Tawas, Michigan
WIOU Kokomo, Indiana
WIOV Reading, Pennsylvania
WIOZ Pinehurst, North Carolina
WIPC Lake Wales, Florida
WIPR San Juan, Puerto Rico
WIQB Conway, South Carolina
WIQR Prattville, Alabama
WIRA Fort Pierce, Florida
WIRB Level Plains, Alabama
WIRD Lake Placid, New York
WIRJ Humboldt, Tennessee
WIRL Peoria, Illinois
WIRO Ironton, Ohio
WIRV Irvine, Kentucky
WIRY Plattsburgh, New York
WISA Isabela, Puerto Rico
WISE Asheville, North Carolina
WISK Lawrenceville, Georgia
WISN Milwaukee, Wisconsin
WISO Ponce, Puerto Rico
WISP Doylestown, Pennsylvania
WISR Butler, Pennsylvania
WISS Berlin, Wisconsin
WISW Columbia, South Carolina
WITA Knoxville, Tennessee
WITK Pittston, Pennsylvania
WITM Marion, Virginia
WITS Sebring, Florida
WITZ Jasper, Indiana
WIVV Island of Vieques, Puerto Rico
WIWA St. Cloud, Florida
WIXC Titusville, Florida
WIXE Monroe, North Carolina
WIXI Jasper, Alabama
WIXK New Richmond, Wisconsin
WIXN Dixon, Illinois
WIXT Little Falls, New York
WIYD Palatka, Florida
WIZD Neon, Kentucky
WIZE Springfield, Ohio
WIZK Bay Springs, Mississippi
WIZM-AM La Crosse, Wisconsin
WIZR Johnstown, New York
WIZS Henderson, North Carolina
WIZZ Greenfield, Massachusetts
WJAG Norfolk, Nebraska
WJAM Selma, Alabama
WJAS Pittsburgh, Pennsylvania
WJAT Swainsboro, Georgia
WJAW St. Marys, West Virginia
WJAX Jacksonville, Florida
WJAY Mullins, South Carolina
WJBC Bloomington, Illinois
WJBD Salem, Illinois
WJBE Powell, Tennessee
WJBI Batesville, Mississippi
WJBM Jerseyville, Illinois
WJBO Baton Rouge, Louisiana
WJBS Holly Hill, South Carolina
WJBW Jupiter, Florida
WJBX North Fort Myers, Florida
WJCM Sebring, Florida
WJCP North Vernon, Indiana
WJCV Jacksonville, North Carolina
WJCW Johnson City, Tennessee
WJDA Quincy, Massachusetts
WJDB Thomasville, Alabama
WJDM Elizabeth, New Jersey
WJDX Jackson, Mississippi
WJDY Salisbury, Maryland
WJEH Gallipolis, Ohio
WJEJ Hagerstown, Maryland
WJEM Valdosta, Georgia
WJER Dover-New Philadelphia, Ohio
WJET Erie, Pennsylvania
WJFC Jefferson City, Tennessee
WJFJ Tryon, North Carolina
WJFK Morningside, District of Columbia
WJHX Lexington, Alabama
WJIB Cambridge, Massachusetts
WJIL Jacksonville, Illinois
WJIM Lansing, Michigan
WJIP Ellenville, New York
WJIT Sabana, Puerto Rico
WJJC Commerce, Georgia
WJJG Elmhurst, Illinois
WJJL Niagara Falls, New York
WJJM Lewisburg, Tennessee
WJJQ Tomahawk, Wisconsin
WJJT Jellico, Tennessee
WJKB Moncks Corner, South Carolina
WJKN Jackson, Michigan
WJKY Jamestown, Kentucky
WJLD(AM) Fairfield, Alabama
WJLE Smithville, Tennessee
WJLG Savannah, Georgia
WJLS Beckley, West Virginia
WJLX Jasper, Alabama
WJMC Rice Lake, Wisconsin
WJML Petoskey, Michigan
WJMO Cleveland, Ohio
WJMP Kent, Ohio
WJMS Ironwood, Michigan
WJMT Merrill, Wisconsin
WJMX Darlington, South Carolina
WJNA Ashland City, Tennessee
WJNC Jacksonville, North Carolina
WJNL Kingsley, Michigan
WJNO West Palm Beach, Florida
WJNT Pearl, Mississippi
WJNX Fort Pierce, Florida
WJOB Hammond, Indiana
WJOC Chattanooga, Tennessee
WJOI Norfolk, Virginia
WJOK Kaukauna, Wisconsin
WJOL Joliet, Illinois
WJON St. Cloud, Minnesota
WJOT Wabash, Indiana
WJOX Birmingham, Alabama
WJOY Burlington, Vermont
WJPA Washington, Pennsylvania
WJPF Herrin, Illinois
WJQS Jackson, Mississippi
WJR Detroit, Michigan
WJRD Tuscaloosa, Alabama
WJRI Lenoir, North Carolina
WJRM Troy, North Carolina
WJRW Grand Rapids, Michigan
WJSB Crestview, Florida
WJSS Havre De Grace, Maryland
WJST New Castle, Pennsylvania
WJTB North Ridgeville, Ohio
WJTH Calhoun, Georgia
WJTI West Allis, Wisconsin
WJTN Jamestown, New York
WJTO Bath, Maine
WJTP Lithia Springs, Georgia
WJUA Pine Island Center, Florida
WJUB Plymouth, Wisconsin
WJUL Hiawassee, Georgia
WJUN Mexico, Pennsylvania
WJUS Marion, Alabama
WJWF Columbus, Mississippi
WJWK Seaford, Delaware
WJWL Georgetown, Delaware
WJXL Jacksonville Beach, Florida
WJYI Milwaukee, Wisconsin
WJYK Chase City, Virginia
WJYM Bowling Green, Ohio
WJYP St. Albans, West Virginia
WJYZ Albany, Georgia
WJZ Baltimore, Maryland
WJZI(AM) Decatur, Indiana
WJZM Clarksville, Tennessee
WJZN Augusta, Maine
WKAC Athens, Alabama
WKAL Rome, New York
WKAM Goshen, Indiana
WKAN Kankakee, Illinois
WKAQ San Juan, Puerto Rico
WKAR East Lansing, Michigan
WKAT North Miami, Florida
WKAV Charlottesville, Virginia
WKAX Russellville, Alabama
WKAZ Charleston, West Virginia
WKBA Vinton, Virginia
WKBC North Wilkesboro, North Carolina
WKBF Rock Island, Illinois
WKBH Holmen, Wisconsin
WKBI St. Marys, Pennsylvania
WKBK Keene, New Hampshire
WKBL Covington, Tennessee
WKBN Youngstown, Ohio
WKBO Harrisburg, Pennsylvania
WKBV Richmond, Indiana
WKBY Chatham, Virginia
WKBZ Muskegon, Michigan
WKCB Hindman, Kentucky
WKCE Maryville, Tennessee
WKCI Waynesboro, Virginia
WKCM Hawesville, Kentucky
WKCT Bowling Green, Kentucky
WKCU Corinth, Mississippi
WKCW Warrenton, Virginia
WKCY Harrisonburg, Virginia
WKDA Lebanon, Tennessee
WKDE Altavista, Virginia
WKDI Denton, Maryland
WKDK Newberry, South Carolina
WKDL Warrenton, Virginia
WKDM New York, New York
WKDN Philadelphia, Pennsylvania
WKDO Liberty, Kentucky
WKDP Corbin, Kentucky
WKDR Berlin, New Hampshire
WKDV Manassas, Virginia
WKDW Staunton, Virginia
WKDX Hamlet, North Carolina
WKDZ Cadiz, Kentucky
WKEI Kewanee, Illinois
WKEU Griffin, Georgia
WKEW Greensboro, North Carolina
WKEX Blacksburg, Virginia
WKEY Covington, Virginia
WKEZ Bluefield, West Virginia
WKFB Jeannette, Pennsylvania
WKFE Yauco, Puerto Rico
WKFI Wilmington, Ohio
WKFL Bushnell, Florida
WKFN Clarksville, Tennessee
WKGC Southport, Florida
WKGE Johnstown, Pennsylvania
WKGM Smithfield, Virginia
WKGN Knoxville, Tennessee
WKGX Lenoir, North Carolina
WKHB Irwin, Pennsylvania
WKHM Jackson, Michigan
WKHZ Easton, Maryland
WKIC(AM) Hazard, Kentucky
WKII Solana, Florida
WKIK La Plata, Maryland
WKIP Poughkeepsie, New York
WKIQ Eustis, Florida
WKIZ Key West, Florida
WKJB Mayaguez, Puerto Rico
WKJG Fort Wayne, Indiana
WKJK Louisville, Kentucky
WKJR Rantoul, Illinois
WKJW Black Mountain, North Carolina
WKJW Black Mountain, North Carolina
WKKP McDonough, Georgia
WKKS Vanceburg, Kentucky
WKKX Wheeling, West Virginia
WKLA Ludington, Michigan
WKLB Manchester, Kentucky
WKLJ Sparta, Wisconsin
WKLK Cloquet, Minnesota
WKLP Keyser, West Virginia
WKLQ Whitehall, Michigan
WKLV Blackstone, Virginia
WKLY Hartwell, Georgia
WKMB Stirling, New Jersey
WKMC Roaring Spring, Pennsylvania
WKMG Newberry, South Carolina
WKMI Kalamazoo, Michigan
WKMQ Tupelo, Mississippi
WKND Windsor, Connecticut
WKNG Tallapoosa, Georgia
WKNR Cleveland, Ohio
WKNV Fairlawn, Virginia
WKNW Sault Sainte Marie, Michigan
WKNY Kingston, New York
WKOK Sunbury, Pennsylvania
WKOX Everett, Massachusetts
WKPA Lynchburg, Virginia
WKPR Kalamazoo, Michigan
WKPT Kingsport, Tennessee
WKQW Oil City, Pennsylvania
WKRA Holly Springs, Mississippi
WKRC Cincinnati, Ohio
WKRD Louisville, Kentucky
WKRK Murphy, North Carolina
WKRM Columbia, Tennessee
WKRO Cairo, Illinois
WKRS Waukegan, Illinois
WKSC Kershaw, South Carolina
WKSH Sussex, Wisconsin
WKSK West Jefferson, North Carolina
WKSN Jamestown, New York
WKSP Hope Valley, Rhode Island
WKSR Pulaski, Tennessee
WKST New Castle, Pennsylvania
WKTA Evanston, Illinois
WKTE King, North Carolina
WKTF Vienna, Georgia
WKTP Jonesborough, Tennessee
WKTQ South Paris, Maine
WKTR Earlysville, Virginia
WKTX Cortland, Ohio
WKTY La Crosse, Wisconsin
WKUN Monroe, Georgia
WKVA Lewistown, Pennsylvania
WKVG Jenkins, Kentucky
WKVI Knox, Indiana
WKVL Knoxville, Tennessee
WKVM San Juan, Puerto Rico
WKVQ Eatonton, Georgia
WKVT Brattleboro, Vermont
WKVX Wooster, Ohio
WKWF Key West, Florida
WKWL Florala, Alabama
WKWN Trenton, Georgia
WKXG Greenwood, Mississippi
WKXL Concord, New Hampshire
WKXM Winfield, Alabama
WKXO Berea, Kentucky
WKXR Asheboro, North Carolina
WKXV Knoxville, Tennessee
WKY Oklahoma City, Oklahoma
WKYH Paintsville, Kentucky
WKYK Burnsville, North Carolina

WKYO Caro, Michigan
WKYW Frankfort, Kentucky
WKYX Paducah, Kentucky
WKZD Priceville, Alabama
WKZI Casey, Illinois
WKZK North Augusta, South Carolina
WKZN West Hazleton, Pennsylvania
WKZO Kalamazoo, Michigan
WLAA Winter Garden, Florida
WLAC Nashville, Tennessee
WLAD Danbury, Connecticut
WLAF La Follette, Tennessee
WLAG La Grange, Georgia
WLAM Lewiston, Maine
WLAN Lancaster, Pennsylvania
WLAP Lexington, Kentucky
WLAQ Rome, Georgia
WLAR Athens, Tennessee
WLAT New Britain, Connecticut
WLAY Muscle Shoals, Alabama
WLBA Gainesville, Georgia
WLBB Carrollton, Georgia
WLBE Leesburg-Eustis, Florida
WLBG Laurens, South Carolina
WLBH Mattoon, Illinois
WLBK Dekalb, Illinois
WLBL Auburndale, Wisconsin
WLBN Lebanon, Kentucky
WLBQ Morgantown, Kentucky
WLBR Lebanon, Pennsylvania
WLBY Saline, Michigan
WLCC Brandon, Florida
WLCK Scottsville, Kentucky
WLCM Holt, Michigan
WLCO Lapeer, Michigan
WLCR Mt Washington, Kentucky
WLDS Jacksonville, Illinois
WLDX Fayette, Alabama
WLDY Ladysmith, Wisconsin
WLEA Hornell, New York
WLEC Sandusky, Ohio
WLEE Richmond, Virginia
WLEM Emporium, Pennsylvania
WLEO Ponce, Puerto Rico
WLES Bon Air, Virginia
WLEW Bad Axe, Michigan
WLEY Cayey, Puerto Rico
WLFJ Greenville, South Carolina
WLFN La Crosse, Wisconsin
WLFZ Fort Campbell, Kentucky
WLGC Greenup, Kentucky
WLGN Logan, Ohio
WLIB New York, New York
WLIE Islip, New York
WLIJ Shelbyville, Tennessee
WLIK Newport, Tennessee
WLIL Lenoir City, Tennessee
WLIM Patchogue, New York
WLIP Kenosha, Wisconsin
WLIQ Quincy, Illinois
WLIS Old Saybrook, Connecticut
WLIV Livingston, Tennessee
WLJN Elmwood Township, Michigan
WLJW Cadillac, Michigan
WLKD Minocqua, Wisconsin
WLKF Lakeland, Florida
WLKR Norwalk, Ohio
WLKS West Liberty, Kentucky
WLKW West Warwick, Rhode Island
WLLH Lowell, Massachusetts
WLLI Somerset, Pennsylvania
WLLL Lynchburg, Virginia
WLLM Lincoln, Illinois
WLLN Lillington, North Carolina
WLLQ Chapel Hill, North Carolina
WLLV Louisville, Kentucky
WLLY Wilson, North Carolina
WLMC Georgetown, South Carolina
WLMR Chattanooga, Tennessee
WLMV Madison, Wisconsin
WLNC Laurinburg, North Carolina
WLNL Horseheads, New York
WLNO New Orleans, Louisiana
WLNR Kinston, North Carolina
WLOA Farrell, Pennsylvania
WLOB Portland, Maine
WLOC Munfordville, Kentucky
WLOD Loudon, Tennessee
WLOE Eden, North Carolina
WLOH Lancaster, Ohio
WLOI La Porte, Indiana
WLOK Memphis, Tennessee
WLOL Minneapolis, Minnesota
WLON Lincolnton, North Carolina
WLOP Jesup, Georgia
WLOR Huntsville, Alabama
WLOU Louisville, Kentucky
WLOV Washington, Georgia
WLOY Rural Retreat, Virginia
WLPA Lancaster, Pennsylvania
WLPK Connersville, Indiana
WLPO Lasalle, Illinois
WLPR Prichard, Alabama
WLPR-AM Mobile, Alabama
WLQH Chiefland, Florida
WLQM Franklin, Virginia
WLQR Toledo, Ohio
WLQV Detroit, Michigan
WLQY Hollywood, Florida
WLRB Macomb, Illinois
WLRC Walnut, Mississippi
WLRM Millington, Tennessee
WLRO Denham Springs, Louisiana
WLRP San Sebastian, Puerto Rico
WLRS Eminence, Kentucky
WLRV Lebanon, Virginia
WLS Chicago, Illinois
WLSC Loris, South Carolina
WLSD Big Stone Gap, Virginia
WLSG Wilmington, North Carolina
WLSH Lansford, Pennsylvania
WLSI Pikeville, Kentucky
WLSS Sarasota, Florida
WLSV Wellsville, New York
WLTA Alpharetta, Georgia
WLTG Panama City, Florida
WLTH Gary, Indiana
WLTI New Castle, Indiana
WLTN Littleton, New Hampshire
WLTP Marietta, Ohio
WLTQ Charleston, South Carolina
WLUV Loves Park, Illinois
WLUX Dunbar, West Virginia
WLVA Lynchburg, Virginia
WLVJ Boynton Beach, Florida
WLVL Lockport, New York
WLVP Gorham, Maine
WLW Cincinnati, Ohio
WLWB New Holstein, Wisconsin
WLWE Roanoke, Alabama
WLWI Montgomery, Alabama
WLWL Rockingham, North Carolina
WLXE Rockville, Maryland
WLXG Lexington, Kentucky
WLXN Lexington, North Carolina
WLYC Williamsport, Pennsylvania
WLYG Centre, Alabama
WLYN Lynn, Massachusetts
WLYV Fort Wayne, Indiana
WLYV-AM Laurel, Delaware
WLYV-AM Georgetown, Delaware
WLYY Copper Hill, Tennessee
WLZR(AM) Melbourne, Florida
WMAC Macon, Georgia
WMAF Madison, Florida
WMAK Lobelville, Tennessee
WMAL Washington, District of Columbia
WMAM Marinette, Wisconsin
WMAN Mansfield, Ohio
WMAX Bay City, Michigan
WMAY Springfield, Illinois
WMBA Ambridge, Pennsylvania
WMBD Peoria, Illinois
WMBG Williamsburg, Virginia
WMBH Joplin, Missouri
WMBI-AM Chicago, Illinois
WMBM Miami Beach, Florida
WMBN Petoskey, Michigan
WMBO Auburn, New York
WMBS Uniontown, Pennsylvania
WMC Memphis, Tennessee
WMCA New York, New York
WMCE North East, Pennsylvania
WMCH Church Hill, Tennessee
WMCJ & WMCJ Cullman, Alabama
WMCL McLeansboro, Illinois
WMCP Columbia, Tennessee
WMCR Oneida, New York
WMCT Mountain City, Tennessee
WMDB Nashville, Tennessee
WMDD Fajardo, Puerto Rico
WMDR Augusta, Maine
WMEJ Bay St. Louis, Mississippi
WMEL Cocoa Beach, Florida
WMEN Royal Palm Beach, Florida
WMEQ Menomonie, Wisconsin
WMER Meridian, Mississippi
WMET Gaithersburg, Maryland
WMFA Raeford, North Carolina
WMFD Wilmington, North Carolina
WMFG-AM Hibbing, Minnesota
WMFJ Daytona Beach, Florida
WMFN Zeeland, Michigan
WMFR High Point, North Carolina
WMGC Murfreesboro, Tennessee
WMGG Egypt Lake, Florida
WMGJ Gadsden, Alabama
WMGO Canton, Mississippi
WMGR Bainbridge, Georgia
WMGW Meadville, Pennsylvania
WMGY Montgomery, Alabama
WMIA Arecibo, Puerto Rico
WMIC Sandusky, Michigan
WMID Atlantic City, New Jersey
WMIK Middlesboro, Kentucky
WMIN Sauk Rapids, Minnesota
WMIQ Iron Mountain, Michigan
WMIR Atlantic Beach, South Carolina
WMIS Natchez, Mississippi
WMIX Mount Vernon, Illinois
WMIZ Vineland, New Jersey
WMJH Rockford, Michigan
WMJL Marion, Kentucky
WMJR Nicholasville, Kentucky
WMKI Boston, Massachusetts
WMKT Charlevoix, Michigan
WMLB Avondale Estates, Georgia
WMLC Monticello, Mississippi
WMLM St. Louis, Michigan
WMLP Milton, Pennsylvania
WMLR Hohenwald, Tennessee
WMLT Dublin, Georgia
WMMB Melbourne, Florida
WMMG Brandenburg, Kentucky
WMMI Shepherd, Michigan
WMML Glens Falls, New York
WMMN Fairmont, West Virginia
WMMV Cocoa, Florida
WMMW Meriden, Connecticut
WMNA Gretna, Virginia
WMNC Morganton, North Carolina
WMNI Columbus, Ohio
WMNT Manati, Puerto Rico
WMNY McKeesport, Pennsylvania
WMNZ Montezuma, Georgia
WMOA Marietta, Ohio
WMOB Mobile, Alabama
WMOH Hamilton, Ohio
WMOK Metropolis, Illinois
WMON Montgomery, West Virginia
WMOP Ocala, Florida
WMOR Morehead, Kentucky
WMOU Berlin, New Hampshire
WMOV Ravenswood, West Virginia
WMOX Meridian, Mississippi
WMPC Lapeer, Michigan
WMPL Hancock, Michigan
WMPM Smithfield, North Carolina
WMPO Middleport-Pomeroy, Ohio
WMPS Bartlett, Tennessee
WMPW Danville, Virginia
WMPX Midland, Michigan
WMQM Lakeland, Tennessee
WMRB Columbia, Tennessee
WMRC Milford, Massachusetts
WMRD Middletown, Connecticut
WMRE Charlestown, West Virginia
WMRI Marion, Indiana
WMRN Marion, Ohio
WMRO Gallatin, Tennessee
WMSA Massena, New York
WMSG Oakland, Maryland
WMSK Morganfield, Kentucky
WMSP Montgomery, Alabama
WMSR Manchester, Tennessee
WMST Mount Sterling, Kentucky
WMSW Hatillo, Puerto Rico
WMSX Brockton, Massachusetts
WMT Cedar Rapids, Iowa
WMTA Central City, Kentucky
WMTD Hinton, West Virginia
WMTE Manistee, Michigan
WMTL Leitchfield, Kentucky
WMTM Moultrie, Georgia
WMTN Morristown, Tennessee
WMTR Morristown, New Jersey
WMTY Farragut, Tennessee
WMUX Hurricane, West Virginia
WMVA Martinsville, Virginia
WMVB Millville, New Jersey
WMVG Milledgeville, Georgia
WMVO Mount Vernon, Ohio
WMVP Chicago, Illinois
WMVX Salem, New Hampshire
WMXB Tuscaloosa, Alabama
WMXF Waynesville, North Carolina
WMYF Portsmouth, New Hampshire
WMYJ Martinsville, Indiana
WMYM Miami, Florida
WMYN Mayodan, North Carolina
WMYR Fort Myers, Florida
WNAE Warren, Pennsylvania
WNAH Nashville, Tennessee
WNAM Neenah-Menasha, Wisconsin
WNAP Norristown, Pennsylvania
WNAT Natchez, Mississippi
WNAU New Albany, Mississippi
WNAV Annapolis, Maryland
WNAW North Adams, Massachusetts
WNAX Yankton, South Dakota
WNBF Binghamton, New York
WNBH New Bedford, Massachusetts
WNBN Meridian, Mississippi
WNBP Newburyport, Massachusetts
WNBS Murray, Kentucky
WNBT Wellsboro, Pennsylvania
WNBY Newberry, Michigan
WNBZ Saranac Lake, New York
WNCA Siler City, North Carolina
WNCC Barnesboro, Pennsylvania
WNCO Ashland, Ohio
WNCT Greenville, North Carolina
WNDA New Albany, Indiana
WNDB Daytona Beach, Florida
WNDE Indianapolis, Indiana
WNDI Sullivan, Indiana
WNDZ Portage, Indiana
WNEA Newnan, Georgia
WNEB Worcester, Massachusetts
WNEG Toccoa, Georgia
WNEL Caguas, Puerto Rico
WNER Watertown, New York
WNES Central City, Kentucky
WNEX Macon, Georgia
WNEZ Manchester, Connecticut
WNFL-AM Green Bay, Wisconsin
WNFO Sun City-Hilton Head, South Carolina
WNGL Mobile, Alabama
WNGO Mayfield, Kentucky
WNIK Arecibo, Puerto Rico
WNIO Youngstown, Ohio
WNIS Norfolk, Virginia
WNIV Atlanta, Georgia
WNIX Greenville, Mississippi
WNJC Vineland, New Jersey
WNJE Trenton, New Jersey
WNLA Indianola, Mississippi
WNLK Norwalk, Connecticut
WNLR Churchville, Virginia
WNMA Miami Springs, Florida
WNMB North Myrtle Beach, South Carolina
WNML Knoxville, Tennessee
WNMT Nashwauk, Minnesota
WNNC Newton, North Carolina
WNNR Jacksonville, Florida
WNNW Lawrence, Massachusetts
WNNZ Westfield, Massachusetts
WNOG Naples, Florida
WNOO Chattanooga, Tennessee
WNOP Newport, Kentucky
WNOS New Bern, North Carolina
WNOV Milwaukee, Wisconsin
WNOW Mint Hill, North Carolina
WNPL Golden Gate, Florida
WNPV Lansdale, Pennsylvania
WNPZ Knoxville, Tennessee
WNQM Nashville, Tennessee
WNRA Eufaula, Alabama
WNRG Grundy, Virginia
WNRI Woonsocket, Rhode Island
WNRP Gulf Breeze, Florida
WNRR North Augusta, South Carolina
WNRS Herkimer, New York
WNRV Narrows-Pearisburg, Virginia

WNSR Brentwood, Tennessee
WNST Towson, Maryland
WNSW Newark, New Jersey
WNTA Rockford, Illinois
WNTD Chicago, Illinois
WNTF Bithlo, Florida
WNTJ Johnstown, Pennsylvania
WNTM Mobile, Alabama
WNTN Newton, Massachusetts
WNTP Philadelphia, Pennsylvania
WNTS Beech Grove, Indiana
WNTT Tazewell, Tennessee
WNTW Chester, Virginia
WNTX Fredericksburg, Virginia
WNVA Norton, Virginia
WNVL Nashville, Tennessee
WNVR Vernon Hills, Illinois
WNVY Cantonment, Florida
WNWC Sun Prairie, Wisconsin
WNWF Destin, Florida
WNWI Oak Lawn, Illinois
WNWN-AM Portage, Michigan
WNWR Philadelphia, Pennsylvania
WNWS Brownsville, Tennessee
WNWT Rossford, Ohio
WNWZ Grand Rapids, Michigan
WNXT Portsmouth, Ohio
WNYC New York, New York
WNYG Medford, New York
WNYH Huntington, New York
WNYM Hackensack, New Jersey
WNYY Ithaca, New York
WNZF Bunnell, Florida
WNZK Dearborn Heights, Michigan
WNZS Veazie, Maine
WNZZ Montgomery, Alabama
WOAD Jackson, Mississippi
WOAI San Antonio, Texas
WOAM Peoria, Illinois
WOAP Owosso, Michigan
WOAY Oak Hill, West Virginia
WOBL Oberlin, Ohio
WOBM Lakewood Township, New Jersey
WOBT Rhinelander, Wisconsin
WOBX Wanchese, North Carolina
WOC Davenport, Iowa
WOCA Ocala, Florida
WOCC Corydon, Indiana
WOCN Miami, Florida
WOCO Oconto, Wisconsin
WOCV Oneida, Tennessee
WODI Brookneal, Virginia
WODJ Big Rapids, Michigan
WODT New Orleans, Louisiana
WODY Fieldale, Virginia
WOEG Hazlehurst, Mississippi
WOEN Olean, New York
WOFC Murray, Kentucky
WOFX Troy, New York
WOGO Hallie, Wisconsin
WOGR Charlotte, North Carolina
WOHI East Liverpool, Ohio
WOHS Shelby, North Carolina
WOI Ames, Iowa
WOIC Columbia, South Carolina
WOIR Homestead, Florida
WOIZ Guayanilla, Puerto Rico
WOKA Douglas, Georgia
WOKB Winter Garden, Florida
WOKC Okeechobee, Florida
WOKS Columbus, Georgia
WOKV(AM) Jacksonville, Quebec
WOKY Milwaukee, Wisconsin
WOL Washington, District of Columbia
WOLA Barranquitas, Puerto Rico
WOLB Baltimore, Maryland
WOLF Syracuse, New York
WOLH Florence, South Carolina
WOLI Spartanburg, South Carolina
WOMI Owensboro, Kentucky
WOMN Franklinton, Louisiana
WOMP Bellaire, Ohio
WOMT Manitowoc, Wisconsin
WONA Winona, Mississippi
WOND Pleasantville, New Jersey
WONE Dayton, Ohio
WONG Canton, Mississippi
WONN Lakeland, Florida
WONQ Oviedo, Florida
WONS Cannonsburg, Kentucky
WONW Defiance, Ohio
WOOD Grand Rapids, Michigan
WOOF Dothan, Alabama
WOON Woonsocket, Rhode Island
WOPI Bristol, Tennessee
WOPP Opp, Alabama
WOQI Adjuntas, Puerto Rico
WOR New York, New York
WORA Mayaguez, Puerto Rico
WORC Worcester, Massachusetts
WORD Spartanburg, South Carolina
WORL Altamonte Springs, Florida
WORM Savannah, Tennessee
WORV Hattiesburg, Mississippi
WOSH Oshkosh, Wisconsin
WOSO San Juan, Puerto Rico
WOSW Fulton, New York
WOTE Clintonville, Wisconsin
WOTS Kissimmee, Florida
WOUB Athens, Ohio
WOWO Niles, Michigan
WOWO Fort Wayne, Indiana
WOWW Germantown, Tennessee
WOWZ Appomattox, Virginia
WOYK York, Pennsylvania
WOZK Ozark, Alabama
WOZN Madison, Wisconsin
WPAB Ponce, Puerto Rico
WPAD Paducah, Kentucky
WPAK Farmville, Virginia
WPAM Pottsville, Pennsylvania
WPAQ Mount Airy, North Carolina
WPAT Paterson, New Jersey
WPAX Thomasville, Georgia
WPAZ Pottstown, Pennsylvania
WPBC Decatur, Georgia
WPBQ Flowood, Mississippi
WPBR Lantana, Florida
WPBS Conyers, Georgia
WPCC Clinton, South Carolina
WPCE Portsmouth, Virginia
WPCF Panama City Beach, Florida
WPCH West Point, Georgia
WPCI Greenville, South Carolina
WPCM Burlington-Graham, North Carolina
WPCN Stevens Point, Wisconsin
WPDC Elizabethtown, Pennsylvania
WPDM Potsdam, New York
WPDR Portage, Wisconsin
WPDX Clarksburg, West Virginia
WPEH Louisville, Georgia
WPEK Fairview, North Carolina
WPEO Peoria, Illinois
WPET Greensboro, North Carolina
WPFB Middletown, Ohio
WPFC Baton Rouge, Louisiana
WPFJ Franklin, North Carolina
WPFP Park Falls, Wisconsin
WPFR Terre Haute, Indiana
WPGA Perry, Georgia
WPGG Atlantic City, New Jersey
WPGR Monroeville, Pennsylvania
WPGS Mims, Florida
WPGW Portland, Indiana
WPGY Ellijay, Georgia
WPHB Philipsburg, Pennsylvania
WPHE Phoenixville, Pennsylvania
WPHM Port Huron, Michigan
WPHT Philadelphia, Pennsylvania
WPIC Sharon, Pennsylvania
WPID Piedmont, Alabama
WPIE Trumansburg, New York
WPIN Dublin, Virginia
WPIP Winston-Salem, North Carolina
WPIT Pittsburgh, Pennsylvania
WPJF Greenville, South Carolina
WPJK Orangeburg, South Carolina
WPJL Raleigh, North Carolina
WPJM Greer, South Carolina
WPJS Conway, South Carolina
WPJX Zion, Illinois
WPKE Pikeville, Kentucky
WPKX Rochester, New Hampshire
WPKY Princeton, Kentucky
WPKZ Fitchburg, Massachusetts
WPLA Dry Branch, Georgia
WPLK Palatka, Florida
WPLM Plymouth, Massachusetts
WPLN Madison, Tennessee
WPLO Grayson, Georgia
WPLV West Point, Georgia
WPMB Vandalia, Illinois
WPMH Portsmouth, Virginia
WPMO Pascagoula-Moss Point, Mississippi
WPMZ East Providence, Rhode Island
WPNA Oak Park, Illinois
WPNH Plymouth, New Hampshire
WPNI Amherst, Massachusetts
WPNN Pensacola, Florida
WPNW Zeeland, Michigan
WPOG St. Matthews, South Carolina
WPOL Winston-Salem, North Carolina
WPON Walled Lake, Michigan
WPOP Hartford, Connecticut
WPPA Pottsville, Pennsylvania
WPPC Penuelas, Puerto Rico
WPRA Mayaguez, Puerto Rico
WPRD Winter Park, Florida
WPRE Prairie Du Chien, Wisconsin
WPRO Providence, Rhode Island
WPRP Ponce, Puerto Rico
WPRR Ada, Michigan
WPRT Prestonsburg, Kentucky
WPRT Pegram, Tennessee
WPRT-HD2 Philpot, Kentucky
WPRV Providence, Rhode Island
WPRX Bristol, Connecticut
WPRY Perry, Florida
WPSE Erie, Pennsylvania
WPSL Port St. Lucie, Florida
WPSN Honesdale, Pennsylvania
WPSO New Port Richey, Florida
WPSP Royal Palm Beach, Florida
WPTB Statesboro, Georgia
WPTF Raleigh, North Carolina
WPTK(AM) Raleigh, North Carolina
WPTL Canton, North Carolina
WPTN Cookeville, Tennessee
WPTR Schenectady, New York
WPTW Piqua, Ohio
WPTX Lexington Park, Maryland
WPUL South Daytona, Florida
WPUT Brewster, New York
WPVL-AM Platteville, Wisconsin
WPWA Chester, Pennsylvania
WPWC Dumfries-Triangle, Virginia
WPWT Colonial Heights, Tennessee
WPYB Benson, North Carolina
WPYR Baton Rouge, Louisiana
WQAL(AM) Pikesville, Maryland
WQAM Miami, Florida
WQBA Miami, Florida
WQBC Vicksburg, Mississippi
WQBN Temple Terrace, Florida
WQBQ Leesburg, Florida
WQBS San Juan, Puerto Rico
WQCH La Fayette, Georgia
WQCR Alabaster, Alabama
WQCT Bryan, Ohio
WQEW New York, New York
WQFX Gulfport, Mississippi
WQHC Hanceville, Alabama
WQHL Live Oak, Florida
WQII San Juan, Puerto Rico
WQIZ St. George, South Carolina
WQKR Portland, Tennessee
WQLA La Follette, Tennessee
WQLR Kalamazoo, Michigan
WQMS Quitman, Mississippi
WQMV Waverly, Tennessee
WQNO New Orleans, Louisiana
WQNT Charleston, South Carolina
WQOH Irondale, Alabama
WQOM Natick, Massachusetts
WQOP Jacksonville, Florida
WQOR Olyphant, Pennsylvania
WQPM Princeton, Minnesota
WQRX Valley Head, Alabama
WQSC Charleston, South Carolina
WQSE White Bluff, Tennessee
WQTM Fair Bluff, North Carolina
WQTT Marysville, Ohio
WQTW Latrobe, Pennsylvania
WQUL Woodruff, South Carolina
WQUL(AM) Woodruff, South Carolina
WQUN Hamden, Connecticut
WQWK State College, Pennsylvania
WQXI Atlanta, Georgia
WQXL Columbia, South Carolina
WQXM Bartow, Florida
WQXO Munising, Michigan
WQXY Hazard, Kentucky
WQZQ Goodlettsville, Tennessee
WRAA Luray, Virginia
WRAB Arab, Alabama
WRAD Radford, Virginia
WRAK Williamsport, Pennsylvania
WRAM Monmouth, Illinois
WRAR Tappahannock, Virginia
WRAW Reading, Pennsylvania
WRAY Princeton, Indiana
WRBS Baltimore, Maryland
WRBZ Wetumpka, Alabama
WRCA Watertown, Massachusetts
WRCE Watkins Glen, New York
WRCG Columbus, Georgia
WRCI Three Rivers, Michigan
WRCK Remsen, New York
WRCO Richland Center, Wisconsin
WRCR Ramapo, New York
WRCS Ahoskie, North Carolina
WRCY Mt. Vernon, Indiana
WRDB Reedsburg, Wisconsin
WRDN Durand, Wisconsin
WRDT Monroe, Michigan
WRDW Augusta, Georgia
WRDZ La Grange, Illinois
WREC Memphis, Tennessee
WRED Westbrook, Maine
WREJ Richmond, Virginia
WREL Lexington, Virginia
WREV Reidsville, North Carolina
WREY St. Paul, Minnesota
WRFC Athens, Georgia
WRFD Columbus-Worthington, Ohio
WRFM Muncie, Indiana
WRFV Valdosta, Georgia
WRGA Rome, Georgia
WRGC Sylva, North Carolina
WRGM Ontario, Ohio
WRGS Rogersville, Tennessee
WRHA(AM) Spring City, Tennessee
WRHC Coral Gables, Florida
WRHI Rock Hill, South Carolina
WRHL Rochelle, Illinois
WRIE Erie, Pennsylvania
WRIG Schofield, Wisconsin
WRIK Brookport, Illinois
WRIN Rensselaer, Indiana
WRIV Riverhead, New York
WRIX Homeland Park, South Carolina
WRJC Mauston, Wisconsin
WRJD Durham, North Carolina
WRJE Dover, Delaware
WRJN Racine, Wisconsin
WRJN Janesville, Wisconsin
WRJR Claremont, Virginia
WRJW Picayune, Mississippi
WRJX Jackson, Alabama
WRJZ Knoxville, Tennessee
WRKB Kannapolis, North Carolina
WRKK Hughesville, Pennsylvania
WRKL New City, New York
WRKM Carthage, Tennessee
WRKO Boston, Massachusetts
WRKQ Madisonville, Tennessee
WRLA West Point, Georgia
WRLL Cicero, Illinois
WRLV Salyersville, Kentucky
WRLZ Eatonville, Florida
WRMG Red Bay, Alabama
WRMN Elgin, Illinois
WRMQ Orlando, Florida
WRMS Beardstown, Illinois
WRMT Rocky Mount, North Carolina
WRNA China Grove, North Carolina
WRNE Gulf Breeze, Florida
WRNI Providence, Rhode Island
WRNJ Hackettstown, New Jersey
WRNL Richmond, Virginia
WRNN Myrtle Beach, South Carolina
WRNR Martinsburg, West Virginia
WRNS Kinston, North Carolina
WRNY Rome, New York
WROA Gulfport, Mississippi
WROC Rochester, New York
WROD Daytona Beach, Florida
WROK Rockford, Illinois
WROL Boston, Massachusetts
WROM Rome, Georgia
WRON Ronceverte, West Virginia
WROS Jacksonville, Florida
WROW Albany, New York
WROX Clarksdale, Mississippi

WROY Carmi, Illinois
WRPM Poplarville, Mississippi
WRPN Ripon, Wisconsin
WRPQ Baraboo, Wisconsin
WRQR(AM) Paris, Tennessee
WRRD Waukesha, Wisconsin
WRRE Juncos, Puerto Rico
WRRL Rainelle, West Virginia
WRRZ Clinton, North Carolina
WRSA St. Albans, Vermont
WRSB Canandaigua, New York
WRSC State College, Pennsylvania
WRSJ Bayamon, Puerto Rico
WRSL Corbin, Kentucky
WRSO(AM) Orlovista, Florida
WRSS San Sebastian, Puerto Rico
WRSW Warsaw, Indiana
WRTA Altoona, Pennsylvania
WRTG Garner, North Carolina
WRTO Chicago, Illinois
WRTZ Roanoke, Virginia
WRUF Gainesville, Florida
WRUS Russellville, Kentucky
WRVA Richmond, Virginia
WRVC Huntington, West Virginia
WRVK Mount Vernon, Kentucky
WRVP Mount Kisco, New York
WRWH Cleveland, Georgia
WRWR Warner Robins, Georgia
WRXB St. Petersburg Beach, Florida
WRXO Roxboro, North Carolina
WRYM New Britain, Connecticut
WRYT Edwardsville, Illinois
WRZN Hernando, Florida
WSAI Cincinnati, Ohio
WSAL Logansport, Indiana
WSAM Saginaw, Michigan
WSAN Allentown, Pennsylvania
WSAO Senatobia, Mississippi
WSAR Fall River, Massachusetts
WSAT Salisbury, North Carolina
WSAU-AM Wausau, Wisconsin
WSB Atlanta, Georgia
WSBA York, Pennsylvania
WSBB New Smyrna Beach, Florida
WSBC Chicago, Illinois
WSBI Static, Tennessee
WSBM Florence, Alabama
WSBR Boca Raton, Florida
WSBS Great Barrington, Massachusetts
WSBT South Bend, Indiana
WSBV South Boston, Virginia
WSCO Appleton, Wisconsin
WSCP Sandy Creek-Pulaski, New York
WSCR Chicago, Illinois
WSCW South Charleston, West Virginia
WSDE Cobleskill, New York
WSDK Bloomfield, Connecticut
WSDO Sanford, Florida
WSDQ Dunlap, Tennessee
WSDR Sterling, Illinois
WSDS Salem Township, Michigan
WSDT Soddy-Daisy, Tennessee
WSDV Sarasota, Florida
WSDZ Belleville, Illinois
WSEG Savannah, Georgia
WSEL Pontotoc, Mississippi
WSEM Donalsonville, Georgia
WSEN Baldwinsville, New York
WSEV Sevierville, Tennessee
WSEZ Paoli, Indiana
WSFB Quitman, Georgia
WSFC Somerset, Kentucky
WSFE Burnside, Kentucky
WSFN Brunswick, Georgia
WSFW Seneca Falls, New York
WSFZ Jackson, Mississippi
WSGB Sutton, West Virginia
WSGC Elberton, Georgia
WSGH Lewisville, North Carolina
WSGI Springfield, Tennessee
WSGO Oswego, New York
WSGW Saginaw, Michigan
WSHO New Orleans, Louisiana
WSHU Westport, Connecticut
WSHV South Hill, Virginia
WSHY Lafayette, Indiana
WSIC Statesville, North Carolina
WSIP Paintsville, Kentucky
WSIR Winter Haven, Florida
WSIV E. Syracuse, New York
WSJC Magee, Mississippi
WSJM-AM Benton Harbor, Michigan
WSJS Winston-Salem, North Carolina
WSKI Montpelier, Vermont
WSKN San Juan, Puerto Rico
WSKO Syracuse, New York
WSKW Skowhegan, Maine
WSKY Asheville, North Carolina
WSLA Slidell, Louisiana
WSLB Ogdensburg, New York
WSLK Moneta, Virginia
WSLM Salem, Indiana
WSLW White Sulphur Spring, West Virginia
WSM Nashville, Tennessee
WSME Camp Lejeune, North Carolina
WSMG Greeneville, Tennessee
WSMI Litchfield, Illinois
WSML Graham, North Carolina
WSMN Nashua, New Hampshire
WSMT Sparta, Tennessee
WSMX Winston-Salem, North Carolina
WSMY Weldon, North Carolina
WSNG Torrington, Connecticut
WSNJ Bridgeton, New Jersey
WSNL Flint, Michigan
WSNO Barre, Vermont
WSNR Jersey City, New Jersey
WSNT Sandersville, Georgia
WSNW Seneca, South Carolina
WSOK Savannah, Georgia
WSOL San German, Puerto Rico
WSOM Salem, Ohio
WSON Henderson, Kentucky
WSOO Sault Ste. Marie, Michigan
WSOS St. Augustine Beach, Florida
WSOY Decatur, Illinois
WSPC Albemarle, North Carolina
WSPD Toledo, Ohio
WSPG Spartanburg, South Carolina
WSPL Streator, Illinois
WSPO Charleston, South Carolina
WSPQ Springville, New York
WSPR Springfield, Massachusetts
WSPY Geneva, Illinois
WSQL Brevard, North Carolina
WSQR Sycamore, Illinois
WSRA Albany, Georgia
WSRF Fort Lauderdale, Florida
WSRO Ashland, Massachusetts
WSRP Jacksonville, North Carolina
WSRQ Sarasota, Florida
WSRW Hillsboro, Ohio
WSRY Elkton, Maryland
WSSC Sumter, South Carolina
WSSG Goldsboro, North Carolina
WSSO Starkville, Mississippi
WSTA Charlotte Amalie, Virgin Islands
WSTC Stamford, Connecticut
WSTJ St. Johnsbury, Vermont
WSTL Providence, Rhode Island
WSTP Salisbury, North Carolina
WSTT Thomasville, Georgia
WSTU Stuart, Florida
WSTX Christiansted, Virgin Islands
WSUA Miami, Florida
WSUI Iowa City, Iowa
WSVA Harrisonburg, Virginia
WSVG Mount Jackson, Virginia
WSVM Valdese, North Carolina
WSVS Crewe, Virginia
WSVU North Palm Beach, Florida
WSVX Shelbyville, Indiana
WSWI Evansville, Indiana
WSWN Belle Glade, Florida
WSWV Pennington Gap, Virginia
WSWW Charleston, West Virginia
WSYB Rutland, Vermont
WSYD Mount Airy, North Carolina
WSYL Sylvania, Georgia
WSYR Syracuse, New York
WSYW Indianapolis, Indiana
WSYY Millinocket, Maine
WTAB Tabor City, North Carolina
WTAD Quincy, Illinois
WTAG Worcester, Massachusetts
WTAL Tallahassee, Florida
WTAM Cleveland, Ohio
WTAN Clearwater, Florida
WTAQ-AM Green Bay, Wisconsin
WTAR Norfolk, Virginia
WTAW College Station, Texas
WTAX Springfield, Illinois
WTAY Robinson, Illinois
WTBC Tuscaloosa, Alabama
WTBF Troy, Alabama
WTBI Pickens, South Carolina
WTBN Pinellas Park, Florida
WTBO Cumberland, Maryland
WTBQ Warwick, New York
WTCA Plymouth, Indiana
WTCH Shawano, Wisconsin
WTCJ Tell City, Indiana
WTCL Chattahoochee, Florida
WTCM Traverse City, Michigan
WTCO Campbellsville, Kentucky
WTCR Kenova, West Virginia
WTCS Fairmont, West Virginia
WTCW Whitesburg, Kentucky
WTDR Gadsden, Alabama
WTEL Philadelphia, Pennsylvania
WTEM Washington, District of Columbia
WTGA Thomaston, Georgia
WTGM Salisbury, Maryland
WTHB Augusta, Georgia
WTHE Mineola, New York
WTHU Thurmont, Maryland
WTHV Hahira, Georgia
WTIC Hartford, Connecticut
WTIF Tifton, Georgia
WTIG Massillon, Ohio
WTIK Durham, North Carolina
WTIL Mayaguez, Puerto Rico
WTIM Assumption, Illinois
WTIQ Manistique, Michigan
WTIS Tampa, Florida
WTIV Titusville, Pennsylvania
WTJH East Point, Georgia
WTJS Jackson, Tennessee
WTJV Deland, Florida
WTJZ Newport News, Virginia
WTKA Ann Arbor, Michigan
WTKD Mobile, Alabama
WTKG Grand Rapids, Michigan
WTKI Huntsville, Alabama
WTKM Hartford, Wisconsin
WTKN Corinth, Mississippi
WTKS Savannah, Georgia
WTKT Harrisburg, Pennsylvania
WTKY Tompkinsville, Kentucky
WTKZ Allentown, Pennsylvania
WTLA North Syracuse, New York
WTLB Utica, New York
WTLC Indianapolis, Indiana
WTLK Taylorsville, North Carolina
WTLM Opelika, Alabama
WTLN Orlando, Florida
WTLO Somerset, Kentucky
WTLS Tallassee, Alabama
WTLY Tallahassee, Florida
WTMA Charleston, South Carolina
WTMC Wilmington, Delaware
WTME Rumford, Maine
WTMJ Milwaukee, Wisconsin
WTMN Gainesville, Florida
WTMP Egypt Lake, Florida
WTMR Camden, New Jersey
WTMY Sarasota, Florida
WTMZ Dorchester Terrace-Brentwood, South Carolina
WTNE Trenton, Tennessee
WTNI Biloxi, Mississippi
WTNK Hartsville, Tennessee
WTNL Reidsville, Georgia
WTNS Coshocton, Ohio
WTNT Alexandria, Virginia
WTNY Watertown, New York
WTOB Winston-Salem, North Carolina
WTOC Newton, New Jersey
WTOD Hartsville, South Carolina
WTOE Spruce Pine, North Carolina
WTOF Bay Minette, Alabama
WTON Staunton, Virginia
WTOR Youngstown, New York
WTOT Marianna, Florida
WTOX Glen Allen, Virginia
WTOY Salem, Virginia
WTPR Paris, Tennessee
WTPS Petersburg, Virginia
WTQS Cameron, South Carolina
WTRB Ripley, Tennessee
WTRC Elkhart, Indiana
WTRE Greensburg, Indiana
WTRI Brunswick, Maryland
WTRN Tyrone, Pennsylvania
WTRO Dyersburg, Tennessee
WTRP LaGrange, Georgia
WTRU Kernersville, North Carolina
WTRX Flint, Michigan
WTSA Brattleboro, Vermont
WTSB Selma, North Carolina
WTSK Tuscaloosa, Alabama
WTSL Hanover, New Hampshire
WTSN Dover, New Hampshire
WTSO Madison, Wisconsin
WTSV Claremont, New Hampshire
WTTB Vero Beach, Florida
WTTC Towanda, Pennsylvania
WTTF Tiffin, Ohio
WTTI Dalton, Georgia
WTTL Madisonville, Kentucky
WTTM Lindenwold, New Jersey
WTTN Columbus, Wisconsin
WTTR Westminster, Maryland
WTUB Lake City, Florida
WTUP Tupelo, Mississippi
WTUV Louisville, Kentucky
WTVB-AM Coldwater, Michigan
WTVL Waterville, Maine
WTVN Columbus, Ohio
WTWA Thomson, Georgia
WTWB Auburndale, Florida
WTWD Plant City, Florida
WTWG Columbus, Mississippi
WTWK Plattsburgh, New York
WTWN Wells River, Vermont
WTWZ Clinton, Mississippi
WTXK Pike Road, Alabama
WTXY Whiteville, North Carolina
WTYL Tylertown, Mississippi
WTYM Kittanning, Pennsylvania
WTYS Marianna, Florida
WTZA Atlanta, Georgia
WTZE Tazewell, Virginia
WTZN Troy, Pennsylvania
WTZQ Fountain Inn, South Carolina
WTZQ Hendersonville, North Carolina
WTZX Sparta, Tennessee
WUAM Watervliet, New York
WUAT Pikeville, Tennessee
WUBR Baton Rouge, Louisiana
WUFE Baxley, Georgia
WUFF Eastman, Georgia
WUFL Sterling Heights, Michigan
WUFO Amherst, New York
WUKQ Ponce, Puerto Rico
WUKZ(AM) Marion, Virginia
WULM Springfield, Ohio
WULR York, South Carolina
WUMP Madison, Alabama
WUMY Memphis, Tennessee
WUMY Turrell, Arkansas
WUNA Ocoee, Florida
WUNN Mason, Michigan
WUNO San Juan, Puerto Rico
WUNR Brookline, Massachusetts
WUPE Pittsfield, Massachusetts
WUPR Utuado, Puerto Rico
WURA Quantico, Virginia
WURD Philadelphia, Pennsylvania
WURL Moody, Alabama
WURN Kendall, Florida
WUSP Utica, New York
WUST Washington, District of Columbia
WUTI Utica, New York
WUVI(AM) Charlotte Amalie, Virgin Islands
WUVR Lebanon, New Hampshire
WVAB Virginia Beach, Virginia
WVAL Sauk Rapids, Minnesota
WVAM Altoona, Pennsylvania
WVAR Richwood, West Virginia
WVAX Charlottesville, Virginia
WVBE Roanoke, Virginia
WVBF Middleborough Center, Massachusetts
WVBG Vicksburg, Mississippi
WVBS Burgaw, North Carolina
WVCB Shallotte, North Carolina
WVCC Hogansville, Georgia
WVCD Bamberg-Denmark, South Carolina
WVCH Chester, Pennsylvania
WVCV Orange, Virginia
WVCY Oshkosh, Wisconsin
WVEI Worcester, Massachusetts
WVEL Pekin, Illinois

WVFN East Lansing, Michigan
WVGB Beaufort, South Carolina
WVGG Lucedale, Mississippi
WVGM Lynchburg, Virginia
WVHF Kentwood, Michigan
WVHI Evansville, Indiana
WVHU Huntington, West Virginia
WVJP Caguas, Puerto Rico
WVJS Owensboro, Kentucky
WVKO Columbus, Ohio
WVLD Valdosta, Georgia
WVLG Wildwood, Florida
WVLK Lexington, Kentucky
WVLN Olney, Illinois
WVLY Moundsville, West Virginia
WVLZ Knoxville, Tennessee
WVMR Frost, West Virginia
WVMT Burlington, Vermont
WVNA Tuscumbia, Alabama
WVNE Leicester, Massachusetts
WVNJ Oakland, New Jersey
WVNN Athens, Alabama
WVNR Poultney, Vermont
WVNT Parkersburg, West Virginia
WVNZ Richmond, Virginia
WVOC Columbia, South Carolina
WVOE Chadbourn, North Carolina
WVOG New Orleans, Louisiana
WVOI Marco Island, Florida
WVOJ Fernandina Beach, Florida
WVOK Oxford, Alabama
WVOL Berry Hill, Tennessee
WVOM Rockland, Maine
WVON Berwyn, Illinois
WVOP Vidalia, Georgia
WVOS Liberty, New York
WVOT Wilson, North Carolina
WVOV Bridgeport, Alabama
WVOW Logan, West Virginia
WVOX New Rochelle, New York
WVOZ San Juan, Puerto Rico
WVPO Stroudsburg, Pennsylvania
WVRC Spencer, West Virginia
WVRQ Viroqua, Wisconsin
WVSA Vernon, Alabama
WVSG Columbus, Ohio
WVSM Rainsville, Alabama
WVTJ Pensacola, Florida
WVTS Dunbar, West Virginia
WVTS(AM) Charleston, West Virginia
WVUS Grafton, West Virginia
WVWI Charlotte Amalie, Virgin Islands
WVXX Norfolk, Virginia
WVZN Columbia, Pennsylvania
WWAB Lakeland, Florida
WWBA Largo, Florida
WWBC Cocoa, Florida
WWBF Bartow, Florida
WWBG Greensboro, North Carolina
WWBJ Martinsburg, Pennsylvania
WWCA Gary, Indiana
WWCB(AM) Corry, Pennsylvania
WWCD Baltimore, Ohio
WWCH Clarion, Pennsylvania
WWCK Flint, Michigan
WWCL Lehigh Acres, Florida
WWCO Waterbury, Connecticut
WWCS Canonsburg, Pennsylvania
WWDB Philadelphia, Pennsylvania
WWDJ Boston, Massachusetts
WWDN Danville, Virginia
WWDR Murfreesboro, North Carolina
WWDX Huntingdon, Tennessee
WWFD Frederick, Maryland
WWFE Miami, Florida
WWFL Clermont, Florida
WWGA(AM) Waycross, Georgia
WWGB Indian Head, Maryland
WWGC Albertville, Alabama
WWGE Loretto, Pennsylvania
WWGK Cleveland, Ohio
WWGP Sanford, North Carolina
WWHM Sumter, South Carolina
WWHN Joliet, Illinois
WWIC Scottsboro, Alabama
WWIL Wilmington, North Carolina
WWIN Baltimore, Maryland
WWIO St. Marys, Georgia
WWIS Black River Falls, Wisconsin
WWJ Detroit, Michigan
WWJB Brooksville, Florida
WWJC Duluth, Minnesota
WWJZ Mount Holly, New Jersey
WWKB Buffalo, New York
WWKU Plum Springs, Kentucky
WWL New Orleans, Louisiana
WWLE Cornwall, New York
WWLX Lawrenceburg, Tennessee
WWLZ Horseheads, New York
WWMI St. Petersburg, Florida
WWMK Cleveland, Ohio
WWNA Aguadilla, Puerto Rico
WWNB New Bern, North Carolina
WWNC Asheville, North Carolina
WWNH Madbury, New Hampshire
WWNL Pittsburgh, Pennsylvania
WWNN Pompano Beach, Florida
WWNR Beckley, West Virginia
WWNS Statesboro, Georgia
WWNT Dothan, Alabama
WWNZ Veazie, Maine
WWOL Forest City, North Carolina
WWON Waynesboro, Tennessee
WWOW Conneaut, Ohio
WWPA Williamsport, Pennsylvania
WWPR Bradenton, Florida
WWRC Washington, District of Columbia
WWRF Lake Worth, Florida
WWRK Florence, South Carolina
WWRL New York, New York
WWRU Jersey City, New Jersey
WWRV New York, New York
WWSC Glens Falls, New York
WWSF Sanford, Maine
WWSJ St. Johns, Michigan
WWSM Annville-Cleona, Pennsylvania
WWTC Minneapolis, Minnesota
WWTF Georgetown, Kentucky
WWTK Lake Placid, Florida
WWTM Decatur, Alabama
WWTR Bridgewater, New Jersey
WWTX Wilmington, Delaware
WWVA Wheeling, West Virginia
WWVT Christiansburg, Virginia
WWWC Wilkesboro, North Carolina
WWWE Hapeville, Georgia
WWWH Haleyville, Alabama
WWWI Baxter, Minnesota
WWWJ Galax, Virginia
WWWL New Orleans, Louisiana
WWWS Buffalo, New York
WWXL Manchester, Kentucky
WWYC Toledo, Ohio
WWYO Pineville, West Virginia
WWZN Boston, Massachusetts
WWZQ Aberdeen, Mississippi
WXAG Athens, Georgia
WXAM Buffalo, Kentucky
WXBD Biloxi, Mississippi
WXBR Brockton, Massachusetts
WXCE Amery, Wisconsin
WXCF Clifton Forge, Virginia
WXCO Wausau, Wisconsin
WXCT Southington, Connecticut
WXEM Buford, Georgia
WXEW Yabucoa, Puerto Rico
WXEX Exeter, New Hampshire
WXFN Muncie, Indiana
WXFO Royston, Georgia
WXGI Richmond, Virginia
WXGM Gloucester, Virginia
WXGO Madison, Indiana
WXIC Waverly, Ohio
WXIT Blowing Rock, North Carolina
WXJC Cordova, Alabama
WXJO Douglasville, Georgia
WXKL Sanford, North Carolina
WXKO Fort Valley, Georgia
WXKS Newton, Massachusetts
WXKX Clarksburg, West Virginia
WXLA Dimondale, Michigan
WXLI Dublin, Georgia
WXLM Groton, Connecticut
WXLW Indianapolis, Indiana
WXLZ St. Paul, Virginia
WXMC Parsippany-Troy Hill, New Jersey
WXME Monticello, Maine
WXMY Saltville, Virginia
WXNC Monroe, North Carolina
WXNT Indianapolis, Indiana
WXOK Port Allen, Louisiana
WXQW Fairhope, Alabama
WXRF Guayama, Puerto Rico
WXRL Lancaster, New York
WXRQ Mount Pleasant, Tennessee
WXRS Swainsboro, Georgia
WXSM Blountville, Tennessee
WXTG Hampton, Virginia
WXTN Benton, Mississippi
WXVA Winchester, Virginia
WXVI Montgomery, Alabama
WXVW Jeffersonville, Indiana
WXXI Rochester, New York
WXYB Indian Rocks Beach, Florida
WXYG Sauk Rapids, Minnesota
WXYT Detroit, Michigan
WYAC Cabo Rojo, Puerto Rico
WYAL Scotland Neck, North Carolina
WYAM Hartselle, Alabama
WYBC New Haven, Connecticut
WYBG Massena, New York
WYBT Blountstown, Florida
WYBY Cortland, New York
WYCB Washington, District of Columbia
WYCK Plains, Pennsylvania
WYCL Niles, Ohio
WYCV Granite Falls, North Carolina
WYDE Birmingham, Alabama
WYEA Sylacauga, Alabama
WYEL Mayaguez, Puerto Rico
WYFN Nashville, Tennessee
WYFQ Charlotte, North Carolina
WYGH Paris, Kentucky
WYGM Orlando, Florida
WYGR Wyoming, Michigan
WYHL Meridian, Mississippi
WYHM Rockwood, Tennessee
WYIS McRae, Georgia
WYKM Rupert, West Virginia
WYKO Sabana Grande, Puerto Rico
WYLD New Orleans, Louisiana
WYLF Penn Yan, New York
WYLL Chicago, Illinois
WYLS York, Alabama
WYMB Manning, South Carolina
WYMC Mayfield, Kentucky
WYMM Jacksonville, Florida
WYNC Yanceyville, North Carolina
WYND Deland, Florida
WYNF Augusta, Georgia
WYNN Florence, South Carolina
WYNY(AM) Ontario, New York
WYNY(AM) Milford, Pennsylvania
WYNY(AM) Milford, New York
WYOS Binghamton, New York
WYPC Wellston, Ohio
WYRD Greenville, South Carolina
WYRE Annapolis, Maryland
WYRM Norfolk, Virginia
WYRN Louisburg, North Carolina
WYRV Cedar Bluff, Virginia
WYSE Canton, North Carolina
WYSH Clinton, Tennessee
WYSL Avon, New York
WYSR High Point, North Carolina
WYTH Madison, Georgia
WYTI Rocky Mount, Virginia
WYTS Columbus, Ohio
WYUS Milford, Delaware
WYVE Wytheville, Virginia
WYWY Barbourville, Kentucky
WYXC Cartersville, Georgia
WYXE Gallatin, Tennessee
WYXI Athens, Tennessee
WYYC York, Pennsylvania
WYYZ Jasper, Georgia
WYZD Dobson, North Carolina
WYZE Atlanta, Georgia
WZAB Sweetwater, Florida
WZAM Ishpeming, Michigan
WZAN Portland, Maine
WZAP Bristol, Virginia
WZAZ Jacksonville, Florida
WZBK Keene, New Hampshire
WZBO Edenton, North Carolina
WZBR Coral Springs, Florida
WZCC Cross City, Florida
WZCT Scottsboro, Alabama
WZEP De Funiak Springs, Florida
WZFG Dilworth, Minnesota
WZGM Black Mountain, North Carolina
WZGV Cramerton, North Carolina
WZGX Bessemer, Alabama
WZHF Arlington, Virginia
WZHR Zephyrhills, Florida
WZJY Mount Pleasant, South Carolina
WZKY Albemarle, North Carolina
WZMF(AM) Nanticoke, Pennsylvania
WZMG Pepperell, Alabama
WZNA Moca, Puerto Rico
WZNG Shelbyville, Tennessee
WZNH Fitzwilliam Depot, New Hampshire
WZNZ Atlantic Beach, Florida
WZNZ Atlantic Beach, Florida
WZOB Fort Payne, Alabama
WZOE Princeton, Illinois
WZON Bangor, Maine
WZOO Asheboro, North Carolina
WZOT Rockmart, Georgia
WZQZ Trion, Georgia
WZRC New York, New York
WZRK Northbrook, Illinois
WZSK Everett, Pennsylvania
WZTA Vero Beach, Florida
WZTI Greenfield, Wisconsin
WZUM Braddock, Pennsylvania
WZYX Cowan, Tennessee
WZZA Tuscumbia, Alabama
WZZB Seymour, Indiana
WZZQ(AM) Gaffney, South Carolina
WZZW Milton, West Virginia
WZZX Lineville, Alabama
XETRA Tijuana, Mexico

U.S. FM Radio Stations by Call Letters

***KFWA(FM)** Weldona, Colorado
K204CE Clifton, Arizona
K216FX Mena, Arkansas
K220EO Hilo, Hawaii
K225BN Oklahoma City, Oklahoma
K243BJ Oklahoma City, Oklahoma
KAAI Palisade, Colorado
KAAK Great Falls, Montana
KAAN-FM Bethany, Missouri
KAAP Rock Island, Washington
KAAQ Alliance, Nebraska
KAAR Butte, Montana
KAAT Oakhurst, California
KAAX Avenal, California
KAAZ-FM Spanish Fork, Utah
KABA Louise, Texas
KABD Ipswich, South Dakota
KABF Little Rock, Arkansas
KABG Los Alamos, New Mexico
KABN-FM Kasilof, Alaska
KABQ-FM Bosque Farms, New Mexico
KABR Alamo Community, New Mexico
KABU Fort Totten, North Dakota
KABW Abilene, Texas
KABX-FM Merced, California
KABZ Little Rock, Arkansas
KACC Alvin, Texas
KACI-FM The Dalles, Oregon
KACL Bismarck, North Dakota
KACO Apache, Oklahoma
KACQ Lometa, Texas
KACS Rainier, Washington
KACT-FM Andrews, Texas
KACU Abilene, Texas
KACV-FM Amarillo, Texas
KACY Arkansas City, Kansas
KACZ Riley, Kansas
KADA-FM Ada, Oklahoma
KADD Logandale, Nevada
KADI-FM Republic, Missouri
KADL Imperial, Nebraska
KADO(FM) Fair Oaks, California
KADQ-FM Evanston, Wyoming
KADS Elk City, Oklahoma
KADU Hibbing, Minnesota
KADV Modesto, California
KAEH Beaumont, California
KAER Mesquite, Nevada
KAFC Anchorage, Alaska
KAFE Bellingham, Washington
KAFF-FM Flagstaff, Arizona
KAFH Great Falls, Montana
KAFM Grand Junction, Colorado
KAFR Conroe, Texas
KAFX-FM Diboll, Texas
KAFZ Ash Fork, Arizona
KAGB Waimea, Hawaii
KAGE-FM Winona, Minnesota
KAGG Madisonville, Texas
KAGH-FM Crossett, Arkansas
KAGJ Ephraim, Utah
KAGL El Dorado, Arkansas
KAGM Los Alamos, New Mexico
KAGO-FM Klamath Falls, Oregon
KAGT Abilene, Texas
KAGU Spokane, Washington
KAGZ(FM) Lufkin, Texas
KAHE Dodge City, Kansas
KAHL-FM Hondo, Texas
KAHM Spring Valley, Arizona
KAHR Poplar Bluff, Missouri
KAHU Pahala, Hawaii
KAIA Bloomfield, Missouri
KAIB Shafter, California
KAIC Tucson, Arizona
KAIG Dodge City, Kansas
KAIH Lake Havasu City, Arizona
KAIK Tillamook, Oregon
KAIM-FM Honolulu, Hawaii
KAIO Idaho Falls, Idaho
KAIP Wapello, Iowa
KAIQ Wolfforth, Texas
KAIR-FM Horton, Kansas
KAIS(FM) Tracy, California
KAIW Laramie, Wyoming
KAIX Cheyenne, Wyoming
KAIZ Mesquite, Nevada
KAJA San Antonio, Texas
KAJC Salem, Oregon
KAJM Camp Verde, Arizona
KAJN-FM Crowley, Louisiana
KAJP Carrizo Springs, Texas
KAJR Indian Wells, California
KAJT Ada, Oklahoma
KAJX Aspen, Colorado
KAJZ Llano, Texas
KAKA Salina, Kansas
KAKI Juneau, Alaska
KAKJ Marianna, Arkansas
KAKL Anchorage, Alaska
KAKN Naknek, Alaska
KAKO Ada, Oklahoma
KAKQ-FM Fairbanks, Alaska
KAKS Goshen, Arkansas
KAKT Phoenix, Oregon
KAKV El Dorado, Arkansas
KAKX Mendocino, California
KALA Davenport, Iowa
KALC Denver, Colorado
KALF Red Bluff, California
KALG Kaltag, Alaska
KALI-FM Santa Ana, California
KALK Winfield, Texas
KALN Dexter, New Mexico
KALP Alpine, Texas
KALQ-FM Alamosa, Colorado
KALR Hot Springs, Arkansas
KALS Kalispell, Montana
KALT-FM Alturas, California
KALU Langston, Oklahoma
KALW San Francisco, California
KALX Berkeley, California
KALZ Fowler, California
KAMA-FM Deer Park, Texas
KAMB Merced, California
KAMD-FM Camden, Arkansas
KAMF Tulare, South Dakota
KAMJ Gosnell, Arkansas
KAML-FM Gillette, Wyoming
KAMO-FM Rogers, Arkansas
KAMP Los Angeles, California
KAMS Mammoth Spring, Arkansas
KAMU-FM College Station, Texas
KAMX Luling, Texas
KAMY Lubbock, Texas
KAMZ Tahoka, Texas
KANC Baker, Oregon
KANH Emporia, Kansas
KANJ Giddings, Texas
KANL Baker, Oregon
KANO Hilo, Hawaii
KANQ Chanute, Kansas
KANS Emporia, Kansas
KANT Guernsey, Wyoming
KANU Lawrence, Kansas
KANV Olsburg, Kansas
KANW Albuquerque, New Mexico
KANX Sheridan, Arkansas
KANY Montesano, Washington
KANZ Garden City, Kansas
KAOC Cavalier, North Dakota
KAOD Babbitt, Minnesota
KAOG Jonesboro, Arkansas
KAOI-FM Wailuku, Hawaii
KAOR Vermillion, South Dakota
KAOS Olympia, Washington
KAOW Fort Smith, Arkansas
KAOX Kemmerer, Wyoming
KAOY Kealakekua, Hawaii
KAPA Hilo, Hawaii
KAPB-FM Marksville, Louisiana
KAPC Butte, Montana
KAPI Ruston, Louisiana
KAPM Alexandria, Louisiana
KAPN Caldwell, Texas
KAPW White Oak, Texas
KAQA Kilauea, Hawaii
KAQD Abilene, Texas
KAQF Clovis, New Mexico
KARA Williams, California
KARB Price, Utah
KARF Independence, Kansas
KARG Poteau, Oklahoma
KARH Forrest City, Arkansas
KARJ Kuna, Idaho
KARL Tracy, Minnesota
KARM Visalia, California
KARN-FM Sheridan, Arkansas
KARO Nyssa, Oregon
KARP-FM Dassel, Minnesota
KARQ San Andreas, California
KARS-FM Laramie, Wyoming
KARU Cache, Oklahoma
KARV-FM Ola, Arkansas
KARX Claude, Texas
KARY-FM Grandview, Washington
KARZ Marshall, Minnesota
KASB Bellevue, Washington
KASD Rapid City, South Dakota
KASE-FM Austin, Texas
KASF Alamosa, Colorado
KASH-FM Anchorage, Alaska
KASK Fairfield, California
KASR Vilonia, Arkansas
KASS Casper, Wyoming
KASU Jonesboro, Arkansas
KASV Borger, Texas
KATB Anchorage, Alaska
KATC Colorado Springs, Colorado
KATF Dubuque, Iowa
KATG Elkhart, Texas
KATI California, Missouri
KATJ-FM George, California
KATK-FM Carlsbad, New Mexico
KATM Modesto, California
KATO-FM New Ulm, Minnesota
KATP Amarillo, Texas
KATQ-FM Plentywood, Montana
KATR-FM Wray, Colorado
KATS Yakima, Washington
KATT Oklahoma City, Oklahoma
KATW Lewiston, Idaho
KATX Eastland, Texas
KATY-FM Idyllwild, California
KAUC West Clarkston, Washington
KAUD Mexico, Missouri
KAUF Kennett, Missouri
KAUG Anchorage, Alaska
KAUJ Grafton, North Dakota
KAUM Colorado City, Texas
KAUR Sioux Falls, South Dakota
KAUS-FM Austin, Minnesota
KAUU Manti, Utah
KAVB Hawthorne, Nevada
KAVE Oakridge, Oregon
KAVH Eudora, Arkansas
KAVK Many, Louisiana
KAVO Pampa, Texas
KAVV Benson, Arizona
KAVW Amarillo, Texas
KAVX Lufkin, Texas
KAWC-FM Yuma, Arizona
KAWK Custer, South Dakota
KAWN Winslow, Arizona
KAWO Boise, Idaho
KAWS Marsing, Idaho
KAWS Marsing, Idaho
KAWV Fort Dodge, Iowa
KAWZ Twin Falls, Idaho
KAXA Mountain Home, Texas
KAXE Grand Rapids, Minnesota
KAXG Gillette, Wyoming
KAXL Greenacres, California
KAXR Arkansas City, Kansas
KAXV Bastrop, Louisiana
KAYA Hubbard, Nebraska
KAYB Sunnyside, Washington
KAYC Durant, Oklahoma
KAYD-FM Silsbee, Texas
KAYE-FM Tonkawa, Oklahoma
KAYH Fayetteville, Arkansas
KAYK Victoria, Texas
KAYL-FM Storm Lake, Iowa
KAYM Weatherford, Oklahoma
KAYO Wasilla, Alaska
KAYP Burlington, Iowa
KAYQ Warsaw, Missouri
KAYT Jena, Louisiana
KAYX Richmond, Missouri
KAZC Healdton, Oklahoma
KAZE Ore City, Texas
KAZI Austin, Texas
KAZR Pella, Iowa
KAZU Pacific Grove, California
KAZX Kirtland, New Mexico
KAZY Cheyenne, Wyoming
KBAA Grass Valley, California
KBAC Las Vegas, New Mexico
KBAH Plainview, Texas
KBAJ Deer River, Minnesota
KBAN DeRidder, Louisiana
KBAQ Phoenix, Arizona
KBAR-FM Victoria, Texas
KBAT Monahans, Texas
KBAY Gilroy, California
KBAZ Hamilton, Montana
KBBC Tishomingo, Oklahoma
KBBD Spokane, Washington
KBBE McPherson, Kansas
KBBF Calistoga, California
KBBG Waterloo, Iowa
KBBK Lincoln, Nebraska
KBBM Jefferson City, Missouri
KBBN-FM Broken Bow, Nebraska
KBBO-FM Houston, Alaska
KBBQ-FM Van Buren, Arkansas
KBBT Schertz, Texas
KBBU Modesto, California
KBBX-FM Nebraska City, Nebraska
KBBY-FM Ventura, California
KBBZ Kalispell, Montana
KBCE Boyce, Louisiana
KBCM Blytheville, Arkansas
KBCN-FM Marshall, Arkansas
KBCO Boulder, Colorado
KBCQ-FM Roswell, New Mexico
KBCR-FM Steamboat Springs, Colorado
KBCS Bellevue, Washington
KBCT Waco, Texas
KBCU North Newton, Kansas
KBCW-FM McAlester, Oklahoma
KBCX Big Spring, Texas
KBCY Tye, Texas
KBDA Great Bend, Kansas
KBDB-FM Forks, Washington
KBDD Winfield, Kansas
KBDE Temple, Texas
KBDG Turlock, California
KBDN Bandon, Oregon
KBDO Des Arc, Arkansas
KBDR Mirando City, Texas
KBDS Taft, California
KBDV Leesville, Louisiana
KBDW Wheeler, Texas
KBDX Blanding, Utah
KBDY Hanna, Wyoming
KBDZ Perryville, Missouri
KBEA-FM Muscatine, Iowa
KBEB Sacramento, California
KBEE Salt Lake City, Utah
KBEF Gibsland, Louisiana
KBEK Mora, Minnesota
KBEL-FM Idabel, Oklahoma
KBEM-FM Minneapolis, Minnesota
KBEN-FM Cowley, Wyoming
KBEQ-FM Kansas City, Missouri
KBER Ogden, Utah
KBES Ceres, California
KBEV-FM Dillon, Montana
KBEW-FM Blue Earth, Minnesota
KBEX Dalhart, Texas
KBEY Burnet, Texas
KBEZ Tulsa, Oklahoma
KBFB Dallas, Texas
KBFF Portland, Oregon
KBFL-FM Buffalo, Missouri
KBFM Edinburg, Texas
KBFO Aberdeen, South Dakota
KBFP-FM Delano, California
KBFR Bismarck, North Dakota
KBFX Anchorage, Alaska
KBGA Missoula, Montana
KBGB Magness, Arkansas
KBGL Larned, Kansas
KBGM Park Hills, Missouri
KBGO Waco, Texas
KBGX Keaau, Hawaii
KBGY Faribault, Minnesota
KBGZ Spring Creek, Nevada
KBHE-FM Rapid City, South Dakota
KBHG Alexandria, Minnesota
KBHH Kerman, California
KBHI Miner, Missouri
KBHL Osakis, Minnesota
KBHM Basin, Wyoming
KBHN Booneville, Arkansas
KBHP Bemidji, Minnesota
KBHR Big Bear City, California
KBHU-FM Spearfish, South Dakota
KBHW International Falls, Minnesota

KBHZ Willmar, Minnesota
KBIA Columbia, Missouri
KBIC Raymondville, Texas
KBIG Los Angeles, California
KBIJ Guymon, Oklahoma
KBIK Independence, Kansas
KBIL Park City, Montana
KBIM-FM Roswell, New Mexico
KBIO Natchitoches, Louisiana
KBIQ Manitou Springs, Colorado
KBIU Lake Charles, Louisiana
KBIY Van Buren, Missouri
KBJF Nephi, Utah
KBJK Concow, California
KBJQ Bronson, Kansas
KBJS Jacksonville, Texas
KBKB-FM Fort Madison, Iowa
KBKC Moberly, Missouri
KBKG Corning, Arkansas
KBKK Ball, Louisiana
KBKL Grand Junction, Colorado
KBKN Lamesa, Texas
KBKO Kodiak, Alaska
KBKS-FM Tacoma, Washington
KBKY Merced, California
KBKZ Raton, New Mexico
KBLB Nisswa, Minnesota
KBLC Fredericksburg, Texas
KBLD Kennewick, Washington
KBLL-FM Helena, Montana
KBLO Corcoran, California
KBLP Lindsay, Oklahoma
KBLQ-FM Logan, Utah
KBLR-FM Blair, Nebraska
KBLS North Fort Riley, Kansas
KBLS North Fort Riley, Kansas
KBLV Tehachapi, California
KBLW Billings, Montana
KBLX-FM Berkeley, California
KBLZ Winona, Texas
KBMC Bozeman, Montana
KBMD Marble Falls, Texas
KBMG Evanston, Wyoming
KBMH Holbrook, Arizona
KBMI-FM East Helena, Montana
KBMJ Heber Springs, Arkansas
KBMK Bismarck, North Dakota
KBMM Odessa, Texas
KBMP Enterprise, Kansas
KBMQ Monroe, Louisiana
KBMV-FM Birch Tree, Missouri
KBMX Proctor, Minnesota
KBNA-FM El Paso, Texas
KBNJ Corpus Christi, Texas
KBNL Laredo, Texas
KBNO-FM White Salmon, Washington
KBNR Brownsville, Texas
KBNU Uvalde, Texas
KBNV Fayetteville, Arkansas
KBOA-FM Piggott, Arkansas
KBOB-FM De Witt, Iowa
KBOC Bridgeport, Texas
KBOD Gainesville, Missouri
KBOE-FM Oskaloosa, Iowa
KBOM Socorro, New Mexico
KBON Mamou, Louisiana
KBOO Portland, Oregon
KBOQ Seaside, California
KBOS-FM Tulare, California
KBOT Pelican Rapids, Minnesota
KBOX Lompoc, California
KBOY-FM Medford, Oregon
KBOZ-FM Bozeman, Montana
KBPA San Marcos, Texas
KBPB Harrison, Arkansas
KBPC Crockett, Texas
KBPG Montevideo, Minnesota
KBPI Denver, Colorado
KBPK Buena Park, California
KBPN Brainerd, Minnesota
KBPR Brainerd, Minnesota
KBPU De Queen, Arkansas
KBPW Hampton, Arkansas
KBQB Chico, California
KBQC Independence, Kansas
KBQF McFarland, California
KBQI Albuquerque, New Mexico
KBQL Las Vegas, New Mexico
KBRB-FM Ainsworth, Nebraska
KBRE Atwater, California
KBRG San Jose, California
KBRJ Anchorage, Alaska
KBRK-FM Brookings, South Dakota
KBRQ Hillsboro, Texas
KBRU Oklahoma City, Oklahoma
KBRW-FM Barrow, Alaska
KBRX-FM O'Neill, Nebraska
KBRY Sargent, Nebraska
KBSA El Dorado, Arkansas
KBSB Bemidji, Minnesota
KBSG Aberdeen, Washington
KBSJ Jackpot, Nevada
KBSK McCall, Idaho
KBSM McCall, Idaho
KBSO Corpus Christi, Texas
KBSQ McCall, Idaho
KBSS Sun Valley, Idaho
KBST-FM Big Spring, Texas
KBSU-FM Boise, Idaho
KBSW Twin Falls, Idaho
KBSX Boise, Idaho
KBSY Burley, Idaho
KBTA-FM Batesville, Arkansas
KBTE Tulia, Texas
KBTK(FM) Kachina Village, Arizona
KBTL El Dorado, Kansas
KBTN-FM Neosho, Missouri
KBTO Bottineau, North Dakota
KBTQ Harlingen, Texas
KBTS Big Spring, Texas
KBTT Haughton, Louisiana
KBTW Lenwood, California
KBUA San Fernando, California
KBUB Brownwood, Texas
KBUC Raymondville, Texas
KBUD Sardis, Mississippi
KBUE Long Beach, California
KBUK La Grange, Texas
KBUL Carson City, Nevada
KBUS Paris, Texas
KBUT Crested Butte, Colorado
KBUW Buffalo, Wyoming
KBUX Quartzsite, Arizona
KBUZ Topeka, Kansas
KBVA Bella Vista, Arkansas
KBVB Barnesville, Minnesota
KBVC Buena Vista, Colorado
KBVM Portland, Oregon
KBVR Corvallis, Oregon
KBVU-FM Alta, Iowa
KBWA Brush, Colorado
KBWC Marshall, Texas
KBWS-FM Sisseton, South Dakota
KBWW Broken Bow, Oklahoma
KBWX Columbia, Illinois
KBXB Sikeston, Missouri
KBXL Caldwell, Idaho
KBXR Columbia, Missouri
KBXT Wixon Valley, Texas
KBXX Houston, Texas
KBYB Hope, Arkansas
KBYI Rexburg, Idaho
KBYN Arnold, California
KBYO-FM Farmerville, Louisiana
KBYR-FM Rexburg, Idaho
KBYU-FM Provo, Utah
KBYZ Bismarck, North Dakota
KBZD Amarillo, Texas
KBZE Berwick, Louisiana
KBZM Big Sky, Montana
KBZN Ogden, Utah
KBZQ Lawton, Oklahoma
KBZR Billings, Montana
KBZS Wichita Falls, Texas
KBZT San Diego, California
KBZU Albuquerque, New Mexico
KCAC Camden, Arkansas
KCAD Dickinson, North Dakota
KCAI Lodi, California
KCAJ-FM Roseau, Minnesota
KCAL-FM Redlands, California
KCAQ Camarillo, California
KCAR-FM Baxter Springs, Kansas
KCAS McCook, Texas
KCAV Marshall, Arkansas
KCAW Sitka, Alaska
KCBI Dallas, Texas
KCBS-FM Los Angeles, California
KCBW Grandin, Missouri
KCBX San Luis Obispo, California
KCCD Moorhead, Minnesota
KCCK-FM Cedar Rapids, Iowa
KCCL Woodland, California
KCCM-FM Moorhead, Minnesota
KCCN-FM Honolulu, Hawaii
KCCS Starkville, Colorado
KCCU Lawton, Oklahoma
KCCV-FM Olathe, Kansas
KCCY-FM Pueblo, Colorado
KCDA Post Falls, Idaho
KCDD Hamlin, Texas
KCDQ Douglas, Arizona
KCDU Carmel, California
KCDV Cordova, Alaska
KCDX Florence, Arizona
KCDY Carlsbad, New Mexico
KCDZ Twentynine Palms, California
KCEA Atherton, California
KCEC-FM Wellton, Arizona
KCED Centralia, Washington
KCEI Red River, New Mexico
KCEL Mojave, California
KCEP Las Vegas, Nevada
KCEU Price, Utah
KCEY Ranchos De Taos, New Mexico
KCEZ Los Molinos, California
KCFA Arnold, California
KCFB St. Cloud, Minnesota
KCFD Crawford, Nebraska
KCFL Westport, Washington
KCFN Wichita, Kansas
KCFP Pueblo, Colorado
KCFR-FM Denver, Colorado
KCFS Sioux Falls, South Dakota
KCFV Ferguson, Missouri
KCFX Harrisonville, Missouri
KCFY Yuma, Arizona
KCGB-FM Columbia River, Oregon
KCGL Powell, Wyoming
KCGM Scobey, Montana
KCGN-FM Ortonville, Minnesota
KCGQ-FM Gordonville, Missouri
KCGR Oran, Missouri
KCGY Laramie, Wyoming
KCHA-FM Charles City, Iowa
KCHB Kaibito, Arizona
KCHE-FM Cherokee, Iowa
KCHG Cedar City, Utah
KCHH Worden, Montana
KCHI-FM Chillicothe, Missouri
KCHK-FM New Prague, Minnesota
KCHO Chico, California
KCHQ Driggs, Idaho
KCHX Midland, Texas
KCHZ Ottawa, Kansas
KCIC Grand Junction, Colorado
KCIE Dulce, New Mexico
KCIF Hilo, Hawaii
KCII-FM Washington, Iowa
KCIJ Atlanta, Louisiana
KCIL Gray, Louisiana
KCIN Cedar City, Utah
KCIR Twin Falls, Idaho
KCIU Columbia, Missouri
KCIV Mount Bullion, California
KCIX Garden City, Idaho
KCJC Dardanelle, Arkansas
KCJF Earle, Arkansas
KCJH Livingston, California
KCJK Garden City, Missouri
KCJX Carbondale, Colorado
KCKC Kansas City, Missouri
KCKJ Sarcoxie, Missouri
KCKL Malakoff, Texas
KCKR Church Point, Louisiana
KCKS Hamilton City, California
KCKT Crockett, Texas
KCKV Kirksville, Missouri
KCLB-FM Coachella, California
KCLC St. Charles, Missouri
KCLD-FM St. Cloud, Minnesota
KCLH Caledonia, Minnesota
KCLI-FM Cordell, Oklahoma
KCLK-FM Clarkston, Washington
KCLL San Angelo, Texas
KCLM Santa Maria, California
KCLQ Lebanon, Missouri
KCLR-FM Boonville, Missouri
KCLS Leeds, Utah
KCLT West Helena, Arkansas
KCLU-FM Thousand Oaks, California
KCLV-FM Clovis, New Mexico
KCLY Clay Center, Kansas
KCLZ Twentynine Palms, California
KCMB Baker City, Oregon
KCMC-FM Viola, Arkansas
KCMD Grants Pass, Oregon
KCME Manitou Springs, Colorado
KCMF Fergus Falls, Minnesota
KCMH Mountain Home, Arkansas
KCMI Terrytown, Nebraska
KCML St. Joseph, Minnesota
KCMM Belgrade, Montana
KCMO-FM Shawnee, Kansas
KCMP Northfield, Minnesota
KCMQ Columbia, Missouri
KCMR Mason City, Iowa
KCMS Edmonds, Washington
KCMT Oro Valley, Arizona
KCMX-FM Ashland, Oregon
KCNA Cave Junction, Oregon
KCNB Chadron, Nebraska
KCND Bismarck, North Dakota
KCNE-FM Chadron, Nebraska
KCNO Alturas, California
KCNP Ada, Oklahoma
KCNQ Kernville, California
KCNT Hastings, Nebraska
KCNV Las Vegas, Nevada
KCNY Greenbrier, Arkansas
KCOB-FM Newton, Iowa
KCOL-FM Groves, Texas
KCON Atkins, Arkansas
KCOO Dunkerton, Iowa
KCOU Columbia, Missouri
KCOZ Point Lookout, Missouri
KCPB-FM Warrenton, Oregon
KCPC Camino, California
KCPI Albert Lea, Minnesota
KCPR San Luis Obispo, California
KCPW-FM Salt Lake City, Utah
KCQQ Davenport, Iowa
KCRB-FM Bemidji, Minnesota
KCRE-FM Crescent City, California
KCRF-FM Lincoln City, Oregon
KCRH Hayward, California
KCRI Indio, California
KCRK-FM Colville, Washington
KCRL Sunrise Beach, Missouri
KCRN-FM San Angelo, Texas
KCRR Grundy Center, Iowa
KCRS-FM Midland, Texas
KCRT-FM Trinidad, Colorado
KCRU Oxnard, California
KCRV-FM Caruthersville, Missouri
KCRW Santa Monica, California
KCRX-FM Seaside, Oregon
KCRY Mojave, California
KCRZ Tipton, California
KCSB-FM Santa Barbara, California
KCSC Edmond, Oklahoma
KCSD Sioux Falls, South Dakota
KCSH Ellensburg, Washington
KCSI Villisca, Iowa
KCSM San Mateo, California
KCSN Northridge, California
KCSP Casper, Wyoming
KCSS Turlock, California
KCST-FM Florence, Oregon
KCSU-FM Fort Collins, Colorado
KCSY Twisp, Washington
KCTN Garnavillo, Iowa
KCTR-FM Billings, Montana
KCTT-FM Yellville, Arkansas
KCTX-FM Childress, Texas
KCTY Emerson, Nebraska
KCUA Naples, Utah
KCUK Chevak, Alaska
KCUL-FM Marshall, Texas
KCUR-FM Kansas City, Missouri
KCVI Blackfoot, Idaho
KCVJ Osceola, Missouri
KCVK Otterville, Missouri
KCVM Hudson, Iowa
KCVN Cozad, Nebraska
KCVO-FM Camdenton, Missouri
KCVQ Knob Noster, Missouri
KCVR-FM Columbia, California
KCVS Salina, Kansas
KCVT Silver Lake, Kansas
KCVW Kingman, Kansas
KCVX Salem, Missouri
KCVY Cabool, Missouri
KCVZ Dixon, Missouri

KCWC-FM Riverton, Wyoming
KCWD Harrison, Arkansas
KCWN New Sharon, Iowa
KCWR Bakersfield, California
KCWU Ellensburg, Washington
KCXR Taft, Oklahoma
KCXX Lake Arrowhead, California
KCXY East Camden, Arkansas
KCYE Boulder City, Nevada
KCYN Moab, Utah
KCYS Seaside, Oregon
KCYT Ozark, Arkansas
KCYY San Antonio, Texas
KCYZ Ames, Iowa
KCZE New Hampton, Iowa
KCZO Carrizo Springs, Texas
KCZQ Cresco, Iowa
KDAA Rolla, Missouri
KDAD Bar Nunn, Wyoming
KDAG Farmington, New Mexico
KDAI Scottsbluff, Nebraska
KDAL-FM Duluth, Minnesota
KDAO-FM Eldora, Iowa
KDAQ Shreveport, Louisiana
KDAR Oxnard, California
KDAT Cedar Rapids, Iowa
KDAY Redondo Beach, California
KDB Santa Barbara, California
KDBB Bonne Terre, Missouri
KDBH-FM Natchitoches, Louisiana
KDBI Emmett, Idaho
KDBL Parachute, Washington
KDBL(FM) Toppenish, Washington
KDBN Parachute, Colorado
KDBQ Rattan, Oklahoma
KDBR Kalispell, Montana
KDBX Clear Lake, South Dakota
KDBZ Anchorage, Alaska
KDCD San Angelo, Texas
KDCQ Coos Bay, Oregon
KDCR Sioux Center, Iowa
KDCZ Eyota, Minnesota
KDDB Waipahu, Hawaii
KDDD-FM Dumas, Texas
KDDG Albany, Minnesota
KDDK Franklin, Louisiana
KDDL Chino Valley, Arizona
KDDQ Comanche, Oklahoma
KDDS-FM Elma, Washington
KDDV-FM Wright, Wyoming
KDDX Spearfish, South Dakota
KDEC-FM Decorah, Iowa
KDEL-FM Arkadelphia, Arkansas
KDEM Deming, New Mexico
KDEP Garibaldi, Oregon
KDES-FM Cathedral City, California
KDEW-FM De Witt, Arkansas
KDEX-FM Dexter, Missouri
KDEY-FM Ontario, California
KDEZ Brandon, South Dakota
KDFC Sunnyvale, California
KDFC Angwin, California
KDFM Falfurrias, Texas
KDFO Delano, California
KDFR Des Moines, Iowa
KDGE Fort Worth-Dallas, Texas
KDGL Yucca Valley, California
KDGS Wichita, Kansas
KDHX Saint Louis, Missouri
KDIM Coweta, Oklahoma
KDIS-FM Little Rock, Arkansas
KDJC Baker, Oregon
KDJE Jacksonville, Arkansas
KDJF Ester, Alaska
KDJK Mariposa, California
KDJM Lindsborg, Kansas
KDJR De Soto, Missouri
KDJS-FM Willmar, Minnesota
KDKA-FM Pittsburgh, Pennsylvania
KDKB Mesa, Arizona
KDKD-FM Clinton, Missouri
KDKE Superior, Wisconsin
KDKK Park Rapids, Minnesota
KDKL Coalinga, California
KDKN Ellington, Missouri
KDKR Decatur, Texas
KDKS-FM Blanchard, Louisiana
KDLC Dulac, Louisiana
KDLD Santa Monica, California
KDLE Newport Beach, California
KDLG-FM Dillingham, Alaska
KDLI Del Rio, Texas
KDLK-FM Del Rio, Texas
KDLL Kenai, Alaska
KDLO-FM Watertown, South Dakota
KDLS-FM Perry, Iowa
KDLW Los Lunas, New Mexico
KDLX Makawao, Hawaii
KDLY Lander, Wyoming
KDMG Burlington, Iowa
KDMX Dallas, Texas
KDNA Yakima, Washington
KDND Sacramento, California
KDNE Crete, Nebraska
KDNG Durango, Colorado
KDNI Duluth, Minnesota
KDNK Glenwood Springs, Colorado
KDNN Honolulu, Hawaii
KDNO Thermopolis, Wyoming
KDNR South Greeley, Wyoming
KDNS Downs, Kansas
KDNW Duluth, Minnesota
KDOE Antlers, Oklahoma
KDOG North Mankato, Minnesota
KDOM-FM Windom, Minnesota
KDON-FM Salinas, California
KDOT Reno, Nevada
KDOV Medford, Oregon
KDPR Dickinson, North Dakota
KDQN-FM De Queen, Arkansas
KDRB Des Moines, Iowa
KDRE Sterling, Colorado
KDRF Albuquerque, New Mexico
KDRH King City, California
KDRI Grants, New Mexico
KDRK-FM Spokane, Washington
KDRM Moses Lake, Washington
KDRS-FM Paragould, Arkansas
KDRX Laughlin Afb, Texas
KDSC Thousand Oaks, California
KDSD-FM Pierpont, South Dakota
KDSK-FM Grants, New Mexico
KDSN-FM Denison, Iowa
KDSP(FM) Greenwood Village, Colorado
KDSR Williston, North Dakota
KDSS Ely, Nevada
KDST Dyersville, Iowa
KDSU Fargo, North Dakota
KDTR Florence, Montana
KDUC Barstow, California
KDUK-FM Eugene, Oregon
KDUP Cedarville, California
KDUQ Ludlow, California
KDUR Durango, Colorado
KDUT Randolph, Utah
KDUV Visalia, California
KDUW Douglas, Wyoming
KDUX-FM Hoquiam, Washington
KDVA Buckeye, Arizona
KDVB Effingham, Kansas
KDVC Loma, Colorado
KDVI Devils Lake, North Dakota
KDVL Devils Lake, North Dakota
KDVS Davis, California
KDVV Topeka, Kansas
KDWB-FM Richfield, Minnesota
KDWG Dillon, Montana
KDWY Diamondville, Wyoming
KDXA Ankeny, Iowa
KDXL St. Louis Park, Minnesota
KDXN South Heart, North Dakota
KDXT Lolo, Montana
KDXX Denton, Texas
KDXY Lake City, Arkansas
KDYN-FM Coal Hill, Arkansas
KDZA-FM Pueblo, Colorado
KDZN Glendive, Montana
KDZY McCall, Idaho
KDZZ St. Charles, Minnesota
KEAF Fort Smith, Arkansas
KEAG Anchorage, Alaska
KEAL Taft, California
KEAN-FM Abilene, Texas
KEAR-FM Sacramento, California
KEAZ Kensett, Arkansas
KEBN Garden Grove, California
KEBT Lost Hills, California
KECC La Junta, Colorado
KECG El Cerrito, California
KECH-FM Sun Valley, Idaho
KECK Eckley, Colorado
KECO Elk City, Oklahoma
KECU Kaibito, Arizona
KEDB Chariton, Iowa
KEDC Hearne, Texas
KEDG Alexandria, Louisiana
KEDJ Jerome, Idaho
KEDM Monroe, Louisiana
KEDP Las Vegas, New Mexico
KEDR Bay City, Texas
KEDR(FM) Butte, Montana
KEDT-FM Corpus Christi, Texas
KEEA Aberdeen, South Dakota
KEEH Spokane, Washington
KEEP Bandera, Texas
KEEY-FM St. Paul, Minnesota
KEEZ-FM Mankato, Minnesota
KEFH Clarendon, Texas
KEFR Le Grand, California
KEFS North Powder, Oregon
KEFX Twin Falls, Idaho
KEGA Oakley, Utah
KEGE Pocatello, Idaho
KEGH Brigham City, Utah
KEGI Jonesboro, Arkansas
KEGK Wahpeton, North Dakota
KEGL Fort Worth, Texas
KEGX Richland, Washington
KEGY San Diego, California
KEHK Brownsville, Oregon
KEIS York, Nebraska
KEJA Cale, Arkansas
KEJJ Gunnison, Colorado
KEJL Eunice, New Mexico
KEJS Lubbock, Texas
KEKA-FM Eureka, California
KEKB Fruita, Colorado
KEKL Mesquite, Nevada
KEKO Hebbronville, Texas
KEKS Olpe, Kansas
KELC Hawthorne, Nevada
KELD-FM Hampton, Arkansas
KELE-FM Mountain Grove, Missouri
KELI San Angelo, Texas
KELN North Platte, Nebraska
KELO-FM Sioux Falls, South Dakota
KELP-FM Mesquite, New Mexico
KELU Clovis, New Mexico
KEMA Three Rivers, Texas
KEMC Billings, Montana
KEMX Locust Grove, Oklahoma
KENA-FM Mena, Arkansas
KEND Roswell, New Mexico
KENM Tucumcari, New Mexico
KENR Superior, Montana
KENU Des Moines, New Mexico
KENW-FM Portales, New Mexico
KENZ Provo, Utah
KENZ Provo, Utah
KEOJ Caney, Kansas
KEOK Tahlequah, Oklahoma
KEOL La Grande, Oregon
KEOM Mesquite, Texas
KEOS College Station, Texas
KEPC Colorado Springs, Colorado
KEPI Eagle Pass, Texas
KEPX Eagle Pass, Texas
KEQX Stephenville, Texas
KERA Dallas, Texas
KERB-FM Kermit, Texas
KERL Cotton Plant, Arkansas
KERM Torrington, Wyoming
KERN Wasco-Greenacres, California
KERP Ingalls, Kansas
KERX Paris, Arkansas
KESA Eureka Springs, Arkansas
KESC Morro Bay, California
KESD Brookings, South Dakota
KESM-FM El Dorado Springs, Missouri
KESN Allen, Texas
KESO South Padre Island, Texas
KESR Shasta Lake City, California
KESS Benbrook, Texas
KESY Baker City, Oregon
KESZ Phoenix, Arizona
KETE Sulphur Bluff, Texas
KETP Enterprise, Oregon
KETR Commerce, Texas
KETT Mitchell, Nebraska
KETX-FM Livingston, Texas
KEUG Veneta, Oregon
KEUL Girdwood, Alaska
KEUN-FM Eunice, Louisiana
KEWB Anderson, California
KEWF Billings, Montana
KEWL-FM New Boston, Texas
KEWS(FM) Sac City, Iowa
KEWU-FM Cheney, Washington
KEXA King City, California
KEXL Pierce, Nebraska
KEXP-FM Seattle, Washington
KEXS-FM Ravenwood, Missouri
KEXX(FM) Gilbert, Arizona
KEYA Belcourt, North Dakota
KEYB Altus, Oklahoma
KEYD Delta, Utah
KEYE-FM Perryton, Texas
KEYF-FM Cheney, Washington
KEYG-FM Grand Coulee, Washington
KEYJ-FM Abilene, Texas
KEYN-FM Wichita, Kansas
KEYP Price, Utah
KEYR Richfield, Utah
KEYU-FM Amarillo, Texas
KEYV Vernal, Utah
KEYW Pasco, Washington
KEZA Fayetteville, Arkansas
KEZB Beaver, Utah
KEZE Spokane, Washington
KEZJ-FM Twin Falls, Idaho
KEZK St. Louis, Missouri
KEZN Palm Desert, California
KEZO-FM Omaha, Nebraska
KEZP Bunkie, Louisiana
KEZQ West Yellowstone, Montana
KEZR San Jose, California
KEZS-FM Cape Girardeau, Missouri
KEZZ Phippsburg, Colorado
KFAE-FM Richland, Washington
KFAI Minneapolis, Minnesota
KFAN-FM Johnson City, Texas
KFAT Anchorage, Alaska
KFAV Warrenton, Missouri
KFBD-FM Waynesville, Missouri
KFBK-FM Pollock Pines, California
KFBN Fargo, North Dakota
KFBR Gerlach, Nevada
KFBT Hanford, California
KFBZ Haysville, Kansas
KFCF Fresno, California
KFCM Ash Flat, Arkansas
KFCO Bennett, Colorado
KFCV Dixon, Missouri
KFDC Shiprock, New Mexico
KFDI-FM Wichita, Kansas
KFEB Campbell, Missouri
KFEG Klamath Falls, Oregon
KFER Santa Cruz, California
KFEZ(FM) Walsenburg, Colorado
KFFA-FM Helena, Arkansas
KFFB Fairfield Bay, Arkansas
KFFF Bennington, Nebraska
KFFF-FM Boone, Iowa
KFFG Los Altos, California
KFFM Yakima, Washington
KFFX Emporia, Kansas
KFGE Milford, Nebraska
KFGI Crosby, Minnesota
KFGY Healdsburg, California
KFH-FM Clearwater, Kansas
KFHC Ponca, Nebraska
KFHL Wasco, California
KFIL-FM Chatfield, Minnesota
KFIN Jonesboro, Arkansas
KFIS Scappoose, Oregon
KFIX Plainville, Kansas
KFJC Los Altos, California
KFJM Grand Forks, North Dakota
KFJS North Platte, Nebraska
KFKF-FM Kansas City, Kansas
KFKX Hastings, Nebraska
KFLB-FM Stanton, Texas
KFLF Somers, Montana
KFLG-FM Big River, California
KFLI Des Arc, Arkansas
KFLO-FM Blanchard, Louisiana
KFLP-FM Floydada, Texas
KFLQ Albuquerque, New Mexico
KFLR-FM Phoenix, Arizona
KFLS-FM Tulelake, California
KFLT-FM Tucson, Arizona
KFLV Wilber, Nebraska
KFLW St. Robert, Missouri
KFLY Eugene, Oregon

KFMA Green Valley, Arizona
KFMB-FM San Diego, California
KFMC-FM Fairmont, Minnesota
KFMF Chico, California
KFMH Belle Fourche, South Dakota
KFMI Eureka, California
KFMJ Ketchikan, Alaska
KFMK Round Rock, Texas
KFML Little Falls, Minnesota
KFMM Thatcher, Arizona
KFMN Lihue, Hawaii
KFMQ Gallup, New Mexico
KFMR Ballard, Utah
KFMT-FM Fremont, Nebraska
KFMU-FM Oak Creek, Colorado
KFMW Waterloo, Iowa
KFMX-FM Lubbock, Texas
KFNC Mont Belvieu, Texas
KFNF Oberlin, Kansas
KFNL Kindred, North Dakota
KFNO Fresno, California
KFNS-FM Troy, Missouri
KFNV-FM Ferriday, Louisiana
KFNW-FM Fargo, North Dakota
KFOG San Francisco, California
KFPR Redding, California
KFPW-FM Barling, Arkansas
KFRB Bakersfield, California
KFRC San Francisco, California
KFRD Butte, Montana
KFRG San Bernardino, California
KFRH North Las Vegas, Nevada
KFRI West Odessa, Texas
KFRJ China Lake, California
KFRO-FM Gilmer, Texas
KFRP Coalinga, California
KFRQ Harlingen, Texas
KFRR Woodlake, California
KFRS Soledad, California
KFRW Great Falls, Montana
KFRX Lincoln, Nebraska
KFRY Pueblo, Colorado
KFRZ Green River, Wyoming
KFSE Kasilof, Alaska
KFSH-FM La Mirada, California
KFSI Rochester, Minnesota
KFSK Petersburg, Alaska
KFSO-FM Visalia, California
KFSR Fresno, California
KFST-FM Fort Stockton, Texas
KFSZ Munds Park, Arizona
KFTE Abbeville, Louisiana
KFTG Pasadena, Texas
KFTI-FM Newton, Kansas
KFTK Florissant, Missouri
KFTT Bagdad, Arizona
KFTX Kingsville, Texas
KFTZ Idaho Falls, Idaho
KFVR-FM Beulah, Colorado
KFWR Jacksboro, Texas
KFXH Marlow, Oklahoma
KFXI Marlow, Oklahoma
KFXJ Augusta, Kansas
KFXN-FM Minneapolis, Minnesota
KFXR-FM Chinle, Arizona
KFXS Rapid City, South Dakota
KFXT Sulphur, Oklahoma
KFXU Chickasha, Oklahoma
KFXX-FM Hugoton, Kansas
KFXZ-FM Opelousas, Louisiana
KFYV Ojai, California
KFYX(FM) Texarkana, Arkansas
KFZE Daniel, Wyoming
KFZO Lewisville, Texas
KFZX Gardendale, Texas
KGAC Saint Peter, Minnesota
KGAM Merced, California
KGAM(FM) Merced, California
KGAP Clarksville, Texas
KGAS-FM Carthage, Texas
KGB-FM San Diego, California
KGBA-FM Holtville, California
KGBB Edwards, California
KGBI-FM Omaha, Nebraska
KGBM Randsburg, California
KGBR Gold Beach, Oregon
KGBT-FM McAllen, Texas
KGBX-FM Nixa, Missouri
KGCB Prescott, Arizona
KGCC Gillette, Wyoming
KGCD Wray, Colorado

KGCL Jordan Valley, Oregon
KGCM Belgrade, Montana
KGCN Roswell, New Mexico
KGCO Fort Collins, Colorado
KGCR Goodland, Kansas
KGCU Port Alsworth, Alaska
KGCX Sidney, Montana
KGDN Pasco, Washington
KGDP-FM Santa Maria, California
KGEE Pecos, Texas
KGEN-FM Hanford, California
KGFA Great Falls, Montana
KGFC Great Falls, Montana
KGFJ Belt, Montana
KGFK East Grand Forks, Minnesota
KGFM Bakersfield, California
KGFT Pueblo, Colorado
KGFX-FM Pierre, South Dakota
KGFY Stillwater, Oklahoma
KGGA Gallup, New Mexico
KGGB Yorktown, Texas
KGGF FM Fredonia, Kansas
KGGI Riverside, California
KGGL Missoula, Montana
KGGM Delhi, Louisiana
KGGO Des Moines, Iowa
KGHE Glenoma, Washington
KGHL(FM) Billings, Montana
KGHP Gig Harbor, Washington
KGHT El Jebel, Colorado
KGHY Beaumont, Texas
KGIL Johannesburg, California
KGIM-FM Redfield, South Dakota
KGIO Astoria, Oregon
KGJX Fruita, Colorado
KGKL-FM San Angelo, Texas
KGKS Scott City, Missouri
KGKV Garberville, California
KGLC Miami, Oklahoma
KGLF Doss, Texas
KGLI Sioux City, Iowa
KGLK Lake Jackson, Texas
KGLK Lake Jackson, Texas
KGLL Gillette, Wyoming
KGLM-FM Anaconda, Montana
KGLP Gallup, New Mexico
KGLT Bozeman, Montana
KGLU Gideon, Missouri
KGLV Manhattan, Kansas
KGLX Gallup, New Mexico
KGLY Tyler, Texas
KGMN Kingman, Arizona
KGMO Cape Girardeau, Missouri
KGMX Lancaster, California
KGMZ(FM) San Francisco, California
KGNA-FM Arnold, Missouri
KGNC-FM Amarillo, Texas
KGNN-FM Cuba, Missouri
KGNR John Day, Oregon
KGNT Smithfield, Utah
KGNU-FM Boulder, Colorado
KGNV Washington, Missouri
KGNX Ballwin, Missouri
KGNZ Abilene, Texas
KGON Portland, Oregon
KGOR Omaha, Nebraska
KGOT Anchorage, Alaska
KGOU Norman, Oklahoma
KGOZ Gallatin, Missouri
KGPQ Monticello, Arkansas
KGPR Great Falls, Montana
KGPZ Coleraine, Minnesota
KGRA Jefferson, Iowa
KGRB(FM) Jackson, California
KGRC Hannibal, Missouri
KGRD Orchard, Nebraska
KGRG-FM Auburn, Washington
KGRI Lebanon, Oregon
KGRK Glenrock, Wyoming
KGRM Grambling, Louisiana
KGRP Grand Rapids, Minnesota
KGRR Epworth, Iowa
KGRS Burlington, Iowa
KGRT-FM Las Cruces, New Mexico
KGRW Friona, Texas
KGSF Hunstville, Arkansas
KGSP Parkville, Missouri
KGSR Cedar Park, Texas
KGTM Rexburg, Idaho
KGTR Albany, Missouri
KGTS College Place, Washington

KGTW Ketchikan, Alaska
KGUA Gualala, California
KGUD Longmont, Colorado
KGUM-FM Dededo, Guam
KGVA Fort Belknap Agency, Montana
KGVB Holliday, Texas
KGVE Grove, Oklahoma
KGVO-FM Frenchtown, Montana
KGVV Goltry, Oklahoma
KGWB Snyder, Texas
KGWP Pittsburg, Texas
KGWT George West, Texas
KGWY Gillette, Wyoming
KGZG-FM Newport, Washington
KGZO Shafter, California
KHAD Upton, Wyoming
KHAI Wahiawa, Hawaii
KHAK Cedar Rapids, Iowa
KHAL Cedarville, California
KHAM Britt, Iowa
KHAN Medicine Bow, Wyoming
KHAP Chico, California
KHAQ Maxwell, Nebraska
KHAY Ventura, California
KHAZ Hays, Kansas
KHBC Hilo, Hawaii
KHBM-FM Monticello, Arkansas
KHBT Humboldt, Iowa
KHBW Brownwood, Texas
KHBZ Harrison, Arkansas
KHCA Wamego, Kansas
KHCB-FM Houston, Texas
KHCC-FM Hutchinson, Kansas
KHCD Salina, Kansas
KHCJ Jefferson, Texas
KHCL Arcadia, Louisiana
KHCM-FM Honolulu, Hawaii
KHCO Hayden, Colorado
KHCP Paris, Texas
KHCR Bismarck, Missouri
KHCS Palm Desert, California
KHCT Great Bend, Kansas
KHDC Chualar, California
KHDK New London, Iowa
KHDR Lenwood, California
KHDV Darby, Montana
KHDX Conway, Arkansas
KHEB Granite, Oklahoma
KHEC Crescent City, California
KHED Arkadelphia, Arkansas
KHEI-FM Kihei, Hawaii
KHER Crystal City, Texas
KHEV Fairview, Oklahoma
KHEW Rocky Boy's Reserv., Montana
KHEY-FM El Paso, Texas
KHFI-FM Georgetown, Texas
KHFM Santa Fe, New Mexico
KHGE Fresno, California
KHGG-FM Waldron, Arkansas
KHHK Yakima, Washington
KHHL Karnes City, Texas
KHHM Sacramento, California
KHHZ Gridley, California
KHIB Bastrop, Texas
KHIC Keno, Oregon
KHID McAllen, Texas
KHIH Estes Park, Colorado
KHII Cloudcroft, New Mexico
KHIM Mangum, Oklahoma
KHIP Gonzales, California
KHIS Jackson, Missouri
KHIT-FM Madera, California
KHIX Carlin, Nevada
KHJC Lihue, Hawaii
KHJJ Shaniko, Oregon
KHJK La Porte, Texas
KHJZ Honolulu, Hawaii
KHKC-FM Atoka, Oklahoma
KHKE Cedar Falls, Iowa
KHKI Des Moines, Iowa
KHKK Modesto, California
KHKL Laytonville, California
KHKN Maumelle, Arkansas
KHKS Denton, Texas
KHKV Kerrville, Texas
KHKX Odessa, Texas
KHKY Akiachak, Alaska
KHKZ San Benito, Texas
KHLA Jennings, Louisiana
KHLB Mason, Texas
KHLL Richwood, Louisiana

KHLR Benton, Arkansas
KHLS Blytheville, Arkansas
KHLT Belle Plaine, Kansas
KHLV Helena, Montana
KHMB Hamburg, Arkansas
KHMC Goliad, Texas
KHMD Mansfield, Louisiana
KHME Winona, Minnesota
KHMG Barrigada, Guam
KHML Madisonville, Texas
KHMS Victorville, California
KHMX Houston, Texas
KHMY Pratt, Kansas
KHNE-FM Hastings, Nebraska
KHNK Columbia Falls, Montana
KHNO Huntington, Oregon
KHNS Haines, Alaska
KHNW Manson, Washington
KHOC Casper, Wyoming
KHOE Fairfield, Iowa
KHOI Story City, Iowa
KHOK Hoisington, Kansas
KHOL Jackson, Wyoming
KHOM Salem, Arkansas
KHOP Oakdale, California
KHOS-FM Sonora, Texas
KHOT-FM Paradise Valley, Arizona
KHOV-FM Wickenburg, Arizona
KHOY Laredo, Texas
KHPA Hope, Arkansas
KHPE Albany, Oregon
KHPO Port O'Connor, Texas
KHPQ Clinton, Arkansas
KHPR Honolulu, Hawaii
KHQT Las Cruces, New Mexico
KHRD Weaverville, California
KHRI Hollister, California
KHRQ Baker, California
KHRS Winthrop, Minnesota
KHRT-FM Minot, North Dakota
KHRV Hood River, Oregon
KHRW Ranchester, Wyoming
KHSK Allen, Nebraska
KHSL-FM Paradise, California
KHSR Crescent City, California
KHSS Athena, Oregon
KHST Lamar, Missouri
KHSU Arcata, California
KHTA Wake Village, Texas
KHTE-FM England, Arkansas
KHTH Santa Rosa, California
KHTN Planada, California
KHTO(FM) Hot Springs, Arkansas
KHTP Tacoma, Washington
KHTQ Hayden, Idaho
KHTR Pullman, Washington
KHTS-FM El Cajon, California
KHTT Muskogee, Oklahoma
KHTZ Ganado, Texas
KHUI Alamosa, Colorado
KHUM Cutten, California
KHUT Hutchinson, Kansas
KHVT Bloomington, Texas
KHWG-FM Crystal, Nevada
KHWI Holualoa, Hawaii
KHWY Essex, California
KHXS Merkel, Texas
KHXT Erath, Louisiana
KHYI Howe, Texas
KHYL Auburn, California
KHYM Copeland, Kansas
KHYS Hays, Kansas
KHYT Tucson, Arizona
KHYY Minatare, Nebraska
KHYZ Mountain Pass, California
KHZR Potosi, Missouri
KHZY Overton, Nebraska
KIAD Dubuque, Iowa
KIAI Mason City, Iowa
KIAK-FM Fairbanks, Alaska
KIAM-FM North Nenana, Alaska
KIAQ Clarion, Iowa
KIBB Haven, Kansas
KIBC Burney, California
KIBG Bigfork, Montana
KIBR Sandpoint, Idaho
KIBS Bishop, California
KIBT Fountain, Colorado
KIBX Bonners Ferry, Idaho
KIBZ Crete, Nebraska
KICA-FM Farwell, Texas

KICB Fort Dodge, Iowa
KICD-FM Spencer, Iowa
KICJ(FM) Mitchellville, Iowa
KICK-FM Palmyra, Missouri
KICL(FM) Pleasantville, Iowa
KICM Healdton, Oklahoma
KICO Rico, Colorado
KICR Coeur D'Alene, Idaho
KICT-FM Wichita, Kansas
KICX-FM McCook, Nebraska
KICY-FM Nome, Alaska
KID-FM Idaho Falls, Idaho
KIDE Hoopa, California
KIDI-FM Lompoc, California
KIDN-FM Burns, Colorado
KIDS Grants, New Mexico
KIDX Ruidoso, New Mexico
KIFG-FM Iowa Falls, Iowa
KIFM San Diego, California
KIFR Alice, Texas
KIFS Medford, Oregon
KIFT(FM) Kremmling, Colorado
KIFX Roosevelt, Utah
KIGC Oskaloosa, Iowa
KIGL Seligman, Missouri
KIGN Burns, Wyoming
KIHI Burns, Wyoming
KIHK Rock Valley, Iowa
KIHS Adel, Iowa
KIIC Albia, Iowa
KIIM Tucson, Arizona
KIIS-FM Los Angeles, California
KIIX-FM Opportunity, Washington
KIIZ-FM Killeen, Texas
KIJI Tumon, Guam
KIJN-FM Farwell, Texas
KIKC-FM Forsyth, Montana
KIKD Lake City, Iowa
KIKF Cascade, Montana
KIKG Licking, Missouri
KIKL Lafayette, Louisiana
KIKN-FM Salem, South Dakota
KIKO Miami, Arizona
KIKO-FM Claypool, Arizona
KIKS-FM Iola, Kansas
KIKT Greenville, Texas
KIKV-FM Sauk Centre, Minnesota
KIKX Ketchum, Idaho
KILE-FM Woodland Park, Colorado
KILI Porcupine, South Dakota
KILJ-FM Mount Pleasant, Iowa
KILO Colorado Springs, Colorado
KILR-FM Estherville, Iowa
KILT-FM Houston, Texas
KILV Castana, Iowa
KILX Hatfield, Arkansas
KIMN Denver, Colorado
KIMO Helena Valley SE, Montana
KIMW Heflin, Louisiana
KIMX Nunn, Colorado
KIMY Watonga, Oklahoma
KINB Kingfisher, Oklahoma
KIND-FM Elk City, Kansas
KINE-FM Honolulu, Hawaii
KINF Gooding, Idaho
KING-FM Seattle, Washington
KINI Crookston, Nebraska
KINK Portland, Oregon
KINL Eagle Pass, Texas
KINS-FM Blue Lake, California
KINT-FM El Paso, Texas
KINU Kotzebue, Alaska
KINX Fairfield, Hawaii
KINZ Humboldt, Kansas
KIOA Des Moines, Iowa
KIOC Orange, Texas
KIOD McCook, Nebraska
KIOI San Francisco, California
KIOK Richland, Washington
KIOO Porterville, California
KIOS-FM Omaha, Nebraska
KIOT Los Lunas, New Mexico
KIOW Forest City, Iowa
KIOX-FM Edna, Texas
KIOZ San Diego, California
KIPO Honolulu, Hawaii
KIPR Pine Bluff, Arkansas
KIQK Rapid City, South Dakota
KIQN-FM Pueblo, Colorado
KIQQ-FM Newberry Springs, California
KIQX Durango, Colorado
KIQZ Rawlins, Wyoming
KIRC Seminole, Oklahoma
KIRK Macon, Missouri
KIRL Osage Beach, Missouri
KIRO-FM Tacoma, Washington
KIRQ Twin Falls, Idaho
KISC Spokane, Washington
KISD Pipestone, Minnesota
KISF Las Vegas, Nevada
KISH Agana, Guam
KISL Avalon, California
KISM Bellingham, Washington
KISN Belgrade, Montana
KISO Omaha, Nebraska
KISQ San Francisco, California
KISR Fort Smith, Arkansas
KISS-FM San Antonio, Texas
KISS-FM San Antonio, Texas
KIST-FM Carpinteria, California
KISU-FM Pocatello, Idaho
KISV Bakersfield, California
KISW Seattle, Washington
KISX Whitehouse, Texas
KISZ-FM Cortez, Colorado
KIT-FM Naches, Washington
KITA Iota, Louisiana
KITE Port Lavaca, Texas
KITF International Falls, Minnesota
KITH Kapaa, Hawaii
KITI-FM Winlock, Washington
KITN Worthington, Minnesota
KITO-FM Vinita, Oklahoma
KITS San Francisco, California
KITT Soda Springs, Idaho
KITX Hugo, Oklahoma
KITY Llano, Texas
KIVY-FM Crockett, Texas
KIWA-FM Sheldon, Iowa
KIWI McFarland, California
KIWR Council Bluffs, Iowa
KIXA Lucerne Valley, California
KIXB El Dorado, Arkansas
KIXF Baker, California
KIXN Hobbs, New Mexico
KIXO Sulphur, Oklahoma
KIXQ Joplin, Missouri
KIXS Victoria, Texas
KIXV(FM) Malvern, Arkansas
KIXW-FM Lenwood, California
KIXX Watertown, South Dakota
KIXX Lebanon, New Hampshire
KIXY-FM San Angelo, Texas
KIYK Saint George, Utah
KIYS Walnut Ridge, Arkansas
KIYU-FM Galena, Alaska
KIYX Sageville, Iowa
KIZN Boise, Idaho
KIZS Collinsville, Oklahoma
KIZZ Minot, North Dakota
KJAB-FM Mexico, Missouri
KJAC Timnath, Colorado
KJAE Leesville, Louisiana
KJAK Slaton, Texas
KJAM-FM Madison, South Dakota
KJAQ Seattle, Washington
KJAS Jasper, Texas
KJAV Alamo, Texas
KJAX Jackson, Wyoming
KJBI Fort Pierre, South Dakota
KJBL Julesburg, Colorado
KJBR Marked Tree, Arkansas
KJBX Cash, Arkansas
KJBX Walnut Ridge, Arkansas
KJBZ Laredo, Texas
KJCC Carnegie, Oklahoma
KJCG Missoula, Montana
KJCH Coos Bay, Oregon
KJCK-FM Junction City, Kansas
KJCM Snyder, Oklahoma
KJCS Nacogdoches, Texas
KJCU Fort Bragg, California
KJCV-FM Country Club, Missouri
KJCY St. Ansgar, Iowa
KJDL-FM Levelland, Texas
KJDR Guymon, Oklahoma
KJDX Susanville, California
KJDY-FM Canyon City, Oregon
KJEE Montecito, California
KJEL Lebanon, Missouri
KJET Raymond, Washington
KJEZ Poplar Bluff, Missouri
KJFA-FM Santa Fe, New Mexico
KJFM Louisiana, Missouri
KJFT Arlee, Montana
KJFX Fresno, California
KJGS Aurora, Nebraska
KJHA Houston, Alaska
KJHK Lawrence, Kansas
KJHL Boise City, Oklahoma
KJHM Strasburg, Colorado
KJIA Spirit Lake, Iowa
KJIH Manhattan, Kansas
KJIK Duncan, Arizona
KJIL Copeland, Kansas
KJIR Hannibal, Missouri
KJIV Reno, Nevada
KJIW-FM Helena, Arkansas
KJJJ Laughlin, Nevada
KJJK-FM Fergus Falls, Minnesota
KJJM Baker, Montana
KJJP Amarillo, Texas
KJJS Zapata, Texas
KJJT Los Ybanez, Texas
KJJY West Des Moines, Iowa
KJJZ Indio, California
KJKE Newcastle, Oklahoma
KJKJ Grand Forks, North Dakota
KJKK Dallas, Texas
KJKL Selma, Oregon
KJKS Kahului, Hawaii
KJKT Spearfish, South Dakota
KJLC-FM Needles, California
KJLF Butte, Montana
KJLG Emporia, Kansas
KJLH Compton, California
KJLJ Scott City, Kansas
KJLO-FM Monroe, Louisiana
KJLP Palmer, Alaska
KJLS Hays, Kansas
KJLT-FM North Platte, Nebraska
KJLU Jefferson City, Missouri
KJLV Hoxie, Arkansas
KJLY Blue Earth, Minnesota
KJMA Floresville, Texas
KJMB-FM Blythe, California
KJMC Des Moines, Iowa
KJMD Pukalani, Hawaii
KJMG Bastrop, Louisiana
KJMH Lake Charles, Louisiana
KJMK Webb City, Missouri
KJML Columbus, Kansas
KJML(FM) Columbus, Kansas
KJMM Bixby, Oklahoma
KJMN Castle Rock, Colorado
KJMO Linn, Missouri
KJMQ Lihue, Hawaii
KJMS Olive Branch, Mississippi
KJMT Calico Rock, Arkansas
KJMX Coos Bay, Oregon
KJMY Bountiful, Utah
KJMZ Cache, Oklahoma
KJNA-FM Jena, Louisiana
KJND-FM Williston, North Dakota
KJNP-FM North Pole, Alaska
KJNW Kansas City, Missouri
KJNZ Hereford, Texas
KJOE Slayton, Minnesota
KJOG Cleveland, Oklahoma
KJOJ-FM Freeport, Texas
KJOK Hollis, Oklahoma
KJOL-FM Montrose, Colorado
KJOR Windsor, California
KJOT Boise, Idaho
KJOV Woodward, Oklahoma
KJOY Stockton, California
KJQY Colorado City, Colorado
KJR-FM Seattle, Washington
KJRF Lawton, Oklahoma
KJRL Herington, Kansas
KJRN Keene, Texas
KJRT Amarillo, Texas
KJRV Wessington Springs, South Dakota
KJSB Jonesboro, Arkansas
KJSM-FM Augusta, Arkansas
KJSN Modesto, California
KJSR Tulsa, Oklahoma
KJSR Sand Springs, Oklahoma
KJTA Flagstaff, Arizona
KJTH Ponca City, Oklahoma
KJTW Jamestown, North Dakota
KJTX Jefferson, Texas
KJTY Topeka, Kansas
KJUG-FM Tulare, California
KJUL Moapa Valley, Nevada
KJVC Mansfield, Louisiana
KJVH Longview, Washington
KJWA Trinidad, Colorado
KJWL Fresno, California
KJWR Windom, Minnesota
KJXJ Franklin, Texas
KJXK San Antonio, Texas
KJXN South Park, Wyoming
KJYL Eagle Grove, Iowa
KJYO Oklahoma City, Oklahoma
KJZA Drake, Arizona
KJZK Kingman, Arizona
KJZN San Joaquin, California
KJZP Prescott, Arizona
KJZY Sebastopol, California
KJZZ Phoenix, Arizona
KKAC Vandalia, Missouri
KKAJ-FM Davis, Oklahoma
KKAL Paso Robles, California
KKAR Wamsutter, Wyoming
KKAW Douglas, Wyoming
KKBA Kingsville, Texas
KKBB Bakersfield, California
KKBC-FM Baker, Oregon
KKBD Sallisaw, Oklahoma
KKBG Hilo, Hawaii
KKBI Broken Bow, Oklahoma
KKBJ-FM Bemidji, Minnesota
KKBL Monett, Missouri
KKBN Twain Harte, California
KKBO Flasher, North Dakota
KKBQ-FM Pasadena, Texas
KKBR Billings, Montana
KKBS Guymon, Oklahoma
KKBW Eatonville, Washington
KKBY Kirby, Wyoming
KKBZ Auberry, California
KKCB Duluth, Minnesota
KKCD Omaha, Nebraska
KKCH Glenwood Springs, Colorado
KKCI Goodland, Kansas
KKCJ Cannon Afb, New Mexico
KKCK Marshall, Minnesota
KKCL Lorenzo, Texas
KKCM Thermal, California
KKCN Ballinger, Texas
KKCQ-FM Bagley, Minnesota
KKCR Hanalei, Hawaii
KKCS(FM) Calhan, Colorado
KKCT Bismarck, North Dakota
KKCV Rozel, Kansas
KKCW Beaverton, Oregon
KKCY Colusa, California
KKDA Dallas, Texas
KKDC Dolores, Colorado
KKDL Dilley, Texas
KKDM Des Moines, Iowa
KKDQ Thief River Falls, Minnesota
KKDT Burdett, Kansas
KKDV Walnut Creek, California
KKDY West Plains, Missouri
KKED Fairbanks, Alaska
KKEE Wheelock, Texas
KKEG Bentonville, Arkansas
KKEN Duncan, Oklahoma
KKER Kerrville, Texas
KKEX Preston, Idaho
KKEZ Fort Dodge, Iowa
KKFC Hart, Texas
KKFD-FM Fairfield, Iowa
KKFG Bloomfield, New Mexico
KKFI Kansas City, Missouri
KKFM Colorado Springs, Colorado
KKFN Longmont, Colorado
KKFR Mayer, Arizona
KKFS Lincoln, California
KKFT Gardnerville-Minden, Nevada
KKGB Sulphur, Louisiana
KKGL Nampa, Idaho
KKGN Ingram, Texas
KKGO Los Angeles, California
KKHA Markham, Texas
KKHB Eureka, California
KKHH Houston, Texas
KKHI Kihei, Hawaii
KKHJ-FM Pago Pago, American Samoa
KKHK Carmel, California
KKHQ-FM Oelwein, Iowa
KKHR Abilene, Texas

KKHT-FM Lumberton, Texas
KKIA Ida Grove, Iowa
KKID Salem, Missouri
KKIK Horseshoe Bend, Arkansas
KKIN-FM Aitkin, Minnesota
KKIQ Livermore, California
KKIS-FM Soldotna, Alaska
KKIT Taos, New Mexico
KKIX Fayetteville, Arkansas
KKJA Redmond, Oregon
KKJD Borrego Springs, California
KKJG San Luis Obispo, California
KKJK Ravenna, Nebraska
KKJM St. Joseph, Minnesota
KKJO-FM St. Joseph, Missouri
KKJQ Garden City, Kansas
KKJZ Long Beach, California
KKKC Central City, Colorado
KKKJ Merrill, Oregon
KKLA-FM Los Angeles, California
KKLB Ruidoso, New Mexico
KKLC Fall River Mills, California
KKLD Cottonwood, Arizona
KKLG Newton, Iowa
KKLH Marshfield, Missouri
KKLI Widefield, Colorado
KKLJ Klamath Falls, Oregon
KKLM Corpus Christi, Texas
KKLN Atwater, Minnesota
KKLP La Pine, Oregon
KKLQ Harwood, North Dakota
KKLR-FM Poplar Bluff, Missouri
KKLS-FM Sioux Falls, South Dakota
KKLT Texarkana, Arkansas
KKLU Lubbock, Texas
KKLV Orem, Utah
KKLV Kaysville, Utah
KKLW Willmar, Minnesota
KKLX Worland, Wyoming
KKLY El Paso, Texas
KKLZ Las Vegas, Nevada
KKMA Le Mars, Iowa
KKMG Pueblo, Colorado
KKMI Burlington, Iowa
KKMJ-FM Austin, Texas
KKMK Rapid City, South Dakota
KKMR Arizona City, Arizona
KKMT Ronan, Montana
KKMV Rupert, Idaho
KKMX Tri City, Oregon
KKMY Orange, Texas
KKND Port Sulphur, Louisiana
KKND Belle Chasse, Louisiana
KKNG-FM Blanchard, Oklahoma
KKNI Sterling, Alaska
KKNL Valentine, Nebraska
KKNM Bovina, Texas
KKNN Delta, Colorado
KKNU Springfield-Eugene, Oregon
KKOA Volcano, Hawaii
KKOB Albuquerque, New Mexico
KKOK-FM Morris, Minnesota
KKOL-FM Aiea, Hawaii
KKOT Columbus, Nebraska
KKOW-FM Pittsburg, Kansas
KKOY-FM Chanute, Kansas
KKOZ-FM Ava, Missouri
KKPK Colorado Springs, Colorado
KKPL Cheyenne, Wyoming
KKPN Rockport, Texas
KKPR-FM Kearney, Nebraska
KKPS Brownsville, Texas
KKPT Little Rock, Arkansas
KKQQ Volga, South Dakota
KKQX Manhattan, Montana
KKQY Hill City, Kansas
KKRB Klamath Falls, Oregon
KKRC Granite Falls, Minnesota
KKRD Enid, Oklahoma
KKRE Hollis, Oklahoma
KKRF Stuart, Iowa
KKRG Albuquerque, New Mexico
KKRH Grangeville, Idaho
KKRI Pocola, Oklahoma
KKRK Whitehall, Montana
KKRL Carroll, Iowa
KKRN Bella Vista, California
KKRO Red Bluff, California
KKRQ Iowa City, Iowa
KKRR Casper, Wyoming
KKRS Davenport, Washington
KKRV Wenatchee, Washington
KKRZ Portland, Oregon
KKSD Milbank, South Dakota
KKSI Eddyville, Iowa
KKSP Bryant, Arkansas
KKSR Walla Walla, Washington
KKSS Santa Fe, New Mexico
KKST Oakdale, Louisiana
KKSW Lawrence, Kansas
KKSY-FM Cedar Rapids, Iowa
KKTC Angel Fire, New Mexico
KKTO Tahoe City, California
KKTR Kirksville, Missouri
KKTS-FM Douglas, Wyoming
KKTU-FM Fallon, Nevada
KKTV Fallon, Nevada
KKTX-FM Kilgore, Texas
KKTY-FM Glendo, Wyoming
KKTZ Lakeview, Arkansas
KKUA Wailuku, Hawaii
KKUP Cupertino, California
KKUS Tyler, Texas
KKUU Indio, California
KKVI Overland, Texas
KKVO Altus, Oklahoma
KKVR Kerrville, Texas
KKVS Truth or Consequences, New Mexico
KKVT Grand Junction, Colorado
KKVU Stevensville, Montana
KKWB Kelliher, Minnesota
KKWD Bethany, Oklahoma
KKWD(FM) Bethany, Colorado
KKWF Seattle, Washington
KKWK Cameron, Missouri
KKWQ Warroad, Minnesota
KKWS Wadena, Minnesota
KKWV Aransas Pass, Texas
KKWW Shelbina, Missouri
KKWY Albin, Wyoming
KKXK Montrose, Colorado
KKXL-FM Grand Forks, North Dakota
KKXS Shingletown, California
KKXX-FM Shafter, California
KKYA Yankton, South Dakota
KKYC Clovis, New Mexico
KKYN-FM Plainview, Texas
KKYR-FM Texarkana, Texas
KKYS Bryan, Texas
KKYY Whiting, Iowa
KKYZ Sierra Vista, Arizona
KKZQ Tehachapi, California
KKZX Spokane, Washington
KKZY Bemidji, Minnesota
KLAA-FM Tioga, Louisiana
KLAD-FM Klamath Falls, Oregon
KLAG Alamogordo, New Mexico
KLAI Laytonville, California
KLAK Tom Bean, Texas
KLAL Wrightsville, Arkansas
KLAN Glasgow, Montana
KLAP Gerlach, Nevada
KLAQ El Paso, Texas
KLAW Lawton, Oklahoma
KLAX-FM East Los Angeles, California
KLAZ Hot Springs, Arkansas
KLBC Durant, Oklahoma
KLBD(FM) Fremont, Texas
KLBJ-FM Austin, Texas
KLBL Pearcy, Arkansas
KLBN Fresno, California
KLBQ El Dorado, Arkansas
KLBR Bend, Oregon
KLBT Beaumont, Texas
KLBU Pecos, New Mexico
KLBU Santa Fe, New Mexico
KLBV Steamboat Springs, Colorado
KLBZ Bozeman, Montana
KLCA Tahoe City, California
KLCC Eugene, Oregon
KLCD Decorah, Iowa
KLCE Blackfoot, Idaho
KLCF Truth or Consequence, New Mexico
KLCH Lake City, Minnesota
KLCI Elk River, Minnesota
KLCK-FM Seattle, Washington
KLCM Lewistown, Montana
KLCO Newport, Oregon
KLCR Lakeview, Oregon
KLCU Ardmore, Oklahoma
KLCV Lincoln, Nebraska
KLCY Vernal, Utah
KLCZ Lewiston, Idaho
KLDB Beaver, Oklahoma
KLDD McCloud, California
KLDE Eldorado, Texas
KLDG Liberal, Kansas
KLDJ Duluth, Minnesota
KLDN Lufkin, Texas
KLDR Harbeck-Fruitdale, Oregon
KLDV Morrison, Colorado
KLDZ Medford, Oregon
KLEA-FM Lovington, New Mexico
KLED Antelope Valley Crestview, Wyoming
KLEF Anchorage, Alaska
KLEJ Rayne, Louisiana
KLEN Cheyenne, Wyoming
KLEO Kahaluu, Hawaii
KLER-FM Orofino, Idaho
KLES Prosser, Washington
KLEU Lewistown, Montana
KLEY-FM Jourdanton, Texas
KLFC Branson, Missouri
KLFF San Luis Obispo, California
KLFH Ojai, California
KLFM Great Falls, Montana
KLFN Sunburg, Minnesota
KLFO Florence, Oregon
KLFR Reedsport, Oregon
KLFS Van Buren, Arkansas
KLFV Grand Junction, Colorado
KLFX Nolanville, Texas
KLGA-FM Algona, Iowa
KLGD Stamford, Texas
KLGS College Station, Texas
KLGT Buffalo, Wyoming
KLHB Portland, Texas
KLHI-FM Kahului, Hawaii
KLIF Haltom City, Texas
KLIL Moreauville, Louisiana
KLIP Monroe, Louisiana
KLIQ Hastings, Nebraska
KLIR Columbus, Nebraska
KLIT Ranchitos Las Lomas, Texas
KLIX-FM Twin Falls, Idaho
KLIZ-FM Brainerd, Minnesota
KLJA Georgetown, Texas
KLJA(FM) Georgetown, North Dakota
KLJH Bayfield, Colorado
KLJR-FM Santa Paula, California
KLJT Jacksonville, Texas
KLJV Scottsbluff, Nebraska
KLJY Clayton, Missouri
KLJZ Yuma, Arizona
KLKA Globe, Arizona
KLKC-FM Parsons, Kansas
KLKI Dolan Springs, Arizona
KLKK Clear Lake, Iowa
KLKL Minden, Louisiana
KLKM Kalispell, Montana
KLKO Elko, Nevada
KLKS Pequot Lakes, Minnesota
KLKV Hunt, Texas
KLKY Stanfield, Oregon
KLLC San Francisco, California
KLLE North Fork, California
KLLL-FM Lubbock, Texas
KLLM(FM) Rawlins, Wyoming
KLLN Newark, Arkansas
KLLP Chubbuck, Idaho
KLLR Dripping Springs, Texas
KLLT Spencer, Iowa
KLLU Gallup, New Mexico
KLLY Oildale, California
KLLZ-FM Walker, Minnesota
KLMA Hobbs, New Mexico
KLMB Roundup, Montana
KLMF Klamath Falls, Oregon
KLMG Esparto, California
KLMI Rock River, Wyoming
KLMJ Hampton, Iowa
KLMK Marvell, Arkansas
KLMM Oceano, California
KLMO-FM Dilley, Texas
KLMP Rapid City, South Dakota
KLMR-FM Lamar, Colorado
KLMT Billings, Montana
KLNB Grand Island, Nebraska
KLNC Lincoln, Nebraska
KLND Little Eagle, South Dakota
KLNE-FM Lexington, Nebraska
KLNI Decorah, Iowa
KLNN Questa, New Mexico
KLNO Fort Worth, Texas
KLNR Panaca, Nevada
KLNV San Diego, California
KLNZ Glendale, Arizona
KLOA Ridgecrest, California
KLOB Thousand Palms, California
KLOF Gillette, Wyoming
KLOK-FM Greenfield, California
KLOL Houston, Texas
KLON Rockaway Beach, Oregon
KLOO-FM Albany, Oregon
KLOQ-FM Winton, California
KLOR-FM Ponca City, Oklahoma
KLOS Los Angeles, California
KLOU St. Louis, Missouri
KLOV Winchester, Oregon
KLOW Reno, Texas
KLOX Creston, Iowa
KLOY Astoria, Oregon
KLOZ Eldon, Missouri
KLPI Ruston, Louisiana
KLPL(FM) Lake Providence, Louisiana
KLPR Kearney, Nebraska
KLPW-FM Steelville, Missouri
KLPX Tucson, Arizona
KLPX Tucsun, Nevada
KLQB Taylor, Texas
KLQL Luverne, Minnesota
KLQP Madison, Minnesota
KLQQ Clearmont, Wyoming
KLQT Corrales, New Mexico
KLQV San Diego, California
KLRB Stuart, Oklahoma
KLRC Siloam Springs, Arkansas
KLRD Yucaipa, California
KLRE-FM Little Rock, Arkansas
KLRF Milton-Freewater, Oregon
KLRH Sparks, Nevada
KLRI Rigby, Idaho
KLRJ Aberdeen, South Dakota
KLRM Melbourne, Arkansas
KLRO Hot Springs, Arkansas
KLRQ Clinton, Missouri
KLRR Redmond, Oregon
KLRV Billings, Montana
KLRW Byrne, Texas
KLRX Lee's Summit, Missouri
KLRY Gypsum, Colorado
KLRZ Larose, Louisiana
KLSA Alexandria, Louisiana
KLSB Norfolk, Nebraska
KLSC Malden, Missouri
KLSE Rochester, Minnesota
KLSK Great Falls, Montana
KLSM Tallulah, Louisiana
KLSP Angola, Louisiana
KLSR-FM Memphis, Texas
KLSS-FM Mason City, Iowa
KLSU Baton Rouge, Louisiana
KLSY Cosmopolis, Washington
KLSZ-FM Fort Smith, Arkansas
KLTA-FM Moorhead, Minnesota
KLTD Temple, Texas
KLTE Kirksville, Missouri
KLTG Corpus Christi, Texas
KLTH Lake Oswego, Oregon
KLTI-FM Ames, Iowa
KLTN Houston, Texas
KLTP San Angelo, Texas
KLTR Brenham, Texas
KLTU Mammoth, Arizona
KLTW-FM Prineville, Oregon
KLTY Arlington, Texas
KLUA Kailua Kona, Hawaii
KLUB Bloomington, Texas
KLUC Las Vegas, Nevada
KLUE Poplar Bluff, Missouri
KLUH Poplar Bluff, Missouri
KLUK Needles, California
KLUN Paso Robles, California
KLUR Wichita Falls, Texas
KLUU Jamestown, North Dakota
KLUV Dallas, Texas
KLUW East Wenatchee, Washington
KLUX Robstown, Texas
KLVA Maricopa, Arizona
KLVB Citrus Heights, California
KLVC Magalia, California
KLVE Los Angeles, California
KLVF Las Vegas, New Mexico
KLVG Garberville, California

KLVH San Luis Obispo, California
KLVJ Julian, California
KLVK Fountain Hills, Arizona
KLVM Prunedale, California
KLVN Livingston, California
KLVO Belen, New Mexico
KLVP Aloha, Oregon
KLVR Middletown, California
KLVS Livermore, California
KLVU Sweet Home, Oregon
KLVV Ponca City, Oklahoma
KLVW Odessa, Texas
KLVY Fairmead, California
KLWA Westport, Washington
KLWB Carencro, Louisiana
KLWC Casper, Wyoming
KLWD Gillette, Wyoming
KLWG Lompoc, California
KLWL Chillicothe, Missouri
KLWO Longview, Washington
KLWS Moses Lake, Washington
KLWV Chugwater, Wyoming
KLXA Alexandria, Louisiana
KLXK Breckenridge, Texas
KLXQ Mountain Pine, Arkansas
KLXS-FM Pierre, South Dakota
KLXV Glenwood Springs, Colorado
KLYD Snyder, Texas
KLYK Kelso, Washington
KLYT Albuquerque, New Mexico
KLYV Dubuque, Iowa
KLYY Riverside, California
KLZA-FM Falls City, Nebraska
KLZK New Deal, Texas
KLZR Westcliffe, Colorado
KLZT Bastrop, Texas
KLZV Brush, Colorado
KLZX Weston, Idaho
KLZZ Waite Park, Minnesota
KMA-FM Clarinda, Iowa
KMAD-FM Whitesboro, Texas
KMAG Fort Smith, Arkansas
KMAJ-FM Carbondale, Kansas
KMAK Orange Cove, California
KMAQ-FM Maquoketa, Iowa
KMAR-FM Winnsboro, Louisiana
KMAT Seadrift, Texas
KMAV-FM Mayville, North Dakota
KMAX-FM Wellington, Colorado
KMBH-FM Harlingen, Texas
KMBI Spokane, Washington
KMBM Polson, Montana
KMBN Las Cruces, New Mexico
KMBQ-FM Wasilla, Alaska
KMBR Butte, Montana
KMBV Valentine, Nebraska
KMBZ-FM Kansas City, Kansas
KMCG McGrath, Alaska
KMCH Manchester, Iowa
KMCJ Colstrip, Montana
KMCK-FM Prarie Grove, Arkansas
KMCM Odessa, Texas
KMCN Clinton, Iowa
KMCO Wilburton, Oklahoma
KMCQ Covington, Washington
KMCR Montgomery City, Missouri
KMCS Muscatine, Iowa
KMCU Wichita Falls, Texas
KMCV High Point, Missouri
KMCX-FM Ogallala, Nebraska
KMDL Kaplan, Louisiana
KMDR McKinleyville, California
KMDX San Angelo, Texas
KMDY Keokuk, Iowa
KMDZ Las Vegas, New Mexico
KMEL San Francisco, California
KMEM-FM Memphis, Missouri
KMEN Mendota, California
KMEO Mertzon, Texas
KMFA Austin, Texas
KMFB(FM) Mendocino, California
KMFC Centralia, Missouri
KMFX-FM Lake City, Minnesota
KMFY Grand Rapids, Minnesota
KMGC Camden, Arkansas
KMGE Eugene, Oregon
KMGI Pocatello, Idaho
KMGJ Grand Junction, Colorado
KMGK Glenwood, Minnesota
KMGL Oklahoma City, Oklahoma
KMGM Montevideo, Minnesota
KMGN Flagstaff, Arizona
KMGO Centerville, Iowa
KMGR Delta, Utah
KMGT Circle, Montana
KMGV Fresno, California
KMGX Bend, Oregon
KMGZ Lawton, Oklahoma
KMHA Four Bears, North Dakota
KMHD Gresham, Oregon
KMHK Billings, Montana
KMHK Billings, Montana
KMHM Lutesville, Missouri
KMHS-FM Coos Bay, Oregon
KMHT-FM Marshall, Texas
KMHX Rohnert Park, California
KMIH Mercer Island, Washington
KMIL Cameron, Texas
KMIQ Robstown, Texas
KMIT Mitchell, South Dakota
KMIX Tracy, California
KMIY Tucson, Arizona
KMJ Fresno, California
KMJE Placerville, California
KMJI Ashdown, Arkansas
KMJJ-FM Shreveport, Louisiana
KMJK North Kansas City, Missouri
KMJO Hope, North Dakota
KMJQ Houston, Texas
KMJR Odem, Texas
KMJV Soledad, California
KMJX Conway, Arkansas
KMKF Manhattan, Kansas
KMKF Manhattan, Kansas
KMKK-FM Kaunakakai, Hawaii
KMKL North Branch, Minnesota
KMKO-FM Lake Crystal, Minnesota
KMKS Bay City, Texas
KMKT Bells, Texas
KMKV Paia, Hawaii
KMKX Willits, California
KMKZ(FM) Red Feather Lakes, Colorado
KMLA El Rio, California
KMLD Casper, Wyoming
KMLE Chandler, Arizona
KMLK El Dorado, Arkansas
KMLL Marysville, Kansas
KMLO Lowry, South Dakota
KMLR Gonzales, Texas
KMLT Jackson, Wyoming
KMLV Ralston, Nebraska
KMLW Moses Lake, Washington
KMME(FM) Cottage Grove, Oregon
KMMG Benton City, Washington
KMML Cimarron, Kansas
KMMO-FM Marshall, Missouri
KMMR Malta, Montana
KMMS-FM Bozeman, Montana
KMMT Mammoth Lakes, California
KMMX Tahoka, Texas
KMMY Soper, Oklahoma
KMMZ Crane, Texas
KMNA Mabton, Washington
KMNB Minneapolis, Minnesota
KMNE-FM Bassett, Nebraska
KMNO Wailuku, Hawaii
KMNR Rolla, Missouri
KMNT Chehalis, Washington
KMOA Nu'uuli, American Samoa
KMOC Wichita Falls, Texas
KMOD-FM Tulsa, Oklahoma
KMOE Butler, Missouri
KMOJ Minneapolis, Minnesota
KMOK Lewiston, Idaho
KMOM Roscoe, South Dakota
KMON-FM Great Falls, Montana
KMOO-FM Mineola, Texas
KMOQ Columbus, Kansas
KMOR Gering, Nebraska
KMOU Roswell, New Mexico
KMOZ-FM Grand Junction, Colorado
KMPA Pittsburg, Texas
KMPB Breckenridge, Colorado
KMPO Modesto, California
KMPQ Roseburg, Oregon
KMPR Minot, North Dakota
KMPS Seattle, Washington
KMPZ Salida, Colorado
KMQA East Porterville, California
KMQX Weatherford, Texas
KMRJ Rancho Mirage, California
KMRK-FM Odessa, Texas
KMRL Buras, Louisiana
KMRO Camarillo, California
KMRQ Riverbank, California
KMRX El Dorado, Arkansas
KMRZ-FM Superior, Wyoming
KMSA Grand Junction, Colorado
KMSC Sioux City, Iowa
KMSE Rochester, Minnesota
KMSI Moore, Oklahoma
KMSK Austin, Minnesota
KMSL Mansfield, Louisiana
KMSM-FM Butte, Montana
KMSO Missoula, Montana
KMST Rolla, Missouri
KMSU Mankato, Minnesota
KMSW The Dalles, Oregon
KMTB Murfreesboro, Arkansas
KMTC Russellville, Arkansas
KMTG San Jose, California
KMTH Maljamar, New Mexico
KMTK Bend, Oregon
KMTN Jackson, Wyoming
KMTS Glenwood Springs, Colorado
KMTX-FM Helena, Montana
KMTY Gibbon, Nebraska
KMTZ Three Forks, Montana
KMUD Garberville, California
KMUE Eureka, California
KMUL-FM Muleshoe, Texas
KMUN Astoria, Oregon
KMUW Wichita, Kansas
KMUZ Turner, Oregon
KMVA Dewey-Humboldt, Arizona
KMVC Marshall, Missouri
KMVE California City, California
KMVK Fort Worth, Texas
KMVL-FM Madisonville, Texas
KMVN Anchorage, Alaska
KMVN Palmer, Alaska
KMVP-FM Phoenix, Arizona
KMVQ San Francisco, California
KMVR Mesilla Park, New Mexico
KMVX Monroe, Louisiana
KMWB Captain Cook, Hawaii
KMWR Brookings, Oregon
KMWS Mount Vernon, Washington
KMWX Abilene, Texas
KMWY Jackson, Wyoming
KMXA-FM Minot, North Dakota
KMXB Henderson, Nevada
KMXC Sioux Falls, South Dakota
KMXD Monroe, Utah
KMXE-FM Red Lodge, Montana
KMXF Lowell, Arkansas
KMXG Clinton, Iowa
KMXH Alexandria, Louisiana
KMXI Chico, California
KMXJ-FM Amarillo, Texas
KMXK Cold Spring, Minnesota
KMXL Carthage, Missouri
KMXM(FM) Helena Valley NE, Montana
KMXN Osage City, Kansas
KMXP Phoenix, Arizona
KMXQ Socorro, New Mexico
KMXR Corpus Christi, Texas
KMXS Anchorage, Alaska
KMXT Kodiak, Alaska
KMXV Kansas City, Missouri
KMXW Sparks, Nevada
KMXX Imperial, California
KMXY Grand Junction, Colorado
KMXZ-FM Tucson, Arizona
KMYI San Diego, California
KMYK Osage Beach, Missouri
KMYO Comfort, Texas
KMYT Temecula, California
KMYX-FM Arvin, California
KMYY Rayville, Louisiana
KMYZ-FM Pryor, Oklahoma
KMZA-FM Seneca, Kansas
KMZE Woodward, Oklahoma
KMZK Clifton, Colorado
KMZL Missoula, Montana
KMZO Hamilton, Montana
KMZQ-FM Payson, Arizona
KMZT-FM Salinas, California
KMZU Carrollton, Missouri
KMZZ Bishop, Texas
KNAA Show Low, Arizona
KNAB-FM Burlington, Colorado
KNAC Earlimart, California
KNAD Page, Arizona
KNAF-FM Fredericksburg, Texas
KNAG Grand Canyon, Arizona
KNAH Mustang, Oklahoma
KNAI Phoenix, Arizona
KNAN Nanakuli, Hawaii
KNAQ Prescott, Arizona
KNAR San Angelo, Texas
KNAS Nashville, Arkansas
KNAU Flagstaff, Arizona
KNBA Anchorage, Alaska
KNBB Dubach, Louisiana
KNBE Beatrice, Nebraska
KNBJ Bemidji, Minnesota
KNBT New Braunfels, Texas
KNBU Baldwin City, Kansas
KNBX San Ardo, California
KNBZ Redfield, South Dakota
KNCA Burney, California
KNCB-FM Vivian, Louisiana
KNCC Elko, Nevada
KNCH(FM) San Angelo, Texas
KNCI Sacramento, California
KNCM Appleton, Minnesota
KNCN Sinton, Texas
KNCO-FM Grass Valley, California
KNCQ Redding, California
KNCT-FM Killeen, Texas
KNCU Newport, Oregon
KNCW Omak, Washington
KNCY-FM Auburn, Nebraska
KNDA Alice, Texas
KNDD Seattle, Washington
KNDE College Station, Texas
KNDH Hettinger, North Dakota
KNDK-FM Langdon, North Dakota
KNDL(FM) Angwin, California
KNDN-FM Teec Nos Pos, Arizona
KNDR Mandan, North Dakota
KNDW Williston, North Dakota
KNDY-FM Marysville, Kansas
KNDZ McKinleyville, California
KNEB-FM Scottsbluff, Nebraska
KNEC Yuma, Colorado
KNEI-FM Waukon, Iowa
KNEK Washington, Louisiana
KNEL-FM Brady, Texas
KNEN Norfolk, Nebraska
KNEO Neosho, Missouri
KNES Fairfield, Texas
KNEV Reno, Nevada
KNEX Laredo, Texas
KNFA Grand Island, Nebraska
KNFM Midland, Texas
KNFO Basalt, Colorado
KNFT-FM Bayard, New Mexico
KNFX-FM Bryan, Texas
KNGA Saint Peter, Minnesota
KNGM Guymon, Oklahoma
KNGS Coalinga, California
KNGT Lake Charles, Louisiana
KNGW Juneau, Alaska
KNHC Seattle, Washington
KNHM Bayside, California
KNHT Rio Dell, California
KNID North Enid, Oklahoma
KNIN-FM Wichita Falls, Texas
KNIS Carson City, Nevada
KNIT Humboldt, Nebraska
KNIV Lyman, Wyoming
KNIX-FM Phoenix, Arizona
KNJT Coldwater, Kansas
KNKI Pinetop, Arizona
KNKK Needles, California
KNKL North Ogden, Utah
KNKN(FM) Pueblo, Colorado
KNKT Armijo, New Mexico
KNLB Lake Havasu City, Arizona
KNLE-FM Round Rock, Texas
KNLF Quincy, California
KNLG New Bloomfield, Missouri
KNLH Cedar Hill, Missouri
KNLK Santa Rosa, New Mexico
KNLL Nashville, Arkansas
KNLN Vienna, Missouri
KNLP Potosi, Missouri
KNLQ Cuba, Missouri
KNLR Bend, Oregon
KNLV-FM Ord, Nebraska
KNLX Prineville, Oregon
KNMA Tularosa, New Mexico

KNMB Cloudcroft, New Mexico
KNMC Havre, Montana
KNMI Farmington, New Mexico
KNMO-FM Nevada, Missouri
KNMZ Alamogordo, New Mexico
KNNB Whiteriver, Arizona
KNNG Sterling, Colorado
KNNK Dimmitt, Texas
KNNN(FM) Shasta Lake City, California
KNNW Columbia, Louisiana
KNOB Healdsburg, California
KNOD Harlan, Iowa
KNOF St. Paul, Minnesota
KNOG Nogales, Arizona
KNOM-FM Nome, Alaska
KNON Dallas, Texas
KNOR Krum, Texas
KNOU St. Louis, Missouri
KNOW-FM Minneapolis-St. Paul, Minnesota
KNPQ Hershey, Nebraska
KNPR Las Vegas, Nevada
KNRB Atlanta, Texas
KNRG New Ulm, Texas
KNRI Bismarck, North Dakota
KNRJ Cordes Lakes, Arizona
KNRK Camas, Washington
KNRQ Harrisburg, Oregon
KNRX Sterling City, Texas
KNSB(FM) Bettendorf, Iowa
KNSC(FM) Carroll, Iowa
KNSE Austin, Minnesota
KNSG Springfield, Minnesota
KNSH(FM) Fort Dodge, Iowa
KNSL(FM) Lamoni, Iowa
KNSM(FM) Mason City, Iowa
KNSQ Mount Shasta, California
KNSR Collegeville, Minnesota
KNSU Thibodaux, Louisiana
KNSW Worthington-Marshall, Minnesota
KNSX(FM) Moville, Iowa
KNSY(FM) Dubuque, Iowa
KNSZ(FM) Ottumwa, Iowa
KNTE Bay City, Texas
KNTI Lakeport, California
KNTK Firth, Nebraska
KNTN Thief River Falls, Minnesota
KNTO Chowchilla, California
KNTU McKinney, Texas
KNTY Shingle Springs, California
KNUE Tyler, Texas
KNUJ-FM Sleepy Eye, Minnesota
KNUL Nulato, Alaska
KNUQ Paauilo, Hawaii
KNUT Tamuning, Guam
KNUW Santa Clara, New Mexico
KNUZ San Saba, Texas
KNVO-FM Port Isabel, Texas
KNWB Hilo, Hawaii
KNWC-FM Sioux Falls, South Dakota
KNWD Natchitoches, Louisiana
KNWF Fergus Falls, Minnesota
KNWI Osceola, Iowa
KNWJ Leone, American Samoa
KNWM Madrid, Iowa
KNWO Cottonwood, Idaho
KNWP Port Angeles, Washington
KNWR Ellensburg, Washington
KNWS-FM Waterloo, Iowa
KNWU Forks, Washington
KNWV Clarkston, Washington
KNWY Yakima, Washington
KNXR Rochester, Minnesota
KNXX Donaldsonville, Louisiana
KNYD Broken Arrow, Oklahoma
KNYE Pahrump, Nevada
KNYN Fort Bridger, Wyoming
KNYR Yreka, California
KNZA-FM Hiawatha, Kansas
KNZR-FM Shafter, California
KNZS Arlington, Kansas
KOAB-FM Bend, Oregon
KOAP Lakeview, Oregon
KOAR Beebe, Arkansas
KOAS Dolan Springs, Arizona
KOAY(FM) Middleton, Idaho
KOBB-FM Bozeman, Montana
KOBC Joplin, Missouri
KOBH Hobbs, New Mexico
KOBK Baker City, Oregon
KOBN Burns, Oregon
KOCN Pacific Grove, California
KOCP Oxnard, California
KOCU Altus, Oklahoma
KODA Houston, Texas
KODJ Salt Lake City, Utah
KODM Odessa, Texas
KODS Carnelian Bay, California
KODV Barstow, California
KODZ Eugene, Oregon
KOEA Doniphan, Missouri
KOEL-FM Cedar Falls, Iowa
KOFG Cody, Wyoming
KOFH Nogales, Arizona
KOFM Enid, Oklahoma
KOFX El Paso, Texas
KOGA-FM Ogallala, Nebraska
KOGB McGrath, Alaska
KOGJ Kenai, Alaska
KOGL Gleneden Beach, Oregon
KOGM Opelousas, Louisiana
KOGW Stratford, Texas
KOHL Fremont, California
KOHN Sells, Arizona
KOHO Leavenworth, Washington
KOHR Sheridan, Wyoming
KOHS Orem, Utah
KOHT Marana, Arizona
KOIA Storm Lake, Iowa
KOIR Edinburg, Texas
KOIT San Francisco, California
KOJB Cass Lake, Minnesota
KOJD John Day, Oregon
KOJI Okoboji, Iowa
KOJO Lake Charles, Louisiana
KOKE-FM Thorndale, Texas
KOKF Edmond, Oklahoma
KOKN Oketo, Kansas
KOKO-FM Kerman, California
KOKR Newport, Arkansas
KOKS Poplar Bluff, Missouri
KOKU Hagatna, Guam
KOKX-FM Keokuk, Iowa
KOKY Sherwood, Arkansas
KOKZ Waterloo, Iowa
KOLA San Bernardino, California
KOLC Carson City, Nevada
KOLI Electra, Texas
KOLJ-FM Warroad, Minnesota
KOLL Lonoke, Arkansas
KOLT-FM Warren Afb, Wyoming
KOLU Pasco, Washington
KOLV Olivia, Minnesota
KOLW Basin City, Washington
KOLY-FM Mobridge, South Dakota
KOLZ Cheyenne, Wyoming
KOMA Oklahoma City, Oklahoma
KOMB Fort Scott, Kansas
KOMC-FM Kimberling City, Missouri
KOME-FM Meridian, Texas
KOMH Marshall, Minnesota
KOMO-FM Oakville, Washington
KOMP Las Vegas, Nevada
KOMR Sun City, Arizona
KOMS Poteau, Oklahoma
KOMT Mountain Home, Arkansas
KOMX Pampa, Texas
KONA-FM Kennewick, Washington
KOND Clovis, California
KONE Lubbock, Texas
KONI Lanai City, Hawaii
KONO-FM Helotes, Texas
KONQ Dodge City, Kansas
KONY St. George, Utah
KOOC(FM) Belton, Texas
KOOI Jacksonville, Texas
KOOK Junction, Texas
KOOL Phoenix, Arizona
KOOO La Vista, Nebraska
KOOP Hornsby, Texas
KOOS North Bend, Oregon
KOOT Hurley, New Mexico
KOOU Hardy, Arkansas
KOOV Kempner, Texas
KOOZ Myrtle Point, Oregon
KOPA(FM) Pala, California
KOPB-FM Portland, Oregon
KOPJ Sebeka, Minnesota
KOPN Columbia, Missouri
KOPR Butte, Montana
KOPW Plattsmouth, Nebraska
KOPY-FM Alice, Texas
KOQL Ashland, Missouri
KORA-FM Bryan, Texas
KORB Hopland, California
KORC(FM) Burns, Oregon
KORD-FM Richland, Washington
KORQ Winters, Texas
KORR American Falls, Idaho
KORT-FM Grangeville, Idaho
KORU Garapan-Saipan, Guam
KORV Lakeview, Oregon
KORV-FM Lakeview, Oregon
KOSB Perry, Oklahoma
KOSF San Francisco, California
KOSG Pawhuska, Oklahoma
KOSI Denver, Colorado
KOSN Ketchum, Oklahoma
KOSO Patterson, California
KOSP Ozark, Missouri
KOST Los Angeles, California
KOSU Stillwater, Oklahoma
KOSY-FM Anamosa, Iowa
KOTD The Dalles, Oregon
KOTE Eureka, Kansas
KOTM-FM Ottumwa, Iowa
KOTN(FM) Gould, Arkansas
KOTO Telluride, Colorado
KOTY Mason, Texas
KOUI Louisville, Mississippi
KOUT Rapid City, South Dakota
KOUW(FM) Island Park, Idaho
KOVA Bovina, Texas
KOVE-FM Galveston, Texas
KOWY Dayton, Wyoming
KOWZ-FM Blooming Prairie, Minnesota
KOXE Brownwood, Texas
KOYA Rosebud, South Dakota
KOYE Frankston, Texas
KOYN Paris, Texas
KOYT(FM) Alberton, Montana
KOYT(FM) Montana City, Montana
KOYU Koyukuk, Alaska
KOYY Fargo, North Dakota
KOZB Livingston, Montana
KOZE-FM Lewiston, Idaho
KOZI-FM Chelan, Washington
KOZO Branson, Missouri
KOZQ-FM Waynesville, Missouri
KOZT Fort Bragg, California
KOZX Cabool, Missouri
KOZY-FM Bridgeport, Nebraska
KOZZ-FM Reno, Nevada
KPAC San Antonio, Texas
KPAE Erwinville, Louisiana
KPAK Alva, Oklahoma
KPAN-FM Hereford, Texas
KPAQ Plaquemine, Louisiana
KPAS Fabens, Texas
KPAT Orcutt, California
KPAU Center, Colorado
KPAW Fort Collins, Colorado
KPBR Poplar Bluff, Missouri
KPBS-FM San Diego, California
KPBX-FM Spokane, Washington
KPBZ Spokane, Washington
KPCC Pasadena, California
KPCH Ruston, Louisiana
KPCL Farmington, New Mexico
KPCP New Roads, Louisiana
KPCR Fowler, Colorado
KPCS Princeton, Minnesota
KPCV Portales, New Mexico
KPCW Park City, Utah
KPDA Mountain Home, Idaho
KPDO Pescadero, California
KPDQ-FM Portland, Oregon
KPDR Wheeler, Texas
KPEK Albuquerque, New Mexico
KPEL-FM Breaux Bridge, Louisiana
KPEN-FM Soldotna, Alaska
KPER Hobbs, New Mexico
KPEZ Austin, Texas
KPFA Berkeley, California
KPFB Berkeley, California
KPFC Callisburg, Texas
KPFK Los Angeles, California
KPFM Mountain Home, Arkansas
KPFR Pine Grove, Oregon
KPFT Houston, Texas
KPFX Fargo, North Dakota
KPFZ-FM Lakeport, California
KPGA Morton, Texas
KPGB Pryor, Montana
KPGG Ashdown, Arkansas
KPGR Pleasant Grove, Utah
KPGS Pagosa Springs, Colorado
KPGT Watertown, South Dakota
KPHF Phoenix, Arizona
KPHR Ortonville, Minnesota
KPHS Plains, Texas
KPHT Rocky Ford, Colorado
KPHW Kaneohe, Hawaii
KPIG-FM Freedom, California
KPIJ Junction City, Oregon
KPIN Pinedale, Wyoming
KPIO-FM Pleasanton, Kansas
KPIT Pittsburg, Texas
KPJH Polson, Montana
KPJP Greenville, California
KPKJ Mentmore, New Mexico
KPKK Amargosa Valley, Nevada
KPKL Deer Park, Washington
KPKO Pecos, Texas
KPKP Harts Bluff, Texas
KPKR Parker, Arizona
KPKY Pocatello, Idaho
KPLA Columbia, Missouri
KPLD Kanab, Utah
KPLG Plains, Montana
KPLI Olympia, Washington
KPLM Palm Springs, California
KPLN Lockwood, Montana
KPLO-FM Reliance, South Dakota
KPLT-FM Paris, Texas
KPLU-FM Tacoma, Washington
KPLV Las Vegas, Nevada
KPLW Wenatchee, Washington
KPLX Fort Worth, Texas
KPLZ-FM Seattle, Washington
KPMB Plainview, Texas
KPMD Evanston, Wyoming
KPMW Haliimaile, Hawaii
KPMX Sterling, Colorado
KPNC Ponca City, Oklahoma
KPND Sandpoint, Idaho
KPNE-FM North Platte, Nebraska
KPNO Norfolk, Nebraska
KPNT Collinsville, Illinois
KPNY Alliance, Nebraska
KPOA Lahaina, Hawaii
KPOC-FM Pocahontas, Arkansas
KPOD-FM Crescent City, California
KPOI-FM Honolulu, Hawaii
KPOO San Francisco, California
KPOR Emporia, Kansas
KPOS Fouke, Arkansas
KPOW-FM La Monte, Missouri
KPOY(FM) Fraser, Colorado
KPPD Devils Lake, North Dakota
KPPL Poplar Bluff, Missouri
KPPR Williston, North Dakota
KPPT-FM Depoe Bay, Oregon
KPPV Prescott Valley, Arizona
KPQ-FM Wenatchee, Washington
KPQX Havre, Montana
KPRA Ukiah, California
KPRB Brush, Colorado
KPRC-FM Salinas, California
KPRD Hays, Kansas
KPRE Vail, Colorado
KPRF Amarillo, Texas
KPRG Agana, Guam
KPRH Montrose, Colorado
KPRI Encinitas, California
KPRJ Jamestown, North Dakota
KPRN Grand Junction, Colorado
KPRQ Sheridan, Wyoming
KPRR El Paso, Texas
KPRS Kansas City, Missouri
KPRU Delta, Colorado
KPRV-FM Heavener, Oklahoma
KPRW Perham, Minnesota
KPRX Bakersfield, California
KPSA-FM Lordsburg, New Mexico
KPSC Palm Springs, California
KPSD-FM Faith, South Dakota
KPSH Coachella, California
KPSI-FM Palm Springs, California
KPSL-FM Bakersfield, California
KPSM Brownwood, Texas
KPSO-FM Falfurrias, Texas
KPST Coachella, California
KPSU Goodwell, Oklahoma
KPTE Durango, Colorado

KPTT Denver, Colorado
KPTX Pecos, Texas
KPTZ Port Townsend, Washington
KPUB Flagstaff, Arizona
KPUL Winterset, Iowa
KPUR-FM Canyon, Texas
KPUS Gregory, Texas
KPUT Mona, Utah
KPVL Postville, Iowa
KPVR Bowling Green, Missouri
KPVS Hilo, Hawaii
KPVU Prairie View, Texas
KPVW Aspen, Colorado
KPWB-FM Piedmont, Missouri
KPWJ Kurten, Texas
KPWR Los Angeles, California
KPWW Hooks, Texas
KPXI Overton, Texas
KPXP Garapan-Saipan, Guam
KPYG Cayucos, California
KPYR Craig, Colorado
KPZA-FM Jal, New Mexico
KPZE-FM Carlsbad, New Mexico
KPZK Cabot, Arkansas
KQAC Portland, Oregon
KQAI Roswell, New Mexico
KQAK Bend, Oregon
KQAL Winona, Minnesota
KQAV Rosamond, California
KQAY-FM Tucumcari, New Mexico
KQAZ Springerville, Arizona
KQBA Los Alamos, New Mexico
KQBB Center, Texas
KQBK Booneville, Arkansas
KQBL Emmett, Idaho
KQBO Rio Grande City, Texas
KQBR Lubbock, Texas
KQBT Houston, Texas
KQBU-FM Port Arthur, Texas
KQBZ Brownwood, Texas
KQCH Omaha, Nebraska
KQCJ Cambridge, Illinois
KQCL Faribault, Minnesota
KQCO Esterbrook, Wyoming
KQCR-FM Parkersburg, Iowa
KQCS Bettendorf, Iowa
KQCV-FM Shawnee, Oklahoma
KQDI-FM Highwood, Montana
KQDJ-FM Valley City, North Dakota
KQDL Hines, Oregon
KQDR Savoy, Texas
KQDS Duluth, Minnesota
KQDY Bismarck, North Dakota
KQED-FM San Francisco, California
KQEG La Crescent, Minnesota
KQEI-FM North Highlands, California
KQEL Alamogordo, New Mexico
KQEO Idaho Falls, Idaho
KQEW Fordyce, Arkansas
KQEZ(FM) Shelley, Idaho
KQFC Boise, Idaho
KQFE Springfield, Oregon
KQFM Hermiston, Oregon
KQFR Rapid City, South Dakota
KQFX Borger, Texas
KQHK McCook, Nebraska
KQHN Waskom, Texas
KQHR The Dalles, Oregon
KQHT Crookston, Minnesota
KQIB Idabel, Oklahoma
KQIC Willmar, Minnesota
KQID-FM Alexandria, Louisiana
KQIK Haileyville, Oklahoma
KQIZ-FM Amarillo, Texas
KQJK Roseville, California
KQKI-FM Bayou Vista, Louisiana
KQKK Walker, Minnesota
KQKL Selma, California
KQKQ-FM Council Bluffs, Iowa
KQKS Lakewood, Colorado
KQKX Norfolk, Nebraska
KQKY Kearney, Nebraska
KQLA Ogden, Kansas
KQLB Los Banos, California
KQLK De Ridder, Louisiana
KQLM Odessa, Texas
KQLP Leupp, Arizona
KQLR Whitehall, Montana
KQLT Casper, Wyoming
KQLV(FM) Bosque Farms, New Mexico
KQLX-FM Lisbon, North Dakota
KQLZ Beulah, North Dakota
KQMA Phillipsburg, Kansas
KQMB Levan, Utah
KQMC Hawthorne, Nevada
KQMG-FM Independence, Iowa
KQMJ(FM) Osceola, Arkansas
KQMN Thief River Falls, Minnesota
KQMO Shell Knob, Missouri
KQMQ-FM Honolulu, Hawaii
KQMR Globe, Arizona
KQMT Denver, Colorado
KQMV Bellevue, Washington
KQMX Lost Hills, California
KQNC Quincy, California
KQNG-FM Lihue, Hawaii
KQNK-FM Norton, Kansas
KQNU(FM) Onawa, Iowa
KQNV Fallon, Nevada
KQNY Quincy, California
KQOB Enid, Oklahoma
KQOC Gleneden Beach, Oregon
KQOD Stockton, California
KQOH Marshfield, Missouri
KQOL Sleepy Hollow, Wyoming
KQOR Mena, Arkansas
KQPD Ardmore, Oklahoma
KQPI Aberdeen, Idaho
KQPM Ukiah, California
KQPR Albert Lea, Minnesota
KQPT Colusa, California
KQQF Coffeyville, Kansas
KQQK Beaumont, Texas
KQQL Anoka, Minnesota
KQQX Hermann, Missouri
KQRA Brookline, Missouri
KQRC-FM Leavenworth, Kansas
KQRI Bosque Farms, New Mexico
KQRK Pablo, Montana
KQRN Mitchell, South Dakota
KQRQ Rapid City, South Dakota
KQRS Golden Valley, Minnesota
KQRT Las Vegas, Nevada
KQRV Deer Lodge, Montana
KQRX Midland, Texas
KQSD-FM Lowry, South Dakota
KQSE Gypsum, Colorado
KQSF Dell Rapids, South Dakota
KQSK Chadron, Nebraska
KQSM-FM Fayetteville, Arkansas
KQSN Ponca City, Oklahoma
KQSR Yuma, Arizona
KQSS Miami, Arizona
KQST Sedona, Arizona
KQSW Rock Springs, Wyoming
KQTA Homedale, Idaho
KQTH Tucson, Arizona
KQTM Rio Rancho, New Mexico
KQTY-FM Borger, Texas
KQTZ Hobart, Oklahoma
KQUL Lake Ozark, Missouri
KQUR Laredo, Texas
KQUS-FM Hot Springs, Arkansas
KQVO Calexico, California
KQVT Victoria, Texas
KQWB-FM Breckenridge, Minnesota
KQWC-FM Webster City, Iowa
KQWS Omak, Washington
KQWY Lusk, Wyoming
KQXB Breckenridge, Texas
KQXC-FM Wichita Falls, Texas
KQXE Eastland, Texas
KQXL New Roads, Louisiana
KQXR Payette, Idaho
KQXS Stephenville, Texas
KQXT-FM San Antonio, Texas
KQXX-FM Mission, Texas
KQXY-FM Beaumont, Texas
KQYB Spring Grove, Minnesota
KQZB Troy, Idaho
KQZQ Kiowa, Kansas
KQZR Hayden, Colorado
KQZZ Devils Lake, North Dakota
KRAB Greenacres, California
KRAI-FM Craig, Colorado
KRAJ Johannesburg, California
KRAN Warren Afb, Wyoming
KRAO-FM Colfax, Washington
KRAQ Jackson, Minnesota
KRAR Espanola, New Mexico
KRAT(FM) Altamont, Oregon
KRAV-FM Tulsa, Oklahoma
KRAY-FM Salinas, California
KRAZ Santa Ynez, California
KRBB Wichita, Kansas
KRBD Ketchikan, Alaska
KRBE Houston, Texas
KRBG Umbarger, Texas
KRBI-FM St. Peter, Minnesota
KRBL Idalou, Texas
KRBM Pendleton, Oregon
KRBO(FM) Millers Ranch, California
KRBP Rock Creek, California
KRBR La Barge, Wyoming
KRBW Ottawa, Kansas
KRBY Ruby, Alaska
KRBZ Kansas City, Missouri
KRCB-FM Windsor, California
KRCC Colorado Springs, Colorado
KRCD Inglewood, California
KRCH Rochester, Minnesota
KRCI Pinetop-Lakeside, Arizona
KRCK-FM Mecca, California
KRCL Salt Lake City, Utah
KRCQ Detroit Lakes, Minnesota
KRCS Sturgis, South Dakota
KRCU Cape Girardeau, Missouri
KRCV West Covina, California
KRCW Royal City, Washington
KRCX-FM Marysville, California
KRCY-FM Lake Havasu City, Arizona
KRDA Hanford, California
KRDE Globe, Arizona
KRDG Shingletown, California
KRDO-FM Security, Colorado
KRDQ Colby, Kansas
KRDX Vail, Arizona
KREC Brian Head, Utah
KRED Eureka, California
KREJ Medicine Lodge, Kansas
KREK Bristow, Oklahoma
KREP Belleville, Kansas
KRES Moberly, Missouri
KREU Roland, Oklahoma
KREV Alameda, California
KREZ Chaffee, Missouri
KRFA-FM Moscow, Idaho
KRFC Fort Collins, Colorado
KRFD(FM) Merino, Colorado
KRFG Glenwood, Minnesota
KRFH Marshalltown, Iowa
KRFI Redwood Falls, Minnesota
KRFM Show Low, Arizona
KRFO-FM Owatonna, Minnesota
KRFS-FM Superior, Nebraska
KRFX Denver, Colorado
KRGI-FM Grand Island, Nebraska
KRGM Marshall, Minnesota
KRGO Alton, Iowa
KRGT Indian Springs, Nevada
KRGX Rio Grande City, Texas
KRGY Aurora, Nebraska
KRHS Overland, Missouri
KRHV Big Pine, California
KRIA Plainview, Texas
KRIG-FM Nowata, Oklahoma
KRIO-FM Roma, Texas
KRIT Parker, Arizona
KRJA Lamesa, Texas
KRJB Ada, Minnesota
KRJC Elko, Nevada
KRJM Mahnomen, Minnesota
KRJT Elgin, Oregon
KRKA Severance, Colorado
KRKC-FM King City, California
KRKG-FM Pasco, Washington
KRKH Wailea-Makena, Hawaii
KRKI Keystone, South Dakota
KRKL Walla Walla, Washington
KRKM Fort Washakie, Wyoming
KRKN Eldon, Iowa
KRKQ Mountain Village, Colorado
KRKR Waverly, Nebraska
KRKS-FM Lafayette, Colorado
KRKT-FM Albany, Oregon
KRKU Wheatland, Wyoming
KRKV Las Animas, Colorado
KRKX Billings, Montana
KRKY-FM Estes Park, Colorado
KRLD-FM Dallas, Texas
KRLE Oberlin, Kansas
KRLF Pullman, Washington
KRLH Hereford, Texas
KRLI Malta Bend, Missouri
KRLP Fairmont, Minnesota
KRLQ Hodge, Louisiana
KRLR Sulphur, Louisiana
KRLS Knoxville, Iowa
KRLT South Lake Tahoe, California
KRLU Roswell, New Mexico
KRLX Northfield, Minnesota
KRMB Bisbee, Arizona
KRMC Douglas, Arizona
KRMD-FM Oil City, Louisiana
KRMG-FM Sand Springs, Oklahoma
KRMH Red Mesa, Arizona
KRMQ-FM Clovis, New Mexico
KRMR Hays, Kansas
KRMW Cedarville, Arizona
KRMX Marlin, Texas
KRMX(FM) Marlin, Texas
KRNA Iowa City, Iowa
KRNB Decatur, Texas
KRNC Steamboat Springs, Colorado
KRNE-FM Merriman, Nebraska
KRNF Montezuma, Iowa
KRNG Fallon, Nevada
KRNH Kerrville, Texas
KRNK Casper, Wyoming
KRNL-FM Mount Vernon, Iowa
KRNM Chalan Kanoa-Saipan, Guam
KRNN Juneau, Alaska
KRNO Incline Village, Nevada
KRNP Sutherland, Nebraska
KRNQ Keokuk, Iowa
KRNU Lincoln, Nebraska
KRNV-FM Reno, Nevada
KRNW Chillicothe, Missouri
KRNY Kearney, Nebraska
KRNZ Gonzales, Texas
KROA Grand Island, Nebraska
KROC-FM Rochester, Minnesota
KROG Grants Pass, Oregon
KROI Seabrook, Texas
KROK South Fort Polk, Louisiana
KROM San Antonio, Texas
KROQ Pasadena, California
KROR Hastings, Nebraska
KROU Spencer, Oklahoma
KROW Cody, Wyoming
KROX-FM Buda, Texas
KRPH Morristown, Arizona
KRPM Billings, Montana
KRPR Rochester, Minnesota
KRPS Pittsburg, Kansas
KRPT Devine, Texas
KRPW(FM) Coarsegold, California
KRPX Wellington, Utah
KRQB San Jacinto, California
KRQK Lompoc, California
KRQN Vinton, Iowa
KRQQ Tucson, Arizona
KRQR Orland, California
KRQT Longview, Washington
KRQU Laramie, Wyoming
KRQX-FM Santa Clara, Utah
KRQZ Lompoc, California
KRRA Paragonah, Utah
KRRE Las Vegas, New Mexico
KRRF Oak View, California
KRRG Laredo, Texas
KRRK Desert Hills, Arizona
KRRL Los Angeles, California
KRRM Rogue River, Oregon
KRRN Moapa Valley, Nevada
KRRO Sioux Falls, South Dakota
KRRQ Lafayette, Louisiana
KRRR Cheyenne, Wyoming
KRRT Arroyo Seco, New Mexico
KRRV-FM Alexandria, Louisiana
KRRW St. James, Minnesota
KRRX Burney, California
KRRY Canton, Missouri
KRSB-FM Roseburg, Oregon
KRSC-FM Claremore, Oklahoma
KRSD Sioux Falls, South Dakota
KRSE Yakima, Washington
KRSF Ridgecrest, California
KRSH Healdsburg, California
KRSI Garapan-Saipan, Guam
KRSJ Durango, Colorado
KRSK Molalla, Oregon
KRSL-FM Russell, Kansas
KRSP-FM Salt Lake City, Utah

KRSQ Laurel, Montana
KRSS Tarkio, Missouri
KRST Albuquerque, New Mexico
KRSU Appleton, Minnesota
KRSV Afton, Wyoming
KRSW Worthington, Minnesota
KRSY-FM La Luz, New Mexico
KRTH Los Angeles, California
KRTI Grinnell, Iowa
KRTM Banning, California
KRTN-FM Raton, New Mexico
KRTO Guadalupe, California
KRTR-FM Kailua, Hawaii
KRTS Marfa, Texas
KRTT Great Bend, Kansas
KRTU-FM San Antonio, Texas
KRTY Los Gatos, California
KRTZ Cortez, Colorado
KRUA Anchorage, Alaska
KRUC Las Cruces, New Mexico
KRUD Newman, California
KRUE Waseca, Minnesota
KRUF Shreveport, Louisiana
KRUI-FM Iowa City, Iowa
KRUP Dillingham, Alaska
KRUX Las Cruces, New Mexico
KRVA-FM Campbell, Texas
KRVB Nampa, Idaho
KRVC Hornbrook, California
KRVE Brusly, Louisiana
KRVF Kerens, Texas
KRVG Glenwood Springs, Colorado
KRVH Rio Vista, California
KRVI Mount Vernon, Missouri
KRVK Vista West, Wyoming
KRVL Kerrville, Texas
KRVM-FM Eugene, Oregon
KRVN-FM Lexington, Nebraska
KRVO Columbia Falls, Montana
KRVQ-FM Lake Isabella, California
KRVR Copperopolis, California
KRVS Lafayette, Louisiana
KRVV Bastrop, Louisiana
KRVX Wimbledon, North Dakota
KRVY-FM Starbuck, Minnesota
KRWA Rye, Colorado
KRWG Las Cruces, New Mexico
KRWK Fargo, North Dakota
KRWM Bremerton, Washington
KRWN Farmington, New Mexico
KRWP Stockton, Missouri
KRWQ Gold Hill, Oregon
KRWR Tyler, Texas
KRWY Rawlins, Wyoming
KRXB Beeville, Texas
KRXF Bend, Oregon
KRXL Kirksville, Missouri
KRXO-FM Oklahoma City, Oklahoma
KRXP Pueblo West, Colorado
KRXQ Sacramento, California
KRXT Rockdale, Texas
KRXV Yermo, California
KRXW Roseau, Minnesota
KRXX Kodiak, Alaska
KRXY Shelton, Washington
KRYD Norwood, Colorado
KRYE Olney Springs, Colorado
KRYK Chinook, Montana
KRYL(FM) Haiku, Hawaii
KRYP Gladstone, Oregon
KRYS-FM Corpus Christi, Texas
KRZA Alamosa, Colorado
KRZK Branson, Missouri
KRZN Billings, Montana
KRZU Batesville, Texas
KRZX Redlands, Colorado
KRZY-FM Santa Fe, New Mexico
KRZZ San Francisco, California
KSAB Robstown, Texas
KSAC-FM Dunnigan, California
KSAG Pearsall, Texas
KSAH-FM Pearsall, Texas
KSAJ-FM Abilene, Kansas
KSAK Walnut, California
KSAL-FM Salina, Kansas
KSAM-FM Huntsville, Texas
KSAN San Mateo, California
KSAQ Charlotte, Texas
KSAR Thayer, Missouri
KSAS-FM Caldwell, Idaho
KSAU Nacogdoches, Texas
KSBA Coos Bay, Oregon
KSBC Nile, Washington
KSBH Coushatta, Louisiana
KSBJ Humble, Texas
KSBL Isla Vista, California
KSBR Mission Viejo, California
KSBS-FM Pago Pago, American Samoa
KSBV Salida, Colorado
KSBX Santa Barbara, California
KSBZ Sitka, Alaska
KSCA Glendale, California
KSCB-FM Liberal, Kansas
KSCH Sulphur Springs, Texas
KSCL Shreveport, Louisiana
KSCN Pittsburg, Texas
KSCQ Silver City, New Mexico
KSCR-FM Benson, Minnesota
KSCS Fort Worth, Texas
KSCU Santa Clara, California
KSCV Springfield, Missouri
KSCY Four Corners, Montana
KSD St. Louis, Missouri
KSDA-FM Agat, Guam
KSDB-FM Manhattan, Kansas
KSDJ Brookings, South Dakota
KSDL Sedalia, Missouri
KSDM International Falls, Minnesota
KSDN-FM Aberdeen, South Dakota
KSDQ Moberly, Missouri
KSDR-FM Watertown, South Dakota
KSDS San Diego, California
KSDZ Gordon, Nebraska
KSEA Greenfield, California
KSEC Bentonville, Arkansas
KSED Sedona, Arizona
KSEF Ste. Genevieve, Missouri
KSEG Sacramento, California
KSEH Brawley, California
KSEK-FM Girard, Kansas
KSEL-FM Portales, New Mexico
KSEM Seminole, Texas
KSEQ Visalia, California
KSER Everett, Washington
KSES-FM Seaside, California
KSEY-FM Seymour, Texas
KSEZ Sioux City, Iowa
KSFC Spokane, Washington
KSFH Mountain View, California
KSFI Salt Lake City, Utah
KSFM Woodland, California
KSFR White Rock, New Mexico
KSFS Sioux Falls, South Dakota
KSFT-FM South Sioux City, Nebraska
KSFX Roswell, New Mexico
KSGF-FM Ash Grove, Missouri
KSGN Riverside, California
KSGR Portland, Texas
KSGU Saint George, Utah
KSHA Redding, California
KSHE Crestwood, Missouri
KSHI Zuni, New Mexico
KSHK Hanamaulu, Hawaii
KSHL Coburg, Oregon
KSHN Liberty, Texas
KSHR-FM Coquille, Oregon
KSHU Huntsville, Texas
KSIB-FM Creston, Iowa
KSID-FM Sidney, Nebraska
KSIH Belcourt, North Dakota
KSII El Paso, Texas
KSIK Fleming, Colorado
KSIL Rincon, New Mexico
KSIT Rock Springs, Wyoming
KSIV-FM St. Louis, Missouri
KSIZ Weed, California
KSJD Cortez, Colorado
KSJE Farmington, New Mexico
KSJI Saint Joseph, Missouri
KSJJ Redmond, Oregon
KSJL Strasburg, Colorado
KSJN Minneapolis, Minnesota
KSJO San Jose, California
KSJP(FM) Ipswich, South Dakota
KSJQ Savannah, Missouri
KSJR-FM Collegeville, Minnesota
KSJS San Jose, California
KSJT-FM San Angelo, Texas
KSJU Friday Harbor, Washington
KSJV Fresno, California
KSJY St. Martinville, Louisiana
KSJZ Jamestown, North Dakota
KSKA Anchorage, Alaska
KSKB Brooklyn, Iowa
KSKD Livingston, California
KSKE-FM Eagle, Colorado
KSKF Klamath Falls, Oregon
KSKG Salina, Kansas
KSKI-FM Sun Valley, Idaho
KSKK Staples, Minnesota
KSKL Scott City, Kansas
KSKR-FM Sutherlin, Oregon
KSKS Fresno, California
KSKU Sterling, Kansas
KSKX Chemult, Oregon
KSKZ Copeland, Kansas
KSL-FM Midvale, Utah
KSLC McMinnville, Oregon
KSLE Wewoka, Oklahoma
KSLG-FM Hydesville, California
KSLO Simmesport, Louisiana
KSLQ-FM Washington, Missouri
KSLT Spearfish, South Dakota
KSLU Hammond, Louisiana
KSLV-FM Del Norte, Colorado
KSLX-FM Scottsdale, Arizona
KSLY-FM San Luis Obispo, California
KSLZ St. Louis, Missouri
KSMA-FM Osage, Iowa
KSMB Lafayette, Louisiana
KSMC Moraga, California
KSMD Pangburn, Arkansas
KSME Greeley, Colorado
KSMF Ashland, Oregon
KSMG San Antonio, Texas
KSML-FM Huntington, Texas
KSMM-FM Liberal, Kansas
KSMR Winona, Minnesota
KSMS-FM Point Lookout, Missouri
KSMT Breckenridge, Colorado
KSMU Springfield, Missouri
KSMW West Plains, Missouri
KSMX-FM Clovis, New Mexico
KSMY Lompoc, California
KSNA Idaho Falls, Idaho
KSNB Norton, Kansas
KSND Monmouth, Oregon
KSNE-FM Las Vegas, Nevada
KSNI-FM Santa Maria, California
KSNN-FM Ridgway, Colorado
KSNO-FM Snowmass Village, Colorado
KSNP Burlington, Kansas
KSNQ Twin Falls, Idaho
KSNR Fisher, Minnesota
KSNS Medicine Lodge, Kansas
KSNX Show Low, Arizona
KSNY-FM Snyder, Texas
KSOB Larned, Kansas
KSOC Gainesville, Texas
KSOF Dinuba, California
KSOH Wapato, Washington
KSOK-FM Winfield, Kansas
KSOL San Francisco, California
KSOM Audubon, Iowa
KSON San Diego, California
KSOO-FM Lennox, South Dakota
KSOP-FM Salt Lake City, Utah
KSOQ-FM Escondido, California
KSOR Ashland, Oregon
KSOS Las Vegas, Nevada
KSOU-FM Sioux Center, Iowa
KSPB Pebble Beach, California
KSPC Claremont, California
KSPE-FM Ellwood, California
KSPI FM Stillwater, Oklahoma
KSPK-FM Walsenburg, Colorado
KSPL Kalispell, Montana
KSPM Sand Point, Alaska
KSPN-FM Aspen, Colorado
KSPO Dishman, Washington
KSPP Rhinelander, Wisconsin
KSPQ West Plains, Missouri
KSPW Sparta, Missouri
KSQL Santa Cruz, California
KSQM Sequim, Washington
KSQN Coalville, Utah
KSQQ Morgan Hill, California
KSQS Ririe, Idaho
KSQX Springtown, Texas
KSQY Deadwood, South Dakota
KSRA-FM Salmon, Idaho
KSRC Loup City, Nebraska
KSRD St. Joseph, Missouri
KSRF Poipu, Hawaii
KSRG Ashland, Oregon
KSRH San Rafael, California
KSRI Santa Cruz, California
KSRN Kings Beach, California
KSRQ Thief River Falls, Minnesota
KSRS Roseburg, Oregon
KSRT Cloverdale, California
KSRV-FM Ontario, Oregon
KSRW Independence, California
KSRX Sterling, Colorado
KSRY Tehachapi, California
KSRZ Omaha, Nebraska
KSSA Ingalls, Kansas
KSSB Calipatria, California
KSSC Ventura, California
KSSD Fallbrook, California
KSSE Arcadia, California
KSSI China Lake, California
KSSK-FM Waipahu, Hawaii
KSSL Post, Texas
KSSM Copperas Cove, Texas
KSSN Little Rock, Arkansas
KSSO Norman, Oklahoma
KSSR-FM Santa Rosa, New Mexico
KSSS Bismarck, North Dakota
KSSU Durant, Oklahoma
KSSW Nashville, Arkansas
KSSX Carlsbad, California
KSSZ Fayette, Missouri
KSTB Crystal Beach, Texas
KSTH Holyoke, Colorado
KSTK Wrangell, Alaska
KSTM Indianola, Iowa
KSTN-FM Redding, California
KSTO Agana, Guam
KSTP-FM St. Paul, Minnesota
KSTR-FM Montrose, Colorado
KSTT Atascadero, California
KSTT-FM Los Osos-Baywood Par, California
KSTV-FM Dublin, Texas
KSTX San Antonio, Texas
KSTY Canon City, Colorado
KSTZ Des Moines, Iowa
KSUA Fairbanks, Alaska
KSUI Iowa City, Iowa
KSUP Juneau, Alaska
KSUT Ignacio, Colorado
KSUU Cedar City, Utah
KSUW Sheridan, Wyoming
KSUX Winnebago, Nebraska
KSVL Smith, Nevada
KSVR Mount Vernon, Washington
KSVU Hamilton, Washington
KSVY Sonoma, California
KSWC Winfield, Kansas
KSWD Los Angeles, California
KSWF Aurora, Missouri
KSWG Wickenburg, Arizona
KSWH-FM Arkadelphia, Arkansas
KSWI Atlantic, Iowa
KSWN McCook, Nebraska
KSWP Lufkin, Texas
KSWS Chehalis, Washington
KSWW Ocean Shores, Washington
KSXY Forestville, California
KSYC-FM Yreka, California
KSYD Reedsport, Oregon
KSYE Frederick, Oklahoma
KSYM-FM San Antonio, Texas
KSYN Joplin, Missouri
KSYR Benton, Louisiana
KSYV Solvang, California
KSYZ-FM Grand Island, Nebraska
KSZR Oro Valley, Arizona
KTAA Big Sandy, Texas
KTAC Ephrata, Washington
KTAD Sterling, Colorado
KTAE Hico, Texas
KTAG Cody, Wyoming
KTAI Kingsville, Texas
KTAK Riverton, Wyoming
KTAL-FM Texarkana, Texas
KTAO Taos, New Mexico
KTAR-FM Glendale, Arizona
KTAW Walsenburg, Colorado
KTBB Troup, Texas
KTBG Warrensburg, Missouri
KTBH-FM Kurtistown, Hawaii
KTBJ Festus, Missouri
KTBQ Nacogdoches, Texas

KTBT Broken Arrow, Oklahoma
KTBZ-FM Houston, Texas
KTCB Tillamook, Oregon
KTCC Colby, Kansas
KTCE Payson, Utah
KTCF Dolores, Colorado
KTCK Flower Mound, Texas
KTCL Wheat Ridge, Colorado
KTCM Madison, Missouri
KTCO Duluth, Minnesota
KTCS-FM Fort Smith, Arkansas
KTCU Fort Worth, Texas
KTCV Kennewick, Washington
KTCX Beaumont, Texas
KTCZ-FM Minneapolis, Minnesota
KTDA Dalhart, Texas
KTDB Ramah, New Mexico
KTDE Gualala, California
KTDL Trinidad, Colorado
KTDR Del Rio, Texas
KTDU Durango, Colorado
KTDV State Center, Iowa
KTDX Laramie, Wyoming
KTDY Lafayette, Louisiana
KTDZ College, Alaska
KTEC Klamath Falls, Oregon
KTED Evansville, Wyoming
KTEE North Bend, Oregon
KTEG Santa Fe, New Mexico
KTEI Placerville, Colorado
KTEP El Paso, Texas
KTER Rudolph, Texas
KTEX Mercedes, Texas
KTEZ Zwolle, Louisiana
KTFC Sioux City, Iowa
KTFG Sioux Rapids, Iowa
KTFM Floresville, Texas
KTFR Chelsea, Oklahoma
KTFW-FM Glen Rose, Texas
KTFX-FM Warner, Oklahoma
KTFY Buhl, Idaho
KTGA Saratoga, Wyoming
KTGL Beatrice, Nebraska
KTGR-FM Fulton, Missouri
KTGS Tishomingo, Oklahoma
KTGV Oracle, Arizona
KTGW Fruitland, New Mexico
KTGX Owasso, Oklahoma
KTHC Sidney, Montana
KTHF Hammon, Oklahoma
KTHI Caldwell, Idaho
KTHK Idaho Falls, Idaho
KTHL Altus, Oklahoma
KTHM Red Bluff, California
KTHN La Junta, Colorado
KTHP Hemphill, Texas
KTHQ Eagar, Arizona
KTHR Wichita, Kansas
KTHS-FM Berryville, Arkansas
KTHT Cleveland, Texas
KTHU Corning, California
KTHX-FM Dayton, Nevada
KTIC-FM West Point, Nebraska
KTIG Pequot Lakes, Minnesota
KTIJ Elk City, Oklahoma
KTIK New Plymouth, Idaho
KTIL-FM Bay City, Oregon
KTIL-FM Bay City, Oregon
KTIS-FM Minneapolis, Minnesota
KTJJ Farmington, Missouri
KTJM Port Arthur, Texas
KTJO-FM Ottawa, Kansas
KTJZ Tallulah, Louisiana
KTKB Dededo, Guam
KTKC Springhill, Louisiana
KTKE Truckee, California
KTKL Stigler, Oklahoma
KTKO Beeville, Texas
KTKS Versailles, Missouri
KTKU Juneau, Alaska
KTKX Terrell Hills, Texas
KTLB Twin Lakes, Iowa
KTLC Canon City, Colorado
KTLF Colorado Springs, Colorado
KTLI El Dorado, Kansas
KTLN Thibodaux, Louisiana
KTLO-FM Mountain Home, Arkansas
KTLS-FM Holdenville, Oklahoma
KTLT Anson, Texas
KTLW Lancaster, California
KTLX Columbus, Nebraska
KTLZ Cuero, Texas
KTMC-FM McAlester, Oklahoma
KTME Reliance, Wyoming
KTMG Prescott, Arizona
KTMH Montrose, Colorado
KTMK Tillamook, Oregon
KTML South Fork, Colorado
KTMO New Madrid, Missouri
KTMQ Temecula, California
KTMT-FM Medford, Oregon
KTMU Muenster, Texas
KTMX York, Nebraska
KTNA Talkeetna, Alaska
KTND Aspen, Colorado
KTNE-FM Alliance, Nebraska
KTNR Kenedy, Texas
KTNT Eufaula, Oklahoma
KTNX Arcadia, Missouri
KTNY Libby, Montana
KTOC-FM Jonesboro, Louisiana
KTOH Kalaheo, Hawaii
KTOL Leadville, Colorado
KTOM-FM Marina, California
KTOO Juneau, Alaska
KTOP-FM Saint Marys, Kansas
KTOR Gerber, California
KTOT Spearman, Texas
KTOY Texarkana, Arkansas
KTOZ-FM Pleasant Hope, Missouri
KTPF Salida, Colorado
KTPH Tonopah, Nevada
KTPI-FM Mojave, California
KTPK Topeka, Kansas
KTPL Pueblo, Colorado
KTPO Kootenai, Idaho
KTPS Pagosa Springs, Colorado
KTPT Rapid City, South Dakota
KTPZ Hazelton, Idaho
KTQM-FM Clovis, New Mexico
KTQQ Elko, Nevada
KTQX Bakersfield, California
KTRA-FM Farmington, New Mexico
KTRI-FM Mansfield, Missouri
KTRM Kirksville, Missouri
KTRN White Hall, Arkansas
KTRQ Colt, Arkansas
KTRR Loveland, Colorado
KTRS-FM Casper, Wyoming
KTRT Winthrop, Washington
KTRU(FM) Houston, Texas
KTRX Dickson, Oklahoma
KTRY(FM) Cazadero, California
KTRZ Riverton, Wyoming
KTSC-FM Pueblo, Colorado
KTSD-FM Reliance, South Dakota
KTSE-FM Patterson, California
KTSG Steamboat Springs, Colorado
KTSL Medical Lake, Washington
KTSM-FM El Paso, Texas
KTSO Glenpool, Oklahoma
KTSR De Quincy, Louisiana
KTST Oklahoma City, Oklahoma
KTSU Houston, Texas
KTSW San Marcos, Texas
KTSY Caldwell, Idaho
KTTA(FM) Jackson, California
KTTE Springfield, Colorado
KTTG Mena, Arkansas
KTTI Yuma, Arizona
KTTK Lebanon, Missouri
KTTN-FM Trenton, Missouri
KTTR FM St. James, Missouri
KTTS-FM Springfield, Missouri
KTTU Brownfield, Texas
KTTX Brenham, Texas
KTTY New Boston, Texas
KTTZ-FM Lubbock, Texas
KTUF Kirksville, Missouri
KTUG Hudson, Wyoming
KTUH Honolulu, Hawaii
KTUI-FM Sullivan, Missouri
KTUM Tatum, New Mexico
KTUN New Castle, Colorado
KTUT Frankfort, South Dakota
KTUX Carthage, Texas
KTUZ-FM Okarche, Oklahoma
KTVR-FM La Grande, Oregon
KTWA Ottumwa, Iowa
KTWB Sioux Falls, South Dakota
KTWD Wallace, Idaho
KTWL Hempstead, Texas
KTWN-FM Edina, Minnesota
KTWS Bend, Oregon
KTWV Los Angeles, California
KTXB Beaumont, Texas
KTXC Lamesa, Texas
KTXG Greenville, Texas
KTXI Ingram, Texas
KTXJ-FM Jasper, Texas
KTXK Texarkana, Texas
KTXM Hallettsville, Texas
KTXN-FM Victoria, Texas
KTXO Goldsmith, Texas
KTXP Bushland, Texas
KTXR Springfield, Missouri
KTXT-FM Lubbock, Texas
KTXX-FM Bee Cave, Texas
KTXY Jefferson City, Missouri
KTYD Santa Barbara, California
KTYL-FM Tyler, Texas
KTYN Thayne, Wyoming
KTZA Artesia, New Mexico
KTZU Velva, North Dakota
KTZZ Conrad, Montana
KUAC Fairbanks, Alaska
KUAD-FM Windsor, Colorado
KUAF Fayetteville, Arkansas
KUAL-FM Brainerd, Minnesota
KUAM-FM Hagatna, Guam
KUAP Pine Bluff, Arkansas
KUAR Little Rock, Arkansas
KUAT-FM Tucson, Arizona
KUAZ-FM Tucson, Arizona
KUBB Mariposa, California
KUBE Seattle, Washington
KUBJ Brenham, Texas
KUBL-FM Salt Lake City, Utah
KUBO Calexico, California
KUBQ La Grande, Oregon
KUBS Newport, Washington
KUCA Conway, Arkansas
KUCB Unalaska, Alaska
KUCC Clarkston, Washington
KUCD Pearl City, Hawaii
KUCI Irvine, California
KUCR Riverside, California
KUCV-FM Lincoln, Nebraska
KUDD Roy, Utah
KUDD Indian Springs, Nevada
KUDE Nephi, Utah
KUDI Choteau, Montana
KUDL Sacramento, Kansas
KUDL Sacramento, California
KUDU Tok, Alaska
KUER-FM Salt Lake City, Utah
KUEU Logan, Utah
KUFL Libby, Montana
KUFM Missoula, Montana
KUFN Hamilton, Montana
KUFR Salt Lake City, Utah
KUFW Phoenix, Arizona
KUFX San Jose, California
KUGS Bellingham, Washington
KUHB-FM St. Paul, Alaska
KUHC Clayton, New Mexico
KUHF Houston, Texas
KUHM Helena, Montana
KUHN Golden Meadow, Louisiana
KUIC Vacaville, California
KUJ-FM Burbank, Washington
KUJZ Creswell, Oregon
KUKA San Diego, Texas
KUKI-FM Ukiah, California
KUKL Kalispell, Montana
KUKN Longview, Washington
KUKU-FM Willow Springs, Missouri
KUKY Wellton, Arizona
KULH Wheeling, Missouri
KULL Abilene, Texas
KULM-FM Columbus, Texas
KULO Alexandria, Minnesota
KULV Ukiah, California
KUMA-FM Pilot Rock, Oregon
KUMD-FM Duluth, Minnesota
KUMM Morris, Minnesota
KUMR Doolittle, Missouri
KUMU-FM Honolulu, Hawaii
KUMX North Fort Polk, Louisiana
KUNA-FM La Quinta, California
KUNC Greeley, Colorado
KUND-FM Grand Forks, North Dakota
KUNI Cedar Falls, Iowa
KUNM Albuquerque, New Mexico
KUNQ Houston, Missouri
KUNR Reno, Nevada
KUNV Las Vegas, Nevada
KUOI-FM Moscow, Idaho
KUOM-FM St. Louis Park, Minnesota
KUOO Spirit Lake, Iowa
KUOP Stockton, California
KUOR-FM Redlands, California
KUOW-FM Seattle, Washington
KUPD Tempe, Arizona
KUPH Mountain View, Missouri
KUPI-FM Rexburg, Idaho
KUPL Portland, Oregon
KUPS Tacoma, Washington
KUQL Ethan, South Dakota
KUQQ Milford, Iowa
KURB Little Rock, Arkansas
KURE Ames, Iowa
KURK Reno, Nevada
KURL(FM) Billings, Montana
KURM-FM Gravette, Arkansas
KURQ Grover Beach, California
KURY-FM Brookings, Oregon
KUSB Hazelton, North Dakota
KUSC Los Angeles, California
KUSD Vermillion, South Dakota
KUSJ Harker Heights, Texas
KUSL Richfield, Utah
KUSN Dearing, Kansas
KUSO Albion, Nebraska
KUSP Santa Cruz, California
KUSQ Worthington, Minnesota
KUSQ-FM Worthington, Minnesota
KUSR Logan, Utah
KUSU-FM Logan, Utah
KUSW Flora Vista, New Mexico
KUSZ Olathe, Colorado
KUT Austin, Texas
KUTC Mount Pleasant, Utah
KUTE Ignacio, Colorado
KUTX Leander, Texas
KUUB Sun Valley, Nevada
KUUL East Moline, Illinois
KUUR Carbondale, Colorado
KUUT Farmington, New Mexico
KUUU South Jordan, Utah
KUUZ Lake Village, Arkansas
KUVA Uvalde, Texas
KUVO Denver, Colorado
KUWA Afton, Wyoming
KUWC Casper, Wyoming
KUWD Sundance, Wyoming
KUWG Gillette, Wyoming
KUWI Rawlins, Wyoming
KUWJ Jackson, Wyoming
KUWL Laramie, Wyoming
KUWN Newcastle, Wyoming
KUWP Powell, Wyoming
KUWR Laramie, Wyoming
KUWS Superior, Wisconsin
KUWT Thermopolis, Wyoming
KUWW Fort Washakie, Wyoming
KUWX Pinedale, Wyoming
KUWY Laramie, Wyoming
KUWZ Rock Springs, Wyoming
KUYI Hotevilla, Arizona
KUYY Emmetsburg, Iowa
KUZN Centerville, Texas
KUZZ-FM Bakersfield, California
KVAB Clarkston, Washington
KVAK-FM Valdez, Alaska
KVAL Cal-Nev-Ari, Nevada
KVAM Goodland, Nebraska
KVAR Pine Ridge, South Dakota
KVAS-FM Ilwaco, Washington
KVAY Lamar, Colorado
KVAZ Henryetta, Oklahoma
KVBL La Grande, Oregon
KVCF Freeman, South Dakota
KVCH Huron, South Dakota
KVCK-FM Wolf Point, Montana
KVCL-FM Winnfield, Louisiana
KVCM Helena, Montana
KVCO Concordia, Kansas
KVCR San Bernardino, California
KVCS Spring Valley, Minnesota
KVCX Gregory, South Dakota
KVCY Fort Scott, Kansas
KVDG Midland, Texas
KVDP Dry Prong, Louisiana

KVDU Houma, Louisiana
KVED Vernon, Texas
KVEG Mesquite, Nevada
KVER El Paso, Texas
KVET-FM Austin, Texas
KVFG Victorville, California
KVFL Pierre, South Dakota
KVFM Beeville, Texas
KVFX Logan, Utah
KVGB-FM Great Bend, Kansas
KVGG Salome, Arizona
KVGO Spring Valley, Minnesota
KVGQ Overton, Nevada
KVGS Meadview, Arizona
KVHR Van Horn, Texas
KVHS Concord, California
KVHT Vermillion, South Dakota
KVHU Judsonia, Arkansas
KVIB Sun City West, Arizona
KVIC Victoria, Texas
KVIL Highland Park-Dallas, Texas
KVIP-FM Redding, California
KVIR Bullhead City, Arizona
KVIX Port Angeles, Washington
KVJC Globe, Arizona
KVJM Hearne, Texas
KVJZ Vail, Colorado
KVKI-FM Shreveport, Louisiana
KVKL Las Vegas, Nevada
KVKR Pine Ridge, South Dakota
KVLB Bend, Oregon
KVLC Hatch, New Mexico
KVLE-FM Gunnison, Colorado
KVLI(FM) Lake Isabella, California
KVLK Milan, New Mexico
KVLL-FM Wells, Texas
KVLO Humnoke, Arkansas
KVLP Tucumcari, New Mexico
KVLR Elgin, Texas
KVLT Temple, Texas
KVLU Beaumont, Texas
KVLW Gatesville, Texas
KVLY Edinburg, Texas
KVLZ Sheridan, Wyoming
KVMA-FM Shreveport, Louisiana
KVMI Arthur, North Dakota
KVMN Cave City, Arkansas
KVMO Fort Benton, Montana
KVMR Nevada City, California
KVMT Montrose, Colorado
KVMV Mc Allen, Texas
KVMX Bakersfield, California
KVMZ Waldo, Arkansas
KVNA-FM Flagstaff, Arizona
KVNC Minturn, Colorado
KVNE Tyler, Texas
KVNF Paonia, Colorado
KVNO Omaha, Nebraska
KVOB Lindsborg, Kansas
KVOD Lakewood, Colorado
KVOE-FM Emporia, Kansas
KVOM-FM Morrilton, Arkansas
KVOO-FM Tulsa, Oklahoma
KVOU-FM Uvalde, Texas
KVOV Carbondale, Colorado
KVOX-FM Moorhead, Minnesota
KVPI-FM Ville Platte, Louisiana
KVPR Fresno, California
KVPW Kingsburg, California
KVRA Sisters, Oregon
KVRD-FM Cottonwood, Arizona
KVRE Hot Springs Village, Arkansas
KVRG Victor, Idaho
KVRH-FM Salida, Colorado
KVRK Sanger, Texas
KVRO Stillwater, Oklahoma
KVRP-FM Haskell, Texas
KVRS Lawton, Oklahoma
KVRT Victoria, Texas
KVRV Monte Rio, California
KVRW Lawton, Oklahoma
KVRX Austin, Texas
KVRZ Libby, Montana
KVSC St. Cloud, Minnesota
KVSF-FM Pecos, New Mexico
KVSP Anadarko, Oklahoma
KVSR Kirksville, Missouri
KVSS Papillion, Nebraska
KVST Willis, Texas
KVSV-FM Beloit, Kansas
KVTI Tacoma, Washington
KVTY Lewiston, Idaho
KVUH Laytonville, California
KVUU Pueblo, Colorado
KVUW Wendover, Nevada
KVVA-FM Apache Junction, Arizona
KVVF Santa Clara, California
KVVL Maryville, Missouri
KVVP Leesville, Louisiana
KVVR Dutton, Montana
KVVS Rosamond, California
KVVZ San Rafael, California
KVWC-FM Vernon, Texas
KVWF Augusta, Kansas
KVWG-FM Dilley, Texas
KVYB Santa Barbara, California
KVYL Mohave Valley, Arizona
KVYN St. Helena, California
KWAK-FM Stuttgart, Arkansas
KWAO Ocean Park, Washington
KWAP(FM) Pine Haven, Wyoming
KWAR Waverly, Iowa
KWAS Borger, Texas
KWAV Monterey, California
KWAW Garapan-Saipan, Guam
KWAX Eugene, Oregon
KWAY-FM Waverly, Iowa
KWBI Great Bend, Kansas
KWBT Bellmead, Texas
KWBU-FM Waco, Texas
KWBX Salem, Oregon
KWBY-FM Ranger, Texas
KWBZ Monroe City, Missouri
KWCA Palo Cedro, California
KWCD Bisbee, Arizona
KWCK-FM Searcy, Arkansas
KWCL-FM Oak Grove, Louisiana
KWCN Pinedale, Wyoming
KWCO-FM Chickasha, Oklahoma
KWCR-FM Ogden, Utah
KWCW Walla Walla, Washington
KWCX-FM Tanque Verde, Arizona
KWDD(FM) Fairbanks, Alaska
KWDF Ball, Louisiana
KWDI Idalia, Colorado
KWDM West Des Moines, Iowa
KWDQ Woodward, Oklahoma
KWDR Royal City, Washington
KWDS Kettleman City, California
KWEN Tulsa, Oklahoma
KWEN Sand Springs, Oklahoma
KWES-FM Ruidoso, New Mexico
KWEY-FM Clinton, Oklahoma
KWFB Holliday, Texas
KWFC Springfield, Missouri
KWFH Parker, Arizona
KWFJ Roy, Washington
KWFL Roswell, New Mexico
KWFP Sparks, Nevada
KWFR San Angelo, Texas
KWFS-FM Wichita Falls, Texas
KWFX Woodward, Oklahoma
KWGB Colby, Kansas
KWGL Ouray, Colorado
KWGO Burlington, North Dakota
KWGS Tulsa, Oklahoma
KWHF Harrisburg, Arkansas
KWHK Hutchinson, Kansas
KWHL Anchorage, Alaska
KWHO Lovell, Wyoming
KWHQ-FM Kenai, Alaska
KWHT Pendleton, Oregon
KWHW-FM Altus, Oklahoma
KWIC Topeka, Kansas
KWID Las Vegas, Nevada
KWIM Window Rock, Arizona
KWIN Lodi, California
KWIQ-FM Moses Lake, Washington
KWIS Plummer, Idaho
KWIT Sioux City, Iowa
KWIZ Santa Ana, California
KWJC Liberty, Missouri
KWJJ-FM Portland, Oregon
KWJK Boonville, Missouri
KWKJ Windsor, Missouri
KWKK Russellville, Arkansas
KWKL Grandfield, Oklahoma
KWKM St. Johns, Arizona
KWKQ Graham, Texas
KWKR Leoti, Kansas
KWKZ Charleston, Missouri
KWLD Plainview, Texas
KWLF Fairbanks, Alaska
KWLK Westwood, California
KWLN Wilson Creek, Washington
KWLR Maumelle, Arkansas
KWLS Winfield, Kansas
KWLT North Crossett, Arkansas
KWLU Chester, California
KWLV Many, Louisiana
KWLZ-FM West Linn, Oregon
KWME Wellington, Kansas
KWML Georgetown, Delaware
KWMR Point Reyes Station, California
KWMU St. Louis, Missouri
KWMW Maljamar, New Mexico
KWMX Williams, Arizona
KWMY Joliet, Montana
KWMZ-FM Empire, Louisiana
KWNA-FM Winnemucca, Nevada
KWND Springfield, Missouri
KWNE Ukiah, California
KWNG Red Wing, Minnesota
KWNM Winnemucca, Nevada
KWNN Lodi, California
KWNO-FM Rushford, Minnesota
KWNR Henderson, Nevada
KWNS Winnsboro, Texas
KWNZ Lovelock, Nevada
KWOF Broomfield, Colorado
KWOL-FM Whitefish, Montana
KWOP(FM) Fort Dodge, North Carolina
KWOW Clifton, Texas
KWOX Woodward, Oklahoma
KWOZ Mountain View, Arkansas
KWPK-FM Sisters, Oregon
KWPR Lund, Nevada
KWPS-FM Caddo Valley, Arkansas
KWPT Fortuna, California
KWPW Robinson, Texas
KWPZ Lynden, Washington
KWQW Boone, Iowa
KWRB Bisbee, Arizona
KWRC Hermosa, South Dakota
KWRD-FM Highland Village, Texas
KWRF-FM Warren, Arkansas
KWRI Bartlesville, Oklahoma
KWRK Window Rock, Arizona
KWRL La Grande, Oregon
KWRQ Clifton, Arizona
KWRR Ethete, Wyoming
KWRV Sun Valley, Idaho
KWRW Rusk, Texas
KWRX Redmond, Oregon
KWRZ Canyonville, Oregon
KWSA Price, Utah
KWSB-FM Gunnison, Colorado
KWSC Wayne, Nebraska
KWSO Warm Springs, Oregon
KWTD Ridgecrest, California
KWTG Vidalia, Louisiana
KWTH Barstow, California
KWTM June Lake, California
KWTO-FM Springfield, Missouri
KWTS Canyon, Texas
KWTU Tulsa, Oklahoma
KWTW Bishop, California
KWTX-FM Waco, Texas
KWTY Cartago, California
KWUF-FM Pagosa Springs, Colorado
KWUP Navasota, Texas
KWUR Clayton, Missouri
KWUT(FM) Elsinore, Utah
KWUZ Poncha Springs, Colorado
KWVA Eugene, Oregon
KWVE-FM San Clemente, California
KWVI Waverly, Iowa
KWVR-FM Enterprise, Oregon
KWVV-FM Homer, Alaska
KWVZ Florence, Oregon
KWWC-FM Columbia, Missouri
KWWK Rochester, Minnesota
KWWR Mexico, Missouri
KWWS Walla Walla, Washington
KWWV Santa Margarita, California
KWWW-FM Quincy, Washington
KWWX Cashmere, Washington
KWXC Grove, Oklahoma
KWXD Asbury, Missouri
KWXR Reliance, Wyoming
KWXX-FM Hilo, Hawaii
KWYD Parma, Idaho
KWYE Fresno, California
KWYI Kawaihae, Hawaii
KWYK-FM Aztec, New Mexico
KWYL South Lake Tahoe, California
KWYN-FM Wynne, Arkansas
KWYR-FM Winner, South Dakota
KWYW Lost Cabin, Wyoming
KWYX Casper, Wyoming
KWYY Midwest, Wyoming
KXAA Cle Elum, Washington
KXAC St. James, Minnesota
KXAI Refugio, Texas
KXAZ Page, Arizona
KXBA Nikiski, Alaska
KXBG Cheyenne, Wyoming
KXBJ El Campo, Texas
KXBL Henryetta, Oklahoma
KXBN Cedar City, Utah
KXBR International Falls, Minnesota
KXBX-FM Lakeport, California
KXBZ Manhattan, Kansas
KXCI Tucson, Arizona
KXCL Rock Creek Park, Colorado
KXCM Joshua Tree, California
KXCS(FM) Coahoma, Texas
KXCV Maryville, Missouri
KXDD Yakima, Washington
KXDG Webb City, Missouri
KXDI Belfield, North Dakota
KXDJ Spearman, Texas
KXDL Browerville, Minnesota
KXDR Pinesdale, Montana
KXDR(FM) Pinesdale, Montana
KXDS Santa Clara, Utah
KXDZ Templeton, California
KXEI Havre, Montana
KXEZ Farmersville, Texas
KXFC Coalgate, Oklahoma
KXFE Dumas, Arkansas
KXFF Colorado City, Arizona
KXFG Menifee, California
KXFM Santa Maria, California
KXFR Socorro, New Mexico
KXFT Manson, Iowa
KXGA Glennallen, Alaska
KXGE Dubuque, Iowa
KXGJ Victoria, Texas
KXGL Amarillo, Texas
KXGM-FM Hiawatha, Iowa
KXGO Arcata, California
KXGR Loveland, Colorado
KXGT Carrington, North Dakota
KXHT Marion, Arkansas
KXIA Marshalltown, Iowa
KXIM Sanborn, Iowa
KXIO Clarksville, Arkansas
KXIX Sunriver, Oregon
KXJM Banks, Oregon
KXJN Moose Wilson Road, Wyoming
KXJO St. Maries, Idaho
KXJS Sutter, California
KXJZ Sacramento, California
KXKC New Iberia, Louisiana
KXKK Park Rapids, Minnesota
KXKL-FM Denver, Colorado
KXKM McCarthy, Alaska
KXKQ Safford, Arizona
KXKS-FM Shreveport, Louisiana
KXKT Glenwood, Iowa
KXKU Lyons, Kansas
KXKX Knob Noster, Missouri
KXKZ Ruston, Louisiana
KXL-FM Portland, Oregon
KXLB Livingston, Montana
KXLC La Crescent, Minnesota
KXLG Milbank, South Dakota
KXLI Moapa, Nevada
KXLL Juneau, Alaska
KXLM Oxnard, California
KXLP Eagle Lake, Minnesota
KXLR Fairbanks, Alaska
KXLS Lahoma, Oklahoma
KXLT-FM Eagle, Idaho
KXLU Los Angeles, California
KXLV Amarillo, Texas
KXLW Houston, Alaska
KXLY-FM Spokane, Washington
KXMG Jean Lafitte, Louisiana
KXML Fairfield, Idaho
KXMO Owensville, Missouri
KXMS Joplin, Missouri
KXMT Taos, New Mexico

KXMX Muldrow, Oklahoma
KXMZ Box Elder, South Dakota
KXNA Springdale, Arkansas
KXNC Ness City, Kansas
KXNE-FM Norfolk, Nebraska
KXNM Encino, New Mexico
KXNP North Platte, Nebraska
KXNT-FM Henderson, Nevada
KXNV Sun Valley, Nevada
KXO-FM El Centro, California
KXOJ-FM Sapulpa, Oklahoma
KXOL-FM Los Angeles, California
KXOO Elk City, Oklahoma
KXOQ Kennett, Missouri
KXOR-FM Thibodaux, Louisiana
KXOT Tacoma, Washington
KXOX-FM Sweetwater, Texas
KXPC Welches, Oregon
KXPK Evergreen, Colorado
KXPN-FM Scotland, Texas
KXPR Sacramento, California
KXPT Las Vegas, Nevada
KXPZ Las Cruces, New Mexico
KXQK Leakey, Texas
KXQQ Henderson, Nevada
KXRA-FM Alexandria, Minnesota
KXRD Victorville, California
KXRI Amarillo, Texas
KXRJ Russellville, Arkansas
KXRK Provo, Utah
KXRL Cherry Valley, Arkansas
KXRQ Roosevelt, Utah
KXRR Monroe, Louisiana
KXRS Hemet, California
KXRT Idabel, Oklahoma
KXRV Cannon Ball, North Dakota
KXRX Walla Walla, Washington
KXRY Portland, Oregon
KXRZ Alexandria, Minnesota
KXSA-FM Dermott, Arkansas
KXSB Big Bear Lake, California
KXSE Davis, California
KXSM Hollister, California
KXSR Groveland, California
KXSS-FM Amarillo, Texas
KXTA-2 Gooding, Idaho
KXTC Thoreau, New Mexico
KXTE Pahrump, Nevada
KXTH Seminole, Oklahoma
KXTN-FM San Antonio, Texas
KXTQ Lubbock, Texas
KXTS Geyserville, California
KXTT Maricopa, California
KXTZ Pismo Beach, California
KXUA Fayetteville, Arkansas
KXUL Monroe, Louisiana
KXUS Springfield, Missouri
KXWA Centennial, Colorado
KXWT Odessa, Texas
KXXE-FM San Augustine, Texas
KXXI Gallup, New Mexico
KXXK Hoquiam, Washington
KXXL Moorcroft, Wyoming
KXXM San Antonio, Texas
KXXN Iowa Park, Texas
KXXO Olympia, Washington
KXXQ Milan, New Mexico
KXXR Minneapolis, Minnesota
KXXY-FM Oklahoma City, Oklahoma
KXXZ Barstow, California
KXYL-FM Coleman, Texas
KXZK Vail, Arizona
KXZM Felton, California
KXZS Wall, South Dakota
KXZT Newell, South Dakota
KYAF Firebaugh, California
KYAI McKee, Kentucky
KYAL-FM Muskogee, Oklahoma
KYAR Lorena, Texas
KYAT Gallup, New Mexico
KYBA Stewartville, Minnesota
KYBB Canton, South Dakota
KYBE Frederick, Oklahoma
KYBG Basile, Louisiana
KYBI Lufkin, Texas
KYBJ Lake Jackson, Texas
KYBR Espanola, New Mexico
KYCC Stockton, California
KYCH-FM Portland, Oregon
KYCI Firebaugh, California
KYCK Crookston, Minnesota
KYCM Alamogordo, New Mexico
KYCO Limon, Colorado
KYCS Rock Springs, Wyoming
KYCU Clinton, Oklahoma
KYDA Azle, Texas
KYDN Monte Vista, Colorado
KYDS Sacramento, California
KYDT Pine Haven, Wyoming
KYEE Alamogordo, New Mexico
KYEL Danville, Arkansas
KYEZ Salina, Kansas
KYFB Denison, Texas
KYFG Omaha, Nebraska
KYFJ New Iberia, Louisiana
KYFL Monroe, Louisiana
KYFM Bartlesville, Oklahoma
KYFO-FM Ogden, Utah
KYFP Palestine, Texas
KYFQ Tacoma, Washington
KYFS San Antonio, Texas
KYFW Wichita, Kansas
KYGA Goleta, California
KYGL Texarkana, Arkansas
KYGO-FM Denver, Colorado
KYGR Alamo, New Mexico
KYHD Valliant, Oklahoma
KYIS Oklahoma City, Oklahoma
KYIX South Oroville, California
KYJC Commerce, Texas
KYJK Missoula, Montana
KYKA Meadow Lakes, Alaska
KYKC Byng, Oklahoma
KYKD Bethel, Alaska
KYKM Yoakum, Texas
KYKR Beaumont, Texas
KYKS Lufkin, Texas
KYKV Selah, Washington
KYKX Longview, Texas
KYKY St. Louis, Missouri
KYKZ Lake Charles, Louisiana
KYLA(FM) Fountain Valley, California
KYLC Lake Charles, Louisiana
KYLD San Francisco, California
KYLF Adrian, Missouri
KYLI Bunkerville, Nevada
KYLK Okemah, Oklahoma
KYLR Hutto, Texas
KYLS-FM Ironton, Missouri
KYLV Oklahoma City, Oklahoma
KYME Rockford, Iowa
KYMG Anchorage, Alaska
KYMK-FM Maurice, Louisiana
KYMN-FM Northfield, Minnesota
KYMS Rathdrum, Idaho
KYMV Woodruff, Utah
KYMX Sacramento, California
KYNU Jamestown, North Dakota
KYNW Centralia, Washington
KYNZ Lone Grove, Oklahoma
KYOE Point Arena, California
KYOO-FM Half Way, Missouri
KYOR Newport, Oregon
KYOT-FM Phoenix, Arizona
KYOX Comanche, Texas
KYOY Hillsdale, Wyoming
KYPB Big Timber, Montana
KYPC Colstrip, Montana
KYPF Stanford, Montana
KYPL Yakima, Washington
KYPM Livingston, Montana
KYPR Miles City, Montana
KYPW Wolf Point, Montana
KYQQ Arkansas City, Kansas
KYQX Weatherford, Texas
KYRA Thousand Oaks, California
KYRA Thousand Oaks, California
KYRK Refugio, Texas
KYRM Yuma, Arizona
KYRN Socorro, New Mexico
KYRQ Natalia, Texas
KYRT Hunt, Texas
KYRV Concordia, Missouri
KYRX Marble Hill, Missouri
KYSC Fairbanks, Alaska
KYSE El Paso, Texas
KYSF Bonanza, Oregon
KYSJ Coos Bay, Oregon
KYSL Frisco, Colorado
KYSM-FM Mankato, Minnesota
KYSN East Wenatchee, Washington
KYSR Los Angeles, California
KYSS-FM Missoula, Montana
KYSX Billings, Montana
KYTC Northwood, Iowa
KYTE Newport, Oregon
KYTI Sheridan, Wyoming
KYTM Corrigan, Texas
KYTN Union City, Tennessee
KYTS Manderson, Wyoming
KYTT-FM Coos Bay, Oregon
KYTZ Walhalla, North Dakota
KYUN Hailey, Idaho
KYUS-FM Miles City, Montana
KYVA-FM Church Rock, New Mexico
KYVT Yakima, Washington
KYWA Wichita, Kansas
KYWD Green Valley, Arizona
KYWH Lockwood, Montana
KYWL Evergreen, Montana
KYXA Homer, Louisiana
KYXK Gurdon, Arkansas
KYXX Ozona, Texas
KYXY San Diego, California
KYYI Burkburnett, Texas
KYYK Palestine, Texas
KYYO McCleary, Washington
KYYT Goldendale, Washington
KYYX Minot, North Dakota
KYYY Bismarck, North Dakota
KYYZ Williston, North Dakota
KYZA Adelanto, California
KYZK Sun Valley, Idaho
KYZQ Mount Pleasant, Texas
KYZZ Big Sur, California
KZAI Superior, Arizona
KZAL Manson, Washington
KZAM Pleasant Valley, Texas
KZAN Hays, Kansas
KZAP Paradise, California
KZAR McQueeney, Texas
KZAT-FM Belle Plaine, Iowa
KZAZ Bellingham, Washington
KZBB Poteau, Oklahoma
KZBD Spokane, Washington
KZBE Omak, Washington
KZBG Lapwai, Idaho
KZBI Elko, Nevada
KZBJ Bay City, Texas
KZBK Brookfield, Missouri
KZBL Natchitoches, Louisiana
KZBQ Pocatello, Idaho
KZBR La Jara, Colorado
KZBS Granite, Oklahoma
KZBT Midland, Texas
KZCD Lawton, Oklahoma
KZCH Derby, Kansas
KZCR Fergus Falls, Minnesota
KZCU Woodward, Oklahoma
KZDX Burley, Idaho
KZDY Cawker City, Kansas
KZEL-FM Eugene, Oregon
KZEN Central City, Nebraska
KZEP-FM San Antonio, Texas
KZET Cortez, Colorado
KZEW Wheatland, Wyoming
KZFM Corpus Christi, Texas
KZFN Moscow, Idaho
KZFR Chico, California
KZFT Fannett, Texas
KZGF Grand Forks, North Dakota
KZGL Flagstaff, Arizona
KZGM Cabool, Missouri
KZGZ Hagatna, Guam
KZHE Stamps, Arkansas
KZHK St. George, Utah
KZHR Dayton, Washington
KZHT Salt Lake City, Utah
KZIA Cedar Rapids, Iowa
KZID Culdesac, Idaho
KZII-FM Lubbock, Texas
KZIN-FM Shelby, Montana
KZIO Two Harbors, Minnesota
KZIQ-FM Ridgecrest, California
KZIU-FM Weston, Oregon
KZJB Pocatello, Idaho
KZJF Jefferson City, Missouri
KZJH Jackson, Wyoming
KZJK St. Louis Park, Minnesota
KZJZ St. Regis, Montana
KZKE Seligman, Arizona
KZKK Huron, South Dakota
KZKL Wichita Falls, Texas
KZKR Jonesville, Louisiana
KZKS Rifle, Colorado
KZKX Seward, Nebraska
KZKY(FM) Ucon, Idaho
KZKZ-FM Greenwood, Arkansas
KZLA Riverdale, California
KZLB Fort Dodge, Iowa
KZLE Batesville, Arkansas
KZLG Mansura, Louisiana
KZLK Rapid City, South Dakota
KZLO Kilgore, Texas
KZLT-FM East Grand Forks, Minnesota
KZLU Inyokern, California
KZLV Lytle, Texas
KZLZ Casas Adobes, Arizona
KZMA Naylor, Missouri
KZMC McCook, Nebraska
KZME Brightwood, Oregon
KZMG Elko, Nevada
KZMI Garapan-Saipan, Guam
KZMK Sierra Vista, Arizona
KZML Quincy, Washington
KZMN Kalispell, Montana
KZMO Roundup, Montana
KZMP-FM Pilot Point, Texas
KZMQ-FM Greybull, Wyoming
KZMT Helena, Montana
KZMU Moab, Utah
KZMX-FM Hot Springs, South Dakota
KZMY Bozeman, Montana
KZMZ Alexandria, Louisiana
KZNA Hill City, Kansas
KZND Houston, Alaska
KZNN Rolla, Missouri
KZNSFM) Coalville, Utah
KZOC Bourbon, Missouri
KZOK Seattle, Washington
KZON Phoenix, Arizona
KZOQ-FM Missoula, Montana
KZOZ San Luis Obispo, California
KZPE Ford City, California
KZPK Paynesville, Minnesota
KZPO Lindsay, California
KZPR Minot, North Dakota
KZPS Dallas, Texas
KZPT Kansas City, Missouri
KZQD Liberal, Kansas
KZQL Mills, Wyoming
KZQX Tatum, Texas
KZRB New Boston, Texas
KZRC Bennington, Oklahoma
KZRD Dodge City, Kansas
KZRI Sandy, Oregon
KZRK-FM Canyon, Texas
KZRM Chama, New Mexico
KZRO Dunsmuir, California
KZRR Albuquerque, New Mexico
KZRS Great Bend, Kansas
KZRV Sartell, Minnesota
KZRX Dickinson, North Dakota
KZRZ West Monroe, Louisiana
KZSC Santa Cruz, California
KZSD-FM Martin, South Dakota
KZSE Rochester, Minnesota
KZSN Hutchinson, Kansas
KZSP South Padre Island, Texas
KZSQ-FM Sonora, California
KZST Santa Rosa, California
KZSU Stanford, California
KZTA Naches, Washington
KZTB Milton-Freewater, Oregon
KZTH Piedmont, Oklahoma
KZTI(FM) Fallon Station, Pennsylvania
KZTL Paxton, Nebraska
KZTQ Sun Valley, Nevada
KZTW Tioga, North Dakota
KZUA Holbrook, Arizona
KZUH Minneapolis, Kansas
KZUL-FM Lake Havasu City, Arizona
KZUM Lincoln, Nebraska
KZUS Ephrata, Washington
KZUU Pullman, Washington
KZUW Reliance, Wyoming
KZWA Moss Bluff, Louisiana
KZWB Green River, Wyoming
KZWV Eldon, Missouri
KZWY Sheridan, Wyoming
KZWY-HD Clearmont, Wyoming
KZXK Doney Park, Arizona
KZXL Hudson, Texas
KZXQ Lake of the Woods, Arizona

KZXT Eureka, Montana
KZXY-FM Apple Valley, California
KZXZ Wyola, Montana
KZYR Avon, Colorado
KZYX Philo, California
KZYZ Willits, California
KZZA Muenster, Texas
KZZI Belle Fourche, South Dakota
KZZK New London, Missouri
KZZL-FM Pullman, Washington
KZZO Sacramento, California
KZZP Mesa, Arizona
KZZS Story, Wyoming
KZZT Moberly, Missouri
KZZU Spokane, Washington
KZZX Alamogordo, New Mexico
KZZY Devils Lake, North Dakota
W245CA Pocomoke City, Maryland
W263BJ Loves Park, Illinois
WAAC Valdosta, Georgia
WAAE New Bern, North Carolina
WAAF Westborough, Massachusetts
WAAF Brockton, Massachusetts
WAAG Galesburg, Illinois
WAAI Hurlock, Maryland
WAAJ Benton, Kentucky
WAAL Binghamton, New York
WAAO-FM Andalusia, Alabama
WAAW Williston, South Carolina
WAAZ-FM Crestview, Florida
WABD Mobile, Alabama
WABE Atlanta, Georgia
WABK Gardiner, Maine
WABO-FM Waynesboro, Mississippi
WABR Tifton, Georgia
WABT(FM) Lehman Township, Pennsylvania
WABX Evansville, Indiana
WACD Antigo, Wisconsin
WACG-FM Augusta, Georgia
WACL Elkton, Virginia
WACO-FM Waco, Texas
WACR-FM Columbus Afb, Mississippi
WACV Coosada, Alabama
WADI Corinth, Mississippi
WAEB-FM Allentown, Pennsylvania
WAEF Cordele, Georgia
WAEG Evans, Georgia
WAEL-FM Maricao, Puerto Rico
WAER Syracuse, New York
WAES Lincolnshire, Illinois
WAEV Savannah, Georgia
WAEZ Greeneville, Tennessee
WAFC-FM Okeechobee, Florida
WAFD Webster Springs, West Virginia
WAFJ Belvedere, South Carolina
WAFL Milford, Delaware
WAFM Amory, Mississippi
WAFN-FM Arab, Alabama
WAFR Tupelo, Mississippi
WAFT Valdosta, Georgia
WAFX Suffolk, Virginia
WAFY Middletown, Maryland
WAFZ-FM Immokalee, Florida
WAGE Dogwood Lakes Estate, Florida
WAGF-FM Dothan, Alabama
WAGH Smiths, Alabama
WAGO Snow Hill, North Carolina
WAGR-FM Lexington, Mississippi
WAGX Manchester, Ohio
WAHR Huntsville, Alabama
WAHS Auburn Hills, Michigan
WAIC Springfield, Massachusetts
WAID Clarksdale, Mississippi
WAIH Potsdam, New York
WAII Hattiesburg, Mississippi
WAIJ Grantsville, Maryland
WAIL Key West, Florida
WAIN-FM Columbia, Kentucky
WAIO Honeoye Falls, New York
WAIR Lake City, Michigan
WAIV Cape May Court House, New Jersey
WAJI Fort Wayne, Indiana
WAJJ McKenzie, Tennessee
WAJK La Salle, Illinois
WAJM Atlantic City, New Jersey
WAJQ-FM Alma, Georgia
WAJR-FM Salem, West Virginia
WAJS Tupelo, Mississippi
WAJV Brooksville, Mississippi
WAJZ Voorheesville, New York
WAKB Hephzibah, Georgia
WAKD Sheffield, Alabama
WAKG Danville, Virginia
WAKH McComb, Mississippi
WAKJ Defuniak Springs, Florida
WAKL Flint, Michigan
WAKO-FM Lawrenceville, Illinois
WAKP Smithboro, Georgia
WAKQ Paris, Tennessee
WAKS Akron, Ohio
WAKT-FM Callaway, Florida
WAKU Crawfordville, Florida
WAKW Cincinnati, Ohio
WAKY Radcliff, Kentucky
WAKZ Sharpsville, Pennsylvania
WALC Charleston, South Carolina
WALF Alfred, New York
WALI Walterboro, South Carolina
WALK-FM Patchogue, New York
WALN Carrollton, Alabama
WALR-FM Palmetto, Georgia
WALS Oglesby, Illinois
WALT-FM Meridian, Mississippi
WALV-FM Lakesite, Tennessee
WALX Orrville, Alabama
WALY Bellwood, Pennsylvania
WALZ-FM Machias, Maine
WAMC-FM Albany, New York
WAMH Amherst, Massachusetts
WAMI-FM Opp, Alabama
WAMJ Roswell, Georgia
WAMK Kingston, New York
WAMP Jackson, Tennessee
WAMQ Great Barrington, Massachusetts
WAMR-FM Miami, Florida
WAMS-FM Snow Hill, Maryland
WAMU Washington, District of Columbia
WAMW-FM Washington, Indiana
WAMX Milton, West Virginia
WAMZ Louisville, Kentucky
WANC Ticonderoga, New York
WANH Meredith, New Hampshire
WANM Tallahassee, Florida
WANT Lebanon, Tennessee
WANV Annville, Kentucky
WANY-FM Albany, Kentucky
WAOA-FM Melbourne, Florida
WAOB-FM Beaver Falls, Pennsylvania
WAOL Ripley, Ohio
WAOQ Goshen, Alabama
WAOX Staunton, Illinois
WAOY Gulfport, Mississippi
WAPB Madison, Florida
WAPD Campbellsville, Kentucky
WAPE-FM Jacksonville, Florida
WAPJ Torrington, Connecticut
WAPL Appleton, Wisconsin
WAPN Holly Hill, Florida
WAPO Mount Vernon, Illinois
WAPR Selma, Alabama
WAPS Akron, Ohio
WAPX-FM Clarksville, Tennessee
WAQB Tupelo, Mississippi
WAQE-FM Barron, Wisconsin
WAQG Ozark, Alabama
WAQL McComb, Mississippi
WAQU Selma, Alabama
WAQV Crystal River, Florida
WAQX Manlius, New York
WAQY Springfield, Massachusetts
WARA New Washington, Indiana
WARC Meadville, Pennsylvania
WARG Summit, Illinois
WARH Granite City, Illinois
WARM York, Pennsylvania
WARN Culpeper, Virginia
WARO Naples, Florida
WARQ Columbia, South Carolina
WARU-FM Roann, Indiana
WARV-FM Petersburg, Virginia
WARW Dorsey, Illinois
WARX Lewiston, Maine
WARY Valhalla, New York
WASG Daphne, Alabama
WASH Washington, District of Columbia
WASJ Panama City Beach, Florida
WASK-FM Battle Ground, Indiana
WASL Dyersburg, Tennessee
WASM Natchez, Mississippi
WASU-FM Boone, North Carolina
WASW Waycross, Georgia
WATD-FM Marshfield, Massachusetts
WATG Trion, Georgia
WATI Vincennes, Indiana
WATP Laurel, Mississippi
WATQ Chetek, Wisconsin
WATU Port Gibson, Mississippi
WATY Folkston, Georgia
WATZ-FM Alpena, Michigan
WAUA Petersburg, West Virginia
WAUH Wautoma, Wisconsin
WAUI Shelby, Ohio
WAUM Duck Hill, Mississippi
WAUN Kewaunee, Wisconsin
WAUO Hohenwald, Tennessee
WAUQ Charles City, Virginia
WAUS Berrien Springs, Michigan
WAUV Ripley, Tennessee
WAUZ Greensburg, Indiana
WAVA-FM Arlington, Virginia
WAVC Mio, Michigan
WAVD Ocean Pines, Maryland
WAVF Hanahan, South Carolina
WAVH Daphne, Alabama
WAVI Oxford, Mississippi
WAVJ Princeton, Kentucky
WAVK Marathon, Florida
WAVM Maynard, Massachusetts
WAVR Waverly, New York
WAVT-FM Pottsville, Pennsylvania
WAVV Naples Park, Florida
WAVW Stuart, Florida
WAWC Syracuse, Indiana
WAWF Kankakee, Illinois
WAWH Dublin, Georgia
WAWI Lawrenceburg, Tennessee
WAWJ Marion, Illinois
WAWN Franklin, Pennsylvania
WAWZ Zarephath, New Jersey
WAXG Mount Sterling, Kentucky
WAXI Rockville, Indiana
WAXJ Frederiksted, Virgin Islands
WAXL Santa Claus, Indiana
WAXM Big Stone Gap, Virginia
WAXQ New York, New York
WAXR Geneseo, Illinois
WAXS Oak Hill, West Virginia
WAXU Troy, Alabama
WAXX Eau Claire, Wisconsin
WAXY-FM Miramar, Florida
WAY New Johnsonville, Tennessee
WAYA-FM Ridgeville, South Carolina
WAYB-FM Graysville, Tennessee
WAYC Bedford, Pennsylvania
WAYD Auburn, Kentucky
WAYF West Palm Beach, Florida
WAYH Harvest, Alabama
WAYJ Naples, Florida
WAYJ(FM) Naples, Florida
WAYL St. Augustine, Florida
WAYM Spring Hill, Tennessee
WAYP Marianna, Florida
WAYQ Clarksville, Tennessee
WAYR-FM Brunswick, Georgia
WAYT Thomasville, Georgia
WAYU Steele, Alabama
WAYV Atlantic City, New Jersey
WAYZ Hagerstown, Maryland
WAZA Liberty, Mississippi
WAZD Savannah, Tennessee
WAZO Southport, North Carolina
WAZQ Islamorada, Florida
WAZR Woodstock, Virginia
WAZU Peoria, Illinois
WAZX-FM Cleveland, Georgia
WAZY-FM Lafayette, Indiana
WBAA-FM West Lafayette, Indiana
WBAB Babylon, New York
WBAD Leland, Mississippi
WBAI New York, New York
WBAK Belfast, Maine
WBAM-FM Montgomery, Alabama
WBAR-FM Lake Luzerne, New York
WBAV-FM Gastonia, North Carolina
WBAW-FM Pembroke, Georgia
WBAZ Bridgehampton, New York
WBBA-FM Pittsfield, Illinois
WBBB Raleigh, North Carolina
WBBC-FM Blackstone, Virginia
WBBE Heyworth, Illinois
WBBG Niles, Ohio
WBBI Endwell, New York
WBBK-FM Blakely, Georgia
WBBL Greenville, Michigan
WBBM-FM Chicago, Illinois
WBBN Taylorsville, Mississippi
WBBO(FM) Ocean Acres, New Jersey
WBBQ-FM Augusta, Georgia
WBBS Fulton, New York
WBBT-FM Powhatan, Virginia
WBBV Vicksburg, Mississippi
WBCG Murdock, Florida
WBCH-FM Hastings, Michigan
WBCI Bath, Maine
WBCJ Spencerville, Ohio
WBCK-FM Battle Creek, Michigan
WBCL Fort Wayne, Indiana
WBCM Boyne City, Michigan
WBCQ-FM Monticello, Maine
WBCR-FM Beloit, Wisconsin
WBCT Grand Rapids, Michigan
WBCV Wausau, Wisconsin
WBCX Gainesville, Georgia
WBCY Archbold, Ohio
WBDC Huntingburg, Indiana
WBDG Indianapolis, Indiana
WBDK Algoma, Wisconsin
WBDL Reedsburg, Wisconsin
WBDR Copenhagen, New York
WBDX Trenton, Georgia
WBEA Southold, New York
WBEB Philadelphia, Pennsylvania
WBEC-FM Pittsfield, Massachusetts
WBEE-FM Rochester, New York
WBEI Reform, Alabama
WBEL Cairo, Illinois
WBEN-FM Philadelphia, Pennsylvania
WBEQ Morris, Illinois
WBER Rochester, New York
WBET-FM Sturgis, Michigan
WBEW Chesterton, Indiana
WBEY-FM Crisfield, Maryland
WBEZ Chicago, Illinois
WBFA Fort Mitchell, Alabama
WBFB Bangor, Maine
WBFE Bar Harbor, Maine
WBFG Parker's Crossroads, Tennessee
WBFH Bloomfield Hills, Michigan
WBFI McDaniels, Kentucky
WBFJ-FM Winston-Salem, North Carolina
WBFK Smiths Grove, Kentucky
WBFM Sheboygan, Wisconsin
WBFO Buffalo, New York
WBFR Birmingham, Alabama
WBFX Grand Rapids, Michigan
WBGA St. Simons Island, Georgia
WBGE Bainbridge, Georgia
WBGF Belle Glade, Florida
WBGG-FM Fort Lauderdale, Florida
WBGI-FM Moundsville, West Virginia
WBGK Newport Village, New York
WBGL Champaign, Illinois
WBGM New Berlin, Pennsylvania
WBGO Newark, New Jersey
WBGQ Bulls Gap, Tennessee
WBGU Bowling Green, Ohio
WBGV Marlette, Michigan
WBGW Fort Branch, Indiana
WBGY Everglades City, Florida
WBHB-FM Waynesboro, Pennsylvania
WBHC-FM Hampton, South Carolina
WBHD Olyphant, Pennsylvania
WBHJ Midfield, Alabama
WBHK Warrior, Alabama
WBHL Harrison, Michigan
WBHM Birmingham, Alabama
WBHQ Beverly Beach, Florida
WBHT Mountain Top, Pennsylvania
WBHV-FM State College, Pennsylvania
WBHW Loogootee, Indiana
WBHX Tuckerton, New Jersey
WBHY-FM Mobile, Alabama
WBHZ Elkins, West Virginia
WBIA Shelbyville, Tennessee
WBIB-FM Forsyth, Georgia
WBIE Delphos, Ohio
WBIG-FM Washington, District of Columbia
WBIK Pleasant City, Ohio
WBIM-FM Bridgewater, Massachusetts
WBIO Philpot, Kentucky
WBIY La Belle, Florida
WBIZ-FM Eau Claire, Wisconsin
WBJB-FM Lincroft, New Jersey
WBJC Baltimore, Maryland

WBJD Atlantic Beach, North Carolina
WBJI Blackduck, Minnesota
WBJV Steubenville, Ohio
WBJW Albion, Illinois
WBJY Americus, Georgia
WBJZ Berlin, Wisconsin
WBKA Bar Harbor, Maine
WBKE-FM North Manchester, Indiana
WBKG Macon, Georgia
WBKL Clinton, Louisiana
WBKN Brookhaven, Mississippi
WBKQ Alexandria, Indiana
WBKR Owensboro, Kentucky
WBKS Columbus Grove, Ohio
WBKT Norwich, New York
WBKU Ahoskie, North Carolina
WBKX Fredonia, New York
WBKY Portage, Wisconsin
WBLD Orchard Lake, Michigan
WBLE Batesville, Mississippi
WBLH Black River, New York
WBLI Patchogue, New York
WBLI Patchogue, New York
WBLJ-FM Shamokin, Pennsylvania
WBLK Depew, New York
WBLM Portland, Maine
WBLS New York, New York
WBLU-FM Grand Rapids, Michigan
WBLV Twin Lake, Michigan
WBLW Gaylord, Michigan
WBLX-FM Mobile, Alabama
WBMF Crete, Illinois
WBMH Grove Hill, Alabama
WBMI West Branch, Michigan
WBMK Morehead, Kentucky
WBMP New York, New York
WBMT Boxford, Massachusetts
WBMV Mount Vernon, Illinois
WBMW Pawcatuck, Connecticut
WBMX Boston, Massachusetts
WBMZ Metter, Georgia
WBNB Equality, Alabama
WBNH Pekin, Illinois
WBNI-FM Roanoke, Indiana
WBNJ Barnegat, New Jersey
WBNK Pine Knoll Shores, North Carolina
WBNN-FM Dillwyn, Virginia
WBNO-FM Bryan, Ohio
WBNQ Bloomington, Illinois
WBNS-FM Columbus, Ohio
WBNT-FM Oneida, Tennessee
WBNV Barnesville, Ohio
WBNW-FM Endicott, New York
WBNY Buffalo, New York
WBNZ Frankfort, Michigan
WBOI Fort Wayne, Indiana
WBOJ Lumpkin, Georgia
WBON Westhampton, New York
WBOO Morganfield, Kentucky
WBOP Buffalo Gap, Virginia
WBOQ Gloucester, Massachusetts
WBOR Brunswick, Maine
WBOS Brookline, Massachusetts
WBOX-FM Varnado, Louisiana
WBOZ Woodbury, Tennessee
WBPC Ebro, Florida
WBPE Brookston, Indiana
WBPM Saugerties, New York
WBPR Worcester, Massachusetts
WBPT Homewood, Alabama
WBPW Presque Isle, Maine
WBQB Fredericksburg, Virginia
WBQK West Point, Virginia
WBQQ Kennebunk, Maine
WBQT Boston, Massachusetts
WBQX Thomaston, Maine
WBRB Buckhannon, West Virginia
WBRF Galax, Virginia
WBRH Baton Rouge, Louisiana
WBRK-FM Pittsfield, Massachusetts
WBRN Holmes Beach, Florida
WBRO Marengo, Indiana
WBRP Baker, Louisiana
WBRQ La Grange, Georgia
WBRR Bradford, Pennsylvania
WBRS Waltham, Massachusetts
WBRU Providence, Rhode Island
WBRV-FM Boonville, New York
WBRW Blacksburg, Virginia
WBRX Cresson, Pennsylvania
WBSB Anderson, Indiana
WBSD Burlington, Wisconsin
WBSH Hagerstown, Indiana
WBSJ Portland, Indiana
WBSL-FM Sheffield, Massachusetts
WBSN-FM New Orleans, Louisiana
WBST Muncie, Indiana
WBSU Brockport, New York
WBSW Marion, Indiana
WBSX Hazleton, Pennsylvania
WBSZ Ashland, Wisconsin
WBT-FM Chester, South Carolina
WBTF Midway, Kentucky
WBTG-FM Sheffield, Alabama
WBTI Lexington, Michigan
WBTJ Richmond, Virginia
WBTN-FM Bennington, Vermont
WBTO Petersburg, Indiana
WBTP Clearwater, Florida
WBTQ Buckhannon, West Virginia
WBTR-FM Carrollton, Georgia
WBTT Naples Park, Florida
WBTU Kendallville, Indiana
WBTY Homerville, Georgia
WBTZ Plattsburgh, New York
WBUA Tisbury, Massachusetts
WBUF Buffalo, New York
WBUG-FM Fort Plain, New York
WBUK Ottawa, Ohio
WBUL-FM Lexington, Kentucky
WBUQ Bloomsburg, Pennsylvania
WBUR-FM Boston, Massachusetts
WBUS Boalsburg, Pennsylvania
WBUV Moss Point, Mississippi
WBUX Buxton, North Carolina
WBUZ La Vergne, Tennessee
WBVB Coal Grove, Ohio
WBVC Pomfret, Connecticut
WBVE Bedford, Pennsylvania
WBVI Fostoria, Ohio
WBVM Tampa, Florida
WBVN Carrier Mills, Illinois
WBVR-FM Auburn, Kentucky
WBVV Guntown, Mississippi
WBVX Carlisle, Kentucky
WBWB Bloomington, Indiana
WBWC Berea, Ohio
WBWI Janesville, Wisconsin
WBWL Lynn, Massachusetts
WBWN LeRoy, Illinois
WBWR Hilliard, Ohio
WBWZ New Paltz, New York
WBXB Edenton, North Carolina
WBXE Baxter, Tennessee
WBXL Baldwinsville, New York
WBXQ Patton, Pennsylvania
WBXX Marshall, Michigan
WBXY La Crosse, Florida
WBYA Islesboro, Maine
WBYB(FM) Eldred, Pennsylvania
WBYG Point Pleasant, West Virginia
WBYH Hawley, Pennsylvania
WBYL Salladasburg, Pennsylvania
WBYN-FM Boyertown, Pennsylvania
WBYO Sellersville, Pennsylvania
WBYP Belzoni, Mississippi
WBYR Woodburn, Indiana
WBYT Elkhart, Indiana
WBYW(FM) Lynn Haven, Florida
WBYX Stroudsburg, Pennsylvania
WBYY Somersworth, New Hampshire
WBYZ Baxley, Georgia
WBZ-FM Boston, Massachusetts
WBZA Rochester, New York
WBZC Pemberton, New Jersey
WBZD Muncy, Pennsylvania
WBZE Tallahassee, Florida
WBZF Hartsville, South Carolina
WBZG Peru, Illinois
WBZJ Goldsboro, North Carolina
WBZL(FM) Greenwood, Mississippi
WBZN Old Town, Maine
WBZO Bay Shore, New York
WBZV Hudson, Michigan
WBZY Bowdon, Georgia
WBZZ New Kensington, Pennsylvania
WCAD San Juan, Puerto Rico
WCAI Woods Hole, Massachusetts
WCAL California, Pennsylvania
WCAN Canajoharie, New York
WCAT-FM Carlisle, Pennsylvania
WCBC-FM Keyser, West Virginia
WCBE Columbus, Ohio
WCBH Casey, Illinois
WCBJ Campton, Kentucky
WCBK-FM Martinsville, Indiana
WCBL-FM Grand Rivers, Kentucky
WCBN-FM Ann Arbor, Michigan
WCBS-FM New York, New York
WCBU Peoria, Illinois
WCBW-FM East St. Louis, Illinois
WCCC-FM Hartford, Connecticut
WCCE Buies Creek, North Carolina
WCCG Hope Mills, North Carolina
WCCH Holyoke, Massachusetts
WCCI Savanna, Illinois
WCCK Calvert City, Kentucky
WCCL Central City, Pennsylvania
WCCN-FM Neillsville, Wisconsin
WCCP-FM Clemson, South Carolina
WCCQ Crest Hill, Illinois
WCCR Clarion, Pennsylvania
WCCV Cartersville, Georgia
WCCW-FM Traverse City, Michigan
WCCX Waukesha, Wisconsin
WCDA Versailles, Kentucky
WCDB Albany, New York
WCDD Canton, Illinois
WCDG Dahlonega, Georgia
WCDK Cadiz, Ohio
WCDO-FM Sidney, New York
WCDQ Crawfordsville, Indiana
WCDW Port Dickinson, New York
WCDX Mechanicsville, Virginia
WCDZ Dresden, Tennessee
WCEF Ripley, West Virginia
WCEH-FM Pinehurst, Georgia
WCEI-FM Easton, Maryland
WCEL Plattsburgh, New York
WCEM-FM Cambridge, Maryland
WCEN-FM Hemlock, Michigan
WCEZ Carthage, Illinois
WCFB Orlando, Florida
WCFF Urbana, Illinois
WCFG Springfield, Michigan
WCFL Morris, Illinois
WCFL(FM) Nashville, Tennessee
WCFM Williamstown, Massachusetts
WCFS Elmwood Park, Illinois
WCFW Chippewa Falls, Wisconsin
WCFX Clare, Michigan
WCGF Cambridge Springs, Pennsylvania
WCGM Wattsburg, Pennsylvania
WCGQ Columbus, Georgia
WCHC Worcester, Massachusetts
WCHD Kettering, Ohio
WCHG Hot Springs, Virginia
WCHO-FM Washington Ct House, Ohio
WCHR-FM Manahawkin, New Jersey
WCHV-FM Charlottesville, Virginia
WCHW-FM Bay City, Michigan
WCHX Lewistown, Pennsylvania
WCHZ-FM Warrenton, Georgia
WCIB Falmouth, Massachusetts
WCIC Pekin, Illinois
WCID Friendship, New York
WCIE New Port Richey, Florida
WCIF Melbourne, Florida
WCIG Dallas, Pennsylvania
WCIH Elmira, New York
WCII Spencer, New York
WCIJ Unadilla, New York
WCIL-FM Carbondale, Illinois
WCIM Shenandoah, Pennsylvania
WCIN-FM Tunkhannock, Pennsylvania
WCIR-FM Beckley, West Virginia
WCIS Laporte, Pennsylvania
WCIT-FM Trout Run, Pennsylvania
WCIY Canandaigua, New York
WCIZ-FM Watertown, New York
WCJC Van Buren, Indiana
WCJK Murfreesboro, Tennessee
WCJL Morgantown, Indiana
WCJM-FM West Point, Georgia
WCJO Jackson, Ohio
WCJU-FM Prentiss, Mississippi
WCJX Five Points, Florida
WCJZ Cannelton, Indiana
WCKC Cadillac, Michigan
WCKF Ashland, Alabama
WCKJ St. Johnsbury, Vermont
WCKM-FM Lake George, New York
WCKN Hollywood, South Carolina
WCKQ Campbellsville, Kentucky
WCKR Hornell, New York
WCKS Fruithurst, Alabama
WCKT Lehigh Acres, Florida
WCKU Clarksburg, West Virginia
WCKX Columbus, Ohio
WCKY-FM Pemberville, Ohio
WCKZ Orland, Indiana
WCLC-FM Jamestown, Tennessee
WCLD-FM Cleveland, Mississippi
WCLE-FM Calhoun, Tennessee
WCLG-FM Morgantown, West Virginia
WCLH Wilkes-Barre, Pennsylvania
WCLI-FM Enon, Ohio
WCLK Atlanta, Georgia
WCLN-FM Clinton, North Carolina
WCLQ Wausau, Wisconsin
WCLR Arlington Heights, Illinois
WCLS Spencer, Indiana
WCLT-FM Newark, Ohio
WCLU-FM Munfordville, Kentucky
WCLV Lorain, Ohio
WCLX Westport, New York
WCLZ North Yarmouth, Maine
WCMB-FM Oscoda, Michigan
WCMC-FM Holly Springs, North Carolina
WCMD-FM Barre, Vermont
WCMF-FM Rochester, New York
WCMG Latta, South Carolina
WCMI-FM Catlettsburg, Kentucky
WCMJ Cambridge, Ohio
WCMK Putney, Vermont
WCML-FM Alpena, Michigan
WCMM Gulliver, Michigan
WCMN-FM Arecibo, Puerto Rico
WCMO Marietta, Ohio
WCMP-FM Pine City, Minnesota
WCMQ-FM Hialeah, Florida
WCMS-FM Hatteras, North Carolina
WCMT Martin, Tennessee
WCMU-FM Mount Pleasant, Michigan
WCMW-FM Harbor Springs, Michigan
WCMZ-FM Sault Ste. Marie, Michigan
WCNA Potts Camp, Mississippi
WCNB Dayton, Indiana
WCNG Murphy, North Carolina
WCNI New London, Connecticut
WCNK Key West, Florida
WCNO Palm City, Florida
WCNR Keswick, Virginia
WCNV Heathsville, Virginia
WCNY-FM Syracuse, New York
WCOA-FM Pensacola, Florida
WCOD-FM Hyannis, Massachusetts
WCOE La Porte, Indiana
WCOF Arcade, New York
WCOG-FM Galeton, Pennsylvania
WCOH-FM Du Bois, Pennsylvania
WCOL-FM Columbus, Ohio
WCOM-FM Silver Creek, New York
WCON-FM Cornelia, Georgia
WCOO Kiawah Island, South Carolina
WCOP Farmington Township, Pennsylvania
WCOQ Colquitt, Georgia
WCOS-FM Columbia, South Carolina
WCOS-FM Columbia, South Carolina
WCOT Jamestown, New York
WCOU Attica, New York
WCOV-FM Clyde, New York
WCOW-FM Sparta, Wisconsin
WCOY Quincy, Illinois
WCOZ Laceyville, Pennsylvania
WCPE Raleigh, North Carolina
WCPI McMinnville, Tennessee
WCPN Cleveland, Ohio
WCPQ Park Forest, Illinois
WCPR-FM D'Iberville, Mississippi
WCPT-FM DeKalb, Illinois
WCPV Essex, New York
WCPY Arlington Heights, Illinois
WCPZ Sandusky, Ohio
WCQL Queensbury, New York
WCQM Park Falls, Wisconsin
WCQR-FM Kingsport, Tennessee
WCQS Asheville, North Carolina
WCRA-FM Effingham, Illinois
WCRB Lowell, Massachusetts
WCRC Effingham, Illinois
WCRF Cleveland, Ohio
WCRG Williamsport, Pennsylvania
WCRH Williamsport, Maryland

WCRJ Jacksonville, Florida
WCRP Guayama, Puerto Rico
WCRQ Dennysville, Maine
WCRT-FM Terre Haute, Indiana
WCRX Chicago, Illinois
WCRZ Flint, Michigan
WCSB Cleveland, Ohio
WCSF Joliet, Illinois
WCSG Grand Rapids, Michigan
WCSJ-FM Morris, Illinois
WCSK Kingsport, Tennessee
WCSM-FM Celina, Ohio
WCSN-FM Orange Beach, Alabama
WCSO Columbus, Mississippi
WCSP-FM Washington, District of Columbia
WCSR-FM Hillsdale, Michigan
WCSU-FM Wilberforce, Ohio
WCSX Birmingham, Michigan
WCSY South Haven, Michigan
WCTB Fairfield, Maine
WCTG Chincoteague, Virginia
WCTH Plantation Key, Florida
WCTK New Bedford, Massachusetts
WCTL Union City, Pennsylvania
WCTO Easton, Pennsylvania
WCTP Gagetown, Michigan
WCTQ Sarasota, Florida
WCTT-FM Corbin, Kentucky
WCTW Catskill, New York
WCTY Norwich, Connecticut
WCUC-FM Clarion, Pennsylvania
WCUP L'Anse, Michigan
WCUR West Chester, Pennsylvania
WCUW Worcester, Massachusetts
WCUZ Bear Lake, Michigan
WCVE-FM Richmond, Virginia
WCVF-FM Fredonia, New York
WCVH Flemington, New Jersey
WCVJ Jefferson, Ohio
WCVK Bowling Green, Kentucky
WCVM Bronson, Michigan
WCVO Gahanna, Ohio
WCVP-FM Robbinsville, North Carolina
WCVQ Fort Campbell, Kentucky
WCVS-FM Virden, Illinois
WCVT Stowe, Vermont
WCVU Solana, Florida
WCVV Belpre, Ohio
WCVY Coventry, Rhode Island
WCWM Williamsburg, Virginia
WCWP Brookville, New York
WCWS-FM Wooster, Ohio
WCWT-FM Centerville, Ohio
WCWV Summersville, West Virginia
WCXB Benton Harbor, Michigan
WCXG Grand Rapids, Michigan
WCXK Kalamazoo, Michigan
WCXL Kill Devil Hills, North Carolina
WCXR Lewisburg, Pennsylvania
WCXT Hartford, Michigan
WCXU Caribou, Maine
WCXV Van Buren, Maine
WCXX Madawaska, Maine
WCYE Three Lakes, Wisconsin
WCYJ-FM Waynesburg, Pennsylvania
WCYK-FM Staunton, Virginia
WCYN-FM Cynthiana, Kentucky
WCYO Irvine, Kentucky
WCYQ Oak Ridge, Tennessee
WCYT Lafayette Township, Indiana
WCYY Biddeford, Maine
WCZE Harbor Beach, Michigan
WCZQ Monticello, Illinois
WCZR Vero Beach, Florida
WCZT Villas, New Jersey
WCZW Charlevoix, Michigan
WCZX Hyde Park, New York
WCZY-FM Mount Pleasant, Michigan
WDAC Lancaster, Pennsylvania
WDAF-FM Mission, Missouri
WDAI Pawleys Island, South Carolina
WDAQ Danbury, Connecticut
WDAR-FM Darlington, South Carolina
WDAS-FM Philadelphia, Pennsylvania
WDAV Davidson, North Carolina
WDBK Blackwood, New Jersey
WDBM East Lansing, Michigan
WDBN Wrightsville, Georgia
WDBO(FM) Orlando, Florida
WDBQ-FM Galena, Illinois
WDBR Springfield, Illinois
WDBS Sutton, West Virginia
WDBT Hartford, Alabama
WDBX Carbondale, Illinois
WDBY Patterson, New York
WDCB Glen Ellyn, Illinois
WDCC Sanford, North Carolina
WDCD-FM Clifton Park, New York
WDCE Richmond, Virginia
WDCG Durham, North Carolina
WDCK Oolitic, Indiana
WDCL-FM Somerset, Kentucky
WDCR Oreana, Illinois
WDCV-FM Carlisle, Pennsylvania
WDCX-FM Buffalo, New York
WDDC Portage, Wisconsin
WDDD-FM Johnston City, Illinois
WDDH St. Marys, Pennsylvania
WDDJ Paducah, Kentucky
WDDK Greensboro, Georgia
WDDQ Adel, Georgia
WDDW Sturtevant, Wisconsin
WDEB-FM Jamestown, Tennessee
WDEC-FM Americus, Georgia
WDEE-FM Reed City, Michigan
WDEF-FM Chattanooga, Tennessee
WDEN-FM Macon, Georgia
WDEO-FM San Carlos Park, Florida
WDEQ-FM De Graff, Ohio
WDER-FM Peterborough, New Hampshire
WDET-FM Detroit, Michigan
WDEV-FM Warren, Vermont
WDEZ Wausau, Wisconsin
WDFB-FM Danville, Kentucky
WDFM Defiance, Ohio
WDFX Cleveland, Mississippi
WDGC-FM Downers Grove, Illinois
WDGG Ashland, Kentucky
WDGL Baton Rouge, Louisiana
WDGM Greensboro, Alabama
WDHA-FM Dover, New Jersey
WDHC Berkeley Springs, West Virginia
WDHI Delhi, New York
WDHR Pikeville, Kentucky
WDHT Urbana, Ohio
WDIC-FM Clinchco, Virginia
WDIH Salisbury, Maryland
WDIN Camuy, Puerto Rico
WDIY Allentown, Pennsylvania
WDJC-FM Birmingham, Alabama
WDJM-FM Framingham, Massachusetts
WDJQ Alliance, Ohio
WDJR Enterprise, Alabama
WDJW Somers, Connecticut
WDJX Louisville, Kentucky
WDKB Dekalb, Illinois
WDKC Covington, Pennsylvania
WDKE Coleraine, Minnesota
WDKL Grafton, West Virginia
WDKM Adams, Wisconsin
WDKR Maroa, Illinois
WDKS Newburgh, Indiana
WDKV Fond Du Lac, Wisconsin
WDKW Maryville, Tennessee
WDKX Rochester, New York
WDLA-FM Walton, New York
WDLD Halfway, Maryland
WDLG Thomasville, Alabama
WDLJ Breese, Illinois
WDLL Dillon, South Carolina
WDLM-FM East Moline, Illinois
WDLT Saraland, Alabama
WDLT-FM Saraland, Alabama
WDLZ Murfreesboro, North Carolina
WDMG-FM Ambrose, Georgia
WDMK Detroit, Michigan
WDML Woodlawn, Illinois
WDMO Baldwin, Wisconsin
WDMP-FM Dodgeville, Wisconsin
WDMS Greenville, Mississippi
WDMX Vienna, West Virginia
WDNA Miami, Florida
WDNB Jeffersonville, New York
WDNE-FM Elkins, West Virginia
WDNH-FM Honesdale, Pennsylvania
WDNJ Hopatcong, New Jersey
WDNL Danville, Illinois
WDNR Chester, Pennsylvania
WDNS Bowling Green, Kentucky
WDNX Olive Hill, Tennessee
WDOD-FM Chattanooga, Tennessee
WDOG-FM Allendale, South Carolina
WDOH Delphos, Ohio
WDOK Cleveland, Ohio
WDOM Providence, Rhode Island
WDOR-FM Sturgeon Bay, Wisconsin
WDOT Danville, Vermont
WDPG Greenville, Ohio
WDPR Dayton, Ohio
WDPS Dayton, Ohio
WDPW Greenville, Michigan
WDQN-FM Duquoin, Illinois
WDRC-FM Hartford, Connecticut
WDRE Susquehanna, Pennsylvania
WDRK Cornell, Wisconsin
WDRM Decatur, Alabama
WDRQ Detroit, Michigan
WDRR Martinez, Georgia
WDRT Viroqua, Wisconsin
WDRV Chicago, Illinois
WDSD Dover, Delaware
WDSJ Greenville, Ohio
WDSN Reynoldsville, Pennsylvania
WDSO Chesterton, Indiana
WDST Woodstock, New York
WDSV Greenville, Mississippi
WDSY Pittsburgh, Pennsylvania
WDTR Imlay City, Michigan
WDTW-FM Detroit, Michigan
WDTX Rothschild, Wisconsin
WDUB Granville, Ohio
WDUK Havana, Illinois
WDUN-FM Clarkesville, Georgia
WDUV New Port Richey, Florida
WDUX-FM Waupaca, Wisconsin
WDUZ-FM Brillion, Wisconsin
WDVD Detroit, Michigan
WDVE Pittsburgh, Pennsylvania
WDVH-FM Trenton, Florida
WDVI Rochester, New York
WDVR Delaware Township, New Jersey
WDVT Rutland, Vermont
WDVV Wilmington, North Carolina
WDVW(FM) Humboldt, Tennessee
WDVX Clinton, Tennessee
WDWG Rocky Mount, North Carolina
WDWN Auburn, New York
WDWQ Terre Haute, Indiana
WDWZ Andalusia, Alabama
WDXB Jasper, Alabama
WDXC Pound, Virginia
WDXE-FM Lawrenceburg, Tennessee
WDXO Hazlehurst, Mississippi
WDYF Dothan, Alabama
WDYK Ridgeley, West Virginia
WDYS Dushore, Pennsylvania
WDZH Detroit, Michigan
WDZN Midland, Maryland
WDZQ Decatur, Illinois
WDZY Colonial Heights, Virginia
WDZZ-FM Flint, Michigan
WEAA Baltimore, Maryland
WEAI Lynnville, Illinois
WEAM-FM Buena Vista, Georgia
WEAN Wakefield-Peacedale, Rhode Island
WEAS-FM Springfield, Georgia
WEAT West Palm Beach, Florida
WEAX Angola, Indiana
WEBB Waterville, Maine
WEBE Westport, Connecticut
WEBF Lerose, Kentucky
WEBG Chicago, Illinois
WEBK Society Hill, South Carolina
WEBL Coldwater, Mississippi
WEBN Cincinnati, Ohio
WEBQ-FM Eldorado, Illinois
WEBT Langdale, Alabama
WEBZ Mexico Beach, Florida
WECB Headland, Alabama
WECC-FM Folkston, Georgia
WECI Richmond, Indiana
WECL Elk Mound, Wisconsin
WECO-FM Wartburg, Tennessee
WECQ Destin, Florida
WECR-FM Beech Mountain, North Carolina
WECS Willimantic, Connecticut
WECV-FM Nashville, Tennessee
WECW Elmira, New York
WEDB East Dublin, Georgia
WEDG Buffalo, New York
WEDJ Danville, Indiana
WEDM Indianapolis, Indiana
WEDR Miami, Florida
WEDW-FM Stamford, Connecticut
WEEC Springfield, Ohio
WEEI(FM) Lawrence, Massachusetts
WEEI-FM Lawrence, Massachusetts
WEEM-FM Pendleton, Indiana
WEEO-FM McConnellsburg, Pennsylvania
WEER Montauk, New York
WEEY Swanzey, New Hampshire
WEFI Effingham, Illinois
WEFM Michigan City, Indiana
WEFR Erie, Pennsylvania
WEFT Champaign, Illinois
WEFX Henderson, New York
WEGB Napeague, New York
WEGC Sasser, Georgia
WEGE Lima, Ohio
WEGH Northumberland, Pennsylvania
WEGI-FM Oak Grove, Kentucky
WEGL Auburn, Alabama
WEGM San German, Puerto Rico
WEGN Kankakee, Illinois
WEGR Arlington, Tennessee
WEGS Milton, Florida
WEGW Wheeling, West Virginia
WEGX Dillon, South Carolina
WEGZ Washburn, Wisconsin
WEHA(FM) Port Republic, New Jersey
WEHC Emory, Virginia
WEHM Manorville, New York
WEHN East Hampton, New York
WEIB Northampton, Massachusetts
WEII Dennis, Massachusetts
WEIO(FM) Huntingdon, Tennessee
WEIU Charleston, Illinois
WEJC White Star, Michigan
WEJF Palm Bay, Florida
WEJK Boonville, Indiana
WEJL-FM Forest City, Pennsylvania
WEJT Shelbyville, Illinois
WEJZ Jacksonville, Florida
WEKF Corbin, Kentucky
WEKH Hazard, Kentucky
WEKI Decatur, Alabama
WEKL Augusta, Georgia
WEKS Zebulon, Georgia
WEKU Richmond, Kentucky
WEKV South Webster, Ohio
WEKX Jellico, Tennessee
WEKZ-FM Monroe, Wisconsin
WELD-FM Moorefield, West Virginia
WELH Providence, Rhode Island
WELJ Montauk, New York
WELK Elkins, West Virginia
WELL-FM Waverly, Alabama
WELR-FM Roanoke, Alabama
WELS-FM Kinston, North Carolina
WELX Isabela, Puerto Rico
WELY-FM Ely, Minnesota
WEMC Harrisonburg, Virginia
WEMI Appleton, Wisconsin
WEMM Huntington, West Virginia
WEMR Pleasant Gap, Pennsylvania
WEMU Ypsilanti, Michigan
WEMX Kentwood, Louisiana
WEMY Green Bay, Wisconsin
WEND Salisbury, North Carolina
WENI-FM Big Flats, New York
WENJ Millville, New Jersey
WENS Wadesville, Indiana
WENY-FM Elmira, New York
WENZ Cleveland, Ohio
WEOS Geneva, New York
WEOW Key West, Florida
WEPC Belton, South Carolina
WEPN-FM New York, New York
WEPR Greenville, South Carolina
WEPS Elgin, Illinois
WEQP Pamplin City, Virginia
WEQR Walnut Creek, North Carolina
WEQX Manchester, Vermont
WERB Berlin, Connecticut
WERC-FM Hoover, Alabama
WERG Erie, Pennsylvania
WERH-FM Hamilton, Alabama
WERK Muncie, Indiana
WERN Madison, Wisconsin
WERO Washington, North Carolina
WERQ-FM Baltimore, Maryland
WERR Vega Alta, Puerto Rico
WERS Boston, Massachusetts
WERU-FM Blue Hill, Maine

WERV-FM Aurora, Illinois
WERX-FM Columbia, North Carolina
WERZ Exeter, New Hampshire
WESA Pittsburgh, Pennsylvania
WESC-FM Greenville, South Carolina
WESE Baldwyn, Mississippi
WESM Princess Anne, Maryland
WESN Bloomington, Illinois
WESP Dothan, Alabama
WESR-FM Onley-Onancock, Virginia
WESS East Stroudsburg, Pennsylvania
WESU Middletown, Connecticut
WETA Washington, District of Columbia
WETD Alfred, New York
WETL South Bend, Indiana
WETN Wheaton, Illinois
WETS-FM Johnson City, Tennessee
WETT Bridgeport, West Virginia
WETZ(FM) New Martinsville, West Virginia
WEUC Morganfield, Kentucky
WEUL Kingsford, Michigan
WEUP-FM Moulton, Alabama
WEUZ Minor Hill, Tennessee
WEVE Eveleth, Minnesota
WEVH Hanover, New Hampshire
WEVI Frederiksted, Virgin Islands
WEVJ Jackson, New Hampshire
WEVL Memphis, Tennessee
WEVN Keene, New Hampshire
WEVO Concord, New Hampshire
WEVO(FM) Concord, New Hampshire
WEVR-FM River Falls, Wisconsin
WEVS Nashua, New Hampshire
WEXP Brandon, Vermont
WEXR Stonewall, Mississippi
WEXT Amsterdam, New York
WEYE Surgoinsville, Tennessee
WEYY Tallapoosa, Georgia
WEZB New Orleans, Louisiana
WEZC Clinton, Illinois
WEZF Burlington, Vermont
WEZI Ponte Vedra Beach, Florida
WEZJ-FM Williamsburg, Kentucky
WEZL Charleston, South Carolina
WEZN-FM Bridgeport, Connecticut
WEZQ Bangor, Maine
WEZV North Myrtle Beach, South Carolina
WEZW Wildwood Crest, New Jersey
WEZX Scranton, Pennsylvania
WEZY Janesville, Wisconsin
WEZZ-FM Gardendale, Alabama
WFAE Charlotte, North Carolina
WFAN-FM New York, New York
WFAR Danbury, Connecticut
WFAS-FM Bronxville, New York
WFAV Kankakee, Illinois
WFAZ Goodwater, Alabama
WFBC-FM Greenville, South Carolina
WFBE Flint, Michigan
WFBF Buffalo, New York
WFBK Fort Mill, South Carolina
WFBQ Indianapolis, Indiana
WFBY Weston, West Virginia
WFBZ Trempealeau, Wisconsin
WFCA Ackerman, Mississippi
WFCC-FM Chatham, Massachusetts
WFCF St. Augustine, Florida
WFCG Tylertown, Mississippi
WFCH Charleston, South Carolina
WFCI Franklin, Indiana
WFCJ Miamisburg, Ohio
WFCM-FM Murfreesboro, Tennessee
WFCO Lancaster, Ohio
WFCR Amherst, Massachusetts
WFCS New Britain, Connecticut
WFCT Apalachicola, Florida
WFCV-FM Bluffton, Indiana
WFCX Leland, Michigan
WFDD Winston-Salem, North Carolina
WFDL-FM Lomira, Wisconsin
WFDM-FM Franklin, Indiana
WFDR-FM Woodbury, Georgia
WFDT Aguada, Puerto Rico
WFDU Teaneck, New Jersey
WFDX Atlanta, Michigan
WFDZ Perry, Florida
WFEN Rockford, Illinois
WFEZ(FM) Miami, Florida
WFFC Ferrum, Virginia
WFFF-FM Columbia, Mississippi
WFFG-FM Corinth, New York
WFFH Smyrna, Tennessee
WFFI Kingston Springs, Tennessee
WFFL Panama City, Florida
WFFM Ashburn, Georgia
WFFN Coaling, Alabama
WFFX Hattiesburg, Mississippi
WFGA Hicksville, Ohio
WFGB Kingston, New York
WFGE State College, Pennsylvania
WFGF Wapakoneta, Ohio
WFGH Fort Gay, West Virginia
WFGI-FM Johnstown, Pennsylvania
WFGM-FM Barrackville, West Virginia
WFGR Grand Rapids, Michigan
WFGS Murray, Kentucky
WFGW(FM) Norris, Tennessee
WFGY Altoona, Pennsylvania
WFHB Bloomington, Indiana
WFHE Hickory, North Carolina
WFHG-FM Bluff City, Tennessee
WFHL New Bedford, Massachusetts
WFHM-FM Cleveland, Ohio
WFHN Fairhaven, Massachusetts
WFHU Henderson, Tennessee
WFIA-FM New Albany, Indiana
WFID Rio Piedras, Puerto Rico
WFIT Melbourne, Florida
WFIU Bloomington, Indiana
WFIV-FM Loudon, Tennessee
WFIW Fairfield, Illinois
WFIX Florence, Alabama
WFIZ Odessa, New York
WFJA Sanford, North Carolina
WFJO Jacksonville Beach, Florida
WFJS-FM Freehold, New Jersey
WFKL Fairport, New York
WFKS Melbourne, Florida
WFKX Henderson, Tennessee
WFKY Frankfort, Kentucky
WFKZ Plantation Key, Florida
WFLA-FM Midway, Florida
WFLB Laurinburg, North Carolina
WFLC Miami, Florida
WFLE-FM Flemingsburg, Kentucky
WFLF-FM Parker, Florida
WFLK Geneva, New York
WFLM White City, Florida
WFLO-FM Farmville, Virginia
WFLQ French Lick, Indiana
WFLS-FM Fredericksburg, Virginia
WFLY Troy, New York
WFLZ-FM Tampa, Florida
WFMB-FM Springfield, Illinois
WFME Mount Kisco, New York
WFMF Baton Rouge, Louisiana
WFMG Richmond, Indiana
WFMH-FM Hackleburg, Alabama
WFMI Southern Shores, North Carolina
WFMK Lansing, Michigan
WFML Vincennes, Indiana
WFMM Sumrall, Mississippi
WFMN Flora, Mississippi
WFMQ Lebanon, Tennessee
WFMR Orleans, Massachusetts
WFMS Fishers, Indiana
WFMT Chicago, Illinois
WFMU East Orange, New Jersey
WFMV South Congaree, South Carolina
WFMX Skowhegan, Maine
WFMZ Hertford, North Carolina
WFNB Brazil, Indiana
WFNK Lewiston, Maine
WFNM Lancaster, Pennsylvania
WFNP Rosendale, New York
WFNQ Nashua, New Hampshire
WFNX Athol, Massachusetts
WFOF Covington, Indiana
WFON Fond Du Lac, Wisconsin
WFOS Chesapeake, Virginia
WFOT Lexington, Ohio
WFOX Norwalk, Connecticut
WFPB-FM Falmouth, Massachusetts
WFPG Atlantic City, New Jersey
WFPK Louisville, Kentucky
WFPL Louisville, Kentucky
WFPS Freeport, Illinois
WFQS Franklin, North Carolina
WFQX Front Royal, Virginia
WFRB-FM Frostburg, Maryland
WFRC Columbus, Georgia
WFRD Hanover, New Hampshire
WFRE Frederick, Maryland
WFRF-FM Monticello, Florida
WFRG-FM Utica, New York
WFRH Kingston, New York
WFRI Winamac, Indiana
WFRJ Johnstown, Pennsylvania
WFRN-FM Elkhart, Indiana
WFRO-FM Fremont, Ohio
WFRP Americus, Georgia
WFRQ Harwich Port, Massachusetts
WFRR Walton, Indiana
WFRS Smithtown, New York
WFRU Quincy, Florida
WFRY-FM Watertown, New York
WFSE Edinboro, Pennsylvania
WFSH-FM Athens, Georgia
WFSK-FM Nashville, Tennessee
WFSL Thomasville, Georgia
WFSO Olivebridge, New York
WFSP-FM Kingwood, West Virginia
WFSQ Tallahassee, Florida
WFSS Fayetteville, North Carolina
WFSU-FM Tallahassee, Florida
WFSW Panama City, Florida
WFSX-FM Estero, Florida
WFSY Panama City, Florida
WFTA Fulton, Mississippi
WFTE Mount Cobb, Pennsylvania
WFTF Rutland, Vermont
WFTI-FM St. Petersburg, Florida
WFTK Lebanon, Ohio
WFTM-FM Maysville, Kentucky
WFTN-FM Franklin, New Hampshire
WFTZ Manchester, Tennessee
WFUM(FM) Flint, Michigan
WFUN-FM Bethalto, Illinois
WFUR-FM Grand Rapids, Michigan
WFUS Gulfport, Florida
WFUV New York, New York
WFVL Lumberton, North Carolina
WFWM Frostburg, Maryland
WFWO Medina, New York
WFWR Attica, Indiana
WFXA-FM Augusta, Georgia
WFXC Durham, North Carolina
WFXD Marquette, Michigan
WFXE Columbus, Georgia
WFXF Dundee, Illinois
WFXH-FM Hilton Head Island, South Carolina
WFXJ-FM North Kingsville, Ohio
WFXK Bunn, North Carolina
WFXM Gordon, Georgia
WFXN-FM Galion, Ohio
WFXO Ashland, Alabama
WFXX Georgiana, Alabama
WFYE Glade Spring, Virginia
WFYI-FM Indianapolis, Indiana
WFYR Elmwood, Illinois
WFYX Walpole, New Hampshire
WFYY Bloomsburg, Pennsylvania
WGAC-FM Harlem, Georgia
WGAO Franklin, Massachusetts
WGAR-FM Cleveland, Ohio
WGBE Bryan, Ohio
WGBF-FM Henderson, Kentucky
WGBG Seaford, Delaware
WGBH(FM) Boston, Massachusetts
WGBJ Auburn, Indiana
WGBK Glenview, Illinois
WGBL Gulfport, Mississippi
WGBQ Lynchburg, Tennessee
WGBZ Cape May, New Jersey
WGCA-FM Quincy, Illinois
WGCC-FM Batavia, New York
WGCF Paducah, Kentucky
WGCI-FM Chicago, Illinois
WGCK-FM Coeburn, Virginia
WGCM-FM Gulfport, Mississippi
WGCN Nashville, Georgia
WGCO Midway, Georgia
WGCP Cadillac, Michigan
WGCS Goshen, Indiana
WGCU-FM Fort Myers, Florida
WGCY Gibson City, Illinois
WGDE Defiance, Ohio
WGDN-FM Gladwin, Michigan
WGDQ Sumrall, Mississippi
WGDR Plainfield, Vermont
WGEE-FM New London, Wisconsin
WGEL Greenville, Illinois
WGEM-FM Quincy, Illinois
WGEN-FM Monee, Illinois
WGER Saginaw, Michigan
WGEX Bainbridge, Georgia
WGFA-FM Watseka, Illinois
WGFB Rockton, Illinois
WGFG Branchville, South Carolina
WGFM Cheboygan, Michigan
WGFN Glen Arbor, Michigan
WGFR Glens Falls, New York
WGFX Gallatin, Tennessee
WGGC Bowling Green, Kentucky
WGGE Parkersburg, West Virginia
WGGI Benton, Pennsylvania
WGGL-FM Houghton, Michigan
WGGN Castalia, Ohio
WGGY Scranton, Pennsylvania
WGH-FM Newport News, Virginia
WGHJ Fair Bluff, 0
WGHL Shepherdsville, Kentucky
WGHN-FM Grand Haven, Michigan
WGHW Lockwoods Folly Town, North Carolina
WGIB Eirmingham, Alabama
WGIE Clarksburg, West Virginia
WGIR-FM Manchester, New Hampshire
WGIW Pilot Mountain, North Carolina
WGKC Mahomet, Illinois
WGKL Gladstone, Michigan
WGKR Grand Gorge, New York
WGKS Paris, Kentucky
WGKV Pulaski, New York
WGKX Memphis, Tennessee
WGKY Wickliffe, Kentucky
WGL-FM Huntington, Indiana
WGLC Mendota, Illinois
WGLE Lima, Ohio
WGLF Tallahassee, Florida
WGLI Hancock, Michigan
WGLM-FM Lakeview, Michigan
WGLO Pekin, Illinois
WGLQ Escanaba, Michigan
WGLR Lancaster, Wisconsin
WGLS-FM Glassboro, New Jersey
WGLT Normal, Illinois
WGLV Woodstock, Vermont
WGLX-FM Wisconsin Rapids, Wisconsin
WGLY-FM Bolton, Vermont
WGLZ West Liberty, West Virginia
WGMC Greece, New York
WGMD Rehoboth Beach, Delaware
WGMG Crawford, Georgia
WGMK Donalsonville, Georgia
WGMM Corning, New York
WGMO Spooner, Wisconsin
WGMR Effingham, Illinois
WGMS Hagerstown, Maryland
WGMT Lyndon, Vermont
WGMX Marathon, Florida
WGMY Thomasville, Georgia
WGMZ Glencoe, Alabama
WGNA-FM Albany, New York
WGNB Zeeland, Michigan
WGNE-FM Middleburg, Florida
WGNG Tchula, Mississippi
WGNI Wilmington, North Carolina
WGNJ St. Joseph, Illinois
WGNK Pennsuco, Florida
WGNL Greenwood, Mississippi
WGNN Fisher, Illinois
WGNR-FM Anderson, Indiana
WGNV Milladore, Wisconsin
WGNX Colchester, Illinois
WGOD-FM Charlotte Amalie, Virgin Islands
WGOG Walhalla, South Carolina
WGOJ Conneaut, Ohio
WGOV-FM Valdosta, Georgia
WGOW Soddy-Daisy, Tennessee
WGPB Rome, Georgia
WGPH Vidalia, Georgia
WGPR Detroit, Michigan
WGQR Rennert, North Carolina
WGRC Lewisburg, Pennsylvania
WGRD-FM Grand Rapids, Michigan
WGRE Greencastle, Indiana
WGRF Buffalo, New York
WGRH Hinckley, Minnesota
WGRK-FM Greensburg, Kentucky
WGRM-FM Greenwood, Mississippi
WGRQ Fairview Beach, Virginia
WGRR Hamilton, Ohio
WGRS Guilford, Connecticut
WGRT Port Huron, Michigan

WGRW Anniston, Alabama
WGRX Falmouth, Virginia
WGRY-FM Roscommon, Michigan
WGSG Mayo, Florida
WGSK South Kent, Connecticut
WGSL Loves Park, Illinois
WGSN Newport, Tennessee
WGSP-FM Pageland, South Carolina
WGSQ Cookeville, Tennessee
WGSU Geneseo, New York
WGSY Phenix City, Alabama
WGTD Kenosha, Wisconsin
WGTE-FM Toledo, Ohio
WGTF Dothan, Alabama
WGTH-FM Richlands, Virginia
WGTI Winfall, North Carolina
WGTK-FM Greenville, South Carolina
WGTN-FM Andrews, South Carolina
WGTR Bucksport, South Carolina
WGTS Takoma Park, Maryland
WGTT Emeralda, Florida
WGTX Truro, Massachusetts
WGTY Gettysburg, Pennsylvania
WGTZ Eaton, Ohio
WGUC Cincinnati, Ohio
WGUF Marco, Florida
WGUR Milledgeville, Georgia
WGUS-FM New Ellenton, South Carolina
WGVE-FM Gary, Indiana
WGVS-FM Whitehall, Michigan
WGVU-FM Allendale, Michigan
WGVX Lakeville, Minnesota
WGVZ Eden Prairie, Minnesota
WGWG Boiling Springs, North Carolina
WGWR Liberty, New York
WGWS St. Mary's City, Maryland
WGXC Acra, New York
WGXL Hanover, New Hampshire
WGY-FM Albany, New York
WGYE Mannington, West Virginia
WGYI Oil City, Pennsylvania
WGYL Vero Beach, Florida
WGYY Meadville, Pennsylvania
WGZB-FM Lanesville, Indiana
WGZS Cloquet, Minnesota
WGZZ Waverly, Alabama
WHAA Adams, Wisconsin
WHAB Acton, Massachusetts
WHAD Delafield, Wisconsin
WHAI Greenfield, Massachusetts
WHAJ Bluefield, West Virginia
WHAK-FM Rogers City, Michigan
WHAL-FM Horn Lake, Mississippi
WHAY Whitley City, Kentucky
WHAZ-FM Hoosick Falls, New York
WHBC-FM Canton, Ohio
WHBJ Barnwell, 0
WHBM Park Falls, Wisconsin
WHBP Harbor Springs, Michigan
WHBQ-FM Germantown, Tennessee
WHBR-FM Parkersburg, West Virginia
WHBS Pittston, Pennsylvania
WHBT-FM Moyock, North Carolina
WHBX Tallahassee, Florida
WHBZ Sheboygan Falls, Wisconsin
WHCB Bristol, Tennessee
WHCC Ellettsville, Indiana
WHCE Highland Springs, Virginia
WHCF Bangor, Maine
WHCJ Savannah, Georgia
WHCL-FM Clinton, New York
WHCM Palatine, Illinois
WHCN Hartford, Connecticut
WHCR-FM New York, New York
WHCY Blairstown, New Jersey
WHDD-FM Sharon, Connecticut
WHDG Rhinelander, Wisconsin
WHDI Sister Bay, Wisconsin
WHDQ Claremont, New Hampshire
WHDX Buxton, North Carolina
WHDZ Buxton, North Carolina
WHEB Portsmouth, New Hampshire
WHEM Eau Claire, Wisconsin
WHEY North Muskegon, Michigan
WHFB-FM Benton Harbor, Michigan
WHFC Bel Air, Maryland
WHFG Broussard, Louisiana
WHFH Flossmoor, Illinois
WHFI Lindside, West Virginia
WHFM Southampton, New York
WHFR Dearborn, Michigan
WHFX Darien, Georgia
WHGL-FM Canton, Pennsylvania
WHGN Crystal River, Florida
WHGO Hertford, North Carolina
WHHB Holliston, Massachusetts
WHHD Clearwater, South Carolina
WHHH Indianapolis, Indiana
WHHI Highland, Wisconsin
WHHL Hazelwood, Missouri
WHHM-FM Henderson, Tennessee
WHHN Hollidaysburg, Pennsylvania
WHHR Vienna, Georgia
WHHS Havertown, Pennsylvania
WHHT(FM) Cave City, Kentucky
WHHY-FM Montgomery, Alabama
WHHZ Newberry, Florida
WHID Green Bay, Wisconsin
WHIF Palatka, Florida
WHIJ Ocala, Florida
WHIL-FM Mobile, Alabama
WHIO-FM Pleasant Hill, Ohio
WHIZ(FM) South Zanesville, Ohio
WHIZ-FM South Zanesville, Ohio
WHJE Carmel, Indiana
WHJL Merrill, Wisconsin
WHJM Anna, Ohio
WHJT Clinton, Mississippi
WHJY Providence, Rhode Island
WHKB Houghton, Michigan
WHKC Columbus, Ohio
WHKF Harrisburg, Pennsylvania
WHKL Crenshaw, Mississippi
WHKN Millen, Georgia
WHKO Dayton, Ohio
WHKR Rockledge, Florida
WHKS Port Allegany, Pennsylvania
WHKU Proctorville, Ohio
WHKV Sylvester, Georgia
WHKX Bluefield, Virginia
WHLA La Crosse, Wisconsin
WHLC Highlands, North Carolina
WHLF South Boston, Virginia
WHLG Port St. Lucie, Florida
WHLH Jackson, Mississippi
WHLJ-FM Statenville, Georgia
WHLK Cleveland, Ohio
WHLM-FM Berwick, Pennsylvania
WHLP Hanna, Indiana
WHLW Luverne, Alabama
WHLZ Marion, South Carolina
WHMA-FM Hobson City, Alabama
WHMC-FM Conway, South Carolina
WHMD Hammond, Louisiana
WHME South Bend, Indiana
WHMF Marianna, Florida
WHMH-FM Sauk Rapids, Minnesota
WHMI-FM Howell, Michigan
WHMJ Franklin, Pennsylvania
WHMO Madison, Indiana
WHMS-FM Champaign, Illinois
WHMX Lincoln, Maine
WHND Sister Bay, Wisconsin
WHNN Bay City, Michigan
WHOD Jackson, Alabama
WHOF North Canton, Ohio
WHOG-FM Ormond-By-The-Sea, Florida
WHOH Rhinelander, Wisconsin
WHOJ Terre Haute, Indiana
WHOK-FM Circleville, Ohio
WHOM Mount Washington, New Hampshire
WHOP-FM Hopkinsville, Kentucky
WHOT-FM Youngstown, Ohio
WHOU-FM Houlton, Maine
WHOV Hampton, Virginia
WHPC Garden City, New York
WHPD Dowagiac, Michigan
WHPE-FM High Point, North Carolina
WHPF Pittston Farm, Maine
WHPH Jemison, Alabama
WHPI Glasford, Illinois
WHPK-FM Chicago, Illinois
WHPL West Lafayette, Indiana
WHPO Hoopeston, Illinois
WHPP Columbia City, Virginia
WHPR-FM Highland Park, Michigan
WHPT Sarasota, Florida
WHPY-FM Bellevue, Tennessee
WHPZ Bremen, Indiana
WHQC Shelby, North Carolina
WHQG Milwaukee, Wisconsin
WHQQ Neoga, Illinois
WHQR Wilmington, North Carolina
WHQT Coral Gables, Florida
WHQX Gary, West Virginia
WHRB Cambridge, Massachusetts
WHRE Eastville, Virginia
WHRJ Gloucester Courthouse, Virginia
WHRK Memphis, Tennessee
WHRM Wausau, Wisconsin
WHRO-FM Norfolk, Virginia
WHRP Gurley, Alabama
WHRS Cookeville, Tennessee
WHRV Norfolk, Virginia
WHRW Binghamton, New York
WHRX Nassawadox, Virginia
WHSA Brule, Wisconsin
WHSB Alpena, Michigan
WHSD Hinsdale, Illinois
WHSL Lisman, Alabama
WHSM-FM Hayward, Wisconsin
WHSN Bangor, Maine
WHSS Hamilton, Ohio
WHST Tawas City, Michigan
WHSX Edmonton, Kentucky
WHTA Hampton, Georgia
WHTD Tallulah Falls, Georgia
WHTE-FM Ruckersville, Virginia
WHTF Havana, Florida
WHTI(FM) Lakeside, Virginia
WHTL-FM Whitehall, Wisconsin
WHTO Iron Mountain, Michigan
WHTP Kennebunkport, Maine
WHTS Coopersville, Michigan
WHTT Buffalo, New York
WHTU Big Island, Virginia
WHTZ Newark, New Jersey
WHUD Peekskill, New York
WHUG Jamestown, New York
WHUR-FM Washington, District of Columbia
WHUS Storrs, Connecticut
WHUZ(FM) Cole, Indiana
WHVE Russell Springs, Kentucky
WHVK New Hope, Alabama
WHVP Hudson, New York
WHVT Clyde, Ohio
WHWC Menomonie, Wisconsin
WHWG Trout Lake, Michigan
WHWK Binghamton, New York
WHWL Marquette, Michigan
WHWY Holt, Florida
WHXR Scarborough, Maine
WHXT Orangeburg, South Carolina
WHYA(FM) Mashpee, Massachusetts
WHYB Menominee, Michigan
WHYI-FM Fort Lauderdale, Florida
WHYN-FM Springfield, Massachusetts
WHYT Goodland Township, Michigan
WHYY-FM Philadelphia, Pennsylvania
WHYZ Palm Coast, Florida
WHYZ(FM) Palm Bay, Florida
WHZN New Whiteland, Indiana
WHZR Royal Center, Indiana
WHZT Williamston, South Carolina
WHZZ Lansing, Michigan
WIAA Interlochen, Michigan
WIAB Mackinaw City, Michigan
WIAD Bethesda, District of Columbia
WIAL Eau Claire, Wisconsin
WIBA-FM Sauk City, Wisconsin
WIBB-FM Fort Valley, Georgia
WIBC Indianapolis, Indiana
WIBD Janesville, Wisconsin
WIBG-FM Avalon, New Jersey
WIBI Carlinville, Illinois
WIBL(FM) Fairbury, Illinois
WIBN Earl Park, Indiana
WIBT Indianola, Mississippi
WIBV Mount Vernon, Illinois
WIBW-FM Topeka, Kansas
WIBZ Wedgefield, South Carolina
WICA Traverse City, Michigan
WICB Ithaca, New York
WICL Williamsport, Maryland
WICN Worcester, Massachusetts
WICO-FM Pocomoke City, Maryland
WICR Indianapolis, Indiana
WICV East Jordan, Michigan
WIDA-FM Carolina, Puerto Rico
WIDI Quebradillas, Puerto Rico
WIDL Cass City, Michigan
WIDR Kalamazoo, Michigan
WIFC Wausau, Wisconsin
WIFE-FM Rushville, Indiana
WIFF Windsor, New York
WIFM-FM Elkin, North Carolina
WIFO-FM Jesup, Georgia
WIFX-FM Jenkins, Kentucky
WIFY Addison, Vermont
WIGH Jackson, Tennessee
WIGO-FM White Stone, Virginia
WIGW Eustis, Florida
WIHB-FM Gray, Georgia
WIHC Newberry, Michigan
WIHG Rockwood, Tennessee
WIHN Normal, Illinois
WIHS Middletown, Connecticut
WIHT Washington, District of Columbia
WIII Cortland, New York
WIIL Union Grove, Wisconsin
WIIS Key West, Florida
WIIT Chicago, Illinois
WIIZ Blackville, South Carolina
WIJD Prichard, Alabama
WIJD Prichard, Alabama
WIJV Harriman, Tennessee
WIKB-FM Iron River, Michigan
WIKI Carrollton, Kentucky
WIKK Newton, Illinois
WIKL(FM) Elwood, Indiana
WIKQ Tusculum, Tennessee
WIKS New Bern, North Carolina
WIKV Plymouth, Indiana
WIKX Charlotte Harbor, Florida
WIKY Evansville, Indiana
WIKZ Chambersburg, Pennsylvania
WIL-FM St. Louis, Missouri
WILA Live Oak, Florida
WILE-FM Byesville, Ohio
WILI-FM Willimantic, Connecticut
WILK-FM Avoca, Pennsylvania
WILL-FM Urbana, Illinois
WILN Panama City, Florida
WILQ Williamsport, Pennsylvania
WILT Wrightsville Beach, North Carolina
WILT Wilmington, North Carolina
WILZ Saginaw, Michigan
WIMC Crawfordsville, Indiana
WIMI Ironwood, Michigan
WIMK Iron Mountain, Michigan
WIMT Lima, Ohio
WIMX Gibsonburg, Ohio
WIMZ Knoxville, Tennessee
WINC-FM Winchester, Virginia
WINK-FM Fort Myers, Florida
WINL Linden, Alabama
WINN Columbus, Indiana
WINO Odessa, New York
WINQ Winchester, New Hampshire
WINX-FM St. Michaels, Maryland
WIOA San Juan, Puerto Rico
WIOB Mayaguez, Puerto Rico
WIOC Ponce, Puerto Rico
WIOG Bay City, Michigan
WIOK Falmouth, Kentucky
WIOL-FM Waverly Hall, Georgia
WIOQ Philadelphia, Pennsylvania
WIOT Toledo, Ohio
WIOV Ephrata, Pennsylvania
WIOX Roxbury, New York
WIOZ Southern Pines, North Carolina
WIP Philadelphia, Pennsylvania
WIPA Pittsfield, Illinois
WIPK-FM Calhoun, Georgia
WIPR-FM San Juan, Puerto Rico
WIQH Concord, Massachusetts
WIQI Chicago, Illinois
WIQO-FM Forest, Virginia
WIQQ Leland, Mississippi
WIRC Ely, Minnesota
WIRE Lebanon, Indiana
WIRK Indiantown, Florida
WIRN Buhl, Minnesota
WIRQ Rochester, New York
WIRR Virginia-Hibbing, Minnesota
WIRX St. Joseph, Michigan
WISE-FM Wise, Virginia
WISH-FM Galatia, Illinois
WISK-FM Americus, Georgia
WISM Altoona, Wisconsin
WISU Terre Haute, Indiana
WISX Philadelphia, Pennsylvania
WITC Cazenovia, New York
WITF-FM Harrisburg, Pennsylvania

WITH Ithaca, New York
WITL Lansing, Michigan
WITR Henrietta, New York
WITT Zionsville, Indiana
WITZ-FM Jasper, Indiana
WIUJ Charlotte Amalie, Virgin Islands
WIUM Macomb, Illinois
WIUP-FM Indiana, Pennsylvania
WIUS Macomb, Illinois
WIUV Castleton, Vermont
WIUW Warsaw, Illinois
WIVA-FM Aguadilla, Puerto Rico
WIVG Tunica, Mississippi
WIVH Christiansted, Virgin Islands
WIVI Charlotte Amalie, Virgin Islands
WIVK Knoxville, Tennessee
WIVL Jasper, Georgia
WIVQ Spring Valley, Illinois
WIVR Kentland, Indiana
WIVY Morehead, Kentucky
WIWC Kokomo, Indiana
WIWF Charleston, South Carolina
WIXM Grand Isle, Vermont
WIXO Peoria, Illinois
WIXQ Millersville, Pennsylvania
WIXV Savannah, Georgia
WIXX Green Bay, Wisconsin
WIXY Champaign, Illinois
WIYN Deposit, New York
WIYY Baltimore, Maryland
WIZB Abbeville, Alabama
WIZF Erlanger, Kentucky
WIZM-FM La Crosse, Wisconsin
WIZN Vergennes, Vermont
WJAA Austin, Indiana
WJAB Huntsville, Alabama
WJAD Leesburg, Georgia
WJAI Pearl, Mississippi
WJAQ Marianna, Florida
WJAW-FM McConnelsville, Ohio
WJAZ Summerdale, Pennsylvania
WJBC Pontiac, Illinois
WJBD-FM Salem, Illinois
WJBE-FM Five Points, Alabama
WJBL Ladysmith, Wisconsin
WJBP Red Bank, Tennessee
WJBQ Portland, Maine
WJBR-FM Wilmington, Delaware
WJBT Callahan, Florida
WJBZ-FM Seymour, Tennessee
WJCA Albion, New York
WJCB Clewiston, Florida
WJCF-FM Morristown, Indiana
WJCH Joliet, Illinois
WJCI Huntington, Indiana
WJCK Piedmont, Alabama
WJCL-FM Savannah, Georgia
WJCO Montpelier, Indiana
WJCR-FM Upton, Kentucky
WJCS Allentown, Pennsylvania
WJCT-FM Jacksonville, Florida
WJCU University Heights, Ohio
WJCX Pittsfield, Maine
WJCY Cicero, Indiana
WJCZ Milford, Illinois
WJDB-FM Thomasville, Alabama
WJDD Carrollton, Ohio
WJDF Orange, Massachusetts
WJDK-FM Seneca, Illinois
WJDQ Meridian, Mississippi
WJDR Prentiss, Mississippi
WJDS Sparta, Georgia
WJDT Rogersville, Tennessee
WJDV Broadway, Virginia
WJDX-FM Kosciusko, Mississippi
WJDZ Pastillo, Puerto Rico
WJEC Vernon, Alabama
WJEF Lafayette, Indiana
WJEK(FM) Rantoul, Illinois
WJEL Indianapolis, Indiana
WJEN Killington, Vermont
WJEQ Macomb, Illinois
WJEZ Dwight, Illinois
WJFD-FM New Bedford, Massachusetts
WJFF Jeffersonville, New York
WJFH Sebring, Florida
WJFK-FM Manassas, District of Columbia
WJFL Tennille, Georgia
WJFM Baton Rouge, Louisiana
WJFP Fort Pierce, Florida
WJFR Jacksonville, Florida
WJFX New Haven, Indiana
WJGA-FM Jackson, Georgia
WJGK(FM) Newburgh, New York
WJGL Jacksonville, Florida
WJGM(FM) Baldwin, Florida
WJGO Tice, Florida
WJGS Norwood, Georgia
WJHD Portsmouth, Rhode Island
WJHO Alexander City, Alabama
WJHS Columbia City, Indiana
WJHT Johnstown, Pennsylvania
WJIA Guntersville, Alabama
WJIC Zanesville, Ohio
WJIE-FM Okolona, Kentucky
WJIF Opp, Alabama
WJIK Fulton, Alabama
WJIM Lansing, Michigan
WJIR Key West, Florida
WJIS Bradenton, Florida
WJIV Cherry Valley, New York
WJIW Greenville, Mississippi
WJIZ-FM Albany, Georgia
WJJB-FM Gray, Maine
WJJE Delaware, Ohio
WJJH Ashland, Wisconsin
WJJJ Beckley, West Virginia
WJJK Noblesville, Indiana
WJJM-FM Lewisburg, Tennessee
WJJN Columbia, Alabama
WJJO Watertown, Wisconsin
WJJQ-FM Tomahawk, Wisconsin
WJJR Rutland, Vermont
WJJS Roanoke, Virginia
WJJW North Adams, Massachusetts
WJJX Appomattox, Virginia
WJJY-FM Brainerd, Minnesota
WJJZ Irasberg, Vermont
WJKA Jacksonville, North Carolina
WJKC Christiansted, Virgin Islands
WJKD Vero Beach, Florida
WJKE Stillwater, New York
WJKG Effingham, Kentucky
WJKI Bethany Beach, Delaware
WJKK Vicksburg, Mississippi
WJKL Glendale Heights, Illinois
WJKN-FM Spring Arbor, Michigan
WJKR Worthington, Ohio
WJKS Canton, New Jersey
WJKW Athens, Ohio
WJKX Ellisville, Mississippi
WJKZ Hanover, Michigan
WJLB Detroit, Michigan
WJLE-FM Smithville, Tennessee
WJLF Gainesville, Florida
WJLH Flagler Beach, Florida
WJLI Metropolis, Illinois
WJLK Asbury Park, New Jersey
WJLR Seymour, Indiana
WJLS-FM Beckley, West Virginia
WJLT Evansville, Indiana
WJLU New Smyrna Beach, Florida
WJLV Jackson, Mississippi
WJLY Ramsey, Illinois
WJLZ Virginia Beach, Virginia
WJMA Culpeper, Virginia
WJMC-FM Rice Lake, Wisconsin
WJMD Hazard, Kentucky
WJMF Smithfield, Rhode Island
WJMG Hattiesburg, Mississippi
WJMH Reidsville, North Carolina
WJMI Jackson, Mississippi
WJMJ Hartford, Connecticut
WJMK Chicago, Illinois
WJMM-FM Keene, Kentucky
WJMN Boston, Massachusetts
WJMQ Clintonville, Wisconsin
WJMR-FM Menomonee Falls, Wisconsin
WJMU Decatur, Illinois
WJMX-FM Cheraw, South Carolina
WJMZ-FM Anderson, South Carolina
WJNG Johnsonburg, Pennsylvania
WJNI Ladson, South Carolina
WJNR-FM Iron Mountain, Michigan
WJNS-FM Bentonia, Mississippi
WJNV Jonesville, Virginia
WJNY Watertown, New York
WJOD Asbury, Iowa
WJOG Good Hart, Michigan
WJOH Raco, Michigan
WJOJ Rust Township, Michigan
WJOM Eagle, Michigan
WJOT-FM Wabash, Indiana
WJOU Huntsville, Alabama
WJOX Birmingham, Alabama
WJPA-FM Washington, Pennsylvania
WJPD Ishpeming, Michigan
WJPG Woodbine, New Jersey
WJPG Cape May Court House, New Jersey
WJPR Jasper, Indiana
WJPS Boonville, Indiana
WJPT Fort Myers, Florida
WJPZ-FM Syracuse, New York
WJQB Spring Hill, Florida
WJQK Zeeland, Michigan
WJQM De Forest, Wisconsin
WJQX Helena, Alabama
WJQZ Wellsville, New York
WJRB Young Harris, Georgia
WJRC Lewistown, Pennsylvania
WJRE Galva, Illinois
WJRF Duluth, Minnesota
WJRH Easton, Pennsylvania
WJRL-FM Slocomb, Alabama
WJRR Cocoa Beach, Florida
WJRS Jamestown, Kentucky
WJRV(FM) Oliver Springs, Tennessee
WJRZ-FM Manahawkin, New Jersey
WJSA-FM Jersey Shore, Pennsylvania
WJSC-FM Johnson, Vermont
WJSE North Cape May, New Jersey
WJSG Hamlet, North Carolina
WJSH Folsom, Louisiana
WJSJ Fernandina Beach, Florida
WJSM-FM Martinsburg, Pennsylvania
WJSN-FM Jackson, Kentucky
WJSO Pikeville, Kentucky
WJSP-FM Warm Springs, Georgia
WJSQ Athens, Tennessee
WJSR Birmingham, Alabama
WJSU-FM Jackson, Mississippi
WJSV Morristown, New Jersey
WJSZ Ashley, Michigan
WJTF Panama City, Florida
WJTG Fort Valley, Georgia
WJTK Columbia City, Florida
WJTL Lancaster, Pennsylvania
WJTT Red Bank, Tennessee
WJTY Lancaster, Wisconsin
WJUC Swanton, Ohio
WJUF Inverness, Florida
WJUN-FM Mexico, Pennsylvania
WJUX Monticello, New York
WJVC Center Moriches, New York
WJVK Owensboro, Kentucky
WJVL Janesville, Wisconsin
WJVL Janesville, Wisconsin
WJVO South Jacksonville, Illinois
WJVP Culebra, Puerto Rico
WJWD Marshall, Wisconsin
WJWJ-FM Beaufort, South Carolina
WJWR Bloomington, Illinois
WJWT Gardner, Massachusetts
WJWV Fort Gaines, Georgia
WJWZ Wetumpka, Alabama
WJXA Nashville, Tennessee
WJXB Knoxville, Tennessee
WJXM De Kalb, Mississippi
WJXN-FM Utica, Mississippi
WJXQ Charlotte, Michigan
WJXR Macclenny, Florida
WJXY-FM Conway, South Carolina
WJYA Emporia, Virginia
WJYE Buffalo, New York
WJYJ Fredericksburg, Virginia
WJYO Fort Myers, Florida
WJYW Union City, Indiana
WJYY Concord, New Hampshire
WJZ-FM Catonsville, Maryland
WJZB Starkville, Mississippi
WJZD-FM Long Beach, Mississippi
WJZE Oak Harbor, Ohio
WJZQ Cadillac, Michigan
WJZR Rochester, New York
WJZS Live Oak, Florida
WJZZ North Salem, New York
WJZZ(FM) North Salem, New York
WKAA Willacoochee, Georgia
WKAD Harrietta, Michigan
WKAI Macomb, Illinois
WKAK Albany, Georgia
WKAO Ashland, Kentucky
WKAQ-FM San Juan, Puerto Rico
WKAR-FM East Lansing, Michigan
WKAY Knoxville, Illinois
WKAZ-FM Miami, West Virginia
WKBB Mantee, Mississippi
WKBC-FM North Wilkesboro, North Carolina
WKBE Warrensburg, New York
WKBH-FM West Salem, Wisconsin
WKBI-FM St. Marys, Pennsylvania
WKBQ Covington, Tennessee
WKBU New Orleans, Louisiana
WKBX Kingsland, Georgia
WKCA Salt Lick, Kentucky
WKCB-FM Hindman, Kentucky
WKCC Kankakee, Illinois
WKCH Whitewater, Wisconsin
WKCI-FM Hamden, Connecticut
WKCL Ladson, South Carolina
WKCN Fort Benning South, Georgia
WKCO Gambier, Ohio
WKCP Miami, Florida
WKCQ Saginaw, Michigan
WKCR-FM New York, New York
WKCS Knoxville, Tennessee
WKCY-FM Harrisonburg, Virginia
WKDC-FM Cedarville, Ohio
WKDD Munroe Falls, Ohio
WKDE-FM Altavista, Virginia
WKDF Nashville, Tennessee
WKDJ-FM Clarksdale, Mississippi
WKDL-FM Brockport, New York
WKDN-FM State College, Pennsylvania
WKDO-FM Liberty, Kentucky
WKDP-FM Corbin, Kentucky
WKDQ Henderson, Kentucky
WKDS Kalamazoo, Michigan
WKDU Philadelphia, Pennsylvania
WKDZ-FM Cadiz, Kentucky
WKEA-FM Scottsboro, Alabama
WKEB Medford, Wisconsin
WKEE-FM Huntington, West Virginia
WKEK Gunflint Lake, Minnesota
WKEL Webster, New York
WKEQ Somerset, Kentucky
WKES Lakeland, Florida
WKET Kettering, Ohio
WKEU-FM The Rock, Georgia
WKEY-FM Key West, Florida
WKEZ-FM Tavernier, Florida
WKFA St. Catherine, Florida
WKFC North Corbin, Kentucky
WKFM Huron, Ohio
WKFP(FM) Navarre, Florida
WKFR-FM Battle Creek, Michigan
WKFS Milford, Ohio
WKFX Rice Lake, Wisconsin
WKGA Goodwater, Alabama
WKGB-FM Conklin, New York
WKGC-FM Panama City, Florida
WKGL-FM Loves Park, Illinois
WKGO Cumberland, Maryland
WKGR Wellington, Florida
WKGS Irondequoit, New York
WKGV Swansboro, North Carolina
WKHF(FM) Lynchburg, Virginia
WKHG Leitchfield, Kentucky
WKHI Fruitland, Maryland
WKHJ Mountain Lake Park, Maryland
WKHK Colonial Heights, Virginia
WKHL West Lafayette, Indiana
WKHM-FM Brooklyn, Michigan
WKHQ-FM Charlevoix, Michigan
WKHR Bainbridge, Ohio
WKHS Worton, Maryland
WKHT Knoxville, Tennessee
WKHX Marietta, Georgia
WKHY Lafayette, Indiana
WKIB Anna, Illinois
WKIC Hyden, Kentucky
WKID Vevay, Indiana
WKIK-FM California, Maryland
WKIM Munford, Tennessee
WKIO Arcola, Illinois
WKIS Boca Raton, Florida
WKIT Brewer, Maine
WKIV Westerly, Rhode Island
WKIW Ironwood, Michigan
WKIX-FM Raleigh, North Carolina
WKJA Brunswick, Ohio
WKJC-FM Tawas City, Michigan
WKJD Columbus, Indiana
WKJL Clarksburg, West Virginia

WKJM Petersburg, Virginia
WKJN Centreville, Mississippi
WKJQ-FM Parsons, Tennessee
WKJS Richmond, Virginia
WKJT Teutopolis, Illinois
WKJX Elizabeth City, North Carolina
WKJY Hempstead, New York
WKJZ Hillman, Michigan
WKKB Middletown, Rhode Island
WKKC Chicago, Illinois
WKKF Ballston Spa, New York
WKKG Columbus, Indiana
WKKI Celina, Ohio
WKKJ Chillicothe, Ohio
WKKL West Barnstable, Massachusetts
WKKN Westminster, Vermont
WKKO Toledo, Ohio
WKKQ Barbourville, Kentucky
WKKR Auburn, Alabama
WKKS-FM Vanceburg, Kentucky
WKKT Statesville, North Carolina
WKKV-FM Racine, Wisconsin
WKKW Fairmont, West Virginia
WKKY Geneva, Ohio
WKKZ Dublin, Georgia
WKLA-FM Ludington, Michigan
WKLB-FM Waltham, Massachusetts
WKLC-FM St. Albans, West Virginia
WKLG Rock Harbor, Florida
WKLH Milwaukee, Wisconsin
WKLI-FM Albany, New York
WKLK-FM Cloquet, Minnesota
WKLL Frankfort, New York
WKLM Millersburg, Ohio
WKLN Wilmington, Ohio
WKLO Hardinsburg, Indiana
WKLR Fort Lee, Virginia
WKLS Southside, Alabama
WKLT Kalkaska, Michigan
WKLU Brownsburg, Indiana
WKLV-FM Port Chester, New York
WKLW-FM Paintsville, Kentucky
WKLX Brownsville, Kentucky
WKLZ-FM Petoskey, Michigan
WKMD Madisonville, Kentucky
WKMJ-FM Hancock, Michigan
WKMK Eatontown, New Jersey
WKML Lumberton, North Carolina
WKMM Kingwood, West Virginia
WKMO Lebanon Junction, Kentucky
WKMS-FM Murray, Kentucky
WKMT Fulton, Kentucky
WKMV Muncie, Indiana
WKMX Enterprise, Alabama
WKMY Winchendon, Massachusetts
WKNA Logan, Ohio
WKNB Clarendon, Pennsylvania
WKNC-FM Raleigh, North Carolina
WKNE Keene, New Hampshire
WKNG-FM Heflin, Alabama
WKNH Keene, New Hampshire
WKNJ-FM Union Township, New Jersey
WKNK(FM) Callaway, Florida
WKNL New London, Connecticut
WKNN-FM Pascagoula, Mississippi
WKNO-FM Memphis, Tennessee
WKNP Jackson, Tennessee
WKNS Kinston, North Carolina
WKNU Brewton, Alabama
WKNZ Harrington, Delaware
WKOA Lafayette, Indiana
WKOL Plattsburgh, New York
WKOM Columbia, Tennessee
WKOR-FM Columbus, Mississippi
WKOS Kingsport, Tennessee
WKOV-FM Wellston, Ohio
WKOY-FM Princeton, West Virginia
WKOZ-FM Carthage, Mississippi
WKPB Henderson, Kentucky
WKPE-FM South Yarmouth, Massachusetts
WKPK Michigamme, Michigan
WKPL Ellwood City, Pennsylvania
WKPO Soldiers Grove, Wisconsin
WKPQ Hornell, New York
WKPS State College, Pennsylvania
WKPW Knightstown, Indiana
WKPX Sunrise, Florida
WKQB Pocahontas, Virginia
WKQC Charlotte, North Carolina
WKQH Marathon, Wisconsin
WKQI Detroit, Michigan
WKQK Germantown, Tennessee
WKQL Brookville, Pennsylvania
WKQQ Winchester, Kentucky
WKQR Mullens, West Virginia
WKQS-FM Negaunee, Michigan
WKQV Cowen, West Virginia
WKQW-FM Oil City, Pennsylvania
WKQX Chicago, Illinois
WKQY Tazewell, Virginia
WKQZ Midland, Michigan
WKRA-FM Holly Springs, Mississippi
WKRB Brooklyn, New York
WKRF Tobyhanna, Pennsylvania
WKRH Minetto, New York
WKRI Cokesbury, South Carolina
WKRJ New Philadelphia, Ohio
WKRK-FM Cleveland Heights, Ohio
WKRL-FM North Syracuse, New York
WKRO-FM Port Orange, Florida
WKRQ Cincinnati, Ohio
WKRR Asheboro, North Carolina
WKRU Allouez, Wisconsin
WKRV Vandalia, Illinois
WKRW Wooster, Ohio
WKRX Roxboro, North Carolina
WKRY Versailles, Indiana
WKRZ Freeland, Pennsylvania
WKSB Williamsport, Pennsylvania
WKSC-FM Chicago, Illinois
WKSD Paulding, Ohio
WKSE Niagara Falls, New York
WKSF Old Fort, North Carolina
WKSG Cedar Creek, Florida
WKSI-FM Stephens City, Virginia
WKSJ-FM Mobile, Alabama
WKSK-FM South Hill, Virginia
WKSL Neptune Beach, Florida
WKSM Fort Walton Beach, Florida
WKSO Natchez, Mississippi
WKSP Aiken, South Carolina
WKSP(AM) Block Island, Rhode Island
WKSQ Ellsworth, Maine
WKSR-FM Loretto, Tennessee
WKSS Hartford-Meriden, Connecticut
WKST-FM Pittsburgh, Pennsylvania
WKSU-FM Kent, Ohio
WKSV Thompson, Ohio
WKSW Cookeville, Tennessee
WKSX-FM Johnston, South Carolina
WKSZ De Pere, Wisconsin
WKTG Madisonville, Kentucky
WKTJ-FM Farmington, Maine
WKTK Crystal River, Florida
WKTL Struthers, Ohio
WKTM Soperton, Georgia
WKTN Kenton, Ohio
WKTO Edgewater, Florida
WKTS Kingston, Tennessee
WKTT Salisbury, Maryland
WKTU Lake Success, New York
WKTZ-FM Jacksonville, Florida
WKUA Moundville, Alabama
WKUB Blackshear, Georgia
WKUE Elizabethtown, Kentucky
WKUL Cullman, Alabama
WKUZ Wabash, Indiana
WKVB Port Matilda, Pennsylvania
WKVC North Myrtle Beach, South Carolina
WKVE Mount Pleasant, Pennsylvania
WKVF Bartlett, Tennessee
WKVH Monticello, Florida
WKVI-FM Knox, Indiana
WKVJ Dannemora, New York
WKVK Semora, North Carolina
WKVN Morganfield, Kentucky
WKVO Georgetown, Kentucky
WKVP Camden, New Jersey
WKVR-FM Huntingdon, Pennsylvania
WKVS Lenoir, North Carolina
WKVT-FM Brattleboro, Vermont
WKVU Utica, New York
WKVV Searsport, Maine
WKVW Marmet, West Virginia
WKVY Somerset, Kentucky
WKVZ Dexter, Maine
WKWC Owensboro, Kentucky
WKWH Liberty, Indiana
WKWI Kilmarnock, Virginia
WKWK-FM Wheeling, West Virginia
WKWM Marathon, Florida
WKWR Key West, Florida
WKWS Charleston, West Virginia
WKWV Watertown, New York
WKWX Savannah, Tennessee
WKWY Tompkinsville, Kentucky
WKWZ Syosset, New York
WKXA-FM Findlay, Ohio
WKXB Boiling Spring Lakes, North Carolina
WKXC-FM Aiken, South Carolina
WKXD-FM Monterey, Tennessee
WKXH St. Johnsbury, Vermont
WKXI-FM Magee, Mississippi
WKXK Pine Hill, Alabama
WKXM-FM Winfield, Alabama
WKXN Fort Deposit, Alabama
WKXP Kingston, New York
WKXQ Rushville, Illinois
WKXS-FM Leland, North Carolina
WKXW Trenton, New Jersey
WKXX Attalla, Alabama
WKXY Merigold, Mississippi
WKXZ Norwich, New York
WKYA Greenville, Kentucky
WKYE Johnstown, Pennsylvania
WKYJ Rouses Point, New York
WKYL Lawrenceburg, Kentucky
WKYM Monticello, Kentucky
WKYN Mount Sterling, Kentucky
WKYP Ledbetter, Kentucky
WKYQ Paducah, Kentucky
WKYR-FM Burkesville, Kentucky
WKYS Washington, District of Columbia
WKYU-FM Bowling Green, Kentucky
WKYV Colonial Heights, Virginia
WKYX-FM Golconda, Illinois
WKYZ Key Colony Beach, Florida
WKZA Lakewood, New York
WKZB Marion, Mississippi
WKZC Scottville, Michigan
WKZE-FM Salisbury, Connecticut
WKZG Seymour, Wisconsin
WKZJ Eufaula, Alabama
WKZL Winston-Salem, North Carolina
WKZM Sarasota, Florida
WKZP Bethany Beach, Delaware
WKZQ-FM Forestbrook, South Carolina
WKZR Milledgeville, Georgia
WKZS Thomasboro, Illinois
WKZU Iuka, Mississippi
WKZW Sandersville, Mississippi
WKZX-FM Lenoir City, Tennessee
WKZY Chilton, Wisconsin
WKZZ Tifton, Georgia
WLAB Fort Wayne, Indiana
WLAI Wilmore, Kentucky
WLAN-FM Lancaster, Pennsylvania
WLAU Heidelberg, Mississippi
WLAV Grand Rapids, Michigan
WLAW Newaygo, Michigan
WLAY-FM Littleville, Alabama
WLAZ Kissimmee, Florida
WLBC Muncie, Indiana
WLBF Montgomery, Alabama
WLBH-FM Mattoon, Illinois
WLBL-FM Wausau, Wisconsin
WLBS Bristol, Pennsylvania
WLBW Fenwick Island, Delaware
WLCA Godfrey, Illinois
WLCE Petersburg, Illinois
WLCH Lancaster, Pennsylvania
WLCL Sellersburg, Indiana
WLCN Atlanta, Illinois
WLCS North Muskegon, Michigan
WLCT Lafayette, Tennessee
WLCU Campbellsville, Kentucky
WLCY Blairsville, Pennsylvania
WLDA Fort Rucker, Alabama
WLDB Milwaukee, Wisconsin
WLDE Fort Wayne, Indiana
WLDI Juno Beach, Florida
WLDR-FM Traverse City, Michigan
WLEG Ligonier, Indiana
WLEL Ellaville, Georgia
WLEN Adrian, Michigan
WLER-FM Butler, Pennsylvania
WLEV Allentown, Pennsylvania
WLEW-FM Bad Axe, Michigan
WLEY-FM Aurora, Illinois
WLFA Asheville, North Carolina
WLFC North Baltimore, Ohio
WLFE-FM Key Largo, Florida
WLFF Georgetown, South Carolina
WLFJ-FM Greenville, South Carolina
WLFK Gouverneur, New York
WLFR Pomona, New Jersey
WLFS Port Wentworth, Georgia
WLFV Midlothian, Virginia
WLFW Chandler, Indiana
WLFX Berea, Kentucky
WLFZ-FM Springfield, Illinois
WLGC-FM Greenup, Kentucky
WLGE Baileys Harbor, Wisconsin
WLGH Leroy Township, Michigan
WLGI Hemingway, South Carolina
WLGP Jacksonville, North Carolina
WLGT Washington, North Carolina
WLGX Louisville, Kentucky
WLGZ-FM Webster, New York
WLHC Robbins, North Carolina
WLHH Ridgeland, South Carolina
WLHI Schnecksville, Pennsylvania
WLHK Shelbyville, Indiana
WLHR-FM Lavonia, Georgia
WLHS West Chester, Ohio
WLHT-FM Grand Rapids, Michigan
WLHW Casey, Illinois
WLIC Frostburg, Maryland
WLIF Baltimore, Maryland
WLIH Whitneyville, Pennsylvania
WLIN-FM Durant, Mississippi
WLIT-FM Chicago, Illinois
WLIV-FM Monterey, Tennessee
WLJA-FM Ellijay, Georgia
WLJC Beattyville, Kentucky
WLJE Valparaiso, Indiana
WLJE-FM Georgetown, Delaware
WLJH Grand Gorge, New York
WLJI Summerton, South Carolina
WLJK Aiken, South Carolina
WLJN-FM Traverse City, Michigan
WLJP Monroe, New York
WLJR Birmingham, Alabama
WLJS-FM Jacksonville, Alabama
WLJY Nekoosa, Wisconsin
WLKA Tafton, Pennsylvania
WLKB Bay City, Michigan
WLKC Campton, New Hampshire
WLKG Lake Geneva, Wisconsin
WLKH Somerset, Pennsylvania
WLKI Angola, Indiana
WLKJ Portage, Pennsylvania
WLKK Wethersfield Twnshp, New York
WLKL Mattoon, Illinois
WLKM-FM Three Rivers, Michigan
WLKN Cleveland, Wisconsin
WLKO Hickory, North Carolina
WLKP Belpre, Ohio
WLKQ-FM Buford, Georgia
WLKR Norwalk, Ohio
WLKS-FM West Liberty, Kentucky
WLKT Lexington-Fayette, Kentucky
WLKU Rock Island, Illinois
WLKV Ripley, West Virginia
WLKX-FM Forest Lake, Minnesota
WLKZ Wolfeboro, New Hampshire
WLLD Lakeland, Florida
WLLE Mayfield, Kentucky
WLLF Mercer, Pennsylvania
WLLG Lowville, New York
WLLJ Etowah, Tennessee
WLLK-FM Somerset, Kentucky
WLLR-FM Davenport, Iowa
WLLT Polo, Illinois
WLLW Seneca Falls, New York
WLLX Lawrenceburg, Tennessee
WLMD Bushnell, Illinois
WLME Lewisport, Kentucky
WLMG New Orleans, Louisiana
WLMI Grand Ledge, Michigan
WLMN Manistee, Michigan
WLMU Harrogate, Tennessee
WLMW Manchester, New Hampshire
WLMX-FM Balsam Lake, Wisconsin
WLMY Williamsport, Pennsylvania
WLND Signal Mountain, Tennessee
WLNF Rapids, New York
WLNG Sag Harbor, New York
WLNH-FM Laconia, New Hampshire
WLNI Lynchburg, Virginia
WLNJ Lakehurst, New Jersey
WLNK Charlotte, North Carolina
WLNQ White Pine, Tennessee
WLNQ-FM Newport, Tennessee

WLNX Lincoln, Illinois
WLNZ Lansing, Michigan
WLOF Elma, New York
WLOG Markleysburg, Pennsylvania
WLOL-FM Star City, West Virginia
WLOQ Indian Lakes Estates, Florida
WLPE Augusta, Georgia
WLPF Ocilla, Georgia
WLPG Florence, South Carolina
WLPR-FM Lowell, Indiana
WLPS-FM Lumberton, North Carolina
WLPT Jesup, Georgia
WLPW Lake Placid, New York
WLQB Ocean Isle Beach, North Carolina
WLQC Sharpsburg, North Carolina
WLQI Rensselaer, Indiana
WLQK Livingston, Tennessee
WLQM-FM Franklin, Virginia
WLQR-FM Delta, Ohio
WLRA Lockport, Illinois
WLRD Willard, Ohio
WLRH Huntsville, Alabama
WLRK Greenville, Mississippi
WLRN-FM Miami, Florida
WLRQ-FM Cocoa, Florida
WLRR Milledgeville, Georgia
WLRW Champaign, Illinois
WLRX Ironton, Ohio
WLRY Rushville, Ohio
WLS Chicago, Illinois
WLSK Lebanon, Kentucky
WLSM-FM Louisville, Mississippi
WLSN Grand Marais, Minnesota
WLSO Sault Ste. Marie, Michigan
WLSR Galesburg, Illinois
WLST Marinette, Wisconsin
WLSU La Crosse, Wisconsin
WLSW Scottdale, Pennsylvania
WLTB Johnson City, New York
WLTC Cusseta, Georgia
WLTF Martinsburg, West Virginia
WLTJ Pittsburgh, Pennsylvania
WLTK New Market, Virginia
WLTL La Grange, Illinois
WLTM Greenville, Mississippi
WLTN-FM Lisbon, New Hampshire
WLTO Nicholasville, Kentucky
WLTQ-FM Venice, Florida
WLTR Columbia, South Carolina
WLTU Manitowoc, Wisconsin
WLTW New York, New York
WLTY Cayce, South Carolina
WLUJ Springfield, Illinois
WLUM-FM Milwaukee, Wisconsin
WLUN Pinconning, Michigan
WLUP-FM Chicago, Illinois
WLUR Lexington, Virginia
WLUS-FM Clarksville, Virginia
WLUW Chicago, Illinois
WLUZ Levittown, Puerto Rico
WLVB Morrisville, Vermont
WLVE Mukwonago, Wisconsin
WLVF-FM Haines City, Florida
WLVG Havelock, North Carolina
WLVH Hardeeville, South Carolina
WLVK Fort Knox, Kentucky
WLVM Chickasaw, Alabama
WLVQ Columbus, Ohio
WLVR-FM Bethlehem, Pennsylvania
WLVS-FM Clifton, Tennessee
WLVU Belle Meade, Tennessee
WLVV Midland, Maryland
WLVW Salisbury, Maryland
WLVX(FM) Greenville, Pennsylvania
WLVY Elmira, New York
WLVZ Collins, Mississippi
WLWF Marseilles, Illinois
WLWI-FM Montgomery, Alabama
WLWJ Petersburg, Illinois
WLWK-FM Milwaukee, Wisconsin
WLXC Columbia, South Carolina
WLXO Stamping Ground, Kentucky
WLXP Savannah, Georgia
WLXR-FM La Crosse, Wisconsin
WLXT Petoskey, Michigan
WLXV Cadillac, Michigan
WLXX Lexington, Kentucky
WLYE-FM Glasgow, Kentucky
WLYF Miami, Florida
WLYJ(FM) Tullahoma, Tennessee
WLYK Cape Vincent, New York
WLYU Lyons, Georgia
WLZA Eupora, Mississippi
WLZK Paris, Tennessee
WLZL Annapolis, District of Columbia
WLZN Macon, Georgia
WLZS Beaver Springs, Pennsylvania
WLZW Utica, New York
WLZX Northampton, Massachusetts
WMAB-FM Mississippi State, Mississippi
WMAD Cross Plains, Wisconsin
WMAE-FM Booneville, Mississippi
WMAG High Point, North Carolina
WMAH-FM Biloxi, Mississippi
WMAJ-FM Centre Hall, Pennsylvania
WMAL Woodbridge, Virginia
WMAN-FM Fredericktown, Ohio
WMAO-FM Greenwood, Mississippi
WMAS Enfield, Connecticut
WMAU-FM Bude, Mississippi
WMAV-FM Oxford, Mississippi
WMAW-FM Meridian, Mississippi
WMAX-FM Holland, Michigan
WMBI-FM Chicago, Illinois
WMBJ Murrells Inlet, South Carolina
WMBL Mitchell, Indiana
WMBR Cambridge, Massachusetts
WMBU Forest, Mississippi
WMBV Dixons Mills, Alabama
WMBW Chattanooga, Tennessee
WMBX Jensen Beach, Florida
WMBZ West Bend, Wisconsin
WMC-FM Memphis, Tennessee
WMCD Claxton, Georgia
WMCE Erie, Pennsylvania
WMCG Milan, Georgia
WMCI Neoga, Illinois
WMCM Rockland, Maine
WMCN St. Paul, Minnesota
WMCO New Concord, Ohio
WMCQ Muskegon, Michigan
WMCR-FM Oneida, New York
WMCX West Long Branch, New Jersey
WMDC Mayville, Wisconsin
WMDH New Castle, Indiana
WMDJ-FM Allen, Kentucky
WMDM Lexington Park, Maryland
WMDR-FM Oakland, Maine
WMEA Portland, Maine
WMEB-FM Orono, Maine
WMED Calais, Maine
WMEE Fort Wayne, Indiana
WMEF Fort Kent, Maine
WMEG Guayama, Puerto Rico
WMEH Bangor, Maine
WMEK Kennebunkport, Maine
WMEM Presque Isle, Maine
WMEP Camden, Maine
WMEQ-FM Menomonie, Wisconsin
WMEV-FM Marion, Virginia
WMEW Waterville, Maine
WMEZ Pensacola, Florida
WMFC Monroeville, Alabama
WMFD Mansfield, Ohio
WMFE-FM Orlando, Florida
WMFG-FM Hibbing, Minnesota
WMFL Florida City, Florida
WMFM Key West, Florida
WMFO Medford, Massachusetts
WMFQ Ocala, Florida
WMFS-FM Bartlett, Tennessee
WMFT Tuscaloosa, Alabama
WMFU(FM) Mount Hope, New York
WMFX St. Andrews, South Carolina
WMGA Kenova, West Virginia
WMGB Montezuma, Georgia
WMGC-FM Detroit, Michigan
WMGE Miami Beach, Florida
WMGF Mount Dora, Florida
WMGH-FM Tamaqua, Pennsylvania
WMGI Terre Haute, Indiana
WMGK Philadelphia, Pennsylvania
WMGL Ravenel, South Carolina
WMGM Atlantic City, New Jersey
WMGN Madison, Wisconsin
WMGP Hogansville, Georgia
WMGQ New Brunswick, New Jersey
WMGS Wilkes-Barre, Pennsylvania
WMGU Southern Pines, North Carolina
WMGV Newport, North Carolina
WMGX Portland, Maine
WMGZ Eatonton, Georgia
WMHB Waterville, Maine
WMHC South Hadley, Massachusetts
WMHI Cape Vincent, New York
WMHK Columbia, South Carolina
WMHN Webster, New York
WMHQ Malone, New York
WMHR Syracuse, New York
WMHS Pike Creek, Delaware
WMHT-FM Schenectady, New York
WMHU Cold Brook, New York
WMHW-FM Mount Pleasant, Michigan
WMHX Waunakee, Wisconsin
WMIA-FM Miami Beach, Florida
WMIB Fort Lauderdale, Florida
WMIE-FM Cocoa, Florida
WMIK-FM Middlesboro, Kentucky
WMIL-FM Waukesha, Wisconsin
WMIM Luna Pier, Michigan
WMIO Cabo Rojo, Puerto Rico
WMIS-FM Blackduck, Minnesota
WMIT Black Mountain, North Carolina
WMIX-FM Mount Vernon, Illinois
WMJC Richland, Michigan
WMJD Grundy, Virginia
WMJI Cleveland, Ohio
WMJJ Birmingham, Alabama
WMJK Clyde, Ohio
WMJL-FM Marion, Kentucky
WMJM Jeffersontown, Kentucky
WMJO Essexville, Michigan
WMJT McMillan, Michigan
WMJU Bude, Mississippi
WMJW Rosedale, Mississippi
WMJX Boston, Massachusetts
WMJY Biloxi, Mississippi
WMJZ-FM Gaylord, Michigan
WMKB Earlville, Illinois
WMKC Indian River, Michigan
WMKD Pickford, Michigan
WMKL Hammocks, Florida
WMKO Marco, Florida
WMKR Pana, Illinois
WMKS Clemmons, North Carolina
WMKV Reading, Ohio
WMKW Crossville, Tennessee
WMKX Brookville, Pennsylvania
WMKY Morehead, Kentucky
WMKZ Monticello, Kentucky
WMLJ Summersville, West Virginia
WMLL Bedford, New Hampshire
WMLN-FM Milton, Massachusetts
WMLQ Manistee, Michigan
WMLS Grand Marais, Minnesota
WMLU Farmville, Virginia
WMLV Butler, Alabama
WMLX St. Marys, Ohio
WMMA Nekoosa, Wisconsin
WMMC Marshall, Illinois
WMME-FM Augusta, Maine
WMMG-FM Brandenburg, Kentucky
WMMJ Bethesda, Maryland
WMMM-FM Verona, Wisconsin
WMMO Orlando, Florida
WMMQ Lansing, Michigan
WMMR Philadelphia, Pennsylvania
WMMS Cleveland, Ohio
WMMT Whitesburg, Kentucky
WMMX Dayton, Ohio
WMMY Boone, North Carolina
WMNA-FM Gretna, Virginia
WMNC-FM Morganton, North Carolina
WMNF Tampa, Florida
WMNG Christiansted, Virgin Islands
WMNP Block Island, Rhode Island
WMNR Monroe, Connecticut
WMNV Rupert, Vermont
WMNX Wilmington, North Carolina
WMOC Lumber City, Georgia
WMOD Bolivar, Tennessee
WMOI Monmouth, Illinois
WMOM Pentwater, Michigan
WMOO Derby Center, Vermont
WMOQ Bostwick, Georgia
WMOR-FM Morehead, Kentucky
WMOS Stonington, Connecticut
WMOT Murfreesboro, Tennessee
WMOV-FM Norfolk, Virginia
WMOZ Moose Lake, Minnesota
WMPG Gorham, Maine
WMPH Wilmington, Delaware
WMPI Scottsburg, Indiana
WMPN-FM Jackson, Mississippi
WMPR Jackson, Mississippi
WMPZ Harrison, Tennessee
WMQA-FM Minocqua, Wisconsin
WMQT-FM Ishpeming, Michigan
WMQZ Colchester, Illinois
WMRA Harrisonburg, Virginia
WMRF Huntingdon, Pennsylvania
WMRF-FM Lewistown, Pennsylvania
WMRG Albany, Georgia
WMRK-FM Shorter, Alabama
WMRL Lexington, Virginia
WMRN-FM Marion, Ohio
WMRQ-FM Waterbury, Connecticut
WMRR Muskegon Heights, Michigan
WMRS Monticello, Indiana
WMRT Marietta, Ohio
WMRV Dansville, New York
WMRX-FM Beaverton, Michigan
WMRY Crozet, Virginia
WMRZ Dawson, Georgia
WMSB Byhalia, Mississippi
WMSC Upper Montclair, New Jersey
WMSD Rose Township, Michigan
WMSE Milwaukee, Wisconsin
WMSI-FM Jackson, Mississippi
WMSJ Freeport, Maine
WMSK-FM Sturgis, Kentucky
WMSL Athens, Georgia
WMSO Quitman, Mississippi
WMSR-FM Collinwood, Tennessee
WMSS Middletown, Pennsylvania
WMSU Starkville, Mississippi
WMSV Starkville, Mississippi
WMTB-FM Emmitsburg, Maryland
WMTC-FM Vancleve, Kentucky
WMTD-FM Hinton, West Virginia
WMTE-FM Manistee, Michigan
WMTH Park Ridge, Illinois
WMTK Littleton, New Hampshire
WMTM-FM Moultrie, Georgia
WMTP Conway, Pennsylvania
WMTR-FM Archbold, Ohio
WMTS-FM Murfreesboro, Tennessee
WMTT Tioga, Pennsylvania
WMTU-FM Houghton, Michigan
WMTX Tampa, Florida
WMTY-FM Sweetwater, Tennessee
WMUA Amherst, Massachusetts
WMUB Oxford, Ohio
WMUC-FM College Park, Maryland
WMUF Henry, Tennessee
WMUH Allentown, Pennsylvania
WMUK Kalamazoo, Michigan
WMUL Huntington, West Virginia
WMUM-FM Cochran, Georgia
WMUS Muskegon, Michigan
WMUT Grenada, Mississippi
WMUV Brunswick, Georgia
WMUV Brunswick, Florida
WMUW Columbus, Mississippi
WMUZ Detroit, Michigan
WMVE Chase City, Virginia
WMVL Linesville, Pennsylvania
WMVM Goodman, Wisconsin
WMVN Sylvan Beach, New York
WMVR-FM Sidney, Ohio
WMVV Griffin, Georgia
WMVW Peachtree City, Georgia
WMWI Demopolis, Alabama
WMWK Milwaukee, Wisconsin
WMWM Salem, Massachusetts
WMWV Conway, New Hampshire
WMWX Miamitown, Ohio
WMXA Opelika, Alabama
WMXC Mobile, Alabama
WMXD Detroit, Michigan
WMXE South Charleston, West Virginia
WMXG Stephenson, Michigan
WMXH-FM Luray, Virginia
WMXI Laurel, Mississippi
WMXJ Pompano Beach, Florida
WMXK Morristown, Tennessee
WMXL Lexington, Kentucky
WMXM Lake Forest, Illinois
WMXN-FM Stevenson, Alabama
WMXO Olean, New York
WMXQ Hartford City, Indiana
WMXS Montgomery, Alabama
WMXT Pamplico, South Carolina
WMXU Starkville, Mississippi

WMXV St. Joseph, Tennessee
WMXW Vestal, New York
WMXX-FM Jackson, Tennessee
WMXY Youngstown, Ohio
WMXZ Isle of Palms, South Carolina
WMYB Myrtle Beach, South Carolina
WMYE Fort Myers, Florida
WMYI Hendersonville, North Carolina
WMYJ-FM Bloomfield, Indiana
WMYK Peru, Indiana
WMYL Halls Crossroads, Tennessee
WMYP Frederiksted, Virgin Islands
WMYQ South Whitley, Indiana
WMYT Carolina Beach, North Carolina
WMYV Hartford, Vermont
WMYX-FM Milwaukee, Wisconsin
WMYY Schoharie, New York
WMYZ Clermont, Florida
WMZK Merrill, Wisconsin
WMZQ-FM Washington, District of Columbia
WNAA Greensboro, North Carolina
WNAN Nantucket, Massachusetts
WNAS New Albany, Indiana
WNAX-FM Yankton, South Dakota
WNBB Bayboro, North Carolina
WNBK Whitmire, South Carolina
WNBL South Bristol Township, New York
WNBQ Mansfield, Pennsylvania
WNBR-FM Bethel, North Carolina
WNBT-FM Wellsboro, Pennsylvania
WNBU(FM) Oriental, North Carolina
WNBV Grundy, Virginia
WNBY-FM Newberry, Michigan
WNCB Cary, North Carolina
WNCC Franklin, North Carolina
WNCD Youngstown, Ohio
WNCH Norwich, Vermont
WNCI Columbus, Ohio
WNCK Nantucket, Massachusetts
WNCL Milford, Delaware
WNCO-FM Ashland, Ohio
WNCQ-FM Canton, New York
WNCS Montpelier, Vermont
WNCT-FM Greenville, North Carolina
WNCU Durham, North Carolina
WNCV Shalimar, Florida
WNCW Spindale, North Carolina
WNCX Cleveland, Ohio
WNCY Neenah-Menasha, Wisconsin
WNDD Silver Springs, Florida
WNDH Napoleon, Ohio
WNDI-FM Sullivan, Indiana
WNDN Chiefland, Florida
WNDR-FM Mexico, New York
WNDT Alachua, Florida
WNDV-FM South Bend, Indiana
WNDY Crawfordsville, Indiana
WNEC-FM Henniker, New Hampshire
WNED-FM Buffalo, New York
WNEE Patterson, Georgia
WNEF Newburyport, Massachusetts
WNEK-FM Springfield, Massachusetts
WNEV Friars Point, Mississippi
WNEW Bowie, District of Columbia
WNFA Port Huron, Michigan
WNFB Lake City, Florida
WNFC Paducah, Kentucky
WNFK Perry, Florida
WNFM Reedsburg, Wisconsin
WNFN Millersville, Tennessee
WNFR Sandusky, Michigan
WNFZ Powell, Tennessee
WNGA Clermont, Georgia
WNGB Petersham, Massachusetts
WNGC Arcade, Georgia
WNGE Negaunee, Michigan
WNGF Swanton, Vermont
WNGH-FM Chatsworth, Georgia
WNGM(FM) Tallulah Falls, Georgia
WNGM(FM) Tallulah Falls, Georgia
WNGN Argyle, New York
WNGU Dahlonega, Georgia
WNGY Morton, Illinois
WNGZ Montour Falls, New York
WNHI Farmington, New Hampshire
WNHT Churubusco, Indiana
WNHU West Haven, Connecticut
WNHW Belmont, New Hampshire
WNIC Dearborn, Michigan
WNIE Freeport, Illinois
WNIJ Dekalb, Illinois
WNIK-FM Arecibo, Puerto Rico
WNIN-FM Evansville, Indiana
WNIQ Sterling, Illinois
WNIR Kent, Ohio
WNIU Rockford, Illinois
WNIW La Salle, Illinois
WNJA Jamestown, New York
WNJB-FM Bridgeton, New Jersey
WNJM Manahawkin, New Jersey
WNJN-FM Atlantic City, New Jersey
WNJO Toms River, New Jersey
WNJP Sussex, New Jersey
WNJR Washington, Pennsylvania
WNJS-FM Berlin, New Jersey
WNJT-FM Trenton, New Jersey
WNJY Netcong, New Jersey
WNJZ Cape May Court House, New Jersey
WNKE New Boston, Ohio
WNKI Corning, New York
WNKJ Hopkinsville, Kentucky
WNKL Wauseon, Ohio
WNKN Middletown, Ohio
WNKO New Albany, Ohio
WNKR Williamstown, Kentucky
WNKS Charlotte, North Carolina
WNKT Eastover, South Carolina
WNKU Highland Heights, Kentucky
WNKV Norco, Louisiana
WNKX-FM Centerville, Tennessee
WNLC East Lyme, Connecticut
WNLF Macomb, Illinois
WNLI Sturgeon Bay, Wisconsin
WNLT Delhi Hills, Ohio
WNMC-FM Traverse City, Michigan
WNML Friendsville, Tennessee
WNMQ Columbus, Mississippi
WNMR Dannemora, New York
WNMU-FM Marquette, Michigan
WNMX Christiansburg, Virginia
WNND Pickerington, Ohio
WNNF Cincinnati, Ohio
WNNG-FM Unadilla, Georgia
WNNH Henniker, New Hampshire
WNNJ Newton, New Jersey
WNNK Harrisburg, Pennsylvania
WNNL Fuquay-Varina, North Carolina
WNNO Wisconsin Dells, Wisconsin
WNNP Richwood, Ohio
WNNS Springfield, Illinois
WNNT-FM Warsaw, Virginia
WNNV San German, Puerto Rico
WNNX College Park, Georgia
WNNZ-FM Westfield, Massachusetts
WNOB Chesapeake, Virginia
WNOC Bowling Green, Ohio
WNOD Mayaguez, Puerto Rico
WNOE-FM New Orleans, Louisiana
WNOH Windsor, Virginia
WNOI Flora, Illinois
WNOK Columbia, South Carolina
WNON Warfield, Kentucky
WNOR Norfolk, Virginia
WNOW Speedway, Indiana
WNOX Karns, Tennessee
WNPQ New Philadelphia, Ohio
WNPR Meriden, Connecticut
WNPT-FM Marion, Alabama
WNRK Norwalk, Ohio
WNRN Charlottesville, Virginia
WNRQ Nashville, Tennessee
WNRS-FM Sweet Briar, Virginia
WNRT Manati, Puerto Rico
WNRW Salem, Indiana
WNRX Jefferson City, Tennessee
WNRZ Dickson, Tennessee
WNSB Norfolk, Virginia
WNSC-FM Rock Hill, South Carolina
WNSH Newark, New Jersey
WNSL Laurel, Mississippi
WNSN South Bend, Indiana
WNSP Bay Minette, Alabama
WNSV Nashville, Illinois
WNSX Winter Harbor, Maine
WNSY Talking Rock, Georgia
WNTB Topsail Beach, North Carolina
WNTC Drakesboro, Kentucky
WNTE Mansfield, Pennsylvania
WNTH Winnetka, Illinois
WNTI Hackettstown, New Jersey
WNTK-FM New London, New Hampshire
WNTO Racine, Ohio
WNTQ Syracuse, New York
WNTR Indianapolis, Indiana
WNUB-FM Northfield, Vermont
WNUE-FM Deltona, Florida
WNUQ Sylvester, Georgia
WNUR-FM Evanston, Illinois
WNUS Belpre, Ohio
WNUZ Mercersburg, Pennsylvania
WNVM Cidra, Puerto Rico
WNVZ Norfolk, Virginia
WNWC-FM Madison, Wisconsin
WNWN-FM Coldwater, Michigan
WNWS-FM Jackson, Tennessee
WNWV Elyria, Ohio
WNXR Iron River, Wisconsin
WNXT-FM Portsmouth, Ohio
WNXX Jackson, Louisiana
WNYC-FM New York, New York
WNYE New York, New York
WNYK Nyack, New York
WNYN-FM Whitefield, New Hampshire
WNYO Oswego, New York
WNYQ Hudson Falls, New York
WNYR Waterloo, New York
WNYU-FM New York, New York
WNYV Whitehall, New York
WNZN Lorain, Ohio
WNZR Mount Vernon, Ohio
WOAB Ozark, Alabama
WOAH Glennville, Georgia
WOAK La Grange, Georgia
WOAR South Vienna, Ohio
WOAS Ontonagon, Michigan
WOBB Tifton, Georgia
WOBC-FM Oberlin, Ohio
WOBE Crystal Falls, Michigan
WOBG-FM Salem, West Virginia
WOBM-FM Toms River, New Jersey
WOBN Westerville, Ohio
WOBO Batavia, Ohio
WOBR-FM Wanchese, North Carolina
WOBX-FM Manteo, North Carolina
WOCE Ringgold, Georgia
WOCL Deland, Florida
WOCM Selbyville, Delaware
WOCN-FM Orleans, Massachusetts
WOCO-FM Oconto, Wisconsin
WOCQ Berlin, Maryland
WOCR Olivet, Michigan
WOCY Carrabelle, Florida
WODA Bayamon, Puerto Rico
WODC Ashville, Ohio
WODE-FM Easton, Pennsylvania
WODR Fair Bluff, North Carolina
WODS Boston, Massachusetts
WODZ-FM Rome, New York
WOEL-FM Elkton, Maryland
WOES Ovid-Elsie, Michigan
WOFN Beach City, Ohio
WOFR Schoolcraft, Michigan
WOFX-FM Cincinnati, Ohio
WOGB Reedsville, Wisconsin
WOGG Oliver, Pennsylvania
WOGH Burgettstown, Pennsylvania
WOGI Moon Township, Pennsylvania
WOGK Ocala, Florida
WOGL Philadelphia, Pennsylvania
WOGR-FM Salisbury, North Carolina
WOGT East Ridge, Tennessee
WOGY Jackson, Tennessee
WOHA Ashtabula, Ohio
WOHC Chillicothe, Ohio
WOHF Bellevue, Ohio
WOHT Grenada, Mississippi
WOI-FM Ames, Iowa
WOJB Reserve, Wisconsin
WOJC Crothersville, Indiana
WOJG Bolivar, Tennessee
WOJL Louisa, Virginia
WOJO Evanston, Illinois
WOKA-FM Douglas, Georgia
WOKD-FM Danville, Virginia
WOKE Garrison, Kentucky
WOKG Galax, Virginia
WOKI Oliver Springs, Tennessee
WOKK Meridian, Mississippi
WOKN Southport, New York
WOKO Burlington, Vermont
WOKQ Dover, New Hampshire
WOKR Remsen, New York
WOKV-FM Atlantic Beach, Florida
WOKW Curwensville, Pennsylvania
WOKZ Fairfield, Illinois
WOLC Princess Anne, Maryland
WOLD-FM Marion, Virginia
WOLF-FM DeRuyter, New York
WOLF-FM DeRuyter, New York
WOLG Carlinville, Illinois
WOLI-FM Easley, South Carolina
WOLL Hobe Sound, Florida
WOLN Olean, New York
WOLR Lake City, Florida
WOLS Waxhaw, North Carolina
WOLT Indianapolis, South Carolina
WOLV Houghton, Michigan
WOLW Cadillac, Michigan
WOLX-FM Baraboo, Wisconsin
WOLZ Fort Myers, Florida
WOMC Detroit, Michigan
WOMG Lexington, South Carolina
WOMR Provincetown, Massachusetts
WOMX Orlando, Florida
WONA-FM Winona, Mississippi
WONB Ada, Ohio
WONC Naperville, Illinois
WONE-FM Akron, Ohio
WONU Kankakee, Illinois
WONY Oneonta, New York
WOOD-FM Muskegon, Michigan
WOOF-FM Dothan, Alabama
WOOZ-FM Harrisburg, Illinois
WOPC Linden, Tennessee
WORC Webster, Massachusetts
WORD-FM Pittsburgh, Pennsylvania
WORG Elloree, South Carolina
WORI Harrison, Ohio
WORM-FM Savannah, Tennessee
WORO Corozal, Puerto Rico
WORQ Green Bay, Wisconsin
WORT Madison, Wisconsin
WORW Port Huron, Michigan
WORX-FM Madison, Indiana
WOSA Grove City, Ohio
WOSB Marion, Ohio
WOSE Coshocton, Ohio
WOSF Gaffney, South Carolina
WOSL Norwood, Ohio
WOSM Ocean Springs, Mississippi
WOSN Indian River Shores, Florida
WOSP Portsmouth, Ohio
WOSQ Spencer, Wisconsin
WOSR Middletown, New York
WOSS Ossining, New York
WOSU-FM Columbus, Ohio
WOSV Mansfield, Ohio
WOTC Edinburg, Virginia
WOTJ Morehead City, North Carolina
WOTL Toledo, Ohio
WOTR(FM) Lost Creek, West Virginia
WOTT Calcium, New York
WOTW Windermere, Florida
WOTX Lunenburg, Vermont
WOUB-FM Athens, Ohio
WOUC-FM Cambridge, Ohio
WOUF Beulah, Michigan
WOUH-FM Chillicothe, Ohio
WOUL-FM Ironton, Ohio
WOUR Utica, New York
WOUZ-FM Zanesville, Ohio
WOVI Novi, Michigan
WOVK Wheeling, West Virginia
WOVM Appleton, Wisconsin
WOVO Horse Cave, Kentucky
WOVV Ocracoke, North Carolina
WOWB Brewton, Alabama
WOWC Morrison, Tennessee
WOWE Vassar, Michigan
WOWF Crossville, Tennessee
WOWI Norfolk, Virginia
WOWL Burnsville, Mississippi
WOWN Shawano, Wisconsin
WOWO-FM Fort Wayne, Indiana
WOWQ Du Bois, Pennsylvania
WOWY University Park, Pennsylvania
WOXD Oxford, Mississippi
WOXL-FM Biltmore Forest, North Carolina
WOXM Middlebury, Vermont
WOXO-FM Norway, Maine
WOXR Schuyler Falls, New York
WOXY Mason, Ohio
WOYE Rio Grande, Puerto Rico
WOYS Apalachicola, Florida

WOZI Presque Isle, Maine
WOZN-FM Mount Horeb, Wisconsin
WOZQ Northampton, Massachusetts
WOZZ Mosinee, Wisconsin
WPAC Ogdensburg, New York
WPAE Centreville, Mississippi
WPAI Nanty Glo, Pennsylvania
WPAL Laporte, Pennsylvania
WPAL(FM) Laporte, Pennsylvania
WPAP Panama City, Florida
WPAR Salem, Virginia
WPAS Pascagoula, Mississippi
WPAT-FM Paterson, New Jersey
WPAW Winston-Salem, North Carolina
WPBD Lewes, Delaware
WPBG Peoria, Illinois
WPBI(FM) West Palm Beach, Florida
WPBK Crab Orchard, Kentucky
WPBX Crossville, Tennessee
WPCD Champaign, Illinois
WPCJ Pittsford, Michigan
WPCK Denmark, Wisconsin
WPCL Northern Cambria, Pennsylvania
WPCN(FM) Point Pleasant, West Virginia
WPCR-FM Plymouth, New Hampshire
WPCS Pensacola, Florida
WPCV Winter Haven, Florida
WPDA Jeffersonville, New York
WPDH Poughkeepsie, New York
WPDI Hazlet, New Jersey
WPDT Coward, South Carolina
WPDX-FM Clarksburg, West Virginia
WPEA Exeter, New Hampshire
WPEB Philadelphia, Pennsylvania
WPEF Kentwood, Louisiana
WPEG Concord, North Carolina
WPEH-FM Louisville, Georgia
WPEI Saco, Maine
WPEL Montrose, Pennsylvania
WPEN-FM Burlington, New Jersey
WPER Culpeper, Virginia
WPEZ Jeffersonville, Georgia
WPFF Sturgeon Bay, Wisconsin
WPFL Century, Florida
WPFM-FM Panama City, Florida
WPFR-FM Clinton, Indiana
WPFT Pigeon Forge, Tennessee
WPFW Washington, District of Columbia
WPFX-FM Luckey, Ohio
WPGA-FM Perry, Georgia
WPGB Pittsburgh, Pennsylvania
WPGC Morningside, District of Columbia
WPGI Horseheads, New York
WPGL Pattersonville, New York
WPGM Danville, Pennsylvania
WPGU Urbana, Illinois
WPGW-FM Portland, Indiana
WPHD South Waverly, Pennsylvania
WPHI-FM Pennsauken, New Jersey
WPHK Blountstown, Florida
WPHN Gaylord, Michigan
WPHP Wheeling, West Virginia
WPHR-FM Gifford, Florida
WPHS Warren, Michigan
WPHZ Orleans, Indiana
WPIA Eureka, Illinois
WPIB Bluefield, West Virginia
WPIG Olean, New York
WPIK Summerland Key, Florida
WPIL Heflin, Alabama
WPIM Martinsville, Virginia
WPIN-FM Dublin, Virginia
WPIO Titusville, Florida
WPIR Hickory, North Carolina
WPJC Pontiac, Illinois
WPJN Jemison, Alabama
WPJP Port Washington, Wisconsin
WPJW Hurricane, West Virginia
WPJY Blennerhassett, West Virginia
WPKE-FM Coal Run, Kentucky
WPKF Poughkeepsie, New York
WPKG Neillsville, Wisconsin
WPKL Uniontown, Pennsylvania
WPKN Bridgeport, Connecticut
WPKO-FM Bellefontaine, Ohio
WPKQ North Conway, New Hampshire
WPKR Omro, Wisconsin
WPKT Norwich, Connecticut
WPLB Plattsburgh West, New York
WPLH Tifton, Georgia
WPLJ New York, New York
WPLL Cross City, Florida
WPLM-FM Plymouth, Massachusetts
WPLN-FM Nashville, Tennessee
WPLR New Haven, Connecticut
WPLT Sarona, Wisconsin
WPLW Hillsborough, North Carolina
WPLZ Ooltewah, Tennessee
WPMA Greensboro, Georgia
WPMJ Chillicothe, Illinois
WPMW Bayview, Massachusetts
WPMX Statesboro, Georgia
WPNC-FM Plymouth, North Carolina
WPNE-FM Green Bay, Wisconsin
WPNH-FM Plymouth, New Hampshire
WPNR-FM Utica, New York
WPOB Plainview, New York
WPOC Baltimore, Maryland
WPOI St. Petersburg, Florida
WPOR Portland, Maine
WPOS-FM Holland, Ohio
WPOW Miami, Florida
WPOZ Union Park, Florida
WPPB Southampton, New York
WPPG Repton, Alabama
WPPI Topsham, Maine
WPPL Blue Ridge, Georgia
WPPN Des Plaines, Illinois
WPPR Demorest, Georgia
WPPZ-FM Jenkintown, Pennsylvania
WPRB Princeton, New Jersey
WPRC Sheffield, Illinois
WPRF Reserve, Louisiana
WPRG Columbia, Mississippi
WPRH Paris, Tennessee
WPRJ Coleman, Michigan
WPRK Winter Park, Florida
WPRL Lorman, Mississippi
WPRM-FM San Juan, Puerto Rico
WPRO Providence, Rhode Island
WPRR-FM Clyde Township, Michigan
WPRS-FM Waldorf, Maryland
WPRT-FM Pegram, Tennessee
WPRW-FM Martinez, Georgia
WPRZ-FM Brandy Station, Virginia
WPSC-FM Wayne, New Jersey
WPSF Clewiston, Florida
WPSK-FM Pulaski, Virginia
WPSM Fort Walton Beach, Florida
WPSR Evansville, Indiana
WPST Trenton, New Jersey
WPSU State College, Pennsylvania
WPSX Kane, Pennsylvania
WPTC Williamsport, Pennsylvania
WPTE Virginia Beach, Virginia
WPTH Olney, Illinois
WPTI Eden, North Carolina
WPTJ Paris, Kentucky
WPTM Roanoke Rapids, North Carolina
WPTQ Glasgow, Kentucky
WPTS-FM Pittsburgh, Pennsylvania
WPTY Calverton-Roanoke, New York
WPUB-FM Camden, South Carolina
WPUC-FM Ponce, Puerto Rico
WPUM Rensselaer, Indiana
WPUP Watkinsville, Georgia
WPUR Atlantic City, New Jersey
WPVA Waynesboro, Virginia
WPVL-FM Platteville, Wisconsin
WPVQ Greenfield, Massachusetts
WPWB Byron, Georgia
WPWQ Mount Sterling, Illinois
WPWV Princeton, West Virginia
WPWX Hammond, Indiana
WPWZ Pinetops, North Carolina
WPXC Hyannis, Massachusetts
WPXN Paxton, Illinois
WPXY-FM Rochester, New York
WPXZ-FM Punxsutawney, Pennsylvania
WPYO Maitland, Florida
WPYX Albany, New York
WPZE Mableton, Georgia
WPZR Mount Clemens, Michigan
WPZS Harrisburg, North Carolina
WPZX Pocono Pines, Pennsylvania
WPZZ Crewe, Virginia
WQAB Philippi, West Virginia
WQAC Alma, Michigan
WQAH-FM Addison, Alabama
WQAI Thomson, Georgia
WQAK Union City, Tennessee
WQAL Cleveland, Ohio
WQAQ Hamden, Connecticut
WQBB Pascagoula, Mississippi
WQBE-FM Charleston, West Virginia
WQBJ Cobleskill, New York
WQBK-FM Rensselaer, New York
WQBR Avis, Pennsylvania
WQBT Savannah, Georgia
WQBU-FM Garden City, New York
WQBX Fowler, Michigan
WQBZ Fort Valley, Georgia
WQCB Brewer, Maine
WQCC La Crosse, Wisconsin
WQCK(FM) Philipsburg, Pennsylvania
WQCM Greencastle, Pennsylvania
WQCS Fort Pierce, Florida
WQCY Quincy, Illinois
WQDC Sturgeon Bay, Wisconsin
WQDK Gatesville, North Carolina
WQDR-FM Raleigh, North Carolina
WQDY-FM Calais, Maine
WQED-FM Pittsburgh, Pennsylvania
WQEJ Johnstown, Pennsylvania
WQEL Bucyrus, Ohio
WQEM Columbiana, Alabama
WQEN Trussville, Alabama
WQFL Rockford, Illinois
WQFS Greensboro, North Carolina
WQFX-FM Russell, Pennsylvania
WQGA Waycross, Georgia
WQGN-FM Groton, Connecticut
WQHH DeWitt, Michigan
WQHK-FM Huntertown, Indiana
WQHL-FM Live Oak, Florida
WQHQ Ocean City-Salisbury, Maryland
WQHR Presque Isle, Maine
WQHT New York, New York
WQHY Prestonsburg, Kentucky
WQHZ Erie, Pennsylvania
WQIC Lebanon, Pennsylvania
WQIK-FM Jacksonville, Florida
WQIL Chauncey, Georgia
WQIO Mount Vernon, Ohio
WQIQ Spotsylvania, Virginia
WQJB State College, Mississippi
WQJQ Barton, Vermont
WQJU Mifflintown, Pennsylvania
WQKE Plattsburgh, New York
WQKI-FM Orangeburg, South Carolina
WQKK(FM) Renovo, Pennsylvania
WQKL Ann Arbor, Michigan
WQKO Howe, Indiana
WQKQ Carthage, Illinois
WQKS-FM Montgomery, Alabama
WQKT Wooster, Ohio
WQKV Warsaw, Indiana
WQKX Sunbury, Pennsylvania
WQKY Emporium, Pennsylvania
WQKZ Ferdinand, Indiana
WQLB Tawas City, Michigan
WQLC Watertown, Florida
WQLF Lena, Illinois
WQLH Green Bay, Wisconsin
WQLI Meigs, Georgia
WQLJ Oxford, Mississippi
WQLK Richmond, Indiana
WQLN-FM Erie, Pennsylvania
WQLQ Benton Harbor, Michigan
WQLS Camden, Alabama
WQLT-FM Florence, Alabama
WQLU Lynchburg, Virginia
WQLV Millersburg, Pennsylvania
WQLX Chillicothe, Ohio
WQLZ Petersburg, Illinois
WQME Anderson, Indiana
WQMF Jeffersonville, Indiana
WQMG Greensboro, North Carolina
WQMJ Forsyth, Georgia
WQML Ceiba, Puerto Rico
WQMU Indiana, Pennsylvania
WQMX Medina, Ohio
WQMZ Charlottesville, Virginia
WQNA Springfield, Illinois
WQNC Harrisburg, North Carolina
WQNQ Fletcher, North Carolina
WQNR Tallassee, Alabama
WQNS Waynesville, North Carolina
WQNU Lyndon, Kentucky
WQNY Ithaca, New York
WQNZ Natchez, Mississippi
WQOK Carrboro, North Carolina
WQOL Vero Beach, Florida
WQON Grayling, Michigan
WQOX Memphis, Tennessee
WQPC Prairie Du Chien, Wisconsin
WQPO Harrisonburg, Virginia
WQPR Muscle Shoals, Alabama
WQPW Valdosta, Georgia
WQQB Rantoul, Illinois
WQQK Goodlettsville, Tennessee
WQQL Sherman, Illinois
WQQQ Sharon, Connecticut
WQQR Clinton, Kentucky
WQRA Greencastle, Indiana
WQRB Bloomer, Wisconsin
WQRC Barnstable, Massachusetts
WQRI Bristol, Rhode Island
WQRK Bedford, Indiana
WQRL Benton, Illinois
WQRN Cook, Minnesota
WQRP Dayton, Ohio
WQRS Salamanca, New York
WQRV Meridianville, Alabama
WQRW Wellsville, New York
WQSB Albertville, Alabama
WQSG Lafayette, Indiana
WQSH Malta, New York
WQSI Tuskegee, Alabama
WQSK Madison, Maine
WQSL Jacksonville, North Carolina
WQSM Fayetteville, North Carolina
WQSO Rochester, New Hampshire
WQSR Baltimore, Maryland
WQSS Camden, Maine
WQST Forest, Mississippi
WQSU Selinsgrove, Pennsylvania
WQTC-FM Manitowoc, Wisconsin
WQTE Adrian, Michigan
WQTK Ogdensburg, New York
WQTL Tallahassee, Florida
WQTQ Hartford, Connecticut
WQTU Rome, Georgia
WQTX St. Johns, Michigan
WQTY Linton, Indiana
WQUA Citronelle, Alabama
WQUB Quincy, Illinois
WQUE-FM New Orleans, Louisiana
WQUS Lapeer, Michigan
WQUT Johnson City, Tennessee
WQVE Albany, Georgia
WQVI Madison, Mississippi
WQWV Fisher, West Virginia
WQXA York, Pennsylvania
WQXB Grenada, Mississippi
WQXC-FM Otsego, Michigan
WQXE Elizabethtown, Kentucky
WQXJ Blackduck, Minnesota
WQXK Salem, Ohio
WQXQ Central City, Kentucky
WQXR-FM Newark, New Jersey
WQXW Ossining, New York
WQXZ Hawkinsville, Georgia
WQYK-FM St. Petersburg, Florida
WQYX Clearfield, Pennsylvania
WQYZ Ocean Springs, Mississippi
WQZK-FM Keyser, West Virginia
WQZL Belhaven, North Carolina
WQZQ-FM Goodlettsville, Tennessee
WQZS Meyersdale, Pennsylvania
WQZX Greenville, Alabama
WQZY Dublin, Georgia
WQZZ Boligee, Alabama
WRAC Georgetown, Ohio
WRAE Raeford, North Carolina
WRAF Toccoa Falls, Georgia
WRAL Raleigh, North Carolina
WRAN Taylorville, Illinois
WRAO Wisconsin Rapids, Wisconsin
WRAR-FM Tappahannock, Virginia
WRAS Atlanta, Georgia
WRAT Point Pleasant, New Jersey
WRAU Ocean City, Maryland
WRAX Lake Isabella, Michigan
WRAY-FM Princeton, Indiana
WRAZ-FM Leisure City, Florida
WRBA Springfield, Florida
WRBB Boston, Massachusetts
WRBC Lewiston, Maine
WRBE-FM Lucedale, Mississippi
WRBF Plainville, Georgia
WRBH New Orleans, Louisiana
WRBI Batesville, Indiana
WRBJ Brandon, Mississippi

WRBK Richburg, South Carolina
WRBN Clayton, Georgia
WRBO Como, Mississippi
WRBQ-FM Tampa, Florida
WRBR-FM South Bend, Indiana
WRBS-FM Baltimore, Maryland
WRBT Harrisburg, Pennsylvania
WRBV Warner Robins, Georgia
WRBX Reidsville, Georgia
WRCC Dibrell, Tennessee
WRCD Canton, New York
WRCH New Britain, Connecticut
WRCJ-FM Detroit, Michigan
WRCL Frankenmuth, Michigan
WRCM Wingate, North Carolina
WRCN-FM Riverhead, New York
WRCO-FM Richland Center, Wisconsin
WRCQ Dunn, North Carolina
WRCT Pittsburgh, Pennsylvania
WRCT(FM) Pittsburgh, Pennsylvania
WRCU-FM Hamilton, New York
WRCV Dixon, Illinois
WRDA-FM Canton, Georgia
WRDG Peachtree City, Georgia
WRDI Nappanee, Indiana
WRDK Bladenboro, North Carolina
WRDL Ashland, Ohio
WRDO Fitzgerald, Georgia
WRDR Freehold Township, New Jersey
WRDU Wake Forest, North Carolina
WRDV Warminster, Pennsylvania
WRDX Smyrna, Delaware
WRDZ-FM Plainfield, Indiana
WREB Greencastle, Indiana
WREH Cypress Quarters, Florida
WREK Atlanta, Georgia
WREM Canton, New York
WREO-FM Ashtabula, Ohio
WREZ Metropolis, Illinois
WRFE Chesterfield, South Carolina
WRFF Philadelphia, Pennsylvania
WRFG Atlanta, Georgia
WRFI Watkins Glen, New York
WRFK Barre, Vermont
WRFL Lexington, Kentucky
WRFQ Mount Pleasant, South Carolina
WRFT Indianapolis, Indiana
WRFW River Falls, Wisconsin
WRFX Kannapolis, North Carolina
WRFY-FM Reading, Pennsylvania
WRGC-FM Milledgeville, Georgia
WRGF Greenfield, Indiana
WRGN Sweet Valley, Pennsylvania
WRGO Cedar Key, Florida
WRGP Homestead, Florida
WRGR Tupper Lake, New York
WRGV Pensacola, Florida
WRGZ Rogers City, Michigan
WRHD Farmville, North Carolina
WRHK Danville, Illinois
WRHL-FM Rochelle, Illinois
WRHM Lancaster, South Carolina
WRHN Rhinelander, Wisconsin
WRHO Oneonta, New York
WRHQ Richmond Hill, Georgia
WRHT Morehead City, North Carolina
WRHU Hempstead, New York
WRHV Poughkeepsie, New York
WRIC-FM Richlands, Virginia
WRIF Detroit, Michigan
WRIH Richmond, Virginia
WRIJ Masontown, Pennsylvania
WRIL Pineville, Kentucky
WRIO Ponce, Puerto Rico
WRIP Windham, New York
WRIQ Lexington, Virginia
WRIT-FM Milwaukee, Wisconsin
WRIU Kingston, Rhode Island
WRIX-FM Honea Path, South Carolina
WRJA-FM Sumter, South Carolina
WRJB Camden, Tennessee
WRJC-FM Mauston, Wisconsin
WRJJ La Center, Kentucky
WRJL-FM Eva, Alabama
WRJO Eagle River, Wisconsin
WRJT Royalton, Vermont
WRJY Brunswick, Georgia
WRKA Louisville, Kentucky
WRKC Wilkes-Barre, Pennsylvania
WRKF Baton Rouge, Louisiana
WRKH Mobile, Alabama
WRKI Brookfield, Connecticut
WRKJ Westbrook, Maine
WRKN LaPlace, Louisiana
WRKR Portage, Michigan
WRKS Pickens, Mississippi
WRKT North East, Pennsylvania
WRKU Forestville, Wisconsin
WRKW Ebensburg, Pennsylvania
WRKX Ottawa, Illinois
WRKY-FM Hollidaysburg, Pennsylvania
WRKZ Columbus, Ohio
WRLB Rainelle, West Virginia
WRLC Williamsport, Pennsylvania
WRLD Valley, Alabama
WRLF Fairmont, West Virginia
WRLI-FM Southampton, New York
WRLN Rushville, Indiana
WRLO-FM Antigo, Wisconsin
WRLS-FM Hayward, Wisconsin
WRLT Franklin, Tennessee
WRLU Algoma, Wisconsin
WRLV-FM Salyersville, Kentucky
WRLX West Palm Beach, Florida
WRMA Fort Lauderdale, Florida
WRMB Boynton Beach, Florida
WRMC-FM Middlebury, Vermont
WRMF Palm Beach, Florida
WRMJ Aledo, Illinois
WRMM-FM Rochester, New York
WRMO Milbridge, Maine
WRMR Jacksonville, North Carolina
WRMS-FM Beardstown, Illinois
WRMU-FM Alliance, Ohio
WRNB Media, Pennsylvania
WRNF Selma, Alabama
WRNI-FM Narragansett Pier, Rhode Island
WRNN-FM Socastee, South Carolina
WRNO-FM New Orleans, Louisiana
WRNQ Poughkeepsie, New York
WRNR-FM Grasonville, Maryland
WRNS-FM Kinston, North Carolina
WRNW Milwaukee, Wisconsin
WRNX Amherst, Massachusetts
WRNZ Lancaster, Kentucky
WROI Rochester, Indiana
WROK-FM Macon, Georgia
WRON-FM Lewisburg, West Virginia
WROQ Anderson, South Carolina
WROR-FM Framingham, Massachusetts
WROU-FM West Carrollton, Ohio
WROV-FM Martinsville, Virginia
WROX-FM Exmore, Virginia
WROZ Lancaster, Pennsylvania
WRPB Benedicta, Maine
WRPI Troy, New York
WRPJ Port Jervis, New York
WRPN-FM Ripon, Wisconsin
WRPR Mahwah, New Jersey
WRPS Rockland, Massachusetts
WRPW Colfax, Illinois
WRQK-FM Canton, Ohio
WRQM Rocky Mount, North Carolina
WRQN Bowling Green, Ohio
WRQO Monticello, Mississippi
WRQQ Hammond, Louisiana
WRQT La Crosse, Wisconsin
WRQX Washington, District of Columbia
WRQY-FM Bellaire, Ohio
WRR Dallas, Texas
WRRB Arlington, New York
WRRC Lawrenceville, New Jersey
WRRG River Grove, Illinois
WRRH Hormigueros, Puerto Rico
WRRK Braddock, Pennsylvania
WRRM Cincinnati, Ohio
WRRN Warren, Pennsylvania
WRRR-FM St. Marys, West Virginia
WRRV Middletown, New York
WRRX Gulf Breeze, Florida
WRSA-FM Holly Pond, Alabama
WRSC-FM State College, Pennsylvania
WRSD Folsom, Pennsylvania
WRSE Elmhurst, Illinois
WRSF Columbia, North Carolina
WRSG Middlebourne, West Virginia
WRSH Rockingham, North Carolina
WRSI Turners Falls, Massachusetts
WRSN Lebanon, Tennessee
WRSR Owosso, Michigan
WRST-FM Oshkosh, Wisconsin
WRSU-FM New Brunswick, New Jersey
WRSV Elm City, North Carolina
WRSW Niles, Michigan
WRSW-FM Warsaw, Indiana
WRSY Marlboro, Vermont
WRTB Winnebago, Illinois
WRTC-FM Hartford, Connecticut
WRTE Chicago, Illinois
WRTH-FM Greer, 0
WRTI Philadelphia, Pennsylvania
WRTI Ephrata, Pennsylvania
WRTI Coatesville, Pennsylvania
WRTK Paxton, Illinois
WRTM-FM Sharon, Mississippi
WRTO-FM Goulds, Florida
WRTP Franklinton, North Carolina
WRTQ Ocean City, New Jersey
WRTR Brookwood, Alabama
WRTS Erie, Pennsylvania
WRTT-FM Huntsville, Alabama
WRTU San Juan, Puerto Rico
WRTW Crown Point, Indiana
WRTX Dover, Delaware
WRTY Jackson Township, Pennsylvania
WRUC Schenectady, New York
WRUF-FM Gainesville, Florida
WRUL Carmi, Illinois
WRUM Orlando, Florida
WRUN Remsen, New York
WRUO Mayaguez, Puerto Rico
WRUP Palmer, Michigan
WRUR-FM Rochester, New York
WRUV Burlington, Vermont
WRUW-FM Cleveland, Ohio
WRVB Marietta, Ohio
WRVD Syracuse, New York
WRVE Schenectady, New York
WRVF Toledo, Ohio
WRVH Clayton, New York
WRVJ Watertown, New York
WRVL Lynchburg, Virginia
WRVM Suring, Wisconsin
WRVN Utica, New York
WRVO Oswego, New York
WRVQ Richmond, Virginia
WRVR Memphis, Tennessee
WRVS-FM Elizabeth City, North Carolina
WRVT Rutland, Vermont
WRVV Harrisburg, Pennsylvania
WRVW Lebanon, Tennessee
WRVX Cameron, Missouri
WRVY-FM Henry, Illinois
WRVZ Pocatalico, West Virginia
WRWA Dothan, Alabama
WRWB-FM Ellenville, New York
WRWD-FM Highland, New York
WRWJ Murrysville, Pennsylvania
WRWM Lawrence, Indiana
WRWM(FM) Lawrence, Indiana
WRWN Port Royal, South Carolina
WRXC Shelton, Connecticut
WRXD Fajardo, Puerto Rico
WRXK-FM Bonita Springs, Florida
WRXL Richmond, Virginia
WRXP Cambridge, Minnesota
WRXQ Coal City, Illinois
WRXR-FM Rossville, Georgia
WRXT Roanoke, Virginia
WRXV State College, Pennsylvania
WRXX Centralia, Illinois
WRXZ Briarcliff Acres, South Carolina
WRYN Hickory, North Carolina
WRYP Wellfleet, Massachusetts
WRYV Milroy, Pennsylvania
WRZE Kingstree, South Carolina
WRZI Hodgenville, Kentucky
WRZK Colonial Heights, Tennessee
WRZQ-FM Greensburg, Indiana
WRZR Loogootee, Indiana
WRZX Greenville, Indiana
WRZZ Parkersburg, West Virginia
WSAA Benton, Tennessee
WSAG Linwood, Michigan
WSAJ-FM Grove City, Pennsylvania
WSAK Hampton, New Hampshire
WSAQ Port Huron, Michigan
WSAU-FM Rudolph, Wisconsin
WSB(FM) Clemson, Georgia
WSB-FM Atlanta, Georgia
WSBF-FM Clemson, South Carolina
WSBG Stroudsburg, Pennsylvania
WSBH Satellite Beach, Florida
WSBW Ephraim, Wisconsin
WSBY-FM Salisbury, Maryland
WSBZ Miramar Beach, Florida
WSCB Springfield, Massachusetts
WSCC-FM Goose Creek, South Carolina
WSCD-FM Duluth, Minnesota
WSCF-FM Vero Beach, Florida
WSCG Augusta, Georgia
WSCH Aurora, Indiana
WSCI Charleston, South Carolina
WSCL Salisbury, Maryland
WSCN Cloquet, Minnesota
WSCS New London, New Hampshire
WSCT Springfield, Illinois
WSCY Moultonborough, New Hampshire
WSCZ Winnsboro, South Carolina
WSDH Sandwich, Massachusetts
WSDL Ocean City, Maryland
WSDM-FM Brazil, Indiana
WSDP Plymouth, Michigan
WSEA Atlantic Beach, South Carolina
WSEB Englewood, Florida
WSEI Olney, Illinois
WSEK Burnside, Kentucky
WSEL-FM Pontotoc, Mississippi
WSEN-FM Baldwinsville, New York
WSEO Nelsonville, Ohio
WSEV-FM Gatlinburg, Tennessee
WSEW Sanford, Maine
WSEY Oregon, Illinois
WSFF Vinton, Virginia
WSFL-FM New Bern, North Carolina
WSFP Harrisville, Michigan
WSFQ Peshtigo, Wisconsin
WSFR Corydon, Indiana
WSFX Nanticoke, Pennsylvania
WSGA Hinesville, Georgia
WSGC-FM Tignall, Georgia
WSGE Dallas, North Carolina
WSGG Norfolk, Connecticut
WSGL Naples, Florida
WSGM Coalmont, Tennessee
WSGN Gadsden, Alabama
WSGP Glasgow, Kentucky
WSGR-FM Port Huron, Michigan
WSGS Hazard, Kentucky
WSGW-FM Carrollton, Michigan
WSHA Raleigh, North Carolina
WSHC Shepherdstown, West Virginia
WSHD Eastport, Maine
WSHE-FM Chicago, Illinois
WSHH Pittsburgh, Pennsylvania
WSHJ Southfield, Michigan
WSHK Kittery, Maine
WSHL-FM Easton, Massachusetts
WSHM Wixom, Michigan
WSHN Munising, Michigan
WSHP Attica, Indiana
WSHR Lake Ronkonkoma, New York
WSHS Sheboygan, Wisconsin
WSHU-FM Fairfield, Connecticut
WSHW Frankfort, Indiana
WSIA Staten Island, New York
WSIB Selmer, Tennessee
WSIE Edwardsville, Illinois
WSIF Wilkesboro, North Carolina
WSIG Mount Jackson, Virginia
WSIM Lamar, South Carolina
WSIP-FM Paintsville, Kentucky
WSIS Riverside, Michigan
WSIU Carbondale, Illinois
WSIX-FM Nashville, Tennessee
WSIZ-FM Jacksonville, Georgia
WSJA York, Georgia
WSJD Princeton, Indiana
WSJE Summersville, West Virginia
WSJK(FM) Tuscola, Illinois
WSJL Bessemer, Alabama
WSJM-FM Benton Harbor, Michigan
WSJO Egg Harbor City, New Jersey
WSJR Dallas, Pennsylvania
WSJY Fort Atkinson, Wisconsin
WSJZ-FM Sebastian, Florida
WSKB Westfield, Massachusetts
WSKE Everett, Pennsylvania
WSKG-FM Binghamton, New York
WSKK Ripley, Mississippi
WSKL Veedersburg, Indiana
WSKQ-FM New York, New York
WSKS Whitesboro, New York
WSKU Little Falls, New York

WSKV-FM Stanton, Kentucky
WSKY-FM Micanopy, Florida
WSKZ Chattanooga, Tennessee
WSLC-FM Roanoke, Virginia
WSLD Whitewater, Wisconsin
WSLE Salem, Illinois
WSLG Gouverneur, New York
WSLI Belding, Michigan
WSLJ Watertown, New York
WSLL Saranac Lake, New York
WSLM-FM Salem, Indiana
WSLO Malone, New York
WSLP Saranac Lake, New York
WSLQ Roanoke, Virginia
WSLT Statesboro, Georgia
WSLU Canton, New York
WSLX New Canaan, Connecticut
WSLY York, Alabama
WSLZ Cape Vincent, New York
WSM-FM Nashville, Tennessee
WSMA Scituate, Massachusetts
WSMB Harbor Beach, Michigan
WSMC-FM Collegedale, Tennessee
WSMD-FM Mechanicsville, Maryland
WSMF Monroe, Michigan
WSMI-FM Litchfield, Illinois
WSMJ(FM) Wilkinson, Indiana
WSMK Buchanan, Michigan
WSMM New Carlisle, Indiana
WSMP New Hebron, Mississippi
WSMR Sarasota, Florida
WSMS Artesia, Mississippi
WSMW Greensboro, North Carolina
WSNC Winston-Salem, North Carolina
WSND-FM Notre Dame, Indiana
WSNE-FM Taunton, Massachusetts
WSNI Keene, New Hampshire
WSNN Potsdam, New York
WSNN Potsdam, New York
WSNT-FM Sandersville, Georgia
WSNV Salem, Virginia
WSNX-FM Muskegon, Michigan
WSNY Columbus, Ohio
WSNZ Lynchburg, Virginia
WSOC-FM Charlotte, North Carolina
WSOE Elon College, North Carolina
WSOF-FM Madisonville, Kentucky
WSOG Spring Valley, Illinois
WSOL-FM Brunswick, Georgia
WSOR Naples, Florida
WSOS-FM Fruit Cove, Florida
WSOU South Orange, New Jersey
WSOX Red Lion, Pennsylvania
WSOY-FM Decatur, Illinois
WSPA-FM Spartanburg, South Carolina
WSPI Ellsworth, Illinois
WSPK Poughkeepsie, New York
WSPM Cloverdale, Indiana
WSPN Saratoga Springs, New York
WSPS Concord, New Hampshire
WSPT Stevens Point, Wisconsin
WSPX Bowman, South Carolina
WSPY-FM Plano, Illinois
WSQA Hornell, New York
WSQC-FM Oneonta, New York
WSQE Corning, New York
WSQG-FM Ithaca, New York
WSQH Decatur, Mississippi
WSQV(FM) Lock Haven, Pennsylvania
WSQX-FM Binghamton, New York
WSRB Lansing, Illinois
WSRC(FM) Waynetown, Indiana
WSRI Sugar Grove, Illinois
WSRJ Honor, Michigan
WSRK Oneonta, New York
WSRM Coosa, Georgia
WSRN-FM Swarthmore, Pennsylvania
WSRS Worcester, Massachusetts
WSRT Gaylord, Michigan
WSRU Slippery Rock, Pennsylvania
WSRV Gainesville, Georgia
WSRW-FM Grand Rapids, Michigan
WSRZ-FM Coral Cove, Florida
WSSB-FM Orangeburg, South Carolina
WSSD Chicago, Illinois
WSSJ Rincon, Georgia
WSSK Saratoga Springs, New York
WSSL-FM Gray Court, South Carolina
WSSM(FM) Goshen, Indiana
WSSP Milwaukee, Wisconsin
WSSQ Sterling, Illinois
WSSR Joliet, Illinois
WSSW Platteville, Wisconsin
WSSX Charleston, South Carolina
WSTB Streetsboro, Ohio
WSTF Andalusia, Alabama
WSTG Princeton, West Virginia
WSTH-FM Alexander City, Alabama
WSTI-FM Quitman, Georgia
WSTK Aurora, North Carolina
WSTM Kiel, Wisconsin
WSTO Owensboro, Kentucky
WSTQ Streator, Illinois
WSTR Smyrna, Georgia
WSTS Fairmont, North Carolina
WSTV-FM Frankfort, Kentucky
WSTW Wilmington, Delaware
WSTX-FM Christiansted, Virgin Islands
WSTZ-FM Vicksburg, Mississippi
WSUC-FM Cortland, New York
WSUE Sault Ste. Marie, Michigan
WSUF Noyack, New York
WSUL Monticello, New York
WSUM Madison, Wisconsin
WSUN-FM Holiday, Florida
WSUP Platteville, Wisconsin
WSUS Franklin, New Jersey
WSUW Whitewater, Wisconsin
WSVH Savannah, Georgia
WSVO Staunton, Virginia
WSVZ Tower Hill, Illinois
WSWR Shelby, Ohio
WSWS(FM) Smithboro, Illinois
WSWT Peoria, Illinois
WSWV-FM Pennington Gap, Virginia
WSWW-FM Craigsville, West Virginia
WSYC-FM Shippensburg, Pennsylvania
WSYE Houston, Mississippi
WSYI Valley Station, Kentucky
WSYN Surfside Beach, South Carolina
WSYR Solvay, New York
WSYY-FM Millinocket, Maine
WTAC Burton, Michigan
WTAI Union City, Tennessee
WTAK-FM Hartselle, Alabama
WTAO-FM Herrin, Illinois
WTAW-FM Buffalo, Texas
WTBB Gadsden, Alabama
WTBD-FM Delhi, New York
WTBF-FM Brundidge, Alabama
WTBG Brownsville, Tennessee
WTBI-FM Greenville, South Carolina
WTBJ Oxford, Alabama
WTBK Manchester, Kentucky
WTBM Mexico, Maine
WTBP Bath, Maine
WTBU York Center, Maine
WTBX Hibbing, Minnesota
WTCB Orangeburg, South Carolina
WTCC Springfield, Massachusetts
WTCD Indianola, Mississippi
WTCF Wardensville, West Virginia
WTCK Charlevoix, Michigan
WTCM-FM Traverse City, Michigan
WTCQ Vidalia, Georgia
WTCR-FM Huntington, West Virginia
WTCX Ripon, Wisconsin
WTDK Federalsburg, Maryland
WTDR-FM Talladega, Alabama
WTEB New Bern, North Carolina
WTFH Helen, Georgia
WTFM Kingsport, Tennessee
WTFX-FM Clarksville, Indiana
WTGA-FM Thomaston, Georgia
WTGD Bridgewater, Virginia
WTGE Baton Rouge, Louisiana
WTGG Amite, Louisiana
WTGN Lima, Ohio
WTGR Union City, Ohio
WTGV-FM Sandusky, Michigan
WTGY Charleston, Mississippi
WTGZ Union Springs, Alabama
WTHB-FM Wrens, Georgia
WTHD Lagrange, Indiana
WTHG Hinesville, Georgia
WTHI-FM Terre Haute, Indiana
WTHK Wilmington, Vermont
WTHL Somerset, Kentucky
WTHN Sault Ste. Marie, Michigan
WTHO-FM Thomson, Georgia
WTHP Gibson, Georgia
WTHS Holland, Michigan
WTHT Auburn, Maine
WTHX Vine Grove, Kentucky
WTIB Williamston, North Carolina
WTIC-FM Hartford, Connecticut
WTID Thomaston, Alabama
WTIF-FM Omega, Georgia
WTIM Taylorville, Illinois
WTIM Taylorville, Illinois
WTIP Grand Marais, Minnesota
WTIX-FM Galliano, Louisiana
WTJB Columbus, Georgia
WTJJ Dyer, Tennessee
WTJT Baker, Florida
WTJU Charlottesville, Virginia
WTJY Asheboro, North Carolina
WTKB-FM Atwood, Tennessee
WTKC Findlay, Ohio
WTKE-FM Niceville, Florida
WTKF Atlantic, North Carolina
WTKI Huntsville, Alabama
WTKK Knightdale, North Carolina
WTKL North Dartmouth, Massachusetts
WTKM-FM Hartford, Wisconsin
WTKS-FM Cocoa Beach, Florida
WTKU-FM Petersburg, New Jersey
WTKV Oswego, New York
WTKW Bridgeport, New York
WTKX-FM Pensacola, Florida
WTKY-FM Tompkinsville, Kentucky
WTLC-FM Greenwood, Indiana
WTLD Jesup, Georgia
WTLG Starke, Florida
WTLI Bear Creek Township, Michigan
WTLP Braddock Heights, Maryland
WTLQ-FM Punta Rassa, Florida
WTLR State College, Pennsylvania
WTLX Monona, Wisconsin
WTLZ Saginaw, Michigan
WTMB Tomah, Wisconsin
WTMD Towson, Maryland
WTMG Williston, Florida
WTMK Wanatah, Indiana
WTML Tullahoma, Tennessee
WTMM-FM Mechanicville, New York
WTMP-FM Dade City, Florida
WTMT Weaverville, North Carolina
WTMX Skokie, Illinois
WTMY(FM) Coon Rapids, Minnesota
WTNJ Mount Hope, West Virginia
WTNM Water Valley, Mississippi
WTNN Bristol, Vermont
WTNQ La Follette, Tennessee
WTNR Holland, Michigan
WTNS-FM Coshocton, Ohio
WTNT-FM Tallahassee, Florida
WTNV Tiptonville, Tennessee
WTOH Upper Arlington, Ohio
WTOJ Carthage, New York
WTOK-FM San Juan, Puerto Rico
WTON-FM Staunton, Virginia
WTOP-FM Washington, District of Columbia
WTOS-FM Skowhegan, Maine
WTOT-FM Graceville, Florida
WTPA Palmyra, Pennsylvania
WTPG Whitehouse, Ohio
WTPL Hillsboro, New Hampshire
WTPM Aguadilla, Puerto Rico
WTPN Westby, Wisconsin
WTPO New Albany, Mississippi
WTPR-FM McKinnon, Tennessee
WTPT Forest City, North Carolina
WTQR Winston-Salem, North Carolina
WTQX Boothbay Harbor, Maine
WTRE(FM) Greensburg, Indiana
WTRG Gaston, North Carolina
WTRH Ramsey, Illinois
WTRK Freeland, Michigan
WTRM Winchester, Virginia
WTRS Dunnellon, Florida
WTRT Benton, Kentucky
WTRV Walker, Michigan
WTRW(FM) Carbondale, Pennsylvania
WTRY-FM Rotterdam, New York
WTRZ Spencer, Tennessee
WTSA-FM Brattleboro, Vermont
WTSC-FM Potsdam, New York
WTSE Benton, Tennessee
WTSG Carlinville, Illinois
WTSH-FM Aragon, Georgia
WTSM(FM) Woodville, Florida
WTSR Trenton, New Jersey
WTSS Buffalo, New York
WTSU Montgomery-Troy, Alabama
WTTC-FM Towanda, Pennsylvania
WTTH Margate City, New Jersey
WTTL-FM Madisonville, Kentucky
WTTS Bloomington, Indiana
WTTU Cookeville, Tennessee
WTTX-FM Appomattox, Virginia
WTUA Pinopolis, South Carolina
WTUE Dayton, Ohio
WTUF Boston, Georgia
WTUG-FM Northport, Alabama
WTUK Harlan, Kentucky
WTUL New Orleans, Louisiana
WTUR Upland, Indiana
WTUV-FM Eminence, Kentucky
WTUZ Uhrichsville, Ohio
WTVR-FM Richmond, Virginia
WTVY-FM Dothan, Alabama
WTWF Fairview, Pennsylvania
WTWS Houghton Lake, Michigan
WTWT Bradford, Pennsylvania
WTWX-FM Guntersville, Alabama
WTXR Toccoa Falls, Georgia
WTXT Fayette, Alabama
WTYB Bluffon, South Carolina
WTYD Deltaville, Virginia
WTYE Robinson, Illinois
WTYG Sparr, Florida
WTYJ Fayette, Mississippi
WTYL-FM Tylertown, Mississippi
WTYS-FM Marianna, Florida
WTZB Englewood, Florida
WTZI Rosemont, Illinois
WTZR Elizabethton, Tennessee
WTZY Wonder Lake, Illinois
WUAG Greensboro, North Carolina
WUAL-FM Tuscaloosa, Alabama
WUAW Erwin, North Carolina
WUBA High Springs, Florida
WUBB Bluffton, South Carolina
WUBE-FM Cincinnati, Ohio
WUBG Plainfield, South Carolina
WUBJ Jamestown, New York
WUBK(FM) Enoree, South Carolina
WUBL Atlanta, Georgia
WUBS South Bend, Indiana
WUBT Russellville, Kentucky
WUBU South Bend, Indiana
WUCF-FM Orlando, Florida
WUCL Newton, Mississippi
WUCS Windsor Locks, Connecticut
WUCX-FM Bay City, Michigan
WUCZ Carthage, Tennessee
WUDE Bolivia, North Carolina
WUDR Dayton, Ohio
WUEC Eau Claire, Wisconsin
WUEV Evansville, Indiana
WUEZ Carterville, Illinois
WUFF-FM Eastman, Georgia
WUFM Columbus, Ohio
WUFN Albion, Michigan
WUFR Bedford, Pennsylvania
WUFT-FM Gainesville, Florida
WUGA Athens, Georgia
WUGN Midland, Michigan
WUGO Grayson, Kentucky
WUHT Birmingham, Alabama
WUHU Smiths Grove, Kentucky
WUIN Oak Island, North Carolina
WUIS Springfield, Illinois
WUJC St. Marks, Florida
WUKL Bethlehem, West Virginia
WUKQ-FM Mayaguez, Puerto Rico
WUKS St. Pauls, North Carolina
WUKV Portsmouth, Ohio
WUKY Lexington, Kentucky
WULF Hardinsburg, Kentucky
WULS Broxton, Georgia
WUMB-FM Boston, Massachusetts
WUMC Elizabethton, Tennessee
WUMD North Dartmouth, Massachusetts
WUME-FM Paoli, Indiana
WUMI Newberry, Michigan
WUMJ Fayetteville, Georgia
WUML Lowell, Massachusetts
WUMM Machias, Maine
WUMR Memphis, Tennessee
WUMS University, Mississippi
WUMX Rome, New York
WUNC Chapel Hill, North Carolina

WUND-FM Manteo, North Carolina
WUNH Durham, New Hampshire
WUNV Albany, Georgia
WUNY Utica, New York
WUOG Athens, Georgia
WUOL-FM Louisville, Kentucky
WUOM Ann Arbor, Michigan
WUOT Knoxville, Tennessee
WUOW Milford, New York
WUPE-FM North Adams, Massachusetts
WUPF Powers, Michigan
WUPG Republic, Michigan
WUPI Presque Isle, Maine
WUPJ Escanaba, Michigan
WUPK Marquette, Michigan
WUPM Ironwood, Michigan
WUPN Paradise, Michigan
WUPS Houghton Lake, Michigan
WUPT Gwinn, Michigan
WUPX Marquette, Michigan
WUPY Ontonagon, Michigan
WUPZ Chocolay Township, Michigan
WURB Cross City, Florida
WURC Holly Springs, Mississippi
WURI Manteo, North Carolina
WURV(FM) Richmond, Virginia
WUSB Stony Brook, New York
WUSC-FM Columbia, South Carolina
WUSF Tampa, Florida
WUSH Poquoson, Virginia
WUSI Olney, Illinois
WUSJ Madison, Mississippi
WUSL Philadelphia, Pennsylvania
WUSM-FM Hattiesburg, Mississippi
WUSN Chicago, Illinois
WUSO Springfield, Ohio
WUSQ-FM Winchester, Virginia
WUSR Scranton, Pennsylvania
WUSW Taylorville, Illinois
WUSY Cleveland, Tennessee
WUSZ Virginia, Minnesota
WUTC Chattanooga, Tennessee
WUTK-FM Knoxville, Tennessee
WUTM Martin, Tennessee
WUTQ-FM Utica, New York
WUTS Sewanee, Tennessee
WUUB Jupiter, Florida
WUUF Sodus, New York
WUUQ South Pittsburg, Tennessee
WUUU Franklinton, Louisiana
WUUZ Cooperstown, Pennsylvania
WUVA Charlottesville, Virginia
WUVT-FM Blacksburg, Virginia
WUWF Pensacola, Florida
WUWG Carrollton, Georgia
WUWM Milwaukee, Wisconsin
WUWS Ashland, Wisconsin
WUZR Bicknell, Indiana
WUZZ Saegertown, Pennsylvania
WVAC-FM Adrian, Michigan
WVAF Charleston, West Virginia
WVAQ Morgantown, West Virginia
WVAS Montgomery, Alabama
WVAZ Oak Park, Illinois
WVBB(FM) Elliston-Lafayette, Virginia
WVBD Fayetteville, West Virginia
WVBE-FM Lynchburg, Virginia
WVBG-FM Redwood, Mississippi
WVBH Beach Haven West, New Jersey
WVBO Winneconne, Wisconsin
WVBR-FM Ithaca, New York
WVBU-FM Lewisburg, Pennsylvania
WVBV Medford Lakes, New Jersey
WVBW Suffolk, Virginia
WVBX Spotsylvania, Virginia
WVBZ High Point, North Carolina
WVCF Eau Claire, Wisconsin
WVCM Iron Mountain, Michigan
WVCN Baraga, Michigan
WVCO Loris, South Carolina
WVCP Gallatin, Tennessee
WVCR-FM Loudonville, New York
WVCS Owen, Wisconsin
WVCT Keavy, Kentucky
WVCX Tomah, Wisconsin
WVCY-FM Milwaukee, Wisconsin
WVDA Valdosta, Georgia
WVEE Atlanta, Georgia
WVEK-FM Weber City, Virginia
WVEP Martinsburg, West Virginia
WVES Accomac, Virginia
WVEZ St. Matthews, Kentucky
WVFA Lebanon, New Hampshire
WVFB Celina, Tennessee
WVFJ-FM Manchester, Georgia
WVFL Fond Du Lac, Wisconsin
WVFM Kalamazoo, Michigan
WVFS Tallahassee, Florida
WVFT Gretna, Florida
WVGA Lakeland, Georgia
WVGN Charlotte Amalie, Virgin Islands
WVGO Terre Haute, Illinois
WVGR Grand Rapids, Michigan
WVGS Statesboro, Georgia
WVGV West Union, West Virginia
WVHC Herkimer, New York
WVHL Farmville, Virginia
WVHM Benton, Kentucky
WVHT Norfolk, Virginia
WVIA-FM Scranton, Pennsylvania
WVIB Holton, Michigan
WVIJ Port Charlotte, Florida
WVIK Rock Island, Illinois
WVIL Virginia, Illinois
WVIN-FM Bath, New York
WVIP New Rochelle, New York
WVIQ Christiansted, Virgin Islands
WVIS Vieques, Puerto Rico
WVIV-FM Highland Park, Illinois
WVIX Lemont, Illinois
WVJC Mount Carmel, Illinois
WVJP-FM Caguas, Puerto Rico
WVJZ Charlotte Amalie, Virgin Islands
WVKC Galesburg, Illinois
WVKF Shadyside, Ohio
WVKL Norfolk, Virginia
WVKM Matewan, West Virginia
WVKO-FM Johnstown, Ohio
WVKR-FM Poughkeepsie, New York
WVKS Toledo, Ohio
WVKV Nashville, Georgia
WVKX Irwinton, Georgia
WVKY Shelbyville, Kentucky
WVKY(FM) Shelbyville, Kentucky
WVLC Mannsville, Kentucky
WVLE Scottsville, Kentucky
WVLF Norwood, New York
WVLI Kankakee, Illinois
WVLK-FM Richmond, Kentucky
WVLO Cridersville, Ohio
WVLS Monterey, Virginia
WVLT Vineland, New Jersey
WVLY-FM Milton, Pennsylvania
WVMC-FM Mansfield, Ohio
WVMD Romney, West Virginia
WVME Meadville, Pennsylvania
WVMJ Conway, New Hampshire
WVML Millersburg, Ohio
WVMM Grantham, Pennsylvania
WVMN New Castle, Pennsylvania
WVMP Vinton, Virginia
WVMR Marlinton, West Virginia
WVMR-FM Hillsboro, West Virginia
WVMS Sandusky, Ohio
WVMU Ashtabula, Ohio
WVMW-FM Scranton, Pennsylvania
WVMX Westerville, Ohio
WVNA-FM Muscle Shoals, Alabama
WVNC Lawrenceville, Virginia
WVNH Concord, New Hampshire
WVNI Nashville, Indiana
WVNK Manchester, Vermont
WVNL Vandalia, Illinois
WVNN-FM Trinity, Alabama
WVNP Wheeling, West Virginia
WVNU Greenfield, Ohio
WVNV Malone, New York
WVNW Burnham, Pennsylvania
WVOB Dothan, Alabama
WVOD Manteo, North Carolina
WVOF Fairfield, Connecticut
WVOH-FM Nicholls, Georgia
WVOK-FM Oxford, Alabama
WVOM-FM Howland, Maine
WVOR Canandaigua, New York
WVOS-FM Liberty, New York
WVOW-FM Logan, West Virginia
WVOZ-FM Carolina, Puerto Rico
WVPA St. Johnsbury, Vermont
WVPB Beckley, West Virginia
WVPC Franklin, West Virginia
WVPE Elkhart, Indiana
WVPG Parkersburg, West Virginia
WVPH Piscataway, New Jersey
WVPL Dozier, Alabama
WVPM Morgantown, West Virginia
WVPN Charleston, West Virginia
WVPR Windsor, Vermont
WVPS Burlington, Vermont
WVPW Buckhannon, West Virginia
WVQM Augusta, Maine
WVRA Enfield, North Carolina
WVRB Wilmore, Kentucky
WVRC-FM Spencer, West Virginia
WVRD Zebulon, North Carolina
WVRE Dickeyville, Wisconsin
WVRH Norlina, North Carolina
WVRI Clifton Forge, Virginia
WVRK Columbus, Georgia
WVRL Elizabeth City, North Carolina
WVRN Wittenberg, Wisconsin
WVRP Roanoke Rapids, North Carolina
WVRQ-FM Viroqua, Wisconsin
WVRT Mill Hall, Pennsylvania
WVRU-FM Radford, Virginia
WVRV Pine Level, Alabama
WVRW Glenville, West Virginia
WVRX Maryville, Tennessee
WVRY Waverly, Tennessee
WVRZ Mount Carmel, Pennsylvania
WVSB Romney, West Virginia
WVSC Port Royal, South Carolina
WVSD Itta Bena, Mississippi
WVSE Christiansted, Virgin Islands
WVSH Huntington, Indiana
WVSI Mt. Vernon, Illinois
WVSL-FM Riverside, Pennsylvania
WVSP-FM Yorktown, Virginia
WVSR-FM Charleston, West Virginia
WVSS Menomonie, Wisconsin
WVST-FM Petersburg, Virginia
WVSU-FM Birmingham, Alabama
WVSZ Chesterfield, South Carolina
WVTC Randolph Center, Vermont
WVTF Roanoke, Virginia
WVTI Brighton, Vermont
WVTK Port Henry, New York
WVTL Amsterdam, New York
WVTQ Sunderland, Vermont
WVTR Marion, Virginia
WVTS-FM Dunbar, West Virginia
WVTT Portville, New York
WVTU Charlottesville, Virginia
WVTW Charlottesville, Virginia
WVTY Racine, Wisconsin
WVUA-FM Tuscaloosa, Alabama
WVUB Vincennes, Indiana
WVUD Newark, Delaware
WVUM Coral Gables, Florida
WVUR-FM Valparaiso, Indiana
WVUV-FM Fagaitua, American Samoa
WVVE Panama City Beach, Florida
WVVI-FM Christiansted, Virgin Islands
WVVL Elba, Alabama
WVVR Hopkinsville, Kentucky
WVVS-FM Valdosta, Georgia
WVVV Williamstown, West Virginia
WVWC Buckhannon, West Virginia
WVWG Seelyville, Indiana
WVWV Huntington, West Virginia
WVXG Mount Gilead, Ohio
WVXR Randolph, Vermont
WVXU Cincinnati, Ohio
WVYA Williamsport, Pennsylvania
WVYB Holly Hill, Florida
WVYC York, Pennsylvania
WVYN Bluford, Illinois
WVYS Ridgebury, Pennsylvania
WVYS-FM2 Towanda, Pennsylvania
WVZA Murphysboro, Illinois
WWAC Ocean City, New Jersey
WWAG McKee, Kentucky
WWAV Santa Rosa Beach, Florida
WWAX Hermantown, Minnesota
WWBB Providence, Rhode Island
WWBD Sumter, South Carolina
WWBE Mifflinburg, Pennsylvania
WWBL Washington, Indiana
WWBN Tuscola, Michigan
WWBR Big Rapids, Michigan
WWBU Radford, Virginia
WWCF McConnellsburg, Pennsylvania
WWCJ Cape May, New Jersey
WWCK-FM Flint, Michigan
WWCM Standish, Michigan
WWCN Fort Myers Beach, Florida
WWCT Bartonville, Illinois
WWCU Cullowhee, North Carolina
WWDC Washington, District of Columbia
WWDE-FM Hampton, Virginia
WWDK Jackson, Michigan
WWDL Plainfield, Indiana
WWDM Sumter, South Carolina
WWDV Zion, Illinois
WWDW Alberta, Virginia
WWEB Wallingford, Connecticut
WWED Spotsylvania, Virginia
WWEG Myersville, Maryland
WWEI Easthampton, Massachusetts
WWEL London, Kentucky
WWEM Rustburg, Virginia
WWES Mount Kisco, New York
WWET Valdosta, Georgia
WWEV-FM Cumming, Georgia
WWFA St. Florian, Alabama
WWFF-FM New Market, Alabama
WWFG Ocean City, Maryland
WWFJ East Fayetteville, North Carolina
WWFM Trenton, New Jersey
WWFN-FM Lake City, South Carolina
WWFP Brigantine, New Jersey
WWFR Stuart, Florida
WWFX Southbridge, Massachusetts
WWFY Berlin, Vermont
WWGF Donalsonville, Georgia
WWGM Alamo, Tennessee
WWGN Ottawa, Illinois
WWGO Charleston, Illinois
WWGO-HD2 Casey, Illinois
WWGR Fort Myers, Florida
WWGV Grove City, Ohio
WWGY Grove City, Pennsylvania
WWHG Evansville/Rockten, Wisconsin
WWHI Muncie, Indiana
WWHK Concord, New Hampshire
WWHP Farmer City, Illinois
WWHQ Oakland, Maryland
WWHR Bowling Green, Kentucky
WWHS-FM Hampden-Sydney, Virginia
WWHT Syracuse, New York
WWIB Hallie, Wisconsin
WWIK McClellanville, South Carolina
WWIL-FM Wilmington, North Carolina
WWIN-FM Glen Burnie, Maryland
WWIO-FM Brunswick, Georgia
WWIP Cheriton, Virginia
WWIP Chesapeake, Virginia
WWIS-FM Black River Falls, Wisconsin
WWIZ West Middlesex, Pennsylvania
WWJD Pippa Passes, Kentucky
WWJK Green Cove Springs, Florida
WWJM New Lexington, Ohio
WWJO St. Cloud, Minnesota
WWKA Orlando, Florida
WWKC Caldwell, Ohio
WWKF Fulton, Kentucky
WWKI Kokomo, Indiana
WWKL Mechanicsburg, Pennsylvania
WWKM Rochelle, Georgia
WWKN Morgantown, Kentucky
WWKR Hart, Michigan
WWKS Cruz Bay, Virgin Islands
WWKT-FM Kingstree, South Carolina
WWKX Woonsocket, Rhode Island
WWKY Providence, Kentucky
WWKZ Okolona, Mississippi
WWL-FM Kenner, Louisiana
WWLA South Charleston, West Virginia
WWLB Ettrick, Virginia
WWLC Cross City, Florida
WWLD Cairo, Georgia
WWLF-FM Oswego, New York
WWLI Providence, Rhode Island
WWLL Sebring, Florida
WWLN Lincoln, Maine
WWLR Lyndonville, Vermont
WWLT Manchester, Kentucky
WWLU Lincoln University, Pennsylvania
WWLV(FM) Lexington, North Carolina
WWLW Clarksburg, West Virginia
WWMC Lynchburg, Virginia
WWMG Millbrook, Alabama
WWMJ Ellsworth, Maine
WWMK Onaway, Michigan

WWMP Waterbury, Vermont
WWMR Saltillo, Mississippi
WWMS Oxford, Mississippi
WWMX Baltimore, Maryland
WWNJ Toms River Township, New Jersey
WWNO New Orleans, Louisiana
WWNQ Forest Acres, South Carolina
WWNU Irmo, South Carolina
WWNW New Wilmington, Pennsylvania
WWOD Woodstock, Vermont
WWOF(FM) Tallahassee, Florida
WWOG Cookeville, Tennessee
WWOJ Avon Park, Florida
WWOT Altoona, Pennsylvania
WWOZ New Orleans, Louisiana
WWPG Eutaw, Alabama
WWPH Princeton Junction, New Jersey
WWPJ Pen Argyl, Pennsylvania
WWPL Smithfield, North Carolina
WWPN Westernport, Maryland
WWPR-FM New York, New York
WWPT Westport, Connecticut
WWPV-FM Colchester, Vermont
WWPW Atlanta, Georgia
WWQA North Granby, Connecticut
WWQM-FM Middleton, Wisconsin
WWQQ-FM Wilmington, North Carolina
WWQW(FM) Wartburg, Tennessee
WWQY Yadkin, North Carolina
WWQZ Baptist Village, Massachusetts
WWRA Clinton, Louisiana
WWRM Tampa, Florida
WWRQ-FM Valdosta, Georgia
WWRR Scranton, Pennsylvania
WWRW Mt. Sterling, Kentucky
WWRX Ledyard, Connecticut
WWRZ Fort Meade, Florida
WWSE Jamestown, New York
WWSK Smithtown, New York
WWSL Philadelphia, Mississippi
WWSN Whitehall, Michigan
WWSP Stevens Point, Wisconsin
WWSR Lima, Ohio
WWSS Tuscarora Township, Michigan
WWST Sevierville, Tennessee
WWSU Fairborn, Ohio
WWSW-FM Pittsburgh, Pennsylvania
WWTA Marion, Massachusetts
WWTG Carpentersville, Illinois
WWTH Oscoda, Michigan
WWTN Hendersonville, Tennessee
WWTP Augusta, Maine
WWUF Waycross, Georgia
WWUH West Hartford, Connecticut
WWUN-FM Friar's Point, Mississippi
WWUS Big Pine Key, Florida
WWUU Washington, Mississippi
WWUZ Bowling Green, Virginia
WWVO Albany, Georgia
WWVR Paris, Indiana
WWVU-FM Morgantown, West Virginia
WWWA Winslow, Maine
WWWD Bolingbroke, Georgia
WWWH-FM Haleyville, Alabama
WWWI-FM Pillager, Minnesota
WWWK Islamorada, Florida
WWWM-FM Sylvania, Ohio
WWWQ Atlanta, Georgia
WWWT-FM Manassas, Virginia
WWWV Charlottesville, Virginia
WWWW-FM Ann Arbor, Michigan
WWWX Oshkosh, Wisconsin
WWWY North Vernon, Indiana
WWWZ Summerville, South Carolina
WWXM Garden City, South Carolina
WWXT Prince Frederick, Maryland
WWXX Warrenton, Virginia
WWYL Chenango Bridge, New York
WWYN McKenzie, Tennessee
WWYY Belvidere, New Jersey
WWYZ Waterbury, Connecticut
WWZD-FM New Albany, Mississippi
WWZW Buena Vista, Virginia
WWZY Long Branch, New Jersey
WXAC Reading, Pennsylvania
WXAF Charleston, West Virginia
WXAJ Hillsboro, Illinois
WXAN Ava, Illinois
WXBA Brentwood, New York
WXBB Erie, Pennsylvania
WXBC Hardinsburg, Kentucky
WXBE Beaufort, North Carolina
WXBM-FM Milton, Florida
WXBN Berryville, Virginia
WXBP Augusta, Maine
WXBQ-FM Bristol, Virginia
WXBT West Columbia, South Carolina
WXBW Gallipolis, Ohio
WXBX Rural Retreat, Virginia
WXCC Williamson, West Virginia
WXCH Columbus, Indiana
WXCI Danbury, Connecticut
WXCL Pekin, Illinois
WXCM Whitesville, Kentucky
WXCR New Martinsville, West Virginia
WXCV Homosassa Springs, Florida
WXCX Siren, Wisconsin
WXCY Havre De Grace, Maryland
WXDE Lewes, Delaware
WXDJ North Miami Beach, Florida
WXDU Durham, North Carolina
WXDX-FM Pittsburgh, Pennsylvania
WXEF Effingham, Illinois
WXER Plymouth, Wisconsin
WXEX-FM Sanford, Maine
WXFL Florence, Alabama
WXFM-FM Mount Zion, Illinois
WXFX Prattville, Alabama
WXGL St. Petersburg, Florida
WXGM-FM Gloucester, Virginia
WXGN Somers Point, New Jersey
WXHB Richton, Mississippi
WXHC Homer, New York
WXHL-FM Christiana, Delaware
WXHM Middletown, Delaware
WXHT Madison, Florida
WXIL Elizabeth, West Virginia
WXIV Lumpkin, Georgia
WXIZ Waverly, Ohio
WXJC-FM Cordova, Alabama
WXJM Harrisonburg, Virginia
WXJY Georgetown, South Carolina
WXJZ Gainesville, Florida
WXKB Cape Coral, Florida
WXKC Erie, Pennsylvania
WXKE Fort Wayne, Indiana
WXKE-FM Pocomoke City, Maryland
WXKQ-FM Whitesburg, Kentucky
WXKR Port Clinton, Ohio
WXKS-FM Medford, Massachusetts
WXKT Maysville, Georgia
WXKU-FM Austin, Indiana
WXKV Selmer, Tennessee
WXKY-FM Stanford, Kentucky
WXKZ-FM Prestonsburg, Kentucky
WXLB Boonville, New York
WXLC Waukegan, Illinois
WXLF Hartford, Vermont
WXLG North Creek, New York
WXLH Blue Mountain Lake, New York
WXLK Roanoke, Virginia
WXLO Fitchburg, Massachusetts
WXLP Moline, Illinois
WXLQ Bristol, Vermont
WXLR Harold, Kentucky
WXLS Tupper Lake, New York
WXLT Christopher, Illinois
WXLU Peru, New York
WXLX Lajas, Puerto Rico
WXLZ-FM Lebanon, Virginia
WXMA Louisville, Kentucky
WXMF Marion, Ohio
WXMG London, Ohio
WXMJ Cambridge Springs, Pennsylvania
WXMK Dock Junction, Georgia
WXML Upper Sandusky, Ohio
WXMT Smethport, Pennsylvania
WXMX Millington, Tennessee
WXMZ Hartford, Kentucky
WXNR Grifton, North Carolina
WXNU St. Anne, Illinois
WXNX Sanibel, Florida
WXNY-FM New York, New York
WXOF Yankeetown, Florida
WXOQ Selmer, Tennessee
WXOS East St. Louis, Illinois
WXOU Auburn Hills, Michigan
WXPH Middletown, Pennsylvania
WXPK Briarcliff Manor, New York
WXPL Fitchburg, Massachusetts
WXPN Philadelphia, Pennsylvania
WXPR Rhinelander, Wisconsin
WXPW Wausau, Wisconsin
WXQR-FM Jacksonville, North Carolina
WXRA Inglis, Florida
WXRB Dudley, Massachusetts
WXRC Hickory, North Carolina
WXRD Crown Point, Indiana
WXRD-FM Georgetown, Delaware
WXRI Winston-Salem, North Carolina
WXRO Beaver Dam, Wisconsin
WXRR Hattiesburg, Mississippi
WXRS-FM Portal, Georgia
WXRT Chicago, Illinois
WXRV Andover, Massachusetts
WXRX Belvidere, Illinois
WXRZ Corinth, Mississippi
WXSH Pocomoke City, Maryland
WXSR Quincy, Florida
WXSS Wauwatosa, Wisconsin
WXST Hollywood, South Carolina
WXTA Edinboro, Pennsylvania
WXTB Clearwater, Florida
WXTC Greenville, Pennsylvania
WXTG-FM Virginia Beach, Virginia
WXTK West Yarmouth, Massachusetts
WXTL Syracuse, New York
WXTP North Windham, Maine
WXTQ Athens, Ohio
WXTS-FM Toledo, Ohio
WXTU Philadelphia, Pennsylvania
WXUR Herkimer, New York
WXUT Toledo, Ohio
WXVS Waycross, Georgia
WXVU Villanova, Pennsylvania
WXWX Marietta, Mississippi
WXXB Delphi, Indiana
WXXC Marion, Indiana
WXXE Fenner, New York
WXXF Loudonville, Ohio
WXXI-FM Rochester, New York
WXXJ Jacksonville, Florida
WXXL Tavares, Florida
WXXM Sun Prairie, Wisconsin
WXXQ Freeport, Illinois
WXXS Lancaster, New Hampshire
WXXX South Burlington, Vermont
WXXY Houghton, New York
WXXZ Grand Marais, Minnesota
WXYC Chapel Hill, North Carolina
WXYK Gulfport, Mississippi
WXYM Tomah, Wisconsin
WXYT-FM Detroit, Michigan
WXYX Bayamon, Puerto Rico
WXZO Willsboro, New York
WXZQ Piketon, Ohio
WXZZ Georgetown, Kentucky
WYAB Flora, Mississippi
WYAD Benton, Mississippi
WYAI Scotia, New York
WYAJ Sudbury, Massachusetts
WYAR Yarmouth, Maine
WYAS Luquillo, Puerto Rico
WYAV Myrtle Beach, South Carolina
WYAY Gainesville, Georgia
WYAZ Yazoo City, Mississippi
WYBA Coldwater, Michigan
WYBB Folly Beach, South Carolina
WYBC-FM New Haven, Connecticut
WYBF Radnor Township, Pennsylvania
WYBH Fayetteville, North Carolina
WYBJ Newton Grove, North Carolina
WYBK Chattanooga, Tennessee
WYBL Ashtabula, Ohio
WYBP Fort Lauderdale, Florida
WYBQ Leesport, Pennsylvania
WYBR Big Rapids, Michigan
WYBV Wakarusa, Indiana
WYBW Key Colony Beach, Florida
WYBX Key West, Florida
WYBZ Crooksville, Ohio
WYCA Crete, Illinois
WYCD Detroit, Michigan
WYCE Wyoming, Michigan
WYCR York-Hanover, Pennsylvania
WYCS Yorktown, Virginia
WYCT Pensacola, Florida
WYCY Hawley, Pennsylvania
WYDA Troy, Ohio
WYDB Englewood, Ohio
WYDE-FM Cullman, Alabama
WYDK Eufaula, Alabama
WYDL Middleton, Tennessee
WYDM Monroe, Michigan
WYDR Neenah-Menasha, Wisconsin
WYDS Decatur, Illinois
WYDS-HD2 Decatur, Illinois
WYEP-FM Pittsburgh, Pennsylvania
WYER Carmi, Illinois
WYEZ Murrells Inlet, South Carolina
WYFA Waynesboro, Georgia
WYFB Gainesville, Florida
WYFC Clinton, Tennessee
WYFD Decatur, Alabama
WYFE Tarpon Springs, Florida
WYFG Gaffney, South Carolina
WYFH North Charleston, South Carolina
WYFI Norfolk, Virginia
WYFJ Ashland, Virginia
WYFK Columbus, Georgia
WYFL Henderson, North Carolina
WYFM Sharon, Pennsylvania
WYFO Lakeland, Florida
WYFP Harpswell, Maine
WYFQ-FM Wadesboro, North Carolina
WYFS Savannah, Georgia
WYFT Luray, Virginia
WYFU Masontown, Pennsylvania
WYFV Cayce, South Carolina
WYFW Winder, Georgia
WYFX Mount Vernon, Indiana
WYFY Cambridge, Ohio
WYFZ Belleview, Florida
WYGB Edinburgh, Indiana
WYGC High Springs, Florida
WYGE London, Kentucky
WYGG Asbury Park, New Jersey
WYGL-FM Elizabethville, Pennsylvania
WYGO Madisonville, Tennessee
WYGS Hope, Indiana
WYGY Fort Thomas, Kentucky
WYHT Mansfield, Ohio
WYJB Albany, New York
WYJJ Trenton, Tennessee
WYJZ Fearsville, Kentucky
WYKE(FM) Inglis, Florida
WYKL Crestline, Ohio
WYKR-FM Haverhill, New Hampshire
WYKS Gainesville, Florida
WYKT Wilmington, Illinois
WYKV Ravena, New York
WYKX Escanaba, Michigan
WYKY Science Hill, Kentucky
WYKZ Beaufort, South Carolina
WYLC Jackson, Kentucky
WYLD-FM New Orleans, Louisiana
WYLK Lacombe, Louisiana
WYLV Maynardville, Tennessee
WYLV(FM) Maynardville, Tennessee
WYMG Chatham, Illinois
WYMJ New Martinsville, West Virginia
WYMS Milwaukee, Wisconsin
WYMX Greenwood, Mississippi
WYMY Burlington, North Carolina
WYNA Calabash, North Carolina
WYND-FM Hatteras, North Carolina
WYNG Mount Carmel, Illinois
WYNJ Blackduck, Minnesota
WYNK-FM Baton Rouge, Louisiana
WYNN-FM Florence, South Carolina
WYNR Waycross, Georgia
WYNS Waynesville, Ohio
WYNT Caledonia, Ohio
WYNU Milan, Tennessee
WYNW Birnamwood, Wisconsin
WYNZ South Portland, Maine
WYOO Springfield, Florida
WYOR Republic, Ohio
WYOY Gluckstadt, Mississippi
WYPA Cherry Hill, New Jersey
WYPF Frederick, Maryland
WYPL Memphis, Tennessee
WYPO Ocean City, Maryland
WYPR Baltimore, Maryland
WYPV Mackinaw City, Michigan
WYPZ Cochran, Georgia
WYQE Naguabo, Puerto Rico
WYQQ Charlton, Massachusetts
WYQS Mars Hill, North Carolina
WYRB Genoa, Illinois
WYRD-FM Simpsonville, South Carolina
WYRE-FM Saint Augustine Beach, Florida
WYRK Buffalo, New York
WYRO McArthur, Ohio

WYRQ-FM Little Falls, Minnesota
WYRR Lakewood, New York
WYRS Manahawkin, New Jersey
WYRY Hinsdale, New Hampshire
WYSA Wauseon, Ohio
WYSB Springfield, Kentucky
WYSM Lima, Ohio
WYSO Yellow Springs, Ohio
WYSS Sault Ste. Marie, Michigan
WYSU Youngstown, Ohio
WYSX Morristown, New York
WYSZ Maumee, Ohio
WYTE Marshfield, Wisconsin
WYTF Indianola, Mississippi
WYTJ Linton, Indiana
WYTK Rogersville, Alabama
WYTL Wyomissing, Pennsylvania
WYTM-FM Fayetteville, Tennessee
WYTN Youngstown, Ohio
WYTT Emporia, Virginia
WYTZ Bridgman, Michigan
WYUL Chateaugay, New York
WYUM Mount Vernon, Georgia
WYUR Gilman, Illinois
WYUU Safety Harbor, Florida
WYVK Middleport, Ohio
WYVL(FM) Youngsville, Pennsylvania
WYVN Saugatuck, Michigan
WYVS Spectacular, New York
WYXB Indianapolis, Indiana
WYXL Ithaca, New York
WYXY(FM) Danville, Illinois
WYYD Amherst, Virginia
WYYS Streator, Illinois
WYYU Dalton, Georgia
WYYX Bonifay, Florida
WYYY Syracuse, New York
WYZB Mary Esther, Florida
WYZR Bethany, West Virginia
WYZY Saranac, New York
WZAC-FM Danville, West Virginia
WZAD Wurtsboro, New York
WZAE Wadley, Georgia
WZAI Brewster, Massachusetts
WZAK Cleveland, Ohio
WZAQ Louisa, Kentucky
WZAR Ponce, Puerto Rico
WZAT Tybee Island, Georgia
WZAX Nashville, North Carolina
WZBA Westminster, Maryland
WZBB Stanleytown, Virginia
WZBC Newton, Massachusetts
WZBD Berne, Indiana
WZBG Litchfield, Connecticut
WZBH Georgetown, Delaware
WZBN Camilla, Georgia
WZBQ Carrollton, Alabama
WZBT Gettysburg, Pennsylvania
WZBX Rocky Ford, Georgia
WZBZ Pleasantville, New Jersey
WZCA Quebradillas, Puerto Rico
WZCB Dublin, Ohio
WZCH Warner Robins, Georgia
WZCP Chillicothe, Ohio
WZCR Hudson, New York
WZCY Hershey, Pennsylvania
WZDA Beavercreek, Ohio
WZDB Sykesville, Pennsylvania
WZDG Scotts Hill, North Carolina
WZDM Vincennes, Indiana
WZDQ Humboldt, Tennessee
WZEB Ocean View, Delaware
WZEC Strasburg, Mississippi
WZEE Madison, Wisconsin
WZEI Meredith, New Hampshire
WZET Hormigueros, Puerto Rico
WZEV Lineville, Alabama
WZEW Fairhope, Alabama
WZEZ Goochland, Virginia
WZFC Strasburg, Virginia
WZFJ(FM) Breezy Point, Minnesota
WZFL Islamorada, Florida
WZFM Narrows, Virginia
WZFT Baltimore, Maryland
WZFX Whiteville, North Carolina
WZGC Atlanta, Georgia
WZGL Charleston, Illinois
WZGN Crozet, Virginia
WZGO Aurora, North Carolina
WZHD Canaseraga, 0
WZHL New Augusta, Mississippi
WZHT Troy, Alabama
WZID Manchester, New Hampshire
WZIM(FM) Lexington, Illinois
WZIN Charlotte Amalie, Virgin Islands
WZIP Akron, Ohio
WZIQ Smithville, Georgia
WZIS(FM) Terre Haute, Indiana
WZJK West Terre Haute, Illinois
WZJS Banner Elk, North Carolina
WZJZ Port Charlotte, Florida
WZKL Woodstock, Illinois
WZKR Collinsville, Mississippi
WZKS Union, Mississippi
WZKV Dyersburg, Tennessee
WZKX Bay St. Louis, Mississippi
WZKZ Alfred, New York
WZKZ(FM) Alfred, New York
WZLA-FM Abbeville, South Carolina
WZLB Santa Rosa Beach, Florida
WZLD Petal, Mississippi
WZLF Bellows Falls, Vermont
WZLK Virgie, Kentucky
WZLO Dover-Foxcroft, Maine
WZLQ Tupelo, Mississippi
WZLR Xenia, Ohio
WZLT Lexington, Tennessee
WZLX Boston, Massachusetts
WZLY Wellesley, Massachusetts
WZMB Greenville, North Carolina
WZMJ Batesburg, South Carolina
WZMP Philadelphia, Pennsylvania
WZMR Altamont, New York
WZMT Ponce, Puerto Rico
WZMX Hartford, Connecticut
WZNB New Bern, North Carolina
WZNE Brighton, New York
WZNF Lumberton, Mississippi
WZNJ Demopolis, Alabama
WZNL Norway, Michigan
WZNP Newark, Ohio
WZNS Fort Walton Beach, Florida
WZNT San Juan, Puerto Rico
WZNX Sullivan, Illinois
WZOC Plymouth, Indiana
WZOE-FM Princeton, Illinois
WZOH-FM Lancaster, Ohio
WZOK Rockford, Illinois
WZOL Las Piedras, Puerto Rico
WZOM Defiance, Ohio
WZOO-FM Edgewood, Ohio
WZOR Mishicot, Wisconsin
WZOX Portage, Michigan
WZOZ Oneonta, New York
WZPE Bath, North Carolina
WZPL Greenfield, Indiana
WZPN Farmington, Illinois
WZPR Nags Head, North Carolina
WZPW Peoria, Illinois
WZRD Chicago, Illinois
WZRG(FM) Kulpmont, Pennsylvania
WZRH Picayune, Mississippi
WZRI Spring Lake, North Carolina
WZRN Norlina, North Carolina
WZRR Birmingham, Alabama
WZRT Rutland, Vermont
WZRU Garysburg, North Carolina
WZRV Front Royal, Virginia
WZRX-FM Fort Shawnee, Ohio
WZSN Greenwood, South Carolina
WZSP Nocatee, Florida
WZSR Woodstock, Illinois
WZST Westover, West Virginia
WZTF Scranton, South Carolina
WZTH Tusculum, Tennessee
WZTK Alpena, Michigan
WZTR Dahlonega, Georgia
WZUN Phoenix, New York
WZUP La Grange, North Carolina
WZUS Macon, Illinois
WZUU Mattawan, Michigan
WZVA Marion, Virginia
WZVN Lowell, Indiana
WZVN-FM Georgetown, Delaware
WZWP West Union, Ohio
WZWW Bellefonte, Pennsylvania
WZWZ Kokomo, Indiana
WZXE East Nottingham, Pennsylvania
WZXH Hagerstown, Maryland
WZXL Wildwood, New Jersey
WZXM Harrisburg, Pennsylvania
WZXP Au Sable, New York
WZXQ Chambersburg, Pennsylvania
WZXR South Williamsport, Pennsylvania
WZXV Palmyra, New York
WZXX Lawrenceburg, Tennessee
WZYP Athens, Alabama
WZYZ Spencer, Tennessee
WZZD Warwick, Pennsylvania
WZZE Glen Mills, Pennsylvania
WZZG Toomsboro, Georgia
WZZH Honesdale, Pennsylvania
WZZI(FM) Bedford, Virginia
WZZK-FM Birmingham, Alabama
WZZL Reidland, Kentucky
WZZN Oneonta, Alabama
WZZO Bethlehem, Pennsylvania
WZZP Hopkinsville, Kentucky
WZZR Riviera Beach, Florida
WZZS Zolfo Springs, Florida
WZZT Morrison, Illinois
WZZU Lynchburg, Virginia
WZZY Winchester, Indiana
WZZZ Portsmouth, Ohio
XETRAFM Tijuana, Mexico
XHRMFM Tijuana, Mexico

U.S. AM Stations by Frequency

1000 kHz

KBIB Marion, Texas
KCEO Vista, California
KFLG Bullhead City, Arizona
KKIM Albuquerque, New Mexico
KOMO Seattle, Washington
KSTA Coleman, Texas
KTOK Oklahoma City, Oklahoma
KXRB Sioux Falls, South Dakota
WCCD Parma, Ohio
WCMX Leominster, Massachusetts
WJBW Jupiter, Florida
WDJL Huntsville, Alabama
WIOO Carlisle, Pennsylvania
WKDE Altavista, Virginia
WKVG Jenkins, Kentucky
WLNL Horseheads, New York
WRQR(AM) Paris, Tennessee
WMVP Chicago, Illinois
WRAR Tappahannock, Virginia
WRTG Garner, North Carolina
WVWI Charlotte Amalie, Virgin Islands
WXTN Benton, Mississippi
WDXZ Robertsdale, Alabama
WYBT Blountstown, Florida

1010 kHz

KBBW Waco, Texas
KCHI Chillicothe, Missouri
KCHJ Delano, California
KDLA De Ridder, Louisiana
KIND Independence, Kansas
KIQI San Francisco, California
KLAT Houston, Texas
KXPS Thousand Palms, California
KRNI Mason City, Iowa
KSIR Brush, Colorado
KTNZ Amarillo, Texas
KXXT Tolleson, Arizona
KXEN St. Louis, Missouri
KOOR Milwaukie, Oregon
WCKW Garyville, Louisiana
WCSI Columbus, Indiana
WCST Berkeley Springs, West Virginia
WELS Kinston, North Carolina
WKJW Black Mountain, North Carolina
WTZA Atlanta, Georgia
WHIN Gallatin, Tennessee
WINS New York, New York
WIOI New Boston, Ohio
WJXL Jacksonville Beach, Florida
WUKZ(AM) Marion, Virginia
WMOX Meridian, Mississippi
WCNL Newport, New Hampshire
WOLB Baltimore, Maryland
WORM Savannah, Tennessee
WPMH Portsmouth, Virginia
WCOC Dora, Alabama
WHFS Seffner, Florida
WSPC Albemarle, North Carolina
WPCN Stevens Point, Wisconsin
WMIN Sauk Rapids, Minnesota
WKJW Black Mountain, North Carolina

1020 kHz

KCKN Roswell, New Mexico
KDKA Pittsburgh, Pennsylvania
KJJK Fergus Falls, Minnesota
KOKP Perry, Oklahoma
KMMQ Plattsmouth, Nebraska
KTNQ Los Angeles, California
KWIQ Moses Lake North, Washington
KDYK Union Gap, Washington
WCIL Carbondale, Illinois
WIBG Ocean City/Somers Po, New Jersey
WHDD Sharon, Connecticut
WPEO Peoria, Illinois
WOQI Adjuntas, Puerto Rico
WURN Kendall, Florida
WRIX Homeland Park, South Carolina
KVNT Eagle River, Alaska

1030 kHz

KBUF Holcomb, Kansas
KCTA Corpus Christi, Texas
KCWJ Blue Springs, Missouri
KFAY Farmington, Arkansas
KJDJ San Luis Obispo, California
KDUN Reedsport, Oregon
KMAS Shelton, Washington
KTWO Casper, Wyoming
KVOI Cortaro, Arizona
WBGS Point Pleasant, West Virginia
WBZ Boston, Massachusetts
WCTS Maplewood, Minnesota
WEBS Calhoun, Georgia
WDRU Creedmore, North Carolina
WGFC Floyd, Virginia
WNOW Mint Hill, North Carolina
WNVR Vernon Hills, Illinois
WONQ Oviedo, Florida
WOSO San Juan, Puerto Rico
WQSE White Bluff, Tennessee
WGSF Memphis, Tennessee
WUFL Sterling Heights, Michigan
WWGB Indian Head, Maryland
KWFA Tye, Texas

1040 kHz

KCBR Monument, Colorado
KGGR Dallas, Texas
KLHT Honolulu, Hawaii
KXPD Tigard, Oregon
KURS San Diego, California
WHO Des Moines, Iowa
WCHR Flemington, New Jersey
WLVJ Boynton Beach, Florida
WJTB North Ridgeville, Ohio
WLCR Mt Washington, Kentucky
WPBS Conyers, Georgia
WJBE Powell, Tennessee
WSGH Lewisville, North Carolina
WZSK Everett, Pennsylvania
WHBO Pinellas Park, Florida
WYSL Avon, New York
WZNA Moca, Puerto Rico

1050 kHz

KCAA Loma Linda, California
KBLE Seattle, Washington
KCHN Brookshire, Texas
KEYF Dishman, Washington
KGTO Tulsa, Oklahoma
KJBN Little Rock, Arkansas
KLOH Pipestone, Minnesota
KLPL(AM) Lake Providence, Louisiana
KMIS-AM Portageville, Missouri
KMTA Miles City, Montana
KTBL Los Ranchos, New Mexico
KORE Springfield-Eugene, Oregon
KRMY Killeen, Texas
KSIS Sedalia, Missouri
KTCT San Francisco, California
KJPG Frazier Park, California
KVPI Ville Platte, Louisiana
WTWG Columbus, Mississippi
WADC Parkersburg, West Virginia
WAMN Green Valley, West Virginia
WBRG Lynchburg, Virginia
WBUT Butler, Pennsylvania
WVXX Norfolk, Virginia
WDZ Decatur, Illinois
WDVM Eau Claire, Wisconsin
WEPN New York, New York
WFAM Augusta, Georgia
WSEN Baldwinsville, New York
WFSC Franklin, North Carolina
WGAT Gate City, Virginia
WJCM Sebring, Florida
WJOK Kaukauna, Wisconsin
WJSB Crestview, Florida
WIQB Conway, South Carolina
WBQH Silver Spring, Maryland
WLIP Kenosha, Wisconsin
WLON Lincolnton, North Carolina
WLYC Williamsport, Pennsylvania
WMNZ Montezuma, Georgia
WMSG Oakland, Maryland
WNES Central City, Kentucky
WBNM Alexander City, Alabama
WROS Jacksonville, Florida
WSMT Sparta, Tennessee
WTCA Plymouth, Indiana
WTKA Ann Arbor, Michigan
WGRI Cincinnati, Ohio
WWGP Sanford, North Carolina
WWIC Scottsboro, Alabama
WYBG Massena, New York

1060 kHz

KBGN Caldwell, Idaho
KDUS Tempe, Arizona
KFIL Preston, Minnesota
KFIT Lockhart, Texas
KFIT EXP S San Antonio, Texas
KXPL El Paso, Texas
KGFX Pierre, South Dakota
KIJN Farwell, Texas
KDYL South Salt Lake, Utah
KKVV Las Vegas, Nevada
KRCN Longmont, Colorado
KNLV Ord, Nebraska
KTNS Oakhurst, California
KBFL-AM Springfield, Missouri
KYW Philadelphia, Pennsylvania
WIXC Titusville, Florida
WCGB Juana Diaz, Puerto Rico
WCOK Sparta, North Carolina
WFLE Flemingsburg, Kentucky
WGSB Mebane, North Carolina
WHFB Benton Harbor-St. Jo, Michigan
WJKY Jamestown, Kentucky
WQOM Natick, Massachusetts
WKNG Tallapoosa, Georgia
WXNC Monroe, North Carolina
WLNO New Orleans, Louisiana
WMCL McLeansboro, Illinois
WKMQ Tupelo, Mississippi
WQMV Waverly, Tennessee
WILB Canton, Ohio
WRHL Rochelle, Illinois
WMEL Cocoa Beach, Florida
KIPA Hilo, Hawaii

1070 kHz

KATQ Plentywood, Montana
KBCL Bossier City, Louisiana
KNTH Houston, Texas
KLIO Wichita, Kansas
KHMO Hannibal, Missouri
KILR Estherville, Iowa
KNX Los Angeles, California
KOPY Alice, Texas
KWEL Midland, Texas
WAPI Birmingham, Alabama
WDIA Memphis, Tennessee
WTWK Plattsburgh, New York
WEKT Elkton, Kentucky
WFLI Lookout Mountain, Tennessee
WFRF Tallahassee, Florida
WGOS High Point, North Carolina
WCSZ Sans Souci, South Carolina
WFNI Indianapolis, Indiana
WINA Charlottesville, Virginia
WBKW(AM) Beckley, West Virginia
WKII Solana, Florida
WKMB Stirling, New Jersey
WKOK Sunbury, Pennsylvania
WMIA Arecibo, Puerto Rico
WNCT Greenville, North Carolina
WNVY Cantonment, Florida
WSCP Sandy Creek-Pulaski, New York
WTSO Madison, Wisconsin
KVKK Verndale, Minnesota
WBKW Beckley, West Virginia

1080 kHz

KOAN Anchorage, Alaska
KCNM Saipan, Guam
KGVY Green Valley, Arizona
KNDK Langdon, North Dakota
KOAK Red Oak, Iowa
KFXX Portland, Oregon
KRLD Dallas, Texas
KSLL Price, Utah
KSCO Santa Cruz, California
KVNI Coeur D'Alene, Idaho
KWAI Honolulu, Hawaii
KYMN-AM Northfield, Minnesota
KYMO East Prairie, Missouri
WALD Johnsonville, South Carolina
WHOO Kissimmee, Florida
WFTD Marietta, Georgia
WHIM Coral Gables, Florida
WKAC Athens, Alabama
WKBY Chatham, Virginia
WKGX Lenoir, North Carolina
WKJK Louisville, Kentucky
WLEY Cayey, Puerto Rico
WNWI Oak Lawn, Illinois
WOAP Owosso, Michigan
WONS Cannonsburg, Kentucky
WWNL Pittsburgh, Pennsylvania
WRYT Edwardsville, Illinois
WTIC Hartford, Connecticut
WUFO Amherst, New York
WHIM(AM) Coral Gables, Florida
WWDR Murfreesboro, North Carolina
KOAN Anchorage, Alaska

1090 kHz

KAAY Little Rock, Arkansas
KBOZ Bozeman, Montana
KEXS Excelsior Springs, Missouri
KVOP Plainview, Texas
KLWJ(AM) Umatilla, Oregon
KFNQ Seattle, Washington
KMXA Aurora, Colorado
KNCR Fortuna, California
KULF Bellville, Texas
KNWS Waterloo, Iowa
KQNM Milan, New Mexico
KSOU Sioux Center, Iowa
KTGO Tioga, North Dakota
WAQE Rice Lake, Wisconsin
WBAF Barnesville, Georgia
WBAL Baltimore, Maryland
WTSB Selma, North Carolina
WCAR Livonia, Michigan
WCRA Effingham, Illinois
WENR Englewood, Tennessee
WFCV Fort Wayne, Indiana
WUVI(AM) Charlotte Amalie, Virgin Islands
WILD Boston, Massachusetts
WTNK Hartsville, Tennessee
WHGG Kingsport, Tennessee
WKFI Wilmington, Ohio
WKTE King, North Carolina
WCZZ Greenwood, South Carolina
WKBZ Muskegon, Michigan
WSOL San German, Puerto Rico
WWGC Albertville, Alabama

1100 kHz

KRKE Milan, New Mexico
KDRY Alamo Heights, Texas
KFAX San Francisco, California
KFNX Cave Creek, Arizona
KKLL Webb City, Missouri
KNZZ Grand Junction, Colorado
KAFY Bakersfield, California
WCGA Woodbine, Georgia
WGPA Bethlehem, Pennsylvania
WHLI Hempstead, New York
WISS Berlin, Wisconsin
WSGI Springfield, Tennessee
WTAM Cleveland, Ohio
WTWN Wells River, Vermont
WWWE Hapeville, Georgia
KWWN Las Vegas, Nevada
WZFG Dilworth, Minnesota

1110 kHz

KAOI Kihei, Hawaii
KBND Bend, Oregon
KFAB Omaha, Nebraska
KGFL Clinton, Arkansas
KRPA Oak Harbor, Washington
KLIB Roseville, California
KDIS Pasadena, California
KTEK Alvin, Texas
KTTP Pineville, Louisiana
KYKK Humble City, New Mexico
WTOF Bay Minette, Alabama
WBIB Centreville, Alabama
WBT Charlotte, North Carolina
WCBR Richmond, Kentucky
WYRM Norfolk, Virginia
WOMN Franklinton, Louisiana
WGNZ Fairborn, Ohio
WJML Petoskey, Michigan
WWBJ Martinsburg, Pennsylvania
WKDZ Cadiz, Kentucky
WKRA Holly Springs, Mississippi
WMBI-AM Chicago, Illinois
WNAP Norristown, Pennsylvania
WMVX Salem, New Hampshire
WMUX Hurricane, West Virginia
WPMZ East Providence, Rhode Island

WSFW Seneca Falls, New York
WTBQ Warwick, New York
WTIS Tampa, Florida
WUAT Pikeville, Tennessee
WUPE Pittsfield, Massachusetts
WUNN Mason, Michigan
WVJP Caguas, Puerto Rico
KAGV Big Lake, Alaska

1120 kHz

KANN Roy, Utah
KEOR Catoosa, Oklahoma
KVTT Mineral Wells, Texas
KLIM Black Forest, Colorado
KMOX St. Louis, Missouri
KPNW Eugene, Oregon
KZSJ San Martin, California
WEAF Saint Stephen, South Carolina
WXJO Douglasville, Georgia
WBNW Concord, Massachusetts
WNWF Destin, Florida
WHOG Hobson City, Alabama
WKCE Maryville, Tennessee
WKQW Oil City, Pennsylvania
WBBF Buffalo, New York
WMSW Hatillo, Puerto Rico
WPRX Bristol, Connecticut
WTWZ Clinton, Mississippi
WUST Washington, District of Columbia
WSME Camp Lejeune, North Carolina
KTXW Manor, Texas
WZBR Coral Springs, Florida

1130 kHz

KAAB Batesville, Arkansas
KBMR Bismarck, North Dakota
KILJ Mount Pleasant, Iowa
KLEY Wellington, Kansas
KQNA Prescott Valley, Arizona
KRDU Dinuba, California
KSDO San Diego, California
KTMR Converse, Texas
KWKH Shreveport, Louisiana
KTLK Minneapolis, Minnesota
WBBR New York, New York
WCLW Eden, North Carolina
WEDI Eaton, Ohio
WDFN Detroit, Michigan
WECR Newland, North Carolina
WHHW Hilton Head Island, South Carolina
WISN Milwaukee, Wisconsin
WLBA Gainesville, Georgia
WOIZ Guayanilla, Puerto Rico
WPYB Benson, North Carolina
WQFX Gulfport, Mississippi
WRRL Rainelle, West Virginia
WAMB Brazil, Indiana
WOFC Murray, Kentucky
WWBF Bartow, Florida
WYXE Gallatin, Tennessee
KPHI Honolulu, Hawaii
WFNF Brazil, Indiana

1140 kHz

KYOK Conroe, Texas
KHFX Cleburne, Texas
KNWQ Palm Springs, California
KCXL Liberty, Missouri
KGEM Boise, Idaho
KHTK Sacramento, California
KLTK Centerton, Arkansas
KNAB Burlington, Colorado
KPWB Piedmont, Missouri
KQAB(AM) Lake Isabella, California
KXST North Las Vegas, Nevada
KSLD Soldotna, Alaska
KSOO Sioux Falls, South Dakota
KZMQ Ten Sleep, Wyoming
WAPF McComb, Mississippi
WAWK Kendallville, Indiana
WBXR Hazel Green, Alabama
WCJW Warsaw, New York
WVHF Kentwood, Michigan
WLOD Loudon, Tennessee
WMMG Brandenburg, Kentucky
WQBA Miami, Florida
WQII San Juan, Puerto Rico
WRLV Salyersville, Kentucky
WRMQ Orlando, Florida
WRNA China Grove, North Carolina
WRVA Richmond, Virginia
WSAO Senatobia, Mississippi
WVEL Pekin, Illinois
WXLZ St. Paul, Virginia

1150 kHz

KAGO Klamath Falls, Oregon
KASM Albany, Minnesota
KCCT Corpus Christi, Texas
KCKY Coolidge, Arizona
KCPS Burlington, Iowa
KNRV Englewood, Colorado
KDEF Albuquerque, New Mexico
KIMM Rapid City, South Dakota
KLPF Midland, Texas
KNED McAlester, Oklahoma
KQQQ Pullman, Washington
KRMS Osage Beach, Missouri
KSAL Salina, Kansas
KSEN Shelby, Montana
KKNW Seattle, Washington
KHRO El Paso, Texas
KBPO Port Neches, Texas
KWKY Des Moines, Iowa
WAVO Rock Hill, South Carolina
WBAG Burlington-Graham, North Carolina
WCRK Morristown, Tennessee
WCUE Cuyahoga Falls, Ohio
WDEL Wilmington, Delaware
WDTM Selmer, Tennessee
WEAQ Chippewa Falls, Wisconsin
WELC Welch, West Virginia
WGBN New Kensington, Pennsylvania
WGBR Goldsboro, North Carolina
WGEA Geneva, Alabama
WGGH Marion, Illinois
WGOW Chattanooga, Tennessee
WHBY Kimberly, Wisconsin
WHUN Huntingdon, Pennsylvania
WHUN Huntingdon, Pennsylvania
WIMA Lima, Ohio
WJBO Baton Rouge, Louisiana
WLOC Munfordville, Kentucky
WMRD Middletown, Connecticut
WMST Mount Sterling, Kentucky
WNDB Daytona Beach, Florida
WWDJ Boston, Massachusetts
WNLR Churchville, Virginia
WONG Canton, Mississippi
WUTI Utica, New York
WSNW Seneca, South Carolina
WJRD Tuscaloosa, Alabama
KZNE College Station, Texas
WTMP Egypt Lake, Florida
WXKO Fort Valley, Georgia
WJEM Valdosta, Georgia
KXET(AM) Portland, Oregon
KEIB Los Angeles, California

1160 kHz

KVCE Highland Park, Texas
KRDY San Antonio, Texas
KSL Salt Lake City, Utah
WCRT Donelson, Tennessee
WCVX Florence, Kentucky
WBQN Barceloneta-Manati, Puerto Rico
WCCS Homer City, Pennsylvania
WEWC Callahan, Florida
WJFJ Tryon, North Carolina
WKCM Hawesville, Kentucky
WCFO East Point, Georgia
WMET Gaithersburg, Maryland
WOBM Lakewood Township, New Jersey
WODY Fieldale, Virginia
WPIE Trumansburg, New York
WYLL Chicago, Illinois
WSKW Skowhegan, Maine
WVNJ Oakland, New Jersey
WCXI Fenton, Michigan
WBYN Lehighton, Pennsylvania
WIWA St. Cloud, Florida
KCTO Cleveland, Missouri
KHPP(AM) Waukon, Iowa

1170 kHz

KCBQ San Diego, California
KJNP North Pole, Alaska
KJOC Davenport, Iowa
KLOK San Jose, California
KRUE Waseca, Minnesota
KPUG Bellingham, Washington
KJXX Jackson, Missouri
KFAQ Tulsa, Oklahoma
KJJD Windsor, Colorado
KYET Golden Valley, Arizona
WGMP Montgomery, Alabama
WAVS Davie, Florida
WCLN Clinton, North Carolina
WCTF Vernon, Connecticut
WCXN Claremont, North Carolina
WDFB Junction City, Kentucky
WDIS Norfolk, Massachusetts
WFPB Orleans, Massachusetts
WKFL Bushnell, Florida
WSOS St. Augustine Beach, Florida
WLBH Mattoon, Illinois
WDEK(AM) Lexington, South Carolina
WFDL Waupun, Wisconsin
WRPM Poplarville, Mississippi
WWLE Cornwall, New York
WWTR Bridgewater, New Jersey
WWVA Wheeling, West Virginia
WQHC Hanceville, Alabama
WLEO Ponce, Puerto Rico

1180 kHz

KERN Wasco-Greenacres, California
KGOL Humble, Texas
KLAY Lakewood, Washington
KOFI Kalispell, Montana
KORL Honolulu, Hawaii
KZOT Bellevue, Nebraska
WFGN Gaffney, South Carolina
WGAB Newburgh, Indiana
WHAM Rochester, New York
WVLZ Knoxville, Tennessee
WKSP Hope Valley, Rhode Island
WJNT Pearl, Mississippi
WLDS Jacksonville, Illinois
WFYL King of Prussia, Pennsylvania
WUMY Turrell, Arkansas
WZQZ Trion, Georgia
WSQR Sycamore, Illinois
WXLA Dimondale, Michigan
KYES Rockville, Minnesota

1190 kHz

KDAO Marshalltown, Iowa
KDYA Vallejo, California
KREB Bentonville-Bella, Arkansas
KEX Portland, Oregon
KQQZ Fairview Heights, Missouri
KKOJ Jackson, Minnesota
KFXR Dallas, Texas
WBHA Wabasha, Minnesota
KNUV Tolleson, Arizona
KNEK Washington, Louisiana
KPHN Kansas City, Missouri
KVCU Boulder, Colorado
KVSV Beloit, Kansas
KXKS Albuquerque, New Mexico
WCRW(AM) Leesburg, Virginia
WAMT Pine Castle Sky Lake, Florida
WBMJ San Juan, Puerto Rico
WWIO St. Marys, Georgia
WAFS Atlanta, Georgia
WEUV Moulton, Alabama
WIXE Monroe, North Carolina
WLIB New York, New York
WNWC Sun Prairie, Wisconsin
WOWO Fort Wayne, Indiana
WPSP Royal Palm Beach, Florida
WSDQ Dunlap, Tennessee
WVUS Grafton, West Virginia
WSDE Cobleskill, New York
WMEJ Bay St. Louis, Mississippi

1200 kHz

KFNW West Fargo, North Dakota
KYAA Soquel, California
KYOO Bolivar, Missouri
WGRK Jeffersontown, Kentucky
WBCE Wickliffe, Kentucky
WCHB Taylor, Michigan
WFCN Nashville, Tennessee
WGDL Lares, Puerto Rico
WJUA Pine Island Center, Florida
WAMB Nashville, Tennessee
WXKS Newton, Massachusetts
WRTO Chicago, Illinois
WMIR Atlantic Beach, South Carolina
WOAI San Antonio, Texas
WRKK Hughesville, Pennsylvania
WSML Graham, North Carolina
WTLA North Syracuse, New York
WXIT Blowing Rock, North Carolina
WKST New Castle, Pennsylvania

1210 kHz

KMIA Auburn-Federal Way, Washington
KEBR Rocklin, California
KGYN Guymon, Oklahoma
KHAT Laramie, Wyoming
KOKK Huron, South Dakota
KHKR Washington, Utah
KPRZ San Marcos-Poway, California
KQEQ Fowler, California
KEVT Sahuarita, Arizona
KRSV Afton, Wyoming
KUBR San Juan, Texas
KZOO Honolulu, Hawaii
WANB Waynesburg, Pennsylvania
WDAO Dayton, Ohio
WDGR Dahlonega, Georgia
WMPS Bartlett, Tennessee
WHOY Salinas, Puerto Rico
WILY Centralia, Illinois
WJNL Kingsley, Michigan
WNMA Miami Springs, Florida
WPHT Philadelphia, Pennsylvania
WTXK Pike Road, Alabama
WSBI Static, Tennessee
WLRO Denham Springs, Louisiana

1220 kHz

KHTS Canyon Country, California
KLDC Denver, Colorado
KDOW Palo Alto, California
KPJC Salem, Oregon
KDDR Oakes, North Dakota
KGIR Cape Girardeau, Missouri
KJAN Atlantic, Iowa
KLPW Union, Missouri
KMVL Madisonville, Texas
KOFO Ottawa, Kansas
KOMC Branson, Missouri
KQMG Independence, Iowa
KTLV Midwest City, Oklahoma
KVSA McGehee, Arkansas
KWKU Pomona, California
KZEE Weatherford, Texas
WABF Fairhope, Alabama
WAXO Lewisburg, Tennessee
WAYE Birmingham, Alabama
WBCH Hastings, Michigan
WCPH Etowah, Tennessee
WENC Whiteville, North Carolina
WERT Van Wert, Ohio
KLBB Stillwater, Minnesota
WFAX Falls Church, Virginia
WFKN Franklin, Kentucky
WFWL Camden, Tennessee
WGNY Newburgh, New York
WJAX Jacksonville, Florida
WJUN Mexico, Pennsylvania
WZBK Keene, New Hampshire
WDYT Kings Mountain, North Carolina
WHKW Cleveland, Ohio
WKRS Waukegan, Illinois
WLPO Lasalle, Illinois
WLSD Big Stone Gap, Virginia
WOEG Hazlehurst, Mississippi
WOTS Kissimmee, Florida
WSRQ Sarasota, Florida
WQUN Hamden, Connecticut
WREV Reidsville, North Carolina
WSTL Providence, Rhode Island
WSLM Salem, Indiana
WWSF Sanford, Maine
WZOT Rockmart, Georgia

1230 kHz

KAAA Kingman, Arizona
KADA Ada, Oklahoma
KATO Safford, Arizona
KBAR Burley, Idaho
KBCR Steamboat Springs, Colorado
KBOV Bishop, California
KBTM Jonesboro, Arkansas
KSGG Reno, Nevada

KDIX Dickinson, North Dakota
KELY Ely, Nevada
KERV Kerrville, Texas
KEXO Grand Junction, Colorado
KFJB Marshalltown, Iowa
KFPW Fort Smith, Arkansas
KFUN Las Vegas, New Mexico
KGEO Bakersfield, California
KGHS International Falls, Minnesota
KGRO Pampa, Texas
KHAS Hastings, Nebraska
KHDN Hardin, Montana
KHSN Coos Bay, Oregon
KIFW Sitka, Alaska
KINO Winslow, Arizona
KKPC Pueblo, Colorado
KLAV Las Vegas, Nevada
KLCB Libby, Montana
KLIC Richwood, Louisiana
KLVT Levelland, Texas
KLWT Lebanon, Missouri
KLXR Redding, California
KMRS Morris, Minnesota
KSZN(AM) Gresham, Oregon
KRSY Alamogordo, New Mexico
KOBB Bozeman, Montana
KORT Grangeville, Idaho
KOTS Deming, New Mexico
KOY Phoenix, Arizona
KOZA Odessa, Texas
KOZI Chelan, Washington
KCUP Toledo, Oregon
KPRL Paso Robles, California
KDYM Sunnyside, Washington
KBCQ Roswell, New Mexico
KRXK Rexburg, Idaho
KSBN Spokane, Washington
KSEY Seymour, Texas
KSIX Corpus Christi, Texas
KSJK Talent, Oregon
KSLO Opelousas, Louisiana
KSST Sulphur Springs, Texas
KSTC Sterling, Colorado
KSZL Barstow, California
KYVA Gallup, New Mexico
KLTO Del Rio, Texas
KTNC Falls City, Nebraska
KTRF Thief River Falls, Minnesota
KVAK Valdez, Alaska
KVOC Casper, Wyoming
KZYM Joplin, Missouri
KWG Stockton, California
KWIX Moberly, Missouri
KWNO Winona, Minnesota
KWSN Sioux Falls, South Dakota
KWTX Waco, Texas
KJQS Murray, Utah
KWYZ Everett, Washington
KXLO Lewistown, Montana
KXO El Centro, California
KYPA Los Angeles, California
KFSP Mankato, Minnesota
WABN Abingdon, Virginia
WIBQ Terre Haute, Indiana
WAIM Anderson, South Carolina
WAKI McMinnville, Tennessee
WAMM Woodstock, Virginia
WANO Pineville, Kentucky
WAUD Auburn, Alabama
WBBZ Ponca City, Oklahoma
WBHP Huntsville, Alabama
WBLJ Dalton, Georgia
WBOK New Orleans, Louisiana
WBPZ Lock Haven, Pennsylvania
WBVP Beaver Falls, Pennsylvania
WCBT Roanoke Rapids, North Carolina
WCLO Janesville, Wisconsin
WTKN Corinth, Mississippi
WCMC Wildwood, New Jersey
WCRO Johnstown, Pennsylvania
WCWA Toledo, Ohio
WECK Cheektowaga, New York
WEEX Easton, Pennsylvania
WENY Elmira, New York
WESX Nahant, Massachusetts
WFAY Fayetteville, North Carolina
WFAS White Plains, New York
WYTS Columbus, Ohio
WFOM Marietta, Georgia
WFVA Fredericksburg, Virginia
WGGG Gainesville, Florida
WGRY Grayling, Michigan
WHCO Sparta, Illinois
WHIR Danville, Kentucky
WRJX Jackson, Alabama
WHOP Hopkinsville, Kentucky
WHUC Hudson, New York
WFER Iron River, Michigan
WIRO Ironton, Ohio
WRBS Baltimore, Maryland
WWWH Haleyville, Alabama
WJBC Bloomington, Illinois
WBZT West Palm Beach, Florida
WJOB Hammond, Indiana
WJOI Norfolk, Virginia
WJOY Burlington, Vermont
WKBO Harrisburg, Pennsylvania
WEZO Augusta, Georgia
WKLK Cloquet, Minnesota
WKWL Florala, Alabama
WVNT Parkersburg, West Virginia
WNEZ Manchester, Connecticut
WIXT Little Falls, New York
WFXN Moline, Illinois
WLNR Kinston, North Carolina
WMAF Madison, Florida
WMFR High Point, North Carolina
WMLR Hohenwald, Tennessee
WMML Glens Falls, New York
WMOU Berlin, New Hampshire
WMPC Lapeer, Michigan
WBET Sturgis, Michigan
WNAW North Adams, Massachusetts
WNEB Worcester, Massachusetts
WNIK Arecibo, Puerto Rico
WNNC Newton, North Carolina
WCMD Cumberland, Maryland
WODI Brookneal, Virginia
WOIC Columbia, South Carolina
WOLH Florence, South Carolina
WONN Lakeland, Florida
WSAL Logansport, Indiana
WSBB New Smyrna Beach, Florida
WSKY Asheville, North Carolina
WSOK Savannah, Georgia
WSOO Sault Ste. Marie, Michigan
WSSO Starkville, Mississippi
WTBC Tuscaloosa, Alabama
WTCJ Tell City, Indiana
WTIV Titusville, Pennsylvania
WTKG Grand Rapids, Michigan
WTSV Claremont, New Hampshire
WDBZ Cincinnati, Ohio
WXCF Clifton Forge, Virginia
WXCO Wausau, Wisconsin
WXLI Dublin, Georgia
WBLQ(AM) Westerly, Rhode Island
WDWR Pensacola, Florida
WWGA(AM) Waycross, Georgia
WCDS Glasgow, Kentucky
WJUL Hiawassee, Georgia
KRYN(AM) Gresham, Oregon

1240 kHz

KDSK Los Ranchos De Albuquerque, New Mexico
KAMQ Carlsbad, New Mexico
KANE New Iberia, Louisiana
KASL Newcastle, Wyoming
KASO Minden, Louisiana
KBIZ Ottumwa, Iowa
KBLL Helena, Montana
KCCR Pierre, South Dakota
KCLV Clovis, New Mexico
KCRT Trinidad, Colorado
KCVL Colville, Washington
KDEC Decorah, Iowa
KDGO Durango, Colorado
KDLR Devils Lake, North Dakota
KEJO Albany, Oregon
KELK Elko, Nevada
KEVA Evanston, Wyoming
KFBC Cheyenne, Wyoming
KFMO Park Hills, Missouri
KFOR Lincoln, Nebraska
KGY Olympia, Washington
KICD Spencer, Iowa
KIUL Garden City, Kansas
KJAA Globe, Arizona
KJOP Lemoore, California
KEZY San Bernardino, California
KLOA Ridgecrest, California
KLTZ Glasgow, Montana
KLYQ Hamilton, Montana
KMCL(AM) Donnelly, Idaho
KMHI Mountain Home, Idaho
KNEM Nevada, Missouri
KNRY Monterey Bay, California
KFH Wichita, Kansas
KODY North Platte, Nebraska
KOFE St. Maries, Idaho
KOKL Okmulgee, Oklahoma
KPOD Crescent City, California
KQEN Roseburg, Oregon
KRAL Rawlins, Wyoming
KRDO Colorado Springs, Colorado
KSLV Monte Vista, Colorado
KSMX Santa Maria, California
KSNN San Diego, California
KSOX Raymondville, Texas
KSUE Susanville, California
KTAM Bryan, Texas
KTHE Thermopolis, Wyoming
KTIX Pendleton, Oregon
KTLO Mountain Home, Arkansas
KSMA Santa Maria, California
KVLF Alpine, Texas
KVRC Arkadelphia, Arkansas
KVSO Ardmore, Oklahoma
KWAK Stuttgart, Arkansas
KWIK Pocatello, Idaho
KWLC Decorah, Iowa
KLIK Jefferson City, Missouri
KXIT Dalhart, Texas
KXLE Ellensburg, Washington
KXOX Sweetwater, Texas
KQBZ Brownwood, Texas
WALO Humacao, Puerto Rico
WJLX Jasper, Alabama
WATN Watertown, New York
WATT Cadillac, Michigan
WAVN Southaven, Mississippi
WBAX Wilkes-Barre, Pennsylvania
WBBW Youngstown, Ohio
WBCF Florence, Alabama
WBEJ Elizabethton, Tennessee
WBGC Chipley, Florida
WBHB Fitzgerald, Georgia
WBUR West Yarmouth, Massachusetts
WCBY Cheboygan, Michigan
WCEM Cambridge, Maryland
WCNC Elizabeth City, North Carolina
WDDO Macon, Georgia
WZCC Cross City, Florida
WDNE Elkins, West Virginia
WDXY Sumter, South Carolina
WEBJ Brewton, Alabama
WEBQ Harrisburg, Illinois
WEKR Fayetteville, Tennessee
WENK Union City, Tennessee
WFOY St. Augustine, Florida
WFTM Maysville, Kentucky
WFTN Franklin, New Hampshire
WGBB Freeport, New York
WGCM Gulfport, Mississippi
WTPS Petersburg, Virginia
WGGA Gainesville, Georgia
WGMN Roanoke, Virginia
WGRM Greenwood, Mississippi
WGVA Geneva, New York
WHMQ Greenfield, Massachusetts
WHBU Anderson, Indiana
WWCD Baltimore, Ohio
WHVN Charlotte, North Carolina
WIAN Ishpeming, Michigan
WHFA Poynette, Wisconsin
WIFA Knoxville, Tennessee
WIOV Reading, Pennsylvania
WJEJ Hagerstown, Maryland
WJIM Lansing, Michigan
WJMC Rice Lake, Wisconsin
WJNC Jacksonville, North Carolina
WJON St. Cloud, Minnesota
WJTN Jamestown, New York
WKDK Newberry, South Carolina
WKEZ Bluefield, West Virginia
WKIQ Eustis, Florida
WLAG La Grange, Georgia
WLLV Louisville, Kentucky
WLSC Loris, South Carolina
WMFG-AM Hibbing, Minnesota
WMGJ Gadsden, Alabama
WMIS Natchez, Mississippi
WMMB Melbourne, Florida
WNBZ Saranac Lake, New York
WNVL Nashville, Tennessee
WOBT Rhinelander, Wisconsin
WOMT Manitowoc, Wisconsin
WOON Woonsocket, Rhode Island
WPAX Thomasville, Georgia
WPBQ Flowood, Mississippi
WPJL Raleigh, North Carolina
WPKE Pikeville, Kentucky
WRTA Altoona, Pennsylvania
WSBC Chicago, Illinois
WSDR Sterling, Illinois
WSDT Soddy-Daisy, Tennessee
WSFC Somerset, Kentucky
WSKI Montpelier, Vermont
WSNJ Bridgeton, New Jersey
WSQL Brevard, North Carolina
WSYY Millinocket, Maine
WTAX Springfield, Illinois
WEZR Lewiston, Maine
WTON Staunton, Virginia
WTWA Thomson, Georgia
WNRA Eufaula, Alabama
WPTR Schenectady, New York
WVOS Liberty, New York
WVTS Dunbar, West Virginia
WWCO Waterbury, Connecticut
WWNS Statesboro, Georgia
WWWC Wilkesboro, North Carolina
WWZQ Aberdeen, Mississippi
KRDM Redmond, Oregon
KSAM Whitefish, Montana
WVTS(AM) Charleston, West Virginia
WFWN Fort Myers, Florida

1250 kHz

KDEI Port Arthur, Texas
KBRF Fergus Falls, Minnesota
KBTC Houston, Missouri
KCFI(AM) Cedar Falls, Iowa
KCFM(AM) Florence, Oregon
KCUE Red Wing, Minnesota
KZER Santa Barbara, California
KZHN Paris, Texas
KHIL Willcox, Arizona
KHOT Madera, California
KIKC Forsyth, Montana
KIKZ Seminole, Texas
KKDZ Seattle, Washington
KPZK Little Rock, Arkansas
KNEU Roosevelt, Utah
KOFC Fayetteville, Arkansas
KNWH Yucca Valley, California
KTFJ Dakota City, Nebraska
KWSU Pullman, Washington
KZDC San Antonio, Texas
WSRA Albany, Georgia
WRBZ Wetumpka, Alabama
WARE Ware, Massachusetts
WBRM Marion, North Carolina
WCHO Washington Ct House, Ohio
WHNZ Tampa, Florida
WDVA Danville, Virginia
WGHB Farmville, North Carolina
WGL Fort Wayne, Indiana
WSPL Streator, Illinois
WJIT Sabana, Puerto Rico
WKBL Covington, Tennessee
WGAM Manchester, New Hampshire
WKDX Hamlet, North Carolina
WHHQ Bridgeport, Michigan
WLCK Scottsville, Kentucky
WLEM Emporium, Pennsylvania
WDDZ Pittsburgh, Pennsylvania
WLQM Franklin, Virginia
WMTR Morristown, New Jersey
WNTT Tazewell, Tennessee
WKDL Warrenton, Virginia
WQHL Live Oak, Florida
WYYC York, Pennsylvania
WRAY Princeton, Indiana
KYYS Kansas City, Kansas
WRKQ Madisonville, Tennessee
WTMA Charleston, South Carolina
WYKM Rupert, West Virginia
WYTH Madison, Georgia
WZOB Fort Payne, Alabama
WGAM(AM) Manchester, New Hampshire

1260 kHz

KBHC Nashville, Arkansas
KBRH Baton Rouge, Louisiana
KBSZ Apache Junction, Arizona
KCCB Corning, Arkansas
KDUZ Hutchinson, Minnesota
KFFF(AM) Boone, Iowa
KBLY Idaho Falls, Idaho
KIMB Kimball, Nebraska
KKSA San Angelo, Texas
KLDS Falfurrias, Texas
KLYC McMinnville, Oregon
KSFB San Francisco, California
KPOW Powell, Wyoming
KROX Crookston, Minnesota
KSML Diboll, Texas
KWNX Elgin, Texas
KSGF Springfield, Missouri
KTRC Santa Fe, New Mexico
KWSH Wewoka, Oklahoma
KWYR Winner, South Dakota
WBNR Beacon, New York
WFJS Trenton, New Jersey
WCHV Charlottesville, Virginia
WCLC Jamestown, Tennessee
WCSA Ripley, Mississippi
WYDE Birmingham, Alabama
WDKN Dickson, Tennessee
WEKZ Monroe, Wisconsin
WFTW Fort Walton Beach, Florida
WWRC Washington, District of Columbia
WGVM Greenville, Mississippi
WHYM Lake City, South Carolina
WISO Ponce, Puerto Rico
WIYD Palatka, Florida
WKXR Asheboro, North Carolina
WMCH Church Hill, Tennessee
WSHU Westport, Connecticut
WPJF Greenville, South Carolina
WNDE Indianapolis, Indiana
WNOO Chattanooga, Tennessee
WSKO Syracuse, New York
WNXT Portsmouth, Ohio
WOCO Oconto, Wisconsin
WPHB Philipsburg, Pennsylvania
WMKI Boston, Massachusetts
WRIE Erie, Pennsylvania
WSDZ Belleville, Illinois
WSUA Miami, Florida
WTJH East Point, Georgia
WUFE Baxley, Georgia
WWIS Black River Falls, Wisconsin
WPNW Zeeland, Michigan
WWMK Cleveland, Ohio
WWVT Christiansburg, Virginia
WXCE Amery, Wisconsin
WZBO Edenton, North Carolina
KTRP Weiser, Idaho

1270 kHz

KAJO Grants Pass, Oregon
KBAM Longview, Washington
KDJI Holbrook, Arizona
KEPS Eagle Pass, Texas
KFLC Benbrook, Texas
KGNM St. Joseph, Missouri
KIML Gillette, Wyoming
KINN Alamogordo, New Mexico
KJUG Tulare, California
KLXX Bismarck-Mandan, North Dakota
KNDI Honolulu, Hawaii
KNWC Sioux Falls, South Dakota
KIIK Waynesville, Missouri
KBZZ Sparks, Nevada
KSCB Liberal, Kansas
KRVT Claremore, Oklahoma
KFAN Rochester, Minnesota
KXBX Ukiah, California
KFSQ Thousand Palms, California
WAIN Columbia, Kentucky
WHGS Hampton, South Carolina
WCBC Cumberland, Maryland
WCGC Belmont, North Carolina
WDLA Walton, New York
WCMR Elkhart, Indiana
WGSV Guntersville, Alabama
WHEO Stuart, Virginia
WHLD Niagara Falls, New York
WILE Cambridge, Ohio
WJJC Commerce, Georgia
WKBF Rock Island, Illinois
WIJD Prichard, Alabama
WLBR Lebanon, Pennsylvania
WLIK Newport, Tennessee
WMIZ Vineland, New Jersey
WMKT Charlevoix, Michigan
WBOJ Columbus, Georgia
WMPM Smithfield, North Carolina
WTLY Tallahassee, Florida
WNOG Naples, Florida
WQKR Portland, Tennessee
WRJC Mauston, Wisconsin
WRLZ Eatonville, Florida
WSPR Springfield, Massachusetts
WTJZ Newport News, Virginia
WTSN Dover, New Hampshire
WQTT Marysville, Ohio
WWCA Gary, Indiana
WWWI Baxter, Minnesota
WXGO Madison, Indiana
WXYT Detroit, Michigan
WYXC Cartersville, Georgia
WMLC Monticello, Mississippi

1280 kHz

KCNI Broken Bow, Nebraska
KCOB Newton, Iowa
KDKD Clinton, Missouri
KQLL Henderson, Nevada
KZNS Salt Lake City, Utah
KFRN Long Beach, California
KSLI Abilene, Texas
KIT Yakima, Washington
KWSX Stockton, California
KXTK Arroyo Grande, California
KLDY Lacey, Washington
KNBY Newport, Arkansas
KPRV Poteau, Oklahoma
KRVM Eugene, Oregon
KSOK Arkansas City, Kansas
KXEG Phoenix, Arizona
KZFS Spokane, Washington
KBNO Denver, Colorado
KVXR Moorhead, Minnesota
KMFR Pearsall, Texas
KWHI Brenham, Texas
KYRO Troy, Missouri
WADO New York, New York
WANS Anderson, South Carolina
WBIG Aurora, Illinois
WCMN Arecibo, Puerto Rico
WCPM Cumberland, Kentucky
WDNT Dayton, Tennessee
WPKZ Fitchburg, Massachusetts
WFAU Gardiner, Maine
WFYC Alma, Michigan
WGBF Evansville, Indiana
WDSP De Funiak Springs, Florida
WHTK Rochester, New York
WHVR Hanover, Pennsylvania
WIPC Lake Wales, Florida
WJAY Mullins, South Carolina
WJWK Seaford, Delaware
WJST New Castle, Pennsylvania
WIHB Macon, Georgia
WMCP Columbia, Tennessee
WNAM Neenah-Menasha, Wisconsin
WODT New Orleans, Louisiana
WONW Defiance, Ohio
WPID Piedmont, Alabama
WSAT Salisbury, North Carolina
WBWX(AM) Berwick, Pennsylvania
WTMY Sarasota, Florida
WOWZ Appomattox, Virginia
WMXB Tuscaloosa, Alabama
WWTC Minneapolis, Minnesota
WYAL Scotland Neck, North Carolina
WYVE Wytheville, Virginia

1290 kHz

KALM Thayer, Missouri
KAZA Gilroy, California
KCUB Tucson, Arizona
KDMS El Dorado, Arkansas
KGVO Missoula, Montana
KIVY Crockett, Texas
KJEF Jennings, Louisiana
KOIL Omaha, Nebraska
KKDD San Bernardino, California
KOUU Pocatello, Idaho
KOWB Laramie, Wyoming
KPAY Chico, California
KRGE Weslaco, Texas
KBMO Benson, Minnesota
KUMA Pendleton, Oregon
KUOA Siloam Springs, Arkansas
KWFS Wichita Falls, Texas
KMMM Pratt, Kansas
KZSB Santa Barbara, California
WBTG Sheffield, Alabama
WJNO West Palm Beach, Florida
WCBL Benton, Kentucky
WCCC West Hartford, Connecticut
WCHK Canton, Georgia
WTKS Savannah, Georgia
WLBY Saline, Michigan
WPCF Panama City Beach, Florida
WDZY Colonial Heights, Virginia
WFBG Altoona, Pennsylvania
WHIO Dayton, Ohio
WHKY Hickory, North Carolina
WIRL Peoria, Illinois
WJBI Batesville, Mississippi
WWTX Wilmington, Delaware
WJCV Jacksonville, North Carolina
WKLB Manchester, Kentucky
WKLJ Sparta, Wisconsin
WKBK Keene, New Hampshire
WZTI Greenfield, Wisconsin
WNBF Binghamton, New York
WNBN Meridian, Mississippi
WOWO Niles, Michigan
WOMP Bellaire, Ohio
WOPP Opp, Alabama
WWHM Sumter, South Carolina
WRNI Providence, Rhode Island
WTYL Tylertown, Mississippi
WVOW Logan, West Virginia
WXKL Sanford, North Carolina
WYEA Sylacauga, Alabama

1300 kHz

KACI The Dalles, Oregon
KAKC Tulsa, Oklahoma
KAPL Phoenix, Oregon
KAZN Pasadena, California
KBRL McCook, Nebraska
KSYB Shreveport, Louisiana
KGLO Mason City, Iowa
KSET Lumberton, Texas
KKOL Seattle, Washington
KROP Brawley, California
KKUB Brownfield, Texas
KLAR Laredo, Texas
KLER Orofino, Idaho
KMMO Marshall, Missouri
KOLY Mobridge, South Dakota
KPMO Mendocino, California
KCMY Carson City, Nevada
KCSF Colorado Springs, Colorado
KVET Austin, Texas
KWCK Searcy, Arkansas
KYNO Fresno, California
WAVZ New Haven, Connecticut
WBSA Boaz, Alabama
WBZQ Huntington, Indiana
WCKI Greer, South Carolina
WCLG Morgantown, West Virginia
WJYP St. Albans, West Virginia
WJMO Cleveland, Ohio
WFFG Marathon, Florida
WFRX West Frankfort, Illinois
WIBR Baton Rouge, Louisiana
WKZN West Hazleton, Pennsylvania
WIMG Ewing, New Jersey
WIMO Winder, Georgia
WJDA Quincy, Massachusetts
WJZ Baltimore, Maryland
WBOW Terre Haute, Indiana
WKCY Harrisonburg, Virginia
WKSC Kershaw, South Carolina
WKXM Winfield, Alabama
WLNC Laurinburg, North Carolina
WLXG Lexington, Kentucky
WMTM Moultrie, Georgia
WMTN Morristown, Tennessee
WMVO Mount Vernon, Ohio
WNEA Newnan, Georgia
WNQM Nashville, Tennessee
WOAD Jackson, Mississippi
WOOD Grand Rapids, Michigan
WPNH Plymouth, New Hampshire
WQBN Temple Terrace, Florida
WQPM Princeton, Minnesota
WRDZ La Grange, Illinois
WSYD Mount Airy, North Carolina
WTIL Mayaguez, Puerto Rico
WTLS Tallassee, Alabama
WGDJ Rensselaer, New York
WWCH Clarion, Pennsylvania
WXRL Lancaster, New York
WOSW Fulton, New York
WSSG Goldsboro, North Carolina

1310 kHz

KBOK Malvern, Arkansas
KDLS Perry, Iowa
KEIN Great Falls, Montana
KEZM Sulphur, Louisiana
KFKA Greeley, Colorado
KYUL Scott City, Kansas
KFVR Crescent City, California
KGMT Fairbury, Nebraska
KIQQ Barstow, California
KKNS Corrales, New Mexico
KLIX Twin Falls, Idaho
KMBS West Monroe, Louisiana
KMKY Oakland, California
KNOX Grand Forks, North Dakota
KNPT Newport, Oregon
KZRG Joplin, Missouri
KOKX Keokuk, Iowa
KGLB Glencoe, Minnesota
KTCK Dallas, Texas
KIHP Mesa, Arizona
KAHL San Antonio, Texas
KZIP Amarillo, Texas
KZXR Prosser, Washington
WADB(AM) Asbury Park, New Jersey
WAUC Wauchula, Florida
WCCW Traverse City, Michigan
WDCT Fairfax, Virginia
WDKD Kingstree, South Carolina
WDOC Prestonsburg, Kentucky
WDPN Alliance, Ohio
WDXI Jackson, Tennessee
WGH Newport News, Virginia
WGSP Charlotte, North Carolina
WHEP Foley, Alabama
WTZN Troy, Pennsylvania
WIBA Madison, Wisconsin
WICH Norwich, Connecticut
WISE Asheville, North Carolina
WKZD Priceville, Alabama
WJUS Marion, Alabama
WLOB Portland, Maine
WNAE Warren, Pennsylvania
WOCV Oneida, Tennessee
WOKA Douglas, Georgia
WBFD Bedford, Pennsylvania
WORC Worcester, Massachusetts
WPBC Decatur, Georgia
WPLV West Point, Georgia
WRSB Canandaigua, New York
WSLW White Sulphur Spring, West Virginia
WEMG Camden, New Jersey
WTIK Durham, North Carolina
WTLB Utica, New York
WTLC Indianapolis, Indiana
WTTL Madisonville, Kentucky
WRVP Mount Kisco, New York
WXMC Parsippany-Troy Hill, New Jersey
WYND Deland, Florida
WDTW Dearborn, Michigan
WPCH West Point, Georgia

1320 kHz

KAWC Yuma, Arizona
KCLI Clinton, Oklahoma
KIFM West Sacramento, California
KFNZ Salt Lake City, Utah
KGDC Walla Walla, Washington
KHRT Minot, North Dakota
KKSM Oceanside, California
KLWN Lawrence, Kansas
KMAQ Maquoketa, Iowa
KNCB Vivian, Louisiana
KNIA Knoxville, Iowa
KSCR Eugene, Oregon
KOLT Scottsbluff, Nebraska
KOZY Grand Rapids, Minnesota
KRDD Roswell, New Mexico
KRLW Walnut Ridge, Arkansas

KSDT Hemet, California
KSIV Clayton, Missouri
KVMC Colorado City, Texas
KWHN Fort Smith, Arkansas
KXRO Aberdeen, Washington
KXYZ Houston, Texas
WAGF Dothan, Alabama
WDDV Venice, Florida
WATR Waterbury, Connecticut
WBRT Bardstown, Kentucky
WCOG Greensboro, North Carolina
WCVG Covington, Kentucky
WDER Derry, New Hampshire
WDMJ Marquette, Michigan
WENN Birmingham, Alabama
WFHR Wisconsin Rapids, Wisconsin
WGET Gettysburg, Pennsylvania
WHIE Griffin, Georgia
WICO Salisbury, Maryland
WILS Lansing, Michigan
WISW Columbia, South Carolina
WNGO Mayfield, Kentucky
WJAS Pittsburgh, Pennsylvania
WARL Attleboro, Massachusetts
WKAN Kankakee, Illinois
WGOC Kingsport, Tennessee
WKRK Murphy, North Carolina
WVNZ Richmond, Virginia
WLOH Lancaster, Ohio
WLQY Hollywood, Florida
WMSR Manchester, Tennessee
WOBL Oberlin, Ohio
WRJW Picayune, Mississippi
WTKZ Allentown, Pennsylvania
WSKN San Juan, Puerto Rico
WVGM Lynchburg, Virginia
WCVR(AM) Randolph, Vermont
WAGY Forest City, North Carolina
KELO-AM Sioux Falls, South Dakota

1330 kHz

KGRG Enumclaw, Washington
KNSS Wichita, Kansas
KGAK Gallup, New Mexico
KGLD Tyler, Texas
KINE Kingsville, Texas
KWFM(AM) South Tucson, Arizona
KKPZ Portland, Oregon
KCKM Monahans, Texas
KLBS Los Banos, California
KTON Cameron, Texas
KOVE Lander, Wyoming
KSWA Graham, Texas
KXXA(AM) Conway, Arkansas
KUKU Willow Springs, Missouri
KVOL Lafayette, Louisiana
KWKW Los Angeles, California
KWLO Waterloo, Iowa
WAEW Crossville, Tennessee
WANG Havelock, North Carolina
WJSS Havre De Grace, Maryland
WGFT Campbell, Ohio
WBTM Danville, Virginia
WLBB Carrollton, Georgia
WCVC Tallahassee, Florida
WEBO Owego, New York
WEBY Milton, Florida
WINT Willoughby, Ohio
WENA Yauco, Puerto Rico
WESR Onley-Onancock, Virginia
WETZ New Martinsville, West Virginia
WFIN Findlay, Ohio
WFNN Erie, Pennsylvania
WHAZ Troy, New York
WHBL Sheboygan, Wisconsin
WJNX Fort Pierce, Florida
WKDP Corbin, Kentucky
WKTA Evanston, Illinois
WGTJ Murrayville, Georgia
WMLT Dublin, Georgia
WLOL Minneapolis, Minnesota
WMOR Morehead, Kentucky
WNIX Greenville, Mississippi
WNTA Rockford, Illinois
WITM Marion, Virginia
WPJS Conway, South Carolina
WRAA Luray, Virginia
WRAM Monmouth, Illinois
WRCA Watertown, Massachusetts
WSPQ Springville, New York
WTRE Greensburg, Indiana
WTRX Flint, Michigan
WVHI Evansville, Indiana
WWAB Lakeland, Florida
WWRV New York, New York
WYPC Wellston, Ohio
WYRD Greenville, South Carolina
WZCT Scottsboro, Alabama
KJPR Shasta Lake City, California
KXXJ Juneau, Alaska

1340 kHz

KACH Preston, Idaho
KVNN Victoria, Texas
KAND Corsicana, Texas
KATA Eureka, California
KTPI Mojave, California
KBBR Coos Bay, Oregon
KBTA Batesville, Arkansas
KCAP Helena, Montana
KCAT Pine Bluff, Arkansas
KCBL Fresno, California
KCQL Aztec, New Mexico
KCRN San Angelo, Texas
KDLM Detroit Lakes, Minnesota
KGHM Midwest City, Oklahoma
KDTD Kansas City, Kansas
KGFW Kearney, Nebraska
KYNS San Luis Obispo, California
KHUB Fremont, Nebraska
KADI Springfield, Missouri
KIHR Hood River, Oregon
KIJV Huron, South Dakota
KNTF Oroville, California
KKAM Lubbock, Texas
KVOQ(AM) Denver, Colorado
KLID Poplar Bluff, Missouri
KWLE Anacortes, Washington
KLOO Albany, Oregon
KOLE Port Arthur, Texas
KOMY La Selva Beach, California
KPGE Page, Arizona
KPOK Bowman, North Dakota
KPRK Livingston, Montana
KTMM Grand Junction, Colorado
KRBA Lufkin, Texas
KRBT Eveleth, Minnesota
KRLV Las Vegas, Nevada
KRMD Shreveport, Louisiana
KROC Rochester, Minnesota
KROS Clinton, Iowa
KSEK Pittsburg, Kansas
KSGT Jackson, Wyoming
KSID Sidney, Nebraska
KSMO Salem, Missouri
KJOX Kennewick, Washington
KTFI Wendell, Idaho
KJMU Sand Springs, Oklahoma
KTOQ Rapid City, South Dakota
KTOX Needles, California
KTSN Elko, Nevada
KVBR Brainerd, Minnesota
KVIV El Paso, Texas
KVRH Salida, Colorado
KUOW Tumwater, Washington
KWKC Abilene, Texas
KWLM Willmar, Minnesota
KWOR Worland, Wyoming
KWVR Enterprise, Oregon
KZNW Wenatchee, Washington
KWXY AM Cathedral City, California
KXEO Mexico, Missouri
KXEQ Reno, Nevada
KXPO Grafton, North Dakota
KCLU Santa Barbara, California
KYCN Wheatland, Wyoming
KYLT Missoula, Montana
KZNG Hot Springs, Arkansas
WADE Wadesboro, North Carolina
WAGN Menominee, Michigan
WAGR Lumberton, North Carolina
WLSG Wilmington, North Carolina
WALL Middletown, New York
WIFN Atlanta, Georgia
WAML Laurel, Mississippi
WBAC Cleveland, Tennessee
WYNF Augusta, Georgia
WBBT Lyons, Georgia
WBGN Bowling Green, Kentucky
WBIW Bedford, Indiana
WBRK Pittsfield, Massachusetts
WCBQ Oxford, North Carolina
WCDT Winchester, Tennessee
WCMI Ashland, Kentucky
WCSR Hillsdale, Michigan
WDSR Lake City, Florida
WEKY Richmond, Kentucky
WENT Gloversville, New York
WEPM Martinsburg, West Virginia
WEXL Royal Oak, Michigan
WFEB Sylacauga, Alabama
WGAU Athens, Georgia
WGAW Gardner, Massachusetts
WGRV Greeneville, Tennessee
WHAP Hopewell, Virginia
WXKX Clarksburg, West Virginia
WHAT Philadelphia, Pennsylvania
WIRY Plattsburgh, New York
WITS Sebring, Florida
WIZE Springfield, Ohio
WJOL Joliet, Illinois
WJPF Herrin, Illinois
WJRI Lenoir, North Carolina
WJYI Milwaukee, Wisconsin
WKCB Hindman, Kentucky
WKEY Covington, Virginia
WMBO Auburn, New York
WKGN Knoxville, Tennessee
WKRM Columbia, Tennessee
WKSN Jamestown, New York
WLDY Ladysmith, Wisconsin
WLEW Bad Axe, Michigan
WLOK Memphis, Tennessee
WLVL Lockport, New York
WMBN Petoskey, Michigan
WMDR Augusta, Maine
WMID Atlantic City, New Jersey
WMON Montgomery, West Virginia
WJAM Selma, Alabama
WMSA Massena, New York
WMTE Manistee, Michigan
WNBH New Bedford, Massachusetts
WNBS Murray, Kentucky
WNCO Ashland, Ohio
WWNA Aguadilla, Puerto Rico
WOKS Columbus, Georgia
WOUB Athens, Ohio
WPBR Lantana, Florida
WPOL Winston-Salem, North Carolina
WQSC Charleston, South Carolina
WRAW Reading, Pennsylvania
WRHI Rock Hill, South Carolina
WROD Daytona Beach, Florida
WSBM Florence, Alabama
WSOY Decatur, Illinois
WSSC Sumter, South Carolina
WSTA Charlotte Amalie, Virgin Islands
WSTJ St. Johnsbury, Vermont
WTAN Clearwater, Florida
WTIF Tifton, Georgia
WTRC Elkhart, Indiana
WTRN Tyrone, Pennsylvania
WTYS Marianna, Florida
WVCV Orange, Virginia
WVNR Poultney, Vermont
WWFL Clermont, Florida
WWNH Madbury, New Hampshire
WWPA Williamsport, Pennsylvania
WXFN Muncie, Indiana
WFMH Cullman, Alabama
WYBC New Haven, Connecticut
WYCB Washington, District of Columbia
WYCK Plains, Pennsylvania
WNZS Veazie, Maine
KVOT Taos, New Mexico
KBNW Bend, Oregon
WJRW Grand Rapids, Michigan

1350 kHz

KABQ Albuquerque, New Mexico
KZTD Cabot, Arkansas
KLHC Bakersfield, California
KBRX O'Neill, Nebraska
KCAR Clarksville, Texas
KCHK New Prague, Minnesota
KCHR Charleston, Missouri
KTDD San Bernardino, California
KCOR San Antonio, Texas
KDIO Ortonville, Minnesota
KCCY Pueblo, Colorado
KPNS Duncan, Oklahoma
KMAN Manhattan, Kansas
KRLC Lewiston-Clarkston, Idaho
KRNT Des Moines, Iowa
KSRO Santa Rosa, California
KTIK Nampa, Idaho
KTLQ Tahlequah, Oklahoma
KCOX Jasper, Texas
KWMO Washington, Missouri
WCBA Corning, New York
WCHI Chillicothe, Ohio
WCMP Pine City, Minnesota
WRWR Warner Robins, Georgia
WCRM Fort Myers, Florida
WCSM Celina, Ohio
WDCF Dade City, Florida
WEGA Vega Baja, Puerto Rico
WELB Elba, Alabama
WEZS Laconia, New Hampshire
WTDR Gadsden, Alabama
WGDN Gladwin, Michigan
WFNS Blackshear, Georgia
WGPL Portsmouth, Virginia
WHIP Mooresville, North Carolina
WHWH Princeton, New Jersey
WINY Putnam, Connecticut
WIOU Kokomo, Indiana
WJBD Salem, Illinois
WKCU Corinth, Mississippi
WLLY Wilson, North Carolina
WLOU Louisville, Kentucky
WMMV Cocoa, Florida
WNLK Norwalk, Connecticut
WNVA Norton, Virginia
WOAM Peoria, Illinois
WOYK York, Pennsylvania
WPDR Portage, Wisconsin
WRKM Carthage, Tennessee
WRNY Rome, New York
WRWH Cleveland, Georgia
WWWL New Orleans, Louisiana
WARF Akron, Ohio
WZGM Black Mountain, North Carolina
WNTX Fredericksburg, Virginia
WBLT Bedford, Virginia

1360 kHz

KACT Andrews, Texas
KMNY Hurst, Texas
KBKB Fort Madison, Iowa
KBUY Ruidoso, New Mexico
KBYO Tallulah, Louisiana
KDJW Amarillo, Texas
KELE Mountain Grove, Missouri
KPXQ Glendale, Arizona
KFFA Helena, Arkansas
KFIV Modesto, California
KHNC Johnstown, Colorado
KKBJ Bemidji, Minnesota
KKMO Tacoma, Washington
KLYR Clarksville, Arkansas
KMRN Cameron, Missouri
KNGN McCook, Nebraska
KNIR New Iberia, Louisiana
KOHU Hermiston, Oregon
KLSD San Diego, California
KRKK Rock Springs, Wyoming
KRWC Buffalo, Minnesota
KKTX Corpus Christi, Texas
KSCJ Sioux City, Iowa
KAHS El Dorado, Kansas
KMJM Cedar Rapids, Iowa
KUIK Hillsboro, Oregon
KWWJ Baytown, Texas
KWDJ Ridgecrest, California
WBLC Lenoir City, Tennessee
WCGL Jacksonville, Florida
WCHL Chapel Hill, North Carolina
WSAI Cincinnati, Ohio
WDRC Hartford, Connecticut
WELP Easley, South Carolina
WLWE Roanoke, Alabama
WFFF Columbia, Mississippi
WFLW Monticello, Kentucky
WTAQ-AM Green Bay, Wisconsin
WGFA Watseka, Illinois
WHBG Harrisonburg, Virginia
WHCG Metter, Georgia
WHJC Matewan, West Virginia
WHNR Cypress Gardens, Florida
WKAT North Miami, Florida
WKMI Kalamazoo, Michigan
WYOS Binghamton, New York
WKYO Caro, Michigan

WLBK Dekalb, Illinois
WLYN Lynn, Massachusetts
WOEN Olean, New York
WMOB Mobile, Alabama
WMOV Ravenswood, West Virginia
WNAH Nashville, Tennessee
WNJC Vineland, New Jersey
WTOC Newton, New Jersey
WPPA Pottsville, Pennsylvania
WMNY McKeesport, Pennsylvania
WGJK Rome, Georgia
WVRQ Viroqua, Wisconsin
WWOW Conneaut, Ohio
WWWJ Galax, Virginia
WIXI Jasper, Alabama

1370 kHz

KIOL Iola, Kansas
KAST Astoria, Oregon
KAWL York, Nebraska
KAWW Heber Springs, Arkansas
KCRV-AM Caruthersville, Missouri
KDTH Dubuque, Iowa
KFRO Longview, Texas
KGEN Tulare, California
KGNO Dodge City, Kansas
KUPA Pearl City, Hawaii
KJCE Rollingwood, Texas
KRAC Quincy, California
KSOP South Salt Lake, Utah
KSUM Fairmont, Minnesota
KTPA Prescott, Arkansas
KWTL Grand Forks, North Dakota
KWNC Quincy, Washington
KWRM Corona, California
KWRT Boonville, Missouri
KXTL Butte, Montana
KZSF San Jose, California
WLFZ Fort Campbell, Kentucky
WALK Patchogue, New York
WAXE Vero Beach, Florida
WBTN Bennington, Vermont
WCCN Neillsville, Wisconsin
WCOA Pensacola, Florida
WDEA Ellsworth, Maine
WDEF Chattanooga, Tennessee
WDXE Lawrenceburg, Tennessee
WJIP Ellenville, New York
WFDR Manchester, Georgia
WFEA Manchester, New Hampshire
WGCL Bloomington, Indiana
WGHN Grand Haven, Michigan
WGOH Grayson, Kentucky
WHEE Martinsville, Virginia
WIVV Island of Vieques, Puerto Rico
WSHV South Hill, Virginia
WLJW Cadillac, Michigan
WKMC Roaring Spring, Pennsylvania
WLLM Lincoln, Illinois
WLLN Lillington, North Carolina
WLOP Jesup, Georgia
WLOV Washington, Georgia
WGIV Pineville, North Carolina
WLTH Gary, Indiana
WMGO Canton, Mississippi
WVLY Moundsville, West Virginia
WOCA Ocala, Florida
WPAZ Pottstown, Pennsylvania
WRGS Rogersville, Tennessee
WSPD Toledo, Ohio
WTAB Tabor City, North Carolina
WTKY Tompkinsville, Kentucky
WVMR Frost, West Virginia
WWCB(AM) Corry, Pennsylvania
WQAL(AM) Pikesville, Maryland
WXXI Rochester, New York
KPWL Newport, Washington
WZTA Vero Beach, Florida

1380 kHz

KAGE Winona, Minnesota
KBWD Brownwood, Texas
KCII Washington, Iowa
KCIM Carroll, Iowa
KCNW Fairway, Kansas
KWMF Pleasanton, Texas
KOSS Lancaster, California
KJUA Cheyenne, Wyoming
KLIZ Brainerd, Minnesota
KLPZ Parker, Arizona
KMUS Sperry, Oklahoma
KOTA Rapid City, South Dakota
KQKD Redfield, South Dakota
KRCM Shanandoah, Texas
KRKO Everett, Washington
KDXE North Little Rock, Arkansas
KSRV Ontario, Oregon
KTKZ Sacramento, California
KHEY El Paso, Texas
KUVR Holdrege, Nebraska
KXCA Lawton, Oklahoma
KXFN Saint Louis, Missouri
WABH Bath, New York
WAGS Bishopville, South Carolina
WTMC Wilmington, Delaware
WAOK Atlanta, Georgia
WDLW Lorain, Ohio
WELE Ormond Beach, Florida
WOTE Clintonville, Wisconsin
WPYR Baton Rouge, Louisiana
WFNW Naugatuck, Connecticut
WNRR North Augusta, South Carolina
WGYV Greenville, Alabama
WCBG Waynesboro, Pennsylvania
WKJG Fort Wayne, Indiana
WKDM New York, New York
WLRV Lebanon, Virginia
WWRF Lake Worth, Florida
WMJR Nicholasville, Kentucky
WMLP Milton, Pennsylvania
WMTA Central City, Kentucky
WMTD Hinton, West Virginia
WMYF Portsmouth, New Hampshire
WNLA Indianola, Mississippi
WNRI Woonsocket, Rhode Island
WOLA Barranquitas, Puerto Rico
WLRM Millington, Tennessee
WPHM Port Huron, Michigan
WGLM Greenville, Michigan
WRAB Arab, Alabama
WSYB Rutland, Vermont
WTOB Winston-Salem, North Carolina
WBTK Richmond, Virginia
WTYM Kittanning, Pennsylvania
WVSA Vernon, Alabama
WWMI St. Petersburg, Florida
WYSH Clinton, Tennessee
WHEW Franklin, Tennessee

1390 kHz

KTCR Yakima, Washington
KBEC Waxahachie, Texas
KCLN Clinton, Iowa
KCRC Enid, Oklahoma
KDQN De Queen, Arkansas
KENN Farmington, New Mexico
KFRA Franklin, Louisiana
KHOB Hobbs, New Mexico
KJAM Madison, South Dakota
KGNU Denver, Colorado
KJPW Waynesville, Missouri
KLGN Logan, Utah
KLTX Long Beach, California
KNCK Concordia, Kansas
KFFK Rogers, Arkansas
KRFO Owatonna, Minnesota
KRRZ Minot, North Dakota
KULP El Campo, Texas
KLOC Turlock, California
KXSS Waite Park, Minnesota
WOHS Shelby, North Carolina
WAJD Gainesville, Florida
WANY Albany, Kentucky
WFHT Avon Park, Florida
WBLL Bellefontaine, Ohio
WFBL Syracuse, New York
WEED Rocky Mount, North Carolina
WEGP Presque Isle, Maine
WEOK Poughkeepsie, New York
WFIW Fairfield, Illinois
WGRB Chicago, Illinois
WHMA Anniston, Alabama
WABB Belton, South Carolina
WISA Isabela, Puerto Rico
WJRM Troy, North Carolina
WCAT Burlington, Vermont
WKIC(AM) Hazard, Kentucky
WKLP Keyser, West Virginia
WKPA Lynchburg, Virginia
WLAN Lancaster, Pennsylvania
WLCM Holt, Michigan
WMCT Mountain City, Tennessee
WMER Meridian, Mississippi
WMPO Middleport-Pomeroy, Ohio
WPLM Plymouth, Massachusetts
WRIG Schofield, Wisconsin
WRIV Riverhead, New York
WROA Gulfport, Mississippi
WRSC State College, Pennsylvania
WNIO Youngstown, Ohio
WTJS Jackson, Tennessee
WTNL Reidsville, Georgia
WSPO Charleston, South Carolina
WYXI Athens, Tennessee
WZHF Arlington, Virginia
WZZB Seymour, Indiana

1400 Hz

WRJN Janesville, Wisconsin

1400 kHz

KADR Elkader, Iowa
KAOK Lake Charles, Louisiana
KART Jerome, Idaho
KAYS Hays, Kansas
KNRO Redding, California
KBCH Lincoln City, Oregon
KBJM Lemmon, South Dakota
KBRB Ainsworth, Nebraska
KBYG Big Spring, Texas
KBLJ La Junta, Colorado
KCHS Truth or Consequences, New Mexico
KCOG Centerville, Iowa
KCOW Alliance, Nebraska
KBCK Deer Lodge, Montana
KDTA Delta, Colorado
KEBE Jacksonville, Texas
KEDO Longview, Washington
KELD El Dorado, Arkansas
KESQ Indio, California
KKTK Texarkana, Texas
KEYL Long Prairie, Minnesota
KFRU Columbia, Missouri
KFTM Fort Morgan, Colorado
KGMY Springfield, Missouri
KGVL Greenville, Texas
KHCB League City, Texas
KITZ Silverdale, Washington
KIUN Pecos, Texas
KJDY John Day, Oregon
KJFF Festus, Missouri
KCYK Yuma, Arizona
KKJL San Luis Obispo, California
KKTL Casper, Wyoming
KMNV St. Paul, Minnesota
KLCK Goldendale, Washington
KLIN Lincoln, Nebraska
KMHL Marshall, Minnesota
KNND Cottage Grove, Oregon
KREF Norman, Oklahoma
KODI Cody, Wyoming
KQDJ Jamestown, North Dakota
KQMS Redding, California
KRAM Vernal, Utah
KRLN Canon City, Colorado
KRPL Moscow, Idaho
KRSC Othello, Washington
KRUN Ballinger, Texas
KRVZ Springerville, Arizona
KRZR Visalia, California
KSHP North Las Vegas, Nevada
KSIM Sikeston, Missouri
KSPT Sandpoint, Idaho
KSRR Provo, Utah
KTEM Temple, Texas
KTMC McAlester, Oklahoma
KTNM Tucumcari, New Mexico
KVSF Santa Fe, New Mexico
KTUC Tucson, Arizona
KUKI Ukiah, California
KUNO Corpus Christi, Texas
KVFD Fort Dodge, Iowa
KVOE Emporia, Kansas
KREW Plainview, Texas
KGWU Uvalde, Texas
KVRP Stamford, Texas
KUNX Santa Paula, California
KVTO Berkeley, California
KWNA Winnemucca, Nevada
KWON Bartlesville, Oklahoma
KWUF Pagosa Springs, Colorado
KWYN Wynne, Arkansas
KXGF Great Falls, Montana
KXGN Glendive, Montana
WAMC Albany, New York
WAWO Alma, Georgia
WANI Opelika, Alabama
WATW Ashland, Wisconsin
WBAT Marion, Indiana
WBBD Wheeling, West Virginia
WBIP Booneville, Mississippi
WBIZ Eau Claire, Wisconsin
WBTH Williamson, West Virginia
WCCY Houghton, Michigan
WCOH Newnan, Georgia
WCOS Columbia, South Carolina
WCYN Cynthiana, Kentucky
WDNY Dansville, New York
WDUZ Green Bay, Wisconsin
WDWS Champaign, Illinois
WWGE Loretto, Pennsylvania
WEOA Evansville, Indiana
WEST Easton, Pennsylvania
WJZN Augusta, Maine
WEDM(AM) Fort Walton Beach, Florida
WFOR Hattiesburg, Mississippi
WFPR Hammond, Louisiana
WFTG London, Kentucky
WFLL Fort Lauderdale, Florida
WGAP Maryville, Tennessee
WGIL Galesburg, Illinois
WGTN Georgetown, South Carolina
WMXF Waynesville, North Carolina
WHHV Hillsville, Virginia
WHMP Northampton, Massachusetts
WHTB Fall River, Massachusetts
WHUB Cookeville, Tennessee
WICK Scranton, Pennsylvania
WIDA Carolina, Puerto Rico
WGIN Biddeford, Maine
WIEL Elizabethtown, Kentucky
WILI Willimantic, Connecticut
WINC Winchester, Virginia
WIRA Fort Pierce, Florida
WJLD(AM) Fairfield, Alabama
WJWF Columbus, Mississippi
WJZM Clarksville, Tennessee
WKAV Charlottesville, Virginia
WKBI St. Marys, Pennsylvania
WSPG Spartanburg, South Carolina
WKEW Greensboro, North Carolina
WKNW Sault Sainte Marie, Michigan
WKPT Kingsport, Tennessee
WJQS Jackson, Mississippi
WLJN Elmwood Township, Michigan
WJET Erie, Pennsylvania
WLLH Lowell, Massachusetts
WLYY Copper Hill, Tennessee
WLTA Alpharetta, Georgia
WLTN Littleton, New Hampshire
WMAN Mansfield, Ohio
WMFA Raeford, North Carolina
WFPA Fort Payne, Alabama
WNEX Macon, Georgia
WOND Pleasantville, New Jersey
WPCE Portsmouth, Virginia
WJMX Darlington, South Carolina
WPRY Perry, Florida
WDTK Detroit, Michigan
WQXO Munising, Michigan
WRAK Williamsport, Pennsylvania
WBFN Battle Creek, Michigan
WRDB Reedsburg, Wisconsin
WRJN Racine, Wisconsin
WRON Ronceverte, West Virginia
WSAM Saginaw, Michigan
WSEG Savannah, Georgia
WSIC Statesville, North Carolina
WSJM-AM Benton Harbor, Michigan
WSLB Ogdensburg, New York
WSMY Weldon, North Carolina
WSTC Stamford, Connecticut
WHGB Harrisburg, Pennsylvania
WSDO Sanford, Florida
WTSL Hanover, New Hampshire
WVRC Spencer, West Virginia
WWIN Baltimore, Maryland
WSGC Elberton, Georgia
WWWS Buffalo, New York
WZAZ Jacksonville, Florida
WZHR Zephyrhills, Florida
WZNG Shelbyville, Tennessee
KENT Parowan, Utah
WHLJ(AM) Moultrie, Georgia

WWNZ Veazie, Maine
KNNR Sparks, Nevada
WWTM Decatur, Alabama
WAJL South Boston, Virginia
KIHH Eureka, California
WYNY(AM) Milford, New York
WAVQ Jacksonville, North Carolina
KFJL Central Point, Oregon

1410 kHz

KBNP Portland, Oregon
KCAL(AM) Redlands, California
KIIX Fort Collins, Colorado
KCUL Marshall, Texas
KDBS Alexandria, Louisiana
KERI Bakersfield, California
KGRN Grinnell, Iowa
KHCH Huntsville, Texas
KDKT Beulah, North Dakota
KKLO Leavenworth, Kansas
KLEM Le Mars, Iowa
KLFD Litchfield, Minnesota
KLVQ Athens, Texas
KMYC Marysville, California
KGSO Wichita, Kansas
KOOQ North Platte, Nebraska
KQV Pittsburgh, Pennsylvania
KRIL Odessa, Texas
KNTX Bowie, Texas
KRML Carmel, California
KRWB Roseau, Minnesota
KTCS Fort Smith, Arkansas
KWYO Sheridan, Wyoming
KNAL Victoria, Texas
WSHY Lafayette, Indiana
WBBX Kingston, Tennessee
WENU South Glen Falls, New York
WCMT Martin, Tennessee
WDOE Dunkirk, New York
WDOV Dover, Delaware
WELM Elmira, New York
WHAG Halfway, Maryland
WHBT Tallahassee, Florida
WHLN Harlan, Kentucky
WHTG Eatontown, New Jersey
WIHM Taylorville, Illinois
WING Dayton, Ohio
WIQR Prattville, Alabama
WIZM-AM La Crosse, Wisconsin
WKKP McDonough, Georgia
WLAQ Rome, Georgia
WLSH Lansford, Pennsylvania
WNGL Mobile, Alabama
WMSX Brockton, Massachusetts
WMYR Fort Myers, Florida
WNWZ Grand Rapids, Michigan
WPCC Clinton, South Carolina
WPOP Hartford, Connecticut
WQBQ Leesburg, Florida
WRTZ Roanoke, Virginia
WRMN Elgin, Illinois
WRSS San Sebastian, Puerto Rico
WSCW South Charleston, West Virginia
WRJD Durham, North Carolina
WNER Watertown, New York
WVCB Shallotte, North Carolina
WYIS McRae, Georgia
WZZA Tuscumbia, Alabama
KNVR San Saba, Texas

1420 kHz

KOTK Omaha, Nebraska
KBTN Neosho, Missouri
KKEA Honolulu, Hawaii
KFYN Bonham, Texas
KGIM Aberdeen, South Dakota
KGNB New Braunfels, Texas
KIGO St. Anthony, Idaho
KITI Chehalis-Centralia, Washington
KJCK Junction City, Kansas
KJDL Lubbock, Texas
KMHS Coos Bay, Oregon
KMOG Payson, Arizona
KPIR Granbury, Texas
KPEL Lafayette, Louisiana
KPOC Pocahontas, Arkansas
KRLL California, Missouri
KRIZ Renton, Washington
KSTN Stockton, California
KTAN Sierra Vista, Arizona
KTJS Hobart, Oklahoma
KTOE Mankato, Minnesota
KUJ Walla Walla, Washington
KULY Ulysses, Kansas
KBHS Hot Springs, Arkansas
WACK Newark, New York
WACT Tuscaloosa, Alabama
WVOT Wilson, North Carolina
WAMV Amherst, Virginia
WAOC Saint Augustine, Florida
WASR Wolfeboro, New Hampshire
WATB Decatur, Georgia
WBEC Pittsfield, Massachusetts
WBRD Palmetto, Florida
WBSM New Bedford, Massachusetts
WCED Du Bois, Pennsylvania
WCOJ Coatesville, Pennsylvania
WCRE Cheraw, South Carolina
WDJA Delray Beach, Florida
WEMB Erwin, Tennessee
WUKQ Ponce, Puerto Rico
WFLT Flint, Michigan
WGAS South Gastonia, North Carolina
WHBN Harrodsburg, Kentucky
WHK Cleveland, Ohio
WIMS Michigan City, Indiana
WINI Murphysboro, Illinois
WJUB Plymouth, Wisconsin
WKCW Warrenton, Virginia
WKSR Pulaski, Tennessee
WKWN Trenton, Georgia
WLIS Old Saybrook, Connecticut
WMYN Mayodan, North Carolina
WNRS Herkimer, New York
WOC Davenport, Iowa
WPEH Louisville, Georgia
WQBC Vicksburg, Mississippi
WRCG Columbus, Georgia
WTCR Kenova, West Virginia
WVJS Owensboro, Kentucky
WRSA St. Albans, Vermont
WXGM Gloucester, Virginia

1430 kHz

KALV Alva, Oklahoma
KWST El Centro, California
KAOL Carrollton, Missouri
KASI Ames, Iowa
KBRC Mount Vernon, Washington
KBRK Brookings, South Dakota
KCLK Asotin, Washington
KSHJ Houston, Texas
KEZW Aurora, Colorado
KFIG Fresno, California
KHBM Monticello, Arkansas
KJAY Sacramento, California
KKOZ Ava, Missouri
KLO Ogden, Utah
KMRB San Gabriel, California
KMRC Morgan City, Louisiana
KNSP Staples, Minnesota
KTBZ Tulsa, Oklahoma
KSHJ Houston, Texas
KRGI Grand Island, Nebraska
KROO Breckenridge, Texas
KVVN Santa Clara, California
KYKN Keizer, Oregon
WBEV Beaver Dam, Wisconsin
WBLR Batesburg, South Carolina
WCLT Newark, Ohio
WCMY Ottawa, Illinois
WDAL Dalton, Georgia
WDEX Monroe, North Carolina
WDIC Clinchco, Virginia
WDJS Mount Olive, North Carolina
WEEF Deerfield, Illinois
WEIR Weirton, West Virginia
WENE Endicott, New York
WCWC Williamsburg, Kentucky
WFHK Pell City, Alabama
WFOB Fostoria, Ohio
WGFS Covington, Georgia
WION Ionia, Michigan
WKEX Blacksburg, Virginia
WLKF Lakeland, Florida
WLTG Panama City, Florida
WPLN Madison, Tennessee
WMNC Morganton, North Carolina
WXNT Indianapolis, Indiana
WNAV Annapolis, Maryland
WNEL Caguas, Puerto Rico
WNFO Sun City-Hilton Head, South Carolina
WNSW Newark, New Jersey
WOIR Homestead, Florida
WOWW Germantown, Tennessee
WRDN Durand, Wisconsin
WRMG Red Bay, Alabama
KZQZ St. Louis, Missouri
WRXO Roxboro, North Carolina
WPNI Amherst, Massachusetts
WVAM Altoona, Pennsylvania
WTMN Gainesville, Florida
WXAM Buffalo, Kentucky
WKOX Everett, Massachusetts
WYMC Mayfield, Kentucky
KWAP Wasilla, Alaska

1440 kHz

KCHE Cherokee, Iowa
KDIZ Golden Valley, Minnesota
KETX Livingston, Texas
KEYS Corpus Christi, Texas
KTUV Little Rock, Arkansas
KKXL Grand Forks, North Dakota
KMAJ Topeka, Kansas
KMED Medford, Oregon
KODL The Dalles, Oregon
KPUR Amarillo, Texas
KRDZ Wray, Colorado
KAZG Scottsdale, Arizona
KTNO University Park, Texas
KUHL Santa Maria, California
KVON Napa, California
WAJR Morgantown, West Virginia
WBLA Elizabethtown, North Carolina
WGEM Quincy, Illinois
WGIG Brunswick, Georgia
WGMI Bremen, Georgia
WGVL Greenville, South Carolina
WHDM McKenzie, Tennessee
WLWI Montgomery, Alabama
WHIS Bluefield, West Virginia
WIBH Anna, Illinois
WRED Westbrook, Maine
WJBS Holly Hill, South Carolina
WJJL Niagara Falls, New York
WCDL Carbondale, Pennsylvania
WKLV Blackstone, Virginia
WKPR Kalamazoo, Michigan
WLXN Lexington, North Carolina
WMAX Bay City, Michigan
WDRJ Inkster, Michigan
WMVB Millville, New Jersey
WNFL-AM Green Bay, Wisconsin
WNPV Lansdale, Pennsylvania
WNYG Medford, New York
WPGW Portland, Indiana
WPRD Winter Park, Florida
WVGG Lucedale, Mississippi
WHKZ Warren, Ohio
WRGM Ontario, Ohio
WROK Rockford, Illinois
WSEL Pontotoc, Mississippi
WSGO Oswego, New York
WGLD Manchester Township, Pennsylvania
WDXQ Cochran, Georgia
WWCL Lehigh Acres, Florida
WVEI Worcester, Massachusetts
WYGH Paris, Kentucky
WZYX Cowan, Tennessee
WFNY Gloversville, New York
KPTO Pocatello, Idaho
KELG Manor, Texas
KFNY Riverside, California

1449 kHz

V6AH(AM) Pohnpei, 66

1450 kHz

KATE Albert Lea, Minnesota
KAVP Colona, Colorado
KBBS Buffalo, Wyoming
KBEN Carrizo Springs, Texas
KBFI Bonners Ferry, Idaho
KBFS Belle Fourche, South Dakota
KBKW Aberdeen, Washington
KBMW Breckenridge, Minnesota
KBPS Portland, Oregon
KBUN Bemidji, Minnesota
KCLX Colfax, Washington
KCTI Gonzales, Texas
KCYL Lampasas, Texas
KDAP Douglas, Arizona
KSKE Buena Vista, Colorado
KENA Fort Smith, Arkansas
KEST San Francisco, California
KEYY Provo, Utah
KEZJ Twin Falls, Idaho
KFIZ Fond Du Lac, Wisconsin
KFLS Klamath Falls, Oregon
KGFF Shawnee, Oklahoma
KGIW Alamosa, Colorado
KGRE Greeley, Colorado
KGRZ Missoula, Montana
KHIT Reno, Nevada
KIKR Beaumont, Texas
KWEI(AM) Payette, Idaho
KIRX Kirksville, Missouri
KLZS Eugene, Oregon
KLAM Cordova, Alaska
KLBM La Grande, Oregon
KLMX Clayton, New Mexico
KMBL Junction, Texas
KMHT Marshall, Texas
KMMS Bozeman, Montana
KMRY Cedar Rapids, Iowa
KNET Palestine, Texas
KNHD Camden, Arkansas
KNOC Natchitoches, Louisiana
KNOT Prescott, Arizona
KNSI St. Cloud, Minnesota
KOBE Las Cruces, New Mexico
KOBO Yuba City, California
KOKO Warrensburg, Missouri
KONP Port Angeles, Washington
KQDI Great Falls, Montana
KRZY Albuquerque, New Mexico
KSEL Portales, New Mexico
KSIG Crowley, Louisiana
KSIW Woodward, Oklahoma
KSNY Snyder, Texas
KFSD Escondido, California
KSUH Puyallup, Washington
KTIP Porterville, California
KZNU St. George, Utah
KTZR Tucson, Arizona
KVCK Wolf Point, Montana
KVEN Ventura, California
KVML Sonora, California
KVOW Riverton, Wyoming
KVSI Montpelier, Idaho
KVSL Show Low, Arizona
KWBE Beatrice, Nebraska
KWBW Hutchinson, Kansas
KWEI Notus, Idaho
KWHW Altus, Oklahoma
KWPM West Plains, Missouri
KPTR Palm Springs, California
KYLS Fredericktown, Missouri
KYNT Yankton, South Dakota
KZZJ Rugby, North Dakota
WAOV Vincennes, Indiana
WASK Lafayette, Indiana
WATA Boone, North Carolina
WXVW Jeffersonville, Indiana
WBHF Cartersville, Georgia
WBSR Pensacola, Florida
WBVA Bayside, Virginia
WWKU Plum Springs, Kentucky
WCEV Cicero, Illinois
WFBX Spring Lake, North Carolina
WCJU Columbia, Mississippi
WENI Corning, New York
WCLM Highland Springs, Virginia
WCON Cornelia, Georgia
WCPR Coamo, Puerto Rico
WCRS Greenwood, South Carolina
WCTC New Brunswick, New Jersey
WCUM Bridgeport, Connecticut
WDAD Indiana, Pennsylvania
WDLB Marshfield, Wisconsin
WDNG Anniston, Alabama
WDXR Paducah, Kentucky
WLKW West Warwick, Rhode Island
WELY Ely, Minnesota
WYHL Meridian, Mississippi
WFMB Springfield, Illinois
WPGG Atlantic City, New Jersey
WFRA Franklin, Pennsylvania
WFTR Front Royal, Virginia
WGNC Gastonia, North Carolina
WGNS Murfreesboro, Tennessee
WGPC Albany, Georgia

WHDL Olean, New York
WHKP Hendersonville, North Carolina
WHLS Port Huron, Michigan
WHRY Hurley, Wisconsin
WHTC Holland, Michigan
WIBM Jackson, Michigan
WILM Wilmington, Delaware
WIZS Henderson, North Carolina
WJER Dover-New Philadelphia, Ohio
WJPA Washington, Pennsylvania
WKEI Kewanee, Illinois
WKEU Griffin, Georgia
WKIP Poughkeepsie, New York
WKLA Ludington, Michigan
WKTQ South Paris, Maine
WKXL Concord, New Hampshire
WRNN Myrtle Beach, South Carolina
WLAF La Follette, Tennessee
WLAR Athens, Tennessee
WLAY Muscle Shoals, Alabama
WLEC Sandusky, Ohio
WLKS West Liberty, Kentucky
WLMR Chattanooga, Tennessee
WHNK Parkersburg, West Virginia
WLYV Fort Wayne, Indiana
WQWK State College, Pennsylvania
WHLL Springfield, Massachusetts
KQYX Galena, Kansas
WMFJ Daytona Beach, Florida
WMIQ Iron Mountain, Michigan
WMOH Hamilton, Ohio
WMVG Milledgeville, Georgia
WNAT Natchez, Mississippi
WNBP Newburyport, Massachusetts
WNBY Newberry, Michigan
WNOS New Bern, North Carolina
WOCN Miami, Florida
WOL Washington, District of Columbia
WPAM Pottsville, Pennsylvania
WPSE Erie, Pennsylvania
WQNT Charleston, South Carolina
WRCO Richland Center, Wisconsin
WREL Lexington, Virginia
WVOM Rockland, Maine
WROX Clarksdale, Mississippi
WSMG Greeneville, Tennessee
WZGX Bessemer, Alabama
WSNO Barre, Vermont
WSDV Sarasota, Florida
WSTU Stuart, Florida
WTAL Tallahassee, Florida
WTBO Cumberland, Maryland
WTCO Campbellsville, Kentucky
WTKI Huntsville, Alabama
WTRO Dyersburg, Tennessee
WTSA Brattleboro, Vermont
WVLD Valdosta, Georgia
WRLL Cicero, Illinois
WWJB Brooksville, Florida
WWNT Dothan, Alabama
WWSC Glens Falls, New York
WWXL Manchester, Kentucky
WKAL Rome, New York
KYLW Lockwood, Montana
WMVA Martinsville, Virginia
WVAX Charlottesville, Virginia
WYNY(AM) Ontario, New York
KWES Ruidoso, New Mexico
DWKEL Myrtle Beach, South Carolina
WTHU Thurmont, Maryland
WYNY(AM) Milford, Pennsylvania
WLUX Dunbar, West Virginia
WTOD Hartsville, South Carolina
KJCV Jackson, Wyoming

1460 kHz

KARR Kirkland, Washington
KBRZ Missouri City, Texas
KTKC Springhill, Louisiana
KBZO Lubbock, Texas
KCKX Stayton, Oregon
KCWM Hondo, Texas
KDMA Montevideo, Minnesota
KXNO Des Moines, Iowa
KDWA Hastings, Minnesota
KENO Las Vegas, Nevada
KHRA Honolulu, Hawaii
KHOJ St. Charles, Missouri
KKAQ Thief River Falls, Minnesota
KZNT Colorado Springs, Colorado
KKOY Chanute, Kansas
KXPN Kearney, Nebraska
KCLE Burleson, Texas
KLTC Dickinson, North Dakota
KCNR Shasta, California
KUTI Yakima, Washington
KRRS Santa Rosa, California
KION Salinas, California
KTYM Inglewood, California
KZUE El Reno, Oklahoma
WQXM Bartow, Florida
WBCU Union, South Carolina
WXBR Brockton, Massachusetts
WJTI West Allis, Wisconsin
WABQ Painesville, Ohio
WBNS Columbus, Ohio
WEKB Elkhorn City, Kentucky
WBRN Big Rapids, Michigan
WBUC Buckhannon, West Virginia
WKHZ Easton, Maryland
WDOG Barnwell, South Carolina
WEEN Lafayette, Tennessee
WELZ Belzoni, Mississippi
WEWO Laurinburg, North Carolina
WMCJ & WMCJ Cullman, Alabama
WDDY Albany, New York
WHBK Marshall, North Carolina
WIFI Florence, New Jersey
WIXN Dixon, Illinois
WKJR Rantoul, Illinois
WKAM Goshen, Indiana
WKDV Manassas, Virginia
WLRP San Sebastian, Puerto Rico
WMBA Ambridge, Pennsylvania
WJCP North Vernon, Indiana
WHAL Phenix City/Columbus, Alabama
WPON Walled Lake, Michigan
WQOP Jacksonville, Florida
WRAD Radford, Virginia
WRKB Kannapolis, North Carolina
WROY Carmi, Illinois
WRRE Juncos, Puerto Rico
WRVK Mount Vernon, Kentucky
WBOG Tomah, Wisconsin
WVOX New Rochelle, New York
WTKT Harrisburg, Pennsylvania
WHIC Rochester, New York
WXEM Buford, Georgia
WXOK Port Allen, Louisiana
WXRQ Mount Pleasant, Tennessee
WZEP De Funiak Springs, Florida
WNPL Golden Gate, Florida
WGMF Tunkhannock, Pennsylvania

1470 kHz

KAIR Atchison, Kansas
KYYW Abilene, Texas
KBSN Moses Lake, Washington
KDHN Dimmitt, Texas
KELA Centralia-Chehalis, Washington
KDEB(AM) Estes Park, Colorado
KHND Harvey, North Dakota
KGND Vinita, Oklahoma
KKTY Douglas, Wyoming
KLCL Lake Charles, Louisiana
KNXN Sierra Vista, Arizona
KIID Sacramento, California
KMAL Malden, Missouri
KUTY Palmdale, California
KWAY Waverly, Iowa
KWRD Henderson, Texas
KWSL Sioux City, Iowa
KSMM Liberal, Kansas
KFMZ Brookfield, Missouri
WBCR Alcoa, Tennessee
WBFC Stanton, Kentucky
WBKV West Bend, Wisconsin
WBTX Broadway-Timberville, Virginia
WCHJ Brookhaven, Mississippi
WCLA Claxton, Georgia
WFNT Flint, Michigan
WGNR-AM Anderson, Indiana
WEVG Evergreen, Alabama
WJDY Salisbury, Maryland
WSAN Allentown, Pennsylvania
WLMC Georgetown, South Carolina
KMNQ Brooklyn Park, Minnesota
WLQR Toledo, Ohio
WMBD Peoria, Illinois
WMMW Meriden, Connecticut
WNAU New Albany, Mississippi
WLOA Farrell, Pennsylvania
WPDM Potsdam, New York
WQXL Columbia, South Carolina
WRGA Rome, Georgia
WAZN Watertown, Massachusetts
WMGG Egypt Lake, Florida
WNYY Ithaca, New York
WTOE Spruce Pine, North Carolina
WTTR Westminster, Maryland
WTZE Tazewell, Virginia
WVBS Burgaw, North Carolina
WVOL Berry Hill, Tennessee
WWBG Greensboro, North Carolina
WWNN Pompano Beach, Florida
WXAG Athens, Georgia
WLAM Lewiston, Maine
WTQS Cameron, South Carolina

1480 kHz

KAUS Austin, Minnesota
KAVA Pueblo, Colorado
KBMS Vancouver, Washington
KCHL San Antonio, Texas
KBXD Dallas, Texas
KGOE Eureka, California
KHQN Spanish Fork, Utah
KIOU Shreveport, Louisiana
KKCQ Fosston, Minnesota
KLEE Ottumwa, Iowa
KLMS Lincoln, Nebraska
KLVL Pasadena, Texas
KNTB Lakewood, Washington
KPHX Phoenix, Arizona
KQAM Wichita, Kansas
KRAE Cheyenne, Wyoming
KRXR Gooding, Idaho
KSBQ Santa Maria, California
KSDR Watertown, South Dakota
KTHS Green Forest, Arkansas
KCZZ Mission, Kansas
KVNR Santa Ana, California
KYOS Merced, California
WTKD Mobile, Alabama
WRCK Remsen, New York
WBBP Memphis, Tennessee
WCNS Latrobe, Pennsylvania
WIZD Neon, Kentucky
WSPY Geneva, Illinois
WGFY Charlotte, North Carolina
WGVU Kentwood, Michigan
WHBC Canton, Ohio
WIOS Tawas City-East Tawas, Michigan
WJBM Jerseyville, Illinois
WJFC Jefferson City, Tennessee
WJLE Smithville, Tennessee
WVOV Bridgeport, Alabama
WKGC Southport, Florida
WKND Windsor, Connecticut
WLEA Hornell, New York
WQOH Irondale, Alabama
WMDD Fajardo, Puerto Rico
WCFR Springfield, Vermont
WQTM Fair Bluff, North Carolina
WVOI Marco Island, Florida
WPFJ Franklin, North Carolina
WPWC Dumfries-Triangle, Virginia
WHVO Hopkinsville, Kentucky
WRSW Warsaw, Indiana
WSAR Fall River, Massachusetts
WSDS Salem Township, Michigan
WEEO Shippensburg, Pennsylvania
WLMV Madison, Wisconsin
WPFR Terre Haute, Indiana
WTLO Somerset, Kentucky
WTOY Salem, Virginia
WUNA Ocoee, Florida
WYRN Louisburg, North Carolina
WYZE Atlanta, Georgia
WZJY Mount Pleasant, South Carolina
WZRC New York, New York
WFLN Arcadia, Florida
WTOX Glen Allen, Virginia

1490 kHz

KZZZ Bullhead City, Arizona
KBIX Muskogee, Oklahoma
KBKR Baker, Oregon
KBLF Red Bluff, California
KBRO Bremerton, Washington
KBSR Laurel, Montana
KBST Big Spring, Texas
KBUR Burlington, Iowa
KBZY Salem, Oregon
KCID Caldwell, Idaho
KCUZ Clifton, Arizona
KDBM Dillon, Montana
KDMO Carthage, Missouri
KDRO Sedalia, Missouri
KDRS Paragould, Arkansas
KYNR Toppenish, Washington
KEUN Eunice, Louisiana
KEYG Grand Coulee, Washington
KFCR Custer, South Dakota
KFFN Tucson, Arizona
KLGO Austin, Texas
KWOK Aberdeen, Washington
KGOS Torrington, Wyoming
KIBL Beeville, Texas
KGBA Heber, California
KJIN Houma, Louisiana
KKAN Phillipsburg, Kansas
KLGR Redwood Falls, Minnesota
KLNT Laredo, Texas
KLOG Kelso, Washington
KMET Banning, California
KNDC Hettinger, North Dakota
KNEL Brady, Texas
KMFS Guthrie, Oklahoma
KORN Mitchell, South Dakota
KOMJ Omaha, Nebraska
KOVC Valley City, North Dakota
KPKE Gunnison, Colorado
KPLT Paris, Texas
KQTY Borger, Texas
KRIB Mason City, Iowa
KRKC King City, California
KSKR Roseburg, Oregon
KRSN Los Alamos, New Mexico
KRTK Chubbuck, Idaho
KRTN Raton, New Mexico
KRUI Ruidoso Downs, New Mexico
KRUS Ruston, Louisiana
KHVL Huntsville, Texas
KSYC Yreka, California
KTEL Walla Walla, Washington
KTOB Petaluma, California
KTOP Topeka, Kansas
KTTR AM Rolla, Missouri
KUGR Green River, Wyoming
KFKB Forks, Washington
KWUD Woodville, Texas
KVWC Vernon, Texas
KCFC Boulder, Colorado
KWAC Bakersfield, California
KWMC Del Rio, Texas
KWXT Dardanelle, Arkansas
KXAR Hope, Arkansas
KXLQ Indianola, Iowa
KXRA Alexandria, Minnesota
KXRE Manitou Springs, Colorado
KYCA Prescott, Arizona
KOGN Ogden, Utah
KYZS Tyler, Texas
KZZN Littlefield, Texas
WABJ Adrian, Michigan
WACM West Springfield, Massachusetts
WAEY Princeton, West Virginia
WAFZ Immokalee, Florida
WFZX Anniston, Alabama
WARK Hagerstown, Maryland
WAZL Hazleton, Pennsylvania
WAZZ Fayetteville, North Carolina
WBAE Portland, Maine
WBCB Levittown, Pennsylvania
WBEX Chillicothe, Ohio
WBTA Batavia, New York
WXTG Hampton, Virginia
WCDO Sidney, New York
WCHM Clarkesville, Georgia
WCLD Cleveland, Mississippi
WCLU Glasgow, Kentucky
WCSS Amsterdam, New York
WCSV Crossville, Tennessee
WCVA Culpeper, Virginia
WDAN Danville, Illinois
WDBQ Dubuque, Iowa
WDLC Port Jervis, New York
WDUR Durham, North Carolina
WRLA West Point, Georgia
WDXL Lexington, Tennessee
WEMJ Laconia, New Hampshire
WESB Bradford, Pennsylvania
WFFX(AM) Hattiesburg, Illinois

WFAD Middlebury, Vermont
WKYW Frankfort, Kentucky
WFXY Middlesboro, Kentucky
WGCD Chester, South Carolina
WGCH Greenwich, Connecticut
WGEZ Beloit, Wisconsin
WRCE Watkins Glen, New York
WBSS(AM) Pleasantville, New Jersey
WCEC Haverhill, Massachusetts
WHBB Selma, Alabama
WHOC Philadelphia, Mississippi
WIGM Medford, Wisconsin
WIKE Newport, Vermont
WITA Knoxville, Tennessee
WJJM Lewisburg, Tennessee
WERE Cleveland Heights, Ohio
WJOC Chattanooga, Tennessee
WKBV Richmond, Indiana
WKNY Kingston, New York
WKRO Cairo, Illinois
WKUN Monroe, Georgia
WKVT Brattleboro, Vermont
WDEP Ponce, Puerto Rico
WLFN La Crosse, Wisconsin
WLOE Eden, North Carolina
WLPA Lancaster, Pennsylvania
WMBM Miami Beach, Florida
WMGW Meadville, Pennsylvania
WMOA Marietta, Ohio
WBGA Brunswick, Georgia
WMPX Midland, Michigan
WMRC Milford, Massachusetts
WMRN Marion, Ohio
WNBT Wellsboro, Pennsylvania
WNTJ Johnstown, Pennsylvania
WKLQ Whitehall, Michigan
WOHI East Liverpool, Ohio
WOLF Syracuse, New York
WOMI Owensboro, Kentucky
WOPI Bristol, Tennessee
WOSH Oshkosh, Wisconsin
WPAK Farmville, Virginia
WPCI Greenville, South Carolina
WPNA Oak Park, Illinois
WBSS Pleasantville, New Jersey
WRMT Rocky Mount, North Carolina
WVBG Vicksburg, Mississippi
WSFB Quitman, Georgia
WSGB Sutton, West Virginia
WSIP Paintsville, Kentucky
WSIR Winter Haven, Florida
WSTP Salisbury, North Carolina
WSVM Valdese, North Carolina
WSWW Charleston, West Virginia
WSYL Sylvania, Georgia
WTCS Fairmont, West Virginia
WTIQ Manistique, Michigan
WTTB Vero Beach, Florida
WTUP Tupelo, Mississippi
WTVL Waterville, Maine
WVGB Beaufort, South Carolina
WWIL Wilmington, North Carolina
WWNB New Bern, North Carolina
WWPR Bradenton, Florida
WXBD Biloxi, Mississippi
WTJV Deland, Florida
WYYZ Jasper, Georgia
WZOE Princeton, Illinois
WCOR Lebanon, Tennessee
WIRB Level Plains, Alabama
KOWL South Lake Tahoe, California
WUVR Lebanon, New Hampshire
KLZN Susanville, California
KCPX Spanish Valley, Utah
WKDR Berlin, New Hampshire
WSNT Sandersville, Georgia
WEKI Decatur, Alabama

1500 kHz

KANI Wharton, Texas
KBRN Boerne, Texas
KDFN Doniphan, Missouri
KJIM Sherman, Texas
KPGM Pawhuska, Oklahoma
KIEV Burbank, California
KSJX San Jose, California
KSTP St. Paul, Minnesota
KHKA(AM) Honolulu, Hawaii
WAKE Valparaiso, Indiana
WQMS Quitman, Mississippi
WBRI Indianapolis, Indiana
WBZI Xenia, Ohio
WPJX Zion, Illinois
WDEB Jamestown, Tennessee
WAYS Macon, Georgia
WDPC Dallas, Georgia
WZZQ(AM) Gaffney, South Carolina
WFIF Milford, Connecticut
WGHT Pompton Lakes, New Jersey
WQCR Alabaster, Alabama
WICY Malone, New York
WKAX Russellville, Alabama
WKIZ Key West, Florida
WKXO Berea, Kentucky
WLQV Detroit, Michigan
WMJL Marion, Kentucky
WMNT Manati, Puerto Rico
WPMB Vandalia, Illinois
WPSO New Port Richey, Florida
WSEM Donalsonville, Georgia
WSMX Winston-Salem, North Carolina
WTNE Trenton, Tennessee
WFED Washington, District of Columbia
WVSM Rainsville, Alabama
KMXO Merkel, Texas
KCLF New Roads, Louisiana

1510 kHz

KOAZ Isleta, New Mexico
KAGC Bryan, Texas
KAGY Port Sulphur, Louisiana
KCTE Independence, Missouri
KCTX Childress, Texas
KCKK Littleton, Colorado
KFNN Mesa, Arizona
KGA Spokane, Washington
KROB Robstown, Texas
KIFG Iowa Falls, Iowa
KIRV Fresno, California
KSFN Piedmont, California
KLLB West Jordan, Utah
KMND Midland, Texas
KMRF Marshfield, Missouri
KMSD Mibank, South Dakota
KSPA Ontario, California
KNNS Larned, Kansas
KBED Nederland, Texas
KSTV Stephenville, Texas
KTTT Columbus, Nebraska
KWJB Canton, Texas
WRRD Waukesha, Wisconsin
WBSG Lajas, Puerto Rico
WEAL Greensboro, North Carolina
WJKN Jackson, Michigan
WJOT Wabash, Indiana
WLAC Nashville, Tennessee
WLGN Logan, Ohio
WLRB Macomb, Illinois
WFAI Salem, New Jersey
WWZN Boston, Massachusetts
WPUT Brewster, New York
WQUL Woodruff, South Carolina
WRNJ Hackettstown, New Jersey
WTTN Columbus, Wisconsin
WLKR Norwalk, Ohio
WWBC Cocoa, Florida
WWHN Joliet, Illinois
WWSM Annville-Cleona, Pennsylvania
WPGR Monroeville, Pennsylvania
WQUL(AM) Woodruff, South Carolina

1520 kHz

KFXZ Lafayette, Louisiana
KQQB Stockdale, Texas
KGDD Oregon City, Oregon
KKZZ Port Hueneme, California
KMSR Mayville, North Dakota
KMPG Hollister, California
KOLM Rochester, Minnesota
KOKC Oklahoma City, Oklahoma
KRHW Sikeston, Missouri
KZOY(AM) Sioux Falls, South Dakota
KSIB Creston, Iowa
KYND Cypress, Texas
WARR Warrenton, North Carolina
WCHE West Chester, Pennsylvania
WDCY Douglasville, Georgia
WNWT Rossford, Ohio
WDSL Mocksville, North Carolina
WEXY Wilton Manors, Florida
WIZZ Greenfield, Massachusetts
WGMA Spindale, North Carolina
WHOW Clinton, Illinois
WINW Canton, Ohio
WJMP Kent, Ohio
WKMG Newberry, South Carolina
WKVI Knox, Indiana
WLGC Greenup, Kentucky
WRCI Three Rivers, Michigan
WLUV Loves Park, Illinois
WMLM St. Louis, Michigan
WNWS Brownsville, Tennessee
WSVX Shelbyville, Indiana
WQCT Bryan, Ohio
WTHE Mineola, New York
WTLM Opelika, Alabama
WTRI Brunswick, Maryland
WVOZ San Juan, Puerto Rico
WWKB Buffalo, New York
WXYB Indian Rocks Beach, Florida

1530 kHz

KDSN Denison, Iowa
KQSC Santa Barbara, California
KFBK Sacramento, California
KGBT Harlingen, Texas
KVDW England, Arkansas
KMAM Butler, Missouri
KLBW New Boston, Texas
WLIQ Quincy, Illinois
KQNK Norton, Kansas
KQSP Shakopee, Minnesota
KXTD Wagoner, Oklahoma
WASC Spartanburg, South Carolina
WCTR Chestertown, Maryland
WWDX Huntingdon, Tennessee
WDJZ Bridgeport, Connecticut
WENG Englewood, Florida
WMCE North East, Pennsylvania
WFIC Collinsville, Virginia
WJDM Elizabeth, New Jersey
WJJG Elmhurst, Illinois
WLCO Lapeer, Michigan
WLWB New Holstein, Wisconsin
WOBX Wanchese, North Carolina
WYMM Jacksonville, Florida
WLLQ Chapel Hill, North Carolina
WCKY Cincinnati, Ohio
WUPR Utuado, Puerto Rico
WVBF Middleborough Center, Massachusetts
WYGR Wyoming, Michigan
KVOG Agana, Guam
WTTI Dalton, Georgia

1540 kHz

KASA Phoenix, Arizona
KBOA-AM Kennett, Missouri
KMPC Los Angeles, California
KDYN Ozark, Arkansas
KEDA San Antonio, Texas
KGBC Galveston, Texas
KGLA Gretna, Louisiana
KREA Honolulu, Hawaii
KLKC Parsons, Kansas
KNGL McPherson, Kansas
KTGG Okemos, Michigan
KXEL Waterloo, Iowa
KXPA Bellevue, Washington
KZMP University Park, Texas
WWGK Cleveland, Ohio
WACA Wheaton, Maryland
WADK Newport, Rhode Island
WJZI(AM) Decatur, Indiana
WBCO Bucyrus, Ohio
WBIN Benton, Tennessee
WBNL Boonville, Indiana
WBTC Uhrichsville, Ohio
WECZ Punxsutawney, Pennsylvania
WXEX Exeter, New Hampshire
WIBS Guayama, Puerto Rico
WJJT Jellico, Tennessee
WKVQ Eatonton, Georgia
WKXG Greenwood, Mississippi
WLOI La Porte, Indiana
WMYJ Martinsville, Indiana
WNWR Philadelphia, Pennsylvania
WOGR Charlotte, North Carolina
WREJ Richmond, Virginia
WSIV E. Syracuse, New York
WSMI Litchfield, Illinois
WTBI Pickens, South Carolina
WTKM Hartford, Wisconsin
WTXY Whiteville, North Carolina
WYCL Niles, Ohio
WYNC Yanceyville, North Carolina

1550 kHz

KAPE Cape Girardeau, Missouri
KRPI Ferndale, Washington
KCOM Comanche, Texas
KDCC Dodge City, Kansas
KICS Hastings, Nebraska
KIWA Sheldon, Iowa
KKLE Winfield, Kansas
KLFJ Springfield, Missouri
KMAD Madill, Oklahoma
KMRI West Valley City, Utah
KESJ St. Joseph, Missouri
KUAZ Tucson, Arizona
KKOV Vancouver, Washington
KWBC College Station, Texas
KWRN Apple Valley, California
KXEX Fresno, California
KYAL Sapulpa, Oklahoma
KXTO Reno, Nevada
KZDG San Francisco, California
KNSH Canyon, Texas
WAMA Tampa, Florida
WZRK Northbrook, Illinois
WAZX Smyrna, Georgia
WIGN Bristol, Tennessee
WBFJ Winston-Salem, North Carolina
WBSC Bennettsville, South Carolina
WCGR Canandaigua, New York
WCLY Raleigh, North Carolina
WCSJ Morris, Illinois
WCVL Crawfordsville, Indiana
WDLR Delaware, Ohio
WSDK Bloomfield, Connecticut
WEVR River Falls, Wisconsin
WHIT Madison, Wisconsin
WIRV Irvine, Kentucky
WJIL Jacksonville, Illinois
WKBA Vinton, Virginia
WKFE Yauco, Puerto Rico
WITK Pittston, Pennsylvania
WLOR Huntsville, Alabama
WLTI New Castle, Indiana
WMRE Charlestown, West Virginia
WNDI Sullivan, Indiana
WNTN Newton, Massachusetts
WOCC Corydon, Indiana
WPFC Baton Rouge, Louisiana
WRHC Coral Gables, Florida
WSRY Elkton, Maryland
WTHB Augusta, Georgia
WTTC Towanda, Pennsylvania
WUSP Utica, New York
WVAB Virginia Beach, Virginia
WKTF Vienna, Georgia
WMSK Morganfield, Kentucky
WNZF Bunnell, Florida
WZUM Braddock, Pennsylvania

1560 kHz

KABI Abilene, Kansas
KBEW Blue Earth, Minnesota
KNGR Daingerfield, Texas
KHBR Hillsboro, Texas
KGOW Bellaire, Texas
KIQS Willows, California
KKAA Aberdeen, South Dakota
KLNG Council Bluffs, Iowa
KLTI Macon, Missouri
KZQQ Abilene, Texas
KNZR Bakersfield, California
WMBH Joplin, Missouri
KTUI Sullivan, Missouri
KEBC Del City, Oklahoma
KZIZ Pacific, Washington
WLYG Centre, Alabama
WAGL Lancaster, South Carolina
WAHT Clemson, South Carolina
WBOL Bolivar, Tennessee
WBYS Canton, Illinois
WCNW Fairfield, Ohio
WFSP Kingwood, West Virginia
WGLB Elm Grove, Wisconsin
WKDO Liberty, Kentucky
WKIK La Plata, Maryland
WMRO Gallatin, Tennessee
WNWN-AM Portage, Michigan
WPAD Paducah, Kentucky
WQEW New York, New York

WQXY Hazard, Kentucky
WRIN Rensselaer, Indiana
WRSJ Bayamon, Puerto Rico
WSBV South Boston, Virginia
WSEZ Paoli, Indiana
WSLA Slidell, Louisiana
WLZR(AM) Melbourne, Florida
WTNS Coshocton, Ohio
WWYC Toledo, Ohio
WYZD Dobson, North Carolina
KVAN Burbank, Washington
KGOW(AM) Bellaire, Hawaii
KTXZ West Lake Hills, Texas

1570 kHz

KBRI Brinkley, Arkansas
KCVR Lodi, California
KPIO Loveland, Colorado
KLEX Lexington, Missouri
KLLA Leesville, Louisiana
KAKK Walker, Minnesota
KMCD Fairfield, Iowa
KZLI Catoosa, Oklahoma
KNDY Marysville, Kansas
KVTK Vermillion, South Dakota
KPRO Riverside, California
KPYK Terrell, Texas
KQWC Webster City, Iowa
KTAT Frederick, Oklahoma
KTGE Salinas, California
KUAU Haiku, Hawaii
KVLG La Grange, Texas
KYCR Golden Valley, Minnesota
WABL Amite, Louisiana
WHTX Warren, Ohio
WBGX Harvey, Illinois
WBGZ Alton, Illinois
WCLE Cleveland, Tennessee
WCRL Oneonta, Alabama
WFLR Dundee, New York
WFRL Freeport, Illinois
WFUR Grand Rapids, Michigan
WGLL Auburn, Indiana
WVOJ Fernandina Beach, Florida
WILO Frankfort, Indiana
WISP Doylestown, Pennsylvania
WIZK Bay Springs, Mississippi
WKBH Holmen, Wisconsin
WKKS Vanceburg, Kentucky
WLBQ Morgantown, Kentucky
WLKD Minocqua, Wisconsin
WNCA Siler City, North Carolina
WMAK Lobelville, Tennessee
WNST Towson, Maryland
WOKC Okeechobee, Florida
WONA Winona, Mississippi
WPPC Penuelas, Puerto Rico
WPTW Piqua, Ohio
WQTW Latrobe, Pennsylvania
WFTU Riverhead, New York
WSCO Appleton, Wisconsin
WIGO Morrow, Georgia
WSWV Pennington Gap, Virginia
WTAY Robinson, Illinois
WTLK Taylorsville, North Carolina
WTRB Ripley, Tennessee
WTWB Auburndale, Florida
WWCK Flint, Michigan
WNDA New Albany, Indiana
WYTI Rocky Mount, Virginia
KBCV Hollister, Missouri
WECU Winterville, North Carolina
WCCM Methuen, Virgin Islands

1580 kHz

KAMI Cozad, Nebraska
KBLA Santa Monica, California
KCHA Charles City, Iowa
KDOM Windom, Minnesota
KESM Eldorado Springs, Missouri
KHGG Van Buren, Arkansas
KGAF Gainesville, Texas
KGAL Lebanon, Oregon
KIRT Mission, Texas
KMIK Tempe, Arizona
KNIM Maryville, Missouri
KOKB Blackwell, Oklahoma
KTGR Columbia, Missouri
KTLU Rusk, Texas
KREL Colorado Springs, Colorado
KWED Seguin, Texas
KXZZ Lake Charles, Louisiana
WNPZ Knoxville, Tennessee
WAMW-AM Washington, Indiana
WAMY Amory, Mississippi
WBCP Urbana, Illinois
WCCF Punta Gorda, Florida
WLPK Connersville, Indiana
WDQN Duquoin, Illinois
WIOL Columbus, Georgia
WESY Leland, Mississippi
WWDN Danville, Virginia
WHLY South Bend, Indiana
WLIJ Shelbyville, Tennessee
WLIM Patchogue, New York
WPGY Ellijay, Georgia
WEKO Morovis, Puerto Rico
WNTF Bithlo, Florida
WGYM Hammonton, New Jersey
WORV Hattiesburg, Mississippi
WVOK Oxford, Alabama
WJFK Morningside, District of Columbia
WPJK Orangeburg, South Carolina
WPKY Princeton, Kentucky
WSRF Fort Lauderdale, Florida
WTCL Chattahoochee, Florida
WWTF Georgetown, Kentucky
WVKO Columbus, Ohio
WVZN Columbia, Pennsylvania
WWSJ St. Johns, Michigan
WZKY Albemarle, North Carolina
WPMO Pascagoula-Moss Point, Mississippi
DKEZD Windsor, California

1590 kHz

KBJT Fordyce, Arkansas
KDAE Sinton, Texas
KDAV Lubbock, Texas
KDEX Dexter, Missouri
KDJS Willmar, Minnesota
KELP El Paso, Texas
KGAS Carthage, Texas
KKAY White Castle, Louisiana
KLFE Seattle, Washington
KLIV San Jose, California
KTIL(AM) Netarts, Oregon
KMOZ Rolla, Missouri
KPRT Kansas City, Missouri
KLRK Mexia, Texas
KCTY Wayne, Nebraska
KVTA Ventura, California
KVGB Great Bend, Kansas
KWBG Boone, Iowa
KWEY Weatherford, Oklahoma
KMIC Houston, Texas
KYNG Springdale, Arkansas
WABV Abbeville, South Carolina
WAIK Galesburg, Illinois
WAKR Akron, Ohio
WALG Albany, Georgia
WARV Warwick, Rhode Island
WASB Brockport, New York
WAUB Auburn, New York
WBHN Bryson City, North Carolina
WCAM Camden, South Carolina
WCSL Cherryville, North Carolina
WDBL Springfield, Tennessee
WIJK(AM) Ocean City, Maryland
WFTH Richmond, Virginia
WGGO Salamanca, New York
WHPY Clayton, North Carolina
WHLX Marine City, Michigan
WIXK New Richmond, Wisconsin
WFBR Glen Burnie, Maryland
WKTP Jonesborough, Tennessee
WLBN Lebanon, Kentucky
WNTS Beech Grove, Indiana
WYSR High Point, North Carolina
WCGO Evanston, Illinois
WRCY Mt. Vernon, Indiana
WPSL Port St. Lucie, Florida
WPUL South Daytona, Florida
WPVL-AM Platteville, Wisconsin
WPWA Chester, Pennsylvania
WQCH La Fayette, Georgia
WRXB St. Petersburg Beach, Florida
WSMN Nashua, New Hampshire
WSRW Hillsboro, Ohio
WTGA Thomaston, Georgia
WGBW Denmark, Wisconsin
WTVB-AM Coldwater, Michigan
WODJ Big Rapids, Michigan
WVNA Tuscumbia, Alabama
WVOE Chadbourn, North Carolina
WPSN Honesdale, Pennsylvania
WXRF Guayama, Puerto Rico
WXRS Swainsboro, Georgia
WHGT Maugansville, Maryland

1600 kHz

KATZ St. Louis, Missouri
KVRI Blaine, Washington
KEPN Lakewood, Colorado
KGYM Cedar Rapids, Iowa
KDAK Carrington, North Dakota
KIVA Albuquerque, New Mexico
KOPB Eugene, Oregon
KGST Fresno, California
KLEB Golden Meadow, Louisiana
KLGA Algona, Iowa
KMDO Fort Scott, Kansas
KAHZ Pomona, California
KNCY Nebraska City, Nebraska
KNWA Bellefonte, Arkansas
KOGT Orange, Texas
KOHI St. Helens, Oregon
KRFS Superior, Nebraska
KRVA Cockrell Hill, Texas
KTUB Centerville, Utah
KTAP Santa Maria, California
KTTN Trenton, Missouri
KUBA Yuba City, California
KPNP Watertown, Minnesota
KXEW South Tucson, Arizona
KYBC Cottonwood, Arizona
WAAM Ann Arbor, Michigan
WAOS Austell, Georgia
WARU Peru, Indiana
WATX Algood, Tennessee
WAYC Bedford, Pennsylvania
WULM Springfield, Ohio
WCPK Chesapeake, Virginia
WEHH Elmira Hts-Horsehds, New York
WHIY Huntsville, Alabama
WTZQ Fountain Inn, South Carolina
WHOL Allentown, Pennsylvania
WIDU Fayetteville, North Carolina
WLXE Rockville, Maryland
WEJS Jersey Shore, Pennsylvania
WMQM Lakeland, Tennessee
WKWF Key West, Florida
WLRS Eminence, Kentucky
WKZK North Augusta, South Carolina
WCMA(AM) Bayamon, Puerto Rico
WMCR Oneida, New York
WKKX Wheeling, West Virginia
WLAA Winter Garden, Florida
WPDC Elizabethtown, Pennsylvania
WHNP East Longmeadow, Massachusetts
WHTY(AM) Riviera Beach, Florida
WRSL Corbin, Kentucky
WTTF Tiffin, Ohio
WTZQ Hendersonville, North Carolina
WUNR Brookline, Massachusetts
WWRL New York, New York
WXMY Saltville, Virginia
WXVI Montgomery, Alabama
WZNZ Atlantic Beach, Florida
WZZW Milton, West Virginia
WRPN Ripon, Wisconsin
KUSH Cushing, Oklahoma
WRJE Dover, Delaware
KOKE Pflugerville, Texas
WZNZ Atlantic Beach, Florida

1620 kHz

KOZN Bellevue, Nebraska
WTAW College Station, Texas
KSMH West Sacramento, California
KYIZ Renton, Washington
WDHP Frederiksted, Virgin Islands
WDND South Bend, Indiana
WNRP Gulf Breeze, Florida

1630 kHz

KCJJ Iowa City, Iowa
KRND Fox Farm, Wyoming
KKGM Fort Worth, Texas
WRDW Augusta, Georgia

1640 kHz

KZLS Enid, Oklahoma
KBJA Sandy, Utah
KDIA Vallejo, California
KDZR Lake Oswego, Oregon
WKSH Sussex, Wisconsin
WTNI Biloxi, Mississippi

1650 kHz

KSVE El Paso, Texas
KBJD Denver, Colorado
KCNZ Cedar Falls, Iowa
KFOX Torrance, California
KFSW Fort Smith, Arkansas
WHKT Portsmouth, Virginia

1660 kHz

KBRE Merced, California
KRZI Waco, Texas
KQWB West Fargo, North Dakota
KXOL Brigham City, Utah
WBCN Charlotte, North Carolina
WCNZ Marco Island, Florida
WWRU Jersey City, New Jersey
WGIT Canovanas, Puerto Rico
WQLR Kalamazoo, Michigan

1670 kHz

KHPY Moreno Valley, California
WPLA Dry Branch, Georgia
WOZN Madison, Wisconsin

1680 kHz

KGED Fresno, California
KNTS Seattle, Washington
KRJO Monroe, Louisiana
WPRR Ada, Michigan
WOKB Winter Garden, Florida
WTTM Lindenwold, New Jersey

1690 kHz

KDDZ Arvada, Colorado
KFSG Roseville, California
WMLB Avondale Estates, Georgia
WVON Berwyn, Illinois
WPTX Lexington Park, Maryland

1700 kHz

KBGG Des Moines, Iowa
KVNS Brownsville, Texas
KKLF Richardson, Texas
WRCR Ramapo, New York
WEUP Huntsville, Alabama

1kHz

KQRR(AM) Mount Angel, Oregon

540 kHz

KDFT Ferris, Texas
KRXA Carmel Valley, California
KYAH Delta, Utah
KNMX Las Vegas, New Mexico
KMLB Monroe, Louisiana
KVIP Redding, California
KWMT Fort Dodge, Iowa
WASG Daphne, Alabama
WDAK Columbus, Georgia
WGOP Pocomoke City, Maryland
WKFN Clarksville, Tennessee
WETC Wendell-Zebulon, North Carolina
WGTH Richlands, Virginia
WLIE Islip, New York
WFLF Pine Hills, Florida
WRGC Sylva, North Carolina
WWCS Canonsburg, Pennsylvania
WYNN Florence, South Carolina
WAUK Jackson, Wisconsin
WXYG Sauk Rapids, Minnesota

550 kHz

KARI Blaine, Washington
KBOW Butte, Montana
KCRS Midland, Texas
KFRM Salina, Kansas
KFYR Bismarck, North Dakota
KFYI Phoenix, Arizona
KMVI Kahului, Hawaii
KOAC Corvallis, Oregon
KRAI Craig, Colorado
KTRS St. Louis, Missouri
KTSA San Antonio, Texas
KTZN Anchorage, Alaska

KUZZ Bakersfield, California
WAYR Orange Park, Florida
WDEV Waterbury, Vermont
WDUN Gainesville, Georgia
WGR Buffalo, New York
WIOZ Pinehurst, North Carolina
WAME Statesville, North Carolina
WKRC Cincinnati, Ohio
WPAB Ponce, Puerto Rico
WSAU-AM Wausau, Wisconsin
WSVA Harrisonburg, Virginia
KLLV Breen, Colorado

560 kHz

KBLU Yuma, Arizona
KLVI Beaumont, Texas
KLZ Denver, Colorado
KMON Great Falls, Montana
KPQ Wenatchee, Washington
KSFO San Francisco, California
KVOK Kodiak, Alaska
KWTO-AM Springfield, Missouri
WCKL Catskill, New York
WEBC Duluth, Minnesota
WFIL Philadelphia, Pennsylvania
WFRB Frostburg, Maryland
WGAI Elizabeth City, North Carolina
WGAN Portland, Maine
WHBQ Memphis, Tennessee
WHYN Springfield, Massachusetts
WIND Chicago, Illinois
WJLS Beckley, West Virginia
WRDT Monroe, Michigan
WMIK Middlesboro, Kentucky
WNSR Brentwood, Tennessee
WOOF Dothan, Alabama
WQAM Miami, Florida
WVOC Columbia, South Carolina

567 kHz

KGUM Hagatna, Guam

570 kHz

KSNM Las Cruces, New Mexico
KCFJ Alturas, California
KLAC Los Angeles, California
KLIF Dallas, Texas
KNRS Salt Lake City, Utah
KQNG Eleele, Hawaii
KVI Seattle, Washington
WAAX Gadsden, Alabama
WTBN Pinellas Park, Florida
WIDS Russell Springs, Kentucky
WKBN Youngstown, Ohio
WKYX Paducah, Kentucky
WMAM Marinette, Wisconsin
WMCA New York, New York
WNAX Yankton, South Dakota
WFNL Raleigh, North Carolina
WSYR Syracuse, New York
WWNC Asheville, North Carolina

580 kHz

KIDO Nampa, Idaho
KJMJ Alexandria, Louisiana
KMJ Fresno, California
KRFE Lubbock, Texas
KSAZ Marana, Arizona
KUBC Montrose, Colorado
KZMX Hot Springs, South Dakota
WACQ Tuskegee, Alabama
WCHS Charleston, West Virginia
WDBO Orlando, Florida
WELO Tupelo, Mississippi
WGAC Augusta, Georgia
WHP Harrisburg, Pennsylvania
WIBW Topeka, Kansas
WILL Urbana, Illinois
WKAQ San Juan, Puerto Rico
WKSK West Jefferson, North Carolina
WKTY La Crosse, Wisconsin
WLVA Lynchburg, Virginia
WYHM Rockwood, Tennessee
WTAG Worcester, Massachusetts
WTCM Traverse City, Michigan
KANA Anaconda, Montana

585 kHz

KJAL Tafuna, American Samoa

590 kHz

KQNT Spokane, Washington
KZHS Hot Springs, Arkansas
KCSJ Pueblo, Colorado
KFNS Wood River, Illinois
KGLE Glendive, Montana
KHAR Anchorage, Alaska
KID Idaho Falls, Idaho
KLBJ Austin, Texas
KSSK Honolulu, Hawaii
KSUB Cedar City, Utah
KTIE San Bernardino, California
KTHO South Lake Tahoe, California
KUGN Eugene, Oregon
WAFC Clewiston, Florida
WARM Scranton, Pennsylvania
WCAB Rutherfordton, North Carolina
WDIZ Panama City, Florida
WDWD Atlanta, Georgia
WEZE Boston, Massachusetts
WJMS Ironwood, Michigan
WKZO Kalamazoo, Michigan
WLES Bon Air, Virginia
WMBS Uniontown, Pennsylvania
KXSP Omaha, Nebraska
WROW Albany, New York
WVLK Lexington, Kentucky
WWLX Lawrenceburg, Tennessee

600 kHz

KGEZ Kalispell, Montana
KCOL Wellington, Colorado
KOGO San Diego, California
KROD El Paso, Texas
KSJB Jamestown, North Dakota
KTBB Tyler, Texas
KVNA Flagstaff, Arizona
WYEL Mayaguez, Puerto Rico
WCAO Baltimore, Maryland
WCHT Escanaba, Michigan
WCVP Murphy, North Carolina
WFRM Coudersport, Pennsylvania
WFST Caribou, Maine
WICC Bridgeport, Connecticut
WBOB(AM) Jacksonville, Florida
WKYH Paintsville, Kentucky
WMT Cedar Rapids, Iowa
WREC Memphis, Tennessee
WSJS Winston-Salem, North Carolina
WSNL Flint, Michigan
WSOM Salem, Ohio
WVAR Richwood, West Virginia
WVOG New Orleans, Louisiana

610 kHz

KARV Russellville, Arkansas
KAVL Lancaster, California
KCSR Chadron, Nebraska
KDAL-AM Duluth, Minnesota
KEAR San Francisco, California
KNML Albuquerque, New Mexico
KILT Houston, Texas
KOJM Havre, Montana
KONA Kennewick-Richland-P, Washington
KRTA Medford, Oregon
KVLE Vail, Colorado
KVNU Logan, Utah
WAGG Birmingham, Alabama
WCEH Hawkinsville, Georgia
KCSP Kansas City, Missouri
WEXS Patillas, Puerto Rico
WFNZ Charlotte, North Carolina
WGIR Manchester, New Hampshire
WIOD Miami, Florida
WXVA Winchester, Virginia
WPLO Grayson, Georgia
WRUS Russellville, Kentucky
WVBE Roanoke, Virginia
WSNG Torrington, Connecticut
WTEL Philadelphia, Pennsylvania
WTVN Columbus, Ohio
WVTJ Pensacola, Florida

620 kHz

KPOJ Portland, Oregon
KGTL Homer, Alaska
KIGS Hanford, California
KHNU Hilo, Hawaii
KMJC Mount Shasta, California
KMKI Plano, Texas
KMNS Sioux City, Iowa
KJOL Grand Junction, Colorado
KTAR Phoenix, Arizona
KWAL Wallace, Idaho
WDNC Durham, North Carolina
WHEN Syracuse, New York
WJDX Jackson, Mississippi
WSNR Jersey City, New Jersey
WJHX Lexington, Alabama
WKHB Irwin, Pennsylvania
WRJZ Knoxville, Tennessee
WDAE St. Petersburg, Florida
WGCV Cayce, South Carolina
WTMJ Milwaukee, Wisconsin
WTUV Louisville, Kentucky
WTRP LaGrange, Georgia
WVMT Burlington, Vermont
WWNR Beckley, West Virginia
WZON Bangor, Maine
KHNU(AM) Hilo, Hawaii
KGTL(AM) Homer, Alaska
WAKY Radcliff, Kentucky

630 kHz

KCIS Edmonds, Washington
KHOW Denver, Colorado
KIAM Nenana, Alaska
KIDD Monterey, California
KFXD Boise, Idaho
KJNO Juneau, Alaska
KYFI St. Louis, Missouri
KTRW Opportunity, Washington
KLEA Lovington, New Mexico
KPLY Reno, Nevada
KSLR San Antonio, Texas
KTKK Sandy, Utah
KUAM Agana, Guam
KVMA Magnolia, Arkansas
KWRO Coquille, Oregon
WAVU Albertville, Alabama
WBMQ Savannah, Georgia
WREY St. Paul, Minnesota
WEJL Scranton, Pennsylvania
WAIZ Hickory, North Carolina
WJDB Thomasville, Alabama
WLAP Lexington, Kentucky
WMAL Washington, District of Columbia
WMFD Wilmington, North Carolina
WNEG Toccoa, Georgia
WPRO Providence, Rhode Island
WUNO San Juan, Puerto Rico
WJAW St. Marys, West Virginia

640 kHz

KFI Los Angeles, California
KTIB Thibodaux, Louisiana
KYUK Bethel, Alaska
WCRV Collierville, Tennessee
WFNC Fayetteville, North Carolina
WXSM Blountville, Tennessee
WGST Atlanta, Georgia
WHLO Akron, Ohio
WVLG Wildwood, Florida
WMEN Royal Palm Beach, Florida
WMFN Zeeland, Michigan
WNNZ Westfield, Massachusetts
WOI Ames, Iowa
WWJZ Mount Holly, New Jersey
KWPN Moore, Oklahoma

650 kHz

KENI Anchorage, Alaska
KGAB Orchard Valley, Wyoming
KPRP Honolulu, Hawaii
KIKK Pasadena, Texas
KMTI Manti, Utah
KSTE Rancho Cordova, California
WHAN Ashland, Virginia
WNMT Nashwauk, Minnesota
WSRO Ashland, Massachusetts
WSM Nashville, Tennessee

660 kHz

KAPS Mount Vernon, Washington
KCRO Omaha, Nebraska
KEYZ Williston, North Dakota
KFAR Fairbanks, Alaska
KWVE(AM) Oildale, California
KSKY Balch Springs, Texas
KTNN Window Rock, Arizona
KXOR Junction City, Oregon
WAMO Wilkinsburg, Pennsylvania
WBHR Sauk Rapids, Minnesota
WLOY Rural Retreat, Virginia
WXQW Fairhope, Alabama
WLFJ Greenville, South Carolina
WFAN New York, New York
WMIC Sandusky, Michigan
WORL Altamonte Springs, Florida
WXIC Waverly, Ohio
WAMO Wilkinsburg, Pennsylvania

670 kHz

KBOI Boise, Idaho
KDLG Dillingham, Alaska
KLTT Commerce City, Colorado
KPUA Hilo, Hawaii
KIRN Simi Valley, California
KHGZ Glenwood, Arkansas
WIEZ Lewistown, Pennsylvania
WMTY Farragut, Tennessee
WSCR Chicago, Illinois
WRJR Claremont, Virginia
WWFE Miami, Florida
WYLS York, Alabama
KMZQ Las Vegas, Nevada

680 kHz

KBRD Lacey, Washington
KBRW Barrow, Alaska
KFEQ St. Joseph, Missouri
KKGR East Helena, Montana
KKYX San Antonio, Texas
KNBR San Francisco, California
KOMW Omak, Washington
KWKA Clovis, New Mexico
WAPA San Juan, Puerto Rico
WKAZ Charleston, West Virginia
WCBM Baltimore, Maryland
WCNN North Atlanta, Georgia
WCTT Corbin, Kentucky
WDBC Escanaba, Michigan
WINR Binghamton, New York
WISR Butler, Pennsylvania
WHBE Newburg, Kentucky
WOGO Hallie, Wisconsin
WPTF Raleigh, North Carolina
WRKO Boston, Massachusetts
WGES St. Petersburg, Florida

690 kHz

KBLI Blackfoot, Idaho
KCEE Tucson, Arizona
KEWI Benton, Arkansas
KFXN Minneapolis, Minnesota
KGGF AM Coffeyville, Kansas
KTSM El Paso, Texas
KOAQ Terrytown, Nebraska
KPET Lamesa, Texas
KHNR Honolulu, Hawaii
KRCO Prineville, Oregon
KRGS Rifle, Colorado
KSTL St. Louis, Missouri
WADS Ansonia, Connecticut
WELD Fisher, West Virginia
WJOX Birmingham, Alabama
WNZK Dearborn Heights, Michigan
WOKV(AM) Jacksonville, Quebec
WPHE Phoenixville, Pennsylvania
WQNO New Orleans, Louisiana
WVCY Oshkosh, Wisconsin
WZAP Bristol, Virginia
XETRA Tijuana, Mexico

700 kHz

KBYR Anchorage, Alaska
KGRV Winston, Oregon
KXLX Airway Heights, Washington
KSEV Tomball, Texas
KMBX Soledad, California
KALL North Salt Lake City, Utah
WTUB Lake City, Florida
WCNF Dothan, Alabama
WLW Cincinnati, Ohio
WDMV Walkersville, Maryland
KHSE Wylie, Texas
KNAX McCook, Nebraska

710 kHz

KCMO Kansas City, Missouri

KSPN Los Angeles, California
KEEL Shreveport, Louisiana
KFIA Carmichael, California
KGNC Amarillo, Texas
KIRO Seattle, Washington
KNUS Denver, Colorado
KBMB Black Canyon City, Arizona
KURV Edinburg, Texas
KXMR Bismarck, North Dakota
WAQI Miami, Florida
WDSM Superior, Wisconsin
WEGG Rose Hill, North Carolina
WEKC Williamsburg, Kentucky
WFNR Blacksburg, Virginia
WKJB Mayaguez, Puerto Rico
WNTM Mobile, Alabama
WOR New York, New York
WPOG St. Matthews, South Carolina
WROM Rome, Georgia
WTPR Paris, Tennessee
WUFF Eastman, Georgia
WZOO Asheboro, North Carolina

720 kHz

KDWN Las Vegas, Nevada
KFIR Sweet Home, Oregon
KOTZ Kotzebue, Alaska
KSAH Universal City, Texas
KUAI Kekaha, Hawaii
WGCR Pisgah Forest, North Carolina
WGN(AM) Chicago, Illinois
WVCC Hogansville, Georgia
WRZN Hernando, Florida
WHYF(AM) Shiremanstown, Pennsylvania

730 kHz

KBSU-FM Boise, Idaho
KDAZ Albuquerque, New Mexico
KKDA Grand Prairie, Texas
KLOE Goodland, Kansas
KEZX Medford, Oregon
KQPN West Memphis, Arkansas
KSVN Ogden, Utah
KULE Ephrata, Washington
KYYA Billings, Montana
KWOA Worthington, Minnesota
KWRE Warrenton, Missouri
WACE Chicopee, Massachusetts
WTNT Alexandria, Virginia
WDOS Oneonta, New York
WFMC Goldsboro, North Carolina
WFMW Madisonville, Kentucky
WJMT Merrill, Wisconsin
WJTO Bath, Maine
WJYM Bowling Green, Ohio
WLIL Lenoir City, Tennessee
WMNA Gretna, Virginia
WZMF(AM) Nanticoke, Pennsylvania
WZGV Cramerton, North Carolina
WPIT Pittsburgh, Pennsylvania
WLTQ Charleston, South Carolina
WSTT Thomasville, Georgia
WUMP Madison, Alabama
WVFN East Lansing, Michigan
WWTK Lake Placid, Florida
KBQX Big Spring, Texas

740 kHz

KATK Carlsbad, New Mexico
KBOE Oskaloosa, Iowa
KBRT Avalon, California
KCBS San Francisco, California
KCMC Texarkana, Texas
KIDR Phoenix, Arizona
KRMG Tulsa, Oklahoma
KTRH Houston, Texas
KVFC Cortez, Colorado
KVOR Colorado Springs, Colorado
WNYH Huntington, New York
WIAC San Juan, Puerto Rico
WIRJ Humboldt, Tennessee
WJIB Cambridge, Massachusetts
WHMT(AM) Tullahoma, Tennessee
WMBG Williamsburg, Virginia
WDGY Hudson, Wisconsin
WMSP Montgomery, Alabama
WNOP Newport, Kentucky
WPAQ Mount Airy, North Carolina
WRNR Martinsburg, West Virginia
WRPQ Baraboo, Wisconsin
WCXZ Harrogate, Tennessee
WSBR Boca Raton, Florida
WVCH Chester, Pennsylvania
WVLN Olney, Illinois
WYGM Orlando, Florida
KNFL Fargo, North Dakota

750 kHz

KAMA El Paso, Texas
KBNN Lebanon, Missouri
KERR Polson, Montana
KFQD Anchorage, Alaska
KKNO Gretna, Louisiana
KMMJ Grand Island, Nebraska
KOAL Price, Utah
KSEO Durant, Oklahoma
KXTG Portland, Oregon
WQOR Olyphant, Pennsylvania
WAUG New Hope, North Carolina
WBMD Baltimore, Maryland
WARD Petoskey, Michigan
WNDZ Portage, Indiana
WPDX Clarksburg, West Virginia
WRIK Brookport, Illinois
WSB Atlanta, Georgia
KHWG Fallon, Nevada

760 kHz

KCCV Overland Park, Kansas
KFMB San Diego, California
KGU Honolulu, Hawaii
KMTL Sherwood, Arkansas
KTBA Tuba City, Arizona
KTKR San Antonio, Texas
KKZN Thornton, Colorado
WCHP Champlain, New York
WCIS Morganton, North Carolina
WCPS Tarboro, North Carolina
WENO Nashville, Tennessee
WJR Detroit, Michigan
WLCC Brandon, Florida
WETR Knoxville, Tennessee
WORA Mayaguez, Puerto Rico
WURL Moody, Alabama
WVNE Leicester, Massachusetts

770 kHz

KATL Miles City, Montana
KCBC Manteca, California
KCHU Valdez, Alaska
KJCB Lafayette, Louisiana
KKOB Albuquerque, New Mexico
KKOB Exp S Santa Fe, New Mexico
KTTH Seattle, Washington
KAAM Garland, Texas
KUOM Minneapolis, Minnesota
WABC New York City, New York
WAIS Buchtel, Ohio
WKFB Jeannette, Pennsylvania
WCGW Nicholasville, Kentucky
WEW St. Louis, Missouri
WLWL Rockingham, North Carolina
WTOR Youngstown, New York
WVNN Athens, Alabama
WJBX North Fort Myers, Florida
WYRV Cedar Bluff, Virginia

780 kHz

KAZM Sedona, Arizona
KKOH Reno, Nevada
KNOM Nome, Alaska
KSPI AM Stillwater, Oklahoma
WAVA Arlington, Virginia
WBBM Chicago, Illinois
WCKB Dunn, North Carolina
WIIN Ridgeland, Mississippi
WJAG Norfolk, Nebraska
WTME Rumford, Maine
WPTN Cookeville, Tennessee
WXME Monticello, Maine
WWOL Forest City, North Carolina
WZZX Lineville, Alabama

790 kHz

KABC Los Angeles, California
KBME Houston, Texas
KCAM Glennallen, Alaska
KFGO Fargo, North Dakota
KFYO Lubbock, Texas
KGHL Billings, Montana
KGMI Bellingham, Washington
KJRB Spokane, Washington
KKON Kealakekua, Hawaii
KOSY Texarkana, Arkansas
KNST Tucson, Arizona
KFPT Clovis, California
KSPD Boise, Idaho
KURM Rogers, Arkansas
KWIL Albany, Oregon
KXXX Colby, Kansas
WAEB Allentown, Pennsylvania
WAXY South Miami, Florida
WAYY Eau Claire, Wisconsin
WETB Johnson City, Tennessee
WGRA Cairo, Georgia
WHTH Heath, Ohio
WLBE Leesburg-Eustis, Florida
WLSV Wellsville, New York
WMC Memphis, Tennessee
WNIS Norfolk, Virginia
WPIC Sharon, Pennsylvania
WJNA Ashland City, Tennessee
WQXI Atlanta, Georgia
WVCD Bamberg-Denmark, South Carolina
WRMS Beardstown, Illinois
WSFN Brunswick, Georgia
WSGW Saginaw, Michigan
WPRV Providence, Rhode Island
WSVG Mount Jackson, Virginia
WPNN Pensacola, Florida
WBLO Thomasville, North Carolina
WTNY Watertown, New York
WTSK Tuscaloosa, Alabama
WKRD Louisville, Kentucky
KEJY Eureka, California

800 kHz

KAGH Crossett, Arkansas
KBRV Soda Springs, Idaho
KDDD Dumas, Texas
KBFP Bakersfield, California
KINY Juneau, Alaska
KPDQ Portland, Oregon
KQAD Luverne, Minnesota
KQCV Oklahoma City, Oklahoma
KREI Farmington, Missouri
KVOM Morrilton, Arkansas
KXIC Iowa City, Iowa
WNNW Lawrence, Massachusetts
WCHA Chambersburg, Pennsylvania
WDEH Sweetwater, Tennessee
WDSC Dillon, South Carolina
WDUX Waupaca, Wisconsin
WHOS Decatur, Alabama
WJAT Swainsboro, Georgia
WKBC North Wilkesboro, North Carolina
WVHU Huntington, West Virginia
WKZI Casey, Illinois
WLAD Danbury, Connecticut
WMGY Montgomery, Alabama
WPJM Greer, South Carolina
WPLK Palatka, Florida
WSHO New Orleans, Louisiana
WSVS Crewe, Virginia
WTMR Camden, New Jersey
WVAL Sauk Rapids, Minnesota

801 kHz

KTWG Agana, Guam

810 kHz

KBHB Sturgis, South Dakota
KGO San Francisco, California
KLVZ Brighton, Colorado
KYTY Somerset, Texas
KSWV Santa Fe, New Mexico
KTBI Ephrata, Washington
KXOI Crane, Texas
WXFO Royston, Georgia
WDMP Dodgeville, Wisconsin
WEDO McKeesport, Pennsylvania
WEKG Jackson, Kentucky
WGY Schenectady, New York
WHB Kansas City, Missouri
WJJQ Tomahawk, Wisconsin
WKVM San Juan, Puerto Rico
WMGC Murfreesboro, Tennessee
WMJH Rockford, Michigan
WCKA Jacksonville, Alabama
WPIN Dublin, Virginia
WQIZ St. George, South Carolina
WSJC Magee, Mississippi
WSYW Indianapolis, Indiana
WTHV Hahira, Georgia
WYRE Annapolis, Maryland
WRSO(AM) Orlovista, Florida

820 kHz

KCBF Fairbanks, Alaska
KGNW Burien-Seattle, Washington
DKORC Anacortes, Washington
WBAP Fort Worth, Texas
WNTW Chester, Virginia
WNYC New York, New York
WVSG Columbus, Ohio
WSWI Evansville, Indiana
WWLZ Horseheads, New York
WWFD Frederick, Maryland
WCPT-AM Willow Springs, Illinois
WWBA Largo, Florida
KUTR Taylorsville, Utah
WBKK Wilton, Minnesota

830 kHz

KFLT Tucson, Arizona
KHVH Honolulu, Hawaii
KMUL Farwell, Texas
KNCO Grass Valley, California
WUMY Memphis, Tennessee
KLAA Orange, California
KSDP Sand Point, Alaska
KUYO Evansville, Wyoming
WACC Hialeah, Florida
WCCO Minneapolis, Minnesota
WCRN Worcester, Massachusetts
WQZQ Goodlettsville, Tennessee
WEEU Reading, Pennsylvania
WFNO Norco, Louisiana
WKTX Cortland, Ohio
WMMI Shepherd, Michigan
WTRU Kernersville, North Carolina

840 kHz

KARS Belen, New Mexico
KKNX Eugene, Oregon
KMAX Colfax, Washington
KSWB Seaside, Oregon
KTIC West Point, Nebraska
KVJY Pharr, Texas
KWDF Ball, Louisiana
KXNT North Las Vegas, Nevada
WBHY Mobile, Alabama
WCEO Columbia, South Carolina
WHAS Louisville, Kentucky
WKDI Denton, Maryland
WKTR Earlysville, Virginia
WPGS Mims, Florida
WRYM New Britain, Connecticut
WVPO Stroudsburg, Pennsylvania
WXEW Yabucoa, Puerto Rico
KMPH Modesto, California

850 kHz

KEYH Houston, Texas
KFUO Clayton, Missouri
KHHO Tacoma, Washington
KHLO Hilo, Hawaii
KICY Nome, Alaska
KJON Carrollton, Texas
KOA Denver, Colorado
WABA Aguadilla, Puerto Rico
WAIT Crystal Lake, Illinois
WFTL West Palm Beach, Florida
WEEI Boston, Massachusetts
WGVS Muskegon, Michigan
WKVL Knoxville, Tennessee
WLRC Walnut, Mississippi
WPTB Statesboro, Georgia
WPTK(AM) Raleigh, North Carolina
WAXB Ridgefield, Connecticut
WKNR Cleveland, Ohio
WRUF Gainesville, Florida
WTAR Norfolk, Virginia
WWJC Duluth, Minnesota
WYLF Penn Yan, New York
WKGE Johnstown, Pennsylvania

860 Hz

KONO San Antonio, Texas

860 kHz

KKAT Salt Lake City, Utah
KFST Fort Stockton, Texas
KKOW Pittsburg, Kansas
KMVP Phoenix, Arizona
KNUJ New Ulm, Minnesota
KOSE Wilson, Arkansas
KPAM Troutdale, Oregon
KPAN Hereford, Texas
KSFA Nacogdoches, Texas
KTRB San Francisco, California
KWPC Muscatine, Iowa
KWRF Warren, Arkansas
WACB Taylorsville, North Carolina
WAEC Atlanta, Georgia
WAMI Opp, Alabama
WFSI Baltimore, Maryland
WDMG Douglas, Georgia
WEVA Emporia, Virginia
WFMO Fairmont, North Carolina
WMRI Marion, Indiana
WGUL Dunedin, Florida
WLBG Laurens, South Carolina
WNOV Milwaukee, Wisconsin
WOAY Oak Hill, West Virginia
WSBS Great Barrington, Massachusetts
WSON Henderson, Kentucky
WTZX Sparta, Tennessee
WWDB Philadelphia, Pennsylvania

870 kHz

KAAN Bethany, Missouri
KFJZ Fort Worth, Texas
KFLD Pasco, Washington
KRLA Glendale, California
KLSQ Whitney, Nevada
KPRM Park Rapids, Minnesota
WINU Shelbyville, Illinois
WFLO Farmville, Virginia
WHCU Ithaca, New York
WKAR East Lansing, Michigan
WLVP Gorham, Maine
WMTL Leitchfield, Kentucky
WPWT Colonial Heights, Tennessee
WQBS San Juan, Puerto Rico
WQRX Valley Head, Alabama
WTIM Assumption, Illinois
WWL New Orleans, Louisiana
KJMP Pierce, Colorado
WZNH Fitzwilliam Depot, New Hampshire

880 kHz

KHCM Honolulu, Hawaii
KCMX Phoenix, Oregon
KHAC Tse Bonito, New Mexico
KIXI Mercer Island/Seattl, Washington
KJJR Whitefish, Montana
KJOZ Conroe, Texas
KKMC Gonzales, California
KRVN Lexington, Nebraska
KWIP Dallas, Oregon
WCBS New York, New York
WIJR Highland, Illinois
WMDB Nashville, Tennessee
WMEQ Menomonie, Wisconsin
WPIP Winston-Salem, North Carolina
WRFD Columbus-Worthington, Ohio
WRRZ Clinton, North Carolina
WPEK Fairview, North Carolina
WSLK Moneta, Virginia
WYKO Sabana Grande, Puerto Rico
WZAB Sweetwater, Florida

890 kHz

KBBI Homer, Alaska
KTLR Oklahoma City, Oklahoma
KDXU St. George, Utah
KGGN Gladstone, Missouri
KQLX Lisbon, North Dakota
KVOZ Del Mar Hills, Texas
WBAJ Blythewood, South Carolina
WAMG Dedham, Massachusetts
WHJA Laurel, Mississippi
WFAB Ceiba, Puerto Rico
WFKJ Cashtown, Pennsylvania
WJTP Lithia Springs, Georgia
WHNC Henderson, North Carolina
WKNV Fairlawn, Virginia
WLS Chicago, Illinois
WYAM Hartselle, Alabama
KIHC Arroyo Grande, California
KTXV Mabank, Texas
KJME Fountain, Colorado

900 kHz

KALI West Covina, California
KPYN Atlanta, Texas
KBIF Fresno, California
KCLW Hamilton, Texas
KFAL Fulton, Missouri
KFLP Floydada, Texas
KHOZ Harrison, Arkansas
KJSK Columbus, Nebraska
KKRT Wenatchee, Washington
KREH Pecan Grove, Texas
KSGL Wichita, Kansas
KTIS Minneapolis, Minnesota
KZPA Fort Yukon, Alaska
WATK Antigo, Wisconsin
WATV Birmingham, Alabama
WAYN Rockingham, North Carolina
WBML Macon, Georgia
WBRV Boonville, New York
WCBX Bassett, Virginia
WKDA Lebanon, Tennessee
WCPA Clearfield, Pennsylvania
WDLS Wisconsin Dells, Wisconsin
WURD Philadelphia, Pennsylvania
WFIA Louisville, Kentucky
WGOK Mobile, Alabama
WNMB North Myrtle Beach, South Carolina
WIAM Williamston, North Carolina
WILC Laurel, Maryland
WCME(AM) Brunswick, Maine
WJLG Savannah, Georgia
WJTH Calhoun, Georgia
WJWL Georgetown, Delaware
WUAM Watervliet, New York
WKDW Staunton, Virginia
WKXV Knoxville, Tennessee
WLSI Pikeville, Kentucky
WMOP Ocala, Florida
WABY Watervliet, New York
WGHM Nashua, New Hampshire
WOZK Ozark, Alabama
WSWN Belle Glade, Florida
WYCV Granite Falls, North Carolina

910 kHz

KWDZ Salt Lake City, Utah
KBIM Roswell, New Mexico
KBLG Billings, Montana
KCJB Minot, North Dakota
KECR El Cajon, California
KMTT Vancouver, Washington
KGME Phoenix, Arizona
KINA Salina, Kansas
KIYU Galena, Alaska
KJJQ Volga, South Dakota
KKSF Oakland, California
KLCN Blytheville, Arkansas
KNAF Fredericksburg, Texas
KOXR Oxnard, California
KPOF Denver, Colorado
KRIO McAllen, Texas
KURY Brookings, Oregon
KVIS Miami, Oklahoma
KRAK Hesperia, California
KATH Frisco, Texas
WAEI Bangor, Maine
WAKO Lawrenceville, Illinois
WALT Meridian, Mississippi
WAVL Apollo, Pennsylvania
WDOR Sturgeon Bay, Wisconsin
WEPG South Pittsburg, Tennessee
WFDF Farmington Hills, Michigan
WRFV Valdosta, Georgia
WBZU Scranton, Pennsylvania
WGTO Cassopolis, Michigan
WHSM Hayward, Wisconsin
WJCW Johnson City, Tennessee
WSFE Burnside, Kentucky
WMRB Columbia, Tennessee
WUBR Baton Rouge, Louisiana
WLAT New Britain, Connecticut
WOLI Spartanburg, South Carolina
WPFB Middletown, Ohio
WPRP Ponce, Puerto Rico
WRKL New City, New York
WRNL Richmond, Virginia
WSBA York, Pennsylvania
WSRP Jacksonville, North Carolina
WSUI Iowa City, Iowa
WTWD Plant City, Florida
WTMZ Dorchester Terrace-Brentwood, South Carolina
WFJX Roanoke, Virginia
WLTP Marietta, Ohio
WZMG Pepperell, Alabama

92.5 kHz

WXJC Cordova, Alabama

920 kHz

KARN Little Rock, Arkansas
KGTK Olympia, Washington
KBAD Las Vegas, Nevada
KQBU El Paso, Texas
KDHL Faribault, Minnesota
KFLB Odessa, Texas
KIHM Reno, Nevada
KKLS Rapid City, South Dakota
KLMR Lamar, Colorado
KVIN Ceres, California
KPSI Palm Springs, California
KSHO Lebanon, Oregon
KSRM Soldotna, Alaska
KSVA Albuquerque, New Mexico
KVEC San Luis Obispo, California
KVEL Vernal, Utah
KWAD Wadena, Minnesota
KWYS West Yellowstone, Montana
KXLY-AM Spokane, Washington
KYFR Shenandoah, Iowa
KYST Texas City, Texas
WGKA Atlanta, Georgia
WBOX Bogalusa, Louisiana
WNJE Trenton, New Jersey
WGHQ Kingston, New York
WGNU Granite City, Illinois
WGOL Russellville, Alabama
WHJJ Providence, Rhode Island
WIRD Lake Placid, New York
WYBY Cortland, New York
WKVA Lewistown, Pennsylvania
WLIV Livingston, Tennessee
WDMC Melbourne, Florida
WMMN Fairmont, West Virginia
WMNI Columbus, Ohio
WMOK Metropolis, Illinois
WMPL Hancock, Michigan
WOKY Milwaukee, Wisconsin
WPCM Burlington-Graham, North Carolina
WPTL Canton, North Carolina
WTCW Whitesburg, Kentucky
WHJD Hazlehurst, Georgia
WYMB Manning, South Carolina
WEZZ Brantley, Alabama
WBAA West Lafayette, Indiana
WURA Quantico, Virginia

93.7 kHz

KEYE Perryton, Texas

930 kHz

KAFF Flagstaff, Arizona
KAGI Grants Pass, Oregon
KAPR Douglas, Arizona
KCCC Carlsbad, New Mexico
KDET Center, Texas
KIUP Durango, Colorado
KBAI Bellingham, Washington
KHJ Los Angeles, California
KKIN Aitkin, Minnesota
KKXX Paradise, California
KMPT East Missoula, Montana
KLUP Terrell Hills, Texas
KNSA Unalakleet, Alaska
KOGA Ogallala, Nebraska
KRKY Granby, Colorado
KROE Sheridan, Wyoming
KSDN Aberdeen, South Dakota
KSEI Pocatello, Idaho
KTKN Ketchikan, Alaska
KWOC Poplar Bluff, Missouri
KYAK Yakima, Washington
WAUR Sandwich, Illinois
WBCK Battle Creek, Michigan
WBEN Buffalo, New York
WHLM Bloomsburg, Pennsylvania
WDLX Washington, North Carolina
WYAC Cabo Rojo, Puerto Rico
WEOL Elyria, Ohio
WFMD Frederick, Maryland
WPKX Rochester, New Hampshire
WHON Centerville, Indiana
WIZR Johnstown, New York
WGAD Rainbow City, Alabama
WKCT Bowling Green, Kentucky
WLSS Sarasota, Florida
WKY Oklahoma City, Oklahoma
WLBL Auburndale, Wisconsin
WLLL Lynchburg, Virginia
WMGR Bainbridge, Georgia
WFXJ Jacksonville, Florida
WPAT Paterson, New Jersey
WRVC Huntington, West Virginia
WSEV Sevierville, Tennessee
WSFZ Jackson, Mississippi
WTAD Quincy, Illinois
WWON Waynesboro, Tennessee
WYFQ Charlotte, North Carolina
WYUS Milford, Delaware

940 kHz

KGMS Tucson, Arizona
KWRU Fresno, California
KIXZ Amarillo, Texas
KKNE Waipahu, Hawaii
KMER Kemmerer, Wyoming
KSWM Aurora, Missouri
KTFS Texarkana, Texas
KVSH Valentine, Nebraska
KWBY Woodburn, Oregon
KPSZ Des Moines, Iowa
KICE Bend, Oregon
WADV Lebanon, Pennsylvania
WCND Shelbyville, Kentucky
WCPC Houston, Mississippi
WCSW Shell Lake, Wisconsin
WECO Wartburg, Tennessee
WFAW Fort Atkinson, Wisconsin
WGFP Webster, Massachusetts
WGRP Greenville, Pennsylvania
WIDG St. Ignace, Michigan
WINE Brookfield, Connecticut
WINZ Miami, Florida
WIPR San Juan, Puerto Rico
WKGM Smithfield, Virginia
WKYK Burnsville, North Carolina
WCIT(AM) Lima, Ohio
WLQH Chiefland, Florida
WMAC Macon, Georgia
WMIX Mount Vernon, Illinois
WNRG Grundy, Virginia
WYLD New Orleans, Louisiana
KDIL Jerome, Idaho

950 kHz

KAHI Auburn, California
KDCE Espanola, New Mexico
KFSA Fort Smith, Arkansas
KJR Seattle, Washington
KJRG Newton, Kansas
KMHR(AM) Boise, Idaho
KWOS Jefferson City, Missouri
KMTX Helena, Montana
KNFT Bayard, New Mexico
KOEL Oelwein, Iowa
KOZE Lewiston, Idaho
KPRC Houston, Texas
KTNF St. Louis Park, Minnesota
KSEW Seward, Alaska
KTBR Roseburg, Oregon
KWAT Watertown, South Dakota
KXJK Forrest City, Arkansas
KJTV Lubbock, Texas
WAKM Franklin, Tennessee
WHSY Hattiesburg, Mississippi
WCLB Sheboygan, Wisconsin
WCTN Potomac-Cabin John, Maryland
WDIG Steubenville, Ohio
WERL Eagle River, Wisconsin
WROC Rochester, New York
WGUN Valdosta, Georgia
WGTA Summerville, Georgia
WHVW Hyde Park, New York
WIBX Utica, New York
WJKB Moncks Corner, South Carolina
WNCC Barnesboro, Pennsylvania
WNTD Chicago, Illinois
WNZZ Montgomery, Alabama

WKDN Philadelphia, Pennsylvania
WPET Greensboro, North Carolina
WBES Charleston, West Virginia
WROL Boston, Massachusetts
WORD Spartanburg, South Carolina
WTLN Orlando, Florida
WWJ Detroit, Michigan
WXGI Richmond, Virginia
WXLW Indianapolis, Indiana
WYWY Barbourville, Kentucky
KRRP Coushatta, Louisiana

960 kHz

KALE Richland, Washington
KCGS Marshall, Arkansas
KFLN Baker, Montana
KGKL San Angelo, Texas
KGWA Enid, Oklahoma
KIMP Mount Pleasant, Texas
KIXW Apple Valley, California
KLAD Klamath Falls, Oregon
KLTF Little Falls, Minnesota
KMA Shenandoah, Iowa
KNDN Farmington, New Mexico
KNEB Scottsbluff, Nebraska
KNEW Oakland, California
KOVO Provo, Utah
KKNT Phoenix, Arizona
KROF Abbeville, Louisiana
KSRA Salmon, Idaho
KZIM Cape Girardeau, Missouri
WCRU Dallas, North Carolina
WABG Greenwood, Mississippi
WATS Sayre, Pennsylvania
WBMC McMinnville, Tennessee
WDLM-AM East Moline, Illinois
WEAV Plattsburgh, New York
WELI New Haven, Connecticut
WERC Birmingham, Alabama
WFGL Fitchburg, Massachusetts
WFIR Roanoke, Virginia
WQLA La Follette, Tennessee
WGRO Lake City, Florida
WHAK Rogers City, Michigan
WHYL Carlisle, Pennsylvania
WJYZ Albany, Georgia
WDNO Quebradillas, Puerto Rico
WKVX Wooster, Ohio
WLPR Prichard, Alabama
WPRT Prestonsburg, Kentucky
WRFC Athens, Georgia
WRNS Kinston, North Carolina
WSBT South Bend, Indiana
WTCH Shawano, Wisconsin
WTGM Salisbury, Maryland
WSVU North Palm Beach, Florida

970 kHz

KHTY Bakersfield, California
KESP Modesto, California
KFTA Rupert, Idaho
KBUL Billings, Montana
KCFO Tulsa, Oklahoma
KNWZ Coachella, California
KFEL Pueblo, Colorado
KHVN Fort Worth, Texas
KFBX Fairbanks, Alaska
KIXL Del Valle, Texas
KJLT North Platte, Nebraska
KXTA Rupert, Idaho
KNEA Jonesboro, Arkansas
KQAQ Austin, Minnesota
KNIH Paradise, Nevada
KSYL Alexandria, Louisiana
KTTO Spokane, Washington
KVWM Show Low, Arizona
WAMD Aberdeen, Maryland
WATH Athens, Ohio
WBLF Bellefonte, Pennsylvania
WCHN Norwich, New York
WDAY Fargo, North Dakota
WERH Hamilton, Alabama
WESO Southbridge, Massachusetts
WFLA Tampa, Florida
WFSR Harlan, Kentucky
WFUN Ashtabula, Ohio
WHA Madison, Wisconsin
WKCI Waynesboro, Virginia
WWRK Florence, South Carolina
WKHM Jackson, Michigan
WGTK Louisville, Kentucky
WMAY Springfield, Illinois
WDCZ Buffalo, New York
WNIV Atlanta, Georgia
WRCS Ahoskie, North Carolina
WFQY Brandon, Mississippi
WTBF Troy, Alabama
WNNR Jacksonville, Florida
WVOP Vidalia, Georgia
WNYM Hackensack, New Jersey
WYSE Canton, North Carolina
WBGG Pittsburgh, Pennsylvania
WWYO Pineville, West Virginia
WRHA(AM) Spring City, Tennessee
WZAM Ishpeming, Michigan
WZAN Portland, Maine
WSTX Christiansted, Virgin Islands
WMPW Danville, Virginia
KUFO Portland, Oregon
WDUL Superior, Wisconsin

980 kHz

KNTR Lake Havasu City, Arizona
KCAB Dardanelle, Arkansas
KDBV Salinas, California
KDSJ Deadwood, South Dakota
KEYQ Fresno, California
KGLN Glenwood Springs, Colorado
KICA Clovis, New Mexico
KWSW Eureka, California
KTCR Selah, Washington
KKMS Richfield, Minnesota
KMBZ Kansas City, Missouri
KMIN Grants, New Mexico
KOKA Shreveport, Louisiana
KQUE Rosenberg-Richmond, Texas
KSGM Chester, Illinois
KSVC Richfield, Utah
KSPZ Ammon, Idaho
KVLV Fallon, Nevada
WEGO(AM) Winston-Salem, North Carolina
WAAV Leland, North Carolina
WAKV Otsego, Michigan
WAKK McComb, Mississippi
WAZS Summerville, South Carolina
WULR York, South Carolina
WCAP Lowell, Massachusetts
WCUB Two Rivers, Wisconsin
WGWM London, Kentucky
WHAW Lost Creek, West Virginia
WHSR Pompano Beach, Florida
WILK Wilkes-Barre, Pennsylvania
WKLY Hartwell, Georgia
WDYN Rossville, Georgia
WDVH Gainesville, Florida
WPFP Park Falls, Wisconsin
WONE Dayton, Ohio
WPGA Perry, Georgia
WPRE Prairie Du Chien, Wisconsin
WRNE Gulf Breeze, Florida
WXLM Groton, Connecticut
WTEM Washington, District of Columbia
WTOT Marianna, Florida
WOFX Troy, New York
WFHG Bristol, Virginia
WYFN Nashville, Tennessee
WJYK Chase City, Virginia
KBBO Selah, Washington

990 kHz

KAML Kenedy-Karnes City, Texas
KATD Pittsburg, California
KAYL Storm Lake, Iowa
KIKI Honolulu, Hawaii
KRKS Denver, Colorado
KTHH Albany, Oregon
KRMO Cassville, Missouri
KRSL Russell, Kansas
KSVP Artesia, New Mexico
KTKT Tucson, Arizona
KTMS Santa Barbara, California
KFCD Farmersville, Texas
KWAM Memphis, Tennessee
KZZB Beaumont, Texas
WABO Waynesboro, Mississippi
WALE Greenville, Rhode Island
WBTE Windsor, North Carolina
WCAZ Carthage, Illinois
WDCX Rochester, New York
WEEB Southern Pines, North Carolina
WEIS Centre, Alabama
WMYM Miami, Florida
WGML Hinesville, Georgia
WGSO New Orleans, Louisiana
WDYZ Orlando, Florida
WISK Lawrenceville, Georgia
WITZ Jasper, Indiana
WJEH Gallipolis, Ohio
WLDX Fayette, Alabama
WRFM Muncie, Indiana
WNML Knoxville, Tennessee
WNRV Narrows-Pearisburg, Virginia
WXCT Southington, Connecticut
WPRA Mayaguez, Puerto Rico
WTIG Massillon, Ohio
WLEE Richmond, Virginia
WDEO Ypsilanti, Michigan
WNTP Philadelphia, Pennsylvania
WLLI Somerset, Pennsylvania

U.S. FM Stations by Frequency

100.1 MHz

KATQ-FM Plentywood, Montana
KCTN Garnavillo, Iowa
KDJR De Soto, Missouri
KUYY Emmetsburg, Iowa
KITT Soda Springs, Idaho
KGBA-FM Holtville, California
KGMN Kingman, Arizona
KBBM Jefferson City, Missouri
KKZQ Tehachapi, California
KVNA-FM Flagstaff, Arizona
KLVJ Julian, California
KMMR Malta, Montana
KMXT Kodiak, Alaska
KNGS Coalinga, California
KKWK Cameron, Missouri
KOLV Olivia, Minnesota
KOMC-FM Kimberling City, Missouri
KWSA Price, Utah
KNRB Atlanta, Texas
KQFM Hermiston, Oregon
KQOD Stockton, California
KRVV Bastrop, Louisiana
KTHX-FM Dayton, Nevada
KYBI Lufkin, Texas
KKTY-FM Glendo, Wyoming
KWFX Woodward, Oklahoma
KWHQ-FM Kenai, Alaska
KYFM Bartlesville, Oklahoma
KYKC Byng, Oklahoma
KYKD Bethel, Alaska
KCLL San Angelo, Texas
KZOQ-FM Missoula, Montana
KZRO Dunsmuir, California
KZST Santa Rosa, California
WASL Dyersburg, Tennessee
WBCH-FM Hastings, Michigan
WBRR Bradford, Pennsylvania
WBRS Waltham, Massachusetts
WBXB Edenton, North Carolina
WCLG-FM Morgantown, West Virginia
WDDC Portage, Wisconsin
WDMX Vienna, West Virginia
WDST Woodstock, New York
WFLQ French Lick, Indiana
WFRI Winamac, Indiana
WQMJ Forsyth, Georgia
WPJP Port Washington, Wisconsin
WGLC Mendota, Illinois
WGSY Phenix City, Alabama
WHOU-FM Houlton, Maine
WJBD-FM Salem, Illinois
WJRZ-FM Manahawkin, New Jersey
WKAI Macomb, Illinois
WKBH-FM West Salem, Wisconsin
WKQQ Winchester, Kentucky
WKQY Tazewell, Virginia
WVBE-FM Lynchburg, Virginia
WSSJ Rincon, Georgia
WMDJ-FM Allen, Kentucky
WUPE-FM North Adams, Massachusetts
WNIR Kent, Ohio
WNSY Talking Rock, Georgia
WZJZ Port Charlotte, Florida
WVVE Panama City Beach, Florida
WPNH-FM Plymouth, New Hampshire
WWOT Altoona, Pennsylvania
WEJL-FM Forest City, Pennsylvania
WQIC Lebanon, Pennsylvania
WQXB Grenada, Mississippi
WRHN Rhinelander, Wisconsin
WRLT Franklin, Tennessee
WVIB Holton, Michigan
WCUZ Bear Lake, Michigan
WSWR Shelby, Ohio
WWFN-FM Lake City, South Carolina
WWFX Southbridge, Massachusetts
WPUP Watkinsville, Georgia
WXZQ Piketon, Ohio
KLKS Pequot Lakes, Minnesota
WVMD Romney, West Virginia
KJBI Fort Pierre, South Dakota
KDEZ Brandon, South Dakota
KSIK Fleming, Colorado
KHWG-FM Crystal, Nevada
WILA Live Oak, Florida
KZMO Roundup, Montana
WFCV-FM Bluffton, Indiana
WXBT West Columbia, South Carolina

100.3 MHz

KBRG San Jose, California
KCCN-FM Honolulu, Hawaii
KSWD Los Angeles, California
KCVJ Osceola, Missouri
KCYY San Antonio, Texas
KQMR Globe, Arizona
KZQX Tatum, Texas
KDVV Topeka, Kansas
KFXS Rapid City, South Dakota
KCXR Taft, Oklahoma
KAPA Hilo, Hawaii
KICY-FM Nome, Alaska
KILT-FM Houston, Texas
KIMN Denver, Colorado
KJCM Snyder, Oklahoma
KJMB-FM Blythe, California
KJNP-FM North Pole, Alaska
KKRZ Portland, Oregon
KLRZ Larose, Louisiana
KMAK Orange Cove, California
KMMX Tahoka, Texas
KDRB Des Moines, Iowa
KOKU Hagatna, Guam
KOMX Pampa, Texas
KPEK Albuquerque, New Mexico
KDJE Jacksonville, Arkansas
KWPT Fortuna, California
KRDQ Colby, Kansas
KQXR Payette, Idaho
KJKK Dallas, Texas
KRQK Lompoc, California
KRRV-FM Alexandria, Louisiana
KRWQ Gold Hill, Oregon
KSFI Salt Lake City, Utah
KBJK Concow, California
KSNR Fisher, Minnesota
KSWC Winfield, Kansas
KNZS Arlington, Kansas
KTEX Mercedes, Texas
KUKU-FM Willow Springs, Missouri
KWAW Garapan-Saipan, Guam
KURM-FM Gravette, Arkansas
KZEN Central City, Nebraska
KZMQ-FM Greybull, Wyoming
WAFD Webster Springs, West Virginia
WAOQ Goshen, Alabama
WYDL Middleton, Tennessee
WMVN Sylvan Beach, New York
WBIG-FM Washington, District of Columbia
WCCI Savanna, Illinois
WCLT-FM Newark, Ohio
WCTH Plantation Key, Florida
WDHI Delhi, New York
WQON Grayling, Michigan
WHEB Portsmouth, New Hampshire
WHGL-FM Canton, Pennsylvania
WKKB Middletown, Rhode Island
WHTZ Newark, New Jersey
WOSL Norwood, Ohio
WIVA-FM Aguadilla, Puerto Rico
WIXY Champaign, Illinois
WKBE Warrensburg, New York
WKIT Brewer, Maine
WLGP Jacksonville, North Carolina
WLKI Angola, Indiana
WNCY Neenah-Menasha, Wisconsin
WNIC Dearborn, Michigan
WSHE-FM Chicago, Illinois
WNSL Laurel, Mississippi
WOBB Tifton, Georgia
WCYQ Oak Ridge, Tennessee
WORG Elloree, South Carolina
KFXN-FM Minneapolis, Minnesota
WSEA Atlantic Beach, South Carolina
WRUM Orlando, Florida
WRNB Media, Pennsylvania
WARV-FM Petersburg, Virginia
WTKE-FM Niceville, Florida
WQRV Meridianville, Alabama
WVVR Hopkinsville, Kentucky
WYGB Edinburgh, Indiana
WGYY Meadville, Pennsylvania
KXAA Cle Elum, Washington
KLSK Great Falls, Montana
WQJQ Barton, Vermont
WSTX-FM Christiansted, Virgin Islands
WUPT Gwinn, Michigan

100.5 MHz

KATT Oklahoma City, Oklahoma
KBDR Mirando City, Texas
KBFX Anchorage, Alaska
KMME(FM) Cottage Grove, Oregon
KDEC-FM Decorah, Iowa
KQBB Center, Texas
KEGI Jonesboro, Arkansas
KGHT El Jebel, Colorado
KSWF Aurora, Missouri
KIKN-FM Salem, South Dakota
KJJM Baker, Montana
KTGR-FM Fulton, Missouri
KMEM-FM Memphis, Missouri
KMQA East Porterville, California
KMVL-FM Madisonville, Texas
KXNT-FM Henderson, Nevada
KNNK Dimmitt, Texas
KPSI-FM Palm Springs, California
KRSJ Durango, Colorado
KSFX Roswell, New Mexico
KTDE Gualala, California
KWIQ-FM Moses Lake, Washington
KXAC St. James, Minnesota
KZHE Stamps, Arkansas
KZZO Sacramento, California
WALC Charleston, South Carolina
WBLE Batesville, Mississippi
WDRE Susquehanna, Pennsylvania
WVHT Norfolk, Virginia
WHLZ Marion, South Carolina
WNNX College Park, Georgia
WJNG Johnsonburg, Pennsylvania
WKEE-FM Huntington, West Virginia
WKXA-FM Findlay, Ohio
WJQX Helena, Alabama
WOYS Apalachicola, Florida
WRCH New Britain, Connecticut
WHHZ Newberry, Florida
WRTM-FM Sharon, Mississippi
WRVY-FM Henry, Illinois
WSCN Cloquet, Minnesota
WSJD Princeton, Indiana
WSSL-FM Gray Court, South Carolina
WSGW-FM Carrollton, Michigan
WLGX Louisville, Kentucky
WTLX Monona, Wisconsin
WTRV Walker, Michigan
WDVI Rochester, New York
WWKI Kokomo, Indiana
WXRS-FM Portal, Georgia
WJRL-FM Slocomb, Alabama
KIXX Lebanon, New Hampshire
WYGL-FM Elizabethville, Pennsylvania
WYMG Chatham, Illinois
KMEN Mendota, California
WZEZ Goochland, Virginia
KXDZ Templeton, California
KTED Evansville, Wyoming
WDYK Ridgeley, West Virginia
KQZB Troy, Idaho
KVWF Augusta, Kansas
WFYE Glade Spring, Virginia
KMXD Monroe, Utah
WDTX Rothschild, Wisconsin
KXQQ Henderson, Nevada
W263BJ Loves Park, Illinois

100.7 MHz

KSNA Idaho Falls, Idaho
KXLL Juneau, Alaska
KASE-FM Austin, Texas
KATJ-FM George, California
KEAZ Kensett, Arkansas
KLSZ-FM Fort Smith, Arkansas
KTHU Corning, California
KFMB-FM San Diego, California
KGBI-FM Omaha, Nebraska
KGFT Pueblo, Colorado
KGMO Cape Girardeau, Missouri
KGWY Gillette, Wyoming
KHAY Ventura, California
KHOK Hoisington, Kansas
KHSS Athena, Oregon
KIBS Bishop, California
KMGX Bend, Oregon
KIKV-FM Sauk Centre, Minnesota
KVVZ San Rafael, California
KJYL Eagle Grove, Iowa
KKRQ Iowa City, Iowa
KLVF Las Vegas, New Mexico
KMLO Lowry, South Dakota
KINF Gooding, Idaho
KMZU Carrollton, Missouri
KOLZ Cheyenne, Wyoming
KULL Abilene, Texas
KPNC Ponca City, Oklahoma
KPPT-FM Depoe Bay, Oregon
KPXI Overton, Texas
KKWF Seattle, Washington
KXXQ Milan, New Mexico
KWRD-FM Highland Village, Texas
KKLQ Harwood, North Dakota
KRRK Desert Hills, Arizona
KKHT-FM Lumberton, Texas
KIBG Bigfork, Montana
KSLX-FM Scottsdale, Arizona
KKVT Grand Junction, Colorado
KPDA Mountain Home, Idaho
KTFR Chelsea, Oklahoma
KPRC-FM Salinas, California
KZBL Natchitoches, Louisiana
KFNS-FM Troy, Missouri
WMTX Tampa, Florida
WBGQ Bulls Gap, Tennessee
WBIZ-FM Eau Claire, Wisconsin
WRXQ Coal City, Illinois
WBYT Elkhart, Indiana
WNMX Christiansburg, Virginia
WWTH Oscoda, Michigan
WCOG-FM Galeton, Pennsylvania
WCYO Irvine, Kentucky
WDMS Greenville, Mississippi
WEEC Springfield, Ohio
WZBA Westminster, Maryland
WGTN-FM Andrews, South Carolina
WHUD Peekskill, New York
WHYI-FM Fort Lauderdale, Florida
WITL Lansing, Michigan
WFLA-FM Midway, Florida
WKKV-FM Racine, Wisconsin
WKLX Brownsville, Kentucky
WLEV Allentown, Pennsylvania
WLRR Milledgeville, Georgia
WMGI Terre Haute, Indiana
WMJD Grundy, Virginia
WMMS Cleveland, Ohio
WTHK Wilmington, Vermont
WOBE Crystal Falls, Michigan
WEFX Henderson, New York
WQPO Harrisonburg, Virginia
WTBM Mexico, Maine
WRDU Wake Forest, North Carolina
WUSY Cleveland, Tennessee
WUTQ-FM Utica, New York
WCOA-FM Pensacola, Florida
WMUV Brunswick, Georgia
WTGE Baton Rouge, Louisiana
WXYX Bayamon, Puerto Rico
WZJS Banner Elk, North Carolina
WZLX Boston, Massachusetts
WBZZ New Kensington, Pennsylvania
WZXL Wildwood, New Jersey
KXLB Livingston, Montana
KYMV Woodruff, Utah
KJIK Duncan, Arizona
WVBD Fayetteville, West Virginia
WCKF Ashland, Alabama
KRNP Sutherland, Nebraska
WPLB Plattsburgh West, New York
WMUV Brunswick, Florida

100.9 MHz

KAEH Beaumont, California
KAKN Naknek, Alaska
KARY-FM Grandview, Washington
KCDV Cordova, Alaska
KCLY Clay Center, Kansas
KDEL-FM Arkadelphia, Arkansas
KEJL Eunice, New Mexico
KBAR-FM Victoria, Texas
KFSK Petersburg, Alaska
KGLC Miami, Oklahoma
KSXY Forestville, California
KHLL Richwood, Louisiana
KWFB Holliday, Texas
KMIX Tracy, California
KNEC Yuma, Colorado
KOWZ-FM Blooming Prairie, Minnesota
KXGL Amarillo, Texas
KRAJ Johannesburg, California

KRRY Canton, Missouri
KMXW Sparks, Nevada
KHOM Salem, Arkansas
KSSB Calipatria, California
KESA Eureka Springs, Arkansas
KKEE Wheelock, Texas
KWKK Russellville, Arkansas
KXOJ-FM Sapulpa, Oklahoma
KAUJ Grafton, North Dakota
KQSR Yuma, Arizona
KZMK Sierra Vista, Arizona
WAAI Hurlock, Maryland
WQNC Harrisburg, North Carolina
WAKB Hephzibah, Georgia
WALX Orrville, Alabama
WANY-FM Albany, Kentucky
WAYA-FM Ridgeville, South Carolina
WAYC Bedford, Pennsylvania
WBDC Huntingburg, Indiana
WBNO-FM Bryan, Ohio
WWBR Big Rapids, Michigan
WPZS Harrisburg, North Carolina
WCDO-FM Sidney, New York
WCJM-FM West Point, Georgia
WCMP-FM Pine City, Minnesota
WMJK Clyde, Ohio
WHTI(FM) Lakeside, Virginia
WHPO Hoopeston, Illinois
WIFM-FM Elkin, North Carolina
WIQO-FM Forest, Virginia
WICV East Jordan, Michigan
WJAQ Marianna, Florida
WJAW-FM McConnelsville, Ohio
WJXN-FM Utica, Mississippi
WMXE South Charleston, West Virginia
WKBB Mantee, Mississippi
WKLI-FM Albany, New York
WKOY-FM Princeton, West Virginia
WKRL-FM North Syracuse, New York
WBZG Peru, Illinois
WLSK Lebanon, Kentucky
WLYU Lyons, Georgia
WPGA-FM Perry, Georgia
WPGI Horseheads, New York
WPGW-FM Portland, Indiana
WQFL Rockford, Illinois
WQXC-FM Otsego, Michigan
WRCO-FM Richland Center, Wisconsin
WRKT North East, Pennsylvania
WRNX Amherst, Massachusetts
WSTS Fairmont, North Carolina
WKNL New London, Connecticut
WEIO(FM) Huntingdon, Tennessee
WVLY-FM Milton, Pennsylvania
WWFY Berlin, Vermont
WXIZ Waverly, Ohio
WZUS Macon, Illinois
WXJZ Gainesville, Florida
WNOW Speedway, Indiana
WLUN Pinconning, Michigan
WYNZ South Portland, Maine
WZST Westover, West Virginia
WFMI Southern Shores, North Carolina
KHSK Allen, Nebraska
KAYO Wasilla, Alaska

101.1 MHz

KAKQ-FM Fairbanks, Alaska
KSKR-FM Sutherlin, Oregon
KBER Ogden, Utah
KBHP Bemidji, Minnesota
KNUT Tamuning, Guam
KBON Mamou, Louisiana
KCFX Harrisonville, Missouri
KDDX Spearfish, South Dakota
KDSR Williston, North Dakota
KEOJ Caney, Kansas
KNRJ Cordes Lakes, Arizona
KEYF-FM Cheney, Washington
KFNF Oberlin, Kansas
KHME Winona, Minnesota
KHYL Auburn, California
KJMS Olive Branch, Mississippi
KLIR Columbus, Nebraska
KLOL Houston, Texas
KLQL Luverne, Minnesota
KOHO Leavenworth, Washington
KWYD Parma, Idaho
KONE Lubbock, Texas
KONO-FM Helotes, Texas
KOSI Denver, Colorado
KPIN Pinedale, Wyoming
KQDJ-FM Valley City, North Dakota
KRMD-FM Oil City, Louisiana
KRTH Los Angeles, California
KRXX Kodiak, Alaska
KSFR White Rock, New Mexico
KVLC Hatch, New Mexico
KNVO-FM Port Isabel, Texas
KVRO Stillwater, Oklahoma
KWYE Fresno, California
KWOX Woodward, Oklahoma
KXIA Marshalltown, Iowa
KZMT Helena, Montana
WAFT Valdosta, Georgia
WQZL Belhaven, North Carolina
WAVV Naples Park, Florida
WHPI Glasford, Illinois
WBEB Philadelphia, Pennsylvania
WBUG-FM Fort Plain, New York
WCBS-FM New York, New York
WGIR-FM Manchester, New Hampshire
WFGE State College, Pennsylvania
WHOT-FM Youngstown, Ohio
WHSM-FM Hayward, Wisconsin
WIXX Green Bay, Wisconsin
WIZF Erlanger, Kentucky
WJRR Cocoa Beach, Florida
WUBT Russellville, Kentucky
WYMY Burlington, North Carolina
WLIN-FM Durant, Mississippi
WLJA-FM Ellijay, Georgia
WLVH Hardeeville, South Carolina
WMYQ South Whitley, Indiana
WNOE-FM New Orleans, Louisiana
WGRY-FM Roscommon, Michigan
WRIF Detroit, Michigan
WRIO Ponce, Puerto Rico
WROQ Anderson, South Carolina
WRR Dallas, Texas
WYDE-FM Cullman, Alabama
WSGS Hazard, Kentucky
WTGA-FM Thomaston, Georgia
WUPY Ontonagon, Michigan
WXOS East St. Louis, Illinois
WOSA Grove City, Ohio
WWDC Washington, District of Columbia
WHYA(FM) Mashpee, Massachusetts
WWPN Westernport, Maryland
WPPG Repton, Alabama
WYOO Springfield, Florida
WVVL Elba, Alabama
WAMS-FM Snow Hill, Maryland
KPKK Amargosa Valley, Nevada
KWCA Palo Cedro, California
WVRE Dickeyville, Wisconsin
KDBL Parachute, Washington
KDBN Parachute, Colorado
WMYJ-FM Bloomfield, Indiana
WIQI Chicago, Illinois
KXL-FM Portland, Oregon

101.3 Hz

WIBD Janesville, Wisconsin

101.3 MHz

KARV-FM Ola, Arkansas
KATY-FM Idyllwild, California
KOZY-FM Bridgeport, Nebraska
KJFA-FM Santa Fe, New Mexico
KDWB-FM Richfield, Minnesota
KFDI-FM Wichita, Kansas
KGDN Pasco, Washington
KGOT Anchorage, Alaska
KIKC-FM Forsyth, Montana
KIOI San Francisco, California
KIQX Durango, Colorado
KKYY Whiting, Iowa
KKGB Sulphur, Louisiana
KMMZ Crane, Texas
KLAW Lawton, Oklahoma
KLZA-FM Falls City, Nebraska
KMCO Wilburton, Oklahoma
KNCN Sinton, Texas
KOXE Brownwood, Texas
KRNG Fallon, Nevada
KRYK Chinook, Montana
KSIB-FM Creston, Iowa
KSTT-FM Los Osos-Baywood Par, California
KTXR Springfield, Missouri
KUUL East Moline, Illinois
WAGF-FM Dothan, Alabama
WAGX Manchester, Ohio
WBBV Vicksburg, Mississippi
WAGH Smiths, Alabama
WBRB Buckhannon, West Virginia
WBRV-FM Boonville, New York
WCMT Martin, Tennessee
WCPV Essex, New York
WBFX Grand Rapids, Michigan
WECO-FM Wartburg, Tennessee
WFMG Richmond, Indiana
WGGY Scranton, Pennsylvania
WHLG Port St. Lucie, Florida
WJDQ Meridian, Mississippi
WVQM Augusta, Maine
WKCI-FM Hamden, Connecticut
WMCI Neoga, Illinois
WMJM Jeffersontown, Kentucky
WNCO-FM Ashland, Ohio
WJKE Stillwater, New York
WQIL Chauncey, Georgia
WRMM-FM Rochester, New York
WROZ Lancaster, Pennsylvania
WSUE Sault Ste. Marie, Michigan
WTMG Williston, Florida
WVIL Virginia, Illinois
WWDE-FM Hampton, Virginia
WWDM Sumter, South Carolina
WWKS Cruz Bay, Virgin Islands
WWQQ-FM Wilmington, North Carolina
WNCL Milford, Delaware
WYKR-FM Haverhill, New Hampshire
WMUT Grenada, Mississippi
WMSK-FM Sturgis, Kentucky
KLWA Westport, Washington
KFEZ(FM) Walsenburg, Colorado
WZFM Narrows, Virginia
WBAA-FM West Lafayette, Indiana
WOPC Linden, Tennessee

101.5 MHz

KAMB Merced, California
KAOY Kealakekua, Hawaii
KATW Lewiston, Idaho
KAVH Eudora, Arkansas
KCGN-FM Ortonville, Minnesota
KCLS Leeds, Utah
KCVI Blackfoot, Idaho
KEKA-FM Eureka, California
KFLY Eugene, Oregon
KGB-FM San Diego, California
KGFM Bakersfield, California
KMLK El Dorado, Arkansas
KIKS-FM Iola, Kansas
KIXV(FM) Malvern, Arkansas
KIXF Baker, California
KKSI Eddyville, Iowa
KCCL Woodland, California
KMKF Manhattan, Kansas
KIZS Collinsville, Oklahoma
KNUE Tyler, Texas
KOAR Beebe, Arkansas
KPLA Columbia, Missouri
KPLZ-FM Seattle, Washington
KROR Hastings, Nebraska
KROX-FM Buda, Texas
KRRW St. James, Minnesota
KSMM-FM Liberal, Kansas
KSNY-FM Snyder, Texas
KSSS Bismarck, North Dakota
KSTB Crystal Beach, Texas
KFGI Crosby, Minnesota
KVCX Gregory, South Dakota
KZON Phoenix, Arizona
WBHB-FM Waynesboro, Pennsylvania
WBGW Fort Branch, Indiana
WZEI Meredith, New Hampshire
WBNQ Bloomington, Illinois
WBQB Fredericksburg, Virginia
WCIL-FM Carbondale, Illinois
WDKC Covington, Pennsylvania
WEXP Brandon, Vermont
WPOI St. Petersburg, Florida
WFTZ Manchester, Tennessee
WIBA-FM Sauk City, Wisconsin
WJNR-FM Iron Mountain, Michigan
WMXV St. Joseph, Tennessee
WKHX Marietta, Georgia
WKKG Columbus, Indiana
WELX Isabela, Puerto Rico
WCLI-FM Enon, Ohio
WKXW Trenton, New Jersey
WVLK-FM Richmond, Kentucky
WLYF Miami, Florida
WMJZ-FM Gaylord, Michigan
WMXO Olean, New York
WNSN South Bend, Indiana
WNWS-FM Jackson, Tennessee
WORD-FM Pittsburgh, Pennsylvania
WPDH Poughkeepsie, New York
WQEM Columbiana, Alabama
WQUT Johnson City, Tennessee
WRAL Raleigh, North Carolina
WRCD Canton, New York
WRVF Toledo, Ohio
WXBW Gallipolis, Ohio
WTHX Vine Grove, Kentucky
WSOL-FM Brunswick, Georgia
WRSY Marlboro, Vermont
WTKX-FM Pensacola, Florida
WVFB Celina, Tennessee
WWBB Providence, Rhode Island
WWBN Tuscola, Michigan
WWUN-FM Friar's Point, Mississippi
WXHC Homer, New York
WXSR Quincy, Florida
WMTE-FM Manistee, Michigan
WYNK-FM Baton Rouge, Louisiana
WVMP Vinton, Virginia
KIDX Ruidoso, New Mexico
KEGA Oakley, Utah
KRJM Mahnomen, Minnesota
KVSF-FM Pecos, New Mexico
KRMQ-FM Clovis, New Mexico
KTKE Truckee, California
WHDZ Buxton, North Carolina
KQLP Leupp, Arizona
WTPO New Albany, Mississippi
KDDV-FM Wright, Wyoming
KGVO-FM Frenchtown, Montana
KGJX Fruita, Colorado
KJHM Strasburg, Colorado
KMKF Manhattan, Kansas

101.7 MHz

KAYL-FM Storm Lake, Iowa
KDNO Thermopolis, Wyoming
KBKB-FM Fort Madison, Iowa
KCDU Carmel, California
KCKS Hamilton City, California
KCTT-FM Yellville, Arkansas
KEKO Hebbronville, Texas
KGOZ Gallatin, Missouri
KHST Lamar, Missouri
KIYS Walnut Ridge, Arkansas
KKIQ Livermore, California
KVLO Humnoke, Arkansas
KKYZ Sierra Vista, Arizona
KLDJ Duluth, Minnesota
KLEA-FM Lovington, New Mexico
KLRR Redmond, Oregon
KLTD Temple, Texas
KPEN-FM Soldotna, Alaska
KQAZ Springerville, Arizona
KRCH Rochester, Minnesota
KREJ Medicine Lodge, Kansas
KSAM-FM Huntsville, Texas
KSBL Isla Vista, California
KSKE-FM Eagle, Colorado
KSTK Wrangell, Alaska
KTFX-FM Warner, Oklahoma
KTNY Libby, Montana
KVOE-FM Emporia, Kansas
KVOM-FM Morrilton, Arkansas
KAYD-FM Silsbee, Texas
KBYB Hope, Arkansas
KNTE Bay City, Texas
KXSB Big Bear Lake, California
KZEW Wheatland, Wyoming
KQTM Rio Rancho, New Mexico
KYDA Azle, Texas
KLES Prosser, Washington
WBEA Southold, New York
WCZR Vero Beach, Florida
WBRK-FM Pittsfield, Massachusetts
WWBU Radford, Virginia
WKVV Searsport, Maine
WCVT Stowe, Vermont
WDVH-FM Trenton, Florida
WELD-FM Moorefield, West Virginia
WNYQ Hudson Falls, New York
WFLK Geneva, New York
WBWL Lynn, Massachusetts

WGEL Greenville, Illinois
WGOG Walhalla, South Carolina
WHMH-FM Sauk Rapids, Minnesota
WHZZ Lansing, Michigan
WRCV Dixon, Illinois
WHOF North Canton, Ohio
WSNZ Lynchburg, Virginia
WJKS Canton, New Jersey
WJLE-FM Smithville, Tennessee
WJSQ Athens, Tennessee
WKOM Columbia, Tennessee
WKWI Kilmarnock, Virginia
WKYM Monticello, Kentucky
WKYZ Key Colony Beach, Florida
WAVF Hanahan, South Carolina
WLDE Fort Wayne, Indiana
WLQM-FM Franklin, Virginia
WLTB Johnson City, New York
WMRR Muskegon Heights, Michigan
WMXN-FM Stevenson, Alabama
WNKO New Albany, Ohio
WQVE Albany, Georgia
WORM-FM Savannah, Tennessee
WPRJ Coleman, Michigan
WZEB Ocean View, Delaware
WRBV Warner Robins, Georgia
WGKV Pulaski, New York
WCCL Central City, Pennsylvania
WTHO-FM Thomson, Georgia
WVKY(FM) Shelbyville, Kentucky
WBEI Reform, Alabama
WTPR-FM McKinnon, Tennessee
WTYE Robinson, Illinois
WVKY Shelbyville, Kentucky
WIKL(FM) Elwood, Indiana
WMVL Linesville, Pennsylvania
WLOF Elma, New York
WQML Ceiba, Puerto Rico
WTOT-FM Graceville, Florida
WYOY Gluckstadt, Mississippi
WYUM Mount Vernon, Georgia
WIVR Kentland, Indiana
WZHL New Augusta, Mississippi
KMXM(FM) Helena Valley NE, Montana
KDJM Lindsborg, Kansas
KXCL Rock Creek Park, Colorado
KHTH Santa Rosa, California

101.9 MHz

KACQ Lometa, Texas
KATP Amarillo, Texas
KBTO Bottineau, North Dakota
KBUS Paris, Texas
KCMX-FM Ashland, Oregon
KRWK Fargo, North Dakota
KWID Las Vegas, Nevada
KINK Portland, Oregon
KDBI Emmett, Idaho
KKQY Hill City, Kansas
KIGN Burns, Wyoming
KMXF Lowell, Arkansas
KMVX Monroe, Louisiana
KNWS-FM Waterloo, Iowa
KLBN Fresno, California
KQKK Walker, Minnesota
KQSS Miami, Arizona
KQXT-FM San Antonio, Texas
KNTY Shingle Springs, California
KRSQ Laurel, Montana
KSCA Glendale, California
KTAO Taos, New Mexico
KTSL Medical Lake, Washington
KTST Oklahoma City, Oklahoma
KELO-FM Sioux Falls, South Dakota
KUCD Pearl City, Hawaii
KWFR San Angelo, Texas
KSML-FM Huntington, Texas
KLXQ Mountain Pine, Arkansas
KOOO La Vista, Nebraska
KBXT Wixon Valley, Texas
KZIU-FM Weston, Oregon
WAVT-FM Pottsville, Pennsylvania
WAZX-FM Cleveland, Georgia
WBAV-FM Gastonia, North Carolina
WARU-FM Roann, Indiana
WCIB Falmouth, Massachusetts
WDET-FM Detroit, Michigan
WDEZ Wausau, Wisconsin
WFTA Fulton, Mississippi
WHHY-FM Montgomery, Alabama
WHUG Jamestown, New York
WIKS New Bern, North Carolina
WJFL Tennille, Georgia
WJIV Cherry Valley, New York
WKLU Brownsburg, Indiana
WKQS-FM Negaunee, Michigan
WKRQ Cincinnati, Ohio
WLDR-FM Traverse City, Michigan
WLIF Baltimore, Maryland
WLMG New Orleans, Louisiana
WOZI Presque Isle, Maine
KTKB Dededo, Guam
WPOR Portland, Maine
WFAN-FM New York, New York
WLFZ-FM Springfield, Illinois
WQXQ Central City, Kentucky
WOCE Ringgold, Georgia
WKSK-FM South Hill, Virginia
WTMX Skokie, Illinois
WVAQ Morgantown, West Virginia
WVOW-FM Logan, West Virginia
WKKN Westminster, Vermont
WHTE-FM Ruckersville, Virginia
WWGR Fort Myers, Florida
WZAR Ponce, Puerto Rico
WZKZ Alfred, New York
WBGE Bainbridge, Georgia
KFMH Belle Fourche, South Dakota
KXWA Centennial, Colorado
KZWV Eldon, Missouri
WKFC North Corbin, Kentucky
KVGG Salome, Arizona
WZKZ(FM) Alfred, New York
KQBL Emmett, Idaho

102.1 MHz

KAHM Spring Valley, Arizona
KBMC Bozeman, Montana
KCAJ-FM Roseau, Minnesota
KEEY-FM St. Paul, Minnesota
KENA-FM Mena, Arkansas
KEOK Tahlequah, Oklahoma
KFZX Gardendale, Texas
KHKC-FM Atoka, Oklahoma
KBUC Raymondville, Texas
KJFM Louisiana, Missouri
KDBZ Anchorage, Alaska
KMJQ Houston, Texas
KOKY Sherwood, Arkansas
KPNY Alliance, Nebraska
KPQ-FM Wenatchee, Washington
KPRR El Paso, Texas
KYBG Basile, Louisiana
KRKC-FM King City, California
KRKY-FM Estes Park, Colorado
KRNV-FM Reno, Nevada
KDKS-FM Blanchard, Louisiana
KSMT Breckenridge, Colorado
KCKC Kansas City, Missouri
KSWW Ocean Shores, Washington
KCEZ Los Molinos, California
KTRA-FM Farmington, New Mexico
KTUI-FM Sullivan, Missouri
KDGE Fort Worth-Dallas, Texas
KUQQ Milford, Iowa
KPRI Encinitas, California
KZPE Ford City, California
KZSN Hutchinson, Kansas
WIBV Mount Vernon, Illinois
WALS Oglesby, Illinois
WXTG-FM Virginia Beach, Virginia
WAQY Springfield, Massachusetts
WJCA Albion, New York
WLLE Mayfield, Kentucky
WVXR Randolph, Vermont
WDNL Danville, Illinois
WDOK Cleveland, Ohio
WDRM Decatur, Alabama
WGMG Crawford, Georgia
WKVZ Dexter, Maine
WIMT Lima, Ohio
WIOQ Philadelphia, Pennsylvania
WJMH Reidsville, North Carolina
WKLG Rock Harbor, Florida
WKYL Lawrenceburg, Kentucky
WLCT Lafayette, Tennessee
WLEW-FM Bad Axe, Michigan
WLJC Beattyville, Kentucky
WLUM-FM Milwaukee, Wisconsin
WALT-FM Meridian, Mississippi
WMUK Kalamazoo, Michigan
WMXT Pamplico, South Carolina
WWST Sevierville, Tennessee
WOWQ Du Bois, Pennsylvania
WQLC Watertown, Florida
WQUA Citronelle, Alabama
WZUN Phoenix, New York
WRGR Tupper Lake, New York
WRKU Forestville, Wisconsin
WRQO Monticello, Mississippi
WRVB Marietta, Ohio
WRXL Richmond, Virginia
WWAV Santa Rosa Beach, Florida
WDNB Jeffersonville, New York
WNUQ Sylvester, Georgia
WSAK Hampton, New Hampshire
WZAT Tybee Island, Georgia
KCMT Oro Valley, Arizona
KBUD Sardis, Mississippi
WQLF Lena, Illinois
WEVI Frederiksted, Virgin Islands
KQRA Brookline, Missouri
KCHQ Driggs, Idaho
WWWD Bolingbroke, Georgia
KTBH-FM Kurtistown, Hawaii
KIRQ Twin Falls, Idaho
KZMC McCook, Nebraska
KBDY Hanna, Wyoming
KYRN Socorro, New Mexico
KAXA Mountain Home, Texas

102.3 MHz

KDSP(FM) Greenwood Village, Colorado
KDUT Randolph, Utah
KBCE Boyce, Louisiana
KICR Coeur D'Alene, Idaho
KKPN Rockport, Texas
KBXR Columbia, Missouri
KCJC Dardanelle, Arkansas
KCZQ Cresco, Iowa
KDEX-FM Dexter, Missouri
KEHK Brownsville, Oregon
KHNS Haines, Alaska
KJJJ Laughlin, Nevada
KJJZ Indio, California
KJLH Compton, California
KOZQ-FM Waynesville, Missouri
KJSN Modesto, California
KKQQ Volga, South Dakota
KKYC Clovis, New Mexico
KLJT Jacksonville, Texas
KPEZ Austin, Texas
KQEW Fordyce, Arkansas
KRCQ Detroit Lakes, Minnesota
KRNY Kearney, Nebraska
KRMG-FM Sand Springs, Oklahoma
KSPK-FM Walsenburg, Colorado
KTRQ Colt, Arkansas
KCRX-FM Seaside, Oregon
KUVA Uvalde, Texas
KVLE-FM Gunnison, Colorado
KWDQ Woodward, Oklahoma
KWFS-FM Wichita Falls, Texas
KSIZ Weed, California
KWRQ Clifton, Arizona
KXGE Dubuque, Iowa
KXYL-FM Coleman, Texas
KYYT Goldendale, Washington
KQNU(FM) Onawa, Iowa
KZXY-FM Apple Valley, California
WAMI-FM Opp, Alabama
WAVR Waverly, New York
WBAB Babylon, New York
WCBK-FM Martinsville, Indiana
WGTX Truro, Massachusetts
WGBJ Auburn, Indiana
WCLU-FM Munfordville, Kentucky
WCXX Madawaska, Maine
WCYN-FM Cynthiana, Kentucky
WDXC Pound, Virginia
WEBQ-FM Eldorado, Illinois
WECR-FM Beech Mountain, North Carolina
WEKL Augusta, Georgia
WELR-FM Roanoke, Alabama
WWPL Smithfield, North Carolina
WFVL Lumberton, North Carolina
WBTO Petersburg, Indiana
WGCM-FM Gulfport, Mississippi
WFXN-FM Galion, Ohio
WGOW Soddy-Daisy, Tennessee
WGRT Port Huron, Michigan
WSMM New Carlisle, Indiana
WHKB Houghton, Michigan
WHTL-FM Whitehall, Wisconsin
WCAT-FM Carlisle, Pennsylvania
WIQQ Leland, Mississippi
WVOR Canandaigua, New York
WQHZ Erie, Pennsylvania
WGBZ Cape May, New Jersey
WKJT Teutopolis, Illinois
WWHK Concord, New Hampshire
WKZR Milledgeville, Georgia
WSKK Ripley, Mississippi
WIXM Grand Isle, Vermont
WLKQ-FM Buford, Georgia
WLLK-FM Somerset, Kentucky
WXMA Louisville, Kentucky
WMBX Jensen Beach, Florida
WMFX St. Andrews, South Carolina
WMIO Cabo Rojo, Puerto Rico
WMMJ Bethesda, Maryland
WMTD-FM Hinton, West Virginia
WPOS-FM Holland, Ohio
WPTM Roanoke Rapids, North Carolina
WQTC-FM Manitowoc, Wisconsin
WQTU Rome, Georgia
WRHL-FM Rochelle, Illinois
WRMJ Aledo, Illinois
WGSP-FM Pageland, South Carolina
WHBS Pittston, Pennsylvania
WWLD Cairo, Georgia
WFBY Weston, West Virginia
WSUS Franklin, New Jersey
WKLN Wilmington, Ohio
WNGY Morton, Illinois
WTRS Dunnellon, Florida
WZGN Crozet, Virginia
WVRQ-FM Viroqua, Wisconsin
WMOS Stonington, Connecticut
WWSL Philadelphia, Mississippi
WKKF Ballston Spa, New York
WXLC Waukegan, Illinois
WXXS Lancaster, New Hampshire
WYCA Crete, Illinois
WYBR Big Rapids, Michigan
WZDQ Humboldt, Tennessee
WAUH Wautoma, Wisconsin
KVUW Wendover, Nevada
WTHN Sault Ste. Marie, Michigan
KYOE Point Arena, California
KBLO Corcoran, California
KDOE Antlers, Oklahoma
KMKK-FM Kaunakakai, Hawaii
KSAQ Charlotte, Texas
KNDH Hettinger, North Dakota
WSIZ-FM Jacksonville, Georgia
KOWY Dayton, Wyoming

102.5 MHz

KOTN(FM) Gould, Arkansas
KPZK Cabot, Arkansas
KBLS North Fort Riley, Kansas
KBRQ Hillsboro, Texas
KCNQ Kernville, California
KDON-FM Salinas, California
KDUQ Ludlow, California
KDVL Devils Lake, North Dakota
KEZK St. Louis, Missouri
KHOC Casper, Wyoming
KIAK-FM Fairbanks, Alaska
KIBR Sandpoint, Idaho
KIOT Los Lunas, New Mexico
KIXQ Joplin, Missouri
KKCI Goodland, Kansas
KKDY West Plains, Missouri
KKYR-FM Texarkana, Texas
KACY Arkansas City, Kansas
KMAD-FM Whitesboro, Texas
KMFX-FM Lake City, Minnesota
KMGI Pocatello, Idaho
KMKS Bay City, Texas
KMSO Missoula, Montana
KNIX-FM Phoenix, Arizona
KQIC Willmar, Minnesota
KRAO-FM Colfax, Washington
KSFM Woodland, California
KSNI-FM Santa Maria, California
KSTZ Des Moines, Iowa
KTCX Beaumont, Texas
KTNT Eufaula, Oklahoma
KTRR Loveland, Colorado
KZII-FM Lubbock, Texas
KZOK Seattle, Washington
KZSD-FM Martin, South Dakota

WAGR-FM Lexington, Mississippi
WPZE Mableton, Georgia
WYNR Waycross, Georgia
WBAZ Bridgehampton, New York
WCMM Gulliver, Michigan
WKLB-FM Waltham, Massachusetts
WDVE Pittsburgh, Pennsylvania
WERX-FM Columbia, North Carolina
WESP Dothan, Alabama
WGNN Fisher, Illinois
WJRE Galva, Illinois
WPLW Hillsborough, North Carolina
WHPT Sarasota, Florida
WTOK-FM San Juan, Puerto Rico
WIOG Bay City, Michigan
WIOZ Southern Pines, North Carolina
WJKX Ellisville, Mississippi
WZCH Warner Robins, Georgia
WFMF Baton Rouge, Louisiana
WLTO Nicholasville, Kentucky
WMDH New Castle, Indiana
WTSS Buffalo, New York
WBZV Hudson, Michigan
WMYI Hendersonville, North Carolina
WNWC-FM Madison, Wisconsin
WOLC Princess Anne, Maryland
WOLD-FM Marion, Virginia
WDXB Jasper, Alabama
WOWF Crossville, Tennessee
WPIK Summerland Key, Florida
WQSS Camden, Maine
WRFY-FM Reading, Pennsylvania
WUMX Rome, New York
WUSQ-FM Winchester, Virginia
WPHZ Orleans, Indiana
WZOO-FM Edgewood, Ohio
KHLB Mason, Texas
KQSE Gypsum, Colorado
KKCV Rozel, Kansas
KDVC Loma, Colorado
KKWB Kelliher, Minnesota
KDKE Superior, Wisconsin
KBLS North Fort Riley, Kansas

102.7 MHz

KRNN Juneau, Alaska
KHGE Fresno, California
KBIQ Manitou Springs, Colorado
KBLZ Winona, Texas
KCNA Cave Junction, Oregon
KHXS Merkel, Texas
KIIS-FM Los Angeles, California
KJNA-FM Jena, Louisiana
KCYE Boulder City, Nevada
KJYO Oklahoma City, Oklahoma
KDDB Waipahu, Hawaii
KLDG Liberal, Kansas
KBBQ-FM Van Buren, Arkansas
KNTN Thief River Falls, Minnesota
KORD-FM Richland, Washington
KQEG La Crescent, Minnesota
KSL-FM Midvale, Utah
KQUL Lake Ozark, Missouri
KSSI China Lake, California
KJXK San Antonio, Texas
KTIG Pequot Lakes, Minnesota
KVSS Papillion, Nebraska
KWLT North Crossett, Arkansas
KTXJ-FM Jasper, Texas
KYBB Canton, South Dakota
KYTC Northwood, Iowa
KYTE Newport, Oregon
WGUS-FM New Ellenton, South Carolina
WRNI-FM Narragansett Pier, Rhode Island
WYSB Springfield, Kentucky
WLYK Cape Vincent, New York
WBDX Trenton, Georgia
WCKS Fruithurst, Alabama
WCNG Murphy, North Carolina
WLGZ-FM Webster, New York
WPZR Mount Clemens, Michigan
WEBN Cincinnati, Ohio
WEGR Arlington, Tennessee
WEKX Jellico, Tennessee
WEQX Manchester, Vermont
WGNI Wilmington, North Carolina
WHKR Rockledge, Florida
WJEQ Macomb, Illinois
WWAC Ocean City, New Jersey
WKSB Williamsport, Pennsylvania
WJJX Appomattox, Virginia
WLME Lewisport, Kentucky
WLEG Ligonier, Indiana
WMJL-FM Marion, Kentucky
WMOM Pentwater, Michigan
WCPZ Sandusky, Ohio
WMXJ Pompano Beach, Florida
WPHK Blountstown, Florida
WPMA Greensboro, Georgia
WPUB-FM Camden, South Carolina
WRGO Cedar Key, Florida
WRVM Suring, Wisconsin
WVEK-FM Weber City, Virginia
WGYE Mannington, West Virginia
WVAZ Oak Park, Illinois
WVSR-FM Charleston, West Virginia
WXBM-FM Milton, Florida
WQSR Baltimore, Maryland
WXHT Madison, Florida
KKRO Red Bluff, California
WKWY Tompkinsville, Kentucky
KINX Fairfield, Hawaii
WWFA St. Florian, Alabama
KXMZ Box Elder, South Dakota
KJOK Hollis, Oklahoma
WCGM Wattsburg, Pennsylvania
WDWQ Terre Haute, Indiana

102.9 Hz

KUDL Sacramento, Kansas

102.9 MHz

KAJN-FM Crowley, Louisiana
KAZX Kirtland, New Mexico
KVMA-FM Shreveport, Louisiana
KBLX-FM Berkeley, California
KBRX-FM O'Neill, Nebraska
KBWS-FM Sisseton, South Dakota
KCTR-FM Billings, Montana
KDMX Dallas, Texas
KEZS-FM Cape Girardeau, Missouri
KHBZ Harrison, Arkansas
KHUT Hutchinson, Kansas
KBIK Independence, Kansas
KIXN Hobbs, New Mexico
KKND Port Sulphur, Louisiana
KLQV San Diego, California
KLTN Houston, Texas
KKND Belle Chasse, Louisiana
KMMO-FM Marshall, Missouri
KYNW Centralia, Washington
KNDA Alice, Texas
KNFT-FM Bayard, New Mexico
KQIB Idabel, Oklahoma
KQST Sedona, Arizona
KTOP-FM Saint Marys, Kansas
KEYU-FM Amarillo, Texas
KARS-FM Laramie, Wyoming
KSJJ Redmond, Oregon
KIWI McFarland, California
KTFG Sioux Rapids, Iowa
KLBU Pecos, New Mexico
KVAB Clarkston, Washington
KARN-FM Sheridan, Arkansas
KOUW(FM) Island Park, Idaho
KXLM Oxnard, California
KYSF Bonanza, Oregon
KZIA Cedar Rapids, Iowa
KWYL South Lake Tahoe, California
WJGO Tice, Florida
WBDL Reedsburg, Wisconsin
WLTK New Market, Virginia
WBLM Portland, Maine
WCLX Westport, New York
WCRQ Dennysville, Maine
WDIN Camuy, Puerto Rico
WDRC-FM Hartford, Connecticut
WKQB Pocahontas, Virginia
WELS-FM Kinston, North Carolina
WGL-FM Huntington, Indiana
WFUR-FM Grand Rapids, Michigan
WQKI-FM Orangeburg, South Carolina
WDHT Urbana, Ohio
WWWW-FM Ann Arbor, Michigan
WIUJ Charlotte Amalie, Virgin Islands
WKIK-FM California, Maryland
WKXX Attalla, Alabama
WLKS-FM West Liberty, Kentucky
KMNB Minneapolis, Minnesota
WLKO Hickory, North Carolina
WHQG Milwaukee, Wisconsin
WMGK Philadelphia, Pennsylvania
WMHR Syracuse, New York
WDUN-FM Clarkesville, Georgia
WMKC Indian River, Michigan
WMSI-FM Jackson, Mississippi
WXXJ Jacksonville, Florida
WXXB Delphi, Indiana
WNPT-FM Marion, Alabama
WOKW Curwensville, Pennsylvania
WOWI Norfolk, Virginia
WPMX Statesboro, Georgia
WPXC Hyannis, Massachusetts
WSOY-FM Decatur, Illinois
WZTF Scranton, South Carolina
WNCQ-FM Canton, New York
WVRK Columbus, Georgia
WKIX-FM Raleigh, North Carolina
WXCH Columbus, Indiana
WYFM Sharon, Pennsylvania
WBUZ La Vergne, Tennessee
WMKB Earlville, Illinois
KADL Imperial, Nebraska
KITY Llano, Texas
KISH Agana, Guam
KWGO Burlington, North Dakota
KMKV Paia, Hawaii
WWMR Saltillo, Mississippi
WPBK Crab Orchard, Kentucky
WJCI Huntington, Indiana

103.1 MHz

KAAT Oakhurst, California
KDLD Santa Monica, California
KHRD Weaverville, California
KDLE Newport Beach, California
KLUN Paso Robles, California
KCDA Post Falls, Idaho
KCDX Florence, Arizona
KNNW Columbia, Louisiana
KDAA Rolla, Missouri
KDMG Burlington, Iowa
KEEP Bandera, Texas
KEZN Palm Desert, California
KFFA-FM Helena, Arkansas
KFIL-FM Chatfield, Minnesota
KVFG Victorville, California
KJAM-FM Madison, South Dakota
KKCN Ballinger, Texas
KKCY Colusa, California
KMUL-FM Muleshoe, Texas
KMXS Anchorage, Alaska
KNCY-FM Auburn, Nebraska
KOFM Enid, Oklahoma
KSSM Copperas Cove, Texas
KPAS Fabens, Texas
KYKV Selah, Washington
KRSB-FM Roseburg, Oregon
KHGG-FM Waldron, Arkansas
KSBZ Sitka, Alaska
KSHK Hanamaulu, Hawaii
KSPN-FM Aspen, Colorado
KSRY Tehachapi, California
KVCM Helena, Montana
KVJM Hearne, Texas
KVWC-FM Vernon, Texas
KMPA Pittsburg, Texas
KHQT Las Cruces, New Mexico
KXSA-FM Dermott, Arkansas
KYDT Pine Haven, Wyoming
WAFY Middletown, Maryland
WWOF(FM) Tallahassee, Florida
WAKO-FM Lawrenceville, Illinois
WKVE Mount Pleasant, Pennsylvania
WBZO Bay Shore, New York
WJMA Culpeper, Virginia
WLLJ Etowah, Tennessee
WFKZ Plantation Key, Florida
WFXA-FM Augusta, Georgia
WGBF-FM Henderson, Kentucky
WGDN-FM Gladwin, Michigan
WJGK(FM) Newburgh, New York
WVSC Port Royal, South Carolina
WHBR-FM Parkersburg, West Virginia
WHME South Bend, Indiana
WGY-FM Albany, New York
WIRK Indiantown, Florida
WRON-FM Lewisburg, West Virginia
WNMQ Columbus, Mississippi
WMXX-FM Jackson, Tennessee
WNDH Napoleon, Ohio
WOGB Reedsville, Wisconsin
WLXC Columbia, South Carolina
WOSM Ocean Springs, Mississippi
WPKE-FM Coal Run, Kentucky
WPLH Tifton, Georgia
WRAC Georgetown, Ohio
WRIX-FM Honea Path, South Carolina
WRJT Royalton, Vermont
WQNU Lyndon, Kentucky
WQFX-FM Russell, Pennsylvania
WRNR-FM Grasonville, Maryland
WGFB Rockton, Illinois
WQUS Lapeer, Michigan
WIKQ Tusculum, Tennessee
WVKO-FM Johnstown, Ohio
WTOJ Carthage, New York
WUAG Greensboro, North Carolina
WILK-FM Avoca, Pennsylvania
WWLT Manchester, Kentucky
WEUP-FM Moulton, Alabama
WVIV-FM Highland Park, Illinois
WSYN Surfside Beach, South Carolina
WCSJ-FM Morris, Illinois
WZOZ Oneonta, New York
KSQN Coalville, Utah
KHAM Britt, Iowa
KHHL Karnes City, Texas
WLHC Robbins, North Carolina
KKJK Ravenna, Nebraska
KRVX Wimbledon, North Dakota
WVUV-FM Fagaitua, American Samoa
KRVO Columbia Falls, Montana
KEKS Olpe, Kansas
WLQC Sharpsburg, North Carolina
***KFWA(FM)** Weldona, Colorado
KEDJ Jerome, Idaho
WOTW Windermere, Florida
WZLO Dover-Foxcroft, Maine
WRSC-FM State College, Pennsylvania
WZLB Santa Rosa Beach, Florida

103.3 MHz

KSAS-FM Caldwell, Idaho
KATM Modesto, California
KAZR Pella, Iowa
KBIU Lake Charles, Louisiana
KCRS-FM Midland, Texas
KDFM Falfurrias, Texas
KESN Allen, Texas
KFTZ Idaho Falls, Idaho
KIXB El Dorado, Arkansas
KJCS Nacogdoches, Texas
KJLS Hays, Kansas
KJOJ-FM Freeport, Texas
KJSR Tulsa, Oklahoma
KKCW Beaverton, Oregon
KLOU St. Louis, Missouri
KPRS Kansas City, Missouri
KPRU Delta, Colorado
KVYB Santa Barbara, California
KSCU Santa Clara, California
KDRF Albuquerque, New Mexico
KTFC Sioux City, Iowa
KUKI-FM Ukiah, California
KUMD-FM Duluth, Minnesota
KWLN Wilson Creek, Washington
KWBU-FM Waco, Texas
KWOZ Mountain View, Arkansas
KZCR Fergus Falls, Minnesota
KZKE Seligman, Arizona
KZPO Lindsay, California
WIVQ Spring Valley, Illinois
WAKG Danville, Virginia
WARM York, Pennsylvania
WAXL Santa Claus, Indiana
WKQL Brookville, Pennsylvania
WRQQ Hammond, Louisiana
WCRF Cleveland, Ohio
WEDG Buffalo, New York
WESR-FM Onley-Onancock, Virginia
WFXD Marquette, Michigan
WGLX-FM Wisconsin Rapids, Wisconsin
WWMP Waterbury, Vermont
WJMX-FM Cheraw, South Carolina
WJOD Asbury, Iowa
WKDF Nashville, Tennessee
WKFR-FM Battle Creek, Michigan
WKVS Lenoir, North Carolina
WKZS Thomasboro, Illinois
WMCM Rockland, Maine
WMGV Newport, North Carolina
WMLX St. Marys, Ohio
WMXS Montgomery, Alabama

WMXW Vestal, New York
WODS Boston, Massachusetts
WOLT Indianapolis, South Carolina
WPRB Princeton, New Jersey
WQLB Tawas City, Michigan
WQQQ Sharon, Connecticut
WTCR-FM Huntington, West Virginia
WVEE Atlanta, Georgia
WVJP-FM Caguas, Puerto Rico
WVYB Holly Hill, Florida
WQGA Waycross, Georgia
WXZZ Georgetown, Kentucky
WZKR Collinsville, Mississippi
KTMQ Temecula, California
KBAA Grass Valley, California
KDTR Florence, Montana
KUSB Hazelton, North Dakota
KSAG Pearsall, Texas
KRAN Warren Afb, Wyoming
KBEN-FM Cowley, Wyoming
KJQY Colorado City, Colorado
WAJR-FM Salem, West Virginia
WBZL(FM) Greenwood, Mississippi
WTCF Wardensville, West Virginia
WRTH-FM Greer, 0
WDZY Colonial Heights, Virginia

103.3Hz

KJSR Sand Springs, Oklahoma

103.5 MHz

KAMZ Tahoka, Texas
KHHM Sacramento, California
KBPA San Marcos, Texas
KUAL-FM Brainerd, Minnesota
KJNZ Hereford, Texas
KHSL-FM Paradise, California
KISF Las Vegas, Nevada
KLAA-FM Tioga, Louisiana
KLDZ Medford, Oregon
KLNZ Glendale, Arizona
KNEI-FM Waukon, Iowa
KOST Los Angeles, California
KQLA Ogden, Kansas
KTWD Wallace, Idaho
KRAY-FM Salinas, California
KRFX Denver, Colorado
KVSP Anadarko, Oklahoma
KRSP-FM Salt Lake City, Utah
KWHT Pendleton, Oregon
KWVV-FM Homer, Alaska
KWXD Asbury, Missouri
KXNP North Platte, Nebraska
KYSM-FM Mankato, Minnesota
KLUE Poplar Bluff, Missouri
KZRB New Boston, Texas
KZZY Devils Lake, North Dakota
WAKY Radcliff, Kentucky
WAWC Syracuse, Indiana
WAXJ Frederiksted, Virgin Islands
WCCH Holyoke, Massachusetts
WEZL Charleston, South Carolina
WTOP-FM Washington, District of Columbia
WGRR Hamilton, Ohio
WIKK Newton, Illinois
WIMZ Knoxville, Tennessee
WJAD Leesburg, Georgia
WJQZ Wellsville, New York
WJKI Bethany Beach, Delaware
WNND Pickerington, Ohio
WHLM-FM Berwick, Pennsylvania
WLAY-FM Littleville, Alabama
WKTU Lake Success, New York
WMRF Huntingdon, Pennsylvania
WMRY Crozet, Virginia
WMUZ Detroit, Michigan
WAKT-FM Callaway, Florida
WUUF Sodus, New York
WMIB Fort Lauderdale, Florida
WQBJ Cobleskill, New York
WRBO Como, Mississippi
WRCQ Dunn, North Carolina
WOGH Burgettstown, Pennsylvania
WFUS Gulfport, Florida
WTCM-FM Traverse City, Michigan
WKSC-FM Chicago, Illinois
WXLT Christopher, Illinois
WZSN Greenwood, South Carolina
WZVA Marion, Virginia
KZMY Bozeman, Montana
KHAI Wahiawa, Hawaii
KRXW Roseau, Minnesota
WHVK New Hope, Alabama
KPAU Center, Colorado
WTAW-FM Buffalo, Texas
WKNK(FM) Callaway, Florida
KPST Coachella, California

103.7 MHz

KIQQ-FM Newberry Springs, California
KMHK Billings, Montana
KSNN-FM Ridgway, Colorado
KCDD Hamlin, Texas
KBTT Haughton, Louisiana
KEYN-FM Wichita, Kansas
KGIM-FM Redfield, South Dakota
KJEL Lebanon, Missouri
KKBJ-FM Bemidji, Minnesota
KLKK Clear Lake, Iowa
KLVG Garberville, California
KLZZ Waite Park, Minnesota
KMHK Billings, Montana
KMLA El Rio, California
KHTP Tacoma, Washington
KNUQ Paauilo, Hawaii
KODS Carnelian Bay, California
KXAI Refugio, Texas
KEGY San Diego, California
KNMZ Alamogordo, New Mexico
KPZA-FM Jal, New Mexico
KQLT Casper, Wyoming
KRRO Sioux Falls, South Dakota
KABZ Little Rock, Arkansas
KVIL Highland Park-Dallas, Texas
KHJK La Porte, Texas
KXKT Glenwood, Iowa
KNRQ Harrisburg, Oregon
KYVA-FM Church Rock, New Mexico
WCBJ Campton, Kentucky
WTIB Williamston, North Carolina
WCIR-FM Beckley, West Virginia
WCKY-FM Pemberville, Ohio
WCXR Lewisburg, Pennsylvania
WDBR Springfield, Illinois
WEEO-FM McConnellsburg, Pennsylvania
WFGS Murray, Kentucky
WFIU Bloomington, Indiana
WHYB Menominee, Michigan
WHZR Royal Center, Indiana
WSTV-FM Frankfort, Kentucky
WKNE Keene, New Hampshire
WLLR-FM Davenport, Iowa
WILT Wrightsville Beach, North Carolina
WMGM Atlantic City, New Jersey
WURV(FM) Richmond, Virginia
WNNJ Newton, New Jersey
WPKQ North Conway, New Hampshire
WHHT(FM) Cave City, Kentucky
WXKT Maysville, Georgia
WQEN Trussville, Alabama
WQNY Ithaca, New York
WQOL Vero Beach, Florida
WQWV Fisher, West Virginia
WRTS Erie, Pennsylvania
WRUF-FM Gainesville, Florida
WSOC-FM Charlotte, North Carolina
WULS Broxton, Georgia
WFFX Hattiesburg, Mississippi
WVKX Irwinton, Georgia
WWIB Hallie, Wisconsin
WXCY Havre De Grace, Maryland
WXLX Lajas, Puerto Rico
WXSS Wauwatosa, Wisconsin
WCSY South Haven, Michigan
KYLK Okemah, Oklahoma
WCZE Harbor Beach, Michigan
KVRG Victor, Idaho
KLNN Questa, New Mexico
WYUR Gilman, Illinois
KZGL Flagstaff, Arizona
WLTC Cusseta, Georgia
KXZK Vail, Arizona
KLWB Carencro, Louisiana
KFBT Hanford, California
KOSF San Francisco, California

103.9 MHz

KRCD Inglewood, California
KBHL Osakis, Minnesota
KVAS-FM Ilwaco, Washington
KBEY Burnet, Texas
KOSG Pawhuska, Oklahoma
KCXX Lake Arrowhead, California
KDJK Mariposa, California
KGBB Edwards, California
KGRT-FM Las Cruces, New Mexico
KJXJ Franklin, Texas
KPGG Ashdown, Arkansas
KHYM Copeland, Kansas
KBOQ Seaside, California
KKIX Fayetteville, Arkansas
KMCR Montgomery City, Missouri
KMSM-FM Butte, Montana
KBDS Taft, California
KNLV-FM Ord, Nebraska
KNYN Fort Bridger, Wyoming
KNZA-FM Hiawatha, Kansas
KVMI Arthur, North Dakota
KZMN Kalispell, Montana
KOMB Fort Scott, Kansas
KEXX(FM) Gilbert, Arizona
KQXC-FM Wichita Falls, Texas
KRFS-FM Superior, Nebraska
KRLI Malta Bend, Missouri
KSNO-FM Snowmass Village, Colorado
KSYC-FM Yreka, California
KUOO Spirit Lake, Iowa
KTDZ College, Alaska
KRIA Plainview, Texas
KBBD Spokane, Washington
KKFS Lincoln, California
KUDE Nephi, Utah
KRXP Pueblo West, Colorado
KMHT-FM Marshall, Texas
KZMI Garapan-Saipan, Guam
WWKZ Okolona, Mississippi
WALY Bellwood, Pennsylvania
WANC Ticonderoga, New York
WTID Thomaston, Alabama
WCLD-FM Cleveland, Mississippi
WCMW-FM Harbor Springs, Michigan
WPDI Hazlet, New Jersey
WDDK Greensboro, Georgia
WDEB-FM Jamestown, Tennessee
WDKX Rochester, New York
WJKR Worthington, Ohio
WETZ(FM) New Martinsville, West Virginia
WFAS-FM Bronxville, New York
WHXT Orangeburg, South Carolina
WIMC Crawfordsville, Indiana
WLEN Adrian, Michigan
WBYB(FM) Eldred, Pennsylvania
WLSW Scottdale, Pennsylvania
WYAB Flora, Mississippi
WRKA Louisville, Kentucky
WQCY Quincy, Illinois
WNNL Fuquay-Varina, North Carolina
WNOI Flora, Illinois
WNTC Drakesboro, Kentucky
WKPE-FM South Yarmouth, Massachusetts
WOCQ Berlin, Maryland
WOLI-FM Easley, South Carolina
WPPZ-FM Jenkintown, Pennsylvania
WPPL Blue Ridge, Georgia
WQBK-FM Rensselaer, New York
WLDA Fort Rucker, Alabama
WQXZ Hawkinsville, Georgia
WRBI Batesville, Indiana
WRBR-FM South Bend, Indiana
WRCN-FM Riverhead, New York
WDYS Dushore, Pennsylvania
WRSR Owosso, Michigan
WTYB Bluffon, South Carolina
WSRK Oneonta, New York
WVBO Winneconne, Wisconsin
WVOM-FM Howland, Maine
WNDR-FM Mexico, New York
WWEL London, Kentucky
WWIZ West Middlesex, Pennsylvania
WTLP Braddock Heights, Maryland
WXAN Ava, Illinois
WHTU Big Island, Virginia
WZDA Beavercreek, Ohio
WXKB Cape Coral, Florida
WXKE Fort Wayne, Indiana
WXKQ-FM Whitesburg, Kentucky
WXRD Crown Point, Indiana
WYFT Luray, Virginia
WXFF Dundee, Illinois
KCJF Earle, Arkansas
KTHP Hemphill, Texas
KTNX Arcadia, Missouri
KGLU Gideon, Missouri
KCOO Dunkerton, Iowa
WTPN Westby, Wisconsin
KBGZ Spring Creek, Nevada
KRKA Severance, Colorado
KDCZ Eyota, Minnesota
KJJS Zapata, Texas
KQHK McCook, Nebraska
WWUU Washington, Mississippi
WWGO-HD2 Casey, Illinois
WXRD-FM Georgetown, Delaware

104.1 MHz

KAFE Bellingham, Washington
KBFM Edinburg, Texas
KILX Hatfield, Arkansas
KBOT Pelican Rapids, Minnesota
KBOX Lompoc, California
KBRJ Anchorage, Alaska
KBVC Buena Vista, Colorado
KCDY Carlsbad, New Mexico
WNAX-FM Yankton, South Dakota
KFMU-FM Oak Creek, Colorado
KFRR Woodlake, California
KGGF FM Fredonia, Kansas
KHKK Modesto, California
KBMI-FM East Helena, Montana
KIQK Rapid City, South Dakota
KJLO-FM Monroe, Louisiana
KFIS Scappoose, Oregon
KIBZ Crete, Nebraska
KKUS Tyler, Texas
KTEG Santa Fe, New Mexico
KLTI-FM Ames, Iowa
KMGL Oklahoma City, Oklahoma
KMHM Lutesville, Missouri
KJOR Windsor, California
KNAB-FM Burlington, Colorado
KORR American Falls, Idaho
KPOC-FM Pocahontas, Arkansas
KWPK-FM Sisters, Oregon
KRBE Houston, Texas
KSDM International Falls, Minnesota
KVDU Houma, Louisiana
KWOW Clifton, Texas
KXDD Yakima, Washington
KQTH Tucson, Arizona
KSGF-FM Ash Grove, Missouri
WAEB-FM Allentown, Pennsylvania
WBMX Boston, Massachusetts
WBWN LeRoy, Illinois
WCKQ Campbellsville, Kentucky
WCLE-FM Calhoun, Tennessee
WCXL Kill Devil Hills, North Carolina
WETT Bridgeport, West Virginia
WERR Vega Alta, Puerto Rico
WGLF Tallahassee, Florida
WHTT Buffalo, New York
WIKY Evansville, Indiana
WVSB Romney, West Virginia
WALR-FM Palmetto, Georgia
WLBC Muncie, Indiana
WMNV Rupert, Vermont
WMQZ Colchester, Illinois
WMRQ-FM Waterbury, Connecticut
WMZK Merrill, Wisconsin
WNNK Harrisburg, Pennsylvania
WNKE New Boston, Ohio
WPXZ-FM Punxsutawney, Pennsylvania
WQAL Cleveland, Ohio
WRBX Reidsville, Georgia
WNCC Franklin, North Carolina
WRLU Algoma, Wisconsin
WRJY Brunswick, Georgia
WTKS-FM Cocoa Beach, Florida
WOGY Jackson, Tennessee
WTQR Winston-Salem, North Carolina
WUCZ Carthage, Tennessee
WVGR Grand Rapids, Michigan
WWUS Big Pine Key, Florida
WPRS-FM Waldorf, Maryland
KZJK St. Louis Park, Minnesota
WHHL Hazelwood, Missouri
WYAV Myrtle Beach, South Carolina
WDLT-FM Saraland, Alabama
WWYL Chenango Bridge, New York
WZEE Madison, Wisconsin
WZKS Union, Mississippi
WKGV Swansboro, North Carolina
KZJF Jefferson City, Missouri
KCGL Powell, Wyoming
WSAG Linwood, Michigan

KSAH-FM Pearsall, Texas
KANT Guernsey, Wyoming
WDLT Saraland, Alabama
KZTW Tioga, North Dakota

104.3 MHz

KBCN-FM Marshall, Arkansas
KBEQ-FM Kansas City, Missouri
KCAR-FM Baxter Springs, Kansas
KBIG Los Angeles, California
KXQK Leakey, Texas
KAJM Camp Verde, Arizona
KKFN Longmont, Colorado
KDBB Bonne Terre, Missouri
KEZP Bunkie, Louisiana
KGAS-FM Carthage, Texas
KHTR Pullman, Washington
KXSE Davis, California
KKMX Tri City, Oregon
KKSD Milbank, South Dakota
WZFJ(FM) Breezy Point, Minnesota
KPOS Fouke, Arkansas
KAWO Boise, Idaho
KTTU Brownfield, Texas
KHIP Gonzales, California
KMXY Grand Junction, Colorado
KLQB Taylor, Texas
KQFX Borger, Texas
KRKN Eldon, Iowa
KSHA Redding, California
KSOP-FM Salt Lake City, Utah
KFRH North Las Vegas, Nevada
KTOO Juneau, Alaska
KVGB-FM Great Bend, Kansas
KVGO Spring Valley, Minnesota
KPHW Kaneohe, Hawaii
KXOQ Kennett, Missouri
KZBE Omak, Washington
KZIO Two Harbors, Minnesota
KZLT-FM East Grand Forks, Minnesota
WABK Gardiner, Maine
WAJQ-FM Alma, Georgia
WAXQ New York, New York
WBBQ-FM Augusta, Georgia
WVCN Baraga, Michigan
WCBH Casey, Illinois
WCZY-FM Mount Pleasant, Michigan
WKZG Seymour, Wisconsin
WOGI Moon Township, Pennsylvania
WEYE Surgoinsville, Tennessee
WEZJ-FM Williamsburg, Kentucky
WFRG-FM Utica, New York
WFXK Bunn, North Carolina
WMYV Hartford, Vermont
WGNL Greenwood, Mississippi
WYKE(FM) Inglis, Florida
WJMK Chicago, Illinois
WJSG Hamlet, North Carolina
WKCY-FM Harrisonburg, Virginia
WZTR Dahlonega, Georgia
WKNB Clarendon, Pennsylvania
WKZM Sarasota, Florida
WMJU Bude, Mississippi
WQNQ Fletcher, North Carolina
WNLT Delhi Hills, Ohio
WZFT Baltimore, Maryland
WOMC Detroit, Michigan
WHLW Luverne, Alabama
WWPG Eutaw, Alabama
WSKE Everett, Pennsylvania
WZIN Charlotte Amalie, Virgin Islands
WXBC Hardinsburg, Kentucky
WNNP Richwood, Ohio
WZYP Athens, Alabama
KKAC Vandalia, Missouri
KIJI Tumon, Guam
KMNT Chehalis, Washington
KFZE Daniel, Wyoming
KBQF McFarland, California
WBYW(FM) Lynn Haven, Florida
KZBS Granite, Oklahoma
WRJJ La Center, Kentucky
WAXY-FM Miramar, Florida

104.5 MHz

KCVN Cozad, Nebraska
KBEF Gibsland, Louisiana
KCEC-FM Wellton, Arizona
KWMZ-FM Empire, Louisiana
KBTW Lenwood, California
KLSM Tallulah, Louisiana
KDAT Cedar Rapids, Iowa
KDOT Reno, Nevada
KFOG San Francisco, California
KSTT Atascadero, California
KJLY Blue Earth, Minnesota
KJTX Jefferson, Texas
KKDA Dallas, Texas
KKFG Bloomfield, New Mexico
KKMY Orange, Texas
KPUS Gregory, Texas
KFXJ Augusta, Kansas
KMCQ Covington, Washington
KMGC Camden, Arkansas
KGZG-FM Newport, Washington
KMYZ-FM Pryor, Oklahoma
KZXQ Lake of the Woods, Arizona
KSLQ-FM Washington, Missouri
KSRZ Omaha, Nebraska
KSTY Canon City, Colorado
KTRN White Hall, Arkansas
KVLI(FM) Lake Isabella, California
KLBL Pearcy, Arkansas
KZEP-FM San Antonio, Texas
KZUL-FM Lake Havasu City, Arizona
WTMM-FM Mechanicville, New York
WXMJ Cambridge Springs, Pennsylvania
WAXX Eau Claire, Wisconsin
WNXX Jackson, Louisiana
WVMJ Conway, New Hampshire
WBVN Carrier Mills, Illinois
WCCG Hope Mills, North Carolina
WCCX Waukesha, Wisconsin
WGRX Falmouth, Virginia
WFMB-FM Springfield, Illinois
WSTK Aurora, North Carolina
WOKV-FM Atlantic Beach, Florida
WGFX Gallatin, Tennessee
WJJK Noblesville, Indiana
WHAJ Bluefield, West Virginia
WHLC Highlands, North Carolina
WILZ Saginaw, Michigan
WKAK Albany, Georgia
WKHJ Mountain Lake Park, Maryland
WLKT Lexington-Fayette, Kentucky
WNBT-FM Wellsboro, Pennsylvania
WNVZ Norfolk, Virginia
WKHT Knoxville, Tennessee
WQKT Wooster, Ohio
WRFQ Mount Pleasant, South Carolina
WILT Wilmington, North Carolina
WRVR Memphis, Tennessee
WSLD Whitewater, Wisconsin
WSNX-FM Muskegon, Michigan
WXER Plymouth, Wisconsin
WXLO Fitchburg, Massachusetts
WXRR Hattiesburg, Mississippi
WRFF Philadelphia, Pennsylvania
WYYU Dalton, Georgia
WQJB State College, Mississippi
KRVQ-FM Lake Isabella, California
KKVU Stevensville, Montana
KHAD Upton, Wyoming
KUMR Doolittle, Missouri
KZKY(FM) Ucon, Idaho
WQXJ Blackduck, Minnesota
KCBW Grandin, Missouri
KWML Georgetown, Delaware

104.7 MHz

KBZM Big Sky, Montana
KJUL Moapa Valley, Nevada
KCAW Sitka, Alaska
KCLD-FM St. Cloud, Minnesota
KCMB Baker City, Oregon
KDUK-FM Eugene, Oregon
KABQ-FM Bosque Farms, New Mexico
KQBK Booneville, Arkansas
KNWJ Leone, American Samoa
KHTN Planada, California
KHUM Cutten, California
KIKX Ketchum, Idaho
KQSN Ponca City, Oklahoma
KKED Fairbanks, Alaska
KKLH Marshfield, Missouri
KKLS-FM Sioux Falls, South Dakota
KKRV Wenatchee, Washington
KKYS Bryan, Texas
KMOU Roswell, New Mexico
KNDR Mandan, North Dakota
KNEK Washington, Louisiana
KNIV Lyman, Wyoming
KNNG Sterling, Colorado
KOCP Oxnard, California
KONI Lanai City, Hawaii
KOOU Hardy, Arkansas
KHMD Mansfield, Louisiana
KRES Moberly, Missouri
KTRS-FM Casper, Wyoming
KTXC Lamesa, Texas
KVCY Fort Scott, Kansas
KVIC Victoria, Texas
KWNS Winnsboro, Texas
KSLE Wewoka, Oklahoma
KXBZ Manhattan, Kansas
KREZ Chaffee, Missouri
KYYI Burkburnett, Texas
KHTZ Ganado, Texas
KZZP Mesa, Arizona
WAAZ-FM Crestview, Florida
WFSH-FM Athens, Georgia
WBBS Fulton, New York
WELJ Montauk, New York
WBAK Belfast, Maine
WBJZ Berlin, Wisconsin
WZUP La Grange, North Carolina
WCFL Morris, Illinois
WDDW Sturtevant, Wisconsin
WFLM White City, Florida
WFRN-FM Elkhart, Indiana
WTHG Hinesville, Georgia
WIOT Toledo, Ohio
WITZ-FM Jasper, Indiana
WPGB Pittsburgh, Pennsylvania
WJMD Hazard, Kentucky
WKAQ-FM San Juan, Puerto Rico
WKJC-FM Tawas City, Michigan
WPZZ Crewe, Virginia
WKKY Geneva, Ohio
WOCN-FM Orleans, Massachusetts
WLIV-FM Monterey, Tennessee
WLMD Bushnell, Illinois
WMUF Henry, Tennessee
WNCS Montpelier, Vermont
WNOK Columbia, South Carolina
WNSV Nashville, Illinois
WQBX Fowler, Michigan
WHTP Kennebunkport, Maine
WQHQ Ocean City-Salisbury, Maryland
WRBQ-FM Tampa, Florida
WSGL Naples, Florida
WSGM Coalmont, Tennessee
WSPK Poughkeepsie, New York
WKQC Charlotte, North Carolina
WTUE Dayton, Ohio
WVRC-FM Spencer, West Virginia
WAYZ Hagerstown, Maryland
WYKX Escanaba, Michigan
WJSH Folsom, Louisiana
WZZK-FM Birmingham, Alabama
KFEG Klamath Falls, Oregon
KMJO Hope, North Dakota
KFLI Des Arc, Arkansas
WJIW Greenville, Mississippi
KTOY Texarkana, Arkansas
KXNC Ness City, Kansas
WLNQ White Pine, Tennessee
KWTG Vidalia, Louisiana
KEWS(FM) Sac City, Iowa
KKCS(FM) Calhan, Colorado
KDUX-FM Hoquiam, Washington

104.9 MHz

KAGH-FM Crossett, Arkansas
KTXX-FM Bee Cave, Texas
KBOE-FM Oskaloosa, Iowa
KXNA Springdale, Arkansas
KBUK La Grange, Texas
KCLT West Helena, Arkansas
KDFC Sunnyvale, California
KCRZ Tipton, California
KDXY Lake City, Arkansas
KEEH Spokane, Washington
KFFX Emporia, Kansas
KHPA Hope, Arkansas
KLLT Spencer, Iowa
KJAV Alamo, Texas
KNXX Donaldsonville, Louisiana
KKBW Eatonville, Washington
KBTE Tulia, Texas
KLMJ Hampton, Iowa
KLOA Ridgecrest, California
KMIQ Robstown, Texas
KBWX Columbia, Illinois
KMVR Mesilla Park, New Mexico
KKWD Bethany, Oklahoma
KAMA-FM Deer Park, Texas
KPWB-FM Piedmont, Missouri
KBOB-FM De Witt, Iowa
KREK Bristow, Oklahoma
KRFO-FM Owatonna, Minnesota
KRIG-FM Nowata, Oklahoma
KMHX Rohnert Park, California
KRYD Norwood, Colorado
KCTY Emerson, Nebraska
KZMP-FM Pilot Point, Texas
KTMX York, Nebraska
KTOC-FM Jonesboro, Louisiana
KWCX-FM Tanque Verde, Arizona
KWIM Window Rock, Arizona
KWBT Bellmead, Texas
KYIX South Oroville, California
KVOU-FM Uvalde, Texas
KSAL-FM Salina, Kansas
KRRR Cheyenne, Wyoming
KZWA Moss Bluff, Louisiana
WEGE Lima, Ohio
WAVJ Princeton, Kentucky
WAXI Rockville, Indiana
WCJU-FM Prentiss, Mississippi
WBMZ Metter, Georgia
WBOQ Gloucester, Massachusetts
WBOZ Woodbury, Tennessee
WZEC Strasburg, Mississippi
WCCP-FM Clemson, South Carolina
WCVO Gahanna, Ohio
WCVU Solana, Florida
WBUV Moss Point, Mississippi
WSJO Egg Harbor City, New Jersey
WERK Muncie, Indiana
WFIW Fairfield, Illinois
WFMZ Hertford, North Carolina
WFXE Columbus, Georgia
WKZU Iuka, Mississippi
WLHH Ridgeland, South Carolina
WHTF Havana, Florida
WIHS Middletown, Connecticut
WJRH Easton, Pennsylvania
WJRS Jamestown, Kentucky
WKHG Leitchfield, Kentucky
WKKS-FM Vanceburg, Kentucky
WKOS Kingsport, Tennessee
WKQH Marathon, Wisconsin
WFKY Frankfort, Kentucky
WLKZ Wolfeboro, New Hampshire
WLXR-FM La Crosse, Wisconsin
WMCG Milan, Georgia
WMNG Christiansted, Virgin Islands
WRKY-FM Hollidaysburg, Pennsylvania
WIGO-FM White Stone, Virginia
WNFM Reedsburg, Wisconsin
WNGZ Montour Falls, New York
WOAB Ozark, Alabama
WPCK Denmark, Wisconsin
WPDX-FM Clarksburg, West Virginia
WPXN Paxton, Illinois
WTNQ La Follette, Tennessee
WRBB Boston, Massachusetts
WJJS Roanoke, Virginia
WKDL-FM Brockport, New York
WSKV-FM Stanton, Kentucky
WSLY York, Alabama
WTKM-FM Hartford, Wisconsin
WWRR Scranton, Pennsylvania
WWKC Caldwell, Ohio
WBXX Marshall, Michigan
WLMX-FM Balsam Lake, Wisconsin
WINN Columbus, Indiana
WXCL Pekin, Illinois
WYGC High Springs, Florida
WXLR Harold, Kentucky
WXRX Belvidere, Illinois
WYNA Calabash, North Carolina
WYRY Hinsdale, New Hampshire
KYTN Union City, Tennessee
WCLV Lorain, Ohio
WZMR Altamont, New York
KIKF Cascade, Montana
WAIR Lake City, Michigan
KRYE Olney Springs, Colorado
WKJN Centreville, Mississippi
KNLX Prineville, Oregon
KLQQ Clearmont, Wyoming
KKAR Wamsutter, Wyoming

KLDE Eldorado, Texas
KVAL Cal-Nev-Ari, Nevada
WRBF Plainville, Georgia
KKWD(FM) Bethany, Colorado
WZFC Strasburg, Virginia
KYKA Meadow Lakes, Alaska

105 MHz

WEAM-FM Buena Vista, Georgia

105.1 MHz

KAKT Phoenix, Oregon
KAOC Cavalier, North Dakota
KIDI-FM Lompoc, North California
KARL Tracy, Minnesota
KAWK Custer, South Dakota
KYSX Billings, Montana
KBLP Lindsay, Oklahoma
KCYZ Ames, Iowa
KEAN-FM Abilene, Texas
KXMX Muldrow, Oklahoma
KBTK(FM) Kachina Village, Arizona
KCJK Garden City, Missouri
KGUM-FM Dededo, Guam
KMIL Cameron, Texas
KINE-FM Honolulu, Hawaii
KJOT Boise, Idaho
KKCB Duluth, Minnesota
KKGO Los Angeles, California
KKBZ Auberry, California
KCRV-FM Caruthersville, Missouri
KQWB-FM Breckenridge, Minnesota
KMAT Seadrift, Texas
KMJX Conway, Arkansas
KAUU Manti, Utah
KNCI Sacramento, California
KOCN Pacific Grove, California
KPLD Kanab, Utah
KOSB Perry, Oklahoma
KFTE Abbeville, Louisiana
KKRG Albuquerque, New Mexico
KRSK Molalla, Oregon
KTKU Juneau, Alaska
KTMC-FM McAlester, Oklahoma
KZKR Jonesville, Louisiana
KQRT Las Vegas, Nevada
KVTY Lewiston, Idaho
KWMW Maljamar, New Mexico
KXKL-FM Denver, Colorado
KYKS Lufkin, Texas
KZKK Huron, South Dakota
WGVX Lakeville, Minnesota
KZQD Liberal, Kansas
WASJ Panama City Beach, Florida
WTGD Bridgewater, Virginia
WAMQ Great Barrington, Massachusetts
WLVG Havelock, North Carolina
WAVA-FM Arlington, Virginia
WCLC-FM Jamestown, Tennessee
WDCG Durham, North Carolina
WALV-FM Lakesite, Tennessee
WEJT Shelbyville, Illinois
WHCC Ellettsville, Indiana
WGEM-FM Quincy, Illinois
WGFM Cheboygan, Michigan
WNGA Clermont, Georgia
WHQT Coral Gables, Florida
WILQ Williamsport, Pennsylvania
WIOC Ponce, Puerto Rico
WIOV Ephrata, Pennsylvania
WKLC-FM St. Albans, West Virginia
WKOL Plattsburgh, New York
WKUB Blackshear, Georgia
WNEK-FM Springfield, Massachusetts
WOJO Evanston, Illinois
WOMX Orlando, Florida
WPDT Coward, South Carolina
WPFL Century, Florida
WQHK-FM Huntertown, Indiana
WJDX-FM Kosciusko, Mississippi
WQNS Waynesville, North Carolina
WQSB Albertville, Alabama
WQXK Salem, Ohio
WRNZ Lancaster, Kentucky
WWPR-FM New York, New York
WTOS-FM Skowhegan, Maine
WTUK Harlan, Kentucky
WUBE-FM Cincinnati, Ohio
WOLF-FM DeRuyter, New York
WVRY Waverly, Tennessee
WVZA Murphysboro, Illinois
WWLI Providence, Rhode Island
WMGC-FM Detroit, Michigan
WGHL Shepherdsville, Kentucky
WMHX Waunakee, Wisconsin
KJXN South Park, Wyoming
KWOL-FM Whitefish, Montana
WSBW Ephraim, Wisconsin
KTTY New Boston, Texas
KTUG Hudson, Wyoming
KUDD Indian Springs, Nevada
WOLF-FM DeRuyter, New York

105.3 MHz

KAKJ Marianna, Arkansas
KDWY Diamondville, Wyoming
KQOR Mena, Arkansas
KCMS Edmonds, Washington
KDDQ Comanche, Oklahoma
KEDB Chariton, Iowa
KTWL Hempstead, Texas
KGRD Orchard, Nebraska
KIOD McCook, Nebraska
KIOZ San Diego, California
KITS San Francisco, California
KIWA-FM Sheldon, Iowa
KMOQ Columbus, Kansas
KJMM Bixby, Oklahoma
KBFP-FM Delano, California
KQOL Sleepy Hollow, Wyoming
KLNC Lincoln, Nebraska
KLIP Monroe, Louisiana
KLSR-FM Memphis, Texas
KJDL-FM Levelland, Texas
KLYV Dubuque, Iowa
KMTX-FM Helena, Montana
KHOV-FM Wickenburg, Arizona
KNCB-FM Vivian, Louisiana
KNOD Harlan, Iowa
KJLV Hoxie, Arkansas
KONA-FM Kennewick, Washington
KKNI Sterling, Alaska
KRBD Ketchikan, Alaska
KRDG Shingletown, California
KSMG San Antonio, Texas
KFBZ Haysville, Kansas
KYBA Stewartville, Minnesota
KRLD-FM Dallas, Texas
KZKS Rifle, Colorado
KZLZ Casas Adobes, Arizona
KZNN Rolla, Missouri
WRXP Cambridge, Minnesota
KZPR Minot, North Dakota
KZZX Alamogordo, New Mexico
WOSF Gaffney, South Carolina
WAOX Staunton, Illinois
WECB Headland, Alabama
WKAY Knoxville, Illinois
WBNN-FM Dillwyn, Virginia
WBRW Blacksburg, Virginia
WHTS Coopersville, Michigan
WDAS-FM Philadelphia, Pennsylvania
WJEN Killington, Vermont
WSGC-FM Tignall, Georgia
WFIV-FM Loudon, Tennessee
WFRB-FM Frostburg, Maryland
WGFG Branchville, South Carolina
WGKR Grand Gorge, New York
WNOH Windsor, Virginia
WKHM-FM Brooklyn, Michigan
WKOA Lafayette, Indiana
WKPQ Hornell, New York
WDVW(FM) Humboldt, Tennessee
WWL-FM Kenner, Louisiana
WMPI Scottsburg, Indiana
WPTQ Glasgow, Kentucky
WRHQ Richmond Hill, Georgia
WRLO-FM Antigo, Wisconsin
WOWC Morrison, Tennessee
WSTI-FM Quitman, Georgia
WVJZ Charlotte Amalie, Virgin Islands
WACR-FM Columbus Afb, Mississippi
WSHK Kittery, Maine
WXKZ-FM Prestonsburg, Kentucky
WPTY Calverton-Roanoke, New York
WBZY Bowdon, Georgia
WYCY Hawley, Pennsylvania
WYHT Mansfield, Ohio
WYKS Gainesville, Florida
WJLT Evansville, Indiana
WZSP Nocatee, Florida
WJSJ Fernandina Beach, Florida
WODR Fair Bluff, North Carolina
WLVE Mukwonago, Wisconsin
KINB Kingfisher, Oklahoma
KBGX Keaau, Hawaii
KSLO Simmesport, Louisiana
KZTI(FM) Fallon Station, Pennsylvania

105.3 Mhz

WGHJ Fair Bluff, 0

105.5 MHz

KACT-FM Andrews, Texas
KXFC Coalgate, Oklahoma
KBAJ Deer River, Minnesota
KBOA-FM Piggott, Arkansas
KBUE Long Beach, California
KCGB-FM Columbia River, Oregon
KDDG Albany, Minnesota
KDEP Garibaldi, Oregon
KDLS-FM Perry, Iowa
KESM-FM El Dorado Springs, Missouri
KEUG Veneta, Oregon
KFMT-FM Fremont, Nebraska
KDDK Franklin, Louisiana
KGFY Stillwater, Oklahoma
KBKK Ball, Louisiana
KILJ-FM Mount Pleasant, Iowa
KJAC Timnath, Colorado
KEUN-FM Eunice, Louisiana
KFYV Ojai, California
KKHB Eureka, California
KKJO-FM St. Joseph, Missouri
KKOY-FM Chanute, Kansas
KLCY Vernal, Utah
KSAC-FM Dunnigan, California
KLVA Maricopa, Arizona
KUKN Longview, Washington
KMAV-FM Mayville, North Dakota
KMGM Montevideo, Minnesota
KNAS Nashville, Arkansas
KVVS Rosamond, California
KTHK Idaho Falls, Idaho
KPFM Mountain Home, Arkansas
KPMW Haliimaile, Hawaii
KQLV(FM) Bosque Farms, New Mexico
KLHB Portland, Texas
KRBI-FM St. Peter, Minnesota
KRVR Copperopolis, California
KRDO-FM Security, Colorado
KQXX-FM Mission, Texas
KWCO-FM Chickasha, Oklahoma
KJZN San Joaquin, California
KVSV-FM Beloit, Kansas
KWAK-FM Stuttgart, Arkansas
KWRF-FM Warren, Arkansas
KUSJ Harker Heights, Texas
KZZT Moberly, Missouri
WABO-FM Waynesboro, Mississippi
WSRJ Honor, Michigan
WAKQ Paris, Tennessee
WXBN Berryville, Virginia
WWWK Islamorada, Florida
WDBY Patterson, New York
WBYA Islesboro, Maine
WWEI Easthampton, Massachusetts
WBMI West Branch, Michigan
WBNT-FM Oneida, Tennessee
WCHO-FM Washington Ct House, Ohio
WCHX Lewistown, Pennsylvania
WCOO Kiawah Island, South Carolina
WCZQ Monticello, Illinois
WDAR-FM Darlington, South Carolina
WROK-FM Macon, Georgia
WDHA-FM Dover, New Jersey
WSEV-FM Gatlinburg, Tennessee
WDUV New Port Richey, Florida
WFBZ Trempealeau, Wisconsin
WFJA Sanford, North Carolina
WGKL Gladstone, Michigan
WGOJ Conneaut, Ohio
WGTH-FM Richlands, Virginia
WVNC Lawrenceville, Virginia
WIFO-FM Jesup, Georgia
WYRE-FM Saint Augustine Beach, Florida
WJVO South Jacksonville, Illinois
WJYY Concord, New Hampshire
WKDE-FM Altavista, Virginia
WKXH St. Johnsbury, Vermont
WKYA Greenville, Kentucky
WVNA-FM Muscle Shoals, Alabama
WLJE Valparaiso, Indiana
WRXR-FM Rossville, Georgia
WLPW Lake Placid, New York
WTNM Water Valley, Mississippi
WOJL Louisa, Virginia
WLVK Fort Knox, Kentucky
WLVW Salisbury, Maryland
WMGH-FM Tamaqua, Pennsylvania
WMKX Brookville, Pennsylvania
WMMM-FM Verona, Wisconsin
WWRW Mt. Sterling, Kentucky
WMVR-FM Sidney, Ohio
WIBT Indianola, Mississippi
WFDT Aguada, Puerto Rico
WNSP Bay Minette, Alabama
WOLL Hobe Sound, Florida
WSKU Little Falls, New York
WQGN-FM Groton, Connecticut
WBTT Naples Park, Florida
WQRK Bedford, Indiana
WZBN Camilla, Georgia
WRAR-FM Tappahannock, Virginia
WREZ Metropolis, Illinois
WSWV-FM Pennington Gap, Virginia
WTHD Lagrange, Indiana
WTKV Oswego, New York
WWCK-FM Flint, Michigan
WWWM-FM Sylvania, Ohio
WFCT Apalachicola, Florida
WXOQ Selmer, Tennessee
WXQR-FM Jacksonville, North Carolina
WXTQ Athens, Ohio
WYKT Wilmington, Illinois
WYTM-FM Fayetteville, Tennessee
WYZB Mary Esther, Florida
WAIV Cape May Court House, New Jersey
WUKL Bethlehem, West Virginia
WZSR Woodstock, Illinois
KYEL Danville, Arkansas
WMKD Pickford, Michigan
KQRI Bosque Farms, New Mexico
WLJY Nekoosa, Wisconsin
KSIL Rincon, New Mexico
WVBG-FM Redwood, Mississippi
KZQL Mills, Wyoming
WKQV Cowen, West Virginia
KOYT(FM) Alberton, Montana
KXCS(FM) Coahoma, Texas
KMOM Roscoe, South Dakota
KKKJ Merrill, Oregon
WERC-FM Hoover, Alabama
WJKG Effingham, Kentucky
WLJE-FM Georgetown, Delaware
KIMW Heflin, Louisiana
WZJK West Terre Haute, Illinois

105.7 MHz

KZBD Spokane, Washington
KJJP Amarillo, Texas
KVVF Santa Clara, California
KBIC Raymondville, Texas
KJRL Herington, Kansas
KOAS Dolan Springs, Arizona
KHCB-FM Houston, Texas
KJET Raymond, Washington
KMCK-FM Prarie Grove, Arkansas
KMVN Anchorage, Alaska
KOKZ Waterloo, Iowa
KOZZ-FM Reno, Nevada
KPMX Sterling, Colorado
KPNT Collinsville, Illinois
KQAK Bend, Oregon
KRAQ Jackson, Minnesota
KRBL Idalou, Texas
KRNB Decatur, Texas
KROU Spencer, Oklahoma
KRSE Yakima, Washington
KSUX Winnebago, Nebraska
KTKO Beeville, Texas
KVAY Lamar, Colorado
KVRD-FM Cottonwood, Arizona
KVVP Leesville, Louisiana
KWGL Ouray, Colorado
KXKX Knob Noster, Missouri
KXRS Hemet, California
KYKX Longview, Texas
WGVZ Eden Prairie, Minnesota
WAKH McComb, Mississippi
WAPL Appleton, Wisconsin
WZTK Alpena, Michigan
WXCX Siren, Wisconsin
WCAD San Juan, Puerto Rico

RADIO - U.S.

WCFW Chippewa Falls, Wisconsin
WCHR-FM Manahawkin, New Jersey
WCSN-FM Orange Beach, Alabama
WCUP L'Anse, Michigan
WSSP Milwaukee, Wisconsin
WFFM Ashburn, Georgia
WLKJ Portage, Pennsylvania
WMKS Clemmons, North Carolina
WGQR Rennert, North Carolina
WGRK-FM Greensburg, Kentucky
WRDA-FM Canton, Georgia
WHMX Lincoln, Maine
WVBZ High Point, North Carolina
WKJS Richmond, Virginia
WJXM De Kalb, Mississippi
WLGC-FM Greenup, Kentucky
WMJI Cleveland, Ohio
WBNW-FM Endicott, New York
WMXH-FM Luray, Virginia
WQSH Malta, New York
WOBG-FM Salem, West Virginia
WIHG Rockwood, Tennessee
WSRW-FM Grand Rapids, Michigan
WQAK Union City, Tennessee
WJZ-FM Catonsville, Maryland
WQXA York, Pennsylvania
WROR-FM Framingham, Massachusetts
WRSF Columbia, North Carolina
WTBK Manchester, Kentucky
WYXB Indianapolis, Indiana
WUZR Bicknell, Indiana
WLKC Campton, New Hampshire
WFRF-FM Monticello, Florida
WIXO Peoria, Illinois
WWLL Sebring, Florida
WTUV-FM Eminence, Kentucky
WJGM(FM) Baldwin, Florida
WQAH-FM Addison, Alabama
WBWR Hilliard, Ohio
WZHT Troy, Alabama
WSCG Augusta, Georgia
WZOM Defiance, Ohio
WCJZ Cannelton, Indiana
KNAF-FM Fredericksburg, Texas
KKQX Manhattan, Montana
KBGB Magness, Arkansas
KQMX Lost Hills, California
KYTS Manderson, Wyoming
KRMR Hays, Kansas
KDXN South Heart, North Dakota

105.9 MHz

KAAQ Alliance, Nebraska
KUZN Centerville, Texas
KALC Denver, Colorado
KBZE Berwick, Louisiana
KCIX Garden City, Idaho
KFMK Round Rock, Texas
KGBX-FM Nixa, Missouri
KHOT-FM Paradise Valley, Arizona
KIRC Seminole, Oklahoma
KKCD Omaha, Nebraska
KKWS Wadena, Minnesota
KLAZ Hot Springs, Arkansas
KKSW Lawrence, Kansas
KWMY Joliet, Montana
KMIT Mitchell, South Dakota
KPOI-FM Honolulu, Hawaii
KPWR Los Angeles, California
KQKY Kearney, Nebraska
KQPM Ukiah, California
KQTZ Hobart, Oklahoma
KRAZ Santa Ynez, California
KAHL-FM Hondo, Texas
KMJ Fresno, California
KRZY-FM Santa Fe, New Mexico
KSEL-FM Portales, New Mexico
KSSA Ingalls, Kansas
KTLB Twin Lakes, Iowa
KUKA San Diego, Texas
KULH Wheeling, Missouri
KFXZ-FM Opelousas, Louisiana
KWNG Red Wing, Minnesota
KYSJ Coos Bay, Oregon
KZZK New London, Missouri
WBCI Bath, Maine
WBGG-FM Fort Lauderdale, Florida
WQXR-FM Newark, New Jersey
WCFS Elmwood Park, Illinois
WTMT Weaverville, North Carolina
WDMK Detroit, Michigan
WEGZ Washburn, Wisconsin
WGKC Mahomet, Illinois
WGKX Memphis, Tennessee
WHCN Hartford, Connecticut
WVGA Lakeland, Georgia
WILN Panama City, Florida
WJOT-FM Wabash, Indiana
WJZR Rochester, New York
WMAL Woodbridge, Virginia
WKHQ-FM Charlevoix, Michigan
WWHG Evansville/Rockten, Wisconsin
WLNI Lynchburg, Virginia
WXTL Syracuse, New York
WMMC Marshall, Illinois
WEZV North Myrtle Beach, South Carolina
WNRQ Nashville, Tennessee
WOCL Deland, Florida
WOKZ Fairfield, Illinois
WNKN Middletown, Ohio
WKLS Southside, Alabama
WRTR Brookwood, Alabama
WSYI Valley Station, Kentucky
WTNJ Mount Hope, West Virginia
WTUA Pinopolis, South Carolina
WQCK(FM) Philipsburg, Pennsylvania
WXDX-FM Pittsburgh, Pennsylvania
WXDE Lewes, Delaware
WXMK Dock Junction, Georgia
WTZB Englewood, Florida
WPZX Pocono Pines, Pennsylvania
KYJK Missoula, Montana
KRJT Elgin, Oregon
KHRS Winthrop, Minnesota
WKPO Soldiers Grove, Wisconsin
KKBO Flasher, North Dakota
WRKS Pickens, Mississippi
WQBB Pascagoula, Mississippi
KZWY-HD Clearmont, Wyoming
KQIK Haileyville, Oklahoma

106.1 Hz

WASG Daphne, Alabama

106.1 MHz

KNUZ San Saba, Texas
KPZE-FM Carlsbad, New Mexico
KBKS-FM Tacoma, Washington
KXFF Colorado City, Arizona
KCFA Arnold, California
KCII-FM Washington, Iowa
KFFB Fairfield Bay, Arkansas
KFLP-FM Floydada, Texas
KFMQ Gallup, New Mexico
KHKS Denton, Texas
KIOC Orange, Texas
KIXO Sulphur, Oklahoma
KIYX Sageville, Iowa
KJOE Slayton, Minnesota
KWWV Santa Margarita, California
KKBI Broken Bow, Oklahoma
KKMV Rupert, Idaho
KLCI Elk River, Minnesota
KLEO Kahaluu, Hawaii
KLSS-FM Mason City, Iowa
KMDX San Angelo, Texas
KMEL San Francisco, California
KXRR Monroe, Louisiana
KNEX Laredo, Texas
KNFO Basalt, Colorado
KOQL Ashland, Missouri
KPLM Palm Springs, California
KQDI-FM Highwood, Montana
KTGX Owasso, Oklahoma
KQLX-FM Lisbon, North Dakota
KRAB Greenacres, California
KRRX Burney, California
KYRK Refugio, Texas
KTTX Brenham, Texas
KWKZ Charleston, Missouri
KXKU Lyons, Kansas
KZFN Moscow, Idaho
WACD Antigo, Wisconsin
WAFC-FM Okeechobee, Florida
WMMY Boone, North Carolina
WBLI Patchogue, New York
WCNR Keswick, Virginia
WCOD-FM Hyannis, Massachusetts
WDKM Adams, Wisconsin
WDKS Newburgh, Indiana
WBMH Grove Hill, Alabama
WFXH-FM Hilton Head Island, South Carolina
WHDQ Claremont, New Hampshire
WHST Tawas City, Michigan
WWWY North Vernon, Indiana
WSFF Vinton, Virginia
WISX Philadelphia, Pennsylvania
WJXQ Charlotte, Michigan
WKGO Cumberland, Maryland
WXSH Pocomoke City, Maryland
WJGL Jacksonville, Florida
WZRH Picayune, Mississippi
WKTM Soperton, Georgia
WLZS Beaver Springs, Pennsylvania
WMEM Presque Isle, Maine
WMIL-FM Waukesha, Wisconsin
WMOR-FM Morehead, Kentucky
WMXU Starkville, Mississippi
WBBG Niles, Ohio
WNKI Corning, New York
WOLS Waxhaw, North Carolina
WPDA Jeffersonville, New York
WTKK Knightdale, North Carolina
WRRH Hormigueros, Puerto Rico
WHKV Sylvester, Georgia
WRZZ Parkersburg, West Virginia
WSMI-FM Litchfield, Illinois
WNGC Arcade, Georgia
WSTH-FM Alexander City, Alabama
WTAK-FM Hartselle, Alabama
WMFD Mansfield, Ohio
WQTL Tallahassee, Florida
WYYS Streator, Illinois
WRRX Gulf Breeze, Florida
WUSH Poquoson, Virginia
KLMI Rock River, Wyoming
KFSZ Munds Park, Arizona
KRZX Redlands, Colorado
KKVR Kerrville, Texas
WVIS Vieques, Puerto Rico
WYKY Science Hill, Kentucky
KXXL Moorcroft, Wyoming
KEXS-FM Ravenwood, Missouri
WJRV(FM) Oliver Springs, Tennessee
WCOP Farmington Township, Pennsylvania
WJZS Live Oak, Florida

106.1 kHz

WBLI Patchogue, New York

106.3 MHz

KALI-FM Santa Ana, California
KQEZ(FM) Shelley, Idaho
KQTA Homedale, Idaho
KMLR Gonzales, Texas
KDBR Kalispell, Montana
KOMR Sun City, Arizona
KERB-FM Kermit, Texas
KYMK-FM Maurice, Louisiana
KGAM Merced, California
KTGV Oracle, Arizona
KGMX Lancaster, California
KGOU Norman, Oklahoma
KOLL Lonoke, Arkansas
KGAM(FM) Merced, California
KFRX Lincoln, Nebraska
KJBX Cash, Arkansas
KKHR Abilene, Texas
KKLI Widefield, Colorado
KRRF Oak View, California
KLBC Durant, Oklahoma
KLEN Cheyenne, Wyoming
KLOO-FM Albany, Oregon
KMJV Soledad, California
KVPW Kingsburg, California
KOOC(FM) Belton, Texas
KBMG Evanston, Wyoming
KPAN-FM Hereford, Texas
KPHR Ortonville, Minnesota
KPRB Brush, Colorado
KPSO-FM Falfurrias, Texas
KIFT(FM) Kremmling, Colorado
KJBX Walnut Ridge, Arkansas
KRZK Branson, Missouri
KSEM Seminole, Texas
KSUP Juneau, Alaska
KHKZ San Benito, Texas
KBZS Wichita Falls, Texas
KVHT Vermillion, South Dakota
KCSY Twisp, Washington
KWUF-FM Pagosa Springs, Colorado
KXOR-FM Thibodaux, Louisiana
KYGL Texarkana, Arkansas
KDLW Los Lunas, New Mexico
KDXA Ankeny, Iowa
KZKZ-FM Greenwood, Arkansas
WAMX Milton, West Virginia
WHXR Scarborough, Maine
WBTG-FM Sheffield, Alabama
WUDE Bolivia, North Carolina
WCDA Versailles, Kentucky
WCDK Cadiz, Ohio
WCEM-FM Cambridge, Maryland
WCIF Melbourne, Florida
WCTL Union City, Pennsylvania
WXMG London, Ohio
WYRD-FM Simpsonville, South Carolina
WEIB Northampton, Massachusetts
WEVR-FM River Falls, Wisconsin
WGCY Gibson City, Illinois
WGER Saginaw, Michigan
WGMK Donalsonville, Georgia
WGNG Tchula, Mississippi
WJQB Spring Hill, Florida
WHCY Blairstown, New Jersey
WOVO Horse Cave, Kentucky
WHKX Bluefield, Virginia
WFNQ Nashua, New Hampshire
WKMK Eatontown, New Jersey
WJNI Ladson, South Carolina
WJSE North Cape May, New Jersey
WJPT Fort Myers, Florida
WWMK Onaway, Michigan
WKBX Kingsland, Georgia
WOAH Glennville, Georgia
WKLA-FM Ludington, Michigan
WKNU Brewton, Alabama
WLCY Blairsville, Pennsylvania
WMCR-FM Oneida, New York
WMFG-FM Hibbing, Minnesota
WZLD Petal, Mississippi
WMNA-FM Gretna, Virginia
WMTK Littleton, New Hampshire
WYRB Genoa, Illinois
WGLM-FM Lakeview, Michigan
WQBZ Fort Valley, Georgia
WQCC La Crosse, Wisconsin
WQRL Benton, Illinois
WXMT Smethport, Pennsylvania
WBUK Ottawa, Ohio
WRIL Pineville, Kentucky
WSBZ Miramar Beach, Florida
WHPP Columbia City, Virginia
WYZY Saranac, New York
WTUF Boston, Georgia
WUBU South Bend, Indiana
WCDQ Crawfordsville, Indiana
WMXG Stephenson, Michigan
WWJM New Lexington, Ohio
WWKX Woonsocket, Rhode Island
WWQM-FM Middleton, Wisconsin
WSRB Lansing, Illinois
WYNN-FM Florence, South Carolina
WRAZ-FM Leisure City, Florida
WFME Mount Kisco, New York
KZLK Rapid City, South Dakota
WPLT Sarona, Wisconsin
WPFT Pigeon Forge, Tennessee
KWNZ Lovelock, Nevada
WUUB Jupiter, Florida
KTRY(FM) Cazadero, California
KINS-FM Blue Lake, California

106.5 MHz

KALT-FM Alturas, California
KBVA Bella Vista, Arkansas
KKMR Arizona City, Arizona
WDAF-FM Mission, Missouri
KCQQ Davenport, Iowa
KDXL St. Louis Park, Minnesota
KEGX Richland, Washington
KEJS Lubbock, Texas
KEND Roswell, New Mexico
KEZR San Jose, California
KFMC-FM Fairmont, Minnesota
KIXA Lucerne Valley, California
KLNV San Diego, California
KMCX-FM Ogallala, Nebraska
KTMO New Madrid, Missouri
KMMT Mammoth Lakes, California
KOOI Jacksonville, Texas
KOVE-FM Galveston, Texas
KQXL New Roads, Louisiana
KRJB Ada, Minnesota

KUSZ Olathe, Colorado
KSNE-FM Las Vegas, Nevada
KSPO Dishman, Washington
KTLS-FM Holdenville, Oklahoma
KWHL Anchorage, Alaska
KUDL Sacramento, California
KWPZ Lynden, Washington
KYQQ Arkansas City, Kansas
WAID Clarksdale, Mississippi
WAVH Daphne, Alabama
WEZI Ponte Vedra Beach, Florida
WDSJ Greenville, Ohio
WBMW Pawcatuck, Connecticut
WLQR-FM Delta, Ohio
WCJX Five Points, Florida
WCTQ Sarasota, Florida
WDSN Reynoldsville, Pennsylvania
WEND Salisbury, North Carolina
WWLW Clarksburg, West Virginia
WFYY Bloomsburg, Pennsylvania
WJDT Rogersville, Tennessee
WJEC Vernon, Alabama
WKCH Whitewater, Wisconsin
WKDZ-FM Cadiz, Kentucky
WARH Granite City, Illinois
WKRH Minetto, New York
WYTE Marshfield, Wisconsin
WMEF Fort Kent, Maine
WHLK Cleveland, Ohio
WNIK-FM Arecibo, Puerto Rico
WOCY Carrabelle, Florida
WPYX Albany, New York
WQCB Brewer, Maine
WVFM Kalamazoo, Michigan
WBTJ Richmond, Virginia
WRLV-FM Salyersville, Kentucky
WRZX Greenville, Indiana
WSFL-FM New Bern, North Carolina
WSKZ Chattanooga, Tennessee
WLFF Georgetown, South Carolina
WWBL Washington, Indiana
WHBZ Sheboygan Falls, Wisconsin
WWMX Baltimore, Maryland
WYRK Buffalo, New York
WZBX Rocky Ford, Georgia
WNHI Farmington, New Hampshire
WZIQ Smithville, Georgia
WZNJ Demopolis, Alabama
WLVS-FM Clifton, Tennessee
KLFN Sunburg, Minnesota
KAJZ Llano, Texas
KCIJ Atlanta, Louisiana
KUOM-FM St. Louis Park, Minnesota
KKIK Horseshoe Bend, Arkansas
KEAL Taft, California
WXNU St. Anne, Illinois
KRYL(FM) Haiku, Hawaii
KRKU Wheatland, Wyoming
KKRK Whitehall, Montana
WQLX Chillicothe, Ohio

106.7 MHz

KSMY Lompoc, California
KAOD Babbitt, Minnesota
KYTZ Walhalla, North Dakota
KDKN Ellington, Missouri
KBFO Aberdeen, South Dakota
KAGM Los Alamos, New Mexico
KBPI Denver, Colorado
KCHX Midland, Texas
KUMX North Fort Polk, Louisiana
KTKX Terrell Hills, Texas
KTUZ-FM Okarche, Oklahoma
KQKX Norfolk, Nebraska
KFXX-FM Hugoton, Kansas
KGTW Ketchikan, Alaska
KRVI Mount Vernon, Missouri
KIKD Lake City, Iowa
KJUG-FM Tulare, California
KLTH Lake Oswego, Oregon
KLEJ Rayne, Louisiana
KHLR Benton, Arkansas
KAAZ-FM Spanish Fork, Utah
KPPV Prescott Valley, Arizona
KQNK-FM Norton, Kansas
KQTY-FM Borger, Texas
KROQ Pasadena, California
KRQR Orland, California
KRTI Grinnell, Iowa
KXDR Pinesdale, Montana
KZZA Muenster, Texas
KYXA Homer, Louisiana
KWWX Cashmere, Washington
WAOB-FM Beaver Falls, Pennsylvania
WATQ Chetek, Wisconsin
WFGW(FM) Norris, Tennessee
WTLC-FM Greenwood, Indiana
WYFX Mount Vernon, Indiana
WKHL West Lafayette, Indiana
WHFI Lindside, West Virginia
WIZN Vergennes, Vermont
WJFK-FM Manassas, District of Columbia
WJJY-FM Brainerd, Minnesota
WKRU Allouez, Wisconsin
WKGS Irondequoit, New York
WKMX Enterprise, Alabama
WSRT Gaylord, Michigan
WLFX Berea, Kentucky
WXTP North Windham, Maine
WMYT Carolina Beach, North Carolina
WPWQ Mount Sterling, Illinois
WLTW New York, New York
WMJX Boston, Massachusetts
WZCB Dublin, Ohio
WNKR Williamstown, Kentucky
WNFN Millersville, Tennessee
WOKA-FM Douglas, Georgia
WKVK Semora, North Carolina
WZCY Hershey, Pennsylvania
WRMA Fort Lauderdale, Florida
WSTZ-FM Vicksburg, Mississippi
WTCB Orangeburg, South Carolina
WVKM Matewan, West Virginia
WBDR Copenhagen, New York
WWZD-FM New Albany, Mississippi
WXXL Tavares, Florida
WYAY Gainesville, Georgia
WPPN Des Plaines, Illinois
WZNX Sullivan, Illinois
WZZL Reidland, Kentucky
WFGA Hicksville, Ohio
WDTW-FM Detroit, Michigan
KXDR(FM) Pinesdale, Montana
WHTO Iron Mountain, Michigan
KTPO Kootenai, Idaho
WOZN-FM Mount Horeb, Wisconsin
KPLN Lockwood, Montana
KYUN Hailey, Idaho
WCDW Port Dickinson, New York
KNAN Nanakuli, Hawaii
KMRZ-FM Superior, Wyoming
KNKI Pinetop, Arizona

106.9 MHz

KAAX Avenal, California
KASS Casper, Wyoming
WMOZ Moose Lake, Minnesota
KBGL Larned, Kansas
KMVE California City, California
KCST-FM Florence, Oregon
KFRC San Francisco, California
KEDG Alexandria, Louisiana
KMZZ Bishop, Texas
KEGK Wahpeton, North Dakota
KOOV Kempner, Texas
KHTT Muskogee, Oklahoma
KIHK Rock Valley, Iowa
KARP-FM Dassel, Minnesota
KAZE Ore City, Texas
KKRB Klamath Falls, Oregon
KKYN-FM Plainview, Texas
KLUB Bloomington, Texas
KDVA Buckeye, Arizona
KMOK Lewiston, Idaho
KMZK Clifton, Colorado
KNKN(FM) Pueblo, Colorado
KLGD Stamford, Texas
KOPW Plattsmouth, Nebraska
KQLB Los Banos, California
KEGH Brigham City, Utah
KRNO Incline Village, Nevada
KROC-FM Rochester, Minnesota
KRWM Bremerton, Washington
KTIJ Elk City, Oklahoma
KTPK Topeka, Kansas
KTXY Jefferson City, Missouri
KWYI Kawaihae, Hawaii
KXFE Dumas, Arkansas
KXIO Clarksville, Arkansas
KDGL Yucca Valley, California
KYXK Gurdon, Arkansas
KRVF Kerens, Texas
WAFX Suffolk, Virginia
WWEG Myersville, Maryland
WBQX Thomaston, Maine
WCCC-FM Hartford, Connecticut
WDML Woodlawn, Illinois
WEZX Scranton, Pennsylvania
WHKL Crenshaw, Mississippi
WKVP Camden, New Jersey
WMGU Southern Pines, North Carolina
WKXD-FM Monterey, Tennessee
WPLL Cross City, Florida
WZZI(FM) Bedford, Virginia
WMEG Guayama, Puerto Rico
WMIT Black Mountain, North Carolina
WEXR Stonewall, Mississippi
WXXC Marion, Indiana
WOOD-FM Muskegon, Michigan
WNNO Wisconsin Dells, Wisconsin
WBPT Homewood, Alabama
WRBE-FM Lucedale, Mississippi
WRIJ Masontown, Pennsylvania
WRQK-FM Canton, Ohio
WYPO Ocean City, Maryland
WSCY Moultonborough, New Hampshire
WSWT Peoria, Illinois
WUPM Ironwood, Michigan
WVEZ St. Matthews, Kentucky
WWSU Fairborn, Ohio
WUBB Bluffton, South Carolina
WWYN McKenzie, Tennessee
WTTL-FM Madisonville, Kentucky
WQKK(FM) Renovo, Pennsylvania
WZZS Zolfo Springs, Florida
WKZA Lakewood, New York
KHRT-FM Minot, North Dakota
KSCY Four Corners, Montana
KHYY Minatare, Nebraska
KFSE Kasilof, Alaska
KVGQ Overton, Nevada
KDRX Laughlin Afb, Texas
WVTI Brighton, Vermont
WLGE Baileys Harbor, Wisconsin
KIQN-FM Pueblo, Colorado
WSYR Solvay, New York

107.1 MHz

KAUM Colorado City, Texas
KPKL Deer Park, Washington
KDBX Clear Lake, South Dakota
KBHI Miner, Missouri
KBMV-FM Birch Tree, Missouri
KSRT Cloverdale, California
KTHI Caldwell, Idaho
KCWR Bakersfield, California
KDRS-FM Paragould, Arkansas
KDSN-FM Denison, Iowa
KESS Benbrook, Texas
WFON Fond Du Lac, Wisconsin
KFNV-FM Ferriday, Louisiana
KESR Shasta Lake City, California
KNWI Osceola, Iowa
KELD-FM Hampton, Arkansas
KCNY Greenbrier, Arkansas
KLVU Sweet Home, Oregon
KSSE Arcadia, California
KMGK Glenwood, Minnesota
KHIT-FM Madera, California
KJML(FM) Columbus, Kansas
KNKT Armijo, New Mexico
KOGM Opelousas, Louisiana
KPUR-FM Canyon, Texas
KRQT Longview, Washington
KSFT-FM South Sioux City, Nebraska
KFCO Bennett, Colorado
KSLT Spearfish, South Dakota
KSSD Fallbrook, California
KTHS-FM Berryville, Arkansas
KFYX(FM) Texarkana, Arkansas
KSES-FM Seaside, California
KVVA-FM Apache Junction, Arizona
KSSC Ventura, California
KWLV Many, Louisiana
KXHT Marion, Arkansas
KYNZ Lone Grove, Oklahoma
KRXB Beeville, Texas
KRVA-FM Campbell, Texas
WFXM Gordon, Georgia
WAOA-FM Melbourne, Florida
WHOK-FM Circleville, Ohio
WUHU Smiths Grove, Kentucky
WEJK Boonville, Indiana
WBYP Belzoni, Mississippi
WCBC-FM Keyser, West Virginia
WCHG Hot Springs, Virginia
WCKC Cadillac, Michigan
WCKT Lehigh Acres, Florida
WDOH Delphos, Ohio
WEAI Lynnville, Illinois
WERZ Exeter, New Hampshire
WLVX(FM) Greenville, Pennsylvania
WFHN Fairhaven, Massachusetts
WFXC Durham, North Carolina
WLRX Ironton, Ohio
WLAI Wilmore, Kentucky
WHMD Hammond, Louisiana
WFFG-FM Corinth, New York
WIIS Key West, Florida
WIRX St. Joseph, Michigan
WTMY(FM) Coon Rapids, Minnesota
WKCB-FM Hindman, Kentucky
WKFS Milford, Ohio
WLVZ Collins, Mississippi
WKRV Vandalia, Illinois
WLIH Whitneyville, Pennsylvania
WLSM-FM Louisville, Mississippi
WNUS Belpre, Ohio
WOCO-FM Oconto, Wisconsin
WRFK Barre, Vermont
WPGU Urbana, Illinois
WPSK-FM Pulaski, Virginia
WPVL-FM Platteville, Wisconsin
WQJU Mifflintown, Pennsylvania
WQKL Ann Arbor, Michigan
WRHM Lancaster, South Carolina
WSAQ Port Huron, Michigan
WSPY-FM Plano, Illinois
WEDJ Danville, Indiana
WTDK Federalsburg, Maryland
WTKF Atlantic, North Carolina
WTLZ Saginaw, Michigan
WTSH-FM Aragon, Georgia
WTTX-FM Appomattox, Virginia
WRXZ Briarcliff Acres, South Carolina
WWYY Belvidere, New Jersey
WWZY Long Branch, New Jersey
WXYK Gulfport, Mississippi
WYFA Waynesboro, Georgia
WXPK Briarcliff Manor, New York
WZLF Bellows Falls, Vermont
WZVN Lowell, Indiana
KLJH Bayfield, Colorado
KTUM Tatum, New Mexico
KQEO Idaho Falls, Idaho
KNKK Needles, California
KPVW Aspen, Colorado
KRQN Vinton, Iowa
KWHO Lovell, Wyoming
WGMY Thomasville, Georgia
WNMR Dannemora, New York
KNID North Enid, Oklahoma
KJML Columbus, Kansas
WJPS Boonville, Indiana
KLZT Bastrop, Texas
WZVN-FM Georgetown, Delaware

107.3 Hz

WRSW Niles, Michigan

107.3 MHz

KOOS North Bend, Oregon
KAOX Kemmerer, Wyoming
KQZR Hayden, Colorado
KBBK Lincoln, Nebraska
KFFM Yakima, Washington
KFXR-FM Chinle, Arizona
KGRS Burlington, Iowa
KIOW Forest City, Iowa
KISX Whitehouse, Texas
KIXW-FM Lenwood, California
KJAS Jasper, Texas
KKWY Albin, Wyoming
KTHR Wichita, Kansas
KLFX Nolanville, Texas
KLPW-FM Steelville, Missouri
KAPN Caldwell, Texas
KLVS Livermore, California
KNHT Rio Dell, California
KMJK North Kansas City, Missouri
KNUJ-FM Sleepy Eye, Minnesota
KSSL Post, Texas
KOMS Poteau, Oklahoma
KQMJ(FM) Osceola, Arkansas

RADIO - U.S.

KURQ Grover Beach, California
KQRN Mitchell, South Dakota
KIYK Saint George, Utah
KVRW Lawton, Oklahoma
WAAF Westborough, Massachusetts
WBZN Old Town, Maine
WCGQ Columbus, Georgia
WMCD Claxton, Georgia
WCLN-FM Clinton, North Carolina
WCMN-FM Arecibo, Puerto Rico
WXGL St. Petersburg, Florida
WCTT-FM Corbin, Kentucky
WCWT-FM Centerville, Ohio
WCOH-FM Du Bois, Pennsylvania
WDDD-FM Johnston City, Illinois
WDKR Maroa, Illinois
WEGH Northumberland, Pennsylvania
WJMZ-FM Anderson, South Carolina
WJUC Swanton, Ohio
WKAZ-FM Miami, West Virginia
WRZI Hodgenville, Kentucky
WNBL South Bristol Township, New York
WMGL Ravenel, South Carolina
WNWV Elyria, Ohio
WNXR Iron River, Wisconsin
WPUR Atlantic City, New Jersey
WQLT-FM Florence, Alabama
WKVU Utica, New York
WRQX Washington, District of Columbia
WRSW-FM Warsaw, Indiana
WRWD-FM Highland, New York
WRZQ-FM Greensburg, Indiana
WSJY Fort Atkinson, Wisconsin
WBRP Baker, Louisiana
WVGN Charlotte Amalie, Virgin Islands
WVSZ Chesterfield, South Carolina
WTRZ Spencer, Tennessee
WXLZ-FM Lebanon, Virginia
WBBT-FM Powhatan, Virginia
WYBZ Crooksville, Ohio
KIMO Helena Valley SE, Montana
WFCG Tylertown, Mississippi
KRKV Las Animas, Colorado
WVRA Enfield, North Carolina
KLSY Cosmopolis, Washington
WUPF Powers, Michigan
KQDR Savoy, Texas
KNPQ Hershey, Nebraska
WQZZ Boligee, Alabama
WWJK Green Cove Springs, Florida
WRGV Pensacola, Florida

107.5 MHz

KKLV Orem, Utah
KARZ Marshall, Minnesota
KASH-FM Anchorage, Alaska
KXJM Banks, Oregon
KBGY Faribault, Minnesota
KXMG Jean Lafitte, Louisiana
KQBO Rio Grande City, Texas
KWBZ Monroe City, Missouri
KQBA Los Alamos, New Mexico
KKLV Kaysville, Utah
KFEB Campbell, Missouri
KOSN Ketchum, Oklahoma
KHYT Tucson, Arizona
KJKJ Grand Forks, North Dakota
KKDM Des Moines, Iowa
KGLK Lake Jackson, Texas
KIFS Medford, Oregon
KOMT Mountain Home, Arkansas
KLIZ-FM Brainerd, Minnesota
KLVE Los Angeles, California
KILV Castana, Iowa
KRDA Hanford, California
KMVK Fort Worth, Texas
KPIG-FM Freedom, California
KQPT Colusa, California
KQKS Lakewood, Colorado
KJMH Lake Charles, Louisiana
KENR Superior, Montana
KSCB-FM Liberal, Kansas
KSED Sedona, Arizona
KSJT-FM San Angelo, Texas
KSMX-FM Clovis, New Mexico
KGLK Lake Jackson, Texas
KXKZ Ruston, Louisiana
KXO-FM El Centro, California
KXTE Pahrump, Nevada
KXTN-FM San Antonio, Texas
WABX Evansville, Indiana
WAMJ Roswell, Georgia
WAMR-FM Miami, Florida
WBBI Endwell, New York
WBLS New York, New York
WZRX-FM Fort Shawnee, Ohio
WBYN-FM Boyertown, Pennsylvania
WCCN-FM Neillsville, Wisconsin
WCCW-FM Traverse City, Michigan
WCKX Columbus, Ohio
WDBQ-FM Galena, Illinois
WEGW Wheeling, West Virginia
WFCC-FM Chatham, Massachusetts
WGCI-FM Chicago, Illinois
WGPR Detroit, Michigan
WIOK Falmouth, Kentucky
WHBQ-FM Germantown, Tennessee
WKXI-FM Magee, Mississippi
WKZL Winston-Salem, North Carolina
WMJW Rosedale, Mississippi
WNKT Eastover, South Carolina
WNNT-FM Warsaw, Virginia
WRVW Lebanon, Tennessee
WAZO Southport, North Carolina
WFNK Lewiston, Maine
WTIF-FM Omega, Georgia
WCHV-FM Charlottesville, Virginia
WYPZ Cochran, Georgia
WBVE Bedford, Pennsylvania
WWGF Donalsonville, Georgia
WDUZ-FM Brillion, Wisconsin
WZLK Virgie, Kentucky
WFXJ-FM North Kingsville, Ohio
WZZZ Portsmouth, Ohio
KRPM Billings, Montana
KYZK Sun Valley, Idaho
KLLM(FM) Rawlins, Wyoming
KHEI-FM Kihei, Hawaii
KXZS Wall, South Dakota
KXRV Cannon Ball, North Dakota
KABR Alamo Community, New Mexico
WTIM Taylorville, Illinois

107.7 MHz

KLJA Georgetown, Texas
KFTT Bagdad, Arizona
KCDZ Twentynine Palms, California
KGCR Goodland, Kansas
KSRN Kings Beach, California
KICD-FM Spencer, Iowa
KIST-FM Carpinteria, California
KKHI Kihei, Hawaii
KKOA Volcano, Hawaii
KLAL Wrightsville, Arkansas
KDZZ St. Charles, Minnesota
KMAJ-FM Carbondale, Kansas
KNDD Seattle, Washington
KCVK Otterville, Missouri
KPLT-FM Paris, Texas
KRWP Stockton, Missouri
KRXO-FM Oklahoma City, Oklahoma
KSAN San Mateo, California
KSLZ St. Louis, Missouri
KSYZ-FM Grand Island, Nebraska
KTBQ Nacogdoches, Texas
KBMX Proctor, Minnesota
WWDW Alberta, Virginia
WAZA Liberty, Mississippi
WXXF Loudonville, Ohio
WECW Elmira, New York
WEGC Sasser, Georgia
WFCS New Britain, Connecticut
WFSP-FM Kingwood, West Virginia
WFXX Georgiana, Alabama
WGNA-FM Albany, New York
WGTY Gettysburg, Pennsylvania
WHHM-FM Henderson, Tennessee
WHQX Gary, West Virginia
WHSB Alpena, Michigan
WPFX-FM Luckey, Ohio
WIVK Knoxville, Tennessee
WKYN Mount Sterling, Kentucky
WWRX Ledyard, Connecticut
WKHI Fruitland, Maryland
WLLT Polo, Illinois
WBKA Bar Harbor, Maine
WMGF Mount Dora, Florida
WMMX Dayton, Ohio
WMQT-FM Ishpeming, Michigan
WMRS Monticello, Indiana
WLKK Wethersfield Twnshp, New York
WHSL Lisman, Alabama
WUHT Birmingham, Alabama
WTPL Hillsboro, New Hampshire
WRKR Portage, Michigan
WRRC Lawrenceville, New Jersey
WSEO Nelsonville, Ohio
WSFR Corydon, Indiana
WWWT-FM Manassas, Virginia
WUKS St. Pauls, North Carolina
WPRW-FM Martinez, Georgia
WVCY-FM Milwaukee, Wisconsin
WVOZ-FM Carolina, Puerto Rico
WHFX Darien, Georgia
WUUZ Cooperstown, Pennsylvania
WIBL(FM) Fairbury, Illinois
WCIG Dallas, Pennsylvania
KMTZ Three Forks, Montana
KABD Ipswich, South Dakota
KPWJ Kurten, Texas
WVRW Glenville, West Virginia
KLJA(FM) Georgetown, North Dakota
KTAE Hico, Texas
K243BJ Oklahoma City, Oklahoma
WMOV-FM Norfolk, Virginia

107.9 MHz

KLLE North Fork, California
KBKL Grand Junction, Colorado
KCLQ Lebanon, Missouri
KDND Sacramento, California
KFZO Lewisville, Texas
KWPW Robinson, Texas
KDZA-FM Pueblo, Colorado
KEYB Altus, Oklahoma
KEYJ-FM Abilene, Texas
KEZA Fayetteville, Arkansas
KFAN-FM Johnson City, Texas
KFIN Jonesboro, Arkansas
KFMW Waterloo, Iowa
KKOL-FM Aiea, Hawaii
KHPE Albany, Oregon
KIXS Victoria, Texas
KKRF Stuart, Iowa
KLTE Kirksville, Missouri
KVGS Meadview, Arizona
KMBI Spokane, Washington
KKLC Fall River Mills, California
KMLE Chandler, Arizona
KPAW Fort Collins, Colorado
KPFX Fargo, North Dakota
KQLM Odessa, Texas
KQQL Anoka, Minnesota
KRVK Vista West, Wyoming
KHXT Erath, Louisiana
KSEA Greenfield, California
KUDD Roy, Utah
KWLS Winfield, Kansas
KBQI Albuquerque, New Mexico
KUZZ-FM Bakersfield, California
KVLY Edinburg, Texas
KTIC-FM West Point, Nebraska
KWVE-FM San Clemente, California
KXLT-FM Eagle, Idaho
KQQK Beaumont, Texas
KZRS Great Bend, Kansas
KZRK-FM Canyon, Texas
WAMW-FM Washington, Indiana
WBTF Midway, Kentucky
WCDD Canton, Illinois
WCRZ Flint, Michigan
WCVQ Fort Campbell, Kentucky
WDBN Wrightsville, Georgia
WDSY Pittsburgh, Pennsylvania
WEAT West Palm Beach, Florida
WEBE Westport, Connecticut
WEMM Huntington, West Virginia
WENZ Cleveland, Ohio
WFCA Ackerman, Mississippi
WLZL Annapolis, District of Columbia
WGTR Bucksport, South Carolina
WFMX Skowhegan, Maine
WMRK-FM Shorter, Alabama
WJFX New Haven, Indiana
WKRF Tobyhanna, Pennsylvania
WKYR-FM Burkesville, Kentucky
WLEY-FM Aurora, Illinois
WPFM-FM Panama City, Florida
WLNK Charlotte, North Carolina
WRWN Port Royal, South Carolina
WNDN Chiefland, Florida
WKVB Port Matilda, Pennsylvania
WNCT-FM Greenville, North Carolina
WOGT East Ridge, Tennessee
WHTA Hampton, Georgia
WPHI-FM Pennsauken, New Jersey
WBQK West Point, Virginia
WMUS Muskegon, Michigan
WSRZ-FM Coral Cove, Florida
WNTR Indianapolis, Indiana
WVAC-FM Adrian, Michigan
WMFM Key West, Florida
WVPS Burlington, Vermont
WWAG McKee, Kentucky
WWHT Syracuse, New York
WWPH Princeton Junction, New Jersey
WWRQ-FM Valdosta, Georgia
WKIO Arcola, Illinois
WXKS-FM Medford, Massachusetts
WVMX Westerville, Ohio
WBCV Wausau, Wisconsin
WYYD Amherst, Virginia
WZKX Bay St. Louis, Mississippi
WCZW Charlevoix, Michigan
KQEL Alamogordo, New Mexico
KHDV Darby, Montana
KXZT Newell, South Dakota
KBHM Basin, Wyoming
WLMY Williamsport, Pennsylvania

1090 MHz

WCRA-FM Effingham, Illinois

10MHz

WVTL Amsterdam, New York

1240 kHz

KADS Elk City, Oklahoma

87.9 MHz

KSFH Mountain View, California

88.1 MHz

KAFM Grand Junction, Colorado
KARH Forrest City, Arkansas
KAYB Sunnyside, Washington
KAYT Jena, Louisiana
KBBG Waterloo, Iowa
KBCU North Newton, Kansas
KBTL El Dorado, Kansas
KCEP Las Vegas, Nevada
KCFY Yuma, Arizona
KCNT Hastings, Nebraska
KCOU Columbia, Missouri
KCRY Mojave, California
KPMD Evanston, Wyoming
KCUK Chevak, Alaska
KCWC-FM Riverton, Wyoming
KCWU Ellensburg, Washington
KDHX Saint Louis, Missouri
KECG El Cerrito, California
KEAR-FM Sacramento, California
KFLB-FM Stanton, Texas
KFCF Fresno, California
KFTG Pasadena, Texas
KGNZ Abilene, Texas
KGVA Fort Belknap Agency, Montana
KHID McAllen, Texas
KHMG Barrigada, Guam
KHOY Laredo, Texas
KHPR Honolulu, Hawaii
KICB Fort Dodge, Iowa
KJTY Topeka, Kansas
KLFC Branson, Missouri
KLFO Florence, Oregon
KKJZ Long Beach, California
KMLV Ralston, Nebraska
KMSI Moore, Oklahoma
KMUE Eureka, California
KNLE-FM Round Rock, Texas
KNNB Whiteriver, Arizona
KNSQ Mount Shasta, California
KNTU McKinney, Texas
KPGR Pleasant Grove, Utah
KRLX Northfield, Minnesota
KRNM Chalan Kanoa-Saipan, Guam
KRSD Sioux Falls, South Dakota
KRTM Banning, California
KRUA Anchorage, Alaska
KSRH San Rafael, California
KTCV Kennewick, Washington
KTXT-FM Lubbock, Texas
KUYI Hotevilla, Arizona

KVSC St. Cloud, Minnesota
KWCR-FM Ogden, Utah
KWVA Eugene, Oregon
KYRV Concordia, Missouri
KZSC Santa Cruz, California
WAES Lincolnshire, Illinois
WAMP Jackson, Tennessee
WARY Valhalla, New York
WAXG Mount Sterling, Kentucky
WAXR Geneseo, Illinois
WAYF West Palm Beach, Florida
WAZD Savannah, Tennessee
WBCJ Spencerville, Ohio
WBFH Bloomfield Hills, Michigan
WBGM New Berlin, Pennsylvania
WBGU Bowling Green, Ohio
WBGY Everglades City, Florida
WKIV Westerly, Rhode Island
WBLW Gaylord, Michigan
WBMF Crete, Illinois
WCHC Worcester, Massachusetts
WCQS Asheville, North Carolina
WCRP Guayama, Puerto Rico
WCRX Chicago, Illinois
WCWP Brookville, New York
WUBA High Springs, Florida
WDFB-FM Danville, Kentucky
WDIY Allentown, Pennsylvania
WDPR Dayton, Ohio
WEFR Erie, Pennsylvania
WELH Providence, Rhode Island
WESN Bloomington, Illinois
WESU Middletown, Connecticut
WETN Wheaton, Illinois
WKEL Webster, New York
WFSK-FM Nashville, Tennessee
WGWR Liberty, New York
WHID Green Bay, Wisconsin
WHIJ Ocala, Florida
WHOV Hampton, Virginia
WHPR-FM Highland Park, Michigan
WYPR Baltimore, Maryland
WJIS Bradenton, Florida
WJSP-FM Warm Springs, Georgia
WYPF Frederick, Maryland
WJTY Lancaster, Wisconsin
WKJL Clarksburg, West Virginia
WKNC-FM Raleigh, North Carolina
WLGH Leroy Township, Michigan
WLRA Lockport, Illinois
WLTL La Grange, Illinois
WLXP Savannah, Georgia
WMAW-FM Meridian, Mississippi
WMBR Cambridge, Massachusetts
WMNR Monroe, Connecticut
WMUC-FM College Park, Maryland
WMUL Huntington, West Virginia
WMWK Milwaukee, Wisconsin
WNAS New Albany, Indiana
WCRJ Jacksonville, Florida
WNJS-FM Berlin, New Jersey
WNJT-FM Trenton, New Jersey
WNTH Winnetka, Illinois
WPCN(FM) Point Pleasant, West Virginia
WPEB Philadelphia, Pennsylvania
WPIR Hickory, North Carolina
WPTC Williamsport, Pennsylvania
WPTH Olney, Illinois
WRFL Lexington, Kentucky
WRGN Sweet Valley, Pennsylvania
WRGP Homestead, Florida
WRJA-FM Sumter, South Carolina
WSRU Slippery Rock, Pennsylvania
WRWJ Murrysville, Pennsylvania
WSBF-FM Clemson, South Carolina
WSDP Plymouth, Michigan
WSSD Chicago, Illinois
WTRT Benton, Kentucky
WUBJ Jamestown, New York
WURC Holly Springs, Mississippi
WUTC Chattanooga, Tennessee
WUWF Pensacola, Florida
WYZR Bethany, West Virginia
WVPE Elkhart, Indiana
WVYC York, Pennsylvania
WXBA Brentwood, New York
WXLU Peru, New York
WXZM Harrisburg, Pennsylvania
WXTC Greenville, Pennsylvania
WYCE Wyoming, Michigan
WYGG Asbury Park, New Jersey
WZIP Akron, Ohio
KBPW Hampton, Arkansas
WMHS Pike Creek, Delaware
WZZD Warwick, Pennsylvania
WSMF Monroe, Michigan
WJCF-FM Morristown, Indiana
WKRY Versailles, Indiana
WLWJ Petersburg, Illinois
KQHR The Dalles, Oregon
WMBL Mitchell, Indiana
KKRI Pocola, Oklahoma
WSOG Spring Valley, Illinois
KDNK Glenwood Springs, Colorado
KEDR(FM) Butte, Montana
WAYH Harvest, Alabama
WFHL New Bedford, Massachusetts
WAYT Thomasville, Georgia
KVOD Lakewood, Colorado
KGLF Doss, Texas
WAYD Auburn, Kentucky
KDJC Baker, Oregon
KTFY Buhl, Idaho
KGRI Lebanon, Oregon
WKVY Somerset, Kentucky
WHYT Goodland Township, Michigan
KDIM Coweta, Oklahoma
KLBT Beaumont, Texas
KVLW Gatesville, Texas
KQNC Quincy, California
WNCH Norwich, Vermont
KWAO Ocean Park, Washington
KMPQ Roseburg, Oregon
WJPG Cape May Court House, New Jersey
KEDR Bay City, Texas
KPAQ Plaquemine, Louisiana
KAIX Cheyenne, Wyoming
WRIH Richmond, Virginia
KLTU Mammoth, Arizona
KLWG Lompoc, California
KRNZ Gonzales, Texas
KLUW East Wenatchee, Washington
WSJL Bessemer, Alabama
KPRQ Sheridan, Wyoming
KNMA Tularosa, New Mexico
WGHW Lockwoods Folly Town, North Carolina
KPGS Pagosa Springs, Colorado
KGGA Gallup, New Mexico
KLBR Bend, Oregon
KATG Elkhart, Texas
KIDS Grants, New Mexico
KKWV Aransas Pass, Texas
WPRZ-FM Brandy Station, Virginia
KRLP Fairmont, Minnesota
KUSW Flora Vista, New Mexico
WSFP Harrisville, Michigan
KQOC Gleneden Beach, Oregon
WSRC(FM) Waynetown, Indiana
WJJJ Beckley, West Virginia
WWGV Grove City, Ohio
WWTG Carpentersville, Illinois
KFHC Ponca, Nebraska
WZGL Charleston, Illinois
WTZI Rosemont, Illinois
KZGM Cabool, Missouri
KGLL Gillette, Wyoming
WDNJ Hopatcong, New Jersey
KSRC Loup City, Nebraska
KRFI Redwood Falls, Minnesota
KOYA Rosebud, South Dakota
KPFZ-FM Lakeport, California
KDUP Cedarville, California
WHHN Hollidaysburg, Pennsylvania
KMPZ Salida, Colorado
WNEE Patterson, Georgia
WGWS St. Mary's City, Maryland
WHUZ(FM) Cole, Indiana
KGFJ Belt, Montana
WSLZ Cape Vincent, New York
WUBK(FM) Enoree, South Carolina
WWFJ East Fayetteville, North Carolina
KAKI Juneau, Alaska
WNBV Grundy, Virginia
WHJL Merrill, Wisconsin
WRSN Lebanon, Tennessee
KYGR Alamo, New Mexico
KRTT Great Bend, Kansas
KOOT Hurley, New Mexico
KOIA Storm Lake, Iowa
KUCC Clarkston, Washington
KCFD Crawford, Nebraska
WHPF Pittston Farm, Maine
KLBD(FM) Fremont, Texas
WYFY Cambridge, Ohio
KTQQ Elko, Nevada
KLWL Chillicothe, Missouri
KOGJ Kenai, Alaska
KJDR Guymon, Oklahoma
KCIU Columbia, Missouri

88.3 MHz

KABF Little Rock, Arkansas
KAPI Ruston, Louisiana
KAFR Conroe, Texas
KAXL Greenacres, California
KDKL Coalinga, California
KTGS Tishomingo, Oklahoma
KBCM Blytheville, Arkansas
KBJQ Bronson, Kansas
KBNR Brownsville, Texas
KBVM Portland, Oregon
KCCK-FM Cedar Rapids, Iowa
KCLU-FM Thousand Oaks, California
KCPW-FM Salt Lake City, Utah
KESD Brookings, South Dakota
KJAB-FM Mexico, Missouri
KJRN Keene, Texas
KJRT Amarillo, Texas
KSBC Nile, Washington
KLVC Magalia, California
KLVN Livingston, California
KLYT Albuquerque, New Mexico
KMLW Moses Lake, Washington
KNAI Phoenix, Arizona
KPAC San Antonio, Texas
KPHF Phoenix, Arizona
KPRH Montrose, Colorado
KSDS San Diego, California
KSRG Ashland, Oregon
KUCR Riverside, California
KVCO Concordia, Kansas
KWND Springfield, Missouri
KXUA Fayetteville, Arkansas
KYFW Wichita, Kansas
WAER Syracuse, New York
WAFJ Belvedere, South Carolina
WAFR Tupelo, Mississippi
WAPR Selma, Alabama
WYLV(FM) Maynardville, Tennessee
WAUI Shelby, Ohio
WAWF Kankakee, Illinois
WAWH Dublin, Georgia
WCXK Kalamazoo, Michigan
WBGO Newark, New Jersey
WBIA Shelbyville, Tennessee
WBIY La Belle, Florida
WBMT Boxford, Massachusetts
WBWC Berea, Ohio
WCBN-FM Ann Arbor, Michigan
WCOU Attica, New York
WCQR-FM Kingsport, Tennessee
WDCV-FM Carlisle, Pennsylvania
WDGC-FM Downers Grove, Illinois
WDSO Chesterton, Indiana
WEAX Angola, Indiana
WEJC White Star, Michigan
WFEN Rockford, Illinois
WFSO Olivebridge, New York
WGAO Franklin, Massachusetts
WGWG Boiling Springs, North Carolina
WMBJ Murrells Inlet, South Carolina
WHWC Menomonie, Wisconsin
WIQH Concord, Massachusetts
WGNK Pennsuco, Florida
WIUS Macomb, Illinois
WJCK Piedmont, Alabama
WJLY Ramsey, Illinois
WAYP Marianna, Florida
WLAB Fort Wayne, Indiana
WLFC North Baltimore, Ohio
WLPT Jesup, Georgia
WMRT Marietta, Ohio
WMTS-FM Murfreesboro, Tennessee
WIVL Jasper, Georgia
WNFA Port Huron, Michigan
WNIN-FM Evansville, Indiana
WNUB-FM Northfield, Vermont
WUKV Portsmouth, Ohio
WOTC Edinburg, Virginia
WPPB Southampton, New York
WPOZ Union Park, Florida
WPPR Demorest, Georgia
WQNA Springfield, Illinois
WQRI Bristol, Rhode Island
WRBH New Orleans, Louisiana
WRCT Pittsburgh, Pennsylvania
WRPS Rockland, Massachusetts
WRUO Mayaguez, Puerto Rico
WRVL Lynchburg, Virginia
WSHJ Southfield, Michigan
WARA New Washington, Indiana
WEBF Lerose, Kentucky
WTLG Starke, Florida
WUAW Erwin, North Carolina
WVCR-FM Loudonville, New York
WXOU Auburn Hills, Michigan
WXTS-FM Toledo, Ohio
WXUT Toledo, Ohio
WYAR Yarmouth, Maine
WYLV Maynardville, Tennessee
WZRD Chicago, Illinois
KPGB Pryor, Montana
WVBH Beach Haven West, New Jersey
WLKA Tafton, Pennsylvania
WPJC Pontiac, Illinois
WHCM Palatine, Illinois
WCLR Arlington Heights, Illinois
WVRL Elizabeth City, North Carolina
WAYQ Clarksville, Tennessee
KBPN Brainerd, Minnesota
KGCO Fort Collins, Colorado
KTPL Pueblo, Colorado
KLNB Grand Island, Nebraska
WYBX Key West, Florida
KARJ Kuna, Idaho
KLJV Scottsbluff, Nebraska
WZXQ Chambersburg, Pennsylvania
KKLG Newton, Iowa
WSGP Glasgow, Kentucky
WXBE Beaufort, North Carolina
KBMK Bismarck, North Dakota
KPYR Craig, Colorado
KLRH Sparks, Nevada
WEVS Nashua, New Hampshire
KLMP Rapid City, South Dakota
WOAR South Vienna, Ohio
KMLT Jackson, Wyoming
WKMV Muncie, Indiana
WKIW Ironwood, Michigan
KCPC Camino, California
WKDN-FM State College, Pennsylvania
WKPK Michigamme, Michigan
WHZN New Whiteland, Indiana
KIFR Alice, Texas
KJCG Missoula, Montana
WRAU Ocean City, Maryland
KPCP New Roads, Louisiana
KJSB Jonesboro, Arkansas
WRCC Dibrell, Tennessee
KITF International Falls, Minnesota
WYAD Benton, Mississippi
KVAM Goodland, Nebraska
WSHM Wixom, Michigan
KYZQ Mount Pleasant, Texas
KGUA Gualala, California
KKRR Casper, Wyoming
WZXE East Nottingham, Pennsylvania
WRGC-FM Milledgeville, Georgia
KLMB Roundup, Montana
KVKR Pine Ridge, South Dakota
WXLS Tupper Lake, New York
WMEK Kennebunkport, Maine
KBWW Broken Bow, Oklahoma
WLVV Midland, Maryland
KWIS Plummer, Idaho
KHNW Manson, Washington
KYPW Wolf Point, Montana
KBKO Kodiak, Alaska
WQIQ Spotsylvania, Virginia
WRCT(FM) Pittsburgh, Pennsylvania
WYBW Key Colony Beach, Florida
WYBQ Leesport, Pennsylvania

88.5 MHz

KAKA Salina, Kansas
KALA Davenport, Iowa
KAYK Victoria, Texas
KBEM-FM Minneapolis, Minnesota
KBMD Marble Falls, Texas
KBSY Burley, Idaho
KCIC Grand Junction, Colorado
KCRB-FM Bemidji, Minnesota
KCSN Northridge, California
KDCR Sioux Center, Iowa

KEOM Mesquite, Texas
KEYA Belcourt, North Dakota
KBZR Billings, Montana
KGNU-FM Boulder, Colorado
KHMS Victorville, California
KLCV Lincoln, Nebraska
KJNW Kansas City, Missouri
KLRF Milton-Freewater, Oregon
KLVH San Luis Obispo, California
KRSU Appleton, Minnesota
KOIR Edinburg, Texas
KPLU-FM Tacoma, Washington
KPSC Palm Springs, California
KQED-FM San Francisco, California
KRLF Pullman, Washington
KSBA Coos Bay, Oregon
KSBR Mission Viejo, California
KTEP El Paso, Texas
KMST Rolla, Missouri
KURE Ames, Iowa
KWTW Bishop, California
KHIB Bastrop, Texas
KYVT Yakima, Washington
WIAB Mackinaw City, Michigan
WAMU Washington, District of Columbia
WLYJ(FM) Tullahoma, Tennessee
WYOR Republic, Ohio
WBEL Cairo, Illinois
WBHY-FM Mobile, Alabama
WBMK Morehead, Kentucky
WBNH Pekin, Illinois
WCII Spencer, New York
WCRT-FM Terre Haute, Indiana
WEDW-FM Stamford, Connecticut
WEPC Belton, South Carolina
WFCF St. Augustine, Florida
WFCH Charleston, South Carolina
WFCR Amherst, Massachusetts
WFDD Winston-Salem, North Carolina
WGBK Glenview, Illinois
WGCA-FM Quincy, Illinois
WGNV Milladore, Wisconsin
WGVU-FM Allendale, Michigan
WHCF Bangor, Maine
WHFH Flossmoor, Illinois
WHPK-FM Chicago, Illinois
WHSD Hinsdale, Illinois
WJFM Baton Rouge, Louisiana
WJIA Guntersville, Alabama
WJIE-FM Okolona, Kentucky
WJSU-FM Jackson, Mississippi
WKPX Sunrise, Florida
WLUZ Levittown, Puerto Rico
WKWZ Syosset, New York
WLJR Birmingham, Alabama
WMCE Erie, Pennsylvania
WMFL Florida City, Florida
WMNF Tampa, Florida
WMUB Oxford, Ohio
WNJP Sussex, New Jersey
WOAS Ontonagon, Michigan
WJLZ Virginia Beach, Virginia
WPOB Plainview, New York
WQOX Memphis, Tennessee
WRAS Atlanta, Georgia
WNLI Sturgeon Bay, Wisconsin
WRKC Wilkes-Barre, Pennsylvania
WRUR-FM Rochester, New York
WYVL(FM) Youngsville, Pennsylvania
WTTU Cookeville, Tennessee
WUSM-FM Hattiesburg, Mississippi
WVCP Gallatin, Tennessee
WVOF Fairfield, Connecticut
WVPA St. Johnsbury, Vermont
WVPN Charleston, West Virginia
WVTW Charlottesville, Virginia
WHYZ(FM) Palm Bay, Florida
WWTA Marion, Massachusetts
WXPN Philadelphia, Pennsylvania
WYFU Masontown, Pennsylvania
WYFV Cayce, South Carolina
WYSA Wauseon, Ohio
WYSU Youngstown, Ohio
WRTP Franklinton, North Carolina
KPMB Plainview, Texas
KBQC Independence, Kansas
KCKT Crockett, Texas
WJCB Clewiston, Florida
KIHS Adel, Iowa
KWRX Redmond, Oregon
WZXX Lawrenceburg, Tennessee
KVUH Laytonville, California
KQKL Selma, California
KTKL Stigler, Oklahoma
KTDU Durango, Colorado
WBOJ Lumpkin, Georgia
KAKL Anchorage, Alaska
WZNB New Bern, North Carolina
KLMF Klamath Falls, Oregon
KMQX Weatherford, Texas
WVDA Valdosta, Georgia
KVLT Temple, Texas
WWLC Cross City, Florida
WTMK Wanatah, Indiana
KLRW Byrne, Texas
WEKF Corbin, Kentucky
KRNC Steamboat Springs, Colorado
WJOM Eagle, Michigan
KWLK Westwood, California
KAIK Tillamook, Oregon
KAVE Oakridge, Oregon
KEKL Mesquite, Nevada
KFLT-FM Tucson, Arizona
KIAD Dubuque, Iowa
KLKA Globe, Arizona
KZLU Inyokern, California
KPIJ Junction City, Oregon
KPKJ Mentmore, New Mexico
WCTP Gagetown, Michigan
WMUW Columbus, Mississippi
WZDG Scotts Hill, North Carolina
KUWY Laramie, Wyoming
KGHY Beaumont, Texas
KZTH Piedmont, Oklahoma
KVJZ Vail, Colorado
WJBE-FM Five Points, Alabama
KECU Kaibito, Arizona
WSLT Statesboro, Georgia
KKRN Bella Vista, California
WRKJ Westbrook, Maine
KMUZ Turner, Oregon
WGRH Hinckley, Minnesota
WVMR Marlinton, West Virginia
KZUW Reliance, Wyoming
KJLJ Scott City, Kansas
KHEW Rocky Boy's Reserv., Montana
KEDC Hearne, Texas
WPMW Bayview, Massachusetts
KENU Des Moines, New Mexico
WKUA Moundville, Alabama
WUOW Milford, New York
Minooka, Virginia
KVED Vernon, Texas

88.7 MHz

KAGU Spokane, Washington
KASV Borger, Texas
KAZI Austin, Texas
KKER Kerrville, Texas
KBMQ Monroe, Louisiana
KBPU De Queen, Arkansas
KBVR Corvallis, Oregon
KCME Manitou Springs, Colorado
KEPI Eagle Pass, Texas
KFBN Fargo, North Dakota
KKLM Corpus Christi, Texas
KIGC Oskaloosa, Iowa
KISL Avalon, California
KJHA Houston, Alaska
KLNE-FM Lexington, Nebraska
KLNI Decorah, Iowa
KZRI Sandy, Oregon
KLVV Ponca City, Oklahoma
KMPO Modesto, California
KMSE Rochester, Minnesota
KNAU Flagstaff, Arizona
KRVS Lafayette, Louisiana
KRZA Alamosa, Colorado
KSPC Claremont, California
KTCU Fort Worth, Texas
KZLO Kilgore, Texas
KTRM Kirksville, Missouri
KUBO Calexico, California
KUHF Houston, Texas
KUNR Reno, Nevada
KWDM West Des Moines, Iowa
KWPR Lund, Nevada
KXMS Joplin, Missouri
WAGO Snow Hill, North Carolina
WAYM Spring Hill, Tennessee
WBFO Buffalo, New York
WBHW Loogootee, Indiana
WBYX Stroudsburg, Pennsylvania
WCSF Joliet, Illinois
WELL-FM Waverly, Alabama
WERN Madison, Wisconsin
WFNP Rosendale, New York
WFOS Chesapeake, Virginia
WGVE-FM Gary, Indiana
WHCL-FM Clinton, New York
WIAA Interlochen, Michigan
WICR Indianapolis, Indiana
WIGH Jackson, Tennessee
WJCU University Heights, Ohio
WJFR Jacksonville, Florida
WJMF Smithfield, Rhode Island
WJZB Starkville, Mississippi
WMYZ Clermont, Florida
WWLU Lincoln University, Pennsylvania
WLOQ Indian Lakes Estates, Florida
WLUW Chicago, Illinois
WMMT Whitesburg, Kentucky
WMOC Lumber City, Georgia
WNCW Spindale, North Carolina
WNHU West Haven, Connecticut
WNYK Nyack, New York
WOBO Batavia, Ohio
WOFN Beach City, Ohio
WPCD Champaign, Illinois
WPSC-FM Wayne, New Jersey
WQPR Muscle Shoals, Alabama
WRFW River Falls, Wisconsin
WRHU Hempstead, New York
WRHV Poughkeepsie, New York
WRSE Elmhurst, Illinois
WRSU-FM New Brunswick, New Jersey
WRVT Rutland, Vermont
WRWA Dothan, Alabama
WSEW Sanford, Maine
WSIE Edwardsville, Illinois
WSQA Hornell, New York
WSYC-FM Shippensburg, Pennsylvania
WUFM Columbus, Ohio
WWPV-FM Colchester, Vermont
WXDU Durham, North Carolina
WXJM Harrisonburg, Virginia
WJDS Sparta, Georgia
WEHA(FM) Port Republic, New Jersey
WMLS Grand Marais, Minnesota
KOAP Lakeview, Oregon
KMCU Wichita Falls, Texas
WSRI Sugar Grove, Illinois
KJKL Selma, Oregon
KDNR South Greeley, Wyoming
WFRP Americus, Georgia
KNKL North Ogden, Utah
WPRC Sheffield, Illinois
KFRI West Odessa, Texas
KXJS Sutter, California
KLKM Kalispell, Montana
KAJT Ada, Oklahoma
KWTU Tulsa, Oklahoma
WYTF Indianola, Mississippi
WQKV Warsaw, Indiana
WXPH Middletown, Pennsylvania
KLOY Astoria, Oregon
WWCF McConnellsburg, Pennsylvania
WEER Montauk, New York
WRAE Raeford, North Carolina
WKYJ Rouses Point, New York
KORB Hopland, California
KBLV Tehachapi, California
KGSF Hunstville, Arkansas
KRBG Umbarger, Texas
WPJY Blennerhassett, West Virginia
WHJM Anna, Ohio
KRFH Marshalltown, Iowa
KOAY(FM) Middleton, Idaho
KBOM Socorro, New Mexico
KETP Enterprise, Oregon
WEGN Kankakee, Illinois
KVCH Huron, South Dakota
WLCU Campbellsville, Kentucky
WEYY Tallapoosa, Georgia
KMKZ(FM) Red Feather Lakes, Colorado
KFXH Marlow, Oklahoma
KSDQ Moberly, Missouri
WREM Canton, New York
WKNZ Harrington, Delaware
WEUC Morganfield, Kentucky
KXNM Encino, New Mexico
WRIQ Lexington, Virginia
KHIH Estes Park, Colorado
KUDI Choteau, Montana
WSIS Riverside, Michigan
KKAW Douglas, Wyoming
KTMU Muenster, Texas
KOKN Oketo, Kansas
WMWI Demopolis, Alabama
WRYV Milroy, Pennsylvania
KWOP(FM) Fort Dodge, North Carolina
WCDG Dahlonega, Georgia
KWAS Borger, Texas
K204CE Clifton, Arizona

88.9 MHz

KAOW Fort Smith, Arkansas
KAWC-FM Yuma, Arizona
KHII Cloudcroft, New Mexico
KCSH Ellensburg, Washington
KDUV Visalia, California
KEFX Twin Falls, Idaho
KETR Commerce, Texas
KEUL Girdwood, Alaska
KFPR Redding, California
KGFC Great Falls, Montana
KJLU Jefferson City, Missouri
KLDN Lufkin, Texas
KLCZ Lewiston, Idaho
KMBH-FM Harlingen, Texas
KMIH Mercer Island, Washington
KMPR Minot, North Dakota
KNMI Farmington, New Mexico
KNSR Collegeville, Minnesota
KPRD Hays, Kansas
KQFE Springfield, Oregon
KRNW Chillicothe, Missouri
KRUC Las Cruces, New Mexico
KSTM Indianola, Iowa
KTJO-FM Ottawa, Kansas
KTLW Lancaster, California
KTNA Talkeetna, Alaska
KUCI Irvine, California
KUSP Santa Cruz, California
KXPR Sacramento, California
KXLU Los Angeles, California
KYLV Oklahoma City, Oklahoma
WAJM Atlantic City, New Jersey
WARG Summit, Illinois
WBJV Steubenville, Ohio
WBKG Macon, Georgia
WBLU-FM Grand Rapids, Michigan
WBYO Sellersville, Pennsylvania
WBZC Pemberton, New Jersey
WCIY Canandaigua, New York
WCSU-FM Wilberforce, Ohio
WCVE-FM Richmond, Virginia
WCVF-FM Fredonia, New York
WDBM East Lansing, Michigan
WDCR Oreana, Illinois
WDNA Miami, Florida
WEAA Baltimore, Maryland
WEIU Charleston, Illinois
WEKU Richmond, Kentucky
WEPS Elgin, Illinois
WERS Boston, Massachusetts
WPUC-FM Ponce, Puerto Rico
WFRJ Johnstown, Pennsylvania
WFRS Smithtown, New York
WFSE Edinboro, Pennsylvania
WFSU-FM Tallahassee, Florida
WAKL Flint, Michigan
WITC Cazenovia, New York
WGEN-FM Monee, Illinois
WJMJ Hartford, Connecticut
WJYW Union City, Indiana
WKEU-FM The Rock, Georgia
WMSB Byhalia, Mississippi
WKTO Edgewater, Florida
WKYU-FM Bowling Green, Kentucky
WLNX Lincoln, Illinois
WLRY Rushville, Ohio
WLSU La Crosse, Wisconsin
WMAU-FM Bude, Mississippi
WMBW Chattanooga, Tennessee
WMCX West Long Branch, New Jersey
WKVC North Myrtle Beach, South Carolina
WMSL Athens, Georgia
WMXM Lake Forest, Illinois
WNSC-FM Rock Hill, South Carolina
WNYO Oswego, New York
WOJB Reserve, Wisconsin
WIIT Chicago, Illinois
WQCS Fort Pierce, Florida

WQSU Selinsgrove, Pennsylvania
WRDL Ashland, Ohio
WRPJ Port Jervis, New York
WRRG River Grove, Illinois
WSHA Raleigh, North Carolina
WSIA Staten Island, New York
WSLJ Watertown, New York
WSND-FM Notre Dame, Indiana
WSTB Streetsboro, Ohio
WVEP Martinsburg, West Virginia
WVPW Buckhannon, West Virginia
WWGN Ottawa, Illinois
WWIO-FM Brunswick, Georgia
WWNW New Wilmington, Pennsylvania
WYFE Tarpon Springs, Florida
WYMS Milwaukee, Wisconsin
KAGJ Ephraim, Utah
KHJC Lihue, Hawaii
KJIA Spirit Lake, Iowa
WVSI Mt. Vernon, Illinois
WUND-FM Manteo, North Carolina
KAKV El Dorado, Arkansas
KARU Cache, Oklahoma
KRFC Fort Collins, Colorado
WTAI Union City, Tennessee
KAIP Wapello, Iowa
WDCK Oolitic, Indiana
KKLJ Klamath Falls, Oregon
KNPR Las Vegas, Nevada
KOHR Sheridan, Wyoming
KJLP Palmer, Alaska
KOBK Baker City, Oregon
KABN-FM Kasilof, Alaska
KYWH Lockwood, Montana
KSEF Ste. Genevieve, Missouri
KCJX Carbondale, Colorado
KICJ(FM) Mitchellville, Iowa
WMFT Tuscaloosa, Alabama
KAIC Tucson, Arizona
WMDR-FM Oakland, Maine
KFRD Butte, Montana
WVRN Wittenberg, Wisconsin
KAIW Laramie, Wyoming
KYOR Newport, Oregon
KWXC Grove, Oklahoma
KWVI Waverly, Iowa
KLLU Gallup, New Mexico
KNBE Beatrice, Nebraska
KGLV Manhattan, Kansas
WMWX Miamitown, Ohio
KLOF Gillette, Wyoming
KSWS Chehalis, Washington
WWES Mount Kisco, New York
WHEY North Muskegon, Michigan
KVRZ Libby, Montana
KSJP(FM) Ipswich, South Dakota
KIHI Burns, Wyoming
WQRN Cook, Minnesota
KNGM Guymon, Oklahoma
KNGW Juneau, Alaska
KUHN Golden Meadow, Louisiana
KENM Tucumcari, New Mexico
KCHG Cedar City, Utah
WYRR Lakewood, New York
KKKC Central City, Colorado
WTPG Whitehouse, Ohio
WCIJ Unadilla, New York
KRJA Lamesa, Texas
KRBR La Barge, Wyoming
KYLF Adrian, Missouri
KYFG Omaha, Nebraska
WVWG Seelyville, Indiana

89.1 MHz

KANW Albuquerque, New Mexico
KLFR Reedsport, Oregon
KAUR Sioux Falls, South Dakota
KBBF Calistoga, California
KBHU-FM Spearfish, South Dakota
KLVK Fountain Hills, Arizona
KBYU-FM Provo, Utah
KCEA Atherton, California
KCLC St. Charles, Missouri
KCRU Oxnard, California
KEOS College Station, Texas
KFAE-FM Richland, Washington
KHAP Chico, California
KHNE-FM Hastings, Nebraska
KXLV Amarillo, Texas
KLPI Ruston, Louisiana
KMHD Gresham, Oregon
KSQX Springtown, Texas
KMUW Wichita, Kansas
KTTZ-FM Lubbock, Texas
KHUI Alamosa, Colorado
KPRX Bakersfield, California
KSMF Ashland, Oregon
KSTX San Antonio, Texas
KTLC Canon City, Colorado
KUAR Little Rock, Arkansas
KUAZ-FM Tucson, Arizona
KUFM Missoula, Montana
KVDP Dry Prong, Louisiana
KVMT Montrose, Colorado
KWFC Springfield, Missouri
KCJH Livingston, California
KYFP Palestine, Texas
WAUZ Greensburg, Indiana
WBCX Gainesville, Georgia
WBOI Fort Wayne, Indiana
WBSD Burlington, Wisconsin
WBSN-FM New Orleans, Louisiana
WBSU Brockport, New York
WCID Friendship, New York
WDNX Olive Hill, Tennessee
WDWN Auburn, New York
WEMU Ypsilanti, Michigan
WGMS Hagerstown, Maryland
WEVO(FM) Concord, New Hampshire
WFDU Teaneck, New Jersey
WFNM Lancaster, Pennsylvania
WFSW Panama City, Florida
WGLT Normal, Illinois
WHAB Acton, Massachusetts
WIDR Kalamazoo, Michigan
WJPZ-FM Syracuse, New York
WKSV Thompson, Ohio
WLBF Montgomery, Alabama
WLJK Aiken, South Carolina
WMBU Forest, Mississippi
WMHT-FM Schenectady, New York
WECV-FM Nashville, Tennessee
WNIE Freeport, Illinois
WPKT Norwich, Connecticut
WNYU-FM New York, New York
WNZN Lorain, Ohio
WOCR Olivet, Michigan
WONC Naperville, Illinois
WOUC-FM Cambridge, Ohio
WOUL-FM Ironton, Ohio
WPHS Warren, Michigan
WSFX Nanticoke, Pennsylvania
WSMR Sarasota, Florida
WLKB Bay City, Michigan
WUFT-FM Gainesville, Florida
WUSO Springfield, Ohio
WVJC Mount Carmel, Illinois
WVTF Roanoke, Virginia
WWCJ Cape May, New Jersey
WWFM Trenton, New Jersey
WLAZ Kissimmee, Florida
WXHL-FM Christiana, Delaware
WEVO Concord, New Hampshire
WXVU Villanova, Pennsylvania
WYBF Radnor Township, Pennsylvania
KECC La Junta, Colorado
KPGT Watertown, South Dakota
WBYH Hawley, Pennsylvania
WDTR Imlay City, Michigan
KXTH Seminole, Oklahoma
KWRI Bartlesville, Oklahoma
KYCU Clinton, Oklahoma
WLOG Markleysburg, Pennsylvania
WPAS Pascagoula, Mississippi
KQXS Stephenville, Texas
KLWC Casper, Wyoming
KXGM-FM Hiawatha, Iowa
WSPM Cloverdale, Indiana
WJJE Delaware, Ohio
WRXV State College, Pennsylvania
WCNV Heathsville, Virginia
WWIP Cheriton, Virginia
KQAI Roswell, New Mexico
KAWS Marsing, Idaho
WKNG-FM Heflin, Alabama
KBWA Brush, Colorado
KHOL Jackson, Wyoming
KRLR Sulphur, Louisiana
KDAI Scottsbluff, Nebraska
KODV Barstow, California
KFLO-FM Blanchard, Louisiana
KLUU Jamestown, North Dakota
KVFL Pierre, South Dakota
WLPR-FM Lowell, Indiana
KGKV Garberville, California
WSSW Platteville, Wisconsin
KUOR-FM Redlands, California
WHAA Adams, Wisconsin
WRYN Hickory, North Carolina
KVCS Spring Valley, Minnesota
KPVL Postville, Iowa
KNSZ(FM) Ottumwa, Iowa
WBIB-FM Forsyth, Georgia
KGHE Glenoma, Washington
WSMJ(FM) Wilkinson, Indiana
KYCO Limon, Colorado
KQDL Hines, Oregon
KPKP Harts Bluff, Texas
WAKP Smithboro, Georgia
WGZS Cloquet, Minnesota
KHOI Story City, Iowa
KXNV Sun Valley, Nevada
KSPP Rhinelander, Wisconsin
WKEK Gunflint Lake, Minnesota
KKWW Shelbina, Missouri
WWIP Chesapeake, Virginia
KAWS Marsing, Idaho

89.3 MHz

KAKX Mendocino, California
KALU Langston, Oklahoma
KAOS Olympia, Washington
KATB Anchorage, Alaska
KAVK Many, Louisiana
KAYH Fayetteville, Arkansas
KHCP Paris, Texas
KBHE-FM Rapid City, South Dakota
KCCU Lawton, Oklahoma
KCRI Indio, California
KCUR-FM Kansas City, Missouri
KQEI-FM North Highlands, California
KIPO Honolulu, Hawaii
KJMC Des Moines, Iowa
KMTG San Jose, California
KLFF San Luis Obispo, California
KLOV Winchester, Oregon
KNON Dallas, Texas
KOHL Fremont, California
KPCC Pasadena, California
KPFB Berkeley, California
KPRG Agana, Guam
KNAQ Prescott, Arizona
KRSW Worthington, Minnesota
KSBJ Humble, Texas
KTBJ Festus, Missouri
KUGS Bellingham, Washington
KUND-FM Grand Forks, North Dakota
KUOI-FM Moscow, Idaho
KUVO Denver, Colorado
KVPR Fresno, California
KXGJ Victoria, Texas
KXNE-FM Norfolk, Nebraska
KZUM Lincoln, Nebraska
WAII Hattiesburg, Mississippi
WALN Carrollton, Alabama
WAMH Amherst, Massachusetts
WATU Port Gibson, Mississippi
WBFJ-FM Winston-Salem, North Carolina
WBJY Americus, Georgia
WBLD Orchard Lake, Michigan
KCMP Northfield, Minnesota
WCSB Cleveland, Ohio
WDLM-FM East Moline, Illinois
WECC-FM Folkston, Georgia
WFPL Louisville, Kentucky
WGCF Paducah, Kentucky
WGNB Zeeland, Michigan
WGNJ St. Joseph, Illinois
WGSU Geneseo, New York
WHFR Dearborn, Michigan
WHSN Bangor, Maine
WIPA Pittsfield, Illinois
WSMB Harbor Beach, Michigan
WJCS Allentown, Pennsylvania
WJEL Indianapolis, Indiana
WJVP Culebra, Puerto Rico
WJYA Emporia, Virginia
WKKC Chicago, Illinois
WKRW Wooster, Ohio
WLFJ-FM Greenville, South Carolina
WLJP Monroe, New York
WLRH Huntsville, Alabama
WMHN Webster, New York
WMKV Reading, Ohio
WMKW Crossville, Tennessee
WMSJ Freeport, Maine
WNJB-FM Bridgeton, New Jersey
WNKJ Hopkinsville, Kentucky
WNUR-FM Evanston, Illinois
WPFW Washington, District of Columbia
WPIO Titusville, Florida
WPNE-FM Green Bay, Wisconsin
WQED-FM Pittsburgh, Pennsylvania
WRDV Warminster, Pennsylvania
WRFG Atlanta, Georgia
WRKF Baton Rouge, Louisiana
WRMB Boynton Beach, Florida
WRTC-FM Hartford, Connecticut
WSCI Charleston, South Carolina
WRVH Clayton, New York
WSKG-FM Binghamton, New York
WSOE Elon College, North Carolina
WTEB New Bern, North Carolina
WTLI Bear Creek Township, Michigan
WVTU Charlottesville, Virginia
WZCP Chillicothe, Ohio
WXYC Chapel Hill, North Carolina
WYPL Memphis, Tennessee
WYSZ Maumee, Ohio
KBNO-FM White Salmon, Washington
WAJJ McKenzie, Tennessee
WYSM Lima, Ohio
KELP-FM Mesquite, New Mexico
WSGG Norfolk, Connecticut
KARQ San Andreas, California
KLMT Billings, Montana
KLBV Steamboat Springs, Colorado
KKLT Texarkana, Arkansas
WIKV Plymouth, Indiana
WYTJ Linton, Indiana
WJKN-FM Spring Arbor, Michigan
WZRI Spring Lake, North Carolina
KPJP Greenville, California
KAER Mesquite, Nevada
KPDO Pescadero, California
WKFA St. Catherine, Florida
KVIX Port Angeles, Washington
KOPJ Sebeka, Minnesota
KAIH Lake Havasu City, Arizona
KNAR San Angelo, Texas
WRFE Chesterfield, South Carolina
KYAI McKee, Kentucky
KLBZ Bozeman, Montana
WWLA South Charleston, West Virginia
KSSO Norman, Oklahoma
KVRA Sisters, Oregon
KTAW Walsenburg, Colorado
KOGL Gleneden Beach, Oregon
KNDZ McKinleyville, California
WUMD North Dartmouth, Massachusetts
WJIK Fulton, Alabama
WRTI Coatesville, Pennsylvania
KDNG Durango, Colorado
KUSL Richfield, Utah
KKNL Valentine, Nebraska
WZNP Newark, Ohio
KRSF Ridgecrest, California
WNJY Netcong, New Jersey
KIRL Osage Beach, Missouri
KTDX Laramie, Wyoming
WPJN Jemison, Alabama
WIRC Ely, Minnesota
WAZQ Islamorada, Florida
KTHL Altus, Oklahoma
WYNS Waynesville, Ohio
KRWY Rawlins, Wyoming
KAZC Healdton, Oklahoma
WRPB Benedicta, Maine
KKFC Hart, Texas
KYPB Big Timber, Montana
WFJS-FM Freehold, New Jersey
WCOM-FM Silver Creek, New York
WDWZ Andalusia, Alabama
KRBO(FM) Millers Ranch, California

89.5 MHz

KBAQ Phoenix, Arizona
KBES Ceres, California
KBHG Alexandria, Minnesota
KBMJ Heber Springs, Arkansas
KBMM Odessa, Texas
KBPG Montevideo, Minnesota
KCAC Camden, Arkansas
KCFV Ferguson, Missouri

KENW-FM Portales, New Mexico
KEPX Eagle Pass, Texas
KEWU-FM Cheney, Washington
KHCD Salina, Kansas
KHKE Cedar Falls, Iowa
KJVH Longview, Washington
KLCD Decorah, Iowa
KLND Little Eagle, South Dakota
KLUX Robstown, Texas
KMFA Austin, Texas
KMOC Wichita Falls, Texas
KNHC Seattle, Washington
KNLH Cedar Hill, Missouri
KCNV Las Vegas, Nevada
KOKS Poplar Bluff, Missouri
KOPN Columbia, Missouri
KPBS-FM San Diego, California
KPOO San Francisco, California
KPPR Williston, North Dakota
KPRA Ukiah, California
KPRN Grand Junction, Colorado
KQAL Winona, Minnesota
KSMC Moraga, California
KSOH Wapato, Washington
KTEC Klamath Falls, Oregon
KCNP Ada, Oklahoma
KTSC-FM Pueblo, Colorado
KTSY Caldwell, Idaho
KUSR Logan, Utah
KVMR Nevada City, California
KVNE Tyler, Texas
KWGS Tulsa, Oklahoma
KWRR Ethete, Wyoming
KKLY El Paso, Texas
KXRD Victorville, California
KYFL Monroe, Louisiana
KYQX Weatherford, Texas
WAHS Auburn Hills, Michigan
WBEW Chesterton, Indiana
WAUA Petersburg, West Virginia
WAWN Franklin, Pennsylvania
WAYJ Naples, Florida
WBCY Archbold, Ohio
WBFR Birmingham, Alabama
WBKE-FM North Manchester, Indiana
WBSB Anderson, Indiana
WCLQ Wausau, Wisconsin
WCMU-FM Mount Pleasant, Michigan
WCVV Belpre, Ohio
WDNR Chester, Pennsylvania
WDPS Dayton, Ohio
WETS-FM Johnson City, Tennessee
WFCI Franklin, Indiana
WFIT Melbourne, Florida
WGSG Mayo, Florida
WGTF Dothan, Alabama
WHRV Norfolk, Virginia
WHSS Hamilton, Ohio
WITF-FM Harrisburg, Pennsylvania
WIUW Warsaw, Illinois
WJMU Decatur, Illinois
WKPB Henderson, Kentucky
WKSG Cedar Creek, Florida
WMAE-FM Booneville, Mississippi
WMOT Murfreesboro, Tennessee
WJRF Duluth, Minnesota
WNGU Dahlonega, Georgia
WNIJ Dekalb, Illinois
WNTE Mansfield, Pennsylvania
WOVI Novi, Michigan
WPCS Pensacola, Florida
WPKN Bridgeport, Connecticut
WQRP Dayton, Ohio
WSCL Salisbury, Maryland
WYPA Cherry Hill, New Jersey
WSKB Westfield, Massachusetts
WSLU Canton, New York
WSOU South Orange, New Jersey
WAYJ(FM) Naples, Florida
WTJY Asheboro, North Carolina
WUNY Utica, New York
WVMS Sandusky, Ohio
WVPR Windsor, Vermont
WZWP West Union, Ohio
WYFK Columbus, Georgia
WYFS Savannah, Georgia
WYFW Winder, Georgia
WOFR Schoolcraft, Michigan
WWPJ Pen Argyl, Pennsylvania
KJZA Drake, Arizona
WPRG Columbia, Mississippi
WNCK Nantucket, Massachusetts
KTOT Spearman, Texas
WCOF Arcade, New York
KAWV Fort Dodge, Iowa
KPFR Pine Grove, Oregon
KTCF Dolores, Colorado
KLRI Rigby, Idaho
KSBX Santa Barbara, California
KJCC Carnegie, Oklahoma
KLFH Ojai, California
WARW Dorsey, Illinois
KZBJ Bay City, Texas
WYAZ Yazoo City, Mississippi
KAIB Shafter, California
KVLK Milan, New Mexico
KTCB Tillamook, Oregon
KITA Iota, Louisiana
KEFS North Powder, Oregon
WRNF Selma, Alabama
WWED Spotsylvania, Virginia
WEFI Effingham, Illinois
WQAI Thomson, Georgia
WLPS-FM Lumberton, North Carolina
WFOT Lexington, Ohio
KJIV Reno, Nevada
KICO Rico, Colorado
KQCO Esterbrook, Wyoming
WKMT Fulton, Kentucky
KLAP Gerlach, Nevada
WYNJ Blackduck, Minnesota
KCKJ Sarcoxie, Missouri
WSPI Ellsworth, Illinois
KSKX Chemult, Oregon
KILE-FM Woodland Park, Colorado
KPJH Polson, Montana
WWQZ Baptist Village, Massachusetts
KTUT Frankfort, South Dakota
KRCI Pinetop-Lakeside, Arizona
KYPF Stanford, Montana
KCEY Ranchos De Taos, New Mexico
WWTP Augusta, Maine
KTME Reliance, Wyoming

89.7 MHz

KACC Alvin, Texas
KACU Abilene, Texas
KARM Visalia, California
KAXG Gillette, Wyoming
KBDA Great Bend, Kansas
KBIO Natchitoches, Louisiana
KMBN Las Cruces, New Mexico
KKTR Kirksville, Missouri
KBSB Bemidji, Minnesota
KCVQ Knob Noster, Missouri
KEPC Colorado Springs, Colorado
KFJC Los Altos, California
KIWR Council Bluffs, Iowa
KLCC Eugene, Oregon
KLVM Prunedale, California
KMNR Rolla, Missouri
KMSU Mankato, Minnesota
KNBU Baldwin City, Kansas
KNCA Burney, California
KNLP Potosi, Missouri
KOZO Branson, Missouri
KRMH Red Mesa, Arizona
KRNL-FM Mount Vernon, Iowa
KRUI-FM Iowa City, Iowa
KSGN Riverside, California
KMWS Mount Vernon, Washington
KTDB Ramah, New Mexico
KVRK Sanger, Texas
KTXB Beaumont, Texas
KUAP Pine Bluff, Arkansas
KUMM Morris, Minnesota
KUSD Vermillion, South Dakota
KJMA Floresville, Texas
KWFJ Roy, Washington
KWWS Walla Walla, Washington
KXKM McCarthy, Alaska
KGNX Ballwin, Missouri
WAAJ Benton, Kentucky
WALF Alfred, New York
WAUQ Charles City, Virginia
WAUV Ripley, Tennessee
WAWI Lawrenceburg, Tennessee
WSHN Munising, Michigan
WBMV Mount Vernon, Illinois
WCBW-FM East St. Louis, Illinois
WCPE Raleigh, North Carolina
WDCL-FM Somerset, Kentucky
WMUM-FM Cochran, Georgia
WDJW Somers, Connecticut
WDVR Delaware Township, New Jersey
WDVV Wilmington, North Carolina
WYBK Chattanooga, Tennessee
WEOS Geneva, New York
WFGB Kingston, New York
WGBH(FM) Boston, Massachusetts
WGLS-FM Glassboro, New Jersey
WHND Sister Bay, Wisconsin
WISU Terre Haute, Indiana
WITR Henrietta, New York
WJLU New Smyrna Beach, Florida
WKSU-FM Kent, Ohio
WLUJ Springfield, Illinois
WLNZ Lansing, Michigan
WKCP Miami, Florida
WMED Calais, Maine
WMHB Waterville, Maine
WMHK Columbia, South Carolina
WJOJ Rust Township, Michigan
WNJA Jamestown, New York
WNJN-FM Atlantic City, New Jersey
WNKU Highland Heights, Kentucky
WONU Kankakee, Illinois
WOSU-FM Columbus, Ohio
WPAE Centreville, Mississippi
WRDR Freehold Township, New Jersey
WQEJ Johnstown, Pennsylvania
WRGF Greenfield, Indiana
WRHO Oneonta, New York
WRTU San Juan, Puerto Rico
WRUC Schenectady, New York
WSHC Shepherdstown, West Virginia
WSSK Saratoga Springs, New York
WTMD Towson, Maryland
WTUR Upland, Indiana
WTXR Toccoa Falls, Georgia
WUBS South Bend, Indiana
WUEC Eau Claire, Wisconsin
WUSF Tampa, Florida
WUWM Milwaukee, Wisconsin
WVFS Tallahassee, Florida
WVLS Monterey, Virginia
WLSN Grand Marais, Minnesota
KCMF Fergus Falls, Minnesota
WVYA Williamsport, Pennsylvania
KGBM Randsburg, California
KANH Emporia, Kansas
KJCV-FM Country Club, Missouri
KBIL Park City, Montana
KTPS Pagosa Springs, Colorado
KCLM Santa Maria, California
WOJC Crothersville, Indiana
KEQX Stephenville, Texas
WKVJ Dannemora, New York
KNRI Bismarck, North Dakota
KJTH Ponca City, Oklahoma
KBHN Booneville, Arkansas
KNSY(FM) Dubuque, Iowa
KJWA Trinidad, Colorado
KQLR Whitehall, Montana
WTKC Findlay, Ohio
KUUT Farmington, New Mexico
KUBJ Brenham, Texas
KRLE Oberlin, Kansas
KHYS Hays, Kansas
KGRP Grand Rapids, Minnesota
KCAI Lodi, California
WTAC Burton, Michigan
KPCS Princeton, Minnesota
WJHO Alexander City, Alabama
KCEU Price, Utah
KDBQ Rattan, Oklahoma
KOTD The Dalles, Oregon
KUCB Unalaska, Alaska
KWNM Winnemucca, Nevada
WKWH Liberty, Indiana
WLMN Manistee, Michigan
WGIW Pilot Mountain, North Carolina
KRNF Montezuma, Iowa
KOJD John Day, Oregon
WLOL-FM Star City, West Virginia
WVGV West Union, West Virginia
WNOC Bowling Green, Ohio
KAUC West Clarkston, Washington
KMOA Nu'uuli, American Samoa
WFWO Medina, New York
WYLC Jackson, Kentucky
KXGR Loveland, Colorado
WTBP Bath, Maine

89.9 MHz

KACV-FM Amarillo, Texas
KSJY St. Martinville, Louisiana
KASB Bellevue, Washington
KAUF Kennett, Missouri
KAWZ Twin Falls, Idaho
KAYP Burlington, Iowa
KBDE Temple, Texas
KBGA Missoula, Montana
KMCV High Point, Missouri
KBNL Laredo, Texas
KBSK McCall, Idaho
KQAC Portland, Oregon
KCRH Hayward, California
KCRW Santa Monica, California
KGNA-FM Arnold, Missouri
KDAQ Shreveport, Louisiana
KDFC Angwin, California
KDPR Dickinson, North Dakota
KEFR Le Grand, California
KFER Santa Cruz, California
KFLV Wilber, Nebraska
KFRS Soledad, California
KGHP Gig Harbor, Washington
KGNV Washington, Missouri
KGPR Great Falls, Montana
KGRG-FM Auburn, Washington
KJTA Flagstaff, Arizona
KMOJ Minneapolis, Minnesota
KNDL(FM) Angwin, California
KLXA Alexandria, Louisiana
KPLW Wenatchee, Washington
KPRE Vail, Colorado
KRPR Rochester, Minnesota
KRPS Pittsburg, Kansas
KTSW San Marcos, Texas
KUAC Fairbanks, Alaska
KUNM Albuquerque, New Mexico
KVMN Cave City, Arkansas
WAKD Sheffield, Alabama
WAPJ Torrington, Connecticut
WATI Vincennes, Indiana
WCXG Grand Rapids, Michigan
WCBU Peoria, Illinois
WCMD-FM Barre, Vermont
WCNO Palm City, Florida
WDAV Davidson, North Carolina
WDPG Greenville, Ohio
WDVX Clinton, Tennessee
WERU-FM Blue Hill, Maine
WEVL Memphis, Tennessee
WFBF Buffalo, New York
WFFC Ferrum, Virginia
WHPL West Lafayette, Indiana
WHSA Brule, Wisconsin
WHWG Trout Lake, Michigan
WIVH Christiansted, Virgin Islands
WJCT-FM Jacksonville, Florida
WJPG Woodbine, New Jersey
WJTF Panama City, Florida
WJWJ-FM Beaufort, South Carolina
WKCR-FM New York, New York
WKDS Kalamazoo, Michigan
WBRO Marengo, Indiana
WLCA Godfrey, Illinois
WLHS West Chester, Ohio
WLJN-FM Traverse City, Michigan
WLKL Mattoon, Illinois
WMAB-FM Mississippi State, Mississippi
WMRL Lexington, Virginia
WMTB-FM Emmitsburg, Maryland
WNJM Manahawkin, New Jersey
WOEL-FM Elkton, Maryland
WORT Madison, Wisconsin
WPER Culpeper, Virginia
WQTQ Hartford, Connecticut
WKVO Georgetown, Kentucky
WRVO Oswego, New York
WRVS-FM Elizabeth City, North Carolina
WSCB Springfield, Massachusetts
WSOF-FM Madisonville, Kentucky
WSUF Noyack, New York
WTBB Gadsden, Alabama
WTFH Helen, Georgia
WTHS Holland, Michigan
WTLR State College, Pennsylvania
WTSU Montgomery-Troy, Alabama
WUCF-FM Orlando, Florida
WVIA-FM Scranton, Pennsylvania
WVNP Wheeling, West Virginia

WVRU-FM Radford, Virginia
WVWV Huntington, West Virginia
WWEB Wallingford, Connecticut
WWNO New Orleans, Louisiana
WWSP Stevens Point, Wisconsin
WXLG North Creek, New York
WNRS-FM Sweet Briar, Virginia
WAY New Johnsonville, Tennessee
KCVY Cabool, Missouri
KWKL Grandfield, Oklahoma
WHLP Hanna, Indiana
KTLZ Cuero, Texas
KLRB Stuart, Oklahoma
KTMH Montrose, Colorado
KQFR Rapid City, South Dakota
KJCU Fort Bragg, California
KTAD Sterling, Colorado
KYMS Rathdrum, Idaho
KZAI Superior, Arizona
KFRY Pueblo, Colorado
WVFL Fond Du Lac, Wisconsin
KAIG Dodge City, Kansas
KKJA Redmond, Oregon
KWDS Kettleman City, California
WYBV Wakarusa, Indiana
KLGS College Station, Texas
KDVI Devils Lake, North Dakota
KVIR Bullhead City, Arizona
KDLI Del Rio, Texas
KYCM Alamogordo, New Mexico
KJTW Jamestown, North Dakota
KWAR Waverly, Iowa
WCXB Benton Harbor, Michigan
KAUG Anchorage, Alaska
KINU Kotzebue, Alaska
WSWS(FM) Smithboro, Illinois
KGTR Albany, Missouri
KANC Baker, Oregon
KDLG-FM Dillingham, Alaska
KKVI Overland, Texas
KQXB Breckenridge, Texas
KJIH Manhattan, Kansas
KUWI Rawlins, Wyoming
KQNV Fallon, Nevada
KORU Garapan-Saipan, Guam
KYPM Livingston, Montana
WNGF Swanton, Vermont
KTHF Hammon, Oklahoma
KRGM Marshall, Minnesota
WINO Odessa, New York
KYPC Colstrip, Montana
WWQA North Granby, Connecticut
KWCN Pinedale, Wyoming
WHRJ Gloucester Courthouse, Virginia
KHIS Jackson, Missouri
WTRE(FM) Greensburg, Indiana
WCGF Cambridge Springs, Pennsylvania

90.1 MHz

KSCV Springfield, Missouri
KAMY Lubbock, Texas
KBKC Moberly, Missouri
KBNV Fayetteville, Arkansas
KBPK Buena Park, California
KCBX San Luis Obispo, California
KCFR-FM Denver, Colorado
KYCC Stockton, California
KCSC Edmond, Oklahoma
KERA Dallas, Texas
KFKX Hastings, Nebraska
KHCC-FM Hutchinson, Kansas
KKFI Kansas City, Missouri
KLRD Yucaipa, California
KNMC Havre, Montana
KNWO Cottonwood, Idaho
KNWP Port Angeles, Washington
KOLU Pasco, Washington
KPFT Houston, Texas
KQWS Omak, Washington
KCEI Red River, New Mexico
KRHS Overland, Missouri
KRMB Bisbee, Arizona
KSAK Walnut, California
KSAU Nacogdoches, Texas
KLRO Hot Springs, Arkansas
KSJR-FM Collegeville, Minnesota
KSOR Ashland, Oregon
KSRQ Thief River Falls, Minnesota
KSYM-FM San Antonio, Texas
KTQX Bakersfield, California
KTRU(FM) Houston, Texas
KTXI Ingram, Texas
KUER-FM Salt Lake City, Utah
KUKL Kalispell, Montana
KUPS Tacoma, Washington
KUTE Ignacio, Colorado
KNCH(FM) San Angelo, Texas
KZFR Chico, California
KZMU Moab, Utah
KZSU Stanford, California
WABE Atlanta, Georgia
WAWJ Marion, Illinois
WCAI Woods Hole, Massachusetts
WCCE Buies Creek, North Carolina
WCSP-FM Washington, District of Columbia
WDCE Richmond, Virginia
WECS Willimantic, Connecticut
WEFT Champaign, Illinois
WEPR Greenville, South Carolina
WFYI-FM Indianapolis, Indiana
WGCU-FM Fort Myers, Florida
WGMC Greece, New York
WGSK South Kent, Connecticut
WZRU Garysburg, North Carolina
WHMC-FM Conway, South Carolina
WIUP-FM Indiana, Pennsylvania
WJCR-FM Upton, Kentucky
WIFF Windsor, New York
WJSO Pikeville, Kentucky
WJUF Inverness, Florida
WORI Harrison, Ohio
WKNP Jackson, Tennessee
WLSO Sault Ste. Marie, Michigan
WMBI-FM Chicago, Illinois
WMEA Portland, Maine
WMPR Jackson, Mississippi
WNAA Greensboro, North Carolina
WNMU-FM Marquette, Michigan
WJOU Huntsville, Alabama
WOHC Chillicothe, Ohio
WOI-FM Ames, Iowa
WORQ Green Bay, Wisconsin
WOUZ-FM Zanesville, Ohio
WPSX Kane, Pennsylvania
WPVA Waynesboro, Virginia
WRCU-FM Hamilton, New York
WRPN-FM Ripon, Wisconsin
WRTI Philadelphia, Pennsylvania
WRUV Burlington, Vermont
WRXC Shelton, Connecticut
WTJT Baker, Florida
WTSG Carlinville, Illinois
WUCX-FM Bay City, Michigan
WUSB Stony Brook, New York
WVMN New Castle, Pennsylvania
WMFU(FM) Mount Hope, New York
WXML Upper Sandusky, Ohio
WXVS Waycross, Georgia
KUWP Powell, Wyoming
WKWV Watertown, New York
WKTS Kingston, Tennessee
WCIT-FM Trout Run, Pennsylvania
WZYZ Spencer, Tennessee
KOCU Altus, Oklahoma
WPWV Princeton, West Virginia
KBLW Billings, Montana
WENS Wadesville, Indiana
KKLP La Pine, Oregon
KNSE Austin, Minnesota
WMHQ Malone, New York
WKYP Ledbetter, Kentucky
KHCO Hayden, Colorado
KAJC Salem, Oregon
WKWR Key West, Florida
KHLV Helena, Montana
WJDZ Pastillo, Puerto Rico
KQMC Hawthorne, Nevada
WRYP Wellfleet, Massachusetts
WYQQ Charlton, Massachusetts
KRLU Roswell, New Mexico
KPLI Olympia, Washington
KADU Hibbing, Minnesota
WZPE Bath, North Carolina
WMVE Chase City, Virginia
WJKA Jacksonville, North Carolina
KSFS Sioux Falls, South Dakota
WPRR-FM Clyde Township, Michigan
KXRL Cherry Valley, Arkansas
WYBA Coldwater, Michigan
KILI Porcupine, South Dakota
WDLG Thomasville, Alabama
KUWL Laramie, Wyoming
WFRU Quincy, Florida
WITH Ithaca, New York
KOBN Burns, Oregon
KEEA Aberdeen, South Dakota
WCKU Clarksburg, West Virginia
WOVV Ocracoke, North Carolina
KHRV Hood River, Oregon
WJZZ North Salem, New York
WHBP Harbor Springs, Michigan
KSIH Belcourt, North Dakota
WXIV Lumpkin, Georgia
KSVU Hamilton, Washington
WOXM Middlebury, Vermont
WKYV Colonial Heights, Virginia
KCHB Kaibito, Arizona
WJZZ(FM) North Salem, New York
KNIT Humboldt, Nebraska
WVCS Owen, Wisconsin
KJZP Prescott, Arizona
KOJB Cass Lake, Minnesota
KFJS North Platte, Nebraska

90.3 MHz

KABA Louise, Texas
KAZU Pacific Grove, California
KBJS Jacksonville, Texas
KBMH Holbrook, Arizona
KBSU-FM Boise, Idaho
KBUB Brownwood, Texas
KBUT Crested Butte, Colorado
KBUZ Topeka, Kansas
KCCD Moorhead, Minnesota
KCIF Hilo, Hawaii
KEXP-FM Seattle, Washington
KCRL Sunrise Beach, Missouri
KDVS Davis, California
KEDM Monroe, Louisiana
KEDT-FM Corpus Christi, Texas
KFAI Minneapolis, Minnesota
KFLR-FM Phoenix, Arizona
KFNO Fresno, California
KGNN-FM Cuba, Missouri
KLFV Grand Junction, Colorado
KLCU Ardmore, Oklahoma
KLUH Poplar Bluff, Missouri
KMNE-FM Bassett, Nebraska
KMRO Camarillo, California
KNBA Anchorage, Alaska
KNLG New Bloomfield, Missouri
KNWY Yakima, Washington
KPDR Wheeler, Texas
KPHS Plains, Texas
KRNU Lincoln, Nebraska
KSLC McMinnville, Oregon
KTUH Honolulu, Hawaii
KUWJ Jackson, Wyoming
KVRS Lawton, Oklahoma
KWFH Parker, Arizona
KWIT Sioux City, Iowa
KWUR Clayton, Missouri
KLWO Longview, Washington
WAEF Cordele, Georgia
WYBP Fort Lauderdale, Florida
WAIH Potsdam, New York
WAIJ Grantsville, Maryland
WAMC-FM Albany, New York
WARC Meadville, Pennsylvania
WBCL Fort Wayne, Indiana
WBCR-FM Beloit, Wisconsin
WBHM Birmingham, Alabama
WBLV Twin Lake, Michigan
WBRH Baton Rouge, Louisiana
WKDC-FM Cedarville, Ohio
WCIH Elmira, New York
WCPN Cleveland, Ohio
WCSK Kingsport, Tennessee
WQXW Ossining, New York
WDIH Salisbury, Maryland
WEJF Palm Bay, Florida
WESS East Stroudsburg, Pennsylvania
WFHE Hickory, North Carolina
WFOF Covington, Indiana
WHBM Park Falls, Wisconsin
WHCJ Savannah, Georgia
WHCR-FM New York, New York
WHLA La Crosse, Wisconsin
WHPC Garden City, New York
WHRO-FM Norfolk, Virginia
WJLH Flagler Beach, Florida
WJTL Lancaster, Pennsylvania
WKNJ-FM Union Township, New Jersey
WKNS Kinston, North Carolina
WKRB Brooklyn, New York
WKWC Owensboro, Kentucky
WLVF-FM Haines City, Florida
WMAH-FM Biloxi, Mississippi
WMAV-FM Oxford, Mississippi
WMKY Morehead, Kentucky
WMSC Upper Montclair, New Jersey
WNJZ Cape May Court House, New Jersey
WOTL Toledo, Ohio
WPLN-FM Nashville, Tennessee
WQUB Quincy, Illinois
WXXY Houghton, New York
WRBK Richburg, South Carolina
WRIU Kingston, Rhode Island
WRPR Mahwah, New Jersey
WRST-FM Oshkosh, Wisconsin
WRVD Syracuse, New York
WRXT Roanoke, Virginia
WSSB-FM Orangeburg, South Carolina
WUSI Olney, Illinois
WUTK-FM Knoxville, Tennessee
WUTM Martin, Tennessee
WVIK Rock Island, Illinois
WVPG Parkersburg, West Virginia
WVPH Piscataway, New Jersey
WWPT Westport, Connecticut
WLHI Schnecksville, Pennsylvania
WZBC Newton, Massachusetts
KYLC Lake Charles, Louisiana
KXPC Welches, Oregon
WDYF Dothan, Alabama
KNAG Grand Canyon, Arizona
KMKL North Branch, Minnesota
WJWD Marshall, Wisconsin
KSMW West Plains, Missouri
KWBX Salem, Oregon
KLFS Van Buren, Arkansas
WOKG Galax, Virginia
KTVR-FM La Grande, Oregon
KZJB Pocatello, Idaho
WHRX Nassawadox, Virginia
KGCD Wray, Colorado
KLON Rockaway Beach, Oregon
KELU Clovis, New Mexico
KSGU Saint George, Utah
KJFT Arlee, Montana
KLAI Laytonville, California
KASD Rapid City, South Dakota
KDRI Grants, New Mexico
WKJD Columbus, Indiana
KVLZ Sheridan, Wyoming
WRUN Remsen, New York
WJWR Bloomington, Illinois
WFTE Mount Cobb, Pennsylvania
KSPM Sand Point, Alaska
KMCG McGrath, Alaska
WBOO Morganfield, Kentucky
KYRQ Natalia, Texas
KGCU Port Alsworth, Alaska
WUMI Newberry, Michigan
WWQW(FM) Wartburg, Tennessee
KEIS York, Nebraska
WNJO Toms River, New Jersey
WNGM(FM) Tallulah Falls, Georgia
KPOY(FM) Fraser, Colorado
KBSG Aberdeen, Washington
KPBZ Spokane, Washington
KHEV Fairview, Oklahoma
KANQ Chanute, Kansas
KNJT Coldwater, Kansas
KMGT Circle, Montana
WIGW Eustis, Florida
KCAV Marshall, Arkansas
WWQY Yadkin, North Carolina
WXBP Augusta, Maine
KCSP Casper, Wyoming

90.5 MHz

KACS Rainier, Washington
KADV Modesto, California
KAOG Jonesboro, Arkansas
KAYM Weatherford, Oklahoma
KBAH Plainview, Texas
KBMP Enterprise, Kansas
KBUW Buffalo, Wyoming
KCIE Dulce, New Mexico
KCND Bismarck, North Dakota
KCSU-FM Fort Collins, Colorado
KDNI Duluth, Minnesota
KVOV Carbondale, Colorado

KNGA Saint Peter, Minnesota
KGSP Parkville, Missouri
KHOE Fairfield, Iowa
KHSU Arcata, California
KIBC Burney, California
KSOS Las Vegas, Nevada
KKTO Tahoe City, California
KLCO Newport, Oregon
KLRE-FM Little Rock, Arkansas
KNWV Clarkston, Washington
KNYD Broken Arrow, Oklahoma
KRBW Ottawa, Kansas
KSHU Huntsville, Texas
KSJS San Jose, California
KSMS-FM Point Lookout, Missouri
KZKL Wichita Falls, Texas
KTLF Colorado Springs, Colorado
KTLN Thibodaux, Louisiana
KUAT-FM Tucson, Arizona
KUT Austin, Texas
KUWN Newcastle, Wyoming
KUWZ Rock Springs, Wyoming
KVHS Concord, California
KWCW Walla Walla, Washington
KWMR Point Reyes Station, California
KWWC-FM Columbia, Missouri
KXCV Maryville, Missouri
KXGA Glennallen, Alaska
KZNA Hill City, Kansas
WVRD Zebulon, North Carolina
WANM Tallahassee, Florida
WAPO Mount Vernon, Illinois
WAQL McComb, Mississippi
WASU-FM Boone, North Carolina
WBER Rochester, New York
WBJB-FM Lincroft, New Jersey
WTLD Jesup, Georgia
WBVM Tampa, Florida
WBXL Baldwinsville, New York
WCBE Columbus, Ohio
WCKJ St. Johnsbury, Vermont
WCRH Williamsport, Maryland
WCVH Flemington, New Jersey
WDCC Sanford, North Carolina
WESA Pittsburgh, Pennsylvania
WERG Erie, Pennsylvania
WFRC Columbus, Georgia
WFTF Rutland, Vermont
WHRW Binghamton, New York
WHVT Clyde, Ohio
WICN Worcester, Massachusetts
WIDA-FM Carolina, Puerto Rico
WISE-FM Wise, Virginia
WJFF Jeffersonville, New York
WJSV Morristown, New Jersey
WJYJ Fredericksburg, Virginia
WKAR-FM East Lansing, Michigan
WKHS Worton, Maryland
WMLJ Summersville, West Virginia
WMTH Park Ridge, Illinois
WRTK Paxton, Illinois
WNIU Rockford, Illinois
WPEA Exeter, New Hampshire
WPFF Sturgeon Bay, Wisconsin
WPHN Gaylord, Michigan
WPIM Martinsville, Virginia
WNPR Meriden, Connecticut
WPWB Byron, Georgia
WRTE Chicago, Illinois
WSCT Springfield, Illinois
WSLL Saranac Lake, New York
WSMC-FM Collegedale, Tennessee
WSNC Winston-Salem, North Carolina
WSPS Concord, New Hampshire
WSUC-FM Cortland, New York
WSUP Platteville, Wisconsin
WTHL Somerset, Kentucky
WUMC Elizabethton, Tennessee
WUOG Athens, Georgia
WUOL-FM Louisville, Kentucky
WUSC-FM Columbia, South Carolina
WVBU-FM Lewisburg, Pennsylvania
WVCF Eau Claire, Wisconsin
WVHM Benton, Kentucky
WYQS Mars Hill, North Carolina
WVUM Coral Gables, Florida
WWCU Cullowhee, North Carolina
WWIL-FM Wilmington, North Carolina
WXGN Somers Point, New Jersey
WXXE Fenner, New York
WYFB Gainesville, Florida
WMEP Camden, Maine
KLVW Odessa, Texas
WREH Cypress Quarters, Florida
WVFA Lebanon, New Hampshire
WVML Millersburg, Ohio
KVLB Bend, Oregon
WZRN Norlina, North Carolina
KAGT Abilene, Texas
KZFT Fannett, Texas
WVBV Medford Lakes, New Jersey
WQVI Madison, Mississippi
WQRA Greencastle, Indiana
WGCN Nashville, Georgia
WBUX Buxton, North Carolina
WSMA Scituate, Massachusetts
KGDP-FM Santa Maria, California
WWFP Brigantine, New Jersey
KGIO Astoria, Oregon
WCSO Columbus, Mississippi
KTXG Greenville, Texas
KVCF Freeman, South Dakota
KUEU Logan, Utah
WXKV Selmer, Tennessee
KAIO Idaho Falls, Idaho
KFXU Chickasha, Oklahoma
KNLL Nashville, Arkansas
KJLF Butte, Montana
WDLL Dillon, South Carolina
WRTW Crown Point, Indiana
KRFG Glenwood, Minnesota
WCOQ Colquitt, Georgia
KYCI Firebaugh, California
KCGR Oran, Missouri
WYER Carmi, Illinois
WSLG Gouverneur, New York
WXLQ Bristol, Vermont
WEQP Pamplin City, Virginia
KUFL Libby, Montana
KUHC Clayton, New Mexico
WLNF Rapids, New York
WCOZ Laceyville, Pennsylvania
KBJF Nephi, Utah
WWLN Lincoln, Maine
WTWT Bradford, Pennsylvania
KGVV Goltry, Oklahoma
KKBY Kirby, Wyoming
KFDC Shiprock, New Mexico
KZET Cortez, Colorado
KAUD Mexico, Missouri
WVPL Dozier, Alabama
WZEV Lineville, Alabama
WQLS Camden, Alabama
KFCV Dixon, Missouri
KUFW Phoenix, Arizona

90.7 MHz

KABU Fort Totten, North Dakota
KALX Berkeley, California
KAVW Amarillo, Texas
KAYE-FM Tonkawa, Oklahoma
KTAA Big Sandy, Texas
KBOO Portland, Oregon
KTER Rudolph, Texas
KBPR Brainerd, Minnesota
KGUD Longmont, Colorado
KCIR Twin Falls, Idaho
KYPR Miles City, Montana
KFJM Grand Forks, North Dakota
KFSR Fresno, California
KFXT Sulphur, Oklahoma
KVSR Kirksville, Missouri
KJHK Lawrence, Kansas
KJOV Woodward, Oklahoma
KKUA Wailuku, Hawaii
KLSA Alexandria, Louisiana
KSRI Santa Cruz, California
KNAA Show Low, Arizona
KNOG Nogales, Arizona
KNWR Ellensburg, Washington
KOBC Joplin, Missouri
KPFK Los Angeles, California
KPOR Emporia, Kansas
KRWG Las Cruces, New Mexico
KSDJ Brookings, South Dakota
KSER Everett, Washington
KVNO Omaha, Nebraska
KLMK Marvell, Arkansas
KVRT Victoria, Texas
KWMU St. Louis, Missouri
KLSE Rochester, Minnesota
KZUU Pullman, Washington
KZYX Philo, California
KYWA Wichita, Kansas
WACG-FM Augusta, Georgia
WAUO Hohenwald, Tennessee
WAUS Berrien Springs, Michigan
WAYR-FM Brunswick, Georgia
WCLH Wilkes-Barre, Pennsylvania
WCVK Bowling Green, Kentucky
WEHC Emory, Virginia
WETD Alfred, New York
WEVN Keene, New Hampshire
WFAE Charlotte, North Carolina
WFGH Fort Gay, West Virginia
WFUV New York, New York
WMVM Goodman, Wisconsin
WGCC-FM Batavia, New York
WGLE Lima, Ohio
WWVO Albany, Georgia
WGRW Anniston, Alabama
WHAD Delafield, Wisconsin
WJHD Portsmouth, Rhode Island
WJSC-FM Johnson, Vermont
WKGC-FM Panama City, Florida
WKKL West Barnstable, Massachusetts
WZKV Dyersburg, Tennessee
WKPS State College, Pennsylvania
WKPW Knightstown, Indiana
WKTL Struthers, Ohio
WLJH Grand Gorge, New York
WLMW Manchester, New Hampshire
WMCO New Concord, Ohio
WMFE-FM Orlando, Florida
WZIS(FM) Terre Haute, Indiana
WMRA Harrisonburg, Virginia
WMVV Griffin, Georgia
WNCU Durham, North Carolina
WNFR Sandusky, Michigan
WNMC-FM Traverse City, Michigan
WOTJ Morehead City, North Carolina
WPGL Pattersonville, New York
WPNR-FM Utica, New York
WPSR Evansville, Indiana
WSDL Ocean City, Maryland
WTCC Springfield, Massachusetts
WTIP Grand Marais, Minnesota
WUVT-FM Blacksburg, Virginia
WVAS Montgomery, Alabama
WVKC Galesburg, Illinois
WVMC-FM Mansfield, Ohio
WVMM Grantham, Pennsylvania
WLKV Ripley, West Virginia
WVSS Menomonie, Wisconsin
WVTC Randolph Center, Vermont
WVUA-FM Tuscaloosa, Alabama
WUWG Carrollton, Georgia
WWOZ New Orleans, Louisiana
WPBI(FM) West Palm Beach, Florida
WYFH North Charleston, South Carolina
WYRS Manahawkin, New Jersey
KBSQ McCall, Idaho
WPTJ Paris, Kentucky
KHRI Hollister, California
KAIS(FM) Tracy, California
WCRG Williamsport, Pennsylvania
WRTI Ephrata, Pennsylvania
KOJI Okoboji, Iowa
KMWR Brookings, Oregon
KNSC(FM) Carroll, Iowa
KANL Baker, Oregon
KTEI Placerville, Colorado
KMZO Hamilton, Montana
WFSL Thomasville, Georgia
WBEQ Morris, Illinois
WNRK Norwalk, Ohio
KFRP Coalinga, California
KDRE Sterling, Colorado
KTTK Lebanon, Missouri
WQSG Lafayette, Indiana
KKCJ Cannon Afb, New Mexico
KGFA Great Falls, Montana
WPAI Nanty Glo, Pennsylvania
KNFA Grand Island, Nebraska
KLRM Melbourne, Arkansas
KMPB Breckenridge, Colorado
KTDL Trinidad, Colorado
KEAF Fort Smith, Arkansas
KJKT Spearfish, South Dakota
WYBJ Newton Grove, North Carolina
KTHM Red Bluff, California
WAZU Peoria, Illinois
WGSN Newport, Tennessee
KEZB Beaver, Utah
KOMH Marshall, Minnesota
WRDK Bladenboro, North Carolina
WBHL Harrison, Michigan
WEGB Napeague, New York
KMBV Valentine, Nebraska
WGXC Acra, New York
KOUI Louisville, Mississippi
KJND-FM Williston, North Dakota
KJZK Kingman, Arizona
KMBM Polson, Montana
KRZU Batesville, Texas
KJLC-FM Needles, California
KRBP Rock Creek, California
KRUD Newman, California

90.9 MHz

KAMU-FM College Station, Texas
KASF Alamosa, Colorado
KAVO Pampa, Texas
KBDG Turlock, California
KBSA El Dorado, Arkansas
KCBI Dallas, Texas
KTBG Warrensburg, Missouri
KCSD Sioux Falls, South Dakota
KDSD-FM Pierpont, South Dakota
KGCB Prescott, Arizona
KGZO Shafter, California
KHCT Great Bend, Kansas
KHDC Chualar, California
KWTM June Lake, California
KKCR Hanalei, Hawaii
KKVO Altus, Oklahoma
KLLN Newark, Arkansas
KMDY Keokuk, Iowa
KOKF Edmond, Oklahoma
KPNO Norfolk, Nebraska
KRBM Pendleton, Oregon
KRCL Salt Lake City, Utah
KRCU Cape Girardeau, Missouri
KSHI Zuni, New Mexico
KSJE Farmington, New Mexico
KIKL Lafayette, Louisiana
KSKF Klamath Falls, Oregon
KSLU Hammond, Louisiana
KSPL Kalispell, Montana
KSWP Lufkin, Texas
KTSU Houston, Texas
KUNI Cedar Falls, Iowa
KUWG Gillette, Wyoming
KVNF Paonia, Colorado
KVTI Tacoma, Washington
KWRB Bisbee, Arizona
KXJZ Sacramento, California
KYFS San Antonio, Texas
KKLU Lubbock, Texas
WAMK Kingston, New York
WAQB Tupelo, Mississippi
WAQV Crystal River, Florida
WATP Laurel, Mississippi
WBDG Indianapolis, Indiana
WBSW Marion, Indiana
WBUR-FM Boston, Massachusetts
WCDB Albany, New York
WCNI New London, Connecticut
WCOT Jamestown, New York
WCVJ Jefferson, Ohio
WCWM Williamsburg, Virginia
WCWS-FM Wooster, Ohio
WDCB Glen Ellyn, Illinois
WRCJ-FM Detroit, Michigan
WEKH Hazard, Kentucky
WETA Washington, District of Columbia
WFCO Lancaster, Ohio
WGBE Bryan, Ohio
WGUC Cincinnati, Ohio
WHRM Wausau, Wisconsin
WHYY-FM Philadelphia, Pennsylvania
WILL-FM Urbana, Illinois
WIRQ Rochester, New York
WIRR Virginia-Hibbing, Minnesota
WJAB Huntsville, Alabama
WJIR Key West, Florida
WJNY Watertown, New York
WJRC Lewistown, Pennsylvania
WJWV Fort Gaines, Georgia
WKTZ-FM Jacksonville, Florida
WKUE Elizabethtown, Kentucky
WLGI Hemingway, South Carolina
WMAO-FM Greenwood, Mississippi
WMEH Bangor, Maine

WMPG Gorham, Maine
WNZR Mount Vernon, Ohio
WOAK La Grange, Georgia
WONY Oneonta, New York
WOWB Brewton, Alabama
WQAC Alma, Michigan
WQFS Greensboro, North Carolina
WRAF Toccoa Falls, Georgia
WRQM Rocky Mount, North Carolina
WSCS New London, New Hampshire
WSIF Wilkesboro, North Carolina
WSLO Malone, New York
WSOR Naples, Florida
WSQG-FM Ithaca, New York
WVPM Morgantown, West Virginia
WVVS-FM Valdosta, Georgia
WWMC Lynchburg, Virginia
WWOG Cookeville, Tennessee
KNLN Vienna, Missouri
KUWX Pinedale, Wyoming
KXRT Idabel, Oklahoma
WMSD Rose Township, Michigan
WURI Manteo, North Carolina
KDWG Dillon, Montana
WLFE-FM Key Largo, Florida
WTRK Freeland, Michigan
KLWV Chugwater, Wyoming
KLRV Billings, Montana
KGCL Jordan Valley, Oregon
KAIZ Mesquite, Nevada
KKLW Willmar, Minnesota
KJCH Coos Bay, Oregon
KLOX Creston, Iowa
WCJL Morgantown, Indiana
KPSH Coachella, California
WTCK Charlevoix, Michigan
WOXR Schuyler Falls, New York
KWRC Hermosa, South Dakota
KLTP San Angelo, Texas
KRWA Rye, Colorado
KGCM Belgrade, Montana
WZZH Honesdale, Pennsylvania
KCPB-FM Warrenton, Oregon
KTOL Leadville, Colorado
WCFG Springfield, Michigan
KVDG Midland, Texas
KRLH Hereford, Texas
WSLI Belding, Michigan
WPRH Paris, Tennessee
KRRT Arroyo Seco, New Mexico
KKRH Grangeville, Idaho
KGVB Holliday, Texas
KJWR Windom, Minnesota
KHJJ Shaniko, Oregon
WKMD Madisonville, Kentucky
WNBK Whitmire, South Carolina
WJKZ Hanover, Michigan
WXAF Charleston, West Virginia
WJDD Carrollton, Ohio
WVYN Bluford, Illinois
KJHL Boise City, Oklahoma
KZXZ Wyola, Montana
KOVA Bovina, Texas
WVRI Clifton Forge, Virginia
WUWS Ashland, Wisconsin
KUWW Fort Washakie, Wyoming
WUPJ Escanaba, Michigan
KVNC Mintum, Colorado
WCIS Laporte, Pennsylvania
WQLU Lynchburg, Virginia

91.1 MHz

KANJ Giddings, Texas
KANO Hilo, Hawaii
KANX Sheridan, Arkansas
KANZ Garden City, Kansas
KAOR Vermillion, South Dakota
KAQF Clovis, New Mexico
KAYC Durant, Oklahoma
KBGM Park Hills, Missouri
KKRD Enid, Oklahoma
KBWC Marshall, Texas
KCCM-FM Moorhead, Minnesota
KCFN Wichita, Kansas
KDSC Thousand Oaks, California
KCSM San Mateo, California
KEDP Las Vegas, New Mexico
KISU-FM Pocatello, Idaho
KHKV Kerrville, Texas
KLPR Kearney, Nebraska
KLSU Baton Rouge, Louisiana
KLVY Fairmead, California
KMTC Russellville, Arkansas
KMUD Garberville, California
KMZL Missoula, Montana
KNLB Lake Havasu City, Arizona
KXUL Monroe, Louisiana
KNOW-FM Minneapolis-St. Paul, Minnesota
KOJO Lake Charles, Louisiana
KPBX-FM Spokane, Washington
KRCB-FM Windsor, California
KXRY Portland, Oregon
KSGR Portland, Texas
KSKA Anchorage, Alaska
KSMU Springfield, Missouri
KLCF Truth or Consequence, New Mexico
KSUU Cedar City, Utah
KSWH-FM Arkadelphia, Arkansas
KTAI Kingsville, Texas
KTNE-FM Alliance, Nebraska
KNSH(FM) Fort Dodge, Iowa
KTSD-FM Reliance, South Dakota
KUCV-FM Lincoln, Nebraska
KVER El Paso, Texas
KWAX Eugene, Oregon
KLDV Morrison, Colorado
KWSB-FM Gunnison, Colorado
KWTS Canyon, Texas
KXLC La Crescent, Minnesota
KYBJ Lake Jackson, Texas
KYPL Yakima, Washington
WABR Tifton, Georgia
WAQU Selma, Alabama
WASM Natchez, Mississippi
WAXU Troy, Alabama
WBOR Brunswick, Maine
WBSH Hagerstown, Indiana
WBUQ Bloomsburg, Pennsylvania
WBVC Pomfret, Connecticut
WCYT Lafayette Township, Indiana
WDBX Carbondale, Illinois
WDUB Granville, Ohio
WEDM Indianapolis, Indiana
WEGL Auburn, Alabama
WFMU East Orange, New Jersey
WFUM(FM) Flint, Michigan
WGCS Goshen, Indiana
WGDR Plainfield, Vermont
WGGL-FM Houghton, Michigan
WGSL Loves Park, Illinois
WGTD Kenosha, Wisconsin
WHFC Bel Air, Maryland
WHVP Hudson, New York
WIBI Carlinville, Illinois
WIRE Lebanon, Indiana
WAGE Dogwood Lakes Estate, Florida
WJFP Fort Pierce, Florida
WJJW North Adams, Massachusetts
WJSR Birmingham, Alabama
WKCS Knoxville, Tennessee
WKES Lakeland, Florida
WKNO-FM Memphis, Tennessee
WOVM Appleton, Wisconsin
WMSS Middletown, Pennsylvania
WMSV Starkville, Mississippi
WMUA Amherst, Massachusetts
WNAN Nantucket, Massachusetts
WNSB Norfolk, Virginia
WOKD-FM Danville, Virginia
WOLW Cadillac, Michigan
WOSB Marion, Ohio
WOSE Coshocton, Ohio
WOSS Ossining, New York
WPCJ Pittsford, Michigan
WPIB Bluefield, West Virginia
WPSM Fort Walton Beach, Florida
WREK Atlanta, Georgia
WRMC-FM Middlebury, Vermont
WRMU-FM Alliance, Ohio
WRSH Rockingham, North Carolina
WRTY Jackson Township, Pennsylvania
WRUW-FM Cleveland, Ohio
WCFL(FM) Nashville, Tennessee
WSAJ-FM Grove City, Pennsylvania
WSHU-FM Fairfield, Connecticut
WTKL North Dartmouth, Massachusetts
WSPN Saratoga Springs, New York
WSQE Corning, New York
WSVH Savannah, Georgia
WTJU Charlottesville, Virginia
WKCC Kankakee, Illinois
WTSC-FM Potsdam, New York
WVNH Concord, New Hampshire
WVSU-FM Birmingham, Alabama
WVUB Vincennes, Indiana
WWNJ Toms River Township, New Jersey
WVRP Roanoke Rapids, North Carolina
WYFG Gaffney, South Carolina
WZBT Gettysburg, Pennsylvania
XETRAFM Tijuana, Mexico
KJRF Lawton, Oklahoma
KQPD Ardmore, Oklahoma
KLEU Lewistown, Montana
KBSS Sun Valley, Idaho
KFRJ China Lake, California
WUJC St. Marks, Florida
KGWP Pittsburg, Texas
WYGS Hope, Indiana
KTMK Tillamook, Oregon
WHCE Highland Springs, Virginia
WTSE Benton, Tennessee
WNKV Norco, Louisiana
WKMY Winchendon, Massachusetts
KVKL Las Vegas, Nevada
WUFR Bedford, Pennsylvania
KQXE Eastland, Texas
WZGO Aurora, North Carolina
WYBH Fayetteville, North Carolina
WKAO Ashland, Kentucky
KNSB(FM) Bettendorf, Iowa
KMWY Jackson, Wyoming
WFAZ Goodwater, Alabama
WVPC Franklin, West Virginia
WHMO Madison, Indiana
KHEC Crescent City, California
KZME Brightwood, Oregon
KOFG Cody, Wyoming
KGWB Snyder, Texas
KJOG Cleveland, Oklahoma
WEBK Society Hill, South Carolina
KSJI Saint Joseph, Missouri
WAYU Steele, Alabama
WHYZ Palm Coast, Florida
WVNK Manchester, Vermont
KIKG Licking, Missouri
KOGW Stratford, Texas
WZTH Tusculum, Tennessee
WHMF Marianna, Florida
WBFK Smiths Grove, Kentucky
KCFL Westport, Washington
WMHU Cold Brook, New York
K216FX Mena, Arkansas

91.3 MHz

KAPC Butte, Montana
KAQD Abilene, Texas
KAXR Arkansas City, Kansas
KAYA Hubbard, Nebraska
KDRH King City, California
KBCS Bellevue, Washington
KBIA Columbia, Missouri
KBIY Van Buren, Missouri
KBKN Lamesa, Texas
KCED Centralia, Washington
KCPR San Luis Obispo, California
KDFR Des Moines, Iowa
KDKR Decatur, Texas
KFRB Bakersfield, California
KGLY Tyler, Texas
KGTS College Place, Washington
KIDE Hoopa, California
KMHA Four Bears, North Dakota
KMSA Grand Junction, Colorado
KMSK Austin, Minnesota
KNBJ Bemidji, Minnesota
KNCT-FM Killeen, Texas
KNIS Carson City, Nevada
KOAB-FM Bend, Oregon
KXWT Odessa, Texas
KPVU Prairie View, Texas
KRSC-FM Claremore, Oklahoma
KNCM Appleton, Minnesota
KSCL Shreveport, Louisiana
KSUT Ignacio, Colorado
KSUW Sheridan, Wyoming
KTLX Columbus, Nebraska
KUAF Fayetteville, Arkansas
KUCA Conway, Arkansas
KUOP Stockton, California
KUWA Afton, Wyoming
KUWC Casper, Wyoming
KUWS Superior, Wisconsin
KVFM Beeville, Texas
KVLU Beaumont, Texas
KXCI Tucson, Arizona
KZLV Lytle, Texas
WAKJ Defuniak Springs, Florida
WAPS Akron, Ohio
WATY Folkston, Georgia
WFIX Florence, Alabama
WBNY Buffalo, New York
WCHW-FM Bay City, Michigan
WCNY-FM Syracuse, New York
WCPI McMinnville, Tennessee
WCSG Grand Rapids, Michigan
WCUW Worcester, Massachusetts
WDJM-FM Framingham, Massachusetts
WDOM Providence, Rhode Island
WESM Princess Anne, Maryland
WEVH Hanover, New Hampshire
WFHB Bloomington, Indiana
WFQS Franklin, North Carolina
WGRC Lewisburg, Pennsylvania
WGTE-FM Toledo, Ohio
WHEM Eau Claire, Wisconsin
WHHI Highland, Wisconsin
WHIF Palatka, Florida
WHIL-FM Mobile, Alabama
WHJE Carmel, Indiana
WHQR Wilmington, North Carolina
WIPR-FM San Juan, Puerto Rico
WIUM Macomb, Illinois
WIUV Castleton, Vermont
WJTG Fort Valley, Georgia
WKMS-FM Murray, Kentucky
WKNH Keene, New Hampshire
WLCH Lancaster, Pennsylvania
WMLU Farmville, Virginia
WLFA Asheville, North Carolina
WLMU Harrogate, Tennessee
WLRN-FM Miami, Florida
WLTR Columbia, South Carolina
WLVR-FM Bethlehem, Pennsylvania
WMEW Waterville, Maine
WMPN-FM Jackson, Mississippi
WNDY Crawfordsville, Indiana
WNIW La Salle, Illinois
WOES Ovid-Elsie, Michigan
WOLN Olean, New York
WOLR Lake City, Florida
WOUB-FM Athens, Ohio
WPAR Salem, Virginia
WQAB Philippi, West Virginia
WQLN-FM Erie, Pennsylvania
WRLI-FM Southampton, New York
WRTQ Ocean City, New Jersey
WSEB Englewood, Florida
WSGR-FM Port Huron, Michigan
WSHL-FM Easton, Massachusetts
WTBJ Oxford, Alabama
WTRM Winchester, Virginia
WTSR Trenton, New Jersey
WUKY Lexington, Kentucky
WUNH Durham, New Hampshire
WUTS Sewanee, Tennessee
WVKR-FM Poughkeepsie, New York
WVOB Dothan, Alabama
WVST-FM Petersburg, Virginia
WVUD Newark, Delaware
WWHI Muncie, Indiana
WYFZ Belleview, Florida
WWUH West Hartford, Connecticut
WXAC Reading, Pennsylvania
WXLH Blue Mountain Lake, New York
WXPL Fitchburg, Massachusetts
WHGO Hertford, North Carolina
WXRI Winston-Salem, North Carolina
WYEP-FM Pittsburgh, Pennsylvania
WYSO Yellow Springs, Ohio
WZMB Greenville, North Carolina
KBSJ Jackpot, Nevada
WCKZ Orland, Indiana
KUWT Thermopolis, Wyoming
KANV Olsburg, Kansas
WJCO Montpelier, Indiana
WJCZ Milford, Illinois
WSTM Kiel, Wisconsin
KNYR Yreka, California
KLZV Brush, Colorado
KWTH Barstow, California
KYJC Commerce, Texas
WJOG Good Hart, Michigan
WSLE Salem, Illinois
KLRY Gypsum, Colorado

KSVY Sonoma, California
KAKO Ada, Oklahoma
WHFG Broussard, Louisiana
KTPF Salida, Colorado
WWDL Plainfield, Indiana
KKLB Ruidoso, New Mexico
WFMR Orleans, Massachusetts
KFLF Somers, Montana
KAWN Winslow, Arizona
WNON Warfield, Kentucky
KMHS-FM Coos Bay, Oregon
WIOX Roxbury, New York
WSJE Summersville, West Virginia
WBNB Equality, Alabama
KOGB McGrath, Alaska
KPKO Pecos, Texas
WNGB Petersham, Massachusetts
KRRA Paragonah, Utah
KXDS Santa Clara, Utah
KOPA(FM) Pala, California
WGMR Effingham, Illinois
KKJD Borrego Springs, California
WCIN-FM Tunkhannock, Pennsylvania
WTZY Wonder Lake, Illinois
WSJA York, Georgia

91.5 MHz

KAJX Aspen, Colorado
KALR Hot Springs, Arkansas
KANU Lawrence, Kansas
KARF Independence, Kansas
KASK Fairfield, California
KBAN DeRidder, Louisiana
KBCX Big Spring, Texas
KBSX Boise, Idaho
KCAS McCook, Texas
KCFB St. Cloud, Minnesota
KCMH Mountain Home, Arkansas
KFLQ Albuquerque, New Mexico
KGRM Grambling, Louisiana
KIOS-FM Omaha, Nebraska
KJZZ Phoenix, Arizona
KKUP Cupertino, California
KLWS Moses Lake, Washington
KNCC Elko, Nevada
KGAC Saint Peter, Minnesota
KNSU Thibodaux, Louisiana
KOPB-FM Portland, Oregon
KPAE Erwinville, Louisiana
KPLG Plains, Montana
KPRJ Jamestown, North Dakota
KQMN Thief River Falls, Minnesota
KRCC Colorado Springs, Colorado
KRNE-FM Merriman, Nebraska
KRUX Las Cruces, New Mexico
KRVH Rio Vista, California
KSIV-FM St. Louis, Missouri
KSJD Cortez, Colorado
KSJV Fresno, California
KSNS Medicine Lodge, Kansas
KSRS Roseburg, Oregon
KSTN-FM Redding, California
KSUA Fairbanks, Alaska
KSYE Frederick, Oklahoma
KTXK Texarkana, Texas
KUBS Newport, Washington
KUNC Greeley, Colorado
KUNV Las Vegas, Nevada
KNSM(FM) Mason City, Iowa
KUSC Los Angeles, California
KUSU-FM Logan, Utah
KVAZ Henryetta, Oklahoma
KBYR-FM Rexburg, Idaho
KWLD Plainview, Texas
KWVZ Florence, Oregon
KYDS Sacramento, California
KNHM Bayside, California
KZYZ Willits, California
WAPN Holly Hill, Florida
WARN Culpeper, Virginia
WAVI Oxford, Mississippi
WJBP Red Bank, Tennessee
WBEZ Chicago, Illinois
WBFI McDaniels, Kentucky
WBIE Delphos, Ohio
WBIM-FM Bridgewater, Massachusetts
WBJC Baltimore, Maryland
WBJD Atlantic Beach, North Carolina
WCIC Pekin, Illinois
WGLY-FM Bolton, Vermont
WCVY Coventry, Rhode Island
WDBK Blackwood, New Jersey
WEBT Langdale, Alabama
WECI Richmond, Indiana
WEMY Green Bay, Wisconsin
WFHU Henderson, Tennessee
WFMQ Lebanon, Tennessee
WFSQ Tallahassee, Florida
WGLZ West Liberty, West Virginia
WGPH Vidalia, Georgia
WGRE Greencastle, Indiana
WGRS Guilford, Connecticut
WHCB Bristol, Tennessee
WICA Traverse City, Michigan
WJHS Columbia City, Indiana
WJLR Seymour, Indiana
WUML Lowell, Massachusetts
WJYO Fort Myers, Florida
WKCL Ladson, South Carolina
WKHR Bainbridge, Ohio
WKRJ New Philadelphia, Ohio
WCIE New Port Richey, Florida
WLUR Lexington, Virginia
WMFO Medford, Massachusetts
WMHC South Hadley, Massachusetts
WMHW-FM Mount Pleasant, Michigan
WMIE-FM Cocoa, Florida
WMLN-FM Milton, Massachusetts
WNIQ Sterling, Illinois
WNRZ Dickson, Tennessee
WNYE New York, New York
WOBC-FM Oberlin, Ohio
WOSP Portsmouth, Ohio
WPIN-FM Dublin, Virginia
WPRK Winter Park, Florida
WPSU State College, Pennsylvania
WRBC Lewiston, Maine
WRFT Indianapolis, Indiana
WRPI Troy, New York
WSDH Sandwich, Massachusetts
WSGN Gadsden, Alabama
WSQX-FM Binghamton, New York
WSRN-FM Swarthmore, Pennsylvania
WSTF Andalusia, Alabama
WTBI-FM Greenville, South Carolina
WTUL New Orleans, Louisiana
WUAL-FM Tuscaloosa, Alabama
WUEV Evansville, Indiana
WUNC Chapel Hill, North Carolina
WUPX Marquette, Michigan
WVCT Keavy, Kentucky
WVHC Herkimer, New York
WWEV-FM Cumming, Georgia
WWLR Lyndonville, Vermont
WXXI-FM Rochester, New York
WYCS Yorktown, Virginia
WZLY Wellesley, Massachusetts
KUWD Sundance, Wyoming
WVCM Iron Mountain, Michigan
WFWR Attica, Indiana
WTML Tullahoma, Tennessee
KRQZ Lompoc, California
KNWF Fergus Falls, Minnesota
WRSG Middlebourne, West Virginia
KTXP Bushland, Texas
WJCY Cicero, Indiana
KAIA Bloomfield, Missouri
KHVT Bloomington, Texas
WLRK Greenville, Mississippi
WJOH Raco, Michigan
WLHW Casey, Illinois
KAFH Great Falls, Montana
KHML Madisonville, Texas
WHKC Columbus, Ohio
WKWM Marathon, Florida
WCIM Shenandoah, Pennsylvania
WGTT Emeralda, Florida
KBLC Fredericksburg, Texas
KYFB Denison, Texas
WPJW Hurricane, West Virginia
WPSF Clewiston, Florida
WCNB Dayton, Indiana
KRGO Alton, Iowa
KVHR Van Horn, Texas
KSNB Norton, Kansas
WFBK Fort Mill, South Carolina
KNWU Forks, Washington
KSQM Sequim, Washington
WANH Meredith, New Hampshire
KBDW Wheeler, Texas
WPEF Kentwood, Louisiana
WTYG Sparr, Florida
KTML South Fork, Colorado
WPBD Lewes, Delaware
KFBR Gerlach, Nevada
WJGS Norwood, Georgia

91.6 kHz

KLPX Tucsun, Nevada

91.7 MHz

KALW San Francisco, California
KAPM Alexandria, Louisiana
KARG Poteau, Oklahoma
KAXE Grand Rapids, Minnesota
KNBX San Ardo, California
KBDO Des Arc, Arkansas
KBLD Kennewick, Washington
KBNJ Corpus Christi, Texas
KBSM McCall, Idaho
KBSW Twin Falls, Idaho
KXOT Tacoma, Washington
KCHO Chico, California
KCOZ Point Lookout, Missouri
KCVO-FM Camdenton, Missouri
KCVS Salina, Kansas
KDOV Medford, Oregon
KEMC Billings, Montana
KEOL La Grande, Oregon
KGLP Gallup, New Mexico
KHCS Palm Desert, California
KHBW Brownwood, Texas
KJIR Hannibal, Missouri
KLNR Panaca, Nevada
KZSE Rochester, Minnesota
KLSP Angola, Louisiana
KMVC Marshall, Missouri
KNAD Page, Arizona
KPUB Flagstaff, Arizona
KNEO Neosho, Missouri
KNWD Natchitoches, Louisiana
KOHS Orem, Utah
KOOP Hornsby, Texas
KOSU Stillwater, Oklahoma
KOTO Telluride, Colorado
KPNE-FM North Platte, Nebraska
KPSU Goodwell, Oklahoma
KRFA-FM Moscow, Idaho
KRMC Douglas, Arizona
KRTU-FM San Antonio, Texas
KSUI Iowa City, Iowa
KTPH Tonopah, Nevada
KUFR Salt Lake City, Utah
KUHM Helena, Montana
KLAG Alamogordo, New Mexico
KVRX Austin, Texas
KXSR Groveland, California
KZAZ Bellingham, Washington
WAJS Tupelo, Mississippi
WAOY Gulfport, Mississippi
WAPD Campbellsville, Kentucky
WAQG Ozark, Alabama
WAVM Maynard, Massachusetts
WBGL Champaign, Illinois
WBJW Albion, Illinois
WBKU Ahoskie, North Carolina
WBSJ Portland, Indiana
WBSL-FM Sheffield, Massachusetts
WCCV Cartersville, Georgia
WGLV Woodstock, Vermont
WCML-FM Alpena, Michigan
WCUC-FM Clarion, Pennsylvania
WCUR West Chester, Pennsylvania
WDEQ-FM De Graff, Ohio
WEEM-FM Pendleton, Indiana
WEGS Milton, Florida
WEMC Harrisonburg, Virginia
WETL South Bend, Indiana
WFCM-FM Murfreesboro, Tennessee
WFRH Kingston, New York
WFTI-FM St. Petersburg, Florida
WNNZ-FM Westfield, Massachusetts
WHRS Cookeville, Tennessee
WHUS Storrs, Connecticut
WICB Ithaca, New York
WIWC Kokomo, Indiana
WIXQ Millersville, Pennsylvania
WJAZ Summerdale, Pennsylvania
WJIC Zanesville, Ohio
WJLF Gainesville, Florida
WKDU Philadelphia, Pennsylvania
WLBS Bristol, Pennsylvania
WLFR Pomona, New Jersey
WLPE Augusta, Georgia
WLPG Florence, South Carolina
WMCN St. Paul, Minnesota
WMKO Marco, Florida
WMPH Wilmington, Delaware
WMSE Milwaukee, Wisconsin
WMUH Allentown, Pennsylvania
WMWM Salem, Massachusetts
WNEC-FM Henniker, New Hampshire
WOSR Middletown, New York
WOSV Mansfield, Ohio
WPAL Laporte, Pennsylvania
WPCR-FM Plymouth, New Hampshire
WPRL Lorman, Mississippi
WRLC Williamsport, Pennsylvania
WRTX Dover, Delaware
WRVJ Watertown, New York
WSGE Dallas, North Carolina
WSHD Eastport, Maine
WSHS Sheboygan, Wisconsin
WSQC-FM Oneonta, New York
WSUM Madison, Wisconsin
WSUW Whitewater, Wisconsin
WTJB Columbus, Georgia
WUGA Athens, Georgia
WUMR Memphis, Tennessee
WUNV Albany, Georgia
WUOM Ann Arbor, Michigan
WVIJ Port Charlotte, Florida
WVMW-FM Scranton, Pennsylvania
WVPB Beckley, West Virginia
WVSD Itta Bena, Mississippi
WVXU Cincinnati, Ohio
WWET Valdosta, Georgia
WWFR Stuart, Florida
WWHR Bowling Green, Kentucky
WWJD Pippa Passes, Kentucky
WWVU-FM Morgantown, West Virginia
WXCI Danbury, Connecticut
WNJR Washington, Pennsylvania
WXPR Rhinelander, Wisconsin
WYFD Decatur, Alabama
WYTN Youngstown, Ohio
WNNV San German, Puerto Rico
KTGW Fruitland, New Mexico
KDUW Douglas, Wyoming
KSVR Mount Vernon, Washington
WMCQ Muskegon, Michigan
WVNL Vandalia, Illinois
WNEF Newburyport, Massachusetts
KCVX Salem, Missouri
KZAN Hays, Kansas
KBFR Bismarck, North Dakota
WAPB Madison, Florida
WPIL Heflin, Alabama
WJVK Owensboro, Kentucky
WDKV Fond Du Lac, Wisconsin
WSQH Decatur, Mississippi
KPCV Portales, New Mexico
KFHL Wasco, California
WJWT Gardner, Massachusetts
WYTL Wyomissing, Pennsylvania
WJPR Jasper, Indiana
KNSW Worthington-Marshall, Minnesota
KMSL Mansfield, Louisiana
WFFL Panama City, Florida
KTSG Steamboat Springs, Colorado
KSQS Ririe, Idaho
KPBR Poplar Bluff, Missouri
KVLP Tucumcari, New Mexico
KTDA Dalhart, Texas
WJFH Sebring, Florida
WZXH Hagerstown, Maryland
KOBH Hobbs, New Mexico
WWEM Rustburg, Virginia
WMVW Peachtree City, Georgia
KGCN Roswell, New Mexico
KCCS Starkville, Colorado
WYJZ Fearsville, Kentucky
KPIT Pittsburg, Texas
KAHU Pahala, Hawaii
KMLL Marysville, Kansas
KRKM Fort Washakie, Wyoming
KNDW Williston, North Dakota
WNFC Paducah, Kentucky
KOLJ-FM Warroad, Minnesota
WXLB Boonville, New York
WZKL Woodstock, Illinois
WNGM(FM) Tallulah Falls, Georgia
WUMM Machias, Maine
KEJA Cale, Arkansas

KLSB Norfolk, Nebraska
KAMF Tulare, South Dakota
WRVX Cameron, Missouri
WPAL(FM) Laporte, Pennsylvania
KEYV Vernal, Utah
KEYR Richfield, Utah
WLNJ Lakehurst, New Jersey
KPPD Devils Lake, North Dakota
WHTD Tallulah Falls, Georgia
WZCA Quebradillas, Puerto Rico
KMNO Wailuku, Hawaii
KYFQ Tacoma, Washington
WVMU Ashtabula, Ohio

91.9 MHz

KAQA Kilauea, Hawaii
KASU Jonesboro, Arkansas
KAVX Lufkin, Texas
KAXV Bastrop, Louisiana
KBCW-FM McAlester, Oklahoma
KBDD Winfield, Kansas
KBHZ Willmar, Minnesota
KXBR International Falls, Minnesota
KBPB Harrison, Arkansas
KBRW-FM Barrow, Alaska
KCFP Pueblo, Colorado
KCNE-FM Chadron, Nebraska
KCSB-FM Santa Barbara, California
KCSS Turlock, California
KDLL Kenai, Alaska
KDNA Yakima, Washington
KDNE Crete, Nebraska
KLXV Glenwood Springs, Colorado
KDSU Fargo, North Dakota
KDUR Durango, Colorado
KGLT Bozeman, Montana
KHSR Crescent City, California
KLVR Middletown, California
KLWD Gillette, Wyoming
KMRL Buras, Louisiana
KMUN Astoria, Oregon
KJLG Emporia, Kansas
KQOH Marshfield, Missouri
KONQ Dodge City, Kansas
KPCW Park City, Utah
KPFC Callisburg, Texas
KRVM-FM Eugene, Oregon
KSDA-FM Agat, Guam
KSDB-FM Manhattan, Kansas
KSFC Spokane, Washington
KSPB Pebble Beach, California
KQSD-FM Lowry, South Dakota
KSSU Durant, Oklahoma
KTCC Colby, Kansas
KUDU Tok, Alaska
KUFN Hamilton, Montana
KUHB-FM St. Paul, Alaska
KUWR Laramie, Wyoming
KVCR San Bernardino, California
KWJC Liberty, Missouri
KWRV Sun Valley, Idaho
KWSC Wayne, Nebraska
KWSO Warm Springs, Oregon
KXRJ Russellville, Arkansas
KXRI Amarillo, Texas
KYRM Yuma, Arizona
WAAE New Bern, North Carolina
WAIC Springfield, Massachusetts
WHOJ Terre Haute, Indiana
WAPX-FM Clarksville, Tennessee
WASW Waycross, Georgia
WAUM Duck Hill, Mississippi
WLFS Port Wentworth, Georgia
WAYL St. Augustine, Florida
WBHZ Elkins, West Virginia
WBPR Worcester, Massachusetts
WCEL Plattsburgh, New York
WCLK Atlanta, Georgia
WEMI Appleton, Wisconsin
WFPB-FM Falmouth, Massachusetts
WFPK Louisville, Kentucky
WFSS Fayetteville, North Carolina
WFWM Frostburg, Maryland
WGDE Defiance, Ohio
WGIB Eirmingham, Alabama
WGTS Takoma Park, Maryland
WHDI Sister Bay, Wisconsin
WJCH Joliet, Illinois
WJEF Lafayette, Indiana
WJIF Opp, Alabama
WKCO Gambier, Ohio
WLBL-FM Wausau, Wisconsin
WLJS-FM Jacksonville, Alabama
WLKP Belpre, Ohio
WMBV Dixons Mills, Alabama
WMEB-FM Orono, Maine
WHKU Proctorville, Ohio
WMKL Hammocks, Florida
WMTU-FM Houghton, Michigan
WNGN Argyle, New York
WNRN Charlottesville, Virginia
WNTI Hackettstown, New Jersey
WORW Port Huron, Michigan
WOUH-FM Chillicothe, Ohio
WOWL Burnsville, Mississippi
WOZQ Northampton, Massachusetts
WPHP Wheeling, West Virginia
WQKO Howe, Indiana
WRCM Wingate, North Carolina
WRVN Utica, New York
WSCF-FM Vero Beach, Florida
WSHR Lake Ronkonkoma, New York
WSIU Carbondale, Illinois
WSLX New Canaan, Connecticut
WUIS Springfield, Illinois
WUMB-FM Boston, Massachusetts
WUOT Knoxville, Tennessee
WCAL California, Pennsylvania
WVGS Statesboro, Georgia
WVSH Huntington, Indiana
WVTR Marion, Virginia
WHGN Crystal River, Florida
WXPW Wausau, Wisconsin
WYFO Lakeland, Florida
WYFP Harpswell, Maine
WVME Meadville, Pennsylvania
WCMK Putney, Vermont
KOHN Sells, Arizona
KWBI Great Bend, Kansas
KESY Baker City, Oregon
KSRD St. Joseph, Missouri
KHKL Laytonville, California
KHCJ Jefferson, Texas
WKVH Monticello, Florida
KWTD Ridgecrest, California
KNLK Santa Rosa, New Mexico
KVJC Globe, Arizona
KNLQ Cuba, Missouri
KFRW Great Falls, Montana
KLLR Dripping Springs, Texas
KMEO Mertzon, Texas
WCFM Williamstown, Massachusetts
WDPW Greenville, Michigan
KCKR Church Point, Louisiana
KTDV State Center, Iowa
WMJC Richland, Michigan
KXFR Socorro, New Mexico
KHPO Port O'Connor, Texas
KLKI Dolan Springs, Arizona
WITT Zionsville, Indiana
KHED Arkadelphia, Arkansas
WXMF Marion, Ohio
KRRE Las Vegas, New Mexico
WBNJ Barnegat, New Jersey
KRAR Espanola, New Mexico
KPGA Morton, Texas
KTYN Thayne, Wyoming
WMYE Fort Myers, Florida
WWRA Clinton, Louisiana
WHDD-FM Sharon, Connecticut
KIAM-FM North Nenana, Alaska
KJOL-FM Montrose, Colorado
WKJA Brunswick, Ohio
WRAO Wisconsin Rapids, Wisconsin
KTTE Springfield, Colorado
KLDB Beaver, Oklahoma
WBRQ La Grange, Georgia
WZRG(FM) Kulpmont, Pennsylvania
KELC Hawthorne, Nevada
WVMR-FM Hillsboro, West Virginia
KLDD McCloud, California
WRFI Watkins Glen, New York
WXHM Middletown, Delaware
WKRI Cokesbury, South Carolina
KPTZ Port Townsend, Washington
KCKV Kirksville, Missouri
KQNY Quincy, California
WGCP Cadillac, Michigan
WGBQ Lynchburg, Tennessee
KEYD Delta, Utah
WRLN Rushville, Indiana
KEYP Price, Utah
WZZG Toomsboro, Georgia
WSMP New Hebron, Mississippi
KSJU Friday Harbor, Washington
KHEB Granite, Oklahoma
WDRT Viroqua, Wisconsin
WDSV Greenville, Mississippi
WHRE Eastville, Virginia
WVSE Christiansted, Virgin Islands
KJGS Aurora, Nebraska
KLZR Westcliffe, Colorado
KGNR John Day, Oregon
K220EO Hilo, Hawaii

92.1 Hz

WEZY Janesville, Wisconsin

92.1 MHz

KHWI Holualoa, Hawaii
KATK-FM Carlsbad, New Mexico
KTHN La Junta, Colorado
KCHE-FM Cherokee, Iowa
KCRK-FM Colville, Washington
KCZO Carrizo Springs, Texas
KKCM Thermal, California
KDQN-FM De Queen, Arkansas
KQSM-FM Fayetteville, Arkansas
KKDV Walnut Creek, California
KFMA Green Valley, Arizona
KFRZ Green River, Wyoming
KSOQ-FM Escondido, California
KFXI Marlow, Oklahoma
KHOS-FM Sonora, Texas
KHPQ Clinton, Arkansas
KJMN Castle Rock, Colorado
KKOZ-FM Ava, Missouri
KVMX Bakersfield, California
KLIL Moreauville, Louisiana
KSYR Benton, Louisiana
KLQP Madison, Minnesota
KMFC Centralia, Missouri
KMOE Butler, Missouri
KMZA-FM Seneca, Kansas
KMZE Woodward, Oklahoma
KNBT New Braunfels, Texas
KTBT Broken Arrow, Oklahoma
KOPY-FM Alice, Texas
KBBO-FM Houston, Alaska
KYLR Hutto, Texas
KREP Belleville, Kansas
KRLS Knoxville, Iowa
KTSR De Quincy, Louisiana
KROI Seabrook, Texas
KRUE Waseca, Minnesota
KSBS-FM Pago Pago, American Samoa
KWFP Sparks, Nevada
KXBN Cedar City, Utah
KSYD Reedsport, Oregon
KTCE Payson, Utah
KTFW-FM Glen Rose, Texas
KTNR Kenedy, Texas
KZLB Fort Dodge, Iowa
KUMA-FM Pilot Rock, Oregon
KVCL-FM Winnfield, Louisiana
KWVR-FM Enterprise, Oregon
KXEZ Farmersville, Texas
KOND Clovis, California
KZRX Dickinson, North Dakota
KMJE Placerville, California
KZUA Holbrook, Arizona
WBHC-FM Hampton, South Carolina
WBIK Pleasant City, Ohio
WBKN Brookhaven, Mississippi
WBST Muncie, Indiana
WBTR-FM Carrollton, Georgia
WXEX-FM Sanford, Maine
WCDX Mechanicsville, Virginia
WCKR Hornell, New York
WCSR-FM Hillsdale, Michigan
WDDQ Adel, Georgia
WLTQ-FM Venice, Florida
WDIC-FM Clinchco, Virginia
WDLA-FM Walton, New York
WZET Hormigueros, Puerto Rico
WERH-FM Hamilton, Alabama
WEUZ Minor Hill, Tennessee
WVTY Racine, Wisconsin
WFGF Wapakoneta, Ohio
WFPS Freeport, Illinois
WAFZ-FM Immokalee, Florida
WGHN-FM Grand Haven, Michigan
WJHT Johnstown, Pennsylvania
WIDL Cass City, Michigan
WWNU Irmo, South Carolina
WJGA-FM Jackson, Georgia
WJJN Columbia, Alabama
WJMG Hattiesburg, Mississippi
WJNS-FM Bentonia, Mississippi
WJXR Macclenny, Florida
WMYB Myrtle Beach, South Carolina
WTWS Houghton Lake, Michigan
WKPL Ellwood City, Pennsylvania
WKUL Cullman, Alabama
WLBW Fenwick Island, Delaware
WLNG Sag Harbor, New York
WLTU Manitowoc, Wisconsin
WXXM Sun Prairie, Wisconsin
WMEQ-FM Menomonie, Wisconsin
WECQ Destin, Florida
WMNC-FM Morganton, North Carolina
WMOO Derby Center, Vermont
WYVK Middleport, Ohio
WMSU Starkville, Mississippi
WNFK Perry, Florida
WDER-FM Peterborough, New Hampshire
WQKQ Carthage, Illinois
WOHF Bellevue, Ohio
WNUZ Mercersburg, Pennsylvania
WOMR Provincetown, Massachusetts
WPEH-FM Louisville, Georgia
WPTS-FM Pittsburgh, Pennsylvania
WQQK Goodlettsville, Tennessee
WRJC-FM Mauston, Wisconsin
WRLX West Palm Beach, Florida
WRNQ Poughkeepsie, New York
WROI Rochester, Indiana
WROU-FM West Carrollton, Ohio
WRSV Elm City, North Carolina
WSEN-FM Baldwinsville, New York
WSQV(FM) Lock Haven, Pennsylvania
WBVX Carlisle, Kentucky
WHBT-FM Moyock, North Carolina
WTKY-FM Tompkinsville, Kentucky
WTPA Palmyra, Pennsylvania
WUMS University, Mississippi
WUPI Presque Isle, Maine
WHPD Dowagiac, Michigan
WVLT Vineland, New Jersey
WVWC Buckhannon, West Virginia
WWAX Hermantown, Minnesota
WQTX St. Johns, Michigan
WWGO Charleston, Illinois
WWHS-FM Hampden-Sydney, Virginia
WLHR-FM Lavonia, Georgia
WVTK Port Henry, New York
WYRQ-FM Little Falls, Minnesota
WZDM Vincennes, Indiana
WZEW Fairhope, Alabama
KIBX Bonners Ferry, Idaho
KCVZ Dixon, Missouri
KEGE Pocatello, Idaho
WYAS Luquillo, Puerto Rico
WKXY Merigold, Mississippi
KBRY Sargent, Nebraska
WHHR Vienna, Georgia
WMIS-FM Blackduck, Minnesota
KXJO St. Maries, Idaho
KRWR Tyler, Texas

92.3 MHz

KWRZ Canyonville, Oregon
KYOY Hillsdale, Wyoming
KCCV-FM Olathe, Kansas
KCUL-FM Marshall, Texas
KETX-FM Livingston, Texas
KEZO-FM Omaha, Nebraska
KGON Portland, Oregon
KIIZ-FM Killeen, Texas
KIJN-FM Farwell, Texas
KIPR Pine Bluff, Arkansas
KRNH Kerrville, Texas
KIZN Boise, Idaho
KMOZ-FM Grand Junction, Colorado
KRRL Los Angeles, California
KTAR-FM Glendale, Arizona
KYUS-FM Miles City, Montana
KSTH Holyoke, Colorado
KNRG New Ulm, Texas
KNFM Midland, Texas
KKHQ-FM Oelwein, Iowa
KFTI-FM Newton, Kansas
KOFX El Paso, Texas
KOMP Las Vegas, Nevada

KKMT Ronan, Montana
KRED Eureka, California
KREU Roland, Oklahoma
KRST Albuquerque, New Mexico
KSDL Sedalia, Missouri
KSJO San Jose, California
KSSK-FM Waipahu, Hawaii
KSVL Smith, Nevada
KMYY Rayville, Louisiana
KTTN-FM Trenton, Missouri
KZUS Ephrata, Washington
KQVT Victoria, Texas
KVRH-FM Salida, Colorado
KWCD Bisbee, Arizona
KXRA-FM Alexandria, Minnesota
WAEG Evans, Georgia
WZPW Peoria, Illinois
WBNZ Frankfort, Michigan
WRKN LaPlace, Louisiana
WCMQ-FM Hialeah, Florida
WCOL-FM Columbus, Ohio
WDEF-FM Chattanooga, Tennessee
WERQ-FM Baltimore, Maryland
WFLY Troy, New York
WOWO-FM Fort Wayne, Indiana
WGXL Hanover, New Hampshire
WIL-FM St. Louis, Missouri
WJMQ Clintonville, Wisconsin
WJPD Ishpeming, Michigan
WKRR Asheboro, North Carolina
WKVR-FM Huntingdon, Pennsylvania
WLWI-FM Montgomery, Alabama
WMME-FM Augusta, Maine
WMOQ Bostwick, Georgia
WMXD Detroit, Michigan
WNBQ Mansfield, Pennsylvania
WZPR Nags Head, North Carolina
WOSQ Spencer, Wisconsin
WLZN Macon, Georgia
WPRO Providence, Rhode Island
WQSL Jacksonville, North Carolina
WRLS-FM Hayward, Wisconsin
WRRN Warren, Pennsylvania
WZAQ Louisa, Kentucky
WSGA Hinesville, Georgia
WTYD Deltaville, Virginia
WTTS Bloomington, Indiana
WWHQ Oakland, Maryland
WWKA Orlando, Florida
WXLK Roanoke, Virginia
WPWX Hammond, Indiana
WYGE London, Kentucky
WYNU Milan, Tennessee
WKRK-FM Cleveland Heights, Ohio
WXCR New Martinsville, West Virginia
WQLI Meigs, Georgia
KSAR Thayer, Missouri
WOHT Grenada, Mississippi
KQRQ Rapid City, South Dakota
WBMP New York, New York
WVSL-FM Riverside, Pennsylvania

92.5 Hz

WBWI Janesville, Wisconsin

92.5 MHz

KAAR Butte, Montana
KAYX Richmond, Missouri
KMYX-FM Arvin, California
KHTA Wake Village, Texas
KXXE-FM San Augustine, Texas
KCRT-FM Trinidad, Colorado
KCUA Naples, Utah
KCVT Silver Lake, Kansas
KSRW Independence, California
KKAL Paso Robles, California
KWOF Broomfield, Colorado
KELE-FM Mountain Grove, Missouri
KTWB Sioux Falls, South Dakota
KKHA Markham, Texas
KBEB Sacramento, California
KJJY West Des Moines, Iowa
KBRE Atwater, California
KKWQ Warroad, Minnesota
KLAD-FM Klamath Falls, Oregon
KQMV Bellevue, Washington
KWUP Navasota, Texas
KOMA Oklahoma City, Oklahoma
KPQX Havre, Montana
KPRV-FM Heavener, Oklahoma
KQMA Phillipsburg, Kansas
KQRS Golden Valley, Minnesota
KRPT Devine, Texas
KSMR Winona, Minnesota
KSYN Joplin, Missouri
KCOL-FM Groves, Texas
KTHQ Eagar, Arizona
KMWX Abilene, Texas
KUUU South Jordan, Utah
KVPI-FM Ville Platte, Louisiana
KWYN-FM Wynne, Arkansas
KXKK Park Rapids, Minnesota
KYKM Yoakum, Texas
KZHR Dayton, Washington
KZPS Dallas, Texas
WBEE-FM Rochester, New York
WBGV Marlette, Michigan
WBKR Owensboro, Kentucky
WMBZ West Bend, Wisconsin
WFDX Atlanta, Michigan
WEKS Zebulon, Georgia
WESC-FM Greenville, South Carolina
WESE Baldwyn, Mississippi
WINC-FM Winchester, Virginia
WIRN Buhl, Minnesota
WJJQ-FM Tomahawk, Wisconsin
WJSZ Ashley, Michigan
WJUN-FM Mexico, Pennsylvania
WKGB-FM Conklin, New York
WCPT-FM DeKalb, Illinois
WCFF Urbana, Illinois
WKXQ Rushville, Illinois
WKZZ Tifton, Georgia
WNDT Alachua, Florida
WOFX-FM Cincinnati, Ohio
WFJO Jacksonville Beach, Florida
WORO Corozal, Puerto Rico
WPAP Panama City, Florida
WQMU Indiana, Pennsylvania
WQYZ Ocean Springs, Mississippi
WVKS Toledo, Ohio
WFSX-FM Estero, Florida
WVNN-FM Trinity, Alabama
WWYZ Waterbury, Connecticut
WXRV Andover, Massachusetts
WXTU Philadelphia, Pennsylvania
WYFL Henderson, North Carolina
WYUU Safety Harbor, Florida
WZAC-FM Danville, West Virginia
WXJC-FM Cordova, Alabama
WDJQ Alliance, Ohio
WZUU Mattawan, Michigan
WZWZ Kokomo, Indiana
XHRMFM Tijuana, Mexico
WICO-FM Pocomoke City, Maryland
KHCL Arcadia, Louisiana
KPPL Poplar Bluff, Missouri
WLAW Newaygo, Michigan
KKRE Hollis, Oklahoma
KDAD Bar Nunn, Wyoming
KLHI-FM Kahului, Hawaii
WBLH Black River, New York
KVLR Elgin, Texas
WQST Forest, Mississippi
WCKN Hollywood, South Carolina

92.7 MHz

KHBC Hilo, Hawaii
KDSK-FM Grants, New Mexico
KALP Alpine, Texas
KASR Vilonia, Arkansas
KNCU Newport, Oregon
KBRB-FM Ainsworth, Nebraska
KDSS Ely, Nevada
KESO South Padre Island, Texas
KGBR Gold Beach, Oregon
KGFX-FM Pierre, South Dakota
KZUH Minneapolis, Kansas
KINL Eagle Pass, Texas
KIQZ Rawlins, Wyoming
KIVY-FM Crockett, Texas
KJAK Slaton, Texas
KJBZ Laredo, Texas
KJVC Mansfield, Louisiana
KKBA Kingsville, Texas
KKBS Guymon, Oklahoma
KKCH Glenwood Springs, Colorado
KKUU Indio, California
KLGA-FM Algona, Iowa
KYLA(FM) Fountain Valley, California
KLOZ Eldon, Missouri
KLPL(FM) Lake Providence, Louisiana
KBQB Chico, California
KDYN-FM Coal Hill, Arkansas
KMFB(FM) Mendocino, California
KYRA Thousand Oaks, California
KNCW Omak, Washington
KORT-FM Grangeville, Idaho
KFNL Kindred, North Dakota
KRSY-FM La Luz, New Mexico
KQAY-FM Tucumcari, New Mexico
KORC(FM) Burns, Oregon
KRRN Moapa Valley, Nevada
KTOM-FM Marina, California
KSJQ Savannah, Missouri
KSRA-FM Salmon, Idaho
KTWA Ottumwa, Iowa
KUSO Albion, Nebraska
KVCK-FM Wolf Point, Montana
KBYO-FM Farmerville, Louisiana
KWME Wellington, Kansas
KWNA-FM Winnemucca, Nevada
KREV Alameda, California
KZIQ-FM Ridgecrest, California
KZSQ-FM Sonora, California
WAFN-FM Arab, Alabama
WAUN Kewaunee, Wisconsin
WCCR Clarion, Pennsylvania
WHIZ(FM) South Zanesville, Ohio
WCPY Arlington Heights, Illinois
WDUX-FM Waupaca, Wisconsin
WDZZ-FM Flint, Michigan
WENY-FM Elmira, New York
WEOW Key West, Florida
WYVN Saugatuck, Michigan
WTDR-FM Talladega, Alabama
WGFR Glens Falls, New York
WGMD Rehoboth Beach, Delaware
WBGA St. Simons Island, Georgia
WHIZ-FM South Zanesville, Ohio
WHVE Russell Springs, Kentucky
WKZJ Eufaula, Alabama
WWWH-FM Haleyville, Alabama
WBHQ Beverly Beach, Florida
WXKU-FM Austin, Indiana
WJSM-FM Martinsburg, Pennsylvania
WVLI Kankakee, Illinois
WKKZ Dublin, Georgia
WKRA-FM Holly Springs, Mississippi
WKSX-FM Johnston, South Carolina
WKVT-FM Brattleboro, Vermont
WQBU-FM Garden City, New York
WLSR Galesburg, Illinois
WMIK-FM Middlesboro, Kentucky
WWXT Prince Frederick, Maryland
WBUA Tisbury, Massachusetts
WOBM-FM Toms River, New Jersey
WOXO-FM Norway, Maine
WQTK Ogdensburg, New York
WKQR Mullens, West Virginia
WBKL Clinton, Louisiana
WQDY-FM Calais, Maine
WQEL Bucyrus, Ohio
WRRV Middletown, New York
WCMI-FM Catlettsburg, Kentucky
WSDM-FM Brazil, Indiana
WTAO-FM Herrin, Illinois
WIJV Harriman, Tennessee
WUVA Charlottesville, Virginia
WGIE Clarksburg, West Virginia
WXUR Herkimer, New York
WZBD Berne, Indiana
WAVW Stuart, Florida
WPKG Neillsville, Wisconsin
KMSW The Dalles, Oregon
KBDX Blanding, Utah
KTRX Dickson, Oklahoma
KYRA Thousand Oaks, California
KTPZ Hazelton, Idaho
KHRW Ranchester, Wyoming
KHKY Akiachak, Alaska
WBNK Pine Knoll Shores, North Carolina
KBQL Las Vegas, New Mexico
KBDV Leesville, Louisiana
KYZA Adelanto, California
WFNB Brazil, Indiana
WUSW Taylorville, Illinois

92.9 MHz

KAFF-FM Flagstaff, Arizona
KMXN Osage City, Kansas
KATF Dubuque, Iowa
KBEZ Tulsa, Oklahoma
KBLQ-FM Logan, Utah
KOSP Ozark, Missouri
KDCD San Angelo, Texas
KDCQ Coos Bay, Oregon
KRMX(FM) Marlin, Texas
KEZQ West Yellowstone, Montana
KFAT Anchorage, Alaska
KFGY Healdsburg, California
KFSI Rochester, Minnesota
KFSO-FM Visalia, California
KGRC Hannibal, Missouri
KISM Bellingham, Washington
KJEE Montecito, California
KHLA Jennings, Louisiana
KKIA Ida Grove, Iowa
KKID Salem, Missouri
KKJM St. Joseph, Minnesota
KKXL-FM Grand Forks, North Dakota
KLFM Great Falls, Montana
KLSC Malden, Missouri
KOLT-FM Warren Afb, Wyoming
KMSC Sioux City, Iowa
KMXQ Socorro, New Mexico
KURK Reno, Nevada
KNIN-FM Wichita Falls, Texas
KOSO Patterson, California
KDBL(FM) Toppenish, Washington
KRMX Marlin, Texas
KROM San Antonio, Texas
KRWN Farmington, New Mexico
KSCQ Silver City, New Mexico
KSDR-FM Watertown, South Dakota
KKPK Colorado Springs, Colorado
KTGL Beatrice, Nebraska
KTKC Springhill, Louisiana
KTZA Artesia, New Mexico
KVRE Hot Springs Village, Arkansas
KMIY Tucson, Arizona
KXFG Menifee, California
KYBR Espanola, New Mexico
KYYY Bismarck, North Dakota
KZZU Spokane, Washington
WAAC Valdosta, Georgia
WFHG-FM Bluff City, Tennessee
WBLX-FM Mobile, Alabama
WBOS Brookline, Massachusetts
WBOX-FM Varnado, Louisiana
WCWV Summersville, West Virginia
WDHC Berkeley Springs, West Virginia
WRDX Smyrna, Delaware
WDXO Hazlehurst, Mississippi
WECL Elk Mound, Wisconsin
WEGX Dillon, South Carolina
WEZF Burlington, Vermont
WEZQ Bangor, Maine
WVBW Suffolk, Virginia
WGTZ Eaton, Ohio
WIKX Charlotte Harbor, Florida
WJXA Nashville, Tennessee
WJZQ Cadillac, Michigan
WBUF Buffalo, New York
WLTJ Pittsburgh, Pennsylvania
WMFQ Ocala, Florida
WMFS-FM Bartlett, Tennessee
WMGS Wilkes-Barre, Pennsylvania
WNDV-FM South Bend, Indiana
WLNQ-FM Newport, Tennessee
WBPM Saugerties, New York
WSCD-FM Duluth, Minnesota
WSEI Olney, Illinois
WSKL Veedersburg, Indiana
WRPW Colfax, Illinois
WTPM Aguadilla, Puerto Rico
WTUG-FM Northport, Alabama
WVHL Farmville, Virginia
WLMI Grand Ledge, Michigan
WLXX Lexington, Kentucky
WYQE Naguabo, Puerto Rico
WZGC Atlanta, Georgia
WZLA-FM Abbeville, South Carolina
WYNW Birnamwood, Wisconsin
WEHM Manorville, New York
KRXF Bend, Oregon
KMML Cimarron, Kansas
KYME Rockford, Iowa
KPUT Mona, Utah
WKZY Chilton, Wisconsin
WTKI Huntsville, Alabama
K225BN Oklahoma City, Oklahoma

93.1 MHz

KRYP Gladstone, Oregon
KBDZ Perryville, Missouri
KWJK Boonville, Missouri
KCBS-FM Los Angeles, California
KXSM Hollister, California
KKXX-FM Shafter, California
KHMY Pratt, Kansas
KFBK-FM Pollock Pines, California
KHDX Conway, Arkansas
KKHJ-FM Pago Pago, American Samoa
KKYA Yankton, South Dakota
KLJZ Yuma, Arizona
KMKT Bells, Texas
KQID-FM Alexandria, Louisiana
KMGJ Grand Junction, Colorado
KQIZ-FM Amarillo, Texas
KQMQ-FM Honolulu, Hawaii
KPLV Las Vegas, Nevada
KRCS Sturgis, South Dakota
KRVN-FM Lexington, Nebraska
KSII El Paso, Texas
KSTV-FM Dublin, Texas
KTRZ Riverton, Wyoming
KTYL-FM Tyler, Texas
KMCS Muscatine, Iowa
KXGO Arcata, California
KATO-FM New Ulm, Minnesota
KZLE Batesville, Arkansas
WBBK-FM Blakely, Georgia
WEZW Wildwood Crest, New Jersey
WDHR Pikeville, Kentucky
WDRQ Detroit, Michigan
WEAS-FM Springfield, Georgia
WGMZ Glencoe, Alabama
WHYN-FM Springfield, Massachusetts
WIMK Iron Mountain, Michigan
WJBL Ladysmith, Wisconsin
WKRO-FM Port Orange, Florida
WMGX Portland, Maine
WMKZ Monticello, Kentucky
WNTO Racine, Ohio
WPAW Winston-Salem, North Carolina
WIBC Indianapolis, Indiana
WNTQ Syracuse, New York
WSAA Benton, Tennessee
WPAT-FM Paterson, New Jersey
WPOC Baltimore, Maryland
WTFX-FM Clarksville, Indiana
WQYX Clearfield, Pennsylvania
WCHZ-FM Warrenton, Georgia
WSVO Staunton, Virginia
WFEZ(FM) Miami, Florida
WFGM-FM Barrackville, West Virginia
WWGM Alamo, Tennessee
WNOX Karns, Tennessee
WXRT Chicago, Illinois
WYDS Decatur, Illinois
WZAK Cleveland, Ohio
WZMJ Batesburg, South Carolina
WWSR Lima, Ohio
WJQM De Forest, Wisconsin
KGCX Sidney, Montana
WGDQ Sumrall, Mississippi
KMWB Captain Cook, Hawaii
WACV Coosada, Alabama
WWKM Rochelle, Georgia
KTIK New Plymouth, Idaho

93.3 MHz

KAGL El Dorado, Arkansas
KMJI Ashdown, Arkansas
KZBT Midland, Texas
KLIT Ranchitos Las Lomas, Texas
KBHR Big Bear City, California
KBLB Nisswa, Minnesota
KDKB Mesa, Arizona
KGGL Missoula, Montana
KJDX Susanville, California
KHTS-FM El Cajon, California
KIOA Des Moines, Iowa
KIGL Seligman, Missouri
KJKE Newcastle, Oklahoma
KKNU Springfield-Eugene, Oregon
KKOB Albuquerque, New Mexico
KLIF Haltom City, Texas
KGSR Cedar Park, Texas
KKSP Bryant, Arkansas
KMXV Kansas City, Missouri
KQQX Hermann, Missouri
KMOR Gering, Nebraska
KQBU-FM Port Arthur, Texas
KITE Port Lavaca, Texas
KRHV Big Pine, California
KSJZ Jamestown, North Dakota
KNTO Chowchilla, California
KTCL Wheat Ridge, Colorado
KFFF Bennington, Nebraska
KRKL Walla Walla, Washington
KUBE Seattle, Washington
KUBL-FM Salt Lake City, Utah
KVAK-FM Valdez, Alaska
KXAZ Page, Arizona
KXBA Nikiski, Alaska
KRZZ San Francisco, California
KURL(FM) Billings, Montana
KZOZ San Luis Obispo, California
WAKW Cincinnati, Ohio
WNCD Youngstown, Ohio
WBSZ Ashland, Wisconsin
WBTU Kendallville, Indiana
WBWZ New Paltz, New York
WCAN Canajoharie, New York
WCIZ-FM Watertown, New York
WDNS Bowling Green, Kentucky
WERO Washington, North Carolina
WFAR Danbury, Connecticut
WFLS-FM Fredericksburg, Virginia
WFLZ-FM Tampa, Florida
WVFT Gretna, Florida
WBZD Muncy, Pennsylvania
WIZM-FM La Crosse, Wisconsin
WLDB Milwaukee, Wisconsin
WODC Ashville, Ohio
WKQZ Midland, Michigan
WKYQ Paducah, Kentucky
WMMR Philadelphia, Pennsylvania
WNHW Belmont, New Hampshire
WOGR-FM Salisbury, North Carolina
WPBG Peoria, Illinois
WNCV Shalimar, Florida
WJBT Callahan, Florida
WPUM Rensselaer, Indiana
WWFF-FM New Market, Alabama
WFKL Fairport, New York
WQTY Linton, Indiana
WQUE-FM New Orleans, Louisiana
WQZS Meyersdale, Pennsylvania
WSNE-FM Taunton, Massachusetts
WSYE Houston, Mississippi
WTPT Forest City, North Carolina
WTRH Ramsey, Illinois
WVFJ-FM Manchester, Georgia
WWSE Jamestown, New York
WWWZ Summerville, South Carolina
WKVW Marmet, West Virginia
WZMT Ponce, Puerto Rico
KKDC Dolores, Colorado
KJRV Wessington Springs, South Dakota
WSLP Saranac Lake, New York
KLED Antelope Valley Crestview, Wyoming
WZAE Wadley, Georgia

93.3 kHz

WQZQ-FM Goodlettsville, Tennessee

93.5 MHz

KADD Logandale, Nevada
KALQ-FM Alamosa, Colorado
KKTZ Lakeview, Arkansas
KJAX Jackson, Wyoming
KBPC Crockett, Texas
KBKG Corning, Arkansas
KCVM Hudson, Iowa
KDAY Redondo Beach, California
KGGM Delhi, Louisiana
KIKT Greenville, Texas
KITN Worthington, Minnesota
KJAE Leesville, Louisiana
KKBN Twain Harte, California
KKMI Burlington, Iowa
KKOT Columbus, Nebraska
KLAN Glasgow, Montana
KLKC-FM Parsons, Kansas
KQAV Rosamond, California
KMKX Willits, California
KLXK Breckenridge, Texas
KNAC Earlimart, California
KOOK Junction, Texas
KQCS Bettendorf, Iowa
KOTE Eureka, Kansas
KOZI-FM Chelan, Washington
KPOA Lahaina, Hawaii
KORV-FM Lakeview, Oregon
KQNG-FM Lihue, Hawaii
KDEY-FM Ontario, California
KWHW-FM Altus, Oklahoma
KMYK Osage Beach, Missouri
KRSS Tarkio, Missouri
KSCR-FM Benson, Minnesota
KLMR-FM Lamar, Colorado
KSNX Show Low, Arizona
KWES-FM Ruidoso, New Mexico
WAIN-FM Columbia, Kentucky
WARQ Columbia, South Carolina
WAXM Big Stone Gap, Virginia
WBBC-FM Blackstone, Virginia
WBCM Boyne City, Michigan
WBGF Belle Glade, Florida
WBNV Barnesville, Ohio
WBTQ Buckhannon, West Virginia
WEEY Swanzey, New Hampshire
WCTB Fairfield, Maine
WDOG-FM Allendale, South Carolina
WLQB Ocean Isle Beach, North Carolina
WSJK(FM) Tuscola, Illinois
WHJT Clinton, Mississippi
WHMI-FM Howell, Michigan
WSNV Salem, Virginia
WLFW Chandler, Indiana
WVIX Lemont, Illinois
WKBQ Covington, Tennessee
WKHY Lafayette, Indiana
WKWX Savannah, Tennessee
WMLV Butler, Alabama
WKZX-FM Lenoir City, Tennessee
WMMG-FM Brandenburg, Kentucky
WKMJ-FM Hancock, Michigan
WMPZ Harrison, Tennessee
WMWV Conway, New Hampshire
WWKL Mechanicsburg, Pennsylvania
WGEE-FM New London, Wisconsin
WOKR Remsen, New York
WRQN Bowling Green, Ohio
WVIP New Rochelle, New York
WSBG Stroudsburg, Pennsylvania
WZCR Hudson, New York
WVBR-FM Ithaca, New York
WVOH-FM Nicholls, Georgia
WVVI-FM Christiansted, Virgin Islands
WYFQ-FM Wadesboro, North Carolina
WZBH Georgetown, Delaware
WSRM Coosa, Georgia
KDJF Ester, Alaska
KZXT Eureka, Montana
KWYX Casper, Wyoming
KWDR Royal City, Washington
WQRW Wellsville, New York
KRTS Marfa, Texas
KZTL Paxton, Nebraska
KKDT Burdett, Kansas
WFDZ Perry, Florida
KGWT George West, Texas
KORV Lakeview, Oregon
KAJP Carrizo Springs, Texas
WMRG Albany, Georgia
WZFL Islamorada, Florida
KHNO Huntington, Oregon
WFRQ Harwich Port, Massachusetts
KTND Aspen, Colorado
WMXQ Hartford City, Indiana

93.7

WAAO-FM Andalusia, Alabama

93.7 MHz

KAFC Anchorage, Alaska
KAIR-FM Horton, Kansas
KZTQ Sun Valley, Nevada
KBRK-FM Brookings, South Dakota
KCLB-FM Coachella, California
KUTC Mount Pleasant, Utah
KDB Santa Barbara, California
KDRK-FM Spokane, Washington
KTZZ Conrad, Montana
KEYE-FM Perryton, Texas
KRKG-FM Pasco, Washington
KHBM-FM Monticello, Arkansas
KXZM Felton, California
KNOR Krum, Texas
KISR Fort Smith, Arkansas
KXKS-FM Shreveport, Louisiana
KIZZ Minot, North Dakota
KJBR Marked Tree, Arkansas
KJZY Sebastopol, California
KKBQ-FM Pasadena, Texas
KKRL Carroll, Iowa
KQBT Houston, Texas
KLBJ-FM Austin, Texas
KLKO Elko, Nevada
KOBB-FM Bozeman, Montana
KYFJ New Iberia, Louisiana
KRAI-FM Craig, Colorado
KRQQ Tucson, Arizona
KSD St. Louis, Missouri
KSKS Fresno, California
KSPI FM Stillwater, Oklahoma
KTMT-FM Medford, Oregon
KTUF Kirksville, Missouri
KWYR-FM Winner, South Dakota
KQJK Roseville, California
KXTQ Lubbock, Texas
KXXI Gallup, New Mexico
KXXR Minneapolis, Minnesota
KYEZ Salina, Kansas
KYTI Sheridan, Wyoming
KZBQ Pocatello, Idaho
WALI Walterboro, South Carolina
WAZR Woodstock, Virginia
WBCT Grand Rapids, Michigan
WBFM Sheboygan, Wisconsin
WBLK Depew, New York
WBUS Boalsburg, Pennsylvania
WBXE Baxter, Tennessee
KDKA-FM Pittsburgh, Pennsylvania
WSJR Dallas, Pennsylvania
WDGG Ashland, Kentucky
WDJC-FM Birmingham, Alabama
WEKZ-FM Monroe, Wisconsin
WFBC-FM Greenville, South Carolina
WFCJ Miamisburg, Ohio
WFRR Walton, Indiana
WGYL Vero Beach, Florida
WCYE Three Lakes, Wisconsin
WSIM Lamar, South Carolina
WNOB Chesapeake, Virginia
WKEY-FM Key West, Florida
WCOV-FM Clyde, New York
WPEZ Jeffersonville, Georgia
WMJY Biloxi, Mississippi
WJBC Pontiac, Illinois
WOGK Ocala, Florida
WPFR-FM Clinton, Indiana
WQIO Mount Vernon, Ohio
WQLJ Oxford, Mississippi
WEEI(FM) Lawrence, Massachusetts
WDBT Hartford, Alabama
WIFY Addison, Vermont
WSTW Wilmington, Delaware
WTKB-FM Atwood, Tennessee
WXNX Sanibel, Florida
WEEI-FM Lawrence, Massachusetts
WXJY Georgetown, South Carolina
WFFI Kingston Springs, Tennessee
WZMX Hartford, Connecticut
WZNT San Juan, Puerto Rico
WYAI Scotia, New York
WNTB Topsail Beach, North Carolina
KSBV Salida, Colorado
WRCL Frankenmuth, Michigan
WKAD Harrietta, Michigan
WRMO Milbridge, Maine
KAZY Cheyenne, Wyoming
KVAR Pine Ridge, South Dakota
KANY Montesano, Washington
WOTX Lunenburg, Vermont
KNTK Firth, Nebraska
KKDL Dilley, Texas
KVYL Mohave Valley, Arizona
KPIO-FM Pleasanton, Kansas
WKHF(FM) Lynchburg, Virginia
KOYY Fargo, North Dakota

93.9 MHz

KAMJ Gosnell, Arkansas
KBNU Uvalde, Texas
KCRN-FM San Angelo, Texas
KDGS Wichita, Kansas
KBBU Modesto, California
KMXH Alexandria, Louisiana
KFMF Chico, California
KGKS Scott City, Missouri
KIAI Mason City, Iowa

KIMY Watonga, Oklahoma
KINT-FM El Paso, Texas
KJMK Webb City, Missouri
KKMK Rapid City, South Dakota
KKRC Granite Falls, Minnesota
KSSZ Fayette, Missouri
KLUA Kailua Kona, Hawaii
KMGN Flagstaff, Arizona
KMXR Corpus Christi, Texas
KOYN Paris, Texas
KPDQ-FM Portland, Oregon
KRLT South Lake Tahoe, California
KZRD Dodge City, Kansas
KRTN-FM Raton, New Mexico
KSOU-FM Sioux Center, Iowa
KSPQ West Plains, Missouri
KSWN McCook, Nebraska
KTAC Ephrata, Washington
KTAK Riverton, Wyoming
KUAM-FM Hagatna, Guam
KYSL Frisco, Colorado
KEXA King City, California
WAVC Mio, Michigan
WLCL Sellersburg, Indiana
WARX Lewiston, Maine
WMRV Dansville, New York
WDOR-FM Sturgeon Bay, Wisconsin
WYTK Rogersville, Alabama
WDRR Martinez, Georgia
WRWM Lawrence, Indiana
WGRM-FM Greenwood, Mississippi
KQCJ Cambridge, Illinois
WJXY-FM Conway, South Carolina
WKBI-FM St. Marys, Pennsylvania
WKTG Madisonville, Kentucky
WKXZ Norwich, New York
WKYS Washington, District of Columbia
WLIT-FM Chicago, Illinois
WLVB Morrisville, Vermont
WMIA-FM Miami Beach, Florida
WMEV-FM Marion, Virginia
WMTM-FM Moultrie, Georgia
WWOD Woodstock, Vermont
WNBY-FM Newberry, Michigan
WNYC-FM New York, New York
WRSI Turners Falls, Massachusetts
WQKE Plattsburgh, New York
WSCZ Winnsboro, South Carolina
WRRR-FM St. Marys, West Virginia
WNCB Cary, North Carolina
WTGZ Union Springs, Alabama
WSIB Selmer, Tennessee
WTBX Hibbing, Minnesota
WJAI Pearl, Mississippi
WSEK Burnside, Kentucky
WMMA Nekoosa, Wisconsin
WQQL Sherman, Illinois
WCEZ Carthage, Illinois
WTWF Fairview, Pennsylvania
WBKS Columbus Grove, Ohio
KRIT Parker, Arizona
KAGZ(FM) Lufkin, Texas
WRWM(FM) Lawrence, Indiana
KXDI Belfield, North Dakota
KHJZ Honolulu, Hawaii

94.1 MHz

KSLG-FM Hydesville, California
KBKY Merced, California
KMXJ-FM Amarillo, Texas
KBXL Caldwell, Idaho
KLMM Oceano, California
KTSO Glenpool, Oklahoma
KCLK-FM Clarkston, Washington
KDLK-FM Del Rio, Texas
KDNS Downs, Kansas
KFKF-FM Kansas City, Kansas
KFML Little Falls, Minnesota
KISV Bakersfield, California
KMYI San Diego, California
KKLN Atwater, Minnesota
KKPT Little Rock, Arkansas
KKXK Montrose, Colorado
KTFM Floresville, Texas
KLNO Fort Worth, Texas
KMPS Seattle, Washington
KMXB Henderson, Nevada
KNCO-FM Grass Valley, California
KNEB-FM Scottsbluff, Nebraska
KODJ Salt Lake City, Utah
KOPR Butte, Montana
KPVR Bowling Green, Missouri
KPFA Berkeley, California
KQXY-FM Beaumont, Texas
KRKX Billings, Montana
KRNA Iowa City, Iowa
KRDE Globe, Arizona
KSDN-FM Aberdeen, South Dakota
KOOZ Myrtle Point, Oregon
KLTR Brenham, Texas
KXIX Sunriver, Oregon
KXKQ Safford, Arizona
KZCD Lawton, Oklahoma
KZRR Albuquerque, New Mexico
WAKU Crawfordville, Florida
WAXS Oak Hill, West Virginia
WTYS-FM Marianna, Florida
WEMX Kentwood, Louisiana
WFTN-FM Franklin, New Hampshire
WLYE-FM Glasgow, Kentucky
WGFA-FM Watseka, Illinois
WRZE Kingstree, South Carolina
WHBC-FM Canton, Ohio
WHJY Providence, Rhode Island
WIAL Eau Claire, Wisconsin
WIP Philadelphia, Pennsylvania
WJJO Watertown, Wisconsin
WLLD Lakeland, Florida
WLZK Paris, Tennessee
WMEZ Pensacola, Florida
WMIX-FM Mount Vernon, Illinois
WMXK Morristown, Tennessee
WNBU(FM) Oriental, North Carolina
WNYV Whitehall, New York
WKQK Germantown, Tennessee
KQCH Omaha, Nebraska
WNOD Mayaguez, Puerto Rico
WQKX Sunbury, Pennsylvania
WQZK-FM Keyser, West Virginia
WFFH Smyrna, Tennessee
WQBT Savannah, Georgia
WSOS-FM Fruit Cove, Florida
WSTR Smyrna, Georgia
WUPK Marquette, Michigan
WNNF Cincinnati, Ohio
WWLV(FM) Lexington, North Carolina
WWKR Hart, Michigan
WVSP-FM Yorktown, Virginia
WWDK Jackson, Michigan
WHRP Gurley, Alabama
WBNI-FM Roanoke, Indiana
WZBQ Carrollton, Alabama
WZNE Brighton, New York
KWDI Idalia, Colorado
WOTT Calcium, New York
KRLQ Hodge, Louisiana
KEZZ Phippsburg, Colorado
KXLP Eagle Lake, Minnesota
KZOC Bourbon, Missouri

94.3 MHz

KAMO-FM Rogers, Arkansas
KATI California, Missouri
KBTS Big Spring, Texas
KBUA San Fernando, California
KBUX Quartzsite, Arizona
KCRE-FM Crescent City, California
KCVW Kingman, Kansas
KDEM Deming, New Mexico
KDLX Makawao, Hawaii
KDOM-FM Windom, Minnesota
KDUC Barstow, California
KFST-FM Fort Stockton, Texas
KHER Crystal City, Texas
KEBN Garden Grove, California
KILO Colorado Springs, Colorado
KKIN-FM Aitkin, Minnesota
KOKO-FM Kerman, California
KULO Alexandria, Minnesota
KTTA(FM) Jackson, California
KDDL Chino Valley, Arizona
KBYI Rexburg, Idaho
KRVL Kerrville, Texas
KSEY-FM Seymour, Texas
KXOO Elk City, Oklahoma
KXRQ Roosevelt, Utah
KYEE Alamogordo, New Mexico
KYOX Comanche, Texas
KYXX Ozona, Texas
WBAD Leland, Mississippi
WVRH Norlina, North Carolina
WKXP Kingston, New York
WBXQ Patton, Pennsylvania
WBTN-FM Bennington, Vermont
WFCX Leland, Michigan
WQCM Greencastle, Pennsylvania
WCMG Latta, South Carolina
WTRW(FM) Carbondale, Pennsylvania
WCYY Biddeford, Maine
WIBG-FM Avalon, New Jersey
WEGI-FM Oak Grove, Kentucky
WMRN-FM Marion, Ohio
WKYX-FM Golconda, Illinois
WINX-FM St. Michaels, Maryland
WKKJ Chillicothe, Ohio
WPMJ Chillicothe, Illinois
WGMX Marathon, Florida
WRHD Farmville, North Carolina
WIFX-FM Jenkins, Kentucky
WIZB Abbeville, Alabama
WJJM-FM Lewisburg, Tennessee
WJKL Glendale Heights, Illinois
WJLK Asbury Park, New Jersey
WJTT Red Bank, Tennessee
WKKI Celina, Ohio
WKZW Sandersville, Mississippi
WTJJ Dyer, Tennessee
WLVY Elmira, New York
WUZZ Saegertown, Pennsylvania
WWSK Smithtown, New York
WMKR Pana, Illinois
WNFB Lake City, Florida
WNFZ Powell, Tennessee
WWXX Warrenton, Virginia
WQPC Prairie Du Chien, Wisconsin
WQZX Greenville, Alabama
WIFE-FM Rushville, Indiana
WREB Greencastle, Indiana
WRLF Fairmont, West Virginia
WRMS-FM Beardstown, Illinois
WYDR Neenah-Menasha, Wisconsin
WSCC-FM Goose Creek, South Carolina
WSSQ Sterling, Illinois
WTIX-FM Galliano, Louisiana
WTON-FM Staunton, Virginia
WULF Hardinsburg, Kentucky
WZZR Riviera Beach, Florida
WXRZ Corinth, Mississippi
WYBC-FM New Haven, Connecticut
WGZZ Waverly, Alabama
WZNL Norway, Michigan
WZOC Plymouth, Indiana
KMAX-FM Wellington, Colorado
WWNQ Forest Acres, South Carolina
WZAI Brewster, Massachusetts
WTHP Gibson, Georgia
KCMC-FM Viola, Arkansas
WLEL Ellaville, Georgia
KWDD(FM) Fairbanks, Alaska
KGRB(FM) Jackson, California
WQLQ Benton Harbor, Michigan

94.5 MHz

KATS Yakima, Washington
KBAY Gilroy, California
KBCT Waco, Texas
KLIQ Hastings, Nebraska
KEMA Three Rivers, Texas
KCFS Sioux Falls, South Dakota
KCNO Alturas, California
KSOC Gainesville, Texas
KEMX Locust Grove, Oklahoma
KFMX-FM Lubbock, Texas
KFRQ Harlingen, Texas
KGEN-FM Hanford, California
KHTQ Hayden, Idaho
KUUB Sun Valley, Nevada
KJDY-FM Canyon City, Oregon
KJIW-FM Helena, Arkansas
KKEZ Fort Dodge, Iowa
KKLR-FM Poplar Bluff, Missouri
KYAT Gallup, New Mexico
KTBZ-FM Houston, Texas
KMGE Eugene, Oregon
KMLD Casper, Wyoming
KMON-FM Great Falls, Montana
KFPW-FM Barling, Arkansas
KOOL Phoenix, Arizona
KPLO-FM Reliance, South Dakota
KQDY Bismarck, North Dakota
KRUF Shreveport, Louisiana
KRXL Kirksville, Missouri
KRXY Shelton, Washington
KSKI-FM Sun Valley, Idaho
KSKL Scott City, Kansas
KSMB Lafayette, Louisiana
KSPE-FM Ellwood, California
KSTP-FM St. Paul, Minnesota
KTUN New Castle, Colorado
KLYK Kelso, Washington
KVFX Logan, Utah
KWNE Ukiah, California
KSEH Brawley, California
KWTY Cartago, California
WKXS-FM Leland, North Carolina
WYKV Ravena, New York
WARO Naples, Florida
WVTS-FM Dunbar, West Virginia
WTMB Tomah, Wisconsin
WBYZ Baxley, Georgia
WCEN-FM Hemlock, Michigan
WCFB Orlando, Florida
WDAC Lancaster, Pennsylvania
WELY-FM Ely, Minnesota
WERB Berlin, Connecticut
WBHV-FM State College, Pennsylvania
WHPY-FM Bellevue, Tennessee
WHOD Jackson, Alabama
WIBW-FM Topeka, Kansas
WDVT Rutland, Vermont
WJMN Boston, Massachusetts
WJZD-FM Long Beach, Mississippi
WTNR Holland, Michigan
WKSQ Ellsworth, Maine
WLWK-FM Milwaukee, Wisconsin
WYPV Mackinaw City, Michigan
WYDB Englewood, Ohio
WLRW Champaign, Illinois
WGTK-FM Greenville, South Carolina
WMXL Lexington, Kentucky
WNED-FM Buffalo, New York
WPST Trenton, New Jersey
WFLF-FM Parker, Florida
WRJO Eagle River, Wisconsin
WYEZ Murrells Inlet, South Carolina
WRVQ Richmond, Virginia
WRZR Loogootee, Indiana
WSPX Bowman, South Carolina
WCMS-FM Hatteras, North Carolina
WWSW-FM Pittsburgh, Pennsylvania
WXKR Port Clinton, Ohio
WPTI Eden, North Carolina
WJOX Birmingham, Alabama
WYYY Syracuse, New York
KMYT Temecula, California
KZBI Elko, Nevada
KXLI Moapa, Nevada
WFDR-FM Woodbury, Georgia
KRPW(FM) Coarsegold, California
KRFD(FM) Merino, Colorado
WJJZ Irasberg, Vermont
WIPK-FM Calhoun, Georgia

94.7 MHz

KZND Houston, Alaska
KYAF Firebaugh, California
KAMX Luling, Texas
KYSE El Paso, Texas
KBSO Corpus Christi, Texas
KEWB Anderson, California
KSKU Sterling, Kansas
KGRW Friona, Texas
KIXY-FM San Angelo, Texas
KFVR-FM Beulah, Colorado
KLOB Thousand Palms, California
KMCH Manchester, Iowa
KNEN Norfolk, Nebraska
KZGF Grand Forks, North Dakota
KNRK Camas, Washington
KNSG Springfield, Minnesota
KBRU Oklahoma City, Oklahoma
KRKS-FM Lafayette, Colorado
KRRM Rogue River, Oregon
KCLH Caledonia, Minnesota
KSHE Crestwood, Missouri
KSKK Staples, Minnesota
KADO(FM) Fair Oaks, California
KTTS-FM Springfield, Missouri
KTWV Los Angeles, California
KUMU-FM Honolulu, Hawaii
KVLL-FM Wells, Texas
KWKQ Graham, Texas
KWXX-FM Hilo, Hawaii
KMCN Clinton, Iowa

KLBU Santa Fe, New Mexico
KFLG-FM Big River, California
WAAW Williston, South Carolina
WIAD Bethesda, District of Columbia
WPHR-FM Gifford, Florida
WBAR-FM Lake Luzerne, New York
WBIO Philpot, Kentucky
WBRX Cresson, Pennsylvania
WODA Bayamon, Puerto Rico
WCSX Birmingham, Michigan
WCVM Bronson, Michigan
WDEC-FM Americus, Georgia
WELK Elkins, West Virginia
WFBQ Indianapolis, Indiana
WXBB Erie, Pennsylvania
WNSH Newark, New Jersey
WZOR Mishicot, Wisconsin
WGSQ Cookeville, Tennessee
WWBD Sumter, South Carolina
WQQR Clinton, Kentucky
WIYN Deposit, New York
WKLW-FM Paintsville, Kentucky
WFIA-FM New Albany, Indiana
WMAS Enfield, Connecticut
WMHI Cape Vincent, New York
WOZZ Mosinee, Wisconsin
WOJG Bolivar, Tennessee
WMTT Tioga, Pennsylvania
WQDR-FM Raleigh, North Carolina
WDSD Dover, Delaware
WSNY Columbus, Ohio
WTBF-FM Brundidge, Alabama
WJLV Jackson, Mississippi
WLS Chicago, Illinois
WYLK Lacombe, Louisiana
WYUL Chateaugay, New York
KZAL Manson, Washington
KTXO Goldsmith, Texas
KCNB Chadron, Nebraska
WBCQ-FM Monticello, Maine
WEKI Decatur, Alabama
KYHD Valliant, Oklahoma

94.9 MHz

KBIM-FM Roswell, New Mexico
KBOS-FM Tulare, California
KCIN Cedar City, Utah
KBZT San Diego, California
KCMO-FM Shawnee, Kansas
KCPI Albert Lea, Minnesota
KHKN Maumelle, Arkansas
KRVB Nampa, Idaho
KGGO Des Moines, Iowa
KIOK Richland, Washington
KJLT-FM North Platte, Nebraska
KENZ Provo, Utah
KMXK Cold Spring, Minnesota
KMXZ-FM Tucson, Arizona
KOLI Electra, Texas
KTEE North Bend, Oregon
KPYG Cayucos, California
KQUR Laredo, Texas
KPKY Pocatello, Idaho
KLRJ Aberdeen, South Dakota
KQDS Duluth, Minnesota
KSBH Coushatta, Louisiana
KUOW-FM Seattle, Washington
KLTY Arlington, Texas
KWYK-FM Aztec, New Mexico
KYLD San Francisco, California
KYSS-FM Missoula, Montana
KENZ Provo, Utah
KZWY Sheridan, Wyoming
WAAG Galesburg, Illinois
WPRF Reserve, Louisiana
WOGG Oliver, Pennsylvania
WSJM-FM Benton Harbor, Michigan
WDKB Dekalb, Illinois
WHKN Millen, Georgia
WHKS Port Allegany, Pennsylvania
WHOM Mount Washington, New Hampshire
WAEZ Greeneville, Tennessee
WKJZ Hillman, Michigan
WKLL Frankfort, New York
WKOR-FM Columbus, Mississippi
WKSJ-FM Mobile, Alabama
WKZC Scottville, Michigan
WMMQ Lansing, Michigan
WMSR-FM Collinwood, Tennessee
WOLX-FM Baraboo, Wisconsin
WONB Ada, Ohio
WUBL Atlanta, Georgia
WPTE Virginia Beach, Virginia
WSLC-FM Roanoke, Virginia
WQMX Medina, Ohio
WRBT Harrisburg, Pennsylvania
WRHK Danville, Illinois
WRSD Folsom, Pennsylvania
WSYY-FM Millinocket, Maine
WTNT-FM Tallahassee, Florida
WYNG Mount Carmel, Illinois
WVCO Loris, South Carolina
WWRM Tampa, Florida
WKVF Bartlett, Tennessee
WEKV South Webster, Ohio
WMGE Miami Beach, Florida
KLCH Lake City, Minnesota
KHRQ Baker, California
KTZU Velva, North Dakota
KXTT Maricopa, California
WUPZ Chocolay Township, Michigan
KIND-FM Elk City, Kansas
KRMW Cedarville, Arizona
WPRT-FM Pegram, Tennessee

95.1 MHz

KAMS Mammoth Spring, Arkansas
KAOI-FM Wailuku, Hawaii
KABW Abilene, Texas
KBBY-FM Ventura, California
KCGY Laramie, Wyoming
KCZE New Hampton, Iowa
KEWL-FM New Boston, Texas
KBVB Barnesville, Minnesota
KVIB Sun City West, Arizona
KFRG San Bernardino, California
KHOP Oakdale, California
KICT-FM Wichita, Kansas
KITI-FM Winlock, Washington
KKNN Delta, Colorado
KLER-FM Orofino, Idaho
KMAQ-FM Maquoketa, Iowa
KMMS-FM Bozeman, Montana
KMXI Chico, California
KMXL Carthage, Missouri
KNUW Santa Clara, New Mexico
KQCV-FM Shawnee, Oklahoma
KQRX Midland, Texas
KATC Colorado Springs, Colorado
KRKR Waverly, Nebraska
KMYO Comfort, Texas
KSND Monmouth, Oregon
KSQY Deadwood, South Dakota
KLQT Corrales, New Mexico
KTHC Sidney, Montana
KTKS Versailles, Missouri
KNDE College Station, Texas
KTTI Yuma, Arizona
KUSQ-FM Worthington, Minnesota
KXEI Havre, Montana
KYCS Rock Springs, Wyoming
KYKR Beaumont, Texas
WAJI Fort Wayne, Indiana
WAPE-FM Jacksonville, Florida
WAYV Atlantic City, New Jersey
WFKS Melbourne, Florida
WCDZ Dresden, Tennessee
WGAC-FM Harlem, Georgia
WEGM San German, Puerto Rico
WDZQ Decatur, Illinois
WFBE Flint, Michigan
WFLE-FM Flemingsburg, Kentucky
WGGC Bowling Green, Kentucky
WWGY Grove City, Pennsylvania
WIIL Union Grove, Wisconsin
WIKZ Chambersburg, Pennsylvania
WVTQ Sunderland, Vermont
WJKC Christiansted, Virgin Islands
WLST Marinette, Wisconsin
WRTT-FM Huntsville, Alabama
WNKS Charlotte, North Carolina
WXRB Dudley, Massachusetts
WAIO Honeoye Falls, New York
WONA-FM Winona, Mississippi
WQMZ Charlottesville, Virginia
WQNZ Natchez, Mississippi
WQRB Bloomer, Wisconsin
WRBS-FM Baltimore, Maryland
WRKI Brookfield, Connecticut
WRNS-FM Kinston, North Carolina
WSSX Charleston, South Carolina
WFAV Kankakee, Illinois
WVNI Nashville, Indiana
WVUR-FM Valparaiso, Indiana
WVXG Mount Gilead, Ohio
WXFX Prattville, Alabama
WXIL Elizabeth, West Virginia
WUEZ Carterville, Illinois
WXTK West Yarmouth, Massachusetts
WKZB Marion, Mississippi
WZZO Bethlehem, Pennsylvania
WZZT Morrison, Illinois
WMGB Montezuma, Georgia
KNYE Pahrump, Nevada
WBPC Ebro, Florida
WJRB Young Harris, Georgia
KMDR McKinleyville, California
KUSQ Worthington, Minnesota
WUPN Paradise, Michigan
KRGX Rio Grande City, Texas
KYMN-FM Northfield, Minnesota

95.3 MHz

KAGE-FM Winona, Minnesota
KBBN-FM Broken Bow, Nebraska
KBHH Kerman, California
KCSI Villisca, Iowa
KCXY East Camden, Arkansas
KDJS-FM Willmar, Minnesota
KDKD-FM Clinton, Missouri
KCDQ Douglas, Arizona
KECH-FM Sun Valley, Idaho
KERX Paris, Arkansas
KFRO-FM Gilmer, Texas
KXXK Hoquiam, Washington
KHCA Wamego, Kansas
KHYI Howe, Texas
KIFG-FM Iowa Falls, Iowa
KINZ Humboldt, Kansas
KKBC-FM Baker, Oregon
KLCR Lakeview, Oregon
KLLY Oildale, California
KLXS-FM Pierre, South Dakota
KMGZ Lawton, Oklahoma
KDDD-FM Dumas, Texas
KNEL-FM Brady, Texas
KNOF St. Paul, Minnesota
KUJZ Creswell, Oregon
KOKX-FM Keokuk, Iowa
KOZT Fort Bragg, California
KPND Sandpoint, Idaho
KQKI-FM Bayou Vista, Louisiana
KQMG-FM Independence, Iowa
KRJC Elko, Nevada
KRTY Los Gatos, California
KYDN Monte Vista, Colorado
KUIC Vacaville, California
KURY-FM Brookings, Oregon
KVWG-FM Dilley, Texas
KXTZ Pismo Beach, California
KZJH Jackson, Wyoming
KZSP South Padre Island, Texas
WADI Corinth, Mississippi
WPLZ Ooltewah, Tennessee
WALZ-FM Machias, Maine
WBKT Norwich, New York
WBCK-FM Battle Creek, Michigan
WCFX Clare, Michigan
WDNH-FM Honesdale, Pennsylvania
WFFN Coaling, Alabama
WFMV South Congaree, South Carolina
WZRV Front Royal, Virginia
WLFK Gouverneur, New York
WGMO Spooner, Wisconsin
WGUR Milledgeville, Georgia
WGVS-FM Whitehall, Michigan
WHFM Southampton, New York
WHLF South Boston, Virginia
WHOP-FM Hopkinsville, Kentucky
WHRB Cambridge, Massachusetts
WIKI Carrollton, Kentucky
WBLJ-FM Shamokin, Pennsylvania
WJPA-FM Washington, Pennsylvania
WVKV Nashville, Georgia
WKHK Colonial Heights, Virginia
WKLM Millersburg, Ohio
WRTB Winnebago, Illinois
WKTN Kenton, Ohio
WBPE Brookston, Indiana
WLKR Norwalk, Ohio
WZNF Lumberton, Mississippi
WKVN Morganfield, Kentucky
WNDI-FM Sullivan, Indiana
WOBR-FM Wanchese, North Carolina
WOLZ Fort Myers, Florida
WPYO Maitland, Florida
WQTE Adrian, Michigan
WRKX Ottawa, Illinois
WRLB Rainelle, West Virginia
WRLD Valley, Alabama
WPVQ Greenfield, Massachusetts
WRXX Centralia, Illinois
WTBG Brownsville, Tennessee
WTTC-FM Towanda, Pennsylvania
WTBU York Center, Maine
WUME-FM Paoli, Indiana
WEBL Coldwater, Mississippi
WVRB Wilmore, Kentucky
WXLF Hartford, Vermont
WWWA Winslow, Maine
WXBX Rural Retreat, Virginia
WXCV Homosassa Springs, Florida
WXRO Beaver Dam, Wisconsin
WXXZ Grand Marais, Minnesota
WYFC Clinton, Tennessee
WZLR Xenia, Ohio
WJEK(FM) Rantoul, Illinois
WZWW Bellefonte, Pennsylvania
KXMO Owensville, Missouri
KRPX Wellington, Utah
KVHU Judsonia, Arkansas
KOME-FM Meridian, Texas
KECK Eckley, Colorado
WWSS Tuscarora Township, Michigan

95.5 MHz

KAAN-FM Bethany, Missouri
KAFX-FM Diboll, Texas
KAIM-FM Honolulu, Hawaii
KBEK Mora, Minnesota
KHKK Carmel, California
KCHK-FM New Prague, Minnesota
KGLI Sioux City, Iowa
KJCY St. Ansgar, Iowa
KJEZ Poplar Bluff, Missouri
KXPN-FM Scotland, Texas
KKMJ-FM Austin, Texas
KKZY Bemidji, Minnesota
KLAQ El Paso, Texas
KLOS Los Angeles, California
KMBR Butte, Montana
KHFM Santa Fe, New Mexico
KNDY-FM Marysville, Kansas
KNEV Reno, Nevada
KAHE Dodge City, Kansas
KPHT Rocky Ford, Colorado
KWEY-FM Clinton, Oklahoma
KVOB Lindsborg, Kansas
KRRQ Lafayette, Louisiana
KSDZ Gordon, Nebraska
KSTO Agana, Guam
KTOZ-FM Pleasant Hope, Missouri
KWEN Tulsa, Oklahoma
KWNR Henderson, Nevada
KWYY Midwest, Wyoming
KYNU Jamestown, North Dakota
KYFO-FM Ogden, Utah
KCLZ Twentynine Palms, California
KYOT-FM Phoenix, Arizona
KZAT-FM Belle Plaine, Iowa
KZFM Corpus Christi, Texas
KMVN Palmer, Alaska
WHMA-FM Hobson City, Alabama
WBRU Providence, Rhode Island
WFHM-FM Cleveland, Ohio
WFIZ Odessa, New York
WFMH-FM Hackleburg, Alabama
WFMS Fishers, Indiana
WFUN-FM Bethalto, Illinois
WGLO Pekin, Illinois
WZOH-FM Lancaster, Ohio
WHPE-FM High Point, North Carolina
WIBZ Wedgefield, South Carolina
WIFC Wausau, Wisconsin
WIXV Savannah, Georgia
WJDB-FM Thomasville, Alabama
WKQI Detroit, Michigan
WPWZ Pinetops, North Carolina
WHLH Jackson, Mississippi
WFGI-FM Johnstown, Pennsylvania
WLDI Juno Beach, Florida
WBYL Salladasburg, Pennsylvania
WNDD Silver Springs, Florida
WEBG Chicago, Illinois

WOXD Oxford, Mississippi
WPGC Morningside, District of Columbia
WPLJ New York, New York
WQHY Prestonsburg, Kentucky
WSM-FM Nashville, Tennessee
WTVY-FM Dothan, Alabama
WPPI Topsham, Maine
WXXX South Burlington, Vermont
WYJB Albany, New York
WBOP Buffalo Gap, Virginia
KRVG Glenwood Springs, Colorado
KAIQ Wolfforth, Texas
KHAL Cedarville, California
KFMR Ballard, Utah
KRKQ Mountain Village, Colorado
KITX Hugo, Oklahoma
KCHH Worden, Montana
KBFF Portland, Oregon
WYDS-HD2 Decatur, Illinois

95.5Hz

KWEN Sand Springs, Oklahoma

95.7 MHz

KALF Red Bluff, California
KARX Claude, Texas
KLEY-FM Jourdanton, Texas
KBOY-FM Medford, Oregon
KBST-FM Big Spring, Texas
KCGM Scobey, Montana
KCHZ Ottawa, Kansas
KBGO Waco, Texas
KDAL-FM Duluth, Minnesota
KEZJ-FM Twin Falls, Idaho
KPTT Denver, Colorado
KLTW-FM Prineville, Oregon
KKHH Houston, Texas
KJFX Fresno, California
KJR-FM Seattle, Washington
KKAJ-FM Davis, Oklahoma
KKOK-FM Morris, Minnesota
KXLS Lahoma, Oklahoma
KSSX Carlsbad, California
KNDK-FM Langdon, North Dakota
KKSR Walla Walla, Washington
KPAT Orcutt, California
KPCL Farmington, New Mexico
KPER Hobbs, New Mexico
KQWC-FM Webster City, Iowa
KROA Grand Island, Nebraska
KQSF Dell Rapids, South Dakota
KSSN Little Rock, Arkansas
KLKL Minden, Louisiana
KWKM St. Johns, Arizona
KWWR Mexico, Missouri
KYBE Frederick, Oklahoma
KGMZ(FM) San Francisco, California
WAFM Amory, Mississippi
WAQX Manlius, New York
WATG Trion, Georgia
WAYB-FM Graysville, Tennessee
WBHJ Midfield, Alabama
WCCK Calvert City, Kentucky
WHIO-FM Pleasant Hill, Ohio
WCMB-FM Oscoda, Michigan
WCRC Effingham, Illinois
WVKF Shadyside, Ohio
WFID Rio Piedras, Puerto Rico
WFKX Henderson, Tennessee
WFLO-FM Farmville, Virginia
WSHP Attica, Indiana
WKFP(FM) Navarre, Florida
WHOG-FM Ormond-By-The-Sea, Florida
WHWL Marquette, Michigan
WIMX Gibsonburg, Ohio
WJDK-FM Seneca, Illinois
WKML Lumberton, North Carolina
WKSS Hartford-Meriden, Connecticut
WKXN Fort Deposit, Alabama
WIOL-FM Waverly Hall, Georgia
WLHT-FM Grand Rapids, Michigan
WRDI Nappanee, Indiana
WMRF-FM Lewistown, Pennsylvania
WHAL-FM Horn Lake, Mississippi
WPIG Olean, New York
WQMF Jeffersonville, Indiana
WQPW Valdosta, Georgia
WDMO Baldwin, Wisconsin
WRQT La Crosse, Wisconsin
WSEY Oregon, Illinois
WDOT Danville, Vermont
WBTP Clearwater, Florida
WTGY Charleston, Mississippi
WKBU New Orleans, Louisiana
WVRX Maryville, Tennessee
WVKL Norfolk, Virginia
WWMJ Ellsworth, Maine
WBHD Olyphant, Pennsylvania
WXDJ North Miami Beach, Florida
WXRC Hickory, North Carolina
WBEN-FM Philadelphia, Pennsylvania
WZID Manchester, New Hampshire
WRIT-FM Milwaukee, Wisconsin
KSWI Atlantic, Iowa
KSEC Bentonville, Arkansas
KOTY Mason, Texas
KROK South Fort Polk, Louisiana
KMKO-FM Lake Crystal, Minnesota
KQLZ Beulah, North Dakota
WSWW-FM Craigsville, West Virginia
WIJD Prichard, Alabama
KOSY-FM Anamosa, Iowa
WDKW Maryville, Tennessee

95.7 kHz

KGFK East Grand Forks, Minnesota

95.9 MHz

KSOK-FM Winfield, Kansas
WWWI-FM Pillager, Minnesota
KBYN Arnold, California
KCAQ Camarillo, California
KRSL-FM Russell, Kansas
KCHA-FM Charles City, Iowa
KCKL Malakoff, Texas
KCOB-FM Newton, Iowa
KZML Quincy, Washington
KHMC Goliad, Texas
KIDN-FM Burns, Colorado
KKFD-FM Fairfield, Iowa
KILR-FM Estherville, Iowa
KKBL Monett, Missouri
KWHF Harrisburg, Arkansas
KHNK Columbia Falls, Montana
KLCM Lewistown, Montana
KMAR-FM Winnsboro, Louisiana
KZCU Woodward, Oklahoma
KKBD Sallisaw, Oklahoma
KNLF Quincy, California
KSKD Livingston, California
KPVS Hilo, Hawaii
KPWW Hooks, Texas
KQCL Faribault, Minnesota
KSSR-FM Santa Rosa, New Mexico
KSCN Pittsburg, Texas
KSRF Poipu, Hawaii
KRSH Healdsburg, California
KTIL-FM Bay City, Oregon
KTRI-FM Mansfield, Missouri
KUUZ Lake Village, Arkansas
KXLR Fairbanks, Alaska
KFSH-FM La Mirada, California
KXXZ Barstow, California
KYLS-FM Ironton, Missouri
KFWR Jacksboro, Texas
KMGR Delta, Utah
KKLD Cottonwood, Arizona
KZHK St. George, Utah
KZZI Belle Fourche, South Dakota
WATD-FM Marshfield, Massachusetts
WBBN Taylorsville, Mississippi
WSJZ-FM Sebastian, Florida
WBKY Portage, Wisconsin
WCNA Potts Camp, Mississippi
WCQL Queensbury, New York
WKSP(AM) Block Island, Rhode Island
WCVP-FM Robbinsville, North Carolina
WDQN-FM Duquoin, Illinois
WEFM Michigan City, Indiana
WFOX Norwalk, Connecticut
WFTM-FM Maysville, Kentucky
WGGI Benton, Pennsylvania
WGKY Wickliffe, Kentucky
WGRQ Fairview Beach, Virginia
WEZC Clinton, Illinois
WJKW Athens, Ohio
WKID Vevay, Indiana
WERV-FM Aurora, Illinois
WKQX Chicago, Illinois
WKSZ De Pere, Wisconsin
WKUZ Wabash, Indiana
WLKM-FM Three Rivers, Michigan
WLKX-FM Forest Lake, Minnesota
WMQA-FM Minocqua, Wisconsin
WMXZ Isle of Palms, South Carolina
WNPQ New Philadelphia, Ohio
WOLG Carlinville, Illinois
WKZP Bethany Beach, Delaware
WPNC-FM Plymouth, North Carolina
WFDM-FM Franklin, Indiana
WQZY Dublin, Georgia
WRAT Point Pleasant, New Jersey
WRBA Springfield, Florida
WPEI Saco, Maine
WRJB Camden, Tennessee
WRZK Colonial Heights, Tennessee
WSTG Princeton, West Virginia
WDKL Grafton, West Virginia
WQSI Tuskegee, Alabama
WAKZ Sharpsville, Pennsylvania
WTWX-FM Guntersville, Alabama
WBEC-FM Pittsfield, Massachusetts
WLQK Livingston, Tennessee
WVOS-FM Liberty, New York
WWIN-FM Glen Burnie, Maryland
WICL Williamsport, Maryland
WYNT Caledonia, Ohio
KLZX Weston, Idaho
KZLG Mansura, Louisiana
WNLF Macomb, Illinois
KTIL-FM Bay City, Oregon
KKIT Taos, New Mexico
KWHK Hutchinson, Kansas
KAJR Indian Wells, California
WZDB Sykesville, Pennsylvania
KVMO Fort Benton, Montana
KUKY Wellton, Arizona
KYZZ Big Sur, California
WVGO Terre Haute, Illinois

96.1 MHz

KAGG Madisonville, Texas
KORQ Winters, Texas
KKXS Shingletown, California
KMRX El Dorado, Arkansas
KCWD Harrison, Arkansas
KISO Omaha, Nebraska
KZRC Bennington, Oklahoma
KSME Greeley, Colorado
KGPZ Coleraine, Minnesota
KIOX-FM Edna, Texas
KICX-FM McCook, Nebraska
KID-FM Idaho Falls, Idaho
KINI Crookston, Nebraska
KITO-FM Vinita, Oklahoma
KBTQ Harlingen, Texas
KIXX Watertown, South Dakota
KKLX Worland, Wyoming
KKTX-FM Kilgore, Texas
KLPX Tucson, Arizona
KLRQ Clinton, Missouri
KNWM Madrid, Iowa
KMRK-FM Odessa, Texas
KMXG Clinton, Iowa
KIIX-FM Opportunity, Washington
KNOM-FM Nome, Alaska
KIBT Fountain, Colorado
KQHT Crookston, Minnesota
KQPR Albert Lea, Minnesota
KRVE Brusly, Louisiana
KANS Emporia, Kansas
KSLY-FM San Luis Obispo, California
KSQQ Morgan Hill, California
KSRV-FM Ontario, Oregon
KCTX-FM Childress, Texas
KSTR-FM Montrose, Colorado
KWRK Window Rock, Arizona
KRQB San Jacinto, California
KXXM San Antonio, Texas
KXXO Olympia, Washington
KXXY-FM Oklahoma City, Oklahoma
KZRM Chama, New Mexico
KYKZ Lake Charles, Louisiana
KYMX Sacramento, California
KYYZ Williston, North Dakota
KZEL-FM Eugene, Oregon
WAEL-FM Maricao, Puerto Rico
WKZQ-FM Forestbrook, South Carolina
WVLF Norwood, New York
WBBB Raleigh, North Carolina
WCTO Easton, Pennsylvania
WDEV-FM Warren, Vermont
WEJZ Jacksonville, Florida
WHBX Tallahassee, Florida
WHNN Bay City, Michigan
WIVI Charlotte Amalie, Virgin Islands
WJMC-FM Rice Lake, Wisconsin
WJYE Buffalo, New York
WKFM Huron, Ohio
WWPW Atlanta, Georgia
WKWS Charleston, West Virginia
WLXO Stamping Ground, Kentucky
WLKG Lake Geneva, Wisconsin
WJDV Broadway, Virginia
WJVC Center Moriches, New York
WLZA Eupora, Mississippi
WTMP-FM Dade City, Florida
WIVG Tunica, Mississippi
WMTR-FM Archbold, Ohio
WODZ-FM Rome, New York
WMTP Conway, Pennsylvania
WQHR Presque Isle, Maine
WQKS-FM Montgomery, Alabama
WQLK Richmond, Indiana
WQQB Rantoul, Illinois
WRKH Mobile, Alabama
WROX-FM Exmore, Virginia
WRXK-FM Bonita Springs, Florida
WSOX Red Lion, Pennsylvania
WSRS Worcester, Massachusetts
WSTO Owensboro, Kentucky
WTCX Ripon, Wisconsin
WDKE Coleraine, Minnesota
WPKF Poughkeepsie, New York
WTTH Margate City, New Jersey
WXYM Tomah, Wisconsin
WMAX-FM Holland, Michigan
WHQC Shelby, North Carolina
WXFL Florence, Alabama
WKKQ Barbourville, Kentucky
WPHD South Waverly, Pennsylvania
KLKY Stanfield, Oregon
KCEL Mojave, California
KALN Dexter, New Mexico
WOHA Ashtabula, Ohio
WKST-FM Pittsburgh, Pennsylvania
WTIM Taylorville, Illinois
KERN Wasco-Greenacres, California

96.3 MHz

KTWN-FM Edina, Minnesota
KERP Ingalls, Kansas
KBAZ Hamilton, Montana
KRZN Billings, Montana
KFMI Eureka, California
KXOL-FM Los Angeles, California
KHEY-FM El Paso, Texas
KBZU Albuquerque, New Mexico
KHLS Blytheville, Arkansas
KNOU St. Louis, Missouri
KXCM Joshua Tree, California
KKLZ Las Vegas, Nevada
KLLL-FM Lubbock, Texas
KRCW Royal City, Washington
KRNQ Keokuk, Iowa
KRTR-FM Kailua, Hawaii
KZCH Derby, Kansas
KSCS Fort Worth, Texas
KSWG Wickenburg, Arizona
KTDR Del Rio, Texas
KTTG Mena, Arkansas
KUBB Mariposa, California
KWLZ-FM West Linn, Oregon
KBEX Dalhart, Texas
KXRK Provo, Utah
KZDY Cawker City, Kansas
WAJZ Voorheesville, New York
WBBM-FM Chicago, Illinois
WNHT Churubusco, Indiana
WHHH Indianapolis, Indiana
WHUR-FM Washington, District of Columbia
WIVY Morehead, Kentucky
WJAA Austin, Indiana
WJBZ-FM Seymour, Tennessee
WJIZ-FM Albany, Georgia
WJSA-FM Jersey Shore, Pennsylvania
WKQW-FM Oil City, Pennsylvania
WUSJ Madison, Mississippi
WJJB-FM Gray, Maine
WLVQ Columbus, Ohio
WLXT Petoskey, Michigan
WMAD Cross Plains, Wisconsin
WLCN Atlanta, Illinois
WOTR(FM) Lost Creek, West Virginia

WDVD Detroit, Michigan
WXNY-FM New York, New York
WRBN Clayton, Georgia
WRHT Morehead City, North Carolina
WCJK Murfreesboro, Tennessee
WROV-FM Martinsville, Virginia
WXKY-FM Stanford, Kentucky
WKSP Aiken, South Carolina
WEII Dennis, Massachusetts
WSFQ Peshtigo, Wisconsin
KXLW Houston, Alaska
WFYX Walpole, New Hampshire
KZXL Hudson, Texas
KACZ Riley, Kansas
KGGB Yorktown, Texas
KXXN Iowa Park, Texas
KQWY Lusk, Wyoming
KICL(FM) Pleasantville, Iowa
WXWX Marietta, Mississippi
WXKE-FM Pocomoke City, Maryland

96.5 MHz

KBDN Bandon, Oregon
KBKZ Raton, New Mexico
KBYZ Bismarck, North Dakota
KNRX Sterling City, Texas
KCYS Seaside, Oregon
KDZN Glendive, Montana
KECO Elk City, Oklahoma
KFLS-FM Tulelake, California
KPEL-FM Breaux Bridge, Louisiana
KHMX Houston, Texas
KPSL-FM Bakersfield, California
KJJK-FM Fergus Falls, Minnesota
KKIS-FM Soldotna, Alaska
KLCA Tahoe City, California
KHTE-FM England, Arkansas
KLGT Buffalo, Wyoming
KLIX-FM Twin Falls, Idaho
KLMA Hobbs, New Mexico
KLTG Corpus Christi, Texas
KSPW Sparta, Missouri
KNWC-FM Sioux Falls, South Dakota
KOIT San Francisco, California
KOZE-FM Lewiston, Idaho
KQSW Rock Springs, Wyoming
KRAV-FM Tulsa, Oklahoma
KRFM Show Low, Arizona
KRGI-FM Grand Island, Nebraska
KSOM Audubon, Iowa
KVKI-FM Shreveport, Louisiana
KWWK Rochester, Minnesota
KXPK Evergreen, Colorado
KRBZ Kansas City, Missouri
KJAQ Seattle, Washington
KYXY San Diego, California
WAZY-FM Lafayette, Indiana
WBFG Parker's Crossroads, Tennessee
WCMF-FM Rochester, New York
WBKX Fredonia, New York
WDOD-FM Chattanooga, Tennessee
WRXD Fajardo, Puerto Rico
WZOX Portage, Michigan
WFLB Laurinburg, North Carolina
WGZB-FM Lanesville, Indiana
WDBO(FM) Orlando, Florida
WJCL-FM Savannah, Georgia
WZPN Farmington, Illinois
WAKS Akron, Ohio
WKDJ-FM Clarksdale, Mississippi
WKIB Anna, Illinois
WKLH Milwaukee, Wisconsin
WKLK-FM Cloquet, Minnesota
WKLR Fort Lee, Virginia
WLWF Marseilles, Illinois
WMJJ Birmingham, Alabama
WKYE Johnstown, Pennsylvania
WRQY-FM Bellaire, Ohio
WPEL Montrose, Pennsylvania
WPOW Miami, Florida
WQHH DeWitt, Michigan
WMLL Bedford, New Hampshire
WBGI-FM Moundsville, West Virginia
WIHB-FM Gray, Georgia
WTGG Amite, Louisiana
WTIC-FM Hartford, Connecticut
WVNV Malone, New York
WXCC Williamson, West Virginia
WXHB Richton, Mississippi
WFTK Lebanon, Ohio
WZNS Fort Walton Beach, Florida
WOXL-FM Biltmore Forest, North Carolina
WCTG Chincoteague, Virginia
KJBL Julesburg, Colorado
KMMY Soper, Oklahoma
WJTK Columbia City, Florida
KKGN Ingram, Texas
KKSY-FM Cedar Rapids, Iowa
KSLV-FM Del Norte, Colorado
KKNM Bovina, Texas
KNDN-FM Teec Nos Pos, Arizona
WYVS Spectacular, New York
WHOH Rhinelander, Wisconsin
WZMP Philadelphia, Pennsylvania

96.7 MHz

KAHR Poplar Bluff, Missouri
KRCY-FM Lake Havasu City, Arizona
KBBE McPherson, Kansas
KBEL-FM Idabel, Oklahoma
KQMB Levan, Utah
KCAL-FM Redlands, California
KCMQ Columbia, Missouri
KCRF-FM Lincoln City, Oregon
KLJR-FM Santa Paula, California
KDOG North Mankato, Minnesota
KCYT Ozark, Arkansas
KALZ Fowler, California
KCIL Gray, Louisiana
KSOB Larned, Kansas
KHFI-FM Georgetown, Texas
KHIX Carlin, Nevada
KKCQ-FM Bagley, Minnesota
KKEX Preston, Idaho
KMRQ Riverbank, California
KZRV Sartell, Minnesota
KIIC Albia, Iowa
KOYE Frankston, Texas
KBDB-FM Forks, Washington
KHTO(FM) Hot Springs, Arkansas
KTCK Flower Mound, Texas
KRNK Casper, Wyoming
KOKR Newport, Arkansas
KQZZ Devils Lake, North Dakota
KISN Belgrade, Montana
KSYV Solvang, California
KUNA-FM La Quinta, California
KWCL-FM Oak Grove, Louisiana
KWIZ Santa Ana, California
KWMX Williams, Arizona
KWWW-FM Quincy, Washington
KXOX-FM Sweetwater, Texas
KZAP Paradise, California
KZIN-FM Shelby, Montana
KZMX-FM Hot Springs, South Dakota
KMMG Benton City, Washington
WBDK Algoma, Wisconsin
WBVI Fostoria, Ohio
WBVR-FM Auburn, Kentucky
WBWB Bloomington, Indiana
WCEI-FM Easton, Maryland
WTQX Boothbay Harbor, Maine
WCMJ Cambridge, Ohio
WCOE La Porte, Indiana
WCSM-FM Celina, Ohio
WCVS-FM Virden, Illinois
WDCD-FM Clifton Park, New York
WFFF-FM Columbia, Mississippi
WFML Vincennes, Indiana
WIHN Normal, Illinois
WJJH Ashland, Wisconsin
WKLV-FM Port Chester, New York
WKJX Elizabeth City, North Carolina
WKMM Kingwood, West Virginia
WKOV-FM Wellston, Ohio
WKRX Roxboro, North Carolina
WKXK Pine Hill, Alabama
WLLF Mercer, Pennsylvania
WSSR Joliet, Illinois
WGBL Gulfport, Mississippi
WLTN-FM Lisbon, New Hampshire
WLTY Cayce, South Carolina
WKGL-FM Loves Park, Illinois
WLXV Cadillac, Michigan
WRDG Peachtree City, Georgia
WMOD Bolivar, Tennessee
WMXA Opelika, Alabama
WYSX Morristown, New York
WNKX-FM Centerville, Tennessee
WWLF-FM Oswego, New York
WORX-FM Madison, Indiana
WPGM Danville, Pennsylvania
WDLD Halfway, Maryland
WQSO Rochester, New Hampshire
WWZW Buena Vista, Virginia
WSEL-FM Pontotoc, Mississippi
WTSA-FM Brattleboro, Vermont
WABT(FM) Lehman Township, Pennsylvania
WUFN Albion, Michigan
WVNW Burnham, Pennsylvania
WRGZ Rogers City, Michigan
WMYL Halls Crossroads, Tennessee
WXOF Yankeetown, Florida
WXZO Willsboro, New York
WGOV-FM Valdosta, Georgia
KMDZ Las Vegas, New Mexico
KNMB Cloudcroft, New Mexico
KNOB Healdsburg, California
KUUR Carbondale, Colorado
WANV Annville, Kentucky
WMJT McMillan, Michigan
KROW Cody, Wyoming
WUPG Republic, Michigan
WGNX Colchester, Illinois
KYLI Bunkerville, Nevada
WVTT Portville, New York
WBKQ Alexandria, Indiana

96.9 MHz

KBCR-FM Steamboat Springs, Colorado
KIMX Nunn, Colorado
KCCY-FM Pueblo, Colorado
KCMI Terrytown, Nebraska
KDAG Farmington, New Mexico
KDLO-FM Watertown, South Dakota
KEZE Spokane, Washington
KFIX Plainville, Kansas
KFMN Lihue, Hawaii
KYYO McCleary, Washington
KIAQ Clarion, Iowa
KXBJ El Campo, Texas
KKGL Nampa, Idaho
KKOW-FM Pittsburg, Kansas
KMCM Odessa, Texas
KMFY Grand Rapids, Minnesota
KXSS-FM Amarillo, Texas
KMTN Jackson, Wyoming
KMXP Phoenix, Arizona
KQOB Enid, Oklahoma
KQRV Deer Lodge, Montana
KROG Grants Pass, Oregon
KSCH Sulphur Springs, Texas
KSEG Sacramento, California
KUPH Mountain View, Missouri
KVMV Mc Allen, Texas
KWAV Monterey, California
KWLR Maumelle, Arkansas
KEBT Lost Hills, California
KZBK Brookfield, Missouri
KZKX Seward, Nebraska
KZMZ Alexandria, Louisiana
KZTA Naches, Washington
WTHB-FM Wrens, Georgia
WBPW Presque Isle, Maine
WBTI Lexington, Michigan
WDDJ Paducah, Kentucky
WDJR Enterprise, Alabama
WRRB Arlington, New York
WEHN East Hampton, New York
WFPG Atlantic City, New Jersey
WGKS Paris, Kentucky
WGRF Buffalo, New York
WHPZ Bremen, Indiana
WINK-FM Fort Myers, Florida
WKEZ-FM Tavernier, Florida
WBZJ Goldsboro, North Carolina
WKKT Statesville, North Carolina
WLAN-FM Lancaster, Pennsylvania
WLAV Grand Rapids, Michigan
WLBH-FM Mattoon, Illinois
WLRD Willard, Ohio
WWDV Zion, Illinois
WNRT Manati, Puerto Rico
WOUR Utica, New York
WRDO Fitzgerald, Georgia
WVYS Ridgebury, Pennsylvania
WYDA Troy, Ohio
WRRK Braddock, Pennsylvania
WRSA-FM Holly Pond, Alabama
WSIG Mount Jackson, Virginia
WBQT Boston, Massachusetts
WWCM Standish, Michigan
WIWF Charleston, South Carolina
WTCD Indianola, Mississippi
WWUZ Bowling Green, Virginia
WWWX Oshkosh, Wisconsin
WXBQ-FM Bristol, Virginia
WXLP Moline, Illinois
WVVV Williamstown, West Virginia
WNKL Wauseon, Ohio
WKLO Hardinsburg, Indiana
KYSC Fairbanks, Alaska
KSSW Nashville, Arkansas
KHDR Lenwood, California
KDVB Effingham, Kansas
W245CA Pocomoke City, Maryland
WVYS-FM2 Towanda, Pennsylvania
KQBZ Brownwood, Texas

97.1 MHz

KALS Kalispell, Montana
KAMD-FM Camden, Arkansas
KAYQ Warsaw, Missouri
KBCQ-FM Roswell, New Mexico
KCYN Moab, Utah
KEGL Fort Worth, Texas
KELN North Platte, Nebraska
KYWD Green Valley, Arizona
KRTO Guadalupe, California
KZHT Salt Lake City, Utah
KKBR Billings, Montana
KKEN Duncan, Oklahoma
KYCH-FM Portland, Oregon
KTHT Cleveland, Texas
KYAL-FM Muskogee, Oklahoma
KVVL Maryville, Missouri
KNWB Hilo, Hawaii
KPSD-FM Faith, South Dakota
KSEQ Visalia, California
KIBB Haven, Kansas
KTCZ-FM Minneapolis, Minnesota
KVRP-FM Haskell, Texas
KFTK Florissant, Missouri
KXPT Las Vegas, Nevada
KXRX Walla Walla, Washington
KYCK Crookston, Minnesota
KYYX Minot, North Dakota
KTSE-FM Patterson, California
WASH Washington, District of Columbia
WBHT Mountain Top, Pennsylvania
WBNS-FM Columbus, Ohio
WBVB Coal Grove, Ohio
WDBS Sutton, West Virginia
WCOW-FM Sparta, Wisconsin
WLHK Shelbyville, Indiana
WEZB New Orleans, Louisiana
WSRV Gainesville, Georgia
WGLQ Escanaba, Michigan
WHRK Memphis, Tennessee
WXYT-FM Detroit, Michigan
WLIC Frostburg, Maryland
WWMG Millbrook, Alabama
WDRV Chicago, Illinois
WOKK Meridian, Mississippi
WOSN Indian River Shores, Florida
WQHT New York, New York
WAVD Ocean Pines, Maryland
WQMG Greensboro, North Carolina
WOWY University Park, Pennsylvania
WREO-FM Ashtabula, Ohio
WKEQ Somerset, Kentucky
WSUN-FM Holiday, Florida
WBFB Bangor, Maine
WXCM Whitesville, Kentucky
WYND-FM Hatteras, North Carolina
WZRT Rutland, Vermont
KULV Ukiah, California
KJMT Calico Rock, Arkansas
WLVU Belle Meade, Tennessee
KZBR La Jara, Colorado
KIYU-FM Galena, Alaska
KNSX(FM) Moville, Iowa
WZHD Canaseraga, 0
KAMP Los Angeles, California

97.3 MHz

KAJA San Antonio, Texas
KAML-FM Gillette, Wyoming
KRVY-FM Starbuck, Minnesota
KBCO Boulder, Colorado
KYRX Marble Hill, Missouri
KIRO-FM Tacoma, Washington
KLRX Lee's Summit, Missouri
KDEW-FM De Witt, Arkansas

KDNW Duluth, Minnesota
KEAG Anchorage, Alaska
KGRR Epworth, Iowa
KLZK New Deal, Texas
KHKI Des Moines, Iowa
KIKO Miami, Arizona
KIKO-FM Claypool, Arizona
KJMG Bastrop, Louisiana
KKJQ Garden City, Kansas
KGEE Pecos, Texas
KKRS Davenport, Washington
KKSS Santa Fe, New Mexico
KLCE Blackfoot, Idaho
KLLC San Francisco, California
KRGY Aurora, Nebraska
KMDL Kaplan, Louisiana
KMXC Sioux Falls, South Dakota
KNCQ Redding, California
KSHR-FM Coquille, Oregon
KSON San Diego, California
KQHN Waskom, Texas
KKNG-FM Blanchard, Oklahoma
KOLC Carson City, Nevada
KXUS Springfield, Missouri
WAEV Savannah, Georgia
WDEE-FM Reed City, Michigan
WMJO Essexville, Michigan
WFLC Miami, Florida
WFMM Sumrall, Mississippi
WFMN Flora, Mississippi
WFYR Elmwood, Illinois
WGH-FM Newport News, Virginia
WHDG Rhinelander, Wisconsin
WJDF Orange, Massachusetts
WJFD-FM New Bedford, Massachusetts
WJSN-FM Jackson, Kentucky
WJZE Oak Harbor, Ohio
WKBC-FM North Wilkesboro, North Carolina
WKJQ-FM Parsons, Tennessee
WKWK-FM Wheeling, West Virginia
WUUQ South Pittsburg, Tennessee
WRNW Milwaukee, Wisconsin
WMEE Fort Wayne, Indiana
WGEX Bainbridge, Georgia
WMNX Wilmington, North Carolina
WYGY Fort Thomas, Kentucky
WMYY Schoharie, New York
WPCL Northern Cambria, Pennsylvania
WRAN Taylorville, Illinois
WRUL Carmi, Illinois
WRVV Harrisburg, Pennsylvania
WSKY-FM Micanopy, Florida
WKSO Natchez, Mississippi
WYXL Ithaca, New York
WZAD Wurtsboro, New York
WZBG Litchfield, Connecticut
WZZE Glen Mills, Pennsylvania
WOYE Rio Grande, Puerto Rico
KHDK New London, Iowa
KBLR-FM Blair, Nebraska
WTNV Tiptonville, Tennessee
KTCM Madison, Missouri
KPKR Parker, Arizona
KRKH Wailea-Makena, Hawaii
WENJ Millville, New Jersey
WEZZ-FM Gardendale, Alabama

97.5 MHz

KABX-FM Merced, California
KFNC Mont Belvieu, Texas
KVEG Mesquite, Nevada
KBNA-FM El Paso, Texas
KBVU-FM Alta, Iowa
KDBH-FM Natchitoches, Louisiana
KDKK Park Rapids, Minnesota
KDLY Lander, Wyoming
KTBB Troup, Texas
KFTX Kingsville, Texas
KGKL-FM San Angelo, Texas
KJCK-FM Junction City, Kansas
KKCT Bismarck, North Dakota
KLAK Tom Bean, Texas
KYGA Goleta, California
KMOD-FM Tulsa, Oklahoma
KNLR Bend, Oregon
KNMO-FM Nevada, Missouri
KNXR Rochester, Minnesota
KSZR Oro Valley, Arizona
KOEA Doniphan, Missouri
KOZB Livingston, Montana
KHCM-FM Honolulu, Hawaii
KQSK Chadron, Nebraska
KQUS-FM Hot Springs, Arkansas
KLYY Riverside, California
KMVA Dewey-Humboldt, Arizona
KWTX-FM Waco, Texas
KZGZ Hagatna, Guam
KOLW Basin City, Washington
WABD Mobile, Alabama
WALK-FM Patchogue, New York
WAMZ Louisville, Kentucky
WBBA-FM Pittsfield, Illinois
WCOS-FM Columbia, South Carolina
WWSN Whitehall, Michigan
WYDM Monroe, Michigan
WFRY-FM Watertown, New York
WHLJ-FM Statenville, Georgia
WHMS-FM Champaign, Illinois
WUMJ Fayetteville, Georgia
WKTT Salisbury, Maryland
WQSK Madison, Maine
WIOB Mayaguez, Puerto Rico
WJIM Lansing, Michigan
WJXB Knoxville, Tennessee
WKLT Kalkaska, Michigan
WLTF Martinsburg, West Virginia
WLLX Lawrenceburg, Tennessee
WOBN Westerville, Ohio
WOKQ Dover, New Hampshire
WONE-FM Akron, Ohio
WPCV Winter Haven, Florida
WDDH St. Marys, Pennsylvania
WPEN-FM Burlington, New Jersey
WQBE-FM Charleston, West Virginia
WQOK Carrboro, North Carolina
WKGA Goodwater, Alabama
WTGR Union City, Ohio
WUFF-FM Eastman, Georgia
WVNU Greenfield, Ohio
WWMS Oxford, Mississippi
WWWV Charlottesville, Virginia
WYTZ Bridgman, Michigan
WHAZ-FM Hoosick Falls, New York
WZOK Rockford, Illinois
WDLJ Breese, Illinois
WZZP Hopkinsville, Kentucky
KPAK Alva, Oklahoma
KZNSFM) Coalville, Utah
KTJZ Tallulah, Louisiana
KTRT Winthrop, Washington
KZMG Elko, Nevada
KWUZ Poncha Springs, Colorado
KJMO Linn, Missouri
WTNN Bristol, Vermont
KSRX Sterling, Colorado
WTBD-FM Delhi, New York
WVRV Pine Level, Alabama
KEXL Pierce, Nebraska
KXTA-2 Gooding, Idaho
WCOS-FM Columbia, South Carolina

97.7 MHz

KJSM-FM Augusta, Arkansas
KACI-FM The Dalles, Oregon
KALK Winfield, Texas
KAPB-FM Marksville, Louisiana
KTPI-FM Mojave, California
KAVV Benson, Arizona
KRIO-FM Roma, Texas
KCRR Grundy Center, Iowa
KATX Eastland, Texas
KFFG Los Altos, California
KOMO-FM Oakville, Washington
KGLM-FM Anaconda, Montana
KICM Healdton, Oklahoma
KHBT Humboldt, Iowa
KHZR Potosi, Missouri
KHIM Mangum, Oklahoma
KLVO Belen, New Mexico
KVRV Monte Rio, California
KMTY Gibbon, Nebraska
KNBZ Redfield, South Dakota
KOTM-FM Ottumwa, Iowa
KNBB Dubach, Louisiana
KPOW-FM La Monte, Missouri
KBBX-FM Nebraska City, Nebraska
KQMO Shell Knob, Missouri
KQVO Calexico, California
KRAT(FM) Altamont, Oregon
KRCK-FM Mecca, California
KWUT(FM) Elsinore, Utah
KNZR-FM Shafter, California
KSHL Coburg, Oregon
KSNP Burlington, Kansas
KZAR McQueeney, Texas
KWIN Lodi, California
KWRW Rusk, Texas
KYSN East Wenatchee, Washington
KHHZ Gridley, California
KZYR Avon, Colorado
WAFL Milford, Delaware
WNSX Winter Harbor, Maine
WKFX Rice Lake, Wisconsin
WKCA Salt Lick, Kentucky
WEXT Amsterdam, New York
WNVM Cidra, Puerto Rico
WAAF Brockton, Massachusetts
WTLQ-FM Punta Rassa, Florida
WCJO Jackson, Ohio
WCTY Norwich, Connecticut
WCXU Caribou, Maine
WCZX Hyde Park, New York
WHPH Jemison, Alabama
WFDL-FM Lomira, Wisconsin
WGGN Castalia, Ohio
WGLR Lancaster, Wisconsin
WENI-FM Big Flats, New York
WGMT Lyndon, Vermont
WWKY Providence, Kentucky
WILE-FM Byesville, Ohio
WSNI Keene, New Hampshire
WGPB Rome, Georgia
WAQE-FM Barron, Wisconsin
WKKR Auburn, Alabama
WZZN Oneonta, Alabama
WAVK Marathon, Florida
WKXM-FM Winfield, Alabama
WLER-FM Butler, Pennsylvania
WLQI Rensselaer, Indiana
WLCE Petersburg, Illinois
WMDM Lexington Park, Maryland
WMGZ Eatonton, Georgia
WMOI Monmouth, Illinois
WMRX-FM Beaverton, Michigan
WOLV Houghton, Michigan
WOXY Mason, Ohio
WQLZ Petersburg, Illinois
WRIC-FM Richlands, Virginia
WRBJ Brandon, Mississippi
WVBB(FM) Elliston-Lafayette, Virginia
WLKH Somerset, Pennsylvania
WCLS Spencer, Indiana
WQDC Sturgeon Bay, Wisconsin
WSTQ Streator, Illinois
WTCQ Vidalia, Georgia
WTGN Lima, Ohio
WTGV-FM Sandusky, Michigan
WTYJ Fayette, Mississippi
WTYL-FM Tylertown, Mississippi
WGTI Winfall, North Carolina
WVRT Mill Hall, Pennsylvania
WMLQ Manistee, Michigan
WWUF Waycross, Georgia
WWXM Garden City, South Carolina
WYAJ Sudbury, Massachusetts
WYYX Bonifay, Florida
WEQR Walnut Creek, North Carolina
WSSM(FM) Goshen, Indiana
KZBG Lapwai, Idaho
KSJL Strasburg, Colorado
WURB Cross City, Florida
KDLC Dulac, Louisiana
WYJJ Trenton, Tennessee

97.9 MHz

KBFB Dallas, Texas
KBXB Sikeston, Missouri
KBXX Houston, Texas
KBZN Ogden, Utah
KCMR Mason City, Iowa
KQLK De Ridder, Louisiana
KFBD-FM Waynesville, Missouri
KFNW-FM Fargo, North Dakota
KGNC-FM Amarillo, Texas
KICK-FM Palmyra, Missouri
KXBG Cheyenne, Wyoming
KNSL(FM) Lamoni, Iowa
KISZ-FM Cortez, Colorado
KJMZ Cache, Oklahoma
KKBG Hilo, Hawaii
KLVP Aloha, Oregon
KLAX-FM East Los Angeles, California
KVVR Dutton, Montana
KTPT Rapid City, South Dakota
KMZT-FM Salinas, California
KMGV Fresno, California
KLUK Needles, California
KODM Odessa, Texas
KPOD-FM Crescent City, California
KQFC Boise, Idaho
KPSA-FM Lordsburg, New Mexico
KRBB Wichita, Kansas
KRSI Garapan-Saipan, Guam
KSEZ Sioux City, Iowa
KTAG Cody, Wyoming
KZTB Milton-Freewater, Oregon
KTLO-FM Mountain Home, Arkansas
KLMG Esparto, California
KUPD Tempe, Arizona
KWGB Colby, Kansas
KXDG Webb City, Missouri
KZBB Poteau, Oklahoma
WLTM Greenville, Mississippi
WBEY-FM Crisfield, Maryland
WNBB Bayboro, North Carolina
WCPR-FM D'Iberville, Mississippi
WYDK Eufaula, Alabama
WEVE Eveleth, Minnesota
WGNR-FM Anderson, Indiana
WGOD-FM Charlotte Amalie, Virgin Islands
WGRD-FM Grand Rapids, Michigan
WIBB-FM Fort Valley, Georgia
WIHC Newberry, Michigan
WIIZ Blackville, South Carolina
WIYY Baltimore, Maryland
WJBQ Portland, Maine
WJLB Detroit, Michigan
WJWZ Wetumpka, Alabama
WDMG-FM Ambrose, Georgia
WKKW Fairmont, West Virginia
WTRG Gaston, North Carolina
WLUP-FM Chicago, Illinois
WUCL Newton, Mississippi
WNCI Columbus, Ohio
WSKS Whitesboro, New York
WPEG Concord, North Carolina
WUCS Windsor Locks, Connecticut
WPXY-FM Rochester, New York
WRIP Windham, New York
WRMF Palm Beach, Florida
WZZU Lynchburg, Virginia
WSIX-FM Nashville, Tennessee
WSKQ-FM New York, New York
WSLM-FM Salem, Indiana
WSPT Stevens Point, Wisconsin
WVOK-FM Oxford, Alabama
WBSX Hazleton, Pennsylvania
WXEF Effingham, Illinois
WXTA Edinboro, Pennsylvania
WXTB Clearwater, Florida
WKIC Hyden, Kentucky
WTSM(FM) Woodville, Florida
KZWB Green River, Wyoming
WBBE Heyworth, Illinois
WMGA Kenova, West Virginia
KDXT Lolo, Montana
WZXP Au Sable, New York
KYRT Hunt, Texas
WKSL Neptune Beach, Florida

97.9 kHz

KYWL Evergreen, Montana
WIJD Prichard, Alabama

98.1 MHz

KJMQ Lihue, Hawaii
KBAC Las Vegas, New Mexico
KBEW-FM Blue Earth, Minnesota
KBUL Carson City, Nevada
KFGE Milford, Nebraska
KTLT Anson, Texas
KGTM Rexburg, Idaho
KHAK Cedar Rapids, Iowa
KIFM San Diego, California
KING-FM Seattle, Washington
KISC Spokane, Washington
KISQ San Francisco, California
KKCL Lorenzo, Texas
KKFM Colorado Springs, Colorado
KKJG San Luis Obispo, California
KUSN Dearing, Kansas
KLEF Anchorage, Alaska
KOZX Cabool, Missouri
KREC Brian Head, Utah

KRRG Laredo, Texas
KRXV Yermo, California
KTAL-FM Texarkana, Texas
KMBZ-FM Kansas City, Kansas
KVET-FM Austin, Texas
KVIP-FM Redding, California
KWLF Fairbanks, Alaska
KSKZ Copeland, Kansas
KYKY St. Louis, Missouri
WOBX-FM Manteo, North Carolina
WBRF Galax, Virginia
WBUL-FM Lexington, Kentucky
WCTK New Bedford, Massachusetts
WDFM Defiance, Ohio
WDGL Baton Rouge, Louisiana
WEDB East Dublin, Georgia
WEUL Kingsford, Michigan
WFGY Altoona, Pennsylvania
WGFN Glen Arbor, Michigan
WNUE-FM Deltona, Florida
WKDD Munroe Falls, Ohio
WHWK Binghamton, New York
WIBN Earl Park, Indiana
WISM Altoona, Wisconsin
WJJR Rutland, Vermont
WKCQ Saginaw, Michigan
WLKN Cleveland, Wisconsin
WKZE-FM Salisbury, Connecticut
WLND Signal Mountain, Tennessee
WMGN Madison, Wisconsin
WMXI Laurel, Mississippi
WOGL Philadelphia, Pennsylvania
WHZT Williamston, South Carolina
WQAQ Hamden, Connecticut
WQHL-FM Live Oak, Florida
WQSM Fayetteville, North Carolina
WRAY-FM Princeton, Indiana
WOCM Selbyville, Delaware
WXMX Millington, Tennessee
WTVR-FM Richmond, Virginia
WTXT Fayette, Alabama
WWJO St. Cloud, Minnesota
WYBB Folly Beach, South Carolina
WMGP Hogansville, Georgia
WZOE-FM Princeton, Illinois
WMRZ Dawson, Georgia
WUDR Dayton, Ohio
WCXV Van Buren, Maine
KRBY Ruby, Alaska
KALG Kaltag, Alaska
KOYU Koyukuk, Alaska
WHWY Holt, Florida

98.3 MHz

KARB Price, Utah
KATR-FM Wray, Colorado
KBEV-FM Dillon, Montana
KBOC Bridgeport, Texas
KDAR Oxnard, California
KDZY McCall, Idaho
KEJJ Gunnison, Colorado
KERM Torrington, Wyoming
KEYW Pasco, Washington
KFCM Ash Flat, Arkansas
KUQL Ethan, South Dakota
KICA-FM Farwell, Texas
KKEG Bentonville, Arkansas
KKFR Mayer, Arizona
KLDR Harbeck-Fruitdale, Oregon
KMJR Odem, Texas
KJMD Pukalani, Hawaii
KOHT Marana, Arizona
KORA-FM Bryan, Texas
KPTX Pecos, Texas
KQYB Spring Grove, Minnesota
KXDJ Spearman, Texas
KWQW Boone, Iowa
KRCV West Covina, California
KYAR Lorena, Texas
KTWS Bend, Oregon
KULM-FM Columbus, Texas
KWNN Lodi, California
KXBX-FM Lakeport, California
KZRZ West Monroe, Louisiana
KXGT Carrington, North Dakota
KYYK Palestine, Texas
WBFA Fort Mitchell, Alabama
WFXO Ashland, Alabama
WUIN Oak Island, North Carolina
WBJI Blackduck, Minnesota
WCCQ Crest Hill, Illinois
WCEF Ripley, West Virginia
WCMZ-FM Sault Ste. Marie, Michigan
WCQM Park Falls, Wisconsin
WCXT Hartford, Michigan
WLGT Washington, North Carolina
WDAQ Danbury, Connecticut
WMTY-FM Sweetwater, Tennessee
WDFX Cleveland, Mississippi
WDLZ Murfreesboro, North Carolina
WDXE-FM Lawrenceburg, Tennessee
WJMR-FM Menomonee Falls, Wisconsin
WGCO Midway, Georgia
WHAI Greenfield, Massachusetts
WHAY Whitley City, Kentucky
WRUP Palmer, Michigan
WILI-FM Willimantic, Connecticut
WJDR Prentiss, Mississippi
WLUS-FM Clarksville, Virginia
WKEA-FM Scottsboro, Alabama
WKET Kettering, Ohio
WKJY Hempstead, New York
WCEH-FM Pinehurst, Georgia
WKSR-FM Loretto, Tennessee
WLCS North Muskegon, Michigan
WKNA Logan, Ohio
WLJI Summerton, South Carolina
WLNH-FM Laconia, New Hampshire
WMGQ New Brunswick, New Jersey
WOKE Garrison, Kentucky
WPKO-FM Bellefontaine, Ohio
WQRS Salamanca, New York
WQXE Elizabethtown, Kentucky
WMYP Frederiksted, Virgin Islands
WJLI Metropolis, Illinois
WRTO-FM Goulds, Florida
WZOL Las Piedras, Puerto Rico
WHHD Clearwater, South Carolina
WSMD-FM Mechanicsville, Maryland
WKOZ-FM Carthage, Mississippi
WSUL Monticello, New York
WTKU-FM Petersburg, New Jersey
WTRY-FM Rotterdam, New York
WMIM Luna Pier, Michigan
WVIN-FM Bath, New York
WWBE Mifflinburg, Pennsylvania
WMAN-FM Fredericktown, Ohio
WWHP Farmer City, Illinois
WWRZ Fort Meade, Florida
WRDZ-FM Plainfield, Indiana
WKSI-FM Stephens City, Virginia
WZZY Winchester, Indiana
KZZS Story, Wyoming
KSNQ Twin Falls, Idaho
WYBL Ashtabula, Ohio
KZLA Riverdale, California
KADQ-FM Evanston, Wyoming
KQZQ Kiowa, Kansas
KXIM Sanborn, Iowa
WLVM Chickasaw, Alabama
WUBG Plainfield, South Carolina
WSVZ Tower Hill, Illinois

98.5 MHz

KABG Los Alamos, New Mexico
KACO Apache, Oklahoma
KBBZ Kalispell, Montana
KBBT Schertz, Texas
KCHI-FM Chillicothe, Missouri
KWBY-FM Ranger, Texas
KDES-FM Cathedral City, California
KEYG-FM Grand Coulee, Washington
KGAP Clarksville, Texas
KGBT-FM McAllen, Texas
KGIL Johannesburg, California
KGHL(FM) Billings, Montana
KIFX Roosevelt, Utah
KOEL-FM Cedar Falls, Iowa
KDNN Honolulu, Hawaii
KLLP Chubbuck, Idaho
KLUC Las Vegas, Nevada
KQKQ-FM Council Bluffs, Iowa
KRXQ Sacramento, California
KRXT Rockdale, Texas
KSAJ-FM Abilene, Kansas
KDFO Delano, California
KTIS-FM Minneapolis, Minnesota
KTJJ Farmington, Missouri
KTJM Port Arthur, Texas
KUFX San Jose, California
KURB Little Rock, Arkansas
KVOO-FM Tulsa, Oklahoma
KYGO-FM Denver, Colorado
KJJT Los Ybanez, Texas
KRDX Vail, Arizona
WACL Elkton, Virginia
WMYK Peru, Indiana
WBBO(FM) Ocean Acres, New Jersey
WBZF Hartsville, South Carolina
WCKM-FM Lake George, New York
WCMO Marietta, Ohio
WCTW Catskill, New York
WDAI Pawleys Island, South Carolina
WBON Westhampton, New York
WDEO-FM San Carlos Park, Florida
WEBB Waterville, Maine
WPIA Eureka, Illinois
WFSY Panama City, Florida
WKSW Cookeville, Tennessee
WINL Linden, Alabama
WKRZ Freeland, Pennsylvania
WKSE Niagara Falls, New York
WKTK Crystal River, Florida
WLPF Ocilla, Georgia
WOMG Lexington, South Carolina
WNCX Cleveland, Ohio
WSB(FM) Clemson, Georgia
WNWN-FM Coldwater, Michigan
WNYR Waterloo, New York
WGYI Oil City, Pennsylvania
WQKZ Ferdinand, Indiana
WQLH Green Bay, Wisconsin
WRRM Cincinnati, Ohio
WDWG Rocky Mount, North Carolina
WSB-FM Atlanta, Georgia
WTFM Kingsport, Tennessee
WUPS Houghton Lake, Michigan
WWVR Paris, Indiana
WXXQ Freeport, Illinois
WYCR York-Hanover, Pennsylvania
WYLD-FM New Orleans, Louisiana
WZLQ Tupelo, Mississippi
KHAQ Maxwell, Nebraska
KWKJ Windsor, Missouri
KZID Culdesac, Idaho
KGRK Glenrock, Wyoming
WSBH Satellite Beach, Florida
KAAI Palisade, Colorado
KOYT(FM) Montana City, Montana
KXJN Moose Wilson Road, Wyoming
KEWF Billings, Montana
KHIC Keno, Oregon
WBZ-FM Boston, Massachusetts

98.5 mhz

WGBG Seaford, Delaware

98.7 MHz

KACL Bismarck, North Dakota
KFH-FM Clearwater, Kansas
KBEE Salt Lake City, Utah
KELI San Angelo, Texas
KARO Nyssa, Oregon
KISD Pipestone, Minnesota
KMVP-FM Phoenix, Arizona
KKST Oakdale, Louisiana
KLBQ El Dorado, Arkansas
KMNA Mabton, Washington
KLOQ-FM Winton, California
KLUV Dallas, Texas
KMGO Centerville, Iowa
KMTH Maljamar, New Mexico
KPRF Amarillo, Texas
KOUT Rapid City, South Dakota
KLTA-FM Moorhead, Minnesota
KXTS Geyserville, California
KRSV Afton, Wyoming
KRTZ Cortez, Colorado
KSID-FM Sidney, Nebraska
KKVS Truth or Consequences, New Mexico
KTXN-FM Victoria, Texas
KUBQ La Grande, Oregon
KUPL Portland, Oregon
KSMA-FM Osage, Iowa
KWTO-FM Springfield, Missouri
KYSR Los Angeles, California
KYTT-FM Coos Bay, Oregon
WASK-FM Battle Ground, Indiana
WYCT Pensacola, Florida
WBHK Warrior, Alabama
WBTY Homerville, Georgia
WBYY Somersworth, New Hampshire
WGMM Corning, New York
WCNK Key West, Florida
WEMR Pleasant Gap, Pennsylvania
WFGR Grand Rapids, Michigan
WFMT Chicago, Illinois
WISK-FM Americus, Georgia
WJKK Vicksburg, Mississippi
WYRO McArthur, Ohio
WKDO-FM Liberty, Kentucky
WKGR Wellington, Florida
WRMR Jacksonville, North Carolina
WSMW Greensboro, North Carolina
WLZW Utica, New York
WMDC Mayville, Wisconsin
WMZQ-FM Washington, District of Columbia
WNLC East Lyme, Connecticut
WNNS Springfield, Illinois
WNOR Norfolk, Virginia
WOVK Wheeling, West Virginia
WQME Anderson, Indiana
WEPN-FM New York, New York
WRVZ Pocatalico, West Virginia
WOKI Oliver Springs, Tennessee
WUKQ-FM Mayaguez, Puerto Rico
WDZH Detroit, Michigan
WCZT Villas, New Jersey
WINQ Winchester, New Hampshire
WYKZ Beaufort, South Carolina
WPAC Ogdensburg, New York
WYKL Crestline, Ohio
WGLI Hancock, Michigan
KRQU Laramie, Wyoming
WNEV Friars Point, Mississippi
KZAM Pleasant Valley, Texas
KAVB Hawthorne, Nevada
KWXR Reliance, Wyoming
WBRN Holmes Beach, Florida

98.9 MHz

KAAK Great Falls, Montana
KITH Kapaa, Hawaii
KWLU Chester, California
KRQX-FM Santa Clara, Utah
KFLW St. Robert, Missouri
KGRA Jefferson, Iowa
KHWY Essex, California
KUTX Leander, Texas
KKMG Pueblo, Colorado
KKPR-FM Kearney, Nebraska
KKZX Spokane, Washington
KQRC-FM Leavenworth, Kansas
KSOF Dinuba, California
KSOL San Francisco, California
KTCO Duluth, Minnesota
KCVR-FM Columbia, California
WKIM Munford, Tennessee
KTUX Carthage, Texas
KQQF Coffeyville, Kansas
KLCK-FM Seattle, Washington
KYIS Oklahoma City, Oklahoma
KYMG Anchorage, Alaska
KZPK Paynesville, Minnesota
WAJV Brooksville, Mississippi
WANT Lebanon, Tennessee
WBAM-FM Montgomery, Alabama
WBZA Rochester, New York
WBYR Woodburn, Indiana
WBZE Tallahassee, Florida
WCLZ North Yarmouth, Maine
WDNE-FM Elkins, West Virginia
WNBR-FM Bethel, North Carolina
WUUU Franklinton, Louisiana
WGUF Marco, Florida
WBCG Murdock, Florida
WNRW Salem, Indiana
WHQQ Neoga, Illinois
WLKU Rock Island, Illinois
WWLB Ettrick, Virginia
WMXY Youngstown, Ohio
WKLZ-FM Petoskey, Michigan
WJEZ Dwight, Illinois
WMMO Orlando, Florida
WOKO Burlington, Vermont
WORC Webster, Massachusetts
WOWE Vassar, Michigan
WQKY Emporium, Pennsylvania
WQLV Millersburg, Pennsylvania
WNGH-FM Chatsworth, Georgia
WSBY-FM Salisbury, Maryland
WSIP-FM Paintsville, Kentucky
WSPA-FM Spartanburg, South Carolina
WUSL Philadelphia, Pennsylvania

WVCX Tomah, Wisconsin
WWIK McClellanville, South Carolina
WTOH Upper Arlington, Ohio
WMSO Quitman, Mississippi
KQCR-FM Parkersburg, Iowa
KLMO-FM Dilley, Texas
WISH-FM Galatia, Illinois
KLYD Snyder, Texas
WLFV Midlothian, Virginia
KLOW Reno, Texas
KRVC Hornbrook, California
WRAX Lake Isabella, Michigan
KZXK Doney Park, Arizona

99 MHz

WEDR Miami, Florida

99.1 MHz

KAGB Waimea, Hawaii
KCAD Dickinson, North Dakota
KCLV-FM Clovis, New Mexico
KEEZ-FM Mankato, Minnesota
KFMM Thatcher, Arizona
KLJY Clayton, Missouri
KGGI Riverside, California
KGLX Gallup, New Mexico
KGNT Smithfield, Utah
KKFT Gardnerville-Minden, Nevada
KDXX Denton, Texas
KXMT Taos, New Mexico
KJIL Copeland, Kansas
KMA-FM Clarinda, Iowa
KLLZ-FM Walker, Minnesota
KHKX Odessa, Texas
KMAG Fort Smith, Arkansas
KMTS Glenwood Springs, Colorado
KNES Fairfield, Texas
KTMG Prescott, Arizona
KODA Houston, Texas
KODZ Eugene, Oregon
KOFH Nogales, Arizona
KRUP Dillingham, Alaska
KRYS-FM Corpus Christi, Texas
KSEK-FM Girard, Kansas
KSKB Brooklyn, Iowa
KTLI El Dorado, Kansas
KUAD-FM Windsor, Colorado
KUJ-FM Burbank, Washington
KUPI-FM Rexburg, Idaho
KXFM Santa Maria, California
KXKC New Iberia, Louisiana
KYOO-FM Half Way, Missouri
KXLG Milbank, South Dakota
KSQL Santa Cruz, California
WAAL Binghamton, New York
WAHR Huntsville, Alabama
WAWZ Zarephath, New Jersey
WDEN-FM Macon, Georgia
WCBL-FM Grand Rivers, Kentucky
WFMK Lansing, Michigan
WFRO-FM Fremont, Ohio
WNEW Bowie, District of Columbia
WHKO Dayton, Ohio
WYXY(FM) Danville, Illinois
WIKB-FM Iron River, Michigan
WJMM-FM Keene, Kentucky
WJNV Jonesville, Virginia
WHSX Edmonton, Kentucky
WKNN-FM Pascagoula, Mississippi
WBFE Bar Harbor, Maine
WMYX-FM Milwaukee, Wisconsin
WNNH Henniker, New Hampshire
WNML Friendsville, Tennessee
WPLM-FM Plymouth, Massachusetts
WPLR New Haven, Connecticut
WPRM-FM San Juan, Puerto Rico
WQIK-FM Jacksonville, Florida
WRKW Ebensburg, Pennsylvania
WSLQ Roanoke, Virginia
WSMK Buchanan, Michigan
WVOD Manteo, North Carolina
WWOJ Avon Park, Florida
WXGM-FM Gloucester, Virginia
WGGE Parkersburg, West Virginia
WYMX Greenwood, Mississippi
WZFX Whiteville, North Carolina
KWYW Lost Cabin, Wyoming
KCMM Belgrade, Montana
WDGM Greensboro, Alabama
KVMZ Waldo, Arkansas
KARA Williams, California
KSMD Pangburn, Arkansas
KZJZ St. Regis, Montana
KWAP(FM) Pine Haven, Wyoming
WNYN-FM Whitefield, New Hampshire
WWKN Morgantown, Kentucky
KSOO-FM Lennox, South Dakota
KNUL Nulato, Alaska
WHBJ Barnwell, 0

99.3 MHz

KADA-FM Ada, Oklahoma
KDDS-FM Elma, Washington
KCLI-FM Cordell, Oklahoma
KCGQ-FM Gordonville, Missouri
KCLR-FM Boonville, Missouri
KDRM Moses Lake, Washington
KDST Dyersville, Iowa
KEFH Clarendon, Texas
KFFF-FM Boone, Iowa
KGVE Grove, Oklahoma
KAPW White Oak, Texas
KJOY Stockton, California
KJWL Fresno, California
KKBB Bakersfield, California
KKDQ Thief River Falls, Minnesota
KKTS-FM Douglas, Wyoming
KLOR-FM Ponca City, Oklahoma
KMXE-FM Red Lodge, Montana
KMXX Imperial, California
KPCH Ruston, Louisiana
KNNN(FM) Shasta Lake City, California
KPSM Brownwood, Texas
KRGT Indian Springs, Nevada
KIT-FM Naches, Washington
KCON Atkins, Arkansas
KXRZ Alexandria, Minnesota
KUNQ Houston, Missouri
KCMD Grants Pass, Oregon
KVYN St. Helena, California
KWAY-FM Waverly, Iowa
KWFL Roswell, New Mexico
KWIC Topeka, Kansas
KWNO-FM Rushford, Minnesota
WTZR Elizabethton, Tennessee
WAJK La Salle, Illinois
WATZ-FM Alpena, Michigan
WBAW-FM Pembroke, Georgia
WBVV Guntown, Mississippi
WBQQ Kennebunk, Maine
WBT-FM Chester, South Carolina
WOUF Beulah, Michigan
WCJC Van Buren, Indiana
WCON-FM Cornelia, Georgia
WDMP-FM Dodgeville, Wisconsin
WDUK Havana, Illinois
WMNP Block Island, Rhode Island
WNRX Jefferson City, Tennessee
WFQX Front Royal, Virginia
WHMJ Franklin, Pennsylvania
WFRD Hanover, New Hampshire
WLAU Heidelberg, Mississippi
WLZX Northampton, Massachusetts
WWCN Fort Myers Beach, Florida
WJQK Zeeland, Michigan
WKCN Fort Benning South, Georgia
WKEB Medford, Wisconsin
WKTJ-FM Farmington, Maine
WKVI-FM Knox, Indiana
WLLG Lowville, New York
WMFC Monroeville, Alabama
WBET-FM Sturgis, Michigan
WNXT-FM Portsmouth, Ohio
WKMO Lebanon Junction, Kentucky
WOWN Shawano, Wisconsin
WKJM Petersburg, Virginia
WPKL Uniontown, Pennsylvania
WQDK Gatesville, North Carolina
WZBZ Pleasantville, New Jersey
WSCH Aurora, Indiana
WLLW Seneca Falls, New York
WEBZ Mexico Beach, Florida
WSNN Potsdam, New York
WRWB-FM Ellenville, New York
WTNS-FM Coshocton, Ohio
WVES Accomac, Virginia
WVLE Scottsville, Kentucky
WWKF Fulton, Kentucky
WHKF Harrisburg, Pennsylvania
WWKT-FM Kingstree, South Carolina
WXFM-FM Mount Zion, Illinois
WPBX Crossville, Tennessee
WZAX Nashville, North Carolina
WZLT Lexington, Tennessee
WZXR South Williamsport, Pennsylvania
KOKE-FM Thorndale, Texas
KTGA Saratoga, Wyoming
KMZQ-FM Payson, Arizona
KERL Cotton Plant, Arkansas
KETT Mitchell, Nebraska
KHZY Overton, Nebraska
WXRA Inglis, Florida
KPCR Fowler, Colorado
KYTM Corrigan, Texas
WVLO Cridersville, Ohio
KKTU-FM Fallon, Nevada
WVBX Spotsylvania, Virginia
WLRQ-FM Cocoa, Florida
WSNN Potsdam, New York

99.5 MHz

KADI-FM Republic, Missouri
KAGO-FM Klamath Falls, Oregon
KBHW International Falls, Minnesota
KBLL-FM Helena, Montana
KNFX-FM Bryan, Texas
KBTA-FM Batesville, Arkansas
KBZQ Lawton, Oklahoma
KXBL Henryetta, Oklahoma
KQBR Lubbock, Texas
KDAO-FM Eldora, Iowa
KLVB Citrus Heights, California
KHAZ Hays, Kansas
KNGT Lake Charles, Louisiana
KHMB Hamburg, Arkansas
KIIM Tucson, Arizona
KISS-FM San Antonio, Texas
KQMT Denver, Colorado
KKLA-FM Los Angeles, California
KKMA Le Mars, Iowa
KKPS Brownsville, Texas
KLOK-FM Greenfield, California
KMRJ Rancho Mirage, California
KMTB Murfreesboro, Arkansas
KNTI Lakeport, California
KOLY-FM Mobridge, South Dakota
KPLX Fort Worth, Texas
KPRW Perham, Minnesota
KPXP Garapan-Saipan, Guam
KJMX Coos Bay, Oregon
KAKS Goshen, Arkansas
KXPZ Las Cruces, New Mexico
KSJN Minneapolis, Minnesota
KJMY Bountiful, Utah
KKTV Fallon, Nevada
KWJJ-FM Portland, Oregon
KAAP Rock Island, Washington
KDIS-FM Little Rock, Arkansas
KZZL-FM Pullman, Washington
KPUL Winterset, Iowa
WAIL Key West, Florida
WAOL Ripley, Ohio
WBAI New York, New York
WBXY La Crosse, Florida
WBYG Point Pleasant, West Virginia
WCYJ-FM Waynesburg, Pennsylvania
WDCX-FM Buffalo, New York
WKAA Willacoochee, Georgia
WDZN Midland, Maryland
WGAR-FM Cleveland, Ohio
WJBR-FM Wilmington, Delaware
WJCX Pittsfield, Maine
WJLS-FM Beckley, West Virginia
WIHT Washington, District of Columbia
WKDP-FM Corbin, Kentucky
WKDQ Henderson, Kentucky
WCRB Lowell, Massachusetts
WKSM Fort Walton Beach, Florida
WKXC-FM Aiken, South Carolina
WMAG High Point, North Carolina
WRNN-FM Socastee, South Carolina
WNGE Negaunee, Michigan
WOKN Southport, New York
WPKR Omro, Wisconsin
WCOY Quincy, Illinois
WIDI Quebradillas, Puerto Rico
WQYK-FM St. Petersburg, Florida
WRNO-FM New Orleans, Louisiana
WRVE Schenectady, New York
WTKW Bridgeport, New York
WUSN Chicago, Illinois
WUSR Scranton, Pennsylvania
WVIQ Christiansted, Virgin Islands
WMAJ-FM Centre Hall, Pennsylvania
WXNR Grifton, North Carolina
WYCD Detroit, Michigan
WYGO Madisonville, Tennessee
WYSS Sault Ste. Marie, Michigan
WZPL Greenfield, Indiana
WZRR Birmingham, Alabama
KMCJ Colstrip, Montana
KRKI Keystone, South Dakota
WYMJ New Martinsville, West Virginia
WZIM(FM) Lexington, Illinois
WEVJ Jackson, New Hampshire
WYTT Emporia, Virginia
KHCR Bismarck, Missouri
KBIJ Guymon, Oklahoma
KQPI Aberdeen, Idaho
KRPH Morristown, Arizona
KISS-FM San Antonio, Texas

99.7 MHz

KHLT Belle Plaine, Kansas
KBCY Tye, Texas
KBEA-FM Muscatine, Iowa
KBTN-FM Neosho, Missouri
KBZD Amarillo, Texas
KMVQ San Francisco, California
KHHK Yakima, Washington
KHYZ Mountain Pass, California
KIOO Porterville, California
KKCK Marshall, Minnesota
KBOD Gainesville, Missouri
KMBQ-FM Wasilla, Alaska
KMJJ-FM Shreveport, Louisiana
KSIT Rock Springs, Wyoming
KOGA-FM Ogallala, Nebraska
KPTE Durango, Colorado
KTTR FM St. James, Missouri
KVST Willis, Texas
KESC Morro Bay, California
KXDL Browerville, Minnesota
KNAH Mustang, Oklahoma
KZPT Kansas City, Missouri
WBGK Newport Village, New York
WBHX Tuckerton, New Jersey
WRKZ Columbus, Ohio
WCYK-FM Staunton, Virginia
WDJX Louisville, Kentucky
WXST Hollywood, South Carolina
WIMI Ironwood, Michigan
WJMI Jackson, Mississippi
WJUX Monticello, New York
WKSD Paulding, Ohio
WMC-FM Memphis, Tennessee
WWWQ Atlanta, Georgia
WNTK-FM New London, New Hampshire
WOOF-FM Dothan, Alabama
WJKD Vero Beach, Florida
WRFX Kannapolis, North Carolina
WSHH Pittsburgh, Pennsylvania
WSHW Frankfort, Indiana
WVRZ Mount Carmel, Pennsylvania
WUGN Midland, Michigan
WWIS-FM Black River Falls, Wisconsin
WWTN Hendersonville, Tennessee
WXAJ Hillsboro, Illinois
WEAN Wakefield-Peacedale, Rhode Island
WYFI Norfolk, Virginia
WGCK-FM Coeburn, Virginia
WZXV Palmyra, New York
KMTK Bend, Oregon
KTOR Gerber, California
KHAN Medicine Bow, Wyoming
KQRK Pablo, Montana
KXFT Manson, Iowa
KETE Sulphur Bluff, Texas
KBBC Tishomingo, Oklahoma
KAFZ Ash Fork, Arizona
KWPS-FM Caddo Valley, Arkansas

99.7 kHz

KWDF Ball, Louisiana

99.9 Hz

WJVL Janesville, Wisconsin

99.9 MHz

KAUS-FM Austin, Minnesota
KTOH Kalaheo, Hawaii
KBFL-FM Buffalo, Missouri
KCIV Mount Bullion, California

KCML St. Joseph, Minnesota
KCWN New Sharon, Iowa
KEKB Fruita, Colorado
KONY St. George, Utah
KESZ Phoenix, Arizona
KFAV Warrenton, Missouri
KFMJ Ketchikan, Alaska
KBAT Monahans, Texas
KGOR Omaha, Nebraska
KGPQ Monticello, Arkansas
KTEZ Zwolle, Louisiana
KIRK Macon, Missouri
KISW Seattle, Washington
KKTC Angel Fire, New Mexico
KLUR Wichita Falls, Texas
KMOO-FM Mineola, Texas
KMXA-FM Minot, North Dakota
KJKS Kahului, Hawaii
KOLA San Bernardino, California
KRCX-FM Marysville, California
KRKT-FM Albany, Oregon
KKPL Cheyenne, Wyoming
KSAB Robstown, Texas
KSHN Liberty, Texas
KSKG Salina, Kansas
KWKR Leoti, Kansas
KTCS-FM Fort Smith, Arkansas
KTDY Lafayette, Louisiana
KTQM-FM Clovis, New Mexico
KTSM-FM El Paso, Texas
KTXM Hallettsville, Texas
KTYD Santa Barbara, California
KVOX-FM Moorhead, Minnesota
KVUU Pueblo, Colorado
KWCK-FM Searcy, Arkansas
KWRL La Grande, Oregon
KXLY-FM Spokane, Washington
KXTC Thoreau, New Mexico
KZDX Burley, Idaho
KBOZ-FM Bozeman, Montana
WACO-FM Waco, Texas
WQNR Tallassee, Alabama
WNNG-FM Unadilla, Georgia
WBTZ Plattsburgh, New York
WFNX Athol, Massachusetts
WEZN-FM Bridgeport, Connecticut
WGNE-FM Middleburg, Florida
WFRE Frederick, Maryland
WCMC-FM Holly Springs, North Carolina
WHAK-FM Rogers City, Michigan
WHFB-FM Benton Harbor, Michigan
WHHB Holliston, Massachusetts
WHHS Havertown, Pennsylvania
WIII Cortland, New York
WIOA San Juan, Puerto Rico
WWCT Bartonville, Illinois
WSAU-FM Rudolph, Wisconsin
WJVL Janesville, Wisconsin
WKIS Boca Raton, Florida
WKKO Toledo, Ohio
WKSF Old Fort, North Carolina
WKXB Boiling Spring Lakes, North Carolina
WMTC-FM Vancleve, Kentucky
WTHT Auburn, Maine
WMXC Mobile, Alabama
WODE-FM Easton, Pennsylvania
WOOZ-FM Harrisburg, Illinois
WQBR Avis, Pennsylvania
WQRC Barnstable, Massachusetts
WRJL-FM Eva, Alabama
WCPQ Park Forest, Illinois
WTHI-FM Terre Haute, Indiana
WTUZ Uhrichsville, Ohio
WUSZ Virginia, Minnesota
WVAF Charleston, West Virginia
WVLC Mannsville, Kentucky
WWFG Ocean City, Maryland
WXKC Erie, Pennsylvania
WXMZ Hartford, Kentucky
WYFJ Ashland, Virginia
WZBB Stanleytown, Virginia
WDRK Cornell, Wisconsin
KGCC Gillette, Wyoming
WSMS Artesia, Mississippi
KZMA Naylor, Missouri
WHDX Buxton, North Carolina
WSNT-FM Sandersville, Georgia
KXML Fairfield, Idaho
KLKV Hunt, Texas
KVBL La Grande, Oregon
WCHD Kettering, Ohio

9MHz

KLRC Siloam Springs, Arkansas
WUGO Grayson, Kentucky

MHz

WBBL Greenville, Michigan

Radio Formats Defined

AAA (or Triple A)—Adult Album Alternative. Eclectic choice of music ranging from hard rock to folk music.

Adult Contemporary—Recent popular songs, with a few oldies. The songs tend to be upbeat and soft. News and talk segments are prominent during rush hour "drive times." Also known as Light Rock.

Agriculture & Farm—News, weather and features of interest to farmers and others involved in agriculture.

Album-Oriented Rock—Popular rock music from past and present rock albums. Also see Rock/AOR.

Alternative—Rock music first popularized in the late 80s and early 90s. Also known as Progressive.

American Indian—Programming for North American Indians; includes native language (i.e. Navajo) broadcasts.

Arabic.

Beautiful Music—Uninterrupted, instrumental soft music. There is usually very little talk and few commercials. Also known as Easy Listening.

Big Band—Popular music from the 30s and 40s. Primarily instrumental works by bands such as Glen Miller's Orchestra and Tommy Dorsey. Also see Nostalgia.

Black—Music, talk and news targeted at Black listeners. Music at these stations is similar to Urban Contemporary stations, but this format caters more directly to the interests and tastes of Black audiences.

Bluegrass—Related formats are Country and Folk.

Blues—Some Jazz and Progressive stations also program blues music.

Children—Programming for children, usually for educational purposes. Includes music, informational programming, and news presented for young people.

Chinese.

Christian.

Classic Rock—Popular rock music of the 60s, 70s and 80s. Also see Rock/AOR.

Classical—Classical music, often long pieces played without interruption. Announcers provide extended commentary and criticism on the pieces. Special features, such as live concerts, are common. Primarily a noncommercial FM format.

Comedy—Recorded stand-up comics and/or old radio comedy series. A rare format.

Contemporary Hit/Top-40—Current hot selling records. Usually a playlist of 20 to 40 songs continuously played throughout the day. DJs are often upbeat "personalities." News and information are given light coverage.

Country—Country music, ranging from older traditional country and western to today's "Hit Country" sounds. The amount of news and talk on country stations varies widely from station to station.

Disco—High-energy dance music first popular in the 70s. Also see Black and Urban Contemporary.

Diversified—See Variety/Diverse.

Easy Listening—Similar to Beautiful Music, but may include some soft rock.

Ethnic—Programming for ethnic minorities, mostly in foreign languages.

Farsi.

Filipino.

Folk—Played full-time on very few stations, American folk music is also heard on noncommercial Variety stations. Also see Bluegrass.

Foreign Language/Ethnic—In addition to the specific language categories (i.e. French, German), this format denotes multilingual stations and others catering to ethnic minorities.

French.

Golden Oldies—Hit songs of the 50s. Also see Oldies.

Gospel—Especially popular in the South, evangelical music is programmed on many Religious format stations.

Greek.

Italian.

Japanese.

Jazz—Primarily a noncommercial FM format. Some Classical stations program jazz music features.

Korean.

Light Rock—See Adult Contemporary.

MOR (Middle-of-the-Road)—Traditional AM format featuring a balanced mix of music, news and talk. Songs are usually popular standards. Announcers are often personalities who try to keep the listener interested and informed. News, both local and national, plays an important role at most MOR stations; coverage of sporting events and other features of interest to the community is common.

Native American.

News—Continous coverage of local, national and international news, including sports, weather forecasts and features.

News/Talk—Combination of news and talk formats. One of these elements may receive more emphasis. Also see News and Talk.

Oldies—Hit songs from the 50s, 60s and 70s. Usually played by upbeat DJs, with news, talk and special features (chart countdowns, trivia contests, etc.) playing an important role.

Polish.

Polka—Music for the traditional dance. Most polka format stations are located in Wisconsin.

Portuguese.

Public Affairs—Community interest programming (ie: broadcasts of city council meetings.) Many noncommercial, News, and Talk stations cover local issues on news features or talk shows.

Reggae—Jamaican music. Often played on Progressive stations.

Religious—Inspirational/spiritual talk and music. Most religious stations air Christian sermons or songs. Also see Gospel.

Rock/AOR—Rock music from the 60s to the present. Album-oriented rock features music "sweeps" or uninterrrupted sets. News plays a secondary role. Also see Classic Rock.

Russian.

Spanish.

Sports—Play-by-play and taped coverage, sports news, interviews, discussion.

Talk—Topical programs on various subjects. Includes health, finance, and community issues. Listener call-in and interview shows are common, and the host's personality tends to be an important element. Many talk stations air national satellite-delivered talk programs. News, sports and weather are usually emphasized during "drive times." Also see News and News/Talk.

Tejano—Bicultural programming including Spanish programming, popular in Texas, particularly near the Mexican border. Interest surged in this type of Spanish music during the early 90s.

Top-40—See Contemporary Hit/Top-40.

Urban Contemporary—Dance music, often from a variety of genres (i.e. rhythm & blues, rap). Most Urban Contemporary stations emphasize music by Black artists. Also see Black and Disco.

Variety/Diverse—A station listing four or more formats. Typical of noncommerical stations.

Vietnamese.

Programming on Radio Stations in the U.S.

Adult Contemp

KDBZ Anchorage, Alaska
KMXS Anchorage, Alaska
KYMG Anchorage, Alaska
KBRW-FM Barrow, Alaska
KTDZ College, Alaska
KCDV Cordova, Alaska
KDLG Dillingham, Alaska
KYSC Fairbanks, Alaska
KGTL Homer, Alaska
KWVV-FM Homer, Alaska
KBBO-FM Houston, Alaska
KINY Juneau, Alaska
KTKN Ketchikan, Alaska
KAKN Naknek, Alaska
KMVN Palmer, Alaska
KIFW Sitka, Alaska
KKIS-FM Soldotna, Alaska
KUHB-FM St. Paul, Alaska
KVAK-FM Valdez, Alaska
WSTF Andalusia, Alabama
WKXX Attalla, Alabama
WAYE Birmingham, Alabama
WMJJ Birmingham, Alabama
WUHT Birmingham, Alabama
WQZZ Boligee, Alabama
WMLV Butler, Alabama
WYDE-FM Cullman, Alabama
WDYF Dothan, Alabama
WKZJ Eufaula, Alabama
WFIX Florence, Alabama
WQLT-FM Florence, Alabama
WHEP Foley, Alabama
WCKS Fruithurst, Alabama
WFXX Georgiana, Alabama
WHOG Hobson City, Alabama
WAHR Huntsville, Alabama
WHOD Jackson, Alabama
WLBF Montgomery, Alabama
WMXS Montgomery, Alabama
WEUP-FM Moulton, Alabama
WMXA Opelika, Alabama
WCSN-FM Orange Beach, Alabama
WALX Orrville, Alabama
WOZK Ozark, Alabama
WGSY Phenix City, Alabama
WPID Piedmont, Alabama
WDLT-FM Saraland, Alabama
WJAM Selma, Alabama
WJRL-FM Slocomb, Alabama
WAGH Smiths, Alabama
WWFA St. Florian, Alabama
WQNR Tallassee, Alabama
WACT Tuscaloosa, Alabama
KMJI Ashdown, Arkansas
KBTA-FM Batesville, Arkansas
KHLR Benton, Arkansas
KJBX Cash, Arkansas
KBKG Corning, Arkansas
KDMS El Dorado, Arkansas
KLBQ El Dorado, Arkansas
KMLK El Dorado, Arkansas
KMRX El Dorado, Arkansas
KESA Eureka Springs, Arkansas
KFFB Fairfield Bay, Arkansas
KEZA Fayetteville, Arkansas
KCNY Greenbrier, Arkansas
KHMB Hamburg, Arkansas
KOOU Hardy, Arkansas
KILX Hatfield, Arkansas
KFFA-FM Helena, Arkansas
KBYB Hope, Arkansas
KBHS Hot Springs, Arkansas
KHTO(FM) Hot Springs, Arkansas
KLAZ Hot Springs, Arkansas
KVRE Hot Springs Village, Arkansas
KVLO Humnoke, Arkansas
KEAZ Kensett, Arkansas
KKTZ Lakeview, Arkansas
KKPT Little Rock, Arkansas
KURB Little Rock, Arkansas
KOLL Lonoke, Arkansas
KBGB Magness, Arkansas
KHKN Maumelle, Arkansas
KGPQ Monticello, Arkansas
KHBM-FM Monticello, Arkansas
KOMT Mountain Home, Arkansas
KTLO-FM Mountain Home, Arkansas
KQMJ(FM) Osceola, Arkansas
KBOA-FM Piggott, Arkansas
KPOC Pocahontas, Arkansas
KPOC-FM Pocahontas, Arkansas
KWKK Russellville, Arkansas
KTOY Texarkana, Arkansas
KKHJ-FM Pago Pago, American Samoa
KVVA-FM Apache Junction, Arizona
KFTT Bagdad, Arizona
KIKO-FM Claypool, Arizona
KWRQ Clifton, Arizona
KYBC Cottonwood, Arizona
KOAS Dolan Springs, Arizona
KJIK Duncan, Arizona
KVNA-FM Flagstaff, Arizona
KZUL-FM Lake Havasu City, Arizona
KVGS Meadview, Arizona
KESZ Phoenix, Arizona
KMXP Phoenix, Arizona
KYOT-FM Phoenix, Arizona
KTMG Prescott, Arizona
KPPV Prescott Valley, Arizona
KRFM Show Low, Arizona
KZMK Sierra Vista, Arizona
KQAZ Springerville, Arizona
KWKM St. Johns, Arizona
KTBA Tuba City, Arizona
KHYT Tucson, Arizona
KMIY Tucson, Arizona
KMXZ-FM Tucson, Arizona
KTUC Tucson, Arizona
KWIM Window Rock, Arizona
KLJZ Yuma, Arizona
KQSR Yuma, Arizona
XETRA Tijuana, Mexico
XHRMFM Tijuana, Mexico
KYZA Adelanto, California
KZXY-FM Apple Valley, California
KSTT Atascadero, California
KGFM Bakersfield, California
KBLX-FM Berkeley, California
KJMB-FM Blythe, California
KSEH Brawley, California
KBPK Buena Park, California
KCDU Carmel, California
KWXY AM Cathedral City, California
KVIN Ceres, California
KBQB Chico, California
KMXI Chico, California
KPST Coachella, California
KXSE Davis, California
KGBB Edwards, California
KWST El Centro, California
KXO-FM El Centro, California
KFSD Escondido, California
KHWY Essex, California
KFMI Eureka, California
KSXY Forestville, California
KWPT Fortuna, California
KYLA(FM) Fountain Valley, California
KWYE Fresno, California
KBAY Gilroy, California
KNCO-FM Grass Valley, California
KTDE Gualala, California
KFBT Hanford, California
KRDA Hanford, California
KCRH Hayward, California
KNOB Healdsburg, California
KATY-FM Idyllwild, California
KSRW Independence, California
KAJR Indian Wells, California
KRCD Inglewood, California
KRKC-FM King City, California
KNTI Lakeport, California
KXBX-FM Lakeport, California
KGMX Lancaster, California
KKIQ Livermore, California
KCJH Livingston, California
KSKD Livingston, California
KBOX Lompoc, California
KBIG Los Angeles, California
KCBS-FM Los Angeles, California
KLVE Los Angeles, California
KOST Los Angeles, California
KTWV Los Angeles, California
KYSR Los Angeles, California
KSTT-FM Los Osos-Baywood Par, California
KMMT Mammoth Lakes, California
KMDR McKinleyville, California
KBKY Merced, California
KJSN Modesto, California
KTPI Mojave, California
KWAV Monterey, California
KHYZ Mountain Pass, California
KLLE North Fork, California
KRRF Oak View, California
KTNS Oakhurst, California
KLMM Oceano, California
KFYV Ojai, California
KSPA Ontario, California
KXLM Oxnard, California
KEZN Palm Desert, California
KKAL Paso Robles, California
KTSE-FM Patterson, California
KXTZ Pismo Beach, California
KLXR Redding, California
KSHA Redding, California
KLYY Riverside, California
KMHX Rohnert Park, California
KQJK Roseville, California
KUDL Sacramento, California
KYMX Sacramento, California
KZZO Sacramento, California
KDON-FM Salinas, California
KFMB-FM San Diego, California
KMYI San Diego, California
KYXY San Diego, California
KIOI San Francisco, California
KLLC San Francisco, California
KOIT San Francisco, California
KBRG San Jose, California
KEZR San Jose, California
KKJL San Luis Obispo, California
KVYB Santa Barbara, California
KLJR-FM Santa Paula, California
KZST Santa Rosa, California
KSES-FM Seaside, California
KKXX-FM Shafter, California
KESR Shasta Lake City, California
KIRN Simi Valley, California
KSYV Solvang, California
KZSQ-FM Sonora, California
KVYN St. Helena, California
KYCC Stockton, California
KLZN Susanville, California
KLCA Tahoe City, California
KXDZ Templeton, California
KYRA Thousand Oaks, California
KYRA Thousand Oaks, California
KLOB Thousand Palms, California
KCRZ Tipton, California
KFOX Torrance, California
KCDZ Twentynine Palms, California
KWNE Ukiah, California
KXBX Ukiah, California
KUIC Vacaville, California
KBBY-FM Ventura, California
KHMS Victorville, California
KKDV Walnut Creek, California
KSIZ Weed, California
KCCL Woodland, California
KRXV Yermo, California
KDGL Yucca Valley, California
KGIW Alamosa, Colorado
KTND Aspen, Colorado
KMXA Aurora, Colorado
KPRB Brush, Colorado
KNAB Burlington, Colorado
KJMN Castle Rock, Colorado
KRTZ Cortez, Colorado
KALC Denver, Colorado
KIMN Denver, Colorado
KOSI Denver, Colorado
KIQX Durango, Colorado
KPTE Durango, Colorado
KFTM Fort Morgan, Colorado
KDSP(FM) Greenwood Village, Colorado
KVLE-FM Gunnison, Colorado
KSTH Holyoke, Colorado
KBLJ La Junta, Colorado
KTRR Loveland, Colorado
KBIQ Manitou Springs, Colorado
KIMX Nunn, Colorado
KWUF-FM Pagosa Springs, Colorado
KWUZ Poncha Springs, Colorado
KVUU Pueblo, Colorado
KVRH Salida, Colorado
KVRH-FM Salida, Colorado
KPMX Sterling, Colorado
KJHM Strasburg, Colorado

KKLI Widefield, Colorado
KNEC Yuma, Colorado
WEZN-FM Bridgeport, Connecticut
WDAQ Danbury, Connecticut
WMAS Enfield, Connecticut
WZBG Litchfield, Connecticut
WRCH New Britain, Connecticut
WBMW Pawcatuck, Connecticut
WINY Putnam, Connecticut
WQQQ Sharon, Connecticut
WMRQ-FM Waterbury, Connecticut
WEBE Westport, Connecticut
WILI Willimantic, Connecticut
WASH Washington, District of Columbia
WHUR-FM Washington, District of Columbia
WXRD-FM Georgetown, Delaware
WZVN-FM Georgetown, Delaware
WLYV-AM Laurel, Delaware
WAFL Milford, Delaware
WRDX Smyrna, Delaware
WJBR-FM Wilmington, Delaware
WSTW Wilmington, Delaware
WFCT Apalachicola, Florida
WWUS Big Pine Key, Florida
WJIS Bradenton, Florida
WKSG Cedar Creek, Florida
WWFL Clermont, Florida
WHQT Coral Gables, Florida
WPLL Cross City, Florida
WURB Cross City, Florida
WAQV Crystal River, Florida
WKTK Crystal River, Florida
WROD Daytona Beach, Florida
WTJV Deland, Florida
WTMP Egypt Lake, Florida
WWRZ Fort Meade, Florida
WINK-FM Fort Myers, Florida
WJPT Fort Myers, Florida
WSOS-FM Fruit Cove, Florida
WXJZ Gainesville, Florida
WNPL Golden Gate, Florida
WTOT-FM Graceville, Florida
WWJK Green Cove Springs, Florida
WRZN Hernando, Florida
WCMQ-FM Hialeah, Florida
WOLL Hobe Sound, Florida
WVYB Holly Hill, Florida
WOSN Indian River Shores, Florida
WYKE(FM) Inglis, Florida
WAZQ Islamorada, Florida
WEJZ Jacksonville, Florida
WJAX Jacksonville, Florida
WJGL Jacksonville, Florida
WKEY-FM Key West, Florida
WNFB Lake City, Florida
WQBQ Leesburg, Florida
WQHL Live Oak, Florida
WAVK Marathon, Florida
WGMX Marathon, Florida
WAMR-FM Miami, Florida
WLYF Miami, Florida
WMIA-FM Miami Beach, Florida
WSBZ Miramar Beach, Florida
WMGF Mount Dora, Florida
WBCG Murdock, Florida
WSGL Naples, Florida
WCIE New Port Richey, Florida
WDUV New Port Richey, Florida
WSVU North Palm Beach, Florida
WHIJ Ocala, Florida
WMFQ Ocala, Florida
WOMX Orlando, Florida
WHIF Palatka, Florida
WEJF Palm Bay, Florida
WRMF Palm Beach, Florida
WCNO Palm City, Florida
WFSY Panama City, Florida
WVVE Panama City Beach, Florida
WBSR Pensacola, Florida
WMEZ Pensacola, Florida
WPRY Perry, Florida
WJUA Pine Island Center, Florida
WHLG Port St. Lucie, Florida
WKLG Rock Harbor, Florida
WWAV Santa Rosa Beach, Florida
WSDV Sarasota, Florida
WTMY Sarasota, Florida
WITS Sebring, Florida
WWLL Sebring, Florida
WNCV Shalimar, Florida
WCVU Solana, Florida
WXGL St. Petersburg, Florida
WBZE Tallahassee, Florida
WTLY Tallahassee, Florida
WMTX Tampa, Florida
WWRM Tampa, Florida
WJGO Tice, Florida
WDDV Venice, Florida
WLTQ-FM Venice, Florida
WGYL Vero Beach, Florida
WJKD Vero Beach, Florida
WEAT West Palm Beach, Florida
WTMG Williston, Florida
WDEC-FM Americus, Georgia
WQXI Atlanta, Georgia
WSB-FM Atlanta, Georgia
WBBQ-FM Augusta, Georgia
WBGE Bainbridge, Georgia
WBAF Barnesville, Georgia
WLKQ-FM Buford, Georgia
WCHK Canton, Georgia
WMCD Claxton, Georgia
WRBN Clayton, Georgia
WNGA Clermont, Georgia
WGMG Crawford, Georgia
WYYU Dalton, Georgia
WXMK Dock Junction, Georgia
WGMK Donalsonville, Georgia
WKVQ Eatonton, Georgia
WMGZ Eatonton, Georgia
WSGC Elberton, Georgia
WLEL Ellaville, Georgia
WRDO Fitzgerald, Georgia
WSRV Gainesville, Georgia
WSGA Hinesville, Georgia
WMGP Hogansville, Georgia
WBTY Homerville, Georgia
WJGA-FM Jackson, Georgia
WIVL Jasper, Georgia
WLHR-FM Lavonia, Georgia
WYTH Madison, Georgia
WDRR Martinez, Georgia
WXKT Maysville, Georgia
WQLI Meigs, Georgia
WBMZ Metter, Georgia
WLRR Milledgeville, Georgia
WALR-FM Palmetto, Georgia
WPGA-FM Perry, Georgia
WCEH-FM Pinehurst, Georgia
WSFB Quitman, Georgia
WQTU Rome, Georgia
WAMJ Roswell, Georgia
WEGC Sasser, Georgia
WSEG Savannah, Georgia
WPMX Statesboro, Georgia
WTGA Thomaston, Georgia
WTWA Thomson, Georgia
WKZZ Tifton, Georgia
WRAF Toccoa Falls, Georgia
WNNG-FM Unadilla, Georgia
WQPW Valdosta, Georgia
WTCQ Vidalia, Georgia
WZCH Warner Robins, Georgia
WQGA Waycross, Georgia
WWUF Waycross, Georgia
KSTO Agana, Guam
KUAM Agana, Guam
KTKB Dededo, Guam
KMWB Captain Cook, Hawaii
KKBG Hilo, Hawaii
KNWB Hilo, Hawaii
KWXX-FM Hilo, Hawaii
KHWI Holualoa, Hawaii
KHJZ Honolulu, Hawaii
KSSK Honolulu, Hawaii
KUMU-FM Honolulu, Hawaii
KLEO Kahaluu, Hawaii
KJKS Kahului, Hawaii
KRTR-FM Kailua, Hawaii
KLUA Kailua Kona, Hawaii
KTOH Kalaheo, Hawaii
KMKK-FM Kaunakakai, Hawaii
KWYI Kawaihae, Hawaii
KAOY Kealakekua, Hawaii
KUAI Kekaha, Hawaii
KKHI Kihei, Hawaii
KTBH-FM Kurtistown, Hawaii
KPOA Lahaina, Hawaii
KAOI-FM Wailuku, Hawaii
KSSK-FM Waipahu, Hawaii
KLGA Algona, Iowa
KCYZ Ames, Iowa
KLTI-FM Ames, Iowa
KJAN Atlantic, Iowa
KSWI Atlantic, Iowa
KZAT-FM Belle Plaine, Iowa
KSKB Brooklyn, Iowa
KGRS Burlington, Iowa
KKMI Burlington, Iowa
KDAT Cedar Rapids, Iowa
KMRY Cedar Rapids, Iowa
KCOG Centerville, Iowa
KEDB Chariton, Iowa
KCHA Charles City, Iowa
KCHA-FM Charles City, Iowa
KCHE-FM Cherokee, Iowa
KMA-FM Clarinda, Iowa
KCLN Clinton, Iowa
KMCN Clinton, Iowa
KMXG Clinton, Iowa
KQKQ-FM Council Bluffs, Iowa
KCZQ Cresco, Iowa
KLOX Creston, Iowa
KDSN Denison, Iowa
KDSN-FM Denison, Iowa
KDRB Des Moines, Iowa
KRNT Des Moines, Iowa
KSTZ Des Moines, Iowa
KATF Dubuque, Iowa
KDAO-FM Eldora, Iowa
KADR Elkader, Iowa
KUYY Emmetsburg, Iowa
KGRR Epworth, Iowa
KIOW Forest City, Iowa
KKEZ Fort Dodge, Iowa
KLMJ Hampton, Iowa
KCVM Hudson, Iowa
KHBT Humboldt, Iowa
KIFG Iowa Falls, Iowa
KOKX Keokuk, Iowa
KRLS Knoxville, Iowa
KLEM Le Mars, Iowa
KMCH Manchester, Iowa
KDAO Marshalltown, Iowa
KLSS-FM Mason City, Iowa
KCWN New Sharon, Iowa
KYTC Northwood, Iowa
KSMA-FM Osage, Iowa
KTWA Ottumwa, Iowa
KQCR-FM Parkersburg, Iowa
KYME Rockford, Iowa
KSOU-FM Sioux Center, Iowa
KGLI Sioux City, Iowa
KUOO Spirit Lake, Iowa
KTDV State Center, Iowa
KAYL-FM Storm Lake, Iowa
KCII Washington, Iowa
KNWS-FM Waterloo, Iowa
KOKZ Waterloo, Iowa
KWAY-FM Waverly, Iowa
KORR American Falls, Idaho
KLCE Blackfoot, Idaho
KZDX Burley, Idaho
KLLP Chubbuck, Idaho
KVNI Coeur D'Alene, Idaho
KXLT-FM Eagle, Idaho
KQEO Idaho Falls, Idaho
KATW Lewiston, Idaho
KLER-FM Orofino, Idaho
KCDA Post Falls, Idaho
KBYR-FM Rexburg, Idaho
KGTM Rexburg, Idaho
KSQS Ririe, Idaho
KSRA Salmon, Idaho
KOFE St. Maries, Idaho
WERV-FM Aurora, Illinois
WKRO Cairo, Illinois
KQCJ Cambridge, Illinois
WIBI Carlinville, Illinois
WUEZ Carterville, Illinois
WCEZ Carthage, Illinois
WHMS-FM Champaign, Illinois
WLRW Champaign, Illinois
WLIT-FM Chicago, Illinois
WLS Chicago, Illinois
WSHE-FM Chicago, Illinois
WEZC Clinton, Illinois
KBWX Columbia, Illinois
WDNL Danville, Illinois
WDKB Dekalb, Illinois
WPPN Des Plaines, Illinois
WDQN Duquoin, Illinois
WJEZ Dwight, Illinois

WXEF Effingham, Illinois
WEBQ-FM Eldorado, Illinois
WIBL(FM) Fairbury, Illinois
WFIW Fairfield, Illinois
WNOI Flora, Illinois
WISH-FM Galatia, Illinois
WDBQ-FM Galena, Illinois
WSPY Geneva, Illinois
WPWX Hammond, Indiana
WLDS Jacksonville, Illinois
WSSR Joliet, Illinois
WAJK La Salle, Illinois
WAKO Lawrenceville, Illinois
WQLF Lena, Illinois
WKAI Macomb, Illinois
WLWF Marseilles, Illinois
WLBH Mattoon, Illinois
WLBH-FM Mattoon, Illinois
WJLI Metropolis, Illinois
WREZ Metropolis, Illinois
WMOI Monmouth, Illinois
WCSJ Morris, Illinois
WCSJ-FM Morris, Illinois
WYNG Mount Carmel, Illinois
WBMV Mount Vernon, Illinois
WMIX Mount Vernon, Illinois
WVZA Murphysboro, Illinois
WNSV Nashville, Illinois
WCMY Ottawa, Illinois
WRKX Ottawa, Illinois
WCIC Pekin, Illinois
WPBG Peoria, Illinois
WSWT Peoria, Illinois
WBBA-FM Pittsfield, Illinois
WLLT Polo, Illinois
WZOE-FM Princeton, Illinois
WLIQ Quincy, Illinois
WTAY Robinson, Illinois
WTYE Robinson, Illinois
WRHL-FM Rochelle, Illinois
WGFB Rockton, Illinois
WJBD-FM Salem, Illinois
WJDK-FM Seneca, Illinois
WEJT Shelbyville, Illinois
WQQL Sherman, Illinois
WNNS Springfield, Illinois
WAOX Staunton, Illinois
WSSQ Sterling, Illinois
WYYS Streator, Illinois
WSQR Sycamore, Illinois
WKRV Vandalia, Illinois
WPMB Vandalia, Illinois
WXLC Waukegan, Illinois
WRTB Winnebago, Illinois
WZSR Woodstock, Illinois
WQME Anderson, Indiana
WLKI Angola, Indiana
WZBD Berne, Indiana
WBNL Boonville, Indiana
WJPS Boonville, Indiana
WFNB Brazil, Indiana
WBPE Brookston, Indiana
WHON Centerville, Indiana
WHPP Columbia City, Virginia
WINN Columbus, Indiana
WIMC Crawfordsville, Indiana
WEOA Evansville, Indiana
WIKY Evansville, Indiana
WVHI Evansville, Indiana
WAJI Fort Wayne, Indiana
WGL Fort Wayne, Indiana
WLAB Fort Wayne, Indiana
WLDE Fort Wayne, Indiana
WMEE Fort Wayne, Indiana
WSHW Frankfort, Indiana
WKAM Goshen, Indiana
WZPL Greenfield, Indiana
WRZQ-FM Greensburg, Indiana
WKLO Hardinsburg, Indiana
WGL-FM Huntington, Indiana
WNTR Indianapolis, Indiana
WITZ-FM Jasper, Indiana
WKVI Knox, Indiana
WZWZ Kokomo, Indiana
WLOI La Porte, Indiana
WIRE Lebanon, Indiana
WSAL Logansport, Indiana
WZVN Lowell, Indiana
WORX-FM Madison, Indiana
WXGO Madison, Indiana
WXXC Marion, Indiana
WEFM Michigan City, Indiana
WMRS Monticello, Indiana
WERK Muncie, Indiana
WLBC Muncie, Indiana
WRDI Nappanee, Indiana
WJJK Noblesville, Indiana
WPHZ Orleans, Indiana
WTCA Plymouth, Indiana
WPGW Portland, Indiana
WLQI Rensselaer, Indiana
WRIN Rensselaer, Indiana
WFMG Richmond, Indiana
WARU-FM Roann, Indiana
WAXL Santa Claus, Indiana
WNSN South Bend, Indiana
WUBU South Bend, Indiana
WMYQ South Whitley, Indiana
WCLS Spencer, Indiana
WVUB Vincennes, Indiana
WZDM Vincennes, Indiana
WTMK Wanatah, Indiana
WRSW-FM Warsaw, Indiana
WAMW-AM Washington, Indiana
WAMW-FM Washington, Indiana
WHPL West Lafayette, Indiana
WZZY Winchester, Indiana
KABI Abilene, Kansas
KVSV Beloit, Kansas
KKDT Burdett, Kansas
KMAJ-FM Carbondale, Kansas
KZDY Cawker City, Kansas
KKOY-FM Chanute, Kansas
KCLY Clay Center, Kansas
KRDQ Colby, Kansas
KSKZ Copeland, Kansas
KONQ Dodge City, Kansas
KTLI El Dorado, Kansas
KFFX Emporia, Kansas
KVOE Emporia, Kansas
KOMB Fort Scott, Kansas
KKJQ Garden City, Kansas
KZRS Great Bend, Kansas
KIBB Haven, Kansas
KJLS Hays, Kansas
KFBZ Haysville, Kansas
KIND Independence, Kansas
KSCB-FM Liberal, Kansas
KBLS North Fort Riley, Kansas
KHMY Pratt, Kansas
KRSL Russell, Kansas
KRSL-FM Russell, Kansas
KWIC Topeka, Kansas
KHCA Wamego, Kansas
KRBB Wichita, Kansas
WANV Annville, Kentucky
WKKQ Barbourville, Kentucky
WLJC Beattyville, Kentucky
WTRT Benton, Kentucky
WCVK Bowling Green, Kentucky
WKLX Brownsville, Kentucky
WCKQ Campbellsville, Kentucky
WCBJ Campton, Kentucky
WBVX Carlisle, Kentucky
WQXQ Central City, Kentucky
WCTT Corbin, Kentucky
WCTT-FM Corbin, Kentucky
WQXE Elizabethtown, Kentucky
WCVQ Fort Campbell, Kentucky
WLFZ Fort Campbell, Kentucky
WSTV-FM Frankfort, Kentucky
WSON Henderson, Kentucky
WOVO Horse Cave, Kentucky
WKHG Leitchfield, Kentucky
WMXL Lexington, Kentucky
WZAQ Louisa, Kentucky
WLGX Louisville, Kentucky
WXMA Louisville, Kentucky
WYMC Mayfield, Kentucky
WBFI McDaniels, Kentucky
WFXY Middlesboro, Kentucky
WIVY Morehead, Kentucky
WMOR-FM Morehead, Kentucky
WMST Mount Sterling, Kentucky
WCLU-FM Munfordville, Kentucky
WEGI-FM Oak Grove, Kentucky
WKLW-FM Paintsville, Kentucky
WGKS Paris, Kentucky
WWJD Pippa Passes, Kentucky
WHVE Russell Springs, Kentucky
WYKY Science Hill, Kentucky
WUHU Smiths Grove, Kentucky
WLLK-FM Somerset, Kentucky
WYSB Springfield, Kentucky
WVEZ St. Matthews, Kentucky
WCDA Versailles, Kentucky
WABL Amite, Louisiana
KCIJ Atlanta, Louisiana
KJMG Bastrop, Louisiana
KBZE Berwick, Louisiana
KRVE Brusly, Louisiana
KQLK De Ridder, Louisiana
KBYO-FM Farmerville, Louisiana
KFNV-FM Ferriday, Louisiana
WRQQ Hammond, Louisiana
KHLA Jennings, Louisiana
KFXZ Lafayette, Louisiana
KTDY Lafayette, Louisiana
KBIU Lake Charles, Louisiana
KBDV Leesville, Louisiana
KZLG Mansura, Louisiana
KYMK-FM Maurice, Louisiana
KASO Minden, Louisiana
KLIP Monroe, Louisiana
KMRC Morgan City, Louisiana
WLMG New Orleans, Louisiana
WYLD-FM New Orleans, Louisiana
KPCP New Roads, Louisiana
KUMX North Fort Polk, Louisiana
KAGY Port Sulphur, Louisiana
KVKI-FM Shreveport, Louisiana
KLSM Tallulah, Louisiana
KZRZ West Monroe, Louisiana
KTEZ Zwolle, Louisiana
WXRV Andover, Massachusetts
WQRC Barnstable, Massachusetts
WBMX Boston, Massachusetts
WMJX Boston, Massachusetts
WJIB Cambridge, Massachusetts
WCIB Falmouth, Massachusetts
WXLO Fitchburg, Massachusetts
WROR-FM Framingham, Massachusetts
WSBS Great Barrington, Massachusetts
WHAI Greenfield, Massachusetts
WCOD-FM Hyannis, Massachusetts
WATD-FM Marshfield, Massachusetts
WMRC Milford, Massachusetts
WMLN-FM Milton, Massachusetts
WNBP Newburyport, Massachusetts
WNAW North Adams, Massachusetts
WJDF Orange, Massachusetts
WBEC-FM Pittsfield, Massachusetts
WBRK-FM Pittsfield, Massachusetts
WPLM Plymouth, Massachusetts
WPLM-FM Plymouth, Massachusetts
WRPS Rockland, Massachusetts
WWFX Southbridge, Massachusetts
WHYN-FM Springfield, Massachusetts
WSNE-FM Taunton, Massachusetts
WSRS Worcester, Massachusetts
WNAV Annapolis, Maryland
WLIF Baltimore, Maryland
WQSR Baltimore, Maryland
WWMX Baltimore, Maryland
WIAD Bethesda, District of Columbia
WCEM Cambridge, Maryland
WCEI-FM Easton, Maryland
WLIC Frostburg, Maryland
WILC Laurel, Maryland
WAFY Middletown, Maryland
WDZN Midland, Maryland
WKHJ Mountain Lake Park, Maryland
WWEG Myersville, Maryland
WQHQ Ocean City-Salisbury, Maryland
WTTR Westminster, Maryland
WJTO Bath, Maine
WGIN Biddeford, Maine
WQSS Camden, Maine
WCXU Caribou, Maine
WCRQ Dennysville, Maine
WZLO Dover-Foxcroft, Maine
WKSQ Ellsworth, Maine
WWMJ Ellsworth, Maine
WABK Gardiner, Maine
WHOU-FM Houlton, Maine
WSHK Kittery, Maine
WALZ-FM Machias, Maine
WCXX Madawaska, Maine
WRMO Milbridge, Maine
WMGX Portland, Maine
WFMX Skowhegan, Maine
WCXV Van Buren, Maine
WHSB Alpena, Michigan

RADIO - U.S.

WJSZ Ashley, Michigan
WFDX Atlanta, Michigan
WHNN Bay City, Michigan
WMRX-FM Beaverton, Michigan
WYBR Big Rapids, Michigan
WKHM-FM Brooklyn, Michigan
WSMK Buchanan, Michigan
WLXV Cadillac, Michigan
WIDL Cass City, Michigan
WPRJ Coleman, Michigan
WNIC Dearborn, Michigan
WDVD Detroit, Michigan
WMGC-FM Detroit, Michigan
WXLA Dimondale, Michigan
WGLQ Escanaba, Michigan
WMJO Essexville, Michigan
WCRZ Flint, Michigan
WQBX Fowler, Michigan
WSRT Gaylord, Michigan
WGHN-FM Grand Haven, Michigan
WLHT-FM Grand Rapids, Michigan
WSRW-FM Grand Rapids, Michigan
WUPT Gwinn, Michigan
WKMJ-FM Hancock, Michigan
WCXT Hartford, Michigan
WBCH Hastings, Michigan
WCSR Hillsdale, Michigan
WCCY Houghton, Michigan
WHMI-FM Howell, Michigan
WIKB-FM Iron River, Michigan
WIMI Ironwood, Michigan
WUPM Ironwood, Michigan
WMQT-FM Ishpeming, Michigan
WFMK Lansing, Michigan
WHZZ Lansing, Michigan
WFCX Leland, Michigan
WKLA-FM Ludington, Michigan
WMLQ Manistee, Michigan
WBXX Marshall, Michigan
WMJT McMillan, Michigan
WMPX Midland, Michigan
WCZY-FM Mount Pleasant, Michigan
WLCS North Muskegon, Michigan
WZNL Norway, Michigan
WMOM Pentwater, Michigan
WLXT Petoskey, Michigan
WHAK-FM Rogers City, Michigan
WGRY-FM Roscommon, Michigan
WGER Saginaw, Michigan
WSAM Saginaw, Michigan
WTGV-FM Sandusky, Michigan
WSOO Sault Ste. Marie, Michigan
WLKM-FM Three Rivers, Michigan
WTRV Walker, Michigan
KDDG Albany, Minnesota
KCPI Albert Lea, Minnesota
KKBJ-FM Bemidji, Minnesota
KKZY Bemidji, Minnesota
KSCR-FM Benson, Minnesota
KOWZ-FM Blooming Prairie, Minnesota
WJJY-FM Brainerd, Minnesota
WZFJ(FM) Breezy Point, Minnesota
KXDL Browerville, Minnesota
KRWC Buffalo, Minnesota
WKLK-FM Cloquet, Minnesota
KMXK Cold Spring, Minnesota
KDLM Detroit Lakes, Minnesota
KZLT-FM East Grand Forks, Minnesota
WEVE Eveleth, Minnesota
WLKX-FM Forest Lake, Minnesota
WTIP Grand Marais, Minnesota
KMFY Grand Rapids, Minnesota
KLCH Lake City, Minnesota
KFML Little Falls, Minnesota
KQAD Luverne, Minnesota
KKCK Marshall, Minnesota
KTCZ-FM Minneapolis, Minnesota
KMRS Morris, Minnesota
KCGN-FM Ortonville, Minnesota
KBMX Proctor, Minnesota
KWNG Red Wing, Minnesota
KFSI Rochester, Minnesota
WMIN Sauk Rapids, Minnesota
KNUJ-FM Sleepy Eye, Minnesota
KNSG Springfield, Minnesota
KKJM St. Joseph, Minnesota
KZJK St. Louis Park, Minnesota
KSTP-FM St. Paul, Minnesota
KRBI-FM St. Peter, Minnesota
KRVY-FM Starbuck, Minnesota
KYBA Stewartville, Minnesota
KLBB Stillwater, Minnesota
KTRF Thief River Falls, Minnesota
KQKK Walker, Minnesota
KQIC Willmar, Minnesota
KAGE-FM Winona, Minnesota
KITN Worthington, Minnesota
KBMV-FM Birch Tree, Missouri
KWJK Boonville, Missouri
KFMZ Brookfield, Missouri
KZBK Brookfield, Missouri
KOZX Cabool, Missouri
KNLH Cedar Hill, Missouri
KREZ Chaffee, Missouri
KPLA Columbia, Missouri
KLOZ Eldon, Missouri
KZWV Eldon, Missouri
KCFV Ferguson, Missouri
KCJK Garden City, Missouri
KGLU Gideon, Missouri
KYOO-FM Half Way, Missouri
KTXY Jefferson City, Missouri
KCKC Kansas City, Missouri
KZPT Kansas City, Missouri
KBOA-AM Kennett, Missouri
KCXL Liberty, Missouri
KIRK Macon, Missouri
KTRI-FM Mansfield, Missouri
KXEO Mexico, Missouri
KMCR Montgomery City, Missouri
KUPH Mountain View, Missouri
KZMA Naylor, Missouri
KGBX-FM Nixa, Missouri
KTOZ-FM Pleasant Hope, Missouri
KAHR Poplar Bluff, Missouri
KNLP Potosi, Missouri
KADI-FM Republic, Missouri
KDAA Rolla, Missouri
KSDL Sedalia, Missouri
KWND Springfield, Missouri
KGNM St. Joseph, Missouri
KEZK St. Louis, Missouri
KNOU St. Louis, Missouri
KYKY St. Louis, Missouri
KFLW St. Robert, Missouri
KTTN Trenton, Missouri
KBIY Van Buren, Missouri
KSLQ-FM Washington, Missouri
KFBD-FM Waynesville, Missouri
KJMK Webb City, Missouri
KULH Wheeling, Missouri
KZMI Garapan-Saipan, Guam
WJBI Batesville, Mississippi
WMJY Biloxi, Mississippi
WMJU Bude, Mississippi
WOWL Burnsville, Mississippi
WFFF-FM Columbia, Mississippi
WTWG Columbus, Mississippi
WLIN-FM Durant, Mississippi
WLZA Eupora, Mississippi
WFTA Fulton, Mississippi
WGNL Greenwood, Mississippi
WKRA-FM Holly Springs, Mississippi
WSYE Houston, Mississippi
WIQQ Leland, Mississippi
WJZD-FM Long Beach, Mississippi
WLSM-FM Louisville, Mississippi
WKSO Natchez, Mississippi
WOXD Oxford, Mississippi
WQLJ Oxford, Mississippi
WHOC Philadelphia, Mississippi
WWSL Philadelphia, Mississippi
WCNA Potts Camp, Mississippi
WSKK Ripley, Mississippi
WKZW Sandersville, Mississippi
WZLQ Tupelo, Mississippi
WUMS University, Mississippi
WJKK Vicksburg, Mississippi
WVBG Vicksburg, Mississippi
KGLM-FM Anaconda, Montana
KMHK Billings, Montana
KOBB Bozeman, Montana
KZMY Bozeman, Montana
KOPR Butte, Montana
KRYK Chinook, Montana
KVVR Dutton, Montana
KVMO Fort Benton, Montana
KLAN Glasgow, Montana
KXGN Glendive, Montana
KAAK Great Falls, Montana
KEIN Great Falls, Montana
KHDN Hardin, Montana
KOJM Havre, Montana
KMTX-FM Helena, Montana
KWMY Joliet, Montana
KALS Kalispell, Montana
KLCM Lewistown, Montana
KPLN Lockwood, Montana
KMMR Malta, Montana
KKQX Manhattan, Montana
KATL Miles City, Montana
KYUS-FM Miles City, Montana
KMSO Missoula, Montana
KMZL Missoula, Montana
KYJK Missoula, Montana
KQRK Pablo, Montana
KTHC Sidney, Montana
KKVU Stevensville, Montana
KEZQ West Yellowstone, Montana
WECR-FM Beech Mountain, North Carolina
WSQL Brevard, North Carolina
WBHN Bryson City, North Carolina
WKQC Charlotte, North Carolina
WLNK Charlotte, North Carolina
WKJX Elizabeth City, North Carolina
WAZZ Fayetteville, North Carolina
WZRU Garysburg, North Carolina
WBAV-FM Gastonia, North Carolina
WSMW Greensboro, North Carolina
WMYI Hendersonville, North Carolina
WFMZ Hertford, North Carolina
WHGO Hertford, North Carolina
WLKO Hickory, North Carolina
WMAG High Point, North Carolina
WQSL Jacksonville, North Carolina
WCXL Kill Devil Hills, North Carolina
WFLB Laurinburg, North Carolina
WLNC Laurinburg, North Carolina
WKGX Lenoir, North Carolina
WWLV(FM) Lexington, North Carolina
WDLZ Murfreesboro, North Carolina
WCVP Murphy, North Carolina
WIKS New Bern, North Carolina
WMGV Newport, North Carolina
WNNC Newton, North Carolina
WLQB Ocean Isle Beach, North Carolina
WIOZ Pinehurst, North Carolina
WPNC-FM Plymouth, North Carolina
WBBB Raleigh, North Carolina
WKIX-FM Raleigh, North Carolina
WRAL Raleigh, North Carolina
WJMH Reidsville, North Carolina
WVRP Roanoke Rapids, North Carolina
WLHC Robbins, North Carolina
WAYN Rockingham, North Carolina
WIOZ Southern Pines, North Carolina
WEQR Walnut Creek, North Carolina
WMXF Waynesville, North Carolina
WGNI Wilmington, North Carolina
WILT Wilmington, North Carolina
WWIL-FM Wilmington, North Carolina
WRCM Wingate, North Carolina
KYYY Bismarck, North Dakota
KWGO Burlington, North Dakota
KXRV Cannon Ball, North Dakota
KXGT Carrington, North Dakota
KQZZ Devils Lake, North Dakota
KDIX Dickinson, North Dakota
KRWK Fargo, North Dakota
KKBO Flasher, North Dakota
KHND Harvey, North Dakota
KSJZ Jamestown, North Dakota
KNDK-FM Langdon, North Dakota
KNDR Mandan, North Dakota
KMXA-FM Minot, North Dakota
KRRZ Minot, North Dakota
KYTZ Walhalla, North Dakota
KBRB Ainsworth, Nebraska
KBRB-FM Ainsworth, Nebraska
KRGY Aurora, Nebraska
KWBE Beatrice, Nebraska
KLIR Columbus, Nebraska
KINI Crookston, Nebraska
KLZA-FM Falls City, Nebraska
KMTY Gibbon, Nebraska
KHAS Hastings, Nebraska
KLIQ Hastings, Nebraska
KNIT Humboldt, Nebraska
KBBK Lincoln, Nebraska
KSRC Loup City, Nebraska
KSWN McCook, Nebraska
KJLT-FM North Platte, Nebraska
KOMJ Omaha, Nebraska

KQCH Omaha, Nebraska
KSRZ Omaha, Nebraska
KSID-FM Sidney, Nebraska
KRFS Superior, Nebraska
KRKR Waverly, Nebraska
KTMX York, Nebraska
WKDR Berlin, New Hampshire
WMOU Berlin, New Hampshire
WVMJ Conway, New Hampshire
WFTN-FM Franklin, New Hampshire
WSAK Hampton, New Hampshire
WGXL Hanover, New Hampshire
WNEC-FM Henniker, New Hampshire
WKNE Keene, New Hampshire
WSNI Keene, New Hampshire
WLNH-FM Laconia, New Hampshire
WXXS Lancaster, New Hampshire
WLTN-FM Lisbon, New Hampshire
WWNH Madbury, New Hampshire
WFEA Manchester, New Hampshire
WZID Manchester, New Hampshire
WHOM Mount Washington, New Hampshire
WFNQ Nashua, New Hampshire
WBYY Somersworth, New Hampshire
WNYN-FM Whitefield, New Hampshire
WASR Wolfeboro, New Hampshire
WLKZ Wolfeboro, New Hampshire
WJLK Asbury Park, New Jersey
WFPG Atlantic City, New Jersey
WVBH Beach Haven West, New Jersey
WGBZ Cape May, New Jersey
WSJO Egg Harbor City, New Jersey
WIMG Ewing, New Jersey
WSUS Franklin, New Jersey
WWZY Long Branch, New Jersey
WJRZ-FM Manahawkin, New Jersey
WTTH Margate City, New Jersey
WMGQ New Brunswick, New Jersey
WPAT-FM Paterson, New Jersey
WBZC Pemberton, New Jersey
WBHX Tuckerton, New Jersey
WCZT Villas, New Jersey
WCMC Wildwood, New Jersey
WEZW Wildwood Crest, New Jersey
KYCM Alamogordo, New Mexico
KDEF Albuquerque, New Mexico
KDRF Albuquerque, New Mexico
KPEK Albuquerque, New Mexico
KWYK-FM Aztec, New Mexico
KLVO Belen, New Mexico
KAMQ Carlsbad, New Mexico
KATK Carlsbad, New Mexico
KCDY Carlsbad, New Mexico
KSMX-FM Clovis, New Mexico
KTQM-FM Clovis, New Mexico
KLQT Corrales, New Mexico
KDEM Deming, New Mexico
KLVF Las Vegas, New Mexico
KABG Los Alamos, New Mexico
KMVR Mesilla Park, New Mexico
KQNM Milan, New Mexico
KLBU Pecos, New Mexico
KLNN Questa, New Mexico
KRTN Raton, New Mexico
KBIM-FM Roswell, New Mexico
KSFX Roswell, New Mexico
KKLB Ruidoso, New Mexico
KKOB Exp S Santa Fe, New Mexico
KSCQ Silver City, New Mexico
KKIT Taos, New Mexico
KVAL Cal-Nev-Ari, Nevada
KHIX Carlin, Nevada
KELK Elko, Nevada
KMXB Henderson, Nevada
KXQQ Henderson, Nevada
KRNO Incline Village, Nevada
KKLZ Las Vegas, Nevada
KKVV Las Vegas, Nevada
KSNE-FM Las Vegas, Nevada
KXPT Las Vegas, Nevada
KADD Logandale, Nevada
KJUL Moapa Valley, Nevada
KFRH North Las Vegas, Nevada
WKLI-FM Albany, New York
WYJB Albany, New York
WSEN-FM Baldwinsville, New York
WVIN-FM Bath, New York
WBAZ Bridgehampton, New York
WFAS-FM Bronxville, New York
WHTT Buffalo, New York
WJYE Buffalo, New York
WVOR Canandaigua, New York
WTOJ Carthage, New York
WCTW Catskill, New York
WRVH Clayton, New York
WGMM Corning, New York
WNKI Corning, New York
WMRV Dansville, New York
WENY-FM Elmira, New York
WLVY Elmira, New York
WEHH Elmira Hts-Horsehds, New York
WHPC Garden City, New York
WHLI Hempstead, New York
WKJY Hempstead, New York
WXUR Herkimer, New York
WKPQ Hornell, New York
WHUC Hudson, New York
WNYQ Hudson Falls, New York
WCZX Hyde Park, New York
WYXL Ithaca, New York
WWSE Jamestown, New York
WLTB Johnson City, New York
WIZR Johnstown, New York
WKNY Kingston, New York
WKTU Lake Success, New York
WMSA Massena, New York
WSUL Monticello, New York
WLTW New York, New York
WPLJ New York, New York
WKXZ Norwich, New York
WMXO Olean, New York
WSRK Oneonta, New York
WALK Patchogue, New York
WALK-FM Patchogue, New York
WHUD Peekskill, New York
WYLF Penn Yan, New York
WZUN Phoenix, New York
WKOL Plattsburgh, New York
WKLV-FM Port Chester, New York
WCDW Port Dickinson, New York
WPDM Potsdam, New York
WRNQ Poughkeepsie, New York
WRCR Ramapo, New York
WRIV Riverhead, New York
WDVI Rochester, New York
WRMM-FM Rochester, New York
WSLP Saranac Lake, New York
WBPM Saugerties, New York
WRVE Schenectady, New York
WCDO Sidney, New York
WCDO-FM Sidney, New York
WHFM Southampton, New York
WSPQ Springville, New York
WJKE Stillwater, New York
WYYY Syracuse, New York
WRGR Tupper Lake, New York
WLZW Utica, New York
WTLB Utica, New York
WMXW Vestal, New York
WNYR Waterloo, New York
WABY Watervliet, New York
WFAS White Plains, New York
WDJQ Alliance, Ohio
WBCY Archbold, Ohio
WREO-FM Ashtabula, Ohio
WATH Athens, Ohio
WJKW Athens, Ohio
WOUB-FM Athens, Ohio
WXTQ Athens, Ohio
WBNV Barnesville, Ohio
WPKO-FM Bellefontaine, Ohio
WBNO-FM Bryan, Ohio
WBCO Bucyrus, Ohio
WILE-FM Byesville, Ohio
WYNT Caledonia, Ohio
WCMJ Cambridge, Ohio
WHBC-FM Canton, Ohio
WGGN Castalia, Ohio
WQLX Chillicothe, Ohio
WNNF Cincinnati, Ohio
WRRM Cincinnati, Ohio
WDOK Cleveland, Ohio
WFHM-FM Cleveland, Ohio
WHLK Cleveland, Ohio
WQAL Cleveland, Ohio
WSNY Columbus, Ohio
WTNS-FM Coshocton, Ohio
WMMX Dayton, Ohio
WDFM Defiance, Ohio
WGTZ Eaton, Ohio
WNWV Elyria, Ohio
WYDB Englewood, Ohio
WKXA-FM Findlay, Ohio
WBVI Fostoria, Ohio
WFRO-FM Fremont, Ohio
WCVO Gahanna, Ohio
WXBW Gallipolis, Ohio
WIMX Gibsonburg, Ohio
WVNU Greenfield, Ohio
WGRR Hamilton, Ohio
WKTN Kenton, Ohio
WKNA Logan, Ohio
WMFD Mansfield, Ohio
WYHT Mansfield, Ohio
WMOA Marietta, Ohio
WKLM Millersburg, Ohio
WQIO Mount Vernon, Ohio
WIOI New Boston, Ohio
WWJM New Lexington, Ohio
WHOF North Canton, Ohio
WLKR Norwalk, Ohio
WLKR Norwalk, Ohio
WNTO Racine, Ohio
WAOL Ripley, Ohio
WCPZ Sandusky, Ohio
WMVR-FM Sidney, Ohio
WHIZ-FM South Zanesville, Ohio
WBCJ Spencerville, Ohio
WMLX St. Marys, Ohio
WKTL Struthers, Ohio
WJUC Swanton, Ohio
WWWM-FM Sylvania, Ohio
WRVF Toledo, Ohio
WERT Van Wert, Ohio
WKOV-FM Wellston, Ohio
WVMX Westerville, Ohio
WZLR Xenia, Ohio
WMXY Youngstown, Ohio
KKWD Bethany, Oklahoma
KZLI Catoosa, Oklahoma
KXOO Elk City, Oklahoma
KTSO Glenpool, Oklahoma
KQTZ Hobart, Oklahoma
KQIB Idabel, Oklahoma
KXLS Lahoma, Oklahoma
KMGZ Lawton, Oklahoma
KVRW Lawton, Oklahoma
KMGL Oklahoma City, Oklahoma
KOMA Oklahoma City, Oklahoma
KYIS Oklahoma City, Oklahoma
KZBB Poteau, Oklahoma
KXTH Seminole, Oklahoma
KJCM Snyder, Oklahoma
KSPI AM Stillwater, Oklahoma
KSPI FM Stillwater, Oklahoma
KBEZ Tulsa, Oklahoma
KGTO Tulsa, Oklahoma
KRAV-FM Tulsa, Oklahoma
KMZE Woodward, Oklahoma
KCMX-FM Ashland, Oregon
KTIL-FM Bay City, Oregon
KKCW Beaverton, Oregon
KMGX Bend, Oregon
KNLR Bend, Oregon
KQAK Bend, Oregon
KEHK Brownsville, Oregon
KORC(FM) Burns, Oregon
KCNA Cave Junction, Oregon
KCGB-FM Columbia River, Oregon
KDCQ Coos Bay, Oregon
KMGE Eugene, Oregon
KODZ Eugene, Oregon
KCST-FM Florence, Oregon
KAJO Grants Pass, Oregon
KLDR Harbeck-Fruitdale, Oregon
KQFM Hermiston, Oregon
KWRL La Grande, Oregon
KORV Lakeview, Oregon
KSHO Lebanon, Oregon
KBCH Lincoln City, Oregon
KTMT-FM Medford, Oregon
KKKJ Merrill, Oregon
KOOR Milwaukie, Oregon
KRSK Molalla, Oregon
KSND Monmouth, Oregon
KSRV-FM Ontario, Oregon
KUMA-FM Pilot Rock, Oregon
KYCH-FM Portland, Oregon
KLTW-FM Prineville, Oregon
KWPK-FM Sisters, Oregon
KODL The Dalles, Oregon
KKMX Tri City, Oregon
KEUG Veneta, Oregon

KWSO Warm Springs, Oregon
WLEV Allentown, Pennsylvania
WNCC Barnesboro, Pennsylvania
WAYC Bedford, Pennsylvania
WAYC Bedford, Pennsylvania
WALY Bellwood, Pennsylvania
WHLM-FM Berwick, Pennsylvania
WFYY Bloomsburg, Pennsylvania
WBYN-FM Boyertown, Pennsylvania
WRRK Braddock, Pennsylvania
WXMJ Cambridge Springs, Pennsylvania
WTRW(FM) Carbondale, Pennsylvania
WIKZ Chambersburg, Pennsylvania
WCCR Clarion, Pennsylvania
WQYX Clearfield, Pennsylvania
WUUZ Cooperstown, Pennsylvania
WFRM Coudersport, Pennsylvania
WBRX Cresson, Pennsylvania
WDYS Dushore, Pennsylvania
WKPL Ellwood City, Pennsylvania
WQKY Emporium, Pennsylvania
WXBB Erie, Pennsylvania
WXKC Erie, Pennsylvania
WRSD Folsom, Pennsylvania
WEJL-FM Forest City, Pennsylvania
WHMJ Franklin, Pennsylvania
WGET Gettysburg, Pennsylvania
WNNK Harrisburg, Pennsylvania
WCCS Homer City, Pennsylvania
WDNH-FM Honesdale, Pennsylvania
WMRF Huntingdon, Pennsylvania
WQMU Indiana, Pennsylvania
WCRO Johnstown, Pennsylvania
WKYE Johnstown, Pennsylvania
WROZ Lancaster, Pennsylvania
WLSH Lansford, Pennsylvania
WQTW Latrobe, Pennsylvania
WQIC Lebanon, Pennsylvania
WGRC Lewisburg, Pennsylvania
WMRF-FM Lewistown, Pennsylvania
WSQV(FM) Lock Haven, Pennsylvania
WNBQ Mansfield, Pennsylvania
WRIJ Masontown, Pennsylvania
WLLF Mercer, Pennsylvania
WMSS Middletown, Pennsylvania
WVRT Mill Hall, Pennsylvania
WQLV Millersburg, Pennsylvania
WVLY-FM Milton, Pennsylvania
WBZZ New Kensington, Pennsylvania
WPCL Northern Cambria, Pennsylvania
WEGH Northumberland, Pennsylvania
WKQW-FM Oil City, Pennsylvania
WBEN-FM Philadelphia, Pennsylvania
WDAS-FM Philadelphia, Pennsylvania
WISX Philadelphia, Pennsylvania
WJAS Pittsburgh, Pennsylvania
WLTJ Pittsburgh, Pennsylvania
WSHH Pittsburgh, Pennsylvania
WWSW-FM Pittsburgh, Pennsylvania
WHKS Port Allegany, Pennsylvania
WPPA Pottsville, Pennsylvania
WPXZ-FM Punxsutawney, Pennsylvania
WSOX Red Lion, Pennsylvania
WDSN Reynoldsville, Pennsylvania
WVYS Ridgebury, Pennsylvania
WKMC Roaring Spring, Pennsylvania
WATS Sayre, Pennsylvania
WLSW Scottdale, Pennsylvania
WWRR Scranton, Pennsylvania
WKBI St. Marys, Pennsylvania
WKBI-FM St. Marys, Pennsylvania
WQKX Sunbury, Pennsylvania
WMGH-FM Tamaqua, Pennsylvania
WTTC-FM Towanda, Pennsylvania
WVYS-FM2 Towanda, Pennsylvania
WTRN Tyrone, Pennsylvania
WCTL Union City, Pennsylvania
WMBS Uniontown, Pennsylvania
WCYJ-FM Waynesburg, Pennsylvania
WNBT Wellsboro, Pennsylvania
WNBT-FM Wellsboro, Pennsylvania
WMGS Wilkes-Barre, Pennsylvania
WKSB Williamsport, Pennsylvania
WLMY Williamsport, Pennsylvania
WWPA Williamsport, Pennsylvania
WARM York, Pennsylvania
WYCR York-Hanover, Pennsylvania
WFDT Aguada, Puerto Rico
WABA Aguadilla, Puerto Rico
WTPM Aguadilla, Puerto Rico
WVJP Caguas, Puerto Rico
WVOZ-FM Carolina, Puerto Rico
WCPR Coamo, Puerto Rico
WALO Humacao, Puerto Rico
WISA Isabela, Puerto Rico
WIVV Island of Vieques, Puerto Rico
WTIL Mayaguez, Puerto Rico
WEXS Patillas, Puerto Rico
WPPC Penuelas, Puerto Rico
WIOC Ponce, Puerto Rico
WPUC-FM Ponce, Puerto Rico
WZAR Ponce, Puerto Rico
WFID Rio Piedras, Puerto Rico
WBMJ San Juan, Puerto Rico
WIOA San Juan, Puerto Rico
WLRP San Sebastian, Puerto Rico
WERR Vega Alta, Puerto Rico
WVIS Vieques, Puerto Rico
WXEW Yabucoa, Puerto Rico
WENA Yauco, Puerto Rico
WMNP Block Island, Rhode Island
WWBB Providence, Rhode Island
WWLI Providence, Rhode Island
WWKX Woonsocket, Rhode Island
WGTN-FM Andrews, South Carolina
WYKZ Beaufort, South Carolina
WEPC Belton, South Carolina
WARQ Columbia, South Carolina
WWNQ Forest Acres, South Carolina
WFBC-FM Greenville, South Carolina
WCRS Greenwood, South Carolina
WZSN Greenwood, South Carolina
WAVF Hanahan, South Carolina
WMXZ Isle of Palms, South Carolina
WDKD Kingstree, South Carolina
WKCL Ladson, South Carolina
WSIM Lamar, South Carolina
WMYB Myrtle Beach, South Carolina
WKDK Newberry, South Carolina
WTCB Orangeburg, South Carolina
WVSC Port Royal, South Carolina
WMGL Ravenel, South Carolina
WSNW Seneca, South Carolina
WSPA-FM Spartanburg, South Carolina
WWHM Sumter, South Carolina
WIBZ Wedgefield, South Carolina
WSCZ Winnsboro, South Carolina
KBFO Aberdeen, South Dakota
KBRK-FM Brookings, South Dakota
KDBX Clear Lake, South Dakota
KFCR Custer, South Dakota
KQSF Dell Rapids, South Dakota
KJBI Fort Pierre, South Dakota
KZKK Huron, South Dakota
KQRN Mitchell, South Dakota
KGFX-FM Pierre, South Dakota
KLXS-FM Pierre, South Dakota
KKMK Rapid City, South Dakota
KQRQ Rapid City, South Dakota
KNBZ Redfield, South Dakota
KELO-FM Sioux Falls, South Dakota
KMXC Sioux Falls, South Dakota
KIXX Watertown, South Dakota
KWYR-FM Winner, South Dakota
KYNT Yankton, South Dakota
WBGQ Bulls Gap, Tennessee
WCLE-FM Calhoun, Tennessee
WRJB Camden, Tennessee
WDEF-FM Chattanooga, Tennessee
WKRM Columbia, Tennessee
WKSW Cookeville, Tennessee
WPBX Crossville, Tennessee
WDNT Dayton, Tennessee
WCDZ Dresden, Tennessee
WLLJ Etowah, Tennessee
WMRO Gallatin, Tennessee
WSEV-FM Gatlinburg, Tennessee
WMPZ Harrison, Tennessee
WHHM-FM Henderson, Tennessee
WTFM Kingsport, Tennessee
WIFA Knoxville, Tennessee
WJXB Knoxville, Tennessee
WDXE-FM Lawrenceburg, Tennessee
WZLT Lexington, Tennessee
WYGO Madisonville, Tennessee
WFTZ Manchester, Tennessee
WCMT Martin, Tennessee
WMC-FM Memphis, Tennessee
WQOX Memphis, Tennessee
WRVR Memphis, Tennessee
WCJK Murfreesboro, Tennessee
WAMB Nashville, Tennessee
WJXA Nashville, Tennessee
WNRQ Nashville, Tennessee
WBNT-FM Oneida, Tennessee
WLZK Paris, Tennessee
WPRT Pegram, Tennessee
WPRT-FM Pegram, Tennessee
WSEV Sevierville, Tennessee
WLND Signal Mountain, Tennessee
WUUQ South Pittsburg, Tennessee
WAYM Spring Hill, Tennessee
WMXV St. Joseph, Tennessee
WTNE Trenton, Tennessee
KACU Abilene, Texas
KGNZ Abilene, Texas
KJAV Alamo, Texas
KMXJ-FM Amarillo, Texas
KPRF Amarillo, Texas
KLTY Arlington, Texas
KKMJ-FM Austin, Texas
KOOC(FM) Belton, Texas
KBTS Big Spring, Texas
KROO Breckenridge, Texas
KLTR Brenham, Texas
KBOC Bridgeport, Texas
KBWD Brownwood, Texas
KKYS Bryan, Texas
KAPN Caldwell, Texas
KGSR Cedar Park, Texas
KETR Commerce, Texas
KSSM Copperas Cove, Texas
KLTG Corpus Christi, Texas
KDMX Dallas, Texas
KJKK Dallas, Texas
KTDR Del Rio, Texas
KAFX-FM Diboll, Texas
KXBJ El Campo, Texas
KINT-FM El Paso, Texas
KSII El Paso, Texas
KSVE El Paso, Texas
KTSM-FM El Paso, Texas
KFST Fort Stockton, Texas
KGAF Gainesville, Texas
KLJA Georgetown, Texas
KTWL Hempstead, Texas
KVIL Highland Park-Dallas, Texas
KHMX Houston, Texas
KODA Houston, Texas
KKGN Ingram, Texas
KLJT Jacksonville, Texas
KOOI Jacksonville, Texas
KJAS Jasper, Texas
KKVR Kerrville, Texas
KQUR Laredo, Texas
KBZO Lubbock, Texas
KYBI Lufkin, Texas
KAMX Luling, Texas
KZLV Lytle, Texas
KKHA Markham, Texas
KBWC Marshall, Texas
KCHX Midland, Texas
KCRS-FM Midland, Texas
KQRX Midland, Texas
KLBW New Boston, Texas
KZRB New Boston, Texas
KLZK New Deal, Texas
KNRG New Ulm, Texas
KMCM Odessa, Texas
KODM Odessa, Texas
KKMY Orange, Texas
KGRO Pampa, Texas
KPLT-FM Paris, Texas
KPTX Pecos, Texas
KNVO-FM Port Isabel, Texas
KNLE-FM Round Rock, Texas
KELI San Angelo, Texas
KIXY-FM San Angelo, Texas
KMDX San Angelo, Texas
KAHL San Antonio, Texas
KQXT-FM San Antonio, Texas
KSMG San Antonio, Texas
KHKZ San Benito, Texas
KBPA San Marcos, Texas
KNVR San Saba, Texas
KDAE Sinton, Texas
KSST Sulphur Springs, Texas
KLAK Tom Bean, Texas
KTYL-FM Tyler, Texas
KNAL Victoria, Texas
KQVT Victoria, Texas
KTXN-FM Victoria, Texas
KVIC Victoria, Texas

KQHN Waskom, Texas
KAPW White Oak, Texas
KBZS Wichita Falls, Texas
KALK Winfield, Texas
KJMY Bountiful, Utah
KREC Brian Head, Utah
KQMB Levan, Utah
KBLQ-FM Logan, Utah
KLGN Logan, Utah
KUDE Nephi, Utah
KBZN Ogden, Utah
KOGN Ogden, Utah
KTCE Payson, Utah
KSRR Provo, Utah
KIFX Roosevelt, Utah
KXRQ Roosevelt, Utah
KANN Roy, Utah
KUDD Roy, Utah
KBEE Salt Lake City, Utah
KSFI Salt Lake City, Utah
KAAZ-FM Spanish Fork, Utah
KYMV Woodruff, Utah
WWDW Alberta, Virginia
WAVA-FM Arlington, Virginia
WJDV Broadway, Virginia
WWZW Buena Vista, Virginia
WQMZ Charlottesville, Virginia
WWIP Chesapeake, Virginia
WNLR Churchville, Virginia
WVRI Clifton Forge, Virginia
WGCK-FM Coeburn, Virginia
WZGN Crozet, Virginia
WCVA Culpeper, Virginia
WPIN-FM Dublin, Virginia
WEVA Emporia, Virginia
WFLO-FM Farmville, Virginia
WBQB Fredericksburg, Virginia
WXGM Gloucester, Virginia
WXGM-FM Gloucester, Virginia
WWDE-FM Hampton, Virginia
WKWI Kilmarnock, Virginia
WOJL Louisa, Virginia
WMXH-FM Luray, Virginia
WRVL Lynchburg, Virginia
WSNZ Lynchburg, Virginia
WZVA Marion, Virginia
WPIM Martinsville, Virginia
WJOI Norfolk, Virginia
WMOV-FM Norfolk, Virginia
WNVZ Norfolk, Virginia
WESR-FM Onley-Onancock, Virginia
WVCV Orange, Virginia
WRIC-FM Richlands, Virginia
WTVR-FM Richmond, Virginia
WSLQ Roanoke, Virginia
WPAR Salem, Virginia
WSNV Salem, Virginia
WHLF South Boston, Virginia
WSVO Staunton, Virginia
WTON-FM Staunton, Virginia
WRAR-FM Tappahannock, Virginia
WSFF Vinton, Virginia
WMBG Williamsburg, Virginia
WINC-FM Winchester, Virginia
WIUJ Charlotte Amalie, Virgin Islands
WVIQ Christiansted, Virgin Islands
WKVT-FM Brattleboro, Vermont
WTSA-FM Brattleboro, Vermont
WEZF Burlington, Vermont
WMOO Derby Center, Vermont
WGMT Lyndon, Vermont
WVNR Poultney, Vermont
WDVT Rutland, Vermont
WJJR Rutland, Vermont
WZRT Rutland, Vermont
WCFR Springfield, Vermont
WSTJ St. Johnsbury, Vermont
KWLE Anacortes, Washington
KOLW Basin City, Washington
KQMV Bellevue, Washington
KAFE Bellingham, Washington
KRWM Bremerton, Washington
KOZI Chelan, Washington
KOZI-FM Chelan, Washington
KCLK-FM Clarkston, Washington
KXAA Cle Elum, Washington
KRAO-FM Colfax, Washington
KCRK-FM Colville, Washington
KMCQ Covington, Washington
KEYF Dishman, Washington
KCMS Edmonds, Washington
KEYG-FM Grand Coulee, Washington
KLOG Kelso, Washington
KLYK Kelso, Washington
KONA-FM Kennewick, Washington
KIXI Mercer Island/Seattl, Washington
KSWW Ocean Shores, Washington
KGY Olympia, Washington
KOMW Omak, Washington
KZBE Omak, Washington
KEYW Pasco, Washington
KJET Raymond, Washington
KRIZ Renton, Washington
KAAP Rock Island, Washington
KJAQ Seattle, Washington
KJR-FM Seattle, Washington
KPLZ-FM Seattle, Washington
KAGU Spokane, Washington
KISC Spokane, Washington
KZZU Spokane, Washington
WDKM Adams, Wisconsin
WATK Antigo, Wisconsin
WOVM Appleton, Wisconsin
WLBL Auburndale, Wisconsin
WRPQ Baraboo, Wisconsin
WBEV Beaver Dam, Wisconsin
WBCR-FM Beloit, Wisconsin
WBJZ Berlin, Wisconsin
WWIS-FM Black River Falls, Wisconsin
WCFW Chippewa Falls, Wisconsin
WIAL Eau Claire, Wisconsin
WSBW Ephraim, Wisconsin
WFON Fond Du Lac, Wisconsin
WSJY Fort Atkinson, Wisconsin
WQLH Green Bay, Wisconsin
WRLS-FM Hayward, Wisconsin
WEZY Janesville, Wisconsin
WLXR-FM La Crosse, Wisconsin
WLKG Lake Geneva, Wisconsin
WFDL-FM Lomira, Wisconsin
WMGN Madison, Wisconsin
WZEE Madison, Wisconsin
WRJC-FM Mauston, Wisconsin
WJMT Merrill, Wisconsin
WKLH Milwaukee, Wisconsin
WLWK-FM Milwaukee, Wisconsin
WMYX-FM Milwaukee, Wisconsin
WRIT-FM Milwaukee, Wisconsin
WMQA-FM Minocqua, Wisconsin
WEKZ-FM Monroe, Wisconsin
WNAM Neenah-Menasha, Wisconsin
WPKG Neillsville, Wisconsin
WJUB Plymouth, Wisconsin
WRJN Racine, Wisconsin
WVTY Racine, Wisconsin
WBDL Reedsburg, Wisconsin
WRHN Rhinelander, Wisconsin
WKFX Rice Lake, Wisconsin
WRCO Richland Center, Wisconsin
WTCX Ripon, Wisconsin
WEVR River Falls, Wisconsin
WEVR-FM River Falls, Wisconsin
WOWN Shawano, Wisconsin
WSHS Sheboygan, Wisconsin
WXCX Siren, Wisconsin
WKPO Soldiers Grove, Wisconsin
WQDC Sturgeon Bay, Wisconsin
WXYM Tomah, Wisconsin
WFDL Waupun, Wisconsin
WAUH Wautoma, Wisconsin
WBKV West Bend, Wisconsin
WNNO Wisconsin Dells, Wisconsin
WHAJ Bluefield, West Virginia
WPIB Bluefield, West Virginia
WVAF Charleston, West Virginia
WWLW Clarksburg, West Virginia
WXIL Elizabeth, West Virginia
WELK Elkins, West Virginia
WELD Fisher, West Virginia
WVUS Grafton, West Virginia
WMGA Kenova, West Virginia
WHFI Lindside, West Virginia
WVOW Logan, West Virginia
WVOW-FM Logan, West Virginia
WLTF Martinsburg, West Virginia
WKAZ-FM Miami, West Virginia
WYMJ New Martinsville, West Virginia
WADC Parkersburg, West Virginia
WQAB Philippi, West Virginia
WVAR Richwood, West Virginia
WDYK Ridgeley, West Virginia
WMXE South Charleston, West Virginia
WRRR-FM St. Marys, West Virginia
WCWV Summersville, West Virginia
WSGB Sutton, West Virginia
WAFD Webster Springs, West Virginia
WEIR Weirton, West Virginia
WELC Welch, West Virginia
WZST Westover, West Virginia
WKWK-FM Wheeling, West Virginia
KHOC Casper, Wyoming
KJUA Cheyenne, Wyoming
KTAG Cody, Wyoming
KNYN Fort Bridger, Wyoming
KAML-FM Gillette, Wyoming
KUGR Green River, Wyoming
KZWB Green River, Wyoming
KAOX Kemmerer, Wyoming
KZQL Mills, Wyoming
KHRW Ranchester, Wyoming
KRAL Rawlins, Wyoming
KTRZ Riverton, Wyoming
KWYO Sheridan, Wyoming
KTHE Thermopolis, Wyoming
KZEW Wheatland, Wyoming
KDDV-FM Wright, Wyoming

Agriculture

KSIR Brush, Colorado
WHOW Clinton, Illinois
KSUM Fairmont, Minnesota
KQLX Lisbon, North Dakota
KNEB-FM Scottsbluff, Nebraska
WCJW Warsaw, New York
KWHW Altus, Oklahoma
KBHB Sturgis, South Dakota
KJJQ Volga, South Dakota
KFLP-FM Floydada, Texas

Alternative

KRUA Anchorage, Alaska
KSUA Fairbanks, Alaska
KXLL Juneau, Alaska
KUHB-FM St. Paul, Alaska
WEGL Auburn, Alabama
WZEW Fairhope, Alabama
WVUA-FM Tuscaloosa, Alabama
KCAC Camden, Arkansas
KPOS Fouke, Arkansas
KALR Hot Springs, Arkansas
KJBR Marked Tree, Arkansas
KXNA Springdale, Arkansas
KFMA Green Valley, Arizona
KAIH Lake Havasu City, Arizona
KZAI Superior, Arizona
KAIC Tucson, Arizona
XETRAFM Tijuana, Mexico
KSPC Claremont, California
KKUP Cupertino, California
KHRI Hollister, California
KDRH King City, California
KFFG Los Altos, California
KPTR Palm Springs, California
KROQ Pasadena, California
KOSO Patterson, California
KSPB Pebble Beach, California
KGBM Randsburg, California
KKRO Red Bluff, California
KUCR Riverside, California
KARQ San Andreas, California
KBZT San Diego, California
KFOG San Francisco, California
KITS San Francisco, California
KSJO San Jose, California
KYNS San Luis Obispo, California
KSCU Santa Clara, California
KSRI Santa Cruz, California
KAIB Shafter, California
KYIX South Oroville, California
KKZQ Tehachapi, California
KSRY Tehachapi, California
KXRD Victorville, California
KARA Williams, California
KFRR Woodlake, California
KLRD Yucaipa, California
KCSU-FM Fort Collins, Colorado
KMSA Grand Junction, Colorado
KHCO Hayden, Colorado
KAAI Palisade, Colorado
KRXP Pueblo West, Colorado
KDRE Sterling, Colorado
KTCL Wheat Ridge, Colorado

WXCI Danbury, Connecticut
WQAQ Hamden, Connecticut
WDJW Somers, Connecticut
WVUM Coral Gables, Florida
WTZB Englewood, Florida
WSUN-FM Holiday, Florida
WIIS Key West, Florida
WAYJ Naples, Florida
WAYR Orange Park, Florida
WUWF Pensacola, Florida
WHPT Sarasota, Florida
WKPX Sunrise, Florida
WVFS Tallahassee, Florida
WUOG Athens, Georgia
WRDA-FM Canton, Georgia
WRDG Peachtree City, Georgia
WVGS Statesboro, Georgia
WQAI Thomson, Georgia
WPLH Tifton, Georgia
WVVS-FM Valdosta, Georgia
KUCD Pearl City, Hawaii
KHAI Wahiawa, Hawaii
KBVU-FM Alta, Iowa
KIWR Council Bluffs, Iowa
KICB Fort Dodge, Iowa
KSTM Indianola, Iowa
KIGC Oskaloosa, Iowa
KMSC Sioux City, Iowa
KAIP Wapello, Iowa
KWDM West Des Moines, Iowa
KAIO Idaho Falls, Idaho
KARJ Kuna, Idaho
KSKI-FM Sun Valley, Idaho
WCLR Arlington Heights, Illinois
WPCD Champaign, Illinois
WKQX Chicago, Illinois
WRTE Chicago, Illinois
WXRT Chicago, Illinois
WJMU Decatur, Illinois
WARW Dorsey, Illinois
WRSE Elmhurst, Illinois
WGBK Glenview, Illinois
WIUS Macomb, Illinois
WVJC Mount Carmel, Illinois
WONC Naperville, Illinois
WRRG River Grove, Illinois
WSRI Sugar Grove, Illinois
WARG Summit, Illinois
WSJK(FM) Tuscola, Illinois
WPGU Urbana, Illinois
WEAX Angola, Indiana
WHJE Carmel, Indiana
WJHS Columbia City, Indiana
WSWI Evansville, Indiana
WGRE Greencastle, Indiana
WQRA Greencastle, Indiana
WOLT Indianapolis, South Carolina
WCYT Lafayette Township, Indiana
WARA New Washington, Indiana
KAIG Dodge City, Kansas
KSDB-FM Manhattan, Kansas
KTHR Wichita, Kansas
WFPK Louisville, Kentucky
KSLU Hammond, Louisiana
KITA Iota, Louisiana
WNXX Jackson, Louisiana
KXUL Monroe, Louisiana
WTUL New Orleans, Louisiana
KLPI Ruston, Louisiana
KSCL Shreveport, Louisiana
KROK South Fort Polk, Louisiana
KNSU Thibodaux, Louisiana
WDJM-FM Framingham, Massachusetts
WZBC Newton, Massachusetts
WKKL West Barnstable, Massachusetts
WCHC Worcester, Massachusetts
WMTB-FM Emmitsburg, Maryland
WRNR-FM Grasonville, Maryland
WHSN Bangor, Maine
WZLO Dover-Foxcroft, Maine
WQAC Alma, Michigan
WDTW Dearborn, Michigan
WDBM East Lansing, Michigan
WTRK Freeland, Michigan
WGRD-FM Grand Rapids, Michigan
WUPX Marquette, Michigan
WMHW-FM Mount Pleasant, Michigan
WOVI Novi, Michigan
WZOX Portage, Michigan
WYCE Wyoming, Michigan
KUMM Morris, Minnesota
KVSC St. Cloud, Minnesota
KSRQ Thief River Falls, Minnesota
KAIA Bloomfield, Missouri
KWUR Clayton, Missouri
KCOU Columbia, Missouri
KQQX Hermann, Missouri
KTRM Kirksville, Missouri
KMVC Marshall, Missouri
KZZK New London, Missouri
KGSP Parkville, Missouri
WCPR-FM D'Iberville, Mississippi
WZRH Picayune, Mississippi
WMSV Starkville, Mississippi
WUMS University, Mississippi
WABO-FM Waynesboro, Mississippi
KMSM-FM Butte, Montana
KRVO Columbia Falls, Montana
KMPT East Missoula, Montana
KGFA Great Falls, Montana
KBAZ Hamilton, Montana
KBIL Park City, Montana
WASU-FM Boone, North Carolina
WSOE Elon College, North Carolina
WZMB Greenville, North Carolina
WEND Salisbury, North Carolina
WDCC Sanford, North Carolina
WZDG Scotts Hill, North Carolina
WZRI Spring Lake, North Carolina
KNRI Bismarck, North Dakota
KDNE Crete, Nebraska
KDAI Scottsbluff, Nebraska
KWSC Wayne, Nebraska
WUNH Durham, New Hampshire
WKNH Keene, New Hampshire
WPNH-FM Plymouth, New Hampshire
WADB(AM) Asbury Park, New Jersey
WDBK Blackwood, New Jersey
WLFR Pomona, New Jersey
WTSR Trenton, New Jersey
WPSC-FM Wayne, New Jersey
KGGA Gallup, New Mexico
KQAI Roswell, New Mexico
KTEG Santa Fe, New Mexico
KTRC Santa Fe, New Mexico
KAER Mesquite, Nevada
KAIZ Mesquite, Nevada
KXTE Pahrump, Nevada
WRRB Arlington, New York
WZNE Brighton, New York
WBNY Buffalo, New York
WITC Cazenovia, New York
WEHN East Hampton, New York
WGSU Geneseo, New York
WNYH Huntington, New York
WNYY Ithaca, New York
WRRV Middletown, New York
WKRH Minetto, New York
WBAI New York, New York
WWRL New York, New York
WDBY Patterson, New York
WBTZ Plattsburgh, New York
WQKE Plattsburgh, New York
WTSC-FM Potsdam, New York
WBER Rochester, New York
WYAI Scotia, New York
WDST Woodstock, New York
WZDA Beavercreek, Ohio
WCSB Cleveland, Ohio
WLQR-FM Delta, Ohio
WBWR Hilliard, Ohio
WCVJ Jefferson, Ohio
WOXY Mason, Ohio
WOAR South Vienna, Ohio
WUSO Springfield, Ohio
WXUT Toledo, Ohio
KPAK Alva, Oklahoma
KWRI Bartlesville, Oklahoma
KARU Cache, Oklahoma
KRSC-FM Claremore, Oklahoma
KOKF Edmond, Oklahoma
KKRD Enid, Oklahoma
KKRI Pocola, Oklahoma
WBBZ Ponca City, Oklahoma
KMYZ-FM Pryor, Oklahoma
KLVP Aloha, Oregon
KBVR Corvallis, Oregon
KGRI Lebanon, Oregon
KSLC McMinnville, Oregon
KARO Nyssa, Oregon
KVRA Sisters, Oregon
KAIK Tillamook, Oregon
KXPC Welches, Oregon
WBUQ Bloomsburg, Pennsylvania
WESS East Stroudsburg, Pennsylvania
WFSE Edinboro, Pennsylvania
WERG Erie, Pennsylvania
WZBT Gettysburg, Pennsylvania
WARC Meadville, Pennsylvania
WXPH Middletown, Pennsylvania
WPAI Nanty Glo, Pennsylvania
WKDU Philadelphia, Pennsylvania
WXPN Philadelphia, Pennsylvania
WQCK(FM) Philipsburg, Pennsylvania
WXDX-FM Pittsburgh, Pennsylvania
WUSR Scranton, Pennsylvania
WVMW-FM Scranton, Pennsylvania
WCHE West Chester, Pennsylvania
WCLH Wilkes-Barre, Pennsylvania
WRLC Williamsport, Pennsylvania
WBRU Providence, Rhode Island
WDOM Providence, Rhode Island
WJMF Smithfield, Rhode Island
WSBF-FM Clemson, South Carolina
WHHW Hilton Head Island, South Carolina
KSDJ Brookings, South Dakota
KAUR Sioux Falls, South Dakota
KBHU-FM Spearfish, South Dakota
WTTU Cookeville, Tennessee
WTZR Elizabethton, Tennessee
WBBP Memphis, Tennessee
WNFZ Powell, Tennessee
WQAK Union City, Tennessee
WTAI Union City, Tennessee
KAGT Abilene, Texas
KEYJ-FM Abilene, Texas
KACV-FM Amarillo, Texas
KXRI Amarillo, Texas
KTLT Anson, Texas
KKWV Aransas Pass, Texas
KVRX Austin, Texas
KROX-FM Buda, Texas
KGSR Cedar Park, Texas
KDGE Fort Worth-Dallas, Texas
KYAR Lorena, Texas
KPGA Morton, Texas
KNAR San Angelo, Texas
KSYM-FM San Antonio, Texas
KTSW San Marcos, Texas
KFRI West Odessa, Texas
KOHS Orem, Utah
KXRK Provo, Utah
KXDS Santa Clara, Utah
WNRN Charlottesville, Virginia
WXJM Harrisonburg, Virginia
WHRV Norfolk, Virginia
WRXL Richmond, Virginia
WCWM Williamsburg, Virginia
WZIN Charlotte Amalie, Virgin Islands
WIUV Castleton, Vermont
WJSC-FM Johnson, Vermont
WEQX Manchester, Vermont
WVTC Randolph Center, Vermont
KBAI Bellingham, Washington
KNRK Camas, Washington
KKBW Eatonville, Washington
KCWU Ellensburg, Washington
KGRG Enumclaw, Washington
KTCV Kennewick, Washington
KTSL Medical Lake, Washington
KEXP-FM Seattle, Washington
KNDD Seattle, Washington
KZBD Spokane, Washington
KUPS Tacoma, Washington
KYVT Yakima, Washington
WBSD Burlington, Wisconsin
WLUM-FM Milwaukee, Wisconsin
WMSE Milwaukee, Wisconsin
WSUW Whitewater, Wisconsin
WGLZ West Liberty, West Virginia
KAIX Cheyenne, Wyoming
KAIW Laramie, Wyoming

Big Band

KBRW-FM Barrow, Alaska
KCEA Atherton, California
KEZW Aurora, Colorado
WTMY Sarasota, Florida
WFRX West Frankfort, Illinois
WICN Worcester, Massachusetts
WYAR Yarmouth, Maine
WCBY Cheboygan, Michigan

WIOS Tawas City-East Tawas, Michigan
WZFJ(FM) Breezy Point, Minnesota
KRLI Malta Bend, Missouri
WELO Tupelo, Mississippi
WPAQ Mount Airy, North Carolina
WPNH Plymouth, New Hampshire
KNCC Elko, Nevada
WNYC New York, New York
WNYV Whitehall, New York
WKHR Bainbridge, Ohio
WMKV Reading, Ohio
WJAS Pittsburgh, Pennsylvania
KSQX Springtown, Texas
KQXS Stephenville, Texas
KPYK Terrell, Texas
WFOS Chesapeake, Virginia
WIUJ Charlotte Amalie, Virgin Islands
KTRW Opportunity, Washington
WCCN Neillsville, Wisconsin

Black

WATV Birmingham, Alabama
WOOF Dothan, Alabama
WRJX Jackson, Alabama
WEUV Moulton, Alabama
WOPP Opp, Alabama
WZZA Tuscumbia, Alabama
WBHK Warrior, Alabama
KABF Little Rock, Arkansas
KAKJ Marianna, Arkansas
KTYM Inglewood, California
KSRH San Rafael, California
KJQY Colorado City, Colorado
WOCA Ocala, Florida
WYZE Atlanta, Georgia
WFXA-FM Augusta, Georgia
WBHB Fitzgerald, Georgia
WJGA-FM Jackson, Georgia
WDDO Macon, Georgia
WIGO Morrow, Georgia
KIGC Oskaloosa, Iowa
WYRB Genoa, Illinois
WPWX Hammond, Indiana
WSRB Lansing, Illinois
WLLV Louisville, Kentucky
KXZZ Lake Charles, Louisiana
KRUS Ruston, Louisiana
WOMR Provincetown, Massachusetts
WFLT Flint, Michigan
WELZ Belzoni, Mississippi
WCHJ Brookhaven, Mississippi
WCLD Cleveland, Mississippi
WACR-FM Columbus Afb, Mississippi
WNLA Indianola, Mississippi
WFMO Fairmont, North Carolina
WIDU Fayetteville, North Carolina
WQMG Greensboro, North Carolina
WEGG Rose Hill, North Carolina
WARR Warrenton, North Carolina
WWIL Wilmington, North Carolina
WNEC-FM Henniker, New Hampshire
KCEP Las Vegas, Nevada
WXXY Houghton, New York
WTHE Mineola, New York
WBLS New York, New York
WHCR-FM New York, New York
WNYU-FM New York, New York
WNYK Nyack, New York
WBGU Bowling Green, Ohio
WOHC Chillicothe, Ohio
WXTC Greenville, Pennsylvania
WIXQ Millersville, Pennsylvania
WNAP Norristown, Pennsylvania
WAMO Wilkinsburg, Pennsylvania
WOON Woonsocket, Rhode Island
WDOG Barnwell, South Carolina
WPJS Conway, South Carolina
WYNN Florence, South Carolina
WBZF Hartsville, South Carolina
WLGI Hemingway, South Carolina
WKZK North Augusta, South Carolina
WASC Spartanburg, South Carolina
WFKX Henderson, Tennessee
KGGR Dallas, Texas
KSHJ Houston, Texas
WSHV South Hill, Virginia

Blues

WAGF-FM Dothan, Alabama
WJLD(AM) Fairfield, Alabama
WZEW Fairhope, Alabama
WKXN Fort Deposit, Alabama
WHIY Huntsville, Alabama
WJAB Huntsville, Alabama
WBHJ Midfield, Alabama
WKXK Pine Hill, Alabama
WDLT Saraland, Alabama
WZZA Tuscumbia, Alabama
WBHK Warrior, Alabama
KAJM Camp Verde, Arizona
KOHT Marana, Arizona
KPKR Parker, Arizona
KJLH Compton, California
KKUP Cupertino, California
KPIG-FM Freedom, California
KQNY Quincy, California
KTSC-FM Pueblo, Colorado
WKND Windsor, Connecticut
WMIB Fort Lauderdale, Florida
WWAB Lakeland, Florida
WFLM White City, Florida
WMRZ Dawson, Georgia
WIBB-FM Fort Valley, Georgia
WVKX Irwinton, Georgia
WNUQ Sylvester, Georgia
WGUN Valdosta, Georgia
WRBV Warner Robins, Georgia
KBBG Waterloo, Iowa
WSSD Chicago, Illinois
WYRB Genoa, Illinois
WYRB Genoa, Illinois
WFFX(AM) Hattiesburg, Illinois
WSRB Lansing, Illinois
WGLT Normal, Illinois
KBRH Baton Rouge, Louisiana
KRVS Lafayette, Louisiana
WWOZ New Orleans, Louisiana
KTJZ Tallulah, Louisiana
WATD-FM Marshfield, Massachusetts
WESM Princess Anne, Maryland
WUCX-FM Bay City, Michigan
WLNZ Lansing, Michigan
WTLZ Saginaw, Michigan
WNMC-FM Traverse City, Michigan
WEMU Ypsilanti, Michigan
KMVC Marshall, Missouri
KCOZ Point Lookout, Missouri
WELZ Belzoni, Mississippi
WTWZ Clinton, Mississippi
WACR-FM Columbus Afb, Mississippi
WNEV Friars Point, Mississippi
WURC Holly Springs, Mississippi
WHJA Laurel, Mississippi
WESY Leland, Mississippi
WNBN Meridian, Mississippi
WQYZ Ocean Springs, Mississippi
WQZL Belhaven, North Carolina
WQMG Greensboro, North Carolina
WNCT Greenville, North Carolina
WCCG Hope Mills, North Carolina
WGIV Pineville, North Carolina
WENC Whiteville, North Carolina
KCEP Las Vegas, Nevada
WJZR Rochester, New York
WDAO Dayton, Ohio
WYOR Republic, Ohio
WJUC Swanton, Ohio
KROU Spencer, Oklahoma
KMHD Gresham, Oregon
WUSR Scranton, Pennsylvania
WAMO Wilkinsburg, Pennsylvania
WKSP Aiken, South Carolina
WYNN Florence, South Carolina
WWHM Sumter, South Carolina
WSCZ Winnsboro, South Carolina
WVOL Berry Hill, Tennessee
WBOL Bolivar, Tennessee
WEVL Memphis, Tennessee
WEUZ Minor Hill, Tennessee
KNDA Alice, Texas
KGEE Pecos, Texas
KUUU South Jordan, Utah
WFOS Chesapeake, Virginia
WNRV Narrows-Pearisburg, Virginia
WVKL Norfolk, Virginia
WBTJ Richmond, Virginia
WWED Spotsylvania, Virginia
KVIX Port Angeles, Washington
KRIZ Renton, Washington
KYIZ Renton, Washington
KPLU-FM Tacoma, Washington
WKKV-FM Racine, Wisconsin

Children

KDIS-FM Little Rock, Arkansas
KIDR Phoenix, Arizona
KMIK Tempe, Arizona
KMKY Oakland, California
KIID Sacramento, California
KDDZ Arvada, Colorado
WAJD Gainesville, Florida
WDYZ Orlando, Florida
WHTY(AM) Riviera Beach, Florida
WWMI St. Petersburg, Florida
WDWD Atlanta, Georgia
WPGA Perry, Georgia
WRDZ La Grange, Illinois
WYLC Jackson, Kentucky
WMKI Boston, Massachusetts
WFDF Farmington Hills, Michigan
KDIZ Golden Valley, Minnesota
KPHN Kansas City, Missouri
WGFY Charlotte, North Carolina
WCOG Greensboro, North Carolina
KMMQ Plattsmouth, Nebraska
WYRS Manahawkin, New Jersey
WWJZ Mount Holly, New Jersey
KDSK Los Ranchos De Albuquerque, New Mexico
WDDY Albany, New York
WMBO Auburn, New York
WALL Middletown, New York
WQEW New York, New York
WWMK Cleveland, Ohio
KMUS Sperry, Oklahoma
KDZR Lake Oswego, Oregon
KBPS Portland, Oregon
WWCF McConnellsburg, Pennsylvania
WDDZ Pittsburgh, Pennsylvania
WOWW Germantown, Tennessee
KMIC Houston, Texas
KRDY San Antonio, Texas
WHKT Portsmouth, Virginia
KKDZ Seattle, Washington
WKSH Sussex, Wisconsin
WMLJ Summersville, West Virginia

Chinese

KVTO Berkeley, California
KAZN Pasadena, California
KAHZ Pomona, California
KNSN San Diego, California
KMRB San Gabriel, California
KALI-FM Santa Ana, California
KHCM Honolulu, Hawaii
WKDM New York, New York
WZRC New York, New York
KGBC Galveston, Texas
KREH Pecan Grove, Texas

Christian

KHKY Akiachak, Alaska
KAFC Anchorage, Alaska
KAKL Anchorage, Alaska
KFAT Anchorage, Alaska
KAGV Big Lake, Alaska
KNGW Juneau, Alaska
KOGJ Kenai, Alaska
KAKN Naknek, Alaska
KIAM Nenana, Alaska
KICY-FM Nome, Alaska
KIAM-FM North Nenana, Alaska
KJLP Palmer, Alaska
WIZB Abbeville, Alabama
WGRW Anniston, Alabama
WBFR Birmingham, Alabama
WDJC-FM Birmingham, Alabama
WVOV Bridgeport, Alabama
WALN Carrollton, Alabama
WQUA Citronelle, Alabama
WXJC Cordova, Alabama
WXJC-FM Cordova, Alabama
WAVH Daphne, Alabama
WYFD Decatur, Alabama
WMBV Dixons Mills, Alabama
WGIB Eirmingham, Alabama
WKWL Florala, Alabama
WBCF Florence, Alabama
WFIX Florence, Alabama
WJIK Fulton, Alabama
WJIA Guntersville, Alabama

WAYH Harvest, Alabama
WBXR Hazel Green, Alabama
WQOH Irondale, Alabama
WIXI Jasper, Alabama
WBHY Mobile, Alabama
WBHY-FM Mobile, Alabama
WBAM-FM Montgomery, Alabama
WXVI Montgomery, Alabama
WAQG Ozark, Alabama
WIJD Prichard, Alabama
WIJD Prichard, Alabama
WIJD Prichard, Alabama
WAQU Selma, Alabama
WAKD Sheffield, Alabama
WAYU Steele, Alabama
WYEA Sylacauga, Alabama
WTID Thomaston, Alabama
WDLG Thomasville, Alabama
WAXU Troy, Alabama
WMFT Tuscaloosa, Alabama
WELL-FM Waverly, Alabama
KJSM-FM Augusta, Arkansas
KOAR Beebe, Arkansas
KBCM Blytheville, Arkansas
KBHN Booneville, Arkansas
KKSP Bryant, Arkansas
KEJA Cale, Arkansas
KXRL Cherry Valley, Arkansas
KWXT Dardanelle, Arkansas
KBPU De Queen, Arkansas
KAKV El Dorado, Arkansas
KAYH Fayetteville, Arkansas
KBNV Fayetteville, Arkansas
KOFC Fayetteville, Arkansas
KEAF Fort Smith, Arkansas
KPOS Fouke, Arkansas
KZKZ-FM Greenwood, Arkansas
KBPW Hampton, Arkansas
KBPB Harrison, Arkansas
KBMJ Heber Springs, Arkansas
KALR Hot Springs, Arkansas
KLRO Hot Springs, Arkansas
KJLV Hoxie, Arkansas
KGSF Hunstville, Arkansas
KJSB Jonesboro, Arkansas
KAAY Little Rock, Arkansas
KJBR Marked Tree, Arkansas
KLMK Marvell, Arkansas
KLRM Melbourne, Arkansas
K216FX Mena, Arkansas
KNLL Nashville, Arkansas
KLRC Siloam Springs, Arkansas
KKLT Texarkana, Arkansas
KLFS Van Buren, Arkansas
KNWJ Leone, American Samoa
KJAL Tafuna, American Samoa
KRMB Bisbee, Arizona
KWRB Bisbee, Arizona
KVIR Bullhead City, Arizona
K204CE Clifton, Arizona
KCKY Coolidge, Arizona
KLKI Dolan Springs, Arizona
KJTA Flagstaff, Arizona
KLVK Fountain Hills, Arizona
KLKA Globe, Arizona
KVJC Globe, Arizona
KBMH Holbrook, Arizona
KAIH Lake Havasu City, Arizona
KNLB Lake Havasu City, Arizona
KLTU Mammoth, Arizona
KLVA Maricopa, Arizona
KFLR-FM Phoenix, Arizona
KPHF Phoenix, Arizona
KXEG Phoenix, Arizona
KNXN Sierra Vista, Arizona
KZAI Superior, Arizona
KAIC Tucson, Arizona
KFLT Tucson, Arizona
KFLT-FM Tucson, Arizona
KGMS Tucson, Arizona
KWIM Window Rock, Arizona
KAWN Winslow, Arizona
KCFY Yuma, Arizona
KYRM Yuma, Arizona
KNDL(FM) Angwin, California
KERI Bakersfield, California
KFRB Bakersfield, California
KRTM Banning, California
KWTH Barstow, California
KWTW Bishop, California
KWLU Chester, California
KHAP Chico, California
KFRJ China Lake, California
KLVB Citrus Heights, California
KPSH Coachella, California
KDKL Coalinga, California
KFRP Coalinga, California
KRDU Dinuba, California
KLMG Esparto, California
KIHH Eureka, California
KLVY Fairmead, California
KKLC Fall River Mills, California
KJCU Fort Bragg, California
KJPG Frazier Park, California
KGED Fresno, California
KIRV Fresno, California
KWRU Fresno, California
KGKV Garberville, California
KLVG Garberville, California
KKMC Gonzales, California
KGBA Heber, California
KSDT Hemet, California
KHRI Hollister, California
KORB Hopland, California
KZLU Inyokern, California
KLVJ Julian, California
KWTM June Lake, California
KWDS Kettleman City, California
KDRH King City, California
KVPW Kingsburg, California
KFSH-FM La Mirada, California
KHKL Laytonville, California
KEFR Le Grand, California
KJOP Lemoore, California
KKFS Lincoln, California
KLVS Livermore, California
KLVN Livingston, California
KRQZ Lompoc, California
KFRN Long Beach, California
KHJ Los Angeles, California
KKLA-FM Los Angeles, California
KLVC Magalia, California
KCBC Manteca, California
KNDZ McKinleyville, California
KAMB Merced, California
KBRE Merced, California
KLVR Middletown, California
KCIV Mount Bullion, California
KWVE(AM) Oildale, California
KDAR Oxnard, California
KHCS Palm Desert, California
KLVM Prunedale, California
KGBM Randsburg, California
KKRO Red Bluff, California
KVIP Redding, California
KVIP-FM Redding, California
KWTD Ridgecrest, California
KPRO Riverside, California
KSGN Riverside, California
KDBV Salinas, California
KARQ San Andreas, California
KWVE-FM San Clemente, California
KEAR San Francisco, California
KSFB San Francisco, California
KLFF San Luis Obispo, California
KLVH San Luis Obispo, California
KPRZ San Marcos-Poway, California
KSRI Santa Cruz, California
KCLM Santa Maria, California
KGDP-FM Santa Maria, California
KSBQ Santa Maria, California
KBLA Santa Monica, California
KQKL Selma, California
KAIB Shafter, California
KFRS Soledad, California
KYIX South Oroville, California
KWG Stockton, California
KBLV Tehachapi, California
KAIS(FM) Tracy, California
KPRA Ukiah, California
KULV Ukiah, California
KHMS Victorville, California
KXRD Victorville, California
KARM Visalia, California
KDUV Visalia, California
KSAK Walnut, California
KFHL Wasco, California
KARA Williams, California
KIQS Willows, California
KLRD Yucaipa, California
KLJH Bayfield, Colorado
KLLV Breen, Colorado
KBWA Brush, Colorado
KLZV Brush, Colorado
KTLC Canon City, Colorado
KXWA Centennial, Colorado
KMZK Clifton, Colorado
KKPK Colorado Springs, Colorado
KTLF Colorado Springs, Colorado
KLZ Denver, Colorado
KPOF Denver, Colorado
KRKS Denver, Colorado
KTCF Dolores, Colorado
KTDU Durango, Colorado
KSIK Fleming, Colorado
KGCO Fort Collins, Colorado
KLXV Glenwood Springs, Colorado
KJOL Grand Junction, Colorado
KLFV Grand Junction, Colorado
KLRY Gypsum, Colorado
KHCO Hayden, Colorado
KRKS-FM Lafayette, Colorado
KTOL Leadville, Colorado
KRCN Longmont, Colorado
KPIO Loveland, Colorado
KXGR Loveland, Colorado
KBIQ Manitou Springs, Colorado
KTMH Montrose, Colorado
KCBR Monument, Colorado
KLDV Morrison, Colorado
KTPS Pagosa Springs, Colorado
KAAI Palisade, Colorado
KTEI Placerville, Colorado
KFRY Pueblo, Colorado
KGFT Pueblo, Colorado
KTPL Pueblo, Colorado
KRWA Rye, Colorado
KTPF Salida, Colorado
KTML South Fork, Colorado
KLBV Steamboat Springs, Colorado
KTSG Steamboat Springs, Colorado
KDRE Sterling, Colorado
KTAD Sterling, Colorado
KJWA Trinidad, Colorado
KTDL Trinidad, Colorado
KTAW Walsenburg, Colorado
WADS Ansonia, Connecticut
WSGG Norfolk, Connecticut
WXCT Southington, Connecticut
WXHL-FM Christiana, Delaware
WLJH Grand Gorge, New York
WZNZ Atlantic Beach, Florida
WTWB Auburndale, Florida
WTJT Baker, Florida
WRMB Boynton Beach, Florida
WJIS Bradenton, Florida
WNVY Cantonment, Florida
WKSG Cedar Creek, Florida
WMYZ Clermont, Florida
WPSF Clewiston, Florida
WHIM Coral Gables, Florida
WHIM(AM) Coral Gables, Florida
WAKU Crawfordville, Florida
WAQV Crystal River, Florida
WHGN Crystal River, Florida
WREH Cypress Quarters, Florida
WAKJ Defuniak Springs, Florida
WYND Deland, Florida
WIGW Eustis, Florida
WVOJ Fernandina Beach, Florida
WJLH Flagler Beach, Florida
WMFL Florida City, Florida
WYBP Fort Lauderdale, Florida
WCRM Fort Myers, Florida
WJYO Fort Myers, Florida
WMYE Fort Myers, Florida
WPSM Fort Walton Beach, Florida
WJLF Gainesville, Florida
WPHR-FM Gifford, Florida
WMKL Hammocks, Florida
WXRA Inglis, Florida
WCRJ Jacksonville, Florida
WROS Jacksonville, Florida
WYBW Key Colony Beach, Florida
WLFE-FM Key Largo, Florida
WJIR Key West, Florida
WKWR Key West, Florida
WYBX Key West, Florida
WLAZ Kissimmee, Florida
WBIY La Belle, Florida
WKES Lakeland, Florida
WYFO Lakeland, Florida
WWCL Lehigh Acres, Florida

WAYP Marianna, Florida
WTOT Marianna, Florida
WDMC Melbourne, Florida
WEGS Milton, Florida
WKVH Monticello, Florida
WAYJ Naples, Florida
WAYJ(FM) Naples, Florida
WSOR Naples, Florida
WKFP(FM) Navarre, Florida
WCIE New Port Richey, Florida
WHIJ Ocala, Florida
WAYR Orange Park, Florida
WTLN Orlando, Florida
WHIF Palatka, Florida
WEJF Palm Bay, Florida
WHYZ(FM) Palm Bay, Florida
WCNO Palm City, Florida
WHYZ Palm Coast, Florida
WFFL Panama City, Florida
WJTF Panama City, Florida
WGNK Pennsuco, Florida
WDWR Pensacola, Florida
WTBN Pinellas Park, Florida
WTWD Plant City, Florida
WEZI Ponte Vedra Beach, Florida
WDEO-FM San Carlos Park, Florida
WSMR Sarasota, Florida
WJFH Sebring, Florida
WUJC St. Marks, Florida
WTLG Starke, Florida
WWFR Stuart, Florida
WFRF Tallahassee, Florida
WTAL Tallahassee, Florida
WBVM Tampa, Florida
WPOZ Union Park, Florida
WBJY Americus, Georgia
WFRP Americus, Georgia
WFSH-FM Athens, Georgia
WMSL Athens, Georgia
WAEC Atlanta, Georgia
WNIV Atlanta, Georgia
WFAM Augusta, Georgia
WLPE Augusta, Georgia
WBBK-FM Blakely, Georgia
WGMI Bremen, Georgia
WULS Broxton, Georgia
WPWB Byron, Georgia
WCHM Clarkesville, Georgia
WNGA Clermont, Georgia
WPBS Conyers, Georgia
WGFS Covington, Georgia
WCDG Dahlonega, Georgia
WTTI Dalton, Georgia
WWGF Donalsonville, Georgia
WAWH Dublin, Georgia
WECC-FM Folkston, Georgia
WBIB-FM Forsyth, Georgia
WJTG Fort Valley, Georgia
WTHP Gibson, Georgia
WPLO Grayson, Georgia
WPMA Greensboro, Georgia
WMVV Griffin, Georgia
WTFH Helen, Georgia
WLPT Jesup, Georgia
WDEN-FM Macon, Georgia
WVFJ-FM Manchester, Georgia
WGTJ Murrayville, Georgia
WVKV Nashville, Georgia
WJGS Norwood, Georgia
WLPF Ocilla, Georgia
WMVW Peachtree City, Georgia
WLFS Port Wentworth, Georgia
WLXP Savannah, Georgia
WYFS Savannah, Georgia
WAYT Thomasville, Georgia
WQAI Thomson, Georgia
WTXR Toccoa Falls, Georgia
WBDX Trenton, Georgia
WVDA Valdosta, Georgia
WGPH Vidalia, Georgia
WKTF Vienna, Georgia
WASW Waycross, Georgia
WYFW Winder, Georgia
WFDR-FM Woodbury, Georgia
KSDA-FM Agat, Guam
K220EO Hilo, Hawaii
KCIF Hilo, Hawaii
KAIM-FM Honolulu, Hawaii
KGU Honolulu, Hawaii
KHJC Lihue, Hawaii
KHAI Wahiawa, Hawaii

KIHS Adel, Iowa
KRGO Alton, Iowa
KSKB Brooklyn, Iowa
KAYP Burlington, Iowa
KILV Castana, Iowa
KLNG Council Bluffs, Iowa
KLOX Creston, Iowa
KPSZ Des Moines, Iowa
KWKY Des Moines, Iowa
KIAD Dubuque, Iowa
KJYL Eagle Grove, Iowa
KXGM-FM Hiawatha, Iowa
KMDY Keokuk, Iowa
KNWM Madrid, Iowa
KCWN New Sharon, Iowa
KKLG Newton, Iowa
KNWI Osceola, Iowa
KYFR Shenandoah, Iowa
KSOU Sioux Center, Iowa
KTFC Sioux City, Iowa
KTFG Sioux Rapids, Iowa
KJIA Spirit Lake, Iowa
KJCY St. Ansgar, Iowa
KTDV State Center, Iowa
KAIP Wapello, Iowa
KNWS Waterloo, Iowa
KNWS-FM Waterloo, Iowa
KWVI Waverly, Iowa
KPUL Winterset, Iowa
KGEM Boise, Idaho
KSPD Boise, Idaho
KTFY Buhl, Idaho
KBGN Caldwell, Idaho
KBXL Caldwell, Idaho
KTSY Caldwell, Idaho
KRTK Chubbuck, Idaho
KKRH Grangeville, Idaho
KTPZ Hazelton, Idaho
KAIO Idaho Falls, Idaho
KARJ Kuna, Idaho
KAWS Marsing, Idaho
KAWS Marsing, Idaho
KMHI Mountain Home, Idaho
KZJB Pocatello, Idaho
KYMS Rathdrum, Idaho
KLRI Rigby, Idaho
KSQS Ririe, Idaho
KAWZ Twin Falls, Idaho
KCIR Twin Falls, Idaho
KEFX Twin Falls, Idaho
KTWD Wallace, Idaho
WKIO Arcola, Illinois
WCLR Arlington Heights, Illinois
WRMS Beardstown, Illinois
WIBI Carlinville, Illinois
WBVN Carrier Mills, Illinois
WLHW Casey, Illinois
WZGL Charleston, Illinois
WMBI-AM Chicago, Illinois
WMBI-FM Chicago, Illinois
WBMF Crete, Illinois
WYCA Crete, Illinois
WAIT Crystal Lake, Illinois
WARW Dorsey, Illinois
WDQN-FM Duquoin, Illinois
WDLM-AM East Moline, Illinois
WDLM-FM East Moline, Illinois
WEFI Effingham, Illinois
WGMR Effingham, Illinois
WSPI Ellsworth, Illinois
WYRB Genoa, Illinois
WJKL Glendale Heights, Illinois
WGNU Granite City, Illinois
WBGX Harvey, Illinois
WKAY Knoxville, Illinois
WLLM Lincoln, Illinois
WAWJ Marion, Illinois
WJCZ Milford, Illinois
WGEN-FM Monee, Illinois
WAPO Mount Vernon, Illinois
WBMV Mount Vernon, Illinois
WPTH Olney, Illinois
WRTK Paxton, Illinois
WCIC Pekin, Illinois
WLWJ Petersburg, Illinois
WGCA-FM Quincy, Illinois
WJLY Ramsey, Illinois
WLKU Rock Island, Illinois
WFEN Rockford, Illinois
WQFL Rockford, Illinois
WSLE Salem, Illinois

WAUR Sandwich, Illinois
WPRC Sheffield, Illinois
WINU Shelbyville, Illinois
WSOG Spring Valley, Illinois
WLUJ Springfield, Illinois
WGNJ St. Joseph, Illinois
WSRI Sugar Grove, Illinois
WIHM Taylorville, Illinois
WVNL Vandalia, Illinois
WETN Wheaton, Illinois
WTZY Wonder Lake, Illinois
WGNR-AM Anderson, Indiana
WGNR-FM Anderson, Indiana
WQME Anderson, Indiana
WFCV-FM Bluffton, Indiana
WHPZ Bremen, Indiana
WNHT Churubusco, Indiana
WJCY Cicero, Indiana
WFOF Covington, Indiana
WOJC Crothersville, Indiana
WRTW Crown Point, Indiana
WCMR Elkhart, Indiana
WFRN-FM Elkhart, Indiana
WFCV Fort Wayne, Indiana
WLAB Fort Wayne, Indiana
WLYV Fort Wayne, Indiana
WQRA Greencastle, Indiana
WAUZ Greensburg, Indiana
WQKO Howe, Indiana
WJCI Huntington, Indiana
WBDG Indianapolis, Indiana
WBRI Indianapolis, Indiana
WAWK Kendallville, Indiana
WIWC Kokomo, Indiana
WAZY-FM Lafayette, Indiana
WQSG Lafayette, Indiana
WSHY Lafayette, Indiana
WBAT Marion, Indiana
WMBL Mitchell, Indiana
WJCO Montpelier, Indiana
WCJL Morgantown, Indiana
WJCF-FM Morristown, Indiana
WKMV Muncie, Indiana
WVNI Nashville, Indiana
WARA New Washington, Indiana
WHZN New Whiteland, Indiana
WGAB Newburgh, Indiana
WRDZ-FM Plainfield, Indiana
WIKV Plymouth, Indiana
WAXI Rockville, Indiana
WVWG Seelyville, Indiana
WJLR Seymour, Indiana
WHLY South Bend, Indiana
WHME South Bend, Indiana
WHOJ Terre Haute, Indiana
WJYW Union City, Indiana
WTUR Upland, Indiana
WATI Vincennes, Indiana
WENS Wadesville, Indiana
WYBV Wakarusa, Indiana
WFRR Walton, Indiana
WTMK Wanatah, Indiana
WQKV Warsaw, Indiana
WHPL West Lafayette, Indiana
WKHL West Lafayette, Indiana
WFRI Winamac, Indiana
KAXR Arkansas City, Kansas
KEOJ Caney, Kansas
KHYM Copeland, Kansas
KJIL Copeland, Kansas
KAIG Dodge City, Kansas
KTLI El Dorado, Kansas
KBMP Enterprise, Kansas
KCNW Fairway, Kansas
KVCY Fort Scott, Kansas
KGCR Goodland, Kansas
KBDA Great Bend, Kansas
KWBI Great Bend, Kansas
KHYS Hays, Kansas
KARF Independence, Kansas
KBQC Independence, Kansas
KCVW Kingman, Kansas
KKLO Leavenworth, Kansas
KZQD Liberal, Kansas
KGLV Manhattan, Kansas
KMLL Marysville, Kansas
KSNS Medicine Lodge, Kansas
KJRG Newton, Kansas
KSNB Norton, Kansas
KRLE Oberlin, Kansas
KCCV-FM Olathe, Kansas

KRBW Ottawa, Kansas
KTJO-FM Ottawa, Kansas
KCCV Overland Park, Kansas
KPIO-FM Pleasanton, Kansas
KKCV Rozel, Kansas
KCVS Salina, Kansas
KJLJ Scott City, Kansas
KCVT Silver Lake, Kansas
KHCA Wamego, Kansas
KCFN Wichita, Kansas
KYFW Wichita, Kansas
KYWA Wichita, Kansas
KBDD Winfield, Kansas
WAYD Auburn, Kentucky
WTRT Benton, Kentucky
WCVK Bowling Green, Kentucky
WAPD Campbellsville, Kentucky
WONS Cannonsburg, Kentucky
WOKE Garrison, Kentucky
WKCB Hindman, Kentucky
WJMM-FM Keene, Kentucky
WFIA Louisville, Kentucky
WSOF-FM Madisonville, Kentucky
WWLT Manchester, Kentucky
WBFI McDaniels, Kentucky
WBTF Midway, Kentucky
WBMK Morehead, Kentucky
WEUC Morganfield, Kentucky
WKVN Morganfield, Kentucky
WAXG Mount Sterling, Kentucky
WNOP Newport, Kentucky
WJIE-FM Okolona, Kentucky
WJVK Owensboro, Kentucky
WGCF Paducah, Kentucky
WJSO Pikeville, Kentucky
WWJD Pippa Passes, Kentucky
WAVJ Princeton, Kentucky
WKVY Somerset, Kentucky
WXKY-FM Stanford, Kentucky
WMTC-FM Vancleve, Kentucky
WBCE Wickliffe, Kentucky
WVRB Wilmore, Kentucky
KAPM Alexandria, Louisiana
KJMJ Alexandria, Louisiana
KLXA Alexandria, Louisiana
KHCL Arcadia, Louisiana
KWDF Ball, Louisiana
KWDF Ball, Louisiana
KAXV Bastrop, Louisiana
WJFM Baton Rouge, Louisiana
WPYR Baton Rouge, Louisiana
KBCL Bossier City, Louisiana
WBKL Clinton, Louisiana
KBAN DeRidder, Louisiana
KVDP Dry Prong, Louisiana
KBEF Gibsland, Louisiana
KKNO Gretna, Louisiana
KIMW Heflin, Louisiana
KYXA Homer, Louisiana
KITA Iota, Louisiana
KTOC-FM Jonesboro, Louisiana
WYLK Lacombe, Louisiana
KIKL Lafayette, Louisiana
KOJO Lake Charles, Louisiana
KYLC Lake Charles, Louisiana
KHMD Mansfield, Louisiana
KMSL Mansfield, Louisiana
KAVK Many, Louisiana
KBMQ Monroe, Louisiana
KYFL Monroe, Louisiana
KBIO Natchitoches, Louisiana
KNIR New Iberia, Louisiana
WBSN-FM New Orleans, Louisiana
WLNO New Orleans, Louisiana
WVOG New Orleans, Louisiana
WNKV Norco, Louisiana
KUMX North Fort Polk, Louisiana
KPAQ Plaquemine, Louisiana
KHLL Richwood, Louisiana
KIOU Shreveport, Louisiana
KSYB Shreveport, Louisiana
KSJY St. Martinville, Louisiana
KRLR Sulphur, Louisiana
WPMW Bayview, Massachusetts
WROL Boston, Massachusetts
WWDJ Boston, Massachusetts
WYQQ Charlton, Massachusetts
WFGL Fitchburg, Massachusetts
WJWT Gardner, Massachusetts
WVNE Leicester, Massachusetts
WCMX Leominster, Massachusetts
WTKL North Dartmouth, Massachusetts
WNGB Petersham, Massachusetts
WSMA Scituate, Massachusetts
WRYP Wellfleet, Massachusetts
WKMY Winchendon, Massachusetts
WFSI Baltimore, Maryland
WKDI Denton, Maryland
WLIC Frostburg, Maryland
WAIJ Grantsville, Maryland
WWGB Indian Head, Maryland
WHGT Maugansville, Maryland
WDIH Salisbury, Maryland
WGWS St. Mary's City, Maryland
WWPN Westernport, Maryland
WHCF Bangor, Maine
WRPB Benedicta, Maine
WFST Caribou, Maine
WKVZ Dexter, Maine
WMSJ Freeport, Maine
WARX Lewiston, Maine
WRBC Lewiston, Maine
WHMX Lincoln, Maine
WMDR-FM Oakland, Maine
WJCX Pittsfield, Maine
WHPF Pittston Farm, Maine
WBAE Portland, Maine
WKVV Searsport, Maine
WRKJ Westbrook, Maine
WWWA Winslow, Maine
WUFN Albion, Michigan
WAAM Ann Arbor, Michigan
WVCN Baraga, Michigan
WBFN Battle Creek, Michigan
WLKB Bay City, Michigan
WMAX Bay City, Michigan
WTLI Bear Creek Township, Michigan
WSLI Belding, Michigan
WCXB Benton Harbor, Michigan
WCVM Bronson, Michigan
WTAC Burton, Michigan
WLJW Cadillac, Michigan
WTCK Charlevoix, Michigan
WCFX Clare, Michigan
WYBA Coldwater, Michigan
WPRJ Coleman, Michigan
WMUZ Detroit, Michigan
WHPD Dowagiac, Michigan
WJOM Eagle, Michigan
WAKL Flint, Michigan
WSNL Flint, Michigan
WRCL Frankenmuth, Michigan
WTRK Freeland, Michigan
WBLW Gaylord, Michigan
WPHN Gaylord, Michigan
WHYT Goodland Township, Michigan
WCSG Grand Rapids, Michigan
WCZE Harbor Beach, Michigan
WSFP Harrisville, Michigan
WVCM Iron Mountain, Michigan
WCXK Kalamazoo, Michigan
WAIR Lake City, Michigan
WLGH Leroy Township, Michigan
WUNN Mason, Michigan
WKPK Michigamme, Michigan
WUGN Midland, Michigan
WRDT Monroe, Michigan
WMCQ Muskegon, Michigan
WHEY North Muskegon, Michigan
WPCJ Pittsford, Michigan
WJOH Raco, Michigan
WMJC Richland, Michigan
WSIS Riverside, Michigan
WEXL Royal Oak, Michigan
WJOJ Rust Township, Michigan
WTHN Sault Ste. Marie, Michigan
WOFR Schoolcraft, Michigan
WJKN-FM Spring Arbor, Michigan
WCFG Springfield, Michigan
WIDG St. Ignace, Michigan
WUFL Sterling Heights, Michigan
WHST Tawas City, Michigan
WLJN-FM Traverse City, Michigan
WEJC White Star, Michigan
WDEO Ypsilanti, Michigan
WGNB Zeeland, Michigan
WJQK Zeeland, Michigan
KBHG Alexandria, Minnesota
WYNJ Blackduck, Minnesota
WQRN Cook, Minnesota
KDNW Duluth, Minnesota
WJRF Duluth, Minnesota
KRLP Fairmont, Minnesota
KBGY Faribault, Minnesota
WLKX-FM Forest Lake, Minnesota
KRFG Glenwood, Minnesota
KADU Hibbing, Minnesota
KBHW International Falls, Minnesota
KXBR International Falls, Minnesota
WCTS Maplewood, Minnesota
KTIS Minneapolis, Minnesota
WLOL Minneapolis, Minnesota
KVXR Moorhead, Minnesota
KMKL North Branch, Minnesota
KCGN-FM Ortonville, Minnesota
KBHL Osakis, Minnesota
KKMS Richfield, Minnesota
KFSI Rochester, Minnesota
KYES Rockville, Minnesota
KKJM St. Joseph, Minnesota
KKLW Willmar, Minnesota
KJWR Windom, Minnesota
KUSQ Worthington, Minnesota
KYLF Adrian, Missouri
KHCR Bismarck, Missouri
KAIA Bloomfield, Missouri
KCWJ Blue Springs, Missouri
KPVR Bowling Green, Missouri
KCVY Cabool, Missouri
KCVO-FM Camdenton, Missouri
KLWL Chillicothe, Missouri
KSIV Clayton, Missouri
KLRQ Clinton, Missouri
KJCV-FM Country Club, Missouri
KCVZ Dixon, Missouri
KFCV Dixon, Missouri
KEXS Excelsior Springs, Missouri
KTBJ Festus, Missouri
KMCV High Point, Missouri
KBCV Hollister, Missouri
KOBC Joplin, Missouri
KJNW Kansas City, Missouri
KAUF Kennett, Missouri
KLTE Kirksville, Missouri
KCVQ Knob Noster, Missouri
KTTK Lebanon, Missouri
KLRX Lee's Summit, Missouri
KLEX Lexington, Missouri
KQOH Marshfield, Missouri
KBKC Moberly, Missouri
KCGR Oran, Missouri
KCVJ Osceola, Missouri
KCVK Otterville, Missouri
KBGM Park Hills, Missouri
KHZR Potosi, Missouri
KADI-FM Republic, Missouri
KAYX Richmond, Missouri
KMOZ Rolla, Missouri
KCVX Salem, Missouri
KSCV Springfield, Missouri
KWFC Springfield, Missouri
KWND Springfield, Missouri
KGNM St. Joseph, Missouri
KSRD St. Joseph, Missouri
KSIV-FM St. Louis, Missouri
KSTL St. Louis, Missouri
KYFI St. Louis, Missouri
KCRL Sunrise Beach, Missouri
KRSS Tarkio, Missouri
KKLL Webb City, Missouri
KULH Wheeling, Missouri
WXTN Benton, Mississippi
WMSB Byhalia, Mississippi
WDFX Cleveland, Mississippi
WLVZ Collins, Mississippi
WPRG Columbia, Mississippi
WCSO Columbus, Mississippi
WRBO Como, Mississippi
WKCU Corinth, Mississippi
WSQH Decatur, Mississippi
WAUM Duck Hill, Mississippi
WMBU Forest, Mississippi
WQST Forest, Mississippi
WWUN-FM Friar's Point, Mississippi
WLRK Greenville, Mississippi
WABG Greenwood, Mississippi
WAOY Gulfport, Mississippi
WCPC Houston, Mississippi
WYTF Indianola, Mississippi
WBAD Leland, Mississippi
WQVI Madison, Mississippi
WPAS Pascagoula, Mississippi
WAFR Tupelo, Mississippi

WAJS Tupelo, Mississippi
WAQB Tupelo, Mississippi
WJXN-FM Utica, Mississippi
WLRC Walnut, Mississippi
WABO-FM Waynesboro, Mississippi
WYAZ Yazoo City, Mississippi
KJFT Arlee, Montana
KCMM Belgrade, Montana
KGFJ Belt, Montana
KBZR Billings, Montana
KLMT Billings, Montana
KLRV Billings, Montana
KLBZ Bozeman, Montana
KEDR(FM) Butte, Montana
KFRD Butte, Montana
KJLF Butte, Montana
KUDI Choteau, Montana
KMCJ Colstrip, Montana
KAFH Great Falls, Montana
KFRW Great Falls, Montana
KGFA Great Falls, Montana
KGFC Great Falls, Montana
KMZO Hamilton, Montana
KXEI Havre, Montana
KHLV Helena, Montana
KVCM Helena, Montana
KALS Kalispell, Montana
KLKM Kalispell, Montana
KSPL Kalispell, Montana
KLEU Lewistown, Montana
KYWH Lockwood, Montana
KJCG Missoula, Montana
KMZL Missoula, Montana
KBIL Park City, Montana
KQLR Whitehall, Montana
WBKU Ahoskie, North Carolina
WSKY Asheville, North Carolina
WZGO Aurora, North Carolina
WXBE Beaufort, North Carolina
WKJW Black Mountain, North Carolina
WMIT Black Mountain, North Carolina
WVBS Burgaw, North Carolina
WYFQ Charlotte, North Carolina
WCSL Cherryville, North Carolina
WHPY Clayton, North Carolina
WCLN-FM Clinton, North Carolina
WDRU Creedmore, North Carolina
WWFJ East Fayetteville, North Carolina
WVRL Elizabeth City, North Carolina
WVRA Enfield, North Carolina
WYBH Fayetteville, North Carolina
WRTP Franklinton, North Carolina
WSSG Goldsboro, North Carolina
WJSG Hamlet, North Carolina
WRYN Hickory, North Carolina
WJKA Jacksonville, North Carolina
WLGP Jacksonville, North Carolina
WTRU Kernersville, North Carolina
WGHW Lockwoods Folly Town, North Carolina
WDJS Mount Olive, North Carolina
WVRH Norlina, North Carolina
WBNK Pine Knoll Shores, North Carolina
WRAE Raeford, North Carolina
WPJL Raleigh, North Carolina
WVRP Roanoke Rapids, North Carolina
WXKL Sanford, North Carolina
WZDG Scotts Hill, North Carolina
WKVK Semora, North Carolina
WNCA Siler City, North Carolina
WMPM Smithfield, North Carolina
WAGO Snow Hill, North Carolina
WZRI Spring Lake, North Carolina
WKGV Swansboro, North Carolina
WJRM Troy, North Carolina
WJFJ Tryon, North Carolina
WDVV Wilmington, North Carolina
WWIL-FM Wilmington, North Carolina
WVOT Wilson, North Carolina
WRCM Wingate, North Carolina
WBFJ Winston-Salem, North Carolina
WBFJ-FM Winston-Salem, North Carolina
WPIP Winston-Salem, North Carolina
WVRD Zebulon, North Carolina
KBFR Bismarck, North Dakota
KBMK Bismarck, North Dakota
KNRI Bismarck, North Dakota
KDVI Devils Lake, North Dakota
KFNW-FM Fargo, North Dakota
KWTL Grand Forks, North Dakota
KKLQ Harwood, North Dakota
KJTW Jamestown, North Dakota
KLUU Jamestown, North Dakota
KNDR Mandan, North Dakota
KHRT-FM Minot, North Dakota
KNDW Williston, North Dakota
KNBE Beatrice, Nebraska
KCVN Cozad, Nebraska
KLNB Grand Island, Nebraska
KMMJ Grand Island, Nebraska
KNFA Grand Island, Nebraska
KAYA Hubbard, Nebraska
KLCV Lincoln, Nebraska
KJLT North Platte, Nebraska
KCRO Omaha, Nebraska
KGBI-FM Omaha, Nebraska
KYFG Omaha, Nebraska
KGRD Orchard, Nebraska
KHZY Overton, Nebraska
KVSS Papillion, Nebraska
KFHC Ponca, Nebraska
KMLV Ralston, Nebraska
KBRY Sargent, Nebraska
KDAI Scottsbluff, Nebraska
KLJV Scottsbluff, Nebraska
KKNL Valentine, Nebraska
KRKR Waverly, Nebraska
KFLV Wilber, Nebraska
KEIS York, Nebraska
WVNH Concord, New Hampshire
WMTP Conway, Pennsylvania
WNHI Farmington, New Hampshire
WADB(AM) Asbury Park, New Jersey
WWFP Brigantine, New Jersey
WRDR Freehold Township, New Jersey
WDNJ Hopatcong, New Jersey
WVBV Medford Lakes, New Jersey
WNSW Newark, New Jersey
WIBG Ocean City/Somers Po, New Jersey
WHWH Princeton, New Jersey
WXGN Somers Point, New Jersey
WKMB Stirling, New Jersey
WFJS Trenton, New Jersey
KFLQ Albuquerque, New Mexico
KKIM Albuquerque, New Mexico
KLYT Albuquerque, New Mexico
KSVA Albuquerque, New Mexico
KXKS Albuquerque, New Mexico
KQLV(FM) Bosque Farms, New Mexico
KQRI Bosque Farms, New Mexico
KKCJ Cannon Afb, New Mexico
KAMQ Carlsbad, New Mexico
KAQF Clovis, New Mexico
KELU Clovis, New Mexico
KNMI Farmington, New Mexico
KPCL Farmington, New Mexico
KTGW Fruitland, New Mexico
KGGA Gallup, New Mexico
KLLU Gallup, New Mexico
KOBH Hobbs, New Mexico
KMBN Las Cruces, New Mexico
KPKJ Mentmore, New Mexico
KELP-FM Mesquite, New Mexico
KVLK Milan, New Mexico
KXXQ Milan, New Mexico
KGCN Roswell, New Mexico
KQAI Roswell, New Mexico
KRLU Roswell, New Mexico
KWFL Roswell, New Mexico
KLBU Santa Fe, New Mexico
KXFR Socorro, New Mexico
KHAC Tse Bonito, New Mexico
KVLP Tucumcari, New Mexico
KNMA Tularosa, New Mexico
KNIS Carson City, Nevada
KAER Mesquite, Nevada
KAIZ Mesquite, Nevada
KEKL Mesquite, Nevada
KIHM Reno, Nevada
KLRH Sparks, Nevada
WAMC Albany, New York
WJCA Albion, New York
WCOF Arcade, New York
WNGN Argyle, New York
WCOU Attica, New York
WABH Bath, New York
WAAL Binghamton, New York
WXBA Brentwood, New York
WASB Brockport, New York
WKDL-FM Brockport, New York
WDCX-FM Buffalo, New York
WFBF Buffalo, New York
WCIY Canandaigua, New York
WRSB Canandaigua, New York
WLYK Cape Vincent, New York
WMHI Cape Vincent, New York
WDCD-FM Clifton Park, New York
WCOV-FM Clyde, New York
WMHU Cold Brook, New York
WKVJ Dannemora, New York
WCIH Elmira, New York
WCID Friendship, New York
WGKR Grand Gorge, New York
WHAZ-FM Hoosick Falls, New York
WHVP Hudson, New York
WCOT Jamestown, New York
WFGB Kingston, New York
WGWR Liberty, New York
WMHQ Malone, New York
WLJP Monroe, New York
WFME Mount Kisco, New York
WRVP Mount Kisco, New York
WBAI New York, New York
WBBR New York, New York
WMCA New York, New York
WWRV New York, New York
WZXV Palmyra, New York
WDBY Patterson, New York
WPGL Pattersonville, New York
WRPJ Port Jervis, New York
WDCX Rochester, New York
WHIC Rochester, New York
WKYJ Rouses Point, New York
WSSK Saratoga Springs, New York
WMYY Schoharie, New York
WYAI Scotia, New York
WSFW Seneca Falls, New York
WCOM-FM Silver Creek, New York
WFRS Smithtown, New York
WCII Spencer, New York
WMHR Syracuse, New York
WHAZ Troy, New York
WCIJ Unadilla, New York
WAJZ Voorheesville, New York
WKWV Watertown, New York
WMHN Webster, New York
WHJM Anna, Ohio
WBCY Archbold, Ohio
WVMU Ashtabula, Ohio
WJKW Athens, Ohio
WCVV Belpre, Ohio
WLKP Belpre, Ohio
WKJA Brunswick, Ohio
WYFY Cambridge, Ohio
WILB Canton, Ohio
WGGN Castalia, Ohio
WZCP Chillicothe, Ohio
WAKW Cincinnati, Ohio
WCRF Cleveland, Ohio
WFHM-FM Cleveland, Ohio
WHKW Cleveland, Ohio
WVKO Columbus, Ohio
WGOJ Conneaut, Ohio
WYKL Crestline, Ohio
WQRP Dayton, Ohio
WNLT Delhi Hills, Ohio
WBIE Delphos, Ohio
WTKC Findlay, Ohio
WCVO Gahanna, Ohio
WWGV Grove City, Ohio
WPOS-FM Holland, Ohio
WCVJ Jefferson, Ohio
WFCO Lancaster, Ohio
WFOT Lexington, Ohio
WTGN Lima, Ohio
WXMF Marion, Ohio
WYSZ Maumee, Ohio
WFCJ Miamisburg, Ohio
WVML Millersburg, Ohio
WZNP Newark, Ohio
WCCD Parma, Ohio
WHKU Proctorville, Ohio
WNWT Rossford, Ohio
WLRY Rushville, Ohio
WVMS Sandusky, Ohio
WAUI Shelby, Ohio
WOAR South Vienna, Ohio
WEKV South Webster, Ohio
WBCJ Spencerville, Ohio
WEEC Springfield, Ohio
WULM Springfield, Ohio
WBJV Steubenville, Ohio
WYDA Troy, Ohio
WHKZ Warren, Ohio

WNKL Wauseon, Ohio
WYSA Wauseon, Ohio
WTPG Whitehouse, Ohio
WKLN Wilmington, Ohio
WJIC Zanesville, Ohio
KAKO Ada, Oklahoma
KKVO Altus, Oklahoma
KQPD Ardmore, Oklahoma
KVSO Ardmore, Oklahoma
KWRI Bartlesville, Oklahoma
KKWD(FM) Bethany, Colorado
KJHL Boise City, Oklahoma
KARU Cache, Oklahoma
KJCC Carnegie, Oklahoma
KTFR Chelsea, Oklahoma
KAYC Durant, Oklahoma
KSEO Durant, Oklahoma
KOKF Edmond, Oklahoma
KXOO Elk City, Oklahoma
KKRD Enid, Oklahoma
KSYE Frederick, Oklahoma
KWKL Grandfield, Oklahoma
KBIJ Guymon, Oklahoma
KXRT Idabel, Oklahoma
KJRF Lawton, Oklahoma
KVRS Lawton, Oklahoma
KEMX Locust Grove, Oklahoma
KTLV Midwest City, Oklahoma
KQCV Oklahoma City, Oklahoma
KYLV Oklahoma City, Oklahoma
KPGM Pawhuska, Oklahoma
KZTH Piedmont, Oklahoma
KKRI Pocola, Oklahoma
KJTH Ponca City, Oklahoma
KLVV Ponca City, Oklahoma
WBBZ Ponca City, Oklahoma
KARG Poteau, Oklahoma
KXOJ-FM Sapulpa, Oklahoma
KXTH Seminole, Oklahoma
KQCV-FM Shawnee, Oklahoma
KTKL Stigler, Oklahoma
KLRB Stuart, Oklahoma
KCXR Taft, Oklahoma
KAYM Weatherford, Oklahoma
KJOV Woodward, Oklahoma
KHPE Albany, Oregon
KWIL Albany, Oregon
KLOY Astoria, Oregon
KHSS Athena, Oregon
KANC Baker, Oregon
KANL Baker, Oregon
KDJC Baker, Oregon
KNLR Bend, Oregon
KVLB Bend, Oregon
KMWR Brookings, Oregon
KJCH Coos Bay, Oregon
KYTT-FM Coos Bay, Oregon
KQDL Hines, Oregon
KGNR John Day, Oregon
KGCL Jordan Valley, Oregon
KPIJ Junction City, Oregon
KKLJ Klamath Falls, Oregon
KKLP La Pine, Oregon
KGRI Lebanon, Oregon
KYOR Newport, Oregon
KTEE North Bend, Oregon
KEFS North Powder, Oregon
KARO Nyssa, Oregon
KAPL Phoenix, Oregon
KPFR Pine Grove, Oregon
KKPZ Portland, Oregon
KPDQ Portland, Oregon
KPDQ-FM Portland, Oregon
KNLX Prineville, Oregon
KKJA Redmond, Oregon
KLON Rockaway Beach, Oregon
KAJC Salem, Oregon
KPJC Salem, Oregon
KWBX Salem, Oregon
KZRI Sandy, Oregon
KFIS Scappoose, Oregon
KJKL Selma, Oregon
KVRA Sisters, Oregon
KQFE Springfield, Oregon
KORE Springfield-Eugene, Oregon
KLVU Sweet Home, Oregon
KAIK Tillamook, Oregon
KLWJ(AM) Umatilla, Oregon
KXPC Welches, Oregon
KLOV Winchester, Oregon
KGRV Winston, Oregon
WJCS Allentown, Pennsylvania
WTWT Bradford, Pennsylvania
WCGF Cambridge Springs, Pennsylvania
WPWA Chester, Pennsylvania
WVCH Chester, Pennsylvania
WCOJ Coatesville, Pennsylvania
WCIG Dallas, Pennsylvania
WCOH-FM Du Bois, Pennsylvania
WEFR Erie, Pennsylvania
WCOP Farmington Township, Pennsylvania
WCOG-FM Galeton, Pennsylvania
WVMM Grantham, Pennsylvania
WLVX(FM) Greenville, Pennsylvania
WKBO Harrisburg, Pennsylvania
WHHN Hollidaysburg, Pennsylvania
WFRJ Johnstown, Pennsylvania
WDAC Lancaster, Pennsylvania
WCIS Laporte, Pennsylvania
WPAL Laporte, Pennsylvania
WYBQ Leesport, Pennsylvania
WBCB Levittown, Pennsylvania
WGRC Lewisburg, Pennsylvania
WJRC Lewistown, Pennsylvania
WLOG Markleysburg, Pennsylvania
WRIJ Masontown, Pennsylvania
WYFU Masontown, Pennsylvania
WVME Meadville, Pennsylvania
WQJU Mifflintown, Pennsylvania
WRYV Milroy, Pennsylvania
WPGR Monroeville, Pennsylvania
WPAI Nanty Glo, Pennsylvania
WBGM New Berlin, Pennsylvania
WVMN New Castle, Pennsylvania
WPCL Northern Cambria, Pennsylvania
WPIT Pittsburgh, Pennsylvania
WWNL Pittsburgh, Pennsylvania
WITK Pittston, Pennsylvania
WLKJ Portage, Pennsylvania
WCIM Shenandoah, Pennsylvania
WHYF(AM) Shiremanstown, Pennsylvania
WBHV-FM State College, Pennsylvania
WRXV State College, Pennsylvania
WTLR State College, Pennsylvania
WLKA Tafton, Pennsylvania
WCIT-FM Trout Run, Pennsylvania
WCIN-FM Tunkhannock, Pennsylvania
WCTL Union City, Pennsylvania
WCGM Wattsburg, Pennsylvania
WLIH Whitneyville, Pennsylvania
WYYC York, Pennsylvania
WYVL(FM) Youngsville, Pennsylvania
WABA Aguadilla, Puerto Rico
WNIK-FM Arecibo, Puerto Rico
WQML Ceiba, Puerto Rico
WNVM Cidra, Puerto Rico
WMEG Guayama, Puerto Rico
WRRH Hormigueros, Puerto Rico
WNRT Manati, Puerto Rico
WAEL-FM Maricao, Puerto Rico
WZNA Moca, Puerto Rico
WJDZ Pastillo, Puerto Rico
WNNV San German, Puerto Rico
WERR Vega Alta, Puerto Rico
WSTL Providence, Rhode Island
WKIV Westerly, Rhode Island
WZMJ Batesburg, South Carolina
WEPC Belton, South Carolina
WAFJ Belvedere, South Carolina
WYFV Cayce, South Carolina
WALC Charleston, South Carolina
WMHK Columbia, South Carolina
WDAR-FM Darlington, South Carolina
WDLL Dillon, South Carolina
WELP Easley, South Carolina
WLPG Florence, South Carolina
WKZQ-FM Forestbrook, South Carolina
WYFG Gaffney, South Carolina
WLMC Georgetown, South Carolina
WLFJ Greenville, South Carolina
WMBJ Murrells Inlet, South Carolina
DWKEL Myrtle Beach, South Carolina
WYFH North Charleston, South Carolina
WTBI Pickens, South Carolina
WAYA-FM Ridgeville, South Carolina
WQIZ St. George, South Carolina
WAZS Summerville, South Carolina
WSSC Sumter, South Carolina
WULR York, South Carolina
KEEA Aberdeen, South Dakota
KKAA Aberdeen, South Dakota
KLRJ Aberdeen, South Dakota
KVCF Freeman, South Dakota
KWRC Hermosa, South Dakota
KVFL Pierre, South Dakota
KASD Rapid City, South Dakota
KQFR Rapid City, South Dakota
KTPT Rapid City, South Dakota
KQKD Redfield, South Dakota
KNWC-FM Sioux Falls, South Dakota
KSFS Sioux Falls, South Dakota
WWGM Alamo, Tennessee
WATX Algood, Tennessee
WTKB-FM Atwood, Tennessee
WKVF Bartlett, Tennessee
WLVU Belle Meade, Tennessee
WHPY-FM Bellevue, Tennessee
WFHG-FM Bluff City, Tennessee
WHCB Bristol, Tennessee
WIGN Bristol, Tennessee
WJOC Chattanooga, Tennessee
WLMR Chattanooga, Tennessee
WMBW Chattanooga, Tennessee
WAYQ Clarksville, Tennessee
WYFC Clinton, Tennessee
WCRV Collierville, Tennessee
WMKW Crossville, Tennessee
WNRZ Dickson, Tennessee
WCRT Donelson, Tennessee
WZKV Dyersburg, Tennessee
WUMC Elizabethton, Tennessee
WLLJ Etowah, Tennessee
WIJV Harriman, Tennessee
WAUO Hohenwald, Tennessee
WAMP Jackson, Tennessee
WIGH Jackson, Tennessee
WCQR-FM Kingsport, Tennessee
WKTS Kingston, Tennessee
WFFI Kingston Springs, Tennessee
WIFA Knoxville, Tennessee
WITA Knoxville, Tennessee
WRJZ Knoxville, Tennessee
WZXX Lawrenceburg, Tennessee
WRSN Lebanon, Tennessee
WBLC Lenoir City, Tennessee
WAXO Lewisburg, Tennessee
WGBQ Lynchburg, Tennessee
WYLV Maynardville, Tennessee
WYLV(FM) Maynardville, Tennessee
WAJJ McKenzie, Tennessee
WBBP Memphis, Tennessee
WMXK Morristown, Tennessee
WFCM-FM Murfreesboro, Tennessee
WECV-FM Nashville, Tennessee
WENO Nashville, Tennessee
WFCN Nashville, Tennessee
WAY New Johnsonville, Tennessee
WDNX Olive Hill, Tennessee
WPRH Paris, Tennessee
WPRT-HD2 Philpot, Kentucky
WJBP Red Bank, Tennessee
WAZD Savannah, Tennessee
WDTM Selmer, Tennessee
WXKV Selmer, Tennessee
WBIA Shelbyville, Tennessee
WFFH Smyrna, Tennessee
WDBL Springfield, Tennessee
WHMT(AM) Tullahoma, Tennessee
WTAI Union City, Tennessee
WBOZ Woodbury, Tennessee
KAGT Abilene, Texas
KGNZ Abilene, Texas
KAVW Amarillo, Texas
KJJP Amarillo, Texas
KTNZ Amarillo, Texas
KXLV Amarillo, Texas
KXRI Amarillo, Texas
KKWV Aransas Pass, Texas
KNRB Atlanta, Texas
KPYN Atlanta, Texas
KHIB Bastrop, Texas
KLBT Beaumont, Texas
KTXB Beaumont, Texas
KIBL Beeville, Texas
KTAA Big Sandy, Texas
KBCX Big Spring, Texas
KBQX Big Spring, Texas
KHVT Bloomington, Texas
KUBJ Brenham, Texas
KBUB Brownwood, Texas
KHBW Brownwood, Texas
KPSM Brownwood, Texas
KAGC Bryan, Texas

KLRW Byrne, Texas
KCZO Carrizo Springs, Texas
KJON Carrollton, Texas
KXCS(FM) Coahoma, Texas
KLGS College Station, Texas
KYJC Commerce, Texas
KAFR Conroe, Texas
KKLM Corpus Christi, Texas
KCKT Crockett, Texas
KTLZ Cuero, Texas
KTDA Dalhart, Texas
KCBI Dallas, Texas
KDKR Decatur, Texas
KDLI Del Rio, Texas
KIXL Del Valle, Texas
KYFB Denison, Texas
KGLF Doss, Texas
KLLR Dripping Springs, Texas
KEPI Eagle Pass, Texas
KEPX Eagle Pass, Texas
KXBJ El Campo, Texas
KELP El Paso, Texas
KKLY El Paso, Texas
KATG Elkhart, Texas
KLDS Falfurrias, Texas
KZFT Fannett, Texas
KIJN Farwell, Texas
KIJN-FM Farwell, Texas
KDFT Ferris, Texas
KJMA Floresville, Texas
KBLC Fredericksburg, Texas
KAAM Garland, Texas
KANJ Giddings, Texas
KMLR Gonzales, Texas
KTXG Greenville, Texas
KEDC Hearne, Texas
KEKO Hebbronville, Texas
KRLH Hereford, Texas
KWRD-FM Highland Village, Texas
KHCB-FM Houston, Texas
KSHJ Houston, Texas
KSBJ Humble, Texas
KHCH Huntsville, Texas
KYLR Hutto, Texas
KXXN Iowa Park, Texas
KBJS Jacksonville, Texas
KCOX Jasper, Texas
KHCJ Jefferson, Texas
KJTX Jefferson, Texas
KHKV Kerrville, Texas
KKER Kerrville, Texas
KZLO Kilgore, Texas
KPWJ Kurten, Texas
KHJK La Porte, Texas
KBKN Lamesa, Texas
KLAR Laredo, Texas
KHCB League City, Texas
KXQK Leakey, Texas
KFRO Longview, Texas
KYAR Lorena, Texas
KAMY Lubbock, Texas
KKLU Lubbock, Texas
KSWP Lufkin, Texas
KKHT-FM Lumberton, Texas
KZLV Lytle, Texas
KHML Madisonville, Texas
KBMD Marble Falls, Texas
KVMV Mc Allen, Texas
KRIO McAllen, Texas
KZAR McQueeney, Texas
KMXO Merkel, Texas
KMEO Mertzon, Texas
KLPF Midland, Texas
KBRZ Missouri City, Texas
KPGA Morton, Texas
KYRQ Natalia, Texas
KLBW New Boston, Texas
KTTY New Boston, Texas
KBMM Odessa, Texas
KFLB Odessa, Texas
KLVW Odessa, Texas
KKVI Overland, Texas
KAVO Pampa, Texas
KHCP Paris, Texas
KLVL Pasadena, Texas
KPKO Pecos, Texas
KGWP Pittsburg, Texas
KBAH Plainview, Texas
KWLD Plainview, Texas
KWMF Pleasanton, Texas
KDEI Port Arthur, Texas
KHPO Port O'Connor, Texas
KLIT Ranchitos Las Lomas, Texas
KLOW Reno, Texas
KFMK Round Rock, Texas
KTER Rudolph, Texas
KCRN-FM San Angelo, Texas
KLTP San Angelo, Texas
KNAR San Angelo, Texas
KSLR San Antonio, Texas
KYFS San Antonio, Texas
KUBR San Juan, Texas
KDAE Sinton, Texas
KJAK Slaton, Texas
KFLB-FM Stanton, Texas
KBDE Temple, Texas
KVLT Temple, Texas
KTNO University Park, Texas
KVHR Van Horn, Texas
KAYK Victoria, Texas
KBBW Waco, Texas
KHTA Wake Village, Texas
KZEE Weatherford, Texas
KRGE Weslaco, Texas
KFRI West Odessa, Texas
KANI Wharton, Texas
KMOC Wichita Falls, Texas
KZKL Wichita Falls, Texas
KKLV Kaysville, Utah
KNKL North Ogden, Utah
KYFO-FM Ogden, Utah
KKLV Orem, Utah
KANN Roy, Utah
KUFR Salt Lake City, Utah
KUTR Taylorsville, Utah
KMRI West Valley City, Utah
WYFJ Ashland, Virginia
WAXM Big Stone Gap, Virginia
WLES Bon Air, Virginia
WPRZ-FM Brandy Station, Virginia
WBOP Buffalo Gap, Virginia
WAUQ Charles City, Virginia
WJYK Chase City, Virginia
WVRI Clifton Forge, Virginia
WDZY Colonial Heights, Virginia
WDZY Colonial Heights, Virginia
WKYV Colonial Heights, Virginia
WARN Culpeper, Virginia
WPER Culpeper, Virginia
WPIN-FM Dublin, Virginia
WJYA Emporia, Virginia
WKNV Fairlawn, Virginia
WJYJ Fredericksburg, Virginia
WOKG Galax, Virginia
WQLU Lynchburg, Virginia
WRVL Lynchburg, Virginia
WPIM Martinsville, Virginia
WRIH Richmond, Virginia
WPAR Salem, Virginia
WTZE Tazewell, Virginia
WVAB Virginia Beach, Virginia
WPVA Waynesboro, Virginia
WEVI Frederiksted, Virgin Islands
WCMD-FM Barre, Vermont
WCMK Putney, Vermont
WMNV Rupert, Vermont
WFTF Rutland, Vermont
WCKJ St. Johnsbury, Vermont
WNGF Swanton, Vermont
WGLV Woodstock, Vermont
KARI Blaine, Washington
KGNW Burien-Seattle, Washington
KGTS College Place, Washington
KKRS Davenport, Washington
KLUW East Wenatchee, Washington
KCIS Edmonds, Washington
KCMS Edmonds, Washington
KBLD Kennewick, Washington
KARR Kirkland, Washington
KJVH Longview, Washington
KWPZ Lynden, Washington
KTSL Medical Lake, Washington
KMLW Moses Lake, Washington
KSBC Nile, Washington
KOMO-FM Oakville, Washington
KGDN Pasco, Washington
KRLF Pullman, Washington
KWWW-FM Quincy, Washington
KWFJ Roy, Washington
KWDR Royal City, Washington
KLFE Seattle, Washington
KNTS Seattle, Washington
KYKV Selah, Washington
KEEH Spokane, Washington
KMBI Spokane, Washington
KTTO Spokane, Washington
KZFS Spokane, Washington
KAYB Sunnyside, Washington
KYFQ Tacoma, Washington
KRKL Walla Walla, Washington
KPLW Wenatchee, Washington
KYAK Yakima, Washington
KYPL Yakima, Washington
WYNW Birnamwood, Wisconsin
WHEM Eau Claire, Wisconsin
WDKV Fond Du Lac, Wisconsin
WVFL Fond Du Lac, Wisconsin
WMVM Goodman, Wisconsin
WWIB Hallie, Wisconsin
WKBH Holmen, Wisconsin
WJOK Kaukauna, Wisconsin
WSTM Kiel, Wisconsin
WJTY Lancaster, Wisconsin
WHJL Merrill, Wisconsin
WJYI Milwaukee, Wisconsin
WMWK Milwaukee, Wisconsin
WVCY-FM Milwaukee, Wisconsin
WVCS Owen, Wisconsin
WHFA Poynette, Wisconsin
WNLI Sturgeon Bay, Wisconsin
WPFF Sturgeon Bay, Wisconsin
WVCX Tomah, Wisconsin
WEGZ Washburn, Wisconsin
WPJY Blennerhassett, West Virginia
WPIB Bluefield, West Virginia
WCKU Clarksburg, West Virginia
WKJL Clarksburg, West Virginia
WBHZ Elkins, West Virginia
WDKL Grafton, West Virginia
WKVW Marmet, West Virginia
WZZW Milton, West Virginia
WPWV Princeton, West Virginia
WRLB Rainelle, West Virginia
WRRL Rainelle, West Virginia
WLKV Ripley, West Virginia
WTCF Wardensville, West Virginia
KCSP Casper, Wyoming
KLWC Casper, Wyoming
KAIX Cheyenne, Wyoming
KLWV Chugwater, Wyoming
KPMD Evanston, Wyoming
KUYO Evansville, Wyoming
KRKM Fort Washakie, Wyoming
KAXG Gillette, Wyoming
KGLL Gillette, Wyoming
KLOF Gillette, Wyoming
KLWD Gillette, Wyoming
KTUG Hudson, Wyoming
KJCV Jackson, Wyoming
KMLT Jackson, Wyoming
KMWY Jackson, Wyoming
KAIW Laramie, Wyoming
KTDX Laramie, Wyoming
KOHR Sheridan, Wyoming
KVLZ Sheridan, Wyoming

Classic Rock

KBFX Anchorage, Alaska
KLAM Cordova, Alaska
KXLR Fairbanks, Alaska
KSUP Juneau, Alaska
KSLD Soldotna, Alaska
KUHB-FM St. Paul, Alaska
WJSR Birmingham, Alabama
WERH-FM Hamilton, Alabama
WTAK-FM Hartselle, Alabama
WRKH Mobile, Alabama
WVNA-FM Muscle Shoals, Alabama
WPPG Repton, Alabama
KDEL-FM Arkadelphia, Arkansas
KCON Atkins, Arkansas
KKEG Bentonville, Arkansas
KCCB Corning, Arkansas
KAGL El Dorado, Arkansas
KXJK Forrest City, Arkansas
KCWD Harrison, Arkansas
KLXQ Mountain Pine, Arkansas
KWLT North Crossett, Arkansas
KYGL Texarkana, Arkansas
KWRF Warren, Arkansas
KTRN White Hall, Arkansas
KCUZ Clifton, Arizona

RADIO - U.S.

KMGN Flagstaff, Arizona
KCDX Florence, Arizona
KZUL-FM Lake Havasu City, Arizona
KPKR Parker, Arizona
KSLX-FM Scottsdale, Arizona
KLPX Tucson, Arizona
KLPX Tucsun, Nevada
KWMX Williams, Arizona
KALT-FM Alturas, California
KKBZ Auberry, California
KHRQ Baker, California
KVMX Bakersfield, California
KRHV Big Pine, California
KWTY Cartago, California
KTHU Corning, California
KDFO Delano, California
KZRO Dunsmuir, California
KJFX Fresno, California
KJWL Fresno, California
KTOR Gerber, California
KHIP Gonzales, California
KRVQ-FM Lake Isabella, California
KHDR Lenwood, California
KSWD Los Angeles, California
KIXA Lucerne Valley, California
KDJK Mariposa, California
KHKK Modesto, California
KVRV Monte Rio, California
KLUK Needles, California
KIOO Porterville, California
KMRJ Rancho Mirage, California
KRVH Rio Vista, California
KQAV Rosamond, California
KSEG Sacramento, California
KGB-FM San Diego, California
KUFX San Jose, California
KZOZ San Luis Obispo, California
KXFM Santa Maria, California
KHRD Weaverville, California
KKFM Colorado Springs, Colorado
KQMT Denver, Colorado
KRFX Denver, Colorado
KPAW Fort Collins, Colorado
KRVG Glenwood Springs, Colorado
KQZR Hayden, Colorado
KLMR-FM Lamar, Colorado
KTUN New Castle, Colorado
KDZA-FM Pueblo, Colorado
KSBV Salida, Colorado
KRKA Severance, Colorado
KCRT-FM Trinidad, Colorado
KMAX-FM Wellington, Colorado
WRKI Brookfield, Connecticut
WDRC-FM Hartford, Connecticut
WFOX Norwalk, Connecticut
WMOS Stonington, Connecticut
WBIG-FM Washington, District of Columbia
WJKI Bethany Beach, Delaware
KSNM-FM Georgetown, Delaware
WGBG Seaford, Delaware
WCJX Five Points, Florida
WBGG-FM Fort Lauderdale, Florida
WXCV Homosassa Springs, Florida
WKYZ Key Colony Beach, Florida
WAIL Key West, Florida
WARO Naples, Florida
WMMO Orlando, Florida
WHOG-FM Ormond-By-The-Sea, Florida
WFKZ Plantation Key, Florida
WNDD Silver Springs, Florida
WRBA Springfield, Florida
WGLF Tallahassee, Florida
WKGR Wellington, Florida
WAYF West Palm Beach, Florida
WXOF Yankeetown, Florida
WDMG-FM Ambrose, Georgia
WNNX College Park, Georgia
WVRK Columbus, Georgia
WZTR Dahlonega, Georgia
WQBZ Fort Valley, Georgia
WTHG Hinesville, Georgia
WSIZ-FM Jacksonville, Georgia
WYYZ Jasper, Georgia
WPEZ Jeffersonville, Georgia
WBAW-FM Pembroke, Georgia
WRBF Plainville, Georgia
WZBX Rocky Ford, Georgia
WIXV Savannah, Georgia
WKEU-FM The Rock, Georgia
WTIF Tifton, Georgia
WWRQ-FM Valdosta, Georgia
WLOV Washington, Georgia
KIPA Hilo, Hawaii
KPOI-FM Honolulu, Hawaii
KRKH Wailea-Makena, Hawaii
KLKK Clear Lake, Iowa
KCQQ Davenport, Iowa
KGGO Des Moines, Iowa
KXGE Dubuque, Iowa
KKSI Eddyville, Iowa
KGRR Epworth, Iowa
KKFD-FM Fairfield, Iowa
KZLB Fort Dodge, Iowa
KCRR Grundy Center, Iowa
KKRQ Iowa City, Iowa
KGRA Jefferson, Iowa
KUQQ Milford, Iowa
KSEZ Sioux City, Iowa
KJOT Boise, Idaho
KOUW(FM) Island Park, Idaho
KTPO Kootenai, Idaho
KKGL Nampa, Idaho
KRVB Nampa, Idaho
KMGI Pocatello, Idaho
KPKY Pocatello, Idaho
KQEZ(FM) Shelley, Idaho
KECH-FM Sun Valley, Idaho
KSNQ Twin Falls, Idaho
KLZX Weston, Idaho
WDLJ Breese, Illinois
WWGO Charleston, Illinois
WYMG Chatham, Illinois
WDRV Chicago, Illinois
WLS Chicago, Illinois
WRXQ Coal City, Illinois
WRHK Danville, Illinois
WYXY(FM) Danville, Illinois
KUUL East Moline, Illinois
WJKG Effingham, Kentucky
WMXM Lake Forest, Illinois
WKGL-FM Loves Park, Illinois
WJEQ Macomb, Illinois
WGKC Mahomet, Illinois
WXLP Moline, Illinois
WZZT Morrison, Illinois
WIKK Newton, Illinois
WWVR Paris, Indiana
WGLO Pekin, Illinois
WEJT Shelbyville, Illinois
WQQL Sherman, Illinois
WZNX Sullivan, Illinois
WKRV Vandalia, Illinois
WWDV Zion, Illinois
WSHP Attica, Indiana
WJAA Austin, Indiana
WCJZ Cannelton, Indiana
WHJE Carmel, Indiana
WXRD Crown Point, Indiana
WABX Evansville, Indiana
WXKE Fort Wayne, Indiana
WSSM(FM) Goshen, Indiana
WRGF Greenfield, Indiana
WMXQ Hartford City, Indiana
WFBQ Indianapolis, Indiana
WQMF Jeffersonville, Indiana
WKHY Lafayette, Indiana
WRZR Loogootee, Indiana
WERK Muncie, Indiana
WSMM New Carlisle, Indiana
WMYK Peru, Indiana
WBTO Petersburg, Indiana
WTCJ Tell City, Indiana
KNZS Arlington, Kansas
KFXJ Augusta, Kansas
KCAR-FM Baxter Springs, Kansas
KSNP Burlington, Kansas
KANS Emporia, Kansas
KOTE Eureka, Kansas
KSEK-FM Girard, Kansas
KKCI Goodland, Kansas
KVGB-FM Great Bend, Kansas
KINZ Humboldt, Kansas
KWKR Leoti, Kansas
KFIX Plainville, Kansas
WDNS Bowling Green, Kentucky
WHHT(FM) Cave City, Kentucky
WQQR Clinton, Kentucky
WPKE-FM Coal Run, Kentucky
WWEL London, Kentucky
WTBK Manchester, Kentucky
WFTM-FM Maysville, Kentucky
WKYM Monticello, Kentucky
WKEQ Somerset, Kentucky
WKQQ Winchester, Kentucky
WDGL Baton Rouge, Louisiana
WKBU New Orleans, Louisiana
KKGB Sulphur, Louisiana
WFNX Athol, Massachusetts
WZLX Boston, Massachusetts
WGAO Franklin, Massachusetts
WOCN-FM Orleans, Massachusetts
WAQY Springfield, Massachusetts
WKGO Cumberland, Maryland
WMDM Lexington Park, Maryland
WZBA Westminster, Maryland
WKIT Brewer, Maine
WQDY-FM Calais, Maine
WFNK Lewiston, Maine
WBLM Portland, Maine
WNSX Winter Harbor, Maine
WCSX Birmingham, Michigan
WCKC Cadillac, Michigan
WGFM Cheboygan, Michigan
WDTW-FM Detroit, Michigan
WBNZ Frankfort, Michigan
WGFN Glen Arbor, Michigan
WBFX Grand Rapids, Michigan
WLAV Grand Rapids, Michigan
WGLI Hancock, Michigan
WWKR Hart, Michigan
WSRJ Honor, Michigan
WBZV Hudson, Michigan
WIMK Iron Mountain, Michigan
WMMQ Lansing, Michigan
WUPK Marquette, Michigan
WMRR Muskegon Heights, Michigan
WIHC Newberry, Michigan
WRSW Niles, Michigan
WOVI Novi, Michigan
WWTH Oscoda, Michigan
WRSR Owosso, Michigan
WRUP Palmer, Michigan
WRKR Portage, Michigan
WUPF Powers, Michigan
WILZ Saginaw, Michigan
WSUE Sault Ste. Marie, Michigan
KAOD Babbitt, Minnesota
KLIZ-FM Brainerd, Minnesota
KBAJ Deer River, Minnesota
KQDS Duluth, Minnesota
KXLP Eagle Lake, Minnesota
KFMC-FM Fairmont, Minnesota
KMGK Glenwood, Minnesota
KQRS Golden Valley, Minnesota
WXXZ Grand Marais, Minnesota
KOZY Grand Rapids, Minnesota
WMFG-FM Hibbing, Minnesota
KARZ Marshall, Minnesota
KMGM Montevideo, Minnesota
KLTA-FM Moorhead, Minnesota
KPHR Ortonville, Minnesota
KRCH Rochester, Minnesota
KRWB Roseau, Minnesota
KDXL St. Louis Park, Minnesota
KLFN Sunburg, Minnesota
KLZZ Waite Park, Minnesota
KLLZ-FM Walker, Minnesota
KHME Winona, Minnesota
KHRS Winthrop, Minnesota
KGMO Cape Girardeau, Missouri
KCFX Harrisonville, Missouri
KRXL Kirksville, Missouri
KKLH Marshfield, Missouri
KZZT Moberly, Missouri
KZZK New London, Missouri
KJEZ Poplar Bluff, Missouri
KIGL Seligman, Missouri
KXUS Springfield, Missouri
KXDG Webb City, Missouri
KSPQ West Plains, Missouri
KRSI Garapan-Saipan, Guam
WXRR Hattiesburg, Mississippi
WSTZ-FM Vicksburg, Mississippi
KFLN Baker, Montana
KJJM Baker, Montana
KBZM Big Sky, Montana
KURL(FM) Billings, Montana
KMBR Butte, Montana
KTZZ Conrad, Montana
KGVO-FM Frenchtown, Montana
KZMT Helena, Montana
KBBZ Kalispell, Montana
KZMN Kalispell, Montana

KOZB Livingston, Montana
KKQX Manhattan, Montana
KMTA Miles City, Montana
WKRR Asheboro, North Carolina
WZJS Banner Elk, North Carolina
WTZQ Hendersonville, North Carolina
WRFX Kannapolis, North Carolina
WCNG Murphy, North Carolina
WZAX Nashville, North Carolina
WSFL-FM New Bern, North Carolina
WBBB Raleigh, North Carolina
WKIX-FM Raleigh, North Carolina
WNTB Topsail Beach, North Carolina
WRDU Wake Forest, North Carolina
WQNS Waynesville, North Carolina
WILT Wrightsville Beach, North Carolina
KBYZ Bismarck, North Dakota
KSSS Bismarck, North Dakota
KPFX Fargo, North Dakota
KRWK Fargo, North Dakota
KZPR Minot, North Dakota
KTZU Velva, North Dakota
KTGL Beatrice, Nebraska
KBBN-FM Broken Bow, Nebraska
KCFD Crawford, Nebraska
KFMT-FM Fremont, Nebraska
KQHK McCook, Nebraska
KNEN Norfolk, Nebraska
KBRX O'Neill, Nebraska
KKCD Omaha, Nebraska
WMLL Bedford, New Hampshire
WHDQ Claremont, New Hampshire
WZEI Meredith, New Hampshire
WDHA-FM Dover, New Jersey
WCHR-FM Manahawkin, New Jersey
WZXL Wildwood, New Jersey
KZRM Chama, New Mexico
KEJL Eunice, New Mexico
KRWN Farmington, New Mexico
KXXI Gallup, New Mexico
KMDZ Las Vegas, New Mexico
KPSA-FM Lordsburg, New Mexico
KIDX Ruidoso, New Mexico
KTUM Tatum, New Mexico
KOZZ-FM Reno, Nevada
KURK Reno, Nevada
WPYX Albany, New York
WBNR Beacon, New York
WTKW Bridgeport, New York
WGRF Buffalo, New York
WSDE Cobleskill, New York
WKGB-FM Conklin, New York
WIII Cortland, New York
WNMR Dannemora, New York
WECW Elmira, New York
WCPV Essex, New York
WAIO Honeoye Falls, New York
WLPW Lake Placid, New York
WNGZ Montour Falls, New York
WBWZ New Paltz, New York
WAXQ New York, New York
WCHN Norwich, New York
WRHO Oneonta, New York
WTKV Oswego, New York
WPDH Poughkeepsie, New York
WBZA Rochester, New York
WCMF-FM Rochester, New York
WQRS Salamanca, New York
WLLW Seneca Falls, New York
WXTL Syracuse, New York
WRGR Tupper Lake, New York
WLGZ-FM Webster, New York
WQEL Bucyrus, Ohio
WCWT-FM Centerville, Ohio
WNCX Cleveland, Ohio
WLVQ Columbus, Ohio
WDOH Delphos, Ohio
WFXN-FM Galion, Ohio
WDUB Granville, Ohio
WKET Kettering, Ohio
WEGE Lima, Ohio
WXXF Loudonville, Ohio
WYRO McArthur, Ohio
WMWX Miamitown, Ohio
WVXG Mount Gilead, Ohio
WYCL Niles, Ohio
WFXJ-FM North Kingsville, Ohio
WBUK Ottawa, Ohio
WBIK Pleasant City, Ohio
WXKR Port Clinton, Ohio
WZZZ Portsmouth, Ohio

WKTL Struthers, Ohio
WNCD Youngstown, Ohio
KFXU Chickasha, Oklahoma
KDDQ Comanche, Oklahoma
KTRX Dickson, Oklahoma
KTLS-FM Holdenville, Oklahoma
KJOK Hollis, Oklahoma
KTMC McAlester, Oklahoma
KTMC-FM McAlester, Oklahoma
KLOR-FM Ponca City, Oklahoma
KKBD Sallisaw, Oklahoma
KVRO Stillwater, Oklahoma
KJSR Tulsa, Oklahoma
KLOO-FM Albany, Oregon
KTWS Bend, Oregon
KJMX Coos Bay, Oregon
KZEL-FM Eugene, Oregon
KDEP Garibaldi, Oregon
KAGO-FM Klamath Falls, Oregon
KFEG Klamath Falls, Oregon
KUBQ La Grande, Oregon
KLCR Lakeview, Oregon
KCRF-FM Lincoln City, Oregon
KBOY-FM Medford, Oregon
KGON Portland, Oregon
KCRX-FM Seaside, Oregon
KMSW The Dalles, Oregon
WBVE Bedford, Pennsylvania
WBUS Boalsburg, Pennsylvania
WUUZ Cooperstown, Pennsylvania
WWCB(AM) Corry, Pennsylvania
WRKW Ebensburg, Pennsylvania
WQHZ Erie, Pennsylvania
WRVV Harrisburg, Pennsylvania
WKVR-FM Huntingdon, Pennsylvania
WJNG Johnsonburg, Pennsylvania
WRKT North East, Pennsylvania
WHAT Philadelphia, Pennsylvania
WDVE Pittsburgh, Pennsylvania
WPZX Pocono Pines, Pennsylvania
WPAM Pottsville, Pennsylvania
WQKK(FM) Renovo, Pennsylvania
WQFX-FM Russell, Pennsylvania
WUZZ Saegertown, Pennsylvania
WYFM Sharon, Pennsylvania
WSRU Slippery Rock, Pennsylvania
WXMT Smethport, Pennsylvania
WZXR South Williamsport, Pennsylvania
WZDB Sykesville, Pennsylvania
WMTT Tioga, Pennsylvania
WBAX Wilkes-Barre, Pennsylvania
WVJP-FM Caguas, Puerto Rico
WROQ Anderson, South Carolina
WVGB Beaufort, South Carolina
WBAJ Blythewood, South Carolina
WRFQ Mount Pleasant, South Carolina
WYAV Myrtle Beach, South Carolina
WMFX St. Andrews, South Carolina
WQUL Woodruff, South Carolina
KSDN-FM Aberdeen, South Dakota
KYBB Canton, South Dakota
KQSF Dell Rapids, South Dakota
KFXS Rapid City, South Dakota
KJRV Wessington Springs, South Dakota
WEGR Arlington, Tennessee
WOPI Bristol, Tennessee
WKOM Columbia, Tennessee
WQZQ Goodlettsville, Tennessee
WQZQ-FM Goodlettsville, Tennessee
WFHU Henderson, Tennessee
WNRX Jefferson City, Tennessee
WEKX Jellico, Tennessee
WQUT Johnson City, Tennessee
WIMZ Knoxville, Tennessee
WKHT Knoxville, Tennessee
WQLA La Follette, Tennessee
WLQK Livingston, Tennessee
WYNU Milan, Tennessee
WOWC Morrison, Tennessee
WJBE Powell, Tennessee
KRXB Beeville, Texas
KLUB Bloomington, Texas
KNFX-FM Bryan, Texas
KYYI Burkburnett, Texas
KARX Claude, Texas
KZPS Dallas, Texas
KATX Eastland, Texas
KICA-FM Farwell, Texas
KFZX Gardendale, Texas
KWKQ Graham, Texas
KPUS Gregory, Texas

KBRQ Hillsboro, Texas
KKTX-FM Kilgore, Texas
KONE Lubbock, Texas
KHXS Merkel, Texas
KTBQ Nacogdoches, Texas
KBUS Paris, Texas
KRIA Plainview, Texas
KWFR San Angelo, Texas
KISS-FM San Antonio, Texas
KZEP-FM San Antonio, Texas
KXPN-FM Scotland, Texas
KNRX Sterling City, Texas
KTKX Terrell Hills, Texas
KTAL-FM Texarkana, Texas
KYQX Weatherford, Texas
KMAD-FM Whitesboro, Texas
KAGJ Ephraim, Utah
KCUA Naples, Utah
KWCR-FM Ogden, Utah
KWSA Price, Utah
KRSP-FM Salt Lake City, Utah
KZHK St. George, Utah
WWUZ Bowling Green, Virginia
WKLR Fort Lee, Virginia
WUKZ(AM) Marion, Virginia
WZFM Narrows, Virginia
WAFX Suffolk, Virginia
WIVI Charlotte Amalie, Virgin Islands
WEXP Brandon, Vermont
WOTX Lunenburg, Vermont
KISM Bellingham, Washington
KWWX Cashmere, Washington
KVAB Clarkston, Washington
KLSY Cosmopolis, Washington
KDUX-FM Hoquiam, Washington
KZOK Seattle, Washington
KKZX Spokane, Washington
KYNR Toppenish, Washington
KPQ-FM Wenatchee, Washington
WRLO-FM Antigo, Wisconsin
WJJH Ashland, Wisconsin
WOLX-FM Baraboo, Wisconsin
WMEQ-FM Menomonie, Wisconsin
WLDB Milwaukee, Wisconsin
WRPN-FM Ripon, Wisconsin
WIBA-FM Sauk City, Wisconsin
WGMO Spooner, Wisconsin
WTMB Tomah, Wisconsin
WJJO Watertown, Wisconsin
WMHX Waunakee, Wisconsin
WKBH-FM West Salem, Wisconsin
WGLX-FM Wisconsin Rapids, Wisconsin
WFGM-FM Barrackville, West Virginia
WVWC Buckhannon, West Virginia
WKQV Cowen, West Virginia
WRLF Fairmont, West Virginia
WVKM Matewan, West Virginia
WCLG-FM Morgantown, West Virginia
WETZ New Martinsville, West Virginia
WXCR New Martinsville, West Virginia
WRZZ Parkersburg, West Virginia
WKOY-FM Princeton, West Virginia
WFBY Weston, West Virginia
KASS Casper, Wyoming
KGCC Gillette, Wyoming
KZJH Jackson, Wyoming
KDLY Lander, Wyoming
KXXL Moorcroft, Wyoming
KCGL Powell, Wyoming
KSIT Rock Springs, Wyoming
KZWY Sheridan, Wyoming
KRVK Vista West, Wyoming

Classical

WHIL-FM Mobile, Alabama
WTSU Montgomery-Troy, Alabama
KBSA El Dorado, Arkansas
KASU Jonesboro, Arkansas
KJZP Prescott, Arizona
KUAT-FM Tucson, Arizona
KGIL Johannesburg, California
KLDD McCloud, California
KESC Morro Bay, California
KPSC Palm Springs, California
KNHT Rio Dell, California
KXPR Sacramento, California
KVOV Carbondale, Colorado
KMPZ Salida, Colorado
WJUF Inverness, Florida
WKAT North Miami, Florida

RADIO - U.S.

WWIO-FM Brunswick, Georgia
WUWG Carrollton, Georgia
WNGH-FM Chatsworth, Georgia
WAZX-FM Cleveland, Georgia
WMUM-FM Cochran, Georgia
WNGU Dahlonega, Georgia
WSRV Gainesville, Georgia
WGPB Rome, Georgia
WWIO St. Marys, Georgia
WXVS Waycross, Georgia
KHOE Fairfield, Iowa
KIBX Bonners Ferry, Idaho
WNIW La Salle, Illinois
WCBU Peoria, Illinois
WNIU Rockford, Illinois
WETN Wheaton, Illinois
WBST Muncie, Indiana
WSND-FM Notre Dame, Indiana
WCKZ Orland, Indiana
WBNI-FM Roanoke, Indiana
WBAA-FM West Lafayette, Indiana
WEKF Corbin, Kentucky
KLSA Alexandria, Louisiana
KEDM Monroe, Louisiana
KDAQ Shreveport, Louisiana
WFCC-FM Chatham, Massachusetts
WCRB Lowell, Massachusetts
WBJC Baltimore, Maryland
WFWM Frostburg, Maryland
WICV East Jordan, Michigan
WIAA Interlochen, Michigan
WSCD-FM Duluth, Minnesota
WMLS Grand Marais, Minnesota
WVAL Sauk Rapids, Minnesota
KQMN Thief River Falls, Minnesota
KRCU Cape Girardeau, Missouri
KAUD Mexico, Missouri
KSMS-FM Point Lookout, Missouri
KSMU Springfield, Missouri
KSEF Ste. Genevieve, Missouri
WWSL Philadelphia, Mississippi
KAPC Butte, Montana
KUFN Hamilton, Montana
KUHM Helena, Montana
KUKL Kalispell, Montana
WZPE Bath, North Carolina
WBUX Buxton, North Carolina
WURI Manteo, North Carolina
WCPE Raleigh, North Carolina
WWCJ Cape May, New Jersey
WQXR-FM Newark, New Jersey
WWNJ Toms River Township, New Jersey
WWFM Trenton, New Jersey
KSJE Farmington, New Mexico
KHFM Santa Fe, New Mexico
KQMC Hawthorne, Nevada
KBSJ Jackpot, Nevada
KTPH Tonopah, Nevada
WEXT Amsterdam, New York
WQXW Ossining, New York
WOXR Schuyler Falls, New York
WCNY-FM Syracuse, New York
WCLV Lorain, Ohio
WOSV Mansfield, Ohio
WOSP Portsmouth, Ohio
KOCU Altus, Oklahoma
KLCU Ardmore, Oklahoma
KYCU Clinton, Oklahoma
KCCU Lawton, Oklahoma
KWTU Tulsa, Oklahoma
KSRG Ashland, Oregon
KWVZ Florence, Oregon
KQOC Gleneden Beach, Oregon
KQAC Portland, Oregon
KWRX Redmond, Oregon
KQHR The Dalles, Oregon
WRTI Coatesville, Pennsylvania
WRTI Ephrata, Pennsylvania
WQLN-FM Erie, Pennsylvania
WQEJ Johnstown, Pennsylvania
WWPJ Pen Argyl, Pennsylvania
WJAZ Summerdale, Pennsylvania
KQSD-FM Lowry, South Dakota
KZSD-FM Martin, South Dakota
KBHE-FM Rapid City, South Dakota
KTSD-FM Reliance, South Dakota
KUSD Vermillion, South Dakota
WFHU Henderson, Tennessee
WKNP Jackson, Tennessee
WUOT Knoxville, Tennessee
WKNO-FM Memphis, Tennessee
WTML Tullahoma, Tennessee
WRR Dallas, Texas
KLDN Lufkin, Texas
KMCU Wichita Falls, Texas
KUSR Logan, Utah
WMVE Chase City, Virginia
WEMC Harrisonburg, Virginia
WRIQ Lexington, Virginia
WCVE-FM Richmond, Virginia
WBQK West Point, Virginia
WBTN-FM Bennington, Vermont
WVTI Brighton, Vermont
WVNK Manchester, Vermont
WOXM Middlebury, Vermont
WCVT Stowe, Vermont
WVTQ Sunderland, Vermont
KSWS Chehalis, Washington
KNWU Forks, Washington
KNWP Port Angeles, Washington
WPNE-FM Green Bay, Wisconsin
WGTD Kenosha, Wisconsin
WERN Madison, Wisconsin
WSSW Platteville, Wisconsin
WHND Sister Bay, Wisconsin
KZUW Reliance, Wyoming
KPRQ Sheridan, Wyoming

Comedy

KBFP Bakersfield, California
WMVP Chicago, Illinois
KTHH Albany, Oregon

Contemporary Hits/Top 40

WIPK-FM Calhoun, Georgia
KGOT Anchorage, Alaska
KAKQ-FM Fairbanks, Alaska
KWLF Fairbanks, Alaska
KSUP Juneau, Alaska
KUHB-FM St. Paul, Alaska
WZYP Athens, Alabama
WZBQ Carrollton, Alabama
WKMX Enterprise, Alabama
WABD Mobile, Alabama
WHHY-FM Montgomery, Alabama
WWFA St. Florian, Alabama
WMXN-FM Stevenson, Alabama
WQNR Tallassee, Alabama
WJDB-FM Thomasville, Alabama
WQEN Trussville, Alabama
WACQ Tuskegee, Alabama
KLBQ El Dorado, Arkansas
KHTE-FM England, Arkansas
KISR Fort Smith, Arkansas
KKPT Little Rock, Arkansas
KMXF Lowell, Arkansas
KHBM Monticello, Arkansas
KHBM-FM Monticello, Arkansas
KQMJ(FM) Osceola, Arkansas
KFYX(FM) Texarkana, Arkansas
KBBQ-FM Van Buren, Arkansas
KIYS Walnut Ridge, Arkansas
KJBX Walnut Ridge, Arkansas
KLAL Wrightsville, Arkansas
KCDQ Douglas, Arizona
KZZP Mesa, Arizona
KFSZ Munds Park, Arizona
KOFH Nogales, Arizona
KXAZ Page, Arizona
KZON Phoenix, Arizona
KQST Sedona, Arizona
KRQQ Tucson, Arizona
KREV Alameda, California
KEWB Anderson, California
KWRN Apple Valley, California
KSSE Arcadia, California
KISV Bakersfield, California
KDUC Barstow, California
KXSB Big Bear Lake, California
KCAQ Camarillo, California
KCVR-FM Columbia, California
KQPT Colusa, California
KHTS-FM El Cajon, California
KSSD Fallbrook, California
KWPT Fortuna, California
KOHL Fremont, California
KRTO Guadalupe, California
KRVC Hornbrook, California
KKUU Indio, California
KRAJ Johannesburg, California
KNTI Lakeport, California
KCVR Lodi, California
KAMP Los Angeles, California
KIIS-FM Los Angeles, California
KDUQ Ludlow, California
KRCK-FM Mecca, California
KSMC Moraga, California
KNKK Needles, California
KDLE Newport Beach, California
KHOP Oakdale, California
KLLY Oildale, California
KFYV Ojai, California
KLFH Ojai, California
KSPA Ontario, California
KPAT Orcutt, California
KDIS Pasadena, California
KXTZ Pismo Beach, California
KHTN Planada, California
KGGI Riverside, California
KVVS Rosamond, California
KDND Sacramento, California
KUDL Sacramento, Kansas
KMZT-FM Salinas, California
KEGY San Diego, California
KMVQ San Francisco, California
KYLD San Francisco, California
KWWV Santa Margarita, California
KDLD Santa Monica, California
KKXX-FM Shafter, California
KRLT South Lake Tahoe, California
KWYL South Lake Tahoe, California
KLCA Tahoe City, California
KXDZ Templeton, California
KBOS-FM Tulare, California
KSSC Ventura, California
KSEQ Visalia, California
KSIZ Weed, California
KSFM Woodland, California
KDGL Yucca Valley, California
KASF Alamosa, Colorado
KLVZ Brighton, Colorado
KIDN-FM Burns, Colorado
KPTT Denver, Colorado
KPTE Durango, Colorado
KGHT El Jebel, Colorado
KIBT Fountain, Colorado
KMGJ Grand Junction, Colorado
KSME Greeley, Colorado
KIFT(FM) Kremmling, Colorado
KBLJ La Junta, Colorado
KQKS Lakewood, Colorado
KWUZ Poncha Springs, Colorado
KKMG Pueblo, Colorado
KRDZ Wray, Colorado
WNLC East Lyme, Connecticut
WQGN-FM Groton, Connecticut
WKCI-FM Hamden, Connecticut
WTIC-FM Hartford, Connecticut
WKSS Hartford-Meriden, Connecticut
WWRX Ledyard, Connecticut
WAXB Ridgefield, Connecticut
WILI-FM Willimantic, Connecticut
WIHT Washington, District of Columbia
WRQX Washington, District of Columbia
WKZP Bethany Beach, Delaware
WAKE-AM Georgetown, Delaware
WLJE-FM Georgetown, Delaware
WZBH Georgetown, Delaware
WRDX Smyrna, Delaware
WXKB Cape Coral, Florida
WLQH Chiefland, Florida
WROD Daytona Beach, Florida
WECQ Destin, Florida
WHYI-FM Fort Lauderdale, Florida
WZNS Fort Walton Beach, Florida
WRUF-FM Gainesville, Florida
WYKS Gainesville, Florida
WHTF Havana, Florida
WAPE-FM Jacksonville, Florida
WJGL Jacksonville, Florida
WMBX Jensen Beach, Florida
WLDI Juno Beach, Florida
WEOW Key West, Florida
WLLD Lakeland, Florida
WQHL Live Oak, Florida
WXHT Madison, Florida
WAOA-FM Melbourne, Florida
WFKS Melbourne, Florida
WMYM Miami, Florida
WPOW Miami, Florida
WBTT Naples Park, Florida
WKSL Neptune Beach, Florida

WMFQ Ocala, Florida
WCFB Orlando, Florida
WILN Panama City, Florida
WPFM-FM Panama City, Florida
WRGV Pensacola, Florida
WPRY Perry, Florida
WMXJ Pompano Beach, Florida
WZJZ Port Charlotte, Florida
WPOI St. Petersburg, Florida
WXGL St. Petersburg, Florida
WFLZ-FM Tampa, Florida
WXXL Tavares, Florida
V6AH(AM) Pohnpei, 66
WQVE Albany, Georgia
WQXI Atlanta, Georgia
WWPW Atlanta, Georgia
WWWQ Atlanta, Georgia
WGEX Bainbridge, Georgia
WCHK Canton, Georgia
WSB(FM) Clemson, Georgia
WCGQ Columbus, Georgia
WXMK Dock Junction, Georgia
WKKZ Dublin, Georgia
WEDB East Dublin, Georgia
WLEL Ellaville, Georgia
WMGP Hogansville, Georgia
WBTY Homerville, Georgia
WBMZ Metter, Georgia
WMGB Montezuma, Georgia
WMTM-FM Moultrie, Georgia
WSFB Quitman, Georgia
WAEV Savannah, Georgia
WSEG Savannah, Georgia
WSTR Smyrna, Georgia
WJFL Tennille, Georgia
WGMY Thomasville, Georgia
WPAX Thomasville, Georgia
WZAT Tybee Island, Georgia
WKTF Vienna, Georgia
WZCH Warner Robins, Georgia
WPUP Watkinsville, Georgia
WWUF Waycross, Georgia
KTKB Dededo, Guam
KOKU Hagatna, Guam
KMWB Captain Cook, Hawaii
KPMW Haliimaile, Hawaii
KSHK Hanamaulu, Hawaii
KNWB Hilo, Hawaii
KINE-FM Honolulu, Hawaii
KLHI-FM Kahului, Hawaii
KTOH Kalaheo, Hawaii
KPHW Kaneohe, Hawaii
KJMQ Lihue, Hawaii
KQNG-FM Lihue, Hawaii
KJMD Pukalani, Hawaii
KDDB Waipahu, Hawaii
KOSY-FM Anamosa, Iowa
KSWI Atlantic, Iowa
KZAT-FM Belle Plaine, Iowa
KKDM Des Moines, Iowa
KRTI Grinnell, Iowa
KIFG Iowa Falls, Iowa
KBEA-FM Muscatine, Iowa
KHDK New London, Iowa
KOTM-FM Ottumwa, Iowa
KRQN Vinton, Iowa
KOKZ Waterloo, Iowa
KWAR Waverly, Iowa
KSAS-FM Caldwell, Idaho
KXTA-2 Gooding, Idaho
KFTZ Idaho Falls, Idaho
KQEO Idaho Falls, Idaho
KSNA Idaho Falls, Idaho
KVTY Lewiston, Idaho
KZFN Moscow, Idaho
KWYD Parma, Idaho
KGTM Rexburg, Idaho
KOFE St. Maries, Idaho
WKIB Anna, Illinois
WERV-FM Aurora, Illinois
WSDZ Belleville, Illinois
WBNQ Bloomington, Illinois
WCIL-FM Carbondale, Illinois
WCBH Casey, Illinois
WBBM-FM Chicago, Illinois
WKSC-FM Chicago, Illinois
WRPW Colfax, Illinois
WSOY-FM Decatur, Illinois
WJKG Effingham, Kentucky
WPIA Eureka, Illinois
WISH-FM Galatia, Illinois
WDBQ-FM Galena, Illinois
WYUR Gilman, Illinois
WARH Granite City, Illinois
WXAJ Hillsboro, Illinois
WFAV Kankakee, Illinois
WQLF Lena, Illinois
WLRB Macomb, Illinois
WLWF Marseilles, Illinois
WNGY Morton, Illinois
WPBG Peoria, Illinois
WZPW Peoria, Illinois
WQQB Rantoul, Illinois
WRRG River Grove, Illinois
WZOK Rockford, Illinois
WGFB Rockton, Illinois
WEJT Shelbyville, Illinois
WTMX Skokie, Illinois
WIVQ Spring Valley, Illinois
WDBR Springfield, Illinois
WSTQ Streator, Illinois
WBWB Bloomington, Indiana
WINN Columbus, Indiana
WIMC Crawfordsville, Indiana
WXXB Delphi, Indiana
WLDE Fort Wayne, Indiana
WFCI Franklin, Indiana
WVSH Huntington, Indiana
WEDM Indianapolis, Indiana
WXXC Marion, Indiana
WERK Muncie, Indiana
WNAS New Albany, Indiana
WJFX New Haven, Indiana
WDKS Newburgh, Indiana
WUME-FM Paoli, Indiana
WTCA Plymouth, Indiana
WLQI Rensselaer, Indiana
WNRW Salem, Indiana
WDND South Bend, Indiana
WNDV-FM South Bend, Indiana
WNOW Speedway, Indiana
WCLS Spencer, Indiana
WMGI Terre Haute, Indiana
WRSW-FM Warsaw, Indiana
WAMW-FM Washington, Indiana
KQQF Coffeyville, Kansas
KTCC Colby, Kansas
KMOQ Columbus, Kansas
KZCH Derby, Kansas
KOMB Fort Scott, Kansas
KRMR Hays, Kansas
KJCK-FM Junction City, Kansas
KBGL Larned, Kansas
KXNC Ness City, Kansas
KQNK Norton, Kansas
KQNK-FM Norton, Kansas
KCHZ Ottawa, Kansas
KHMY Pratt, Kansas
KACZ Riley, Kansas
KRSL Russell, Kansas
KRSL-FM Russell, Kansas
KSAL-FM Salina, Kansas
KSKU Sterling, Kansas
KWIC Topeka, Kansas
KDGS Wichita, Kansas
WANV Annville, Kentucky
WLFX Berea, Kentucky
WBVX Carlisle, Kentucky
WWKF Fulton, Kentucky
WLKT Lexington-Fayette, Kentucky
WDJX Louisville, Kentucky
WFTM Maysville, Kentucky
WLTO Nicholasville, Kentucky
WEGI-FM Oak Grove, Kentucky
WSTO Owensboro, Kentucky
WDDJ Paducah, Kentucky
WQHY Prestonsburg, Kentucky
WKKS-FM Vanceburg, Kentucky
WZLK Virgie, Kentucky
WXKQ-FM Whitesburg, Kentucky
KQID-FM Alexandria, Louisiana
WABL Amite, Louisiana
KCIJ Atlanta, Louisiana
WFMF Baton Rouge, Louisiana
KKND Belle Chasse, Louisiana
KTSR De Quincy, Louisiana
KFNV-FM Ferriday, Louisiana
KVDU Houma, Louisiana
KHLA Jennings, Louisiana
WEMX Kentwood, Louisiana
KSMB Lafayette, Louisiana
KLIP Monroe, Louisiana
KMVX Monroe, Louisiana
WEZB New Orleans, Louisiana
KKND Port Sulphur, Louisiana
KRUF Shreveport, Louisiana
WJMN Boston, Massachusetts
WODS Boston, Massachusetts
WFHN Fairhaven, Massachusetts
WCIB Falmouth, Massachusetts
WROR-FM Framingham, Massachusetts
WXKS-FM Medford, Massachusetts
WAMD Aberdeen, Maryland
WZFT Baltimore, Maryland
WCEM-FM Cambridge, Maryland
WDLD Halfway, Maryland
WSMD-FM Mechanicsville, Maryland
WPGC Morningside, District of Columbia
WWEG Myersville, Maryland
WTTR Westminster, Maryland
WMME-FM Augusta, Maine
WWMJ Ellsworth, Maine
WALZ-FM Machias, Maine
WJBQ Portland, Maine
WFDX Atlanta, Michigan
WAHS Auburn Hills, Michigan
WKFR-FM Battle Creek, Michigan
WIOG Bay City, Michigan
WQLQ Benton Harbor, Michigan
WJZQ Cadillac, Michigan
WCZW Charlevoix, Michigan
WKHQ-FM Charlevoix, Michigan
WUPZ Chocolay Township, Michigan
WHTS Coopersville, Michigan
WDZH Detroit, Michigan
WKQI Detroit, Michigan
WWCK-FM Flint, Michigan
WLMI Grand Ledge, Michigan
WGRY Grayling, Michigan
WUPT Gwinn, Michigan
WHMI-FM Howell, Michigan
WJIM Lansing, Michigan
WFCX Leland, Michigan
WBTI Lexington, Michigan
WSNX-FM Muskegon, Michigan
WKQS-FM Negaunee, Michigan
WSDP Plymouth, Michigan
WYVN Saugatuck, Michigan
WYSS Sault Ste. Marie, Michigan
WMXG Stephenson, Michigan
WLKM-FM Three Rivers, Michigan
KBSB Bemidji, Minnesota
KBMO Benson, Minnesota
KSCR-FM Benson, Minnesota
WKLK Cloquet, Minnesota
KQHT Crookston, Minnesota
KDAL-FM Duluth, Minnesota
WTBX Hibbing, Minnesota
KEEZ-FM Mankato, Minnesota
KDOG North Mankato, Minnesota
KDKK Park Rapids, Minnesota
KWNG Red Wing, Minnesota
KDWB-FM Richfield, Minnesota
KROC-FM Rochester, Minnesota
KCAJ-FM Roseau, Minnesota
KCLD-FM St. Cloud, Minnesota
KCML St. Joseph, Minnesota
KTNX Arcadia, Missouri
KOQL Ashland, Missouri
KOZX Cabool, Missouri
KFEB Campbell, Missouri
KRRY Canton, Missouri
KGRC Hannibal, Missouri
KSYN Joplin, Missouri
KMXV Kansas City, Missouri
KZPT Kansas City, Missouri
KWJC Liberty, Missouri
KOSP Ozark, Missouri
KDAA Rolla, Missouri
KTTR AM Rolla, Missouri
KGKS Scott City, Missouri
KSPW Sparta, Missouri
KKJO-FM St. Joseph, Missouri
KNOU St. Louis, Missouri
KSLZ St. Louis, Missouri
KPXP Garapan-Saipan, Guam
WHJT Clinton, Mississippi
WYOY Gluckstadt, Mississippi
WROA Gulfport, Mississippi
WXYK Gulfport, Mississippi
WNSL Laurel, Mississippi
WAZA Liberty, Mississippi
WZNF Lumberton, Mississippi

WWKZ Okolona, Mississippi
WOXD Oxford, Mississippi
WQBB Pascagoula, Mississippi
WSKK Ripley, Mississippi
KBUD Sardis, Mississippi
WIVG Tunica, Mississippi
WBBV Vicksburg, Mississippi
WVBG Vicksburg, Mississippi
KISN Belgrade, Montana
KMXM(FM) Helena Valley NE, Montana
KWMY Joliet, Montana
KLCM Lewistown, Montana
KPLN Lockwood, Montana
KQRK Pablo, Montana
KXDR Pinesdale, Montana
KENR Superior, Montana
WBHN Bryson City, North Carolina
WNKS Charlotte, North Carolina
WMKS Clemmons, North Carolina
WDCG Durham, North Carolina
WQSM Fayetteville, North Carolina
WQNQ Fletcher, North Carolina
WFMZ Hertford, North Carolina
WHGO Hertford, North Carolina
WRHT Morehead City, North Carolina
WZPR Nags Head, North Carolina
WKBC-FM North Wilkesboro, North Carolina
WDCC Sanford, North Carolina
WHQC Shelby, North Carolina
WAZO Southport, North Carolina
WERO Washington, North Carolina
WKZL Winston-Salem, North Carolina
KKCT Bismarck, North Dakota
KXRV Cannon Ball, North Dakota
KOYY Fargo, North Dakota
KKXL-FM Grand Forks, North Dakota
KQDJ Jamestown, North Dakota
KIZZ Minot, North Dakota
KQDJ-FM Valley City, North Dakota
KCNB Chadron, Nebraska
KCNT Hastings, Nebraska
KQKY Kearney, Nebraska
KFRX Lincoln, Nebraska
KELN North Platte, Nebraska
KGOR Omaha, Nebraska
KISO Omaha, Nebraska
KOPW Plattsmouth, Nebraska
KSFT-FM South Sioux City, Nebraska
WJYY Concord, New Hampshire
WERZ Exeter, New Hampshire
WFTN Franklin, New Hampshire
WKNE Keene, New Hampshire
WMTK Littleton, New Hampshire
WLKZ Wolfeboro, New Hampshire
WHCY Blairstown, New Jersey
WAIV Cape May Court House, New Jersey
WHTG Eatontown, New Jersey
WRPR Mahwah, New Jersey
WJRZ-FM Manahawkin, New Jersey
WHTZ Newark, New Jersey
WWAC Ocean City, New Jersey
WPST Trenton, New Jersey
KYEE Alamogordo, New Mexico
KKOB Albuquerque, New Mexico
KKYC Clovis, New Mexico
KAZX Kirtland, New Mexico
KHQT Las Cruces, New Mexico
KAGM Los Alamos, New Mexico
KDLW Los Lunas, New Mexico
KLEA Lovington, New Mexico
KBCQ-FM Roswell, New Mexico
KSFX Roswell, New Mexico
KKSS Santa Fe, New Mexico
KXTC Thoreau, New Mexico
KKLZ Las Vegas, Nevada
KLUC Las Vegas, Nevada
KPLV Las Vegas, Nevada
KXPT Las Vegas, Nevada
KVEG Mesquite, Nevada
KRRN Moapa Valley, Nevada
WBXL Baldwinsville, New York
WSEN-FM Baldwinsville, New York
WKKF Ballston Spa, New York
WPTY Calverton-Roanoke, New York
WYUL Chateaugay, New York
WWYL Chenango Bridge, New York
WBDR Copenhagen, New York
WDNY Dansville, New York
WDHI Delhi, New York
WECW Elmira, New York
WLVY Elmira, New York
WBNW-FM Endicott, New York
WITR Henrietta, New York
WXUR Herkimer, New York
WKGS Irondequoit, New York
WKZA Lakewood, New York
WSKU Little Falls, New York
WYSX Morristown, New York
WBMP New York, New York
WKSE Niagara Falls, New York
WFIZ Odessa, New York
WMCR-FM Oneida, New York
WOSS Ossining, New York
WBLI Patchogue, New York
WBLI Patchogue, New York
WKOL Plattsburgh, New York
WSNN Potsdam, New York
WPKF Poughkeepsie, New York
WSPK Poughkeepsie, New York
WPXY-FM Rochester, New York
WYZY Saranac, New York
WBPM Saugerties, New York
WENU South Glen Falls, New York
WJPZ-FM Syracuse, New York
WNTQ Syracuse, New York
WWHT Syracuse, New York
WFLY Troy, New York
WKBE Warrensburg, New York
WQRW Wellsville, New York
WAKS Akron, Ohio
WZIP Akron, Ohio
WOHF Bellevue, Ohio
WBNO-FM Bryan, Ohio
WCDK Cadiz, Ohio
WKRQ Cincinnati, Ohio
WMJI Cleveland, Ohio
WNCI Columbus, Ohio
WOSU-FM Columbus, Ohio
WUFM Columbus, Ohio
WBKS Columbus Grove, Ohio
WKXA-FM Findlay, Ohio
WJEH Gallipolis, Ohio
WCHD Kettering, Ohio
WWSR Lima, Ohio
WRVB Marietta, Ohio
WYVK Middleport, Ohio
WKFS Milford, Ohio
WKDD Munroe Falls, Ohio
WNKO New Albany, Ohio
WJZE Oak Harbor, Ohio
WXZQ Piketon, Ohio
WVKF Shadyside, Ohio
WVKS Toledo, Ohio
WKOV-FM Wellston, Ohio
WZWP West Union, Ohio
WZLR Xenia, Ohio
KTBT Broken Arrow, Oklahoma
KXFC Coalgate, Oklahoma
KTIJ Elk City, Oklahoma
KTSO Glenpool, Oklahoma
KGLC Miami, Oklahoma
KHTT Muskogee, Oklahoma
K225BN Oklahoma City, Oklahoma
KJYO Oklahoma City, Oklahoma
KTGX Owasso, Oklahoma
KAYE-FM Tonkawa, Oklahoma
KZME Brightwood, Oregon
KWRZ Canyonville, Oregon
KCNA Cave Junction, Oregon
KDCQ Coos Bay, Oregon
KMHS-FM Coos Bay, Oregon
KMME(FM) Cottage Grove, Oregon
KDUK-FM Eugene, Oregon
KCFM(AM) Florence, Oregon
KEOL La Grande, Oregon
KORV-FM Lakeview, Oregon
KIFS Medford, Oregon
KLDZ Medford, Oregon
KOOS North Bend, Oregon
KBFF Portland, Oregon
KKRZ Portland, Oregon
KLKY Stanfield, Oregon
KXIX Sunriver, Oregon
KSKR-FM Sutherlin, Oregon
WAEB-FM Allentown, Pennsylvania
WHOL Allentown, Pennsylvania
WWOT Altoona, Pennsylvania
WHLM-FM Berwick, Pennsylvania
WBYN-FM Boyertown, Pennsylvania
WCUC-FM Clarion, Pennsylvania
WRTS Erie, Pennsylvania
WKRZ Freeland, Pennsylvania
WZZE Glen Mills, Pennsylvania
WHKF Harrisburg, Pennsylvania
WJHT Johnstown, Pennsylvania
WLAN-FM Lancaster, Pennsylvania
WBYN Lehighton, Pennsylvania
WNBQ Mansfield, Pennsylvania
WNTE Mansfield, Pennsylvania
WWKL Mechanicsburg, Pennsylvania
WNUZ Mercersburg, Pennsylvania
WVRZ Mount Carmel, Pennsylvania
WBHT Mountain Top, Pennsylvania
WEGH Northumberland, Pennsylvania
WBHD Olyphant, Pennsylvania
WIOQ Philadelphia, Pennsylvania
WZMP Philadelphia, Pennsylvania
WKST-FM Pittsburgh, Pennsylvania
WWSW-FM Pittsburgh, Pennsylvania
WWRR Scranton, Pennsylvania
WAKZ Sharpsville, Pennsylvania
WRSC-FM State College, Pennsylvania
WKRF Tobyhanna, Pennsylvania
WTTC-FM Towanda, Pennsylvania
WNBT-FM Wellsboro, Pennsylvania
WLMY Williamsport, Pennsylvania
WYCR York-Hanover, Pennsylvania
WCMN-FM Arecibo, Puerto Rico
WBQN Barceloneta-Manati, Puerto Rico
WODA Bayamon, Puerto Rico
WXYX Bayamon, Puerto Rico
WMIO Cabo Rojo, Puerto Rico
WNOD Mayaguez, Puerto Rico
WPRA Mayaguez, Puerto Rico
WUKQ-FM Mayaguez, Puerto Rico
WEGM San German, Puerto Rico
WKAQ-FM San Juan, Puerto Rico
WCVY Coventry, Rhode Island
WPRO Providence, Rhode Island
WWBB Providence, Rhode Island
WSEA Atlantic Beach, South Carolina
WSSX Charleston, South Carolina
WJMX-FM Cheraw, South Carolina
WHHD Clearwater, South Carolina
WNOK Columbia, South Carolina
WWNQ Forest Acres, South Carolina
WWXM Garden City, South Carolina
WYMB Manning, South Carolina
WAVO Rock Hill, South Carolina
WIBZ Wedgefield, South Carolina
KXMZ Box Elder, South Dakota
KJBI Fort Pierre, South Dakota
KQRQ Rapid City, South Dakota
KKLS-FM Sioux Falls, South Dakota
KRCS Sturgis, South Dakota
WMPS Bartlett, Tennessee
WDOD-FM Chattanooga, Tennessee
WMSR-FM Collinwood, Tennessee
WUMC Elizabethton, Tennessee
WHBQ-FM Germantown, Tennessee
WAYB-FM Graysville, Tennessee
WAEZ Greeneville, Tennessee
WRVW Lebanon, Tennessee
WUTM Martin, Tennessee
WBMC McMinnville, Tennessee
WNFN Millersville, Tennessee
WCRK Morristown, Tennessee
WPLZ Ooltewah, Tennessee
WAKQ Paris, Tennessee
WWST Sevierville, Tennessee
WTRZ Spencer, Tennessee
KQIZ-FM Amarillo, Texas
KXGL Amarillo, Texas
KXSS-FM Amarillo, Texas
KPEZ Austin, Texas
KGHY Beaumont, Texas
KQXY-FM Beaumont, Texas
KPFC Callisburg, Texas
KNDE College Station, Texas
KZFM Corpus Christi, Texas
KMMZ Crane, Texas
KHKS Denton, Texas
KBFM Edinburg, Texas
KVLY Edinburg, Texas
KPRR El Paso, Texas
KTFM Floresville, Texas
KHFI-FM Georgetown, Texas
KLIF Haltom City, Texas
KCDD Hamlin, Texas
KVJM Hearne, Texas
KPWW Hooks, Texas
KKHH Houston, Texas
KRBE Houston, Texas

KKVR Kerrville, Texas
KNEX Laredo, Texas
KZII-FM Lubbock, Texas
KKHA Markham, Texas
KZBT Midland, Texas
KNRG New Ulm, Texas
KMCM Odessa, Texas
KWLD Plainview, Texas
KMKI Plano, Texas
KWPW Robinson, Texas
KKPN Rockport, Texas
KIXY-FM San Angelo, Texas
KJXK San Antonio, Texas
KONO San Antonio, Texas
KXXM San Antonio, Texas
KQDR Savoy, Texas
KMMX Tahoka, Texas
KWTX-FM Waco, Texas
KISX Whitehouse, Texas
KNIN-FM Wichita Falls, Texas
KQXC-FM Wichita Falls, Texas
KCIN Cedar City, Utah
KSUU Cedar City, Utah
KVFX Logan, Utah
KUTC Mount Pleasant, Utah
KWCR-FM Ogden, Utah
KXRQ Roosevelt, Utah
KZHT Salt Lake City, Utah
KXDS Santa Clara, Utah
WJJX Appomattox, Virginia
WZGN Crozet, Virginia
WQPO Harrisonburg, Virginia
WHCE Highland Springs, Virginia
WZVA Marion, Virginia
WVHT Norfolk, Virginia
WKQB Pocahontas, Virginia
WRVQ Richmond, Virginia
WJJS Roanoke, Virginia
WXLK Roanoke, Virginia
WHTE-FM Ruckersville, Virginia
WVBX Spotsylvania, Virginia
WTON-FM Staunton, Virginia
WKSI-FM Stephens City, Virginia
WVBW Suffolk, Virginia
WNOH Windsor, Virginia
WAZR Woodstock, Virginia
WMNG Christiansted, Virgin Islands
WKVT-FM Brattleboro, Vermont
WDVT Rutland, Vermont
WXXX South Burlington, Vermont
WCFR Springfield, Vermont
WWOD Woodstock, Vermont
KOLW Basin City, Washington
KYNW Centralia, Washington
KXAA Cle Elum, Washington
KBDB-FM Forks, Washington
KEYG-FM Grand Coulee, Washington
KMIH Mercer Island, Washington
KHTR Pullman, Washington
KING-FM Seattle, Washington
KJR-FM Seattle, Washington
KNHC Seattle, Washington
KUBE Seattle, Washington
KRXY Shelton, Washington
KEZE Spokane, Washington
KZZU Spokane, Washington
KBKS-FM Tacoma, Washington
KFFM Yakima, Washington
WDKM Adams, Wisconsin
WEAQ Chippewa Falls, Wisconsin
WJQM De Forest, Wisconsin
WKSZ De Pere, Wisconsin
WBIZ-FM Eau Claire, Wisconsin
WIXX Green Bay, Wisconsin
WIZM-FM La Crosse, Wisconsin
WMDC Mayville, Wisconsin
WKEB Medford, Wisconsin
WKLH Milwaukee, Wisconsin
WRNW Milwaukee, Wisconsin
WLKD Minocqua, Wisconsin
WYDR Neenah-Menasha, Wisconsin
WPVL-FM Platteville, Wisconsin
WXER Plymouth, Wisconsin
WKFX Rice Lake, Wisconsin
WOWN Shawano, Wisconsin
WCLQ Wausau, Wisconsin
WIFC Wausau, Wisconsin
WAUH Wautoma, Wisconsin
WXSS Wauwatosa, Wisconsin
WHTL-FM Whitehall, Wisconsin
WCIR-FM Beckley, West Virginia
WVSR-FM Charleston, West Virginia
WXIL Elizabeth, West Virginia
WELD Fisher, West Virginia
WQWV Fisher, West Virginia
WMTD Hinton, West Virginia
WKEE-FM Huntington, West Virginia
WQZK-FM Keyser, West Virginia
WVAQ Morgantown, West Virginia
WKQR Mullens, West Virginia
WRVZ Pocatalico, West Virginia
WSTG Princeton, West Virginia
WVAR Richwood, West Virginia
WSGB Sutton, West Virginia
WPHP Wheeling, West Virginia
KTRS-FM Casper, Wyoming
KLQQ Clearmont, Wyoming
KZWB Green River, Wyoming
KHRW Ranchester, Wyoming
KLMI Rock River, Wyoming
KYCS Rock Springs, Wyoming
KZZS Story, Wyoming
KDDV-FM Wright, Wyoming

Country

KASH-FM Anchorage, Alaska
KBRJ Anchorage, Alaska
KLAM Cordova, Alaska
KDLG Dillingham, Alaska
KIAK-FM Fairbanks, Alaska
KJHA Houston, Alaska
KTKU Juneau, Alaska
KWHQ-FM Kenai, Alaska
KGTW Ketchikan, Alaska
KVOK Kodiak, Alaska
KJNP North Pole, Alaska
KSEW Seward, Alaska
KPEN-FM Soldotna, Alaska
KVAK Valdez, Alaska
KAYO Wasilla, Alaska
WQAH-FM Addison, Alabama
WQSB Albertville, Alabama
WSTH-FM Alexander City, Alabama
WAAO-FM Andalusia, Alabama
WFZX Anniston, Alabama
WRAB Arab, Alabama
WKKR Auburn, Alabama
WZRR Birmingham, Alabama
WZZK-FM Birmingham, Alabama
WKNU Brewton, Alabama
WEIS Centre, Alabama
WBIB Centreville, Alabama
WAVH Daphne, Alabama
WDRM Decatur, Alabama
WTVY-FM Dothan, Alabama
WELB Elba, Alabama
WVVL Elba, Alabama
WDJR Enterprise, Alabama
WABF Fairhope, Alabama
WLDX Fayette, Alabama
WTXT Fayette, Alabama
WKWL Florala, Alabama
WXFL Florence, Alabama
WZOB Fort Payne, Alabama
WGEA Geneva, Alabama
WKGA Goodwater, Alabama
WAOQ Goshen, Alabama
WQZX Greenville, Alabama
WBMH Grove Hill, Alabama
WTWX-FM Guntersville, Alabama
WFMH-FM Hackleburg, Alabama
WERH Hamilton, Alabama
WPIL Heflin, Alabama
WHMA-FM Hobson City, Alabama
WCKA Jacksonville, Alabama
WDXB Jasper, Alabama
WINL Linden, Alabama
WZZX Lineville, Alabama
WNPT-FM Marion, Alabama
WKSJ-FM Mobile, Alabama
WLWI-FM Montgomery, Alabama
WWFF-FM New Market, Alabama
WTLM Opelika, Alabama
WFHK Pell City, Alabama
WHAL Phenix City/Columbus, Alabama
WRMG Red Bay, Alabama
WELR-FM Roanoke, Alabama
WGOL Russellville, Alabama
WKEA-FM Scottsboro, Alabama
WWIC Scottsboro, Alabama
WYEA Sylacauga, Alabama
WJDB-FM Thomasville, Alabama
WGZZ Waverly, Alabama
KPGG Ashdown, Arkansas
KEWI Benton, Arkansas
KTHS-FM Berryville, Arkansas
KHLS Blytheville, Arkansas
KRMW Cedarville, Arizona
KLYR Clarksville, Arkansas
KXIO Clarksville, Arkansas
KHPQ Clinton, Arkansas
KDYN-FM Coal Hill, Arkansas
KMJX Conway, Arkansas
KAGH Crossett, Arkansas
KAGH-FM Crossett, Arkansas
KYEL Danville, Arkansas
KCJC Dardanelle, Arkansas
KWXT Dardanelle, Arkansas
KDQN-FM De Queen, Arkansas
KDEW-FM De Witt, Arkansas
KXSA-FM Dermott, Arkansas
KIXB El Dorado, Arkansas
KKIX Fayetteville, Arkansas
KQSM-FM Fayetteville, Arkansas
KMAG Fort Smith, Arkansas
KTCS-FM Fort Smith, Arkansas
KOTN(FM) Gould, Arkansas
KYXK Gurdon, Arkansas
KWHF Harrisburg, Arkansas
KHBZ Harrison, Arkansas
KHOZ Harrison, Arkansas
KFFA Helena, Arkansas
KHPA Hope, Arkansas
KFIN Jonesboro, Arkansas
KSSN Little Rock, Arkansas
KVMA Magnolia, Arkansas
KBOK Malvern, Arkansas
KAMS Mammoth Spring, Arkansas
KENA-FM Mena, Arkansas
KVOM Morrilton, Arkansas
KVOM-FM Morrilton, Arkansas
KPFM Mountain Home, Arkansas
KTLO Mountain Home, Arkansas
KWOZ Mountain View, Arkansas
KMTB Murfreesboro, Arkansas
KOKR Newport, Arkansas
KDYN Ozark, Arkansas
KLBL Pearcy, Arkansas
KHOM Salem, Arkansas
KWCK-FM Searcy, Arkansas
KZHE Stamps, Arkansas
KOSY Texarkana, Arkansas
WUMY Turrell, Arkansas
KVMZ Waldo, Arkansas
KWYN-FM Wynne, Arkansas
KWCD Bisbee, Arizona
KFLG Bullhead City, Arizona
KMLE Chandler, Arizona
KFXR-FM Chinle, Arizona
KDDL Chino Valley, Arizona
KVRD-FM Cottonwood, Arizona
KTHQ Eagar, Arizona
KYWD Green Valley, Arizona
KZUA Holbrook, Arizona
KGMN Kingman, Arizona
KSAZ Marana, Arizona
KQSS Miami, Arizona
KPGE Page, Arizona
KLPZ Parker, Arizona
KMOG Payson, Arizona
KNIX-FM Phoenix, Arizona
KNOT Prescott, Arizona
KBUX Quartzsite, Arizona
KSED Sedona, Arizona
KIIM Tucson, Arizona
KSWG Wickenburg, Arizona
KHIL Willcox, Arizona
KTNN Window Rock, Arizona
KWRK Window Rock, Arizona
KINO Winslow, Arizona
KTTI Yuma, Arizona
KCNO Alturas, California
KIXF Baker, California
KCWR Bakersfield, California
KUZZ-FM Bakersfield, California
KFLG-FM Big River, California
KIBS Bishop, California
KROP Brawley, California
KKHK Carmel, California
KKCY Colusa, California
KSOQ-FM Escondido, California
KEKA-FM Eureka, California

KRED Eureka, California
KPIG-FM Freedom, California
KHGE Fresno, California
KSKS Fresno, California
KATJ-FM George, California
KFGY Healdsburg, California
KXCM Joshua Tree, California
KCNQ Kernville, California
KRKC King City, California
KIXW-FM Lenwood, California
KKGO Los Angeles, California
KRTY Los Gatos, California
KTOM-FM Marina, California
KUBB Mariposa, California
KXFG Menifee, California
KGAM(FM) Merced, California
KATM Modesto, California
KTPI-FM Mojave, California
KSMC Moraga, California
KPLM Palm Springs, California
KHSL-FM Paradise, California
KYOE Point Arena, California
KALF Red Bluff, California
KNCQ Redding, California
KZIQ-FM Ridgecrest, California
KBEB Sacramento, California
KNCI Sacramento, California
KFRG San Bernardino, California
KSON San Diego, California
KKJG San Luis Obispo, California
KSLY-FM San Luis Obispo, California
KSNI-FM Santa Maria, California
KRAZ Santa Ynez, California
KNNN(FM) Shasta Lake City, California
KNTY Shingle Springs, California
KJDX Susanville, California
KJUG Tulare, California
KJUG-FM Tulare, California
KFLS-FM Tulelake, California
KKBN Twain Harte, California
KQPM Ukiah, California
KUKI-FM Ukiah, California
KHAY Ventura, California
KSYC-FM Yreka, California
KALQ-FM Alamosa, Colorado
KWOF Broomfield, Colorado
KBVC Buena Vista, Colorado
KNAB-FM Burlington, Colorado
KSTY Canon City, Colorado
KAVP Colona, Colorado
KATC Colorado Springs, Colorado
KREL Colorado Springs, Colorado
KISZ-FM Cortez, Colorado
KRAI Craig, Colorado
KPRU Delta, Colorado
KYGO-FM Denver, Colorado
KRSJ Durango, Colorado
KSKE-FM Eagle, Colorado
KIIX Fort Collins, Colorado
KMTS Glenwood Springs, Colorado
KRKY Granby, Colorado
KKVT Grand Junction, Colorado
KPKE Gunnison, Colorado
KJBL Julesburg, Colorado
KTHN La Junta, Colorado
KLMR Lamar, Colorado
KVAY Lamar, Colorado
KSLV Monte Vista, Colorado
KYDN Monte Vista, Colorado
KKXK Montrose, Colorado
KRYD Norwood, Colorado
KWGL Ouray, Colorado
KWUF Pagosa Springs, Colorado
KCCY-FM Pueblo, Colorado
KNNG Sterling, Colorado
KCRT Trinidad, Colorado
KSPK-FM Walsenburg, Colorado
KUAD-FM Windsor, Colorado
KATR-FM Wray, Colorado
KGCD Wray, Colorado
WCTY Norwich, Connecticut
WWYZ Waterbury, Connecticut
WMZQ-FM Washington, District of Columbia
WDSD Dover, Delaware
WWOJ Avon Park, Florida
WQXM Bartow, Florida
WPHK Blountstown, Florida
WKIS Boca Raton, Florida
WAKT-FM Callaway, Florida
WIKX Charlotte Harbor, Florida
WJSB Crestview, Florida
WZCC Cross City, Florida
WDSP De Funiak Springs, Florida
WTRS Dunnellon, Florida
WBGY Everglades City, Florida
WWGR Fort Myers, Florida
WVFT Gretna, Florida
WFUS Gulfport, Florida
WHWY Holt, Florida
WIRK Indiantown, Florida
WWWK Islamorada, Florida
WQIK-FM Jacksonville, Florida
WCNK Key West, Florida
WGRO Lake City, Florida
WCKT Lehigh Acres, Florida
WQHL-FM Live Oak, Florida
WMAF Madison, Florida
WJAQ Marianna, Florida
WTYS Marianna, Florida
WYZB Mary Esther, Florida
WGNE-FM Middleburg, Florida
WXBM-FM Milton, Florida
WOGK Ocala, Florida
WWKA Orlando, Florida
WIYD Palatka, Florida
WPAP Panama City, Florida
WPCF Panama City Beach, Florida
WYCT Pensacola, Florida
WNFK Perry, Florida
WCTH Plantation Key, Florida
WKRO-FM Port Orange, Florida
WHKR Rockledge, Florida
WCTQ Sarasota, Florida
WQYK-FM St. Petersburg, Florida
WAVW Stuart, Florida
WTNT-FM Tallahassee, Florida
WWOF(FM) Tallahassee, Florida
WDVH-FM Trenton, Florida
WQLC Watertown, Florida
WOTW Windermere, Florida
WPCV Winter Haven, Florida
WZZS Zolfo Springs, Florida
WKAK Albany, Georgia
WAJQ-FM Alma, Georgia
WISK-FM Americus, Georgia
WNGC Arcade, Georgia
WFFM Ashburn, Georgia
WUBL Atlanta, Georgia
WSCG Augusta, Georgia
WKUB Blackshear, Georgia
WPPL Blue Ridge, Georgia
WTUF Boston, Georgia
WMOQ Bostwick, Georgia
WMUV Brunswick, Georgia
WRJY Brunswick, Georgia
WBTR-FM Carrollton, Georgia
WRCG Columbus, Georgia
WCON Cornelia, Georgia
WCON-FM Cornelia, Georgia
WZTR Dahlonega, Georgia
WQZY Dublin, Georgia
WXLI Dublin, Georgia
WUFF Eastman, Georgia
WLJA-FM Ellijay, Georgia
WPGY Ellijay, Georgia
WKCN Fort Benning South, Georgia
WXKO Fort Valley, Georgia
WIHB-FM Gray, Georgia
WHIE Griffin, Georgia
WKLY Hartwell, Georgia
WIFO-FM Jesup, Georgia
WKBX Kingsland, Georgia
WLHR-FM Lavonia, Georgia
WPEH Louisville, Georgia
WLYU Lyons, Georgia
WIHB Macon, Georgia
WKHX Marietta, Georgia
WKKP McDonough, Georgia
WGCO Midway, Georgia
WMCG Milan, Georgia
WKZR Milledgeville, Georgia
WHKN Millen, Georgia
WMNZ Montezuma, Georgia
WYUM Mount Vernon, Georgia
WGCN Nashville, Georgia
WTIF-FM Omega, Georgia
WXRS-FM Portal, Georgia
WJCL-FM Savannah, Georgia
WKNG Tallapoosa, Georgia
WTHO-FM Thomson, Georgia
WABR Tifton, Georgia
WOBB Tifton, Georgia
WSGC-FM Tignall, Georgia
WAAC Valdosta, Georgia
WYNR Waycross, Georgia
WCJM-FM West Point, Georgia
WKAA Willacoochee, Georgia
WEKS Zebulon, Georgia
KUAI Kekaha, Hawaii
KDLX Makawao, Hawaii
KKOA Volcano, Hawaii
KKNE Waipahu, Hawaii
KIIC Albia, Iowa
WJOD Asbury, Iowa
KSOM Audubon, Iowa
KDMG Burlington, Iowa
KOEL-FM Cedar Falls, Iowa
KHAK Cedar Rapids, Iowa
KKSY-FM Cedar Rapids, Iowa
KMJM Cedar Rapids, Iowa
KMGO Centerville, Iowa
KIAQ Clarion, Iowa
KSIB Creston, Iowa
KSIB-FM Creston, Iowa
WLLR-FM Davenport, Iowa
KDSN Denison, Iowa
KHKI Des Moines, Iowa
KDST Dyersville, Iowa
KRKN Eldon, Iowa
KILR Estherville, Iowa
KILR-FM Estherville, Iowa
KMCD Fairfield, Iowa
KIOW Forest City, Iowa
KWMT Fort Dodge, Iowa
KBKB Fort Madison, Iowa
KBKB-FM Fort Madison, Iowa
KCTN Garnavillo, Iowa
KXKT Glenwood, Iowa
KLMJ Hampton, Iowa
KKIA Ida Grove, Iowa
KNIA Knoxville, Iowa
KIKD Lake City, Iowa
KMCH Manchester, Iowa
KXFT Manson, Iowa
KMAQ Maquoketa, Iowa
KXIA Marshalltown, Iowa
KIAI Mason City, Iowa
KRNF Montezuma, Iowa
KILJ Mount Pleasant, Iowa
KILJ-FM Mount Pleasant, Iowa
KWPC Muscatine, Iowa
KCZE New Hampton, Iowa
KCOB Newton, Iowa
KCOB-FM Newton, Iowa
KBOE Oskaloosa, Iowa
KBOE-FM Oskaloosa, Iowa
KICL(FM) Pleasantville, Iowa
KOAK Red Oak, Iowa
KIHK Rock Valley, Iowa
KICD-FM Spencer, Iowa
KKRF Stuart, Iowa
KCSI Villisca, Iowa
KNEI-FM Waukon, Iowa
KWAY Waverly, Iowa
KJJY West Des Moines, Iowa
KKYY Whiting, Iowa
KQPI Aberdeen, Idaho
KAWO Boise, Idaho
KIZN Boise, Idaho
KQFC Boise, Idaho
KICR Coeur D'Alene, Idaho
KQBL Emmett, Idaho
KYUN Hailey, Idaho
KID-FM Idaho Falls, Idaho
KTHK Idaho Falls, Idaho
KZBG Lapwai, Idaho
KMOK Lewiston, Idaho
KRLC Lewiston-Clarkston, Idaho
KDZY McCall, Idaho
KVSI Montpelier, Idaho
KLER Orofino, Idaho
KOUU Pocatello, Idaho
KZBQ Pocatello, Idaho
KKEX Preston, Idaho
KUPI-FM Rexburg, Idaho
KKMV Rupert, Idaho
KSRA Salmon, Idaho
KIBR Sandpoint, Idaho
KBRV Soda Springs, Idaho
KITT Soda Springs, Idaho
KQZB Troy, Idaho
KEZJ-FM Twin Falls, Idaho
KVRG Victor, Idaho

KWAL Wallace, Idaho
WRMJ Aledo, Illinois
WIBH Anna, Illinois
WLCN Atlanta, Illinois
WRMS-FM Beardstown, Illinois
WLMD Bushnell, Illinois
WCDD Canton, Illinois
WRUL Carmi, Illinois
WIXY Champaign, Illinois
KSGM Chester, Illinois
WEBG Chicago, Illinois
WUSN Chicago, Illinois
WCCQ Crest Hill, Illinois
WDZQ Decatur, Illinois
WRCV Dixon, Illinois
WDQN Duquoin, Illinois
WCRC Effingham, Illinois
WFYR Elmwood, Illinois
WOKZ Fairfield, Illinois
WFPS Freeport, Illinois
WXXQ Freeport, Illinois
WAAG Galesburg, Illinois
WJRE Galva, Illinois
WGEL Greenville, Illinois
WEBQ Harrisburg, Illinois
WOOZ-FM Harrisburg, Illinois
WDUK Havana, Illinois
WRVY-FM Henry, Illinois
WHPO Hoopeston, Illinois
WDDD-FM Johnston City, Illinois
WAKO Lawrenceville, Illinois
WBWN LeRoy, Illinois
WSMI Litchfield, Illinois
WLUV Loves Park, Illinois
WGGH Marion, Illinois
WMCL McLeansboro, Illinois
WGLC Mendota, Illinois
WMOK Metropolis, Illinois
WRAM Monmouth, Illinois
WIBV Mount Vernon, Illinois
WMIX-FM Mount Vernon, Illinois
WALS Oglesby, Illinois
WSEI Olney, Illinois
WMKR Pana, Illinois
WXCL Pekin, Illinois
WJBC Pontiac, Illinois
WCOY Quincy, Illinois
WJEK(FM) Rantoul, Illinois
WJBD Salem, Illinois
WCCI Savanna, Illinois
WJVO South Jacksonville, Illinois
WFMB-FM Springfield, Illinois
WXNU St. Anne, Illinois
WUSW Taylorville, Illinois
WKJT Teutopolis, Illinois
WKZS Thomasboro, Illinois
WSVZ Tower Hill, Illinois
WRTB Winnebago, Illinois
WBKQ Alexandria, Indiana
WSCH Aurora, Indiana
WXKU-FM Austin, Indiana
WUZR Bicknell, Indiana
WLFW Chandler, Indiana
WKKG Columbus, Indiana
WXCH Columbus, Indiana
WCDQ Crawfordsville, Indiana
WYGB Edinburgh, Indiana
WBYT Elkhart, Indiana
WHCC Ellettsville, Indiana
WQKZ Ferdinand, Indiana
WFMS Fishers, Indiana
WFLQ French Lick, Indiana
WTRE Greensburg, Indiana
WQHK-FM Huntertown, Indiana
WBDC Huntingburg, Indiana
WBTU Kendallville, Indiana
WIVR Kentland, Indiana
WKPW Knightstown, Indiana
WWKI Kokomo, Indiana
WCOE La Porte, Indiana
WKOA Lafayette, Indiana
WTHD Lagrange, Indiana
WRCY Mt. Vernon, Indiana
WERK Muncie, Indiana
WLTI New Castle, Indiana
WMDH New Castle, Indiana
WARU Peru, Indiana
WUBG Plainfield, South Carolina
WPGW-FM Portland, Indiana
WRAY-FM Princeton, Indiana
WECI Richmond, Indiana
WQLK Richmond, Indiana
WHZR Royal Center, Indiana
WIFE-FM Rushville, Indiana
WMPI Scottsburg, Indiana
WLHK Shelbyville, Indiana
WNDI Sullivan, Indiana
WDWQ Terre Haute, Indiana
WTHI-FM Terre Haute, Indiana
WLJE Valparaiso, Indiana
WCJC Van Buren, Indiana
WKID Vevay, Indiana
WFML Vincennes, Indiana
WWBL Washington, Indiana
KAIR Atchison, Kansas
KVWF Augusta, Kansas
KREP Belleville, Kansas
KKOY Chanute, Kansas
KWGB Colby, Kansas
KXXX Colby, Kansas
KNCK Concordia, Kansas
KUSN Dearing, Kansas
KDNS Downs, Kansas
KIND-FM Elk City, Kansas
KVOE-FM Emporia, Kansas
KOTE Eureka, Kansas
KKJQ Garden City, Kansas
KHAZ Hays, Kansas
KNZA-FM Hiawatha, Kansas
KKQY Hill City, Kansas
KHOK Hoisington, Kansas
KBUF Holcomb, Kansas
KAIR-FM Horton, Kansas
KHUT Hutchinson, Kansas
KZSN Hutchinson, Kansas
KERP Ingalls, Kansas
KIKS-FM Iola, Kansas
KFKF-FM Kansas City, Kansas
KQZQ Kiowa, Kansas
KLDG Liberal, Kansas
KDJM Lindsborg, Kansas
KXKU Lyons, Kansas
KXBZ Manhattan, Kansas
KNDY Marysville, Kansas
KNDY-FM Marysville, Kansas
KFTI-FM Newton, Kansas
KFNF Oberlin, Kansas
KQLA Ogden, Kansas
KKOW Pittsburg, Kansas
KKOW-FM Pittsburg, Kansas
KSKG Salina, Kansas
KYEZ Salina, Kansas
KMZA-FM Seneca, Kansas
KTPK Topeka, Kansas
WIBW-FM Topeka, Kansas
KULY Ulysses, Kansas
KFDI-FM Wichita, Kansas
KWLS Winfield, Kansas
WANY Albany, Kentucky
WANY-FM Albany, Kentucky
WMDJ-FM Allen, Kentucky
WDGG Ashland, Kentucky
WBVR-FM Auburn, Kentucky
WGGC Bowling Green, Kentucky
WMMG Brandenburg, Kentucky
WKYR-FM Burkesville, Kentucky
WSEK Burnside, Kentucky
WKDZ-FM Cadiz, Kentucky
WCCK Calvert City, Kentucky
WIKI Carrollton, Kentucky
WAIN-FM Columbia, Kentucky
WKDP-FM Corbin, Kentucky
WCPM Cumberland, Kentucky
WCYN-FM Cynthiana, Kentucky
WHSX Edmonton, Kentucky
WFLE Flemingsburg, Kentucky
WFLE-FM Flemingsburg, Kentucky
WLVK Fort Knox, Kentucky
WYGY Fort Thomas, Kentucky
WFKY Frankfort, Kentucky
WFKN Franklin, Kentucky
WLYE-FM Glasgow, Kentucky
WGOH Grayson, Kentucky
WGRK-FM Greensburg, Kentucky
WLGC-FM Greenup, Kentucky
WULF Hardinsburg, Kentucky
WXBC Hardinsburg, Kentucky
WTUK Harlan, Kentucky
WXLR Harold, Kentucky
WHBN Harrodsburg, Kentucky
WKCM Hawesville, Kentucky
WSGS Hazard, Kentucky
WKDQ Henderson, Kentucky
WVVR Hopkinsville, Kentucky
WCYO Irvine, Kentucky
WJSN-FM Jackson, Kentucky
WJKY Jamestown, Kentucky
WJRS Jamestown, Kentucky
WGRK Jeffersontown, Kentucky
WMTL Leitchfield, Kentucky
WBUL-FM Lexington, Kentucky
WLXX Lexington, Kentucky
WKDO Liberty, Kentucky
WAMZ Louisville, Kentucky
WRKA Louisville, Kentucky
WQNU Lyndon, Kentucky
WFMW Madisonville, Kentucky
WKLB Manchester, Kentucky
WVLC Mannsville, Kentucky
WLLE Mayfield, Kentucky
WWAG McKee, Kentucky
WMKZ Monticello, Kentucky
WLBQ Morgantown, Kentucky
WKYN Mount Sterling, Kentucky
WRVK Mount Vernon, Kentucky
WLOC Munfordville, Kentucky
WFGS Murray, Kentucky
WKFC North Corbin, Kentucky
WBKR Owensboro, Kentucky
WKYQ Paducah, Kentucky
WSIP-FM Paintsville, Kentucky
WBIO Philpot, Kentucky
WDHR Pikeville, Kentucky
WRIL Pineville, Kentucky
WKCA Salt Lick, Kentucky
WRLV Salyersville, Kentucky
WRLV-FM Salyersville, Kentucky
WVLE Scottsville, Kentucky
WKWY Tompkinsville, Kentucky
WTKY Tompkinsville, Kentucky
WTKY-FM Tompkinsville, Kentucky
WKKS Vanceburg, Kentucky
WLKS-FM West Liberty, Kentucky
WTCW Whitesburg, Kentucky
WEZJ-FM Williamsburg, Kentucky
WNKR Williamstown, Kentucky
KRRV-FM Alexandria, Louisiana
KBKK Ball, Louisiana
WYNK-FM Baton Rouge, Louisiana
KQKI-FM Bayou Vista, Louisiana
WBOX Bogalusa, Louisiana
KSBH Coushatta, Louisiana
KEUN-FM Eunice, Louisiana
WOMN Franklinton, Louisiana
KLEB Golden Meadow, Louisiana
WFPR Hammond, Louisiana
WHMD Hammond, Louisiana
KRLQ Hodge, Louisiana
KJNA-FM Jena, Louisiana
KMDL Kaplan, Louisiana
WRKN LaPlace, Louisiana
KNGT Lake Charles, Louisiana
KYKZ Lake Charles, Louisiana
KJAE Leesville, Louisiana
KLLA Leesville, Louisiana
KVVP Leesville, Louisiana
KBON Mamou, Louisiana
KJVC Mansfield, Louisiana
KWLV Many, Louisiana
KAPB-FM Marksville, Louisiana
KJLO-FM Monroe, Louisiana
KDBH-FM Natchitoches, Louisiana
KXKC New Iberia, Louisiana
WNOE-FM New Orleans, Louisiana
KOGM Opelousas, Louisiana
KMYY Rayville, Louisiana
KXKZ Ruston, Louisiana
KWKH Shreveport, Louisiana
KXKS-FM Shreveport, Louisiana
KTKC Springhill, Louisiana
KLAA-FM Tioga, Louisiana
WBOX-FM Varnado, Louisiana
KWTG Vidalia, Louisiana
KNCB Vivian, Louisiana
KNCB-FM Vivian, Louisiana
KVCL-FM Winnfield, Louisiana
KMAR-FM Winnsboro, Louisiana
WRNX Amherst, Massachusetts
WPVQ Greenfield, Massachusetts
WBWL Lynn, Massachusetts
WESO Southbridge, Massachusetts
WKLB-FM Waltham, Massachusetts
WGFP Webster, Massachusetts

WORC Webster, Massachusetts
WPOC Baltimore, Maryland
WTRI Brunswick, Maryland
WKIK-FM California, Maryland
WBEY-FM Crisfield, Maryland
WFRE Frederick, Maryland
WFRB-FM Frostburg, Maryland
WKHI Fruitland, Maryland
WAYZ Hagerstown, Maryland
WXCY Havre De Grace, Maryland
WAAI Hurlock, Maryland
WKIK La Plata, Maryland
WWHQ Oakland, Maryland
WWFG Ocean City, Maryland
WKTT Salisbury, Maryland
WINX-FM St. Michaels, Maryland
WICL Williamsport, Maryland
WTHT Auburn, Maine
WBFE Bar Harbor, Maine
WQCB Brewer, Maine
WTBM Mexico, Maine
WBCQ-FM Monticello, Maine
WOXO-FM Norway, Maine
WMDR-FM Oakland, Maine
WPOR Portland, Maine
WMCM Rockland, Maine
WSKW Skowhegan, Maine
WTBU York Center, Maine
WQTE Adrian, Michigan
WATZ-FM Alpena, Michigan
WWWW-FM Ann Arbor, Michigan
WLEW Bad Axe, Michigan
WCUZ Bear Lake, Michigan
WHFB-FM Benton Harbor, Michigan
WOUF Beulah, Michigan
WWBR Big Rapids, Michigan
WBCM Boyne City, Michigan
WYTZ Bridgman, Michigan
WNWN-FM Coldwater, Michigan
WDRQ Detroit, Michigan
WYCD Detroit, Michigan
WYKX Escanaba, Michigan
WFBE Flint, Michigan
WGDN-FM Gladwin, Michigan
WBCT Grand Rapids, Michigan
WQON Grayling, Michigan
WCMM Gulliver, Michigan
WCEN-FM Hemlock, Michigan
WTNR Holland, Michigan
WHKB Houghton, Michigan
WTWS Houghton Lake, Michigan
WMKC Indian River, Michigan
WJNR-FM Iron Mountain, Michigan
WJMS Ironwood, Michigan
WJPD Ishpeming, Michigan
WWDK Jackson, Michigan
WCUP L'Anse, Michigan
WGLM-FM Lakeview, Michigan
WITL Lansing, Michigan
WLCO Lapeer, Michigan
WYPV Mackinaw City, Michigan
WBGV Marlette, Michigan
WFXD Marquette, Michigan
WMUS Muskegon, Michigan
WLAW Newaygo, Michigan
WNBY Newberry, Michigan
WUPY Ontonagon, Michigan
WARD Petoskey, Michigan
WSAQ Port Huron, Michigan
WHAK Rogers City, Michigan
WRGZ Rogers City, Michigan
WKCQ Saginaw, Michigan
WMIC Sandusky, Michigan
WKZC Scottville, Michigan
WMLM St. Louis, Michigan
WKJC-FM Tawas City, Michigan
WRCI Three Rivers, Michigan
WLDR-FM Traverse City, Michigan
WTCM-FM Traverse City, Michigan
KRJB Ada, Minnesota
KKIN-FM Aitkin, Minnesota
KASM Albany, Minnesota
KAUS-FM Austin, Minnesota
KQAQ Austin, Minnesota
KKCQ-FM Bagley, Minnesota
KBVB Barnesville, Minnesota
KBHP Bemidji, Minnesota
KBMW Breckenridge, Minnesota
KRWC Buffalo, Minnesota
KFIL-FM Chatfield, Minnesota
KGPZ Coleraine, Minnesota
WDKE Coleraine, Minnesota
KARP-FM Dassel, Minnesota
KRCQ Detroit Lakes, Minnesota
KTCO Duluth, Minnesota
KLCI Elk River, Minnesota
KJJK-FM Fergus Falls, Minnesota
KSNR Fisher, Minnesota
KGRP Grand Rapids, Minnesota
KSDM International Falls, Minnesota
KKOJ Jackson, Minnesota
KKWB Kelliher, Minnesota
KMFX-FM Lake City, Minnesota
KEYL Long Prairie, Minnesota
KLQL Luverne, Minnesota
KYSM-FM Mankato, Minnesota
KMHL Marshall, Minnesota
KMNB Minneapolis, Minnesota
KVOX-FM Moorhead, Minnesota
KKOK-FM Morris, Minnesota
KATO-FM New Ulm, Minnesota
KNUJ New Ulm, Minnesota
KBLB Nisswa, Minnesota
KOLV Olivia, Minnesota
KDIO Ortonville, Minnesota
KRFO-FM Owatonna, Minnesota
KPRM Park Rapids, Minnesota
KXKK Park Rapids, Minnesota
KZPK Paynesville, Minnesota
KBOT Pelican Rapids, Minnesota
KFIL Preston, Minnesota
WQPM Princeton, Minnesota
KCUE Red Wing, Minnesota
KLGR Redwood Falls, Minnesota
KWWK Rochester, Minnesota
KWNO-FM Rushford, Minnesota
KIKV-FM Sauk Centre, Minnesota
WVAL Sauk Rapids, Minnesota
KJOE Slayton, Minnesota
KQYB Spring Grove, Minnesota
WWJO St. Cloud, Minnesota
KRRW St. James, Minnesota
KEEY-FM St. Paul, Minnesota
KNSP Staples, Minnesota
KKDQ Thief River Falls, Minnesota
KARL Tracy, Minnesota
KVKK Verndale, Minnesota
WUSZ Virginia, Minnesota
KKWS Wadena, Minnesota
KWAD Wadena, Minnesota
KKWQ Warroad, Minnesota
KRUE Waseca, Minnesota
KRUE Waseca, Minnesota
KDOM Windom, Minnesota
KDOM-FM Windom, Minnesota
KAGE Winona, Minnesota
KSWF Aurora, Missouri
KAAN Bethany, Missouri
KYOO Bolivar, Missouri
KCLR-FM Boonville, Missouri
KWRT Boonville, Missouri
KMAM Butler, Missouri
KATI California, Missouri
KRLL California, Missouri
KEZS-FM Cape Girardeau, Missouri
KAOL Carrollton, Missouri
KCRV-AM Caruthersville, Missouri
KRMO Cassville, Missouri
KWKZ Charleston, Missouri
KDKD-FM Clinton, Missouri
KDEX Dexter, Missouri
KDEX-FM Dexter, Missouri
KOEA Doniphan, Missouri
KESM Eldorado Springs, Missouri
KTJJ Farmington, Missouri
KFAL Fulton, Missouri
KBOD Gainesville, Missouri
KGOZ Gallatin, Missouri
KUNQ Houston, Missouri
KYLS-FM Ironton, Missouri
KZJF Jefferson City, Missouri
KIXQ Joplin, Missouri
KBEQ-FM Kansas City, Missouri
KTUF Kirksville, Missouri
KXKX Knob Noster, Missouri
KHST Lamar, Missouri
KCLQ Lebanon, Missouri
KJEL Lebanon, Missouri
KLWT Lebanon, Missouri
KJFM Louisiana, Missouri
KLTI Macon, Missouri
KMMO-FM Marshall, Missouri
KMEM-FM Memphis, Missouri
KWWR Mexico, Missouri
KRES Moberly, Missouri
KELE Mountain Grove, Missouri
KELE-FM Mountain Grove, Missouri
KBTN Neosho, Missouri
KBTN-FM Neosho, Missouri
KNEM Nevada, Missouri
KTMO New Madrid, Missouri
KICK-FM Palmyra, Missouri
KBDZ Perryville, Missouri
KPWB-FM Piedmont, Missouri
KKLR-FM Poplar Bluff, Missouri
KPBR Poplar Bluff, Missouri
KPPL Poplar Bluff, Missouri
KZNN Rolla, Missouri
KKID Salem, Missouri
KSMO Salem, Missouri
KSJQ Savannah, Missouri
KDRO Sedalia, Missouri
KBXB Sikeston, Missouri
KRHW Sikeston, Missouri
KTTS-FM Springfield, Missouri
KSD St. Louis, Missouri
WIL-FM St. Louis, Missouri
KLPW-FM Steelville, Missouri
KTUI-FM Sullivan, Missouri
KSAR Thayer, Missouri
KTTN-FM Trenton, Missouri
KKAC Vandalia, Missouri
KTKS Versailles, Missouri
KFAV Warrenton, Missouri
KWRE Warrenton, Missouri
KAYQ Warsaw, Missouri
KKDY West Plains, Missouri
KWKJ Windsor, Missouri
WBLE Batesville, Mississippi
WIZK Bay Springs, Mississippi
WZKX Bay St. Louis, Mississippi
WBYP Belzoni, Mississippi
WBKN Brookhaven, Mississippi
WKJN Centreville, Mississippi
WKDJ-FM Clarksdale, Mississippi
WEBL Coldwater, Mississippi
WZKR Collinsville, Mississippi
WFFF Columbia, Mississippi
WKOR-FM Columbus, Mississippi
WDMS Greenville, Mississippi
WQXB Grenada, Mississippi
WGBL Gulfport, Mississippi
WGCM Gulfport, Mississippi
WKZU Iuka, Mississippi
WMSI-FM Jackson, Mississippi
WAGR-FM Lexington, Mississippi
WRBE-FM Lucedale, Mississippi
WUSJ Madison, Mississippi
WAKH McComb, Mississippi
WKXY Merigold, Mississippi
WQNZ Natchez, Mississippi
WWZD-FM New Albany, Mississippi
WWMS Oxford, Mississippi
WKNN-FM Pascagoula, Mississippi
WJDR Prentiss, Mississippi
WMJW Rosedale, Mississippi
WQJB State College, Mississippi
WBBN Taylorsville, Mississippi
WTYL Tylertown, Mississippi
KGCM Belgrade, Montana
KCTR-FM Billings, Montana
KEWF Billings, Montana
KGHL Billings, Montana
KGHL(FM) Billings, Montana
KRKX Billings, Montana
KRPM Billings, Montana
KBOZ-FM Bozeman, Montana
KAAR Butte, Montana
KIKF Cascade, Montana
KHNK Columbia Falls, Montana
KQRV Deer Lodge, Montana
KDBM Dillon, Montana
KBMI-FM East Helena, Montana
KIKC-FM Forsyth, Montana
KSCY Four Corners, Montana
KLTZ Glasgow, Montana
KDZN Glendive, Montana
KMON Great Falls, Montana
KMON-FM Great Falls, Montana
KPQX Havre, Montana
KBLL-FM Helena, Montana
KDBR Kalispell, Montana
KXLO Lewistown, Montana

KLCB Libby, Montana
KXLB Livingston, Montana
KDXT Lolo, Montana
KMMR Malta, Montana
KGGL Missoula, Montana
KYSS-FM Missoula, Montana
KATQ Plentywood, Montana
KATQ-FM Plentywood, Montana
KERR Polson, Montana
KCGM Scobey, Montana
KZIN-FM Shelby, Montana
KVCK-FM Wolf Point, Montana
WKXR Asheboro, North Carolina
WNBB Bayboro, North Carolina
WPYB Benson, North Carolina
WMMY Boone, North Carolina
WKYK Burnsville, North Carolina
WSME Camp Lejeune, North Carolina
WPTL Canton, North Carolina
WNCB Cary, North Carolina
WSOC-FM Charlotte, North Carolina
WRSF Columbia, North Carolina
WAGY Forest City, North Carolina
WNCC Franklin, North Carolina
WQDK Gatesville, North Carolina
WJSG Hamlet, North Carolina
WCMS-FM Hatteras, North Carolina
WYND-FM Hatteras, North Carolina
WIZS Henderson, North Carolina
WKTE King, North Carolina
WRNS Kinston, North Carolina
WRNS-FM Kinston, North Carolina
WKVS Lenoir, North Carolina
WKML Lumberton, North Carolina
WBRM Marion, North Carolina
WDSL Mocksville, North Carolina
WIXE Monroe, North Carolina
WMNC Morganton, North Carolina
WMNC-FM Morganton, North Carolina
WKRK Murphy, North Carolina
WECR Newland, North Carolina
WKBC North Wilkesboro, North Carolina
WKSF Old Fort, North Carolina
WPTM Roanoke Rapids, North Carolina
WCVP-FM Robbinsville, North Carolina
WDWG Rocky Mount, North Carolina
WRXO Roxboro, North Carolina
WCAB Rutherfordton, North Carolina
WWGP Sanford, North Carolina
WTSB Selma, North Carolina
WCOK Sparta, North Carolina
WAME Statesville, North Carolina
WKKT Statesville, North Carolina
WTAB Tabor City, North Carolina
WWQQ-FM Wilmington, North Carolina
WPAW Winston-Salem, North Carolina
WTQR Winston-Salem, North Carolina
KVMI Arthur, North Dakota
KEYA Belcourt, North Dakota
KBMR Bismarck, North Dakota
KQDY Bismarck, North Dakota
KBTO Bottineau, North Dakota
KPOK Bowman, North Dakota
KDAK Carrington, North Dakota
KAOC Cavalier, North Dakota
KDLR Devils Lake, North Dakota
KZZY Devils Lake, North Dakota
KCAD Dickinson, North Dakota
KLTC Dickinson, North Dakota
KXPO Grafton, North Dakota
KUSB Hazelton, North Dakota
KNDC Hettinger, North Dakota
KMJO Hope, North Dakota
KSJB Jamestown, North Dakota
KYNU Jamestown, North Dakota
KNDK Langdon, North Dakota
KQLX-FM Lisbon, North Dakota
KCJB Minot, North Dakota
KYYX Minot, North Dakota
KDDR Oakes, North Dakota
KZZJ Rugby, North Dakota
KDXN South Heart, North Dakota
KTGO Tioga, North Dakota
KOVC Valley City, North Dakota
KEYZ Williston, North Dakota
KYYZ Williston, North Dakota
KBRB Ainsworth, Nebraska
KUSO Albion, Nebraska
KAAQ Alliance, Nebraska
KNCY-FM Auburn, Nebraska
KFFF Bennington, Nebraska
KBLR-FM Blair, Nebraska
KCNI Broken Bow, Nebraska
KZEN Central City, Nebraska
KCSR Chadron, Nebraska
KAMI Cozad, Nebraska
KSDZ Gordon, Nebraska
KRGI-FM Grand Island, Nebraska
KNPQ Hershey, Nebraska
KRNY Kearney, Nebraska
KICX-FM McCook, Nebraska
KFGE Milford, Nebraska
KHYY Minatare, Nebraska
KXNP North Platte, Nebraska
KMCX-FM Ogallala, Nebraska
KZTL Paxton, Nebraska
KNEB Scottsbluff, Nebraska
KNEB-FM Scottsbluff, Nebraska
KZKX Seward, Nebraska
KSID Sidney, Nebraska
KRFS-FM Superior, Nebraska
KMBV Valentine, Nebraska
KVSH Valentine, Nebraska
KTIC West Point, Nebraska
KTIC-FM West Point, Nebraska
KSUX Winnebago, Nebraska
WNHW Belmont, New Hampshire
WOKQ Dover, New Hampshire
WYKR-FM Haverhill, New Hampshire
WYRY Hinsdale, New Hampshire
KIXX Lebanon, New Hampshire
WSCY Moultonborough, New Hampshire
WCNL Newport, New Hampshire
WPKQ North Conway, New Hampshire
WMYF Portsmouth, New Hampshire
WINQ Winchester, New Hampshire
WPUR Atlantic City, New Jersey
WCVH Flemington, New Jersey
WNSH Newark, New Jersey
KLAG Alamogordo, New Mexico
KZZX Alamogordo, New Mexico
KBQI Albuquerque, New Mexico
KRST Albuquerque, New Mexico
KKTC Angel Fire, New Mexico
KTZA Artesia, New Mexico
KNFT-FM Bayard, New Mexico
KARS Belen, New Mexico
KABQ-FM Bosque Farms, New Mexico
KATK-FM Carlsbad, New Mexico
KLMX Clayton, New Mexico
KNMB Cloudcroft, New Mexico
KCLV-FM Clovis, New Mexico
KOTS Deming, New Mexico
KTRA-FM Farmington, New Mexico
KGLX Gallup, New Mexico
KYVA Gallup, New Mexico
KIXN Hobbs, New Mexico
KPER Hobbs, New Mexico
KRSY-FM La Luz, New Mexico
KGRT-FM Las Cruces, New Mexico
KFUN Las Vegas, New Mexico
KQBA Los Alamos, New Mexico
KWMW Maljamar, New Mexico
KSEL-FM Portales, New Mexico
KTDB Ramah, New Mexico
KBKZ Raton, New Mexico
KCKN Roswell, New Mexico
KMOU Roswell, New Mexico
KWES-FM Ruidoso, New Mexico
KMXQ Socorro, New Mexico
KQAY-FM Tucumcari, New Mexico
KTNM Tucumcari, New Mexico
KCYE Boulder City, Nevada
KBUL Carson City, Nevada
KCMY Carson City, Nevada
KOLC Carson City, Nevada
KRJC Elko, Nevada
KDSS Ely, Nevada
KHWG Fallon, Nevada
KVLV Fallon, Nevada
KLAP Gerlach, Nevada
KWNR Henderson, Nevada
KJJJ Laughlin, Nevada
KJUL Moapa Valley, Nevada
KSGG Reno, Nevada
KWNA-FM Winnemucca, Nevada
WGNA-FM Albany, New York
WZKZ Alfred, New York
WHWK Binghamton, New York
WINR Binghamton, New York
WBRV Boonville, New York
WYRK Buffalo, New York
WJVC Center Moriches, New York
WFFG-FM Corinth, New York
WOLF-FM DeRuyter, New York
WFLR Dundee, New York
WRWB-FM Ellenville, New York
WBBI Endwell, New York
WBUG-FM Fort Plain, New York
WBKX Fredonia, New York
WBBS Fulton, New York
WFLK Geneva, New York
WRWD-FM Highland, New York
WCKR Hornell, New York
WPGI Horseheads, New York
WQNY Ithaca, New York
WHUG Jamestown, New York
WDNB Jeffersonville, New York
WKXP Kingston, New York
WXRL Lancaster, New York
WVOS Liberty, New York
WLLG Lowville, New York
WVNV Malone, New York
WELJ Montauk, New York
WBGK Newport Village, New York
WBKT Norwich, New York
WPIG Olean, New York
WDOS Oneonta, New York
WDLC Port Jervis, New York
WSNN Potsdam, New York
WOKR Remsen, New York
WUUF Sodus, New York
WNBL South Bristol Township, New York
WSPQ Springville, New York
WFRG-FM Utica, New York
WCJW Warsaw, New York
WFRY-FM Watertown, New York
WRCE Watkins Glen, New York
WAVR Waverly, New York
WLSV Wellsville, New York
WZAD Wurtsboro, New York
WNCO-FM Ashland, Ohio
WNUS Belpre, Ohio
WWKC Caldwell, Ohio
WKKJ Chillicothe, Ohio
WUBE-FM Cincinnati, Ohio
WGAR-FM Cleveland, Ohio
WMJK Clyde, Ohio
WCOL-FM Columbus, Ohio
WTNS Coshocton, Ohio
WHKO Dayton, Ohio
WZOM Defiance, Ohio
WEDI Eaton, Ohio
WCLI-FM Enon, Ohio
WRAC Georgetown, Ohio
WDSJ Greenville, Ohio
WSRW Hillsboro, Ohio
WKFM Huron, Ohio
WCJO Jackson, Ohio
WIMT Lima, Ohio
WMRN-FM Marion, Ohio
WQMX Medina, Ohio
WPFB Middletown, Ohio
WSEO Nelsonville, Ohio
WCKY-FM Pemberville, Ohio
WQXK Salem, Ohio
WIZE Springfield, Ohio
WTUZ Uhrichsville, Ohio
WTGR Union City, Ohio
WFGF Wapakoneta, Ohio
WCHO-FM Washington Ct House, Ohio
WXIZ Waverly, Ohio
WKFI Wilmington, Ohio
WQKT Wooster, Ohio
WBZI Xenia, Ohio
KADA-FM Ada, Oklahoma
KEYB Altus, Oklahoma
KWHW Altus, Oklahoma
KACO Apache, Oklahoma
KHKC-FM Atoka, Oklahoma
KREK Bristow, Oklahoma
KKBI Broken Bow, Oklahoma
KWEY-FM Clinton, Oklahoma
KKAJ-FM Davis, Oklahoma
KKEN Duncan, Oklahoma
KLBC Durant, Oklahoma
KECO Elk City, Oklahoma
KOFM Enid, Oklahoma
KTNT Eufaula, Oklahoma
KYBE Frederick, Oklahoma
KGVE Grove, Oklahoma
KGYN Guymon, Oklahoma
KICM Healdton, Oklahoma

KPRV-FM Heavener, Oklahoma
KXBL Henryetta, Oklahoma
KTJS Hobart, Oklahoma
KITX Hugo, Oklahoma
KBEL-FM Idabel, Oklahoma
KLAW Lawton, Oklahoma
KBLP Lindsay, Oklahoma
KMAD Madill, Oklahoma
KFXI Marlow, Oklahoma
KNED McAlester, Oklahoma
KNAH Mustang, Oklahoma
KJKE Newcastle, Oklahoma
KNID North Enid, Oklahoma
KRIG-FM Nowata, Oklahoma
KTST Oklahoma City, Oklahoma
KXXY-FM Oklahoma City, Oklahoma
KOKL Okmulgee, Oklahoma
KPNC Ponca City, Oklahoma
KOMS Poteau, Oklahoma
KPRV Poteau, Oklahoma
KIRC Seminole, Oklahoma
KGFY Stillwater, Oklahoma
KLRB Stuart, Oklahoma
KIXO Sulphur, Oklahoma
KEOK Tahlequah, Oklahoma
KTLQ Tahlequah, Oklahoma
KVOO-FM Tulsa, Oklahoma
KWEN Tulsa, Oklahoma
KITO-FM Vinita, Oklahoma
KTFX-FM Warner, Oklahoma
KWEY Weatherford, Oklahoma
KWSH Wewoka, Oklahoma
KMCO Wilburton, Oklahoma
KWFX Woodward, Oklahoma
KRKT-FM Albany, Oregon
KCMB Baker City, Oregon
KESY Baker City, Oregon
KBDN Bandon, Oregon
KMTK Bend, Oregon
KJDY-FM Canyon City, Oregon
KSHL Coburg, Oregon
KMHS Coos Bay, Oregon
KSHR-FM Coquille, Oregon
KNND Cottage Grove, Oregon
KWVR-FM Enterprise, Oregon
KCST-FM Florence, Oregon
KRWQ Gold Hill, Oregon
KCMD Grants Pass, Oregon
KOHU Hermiston, Oregon
KIHR Hood River, Oregon
KJDY John Day, Oregon
KLAD-FM Klamath Falls, Oregon
KNCU Newport, Oregon
KSRV Ontario, Oregon
KWHT Pendleton, Oregon
KAKT Phoenix, Oregon
KUPL Portland, Oregon
KWJJ-FM Portland, Oregon
KRCO Prineville, Oregon
KSJJ Redmond, Oregon
KRSB-FM Roseburg, Oregon
KKNU Springfield-Eugene, Oregon
KCKX Stayton, Oregon
WFGY Altoona, Pennsylvania
WWSM Annville-Cleona, Pennsylvania
WGGI Benton, Pennsylvania
WLCY Blairsville, Pennsylvania
WVNW Burnham, Pennsylvania
WBUT Butler, Pennsylvania
WHGL-FM Canton, Pennsylvania
WCAT-FM Carlisle, Pennsylvania
WIOO Carlisle, Pennsylvania
WKNB Clarendon, Pennsylvania
WWCH Clarion, Pennsylvania
WDKC Covington, Pennsylvania
WSJR Dallas, Pennsylvania
WOWQ Du Bois, Pennsylvania
WCTO Easton, Pennsylvania
WXTA Edinboro, Pennsylvania
WBYB(FM) Eldred, Pennsylvania
WYGL-FM Elizabethville, Pennsylvania
WLEM Emporium, Pennsylvania
WIOV Ephrata, Pennsylvania
WSKE Everett, Pennsylvania
WTWF Fairview, Pennsylvania
WLOA Farrell, Pennsylvania
WGTY Gettysburg, Pennsylvania
WGRP Greenville, Pennsylvania
WWGY Grove City, Pennsylvania
WHVR Hanover, Pennsylvania
WRBT Harrisburg, Pennsylvania
WZCY Hershey, Pennsylvania
WHUN Huntingdon, Pennsylvania
WFGI-FM Johnstown, Pennsylvania
WGYY Meadville, Pennsylvania
WJUN-FM Mexico, Pennsylvania
WWBE Mifflinburg, Pennsylvania
WOGI Moon Township, Pennsylvania
WKVE Mount Pleasant, Pennsylvania
WGYI Oil City, Pennsylvania
WOGG Oliver, Pennsylvania
WQOR Olyphant, Pennsylvania
WBXQ Patton, Pennsylvania
WXTU Philadelphia, Pennsylvania
WPHB Philipsburg, Pennsylvania
WDSY Pittsburgh, Pennsylvania
WPGB Pittsburgh, Pennsylvania
WBYL Salladasburg, Pennsylvania
WGGY Scranton, Pennsylvania
WBLJ-FM Shamokin, Pennsylvania
WEEO Shippensburg, Pennsylvania
WDDH St. Marys, Pennsylvania
WFGE State College, Pennsylvania
WCBG Waynesboro, Pennsylvania
WILQ Williamsport, Pennsylvania
WKXC-FM Aiken, South Carolina
WDOG Barnwell, South Carolina
WUBB Bluffton, South Carolina
WGFG Branchville, South Carolina
WGTR Bucksport, South Carolina
WEZL Charleston, South Carolina
WIWF Charleston, South Carolina
WVSZ Chesterfield, South Carolina
WCOS-FM Columbia, South Carolina
WCOS-FM Columbia, South Carolina
WEGX Dillon, South Carolina
WZZQ(AM) Gaffney, South Carolina
WSSL-FM Gray Court, South Carolina
WESC-FM Greenville, South Carolina
WCKN Hollywood, South Carolina
WWNU Irmo, South Carolina
WWKT-FM Kingstree, South Carolina
WRHM Lancaster, South Carolina
WOMG Lexington, South Carolina
WHLZ Marion, South Carolina
WSYN Surfside Beach, South Carolina
WGOG Walhalla, South Carolina
WALI Walterboro, South Carolina
KBFS Belle Fourche, South Dakota
KZZI Belle Fourche, South Dakota
KZMX Hot Springs, South Dakota
KZMX-FM Hot Springs, South Dakota
KOKK Huron, South Dakota
KBJM Lemmon, South Dakota
KMLO Lowry, South Dakota
KJAM-FM Madison, South Dakota
KXLG Milbank, South Dakota
KMIT Mitchell, South Dakota
KGFX Pierre, South Dakota
KIQK Rapid City, South Dakota
KOUT Rapid City, South Dakota
KGIM-FM Redfield, South Dakota
KPLO-FM Reliance, South Dakota
KMOM Roscoe, South Dakota
KIKN-FM Salem, South Dakota
KTWB Sioux Falls, South Dakota
KXRB Sioux Falls, South Dakota
KBWS-FM Sisseton, South Dakota
KKQQ Volga, South Dakota
KDLO-FM Watertown, South Dakota
KSDR-FM Watertown, South Dakota
KWYR Winner, South Dakota
KKYA Yankton, South Dakota
WNAX-FM Yankton, South Dakota
WJSQ Athens, Tennessee
WLAR Athens, Tennessee
WMOD Bolivar, Tennessee
WTBG Brownsville, Tennessee
WFWL Camden, Tennessee
WUCZ Carthage, Tennessee
WVFB Celina, Tennessee
WNKX-FM Centerville, Tennessee
WUSY Cleveland, Tennessee
WLVS-FM Clifton, Tennessee
WYSH Clinton, Tennessee
WMCP Columbia, Tennessee
WGSQ Cookeville, Tennessee
WHUB Cookeville, Tennessee
WLYY Copper Hill, Tennessee
WZYX Cowan, Tennessee
WOWF Crossville, Tennessee
WSDQ Dunlap, Tennessee
WOGT East Ridge, Tennessee
WEMB Erwin, Tennessee
WEKR Fayetteville, Tennessee
WYTM-FM Fayetteville, Tennessee
WAKM Franklin, Tennessee
WHIN Gallatin, Tennessee
WMYL Halls Crossroads, Tennessee
WLMU Harrogate, Tennessee
WMUF Henry, Tennessee
WMLR Hohenwald, Tennessee
WEIO(FM) Huntingdon, Tennessee
WWDX Huntingdon, Tennessee
WOGY Jackson, Tennessee
WDEB Jamestown, Tennessee
WDEB-FM Jamestown, Tennessee
WJFC Jefferson City, Tennessee
WNOX Karns, Tennessee
WKOS Kingsport, Tennessee
WIVK Knoxville, Tennessee
WTNQ La Follette, Tennessee
WLCT Lafayette, Tennessee
WDXE Lawrenceburg, Tennessee
WLLX Lawrenceburg, Tennessee
WWLX Lawrenceburg, Tennessee
WANT Lebanon, Tennessee
WLIL Lenoir City, Tennessee
WJJM-FM Lewisburg, Tennessee
WKSR-FM Loretto, Tennessee
WDKW Maryville, Tennessee
WGAP Maryville, Tennessee
WWYN McKenzie, Tennessee
WBMC McMinnville, Tennessee
WGKX Memphis, Tennessee
WLIV-FM Monterey, Tennessee
WMTN Morristown, Tennessee
WMCT Mountain City, Tennessee
WKDF Nashville, Tennessee
WSIX-FM Nashville, Tennessee
WSM Nashville, Tennessee
WSM-FM Nashville, Tennessee
WBNT-FM Oneida, Tennessee
WRQR(AM) Paris, Tennessee
WKJQ-FM Parsons, Tennessee
WUAT Pikeville, Tennessee
WTRB Ripley, Tennessee
WJDT Rogersville, Tennessee
WKWX Savannah, Tennessee
WXOQ Selmer, Tennessee
WLIJ Shelbyville, Tennessee
WJLE Smithville, Tennessee
WJLE-FM Smithville, Tennessee
WUUQ South Pittsburg, Tennessee
WTZX Sparta, Tennessee
WSBI Static, Tennessee
WEYE Surgoinsville, Tennessee
WNTT Tazewell, Tennessee
WTNV Tiptonville, Tennessee
WIKQ Tusculum, Tennessee
KYTN Union City, Tennessee
WECO-FM Wartburg, Tennessee
WLNQ White Pine, Tennessee
WBOZ Woodbury, Tennessee
KEAN-FM Abilene, Texas
KSLI Abilene, Texas
KOPY Alice, Texas
KALP Alpine, Texas
KATP Amarillo, Texas
KDJW Amarillo, Texas
KGNC-FM Amarillo, Texas
KACT-FM Andrews, Texas
KASE-FM Austin, Texas
KVET-FM Austin, Texas
KRUN Ballinger, Texas
KMKS Bay City, Texas
KYKR Beaumont, Texas
KTKO Beeville, Texas
KMKT Bells, Texas
KBST-FM Big Spring, Texas
KNEL-FM Brady, Texas
KLXK Breckenridge, Texas
KTTX Brenham, Texas
KWHI Brenham, Texas
KKUB Brownfield, Texas
KOXE Brownwood, Texas
KORA-FM Bryan, Texas
KCLE Burleson, Texas
KMIL Cameron, Texas
KTON Cameron, Texas
KPUR-FM Canyon, Texas
KGAS-FM Carthage, Texas
KQBB Center, Texas

KCTX-FM Childress, Texas
KCAR Clarksville, Texas
KHFX Cleburne, Texas
KTHT Cleveland, Texas
KSTA Coleman, Texas
KAUM Colorado City, Texas
KVMC Colorado City, Texas
KULM-FM Columbus, Texas
KCOM Comanche, Texas
KYOX Comanche, Texas
KRYS-FM Corpus Christi, Texas
KBPC Crockett, Texas
KIVY-FM Crockett, Texas
KSTB Crystal Beach, Texas
KNGR Daingerfield, Texas
KXIT Dalhart, Texas
KRPT Devine, Texas
KDHN Dimmitt, Texas
KSTV-FM Dublin, Texas
KDDD Dumas, Texas
KIOX-FM Edna, Texas
KULP El Campo, Texas
KHEY-FM El Paso, Texas
KOLI Electra, Texas
KNES Fairfield, Texas
KXEZ Farmersville, Texas
KFLP Floydada, Texas
KFST-FM Fort Stockton, Texas
KPLX Fort Worth, Texas
KSCS Fort Worth, Texas
KNAF Fredericksburg, Texas
KNAF-FM Fredericksburg, Texas
KHTZ Ganado, Texas
KGWT George West, Texas
KTFW-FM Glen Rose, Texas
KCTI Gonzales, Texas
KSWA Graham, Texas
KPIR Granbury, Texas
KGVL Greenville, Texas
KIKT Greenville, Texas
KTXM Hallettsville, Texas
KCLW Hamilton, Texas
KUSJ Harker Heights, Texas
KTHP Hemphill, Texas
KHBR Hillsboro, Texas
KILT-FM Houston, Texas
KHYI Howe, Texas
KSAM-FM Huntsville, Texas
KFWR Jacksboro, Texas
KEBE Jacksonville, Texas
KMBL Junction, Texas
KOOK Junction, Texas
KAML Kenedy-Karnes City, Texas
KRNH Kerrville, Texas
KFTX Kingsville, Texas
KVLG La Grange, Texas
KPET Lamesa, Texas
KCYL Lampasas, Texas
KRRG Laredo, Texas
KDRX Laughlin Afb, Texas
KJDL-FM Levelland, Texas
KLVT Levelland, Texas
KZZN Littlefield, Texas
KETX Livingston, Texas
KETX-FM Livingston, Texas
KACQ Lometa, Texas
KYKX Longview, Texas
KLLL-FM Lubbock, Texas
KQBR Lubbock, Texas
KRBA Lufkin, Texas
KYKS Lufkin, Texas
KAGG Madisonville, Texas
KMVL-FM Madisonville, Texas
KCKL Malakoff, Texas
KRMX Marlin, Texas
KCUL Marshall, Texas
KMHT-FM Marshall, Texas
KHLB Mason, Texas
KLSR-FM Memphis, Texas
KTEX Mercedes, Texas
KNFM Midland, Texas
KMOO-FM Mineola, Texas
KMUL-FM Muleshoe, Texas
KJCS Nacogdoches, Texas
KGNB New Braunfels, Texas
KHKX Odessa, Texas
KMRK-FM Odessa, Texas
KRIL Odessa, Texas
KOGT Orange, Texas
KPXI Overton, Texas
KYXX Ozona, Texas
KOYN Paris, Texas
KPLT Paris, Texas
KZHN Paris, Texas
KKBQ-FM Pasadena, Texas
KIUN Pecos, Texas
KVJY Pharr, Texas
KSCN Pittsburg, Texas
KKYN-FM Plainview, Texas
KXAI Refugio, Texas
KRXT Rockdale, Texas
KDCD San Angelo, Texas
KGKL-FM San Angelo, Texas
KAJA San Antonio, Texas
KCYY San Antonio, Texas
KKYX San Antonio, Texas
KXXE-FM San Augustine, Texas
KWED Seguin, Texas
KIKZ Seminole, Texas
KAYD-FM Silsbee, Texas
KHOS-FM Sonora, Texas
KXDJ Spearman, Texas
KLGD Stamford, Texas
KEQX Stephenville, Texas
KSCH Sulphur Springs, Texas
KXOX Sweetwater, Texas
KKYR-FM Texarkana, Texas
KBCY Tye, Texas
KKUS Tyler, Texas
KNUE Tyler, Texas
KBNU Uvalde, Texas
KVOU-FM Uvalde, Texas
KIXS Victoria, Texas
KVNN Victoria, Texas
WACO-FM Waco, Texas
KBEC Waxahachie, Texas
KLUR Wichita Falls, Texas
KWFS-FM Wichita Falls, Texas
KVST Willis, Texas
KWUD Woodville, Texas
KYKM Yoakum, Texas
KEGH Brigham City, Utah
KWUT(FM) Elsinore, Utah
KMTI Manti, Utah
KCYN Moab, Utah
KEGA Oakley, Utah
KARB Price, Utah
KSLL Price, Utah
KNEU Roosevelt, Utah
KKAT Salt Lake City, Utah
KSOP-FM Salt Lake City, Utah
KUBL-FM Salt Lake City, Utah
KSOP South Salt Lake, Utah
KONY St. George, Utah
KLCY Vernal, Utah
WVES Accomac, Virginia
WYYD Amherst, Virginia
WHKX Bluefield, Virginia
WXBQ-FM Bristol, Virginia
WLUS-FM Clarksville, Virginia
WDIC Clinchco, Virginia
WKHK Colonial Heights, Virginia
WSVS Crewe, Virginia
WAKG Danville, Virginia
WBNN-FM Dillwyn, Virginia
WKTR Earlysville, Virginia
WWLB Ettrick, Virginia
WGRX Falmouth, Virginia
WFLO Farmville, Virginia
WLQM-FM Franklin, Virginia
WFLS-FM Fredericksburg, Virginia
WFTR Front Royal, Virginia
WBRF Galax, Virginia
WMJD Grundy, Virginia
WKCY-FM Harrisonburg, Virginia
WJNV Jonesville, Virginia
WLRV Lebanon, Virginia
WXLZ-FM Lebanon, Virginia
WRAA Luray, Virginia
WMEV-FM Marion, Virginia
WLFV Midlothian, Virginia
WSIG Mount Jackson, Virginia
WGH-FM Newport News, Virginia
WESR Onley-Onancock, Virginia
WSWV-FM Pennington Gap, Virginia
WARV-FM Petersburg, Virginia
WUSH Poquoson, Virginia
WDXC Pound, Virginia
WPSK-FM Pulaski, Virginia
WSLC-FM Roanoke, Virginia
WKSK-FM South Hill, Virginia
WXLZ St. Paul, Virginia
WZBB Stanleytown, Virginia
WCYK-FM Staunton, Virginia
WKDW Staunton, Virginia
WKDL Warrenton, Virginia
WNNT-FM Warsaw, Virginia
WIGO-FM White Stone, Virginia
WUSQ-FM Winchester, Virginia
WYVE Wytheville, Virginia
WVVI-FM Christiansted, Virgin Islands
WZLF Bellows Falls, Vermont
WWFY Berlin, Vermont
WTNN Bristol, Vermont
WXLF Hartford, Vermont
WJEN Killington, Vermont
WLVB Morrisville, Vermont
WIKE Newport, Vermont
WVNR Poultney, Vermont
WKXH St. Johnsbury, Vermont
KMNT Chehalis, Washington
KCLX Colfax, Washington
KCVL Colville, Washington
KYSN East Wenatchee, Washington
KZUS Ephrata, Washington
KYYT Goldendale, Washington
KEYG Grand Coulee, Washington
KXXK Hoquiam, Washington
KBAM Longview, Washington
KUKN Longview, Washington
KZAL Manson, Washington
KYYO McCleary, Washington
KANY Montesano, Washington
KWIQ-FM Moses Lake, Washington
KAPS Mount Vernon, Washington
KNCW Omak, Washington
KIIX-FM Opportunity, Washington
KZZL-FM Pullman, Washington
KORD-FM Richland, Washington
KKWF Seattle, Washington
KMPS Seattle, Washington
KDRK-FM Spokane, Washington
KXLY-FM Spokane, Washington
KDBL(FM) Toppenish, Washington
KYNR Toppenish, Washington
KKRV Wenatchee, Washington
KUTI Yakima, Washington
WBDK Algoma, Wisconsin
WRLU Algoma, Wisconsin
WBSZ Ashland, Wisconsin
WDMO Baldwin, Wisconsin
WLMX-FM Balsam Lake, Wisconsin
WXRO Beaver Dam, Wisconsin
WISS Berlin, Wisconsin
WQRB Bloomer, Wisconsin
WATQ Chetek, Wisconsin
WJMQ Clintonville, Wisconsin
WMAD Cross Plains, Wisconsin
WPCK Denmark, Wisconsin
WVRE Dickeyville, Wisconsin
WDMP Dodgeville, Wisconsin
WAXX Eau Claire, Wisconsin
WBWI Janesville, Wisconsin
WCLO Janesville, Wisconsin
WJVL Janesville, Wisconsin
WJVL Janesville, Wisconsin
WQCC La Crosse, Wisconsin
WLDY Ladysmith, Wisconsin
WGLR Lancaster, Wisconsin
WHIT Madison, Wisconsin
WKQH Marathon, Wisconsin
WLST Marinette, Wisconsin
WYTE Marshfield, Wisconsin
WWQM-FM Middleton, Wisconsin
WEKZ Monroe, Wisconsin
WNCY Neenah-Menasha, Wisconsin
WGEE-FM New London, Wisconsin
WIXK New Richmond, Wisconsin
WPKR Omro, Wisconsin
WCQM Park Falls, Wisconsin
WBKY Portage, Wisconsin
WDDC Portage, Wisconsin
WQPC Prairie Du Chien, Wisconsin
WNFM Reedsburg, Wisconsin
WHDG Rhinelander, Wisconsin
WJMC-FM Rice Lake, Wisconsin
WRCO-FM Richland Center, Wisconsin
WPLT Sarona, Wisconsin
WTCH Shawano, Wisconsin
WBFM Sheboygan, Wisconsin
WCOW-FM Sparta, Wisconsin
KDKE Superior, Wisconsin
WCYE Three Lakes, Wisconsin

WCUB Two Rivers, Wisconsin
WVRQ-FM Viroqua, Wisconsin
WMIL-FM Waukesha, Wisconsin
WDUX Waupaca, Wisconsin
WDEZ Wausau, Wisconsin
WMBZ West Bend, Wisconsin
WSLD Whitewater, Wisconsin
WDLS Wisconsin Dells, Wisconsin
WJLS-FM Beckley, West Virginia
WKEZ Bluefield, West Virginia
WBRB Buckhannon, West Virginia
WKWS Charleston, West Virginia
WGIE Clarksburg, West Virginia
WPDX Clarksburg, West Virginia
WZAC-FM Danville, West Virginia
WDNE Elkins, West Virginia
WDNE-FM Elkins, West Virginia
WKKW Fairmont, West Virginia
WVBD Fayetteville, West Virginia
WFGH Fort Gay, West Virginia
WVMR Frost, West Virginia
WHQX Gary, West Virginia
WAMN Green Valley, West Virginia
WVMR-FM Hillsboro, West Virginia
WTCR-FM Huntington, West Virginia
WKMM Kingwood, West Virginia
WRON-FM Lewisburg, West Virginia
WGYE Mannington, West Virginia
WELD-FM Moorefield, West Virginia
WTNJ Mount Hope, West Virginia
WGGE Parkersburg, West Virginia
WHNK Parkersburg, West Virginia
WCEF Ripley, West Virginia
WVMD Romney, West Virginia
WVSB Romney, West Virginia
WYKM Rupert, West Virginia
WSCW South Charleston, West Virginia
WVRC-FM Spencer, West Virginia
WDBS Sutton, West Virginia
WOVK Wheeling, West Virginia
WXCC Williamson, West Virginia
KRSV Afton, Wyoming
KRSV Afton, Wyoming
KKWY Albin, Wyoming
KLGT Buffalo, Wyoming
KQLT Casper, Wyoming
KLEN Cheyenne, Wyoming
KOLZ Cheyenne, Wyoming
KXBG Cheyenne, Wyoming
KDWY Diamondville, Wyoming
KEVA Evanston, Wyoming
KRND Fox Farm, Wyoming
KGWY Gillette, Wyoming
KFRZ Green River, Wyoming
KZMQ-FM Greybull, Wyoming
KBDY Hanna, Wyoming
KJAX Jackson, Wyoming
KSGT Jackson, Wyoming
KOVE Lander, Wyoming
KCGY Laramie, Wyoming
KWYW Lost Cabin, Wyoming
KWYY Midwest, Wyoming
KASL Newcastle, Wyoming
KYDT Pine Haven, Wyoming
KPIN Pinedale, Wyoming
KPOW Powell, Wyoming
KTAK Riverton, Wyoming
KQSW Rock Springs, Wyoming
KTGA Saratoga, Wyoming
KYTI Sheridan, Wyoming
KDNO Thermopolis, Wyoming
KERM Torrington, Wyoming
KRAN Warren Afb, Wyoming
KYCN Wheatland, Wyoming

Disco

KUHB-FM St. Paul, Alaska
KLVZ Brighton, Colorado

Easy Listening

KIXV(FM) Malvern, Arkansas
KTLO-FM Mountain Home, Arkansas
KAHM Spring Valley, Arizona
KGBA-FM Holtville, California
KIDE Hoopa, California
KGNU Denver, Colorado
KRKQ Mountain Village, Colorado
WYBC New Haven, Connecticut
WKTZ-FM Jacksonville, Florida
WKGC Southport, Florida
WKEZ-FM Tavernier, Florida
WGPC Albany, Georgia
WRFG Atlanta, Georgia
WJKG Effingham, Kentucky
WGCY Gibson City, Illinois
WLLM Lincoln, Illinois
W263BJ Loves Park, Illinois
KVSV-FM Beloit, Kansas
WJEJ Hagerstown, Maryland
WBCH-FM Hastings, Michigan
WMLQ Manistee, Michigan
WCZY-FM Mount Pleasant, Michigan
WSAM Saginaw, Michigan
KUMR Doolittle, Missouri
KYMO East Prairie, Missouri
KTXR Springfield, Missouri
WGCM-FM Gulfport, Mississippi
KZJZ St. Regis, Montana
WHLC Highlands, North Carolina
KTAT Frederick, Oklahoma
KMUN Astoria, Oregon
WSBG Stroudsburg, Pennsylvania
WFDT Aguada, Puerto Rico
WFID Rio Piedras, Puerto Rico
WGTK-FM Greenville, South Carolina
WEZV North Myrtle Beach, South Carolina
KDEZ Brandon, South Dakota
WCPH Etowah, Tennessee
WQZQ Goodlettsville, Tennessee
WQZQ-FM Goodlettsville, Tennessee
DKORC Anacortes, Washington
KGHP Gig Harbor, Washington
WBDK Algoma, Wisconsin

Ethnic

KTQX Bakersfield, California
KUBO Calexico, California
KBES Ceres, California
KHDC Chualar, California
KBIF Fresno, California
KSJV Fresno, California
KVUH Laytonville, California
KMPO Modesto, California
KSQQ Morgan Hill, California
KFSG Roseville, California
KLIB Roseville, California
KEST San Francisco, California
KZDG San Francisco, California
KLOK San Jose, California
KYAA Soquel, California
KOBO Yuba City, California
KHUI Alamosa, Colorado
WDJZ Bridgeport, Connecticut
WUST Washington, District of Columbia
WRMA Fort Lauderdale, Florida
WLQY Hollywood, Florida
WXYB Indian Rocks Beach, Florida
WURN Kendall, Florida
WMGE Miami Beach, Florida
WHSR Pompano Beach, Florida
WPIK Summerland Key, Florida
WTIS Tampa, Florida
WREK Atlanta, Georgia
WGFS Covington, Georgia
WATB Decatur, Georgia
KISH Agana, Guam
KKCR Hanalei, Hawaii
KAPA Hilo, Hawaii
KHBC Hilo, Hawaii
KCCN-FM Honolulu, Hawaii
KDNN Honolulu, Hawaii
KINE-FM Honolulu, Hawaii
KNDI Honolulu, Hawaii
KORL Honolulu, Hawaii
KPHI Honolulu, Hawaii
KITH Kapaa, Hawaii
KHEI-FM Kihei, Hawaii
KAQA Kilauea, Hawaii
KNUQ Paauilo, Hawaii
KAHU Pahala, Hawaii
KSRF Poipu, Hawaii
KAGB Waimea, Hawaii
WEEF Deerfield, Illinois
WKTA Evanston, Illinois
WNWI Oak Lawn, Illinois
WPNA Oak Park, Illinois
WNVR Vernon Hills, Illinois
KJEF Jennings, Louisiana
KLCL Lake Charles, Louisiana
KLRZ Larose, Louisiana
KANE New Iberia, Louisiana
WUNR Brookline, Massachusetts
WHTB Fall River, Massachusetts
WLYN Lynn, Massachusetts
WESX Nahant, Massachusetts
WJFD-FM New Bedford, Massachusetts
WJDA Quincy, Massachusetts
WRCA Watertown, Massachusetts
WNZK Dearborn Heights, Michigan
KFXN Minneapolis, Minnesota
KCCM-FM Moorhead, Minnesota
KPNP Watertown, Minnesota
WKRA Holly Springs, Mississippi
WABO Waynesboro, Mississippi
WWTR Bridgewater, New Jersey
WTTM Lindenwold, New Jersey
WPAT Paterson, New Jersey
WLIE Islip, New York
WRKL New City, New York
WLIM Patchogue, New York
WTOR Youngstown, New York
WOBO Batavia, Ohio
WOMP Bellaire, Ohio
KCHN Brookshire, Texas
KRVA Cockrell Hill, Texas
KYND Cypress, Texas
KZMP-FM Pilot Point, Texas
KQBO Rio Grande City, Texas
KHSE Wylie, Texas
WBBC-FM Blackstone, Virginia
WAMM Woodstock, Virginia
WSTX Christiansted, Virgin Islands
WNCH Norwich, Vermont
KXPA Bellevue, Washington
KVRI Blaine, Washington
KRPI Ferndale, Washington

Farsi

KIRN Simi Valley, California

Filipino

KNDI Honolulu, Hawaii

Gospel

KJHA Houston, Alaska
KICY Nome, Alaska
WBNM Alexander City, Alabama
WJHO Alexander City, Alabama
WHMA Anniston, Alabama
WRAB Arab, Alabama
WAGG Birmingham, Alabama
WBSA Boaz, Alabama
WQLS Camden, Alabama
WEIS Centre, Alabama
WBIB Centreville, Alabama
WQEM Columbiana, Alabama
WXJC-FM Cordova, Alabama
WMCJ & WMCJ Cullman, Alabama
WASG Daphne, Alabama
WASG Daphne, Alabama
WAGF-FM Dothan, Alabama
WOOF Dothan, Alabama
WVOB Dothan, Alabama
WRJL-FM Eva, Alabama
WJLD(AM) Fairfield, Alabama
WXQW Fairhope, Alabama
WKWL Florala, Alabama
WGEA Geneva, Alabama
WERH Hamilton, Alabama
WQHC Hanceville, Alabama
WKNG-FM Heflin, Alabama
WPIL Heflin, Alabama
WDJL Huntsville, Alabama
WEUP Huntsville, Alabama
WRJX Jackson, Alabama
WIXI Jasper, Alabama
WJLX Jasper, Alabama
WEBT Langdale, Alabama
WIRB Level Plains, Alabama
WHLW Luverne, Alabama
WGOK Mobile, Alabama
WLPR-AM Mobile, Alabama
WMGY Montgomery, Alabama
WURL Moody, Alabama
WEUV Moulton, Alabama
WJIF Opp, Alabama
WOPP Opp, Alabama
WKXK Pine Hill, Alabama
WLPR Prichard, Alabama

WVSM Rainsville, Alabama
WRMG Red Bay, Alabama
WKAX Russellville, Alabama
WZCT Scottsboro, Alabama
WZZA Tuscumbia, Alabama
WJEC Vernon, Alabama
WYLS York, Alabama
KNWA Bellefonte, Arkansas
KBRI Brinkley, Arkansas
KPZK Cabot, Arkansas
KEJA Cale, Arkansas
KNHD Camden, Arkansas
KWXT Dardanelle, Arkansas
KVDW England, Arkansas
KAOW Fort Smith, Arkansas
KENA Fort Smith, Arkansas
KTCS Fort Smith, Arkansas
KHGZ Glenwood, Arkansas
KBPB Harrison, Arkansas
KJIW-FM Helena, Arkansas
KNEA Jonesboro, Arkansas
KABF Little Rock, Arkansas
KJBN Little Rock, Arkansas
KCGS Marshall, Arkansas
KLLN Newark, Arkansas
KCAT Pine Bluff, Arkansas
KTPA Prescott, Arkansas
KOSE Wilson, Arkansas
KLTU Mammoth, Arizona
KMVP Phoenix, Arizona
KIBC Burney, California
KCPC Camino, California
KYCI Firebaugh, California
KCJH Livingston, California
KYCC Stockton, California
KDYA Vallejo, California
KLLV Breen, Colorado
KGCD Wray, Colorado
WDJZ Bridgeport, Connecticut
WQTQ Hartford, Connecticut
WYCB Washington, District of Columbia
WTJT Baker, Florida
WTCL Chattahoochee, Florida
WJCB Clewiston, Florida
WWBC Cocoa, Florida
WAGE Dogwood Lakes Estate, Florida
WIRA Fort Pierce, Florida
WTMN Gainesville, Florida
WRNE Gulf Breeze, Florida
WLVF-FM Haines City, Florida
WZAZ Jacksonville, Florida
WGRO Lake City, Florida
WTYS-FM Marianna, Florida
WRMQ Orlando, Florida
WVTJ Pensacola, Florida
WPUL South Daytona, Florida
WRXB St. Petersburg Beach, Florida
WHBT Tallahassee, Florida
WEXY Wilton Manors, Florida
WZHR Zephyrhills, Florida
WJYZ Albany, Georgia
WXAG Athens, Georgia
WAFS Atlanta, Georgia
WYZE Atlanta, Georgia
WTHB Augusta, Georgia
WGMI Bremen, Georgia
WULS Broxton, Georgia
WEAM-FM Buena Vista, Georgia
WQIL Chauncey, Georgia
WCON Cornelia, Georgia
WDPC Dallas, Georgia
WOKA-FM Douglas, Georgia
WMLT Dublin, Georgia
WXLI Dublin, Georgia
WTJH East Point, Georgia
WUFF-FM Eastman, Georgia
WLJA-FM Ellijay, Georgia
WBHB Fitzgerald, Georgia
WKLY Hartwell, Georgia
WGML Hinesville, Georgia
WVKX Irwinton, Georgia
WTLD Jesup, Georgia
WMOC Lumber City, Georgia
WPZE Mableton, Georgia
WDDO Macon, Georgia
WNEX Macon, Georgia
WFDR Manchester, Georgia
WHCG Metter, Georgia
WKUN Monroe, Georgia
WMNZ Montezuma, Georgia
WIGO Morrow, Georgia
WMTM Moultrie, Georgia
WGCN Nashville, Georgia
WRBX Reidsville, Georgia
WTNL Reidsville, Georgia
WSSJ Rincon, Georgia
WZOT Rockmart, Georgia
WROM Rome, Georgia
WSOK Savannah, Georgia
WSTT Thomasville, Georgia
WIMO Winder, Georgia
WTHB-FM Wrens, Georgia
KBBG Waterloo, Iowa
WXAN Ava, Illinois
WTSG Carlinville, Illinois
WGRB Chicago, Illinois
WSSD Chicago, Illinois
WYDS-HD2 Decatur, Illinois
WFFX(AM) Hattiesburg, Illinois
WWHN Joliet, Illinois
WSRB Lansing, Illinois
WRTK Paxton, Illinois
WVEL Pekin, Illinois
WAUZ Greensburg, Indiana
WYGS Hope, Indiana
WTLC Indianapolis, Indiana
WMYJ Martinsville, Indiana
WRFM Muncie, Indiana
WDCK Oolitic, Indiana
WYWY Barbourville, Kentucky
WAAJ Benton, Kentucky
WVHM Benton, Kentucky
WKXO Berea, Kentucky
WCVG Covington, Kentucky
WEKT Elkton, Kentucky
WIOK Falmouth, Kentucky
WFSR Harlan, Kentucky
WHBN Harrodsburg, Kentucky
WEKG Jackson, Kentucky
WKVG Jenkins, Kentucky
WVCT Keavy, Kentucky
WGWM London, Kentucky
WLLV Louisville, Kentucky
WLOU Louisville, Kentucky
WMIK Middlesboro, Kentucky
WFLW Monticello, Kentucky
WRVK Mount Vernon, Kentucky
WLOC Munfordville, Kentucky
WCGW Nicholasville, Kentucky
WYGH Paris, Kentucky
WDOC Prestonsburg, Kentucky
WCBR Richmond, Kentucky
WIDS Russell Springs, Kentucky
WBFC Stanton, Kentucky
WJCR-FM Upton, Kentucky
WEKC Williamsburg, Kentucky
WPFC Baton Rouge, Louisiana
KDLA De Ridder, Louisiana
KGGM Delhi, Louisiana
KGRM Grambling, Louisiana
KKNO Gretna, Louisiana
KJCB Lafayette, Louisiana
WBOK New Orleans, Louisiana
WYLD New Orleans, Louisiana
KTTP Pineville, Louisiana
WXOK Port Allen, Louisiana
KRUS Ruston, Louisiana
KOKA Shreveport, Louisiana
KSYB Shreveport, Louisiana
KTJZ Tallulah, Louisiana
KNCB Vivian, Louisiana
WNGB Petersham, Massachusetts
WSMA Scituate, Massachusetts
WCAO Baltimore, Maryland
WWIN Baltimore, Maryland
WLIC Frostburg, Maryland
WAIJ Grantsville, Maryland
WPRS-FM Waldorf, Maryland
WHCF Bangor, Maine
WFST Caribou, Maine
WFLT Flint, Michigan
WCTP Gagetown, Michigan
WJOG Good Hart, Michigan
WPZR Mount Clemens, Michigan
WEXL Royal Oak, Michigan
WWSJ St. Johns, Michigan
KNOF St. Paul, Minnesota
KGNA-FM Arnold, Missouri
KCWJ Blue Springs, Missouri
KNLH Cedar Hill, Missouri
KYRV Concordia, Missouri
KGNN-FM Cuba, Missouri
KNLQ Cuba, Missouri
KGGN Gladstone, Missouri
KJIR Hannibal, Missouri
KMHM Lutesville, Missouri
KMRF Marshfield, Missouri
KJAB-FM Mexico, Missouri
KNLG New Bloomfield, Missouri
KPWB Piedmont, Missouri
KNLP Potosi, Missouri
KATZ St. Louis, Missouri
KSTL St. Louis, Missouri
KALM Thayer, Missouri
KBIY Van Buren, Missouri
KGNV Washington, Missouri
WBYP Belzoni, Mississippi
WELZ Belzoni, Mississippi
WXTN Benton, Mississippi
WCHJ Brookhaven, Mississippi
WAJV Brooksville, Mississippi
WCLD Cleveland, Mississippi
WFFF Columbia, Mississippi
WNEV Friars Point, Mississippi
WJIW Greenville, Mississippi
WGRM Greenwood, Mississippi
WGRM-FM Greenwood, Mississippi
WQFX Gulfport, Mississippi
WURC Holly Springs, Mississippi
WHAL-FM Horn Lake, Mississippi
WCPC Houston, Mississippi
WNLA Indianola, Mississippi
WVSD Itta Bena, Mississippi
WHLH Jackson, Mississippi
WOAD Jackson, Mississippi
WESY Leland, Mississippi
WAKK McComb, Mississippi
WMER Meridian, Mississippi
WNBN Meridian, Mississippi
WYHL Meridian, Mississippi
WOSM Ocean Springs, Mississippi
WXHB Richton, Mississippi
WFCG Tylertown, Mississippi
KGCM Belgrade, Montana
WRCS Ahoskie, North Carolina
WTJY Asheboro, North Carolina
WZOO Asheboro, North Carolina
WPYB Benson, North Carolina
WZGM Black Mountain, North Carolina
WVOE Chadbourn, North Carolina
WRNA China Grove, North Carolina
WYZD Dobson, North Carolina
WCKB Dunn, North Carolina
WRJD Durham, North Carolina
WBXB Edenton, North Carolina
WGAI Elizabeth City, North Carolina
WFMO Fairmont, North Carolina
WSTS Fairmont, North Carolina
WIDU Fayetteville, North Carolina
WWOL Forest City, North Carolina
WNNL Fuquay-Varina, North Carolina
WYCV Granite Falls, North Carolina
WEAL Greensboro, North Carolina
WKEW Greensboro, North Carolina
WNAA Greensboro, North Carolina
WPET Greensboro, North Carolina
WKDX Hamlet, North Carolina
WPZS Harrisburg, North Carolina
WHNC Henderson, North Carolina
WPIR Hickory, North Carolina
WRKB Kannapolis, North Carolina
WKTE King, North Carolina
WELS Kinston, North Carolina
WEWO Laurinburg, North Carolina
WAGR Lumberton, North Carolina
WLPS-FM Lumberton, North Carolina
WHBK Marshall, North Carolina
WDSL Mocksville, North Carolina
WDEX Monroe, North Carolina
WIXE Monroe, North Carolina
WCIS Morganton, North Carolina
WSYD Mount Airy, North Carolina
WWDR Murfreesboro, North Carolina
WCVP Murphy, North Carolina
WAUG New Hope, North Carolina
WECR Newland, North Carolina
WCBQ Oxford, North Carolina
WGIW Pilot Mountain, North Carolina
WMFA Raeford, North Carolina
WGQR Rennert, North Carolina
WEGG Rose Hill, North Carolina
WXKL Sanford, North Carolina
WYAL Scotland Neck, North Carolina

RADIO - U.S.

WVCB Shallotte, North Carolina
WGAS South Gastonia, North Carolina
WFMI Southern Shores, North Carolina
WTAB Tabor City, North Carolina
WTLK Taylorsville, North Carolina
WJRM Troy, North Carolina
WARR Warrenton, North Carolina
WLGT Washington, North Carolina
WENC Whiteville, North Carolina
WIAM Williamston, North Carolina
WLSG Wilmington, North Carolina
WWIL Wilmington, North Carolina
WLLY Wilson, North Carolina
WBTE Windsor, North Carolina
WPOL Winston-Salem, North Carolina
WSMX Winston-Salem, North Carolina
WXRI Winston-Salem, North Carolina
WECU Winterville, North Carolina
WYNC Yanceyville, North Carolina
KHRT Minot, North Dakota
KTFJ Dakota City, Nebraska
KJLT-FM North Platte, Nebraska
KEIS York, Nebraska
WIMG Ewing, New Jersey
WEHA(FM) Port Republic, New Jersey
WFAI Salem, New Jersey
WNJC Vineland, New Jersey
KLAG Alamogordo, New Mexico
KYCM Alamogordo, New Mexico
KHII Cloudcroft, New Mexico
KKLB Ruidoso, New Mexico
KLCF Truth or Consequence, New Mexico
KEKL Mesquite, Nevada
WUFO Amherst, New York
WXXY Houghton, New York
WFWO Medina, New York
WTHE Mineola, New York
WLIB New York, New York
WOKR Remsen, New York
WKYJ Rouses Point, New York
WINW Canton, Ohio
WDBZ Cincinnati, Ohio
WHOK-FM Circleville, Ohio
WJMO Cleveland, Ohio
WGNZ Fairborn, Ohio
WCNW Fairfield, Ohio
WJTB North Ridgeville, Ohio
WABQ Painesville, Ohio
WCCD Parma, Ohio
WXIC Waverly, Ohio
WLRD Willard, Ohio
KAJT Ada, Oklahoma
KZBS Granite, Oklahoma
KPRV-FM Heavener, Oklahoma
KVAZ Henryetta, Oklahoma
KVIS Miami, Oklahoma
KTLV Midwest City, Oklahoma
KOSG Pawhuska, Oklahoma
KPRV Poteau, Oklahoma
KLRB Stuart, Oklahoma
KFXT Sulphur, Oklahoma
KTGS Tishomingo, Oklahoma
KIMY Watonga, Oklahoma
WPWA Chester, Pennsylvania
WXTC Greenville, Pennsylvania
WPPZ-FM Jenkintown, Pennsylvania
WADV Lebanon, Pennsylvania
WJSM-FM Martinsburg, Pennsylvania
WRIJ Masontown, Pennsylvania
WNAP Norristown, Pennsylvania
WPCL Northern Cambria, Pennsylvania
WOON Woonsocket, Rhode Island
WBSC Bennettsville, South Carolina
WSPX Bowman, South Carolina
WGCV Cayce, South Carolina
WGCD Chester, South Carolina
WRFE Chesterfield, South Carolina
WPJS Conway, South Carolina
WPDT Coward, South Carolina
WYNN Florence, South Carolina
WLMC Georgetown, South Carolina
WTBI-FM Greenville, South Carolina
WCZZ Greenwood, South Carolina
WPJM Greer, South Carolina
WLGI Hemingway, South Carolina
WJBS Holly Hill, South Carolina
WALD Johnsonville, South Carolina
WJNI Ladson, South Carolina
WKCL Ladson, South Carolina
WAGL Lancaster, South Carolina
WJAY Mullins, South Carolina
WGUS-FM New Ellenton, South Carolina
WKZK North Augusta, South Carolina
WPJK Orangeburg, South Carolina
WSSB-FM Orangeburg, South Carolina
WTUA Pinopolis, South Carolina
WCSZ Sans Souci, South Carolina
WPOG St. Matthews, South Carolina
WLJI Summerton, South Carolina
WWGM Alamo, Tennessee
WTKB-FM Atwood, Tennessee
WJOC Chattanooga, Tennessee
WNOO Chattanooga, Tennessee
WHUB Cookeville, Tennessee
WWOG Cookeville, Tennessee
WBEJ Elizabethton, Tennessee
WENR Englewood, Tennessee
WEMB Erwin, Tennessee
WEKR Fayetteville, Tennessee
WDEB-FM Jamestown, Tennessee
WJJT Jellico, Tennessee
WETB Johnson City, Tennessee
WKGN Knoxville, Tennessee
WKXV Knoxville, Tennessee
WLAF La Follette, Tennessee
WEEN Lafayette, Tennessee
WDXL Lexington, Tennessee
WFLI Lookout Mountain, Tennessee
WBMC McMinnville, Tennessee
WXRQ Mount Pleasant, Tennessee
WMDB Nashville, Tennessee
WNAH Nashville, Tennessee
WPRT-HD2 Philpot, Kentucky
WUAT Pikeville, Tennessee
WJBZ-FM Seymour, Tennessee
WLIJ Shelbyville, Tennessee
WSMT Sparta, Tennessee
WDEH Sweetwater, Tennessee
WECO Wartburg, Tennessee
WQSE White Bluff, Tennessee
WBOZ Woodbury, Tennessee
KAQD Abilene, Texas
KAZI Austin, Texas
KWWJ Baytown, Texas
KGHY Beaumont, Texas
KZZB Beaumont, Texas
KCOM Comanche, Texas
KYJC Commerce, Texas
KYOK Conroe, Texas
KBXD Dallas, Texas
KVOZ Del Mar Hills, Texas
KHVN Fort Worth, Texas
KKGM Fort Worth, Texas
KTXJ-FM Jasper, Texas
KJTX Jefferson, Texas
KRMY Killeen, Texas
KZZN Littlefield, Texas
KFIT Lockhart, Texas
KCHL San Antonio, Texas
KFIT EXP S San Antonio, Texas
KGLD Tyler, Texas
KZEE Weatherford, Texas
KANI Wharton, Texas
KWNS Winnsboro, Texas
KLLB West Jordan, Utah
WAMV Amherst, Virginia
WTTX-FM Appomattox, Virginia
WBTX Broadway-Timberville, Virginia
WKBY Chatham, Virginia
WCPK Chesapeake, Virginia
WXCF Clifton Forge, Virginia
WFIC Collinsville, Virginia
WKYV Colonial Heights, Virginia
WPZZ Crewe, Virginia
WKNV Fairlawn, Virginia
WGFC Floyd, Virginia
WLQM Franklin, Virginia
WWWJ Galax, Virginia
WGAT Gate City, Virginia
WNRG Grundy, Virginia
WHHV Hillsville, Virginia
WHAP Hopewell, Virginia
WLRV Lebanon, Virginia
WLLL Lynchburg, Virginia
WGH Newport News, Virginia
WTJZ Newport News, Virginia
WNVA Norton, Virginia
WSWV Pennington Gap, Virginia
WGPL Portsmouth, Virginia
WPCE Portsmouth, Virginia
WGTH-FM Richlands, Virginia
WFTH Richmond, Virginia
WNGF Swanton, Vermont
KZIZ Pacific, Washington
WGLB Elm Grove, Wisconsin
WJLS Beckley, West Virginia
WKJL Clarksburg, West Virginia
WFGH Fort Gay, West Virginia
WEMM Huntington, West Virginia
WOTR(FM) Lost Creek, West Virginia
WHJC Matewan, West Virginia
WBGS Point Pleasant, West Virginia
WPCN(FM) Point Pleasant, West Virginia
WAEY Princeton, West Virginia
WRRL Rainelle, West Virginia
WYKM Rupert, West Virginia
WVRC Spencer, West Virginia
WMLJ Summersville, West Virginia
WVGV West Union, West Virginia
KOFG Cody, Wyoming
KRKM Fort Washakie, Wyoming

Greek

WXYB Indian Rocks Beach, Florida
WPSO New Port Richey, Florida
WCGO Evanston, Illinois
WNTN Newton, Massachusetts

Japanese

KVTO Berkeley, California
KALI-FM Santa Ana, California
KZOO Honolulu, Hawaii
KREH Pecan Grove, Texas

Jazz

WJAB Huntsville, Alabama
WVAS Montgomery, Alabama
WQPR Muscle Shoals, Alabama
WAPR Selma, Alabama
WUAL-FM Tuscaloosa, Alabama
WZZA Tuscumbia, Alabama
KBSA El Dorado, Arkansas
KUAF Fayetteville, Arkansas
KASU Jonesboro, Arkansas
KABF Little Rock, Arkansas
KUAR Little Rock, Arkansas
KUAP Pine Bluff, Arkansas
KXRJ Russellville, Arkansas
KJZA Drake, Arizona
KJZZ Phoenix, Arizona
KJZP Prescott, Arizona
KUAZ Tucson, Arizona
KUAZ-FM Tucson, Arizona
KAWC-FM Yuma, Arizona
KNCA Burney, California
KRML Carmel, California
KCHO Chico, California
KSPC Claremont, California
KECG El Cerrito, California
KADO(FM) Fair Oaks, California
KFSR Fresno, California
KJJZ Indio, California
KKJZ Long Beach, California
KNSQ Mount Shasta, California
KRRF Oak View, California
KQNC Quincy, California
KFPR Redding, California
KXJZ Sacramento, California
KIFM San Diego, California
KCBX San Luis Obispo, California
KCSM San Mateo, California
KSBX Santa Barbara, California
KJZY Sebastopol, California
KKXS Shingletown, California
KXJS Sutter, California
KRZA Alamosa, Colorado
KAJX Aspen, Colorado
KCJX Carbondale, Colorado
KUVO Denver, Colorado
WQTQ Hartford, Connecticut
WDJW Somers, Connecticut
WPFW Washington, District of Columbia
WRTX Dover, Delaware
WUFT-FM Gainesville, Florida
WLOQ Indian Lakes Estates, Florida
WJUF Inverness, Florida
WCNZ Marco Island, Florida
WDNA Miami, Florida
WFLC Miami, Florida
WUCF-FM Orlando, Florida
WUSF Tampa, Florida

WTSM(FM) Woodville, Florida
WCLK Atlanta, Georgia
WAZX-FM Cleveland, Georgia
WSVH Savannah, Georgia
KPRG Agana, Guam
KIPO Honolulu, Hawaii
KCCK-FM Cedar Rapids, Iowa
KALA Davenport, Iowa
KJMC Des Moines, Iowa
KBSU-FM Boise, Idaho
KIBX Bonners Ferry, Idaho
KBSK McCall, Idaho
KISU-FM Pocatello, Idaho
KYZK Sun Valley, Idaho
KEZJ Twin Falls, Idaho
WBEZ Chicago, Illinois
WHPK-FM Chicago, Illinois
WNIJ Dekalb, Illinois
WSIE Edwardsville, Illinois
WNUR-FM Evanston, Illinois
WBEQ Morris, Illinois
WGLT Normal, Illinois
WIPA Pittsfield, Illinois
WQUB Quincy, Illinois
WUIS Springfield, Illinois
WFIU Bloomington, Indiana
WBEW Chesterton, Indiana
WVPE Elkhart, Indiana
WUEV Evansville, Indiana
WBOI Fort Wayne, Indiana
WICR Indianapolis, Indiana
WBAA West Lafayette, Indiana
KANH Emporia, Kansas
KANU Lawrence, Kansas
KJHK Lawrence, Kansas
WDAF-FM Mission, Missouri
KANV Olsburg, Kansas
KMUW Wichita, Kansas
WKYL Lawrenceburg, Kentucky
KLSA Alexandria, Louisiana
WBRH Baton Rouge, Louisiana
KRVS Lafayette, Louisiana
KEDM Monroe, Louisiana
WWNO New Orleans, Louisiana
WWOZ New Orleans, Louisiana
KDAQ Shreveport, Louisiana
KTLN Thibodaux, Louisiana
WGBH(FM) Boston, Massachusetts
WHRB Cambridge, Massachusetts
WEIB Northampton, Massachusetts
WICN Worcester, Massachusetts
WEAA Baltimore, Maryland
WYPR Baltimore, Maryland
WFWM Frostburg, Maryland
WYPO Ocean City, Maryland
WESM Princess Anne, Maryland
WMEH Bangor, Maine
WMED Calais, Maine
WMEP Camden, Maine
WMEF Fort Kent, Maine
WMEM Presque Isle, Maine
WMEW Waterville, Maine
WGVU-FM Allendale, Michigan
WCML-FM Alpena, Michigan
WUCX-FM Bay City, Michigan
WRCJ-FM Detroit, Michigan
WBLU-FM Grand Rapids, Michigan
WCMW-FM Harbor Springs, Michigan
WMUK Kalamazoo, Michigan
WLNZ Lansing, Michigan
WNMU-FM Marquette, Michigan
WCMU-FM Mount Pleasant, Michigan
WCMB-FM Oscoda, Michigan
WSGR-FM Port Huron, Michigan
WCMZ-FM Sault Ste. Marie, Michigan
WWCM Standish, Michigan
WNMC-FM Traverse City, Michigan
WBLV Twin Lake, Michigan
WGVS-FM Whitehall, Michigan
WEMU Ypsilanti, Michigan
KBEM-FM Minneapolis, Minnesota
KRCU Cape Girardeau, Missouri
KWWC-FM Columbia, Missouri
KZWV Eldon, Missouri
KJLU Jefferson City, Missouri
KRLI Malta Bend, Missouri
KXCV Maryville, Missouri
KCOZ Point Lookout, Missouri
KSEF Ste. Genevieve, Missouri
WURC Holly Springs, Mississippi
WVSD Itta Bena, Mississippi
WJSU-FM Jackson, Mississippi
KEMC Billings, Montana
KBMC Bozeman, Montana
KAPC Butte, Montana
KYWL Evergreen, Montana
KUFN Hamilton, Montana
KNMC Havre, Montana
KUHM Helena, Montana
KUKL Kalispell, Montana
KUFM Missoula, Montana
WCQS Asheville, North Carolina
WCCE Buies Creek, North Carolina
WNCU Durham, North Carolina
WFSS Fayetteville, North Carolina
WFQS Franklin, North Carolina
WNAA Greensboro, North Carolina
WSHA Raleigh, North Carolina
WSNC Winston-Salem, North Carolina
KCND Bismarck, North Dakota
KPPD Devils Lake, North Dakota
KDPR Dickinson, North Dakota
KFJM Grand Forks, North Dakota
KPRJ Jamestown, North Dakota
KMPR Minot, North Dakota
KLPR Kearney, Nebraska
KZUM Lincoln, Nebraska
KIOS-FM Omaha, Nebraska
WNEC-FM Henniker, New Hampshire
WBGO Newark, New Jersey
WRTQ Ocean City, New Jersey
WPRB Princeton, New Jersey
WNJO Toms River, New Jersey
KSJE Farmington, New Mexico
KRWG Las Cruces, New Mexico
KNCC Elko, Nevada
KBSJ Jackpot, Nevada
KUNV Las Vegas, Nevada
KUNR Reno, Nevada
WSQX-FM Binghamton, New York
WCWP Brookville, New York
WBFO Buffalo, New York
WEOS Geneva, New York
WGMC Greece, New York
WRCU-FM Hamilton, New York
WVHC Herkimer, New York
WSQA Hornell, New York
WUBJ Jamestown, New York
WHCR-FM New York, New York
WKCR-FM New York, New York
WNYC-FM New York, New York
WJZR Rochester, New York
WAER Syracuse, New York
WRMU-FM Alliance, Ohio
WBGU Bowling Green, Ohio
WCPN Cleveland, Ohio
WDPS Dayton, Ohio
WMRT Marietta, Ohio
WOBC-FM Oberlin, Ohio
WMUB Oxford, Ohio
WXTS-FM Toledo, Ohio
WCSU-FM Wilberforce, Ohio
KALU Langston, Oklahoma
KROU Spencer, Oklahoma
KSMF Ashland, Oregon
KSBA Coos Bay, Oregon
KYSJ Coos Bay, Oregon
KBVR Corvallis, Oregon
KMHD Gresham, Oregon
KSKF Klamath Falls, Oregon
KLCO Newport, Oregon
KZIU-FM Weston, Oregon
WRTI Coatesville, Pennsylvania
WRTI Ephrata, Pennsylvania
WQLN-FM Erie, Pennsylvania
WRTY Jackson Township, Pennsylvania
WRTI Philadelphia, Pennsylvania
WXAC Reading, Pennsylvania
WUSR Scranton, Pennsylvania
WVIA-FM Scranton, Pennsylvania
WJAZ Summerdale, Pennsylvania
WVYA Williamsport, Pennsylvania
WOLA Barranquitas, Puerto Rico
WELH Providence, Rhode Island
WSSB-FM Orangeburg, South Carolina
KPSD-FM Faith, South Dakota
KQSD-FM Lowry, South Dakota
KZSD-FM Martin, South Dakota
KDSD-FM Pierpont, South Dakota
KBHE-FM Rapid City, South Dakota
KTSD-FM Reliance, South Dakota
KAUR Sioux Falls, South Dakota
KUSD Vermillion, South Dakota
WBOL Bolivar, Tennessee
WFHU Henderson, Tennessee
WUOT Knoxville, Tennessee
WFMQ Lebanon, Tennessee
WUMR Memphis, Tennessee
WMOT Murfreesboro, Tennessee
WFSK-FM Nashville, Tennessee
KVLU Beaumont, Texas
KAMU-FM College Station, Texas
KETR Commerce, Texas
KEDT-FM Corpus Christi, Texas
KTEP El Paso, Texas
KMBH-FM Harlingen, Texas
KTSU Houston, Texas
KERV Kerrville, Texas
KLDN Lufkin, Texas
KHID McAllen, Texas
KNTU McKinney, Texas
KSAU Nacogdoches, Texas
KWLD Plainview, Texas
KRTU-FM San Antonio, Texas
KVRT Victoria, Texas
KMCU Wichita Falls, Texas
KUER-FM Salt Lake City, Utah
WVTU Charlottesville, Virginia
WVTW Charlottesville, Virginia
WRIQ Lexington, Virginia
WVTR Marion, Virginia
WHRV Norfolk, Virginia
WVST-FM Petersburg, Virginia
WVRU-FM Radford, Virginia
WVTF Roanoke, Virginia
WISE-FM Wise, Virginia
WRUV Burlington, Vermont
WVPS Burlington, Vermont
WRVT Rutland, Vermont
WVPA St. Johnsbury, Vermont
WVPR Windsor, Vermont
KBCS Bellevue, Washington
KZAZ Bellingham, Washington
KEWU-FM Cheney, Washington
KVIX Port Angeles, Washington
KZUU Pullman, Washington
KPBX-FM Spokane, Washington
KPLU-FM Tacoma, Washington
KYNR Toppenish, Washington
WLSU La Crosse, Wisconsin
WORT Madison, Wisconsin
WWSP Stevens Point, Wisconsin
WVPB Beckley, West Virginia
WVPW Buckhannon, West Virginia
WVPN Charleston, West Virginia
WVWV Huntington, West Virginia
WVEP Martinsburg, West Virginia
WVPM Morgantown, West Virginia
WVPG Parkersburg, West Virginia
WVNP Wheeling, West Virginia
KUWL Laramie, Wyoming
KUWY Laramie, Wyoming
KCWC-FM Riverton, Wyoming
KPRQ Sheridan, Wyoming

Korean

KVTO Berkeley, California
KMPC Los Angeles, California
KYPA Los Angeles, California
KALI-FM Santa Ana, California
KFOX Torrance, California
KHRA Honolulu, Hawaii
KREA Honolulu, Hawaii
WWRU Jersey City, New Jersey
KKDA Grand Prairie, Texas
KREH Pecan Grove, Texas
WDCT Fairfax, Virginia
KWYZ Everett, Washington
KSUH Puyallup, Washington

Light Rock

WMXC Mobile, Alabama
KRRK Desert Hills, Arizona
KSOF Dinuba, California
KJOY Stockton, California
WNDT Alachua, Florida
WLRQ-FM Cocoa, Florida
KRNQ Keokuk, Iowa
KLLT Spencer, Iowa
WQCY Quincy, Illinois
WYXB Indianapolis, Indiana
KQPR Albert Lea, Minnesota

KQCL Faribault, Minnesota
KRVY-FM Starbuck, Minnesota
KMYK Osage Beach, Missouri
WOXL-FM Biltmore Forest, North Carolina
KEXL Pierce, Nebraska
WFPG Atlantic City, New Jersey
WMKX Brookville, Pennsylvania
WZMF(AM) Nanticoke, Pennsylvania
WMXT Pamplico, South Carolina
WSNW Seneca, South Carolina
KRPX Wellington, Utah
WTHK Wilmington, Vermont
KRQT Longview, Washington

Native American

KOHN Sells, Arizona
KSUT Ignacio, Colorado
KOJB Cass Lake, Minnesota
KHEW Rocky Boy's Reserv., Montana
KINI Crookston, Nebraska
KNDN Farmington, New Mexico
KUSW Flora Vista, New Mexico
KGAK Gallup, New Mexico
KWSO Warm Springs, Oregon
KILI Porcupine, South Dakota
KWRR Ethete, Wyoming

News

KBYR Anchorage, Alaska
KENI Anchorage, Alaska
KFQD Anchorage, Alaska
KSKA Anchorage, Alaska
KAGV Big Lake, Alaska
KLAM Cordova, Alaska
KFAR Fairbanks, Alaska
KFBX Fairbanks, Alaska
KUAC Fairbanks, Alaska
KTOO Juneau, Alaska
KTKN Ketchikan, Alaska
KMXT Kodiak, Alaska
KIAM Nenana, Alaska
KNOM Nome, Alaska
KFSK Petersburg, Alaska
KCAW Sitka, Alaska
KIFW Sitka, Alaska
KSRM Soldotna, Alaska
KUHB-FM St. Paul, Alaska
KTNA Talkeetna, Alaska
KUCB Unalaska, Alaska
WDNG Anniston, Alabama
WBHM Birmingham, Alabama
WERC Birmingham, Alabama
WYDE Birmingham, Alabama
WRTR Brookwood, Alabama
WACV Coosada, Alabama
WFMH Cullman, Alabama
WHOS Decatur, Alabama
WRWA Dothan, Alabama
WWNT Dothan, Alabama
WHEP Foley, Alabama
WFPA Fort Payne, Alabama
WAAX Gadsden, Alabama
WSGN Gadsden, Alabama
WGEA Geneva, Alabama
WGYV Greenville, Alabama
WGSV Guntersville, Alabama
WERC-FM Hoover, Alabama
WBHP Huntsville, Alabama
WLRH Huntsville, Alabama
WNTM Mobile, Alabama
WLWI Montgomery, Alabama
WTSU Montgomery-Troy, Alabama
WQPR Muscle Shoals, Alabama
WAPR Selma, Alabama
WHBB Selma, Alabama
WFEB Sylacauga, Alabama
WVNN-FM Trinity, Alabama
WTBC Tuscaloosa, Alabama
WUAL-FM Tuscaloosa, Alabama
WVNA Tuscumbia, Alabama
KVRC Arkadelphia, Arkansas
KEWI Benton, Arkansas
KLCN Blytheville, Arkansas
KJMT Calico Rock, Arkansas
KCAB Dardanelle, Arkansas
KBSA El Dorado, Arkansas
KFAY Farmington, Arkansas
KUAF Fayetteville, Arkansas
KBJT Fordyce, Arkansas
KQEW Fordyce, Arkansas
KXJK Forrest City, Arkansas
KFPW Fort Smith, Arkansas
KFSW Fort Smith, Arkansas
KWHN Fort Smith, Arkansas
KURM-FM Gravette, Arkansas
KELD-FM Hampton, Arkansas
KAWW Heber Springs, Arkansas
KZHS Hot Springs, Arkansas
KZNG Hot Springs, Arkansas
KASU Jonesboro, Arkansas
KBTM Jonesboro, Arkansas
KUAR Little Rock, Arkansas
KBOK Malvern, Arkansas
KNBY Newport, Arkansas
KARV-FM Ola, Arkansas
KSMD Pangburn, Arkansas
KFFK Rogers, Arkansas
KARN-FM Sheridan, Arkansas
KWAK Stuttgart, Arkansas
KVOI Cortaro, Arizona
KAPR Douglas, Arizona
KNAU Flagstaff, Arizona
KPUB Flagstaff, Arizona
KVNA Flagstaff, Arizona
KTAR-FM Glendale, Arizona
KJAA Globe, Arizona
KNAG Grand Canyon, Arizona
KDJI Holbrook, Arizona
KUYI Hotevilla, Arizona
KNTR Lake Havasu City, Arizona
KFNN Mesa, Arizona
KNAD Page, Arizona
KLPZ Parker, Arizona
KBAQ Phoenix, Arizona
KFYI Phoenix, Arizona
KJZZ Phoenix, Arizona
KKNT Phoenix, Arizona
KNAQ Prescott, Arizona
KYCA Prescott, Arizona
KQNA Prescott Valley, Arizona
KNAA Show Low, Arizona
KTAN Sierra Vista, Arizona
KNST Tucson, Arizona
KQTH Tucson, Arizona
KUAZ Tucson, Arizona
KUAZ-FM Tucson, Arizona
KAWC Yuma, Arizona
KAWC-FM Yuma, Arizona
KBLU Yuma, Arizona
KHSU Arcata, California
KGEO Bakersfield, California
KNZR Bakersfield, California
KPRX Bakersfield, California
KSZL Barstow, California
KINS-FM Blue Lake, California
KNCA Burney, California
KCHO Chico, California
KPAY Chico, California
KZFR Chico, California
KNWZ Coachella, California
KHSR Crescent City, California
KGOE Eureka, California
KWSW Eureka, California
KVPR Fresno, California
KRLA Glendale, California
KNCO Grass Valley, California
KCRI Indio, California
KQAB(AM) Lake Isabella, California
KOSS Lancaster, California
KCAA Loma Linda, California
KFRN Long Beach, California
KFI Los Angeles, California
KNX Los Angeles, California
KPFK Los Angeles, California
KTNQ Los Angeles, California
KLDD McCloud, California
KPMO Mendocino, California
KGAM Merced, California
KYOS Merced, California
KFIV Modesto, California
KMPH Modesto, California
KCRY Mojave, California
KNRY Monterey Bay, California
KSMC Moraga, California
KMJC Mount Shasta, California
KNSQ Mount Shasta, California
KVON Napa, California
KTOX Needles, California
KQEI-FM North Highlands, California
KKSF Oakland, California
KNEW Oakland, California
KLAA Orange, California
KCRU Oxnard, California
KAZU Pacific Grove, California
KNWQ Palm Springs, California
KPSI Palm Springs, California
KDOW Palo Alto, California
KKXX Paradise, California
KPRL Paso Robles, California
KZYX Philo, California
KFBK-FM Pollock Pines, California
KWKU Pomona, California
KTIP Porterville, California
KQNC Quincy, California
KFPR Redding, California
KQMS Redding, California
KWDJ Ridgecrest, California
KNHT Rio Dell, California
KFNY Riverside, California
KQAV Rosamond, California
KFBK Sacramento, California
KXJZ Sacramento, California
KION Salinas, California
KTIE San Bernardino, California
KVCR San Bernardino, California
KCBQ San Diego, California
KFMB San Diego, California
KOGO San Diego, California
KPBS-FM San Diego, California
KCBS San Francisco, California
KFRC San Francisco, California
KLIV San Jose, California
KCBX San Luis Obispo, California
KVEC San Luis Obispo, California
KYNS San Luis Obispo, California
KCLU Santa Barbara, California
KZSB Santa Barbara, California
KSCO Santa Cruz, California
KSMA Santa Maria, California
KSMX Santa Maria, California
KUHL Santa Maria, California
KCRW Santa Monica, California
KUNX Santa Paula, California
KSRO Santa Rosa, California
KNZR-FM Shafter, California
KJPR Shasta Lake City, California
KIRN Simi Valley, California
KVML Sonora, California
KOWL South Lake Tahoe, California
KUOP Stockton, California
KWSX Stockton, California
KSUE Susanville, California
KXJS Sutter, California
KKTO Tahoe City, California
KCLU-FM Thousand Oaks, California
KVTA Ventura, California
KRZR Visalia, California
KERN Wasco-Greenacres, California
KERN Wasco-Greenacres, California
KZYZ Willits, California
KRCB-FM Windsor, California
KNYR Yreka, California
KUBA Yuba City, California
KNWH Yucca Valley, California
KRZA Alamosa, Colorado
KAJX Aspen, Colorado
KNFO Basalt, Colorado
KCFC Boulder, Colorado
KRLN Canon City, Colorado
KCJX Carbondale, Colorado
KRDO Colorado Springs, Colorado
KZNT Colorado Springs, Colorado
KVFC Cortez, Colorado
KPYR Craig, Colorado
KRAI Craig, Colorado
KCFR-FM Denver, Colorado
KHOW Denver, Colorado
KNUS Denver, Colorado
KOA Denver, Colorado
KVOQ(AM) Denver, Colorado
KDGO Durango, Colorado
KFTM Fort Morgan, Colorado
KDNK Glenwood Springs, Colorado
KNZZ Grand Junction, Colorado
KPRN Grand Junction, Colorado
KFKA Greeley, Colorado
KUNC Greeley, Colorado
KHNC Johnstown, Colorado
KECC La Junta, Colorado
KPRH Montrose, Colorado
KVMT Montrose, Colorado
KWUF Pagosa Springs, Colorado

KVNF Paonia, Colorado
KCFP Pueblo, Colorado
KCSJ Pueblo, Colorado
KGFT Pueblo, Colorado
KKPC Pueblo, Colorado
KRDO-FM Security, Colorado
KRNC Steamboat Springs, Colorado
KPRE Vail, Colorado
KCOL Wellington, Colorado
WPRX Bristol, Connecticut
WSHU-FM Fairfield, Connecticut
WGCH Greenwich, Connecticut
WQAQ Hamden, Connecticut
WQUN Hamden, Connecticut
WDRC Hartford, Connecticut
WPOP Hartford, Connecticut
WTIC Hartford, Connecticut
WZBG Litchfield, Connecticut
WNEZ Manchester, Connecticut
WMMW Meriden, Connecticut
WELI New Haven, Connecticut
WNLK Norwalk, Connecticut
WHDD-FM Sharon, Connecticut
WEDW-FM Stamford, Connecticut
WSTC Stamford, Connecticut
WSNG Torrington, Connecticut
WATR Waterbury, Connecticut
WWCO Waterbury, Connecticut
WSHU Westport, Connecticut
WILI Willimantic, Connecticut
WAMU Washington, District of Columbia
WFED Washington, District of Columbia
WPFW Washington, District of Columbia
WTOP-FM Washington, District of Columbia
WDOV Dover, Delaware
WGMD Rehoboth Beach, Delaware
WDEL Wilmington, Delaware
WILM Wilmington, Delaware
WFLN Arcadia, Florida
WTWB Auburndale, Florida
WWJB Brooksville, Florida
WNZF Bunnell, Florida
WKFL Bushnell, Florida
WTAN Clearwater, Florida
WMMV Cocoa, Florida
WJTK Columbia City, Florida
WNDB Daytona Beach, Florida
WYND Deland, Florida
WNWF Destin, Florida
WENG Englewood, Florida
WMYR Fort Myers, Florida
WJNX Fort Pierce, Florida
WQCS Fort Pierce, Florida
WFTW Fort Walton Beach, Florida
WDVH Gainesville, Florida
WRUF Gainesville, Florida
WNRP Gulf Breeze, Florida
WXYB Indian Rocks Beach, Florida
WJUF Inverness, Florida
WBOB(AM) Jacksonville, Florida
WJCT-FM Jacksonville, Florida
WJBW Jupiter, Florida
WYBX Key West, Florida
WBXY La Crosse, Florida
WLKF Lakeland, Florida
WPBR Lantana, Florida
WWBA Largo, Florida
WFFG Marathon, Florida
WKWM Marathon, Florida
WGUF Marco, Florida
WMMB Melbourne, Florida
WAQI Miami, Florida
WIOD Miami, Florida
WLRN-FM Miami, Florida
WQBA Miami, Florida
WSUA Miami, Florida
WSKY-FM Micanopy, Florida
WEBY Milton, Florida
WPSO New Port Richey, Florida
WKAT North Miami, Florida
WDBO Orlando, Florida
WMFE-FM Orlando, Florida
WELE Ormond Beach, Florida
WFSW Panama City, Florida
WKGC-FM Panama City, Florida
WLTG Panama City, Florida
WFLF-FM Parker, Florida
WCOA Pensacola, Florida
WCOA-FM Pensacola, Florida
WUWF Pensacola, Florida
WAMT Pine Castle Sky Lake, Florida
WFLF Pine Hills, Florida
WPSL Port St. Lucie, Florida
WCCF Punta Gorda, Florida
WDEO-FM San Carlos Park, Florida
WLSS Sarasota, Florida
WSRQ Sarasota, Florida
WFOY St. Augustine, Florida
WIWA St. Cloud, Florida
WSTU Stuart, Florida
WZAB Sweetwater, Florida
WANM Tallahassee, Florida
WFSU-FM Tallahassee, Florida
WTAL Tallahassee, Florida
WFLA Tampa, Florida
WHNZ Tampa, Florida
WUSF Tampa, Florida
WIXC Titusville, Florida
WAXE Vero Beach, Florida
WZTA Vero Beach, Florida
WBZT West Palm Beach, Florida
WJNO West Palm Beach, Florida
WPBI(FM) West Palm Beach, Florida
WALG Albany, Georgia
WUNV Albany, Georgia
WLTA Alpharetta, Georgia
WUGA Athens, Georgia
WAOK Atlanta, Georgia
WGKA Atlanta, Georgia
WGST Atlanta, Georgia
WSB Atlanta, Georgia
WGAC Augusta, Georgia
WGIG Brunswick, Georgia
WWIO-FM Brunswick, Georgia
WGRA Cairo, Georgia
WLBB Carrollton, Georgia
WUWG Carrollton, Georgia
WBHF Cartersville, Georgia
WYXC Cartersville, Georgia
WNGH-FM Chatsworth, Georgia
WRBN Clayton, Georgia
WAZX-FM Cleveland, Georgia
WMUM-FM Cochran, Georgia
WDAK Columbus, Georgia
WTJB Columbus, Georgia
WSRM Coosa, Georgia
WNGU Dahlonega, Georgia
WBLJ Dalton, Georgia
WPPR Demorest, Georgia
WSEM Donalsonville, Georgia
WCFO East Point, Georgia
WUFF-FM Eastman, Georgia
WJWV Fort Gaines, Georgia
WDUN Gainesville, Georgia
WHIE Griffin, Georgia
WKEU Griffin, Georgia
WGAC-FM Harlem, Georgia
WCEH Hawkinsville, Georgia
WVCC Hogansville, Georgia
WSIZ-FM Jacksonville, Georgia
WVGA Lakeland, Georgia
WLHR-FM Lavonia, Georgia
WMAC Macon, Georgia
WMVG Milledgeville, Georgia
WMTM Moultrie, Georgia
WCNN North Atlanta, Georgia
WGPB Rome, Georgia
WLAQ Rome, Georgia
WRGA Rome, Georgia
WBMQ Savannah, Georgia
WSVH Savannah, Georgia
WTKS Savannah, Georgia
WWIO St. Marys, Georgia
WWNS Statesboro, Georgia
WJAT Swainsboro, Georgia
WNEG Toccoa, Georgia
WKWN Trenton, Georgia
WWET Valdosta, Georgia
WJSP-FM Warm Springs, Georgia
WWGA(AM) Waycross, Georgia
WXVS Waycross, Georgia
WCGA Woodbine, Georgia
KGUM Hagatna, Guam
KQNG Eleele, Hawaii
KHNU Hilo, Hawaii
KPUA Hilo, Hawaii
KHPR Honolulu, Hawaii
KHVH Honolulu, Hawaii
KIKI Honolulu, Hawaii
KIPO Honolulu, Hawaii
KPRP Honolulu, Hawaii
KWAI Honolulu, Hawaii
KAOI Kihei, Hawaii
KKUA Wailuku, Hawaii
KASI Ames, Iowa
KJAN Atlantic, Iowa
KWBG Boone, Iowa
KUNI Cedar Falls, Iowa
WMT Cedar Rapids, Iowa
WOC Davenport, Iowa
KLNI Decorah, Iowa
WHO Des Moines, Iowa
WDBQ Dubuque, Iowa
KIOW Forest City, Iowa
KGRN Grinnell, Iowa
KXIC Iowa City, Iowa
WSUI Iowa City, Iowa
KIFG-FM Iowa Falls, Iowa
KOKX Keokuk, Iowa
KLEM Le Mars, Iowa
KFJB Marshalltown, Iowa
KRNI Mason City, Iowa
KICJ(FM) Mitchellville, Iowa
KCOB Newton, Iowa
KOEL Oelwein, Iowa
KOJI Okoboji, Iowa
KPVL Postville, Iowa
KIWA Sheldon, Iowa
KMA Shenandoah, Iowa
KSCJ Sioux City, Iowa
KWIT Sioux City, Iowa
KCII Washington, Iowa
KCII-FM Washington, Iowa
KXEL Waterloo, Iowa
KBSU-FM Boise, Idaho
KBSX Boise, Idaho
KBFI Bonners Ferry, Idaho
KIBX Bonners Ferry, Idaho
KBSY Burley, Idaho
KNWO Cottonwood, Idaho
KID Idaho Falls, Idaho
KIKX Ketchum, Idaho
KBSM McCall, Idaho
KBSQ McCall, Idaho
KRFA-FM Moscow, Idaho
KIDO Nampa, Idaho
KWEI Notus, Idaho
KEGE Pocatello, Idaho
KISU-FM Pocatello, Idaho
KWIK Pocatello, Idaho
KSPT Sandpoint, Idaho
KBSS Sun Valley, Idaho
KEZJ Twin Falls, Idaho
KLIX Twin Falls, Idaho
WRMJ Aledo, Illinois
WBGZ Alton, Illinois
WTIM Assumption, Illinois
WCIL Carbondale, Illinois
WDWS Champaign, Illinois
KSGM Chester, Illinois
WBBM Chicago, Illinois
WBEZ Chicago, Illinois
WCRX Chicago, Illinois
WGN(AM) Chicago, Illinois
WIND Chicago, Illinois
WRTO Chicago, Illinois
WHOW Clinton, Illinois
WDAN Danville, Illinois
WSOY Decatur, Illinois
WLBK Dekalb, Illinois
WNIJ Dekalb, Illinois
WIXN Dixon, Illinois
WCRA Effingham, Illinois
WCRA Effingham, Illinois
WCRA-FM Effingham, Illinois
WCFS Elmwood Park, Illinois
WGNN Fisher, Illinois
WNIE Freeport, Illinois
WKYX-FM Golconda, Illinois
WJPF Herrin, Illinois
WJIL Jacksonville, Illinois
WLDS Jacksonville, Illinois
WVLI Kankakee, Illinois
WKEI Kewanee, Illinois
WNIW La Salle, Illinois
WLPO Lasalle, Illinois
WSMI Litchfield, Illinois
WIUM Macomb, Illinois
WGGH Marion, Illinois
WLBH Mattoon, Illinois
WBEQ Morris, Illinois
WCSJ Morris, Illinois
WCSJ-FM Morris, Illinois

WVSI Mt. Vernon, Illinois
WINI Murphysboro, Illinois
WUSI Olney, Illinois
WCMY Ottawa, Illinois
WCBU Peoria, Illinois
WMBD Peoria, Illinois
WIPA Pittsfield, Illinois
WGEM Quincy, Illinois
WGEM-FM Quincy, Illinois
WQUB Quincy, Illinois
WTAD Quincy, Illinois
WRHL Rochelle, Illinois
WVIK Rock Island, Illinois
WROK Rockford, Illinois
WJBD-FM Salem, Illinois
WCCI Savanna, Illinois
WHCO Sparta, Illinois
WTAX Springfield, Illinois
WUIS Springfield, Illinois
WNIQ Sterling, Illinois
WSDR Sterling, Illinois
WTIM Taylorville, Illinois
WTIM Taylorville, Illinois
WILL Urbana, Illinois
WIUW Warsaw, Illinois
WKRS Waukegan, Illinois
WFRX West Frankfort, Illinois
WBSB Anderson, Indiana
WHBU Anderson, Indiana
WBIW Bedford, Indiana
WZBD Berne, Indiana
WFHB Bloomington, Indiana
WFIU Bloomington, Indiana
WGCL Bloomington, Indiana
WBEW Chesterton, Indiana
WCSI Columbus, Indiana
WTRC Elkhart, Indiana
WVPE Elkhart, Indiana
WGBF Evansville, Indiana
WNIN-FM Evansville, Indiana
WBOI Fort Wayne, Indiana
WOWO Fort Wayne, Indiana
WOWO-FM Fort Wayne, Indiana
WLTH Gary, Indiana
WTRE Greensburg, Indiana
WBSH Hagerstown, Indiana
WJOB Hammond, Indiana
WFYI-FM Indianapolis, Indiana
WIBC Indianapolis, Indiana
WIOU Kokomo, Indiana
WSAL Logansport, Indiana
WLPR-FM Lowell, Indiana
WBSW Marion, Indiana
WBST Muncie, Indiana
WFIA-FM New Albany, Indiana
WNDA New Albany, Indiana
WBSJ Portland, Indiana
WRAY Princeton, Indiana
WZZB Seymour, Indiana
WAKE Valparaiso, Indiana
WBAA West Lafayette, Indiana
WBAA-FM West Lafayette, Indiana
KGGF AM Coffeyville, Kansas
KDCC Dodge City, Kansas
KGNO Dodge City, Kansas
KVOE Emporia, Kansas
KIUL Garden City, Kansas
KHCT Great Bend, Kansas
KVGB Great Bend, Kansas
KZAN Hays, Kansas
KZNA Hill City, Kansas
KHCC-FM Hutchinson, Kansas
KLWN Lawrence, Kansas
KSCB Liberal, Kansas
KMAN Manhattan, Kansas
KKAN Phillipsburg, Kansas
KHCD Salina, Kansas
KSAL Salina, Kansas
KYUL Scott City, Kansas
KMAJ Topeka, Kansas
WIBW Topeka, Kansas
KLEY Wellington, Kansas
KMUW Wichita, Kansas
KNSS Wichita, Kansas
KQAM Wichita, Kansas
WKCT Bowling Green, Kentucky
WKYU-FM Bowling Green, Kentucky
WSFE Burnside, Kentucky
WCTT Corbin, Kentucky
WEKF Corbin, Kentucky
WKDP Corbin, Kentucky
WCPM Cumberland, Kentucky
WHIR Danville, Kentucky
WKUE Elizabethtown, Kentucky
WEKH Hazard, Kentucky
WKPB Henderson, Kentucky
WNKU Highland Heights, Kentucky
WHOP Hopkinsville, Kentucky
WLAP Lexington, Kentucky
WUKY Lexington, Kentucky
WVLK Lexington, Kentucky
WFPL Louisville, Kentucky
WGTK Louisville, Kentucky
WHAS Louisville, Kentucky
WKJK Louisville, Kentucky
WTTL Madisonville, Kentucky
WNGO Mayfield, Kentucky
WKMS-FM Murray, Kentucky
WNBS Murray, Kentucky
WVJS Owensboro, Kentucky
WKYX Paducah, Kentucky
WKYH Paintsville, Kentucky
WEKU Richmond, Kentucky
WVKY Shelbyville, Kentucky
WDCL-FM Somerset, Kentucky
KLSA Alexandria, Louisiana
WJBO Baton Rouge, Louisiana
WRKF Baton Rouge, Louisiana
KEUN Eunice, Louisiana
WWL-FM Kenner, Louisiana
KVOL Lafayette, Louisiana
KAOK Lake Charles, Louisiana
KEDM Monroe, Louisiana
KMLB Monroe, Louisiana
KNOC Natchitoches, Louisiana
WGSO New Orleans, Louisiana
WRBH New Orleans, Louisiana
WRNO-FM New Orleans, Louisiana
WWL New Orleans, Louisiana
WWNO New Orleans, Louisiana
KSLO Opelousas, Louisiana
KDAQ Shreveport, Louisiana
KEEL Shreveport, Louisiana
KTLN Thibodaux, Louisiana
KNCB Vivian, Louisiana
WHAB Acton, Massachusetts
WPNI Amherst, Massachusetts
WARL Attleboro, Massachusetts
WBUR-FM Boston, Massachusetts
WBZ Boston, Massachusetts
WGBH(FM) Boston, Massachusetts
WILD Boston, Massachusetts
WXBR Brockton, Massachusetts
WBNW Concord, Massachusetts
WHNP East Longmeadow, Massachusetts
WSAR Fall River, Massachusetts
WGAW Gardner, Massachusetts
WBOQ Gloucester, Massachusetts
WAMQ Great Barrington, Massachusetts
WCAP Lowell, Massachusetts
WVBF Middleborough Center, Massachusetts
WMLN-FM Milton, Massachusetts
WNAN Nantucket, Massachusetts
WBSM New Bedford, Massachusetts
WXKS Newton, Massachusetts
WDIS Norfolk, Massachusetts
WESO Southbridge, Massachusetts
WHYN Springfield, Massachusetts
WGTX Truro, Massachusetts
WBUR West Yarmouth, Massachusetts
WXTK West Yarmouth, Massachusetts
WNNZ Westfield, Massachusetts
WCAI Woods Hole, Massachusetts
WTAG Worcester, Massachusetts
WEAA Baltimore, Maryland
WYPR Baltimore, Maryland
WNEW Bowie, District of Columbia
WTLP Braddock Heights, Maryland
WCBC Cumberland, Maryland
WFMD Frederick, Maryland
WYPF Frederick, Maryland
WJSS Havre De Grace, Maryland
WSDL Ocean City, Maryland
WYPO Ocean City, Maryland
WICO Salisbury, Maryland
WJDY Salisbury, Maryland
WVQM Augusta, Maine
WMEH Bangor, Maine
WMED Calais, Maine
WMEP Camden, Maine
WCXU Caribou, Maine
WMEF Fort Kent, Maine
WVOM-FM Howland, Maine
WCXX Madawaska, Maine
WJCX Pittsfield, Maine
WGAN Portland, Maine
WMEA Portland, Maine
WEGP Presque Isle, Maine
WMEM Presque Isle, Maine
WCXV Van Buren, Maine
WNZS Veazie, Maine
WMEW Waterville, Maine
WABJ Adrian, Michigan
WGVU-FM Allendale, Michigan
WCML-FM Alpena, Michigan
WZTK Alpena, Michigan
WUOM Ann Arbor, Michigan
WBCK-FM Battle Creek, Michigan
WUCX-FM Bay City, Michigan
WHFB Benton Harbor-St. Jo, Michigan
WBRN Big Rapids, Michigan
WMKT Charlevoix, Michigan
WDET-FM Detroit, Michigan
WDTK Detroit, Michigan
WWJ Detroit, Michigan
WICV East Jordan, Michigan
WKAR East Lansing, Michigan
WKAR-FM East Lansing, Michigan
WCHT Escanaba, Michigan
WWCK Flint, Michigan
WBLU-FM Grand Rapids, Michigan
WOOD Grand Rapids, Michigan
WVGR Grand Rapids, Michigan
WGLM Greenville, Michigan
WMPL Hancock, Michigan
WCMW-FM Harbor Springs, Michigan
WGGL-FM Houghton, Michigan
WIAA Interlochen, Michigan
WMIQ Iron Mountain, Michigan
WIAN Ishpeming, Michigan
WKMI Kalamazoo, Michigan
WMUK Kalamazoo, Michigan
WGVU Kentwood, Michigan
WJNL Kingsley, Michigan
WILS Lansing, Michigan
WLMN Manistee, Michigan
WDMJ Marquette, Michigan
WNMU-FM Marquette, Michigan
WAVC Mio, Michigan
WCMU-FM Mount Pleasant, Michigan
WSHN Munising, Michigan
WGVS Muskegon, Michigan
WKBZ Muskegon, Michigan
WOOD-FM Muskegon, Michigan
WCMB-FM Oscoda, Michigan
WSGW Saginaw, Michigan
WMIC Sandusky, Michigan
WKNW Sault Sainte Marie, Michigan
WCMZ-FM Sault Ste. Marie, Michigan
WWCM Standish, Michigan
WICA Traverse City, Michigan
WTCM Traverse City, Michigan
WBLV Twin Lake, Michigan
WGVS-FM Whitehall, Michigan
WEMU Ypsilanti, Michigan
WPNW Zeeland, Michigan
KASM Albany, Minnesota
KNSE Austin, Minnesota
WWWI Baxter, Minnesota
KNBJ Bemidji, Minnesota
KBPN Brainerd, Minnesota
KRWC Buffalo, Minnesota
WIRN Buhl, Minnesota
WSCN Cloquet, Minnesota
KNSR Collegeville, Minnesota
KDLM Detroit Lakes, Minnesota
WEBC Duluth, Minnesota
WIRC Ely, Minnesota
KSUM Fairmont, Minnesota
KDHL Faribault, Minnesota
KBRF Fergus Falls, Minnesota
KNWF Fergus Falls, Minnesota
WLSN Grand Marais, Minnesota
KDWA Hastings, Minnesota
WGRH Hinckley, Minnesota
KDUZ Hutchinson, Minnesota
KXLC La Crescent, Minnesota
KLTF Little Falls, Minnesota
KTIS Minneapolis, Minnesota
KTLK Minneapolis, Minnesota
WCCO Minneapolis, Minnesota
WWTC Minneapolis, Minnesota
KNOW-FM Minneapolis-St. Paul, Minnesota

KCCD Moorhead, Minnesota
KMRS Morris, Minnesota
KCHK New Prague, Minnesota
WWWI-FM Pillager, Minnesota
WCMP Pine City, Minnesota
WCMP-FM Pine City, Minnesota
KLOH Pipestone, Minnesota
KRFI Redwood Falls, Minnesota
KROC Rochester, Minnesota
KRXW Roseau, Minnesota
KNSI St. Cloud, Minnesota
WJON St. Cloud, Minnesota
KKAQ Thief River Falls, Minnesota
KNTN Thief River Falls, Minnesota
KTRF Thief River Falls, Minnesota
KWLM Willmar, Minnesota
KDOM Windom, Minnesota
KDOM-FM Windom, Minnesota
KWNO Winona, Minnesota
KWOA Worthington, Minnesota
KNSW Worthington-Marshall, Minnesota
KGNA-FM Arnold, Missouri
KSGF-FM Ash Grove, Missouri
KSWM Aurora, Missouri
KKOZ-FM Ava, Missouri
KAAN Bethany, Missouri
KYOO Bolivar, Missouri
KAPE Cape Girardeau, Missouri
KRCU Cape Girardeau, Missouri
KZIM Cape Girardeau, Missouri
KCHI Chillicothe, Missouri
KRNW Chillicothe, Missouri
KBIA Columbia, Missouri
KCIU Columbia, Missouri
KFRU Columbia, Missouri
KOPN Columbia, Missouri
KGNN-FM Cuba, Missouri
KREI Farmington, Missouri
KSSZ Fayette, Missouri
KJFF Festus, Missouri
KHMO Hannibal, Missouri
KLIK Jefferson City, Missouri
KWOS Jefferson City, Missouri
KCUR-FM Kansas City, Missouri
KKFI Kansas City, Missouri
KMBZ Kansas City, Missouri
KLWT Lebanon, Missouri
KNIM Maryville, Missouri
KXCV Maryville, Missouri
KXEO Mexico, Missouri
KRMS Osage Beach, Missouri
KFMO Park Hills, Missouri
KBDZ Perryville, Missouri
KCOZ Point Lookout, Missouri
KSMS-FM Point Lookout, Missouri
KWOC Poplar Bluff, Missouri
KMST Rolla, Missouri
KSMO Salem, Missouri
KSIS Sedalia, Missouri
KQMO Shell Knob, Missouri
KSIM Sikeston, Missouri
KLFJ Springfield, Missouri
KSGF Springfield, Missouri
KSMU Springfield, Missouri
KTTR FM St. James, Missouri
KMOX St. Louis, Missouri
KTRS St. Louis, Missouri
KWMU St. Louis, Missouri
KSEF Ste. Genevieve, Missouri
KTUI Sullivan, Missouri
KSAR Thayer, Missouri
KTTN-FM Trenton, Missouri
KGNV Washington, Missouri
KSMW West Plains, Missouri
KWPM West Plains, Missouri
KUKU Willow Springs, Missouri
WAMY Amory, Mississippi
WMAH-FM Biloxi, Mississippi
WMAE-FM Booneville, Mississippi
WMAU-FM Bude, Mississippi
WCJU Columbia, Mississippi
WADI Corinth, Mississippi
WMAO-FM Greenwood, Mississippi
WHSY Hattiesburg, Mississippi
WLAU Heidelberg, Mississippi
WURC Holly Springs, Mississippi
WTCD Indianola, Mississippi
WJDX Jackson, Mississippi
WJSU-FM Jackson, Mississippi
WMPN-FM Jackson, Mississippi
WMXI Laurel, Mississippi
WJZD-FM Long Beach, Mississippi
WKBB Mantee, Mississippi
WALT Meridian, Mississippi
WMAW-FM Meridian, Mississippi
WMOX Meridian, Mississippi
WMAB-FM Mississippi State, Mississippi
WBUV Moss Point, Mississippi
WNAT Natchez, Mississippi
WNAU New Albany, Mississippi
WMAV-FM Oxford, Mississippi
WJNT Pearl, Mississippi
WFMM Sumrall, Mississippi
KBLG Billings, Montana
KBUL Billings, Montana
KEMC Billings, Montana
KBMC Bozeman, Montana
KMMS Bozeman, Montana
KAPC Butte, Montana
KGVA Fort Belknap Agency, Montana
KGPR Great Falls, Montana
KQDI Great Falls, Montana
KLYQ Hamilton, Montana
KUFN Hamilton, Montana
KHDN Hardin, Montana
KBLL Helena, Montana
KCAP Helena, Montana
KUHM Helena, Montana
KGEZ Kalispell, Montana
KOFI Kalispell, Montana
KUKL Kalispell, Montana
KBSR Laurel, Montana
KYPF Stanford, Montana
WSPC Albemarle, North Carolina
WZKY Albemarle, North Carolina
WCQS Asheville, North Carolina
WWNC Asheville, North Carolina
WTKF Atlantic, North Carolina
WBJD Atlantic Beach, North Carolina
WXIT Blowing Rock, North Carolina
WUDE Bolivia, North Carolina
WATA Boone, North Carolina
WCHL Chapel Hill, North Carolina
WUNC Chapel Hill, North Carolina
WBT Charlotte, North Carolina
WFAE Charlotte, North Carolina
WNCU Durham, North Carolina
WFNC Fayetteville, North Carolina
WFSS Fayetteville, North Carolina
WIDU Fayetteville, North Carolina
WFQS Franklin, North Carolina
WFSC Franklin, North Carolina
WGBR Goldsboro, North Carolina
WSML Graham, North Carolina
WHKY Hickory, North Carolina
WJNC Jacksonville, North Carolina
WKNS Kinston, North Carolina
WJRI Lenoir, North Carolina
WLXN Lexington, North Carolina
WOBX-FM Manteo, North Carolina
WUND-FM Manteo, North Carolina
WYQS Mars Hill, North Carolina
WCVP Murphy, North Carolina
WTEB New Bern, North Carolina
WZNB New Bern, North Carolina
WAUG New Hope, North Carolina
WGCR Pisgah Forest, North Carolina
WFNL Raleigh, North Carolina
WPTF Raleigh, North Carolina
WRQM Rocky Mount, North Carolina
WCAB Rutherfordton, North Carolina
WSTP Salisbury, North Carolina
WNCA Siler City, North Carolina
WEEB Southern Pines, North Carolina
WNCW Spindale, North Carolina
WSIC Statesville, North Carolina
WTXY Whiteville, North Carolina
WHQR Wilmington, North Carolina
WFDD Winston-Salem, North Carolina
WSJS Winston-Salem, North Carolina
WSNC Winston-Salem, North Carolina
KCND Bismarck, North Dakota
KFYR Bismarck, North Dakota
KLXX Bismarck-Mandan, North Dakota
KDAK Carrington, North Dakota
KDLR Devils Lake, North Dakota
KDPR Dickinson, North Dakota
KFBN Fargo, North Dakota
WDAY Fargo, North Dakota
KNOX Grand Forks, North Dakota
KPRJ Jamestown, North Dakota
KNDK Langdon, North Dakota
KQLX Lisbon, North Dakota
KHRT Minot, North Dakota
KMPR Minot, North Dakota
KDDR Oakes, North Dakota
KOVC Valley City, North Dakota
KEYZ Williston, North Dakota
KNCY-FM Auburn, Nebraska
KWBE Beatrice, Nebraska
KGMT Fairbury, Nebraska
KHUB Fremont, Nebraska
KRGI Grand Island, Nebraska
KGFW Kearney, Nebraska
KLIN Lincoln, Nebraska
WJAG Norfolk, Nebraska
KODY North Platte, Nebraska
KFAB Omaha, Nebraska
KIOS-FM Omaha, Nebraska
KNEB Scottsbluff, Nebraska
KTIC West Point, Nebraska
WEVO(FM) Concord, New Hampshire
WKXL Concord, New Hampshire
WTSN Dover, New Hampshire
WXEX Exeter, New Hampshire
WEVH Hanover, New Hampshire
WTSL Hanover, New Hampshire
WTPL Hillsboro, New Hampshire
WEVJ Jackson, New Hampshire
WEVN Keene, New Hampshire
WKBK Keene, New Hampshire
WZBK Keene, New Hampshire
WUVR Lebanon, New Hampshire
WGIR Manchester, New Hampshire
WEVS Nashua, New Hampshire
WSMN Nashua, New Hampshire
WNTK-FM New London, New Hampshire
WPKX Rochester, New Hampshire
WQSO Rochester, New Hampshire
WMVX Salem, New Hampshire
WASR Wolfeboro, New Hampshire
WNJN-FM Atlantic City, New Jersey
WNJS-FM Berlin, New Jersey
WNJB-FM Bridgeton, New Jersey
WNJZ Cape May Court House, New Jersey
WNYM Hackensack, New Jersey
WRNJ Hackettstown, New Jersey
WBJB-FM Lincroft, New Jersey
WNJM Manahawkin, New Jersey
WNJY Netcong, New Jersey
WVNJ Oakland, New Jersey
WIBG Ocean City/Somers Po, New Jersey
WVPH Piscataway, New Jersey
WOND Pleasantville, New Jersey
WNJP Sussex, New Jersey
WNJT-FM Trenton, New Jersey
KDEF Albuquerque, New Mexico
KUNM Albuquerque, New Mexico
KRRT Arroyo Seco, New Mexico
KWKA Clovis, New Mexico
KENN Farmington, New Mexico
KSJE Farmington, New Mexico
KUSW Flora Vista, New Mexico
KGLP Gallup, New Mexico
KYKK Humble City, New Mexico
KPZA-FM Jal, New Mexico
KOBE Las Cruces, New Mexico
KRWG Las Cruces, New Mexico
KSNM Las Cruces, New Mexico
KNMX Las Vegas, New Mexico
KRSN Los Alamos, New Mexico
KMTH Maljamar, New Mexico
KSEL Portales, New Mexico
KBIM Roswell, New Mexico
KRUI Ruidoso Downs, New Mexico
KLBU Santa Fe, New Mexico
KTRC Santa Fe, New Mexico
KNCC Elko, Nevada
KTSN Elko, Nevada
KDWN Las Vegas, Nevada
KWPR Lund, Nevada
KXNT North Las Vegas, Nevada
KLNR Panaca, Nevada
KNIH Paradise, Nevada
KUNR Reno, Nevada
KBZZ Sparks, Nevada
KTPH Tonopah, Nevada
KWNA Winnemucca, Nevada
WAMC-FM Albany, New York
WGY-FM Albany, New York
WROW Albany, New York
WVTL Amsterdam, New York
WAUB Auburn, New York

WYSL Avon, New York
WBTA Batavia, New York
WNBF Binghamton, New York
WSKG-FM Binghamton, New York
WSQX-FM Binghamton, New York
WCWP Brookville, New York
WBEN Buffalo, New York
WDCZ Buffalo, New York
WCAN Canajoharie, New York
WCGR Canandaigua, New York
WENI Corning, New York
WSQE Corning, New York
WWLE Cornwall, New York
WDOE Dunkirk, New York
WJIP Ellenville, New York
WENY Elmira, New York
WGSU Geneseo, New York
WEOS Geneva, New York
WGVA Geneva, New York
WWSC Glens Falls, New York
WLEA Hornell, New York
WSQA Hornell, New York
WWLZ Horseheads, New York
WHCU Ithaca, New York
WSQG-FM Ithaca, New York
WJTN Jamestown, New York
WUBJ Jamestown, New York
WJFF Jeffersonville, New York
WAMK Kingston, New York
WGHQ Kingston, New York
WLVL Lockport, New York
WLLG Lowville, New York
WOSR Middletown, New York
WADO New York, New York
WCBS New York, New York
WFUV New York, New York
WINS New York, New York
WOR New York, New York
WSUF Noyack, New York
WOEN Olean, New York
WMCR Oneida, New York
WSQC-FM Oneonta, New York
WNYO Oswego, New York
WEBO Owego, New York
WCEL Plattsburgh, New York
WKIP Poughkeepsie, New York
WRCR Ramapo, New York
WRCN-FM Riverhead, New York
WBEE-FM Rochester, New York
WHAM Rochester, New York
WKAL Rome, New York
WNBZ Saranac Lake, New York
WGY Schenectady, New York
WSYR Solvay, New York
WRLI-FM Southampton, New York
WUSB Stony Brook, New York
WAER Syracuse, New York
WSYR Syracuse, New York
WANC Ticonderoga, New York
WIBX Utica, New York
WCJW Warsaw, New York
WTNY Watertown, New York
WUAM Watervliet, New York
WAKR Akron, Ohio
WHLO Akron, Ohio
WYBL Ashtabula, Ohio
WATH Athens, Ohio
WOUB Athens, Ohio
WBLL Bellefontaine, Ohio
WCVV Belpre, Ohio
WGBE Bryan, Ohio
WAIS Buchtel, Ohio
WOUC-FM Cambridge, Ohio
WBEX Chillicothe, Ohio
WOUH-FM Chillicothe, Ohio
WKRC Cincinnati, Ohio
WLW Cincinnati, Ohio
WVXU Cincinnati, Ohio
WCPN Cleveland, Ohio
WTAM Cleveland, Ohio
WCBE Columbus, Ohio
WMNI Columbus, Ohio
WTVN Columbus, Ohio
WWOW Conneaut, Ohio
WHIO Dayton, Ohio
WGDE Defiance, Ohio
WONW Defiance, Ohio
WFIN Findlay, Ohio
WMAN-FM Fredericktown, Ohio
WMOH Hamilton, Ohio
WIRO Ironton, Ohio
WOUL-FM Ironton, Ohio
WFCO Lancaster, Ohio
WGLE Lima, Ohio
WIMA Lima, Ohio
WMAN Mansfield, Ohio
WLTP Marietta, Ohio
WMOA Marietta, Ohio
WMRT Marietta, Ohio
WMRN Marion, Ohio
WMVO Mount Vernon, Ohio
WKRJ New Philadelphia, Ohio
WCLT Newark, Ohio
WMUB Oxford, Ohio
WGTE-FM Toledo, Ohio
WSPD Toledo, Ohio
WBTC Uhrichsville, Ohio
WYSO Yellow Springs, Ohio
WKBN Youngstown, Ohio
WYSU Youngstown, Ohio
WOUZ-FM Zanesville, Ohio
KOCU Altus, Oklahoma
KWHW Altus, Oklahoma
KWON Bartlesville, Oklahoma
KCLI Clinton, Oklahoma
KYCU Clinton, Oklahoma
KUSH Cushing, Oklahoma
KCRC Enid, Oklahoma
KGWA Enid, Oklahoma
KTJS Hobart, Oklahoma
KOSN Ketchum, Oklahoma
KCCU Lawton, Oklahoma
KGOU Norman, Oklahoma
KTOK Oklahoma City, Oklahoma
KOKL Okmulgee, Oklahoma
KPGM Pawhuska, Oklahoma
KJSR Sand Springs, Oklahoma
KWEN Sand Springs, Oklahoma
KOSU Stillwater, Oklahoma
KRMG Tulsa, Oklahoma
KWGS Tulsa, Oklahoma
KLOO Albany, Oregon
KSMF Ashland, Oregon
KSOR Ashland, Oregon
KAST Astoria, Oregon
KBKR Baker, Oregon
KOBK Baker City, Oregon
KBND Bend, Oregon
KBNW Bend, Oregon
KOAB-FM Bend, Oregon
KBBR Coos Bay, Oregon
KSBA Coos Bay, Oregon
KWRO Coquille, Oregon
KOAC Corvallis, Oregon
KNND Cottage Grove, Oregon
KWVR Enterprise, Oregon
KOPB Eugene, Oregon
KPNW Eugene, Oregon
KUGN Eugene, Oregon
KOGL Gleneden Beach, Oregon
KAGI Grants Pass, Oregon
KAJO Grants Pass, Oregon
KUIK Hillsboro, Oregon
KAGO Klamath Falls, Oregon
KFLS Klamath Falls, Oregon
KLMF Klamath Falls, Oregon
KSKF Klamath Falls, Oregon
KLBM La Grande, Oregon
KTVR-FM La Grande, Oregon
KOAP Lakeview, Oregon
KGAL Lebanon, Oregon
KDOV Medford, Oregon
KMED Medford, Oregon
KOOZ Myrtle Point, Oregon
KTIL(AM) Netarts, Oregon
KLCO Newport, Oregon
KSRV Ontario, Oregon
KRBM Pendleton, Oregon
KUMA Pendleton, Oregon
KAPL Phoenix, Oregon
KCMX Phoenix, Oregon
KBNP Portland, Oregon
KEX Portland, Oregon
KOPB-FM Portland, Oregon
KXL-FM Portland, Oregon
KDUN Reedsport, Oregon
KSRS Roseburg, Oregon
KTBR Roseburg, Oregon
KOHI St. Helens, Oregon
KSJK Talent, Oregon
KACI The Dalles, Oregon
KTMK Tillamook, Oregon
KCUP Toledo, Oregon
KPAM Troutdale, Oregon
KLWJ(AM) Umatilla, Oregon
KWLZ-FM West Linn, Oregon
WAEB Allentown, Pennsylvania
WDIY Allentown, Pennsylvania
WJCS Allentown, Pennsylvania
WFBG Altoona, Pennsylvania
WRTA Altoona, Pennsylvania
WILK-FM Avoca, Pennsylvania
WBVP Beaver Falls, Pennsylvania
WBLF Bellefonte, Pennsylvania
WGPA Bethlehem, Pennsylvania
WHLM Bloomsburg, Pennsylvania
WHYL Carlisle, Pennsylvania
WWCH Clarion, Pennsylvania
WJET Erie, Pennsylvania
WPSE Erie, Pennsylvania
WQLN-FM Erie, Pennsylvania
WZSK Everett, Pennsylvania
WFRA Franklin, Pennsylvania
WGET Gettysburg, Pennsylvania
WHP Harrisburg, Pennsylvania
WITF-FM Harrisburg, Pennsylvania
WAZL Hazleton, Pennsylvania
WNTJ Johnstown, Pennsylvania
WNPV Lansdale, Pennsylvania
WLBR Lebanon, Pennsylvania
WIEZ Lewistown, Pennsylvania
WWGE Loretto, Pennsylvania
WJSM-FM Martinsburg, Pennsylvania
WWBJ Martinsburg, Pennsylvania
WEEO-FM McConnellsburg, Pennsylvania
WMGW Meadville, Pennsylvania
WKST New Castle, Pennsylvania
KYW Philadelphia, Pennsylvania
WPHB Philipsburg, Pennsylvania
KDKA Pittsburgh, Pennsylvania
KQV Pittsburgh, Pennsylvania
WEMR Pleasant Gap, Pennsylvania
WPAZ Pottstown, Pennsylvania
WECZ Punxsutawney, Pennsylvania
WYBF Radnor Township, Pennsylvania
WEEU Reading, Pennsylvania
WBZU Scranton, Pennsylvania
WVIA-FM Scranton, Pennsylvania
WPIC Sharon, Pennsylvania
WRSC State College, Pennsylvania
WKOK Sunbury, Pennsylvania
WTIV Titusville, Pennsylvania
WKZN West Hazleton, Pennsylvania
WLIH Whitneyville, Pennsylvania
WILK Wilkes-Barre, Pennsylvania
WLMY Williamsport, Pennsylvania
WRAK Williamsport, Pennsylvania
WVYA Williamsport, Pennsylvania
WCMN Arecibo, Puerto Rico
WYAC Cabo Rojo, Puerto Rico
WLEY Cayey, Puerto Rico
WRXD Fajardo, Puerto Rico
WMSW Hatillo, Puerto Rico
WALO Humacao, Puerto Rico
WMNT Manati, Puerto Rico
WKJB Mayaguez, Puerto Rico
WORA Mayaguez, Puerto Rico
WEKO Morovis, Puerto Rico
WEXS Patillas, Puerto Rico
WDEP Ponce, Puerto Rico
WISO Ponce, Puerto Rico
WPAB Ponce, Puerto Rico
WPRP Ponce, Puerto Rico
WUKQ Ponce, Puerto Rico
WSOL San German, Puerto Rico
WAPA San Juan, Puerto Rico
WIAC San Juan, Puerto Rico
WIPR San Juan, Puerto Rico
WKAQ San Juan, Puerto Rico
WSKN San Juan, Puerto Rico
WUNO San Juan, Puerto Rico
WUPR Utuado, Puerto Rico
WENA Yauco, Puerto Rico
WKFE Yauco, Puerto Rico
WKSP Hope Valley, Rhode Island
WRNI-FM Narragansett Pier, Rhode Island
WHJJ Providence, Rhode Island
WRNI Providence, Rhode Island
WBLQ(AM) Westerly, Rhode Island
WNRI Woonsocket, Rhode Island
WAIM Anderson, South Carolina
WZMJ Batesburg, South Carolina
WTQS Cameron, South Carolina

WBT-FM Chester, South Carolina
WVOC Columbia, South Carolina
WGTN Georgetown, South Carolina
WSCC-FM Goose Creek, South Carolina
WYRD Greenville, South Carolina
WCRS Greenwood, South Carolina
WHGS Hampton, South Carolina
WRIX-FM Honea Path, South Carolina
WHYM Lake City, South Carolina
WRHM Lancaster, South Carolina
WSNW Seneca, South Carolina
WYRD-FM Simpsonville, South Carolina
WORD Spartanburg, South Carolina
WSPG Spartanburg, South Carolina
WDXY Sumter, South Carolina
WRJA-FM Sumter, South Carolina
WGOG Walhalla, South Carolina
KBFS Belle Fourche, South Dakota
KESD Brookings, South Dakota
KDSJ Deadwood, South Dakota
KPSD-FM Faith, South Dakota
KSOO-FM Lennox, South Dakota
KQSD-FM Lowry, South Dakota
KZSD-FM Martin, South Dakota
KMSD Mibank, South Dakota
KORN Mitchell, South Dakota
KDSD-FM Pierpont, South Dakota
KCCR Pierre, South Dakota
KBHE-FM Rapid City, South Dakota
KOTA Rapid City, South Dakota
KTSD-FM Reliance, South Dakota
KNWC Sioux Falls, South Dakota
KRSD Sioux Falls, South Dakota
KSOO Sioux Falls, South Dakota
KUSD Vermillion, South Dakota
WNAX Yankton, South Dakota
WTBG Brownsville, Tennessee
WJZM Clarksville, Tennessee
WBAC Cleveland, Tennessee
WCLE Cleveland, Tennessee
WSMC-FM Collegedale, Tennessee
WHRS Cookeville, Tennessee
WPTN Cookeville, Tennessee
WTJJ Dyer, Tennessee
WCPH Etowah, Tennessee
WAKM Franklin, Tennessee
WWTN Hendersonville, Tennessee
WDXI Jackson, Tennessee
WKNP Jackson, Tennessee
WETS-FM Johnson City, Tennessee
WGOC Kingsport, Tennessee
WETR Knoxville, Tennessee
WUOT Knoxville, Tennessee
WCOR Lebanon, Tennessee
WLIV Livingston, Tennessee
WLOD Loudon, Tennessee
WPLN Madison, Tennessee
WRKQ Madisonville, Tennessee
WAKI McMinnville, Tennessee
WKAM Memphis, Tennessee
WKNO-FM Memphis, Tennessee
WREC Memphis, Tennessee
WYPL Memphis, Tennessee
WGNS Murfreesboro, Tennessee
WLAC Nashville, Tennessee
WPLN-FM Nashville, Tennessee
WRHA(AM) Spring City, Tennessee
WNTT Tazewell, Tennessee
WTML Tullahoma, Tennessee
KACU Abilene, Texas
KWKC Abilene, Texas
KGNC Amarillo, Texas
KIXZ Amarillo, Texas
KACT Andrews, Texas
KUT Austin, Texas
KSKY Balch Springs, Texas
KLVI Beaumont, Texas
KVLU Beaumont, Texas
KFLC Benbrook, Texas
KBST-FM Big Spring, Texas
KWHI Brenham, Texas
WTAW-FM Buffalo, Texas
KTXP Bushland, Texas
KDET Center, Texas
KXYL-FM Coleman, Texas
KAMU-FM College Station, Texas
KWBC College Station, Texas
WTAW College Station, Texas
KETR Commerce, Texas
KEDT-FM Corpus Christi, Texas
KEYS Corpus Christi, Texas
KKTX Corpus Christi, Texas
KHER Crystal City, Texas
KERA Dallas, Texas
KFXR Dallas, Texas
KLIF Dallas, Texas
KRLD Dallas, Texas
KURV Edinburg, Texas
KULP El Campo, Texas
KAMA El Paso, Texas
KBNA-FM El Paso, Texas
KTEP El Paso, Texas
KTSM El Paso, Texas
KXPL El Paso, Texas
KFLP-FM Floydada, Texas
KGAF Gainesville, Texas
KMBH-FM Harlingen, Texas
KLAT Houston, Texas
KNTH Houston, Texas
KPFT Houston, Texas
KPRC Houston, Texas
KTRH Houston, Texas
KUHF Houston, Texas
KTXI Ingram, Texas
KAML Kenedy-Karnes City, Texas
KNCT-FM Killeen, Texas
KFYO Lubbock, Texas
KJDL Lubbock, Texas
KRFE Lubbock, Texas
KLDN Lufkin, Texas
KCUL Marshall, Texas
KHID McAllen, Texas
KCRS Midland, Texas
KWEL Midland, Texas
KSFA Nacogdoches, Texas
KGNB New Braunfels, Texas
KOGT Orange, Texas
KOLE Port Arthur, Texas
KGKL San Angelo, Texas
KKSA San Angelo, Texas
KCOR San Antonio, Texas
KSTX San Antonio, Texas
KTSA San Antonio, Texas
WOAI San Antonio, Texas
KTSW San Marcos, Texas
KWED Seguin, Texas
KJIM Sherman, Texas
KZSP South Padre Island, Texas
KTOT Spearman, Texas
KSQX Springtown, Texas
KQXS Stephenville, Texas
KTEM Temple, Texas
KLUP Terrell Hills, Texas
KTFS Texarkana, Texas
KTXK Texarkana, Texas
KSEV Tomball, Texas
KTBB Tyler, Texas
KVRT Victoria, Texas
KBCT Waco, Texas
KWTX Waco, Texas
KMQX Weatherford, Texas
KMCU Wichita Falls, Texas
KWFS Wichita Falls, Texas
KSUB Cedar City, Utah
KUSR Logan, Utah
KUSU-FM Logan, Utah
KVNU Logan, Utah
KMTI Manti, Utah
KSL-FM Midvale, Utah
KLO Ogden, Utah
KOGN Ogden, Utah
KOAL Price, Utah
KBYU-FM Provo, Utah
KSVC Richfield, Utah
KCPW-FM Salt Lake City, Utah
KNRS Salt Lake City, Utah
KSL Salt Lake City, Utah
KUER-FM Salt Lake City, Utah
KHQN Spanish Fork, Utah
KDXU St. George, Utah
KZNU St. George, Utah
KVEL Vernal, Utah
WOWZ Appomattox, Virginia
WZHF Arlington, Virginia
WBVA Bayside, Virginia
WFNR Blacksburg, Virginia
WCHV Charlottesville, Virginia
WINA Charlottesville, Virginia
WMVE Chase City, Virginia
WDIC-FM Clinchco, Virginia
WMRY Crozet, Virginia
WPIN Dublin, Virginia
WOTC Edinburg, Virginia
WFLO Farmville, Virginia
WFVA Fredericksburg, Virginia
WNTX Fredericksburg, Virginia
WMNA Gretna, Virginia
WEMC Harrisonburg, Virginia
WKCY Harrisonburg, Virginia
WMRA Harrisonburg, Virginia
WSVA Harrisonburg, Virginia
WCNV Heathsville, Virginia
WMRL Lexington, Virginia
WBRG Lynchburg, Virginia
WLNI Lynchburg, Virginia
WWWT-FM Manassas, Virginia
WHRO-FM Norfolk, Virginia
WHRV Norfolk, Virginia
WNIS Norfolk, Virginia
WCVE-FM Richmond, Virginia
WLEE Richmond, Virginia
WRVA Richmond, Virginia
WFIR Roanoke, Virginia
WLOY Rural Retreat, Virginia
WHEO Stuart, Virginia
WKCI Waynesboro, Virginia
WINC Winchester, Virginia
WYVE Wytheville, Virginia
WVGN Charlotte Amalie, Virgin Islands
WVWI Charlotte Amalie, Virgin Islands
WSNO Barre, Vermont
WBTN Bennington, Vermont
WKVT Brattleboro, Vermont
WXLQ Bristol, Vermont
WJOY Burlington, Vermont
WVMT Burlington, Vermont
WVPS Burlington, Vermont
WCVR(AM) Randolph, Vermont
WSYB Rutland, Vermont
WVPA St. Johnsbury, Vermont
WDEV-FM Warren, Vermont
WDEV Waterbury, Vermont
WVPR Windsor, Vermont
KXRO Aberdeen, Washington
KGMI Bellingham, Washington
KUGS Bellingham, Washington
KZAZ Bellingham, Washington
KVAN Burbank, Washington
KELA Centralia-Chehalis, Washington
KNWV Clarkston, Washington
KNWR Ellensburg, Washington
KXLE Ellensburg, Washington
KULE Ephrata, Washington
KONA Kennewick-Richland-P, Washington
KEDO Longview, Washington
KBSN Moses Lake, Washington
KLWS Moses Lake, Washington
KMWS Mount Vernon, Washington
KSVR Mount Vernon, Washington
KQWS Omak, Washington
KFLD Pasco, Washington
KNWP Port Angeles, Washington
KONP Port Angeles, Washington
KVIX Port Angeles, Washington
KQQQ Pullman, Washington
KWSU Pullman, Washington
KWNC Quincy, Washington
KFAE-FM Richland, Washington
KKNW Seattle, Washington
KKOL Seattle, Washington
KOMO Seattle, Washington
KUOW-FM Seattle, Washington
KJRB Spokane, Washington
KPBX-FM Spokane, Washington
KQNT Spokane, Washington
KSFC Spokane, Washington
KXLY-AM Spokane, Washington
KIRO-FM Tacoma, Washington
KPLU-FM Tacoma, Washington
KXOT Tacoma, Washington
KYNR Toppenish, Washington
KUOW Tumwater, Washington
KGDC Walla Walla, Washington
KUJ Walla Walla, Washington
KWWS Walla Walla, Washington
KPLW Wenatchee, Washington
KPQ Wenatchee, Washington
KIT Yakima, Washington
KNWY Yakima, Washington
WXCE Amery, Wisconsin
WLBL Auburndale, Wisconsin
WBEV Beaver Dam, Wisconsin
WHSA Brule, Wisconsin

WHAD Delafield, Wisconsin
KFIZ Fond Du Lac, Wisconsin
WPNE-FM Green Bay, Wisconsin
WTAQ-AM Green Bay, Wisconsin
WHHI Highland, Wisconsin
WGTD Kenosha, Wisconsin
WHBY Kimberly, Wisconsin
WLSU La Crosse, Wisconsin
WLDY Ladysmith, Wisconsin
WERN Madison, Wisconsin
WHA Madison, Wisconsin
WIBA Madison, Wisconsin
WOMT Manitowoc, Wisconsin
WMEQ Menomonie, Wisconsin
WVSS Menomonie, Wisconsin
WISN Milwaukee, Wisconsin
WTMJ Milwaukee, Wisconsin
WOSH Oshkosh, Wisconsin
WHBM Park Falls, Wisconsin
WRCO-FM Richland Center, Wisconsin
WRPN Ripon, Wisconsin
WEVR-FM River Falls, Wisconsin
WHND Sister Bay, Wisconsin
WPCN Stevens Point, Wisconsin
KUWS Superior, Wisconsin
WJJQ-FM Tomahawk, Wisconsin
WHRM Wausau, Wisconsin
WXPW Wausau, Wisconsin
WFHR Wisconsin Rapids, Wisconsin
WVPB Beckley, West Virginia
WWNR Beckley, West Virginia
WCST Berkeley Springs, West Virginia
WHIS Bluefield, West Virginia
WBTQ Buckhannon, West Virginia
WBUC Buckhannon, West Virginia
WVPW Buckhannon, West Virginia
WCHS Charleston, West Virginia
WVPN Charleston, West Virginia
WTCS Fairmont, West Virginia
WVHU Huntington, West Virginia
WVWV Huntington, West Virginia
WFSP Kingwood, West Virginia
WRNR Martinsburg, West Virginia
WVEP Martinsburg, West Virginia
WAJR Morgantown, West Virginia
WVPM Morgantown, West Virginia
WVLY Moundsville, West Virginia
WVNT Parkersburg, West Virginia
WVPG Parkersburg, West Virginia
WAUA Petersburg, West Virginia
WRRL Rainelle, West Virginia
WMOV Ravenswood, West Virginia
WRON Ronceverte, West Virginia
WVNP Wheeling, West Virginia
WWVA Wheeling, West Virginia
KRSV Afton, Wyoming
KUWA Afton, Wyoming
KBBS Buffalo, Wyoming
KBUW Buffalo, Wyoming
KUWC Casper, Wyoming
KFBC Cheyenne, Wyoming
KODI Cody, Wyoming
KDUW Douglas, Wyoming
KIML Gillette, Wyoming
KUWG Gillette, Wyoming
KUWJ Jackson, Wyoming
KOWB Laramie, Wyoming
KUWR Laramie, Wyoming
KUWN Newcastle, Wyoming
KGAB Orchard Valley, Wyoming
KYDT Pine Haven, Wyoming
KUWX Pinedale, Wyoming
KPOW Powell, Wyoming
KUWP Powell, Wyoming
KUWZ Rock Springs, Wyoming
KPRQ Sheridan, Wyoming
KROE Sheridan, Wyoming
KSUW Sheridan, Wyoming
KUWD Sundance, Wyoming
KUWT Thermopolis, Wyoming

News/Talk

KBYR Anchorage, Alaska
KENI Anchorage, Alaska
KFQD Anchorage, Alaska
KAGV Big Lake, Alaska
KVNT Eagle River, Alaska
KFAR Fairbanks, Alaska
KFBX Fairbanks, Alaska
KUAC Fairbanks, Alaska
KBBI Homer, Alaska
KTKN Ketchikan, Alaska
KIAM Nenana, Alaska
KNOM Nome, Alaska
KFSK Petersburg, Alaska
KIFW Sitka, Alaska
KSRM Soldotna, Alaska
KTNA Talkeetna, Alaska
WDNG Anniston, Alabama
WVNN Athens, Alabama
WAPI Birmingham, Alabama
WERC Birmingham, Alabama
WYDE Birmingham, Alabama
WRTR Brookwood, Alabama
WACV Coosada, Alabama
WFMH Cullman, Alabama
WHOS Decatur, Alabama
WHEP Foley, Alabama
WFPA Fort Payne, Alabama
WAAX Gadsden, Alabama
WGEA Geneva, Alabama
WGYV Greenville, Alabama
WGSV Guntersville, Alabama
WERC-FM Hoover, Alabama
WBHP Huntsville, Alabama
WNTM Mobile, Alabama
WLWI Montgomery, Alabama
WHBB Selma, Alabama
WFEB Sylacauga, Alabama
WVNN-FM Trinity, Alabama
WTBC Tuscaloosa, Alabama
WUAL-FM Tuscaloosa, Alabama
WVNA Tuscumbia, Alabama
KVRC Arkadelphia, Arkansas
KLCN Blytheville, Arkansas
KJMT Calico Rock, Arkansas
KCAB Dardanelle, Arkansas
KFAY Farmington, Arkansas
KBJT Fordyce, Arkansas
KXJK Forrest City, Arkansas
KFSW Fort Smith, Arkansas
KWHN Fort Smith, Arkansas
KURM-FM Gravette, Arkansas
KELD-FM Hampton, Arkansas
KAWW Heber Springs, Arkansas
KZHS Hot Springs, Arkansas
KZNG Hot Springs, Arkansas
KBTM Jonesboro, Arkansas
KUAR Little Rock, Arkansas
KNBY Newport, Arkansas
KARV-FM Ola, Arkansas
KSMD Pangburn, Arkansas
KFFK Rogers, Arkansas
KZZZ Bullhead City, Arizona
KAPR Douglas, Arizona
KVNA Flagstaff, Arizona
KTAR-FM Glendale, Arizona
KJAA Globe, Arizona
KDJI Holbrook, Arizona
KAAA Kingman, Arizona
KNTR Lake Havasu City, Arizona
KFNN Mesa, Arizona
KLPZ Parker, Arizona
KFYI Phoenix, Arizona
KKNT Phoenix, Arizona
KNKI Pinetop, Arizona
KYCA Prescott, Arizona
KQNA Prescott Valley, Arizona
KVWM Show Low, Arizona
KTAN Sierra Vista, Arizona
KNST Tucson, Arizona
KUAZ-FM Tucson, Arizona
KAWC Yuma, Arizona
KBLU Yuma, Arizona
KGEO Bakersfield, California
KNZR Bakersfield, California
KINS-FM Blue Lake, California
KPAY Chico, California
KZFR Chico, California
KNWZ Coachella, California
KGOE Eureka, California
KWSW Eureka, California
KMJ Fresno, California
KMJ Fresno, California
KRLA Glendale, California
KNCO Grass Valley, California
KOSS Lancaster, California
KABC Los Angeles, California
KFI Los Angeles, California
KPFK Los Angeles, California
KTNQ Los Angeles, California
KYPA Los Angeles, California
KPMO Mendocino, California
KGAM Merced, California
KYOS Merced, California
KFIV Modesto, California
KMPH Modesto, California
KNRY Monterey Bay, California
KMJC Mount Shasta, California
KVON Napa, California
KTOX Needles, California
KKSF Oakland, California
KNEW Oakland, California
KNWQ Palm Springs, California
KPSC Palm Springs, California
KKXX Paradise, California
KPRL Paso Robles, California
KFBK-FM Pollock Pines, California
KWKU Pomona, California
KKZZ Port Hueneme, California
KTIP Porterville, California
KQMS Redding, California
KFNY Riverside, California
KFBK Sacramento, California
KION Salinas, California
KTIE San Bernardino, California
KCBQ San Diego, California
KFMB San Diego, California
KOGO San Diego, California
KPBS-FM San Diego, California
KGO San Francisco, California
KSFO San Francisco, California
KVEC San Luis Obispo, California
KYNS San Luis Obispo, California
KCLU Santa Barbara, California
KZSB Santa Barbara, California
KSCO Santa Cruz, California
KSMA Santa Maria, California
KSMX Santa Maria, California
KUHL Santa Maria, California
KUNX Santa Paula, California
KSRO Santa Rosa, California
KNZR-FM Shafter, California
KIRN Simi Valley, California
KVML Sonora, California
KOWL South Lake Tahoe, California
KWSX Stockton, California
KSUE Susanville, California
KVTA Ventura, California
KRZR Visalia, California
KERN Wasco-Greenacres, California
KERN Wasco-Greenacres, California
KRCB-FM Windsor, California
KUBA Yuba City, California
KNWH Yucca Valley, California
KSKE Buena Vista, Colorado
KRLN Canon City, Colorado
KRCC Colorado Springs, Colorado
KRDO Colorado Springs, Colorado
KVOR Colorado Springs, Colorado
KZNT Colorado Springs, Colorado
KVFC Cortez, Colorado
KCFR-FM Denver, Colorado
KHOW Denver, Colorado
KNUS Denver, Colorado
KOA Denver, Colorado
KDGO Durango, Colorado
KFTM Fort Morgan, Colorado
KNZZ Grand Junction, Colorado
KFKA Greeley, Colorado
KHNC Johnstown, Colorado
KWUF Pagosa Springs, Colorado
KCSJ Pueblo, Colorado
KGFT Pueblo, Colorado
KRDO-FM Security, Colorado
KVLE Vail, Colorado
KCOL Wellington, Colorado
WPRX Bristol, Connecticut
WLAD Danbury, Connecticut
WXLM Groton, Connecticut
WQAQ Hamden, Connecticut
WDRC Hartford, Connecticut
WPOP Hartford, Connecticut
WTIC Hartford, Connecticut
WNEZ Manchester, Connecticut
WELI New Haven, Connecticut
WNLK Norwalk, Connecticut
WEDW-FM Stamford, Connecticut
WSTC Stamford, Connecticut
WSNG Torrington, Connecticut
WATR Waterbury, Connecticut
WWCO Waterbury, Connecticut

WSHU Westport, Connecticut
WAMU Washington, District of Columbia
WFED Washington, District of Columbia
WMAL Washington, District of Columbia
WPFW Washington, District of Columbia
WDOV Dover, Delaware
WGMD Rehoboth Beach, Delaware
WJWK Seaford, Delaware
WDEL Wilmington, Delaware
WILM Wilmington, Delaware
WFLN Arcadia, Florida
WOKV-FM Atlantic Beach, Florida
WTWB Auburndale, Florida
WWJB Brooksville, Florida
WNZF Bunnell, Florida
WKFL Bushnell, Florida
WMMV Cocoa, Florida
WJTK Columbia City, Florida
WNDB Daytona Beach, Florida
WYND Deland, Florida
WNWF Destin, Florida
WENG Englewood, Florida
WFSX-FM Estero, Florida
WJNX Fort Pierce, Florida
WFTW Fort Walton Beach, Florida
WDVH Gainesville, Florida
WRUF Gainesville, Florida
WNRP Gulf Breeze, Florida
WXYB Indian Rocks Beach, Florida
WBOB(AM) Jacksonville, Florida
WJCT-FM Jacksonville, Florida
WOKV(AM) Jacksonville, Quebec
WJBW Jupiter, Florida
WYBX Key West, Florida
WLKF Lakeland, Florida
WPBR Lantana, Florida
WWBA Largo, Florida
WFFG Marathon, Florida
WKWM Marathon, Florida
WGUF Marco, Florida
WMMB Melbourne, Florida
WAQI Miami, Florida
WIOD Miami, Florida
WLRN-FM Miami, Florida
WQBA Miami, Florida
WSUA Miami, Florida
WSKY-FM Micanopy, Florida
WPSO New Port Richey, Florida
WKAT North Miami, Florida
WDBO Orlando, Florida
WDBO(FM) Orlando, Florida
WELE Ormond Beach, Florida
WLTG Panama City, Florida
WFLF-FM Parker, Florida
WCOA Pensacola, Florida
WCOA-FM Pensacola, Florida
WAMT Pine Castle Sky Lake, Florida
WFLF Pine Hills, Florida
WPSL Port St. Lucie, Florida
WCCF Punta Gorda, Florida
WDEO-FM San Carlos Park, Florida
WLSS Sarasota, Florida
WSRQ Sarasota, Florida
WFOY St. Augustine, Florida
WIWA St. Cloud, Florida
WSTU Stuart, Florida
WZAB Sweetwater, Florida
WFSU-FM Tallahassee, Florida
WTAL Tallahassee, Florida
WFLA Tampa, Florida
WHNZ Tampa, Florida
WIXC Titusville, Florida
WAXE Vero Beach, Florida
WTTB Vero Beach, Florida
WZTA Vero Beach, Florida
WBZT West Palm Beach, Florida
WFTL West Palm Beach, Florida
WJNO West Palm Beach, Florida
WALG Albany, Georgia
WGAU Athens, Georgia
WAOK Atlanta, Georgia
WGKA Atlanta, Georgia
WGST Atlanta, Georgia
WSB Atlanta, Georgia
WGAC Augusta, Georgia
WGIG Brunswick, Georgia
WGRA Cairo, Georgia
WLBB Carrollton, Georgia
WRCG Columbus, Georgia
WSRM Coosa, Georgia
WBLJ Dalton, Georgia
WCFO East Point, Georgia
WDUN Gainesville, Georgia
WYAY Gainesville, Georgia
WHIE Griffin, Georgia
WGAC-FM Harlem, Georgia
WVCC Hogansville, Georgia
WVGA Lakeland, Georgia
WMAC Macon, Georgia
WLAQ Rome, Georgia
WRGA Rome, Georgia
WBMQ Savannah, Georgia
WTKS Savannah, Georgia
WWNS Statesboro, Georgia
WSGC-FM Tignall, Georgia
WKWN Trenton, Georgia
WVOP Vidalia, Georgia
WWGA(AM) Waycross, Georgia
WCGA Woodbine, Georgia
KGUM Hagatna, Guam
KQNG Eleele, Hawaii
KHVH Honolulu, Hawaii
KIKI Honolulu, Hawaii
KWAI Honolulu, Hawaii
KASI Ames, Iowa
KWBG Boone, Iowa
WMT Cedar Rapids, Iowa
WOC Davenport, Iowa
WHO Des Moines, Iowa
KGRN Grinnell, Iowa
KXIC Iowa City, Iowa
WSUI Iowa City, Iowa
KOKX Keokuk, Iowa
KFJB Marshalltown, Iowa
KGLO Mason City, Iowa
KOEL Oelwein, Iowa
KOJI Okoboji, Iowa
KBIZ Ottumwa, Iowa
KIWA Sheldon, Iowa
KMA Shenandoah, Iowa
KSCJ Sioux City, Iowa
KWIT Sioux City, Iowa
KXEL Waterloo, Iowa
KBOI Boise, Idaho
KBSU-FM Boise, Idaho
KBFI Bonners Ferry, Idaho
KBAR Burley, Idaho
KBSY Burley, Idaho
KID Idaho Falls, Idaho
KRFA-FM Moscow, Idaho
KWEI Notus, Idaho
KWIK Pocatello, Idaho
KSPT Sandpoint, Idaho
KEZJ Twin Falls, Idaho
KLIX Twin Falls, Idaho
WBGZ Alton, Illinois
WTIM Assumption, Illinois
WJBC Bloomington, Illinois
WBYS Canton, Illinois
WCIL Carbondale, Illinois
WDWS Champaign, Illinois
KSGM Chester, Illinois
WGN(AM) Chicago, Illinois
WIND Chicago, Illinois
WLS Chicago, Illinois
WRTO Chicago, Illinois
WHOW Clinton, Illinois
WDAN Danville, Illinois
WSOY Decatur, Illinois
WLBK Dekalb, Illinois
WCRA Effingham, Illinois
WCRA Effingham, Illinois
WCRA-FM Effingham, Illinois
WRMN Elgin, Illinois
WKTA Evanston, Illinois
WFIW Fairfield, Illinois
WGNN Fisher, Illinois
WAIK Galesburg, Illinois
WGIL Galesburg, Illinois
WKYX-FM Golconda, Illinois
WJPF Herrin, Illinois
WJIL Jacksonville, Illinois
WLDS Jacksonville, Illinois
WKEI Kewanee, Illinois
WLPO Lasalle, Illinois
WSMI Litchfield, Illinois
WGGH Marion, Illinois
WLBH Mattoon, Illinois
WBEQ Morris, Illinois
WCSJ Morris, Illinois
WCSJ-FM Morris, Illinois
WINI Murphysboro, Illinois
WCMY Ottawa, Illinois
WMBD Peoria, Illinois
WZOE Princeton, Illinois
WGEM Quincy, Illinois
WGEM-FM Quincy, Illinois
WTAD Quincy, Illinois
WRHL Rochelle, Illinois
WROK Rockford, Illinois
WHCO Sparta, Illinois
WMAY Springfield, Illinois
WTAX Springfield, Illinois
WNIQ Sterling, Illinois
WSPL Streator, Illinois
WTIM Taylorville, Illinois
WTIM Taylorville, Illinois
WILL Urbana, Illinois
WKRS Waukegan, Illinois
WHBU Anderson, Indiana
WGCL Bloomington, Indiana
WCSI Columbus, Indiana
WTRC Elkhart, Indiana
WVPE Elkhart, Indiana
WGBF Evansville, Indiana
WBOI Fort Wayne, Indiana
WOWO Fort Wayne, Indiana
WLTH Gary, Indiana
WREB Greencastle, Indiana
WTRE Greensburg, Indiana
WJOB Hammond, Indiana
WFYI-FM Indianapolis, Indiana
WXNT Indianapolis, Indiana
WIOU Kokomo, Indiana
WSAL Logansport, Indiana
WLPR-FM Lowell, Indiana
WYFX Mount Vernon, Indiana
WNDA New Albany, Indiana
WSBT South Bend, Indiana
WIBQ Terre Haute, Indiana
WAOV Vincennes, Indiana
WBAA West Lafayette, Indiana
KGGF AM Coffeyville, Kansas
KIUL Garden City, Kansas
KLOE Goodland, Kansas
KZAN Hays, Kansas
KZNA Hill City, Kansas
KWBW Hutchinson, Kansas
KJCK Junction City, Kansas
KLWN Lawrence, Kansas
KSCB Liberal, Kansas
KMAN Manhattan, Kansas
KINA Salina, Kansas
KSAL Salina, Kansas
KYUL Scott City, Kansas
KMAJ Topeka, Kansas
WIBW Topeka, Kansas
KNSS Wichita, Kansas
KQAM Wichita, Kansas
WKCT Bowling Green, Kentucky
WSFE Burnside, Kentucky
WCTT Corbin, Kentucky
WKDP Corbin, Kentucky
WHIR Danville, Kentucky
WHOP Hopkinsville, Kentucky
WIRV Irvine, Kentucky
WLAP Lexington, Kentucky
WVLK Lexington, Kentucky
WFPL Louisville, Kentucky
WGTK Louisville, Kentucky
WHAS Louisville, Kentucky
WKJK Louisville, Kentucky
WNGO Mayfield, Kentucky
WKYX Paducah, Kentucky
WKYH Paintsville, Kentucky
WEKY Richmond, Kentucky
WVKY Shelbyville, Kentucky
WRKF Baton Rouge, Louisiana
KEUN Eunice, Louisiana
KAOK Lake Charles, Louisiana
KNOC Natchitoches, Louisiana
WGSO New Orleans, Louisiana
WRNO-FM New Orleans, Louisiana
WWL New Orleans, Louisiana
KNCB Vivian, Louisiana
WPNI Amherst, Massachusetts
WARL Attleboro, Massachusetts
WILD Boston, Massachusetts
WXBR Brockton, Massachusetts
WHNP East Longmeadow, Massachusetts
WSAR Fall River, Massachusetts
WGAW Gardner, Massachusetts
WAMQ Great Barrington, Massachusetts

WMLN-FM Milton, Massachusetts
WNAN Nantucket, Massachusetts
WBSM New Bedford, Massachusetts
WXKS Newton, Massachusetts
WDIS Norfolk, Massachusetts
WBEC Pittsfield, Massachusetts
WESO Southbridge, Massachusetts
WHYN Springfield, Massachusetts
WGTX Truro, Massachusetts
WBUR West Yarmouth, Massachusetts
WXTK West Yarmouth, Massachusetts
WCAI Woods Hole, Massachusetts
WTAG Worcester, Massachusetts
WEAA Baltimore, Maryland
WYPR Baltimore, Maryland
WCBC Cumberland, Maryland
WFMD Frederick, Maryland
WYPF Frederick, Maryland
WJSS Havre De Grace, Maryland
WPTX Lexington Park, Maryland
WYPO Ocean City, Maryland
WICO Salisbury, Maryland
WJDY Salisbury, Maryland
WVQM Augusta, Maine
WVOM-FM Howland, Maine
WJCX Pittsfield, Maine
WGAN Portland, Maine
WNZS Veazie, Maine
WABJ Adrian, Michigan
WZTK Alpena, Michigan
WUOM Ann Arbor, Michigan
WBCK-FM Battle Creek, Michigan
WSJM-FM Benton Harbor, Michigan
WHFB Benton Harbor-St. Jo, Michigan
WBRN Big Rapids, Michigan
WMKT Charlevoix, Michigan
WTVB-AM Coldwater, Michigan
WDTK Detroit, Michigan
WJR Detroit, Michigan
WKAR East Lansing, Michigan
WCHT Escanaba, Michigan
WWCK Flint, Michigan
WJRW Grand Rapids, Michigan
WOOD Grand Rapids, Michigan
WVGR Grand Rapids, Michigan
WHTC Holland, Michigan
WMIQ Iron Mountain, Michigan
WIAN Ishpeming, Michigan
WKHM Jackson, Michigan
WKMI Kalamazoo, Michigan
WKZO Kalamazoo, Michigan
WILS Lansing, Michigan
WJIM Lansing, Michigan
WMTE Manistee, Michigan
WDMJ Marquette, Michigan
WAVC Mio, Michigan
WSHN Munising, Michigan
WKBZ Muskegon, Michigan
WOOD-FM Muskegon, Michigan
WPHM Port Huron, Michigan
WSGW Saginaw, Michigan
WMIC Sandusky, Michigan
WKNW Sault Sainte Marie, Michigan
WCHB Taylor, Michigan
WTCM Traverse City, Michigan
KATE Albert Lea, Minnesota
KAUS Austin, Minnesota
WWWI Baxter, Minnesota
KRWC Buffalo, Minnesota
KDLM Detroit Lakes, Minnesota
KDAL-AM Duluth, Minnesota
WEBC Duluth, Minnesota
KBRF Fergus Falls, Minnesota
KLTF Little Falls, Minnesota
KTOE Mankato, Minnesota
KMHL Marshall, Minnesota
KTLK Minneapolis, Minnesota
WCCO Minneapolis, Minnesota
WWTC Minneapolis, Minnesota
KDMA Montevideo, Minnesota
KMRS Morris, Minnesota
WNMT Nashwauk, Minnesota
KCHK New Prague, Minnesota
WWWI-FM Pillager, Minnesota
KROC Rochester, Minnesota
KNSI St. Cloud, Minnesota
WJON St. Cloud, Minnesota
KQMN Thief River Falls, Minnesota
KWLM Willmar, Minnesota
KDOM Windom, Minnesota
KDOM-FM Windom, Minnesota
KWNO Winona, Minnesota
KWOA Worthington, Minnesota
KNSW Worthington-Marshall, Minnesota
KGNA-FM Arnold, Missouri
KSWM Aurora, Missouri
KKOZ-FM Ava, Missouri
KZIM Cape Girardeau, Missouri
KRNW Chillicothe, Missouri
KFRU Columbia, Missouri
KOPN Columbia, Missouri
KGNN-FM Cuba, Missouri
KREI Farmington, Missouri
KSSZ Fayette, Missouri
KJFF Festus, Missouri
KFTK Florissant, Missouri
KHMO Hannibal, Missouri
KLIK Jefferson City, Missouri
KWOS Jefferson City, Missouri
KZRG Joplin, Missouri
KZYM Joplin, Missouri
KLWT Lebanon, Missouri
KRMS Osage Beach, Missouri
KFMO Park Hills, Missouri
KCOZ Point Lookout, Missouri
KWOC Poplar Bluff, Missouri
KSMO Salem, Missouri
KSIS Sedalia, Missouri
KSIM Sikeston, Missouri
KSGF Springfield, Missouri
KWTO-AM Springfield, Missouri
KTTR FM St. James, Missouri
KFEQ St. Joseph, Missouri
KMOX St. Louis, Missouri
KTRS St. Louis, Missouri
KTUI Sullivan, Missouri
KGNV Washington, Missouri
KWPM West Plains, Missouri
KUKU Willow Springs, Missouri
WCJU Columbia, Mississippi
WLAU Heidelberg, Mississippi
WURC Holly Springs, Mississippi
WTCD Indianola, Mississippi
WJDX Jackson, Mississippi
WMXI Laurel, Mississippi
WJZD-FM Long Beach, Mississippi
WKBB Mantee, Mississippi
WALT Meridian, Mississippi
WBUV Moss Point, Mississippi
WNAT Natchez, Mississippi
WJNT Pearl, Mississippi
WFMM Sumrall, Mississippi
KBLG Billings, Montana
KMMS Bozeman, Montana
KGVA Fort Belknap Agency, Montana
KQDI Great Falls, Montana
KLYQ Hamilton, Montana
KBLL Helena, Montana
KCAP Helena, Montana
KGEZ Kalispell, Montana
KOFI Kalispell, Montana
KJJR Whitefish, Montana
WSPC Albemarle, North Carolina
WWNC Asheville, North Carolina
WTKF Atlantic, North Carolina
WXIT Blowing Rock, North Carolina
WUDE Bolivia, North Carolina
WCHL Chapel Hill, North Carolina
WBT Charlotte, North Carolina
WFAE Charlotte, North Carolina
WNCU Durham, North Carolina
WFNC Fayetteville, North Carolina
WIDU Fayetteville, North Carolina
WGBR Goldsboro, North Carolina
WSML Graham, North Carolina
WFHE Hickory, North Carolina
WHKY Hickory, North Carolina
WJNC Jacksonville, North Carolina
WJRI Lenoir, North Carolina
WLXN Lexington, North Carolina
WYQS Mars Hill, North Carolina
WAUG New Hope, North Carolina
WFNL Raleigh, North Carolina
WPTF Raleigh, North Carolina
WCAB Rutherfordton, North Carolina
WSTP Salisbury, North Carolina
WNCA Siler City, North Carolina
WEEB Southern Pines, North Carolina
WTXY Whiteville, North Carolina
KFYR Bismarck, North Dakota
KLXX Bismarck-Mandan, North Dakota
KFGO Fargo, North Dakota
WDAY Fargo, North Dakota
KNOX Grand Forks, North Dakota
KNDK Langdon, North Dakota
KQLX Lisbon, North Dakota
KHRT Minot, North Dakota
KEYZ Williston, North Dakota
KWBE Beatrice, Nebraska
KJSK Columbus, Nebraska
KTTT Columbus, Nebraska
KHUB Fremont, Nebraska
KRGI Grand Island, Nebraska
KGFW Kearney, Nebraska
KFOR Lincoln, Nebraska
KLIN Lincoln, Nebraska
WJAG Norfolk, Nebraska
KODY North Platte, Nebraska
KFAB Omaha, Nebraska
KNEB Scottsbluff, Nebraska
WEVO(FM) Concord, New Hampshire
WKXL Concord, New Hampshire
WTSN Dover, New Hampshire
WXEX Exeter, New Hampshire
WEVH Hanover, New Hampshire
WTSL Hanover, New Hampshire
WTPL Hillsboro, New Hampshire
WEVJ Jackson, New Hampshire
WEVN Keene, New Hampshire
WZBK Keene, New Hampshire
WUVR Lebanon, New Hampshire
WGIR Manchester, New Hampshire
WEVS Nashua, New Hampshire
WSMN Nashua, New Hampshire
WPKX Rochester, New Hampshire
WQSO Rochester, New Hampshire
WMVX Salem, New Hampshire
WNJN-FM Atlantic City, New Jersey
WNJS-FM Berlin, New Jersey
WNJB-FM Bridgeton, New Jersey
WNJZ Cape May Court House, New Jersey
WNYM Hackensack, New Jersey
WRNJ Hackettstown, New Jersey
WNJM Manahawkin, New Jersey
WNJY Netcong, New Jersey
WOND Pleasantville, New Jersey
WNJP Sussex, New Jersey
WNJT-FM Trenton, New Jersey
KINN Alamogordo, New Mexico
KKOB Albuquerque, New Mexico
KUNM Albuquerque, New Mexico
KRRT Arroyo Seco, New Mexico
KWKA Clovis, New Mexico
KENN Farmington, New Mexico
KYKK Humble City, New Mexico
KOBE Las Cruces, New Mexico
KNMX Las Vegas, New Mexico
KTBL Los Ranchos, New Mexico
KSEL Portales, New Mexico
KBIM Roswell, New Mexico
KLBU Santa Fe, New Mexico
KDWN Las Vegas, Nevada
KXNT North Las Vegas, Nevada
KNIH Paradise, Nevada
KKOH Reno, Nevada
KBZZ Sparks, Nevada
KWNA Winnemucca, Nevada
WGY-FM Albany, New York
WROW Albany, New York
WBTA Batavia, New York
WNBF Binghamton, New York
WBEN Buffalo, New York
WDCZ Buffalo, New York
WCGR Canandaigua, New York
WENI Corning, New York
WWLE Cornwall, New York
WDOE Dunkirk, New York
WJIP Ellenville, New York
WENY Elmira, New York
WEOS Geneva, New York
WGVA Geneva, New York
WWSC Glens Falls, New York
WLEA Hornell, New York
WWLZ Horseheads, New York
WHCU Ithaca, New York
WJFF Jeffersonville, New York
WAMK Kingston, New York
WGHQ Kingston, New York
WLVL Lockport, New York
WADO New York, New York
WOR New York, New York
WABC New York City, New York
WSUF Noyack, New York

WOEN Olean, New York
WMCR Oneida, New York
WNYO Oswego, New York
WKIP Poughkeepsie, New York
WRCN-FM Riverhead, New York
WBEE-FM Rochester, New York
WHAM Rochester, New York
WKAL Rome, New York
WNBZ Saranac Lake, New York
WGY Schenectady, New York
WSYR Solvay, New York
WRLI-FM Southampton, New York
WUSB Stony Brook, New York
WSYR Syracuse, New York
WIBX Utica, New York
WHLO Akron, Ohio
WATH Athens, Ohio
WOUB Athens, Ohio
WBLL Bellefontaine, Ohio
WAIS Buchtel, Ohio
WOUC-FM Cambridge, Ohio
WBEX Chillicothe, Ohio
WOUH-FM Chillicothe, Ohio
WKRC Cincinnati, Ohio
WLW Cincinnati, Ohio
WTAM Cleveland, Ohio
WERE Cleveland Heights, Ohio
WTVN Columbus, Ohio
WWOW Conneaut, Ohio
WHIO Dayton, Ohio
WONW Defiance, Ohio
WEOL Elyria, Ohio
WFIN Findlay, Ohio
WMAN-FM Fredericktown, Ohio
WMOH Hamilton, Ohio
WIRO Ironton, Ohio
WOUL-FM Ironton, Ohio
WFCO Lancaster, Ohio
WIMA Lima, Ohio
WMAN Mansfield, Ohio
WLTP Marietta, Ohio
WMRT Marietta, Ohio
WMRN Marion, Ohio
WMVO Mount Vernon, Ohio
WCLT Newark, Ohio
WMUB Oxford, Ohio
WSPD Toledo, Ohio
WBTC Uhrichsville, Ohio
WKBN Youngstown, Ohio
WOUZ-FM Zanesville, Ohio
KWHW Altus, Oklahoma
KWON Bartlesville, Oklahoma
KUSH Cushing, Oklahoma
KGWA Enid, Oklahoma
KTJS Hobart, Oklahoma
KOSN Ketchum, Oklahoma
KGOU Norman, Oklahoma
KOKC Oklahoma City, Oklahoma
KTOK Oklahoma City, Oklahoma
KOKL Okmulgee, Oklahoma
KJSR Sand Springs, Oklahoma
KRMG-FM Sand Springs, Oklahoma
KRMG-FM Sand Springs, Oklahoma
KWEN Sand Springs, Oklahoma
KRMG Tulsa, Oklahoma
KLOO Albany, Oregon
KAST Astoria, Oregon
KBKR Baker, Oregon
KOBK Baker City, Oregon
KBNW Bend, Oregon
KBBR Coos Bay, Oregon
KWRO Coquille, Oregon
KOAC Corvallis, Oregon
KNND Cottage Grove, Oregon
KWVR Enterprise, Oregon
KOPB Eugene, Oregon
KPNW Eugene, Oregon
KUGN Eugene, Oregon
KAJO Grants Pass, Oregon
KUIK Hillsboro, Oregon
KAGO Klamath Falls, Oregon
KFLS Klamath Falls, Oregon
KLBM La Grande, Oregon
KVBL La Grande, Oregon
KBCH Lincoln City, Oregon
KDOV Medford, Oregon
KMED Medford, Oregon
KTIL(AM) Netarts, Oregon
KRBM Pendleton, Oregon
KAPL Phoenix, Oregon
KEX Portland, Oregon
KXL-FM Portland, Oregon
KQEN Roseburg, Oregon
KACI The Dalles, Oregon
KTMK Tillamook, Oregon
KPAM Troutdale, Oregon
KLWJ(AM) Umatilla, Oregon
KWLZ-FM West Linn, Oregon
WAEB Allentown, Pennsylvania
WJCS Allentown, Pennsylvania
WFBG Altoona, Pennsylvania
WRTA Altoona, Pennsylvania
WILK-FM Avoca, Pennsylvania
WBFD Bedford, Pennsylvania
WBLF Bellefonte, Pennsylvania
WGPA Bethlehem, Pennsylvania
WBUT Butler, Pennsylvania
WISR Butler, Pennsylvania
WHYL Carlisle, Pennsylvania
WWCH Clarion, Pennsylvania
WCED Du Bois, Pennsylvania
WJET Erie, Pennsylvania
WZSK Everett, Pennsylvania
WFRA Franklin, Pennsylvania
WHP Harrisburg, Pennsylvania
WITF-FM Harrisburg, Pennsylvania
WAZL Hazleton, Pennsylvania
WNTJ Johnstown, Pennsylvania
WNPV Lansdale, Pennsylvania
WLBR Lebanon, Pennsylvania
WWGE Loretto, Pennsylvania
WJSM-FM Martinsburg, Pennsylvania
WEEO-FM McConnellsburg, Pennsylvania
WMGW Meadville, Pennsylvania
WKST New Castle, Pennsylvania
WPHB Philipsburg, Pennsylvania
KDKA Pittsburgh, Pennsylvania
WEMR Pleasant Gap, Pennsylvania
WPAZ Pottstown, Pennsylvania
WYBF Radnor Township, Pennsylvania
WEEU Reading, Pennsylvania
WBZU Scranton, Pennsylvania
WPIC Sharon, Pennsylvania
WRSC State College, Pennsylvania
WKOK Sunbury, Pennsylvania
WTIV Titusville, Pennsylvania
WKZN West Hazleton, Pennsylvania
WILK Wilkes-Barre, Pennsylvania
WRAK Williamsport, Pennsylvania
WWPA Williamsport, Pennsylvania
WSBA York, Pennsylvania
WYAC Cabo Rojo, Puerto Rico
WMSW Hatillo, Puerto Rico
WALO Humacao, Puerto Rico
WMNT Manati, Puerto Rico
WKJB Mayaguez, Puerto Rico
WORA Mayaguez, Puerto Rico
WDEP Ponce, Puerto Rico
WISO Ponce, Puerto Rico
WPAB Ponce, Puerto Rico
WPRP Ponce, Puerto Rico
WUKQ Ponce, Puerto Rico
WAPA San Juan, Puerto Rico
WKAQ San Juan, Puerto Rico
WSKN San Juan, Puerto Rico
WUNO San Juan, Puerto Rico
WUPR Utuado, Puerto Rico
WENA Yauco, Puerto Rico
WKFE Yauco, Puerto Rico
WRNI-FM Narragansett Pier, Rhode Island
WHJJ Providence, Rhode Island
WPRO Providence, Rhode Island
WPRV Providence, Rhode Island
WRNI Providence, Rhode Island
WEAN Wakefield-Peacedale, Rhode Island
WNRI Woonsocket, Rhode Island
WAIM Anderson, South Carolina
WTQS Cameron, South Carolina
WQSC Charleston, South Carolina
WTMA Charleston, South Carolina
WBT-FM Chester, South Carolina
WVOC Columbia, South Carolina
WJMX Darlington, South Carolina
WORG Elloree, South Carolina
WGTN Georgetown, South Carolina
WSCC-FM Goose Creek, South Carolina
WYRD Greenville, South Carolina
WCRS Greenwood, South Carolina
WRIX-FM Honea Path, South Carolina
WHYM Lake City, South Carolina
WRHI Rock Hill, South Carolina
WYRD-FM Simpsonville, South Carolina
WORD Spartanburg, South Carolina
WSPG Spartanburg, South Carolina
WDXY Sumter, South Carolina
KSOO-FM Lennox, South Dakota
KMSD Mibank, South Dakota
KORN Mitchell, South Dakota
KCCR Pierre, South Dakota
KOTA Rapid City, South Dakota
KELO-AM Sioux Falls, South Dakota
KSOO Sioux Falls, South Dakota
KWAT Watertown, South Dakota
WNAX Yankton, South Dakota
WTBG Brownsville, Tennessee
WGOW Chattanooga, Tennessee
WJZM Clarksville, Tennessee
WBAC Cleveland, Tennessee
WCLE Cleveland, Tennessee
WPTN Cookeville, Tennessee
WTJJ Dyer, Tennessee
WCPH Etowah, Tennessee
WAKM Franklin, Tennessee
WGRV Greeneville, Tennessee
WWTN Hendersonville, Tennessee
WETS-FM Johnson City, Tennessee
WJCW Johnson City, Tennessee
WETR Knoxville, Tennessee
WCOR Lebanon, Tennessee
WLOD Loudon, Tennessee
WPLN Madison, Tennessee
WRKQ Madisonville, Tennessee
WCMT Martin, Tennessee
WAKI McMinnville, Tennessee
WREC Memphis, Tennessee
WGNS Murfreesboro, Tennessee
WLAC Nashville, Tennessee
WOKI Oliver Springs, Tennessee
WGOW Soddy-Daisy, Tennessee
WRHA(AM) Spring City, Tennessee
KWKC Abilene, Texas
KGNC Amarillo, Texas
KIXZ Amarillo, Texas
KLBJ Austin, Texas
KLVI Beaumont, Texas
KFLC Benbrook, Texas
KBST-FM Big Spring, Texas
KWHI Brenham, Texas
WTAW-FM Buffalo, Texas
KDET Center, Texas
KXYL-FM Coleman, Texas
KWBC College Station, Texas
WTAW College Station, Texas
KEYS Corpus Christi, Texas
KKTX Corpus Christi, Texas
KHER Crystal City, Texas
KERA Dallas, Texas
KFXR Dallas, Texas
KURV Edinburg, Texas
KULP El Campo, Texas
KAMA El Paso, Texas
KBNA-FM El Paso, Texas
KTSM El Paso, Texas
WBAP Fort Worth, Texas
KGAF Gainesville, Texas
KLAT Houston, Texas
KNTH Houston, Texas
KPRC Houston, Texas
KTRH Houston, Texas
KFYO Lubbock, Texas
KJDL Lubbock, Texas
KRFE Lubbock, Texas
KCRS Midland, Texas
KIMP Mount Pleasant, Texas
KSFA Nacogdoches, Texas
KNET Palestine, Texas
KOLE Port Arthur, Texas
KKSA San Angelo, Texas
KCOR San Antonio, Texas
KTSA San Antonio, Texas
WOAI San Antonio, Texas
KTSW San Marcos, Texas
KWED Seguin, Texas
KZSP South Padre Island, Texas
KTEM Temple, Texas
KLUP Terrell Hills, Texas
KTFS Texarkana, Texas
KSEV Tomball, Texas
KTBB Troup, Texas
KBCT Waco, Texas
KWTX Waco, Texas
KWFS Wichita Falls, Texas
KSUB Cedar City, Utah

KUSR Logan, Utah
KUSU-FM Logan, Utah
KVNU Logan, Utah
KSL-FM Midvale, Utah
KOAL Price, Utah
KBYU-FM Provo, Utah
KSVC Richfield, Utah
KCPW-FM Salt Lake City, Utah
KNRS Salt Lake City, Utah
KSL Salt Lake City, Utah
KHQN Spanish Fork, Utah
KDXU St. George, Utah
KZNU St. George, Utah
KVEL Vernal, Utah
WBVA Bayside, Virginia
WFNR Blacksburg, Virginia
WCHV Charlottesville, Virginia
WINA Charlottesville, Virginia
WMVE Chase City, Virginia
WPIN Dublin, Virginia
WFLO Farmville, Virginia
WFVA Fredericksburg, Virginia
WNTX Fredericksburg, Virginia
WMNA Gretna, Virginia
WKCY Harrisonburg, Virginia
WSVA Harrisonburg, Virginia
WCNV Heathsville, Virginia
WREL Lexington, Virginia
WBRG Lynchburg, Virginia
WLNI Lynchburg, Virginia
WHRV Norfolk, Virginia
WNIS Norfolk, Virginia
WTPS Petersburg, Virginia
WCVE-FM Richmond, Virginia
WLEE Richmond, Virginia
WRVA Richmond, Virginia
WFIR Roanoke, Virginia
WHEO Stuart, Virginia
WKCI Waynesboro, Virginia
WINC Winchester, Virginia
WVGN Charlotte Amalie, Virgin Islands
WVWI Charlotte Amalie, Virgin Islands
WSNO Barre, Vermont
WBTN Bennington, Vermont
WKVT Brattleboro, Vermont
WVMT Burlington, Vermont
WCVR(AM) Randolph, Vermont
WSYB Rutland, Vermont
WDEV-FM Warren, Vermont
KBKW Aberdeen, Washington
KXRO Aberdeen, Washington
KGMI Bellingham, Washington
KUGS Bellingham, Washington
KELA Centralia-Chehalis, Washington
KXLE Ellensburg, Washington
KULE Ephrata, Washington
KONA Kennewick-Richland-P, Washington
KBSN Moses Lake, Washington
KMWS Mount Vernon, Washington
KSVR Mount Vernon, Washington
KQWS Omak, Washington
KFLD Pasco, Washington
KONP Port Angeles, Washington
KQQQ Pullman, Washington
KKNW Seattle, Washington
KQNT Spokane, Washington
KXLY-AM Spokane, Washington
KIRO-FM Tacoma, Washington
KXOT Tacoma, Washington
KGDC Walla Walla, Washington
KUJ Walla Walla, Washington
KWWS Walla Walla, Washington
KPQ Wenatchee, Washington
KIT Yakima, Washington
WXCE Amery, Wisconsin
WATW Ashland, Wisconsin
WLBL Auburndale, Wisconsin
WBEV Beaver Dam, Wisconsin
WHSA Brule, Wisconsin
WHAD Delafield, Wisconsin
WERL Eagle River, Wisconsin
KFIZ Fond Du Lac, Wisconsin
WTAQ-AM Green Bay, Wisconsin
WHHI Highland, Wisconsin
WRJN Janesville, Wisconsin
WHBY Kimberly, Wisconsin
WIZM-AM La Crosse, Wisconsin
WLDY Ladysmith, Wisconsin
WIBA Madison, Wisconsin
WMEQ Menomonie, Wisconsin
WVSS Menomonie, Wisconsin
WISN Milwaukee, Wisconsin
WTMJ Milwaukee, Wisconsin
WOSH Oshkosh, Wisconsin
WHBM Park Falls, Wisconsin
WJMC Rice Lake, Wisconsin
WRPN Ripon, Wisconsin
WSAU-FM Rudolph, Wisconsin
WHBL Sheboygan, Wisconsin
WCSW Shell Lake, Wisconsin
WPCN Stevens Point, Wisconsin
KUWS Superior, Wisconsin
WSAU-AM Wausau, Wisconsin
WFHR Wisconsin Rapids, Wisconsin
WHIS Bluefield, West Virginia
WTCS Fairmont, West Virginia
WVHU Huntington, West Virginia
WEPM Martinsburg, West Virginia
WRNR Martinsburg, West Virginia
WVLY Moundsville, West Virginia
WVNT Parkersburg, West Virginia
WRRL Rainelle, West Virginia
WAJR-FM Salem, West Virginia
WWVA Wheeling, West Virginia
WBTH Williamson, West Virginia
KUWA Afton, Wyoming
KBBS Buffalo, Wyoming
KODI Cody, Wyoming
KIML Gillette, Wyoming
KOWB Laramie, Wyoming
KGAB Orchard Valley, Wyoming
KROE Sheridan, Wyoming

Oldies

KEAG Anchorage, Alaska
KFMJ Ketchikan, Alaska
KXBA Nikiski, Alaska
KIFW Sitka, Alaska
WAFN-FM Arab, Alabama
WKAC Athens, Alabama
WATV Birmingham, Alabama
WEBJ Brewton, Alabama
WTBF-FM Brundidge, Alabama
WZNJ Demopolis, Alabama
WAGF-FM Dothan, Alabama
WGMZ Glencoe, Alabama
WGYV Greenville, Alabama
WLOR Huntsville, Alabama
WHPH Jemison, Alabama
WLAY-FM Littleville, Alabama
WQRV Meridianville, Alabama
WMFC Monroeville, Alabama
WQKS-FM Montgomery, Alabama
WVOK Oxford, Alabama
WPID Piedmont, Alabama
WKZD Priceville, Alabama
WJDB Thomasville, Alabama
WRLD Valley, Alabama
WKXM-FM Winfield, Alabama
KFCM Ash Flat, Arkansas
KEWI Benton, Arkansas
KQBK Booneville, Arkansas
KTRQ Colt, Arkansas
KBKG Corning, Arkansas
KFLI Des Arc, Arkansas
KLSZ-FM Fort Smith, Arkansas
KKIK Horseshoe Bend, Arkansas
KQOR Mena, Arkansas
KAMO-FM Rogers, Arkansas
KWAK-FM Stuttgart, Arkansas
KRLW Walnut Ridge, Arkansas
KCTT-FM Yellville, Arkansas
KXFF Colorado City, Arizona
KKLD Cottonwood, Arizona
KMVA Dewey-Humboldt, Arizona
KGVY Green Valley, Arizona
KRCY-FM Lake Havasu City, Arizona
KVYL Mohave Valley, Arizona
KOOL Phoenix, Arizona
KOY Phoenix, Arizona
KBUX Quartzsite, Arizona
KAZG Scottsdale, Arizona
KZKE Seligman, Arizona
KSNX Show Low, Arizona
KVSL Show Low, Arizona
KKYZ Sierra Vista, Arizona
KCEE Tucson, Arizona
KHYT Tucson, Arizona
KTUC Tucson, Arizona
XHRMFM Tijuana, Mexico
KCEA Atherton, California
KAFY Bakersfield, California
KKBB Bakersfield, California
KBOV Bishop, California
KSSX Carlsbad, California
KODS Carnelian Bay, California
KDES-FM Cathedral City, California
KCHJ Delano, California
KZRO Dunsmuir, California
KXO El Centro, California
KSPE-FM Ellwood, California
KKHB Eureka, California
KYAF Firebaugh, California
KMGV Fresno, California
KAZA Gilroy, California
KOKO-FM Kerman, California
KOMY La Selva Beach, California
KVLI(FM) Lake Isabella, California
KZPO Lindsay, California
KFFG Los Altos, California
KRTH Los Angeles, California
KCEZ Los Molinos, California
KABX-FM Merced, California
KOCP Oxnard, California
KOCN Pacific Grove, California
KKZZ Port Hueneme, California
KBLF Red Bluff, California
KZLA Riverdale, California
KOLA San Bernardino, California
KURS San Diego, California
KALW San Francisco, California
KFOG San Francisco, California
KISQ San Francisco, California
KOSF San Francisco, California
KQSC Santa Barbara, California
KRDG Shingletown, California
KTHO South Lake Tahoe, California
KQOD Stockton, California
KSTN Stockton, California
KXBX Ukiah, California
KVEN Ventura, California
KVFG Victorville, California
KRCV West Covina, California
KJOR Windsor, California
KEZW Aurora, Colorado
KEZW Aurora, Colorado
KLIM Black Forest, Colorado
KLVZ Brighton, Colorado
KXKL-FM Denver, Colorado
KEJJ Gunnison, Colorado
KUSZ Olathe, Colorado
KPHT Rocky Ford, Colorado
KSTC Sterling, Colorado
KSJL Strasburg, Colorado
WKNL New London, Connecticut
WATR Waterbury, Connecticut
WLBW Fenwick Island, Delaware
KSNM-FM Georgetown, Delaware
KWML Georgetown, Delaware
KWML-AM Georgetown, Delaware
WLYV-AM Georgetown, Delaware
WLYV-AM Georgetown, Delaware
WNCL Milford, Delaware
WMHS Pike Creek, Delaware
WZNZ Atlantic Beach, Florida
WWBF Bartow, Florida
WYBT Blountstown, Florida
WRGO Cedar Key, Florida
WPFL Century, Florida
WSRZ-FM Coral Cove, Florida
WAVS Davie, Florida
WOCL Deland, Florida
WBPC Ebro, Florida
WMGG Egypt Lake, Florida
WMYR Fort Myers, Florida
WOLZ Fort Myers, Florida
WEDM(AM) Fort Walton Beach, Florida
WYGC High Springs, Florida
WDSR Lake City, Florida
WTUB Lake City, Florida
WFLC Miami, Florida
WPLK Palatka, Florida
WDIZ Panama City, Florida
WYRE-FM Saint Augustine Beach, Florida
WJCM Sebring, Florida
WJQB Spring Hill, Florida
WAYL St. Augustine, Florida
WRBQ-FM Tampa, Florida
WQOL Vero Beach, Florida
WMGR Bainbridge, Georgia
WMUV Brunswick, Florida
WEBS Calhoun, Georgia

WBHF Cartersville, Georgia
WCLA Claxton, Georgia
WCOQ Colquitt, Georgia
WMRZ Dawson, Georgia
WXJO Douglasville, Georgia
WDDK Greensboro, Georgia
WKEU Griffin, Georgia
WQXZ Hawkinsville, Georgia
WTRP LaGrange, Georgia
WISK Lawrenceville, Georgia
WJTP Lithia Springs, Georgia
WPEH Louisville, Georgia
WAYS Macon, Georgia
WYIS McRae, Georgia
WMNZ Montezuma, Georgia
WAZX Smyrna, Georgia
WXRS Swainsboro, Georgia
WJFL Tennille, Georgia
WNEG Toccoa, Georgia
WATG Trion, Georgia
WRLA West Point, Georgia
KIJI Tumon, Guam
KKOL-FM Aiea, Hawaii
KBGX Keaau, Hawaii
KONI Lanai City, Hawaii
KCIM Carroll, Iowa
KKRL Carroll, Iowa
KCHE Cherokee, Iowa
KJOC Davenport, Iowa
KIOA Des Moines, Iowa
KJMC Des Moines, Iowa
KLMJ Hampton, Iowa
KNOD Harlan, Iowa
KOKX-FM Keokuk, Iowa
KKMA Le Mars, Iowa
KRIB Mason City, Iowa
KIGC Oskaloosa, Iowa
KLEE Ottumwa, Iowa
KIYX Sageville, Iowa
KTLB Twin Lakes, Iowa
KCII-FM Washington, Iowa
KWLO Waterloo, Iowa
KHPP(AM) Waukon, Iowa
KCID Caldwell, Idaho
KTHI Caldwell, Idaho
KSEI Pocatello, Idaho
KLIX-FM Twin Falls, Idaho
KTFI Wendell, Idaho
WQRL Benton, Illinois
WFUN-FM Bethalto, Illinois
WROY Carmi, Illinois
WILY Centralia, Illinois
WJMK Chicago, Illinois
WMQZ Colchester, Illinois
WYDS-HD2 Decatur, Illinois
WIXN Dixon, Illinois
WFXF Dundee, Illinois
WRSE Elmhurst, Illinois
WJBM Jerseyville, Illinois
WEAI Lynnville, Illinois
WDKR Maroa, Illinois
WMMC Marshall, Illinois
WPWQ Mount Sterling, Illinois
WHQQ Neoga, Illinois
WSEY Oregon, Illinois
WPXN Paxton, Illinois
WIRL Peoria, Illinois
WTRH Ramsey, Illinois
WKXQ Rushville, Illinois
WLFZ-FM Springfield, Illinois
WRAN Taylorville, Illinois
WBCP Urbana, Illinois
WCFF Urbana, Illinois
WYKT Wilmington, Illinois
WASK-FM Battle Ground, Indiana
WQRK Bedford, Indiana
WKLU Brownsburg, Indiana
WLPK Connersville, Indiana
WCVL Crawfordsville, Indiana
WIBN Earl Park, Indiana
WIKL(FM) Elwood, Indiana
WJLT Evansville, Indiana
WILO Frankfort, Indiana
WBZQ Huntington, Indiana
WJPR Jasper, Indiana
WJEF Lafayette, Indiana
WQTY Linton, Indiana
WMRI Marion, Indiana
WEFM Michigan City, Indiana
WSEZ Paoli, Indiana
WZOC Plymouth, Indiana
WSJD Princeton, Indiana
WROI Rochester, Indiana
WSKL Veedersburg, Indiana
WJOT-FM Wabash, Indiana
KSAJ-FM Abilene, Kansas
KCAR-FM Baxter Springs, Kansas
KAHE Dodge City, Kansas
KVOE Emporia, Kansas
KMDO Fort Scott, Kansas
KGGF FM Fredonia, Kansas
KQYX Galena, Kansas
KVAM Goodland, Nebraska
KAYS Hays, Kansas
KWHK Hutchinson, Kansas
KIOL Iola, Kansas
KSOB Larned, Kansas
KBBE McPherson, Kansas
KLKC-FM Parsons, Kansas
KMMM Pratt, Kansas
KSKL Scott City, Kansas
KCMO-FM Shawnee, Kansas
KWME Wellington, Kansas
KEYN-FM Wichita, Kansas
WMDJ-FM Allen, Kentucky
WAIN Columbia, Kentucky
WCTT Corbin, Kentucky
WCYN Cynthiana, Kentucky
WEKB Elkhorn City, Kentucky
WCVX Florence, Kentucky
WKYW Frankfort, Kentucky
WPTQ Glasgow, Kentucky
WCBL-FM Grand Rivers, Kentucky
WKYA Greenville, Kentucky
WQXY Hazard, Kentucky
WHVO Hopkinsville, Kentucky
WLBN Lebanon, Kentucky
WMJL-FM Marion, Kentucky
WMOR Morehead, Kentucky
WSIP Paintsville, Kentucky
WPKE Pikeville, Kentucky
WANO Pineville, Kentucky
WXKZ-FM Prestonsburg, Kentucky
WWKY Providence, Kentucky
WAKY Radcliff, Kentucky
WAKY Radcliff, Kentucky
WCND Shelbyville, Kentucky
WTLO Somerset, Kentucky
WLKS West Liberty, Kentucky
WGKY Wickliffe, Kentucky
WTGG Amite, Louisiana
KSIG Crowley, Louisiana
WTIX-FM Galliano, Louisiana
KLEB Golden Meadow, Louisiana
KLKL Minden, Louisiana
KLIL Moreauville, Louisiana
KZBL Natchitoches, Louisiana
WQNO New Orleans, Louisiana
KWCL-FM Oak Grove, Louisiana
KPCH Ruston, Louisiana
KTKC Springhill, Louisiana
WXRB Dudley, Massachusetts
WIZZ Greenfield, Massachusetts
WATD-FM Marshfield, Massachusetts
WAVM Maynard, Massachusetts
WUPE-FM North Adams, Massachusetts
WUPE Pittsfield, Massachusetts
WARE Ware, Massachusetts
WCTR Chestertown, Maryland
WTBO Cumberland, Maryland
WTDK Federalsburg, Maryland
WHAG Halfway, Maryland
WMSG Oakland, Maryland
WCTN Potomac-Cabin John, Maryland
WCXU Caribou, Maine
WCTB Fairfield, Maine
WKTJ-FM Farmington, Maine
WLVP Gorham, Maine
WLAM Lewiston, Maine
WCXX Madawaska, Maine
WCXV Van Buren, Maine
WTVL Waterville, Maine
WYAR Yarmouth, Maine
WMRX-FM Beaverton, Michigan
WKYO Caro, Michigan
WGTO Cassopolis, Michigan
WCBY Cheboygan, Michigan
WOMC Detroit, Michigan
WDBC Escanaba, Michigan
WMJO Essexville, Michigan
WCXI Fenton, Michigan
WFNT Flint, Michigan
WGKL Gladstone, Michigan
WCXG Grand Rapids, Michigan
WFGR Grand Rapids, Michigan
WHPR-FM Highland Park, Michigan
WHTO Iron Mountain, Michigan
WVFM Kalamazoo, Michigan
WSAG Linwood, Michigan
WKLA Ludington, Michigan
WTIQ Manistique, Michigan
WHYB Menominee, Michigan
WMPX Midland, Michigan
WQXO Munising, Michigan
WKQS-FM Negaunee, Michigan
WNGE Negaunee, Michigan
WNBY-FM Newberry, Michigan
WDEE-FM Reed City, Michigan
WCSY South Haven, Michigan
WSHJ Southfield, Michigan
WCCW-FM Traverse City, Michigan
WPON Walled Lake, Michigan
WBMI West Branch, Michigan
KULO Alexandria, Minnesota
KQQL Anoka, Minnesota
WQXJ Blackduck, Minnesota
KUAL-FM Brainerd, Minnesota
KRWC Buffalo, Minnesota
KCLH Caledonia, Minnesota
KLDJ Duluth, Minnesota
KJJK Fergus Falls, Minnesota
KKCQ Fosston, Minnesota
KKRC Granite Falls, Minnesota
WMFG-AM Hibbing, Minnesota
KDUZ Hutchinson, Minnesota
KGHS International Falls, Minnesota
KRAQ Jackson, Minnesota
KQEG La Crescent, Minnesota
KRJM Mahnomen, Minnesota
WMOZ Moose Lake, Minnesota
KBEK Mora, Minnesota
KCHK-FM New Prague, Minnesota
KRFO Owatonna, Minnesota
KISD Pipestone, Minnesota
KVGO Spring Valley, Minnesota
KXAC St. James, Minnesota
KAKK Walker, Minnesota
KWNO Winona, Minnesota
KBFL-FM Buffalo, Missouri
KCRV-FM Caruthersville, Missouri
KCHR Charleston, Missouri
KDKD Clinton, Missouri
KWWC-FM Columbia, Missouri
KDFN Doniphan, Missouri
KESM Eldorado Springs, Missouri
KXOQ Kennett, Missouri
KIRX Kirksville, Missouri
KQUL Lake Ozark, Missouri
KJMO Linn, Missouri
KRLI Malta Bend, Missouri
KYRX Marble Hill, Missouri
KBHI Miner, Missouri
KWBZ Monroe City, Missouri
KXMO Owensville, Missouri
KLID Poplar Bluff, Missouri
KBFL-AM Springfield, Missouri
KLOU St. Louis, Missouri
KZQZ St. Louis, Missouri
KOKO Warrensburg, Missouri
KUKU-FM Willow Springs, Missouri
WWZQ Aberdeen, Mississippi
WAFM Amory, Mississippi
WHKL Crenshaw, Mississippi
WNIX Greenville, Mississippi
WOHT Grenada, Mississippi
WJQS Jackson, Mississippi
WJDX-FM Kosciusko, Mississippi
WAGR-FM Lexington, Mississippi
WNAU New Albany, Mississippi
WCNA Potts Camp, Mississippi
WVBG-FM Redwood, Mississippi
WIIN Ridgeland, Mississippi
WAVN Southaven, Mississippi
WGDQ Sumrall, Mississippi
KANA Anaconda, Montana
KKBR Billings, Montana
KOBB-FM Bozeman, Montana
KXTL Butte, Montana
KKGR East Helena, Montana
KIKC Forsyth, Montana
KXGN Glendive, Montana
KLFM Great Falls, Montana
KMTX Helena, Montana

RADIO - U.S.

KOFI Kalispell, Montana
KTNY Libby, Montana
KXDR(FM) Pinesdale, Montana
KMXE-FM Red Lodge, Montana
KSEN Shelby, Montana
KWYS West Yellowstone, Montana
KWOL-FM Whitefish, Montana
KVCK Wolf Point, Montana
WZKY Albemarle, North Carolina
WKXB Boiling Spring Lakes, North Carolina
WPCM Burlington-Graham, North Carolina
WCLN Clinton, North Carolina
WERX-FM Columbia, North Carolina
WBLA Elizabethtown, North Carolina
WODR Fair Bluff, North Carolina
WFSC Franklin, North Carolina
WTRG Gaston, North Carolina
WGNC Gastonia, North Carolina
WNCT-FM Greenville, North Carolina
WIZS Henderson, North Carolina
WAIZ Hickory, North Carolina
WCCG Hope Mills, North Carolina
WAAV Leland, North Carolina
WLON Lincolnton, North Carolina
WLWL Rockingham, North Carolina
WSAT Salisbury, North Carolina
WFJA Sanford, North Carolina
WTOE Spruce Pine, North Carolina
KEYA Belcourt, North Dakota
KACL Bismarck, North Dakota
KDVL Devils Lake, North Dakota
KDIX Dickinson, North Dakota
KAUJ Grafton, North Dakota
KEGK Wahpeton, North Dakota
KQWB West Fargo, North Dakota
KCOW Alliance, Nebraska
KKOT Columbus, Nebraska
KCTY Emerson, Nebraska
KGMT Fairbury, Nebraska
KTNC Falls City, Nebraska
KSDZ Gordon, Nebraska
KUVR Holdrege, Nebraska
KKPR-FM Kearney, Nebraska
KLNC Lincoln, Nebraska
KBRL McCook, Nebraska
KOGA Ogallala, Nebraska
KNLV Ord, Nebraska
KOAQ Terrytown, Nebraska
KAWL York, Nebraska
WEZS Laconia, New Hampshire
WLTN Littleton, New Hampshire
WFYX Walpole, New Hampshire
WMID Atlantic City, New Jersey
WIBG-FM Avalon, New Jersey
WBNJ Barnegat, New Jersey
WRNJ Hackettstown, New Jersey
WMTR Morristown, New Jersey
WCTC New Brunswick, New Jersey
WTKU-FM Petersburg, New Jersey
WGHT Pompton Lakes, New Jersey
WVLT Vineland, New Jersey
KQEL Alamogordo, New Mexico
KKFG Bloomfield, New Mexico
KCCC Carlsbad, New Mexico
KYVA-FM Church Rock, New Mexico
KRMQ-FM Clovis, New Mexico
KDSK-FM Grants, New Mexico
KVLC Hatch, New Mexico
KEDP Las Vegas, New Mexico
KABG Los Alamos, New Mexico
KLEA-FM Lovington, New Mexico
KRTN-FM Raton, New Mexico
KBCQ Roswell, New Mexico
KBUY Ruidoso, New Mexico
KNYE Pahrump, Nevada
WBAB Babylon, New York
WSEN Baldwinsville, New York
WENI-FM Big Flats, New York
WWWS Buffalo, New York
WIYN Deposit, New York
WDOE Dunkirk, New York
WFKL Fairport, New York
WXHC Homer, New York
WZCR Hudson, New York
WHVW Hyde Park, New York
WKSN Jamestown, New York
WCKM-FM Lake George, New York
WVOS-FM Liberty, New York
WICY Malone, New York
WCBS-FM New York, New York
WJJL Niagara Falls, New York
WHDL Olean, New York
WZOZ Oneonta, New York
WVTK Port Henry, New York
WTRY-FM Rotterdam, New York
WCDO-FM Sidney, New York
WDLA Walton, New York
WTBQ Warwick, New York
WCIZ-FM Watertown, New York
WLGZ-FM Webster, New York
WJQZ Wellsville, New York
WAKR Akron, Ohio
WRMU-FM Alliance, Ohio
WODC Ashville, Ohio
WRQN Bowling Green, Ohio
WQCT Bryan, Ohio
WHBC Canton, Ohio
WCHI Chillicothe, Ohio
WBVB Coal Grove, Ohio
WZOO-FM Edgewood, Ohio
WRZX Greenville, Indiana
WLGN Logan, Ohio
WDLW Lorain, Ohio
WNDH Napoleon, Ohio
WBBG Niles, Ohio
WLKR Norwalk, Ohio
WOSL Norwood, Ohio
WKSD Paulding, Ohio
WPTW Piqua, Ohio
WSOM Salem, Ohio
WSWR Shelby, Ohio
WDIG Steubenville, Ohio
WCHO Washington Ct House, Ohio
WYPC Wellston, Ohio
WKVX Wooster, Ohio
KALV Alva, Oklahoma
KJMZ Cache, Oklahoma
KRVT Claremore, Oklahoma
KKRE Hollis, Oklahoma
KYNZ Lone Grove, Oklahoma
K243BJ Oklahoma City, Oklahoma
KOMA Oklahoma City, Oklahoma
KLOR-FM Ponca City, Oklahoma
KSLE Wewoka, Oklahoma
KRAT(FM) Altamont, Oregon
KKBC-FM Baker, Oregon
KURY Brookings, Oregon
KURY-FM Brookings, Oregon
KRJT Elgin, Oregon
KKNX Eugene, Oregon
KLZS Eugene, Oregon
KCST-FM Florence, Oregon
KLTH Lake Oswego, Oregon
KBZY Salem, Oregon
KSWB Seaside, Oregon
KACI-FM The Dalles, Oregon
WAVL Apollo, Pennsylvania
WNCC Barnesboro, Pennsylvania
WLZS Beaver Springs, Pennsylvania
WBWX(AM) Berwick, Pennsylvania
WHLM Bloomsburg, Pennsylvania
WKQL Brookville, Pennsylvania
WCCL Central City, Pennsylvania
WCHA Chambersburg, Pennsylvania
WCPA Clearfield, Pennsylvania
WWCB(AM) Corry, Pennsylvania
WOKW Curwensville, Pennsylvania
WDAD Indiana, Pennsylvania
WTYM Kittanning, Pennsylvania
WKVA Lewistown, Pennsylvania
WMVL Linesville, Pennsylvania
WBPZ Lock Haven, Pennsylvania
WRNB Media, Pennsylvania
WQZS Meyersdale, Pennsylvania
WBZD Muncy, Pennsylvania
WMCE North East, Pennsylvania
WKQW Oil City, Pennsylvania
WOGL Philadelphia, Pennsylvania
WJAS Pittsburgh, Pennsylvania
WLSW Scottdale, Pennsylvania
WPHD South Waverly, Pennsylvania
WDRE Susquehanna, Pennsylvania
WTTC Towanda, Pennsylvania
WPKL Uniontown, Pennsylvania
WOWY University Park, Pennsylvania
WRRN Warren, Pennsylvania
WJPA Washington, Pennsylvania
WJPA-FM Washington, Pennsylvania
WBHB-FM Waynesboro, Pennsylvania
WRLC Williamsport, Pennsylvania
WMIA Arecibo, Puerto Rico
WNEL Caguas, Puerto Rico
WTIL Mayaguez, Puerto Rico
WLEO Ponce, Puerto Rico
WIDI Quebradillas, Puerto Rico
WOYE Rio Grande, Puerto Rico
WKVM San Juan, Puerto Rico
WRSS San Sebastian, Puerto Rico
WVIS Vieques, Puerto Rico
WZLA-FM Abbeville, South Carolina
WKSP Aiken, South Carolina
WBSC Bennettsville, South Carolina
WCAM Camden, South Carolina
WPUB-FM Camden, South Carolina
WAHT Clemson, South Carolina
WOSF Gaffney, South Carolina
WLFF Georgetown, South Carolina
WPCI Greenville, South Carolina
WKSX-FM Johnston, South Carolina
WKSC Kershaw, South Carolina
WCOO Kiawah Island, South Carolina
WAGL Lancaster, South Carolina
WVCO Loris, South Carolina
WYEZ Murrells Inlet, South Carolina
WKDK Newberry, South Carolina
WRWN Port Royal, South Carolina
WRBK Richburg, South Carolina
WLHH Ridgeland, South Carolina
WNBK Whitmire, South Carolina
KFMH Belle Fourche, South Dakota
KBRK Brookings, South Dakota
KAWK Custer, South Dakota
KDSJ Deadwood, South Dakota
KUQL Ethan, South Dakota
KIJV Huron, South Dakota
KBJM Lemmon, South Dakota
KJAM Madison, South Dakota
KMSD Mibank, South Dakota
KKSD Milbank, South Dakota
KCCR Pierre, South Dakota
KKLS Rapid City, South Dakota
KZOY(AM) Sioux Falls, South Dakota
KVHT Vermillion, South Dakota
WVOL Berry Hill, Tennessee
WBOL Bolivar, Tennessee
WZYX Cowan, Tennessee
WCDZ Dresden, Tennessee
WTRO Dyersburg, Tennessee
WQZQ Goodlettsville, Tennessee
WQZQ-FM Goodlettsville, Tennessee
WSMG Greeneville, Tennessee
WIRJ Humboldt, Tennessee
WMXX-FM Jackson, Tennessee
WHGG Kingsport, Tennessee
WKCS Knoxville, Tennessee
WYGO Madisonville, Tennessee
WMSR Manchester, Tennessee
WTPR-FM McKinnon, Tennessee
WLIK Newport, Tennessee
WTPR Paris, Tennessee
WQKR Portland, Tennessee
WKSR Pulaski, Tennessee
WSDT Soddy-Daisy, Tennessee
WNTT Tazewell, Tennessee
WENK Union City, Tennessee
WQMV Waverly, Tennessee
WWON Waynesboro, Tennessee
KPUR Amarillo, Texas
KBYG Big Spring, Texas
KNEL Brady, Texas
KRVA-FM Campbell, Texas
KCTX Childress, Texas
KEFH Clarendon, Texas
KGAP Clarksville, Texas
KMXR Corpus Christi, Texas
KIVY Crockett, Texas
KLUV Dallas, Texas
KWMC Del Rio, Texas
KDDD-FM Dumas, Texas
KINL Eagle Pass, Texas
KATX Eastland, Texas
KHRO El Paso, Texas
KOFX El Paso, Texas
KLDE Eldorado, Texas
KGAF Gainesville, Texas
KCOL-FM Groves, Texas
KONO-FM Helotes, Texas
KTBZ-FM Houston, Texas
KHVL Huntsville, Texas
KRVF Kerens, Texas
KGLK Lake Jackson, Texas
KGLK Lake Jackson, Texas
KITY Llano, Texas

KKCL Lorenzo, Texas
KDAV Lubbock, Texas
KMVL Madisonville, Texas
KOTY Mason, Texas
KQXX-FM Mission, Texas
KCKM Monahans, Texas
KZRB New Boston, Texas
KEYE-FM Perryton, Texas
KREW Plainview, Texas
KITE Port Lavaca, Texas
KROB Robstown, Texas
KTLU Rusk, Texas
KSQX Springtown, Texas
KQXS Stephenville, Texas
KBGO Waco, Texas
KMQX Weatherford, Texas
KVLL-FM Wells, Texas
KBDX Blanding, Utah
KXBN Cedar City, Utah
KODJ Salt Lake City, Utah
KGNT Smithfield, Utah
KDYL South Salt Lake, Utah
WFOS Chesapeake, Virginia
WDIC-FM Clinchco, Virginia
WKEY Covington, Virginia
WGRQ Fairview Beach, Virginia
WZRV Front Royal, Virginia
WZEZ Goochland, Virginia
WHAP Hopewell, Virginia
WSLK Moneta, Virginia
WZFM Narrows, Virginia
WBBT-FM Powhatan, Virginia
WRAD Radford, Virginia
WXBX Rural Retreat, Virginia
WKQY Tazewell, Virginia
WSTA Charlotte Amalie, Virgin Islands
WMYV Hartford, Vermont
WSKI Montpelier, Vermont
WVNR Poultney, Vermont
KEYF-FM Cheney, Washington
KCLK-FM Clarkston, Washington
KLCK Goldendale, Washington
KBRD Lacey, Washington
KEDO Longview, Washington
KBRC Mount Vernon, Washington
KTRW Opportunity, Washington
KDYM Sunnyside, Washington
KYNR Toppenish, Washington
KCSY Twisp, Washington
KTEL Walla Walla, Washington
WISM Altoona, Wisconsin
WGEZ Beloit, Wisconsin
WISS Berlin, Wisconsin
WWIS Black River Falls, Wisconsin
WOTE Clintonville, Wisconsin
WTTN Columbus, Wisconsin
WRJO Eagle River, Wisconsin
WRKU Forestville, Wisconsin
WDGY Hudson, Wisconsin
WHRY Hurley, Wisconsin
WNXR Iron River, Wisconsin
WJBL Ladysmith, Wisconsin
WLTU Manitowoc, Wisconsin
WRJC Mauston, Wisconsin
WCCN Neillsville, Wisconsin
WLJY Nekoosa, Wisconsin
WSFQ Peshtigo, Wisconsin
WPDR Portage, Wisconsin
WPRE Prairie Du Chien, Wisconsin
WRJN Racine, Wisconsin
WRDB Reedsburg, Wisconsin
WOGB Reedsville, Wisconsin
WSPT Stevens Point, Wisconsin
WBOG Tomah, Wisconsin
WJJQ-FM Tomahawk, Wisconsin
WBKV West Bend, Wisconsin
WKCH Whitewater, Wisconsin
WVBO Winneconne, Wisconsin
WFGM-FM Barrackville, West Virginia
WUKL Bethlehem, West Virginia
WKAZ Charleston, West Virginia
WFGH Fort Gay, West Virginia
WCBC-FM Keyser, West Virginia
WFSP-FM Kingwood, West Virginia
WCLG Morgantown, West Virginia
WDMX Vienna, West Virginia
KBBS Buffalo, Wyoming
KKRR Casper, Wyoming
KMLD Casper, Wyoming
KRRR Cheyenne, Wyoming
KZWY-HD Clearmont, Wyoming
KKTY Douglas, Wyoming
KANT Guernsey, Wyoming
KYOY Hillsdale, Wyoming
KMER Kemmerer, Wyoming
KLLM(FM) Rawlins, Wyoming
KQOL Sleepy Hollow, Wyoming
KTHE Thermopolis, Wyoming
KKAR Wamsutter, Wyoming
KKLX Worland, Wyoming
KWOR Worland, Wyoming

Polish

WCPY Arlington Heights, Illinois
WPNA Oak Park, Illinois
WCPQ Park Forest, Illinois
KASM Albany, Minnesota
WRKL New City, New York
WLIM Patchogue, New York

Portugese

KIGS Hanford, California
KLBS Los Banos, California
WFHL New Bedford, Massachusetts

Public Affairs

KUCB Unalaska, Alaska
WHDD-FM Sharon, Connecticut
WCSP-FM Washington, District of Columbia
WKFA St. Catherine, Florida
WKCC Kankakee, Illinois
WVBF Middleborough Center, Massachusetts
WFMR Orleans, Massachusetts
KMSK Austin, Minnesota
KMSU Mankato, Minnesota
KUFL Libby, Montana
KPJH Polson, Montana
WKNS Kinston, North Carolina
WZNB New Bern, North Carolina
KABU Fort Totten, North Dakota
KRAR Espanola, New Mexico
KRRE Las Vegas, New Mexico
KBOM Socorro, New Mexico
WSLG Gouverneur, New York
WXLS Tupper Lake, New York
WGLE Lima, Ohio
WGTE-FM Toledo, Ohio
KZME Brightwood, Oregon
KTCB Tillamook, Oregon

Reggae

KMSA Grand Junction, Colorado
WQTQ Hartford, Connecticut
WDJA Delray Beach, Florida
KPVS Hilo, Hawaii
KQMQ-FM Honolulu, Hawaii
WNGX Acra, New York
WNYU-FM New York, New York
WVIS Vieques, Puerto Rico
WQKI-FM Orangeburg, South Carolina
WVJZ Charlotte Amalie, Virgin Islands
WJKC Christiansted, Virgin Islands
WSTX-FM Christiansted, Virgin Islands

Religious

KATB Anchorage, Alaska
KDLG-FM Dillingham, Alaska
KNGW Juneau, Alaska
KOGJ Kenai, Alaska
KBKO Kodiak, Alaska
KNOM Nome, Alaska
KJNP North Pole, Alaska
KJNP-FM North Pole, Alaska
KUDU Tok, Alaska
WSTF Andalusia, Alabama
WRAB Arab, Alabama
WATV Birmingham, Alabama
WBFR Birmingham, Alabama
WDJC-FM Birmingham, Alabama
WLJR Birmingham, Alabama
WALN Carrollton, Alabama
WXJC Cordova, Alabama
WXJC-FM Cordova, Alabama
WDYF Dothan, Alabama
WGTF Dothan, Alabama
WVPL Dozier, Alabama
WJIK Fulton, Alabama
WMOB Mobile, Alabama
WLBF Montgomery, Alabama
WTBJ Oxford, Alabama
WAQG Ozark, Alabama
WJCK Piedmont, Alabama
WAQU Selma, Alabama
WRNF Selma, Alabama
WAKD Sheffield, Alabama
WDLG Thomasville, Alabama
KVMN Cave City, Arkansas
KBDO Des Arc, Arkansas
KVDW England, Arkansas
KARH Forrest City, Arkansas
KFSA Fort Smith, Arkansas
KGSF Hunstville, Arkansas
KAOG Jonesboro, Arkansas
KUUZ Lake Village, Arkansas
KCAV Marshall, Arkansas
KWLR Maumelle, Arkansas
KCMH Mountain Home, Arkansas
KSSW Nashville, Arkansas
KANX Sheridan, Arkansas
KMTL Sherwood, Arkansas
KLRC Siloam Springs, Arkansas
KWRB Bisbee, Arizona
KJTA Flagstaff, Arizona
KPXQ Glendale, Arizona
KVJC Globe, Arizona
KNLB Lake Havasu City, Arizona
KASA Phoenix, Arizona
KFLR-FM Phoenix, Arizona
KPHF Phoenix, Arizona
KRCI Pinetop-Lakeside, Arizona
KNXN Sierra Vista, Arizona
KXXT Tolleson, Arizona
KFLT Tucson, Arizona
KFLT-FM Tucson, Arizona
KWIM Window Rock, Arizona
KYRM Yuma, Arizona
KIHC Arroyo Grande, California
KBRT Avalon, California
KFRB Bakersfield, California
KLHC Bakersfield, California
KWTH Barstow, California
KWTW Bishop, California
KMRO Camarillo, California
KCPC Camino, California
KHAP Chico, California
KFRJ China Lake, California
KPSH Coachella, California
KFRP Coalinga, California
KFVR Crescent City, California
KSAC-FM Dunnigan, California
KECR El Cajon, California
KASK Fairfield, California
KYCI Firebaugh, California
KJCU Fort Bragg, California
KJPG Frazier Park, California
KEYQ Fresno, California
KFNO Fresno, California
KGED Fresno, California
KXEX Fresno, California
KGKV Garberville, California
KKMC Gonzales, California
KAXL Greenacres, California
KPJP Greenville, California
KEFR Le Grand, California
KJOP Lemoore, California
KCJH Livingston, California
KLWG Lompoc, California
KLTX Long Beach, California
KHJ Los Angeles, California
KHOT Madera, California
KCBC Manteca, California
KADV Modesto, California
KHPY Moreno Valley, California
KHCS Palm Desert, California
KKXX Paradise, California
KPRO Riverside, California
KSGN Riverside, California
KRBP Rock Creek, California
KEBR Rocklin, California
KEAR-FM Sacramento, California
KJAY Sacramento, California
KEZY San Bernardino, California
KWVE-FM San Clemente, California
KSDO San Diego, California
KEAR San Francisco, California
KFAX San Francisco, California
KJDJ San Luis Obispo, California
KPRZ San Marcos-Poway, California
KCLM Santa Maria, California
KGZO Shafter, California

KFRS Soledad, California
KMBX Soledad, California
KWG Stockton, California
KYCC Stockton, California
KLOC Turlock, California
KPRA Ukiah, California
KDIA Vallejo, California
KARM Visalia, California
KSMH West Sacramento, California
KWLK Westwood, California
KLLV Breen, Colorado
KLTT Commerce City, Colorado
KBJD Denver, Colorado
KLDC Denver, Colorado
KPOF Denver, Colorado
KCIC Grand Junction, Colorado
KFEL Pueblo, Colorado
KFRY Pueblo, Colorado
KGFT Pueblo, Colorado
KTPL Pueblo, Colorado
KTAD Sterling, Colorado
WADS Ansonia, Connecticut
WSDK Bloomfield, Connecticut
WFAR Danbury, Connecticut
WJMJ Hartford, Connecticut
WFIF Milford, Connecticut
WCTF Vernon, Connecticut
WXHL-FM Christiana, Delaware
WYFZ Belleview, Florida
WLVJ Boynton Beach, Florida
WWBC Cocoa, Florida
WHIM(AM) Coral Gables, Florida
WDCF Dade City, Florida
WMFJ Daytona Beach, Florida
WAGE Dogwood Lakes Estate, Florida
WKTO Edgewater, Florida
WSEB Englewood, Florida
WMFL Florida City, Florida
WJFP Fort Pierce, Florida
WYFB Gainesville, Florida
WPHR-FM Gifford, Florida
WAPN Holly Hill, Florida
WWWK Islamorada, Florida
WCGL Jacksonville, Florida
WJFR Jacksonville, Florida
WQOP Jacksonville, Florida
WYBW Key Colony Beach, Florida
WJIR Key West, Florida
WKIZ Key West, Florida
WYBX Key West, Florida
WONN Lakeland, Florida
WYFO Lakeland, Florida
WAPB Madison, Florida
WGSG Mayo, Florida
WCIF Melbourne, Florida
WFRF-FM Monticello, Florida
WJLU New Smyrna Beach, Florida
WRSO(AM) Orlovista, Florida
WJTF Panama City, Florida
WVIJ Port Charlotte, Florida
WFRU Quincy, Florida
WKZM Sarasota, Florida
WKFA St. Catherine, Florida
WUJC St. Marks, Florida
WFTI-FM St. Petersburg, Florida
WTIS Tampa, Florida
WYFE Tarpon Springs, Florida
WPIO Titusville, Florida
WSCF-FM Vero Beach, Florida
WOKB Winter Garden, Florida
WWVO Albany, Georgia
WLTA Alpharetta, Georgia
WFRP Americus, Georgia
WXAG Athens, Georgia
WAEC Atlanta, Georgia
WTZA Atlanta, Georgia
WGMI Bremen, Georgia
WCCV Cartersville, Georgia
WRWH Cleveland, Georgia
WFRC Columbus, Georgia
WYFK Columbus, Georgia
WAEF Cordele, Georgia
WWEV-FM Cumming, Georgia
WDPC Dallas, Georgia
WDCY Douglasville, Georgia
WTJH East Point, Georgia
WJTG Fort Valley, Georgia
WMVV Griffin, Georgia
WAKB Hephzibah, Georgia
WGML Hinesville, Georgia
WBKG Macon, Georgia
WBML Macon, Georgia
WNEA Newnan, Georgia
WOCE Ringgold, Georgia
WYFS Savannah, Georgia
WHKV Sylvester, Georgia
WRAF Toccoa Falls, Georgia
WGUN Valdosta, Georgia
WASW Waycross, Georgia
WYFA Waynesboro, Georgia
WYFW Winder, Georgia
KTWG Agana, Guam
KSDA-FM Agat, Guam
KCIF Hilo, Hawaii
KIHS Adel, Iowa
KFFF-FM Boone, Iowa
KDFR Des Moines, Iowa
KAWV Fort Dodge, Iowa
KCMR Mason City, Iowa
KDCR Sioux Center, Iowa
KNWS Waterloo, Iowa
KNWS-FM Waterloo, Iowa
KGEM Boise, Idaho
KMHR(AM) Boise, Idaho
KBGN Caldwell, Idaho
KBXL Caldwell, Idaho
KAWS Marsing, Idaho
KMHI Mountain Home, Idaho
KZJB Pocatello, Idaho
KYMS Rathdrum, Idaho
KEFX Twin Falls, Idaho
KTWD Wallace, Idaho
WBJW Albion, Illinois
WBIG Aurora, Illinois
WXAN Ava, Illinois
WRMS Beardstown, Illinois
WBEL Cairo, Illinois
WTSG Carlinville, Illinois
WLHW Casey, Illinois
WNTD Chicago, Illinois
WYLL Chicago, Illinois
WCBW-FM East St. Louis, Illinois
WRYT Edwardsville, Illinois
WGNN Fisher, Illinois
WAXR Geneseo, Illinois
WJCH Joliet, Illinois
WAWF Kankakee, Illinois
WSRB Lansing, Illinois
WGSL Loves Park, Illinois
WJCZ Milford, Illinois
WGEN-FM Monee, Illinois
WAPO Mount Vernon, Illinois
WONC Naperville, Illinois
WWGN Ottawa, Illinois
WCIC Pekin, Illinois
WLWJ Petersburg, Illinois
WTZI Rosemont, Illinois
WSCT Springfield, Illinois
WGNJ St. Joseph, Illinois
WIHM Taylorville, Illinois
WTZY Wonder Lake, Illinois
WGLL Auburn, Indiana
WJCY Cicero, Indiana
WSPM Cloverdale, Indiana
WOJC Crothersville, Indiana
WCMR Elkhart, Indiana
WVHI Evansville, Indiana
WBGW Fort Branch, Indiana
WLYV Fort Wayne, Indiana
WHLP Hanna, Indiana
WQKO Howe, Indiana
WJCI Huntington, Indiana
WYTJ Linton, Indiana
WBHW Loogootee, Indiana
WJCO Montpelier, Indiana
WCJL Morgantown, Indiana
WFIA-FM New Albany, Indiana
WSLM Salem, Indiana
WSLM-FM Salem, Indiana
WVWG Seelyville, Indiana
WUBS South Bend, Indiana
WHOJ Terre Haute, Indiana
WKRY Versailles, Indiana
WATI Vincennes, Indiana
KAXR Arkansas City, Kansas
KBJQ Bronson, Kansas
KHYM Copeland, Kansas
KJIL Copeland, Kansas
KPOR Emporia, Kansas
KVCY Fort Scott, Kansas
KGCR Goodland, Kansas
KBDA Great Bend, Kansas
KPRD Hays, Kansas
KREJ Medicine Lodge, Kansas
KCCV Overland Park, Kansas
KAKA Salina, Kansas
KBUZ Topeka, Kansas
KJTY Topeka, Kansas
KJTY Topeka, Kansas
KSGL Wichita, Kansas
WYWY Barbourville, Kentucky
WMTA Central City, Kentucky
WKDP Corbin, Kentucky
WCPM Cumberland, Kentucky
WKVO Georgetown, Kentucky
WSGP Glasgow, Kentucky
WJMD Hazard, Kentucky
WKVG Jenkins, Kentucky
WDFB Junction City, Kentucky
WJMM-FM Keene, Kentucky
WYGE London, Kentucky
WMIK-FM Middlesboro, Kentucky
WLCR Mt Washington, Kentucky
WMJR Nicholasville, Kentucky
WGCF Paducah, Kentucky
WPTJ Paris, Kentucky
WLCK Scottsville, Kentucky
WTHL Somerset, Kentucky
WMTC-FM Vancleve, Kentucky
WEKC Williamsburg, Kentucky
KAPM Alexandria, Louisiana
KJMJ Alexandria, Louisiana
KAXV Bastrop, Louisiana
WPFC Baton Rouge, Louisiana
WPYR Baton Rouge, Louisiana
KBZE Berwick, Louisiana
KFLO-FM Blanchard, Louisiana
KCKR Church Point, Louisiana
WWRA Clinton, Louisiana
KAJN-FM Crowley, Louisiana
KBAN DeRidder, Louisiana
KVDP Dry Prong, Louisiana
KPAE Erwinville, Louisiana
WCKW Garyville, Louisiana
KKNO Gretna, Louisiana
KIMW Heflin, Louisiana
KAYT Jena, Louisiana
KOJO Lake Charles, Louisiana
KYLC Lake Charles, Louisiana
KAVK Many, Louisiana
KBIO Natchitoches, Louisiana
KYFJ New Iberia, Louisiana
WLNO New Orleans, Louisiana
WSHO New Orleans, Louisiana
KAPI Ruston, Louisiana
KSJY St. Martinville, Louisiana
WSRO Ashland, Massachusetts
WEZE Boston, Massachusetts
WFGL Fitchburg, Massachusetts
WJWT Gardner, Massachusetts
WVNE Leicester, Massachusetts
WNEB Worcester, Massachusetts
WBMD Baltimore, Maryland
WFSI Baltimore, Maryland
WSRY Elkton, Maryland
WMET Gaithersburg, Maryland
WGWS St. Mary's City, Maryland
WGTS Takoma Park, Maryland
WWPN Westernport, Maryland
WCRH Williamsport, Maryland
WMDR Augusta, Maine
WWTP Augusta, Maine
WXBP Augusta, Maine
WHCF Bangor, Maine
WBCI Bath, Maine
WTBP Bath, Maine
WFST Caribou, Maine
WYFP Harpswell, Maine
WMEK Kennebunkport, Maine
WJCX Pittsfield, Maine
WBAE Portland, Maine
WSEW Sanford, Maine
WUFN Albion, Michigan
WAAM Ann Arbor, Michigan
WCVM Bronson, Michigan
WGCP Cadillac, Michigan
WLJW Cadillac, Michigan
WMUZ Detroit, Michigan
WLJN Elmwood Township, Michigan
WPHN Gaylord, Michigan
WGDN Gladwin, Michigan
WFUR Grand Rapids, Michigan
WFUR-FM Grand Rapids, Michigan

WDRJ Inkster, Michigan
WJKN Jackson, Michigan
WKPR Kalamazoo, Michigan
WEUL Kingsford, Michigan
WMPC Lapeer, Michigan
WHWL Marquette, Michigan
WUNN Mason, Michigan
WUGN Midland, Michigan
WRDT Monroe, Michigan
WOWO Niles, Michigan
KTGG Okemos, Michigan
WMKD Pickford, Michigan
WPCJ Pittsford, Michigan
WNFA Port Huron, Michigan
WMJC Richland, Michigan
WEXL Royal Oak, Michigan
WNFR Sandusky, Michigan
WTHN Sault Ste. Marie, Michigan
WOFR Schoolcraft, Michigan
WUFL Sterling Heights, Michigan
WHST Tawas City, Michigan
WLJN-FM Traverse City, Michigan
WHWG Trout Lake, Michigan
KJLY Blue Earth, Minnesota
KYCR Golden Valley, Minnesota
WCTS Maplewood, Minnesota
KTIS Minneapolis, Minnesota
KTIS-FM Minneapolis, Minnesota
KBPG Montevideo, Minnesota
KTIG Pequot Lakes, Minnesota
KCFB St. Cloud, Minnesota
KBHZ Willmar, Minnesota
KGNA-FM Arnold, Missouri
KHCR Bismarck, Missouri
KOZO Branson, Missouri
KLWL Chillicothe, Missouri
KFUO Clayton, Missouri
KDJR De Soto, Missouri
KJXX Jackson, Missouri
KAUF Kennett, Missouri
KCKV Kirksville, Missouri
KBGM Park Hills, Missouri
KLUH Poplar Bluff, Missouri
KEXS-FM Ravenwood, Missouri
KWFC Springfield, Missouri
KSIV-FM St. Louis, Missouri
KSTL St. Louis, Missouri
KXEN St. Louis, Missouri
KRSS Tarkio, Missouri
KNLN Vienna, Missouri
KCNM Saipan, Guam
WJNS-FM Bentonia, Mississippi
WTGY Charleston, Mississippi
WWUN-FM Friar's Point, Mississippi
WBVV Guntown, Mississippi
WAII Hattiesburg, Mississippi
WATP Laurel, Mississippi
WESY Leland, Mississippi
WSJC Magee, Mississippi
WAQL McComb, Mississippi
WASM Natchez, Mississippi
WAVI Oxford, Mississippi
WSEL Pontotoc, Mississippi
WSEL-FM Pontotoc, Mississippi
WATU Port Gibson, Mississippi
WSAO Senatobia, Mississippi
WJZB Starkville, Mississippi
KJFT Arlee, Montana
KBLW Billings, Montana
KEDR(FM) Butte, Montana
KFRD Butte, Montana
KJLF Butte, Montana
KMCJ Colstrip, Montana
KGLE Glendive, Montana
KFRW Great Falls, Montana
KGFC Great Falls, Montana
KXEI Havre, Montana
KVCM Helena, Montana
KLEU Lewistown, Montana
KPLG Plains, Montana
KMBM Polson, Montana
KPGB Pryor, Montana
WBKU Ahoskie, North Carolina
WXBE Beaufort, North Carolina
WCGC Belmont, North Carolina
WCCE Buies Creek, North Carolina
WPTL Canton, North Carolina
WHVN Charlotte, North Carolina
WCLN-FM Clinton, North Carolina
WCRU Dallas, North Carolina
WCKB Dunn, North Carolina
WLOE Eden, North Carolina
WFMO Fairmont, North Carolina
WWOL Forest City, North Carolina
WPFJ Franklin, North Carolina
WYCV Granite Falls, North Carolina
WYFL Henderson, North Carolina
WHPE-FM High Point, North Carolina
WMYN Mayodan, North Carolina
WOTJ Morehead City, North Carolina
WDJS Mount Olive, North Carolina
WAAE New Bern, North Carolina
WAUG New Hope, North Carolina
WVRH Norlina, North Carolina
WGCR Pisgah Forest, North Carolina
WEED Rocky Mount, North Carolina
WEGG Rose Hill, North Carolina
WYAL Scotland Neck, North Carolina
WVCB Shallotte, North Carolina
WCOK Sparta, North Carolina
WYFQ-FM Wadesboro, North Carolina
WIAM Williamston, North Carolina
WLSG Wilmington, North Carolina
WVRD Zebulon, North Carolina
KBFR Bismarck, North Dakota
KHRT Minot, North Dakota
KFNW West Fargo, North Dakota
KPNY Alliance, Nebraska
KJGS Aurora, Nebraska
KNBE Beatrice, Nebraska
KTLX Columbus, Nebraska
KNFA Grand Island, Nebraska
KROA Grand Island, Nebraska
KAYA Hubbard, Nebraska
KNGN McCook, Nebraska
KPNO Norfolk, Nebraska
KJLT-FM North Platte, Nebraska
KOTK Omaha, Nebraska
KYFG Omaha, Nebraska
KGRD Orchard, Nebraska
KCMI Terrytown, Nebraska
WDER Derry, New Hampshire
WVFA Lebanon, New Hampshire
WDER-FM Peterborough, New Hampshire
WYGG Asbury Park, New Jersey
WAYV Atlantic City, New Jersey
WTMR Camden, New Jersey
WJPG Cape May Court House, New Jersey
WYPA Cherry Hill, New Jersey
WXMC Parsippany-Troy Hill, New Jersey
WNJE Trenton, New Jersey
WJPG Woodbine, New Jersey
KYCM Alamogordo, New Mexico
KFLQ Albuquerque, New Mexico
KSVA Albuquerque, New Mexico
KNKT Armijo, New Mexico
KKCJ Cannon Afb, New Mexico
KAQF Clovis, New Mexico
KRUC Las Cruces, New Mexico
KCKN Roswell, New Mexico
KWFL Roswell, New Mexico
KKLB Ruidoso, New Mexico
KNMA Tularosa, New Mexico
KKVV Las Vegas, Nevada
KSOS Las Vegas, Nevada
KXTO Reno, Nevada
WNGN Argyle, New York
WDCX-FM Buffalo, New York
WFBF Buffalo, New York
WLYK Cape Vincent, New York
WCHP Champlain, New York
WJIV Cherry Valley, New York
WDCD-FM Clifton Park, New York
WYBY Cortland, New York
WSIV E. Syracuse, New York
WLOF Elma, New York
WHAZ-FM Hoosick Falls, New York
WLNL Horseheads, New York
WFRH Kingston, New York
WBAR-FM Lake Luzerne, New York
WYRR Lakewood, New York
WTHE Mineola, New York
WJUX Monticello, New York
WFME Mount Kisco, New York
WWRV New York, New York
WNYK Nyack, New York
WGKV Pulaski, New York
WDCX Rochester, New York
WMYY Schoharie, New York
WSFW Seneca Falls, New York
WHAZ Troy, New York
WKEL Webster, New York
WNYV Whitehall, New York
WIFF Windsor, New York
WJYM Bowling Green, Ohio
WNOC Bowling Green, Ohio
WKJA Brunswick, Ohio
WYFY Cambridge, Ohio
WGRI Cincinnati, Ohio
WHVT Clyde, Ohio
WRFD Columbus-Worthington, Ohio
WCUE Cuyahoga Falls, Ohio
WJJE Delaware, Ohio
WBIE Delphos, Ohio
WGNZ Fairborn, Ohio
WCNW Fairfield, Ohio
WXMF Marion, Ohio
WFCJ Miamisburg, Ohio
WVMS Sandusky, Ohio
WAUI Shelby, Ohio
WOTL Toledo, Ohio
WWYC Toledo, Ohio
WBBW Youngstown, Ohio
WYTN Youngstown, Ohio
WJIC Zanesville, Ohio
KKWD(FM) Bethany, Colorado
KJHL Boise City, Oklahoma
KNYD Broken Arrow, Oklahoma
KJCC Carnegie, Oklahoma
KDIM Coweta, Oklahoma
KAYC Durant, Oklahoma
KHEV Fairview, Oklahoma
KSYE Frederick, Oklahoma
KMFS Guthrie, Oklahoma
KJDR Guymon, Oklahoma
KALU Langston, Oklahoma
KVRS Lawton, Oklahoma
KMSI Moore, Oklahoma
KLVV Ponca City, Oklahoma
KARG Poteau, Oklahoma
KCFO Tulsa, Oklahoma
KAYM Weatherford, Oklahoma
KGIO Astoria, Oregon
KDJC Baker, Oregon
KJCH Coos Bay, Oregon
KQDL Hines, Oregon
KGNR John Day, Oregon
KPIJ Junction City, Oregon
KDOV Medford, Oregon
KYOR Newport, Oregon
KPFR Pine Grove, Oregon
KBVM Portland, Oregon
KKJA Redmond, Oregon
KAJC Salem, Oregon
KLWJ(AM) Umatilla, Oregon
WJCS Allentown, Pennsylvania
WAOB-FM Beaver Falls, Pennsylvania
WUFR Bedford, Pennsylvania
WFKJ Cashtown, Pennsylvania
WPWA Chester, Pennsylvania
WVCH Chester, Pennsylvania
WPGM Danville, Pennsylvania
WISP Doylestown, Pennsylvania
WEFR Erie, Pennsylvania
WAWN Franklin, Pennsylvania
WHHN Hollidaysburg, Pennsylvania
WEJS Jersey Shore, Pennsylvania
WJSA-FM Jersey Shore, Pennsylvania
WYBQ Leesport, Pennsylvania
WJSM-FM Martinsburg, Pennsylvania
WWBJ Martinsburg, Pennsylvania
WRIJ Masontown, Pennsylvania
WPEL Montrose, Pennsylvania
WRWJ Murrysville, Pennsylvania
WPCL Northern Cambria, Pennsylvania
WPHE Phoenixville, Pennsylvania
WLKH Somerset, Pennsylvania
WKDN-FM State College, Pennsylvania
WRGN Sweet Valley, Pennsylvania
WLIH Whitneyville, Pennsylvania
WFAB Ceiba, Puerto Rico
WJVP Culebra, Puerto Rico
WCRP Guayama, Puerto Rico
WIVV Island of Vieques, Puerto Rico
WCGB Juana Diaz, Puerto Rico
WRRE Juncos, Puerto Rico
WPPC Penuelas, Puerto Rico
WBMJ San Juan, Puerto Rico
WKVM San Juan, Puerto Rico
WARV Warwick, Rhode Island
WMIR Atlantic Beach, South Carolina
WVCD Bamberg-Denmark, South Carolina
WSPX Bowman, South Carolina

WYFV Cayce, South Carolina
WFCH Charleston, South Carolina
WLTQ Charleston, South Carolina
WQXL Columbia, South Carolina
WPDT Coward, South Carolina
WFGN Gaffney, South Carolina
WYFG Gaffney, South Carolina
WLMC Georgetown, South Carolina
WPJF Greenville, South Carolina
WTBI-FM Greenville, South Carolina
WBZF Hartsville, South Carolina
WRIX Homeland Park, South Carolina
WGUS-FM New Ellenton, South Carolina
WKZK North Augusta, South Carolina
WYFH North Charleston, South Carolina
WKVC North Myrtle Beach, South Carolina
WNMB North Myrtle Beach, South Carolina
WPJK Orangeburg, South Carolina
WCSZ Sans Souci, South Carolina
WLJI Summerton, South Carolina
WQUL(AM) Woodruff, South Carolina
KKAA Aberdeen, South Dakota
KVCF Freeman, South Dakota
KWRC Hermosa, South Dakota
KVFL Pierre, South Dakota
KQFR Rapid City, South Dakota
KQKD Redfield, South Dakota
KNWC Sioux Falls, South Dakota
WBIN Benton, Tennessee
WYBK Chattanooga, Tennessee
WMCH Church Hill, Tennessee
WSGM Coalmont, Tennessee
WWOG Cookeville, Tennessee
WBEJ Elizabethton, Tennessee
WYXE Gallatin, Tennessee
WAUO Hohenwald, Tennessee
WCLC Jamestown, Tennessee
WCLC-FM Jamestown, Tennessee
WDEB Jamestown, Tennessee
WKXV Knoxville, Tennessee
WMQM Lakeland, Tennessee
WAWI Lawrenceburg, Tennessee
WBLC Lenoir City, Tennessee
WAXO Lewisburg, Tennessee
WFLI Lookout Mountain, Tennessee
WGBQ Lynchburg, Tennessee
WYDL Middleton, Tennessee
WENO Nashville, Tennessee
WLAC Nashville, Tennessee
WNQM Nashville, Tennessee
WYFN Nashville, Tennessee
WDNX Olive Hill, Tennessee
WPRT-HD2 Philpot, Kentucky
WJBP Red Bank, Tennessee
WAUV Ripley, Tennessee
WAZD Savannah, Tennessee
WSIB Selmer, Tennessee
WZYZ Spencer, Tennessee
WLYJ(FM) Tullahoma, Tennessee
WZTH Tusculum, Tennessee
KDRY Alamo Heights, Texas
KAVW Amarillo, Texas
KEYU-FM Amarillo, Texas
KJRT Amarillo, Texas
KEDR Bay City, Texas
KBCX Big Spring, Texas
KMZZ Bishop, Texas
KASV Borger, Texas
KWAS Borger, Texas
KBNR Brownsville, Texas
KBEN Carrizo Springs, Texas
KUZN Centerville, Texas
KAFR Conroe, Texas
KBNJ Corpus Christi, Texas
KCTA Corpus Christi, Texas
KCBI Dallas, Texas
KGGR Dallas, Texas
KDKR Decatur, Texas
KDHN Dimmitt, Texas
KOIR Edinburg, Texas
KVER El Paso, Texas
KVIV El Paso, Texas
KPAS Fabens, Texas
KIJN Farwell, Texas
KIJN-FM Farwell, Texas
KFST Fort Stockton, Texas
KAAM Garland, Texas
KSHJ Houston, Texas
KRBL Idalou, Texas
KBJS Jacksonville, Texas
KINE Kingsville, Texas
KHOY Laredo, Texas
KAMY Lubbock, Texas
KBMD Marble Falls, Texas
KBIB Marion, Texas
KCAS McCook, Texas
KFLB Odessa, Texas
KYFP Palestine, Texas
KAVO Pampa, Texas
KFTG Pasadena, Texas
KPMB Plainview, Texas
KDEI Port Arthur, Texas
KSGR Portland, Texas
KBIC Raymondville, Texas
KQUE Rosenberg-Richmond, Texas
KCRN-FM San Angelo, Texas
KFLB-FM Stanton, Texas
KGLY Tyler, Texas
KVNE Tyler, Texas
KVED Vernon, Texas
KANI Wharton, Texas
KPDR Wheeler, Texas
KEZB Beaver, Utah
KEYD Delta, Utah
KRRA Paragonah, Utah
KEYP Price, Utah
KEYR Richfield, Utah
KUFR Salt Lake City, Utah
WYFJ Ashland, Virginia
WLSD Big Stone Gap, Virginia
WAUQ Charles City, Virginia
WJYK Chase City, Virginia
WWIP Chesapeake, Virginia
WNLR Churchville, Virginia
WVRI Clifton Forge, Virginia
WFIC Collinsville, Virginia
WARN Culpeper, Virginia
WOTC Edinburg, Virginia
WKNV Fairlawn, Virginia
WFAX Falls Church, Virginia
WPAK Farmville, Virginia
WYFT Luray, Virginia
WKPA Lynchburg, Virginia
WLVA Lynchburg, Virginia
WRVL Lynchburg, Virginia
WYFI Norfolk, Virginia
WYRM Norfolk, Virginia
WNVA Norton, Virginia
WEQP Pamplin City, Virginia
WGTH-FM Richlands, Virginia
WREJ Richmond, Virginia
WRTZ Roanoke, Virginia
WRXT Roanoke, Virginia
WKGM Smithfield, Virginia
WSBV South Boston, Virginia
WXLZ St. Paul, Virginia
WKBA Vinton, Virginia
WTRM Winchester, Virginia
WYCS Yorktown, Virginia
WGOD-FM Charlotte Amalie, Virgin Islands
WIVH Christiansted, Virgin Islands
WCMD-FM Barre, Vermont
WGLY-FM Bolton, Vermont
WMNV Rupert, Vermont
WFTF Rutland, Vermont
WTWN Wells River, Vermont
KGNW Burien-Seattle, Washington
KUCC Clarkston, Washington
KKRS Davenport, Washington
KSPO Dishman, Washington
KCSH Ellensburg, Washington
KTBI Ephrata, Washington
KARR Kirkland, Washington
KJVH Longview, Washington
KWPZ Lynden, Washington
KOLU Pasco, Washington
KACS Rainier, Washington
KWFJ Roy, Washington
KBLE Seattle, Washington
KAYB Sunnyside, Washington
KYFQ Tacoma, Washington
KSOH Wapato, Washington
KPLW Wenatchee, Washington
KBNO-FM White Salmon, Washington
WDVM Eau Claire, Wisconsin
WVFL Fond Du Lac, Wisconsin
WJTY Lancaster, Wisconsin
WJWD Marshall, Wisconsin
WHJL Merrill, Wisconsin
WMWK Milwaukee, Wisconsin
WVCY-FM Milwaukee, Wisconsin
WMMA Nekoosa, Wisconsin
WVCY Oshkosh, Wisconsin
WRVM Suring, Wisconsin
WVCX Tomah, Wisconsin
WEGZ Washburn, Wisconsin
WJJJ Beckley, West Virginia
WHIS Bluefield, West Virginia
WXAF Charleston, West Virginia
WLUX Dunbar, West Virginia
WMUX Hurricane, West Virginia
WFSP-FM Kingwood, West Virginia
WOTR(FM) Lost Creek, West Virginia
WELD-FM Moorefield, West Virginia
WRLB Rainelle, West Virginia
WMXE South Charleston, West Virginia
WJYP St. Albans, West Virginia
KAXG Gillette, Wyoming
KLWD Gillette, Wyoming
KTME Reliance, Wyoming
KOHR Sheridan, Wyoming
KDNR South Greeley, Wyoming

Rock/AOR

KWHL Anchorage, Alaska
KKED Fairbanks, Alaska
KZND Houston, Alaska
KSUP Juneau, Alaska
WRTT-FM Huntsville, Alabama
WTGZ Union Springs, Alabama
KKEG Bentonville, Arkansas
KDJE Jacksonville, Arkansas
KERX Paris, Arkansas
KDKB Mesa, Arizona
KUPD Tempe, Arizona
KLPX Tucsun, Nevada
KBRE Atwater, California
KRRX Burney, California
KFMF Chico, California
KSSI China Lake, California
KCLB-FM Coachella, California
KVHS Concord, California
KRAB Greenacres, California
KURQ Grover Beach, California
KSLG-FM Hydesville, California
KLOS Los Angeles, California
KAKX Mendocino, California
KJEE Montecito, California
KSFH Mountain View, California
KRQR Orland, California
KQNY Quincy, California
KCAL-FM Redlands, California
KMRQ Riverbank, California
KRXQ Sacramento, California
KIOZ San Diego, California
KZOZ San Luis Obispo, California
KSAN San Mateo, California
KTYD Santa Barbara, California
KTMQ Temecula, California
KCLZ Twentynine Palms, California
KMKX Willits, California
KILO Colorado Springs, Colorado
KBPI Denver, Colorado
KKDC Dolores, Colorado
KRKV Las Animas, Colorado
WQAQ Hamden, Connecticut
WCCC-FM Hartford, Connecticut
WHCN Hartford, Connecticut
WPLR New Haven, Connecticut
WECS Willimantic, Connecticut
WWDC Washington, District of Columbia
WBGF Belle Glade, Florida
WYYX Bonifay, Florida
WRXK-FM Bonita Springs, Florida
WNDN Chiefland, Florida
WXTB Clearwater, Florida
WJRR Cocoa Beach, Florida
WAAZ-FM Crestview, Florida
WSUN-FM Holiday, Florida
WBRN Holmes Beach, Florida
WXXJ Jacksonville, Florida
WFEZ(FM) Miami, Florida
WHHZ Newberry, Florida
WHOG-FM Ormond-By-The-Sea, Florida
WTKX-FM Pensacola, Florida
WXSR Quincy, Florida
WXNX Sanibel, Florida
WZLB Santa Rosa Beach, Florida
WHPT Sarasota, Florida
WNDD Silver Springs, Florida
WGLF Tallahassee, Florida
WQTL Tallahassee, Florida

WVRK Columbus, Georgia
WHFX Darien, Georgia
WBCX Gainesville, Georgia
WRXR-FM Rossville, Georgia
WWRQ-FM Valdosta, Georgia
KQCS Bettendorf, Iowa
KBOB-FM De Witt, Iowa
KRNA Iowa City, Iowa
KMCS Muscatine, Iowa
KAZR Pella, Iowa
KCVI Blackfoot, Idaho
KZID Culdesac, Idaho
KHTQ Hayden, Idaho
KEDJ Jerome, Idaho
KOZE-FM Lewiston, Idaho
KEFX Twin Falls, Idaho
WXRX Belvidere, Illinois
WQKQ Carthage, Illinois
WRXX Centralia, Illinois
KPNT Collinsville, Illinois
WLSR Galesburg, Illinois
WHPI Glasford, Illinois
WLCA Godfrey, Illinois
WTAO-FM Herrin, Illinois
WCSF Joliet, Illinois
WLTL La Grange, Illinois
WNLF Macomb, Illinois
WLKL Mattoon, Illinois
WDCR Oreana, Illinois
WIXO Peoria, Illinois
WBZG Peru, Illinois
WQLZ Petersburg, Illinois
WCVS-FM Virden, Illinois
WDML Woodlawn, Illinois
WJAA Austin, Indiana
WTFX-FM Clarksville, Indiana
WSFR Corydon, Indiana
WRGF Greenfield, Indiana
WKHY Lafayette, Indiana
WWHI Muncie, Indiana
WRBR-FM South Bend, Indiana
WISU Terre Haute, Indiana
WBYR Woodburn, Indiana
KACY Arkansas City, Kansas
KQRC-FM Leavenworth, Kansas
KMKF Manhattan, Kansas
KDVV Topeka, Kansas
KICT-FM Wichita, Kansas
WCMI-FM Catlettsburg, Kentucky
WGBF-FM Henderson, Kentucky
WKCB-FM Hindman, Kentucky
WIFX-FM Jenkins, Kentucky
WKTG Madisonville, Kentucky
WZZL Reidland, Kentucky
WXCM Whitesville, Kentucky
KEZP Bunkie, Louisiana
WBMT Boxford, Massachusetts
WAAF Brockton, Massachusetts
WHRB Cambridge, Massachusetts
WIQH Concord, Massachusetts
WLZX Northampton, Massachusetts
WMHC South Hadley, Massachusetts
WBUA Tisbury, Massachusetts
WAAF Westborough, Massachusetts
WIYY Baltimore, Maryland
WCYY Biddeford, Maine
WTOS-FM Skowhegan, Maine
WCHW-FM Bay City, Michigan
WJXQ Charlotte, Michigan
WRIF Detroit, Michigan
WIMK Iron Mountain, Michigan
WKLT Kalkaska, Michigan
WQUS Lapeer, Michigan
WHLX Marine City, Michigan
WUPK Marquette, Michigan
WKQZ Midland, Michigan
WWMK Onaway, Michigan
WKLZ-FM Petoskey, Michigan
WHLS Port Huron, Michigan
WRKR Portage, Michigan
WWBN Tuscola, Michigan
KKLN Atwater, Minnesota
WMIS-FM Blackduck, Minnesota
KMKO-FM Lake Crystal, Minnesota
KUOM Minneapolis, Minnesota
KXXR Minneapolis, Minnesota
KZRV Sartell, Minnesota
KDXL St. Louis Park, Minnesota
KUOM-FM St. Louis Park, Minnesota
KZIO Two Harbors, Minnesota
KSMR Winona, Minnesota
KWXD Asbury, Missouri
KQRA Brookline, Missouri
KBXR Columbia, Missouri
KCMQ Columbia, Missouri
KCOU Columbia, Missouri
KSHE Crestwood, Missouri
KCGQ-FM Gordonville, Missouri
KBBM Jefferson City, Missouri
KRBZ Kansas City, Missouri
KKBL Monett, Missouri
WSMS Artesia, Mississippi
WCPR-FM D'Iberville, Mississippi
WFFX Hattiesburg, Mississippi
KRZN Billings, Montana
KYSX Billings, Montana
KDWG Dillon, Montana
KRSQ Laurel, Montana
KKMT Ronan, Montana
WRCQ Dunn, North Carolina
WTPT Forest City, North Carolina
WXNR Grifton, North Carolina
WVBZ High Point, North Carolina
WRMR Jacksonville, North Carolina
WXQR-FM Jacksonville, North Carolina
WRFX Kannapolis, North Carolina
WSFL-FM New Bern, North Carolina
WBBB Raleigh, North Carolina
KEYA Belcourt, North Dakota
KZRX Dickinson, North Dakota
KJKJ Grand Forks, North Dakota
KFNL Kindred, North Dakota
KIBZ Crete, Nebraska
KLPR Kearney, Nebraska
KRNU Lincoln, Nebraska
KOGA-FM Ogallala, Nebraska
KEZO-FM Omaha, Nebraska
KKJK Ravenna, Nebraska
KWSC Wayne, Nebraska
WGIR-FM Manchester, New Hampshire
WPCR-FM Plymouth, New Hampshire
WHEB Portsmouth, New Hampshire
WMGM Atlantic City, New Jersey
WJSV Morristown, New Jersey
WNNJ Newton, New Jersey
WSOU South Orange, New Jersey
WKNJ-FM Union Township, New Jersey
KZRR Albuquerque, New Mexico
KDAG Farmington, New Mexico
KFMQ Gallup, New Mexico
KXPZ Las Cruces, New Mexico
KIOT Los Lunas, New Mexico
KEND Roswell, New Mexico
KOMP Las Vegas, Nevada
KDOT Reno, Nevada
WCDB Albany, New York
WETD Alfred, New York
WZMR Altamont, New York
WGCC-FM Batavia, New York
WHCL-FM Clinton, New York
WQBJ Cobleskill, New York
WKGB-FM Conklin, New York
WKLL Frankfort, New York
WEFX Henderson, New York
WICB Ithaca, New York
WVBR-FM Ithaca, New York
WPDA Jeffersonville, New York
WAQX Manlius, New York
WJJL Niagara Falls, New York
WKRL-FM North Syracuse, New York
WRHO Oneonta, New York
WPOB Plainview, New York
WRUC Schenectady, New York
WHFM Southampton, New York
WOUR Utica, New York
WPNR-FM Utica, New York
WARY Valhalla, New York
WLGZ-FM Webster, New York
WLKK Wethersfield Twnshp, New York
WZIP Akron, Ohio
WRMU-FM Alliance, Ohio
WRDL Ashland, Ohio
WRQY-FM Bellaire, Ohio
WBWC Berea, Ohio
WRQK-FM Canton, Ohio
WEBN Cincinnati, Ohio
WMMS Cleveland, Ohio
WTUE Dayton, Ohio
WZRX-FM Fort Shawnee, Ohio
WKET Kettering, Ohio
WFTK Lebanon, Ohio
WCMO Marietta, Ohio
WLFC North Baltimore, Ohio
WUSO Springfield, Ohio
WSTB Streetsboro, Ohio
WIOT Toledo, Ohio
WLHS West Chester, Ohio
KKBS Guymon, Oklahoma
KHIM Mangum, Oklahoma
KATT Oklahoma City, Oklahoma
KBRU Oklahoma City, Oklahoma
KMMY Soper, Oklahoma
KMOD-FM Tulsa, Oklahoma
KWDQ Woodward, Oklahoma
KRXF Bend, Oregon
KFLY Eugene, Oregon
KROG Grants Pass, Oregon
KNRQ Harrisburg, Oregon
KUBQ La Grande, Oregon
KEFS North Powder, Oregon
WZZO Bethlehem, Pennsylvania
WBUQ Bloomsburg, Pennsylvania
WLER-FM Butler, Pennsylvania
WCAL California, Pennsylvania
WQCM Greencastle, Pennsylvania
WBSX Hazleton, Pennsylvania
WRKY-FM Hollidaysburg, Pennsylvania
WRKK Hughesville, Pennsylvania
WKVR-FM Huntingdon, Pennsylvania
WCXR Lewisburg, Pennsylvania
WVBU-FM Lewisburg, Pennsylvania
WNTE Mansfield, Pennsylvania
WTPA Palmyra, Pennsylvania
WMMR Philadelphia, Pennsylvania
WRFF Philadelphia, Pennsylvania
WAVT-FM Pottsville, Pennsylvania
WXAC Reading, Pennsylvania
WUSR Scranton, Pennsylvania
WQSU Selinsgrove, Pennsylvania
WZXR South Williamsport, Pennsylvania
WMTT Tioga, Pennsylvania
WWIZ West Middlesex, Pennsylvania
WRKC Wilkes-Barre, Pennsylvania
WQXA York, Pennsylvania
WCAD San Juan, Puerto Rico
WQRI Bristol, Rhode Island
WHJY Providence, Rhode Island
WRXZ Briarcliff Acres, South Carolina
WYBB Folly Beach, South Carolina
WFXH-FM Hilton Head Island, South Carolina
WMFX St. Andrews, South Carolina
WWBD Sumter, South Carolina
KSQY Deadwood, South Dakota
KVAR Pine Ridge, South Dakota
KRRO Sioux Falls, South Dakota
KDDX Spearfish, South Dakota
WRZK Colonial Heights, Tennessee
WUTK-FM Knoxville, Tennessee
WBUZ La Vergne, Tennessee
WXMX Millington, Tennessee
KACC Alvin, Texas
KLBJ-FM Austin, Texas
KZRK-FM Canyon, Texas
KTUX Carthage, Texas
KLAQ El Paso, Texas
KEGL Fort Worth, Texas
KFRQ Harlingen, Texas
KKBA Kingsville, Texas
KHJK La Porte, Texas
KFMX-FM Lubbock, Texas
KKAM Lubbock, Texas
KZAR McQueeney, Texas
KLFX Nolanville, Texas
KIOC Orange, Texas
KISS-FM San Antonio, Texas
KNCN Sinton, Texas
KLYD Snyder, Texas
KBAR-FM Victoria, Texas
KBZS Wichita Falls, Texas
KBER Ogden, Utah
WBRW Blacksburg, Virginia
WACL Elkton, Virginia
WROX-FM Exmore, Virginia
WFQX Front Royal, Virginia
WZZU Lynchburg, Virginia
WROV-FM Martinsville, Virginia
WNOR Norfolk, Virginia
WNRS-FM Sweet Briar, Virginia
WTZE Tazewell, Virginia
WPTE Virginia Beach, Virginia
WEXP Brandon, Vermont
WWLR Lyndonville, Vermont
WNUB-FM Northfield, Vermont

WIZN Vergennes, Vermont
KGRG-FM Auburn, Washington
KISW Seattle, Washington
KATS Yakima, Washington
WAPL Appleton, Wisconsin
WECL Elk Mound, Wisconsin
WCLO Janesville, Wisconsin
WEZY Janesville, Wisconsin
WRQT La Crosse, Wisconsin
WMZK Merrill, Wisconsin
WHQG Milwaukee, Wisconsin
WZOR Mishicot, Wisconsin
WOZZ Mosinee, Wisconsin
WSUP Platteville, Wisconsin
WTCX Ripon, Wisconsin
WSHS Sheboygan, Wisconsin
WNLI Sturgeon Bay, Wisconsin
WJJO Watertown, Wisconsin
WBCV Wausau, Wisconsin
WAMX Milton, West Virginia
WMON Montgomery, West Virginia
WHBR-FM Parkersburg, West Virginia
WOBG-FM Salem, West Virginia
WKLC-FM St. Albans, West Virginia
WEGW Wheeling, West Virginia
KIGN Burns, Wyoming
KAZY Cheyenne, Wyoming
KMTN Jackson, Wyoming

Russian

KICY Nome, Alaska
WZHF Arlington, Virginia

Smooth Jazz

KUAP Pine Bluff, Arkansas
KJZP Prescott, Arizona
KADO(FM) Fair Oaks, California
KJJZ Indio, California
KIFM San Diego, California
KKXS Shingletown, California
WQTQ Hartford, Connecticut
WTSM(FM) Woodville, Florida
WDAF-FM Mission, Missouri
WKYL Lawrenceburg, Kentucky
WJSH Folsom, Louisiana
WEIB Northampton, Massachusetts
KZWV Eldon, Missouri
KYWL Evergreen, Montana
WCCE Buies Creek, North Carolina
WRMU-FM Alliance, Ohio
KYSJ Coos Bay, Oregon
KZIU-FM Weston, Oregon
WFSK-FM Nashville, Tennessee
KERV Kerrville, Texas
KAJZ Llano, Texas

Spanish

WWGC Albertville, Alabama
WYAM Hartselle, Alabama
WCRL Oneonta, Alabama
KTUV Little Rock, Arkansas
KDXE North Little Rock, Arkansas
KFFK Rogers, Arkansas
KVVA-FM Apache Junction, Arizona
KKMR Arizona City, Arizona
KDVA Buckeye, Arizona
KRMC Douglas, Arizona
KQMR Globe, Arizona
KRIT Parker, Arizona
KOMR Sun City, Arizona
KTZR Tucson, Arizona
KSSE Arcadia, California
KBYN Arnold, California
KCFA Arnold, California
KAFY Bakersfield, California
KPSL-FM Bakersfield, California
KXSB Big Bear Lake, California
KSEH Brawley, California
KBBF Calistoga, California
KNTO Chowchilla, California
KPST Coachella, California
KCVR-FM Columbia, California
KFVR Crescent City, California
KXSE Davis, California
KBFP-FM Delano, California
KCHJ Delano, California
KLAX-FM East Los Angeles, California
KLMG Esparto, California
KEJY Eureka, California
KSSD Fallbrook, California
KWRU Fresno, California
KEBN Garden Grove, California
KSCA Glendale, California
KHHZ Gridley, California
KRDA Hanford, California
KMPG Hollister, California
KESQ Indio, California
KRCD Inglewood, California
KBHH Kerman, California
KCVR Lodi, California
KIDI-FM Lompoc, California
KSMY Lompoc, California
KBUE Long Beach, California
KLVE Los Angeles, California
KTNQ Los Angeles, California
KQLB Los Banos, California
KHIT-FM Madera, California
KBQF McFarland, California
KDLE Newport Beach, California
KLLE North Fork, California
KAAT Oakhurst, California
KTSE-FM Patterson, California
KATD Pittsburg, California
KLOA Ridgecrest, California
KLYY Riverside, California
KPRC-FM Salinas, California
KKDD San Bernardino, California
KLQV San Diego, California
KBUA San Fernando, California
KIQI San Francisco, California
KSOL San Francisco, California
KRQB San Jacinto, California
KBRG San Jose, California
KVVZ San Rafael, California
KWIZ Santa Ana, California
KVVF Santa Clara, California
KSQL Santa Cruz, California
KTAP Santa Maria, California
KBLA Santa Monica, California
KDLD Santa Monica, California
KUNX Santa Paula, California
KSES-FM Seaside, California
KLOB Thousand Palms, California
KLOC Turlock, California
KUKI Ukiah, California
KSSC Ventura, California
KFSO-FM Visalia, California
KRCV West Covina, California
KMXA Aurora, Colorado
KJMN Castle Rock, Colorado
KBJD Denver, Colorado
KRKY-FM Estes Park, Colorado
KNKN(FM) Pueblo, Colorado
KJJD Windsor, Colorado
WLAT New Britain, Connecticut
WJWL Georgetown, Delaware
WTMP-FM Dade City, Florida
WRLZ Eatonville, Florida
WVOJ Fernandina Beach, Florida
WRTO-FM Goulds, Florida
WKIZ Key West, Florida
WOTS Kissimmee, Florida
WAMR-FM Miami, Florida
WAQI Miami, Florida
WQBA Miami, Florida
WNMA Miami Springs, Florida
WUNA Ocoee, Florida
WRUM Orlando, Florida
WPSP Royal Palm Beach, Florida
WYUU Safety Harbor, Florida
WSDO Sanford, Florida
WIWA St. Cloud, Florida
WGES St. Petersburg, Florida
WRLX West Palm Beach, Florida
WPRD Winter Park, Florida
WAOS Austell, Georgia
WLKQ-FM Buford, Georgia
WXEM Buford, Georgia
WCHK Canton, Georgia
WPBS Conyers, Georgia
WLBA Gainesville, Georgia
WPLO Grayson, Georgia
WNSY Talking Rock, Georgia
KWSL Sioux City, Iowa
KQTA Homedale, Idaho
KPDA Mountain Home, Idaho
WMBI-AM Chicago, Illinois
WRTO Chicago, Illinois
WAIT Crystal Lake, Illinois
WPPN Des Plaines, Illinois
WVIV-FM Highland Park, Illinois
WVIX Lemont, Illinois
WPJX Zion, Illinois
WEDJ Danville, Indiana
WSYW Indianapolis, Indiana
KGLA Gretna, Louisiana
KFXZ Lafayette, Louisiana
WFNO Norco, Louisiana
KSLO Opelousas, Louisiana
KSLO Simmesport, Louisiana
WMSX Brockton, Massachusetts
WLZL Annapolis, District of Columbia
WLXE Rockville, Maryland
WDMV Walkersville, Maryland
WSDS Salem Township, Michigan
WYGR Wyoming, Michigan
WREY St. Paul, Minnesota
WYMY Burlington, North Carolina
WGSP Charlotte, North Carolina
WTIK Durham, North Carolina
WBZJ Goldsboro, North Carolina
WZUP La Grange, North Carolina
WLLN Lillington, North Carolina
WJDM Elizabeth, New Jersey
WDNJ Hopatcong, New Jersey
WTOC Newton, New Jersey
WHWH Princeton, New Jersey
WMIZ Vineland, New Jersey
KRZY Albuquerque, New Mexico
KLMA Hobbs, New Mexico
KGCN Roswell, New Mexico
KSWV Santa Fe, New Mexico
KAVB Hawthorne, Nevada
KRGT Indian Springs, Nevada
KWID Las Vegas, Nevada
KRRN Moapa Valley, Nevada
KLSQ Whitney, Nevada
WBBF Buffalo, New York
WADO New York, New York
WEPN New York, New York
WKDM New York, New York
WXNY-FM New York, New York
WBON Westhampton, New York
KIZS Collinsville, Oklahoma
K243BJ Oklahoma City, Oklahoma
KREU Roland, Oklahoma
KJMU Sand Springs, Oklahoma
KGIO Astoria, Oregon
WHOL Allentown, Pennsylvania
WEST Easton, Pennsylvania
WLAN Lancaster, Pennsylvania
WRAW Reading, Pennsylvania
WIVA-FM Aguadilla, Puerto Rico
WWNA Aguadilla, Puerto Rico
WNIK-FM Arecibo, Puerto Rico
WBQN Barceloneta-Manati, Puerto Rico
WXRF Guayama, Puerto Rico
WAEL-FM Maricao, Puerto Rico
WIOB Mayaguez, Puerto Rico
WYEL Mayaguez, Puerto Rico
WYQE Naguabo, Puerto Rico
WJDZ Pastillo, Puerto Rico
WRIO Ponce, Puerto Rico
WZMT Ponce, Puerto Rico
WPRM-FM San Juan, Puerto Rico
WKKB Middletown, Rhode Island
WGVL Greenville, South Carolina
WZJY Mount Pleasant, South Carolina
WKMG Newberry, South Carolina
WNFO Sun City-Hilton Head, South Carolina
WULR York, South Carolina
WKDA Lebanon, Tennessee
KYDA Azle, Texas
KLZT Bastrop, Texas
KNTE Bay City, Texas
KQQK Beaumont, Texas
KESS Benbrook, Texas
KJON Carrollton, Texas
KUNO Corpus Christi, Texas
KTLZ Cuero, Texas
KAMA-FM Deer Park, Texas
KDXX Denton, Texas
KLMO-FM Dilley, Texas
KAMA El Paso, Texas
KBNA-FM El Paso, Texas
KINT-FM El Paso, Texas
KQBU El Paso, Texas
KSVE El Paso, Texas
KDFT Ferris, Texas
KMVK Fort Worth, Texas
KJOJ-FM Freeport, Texas

KOVE-FM Galveston, Texas
KLJA Georgetown, Texas
KFRO-FM Gilmer, Texas
KBTQ Harlingen, Texas
KGBT Harlingen, Texas
KEYH Houston, Texas
KLAT Houston, Texas
KLOL Houston, Texas
KGOL Humble, Texas
KMNY Hurst, Texas
KHHL Karnes City, Texas
KNOR Krum, Texas
KBNL Laredo, Texas
KHOY Laredo, Texas
KNEX Laredo, Texas
KBZO Lubbock, Texas
KZZA Muenster, Texas
KYRQ Natalia, Texas
KQLM Odessa, Texas
KFTG Pasadena, Texas
KTJM Port Arthur, Texas
KNVO-FM Port Isabel, Texas
KROB Robstown, Texas
KCOR San Antonio, Texas
KDAE Sinton, Texas
KZMP University Park, Texas
KBJA Sandy, Utah
WVXX Norfolk, Virginia
WKCW Warrenton, Virginia
KMNA Mabton, Washington
KLES Prosser, Washington
KDYM Sunnyside, Washington
KWLN Wilson Creek, Washington
KDNA Yakima, Washington
WLMV Madison, Wisconsin
WORT Madison, Wisconsin
KBMG Evanston, Wyoming

Sports

KHAR Anchorage, Alaska
KTZN Anchorage, Alaska
KCBF Fairbanks, Alaska
WBNM Alexander City, Alabama
WAUD Auburn, Alabama
WNSP Bay Minette, Alabama
WJOX Birmingham, Alabama
WJOX Birmingham, Alabama
WFMH Cullman, Alabama
WEKI Decatur, Alabama
WEKI Decatur, Alabama
WWTM Decatur, Alabama
WZNJ Demopolis, Alabama
WAGF-FM Dothan, Alabama
WSBM Florence, Alabama
WHEP Foley, Alabama
WJQX Helena, Alabama
WTKI Huntsville, Alabama
WTKI Huntsville, Alabama
WUMP Madison, Alabama
WNTM Mobile, Alabama
WTKD Mobile, Alabama
WMSP Montgomery, Alabama
WLAY Muscle Shoals, Alabama
WIQR Prattville, Alabama
WLWE Roanoke, Alabama
WYTK Rogersville, Alabama
WWIC Scottsboro, Alabama
WBTG Sheffield, Alabama
WBTG-FM Sheffield, Alabama
WFEB Sylacauga, Alabama
WTLS Tallassee, Alabama
WTBC Tuscaloosa, Alabama
WVNA Tuscumbia, Alabama
WVSA Vernon, Alabama
WKXM Winfield, Alabama
WSLY York, Alabama
KBTA Batesville, Arkansas
KEWI Benton, Arkansas
KREB Bentonville-Bella, Arkansas
KXXA(AM) Conway, Arkansas
KCJF Earle, Arkansas
KELD El Dorado, Arkansas
KAKS Goshen, Arkansas
KTHS Green Forest, Arkansas
KFFA-FM Helena, Arkansas
KZHS Hot Springs, Arkansas
KARN Little Rock, Arkansas
KTTG Mena, Arkansas
KNAS Nashville, Arkansas
KARV Russellville, Arkansas
KUOA Siloam Springs, Arkansas
KHGG Van Buren, Arkansas
KASR Vilonia, Arkansas
KHGG-FM Waldron, Arkansas
KQPN West Memphis, Arkansas
KBMB Black Canyon City, Arizona
KVNA Flagstaff, Arizona
KGME Phoenix, Arizona
KMVP-FM Phoenix, Arizona
KTAR Phoenix, Arizona
KQNA Prescott Valley, Arizona
KTAN Sierra Vista, Arizona
KDUS Tempe, Arizona
KCUB Tucson, Arizona
KFFN Tucson, Arizona
KTKT Tucson, Arizona
KXTK Arroyo Grande, California
KGEO Bakersfield, California
KHTY Bakersfield, California
KFPT Clovis, California
KBJK Concow, California
KWRM Corona, California
KATA Eureka, California
KCBL Fresno, California
KGST Fresno, California
KCKS Hamilton City, California
KRAK Hesperia, California
KOMY La Selva Beach, California
KAVL Lancaster, California
KLAC Los Angeles, California
KSPN Los Angeles, California
KWKW Los Angeles, California
KMFB(FM) Mendocino, California
KESP Modesto, California
KIDD Monterey, California
KLAA Orange, California
KNTF Oroville, California
KPRL Paso Robles, California
KWKU Pomona, California
KNRO Redding, California
KLOA Ridgecrest, California
KWDJ Ridgecrest, California
KHTK Sacramento, California
KTDD San Bernardino, California
KLSD San Diego, California
KGMZ(FM) San Francisco, California
KNBR San Francisco, California
KTCT San Francisco, California
KTRB San Francisco, California
KKJL San Luis Obispo, California
KCNR Shasta, California
KIRN Simi Valley, California
KXPS Thousand Palms, California
KIFM West Sacramento, California
KNFO Basalt, Colorado
KSIR Brush, Colorado
KCSF Colorado Springs, Colorado
KRAI Craig, Colorado
KOA Denver, Colorado
KIUP Durango, Colorado
KTMM Grand Junction, Colorado
KEPN Lakewood, Colorado
KCKK Littleton, Colorado
KKFN Longmont, Colorado
KWUF Pagosa Springs, Colorado
KJMP Pierce, Colorado
KCCY Pueblo, Colorado
KCSJ Pueblo, Colorado
KRGS Rifle, Colorado
KSBV Salida, Colorado
KBCR Steamboat Springs, Colorado
KSPK-FM Walsenburg, Colorado
WINE Brookfield, Connecticut
WXLM Groton, Connecticut
WAVZ New Haven, Connecticut
WUCS Windsor Locks, Connecticut
WTEM Washington, District of Columbia
WDOV Dover, Delaware
WWTX Wilmington, Delaware
WWJB Brooksville, Florida
WKFL Bushnell, Florida
WNDB Daytona Beach, Florida
WJSJ Fernandina Beach, Florida
WFWN Fort Myers, Florida
WWCN Fort Myers Beach, Florida
WGGG Gainesville, Florida
WRUF Gainesville, Florida
WFXJ Jacksonville, Florida
WNNR Jacksonville, Florida
WJXL Jacksonville Beach, Florida
WUUB Jupiter, Florida
WKWF Key West, Florida
WHOO Kissimmee, Florida
WBXY La Crosse, Florida
WFFG Marathon, Florida
WLZR(AM) Melbourne, Florida
WINZ Miami, Florida
WQAM Miami, Florida
WNMA Miami Springs, Florida
WNOG Naples, Florida
WTKE-FM Niceville, Florida
WJBX North Fort Myers, Florida
WMOP Ocala, Florida
WYGM Orlando, Florida
WLTG Panama City, Florida
WASJ Panama City Beach, Florida
WHBO Pinellas Park, Florida
WPSL Port St. Lucie, Florida
WMEN Royal Palm Beach, Florida
WSRQ Sarasota, Florida
WSJZ-FM Sebastian, Florida
WKII Solana, Florida
WFOY St. Augustine, Florida
WDAE St. Petersburg, Florida
WSTU Stuart, Florida
WANM Tallahassee, Florida
WJNO West Palm Beach, Florida
WGPC Albany, Georgia
WSRA Albany, Georgia
WRFC Athens, Georgia
WZGC Atlanta, Georgia
WGAC Augusta, Georgia
WRDW Augusta, Georgia
WYNF Augusta, Georgia
WFNS Blackshear, Georgia
WSFN Brunswick, Georgia
WBHF Cartersville, Georgia
WYXC Cartersville, Georgia
WBOJ Columbus, Georgia
WIOL Columbus, Georgia
WDMG Douglas, Georgia
WPLA Dry Branch, Georgia
WGGA Gainesville, Georgia
WHIE Griffin, Georgia
WCEH Hawkinsville, Georgia
WLOP Jesup, Georgia
WLAG La Grange, Georgia
WFOM Marietta, Georgia
WMVG Milledgeville, Georgia
WCOH Newnan, Georgia
WCNN North Atlanta, Georgia
WLAQ Rome, Georgia
WJLG Savannah, Georgia
WPTB Statesboro, Georgia
WWNS Statesboro, Georgia
WJAT Swainsboro, Georgia
WSGC-FM Tignall, Georgia
WJEM Valdosta, Georgia
WVLD Valdosta, Georgia
KHLO Hilo, Hawaii
KPUA Hilo, Hawaii
KKEA Honolulu, Hawaii
KMVI Kahului, Hawaii
KKON Kealakekua, Hawaii
KAOI Kihei, Hawaii
KUPA Pearl City, Hawaii
KASI Ames, Iowa
KCNZ Cedar Falls, Iowa
WMT Cedar Rapids, Iowa
KBGG Des Moines, Iowa
KWKY Des Moines, Iowa
KXNO Des Moines, Iowa
WDBQ Dubuque, Iowa
KQMG-FM Independence, Iowa
KXLQ Indianola, Iowa
KXIC Iowa City, Iowa
KIFG-FM Iowa Falls, Iowa
KOKX Keokuk, Iowa
KLEM Le Mars, Iowa
KOEL Oelwein, Iowa
KMNS Sioux City, Iowa
KSCJ Sioux City, Iowa
KBFI Bonners Ferry, Idaho
KCIX Garden City, Idaho
KART Jerome, Idaho
KTIK Nampa, Idaho
KWEI(AM) Payette, Idaho
KWIK Pocatello, Idaho
KRXK Rexburg, Idaho
KSPT Sandpoint, Idaho
WBIG Aurora, Illinois
WCIL Carbondale, Illinois

WWGO-HD2 Casey, Illinois
WDWS Champaign, Illinois
WCRX Chicago, Illinois
WGN(AM) Chicago, Illinois
WMVP Chicago, Illinois
WSCR Chicago, Illinois
WXLT Christopher, Illinois
WDAN Danville, Illinois
WDZ Decatur, Illinois
WSOY Decatur, Illinois
WXOS East St. Louis, Illinois
WFIW Fairfield, Illinois
WZPN Farmington, Illinois
WGBK Glenview, Illinois
WJPF Herrin, Illinois
WLPO Lasalle, Illinois
WLUV Loves Park, Illinois
WFXN Moline, Illinois
WZZT Morrison, Illinois
WVLN Olney, Illinois
WGEM Quincy, Illinois
WKJR Rantoul, Illinois
WNTA Rockford, Illinois
WHCO Sparta, Illinois
WFMB Springfield, Illinois
WTAX Springfield, Illinois
WSDR Sterling, Illinois
WTIM Taylorville, Illinois
WTIM Taylorville, Illinois
KFNS Wood River, Illinois
WBIW Bedford, Indiana
WFNF Brazil, Indiana
WCSI Columbus, Indiana
WKJG Fort Wayne, Indiana
WOWO Fort Wayne, Indiana
WLTH Gary, Indiana
WREB Greencastle, Indiana
WFNI Indianapolis, Indiana
WIBC Indianapolis, Indiana
WNDE Indianapolis, Indiana
WXLW Indianapolis, Indiana
WXNT Indianapolis, Indiana
WIOU Kokomo, Indiana
WASK Lafayette, Indiana
WLEG Ligonier, Indiana
WXFN Muncie, Indiana
WLCL Sellersburg, Indiana
WZZB Seymour, Indiana
WSBT South Bend, Indiana
WBOW Terre Haute, Indiana
WRSW Warsaw, Indiana
KFH-FM Clearwater, Kansas
KGNO Dodge City, Kansas
KIUL Garden City, Kansas
KFXX-FM Hugoton, Kansas
KWBW Hutchinson, Kansas
KNNS Larned, Kansas
KLWN Lawrence, Kansas
KMAN Manhattan, Kansas
KLKC Parsons, Kansas
KSEK Pittsburg, Kansas
KMAJ Topeka, Kansas
KTOP Topeka, Kansas
WIBW Topeka, Kansas
KFH Wichita, Kansas
KGSO Wichita, Kansas
WCBL Benton, Kentucky
WBGN Bowling Green, Kentucky
WXAM Buffalo, Kentucky
WTCO Campbellsville, Kentucky
WNES Central City, Kentucky
WNTC Drakesboro, Kentucky
WIEL Elizabethtown, Kentucky
WWTF Georgetown, Kentucky
WCDS Glasgow, Kentucky
WLME Lewisport, Kentucky
WLXG Lexington, Kentucky
WVLK Lexington, Kentucky
WKRD Louisville, Kentucky
WTTL Madisonville, Kentucky
WWXL Manchester, Kentucky
WNBS Murray, Kentucky
WOFC Murray, Kentucky
WVJS Owensboro, Kentucky
WPAD Paducah, Kentucky
WKYH Paintsville, Kentucky
WLSI Pikeville, Kentucky
WWKU Plum Springs, Kentucky
WPRT Prestonsburg, Kentucky
WPKY Princeton, Kentucky
WVLK-FM Richmond, Kentucky
WSFC Somerset, Kentucky
KDBS Alexandria, Louisiana
WIBR Baton Rouge, Louisiana
WJBO Baton Rouge, Louisiana
KBZE Berwick, Louisiana
KLWB Carencro, Louisiana
KRRP Coushatta, Louisiana
WLRO Denham Springs, Louisiana
KNBB Dubach, Louisiana
KRLQ Hodge, Louisiana
KJIN Houma, Louisiana
KPEL Lafayette, Louisiana
WODT New Orleans, Louisiana
WWL New Orleans, Louisiana
WWWL New Orleans, Louisiana
WSLA Slidell, Louisiana
KEZM Sulphur, Louisiana
KMBS West Monroe, Louisiana
WARL Attleboro, Massachusetts
WBZ-FM Boston, Massachusetts
WEEI Boston, Massachusetts
WXBR Brockton, Massachusetts
WAMG Dedham, Massachusetts
WEII Dennis, Massachusetts
WWEI Easthampton, Massachusetts
WSAR Fall River, Massachusetts
WPKZ Fitchburg, Massachusetts
WBOQ Gloucester, Massachusetts
WEEI(FM) Lawrence, Massachusetts
WEEI-FM Lawrence, Massachusetts
WLLH Lowell, Massachusetts
WBSM New Bedford, Massachusetts
WNBH New Bedford, Massachusetts
WESO Southbridge, Massachusetts
WHLL Springfield, Massachusetts
WXTK West Yarmouth, Massachusetts
WORC Worcester, Massachusetts
WVEI Worcester, Massachusetts
WJZ Baltimore, Maryland
WJZ-FM Catonsville, Maryland
WCMD Cumberland, Maryland
WFMD Frederick, Maryland
WJFK Morningside, District of Columbia
WQAL(AM) Pikesville, Maryland
WGOP Pocomoke City, Maryland
WWXT Prince Frederick, Maryland
WICO Salisbury, Maryland
WTGM Salisbury, Maryland
WNST Towson, Maryland
WCME(AM) Brunswick, Maine
WFAU Gardiner, Maine
WQSK Madison, Maine
WTBM Mexico, Maine
WSYY Millinocket, Maine
WOXO-FM Norway, Maine
WVOM Rockland, Maine
WPEI Saco, Maine
WRED Westbrook, Maine
WFYC Alma, Michigan
WTKA Ann Arbor, Michigan
WSJM-AM Benton Harbor, Michigan
WBRN Big Rapids, Michigan
WBFH Bloomfield Hills, Michigan
WDFN Detroit, Michigan
WJR Detroit, Michigan
WXYT Detroit, Michigan
WXYT-FM Detroit, Michigan
WVFN East Lansing, Michigan
WTRX Flint, Michigan
WBBL Greenville, Michigan
WGLM Greenville, Michigan
WKMJ-FM Hancock, Michigan
WMPL Hancock, Michigan
WSMB Harbor Beach, Michigan
WMAX-FM Holland, Michigan
WCCY Houghton, Michigan
WMIQ Iron Mountain, Michigan
WZAM Ishpeming, Michigan
WIBM Jackson, Michigan
WQLR Kalamazoo, Michigan
WJNL Kingsley, Michigan
WCAR Livonia, Michigan
WMBN Petoskey, Michigan
WLUN Pinconning, Michigan
WPHM Port Huron, Michigan
WKNW Sault Sainte Marie, Michigan
WQTX St. Johns, Michigan
WCCW Traverse City, Michigan
KKIN Aitkin, Minnesota
KBUN Bemidji, Minnesota
WBJI Blackduck, Minnesota
KLIZ Brainerd, Minnesota
KVBR Brainerd, Minnesota
KDLM Detroit Lakes, Minnesota
WEBC Duluth, Minnesota
KRBT Eveleth, Minnesota
KSUM Fairmont, Minnesota
KDHL Faribault, Minnesota
KDWA Hastings, Minnesota
WWAX Hermantown, Minnesota
KDUZ Hutchinson, Minnesota
KFSP Mankato, Minnesota
KFXN-FM Minneapolis, Minnesota
WCMP-FM Pine City, Minnesota
KFAN Rochester, Minnesota
KOLM Rochester, Minnesota
WBHR Sauk Rapids, Minnesota
KKAQ Thief River Falls, Minnesota
KKDQ Thief River Falls, Minnesota
KXSS Waite Park, Minnesota
KDOM Windom, Minnesota
KDOM-FM Windom, Minnesota
KWNO Winona, Minnesota
KAPE Cape Girardeau, Missouri
KGIR Cape Girardeau, Missouri
KTGR Columbia, Missouri
KYLS Fredericktown, Missouri
KHMO Hannibal, Missouri
KBTC Houston, Missouri
KCTE Independence, Missouri
KCSP Kansas City, Missouri
WHB Kansas City, Missouri
KLWT Lebanon, Missouri
KLSC Malden, Missouri
KMAL Malden, Missouri
KNIM Maryville, Missouri
KXEO Mexico, Missouri
KFMO Park Hills, Missouri
KLID Poplar Bluff, Missouri
KMIS-AM Portageville, Missouri
KSMO Salem, Missouri
KGMY Springfield, Missouri
KWTO-FM Springfield, Missouri
KESJ St. Joseph, Missouri
KFEQ St. Joseph, Missouri
KTRS St. Louis, Missouri
KTUI-FM Sullivan, Missouri
KSAR Thayer, Missouri
KTTN-FM Trenton, Missouri
KFNS-FM Troy, Missouri
KOKO Warrensburg, Missouri
WAMY Amory, Mississippi
WTNI Biloxi, Mississippi
WXBD Biloxi, Mississippi
WCJU Columbia, Mississippi
WJWF Columbus, Mississippi
WNMQ Columbus, Mississippi
WFMN Flora, Mississippi
WPBQ Flowood, Mississippi
WMUT Grenada, Mississippi
WFOR Hattiesburg, Mississippi
WDXO Hazlehurst, Mississippi
WJDX Jackson, Mississippi
WSFZ Jackson, Mississippi
WAML Laurel, Mississippi
WXWX Marietta, Mississippi
WAPF McComb, Mississippi
WMOX Meridian, Mississippi
WMLC Monticello, Mississippi
WNAT Natchez, Mississippi
WNAU New Albany, Mississippi
WRKS Pickens, Mississippi
WQMS Quitman, Mississippi
WSSO Starkville, Mississippi
WTUP Tupelo, Mississippi
WQBC Vicksburg, Mississippi
KBLG Billings, Montana
KMMS Bozeman, Montana
KBOW Butte, Montana
KCAP Helena, Montana
KGEZ Kalispell, Montana
KGRZ Missoula, Montana
KYLT Missoula, Montana
KSAM Whitefish, Montana
WZKY Albemarle, North Carolina
WISE Asheville, North Carolina
WTKF Atlantic, North Carolina
WYSE Canton, North Carolina
WBCN Charlotte, North Carolina
WFNZ Charlotte, North Carolina
WWCU Cullowhee, North Carolina
WDNC Durham, North Carolina

WDUR Durham, North Carolina
WGHB Farmville, North Carolina
WFAY Fayetteville, North Carolina
WGNC Gastonia, North Carolina
WMFR High Point, North Carolina
WCMC-FM Holly Springs, North Carolina
WAVQ Jacksonville, North Carolina
WJNC Jacksonville, North Carolina
WLXN Lexington, North Carolina
WLON Lincolnton, North Carolina
WNOS New Bern, North Carolina
WWNB New Bern, North Carolina
WCLY Raleigh, North Carolina
WCBT Roanoke Rapids, North Carolina
WRMT Rocky Mount, North Carolina
WCAB Rutherfordton, North Carolina
WFBX Spring Lake, North Carolina
WSIC Statesville, North Carolina
WBLO Thomasville, North Carolina
WSMY Weldon, North Carolina
WMFD Wilmington, North Carolina
WVOT Wilson, North Carolina
KXMR Bismarck, North Dakota
KLXX Bismarck-Mandan, North Dakota
KNFL Fargo, North Dakota
WDAY Fargo, North Dakota
KKXL Grand Forks, North Dakota
KOVC Valley City, North Dakota
KOZN Bellevue, Nebraska
KICS Hastings, Nebraska
KXPN Kearney, Nebraska
KLMS Lincoln, Nebraska
KSWN McCook, Nebraska
WJAG Norfolk, Nebraska
KOOQ North Platte, Nebraska
KXSP Omaha, Nebraska
WTSV Claremont, New Hampshire
WTSN Dover, New Hampshire
WXEX Exeter, New Hampshire
WTSL Hanover, New Hampshire
WTPL Hillsboro, New Hampshire
WGAM Manchester, New Hampshire
WGIR Manchester, New Hampshire
WGHM Nashua, New Hampshire
WSMN Nashua, New Hampshire
WPKX Rochester, New Hampshire
WEEY Swanzey, New Hampshire
WCHR Flemington, New Jersey
WSNR Jersey City, New Jersey
WBSS Pleasantville, New Jersey
KBZU Albuquerque, New Mexico
KDEF Albuquerque, New Mexico
KNML Albuquerque, New Mexico
KRZY Albuquerque, New Mexico
KCQL Aztec, New Mexico
KNFT Bayard, New Mexico
KCLV Clovis, New Mexico
KENN Farmington, New Mexico
KHOB Hobbs, New Mexico
KYKK Humble City, New Mexico
KPZA-FM Jal, New Mexico
KOBE Las Cruces, New Mexico
KSNM Las Cruces, New Mexico
KRSN Los Alamos, New Mexico
KLEA Lovington, New Mexico
KQTM Rio Rancho, New Mexico
KWES Ruidoso, New Mexico
KRUI Ruidoso Downs, New Mexico
KVSF Santa Fe, New Mexico
KTSN Elko, Nevada
KBAD Las Vegas, Nevada
KENO Las Vegas, Nevada
KLAV Las Vegas, Nevada
KWWN Las Vegas, Nevada
KSHP North Las Vegas, Nevada
KXST North Las Vegas, Nevada
KHIT Reno, Nevada
KPLY Reno, Nevada
KBZZ Sparks, Nevada
KUUB Sun Valley, Nevada
WVTL Amsterdam, New York
WYSL Avon, New York
WYOS Binghamton, New York
WPUT Brewster, New York
WBEN Buffalo, New York
WGR Buffalo, New York
WWKB Buffalo, New York
WCBA Corning, New York
WELM Elmira, New York
WENE Endicott, New York
WMML Glens Falls, New York
WWSC Glens Falls, New York
WNRS Herkimer, New York
WHCU Ithaca, New York
WJTN Jamestown, New York
WIRD Lake Placid, New York
WIXT Little Falls, New York
WLVL Lockport, New York
WEPN New York, New York
WEPN-FM New York, New York
WFAN New York, New York
WFAN-FM New York, New York
WFUV New York, New York
WOR New York, New York
WHLD Niagara Falls, New York
WTLA North Syracuse, New York
WSLB Ogdensburg, New York
WSGO Oswego, New York
WEAV Plattsburgh, New York
WHTK Rochester, New York
WROC Rochester, New York
WKAL Rome, New York
WRNY Rome, New York
WGGO Salamanca, New York
WSCP Sandy Creek-Pulaski, New York
WPTR Schenectady, New York
WSPQ Springville, New York
WAER Syracuse, New York
WSKO Syracuse, New York
WOFX Troy, New York
WPIE Trumansburg, New York
WIBX Utica, New York
WCJW Warsaw, New York
WNER Watertown, New York
WAKR Akron, Ohio
WARF Akron, Ohio
WNCO Ashland, Ohio
WFUN Ashtabula, Ohio
WATH Athens, Ohio
WRQY-FM Bellaire, Ohio
WBLL Bellefontaine, Ohio
WQEL Bucyrus, Ohio
WILE Cambridge, Ohio
WCSM-FM Celina, Ohio
WCKY Cincinnati, Ohio
WSAI Cincinnati, Ohio
WKNR Cleveland, Ohio
WTAM Cleveland, Ohio
WKRK-FM Cleveland Heights, Ohio
WBNS Columbus, Ohio
WBNS-FM Columbus, Ohio
WYTS Columbus, Ohio
WING Dayton, Ohio
WONE Dayton, Ohio
WONW Defiance, Ohio
WEOL Elyria, Ohio
WFOB Fostoria, Ohio
WMOH Hamilton, Ohio
WJMP Kent, Ohio
WIMA Lima, Ohio
WMOA Marietta, Ohio
WTIG Massillon, Ohio
WJAW-FM McConnelsville, Ohio
WMPO Middleport-Pomeroy, Ohio
WLKR Norwalk, Ohio
WRGM Ontario, Ohio
WKSD Paulding, Ohio
WLEC Sandusky, Ohio
WCWA Toledo, Ohio
WLQR Toledo, Ohio
WBTC Uhrichsville, Ohio
WINT Willoughby, Ohio
WQKT Wooster, Ohio
WKBN Youngstown, Ohio
WNIO Youngstown, Ohio
KADA Ada, Oklahoma
KOKB Blackwell, Oklahoma
KUSH Cushing, Oklahoma
KEBC Del City, Oklahoma
KPNS Duncan, Oklahoma
KADS Elk City, Oklahoma
KZLS Enid, Oklahoma
KINB Kingfisher, Oklahoma
KXCA Lawton, Oklahoma
KGHM Midwest City, Oklahoma
KWPN Moore, Oklahoma
KBIX Muskogee, Oklahoma
KYAL-FM Muskogee, Oklahoma
KREF Norman, Oklahoma
KTUZ-FM Okarche, Oklahoma
KRXO-FM Oklahoma City, Oklahoma
KOKL Okmulgee, Oklahoma
KOKP Perry, Oklahoma
KOSB Perry, Oklahoma
KYAL Sapulpa, Oklahoma
KTLQ Tahlequah, Oklahoma
KAKC Tulsa, Oklahoma
KCFO Tulsa, Oklahoma
KTBZ Tulsa, Oklahoma
KGND Vinita, Oklahoma
KSIW Woodward, Oklahoma
KLOO Albany, Oregon
KAST Astoria, Oregon
KICE Bend, Oregon
KUJZ Creswell, Oregon
KSCR Eugene, Oregon
KUIK Hillsboro, Oregon
KFLS Klamath Falls, Oregon
KLAD Klamath Falls, Oregon
KGAL Lebanon, Oregon
KEZX Medford, Oregon
KTIL(AM) Netarts, Oregon
KTIX Pendleton, Oregon
KFXX Portland, Oregon
KPOJ Portland, Oregon
KXTG Portland, Oregon
KSKR Roseburg, Oregon
KOHI St. Helens, Oregon
WSAN Allentown, Pennsylvania
WTKZ Allentown, Pennsylvania
WVAM Altoona, Pennsylvania
WMBA Ambridge, Pennsylvania
WBVP Beaver Falls, Pennsylvania
WBFD Bedford, Pennsylvania
WISR Butler, Pennsylvania
WWCS Canonsburg, Pennsylvania
WWCB(AM) Corry, Pennsylvania
WCED Du Bois, Pennsylvania
WESS East Stroudsburg, Pennsylvania
WEEX Easton, Pennsylvania
WPDC Elizabethtown, Pennsylvania
WFNN Erie, Pennsylvania
WPSE Erie, Pennsylvania
WRIE Erie, Pennsylvania
WFRA Franklin, Pennsylvania
WGET Gettysburg, Pennsylvania
WHGB Harrisburg, Pennsylvania
WTKT Harrisburg, Pennsylvania
WPSN Honesdale, Pennsylvania
WHUN Huntingdon, Pennsylvania
WTYM Kittanning, Pennsylvania
WLPA Lancaster, Pennsylvania
WNPV Lansdale, Pennsylvania
WWGE Loretto, Pennsylvania
WGLD Manchester Township, Pennsylvania
WMGW Meadville, Pennsylvania
WJUN Mexico, Pennsylvania
WJST New Castle, Pennsylvania
WIP Philadelphia, Pennsylvania
WKDN Philadelphia, Pennsylvania
WTEL Philadelphia, Pennsylvania
WPHB Philipsburg, Pennsylvania
KDKA-FM Pittsburgh, Pennsylvania
WBGG Pittsburgh, Pennsylvania
WYCK Plains, Pennsylvania
WEEU Reading, Pennsylvania
WIOV Reading, Pennsylvania
WVSL-FM Riverside, Pennsylvania
WARM Scranton, Pennsylvania
WEJL Scranton, Pennsylvania
WICK Scranton, Pennsylvania
WLLI Somerset, Pennsylvania
WQWK State College, Pennsylvania
WKOK Sunbury, Pennsylvania
WTZN Troy, Pennsylvania
WXVU Villanova, Pennsylvania
WLYC Williamsport, Pennsylvania
WRAK Williamsport, Pennsylvania
WOYK York, Pennsylvania
WGIT Canovanas, Puerto Rico
WALO Humacao, Puerto Rico
WMNT Manati, Puerto Rico
WVOZ San Juan, Puerto Rico
WLKW West Warwick, Rhode Island
WANS Anderson, South Carolina
WABB Belton, South Carolina
WQNT Charleston, South Carolina
WSPO Charleston, South Carolina
WCCP-FM Clemson, South Carolina
WPCC Clinton, South Carolina
WCOS Columbia, South Carolina
WISW Columbia, South Carolina
WOIC Columbia, South Carolina

RADIO - U.S.

WVOC Columbia, South Carolina
WIQB Conway, South Carolina
WDSC Dillon, South Carolina
WTMZ Dorchester Terrace-Brentwood, South Carolina
WNKT Eastover, South Carolina
WOLH Florence, South Carolina
WTZQ Fountain Inn, South Carolina
WXJY Georgetown, South Carolina
WTOD Hartsville, South Carolina
WWFN-FM Lake City, South Carolina
WRHM Lancaster, South Carolina
WWIK McClellanville, South Carolina
WRNN Myrtle Beach, South Carolina
WOLI Spartanburg, South Carolina
WSPG Spartanburg, South Carolina
WALI Walterboro, South Carolina
KGIM Aberdeen, South Dakota
KBFS Belle Fourche, South Dakota
KDSJ Deadwood, South Dakota
KIJV Huron, South Dakota
KRKI Keystone, South Dakota
KSOO-FM Lennox, South Dakota
KORN Mitchell, South Dakota
KTOQ Rapid City, South Dakota
KSOO Sioux Falls, South Dakota
KWSN Sioux Falls, South Dakota
KVTK Vermillion, South Dakota
WMFS-FM Bartlett, Tennessee
WSAA Benton, Tennessee
WXSM Blountville, Tennessee
WNSR Brentwood, Tennessee
WRKM Carthage, Tennessee
WDEF Chattanooga, Tennessee
WJZM Clarksville, Tennessee
WKFN Clarksville, Tennessee
WMRB Columbia, Tennessee
WCSV Crossville, Tennessee
WEMB Erwin, Tennessee
WCPH Etowah, Tennessee
WEKR Fayetteville, Tennessee
WNML Friendsville, Tennessee
WGFX Gallatin, Tennessee
WWTN Hendersonville, Tennessee
WKTP Jonesborough, Tennessee
WKPT Kingsport, Tennessee
WNML Knoxville, Tennessee
WVLZ Knoxville, Tennessee
WTNQ La Follette, Tennessee
WALV-FM Lakesite, Tennessee
WCOR Lebanon, Tennessee
WLIV Livingston, Tennessee
WMSR Manchester, Tennessee
WKCE Maryville, Tennessee
WHBQ Memphis, Tennessee
WMC Memphis, Tennessee
WREC Memphis, Tennessee
WUMR Memphis, Tennessee
WLIV-FM Monterey, Tennessee
WGNS Murfreesboro, Tennessee
WBFG Parker's Crossroads, Tennessee
WPFT Pigeon Forge, Tennessee
KZQQ Abilene, Texas
KESN Allen, Texas
KACT Andrews, Texas
KVET Austin, Texas
KRUN Ballinger, Texas
KIKR Beaumont, Texas
KGOW Bellaire, Texas
KFLC Benbrook, Texas
KTTU Brownfield, Texas
KVNS Brownsville, Texas
KNSH Canyon, Texas
KGAS Carthage, Texas
KZNE College Station, Texas
KEYS Corpus Christi, Texas
KSIX Corpus Christi, Texas
KRLD-FM Dallas, Texas
KTCK Dallas, Texas
KURV Edinburg, Texas
KULP El Campo, Texas
KHEY El Paso, Texas
KROD El Paso, Texas
KWNX Elgin, Texas
KTCK Flower Mound, Texas
KKGM Fort Worth, Texas
KATH Frisco, Texas
KWRD Henderson, Texas
KBME Houston, Texas
KILT Houston, Texas
KGOL Humble, Texas
KHHL Karnes City, Texas
KOOV Kempner, Texas
KAML Kenedy-Karnes City, Texas
KJTV Lubbock, Texas
KSET Lumberton, Texas
KMHT Marshall, Texas
KMND Midland, Texas
KOGT Orange, Texas
KIKK Pasadena, Texas
KLVL Pasadena, Texas
KVOP Plainview, Texas
KBPO Port Neches, Texas
KSOX Raymondville, Texas
KGKL San Angelo, Texas
KKSA San Angelo, Texas
KTKR San Antonio, Texas
KZDC San Antonio, Texas
KTSW San Marcos, Texas
KJIM Sherman, Texas
KLTD Temple, Texas
KTEM Temple, Texas
KCMC Texarkana, Texas
KRWR Tyler, Texas
KTBB Tyler, Texas
KYZS Tyler, Texas
KRZI Waco, Texas
KMQX Weatherford, Texas
KSL-FM Midvale, Utah
KJQS Murray, Utah
KALL North Salt Lake City, Utah
KLO Ogden, Utah
KOAL Price, Utah
KOVO Provo, Utah
KSVC Richfield, Utah
KFNZ Salt Lake City, Utah
KSL Salt Lake City, Utah
KZNS Salt Lake City, Utah
KHQN Spanish Fork, Utah
KVEL Vernal, Utah
KHKR Washington, Utah
WCBX Bassett, Virginia
WBLT Bedford, Virginia
WKEX Blacksburg, Virginia
WKLV Blackstone, Virginia
WFHG Bristol, Virginia
WINA Charlottesville, Virginia
WKAV Charlottesville, Virginia
WDIC-FM Clinchco, Virginia
WODY Fieldale, Virginia
WNTX Fredericksburg, Virginia
WGAT Gate City, Virginia
WMNA-FM Gretna, Virginia
WXTG Hampton, Virginia
WHBG Harrisonburg, Virginia
WREL Lexington, Virginia
WBRG Lynchburg, Virginia
WVGM Lynchburg, Virginia
WJFK-FM Manassas, District of Columbia
WTAR Norfolk, Virginia
WRAD Radford, Virginia
WRNL Richmond, Virginia
WXGI Richmond, Virginia
WGMN Roanoke, Virginia
WLOY Rural Retreat, Virginia
WTON Staunton, Virginia
WXTG-FM Virginia Beach, Virginia
WINC Winchester, Virginia
WYVE Wytheville, Virginia
WVSP-FM Yorktown, Virginia
WVWI Charlotte Amalie, Virgin Islands
WSNO Barre, Vermont
WTSA Brattleboro, Vermont
WCAT Burlington, Vermont
WVMT Burlington, Vermont
WFAD Middlebury, Vermont
WRSA St. Albans, Vermont
WDEV-FM Warren, Vermont
WDEV Waterbury, Vermont
KWOK Aberdeen, Washington
KXLX Airway Heights, Washington
KCLK Asotin, Washington
KPUG Bellingham, Washington
KBRO Bremerton, Washington
KELA Centralia-Chehalis, Washington
KXLE Ellensburg, Washington
KULE Ephrata, Washington
KRKO Everett, Washington
KBSN Moses Lake, Washington
KWIQ Moses Lake North, Washington
KFNQ Seattle, Washington
KIRO Seattle, Washington
KJR Seattle, Washington
KGA Spokane, Washington
KHHO Tacoma, Washington
KIRO-FM Tacoma, Washington
KYNR Toppenish, Washington
KMTT Vancouver, Washington
KUJ Walla Walla, Washington
KKRT Wenatchee, Washington
WSCO Appleton, Wisconsin
WDUZ-FM Brillion, Wisconsin
WAYY Eau Claire, Wisconsin
WBIZ Eau Claire, Wisconsin
KFIZ Fond Du Lac, Wisconsin
WDUZ Green Bay, Wisconsin
WNFL-AM Green Bay, Wisconsin
WHSM Hayward, Wisconsin
WAUK Jackson, Wisconsin
WIBD Janesville, Wisconsin
WKTY La Crosse, Wisconsin
WOZN Madison, Wisconsin
WTSO Madison, Wisconsin
WMAM Marinette, Wisconsin
WIGM Medford, Wisconsin
WMEQ Menomonie, Wisconsin
WOKY Milwaukee, Wisconsin
WSSP Milwaukee, Wisconsin
WTMJ Milwaukee, Wisconsin
WTLX Monona, Wisconsin
WOSH Oshkosh, Wisconsin
WPVL-AM Platteville, Wisconsin
WRDB Reedsburg, Wisconsin
WAQE Rice Lake, Wisconsin
WEVR River Falls, Wisconsin
WEVR-FM River Falls, Wisconsin
WDTX Rothschild, Wisconsin
WRIG Schofield, Wisconsin
WCLB Sheboygan, Wisconsin
WKLJ Sparta, Wisconsin
WOSQ Spencer, Wisconsin
WPCN Stevens Point, Wisconsin
WDUL Superior, Wisconsin
WJJQ Tomahawk, Wisconsin
WJJQ-FM Tomahawk, Wisconsin
WFBZ Trempealeau, Wisconsin
WRRD Waukesha, Wisconsin
WXCO Wausau, Wisconsin
WWNR Beckley, West Virginia
WBTQ Buckhannon, West Virginia
WBUC Buckhannon, West Virginia
WCHS Charleston, West Virginia
WSWW Charleston, West Virginia
WMRE Charlestown, West Virginia
WXKX Clarksburg, West Virginia
WMMN Fairmont, West Virginia
WMTD-FM Hinton, West Virginia
WRVC Huntington, West Virginia
WTCR Kenova, West Virginia
WKLP Keyser, West Virginia
WEPM Martinsburg, West Virginia
WRNR Martinsburg, West Virginia
WAJR Morgantown, West Virginia
WAJR-FM Salem, West Virginia
WJAW St. Marys, West Virginia
WBBD Wheeling, West Virginia
WSLW White Sulphur Spring, West Virginia
WBTH Williamson, West Virginia
KRSV Afton, Wyoming
KBBS Buffalo, Wyoming
KKTL Casper, Wyoming
KFBC Cheyenne, Wyoming
KRAE Cheyenne, Wyoming
KODI Cody, Wyoming
KIML Gillette, Wyoming
KHAT Laramie, Wyoming
KOWB Laramie, Wyoming
KYDT Pine Haven, Wyoming

Talk

KBYR Anchorage, Alaska
KENI Anchorage, Alaska
KFQD Anchorage, Alaska
KOAN Anchorage, Alaska
KOAN Anchorage, Alaska
KYUK Bethel, Alaska
KAGV Big Lake, Alaska
KRUP Dillingham, Alaska
KFAR Fairbanks, Alaska
KFBX Fairbanks, Alaska
KUAC Fairbanks, Alaska
KHNS Haines, Alaska
KJNO Juneau, Alaska

KTKN Ketchikan, Alaska
KVOK Kodiak, Alaska
KIAM Nenana, Alaska
KNOM Nome, Alaska
KFSK Petersburg, Alaska
KIFW Sitka, Alaska
KSRM Soldotna, Alaska
KTNA Talkeetna, Alaska
KUDU Tok, Alaska
KVAK Valdez, Alaska
WDNG Anniston, Alabama
WERC Birmingham, Alabama
WYDE Birmingham, Alabama
WVOV Bridgeport, Alabama
WRTR Brookwood, Alabama
WACV Coosada, Alabama
WXJC Cordova, Alabama
WFMH Cullman, Alabama
WASG Daphne, Alabama
WASG Daphne, Alabama
WEKI Decatur, Alabama
WEKI Decatur, Alabama
WHOS Decatur, Alabama
WAGF Dothan, Alabama
WWNT Dothan, Alabama
WJLD(AM) Fairfield, Alabama
WHEP Foley, Alabama
WFPA Fort Payne, Alabama
WAAX Gadsden, Alabama
WGEA Geneva, Alabama
WGYV Greenville, Alabama
WGSV Guntersville, Alabama
WBXR Hazel Green, Alabama
WERC-FM Hoover, Alabama
WBHP Huntsville, Alabama
WTKI Huntsville, Alabama
WTKI Huntsville, Alabama
WMOB Mobile, Alabama
WNTM Mobile, Alabama
WBAM-FM Montgomery, Alabama
WLWI Montgomery, Alabama
WIJD Prichard, Alabama
WIJD Prichard, Alabama
WIJD Prichard, Alabama
WHBB Selma, Alabama
WFEB Sylacauga, Alabama
WTLS Tallassee, Alabama
WVNN-FM Trinity, Alabama
WTBF Troy, Alabama
WTBC Tuscaloosa, Alabama
WUAL-FM Tuscaloosa, Alabama
WVNA Tuscumbia, Alabama
WQSI Tuskegee, Alabama
WKXM Winfield, Alabama
KVRC Arkadelphia, Arkansas
KEWI Benton, Arkansas
KREB Bentonville-Bella, Arkansas
KLCN Blytheville, Arkansas
KJMT Calico Rock, Arkansas
KCAB Dardanelle, Arkansas
KCJF Earle, Arkansas
KVDW England, Arkansas
KFAY Farmington, Arkansas
KAYH Fayetteville, Arkansas
KOFC Fayetteville, Arkansas
KBJT Fordyce, Arkansas
KQEW Fordyce, Arkansas
KXJK Forrest City, Arkansas
KFPW Fort Smith, Arkansas
KFSW Fort Smith, Arkansas
KWHN Fort Smith, Arkansas
KURM-FM Gravette, Arkansas
KTHS Green Forest, Arkansas
KELD-FM Hampton, Arkansas
KAWW Heber Springs, Arkansas
KXAR Hope, Arkansas
KZHS Hot Springs, Arkansas
KZNG Hot Springs, Arkansas
KBTM Jonesboro, Arkansas
KJSB Jonesboro, Arkansas
KABZ Little Rock, Arkansas
KLRE-FM Little Rock, Arkansas
KUAR Little Rock, Arkansas
KVMA Magnolia, Arkansas
KTTG Mena, Arkansas
KNBY Newport, Arkansas
KARV-FM Ola, Arkansas
KSMD Pangburn, Arkansas
KFFK Rogers, Arkansas
KARV Russellville, Arkansas
KWCK Searcy, Arkansas
KARN-FM Sheridan, Arkansas
KHGG Van Buren, Arkansas
KHGG-FM Waldron, Arkansas
KWYN Wynne, Arkansas
KFNX Cave Creek, Arizona
KVOI Cortaro, Arizona
KAPR Douglas, Arizona
KVNA Flagstaff, Arizona
KPXQ Glendale, Arizona
KTAR-FM Glendale, Arizona
KJAA Globe, Arizona
KDJI Holbrook, Arizona
KNTR Lake Havasu City, Arizona
KZXQ Lake of the Woods, Arizona
KFNN Mesa, Arizona
KLPZ Parker, Arizona
KFYI Phoenix, Arizona
KGME Phoenix, Arizona
KKNT Phoenix, Arizona
KMVP-FM Phoenix, Arizona
KPHX Phoenix, Arizona
KNKI Pinetop, Arizona
KNAQ Prescott, Arizona
KYCA Prescott, Arizona
KQNA Prescott Valley, Arizona
KNXN Sierra Vista, Arizona
KTAN Sierra Vista, Arizona
KCUB Tucson, Arizona
KGMS Tucson, Arizona
KNST Tucson, Arizona
KUAZ Tucson, Arizona
KUAZ-FM Tucson, Arizona
KAWC Yuma, Arizona
KBLU Yuma, Arizona
KDFC Angwin, California
KIXW Apple Valley, California
KBRT Avalon, California
KERI Bakersfield, California
KGEO Bakersfield, California
KNZR Bakersfield, California
KSZL Barstow, California
KINS-FM Blue Lake, California
KRXA Carmel Valley, California
KPAY Chico, California
KZFR Chico, California
KHDC Chualar, California
KNWZ Coachella, California
KDVS Davis, California
KRDU Dinuba, California
KGOE Eureka, California
KMUE Eureka, California
KWSW Eureka, California
KALZ Fowler, California
KMUD Garberville, California
KRLA Glendale, California
KKMC Gonzales, California
KNCO Grass Valley, California
KXSR Groveland, California
KCKS Hamilton City, California
KQAB(AM) Lake Isabella, California
KPFZ-FM Lakeport, California
KOSS Lancaster, California
KCAA Loma Linda, California
KEIB Los Angeles, California
KFI Los Angeles, California
KPFK Los Angeles, California
KTNQ Los Angeles, California
KUSC Los Angeles, California
KMYC Marysville, California
KPMO Mendocino, California
KBRE Merced, California
KGAM Merced, California
KYOS Merced, California
KFIV Modesto, California
KMPH Modesto, California
KIDD Monterey, California
KNRY Monterey Bay, California
KCIV Mount Bullion, California
KMJC Mount Shasta, California
KVON Napa, California
KTOX Needles, California
KKSF Oakland, California
KNEW Oakland, California
KWVE(AM) Oildale, California
KLAA Orange, California
KDAR Oxnard, California
KNWQ Palm Springs, California
KPSI Palm Springs, California
KPTR Palm Springs, California
KDOW Palo Alto, California
KKXX Paradise, California
KPRL Paso Robles, California
KZYX Philo, California
KWMR Point Reyes Station, California
KFBK-FM Pollock Pines, California
KWKU Pomona, California
KTIP Porterville, California
KRAC Quincy, California
KSTE Rancho Cordova, California
KQMS Redding, California
KUOR-FM Redlands, California
KFNY Riverside, California
KFBK Sacramento, California
KION Salinas, California
KTIE San Bernardino, California
KVCR San Bernardino, California
KWVE-FM San Clemente, California
KCBQ San Diego, California
KFMB San Diego, California
KOGO San Diego, California
KPBS-FM San Diego, California
KEST San Francisco, California
KFAX San Francisco, California
KNBR San Francisco, California
KTCT San Francisco, California
KJZN San Joaquin, California
KVEC San Luis Obispo, California
KYNS San Luis Obispo, California
KPRZ San Marcos-Poway, California
KCLU Santa Barbara, California
KTMS Santa Barbara, California
KZSB Santa Barbara, California
KSCO Santa Cruz, California
KGDP-FM Santa Maria, California
KSMA Santa Maria, California
KSMX Santa Maria, California
KUHL Santa Maria, California
KUNX Santa Paula, California
KSRO Santa Rosa, California
KNZR-FM Shafter, California
KCNR Shasta, California
KIRN Simi Valley, California
KSVY Sonoma, California
KVML Sonora, California
KOWL South Lake Tahoe, California
KWSX Stockton, California
KSUE Susanville, California
KDSC Thousand Oaks, California
KFSQ Thousand Palms, California
KXPS Thousand Palms, California
KBDG Turlock, California
KVTA Ventura, California
KRZR Visalia, California
KCEO Vista, California
KFHL Wasco, California
KERN Wasco-Greenacres, California
KERN Wasco-Greenacres, California
KZYZ Willits, California
KRCB-FM Windsor, California
KUBA Yuba City, California
KNWH Yucca Valley, California
KNFO Basalt, Colorado
KSIR Brush, Colorado
KRLN Canon City, Colorado
KRDO Colorado Springs, Colorado
KZNT Colorado Springs, Colorado
KLTT Commerce City, Colorado
KVFC Cortez, Colorado
KBJD Denver, Colorado
KCFR-FM Denver, Colorado
KHOW Denver, Colorado
KLZ Denver, Colorado
KNUS Denver, Colorado
KOA Denver, Colorado
KDGO Durango, Colorado
KDEB(AM) Estes Park, Colorado
KFTM Fort Morgan, Colorado
KGLN Glenwood Springs, Colorado
KAFM Grand Junction, Colorado
KEXO Grand Junction, Colorado
KNZZ Grand Junction, Colorado
KFKA Greeley, Colorado
KHNC Johnstown, Colorado
KRKS-FM Lafayette, Colorado
KCBR Monument, Colorado
KWUF Pagosa Springs, Colorado
KCSJ Pueblo, Colorado
KGFT Pueblo, Colorado
KRDO-FM Security, Colorado
KKZN Thornton, Colorado
KCOL Wellington, Colorado
WPRX Bristol, Connecticut

WGCH Greenwich, Connecticut
WGRS Guilford, Connecticut
WQAQ Hamden, Connecticut
WDRC Hartford, Connecticut
WPOP Hartford, Connecticut
WTIC Hartford, Connecticut
WNEZ Manchester, Connecticut
WMMW Meriden, Connecticut
WMRD Middletown, Connecticut
WMNR Monroe, Connecticut
WAVZ New Haven, Connecticut
WELI New Haven, Connecticut
WNLK Norwalk, Connecticut
WLIS Old Saybrook, Connecticut
WHDD Sharon, Connecticut
WRXC Shelton, Connecticut
WGSK South Kent, Connecticut
WEDW-FM Stamford, Connecticut
WSTC Stamford, Connecticut
WSNG Torrington, Connecticut
WATR Waterbury, Connecticut
WWCO Waterbury, Connecticut
WCCC West Hartford, Connecticut
WSHU Westport, Connecticut
WKND Windsor, Connecticut
WAMU Washington, District of Columbia
WETA Washington, District of Columbia
WFED Washington, District of Columbia
WOL Washington, District of Columbia
WPFW Washington, District of Columbia
WTEM Washington, District of Columbia
WWRC Washington, District of Columbia
WDOV Dover, Delaware
WGMD Rehoboth Beach, Delaware
WDEL Wilmington, Delaware
WILM Wilmington, Delaware
WTMC Wilmington, Delaware
WWTX Wilmington, Delaware
WFLN Arcadia, Florida
WTWB Auburndale, Florida
WTJT Baker, Florida
WJGM(FM) Baldwin, Florida
WSWN Belle Glade, Florida
WSBR Boca Raton, Florida
WWPR Bradenton, Florida
WWJB Brooksville, Florida
WNZF Bunnell, Florida
WKFL Bushnell, Florida
WNVY Cantonment, Florida
WTAN Clearwater, Florida
WMMV Cocoa, Florida
WWBC Cocoa, Florida
WMEL Cocoa Beach, Florida
WTKS-FM Cocoa Beach, Florida
WJTK Columbia City, Florida
WHIM Coral Gables, Florida
WNDB Daytona Beach, Florida
WYND Deland, Florida
WNWF Destin, Florida
WENG Englewood, Florida
WWCN Fort Myers Beach, Florida
WJNX Fort Pierce, Florida
WFTW Fort Walton Beach, Florida
WDVH Gainesville, Florida
WRUF Gainesville, Florida
WNRP Gulf Breeze, Florida
WXYB Indian Rocks Beach, Florida
WBOB(AM) Jacksonville, Florida
WJCT-FM Jacksonville, Florida
WQOP Jacksonville, Florida
WJBW Jupiter, Florida
WYBX Key West, Florida
WHOO Kissimmee, Florida
WBXY La Crosse, Florida
WWTK Lake Placid, Florida
WLKF Lakeland, Florida
WWAB Lakeland, Florida
WPBR Lantana, Florida
WWBA Largo, Florida
WLBE Leesburg-Eustis, Florida
WFFG Marathon, Florida
WKWM Marathon, Florida
WGUF Marco, Florida
WMMB Melbourne, Florida
WAQI Miami, Florida
WIOD Miami, Florida
WKCP Miami, Florida
WLRN-FM Miami, Florida
WQBA Miami, Florida
WSUA Miami, Florida
WSKY-FM Micanopy, Florida
WFLA-FM Midway, Florida
WEBY Milton, Florida
WEGS Milton, Florida
WPGS Mims, Florida
WSOR Naples, Florida
WPSO New Port Richey, Florida
WTKE-FM Niceville, Florida
WJBX North Fort Myers, Florida
WKAT North Miami, Florida
WMOP Ocala, Florida
WDBO Orlando, Florida
WTLN Orlando, Florida
WELE Ormond Beach, Florida
WFSW Panama City, Florida
WLTG Panama City, Florida
WFLF-FM Parker, Florida
WCOA Pensacola, Florida
WCOA-FM Pensacola, Florida
WVTJ Pensacola, Florida
WAMT Pine Castle Sky Lake, Florida
WFLF Pine Hills, Florida
WTBN Pinellas Park, Florida
WTWD Plant City, Florida
WHSR Pompano Beach, Florida
WWNN Pompano Beach, Florida
WPSL Port St. Lucie, Florida
WCCF Punta Gorda, Florida
WZZR Riviera Beach, Florida
WDEO-FM San Carlos Park, Florida
WLSS Sarasota, Florida
WSRQ Sarasota, Florida
WHFS Seffner, Florida
WPUL South Daytona, Florida
WTYG Sparr, Florida
WYOO Springfield, Florida
WFOY St. Augustine, Florida
WIWA St. Cloud, Florida
WSTU Stuart, Florida
WFSQ Tallahassee, Florida
WFSU-FM Tallahassee, Florida
WTAL Tallahassee, Florida
WFLA Tampa, Florida
WHNZ Tampa, Florida
WIXC Titusville, Florida
WAXE Vero Beach, Florida
WCZR Vero Beach, Florida
WZTA Vero Beach, Florida
WBZT West Palm Beach, Florida
WJNO West Palm Beach, Florida
WZHR Zephyrhills, Florida
WDDQ Adel, Georgia
WALG Albany, Georgia
WLTA Alpharetta, Georgia
WRFC Athens, Georgia
WAOK Atlanta, Georgia
WGKA Atlanta, Georgia
WGST Atlanta, Georgia
WNIV Atlanta, Georgia
WRAS Atlanta, Georgia
WSB Atlanta, Georgia
WTZA Atlanta, Georgia
WFAM Augusta, Georgia
WGAC Augusta, Georgia
WRDW Augusta, Georgia
WGIG Brunswick, Georgia
WGRA Cairo, Georgia
WLBB Carrollton, Georgia
WYXC Cartersville, Georgia
WIOL Columbus, Georgia
WJJC Commerce, Georgia
WSRM Coosa, Georgia
WAEF Cordele, Georgia
WBLJ Dalton, Georgia
WSEM Donalsonville, Georgia
WCFO East Point, Georgia
WAEG Evans, Georgia
WDUN Gainesville, Georgia
WGGA Gainesville, Georgia
WDDK Greensboro, Georgia
WHIE Griffin, Georgia
WWWE Hapeville, Georgia
WGAC-FM Harlem, Georgia
WVCC Hogansville, Georgia
WSIZ-FM Jacksonville, Georgia
WVGA Lakeland, Georgia
WJTP Lithia Springs, Georgia
WMAC Macon, Georgia
WJGS Norwood, Georgia
WLAQ Rome, Georgia
WRGA Rome, Georgia
WXFO Royston, Georgia
WBMQ Savannah, Georgia
WTKS Savannah, Georgia
WWNS Statesboro, Georgia
WJAT Swainsboro, Georgia
WFSL Thomasville, Georgia
WKWN Trenton, Georgia
WZQZ Trion, Georgia
WJEM Valdosta, Georgia
WVLD Valdosta, Georgia
WJSP-FM Warm Springs, Georgia
WWGA(AM) Waycross, Georgia
WPLV West Point, Georgia
WIMO Winder, Georgia
WCGA Woodbine, Georgia
KPRG Agana, Guam
KGUM Hagatna, Guam
KQNG Eleele, Hawaii
KANO Hilo, Hawaii
KHNU Hilo, Hawaii
KPUA Hilo, Hawaii
KGU Honolulu, Hawaii
KHKA(AM) Honolulu, Hawaii
KHVH Honolulu, Hawaii
KIKI Honolulu, Hawaii
KKEA Honolulu, Hawaii
KPRP Honolulu, Hawaii
KWAI Honolulu, Hawaii
KAOI Kihei, Hawaii
KASI Ames, Iowa
KFFF(AM) Boone, Iowa
KWBG Boone, Iowa
KBUR Burlington, Iowa
KCNZ Cedar Falls, Iowa
KHKE Cedar Falls, Iowa
WMT Cedar Rapids, Iowa
KLNG Council Bluffs, Iowa
WOC Davenport, Iowa
KLCD Decorah, Iowa
KWKY Des Moines, Iowa
WHO Des Moines, Iowa
WDBQ Dubuque, Iowa
KVFD Fort Dodge, Iowa
KGRN Grinnell, Iowa
KQMG-FM Independence, Iowa
KCJJ Iowa City, Iowa
KXIC Iowa City, Iowa
WSUI Iowa City, Iowa
KOKX Keokuk, Iowa
KFJB Marshalltown, Iowa
KRNL-FM Mount Vernon, Iowa
KOEL Oelwein, Iowa
KOJI Okoboji, Iowa
KPVL Postville, Iowa
KIWA Sheldon, Iowa
KMA Shenandoah, Iowa
KSCJ Sioux City, Iowa
KTFC Sioux City, Iowa
KWIT Sioux City, Iowa
KTFG Sioux Rapids, Iowa
KICD Spencer, Iowa
KHOI Story City, Iowa
KNWS Waterloo, Iowa
KXEL Waterloo, Iowa
KBLI Blackfoot, Idaho
KBSU-FM Boise, Idaho
KBSU-FM Boise, Idaho
KFXD Boise, Idaho
KGEM Boise, Idaho
KSPD Boise, Idaho
KBFI Bonners Ferry, Idaho
KBSY Burley, Idaho
KBGN Caldwell, Idaho
KBXL Caldwell, Idaho
KBLY Idaho Falls, Idaho
KID Idaho Falls, Idaho
KOZE Lewiston, Idaho
KRFA-FM Moscow, Idaho
KIDO Nampa, Idaho
KWEI Notus, Idaho
KEGE Pocatello, Idaho
KISU-FM Pocatello, Idaho
KWIK Pocatello, Idaho
KBYI Rexburg, Idaho
KSPT Sandpoint, Idaho
KWRV Sun Valley, Idaho
KBSW Twin Falls, Idaho
KEZJ Twin Falls, Idaho
KLIX Twin Falls, Idaho
KTRP Weiser, Idaho
WBGZ Alton, Illinois
WTIM Assumption, Illinois

WBIG Aurora, Illinois
WVON Berwyn, Illinois
WRIK Brookport, Illinois
WCIL Carbondale, Illinois
WCAZ Carthage, Illinois
WWGO-HD2 Casey, Illinois
WDWS Champaign, Illinois
KSGM Chester, Illinois
WFMT Chicago, Illinois
WGN(AM) Chicago, Illinois
WIND Chicago, Illinois
WMVP Chicago, Illinois
WRTO Chicago, Illinois
WSSD Chicago, Illinois
WHOW Clinton, Illinois
WVCA Crete, Illinois
WDAN Danville, Illinois
WCPT-FM DeKalb, Illinois
WSOY Decatur, Illinois
WLBK Dekalb, Illinois
WXOS East St. Louis, Illinois
WCRA Effingham, Illinois
WCRA Effingham, Illinois
WCRA-FM Effingham, Illinois
WZPN Farmington, Illinois
WGNN Fisher, Illinois
WKYX-FM Golconda, Illinois
WJPF Herrin, Illinois
WJIL Jacksonville, Illinois
WLDS Jacksonville, Illinois
WJOL Joliet, Illinois
WKAN Kankakee, Illinois
WKEI Kewanee, Illinois
WLPO Lasalle, Illinois
WSMI Litchfield, Illinois
WGGH Marion, Illinois
WLBH Mattoon, Illinois
WBEQ Morris, Illinois
WCSJ Morris, Illinois
WCSJ-FM Morris, Illinois
WINI Murphysboro, Illinois
WPTH Olney, Illinois
WCMY Ottawa, Illinois
WAZU Peoria, Illinois
WMBD Peoria, Illinois
WLWJ Petersburg, Illinois
WPJC Pontiac, Illinois
WGEM Quincy, Illinois
WGEM-FM Quincy, Illinois
WTAD Quincy, Illinois
WTRH Ramsey, Illinois
WRHL Rochelle, Illinois
WROK Rockford, Illinois
WAUR Sandwich, Illinois
WPRC Sheffield, Illinois
WHCO Sparta, Illinois
WLUJ Springfield, Illinois
WTAX Springfield, Illinois
WGNJ St. Joseph, Illinois
WNIQ Sterling, Illinois
WSDR Sterling, Illinois
WTIM Taylorville, Illinois
WTIM Taylorville, Illinois
WILL Urbana, Illinois
WGFA Watseka, Illinois
WKRS Waukegan, Illinois
WCPT-AM Willow Springs, Illinois
WHBU Anderson, Indiana
WBIW Bedford, Indiana
WGCL Bloomington, Indiana
WFCV-FM Bluffton, Indiana
WBEW Chesterton, Indiana
WCSI Columbus, Indiana
WCMR Elkhart, Indiana
WTRC Elkhart, Indiana
WVPE Elkhart, Indiana
WGBF Evansville, Indiana
WBOI Fort Wayne, Indiana
WFCV Fort Wayne, Indiana
WOWO Fort Wayne, Indiana
WOWO-FM Fort Wayne, Indiana
WFDM-FM Franklin, Indiana
WGVE-FM Gary, Indiana
WLTH Gary, Indiana
WWCA Gary, Indiana
WTRE Greensburg, Indiana
WJOB Hammond, Indiana
WBRI Indianapolis, Indiana
WFYI-FM Indianapolis, Indiana
WIBC Indianapolis, Indiana
WNDE Indianapolis, Indiana
WXLW Indianapolis, Indiana
WXNT Indianapolis, Indiana
WAWK Kendallville, Indiana
WIOU Kokomo, Indiana
WSAL Logansport, Indiana
WLPR-FM Lowell, Indiana
WIMS Michigan City, Indiana
WMRS Monticello, Indiana
WCJL Morgantown, Indiana
WFIA-FM New Albany, Indiana
WNDA New Albany, Indiana
WRAY Princeton, Indiana
WETL South Bend, Indiana
WHOJ Terre Haute, Indiana
WBAA West Lafayette, Indiana
KFH-FM Clearwater, Kansas
KGGF AM Coffeyville, Kansas
KGNO Dodge City, Kansas
KBMP Enterprise, Kansas
KCNW Fairway, Kansas
KIUL Garden City, Kansas
KGCR Goodland, Kansas
KVGB Great Bend, Kansas
KZAN Hays, Kansas
KZNA Hill City, Kansas
KBUF Holcomb, Kansas
KFXX-FM Hugoton, Kansas
KARF Independence, Kansas
KCVW Kingman, Kansas
KLWN Lawrence, Kansas
KSCB Liberal, Kansas
KMAN Manhattan, Kansas
KNGL McPherson, Kansas
KJRG Newton, Kansas
KCCV-FM Olathe, Kansas
KCCV Overland Park, Kansas
KLKC Parsons, Kansas
KKCV Rozel, Kansas
KFRM Salina, Kansas
KSAL Salina, Kansas
KYUL Scott City, Kansas
KCVT Silver Lake, Kansas
KMAJ Topeka, Kansas
WIBW Topeka, Kansas
KLEY Wellington, Kansas
KFH Wichita, Kansas
KNSS Wichita, Kansas
KQAM Wichita, Kansas
KKLE Winfield, Kansas
KSWC Winfield, Kansas
WCBL Benton, Kentucky
WKCT Bowling Green, Kentucky
WXAM Buffalo, Kentucky
WSFE Burnside, Kentucky
WONS Cannonsburg, Kentucky
WNES Central City, Kentucky
WCTT Corbin, Kentucky
WKDP Corbin, Kentucky
WHIR Danville, Kentucky
WHOP Hopkinsville, Kentucky
WLME Lewisport, Kentucky
WLAP Lexington, Kentucky
WVLK Lexington, Kentucky
WFTG London, Kentucky
WFIA Louisville, Kentucky
WFPL Louisville, Kentucky
WGTK Louisville, Kentucky
WHAS Louisville, Kentucky
WKJK Louisville, Kentucky
WUOL-FM Louisville, Kentucky
WTTL Madisonville, Kentucky
WWXL Manchester, Kentucky
WNGO Mayfield, Kentucky
WNBS Murray, Kentucky
WNOP Newport, Kentucky
WKYX Paducah, Kentucky
WKYH Paintsville, Kentucky
WLSI Pikeville, Kentucky
WPRT Prestonsburg, Kentucky
WVLK-FM Richmond, Kentucky
WVKY Shelbyville, Kentucky
WLXO Stamping Ground, Kentucky
KROF Abbeville, Louisiana
KJMJ Alexandria, Louisiana
KSYL Alexandria, Louisiana
KWDF Ball, Louisiana
KWDF Ball, Louisiana
WJBO Baton Rouge, Louisiana
WPYR Baton Rouge, Louisiana
WRKF Baton Rouge, Louisiana
KBCL Bossier City, Louisiana
KLWB Carencro, Louisiana
KNBB Dubach, Louisiana
KEUN Eunice, Louisiana
KRLQ Hodge, Louisiana
WWL-FM Kenner, Louisiana
KVOL Lafayette, Louisiana
KAOK Lake Charles, Louisiana
KOJO Lake Charles, Louisiana
KMLB Monroe, Louisiana
KBIO Natchitoches, Louisiana
KNOC Natchitoches, Louisiana
WGSO New Orleans, Louisiana
WQNO New Orleans, Louisiana
WRNO-FM New Orleans, Louisiana
WVOG New Orleans, Louisiana
WWL New Orleans, Louisiana
KEEL Shreveport, Louisiana
KIOU Shreveport, Louisiana
KRMD Shreveport, Louisiana
KNCB Vivian, Louisiana
WPNI Amherst, Massachusetts
WSRO Ashland, Massachusetts
WARL Attleboro, Massachusetts
WBQT Boston, Massachusetts
WBUR-FM Boston, Massachusetts
WEZE Boston, Massachusetts
WILD Boston, Massachusetts
WRKO Boston, Massachusetts
WXBR Brockton, Massachusetts
WBNW Concord, Massachusetts
WHNP East Longmeadow, Massachusetts
WKOX Everett, Massachusetts
WHTB Fall River, Massachusetts
WSAR Fall River, Massachusetts
WPKZ Fitchburg, Massachusetts
WGAW Gardner, Massachusetts
WAMQ Great Barrington, Massachusetts
WSBS Great Barrington, Massachusetts
WCEC Haverhill, Massachusetts
WEEI-FM Lawrence, Massachusetts
WCAP Lowell, Massachusetts
WMLN-FM Milton, Massachusetts
WNAN Nantucket, Massachusetts
WBSM New Bedford, Massachusetts
WXKS Newton, Massachusetts
WDIS Norfolk, Massachusetts
WPLM Plymouth, Massachusetts
WSMA Scituate, Massachusetts
WESO Southbridge, Massachusetts
WHYN Springfield, Massachusetts
WGTX Truro, Massachusetts
WBUR West Yarmouth, Massachusetts
WXTK West Yarmouth, Massachusetts
WCAI Woods Hole, Massachusetts
WCRN Worcester, Massachusetts
WTAG Worcester, Massachusetts
WCBM Baltimore, Maryland
WEAA Baltimore, Maryland
WJZ Baltimore, Maryland
WOLB Baltimore, Maryland
WYPR Baltimore, Maryland
WCBC Cumberland, Maryland
WKDI Denton, Maryland
WFMD Frederick, Maryland
WYPF Frederick, Maryland
WFRB Frostburg, Maryland
WFBR Glen Burnie, Maryland
WARK Hagerstown, Maryland
WGMS Hagerstown, Maryland
WJSS Havre De Grace, Maryland
WYPO Ocean City, Maryland
WICO-FM Pocomoke City, Maryland
WICO Salisbury, Maryland
WJDY Salisbury, Maryland
WSCL Salisbury, Maryland
WTHU Thurmont, Maryland
WVQM Augusta, Maine
WZON Bangor, Maine
WBKA Bar Harbor, Maine
WCME(AM) Brunswick, Maine
WVOM-FM Howland, Maine
WBQQ Kennebunk, Maine
WXME Monticello, Maine
WJCX Pittsfield, Maine
WGAN Portland, Maine
WZAN Portland, Maine
WEGP Presque Isle, Maine
WTME Rumford, Maine
WKTQ South Paris, Maine
WBQX Thomaston, Maine
WNZS Veazie, Maine

WRED Westbrook, Maine
WPRR Ada, Michigan
WABJ Adrian, Michigan
WZTK Alpena, Michigan
WUOM Ann Arbor, Michigan
WBCK-FM Battle Creek, Michigan
WMAX Bay City, Michigan
WHFB Benton Harbor-St. Jo, Michigan
WAUS Berrien Springs, Michigan
WBRN Big Rapids, Michigan
WODJ Big Rapids, Michigan
WBFH Bloomfield Hills, Michigan
WLJW Cadillac, Michigan
WSGW-FM Carrollton, Michigan
WMKT Charlevoix, Michigan
WPRR-FM Clyde Township, Michigan
WDTW Dearborn, Michigan
WNZK Dearborn Heights, Michigan
WDFN Detroit, Michigan
WDTK Detroit, Michigan
WMUZ Detroit, Michigan
WKAR East Lansing, Michigan
WLJN Elmwood Township, Michigan
WCHT Escanaba, Michigan
WCXI Fenton, Michigan
WSNL Flint, Michigan
WWCK Flint, Michigan
WOOD Grand Rapids, Michigan
WTKG Grand Rapids, Michigan
WVGR Grand Rapids, Michigan
WGLM Greenville, Michigan
WMPL Hancock, Michigan
WHPR-FM Highland Park, Michigan
WMIQ Iron Mountain, Michigan
WJMS Ironwood, Michigan
WIAN Ishpeming, Michigan
WZAM Ishpeming, Michigan
WKMI Kalamazoo, Michigan
WJNL Kingsley, Michigan
WILS Lansing, Michigan
WCAR Livonia, Michigan
WDMJ Marquette, Michigan
WAVC Mio, Michigan
WRDT Monroe, Michigan
WSHN Munising, Michigan
WKBZ Muskegon, Michigan
WOOD-FM Muskegon, Michigan
WOWO Niles, Michigan
WLUN Pinconning, Michigan
WSGW Saginaw, Michigan
WLBY Saline, Michigan
WMIC Sandusky, Michigan
WKNW Sault Sainte Marie, Michigan
WMMI Shepherd, Michigan
WIOS Tawas City-East Tawas, Michigan
WICA Traverse City, Michigan
WTCM Traverse City, Michigan
WPON Walled Lake, Michigan
WKLQ Whitehall, Michigan
WDEO Ypsilanti, Michigan
WPNW Zeeland, Michigan
WWWI Baxter, Minnesota
KBUN Bemidji, Minnesota
KCRB-FM Bemidji, Minnesota
KKBJ Bemidji, Minnesota
KBPR Brainerd, Minnesota
KLIZ Brainerd, Minnesota
KRWC Buffalo, Minnesota
KSJR-FM Collegeville, Minnesota
KDLM Detroit Lakes, Minnesota
WZFG Dilworth, Minnesota
KDNI Duluth, Minnesota
WEBC Duluth, Minnesota
KBRF Fergus Falls, Minnesota
KCMF Fergus Falls, Minnesota
KKCQ Fosston, Minnesota
KYCR Golden Valley, Minnesota
KDWA Hastings, Minnesota
KLTF Little Falls, Minnesota
KFXN-FM Minneapolis, Minnesota
KSJN Minneapolis, Minnesota
KTLK Minneapolis, Minnesota
WCCO Minneapolis, Minnesota
WWTC Minneapolis, Minnesota
KMRS Morris, Minnesota
KCHK New Prague, Minnesota
KRLX Northfield, Minnesota
WWWI-FM Pillager, Minnesota
KLOH Pipestone, Minnesota
KKMS Richfield, Minnesota
KFAN Rochester, Minnesota
KROC Rochester, Minnesota
KNSI St. Cloud, Minnesota
WJON St. Cloud, Minnesota
KTNF St. Louis Park, Minnesota
KSTP St. Paul, Minnesota
WIRR Virginia-Hibbing, Minnesota
KWLM Willmar, Minnesota
KDOM Windom, Minnesota
KDOM-FM Windom, Minnesota
KWNO Winona, Minnesota
KRSW Worthington, Minnesota
KWOA Worthington, Minnesota
KNSW Worthington-Marshall, Minnesota
KYLF Adrian, Missouri
KGNA-FM Arnold, Missouri
KSGF-FM Ash Grove, Missouri
KSWM Aurora, Missouri
KKOZ-FM Ava, Missouri
KZGM Cabool, Missouri
KAPE Cape Girardeau, Missouri
KGIR Cape Girardeau, Missouri
KZIM Cape Girardeau, Missouri
KNLH Cedar Hill, Missouri
KCHR Charleston, Missouri
KRNW Chillicothe, Missouri
KFUO Clayton, Missouri
KSIV Clayton, Missouri
KCTO Cleveland, Missouri
KFRU Columbia, Missouri
KOPN Columbia, Missouri
KJCV-FM Country Club, Missouri
KGNN-FM Cuba, Missouri
KFCV Dixon, Missouri
KREI Farmington, Missouri
KSSZ Fayette, Missouri
KJFF Festus, Missouri
KTBJ Festus, Missouri
KHMO Hannibal, Missouri
KMCV High Point, Missouri
KBCV Hollister, Missouri
KBTC Houston, Missouri
KCTE Independence, Missouri
KLIK Jefferson City, Missouri
KWOS Jefferson City, Missouri
KCMO Kansas City, Missouri
KKFI Kansas City, Missouri
WHB Kansas City, Missouri
KLTE Kirksville, Missouri
KPOW-FM La Monte, Missouri
KBNN Lebanon, Missouri
KLWT Lebanon, Missouri
KLEX Lexington, Missouri
KCXL Liberty, Missouri
KWIX Moberly, Missouri
KCGR Oran, Missouri
KRMS Osage Beach, Missouri
KFMO Park Hills, Missouri
KCOZ Point Lookout, Missouri
KLID Poplar Bluff, Missouri
KWOC Poplar Bluff, Missouri
KNLP Potosi, Missouri
KAYX Richmond, Missouri
KMOZ Rolla, Missouri
KSMO Salem, Missouri
KSIS Sedalia, Missouri
KSIM Sikeston, Missouri
KADI Springfield, Missouri
KSCV Springfield, Missouri
KSGF Springfield, Missouri
KWTO-FM Springfield, Missouri
KTTR FM St. James, Missouri
KMOX St. Louis, Missouri
KMOX St. Louis, Missouri
KSIV-FM St. Louis, Missouri
KTRS St. Louis, Missouri
KYFI St. Louis, Missouri
KTUI Sullivan, Missouri
KCRL Sunrise Beach, Missouri
KLPW Union, Missouri
KGNV Washington, Missouri
KWMO Washington, Missouri
KJPW Waynesville, Missouri
KWPM West Plains, Missouri
KUKU Willow Springs, Missouri
WAMY Amory, Mississippi
WCJU Columbia, Mississippi
WXRZ Corinth, Mississippi
WSQH Decatur, Mississippi
WAUM Duck Hill, Mississippi
WFMN Flora, Mississippi
WYAB Flora, Mississippi
WDSV Greenville, Mississippi
WMUT Grenada, Mississippi
WHSY Hattiesburg, Mississippi
WLAU Heidelberg, Mississippi
WURC Holly Springs, Mississippi
WTCD Indianola, Mississippi
WJDX Jackson, Mississippi
WAML Laurel, Mississippi
WMXI Laurel, Mississippi
WJZD-FM Long Beach, Mississippi
WKBB Mantee, Mississippi
WALT Meridian, Mississippi
WMOX Meridian, Mississippi
WRQO Monticello, Mississippi
WBUV Moss Point, Mississippi
WNAT Natchez, Mississippi
WJNT Pearl, Mississippi
WHOC Philadelphia, Mississippi
WWMR Saltillo, Mississippi
WFMM Sumrall, Mississippi
WAJS Tupelo, Mississippi
WKMQ Tupelo, Mississippi
WQBC Vicksburg, Mississippi
WTNM Water Valley, Mississippi
KBLG Billings, Montana
KBOZ Bozeman, Montana
KMMS Bozeman, Montana
KMPT East Missoula, Montana
KGVA Fort Belknap Agency, Montana
KQDI Great Falls, Montana
KLYQ Hamilton, Montana
KBLL Helena, Montana
KCAP Helena, Montana
KGEZ Kalispell, Montana
KOFI Kalispell, Montana
KBSR Laurel, Montana
KPRK Livingston, Montana
KBGA Missoula, Montana
KGRZ Missoula, Montana
WSPC Albemarle, North Carolina
WSKY Asheville, North Carolina
WWNC Asheville, North Carolina
WTKF Atlantic, North Carolina
WCGC Belmont, North Carolina
WKJW Black Mountain, North Carolina
WXIT Blowing Rock, North Carolina
WUDE Bolivia, North Carolina
WSQL Brevard, North Carolina
WYMY Burlington, North Carolina
WCHL Chapel Hill, North Carolina
WBCN Charlotte, North Carolina
WBT Charlotte, North Carolina
WFAE Charlotte, North Carolina
WFNZ Charlotte, North Carolina
WDAV Davidson, North Carolina
WNCU Durham, North Carolina
WRJD Durham, North Carolina
WLOE Eden, North Carolina
WPTI Eden, North Carolina
WPEK Fairview, North Carolina
WGHB Farmville, North Carolina
WFNC Fayetteville, North Carolina
WIDU Fayetteville, North Carolina
WGBR Goldsboro, North Carolina
WSML Graham, North Carolina
WHNC Henderson, North Carolina
WIZS Henderson, North Carolina
WHKY Hickory, North Carolina
WGOS High Point, North Carolina
WCMC-FM Holly Springs, North Carolina
WAVQ Jacksonville, North Carolina
WJNC Jacksonville, North Carolina
WTKK Knightdale, North Carolina
WJRI Lenoir, North Carolina
WLXN Lexington, North Carolina
WYRN Louisburg, North Carolina
WOBX-FM Manteo, North Carolina
WYQS Mars Hill, North Carolina
WMYN Mayodan, North Carolina
WIXE Monroe, North Carolina
WNOS New Bern, North Carolina
WAUG New Hope, North Carolina
WNBU(FM) Oriental, North Carolina
WCBQ Oxford, North Carolina
WCLY Raleigh, North Carolina
WFNL Raleigh, North Carolina
WPTF Raleigh, North Carolina
WCAB Rutherfordton, North Carolina
WSTP Salisbury, North Carolina
WNCA Siler City, North Carolina
WEEB Southern Pines, North Carolina

WFMI Southern Shores, North Carolina
WBLO Thomasville, North Carolina
WSVM Valdese, North Carolina
WDLX Washington, North Carolina
WTXY Whiteville, North Carolina
WBFJ Winston-Salem, North Carolina
KFYR Bismarck, North Dakota
KLXX Bismarck-Mandan, North Dakota
WDAY Fargo, North Dakota
KNOX Grand Forks, North Dakota
KUND-FM Grand Forks, North Dakota
KNDK Langdon, North Dakota
KQLX Lisbon, North Dakota
KHRT Minot, North Dakota
KEYZ Williston, North Dakota
KWBE Beatrice, Nebraska
KCVN Cozad, Nebraska
KHUB Fremont, Nebraska
KRGI Grand Island, Nebraska
KGFW Kearney, Nebraska
KLCV Lincoln, Nebraska
KLIN Lincoln, Nebraska
WJAG Norfolk, Nebraska
KODY North Platte, Nebraska
KCRO Omaha, Nebraska
KFAB Omaha, Nebraska
KVNO Omaha, Nebraska
KNEB Scottsbluff, Nebraska
KAWL York, Nebraska
WEVO(FM) Concord, New Hampshire
WKXL Concord, New Hampshire
WDER Derry, New Hampshire
WTSN Dover, New Hampshire
WXEX Exeter, New Hampshire
WEVH Hanover, New Hampshire
WTSL Hanover, New Hampshire
WNNH Henniker, New Hampshire
WTPL Hillsboro, New Hampshire
WEVJ Jackson, New Hampshire
WEVN Keene, New Hampshire
WKBK Keene, New Hampshire
WZBK Keene, New Hampshire
WEMJ Laconia, New Hampshire
WUVR Lebanon, New Hampshire
WGIR Manchester, New Hampshire
WEVS Nashua, New Hampshire
WSMN Nashua, New Hampshire
WNTK-FM New London, New Hampshire
WPKX Rochester, New Hampshire
WQSO Rochester, New Hampshire
WMVX Salem, New Hampshire
WNJN-FM Atlantic City, New Jersey
WPGG Atlantic City, New Jersey
WNJS-FM Berlin, New Jersey
WNJB-FM Bridgeton, New Jersey
WTMR Camden, New Jersey
WNJZ Cape May Court House, New Jersey
WNYM Hackensack, New Jersey
WRNJ Hackettstown, New Jersey
WOBM Lakewood Township, New Jersey
WNJM Manahawkin, New Jersey
WVBV Medford Lakes, New Jersey
WNJY Netcong, New Jersey
WVNJ Oakland, New Jersey
WIBG Ocean City/Somers Po, New Jersey
WVPH Piscataway, New Jersey
WOND Pleasantville, New Jersey
WGHT Pompton Lakes, New Jersey
WKMB Stirling, New Jersey
WNJP Sussex, New Jersey
WKXW Trenton, New Jersey
WNJT-FM Trenton, New Jersey
WNJC Vineland, New Jersey
KABQ Albuquerque, New Mexico
KKIM Albuquerque, New Mexico
KNML Albuquerque, New Mexico
KUNM Albuquerque, New Mexico
KXKS Albuquerque, New Mexico
KRRT Arroyo Seco, New Mexico
KSVP Artesia, New Mexico
KNFT Bayard, New Mexico
KICA Clovis, New Mexico
KWKA Clovis, New Mexico
KENN Farmington, New Mexico
KNMI Farmington, New Mexico
KTGW Fruitland, New Mexico
KYKK Humble City, New Mexico
KOBE Las Cruces, New Mexico
KSNM Las Cruces, New Mexico
KNMX Las Vegas, New Mexico
KTBL Los Ranchos, New Mexico
KPCV Portales, New Mexico
KSEL Portales, New Mexico
KBIM Roswell, New Mexico
KRUI Ruidoso Downs, New Mexico
KLBU Santa Fe, New Mexico
KTRC Santa Fe, New Mexico
KVOT Taos, New Mexico
KTSN Elko, Nevada
KELY Ely, Nevada
KDWN Las Vegas, Nevada
KKVV Las Vegas, Nevada
KLAV Las Vegas, Nevada
KMZQ Las Vegas, Nevada
KXNT North Las Vegas, Nevada
KNIH Paradise, Nevada
KSVL Smith, Nevada
KBZZ Sparks, Nevada
KUUB Sun Valley, Nevada
KWNA Winnemucca, Nevada
WAMC-FM Albany, New York
WGY-FM Albany, New York
WROW Albany, New York
WVTL Amsterdam, New York
WAUB Auburn, New York
WBTA Batavia, New York
WNBF Binghamton, New York
WXLH Blue Mountain Lake, New York
WXLB Boonville, New York
WBEN Buffalo, New York
WBUF Buffalo, New York
WDCX-FM Buffalo, New York
WDCZ Buffalo, New York
WNED-FM Buffalo, New York
WWKB Buffalo, New York
WCAN Canajoharie, New York
WCGR Canandaigua, New York
WCKL Catskill, New York
WCHP Champlain, New York
WECK Cheektowaga, New York
WJIV Cherry Valley, New York
WENI Corning, New York
WWLE Cornwall, New York
WDOE Dunkirk, New York
WJIP Ellenville, New York
WENY Elmira, New York
WENE Endicott, New York
WEOS Geneva, New York
WGVA Geneva, New York
WWSC Glens Falls, New York
WLEA Hornell, New York
WWLZ Horseheads, New York
WHCU Ithaca, New York
WNYY Ithaca, New York
WJTN Jamestown, New York
WNJA Jamestown, New York
WJFF Jeffersonville, New York
WAMK Kingston, New York
WGHQ Kingston, New York
WLVL Lockport, New York
WOSR Middletown, New York
WADO New York, New York
WMCA New York, New York
WOR New York, New York
WWRL New York, New York
WXLG North Creek, New York
WSUF Noyack, New York
WQTK Ogdensburg, New York
WOEN Olean, New York
WMCR Oneida, New York
WNYO Oswego, New York
WEBO Owego, New York
WXLU Peru, New York
WCEL Plattsburgh, New York
WEAV Plattsburgh, New York
WTWK Plattsburgh, New York
WAIH Potsdam, New York
WKIP Poughkeepsie, New York
WRHV Poughkeepsie, New York
WGDJ Rensselaer, New York
WFTU Riverhead, New York
WRCN-FM Riverhead, New York
WBEE-FM Rochester, New York
WDCX Rochester, New York
WHAM Rochester, New York
WXXI-FM Rochester, New York
WKAL Rome, New York
WFNP Rosendale, New York
WNBZ Saranac Lake, New York
WSPN Saratoga Springs, New York
WGY Schenectady, New York
WMHT-FM Schenectady, New York
WSYR Solvay, New York
WRLI-FM Southampton, New York
WUSB Stony Brook, New York
WFBL Syracuse, New York
WSKO Syracuse, New York
WSYR Syracuse, New York
WANC Ticonderoga, New York
WOFX Troy, New York
WIBX Utica, New York
WUNY Utica, New York
WTBQ Warwick, New York
WATN Watertown, New York
WJNY Watertown, New York
WXZO Willsboro, New York
WARF Akron, Ohio
WHLO Akron, Ohio
WATH Athens, Ohio
WOUB Athens, Ohio
WBLL Bellefontaine, Ohio
WAIS Buchtel, Ohio
WOUC-FM Cambridge, Ohio
WYFY Cambridge, Ohio
WGFT Campbell, Ohio
WILB Canton, Ohio
WBEX Chillicothe, Ohio
WOUH-FM Chillicothe, Ohio
WDBZ Cincinnati, Ohio
WGRI Cincinnati, Ohio
WGUC Cincinnati, Ohio
WKRC Cincinnati, Ohio
WLW Cincinnati, Ohio
WCPN Cleveland, Ohio
WHK Cleveland, Ohio
WHKW Cleveland, Ohio
WTAM Cleveland, Ohio
WBNS Columbus, Ohio
WBNS-FM Columbus, Ohio
WTVN Columbus, Ohio
WRFD Columbus-Worthington, Ohio
WWOW Conneaut, Ohio
WOSE Coshocton, Ohio
WDPR Dayton, Ohio
WHIO Dayton, Ohio
WING Dayton, Ohio
WONW Defiance, Ohio
WFIN Findlay, Ohio
WTKC Findlay, Ohio
WMAN-FM Fredericktown, Ohio
WWGV Grove City, Ohio
WMOH Hamilton, Ohio
WIRO Ironton, Ohio
WOUL-FM Ironton, Ohio
WNIR Kent, Ohio
WFCO Lancaster, Ohio
WLOH Lancaster, Ohio
WIMA Lima, Ohio
WMAN Mansfield, Ohio
WLTP Marietta, Ohio
WMRT Marietta, Ohio
WMRN Marion, Ohio
WMVO Mount Vernon, Ohio
WCLT Newark, Ohio
WMUB Oxford, Ohio
WCCD Parma, Ohio
WEEC Springfield, Ohio
WSPD Toledo, Ohio
WBTC Uhrichsville, Ohio
WHKZ Warren, Ohio
WINT Willoughby, Ohio
WQKT Wooster, Ohio
WKBN Youngstown, Ohio
WOUZ-FM Zanesville, Ohio
KWHW Altus, Oklahoma
KWON Bartlesville, Oklahoma
KOKB Blackwell, Oklahoma
KCLI Clinton, Oklahoma
KUSH Cushing, Oklahoma
KEBC Del City, Oklahoma
KPNS Duncan, Oklahoma
KCSC Edmond, Oklahoma
KGWA Enid, Oklahoma
KWXC Grove, Oklahoma
KTJS Hobart, Oklahoma
KOSN Ketchum, Oklahoma
KXCA Lawton, Oklahoma
KBCW-FM McAlester, Oklahoma
KWPN Moore, Oklahoma
KGOU Norman, Oklahoma
KQCV Oklahoma City, Oklahoma
KTLR Oklahoma City, Oklahoma
KTOK Oklahoma City, Oklahoma

KOKL Okmulgee, Oklahoma
KPGM Pawhuska, Oklahoma
KQSN Ponca City, Oklahoma
KJSR Sand Springs, Oklahoma
KRMG-FM Sand Springs, Oklahoma
KWEN Sand Springs, Oklahoma
KQCV-FM Shawnee, Oklahoma
KCFO Tulsa, Oklahoma
KFAQ Tulsa, Oklahoma
KRMG Tulsa, Oklahoma
KSIW Woodward, Oklahoma
KLOO Albany, Oregon
KAST Astoria, Oregon
KHSS Athena, Oregon
KBKR Baker, Oregon
KOBK Baker City, Oregon
KBND Bend, Oregon
KBNW Bend, Oregon
KBBR Coos Bay, Oregon
KHSN Coos Bay, Oregon
KWRO Coquille, Oregon
KOAC Corvallis, Oregon
KNND Cottage Grove, Oregon
KPPT-FM Depoe Bay, Oregon
KWVR Enterprise, Oregon
KOPB Eugene, Oregon
KPNW Eugene, Oregon
KUGN Eugene, Oregon
KWAX Eugene, Oregon
KAJO Grants Pass, Oregon
KUIK Hillsboro, Oregon
KAGO Klamath Falls, Oregon
KFLS Klamath Falls, Oregon
KLBM La Grande, Oregon
KGAL Lebanon, Oregon
KDOV Medford, Oregon
KMED Medford, Oregon
KTIL(AM) Netarts, Oregon
KRBM Pendleton, Oregon
KUMA Pendleton, Oregon
KAPL Phoenix, Oregon
KCMX Phoenix, Oregon
KEX Portland, Oregon
KKPZ Portland, Oregon
KPDQ Portland, Oregon
KPDQ-FM Portland, Oregon
KUFO Portland, Oregon
KXL-FM Portland, Oregon
KDUN Reedsport, Oregon
KOHI St. Helens, Oregon
KFIR Sweet Home, Oregon
KACI The Dalles, Oregon
KTMK Tillamook, Oregon
KCUP Toledo, Oregon
KPAM Troutdale, Oregon
KLWJ(AM) Umatilla, Oregon
KWLZ-FM West Linn, Oregon
WAEB Allentown, Pennsylvania
WJCS Allentown, Pennsylvania
WFBG Altoona, Pennsylvania
WRTA Altoona, Pennsylvania
WMBA Ambridge, Pennsylvania
WILK-FM Avoca, Pennsylvania
WBVP Beaver Falls, Pennsylvania
WBLF Bellefonte, Pennsylvania
WGPA Bethlehem, Pennsylvania
WWCS Canonsburg, Pennsylvania
WHYL Carlisle, Pennsylvania
WCHA Chambersburg, Pennsylvania
WWCH Clarion, Pennsylvania
WJET Erie, Pennsylvania
WZSK Everett, Pennsylvania
WFRA Franklin, Pennsylvania
WSAJ-FM Grove City, Pennsylvania
WHP Harrisburg, Pennsylvania
WITF-FM Harrisburg, Pennsylvania
WTKT Harrisburg, Pennsylvania
WAZL Hazleton, Pennsylvania
WHHN Hollidaysburg, Pennsylvania
WKFB Jeannette, Pennsylvania
WKGE Johnstown, Pennsylvania
WNTJ Johnstown, Pennsylvania
WFYL King of Prussia, Pennsylvania
WDAC Lancaster, Pennsylvania
WNPV Lansdale, Pennsylvania
WLBR Lebanon, Pennsylvania
WWGE Loretto, Pennsylvania
WGLD Manchester Township, Pennsylvania
WJSM-FM Martinsburg, Pennsylvania
WWBJ Martinsburg, Pennsylvania
WEEO-FM McConnellsburg, Pennsylvania
WEDO McKeesport, Pennsylvania
WMNY McKeesport, Pennsylvania
WMGW Meadville, Pennsylvania
WMLP Milton, Pennsylvania
WFTE Mount Cobb, Pennsylvania
WKST New Castle, Pennsylvania
WPHT Philadelphia, Pennsylvania
WTEL Philadelphia, Pennsylvania
WURD Philadelphia, Pennsylvania
WWDB Philadelphia, Pennsylvania
WPHB Philipsburg, Pennsylvania
KDKA Pittsburgh, Pennsylvania
WQED-FM Pittsburgh, Pennsylvania
WWNL Pittsburgh, Pennsylvania
WEMR Pleasant Gap, Pennsylvania
WKVB Port Matilda, Pennsylvania
WPAZ Pottstown, Pennsylvania
WECZ Punxsutawney, Pennsylvania
WYBF Radnor Township, Pennsylvania
WEEU Reading, Pennsylvania
WIOV Reading, Pennsylvania
WBZU Scranton, Pennsylvania
WPIC Sharon, Pennsylvania
WRSC State College, Pennsylvania
WVPO Stroudsburg, Pennsylvania
WKOK Sunbury, Pennsylvania
WTIV Titusville, Pennsylvania
WXVU Villanova, Pennsylvania
WNAE Warren, Pennsylvania
WCHE West Chester, Pennsylvania
WKZN West Hazleton, Pennsylvania
WILK Wilkes-Barre, Pennsylvania
WRAK Williamsport, Pennsylvania
WWPA Williamsport, Pennsylvania
WYYC York, Pennsylvania
WBQN Barceloneta-Manati, Puerto Rico
WYAC Cabo Rojo, Puerto Rico
WLEY Cayey, Puerto Rico
WMDD Fajardo, Puerto Rico
WMSW Hatillo, Puerto Rico
WALO Humacao, Puerto Rico
WIVV Island of Vieques, Puerto Rico
WMNT Manati, Puerto Rico
WKJB Mayaguez, Puerto Rico
WORA Mayaguez, Puerto Rico
WPRA Mayaguez, Puerto Rico
WTIL Mayaguez, Puerto Rico
WYEL Mayaguez, Puerto Rico
WDEP Ponce, Puerto Rico
WISO Ponce, Puerto Rico
WPAB Ponce, Puerto Rico
WPRP Ponce, Puerto Rico
WUKQ Ponce, Puerto Rico
WAPA San Juan, Puerto Rico
WBMJ San Juan, Puerto Rico
WIPR-FM San Juan, Puerto Rico
WKAQ San Juan, Puerto Rico
WQII San Juan, Puerto Rico
WSKN San Juan, Puerto Rico
WUNO San Juan, Puerto Rico
WRSS San Sebastian, Puerto Rico
WUPR Utuado, Puerto Rico
WXEW Yabucoa, Puerto Rico
WENA Yauco, Puerto Rico
WKFE Yauco, Puerto Rico
WKSP(AM) Block Island, Rhode Island
WRNI-FM Narragansett Pier, Rhode Island
WADK Newport, Rhode Island
WHJJ Providence, Rhode Island
WRNI Providence, Rhode Island
WBLQ(AM) Westerly, Rhode Island
WNRI Woonsocket, Rhode Island
WAIM Anderson, South Carolina
WZMJ Batesburg, South Carolina
WABB Belton, South Carolina
WTQS Cameron, South Carolina
WQNT Charleston, South Carolina
WSPO Charleston, South Carolina
WBT-FM Chester, South Carolina
WISW Columbia, South Carolina
WVOC Columbia, South Carolina
WTMZ Dorchester Terrace-Brentwood, South Carolina
WELP Easley, South Carolina
WNKT Eastover, South Carolina
WTZQ Fountain Inn, South Carolina
WGTN Georgetown, South Carolina
WSCC-FM Goose Creek, South Carolina
WYRD Greenville, South Carolina
WCRS Greenwood, South Carolina
WHGS Hampton, South Carolina
WRIX-FM Honea Path, South Carolina
WHYM Lake City, South Carolina
WWIK McClellanville, South Carolina
WJKB Moncks Corner, South Carolina
WSNW Seneca, South Carolina
WYRD-FM Simpsonville, South Carolina
WRNN-FM Socastee, South Carolina
WORD Spartanburg, South Carolina
WSPG Spartanburg, South Carolina
WDXY Sumter, South Carolina
KSDN Aberdeen, South Dakota
KBFS Belle Fourche, South Dakota
KIJV Huron, South Dakota
KSOO-FM Lennox, South Dakota
KMSD Mibank, South Dakota
KORN Mitchell, South Dakota
KCCR Pierre, South Dakota
KIMM Rapid City, South Dakota
KOTA Rapid City, South Dakota
KCSD Sioux Falls, South Dakota
KSOO Sioux Falls, South Dakota
KSDR Watertown, South Dakota
WNAX Yankton, South Dakota
WYXI Athens, Tennessee
WSAA Benton, Tennessee
WHCB Bristol, Tennessee
WTBG Brownsville, Tennessee
WLMR Chattanooga, Tennessee
WNOO Chattanooga, Tennessee
WMCH Church Hill, Tennessee
WJZM Clarksville, Tennessee
WKFN Clarksville, Tennessee
WBAC Cleveland, Tennessee
WCLE Cleveland, Tennessee
WCRV Collierville, Tennessee
WPWT Colonial Heights, Tennessee
WPTN Cookeville, Tennessee
WZYX Cowan, Tennessee
WAEW Crossville, Tennessee
WCRT Donelson, Tennessee
WTJJ Dyer, Tennessee
WCPH Etowah, Tennessee
WMTY Farragut, Tennessee
WAKM Franklin, Tennessee
WNML Friendsville, Tennessee
WGFX Gallatin, Tennessee
WCXZ Harrogate, Tennessee
WWTN Hendersonville, Tennessee
WAUO Hohenwald, Tennessee
WIRJ Humboldt, Tennessee
WETS-FM Johnson City, Tennessee
WETR Knoxville, Tennessee
WITA Knoxville, Tennessee
WKVL Knoxville, Tennessee
WNML Knoxville, Tennessee
WRJZ Knoxville, Tennessee
WCOR Lebanon, Tennessee
WLOD Loudon, Tennessee
WPLN Madison, Tennessee
WRKQ Madisonville, Tennessee
WMSR Manchester, Tennessee
WAKI McMinnville, Tennessee
KWAM Memphis, Tennessee
WREC Memphis, Tennessee
WGNS Murfreesboro, Tennessee
WFSK-FM Nashville, Tennessee
WLAC Nashville, Tennessee
WPFT Pigeon Forge, Tennessee
WZNG Shelbyville, Tennessee
WRHA(AM) Spring City, Tennessee
KWKC Abilene, Texas
KYYW Abilene, Texas
KZQQ Abilene, Texas
KTEK Alvin, Texas
KGNC Amarillo, Texas
KIXZ Amarillo, Texas
KZIP Amarillo, Texas
KACT Andrews, Texas
KMFA Austin, Texas
KVET Austin, Texas
KSKY Balch Springs, Texas
KLVI Beaumont, Texas
KFLC Benbrook, Texas
KTAA Big Sandy, Texas
KBST-FM Big Spring, Texas
KBYG Big Spring, Texas
KWHI Brenham, Texas
KAGC Bryan, Texas
WTAW-FM Buffalo, Texas
KNSH Canyon, Texas
KDET Center, Texas
KXYL-FM Coleman, Texas

KWBC College Station, Texas
KZNE College Station, Texas
WTAW College Station, Texas
KYJC Commerce, Texas
KTMR Converse, Texas
KCCT Corpus Christi, Texas
KEYS Corpus Christi, Texas
KKTX Corpus Christi, Texas
KAND Corsicana, Texas
KHER Crystal City, Texas
KERA Dallas, Texas
KFXR Dallas, Texas
KGGR Dallas, Texas
KTCK Dallas, Texas
KIXL Del Valle, Texas
KURV Edinburg, Texas
KULP El Campo, Texas
KAMA El Paso, Texas
KBNA-FM El Paso, Texas
KELP El Paso, Texas
KTSM El Paso, Texas
KFCD Farmersville, Texas
KTCK Flower Mound, Texas
KNAF Fredericksburg, Texas
KGAF Gainesville, Texas
KVCE Highland Park, Texas
KWRD-FM Highland Village, Texas
KLAT Houston, Texas
KNTH Houston, Texas
KPRC Houston, Texas
KSHJ Houston, Texas
KTRH Houston, Texas
KXYZ Houston, Texas
KGOL Humble, Texas
KERV Kerrville, Texas
KFRO Longview, Texas
KABA Louise, Texas
KFYO Lubbock, Texas
KJDL Lubbock, Texas
KJTV Lubbock, Texas
KRFE Lubbock, Texas
KAVX Lufkin, Texas
KKHT-FM Lumberton, Texas
KCRS Midland, Texas
KWEL Midland, Texas
KSFA Nacogdoches, Texas
KLVL Pasadena, Texas
KVOP Plainview, Texas
KDEI Port Arthur, Texas
KOLE Port Arthur, Texas
KJCE Rollingwood, Texas
KGKL San Angelo, Texas
KKSA San Angelo, Texas
KCOR San Antonio, Texas
KPAC San Antonio, Texas
KSLR San Antonio, Texas
KTSA San Antonio, Texas
WOAI San Antonio, Texas
KTSW San Marcos, Texas
KWED Seguin, Texas
KZSP South Padre Island, Texas
KSQX Springtown, Texas
KTEM Temple, Texas
KLUP Terrell Hills, Texas
KKTK Texarkana, Texas
KTFS Texarkana, Texas
KSEV Tomball, Texas
KTBB Tyler, Texas
KTNO University Park, Texas
KBCT Waco, Texas
KWTX Waco, Texas
KKEE Wheelock, Texas
KWFS Wichita Falls, Texas
KSUB Cedar City, Utah
KUSR Logan, Utah
KUSU-FM Logan, Utah
KVNU Logan, Utah
KSL-FM Midvale, Utah
KALL North Salt Lake City, Utah
KLO Ogden, Utah
KOAL Price, Utah
KBYU-FM Provo, Utah
KOVO Provo, Utah
KSVC Richfield, Utah
KCPW-FM Salt Lake City, Utah
KNRS Salt Lake City, Utah
KRCL Salt Lake City, Utah
KSL Salt Lake City, Utah
KZNS Salt Lake City, Utah
KTKK Sandy, Utah
KHQN Spanish Fork, Utah
KCPX Spanish Valley, Utah
KDXU St. George, Utah
KZNU St. George, Utah
KVEL Vernal, Utah
KHKR Washington, Utah
WABN Abingdon, Virginia
WHAN Ashland, Virginia
WBVA Bayside, Virginia
WFNR Blacksburg, Virginia
WKEX Blacksburg, Virginia
WCHV Charlottesville, Virginia
WINA Charlottesville, Virginia
WVAX Charlottesville, Virginia
WMVE Chase City, Virginia
WNTW Chester, Virginia
WWVT Christiansburg, Virginia
WDZY Colonial Heights, Virginia
WDZY Colonial Heights, Virginia
WMRY Crozet, Virginia
WPIN Dublin, Virginia
WEVA Emporia, Virginia
WFLO Farmville, Virginia
WFFC Ferrum, Virginia
WFVA Fredericksburg, Virginia
WNTX Fredericksburg, Virginia
WMNA Gretna, Virginia
WKCY Harrisonburg, Virginia
WMRA Harrisonburg, Virginia
WSVA Harrisonburg, Virginia
WCNV Heathsville, Virginia
WMRL Lexington, Virginia
WBRG Lynchburg, Virginia
WLNI Lynchburg, Virginia
WVGM Lynchburg, Virginia
WKDV Manassas, Virginia
WHEE Martinsville, Virginia
WMVA Martinsville, Virginia
WSVG Mount Jackson, Virginia
WHRV Norfolk, Virginia
WNIS Norfolk, Virginia
WESR Onley-Onancock, Virginia
WWBU Radford, Virginia
WCVE-FM Richmond, Virginia
WLEE Richmond, Virginia
WRVA Richmond, Virginia
WFIR Roanoke, Virginia
WLOY Rural Retreat, Virginia
WHEO Stuart, Virginia
WRAR Tappahannock, Virginia
WXTG-FM Virginia Beach, Virginia
WKCI Waynesboro, Virginia
WINC Winchester, Virginia
WTRM Winchester, Virginia
WMAL Woodbridge, Virginia
WVGN Charlotte Amalie, Virgin Islands
WVWI Charlotte Amalie, Virgin Islands
WSNO Barre, Vermont
WBTN Bennington, Vermont
WKVT Brattleboro, Vermont
WVMT Burlington, Vermont
WGDR Plainfield, Vermont
WCVR(AM) Randolph, Vermont
WSYB Rutland, Vermont
WRSA St. Albans, Vermont
WDEV-FM Warren, Vermont
KWOK Aberdeen, Washington
KXRO Aberdeen, Washington
KCLK Asotin, Washington
KBAI Bellingham, Washington
KGMI Bellingham, Washington
KPUG Bellingham, Washington
KUGS Bellingham, Washington
KGNW Burien-Seattle, Washington
KELA Centralia-Chehalis, Washington
KMAX Colfax, Washington
KSPO Dishman, Washington
KXLE Ellensburg, Washington
KTBI Ephrata, Washington
KULE Ephrata, Washington
KONA Kennewick-Richland-P, Washington
KLAY Lakewood, Washington
KBSN Moses Lake, Washington
KMWS Mount Vernon, Washington
KSVR Mount Vernon, Washington
KGTK Olympia, Washington
KQWS Omak, Washington
KTRW Opportunity, Washington
KFLD Pasco, Washington
KONP Port Angeles, Washington
KPTZ Port Townsend, Washington
KQQQ Pullman, Washington
KKNW Seattle, Washington
KLFE Seattle, Washington
KNTS Seattle, Washington
KTTH Seattle, Washington
KVI Seattle, Washington
KITZ Silverdale, Washington
KGA Spokane, Washington
KJRB Spokane, Washington
KQNT Spokane, Washington
KXLY-AM Spokane, Washington
KIRO-FM Tacoma, Washington
KXOT Tacoma, Washington
KBMS Vancouver, Washington
KGDC Walla Walla, Washington
KUJ Walla Walla, Washington
KWWS Walla Walla, Washington
KPQ Wenatchee, Washington
KIT Yakima, Washington
WHAA Adams, Wisconsin
WXCE Amery, Wisconsin
WLBL Auburndale, Wisconsin
WBEV Beaver Dam, Wisconsin
WDUZ-FM Brillion, Wisconsin
WHSA Brule, Wisconsin
WHAD Delafield, Wisconsin
WDVM Eau Claire, Wisconsin
KFIZ Fond Du Lac, Wisconsin
WHID Green Bay, Wisconsin
WTAQ-AM Green Bay, Wisconsin
WZTI Greenfield, Wisconsin
WHHI Highland, Wisconsin
WKBH Holmen, Wisconsin
WIBD Janesville, Wisconsin
WLIP Kenosha, Wisconsin
WHBY Kimberly, Wisconsin
WHLA La Crosse, Wisconsin
WLFN La Crosse, Wisconsin
WLDY Ladysmith, Wisconsin
WHA Madison, Wisconsin
WIBA Madison, Wisconsin
WOZN Madison, Wisconsin
WHWC Menomonie, Wisconsin
WMEQ Menomonie, Wisconsin
WVSS Menomonie, Wisconsin
WJMT Merrill, Wisconsin
WISN Milwaukee, Wisconsin
WTMJ Milwaukee, Wisconsin
WTLX Monona, Wisconsin
WOSH Oshkosh, Wisconsin
WHBM Park Falls, Wisconsin
WAQE Rice Lake, Wisconsin
WRPN Ripon, Wisconsin
WDTX Rothschild, Wisconsin
WHDI Sister Bay, Wisconsin
WPCN Stevens Point, Wisconsin
WXXM Sun Prairie, Wisconsin
KUWS Superior, Wisconsin
WDSM Superior, Wisconsin
WVCX Tomah, Wisconsin
WEGZ Washburn, Wisconsin
WLBL-FM Wausau, Wisconsin
WXCO Wausau, Wisconsin
WFHR Wisconsin Rapids, Wisconsin
WWNR Beckley, West Virginia
WCST Berkeley Springs, West Virginia
WHIS Bluefield, West Virginia
WBTQ Buckhannon, West Virginia
WBUC Buckhannon, West Virginia
WCHS Charleston, West Virginia
WTCS Fairmont, West Virginia
WVHU Huntington, West Virginia
WFSP Kingwood, West Virginia
WRNR Martinsburg, West Virginia
WAJR Morgantown, West Virginia
WVLY Moundsville, West Virginia
WVNT Parkersburg, West Virginia
WRRL Rainelle, West Virginia
WMOV Ravenswood, West Virginia
WRON Ronceverte, West Virginia
WJYP St. Albans, West Virginia
WEIR Weirton, West Virginia
WWVA Wheeling, West Virginia
KUWA Afton, Wyoming
KBBS Buffalo, Wyoming
KTWO Casper, Wyoming
KVOC Casper, Wyoming
KODI Cody, Wyoming
KUYO Evansville, Wyoming
KGLL Gillette, Wyoming
KIML Gillette, Wyoming
KJCV Jackson, Wyoming

KOWB Laramie, Wyoming
KGAB Orchard Valley, Wyoming
KYDT Pine Haven, Wyoming
KPOW Powell, Wyoming
KVOW Riverton, Wyoming
KRKK Rock Springs, Wyoming
KROE Sheridan, Wyoming

Tejano

KAAB Batesville, Arkansas
KSEC Bentonville, Arkansas
KBHC Nashville, Arkansas
KLNZ Glendale, Arizona
KCMT Oro Valley, Arizona
KHOT-FM Paradise Valley, Arizona
KNAI Phoenix, Arizona
KUFW Phoenix, Arizona
KEVT Sahuarita, Arizona
KXEW South Tucson, Arizona
KCEC-FM Wellton, Arizona
KUKY Wellton, Arizona
KHOV-FM Wickenburg, Arizona
KMYX-FM Arvin, California
KWAC Bakersfield, California
KIQQ Barstow, California
KXXZ Barstow, California
KMVE California City, California
KSRT Cloverdale, California
KOND Clovis, California
KMQA East Porterville, California
KWST El Centro, California
KLBN Fresno, California
KXTS Geyserville, California
KSCA Glendale, California
KBAA Grass Valley, California
KLOK-FM Greenfield, California
KSEA Greenfield, California
KGEN-FM Hanford, California
KMPG Hollister, California
KMXX Imperial, California
KESQ Indio, California
KBHH Kerman, California
KEXA King City, California
KSRN Kings Beach, California
KUNA-FM La Quinta, California
KBTW Lenwood, California
KRQK Lompoc, California
KSMY Lompoc, California
KEBT Lost Hills, California
KRCX-FM Marysville, California
KIWI McFarland, California
KRAY-FM Salinas, California
KTGE Salinas, California
KLNV San Diego, California
KSOL San Francisco, California
KZSF San Jose, California
KSQL Santa Cruz, California
KMJV Soledad, California
KDFC Sunnyvale, California
KMIX Tracy, California
KGEN Tulare, California
KLOQ-FM Winton, California
KPVW Aspen, Colorado
KFVR-FM Beulah, Colorado
KXPK Evergreen, Colorado
WKIQ Eustis, Florida
WAFZ-FM Immokalee, Florida
WWRF Lake Worth, Florida
WBRD Palmetto, Florida
WAMA Tampa, Florida
WQBN Temple Terrace, Florida
WAUC Wauchula, Florida
WLAA Winter Garden, Florida
WBZY Bowdon, Georgia
WDAL Dalton, Georgia
KINF Gooding, Idaho
KXTA Rupert, Idaho
WMKB Earlville, Illinois
WOJO Evanston, Illinois
WIJR Highland, Illinois
WJZI(AM) Decatur, Indiana
KYQQ Arkansas City, Kansas
KYYS Kansas City, Kansas
WBQH Silver Spring, Maryland
WMJH Rockford, Michigan
WMFN Zeeland, Michigan
WCXN Claremont, North Carolina
WZBO Edenton, North Carolina
WCNC Elizabeth City, North Carolina
WBZJ Goldsboro, North Carolina
WWBG Greensboro, North Carolina
WREV Reidsville, North Carolina
KBBX-FM Nebraska City, Nebraska
KPZE-FM Carlsbad, New Mexico
KKNS Corrales, New Mexico
KALN Dexter, New Mexico
KJFA-FM Santa Fe, New Mexico
KXMT Taos, New Mexico
KISF Las Vegas, Nevada
KQRT Las Vegas, Nevada
KRLV Las Vegas, Nevada
KRNV-FM Reno, Nevada
KXEQ Reno, Nevada
WQBU-FM Garden City, New York
WVKO-FM Johnstown, Ohio
WKY Oklahoma City, Oklahoma
KXTD Wagoner, Oklahoma
KRTA Medford, Oregon
KRDM Redmond, Oregon
KWBY Woodburn, Oregon
WVJP-FM Caguas, Puerto Rico
WGSP-FM Pageland, South Carolina
KOPY-FM Alice, Texas
KBZD Amarillo, Texas
KQFX Borger, Texas
KKPS Brownsville, Texas
KTAM Bryan, Texas
KAJP Carrizo Springs, Texas
KWOW Clifton, Texas
KBSO Corpus Christi, Texas
KEPS Eagle Pass, Texas
KYSE El Paso, Texas
KPSO-FM Falfurrias, Texas
KLNO Fort Worth, Texas
KOYE Frankston, Texas
KHMC Goliad, Texas
KLTN Houston, Texas
KLEY-FM Jourdanton, Texas
KJBZ Laredo, Texas
KFZO Lewisville, Texas
KEJS Lubbock, Texas
KXTQ Lubbock, Texas
KCUL-FM Marshall, Texas
KGBT-FM McAllen, Texas
KBDR Mirando City, Texas
KBED Nederland, Texas
KSAH-FM Pearsall, Texas
KPIT Pittsburg, Texas
KQBU-FM Port Arthur, Texas
KMIQ Robstown, Texas
KSAB Robstown, Texas
KCLL San Angelo, Texas
KEDA San Antonio, Texas
KROM San Antonio, Texas
KXTN-FM San Antonio, Texas
KESO South Padre Island, Texas
KSTV Stephenville, Texas
KAMZ Tahoka, Texas
KLQB Taylor, Texas
KSAH Universal City, Texas
KUVA Uvalde, Texas
KAIQ Wolfforth, Texas
KXOL Brigham City, Utah
KTUB Centerville, Utah
KSVN Ogden, Utah
KDUT Randolph, Utah
WMYP Frederiksted, Virgin Islands
KZHR Dayton, Washington
KZXR Prosser, Washington
KZML Quincy, Washington
KRCW Royal City, Washington
WAUN Kewaunee, Wisconsin

Triple A

KXLL Juneau, Alaska
KZGL Flagstaff, Arizona
KXCI Tucson, Arizona
KNCA Burney, California
KPYG Cayucos, California
KHUM Cutten, California
KPRI Encinitas, California
KOZT Fort Bragg, California
KRSH Healdsburg, California
KNSQ Mount Shasta, California
KZAP Paradise, California
KSFN Piedmont, California
KMYT Temecula, California
KTKE Truckee, California
KSPN-FM Aspen, Colorado
KZYR Avon, Colorado
KBCO Boulder, Colorado
KSMT Breckenridge, Colorado
KUTE Ignacio, Colorado
KFMU-FM Oak Creek, Colorado
KPGS Pagosa Springs, Colorado
KSNO-FM Snowmass Village, Colorado
WKZE-FM Salisbury, Connecticut
WOCM Selbyville, Delaware
WAYR-FM Brunswick, Georgia
KMKV Paia, Hawaii
KDXA Ankeny, Iowa
KUNI Cedar Falls, Iowa
KICJ(FM) Mitchellville, Iowa
KISU-FM Pocatello, Idaho
KPND Sandpoint, Idaho
WWHP Farmer City, Illinois
WLCE Petersburg, Illinois
WTTS Bloomington, Indiana
WEEM-FM Pendleton, Indiana
KACY Arkansas City, Kansas
KMUW Wichita, Kansas
WNKU Highland Heights, Kentucky
WUKY Lexington, Kentucky
WKWC Owensboro, Kentucky
WHAY Whitley City, Kentucky
WXRV Andover, Massachusetts
WBOS Brookline, Massachusetts
WXPL Fitchburg, Massachusetts
WRSI Turners Falls, Massachusetts
WTMD Towson, Maryland
WCLZ North Yarmouth, Maine
WMEA Portland, Maine
WQKL Ann Arbor, Michigan
WLNZ Lansing, Michigan
KUMD-FM Duluth, Minnesota
WTIP Grand Marais, Minnesota
KCMP Northfield, Minnesota
KPRW Perham, Minnesota
KMSE Rochester, Minnesota
KSRQ Thief River Falls, Minnesota
KCLC St. Charles, Missouri
KTBG Warrensburg, Missouri
WUSM-FM Hattiesburg, Mississippi
KMMS-FM Bozeman, Montana
KDTR Florence, Montana
WGWG Boiling Springs, North Carolina
WSGE Dallas, North Carolina
WVOD Manteo, North Carolina
WUIN Oak Island, North Carolina
WNCW Spindale, North Carolina
WSIF Wilkesboro, North Carolina
KPPD Devils Lake, North Dakota
KFJM Grand Forks, North Dakota
KPPR Williston, North Dakota
WLKC Campton, New Hampshire
WMWV Conway, New Hampshire
WBJB-FM Lincroft, New Jersey
KUUT Farmington, New Mexico
KTAO Taos, New Mexico
KTHX-FM Dayton, Nevada
WXPK Briarcliff Manor, New York
WGFR Glens Falls, New York
WFUV New York, New York
WSIA Staten Island, New York
WDPS Dayton, Ohio
WYSO Yellow Springs, Ohio
KSMF Ashland, Oregon
KSBA Coos Bay, Oregon
KSKF Klamath Falls, Oregon
KTEE North Bend, Oregon
KINK Portland, Oregon
KLRR Redmond, Oregon
KSYD Reedsport, Oregon
WVMM Grantham, Pennsylvania
WYEP-FM Pittsburgh, Pennsylvania
WHBS Pittston, Pennsylvania
WLHI Schnecksville, Pennsylvania
WFBK Fort Mill, South Carolina
WSKZ Chattanooga, Tennessee
WDVX Clinton, Tennessee
WRLT Franklin, Tennessee
WFIV-FM Loudon, Tennessee
KEEP Bandera, Texas
KFAN-FM Johnson City, Texas
KRVL Kerrville, Texas
KRTS Marfa, Texas
KNBT New Braunfels, Texas
KSYM-FM San Antonio, Texas
WNRN Charlottesville, Virginia
WCTG Chincoteague, Virginia
WTYD Deltaville, Virginia

WCNR Keswick, Virginia
WVRU-FM Radford, Virginia
WIVI Charlotte Amalie, Virgin Islands
WRSY Marlboro, Vermont
WNCS Montpelier, Vermont
WNUB-FM Northfield, Vermont
WRJT Royalton, Vermont
KOHO Leavenworth, Washington
KHTP Tacoma, Washington
KTRT Winthrop, Washington
WLGE Baileys Harbor, Wisconsin
WYMS Milwaukee, Wisconsin
WMMM-FM Verona, Wisconsin
KBUW Buffalo, Wyoming
KUWC Casper, Wyoming

Urban Contemporary

KMVN Anchorage, Alaska
WUHT Birmingham, Alabama
WJJN Columbia, Alabama
WAGF Dothan, Alabama
WAGF-FM Dothan, Alabama
WBFA Fort Mitchell, Alabama
WMGJ Gadsden, Alabama
WHRP Gurley, Alabama
WHOG Hobson City, Alabama
WJUS Marion, Alabama
WWMG Millbrook, Alabama
WBLX-FM Mobile, Alabama
WHVK New Hope, Alabama
WZMG Pepperell, Alabama
WDLT Saraland, Alabama
WMRK-FM Shorter, Alabama
WZHT Troy, Alabama
WJWZ Wetumpka, Alabama
KAMJ Gosnell, Arkansas
KPZK Little Rock, Arkansas
KXHT Marion, Arkansas
KIPR Pine Bluff, Arkansas
KOKY Sherwood, Arkansas
KCLT West Helena, Arkansas
KSZR Oro Valley, Arizona
KHYL Auburn, California
KBLX-FM Berkeley, California
KSSX Carlsbad, California
KWIN Lodi, California
KWNN Lodi, California
KPWR Los Angeles, California
KRRL Los Angeles, California
KDEY-FM Ontario, California
KDAY Redondo Beach, California
KHHM Sacramento, California
KDON-FM Salinas, California
KMEL San Francisco, California
KFCO Bennett, Colorado
KMSA Grand Junction, Colorado
WZMX Hartford, Connecticut
WYBC-FM New Haven, Connecticut
WKYS Washington, District of Columbia
WZEB Ocean View, Delaware
WJBT Callahan, Florida
WBTP Clearwater, Florida
WMIE-FM Cocoa, Florida
WHQT Coral Gables, Florida
WURB Cross City, Florida
WHNR Cypress Gardens, Florida
WMIB Fort Lauderdale, Florida
WRRX Gulf Breeze, Florida
WPYO Maitland, Florida
WEBZ Mexico Beach, Florida
WEDR Miami, Florida
WTLQ-FM Punta Rassa, Florida
WHBX Tallahassee, Florida
WPRK Winter Park, Florida
WJIZ-FM Albany, Georgia
WMRG Albany, Georgia
WVEE Atlanta, Georgia
WBGA Brunswick, Georgia
WSOL-FM Brunswick, Georgia
WWLD Cairo, Georgia
WZBN Camilla, Georgia
WFXE Columbus, Georgia
WOKS Columbus, Georgia
WMRZ Dawson, Georgia
WUMJ Fayetteville, Georgia
WQMJ Forsyth, Georgia
WIBB-FM Fort Valley, Georgia
WFXM Gordon, Georgia
WHTA Hampton, Georgia
WLZN Macon, Georgia
WPRW-FM Martinez, Georgia
WALR-FM Palmetto, Georgia
WSTI-FM Quitman, Georgia
WGJK Rome, Georgia
WAMJ Roswell, Georgia
WQBT Savannah, Georgia
WEAS-FM Springfield, Georgia
WBGA St. Simons Island, Georgia
WRBV Warner Robins, Georgia
WCHZ-FM Warrenton, Georgia
WPCH West Point, Georgia
KZGZ Hagatna, Guam
KWQW Boone, Iowa
WPCD Champaign, Illinois
WGCI-FM Chicago, Illinois
WYDS-HD2 Decatur, Illinois
WYRB Genoa, Illinois
WPWX Hammond, Indiana
WIUS Macomb, Illinois
WCZQ Monticello, Illinois
WVAZ Oak Park, Illinois
WTLC-FM Greenwood, Indiana
WHHH Indianapolis, Indiana
WGZB-FM Lanesville, Indiana
WRWM Lawrence, Indiana
KSDB-FM Manhattan, Kansas
WIZF Erlanger, Kentucky
WMJM Jeffersontown, Kentucky
WBTF Midway, Kentucky
WDXR Paducah, Kentucky
WUBT Russellville, Kentucky
WGHL Shepherdsville, Kentucky
KEDG Alexandria, Louisiana
KMXH Alexandria, Louisiana
KRVV Bastrop, Louisiana
KDKS-FM Blanchard, Louisiana
KBCE Boyce, Louisiana
KNNW Columbia, Louisiana
KBTT Haughton, Louisiana
KRRQ Lafayette, Louisiana
KJMH Lake Charles, Louisiana
KZWA Moss Bluff, Louisiana
WQUE-FM New Orleans, Louisiana
WYLD-FM New Orleans, Louisiana
KCLF New Roads, Louisiana
KQXL New Roads, Louisiana
KFXZ-FM Opelousas, Louisiana
KMJJ-FM Shreveport, Louisiana
KOKA Shreveport, Louisiana
KVMA-FM Shreveport, Louisiana
KNEK Washington, Louisiana
KNEK Washington, Louisiana
WERQ-FM Baltimore, Maryland
WMMJ Bethesda, Maryland
WWIN-FM Glen Burnie, Maryland
W245CA Pocomoke City, Maryland
WXKE-FM Pocomoke City, Maryland
WXSH Pocomoke City, Maryland
WSBY-FM Salisbury, Maryland
WQHH DeWitt, Michigan
WDMK Detroit, Michigan
WGPR Detroit, Michigan
WJLB Detroit, Michigan
WMXD Detroit, Michigan
WDZZ-FM Flint, Michigan
WVIB Holton, Michigan
WSNX-FM Muskegon, Michigan
WNWN-AM Portage, Michigan
WOWE Vassar, Michigan
WPHS Warren, Michigan
WRXP Cambridge, Minnesota
WGVZ Eden Prairie, Minnesota
WGVX Lakeville, Minnesota
KMOJ Minneapolis, Minnesota
KMJM-FM Bridgeton, Missouri
WHHL Hazelwood, Missouri
WMBH Joplin, Missouri
KPRS Kansas City, Missouri
KPRT Kansas City, Missouri
KOSP Ozark, Missouri
WESE Baldwyn, Mississippi
WRBJ Brandon, Mississippi
WAID Clarksdale, Mississippi
WCLD-FM Cleveland, Mississippi
WRBO Como, Mississippi
WJXM De Kalb, Mississippi
WJKX Ellisville, Mississippi
WJMG Hattiesburg, Mississippi
WJMI Jackson, Mississippi
WAZA Liberty, Mississippi
WKXI-FM Magee, Mississippi
KJMS Olive Branch, Mississippi
WZLD Petal, Mississippi
WMSU Starkville, Mississippi
WMXU Starkville, Mississippi
WGNG Tchula, Mississippi
WZKS Union, Mississippi
KLSK Great Falls, Montana
WFXK Bunn, North Carolina
WYNA Calabash, North Carolina
WQOK Carrboro, North Carolina
WPEG Concord, North Carolina
WFXC Durham, North Carolina
WRSV Elm City, North Carolina
WQNC Harrisburg, North Carolina
WHBT-FM Moyock, North Carolina
WPWZ Pinetops, North Carolina
WMGU Southern Pines, North Carolina
WUKS St. Pauls, North Carolina
WZFX Whiteville, North Carolina
WMNX Wilmington, North Carolina
KFKX Hastings, Nebraska
WPHI-FM Pennsauken, New Jersey
WZBZ Pleasantville, New Jersey
KKRG Albuquerque, New Mexico
KNEV Reno, Nevada
WYUL Chateaugay, New York
WBLK Depew, New York
WICB Ithaca, New York
WQHT New York, New York
WWPR-FM New York, New York
WDKX Rochester, New York
WHEN Syracuse, New York
WDPN Alliance, Ohio
WENZ Cleveland, Ohio
WZAK Cleveland, Ohio
WCKX Columbus, Ohio
WZCB Dublin, Ohio
WZOH-FM Lancaster, Ohio
WCIT(AM) Lima, Ohio
WXMG London, Ohio
WDHT Urbana, Ohio
WROU-FM West Carrollton, Ohio
KVSP Anadarko, Oklahoma
KJMM Bixby, Oklahoma
KXJM Banks, Oregon
WWLU Lincoln University, Pennsylvania
WDAS-FM Philadelphia, Pennsylvania
WUSL Philadelphia, Pennsylvania
WAMO Wilkinsburg, Pennsylvania
WDIN Camuy, Puerto Rico
WKSP Aiken, South Carolina
WJMZ-FM Anderson, South Carolina
WIIZ Blackville, South Carolina
WLXC Columbia, South Carolina
WWRK Florence, South Carolina
WYNN-FM Florence, South Carolina
WLVH Hardeeville, South Carolina
WXST Hollywood, South Carolina
WRZE Kingstree, South Carolina
WCMG Latta, South Carolina
WHXT Orangeburg, South Carolina
WDAI Pawleys Island, South Carolina
WZTF Scranton, South Carolina
WFMV South Congaree, South Carolina
WLJI Summerton, South Carolina
WWWZ Summerville, South Carolina
WWDM Sumter, South Carolina
WWHM Sumter, South Carolina
WXBT West Columbia, South Carolina
WSCZ Winnsboro, South Carolina
WQQK Goodlettsville, Tennessee
WMPZ Harrison, Tennessee
WDIA Memphis, Tennessee
WHRK Memphis, Tennessee
WKIM Munford, Tennessee
WJTT Red Bank, Tennessee
WMXV St. Joseph, Tennessee
KNDA Alice, Texas
KTCX Beaumont, Texas
KMYO Comfort, Texas
KZFM Corpus Christi, Texas
KBFB Dallas, Texas
KKDA Dallas, Texas
KRNB Decatur, Texas
KSOC Gainesville, Texas
KBXX Houston, Texas
KMJQ Houston, Texas
KQBT Houston, Texas
KIIZ-FM Killeen, Texas
KAZE Ore City, Texas
KPVU Prairie View, Texas

KBBT Schertz, Texas
KROI Seabrook, Texas
KBTE Tulia, Texas
KBLZ Winona, Texas
KENZ Provo, Utah
KENZ Provo, Utah
KUUU South Jordan, Utah
WUVA Charlottesville, Virginia
WYTT Emporia, Virginia
WVBE-FM Lynchburg, Virginia
WCDX Mechanicsville, Virginia
WNSB Norfolk, Virginia
WOWI Norfolk, Virginia
WKJM Petersburg, Virginia
WBTJ Richmond, Virginia
WKJS Richmond, Virginia
WVBE Roanoke, Virginia
WTOY Salem, Virginia
WWKS Cruz Bay, Virgin Islands
KEZE Spokane, Washington
KHHK Yakima, Washington
WEAQ Chippewa Falls, Wisconsin
WJQM De Forest, Wisconsin
WJMR-FM Menomonee Falls, Wisconsin
WNOV Milwaukee, Wisconsin
WKKV-FM Racine, Wisconsin

Variety/Diverse

KAUG Anchorage, Alaska
KNBA Anchorage, Alaska
KBRW Barrow, Alaska
KYUK Bethel, Alaska
KCUK Chevak, Alaska
KUAC Fairbanks, Alaska
KZPA Fort Yukon, Alaska
KIYU Galena, Alaska
KIYU-FM Galena, Alaska
KEUL Girdwood, Alaska
KXGA Glennallen, Alaska
KRNN Juneau, Alaska
KTOO Juneau, Alaska
KALG Kaltag, Alaska
KMXT Kodiak, Alaska
KINU Kotzebue, Alaska
KOTZ Kotzebue, Alaska
KOYU Koyukuk, Alaska
KNOM Nome, Alaska
KCAW Sitka, Alaska
KNSA Unalakleet, Alaska
KCHU Valdez, Alaska
KSTK Wrangell, Alaska
WLJR Birmingham, Alabama
WLJS-FM Jacksonville, Alabama
WHHY-FM Montgomery, Alabama
WVUA-FM Tuscaloosa, Alabama
KVMN Cave City, Arkansas
KHDX Conway, Arkansas
KAVH Eudora, Arkansas
KXUA Fayetteville, Arkansas
KABF Little Rock, Arkansas
KVSA McGehee, Arkansas
KURM Rogers, Arkansas
KXRJ Russellville, Arkansas
KAFZ Ash Fork, Arizona
KBUX Quartzsite, Arizona
KRMH Red Mesa, Arizona
KRDX Vail, Arizona
KNNB Whiteriver, Arizona
KAHI Auburn, California
KISL Avalon, California
KALX Berkeley, California
KPFA Berkeley, California
KRHV Big Pine, California
KDUP Cedarville, California
KZFR Chico, California
KSPC Claremont, California
KWRM Corona, California
KDVS Davis, California
KECG El Cerrito, California
KMUE Eureka, California
KFCF Fresno, California
KMUD Garberville, California
KTDE Gualala, California
KCRH Hayward, California
KTYM Inglewood, California
KLAI Laytonville, California
KFJC Los Altos, California
KPFK Los Angeles, California
KAKX Mendocino, California
KVMR Nevada City, California
KCSN Northridge, California
KKSM Oceanside, California
KOPA(FM) Pala, California
KZYX Philo, California
KKZZ Port Hueneme, California
KTHM Red Bluff, California
KUCR Riverside, California
KYDS Sacramento, California
KNBX San Ardo, California
KALW San Francisco, California
KPOO San Francisco, California
KMTG San Jose, California
KSJS San Jose, California
KCPR San Luis Obispo, California
KSRH San Rafael, California
KCSB-FM Santa Barbara, California
KFER Santa Cruz, California
KUSP Santa Cruz, California
KZSC Santa Cruz, California
KCSS Turlock, California
KZYZ Willits, California
KGNU-FM Boulder, Colorado
KVCU Boulder, Colorado
KMPB Breckenridge, Colorado
KEPC Colorado Springs, Colorado
KSJD Cortez, Colorado
KZET Cortez, Colorado
KBUT Crested Butte, Colorado
KDUR Durango, Colorado
KIQX Durango, Colorado
KRFC Fort Collins, Colorado
KUNC Greeley, Colorado
KWSB-FM Gunnison, Colorado
KZBR La Jara, Colorado
KECC La Junta, Colorado
KRKV Las Animas, Colorado
KRNC Steamboat Springs, Colorado
KOTO Telluride, Colorado
WPKN Bridgeport, Connecticut
WVOF Fairfield, Connecticut
WRTC-FM Hartford, Connecticut
WESU Middletown, Connecticut
WSLX New Canaan, Connecticut
WCNI New London, Connecticut
WBVC Pomfret, Connecticut
WHUS Storrs, Connecticut
WAPJ Torrington, Connecticut
WWEB Wallingford, Connecticut
WWUH West Hartford, Connecticut
WNHU West Haven, Connecticut
WWPT Westport, Connecticut
WVUD Newark, Delaware
WMPH Wilmington, Delaware
WBHQ Beverly Beach, Florida
WBGC Chipley, Florida
WVUM Coral Gables, Florida
WNUE-FM Deltona, Florida
WRGP Homestead, Florida
WZFL Islamorada, Florida
WOTS Kissimmee, Florida
WSDO Sanford, Florida
WFCF St. Augustine, Florida
WQBN Temple Terrace, Florida
WPRD Winter Park, Florida
WREK Atlanta, Georgia
WMLB Avondale Estates, Georgia
WDRR Martinez, Georgia
WHCJ Savannah, Georgia
WZAT Tybee Island, Georgia
KTUH Honolulu, Hawaii
KURE Ames, Iowa
KROS Clinton, Iowa
KWLC Decorah, Iowa
KDTH Dubuque, Iowa
KHOE Fairfield, Iowa
KRUI-FM Iowa City, Iowa
KQNU(FM) Onawa, Iowa
KDLS Perry, Iowa
KLCZ Lewiston, Idaho
KBSQ McCall, Idaho
KUOI-FM Moscow, Idaho
WESN Bloomington, Illinois
WDBX Carbondale, Illinois
WEFT Champaign, Illinois
WEIU Charleston, Illinois
WHPK-FM Chicago, Illinois
WIIT Chicago, Illinois
WLUW Chicago, Illinois
WZRD Chicago, Illinois
WDGC-FM Downers Grove, Illinois
WEPS Elgin, Illinois
WVKC Galesburg, Illinois
WHPI Glasford, Illinois
WDUK Havana, Illinois
WHSD Hinsdale, Illinois
WLTL La Grange, Illinois
WMXM Lake Forest, Illinois
WAES Lincolnshire, Illinois
WLRA Lockport, Illinois
WHCM Palatine, Illinois
WMTH Park Ridge, Illinois
WSPY-FM Plano, Illinois
WQNA Springfield, Illinois
WILL Urbana, Illinois
WILL-FM Urbana, Illinois
WNTH Winnetka, Illinois
WFWR Attica, Indiana
WFHB Bloomington, Indiana
WPSR Evansville, Indiana
WUEV Evansville, Indiana
WGCS Goshen, Indiana
WTRE Greensburg, Indiana
WJEL Indianapolis, Indiana
WRFT Indianapolis, Indiana
WBRO Marengo, Indiana
WMRS Monticello, Indiana
WBKE-FM North Manchester, Indiana
WECI Richmond, Indiana
WZIS(FM) Terre Haute, Indiana
WVUR-FM Valparaiso, Indiana
WITT Zionsville, Indiana
KVCO Concordia, Kansas
KONQ Dodge City, Kansas
KBTL El Dorado, Kansas
KANZ Garden City, Kansas
KBCU North Newton, Kansas
KTJO-FM Ottawa, Kansas
KKAN Phillipsburg, Kansas
KQMA Phillipsburg, Kansas
WWHR Bowling Green, Kentucky
WKMT Fulton, Kentucky
WCLU Glasgow, Kentucky
WLSK Lebanon, Kentucky
WRFL Lexington, Kentucky
WMKY Morehead, Kentucky
WKMS-FM Murray, Kentucky
WRUS Russellville, Kentucky
WMMT Whitesburg, Kentucky
KLSP Angola, Louisiana
KLSU Baton Rouge, Louisiana
KNWD Natchitoches, Louisiana
KKAY White Castle, Louisiana
WHAB Acton, Massachusetts
WAMH Amherst, Massachusetts
WMUA Amherst, Massachusetts
WERS Boston, Massachusetts
WRBB Boston, Massachusetts
WUMB-FM Boston, Massachusetts
WBIM-FM Bridgewater, Massachusetts
WMBR Cambridge, Massachusetts
WSHL-FM Easton, Massachusetts
WFPB-FM Falmouth, Massachusetts
WHHB Holliston, Massachusetts
WCCH Holyoke, Massachusetts
WUML Lowell, Massachusetts
WWTA Marion, Massachusetts
WMFO Medford, Massachusetts
WMLN-FM Milton, Massachusetts
WNCK Nantucket, Massachusetts
WNEF Newburyport, Massachusetts
WUMD North Dartmouth, Massachusetts
WOZQ Northampton, Massachusetts
WFPB Orleans, Massachusetts
WOCN-FM Orleans, Massachusetts
WBRK Pittsfield, Massachusetts
WMWM Salem, Massachusetts
WSDH Sandwich, Massachusetts
WBSL-FM Sheffield, Massachusetts
WAIC Springfield, Massachusetts
WNEK-FM Springfield, Massachusetts
WSCB Springfield, Massachusetts
WTCC Springfield, Massachusetts
WYAJ Sudbury, Massachusetts
WBRS Waltham, Massachusetts
WAZN Watertown, Massachusetts
WZLY Wellesley, Massachusetts
WSKB Westfield, Massachusetts
WBPR Worcester, Massachusetts
WCUW Worcester, Massachusetts
WHFC Bel Air, Maryland
WMUC-FM College Park, Maryland
WWFD Frederick, Maryland

WRNR-FM Grasonville, Maryland
WKHS Worton, Maryland
WERU-FM Blue Hill, Maine
WBOR Brunswick, Maine
WSHD Eastport, Maine
WMPG Gorham, Maine
WUMM Machias, Maine
WSYY-FM Millinocket, Maine
WMEB-FM Orono, Maine
WUPI Presque Isle, Maine
WMHB Waterville, Maine
WVAC-FM Adrian, Michigan
WCBN-FM Ann Arbor, Michigan
WXOU Auburn Hills, Michigan
WMJO Essexville, Michigan
WMJZ-FM Gaylord, Michigan
WKJZ Hillman, Michigan
WMTU-FM Houghton, Michigan
WION Ionia, Michigan
WIDR Kalamazoo, Michigan
WKDS Kalamazoo, Michigan
WYDM Monroe, Michigan
WBLD Orchard Lake, Michigan
WLSO Sault Ste. Marie, Michigan
WQLB Tawas City, Michigan
WNMC-FM Traverse City, Michigan
KQWB-FM Breckenridge, Minnesota
KFGI Crosby, Minnesota
WELY Ely, Minnesota
KAXE Grand Rapids, Minnesota
KLFD Litchfield, Minnesota
KFAI Minneapolis, Minnesota
WMCN St. Paul, Minnesota
KQAL Winona, Minnesota
KWUR Clayton, Missouri
KXMS Joplin, Missouri
KLUE Poplar Bluff, Missouri
KMNR Rolla, Missouri
KMST Rolla, Missouri
KDHX Saint Louis, Missouri
WEW St. Louis, Missouri
KRSI Garapan-Saipan, Guam
WMGO Canton, Mississippi
WUSM-FM Hattiesburg, Mississippi
WMPR Jackson, Mississippi
WPRL Lorman, Mississippi
KYPB Big Timber, Montana
KMSM-FM Butte, Montana
KYPC Colstrip, Montana
KIMO Helena Valley SE, Montana
KYPR Miles City, Montana
WXDU Durham, North Carolina
WRVS-FM Elizabeth City, North Carolina
WUAW Erwin, North Carolina
WQFS Greensboro, North Carolina
WZMB Greenville, North Carolina
WHKP Hendersonville, North Carolina
WFHE Hickory, North Carolina
WOVV Ocracoke, North Carolina
WRGC Sylva, North Carolina
KDSU Fargo, North Dakota
KABU Fort Totten, North Dakota
KMHA Four Bears, North Dakota
KZUM Lincoln, Nebraska
KNCY Nebraska City, Nebraska
WSPS Concord, New Hampshire
WPEA Exeter, New Hampshire
WAJM Atlantic City, New Jersey
WSNJ Bridgeton, New Jersey
WDVR Delaware Township, New Jersey
WFMU East Orange, New Jersey
WGLS-FM Glassboro, New Jersey
WNTI Hackettstown, New Jersey
WRRC Lawrenceville, New Jersey
WMVB Millville, New Jersey
WRSU-FM New Brunswick, New Jersey
WWPH Princeton Junction, New Jersey
WMSC Upper Montclair, New Jersey
KDAZ Albuquerque, New Mexico
KUNM Albuquerque, New Mexico
KRRT Arroyo Seco, New Mexico
KCIE Dulce, New Mexico
KRAR Espanola, New Mexico
KGLP Gallup, New Mexico
KOOT Hurley, New Mexico
KRUX Las Cruces, New Mexico
KRRE Las Vegas, New Mexico
KVSF-FM Pecos, New Mexico
KSIL Rincon, New Mexico
KBOM Socorro, New Mexico
KWPR Lund, Nevada
WCDB Albany, New York
WALF Alfred, New York
WHRW Binghamton, New York
WKRB Brooklyn, New York
WSLU Canton, New York
WHCL-FM Clinton, New York
WSUC-FM Cortland, New York
WXXE Fenner, New York
WCVF-FM Fredonia, New York
WGBB Freeport, New York
WHPC Garden City, New York
WRCU-FM Hamilton, New York
WRHU Hempstead, New York
WSHR Lake Ronkonkoma, New York
WVCR-FM Loudonville, New York
WSLO Malone, New York
WMFU(FM) Mount Hope, New York
WVIP New Rochelle, New York
WVOX New Rochelle, New York
WFUV New York, New York
WKCR-FM New York, New York
WRVO Oswego, New York
WVKR-FM Poughkeepsie, New York
WRUR-FM Rochester, New York
WUMX Rome, New York
WSLL Saranac Lake, New York
WSPQ Springville, New York
WUSB Stony Brook, New York
WKWZ Syosset, New York
WRVD Syracuse, New York
WRPI Troy, New York
WPNR-FM Utica, New York
WRVN Utica, New York
WRVJ Watertown, New York
WSLJ Watertown, New York
WOHA Ashtabula, Ohio
WBGU Bowling Green, Ohio
WRUW-FM Cleveland, Ohio
WUDR Dayton, Ohio
WWSU Fairborn, Ohio
WKCO Gambier, Ohio
WFGA Hicksville, Ohio
WMCO New Concord, Ohio
WJCU University Heights, Ohio
WYNS Waynesville, Ohio
WCWS-FM Wooster, Ohio
KDOE Antlers, Oklahoma
KQOB Enid, Oklahoma
KXMX Muldrow, Oklahoma
KSRG Ashland, Oregon
KWVA Eugene, Oregon
KHNO Huntington, Oregon
KTEC Klamath Falls, Oregon
KEOL La Grande, Oregon
KLCO Newport, Oregon
KBOO Portland, Oregon
KTCB Tillamook, Oregon
WDIY Allentown, Pennsylvania
WMUH Allentown, Pennsylvania
WLVR-FM Bethlehem, Pennsylvania
WLBS Bristol, Pennsylvania
WDCV-FM Carlisle, Pennsylvania
WMAJ-FM Centre Hall, Pennsylvania
WDNR Chester, Pennsylvania
WESS East Stroudsburg, Pennsylvania
WJRH Easton, Pennsylvania
WRSD Folsom, Pennsylvania
WHHS Havertown, Pennsylvania
WIUP-FM Indiana, Pennsylvania
WKHB Irwin, Pennsylvania
WFNM Lancaster, Pennsylvania
WLCH Lancaster, Pennsylvania
WCNS Latrobe, Pennsylvania
WIXQ Millersville, Pennsylvania
WSFX Nanticoke, Pennsylvania
WPEB Philadelphia, Pennsylvania
WPHE Phoenixville, Pennsylvania
WPTS-FM Pittsburgh, Pennsylvania
WRCT Pittsburgh, Pennsylvania
WYBF Radnor Township, Pennsylvania
WRFY-FM Reading, Pennsylvania
WSYC-FM Shippensburg, Pennsylvania
WSRU Slippery Rock, Pennsylvania
WKPS State College, Pennsylvania
WSRN-FM Swarthmore, Pennsylvania
WRDV Warminster, Pennsylvania
WNJR Washington, Pennsylvania
WCUR West Chester, Pennsylvania
WVYC York, Pennsylvania
WOQI Adjuntas, Puerto Rico
WNIK Arecibo, Puerto Rico
WCGB Juana Diaz, Puerto Rico
WJIT Sabana, Puerto Rico
WQBS San Juan, Puerto Rico
WEGA Vega Baja, Puerto Rico
WRIU Kingston, Rhode Island
WJHD Portsmouth, Rhode Island
WELH Providence, Rhode Island
WLTY Cayce, South Carolina
WUSC-FM Columbia, South Carolina
WLBG Laurens, South Carolina
WLSC Loris, South Carolina
KLND Little Eagle, South Dakota
KVAR Pine Ridge, South Dakota
KCFS Sioux Falls, South Dakota
WJNA Ashland City, Tennessee
WAPX-FM Clarksville, Tennessee
WMTS-FM Murfreesboro, Tennessee
WCFL(FM) Nashville, Tennessee
WUTS Sewanee, Tennessee
WSGI Springfield, Tennessee
KVLF Alpine, Texas
KTXP Bushland, Texas
KNON Dallas, Texas
KTCU Fort Worth, Texas
KGRW Friona, Texas
KWFB Holliday, Texas
KOOP Hornsby, Texas
KEYH Houston, Texas
KPFT Houston, Texas
KTSU Houston, Texas
KLKV Hunt, Texas
KTXT-FM Lubbock, Texas
KLSR-FM Memphis, Texas
KEOM Mesquite, Texas
KZAM Pleasant Valley, Texas
KPVU Prairie View, Texas
KSEY-FM Seymour, Texas
KGWB Snyder, Texas
KSST Sulphur Springs, Texas
KWBU-FM Waco, Texas
KZMU Moab, Utah
KPUT Mona, Utah
KPGR Pleasant Grove, Utah
WUVT-FM Blacksburg, Virginia
WTJU Charlottesville, Virginia
WEHC Emory, Virginia
WMLU Farmville, Virginia
WWHS-FM Hampden-Sydney, Virginia
WHOV Hampton, Virginia
WCLM Highland Springs, Virginia
WCHG Hot Springs, Virginia
WLUR Lexington, Virginia
WVLS Monterey, Virginia
WVST-FM Petersburg, Virginia
WDCE Richmond, Virginia
WWEM Rustburg, Virginia
WCWM Williamsburg, Virginia
WSTA Charlotte Amalie, Virgin Islands
WDHP Frederiksted, Virgin Islands
WRUV Burlington, Vermont
WWPV-FM Colchester, Vermont
WDOT Danville, Vermont
WJSC-FM Johnson, Vermont
WRMC-FM Middlebury, Vermont
WGDR Plainfield, Vermont
WDEV Waterbury, Vermont
WWMP Waterbury, Vermont
KXPA Bellevue, Washington
KCED Centralia, Washington
KCWU Ellensburg, Washington
KSER Everett, Washington
KUBS Newport, Washington
KZUU Pullman, Washington
KSUH Puyallup, Washington
KEXP-FM Seattle, Washington
KWCW Walla Walla, Washington
WLMV Madison, Wisconsin
WXPR Rhinelander, Wisconsin
WRPN-FM Ripon, Wisconsin
WRFW River Falls, Wisconsin
KUWS Superior, Wisconsin
WDRT Viroqua, Wisconsin
WCCX Waukesha, Wisconsin
WYZR Bethany, West Virginia
WVWC Buckhannon, West Virginia
WSWW-FM Craigsville, West Virginia
WQWV Fisher, West Virginia
WMUL Huntington, West Virginia
WRSG Middlebourne, West Virginia
WWVU-FM Morgantown, West Virginia
WQAB Philippi, West Virginia

WWYO Pineville, West Virginia
WSHC Shepherdstown, West Virginia
WVVV Williamstown, West Virginia
KWXR Reliance, Wyoming

Vietnamese

KSJX San Jose, California
KZSJ San Martin, California
KVNR Santa Ana, California
KVVN Santa Clara, California
KALI West Covina, California
WNTF Bithlo, Florida
KYND Cypress, Texas

Special Radio Programming on Radio Stations in the U.S.

Adult Contemp

KUAC Fairbanks, Alaska
WBHM Birmingham, Alabama
WSGN Gadsden, Alabama
WQPR Muscle Shoals, Alabama
WUAL-FM Tuscaloosa, Alabama
KUAF Fayetteville, Arkansas
KASU Jonesboro, Arkansas
KABF Little Rock, Arkansas
KUAR Little Rock, Arkansas
KCTT-FM Yellville, Arkansas
KVNA Flagstaff, Arizona
KNCA Burney, California
KXLU Los Angeles, California
KSBR Mission Viejo, California
KMPO Modesto, California
KNSQ Mount Shasta, California
KCBX San Luis Obispo, California
KVYN St. Helena, California
KKDV Walnut Creek, California
KRCB-FM Windsor, California
KGNU-FM Boulder, Colorado
KMSA Grand Junction, Colorado
WXCI Danbury, Connecticut
WSHU-FM Fairfield, Connecticut
WGRS Guilford, Connecticut
WMNR Monroe, Connecticut
WYBC-FM New Haven, Connecticut
WQQQ Sharon, Connecticut
WRXC Shelton, Connecticut
WGSK South Kent, Connecticut
WNHU West Haven, Connecticut
WUFT-FM Gainesville, Florida
WOTS Kissimmee, Florida
WKGC Southport, Florida
WFCF St. Augustine, Florida
WVFS Tallahassee, Florida
WUGA Athens, Georgia
WRAS Atlanta, Georgia
WUWG Carrollton, Georgia
KUNI Cedar Falls, Iowa
KCCK-FM Cedar Rapids, Iowa
KNSY(FM) Dubuque, Iowa
KRNI Mason City, Iowa
KICJ(FM) Mitchellville, Iowa
KRNL-FM Mount Vernon, Iowa
KBSU-FM Boise, Idaho
KRFA-FM Moscow, Idaho
KUOI-FM Moscow, Idaho
WSIU Carbondale, Illinois
WEFT Champaign, Illinois
WEIU Charleston, Illinois
WFMT Chicago, Illinois
WNIJ Dekalb, Illinois
WSIE Edwardsville, Illinois
WNUR-FM Evanston, Illinois
WDCB Glen Ellyn, Illinois
WIUM Macomb, Illinois
WGLT Normal, Illinois
WNIU Rockford, Illinois
WFHB Bloomington, Indiana
WVPE Elkhart, Indiana
KANZ Garden City, Kansas
KZNA Hill City, Kansas
KRPS Pittsburg, Kansas
WKUE Elizabethtown, Kentucky
WDCL-FM Somerset, Kentucky
WGBH(FM) Boston, Massachusetts
WAMQ Great Barrington, Massachusetts
WBSL-FM Sheffield, Massachusetts
WMTB-FM Emmitsburg, Maryland
WMHB Waterville, Maine
WBNZ Frankfort, Michigan
WBLU-FM Grand Rapids, Michigan
WLNZ Lansing, Michigan
WNMC-FM Traverse City, Michigan
WBLV Twin Lake, Michigan
WYCE Wyoming, Michigan
KMSK Austin, Minnesota
KBSB Bemidji, Minnesota
KMSU Mankato, Minnesota
KFAI Minneapolis, Minnesota
KNGA Saint Peter, Minnesota
KVSC St. Cloud, Minnesota
KKFI Kansas City, Missouri
KCOZ Point Lookout, Missouri
KMST Rolla, Missouri
KEMC Billings, Montana
WCQS Asheville, North Carolina
WBUX Buxton, North Carolina
WUNC Chapel Hill, North Carolina
WCKB Dunn, North Carolina
WFQS Franklin, North Carolina
WUND-FM Manteo, North Carolina
WURI Manteo, North Carolina
WNCW Spindale, North Carolina
KCND Bismarck, North Dakota
KDPR Dickinson, North Dakota
KUND-FM Grand Forks, North Dakota
KPRJ Jamestown, North Dakota
KMPR Minot, North Dakota
KPPR Williston, North Dakota
KZUM Lincoln, Nebraska
WEVO Concord, New Hampshire
WEVO(FM) Concord, New Hampshire
WEVH Hanover, New Hampshire
WEVN Keene, New Hampshire
WSNJ Bridgeton, New Jersey
WLFR Pomona, New Jersey
WTSR Trenton, New Jersey
KSJE Farmington, New Mexico
KRWG Las Cruces, New Mexico
KUNR Reno, Nevada
WAMC-FM Albany, New York
WSKG-FM Binghamton, New York
WCAN Canajoharie, New York
WSQE Corning, New York
WSQG-FM Ithaca, New York
WVBR-FM Ithaca, New York
WAMK Kingston, New York
WOSR Middletown, New York
WSUF Noyack, New York
WRHO Oneonta, New York
WSQC-FM Oneonta, New York
WTKV Oswego, New York
WCEL Plattsburgh, New York
WSPN Saratoga Springs, New York
WAER Syracuse, New York
WANC Ticonderoga, New York
WTBQ Warwick, New York
WBGU Bowling Green, Ohio
WGDE Defiance, Ohio
WKSU-FM Kent, Ohio
WGLE Lima, Ohio
WBUK Ottawa, Ohio
WGTE-FM Toledo, Ohio
WKRW Wooster, Ohio
WYSO Yellow Springs, Ohio
WYSU Youngstown, Ohio
KRSC-FM Claremore, Oklahoma
KWOX Woodward, Oklahoma
KSMF Ashland, Oregon
KMUN Astoria, Oregon
KSBA Coos Bay, Oregon
KBVR Corvallis, Oregon
KLCC Eugene, Oregon
KSKF Klamath Falls, Oregon
KTEC Klamath Falls, Oregon
KLCO Newport, Oregon
WQLN-FM Erie, Pennsylvania
WZBT Gettysburg, Pennsylvania
WPSX Kane, Pennsylvania
WHYY-FM Philadelphia, Pennsylvania
WXPN Philadelphia, Pennsylvania
WEEU Reading, Pennsylvania
WPSU State College, Pennsylvania
WKSP(AM) Block Island, Rhode Island
WJMF Smithfield, Rhode Island
WHHD Clearwater, South Carolina
WPCC Clinton, South Carolina
KAUR Sioux Falls, South Dakota
KCSD Sioux Falls, South Dakota
WTTU Cookeville, Tennessee
KUT Austin, Texas
KAMU-FM College Station, Texas
KEOS College Station, Texas
KTEP El Paso, Texas
KOOP Hornsby, Texas
KNCH(FM) San Angelo, Texas
WNRN Charlottesville, Virginia
WMRY Crozet, Virginia
WMRA Harrisonburg, Virginia
WMRL Lexington, Virginia
WHRV Norfolk, Virginia
WCVE-FM Richmond, Virginia
WVBW Suffolk, Virginia
WNCS Montpelier, Vermont
WRVT Rutland, Vermont
WVPR Windsor, Vermont
KZAZ Bellingham, Washington
KNWR Ellensburg, Washington
KAOS Olympia, Washington
KZUU Pullman, Washington
KFAE-FM Richland, Washington
KAGU Spokane, Washington
KPBX-FM Spokane, Washington
WHSA Brule, Wisconsin
WUEC Eau Claire, Wisconsin
WHWC Menomonie, Wisconsin
WVSS Menomonie, Wisconsin
WHND Sister Bay, Wisconsin
WLBL-FM Wausau, Wisconsin
WHAW Lost Creek, West Virginia
WWVU-FM Morgantown, West Virginia
WWYO Pineville, West Virginia
KUWA Afton, Wyoming
KUWJ Jackson, Wyoming
KUWR Laramie, Wyoming
KUWZ Rock Springs, Wyoming

Agriculture

WKAC Athens, Alabama
WLYG Centre, Alabama
WKUL Cullman, Alabama
WTVY-FM Dothan, Alabama
WNRA Eufaula, Alabama
WKWL Florala, Alabama
WHEP Foley, Alabama
WZOB Fort Payne, Alabama
WWWH Haleyville, Alabama
WERH Hamilton, Alabama
WINL Linden, Alabama
WGMP Montgomery, Alabama
WKEA-FM Scottsboro, Alabama
WHBB Selma, Alabama
WTLS Tallassee, Alabama
WTBF Troy, Alabama
KAAB Batesville, Arkansas
KEWI Benton, Arkansas
KXXA(AM) Conway, Arkansas
KVDW England, Arkansas
KXJK Forrest City, Arkansas
KTHS Green Forest, Arkansas
KFIN Jonesboro, Arkansas
KNEA Jonesboro, Arkansas
KVMA Magnolia, Arkansas
KVSA McGehee, Arkansas
KPOC Pocahontas, Arkansas
KURM Rogers, Arkansas
KARV Russellville, Arkansas
KWCK Searcy, Arkansas
KWAK Stuttgart, Arkansas
KOSE Wilson, Arkansas
KWYN Wynne, Arkansas
KDJI Holbrook, Arizona
KLPZ Parker, Arizona
KVSL Show Low, Arizona
KCFJ Alturas, California
KISV Bakersfield, California
KBHR Big Bear City, California
KJMB-FM Blythe, California
KXO El Centro, California
KRKC King City, California
KUBB Mariposa, California
KYOS Merced, California
KBLF Red Bluff, California
KSTN Stockton, California
KJUG Tulare, California
KWNE Ukiah, California
KUBA Yuba City, California
KGIW Alamosa, Colorado
KRAI Craig, Colorado
KRKY Granby, Colorado
KFKA Greeley, Colorado
KSLV Monte Vista, Colorado
KSTC Sterling, Colorado
KCRT Trinidad, Colorado
KRDZ Wray, Colorado
WGMD Rehoboth Beach, Delaware
WGBG Seaford, Delaware
WBGF Belle Glade, Florida
WLBE Leesburg-Eustis, Florida
WTYS Marianna, Florida
WDVH-FM Trenton, Florida
WZZS Zolfo Springs, Florida
V6AH(AM) Pohnpei, 66
WAWO Alma, Georgia

WDEC-FM Americus, Georgia
WGAC Augusta, Georgia
WJTH Calhoun, Georgia
WCLA Claxton, Georgia
WDXQ Cochran, Georgia
WRCG Columbus, Georgia
WAEF Cordele, Georgia
WDMG Douglas, Georgia
WHJD Hazlehurst, Georgia
WQCH La Fayette, Georgia
WMCG Milan, Georgia
WHKN Millen, Georgia
WMTM Moultrie, Georgia
WSTI-FM Quitman, Georgia
WJAT Swainsboro, Georgia
WSYL Sylvania, Georgia
WTHO-FM Thomson, Georgia
KLGA Algona, Iowa
KJAN Atlantic, Iowa
KWBG Boone, Iowa
KBUR Burlington, Iowa
KCPS Burlington, Iowa
KCNZ Cedar Falls, Iowa
WMT Cedar Rapids, Iowa
KCHE Cherokee, Iowa
KCLN Clinton, Iowa
KCZQ Cresco, Iowa
KDSN Denison, Iowa
WHO Des Moines, Iowa
KDTH Dubuque, Iowa
KDST Dyersville, Iowa
KILR Estherville, Iowa
KIOW Forest City, Iowa
KWMT Fort Dodge, Iowa
KLMJ Hampton, Iowa
KNOD Harlan, Iowa
KHBT Humboldt, Iowa
KKIA Ida Grove, Iowa
KIFG Iowa Falls, Iowa
KOKX Keokuk, Iowa
KLEM Le Mars, Iowa
KMCH Manchester, Iowa
KMAQ Maquoketa, Iowa
KWPC Muscatine, Iowa
KCZE New Hampton, Iowa
KCOB Newton, Iowa
KOEL Oelwein, Iowa
KMA Shenandoah, Iowa
KDCR Sioux Center, Iowa
KTFC Sioux City, Iowa
KICD Spencer, Iowa
KKRF Stuart, Iowa
KQWC Webster City, Iowa
KMHR(AM) Boise, Idaho
KORT Grangeville, Idaho
KOZE Lewiston, Idaho
KRLC Lewiston-Clarkston, Idaho
KVSI Montpelier, Idaho
KRPL Moscow, Idaho
KACH Preston, Idaho
KSRA Salmon, Idaho
KLIX Twin Falls, Idaho
KTFI Wendell, Idaho
WTIM Assumption, Illinois
WQRL Benton, Illinois
WLMD Bushnell, Illinois
WKRO Cairo, Illinois
WBYS Canton, Illinois
WCIL Carbondale, Illinois
WROY Carmi, Illinois
WDWS Champaign, Illinois
KSGM Chester, Illinois
WDAN Danville, Illinois
WLBK Dekalb, Illinois
WIXN Dixon, Illinois
WDQN Duquoin, Illinois
KUUL East Moline, Illinois
WGEL Greenville, Illinois
WEBQ Harrisburg, Illinois
WDUK Havana, Illinois
WRVY-FM Henry, Illinois
WIJR Highland, Illinois
WJIL Jacksonville, Illinois
WLDS Jacksonville, Illinois
WJBM Jerseyville, Illinois
WJOL Joliet, Illinois
WKAN Kankakee, Illinois
WKEI Kewanee, Illinois
WSMI Litchfield, Illinois
WSMI-FM Litchfield, Illinois
WLUV Loves Park, Illinois
WJEQ Macomb, Illinois
WLRB Macomb, Illinois
WZUS Macon, Illinois
WFXN Moline, Illinois
WRAM Monmouth, Illinois
WCZQ Monticello, Illinois
WCSJ-FM Morris, Illinois
WMIX Mount Vernon, Illinois
WHQQ Neoga, Illinois
WMCI Neoga, Illinois
WCMY Ottawa, Illinois
WPXN Paxton, Illinois
WMBD Peoria, Illinois
WSPY-FM Plano, Illinois
WZOE Princeton, Illinois
WKXQ Rushville, Illinois
WJBD Salem, Illinois
WAUR Sandwich, Illinois
WHCO Sparta, Illinois
WTAX Springfield, Illinois
WSDR Sterling, Illinois
WSQR Sycamore, Illinois
WILL Urbana, Illinois
WPMB Vandalia, Illinois
WGFA-FM Watseka, Illinois
WRBI Batesville, Indiana
WBIW Bedford, Indiana
WIKY Evansville, Indiana
WILO Frankfort, Indiana
WSHW Frankfort, Indiana
WFLQ French Lick, Indiana
WTRE Greensburg, Indiana
WLOI La Porte, Indiana
WASK Lafayette, Indiana
WKOA Lafayette, Indiana
WSAL Logansport, Indiana
WRZR Loogootee, Indiana
WXGO Madison, Indiana
WMYJ Martinsville, Indiana
WEFM Michigan City, Indiana
WSEZ Paoli, Indiana
WTCA Plymouth, Indiana
WRIN Rensselaer, Indiana
WKBV Richmond, Indiana
WROI Rochester, Indiana
WIFE-FM Rushville, Indiana
WZZB Seymour, Indiana
WNDI Sullivan, Indiana
WKUZ Wabash, Indiana
KAIR Atchison, Kansas
KVSV Beloit, Kansas
KSNP Burlington, Kansas
KGNO Dodge City, Kansas
KDNS Downs, Kansas
KIUL Garden City, Kansas
KGCR Goodland, Kansas
KVGB Great Bend, Kansas
KHAZ Hays, Kansas
KNZA-FM Hiawatha, Kansas
KBUF Holcomb, Kansas
KNNS Larned, Kansas
KSCB Liberal, Kansas
KOFO Ottawa, Kansas
KLKC Parsons, Kansas
KKAN Phillipsburg, Kansas
KRSL Russell, Kansas
KSAL Salina, Kansas
KYUL Scott City, Kansas
KMZA-FM Seneca, Kansas
KULY Ulysses, Kansas
KLEY Wellington, Kansas
WANY Albany, Kentucky
WBRT Bardstown, Kentucky
WKDZ Cadiz, Kentucky
WNES Central City, Kentucky
WAIN Columbia, Kentucky
WCPM Cumberland, Kentucky
WHSX Edmonton, Kentucky
WFKN Franklin, Kentucky
WKCM Hawesville, Kentucky
WSON Henderson, Kentucky
WRZI Hodgenville, Kentucky
WFTM Maysville, Kentucky
WMIK Middlesboro, Kentucky
WMST Mount Sterling, Kentucky
WBKR Owensboro, Kentucky
WVJS Owensboro, Kentucky
WTLO Somerset, Kentucky
WYSB Springfield, Kentucky
WMTC-FM Vancleve, Kentucky
WLKS West Liberty, Kentucky
WDGL Baton Rouge, Louisiana
KSIG Crowley, Louisiana
WFPR Hammond, Louisiana
WSRY Elkton, Maryland
WICO Salisbury, Maryland
WTTR Westminster, Maryland
WFYC Alma, Michigan
WZTK Alpena, Michigan
WTVB-AM Coldwater, Michigan
WCHT Escanaba, Michigan
WGHN-FM Grand Haven, Michigan
WCSR Hillsdale, Michigan
WKZO Kalamazoo, Michigan
WSGW Saginaw, Michigan
WMIC Sandusky, Michigan
WMLM St. Louis, Michigan
WTCM Traverse City, Michigan
WPNW Zeeland, Michigan
KASM Albany, Minnesota
KXRA Alexandria, Minnesota
KKCQ-FM Bagley, Minnesota
KBMO Benson, Minnesota
KBEW Blue Earth, Minnesota
KJLY Blue Earth, Minnesota
KROX Crookston, Minnesota
KDLM Detroit Lakes, Minnesota
KGFK East Grand Forks, Minnesota
KFMC-FM Fairmont, Minnesota
KBRF Fergus Falls, Minnesota
KSNR Fisher, Minnesota
KKCQ Fosston, Minnesota
KDUZ Hutchinson, Minnesota
KKOJ Jackson, Minnesota
KLFD Litchfield, Minnesota
KLTF Little Falls, Minnesota
KEYL Long Prairie, Minnesota
KLQL Luverne, Minnesota
KLQP Madison, Minnesota
KDMA Montevideo, Minnesota
KDIO Ortonville, Minnesota
WCMP Pine City, Minnesota
WQPM Princeton, Minnesota
KROC Rochester, Minnesota
KIKV-FM Sauk Centre, Minnesota
KNSG Springfield, Minnesota
KNSP Staples, Minnesota
KTRF Thief River Falls, Minnesota
KARL Tracy, Minnesota
KWAD Wadena, Minnesota
KDJS Willmar, Minnesota
KWLM Willmar, Minnesota
KAGE Winona, Minnesota
KWOA Worthington, Minnesota
KAAN Bethany, Missouri
KYOO Bolivar, Missouri
KWRT Boonville, Missouri
KMAM Butler, Missouri
KOZX Cabool, Missouri
KRLL California, Missouri
KMRN Cameron, Missouri
KDFN Doniphan, Missouri
KHMO Hannibal, Missouri
KUNQ Houston, Missouri
KWOS Jefferson City, Missouri
KIRX Kirksville, Missouri
KBNN Lebanon, Missouri
KNIM Maryville, Missouri
KMEM-FM Memphis, Missouri
KWWR Mexico, Missouri
KMCR Montgomery City, Missouri
KBTN Neosho, Missouri
KNEM Nevada, Missouri
KBDZ Perryville, Missouri
KSMO Salem, Missouri
KDRO Sedalia, Missouri
KRHW Sikeston, Missouri
KWTO-AM Springfield, Missouri
KFEQ St. Joseph, Missouri
KRWP Stockton, Missouri
KSAR Thayer, Missouri
KTKS Versailles, Missouri
KWRE Warrenton, Missouri
WJNS-FM Bentonia, Mississippi
WLTM Greenville, Mississippi
WROA Gulfport, Mississippi
WTCD Indianola, Mississippi
WJDX Jackson, Mississippi
WMSI-FM Jackson, Mississippi
WIQQ Leland, Mississippi
WRQO Monticello, Mississippi
WWMS Oxford, Mississippi

WHOC Philadelphia, Mississippi
WELO Tupelo, Mississippi
WTYL Tylertown, Mississippi
KFLN Baker, Montana
KBOW Butte, Montana
KXGN Glendive, Montana
KXGF Great Falls, Montana
KOJM Havre, Montana
KPQX Havre, Montana
KXEI Havre, Montana
KXLO Lewistown, Montana
KYUS-FM Miles City, Montana
KATQ Plentywood, Montana
KCGM Scobey, Montana
KSEN Shelby, Montana
KVCK Wolf Point, Montana
KVCK-FM Wolf Point, Montana
WKXR Asheboro, North Carolina
WWNC Asheville, North Carolina
WGAI Elizabeth City, North Carolina
WFMO Fairmont, North Carolina
WQDK Gatesville, North Carolina
WCXL Kill Devil Hills, North Carolina
WKTE King, North Carolina
WHBK Marshall, North Carolina
WPAQ Mount Airy, North Carolina
WWDR Murfreesboro, North Carolina
WCVP Murphy, North Carolina
WPTF Raleigh, North Carolina
WPTM Roanoke Rapids, North Carolina
WEGG Rose Hill, North Carolina
WRXO Roxboro, North Carolina
WWGP Sanford, North Carolina
WYAL Scotland Neck, North Carolina
WKSK West Jefferson, North Carolina
WENC Whiteville, North Carolina
WTXY Whiteville, North Carolina
KBMR Bismarck, North Dakota
KPOK Bowman, North Dakota
KXPO Grafton, North Dakota
KNDC Hettinger, North Dakota
KSJB Jamestown, North Dakota
KNDK Langdon, North Dakota
KQLX Lisbon, North Dakota
KCJB Minot, North Dakota
KZPR Minot, North Dakota
KUSO Albion, Nebraska
KAAQ Alliance, Nebraska
KCOW Alliance, Nebraska
KWBE Beatrice, Nebraska
KCSR Chadron, Nebraska
KQSK Chadron, Nebraska
KGMT Fairbury, Nebraska
KHUB Fremont, Nebraska
KHAS Hastings, Nebraska
KUVR Holdrege, Nebraska
KGFW Kearney, Nebraska
KRVN-FM Lexington, Nebraska
KIOD McCook, Nebraska
KNCY Nebraska City, Nebraska
KNEN Norfolk, Nebraska
KBRX O'Neill, Nebraska
KMCX-FM Ogallala, Nebraska
KOGA Ogallala, Nebraska
KFAB Omaha, Nebraska
KNLV Ord, Nebraska
KNLV-FM Ord, Nebraska
KNEB Scottsbluff, Nebraska
KSID Sidney, Nebraska
KRFS Superior, Nebraska
KCTY Wayne, Nebraska
KTIC-FM West Point, Nebraska
KAWL York, Nebraska
WFAI Salem, New Jersey
KICA Clovis, New Mexico
KOTS Deming, New Mexico
KSEL-FM Portales, New Mexico
KMXQ Socorro, New Mexico
KDSS Ely, Nevada
KWNA Winnemucca, Nevada
WBRV-FM Boonville, New York
WKGB-FM Conklin, New York
WWLE Cornwall, New York
WRWD-FM Highland, New York
WJTN Jamestown, New York
WIXT Little Falls, New York
WLVL Lockport, New York
WLLG Lowville, New York
WICY Malone, New York
WYBG Massena, New York
WEOK Poughkeepsie, New York
WRIV Riverhead, New York
WSPQ Springville, New York
WIBX Utica, New York
WCJW Warsaw, New York
WTNY Watertown, New York
WNCO Ashland, Ohio
WWCD Baltimore, Ohio
WAIS Buchtel, Ohio
WYNT Caledonia, Ohio
WHBC Canton, Ohio
WDOH Delphos, Ohio
WEDI Eaton, Ohio
WFIN Findlay, Ohio
WKTN Kenton, Ohio
WLOH Lancaster, Ohio
WIMA Lima, Ohio
WMOA Marietta, Ohio
WMRN Marion, Ohio
WMPO Middleport-Pomeroy, Ohio
WSEO Nelsonville, Ohio
WHOF North Canton, Ohio
WBUK Ottawa, Ohio
WPTW Piqua, Ohio
WNTO Racine, Ohio
WSOM Salem, Ohio
WEEC Springfield, Ohio
WSPD Toledo, Ohio
WTUZ Uhrichsville, Ohio
WCHO Washington Ct House, Ohio
WBZI Xenia, Ohio
KEYB Altus, Oklahoma
KKBI Broken Bow, Oklahoma
KGWA Enid, Oklahoma
KMAD Madill, Oklahoma
KYAL-FM Muskogee, Oklahoma
KPNC Ponca City, Oklahoma
KFAQ Tulsa, Oklahoma
KBKR Baker, Oregon
KWVR Enterprise, Oregon
KAGO Klamath Falls, Oregon
KLBM La Grande, Oregon
KSRV Ontario, Oregon
KUMA Pendleton, Oregon
KCKX Stayton, Oregon
KODL The Dalles, Oregon
KLWJ(AM) Umatilla, Oregon
WAEB Allentown, Pennsylvania
WHLM Bloomsburg, Pennsylvania
WFRM Coudersport, Pennsylvania
WDAC Lancaster, Pennsylvania
WWBJ Martinsburg, Pennsylvania
WTEL Philadelphia, Pennsylvania
WATS Sayre, Pennsylvania
WSOL San German, Puerto Rico
WVCD Bamberg-Denmark, South Carolina
WJBS Holly Hill, South Carolina
WJAY Mullins, South Carolina
KSDN Aberdeen, South Dakota
KBFS Belle Fourche, South Dakota
KZMX Hot Springs, South Dakota
KMSD Mibank, South Dakota
KMIT Mitchell, South Dakota
KORN Mitchell, South Dakota
KOLY Mobridge, South Dakota
KIMM Rapid City, South Dakota
KTOQ Rapid City, South Dakota
KGIM-FM Redfield, South Dakota
KPLO-FM Reliance, South Dakota
KYNT Yankton, South Dakota
WNAX Yankton, South Dakota
WLAR Athens, Tennessee
WHCB Bristol, Tennessee
WMCP Columbia, Tennessee
WEKR Fayetteville, Tennessee
WHIN Gallatin, Tennessee
WMYL Halls Crossroads, Tennessee
WDXI Jackson, Tennessee
WCLC Jamestown, Tennessee
WDEB Jamestown, Tennessee
WBUZ La Vergne, Tennessee
WEEN Lafayette, Tennessee
WLIL Lenoir City, Tennessee
WLIV Livingston, Tennessee
WMSR Manchester, Tennessee
WAKI McMinnville, Tennessee
WBMC McMinnville, Tennessee
WREC Memphis, Tennessee
WGNS Murfreesboro, Tennessee
WSM Nashville, Tennessee
WDNX Olive Hill, Tennessee
WRQR(AM) Paris, Tennessee
WUAT Pikeville, Tennessee
WLIJ Shelbyville, Tennessee
WDBL Springfield, Tennessee
WSGI Springfield, Tennessee
WCDT Winchester, Tennessee
KFYN Bonham, Texas
KLXK Breckenridge, Texas
KWHI Brenham, Texas
KMIL Cameron, Texas
KCAR Clarksville, Texas
KSTA Coleman, Texas
KZNE College Station, Texas
KXIT Dalhart, Texas
KDDD-FM Dumas, Texas
KMUL Farwell, Texas
KNAF Fredericksburg, Texas
KGAF Gainesville, Texas
KPIR Granbury, Texas
KVRP-FM Haskell, Texas
KPAN Hereford, Texas
KWFB Holliday, Texas
KHYI Howe, Texas
KEBE Jacksonville, Texas
KMBL Junction, Texas
KVLG La Grange, Texas
KZZN Littlefield, Texas
KCUL Marshall, Texas
KLRK Mexia, Texas
KSFA Nacogdoches, Texas
KBUS Paris, Texas
KEYE Perryton, Texas
KVOP Plainview, Texas
KITE Port Lavaca, Texas
KGKL San Angelo, Texas
KWED Seguin, Texas
KDAE Sinton, Texas
KSTV Stephenville, Texas
KQQB Stockdale, Texas
KXOX Sweetwater, Texas
KGWU Uvalde, Texas
KBEC Waxahachie, Texas
KWUD Woodville, Texas
KSUB Cedar City, Utah
KYAH Delta, Utah
KVNU Logan, Utah
KMTI Manti, Utah
KOAL Price, Utah
KSVC Richfield, Utah
KVEL Vernal, Utah
WBTX Broadway-Timberville, Virginia
WPAK Farmville, Virginia
WWWJ Galax, Virginia
WXGM Gloucester, Virginia
WMNA Gretna, Virginia
WNRG Grundy, Virginia
WSVA Harrisonburg, Virginia
WHHV Hillsville, Virginia
WKGM Smithfield, Virginia
WSBV South Boston, Virginia
WKDW Staunton, Virginia
WHEO Stuart, Virginia
WKCW Warrenton, Virginia
WKCI Waynesboro, Virginia
WZLF Bellows Falls, Vermont
KOZI Chelan, Washington
KCLX Colfax, Washington
KYSN East Wenatchee, Washington
KTBI Ephrata, Washington
KULE Ephrata, Washington
KONA Kennewick-Richland-P, Washington
KBRC Mount Vernon, Washington
KOMW Omak, Washington
KQQQ Pullman, Washington
KWNC Quincy, Washington
KGA Spokane, Washington
KTEL Walla Walla, Washington
KPQ Wenatchee, Washington
KIT Yakima, Washington
WBEV Beaver Dam, Wisconsin
WXRO Beaver Dam, Wisconsin
WOTE Clintonville, Wisconsin
KFIZ Fond Du Lac, Wisconsin
WTAQ-AM Green Bay, Wisconsin
WKTY La Crosse, Wisconsin
WGLR Lancaster, Wisconsin
WTSO Madison, Wisconsin
WIGM Medford, Wisconsin
WJMT Merrill, Wisconsin
WCCN Neillsville, Wisconsin
WPKR Omro, Wisconsin
WPVL-AM Platteville, Wisconsin

WJUB Plymouth, Wisconsin
WRCO Richland Center, Wisconsin
WRCO-FM Richland Center, Wisconsin
WEVR River Falls, Wisconsin
WRFW River Falls, Wisconsin
WTCH Shawano, Wisconsin
WHBL Sheboygan, Wisconsin
WCSW Shell Lake, Wisconsin
WDOR-FM Sturgeon Bay, Wisconsin
WVRQ Viroqua, Wisconsin
WVRQ-FM Viroqua, Wisconsin
WDUX Waupaca, Wisconsin
WFDL Waupun, Wisconsin
WDEZ Wausau, Wisconsin
WSAU-AM Wausau, Wisconsin
WVMR Frost, West Virginia
WRON-FM Lewisburg, West Virginia
WGGE Parkersburg, West Virginia
WWVA Wheeling, West Virginia
KHAT Laramie, Wyoming
KASL Newcastle, Wyoming
KPOW Powell, Wyoming
KVOW Riverton, Wyoming
KYCN Wheatland, Wyoming

Alternative

KSWH-FM Arkadelphia, Arkansas
KIDE Hoopa, California
WRUF-FM Gainesville, Florida
WXXL Tavares, Florida
KECH-FM Sun Valley, Idaho
WQUB Quincy, Illinois
KBIK Independence, Kansas
KHCA Wamego, Kansas
WIRQ Rochester, New York
WOBN Westerville, Ohio
WFBC-FM Greenville, South Carolina
KWKQ Graham, Texas
KRLF Pullman, Washington
KYVT Yakima, Washington
WSUP Platteville, Wisconsin
KUWS Superior, Wisconsin

Arabic

KLAV Las Vegas, Nevada
WDIY Allentown, Pennsylvania
WMUH Allentown, Pennsylvania
KARI Blaine, Washington

Big Band

KASU Jonesboro, Arkansas
WGRS Guilford, Connecticut
WQUN Hamden, Connecticut
WMNR Monroe, Connecticut
WRXC Shelton, Connecticut
WGSK South Kent, Connecticut
WTAN Clearwater, Florida
KMRY Cedar Rapids, Iowa
WSIU Carbondale, Illinois
WHPO Hoopeston, Illinois
WXNT Indianapolis, Indiana
KIND Independence, Kansas
KLKC Parsons, Kansas
WESM Princess Anne, Maryland
WHFR Dearborn, Michigan
WBNZ Frankfort, Michigan
WLNZ Lansing, Michigan
KOLV Olivia, Minnesota
KXMS Joplin, Missouri
KPRK Livingston, Montana
WXIT Blowing Rock, North Carolina
WCCE Buies Creek, North Carolina
KUVR Holdrege, Nebraska
WSNJ Bridgeton, New Jersey
WNTI Hackettstown, New Jersey
WMRV Dansville, New York
WDOS Oneonta, New York
WRGR Tupper Lake, New York
WATH Athens, Ohio
WKFI Wilmington, Ohio
WVMM Grantham, Pennsylvania
WNPV Lansdale, Pennsylvania
WLSH Lansford, Pennsylvania
WPHB Philipsburg, Pennsylvania
WJAS Pittsburgh, Pennsylvania
WKSP(AM) Block Island, Rhode Island
WWRK Florence, South Carolina
KNCT-FM Killeen, Texas
KTBB Troup, Texas
WVNR Poultney, Vermont
KEYG Grand Coulee, Washington
WVMR Frost, West Virginia
WKLP Keyser, West Virginia

Black

KSUA Fairbanks, Alaska
WNRA Eufaula, Alabama
WGYV Greenville, Alabama
WHMA-FM Hobson City, Alabama
WJAB Huntsville, Alabama
WMGY Montgomery, Alabama
WGOL Russellville, Alabama
WKAX Russellville, Alabama
WHBB Selma, Alabama
KUAF Fayetteville, Arkansas
KFFA Helena, Arkansas
KOSE Wilson, Arkansas
KTKT Tucson, Arizona
KXCI Tucson, Arizona
KHYL Auburn, California
KPFA Berkeley, California
KMUD Garberville, California
KXLU Los Angeles, California
KMPO Modesto, California
KVMR Nevada City, California
KSPB Pebble Beach, California
KZYX Philo, California
KUCR Riverside, California
KYCC Stockton, California
KDIA Vallejo, California
KDYA Vallejo, California
KGNU-FM Boulder, Colorado
KLDC Denver, Colorado
KCSU-FM Fort Collins, Colorado
KMSA Grand Junction, Colorado
WPKN Bridgeport, Connecticut
WFIF Milford, Connecticut
WCNI New London, Connecticut
WVUD Newark, Delaware
WPHK Blountstown, Florida
WVUM Coral Gables, Florida
WRUF Gainesville, Florida
WUFT-FM Gainesville, Florida
WVFT Gretna, Florida
WDSR Lake City, Florida
WLBE Leesburg-Eustis, Florida
WKGC-FM Panama City, Florida
WLTG Panama City, Florida
WPRY Perry, Florida
WKPX Sunrise, Florida
WVFS Tallahassee, Florida
WBVM Tampa, Florida
WDEC-FM Americus, Georgia
WRFC Athens, Georgia
WBGA Brunswick, Georgia
WGRA Cairo, Georgia
WEBS Calhoun, Georgia
WBTR-FM Carrollton, Georgia
WDXQ Cochran, Georgia
WUFF Eastman, Georgia
WYIS McRae, Georgia
WMVG Milledgeville, Georgia
WNEA Newnan, Georgia
WTGA Thomaston, Georgia
KLNG Council Bluffs, Iowa
KUOI-FM Moscow, Idaho
WESN Bloomington, Illinois
WEFT Champaign, Illinois
WGN(AM) Chicago, Illinois
WVKC Galesburg, Illinois
WCSF Joliet, Illinois
WMXM Lake Forest, Illinois
WLRA Lockport, Illinois
WWVR Paris, Indiana
WFYI-FM Indianapolis, Indiana
WXFN Muncie, Indiana
KONQ Dodge City, Kansas
KWBW Hutchinson, Kansas
KSDB-FM Manhattan, Kansas
WWHR Bowling Green, Kentucky
WCPM Cumberland, Kentucky
WNKJ Hopkinsville, Kentucky
WFXY Middlesboro, Kentucky
WEKY Richmond, Kentucky
KLSP Angola, Louisiana
KAJN-FM Crowley, Louisiana
WBSL-FM Sheffield, Massachusetts
WYAJ Sudbury, Massachusetts
WCHC Worcester, Massachusetts
WKHI Fruitland, Maryland
WUPX Marquette, Michigan
WNMC-FM Traverse City, Michigan
KFAI Minneapolis, Minnesota
KNOF St. Paul, Minnesota
KMFC Centralia, Missouri
KOPN Columbia, Missouri
KCFV Ferguson, Missouri
KMVC Marshall, Missouri
KLID Poplar Bluff, Missouri
KDRO Sedalia, Missouri
WKCU Corinth, Mississippi
WGRM Greenwood, Mississippi
WNBN Meridian, Mississippi
WRJW Picayune, Mississippi
WJDR Prentiss, Mississippi
WSSO Starkville, Mississippi
WKJW Black Mountain, North Carolina
WRRZ Clinton, North Carolina
WGAI Elizabeth City, North Carolina
WRVS-FM Elizabeth City, North Carolina
WBLA Elizabethtown, North Carolina
WSML Graham, North Carolina
WYRN Louisburg, North Carolina
WHIP Mooresville, North Carolina
WDJS Mount Olive, North Carolina
WNNC Newton, North Carolina
WPJL Raleigh, North Carolina
WRXO Roxboro, North Carolina
KWSC Wayne, Nebraska
WUNH Durham, New Hampshire
WGLS-FM Glassboro, New Jersey
WRRC Lawrenceville, New Jersey
WMSC Upper Montclair, New Jersey
KKIM Albuquerque, New Mexico
WXBA Brentwood, New York
WBNY Buffalo, New York
WSLU Canton, New York
WSIV E. Syracuse, New York
WRCU-FM Hamilton, New York
WHLI Hempstead, New York
WKJY Hempstead, New York
WJJL Niagara Falls, New York
WQKE Plattsburgh, New York
WRNY Rome, New York
WFNP Rosendale, New York
WUSB Stony Brook, New York
WJPZ-FM Syracuse, New York
WOUB Athens, Ohio
WKDC-FM Cedarville, Ohio
WVSG Columbus, Ohio
WWSU Fairborn, Ohio
WDUB Granville, Ohio
WFCJ Miamisburg, Ohio
WNPQ New Philadelphia, Ohio
WCCD Parma, Ohio
WUKV Portsmouth, Ohio
WNTO Racine, Ohio
WEEC Springfield, Ohio
WXUT Toledo, Ohio
KYLV Oklahoma City, Oklahoma
KZBB Poteau, Oklahoma
KKNX Eugene, Oregon
KLCC Eugene, Oregon
KRVM-FM Eugene, Oregon
KWVA Eugene, Oregon
KTEC Klamath Falls, Oregon
KEOL La Grande, Oregon
KSLC McMinnville, Oregon
KLCO Newport, Oregon
KXRY Portland, Oregon
WLVR-FM Bethlehem, Pennsylvania
WFSE Edinboro, Pennsylvania
WKVR-FM Huntingdon, Pennsylvania
WIUP-FM Indiana, Pennsylvania
WFNM Lancaster, Pennsylvania
WNTE Mansfield, Pennsylvania
WARC Meadville, Pennsylvania
WJST New Castle, Pennsylvania
WRCT Pittsburgh, Pennsylvania
WRCT(FM) Pittsburgh, Pennsylvania
WYEP-FM Pittsburgh, Pennsylvania
WVMW-FM Scranton, Pennsylvania
WSYC-FM Shippensburg, Pennsylvania
WXVU Villanova, Pennsylvania
WBRU Providence, Rhode Island
WARV Warwick, Rhode Island
WBSC Bennettsville, South Carolina
WCRE Cheraw, South Carolina
WTZQ Fountain Inn, South Carolina
WJBS Holly Hill, South Carolina

WRIX Homeland Park, South Carolina
KSDJ Brookings, South Dakota
WYXI Athens, Tennessee
WMBW Chattanooga, Tennessee
WAPX-FM Clarksville, Tennessee
WKBL Covington, Tennessee
WHIN Gallatin, Tennessee
WITA Knoxville, Tennessee
WLIL Lenoir City, Tennessee
WDXL Lexington, Tennessee
WXRQ Mount Pleasant, Tennessee
WGNS Murfreesboro, Tennessee
WLAC Nashville, Tennessee
WUTS Sewanee, Tennessee
WLIJ Shelbyville, Tennessee
KGNZ Abilene, Texas
KAGC Bryan, Texas
KWTS Canyon, Texas
KNES Fairfield, Texas
KOOP Hornsby, Texas
KPFT Houston, Texas
KHVL Huntsville, Texas
KBJS Jacksonville, Texas
KTAI Kingsville, Texas
KVLG La Grange, Texas
KSHN Liberty, Texas
KFRO Longview, Texas
KLVL Pasadena, Texas
KHKZ San Benito, Texas
KOKE-FM Thorndale, Texas
KZMU Moab, Utah
KRCL Salt Lake City, Utah
WKDE-FM Altavista, Virginia
WTJU Charlottesville, Virginia
WKEY Covington, Virginia
WFAX Falls Church, Virginia
WMNA Gretna, Virginia
WVRU-FM Radford, Virginia
WKBA Vinton, Virginia
WKCI Waynesboro, Virginia
KBSG Aberdeen, Washington
KUGS Bellingham, Washington
KZUU Pullman, Washington
KNHC Seattle, Washington
KSFC Spokane, Washington
KUPS Tacoma, Washington
KTCR Yakima, Washington
WMSE Milwaukee, Wisconsin
WVWC Buckhannon, West Virginia
WQAB Philippi, West Virginia
WPHP Wheeling, West Virginia

Blues

KUAC Fairbanks, Alaska
KTNA Talkeetna, Alaska
WVAS Montgomery, Alabama
WQPR Muscle Shoals, Alabama
KFFA Helena, Arkansas
KASU Jonesboro, Arkansas
KERX Paris, Arkansas
KNCA Burney, California
KSPC Claremont, California
KKJZ Long Beach, California
KSBR Mission Viejo, California
KNSQ Mount Shasta, California
KVMR Nevada City, California
KZYX Philo, California
KRXQ Sacramento, California
KXJZ Sacramento, California
KCPR San Luis Obispo, California
KCSM San Mateo, California
KSCU Santa Clara, California
KCLU-FM Thousand Oaks, California
KASF Alamosa, Colorado
KRCC Colorado Springs, Colorado
KDUR Durango, Colorado
KIBT Fountain, Colorado
KWSB-FM Gunnison, Colorado
KWUF-FM Pagosa Springs, Colorado
KVNF Paonia, Colorado
KOTO Telluride, Colorado
WQTQ Hartford, Connecticut
WESU Middletown, Connecticut
WFCS New Britain, Connecticut
WUCF-FM Orlando, Florida
WFCF St. Augustine, Florida
WKPX Sunrise, Florida
WCLK Atlanta, Georgia
WZBN Camilla, Georgia
KUNI Cedar Falls, Iowa
KCCK-FM Cedar Rapids, Iowa
KROS Clinton, Iowa
KNSY(FM) Dubuque, Iowa
KRNI Mason City, Iowa
KICJ(FM) Mitchellville, Iowa
KOJI Okoboji, Iowa
KWIT Sioux City, Iowa
KECH-FM Sun Valley, Idaho
WEFT Champaign, Illinois
WIUM Macomb, Illinois
WIUS Macomb, Illinois
WPNA Oak Park, Illinois
WQUB Quincy, Illinois
WNIU Rockford, Illinois
WDML Woodlawn, Illinois
WTTS Bloomington, Indiana
WVPE Elkhart, Indiana
WFYI-FM Indianapolis, Indiana
WCYT Lafayette Township, Indiana
WSND-FM Notre Dame, Indiana
WPUM Rensselaer, Indiana
KANU Lawrence, Kansas
KJHK Lawrence, Kansas
WMKY Morehead, Kentucky
KJMG Bastrop, Louisiana
KGRM Grambling, Louisiana
WGBH(FM) Boston, Massachusetts
WESM Princess Anne, Maryland
WBKA Bar Harbor, Maine
WGTO Cassopolis, Michigan
WHFR Dearborn, Michigan
WDET-FM Detroit, Michigan
WDBM East Lansing, Michigan
WKLT Kalkaska, Michigan
WQUS Lapeer, Michigan
WRKR Portage, Michigan
WPHS Warren, Michigan
WTIP Grand Marais, Minnesota
KOPN Columbia, Missouri
KKFI Kansas City, Missouri
KPOW-FM La Monte, Missouri
KGSP Parkville, Missouri
KBFL-AM Springfield, Missouri
KRSI Garapan-Saipan, Guam
WESE Baldwyn, Mississippi
WROX Clarksdale, Mississippi
WJZD-FM Long Beach, Mississippi
WASU-FM Boone, North Carolina
WNAA Greensboro, North Carolina
WVOD Manteo, North Carolina
WSHA Raleigh, North Carolina
WNCW Spindale, North Carolina
KCND Bismarck, North Dakota
KFJM Grand Forks, North Dakota
KZUM Lincoln, Nebraska
KKCD Omaha, Nebraska
KWSC Wayne, Nebraska
WUNH Durham, New Hampshire
WNEC-FM Henniker, New Hampshire
WKNH Keene, New Hampshire
WPCR-FM Plymouth, New Hampshire
WNTI Hackettstown, New Jersey
WBJB-FM Lincroft, New Jersey
WBFO Buffalo, New York
WICB Ithaca, New York
WVBR-FM Ithaca, New York
WUBJ Jamestown, New York
WZOZ Oneonta, New York
WTKV Oswego, New York
WPDH Poughkeepsie, New York
WSPN Saratoga Springs, New York
WAER Syracuse, New York
WCBE Columbus, Ohio
WUSO Springfield, Ohio
WJUC Swanton, Ohio
WXTS-FM Toledo, Ohio
WXUT Toledo, Ohio
WYSO Yellow Springs, Ohio
KGOU Norman, Oklahoma
KROU Spencer, Oklahoma
KSMF Ashland, Oregon
KSBA Coos Bay, Oregon
KLCC Eugene, Oregon
KMHD Gresham, Oregon
KSKF Klamath Falls, Oregon
KLCO Newport, Oregon
WDCV-FM Carlisle, Pennsylvania
WDNR Chester, Pennsylvania
WPSX Kane, Pennsylvania
WKDU Philadelphia, Pennsylvania
WYEP-FM Pittsburgh, Pennsylvania
WSYC-FM Shippensburg, Pennsylvania
WHYF(AM) Shiremanstown, Pennsylvania
WPSU State College, Pennsylvania
WRDV Warminster, Pennsylvania
WRLC Williamsport, Pennsylvania
WRIU Kingston, Rhode Island
WSSB-FM Orangeburg, South Carolina
KAUR Sioux Falls, South Dakota
WEGR Arlington, Tennessee
WRLT Franklin, Tennessee
WETS-FM Johnson City, Tennessee
KAZI Austin, Texas
KUT Austin, Texas
KLUB Bloomington, Texas
KTRU(FM) Houston, Texas
KXWT Odessa, Texas
KNCH(FM) San Angelo, Texas
KSTX San Antonio, Texas
KSUU Cedar City, Utah
KZMU Moab, Utah
WMRY Crozet, Virginia
WWHS-FM Hampden-Sydney, Virginia
WHOV Hampton, Virginia
WMRA Harrisonburg, Virginia
WCLM Highland Springs, Virginia
WMRL Lexington, Virginia
WCVE-FM Richmond, Virginia
WCWM Williamsburg, Virginia
WRMC-FM Middlebury, Vermont
WIZN Vergennes, Vermont
KMCQ Covington, Washington
KSER Everett, Washington
KKZX Spokane, Washington
KUPS Tacoma, Washington
WBSD Burlington, Wisconsin
WUEC Eau Claire, Wisconsin
WPNE-FM Green Bay, Wisconsin
WZTI Greenfield, Wisconsin
WHND Sister Bay, Wisconsin
WWSP Stevens Point, Wisconsin

Children

KLEF Anchorage, Alaska
KTOO Juneau, Alaska
WMBV Dixons Mills, Alabama
WRWA Dothan, Alabama
WFIX Florence, Alabama
WTSU Montgomery-Troy, Alabama
KFMM Thatcher, Arizona
KYRM Yuma, Arizona
KFRB Bakersfield, California
KZRO Dunsmuir, California
KFNO Fresno, California
KPFK Los Angeles, California
KXLU Los Angeles, California
KWVE-FM San Clemente, California
KFAX San Francisco, California
WIHS Middletown, Connecticut
WJYO Fort Myers, Florida
WJLF Gainesville, Florida
WGNK Pennsuco, Florida
WBVM Tampa, Florida
WTJB Columbus, Georgia
KHMG Barrigada, Guam
KHOE Fairfield, Iowa
KIFG-FM Iowa Falls, Iowa
KTFC Sioux City, Iowa
KTFG Sioux Rapids, Iowa
KCIR Twin Falls, Idaho
WUEV Evansville, Indiana
KJTY Topeka, Kansas
WKHS Worton, Maryland
WHCF Bangor, Maine
WBQX Thomaston, Maine
WDBC Escanaba, Michigan
KJLY Blue Earth, Minnesota
KFSI Rochester, Minnesota
KGNN-FM Cuba, Missouri
KGNV Washington, Missouri
WPAE Centreville, Mississippi
WMBU Forest, Mississippi
KABU Fort Totten, North Dakota
WMVB Millville, New Jersey
KFLQ Albuquerque, New Mexico
KHAC Tse Bonito, New Mexico
WYBG Massena, New York
WRHO Oneonta, New York
WMHR Syracuse, New York
WMHN Webster, New York
WFCJ Miamisburg, Ohio

KMUN Astoria, Oregon
WFKJ Cashtown, Pennsylvania
WDNR Chester, Pennsylvania
WXPN Philadelphia, Pennsylvania
WCTL Union City, Pennsylvania
WYVL(FM) Youngsville, Pennsylvania
KLND Little Eagle, South Dakota
KPSM Brownwood, Texas
WRR Dallas, Texas
KFST Fort Stockton, Texas
KFST-FM Fort Stockton, Texas
KNLE-FM Round Rock, Texas
KTER Rudolph, Texas
KVNE Tyler, Texas
WTJU Charlottesville, Virginia
WMYV Hartford, Vermont
WCVT Stowe, Vermont
WWMP Waterbury, Vermont
WTWN Wells River, Vermont
KRLF Pullman, Washington
KDNA Yakima, Washington
WGNV Milladore, Wisconsin
WVPG Parkersburg, West Virginia
WQAB Philippi, West Virginia

Chinese

KEST San Francisco, California
KSJX San Jose, California
WJDA Quincy, Massachusetts
KRNM Chalan Kanoa-Saipan, Guam
WUSB Stony Brook, New York
WJCU University Heights, Ohio
WULR York, South Carolina
KKER Kerrville, Texas
WUVT-FM Blacksburg, Virginia

Christian

KYKD Bethel, Alaska
KNOM Nome, Alaska
KSWH-FM Arkadelphia, Arkansas
KCGS Marshall, Arkansas
KJLH Compton, California
KNCO Grass Valley, California
KFBK-FM Pollock Pines, California
KFAX San Francisco, California
WEBY Milton, Florida
WMGF Mount Dora, Florida
WZHR Zephyrhills, Florida
WROM Rome, Georgia
KEDB Chariton, Iowa
KGEM Boise, Idaho
KIDO Nampa, Idaho
WDML Woodlawn, Illinois
KBIK Independence, Kansas
WCVK Bowling Green, Kentucky
WHFC Bel Air, Maryland
WYFP Harpswell, Maine
WDBM East Lansing, Michigan
WPHS Warren, Michigan
KGGN Gladstone, Missouri
KWJC Liberty, Missouri
KNEM Nevada, Missouri
KKDY West Plains, Missouri
WQLJ Oxford, Mississippi
WTNM Water Valley, Mississippi
KBZR Billings, Montana
WASU-FM Boone, North Carolina
WLHC Robbins, North Carolina
KTNC Falls City, Nebraska
KKVV Las Vegas, Nevada
WITR Henrietta, New York
WFSO Olivebridge, New York
WRIP Windham, New York
WRDL Ashland, Ohio
WKKI Celina, Ohio
WLFC North Baltimore, Ohio
KKPZ Portland, Oregon
KFIR Sweet Home, Oregon
WCAL California, Pennsylvania
WKVR-FM Huntingdon, Pennsylvania
WCYJ-FM Waynesburg, Pennsylvania
WRLC Williamsport, Pennsylvania
WTZQ Fountain Inn, South Carolina
WVCP Gallatin, Tennessee
WNRQ Nashville, Tennessee
KRUN Ballinger, Texas
KHVT Bloomington, Texas
KQTY-FM Borger, Texas
KPSM Brownwood, Texas
KQBZ Brownwood, Texas
KGGR Dallas, Texas
KAVX Lufkin, Texas
KHML Madisonville, Texas
KWMF Pleasanton, Texas
KHKZ San Benito, Texas
WYZR Bethany, West Virginia
WELD-FM Moorefield, West Virginia

Classic Rock

KVHS Concord, California
KMMT Mammoth Lakes, California
KVAY Lamar, Colorado
WSGL Naples, Florida
WCSF Joliet, Illinois
WRRG River Grove, Illinois
WBKE-FM North Manchester, Indiana
WECI Richmond, Indiana
KTCC Colby, Kansas
KICT-FM Wichita, Kansas
KHND Harvey, North Dakota
WPSC-FM Wayne, New Jersey
WQKE Plattsburgh, New York
WMAN-FM Fredericktown, Ohio
WFXN-FM Galion, Ohio
WCYJ-FM Waynesburg, Pennsylvania
WDOM Providence, Rhode Island
WYZR Bethany, West Virginia

Classical

KYUK Bethel, Alaska
KCAM Glennallen, Alaska
KRBD Ketchikan, Alaska
KIAM Nenana, Alaska
KNOM Nome, Alaska
KCAW Sitka, Alaska
KSTK Wrangell, Alaska
KESA Eureka Springs, Arkansas
KQSM-FM Fayetteville, Arkansas
KVHS Concord, California
KMMT Mammoth Lakes, California
KSMC Moraga, California
KUCR Riverside, California
KJDX Susanville, California
KCSS Turlock, California
KCIC Grand Junction, Colorado
KSUT Ignacio, Colorado
KVOD Lakewood, Colorado
KVAY Lamar, Colorado
WPKN Bridgeport, Connecticut
WRTC-FM Hartford, Connecticut
WWEB Wallingford, Connecticut
WVUD Newark, Delaware
WIIS Key West, Florida
WKEY-FM Key West, Florida
WSGL Naples, Florida
WUCF-FM Orlando, Florida
WRAS Atlanta, Georgia
WREK Atlanta, Georgia
WBGA Brunswick, Georgia
KDFR Des Moines, Iowa
KCMR Mason City, Iowa
KSAS-FM Caldwell, Idaho
KSRA Salmon, Idaho
WESN Bloomington, Illinois
WHPK-FM Chicago, Illinois
WEPS Elgin, Illinois
WVKC Galesburg, Illinois
WDCB Glen Ellyn, Illinois
WJCH Joliet, Illinois
WDSO Chesterton, Indiana
WBKE-FM North Manchester, Indiana
WPUM Rensselaer, Indiana
WECI Richmond, Indiana
WZIS(FM) Terre Haute, Indiana
WVUR-FM Valparaiso, Indiana
WVUB Vincennes, Indiana
KTCC Colby, Kansas
KIND Independence, Kansas
KFKF-FM Kansas City, Kansas
WKMS-FM Murray, Kentucky
WYAJ Sudbury, Massachusetts
WBUA Tisbury, Massachusetts
WCHC Worcester, Massachusetts
WKLT Kalkaska, Michigan
WRSR Owosso, Michigan
KNXR Rochester, Minnesota
KQAL Winona, Minnesota
KLJY Clayton, Missouri
KWJC Liberty, Missouri
KMVC Marshall, Missouri
KGNV Washington, Missouri
KMSM-FM Butte, Montana
KNMC Havre, Montana
KALS Kalispell, Montana
WERX-FM Columbia, North Carolina
WFSS Fayetteville, North Carolina
WVOD Manteo, North Carolina
WCVP Murphy, North Carolina
WCPE Raleigh, North Carolina
KHAS Hastings, Nebraska
KLPR Kearney, Nebraska
KCMI Terrytown, Nebraska
WKNH Keene, New Hampshire
WJSE North Cape May, New Jersey
WLFR Pomona, New Jersey
WKNJ-FM Union Township, New Jersey
WPSC-FM Wayne, New Jersey
KUNM Albuquerque, New Mexico
KPCL Farmington, New Mexico
WXLH Blue Mountain Lake, New York
WBFO Buffalo, New York
WHCL-FM Clinton, New York
WRCU-FM Hamilton, New York
WFSO Olivebridge, New York
WSRK Oneonta, New York
WKWZ Syosset, New York
WPNR-FM Utica, New York
WKEL Webster, New York
WBGU Bowling Green, Ohio
WCUE Cuyahoga Falls, Ohio
WMCO New Concord, Ohio
WUSO Springfield, Ohio
WYTN Youngstown, Ohio
KOSN Ketchum, Oklahoma
KBVR Corvallis, Oregon
KXRY Portland, Oregon
WDIY Allentown, Pennsylvania
WMKX Brookville, Pennsylvania
WSKE Everett, Pennsylvania
WZBT Gettysburg, Pennsylvania
WIUP-FM Indiana, Pennsylvania
WEJS Jersey Shore, Pennsylvania
WJSA-FM Jersey Shore, Pennsylvania
WARC Meadville, Pennsylvania
WJST New Castle, Pennsylvania
WHYY-FM Philadelphia, Pennsylvania
WUSR Scranton, Pennsylvania
WVMW-FM Scranton, Pennsylvania
WQSU Selinsgrove, Pennsylvania
WVYC York, Pennsylvania
WYVL(FM) Youngsville, Pennsylvania
WTPM Aguadilla, Puerto Rico
WGTK-FM Greenville, South Carolina
WHCB Bristol, Tennessee
WOPI Bristol, Tennessee
WVCP Gallatin, Tennessee
WFHU Henderson, Tennessee
WFMQ Lebanon, Tennessee
WDNX Olive Hill, Tennessee
KWTS Canyon, Texas
KNTU McKinney, Texas
KSUU Cedar City, Utah
KPCW Park City, Utah
WVRU-FM Radford, Virginia
WDCE Richmond, Virginia
WIUJ Charlotte Amalie, Virgin Islands
WVPS Burlington, Vermont
WJSC-FM Johnson, Vermont
WWLR Lyndonville, Vermont
WDEV Waterbury, Vermont
KGHP Gig Harbor, Washington
KEYG Grand Coulee, Washington
KMLW Moses Lake, Washington
KAGU Spokane, Washington
WSUP Platteville, Wisconsin
WYZR Bethany, West Virginia
WVTS-FM Dunbar, West Virginia

Comedy

WDJL Huntsville, Alabama
KTCL Wheat Ridge, Colorado
WWHP Farmer City, Illinois
WVSD Itta Bena, Mississippi
WPCR-FM Plymouth, New Hampshire
KFLY Eugene, Oregon
KJXJ Franklin, Texas

Contemporary Hits/Top 40

WSBB New Smyrna Beach, Florida
WQLF Lena, Illinois

WSGR-FM Port Huron, Michigan
WYGR Wyoming, Michigan
KOLV Olivia, Minnesota
KATQ Plentywood, Montana
WRRV Middletown, New York
WKBO Harrisburg, Pennsylvania
WSBG Stroudsburg, Pennsylvania
WCLM Highland Springs, Virginia

Country

KYUK Bethel, Alaska
KHNS Haines, Alaska
KRBD Ketchikan, Alaska
KSTK Wrangell, Alaska
WQPR Muscle Shoals, Alabama
KRDE Globe, Arizona
KIIM Tucson, Arizona
KPFA Berkeley, California
KSOQ-FM Escondido, California
KFJC Los Altos, California
KVMR Nevada City, California
KCSN Northridge, California
KAZU Pacific Grove, California
KAJX Aspen, Colorado
KOTO Telluride, Colorado
WWEB Wallingford, Connecticut
WAMU Washington, District of Columbia
WWOJ Avon Park, Florida
WTUF Boston, Georgia
WUWG Carrollton, Georgia
KSTO Agana, Guam
WUIS Springfield, Illinois
WMRS Monticello, Indiana
WPUM Rensselaer, Indiana
WECI Richmond, Indiana
WZIS(FM) Terre Haute, Indiana
KFKF-FM Kansas City, Kansas
KANU Lawrence, Kansas
WLVK Fort Knox, Kentucky
WGOH Grayson, Kentucky
WWAG McKee, Kentucky
WMKY Morehead, Kentucky
WKMS-FM Murray, Kentucky
WTKY Tompkinsville, Kentucky
KLSP Angola, Louisiana
WKHS Worton, Maryland
WBPW Presque Isle, Maine
WDBM East Lansing, Michigan
WMUK Kalamazoo, Michigan
WPHS Warren, Michigan
KBEM-FM Minneapolis, Minnesota
WMCN St. Paul, Minnesota
KMST Rolla, Missouri
WKZU Iuka, Mississippi
WSKK Ripley, Mississippi
KXEI Havre, Montana
WASU-FM Boone, North Carolina
WMMY Boone, North Carolina
WCCE Buies Creek, North Carolina
WYMY Burlington, North Carolina
WUAG Greensboro, North Carolina
WPLW Hillsborough, North Carolina
WCVP Murphy, North Carolina
WECR Newland, North Carolina
WQDR-FM Raleigh, North Carolina
WLHC Robbins, North Carolina
WEGG Rose Hill, North Carolina
WTQR Winston-Salem, North Carolina
WNEC-FM Henniker, New Hampshire
WDVR Delaware Township, New Jersey
WBJB-FM Lincroft, New Jersey
WBZC Pemberton, New Jersey
KRWG Las Cruces, New Mexico
WBFO Buffalo, New York
WLNL Horseheads, New York
WSQG-FM Ithaca, New York
WUBJ Jamestown, New York
WKCR-FM New York, New York
WGGO Salamanca, New York
WKWZ Syosset, New York
WCNY-FM Syracuse, New York
WUNY Utica, New York
WJNY Watertown, New York
WBGU Bowling Green, Ohio
WVSG Columbus, Ohio
KRSC-FM Claremore, Oklahoma
KRVM-FM Eugene, Oregon
KWVA Eugene, Oregon
KXRY Portland, Oregon
KFIR Sweet Home, Oregon
WWSM Annville-Cleona, Pennsylvania
WFKJ Cashtown, Pennsylvania
WCUC-FM Clarion, Pennsylvania
WSKE Everett, Pennsylvania
WNUZ Mercersburg, Pennsylvania
WRCT Pittsburgh, Pennsylvania
WRCT(FM) Pittsburgh, Pennsylvania
WYEP-FM Pittsburgh, Pennsylvania
WLHI Schnecksville, Pennsylvania
WQSU Selinsgrove, Pennsylvania
WBYO Sellersville, Pennsylvania
WBYX Stroudsburg, Pennsylvania
WRDV Warminster, Pennsylvania
WZZD Warwick, Pennsylvania
WCYJ-FM Waynesburg, Pennsylvania
WCHE West Chester, Pennsylvania
WDOM Providence, Rhode Island
WOPI Bristol, Tennessee
WHRS Cookeville, Tennessee
WEMB Erwin, Tennessee
WVCP Gallatin, Tennessee
WCLC Jamestown, Tennessee
WLAF La Follette, Tennessee
WWLX Lawrenceburg, Tennessee
WEVL Memphis, Tennessee
WUTS Sewanee, Tennessee
WSBI Static, Tennessee
WNTT Tazewell, Tennessee
KQTY-FM Borger, Texas
KETR Commerce, Texas
KSWA Graham, Texas
KSHN Liberty, Texas
KXWT Odessa, Texas
KPCW Park City, Utah
WKDE-FM Altavista, Virginia
WCLM Highland Springs, Virginia
WSIG Mount Jackson, Virginia
WKCW Warrenton, Virginia
WMYV Hartford, Vermont
WJSC-FM Johnson, Vermont
WOJB Reserve, Wisconsin
WVRQ-FM Viroqua, Wisconsin
WHAW Lost Creek, West Virginia

Disco

KSWF Aurora, Missouri

Ethnic

KDLG Dillingham, Alaska
KJHA Houston, Alaska
KJNP North Pole, Alaska
KSAZ Marana, Arizona
KKUP Cupertino, California
KMUD Garberville, California
KMYC Marysville, California
KCSN Northridge, California
KMRB San Gabriel, California
KOBO Yuba City, California
WMRD Middletown, Connecticut
WWPT Westport, Connecticut
WUST Washington, District of Columbia
WKWM Marathon, Florida
WLRN-FM Miami, Florida
WPSO New Port Richey, Florida
KWXX-FM Hilo, Hawaii
KKON Kealakekua, Hawaii
KUAI Kekaha, Hawaii
KKUA Wailuku, Hawaii
WCEV Cicero, Illinois
WNKJ Hopkinsville, Kentucky
KEUN Eunice, Louisiana
KEUN-FM Eunice, Louisiana
KVPI Ville Platte, Louisiana
KVPI-FM Ville Platte, Louisiana
WHTB Fall River, Massachusetts
WNBP Newburyport, Massachusetts
WCUW Worcester, Massachusetts
WMPG Gorham, Maine
WCAR Livonia, Michigan
KMSK Austin, Minnesota
KRBT Eveleth, Minnesota
KMSU Mankato, Minnesota
WUMS University, Mississippi
WFMU East Orange, New Jersey
WPRB Princeton, New Jersey
WSOU South Orange, New Jersey
KTAO Taos, New Mexico
KUNR Reno, Nevada
WNDR-FM Mexico, New York
WFUV New York, New York
WMCA New York, New York
WRHV Poughkeepsie, New York
WBEE-FM Rochester, New York
WUSP Utica, New York
WAPS Akron, Ohio
WCPN Cleveland, Ohio
KBOO Portland, Oregon
WDIY Allentown, Pennsylvania
WMUH Allentown, Pennsylvania
WEDO McKeesport, Pennsylvania
KAGC Bryan, Texas
KTEM Temple, Texas
WWKS Cruz Bay, Virgin Islands
KARI Blaine, Washington
KLFE Seattle, Washington
WGTD Kenosha, Wisconsin
WEKZ Monroe, Wisconsin
WXER Plymouth, Wisconsin
WSHS Sheboygan, Wisconsin

Filipino

KBRW Barrow, Alaska
KECG El Cerrito, California
KMPO Modesto, California

French

KTOO Juneau, Alaska
KSRH San Rafael, California
KVPI-FM Ville Platte, Louisiana
WJIB Cambridge, Massachusetts
WMOU Berlin, New Hampshire
WFEA Manchester, New Hampshire
WCHP Champlain, New York

Gospel

KFAR Fairbanks, Alaska
KSDP Sand Point, Alaska
WKNU Brewton, Alabama
WTVY-FM Dothan, Alabama
WELB Elba, Alabama
WZOB Fort Payne, Alabama
WLDA Fort Rucker, Alabama
WAOQ Goshen, Alabama
WDJL Huntsville, Alabama
WCKA Jacksonville, Alabama
WIXI Jasper, Alabama
WEBT Langdale, Alabama
WINL Linden, Alabama
WLWI-FM Montgomery, Alabama
WVAS Montgomery, Alabama
WGOL Russellville, Alabama
WFEB Sylacauga, Alabama
WTLS Tallassee, Alabama
WGZZ Waverly, Alabama
KEWI Benton, Arkansas
KMLK El Dorado, Arkansas
KBJT Fordyce, Arkansas
KFFA Helena, Arkansas
KBOK Malvern, Arkansas
KZHE Stamps, Arkansas
KWRF Warren, Arkansas
KCLT West Helena, Arkansas
KXCI Tucson, Arizona
KMVE California City, California
KRML Carmel, California
KJLH Compton, California
KECG El Cerrito, California
KTDE Gualala, California
KSRN Kings Beach, California
KPFK Los Angeles, California
KYOS Merced, California
KAZU Pacific Grove, California
KZYX Philo, California
KEST San Francisco, California
KISQ San Francisco, California
KDIA Vallejo, California
KDYA Vallejo, California
KUBA Yuba City, California
KASF Alamosa, Colorado
KRTZ Cortez, Colorado
KVAY Lamar, Colorado
KSLV Monte Vista, Colorado
KVNF Paonia, Colorado
KGFT Pueblo, Colorado
WQTQ Hartford, Connecticut
WRTC-FM Hartford, Connecticut
WESU Middletown, Connecticut
WYBC-FM New Haven, Connecticut
WCNI New London, Connecticut

WKND Windsor, Connecticut
WHUR-FM Washington, District of Columbia
WAFL Milford, Delaware
WYBT Blountstown, Florida
WWPR Bradenton, Florida
WZEP De Funiak Springs, Florida
WRNE Gulf Breeze, Florida
WWAB Lakeland, Florida
WLBE Leesburg-Eustis, Florida
WQHL Live Oak, Florida
WMAF Madison, Florida
WTYS Marianna, Florida
WLTG Panama City, Florida
WANM Tallahassee, Florida
WQLC Watertown, Florida
WFLM White City, Florida
WZZS Zolfo Springs, Florida
V6AH(AM) Pohnpei, 66
WFSH-FM Athens, Georgia
WCLK Atlanta, Georgia
WTUF Boston, Georgia
WJTH Calhoun, Georgia
WZBN Camilla, Georgia
WDXQ Cochran, Georgia
WRDO Fitzgerald, Georgia
WJGA-FM Jackson, Georgia
WNEA Newnan, Georgia
WPTB Statesboro, Georgia
WTHO-FM Thomson, Georgia
WGUN Valdosta, Georgia
WVLD Valdosta, Georgia
KSTO Agana, Guam
KROS Clinton, Iowa
KALA Davenport, Iowa
KHOE Fairfield, Iowa
KBOE Oskaloosa, Iowa
KIGC Oskaloosa, Iowa
KLEE Ottumwa, Iowa
KWIK Pocatello, Idaho
WBGZ Alton, Illinois
WKRO Cairo, Illinois
WSSD Chicago, Illinois
WWHP Farmer City, Illinois
WJRE Galva, Illinois
WDCB Glen Ellyn, Illinois
WHPO Hoopeston, Illinois
WJOL Joliet, Illinois
WMXM Lake Forest, Illinois
WPNA Oak Park, Illinois
WVAZ Oak Park, Illinois
WWVR Paris, Indiana
WPMB Vandalia, Illinois
WYKT Wilmington, Illinois
WBNL Boonville, Indiana
WIKL(FM) Elwood, Indiana
WFLQ French Lick, Indiana
WKAM Goshen, Indiana
WXLW Indianapolis, Indiana
WYXB Indianapolis, Indiana
WKPW Knightstown, Indiana
WMRS Monticello, Indiana
WRIN Rensselaer, Indiana
WTCJ Tell City, Indiana
KDNS Downs, Kansas
KHAZ Hays, Kansas
KINZ Humboldt, Kansas
KWBW Hutchinson, Kansas
KNNS Larned, Kansas
KSDB-FM Manhattan, Kansas
KFNF Oberlin, Kansas
KKAN Phillipsburg, Kansas
KFRM Salina, Kansas
KSKG Salina, Kansas
KMUW Wichita, Kansas
WANY Albany, Kentucky
WLFX Berea, Kentucky
WHVO Hopkinsville, Kentucky
WLBN Lebanon, Kentucky
WFTM Maysville, Kentucky
WWAG McKee, Kentucky
WFXY Middlesboro, Kentucky
WMIK Middlesboro, Kentucky
WTHL Somerset, Kentucky
WTKY Tompkinsville, Kentucky
KRVV Bastrop, Louisiana
WFPR Hammond, Louisiana
KJLO-FM Monroe, Louisiana
WJIB Cambridge, Massachusetts
WAIC Springfield, Massachusetts
WEAA Baltimore, Maryland
WMTB-FM Emmitsburg, Maryland
WKHI Fruitland, Maryland
WAAI Hurlock, Maryland
WESM Princess Anne, Maryland
WGTO Cassopolis, Michigan
WDET-FM Detroit, Michigan
WDZZ-FM Flint, Michigan
WLCM Holt, Michigan
WVHF Kentwood, Michigan
WQUS Lapeer, Michigan
WTLZ Saginaw, Michigan
WMLM St. Louis, Michigan
KDUZ Hutchinson, Minnesota
KLQL Luverne, Minnesota
KYOO Bolivar, Missouri
KBFL-FM Buffalo, Missouri
KRLL California, Missouri
KMFC Centralia, Missouri
KOPN Columbia, Missouri
KUNQ Houston, Missouri
KTTK Lebanon, Missouri
KJAB-FM Mexico, Missouri
KGSP Parkville, Missouri
KMIS-AM Portageville, Missouri
KWND Springfield, Missouri
KTTN-FM Trenton, Missouri
WWZQ Aberdeen, Mississippi
WAMY Amory, Mississippi
WESE Baldwyn, Mississippi
WBKN Brookhaven, Mississippi
WPAE Centreville, Mississippi
WCJU Columbia, Mississippi
WKRA Holly Springs, Mississippi
WKZU Iuka, Mississippi
WNAT Natchez, Mississippi
WNAU New Albany, Mississippi
WWZD-FM New Albany, Mississippi
WOXD Oxford, Mississippi
WSKK Ripley, Mississippi
WKXR Asheboro, North Carolina
WWNC Asheville, North Carolina
WGWG Boiling Springs, North Carolina
WATA Boone, North Carolina
WSQL Brevard, North Carolina
WFXK Bunn, North Carolina
WKYK Burnsville, North Carolina
WCLN Clinton, North Carolina
WPEG Concord, North Carolina
WCKB Dunn, North Carolina
WFXC Durham, North Carolina
WRVS-FM Elizabeth City, North Carolina
WBLA Elizabethtown, North Carolina
WFSS Fayetteville, North Carolina
WZRU Garysburg, North Carolina
WYCV Granite Falls, North Carolina
WNAA Greensboro, North Carolina
WTZQ Hendersonville, North Carolina
WLNC Laurinburg, North Carolina
WLON Lincolnton, North Carolina
WBRM Marion, North Carolina
WDJS Mount Olive, North Carolina
WIKS New Bern, North Carolina
WECR Newland, North Carolina
WGCR Pisgah Forest, North Carolina
WPJL Raleigh, North Carolina
WEGG Rose Hill, North Carolina
WRXO Roxboro, North Carolina
WNCA Siler City, North Carolina
WEEB Southern Pines, North Carolina
WACB Taylorsville, North Carolina
WKSK West Jefferson, North Carolina
WYNC Yanceyville, North Carolina
KABU Fort Totten, North Dakota
KXPO Grafton, North Dakota
KQLX Lisbon, North Dakota
KTGO Tioga, North Dakota
KINI Crookston, Nebraska
KUVR Holdrege, Nebraska
KRNU Lincoln, Nebraska
KZUM Lincoln, Nebraska
KRFS Superior, Nebraska
WJPG Cape May Court House, New Jersey
WTTH Margate City, New Jersey
WMVB Millville, New Jersey
WTSR Trenton, New Jersey
WMSC Upper Montclair, New Jersey
WJPG Woodbine, New Jersey
KATK Carlsbad, New Mexico
KIOT Los Lunas, New Mexico
KCEP Las Vegas, Nevada
WCDB Albany, New York
WROW Albany, New York
WXLH Blue Mountain Lake, New York
WSLU Canton, New York
WSIV E. Syracuse, New York
WEOS Geneva, New York
WVCR-FM Loudonville, New York
WDKX Rochester, New York
WRUR-FM Rochester, New York
WAER Syracuse, New York
WRMU-FM Alliance, Ohio
WAIS Buchtel, Ohio
WGRI Cincinnati, Ohio
WEDI Eaton, Ohio
WWSU Fairborn, Ohio
WPOS-FM Holland, Ohio
WXMG London, Ohio
WMPO Middleport-Pomeroy, Ohio
WQIO Mount Vernon, Ohio
WNPQ New Philadelphia, Ohio
WDIG Steubenville, Ohio
WJUC Swanton, Ohio
WERT Van Wert, Ohio
WBZI Xenia, Ohio
KADA Ada, Oklahoma
KYFM Bartlesville, Oklahoma
KKBI Broken Bow, Oklahoma
KDDQ Comanche, Oklahoma
KTNT Eufaula, Oklahoma
KPRV-FM Heavener, Oklahoma
KFXI Marlow, Oklahoma
KTMC McAlester, Oklahoma
KRIG-FM Nowata, Oklahoma
KYLV Oklahoma City, Oklahoma
KFAQ Tulsa, Oklahoma
KAJO Grants Pass, Oregon
KWBY Woodburn, Oregon
WWSM Annville-Cleona, Pennsylvania
WBVP Beaver Falls, Pennsylvania
WCHA Chambersburg, Pennsylvania
WSKE Everett, Pennsylvania
WVMM Grantham, Pennsylvania
WTKT Harrisburg, Pennsylvania
WIUP-FM Indiana, Pennsylvania
WEJS Jersey Shore, Pennsylvania
WJSA-FM Jersey Shore, Pennsylvania
WNUZ Mercersburg, Pennsylvania
WQZS Meyersdale, Pennsylvania
WWBE Mifflinburg, Pennsylvania
WKDU Philadelphia, Pennsylvania
WURD Philadelphia, Pennsylvania
WUSL Philadelphia, Pennsylvania
WPHB Philipsburg, Pennsylvania
WPAM Pottsville, Pennsylvania
WBYO Sellersville, Pennsylvania
WHYF(AM) Shiremanstown, Pennsylvania
WBYX Stroudsburg, Pennsylvania
WZZD Warwick, Pennsylvania
WRLC Williamsport, Pennsylvania
WRIU Kingston, Rhode Island
WJMF Smithfield, Rhode Island
WZLA-FM Abbeville, South Carolina
WBT-FM Chester, South Carolina
WTZQ Fountain Inn, South Carolina
WKMG Newberry, South Carolina
WGOG Walhalla, South Carolina
KLND Little Eagle, South Dakota
KBHB Sturgis, South Dakota
WATX Algood, Tennessee
WVOL Berry Hill, Tennessee
WFWL Camden, Tennessee
WHUB Cookeville, Tennessee
WZYX Cowan, Tennessee
WSDQ Dunlap, Tennessee
WEMB Erwin, Tennessee
WQQK Goodlettsville, Tennessee
WMYL Halls Crossroads, Tennessee
WTNK Hartsville, Tennessee
WFHU Henderson, Tennessee
WFKX Henderson, Tennessee
WHHM-FM Henderson, Tennessee
WMLR Hohenwald, Tennessee
WDXI Jackson, Tennessee
WLIL Lenoir City, Tennessee
WDXL Lexington, Tennessee
WLIV Livingston, Tennessee
WDIA Memphis, Tennessee
WTRB Ripley, Tennessee
WJLE Smithville, Tennessee
WEPG South Pittsburg, Tennessee
WDBL Springfield, Tennessee
WSGI Springfield, Tennessee
WSBI Static, Tennessee

WNTT Tazewell, Tennessee
KGNZ Abilene, Texas
KIXZ Amarillo, Texas
KAZI Austin, Texas
KQTY-FM Borger, Texas
KNTX Bowie, Texas
KLTR Brenham, Texas
KTON Cameron, Texas
KCAR Clarksville, Texas
KSTA Coleman, Texas
KEOS College Station, Texas
KCOM Comanche, Texas
KSSM Copperas Cove, Texas
KBPC Crockett, Texas
KDDD-FM Dumas, Texas
KTEP El Paso, Texas
KNES Fairfield, Texas
KSWA Graham, Texas
KHBR Hillsboro, Texas
KHYI Howe, Texas
KOOK Junction, Texas
KRVL Kerrville, Texas
KTAI Kingsville, Texas
KLRK Mexia, Texas
KCKM Monahans, Texas
KJCS Nacogdoches, Texas
KPLT Paris, Texas
KHKZ San Benito, Texas
KXOX Sweetwater, Texas
KTBB Tyler, Texas
KVNE Tyler, Texas
KVWC Vernon, Texas
KALK Winfield, Texas
KWUD Woodville, Texas
KBLQ-FM Logan, Utah
KWCR-FM Ogden, Utah
WKDE Altavista, Virginia
WKDE-FM Altavista, Virginia
WTJU Charlottesville, Virginia
WKEY Covington, Virginia
WPAK Farmville, Virginia
WUKZ(AM) Marion, Virginia
WSIG Mount Jackson, Virginia
WVCV Orange, Virginia
WVST-FM Petersburg, Virginia
WKGM Smithfield, Virginia
WAJL South Boston, Virginia
WXLZ St. Paul, Virginia
WMBG Williamsburg, Virginia
WYVE Wytheville, Virginia
WMYV Hartford, Vermont
WTWN Wells River, Vermont
KFKB Forks, Washington
KNHC Seattle, Washington
KTCR Yakima, Washington
WATK Antigo, Wisconsin
WZTI Greenfield, Wisconsin
WKKV-FM Racine, Wisconsin
WRCO-FM Richland Center, Wisconsin
WRON-FM Lewisburg, West Virginia
WHAW Lost Creek, West Virginia
WELD-FM Moorefield, West Virginia
WVNT Parkersburg, West Virginia
WCWV Summersville, West Virginia
KJUA Cheyenne, Wyoming

Greek

WJOB Hammond, Indiana
WKTX Cortland, Ohio
WCCD Parma, Ohio
WEDO McKeesport, Pennsylvania
WULR York, South Carolina
WUVT-FM Blacksburg, Virginia

Italian

WICC Bridgeport, Connecticut
WRYM New Britain, Connecticut
WWUH West Hartford, Connecticut
WDUV New Port Richey, Florida
WRTK Paxton, Illinois
WOSW Fulton, New York
WJTN Jamestown, New York
WRUC Schenectady, New York
WNIO Youngstown, Ohio
WFAX Falls Church, Virginia
WTCS Fairmont, West Virginia
WEIR Weirton, West Virginia

Japanese

KTYM Inglewood, California
KEST San Francisco, California
KCSB-FM Santa Barbara, California
KPUA Hilo, Hawaii
KWVA Eugene, Oregon

Jazz

KBRW Barrow, Alaska
KUAC Fairbanks, Alaska
KIYU Galena, Alaska
KBBI Homer, Alaska
KTOO Juneau, Alaska
KRBD Ketchikan, Alaska
KFSK Petersburg, Alaska
KSTK Wrangell, Alaska
WZEW Fairhope, Alabama
WLDA Fort Rucker, Alabama
WMXB Tuscaloosa, Alabama
KEZA Fayetteville, Arkansas
KXRJ Russellville, Arkansas
KNOT Prescott, Arizona
KXCI Tucson, Arizona
KHSU Arcata, California
KPFA Berkeley, California
KHSR Crescent City, California
KHUM Cutten, California
KMUD Garberville, California
KFGY Healdsburg, California
KFJC Los Altos, California
KPFK Los Angeles, California
KMMT Mammoth Lakes, California
KSMC Moraga, California
KUCR Riverside, California
KZDG San Francisco, California
KNNN(FM) Shasta Lake City, California
KTHO South Lake Tahoe, California
KCLU-FM Thousand Oaks, California
KCSS Turlock, California
KRCB-FM Windsor, California
KASF Alamosa, Colorado
KGNU-FM Boulder, Colorado
KVCU Boulder, Colorado
KRCC Colorado Springs, Colorado
KDUR Durango, Colorado
KCSU-FM Fort Collins, Colorado
KMSA Grand Junction, Colorado
KWSB-FM Gunnison, Colorado
KSUT Ignacio, Colorado
KFMU-FM Oak Creek, Colorado
KWUF-FM Pagosa Springs, Colorado
KVNF Paonia, Colorado
KOTO Telluride, Colorado
WPKN Bridgeport, Connecticut
WXCI Danbury, Connecticut
WQTQ Hartford, Connecticut
WZBG Litchfield, Connecticut
WYBC-FM New Haven, Connecticut
WCNI New London, Connecticut
WLIS Old Saybrook, Connecticut
WQQQ Sharon, Connecticut
WNHU West Haven, Connecticut
WECS Willimantic, Connecticut
WKND Windsor, Connecticut
WAMU Washington, District of Columbia
WVUD Newark, Delaware
WGMD Rehoboth Beach, Delaware
WKTO Edgewater, Florida
WJLF Gainesville, Florida
WXCV Homosassa Springs, Florida
WAVV Naples Park, Florida
WSBB New Smyrna Beach, Florida
WMFE-FM Orlando, Florida
WANM Tallahassee, Florida
WFSU-FM Tallahassee, Florida
WFLM White City, Florida
WPRK Winter Park, Florida
WUGA Athens, Georgia
WREK Atlanta, Georgia
WNGH-FM Chatsworth, Georgia
WMUM-FM Cochran, Georgia
WNGU Dahlonega, Georgia
WPPR Demorest, Georgia
WJWV Fort Gaines, Georgia
WFXM Gordon, Georgia
WGPB Rome, Georgia
WWET Valdosta, Georgia
WJSP-FM Warm Springs, Georgia
WQGA Waycross, Georgia
WXVS Waycross, Georgia
KUAI Kekaha, Hawaii
KMXG Clinton, Iowa
KROS Clinton, Iowa
KHOE Fairfield, Iowa
KRNL-FM Mount Vernon, Iowa
KOJI Okoboji, Iowa
KIGC Oskaloosa, Iowa
KSAS-FM Caldwell, Idaho
KBSM McCall, Idaho
KRFA-FM Moscow, Idaho
KUOI-FM Moscow, Idaho
KECH-FM Sun Valley, Idaho
WESN Bloomington, Illinois
WEIU Charleston, Illinois
WFMT Chicago, Illinois
WIIT Chicago, Illinois
WSSD Chicago, Illinois
WEPS Elgin, Illinois
WVKC Galesburg, Illinois
WCSF Joliet, Illinois
WMXM Lake Forest, Illinois
WLRA Lockport, Illinois
WIUM Macomb, Illinois
WIUS Macomb, Illinois
WRRG River Grove, Illinois
WVIK Rock Island, Illinois
WNNS Springfield, Illinois
WGRE Greencastle, Indiana
WNTR Indianapolis, Indiana
WSND-FM Notre Dame, Indiana
WZIS(FM) Terre Haute, Indiana
WVUR-FM Valparaiso, Indiana
KNBU Baldwin City, Kansas
KAHS El Dorado, Kansas
KANZ Garden City, Kansas
KZNA Hill City, Kansas
KSDB-FM Manhattan, Kansas
KMUW Wichita, Kansas
KRBB Wichita, Kansas
WKUE Elizabethtown, Kentucky
WMKY Morehead, Kentucky
WDCL-FM Somerset, Kentucky
KLSP Angola, Louisiana
KGRM Grambling, Louisiana
WAMQ Great Barrington, Massachusetts
WBWL Lynn, Massachusetts
WBSL-FM Sheffield, Massachusetts
WYAJ Sudbury, Massachusetts
WBUA Tisbury, Massachusetts
WCHC Worcester, Massachusetts
WLIF Baltimore, Maryland
WHFC Bel Air, Maryland
WARK Hagerstown, Maryland
WHTP Kennebunkport, Maine
WXEX-FM Sanford, Maine
WBQX Thomaston, Maine
WMHB Waterville, Maine
WHFR Dearborn, Michigan
WDET-FM Detroit, Michigan
WKAR-FM East Lansing, Michigan
WVHF Kentwood, Michigan
WUPX Marquette, Michigan
WKRR Portage, Michigan
KFAI Minneapolis, Minnesota
KVSC St. Cloud, Minnesota
KCFV Ferguson, Missouri
KKFI Kansas City, Missouri
KGSP Parkville, Missouri
KMST Rolla, Missouri
KBFL-AM Springfield, Missouri
KSMU Springfield, Missouri
KMOX St. Louis, Missouri
KRSI Garapan-Saipan, Guam
WGNL Greenwood, Mississippi
KMSM-FM Butte, Montana
WSQL Brevard, North Carolina
WFXK Bunn, North Carolina
WXDU Durham, North Carolina
WRVS-FM Elizabeth City, North Carolina
WZRU Garysburg, North Carolina
WKNS Kinston, North Carolina
WIKS New Bern, North Carolina
WTEB New Bern, North Carolina
WNNC Newton, North Carolina
WLHC Robbins, North Carolina
WNCW Spindale, North Carolina
WFDD Winston-Salem, North Carolina
KIOS-FM Omaha, Nebraska
KKCD Omaha, Nebraska
KWSC Wayne, Nebraska
WUNH Durham, New Hampshire

RADIO - U.S.

WKNH Keene, New Hampshire
WDER-FM Peterborough, New Hampshire
WPCR-FM Plymouth, New Hampshire
WDVR Delaware Township, New Jersey
WBZC Pemberton, New Jersey
WLFR Pomona, New Jersey
WTSR Trenton, New Jersey
WMSC Upper Montclair, New Jersey
WPSC-FM Wayne, New Jersey
WMCX West Long Branch, New Jersey
KKTC Angel Fire, New Mexico
KSJE Farmington, New Mexico
KGLP Gallup, New Mexico
KTAO Taos, New Mexico
KCEP Las Vegas, Nevada
WAMC-FM Albany, New York
WCDB Albany, New York
WVIN-FM Bath, New York
WHRW Binghamton, New York
WSKG-FM Binghamton, New York
WXLH Blue Mountain Lake, New York
WBNY Buffalo, New York
WCAN Canajoharie, New York
WSLU Canton, New York
WHCL-FM Clinton, New York
WKGB-FM Conklin, New York
WSQE Corning, New York
WRCU-FM Hamilton, New York
WITR Henrietta, New York
WICB Ithaca, New York
WSQG-FM Ithaca, New York
WAMK Kingston, New York
WOSR Middletown, New York
WRHO Oneonta, New York
WSQC-FM Oneonta, New York
WZOZ Oneonta, New York
WCEL Plattsburgh, New York
WRHV Poughkeepsie, New York
WDKX Rochester, New York
WRUR-FM Rochester, New York
WFNP Rosendale, New York
WMHT-FM Schenectady, New York
WRUC Schenectady, New York
WSFW Seneca Falls, New York
WKWZ Syosset, New York
WCNY-FM Syracuse, New York
WANC Ticonderoga, New York
WPNR-FM Utica, New York
WUNY Utica, New York
WJNY Watertown, New York
WRIP Windham, New York
WRDL Ashland, Ohio
WGBE Bryan, Ohio
WCBE Columbus, Ohio
WGDE Defiance, Ohio
WWSU Fairborn, Ohio
WVKO-FM Johnstown, Ohio
WCIT(AM) Lima, Ohio
WGLE Lima, Ohio
WCLV Lorain, Ohio
WMCO New Concord, Ohio
WLFC North Baltimore, Ohio
WUSO Springfield, Ohio
WGTE-FM Toledo, Ohio
WRVF Toledo, Ohio
WYSO Yellow Springs, Ohio
KRSC-FM Claremore, Oklahoma
KBZQ Lawton, Oklahoma
KGOU Norman, Oklahoma
KZBB Poteau, Oklahoma
KOAC Corvallis, Oregon
KEOL La Grande, Oregon
WLVR-FM Bethlehem, Pennsylvania
WMKX Brookville, Pennsylvania
WDCV-FM Carlisle, Pennsylvania
WDNR Chester, Pennsylvania
WCUC-FM Clarion, Pennsylvania
WESS East Stroudsburg, Pennsylvania
WJRH Easton, Pennsylvania
WMCE Erie, Pennsylvania
WZBT Gettysburg, Pennsylvania
WKVR-FM Huntingdon, Pennsylvania
WPSX Kane, Pennsylvania
WFNM Lancaster, Pennsylvania
WVBU-FM Lewisburg, Pennsylvania
WNTE Mansfield, Pennsylvania
WARC Meadville, Pennsylvania
WIXQ Millersville, Pennsylvania
WVLY-FM Milton, Pennsylvania
WHYY-FM Philadelphia, Pennsylvania
WRCT Pittsburgh, Pennsylvania
WRCT(FM) Pittsburgh, Pennsylvania
WVMW-FM Scranton, Pennsylvania
WSYC-FM Shippensburg, Pennsylvania
WKPS State College, Pennsylvania
WPSU State College, Pennsylvania
WRDV Warminster, Pennsylvania
WPTC Williamsport, Pennsylvania
WVYC York, Pennsylvania
WWNA Aguadilla, Puerto Rico
WUKQ-FM Mayaguez, Puerto Rico
WBRU Providence, Rhode Island
WEGX Dillon, South Carolina
WYNN Florence, South Carolina
WLGI Hemingway, South Carolina
WSSB-FM Orangeburg, South Carolina
WSPA-FM Spartanburg, South Carolina
KSDJ Brookings, South Dakota
KCSD Sioux Falls, South Dakota
WAPX-FM Clarksville, Tennessee
WTTU Cookeville, Tennessee
WFHU Henderson, Tennessee
WEVL Memphis, Tennessee
WMTS-FM Murfreesboro, Tennessee
WUTS Sewanee, Tennessee
KACU Abilene, Texas
KACV-FM Amarillo, Texas
KWTS Canyon, Texas
KEOS College Station, Texas
KNNK Dimmitt, Texas
KODA Houston, Texas
KTRU(FM) Houston, Texas
KFAN-FM Johnson City, Texas
KNCT-FM Killeen, Texas
KMND Midland, Texas
KXWT Odessa, Texas
KQXT-FM San Antonio, Texas
KSTX San Antonio, Texas
KTXK Texarkana, Texas
KWBU-FM Waco, Texas
KBLQ-FM Logan, Utah
KPCW Park City, Utah
WWHS-FM Hampden-Sydney, Virginia
WXJM Harrisonburg, Virginia
WVRU-FM Radford, Virginia
WCVE-FM Richmond, Virginia
WDCE Richmond, Virginia
WCWM Williamsburg, Virginia
WISE-FM Wise, Virginia
WIUJ Charlotte Amalie, Virgin Islands
WIUV Castleton, Vermont
WWLR Lyndonville, Vermont
WEQX Manchester, Vermont
WRMC-FM Middlebury, Vermont
WNCS Montpelier, Vermont
KNWR Ellensburg, Washington
KSER Everett, Washington
KGHP Gig Harbor, Washington
KBRD Lacey, Washington
KWSU Pullman, Washington
KZUU Pullman, Washington
KFAE-FM Richland, Washington
KUOW-FM Seattle, Washington
KAGU Spokane, Washington
KPBX-FM Spokane, Washington
KUPS Tacoma, Washington
WHSA Brule, Wisconsin
WBSD Burlington, Wisconsin
WPNE-FM Green Bay, Wisconsin
WVSS Menomonie, Wisconsin
WMSE Milwaukee, Wisconsin
WSUP Platteville, Wisconsin
WOJB Reserve, Wisconsin
WXPR Rhinelander, Wisconsin
KUWS Superior, Wisconsin
WSUW Whitewater, Wisconsin
WVWC Buckhannon, West Virginia
WQAB Philippi, West Virginia
WPHP Wheeling, West Virginia
KUWA Afton, Wyoming
KUWJ Jackson, Wyoming
KUWR Laramie, Wyoming
KUWZ Rock Springs, Wyoming

Korean

WNKJ Hopkinsville, Kentucky
KRNM Chalan Kanoa-Saipan, Guam

Light Rock

KTNA Talkeetna, Alaska

Native American

KRUA Anchorage, Alaska
KCAM Glennallen, Alaska
KDLL Kenai, Alaska
KIAM Nenana, Alaska
KABF Little Rock, Arkansas
KNNB Whiteriver, Arizona
KTNN Window Rock, Arizona
KZFR Chico, California
KFCF Fresno, California
KIDE Hoopa, California
KPSI Palm Springs, California
KCSB-FM Santa Barbara, California
KDUR Durango, Colorado
KSUT Ignacio, Colorado
KWIK Pocatello, Idaho
WUEV Evansville, Indiana
WCUP L'Anse, Michigan
WNMC-FM Traverse City, Michigan
KBSB Bemidji, Minnesota
KGVA Fort Belknap Agency, Montana
KEYA Belcourt, North Dakota
KCND Bismarck, North Dakota
KDPR Dickinson, North Dakota
KABU Fort Totten, North Dakota
KMHA Four Bears, North Dakota
KPRJ Jamestown, North Dakota
KMPR Minot, North Dakota
KPPR Williston, North Dakota
KINI Crookston, Nebraska
WNEC-FM Henniker, New Hampshire
KYVA-FM Church Rock, New Mexico
KGLX Gallup, New Mexico
KOAZ Isleta, New Mexico
KTDB Ramah, New Mexico
KXTC Thoreau, New Mexico
KSFR White Rock, New Mexico
WYBG Massena, New York
WNTO Racine, Ohio
KQSN Ponca City, Oklahoma
KIRC Seminole, Oklahoma
KOSU Stillwater, Oklahoma
KWSH Wewoka, Oklahoma
KRVM-FM Eugene, Oregon
KTEC Klamath Falls, Oregon
KOLY Mobridge, South Dakota
KTSD-FM Reliance, South Dakota
KBHB Sturgis, South Dakota
KAOR Vermillion, South Dakota
KUSD Vermillion, South Dakota
KOOP Hornsby, Texas
KZMU Moab, Utah
KRCL Salt Lake City, Utah
WUVT-FM Blacksburg, Virginia
KSER Everett, Washington
KAOS Olympia, Washington
KSFC Spokane, Washington
KYNR Toppenish, Washington
WPNE-FM Green Bay, Wisconsin
WHND Sister Bay, Wisconsin

News

KFBX Fairbanks, Alaska
WOOF-FM Dothan, Alabama
WBPT Homewood, Alabama
WJOU Huntsville, Alabama
WVAS Montgomery, Alabama
WOPP Opp, Alabama
WVNA Tuscumbia, Alabama
KDXE North Little Rock, Arkansas
KBHR Big Bear City, California
KWXY AM Cathedral City, California
KRZA Alamosa, Colorado
KFTM Fort Morgan, Colorado
WOCL Deland, Florida
WOLZ Fort Myers, Florida
WRZN Hernando, Florida
WRGP Homestead, Florida
WOKV(AM) Jacksonville, Quebec
WCNK Key West, Florida
WONN Lakeland, Florida
WVOI Marco Island, Florida
WOCA Ocala, Florida
WOGK Ocala, Florida
WOKC Okeechobee, Florida
WWWE Hapeville, Georgia
WOBB Tifton, Georgia
KLGA Algona, Iowa
WOI-FM Ames, Iowa
KIFG-FM Iowa Falls, Iowa

KTFC Sioux City, Iowa
KID Idaho Falls, Idaho
KID-FM Idaho Falls, Idaho
KITT Soda Springs, Idaho
WILY Centralia, Illinois
WPCD Champaign, Illinois
WCGO Evanston, Illinois
WHFH Flossmoor, Illinois
WLTL La Grange, Illinois
WWVR Paris, Indiana
WNVR Vernon Hills, Illinois
WBIW Bedford, Indiana
WOCC Corydon, Indiana
WGCS Goshen, Indiana
WORX-FM Madison, Indiana
WSVX Shelbyville, Indiana
KCFN Wichita, Kansas
WTUK Harlan, Kentucky
WKMO Lebanon Junction, Kentucky
WFLW Monticello, Kentucky
WCBR Richmond, Kentucky
WODT New Orleans, Louisiana
WOMR Provincetown, Massachusetts
WOCQ Berlin, Maryland
WKIK La Plata, Maryland
WSMD-FM Mechanicsville, Maryland
WOLW Cadillac, Michigan
WNWN-FM Coldwater, Michigan
WOMC Detroit, Michigan
WOOD Grand Rapids, Michigan
WOLV Houghton, Michigan
WOCR Olivet, Michigan
WNWN-AM Portage, Michigan
KMAM Butler, Missouri
KMRN Cameron, Missouri
KBNN Lebanon, Missouri
KCXL Liberty, Missouri
KWWR Mexico, Missouri
KSIM Sikeston, Missouri
KRWP Stockton, Missouri
WJNS-FM Bentonia, Mississippi
WQNQ Fletcher, North Carolina
WPLW Hillsborough, North Carolina
WCBQ Oxford, North Carolina
WMPM Smithfield, North Carolina
KHND Harvey, North Dakota
KLIQ Hastings, Nebraska
WSNJ Bridgeton, New Jersey
WOBM Lakewood Township, New Jersey
WJSV Morristown, New Jersey
KCKN Roswell, New Mexico
KDSS Ely, Nevada
WBAZ Bridgehampton, New York
WITC Cazenovia, New York
WKCR-FM New York, New York
WNYC-FM New York, New York
WNYU-FM New York, New York
WJJL Niagara Falls, New York
WOLN Olean, New York
WJZR Rochester, New York
WFNP Rosendale, New York
WOKN Southport, New York
WCII Spencer, New York
WNYR Waterloo, New York
WNYV Whitehall, New York
WONB Ada, Ohio
WRMU-FM Alliance, Ohio
WOMP Bellaire, Ohio
WOHC Chillicothe, Ohio
WONE Dayton, Ohio
WNWV Elyria, Ohio
WCLV Lorain, Ohio
WOBC-FM Oberlin, Ohio
WOBL Oberlin, Ohio
WNXT Portsmouth, Ohio
WNXT-FM Portsmouth, Ohio
KGFY Stillwater, Oklahoma
KMHD Gresham, Oregon
KSZN(AM) Gresham, Oregon
KYKN Keizer, Oregon
KBNP Portland, Oregon
WOKW Curwensville, Pennsylvania
WESS East Stroudsburg, Pennsylvania
WOGL Philadelphia, Pennsylvania
WIVV Island of Vieques, Puerto Rico
WOLI Spartanburg, South Carolina
WALI Walterboro, South Carolina
WKQK Germantown, Tennessee
WNWS-FM Jackson, Tennessee
WOCV Oneida, Tennessee
WIHG Rockwood, Tennessee
KORA-FM Bryan, Texas
KTAM Bryan, Texas
KCYL Lampasas, Texas
KRFE Lubbock, Texas
WOAI San Antonio, Texas
KSUU Cedar City, Utah
WODI Brookneal, Virginia
WNVZ Norfolk, Virginia
WNVA Norton, Virginia
WVCV Orange, Virginia
WHEO Stuart, Virginia
WJJR Rutland, Vermont
KASB Bellevue, Washington
KQQQ Pullman, Washington
WOLX-FM Baraboo, Wisconsin
WORQ Green Bay, Wisconsin
WOGO Hallie, Wisconsin
WGLR Lancaster, Wisconsin
WNWC-FM Madison, Wisconsin
WORT Madison, Wisconsin
WOMT Manitowoc, Wisconsin
WOKY Milwaukee, Wisconsin
WOBT Rhinelander, Wisconsin
KUWJ Jackson, Wyoming
KMER Kemmerer, Wyoming
KUWR Laramie, Wyoming
KUWZ Rock Springs, Wyoming

News/Talk

WMBV Dixons Mills, Alabama
KIXF Baker, California
KGEO Bakersfield, California
KGBA-FM Holtville, California
KOSS Lancaster, California
KTOX Needles, California
KVEC San Luis Obispo, California
KGLN Glenwood Springs, Colorado
WILM Wilmington, Delaware
WOTS Kissimmee, Florida
WPBR Lantana, Florida
WWWE Hapeville, Georgia
KFXD Boise, Idaho
WHFH Flossmoor, Illinois
KCFN Wichita, Kansas
WFLW Monticello, Kentucky
KNGT Lake Charles, Louisiana
KKWK Cameron, Missouri
KCMO Kansas City, Missouri
KADI Springfield, Missouri
WQNQ Fletcher, North Carolina
WCBQ Oxford, North Carolina
WMPM Smithfield, North Carolina
WJSV Morristown, New Jersey
WITC Cazenovia, New York
WJJL Niagara Falls, New York
WRMU-FM Alliance, Ohio
WONW Defiance, Ohio
KGWA Enid, Oklahoma
KKBS Guymon, Oklahoma
KBNP Portland, Oregon
KPAM Troutdale, Oregon
WESS East Stroudsburg, Pennsylvania
KBFM Edinburg, Texas
KRFE Lubbock, Texas
KAMX Luling, Texas
WFNR Blacksburg, Virginia
WVBW Suffolk, Virginia
KEDO Longview, Washington
KMER Kemmerer, Wyoming

Oldies

WLDA Fort Rucker, Alabama
WJAB Huntsville, Alabama
KEZA Fayetteville, Arkansas
KSPB Pebble Beach, California
KSIZ Weed, California
WQQQ Sharon, Connecticut
WPFW Washington, District of Columbia
WXCV Homosassa Springs, Florida
WMAF Madison, Florida
WGUN Valdosta, Georgia
KMRY Cedar Rapids, Iowa
KCMR Mason City, Iowa
WQUB Quincy, Illinois
WRRG River Grove, Illinois
WKLU Brownsburg, Indiana
WCYT Lafayette Township, Indiana
WEAA Baltimore, Maryland
WKHS Worton, Maryland
WMRX-FM Beaverton, Michigan
WMPX Midland, Michigan
KASM Albany, Minnesota
KXLP Eagle Lake, Minnesota
KNUJ New Ulm, Minnesota
KOLV Olivia, Minnesota
KCHR Charleston, Missouri
KGBX-FM Nixa, Missouri
WVSD Itta Bena, Mississippi
KPRK Livingston, Montana
WUDE Bolivia, North Carolina
WERX-FM Columbia, North Carolina
WZRU Garysburg, North Carolina
WIXE Monroe, North Carolina
KFYR Bismarck, North Dakota
KLIR Columbus, Nebraska
WDVR Delaware Township, New Jersey
KFUN Las Vegas, New Mexico
WVBR-FM Ithaca, New York
WDOS Oneonta, New York
WZOZ Oneonta, New York
WALK-FM Patchogue, New York
WSFW Seneca Falls, New York
WDLA Walton, New York
WRDL Ashland, Ohio
WMBA Ambridge, Pennsylvania
WMKX Brookville, Pennsylvania
WCCS Homer City, Pennsylvania
WLSH Lansford, Pennsylvania
WMNY McKeesport, Pennsylvania
WJAS Pittsburgh, Pennsylvania
WARM Scranton, Pennsylvania
WMGH-FM Tamaqua, Pennsylvania
WYKZ Beaufort, South Carolina
WMXT Pamplico, South Carolina
WSPA-FM Spartanburg, South Carolina
WEGR Arlington, Tennessee
WWLX Lawrenceburg, Tennessee
KULL Abilene, Texas
KFYN Bonham, Texas
KJAS Jasper, Texas
KLSR-FM Memphis, Texas
WEVA Emporia, Virginia
WTSA-FM Brattleboro, Vermont
WIZN Vergennes, Vermont
KITI Chehalis-Centralia, Washington
WLKG Lake Geneva, Wisconsin
WFGH Fort Gay, West Virginia

Polish

KCAA Loma Linda, California
KZAT-FM Belle Plaine, Iowa
KSKB Brooklyn, Iowa
KMRY Cedar Rapids, Iowa
KDSN Denison, Iowa
KMAQ Maquoketa, Iowa
KLEE Ottumwa, Iowa
WLUV Loves Park, Illinois
WPNA Oak Park, Illinois
KRSL Russell, Kansas
WNBH New Bedford, Massachusetts
WHMP Northampton, Massachusetts
WBRK Pittsfield, Massachusetts
WARE Ware, Massachusetts
WIBM Jackson, Michigan
WCUP L'Anse, Michigan
WNBY Newberry, Michigan
WUPY Ontonagon, Michigan
WYGR Wyoming, Michigan
KRBT Eveleth, Minnesota
KDUZ Hutchinson, Minnesota
KLTF Little Falls, Minnesota
WNMT Nashwauk, Minnesota
KWNO Winona, Minnesota
KHND Harvey, North Dakota
WGHT Pompton Lakes, New Jersey
WCVF-FM Fredonia, New York
WKNY Kingston, New York
WXRL Lancaster, New York
WVCR-FM Loudonville, New York
WTLA North Syracuse, New York
WSGO Oswego, New York
WZIP Akron, Ohio
WKTX Cortland, Ohio
WINT Willoughby, Ohio
WKBN Youngstown, Ohio
WVAM Altoona, Pennsylvania
WMBA Ambridge, Pennsylvania
WWSM Annville-Cleona, Pennsylvania
WBVP Beaver Falls, Pennsylvania
WGPA Bethlehem, Pennsylvania

WHYL Carlisle, Pennsylvania
WBYB(FM) Eldred, Pennsylvania
WERG Erie, Pennsylvania
WMCE Erie, Pennsylvania
WEJL-FM Forest City, Pennsylvania
WMNY McKeesport, Pennsylvania
WPHB Philipsburg, Pennsylvania
WYCK Plains, Pennsylvania
WECZ Punxsutawney, Pennsylvania
WHYF(AM) Shiremanstown, Pennsylvania
WDRE Susquehanna, Pennsylvania
WMGH-FM Tamaqua, Pennsylvania
WMBS Uniontown, Pennsylvania
KYNT Yankton, South Dakota
WMTS-FM Murfreesboro, Tennessee
KWHI Brenham, Texas
KULM-FM Columbus, Texas
KNAF Fredericksburg, Texas
KANI Wharton, Texas
KYKM Yoakum, Texas
WDKM Adams, Wisconsin
WLDY Ladysmith, Wisconsin
WCCN Neillsville, Wisconsin
WVRQ Viroqua, Wisconsin
WSAU-AM Wausau, Wisconsin

Portugese

KSTN-FM Redding, California
WSAR Fall River, Massachusetts
WPHE Phoenixville, Pennsylvania

Public Affairs

KAGV Big Lake, Alaska
KNCA Burney, California
KCRH Hayward, California
KYSR Los Angeles, California
KNSQ Mount Shasta, California
KTYD Santa Barbara, California
KIMN Denver, Colorado
KJJD Windsor, Colorado
WESU Middletown, Connecticut
WILM Wilmington, Delaware
WSTW Wilmington, Delaware
WXTB Clearwater, Florida
WIRA Fort Pierce, Florida
WHKR Rockledge, Florida
WWFR Stuart, Florida
WVOP Vidalia, Georgia
KUUL East Moline, Illinois
WFXN Moline, Illinois
WVAZ Oak Park, Illinois
WSNE-FM Taunton, Massachusetts
WCCY Houghton, Michigan
KQAL Winona, Minnesota
KCMO Kansas City, Missouri
WWOL Forest City, North Carolina
WKRK Murphy, North Carolina
WHCY Blairstown, New Jersey
WBJB-FM Lincroft, New Jersey
WRPR Mahwah, New Jersey
WTOC Newton, New Jersey
WSOU South Orange, New Jersey
KNCC Elko, Nevada
KSNE-FM Las Vegas, Nevada
WBSU Brockport, New York
WDCZ Buffalo, New York
WJYE Buffalo, New York
WAQX Manlius, New York
WQXW Ossining, New York
WUMX Rome, New York
WPPB Southampton, New York
WARY Valhalla, New York
WRQN Bowling Green, Ohio
WKKY Geneva, Ohio
WFCO Lancaster, Ohio
KJSR Tulsa, Oklahoma
KSMF Ashland, Oregon
KSOR Ashland, Oregon
KQAK Bend, Oregon
KSBA Coos Bay, Oregon
KSKF Klamath Falls, Oregon
KLTW-FM Prineville, Oregon
KWPK-FM Sisters, Oregon
KWLZ-FM West Linn, Oregon
WWCH Clarion, Pennsylvania
WQLN-FM Erie, Pennsylvania
WIOQ Philadelphia, Pennsylvania
WXTU Philadelphia, Pennsylvania
WSHH Pittsburgh, Pennsylvania
WAGS Bishopville, South Carolina
WKHT Knoxville, Tennessee
KTBZ-FM Houston, Texas
KSWP Lufkin, Texas
KAMX Luling, Texas
KNTU McKinney, Texas
KKYX San Antonio, Texas
KQXT-FM San Antonio, Texas
KVEL Vernal, Utah
WMOO Derby Center, Vermont
WIKE Newport, Vermont
WJJR Rutland, Vermont
KEDO Longview, Washington
WHID Green Bay, Wisconsin
WWSP Stevens Point, Wisconsin

Reggae

WJAB Huntsville, Alabama
KSPC Claremont, California
KSBR Mission Viejo, California
KSPB Pebble Beach, California
KCSB-FM Santa Barbara, California
KSMT Breckenridge, Colorado
KRCC Colorado Springs, Colorado
KWSB-FM Gunnison, Colorado
KTCL Wheat Ridge, Colorado
WXCI Danbury, Connecticut
WIIS Key West, Florida
WFCF St. Augustine, Florida
WANM Tallahassee, Florida
WFLM White City, Florida
WCLK Atlanta, Georgia
WRAS Atlanta, Georgia
KWXX-FM Hilo, Hawaii
WNUR-FM Evanston, Illinois
WSND-FM Notre Dame, Indiana
KJHK Lawrence, Kansas
WLNZ Lansing, Michigan
KRSI Garapan-Saipan, Guam
WVSD Itta Bena, Mississippi
WNAA Greensboro, North Carolina
WVOD Manteo, North Carolina
KKCD Omaha, Nebraska
WBZC Pemberton, New Jersey
WBNY Buffalo, New York
WCVF-FM Fredonia, New York
WEOS Geneva, New York
WITR Henrietta, New York
WICB Ithaca, New York
WPNR-FM Utica, New York
WDUB Granville, Ohio
WVKO-FM Johnstown, Ohio
KEOL La Grande, Oregon
WLVR-FM Bethlehem, Pennsylvania
WJRH Easton, Pennsylvania
WRIU Kingston, Rhode Island
WSSB-FM Orangeburg, South Carolina
KAZI Austin, Texas
KTRU(FM) Houston, Texas
KTSU Houston, Texas
WWHS-FM Hampden-Sydney, Virginia
WHOV Hampton, Virginia
WCWM Williamsburg, Virginia
WIUV Castleton, Vermont
WIZN Vergennes, Vermont
KGHP Gig Harbor, Washington
WBSD Burlington, Wisconsin
WWVU-FM Morgantown, West Virginia

Religious

KHAR Anchorage, Alaska
KYMG Anchorage, Alaska
KBRW Barrow, Alaska
KBKO Kodiak, Alaska
KNOM Nome, Alaska
WKNU Brewton, Alabama
WKWL Florala, Alabama
WBFA Fort Mitchell, Alabama
WZOB Fort Payne, Alabama
WRTT-FM Huntsville, Alabama
WLJS-FM Jacksonville, Alabama
WEUP-FM Moulton, Alabama
WGOL Russellville, Alabama
WKEA-FM Scottsboro, Alabama
WTBC Tuscaloosa, Alabama
KMJI Ashdown, Arkansas
KEWI Benton, Arkansas
KLYR Clarksville, Arkansas
KAVV Benson, Arizona
KCUZ Clifton, Arizona
KFYI Phoenix, Arizona
KTKT Tucson, Arizona
KISV Bakersfield, California
KSSB Calipatria, California
KRXA Carmel Valley, California
KCNQ Kernville, California
KLBS Los Banos, California
KDUQ Ludlow, California
KSMC Moraga, California
KAAT Oakhurst, California
KWKU Pomona, California
KVML Sonora, California
KSTN Stockton, California
KSUE Susanville, California
KXPS Thousand Palms, California
KDIA Vallejo, California
KDYA Vallejo, California
KFSO-FM Visalia, California
KUBA Yuba City, California
KSJD Cortez, Colorado
KGLN Glenwood Springs, Colorado
KFKA Greeley, Colorado
KUBC Montrose, Colorado
KCRT Trinidad, Colorado
KSPK-FM Walsenburg, Colorado
KCOL Wellington, Colorado
WECS Willimantic, Connecticut
WILI Willimantic, Connecticut
WJWL Georgetown, Delaware
WYUS Milford, Delaware
WGMD Rehoboth Beach, Delaware
WSTW Wilmington, Delaware
WYBT Blountstown, Florida
WWPR Bradenton, Florida
WLQH Chiefland, Florida
WVUM Coral Gables, Florida
WHNR Cypress Gardens, Florida
WNDB Daytona Beach, Florida
WMGG Egypt Lake, Florida
WIRA Fort Pierce, Florida
WEDM(AM) Fort Walton Beach, Florida
WWRF Lake Worth, Florida
WQHL Live Oak, Florida
WPSO New Port Richey, Florida
WHIF Palatka, Florida
WIYD Palatka, Florida
WFLF-FM Parker, Florida
WCOA Pensacola, Florida
WPSL Port St. Lucie, Florida
WSDO Sanford, Florida
WSIR Winter Haven, Florida
V6AH(AM) Pohnpei, 66
WJTH Calhoun, Georgia
WCLA Claxton, Georgia
WBLJ Dalton, Georgia
WDMG Douglas, Georgia
WAEG Evans, Georgia
WMAC Macon, Georgia
WHKN Millen, Georgia
WNEA Newnan, Georgia
WTHO-FM Thomson, Georgia
WVOP Vidalia, Georgia
KCQQ Davenport, Iowa
KILR Estherville, Iowa
KNOD Harlan, Iowa
KNIA Knoxville, Iowa
KMCH Manchester, Iowa
KFJB Marshalltown, Iowa
KICD Spencer, Iowa
KXEL Waterloo, Iowa
KFXD Boise, Idaho
KVSI Montpelier, Idaho
KRPL Moscow, Idaho
KIDO Nampa, Idaho
KWIK Pocatello, Idaho
KSPT Sandpoint, Idaho
KTFI Wendell, Idaho
WRMJ Aledo, Illinois
WBGZ Alton, Illinois
WTIM Assumption, Illinois
WDWS Champaign, Illinois
KSGM Chester, Illinois
WIIT Chicago, Illinois
WDKB Dekalb, Illinois
WDQN Duquoin, Illinois
WAIK Galesburg, Illinois
WKYX-FM Golconda, Illinois
WJBM Jerseyville, Illinois
WKEI Kewanee, Illinois
WLBH Mattoon, Illinois
WMOK Metropolis, Illinois
WRAM Monmouth, Illinois

WNGY Morton, Illinois
WINI Murphysboro, Illinois
WLCE Petersburg, Illinois
WKXQ Rushville, Illinois
WJBD Salem, Illinois
WHCO Sparta, Illinois
WZSR Woodstock, Illinois
WQME Anderson, Indiana
WLPK Connersville, Indiana
WBYT Elkhart, Indiana
WFLQ French Lick, Indiana
WTRE Greensburg, Indiana
WJOB Hammond, Indiana
WXGO Madison, Indiana
WEFM Michigan City, Indiana
WTCA Plymouth, Indiana
WRIN Rensselaer, Indiana
WROI Rochester, Indiana
WZZB Seymour, Indiana
WCLS Spencer, Indiana
WCJC Van Buren, Indiana
KABI Abilene, Kansas
KSNP Burlington, Kansas
KVGB Great Bend, Kansas
KFBZ Haysville, Kansas
KHOK Hoisington, Kansas
KNNS Larned, Kansas
KLWN Lawrence, Kansas
KNGL McPherson, Kansas
KLKC Parsons, Kansas
KLEY Wellington, Kansas
WMMG Brandenburg, Kentucky
WFKN Franklin, Kentucky
WHVO Hopkinsville, Kentucky
WRNZ Lancaster, Kentucky
WKYL Lawrenceburg, Kentucky
WFTM Maysville, Kentucky
WFXY Middlesboro, Kentucky
WEKY Richmond, Kentucky
WTLO Somerset, Kentucky
WTKY Tompkinsville, Kentucky
KVVP Leesville, Louisiana
WGAO Franklin, Massachusetts
WBRK Pittsfield, Massachusetts
WCEM Cambridge, Maryland
WSRY Elkton, Maryland
WMTB-FM Emmitsburg, Maryland
WAYZ Hagerstown, Maryland
WXCY Havre De Grace, Maryland
WHGT Maugansville, Maryland
WGIN Biddeford, Maine
WHOU-FM Houlton, Maine
WZTK Alpena, Michigan
WAUS Berrien Springs, Michigan
WYBR Big Rapids, Michigan
WDBC Escanaba, Michigan
WDZZ-FM Flint, Michigan
WCSR Hillsdale, Michigan
WCCY Houghton, Michigan
WKZO Kalamazoo, Michigan
WFCX Leland, Michigan
WMIM Luna Pier, Michigan
WMPX Midland, Michigan
WOWO Niles, Michigan
WUPY Ontonagon, Michigan
WRSR Owosso, Michigan
WJML Petoskey, Michigan
KXRA Alexandria, Minnesota
KXRZ Alexandria, Minnesota
KKCQ-FM Bagley, Minnesota
KDLM Detroit Lakes, Minnesota
KBRF Fergus Falls, Minnesota
KJJK Fergus Falls, Minnesota
WLKX-FM Forest Lake, Minnesota
KKCQ Fosston, Minnesota
KLFD Litchfield, Minnesota
KLTF Little Falls, Minnesota
KEYL Long Prairie, Minnesota
KMHL Marshall, Minnesota
KDIO Ortonville, Minnesota
KLOH Pipestone, Minnesota
KAGE Winona, Minnesota
KAAN Bethany, Missouri
KCRV-AM Caruthersville, Missouri
KCXL Liberty, Missouri
KMVC Marshall, Missouri
KMEM-FM Memphis, Missouri
KJAB-FM Mexico, Missouri
KMCR Montgomery City, Missouri
KELE-FM Mountain Grove, Missouri
KBDZ Perryville, Missouri
KLID Poplar Bluff, Missouri
KMIS-AM Portageville, Missouri
KDRO Sedalia, Missouri
KWTO-AM Springfield, Missouri
KMOX St. Louis, Missouri
KLPW Union, Missouri
KTKS Versailles, Missouri
KJPW Waynesville, Missouri
WAFM Amory, Mississippi
WAMY Amory, Mississippi
WHJT Clinton, Mississippi
WTCD Indianola, Mississippi
WIQQ Leland, Mississippi
WMOX Meridian, Mississippi
WNBN Meridian, Mississippi
WRQO Monticello, Mississippi
WRJW Picayune, Mississippi
WSKK Ripley, Mississippi
KBOW Butte, Montana
KMSM-FM Butte, Montana
KXTL Butte, Montana
KMSO Missoula, Montana
KATQ Plentywood, Montana
WWNC Asheville, North Carolina
WXIT Blowing Rock, North Carolina
WSQL Brevard, North Carolina
WBAG Burlington-Graham, North Carolina
WRRZ Clinton, North Carolina
WGAI Elizabeth City, North Carolina
WBLA Elizabethtown, North Carolina
WBRM Marion, North Carolina
WHIP Mooresville, North Carolina
WECR Newland, North Carolina
WPTM Roanoke Rapids, North Carolina
WNCA Siler City, North Carolina
WTOE Spruce Pine, North Carolina
WMXF Waynesville, North Carolina
WENC Whiteville, North Carolina
WTXY Whiteville, North Carolina
KEYA Belcourt, North Dakota
KXPO Grafton, North Dakota
KNDK Langdon, North Dakota
KEYZ Williston, North Dakota
KINI Crookston, Nebraska
KRVN Lexington, Nebraska
KRFS Superior, Nebraska
WSJO Egg Harbor City, New Jersey
WRDR Freehold Township, New Jersey
WTTH Margate City, New Jersey
WTOC Newton, New Jersey
WGHT Pompton Lakes, New Jersey
WSOU South Orange, New Jersey
WNJC Vineland, New Jersey
KKTC Angel Fire, New Mexico
KARS Belen, New Mexico
KLEA Lovington, New Mexico
KLAV Las Vegas, Nevada
KSNE-FM Las Vegas, Nevada
WYSL Avon, New York
WBNR Beacon, New York
WHRW Binghamton, New York
WBRV-FM Boonville, New York
WHCL-FM Clinton, New York
WMRV Dansville, New York
WFLR Dundee, New York
WELM Elmira, New York
WGBB Freeport, New York
WMML Glens Falls, New York
WLIE Islip, New York
WKSN Jamestown, New York
WGHQ Kingston, New York
WIXT Little Falls, New York
WLVL Lockport, New York
WLLG Lowville, New York
WOR New York, New York
WGNY Newburgh, New York
WTLA North Syracuse, New York
WDOS Oneonta, New York
WEBO Owego, New York
WBLI Patchogue, New York
WQKE Plattsburgh, New York
WEOK Poughkeepsie, New York
WRUR-FM Rochester, New York
WSPQ Springville, New York
WRGR Tupper Lake, New York
WAJZ Voorheesville, New York
WDPN Alliance, Ohio
WBLL Bellefontaine, Ohio
WMNI Columbus, Ohio
WHIO Dayton, Ohio
WDFM Defiance, Ohio
WZOM Defiance, Ohio
WIRO Ironton, Ohio
WLRX Ironton, Ohio
WVKO-FM Johnstown, Ohio
WCIT(AM) Lima, Ohio
WMOA Marietta, Ohio
WTIG Massillon, Ohio
WMPO Middleport-Pomeroy, Ohio
WMVO Mount Vernon, Ohio
WMCO New Concord, Ohio
WHIZ-FM South Zanesville, Ohio
WCWA Toledo, Ohio
WSPD Toledo, Ohio
WBTC Uhrichsville, Ohio
WTUZ Uhrichsville, Ohio
KWON Bartlesville, Oklahoma
KGYN Guymon, Oklahoma
KICM Healdton, Oklahoma
KTJS Hobart, Oklahoma
KYLV Oklahoma City, Oklahoma
KZBB Poteau, Oklahoma
KHSS Athena, Oregon
KNND Cottage Grove, Oregon
KAJO Grants Pass, Oregon
KSZN(AM) Gresham, Oregon
KUIK Hillsboro, Oregon
KSLC McMinnville, Oregon
KNPT Newport, Oregon
KACI The Dalles, Oregon
KWBY Woodburn, Oregon
WAEB Allentown, Pennsylvania
WBVP Beaver Falls, Pennsylvania
WHLM Bloomsburg, Pennsylvania
WISR Butler, Pennsylvania
WIOO Carlisle, Pennsylvania
WCCL Central City, Pennsylvania
WCHA Chambersburg, Pennsylvania
WWCH Clarion, Pennsylvania
WFSE Edinboro, Pennsylvania
WVMM Grantham, Pennsylvania
WHUN Huntingdon, Pennsylvania
WDAD Indiana, Pennsylvania
WTYM Kittanning, Pennsylvania
WNPV Lansdale, Pennsylvania
WCNS Latrobe, Pennsylvania
WWKL Mechanicsburg, Pennsylvania
WJUN Mexico, Pennsylvania
WMSS Middletown, Pennsylvania
WPGR Monroeville, Pennsylvania
WGBN New Kensington, Pennsylvania
WWNW New Wilmington, Pennsylvania
WYCK Plains, Pennsylvania
WHKS Port Allegany, Pennsylvania
WPAZ Pottstown, Pennsylvania
WBZU Scranton, Pennsylvania
WICK Scranton, Pennsylvania
WUSR Scranton, Pennsylvania
WPIC Sharon, Pennsylvania
WSRU Slippery Rock, Pennsylvania
WKBI-FM St. Marys, Pennsylvania
WTRN Tyrone, Pennsylvania
WXVU Villanova, Pennsylvania
WCHE West Chester, Pennsylvania
WKZN West Hazleton, Pennsylvania
WILK Wilkes-Barre, Pennsylvania
WALO Humacao, Puerto Rico
WEXS Patillas, Puerto Rico
WKSP(AM) Block Island, Rhode Island
WJMF Smithfield, Rhode Island
WAGS Bishopville, South Carolina
WQNT Charleston, South Carolina
WGTK-FM Greenville, South Carolina
WBHC-FM Hampton, South Carolina
WKMG Newberry, South Carolina
WSPA-FM Spartanburg, South Carolina
KBFS Belle Fourche, South Dakota
KGIM-FM Redfield, South Dakota
WNAX Yankton, South Dakota
WYXI Athens, Tennessee
WMPS Bartlett, Tennessee
WJZM Clarksville, Tennessee
WYSH Clinton, Tennessee
WKRM Columbia, Tennessee
WZYX Cowan, Tennessee
WAKM Franklin, Tennessee
WMRO Gallatin, Tennessee
WMYL Halls Crossroads, Tennessee
WKTS Kingston, Tennessee
WKGN Knoxville, Tennessee
WLIV Livingston, Tennessee
WREC Memphis, Tennessee

RADIO - U.S.

WGNS Murfreesboro, Tennessee
WMGC Murfreesboro, Tennessee
WLIK Newport, Tennessee
WUAT Pikeville, Tennessee
WJTT Red Bank, Tennessee
WLIJ Shelbyville, Tennessee
WZNG Shelbyville, Tennessee
WSMT Sparta, Tennessee
WSGI Springfield, Tennessee
WCDT Winchester, Tennessee
KQIZ-FM Amarillo, Texas
KFYN Bonham, Texas
KWHI Brenham, Texas
KCTX-FM Childress, Texas
KHER Crystal City, Texas
KTDR Del Rio, Texas
KWMC Del Rio, Texas
KTSM El Paso, Texas
KCLW Hamilton, Texas
KVRP-FM Haskell, Texas
KWFB Holliday, Texas
KTBZ-FM Houston, Texas
KFTX Kingsville, Texas
KVLG La Grange, Texas
KCYL Lampasas, Texas
KSHN Liberty, Texas
KZZN Littlefield, Texas
KCKL Malakoff, Texas
KLSR-FM Memphis, Texas
KBED Nederland, Texas
KNBT New Braunfels, Texas
KEYE Perryton, Texas
KMIQ Robstown, Texas
KDCD San Angelo, Texas
KELI San Angelo, Texas
KQXT-FM San Antonio, Texas
KSTV Stephenville, Texas
KBCY Tye, Texas
KWUD Woodville, Texas
KSUB Cedar City, Utah
KVNU Logan, Utah
KWCR-FM Ogden, Utah
KXRQ Roosevelt, Utah
KHQN Spanish Fork, Utah
KDXU St. George, Utah
KVEL Vernal, Utah
WBNN-FM Dillwyn, Virginia
WFLO Farmville, Virginia
WXGM Gloucester, Virginia
WKCY Harrisonburg, Virginia
WMXH-FM Luray, Virginia
WRAA Luray, Virginia
WZZU Lynchburg, Virginia
WUKZ(AM) Marion, Virginia
WVCV Orange, Virginia
WDCE Richmond, Virginia
WRVA Richmond, Virginia
WYTI Rocky Mount, Virginia
WHEO Stuart, Virginia
WVBW Suffolk, Virginia
WVWI Charlotte Amalie, Virgin Islands
WVVI-FM Christiansted, Virgin Islands
WRMC-FM Middlebury, Vermont
KWLE Anacortes, Washington
KGTS College Place, Washington
KYSN East Wenatchee, Washington
KARY-FM Grandview, Washington
KZIZ Pacific, Washington
KRIZ Renton, Washington
KMAS Shelton, Washington
KDNA Yakima, Washington
WATW Ashland, Wisconsin
WRPQ Baraboo, Wisconsin
WCFW Chippewa Falls, Wisconsin
WTTN Columbus, Wisconsin
WJOK Kaukauna, Wisconsin
WJMT Merrill, Wisconsin
WMYX-FM Milwaukee, Wisconsin
WSSP Milwaukee, Wisconsin
WTMJ Milwaukee, Wisconsin
WPFP Park Falls, Wisconsin
WVRQ Viroqua, Wisconsin
WSAU-AM Wausau, Wisconsin
WKEZ Bluefield, West Virginia
WVWC Buckhannon, West Virginia
WVMR Frost, West Virginia
WRVC Huntington, West Virginia
WRON-FM Lewisburg, West Virginia
WEPM Martinsburg, West Virginia
WRON Ronceverte, West Virginia
WCWV Summersville, West Virginia
WELC Welch, West Virginia
WZST Westover, West Virginia
KLGT Buffalo, Wyoming
KKTY-FM Glendo, Wyoming
KASL Newcastle, Wyoming

Rock/AOR

KVHS Concord, California
KCPR San Luis Obispo, California
KGRR Epworth, Iowa
WBKE-FM North Manchester, Indiana
WWHR Bowling Green, Kentucky
WQUS Lapeer, Michigan
WTIP Grand Marais, Minnesota
WKNC-FM Raleigh, North Carolina
WLFC North Baltimore, Ohio
WNRN Charlottesville, Virginia
KGRG-FM Auburn, Washington

Russian

KTYM Inglewood, California
KNOF St. Paul, Minnesota
WDCV-FM Carlisle, Pennsylvania
KKNW Seattle, Washington
KLFE Seattle, Washington

Smooth Jazz

WMVB Millville, New Jersey
WVLY-FM Milton, Pennsylvania

Spanish

WTBB Gadsden, Alabama
WTBJ Oxford, Alabama
WRBZ Wetumpka, Alabama
KABF Little Rock, Arkansas
KXEG Phoenix, Arizona
KINO Winslow, Arizona
KAWC Yuma, Arizona
KKCY Colusa, California
KTHU Corning, California
KCHJ Delano, California
KBIF Fresno, California
KFCF Fresno, California
KKMC Gonzales, California
KEBT Lost Hills, California
KADV Modesto, California
KVON Napa, California
KFPR Redding, California
KPRZ San Marcos-Poway, California
KXBX Ukiah, California
KRZA Alamosa, Colorado
KUVO Denver, Colorado
KLFV Grand Junction, Colorado
KGRE Greeley, Colorado
WFAR Danbury, Connecticut
WYBC New Haven, Connecticut
WHUS Storrs, Connecticut
WDEL Wilmington, Delaware
WJFP Fort Pierce, Florida
WWRF Lake Worth, Florida
WHTY(AM) Riviera Beach, Florida
WTIS Tampa, Florida
WRFG Atlanta, Georgia
WTHV Hahira, Georgia
WGML Hinesville, Georgia
KCHE Cherokee, Iowa
KBGN Caldwell, Idaho
WPCD Champaign, Illinois
WMBI-AM Chicago, Illinois
WRMN Elgin, Illinois
WWHN Joliet, Illinois
WFEN Rockford, Illinois
WLYV Fort Wayne, Indiana
KVOE Emporia, Kansas
KWKR Leoti, Kansas
KBCU North Newton, Kansas
WFCR Amherst, Massachusetts
WBUR West Yarmouth, Massachusetts
WLEN Adrian, Michigan
WKAR East Lansing, Michigan
WHTC Holland, Michigan
WIBM Jackson, Michigan
WSDS Salem Township, Michigan
WPNW Zeeland, Michigan
KYCR Golden Valley, Minnesota
KCHK New Prague, Minnesota
KRFO Owatonna, Minnesota
KRRW St. James, Minnesota
KSRQ Thief River Falls, Minnesota
KAOL Carrollton, Missouri
KDMO Carthage, Missouri
KCUR-FM Kansas City, Missouri
WMFA Raeford, North Carolina
WSHA Raleigh, North Carolina
KICS Hastings, Nebraska
KJLT North Platte, Nebraska
WFDU Teaneck, New Jersey
KSVA Albuquerque, New Mexico
KCQL Aztec, New Mexico
KLMX Clayton, New Mexico
KVLC Hatch, New Mexico
KFUN Las Vegas, New Mexico
KBUY Ruidoso, New Mexico
KTNM Tucumcari, New Mexico
KKVV Las Vegas, Nevada
KUNV Las Vegas, Nevada
WCVF-FM Fredonia, New York
WFOB Fostoria, Ohio
WXKR Port Clinton, Ohio
WINT Willoughby, Ohio
KBZQ Lawton, Oklahoma
KTLR Oklahoma City, Oklahoma
KBVR Corvallis, Oregon
KAGI Grants Pass, Oregon
KOHU Hermiston, Oregon
KUIK Hillsboro, Oregon
KAGO Klamath Falls, Oregon
KBVM Portland, Oregon
KKPZ Portland, Oregon
WMCE Erie, Pennsylvania
WKJB Mayaguez, Puerto Rico
WVOZ San Juan, Puerto Rico
WKMG Newberry, South Carolina
WNFO Sun City-Hilton Head, South Carolina
WYPL Memphis, Tennessee
WNQM Nashville, Tennessee
KVLF Alpine, Texas
KVLU Beaumont, Texas
KGSR Cedar Park, Texas
KCTA Corpus Christi, Texas
KEDT-FM Corpus Christi, Texas
KDHN Dimmitt, Texas
KULP El Campo, Texas
KELP El Paso, Texas
KSHU Huntsville, Texas
KKER Kerrville, Texas
KLUX Robstown, Texas
KWRW Rusk, Texas
KEDA San Antonio, Texas
KANI Wharton, Texas
KPDR Wheeler, Texas
WWWJ Galax, Virginia
WHOV Hampton, Virginia
WBTK Richmond, Virginia
KEWU-FM Cheney, Washington
KBSN Moses Lake, Washington
KDNA Yakima, Washington
WMLJ Summersville, West Virginia
KRAE Cheyenne, Wyoming
KUGR Green River, Wyoming

Sports

KRUA Anchorage, Alaska
WMBV Dixons Mills, Alabama
WUMP Madison, Alabama
WMGY Montgomery, Alabama
WZZN Oneonta, Alabama
WZCT Scottsboro, Alabama
KYEL Danville, Arkansas
KFPW Fort Smith, Arkansas
KHOZ Harrison, Arkansas
KBCN-FM Marshall, Arkansas
KWKK Russellville, Arkansas
KDJI Holbrook, Arizona
KAAA Kingman, Arizona
KLVA Maricopa, Arizona
KKNT Phoenix, Arizona
KNOT Prescott, Arizona
KNZR Bakersfield, California
KBHR Big Bear City, California
KIBS Bishop, California
KRKC King City, California
KCAA Loma Linda, California
KLAA Orange, California
KTRB San Francisco, California
KLIV San Jose, California
KKJL San Luis Obispo, California
KVEC San Luis Obispo, California
KSLV-FM Del Norte, Colorado

KFTM Fort Morgan, Colorado
KPKE Gunnison, Colorado
KUBC Montrose, Colorado
KCOL Wellington, Colorado
WGCH Greenwich, Connecticut
WXDE Lewes, Delaware
WQXM Bartow, Florida
WWBF Bartow, Florida
WSWN Belle Glade, Florida
WVUM Coral Gables, Florida
WJSB Crestview, Florida
WNDB Daytona Beach, Florida
WDSP De Funiak Springs, Florida
WJXL Jacksonville Beach, Florida
WQHL-FM Live Oak, Florida
WEBY Milton, Florida
WFLF Pine Hills, Florida
WTBN Pinellas Park, Florida
WCTH Plantation Key, Florida
WAOC Saint Augustine, Florida
WFNS Blackshear, Georgia
WGMI Bremen, Georgia
WRBN Clayton, Georgia
WFOM Marietta, Georgia
WJAT Swainsboro, Georgia
KCPS Burlington, Iowa
KGGO Des Moines, Iowa
KICB Fort Dodge, Iowa
KLMJ Hampton, Iowa
KOKX-FM Keokuk, Iowa
KRNQ Keokuk, Iowa
KMCH Manchester, Iowa
KFJB Marshalltown, Iowa
KIHK Rock Valley, Iowa
KWDM West Des Moines, Iowa
KID Idaho Falls, Idaho
KID-FM Idaho Falls, Idaho
KTFI Wendell, Idaho
WCDD Canton, Illinois
WGN(AM) Chicago, Illinois
WXEF Effingham, Illinois
WHFH Flossmoor, Illinois
WAIK Galesburg, Illinois
WGBK Glenview, Illinois
WJBM Jerseyville, Illinois
WLTL La Grange, Illinois
WLRA Lockport, Illinois
WFXN Moline, Illinois
WGFA-FM Watseka, Illinois
WETN Wheaton, Illinois
WYKT Wilmington, Illinois
WSCH Aurora, Indiana
WBIW Bedford, Indiana
WGCS Goshen, Indiana
WJOB Hammond, Indiana
WEEM-FM Pendleton, Indiana
WFMG Richmond, Indiana
WAMW-FM Washington, Indiana
KTCC Colby, Kansas
KONQ Dodge City, Kansas
KSEK Pittsburg, Kansas
WTUK Harlan, Kentucky
WKCM Hawesville, Kentucky
WLME Lewisport, Kentucky
WCBR Richmond, Kentucky
WYSB Springfield, Kentucky
KBKK Ball, Louisiana
WDGL Baton Rouge, Louisiana
WTGE Baton Rouge, Louisiana
KMLB Monroe, Louisiana
KSYB Shreveport, Louisiana
WXRB Dudley, Massachusetts
WGFP Webster, Massachusetts
WTAG Worcester, Massachusetts
WNAV Annapolis, Maryland
WXCY Havre De Grace, Maryland
WKIK La Plata, Maryland
WALZ-FM Machias, Maine
WBPW Presque Isle, Maine
WBFH Bloomfield Hills, Michigan
WKMI Kalamazoo, Michigan
WZUU Mattawan, Michigan
WRSR Owosso, Michigan
WJML Petoskey, Michigan
KKLN Atwater, Minnesota
WBJI Blackduck, Minnesota
KXDL Browerville, Minnesota
KEYL Long Prairie, Minnesota
KCWJ Blue Springs, Missouri
KDKD-FM Clinton, Missouri
KWWR Mexico, Missouri
KBDZ Perryville, Missouri
KSIM Sikeston, Missouri
KTXR Springfield, Missouri
WMXI Laurel, Mississippi
WZLD Petal, Mississippi
WRJW Picayune, Mississippi
KFLN Baker, Montana
KMON Great Falls, Montana
WATA Boone, North Carolina
WCSL Cherryville, North Carolina
WNCC Franklin, North Carolina
WIZS Henderson, North Carolina
WGOS High Point, North Carolina
WPLW Hillsborough, North Carolina
WELS-FM Kinston, North Carolina
WRNS-FM Kinston, North Carolina
WFLB Laurinburg, North Carolina
WKGX Lenoir, North Carolina
WCBQ Oxford, North Carolina
WQDR-FM Raleigh, North Carolina
WNCA Siler City, North Carolina
WEEB Southern Pines, North Carolina
WRGC Sylva, North Carolina
WTQR Winston-Salem, North Carolina
KLXX Bismarck-Mandan, North Dakota
KDLR Devils Lake, North Dakota
KDIX Dickinson, North Dakota
KCJB Minot, North Dakota
KRRZ Minot, North Dakota
KICS Hastings, Nebraska
KGFW Kearney, Nebraska
KIOD McCook, Nebraska
KNCY Nebraska City, Nebraska
WHTG Eatontown, New Jersey
WJSV Morristown, New Jersey
WCTC New Brunswick, New Jersey
WGHT Pompton Lakes, New Jersey
WKNJ-FM Union Township, New Jersey
WMCX West Long Branch, New Jersey
KICA Clovis, New Mexico
KRSY-FM La Luz, New Mexico
KRSN Los Alamos, New Mexico
KELY Ely, Nevada
WBTA Batavia, New York
WBAZ Bridgehampton, New York
WBEN Buffalo, New York
WMRV Dansville, New York
WKCR-FM New York, New York
WEBO Owego, New York
WRUC Schenectady, New York
WHEN Syracuse, New York
WFAS White Plains, New York
WZIP Akron, Ohio
WXTQ Athens, Ohio
WCDK Cadiz, Ohio
WBVB Coal Grove, Ohio
WEOL Elyria, Ohio
WFIN Findlay, Ohio
WFCO Lancaster, Ohio
WMOA Marietta, Ohio
WKLM Millersburg, Ohio
WRGM Ontario, Ohio
WBUK Ottawa, Ohio
WPTW Piqua, Ohio
WHIZ-FM South Zanesville, Ohio
WCWA Toledo, Ohio
WFGF Wapakoneta, Ohio
KRVT Claremore, Oklahoma
KEBC Del City, Oklahoma
KOKL Okmulgee, Oklahoma
KGFF Shawnee, Oklahoma
KGFY Stillwater, Oklahoma
KGND Vinita, Oklahoma
KITO-FM Vinita, Oklahoma
KPNW Eugene, Oregon
KEX Portland, Oregon
KOHI St. Helens, Oregon
KCKX Stayton, Oregon
WRTA Altoona, Pennsylvania
WZWW Bellefonte, Pennsylvania
WFSE Edinboro, Pennsylvania
WCRO Johnstown, Pennsylvania
WFNM Lancaster, Pennsylvania
WNPV Lansdale, Pennsylvania
WBPZ Lock Haven, Pennsylvania
WMSS Middletown, Pennsylvania
WQLV Millersburg, Pennsylvania
WNTP Philadelphia, Pennsylvania
KQV Pittsburgh, Pennsylvania
WHBS Pittston, Pennsylvania
WQSU Selinsgrove, Pennsylvania
WSRU Slippery Rock, Pennsylvania
WMBS Uniontown, Pennsylvania
WWPA Williamsport, Pennsylvania
WMNT Manati, Puerto Rico
WEXS Patillas, Puerto Rico
WLEO Ponce, Puerto Rico
WCVY Coventry, Rhode Island
WDOM Providence, Rhode Island
WGVB Beaufort, South Carolina
WGTR Bucksport, South Carolina
WPCC Clinton, South Carolina
WJKB Moncks Corner, South Carolina
WSNW Seneca, South Carolina
KIMM Rapid City, South Dakota
WNAX Yankton, South Dakota
WHUB Cookeville, Tennessee
WKBQ Covington, Tennessee
WASL Dyersburg, Tennessee
WTRO Dyersburg, Tennessee
WAKM Franklin, Tennessee
WAEZ Greeneville, Tennessee
WDXI Jackson, Tennessee
WFLI Lookout Mountain, Tennessee
WMSR Manchester, Tennessee
WTNE Trenton, Tennessee
WBOZ Woodbury, Tennessee
KSKY Balch Springs, Texas
KTAM Bryan, Texas
KCAR Clarksville, Texas
KRLD Dallas, Texas
KGAF Gainesville, Texas
KSHJ Houston, Texas
KCYL Lampasas, Texas
KSFA Nacogdoches, Texas
KJAK Slaton, Texas
KTBB Troup, Texas
KVOU-FM Uvalde, Texas
KPGR Pleasant Grove, Utah
WKEX Blacksburg, Virginia
WMNA Gretna, Virginia
WRVL Lynchburg, Virginia
WMEV-FM Marion, Virginia
WYTI Rocky Mount, Virginia
WTON Staunton, Virginia
WTON-FM Staunton, Virginia
WBTN Bennington, Vermont
WVNR Poultney, Vermont
KCED Centralia, Washington
KMNT Chehalis, Washington
KCLX Colfax, Washington
KFKB Forks, Washington
KONA Kennewick-Richland-P, Washington
KFLD Pasco, Washington
KKNW Seattle, Washington
KXLY-AM Spokane, Washington
KKOV Vancouver, Washington
WBEV Beaver Dam, Wisconsin
WLKG Lake Geneva, Wisconsin
WGLR Lancaster, Wisconsin
WMAM Marinette, Wisconsin
WPVL-AM Platteville, Wisconsin
WRPN-FM Ripon, Wisconsin
WCOW-FM Sparta, Wisconsin
WWSP Stevens Point, Wisconsin
WDUX-FM Waupaca, Wisconsin
WJLS Beckley, West Virginia
WXKX Clarksburg, West Virginia
WTNJ Mount Hope, West Virginia
WGGE Parkersburg, West Virginia
WWYO Pineville, West Virginia
WMOV Ravenswood, West Virginia
KPIN Pinedale, Wyoming

Talk

KFQD Anchorage, Alaska
KTHS-FM Berryville, Arkansas
KVDW England, Arkansas
KBOK Malvern, Arkansas
KXRJ Russellville, Arkansas
KMLE Chandler, Arizona
KCUZ Clifton, Arizona
KFMA Green Valley, Arizona
KFNN Mesa, Arizona
KGME Phoenix, Arizona
KAHI Auburn, California
KJLH Compton, California
KHSR Crescent City, California
KFMI Eureka, California
KFSR Fresno, California
KCRH Hayward, California

KWTM June Lake, California
KIIS-FM Los Angeles, California
KHOT Madera, California
KFIV Modesto, California
KHOP Oakdale, California
KAZU Pacific Grove, California
KXTZ Pismo Beach, California
KTIP Porterville, California
KGGI Riverside, California
KFMB San Diego, California
KIFM San Diego, California
KLCA Tahoe City, California
KXBX Ukiah, California
KKDV Walnut Creek, California
KFTM Fort Morgan, Colorado
KCOL Wellington, Colorado
KRDZ Wray, Colorado
WGCH Greenwich, Connecticut
WJMJ Hartford, Connecticut
WINY Putnam, Connecticut
WEBE Westport, Connecticut
WPFW Washington, District of Columbia
WWPR Bradenton, Florida
WFTW Fort Walton Beach, Florida
WRNE Gulf Breeze, Florida
WHIF Palatka, Florida
WKGC Southport, Florida
WFOY St. Augustine, Florida
WFRC Columbus, Georgia
WJJC Commerce, Georgia
WWWE Hapeville, Georgia
KGUM Hagatna, Guam
KGYM Cedar Rapids, Iowa
KBLY Idaho Falls, Idaho
KIDO Nampa, Idaho
KRVB Nampa, Idaho
WSDZ Belleville, Illinois
WSSD Chicago, Illinois
WEPS Elgin, Illinois
WAIK Galesburg, Illinois
WGBK Glenview, Illinois
WWDV Zion, Illinois
WAMW-AM Washington, Indiana
KHCC-FM Hutchinson, Kansas
KIKS-FM Iola, Kansas
KHCD Salina, Kansas
KCFN Wichita, Kansas
KEYN-FM Wichita, Kansas
WTBK Manchester, Kentucky
WFLW Monticello, Kentucky
WCBR Richmond, Kentucky
WVEZ St. Matthews, Kentucky
WBRP Baker, Louisiana
KPEL-FM Breaux Bridge, Louisiana
KUMX North Fort Polk, Louisiana
WESX Nahant, Massachusetts
WFWM Frostburg, Maryland
WAMS-FM Snow Hill, Maryland
WMDR Augusta, Maine
WTBM Mexico, Maine
WXEX-FM Sanford, Maine
WDZZ-FM Flint, Michigan
WGLI Hancock, Michigan
WNMU-FM Marquette, Michigan
WLKX-FM Forest Lake, Minnesota
KFXN Minneapolis, Minnesota
KYMN-AM Northfield, Minnesota
KYMN-FM Northfield, Minnesota
KNXR Rochester, Minnesota
KNSG Springfield, Minnesota
KSWF Aurora, Missouri
KMRN Cameron, Missouri
KFRU Columbia, Missouri
KJXX Jackson, Missouri
KSIM Sikeston, Missouri
WTCD Indianola, Mississippi
WNBN Meridian, Mississippi
WUMS University, Mississippi
KXGN Glendive, Montana
WQNQ Fletcher, North Carolina
WRFX Kannapolis, North Carolina
WMPM Smithfield, North Carolina
WTAB Tabor City, North Carolina
WENC Whiteville, North Carolina
KFJM Grand Forks, North Dakota
KCJB Minot, North Dakota
KHRT Minot, North Dakota
KAWL York, Nebraska
WMOU Berlin, New Hampshire
WDER-FM Peterborough, New Hampshire
WPNH Plymouth, New Hampshire
WRNJ Hackettstown, New Jersey
WVNJ Oakland, New Jersey
KWKA Clovis, New Mexico
KBCQ Roswell, New Mexico
KMXQ Socorro, New Mexico
WUFO Amherst, New York
WCSS Amsterdam, New York
WSQX-FM Binghamton, New York
WITC Cazenovia, New York
WENT Gloversville, New York
WCKM-FM Lake George, New York
WEOK Poughkeepsie, New York
WJKE Stillwater, New York
WZIP Akron, Ohio
WPFB Middletown, Ohio
WLRY Rushville, Ohio
WOBN Westerville, Ohio
WCWS-FM Wooster, Ohio
KWOX Woodward, Oklahoma
KHPE Albany, Oregon
KWIP Dallas, Oregon
KYKN Keizer, Oregon
KGAL Lebanon, Oregon
KKPZ Portland, Oregon
KLTW-FM Prineville, Oregon
KOHI St. Helens, Oregon
KFIR Sweet Home, Oregon
KSJK Talent, Oregon
KACI The Dalles, Oregon
WBUQ Bloomsburg, Pennsylvania
WNUZ Mercersburg, Pennsylvania
WPAM Pottsville, Pennsylvania
WPIC Sharon, Pennsylvania
WMBS Uniontown, Pennsylvania
WZAR Ponce, Puerto Rico
WHHD Clearwater, South Carolina
WORG Elloree, South Carolina
WLMC Georgetown, South Carolina
WRIX-FM Honea Path, South Carolina
WPWT Colonial Heights, Tennessee
WZYX Cowan, Tennessee
WRLT Franklin, Tennessee
WQLA La Follette, Tennessee
KIXZ Amarillo, Texas
KMFA Austin, Texas
KAPN Caldwell, Texas
KNES Fairfield, Texas
KMJQ Houston, Texas
KPRC Houston, Texas
KTBZ-FM Houston, Texas
KKCL Lorenzo, Texas
KRFE Lubbock, Texas
KSWP Lufkin, Texas
KIKK Pasadena, Texas
KSTX San Antonio, Texas
KBXT Wixon Valley, Texas
KSUB Cedar City, Utah
KLGN Logan, Utah
WFLO Farmville, Virginia
WPCE Portsmouth, Virginia
WRUV Burlington, Vermont
WVPS Burlington, Vermont
WRVT Rutland, Vermont
WVPR Windsor, Vermont
KGMI Bellingham, Washington
KGNW Burien-Seattle, Washington
KELA Centralia-Chehalis, Washington
KPLZ-FM Seattle, Washington
KXLY-AM Spokane, Washington
KVTI Tacoma, Washington
WPFP Park Falls, Wisconsin
WELD-FM Moorefield, West Virginia
WWYO Pineville, West Virginia
KMER Kemmerer, Wyoming
KOVE Lander, Wyoming

Tejano

KPAN Hereford, Texas

Triple A

KBBI Homer, Alaska
KOJI Okoboji, Iowa
KWIT Sioux City, Iowa
KMUW Wichita, Kansas
WKMS-FM Murray, Kentucky
WHFC Bel Air, Maryland
WEOS Geneva, New York
WRIP Windham, New York
WEQX Manchester, Vermont

Urban Contemporary

KSWH-FM Arkadelphia, Arkansas
KSPC Claremont, California
KSCU Santa Clara, California
KSMT Breckenridge, Colorado
KCSU-FM Fort Collins, Colorado
WRGP Homestead, Florida
WRSE Elmhurst, Illinois
WVUR-FM Valparaiso, Indiana
WEAA Baltimore, Maryland
WMHB Waterville, Maine
WSGR-FM Port Huron, Michigan
WXDU Durham, North Carolina
WUAG Greensboro, North Carolina
KRNU Lincoln, Nebraska
WBUQ Bloomsburg, Pennsylvania
WCAL California, Pennsylvania
WCUC-FM Clarion, Pennsylvania
WUSR Scranton, Pennsylvania
KCFS Sioux Falls, South Dakota
WTTU Cookeville, Tennessee
KPSM Brownwood, Texas
KGLD Tyler, Texas
WIUV Castleton, Vermont
KGRG-FM Auburn, Washington
KYVT Yakima, Washington
WCCX Waukesha, Wisconsin
WSUW Whitewater, Wisconsin

Variety/Diverse

KRUA Anchorage, Alaska
KSUA Fairbanks, Alaska
WEGL Auburn, Alabama
KNOG Nogales, Arizona
KRLA Glendale, California
KGIL Johannesburg, California
KALW San Francisco, California
KGUM Hagatna, Guam
KIWR Council Bluffs, Iowa
WQNA Springfield, Illinois
KLJY Clayton, Missouri
WNND Pickerington, Ohio
KXTD Wagoner, Oklahoma
KUQL Ethan, South Dakota
KZHN Paris, Texas
KNCN Sinton, Texas

Vietnamese

KSJX San Jose, California

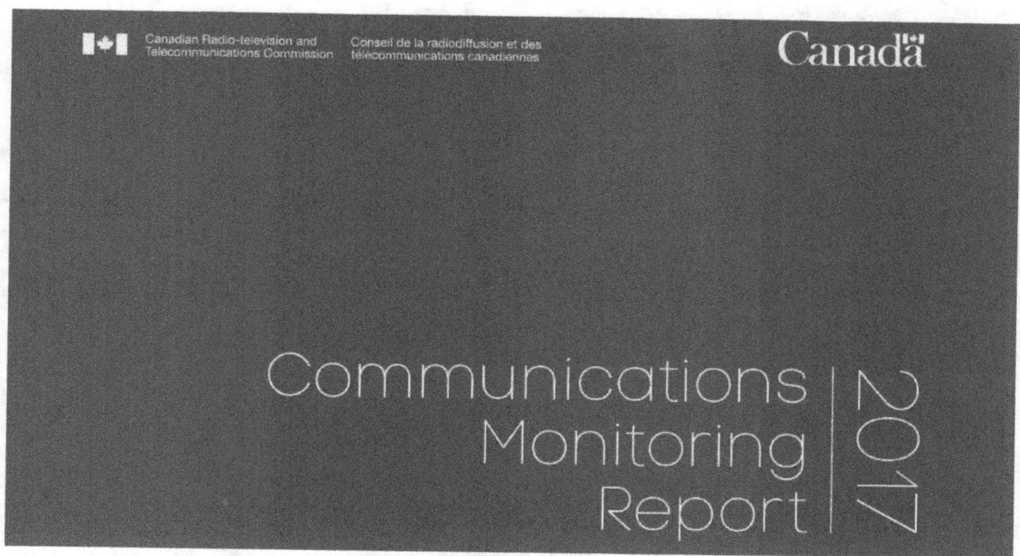

Canadians supplement their content consumption online

- **Canadians continue to use streaming music services to supplement their regular radio listening. In 2016, according to the Media Technology Monitor (MTM), 89% of Canadians 18 years of age or older listened to the radio, while 55% streamed music videos on YouTube and 22% streamed AM/FM radio online.**
- In 2016, 27% of Canadians 18 years of age and older streamed personalized music, while 20% did so in 2015, according to data from MTM.
- Again, according to MTM, in 2016, 16% of Canadians 18 years of age and older subscribed to satellite radio services. This figure is unchanged from 2015 and 2014.
- While 95% of Canadians 18 years of age or older still watched traditional TV in 2016, Internet television's popularity continues to grow, with 58% of reporting streaming Internet TV content compared to 55% in 2015, according to MTM.

Source: *Executive Summary - Canadians supplement their content consumption online*, Communications Monitoring Report 2017, Canadian Radio-television and Telecommunications Commission, https://crtc.gc.ca/eng/publications/reports/PolicyMonitoring/2017/cmr2017.pdf, p. 33. Reproduced with the permission of the Canadian Radio-television and Telecommunications Commission on behalf of Her Majesty the Queen in Right of Canada, 2017.

Table 4.1.9 Average weekly hours of radio tuned per capita by age group for all Canada

Age group	2012	2013	2014	2015	2016	Growth (%) 2015-2016
All persons 12+	16.9	16.4	16.0	15.6	14.5	-7.6
Teens 12 – 17	6.7	6.1	5.7	5.8	4.8	-18.0
18 – 24	11.2	10.8	10.6	9.7	8.7	-11.1
25 – 34	14.9	14.4	14.1	13.8	12.0	-12.6
35 – 49	18.3	18.0	17.1	16.6	15.0	-9.5
50 – 54	20.5	20.0	19.3	19.5	17.6	-9.9
55 – 64	20.0	19.3	19.2	18.5	17.9	-3.5
65 +	20.0	19.3	19.1	18.7	18.0	-3.8

Source: Numeris Radio Diary, Fall surveys, Mo-Su 5a-1a, 12+. Note: Fall 2016 Online Radio Diary (ORD) introduced.

This table shows that over the past 5 years, the average listening hours has decreased by at least 2 hours across all age groups. The average number of hours per week per capita is determined by dividing the total number of hours tuned by the population.

Source: *Table 4.1.9 Average weekly hours of radio tuned per capita by age group for all Canada*, Communications Monitoring Report 2017, Canadian Radio-television and Telecommunications Commission, https://crtc.gc.ca/eng/publications/reports/PolicyMonitoring/2017/cmr2017.pdf, p. 118. Reproduced with the permission of the Canadian Radio-television and Telecommunications Commission on behalf of Her Majesty the Queen in Right of Canada, 2017.

4.1 Radio sector
$1.8 billion

Broadcasting revenues in 2016
$17.9 billion

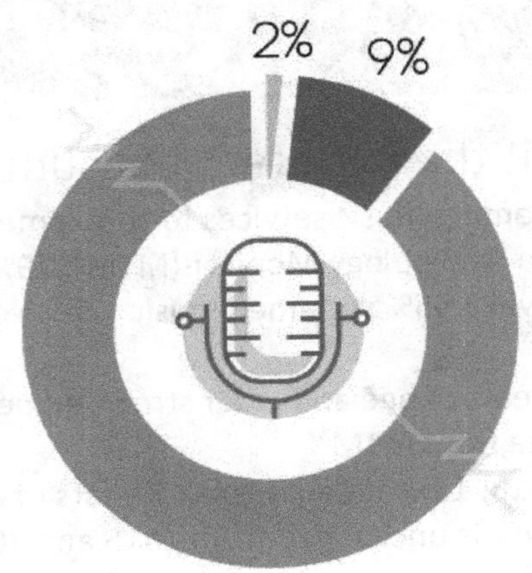

Total radio revenues

$1.8 B

Decrease of 2.0% from 2015

Listening

14.5 HRS

Canadians (12+) listen to radio each week on average

Private commercial radio revenues

$1.6 B

Decrease of 3.2% from 2015

CBC radio revenues

$0.3 B

Increase of 5.1% from 2015

Source: *4.1 Radio sector*, Communications Monitoring Report 2017, Canadian Radio-television and Telecommunications Commission, https://crtc.gc.ca/eng/publications/reports/PolicyMonitoring/2017/cmr2017.pdf, p. 99. Reproduced with the permission of the Canadian Radio-television and Telecommunications Commission on behalf of Her Majesty the Queen in Right of Canada, 2017.

Radio Group Ownership

Acadia Broadcasting Ltd.
58 King St.,3rd Floor, Saint John NB E2L 1G4
(506) 648-2100
www.acadiabroadcastinglimited.ca
info@radioabl.ca
Ownership: Black-Tip Investments Ltd., 50%; Rosa Rugosa Investments Ltd., 50%.

Attraction Radio Inc.
200-5455, avenue De Gasp,, Montr,al QC H2T 3B3
(514) 846-1228; *Fax:*(514) 846-1227
www.attractionradio.ca
info@attractionradio.ca
Ownership: Canada Inc., 55%; Investissment Quebec, 19.75%; F.T.Q., 19.13%.; Others, 6.12%.

Bayshore Broadcasting Corp.
P.O. Box 280, Owen Sound ON N4K 5P5
(519) 376-2030; *Fax:*(519) 371-4242
www.bayshorebroadcasting.ca
info@bayshorebroadcasting.ca
Ownership: C. Douglas Caldwell, 100%.

Bell Media Inc.
299 Queen St. W., Toronto ON M5V 2Z5
(416) 384-8000
www.bellmedia.ca
bellmediapr@bellmedia.ca
Ownership: Bell Canada, 100%.

Canadian Broadcasting Corporation (CBC)
205 Wellington St. W,Room 4E301-B, Toronto ON M5V 3G7
(416) 205-3700
www.cbc.ca
tonews@cbc.ca
Ownership: Government of Canada

Clear Sky Radio Inc.
220 3rd Ave. S.,Suite 400, Lethbridge AB T1J 0G9
(403) 388-2910
www.clearskyradio.com
info@clearskyradio.com
Ownership: Paul Larsen.

Corus Entertainment Inc.
Corus Quay,25 Dockside Dr., Toronto ON M5A 0B5
(416) 479-7000; *Fax:*(416) 479-7006
www.corusent.com
alka.graham@corusent.com
Ownership: JR Shaw and family; Shaw Communications, 39%.

Durham Radio Inc.
1200 Airport Blvd.,Unit 207, Oshawa ON L1J 8P5
(905) 571-0949; *Fax:*(905) 571-1150
powerofradio.ca
Ownership: Douglas Kirk, 82.61%; Mary L. Kirk, 10.85%; Others (Can.), 6.54%.

Evanov Communications Inc.
5312 Dundas St. W, Etobicoke ON M9B 1B3
(416) 213-1035; *Fax:*(416) 233-8617
www.evanovradio.com
info@evanovradio.com
Ownership: William Evanov, 74.26%; Paul Evanov, 25%; And The Bill Evanov Family Trust, 0.74%.

Golden West Broadcasting Ltd.
201-125 Centre Ave., Altona MB R0G 0B0
(204) 324-6464; *Fax:*1-(888)-765-703
www.goldenwestradio.com
help@goldenwestradio.com
Ownership: Elmer Hildebrand Ltd., 53.98%; Airwave Investments Ltd., 26.74%; and others, 19.28%.

Harvard Broadcasting Inc.
1900 Rose St., Regina SK S4P 0A9
(306) 546-6200; *Fax:*(306) 781-7338
www.harvardbroadcasting.com
gbrasil@harvardbroadcasting.com
Ownership: Paul James Hill, 90.91%; Paul James Hill Family Trust, 9.09%.

Larche Communications Inc.
355 Cranston Cres., Midland ON L4R 4L3
(705) 720-1991; *Fax:*(705) 526-3060
larchecom.com
lyoung@larche.com
Ownership: Paul Larche, 100%.

Leclerc Communication Inc.
815 Blvd. Lebourgneuf,Suite 505, Ville de Qu,bec QC G2J 0C1
(418) 688-0919; *Fax:*(418) 682-8430
www.leclerccommunication.ca
nicolas.leclerc@leclerccommunication.ca
Ownership: Jacques Leclerc, 99.7% of voting shares.

Maritime Broadcasting
90 Lovett Lake Ct., Halifax NS B3S 0H6
(902) 425-1225; *Fax:*(902) 423-2093
www.mbsradio.com
mail@mbsradio.com
Ownership: Robert L. Pace, 100%.

MY Broadcasting Corp.
Box 961, Renfrew ON K7V 4H4
(613) 432-6936; *Fax:*(877) 840-6936
www.mybroadcastingcorp.com
jeffd@mbcmedia.ca
Ownership: Andrew Dickson Family Trust, 35.05%; Jon Pole Family Trust, 35.05%; and Blackburn Radio Inc., 29.9%.

NewCap Inc.
8 Basinview Drive, Dartmouth NS B3B 1G4
(902) 468-7557; *Fax:*(902) 468-7558
www.ncc.ca
ncc@ncc.ca
Ownership: Newfoundland Capital Corporation Ltd., 100%.

Newfoundland Broadcasting Co.
446 Logy Bay Rd., St. John's NF A1C 5S2
(709) 722-5015; *Fax:*(709) 726-5107
www.ntv.ca
greetings@ntv.ca
Ownership: G. Scott Stirling, 64.99%; Gregory Stirling, 34.99%; and others, 0.02%.

Quinte Broadcasting Ltd.
10 South Front St.,Box 488, Belleville ON K8N 5B2
(613) 969-5555; *Fax:*(613) 969-8122
www.quintenews.com
billmorton@mix97.com
Ownership: Herbert M. Morton, 66.67%; Joyce Mulock, 33.33%.

Rawlco Radio Ltd.
715 Saskatchewan Cres. W, Saskatoon SK S7M 5V7
(306) 934-2222; *Fax:*(306) 477-0002
www.rawlco.com
kwerner@rawlco.com
Ownership: Gordon S. Rawlinson, 100%.

RNC MEDIA Inc.
1 Place Ville Marie, Suite 1523, Montr,al QC H3B 2B5
(514) 866-8686; *Fax:*(514) 866-8056
www.rncmedia.ca
info@rncmedia.ca
Ownership: Groupe Radio Nord Inc., 100%.

RNC Media Saguenay-Lac-St-Jean
345, Rue des Saguen,ens, Ville de Saguenay QC G7H 6K9
(418) 543-8912
www.rncmedia.ca
info@rncmedia.ca
Ownership: RNC Media Inc., 75% (See Listing); 9150-2898 Quebec inc., 25%.

Rogers Media
1 Ted Rogers Way, Toronto ON M4Y 3B7
(416) 935-8200; *Fax:*(416) 864-2002
www.rogersmedia.com
lvelazquez@impulsemediasales.com
Ownership: Rogers Media Inc., 100%. Note: Rogers Media Inc. is 100% owned by Rogers Communications Inc.

Saskatoon Media Group
366 3rd Ave. S., Saskatoon SK S7K 1M5
(306) 244-1975; *Fax:*(306) 665-8484
www.saskatoonmediagroup.com
tim@saskatoonmediagroup.com
Ownership: Elmer Hildebrand

The Jim Pattison Broadcast Group
460 Pemberton Terrace, Kamloops BC V2C 1T5
(250) 372-3322; *Fax:*(250) 374-0445
www.jpbroadcast.com
info@jpbg.ca
Ownership: James A. Pattison, 100%.

Touch Canada Broadcasting LP.
5316 Calgary Trail NW., Edmonton AB T6H 4J8
(780) 466-4930; *Fax:*(780) 469-5335
www.shinefm.com
105.9@shinefm.com
Ownership: Charles R. Allard, 100%.

Vista Radio Ltd.
201-910 Fitzgerald Ave., Courtenay BC V9N 2R5
(250) 338-1133
www.vistaradio.ca
apersaud@vistaradio.ca
Ownership: Westerkirk Capital Inc.

ZoomerMedia Ltd.
70 Jefferson Ave., Toronto ON M6K 3H4
(416) 367-5353
www.zoomermedia.ca
d.hamilton@mzmedia.com
Ownership: Olympus Management Limited, 61.77%; Fairfac Financial Holdings Limited, 16.47%; other Canadian Shareholders, 13.31%; MRHD Holdings Ltd., 8.12%; otherNon-Canadian shareholders, 0.30%; and Moses Znaimer, 0.02%.

Radio Stations in Canada

Alberta

Airdrie

CFIT-FM
04-12-2007; 106.1 MHz FM; 60 kw; 40 meters; N51 17 35 W113 59 30
105 Main St. N., Suite 30, Airdrie, AB T4B 0R3 Canada
(403) 217-1061
www.discoverairdrie.com
onair@goldenwestradio.com
License: Airdrie, AB held by Golden West Broadcasting Ltd.
Group Owner: Golden West Broadcasting Ltd.
Format: Adult Contemp; *No. News Employees:* 2; *Target Audience:* 25-54.
Ron Zuke, Station Manager
Ron Zuke, General Sales Mgr
Kevin Wallace, Programming Director

Athabasca

CKBA-FM
08-01-1989; 94.1 MHz FM; *Hrs Open:* 24; 9 kw
4902 - 49th St., Suite 1, Athabasca, AB T9S 1C2 Canada
(780) 675-5301; *Fax:* (780) 675-4938
License: Athabasca, AB held by Newcap Inc.
Group Owner: NewCap Inc.; (acq 4-19-2002; grpsl)
Nat'l Reps: Canadian Broadcast Sales; *Wire Services:* BN Wire
Population Served: 10,000; *Format:* Oldies; *No. News Employees:* 1; *Target Audience:* 25-54.; *Adv. Rates:* 33; 26; 26; 20
Dave Schuck, General Manager
Wray Betts, Station Manager
Dave Schuck, General Sales Mgr
Stuart McIntosh, Programming Director
Ron Rimer, News Director
Megan Creaser, Media Marketing Consultant
Jordan Rae, Music Director

Banff

CJXB-FM
107.9 MHz FM; 180 w; -326.4 meters; N51 11 21 W115 32 37
Box 1020, Banff, AB T1L 1H5 Canada
(403) 762-6100; *Fax:* (403) 762-6444
www.banffcentre.ca/radio
License: Banff, AB held by The Banff Centre

Blairmore

CJPR-FM
01-01-2004; 94.9 MHz FM; 760 w; N49 38 02 W114 29 30
P.O. Box 840, 13213 - 20th Ave., Blairmore, AB T0K 0E0 Canada
(403) 562-2807; *Fax:* (403) 562-8114
License: Blairmore, AB held by Newcap Inc.
Group Owner: NewCap Inc.
Population Served: 2,088; *Arbitron Metro Market:* Blairmore, AB; *Format:* Country
Barb Kelly, Station Manager
Jenn Dalen, Programming Director
Randy Spencer, News Director
Crystal Husch, Account Manager

Bonnyville

CJEG-FM
05-19-2006; 101.3 MHz FM; 27 kw
Mailing Address: P.O. Box 8251, Bonnyville, AB T9N 2J5 Canada
Second Address: 4816 50th Ave., Bonnyville, AB 29N 2J5
(780) 812-3058; *Fax:* (780) 812-3363
www.1013koolfm.com
License: Bonnyville, AB held by NewCap Inc.
Group Owner: NewCap Inc.
Population Served: 6,216; *Arbitron Metro Market:* Bonnyville, AB; *Format:* Contemporary Hits/Top 40
Lise Fielding, Station Manager
Leigh Harrison, Marketing Consultant
Morgan Lutzak, Marketing Consultant

CFNA-FM
09-28-2007; 99.7 MHz FM; 22 kw; 121.9 meters
5316 54th Ave., Suite 102, Bonnyville, AB T9N 2C9 Canada
(780) 573-1745; *Fax:* (780) 573-1746
www.mylakelandnow.com
datkinson@vistaradio.ca
License: Bonnyville, AB held by Vista Radio Ltd.
Group Owner: Vista Radio Ltd.; (acq 11-21-2008; C$7.3 million with CKLM-FM Lloydminster)
Population Served: 6,216; *Arbitron Metro Market:* Bonnyville, AB; *Format:* Country
Donnie Atkinson, General Sales Mgr
JD Anderson, Assistant Director of Programming
Chris Hunter, News
Caitlyn Thompson, Integrated Marketing Executive

Brooks

CIXF-FM
10-11-2005; 101.1 MHz FM; 2.2 kw
402 - 2nd Ave. W., Suite 8, Brooks, AB T1R 0S3 Canada
(403) 362-3418; *Fax:* (403) 362-8168
License: Brooks, AB held by Newcap Inc.
Group Owner: NewCap Inc.
Population Served: 593,820; *Format:* Adult Contemp
John Petrie, Station Manager
Jeff Murray, Programming Director

CIBQ-FM
02-16-2011; 105.7 MHz FM; 14 kw; 45.6 meters
402 - 2nd Ave. W., Suite 8, Brooks, AB T1R 0S3 Canada
(403) 362-3418; *Fax:* (403) 362-8168
License: Brooks, AB held by Newcap Inc.
Group Owner: NewCap Inc.
Format: Country
John Petrie, Station Manager
Jenn Dalen, Programming Director

Calgary

CFAC
05-02-1922; 960 kHz AM; *Hrs Open:* 24; 50,000 w; 400 metres
535-7th Ave. SW, Calgary, AB T2P 0Y4 Canada
(416) 935-8200
www.sportsnet.ca
diane.farrell@rci.rogers.com
License: Calgary, AB held by Rogers Media Inc.
Group Owner: Rogers Media Inc.; (acq 12-89)
Format: Sports; *Special Programming:* Agriculture, rural 10 hrs wkly; *Hrs. of News Programming:* news progmg 15 hrs wkly; *No. News Employees:* 3; *Target Audience:* 55 plus.
Kelly Kirch, Programming Director
Leon Tansey, Account Manager

CFFR
01-10-1984; 660 kHz AM; *Hrs Open:* 24; 50,000 w
535 7th Ave. S.W., Calgary, AB T2P 0Y4 Canada
(403) 291-0000
www.660news.com
kevin.usselman@rci.rogers.com
License: Calgary, AB held by Rogers Media Inc.
Group Owner: Rogers Media Inc.; (acq 9-10-99; grpsl).
Format: News; *Special Programming:* Sports 15 hrs wkly; *Hrs. of News Programming:* news progmg 10 hrs wkly; *No. News Employees:* 5; *Target Audience:* 25-49.
Brad Hugel, Retail Sales Manager
Kevin Usselman, News Director
Tanya Blakney, Anchor & Producer

***CHFM-FM**
95.9 MHz FM; *Hrs Open:* 24; 48 kw; 160 meters
535 7th Ave. S.W., Calgary, AB T2P 0Y4 Canada
(403) 246-9696
www.kiss959.com
heike.joshi@rci.rogers.com
License: Calgary, AB held by Rogers Media Inc.
Group Owner: Rogers Media Inc.
Nat'l Reps: Canadian Broadcast Sales
Format: Adult Contemp, Contemporary Hits/Top 40; *No. News Employees:* 1; *Target Audience:* 35-54; females
Angela Reimer, Regional Sales Director
Gayle Zarbatany, Programming Director
Heike Joshi, Sales Associate

CHKF-FM
11-14-1998; 94.7 MHz FM; *Hrs Open:* 24; 53 kw
2723-37 Ave. N.E. #109, Calgary, AB T1Y 5R8 Canada
(403) 717-1940; *Fax:* (403) 717-1945
www.fm947.com
License: Calgary, Calgary County, AB held by Fairchild Radio (Calgary FM) Ltd.
Population Served: 150,000; *Format:* Ethnic; *Hrs. of News Programming:* news progmg 21 hrs wkly; *No. News Employees:* 2; *Target Audience:* General.
Christine Leung, General Manager
Terry Chan, Programming Director

CHQR
08-15-1964; 770 kHz AM; *Hrs Open:* 24; 50 kw
3320 17th Ave. S.W., Suite 200, Calgary, AB T3E 0B4 Canada
(403) 716-6500
www.newstalk770.com
steve.heintz@corusent.com
License: Calgary, AB held by CKIK-FM Ltd.
Group Owner: Corus Entertainment Inc.; (Acq 4-15-70)
Nat'l Reps: Canadian Broadcast Sales; Dora-Clayton
TV Affiliate: CICT-TV affil; *Format:* News, News/Talk, Talk; *Hrs. of News Programming:* news progmg 17 hrs wkly; *No. News Employees:* 11; *Target Audience:* 35 plus.
Steve Heintz, General Sales Mgr
John Vos, Talk & Talent Director
Nikki Harris, Promotions & New Media Manager
Chris Bassett, News Director
Whitney Deane, The Morning News Producer
Joe McFarland, News Manager

***CJAQ-FM**
96.9 MHz FM; *Hrs Open:* 24; 48 kw; 160 meters
535 7th Ave. S.W., Calgary, AB T2P 0Y4 Canada
(403) 250-9797
www.jack969.ca
heike.joshi@rci.rogers.com
License: Calgary, AB held by Rogers Media Inc.
Group Owner: Rogers Media Inc.; (acq 9-10-99; grpsl).
Format: Contemporary Hits/Top 40; *Hrs. of News Programming:* news progmg 6 hrs wkly; *No. News Employees:* 4; *Target Audience:* 25-54.
Angela Reimer, Regional Sales Director
Heike Joshi, Sales Associate

CJAY-FM
06-01-1977; 92.1 MHz FM; *Hrs Open:* 24; 100 kw
1110 Centre St. NE., Suite 300, Calgary, AB T2E 2R2 Canada
(403) 240-5800
www.cjay92.com
stewart.meyers@bellmedia.ca
License: Calgary, AB held by Bell Media Radio G.P.
Group Owner: Bell Media Inc.
Format: Rock/AOR
Stewart Meyers, General Manager
Hilary Whyte, General Sales Mgr
Stewart Meyers, Programming Director
Jason Almeida, Promotions Manager
J Terrence, Music Director

CJSI-FM
12-01-1997; 88.9 MHz FM; 100 kw; Ant 979 ft; N51 03 54 W114 12 47
4510 Macleod Trail S., Calgary, AB T2G 0A4 Canada
(403) 276-1111; *Fax:* (403) 276-1114
www.cjsi.ca
105.9@shinefm.com
License: Calgary, AB held by Touch Canada Broadcasting LP.
Group Owner: Touch Canada Broadcasting LP.
Nat'l Reps: Target Broadcast Sales
Format: Christian; *Target Audience:* a25-54; *Adv. Rates:* 45; 45; 45; 45
Mark Imbach, General Manager
Mike Kelly, Programming Director

***CJSW-FM**
01-15-1985; 90.9 MHz FM; *Hrs Open:* 24; 4 kw
Rm. 312- MacEwan Hall, University Dr. N.W., Calgary, AB Canada
(403) 220-3904; *Fax:* (403) 289-8212
www.cjsw.com
License: Calgary, AB held by The University of Calgary Student Radio Society.
Population Served: 1,000,000; *Special Programming:* Fr one hr, Ger 2 hrs, It one, Sp one hr wkly; *Hrs. of News Programming:* News progmg 5 hrs wkly; *Target Audience:* General; young, trendy & well-heeled
Myke Atkinson, General Manager

CFGQ-FM
04-15-1982; 107.3 MHz FM; 100 kw; N51 03 54 W114 12 47
3320 17th Ave. S.W., Suite 200, Calgary, AB T3E 0B4 Canada
(403) 716-6500; *Fax:* (403) 444-4319
www.q107fm.ca
doug.young@corusent.com
License: Calgary, AB held by CKIK-FM Ltd.
Group Owner: Corus Entertainment Inc.; (acq 7-6-2000; grpsl).
Population Served: 760,000; *Format:* Classic Rock; *Target Audience:* 25-44
Doug Young, Sales Director
Phil Kallsen, Programming Director
Katelyn MacIntyre, Promotions Coordinator

CKMX
05-18-1922; 1060 kHz AM; *Hrs Open:* 24; 50 kw
1110 Centre St. NE., Calgary, AB T2E 2R2 Canada

(403) 240-5800
www.funny1060.com
stewart.meyers@bellmedia.ca
License: Calgary, AB held by Bell Media Radio G.P.
Group Owner: Bell Media Inc.; (acq 10-29-2007; grpsl).
Format: Comedy; *No. News Employees:* 1
Stewart Meyers, General Manager
Hilary Whyte, General Sales Mgr
Stewart Meyers, Programming Director
Jason Almeida, Promotions Manager
J Terrence, Assistant Program Director

***CKRY-FM**
07-09-1982; 105.1 MHz FM; *Hrs Open:* 24; 100 kw
3320 17th Ave. S.W., Suite 200, Calgary, AB T3E 0B4 Canada
(403) 716-6500; *Fax:* (403) 444-4240
www.country105.com
doug.young@corusent.com
License: Calgary, AB held by Corus Radio Co.
Group Owner: Corus Entertainment Inc.
Nat'l Reps: Canadian Broadcast Sales
Format: Country; *Hrs. of News Programming:* news progmg 7 hrs wkly; *No. News Employees:* 6; *Target Audience:* 25-54.
Doug Young, Sales Director
Phil Kallsen, Programming Director
Megan Loomer, Promotions Manager
Scott Phillips, Music Director

***CBRFFM**
01-01-2002; 103.9 MHz FM; kw*Rebroadcasts:* Rebroadcasts CHFA(AM) Edmonton 100%
Mailing Address: Canada
Second Address: 1724 Westmount Blvd. N.W., Calgary, AB T2N 3G7
(866) 306-4636; *Fax:* (780) 468-7849
radio-canada.ca/regions/alberta/index.shtml
License: Calgary, AB held by Canadian Broadcasting Corp.
Nat'l Network: Premiere Chaine
Arbitron Metro Market: Calgary, AB; *Format:* French, News, Talk
Francois Pageau, General Manager

CFXL-FM
08-30-2002; 103.1 MHz FM; 100 kw; Ant 482 ft; N51 03 54 W114 12 51
1110 Centre St. N.E., Suite 100, Calgary, AB T2E 2R2 Canada
(403) 271-6366; *Fax:* (403) 278-6772
www.xl103.ca
feedback@xl103calgary.com
License: Calgary, AB held by Newcap Inc.
Group Owner: NewCap Inc.; (acq 4-19-2002; grpsl)
Wire Services: BN Wire
Population Served: 900,000; *Format:* Oldies; *Hrs. of News Programming:* news progmg 35 hrs wkly; *No. News Employees:* 1; *Target Audience:* 35-54.; *Adv. Rates:* 114; 131; 114; 35
Vinka Dubroja, General Manager

CIBK-FM
09-06-2002; 98.5 MHz FM; 100 kw
1110 Centre St. NE., Suite 300, Calgary, AB T2E 2R2 Canada
(403) 240-5800
www.calgary.virginradio.ca
stewart.meyers@bellmedia.ca
License: Calgary, AB held by Bell Media Radio G.P.
Group Owner: Bell Media Inc.; (acq 10-29-2007; grpsl)
Population Served: 1,096,833; *Arbitron Metro Market:* Calgary, AB; *Format:* Contemporary Hits/Top 40
Stewart Meyers, General Manager
Hilary Whyte, General Sales Mgr
Chad Martin, Programming Director
Jason Almeida, Promotions Manager
Bill Stovold, Engineering Dir
Tyler Hall, Music Director

CFEX-FM
01-01-2007; 92.9 MHz FM; *Hrs Open:* 24; 100 kw
255 17th Ave. S.W., Suite 400, Calgary, AB T2S 2T8 Canada
(403) 670-0210; *Fax:* (403) 212-1399
www.x929.ca
License: Calgary, AB held by Harvard Broadcasting Inc.
Group Owner: Harvard Broadcasting Inc.
Population Served: 1,096,833; *Arbitron Metro Market:* Calgary, AB; *Format:* Alternative
Christian Hall, Operations Manager
Cam Cowie, General Manager
Gary Brasil, General Sales Mgr
Christian Hall, Programming Director
Katie Gerula, Promotions Coordinator
Ginette Ouimet, Marketing Director and Assistant ProgramDirector
Darren Ollinger, Creative Director
Chris McCloy, Production Director
Chad Armstrong, Retail Sales Manager

Bonnie Day, Manager of Interactive
Jenna Ephgrave, Traffic Manager

CKMP-FM
03-19-2007; 90.3 MHz FM; 100 kw; N51 03 37 W114 10 13
1110 Centre St. N.E., Suite 100, Calgary, AB T2E 2R2 Canada
(403) 271-6366; *Fax:* (403) 278-6772
www.ampcalgary.com
License: Calgary, AB held by Newcap Inc.
Group Owner: NewCap Inc.
Population Served: 1,096,833; *Arbitron Metro Market:* Calgary, AB; *Format:* Contemporary Hits/Top 40
Vinka Dubroja, General Manager
Steve Kennedy, Programming Director

CKCE-FM
03-22-2007; 101.5 MHz FM; 48 kw; N51 03 37 W114 10 13
222 58th Ave. S.W., Suite 600, Calgary, AB T2H 2S3 Canada
(403) 508-2222; *Fax:* (403) 508-2224
1015kool.fm
License: Calgary, AB held by 8384835 Canada Inc.
Group Owner: The Jim Pattison Broadcast Group; (acq 6-22-2007; grpsl)
Format: Adult Contemp
Eric Stafford, General Manager
Harold Spicer, General Sales Mgr
Mike Shannon, Programming Director
Christy Hennessy, Promotions Coordinator
Zack Hewitt, Music Director

CKAV-FM-3
88.1 MHz FM; 33 kw; Ant 1,040 ft; N51 03 54 W114 12 47
PO Box 87, Station E, Toronto, ON M6H 4E1 Canada
(416) 703-1287; *Fax:* (416) 703-4328
aboriginalvoices.com
info@aboriginalvoices.com
License: Calgary, AB held by Voices Radio's broadcasting licenses have been revoked by the CRTC. All stations are now broadcasting solely on voicesradio.ca
Group Owner: Voices Radio Inc.
Population Served: 2,615,060; *Arbitron Metro Market:* Toronto, ON; *Format:* Ethnic
Roy Hennessy, Operations Dir
Patrice Mousseau, Programming Director

CHUP-FM
03-06-2008; 97.7 MHz FM; 100 kw; N51 04 24 W114 15 38
#110 - 6807 Railway St. S.E., Calgary, AB T2H 2V6 Canada
(403) 385-4000
www.softrock977.com
License: Calgary, AB held by Rawlco Radio Ltd.
Group Owner: Rawlco Radio Ltd.
Nat'l Reps: Canadian Broadcast Sales
Format: Adult Contemp; *No. News Employees:* 27
Kent Newson, Operations Dir
Glenn Ruskin, Sales Manager
Kent Newson, Programming Director
Marianne Vibert, Promotions Manager

CHPK-FM
04-25-2014; 95.3 MHz FM; 30 kw; 272.9 meters; N51 03 37 W114 10 17
222 58th Ave. S.W., Suite 600, Calgary, AB T2H 2S3 Canada
(403) 536-3866
License: Calgary, AB held by Jim Pattison Broadcast Group Ltd. (the general partner) and Jim Pattison Industries Ltd. (the limited partner), carrying on business as Jim Pattison Broadcast Group L.P.
Group Owner: The Jim Pattison Broadcast Group
Format: Adult Contemp, Alternative
Eric Stafford, General Manager
Kath Thompson, Programming Director

CKYR-FM
106.7 MHz FM; 1.1 kw; 236 meters; N51 04 21 W114 15 38
420-4774 Westwinds Drive NE, Calgary, AB T3J 0L7 Canada
(403) 286-1010; *Fax:* (403) 286-1066
info@redfm.ca
License: Calgary, AB held by Multicultural Broadcasting Corp. Inc.

CJLI
700 kHz AM; *Hrs Open:* 24; 50 kw-D, 20 kw-N
4510 MacLeod Trail S., Calgary, AB T2G 0A4 Canada
(403) 276-1111; *Fax:* (403) 276-1114
www.am700thelight.com
am700@shinefm.com
License: Calgary, AB held by Touch Canada Broadcasting LP.
Group Owner: Touch Canada Broadcasting LP.
Format: Christian
Stan Schmidt, Station Manager

Camrose

CFCW
11-02-1954; 840 kHz AM; *Hrs Open:* 24; 50 kw-U, DA-2; N52 57 37 W112 57 33
5708-48 Ave., Camrose, AB T4V 0K1 Canada
(780) 672-8255; *Fax:* (780) 435-0844
www.cfcw.com
License: Camrose, AB held by Newcap Inc.
Group Owner: NewCap Inc.
Nat'l Reps: imsradio
Population Served: 900,000; *Format:* Country; *Special Programming:* Farm 5 hrs wkly; *Hrs. of News Programming:* News progmg 11 hrs wkly; *Target Audience:* 25-54; country music, sports & hockey listeners in Edmonton rgn
Neil Cunningham, General Manager
Kelly Walter, General Sales Mgr
Jackie Rae Greening, Programming Director
Dean Thorpe, News Director
Rebecca Jayne, Promotions and Marketing
Marisa Jodoin, Promotions and Marketing
Brent Shelton,Promotions and Marketing
Leo Pilon, Retail Sales Manager

CFCW-FM
09-30-2005; 98.1 MHz FM; 50 kw
5708 48th Ave., Camrose, AB T4V 0K1 Canada
(780) 672-8255; *Fax:* (780) 672-4678
www.981camfm.com
License: Camrose, AB held by Newcap Inc.
Group Owner: NewCap Inc.
Wire Services: BN Wire
Format: Adult Contemp, Oldies
Kelly Walter, General Sales Mgr
John Roberts, Programming Director
Leo Pilon, Sales

Canmore

CHMN-FM
106.5 MHz FM; 510 w; -467.6 meters
749 Railway Ave., Canmore, AB T1W 1P2 Canada
(403) 678-2222; *Fax:* (403) 678-6844
www.mountainfm.ca
License: Canmore, AB held by Rogers Media Inc.
Group Owner: Rogers Media Inc.
Nat'l Reps: Canadian Broadcast Sales
Format: Adult Contemp
Brad Hugel, Retail Sales Manager
Kyle Fournier, Promotions Coordinator
Gord Elser, Account Manager

Cold Lake

CJXK-FM
09-03-2004; 95.3 MHz FM; 100 kw; N54 17 26 W110 28 57
B-5412 55th St., Cold Lake, AB T9M 1R5 Canada
(780) 594-2459; *Fax:* (780) 594-3001
www.953krock.com
requests@k-rock953.com
License: Cold Lake, AB held by Newcap Inc.
Group Owner: NewCap Inc.
Population Served: 13,839; *Arbitron Metro Market:* Cold Lake, AB; *Format:* Classic Rock
Chad Tabish, General Manager
Kelli Wispinski, Station Manager
Kelli Wispinski, Sales
Kurt Price, Programming Director
Chris Gill, Marketing Consultant
Leigh Harrison, Marketing Consultant
Morgan Lutzak, Marketing Consultant

Drayton Valley

CIBW-FM
01-01-1994; 92.9 MHz FM; *Hrs Open:* 24; 50 kw
P.O. Bag 929, 5164-52 Ave., Drayton Valley, AB T7A 1V3 Canada
(780) 542-9290; *Fax:* (780) 542-9319
www.bigwestcountry.ca
License: Drayton Valley, Brazeau County, AB held by Jim Pattison Broadcast Group Ltd. (the general partner) and Jim Pattison Industries Ltd. (the limited partner) carrying on business as Jim Pattison Broadcast Group L.P.
Group Owner: The Jim Pattison Broadcast Group; (acq 9-7-95).
Nat'l Reps: Canadian Broadcast Sales; Target Broadcast Sales;
Wire Services: BN Wire
Population Served: 100,000; *Format:* Country; *Hrs. of News Programming:* news progmg 16 hrs wkly; *No. News Employees:* 1; *Target Audience:* General.; *Adv. Rates:* 32; 29; 29; 20

Paul Mason, General Manager
Cassandra Jodoin, News Director
Trevor Stoyko, Music Director

Drumheller

CKDQ

01-01-1958; 910 kHz AM; *Hrs Open:* 24
Mailing Address: P.O. Box 1480, Drumheller, AB T0J 0Y0 Canada
Second Address: 515 Hwy. 10 E., Drumheller, AB T0J 0Y0
(403) 823-3384; *Fax:* (403) 823-7241
www.q91country.com
q91@newcap.ca
License: Drumheller, AB held by Newcap Inc.
Group Owner: NewCap Inc.; (acq 4-19-2002; grpsl)
Nat'l Reps: CBS Radio
Format: Country; *Special Programming:* Farm 8 hrs, relg 2 hrs wkly; *Hrs. of News Programming:* news progmg 11 hrs wkly; *No. News Employees:* 2; *Target Audience:* 25-54.
Al Lucas, Station Manager
Jenn Dalen, Programming Director
Al Redel, News Director

CHOO-FM

04-28-2009; 99.5 MHz FM; 3.6 kw
105 South Railway Ave., Drumheller, AB T0J 0Y6 Canada
(403) 823-9936
www.drumhelleronline.com
License: Drumheller, AB held by Golden West Broadcasting Ltd.
Group Owner: Golden West Broadcasting Ltd.
Format: Adult Contemp
Ryan Semchuk, Station Manager
Ryan Semchuk, General Sales Mgr

Edmonton

CFBR-FM

04-25-1951; 100.3 MHz FM; 100 kw; 482 ft
18520 Stony Plain Rd., Suite 100, Edmonton, AB T5S 2E2 Canada
(780) 486-2800
www.thebearrocks.com
License: Edmonton, AB held by Bell Media Radio G.P.
Group Owner: Bell Media Inc.
Format: Rock/AOR
Susan Reade, General Sales Mgr
Rob Vavrek, Programming Director
Lisa Dickau, Promotions Director

CFMG-FM

08-29-1994; 104.9 MHz FM; *Hrs Open:* 24; 100 kw
18520 Stony Plain Rd., Suite 100, Edmonton, AB T5S 2E2 Canada
(780) 486-2800
www.edmonton.virginradio.ca
License: Edmonton, AB held by Bell Media Radio G.P.
Group Owner: Bell Media Inc.; (acq 10-29-2007; grpsl).
Population Served: 870,000; *Format:* Contemporary Hits/Top 40; *Hrs. of News Programming:* news progmg 4 hrs wkly; *No. News Employees:* 2; *Target Audience:* 25-54; middle to upper income families
Rob Vavrek, Operations Manager
Susan Reade, General Sales Mgr
Mindy Baviello, Promotions Director

CFRN

04-17-1927; 1260 kHz AM; 50 kw
18520 Stony Plain Rd., Edmonton, AB T5S 2E2 Canada
(780) 486-2800
www.tsn.ca/radio/edmonton-1260
License: Edmonton, AB held by Bell Media Radio G.P.
Group Owner: Bell Media Inc.; (acq 10-29-2007; grpsl).
Format: Sports; *Target Audience:* 45 plus.
Susan Reade, General Sales Mgr
Rob Vavrek, Programming Director

CHED

03-03-1954; 630 kHz AM; 50 kw
5204 84th St., Edmonton, AB T6E 5N8 Canada
(780) 440-6300
globalnews.ca/pages/contact-630ched
gisele.sowa@corusent.com
License: Edmonton, AB held by Corus Premium Television Ltd.
Group Owner: Corus Entertainment Inc.; (acq 7-6-00; grpsl).
Format: News, News/Talk, Sports, Talk
Gisele Sowa, General Sales Mgr
Syd Smith, Programming Director
Shaun Tomko, Promotions & New Media Manager
Bob Layton, News Manager
Bryan Hall, Sports Director
Kirby Bourne, Digital Content Coordinator
Alexandra Schwanke,Promotions Coordinator

CHQT

08-19-1965; 880 kHz AM
5204 84th St., Edmonton, AB T6E 5N8 Canada
(780) 440-6300
www.inews880.com
gisele.sowa@corusent.com
License: Edmonton, AB held by Corus Radio Co.
Group Owner: Corus Entertainment Inc.
Format: News
Gisele Sowa, General Sales Mgr
Syd Smith, Programming Director
Shaun Tomko, Promotions & New Media Manager
Bob Layton, News Manager
Alexandra Schwanke, Promotions Coordinator
Kirby Bourne, Digital Content Coordinator

CIRK-FM

01-01-1949; 97.3 MHz FM; 100 kw
2394 West Edmonton Mall, 8882 - 170th St., Edmonton, AB T5T 4M2 Canada
(780) 437-4996; *Fax:* (780) 435-0844
www.k97.fm
License: Edmonton, AB held by NewCap Inc.
Group Owner: NewCap Inc.; (acq 2-17-99; C$10 million)
Nat'l Reps: imsradio
Format: Classic Rock; *Target Audience:* 18-54; mobile adults
Neil Cunningham, General Manager
Kelly Walter, General Sales Mgr
John Roberts, Programming Director
Brent Shelton, Promotions Manager
Doug McCulloch, Retail Sales Manager

CISN-FM

06-05-1982; 103.9 MHz FM; 98 kw; 657 ft
5204 84th St., Edmonton, AB T6E 5N8 Canada
(780) 440-6300; *Fax:* (780) 469-5937
www.cisnfm.com
gisele.sowa@corusent.com
License: Edmonton, AB held by Corus Radio Co.
Group Owner: Corus Entertainment Inc.; (acq 7-6-00; grpsl).
Format: Country
Gisele Sowa, General Sales Mgr
Greg Johnson, Brand Director
Shaun Tomko, Promotions & New Media Manager
Chelsey Jensen, Digital Content Coordinator
Steph Hansen, Music Director
Alexandra Schwanke, Promotions Coordinator

CJCA

05-22-1922; 930 kHz AM; *Hrs Open:* 24; 50 kw; N53 23 00 W113 28 35
5316 Calgary Trail NW., Edmonton, AB T6H 4J8 Canada
(780) 466-4930; *Fax:* (780) 469-5335
www.am930thelight.com
License: Edmonton, AB held by Touch Canada Broadcasting LP.
Group Owner: Touch Canada Broadcasting LP.; (acq 4-12-94).
Format: Christian; *Hrs. of News Programming:* News progmg 6 hrs wkly; *Target Audience:* 25-54.
Stan Schmidt, Station Manager
Johnny Rocket, Programming Director
Len Dehek, Disc Jockey

*CJSR-FM

01-01-1984; 88.5 MHz FM; *Hrs Open:* 24; 900 w
Room 0-09, Students' Union Bldg., Edmonton, AB T6G 2J7 Canada
(780) 492-2577; *Fax:* (780) 492-3121
www.cjsrfm88.blogspot.com
admin@cjsr.com
License: Edmonton, Canada County, AB held by The First Alberta Campus Radio Association.
Population Served: 1,500,000; *Format:* Alternative; *Special Programming:* American Indian 2 hrs, Black 7 hrs, class 2 hrs, f; *Hrs. of News Programming:* 8 hrs wkly; *No. News Employees:* 1; *Target Audience:* Anyonetired with commercial radio; *Adv. Rates:* contact website www.cjsr.com
Chad Brunet, Music Director
Sarah Edwards, Station Manager
Mark Rogers, Programming Director
Sam Power, News Director

CKER-FM

11-01-1980; 101.7 MHz FM; *Hrs Open:* 24; 100 kw
5915 Gateway Blvd., Edmonton, AB T6H 2H3 Canada
(780) 423-2005; *Fax:* (780) 437-5129
www.worldfm.ca
shelley.ruis@rci.rogers.com
License: Edmonton, AB held by Rogers Media Inc.
Group Owner: Rogers Media Inc.; (acq 11-29-2006; grpsl)
Format: Ethnic; *Special Programming:* It 3 hrs, Sp 8 hrs, Por 2 hrs, Ukrainian 10 hrs, D; *Hrs. of News Programming:* news progmg 14 hrs wkly; *No. News Employees:* 2; *Target Audience:* General; ethnic audience (24languages) & Christian
Shelley Ruis, General Sales Mgr
Roman Brytan, Programming Director
Antonio Sorgiovanni, Promotions Coordinator

CKNG-FM

08-11-1982; 92.5 MHz FM; 100 kw
5204-84th St., Edmonton, AB T6E 5N8 Canada
(780) 440-6300; *Fax:* (780) 469-5937
www.925freshradio.ca
gisele.sowa@corusent.com
License: Edmonton, AB held by Corus Premium Television Ltd.
Group Owner: Corus Entertainment Inc.
Format: Adult Contemp
Gisele Sowa, General Sales Mgr
Greg Johnson, Brand Director
Shaun Tomko, Promotions & New Media Manager
Paul O'Neill, Music Director
Alexandra Schwanke, Promotions Coordinator
Chelsey Jensen, Digital Content Coordinator

CKRA-FM

11-15-1979; 96.3 MHz FM; *Hrs Open:* 24; 100 kw; Ant 757 ft
2394 West Edmonton Mall, 8882 170th St., Edmonton, AB T5T 4M2 Canada
(780) 437-4996; *Fax:* (780) 435-0844
www.963capitalfm.com
License: Edmonton, AB held by NewCap Inc.
Group Owner: NewCap Inc.
Nat'l Reps: imsradio
Population Served: 800,000; *Format:* Oldies; *Target Audience:* 25-54; urban young adults
Neil Cunningham, General Manager
Kelly Walter, General Sales Mgr
John Roberts, Programming Director
Brent Shelton, Promotions Manager
Doug McCulloch, Retail Sales Manager

*CKUA-FM

06-28-1948; 94.9 MHz FM; *Hrs Open:* 24 hrs; 100 kw; 400 ft
10526 Jasper Ave., 4th Fl., Edmonton, AB T5J 1Z7 Canada
(780) 428-7595; *Fax:* (780) 428-7624
www.ckua.com
radio@ckua.com
License: Edmonton, AB held by CKUA Radio Foundation.
Population Served: 3,000,000; *Format:* Jazz, Variety/Diverse; *Hrs. of News Programming:* news progmg 6 hrs wkly; *No. News Employees:* 4; *Target Audience:* General; Alberta population; *Adv. Rates:* 100; 70; 50; 50
Natalie O'Toole, Development Director
Ken Regan, General Manager/CEO
Don Barnes, General Sales Mgr
Brian Dunsmore, Programming Director
Sharon Cross, Traffic Manager
Carol Ann Murray, Chief Engineer

CJRY-FM

01-01-2004; 105.9 MHz FM; 100 kw; Ant 633 ft; N53 30 48 W113 17 05
5316 Calgary Trail NW., Edmonton, AB T6H 4J8 Canada
(780) 466-4930; *Fax:* (780) 469-5335
105.9@shinefm.com
License: Edmonton, AB held by Touch Canada Broadcasting LP.
Group Owner: Touch Canada Broadcasting LP.
Population Served: 817,498; *Arbitron Metro Market:* Edmonton, AB; *Format:* Christian
Mark Imbach, General Manager
Stan Schmidt, Station Manager

CHDI-FM

102.9 MHz FM; *Hrs Open:* 24; 64 kw; 53 31 54.7 N 113 46 52.2 W
5915 Gateway Blvd., Edmonton, AB T6H 2H3 Canada
(780) 423-2005; *Fax:* (780) 437-5129
www.sonic1029.com
shelley.ruis@rci.rogers.com
License: Edmonton, AB held by Rogers Media Inc.
Group Owner: Rogers Media Inc.; (acq 11-29-2006; grpsl)
Arbitron Metro Market: Edmonton, AB; *Format:* Rock/AOR, Alternative; *No. News Employees:* 1
Shelley Ruis, General Sales Mgr
Adam Thompson, Programming Director
Brent Shelton, Promotions Manager
Lee Ingram, Account Manager

CHBN-FM

02-17-2005; 91.7 MHz FM; 96 kw; 200.3 meters
5915 Gateway Blvd., Edmonton, AB T6H 2H3 Canada

(780) 423-2005; *Fax:* (780) 437-5129
www.kiss917.com
License: Edmonton, AB held by Rogers Media Inc.
Group Owner: Rogers Media Inc.
Nat'l Reps: CHUM Radio Sales
Format: Contemporary Hits/Top 40; *Target Audience:* 15-39.
Shelley Ruis, General Sales Mgr
Liann Cameron, Programming Director
Mary Megahy, Music Director

CIUP-FM
12-08-2005; 99.3 MHz FM; 100 kw; 272 meters
9894 42nd Ave., Suite 102, Edmonton, AB T6E 5V5 Canada
(780) 433-7877; *Fax:* (780) 438-8484
www.up993.com
chat@up993.com
License: Edmonton, AB held by Jim Pattison Broadcast Group Ltd. (the general partner) and Jim Pattison Industries Ltd. (the limited partner) carrying on business as Jim Pattison Broadcast Group L.P.
Group Owner: The Jim Pattison Broadcast Group
Format: Adult Contemp
Jamie Wall, General Manager
Kurt Leavins, Station Manager
Amanda Au, Director of Social Media and Promotions
Diana McGee, Sales Manager
Michelle Senft, Traffic Manager

CKAV-FM-4
01-01-2007; 89.3 MHz FM; 100 kw; N53 30 53 W113 17 07
PO Box 87, Station E, Toronto, ON M6H 4E1 Canada
(416) 703-1287; *Fax:* (416) 703-4328
License: Edmonton, AB held by Voices Radio's broadcasting licenses have been revoked by the CRTC. All stations are now broadcasting solely on voicesradio.ca
Group Owner: Voices Radio Inc.
Population Served: 2,615,060; *Arbitron Metro Market:* Toronto, ON; *Format:* Ethnic
Roy Hennessy, Operations Dir
Patrice Mousseau, Programming Director

CKNO-FM
02-23-2010; 102.3 MHz FM; 51 kw
9894 42 Ave. N.W., Suite 102, Edmonton, AB T6E 5V5 Canada
(780) 433-7877
www.1023nowradio.com
License: Edmonton, AB held by Jim Pattison Broadcast Group Ltd. (the general partner) and Jim Pattison Industries Ltd. (the limited partner), carrying on business as Jim Pattison Group L.P.
Group Owner: The Jim Pattison Broadcast Group
Format: Adult Contemp, Contemporary Hits/Top 40
Kurt Leavins, General Manager
Shannon Havard, VP of Sales
Amanda Au, Director of Social Media and Promotions

CKEA-FM
09-06-2010; 95.7 MHz FM; 47 kw
Centre 104, Suite 700, 5241 Calgary Trail, Edmonton, AB T6H 5G8 Canada
(780) 435-3023
www.957cruzfm.com
License: Edmonton, AB held by Harvard Broadcasting Inc.
Group Owner: Harvard Broadcasting Inc.
Format: Contemporary Hits/Top 40, Oldies
Tamara Konrad, General Manager
Christian Hall, Programming Director
Lacey Slater, Promotions and Marketing Director

CJNW-FM
10-06-2009; 107.1 MHz FM; 40 kw; 53 31 54.7 N 113 46 52.2 W
Centre 104, Suite 700, 5241 Calgary Trail, Edmonton, AB T6H 5G8 Canada
(780) 435-3023; *Fax:* (780) 988-2387
www.hot107.ca
License: Edmonton, AB held by Harvard Broadcasting Inc.
Group Owner: Harvard Broadcasting Inc.
Format: Contemporary Hits/Top 40
Tamara Konrad, General Manager
Christian Hall, Programming Director
Lacey Slater, Promotions and Marketing Director

Edson

CFXE-FM
07-10-2007; 94.3 MHz FM; *Hrs Open:* 24; 11 kw; N53 38 47 W116 32 26
422 - 50th Street, 2nd Fl., Edson, AB TF7 1T1 Canada
(780) 723-4461; *Fax:* (780) 723-3765
feedback@theeagle.ca
License: Edson, AB held by Newcap Inc.
Group Owner: NewCap Inc.
Nat'l Reps: imsradio; *Wire Services:* Canadian Press
Population Served: 8,475; *Arbitron Metro Market:* Edson, AB; *Format:* Adult Contemp, Contemporary Hits/Top 40; *Special Programming:* Farm 2 hrs wkly; *No. News Employees:* 3; *Target Audience:* 18-55.
Dave Schuck, General Manager
Dave Schuck, General Sales Mgr
Stuart McIntosh, Programming Director
Ron Rimer, News Director
Coady Shay, Creative Director
Jordan Rae, Music Director

Falher

***CKRP-FM**
11-02-1996; 95.7 MHz FM; 671 w; N55 44 07 W117 11 34*Rebroadcasts:* Rebroadcasts CITE-FM Montreal 65%
308 Main Street SE, Falher, AB T0H 1M0 Canada
(780) 837-2346; *Fax:* (780) 837-2092
programmation@ckrp.ca
License: Falher, AB held by Association canadienne-francaise de l'Alberta-Regionale de Riviere-la-Paix.
Format: Adult Contemp; *Target Audience:* Fr population
Julie Cadieux, President

Fort McMurray

CKYX-FM
03-20-1985; 97.9 MHz FM; *Hrs Open:* 24; 43.5 kw; 123 meters
9912 Franklin Ave., Fort McMurray, AB T9H 2K5 Canada
(780) 743-2246
www.979rock.ca
License: Fort McMurray, AB held by Rogers Media Inc.
Group Owner: Rogers Media Inc.; (acq 11-29-2006; grpsl)
Format: Rock/AOR; *Hrs. of News Programming:* news progmg 5 hrs wkly; *No. News Employees:* 3; *Target Audience:* 18-44.; *Adv. Rates:* 75; 65; 75; 50
John Knox, Programming and Promotions Director
Jennifer Ferguson, Sales Coordinator

CJOK-FM
01-01-1973; 93.3 MHz FM; *Hrs Open:* 24; 43.5 kw; 123 meters; 56 41 16 N 111 19 59 W
9912 Franklin Ave., Fort McMurray, AB T9H 2K5 Canada
(780) 743-2246
www.country933.com
rock979.news@rci.rogers.com
License: Fort McMurray, AB held by Rogers Media Inc.
Group Owner: Rogers Media Inc.; (acq 11-29-2006; grpsl)
Arbitron Metro Market: Fort McMurray, AB; *Format:* Country; *Hrs. of News Programming:* news progmg 4 hrs wkly; *No. News Employees:* 3; *Target Audience:* 25-44.
Troy Dickson, Sales Supervisor
John Knox, Programming and Promotions Director

CKOS-FM
01-01-2007; 91.1 MHz FM; 35 w; N56 40 11 W111 19 57
P.O. Box 5512, Fort McMurray, AB T9H 3G5 Canada
(780) 791-5911; *Fax:* (780) 743-1526
kaos911.com
info@kaos911.com
License: Fort McMurray, AB held by King's Kids Promotions Outreach Ministries Inc.
Population Served: 64,773; *Arbitron Metro Market:* Fort McMurray, AB; *Format:* Christian; *Target Audience:* 18-34.
Jill Edwards, Business Manager
Jon Ramer, General Manager
Jonathan Andrews, Music Director
Rick Kirschner, Executive Director
Brittany Pittman, Sales Executive

CFVR-FM
01-14-2008; 103.7 MHz FM; 50 kw; N56 48 29 W111 26 55
9904 Franklin Ave., Fort McMurray, AB T9H 2K5 Canada
(780) 791-0103; *Fax:* (780) 791-1448
www.mix1037fm.com
License: Fort McMurray, AB held by Harvard Broadcasting Inc.
Group Owner: Harvard Broadcasting Inc.
Format: Adult Contemp, Contemporary Hits/Top 40; *No. News Employees:* 3; *Target Audience:* 18-54; women
Don Grose, General Manager
Don Grose, General Sales Mgr
Trent Allen, Programming Director
Marshall Whitsed, Promotions Director
Evan Cooke, News Director
Steve Reeve, Music Director

CHFT-FM
06-16-2008; 100.5 MHz FM; 20 kw; N56 44 00 W111 23 04
9904 Franklin Ave., Fort McMurray, AB T9H 2K5 Canada
(780) 791-0103; *Fax:* (780) 791-1448
License: Fort McMurray, AB held by Harvard Broadcasting Inc.
Group Owner: Harvard Broadcasting Inc.
Population Served: 64,773; *Arbitron Metro Market:* Fort McMurray, AB; *Format:* Adult Contemp, Contemporary Hits/Top 40; *No. News Employees:* 1
Don Grose, General Manager
Don Grose, General Sales Mgr
Andrew Wilcox, Programming Director
Marshall Whitsed, Marketing and Promotions Director

Fort Saskatchewan

CKFT-FM
11-27-2012; 107.9 MHz FM; 11 kw; 70.2 meters; N53 43 04 W113 15 08
9940 - 99 Ave., Suite 200, Fort Saskatchewan, AB T8L 4G8 Canada
(780) 997-1079
www.fortsaskonline.com
License: Fort Saskatchewan, AB held by Golden West Broadcasting Ltd.
Group Owner: Golden West Broadcasting Ltd.
Format: Contemporary Hits/Top 40
Mike LeBlanc, Station Manager

Fort Vermilion

CIAM-FM
01-27-2003; 92.7 MHz FM; *Hrs Open:* 24; 30 w
Mailing Address: Box 609, 4709 River Road, Fort Vermilion, AB T0H 1N0 Canada
Second Address: 4709 River Rd., Fort Vermilion, AB T0H 1N0
(780)-927-2426; *Fax:* (780) 927-2427
www.ciamradio.com
info@ciamradio.com
License: Fort Vermilion, AB held by Care Radio Broadcasting Association.
Population Served: 727; *Arbitron Metro Market:* Fort Vermilion, AB; *Format:* Variety/Diverse
Michael Sandstrom, General Manager
Phil Peters, Programming Director
Kevin Wiebe, News Director

Grande Prairie

CFGP-FM
06-20-1996; 97.7 MHz FM; *Hrs Open:* 24; 70 kw; 55 27 57 N 118 45 37 W
9835-101 Ave., Suite 200, Grande Prairie, AB T8V 5V4 Canada
(780) 539-9700; *Fax:* (780) 532-1600
www.977rock.ca
License: Grande Prairie, AB held by Rogers Media Inc.
Group Owner: Rogers Media Inc.; (acq 11-29-2006; grpsl)
Format: Rock/AOR; *Hrs. of News Programming:* news progmg 4 hrs wkly; *No. News Employees:* 4; *Target Audience:* 25-55.
J.C. Coutts, Programming Director
Lisa Neville, Advertising Account Manager
Shawna Prince, Music Director

CJXX-FM
11-01-2000; 93.1 MHz FM; *Hrs Open:* 24; 100 kw; N55 03 08 W118 51 59
9817 101 Ave., Suite 202, Grande Prairie, AB T8V 0X6 Canada
(780) 532-0840; *Fax:* (780) 538-1266
www.bigcountryxx.com
License: Grande Prairie, AB held by Jim Pattison Broadcast Group Ltd. (the general partner) and Jim Pattison Industries Ltd. (the limited partner) carrying on business as Jim Pattison Broadcast Group L.P.
Group Owner: The Jim Pattison Broadcast Group; (acq 12-21-2000; grpsl)
Wire Services: BN Wire
Population Served: 55,032; *Arbitron Metro Market:* Grand Prairie, AB; *Format:* Country; *Hrs. of News Programming:* news progmg 14 hrs wkly; *No. News Employees:* 5; *Target Audience:* 25-49; adults who love countrymusic; *Adv. Rates:* 93; na; 77; 71
Ken Norman, General Manager
Anne Graham, General Sales Mgr
Suzanne Marceau-Zinterer, Creative Director
Allan Boyd, Sales Representative
Darren Metselaar, Sales Representative

CFRI-FM
03-30-2007; 104.7 MHz FM; 100 kw
11002 104th Ave., Suite 1, Grande Prairie, AB T8V 7W5 Canada
(780) 357-3733; *Fax:* (780) 830-7815
www.mygrandeprairienow.com
cparr@vistaradio.ca
License: Grande Prairie, Canada County, AB held by Vista Radio Ltd.
Group Owner: Vista Radio Ltd.
Nat'l Reps: Canadian Broadcast Sales

Population Served: 55,032; *Arbitron Metro Market:* Grande Prairie, AB; *Format:* Contemporary Hits/Top 40; *No. News Employees:* 3; *Target Audience:* A 25-54
Erica Fisher, News Director
Kyle Phillips, Music Director
Caralee Parr, Integrated Marketing Executive
Evan Degenhardt, Operations Manager

CIKT-FM
04-09-2007; 98.9 MHz FM; 100 kw; Ant 842 ft; N55 28 44 W118 45 04
8716-108th St., Suite 104, Grande Prairie, AB T8V 4C7 Canada
(780) 882-6612; *Fax:* (780) 882-6708
www.q99live.com
License: Grande Prairie, AB held by Jim Pattison Broadcast Group Ltd. (the general partner) and Jim Pattison Industries Ltd. (the limited partner), carrying on business as Jim Pattison Broadcast Group L.P.
Group Owner: The Jim Pattison Broadcast Group
Nat'l Reps: Target Broadcast Sales *Regional Reps:* WTR Media
Population Served: 250,000; *Format:* Adult Contemp; *No. News Employees:* 3; *Target Audience:* 35-54.; *Adv. Rates:* Available on request
Ken Truhn, General Manager
Paul Ouellette, Programming Director
Brittany Meen, Promotions Director
Sheena Roszell, News Director
Barb Shannon, Marketing Manager

CJGY-FM
12-03-2007; 96.3 MHz FM; 70 kw; N55 29 20 W118 44 50
#111, 10530 117 Ave., Grande Prairie, AB T8V 7N7 Canada
(780) 830-7640; *Fax:* (780) 830-7636
www.cjgy.ca
96.3@shinefm.com
License: Grande Prairie, AB held by Grande Prairie Radio Ltd.
No. News Employees: 6
Ed Elias, General Manager
Terry Van Veen, Station Manager
Jane Wheeler, General Sales Mgr
Terry Van Veen, Programming Director
Marco Auriti, Engineering Dir

High Level

CKHL-FM
07-01-1999; 102.1 MHz FM; 8.765 kw
9807 100th Avenue, Floor 2, Fahlman Building, High Level, AB T0H 1Z0 Canada
(780) 624-2535; *Fax:* (780) 624-54a24
www.ylcountry.com
sdale@sawridge.com
License: High Level, AB held by Peace River Broadcasting Corporation
Population Served: 3,641; *Arbitron Metro Market:* High Level, AB; *Format:* Country; *No. News Employees:* 4
Terry Babiy, President/CEO
Kent Schumaker, Operations Dir
Chris Black, General Manager / Sales Manager
Cindy Babiys, Vice President
Chris Black, General Manager / Sales Manager
Don Jennings, Programming Director
Karin Koppitz,News Director
Chris Black, General Sales Manager

High Prairie

CKVH-FM
09-12-2011; 93.5 MHz FM; 25 kw
Mailing Address: P.O. Box 2219, High Prairie, AB T0G 1E0 Canada
Second Address: 4833 52nd Ave., High Prairie, AB T0G 1E0
(780) 523-5120; *Fax:* (780) 523-3360
feedback@prairiefm.ca
License: High Prairie, AB held by Newcap Inc.
Group Owner: NewCap Inc.
Format: Country
Dave Schuck, General Manager
Wray Betts, Station Manager
Dave Schuck, General Sales Mgr
Stuart McIntosh, Programming Director

High River

CHRB
12-05-1977; 1140 kHz AM; *Hrs Open:* 24
11-5th Ave. S.E., High River, AB T1V 1G2 Canada
(403) 652-2472
www.highriveronline.com
License: High River, AB held by Golden West Broadcasting Ltd.
Group Owner: Golden West Broadcasting Ltd.
Nat'l Reps: Canadian Broadcast Sales
Format: Christian, News, Sports; *Special Programming:* Farm 5 hrs hrs wkly; *Hrs. of News Programming:* news progmg 10 hrs wkly; *No. News Employees:* 2; *Target Audience:* General.
Jay Penner, Station Manager
Jay Penner, Programming Director

CKUV-FM
08-29-2003; 100.9 MHz FM; 100 kw
Bay 3, 22 Elizabeth St., P.O. Box 1889, Okotoks, AB T1S 1B7 Canada
(403) 995-9611
www.okotoksonline.com
theeagle1009@goldenwestradio.com
License: High River, AB held by Golden West Broadcasting Ltd.
Group Owner: Golden West Broadcasting Ltd.
Population Served: 12,920; *Arbitron Metro Market:* High River, AB; *Format:* Adult Contemp
Jayme Hall, Programming Director

CFXO-FM
10-30-2007; 99.7 MHz FM; 18 kw; N50 40 01 W113 58 27
11-5th Ave. S.E., High River, AB T1V 1G2 Canada
(403) 652-2472
www.highriveronline.com
License: High River, AB held by Golden West Broadcasting Ltd.
Group Owner: Golden West Broadcasting Ltd.
Population Served: 24,511; *Arbitron Metro Market:* Okotoks, AB; *Format:* Country
Jay Penner, Station Manager
Jay Penner, Programming Director

Hinton

CFXH-FM
07-01-2004; 97.5 MHz FM; 1.2 kw
#102-506 Carmichael Lane, Hinton, AB T7V 1S8 Canada
(780) 865-8804; *Fax:* (780) 865-7792
www.theeagle.ca
feedback@theeagle.ca
License: Hinton, AB held by Newcap Inc.
Group Owner: NewCap Inc.
Population Served: 9,640; *Arbitron Metro Market:* Hinton, AB; *Format:* Contemporary Hits/Top 40, Oldies; *Target Audience:* 18-54.
Dave Schuck, General Manager
Dave Schuck, General Sales Mgr
Stuart McIntosh, Programming Director
Ron Rimer, News Director
Coady Shay, Creative Director

Lac La Biche

CFWE-FM
01-01-1990; 89.9 MHz FM; *Hrs Open:* 24
13245 146th St., Edmonton, AB T5L 4S8 Canada
(780) 447-2393; *Fax:* (780) 454-2820
www.cfweradio.ca
info@cfweradio.ca
License: Lac La Biche, AB held by Aboriginal Multi-Media Society of Alberta.
Format: Country; *Target Audience:* General; Cree, Blackfoot, Stoney, Dene & English language listeners
Bert Crowfoot, CEO
Alan Standerwick, Station Manager

CILB-FM
12-07-2007; 103.5 MHz FM; 1.9 kw
Mailing Address: P.O. Box 86, Lac La Biche, AB T0A 2C0 Canada
Second Address: 10107 - 102 Ave., Suite 201, Lac La Biche, AB T0A 2C0
(780 623-3744; *Fax:* (780) 623-3740
www.1035bigdog.com
License: Lac La Biche, AB held by NewCap Inc.
Group Owner: NewCap Inc.
Arbitron Metro Market: Lac La Biche, AB; *Format:* Contemporary Hits/Top 40, Oldies
Chad Tabish, General Manager
Rick Flumian, Station/Sales Manager
Kurt Price, Programming Director

Lacombe

CJUV-FM
06-28-2006; 94.1 MHz FM; 27 kw
4725 49B Ave, Lacombe, AB T4L 1K1 Canada
(403) 786-0194; *Fax:* (403) 786-0199
www.sunny94.com
sonia@laradiogroup.com
License: Lacombe, AB held by L.A. Radio Group Inc.
Population Served: 11,707; *Arbitron Metro Market:* Lacombe, AB; *Format:* Contemporary Hits/Top 40, Adult Contemp; *Target Audience:* 35-54
Troy Schaab, President/GM
Sonia Sawyer, CFO/Sales Manager
Chelsea Bates, Creative Director
Desirae Grodaes, Promotions Coordinator
Iwalani Post, Operations/Traffic Manager
Mark Crichton, Chief Engineer
Karen McDonnell, BusinessDevelopment Manager

Leduc

CJLD-FM
06-25-2012; 93.1 MHz FM
4111 43a Avenue, Leduc, AB T9E 4S7 Canada
Fax: (780) 986-1244
www.leducfm.com
License: Leduc, AB held by Blackgold Broadcasting Inc
Format: Country
Mark Tamagi, President

Lethbridge

CFRV-FM
08-28-1959; 107.7 MHz FM; *Hrs Open:* 24; 100 kw; 183.4 meters; 49 696 N 112 831 W
1015 3rd Ave S., Lethbridge, AB T1J 0J3 Canada
(403) 320-1220; *Fax:* (403) 380-1539
www.kiss1077.ca
License: Lethbridge, AB held by Rogers Media Inc.
Group Owner: Rogers Media Inc.
Population Served: 98,198; *Format:* Adult Contemp; *Hrs. of News Programming:* news progmg 2 hrs wkly; *No. News Employees:* 1; *Target Audience:* 18-49; males
Christy Ross, Promotions Director
Julie Kosowan, Office Manager
Josh McLean, Music Director
Amanda Hofman, Account Manager

CHLB-FM
03-14-1997; 95.5 MHz FM; *Hrs Open:* 24; 100 kw
401 Mayor Magrath Dr., Lethbridge, AB T1J 3L8 Canada
(403) 329-0955; *Fax:* (403) 329-0195
www.country95.fm
info@country95.fm
License: Lethbridge, AB held by Jim Pattison Broadcast Group Ltd. (the general partner) and Jim Pattison Industries Ltd. (the limited partner) carrying on business as Jim Pattison Broadcast Group L.P.
Group Owner: The Jim Pattison Broadcast Group; (acq 12-21-2000; grpsl)
Format: Country; *No. News Employees:* 5; *Target Audience:* 25-54.
Gary Dorosz, General Manager
Gary Dorosz, General Sales Mgr
Tia Daniels, Director of Programming / Music
Dori Modney, News Director

CJRX-FM
106.7 MHz FM; 100 kw; 183.4 meters; 49 42 23 N 112 43 15 W
1015 3rd Ave. S., Lethbridge, AB T1J 0J3 Canada
(403) 320-1220; *Fax:* (403) 380-1539
www.1067rock.ca
License: Lethbridge, AB held by Rogers Media Inc.
Group Owner: Rogers Media Inc.
Arbitron Metro Market: Lethbridge, AB; *Format:* Rock/AOR; *Hrs. of News Programming:* news progmg 2 hrs wkly; *No. News Employees:* 1; *Target Audience:* 25-44; female
Ann Marie Jacques, Promotions Coordinator

CKBD-FM
09-22-2014; 98.1 MHz FM; *Hrs Open:* 24; 20 kw
220 - 3rd Ave. S., Suite 400, Lethbridge, AB T1J 0G9 Canada
(403) 388-2910; *Fax:* (403) 388-4648
www.981thebridge.ca
License: Lethbridge, AB held by Clear Sky Radio Inc.
Group Owner: Clear Sky Radio Inc.
Nat'l Reps: Canadian Broadcast Sales
Population Served: 83,517; *Arbitron Metro Market:* Lethbridge, AB; *Format:* Rock/AOR; *Hrs. of News Programming:* news progmg 6 hrs wkly; *No. News Employees:* 2; *Adv. Rates:* 33; 27; 33; 23
Peter Deys, General Manager

CKXU-FM
04-08-2004; 88.3 MHz FM; *Hrs Open:* 24; 125 w
SU 164, 4401 University Dr. W., Lethbridge, AB T1K 3M4 Canada
(403) 329-2180; *Fax:* (403) 329-2224
www.ckxu.com
manager@ckxu.com

License: Lethbridge, AB held by CKXU Radio Society.
Population Served: 83,517; *Arbitron Metro Market:* Lethbridge, AB; *Format:* Variety/Diverse, French
Aaron Trozzo, Executive Director
Benjamin Maine, Programming Director
Martine M,nard, Music Director
Branden Hamilton, Digital Music Temp
Chris Hibbard, Volunteer Coordinator

CJOC-FM
07-03-2007; 94.1 MHz FM; 100 kw; Ant 433 ft; N49 43 59 W112 57 36
220 - 3rd Ave. S., Suite 400, Lethbridge, AB T1J 0G9 Canada
(403) 388-2910; *Fax:* (403) 388-4648
www.cjocfm.com
License: Lethbridge, AB held by Clear Sky Radio Inc.
Group Owner: Clear Sky Radio Inc.
Population Served: 83,517; *Arbitron Metro Market:* Lethbridge, AB; *Format:* Adult Contemp, Contemporary Hits/Top 40
Peter Deys, General Manager
Michelle Steele, General Sales Mgr
Patrick Siedlicki, Corporate News Director

Lloydminster

CKLM-FM
05-18-2001; 106.1 MHz FM; *Hrs Open:* 24; 43 kws; 181.9 meters
5012 - 49th St., Lloydminster, AB T9V 0K2 Canada
(780) 875-5400; *Fax:* (780) 875-4628
www.mylloydminsternow.com
datkinson@vistaradio.ca
License: Lloydminster, AB held by Vista Radio Ltd.
Group Owner: Vista Radio Ltd.; (acq 11-21-2008; C$7.3 million with CFNA-FM Bonnyville)
Population Served: 27,804; *Arbitron Metro Market:* Lloydminster, AB; *Format:* Rock/AOR; *No. News Employees:* 3; *Target Audience:* 12-54; male; *Adv. Rates:* 60; 50; 54; 32
Donnie Atkinson, General Sales Mgr
Jesse Tieman, Morning Show Host & Promotion Director
Angie Mellen, News
Kalie MacIntosh, Afternoon Show & Music Director

CKSA-FM
08-29-2003; 95.9 MHz FM; 100 kw
5026 - 50th St., Lloydminster, AB T9V 1P3 Canada
(780) 875-3321; *Fax:* (780) 875-4704
www.959lloydfm.com
License: Lloydminster, AB held by NewCap Inc.
Group Owner: NewCap Inc.; (acq 12-22-2004; C$6,246,000 with CILR-FM Lloydminster).
Population Served: 27,804; *Arbitron Metro Market:* Lloydminster, AB; *Format:* Country
Chad Tabish, General Manager
Bradley Asselstine, Station Manager
Kurt Price, Programming Director
Dean Martin, Creative Director
Heather Klages, Music Director

Medicine Hat

CFMY-FM
02-01-1999; 96.1 MHz FM; 100 kw
Media Centre, 10 Boundary Rd., Redcliff, AB T0J 2P0 Canada
(403) 548-8282; *Fax:* (403) 548-8270
www.my96fm.com
License: Medicine Hat, AB held by Jim Pattison Broadcast Group Ltd. (the general partner) and Jim Pattison Industries Ltd. (the limited partner) carrying on business as Jim Pattison Broadcast Group L.P.
Group Owner: The Jim Pattison Broadcast Group; (acq 12-21-2000; grpsl).
Format: Adult Contemp
Dave Sherwood, General Manager
Tim Weinberger, General Sales Mgr
John Cartwright, Marketing Consultant
Sandy Clemis, Marketing Consultant
Lisa Finkbeiner, Marketing Consultant
Rita Profeta, Marketing Consultant

CJLT-FM
93.7 MHz FM; *Hrs Open:* 8:30am to 4:30pm; 2.3 kw; 99.5 meters
1741 Dunmore Rd. SE., Suite 206, Medicine Hat, AB T1A 1Z8 Canada
(403) 529-9599; *Fax:* (403) 488-5050
www.937praisefm.com
studio@937praisefm.com
License: Medicine Hat, Canada County, AB held by Vista Radio Ltd.
Group Owner: Vista Radio Ltd.
Format: Christian; *No. News Employees:* 6
Warren Affleck, News Director
Megan Pierson, Music Director, Morning News & Promotions

CHAT-FM
01-09-2006; 94.5 MHz FM; *Hrs Open:* 24; 100 kw
Media Centre, 10 Boundary Rd., Redcliff, AB T0J 2P0 Canada
(403) 548-8282; *Fax:* (403) 548-8270
www.chat945.com
chat945@jpbg.com
License: Medicine Hat, AB held by Jim Pattison Broadcast Group Ltd. (the general partner) and Jim Pattison Industries Ltd. (the limited partner) carrying on business as Jim Pattison Broadcast Group Ltd.
Group Owner: The Jim Pattison Broadcast Group
Nat'l Reps: Canadian Broadcast Sales
Population Served: 61,000; *Arbitron Metro Market:* Redcliff, AB *TV Affiliate:* CHAT-TV affil; *Format:* Country; *Hrs. of News Programming:* news progmg 14 hrs wkly; *No. News Employees:* 4; *Target Audience:* General.
Tim Weinberger, General Sales Mgr
John Cartwright, Marketing Consultant
Sandy Clemis, Marketing Consultant
Lisa Finkbeiner, Marketing Consultant
Rita Profeta, Marketing Consultant
Jerry Zacher, Marketing Consultant

CKMH-FM
02-25-2008; 105.3 MHz FM; 100 kw; 49.997 N 110.644 W
7 Strachan Bay SE, Suite 107, Medicine Hat, AB T1B 4Y2 Canada
(403) 548-7581; *Fax:* (403) 548-7598
www.1053rock.ca
License: Medicine Hat, AB held by Rogers Media Inc.
Group Owner: Rogers Media Inc.
Population Served: 61,000; *Arbitron Metro Market:* Medicine Hat, AB; *Format:* Rock/AOR; *Target Audience:* 25-54.
Trapper John, Program and Music Director

CJCY-FM
05-23-2008; 102.1 MHz FM; 40 kw; Ant 686 ft; N50 02 46 W110 37 08
1865 Dunmore Rd. S.E., Suite 104, Medicine Hat, AB T1A 1Z8 Canada
(403) 528-2827; *Fax:* (403) 488-4678
www.cjcyfm.com
info@cjcyfm.com
License: Medicine Hat, AB held by Clear Sky Radio Inc.
Group Owner: Clear Sky Radio Inc.
Population Served: 61,000; *Arbitron Metro Market:* Medicine Hat, AB; *Format:* Adult Contemp, Contemporary Hits/Top 40
Dave Hanni, Station Manager
Dave Hanni, Retail Sales Manager
Kristen Chesson, Promotions/Marketing Consultant

Olds

CKLJ-FM
02-02-2004; 96.5 MHz FM; 35 kw
#6, 4526 49th Ave., Olds, AB T4H 1A4 Canada
(403) 556-2628; *Fax:* (403) 556-2637
cklj@telus.net
License: Olds, AB held by CAB-K Broadcasting Ltd.
Population Served: 8,235; *Arbitron Metro Market:* Olds, AB; *Format:* Country
Brian Hepp, General Manager/General Sales Manager
Galen Hartviksen, News/Sports Director
Brian Stephenson, Programming Director
Lori McNabb, Traffic Manager

CKJX-FM
06-02-2008; 104.5 MHz FM; 12 kw; N51 45 30 W114 05 39
4526 49 Ave.#6, Olds, AB T4H 1A4 Canada
(403) 556-2628; *Fax:* (403) 556-2637
www.rock104.ca
bh_cklj@telus.net
License: Olds, AB held by CAB-K Broadcasting Ltd.
Population Served: 8,235; *Arbitron Metro Market:* Olds, AB; *Format:* Classic Rock
Brian Hepp, General Manager/Sales Manager
Galen Hartviksen, News/Sports Director
Brian Stephenson, Programming Director
Lori McNabb, Traffic Manager

Peace River

CKYL
11-01-1954; 610 kHz AM; 10 kw-U, DA-2
Bag Service No. 300, Peace River, AB Canada
(780) 624-2535; *Fax:* (780) 624-5424
www.ylcountry.com
License: Peace River, AB held by Peace River Broadcasting Ltd.
Nat'l Reps: Target Broadcast Sales
Terry Babiy, President/CEO
Kent Schumaker, Operations Manager
Chris Black, General Manager/Sales Manager

CKKX-FM
07-01-1997; 106.1 MHz FM; 990 w
Mailing Address: Bag Service No. 300, Peace River, AB T8S 1T5 Canada
Second Address: 9807 100th Ave, Peace River, AB T8S 1T5
(780) 624-2535; *Fax:* (780) 624-5424
www.kix106.net
reception@ylcountry.com
License: Peace River, AB held by Peace River Broadcasting, LTD.
Terry Babiy, President/CEO
Kent Schumaker, Operations Manager
Chris Black, General Manager/Sales Manager
Debe Duperron, Traffic Manager

Plamondon

CHPL-FM
06-16-2013; 92.1 MHz FM; 1.215 kw; 128 meters; N54 49 24 W112 19 08
C.P. 487, Plamondon, AB T0A 2T0 Canada
(780) 798-3896; *Fax:* (780) 798-3909
chpl92.1@hotmail.com
License: Plamondon, AB held by Club de la radio communautaire de Plamondon-Lac La Biche

Red Deer

CIZZ-FM
11-02-1987; 98.9 MHz FM; *Hrs Open:* 24; 100 kw; Ant 800 ft
Mailing Address: Bag 5339, Red Deer, AB T4N 6W1 Canada
Second Address: 4920 - 59th St., Red Deer, AB T4N 2N1
(403) 343-0955; *Fax:* (403) 346-1230
www.zed989.com
License: Red Deer, Red Deer County, AB held by Newcap Inc.
Group Owner: NewCap Inc.; (acq 8-10-2005; C$8,392,714 with CKGY-FM Red Deer)
Wire Services: BN Wire
Population Served: 110,000; *Format:* Classic Rock; *No. News Employees:* 6; *Target Audience:* 18-49; male 55%, female 45%
Hilary Montbourquette, General Manager
Al Lucas, General Sales Mgr
Jeff Murray, Programming Director
Natasha Eddy, Promotions Manager
Al Redel, News Director
Travis Currah, Music Director

CHUB-FM
01-01-2000; 105.5 MHz FM; *Hrs Open:* 24; 100 kw
2840 Bremner Ave., Red Deer, AB T4R 1M9 Canada
(403) 343-7105; *Fax:* (403) 343-2573
www.big105.fm
heydj@big105.fm
License: Red Deer, AB held by Jim Pattison Broadcast Group Ltd. (the general partner) and Jim Pattison Industries Ltd. (the limited partner) carrying on business as Jim Pattison Broadcast Group L.P.
Group Owner: The Jim Pattison Broadcast Group; (acq 12-21-2000; grpsl).
Nat'l Reps: Target Broadcast Sales *Regional Reps:* WTR Media Sales; *Wire Services:* BN Wire
Population Served: 91,877; *Arbitron Metro Market:* Red Deer, AB; *Format:* Adult Contemp; *No. News Employees:* 4; *Target Audience:* Adults 25-49; primary demo-females; *Adv. Rates:* 69; 63; 63; 45
Paul Mason, General Manager
Bryn James, General Sales Mgr
Peter Michaels, Programming Director
Alex Skultety, Promotions Manager
Troy Gillard, News Director
Jamie Rankin, Production Manager
Ryan Simmons, Music Director
JoyceRoss, Creative Director

CKGY-FM
05-01-2001; 95.5 MHz FM; *Hrs Open:* 24; 100 kw; Ant 800 ft.
Mailing Address: Bag 5339, Red Deer, AB T4N 6W1 Canada
Second Address: 4920 59th St., Red Deer, AB T4N 2N1
(403) 348-0955; *Fax:* (403) 346-1230
License: Red Deer, Red Deer County, AB held by Newcap Inc.
Group Owner: NewCap Inc.; (acq 8-10-2005; C$8,392,714 with CIZZ-FM Red Deer)
Nat'l Reps: Canadian Broadcast Sales; *Wire Services:* BN Wire
Population Served: 91,877; *Arbitron Metro Market:* Red Deer, AB; *Format:* Country; *No. News Employees:* 6; *Target Audience:* 25-54; 50% male, 50% female
Hilary Montbourquette, General Manager
Al Lucas, General Sales Mgr

Jenn Dalen, Programming Director
Natasha Eddy, Promotions Manager
Al Redel, News Director

CFDV-FM
11-08-2004; 106.7 MHz FM; 100 kw
2840 Bremner Ave., Red Deer, AB T4R 1M9 Canada
(403) 343-7105; *Fax:* (403) 343-2573
www.1067thedrive.fm
License: Red Deer, AB held by Jim Pattison Broadcast Group Ltd. (the general partner) and Jim Pattison Industries Ltd. (the limited partner) carrying on business as Jim Pattison Broadcast Group L.P.
Group Owner: The Jim Pattison Broadcast Group
Nat'l Reps: Target Broadcast Sales *Regional Reps:* WTR Media sales; *Wire Services:* BN Wire
Population Served: 90,564; *Arbitron Metro Market:* Red Deer, AB; *Format:* Classic Rock, Rock/AOR; *Target Audience:* 25-54; adults, primary demo-males
Paul Mason, General Manager
Bryn James, General Sales Mgr
Peter Michaels, Programming Director
Alex Skultety, Promotions Manager
Troy Gillard, News Director
Jamie Rankin, Production Manager
Joyce Ross, Creative Director
RyanSimmons, Music Director

CKRD-FM
04-04-2011; 90.5 MHz FM; 18.4 kw
13-7619 50 Ave., Red Deer, AB T4P 1M6 Canada
(403) 356-9052; *Fax:* (403) 356-1745
www.ckrd.ca
90.5@shinefm.com
License: Red Deer, AB held by Touch Canada Broadcasting LP.
Group Owner: Touch Canada Broadcasting LP.
Format: Christian
Charles Allard, Managing Director

CKRI-FM
08-06-2010; 100.7 MHz FM
3617 50th Ave., Red Deer, AB T4N 3Y5 Canada
(403) 346-8051
www.cruzfm.ca
License: Red Deer, AB held by Harvard Broadcasting Inc.
Group Owner: Harvard Broadcasting Inc.
Format: Adult Contemp, Contemporary Hits/Top 40
Daryl Holien, Programming Director
Travis Kuschminder, Promotions Manager
Eric Tiessen, Retail Sales Supervisor
Cam Webb, Music Director

Rocky Mountain House

CHBW-FM
01-01-1997; 94.5 MHz FM; 720 w
4814B 49th St., Rocky Mountain House, AB T4T 1S8 Canada
(403) 844-9450; *Fax:* (403) 844-4770
www.yourb94.ca
License: Rocky Mountain House, AB held by Jim Pattison Broadcast Group Ltd. (the general partner) and Jim Pattison Industries Ltd. (the limited partner) carrying on business as Jim Pattison Broadcast Group L.P.
Group Owner: The Jim Pattison Broadcast Group
Population Served: 6,933; *Arbitron Metro Market:* Rocky Mountain House, AB; *Format:* Oldies
Paul Mason, General Manager

Siksika

CFXX-FM
01-01-2002; 97.7 MHz FM; 50 w
Box 1490, Siksika, AB T0J 3W0 Canada
(403) 734-5339; *Fax:* (403) 734-5497
siksikamedia@siksikanation.com
License: Siksika, AB held by Siksika Communications Society.
Paul Tallow, General Manager

Slave Lake

CHSL-FM
09-08-2006; 92.7 MHz FM; 5.7 kw; N55 28 18 W114 47 05
229 3rd Ave., Suite 103, Slave Lake, AB T0G 2A1 Canada
(780) 849-2569; *Fax:* (780) 849-4833
License: Slave Lake, Canada County, AB held by Newcap Inc.
Group Owner: NewCap Inc.
Nat'l Reps: Canadian Broadcast Sales; *Wire Services:* BN Wire
Population Served: 10,000; *Format:* Oldies; *No. News Employees:* 1
Wray Betts, Station Manager

St. Paul

CHSP-FM
12-30-2011; 97.7 MHz FM; 22 kw; 80.3 meters
4341 - 50th Ave., Suite 201, St. Paul, AB T0A 3A3 Canada
(780) 645-4425; *Fax:* (780) 645-2383
www.977thespur.com
License: St. Paul, AB held by Newcap Inc.
Group Owner: NewCap Inc.
Format: Country
Chad Tabish, General Manager
Kurt Price, Programming Director
Meredith Gillis, News Director
Kevin Bernhardt, Marketing Consultant
Kriss Fenton, Office Administrator
Geoff Basco, Music Director

Stettler

CKSQ-FM
10-15-2012; 93.3 MHz FM; 11 kw
Mailing Address: PO Box 2050, Stettler, AB T0C 2L0
Second Address: 4812A-50th St., Stettler, AB T0C 2L0
(403) 742-1400; *Fax:* (403) 742-0660
q933@newcap.ca
License: Stettler, AB held by NewCap Inc.
Group Owner: NewCap Inc.
Format: Country
Vicki Leuck, General Manager
Vicki Leuck, General Sales Mgr
Jenn Dalen, Programming Director

Taber

CJBZ-FM
01-01-2000; 93.3 MHz FM; 50 kw
401 Mayor Magrath Dr., Lethbridge, AB T1J 3L8 Canada
(403) 329-0955; *Fax:* (403) 329-0195
www.b93.fm
info@b93.fm
License: Taber, AB held by Jim Pattison Broadcast Group Ltd. (the general partner) and Jim Pattison Industries Ltd. (the limited partner) carrying on business as Jim Pattison Broadcast Group L.P.
Group Owner: The Jim Pattison Broadcast Group; (acq 12-21-2000; grpsl).
Population Served: 83,517; *Arbitron Metro Market:* Lethbridge, AB; *Format:* Contemporary Hits/Top 40, Adult Contemp; *No. News Employees:* 4; *Target Audience:* 18-44; adults
Gary Dorosz, General Manager
Gary Dorosz, General Sales Mgr
Tia Daniels, Director of Programming/Music
Brittany Gerris, Promotions Director
Dori Modney, News Director
Ross Wells, Technical Department

Wainwright

CKKY-FM
02-01-1984; 101.9 MHz FM; *Hrs Open:* 24; 50 kw; 169.5 meters; N52 59 41 W110 31 59
1037 2nd Ave., 2nd Fl., Wainwright, AB T9W 1K7 Canada
(780) 842-4311; *Fax:* (780) 842-4636
www.krock1019.com
License: Wainwright, AB held by Newcap Inc.
Group Owner: NewCap Inc.; (acq 5-20-2002; grpsl)
Population Served: 100,000; *Format:* Rock/AOR; *Special Programming:* Farm 10 hrs wkly; *Hrs. of News Programming:* news progmg 14 hrs wkly; *No. News Employees:* 2; *Target Audience:* 20-45; agriculture-related workingclass
Chad Tabish, General Manager
Hugh MacDonald, Station/Sales Manager
Kurt Price, Programming Director
Kathryn Chase, Music Director

CKWY-FM
01-31-2005; 93.7 MHz FM; 100 kw
1037 2nd Ave., 2nd Fl., Wainwright, AB T9W 1K7 Canada
(780) 842-4311; *Fax:* (780) 842-4636
www.waynefm.com
License: Wainwright, AB held by Newcap Inc.
Group Owner: NewCap Inc.
Population Served: 5,925; *Arbitron Metro Market:* Wainwright, AB; *Format:* Adult Contemp
Chad Tabish, General Manager
Hugh MacDonald, Station/Sales Manager
Kurt Price, Programming Director
Jeff Newland, News Director
Kathy Romanowicz, Administration/Reception/Traffic Coordinator
Kathryn Chase, Music Director
KylePhillips, Web Services

Westlock

CKWB-FM
09-06-2011; 97.9 MHz FM; 27 kw
10030 - 106th St., Suite 17, Westlock, AB T7P 2K4 Canada
(780) 349-4421; *Fax:* (780) 349-6259
feedback@979therange.ca
License: Westlock, AB held by Newcap Inc.
Group Owner: NewCap Inc.
Format: Country
Dave Schuck, General Manager
Wray Betts, Station Manager/Sales Manager
Stuart McIntosh, Programming Director
Jordan Rae, Music Director

Wetaskiwin

CKJR
01-01-1971; 1440 kHz AM
5214A 50th Ave., Wetaskiwin, AB T9A 0S8 Canada
(780) 352-0144; *Fax:* (780) 352-5656
www.w1440.com
License: Wetaskiwin, AB held by Newcap Inc.
Group Owner: NewCap Inc.; (acq 4-19-2002; grpsl)
Format: Oldies; *Special Programming:* Greek 2 hrs wkly
Kelly Walter, General Sales Mgr
Larry Donohue, Programming Director
Leo Pilon, Retail Sales Manager

CIHS-FM
12-01-2000; 93.5 MHz FM; *Hrs Open:* 24; 5.12 kw; Ant 365 ft
207-8334 128th Street, Surrey, BC V3W 4G2 Canada
(780) 361-0245; *Fax:* (866) 409-2797
mail@cihsfm.net
License: Wetaskiwin, AB held by Satnam Media Group
Target Audience: 0-100.
Dave Dhillon, CEO
Lorelei Dubreuil, Operations Dir
Paula Osha, Station Manager

Whitecourt

CFXW-FM
07-01-2005; 96.7 MHz FM; 9 kw
Mailing Address: P.O. Box 2288, Whitecourt, AB T7S 1A1 Canada
Second Address: 5118 50th St., Whitecourt, AB T7S 1A1
(780) 778-5101; *Fax:* (780) 778-5137
License: Whitecourt, AB held by Newcap Inc.
Group Owner: NewCap Inc.
Population Served: 9,605; *Arbitron Metro Market:* Whitecourt, AB; *Format:* Rock/AOR
Dave Schuck, General Manager
Dave Schuck, General Sales Mgr
Stuart McIntosh, Programming Director
M.J. Patterson, Music Director
Magen Steiger, Sales
Shannon Cain, Sales

CIXM-FM
01-01-2006; 105.3 MHz FM; 42.3 kw
Mailing Address: Box 1050, Whitecourt, AB T7S 1N9 Canada
Second Address: 4912A 50th Ave., Whitecourt, AB T7S 1N9
(866) 706-1053; *Fax:* (780) 706-1053
www.xm105.com
info@xm105fm.com
License: Whitecourt, AB held by 1097282 Alberta Ltd.
Group Owner: Fabmar Communications Ltd.; (acq 5-11-2006)
Nat'l Reps: Target Broadcast Sales
Population Served: 9,605; *Arbitron Metro Market:* Whitecourt, AB; *Format:* Country
Ken Singer, Vice President
Neil Shewchuk, Station Manager/General Sales Manager
Jerad Bowes, Programming Director
Cal Gratton, Music Director
Lynden McBeth, News/Sports Director
Kevin Bradley, Promotions Director
Alice McFarlane,Agricultural Information Director
Royal Watson, Production Director
Karen Breiter, Creative Director

British Columbia

100 Mile House

CKBX
840 kHz AM
407 Alder Ave., Suite 3, 100 Mile House, BC V0K 2E0 Canada

(250) 395-3848; *Fax:* (250) 395-4147
www.mycariboonow.com
cverbenkov@vistaradio.ca
License: 100 Mile House, BC held by Vista Radio Ltd.
Group Owner: Vista Radio Ltd.; (acq 1981)
Format: Country; *Special Programming:* Class one hr wkly
Cindy Verbenkov, General Sales Mgr
Carol Gass, Programming Director
Diana Storz, Integrated Marketing Executive
Gary Russell, Regional Cluster Manager

Abbotsford

CKQC-FM
08-20-1962; 107.1 MHz FM; 215 w; 150.5 metres
31935 South Fraser Way, Suite 318, Abbotsford, BC V2T 5N7 Canada
(604) 853-4756; *Fax:* (604) 853-1071
www.country1071.com
License: Abbotsford, BC held by Rogers Media Inc.
Group Owner: Rogers Media Inc.
Arbitron Metro Market: Abbotsford, BC; *Format:* Country
Melanie Green, General Sales Mgr
Curtis Pope, Program and Music Director

CIVL-FM
09-01-2007; 88.5 MHz FM; *Hrs Open:* 24; 520 watts; 104 meters
33844 King Rd., Abbotsford, BC Canada
(604) 851-6306
www.civl.ca
Bob@civl.ca
License: Abbotsford, BC held by UCFV Campus and Community Radio Society.
Target Audience: 18 plus; campus & community radio
Bob Simpson, Station Manager
Swinder Singh, Programming Director

Big White Ski

*CKIQFM
05-26-2003; 98.1 MHz FM; kw
Mailing Address: Canada
Second Address: 1036 Airport Rd., Iqaluit, NU X0A 0H0
(877)-445-2547; *Fax:* (877) 490-2547
icefmiqaluit@gmail.com
License: Big White Ski, BC held by Northern Lights Entertainment Inc.
Nat'l Reps: Target Broadcast Sales
Arbitron Metro Market: Iqaluit, NU; *Format:* Classic Rock
Terri Chegwyn, General Manager

Burnaby

*CJSF-FM
02-06-2003; 90.1 MHz FM; *Hrs Open:* 7 AM-2AM; 450 w
CJSF Radio, TC 216, Simon Fraser University, Burnaby, BC V5A 1S6 Canada
(604) 291-3727; *Fax:* (604) 291-3695
www.cjsf.ca
cjsfmgr@sfu.ca
License: Burnaby, BC held by Simon Fraser Campus Radio Society.
Population Served: 223,218; *Arbitron Metro Market:* Burnaby, BC; *Format:* Variety/Diverse; *Special Programming:* Persian 2 hrs, Portugese 2 hrs, Sp 4 hrs wkly
Frieda Werden, Operations Dir
Magnus Thyvold, Station Manager
Charlotte Bourne, Programming Director
Ed Blake, Music Director
Sarah Buchanan, Programming Coordinator
Frieda Werden, Public Affairs Coordinator
Bonnie Anderson,Music Coordinator
Dave Swanson, Arts & Entertainment Coordinator
Jordan Mitchell, Production Coordinator

Burns Lake

CFLD
760 kHz AM
1139 Queen St., Smithers, BC V0J 2X0 Canada
(250) 847-2521; *Fax:* (250) 847-9411
www.mybulkleylakesnow.com
aangel@vistaradio.ca
License: Burns Lake, BC held by Vista Radio Ltd.
Group Owner: Vista Radio Ltd.
Format: Adult Contemp
Alissa Angel, General Sales Mgr
JD Brown, Programming Director
Daryl Vandenberg, News
Marieke De Jonge, Integrated Marketing Executive

Campbell River

CIQC-FM
09-10-1963; 99.7 MHz FM; 6 kw; 110 meters
470 13th Ave., Campbell River, BC V9W 7J4 Canada
(250) 287-7106; *Fax:* (250) 287-7170
www.mycampbellrivernow.com
amandzuk@vistaradio.ca
License: Campbell River, BC held by Vista Radio Ltd.
Group Owner: Vista Radio Ltd.
Nat'l Reps: Target Broadcast Sales
Population Served: 31,186; *Arbitron Metro Market:* Campbell River, BC; *Format:* Adult Contemp
Allison Mandzuk, General Manager
Mark Tucker, Programming Director
David Boles, News Reporter
Robyn Tymo, Integrated Marketing Executive

Castlegar

CKQR-FM
99.3 MHz FM; *Hrs Open:* 24; 333 w; 366.5 meters
2032 Columbia Ave., Suite 101, Castlegar, BC V1N 2W7 Canada
(250) 365-7600; *Fax:* (250) 365-8480
www.mykootenaynow.com
amartin@vistaradio.ca
License: Castlegar, BC held by Vista Radio Ltd.
Group Owner: Vista Radio Ltd.
Nat'l Reps: Canadian Broadcast Sales
Format: Classic Rock; *Hrs. of News Programming:* news progmg 6 hrs wkly; *No. News Employees:* 1; *Target Audience:* 18-49; median target demo
Alex Martin, Programming Director
Greg Nesteroff, News Director
Marcella Chernoff, Integrated Marketing Executive
LaRae Vig, Integrated Marketing Executive

Chase

CFCH-FM
01-10-2005; 103.5 MHz FM; *Hrs Open:* 8am - 8pm; 4.7 w
Box 1197, Chase, BC V0E 1M0 Canada
(250) 679-8622; *Fax:* (250) 679-3231
www.cablelan.net/ronfair/CFCH.html
License: Chase, BC held by Chase and District Community Radio Society
Population Served: 2,409; *Arbitron Metro Market:* Chase, BC; *Format:* Talk
Ron Fairhurst, General Manager
Susan Parks, Station Manager

Chetwynd

CHET-FM
01-01-1997; 94.5 MHz FM; 25 w
4612 N. Access Rd., Chetwynd, BC V0C 1J0 Canada
(250) 788-9452; *Fax:* (250) 788-9402
www.peacefm.ca
info@peacefm.ca
License: Chetwynd, BC held by Chetwynd Communications Society.
Population Served: 2,635; *Arbitron Metro Market:* Chetwynd, BC; *Format:* Adult Contemp
Leo Sabulsky, General Manager
Jackie Fowler, Secretary Treasurer
Nancy Atchison, Sales & Promotions
Rhianna Ray, Morning Show Host / Music Director
Adam Perrin, Dawson Creek Representative
Justin Morissette, Swing Announcer /Sports Director
Reinisa MacLeod, Afternoon Host / Volunteer Coordinator

Chilliwack

*CKSR-FM
06-27-1927; 98.3 MHz FM; *Hrs Open:* 24; 2.34 kw; 210.1 meters
46167 Yale Rd., Unit 309, Chilliwack, BC V2P 2P2 Canada
(604) 795-5711; *Fax:* (604) 853-1071
www.starfm.com
License: Chilliwack, BC held by Rogers Media Inc.
Group Owner: Rogers Media Inc.
Nat'l Reps: Canadian Broadcast Sales
Format: Adult Contemp; *Special Programming:* Farm 2 hrs wkly; *No. News Employees:* 3; *Target Audience:* 25-54; general
Scott Riley, Music Director

*CKKS-FM
10-01-1986; 107.5 MHz FM; *Hrs Open:* 24; 640 w; 210.1 metres
2440 Ash St., Vancouver, BC V5Z 4J6 Canada
(604) 877-6357
www.kissradio.ca
License: Chilliwack, BC held by Rogers Media Inc.
Group Owner: Rogers Media Inc.
Nat'l Reps: Canadian Broadcast Sales
Format: Contemporary Hits/Top 40; *Special Programming:* Magazine show 3 hrs wkly; *Hrs. of News Programming:* news progmg 16 hrs wkly; *No. News Employees:* 3; *Target Audience:* 25-45.
Shari Craig, Account Manager

CHWK-FM
02-20-2009; 89.5 MHz FM; *Hrs Open:* 6a-6a; 1600 w; Ant 619 ft; N49 06 35 W121 50 52
Box 589 Station Main, Chilliwack, BC V2P 7V5 Canada
(604) 795-2429; *Fax:* (604) 795-9472
License: Chilliwack, BC held by Fabmar Communications Ltd.
Nat'l Reps: Target Broadcast Sales; *Wire Services:* Canadian Press
Population Served: 77,936; *Arbitron Metro Market:* Chilliwack, BC; *Format:* Variety/Diverse; *Special Programming:* Chilliwack Bruins Play by Play; *Hrs. of News Programming:* 14; *No. News Employees:* 4*TargetAudience:* 18-54.
Kevin Gemmell, General Manager
Kevin Gemmell, Station Manager and Sales Manager
Glen Slingerland, Program Director and Music Director
Don Lehn, News Director
Marc Fitzgerald, Sports Director
Steve Fanning, PromotionsCoordinator
Matt Wallace, Production Director
Amanda Romaniuk, Creative Director
Shelley Larson, Marketing Representative
Catherine Farrell, Marketing Representative

Comox Valley

CFCP-FM
99.7 MHz FM; *Hrs Open:* 24; 2.682 kw; 437 meters
910 Fitzgerald Ave., Suite 202, Courtenay, BC V9N 2R5 Canada
(250) 334-2421; *Fax:* (250) 334-1977
www.mycomoxvalleynow.com
amandzuk@vistaradio.ca
License: Comox Valley, BC held by Vista Radio Ltd.
Group Owner: Vista Radio Ltd.
Wire Services: BN Wire
Format: Rock/AOR; *Hrs. of News Programming:* news progmg 16 hrs wkly; *No. News Employees:* 4; *Target Audience:* 25-54; women
Allison Mandzuk, General Manager
Justin Goulet, News
Elizabeth Young, News
Carmen Christensen, Integrated Marketing Executive

Cortes Island

CKTZ-FM
12-30-2011; 89.5 MHz FM; 80 watts; 104.3 meters
Box 210, Manson's Landing, BC V0P 1K0 Canada
(250) 935-0200
www.cortesisland.com
cortesradio@gmail.com
License: Cortes Island, BC held by Cortes Community Radio Society

Courtenay

CKLR-FM
10-01-1998; 97.3 MHz FM; *Hrs Open:* 24; 11.6 kw
801B 29th St., Courtenay, BC V9N 7Z5 Canada
(250) 703-2200; *Fax:* (250) 703-9611
www.973theeagle.com
info@973theeagle.com
License: Courtenay, BC held by Jim Pattison Broadcast Group Ltd. (the general partner) and Jim Pattison Industries Ltd. (the limited partner), carrying on business as Jim Pattison Broadcast Group L.P.
Group Owner: The Jim Pattison Broadcast Group; (acq 6-27-2006; grpsl)
Nat'l Reps: Canadian Broadcast Sales
Population Served: 90,000; *Format:* Adult Contemp; *No. News Employees:* 2; *Target Audience:* 25-54; adult; *Adv. Rates:* 48; 48; 48; 48
Richard Skinner, Operations Manager
Kent Wilson, Programming Director
Linda Thomas, Promotions Director
Bill Nation, News Director
Carla Johnson, APD/Director of Listener Engagement

Cranbrook

CHBZ-FM
10-01-1995; 104.7 MHz FM; *Hrs Open:* 24; 1.26 kw
19 9th Ave. S., Cranbrook, BC V1C 2L Canada

(250) 426-2224; *Fax:* (250) 426-5520
www.b104.ca
License: Cranbrook, BC held by Jim Pattison Broadcast Group Ltd. (the general partner) and Jim Pattison Industries Ltd. (the limited partner) carrying on business as Jim Pattison Broadcast Group L.P.
Group Owner: The Jim Pattison Broadcast Group; (acq 2-1-2001; grpsl).
Nat'l Reps: Target Broadcast Sales
Population Served: 65,000; *Format:* Country; *No. News Employees:* 3; *Target Audience:* 18-54.
Leo Baggio, General Manager
Jason Caven, Sales Manager
Leo Baggio, Programming Director
Jeff Johnson, News Director
Ross Wells, Technical Department

CHDR-FM
09-01-2002; 102.9 MHz FM; *Hrs Open:* 24; 1.6 kw
19 9th Ave. S., Cranbrook, BC V1C 2L9 Canada
(250) 426-2224; *Fax:* (250) 426-5520
www.thedrivefm.ca
info@thedrivefm.ca
License: Cranbrook, BC held by Jim Pattison Broadcast Group Ltd. (the general partner) and Jim Pattison Industries Ltd. (the limited partner) carrying on business as Jim Pattison Broadcast Group L.P.
Group Owner: The Jim Pattison Broadcast Group
Nat'l Reps: Target Broadcast Sales
Population Served: 19,364; *Arbitron Metro Market:* Cranbrook, BC; *Format:* Rock/AOR; *No. News Employees:* 3; *Target Audience:* 25-54.
Leo Baggio, General Manager
Jason Caven, Sales Manager
Jeff Johnson, News Director
Ross Wells, Chief Engineer

CFSM-FM
09-11-2015; 107.5 MHz FM; 1.1 kw
205A Cranbrook St. N., Cranbrook, BC V1C 3R1 Canada
(250) 464-4100; *Fax:* (250) 464-4101
www.summit107.com
License: Cranbrook, BC held by Clear Sky Radio Inc.
Group Owner: Clear Sky Radio Inc.
Population Served: 83,517; *Format:* Adult Contemp
Melissa Hamm, Station Manager
Melissa Hamm, Sales Manager

Crawford Bay

***CBTEFM**
01-01-1988; 89.9 MHz FM; kw*Rebroadcasts:* Rebroadcasts CBTK-FM Kelowna 100%
Canada
(250) 861-3781; *Fax:* (250) 861-6644
kelowna@cbc.ca
License: Crawford Bay, BC held by Canadian Broadcasting Corp.
Format: News
Charlie Cheffins, Operations Dir

Creston

CIDO-FM
97.7 MHz FM; 20 w; Ant 1,092 ft; N49 05 25 W116 22 45
Box 8, Creston, BC V0B 1G0 Canada
(250) 402-6772
www.crestonradio.ca
info@crestonradio.ca
License: Creston, BC held by Creston Community Radio Society.
Population Served: 5,306; *Arbitron Metro Market:* Creston, BC; *Format:* Variety/Diverse

CKCV-FM
08-07-2015; 94.1 MHz FM; 1100 w; 602 meters
1230 Canyon St., Suite 208, Creston, BC V0B 1G5 Canada
(250) 428-9160; *Fax:* (250) 428-0507
www.mycrestonnow.com
amartin@vistaradio.ca
License: Creston, BC held by Vista Radio Ltd.
Group Owner: Vista Radio Ltd.
Format: Adult Contemp
Alex Martin, Programming Director
Greg Nesteroff, News Director
Samantha Martens, Integrated Marketing Executive

Dawson Creek

CJDC
12-15-1947; 890 kHz AM; *Hrs Open:* 24
102 Ave, Suite 901, Dawson Creek, BC V1G 2B6 Canada
(250) 782-3341; *Fax:* (250) 782-3154
www.cjdccountry.com
terry.shepherd@bellmedia.ca
License: Dawson Creek, BC held by Bell Media Radio G.P.
Group Owner: Bell Media Inc.; (acq 10-29-2007; grpsl).
Format: Country; *Hrs. of News Programming:* 4 hours per week; *No. News Employees:* 3; *Target Audience:* General.
Terry Shepherd, General Manager
Greg Evans, Programming Director
Shaun Briltz, Promotions Manager
Shaun Briltz, Brand Director
Greg Evans, Assistant Brand Director
Amy Titley, Sales Supervisor

CHAD-FM
01-01-2003; 104.1 MHz FM; 50 w*Rebroadcasts:* Rebroadcasts CHET-FM Chetwynd 100%
c/o CHET-FM, Box 214, Chetwynd, BC V0C 1J0 Canada
(250) 788-9452; *Fax:* (250) 788-9402
www.chetchad.com
info@peacefm.ca
License: Dawson Creek, BC held by Chetwynd Communications Society.
Population Served: 11,583; *Arbitron Metro Market:* Dawson Creek, BC; *Format:* Adult Contemp, Oldies, Variety/Diverse
Leo Sabulsky, General Manager
Nancy Atchison, Promotions Manager
Mike Sabulsky, Chief Engineer
Jackie Fowler, Secretary Treasurer
Justin Morissette, Sports Director
Caghan Perrin, Dawson Creek Representative

Duncan

CJSU-FM
89.7 MHz FM; *Hrs Open:* 24; 1.862 kw; 506 meters
5380 Trans Canada Hwy., Duncan, BC V9L 6W4 Canada
(250) 746-0897; *Fax:* (250) 748-1517
www.mycowichanvalleynow.com
jwinter@vistaradio.ca
License: Duncan, BC held by Vista Radio Ltd.
Group Owner: Vista Radio Ltd.
Nat'l Reps: Target Broadcast Sales; Canadian Broadcast Sales
Arbitron Metro Market: Duncan, BC; *Format:* Adult Contemp;
Special Programming: Oldies 8 hrs wkly; *Hrs. of News Programming:* news progmg 12 hrs wkly; *No. News Employees:* 2; *Target Audience:* 35-54.
Allison Mandzuk, General Manager
Julie Winter, Sales
Rob Alexander, Programming Director
Sharon Vanhouwe, News Director
Jennifer Metz, Integrated Marketing Executive

Fernie

CJDR-FM
09-01-2002; 99.1 MHz FM; *Hrs Open:* 24; 470 w*Rebroadcasts:* Rebroadcasts CHOR-FM Cranbrook 66%
19 9th Ave. S., Cranbrook, BC V1C 2L9 Canada
(250) 426-2224; *Fax:* (250) 426-5520
www.thedrivefm.ca
info@thedrivefm.ca
License: Fernie, BC held by Jim Pattison Broadcast Group Ltd. (the general partner) and Jim Pattison Industries Ltd. (the limited partner) carrying on business as Jim Pattison Broadcast Group L.P.
Group Owner: The Jim Pattison Broadcast Group
Nat'l Reps: Target Broadcast Sales
Population Served: 4,217; *Arbitron Metro Market:* Fernie, BC; *Format:* Rock/AOR; *No. News Employees:* 1
Leo Baggio, General Manager
Jason Caven, Sales Manager
Jeff Johnson, News Director
Ross Wells, Chief Engineer

Fort Nelson

CKRX-FM
11-21-1967; 102.3 MHz FM; 1.8 kw
5152 Liard St., Fort Nelson, BC V0C 1R0 Canada
(250) 774-2525; *Fax:* (250) 774-2577
www.1023thebear.com
ken.johnson@bellmedia.ca
License: Fort Nelson, BC held by Bell Media Radio G.P.
Group Owner: Bell Media Inc.; (acq 10-29-2007; grpsl).
Format: Rock/AOR
Ken Johnson, Station Manager

Fort St. John

CHRX-FM
01-01-1997; 98.5 MHz FM
10532 Alaska Rd., Fort St. John, BC V1J 1B3 Canada
(250) 785-6634; *Fax:* (250) 785-4544
www.peacesunfm.com
terry.shepherd@bellmedia.ca
License: Fort St. John, BC held by Bell Media Radio G.P.
Group Owner: Bell Media Inc.; (acq 10-29-2007; grpsl).
Format: Adult Contemp
Terry Shepherd, General Manager
Shaun Briltz, Programming Director
Shaun Briltz, Promotions Coordinator
Amy Titley, Sales Supervisor
Dave Lewis, Creative Director

CKFU-FM
09-01-2003; 100.1 MHz FM; *Hrs Open:* 24
10423 101st Ave., Fort St. John, BC V1J 2B7 Canada
(250) 787-7100; *Fax:* (250) 263-9749
www.moosefm.ca
reception@moosefm.ca
License: Fort St. John, Canada County, BC held by 663975 B.C. Ltd.
Nat'l Reps: Canadian Broadcast Sales; *Wire Services:* BN Wire
Population Served: 30,000; *Hrs. of News Programming:* news progmg 5 hours wkly; *No. News Employees:* 3; *Target Audience:* 24-45; female
Russ Beering, General Manager
Adam Reaburn, Promotions Manager

CKNL-FM
06-20-1962; 101.5 MHz FM; 40 kw
10532 Alaska Rd., Fort St. John, BC V1J 1B3 Canada
(250) 785-6634; *Fax:* (250) 785-4544
www.1015thebear.com
License: Fort St. John, BC held by Bell Media Radio G.P.
Group Owner: Bell Media Inc.; (acq 10-29-2007; grpsl)
Population Served: 18,609; *Arbitron Metro Market:* Fort St. John, BC; *Format:* Rock/AOR
Terry Shepherd, General Manager
Amy Titley, Sales Supervisor
Shaun Briltz, Brand Director
Dave Lewis, Creative Director

Gibsons

***CISC-FM**
107.5 MHz FM; *Hrs Open:* 24; 4.6 kw; 287.4 meters*Rebroadcasts:* Rebroadcasts CISQ-FM Squamish
40147 Glenalder Pl., Suite 202, Squamish, BC V8B 0G2 Canada
(604) 892-1021; *Fax:* (604) 892-6383
www.mountainfm.com
news@mountainfm.com
License: Gibsons, BC held by Rogers Media Inc.
Group Owner: Rogers Media Inc.
Format: Adult Contemp; *Special Programming:* Magazine show 3 hrs wkly; *Hrs. of News Programming:* news progmg 16 hrs wkly; *No. News Employees:* 3; *Target Audience:* 25-44.
Darren McPeake, Music Director

CKAY-FM
05-20-2006; 91.7 MHz FM; *Hrs Open:* 24; 260 w; 759 meters; Sunshine Coast/Central Vancouver Island
1877 Field Rd., Suite 1, Sechelt, BC V0N 3A1 Canada
(604) 741-9170; *Fax:* (604) 741-9172
www.mycoastnow.com
amandzuk@vistaradio.ca
License: Gibsons, BC held by Vista Radio Ltd.
Group Owner: Vista Radio Ltd.
Wire Services: BN Wire
Arbitron Metro Market: Gibsons, BC; *Format:* Contemporary Hits/Top 40, Adult Contemp; *Hrs. of News Programming:* news progmg 8 hrs wkly; *No. News Employees:* 3; *Target Audience:* 35 plus; adults
Allison Mandzuk, General Manager
Rob Alexander, Regional Cluster Program Director
Kim Wall, Operations Manager
Vicky Osualdini, Integrated Marketing Executive
Tommy Wang, News Reporter, Sunshine Coast
Sharon Vanhouwe, NewsReporter, Nanaimo

Golden

CKGR-FM
01-01-1974; 106.3 MHz FM; 890 watts
10th Ave. S., Suite 825, Golden, BC V0A 1H0 Canada
(250) 344-7177; *Fax:* (250) 344-7233
www.golden.myezrock.com
bruce.hamlin@bellmedia.ca
License: Golden, BC held by Bell Media Radio G.P.
Group Owner: Bell Media Inc.
TV Affiliate: 24 Hours; *Format:* Adult Contemp

Gord Leighton, General Manager
Gord Leighton, General Sales Mgr

Grand Forks

CKGF-FM
102.3 MHz FM; 0.589 kw; 353 meters
555 Central Ave., Grand Forks, BC V0H 1H0 Canada
(250) 442-2253
www.mygrandforksnow.com
amartin@vistaradio.ca
License: Grand Forks, BC held by Vista Radio Ltd.
Group Owner: Vista Radio Ltd.
Arbitron Metro Market: Castlegar, BC; *Format:* Rock/AOR; *Target Audience:* 25-54.
Alex Martin, Programming Director
Greg Nesteroff, News Director
Michael Kilbride, Integrated Marketing Executive

Hope

CFSR-FM
100.5 MHz FM; 157 kw; -566.4 metres
46167 Yale Rd., Suite 309, Chilliwack, BC V2P 2P2 Canada
(604) 795-5711; *Fax:* (604) 853-1071
www.starfm.com
License: Hope, BC held by Rogers Media Inc.
Group Owner: Rogers Media Inc.
Arbitron Metro Market: Chilliwack, BC; *Format:* Adult Contemp
Scott Riley, Music Director

Kamloops

CHNL
05-01-1970; 610 kHz AM; *Hrs Open:* 24; 25 kw-D, 5 kw-N, DA-N
611 Lansdowne St., Kamloops, BC V2C 1Y6 Canada
(250) 372-2292; *Fax:* (250) 372-2293
www.radionl.com
info@radionl.com
License: Kamloops, BC held by NL Broadcasting Ltd.
Group Owner: Newcap Radio
Regional Network: CRN *Nat'l Reps:* Bell Media Sales *Regional Reps:* Bell Media Sales CHUM Radio Sales; *Wire Services:* Canadian Press
Population Served: 160,000; *Format:* Sports, News/Talk, Oldies; *Hrs. of News Programming:* news progmg 15.5 hrs wkly; *No. News Employees:* 8; *Target Audience:* 25-54; family oriented, middle-upper class income*Adv.Rates:* 852; 732; 732; 528
Garth Buchko, General Manager
Garth Buchko, General Sales Mgr
Howie Reimer, Programming Director
Jim Harrison, News Director
Dave Coulter, Chief Engineer

CIFM-FM
05-21-1962; 98.3 MHz FM; 4.3 kw
460 Pemberton Terrace, Kamloops, BC V2C 1T5 Canada
(250) 372-3322; *Fax:* (250) 374-0445
www.98.3cifm.com
License: Kamloops, BC held by Jim Pattison Broadcast Group Ltd. (the general partner) and Jim Pattison Industries Ltd. (the limited partner) carrying on business as Jim Pattison Broadcast Group L.P.
Group Owner: The Jim Pattison Broadcast Group; (acq 1987).
Population Served: 170,000*TV Affiliate:* CFJC-TV affil.; *Format:* Classic Rock, Rock/AOR; *Hrs. of News Programming:* news progmg 9 hrs wkly; *No. News Employees:* 6; *Target Audience:* 30-40; baby boomers withdisposable income
Rod Schween, President
Rod Schween, General Manager
Bruce Uptigrove, General Sales Mgr
Cheryl Blackwell, Director of Radio Programming and Operations
Doug Collins, Director of News and Information
James Belton, Regional Director ofIT and Engineering
Bill Dinicol, Vice President, Finance

CKRV-FM
01-28-1984; 97.5 MHz FM; *Hrs Open:* 24; 5 kw
611 Lansdowne St., Kamloops, BC V2C 1Y6 Canada
(250) 372-7197; *Fax:* (250) 372-2293
www.975river.com
info@radionl.com
License: Kamloops, BC held by NL Broadcasting Ltd.
Group Owner: Newcap Radio; (acq 6-10-93; $925,000).
Nat'l Reps: CHUM Radio Sales *Regional Reps:* CHUM Radio Sales
Population Served: 80,000; *Format:* Adult Contemp, Contemporary Hits/Top 40; *Hrs. of News Programming:* news progmg 5 hrs wkly; *No. News Employees:* 1; *Target Audience:* 25-54; professionals, office personnel*Adv.Rates:* 816; 732; 744; 528
Garth Buchko, General Manager
Garth Buchko, General Sales Mgr
Jeff Molnar, Programming Director
Jim Harrison, News Director
Dave Coulter, Chief Engineer

CKBZ-FM
09-01-2001; 100.1 MHz FM; 3.5 kw
460 Pemberton Terrace, Kamloops, BC V2C 1T5 Canada
(250) 372-3322; *Fax:* (250) 374-0445
www.b100.ca
License: Kamloops, BC held by Jim Pattison Broadcast Group Ltd. (the general partner) and Jim Pattison Industries Ltd. (the limited partner) carrying on business as Jim Pattison Broadcast Group L.P.
Group Owner: The Jim Pattison Broadcast Group
Population Served: 85,678; *Arbitron Metro Market:* Kamloops, BC*TV Affiliate:* CFJC-TV affil.; *Format:* Adult Contemp; *Hrs. of News Programming:* news progmg 10 hrs wkly; *No. News Employees:* 6; *Target Audience:* 25-44; large, loyal audience with disposable income
Bruce Uptigrove, General Sales Mgr
Doug Collins, News Director
Raffelina Sirianni, Account Manager
Pamela Van Der Woning, Account Manager
Warren Delyzer, Account Manager
Ken Farough, Account Manager

CFBX-FM
04-02-2001; 92.5 MHz FM; 420 w
900 McGill Rd., House 8, Kamloops, BC V2C 0C8 Canada
(250) 377-3988; *Fax:* (250) 852-6350
www.thex.ca
radio@tru.ca
License: Kamloops, BC held by The Kamloops Campus/Community Radio Society.
Population Served: 85,678; *Arbitron Metro Market:* Kamloops, BC; *Format:* Variety/Diverse
Brant Zwicker, Station Manager
Steve Marlow, Programming/Music
Kathy Parkes, Training Coordinator
Julie Niven, Music Librarian

CJKC-FM
01-01-2006; 103.1 MHz FM; *Hrs Open:* 24; 5 kw
611 Lansdowne St., Kamloops, BC V2C 1Y6 Canada
(250) 571-1031; *Fax:* (250) 372-2293
www.country103.ca
info@radionl.com
License: Kamloops, BC held by NL Broadcasting Ltd.
Group Owner: Newcap Radio
Nat'l Reps: CHUM Radio Sales *Regional Reps:* CHUM Radio Sales
Population Served: 85,678; *Arbitron Metro Market:* Kamloops, BC; *Format:* Country; *Hrs. of News Programming:* news progmg 10 hrs wkly; *No. News Employees:* 1; *Target Audience:* 25-54.; *Adv. Rates:* 756; 672; 672;420
Garth Buchko, General Manager
Garth Buchko, General Sales Mgr
TJ Connors, Programming Director
Jim Harrison, News Director
Dave Coulter, Chief Engineer
Tim Tyler, Music Director

Kelowna

***CBTKFM**
11-01-1987; 88.9 MHz FM; kw
Canada
(250) 861-3781; *Fax:* (250) 861-6644
License: Kelowna, BC held by Canadian Broadcasting Corp.
Nat'l Network: CBC Radio One
Format: News
Charlie Cheffins, Operations Dir

CHSU-FM
09-21-1995; 99.9 MHz FM; 11 kw
435 Bernard Ave., Kelowna, BC V1Y 6N8 Canada
(250) 860-8600; *Fax:* (250) 860-8856
www.thesun.net
info@thesun.net
License: Kelowna, BC held by Bell Media Radio G.P.
Group Owner: Bell Media Inc.
Format: Contemporary Hits/Top 40; *No. News Employees:* 3
Ken Kilcullen, General Manager
Peter Angle, Regional Sales Mgr
Mark Burley, Programming Director
Diana Arend, Promotions Director
Howard Alexander, News Director
Tammy Cole, Music Director
Paul Brain, Creative Director

CILK-FM
06-21-1985; 101.5 MHz FM; *Hrs Open:* 24; 10 kw
435 Bernard Ave., Kelowna, BC V1Y 6N8 Canada
(250) 860-8600; *Fax:* (250) 860-8856
www.kelowna.myezrock.com
kelownainfo@myezrock.com
License: Kelowna, BC held by Bell Media Radio G.P.
Group Owner: Bell Media Inc.; (acq 10-29-2007; grpsl).
Format: Adult Contemp; *Hrs. of News Programming:* news progmg 2 hrs wkly; *No. News Employees:* 2; *Target Audience:* 25-54; women
Ken Kilcullen, General Manager
Peter Angle, Regional Sales Mgr
Matt Burley, Programming Director
Diana Arend, Promotions Director
Mark Jeffries, Music Director
Paul Brain, Creative Director

CKFR
11-08-1971; 1150 kHz AM
435 Bernard Ave., Kelowna, BC V1Y 6N8 Canada
(250) 860-8600; *Fax:* (250) 860-8856
www.am1150.ca
info@am1150.ca
License: Kelowna, BC held by Bell Media Radio G.P.
Group Owner: Bell Media Inc.; (acq 10-29-2007; grpsl).
Format: News/Talk, Sports; *No. News Employees:* 3; *Target Audience:* 25-54.; *Adv. Rates:* 28; 18; 22; 12
Ken Kilcullen, General Manager
Peter Angle, General Sales Mgr
Tammy Cole, Programming Director
Diana Arend, Promotions Manager

CKLZ-FM
01-01-1964; 104.7 MHz FM; *Hrs Open:* 24; 2.8 kw; Ant 1,611 ft; N49 46 06 W119 29 59
3805 Lakeshore Rd., Kelowna, BC V1W 3K6 Canada
(250) 763-1047; *Fax:* (250) 762-2141
www.power104.fm
info@power104.fm
License: Kelowna, Central Okanagan County, BC held by Jim Pattison Broadcast Group Ltd. (the general partner) and Jim Pattison Industries Ltd. (the limited partner), carrying on business as Jim Pattison Broadcast Group L.P.
Group Owner: The Jim Pattison Broadcast Group; (acq 6-30-98)
Format: Rock/AOR; *Hrs. of News Programming:* news progmg 4 hrs wkly; *No. News Employees:* 2; *Target Audience:* 25-49.
Stu Crouse, General Sales Mgr
Bob Mills, Programming Director
Don Huculak, Senior Account Manager

***CHIM-FM**
01-01-1996; 104.7 MHz FM; kw
Canada
(705) 264-2150
www.chimfm.com
chimfm@vianet.ca
License: Kelowna, BC held by 1158556 Ontario Ltd.
Arbitron Metro Market: Timmins, ON; *Format:* Christian
Roger de Brabant, Chairman
Roger deBrabant, General Manager/Founder
Karen Turner, Station Manager
Karen Turner, Sales & Marketing Manager
Angela Sommers, Music Director
Paula Gravel, Weather Announcer, Production
Terry Markovich,Red Deer Manager

CKQQ-FM
08-17-2007; 103.1 MHz FM; 11 kw; N49 46 06 W119 29 59
3805 Lakeshore Rd., Kelowna, BC V1W 3K6 Canada
(250) 762-3331; *Fax:* (250) 762-2141
www.q1031.ca
theq@q103.ca
License: Kelowna, BC held by Jim Pattison Broadcast Group Ltd. (the general partner) and Jim Pattison Industries Ltd. (the limited partner), carrying on business as Jim Pattison Broadcast Group L.P.
Group Owner: The Jim Pattison Broadcast Group
Format: Adult Contemp
Stu Crouse, General Manager
Stu Crouse, General Sales Mgr
Jasmin Doobay, News Director

CKKO-FM
11-04-2008; 96.3 MHz FM; 7.1 kw; N49 46 47 W119 30 26
1601 Bertram St., Kelowna, BC V1Y 2G5 Canada
(250) 861-5963; *Fax:* (250) 469-9963
www.k963.fm
License: Kelowna, BC held by NewCap Inc.
Group Owner: NewCap Inc.
Format: Classic Rock

Dallas Gray, General Manager
Dallas Gray, General Sales Mgr
David Larsen, Programming Director
Chris Cleaver, Chief Engineer

Kindersley

CKVX-FM

01-01-2005; 104.9 MHz FM
404 12th Ave. E., P.O. Box 1330, Kindersley, SK S0L 1S0 Canada
(306) 463-2692
www.westcentralonline.com
cjymnews@goldenwestradio.com
License: Kindersley, SK held by Golden West Broadcasting Ltd.
Group Owner: Golden West Broadcasting Ltd.
Format: Adult Contemp
Barbara G. Bell, Station Manager

Kitimat

CKTK-FM

01-01-2004; 97.7 MHz FM; 170 w
4625 Lazelle Ave., Terrace, BC V8G 1S4 Canada
(250) 635-6316; *Fax:* (250) 638-6320
www.kitimat.myezrock.com
grant.scott@bellmedia.ca
License: Kitimat, BC held by Astral Media Radio G.P.
Group Owner: Bell Media Inc.; (acq 10-29-2007; grpsl)
Population Served: 8,335; *Arbitron Metro Market:* Kitimat, BC; *Format:* Contemporary Hits/Top 40
Brian Langston, General Manager
John Crawford, News Director
Janine Kraft, Radio Brand Director

Lake Cowichan

CICV-FM

98.7 MHz FM; 50 w; -82 meters; N48 49 25 W124 03 17
Box 275, Lake Cowichan, BC V0R 2G0 Canada
(250) 932-9000
License: Lake Cowichan, BC held by Cowichan Valley Community Radio Society

Lillooet

CHLS-FM

01-01-2001; 100.5 MHz FM; *Hrs Open:* 24; 5 w; lillooet
#415 Main Street, Lillooet, BC V0K 1V0 Canada
(250) 256-2113; *Fax:* (250) 256-2113
www.radiolillooet.ca
station@radiolillooet.ca
License: Lillooet, BC held by Lillooet Camelfoot T.V. and Radio Association
Population Served: 2,322; *Arbitron Metro Market:* Lillooet, BC; *Format:* Variety/Diverse; *Special Programming:* First nations 16 hrs wkly; *Hrs. of News Programming:* News progmg 5 hrs wkly; *Target Audience:* All ages;community of Lillooet
Kim North, Operations Dir

MacKenzie

CHMM-FM

10-27-2003; 103.5 MHz FM; 900 w
86 Centennial Ave., Box 547, MacKenzie, BC V0J 2C0 Canada
(250) 997-6277; *Fax:* (250) 997-6222
www.chmm.ca
chmm1035@gmail.com
License: MacKenzie, BC held by MacKenzie and Area Community Radio Society.
Population Served: 4,539; *Arbitron Metro Market:* Mackenzie, BC; *Format:* Variety/Diverse
J.D. MacKenzie, Station Manager
Bryan Bezo, General Sales Mgr

Merritt

CKMQ-FM

101.1 MHz FM
Box 1630, 201-2196 Quilchena Avenue, Merrit, BC V1K 1B8 Canada
(250) 378-4288; *Fax:* (250) 378-6979
www.q101.ca
License: Merritt, Thompson-Nicola County, BC held by NL Broadcasting Ltd
Elizabeth Laird, General Manager
Jim Reynolds, Operations Manager

Nanaimo

CKWV-FM

01-02-1995; 102.3 MHz FM; *Hrs Open:* 24; 3 kw; Nanaimo, sc
4550 Wellington Rd., Nanaimo, BC V9T 2H3 Canada
(250) 758-1131; *Fax:* (250) 758-4644
www.1023thewave.com
info@1023thewave.com
License: Nanaimo, BC held by Jim Pattison Broadcast Group Ltd. (the general partner) and Jim Pattison Industries Ltd. (the limited partner), carrying on business as Jim Pattison Broadcast Group L.P.
Group Owner: The Jim Pattison Broadcast Group; (acq 6-27-2006; grpsl)
Nat'l Reps: Canadian Broadcast Sales
Population Served: 125,000; *Format:* Adult Contemp; *No. News Employees:* 2; *Target Audience:* 25-54; general; *Adv. Rates:* 48; 48; 48; 48
Rob Bye, General Manager
Katie O'Connor, Sales Manager
Kent Wilson, Programming Director
Holly Tribble, Promotions Director
Daryl Major, News Director
Barry Mandziak, Chief Engineer
Carla Johnson, APD/Director of ListenerEngagement
Matt Fogarty, Retail Creative Director
Pam Doherty, Traffic Director

*CHLY-FM

09-21-2001; 101.7 MHz FM; *Hrs Open:* 24/7/365; 1.3 kw; Ant 312 ft; N49 13 20 W124 00 07
#2-34 Victoria Crescent, Nanaimo, BC V9R 5B8 Canada
(250) 716-3410; *Fax:* (250) 716-1082
www.chly.ca
programdirector@chly.ca
License: Nanaimo, BC held by Radio Malaspina Society.
Population Served: 500,000; *Target Audience:* campus/community
Dylan Perry, Programming Director

CHWF-FM

10-01-2001; 106.9 MHz FM; *Hrs Open:* 24 hrs; 3 kw; Nanaimo
4550 Wellington Rd., Nanaimo, BC V9T 2H3 Canada
(250) 758-1131; *Fax:* (250) 758-4644
www.1069thewolf.com
info@1069thewolf.com
License: Nanaimo, BC held by Jim Pattison Broadcast Group Ltd. (the general partner) and Jim Pattison Industries Ltd. (the limited partner), carrying on business as Jim Pattison Broadcast Group L.P.
Group Owner: The Jim Pattison Broadcast Group; (acq 6-27-2006; grpsl).
Nat'l Reps: Canadian Broadcast Sales
Population Served: 83,810; *Arbitron Metro Market:* Nanaimo, BC; *Format:* Rock/AOR; *No. News Employees:* 2; *Target Audience:* 25-54; general; *Adv. Rates:* 48; 48; 48; 48
Rob Bye, General Manager
Katie O'Connor, Sales Manager
Kent Wilson, Programming Director
Holly Tribble, Promotions Director
Daryl Major, News Director
Barry Mandziak, Chief Engineer
Carla Johnson, APD/Director of ListenerEngagement
Matt Fogarty, Retail Creative Director
Pat Doherty, Traffic Manager
Graeme Tait, Music Director
Gail Conrad, Account Executive
Shanda Wright, Account Executive

Nelson

CKKC-FM

01-01-1993; 106.9 MHz FM; 13.5
1560 Second Ave., Trail, BC V1R 1M4 Canada
(250) 368-5510; *Fax:* (250) 368-8471
www.kootenays.myezrock.com
License: Nelson, BC held by Bell Media Radio G.P.
Group Owner: Bell Media Inc.; (acq 10-29-2007; grpsl).
Format: Adult Contemp, Oldies
Nicole Beetstra, General Manager
Nicole Beetstra, General Sales Mgr
Jen Zandstra, Promotions Manager
Lea Wilman, Brand Director

*CJLY-FM

01-01-2002; 93.5 MHz FM; 70 w
308a Hall St., Box 767, Nelson, BC V1L 1Y8 Canada
(250) 352-9600; *Fax:* (250) 352-9653
www.kootenaycoopradio.com
km@kootenaycoopradio.com
License: Nelson, BC held by Kootenay Co-operative Radio.
Population Served: 10,203; *Arbitron Metro Market:* Nelson, BC; *Format:* Variety/Diverse
Bill Metcalfe, Operations Dir
Jay Hannley, Station Manager
Terry Brennan, Operations Manager
Zoe Creighton, Sponsorship Producer

CHNV-FM

06-11-2010; 103.5 MHz FM; 1.1 kw; 376 meters
312 Hall St., Nelson, BC V1L 1Y8 Canada
(250) 352-1902; *Fax:* (250) 352-0301
www.mynelsonnow.com
amartin@vistaradio.ca
License: Nelson, BC held by Vista Radio Ltd.
Group Owner: Vista Radio Ltd.
Population Served: 332; *Arbitron Metro Market:* Crawford Bay, BC; *Format:* Variety/Diverse; *No. News Employees:* 2
Alex Martin, Programming Director
Kelsi Balfour, Promotions Manager
Greg Nesteroff, News Director
LaRae Vig, Integrated Marketing Executive

New Westminster

CFMI-FM

03-22-1970; 101.1 MHz FM; 53 kw; 368.4 meters
700 West Georgia St., Suite 2000, Vancouver, BC V7Y 1K9 Canada
(604) 331-2808; *Fax:* (604) 331-2722
www.rock101.com
License: New Westminster, BC held by Corus Premium Television Ltd.
Group Owner: Corus Entertainment Inc.
Format: Classic Rock, Rock/AOR; *Target Audience:* 25-49.
Brad Phillips, General Manager
Paul Ackerman, Sales Director
Dustin Collins, Programming Director
Mike Cohen, Senior Promotions Coordinator
Julie Mangat, Content Coordinator

CKNW

08-15-1944; 980 kHz AM; *Hrs Open:* 24
700 West Georgia St., Suite 2000, Vancouver, BC V7Y 1K9 Canada
(604) 331-2711; *Fax:* (604) 331-2722
www.cknw.com
paul.ackerman@corusent.com
License: New Westminster, BC held by Corus Premium Television Ltd.
Group Owner: Corus Entertainment Inc.; (acq 7-6-2000; grpsl).
Nat'l Reps: Canadian Broadcast Sales
Format: News, News/Talk, Talk; *Hrs. of News Programming:* news progmg 14 hrs wkly; *No. News Employees:* 20; *Target Audience:* General.
Paul Ackerman, Sales Director
Larry Gifford, Programming Director
Monika Coen, Senior Manager, Marketing & Promotions
Terry Schnitz, News Director
Corey McMaster, Promotions Coordinator
Estefania Duran, Content Coordinator

Osoyoos

CJOR

12-01-1966; 1240 kHz AM; 1 kw-U, DA-1
8309 Main St., Suite 203, Osoyoos, BC V0H 1V0 Canada
(250) 492-7226; *Fax:* (250) 495-6841
janet.burley@bellmedia.ca
License: Osoyoos, BC held by Bell Media Radio G.P.
Group Owner: Bell Media Inc.; (acq 10-29-2007; grpsl).
Nat'l Reps: Canadian Broadcast Sales
Format: Adult Contemp; *Special Programming:* Por 3 hrs wkly; *No. News Employees:* 1; *Target Audience:* 25-49.
Mike Mlazgar, Production Director
Janet Burley, General Manager
Janet Burley, General Sales Mgr
Karen Davy, Promotions Manager
Jon Ferebee, News Director
Mark Burley, Brand Director

Parksville

CIBH-FM

01-14-2002; 88.5 MHz FM; *Hrs Open:* 24; 2 kw; Parksville, BC
P.O. Box 1370, 166 E. Isl Hwy., Parksville, BC V9P 2H3 Canada
(250) 248-4211; *Fax:* (250) 248-4210
www.885thebeach.com
info@885thebeach.com
License: Parksville, BC held by Jim Pattison Broadcast Group Ltrd. (the general partner) and Jim Pattison Industries Ltd. (the limited partner), carrying on business as Jim Pattison Broadcast Group L.P.
Group Owner: The Jim Pattison Broadcast Group; (acq 6-27-2006; grpsl).
Population Served: 20,479; *Arbitron Metro Market:* Parksville - Qualicum Beach, BC; *Format:* Adult Contemp, Oldies; *No. News*

Employees: 2; Target Audience: 25-54; Adults; Adv. Rates: 24; 24; 24; 24
Rob Bye, General Manager
Katie O'Connor, Retail Sales Manager
Kent Wilson, Programming Director
Holly Tribble, Promotions Director
Daryl Major, News Director
Barry Mandziak, Chief Engineer
Pam Doherty, Traffic Manager
CarlaJohnson, APD/Director of Listener Engagement
Matt Fogarty, Retail Creative Director

CHPQ-FM
02-11-2005; 99.9 MHz FM; *Hrs Open:* 24; 1.1 kw
166 E. Island Hwy., Parksville, BC V9P 2H3 Canada
(250) 248-4211; *Fax:* (250) 248-4210
www.thelounge999.com
info@thelounge999.com
License: Parksville, BC held by Jim Pattison Broadcast Group Ltd. (the general partner) and Jim Pattison Industries Ltd. (the limited partner), carrying on business as Jim Pattison Broadcast Group L.P.
Group Owner: The Jim Pattison Broadcast Group; (acq 6-27-2006; grpsl).
Nat'l Reps: Canadian Broadcast Sales
Population Served: 26,501; *Format:* Adult Contemp; *No. News Employees:* 1; *Target Audience:* 45 plus; adults; *Adv. Rates:* 24; 24; 24; 24
Rob Bye, General Manager
Katie O'Connor, Retail Sales Manager
Kent Wilson, Programming Director
Ray Evans, Music Director
Gail Conrad, Account Executive
Carolyn Hoare, Account Executive
Felicia Kreutzer, Account Executive
TrishNewton-Segal, Account Executive

Pemberton

CISP-FM
104.5 MHz FM; *Hrs Open:* 24; 400 w; 1,000 ft*Rebroadcasts:* Rebroadcasts CISQ-FM Squamish 100%
40147 Glenalder Pl., Suite 202, Squamish, BC V8B 0G2 Canada
(604) 892-1021; *Fax:* (604) 892-6383
www.mountainfm.com
news@mountainfm.com
License: Pemberton, BC held by Rogers Media Inc.
Group Owner: Rogers Media Inc.
Format: Adult Contemp; *Hrs. of News Programming:* news progmg 16 hrs wkly; *No. News Employees:* 3; *Target Audience:* 25-45.
Rob Michaels, Program and Music Director
Darren McPeake, Music Director

CFPV-FM
98.9 MHz FM; 420 w
McBride Communications & Media Inc., 10760 Fundy Dr., Pemberton, BC V7E 5K7 Canada
(604) 220-8393; *Fax:* (604) 677-6316
info@cimmfm.com
License: Pemberton, BC held by 0749943 BC Ltd. (Matthew G. McBride).
Population Served: 2,369; *Arbitron Metro Market:* Pemberton, BC
Matthew McBride, President

Pender Harbour

CIPN-FM
104.7 MHz FM; *Hrs Open:* 24; 350 w; 297 meters*Rebroadcasts:* Rebroadcasts CISQ-FM Squamish
40147 Glenalder Pl., Suite 202, Squamish, BC V8B 0G2 Canada
(604) 892-1021; *Fax:* (604) 892-6383
www.mountainfm.com
news@mountainfm.com
License: Pender Harbour, BC held by Rogers Media Inc.
Group Owner: Rogers Media Inc.
Format: Adult Contemp, Contemporary Hits/Top 40; *Hrs. of News Programming:* news progmg 16 hrs wkly; *No. News Employees:* 3
Terry Chan, Programming Assistant
Darren McPeake, Music Director

Penticton

***CIGV-FM**
10-18-1981; 100.7 MHz FM; *Hrs Open:* 24
201-1301 Main St., Penticton, BC V2A 5E9 Canada
(250) 493-6767; *Fax:* (250) 487-2851
License: Penticton, BC held by NewCap Inc.
Group Owner: NewCap Inc.
Nat'l Reps: Target Broadcast Sales; *Wire Services:* Broadcast News Ltd.
Format: Country; *Special Programming:* Class 2 hrs, farm one hr wkly; *Hrs. of News Programming:* news progmg 16 hrs wkly; *No. News Employees:* 3; *Target Audience:* 18 plus.
Dallas Gray, General Manager
Dallas Gray, General Sales Mgr
Casey Clarke, Programming Director
Kat Boloten, Promotions Director
Chris Cleaver, Chief Engineer

CJMG-FM
06-01-1965; 97.1 MHz FM; 1.8 kw
33 Carmi Ave., Penticton, BC V2A 3G4 Canada
(250) 492-2800; *Fax:* (250) 493-0370
www.sunonline.ca
mark.burley@bellmedia.ca
License: Penticton, BC held by Bell Media Radio G.P.
Group Owner: Bell Media Inc.
Format: Contemporary Hits/Top 40
Janet Burley, General Manager
Janet Burley, Station Manager
Mark Burley, Programming Director
Karen Davy, Promotions Director
Jon Ferebee, News Director
Tammy Cole, Music Director
Paul Brain, Creative Director

CKOR
09-01-1948; 800 kHz AM
33 Carmi Ave., Penticton, BC V2A 3G4 Canada
(250) 492-2800; *Fax:* (250) 493-0370
www.penticton.myezrock.com
janet.burley@bellmedia.ca
License: Penticton, BC held by Astral Media Radio G.P.
Group Owner: Bell Media Inc.; (acq 10-29-2007; grpsl).
Format: Adult Contemp, Oldies
Nicole Beetstra, General Manager
Nicole Beetstra, General Sales Mgr
Jen Zandstra, Promotions Manager
Lea Wilman, Brand Director

Port Alberni

CJAV-FM
09-02-2005; 93.3 MHz FM; *Hrs Open:* 24; 6 kw
3296 3rd Ave., Port Alberni, BC V9Y 4E1 Canada
(250) 723-2455; *Fax:* (250) 723-0797
www.933thepeak.com
License: Port Alberni, BC held by Jim Pattison Broadcast Group Ltd. (the general partner) and Jim Pattison Industries Ltd. (the limited partner), carrying on business as Jim Pattison Broadcast Group L.P.
Group Owner: The Jim Pattison Broadcast Group; (acq 6-27-2006; grpsl).
Population Served: 21,376; *Format:* Contemporary Hits/Top 40, Adult Contemp; *Target Audience:* 25-54; Adults; *Adv. Rates:* 28; 28; 28; 28
David Wiwchar, Operations Manager
Ashleigh Clark, Promotions
David Wiwchar, News Director
Diane Redlin, Account Executive
Brian Bredesen, Account Executive

Port Hardy

CFNI
1240 kHz AM
7035A Market St., Port Hardy, BC V0N 2P0 Canada
(250) 949-6500; *Fax:* (250) 949-6580
www.mytriportnow.com
amandzuk@vistaradio.ca
License: Port Hardy, BC held by Vista Radio Ltd.
Group Owner: Vista Radio Ltd.
Format: Adult Contemp, Oldies; *No. News Employees:* 1; *Target Audience:* General.
Allison Mandzuk, General Manager
Andrew Davis, Programming Director
Justin Goulet, News

Port Moody

CKPM-FM
98.7 MHz FM
99 Moray Street, Port Moody, BC V3H 3M2 Canada
(604) 917-0188
www.mcmi.ca
info@mcmi.ca
License: Port Moody, Great Vancouver County, BC held by McBride Communications & Media Inc

Powell River

CJMP-FM
01-01-2006; 90.1 MHz FM; 3.6 w
4476 A Marine Ave., Powell River, BC V8A 2K2 Canada
(604) 485-0088; *Fax:* (604) 485-2683
www.cjmp.ca
admin@cjmp.ca
License: Powell River, BC held by Powell River Model Community Project for Persons with Disabilities.
Population Served: 13,165; *Arbitron Metro Market:* Powell River, BC; *Format:* Variety/Diverse
Elaine Hill, General Sales Mgr

CFPW-FM
08-27-2008; 95.7 MHz FM; 1183 w; 416 meters
7074 Westminster St., Unit 103, Powell River, BC V8A 1C5 Canada
(604) 485-4207; *Fax:* (604) 485-4210
www.mypowellrivernow.com
amandzuk@vistaradio.ca
License: Powell River, BC held by Vista Radio Ltd.
Group Owner: Vista Radio Ltd.
Population Served: 13,165; *Arbitron Metro Market:* Powell River, BC; *Format:* Adult Contemp; *No. News Employees:* 4
Allison Mandzuk, General Manager
Andrew Davis, Programming Director
Kim Wall, Operations Manager

Prince George

CIRX-FM
94.3 MHz FM; 11.48 kWs; 69.5 meters
2977 Ferry Ave., Unit 101, Prince George, BC V2N 1L3 Canada
(250) 564-2524; *Fax:* (250) 562-6611
www.myprincegeorgenow.com
License: Prince George, BC held by Vista Radio Ltd.
Group Owner: Vista Radio Ltd.
Format: Rock/AOR; *Target Audience:* 18-34.
Kev Cotter, Programming Director
Kyle Balzer, News Director

CKKN-FM
03-01-1981; 101.3 MHz FM; 9.1 kw; Ant 1,000 ft
1810 3rd Ave., 2nd Fl., Prince George, BC V2M 1G4 Canada
(250) 564-8861; *Fax:* (250) 562-8768
www.1013theriver.com
License: Prince George, BC held by Jim Pattison Broadcast Group Ltd. (the general partner) and Jim Pattison Industries Ltd. (the limited partner) carrying on business as Jim Pattison Broadcast Group L.P.
Group Owner: The Jim Pattison Broadcast Group; (acq 12-21-2000; grpsl).
TV Affiliate: CKPG-TV affil.; *Format:* Adult Contemp
Mike Clotildes, General Manager
Kelli Moorhead, General Sales Mgr
Ron Polillo, Programming Director
Kharah Black, Promotions Director

***CFUR-FM**
01-01-2002; 88.7 MHz FM; 510 w
University of Northern BC, 3333 University Way, Prince George, BC V2N 4Z9 Canada
(250) 960-7664; *Fax:* (250) 960-5995
www.cfur.ca
stationmanager@cfur.ca
License: Prince George, BC held by Education Alternative Radio Society.
Population Served: 71,974; *Arbitron Metro Market:* Prince George, BC; *Format:* Variety/Diverse; *Target Audience:* Community of Prince George.; *Adv. Rates:* 66; 66; 66; 66
Ian Gregg, Station Manager
Glen Yakemchuk, Engineering Dir
Jordan Tucker, Music Director

CKDV-FM
05-30-2003; 99.3 MHz FM; *Hrs Open:* 24; 9.3 kw
1810 3rd Ave., 2nd Fl., Prince George, BC V2M 1G4 Canada
(250) 564-8861; *Fax:* (250) 562-8768
www.993thedrive.com
License: Prince George, BC held by Jim Pattison Broadcast Group Ltd. (the general partner) and Jim Pattison Industries Ltd. (the limited partner) carrying on business as Jim Pattison Broadcast Group L.P.
Group Owner: The Jim Pattison Broadcast Group
Population Served: 71,974; *Arbitron Metro Market:* Prince George, BC; *Format:* Oldies
Mike Clotildes, General Manager
Kelli Moorhead, General Sales Mgr
Ron Polillo, Radio Program Director
Kharah Black, Promotions Director

CJCI-FM
97.3 MHz FM; *Hrs Open:* 24; 12 kw; 63.8 meters
2977 Ferry Ave., Unit 101, Prince George, BC V2N 1L3 Canada
(250) 564-2524; *Fax:* (250) 562-6611
www.myprincegeorgenow.com
License: Prince George, BC held by Vista Radio Ltd.
Group Owner: Vista Radio Ltd.
Population Served: 71,974; *Arbitron Metro Market:* Prince George, BC; *Format:* Country; *No. News Employees:* 3; *Target Audience:* 25-54.
Kyle Balzer, News Director
Gary Russell, Regional Cluster Manager
Brittney Shaw-MacLaren, Integrated Marketing Executive

CFIS-FM
07-03-2007; 93.1 MHz FM; *Hrs Open:* 24; 494 w; -34.5 meters; N53 54 37 W122 46 39
2880 15th Ave., Prince George, BC V2M 1T1 Canada
(250) 563-2347
www.cfisfm.com
cfisfm@yahoo.ca
License: Prince George, Canada County, BC held by Prince George Community Radio Society.
Population Served: 70,000; *Arbitron Metro Market:* Prince George; *Hrs. of News Programming:* 6 hrs wkly; *Target Audience:* 55+; *Adv. Rates:* $10/30 second ad
Corey Walker, President
Reg Feyer, Operations Dir
Reg Feyer, General Manager
Reg Feyer, Station Manager
Howard Foot, General Sales Mgr
Reg Feyer, Programming Director
Reg Feyer, Promotions Manager

Prince Rupert

CIAJ-FM
01-01-2000; 100.7 MHz FM; 26.5 w
Box 1, 531 6th Ave. W., Prince Rupert, BC V8J 3P4 Canada
License: Prince Rupert, BC held by Aboriginal Christian Voice Network.
Population Served: 12,508; *Arbitron Metro Market:* Prince Rupert, BC; *Format:* Christian
Prescott Sandhu, General Manager

CHTK-FM
01-01-1965; 99.1 MHz FM; 160 watts; 278 meters; 54 17 N55 130 23 W10
215 Cowbay Rd., Suite 230, Prince Rupert, BC V8J 1A8 Canada
(250) 624-9111; *Fax:* (250) 624-3100
www.princerupert.myezrock.com
grant.scott@bellmedia.ca
License: Prince Rupert, BC held by Bell Media Radio G.P.
Group Owner: Bell Media Inc.
Format: Contemporary Hits/Top 40
Grant Scott, Programming Director
John Crawford, News Director

Quesnel

CKCQ-FM
100.3 MHz FM; 1.8 kw; 64 meters
410 Kinchant St., Suite 502, Quesnel, BC V2J 7J5 Canada
(250) 992-7046
www.mycariboonow.com
cverbenkov@vistaradio.ca
License: Quesnel, BC held by Vista Radio Ltd.
Group Owner: Vista Radio Ltd.
Population Served: 10,007; *Arbitron Metro Market:* Quesnel, BC; *Format:* Country; *No. News Employees:* 4
Cindy Verbenkov, General Sales Mgr
Carol Gass, Regional Program Director
George Henderson, News
Larissa Mueller, Integrated Marketing Executive
Gary Russell, Regional Cluster Manager

***CFFM-FM-2**
94.9 MHz FM; *Hrs Open:* 24
410 Kinchant St., Suite 502, Quesnel, BC V2J 7J5 Canada
(250) 992-7046
www.mycariboonow.com
cverbenkov@vistaradio.ca
License: Quesnel, BC held by Vista Radio Ltd.
Group Owner: Vista Radio Ltd.
Nat'l Reps: Canadian Broadcast Sales
Format: Rock/AOR; *No. News Employees:* 2; *Target Audience:* 25-54; *Adv. Rates:* 25; 21; 21; 14
Gary Russell, Regional Cluster Manager
Cindy Verbenkov, General Sales Mgr
Carol Gass, Regional Program Director
George Henderson, News
Larissa Mueller, Integrated Marketing Executive

Revelstoke

CKCR-FM
01-01-2009; 106.1 MHz FM
555 Victoria Rd., Suite 207, Revelstoke, BC V0E 2S0 Canada
(250) 837-2149; *Fax:* (250) 837-5577
www.iheartradio.ca/ez-rock/ez-rock-revelstoke
License: Revelstoke, BC held by Bell Media Radio G.P.
Group Owner: Bell Media Inc.
Format: Adult Contemp
Gord Leighton, General Manager
Gord Leighton, General Sales Mgr

Richmond

CHKG-FM
09-06-1997; 96.1 MHz FM; *Hrs Open:* 24; 46 kw; N49 21 12 W122 57 18
2090-4151 Hazelbridge Way, Richmond, BC V6X 4J7 Canada
(604) 295-1234; *Fax:* (604) 295-1201
www.fm961.com
general@fm961.com
License: Richmond, BC held by Fairchild Radio (Vancouver FM) Ltd.
Nat'l Reps: Target Broadcast Sales *Regional Reps:* In House
Population Served: 1,300,000; *Format:* Ethnic; *Hrs. of News Programming:* news progmg 10 hrs wky; *No. News Employees:* 10; *Target Audience:* General.
Thomas Fung, Chairman
Brenda Lo, Operations Dir
Pearl Kwan, General Sales Mgr
Seme Ho, Programming Director
Pearl Kwan, Promotions Manager
Travena Lee, News Director
Alfred Lee, Cantonese Programming
Alan Kwok, OperationsManager
George Lee, Senior Vice President

CISL
05-01-1980; 650 kHz AM; 20 kw
#20 - 11151 Horseshoe Way, Richmond, BC V7A 4S5 Canada
(604) 241-2100; *Fax:* (604) 272-0917
License: Richmond, BC held by 8384886 Canada Inc.
Group Owner: NewCap Inc.; (acq 03-19-2014; grpsl)
Format: Adult Contemp, Oldies
Sherri Pierce, General Manager
Stu Ferguson, Programming Director

Rossland

CHLI-FM
01-01-2009; 101.1 MHz FM; kw
Canada
(250) 362-0080
www.rosslandradio.com
License: Rossland, BC held by Rossland Radio Cooperative.
Arbitron Metro Market: Rossland, BC
Yvon Savoes, President
Francois Morache, Operations Dir
George Daviault, General Manager
Mike Mainville, Programming Director
Mark Andre Halle, News Director

Salmo

CFAD-FM
10-11-2008; 91.1 MHz FM; 5 w; N49 11 45 W117 16 51
Box 549, Salmo, BC Canada
(250) 357-2299
www.salmofm.info
info@salmofm.info
License: Salmo, BC held by Salmo FM Radio Society.
Mariah Davies-Ross, President
Dave Pearce, Vice President

Salmon Arm

CKXR-FM
11-18-1965; 91.5 MHz FM; *Hrs Open:* 24; 400 w
360 Ross St., Box 69, Salmon Arm, BC V1E 4N2 Canada
(250) 832-2161; *Fax:* (250) 832-2240
www.salmonarm.myezrock.com
License: Salmon Arm, BC held by Bell Media Radio G.P.
Group Owner: Bell Media Inc.; (acq 10-29-2007; grpsl)
Population Served: 17,464; *Arbitron Metro Market:* Salmon Arm, BC; *Format:* Adult Contemp; *No. News Employees:* 3; *Target Audience:* 25-54.
Gord Leighton, General Manager
Gord Leighton, General Sales Mgr
Mark Burley, Programming Director

Salt Spring Island

CFSI-FM
107.9 MHz FM; 130 w; 215.6 meters; N48 50 56 W123 31 52
315 Upper Ganges Road, Suite 19A, Salt Spring Island, BC V8K 2X4 Canada
(250) 931-1079
www.greenfm.ca
License: Salt Spring Island, BC held by Salt Spring Island Radio Corp.

Sechelt

CFUN-FM
107.5 MHz FM; *Hrs Open:* 24; 640 w; 210.1 metres; 49.11005 N 121.846396 W
46167 Yale Rd., Suite 309, Chilliwack, BC V2P 2P2 Canada
(604) 877-6357
www.kissradio.ca
License: Sechelt, BC held by Rogers Media Inc.
Group Owner: Rogers Media Inc.; (acq 9-10-99; grpsl)
Format: Contemporary Hits/Top 40; *Hrs. of News Programming:* News progmg 6 hrs wkly; *Target Audience:* 35 plus.
Shari Craig, Account Manager

Smithers

CFBV
870 kHz AM
1139 Queen St., Smithers, BC V0J 2X0 Canada
(250) 847-2521; *Fax:* (250) 847-9411
www.mybulkleylakesnow.com
aangel@vistaradio.ca
License: Smithers, BC held by Vista Radio Ltd.
Group Owner: Vista Radio Ltd.
Format: Adult Contemp
Alissa Angel, General Sales Mgr
JD Brown, Programming Director
Daryl Vandenberg, News
Marieke De Jonge, Integrated Marketing Executive

CICK-FM
93.9 MHz FM; 49.7 w; -73.5 meters; N54 46 47 W127 10 11
Box 834, Smithers, BC V0J 2N0 Canada

www.smithersradio.com
info@smithersradio.com
License: Smithers, BC held by Smithers Community Radio Society
Glen Ingram, Station Manager

Squamish

***CISQ-FM**
107.1 MHz FM; *Hrs Open:* 24; 30 kw; -533.6 m
40147 Glenalder Pl., Suite 202, Squamish, BC V8B 0G2 Canada
(604) 892-1021; *Fax:* (604) 892-6383
www.mountainfm.com
news@mountainfm.com
License: Squamish, BC held by Rogers Media Inc.
Group Owner: Rogers Media Inc.
Nat'l Reps: Canadian Broadcast Sales
Format: Adult Contemp; *Special Programming:* Talk 5 hrs wkly; *Hrs. of News Programming:* news progmg 5 hrs wkly; *No. News Employees:* 3; *Target Audience:* 18-54.
Rob Michaels, Program and Music Director
Darren McPeake, Music Director

Summerland

CHOR-FM
05-21-2010; 98.5 MHz FM; 20 watts; 348 meters
9901 Main St., Suite 200, Summerland, BC V0H 1Z0 Canada
(250) 494-0333; *Fax:* (250) 404-0263
www.summerland.myezrock.com
License: Summerland, BC held by Astral Media Radio G P
Group Owner: Bell Media Inc.
Janet Burley, General Manager
Janet Burley, General Sales Mgr
Karen Davy, Promotions Director
Mark Burley, Brand Director
Jon Ferebee, Assistant Brand Director
Paul Brain, Creative Director

Terrace

CFTK
01-01-1960; 590 kHz AM; 1 kw
4625 Lazelle Ave., Terrace, BC V8G 1S4 Canada
(250) 635-6316; *Fax:* (250) 638-6320
www.terrace.myezrock.com
License: Terrace, BC held by Bell Media Radio G.P.
Group Owner: Bell Media Inc.; (acq 10-29-2007; grpsl).
Format: Adult Contemp
Grant Scott, Programming Director
John Crawford, News Director

CJFW-FM
12-01-1983; 103.1 MHz FM; w
4625 Lazelle Ave., Terrace, BC V8G 1S4 Canada
(250) 635-6316; *Fax:* (250) 638-6320
www.cjfw.ca
grant.scott@bellmedia.ca
License: Terrace, BC held by Bell Media Radio G.P.
Group Owner: Bell Media Inc.
TV Affiliate: CFTK-TV affil.; *Format:* Country
Grant Scott, Programming Director
John Crawford, News Director

CFNR-FM
01-01-1995; 92.1 MHz FM; *Hrs Open:* 24; 43 w
4562 B Queensway Dr., Terrace, BC V8G 3X6 Canada
(250) 638-8137; *Fax:* (250) 638-8027
www.classicrockcfnr.ca
License: Terrace, BC held by Northern Native Broadcasting (Terrace, B.C.).
Population Served: 11,486; *Arbitron Metro Market:* Terrace, BC;
Format: Classic Rock; *Special Programming:* First nations 9 hrs; *Hrs. of News Programming:* News progmg 10 hrs wkly; *Target Audience:* General; 35+
Greg Smith, CEO
Ron Bartlett, Sales Manager
Craig Ellis, Programming Director
Tara Evans, Promotions Manager
Bill Free, News Director
Jillian Milnes, Accounting Manager
Diane Lukasser, Reception
Brent Halfyard, CreativeDirector
Denise Halfyard, Website Coordinator

Tofino

CHMZ-FM
01-01-2005; 90.1 MHz FM; 170 w
Box 1092, Tofino, BC V0R 2Z0 Canada
(250) 725-4411; *Fax:* (250) 725-4411
www.chmzfm.com
License: Tofino, BC held by CHMZ-FM Radio Ltd.
Population Served: 1,876; *Arbitron Metro Market:* Tofino, BC;
Format: Country
Matthew McBride, General Manager

Trail

CJAT-FM
01-01-1993; 95.7 MHz FM; 13.5 kw
1560 Second Ave., Trail, BC V1R 1M4 Canada
(250) 368-5510; *Fax:* (250) 368-8471
www.kootenays.myezrock.com
doreen.stocker@bellmedia.ca
License: Trail, BC held by Bell Media Radio G.P.
Group Owner: Bell Media Inc.; (acq 10-29-2007; grpsl).
Nat'l Reps: Radio Astral
Format: Adult Contemp
Nicole Beetstra, General Manager
Nicole Beetstra, General Sales Mgr
Lea Wilman, Programming Director
Jen Zandstra, Promotions Manager
Jayne Garry, News Director
Lea Wilman, Brand Director

Ucluelet

CIMM-FM
09-01-2006; 99.5 MHz FM; 180 w
10760 Fundy Dr., Richmond, BC V7E 5K7 Canada
(250) 725 4411; *Fax:* (604) 677-6316
www.longbeachradio.ca
info@cimmfm.com
License: Ucluelet, BC held by CIMM-FM Radio Ltd.
Population Served: 1,627; *Arbitron Metro Market:* Ucluelet, BC;
Format: Variety/Diverse
Matthew McBride, General Manager

Vancouver

CBUFFM
12-01-1967; 97.7 MHz FM; 50 kw; Ant 1,823 ft
Mailing Address: 700 Hamilton St., Vancouver, BC Canada
Second Address: Box 4600, Vancouver, BC V6B 4A2
(604) 662-6169; *Fax:* (604) 662-6161
www.radio-canada.ca/c-b
License: Vancouver, BC held by CBC.
Nat'l Network: Premiere Chaine
Pierre Guerin, Station Manager
Mario Deschamps, Programming Director

CFOX-FM
10-15-1964; 99.3 MHz FM; 51 kw; 368.4 meters
700 West Georgia St., Suite 2000, Vancouver, BC V7Y 1K9 Canada
(604) 684-7221; *Fax:* (604) 331-2722
www.cfox.com
webmaster@cfox.com
License: Vancouver, BC held by Corus Radio Co.
Group Owner: Corus Entertainment Inc.
Format: Alternative, Rock/AOR
Paul Ackerman, Sales Director
Dustin Collins, Programming Director
Monika Coen, Promotions Manager
Britters, Music Director
Alanna Koshlay, Promotions Coordinator
Julie Mangat, Content Coordinator

*CFROFM
04-22-1975; 100.5 MHz FM; 5.5 kw; 1,005 ft
110-360 Columbia St., Vancouver, BC Canada
(604) 684-8494
www.coopradio.org
License: Vancouver, BC held by Vancouver Co-Op Radio.
Special Programming: Black 14 hrs, Chinese 2 hrs, Greek one hr, hip hop 17 hrs, jazz 16 hrs, Latin American 7 hrs, Pol 5 hrs wkly; *Target Audience:* General; alternative community
Leela Chinniah, Programming Director
Danjel van Tijn, Engineering Dir
Rob Gauvin, Music Director

CFTE
04-20-1922; 1410 kHz AM; *Hrs Open:* 24; 50 kw-U, DA-2
969 Robson St., Suite 500, Vancouver, BC V6Z 1X5 Canada
(604) 871-9000; *Fax:* (604) 871-2901
www.tsn.ca/radio/vancouver-1040-i-1410
programming@tsn1040.ca
License: Vancouver, BC held by Bell Media British Columbia Radio Partnership
Group Owner: Bell Media Inc.
Format: Sports
John Hinnen, General Manager
Robert Gray, Programming Director

CHMB
12-10-1959; 1320 kHz AM; *Hrs Open:* 24
Canada
(604) 263-1320; *Fax:* (604) 261-0310
www.am1320.com
info@am1320.com
License: Vancouver, BC held by Mainstream Broadcasting Corp.
Nat'l Reps: Canadian Broadcast Sales
Format: Chinese; *Special Programming:* American Indian one hr, Japanese 1 hr, Vietnamese; *Hrs. of News Programming:* news progmg 30 hrs wkly; *No. News Employees:* 8; *Target Audience:* 18-65; multilingual, mainly Chinese
Teresa Wat, CEO
James Ho, President
George Feng, General Sales Mgr
Harry Lee, Programming Director
Trix Chan, News Director
Kay Lai, Sales Manager

CHQM-FM
08-10-1960; 103.5 MHz FM; *Hrs Open:* 24; 100 kw; Ant 2,026 ft
969 Robson St., Suite 500, Vancouver, BC V6Z 1X5 Canada
(604) 871-9000; *Fax:* (604) 871-2901
www.qmfm.com
feedback@qmfm.com
License: Vancouver, BC held by Bell Media British Columbia Radio Partnership
Group Owner: Bell Media Inc.; (acq 6-22-2007; grpsl).
Format: Adult Contemp; *Hrs. of News Programming:* news progmg 2 hrs wkly; *No. News Employees:* 5; *Target Audience:* 25-54.
James Stuart, General Manager
Barry O'Donnell, General Sales Mgr
Clara Carotenuto, Programming Director
Carl LeGrice, Promotions Manager
Dave Youell, Chief Engineer

*CITRFM
04-01-1982; 101.9 MHz FM; *Hrs Open:* 7:30 AM-4 AM; kw
Canada
(604) 822-3017; *Fax:* (604) 822-9364
www.citr.ca
citrmgr@ams.ubc.ca
License: Vancouver, BC held by Student Radio Society of University of British Columbia.
Format: Variety/Diverse; *Hrs. of News Programming:* News progmg 5 hrs wkly; *Target Audience:* General; campus/community
Brenda Grunau, Station Manager
Robin Alam, Programming Director
Bryce Dunn, Program Coordinator

CJJR-FM
07-01-1986; 93.7 MHz FM; *Hrs Open:* 24; 75 kw
1401 West 8th Ave., Suite 300, Vancouver, BC V6H 1C9 Canada
(604) 731-7772; *Fax:* (604) 731-0493
www.jrfm.com
License: Vancouver, BC held by Jim Pattison Broadcast Group Ltd. (the general partner) and Jim Pattison Industries Ltd. (the limited partner), carrying on business as Jim Pattison Group L.P.
Group Owner: The Jim Pattison Broadcast Group
Format: Country; *No. News Employees:* 2; *Target Audience:* 25-54.
Mark Patric, General Manager

CJVB
06-18-1972; 1470 kHz AM; *Hrs Open:* 24; 50 kw-U, DA-2; N49 11 36 W123 01 17
4151 Hazelbridge Way, Unit 2090 Aberdeen Centre, Richmond, BC Canada
(604) 295-1234; *Fax:* (604) 295-1201
www.am1470.com
general@am1470.com
License: Vancouver, BC held by Fairchild Radio Group Ltd.
Nat'l Reps: Target Broadcast Sales *Regional Reps:* In House
Population Served: 1,300,000; *Hrs. of News Programming:* news progmg 23 hrs wkly; *No. News Employees:* 10; *Target Audience:* General.
Thomas Fung, Chairman
Brenda Lo, Operations Dir
Pearl Kwan, General Sales Mgr
Alfred Lee, Programming Director
Pearl Kwan, Promotions Manager
Travena Lee, News Director
Seme Ho, AVP International Programming
Alan Kwok,Operations Manager
George Lee, Senior Vice President

CJAX-FM
03-01-1980; 96.9 MHz FM; *Hrs Open:* 24; 75 kw; 686 metres; 49.357365 N 122.953776 W
2440 Ash St., Vancouver, BC V5Z 4J6 Canada
(604) 872-2557
www.jack969.com
License: Vancouver, BC held by Rogers Media Inc.
Group Owner: Rogers Media Inc.
Format: Adult Contemp, Variety/Diverse
Stephane Lecouteur, Media Sales Supervisor
Kyle Fournier, Promotions Coordinator
Melanie Z Kilpatrick, Promotions and Assistant Music Director

CHMJ
02-03-1955; 730 kHz AM; 50 kw
700 West Georgia St., Suite 2000, Vancouver, BC V7Y 1K9 Canada
(604) 681-7511; *Fax:* (604) 331-2722
www.am730.ca
paul.ackerman@corusent.com
License: Vancouver, BC held by Corus Radio Co.
Group Owner: Corus Entertainment Inc.; (acq 7-6-2000; grpsl).
Format: Talk, News/Talk
Paul Ackerman, Sales Director
Larry Gifford, Programming Director
Monika Coen, Promotions Manager
Corey McMaster, Promotions Assistant
Julie Mangat, Content Coordinator

CKST
01-19-1963; 1040 kHz AM; *Hrs Open:* 24; 50 kw-U, DA-2
969 Robson St., Suite 500, Vancouver, BC Canada
(604) 871-9000; *Fax:* (604) 871-2901
www.tsn.ca/radio/vancouver-1040-i-1410
programming@tsn1040.ca
License: Vancouver, BC held by Bell Media British Columbia Radio Partnership
Group Owner: Bell Media Inc.; (acq 6-22-2007;. grpsl).

Nat'l Reps: Canadian Broadcast Sales
Population Served: 2,000,000; *Format:* Sports; *Hrs. of News Programming:* news progmg 8 hrs wkly; *No. News Employees:* 4; *Target Audience:* 40 plus
James Stuart, General Manager
Robert Gray, Programming Director

CKWX
04-01-1923; 1130 kHz AM; 50 kw
2440 Ash St., Vancouver, BC V5Z 4J6 Canada
(604) 873-2599; *Fax:* (604) 873-0877
www.news1130.com
License: Vancouver, BC held by Rogers Media Inc.
Group Owner: Rogers Media Inc.; acq 1989).
Nat'l Reps: CBS Radio
Format: News; *Hrs. of News Programming:* news progmg 168 hrs wkly; *No. News Employees:* 45; *Target Audience:* 35-54; men
Diana Davies, Sales Manager
Treena Wood, National News Director

CKZZ-FM
05-23-1991; 95.3 MHz FM; 75 kw
#20 - 11151 Horseshoe Way, Richmond, BC V7A 4S5 Canada
(604) 241-2100; *Fax:* (604) 272-0917
www.z953.ca
License: Vancouver, BC held by 8384878 Canada Inc.
Group Owner: NewCap Inc.; (acq 03-19-2014; grpsl)
Format: Adult Contemp
Sherri Pierce, General Manager
Paul Kaye, Programming Director

CFBT-FM
02-15-2002; 94.5 MHz FM; *Hrs Open:* 24; 90 kw
969 Robson St., Vancouver, BC V6Z 1X5 Canada
(604) 871-9000; *Fax:* (604) 871-2901
www.vancouver.virginradio.ca
feedback@945virginradio.ca
License: Vancouver, BC held by Bell Media British Columbia Radio Partnership
Group Owner: Bell Media Inc.; (acq 10-12-2007; C$46,006,717)
Format: Contemporary Hits/Top 40; *Hrs. of News Programming:* news progmg 2 hrs wkly; *No. News Employees:* 1
Robin Haggar, Programming Director

CJRJ
11-01-2006; 1200 kHz AM
Canada
(604) 299-8863; *Fax:* (604) 299-3088
info@rj1200.com
License: Vancouver, BC held by I.T. Productions Ltd.
Arbitron Metro Market: Albuquerque, NM; *Format:* Ethnic
Shushma Datt, CEO
Sudhir Datta, General Manager

CKYE-FM
02-01-2006; 93.1 MHz FM; kw
Canada
(604) 598-9311; *Fax:* (604) 599-6063
redfm.ca
info@redfm.ca
License: Vancouver, BC held by South Asian Broadcasting Corp. Inc.
Arbitron Metro Market: Vancouver, BC; *Format:* Ethnic
Kulwinder Sanghera, CEO
Bijoy Samuel, General Manager
Harjinder Thind, News Director

CKAV-FM-2
01-01-2007; 106.3 MHz FM; 9 kw; Ant 1,968 ft; N49 21 17 W122 57 25
PO Box 87, Station E, Toronto, ON M6H 4E1 Canada
(416) 703-1287; *Fax:* (416) 703-4328
aboriginalvoices.com
info@aboriginalvoices.com
License: Vancouver, BC held by Voices Radio's broadcasting licenses have been revoked by the CRTC. All stations are now broadcasting solely on voicesradio.ca
Group Owner: Voices Radio Inc.
Population Served: 2,615,060; *Arbitron Metro Market:* Toronto, ON; *Format:* Ethnic
Roy Hennessy, Operations Dir
Patrice Mousseau, Programming Director

CKPK-FM
11-13-2008; 102.7 MHz FM; 2.8 kw; Ant 1,932 ft; N49 21 16 W122 57 30
1401 West 8th Ave., Suite 300, Vancouver, BC V6H 1C9 Canada
(604) 731-6111; *Fax:* (604) 731-0493
www.thepeak.fm
License: Vancouver, BC held by Jim Pattison Broadcast Group Ltd. (the general partner) and Jim Pattison Industries Ltd. (the limited partner), carrying on business as Jim Pattison Broadcast Group L.P.
Group Owner: The Jim Pattison Broadcast Group
Nat'l Reps: Canadian Broadcast Sales
Format: Adult Contemp, Alternative; *Target Audience:* 25-49; adults
Mark Patric, General Manager

CHLG-FM
07-01-2009; 104.3 MHz FM; *Hrs Open:* 24/7; 50 kw
#20 - 11151 Horseshoe Way, Richmond, BC V7A 4S5 Canada
(604) 241-2100; *Fax:* (604) 272-0917
www.lg1043.com
License: Vancouver, Canada County, BC held by 8384860 Canada Inc.
Group Owner: NewCap Inc.
Arbitron Metro Market: Vancouver, BC; *Format:* Oldies; *No. News Employees:* 3; *Target Audience:* 25-54.
Sherri Pierce, General Manager

Vanderhoof

CIVH
11-01-1973; 1340 kHz AM; *Hrs Open:* 6-10 AM
150 W. Columbia St., Vanderhoof, BC T0J 3A0 Canada
(250) 567-4914; *Fax:* (250) 567-4982
www.mynechakovalleynow.com
License: Vanderhoof, BC held by Vista Radio Ltd.
Group Owner: Vista Radio Ltd.
Nat'l Reps: Target Broadcast Sales
Format: Country; *Special Programming:* Relg 5 hrs wkly; *Target Audience:* General.
Geoff Poulton, President

CIRX-FM-1
95.9 MHz FM
2977 Ferry Ave., Unit 101, Prince George, BC V2N 1L3 Canada
(250) 564-2524; *Fax:* (250) 562-6611
www.myprincegeorgenow.com
License: Vanderhoof, BC held by Vista Radio Ltd.
Group Owner: Vista Radio Ltd.
Format: Rock/AOR; *Target Audience:* 18-34.
Gary Russell, Regional Cluster Manager
Kyle Balzer, News Director
Don Graham, Production Manager
Brittney Shaw-MacLaren, Integrated Marketing Executive

Vernon

CKIZ-FM
11-15-2001; 107.5 MHz FM; 45 kw
3313 32nd Ave., Vernon, BC V1T 2E1 Canada
(250) 545-2141; *Fax:* (250) 545-9008
www.1075kiss.com
License: Vernon, BC held by Jim Pattison Broadcast Group Ltd. (the general partner) and Jim Pattison Industries Ltd. (the limited partner), carrying on business as Jim Pattison Broadcast Group L.P.
Group Owner: The Jim Pattison Broadcast Group; (acq 10-31-2008; C$4 million)
Nat'l Reps: Canadian Broadcast Sales
Population Served: 38,150; *Arbitron Metro Market:* Vernon, BC; *Format:* Adult Contemp
Stu Crouse, General Manager
Stu Crouse, General Sales Mgr

CICF-FM
10-23-1978; 105.7 MHz FM; 46 kw
31st St., Suite 2800, Vernon, BC V1T 5H4 Canada
(250) 545-9222; *Fax:* (250) 542-2083
www.thesunonline.ca
reception@thesunonline.ca
License: Vernon, BC held by Bell Media Radio G.P.
Group Owner: Bell Media Inc.; (acq 10-29-2007; grpsl)
Population Served: 38,150; *Arbitron Metro Market:* Vernon, BC; *Format:* Contemporary Hits/Top 40; *No. News Employees:* 2
Gord Leighton, General Manager
Gord Leighton, General Sales Mgr
Mark Burley, Programming Director
Kristy Carruthers, Promotions Coordinator
Tammy Cole, Music Director
Brian Martin, Assistant Program Manager

Victoria

CFAX
09-04-1959; 1070 kHz AM; *Hrs Open:* 24; 10 kw
1420 Broad St., Victoria, BC V8W 2B1 Canada
(250) 386-1070; *Fax:* (250) 920-4306
www.cfax1070.com
License: Victoria, BC held by Bell Media British Columbia Radio Partnership
Group Owner: Bell Media Inc.; (acq 10-1-2004;. C$7.5 million with co-located FM).
Nat'l Reps: Target Broadcast Sales; *Wire Services:* BN Wire
Format: News/Talk; *Hrs. of News Programming:* news progmg 21 hrs wkly; *No. News Employees:* 7; *Target Audience:* 45 plus; 50% males, 50% females; *Adv. Rates:* 169; 106; 115; 53
Terry Spence, General Manager
Kevin Bell, General Sales Mgr
Al Ferraby, Programming Director
Astrid Braunschmidt, Meteorologist

*CFUV-FM
12-17-1984; 101.9 MHz FM; *Hrs Open:* 24; kw
Canada
(250) 721-8702
www.cfuv.uvic.ca
cfuvman@uvic.ca
License: Victoria, Canada County, BC held by University of Victoria Student Radio Society.
Format: Variety/Diverse; *Special Programming:* It 2 hrs, American Indian one hrs; Fr 2 hrs, Pol o; *Hrs. of News Programming:* News progmg 8.5 hrs wkly; *Target Audience:* General; people tired of coml radio, on campus & inthe community; *Adv. Rates:* 40; 40; 40; 40
Randy Gelling, Station Manager
Jana Grazley, Programming Director
Justin Lanoue, Music Director

CIOC-FM
98.5 MHz FM; *Hrs Open:* 24; 100 kw; 147.4 meters
817 Fort St., Victoria, BC V8W 1H6 Canada
(250) 382-0900; *Fax:* (250) 382-4358
www.ocean985.com
License: Victoria, BC held by Rogers Media Inc.
Group Owner: Rogers Media Inc.
Population Served: 300,000; *Format:* Adult Contemp; *Hrs. of News Programming:* news progmg 2 hrs wkly; *No. News Employees:* 1; *Target Audience:* 35-54; female
Stephane Lecouteur, Media Sales Supervisor
Rob Michaels, Program and Music Director
Melanie Z Kilpatrick, Promotions Director

CKKQ-FM
12-12-1987; 100.3 MHz FM; *Hrs Open:* 24; 100 kw; Ant 1,620 ft; N48 35 41 W123 32 37
2750 Quadra St., Top Fl., Victoria, BC V8T 4E8 Canada
(250) 475-0100; *Fax:* (250) 475-3299
www.theq.fm
License: Victoria, BC held by Jim Pattison Broadcast Group Ltd. (the general partner) and Jim Pattison Industries Ltd. (the limited partner), carrying on business as Jim Pattison Broadcast Group L.P.
Group Owner: The Jim Pattison Broadcast Group; (acq 11-24-2006; C$15.75 million with CJZN-FM Victoria)
Nat'l Reps: Canadian Broadcast Sales
Format: Classic Rock; *Hrs. of News Programming:* news progmg 4 hrs wkly; *No. News Employees:* 2; *Target Audience:* 25-49.
Rob Bye, General Manager
Mike Jean, Retail Sales Manager
Mark Addams, Programming/On-Air
Tindy Bassi, Promotion/Sponsorship

CHTT-FM
04-01-1923; 103.1 MHz FM; *Hrs Open:* 9 AM-9 PM; 20 kw; 147.4 meters; 48 25 17 N 123 30 40 W
817 Fort St., Victoria, BC V8W 1H6 Canada
(250) 382-0900; *Fax:* (250) 382-4358
www.kiss1031.ca
promotions@kiss1031.ca
License: Victoria, BC held by Rogers Media Inc.
Group Owner: Rogers Media Inc.
Nat'l Reps: Canadian Broadcast Sales
Population Served: 200,000; *Format:* Adult Contemp, Contemporary Hits/Top 40; *Hrs. of News Programming:* News progmg 5 hrs wkly
Nicole Slipetz, Marketing and Promotions Director
Julia Loglisci, Promotions Assistant

CHBE-FM
08-23-2002; 107.3 MHz FM; 20 kw; N48 25 06 W123 30 35
1420 Broad St., Victoria, BC V8W 2B1 Canada
(250) 382-1073; *Fax:* (250) 386-5775
www.1073kool.fm
koolmornings@1073kool.fm
License: Victoria, Victoria County, BC held by Bell Media British Columbia Radio Partnership
Group Owner: Bell Media Inc.
Population Served: 330,088; *Arbitron Metro Market:* Victoria, BC; *Format:* Adult Contemp; *Hrs. of News Programming:* News progmg 2 hrs wkly; *Target Audience:* 35-49.; *Adv. Rates:* 172; 109; 130; 55

Robin Haggar, Programming Director
Coreen Mae, Promotions Manager
Ryan Price, News Director

CJZN-FM
03-20-2000; 91.3 MHz FM; 3.5 kw
2750 Quadra St., Top Fl., Victoria, BC V8T 4E8 Canada
(250) 475-6611; *Fax:* (250) 475-6626
www.thezone.fm
License: Victoria, BC held by Jim Pattison Broadcast Group Ltd. (the general partner) and Jim Pattison Industries Ltd. (the limited partner), carrying on business as Jim Pattison Broadcast Group L.P.
Group Owner: The Jim Pattison Broadcast Group; (acq 11-24-2006; C$15.75 million with CKKQ-FM Victoria)
Population Served: 80,032; *Arbitron Metro Market:* Victoria, BC; *Format:* Rock/AOR; *Target Audience:* 25-64.
Rob Bye, General Manager
Mike Jean, Retail Sales Manager
John Shields, Programming Director
Tindy Bassi, Promotion/Sponsorship
Russell Boorman, Technician
Sheldon Hovde, Creative Director

CILS-FM
11-07-2007; 107.9 MHz FM; 250 w; N48 25 26 W123 20 10
200-535 Yates St., Victoria, BC V8W 2Z6 Canada
(250) 220-4139; *Fax:* (250) 388-6280
www.cilsfm.ca
License: Victoria, BC held by Societe radio communautaire Victoria.
Population Served: 80,032; *Arbitron Metro Market:* Victoria, BC; *Format:* French
Jacques P. Vall,e, President
Jules Desjarlais, Programming Director
Julie Gagnon, Vice President
Fadia Saad, Executive Director
Anne-Marie Breton, Accounting Coordinator
G,rald Montpetit, Brodcasting Chief
William McCarter, ChiefTechnical Officer
Adam Gottlieb, Sales and Promo Counselor

Whistler

CISW-FM
102.1 MHz FM; 1430 w; -306.2 meters
4295 Blackcomb Way, Suite 126, Whistler, BC V0N 1B4 Canada
(604) 892-1021; *Fax:* (604) 892-6383
www.mountainfm.com
news@mountainfm.com
License: Whistler, BC held by Rogers Media Inc.
Group Owner: Rogers Media Inc.
Format: Adult Contemp
Darren McPeake, Music Director

CKEE-FM
101.1 MHz FM; 881 w; N50 04 45 W123 01 00
102-1080 Millar Creek Road, Whistler, BC V0N 1B1 Canada
(604) 935-0004
www.whistlerfm.ca
info@whistlerfm.ca
License: Whistler, BC held by Four Senses Entertainment Inc.
Robert Wilson, General Manager

Williams Lake

***CFFM-FM**
97.5 MHz FM; *Hrs Open:* 24; 125 meters
1st Ave. S, Suite 83, Williams Lake, BC V2G 1H4 Canada
(250) 392-6551; *Fax:* (250) 392-4142
www.mycariboonow.com
cverbenkov@vistaradio.ca
License: Williams Lake, BC held by Vista Radio Ltd.
Group Owner: Vista Radio Ltd.; (Acq 2006)
Nat'l Reps: Canadian Broadcast Sales
Format: Rock/AOR; *No. News Employees:* 2; *Target Audience:* 25-54; *Adv. Rates:* 25; 21; 21; 14
Cindy Verbenkov, General Sales Mgr
Carol Gass, Regional Program Director
Rebecca Dyok, News
Shelley Wiese, Integrated Marketing Executive

CKWL
570 kHz AM; *Hrs Open:* 24
410 Kinchant St., Suite 502, Quesnel, BC V2J 7J5 Canada
(250) 992-7046; *Fax:* (250) 992-2354
www.mycariboonow.com
cverbenkov@vistaradio.ca
License: Williams Lake, BC held by Vista Radio Ltd.
Group Owner: Vista Radio Ltd.
Nat'l Reps: Canadian Broadcast Sales
Format: Country; *No. News Employees:* 1; *Target Audience:* 25-54 plus.; *Adv. Rates:* 25; 21; 21; 14
Cindy Verbenkov, General Sales Mgr
Carol Gass, Regional Program Director
George Henderson, News
Larissa Mueller, Integrated Marketing Executive
Gary Russell, Regional Cluster Manager

CJLJ-FM
02-11-2012; 100.7 MHz FM; 5 watts; -68.8 meters
2672 Indian Drive, Williams Lake, BC V2G 5K9 Canada
(250) 296-3507; *Fax:* (250) 296-4750
www.williamslakeband.ca
License: Williams Lake, BC held by Sugar Cane Community Diversity Association
Heather McKenzie, Station Manager

Manitoba

Altona

CFAM
03-13-1957; 950 kHz AM; *Hrs Open:* 24; 10 kw
227-A 1st St., P.O. Box 399, Winkler, MB R6W 4A6 Canada
(204) 325-9506
www.pembinavalleyonline.com
License: Altona, MB held by Golden West Broadcasting Ltd.
Group Owner: Golden West Broadcasting Ltd.
Nat'l Reps: Canadian Broadcast Sales
Format: Agriculture, News, Variety/Diverse; *Special Programming:* Class 15 hrs wkly; *Hrs. of News Programming:* news progmg 12 hrs wkly; *No. News Employees:* 8; *Target Audience:* General.
Bill Hildebrand, Station Manager
Chuck VanDaele, Programming Director

Boissevain

CJRB
01-01-1973; 1220 kHz AM; *Hrs Open:* 24
420 South Railway, Boissevain, MB R0K 0E0 Canada
(204) 534-6000; *Fax:* (204) 534-6825
www.discoverwestman.com
cjrb@goldenwestradio.com
License: Boissevain, MB held by Golden West Broadcasting Ltd.
Group Owner: Golden West Broadcasting Ltd.
Wire Services: BN Wire
Format: Easy Listening, Variety/Diverse; *No. News Employees:* 1; *Target Audience:* General.
Lyndon Friesen, President

Brandon

CKLQ
10-01-1977; 880 kHz AM; *Hrs Open:* 24
624 14 Street East, Brandon, MB R7A 7E1 Canada
(204) 726-8888; *Fax:* (204) 726-1270
www.cklq.com
qcountry@cklq.mb.ca
License: Brandon, MB held by Riding Mountain Broadcasting Ltd.
Nat'l Reps: Target Broadcast Sales
Format: Country; *Special Programming:* Farm 18 hrs wkly; *No. News Employees:* 7; *Target Audience:* 35 plus.; *Adv. Rates:* 63; 50; 50 38
Cam Clark, General Manager
Steve Antaya, Programming Director

CKX-FM
12-16-1963; 96.1 MHz FM; 88.7 kw; 1,042 ft
2940 Victoria Ave., Brandon, MB R7B 3Y3 Canada
(204) 728-1150; *Fax:* (204) 725-3794
www.961bobfm.ca
License: Brandon, MB held by Bell Media Radio G.P.
Group Owner: Bell Media Inc.; (acq 10-29-2007; grpsl).
Format: Adult Contemp
Donna Smith, Operations Manager
Amanda Navid, Promotions Coordinator
Mike Lamb, Assistant Music Director
Norine Mitchell, Sales Supervisor

CKXA-FM
12-05-1928; 101.1 MHz FM; 100 kw
2940 Victoria Ave., Brandon, MB R7B 3Y3 Canada
(204) 728-1150; *Fax:* (204) 725-3794
www.1011thefarm.com
tim@1011thefarm.com
License: Brandon, MB held by Bell Media Radio G.P.
Group Owner: Bell Media Inc.; (acq 10-29-2007; grpsl)
Population Served: 8,010; *Arbitron Metro Market:* Ruidoso, NM; *Format:* Country
Darcie Morris, Sales Manager
Tim Black, Programming Director
Donna Smith, Promotions Manager

CKLF-FM
06-01-2000; 94.7 MHz FM; *Hrs Open:* 24; 100 kw
624 14th St. E., Brandon, MB R7A 7E1 Canada
(204) 726-8888; *Fax:* (204) 726-1270
www.starfmradio.com
Starfm@starfmradio.com
License: Brandon, MB held by Riding Mountain Broadcasting Ltd.
Population Served: 46,061; *Arbitron Metro Market:* Brandon, MB; *Format:* Adult Contemp; *No. News Employees:* 7; *Target Audience:* 25-54; adults; *Adv. Rates:* 63; 50; 50; 38
Tyler Glen, Programming Director

CJJJ-FM
05-01-2003; 106.5 MHz FM; 930 w
661 24th St., Brandon, MB R7B 1X8 Canada
(204) 725-4474; *Fax:* (204) 726-7014
License: Brandon, MB held by Assiniboine Campus-Community Radio Society Inc.
Population Served: 46,061; *Arbitron Metro Market:* Brandon, MB; *Format:* Variety/Diverse
Jill Ferguson, Station Manager

Cross Lake

CFNC(AM)
01-01-1990; 1490 kHz AM; 50 w
Box 129, Cross Lake, MB R0B 0J0 Canada
(204) 676-2331; *Fax:* (204) 676-2911
License: Cross Lake, MB held by Native Communications Inc.
Format: Talk
Dina Monias, President
Joyce Halcrow, General Manager

Dauphin

CKDM
01-06-1951; 730 kHz AM; *Hrs Open:* 24
27-3rd Avenue NE, Dauphin, MB R7N 0Y5 Canada
(204) 638-3230; *Fax:* (204) 638-8257
www.730ckdm.com
License: Dauphin, MB held by Dauphin Broadcasting Co. Ltd.
Format: Country; *No. News Employees:* 3
Allan Truman, General Manager
Hector Paulhus, General Sales Mgr

Ebb and Flow

CKEB-FM
10-12-2012; 101.3 MHz FM; 50 watts
520 Arena Road GD, Ebb and Flow, MB R0L 0R0 Canada
(204) 448-2146
License: Ebb and Flow, MB held by Ebb and Flow Economic Development Corp

Flin Flon

CFAR
590 kHz AM; *Hrs Open:* 24; 10 kw-D, 1 kw-N, DA-2
316 Green St., Flin Flon, MB Canada
(204) 687-3469; *Fax:* (204) 687-6786
www.flinflononline.com
cfar@arcticradio.ca
License: Flin Flon, MB held by Arctic Radio (1982) Ltd.
Hrs. of News Programming: news progmg 15 hrs wkly; *No. News Employees:* 2; *Target Audience:* General.; *Adv. Rates:* 60; 55; 60; 48
Tom O'Brien, President
Diane O'Brien, Station Manager
Rob Hart, Programming Director
Joe McCormick, News Director
Danny Porter, Engineering Dir

CFAR-FM
102.9 MHz FM; 600 w; 27.7 meters; N54 46 03 W101 51 06
316 Green Street, Flin Flon, MB R8A 0H2 Canada
(204) 687-3469; *Fax:* (204) 687-6786
www.flinflononline.com
License: Flin Flon, MB held by Arctic Radio (1982) Ltd.
Diane O'Brien, Manager

Little Current

CFRM-FM
09-01-2002; 100.7 MHz FM; *Hrs Open:* 24; 27.5 kw; 155 meters; N45 57 14 W81 56 50
Box 358, Little Current, ON P0P 1K0

RADIO - CANADA

(705) 368-1419; *Fax:* (705) 368-1080
www.theislandfm.com
radio@manitoulin.net
License: Little Current, ON held by Manitoulin Radio Communication Inc.
Format: Country; *No. News Employees:* 2; *Target Audience:* General; baby boomer
Craig Timmermans, CEO

Marius

CISB-FM
04-23-2011; 106.3 MHz FM
Box 109, Marius, MB R0H 0T0 Canada
(204) 843-2661
www.sandybayradio.net
License: Marius, MB held by Sandy Bay Radio

Portage La Prairie

CFRY
10-18-1956; 920 kHz AM
2390 Sissons Dr., P.O. Box 130, Portage la Prairie, MB R1N 3B2 Canada
(204) 239-5111
www.portageonline.com
License: Portage La Prairie, MB held by Golden West Broadcasting Ltd.
Group Owner: Golden West Broadcasting Ltd.; (acq 7-26-2000; with co-located FM).
Format: Country; *Special Programming:* Farm 4 hrs wkly
Ryan Simpson, Programming Director

CHPO-FM
93.1 MHz FM; 27 kw
2390 Sissons Dr., P.O. Box 130, Portage la Prairie, MB R1N 3B2 Canada
(204) 239-5111
www.portageonline.com
License: Portage La Prairie, MB held by Golden West Broadcasting Ltd.
Group Owner: Golden West Broadcasting Ltd.
Format: Country
Ryan Simpson, Programming Director

Portage la Prairie

CJPG-FM
05-04-2004; 96.5 MHz FM; 24 kw
2390 Sissons Dr., P.O. Box 130, Portage la Prairie, MB R1N 3B2 Canada
(204) 239-5111
www.portageonline.com
License: Portage la Prairie, MB held by Golden West Broadcasting Ltd.
Group Owner: Golden West Broadcasting Ltd.
Population Served: 12,996; *Arbitron Metro Market:* Portage la Prairie, MB; *Format:* Adult Contemp, Contemporary Hits/Top 40
Ryan Simpson, Programming Director

Pukatawagan

CFPX-FM
09-19-1971; 98.3 MHz FM; 34.8 w
Missinippi River Native, Communications Inc., Pukatawagan, MB R0B 1G0 Canada
(204) 553-2155; *Fax:* (204) 553-2158
License: Pukatawagan, MB held by Missinippi River Native Communications Inc.
Format: Country

Saint Boniface

CKXL-FM
10-01-1991; 91.1 MHz FM; *Hrs Open:* 24; 61 kw
340 Provencher Blvd., Saint-Boniface, MB R2H 0G7 Canada
(204) 233-4243; *Fax:* (204) 233-3646
www.envol91.mb.ca
info@envol91.mb.ca
License: Saint Boniface, MB held by La Radio Communautaire du Manitoba Inc.
Regional Reps: Target Media; George McKringan
Population Served: 600,000; *Format:* Variety/Diverse; *Special Programming:* Folk 2 hrs, jazz 4 hrs, Sp 2 hrs, blues 2 hrs, reg; *Target Audience:* 20-50; Francophone; *Adv. Rates:* 28; 28; 28; 28
Annick Boulet, Station Manager

Selkirk

CFQX-FM
11-09-1981; 104.1 MHz FM; *Hrs Open:* 24; 100 kw; 147.5 meters
177 Lombard Ave., 3rd Fl., Winnipeg, MB R3B 0W5 Canada
(204) 944-1031; *Fax:* (204) 989-5291
www.qx104fm.com
License: Selkirk, MB held by 8384894 Canada Inc.
Group Owner: The Jim Pattison Broadcast Group; (acq 10-29-2007; grpsl)
Format: Country; *No. News Employees:* 2; *Target Audience:* 25-54.
Heidi Rasmussen, General Manager
Kareen McConnell, General Sales Mgr
Janet Trecarten, Programming Director
Dale Davies, Promotions Director
Lonny Bergen, Chief Engineer
Janet Trecarten, Music Director
Jim Van Dusen, CreativeDirector
Jayme Vandenberg, Digital Account Manager

CICY-FM
01-01-2000; 105.5 MHz FM; kw
1507 Inkster Boulevard, Winnipeg, MB R2X 1R2 Canada
(204) 772-8255; *Fax:* (204) 779-5628
www.ncifm.com
info@ncifm.com
License: Selkirk, MB held by Native Communication Inc.
Arbitron Metro Market: Winnipeg, MB; *Format:* Variety/Diverse; *No. News Employees:* 2; *Target Audience:* 25 and up; aboriginal

Skownan

CHWN-FM
05-15-2011; 98.7 MHz FM
Box 106, Skownan, MB R0L 1Y0 Canada
(204) 628-3373; *Fax:* (204) 628-3289
skfo.listen2myradio.com
License: Skownan, MB held by Skownan Band Development Corp

Steinbach

CHSM
03-13-1964; 1250 kHz AM; *Hrs Open:* 24
105-32 Brandt St., Steinbach, MB R5G 2J7 Canada
(204) 326-3737
www.steinbachonline.com
License: Steinbach, MB held by Golden West Broadcasting Ltd.
Group Owner: Golden West Broadcasting Ltd.
Nat'l Reps: Canadian Broadcast Sales
Format: Variety/Diverse; *Hrs. of News Programming:* news progmg 12 hrs wkly; *No. News Employees:* 3; *Target Audience:* General.
Crystal Hildebrandt, Station Manager

CILT-FM
09-26-1998; 96.7 MHz FM; *Hrs Open:* 24; 50 kw
105-32 Brandt St., Steinbach, MB R5G 2J7 Canada
(204) 326-3737
www.steinbachonline.com
License: Steinbach, MB held by Golden West Broadcasting Ltd.
Group Owner: Golden West Broadcasting Ltd.
Format: Adult Contemp
Crystal Hildebrandt, Station Manager

CJXR-FM
107.7 MHz FM; 30 kw; 117.4 meters; N49 31 26 W96 40 02
105-32 Brandt St., Steinbach, MB R5G 2J7 Canada
(204) 326-3737
www.steinbachonline.com
License: Steinbach, MB held by Golden West Braodcasting Ltd.
Group Owner: Golden West Broadcasting Ltd.
Format: Country
Crystal Hildebrandt, Station Manager

Swan River

CJSB-FM
07-01-2006; 104.5 MHz FM; *Hrs Open:* 24; 210 w; N52 06 18 W101 16 10
Canada
(204) 734-5700
www.cj104radio.ca
onair@cj104radio.com
License: Swan River, Swan Valley County, MB held by Stillwater Broadcasting Ltd.
Nat'l Reps: Target Broadcast Sales; *Wire Services:* Canadian Press
Population Served: 390; *Arbitron Metro Market:* Swan River, MB; *Format:* Contemporary Hits/Top 40; *Hrs. of News Programming:* news progmg 20 hrs/week; *No. News Employees:* 2

The Pas

CJAR
01-01-1974; 1240 kHz AM
130 3rd Street West, Box 2980, The Pas, MB Canada
(204) 623-5307; *Fax:* (204) 623-5337
www.thepasonline.com
License: The Pas, MB held by Arctic Radio Corp. Ltd.
Format: Adult Contemp, Rock/AOR, Country; *Special Programming:* Aboriginal 5 hrs wkly
Maureen Kozar, Station Manager

CJAR-FM
102.9 MHz FM; 250 w; 37.7 meters; N53 48 46 W101 16 35
Box 2980, The Pas, MB R9A 1R7 Canada
(204) 623-5307; *Fax:* (204) 623-5337
www.thepasonline.com
License: The Pas, MB held by Arctic Radio (1982) Ltd.
Jeremy Wachal, General Manager

Thompson

CHTM
03-29-1964; 610 kHz AM; *Hrs Open:* 24; 1 kw-U
Canada
(204) 778-7361; *Fax:* (204) 778-5252
www.thompsononline.ca
chtm@arcticradio.ca
License: Thompson, MB held by Arctic Radio (1982) Ltd.
Population Served: 60,000; *Special Programming:* Relg 12 hrs, Cree (American Indian) 10 hrs wkly; *Hrs. of News Programming:* news progmg 15 hrs wkly; *No. News Employees:* 2; *Target Audience:* General.
Tom O'Brien, President

CINC-FM
01-01-1994; 96.3 MHz FM; 86 w*Rebroadcasts:* rebroadcasts CICY-FM Winnipeg 80%
1507 Inkster Boulevard, Thompson, MB R2X 1R2 Canada
(204) 772-8255
www.ncifm.com
info@ncifm.com
License: Thompson, MB held by Native Communications Inc.
Format: Variety/Diverse

CHTM-FM
102.9 MHz FM; 190 w; 95.8 meters; N55 42 08 W97 52 56
103 Cree Road, Thompson, MB R8N 0B9 Canada
(204) 778-7361; *Fax:* (204) 778-5252
www.thompsononline.ca
License: Thompson, MB held by Arctic Radio (1982) Ltd.
Sue O'Brien, General Manager

Winkler

CJEL-FM
10-04-2000; 93.5 MHz FM; *Hrs Open:* 24; 100 kw
277-A 1st St., P.O. Box 399, Winkler, MB R6W 4A6 Canada
(204) 325-9506
www.pembinavalleyonline.com
License: Winkler, MB held by Golden West Broadcasting Ltd.
Group Owner: Golden West Broadcasting Ltd.
Population Served: 10,670; *Arbitron Metro Market:* Winkler, MB; *Format:* Adult Contemp
Bill Hildebrand, Station Manager
Chuck VanDaele, Programming Director

Winkler-Morden

CKMW-FM
06-12-2013; 88.9 MHz FM; 100 kw; 51.7 meters; N49 07 16 W98 04 03
277-A 1st St., P.O. Box 399, Winkler, MB R6W 4A6 Canada
(204) 325-9506
www.pembinavalleyonline.com
License: Winkler-Morden, MB held by Golden West Broadcasting Ltd.
Group Owner: Golden West Broadcasting Ltd.
Format: Country
Bill Hildebrand, Station Manager
Chuck VanDaele, Programming Director

Winnepeg

CHWE-FM
07-29-2011; 106.1 MHz FM; 40 kw
520 Corydon Ave., Winnpeg, MB R3L 0P1 Canada
(204) 477-1221; *Fax:* (204) 453-8244
www.energy106.ca
License: Winnepeg, MB held by Dufferin Communications Inc.
Group Owner: Evanov Communications Inc.
Format: Contemporary Hits/Top 40

Mike Fabian, General Manager
Adam West, Programming Director
Stephanie Harris, Promotions Director

Winnepeg Beach

CJIE-FM

09-22-2011; 107.5 MHz FM; 1.62 kw
515 Main Street, Gimli, MB R0C 1B1 Canada
(204) 642-4387
office@cj107radio.com
License: Winnipeg Beach, MB held by 5777152 Manitoba Ltd
Bill Gade, General Manager

Winnipeg

CFWM-FM

06-13-1996; 99.9 MHz FM; *Hrs Open:* 24; 100 kw
1445 Pembina Hwy., Winnipeg, MB R3T 5C2 Canada
(204) 477-5120; *Fax:* (204) 453-0815
www.999bobfm.com
License: Winnipeg, MB held by Bell Media Canada Radio 2013 Partnership
Group Owner: Bell Media Inc.; (acq 6-22-2007; grpsl).
Population Served: 672,000; *Hrs. of News Programming:* news progmg 5 hrs wkly; *No. News Employees:* 1; *Target Audience:* 25-54.
Jeff Bollenbach, General Manager
Anne Skrynsky, General Sales Mgr
Heather Prosak, Programming Director
Colin Lougheed, Promotions Director

CHIQ-FM

11-01-1963; 94.3 MHz FM; 100 kw; Ant 450 ft; N49 47 58 W97 16 30
177 Lombard Ave., 3rd Fl., Winnipeg, MB R3B 0W5 Canada
(204) 944-1031; *Fax:* (204) 989-5291
www.fab943.com
License: Winnipeg, MB held by 8384843 Canada Inc.
Group Owner: The Jim Pattison Broadcast Group
Format: Oldies
Heidi Rasmussen, General Manager
Kareen McConnell, General Sales Mgr
Janet Trecarten, Programming Director
Dale Davies, Promotions Director
Lonny Bergen, Chief Engineer
Jim Van Dusen, Creative Director
Jayme Vandenberg, DigitalAccount Manager

CFRW

11-01-1963; 1290 kHz AM; 10 kw-U, DA-2
1445 Pembina Hwy., Winnipeg, MB R3T 5C2 Canada
(204) 477-5120; *Fax:* (204) 453-0815
www.tsn.ca/radio/winnipeg-1290
License: Winnipeg, MB held by Bell Media Canada Radio 2013 Partnership
Group Owner: Bell Media Inc.; (acq 6-22-2007; grpsl).
Format: Sports
Jeff Bollenbach, General Manager
Corey Mospanchuk, General Sales Mgr
Heather Prosak, Programming Director
Colin Lougheed, Promotions Director

*CITI-FM

92.1 MHz FM; 100 kw; 206.1 meters
166 Osborne St., Suite 4, Winnipeg, MB R3L 1Y8 Canada
(204) 788-3400
www.921citi.ca
darren.jopka@rci.rogers.com
License: Winnipeg, MB held by Rogers Media Inc.
Group Owner: Rogers Media Inc.; acq 8-20-92).
Format: Rock/AOR, Classic Rock
Darren Jopka, General Manager and Sales
Craig Pfeifer, Programming Director
Stephen Mowat, Account Manager

CJOB

03-11-1946; 680 kHz AM; *Hrs Open:* 24
1440 Jack Blick Ave., Unit 200, Winnipeg, MB R3G 0L4 Canada
(204) 786-2471
www.cjob.com
steve.dubois@corusent.com
License: Winnipeg, MB held by Corus Premium Television Ltd.
Group Owner: Corus Entertainment Inc.; (acq 7-6-2000; grpsl).
Nat'l Reps: Canadian Broadcast Sales
Format: News, News/Talk, Talk; *Hrs. of News Programming:* news progmg 56 hrs wkly; *No. News Employees:* 25; *Target Audience:* 25-54.
Steve Dubois, General Sales Mgr
Brent Bernas, Promotions Director
Kim Lawson, Executive Producer
Kelly Moore, Sports Director
Lauren Robb, Interactive Content Manager

CJUM-FM

09-04-1998; 101.5 MHz FM; *Hrs Open:* 24; 1.2 kw
UMFM, 308 University Center, Winnipeg, MB R3T 2N2 Canada
(204) 474-7027; *Fax:* (204) 269-1299
www.umfm.com
info@umfm.com
License: Winnipeg, MB held by The University of Manitoba Students' Union.
Population Served: 650,000; *Format:* Variety/Diverse; *Hrs. of News Programming:* News progmg 12 hrs wkly; *Target Audience:* 18-58; all genders, all ages who prefer non-coml music & culture; *Adv. Rates:* 18; 18; 18; 18
Jared McKetiak, Station Manager
Michael Elves, Programming Director

CKJS

03-25-1974; 810 kHz AM; 10 kw-U, DA-1
520 Corydon Ave., Winnipeg, MB R3L 0P1 Canada
(204) 477-1221; *Fax:* (204) 453-8244
www.ckjs.com
info@ckjs.com
License: Winnipeg, MB held by Dufferin Communications Inc.
Group Owner: Evanov Communications Inc.; (acq 4-30-2006; C$2.3 million).
Regional Reps: Direct.
Format: Christian, Ethnic; *Special Programming:* Ger 6 hrs, It 5 hrs, Pol 7 hrs, Sp 3 hrs, Por 8 hr; *Target Audience:* General.
Mike Fabian, General Manager
Gido Gigliotti, Programming Director
Heather Milne, Promotions Director

CKMM-FM

02-14-1980; 103.1 MHz FM; 70 kw; Ant 676 ft
1445 Pembina Hwy., Winnipeg, MB R3T 5C2 Canada
(204) 477-5120; *Fax:* (204) 453-0815
www.winnipeg.virginradio.ca
jeff.bollenbach@bellmedia.ca
License: Winnipeg, MB held by Bell Media Radio G.P.
Group Owner: Bell Media Inc.; (acq 10-29-2007; grpsl).
Format: Contemporary Hits/Top 40
Jeff Bollenbach, General Manager
Anne Skyrnsky, General Sales Mgr
Troy Scott, Programming Director
Colin Lougheed, Promotions Director

*CKUW-FM

05-01-1999; 95.9 MHz FM; *Hrs Open:* 24; 450 w; N49 52 51 W97 08 56
515 Portage Ave., Winnipeg, MB R3B 2E9 Canada
(204) 786-9782; *Fax:* (204) 783-7080
www.ckuw.ca
ckuw@uwinnipeg.ca
License: Winnipeg, MB held by The Winnipeg Campus/Community Radio Society.
Population Served: 660,000; *Special Programming:* Children 2 hrs, class 4 hrs, folk 2 hrs, jazz 8 hrs; *Hrs. of News Programming:* News progmg 5 hrs wkly; *Target Audience:* General; Our community; *Adv. Rates:* 30; 30;30; 30
Rob Schmidt, Station Manager
Robin Eriksson, Programming Director
Michael Welch, News Director
David Tymoshchuk, Music Director

CHVN-FM

09-14-2000; 95.1 MHz FM; *Hrs Open:* 24; 100 kw; N49 46 15 W97 30 35
1-741 St. Mary's Rd., Winnipeg, MB R2M 3N5 Canada
(204) 452-9602
www.chvnradio.com
info@chvnradio.com
License: Winnipeg, MB held by Golden West Broadcasting Ltd.
Group Owner: Golden West Broadcasting Ltd.; (acq 2004)
Nat'l Network: Salem Radio Network
Population Served: 684,100; *Arbitron Metro Market:* Winnipeg, MB; *Format:* Christian; *Special Programming:* Children one hr, gospel 4 hrs, teens 6 hrs wkly; *Target Audience:* 18-49; families; *Adv. Rates:* 42; 38; 42;32
Kyle Rudge, Programming Director

CJGV-FM

02-28-2003; 99.1 MHz FM; 63.7 kw; N49 45 20 W97 07 52
1440 Jack Blick Ave., Suite 200, Winnipeg, MB R3G 0L4 Canada
(204) 786-2471; *Fax:* (204) 783-4512
www.peggy991.com
steve.dubois@corusent.com
License: Winnipeg, MB held by Corus Premium Television Ltd.
Group Owner: Corus Entertainment Inc.; (acq 7-6-2007; C$14.5 million with CKBT-FM Kitchener-Waterloo, ON)
Population Served: 684,100; *Arbitron Metro Market:* Winnipeg, MB; *Format:* Adult Contemp; *No. News Employees:* 1; *Target Audience:* 35-45.
Tammy Cole, Brand Manager
Steve Dubois, Market Sales Manager
Brent Bernas, Promotions Director
Lauren Robb, Interactive Content Manager

CFJL-FM

12-07-2002; 100.7 MHz FM; *Hrs Open:* 24; 100 kw; Ant 578 ft
520 Corydon Ave., Winnipeg, MB R3L 0P1 Canada
(204) 477-1221; *Fax:* (204) 453-8244
www.jewelradio.com/new/1005
License: Winnipeg, MB held by Dufferin Communications Inc.
Group Owner: Evanov Communications Inc.; (acq 12-5-2005; C$1,790,000 for stock)
Format: Adult Contemp; *No. News Employees:* 1
Mike Fabian, General Manager
Adam West, Programming Director
Stephanie Harris, Promotions Director

CKCL-FM

10-21-1999; 107.1 MHz FM; 100 kw; 223 meters
2-20 St. Mary's Rd., Winnipeg, MB R2H 1H1 Canada
(204) 256-2525
www.classic107.com
info@classic107.com
License: Winnipeg, MB held by Golden West Broadcasting Ltd.
Group Owner: Golden West Broadcasting Ltd.; (acq 6-27-2008; C$725,000)
Population Served: 750,000; *Format:* Classical, Jazz
Trev Schellenberg, Programming Director

CKY-FM

102.3 MHz FM; 70 kw; 206.1 meters
166 Osborne St., Suite 4, Winnipeg, MB R3L 1Y8 Canada
(204) 788-3400
www.kiss1023.ca
darren.jopka@rci.rogers.com
License: Winnipeg, MB held by Rogers Media Inc.
Group Owner: Rogers Media Inc.
Population Served: 663,617; *Arbitron Metro Market:* Winnipeg, MB; *Format:* Adult Contemp
Darren Jopka, General Manager and Sales
Trina Reid, Marketing Consultant

CJNU-FM

12-01-2006; 93.7 MHz FM; 460 w; 111.6 meters; N49 52 45 W97 09 06
Box 2282, Stn Main, Winnipeg, MB R3C 4A6 Canada
(204) 942-2568
www.cjnu.ca
info@cjnu.ca
License: Winnipeg, MB held by Nostalgia Broadcasting Cooperative
Population Served: 684,100; *Arbitron Metro Market:* Winnipeg, MB; *Format:* Oldies
Bill Stewart, President
Roy Maguire, Chief Engineer

CJKR-FM

05-27-1948; 97.5 MHz FM; 310 kw; 228 ft
1440 Jack Blick Ave., Suite 200, Winnipeg, MB R3G 0L4 Canada
(204) 786-2471; *Fax:* (204) 783-4512
www.power97.com
steve.dubois@corusent.com
License: Winnipeg, MB held by Corus Premium Television Ltd.
Group Owner: Corus Entertainment Inc.
Population Served: 684,100; *Arbitron Metro Market:* Winnipeg, MB; *Format:* Rock/AOR; *Target Audience:* Ages 18-39
Tammy Cole, Brand Director
Steve Dubois, Market Sales Manager
Brent Bernas, Promotions Director
Lauren Robb, Content Coordinator

New Brunswick

Balmoral

CIMS-FM

09-14-1994; 103.9 MHz FM; 7.295 kw
1991 Ave. CP2561, des Pionniers, Balmoral, NB E8E 2W7 Canada
(506) 826-1040; *Fax:* (506) 826-2400
www.cimsfm.com
License: Balmoral, NB held by Cooperative Radio Restigouche Ltee.
Format: Variety/Diverse; *No. News Employees:* 1
Rico Levesque, President
Annie L. Levesque, General Manager

Christian Labrie, General Sales Mgr
Guy Lavoie, Regional Sales Manager

Bathurst

CKBC-FM
04-18-1955; 104.9 MHz FM; *Hrs Open:* 24; 20 kw
640 St. Peter Ave., Unit 1, Bathurst, NB E2A 2Y7 Canada
(506) 547-1360; *Fax:* (506) 547-1367
www.max1049.ca
maxfm@bellmedia.ca
License: Bathurst, NB held by Bell Media Radio Atlantic Inc.
Group Owner: Bell Media Inc.
Nat'l Reps: Canadian Broadcast Sales
Population Served: 12,275; *Arbitron Metro Market:* Bathurst, NB;
Format: Adult Contemp; *Special Programming:* Fr 9 hrs wkly;
Hrs. of News Programming: news progmg 9 hrs wkly; *No. News Employees:* 3*TargetAudience:* 25-49.; *Adv. Rates:* 50; 44; 44; 30
Jacques Parisien, President
Jamie Robichaud, General Manager
Jamie Robichaud, General Sales Mgr
Jeff Long, Program & Music Supervisor
John Eddy, Executive Vice President
Glenn States, Advertising Sales
Ken Comeau, AdvertisingSales
Collette Comeau, Specialty Advertising

Campbellton

CKNB
01-01-1939; 950 kHz AM; *Hrs Open:* 24
74 Water St., Campbellton, NB E3N 1B1 Canada
(506) 753-4415; *Fax:* (506) 789-9505
www.95cknb.ca
License: Campbellton, NB held by Maritime Broadcasting System Ltd.
Group Owner: Maritime Broadcasting
Format: Adult Contemp; *Special Programming:* Fr 18 hrs wkly;
Hrs. of News Programming: News progmg 10 hrs wkly; *Target Audience:* General.
David Montgomery, General Manager
Shelley Comeau, Sales

Caraquet

CJVA
09-15-1977; 810 kHz AM; *Hrs Open:* 18
Canada
(506) 727-4605; *Fax:* (506) 546-6611
www.ckle.fm
superstation@ckle.fm
License: Caraquet, NB held by Radio Acadie Ltd.
Nat'l Reps: Canadian Broadcast Sales
Format: Adult Contemp, Variety/Diverse; *Special Programming:* C&W 15 hrs wkly; *Target Audience:* 25 plus.
Rufino Landry, President
Armand Roussy, General Manager

Edmundston

CFAI-FM
01-15-1991; 10MHz FM; *Hrs Open:* 24; 4 kw; N47 23 22 W68 19 06
161 Boulevard Hebert, Edmundston, NB E3V 2S8 Canada
(506) 737-5060; *Fax:* (506) 737-5084
www.cfai.fm
radio@cfai.fm
License: Edmundston, Madawaska County, NB held by La Cooperative des Montagnes Ltee.
Format: Contemporary Hits/Top 40; *Hrs. of News Programming:* News progmg 6 hrs wkly; *No. News Employees:* 1; *Target Audience:* 12-50.; *Adv. Rates:* 21; 21; 21; 18
Louis G. Plourde, President
Eric Morneault, General Manager
Sheila Desroches, General Sales Mgr

CJEM-FM
07-01-1998; 92.7 MHz FM; *Hrs Open:* 24; 40.75 kw; N47 21 47 W68 17 21
64 Rice St., Edmundston, NB E3V 1K2 Canada
(506) 735-3351; *Fax:* (506) 739-5803
www.cjemfm.com
cjem@cjemfm.com
License: Edmundston, Madawaska County, NB held by Radio Edmundston Inc.
Nat'l Reps: Canadian Broadcast Sales
Population Served: 50,000; *Format:* Adult Contemp; *Hrs. of News Programming:* news progmg 6 hrs wkly; *No. News Employees:* 2; *Target Audience:* 25-54.
Jean Marc Michaud, President
Murillo Soucy, General Manager
Paul Cotter, Programming Director

Fredericton

*CBZ-FM
01-01-1978; 101.5 MHz FM; 100 kw*Rebroadcasts:* Rebroadcasts CBH-FM Halifax, NS 100%
Mailing Address: Box 2200, Fredericton, NB E3B 5G4 Canada
Second Address: 1160 Regent St., Fredericton, NB E3B 5G4
(506) 451-4000; *Fax:* (506) 451-4170
www.cbc.ca
License: Fredericton, NB held by Canadian Broadcasting Corp.
Nat'l Network: CBC Radio Two
Format: News, News/Talk, Talk
Gary Arsenault, General Manager

CBZF-FM
03-04-1964; 99.5 MHz FM; *Hrs Open:* 6:00 am - 8:30 am; 3.2 kw; 82.9 meters
1160 Regent St., P.O. Box 2200, Fredericton, NB E3B 5G4 Canada
(506) 451-4000; *Fax:* (506) 451-4170
www.cbc.ca/news/canada/new-brunswick
infoamfredericton@cbc.ca
License: Fredericton, NB held by Canadian Broadcasting Corp.
Group Owner: CBC
Nat'l Network: CBC Radio One
Format: News/Talk; *Special Programming:* News & Weather Updates
Darrow MacIntyre, Executive Producer of News
Harry Forestell, Host

CHSR-FM
01-24-1961; 97.9 MHz FM; *Hrs Open:* 7 AM-3 AM; 250 w; Ant 157 ft
Box 4400, Student Union Bldg., Fredericton, NB E3B 5A3 Canada
(506) 453-4985; *Fax:* (506) 453-4999
www.unb.ca/chsr
chsr@unb.ca
License: Fredericton, York County, NB held by CHSR Broadcasting Inc.
Format: Alternative, Variety/Diverse; *Special Programming:* Fr 2 hrs, ethnic 5 hrs, American Indian one hr, cl; *Hrs. of News Programming:* News progmg 6 hrs wkly; *Target Audience:* General.
Tim Rayne, Station Manager
Mark Kilfoil, Programming Director

CIBX-FM
08-31-1961; 106.9 MHz FM; *Hrs Open:* 24; 78 kw
206 Rookwood Ave., Fredericton, NB E3B 2M2 Canada
(506) 451-9111; *Fax:* (506) 452-2345
www.capitalfm.ca
feedback@capitalfm.ca
License: Fredericton, NB held by Bell Media Radio Atlantic Inc.
Group Owner: Bell Media Inc.; (acq 7-05-2013; grpsl).
Nat'l Reps: Canadian Broadcast Sales
Format: Contemporary Hits/Top 40; *Hrs. of News Programming:* news progmg 8 hrs wkly; *No. News Employees:* 4; *Target Audience:* 25-54.
John Eddy, President
Pat Brennan, General Manager
Paul Wentzell, General Sales Mgr
Matt Cleveland, Programming Director
Shelby Buckingham, Promotions Manager
James Cormier, Music Director
Greg Toole, Digital Accounts Manager

CKHJ
08-19-1977; 1260 kHz AM; 10 kw-U, DA-N
206 Rookwood Ave., Fredericton, NB E3B 2M2 Canada
(506) 451-9111; *Fax:* (506) 452-2345
www.khj.ca
feedback@khj.ca
License: Fredericton, NB held by Bell Media Radio Atlantic Inc.
Group Owner: Bell Media Inc.; (acq 7-05-2013; grpsl).
Format: Country; *Special Programming:* Fr one hr wkly
Pat Brennan, General Manager
Paul Wentzell, General Sales Mgr
Matt Cleveland, Programming Director
Shelby Buckingham, Promotions Manager
Greg Toole, Digital Accounts Manager

*CJPN-FM
08-01-1997; 90.5 MHz FM; 1.56 kw
715 Priestman St., Fredericton, NB E3B 5W7 Canada
(506) 454-2576; *Fax:* (506) 453-3958
www.cjpn.ca
direction@cjpn.ca
License: Fredericton, NB held by Radio Fredericton Inc.
Format: Adult Contemp
Alexandre Deslongchamps, Director General

CFXY-FM
07-15-1983; 105.3 MHz FM; 78 kw; 800 ft
206 Rookwood Ave., Fredericton, NB E3B 2M2 Canada
(506) 454-2444; *Fax:* (506) 452-2345
www.foxrocks.ca
feedback@foxrocks.ca
License: Fredericton, NB held by Bell Media Radio Atlantic Inc.
Group Owner: Bell Media Inc.; (acq 7-05-2013; grpsl).
Format: Rock/AOR
Pat Brennan, General Manager
Paul Wentzell, General Sales Mgr
Matt Cleveland, Programming Director
Shelby Buckingham, Promotions Manager
Rob Pinnock, Music Director
Greg Toole, Digital Accounts Manager

CIXN-FM
04-08-2001; 96.5 MHz FM; *Hrs Open:* 8:30am-4pm Monday-Friday; 250 w
515 St. Mary St., Fredericton, NB E3B 6A4 Canada
(506) 454-9600
www.joyfm.ca
info@joynetwork.ca
License: Fredericton, NB held by The Joy FM Network Inc.
Population Served: 73,000
Joel Flores, General Manager
Mark Ridley, Marketing & Community Development
Reed Kelsey, Programming Director
Michaels Knolls Jr., Joy Cares Mission Director
Teresa McKnight, Administration & Social Media

CFRK-FM
07-28-2005; 92.3 MHz FM; 93 kw
495-A Prospect St., Fredericton, NB E3B 9M4 Canada
(506) 455-0923; *Fax:* (506) 455-3602
www.newcountry923.com
License: Fredericton, NB held by Newcap Inc.
Group Owner: NewCap Inc.
Format: Country
David Newbury, Station Manager

CJRI-FM
05-18-2005; 104.5 MHz FM; 50 w; N45 56 14 W66 39 19
151 Main St., Fredericton, NB E3A 1C6 Canada
(506) 472-0947; *Fax:* (506) 459-8194
www.cjrifm.com
cjrifm@gmail.com
License: Fredericton, NB held by Faithway Communications Inc.
Population Served: 34,000; *Arbitron Metro Market:* Fredericton, NB; *Format:* Country, Gospel
Ross Ingram, President

CIHI-FM
06-24-2013; 93.1 MHz FM; 93 kw; 150 meters
495-A Prospect St., Fredericton, NB E3B 9M4 Canada
(506) 455-0923; *Fax:* (506) 455-3602
www.up931.com
License: Fredericton, NB held by Newcap Inc.
Group Owner: NewCap Inc.
Format: Adult Contemp
David Newbury, General Manager
Kate Buick, Programming Director

Fredericton Centre

CKTP-FM
01-01-2002; 95.7 MHz FM; 50 w
Kchikhusis Commercial Center, 150 Cliffe St., Box R13, Fredericton, NB E3A 0A1 Canada
(506) 474-2795; *Fax:* (506) 206-330
www.957thewolf.ca
info@957thewolf.ca
License: Fredericton Centre, NB held by Maliseet Nation Radio Inc.
Population Served: 34,000; *Arbitron Metro Market:* Fredericton, NB; *Format:* Contemporary Hits/Top 40
Conrad Mead, Station Manager

Grand Falls

CIKX-FM
07-08-1998; 93.5 MHz FM; 5.3 kw
399 Boul. Broadway Blvd., Grand Falls, NB E3Z 2K5 Canada
(506) 473-9393; *Fax:* (506) 473-3893
www.k93.ca
k93@bellmedia.ca
License: Grand Falls, NB held by Bell Media Radio Atlantic Inc.
Group Owner: Bell Media Inc.; (acq 2003; grpsl).
Population Served: 5,706; *Arbitron Metro Market:* Grand Falls, NB; *Format:* Adult Contemp

Pat Brennan, General Manager
Kirk Davidson, Programming Director
Jennifer Graham, News/Sports

CKMV-FM
08-01-2000; 95.1 MHz FM; *Hrs Open:* 24; 975 w*Rebroadcasts:* Rebroadcasts CJEM-FM Edmundston 100%
174 Church St., Edmundston, NB E3V 1K2 Canada
(506) 735-3351; *Fax:* (506) 739-5803
cjem@nbnet.nb.ca
License: Grand Falls, Victoria County, NB held by Radio Edmundston Inc.
Nat'l Reps: Canadian Broadcast Sales
Target Audience: 25-54.
Murillo Soucy, President
Murillo Soucy, General Manager
Paul Clavette, Programming Director

Inkerman

CKRO-FM
01-01-1988; 97.1 MHz FM; 50 kw; 55 meters; N47 40 45 W64 52 19
142 Route 112, Pokemouche, NB E8P 1K7 Canada
(506) 336-9706; *Fax:* (506) 336-9058
www.ckro.ca
info@ckro.ca
License: Inkerman, NB held by Radio Peninsule Inc.
Format: Adult Contemp; *Target Audience:* General.
Rachel Savoie, Operations Dir
Donald Christmas, General Manager
Rejean Hebert, Programming Director
Marilyne McLaughlin, National Sales Manager

Kedgwick

***CFJU-FM**
01-01-1991; 90.1 MHz FM; *Hrs Open:* 24; 3 kw; N47 35 05 W67 21 47
C.P. 1043, Kedgwick, NB E8B 1Z9 Canada
(506) 235-9000; *Fax:* (506) 235-9001
www.cfjufm.com
License: Kedgwick, NB held by La Radio Communautaire des Hauts-Plateaux Inc.
Population Served: 7,000; *Format:* Variety/Diverse; *Special Programming:* Country 12 hrs wkly; *Hrs. of News Programming:* News progmg 8 hrs wkly; *Target Audience:* 25-55.
M. Victor St- Pierre, President
Lucille Theriault, General Manager

Miramichi

CFAN-FM
01-10-2003; 99.3 MHz FM; *Hrs Open:* 24; 17.8 kw
396 Pleasant St., Miramichi, NB E1V 1X3 Canada
(506) 622-3311; *Fax:* (506) 627-0335
www.993theriver.com
License: Miramichi, Northumberland County, NB held by Maritime Broadcasting System Ltd.
Group Owner: Maritime Broadcasting
Population Served: 50,000; *Format:* Country; *Special Programming:* Relg 4 hrs, folk 2 hrs wkly; *Hrs. of News Programming:* news progmg 8 hrs wkly; *No. News Employees:* 1; *Target Audience:* General.; *Adv. Rates:* 29; 29; 29; 29
Anne Woods, General Manager
Anne Woods, General Sales Mgr
Genna Gouchie, Account Executive

CJFY-FM
01-01-2004; 96.5 MHz FM; 740 w; 35 meters
345 Beaverbrook, Blackville, NB E1V 3L9 Canada
(506) 622-2202; *Fax:* (506) 843-2228
www.liferadio.ca
staff@liferadio.ca
License: Miramichi, NB held by Miramichi Fellowship Center Inc.
John Stewart, CEO
Matt Halihan, General Manager
Scott Underhill, Station Manager
Matt Halihan, Programming Director
Scott Underhill, Promotions Manager
Patrick Dunn, News Director

CKMA-FM
93.7 MHz FM; 11 kw; N47 00 37 W65 35 14
300 chemin Beaverbrook, Miramichi, NB E1V 1A1 Canada
(506) 624-9370; *Fax:* (506) 627-4592
License: Miramichi, NB held by Radio MirAcadie Inc.
Population Served: 18,129; *Arbitron Metro Market:* Miramichi, NB; *Format:* Variety/Diverse
Rick Arnish, President
Bruce Davis, General Manager

Don Huculak, General Sales Mgr
Bob Miller, Programming Director
Dan McFarland, Promotions Manager
Jasmin Doobay, News Director
Craig Foster, Chief Engineer
Michel Savoie,Director of Operations

CHHI-FM
95.9 MHz FM; 25 kw; 86 meters; N47 03 32 W65 34 35
202 Pleasant St., Miramichi, NB E1V 1Y5 Canada
(506) 622-3969; *Fax:* (506) 622-3970
www.959sunfm.com
info@959sunfm.com
License: Miramichi, NB held by Newcap Inc.
Group Owner: NewCap Inc.
Format: Adult Contemp
Dan Gallant, General Manager/Sales Manager
Steve Power, Programming Director
Darcey McLaughlin, News Director
Terry Collette, Account Executive
Paddy Quinn, Music Director

Moncton

CBA-FM
03-01-1982; 95.5 MHz FM; 68 kw*Rebroadcasts:* Rebroadcasts CBH-FM Halifax, NS 100%
PO Box 500, Station A, Toronto, ON M54 1E6 Canada
(506) 853-6666; (866) 306-4636 Canada; *Fax:* (506) 853-6400
www.cbc.ca
License: Moncton, NB held by CBC
Group Owner: Canadian Broadcasting Corporation
Nat'l Network: CBC Radio Two
Format: Talk
Susan Mitton, General Manager

***CBAF-FM**
02-20-1954; 88.5 MHz FM; 21 kw; 211 meters; 45 25'17 N 75 42'00 W
165 Main St., Suite 15, Moncton, NB E1C 1B8 Canada
(506) 853-6666; *Fax:* (506) 853-6400
www.cbc.ca/nb
infoammoncton@cbc.ca
License: Moncton, Westmoreland County, NB held by Ici Radio-Canada PremiŠre
Group Owner: CBC
Format: French, News/Talk
Darrow MacIntyre, Executive Producer of News

***CBAL-FM**
04-15-1983; 98.3 MHz FM; 67.6 kw; 211 meters; 46 08'41 N 64 54'11 W
165 Main St., Bureau 15, Moncton, NB E1C 1B8 Canada
(506) 853-6666; *Fax:* (506) 853-6739
www.cbc.radio-canada.ca
License: Moncton, Westmoreland County, NB held by CBC
Group Owner: CBC
Nat'l Network: Ici Musique
Format: Jazz, Classical
Hubert T. Lacroix, President and CEO
Judith Purves, EVP and Chief Financial Officer

***CFQM-FM**
03-01-1977; 103.9 MHz FM; 70 kw
1000 St. George Blvd., Moncton, NB E1E 4M7 Canada
(506) 858-1220
www.1039maxfm.com
License: Moncton, NB held by Maritime Broadcasting System Ltd.
Group Owner: Maritime Broadcasting
Format: Oldies
Krysta Janssen, Operations Manager
Wayne Keeping, General Sales Mgr
Sandy Mollins, Account Manager

***CJMO-FM**
06-19-1987; 103.1 MHz FM; *Hrs Open:* 24; 46.8 kw
27 Arsenault Ct., Moncton Industrial Park, Moncton, NB E1E 4J8 Canada
(506) 858-5525; *Fax:* (506) 858-5539
www.c103.com
c103@c103.com
License: Moncton, Canada County, NB held by Newcap Inc.
Group Owner: NewCap Inc.
Nat'l Reps: Canadian Broadcast Sales
Format: Classic Rock; *Special Programming:* Jazz 2 hrs wkly; *Hrs. of News Programming:* news progmg 5 hrs wkly; *No. News Employees:* 4; *Target Audience:* 25-54; adults
Dan Fagan, General Manager
Adam McLaren, Programming Director
Cathy Airey, Office Manager

CKUM-FM
01-01-1982; 93.5 MHz FM; *Hrs Open:* 24; 250 w; 98 ft; N46 06 16 W64 46 54
University of Moncton, Student Centre, 2nd Floor, Moncton, NB E1A 3E9 Canada
(506) 858-3750; *Fax:* (506) 858-4524
routierm@umoncton.ca
License: Moncton, NB held by Les Medias Acadiens Universitaires Inc.
Format: Variety/Diverse; *Special Programming:* Jazz 4 hrs wkly; *Hrs. of News Programming:* News progmg one hr wkly; *Target Audience:* 15-30.; *Adv. Rates:* 14; 13; 14; 11
Brian Gallant, President
Justin Robichaud, Operations Dir
Michele Routier, General Manager
Mylene Dugas, Vice President

CHOY-FM
02-19-2001; 99.9 MHz FM; 9.5 kw
1000 St. George Blvd., Moncton, NB E1E 4M7 Canada
(506) 384-2469; *Fax:* (506) 858-1209
www.choix999.com
License: Moncton, NB held by Maritime Broadcasting System Ltd.
Group Owner: Maritime Broadcasting; (acq 12-19-2005).
Population Served: 138,644; *Arbitron Metro Market:* Moncton, NB; *Format:* Country
Krysta Janssen, Operations Manager

CJXL-FM
11-01-2001; 96.9 MHz FM; *Hrs Open:* 24; 100 kw
27 Arsenault Ct., Moncton Industrial Park, Moncton, NB E1E 4J8 Canada
(506) 858-5525; *Fax:* (506) 858-5539
www.xl96.com
License: Moncton, NB held by Newcap Inc.
Group Owner: NewCap Inc.
Population Served: 138,644; *Arbitron Metro Market:* Moncton, NB; *Format:* Country; *Target Audience:* 25-54; adults
Dan Fagan, General Manager
Adam McLaren, Programming Director
Mike Brown, News Director
Cathy Airey, Office Manager

CKCW-FM
01-01-2001; 94.5 MHz FM; 19 kw
1000 St. George Blvd., Moncton, NB E1E 4M7 Canada
(506) 858-1220
www.k945.ca
License: Moncton, NB held by Maritime Broadcasting System Ltd.
Group Owner: Maritime Broadcasting
Population Served: 138,644; *Arbitron Metro Market:* Moncton, NB; *Format:* Contemporary Hits/Top 40; *Target Audience:* 18-44; adults
Krysta Janssen, Operations Manager

CITA-FM
01-01-2001; 105.1 MHz FM; 880 w
645 Pinewood Road, Riverview, NB E1B 5R6 Canada
(902) 468-8854; *Fax:* (902) 468-8851
www.citafm.com
License: Moncton, NB held by International Harvesters for Christ Evangelistic Association Inc.
Population Served: 101,343; *Arbitron Metro Market:* Dartmouth, NS; *Format:* Christian
Jean Brunet, Sales/Advertising

CKOE-FM
11-01-2000; 107.3 MHz FM; 50 w; Ant 82 ft
3030 Mountain Rd., Moncton, NB E1G 2W8 Canada
(506) 384-1009; *Fax:* (506) 383-9699
www.ckoefm.com
info@ckoefm.com
License: Moncton, NB held by Houssen Broadcasting Ltd.
Population Served: 138,074; *Arbitron Metro Market:* Moncton, NB; *Format:* Christian
James Houssen, General Manager
Jim Houssen, Station Manager
Don Houssen, General Sales Mgr
Steve Raye, News Director
Jason Constantine, Production/Music
Steve Meller, Production/Music
Jimmy D Houssen, WebHead

CKNI-FM
10-11-2005; 91.9 MHz FM; 70 kw
220-1600 Main St., Moncton, NB E1E 1G5 Canada
(506) 857-1922
www.919thebend.ca
info@919thebend.ca

License: Moncton, NB held by Acadia Broadcasting Ltd.
Group Owner: Acadia Broadcasting Ltd.
Population Served: 138,644; *Arbitron Metro Market:* Moncton, NB, Canada; *Format:* Adult Contemp
Troy Wallace, Station Manager
Maggie Dalley, Promotions Director

CBAM-FM
04-07-2008; 106.1 MHz FM; *Hrs Open:* 24; 69.5 kw; 211 meters; 46 08'41 N 64 54'11 W
165 Main St., Suite 15, Moncton, NB E1C 1B8 Canada
(506) 853-6666; *Fax:* (506) 853-6400
www.cbc.ca/news/canada/new-brunswick
infoammoncton@cbc.ca
License: Moncton, NB held by CBC Radio One
Group Owner: CBC
Nat'l Network: CBC Radio One
Arbitron Metro Market: Moncton, NB; *Format:* News/Talk
Darrow MacIntyre, Executive Producer

CFBO-FM
01-01-2008; 90.7 MHz FM; 30 kw; N46 11 04 W64 52 52
Cornwall 51, Shediac, NB E4P 8T8 Canada
(506) 532-0080; *Fax:* (506) 532-0120
www.cfbo.ca
cjse@cjse.ca
License: Moncton, NB held by Radio Beausejour Inc.
Population Served: 138,644; *Arbitron Metro Market:* Moncton, NB; *Format:* Adult Contemp
Serge Parent, General Manager

Sackville

***CHMA-FM**
01-01-1985; 106.9 MHz FM; *Hrs Open:* 24; 50 w
62 York Street, Sackville, NB E4L 1E2 Canada
(506) 364-2221
www.mta.ca/chma
chma@mta.ca
License: Sackville, NB held by Attic Broadcasting Ltd.
Population Served: 15,000
Pierre Malloy, Station Manager
Vanessa Blackier, Programming Director

Saint John

CBD-FM
10-15-1964; 91.3 MHz FM; 80 kw; 395 meters
39 King St., Suite A500A, Saint John, NB E2L 4W3 Canada
(506) 632-7710; *Fax:* (506) 632-7761
www.cbc.ca/nb
infoamsaintjohn@cbc.ca
License: Saint John, NB held by CBC Radio One
Group Owner: CBC
Format: News/Talk
Steven Webb, Executive Producer
Elke Semerad, Journalist

CFBC
11-21-1946; 930 kHz AM; *Hrs Open:* 24; 50 kw
226 Union St., Saint John, NB E2L 1B1 Canada
(506) 658-5100
License: Saint John, NB held by Maritime Broadcasting System Ltd.
Group Owner: Maritime Broadcasting; (acq 9-29-98; C$2 million with co-located FM).
Format: Country
Kelly O'Neill, General Sales Mgr

***CHSJ-FM**
01-07-1998; 94.1 MHz FM; *Hrs Open:* 24; kw
58 King St., Saint John, NB E2L 1G4 Canada
(506) 633-3323; *Fax:* (506) 644-3485
www.country94.ca
License: Saint John, NB held by Acadia Broadcasting Ltd.
Group Owner: Acadia Broadcasting Ltd.
Format: Country; *Target Audience:* 25-54.
Dave Boone, General Manager

***CIOK-FM**
08-10-1987; 100.5 MHz FM; *Hrs Open:* 24
226 Union St., Saint John, NB E2L 1B1 Canada
(506) 658-5100
www.k100.ca
License: Saint John, Saint John County, NB held by Maritime Broadcasting System Ltd.
Group Owner: Maritime Broadcasting
Format: Adult Contemp; *Special Programming:* Real radio 4 hrs wkly; *Hrs. of News Programming:* news progmg 7 hrs wkly; *Target Audience:* 25-49; housewives, families, professionals
Kelly O'Neill, General Sales Mgr

CJYC-FM
03-12-1965; 98.9 MHz FM; *Hrs Open:* 24
226 Union St., Saint John, NB E2L 1B1 Canada
(506) 658-5100
www.kool98.fm
License: Saint John, NB held by Maritime Broadcasting System Ltd.
Group Owner: Maritime Broadcasting
Format: Contemporary Hits/Top 40; *Target Audience:* 25-34; young, upwardly, mobile, family oriented
Kelly O'Neill, Advertising General Sales Manager

CINB-FM
11-16-2000; 96.1 MHz FM; 50 w
NewSong FM, Box 96, Saint John, NB E2L 3X1 Canada
(506) 657-9600; *Fax:* (506) 657-7664
www.newsongfm.com
License: Saint John, NB held by New Song Communications Ministries Ltd.
Population Served: 68,000; *Arbitron Metro Market:* Saint John, NB; *Format:* Christian
Don Mabee, Station Manager

CHWV-FM
02-19-2001; 97.3 MHz FM; *Hrs Open:* 24; 55 kw
58 King St., Saint John, NB E2L 1G4 Canada
(506) 633-3323; *Fax:* (506) 644-3485
www.thewave.ca
mail@thewave.ca
License: Saint John, NB held by Acadia Broadcasting Ltd.
Group Owner: Acadia Broadcasting Ltd.
Population Served: 68,000; *Arbitron Metro Market:* Saint John, NB; *Format:* Adult Contemp
Jim MacMullin, President
Dave Boone, Station Manager
Scott Clements, Programming Director

CFMH-FM
01-01-2001; 107.3 MHz FM; 250 w
100 Tucker Park Rd., Thomas J Condon Building RM 235, UNBSJ, Saint John, NB E2L 4L5 Canada
(506) 648-5667; *Fax:* (506) 648-5541
www.localfm.ca
cfmh@unbsj.ca
License: Saint John, NB held by Campus Radio Saint John Inc.
Population Served: 68,000; *Arbitron Metro Market:* Saint John, NB; *Format:* Variety/Diverse
Anthony Enman, Chair
Dan Downes, Vice Chair
Kelly Marino, Secretary

CJEF-FM
10-20-2003; 103.5 MHz FM; *Hrs Open:* 24; 49.6 w; Ant 200 ft; N45 16 31 W65 04 25
177 King Street East, Saint John, NB E2L 1G9 Canada
(506) 214-7571; *Fax:* (506) 642-7408
www.cjrpfm.com
License: Saint John, NB held by TFG Communications Inc.
Population Served: 68,000; *Arbitron Metro Market:* Saint John, NB; *Format:* Comedy; *Target Audience:* 18-34.; *Adv. Rates:* 180; 90; 126; 90
Geoffrey Rivett, CEO
Gary Stackhouse, General Manager
John Kierstead, Sales Manager
Bob Pritchard, Program Director and Owner
John Codner, Program Director and Owner
Graham Brown, News Director
Mark Henwood, Music Director
JudyPritchard, Office Manager
John Codner, Client Relations
Kim Cookson, Sales
John Campbell, Sales
Marc Henwood, Production

CHNI-FM
10-11-2005; 88.9 MHz FM; 79 kw
137 Market Sq., Saint John, NB E2L 4Z6 Canada
(506) 635-6500; *Fax:* (506) 635-6505
www.rock889.com
License: Saint John, NB held by Newcap Inc.
Group Owner: NewCap Inc.
Population Served: 680,004; *Arbitron Metro Market:* Saint John, NB; *Format:* Classic Rock
Dave Newbury, General Manager
Rod Martens, Programming Director

CHQC-FM
01-01-2006; 105.7 MHz FM; *Hrs Open:* 24; 1.85 kw
67 Chemin Ragged Point, Saint John, NB E2K 5C3 Canada
(506) 643-6996; *Fax:* (506) 658-3984
www.chqc.ca
direction@chqc.ca
License: Saint John, NB held by Cooperative radiophonique - La Brise de la Baie Ltee.
Population Served: 68,000; *Arbitron Metro Market:* Saint John, NB; *Format:* Variety/Diverse
Steve Pilotte, President
Nay Saade, General Manager

Saint Stephen

CHTD-FM
05-28-2001; 98.1 MHz FM; *Hrs Open:* 24; 40 kw
112 Milltown Blvd., Saint Stephen, NB E3L 1G6 Canada
(506) 466-1000; *Fax:* (506) 466-4500
www.thetide.ca
mail@thetide.ca
License: Saint Stephen, NB held by Acadia Broadcasting Ltd.
Group Owner: Acadia Broadcasting Ltd.
Population Served: 61,000; *Format:* Country; *No. News Employees:* 2; *Target Audience:* 25-54.
Jim MacMullin, President
Dave Boone, Station Manager

Shediac

CJSEFM
07-26-1994; 89.5 MHz FM; *Hrs Open:* 24; 20.445 kw; N46 11 04 W64 52 52
96 Rue Providence, Shediac, NB Canada
(506) 532-0080; *Fax:* (506) 532-0120
www.cjse.ca
patricia@cjse.ca
License: Shediac, NB held by Radio Beausejour Inc.
Flavian Babineau, President
Serge Parent, General Manager
Marcel Parker Gallant, Programming Director
Jason Oulette, Promotions Manager

Sussex

CJCW
06-01-1975; 590 kHz AM; 1 kw
6 Marble St., Sussex, NB E4E 5M2 Canada
(506) 432-2529; *Fax:* (506) 433-4900
www.590cjcw.com
License: Sussex, NB held by Maritime Broadcasting System Ltd.
Group Owner: Maritime Broadcasting
Format: Adult Contemp; *Special Programming:* Relg 4 hrs wkly; *Target Audience:* General.
Louis McNamara, General Manager
Lisa Graham, Sales

Woodstock

CJCJ-FM
07-01-1959; 104.1 MHz FM
131 Queen St., Unit 2, Woodstock, NB E7M 2M8 Canada
(506) 325-3030; *Fax:* (506) 325-3031
www.cj104.com
cj104@bellmedia.ca
License: Woodstock, NB held by Bell Media Radio Atlantic Inc.
Group Owner: Bell Media Inc.; (acq 4-19-2002; grpsl).
Population Served: 5,254; *Arbitron Metro Market:* Woodstock, NB; *Format:* Adult Contemp
Pat Brennan, General Manager
Rick McGuire, Station Manager

Newfoundland

Argentia

CFOZ-FM
01-01-1980; 100.3 MHz FM; *Hrs Open:* 24; 5 kw*Rebroadcasts:* Rebroadcasts CHOZ-FM St. John's.
Mailing Address: P.O. Box 2020, St. John's, NF A1C 5S2 Canada
Second Address: 446 Logy Bay Rd., St. John's, NF
(709) 726-2922; *Fax:* (709) 726-5107
www.ozfm.com
License: Argentia, Newfoundland County, NF held by Newfoundland Broadcasting Co. Ltd.
Group Owner: Newfoundland Broadcasting Co. Ltd.
Nat'l Reps: Canadian Broadcast Sales
Population Served: 500,000; *Format:* Adult Contemp; *No. News Employees:* 2; *Target Audience:* 18-49.
Ernst Rollmann, Station Manager

Baie Verte

CKIM
01-01-1979; 1240 kHz AM
P.O. Box 620, Grand Falls, NL A2A 2K2 Canada
(709) 489-2192; *Fax:* (709) 489-8626
www.vocm.com
License: Baie Verte, NF held by NewCap Inc.
Group Owner: NewCap Inc.; (acq 6-00; grpsl).
Format: Country, News, News/Talk, Talk
David Hillier, Station Manager
Fred Hutton, News Director

Bonavista Bay

CBGY
08-25-1977; 750 kHz AM*Rebroadcasts:* Rebroadcasts CBG(AM) Gander
Mailing Address: Canada
Second Address: 98 Sullivan Ave., Gander, NF A1V 1W7
(709) 256-4311; *Fax:* (709) 651-2021
www.cbc.ca/hl/
License: Bonavista Bay, NF held by CBC.
Group Owner: Canadian Broadcasting Corp
Format: News
Robert Rabinowitz, CEO
Michael Aucoin, Programming Director

CJOZ-FM
01-01-1979; 92.1 MHz FM; *Hrs Open:* 24; 50 kw*Rebroadcasts:* Rebroadcasts CHOZ-FM, St John's
Mailing Address: P.O. Box 2020, St. John's, NF A1C 5S2 Canada
Second Address: 446 Logy Bay Rd., St. John's, NF
(709) 726-2922; *Fax:* (709) 726-5107
www.ozfm.com
License: Bonavista Bay, Newfoundland County, NL held by Newfoundland Broadcasting Co.
Group Owner: Newfoundland Broadcasting Co.
Nat'l Reps: Canadian Broadcast Sales
Population Served: 500,000; *Format:* Adult Contemp; *No. News Employees:* 2; *Target Audience:* 18-49.
Ernst Rollmann, Station Manager

Burnt Islands

CHBI-FM
01-01-2007; 95.7 MHz FM; *Hrs Open:* 9-5 mon - Fri; 50 w; N47 36 18 W58 52 06
Box 101, Burnt Islands, NF A0M 1B0 Canada
(709) 698-3553; *Fax:* (709) 698-3100
www.burntislandsnl.ca
chbi95.7fm@hotmail.com
License: Burnt Islands, Canada County, NL held by Burnt Islands Economic Development Board.
Population Served: 919; *Arbitron Metro Market:* Burnt Islands, NL; *Format:* Variety/Diverse
Holly Keeping, General Manager

Carbonear

CHVO-FM
01-07-2008; 103.9 MHz FM; 14 kw; N47 43 13 W53 12 50
1 CHVO Dr., Carbonear, NF A1Y 1A2 Canada
(709) 596-1560; *Fax:* (709) 596-8626
www.kixxcountry.ca
License: Carbonear, NL held by Newcap Inc.
Group Owner: NewCap Inc.
Population Served: 4,739; *Arbitron Metro Market:* Carbonear, NL; *Format:* Country; *Target Audience:* 25-54; adults
Mike Campbell, Programming Director

Churchill Falls

CFLC-FM
01-01-1995; 97.9 MHz FM; 8 w; 50 ft
345 O'Connell Dr., Corner Brook, NF A2H 7E5 Canada
(709) 634-6672; *Fax:* (709) 634-4081
www.bigland.fm
info@bigland.fm
License: Churchill Falls, NL held by NewCap Inc.
Group Owner: NewCap Inc.; (acq 4-2-01; grpsl).
Format: News/Talk, Country
Stanley Kruchka, Station Manager
Mike Campbell, Programming Director
Kevin Doyle, Senior Account Manager

Clarenville

CJMY-FM
01-01-1988; 105.3 MHz FM; *Hrs Open:* 24; 2.07 kw
Mailing Address: P.O. Box 2020, St. John's, NF A1C 5S2 Canada
Second Address: 446 Logy Bay Rd., St. John's, NF
(709) 726-2922; *Fax:* (709) 726-5107
www.ozfm.com
License: Clarenville, Newfoundland County, NF held by Newfoundland Broadcasting Co.
Group Owner: Newfoundland Broadcasting Co.
Nat'l Reps: Canadian Broadcast Sales
Population Served: 500,000; *Format:* Adult Contemp; *No. News Employees:* 2; *Target Audience:* 18-49.
Ernst Rollmann, Station Manager

CKVO
11-15-1974; 710 kHz AM*Rebroadcasts:* Rebroadcasts VOCM(AM) St. John's except 9 AM-5 PM (loc progmg)
391 Kenmount Rd., P.O. Box 8-590, St. John's, NL A1B 3P5 Canada
(709) 466-1399; *Fax:* (709) 726-4633
www.vocm.com
License: Clarenville, NF held by NewCap Inc.
Group Owner: NewCap Inc.; (acq 6-00; grpsl).
Format: Country, News, News/Talk, Talk
Mike Murphy, Station Manager
Mike Campbell, Programming Director
Fred Hutton, News Director

Corner Brook

***CBY**
990 kHz AM; 10 kw
PO Box 12010, Station A, St. John's, NL A1B 3T8 Canada
(709) 634-3141; *Fax:* (709) 634-8506
www.cbc.ca/nl
cbrookradio@cbc.ca
License: Corner Brook, NF held by CBC Radio One
Group Owner: CBC
Nat'l Network: CBC Radio One
Format: News, News/Talk, Talk; *Target Audience:* 30 plus; mature
Peter Gullage, Executive Producer
Denise Wilson, Senior Managing Director

CFCB
10-03-1960; 570 kHz AM; *Hrs Open:* 24
345 O'Connell Dr., Corner Brook, NF A2H 7V3 Canada
(709) 634-4570; *Fax:* (709) 634-4081
License: Corner Brook, NF held by Newcap Inc.
Group Owner: NewCap Inc.; (acq 4-2-01; grpsl).
Nat'l Reps: Canadian Broadcast Sales
Format: Country
Robert G. Steele, President

CKOZ-FM
01-01-1979; 92.3 MHz FM; *Hrs Open:* 24; 50 kw*Rebroadcasts:* Rebroadcasts CHOZ-FM St. John's
Mailing Address: P.O. Box 2020, St. John's, NF A1C 5S2 Canada
Second Address: 446 Logy Bay Rd., St. John's, NF
(709) 726-2922; *Fax:* (709) 726-5107
www.ozfm.com
License: Corner Brook, Newfoundland County, NF held by Newfoundland Broadcasting Co.
Group Owner: Newfoundland Broadcasting Co.
Nat'l Reps: Canadian Broadcast Sales
Population Served: 500,000; *Format:* Adult Contemp; *No. News Employees:* 2; *Target Audience:* 18-49.
Ernst Rollmann, Station Manager

CKXX-FM
06-20-1997; 103.9 MHz FM; *Hrs Open:* 24; 40 kw
345 O'Connell Dr., Corner Brook, NF A2H 7E5 Canada
(709) 634-4570; *Fax:* (709) 634-4081
www.k-rock1039.com
License: Corner Brook, NL held by NewCap Inc.
Group Owner: NewCap Inc.; (acq 8-29-90).
Nat'l Reps: Canadian Broadcast Sales
Population Served: 40,000; *Format:* Classic Rock, Rock/AOR; *Special Programming:* Oldies 3 hrs wkly; *No. News Employees:* 2; *Target Audience:* 25-54.; *Adv. Rates:* 32.4; 32.4; 24.3; 10.8
Stanley Kruchka, General Manager
Mike Payne, Program Coordinator/Producer

Gander

***CBG**
1400 kHz AM; 4 kw
PO Box 12010, Station A, St. John's, NL A1B 3T8 Canada
(709) 256-4311; *Fax:* (709) 651-2021
www.cbc.ca/nl
centralmorning@cbc.ca
License: Gander, NF held by CBC Radio One
Group Owner: CBC
Format: News/Talk, News
Peter Gullage, Executive Producer
Victoria King, Senior Manager
Sherry Banfield, Senior Producer, Current Affairs

CKGA
01-01-1969; 650 kHz AM
P.O. Box 650, Gander, NL A1B 1X2 Canada
(709) 651-3650; *Fax:* (709) 651-2542
www.vocm.com
License: Gander, NF held by NewCap Inc.
Group Owner: NewCap Inc.; (acq 6-00; grpsl).
Format: Country, News, Talk
David Hillier, Station Manager
Fred Hutton, News Director

CKXD-FM
11-01-2000; 98.7 MHz FM; 6 kw
P.O. Box 650, Gander, NL A1V 1X2 Canada
(709) 651-3650; *Fax:* (709) 651-2542
www.987krock.com
onair@987krock.com
License: Gander, NL held by Newcap Inc.
Group Owner: NewCap Inc.
Population Served: 196,966; *Arbitron Metro Market:* St. John's, NL; *Format:* Classic Rock; *Special Programming:* Newfoundland & Irish 12 hrs wkly
David Hillier, Station Manager
Mike Hibbs, Programming Director

Goose Bay

CFLN-FM
04-15-2011; 97.9 MHz FM; 50 w; 25.4 meters
345 O'Connell Dr., Corner Brook, NL A2H 7E5 Canada
(709) 634-6672; *Fax:* (709) 634-4081
www.bigland.fm
info@bigland.fm
License: Goose Bay, NF held by NewCap Inc.
Group Owner: NewCap Inc.; (acq 4-2-01; grpsl).
Format: News/Talk
Stanley Kruchka, Station Manager
Mike Campbell, Programming Director
Kevin Doyle, Senior Account Manager

Grand Falls

CKMY-FM
01-01-1979; 95.9 MHz FM; *Hrs Open:* 24; 50 kw*Rebroadcasts:* Rebroadcasts CHOZ-FM St. John's.
Mailing Address: P.O. Box 2020, St. John's, NF A1C 5S2 Canada
Second Address: 446 Logy Bay Rd., St. John's, NF
(709) 726-2922; *Fax:* (709) 726-5107
www.ozfm.com
License: Grand Falls, Newfoundland County, NL held by Newfoundland Broadcasting Co.
Group Owner: Newfoundland Broadcasting Co.
Nat'l Reps: Canadian Broadcast Sales
Population Served: 500,000; *Format:* Adult Contemp; *No. News Employees:* 2; *Target Audience:* 18-49.
Ernst Rollmann, Station Manager

CKCM
07-25-1962; 620 kHz AM; 10 kw
Mailing Address: P.O. Box 620, Grand Falls, NL A2A 2K2 Canada
Second Address: 35A Grenfell Heights, Grand Falls, NL A2A 2K2
(709) 489-2192; *Fax:* (709) 489-8626
www.vocm.com
License: Grand Falls, NF held by NewCap Inc.
Group Owner: NewCap Inc.; (acq 6-00; grpsl).
Format: Country, News/Talk
David Hillier, Station Manager
Richard King, Programming Director
Fred Hutton, News Director

CKXG-FM
01-01-1999; 102.3 MHz FM; *Hrs Open:* 24; 17 kw; 96.6 meters
Mailing Address: P.O. Box 620, Grand Falls, NL A2A 2K2 Canada
Second Address: 35A Grenfell Heights, Grand Falls, NL A2A 2K2
(709) 489-2192; *Fax:* (709) 489-8626
www.krocknl.com
onair@krocknl.com
License: Grand Falls, NL held by NewCap Inc.
Group Owner: NewCap Inc.
Format: Classic Rock

David Hillier, Station Manager
Richard King, Programming Director

Grand Falls-Windsor

CBT
540 kHz AM; 10 kw
2 Harris Ave., Grand Falls-Windsor, NL A2A 2Y2 Canada
(709) 489-2102; *Fax:* (709) 489-1055
www.cbc.ca/nl
chantal.bernard@cbc.ca
License: Grand Falls-Windsor, NF held by CBC
Group Owner: CBC
Nat'l Network: CBC Radio One
Format: News/Talk, News
Peter Gullage, Executive Producer
Victoria King, Senior Manager
Sherry Banfield, Senior Producer, Current Affairs

Happy Valley-Goose Bay

*CFGB-FM
89.5 MHz FM; 4.5 kw; 195.5 meters
PO Box 12010, Station A, St. John's, NL A1B 3T8 Canada
(709) 896-2911; *Fax:* (709) 896-8900
www.cbc.ca/nl
labradormorning@cbc.ca
License: Happy Valley-Goose Bay, NL held by CBC Radio One
Group Owner: CBC
Format: News/Talk, News
Peter Gullage, Executive Producer
Victoria King, Senior Manager

Labrador City

CBDQ-FM
96.3 MHz FM; 255 w*Rebroadcasts:* Rebroadcasts CFGB-FM Happy Valley
500 Vanier Ave., Labrador City, NL A2V 2W7 Canada
(709) 576-5225; *Fax:* (709) 576-5011
www.cbc.ca/nl
peter.gullage@cbc.ca
License: Labrador City, NL held by CBC
Group Owner: CBC
Nat'l Network: CBC Radio One
Format: Talk, News/Talk
Peter Gullage, Executive Producer
Victoria King, Senior Manager

CJRM-FM
09-23-1992; 97.3 MHz FM; 500 w; 1,998 ft; N52 57 01 W66 55 01
65 Ridge Road, St. Johns, NL A1B 4P5 Canada
(709) 722-0627; *Fax:* (709) 722-9904
www.francotnl.ca
cjrm@crrstv.net
License: Labrador City, Labrador County, NL held by Radio Communautaire du Labrador Inc.
Population Served: 17,000; *Format:* Variety/Diverse; *Target Audience:* General; English & Fr speaking audience in Labrador West
Norman Gillespie, President
linda McLean, Station Manager
Dean Baker, Executive Vice President

Lewisporte

CIFX-FM
01-01-2002; 93.7 MHz FM; *Hrs Open:* 24; 50 w; N/A; 37 George Street, Lewisporte, Newfoundland & Labrador,*Rebroadcasts:* N/A
Mailing Address: Box 601, 37 George Street, Lewisporte, NF A0G 3A0 Canada
Second Address: 37 George Street, P.O. Box 601, Lewisporte, NF AOG 3AO
(709) 535-6000; *Fax:* (709) 535-6600
License: Lewisporte, N/A County, NL held by Mix FM Inc.
Population Served: 3,312; *Arbitron Metro Market:* Lewisporte, NL; *Format:* Talk; *Special Programming:* N/A; *No. News Employees:* 2; *Target Audience:* 21-52; *Adv. Rates:* $8.10
Vicki Fudge, Operations Dir
Koren Hurley, General Sales Mgr
Todd Foss, Programming Director
Angela Brenton, Promotions Manager
Peter Ginn, Engineering Dir
Colleen Harris, Administration/Copy
Terry Spurrell, Software Technician

Marystown

CHCM
01-01-1962; 740 kHz AM; 10 kw
P.O. Box 560, Marystown, NL A0E 2M0 Canada
(709) 279-2560; *Fax:* (709) 279-2800
www.vocm.com
License: Marystown, NF held by NewCap Inc.
Group Owner: NewCap Inc.; (acq 5-4-00; grpsl).
Format: Country
Russell Murphy, Station Manager
Gary Myles, Programming Director
Bob Power, News Director

CIOZ-FM
01-01-1979; 96.3 MHz FM; *Hrs Open:* 24; 25 kw*Rebroadcasts:* Rebroadcasts CHOZ-FM St. John's.
Mailing Address: P.O. Box 2020, St. John's, NF A1C 5S2 Canada
Second Address: 446 Logy Bay Rd., St. John's, NF
(709) 726-2922; *Fax:* (709) 726-5107
www.ozfm.com
License: Marystown, Newfoundland County, NF held by Newfoundland Broadcasting Co.
Group Owner: Newfoundland Broadcasting Co.
Nat'l Reps: Canadian Broadcast Sales
Population Served: 500,000; *Format:* Adult Contemp; *No. News Employees:* 2; *Target Audience:* 18-49.
Ernst Rollmann, Station Manager

Saint John's

*CBN-FM
106.9 MHz FM; 100 kw; 221 meters
PO Box 12010, Station A, St. John's, NL A1B 3T8 Canada
(709) 576-5225; *Fax:* (709) 576-5011
www.cbc.ca/nl
victoria.king@cbc.ca
License: Saint John's, NL held by CBC
Group Owner: CBC
Nat'l Network: CBC Radio 2
TV Affiliate: *CBNT-TV affil; *Format:* News, News/Talk, Public Affairs
Victoria King, Senior Manager
Peter Gullage, Executive Producer
Denise Wilson, Senior Managing Director

*CHMR-FM
01-01-1986; 93.5 MHz FM; *Hrs Open:* 24; 50 w; -10 ft
Memorial University, MUNSU, Box A-119, Saint John's, NF A1C 5S7 Canada
(709) 737-4777; *Fax:* (709) 737-7688
www.chmr.ca/
chmr@mun.ca
License: Saint John's, NL held by Memorial University of Newfoundland Radio Society Inc.
Population Served: 200,000; *Format:* Alternative, Variety/Diverse; *Special Programming:* Fr 2 hrs, jazz 6 hrs, relg 4 hrs, blues 6 hrs, rap; *Hrs. of News Programming:* News progmg 7 hrs wkly; *Target Audience:* General.
Kathy Rowe, Station Manager
Bob Earle, Programming Director
Colleen Power, News Director

CKSJ-FM
01-01-2004; 101.1 MHz FM; 20 kw
95 Bonaventure Avenue, Suite 201, Saint John's, NF A1B 2X5 Canada
(709) 754-6748; *Fax:* (709) 754-6749
www.coast1011.com
onair@coast1011.com
License: Saint John's, NL held by Coast Broadcasting Ltd.
Population Served: 106,172; *Arbitron Metro Market:* St. John's, NL; *Format:* Adult Contemp
Andrew Newman, General Manager

St. Andrew's

CFCV-FM
01-01-1974; 97.7 MHz FM*Rebroadcasts:* Rebroadcasts CFGN(AM) Port-aux-Basques
60 West St., Stephenville, NF A2N 1C6 Canada
(709) 643-2191; *Fax:* (709) 643-5025
www.cfsxradio.com
cfsx@vocm.com
License: St. Andrew's, NL held by NewCap Inc.
Group Owner: NewCap Inc.
Format: Country, News/Talk
Katherine Hogan, Station Manager
Katherine Hogan, Sales
Mike Payne, Programming Director

St. John's

*CBN
11-14-1932; 640 kHz AM; *Hrs Open:* 19; 10 kw
PO Box 12010, Station A, St. John's, NL A1B 3T8 Canada
(709) 576-5225; *Fax:* (709) 576-5011
www.cbc.ca/nl
denise.wilson@cbc.ca
License: St. John's, NL held by CBC
Group Owner: CBC
Nat'l Network: CBC Radio One
Format: News/Talk; *Special Programming:* Fisheries 3 hrs wkly; *Hrs. of News Programming:* news progmg 10 hrs wkly; *No. News Employees:* 6; *Target Audience:* General.
Denise Wilson, Senior Managing Director
Peter Gullage, Executive Producer

CHOZ-FM
06-15-1977; 94.7 MHz FM; *Hrs Open:* 24; 100 kw; 821 ft; NN47 31 36 W52 42 50
Mailing Address: P.O. Box 2020, St. John's, NF A1C 5S2 Canada
Second Address: 446 Logy Bay Rd., St. John's, NF
(709) 726-2922; *Fax:* (709) 726-5107
www.ozfm.com
License: St. John's, Newfoundland County, NF held by Newfoundland Broadcasting Co. Ltd.
Group Owner: Newfoundland Broadcasting Co.
Nat'l Reps: Canadian Broadcast Sales
Population Served: 500,000*TV Affiliate:* CJON-TV affil.; *Format:* Adult Contemp; *No. News Employees:* 2; *Target Audience:* 18-49.
Ernst Rollmann, Station Manager

CJYQ
01-01-1951; 930 kHz AM
391 Kenmount Rd., P.O. Box 8-590, St. John's, NL A1B 3P5 Canada
(709) 726-5590; *Fax:* (709) 726-4633
www.thisisnewfoundlandlabrador.ca
License: St. John's, NF held by Newcap Inc.
Group Owner: NewCap Inc.
Format: Light Rock
Mike Murphy, Station Manager
Mike Campbell, Programming Director

CKIX-FM
10-15-1983; 99.1 MHz FM; 100 kw; Ant 930 ft
391 Kenmount Rd., P.O. Box 8-590, St. John's, NL A1B 3P5 Canada
(709) 726-5590; *Fax:* (709) 726-4633
www.991hitsfm.com
hitsmail@991hitsfm.com
License: St. John's, NL held by Newcap Inc.
Group Owner: NewCap Inc.; (acq 1-17-83).
Format: Contemporary Hits/Top 40
Mike Murphy, Station Manager
Mike Campbell, Programming Director
Chris Hanlon, FM Sales Manager

*VOAR
01-01-1930; 1210 kHz AM; *Hrs Open:* 24
1041 Topsail Road, Mount Pearl, NL A1N 5E9 Canada
(709) 745-8627; *Fax:* (709)745-1600
www.voar.org
voar@voar.org
License: St. John's, NF held by Seventh-Day Adventist Church in Newfoundland.
Arbitron Metro Market: St. John's, NL, Canada; *Format:* Gospel, Religious; *Hrs. of News Programming:* News progmg 12 hrs wkly; *Target Audience:* 25-44; individuals interested in family life & traditional values
Gary Hodder, President
Sherry Griffin, Station Manager
Brian Matthews, Chief Engineer
Tina Taylor, Communications Director

VOCM
10-19-1936; 590 kHz AM; *Hrs Open:* 24
391 Kenmount Rd., P.O. Box 8-590, St. John's, NL A1B 3P5 Canada
(709) 726-5590; *Fax:* (709) 726-4633
www.vocm.com
License: St. John's, NF held by NewCap Inc.
Group Owner: NewCap Inc.; (acq 6-00; grpsl).
Nat'l Reps: Canadian Broadcast Sales
Arbitron Metro Market: St. John's, NL, Canada; *Format:* Adult Contemp, Country, News, News/Talk, Talk; *No. News Employees:* 16; *Target Audience:* 25 plus.
Mike Murphy, Station Manager
Mike Campbell, Programming Director
Fred Hutton, News Director

VOCM-FM
09-01-1982; 97.5 MHz FM; *Hrs Open:* 24; 100 kw
391 Kenmount Rd., St. John's, NL A1B 3P5 Canada

(709) 726-5590; *Fax:* (709) 726-4633
www.krockrocks.com
email@krockrocks.com
License: St. John's, NF held by NewCap Inc.
Group Owner: NewCap Inc.
Population Served: 196,966; *Arbitron Metro Market:* St. John's, NL, Canada; *Format:* Classic Rock; *Hrs. of News Programming:* News progmg 7 hrs wkly; *Target Audience:* Adults 25-54.
Mike Murphy, Station Manager
Chris Hanlon, FM Sales Manager
Mike Campbell, Programming Director

***VOWR**
06-20-1924; 800 kHz AM; *Hrs Open:* 24
PO Box 26006, St. Johns, NL A1E 0A5 Canada
(709) 579-9233; *Fax:* (709) 579-9232
www.vowr.org
vowr@vowr.org
License: St. John's, NF held by Wesley United Church Radio Board.
Arbitron Metro Market: St. John's, NL, Canada; *Format:* Oldies, Variety/Diverse; *Special Programming:* Relg 10 hrs, folk 15 hrs wkly; *Target Audience:* 40 plus.
Marvin Barnes, Chairman
John Tessier, General Manager

Stephenville

CFSX
11-13-1964; 870 kHz AM; *Hrs Open:* 24; 500 w
60 West St., Stephenville, NL A2N 1C6 Canada
(709) 643-2191; *Fax:* (709) 643-5025
www.cfsxradio.com
cfsx@vocm.com
License: Stephenville, NF held by NewCap Inc.
Group Owner: NewCap Inc.; (acq 2001; grpsl).
Format: Country, News/Talk; *Special Programming:* Relg one hr wkly; *No. News Employees:* 2; *Target Audience:* General.
Katherine Hogan, Station Manager
Katherine Hogan, Sales
Mike Payne, Programming Director

CIOS-FM
98.5 MHz FM; *Hrs Open:* 24*Rebroadcasts:* Rebroadcasts CHOZ-FM St. John's.
Mailing Address: P.O. Box 2020, St. John's, NF A1C 5S2 Canada
Second Address: 446 Logy Bay Rd., St. John's, NF
(709) 726-2922; *Fax:* (709) 726-5107
www.ozfm.com
License: Stephenville, Newfoundland County, NF held by Newfoundland Broadcasting Co. Ltd.
Group Owner: Newfoundland Broadcasting Co. Ltd.
Nat'l Reps: Canadian Broadcast Sales
Population Served: 500,000; *Format:* Adult Contemp; *No. News Employees:* 2; *Target Audience:* 18-49.
Ernst Rollmann, Station Manager

Wabana

CJBI-FM
93.9 MHz FM; 28 w; 79.5 meters; N47 37 56 W52 56 15
Box 974, Bell Island, NL A0A 4H0 Canada
(709) 488-2901
www.radiobellisland.com
rbi@radiobellisland.com
License: Wabana, NL held by Radio Bell Island Inc.

Northwest Territories

Hay River

CJCD-FM-1
09-15-1986; 100.1 MHz FM; 300 w; 175 ft*Rebroadcasts:* Rebroadcasts CJCD(FM) Yellowknife
Box 218, Yellowknife, NT X1A 2N2 Canada
(867) 920-4636; *Fax:* (867) 920-4033
mix100.ca
info@cjcd.ca
License: Hay River, NT held by CJCD Radio Ltd.
Nat'l Reps: Canadian Broadcast Sales
Format: Adult Contemp; *Target Audience:* 25-49.
Eileen Dent, President
Tim Jaworski, General Sales Mgr
Joanne McKenzie, Programming Director
Kirby Marshall, Chief Engineer
Mandy Church, Traffic Manager

CKHR-FM
01-01-1979; 107.3 MHz FM; 32 w; 185 ft
7000 West Georgia Street, Suite 2000, Vancouver, BC V7Y 1K9 Canada
(604) 331-2808
www.rock101.com
License: Hay River, NT held by Hay River Broadcasting Society.
Format: Adult Contemp
Devon T. Schnitter, Sales Manager

Inuvik

***CHAK**
11-26-1960; 860 kHz AM; 1 kw
100 Mackenzie Rd., Inuvik, NT X0E 0T0 Canada
(867) 920-5431
www.cbc.ca/north
janice.stein@cbc.ca
License: Inuvik, NT held by CBC
Group Owner: CBC
Nat'l Network: CBC Radio One
Format: Public Affairs, News; *Special Programming:* Inuvialuktun 9 hrs, Gwich'in 9 hrs wkly; *Target Audience:* General.
Janice Stein, Managing Director

Tuktoyaktuk

CFCT
01-01-1971; 600 kHz AM
Canada
(867) 777-7600; *Fax:* (867) 777-7640
License: Tuktoyaktuk, NT held by CBC.
Nat'l Network: CBC Radio One
Format: Variety/Diverse; *Special Programming:* Eskimo 5 hrs wkly
Peter Skinner, General Manager

Yellowknife

CJCD-FM
100.1 MHz FM; 400 w; 73 meters; 62 27 13.0 N 114 22 13.0 W
5114 49th St., Yellowknife, NT X1A 1P8 Canada
(867) 920-4636; *Fax:* (867) 920-4033
www.myyellowknifenow.com
rram@vistaradio.ca
License: Yellowknife, NT held by Vista Radio Ltd.
Group Owner: Vista Radio Ltd.; (acq 3-8-00)
Nat'l Reps: Canadian Broadcast Sales
Format: Adult Contemp; *Target Audience:* 25-54.
Robin Ram, General Manager & Sales Manager
Tom Teichroeb, Assistant Program Director
Chris McGee, Integrated Marketing Executive
Trevor Thompson, Integrated Marketing Executive

CKLB-FM
12-11-1985; 101.9 MHz FM; *Hrs Open:* 7 AM-10 PM (M-F); 11 AM-9 PM (S); 130 w; 162 ft*Rebroadcasts:* Rebroadcasts CFWE-FM Lac La Biche, Alberta News
4 Lessard Drive, Box 2193, Yellowknife, NT X1A 2P6 Canada
(320) 295-7686
www.cklbradio.com
denezenakehko@cklbradio.com
License: Yellowknife, Canada County, NT held by Native Communications Society of the Western N.W.T.
Population Served: 30,000; *Format:* Country; *No. News Employees:* 1; *Adv. Rates:* 20; 20; 20; 20
Deneze Nakehko, Director of Radio

***CFYK-FM**
98.9 MHz FM; 5.5 kw; 50 meters
5002 Forrest Dr., Yellowknife, NT X1A 2A9 Canada
(867) 920-5465
www.cbc.ca/north
janice.stein@cbc.ca
License: Yellowknife, NT held by CBC
Group Owner: CBC
Nat'l Network: CBC Radio One
Format: Public Affairs, News
Janice Stein, Managing Director
Mervin Brass, Managing Editor

Nova Scotia

Amherst

CFTA-FM
07-21-2011; 107.9 MHz FM; 6.5 kw; 123 meters
141 Victoria Street E, Suite S, Amherst, NS B4H 1X9 Canada
(902) 660-1079; *Fax:* (902) 660-1080
cftafm.com
License: Amherst, NS held by Tantramar Community Radio Society
Carl Humphrey, Chairman

CKDH-FM
07-20-2011; 101.7 MHz FM; 23 kw; 16 meters
Mailing Address: P.O. Box 670, Amherst, NS B4H 4B8 Canada
Second Address: #38 Hwy. 6, Amherst, NS
(902) 667-3875
www.ckdh.net
License: Amherst, NS held by Maritime Broadcasting System Ltd.
Group Owner: Maritime Broadcasting
Format: Country
Robert Pace, CEO/COO
Leanne Byrnes, Sales
Lonney Bezzina, Sales

Antigonish

CJFX-FM
01-01-2003; 98.9 MHz FM; *Hrs Open:* 24; 75.39 kw
Mailing Address: 5663 Highway #7, PO Box 5800, Antigonish, NS B2G 2J5 Canada
Second Address: 85 Kirk St., Antigonish, NS B2G 2R9
(902) 863-4580; *Fax:* (902) 863-6300
www.989xfm.ca
License: Antigonish, NS held by Atlantic Broadcasters Ltd.
Group Owner: Atlantic Broadcasters Ltd
Nat'l Reps: Canadian Broadcast Sales *Regional Reps:* Canadian Broadcast Sales
Format: Contemporary Hits/Top 40; *Hrs. of News Programming:* news progmg 24 hrs wkly; *No. News Employees:* 3; *Target Audience:* 18 plus.
Ken Farrell, General Manager
Neil Scribner, General Sales Mgr
Barry Mackinnon, Programming Director
Ken Kingston, News Director

CFXU-FM
01-01-2006; 93.3 MHz FM; 50 w; N45 37 10 W61 59 40
Box 948, St. Francis Xavier University, Antigonish, NS B2G 2W5 Canada
(902) 867-2410
www.radiocfxu.ca
cfxv@stfx.ca
License: Antigonish, NS held by Radio CFXU Club.
Population Served: 4,524; *Arbitron Metro Market:* Antigonish, NS;
Format: Variety/Diverse
Rory Macleod, Station Manager
Jess Shanaley, Programming Director

Barrington

CJLS-FM-1
01-01-1982; 96.3 MHz FM; 5.5 kw*Rebroadcasts:* Rebroadcasts CJLS-FM Yarmouth
328 Maint St., Yarmouth, NS B5A 1E4 Canada
(902) 742-7175; *Fax:* (902) 742-3143
www.cjls.com
cjls@cjls.com
License: Barrington, NS held by Radio CJLS Ltd.
Format: Adult Contemp
Ray Zinck, President
Chris Perry, Operations Dir
Dave Hall, General Sales Mgr
Gary Nickerson, News Director

***CJLSFM**
01-01-2003; 96.3 MHz FM; *Hrs Open:* 24; kw
Canada
(902) 742-7175; *Fax:* (902) 742-3143
www.cjls.com
CJLS@cjls.com
License: Barrington, NS held by Radio CJLS Ltd.
Arbitron Metro Market: Yarmouth, NS; *Format:* Adult Contemp
Ray Zinck, General Manager
Dave Hall, General Sales Mgr
Chris Perry, Programming Director
Gary Nickerson, News Director
Jim Harris, Chief Engineer
Sean MacLellan, Sports Director
Carol Sherman, Sales Consultant
Eva Smith, SalesConsultant

Bedford

CHSB-FM
01-01-2007; 99.3 MHz FM; 50 w; N44 44 13 W63 39 13
158 Rocky Lake Drive, PO Box 44073, Bedford, NS B4A 3X5 Canada
(902) 835-5966
www.bedfordbaptist.ca
office@bedfordbaptist.ca
License: Bedford, NS held by Bedford Baptist Church.

Population Served: 18,274; *Arbitron Metro Market:* Bedford, NS; *Format:* Religious
Kevin Haggarty, General Manager

Bridgewater

CKBW-FM
02-01-2002; 98.1 MHz FM; *Hrs Open:* 24; 32 kw
135 North St., Suite 200, Bridgewater, NS B4V 2V7 Canada
(902) 543-2401; *Fax:* (902) 543-1208
www.ckbw.ca
License: Bridgewater, Lunenburg County, NS held by Acadia Broadcasting Ltd.
Group Owner: Acadia Broadcasting Ltd.
Population Served: 8,241; *Arbitron Metro Market:* Bridgewater, NS; *Format:* Adult Contemp; *Hrs. of News Programming:* news progmg 11 hrs wkly; *No. News Employees:* 15; *Target Audience:* General; rural & small townurban
John Wiles, Station Manager
Chris Pearson, General Sales Mgr
Sheldon MacLeod, News Director
Frank Grayney, Chief Engineer
Pamela Smith, Traffic Manager
Greg Lowe, Advertising
Brian Tepper, Creative Director
Eric Whynot,Assistant Sales Manager

CJHK-FM
05-15-2010; 100.7 MHz FM; 10 kw
135 North St., Suite 200, Bridgewater, NS B4V 2V7 Canada
(902) 543-2401; *Fax:* (902) 543-1208
www.cjhk.ca
License: Bridgewater, NS held by Acadia Broadcasting Ltd.
Group Owner: Acadia Broadcasting Ltd.
Format: Country
John Wiles, Station Manager

Cheticamp

*CKJM-FM
06-10-1995; 106.1 MHz FM; *Hrs Open:* 24; 3 kw; N46 36 55 W61 02 52*Rebroadcasts:* Rebroadcasts CFIM-FM Iles-De-La Madeleine, PQ 5%
Box 699, Les Trois Piqnons, Cheticamp, NS B0E 1H0 Canada
(902) 224-1242; *Fax:* (902) 224-1770
www.ckjm.ca
info@ckjm.ca
License: Cheticamp, Inverness County, NS held by La Cooperative Radio Cheticamp Ltee.
Population Served: 5,000; *Format:* Country; *Special Programming:* Gaelic one hr, jazz 3 hrs wkly; *Target Audience:* General.; *Adv. Rates:* 22; 16; 16; 16
Claudie Deveau, President
Angus Lefort, General Manager
Carole Aucoin, General Sales Mgr
Ginette Chiasson, Programming Director

Comeauville

*CIFA-FM
09-28-1990; 104.1 MHz FM; *Hrs Open:* 6am to 10pm; 39.3 w; 475 ft
Box 8, Saulnierville, NS B0W 2Z0 Canada
(902) 769-2432; *Fax:* (902) 769-3101
www.cifa.fm
info@cifafm.ca
License: Comeauville, Digby County, NS held by Association Radio Clare.
Population Served: 60,000; *Format:* News, Variety/Diverse; *Target Audience:* General.
Dave LeBlau, General Manager
Paul Lomberd, General Sales Mgr
Emile Blinn, Engineering Dir

Dartmouth

CFLT-FM
12-05-1962; 92.9 MHz FM; 27 kw; 196 meters
6080 Young St., 9th Fl., Halifax, NS B3K 5L2 Canada
(902) 493-7200
www.jack929.com
scott.bodnarchuk@rci.rogers.com
License: Dartmouth, NS held by Rogers Media Inc.
Group Owner: Rogers Media Inc.
Nat'l Reps: Canadian Broadcast Sales
Format: Adult Contemp, Contemporary Hits/Top 40
Scott Bodnarchuk, General Sales Mgr
Earle Mader, Programming Director
Ferne Wynnyk, Promotions Manager

*CFRQ-FM
11-28-1983; 104.3 MHz FM; 100 kw
3770 Kempt Rd., Suite 200, Halifax, NS B3K 4X8 Canada
(902) 453-4004; *Fax:* (902) 453-3120
www.q104.ca
License: Dartmouth, NS held by Newcap Inc.
Group Owner: NewCap Inc.
Format: Classic Rock, Rock/AOR
Ken Geddes, Station Manager
Trevor Wallworth, Programming Director
Mark Tanner, Sales Manager

Digby

CKDY
02-02-1970; 1420 kHz AM*Rebroadcasts:* Rebroadcasts CKEN-FM Kentville and CKAD(AM) Middleton
P.O. Box 1420, 53 Sydney St., Digby, NS B0V 1A0 Canada
(902) 245-2111; *Fax:* (902) 678-9720
www.avrnetwork.com
License: Digby, NS held by Maritime Broadcasting System Ltd.
Group Owner: Maritime Broadcasting; (acq 8-79).
Format: Country; *Special Programming:* Farm 7 hrs wkly
Andrew Johnson, Kentville, General Sales Mgr

Eastern Passage

*CFEP-FM
01-01-2002; 105.9 MHz FM; *Hrs Open:* 24; 1.68 kw; 37.6 meters; N44 36 46 W63 29 40
Seaside-FM, Box 196, Eastern Passage, NS B3G 1M5 Canada
(902) 469-9231; *Fax:* (902) 469-1935
www.seasidefm.com
info@seasidefm.com
License: Eastern Passage, HRM County, NS held by Seaside Broadcasting Organization.
Population Served: 25,000; *Hrs. of News Programming:* news progmg 50 hrs wkly; *No. News Employees:* 4
Wayne Harrett, Station/General Manager
Jim Coe, General Sales Mgr
Gordon Hefler, Engineering Dir

Eskasoni Indian Reserve

CICU-FM
01-01-1994; 94.1 MHz FM; 1 w
Mailing Address: Box 7100, Eskasoni, NS B1W 1A1 Canada
Second Address: 130 Anslum Rd., Eskasoni Indian Reserve, Eskasoni, NS B1W 1A1
(902) 379-2955; *Fax:* (902) 379-2966
License: Eskasoni Indian Reserve, NS held by Greg Johnson.
Population Served: 3,893; *Arbitron Metro Market:* Eskasoni, NS
Greg Johnson, General Manager
Linda Johnson, Programming Director

Glace Bay

CKOA-FM
12-03-2007; 89.7 MHz FM; *Hrs Open:* 24; 6.0 kw; N46 11 59 W59 58 46
106 Reserve St., Glace Bay, NS B1A 4W5 Canada
(902) 849-4301; *Fax:* (902) 849-1272
www.coastalradio.ca
info@coastalradio.ca
License: Glace Bay, Canada County, NS held by Coastal Community Radio Cooperative Ltd.
Nat'l Reps: Target Broadcast Sales
Population Served: 19,076; *Arbitron Metro Market:* Glace Bay, NS; *Format:* Country; *Hrs. of News Programming:* news progmg 105 hrs wkly; *No. News Employees:* 2; *Target Audience:* 40-65; prime demographic
Karen O'Brien, Operations Dir
Bill MacNeil, General Manager
Dennis Chipman, Music Director

Halifax

*CBH-FM
06-01-1976; 102.7 MHz FM; *Hrs Open:* 24; 92 kw; 714 ft; 44 39'3.6 N 63 39'28.8 W
6940 Mumford Rd., Suite 100, Halifax, NS B3L 0B7 Canada
(902) 420-8311
www.cbc.ca/ns
john.channing@cbc.ca
License: Halifax, NS held by CBC
Group Owner: CBC
Nat'l Network: CBC Radio 2
Format: Public Affairs, News; *Target Audience:* General.
John Channing, Broadcast Sales
Ken MacIntosh, Executive Producer, News and Current Affairs
Chantal Bernard, Senior Communications Officer

CBHA-FM
90.5 MHz FM; 91 kw; 230.5 meters
6940 Mumford Rd., Suite 100, Halifax, NS B3L 0B7 Canada
(902) 420-4100; *Fax:* (902) 420-4137
www.cbc.ca/ns
john.channing@cbc.ca
License: Halifax, NS held by CBC
Group Owner: CBC
Nat'l Network: CBC Radio One
Format: News/Talk, News
John Channing, Broadcast Sales
Ken MacIntosh, Executive Producer, News and Current Affairs
Chantal Bernard, Senior Communications Officer

CHFX-FM
02-09-1970; 101.9 MHz FM; *Hrs Open:* 24
90 Lovett Lake Crt., Halifax, NS B3S 0H6 Canada
(902) 422-1651
www.fx1019.ca
License: Halifax, NS held by Maritime Broadcasting System Ltd.
Group Owner: Maritime Broadcasting; (acq 6-94)
Wire Services: Broadcast News Ltd.
Format: Country; *Hrs. of News Programming:* news progmg 6 hrs wkly; *No. News Employees:* 5; *Target Audience:* 25-44.
Neil Kendall, General Sales Mgr
Gillian Grant, Account Manager

CKUL-FM
08-30-1990; 96.5 MHz FM; *Hrs Open:* 24; 100 kw
3770 Kempt Rd., Suite 200, Halifax, NS B3K 4X8 Canada
(902) 453-4004; *Fax:* (902) 453-3120
License: Halifax, NS held by Newcap Inc.
Group Owner: NewCap Inc.; (acq 12-17-2001)
Nat'l Reps: Canadian Broadcast Sales
Format: Adult Contemp, Triple A; *Hrs. of News Programming:* news progmg 3 hrs wkly; *No. News Employees:* 3; *Target Audience:* 35-54.
Ken Geddes, Station Manager
Christina Fitzgerald, Programming Director

CIOO-FM
11-01-1977; 100.1 MHz FM; *Hrs Open:* 24; 100 kw; 770 ft; N44 39 05 W63 39 51
2900 Agricola St., Halifax, NS B3K 6A7 Canada
(902) 453-2524
www.c100fm.com
License: Halifax, Halifax County, NS held by Bell Media Canada Radio 2013 Partnership
Group Owner: Bell Media Inc.
Format: Adult Contemp
Trent McGrath, General Manager
Trent McGrath, General Sales Mgr
Brad Muir, Programming Director
Zach Bedford, Music Director

*CKDU-FM
02-01-1985; 97.5 MHz FM; *Hrs Open:* 24; 3.2 kw; Ant 300 ft
Dalhousie SUB, 6136 University Ave., Halifax, NS B3H 4J2 Canada
(902) 494-6479
www.ckdu.ca
info@ckdu.ca
License: Halifax, NS held by CKDU-FM Society Ltd.
Population Served: 250,000; *Format:* Variety/Diverse; *Hrs. of News Programming:* news progmg 4 hrs wkly; *No. News Employees:* 1; *Target Audience:* General.
Gianna Lauren, Station Manager
Laura Peek, Programming Director

CBAX-FM
91.5 MHz FM; 77.5 kw; 44 38'34.2 N 63 34'45.1 W
6940 Mumford Rd., Suite 100, Halifax, NS B3L 0B7 Canada
(902) 420-8311
www.cbc.radio-canada.ca
License: Halifax, NS held by CBC
Group Owner: CBC
Nat'l Network: Ici Musique
Arbitron Metro Market: Halifax, NS; *Format:* Classical, Jazz
Hubert T. Lacroix, President and CEO
Judith Purves, EVP and Chief Financial Officer

CJNI-FM
10-11-2005; 95.7 MHz FM; 65 kw; 224.1 meters
6080 Young St., 9th Fl, Halifax, NS B3K 5L2 Canada
(902) 493-7200
www.news957.com
License: Halifax, NS held by Rogers Media Inc.
Group Owner: Rogers Media Inc.
Arbitron Metro Market: Halifax, NS; *Format:* News, News/Talk, Sports, Talk
Mark Campbell, News and Programming Director
Nicole Gnazdowsky, Producer

CKHZ-FM
06-28-2006; 103.5 MHz FM; *Hrs Open:* 24; 100 kw; N44 38 47 W63 39 40
Evanov Radio Group, 5302 Dundas St. W., Toronto, ON M9B 1B2 Canada
(416) 213-1035; *Fax:* (416) 233-8617
www.hotcountry1035.com
info@z103halifax.com
License: Halifax, NS held by HFX Broadcasting Inc.
Group Owner: Evanov Communications Inc.
Population Served: 94,544; *Format:* Country; *Adv. Rates:* 100; 100; 100; 100
Trevor Romkey, General Manager

CHNS-FM
07-19-2006; 89.9 MHz FM; 100 kw
90 Lovett Lake Crt., Halifax, NS B3S 0H6 Canada
(902) 422-1651
www.899thewave.fm
License: Halifax, NS held by Maritime Broadcasting System Ltd.
Group Owner: Maritime Broadcasting
Population Served: 372,858; *Arbitron Metro Market:* Halifax, NS; *Format:* Contemporary Hits/Top 40, Oldies; *Target Audience:* 25-54; adults
Neil Kendall, General Sales Mgr

***CKRH-FM**
09-25-2007; 98.5 MHz FM; 2.35 kw; N44 39 03 W63 39 28
5527 Cogswell St., Halifax, NS B3J 1R2 Canada
(902) 490-2574; *Fax:* (902) 429-2574
www.ckrhfm.ca
License: Halifax, NS held by Cooperative Radio-Halifax-Metro limitee.
Population Served: 372,858; *Arbitron Metro Market:* Halifax, NS; *Format:* French; *No. News Employees:* 3
Nay Saade, General Manager

CJCH-FM
05-30-2008; 101.3 MHz FM; *Hrs Open:* 24; 100 kw; N44 38 47 W63 39 37
2900 Agricola St., Halifax, NS B3K 6A7 Canada
(902) 453-2524
www.1013thebounce.com
License: Halifax, NS held by Bell Media Canada Radio 2013 Partnership
Group Owner: Bell Media Inc.
Format: Contemporary Hits/Top 40
Trent McGrath, General Manager
Brad Muir, Programming Director
Katrina Elliott, Music Director

CKHY-FM
10-01-2010; 105.1 MHz FM; 100 kw; 185.1 meters
5527 Cogswell St., Halifax, NS B3J 1R2 Canada
(902) 429-1035; *Fax:* (902) 425-8637
www.live105.ca
License: Halifax, NS held by HFX Broadcasting Inc.
Group Owner: Evanov Communications Inc.
Format: Rock/AOR
Trevor Romkey, General Sales Mgr
Barry Stewart, Programming Director
Sean Lawson, Promotions Coordinator
Mark Doiron, Producer

***CBAF-FM-5**
92.3 MHz FM; 91 kw; 230.5 meters*Rebroadcasts:* Rebroadcaster of CBAF in Moncton
6940 Mumford Rd., Suite 100, Halifax, NS B3L 4R5 Canada
(902) 420-8311
www.cbc.radio-canada.ca
License: Halifax, NS held by CBC
Group Owner: CBC
Nat'l Network: Ici Radio-Canada PremiŠre
Format: Public Affairs, News
Hubert T. Lacroix, President and CEO
Judith Purves, EVP and Chief Financial Officer

Kentville

CKEN-FM
03-14-1965; 97.7 MHz FM; 18 kw; Ant 680 ft
29 Oakdene Ave., P.O. Box 310, Kentville, NS B4N 1H5 Canada
(902) 678-2111; *Fax:* (902) 678-9894
www.avrnetwork.com
License: Kentville, NS held by Maritime Broadcasting System Ltd.
Group Owner: Maritime Broadcasting; (acq 1998; grpsl).
Nat'l Reps: Canadian Broadcast Sales
Format: Country; *Special Programming:* Farm 5 hrs wkly; *No. News Employees:* 5; *Target Audience:* 18-49.
Andrew Johnson, General Sales Mgr

***CKWM-FM**
01-01-2003; 94.9 MHz FM
29 Oakdene Ave., P.O. Box 310, Kentville, NS B4N 1H5 Canada
(902) 678-2111; *Fax:* (902) 678-9894
www.magic949.ca
License: Kentville, NS held by Maritime Broadcasting System Ltd.
Group Owner: Maritime Broadcasting
Arbitron Metro Market: Kentville, NS; *Format:* Adult Contemp
Andrew Johnson, General Manager

CIJK-FM
06-12-2008; 89.3 MHz FM; 9.9 kw; N45 12 12 W64 24 03
8794 Commercial St., Suite 3, New Minas, NS B4N 3C5 Canada
(902) 365-8930; *Fax:* (902) 365-3360
www.893krock.com
info@893krock.com
License: Kentville, NS held by Newcap Inc.
Group Owner: NewCap Inc.
Population Served: 5,815; *Arbitron Metro Market:* Kentville, NS; *Format:* Classic Rock; *No. News Employees:* 1; *Target Audience:* 24-54.
Randy Skulsky, General Manager
Melanie Sampson, Program and Promotions Director
Dave Chaulk, News Director

Micmac

CIPU-FM
10-07-2012; 97.1 MHz FM; 50 watts; 23 meters
522 Church Street, Micmac, NS B0N 1W0 Canada
(902) 236-3636; *Fax:* (902) 758-3637
www.shubiefm.com
shubiefm@gmail.com
License: Micmac, NS held by Shubenacadie Band Council First Nation
Russell Randall Julian, General Manager

Middleton

CKAD
01-01-1962; 1350 kHz AM*Rebroadcasts:* Rebroadcasts CKEN-FM (Kentville).
10 Bridge St., P.O. Box 550, Middleton, NS B0S 1P0 Canada
(902) 825-3429; *Fax:* (902) 825-6009
www.avrnetwork.com
License: Middleton, NS held by Maritime Broadcasting System Ltd.
Group Owner: Maritime Broadcasting; acq 6-26-79)
Format: Country; *Special Programming:* Farm 3 hrs wkly
Andrew Johnson, Kentville, General Sales Mgr

New Glasgow

CKEC-FM
12-11-2007; 94.1 MHz FM; *Hrs Open:* 24; 36.68 kw; N45 32 24 W62 56 44
Mailing Address: Box 519, 84 Provost Street, New Glasgow, NS B2H 5E7 Canada
Second Address: 84 Provost St., New Glasgow, NS B2H 5E7
(902) 752-4200; *Fax:* (902) 755-2468
ckec941.ca
info@ecfm.ca
License: New Glasgow, NS held by Hector Broadcasting Co. Ltd.
Nat'l Network: BN Audio *Nat'l Reps:* Canadian Broadcast Sales;
Wire Services: BN Wire
Population Served: 20,876; *Arbitron Metro Market:* New Glasgow, NS; *Format:* Adult Contemp; *Special Programming:* Scottish; *Hrs. of News Programming:* news progmg 15 hrs wkly; *No. News Employees:* 3*Target Audience:* General.
Douglas Freeman, CEO
Michael Freeman, Vice President
Ann MacGregor, Music Director
Lynn MacDonald, Accountant / Office Manager
Tom Buffett, Sales Coordinator
Barbara Weir, Account Executive
Eileen Stinson, Account Executive
Ryan Mader, Creative Director

New Tusket

CJLS-FM-2
01-01-1982; 93.5 MHz FM; 3 kw*Rebroadcasts:* Rebroadcasts CJLS-FM Yarmouth
328 Main St., Suite 201, Yarmouth, NS B5A 1E4 Canada
(902) 742-7175; *Fax:* (902) 742-3143
www.cjls.com
cjls@cjls.com
License: New Tusket, NS held by Radio CJLS Ltd.
Format: Adult Contemp
Ray Zinck, President
Chris Perry, Operations Dir
Dave Hall, General Sales Mgr
Gary Nickerson, News Director
Jim Harris, Engineering Dir

Pictou

CKEZ-FM
97.9 MHz FM; 46.72 kw; 246.3 meters
Box 519, New Glasgow, NS B2H 5E7 Canada
(902) 752-4200; *Fax:* (902) 755-2468
License: Pictou, NS held by Hector Broadcasting Co Ltd

Port Hawkesbury

CIGO-FM
01-01-2000; 101.5 MHz FM; 19 kw; N45 39 00 W61 28 00
609 Church St., Ste 201, Port Hawkesbury, NS B9A 2X4 Canada
(902) 625-1220; *Fax:* (902) 625-2664
www.1015thehawk.com
1015thehawk@1015thehawk.com
License: Port Hawkesbury, Inverness County, NS held by MacEachern Broadcasting Ltd.
Wire Services: BN Wire
Population Served: 3,366; *Arbitron Metro Market:* Port Hawkesbury, NS; *Format:* Adult Contemp; *Special Programming:* East Coast 3 hrs, Scottish 1 hrs, Irish one hr wkl; *Hrs. of News Programming:* news progmg 4 hrswkly; *No. News Employees:* 2; *Target Audience:* 18-49; blue collar, high school education, married
Bob MacEachern, President
Bob MacEachern, General Manager
Kevin MacEachern, Sales Manager
Kelly MacMillan, Programming Director
Denise Sampson, Promotions Manager
Greg Morrow, News/Sports Director
Scott Oakley, Music Director

Spryfield

CIRP-FM
05-22-2011; 94.7 MHz FM; 50 w; 22 meters
C/O City Church Halifax, 276 Herring Cove Road, Halifax, NS B3P 1M1 Canada
(902) 479-5433
License: Spryfield, NS held by City Church Halifax
Format: Christian

Sydney

CBI
11-01-1948; 1140 kHz AM; 10 kw
500 George St., Sydney, NS B1P 1K6 Canada
(902) 563-4100; *Fax:* (902) 539-1562
www.cbc.ca/ns
john.channing@cbc.ca
License: Sydney, NS held by CBC
Group Owner: CBC
Nat'l Network: CBC Radio One
Format: Public Affairs, News
John Channing, Broadcast Sales
Ken MacIntosh, Executive Producer, News and Current Affairs
Chantal Bernard, Senior Communications Officer

CBI-FM
105.1 MHz FM; 61.7 kw; 122.5 meters
500 George St., Sydney, NS B1P 1K6 Canada
(902) 563-4100; *Fax:* (902) 539-1562
www.cbc.ca/ns
john.channing@cbc.ca
License: Sydney, NS held by CBC
Group Owner: CBC
Nat'l Network: CBC Radio 2
Format: News, Public Affairs
John Channing, Broadcast Sales
Ken MacIntosh, Executive Producer, News and Current Affairs
Chantal Bernard, Senior Communications Officer

CJCB
02-14-1929; 1270 kHz AM; *Hrs Open:* 24; 10 kw
318 Charlotte St., Sydney, NS B1P 1C8 Canada
(902) 564-5596; *Fax:* (902) 564-1873
www.cjcbradio.com
License: Sydney, NS held by Maritime Broadcasting System Ltd.
Group Owner: Maritime Broadcasting
Format: Country; *No. News Employees:* 3; *Target Audience:* General.
Dwayne Keller, Operations Manager
Alan Peddle, Sales Manager

CKPE-FM
09-01-1962; 94.9 MHz FM; *Hrs Open:* 24; 61 kw; 210 ft

318 Charlotte St., Sydney, NS B1P 1C8 Canada
(902) 564-5596; *Fax:* (902) 564-1873
www.949thecape.com
License: Sydney, NS held by Maritime Broadcasting System Ltd.
Group Owner: Maritime Broadcasting
Population Served: 109,000; *Format:* Adult Contemp; *No. News Employees:* 3
Dwayne Keller, Operations Manager
Alan Peddle, Sales Manager

CJIJ-FM
06-02-2003; 99.9 MHz FM; 50 w; N46 07 01 W60 11 40
Mailing Address: Membertou Radio, 111 Membertou St., Membertou, NS B1S 2M9 Canada
Second Address: 1969 Upper Water St., Suite 1703, Tower II, Purdy's Wharf, Halifax, NS B3J 3R7
(902) 562-0009; *Fax:* (902) 539-6645
c99@membertou.ca
License: Sydney, Cape Breton County, NS held by Membertou Radio Association Inc.
Population Served: 31,597; *Arbitron Metro Market:* Sydney, NS;
Format: Classic Rock, Adult Contemp
Jeff Slivocka, CEO
Dawn Wells, General Manager

CHER-FM
01-01-2007; 98.3 MHz FM; 100 kw
318 Charlotte St., Sydney, NS B1P 1C8 Canada
(902) 564-5596; *Fax:* (902) 564-1873
www.983maxfm.com
License: Sydney, NS held by Maritime Broadcasting System Ltd.
Group Owner: Maritime Broadcasting
Nat'l Reps: Canadian Broadcast Sales
Population Served: 31,597; *Arbitron Metro Market:* Sydney, NS;
Format: Classic Rock; *No. News Employees:* 3
Dwayne Keller, Operations Manager
Alan Peddle, Sales Manager
Jason George, Sales
Steve Gillespie, Sales

***CHRK-FM**
05-27-2008; 101.9 MHz FM; kw
500 Kings Rd., Suite 300, Sydney, NS B1S 1B1 Canada
(902) 270-1019; *Fax:* (902) 270-3566
www.giant1019.com
info@giant1019.com
License: Sydney, NS held by Newcap Inc.
Group Owner: NewCap Inc.
Arbitron Metro Market: Sydney, NS; *Format:* Contemporary Hits/Top 40
Daryl Stevens, Operations Manager
Robert Redshaw, General Manager
Robert Redshaw, General Sales Mgr
Daryl Stevens, Programming Director
Hal Dornadic, News Director
Connie MacDonald, Office Manager

CKCH-FM
06-20-2008; 103.5 MHz FM; 26.5 kw; N46 05 55 W60 18 41
500 Kings Rd., Suite 300, Sydney, NS B1S 1B1 Canada
(902) 563-1035; *Fax:* (902) 270-3566
info@eagle1035.com
License: Sydney, NS held by NewCap Inc.
Group Owner: NewCap Inc.
Population Served: 31,597; *Arbitron Metro Market:* Sydney, NS;
Format: Country
Daryl Stevens, Operations Manager
Rob Redshaw, General Manager
Jay Bedford, Programming Director
Hal Dornadic, News Director
Connie MacDonald, Office Manager

Truro

CKTO-FM
01-01-1965; 100.9 MHz FM; *Hrs Open:* 24; kw
187 Industrial Ave., Truro, ON B2N 6V3 Canada
(902) 893-6060; *Fax:* (902) 893-7771
www.bigdog1009.ca
trureception@bellmedia.ca
License: Truro, NS held by Bell Media Radio Atlantic Inc.
Group Owner: Bell Media Inc.; (acq 7-05-2013; grpsl).
Nat'l Reps: Canadian Broadcast Sales
Format: Rock/AOR; *Hrs. of News Programming:* news progmg 6 hrs wkly; *No. News Employees:* 3; *Target Audience:* 25-49.
John Eddy, President
Mike Worsley, Station Manager
Matt Mossman, General Sales Mgr
Chris VanTassel, Programming Director
Tim Tucker, News Director
Victor Deveau, Chief Engineer
James Cormier, Music Director

CKTY-FM
01-01-2001; 99.5 MHz FM; 16.75 kw
187 Industrial Ave., Truro, NS B2N 6V3 Canada
(902) 893-6060; *Fax:* (902) 893-7771
www.catcountry995.ca
truronewsroom@bellmedia.ca
License: Truro, NS held by Bell Media Radio Atlantic Inc.
Group Owner: Bell Media Inc.; (acq 4-19-2002; grpsl).
Nat'l Reps: Canadian Broadcast Sales
Population Served: 7,847; *Arbitron Metro Market:* Newcastle, OK;
Format: Country
Mike Worsley, General Sales Mgr
Chris VanTassel, Brand Director

CINU-FM
01-01-2004; 98.5 MHz FM; 50 w
Mailing Address: 217 Harmony Ridge Rd, Harmony, NS B6L 3P4 Canada
Second Address: 883 Prince St., Truro, NS B2N 1H2
(902) 843-4673; *Fax:* (902) 662-2879
www.hoperadio.ca
barry@hoperadio.ca
License: Truro, NS held by Hope FM Ministries Ltd.
Population Served: 12,059; *Arbitron Metro Market:* Truro, NS;
Format: Christian
Barry Reid, President

Windsor

CFAB
11-13-1945; 1450 kHz AM; *Hrs Open:* 24
169-A Water St., P.O. Box 278, Windsor, NS B0N 2T0 Canada
(902) 798-2111; *Fax:* (902) 798-8140
www.avrnetwork.com
License: Windsor, NS held by Maritime Broadcasting System Ltd.
Group Owner: Maritime Broadcasting
Format: Country; *Hrs. of News Programming:* news progmg 9 hrs wkly; *No. News Employees:* 5; *Target Audience:* 25-54.
Len Hawley, News Director
Amanda Misner, Music Director

Nunavut

Baker Lake

CKQN-FM
01-01-1973; 99.3 MHz FM; 60 w; -50 ft
Box 13, Baker Lake, NU X0C 0A0 Canada
(867) 793-2962; *Fax:* (867-793-2726)
www.tvradioworld.com
License: Baker Lake, NU held by Qamani'tuap Naalautaa Society.
Nat'l Network: CBC Radio One
Format: Ethnic
Eva Elytuk, President

Iqaluit

CFFB
02-06-1961; 1230 kHz AM; *Hrs Open:* 24; 1 kw
PO Box 490, Iqaluit, NU XOA OHO Canada
(867) 979-6100
cbc.ca/north
cbcnorth@cbc.ca
License: Iqaluit, NU held by CBC
Group Owner: CBC
Nat'l Network: CBC Radio One; CBC North
Format: Public Affairs, News; *No. News Employees:* 9
Joanna Awa, Senior Producer

CFRT-FM
01-01-1994; 107.3 MHz FM; 27 w
C.P. 880, Iqaluit, NU X0A 0H0 Canada
(867) 979-4606; *Fax:* (867) 979-0800
License: Iqaluit, NU held by Association des francophones de Nunavut.
Population Served: 6,699; *Arbitron Metro Market:* Iqaluit, NU;
Format: French
R,jean C"t,, CEO
Daniel Cuerrier, General Manager
Sabrina Bertrand, Programming Director

Rankin Inlet

CBQR-FM
105.1 MHz FM; *Hrs Open:* 24; 87 w; 36.5 meters
Box 130, Rankin Inlet, NU X0C 0G0 Canada
(867) 645-2244; *Fax:* (867) 645-2820
www.cbc.ca/north
janice.stein@cbc.ca
License: Rankin Inlet, NU held by CBC
Group Owner: CBC
Nat'l Network: CBC Radio One
Format: Public Affairs, News; *Special Programming:* Inuktitut 10 hrs wkly
Patrick Nagle, Area Manager

Ontario

Ajax

***CJKX-FM**
01-01-1994; 95.9 MHz FM; *Hrs Open:* 24; 19.96 kw
1200 Airport Blvd., Suite 207, Oshawa, ON L1J 8P5 Canada
(905) 571-0949; *Fax:* (905) 571-1150
www.kx96.fm
kx96@kx96.fm
License: Ajax, ON held by Durham Radio Inc.
Group Owner: Durham Radio Inc.
Format: Country; *Hrs. of News Programming:* news progmg 1.5 hrs wkly; *No. News Employees:* 3; *Target Audience:* 25-54;; *Adv. Rates:* 141; 110; 125; 35
Steve Macaulay, VP, Sales
Steve Kassay, VP, Programming
Adriane Vogel, Promotions
Lisa Walker, Retail Sales Manager
Pete Walker, Music Director

Akwesasne

CKON-FM
10-01-1984; 97.3 MHz FM; 150 w; 150 ft
22 Hilltop Drive, Suite 2, Akwesasne, PQ Canada
(613) 575-2100; *Fax:* (613) 575-2566
www.ckonfm.com
ckon@yahoo.com
License: Akwesasne, ON held by Mohawk Nation Council.
Format: Variety/Diverse; *Special Programming:* Mohawk; *Target Audience:* General.
Diane McDonalds, General Manager
Larry Edwards, Programming Director
Reen Cook, News Director
Gina Jones-Thompson, Finance Officer

Alliston

CIMA-FM
09-19-2013; 92.1 MHz FM; 1.986 kw; 30.5 meters; N44 08 45 W79 50 15
63 Tupper St. W., Alliston, ON L9R 1E4 Canada
(705) 530-6939; *Fax:* (705) 530-1921
License: Alliston, ON held by My Broadcasting Corp.
Group Owner: My Broadcasting Corp.
Format: Adult Contemp
Ellen White, General Manager
Ellen White, General Sales Mgr
D'Arcy Magee, Programming Director
Cindy Clyne, News Director
Marg Tubman, Group Administrator

Apsley

CFSH-FM
92.9 MHz FM; 50 w; N44 45 54 W78 05 27
Attn: John Trotter, 299 McFadden Rd., Apsley, ON K0L 1A0 Canada
(705) 656-1510; *Fax:* (705) 656-1510
www.fish929.com
License: Apsley, ON held by Apsley Community Chapel.
Population Served: 324; *Arbitron Metro Market:* Apsley, ON;
Format: Christian
Joseph Cormier, President

Arnprior

CHMY-FM-1
04-02-2015; 107.7 MHz FM; 128.5 meters
Mailing Address: 160 William St. W., Suite 52, Arnprior, ON K7S 3W4 Canada
Second Address: Kenwood Corporate Centre, Suite 52, Arnprior, ON K7S 3W4
(613) 623-6772; *Fax:* (613) 623-4508
www.arnpriortoday.ca
License: Arnprior, ON held by My Broadcasting Corp.
Group Owner: My Broadcasting Corp.
Format: Adult Contemp
Angela Kluke, General Manager
Angela Kluke, General Sales Mgr
D'Arcy Magee, Programming Director
Cindy Clyne, News Director
Marg Tubman, Group Administrator

Aylmer

CHPD-FM
09-01-2003; 105.9 MHz FM; *Hrs Open:* 7 AM- 8 AM; 5 PM- 8 PM; 250 w; N42 45 40 W80 56 03
16 Talbot St. East, Aylmer, ON N5H 1H4 Canada
(519) 773-8555; *Fax:* (519) 765-3023
www.mcson.org
License: Aylmer, Elgin County, ON held by Alymera Area Inter-Mennonite Community Services.
Population Served: 15,000; *Hrs. of News Programming:* news progmg one hr wkly; *No. News Employees:* 1; *Target Audience:* 5-70; Low German newcomers
Abe Wall, Peple Manager
Jake Wall, Assistant

Bancroft

CHMS-FM
05-01-2001; 97.7 MHz FM; *Hrs Open:* 24; 50 kw; 174.4 m
30674 Hwy. 28E, Bancroft, ON K0L 1C0 Canada
(613) 332-1423; *Fax:* (613) 332-0841
www.mybancroftnow.com
tlamoureux@vistaradio.ca
License: Bancroft, Hastings County, ON held by Vista Radio Ltd.
Group Owner: Vista Radio Ltd.
Population Served: 3,880; *Arbitron Metro Market:* Bancroft, ON;
Format: Adult Contemp; *Target Audience:* General.
Tracy Lamoureux, General Manager and Sales
Drew Hosick, Programming Director
Marie Cassidy, Regional News Director
Mike McAlpine, Integrated Marketing Executive

Barrie

CFJB-FM
10-07-1988; 95.7 MHz FM; *Hrs Open:* 24; 41 kw; Ant 500 ft
431 Huronia Rd., Unit 10, Barrie, ON L4N 9B3 Canada
(705) 725-7304; *Fax:* (705) 792-7858
www.rock95.com
License: Barrie, ON held by Rock 95 Broadcasting (Barrie-Orillia) Ltd.
Population Served: 280,000; *Format:* Classic Rock; *Hrs. of News Programming:* news progmg 4 hrs wkly; *No. News Employees:* 3; *Target Audience:* 18-49; broad-based, well-educated, above-average income
Doug Bingley, CEO
Tom Manton, General Sales Mgr
Dave Carr, Programming Director
Todd Palmer, Promotions Manager

***CHAY-FM**
05-21-1977; 93.1 MHz FM; *Hrs Open:* 24; 100 kw
1125 Bayfield St. N., P.O. Box 937, Barrie, ON L4M 4Y6 Canada
(705) 737-3511
www.931freshradio.ca
kirk.pearson@corusent.com
License: Barrie, Simcoe County, ON held by Corus Radio Co.
Group Owner: Corus Entertainment Inc.
Format: Adult Contemp; *Hrs. of News Programming:* news progmg 13 hrs wkly; *No. News Employees:* 3; *Target Audience:* 25-64; general
Deb James, Brand Director
Kirk Pearson, Sales Manager
Elizabeth Hunter, Promotions Director
Chris Liedtke, Music Director

CIQB-FM
11-12-1994; 101.1 MHz FM; *Hrs Open:* 24; 7 kw
1125 Bayfield St. N., P.O. Box 937, Barrie, ON L4M 4Y6 Canada
(705) 726-1011
www.1011bigfm.com
kirk.pearson@corusent.com
License: Barrie, ON held by 591989 B.C. Ltd.
Group Owner: Corus Entertainment Inc.; (acq 3-24-2000; grpsl).
Format: Classic Rock; *Hrs. of News Programming:* news progmg 11 hrs wkly; *No. News Employees:* 3; *Target Audience:* 25-54; women 35-49 & 25-54 & at work people; *Adv. Rates:* 80; 75; 70; 40
Kirk Pearson, General Sales Mgr
Elizabeth Hunter, Promotions Director
Deb James, Brand Director
Chris Liedtke, Music Director
Chad Fullerton, Interactive Content

CJLF-FM
08-15-1999; 100.3 MHz FM; 18.7 kw
115 Bell Farm Rd, Suite 111, Barrie, ON L4M 5G1 Canada
(705) 735-3370; *Fax:* (705) 735-3301
www.lifeonline.fm
License: Barrie, ON held by Trust Communications Ministries.
Scott Jackson, President
Steve Jones, Programming Director
Tim Maaserany, News Director
Janice Baird, CFO/Office Manager
Pip Lucas, Promotions Director
Evan Duran, Producer
Maria Enqvist, Music Director

CKMB-FM
01-01-2006; 107.5 MHz FM; *Hrs Open:* 24; kw
Canada
(705) 725-7304; *Fax:* (705) 792-7858
www.1075koolfm.com
License: Barrie, ON held by Rock 95 Broadcasting (Barrie-Orillia) Ltd.
Arbitron Metro Market: Barrie, ON; *Format:* Contemporary Hits/Top 40
Doug Bingley, CEO
Tom Manton, General Sales Mgr
Dave Carr, Programming Director
Helen Mathers, Promotions Manager

Barry's Bay

CHBY-FM
10-16-2015; 106.5 MHz FM; 12 kw; 127 meters
41 Bay Street, Barry's Bay, ON K0J 1B0 Canada
(613) 756-9038
www.mybarrysbaynow.com
tlamoureux@vistaradio.ca
License: Barry's Bay, ON held by Vista Radio Ltd.
Group Owner: Vista Radio Ltd.
Format: Adult Contemp, Classic Rock
Tracy Lamoureux, General Manager & Sales Manager
Drew Hosick, Programming Director
Marie Cassidy, Regional News Director
Lesley Ferrier, Integrated Marketing Executive

Belleville

***CIGL-FM**
08-01-1962; 97.1 MHz FM; *Hrs Open:* 24; 50 kw
Box 488, 10 S. Front St., Belleville, ON K8N 5B2 Canada
(613) 969-5555; *Fax:* (613) 969-8122
www.mix97.com
License: Belleville, ON held by Quinte Broadcasting Ltd.
Group Owner: Quinte Broadcasting Ltd.
Format: Adult Contemp
Jody Brooker, General Sales Mgr
Sean Kelly, Programming Director
John Spitters, News Director
Jack Miller, Sports Director

CJBQ
08-12-1946; 800 kHz AM; *Hrs Open:* 24; 10 kw
Box 488, 10 S. Front St., Belleville, ON K8N 5B2 Canada
(613) 969-5555; *Fax:* (613) 969-8122
www.cjbq.com
License: Belleville, ON held by Quinte Broadcasting Ltd.
Group Owner: Quinte Broadcasting Ltd.
Format: Country, Oldies; *Special Programming:* Farm 3 hrs wkly
Bill Morton, General Manager
Jody Brooker, General Sales Mgr
Sean Kelly, Programming Director

CJLX-FM
10-01-1992; 91.3 MHz FM; *Hrs Open:* 24; kw
PO Box 4200, Beleville, OK K8N 5B9 Canada
(613) 966-0923; *Fax:* (613) 962-1376
www.91x.fm
contact@91x.fm
License: Belleville, Hastings County, ON held by Loyalist College Radio Inc.
Nat'l Reps: Target Broadcast Sales; *Wire Services:* BN Wire
Format: Rock/AOR, Public Affairs; *Special Programming:* Folk one hr, jazz 3 hrs, Greek one hr, class 2 hr; *Hrs. of News Programming:* news progmg 6 hrs wkly; *No. News Employees:* 15; *Target Audience:* 18-34; primary,ages 50 plus secondary;
Adv. Rates: 11; 9; 11; 8
Greg Schatzmann, CEO
Sandi Ramsey, General Sales Mgr
Len Arminio, News Director
Tim Rorabeck, Chief Engineer

CJOJ-FM
12-01-1993; 95.5 MHz FM; *Hrs Open:* 24; 42 kw
497 Dundas St. W., Belleville, ON K8P 1B6 Canada
(613) 966-0955
www.955hitsfm.ca
License: Belleville, Canada County, ON held by Starboard Communications Ltd.
Nat'l Reps: CHUM Radio Sales
Population Served: 105,000; *Format:* Contemporary Hits/Top 40, Adult Contemp; *No. News Employees:* 4; *Target Audience:* 25-54; adults-skewed females 60%, males 40%; *Adv. Rates:* 35; 27; 22; 15
John Sherratt, President/Owner
Darren Matassa, General Sales Mgr
Paul Ferguson, Programming Director
Cole Nayler, Promotions Manager
Paul Martin, News Director
Josh Miller, Chief Engineer
Jenn McKay

CHCQ-FM
01-01-2001; 100.1 MHz FM; *Hrs Open:* 24; 21 kw
497 Dundas Street West, Belleville, ON K8P 1B6 Canada
(613) 966-0955
www.cool100.fm
darrenm@cool100.ca
License: Belleville, ON held by Starboard Communications Ltd.
Nat'l Reps: CHUM Radio Sales
Population Served: 49,454; *Arbitron Metro Market:* Belleville, ON;
Format: Country; *No. News Employees:* 4; *Target Audience:* 25-54; adults
John Sherratt, President/Owner
Darren Matassa, General Sales Mgr
Paul Ferguson, Programming Director
Cole Nayler, Promotions Manager
Paul Martin, News Director
Jenn McKay, Music Director
Josh Miller, Chief Engineer/Director ofIT

CKJJ-FM
10-18-2003; 102.3 MHz FM; *Hrs Open:* 24; 45 kw
Box 23095, Belleville, ON K8P 5J3 Canada
(613) 966-4822; *Fax:* (613) 966-3211
www.ucbcanada.com
License: Belleville, ON held by United Christian Broadcasters Canada.
Population Served: 49,454; *Arbitron Metro Market:* Belleville, ON
James Hunt, Executive Director
John Roeper, Station Manager
Brad Linnard, Programming Director
Jake McDonald, Production Manager
Annette Eastcott, Finance
Leland Klassen, IPTV Content Advisor

Bolton

CJFB-FM
105.5 MHz FM; *Hrs Open:* 24/7; 1565 w; -22 metres; 43 52 46N 79 44 18W
30 Martha St., Bolton, ON L7E 5V1 Canada
(905) 951-2899
info@radiocaledon.com
License: Bolton, ON held by Vista Radio Ltd.
Group Owner: Vista Radio Ltd.
Population Served: 26,378; *Arbitron Metro Market:* Bolton, ON;
Format: News
Geoff Poulton, President

Bracebridge

CFBG-FM
99.5 MHz FM; 12 kw
3a Taylor Dr., Bracebridge, ON P1L 1S6 Canada
(705) 645-2218; *Fax:* (705) 645-5798
www.mymuskokanow.com
jhodge@vistaradio.ca
License: Bracebridge, ON held by Vista Radio Ltd.
Group Owner: Vista Radio Ltd.; (acq 12-10-97; C$295,000)
Format: Adult Contemp; *Special Programming:* Jazz 2 hrs, big band one hr, loc magazine one hr w; *Target Audience:* 34-45; older adult contemporary
Jenny Hodge, Regional Cluster and General Sales
Dave Newman, Regional Cluster Program Director
Rachel Detta, Promotions Coordinator
Taylor Ablett, News Director
James Bowler, News
Olivia Guthrie, Promotions Assistant

Brampton

***CFNY-FM**
08-08-1960; 102.1 MHz FM; *Hrs Open:* 24; 35.4 kw; 421 meters
Corus Quay, 25 Dockside Dr., Toronto, ON M5A 0B5 Canada
(416) 479-7000
www.edge.ca
License: Brampton, ON held by Corus Radio Co.
Group Owner: Corus Entertainment Inc.; (acq 1995; C$16.75 million)
Nat'l Reps: Canadian Broadcast Sales

Format: Rock/AOR, Alternative; *Hrs. of News Programming:* news progmg 3 hrs wkly; *No. News Employees:* 2; *Target Audience:* 18-34; self motivated, mus loving, active, young at heart people
Matt Dawson, General Sales Mgr
Ross MacLeod, Programming Director
Sean McNamara, Promotions Coordinator
Chris Santos, New Media Content Manager
Julisa Ly, Music Director

CIAO
12-23-1953; 530 kHz AM; *Hrs Open:* 24
5312 Dundas Street West, Toronto, ON M9B 1B3 Canada
(416) 213-1035; *Fax:* (416) 233-8617
www.am530.ca
info@evanovradio.com
License: Brampton, ON held by Dufferin Communications Inc.
Group Owner: Evanov Communications Inc.; (acq 9-26-83).
Nat'l Reps: Target Broadcast Sales
Format: Ethnic; *Adv. Rates:* 100; 100; 100; 100
Bill Evanov, President
Paul Evanov, Vice President

Brantford

CKPC
12-01-1923; 1380 kHz AM; *Hrs Open:* 24
571 West St., Brantford, ON N3R 7C5 Canada
(519) 759-1000; *Fax:* (519) 753-1470
www.am1380.ca
License: Brantford, ON held by Dufferin Communications Inc.
Group Owner: Evanov Communications Inc.
Nat'l Reps: Target Broadcast Sales
Format: Country, News, Religious; *Hrs. of News Programming:* news progmg 9 hrs wkly; *No. News Employees:* 7; *Target Audience:* 35-64.
Mike Rose, Operations Manager
Amandla Black, Promotions Coordinator
Warren Beck, News Director
Mike Ellsworth, Creative Department

CKPC-FM
05-01-1949; 92.1 MHz FM; *Hrs Open:* 24; 80 kw
571 West St., Brantford, ON N3R 7C5 Canada
(519) 759-1000; *Fax:* (519) 753-1470
www.jewelradio.com/new/92
License: Brantford, ON held by Dufferin Communications Inc.
Group Owner: Evanov Communications Inc.
Nat'l Reps: Target Broadcast Sales
Format: Adult Contemp; *Hrs. of News Programming:* news progmg 7 hrs wkly; *No. News Employees:* 7; *Target Audience:* 25-49.
Mike Rose, Operations Dir
Wendy Rose, Promotions Manager
Warren Beck, News Director
Mike Ellsworth, Creative Department

CFWC-FM
01-01-2002; 93.9 MHz FM; 250 w
271 Greenwich St., Brantford, ON N3S 2X9 Canada
(519) 759-2339; *Fax:* (226) 381-0940
www.brantford.faithfm.org
License: Brantford, ON held by 1486781 Ontario Ltd.
Format: Christian
Peter Jackman, General Manager
Vicki Schleifer, Business Manager
Luke Schleifer, Operations Supervisor

Brighton

*CIYM-FM
05-15-2009; 100.9 MHz FM; *Hrs Open:* 24; kw
Mailing Address: Box 1522, Brighton, ON K0K 1H0 Canada
Second Address: 6 Oliphant St, Unit 5, Brighton, ON K0K 1H0
(613) 475-6936; *Fax:* (613) 475-9026
www.brightontoday.ca
License: Brighton, ON held by My Broadcasting Corp.
Group Owner: My Broadcasting Corp.
Format: Adult Contemp
D'Arcy Magee, Programming Director
Cindy Clyne, News Director

Brockville

CJPT-FM
07-28-1988; 103.7 MHz FM; *Hrs Open:* 24; 100 kw; Ant 495 ft; N44 23 58 W75 58 21
601 Stewart Blvd., Brockville, ON K6V 5T4 Canada
(613) 345-1666; *Fax:* (613) 342-2438
www.bob.fm
License: Brockville, ON held by Bell Media Ontario Regional Radio Partnership
Group Owner: Bell Media Inc.; (acq 6-22-2007; grpsl).
Format: Adult Contemp; *No. News Employees:* 3; *Target Audience:* 18-44; male
Greg Hinton, General Manager
Kim Parker, General Sales Mgr
Pat Kerre, Programming Director
Jaynel White, Promotions Director
Mark LeBel, Music Director

CFJR-FM
01-01-2003; 104.9 MHz FM; *Hrs Open:* 24; 7.7 kw
601 Stewart Blvd., Brockville, ON K6V 5T4 Canada
(613) 345-1666; *Fax:* (613) 342-2438
www.1049jrfm.com
License: Brockville, ON held by Bell Media Ontario Regional Radio Partnership
Group Owner: Bell Media Inc.; (acq 6-22-2007; grpsl)
Format: Adult Contemp; *Hrs. of News Programming:* news progmg 5 hrs wkly; *No. News Employees:* 3; *Target Audience:* 35-54; female slant
Greg Hinton, General Manager
Kim Parker, General Sales Mgr
Pat Kerr, Programming Director
Jaynel White, Promotions Director

CHXL-FM
06-01-2003; 93.5 MHz FM; kw
Canada
(306) 334-3331; *Fax:* (306) 334-2545
License: Brockville, ON held by Okanese Indian Reserve
Arbitron Metro Market: Balcarres, SK; *Format:* Variety/Diverse
William Yuzicapi, Station Manager

Burlington

CJXY-FM
01-01-1948; 107.9 MHz FM; *Hrs Open:* 24; 26.1 kw; Ant 673 ft; N43 23 12 W79 52 34
875 Main St. W., Hamilton, ON L8S 4R1 Canada
(905) 521-9900; *Fax:* (905) 521-1691
www.y108.ca
krista.taaffe@corusent.com
License: Burlington, ON held by Corus Radio Co.
Group Owner: Corus Entertainment Inc.
Format: Rock/AOR; *Hrs. of News Programming:* news progmg 2 hrs wkly; *No. News Employees:* 1; *Target Audience:* 25-39.
Krista Taaffe, General Sales Mgr
Wayne Williams, Programming Director
Olivia Mackay, Promotions Manager
Lisete Culley, Office Manager
Misty Cornell, Creative Supervisor
Chad Fullerton, Interactive Content Manager
Justin Glover,Promotions Coordinator

Caledon

CFGM-FM
102.7 MHz FM; 50 w; 15.3 m
30 Martha St., Suite 210, Bolton, ON L7E 5V1 Canada
(905) 951-2899
License: Caledon, ON held by Vista Radio Ltd.
Group Owner: Vista Radio Ltd.
Format: Adult Contemp
Geoff Poulton, President

Cape Croker (Neyaashiinigmiing)

CHFN-FM
01-01-2003; 100.1 MHz FM; *Hrs Open:* 24; 72 w
67 Community Centre Road, Nevaashiinigmiing, ON N0H 2T0 Canada
(519) 534-1003; *Fax:* (519) 534-4916
www.nawash.ca/chfn
chfn@ymail.com
License: Cape Croker (Neyaashiinigmiing), ON held by Chippewas of Nawash
Population Served: 591; *Arbitron Metro Market:* Neyaashiinigmiing, ON; *Format:* Ethnic, News; *Hrs. of News Programming:* News progmg 12 hrs wkly; *Target Audience:* 18-65; progmg is div
Jake Linklater, President
Peter Akiwenzie, Operations Dir
Jessica Nadjiwon, General Manager
Johnathan Pedoniquotte, Programming Director
Beedahsega Elliott, Promotions Manager

Chatham

CFCO
01-01-1926; 630 kHz AM; *Hrs Open:* 24
Mailing Address: Canada
Second Address: 117 Keil Dr. S., Chatham, ON N7M 3H3
(519) 354-2200; *Fax:* (519) 354-2880
www.country929.com
License: Chatham, Kent County, ON held by Blackburn Radio Inc.
Group Owner: Blackburn Radio Inc.; (acq 3-20-97).
Regional Reps: Rgnl Reps
Format: Country, News; *Special Programming:* Gospel 2 Hrs Wkly; *Hrs. of News Programming:* News Progmg 6 Hrs Wkly; *No. News Employees:* 6; *Target Audience:* 35 plus.
Walter Ploegman, General Manager

CKUE-FM
10-06-1999; 95.1 MHz FM; *Hrs Open:* 24; kw
Mailing Address: Canada
Second Address: 117 Keil Dr. S., Chatham, ON N7M 3H3
(519) 354-2200; *Fax:* (519) 354-2880
0ww.chatham.coolradio.ca
License: Chatham, Kent County, ON held by Blackburn Radio Inc.
Group Owner: Blackburn Radio Inc.
Format: Variety/Diverse; *No. News Employees:* 2; *Target Audience:* 18-49.
Walter Ploegman, General Manager

CKSY-FM
07-01-1986; 94.3 MHz FM; *Hrs Open:* 24; kw
Mailing Address: Canada
Second Address: 117 Keil Dr. S., Chatham, ON N7M 3H3
(519) 354-2200; *Fax:* (519) 354-2880
www.943cksy.com
License: Chatham, Kent County, ON held by Blackburn Radio Inc.
Group Owner: Blackburn Radio Inc.
Format: Adult Contemp; *Special Programming:* Gospel 2 hrs wkly; *Hrs. of News Programming:* news progmg 5 hrs wkly; *No. News Employees:* 5; *Target Audience:* 18-54.
Walter Ploegman, General Manager
Ron Blommers, General Sales Mgr
Jay Poole, Programming Director
Bob Becken, News Director
Walter Ploegman, Marketing Manager

CKGW-FM
01-01-2007; 89.3 MHz FM; *Hrs Open:* 24; 16.7 kw; Ant 436 ft; N42 26 14 W82 06 23
PO Box 985, Chatham, ON N7M 5L3 Canada
(519) 531-1118; *Fax:* (519) 531-0992
www.ucbchathamkent.com
info@ucbcanada.com
License: Chatham, ON held by United Christian Broadcasters Canada.
Population Served: 44,074; *Arbitron Metro Market:* Chatham, ON; *Format:* Christian
James Hunt, COO
Al Baker, Operations Dir
Matt Reaume, Station Manager
James Hunt, Executive Director
Al Baker, Community Engagement/Development Manager
Leland Klassen, IPTV Content Advisor

Christian Island

CKUN-FM
01-01-2003; 101.3 MHz FM; *Hrs Open:* 24; 900 w; Ant 156 ft; N44 49 16 W80 10 24
22 O'Gema Miikean, Christian Island, ON L9M 0A9 Canada
(705) 247-1111; *Fax:* (705) 247-2239
License: Christian Island, Simcoe County, ON held by Beausoleil First Nation
Population Served: 584; *Arbitron Metro Market:* Christian Island, ON; *Format:* Variety/Diverse; *No. News Employees:* 2
Edna King, General Manager
Richard Sutherland, Announcer/Program Director

Clarence-Rockland

CHRC-FM
10-15-2013; 92.5 MHz FM; 300 w; 60 meters; N45 31 27 W75 17 30
8710 County Road 17, Rockland, ON K4K 1T2 Canada
(613) 241-9850
www.jewelradio.com/new/925
License: Clarence-Rockland, ON held by Dufferin Communications Inc.
Group Owner: Evanov Communications Inc.
Format: Adult Contemp
Ted Silver, Programming Director
Vanessa Malloy, Promotions Coordinator

Cobourg

CFMX-FM
01-01-1979; 103.1 MHz FM; *Hrs Open:* 24; 86 kw
1 Queen St., Suite 101, Cobourg, ON K9A 1M8 Canada
(905) 372-4366; *Fax:* (905) 372-1625
www.classical963fm.com
l.gunn@classical1031fm.com
License: Cobourg, ON held by MZ Media Inc.
Group Owner: ZoomerMedia Ltd.; (acq 8-31-2006; C$12 million with CFMZ-FM Toronto).
Nat'l Reps: imsradio
Format: Classical; *Hrs. of News Programming:* news progmg 4 hrs wkly; *No. News Employees:* 3; *Target Audience:* 35 plus; well-educated, upscale, owners/managers/professionals
Dan Hamilton, VP Sales, Broadcast and General Manager
John Van Driel, VP Programming/Operations
Libby Znaimer, VP of News and Information

CKSG-FM
07-18-2002; 93.3 MHz FM; *Hrs Open:* 24; kw
PO Box 520, Cobourg, ON K9A 4J7 Canada
(905) 372-5401; *Fax:* (905) 372-6280
www.star933.com
License: Cobourg, ON held by Pineridge Broadcasting Inc.
Nat'l Reps: Canadian Broadcast Sales
Arbitron Metro Market: Cobourg, ON; *Format:* Adult Contemp; *Hrs. of News Programming:* news progmg one hr wkly; *No. News Employees:* 3; *Target Audience:* 25-54; predominately female
Don Conway, President
Dave Hughes, General Sales Mgr
Joel Scott, Operations Manager
York Bell-Smith, Programming Director
Joe Snider, News Director

CHUC-FM
08-01-2006; 107.9 MHz FM; *Hrs Open:* 24; 6.3 kw
P.O. Box 520, Cobourg, ON K9A 4L3 Canada
(905) 372-5401; *Fax:* (905) 372-6280
License: Cobourg, Northumberland County, ON held by Pineridge Broadcasting Inc.
Nat'l Reps: Canadian Broadcast Sales; *Wire Services:* Canadian Press
Hrs. of News Programming: news prgmg 3.5 hrs per week; *No. News Employees:* 3
Don Conway, President
Joel Scott, Operations Manager
Dave Hughes, General Sales Mgr
York Bell Smith, Programming/Promotions Director
Joe Snider, News Director

Cochrane

CHPB-FM
11-19-2003; 98.1 MHz FM; *Hrs Open:* 24; 50 w; 19 meters
22B 5th Ave., Cochrane, ON P0L 1C0 Canada
(705) 272-6467; *Fax:* (705) 272-2520
www.mycochranenow.com
sarmstrong@vistaradio.ca
License: Cochrane, ON held by Vista Radio Ltd.
Group Owner: Vista Radio Ltd.; (acq 11-19-2003; with CFIF-FM Iroquois Falls).
Arbitron Metro Market: Cochrane, ON; *Format:* Adult Contemp; *Hrs. of News Programming:* news progmg 1.5 hrs wkly; *No. News Employees:* 1; *Target Audience:* 18-65.; *Adv. Rates:* 22.50; 22.50; 22.50; 22.5
Scott Armstrong, Regional Cluster Manager
Shane Button, Regional Cluster Program Director
Rudy Kadlec, Regional News Director

CFDY-FM
01-01-2008; 104.7 MHz FM; 5 w; N49 03 35 W81 01 51
Mailing Address: 34 Aurora Avenue, Cochrane, ON P0L 1C0
Second Address: 286 Main Street, Box 94, Smooth Rock Falls, ON P0L 2B0
(705) 272-2774; *Fax:* (705) 272-2783
www.cpbrfm.com
dyoung@cpbrfm.com
License: Cochrane, ON held by Cochrane Polar Bear Radio Club.
Population Served: 5,487; *Arbitron Metro Market:* Cochrane, ON; *Format:* Variety/Diverse; *Special Programming:* Fr 5 hrs wkly
Douglas Young, Programming Director
L. Oralie, Music/Sales Director

Collingwood

CKCB-FM
03-29-1996; 95.1 MHz FM; *Hrs Open:* 24; 350 w
186 Hurontario St., Suite 200, Collingwood, ON L9Y 4T4 Canada
(705) 446-9510
www.thepeakfm.com
kirk.pearson@corusent.com
License: Collingwood, ON held by 591989 B.C. Ltd.
Group Owner: Corus Entertainment Inc.; (acq 3-24-00; grpsl).
Format: Adult Contemp; *Hrs. of News Programming:* news progmg 11 hrs wkly; *No. News Employees:* 1; *Target Audience:* 25-54.
Kirk Pearson, General Sales Mgr
Elizabeth Hunter, Promotions Director
Deb James, Brand Director
Chad Fullerton, Interactive Content

CFMO-FM
08-30-2015; 102.9 MHz FM; 9.37 kw; 255 meters; N44 28 41 W80 19 40
393 First St., Suite 201, Collingwood, ON L9Y 1B3 Canada
(705) 444-9102
www.classical963fm.com
License: Collingwood, ON held by MZ Media
Group Owner: ZoomerMedia Ltd.
Format: Classical, Talk
Dan Hamilton, VP Sales, Broadcast and General Manager
John Van Driel, VP Programming/Operations
Libby Znaimer, VP of News and Information

Cornwall

*CFLG-FM
02-15-1949; 104.5 MHz FM; *Hrs Open:* 24; 30 kw
709 Cotton Mill St., Cornwall, ON K6H 7K7 Canada
(613) 932-5180; *Fax:* (613) 938-0355
www.1045freshradio.ca
bill.halman@corusent.com
License: Cornwall, Stormont County, ON held by Corus Radio Co.
Group Owner: Corus Entertainment Inc.; (acq 11-19-01; grpsl).
Nat'l Reps: Canadian Broadcast Sales
Format: Adult Contemp; *Hrs. of News Programming:* news progmg 5 hrs wkly; *No. News Employees:* 4; *Target Audience:* 25-54; predominantly female professionals & housewives
Mark Dickie, General Manager
Peter Mayhew, General Sales Mgr
Bill Halman, Programming Director
Holly Wilson, Promotions Director
Mike Lavallee, Music Director
Shannon Lebrun, Retail Sales Manager
Darryl Adams, Brand Director

CHOD-FM
05-01-1994; 92.1 MHz FM; *Hrs Open:* 24; 31.167 kw; 106.7 meters
1111 Montreal Rd., Suite 202, Cornwall, ON K6H 1E1 Canada
(613) 936-2463; *Fax:* (613) 936-2568
chodfm@chodfm.ca
License: Cornwall, ON held by LA Radio Communautaire Cornwall-Alexandria Inc.
Population Served: 45,000; *Special Programming:* Class 4 hrs, jazz 4 hrs wkly; *Hrs. of News Programming:* news progmg 10 hrs wkly; *No. News Employees:* 1; *Target Audience:* 25-54.
Marc Bissonnette, President
Jean Lecompte, VP
Marc Charbonneau, General Manager

CJSS-FM
101.9 MHz FM; *Hrs Open:* 24; 1.42 kw; N45 03 30 W74 44 45
709 Cotton Mill St., Cornwall, ON K6H 7K7 Canada
(613) 932-5180; *Fax:* (613) 938-0355
www.boom1019.com
shannon.lebrun@corusent.com
License: Cornwall, Stormont County, ON held by Corus Radio Co.
Group Owner: Corus Entertainment Inc.; (acq 11-19-01; grpsl).
Nat'l Reps: Canadian Broadcast Sales
Format: Contemporary Hits/Top 40, Oldies; *Special Programming:* Relg one hr wkly; *Hrs. of News Programming:* news progmg 2 hrs wkly; *No. News Employees:* 4; *Target Audience:* 35 -54; males
Shannon Lebrun, Retail Sales Manager
Bill Halman, Programming Director
Krista Datars, Promotions & New Media Manager
Claire Garon, Promotions Assistant

Dryden

CKDR-FM
11-09-2005; 92.7 MHz FM; 36.8 kw
122 King St., Dryden, ON P8N 1C2 Canada
(807) 223-2355; *Fax:* (807) 223-5090
www.ckdr.net
ckdr@radioabl.ca
License: Dryden, ON held by Acadia Broadcasting Ltd.
Group Owner: Acadia Broadcasting Ltd.; (acq 5-1-2007; grpsl)
Population Served: 7,617; *Arbitron Metro Market:* Dryden, ON; *Format:* Adult Contemp; *Target Audience:* 25 plus.
Richard McCarthy, Operations Dir
Bruce Walchuck, Station Manager
Mike Ebbeling, News Director
Chris Pollard, Creative Director
Michelle Nault, Traffic Manager
Roxanne McGee, Sales
Val Artimowich, Sales

Elliot Lake

CKNR-FM
94.1 MHz FM; 90 kw; 193 meters
144 Ontario Ave., Elliot Lake, ON P5A 1Y3 Canada
(705) 848-3608; *Fax:* (705) 848-1378
www.myalgomamanitoulinnow.com
License: Elliot Lake, ON held by Vista Radio Ltd.
Group Owner: Vista Radio Ltd.; (acq 3-12-2004; C$625,000).
Format: Adult Contemp; *No. News Employees:* 1; *Target Audience:* 35-54.
Peter Hobbs, Regional Cluster Manager
Rocco Frangione, News
Erika MacLellan, Integrated Marketing Executive

Englehart

CJBB-FM
01-01-2000; 103.1 MHz FM; *Hrs Open:* 24; 1.6 kw
Box 665, 50 Third St., Englehart, ON P0J 1H0 Canada
(705) 544-1121; *Fax:* (705) 544-2286
cjbb@nt.net
License: Englehart, ON held by 1353151 Ontario Inc.
Nat'l Reps: Target Broadcast Sales
Population Served: 1,519; *Arbitron Metro Market:* Englehart, ON; *Format:* Adult Contemp; *Hrs. of News Programming:* news progmg 5 hrs wkly; *No. News Employees:* 1; *Target Audience:* 18-54; male & female
Boyd Woods, CEO
Rick Stow, Station Manager
Pat Ferris, News Director

Erin

CHES-FM
01-01-2006; 88.1 MHz FM; *Hrs Open:* 24; 250 watts; 63 meters
8 Thompson Crest, Erin, ON N0B 1T0 Canada
(519) 833-9300
www.mix881.com
info@mix881.com
License: Erin, ON held by Erin Community Radio.
Population Served: 11,000
Jay Mowat, Chairman

Espanola

CJJM-FM
99.3 MHz FM; 794 kw; 32.5 meters; 46 2630 N 81 7670 W
90 Gray St., Suite 2, Espanola, ON P5E 1G1 Canada
(705) 869-0758; *Fax:* (705) 869-0758
www.myespanolanow.com
phobbs@vistaradio.ca
License: Espanola, ON held by Vista Radio Ltd.
Group Owner: Vista Radio Ltd.
Population Served: 5,364; *Arbitron Metro Market:* Espanola, ON; *Format:* Adult Contemp
Peter Hobbs, Regional Cluster Manager
Ryan Griffiths, Regional Cluster Program Director
Rocco Frangione, News
Rosalind Russell, Integrated Marketing Executive
Bianca Lazzarino, Integrated Marketing Executive

Exeter

*CKXM-FM
08-31-2009; 90.5 MHz FM; *Hrs Open:* 24; kw
145 Thames Rd. W., Unit 6, Exeter, ON N0M 1S3 Canada
(519) 235-3000; *Fax:* (519) 235-6262
www.exetertoday.ca
License: Exeter, ON held by My Broadcasting Corp.
Group Owner: My Broadcasting Corp.
Format: Adult Contemp
Robin Glenny, General Manager
Robin Glenny, General Sales Mgr
D'Arcy Magee, Group Program Director
Cindy Clyne, Group News Director
Marg Tubman, Group Administrator

Fort Erie

CFLZ-FM
101.1 MHz FM; *Hrs Open:* 24; 19,700 w; 76.5 meters; 42 54 00 N 78 57 08 W
4673 Ontario Ave., Niagara Falls, ON L2E 3R1 Canada
(905) 356-6710; *Fax:* (905) 356-0644
1011.juicefm.ca
License: Fort Erie, Niagara County, ON held by Vista Radio Ltd.
Group Owner: Vista Radio Ltd.; (acq 5-1-2009; with CFLZ-FM Niagara Falls)
Population Served: 1,385,000; *Arbitron Metro Market:* Buffalo-Niagara Falls, NY; *Format:* Contemporary Hits/Top 40; *Target Audience:* 18-44; upper income adults
Chris Barnatt, Producer and News Director

Fort Frances

CFOB-FM
06-04-2002; 93.1 MHz FM; *Hrs Open:* 24; 21 kw
210 Scott St., Fort Frances, ON P9A 1G7 Canada
(807) 275-5341
www.931theborder.ca
info@931theborder.ca
License: Fort Frances, ON held by Acadia Broadcasting Ltd.
Group Owner: Acadia Broadcasting Ltd.; (acq 5-1-2007; grpsl)
Nat'l Reps: TeleRep
Population Served: 7,952; *Arbitron Metro Market:* Fort Frances, ON; *Format:* Adult Contemp; *No. News Employees:* 2; *Target Audience:* 25-54; International Falls/N. Central MN
Barrie Blake, Operations Dir
Ala Dulas, Station Manager
Allan Dearing, News Director

Gananoque

CJGM-FM
09-12-2011; 99.9 MHz FM
Mailing Address: Box 9, Gananoque, ON K7G 2T6 Canada
Second Address: 110 Kate St., Gananoque, ON K7G 2T6
(613) 382-6936; *Fax:* (613) 382-8301
www.gananoquenow.ca
License: Gananoque, ON held by My Broadcasting Corp.
Group Owner: My Broadcasting Corp.
Format: Christian
Terri-Lynn Bayford, General Manager
Terri-Lynn Bayford, General Sales Mgr
D'Arcy Magee, Group Program Director
Cindy Clyne, Group News Director
Marg Tubman, Group Administrator

Georgina Island

CFGI-FM
01-01-2004; 92.3 MHz FM; 650 w; 24 meters
102.7 Nish Radio, Box N-13, Sutton West, ON L0E 1R0 Canada
(705) 437-3748; *Fax:* (705) 437-3748
nish_cfgi@hotmail.com
License: Georgina Island, ON held by Georgina Island First Nations Communications.
Population Served: 353; *Arbitron Metro Market:* Georgina Island, ON; *Format:* Variety/Diverse
Sally Charles, General Manager
Sean Canoe, Programming Director
Morgan Priester, Announcer

Goderich

CHWC-FM
10-15-2007; 104.9 MHz FM; *Hrs Open:* 24; 12.55 kw; N43 40 42 W81 42 31
300 Suncoast Dr., Unit E, Goderich, ON N7A 4N7 Canada
(519) 612-1149; *Fax:* (519) 612-1050
www.1049thebeach.ca
thebeach@1049thebeach.ca
License: Goderich, Huron County, ON held by Bayshore Broadcasting Corp.
Group Owner: Bayshore Broadcasting Corp.
Nat'l Reps: Target Broadcast Sales
Format: Adult Contemp; *No. News Employees:* 14; *Target Audience:* 18-64
Kevin Brown, General Sales Mgr
Ally Anderson, Promotions Director

Guelph

***CFRU-FM**
01-28-1980; 93.3 MHz FM; *Hrs Open:* 24; kw*Rebroadcasts:* BBC World Service Overnight
U.C. Level 2, University of Guelph, Guelph, ON N1G 2W1 Canada
(519) 824-4120 x 53502
www.cfru.ca
cfru.admin@gmail.com
License: Guelph, Wellington County, ON held by University of Guelph Radio-Radio Gryphon.
Format: Variety/Diverse; *Special Programming:* It one hr, relg one hr, Sp; *Hrs. of News Programming:* news progmg 12 hrs wkly; *No. News Employees:* 1; *Target Audience:* General.; *Adv. Rates:* 21/spot start
Vish Khanna, Station Manager
Christopher Currie, Programming Coordinator
Steve Mason, Technical Coordinator
Bryan Webb, Operations Coordinator

CIMJ-FM
07-01-1969; 106.1 MHz FM; *Hrs Open:* 24; 50 kw; 249 ft
75 Speedvale Ave. E., Guelph, ON N1E 6M3 Canada
(519) 824-7000; *Fax:* (519) 824-4118
www.magic106.com
jessica.quackenbush@corusent.com
License: Guelph, Wellington County, ON held by 591989 B.C. Ltd.
Group Owner: Corus Entertainment Inc.
Population Served: 101,000; *Format:* Adult Contemp; *Hrs. of News Programming:* News progmg 6 hrs wkly; *Target Audience:* 25-54.
Lars Wunsche, Corus Radio Central Director
Jessica Quackenbush, General Sales Mgr
Brad Hulme, Programming Director
Lisa Richards, Promotions Coordinator
Darren Baxter, News
Shawn Smith, Chief Engineer
Natasha Hall-Brodie, ContentCoordinator

CJOY
06-14-1948; 1460 kHz AM; *Hrs Open:* 24; 10 kw
75 Speedvale Ave. E., Guelph, ON N1E 6M3 Canada
(519) 824-7000; *Fax:* (519) 824-4118
www.cjoy.com
jessica.quackenbush@corusent.com
License: Guelph, ON held by 591989 B.C. Ltd.
Group Owner: Corus Entertainment Inc.; (acq 3-24-00; grpsl).
Format: Adult Contemp, Contemporary Hits/Top 40; *Hrs. of News Programming:* news progmg 8 hrs wkly; *No. News Employees:* 4; *Target Audience:* 25-54.
Jessica Quackenbush, General Sales Mgr
Larry Mellott, Programming Director
Lisa Richards, Promotions Coordinator
Darren Baxter, News
Shawn Smith, Chief Engineer
Ian Clutton, Senior Sales Representative
Natasha Hall-Brodie,Interactive Content Coordinator

Haliburton

CKHA-FM
07-01-2003; 100.9 MHz FM; 3.4 kw
Box 1125, 739 Mountain Street, Haliburton, ON K0M 1S0 Canada
(705) 457-1009; *Fax:* (705) 457-9522
www.canoefm.com
canoefmadmin@bellnet.ca
License: Haliburton, ON held by Haliburton County Community Radio Association.
Population Served: 17,026; *Arbitron Metro Market:* Haliburton, ON; *Format:* Variety/Diverse; *Target Audience:* 50 plus.
Malcolm Maclean, President
Roxanne Casey, Station Manager
Ron Murphy, Chief Engineer
Dave Allen, Sales Representitive
Jay Bomberry, Vice President
Betty Moffatt, Secretary
Case Bassie, Treasurer/Accounting

CFZN-FM
93.5 MHz FM; *Hrs Open:* 24 Hours; 6 kw; 133.2 meters
152 Highland St., Haliburton, ON K0M 1S0 Canada
(705) 457-3897; *Fax:* (705) 457-3827
www.myhaliburtonnow.com
jhodge@vistaradio.ca
License: Haliburton, ON held by Vista Radio Ltd.
Group Owner: Vista Radio Ltd.
Format: Adult Contemp, Oldies, Rock/AOR
Jenny Hodge, Regional Cluster Manager and General Sales
Dave Newman, Regional Cluster Program Director

Hamilton

***CFMU-FM**
01-13-1978; 93.3 MHz FM; *Hrs Open:* 24; kw
Canada
(905) 525-9140; *Fax:* (905) 529-3208
cfmu.mcmaster.ca
License: Hamilton, ON held by CFMU Radio Inc.
Group Owner: CFMU Radio Inc.; (acq 1978)
Format: Variety/Diverse; *Special Programming:* Class 5 hrs, Sp one hr, blues 5 hrs, Canadian Indi; *Hrs. of News Programming:* News progmg 15 hrs wkly; *Target Audience:* General; univ students, people with an adventurousoutlook towards life
Jamie Tennant, Programming Director
Ben Robinson, Music Director
Amanda MacIntosh, Production Director
Marshall Ferguson, Sports Director

CHAM
11-01-1959; 820 kHz AM; *Hrs Open:* 24; 50 kw-D, 10 kw-N
883 Upper Wentworth St., Suite 401, Hamilton, ON L9A 4Y6 Canada
(905) 574-1150; *Fax:* (905) 575-6429
www.funny820.com
License: Hamilton, ON held by Bell Media Radio G.P.
Group Owner: Bell Media Inc.; (acq 10-29-2007; grpsl).
Wire Services: BN Wire
Format: Comedy; *Hrs. of News Programming:* news progmg 26 hrs wkly; *No. News Employees:* 4; *Target Audience:* 25-54.; *Adv. Rates:* 65; 55; 45; 45
Bob Harris, General Manager
Lisa Peters, Director of Marketing and Promotions
Kristie Boadwin, Promotions Coordinator
Cheryl McFarlane, Promotions Coordinator
Mike Nabuurs, Brand Director

CHML
05-27-1927; 900 kHz AM; *Hrs Open:* 24
875 Main St. W., Hamilton, ON L8S 4R1 Canada
(905) 521-9900; *Fax:* (905) 540-2452
www.900chml.com
news@900chml.com
License: Hamilton, ON held by Corus Premium Television Ltd.
Group Owner: Corus Entertainment Inc.; (acq 7-6-2000; grpsl).
Nat'l Reps: Canadian Broadcast Sales
Format: News, News/Talk, Talk; *Target Audience:* 35 plus.
Krista Taaffe, General Sales Mgr
Jeff Storey, Program & News Director
Olivia Mackay, Promotions Manager
Rick Zamperin, Assistant Program & Sports Director
Lisete Culley, Office Manager
Misty Cornell, Creative Supervisor
JustinGlover, Promotions Coordinator

***CIOI-FM**
01-01-1998; 101.5 MHz FM; *Hrs Open:* 24; 240 w; N43 14 12 W79 53 13
135 Fennell Avenue W., Room F111, Hamilton, ON L8N 3T2 Canada
(905) 575-2175; *Fax:* (905) 575-2420
www.indifm.ca
les.palango@mohawkcollege.ca
License: Hamilton, ON held by The Mohawk College Radio Corp.
Population Served: 400,000; *Format:* Alternative; *Hrs. of News Programming:* News progmg 6 hrs wkly; *Target Audience:* 17-24; college students & the div communities they represent; *Adv. Rates:* 25; 25; 25; 25
Les Palango, Station Manager
Jamie Smith, Programming Director
Jeff Cudahy, Engineering Dir
Sara Heres, Music Director

***CING-FM**
09-24-1976; 95.3 MHz FM; *Hrs Open:* 24; 100 kw
875 Main St. W., Hamilton, ON L8S 4R1 Canada
(905) 521-9900; *Fax:* (905) 521-1691
www.953freshradio.ca
krista.taaffe@corusent.com
License: Hamilton, ON held by Corus Premium Television Ltd.
Group Owner: Corus Entertainment Inc.
Nat'l Reps: Canadian Broadcast Sales
Format: Adult Contemp; *Target Audience:* 25-54; female
Krista Taaffe, General Sales Mgr
Wayne Williams, Programming Director
Olivia Mackay, Promotions Manager
Lisete Culley, Office Manager
Misty Cornell, Creative Supervisor
Chad Fullerton, Interactive Content Manager
Justin Glover,Promotions Coordinator

CKLH-FM
10-07-1986; 102.9 MHz FM; 40.3 kw
883 Upper Wentworth St., Suite 401, Hamilton, L9A 4Y6 Canada
(905) 574-1150; *Fax:* (905) 575-6429
www.k-litefm.com
License: Hamilton, ON held by Bell Media Radio G.P.

Group Owner: Bell Media Inc.
Format: Adult Contemp; *Target Audience:* 25-54; working women, owners, mgrs, professionals
Bob Harris, General Manager
Lisa Peters, Director of Promotions

CKOC
05-01-1922; 1150 kHz AM; *Hrs Open:* 24; 50 kw
883 Upper Wentworth St., Suite 401, Hamilton, ON L9A 4Y6 Canada
(905) 574-1150; *Fax:* (905) 575-6429
www.tsn.ca/radio/hamilton-1150
bob.harris@bellmedia.ca
License: Hamilton, ON held by Bell Media Radio G.P.
Group Owner: Bell Media Inc.; (acq 10-29-2007; grpsl).
Nat'l Reps: Canadian Broadcast Sales; *Wire Services:* Broadcast News Ltd.
Format: Sports; *No. News Employees:* 4; *Target Audience:* 25-54.
Bob Harris, General Manager
Victor Giacomelli, General Sales Mgr
Mike Nabuurs, Programming Director
Lisa Peters, Director of Marketing and Promotions
Kristie Boadwin, Promotions Coordinator
Cheryl McFarlane, PromotionsCoordinator

CHKX-FM
09-01-2000; 94.7 MHz FM; *Hrs Open:* 24; 21.4 kw; Ant 446 ft; N43 12 21 W79 43 50
589 Upper Wellington St., Hamilton, ON L9A 3P8 Canada
(905) 388-8911; *Fax:* (905) 388-7947
www.kx947.fm
License: Hamilton, ON held by Durham Radio Inc.
Group Owner: Durham Radio Inc.; (acq 8-31-2007)
Nat'l Reps: Target Broadcast Sales; *Wire Services:* Broadcast News Ltd.
Population Served: 3,638,000; *Format:* Country; *No. News Employees:* 2; *Target Audience:* 35-64.; *Adv. Rates:* 100; 80; 60; 40
Wally Sollows, General Sales Mgr
Steve Kassay, VP, Programming
Adriane Vogel, Promotions
Steve Macaulay, VP, Sales

Hanover

CFBW-FM
12-31-2001; 91.3 MHz FM; *Hrs Open:* 24; 250 w; Ant 290 ft; N44 08 31 W81 01 47
267 10th St., Hanover, ON N4N 1P1 Canada
(519) 364-0200; *Fax:* (519) 364-5175
www.bluewaterradio.ca
info@bluewaterradio.ca
License: Hanover, Canada County, ON held by Bluewater Community Radio Inc..
Population Served: 150,000; *Special Programming:* Scottish Music, Comedy,Gospel,; *Hrs. of News Programming:* 2; *No. News Employees:* 3; *Target Audience:* 12-75; Ontario audience rural agricultural/urban*Adv. Rates:* Please Call for details & rate
Gary Smith, Chairman
Andrew McBride, CEO/GM
Greg Bolek, Sales/Marketing
Andrew McBride, Programming/Music Director
Craig Smith, Chief Engineer
Brenda Dacey, Accounting

Hawkesbury

CHPR-FM
02-01-1986; 102.1 MHz FM; *Hrs Open:* 24; 789 w; 70 ft; N45 35 01 N45 35 01
11, av Argenteuil, Lachute, QC J8H 1X8 Canada
(480) 562-8862; *Fax:* (450) 562-1902
www.lachute.planeteradio.ca
License: Hawkesbury, ON held by RNC MEDIA Inc.
Group Owner: RNC MEDIA Inc.; (acq 8-22-89)
Format: Adult Contemp; *No. News Employees:* 1; *Target Audience:* 25 plus.
Raynald Briere, President

CKHK-FM
04-02-2008; 107.7 MHz FM; 875 w; N45 39 24 W74 39 43
1320 Main St. E., Hawkesbury, ON K6A 1C5 Canada
(613) 872-1077; *Fax:* (613) 632-4022
www.jewelradio.com/new/1077
info@1077thejewel.com
License: Hawkesbury, ON held by Ottawa Media Inc.
Group Owner: Evanov Communications Inc.
Population Served: 10,551; *Arbitron Metro Market:* Hawkesbury, ON; *Format:* Easy Listening, Adult Contemp; *No. News Employees:* 1

Aron Goodden, General Sales Mgr
Ted Silver, Administration
Vanessa Malloy, Promotions
Dan Chabot, News Director

Hearst

CHYK-FM-3
01-01-1996; 92.9 MHz FM; *Hrs Open:* 24; 140 w*Rebroadcasts:* Rebroadcasts CHYK-FM Timmins
49 Cedar St. S., Timmins, ON P4N 2G5 Canada
(705) 267-6070; *Fax:* (705) 267-6095
License: Hearst, ON held by LE5 Communications Inc.
Nat'l Reps: Canadian Broadcast Sales
Format: Adult Contemp; *Hrs. of News Programming:* news progmg one hrs wkly; *No. News Employees:* 1; *Target Audience:* 18-65.; *Adv. Rates:* 22.50; 22.50; 22.50; 22.50.
Kimberley Grossman, Operations Dir
Christopher Grossman, General Manager
Sylvie Beaulieu, General Sales Mgr
Sylvain Boucher, Programming Director
Gilles Lafortune, News Director
Penny Proulx, Traffic Manager

***CINN-FM**
01-01-1988; 91.1 MHz FM; *Hrs Open:* 6 AM-9 PM; kw
1004 rue Prince, Hearst, ON P0L 1N0 Canada
(705) 372-1011; *Fax:* (705) 362-7411
License: Hearst, Canada County, ON held by Radio de l'Epinette Noire Inc.
Format: Adult Contemp; *No. News Employees:* 2; *Target Audience:* 0-75.
Camire-Lise Laflamme, President
Kathy R. Haberdasher, General Manager

Huntsville

CFBK-FM
105.5 MHz FM; *Hrs Open:* 24; 43,400 w
7 John St., Huntsville, ON P1H 1G1 Canada
(705) 789-4461; *Fax:* (705) 789-1269
www.mymuskokanow.com
tablett@moosefm.com
License: Huntsville, Muskoka County, ON held by Vista Radio Ltd.
Group Owner: Vista Radio Ltd.; (acq 11-7-2007)
Nat'l Network: CHUM Radio Network; *Wire Services:* BN Wire
Population Served: 30,000; *Format:* Adult Contemp, Contemporary Hits/Top 40; *No. News Employees:* 3; *Target Audience:* 21 plus.
Jenny Hodge, Regional Cluster Manager and General Sales
Dave Newman, Regional Cluster Program Director
Rachel Detta, Promotions Coordinator
Taylor Ablett, News Director

Iroquois Falls

CFIF-FM
101.1 MHz FM; *Hrs Open:* 24; 0.033 kw; 32 m
22B 5th Ave., Cochrane, ON P0L 1C0 Canada
(705) 272-6467; *Fax:* (705) 272-2520
www.mycochranenow.com
sarmstrong@vistaradio.ca
License: Iroquois Falls, ON held by Vista Radio Ltd.
Group Owner: Vista Radio Ltd.; (acq 11-19-2003; with CHPB-FM Cochrane)
Population Served: 2,500; *Format:* Adult Contemp; *Hrs. of News Programming:* news progmg 1.5 hrs wkly; *No. News Employees:* 1; *Target Audience:* 25-54.; *Adv. Rates:* 22.50; 22.50; 22.50; 22.50
Scott Armstrong, Regional Cluster Manager
Shane Button, Regional Cluster Program Director
Rudy Kadlec, Regional News Director

Kaministiquia

CFQK-FM
01-01-2002; 104.5 MHz FM; 50 w; N48 30 27 W89 27 28
87 Hill St. N., Thunder Bay, ON P7A 5V6 Canada
(807) 346-2600; *Fax:* (807) 345-9923
www.thethunder.ca
thunder@thethunder.ca
License: Kaministiquia, ON held by Northwest Broadcasting Inc.
Nat'l Reps: Target Broadcast Sales
Population Served: 587; *Arbitron Metro Market:* Kaministiquia, ON; *Format:* Country
Don Caron, President
Bill Malcolm, Energy Programming Director
Leslie Walker-Larson, National Sales Manager
Bill Malcolm, Programming Director
Cora Cambly, Promotions/Marketing Director

Kathy Harris, Director of Local Sales
BryanWyatt, News/Sports

Kapuskasing

CKGN-FM
10-01-1993; 89.7 MHz FM; *Hrs Open:* 24; 3 000 kw
77 chemin Brunelle Nd., Kapuskasing, ON P5N 2M1 Canada
(705) 335-5915; *Fax:* (705) 335-3508
www.ckgn.ca
ckgnfm@nt.net
License: Kapuskasing, ON held by Radio communautaire KapNord Inc.
Population Served: 20,000; *Format:* Variety/Diverse; *No. News Employees:* 1; *Target Audience:* General.
Claude Chabot, General Manager

CKAP-FM
100.9 MHz FM; 12 kw; 83 meters
22 Queen St., Unit 2A, Kapuskasing, ON P5N 1G8 Canada
(705) 335-2379; *Fax:* (705) 337-6391
www.mykapuskasingnow.com
sarmstrong@vistaradio.ca
License: Kapuskasing, ON held by Vista Radio Ltd.
Group Owner: Vista Radio Ltd.
Format: Adult Contemp; *No. News Employees:* 2; *Target Audience:* General.
Scott Armstrong, Regional Cluster Manager
Shane Button, Regional Cluster Program Director

Kawartha Lakes

CKLY-FM
05-16-1998; 91.9 MHz FM; *Hrs Open:* 24; 27.5 kw
249 Kent St. W., Lindsay, ON K9V 2Z3 Canada
(705) 324-9103; *Fax:* (705) 324-4149
www.919bobfm.com
bob@919bobfm.com
License: Kawartha Lakes, ON held by Bell Media Ontario Regional Radio Partnership
Group Owner: Bell Media Inc.; (acq 6-22-2007; grpsl).
Nat'l Reps: Canadian Broadcast Sales
Population Served: 70,000; *Format:* Adult Contemp; *Hrs. of News Programming:* news progmg 14 hrs wkly; *No. News Employees:* 2; *Target Audience:* 30-65.; *Adv. Rates:* 45; 35; na; 10
Harvey Spry, General Sales Mgr
Dave Illman, Programming Director
Mel Hannah, Promotions

Kemptville

CKVV-FM
02-27-2012; 97.5 MHz FM; 2.8 kw; 89 meters
4 Industrial Rd., Unit 4, Kemptville, ON K0G 1J0 Canada
(613) 258-1786
www.mykemptvillenow.com
tlamoureux@vistaradio.ca
License: Kemptville, ON held by Vista Radio Ltd.
Group Owner: Vista Radio Ltd.
Format: Contemporary Hits/Top 40, Variety/Diverse
Tracy Lamoureux, General Manager and Sales
Drew Hosick, Programming Director
Marie Cassidy, Regional News Director
Kapila Ratnayake, Chief Engineer
Michelle Vallee, Integrated Marketing Executive

Kenora

CBQX-FM
03-28-1978; 98.7 MHz FM; kw*Rebroadcasts:* Rebroadcasts CBW(AM) Winnipeg, Man. & CBQT-FM Thunder Bay
213 Miles Street East, Thunder Bay, ON 97C 1J5 Canada
(807) 625-5000; *Fax:* (416) 205-3111
License: Kenora, ON held by CBC/Radio-Canada
Nat'l Network: CBC Radio One
Format: Public Affairs, News
Susan Rogers, Managing Director

CJRL-FM
01-01-2004; 89.5 MHz FM; 40 kw; N49 46 45 W94 27 25
301 1st Ave. S., Kenora, ON P9N 1W2 Canada
(807) 468-3181; *Fax:* (807) 468-4188
www.895thelake.ca
cjrl@cjrl.ca
License: Kenora, ON held by Acadia Broadcasting Ltd.
Group Owner: Acadia Broadcasting Ltd.; (acq 5-1-2007; grpsl)
Population Served: 15,348; *Arbitron Metro Market:* Kenora, ON; *Format:* Adult Contemp; *No. News Employees:* 2; *Target Audience:* 25-54.

Darrell Plummer, Station Manager
Tim Davidson, News Director

Kettle Point

CKTI-FM
04-26-2004; 107.7 MHz FM; *Hrs Open:* 24; 420 w
9111 W. Ipperwash Rd., Kettle + Stony Point, ON N0N 1J1 Canada
(519) 786-3883; *Fax:* (519) 786-2834
www.eaglecountry.ca
info@eaglecountry.ca
License: Kettle Point, ON held by Chippewas of Kettle + Stony Point
Population Served: 936; *Arbitron Metro Market:* Kettle Point, ON; *Format:* Classic Rock, Country
Nadine Buchanan, Co-Manager
Justin Shawnoo, Co-Manager

Killaloe

CHCR-FM
01-01-1998; 102.9 MHz FM; 33 w
14 Lake St. Unit A, PO Box 195, Killaloe, ON K0J 2A0 Canada
(613) 757-0657; *Fax:* (613) 757-0818
www.chcr.org
radio@chcr.org
License: Killaloe, ON held by Homegrown Community Radio.
Population Served: 2,550; *Arbitron Metro Market:* Killaloe, ON; *Format:* Variety/Diverse; *Special Programming:* Canadian fiddle 8 hrs, Fr 8 hrs, Pol one hr, trad
Peter Benner, Chairman
Daryl Andermann, General Manager
Peter Benner, Station Manager
Sabrina Radema, Programming Committee
Tim Rivers Garrett, Secretary
Desiree McGlynn, Treasurer
Jude Bivar, Programming Committee
JuneWalterhouse, Station Management Committee
Div Halliday, Station Management Committee

Kincardine

CIYN-FM
02-27-2006; 95.5 MHz FM; *Hrs Open:* 24
765 Queen St., Kincardine, ON N2Z 2Y2 Canada
(519) 396-7770; *Fax:* (519) 396-7771
www.shorelinetoday.ca
License: Kincardine, ON held by My Broadcasting Corp.
Group Owner: My Broadcasting Corp.
Format: Oldies; *No. News Employees:* 1
Dean Daly, General Manager
D'Arcy Magee, Group Programming Director
Cindy Clyne, News Director

Kingston

***CBBKFM**
05-21-1979; 92.9 MHz FM; *Hrs Open:* 24; kw
Canada
(416) 205-3700; *Fax:* (416) 205-6063
www.cbc.ca
info@cbbk.com
License: Kingston, ON held by Canadian Broadcasting Corp.
Group Owner: Canadian Broadcasting Corporation
Nat'l Network: CBC Radio Two
Robert Raeinobitch, CFO

CFLY-FM
01-01-1963; 98.3 MHz FM; *Hrs Open:* 24; 95.5 kw; 400 ft
993 Princess St., Suite 10, Kingston, ON K7L 1H3 Canada
(613) 650-9800
www.983flyfm.com
heydeejay@983flyfm.com
License: Kingston, ON held by Bell Media Ontario Regional Radio Partnership
Group Owner: Bell Media Inc.; (acq 6-22-2007; grpsl).
Format: Adult Contemp; *Hrs. of News Programming:* news progmg 5 hrs wkly; *No. News Employees:* 2; *Target Audience:* 25-44.
Greg Hinton, General Manager
Kim Parker, General Sales Mgr
Jacquie Beckett, Programming Director
Ali MacLean, Promotions Manager
Matthew Bisson, News Director

***CFMK-FM**
05-14-1947; 96.3 MHz FM; *Hrs Open:* 24; 28 kw; 247.9 meters
170 Queen St., Kingston, ON K7K 1B2 Canada
(613) 544-2340; *Fax:* (613) 544-5508
www.963bigfm.com
brian.bailey@corusent.com
License: Kingston, ON held by 591989 B.C. Ltd.
Group Owner: Corus Entertainment Inc.; (acq 3-24-2000; grpsl)
TV Affiliate: CKWS-TV affil.; *Format:* Classic Rock; *Hrs. of News Programming:* M-F: 6a, 6:30a, 7a,7:30a, 8a, 8:30a, 12p, 4p,; *No. News Employees:* 2; *Target Audience:* 35-64; Male
Dave McCutcheon, General Manager
Peter Mayhew, General Sales Mgr
Brian Bailey, Programming Director
Roger Cole, Chief Engineer

***CFRC-FM**
10-27-2022; 101.9 MHz FM; *Hrs Open:* 24; 3 kw; 295 ft; N44 17 24 W77 25 55
Queens Univ., Lower Carruthers Hall, 62 Fifth Field Company Lane, Kingston, ON K7L 3N6 Canada
(613) 533-2121
www.cfrc.ca
cfrcops@ams.queensu.ca
License: Kingston, Frontenac County, ON held by Radio Queen's University.
Population Served: 150,000; *Hrs. of News Programming:* News progmg 15 hrs wkly; *Target Audience:* General.
Kristiana Clemens, Operations Dir
Eric Beers, Station Manager
Brendon Wilson, Programming Manager
Ayanda Mrigoma, Business Manager

***CKVI-FM**
01-01-1997; 91.9 MHz FM; *Hrs Open:* 8am-6pm; 6.5 w
235 Frontenac St., Kingston, ON K7L 3S7 Canada
(613) 544-7864; *Fax:* (613) 544-8795
www.thecave.ca
rosejf@limestone.on.ca
License: Kingston, Canada County, ON held by KCVI Educational Radio Station Inc.
Format: Variety/Diverse
Fraser Rose, General Manager

CIKR-FM
03-19-2001; 105.7 MHz FM; *Hrs Open:* 24; 24 kw
863 Princess St., Suite 301, Kingston, ON K7L 5N4 Canada
(613) 549-1057; *Fax:* (613) 549-5302
www.krock1057.ca
License: Kingston, ON held by Rogers Broadcasting Ltd.
Group Owner: Rogers Broadcasting Ltd.; (acq 5-4-2009; with CKXC-FM Kingston)
Population Served: 123,363; *Arbitron Metro Market:* Kingston, ON; *Format:* Rock/AOR; *Hrs. of News Programming:* news progmg 2 hrs wkly; *No. News Employees:* 2; *Target Audience:* 25-54; adults; *Adv. Rates:* 75; 70;65; 35
Stephen Peck, General Manager
Stephen Peck, General Sales Mgr
Ian March, Programming Director
John Noon, Promotions/Web Director

CKWS-FM
10-15-2007; 104.3 MHz FM; 8 kw; Ant 813 ft; N44 10 02 W76 25 40
170 Queen St., Kingston, ON K7K 1B2 Canada
(613) 544-2340; *Fax:* (613) 544-5508
www.1043freshradio.ca
peter.mayhew@corusent.com
License: Kingston, ON held by 591989 B.C. Ltd.
Group Owner: Corus Entertainment Inc.
TV Affiliate: CKWS-TV affil; *Format:* Adult Contemp; *Hrs. of News Programming:* Mon-Fri: 6a, 6:30a, 7a, 7:30a, 8a, 8:30a, 12p, 3p, 4p, 5p, 6p; Sat: 8a; *No. News Employees:* 2; *Target Audience:* 35-64; female
Peter Mayhew, General Sales Mgr
Brian Bailey, Programming Director
Roger Cole, Chief Engineer

CKLC-FM
01-01-2007; 98.9 MHz FM; 15 kw; Ant 433 ft; N44 12 36 W76 25 05
993 Princess St., Suite 10, Kingston, ON K7L 1H3 Canada
(613) 544-1380; *Fax:* (613) 546-9751
www.989thedrive.com
onair@989thedrive.com
License: Kingston, ON held by Bell Media Ontario Regional Radio Partnership
Group Owner: Bell Media Inc.
Format: Rock/AOR; *Hrs. of News Programming:* news progmg 3 hrs wkly; *No. News Employees:* 4
Greg Hinton, General Manager
Brian Johnston, General Sales Mgr
Jacquie Beckett, Programming Director
Ali MacLean, Promotions Manager
Matthew Bisson, News Director
Riley Jabour, Music Director

CKXC-FM
01-01-2008; 93.5 MHz FM; 7.5 kw; Ant 371 ft; N44 17 22 W76 28 50
863 Princess St., Suite 301, Kingston, ON K7L 5N4 Canada
(613) 549-1057; *Fax:* (613) 549-5302
www.country935.ca
License: Kingston, Frontenac County, ON held by Rogers Broadcasting Ltd.
Group Owner: Rogers Broadcasting Ltd.; (acq 5-4-2009; with CIKR-FM Kingston)
Population Served: 123,363; *Arbitron Metro Market:* Kingston, ON; *Format:* Country; *Target Audience:* 35-64.
Stephen Peck, General Manager
Stephen Peck, General Sales Mgr
Ian March, Programming Director
John Noon, Promotions/Web Director

Kirkland Lake

CJKL-FM
01-01-1934; 101.5 MHz FM; *Hrs Open:* 24; 23 kw
Mailing Address: Box 430, Kirkland Lake, ON P2N 3J4 Canada
Second Address: 5 Kirkland Street, Kirkland Lake, ON P2N 1N9
(705) 567-3366; *Fax:* (705) 567-6101
www.cjklfm.com
cjkl@cjklfm.com
License: Kirkland Lake, ON held by Connelly Communications Corp.
Nat'l Reps: Canadian Broadcast Sales
Population Served: 8,000; *Arbitron Metro Market:* Kirkland Lake, ON; *Format:* Adult Contemp; *No. News Employees:* 2; *Adv. Rates:* 42; 30; 30; na.
Robin Connelly, President, G.M. & P.D.
Ann Connelly, General Sales Mgr
Elesha Teskey, News Director
Don Elvidge, Engineering Dir
Greg Mackle, News Director
Nathan Evans, Director of Engineering
Corina LaCarte, Sales Manager/CopyDirector
Phil Hutchinson, Account Executive
Michelle Farstad, Account Executive
Luce Moore, Traffic Director

Kitchener

CHYM-FM
01-01-1949; 96.7 MHz FM; *Hrs Open:* 24; 80 kw; Ant 658 ft
305 King St. W., Suite 1101, Kitchener, ON N2G 4E4 Canada
(519) 743-2611
www.chymfm.com
License: Kitchener, ON held by Rogers Broadcasting Ltd.
Group Owner: Rogers Broadcasting Ltd.
Population Served: 500,000; *Format:* Adult Contemp; *Target Audience:* A25-54
Mike Collins, General Manager
Christa Hicks, Promotions Director
Courtney Scott-Schuurs, Promotions Coordinator
Amanda Black, Promotions Coordinator

CJDV-FM
05-28-1998; 107.5 MHz FM; *Hrs Open:* 24; 2.5 kw
50 Sportsworld Crossing Rd., Suite 210, Kitchener, ON N2P 0A4 Canada
(519) 772-1212; *Fax:* (519) 772-1213
www.1075daverocks.com
jessica.quackenbush@corusent.com
License: Kitchener, Waterloo County, ON held by 591989 B.C. Ltd.
Group Owner: Corus Entertainment Inc.; (acq 4-2000; grpsl).
Format: Rock/AOR; *Special Programming:* Por 2 hrs wkly; *No. News Employees:* 2; *Target Audience:* 18-49.
Lars Wunsche, Corus Radio Central Director
Jessica Quackenbush, General Sales Mgr
Steve Kennedy, Programming Director
Jonah Istifan, Promotions Coordinator
Shawn Smith, Chief Engineer
Mike Devine, Music Director
NatashaHall-Brodie, Interactive Content Coordinator
Jaie Tufford, Production Director

CKGL
01-01-1929; 570 kHz AM; *Hrs Open:* 24; 10 kw-U, DA-1
305 King St. W., P.O. Box 936, Kitchener, ON N2G 4E4 Canada
(519) 743-2611
www.570news.com
news570@rogers.com
License: Kitchener, ON held by Rogers Broadcasting Ltd.
Group Owner: Rogers Broadcasting Ltd.
Nat'l Network: CBS
Format: News, News/Talk, Sports, Talk; *Target Audience:* 35 plus.

Mike Collins, General Manager
Mike Collins, General Sales Mgr

CIKZ-FM
02-06-2004; 106.7 MHz FM; 5 kw
305 King St. W., Suite 1101, Kitchener, ON N2G 4E5 Canada
(519) 743-2611
www.country1067.com
License: Kitchener, ON held by Rogers Broadcasting Ltd.
Group Owner: Rogers Broadcasting Ltd.; (acq 12-24-2007; exchange for CICX-FM Orillia)
Arbitron Metro Market: Kitchener, ON; *Format:* Country
Mike Collins, General Manager
Christa Hicks, Program Director/Promotions Director
Dave Bossy, Production/Creative Director
Courtney Scott-Schuurs, Promotions Coordinator
Amanda Black, Promotions Coordinator

CKKW-FM
01-01-2009; 99.5 MHz FM; 1.7 kw; Ant 335 ft; N43 24 13 W80 31 54
255 King St. N., Suite 207, Waterloo, ON N2J 4V2 Canada
(519) 884-4470; *Fax:* (519) 884-6482
www.kfun995.com
websupport@kfun995.com
License: Kitchener, ON held by Bell Media Canada Radio 2013 Partnership
Group Owner: Bell Media Inc.
Population Served: 507,096; *Arbitron Metro Market:* Waterloo, ON; *Format:* Oldies
Tom Fitz-Gerald, General Sales Mgr
Heidi Baiden, Programming Director
Dan Delorme, Music Director
Steve Thompson, Creative Director
Kendra Roberts, Traffic Manager

Kitchener-Waterloo

CKBT-FM
01-31-2004; 91.5 MHz FM; *Hrs Open:* 24; 3.6 kw
50 Sportsworld Crossing Rd., Suite 210, Kitchener, ON N2P 0A4 Canada
(519) 772-1212; *Fax:* (519) 772-1213
www.915thebeat.com
jessica.quackenbush@corusent.com
License: Kitchener-Waterloo, ON held by Corus Premium Television Ltd.
Group Owner: Corus Entertainment Inc.; (acq 7-6-2007; C$14.5 million with CJZZ-FM Winnipeg, MB)
Population Served: 204,668; *Arbitron Metro Market:* Kitchener, ON; *Format:* Contemporary Hits/Top 40; *Target Audience:* 18-34.
Lars Wunsche, Corus Radio Central Director
Jessica Quackenbush, General Sales Mgr
Steve Kennedy, Programming Director
Jonah Istifan, Promotions Coordinator
Shawn Smith, Chief Engineer
Natasha Hall-Brodie, Interactive ContentCoordinator
Elle Dee, Music Director
Jaie Tufford, Production Director

CJTW-FM
02-01-2004; 94.3 MHz FM; *Hrs Open:* 24; 50 w
659 King Street East, Kitchener, ON N2G 2M4 Canada
(519) 575-9090; *Fax:* (519) 575-9119
www.faithfm.org
info@faithfm.org
License: Kitchener-Waterloo, ON held by Sound of Faith Broadcasting.
Special Programming: Religious Spoken Word; *Target Audience:* A25-54; *Adv. Rates:* 40; 35; 40; 20
Tanya Gafoor, Production Manager
Dave MacDonald, General Manager
Barbara Dowling, General Sales Mgr
Brad Loveday, Programming Director
Josh Atkinson, Music Director

Leamington

CHYR-FM
08-23-1993; 96.7 MHz FM; *Hrs Open:* 24; kw
100 Talbot St. E., Leamington, ON N8H 1L3 Canada
(519) 326-6171; *Fax:* (519) 322-1110
www.mix967.ca
License: Leamington, ON held by Blackburn Radio Inc.
Group Owner: Blackburn Radio Inc.; (acq 12-19-94; grpsl).
Format: Adult Contemp; *Target Audience:* 25-54.
Tim O'Neil, General Sales Mgr
Kevin Black, News Director
Cathie Morgan, Sales Director

CJSP-FM
03-03-2008; 92.7 MHz FM; kw*Rebroadcasts:* Simulcasts On CJWF-FM In Windsor
100 Tablot St. E., Leamington, ON N8H 1L3 Canada
(519) 326-6171; *Fax:* (519) 322-1110
www.country959.com
License: Leamington, ON held by Blackburn Radio Inc.
Group Owner: Blackburn Radio Inc.
Arbitron Metro Market: Leamington, ON; *Format:* Country; *Target Audience:* 25-64.
John Weese, General Manager

London

***CBBL-FM**
10-01-1978; 100.5 MHz FM; *Hrs Open:* 24; kw*Rebroadcasts:* Rebroadcasts CBL-FM Toronto
Canada
(416) 205-3700; *Fax:* (416) 205-6063
www.cbc.ca
info@cbbk.com
License: London, ON held by CBC/Radio-Canada
Group Owner: Canadian Broadcasting Corporation
Nat'l Network: CBC Radio Two
Robert Raeinobitch, CFO

***CBCL-FM**
06-01-1998; 93.5 MHz FM; *Hrs Open:* 4 am-6 pm; kw
Canada
(519) 667-1990; *Fax:* (519) 667-1557
www.cbc.ca
License: London, ON held by CBC/Radio-Canada
Group Owner: Canadian Broadcasting Corporation
Nat'l Network: CBC Radio One
Special Programming: News 10 hrs wkly
R,mi Racine, Chairman
Maryse Bertand, VP/General Counsel
William B. Chamers, VP, Brand
Hubert Lacroix, President/CEO
Heather Conway, EVP, English
Steve Guiton, VP, Technology
Louis Lalande, EVP, French
Roula Zaarour, VP,People/Culture
Suzanne Morris, VP/CFO

CFPL
09-30-1922; 980 kHz AM; *Hrs Open:* 24
380 Wellington St., Suite 222, London, ON N6A 5B5 Canada
(519) 931-6000
globalnews.ca/radio/am980
tshaw@am980.ca
License: London, ON held by Corus Radio Co.
Group Owner: Corus Entertainment Inc.
Format: News, News/Talk, Sports, Talk; *Hrs. of News Programming:* news progmg 10 hrs wkly; *No. News Employees:* 5; *Target Audience:* 35-54.
Rob Chiaramida, Regional Sales Manager, Ontario Central
Trudy Shaw, Programming Director
Kent Guy, Promotions & New Media Director
Chelsea Robinson, Promotions Coordinator

***CFPL-FM**
05-15-1948; 95.9 MHz FM; *Hrs Open:* 24; 179 kw
380 Wellington St., Suite 222, London, ON N6A 5B5 Canada
(519) 931-6000; *Fax:* (519) 438-2415
www.fm96.com
robc@corusent.com
License: London, ON held by Corus Radio Co.
Group Owner: Corus Entertainment Inc.
Format: Rock/AOR, Alternative; *Target Audience:* 25-49.
Rob Chiaramida, Regional Sales Manager, Ontario Central
Kent Guy, Promotions Director
Brad Gibb, Brand Director
Mark Cameron, Music Director
Shawn Herman, Promotions Coordinator

***CHRW-FM**
09-02-1980; 94.9 MHz FM; *Hrs Open:* 24; kw
Room 250, University Community Centre, Western University, London, ON N6A 3K7 Canada
(519) 661-3601
www.chrwradio.ca
chrwgm@uwo.ca
License: London, London County, ON held by Radio Western Inc.
Group Owner: CHRW
Format: Alternative, Jazz; *Hrs. of News Programming:* news progmg 5 hrs wkly; *No. News Employees:* 1; *Adv. Rates:* 30; 25; 30; 25
Grant Stein, Station Manager
Allison Brown, Programming Director

Tyler Hetherington, Music Coordinator
Philip Benmore, News Director
Derek Leung, Marketing Director/Production Coordinator

CIQM-FM
06-01-1986; 97.5 MHz FM; *Hrs Open:* 24; 50 kw; 300 ft
743 Wellington Rd. S., London, ON N6C 4R5 Canada
(519) 686-2525
www.london.virginradio.ca
License: London, ON held by Bell Media Radio G.P.
Group Owner: Bell Media Inc.; (acq 10-29-2007; grpsl).
Wire Services: BN Wire
Format: Adult Contemp; *Target Audience:* 25-54; female
Don Mumford, General Manager
Dan MacGillivray, General Sales Mgr
Scott Simpson, Programming Director
Al Smith, Brand Director
Todd Welch, Business Manager

CIXX-FM
10-31-1978; 106.9 MHz FM; *Hrs Open:* 24; kw
1001 Fon Shawe, College Boulevard, London, ON N5Y 5R6 Canada
(519) 453-2810; *Fax:* (519) 452-4153
www.1069thex.com
License: London, Middlesex County, ON held by Radio Fanshawe Inc.
Format: Urban Contemporary; *Special Programming:* Christian 3 hrs, educ 4 hrs hrs wkly; *No. News Employees:* 2; *Target Audience:* 12-34; primarily college, univ., high school
Barry Sutherland, Operations Dir
Steve Andruiak, General Manager
Michael Stoparczyk, Programming Director

CJBK
01-25-1967; 1290 kHz AM; *Hrs Open:* 24; 10 kw
743 Wellington Rd. S., London, ON N6C 4R5 Canada
(519) 686-2525
www.cjbk.com
License: London, ON held by Bell Media Radio G.P.
Group Owner: Bell Media Inc.; (acq 10-29-2007; grpsl).
Format: News/Talk, Sports; *No. News Employees:* 4; *Target Audience:* 35-54.
Don Mumford, General Manager
Dan MacGillivray, General Sales Mgr
Scott Simpson, Programming Director
Todd Welch, Business Manager

CJBX-FM
03-03-1980; 92.7 MHz FM; *Hrs Open:* 24; 50 kw
743 Wellington Rd. S., London, ON N6C 4R5 Canada
(519) 686-2525
www.bx93.com
License: London, ON held by Bell Media Radio G.P.
Group Owner: Bell Media Inc.
Format: Country
Dun Mumford, General Manager
Dan MacGillivray, General Sales Mgr

CKSL
06-01-1956; 1410 kHz AM; *Hrs Open:* 24; 10 kw
743 Wellington Rd. S., London, ON N6C 4R5 Canada
(519) 686-2525
License: London, ON held by Bell Media Radio G.P.
Group Owner: Bell Media Inc.; (acq 10-29-2007; grpsl).
Wire Services: BN Wire
Format: Comedy; *No. News Employees:* 1; *Target Audience:* 35-54; adults
Don Mumford, General Manager
Dan MacGillivray, General Sales Mgr
Todd Welch, Business Manager

CHST-FM
09-01-2000; 102.3 MHz FM; *Hrs Open:* 24; 5.84 kw
1 Communications Rd., London, ON N6J 4Z1 Canada
(519) 690-0102
www.1023jackfm.com
License: London, ON held by Rogers Broadcasting Ltd.
Group Owner: Rogers Broadcasting Ltd.; (acq 6-22-2007; grpsl)
Nat'l Network: CHUM Radio Network; *Wire Services:* BN Wire
Format: Contemporary Hits/Top 40; *Hrs. of News Programming:* weekday mornings; *No. News Employees:* 1; *Target Audience:* 25-54; adults
Mike Collins, General Manager
Brady Kingsbury, Programming Director
Amanda Young, Promotions Director
Gerry Derikx, Creative Director
Matt Loop, Promotions Coordinator
Ann LaRocque, Account Executive
Susan Johnson, AccountExecutive
Michael Testolin, Account Executive

CHJX-FM
01-01-2003; 99.9 MHz FM; *Hrs Open:* 24; 10 w
120 Wellington Street, Suite 100, London, ON N6B 2K6 Canada
(519) 679-2459; *Fax:* (519) 679-8014
www.faithfm.org
License: London, ON held by Sound of Faith Broadcasting.
Population Served: 366,151; *Arbitron Metro Market:* London, ON; *Format:* Christian
Dave Wettlaufer, GM/Programming Director
Josh Atkinson, Music Director
Dave Currie, Engineering

CKLO-FM
07-05-2011; 98.1 MHz FM; 4 kw; 150 meters; N42 56 29 W81 08 03
700 Richmond St, Suite 101, London, ON N6A 5C7 Canada
(519) 679-8680; *Fax:* (519) 679-0711
www.free981.com
License: London, ON held by Blackburn Radio Inc.
Group Owner: Blackburn Radio Inc.
Scott Kitching, News Director

Marathon

***CFNO-FM**
07-17-1982; 93.1 MHz FM; *Hrs Open:* 24; kw
Mailing Address: CFNO Radio, 87 N Hill Street, Thunder Bay, ON P7A 5V6 Canada
Second Address: 93 Evergreen Dr., Marathon, ON P0T 2E0
(888) 621-1989
www.cfno.fm
License: Marathon, ON held by North Superior Broadcasting Ltd.
Format: Adult Contemp; *Special Programming:* C&W 12 hrs wkly
Cora Cambly, Marketing Director
Bill Malcolm, Programming Director
Al Cresswell, News/Sports Director

Markham

CFMS-FM
105.9 MHz FM; 618 w; 21.1 meters
4 Island Grove, Brampton, ON L6X 0W6 Canada
(416) 738-7984; *Fax:* (416) 738-7984
License: Markham, ON held by Markham Radio

Meaford

CJGB-FM
08-01-2014; 99.3 MHz FM; 100 watts; 177 meters
206497 Hwy 26, Unit 7, Meaford, ON N4L 1W7 Canada
(519) 538-0993
www.jewelradio.com/new/993
License: Meaford, ON held by Dufferin Communications Inc.
Group Owner: Evanov Communications Inc.
Format: Adult Contemp, Easy Listening
Veronica Low, General Sales Mgr
Celena Negovetich, Promotions Coordinator
Laura D'Alessio, Assistant Promotions Coordinator

Midland

***CICZ-FM**
09-01-1993; 104.1 MHz FM; 20 kw
355 Cranston Cres., Midland, ON L4R 4L3 Canada
(705) 720-1991; *Fax:* (705) 526-3060
www.1041thedock.com
License: Midland, ON held by Larche Communications Inc.
Group Owner: Larche Communications Inc.
Format: Classic Rock
Linda Young, General Sales Mgr
Ted Roop, Programming Director
Phil Mestre, Promotions Manager
Brian Wicks, News Director
Josh Duncan, News Director
Matt Mise, Director, Digital Media
Shelley Barrey, Director of CreativeServices

Mississauga

CINA
12-22-2008; 1650 kHz AM; 5 kw-D, 680 w-N; N43 37 32 W79 37 52
1515 Britannia Rd. E., Suite 315, Mississauga, ON L4W 4K1 Canada
(416) 777-1650; *Fax:* (905) 795-9030
www.cinaradio.com
cinaradio@gmail.com
License: Mississauga, ON held by 1760791 Ontario Inc.
Neeti Ray, President

Moosonee

***CHMO(AM)**
02-29-1976; 1450 kHz AM; *Hrs Open:* 6 AM-11 PM; 50 w; N51 16 39 W80 38 40
Mailing Address: Box 400, Moosonee, ON P0L 1Y0 Canada
Second Address: 24 First St., Moosonee, ON P0L 1Y0
(705) 336-2466; *Fax:* (705) 336-2186
License: Moosonee, ON held by The James Bay Broadcasting Corp.
Population Served: 5,000; *Format:* Country, Variety/Diverse; *Special Programming:* Cree Indian 5 hrs wkly; *Hrs. of News Programming:* news progmg 10 hrs wkly; *No. News Employees:* 1; *Target Audience:* General.; *Adv. Rates:* 25; 25; 25; 25
John Kirk, President
Ernest Hunter, Station Manager
Jack Williams, Programming Director
George Witham, Chief Engineer

Napanee

CKYM-FM
01-01-2007; 88.7 MHz FM; 5 kw; N44 08 30 W77 04 33
11 Market Sq., Napanee, ON K7R 1J4 Canada
(613) 354-4554; *Fax:* (613) 354-3661
www.napaneetoday.ca
License: Napanee, ON held by My Broadcasting Corp.
Group Owner: My Broadcasting Corp.
Population Served: 15,511; *Arbitron Metro Market:* Greater Napanee, ON; *Format:* Adult Contemp
Pam Oliver, General Manager
Pam Oliver, General Sales Mgr
D'Arcy Magee, Group Program Director
Cindy Clyne, Group News Director
Marg Tubman, Group Administrator

New Liskeard

CJTT-FM
06-26-1998; 104.5 MHz FM; 10 kw
Mailing Address: PO Box 1058, New Liskeard, ON P0J 1P0 Canada
Second Address: 55 Whitewood Ave., New Liskeard, ON P0J 1P0
(705) 647-7334; *Fax:* (705) 647-8660
www.cjttfm.com
cjtt@cjttfm.com
License: New Liskeard, ON held by Connelly Communications Corp.
Nat'l Reps: Canadian Broadcast Sales
Population Served: 20,000; *No. News Employees:* 1
Gail Moore, General Manager

Newmarket

CKDX-FM
09-01-1994; 88.5 MHz FM; 11.3 kw
5312 Dundas St. W., Toronto, ON M9B 1B3 Canada
(416) 213-1035; *Fax:* (416) 233-8617
www.jewelradio.com/new/885
info@885thejewel.com
License: Newmarket, ON held by CKDX Radio Ltd.
Group Owner: Evanov Communications Inc.; (acq 12-21-2000).
Format: Adult Contemp; *Adv. Rates:* 100; 100; 100; 100
Veronica Low, General Sales Mgr
Laura D'Alessio, Promotions Coordinator
Grace Pascucci, Office Manager

***CHOP-FM**
09-28-2007; 102.7 MHz FM; 5 w; N44 02 49 W79 27 08
Pickering College, 16945 Bayview Ave., Newmarket, ON L3Y 4X2 Canada
(905) 895-1700
www.pickeringcollege.on.ca
info@pickeringcollege.on.ca
License: Newmarket, ON held by Pickering College.
Population Served: 80,400; *Arbitron Metro Market:* Newmarket, ON; *Format:* Sports, Talk
Peter Sturrup, General Manager
Kim Bilous, Executive Director of Development

Niagara Falls

CJED-FM
105.1 MHz FM; 406 w; 161 meters
4673 Ontario Ave., Niagara Falls, ON L2E 3R1 Canada
(905) 356-6710; *Fax:* (905) 356-0644
1051.2dayfm.ca
License: Niagara Falls, ON held by Vista Radio Ltd.
Group Owner: Vista Radio Ltd.; (acq 5-1-2009; with CKEY-FM Fort Erie)
Nat'l Reps: Target Broadcast Sales
Arbitron Metro Market: Buffalo-Niagara Falls, NY; *Format:* Contemporary Hits/Top 40; *Hrs. of News Programming:* news progmg 5 hrs wkly; *No. News Employees:* 3; *Target Audience:* 25-54.; *Adv. Rates:* 45; 42; 40; 42
Erica Fisher, News Director
Chris Barnatt, Producer

North Bay

CHUR-FM
01-01-1996; 100.5 MHz FM; 100 kw
273 Main St. E., North Bay, ON P1B 1B2 Canada
(705) 474-2000
www.kissnorthbay.com
License: North Bay, ON held by Rogers Broadcasting Ltd.
Group Owner: Rogers Broadcasting Ltd.; acq 4-19-2002; grpsl).
Format: Adult Contemp; *Target Audience:* 25-54.
Holly Cangiano, General Manager
Kevin Oschefski, Programming Director
Kelsey Richard, Promotions Supervisor
Lynn Larondeau, Sales/Advertising

CKAT
03-03-1931; 600 kHz AM; *Hrs Open:* 24; 10 kw-D, 5 kw-N, DA-1
273 Main St. E., North Bay, ON P1B 1B2 Canada
(705) 474-2000; *Fax:* (705) 476-8400
www.country600.com
License: North Bay, ON held by Rogers Broadcasting Ltd.
Group Owner: Rogers Broadcasting Ltd.; acq 4-19-02; grpsl).
Population Served: 56,000; *Format:* Country; *Hrs. of News Programming:* news progmg 6 hrs wkly; *No. News Employees:* 5; *Target Audience:* 25-54.
Lynn Larondeau, General Sales Mgr
Mike Bissett, Programming Director
Adam Contant, Promotions Manager
Richard Coffin, News Director

CKFX-FM
01-19-1967; 101.9 MHz FM; *Hrs Open:* 24; 100 kw; Ant 350 ft
273 Main St. E., North Bay, ON P1B 1B2 Canada
(705) 474-2000
www.foxradio.ca
License: North Bay, ON held by Rogers Broadcasting Ltd.
Group Owner: Rogers Broadcasting Ltd.
Format: Rock/AOR
Holly Cangiano, General Manager
Lynn Larondeau, Sales Supervisor
Mitch Belanger, Programming Director
Lisa Laporte, Promotions Supervisor

CFXN-FM
07-12-2006; 106.3 MHz FM; *Hrs Open:* 9am-5pm; 10 kw; 145.4 meters; 46 18 10 N 79 24 39 W
118 Main St. E., North Bay, ON P1B 1A8 Canada
(705) 475-9991; *Fax:* (705) 475-9058
www.mynorthbaynow.com
phobbs@vistaradio.ca
License: North Bay, ON held by Vista Radio Ltd.
Group Owner: Vista Radio Ltd.
Population Served: 50,396; *Format:* Contemporary Hits/Top 40, Variety/Diverse; *No. News Employees:* 2
Peter Hobbs, Regional Cluster Manager
Ryan Griffiths, Regional Cluster Program Director
Steph Ferris, Promotions
Stu Campaigne, News
Cindy Charlebois, Integrated Marketing Executive

North York

***CHRY-FM**
01-01-1987; 105.5 MHz FM; *Hrs Open:* 24; 158 w
4700 Keele St., 413 Student Ctr., York University, Toronto, ON M3J 1P3 Canada
(416) 736-5293
www.chry.fm
info@chry.fm
License: North York, ON held by CHRY Community Radio Inc.
Format: Variety/Diverse; *Special Programming:* Afghan, African, Caribbean, French, Hebrew, Jazz,; *Hrs. of News Programming:* 10; *No. News Employees:* 2; *Target Audience:* General; campus community
Danae Peart, Operations Dir
Matthew Fava, Programming Director

Oakville

CJMR
06-17-1974; 1190 kHz AM; *Hrs Open:* 24
284 Church Street, Oakville, ON L6J 7N2 Canada
(905) 271-1320; *Fax:* (905) 845-9171
www.cjmr1320.ca
License: Oakville, ON held by Trafalgar Broadcasting Ltd.

Nat'l Reps: Target Broadcast Sales
Format: Ethnic; *Adv. Rates:* 70 per 30 sec 105 per 60 sec
Michael Caine, President
Harry McDonald, General Manager

CJYE
11-17-1956; 1250 kHz AM; *Hrs Open:* 24
284 Church Street, Oakville, ON L6J 7N2 Canada
(905) 845-2821; *Fax:* (905) 842-1250
www.joy1250.ca
contact@joy1250.ca
License: Oakville, ON held by Trafalgar Broadcasting Ltd.
Nat'l Reps: Western Regional Broadcast Sales
Arbitron Metro Market: Oakville, ON; *Format:* Christian
Michael Caine, President
Harry McDonald, General Manager
Michael Caine, Founder

Ohsweken

***CKRZ-FM**
01-01-1991; 100.3 MHz FM; *Hrs Open:* 6 AM-11 PM; 250 w
Mailing Address: Box 189, Ohsweken, ON N0A 1M0 Canada
Second Address: 1721 Chiefswood Rd., Oashweken, ON
(519) 445-4140; *Fax:* (519) 445-0177
License: Ohsweken, Haldimond County, ON held by Southern Onkwehon: We Nishinabec Indigenous Communications Society.
Format: Country, Variety/Diverse; *Hrs. of News Programming:* news progmg 4.5 hrs wkly; *No. News Employees:* 1; *Target Audience:* General.
Loreen Harris, General Sales Mgr
Kathy Montour, Programming Director

Orangeville

***CIDC-FM**
05-01-1987; 103.5 MHz FM; *Hrs Open:* 24; 30.7 kw
5312 Dundas St. W., Toronto, ON M9B 1B3 Canada
(416) 213-1035; *Fax:* (416) 233-8617
www.z1035.com
License: Orangeville, ON held by Dufferin Communications Inc.
Group Owner: Evanov Communications Inc.; (acq 9-28-94).
Format: Contemporary Hits/Top 40; *No. News Employees:* 1; *Target Audience:* 18-44.; *Adv. Rates:* 180; 180; 180; 180.
Bill Evanov, President
Bruce Campbell, General Manager

CKMO-FM
11-06-2014; 101.5 MHz FM; *Hrs Open:* 24; 338 watts
22 Mill St., Unit 118, Orangeville, ON L9W 2M3 Canada
(226) 790-6936
www.orangevilletoday.ca
License: Orangeville, ON held by My Broadcasting Corp.
Group Owner: My Broadcasting Corp.
Format: Adult Contemp; *No. News Employees:* 1
Gail James, General Manager
Gail James, General Sales Mgr
D'Arcy Magee, Group Program Director
Cindy Clyne, Group News Director
Marg Tubman, Group Administrator

Orillia

CICX-FM
09-07-1943; 105.9 MHz FM; *Hrs Open:* 24; 10.6 kw
7 Progress Dr., RR #1, Orillia, ON L3V 6H1 Canada
(705) 722-5429; *Fax:* (705) 326-1816
www.kicx106.com
License: Orillia, Simcoe County, ON held by Larche Communications Inc.
Group Owner: Larche Communications Inc.; (acq 1-28-2008; exchange for CIKZ-FM Kitchener-Waterloo).
Format: Country; *Hrs. of News Programming:* news progmg 2 hrs wkly; *No. News Employees:* 2; *Adv. Rates:* 35; 31; 33; 20
Paul Larche, President
Linda Young, General Sales Mgr
Jack Latimer, Programming Director
Alex Murdoch, Promotions Manager
Martin Vanderwoude, News Director
Shelley Barry, Creative Director
Trina Ley-Duncan, Promotions Director

CISO-FM
02-24-2011; 89.1 MHz FM
490 West St. N., Suite 2, Orillia, ON L3V 5E8 Canada
(705) 325-9786; *Fax:* (705) 325-2600
www.sunshine89.ca
info@sunshine89.ca
License: Orillia, ON held by Bayshore Broadcasting Corp.
Group Owner: Bayshore Broadcasting Corp.
Format: Adult Contemp

Kevin Brown, VP Sales and Marketing
JD Hunter, Programming Director
Sarah Hewitt, Promotions Co-ordinator
Jim Birchard, News Director

Oshawa

CKDO
10-05-1946; 1580 kHz AM; *Hrs Open:* 24; 10 kw
1200 Airport Blvd., Suite 207, Oshawa, ON L1J 8P5 Canada
(905) 571-0949; *Fax:* (905) 571-1150
www.ckdo.ca
License: Oshawa, ON held by Durham Radio Inc.
Group Owner: Durham Radio Inc.; (acq 4-23-2003; C$3.9 million with co-located FM).
Format: Oldies; *Special Programming:* Relg one hr wkly; *Hrs. of News Programming:* news progmg 9 hrs wkly; *No. News Employees:* 4; *Target Audience:* 45 plus.
Lisa Walker, Retail Sales Mgr
Steve Kassay, VP, Programming
Adriane Vogel, Promotions
Gary Bernarde, Music Director
Steve Macaulay, VP, Sales
Rob Snoek, Sports Director

CKGE-FM
09-12-1957; 94.9 MHz FM; *Hrs Open:* 24; 50 kw; 474 ft; N43 57 15 W78 48 24
1200 Airport Blvd., Suite 207, Oshawa, ON L1J 8P5 Canada
(905) 571-0949; *Fax:* (905) 571-1150
www.therock.fm
therock@therock.fm
License: Oshawa, ON held by Durham Radio Inc.
Group Owner: Durham Radio Inc.
Format: Rock/AOR; *Hrs. of News Programming:* news progmg 5 hrs wkly; *No. News Employees:* 4; *Target Audience:* 35-54.
Lisa Walker, Retail Sales Mgr
Doug Elliot, Programming Director
Adriane Vogel, Promotions
Steve Macaulay, VP, Sales
Steve Kassay, VP, Programming

Ottawa

***CBO-FM**
01-07-1991; 91.5 MHz FM; 20 kw
Mailing Address: Box 3220, Station C, Ottawa, ON K1Y 1E4 Canada
Second Address: Ottawa Broadcast Centre, 181 Queen St., Ottawa, ON K1P 1K9
(613) 288-6000
License: Ottawa, ON held by CBC/Radio Canada
Nat'l Network: CBC Radio One
Remi Rancine, Chairman
Hubert Lacroix, CEO
Ruth Zowdu, Executive Producer
Kim Drummond, Senior Production News
Paula Waddell, Executive Producer
Rhonda Madey, Sales

***CBOFFM**
09-12-1974; 90.7 MHz FM
Box 3220, Station C, Ottawa, ON Canada
(613) 724-1200,(613) 562-8521; *Fax:* (613) 562-8520
www.cbc.radio-canada.ca/regions/ottawa
License: Ottawa, ON held by Societe Radio-Canada.
Nat'l Network: Radio Canada
Patricia Pleszczynska, Operations Dir
Judith Bleier, Operations Manager

***CBOQ-FM**
02-18-1947; 103.3 MHz FM; 70 kw
Mailing Address: PO Box 3220, Station C, Ottawa, ON K1Y 1E4 Canada
Second Address: 181 Queen Street, Ottawa, ON K1P 1K9
(613) 288-6000
www.cbc.ca/news/canada/ottawa
License: Ottawa, ON held by CBC/Radio Canada
Nat'l Network: CBC Radio Two
Jennifer Beard, Web Producer
Ruth Zowdu, Executive Producer, Radio
Paula Waddell, Executive Producer, News
Kim Drummond, Senior Producer
Rhonda Madey, Sales

***CBOX-FM**
01-01-1990; 102.5 MHz FM; 70 kw; Ant 1,077 ft
Box 3220, Station C, Ottawa, ON K1Y 1E4 Canada
(613) 724-1200,(613) 562-8521; *Fax:* (613) 562-8520
www.icimusique.ca
License: Ottawa, ON held by CBC/Radio-Canada
Nat'l Network: Radio Canada

Robert Rabinovitch, CEO
Gilles Tessier, Operations Dir
Miriam Fry, General Manager

CFGO
06-07-1964; 1200 kHz AM; *Hrs Open:* 24; 50 kw-U, DA-2
87 George St., Ottawa, ON K1N 9H7 Canada
(613) 750-1200; *Fax:* (613) 739-4040
www.tsn.ca/radio/ottawa-1200
License: Ottawa, ON held by Bell Media Ottawa Radio Partnership
Group Owner: Bell Media Inc.; (acq 9-10-99; for 87.5%).
Population Served: 1,000,000; *Format:* Sports; *No. News Employees:* 5; *Target Audience:* 18-34; men
Ryan Shortt, Director of Local Sales
Brittany Asselin, Promotions Coordinator
Harrie Jones, Chief Engineer

CFRA
05-03-1947; 580 kHz AM; *Hrs Open:* 24; 50 kw-D, 30 kw-N, DA-2
87 George St., Ottawa, ON K1N 9H7 Canada
(613) 789-2486; *Fax:* (613) 523-6423,(613) 738-5024
www.cfra.com
feedback@cfra.com
License: Ottawa, ON held by Bell Media Ottawa Radio Partnership
Group Owner: Bell Media Inc.
Nat'l Network: ABC
Format: Talk; *Hrs. of News Programming:* News progmg 24 hrs wkly; *Target Audience:* 35-54.
Brittany Asselin, Promotions Coordinator
Harrie Jones, Chief Engineer

***CHEZ-FM**
03-25-1977; 106.1 MHz FM; *Hrs Open:* 24; 100 kw
2001 Thurston Dr., Ottawa, ON K1G 6C9 Canada
(613) 750-1061
www.chez106.com
License: Ottawa, ON held by Rogers Broadcasting Ltd.
Group Owner: Rogers Broadcasting Ltd.; (acq 7-2-99; grpsl)
Format: Rock/AOR; *Hrs. of News Programming:* news progmg 2 hrs wkly; *No. News Employees:* 3; *Target Audience:* 25-54; males
Jenna McQueen, Promotions Coordinator

CHRI-FM
03-06-1997; 99.1 MHz FM; *Hrs Open:* 24; 25.3 kw; 551 ft; N45 13 01 W75 37 51
1010 Thomas Spratt Pl., Suite 3, Ottawa, ON K1G 5L5 Canada
(613) 247-1440; *Fax:* (613) 247-7128
www.chri.ca
chri@chri.ca
License: Ottawa, Canada County, ON held by Christian Hit Radio Inc.
Population Served: 1,300,000; *Special Programming:* Children and Family Programming; *Hrs. of News Programming:* news progmg 2 hrs wkly; *No. News Employees:* 1; *Target Audience:* 18-44.; *Adv. Rates:* 45; 25; 35; na
Ethel Mahoney, President
Bill Stevens, General Manager
Brock Tozer, Programming Director

***CHUO-FM**
05-31-1991; 89.1 MHz FM; *Hrs Open:* 24; 18.2 kw; N45 30 11 W75 51 02
65 University PVT., Suite 0038, Ottawa, ON K1N 9A5 Canada
(613) 562-5965
www.chuo.fm
info@chuo.fm
License: Ottawa, ON held by Radio Ottawa Inc.
Population Served: 900,000; *Format:* French; *Special Programming:* Ger 2 hrs, jazz 5 hrs, relg 2 hrs, Sp 3 hrs, Chine; *Target Audience:* General.
Erin Flynn, Station Manager
Emmanuel Sayer, Programming Director
Olivier Charbonneau, Assistant Programming Director

CIWW
06-01-1949; 1310 kHz AM; *Hrs Open:* 24; 50 kw
2001 Thurston Drive, Ottawa, ON K1G 6C9 Canada
(613) 736-2001
www.1310news.com
License: Ottawa, ON held by Rogers Broadcasting Ltd.
Group Owner: Rogers Broadcasting Ltd.
Format: News, News/Talk, Sports, Talk
Mark Campbell, News Director

CJMJ-FM
08-13-1991; 100.3 MHz FM; *Hrs Open:* 24; 100 kw
87 George St., Ottawa, ON K1N 9H7 Canada
Fax: (613) 789-2486
www.majic100.fm

License: Ottawa, ON held by Bell Media Ottawa Radio Partnership
Group Owner: Bell Media Inc.
Population Served: 1,000,000; *Format:* Adult Contemp; *Target Audience:* 25-44; female
Ryan Shortt, General Sales Mgr
Sarah Gray, Promotions Supervisor
Harrie Jones, Chief Engineer
Candace Drover, Music Director
Jodi Hamilton, Creative Director

CISS-FM
10-29-1969; 105.3 MHz FM; 100 kw; Ant 1,077 ft
2001 Thurston Dr., Ottawa, ON K1G 6C9 Canada
(613) 736-2001
www.1053kissfm.com
License: Ottawa, ON held by Rogers Broadcasting Ltd.
Group Owner: Rogers Broadcasting Ltd.
Format: Adult Contemp, Contemporary Hits/Top 40
Mark Hunter, General Sales Mgr

***CKCUFM**
11-15-1975; 93.1 MHz FM; *Hrs Open:* 24; kw
Room 517 University Centre, 1125 Colonel By Drive, Ottawa, ON K1S 5B6 Canada
(613) 520-2898; *Fax:* (613) 520-4060
www.ckcufm.com
info@ckcufm.com
License: Ottawa, ON held by Radio Carleton Inc.
Format: Variety/Diverse; *Special Programming:* Jazz 15 hrs, Black 12 hrs, Fr 2 hrs, Pol one hr, V; *Hrs. of News Programming:* news progmg 25 hrs wkly; *No. News Employees:* 2; *Target Audience:* General; alternative rock,spoken word, ethnic audience
Matthew Crosier, Station Manager
Dave Aardvark, Programming Director
Dylan Hunter, Production Manager

***CKDJ-FM**
10-03-1994; 107.9 MHz FM; 100 w
1385 Woodroffe Ave., Algonquin College, Ottawa, ON K2G 1V8 Canada
(613) 750-2535
www.ckdj.net
ckdj@algonquincollege.com
License: Ottawa, ON held by CKDJ-FM Algonquin Radio.
Population Served: 300,000; *Format:* Alternative; *Target Audience:* 17-24; collegel students
Don Crockford, General Manager
Ryan Lindsay, Station Manager

CKKL-FM
01-01-1959; 93.9 MHz FM; *Hrs Open:* 24; 95 kw; Ant 1,077 ft
87 George St., Ottawa, ON K1N 9H7 Canada
(613) 789-2486; *Fax:* (613) 739-4040
www.newcountry94.com
License: Ottawa, ON held by Bell Media Ottawa Radio Partnership
Group Owner: Bell Media Inc.
Nat'l Network: ABC
Format: Country; *Hrs. of News Programming:* news progmg one hr wkly; *No. News Employees:* 2; *Target Audience:* 18-34.
Dayna Bourgoin, Program Director
Sarah Gray, Promotions Supervisor
Harrie Jones, Engineering Dir

CKQB-FM
09-01-1994; 106.9 MHz FM; *Hrs Open:* 24; 84 kw
1504 Merivale Rd., Ottawa, ON K2E 6Z5 Canada
(613) 225-1069; *Fax:* (613) 226-3381
www.jumpradio.ca
beth.paris@corusent.com
License: Ottawa, ON held by 8324433 Canada Inc.
Group Owner: Corus Entertainment Inc.; (acq 10-29-2007; grpsl)
Format: Contemporary Hits/Top 40; *Hrs. of News Programming:* news progmg one hr wkly; *No. News Employees:* 3; *Target Audience:* 18-49; professionals
Stephanie Hunter, Brand Director
Alex Stone, Sales Director
Kailey Klempner, Content Coordinator
Krista Datars, Promotions Director
Mike Lavallee, Music Director

CIHT-FM
02-07-2003; 89.9 MHz FM; 27 kw
6 Antares Dr., Suite 100, Ottawa, ON K2E 8A9 Canada
(613) 750-8990; *Fax:* (613) 723-7016
www.hot899.com
License: Ottawa, ON held by NewCap Inc.
Group Owner: NewCap Inc.
Population Served: 812,135; *Arbitron Metro Market:* Ottawa, ON; *Format:* Contemporary Hits/Top 40; *Target Audience:* 25-34; females
Scott Broderick, General Manager
Josie Geuer, Programming Director

CJLL-FM
01-01-2003; 97.9 MHz FM; *Hrs Open:* 24; 6.77 kw
CHIN Radio Ottawa, 30 Murray St., Suite 100, Ottawa, ON K1N 5M4 Canada
(613) 244-0979; *Fax:* (613) 244-3858
www.chinradioottawa.com
License: Ottawa, ON held by Radio 1540 Ltd.
Population Served: 812,135; *Arbitron Metro Market:* Ottawa, ON; *Format:* Ethnic; *Hrs. of News Programming:* 12; *No. News Employees:* 2; *Target Audience:* Ethnic 12 plus; mutlicultural; *Adv. Rates:* 60; 60; 60; 50
Francesco Di Candia, Operations Dir
Gary Michaels, Programming Director

CILV-FM
12-26-2005; 88.5 MHz FM; 2.3 kw
6 Antares Dr., Phase I, Suite 100, Ottawa, ON K2E 8A9 Canada
(613) 688-8888; *Fax:* (613) 723-7016
www.live885.com
License: Ottawa, ON held by NewCap Inc.
Group Owner: NewCap Inc.
Population Served: 812,135; *Arbitron Metro Market:* Ottawa, ON; *Format:* Alternative
Scott Broderick, General Manager
Mark Russett, General Sales Mgr
Dan Youngs, Programming Director
Maggie McAdam, Promotions

CJWL-FM
02-01-2006; 98.5 MHz FM; 485 w
127 York St., Ottawa, ON K1N 5T4 Canada
(613) 241-9850; *Fax:* (613) 241-9852
www.jewelradio.com/new/985
silver@985thejewel.com
License: Ottawa, ON held by Ottawa Media Inc.
Group Owner: Evanov Communications Inc.
Population Served: 812,135; *Arbitron Metro Market:* Ottawa, ON; *Format:* Adult Contemp; *Target Audience:* 45 plus.
Bill Evanov, President
Ted Silver, Programming Director
Vanessa Malloy, Promotions

CKAV-FM-9
01-01-2007; 95.7 MHz FM; 6 kw
PO Box 87, Station E, Toronto, ON M6H 4E1 Canada
(416) 703-1287; *Fax:* (416) 703-4328
aboriginalvoices.com
info@aboriginalvoices.com
License: Ottawa, ON held by Voices Radio's broadcasting licenses have been revoked by the CRTC. All stations are now broadcasting solely on voicesradio.ca
Group Owner: Voices Radio Inc.
Population Served: 2,615,060; *Arbitron Metro Market:* Toronto, ON; *Format:* Ethnic
Roy Hennessy, Operations Dir
Patrice Mousseau, Programming Director

CIDG-FM
06-07-2010; 101.9 MHz FM; *Hrs Open:* 24 hours; 1.793 kw; 98 meters
380 Hunt Club Road, Suite 203, Ottawa, ON K1V 1C1 Canada
(613) 730-1019; *Fax:* (613) 7301092
www.dawgfm.com
License: Ottawa, ON held by Todd Bernard Ottawa Inc
Todd Bernard, General Manager
Yves Trottier, Operations Manager
Alyssa Delle Palme, Promotions Manager
J-Man, Music Director

CJFO-FM
11-15-2010; 94.5 MHz FM; 3.25 kw
245 Avenue McArthur, Ottawa, ON K1L 6P3 Canada
(613) 745-5529; *Fax:* (613) 745-7004
www.cjfofm.com
info@cjfofm.com
License: Ottawa, ON held by La Radio Communautaire Francophone D'Ottawa
Gilles Poulin, CEO
Lucien Bradet, President

CJOT-FM
05-27-2010; 99.7 MHz FM; 45 kw
1504 Merivale Rd., Ottawa, ON K2E 6Z5 Canada
(613) 225-1069; *Fax:* (613) 226-3381
www.boom997.com
alex.stone@corusent.com
License: Ottawa, Renfrew County, ON held by 8324433 Canada Inc.
Group Owner: Corus Entertainment Inc.
Format: Oldies; *Target Audience:* Baby boomers
Stephanie Hunter, Brand Director
Alex Stone, Sales Director
Krista Datars, Promotions Director
Ryan Forsyth, Promotions Assistant
Kailey Klempner, Content Coordinator
Beth Paris, Executive Sales Assistant

Owen Sound

CFOS
03-01-1940; 560 kHz AM; *Hrs Open:* 24
Mailing Address: P.O. Box 280, Owen Sound, ON N4K 5P5 Canada
Second Address: 270 9th St. E., Owen Sound, ON N4K 1N8
(519) 376-2030; *Fax:* (519) 371-4242
www.560cfos.ca
License: Owen Sound, ON held by Bayshore Broadcasting Corp.
Group Owner: Bayshore Broadcasting Corp.
Nat'l Reps: Target Broadcast Sales; *Wire Services:* BN Wire
Format: News, News/Talk, Oldies, Talk; *Hrs. of News Programming:* news progmg 12 hrs wkly; *No. News Employees:* 7; *Target Audience:* 35 plus.
Ross Kentner, General Manager
Kevin Brown, VP Sales and Marketing
Manny Paiva, News Manager

CIXK-FM
01-03-1989; 106.5 MHz FM; *Hrs Open:* 24; 100 kw; 555 ft; N44 44 37 W80 54 16
Mailing Address: P.O. Box 280, Owen Sound, ON N4K 5P5 Canada
Second Address: 270 9th St. E., Owen Sound, ON N4K 1N8
(519) 376-2030; *Fax:* (519) 371-4242
www.mix1065.ca
License: Owen Sound, ON held by Bayshore Broadcasting Corp.
Group Owner: Bayshore Broadcasting Corp.
Nat'l Reps: Target Broadcast Sales; *Wire Services:* BN Wire
Format: Adult Contemp; *No. News Employees:* 7; *Target Audience:* 18-40.
Ross Kentner, General Manager
Kevin Brown, VP Sales and Marketing
Manny Paiva, News Manager

CKYC-FM
09-04-2001; 93.7 MHz FM; *Hrs Open:* 24; 31.6 kw
Mailing Address: P.O. Box 280, Owen Sound, ON N4K 5P5 Canada
Second Address: 270 9th St. E., Owen Sound, ON N4K 1N8
(519) 376-2030; *Fax:* (519) 371-4242
www.country93.ca
License: Owen Sound, ON held by Bayshore Broadcasting Corp.
Group Owner: Bayshore Broadcasting Corp.
Nat'l Reps: Target Broadcast Sales
Population Served: 21,688; *Arbitron Metro Market:* Owen Sound, ON; *Format:* Country; *Target Audience:* 25-54; adult
Ross Kentner, General Manager
Kevin Brown, VP Sales and Marketing

CJOS-FM
07-26-2010; 92.3 MHz FM; 9.4 kw; 214 meters
787 9th Ave. E., Owen Sound, ON N4K 3E6 Canada
(519) 470-7626; *Fax:* (519) 470-7631
www.923thedock.com
License: Owen Sound, ON held by Larche Communications Inc.
Group Owner: Larche Communications Inc.
Format: Contemporary Hits/Top 40
Rebecca Dunphy, General Sales Mgr
Don Vail, Programming Director
Kathleen Scott, Promotions Director
Diana Meder, News Director
Matt Mise, Director of Digital Media

Paris

CJIQ-FM
01-08-2001; 88.3 MHz FM; *Hrs Open:* 24; kw
Canada
(519) 748-5220 x. 3223
www.cjiq.fm
mthurnell@conestogac.on.ca
License: Paris, ON held by Conestoga College Communications Corp.
Arbitron Metro Market: Kitchener, ON; *Format:* Variety/Diverse
Mike Thurnell, Program Director/CJIQ Coordinator

CBLA-FM-2
89.1 MHz FM; 5 kw; 220.5 meters; N43 15 39 W80 26 38
117 King Street West, Kitchener, ON N2G 1A7 Canada
(519) 581-1384
www.cbc.ca/kitchener-waterloo/
License: Paris, ON held by CBC
Nat'l Network: CBC Radio One

Parry Sound

CKLP-FM
103.3 MHz FM; *Hrs Open:* 24
60 James St., Suite 301, Parry Sound, ON P2A 1T5 Canada
(705) 746-2163; *Fax:* (705) 746-4292
www.myparrysoundnow.com
jhodge@vistaradio.ca
License: Parry Sound, ON held by Vista Radio Ltd.
Group Owner: Vista Radio Ltd.; (acq 11-9-01; C$2,025,000).
Nat'l Reps: Target Broadcast
Population Served: 60,000; *Format:* Contemporary Hits/Top 40; *Special Programming:* Canadian First Nation 1 hr feature; *Hrs. of News Programming:* news progmg 12 hrs wkly; *No. News Employees:* 2; *Target Audience:* General.
Jenny Hodge, Regional Cluster Manager and General Sales
Dave Newman, Regional Cluster Program Director
James King, News Director
Kate McCracken, Sales Executive

Pembroke

CHVR-FM
05-06-1996; 96.7 MHz FM; 100 kw
595 Pembroke St. E., Pembroke, ON K8A 3L7 Canada
(613) 735-9670; *Fax:* (613) 735-7748
www.star96.ca
star96@bellmedia.ca
License: Pembroke, ON held by Bell Media Radio G.P.
Group Owner: Bell Media Inc.; (acq 10-29-2007; grpsl).
Population Served: 500,000; *Format:* Country; *Target Audience:* 25-54.
Richard Gray, General Manager
Tracy McBride, General Sales Mgr

CIMY-FM
09-01-2005; 104.9 MHz FM; 16.6 kw; 90.5 meters
84 Isabella St., Pembroke, ON K8A 5S5 Canada
(613) 735-6936; *Fax:* (613) 732-4054
www.pembroketoday.ca
License: Pembroke, ON held by My Broadcasting Corp.
Group Owner: My Broadcasting Corp.
Format: Adult Contemp
Marc Poirier, General Manager
Marc Poirier, General Sales Mgr
D'Arcy Magee, Programming Director
Cindy Clyne, News Director

Penetanguishene

***CFRH-FM**
09-24-1999; 88.1 MHz FM; *Hrs Open:* 24; 8.6 kw; N44 46 10 W79 59 25
63 Main Street, PO Box 5099, Penetanguishene, ON L9M 2G3 Canada
(705) 549-8288; *Fax:* (705) 549-6463
www.vaguefm.ca
License: Penetanguishene, Simcoe County, ON held by La Cle d'la Baie en Huronie
Regional Reps: Radio Unie Target
Population Served: 50,000; *Target Audience:* Francophone; francophone minority in mid-southern Ontario; *Adv. Rates:* 15 per 30 seconds
Pierre Casault, CEO
Melanie Bouchard, Station Manager
Michel Paiement, Host
Marc Lalonde, Music Director

Perth

CHLK-FM
07-01-2007; 88.1 MHz FM; 2.8 kw; 91.5 meters; N44 54 34 W76 16 51
43 Wilson St. W., Perth, ON K7H 2N3 Canada
(613) 264-8811; *Fax:* (613) 264-1119
www.lake88.ca
info@lake88.ca
License: Perth, ON held by Perth FM Radio Inc.
Norm Wright, General Manager

Peterborough

***CFFF-FM**
01-01-1969; 92.7 MHz FM; *Hrs Open:* 24hrs; 700 w
715 George St., N., Peterborough, ON K9H 3T2 Canada
(705) 741-4011
www.trentu.ca/trentradio
info@trentradio.ca
License: Peterborough, Peterborough County, ON held by Trent Radio.
Nat'l Reps: Target Broadcast Sales
Population Served: 120,000; *Target Audience:* General.
John K. Muir, General Manager
James Kerr, Programming Director
Jill Staveley, Production Manager

CKQM-FM
09-16-1977; 105.1 MHz FM; *Hrs Open:* 24; 7.5 kw; Ant 910 ft; N44 17 36 W78 21 20
59 George St. N., Peterborough, ON K9J 6Y8 Canada
(705) 742-8844; *Fax:* (705) 742-1417
www.country105.fm
country105@bellmedia.ca
License: Peterborough, Peterborough County, ON held by Bell Media Ontario Regional Radio Partnership
Group Owner: Bell Media Inc.; (acq 6-22-2007; grpsl).
Hrs. of News Programming: news progmg 4 hrs wkly; *No. News Employees:* 3; *Target Audience:* 25-64.
Steve Fawcett, General Manager
Wanda Bergshoeff, General Sales Mgr
Brian Young, Programming Director
Mel Hannah, Promotions Coordinator
Ray Hebert, Music Director

CKWF-FM
101.5 MHz FM; *Hrs Open:* 24; 15.2 kw
151 King St., Suite 200, Peterborough, ON K9J 2R8 Canada
(705) 748-6101; *Fax:* (705) 742-7708
www.thewolf.ca
brenda.obrien@corusent.com
License: Peterborough, ON held by 591989 B.C. Ltd.
Group Owner: Corus Entertainment Inc.
Format: Rock/AOR; *No. News Employees:* 2
Brian Ellis, Operations Manager
Brenda O'Brien, Sales Manager
Rob Seguin, Programming Director
Carey Walker, Promotions and New Media Director
Ryan Lalonde, Creative Services Producer
Scott Hanes, Music Director

CJMB-FM
11-24-2004; 90.5 MHz FM; *Hrs Open:* 24; 0.125 kw
727 Lansdowne St. W., Unit 201, Peterborough, ON K9J 1Z2 Canada
(705) 874-0905; *Fax:* (705) 748-6936
www.extrapeterborough.ca
License: Peterborough, ON held by My Broadcasting Corp.
Group Owner: My Broadcasting Corp.
Population Served: 112,000; *Format:* Sports, Talk; *No. News Employees:* 5; *Target Audience:* 18-40.; *Adv. Rates:* 18; 14; 16; 10
Brian Armstrong, General Manager
Brian Armstrong, General Sales Mgr
D'Arcy Magee, Programming Director
Cindy Clyne, Group News Director
Marg Tubman, Group Administrator

CKPT-FM
09-10-2007; 99.7 MHz FM; *Hrs Open:* 24; 17 kw; Ant 301 ft; N44 17 36 W78 21 20
59 George St. N., Peterborough, ON K9J 6Y8 Canada
(705) 742-8844; *Fax:* (705) 742-1417
www.energy997.ca
energy997@bellmedia.com
License: Peterborough, ON held by Bell Media Ontario Regional Radio Partnership
Group Owner: Bell Media Inc.
Format: Adult Contemp; *Hrs. of News Programming:* news progmg 2 hrs wkly; *No. News Employees:* 3; *Target Audience:* 18-54; 60% women.
Steve Fawcett, General Manager
Wanda Bergshoeff, General Sales Mgr
Brian Young, Programming Director
Mel Hannah, Promotions Coordinator

CJWV-FM
06-07-2011; 96.7 MHz FM; 6 kw; 233 meters
360 George Street N, Unit 1, Petersburgh, ON K9H 7E7 Canada
(707) 876-7773
License: Peterborough, ON held by Pineridge Broadcasting Inc
Don Conway, President

Petersborough

CKRU-FM
06-15-2009; 100.5 MHz FM; 15 kw; N44 17 36 W78 21 19
151 King St., Suite 200, Petersborough, ON K9J 2R8 Canada
(705) 748-6101; *Fax:* (705) 742-7708
www.1005freshradio.ca
License: Petersborough, ON held by 591989 B.C. Ltd.
Group Owner: Corus Entertainment Inc.
Format: Adult Contemp; *Target Audience:* Women
Brenda O'Brien, General Sales Mgr
Rob Seguin, Programming Director
Carey Walker, Promotions and New Media Director
Gord Gibb, Music Director
Ryan Lablonde, Creative Services, Producer
Sue Korytko, Office Administrator

Port Elgin

CFPS-FM
01-01-2005; 97.9 MHz FM; *Hrs Open:* 24; 3.8 kw
382 Goderich St., Port Elgin, ON N0H 2C1 Canada
(519) 832-9800; *Fax:* (519) 832-9808
www.98thebeach.ca
info@98thebeach.ca
License: Port Elgin, ON held by Bayshore Broadcasting Corp.
Group Owner: Bayshore Broadcasting Corp.
Nat'l Reps: Target Broadcast Sales
Population Served: 95,142; *Format:* Adult Contemp; *Target Audience:* 18-54.
Ross Kentner, General Manager
Kevin Brown, VP Sales and Marketing

Prescott

CKPP-FM
10-22-2015; 107.9 MHz FM
119 King St. W, Prescott, ON K0E 1T0 Canada
(613) 925-9779
www.myprescottnow.com
tlamoureux@vistaradio.ca
License: Prescott, ON held by Vista Radio Ltd.
Group Owner: Vista Radio Ltd.
Format: Adult Contemp
Tracy Lamoureux, General Manager & Sales Manager
Drew Hosick, Programming Director
Marie Cassidy, Regional News Director
Kapila Ratnayake, Chief Engineer
Lisa Campbell, Integrated Marketing Executive

Red Lake

CKDR-5-FM
01-01-2008; 97.1 MHz FM; 420 w; N51 01 12 W93 49
51*Rebroadcasts:* Rebroadcasts CKDR-FM Dryden 99%
122 King St., Dryden, ON P8N 1C2 Canada
(807) 223-2355; *Fax:* (807) 223-5090
www.ckdr.net
ckdr@radioabl.ca
License: Red Lake, Sunset County, ON held by Northwoods Broadcasting Ltd.
Group Owner: Acadia Broadcasting Ltd.; (acq 5-1-2007; grpsl)
Population Served: 7,617; *Arbitron Metro Market:* Dryden, ON; *Format:* Contemporary Hits/Top 40
Richard McCarthy, Operations Dir
Bruce Walchuck, Station Manager
Mike Ebbeling, News Director
Michelle Nault, Traffic Manager
Chris Pollard, Creative Director
Roxanne McGee, Sales
Val Artimowich, Sales

Renfrew

CHMY-FM
08-01-2004; 96.1 MHz FM; 7.1 kw; 128.5 meters
Mailing Address: Box 961, Renfrew, ON K7V 4H4 Canada
Second Address: 321-B Raglan St. S., Renfrew, ON K7V 4H4
(613) 432-6936; *Fax:* (613) 432-1086
www.renfrewtoday.ca
License: Renfrew, ON held by My Broadcasting Corp.
Group Owner: My Broadcasting Corp.
Format: Adult Contemp
Angela Kluke, General Manager
Angela Kluke, General Sales Mgr
D'Arcy Magee, Programming Director
Cindy Clyne, News Director
Marg Tubman, Group Administrator

CJHR-FM
12-11-2006; 98.7 MHz FM; kw
3009 Burnstown Road, Renfrew, ON K7V 4H4 Canada
(613) 432-9873; *Fax:* (613) 432-9103
www.valleyheritageradio.ca
License: Renfrew, ON held by Valley Heritage Radio.
Arbitron Metro Market: Renfrew, ON; *Format:* Country

RADIO - CANADA

Denzil Ferguson, President
Jim Long, Station Manager
Fay Kolpin, Vice President

Richmond Hill

CFMJ
07-01-1957; 640 kHz AM; *Hrs Open:* 24
Corus Quay, 25 Dockside Dr., Toronto, ON M5A 0B5 Canada
(416) 479-7000
www.640toronto.com
License: Richmond Hill, ON held by Corus Premium Television Ltd.
Group Owner: Corus Entertainment Inc.; (acq 7-6-00; grpsl).
Nat'l Network: Premiere Radio Networks *Nat'l Reps:* Canadian Broadcast Sales; *Wire Services:* Broadcast News Ltd.
Format: Sports, News/Talk, Talk; *Special Programming:* NHL hockey; *Hrs. of News Programming:* Hourly 24/7; *No. News Employees:* 10; *Target Audience:* 35-64; upscale, mature, male
Matt Dawson, General Sales Mgr
Maggie Tulecka, Promotions Manager
Kerri Breen, Digital Content Coordinator
Nathan Smith, Brand Director
Scott Guest, Assistant Brand Director

Saint Catharines

CFBU-FM
01-01-1997; 103.7 MHz FM; *Hrs Open:* 24; 250 w
500 Glenridge Ave., St. Catharines, ON L2S 3A1 Canada
(905) 346-2645
www.cfbu.ca
License: Saint Catharines, ON held by Brock University Student Radio.
Population Served: 300,000; *Format:* Variety/Diverse; *Special Programming:* American Indian one hr, jazz 4 hrs, Sp 4 hrs, Por; *Adv. Rates:* 20; 20; 20; 20.
Deborah Cartmer, Programming Director
Jordy Yack, Music Director

Sarnia

***CBEG-FM**
11-27-1977; 90.3 MHz FM; kw*Rebroadcasts:* Rebroadcasts CBEW-FM 97.5
825 Riverside Drive West, Windsor, ON N9A 5K9 Canada
(519) 255-3411
www.cbc.ca/windsor
License: Sarnia, ON held by CBC/Radio-Canada
Group Owner: Canadian Broadcasters Corp
Nat'l Network: CBC Radio One
Format: Public Affairs, News
Shawna Kelly, Managing Director

CFGX-FM
09-14-1981; 99.9 MHz FM; *Hrs Open:* 24; 26 kw; N42 52 12 W82 23 50
1415 London Rd., Sarnia, ON N7S 1P6 Canada
(519) 542-5500; *Fax:* (519) 542-1520
www.foxfm.com
License: Sarnia, Lambton County, ON held by Blackburn Radio Inc.
Group Owner: Blackburn Radio Inc.; (acq 12-19-94; grpsl).
Format: Adult Contemp; *Special Programming:* New age 7 hrs wkly; *Target Audience:* 25-54; females in the workplace
Kevin Begley, Programming Director

CHOK
07-26-1946; 1070 kHz AM; *Hrs Open:* 24
1415 London Rd., Sarnia, ON N7S 1P6 Canada
(519) 542-5500; *Fax:* (519) 542-1520
www.chok.com
License: Sarnia, ON held by Blackburn Radio Inc.
Group Owner: Blackburn Radio Inc.; (acq 12-18-98; C$902,600).
Nat'l Reps: Canadian Broadcast Sales
Format: Adult Contemp, Variety/Diverse; *Special Programming:* Toronto Blue Jays baseball, Toronto Maple Leaf hoc; *Hrs. of News Programming:* news progmg 11 hrs wkly; *No. News Employees:* 3; *Target Audience:* 25-54.
Jeff Telois, Sales Director
Dave Dentinger, News Director

CHKS-FM
08-03-1968; 106.3 MHz FM; 35 kw
1415 London Rd., Sarnia, ON N7S 1P6 Canada
(519) 542-5500; *Fax:* (519) 542-1520
www.k106fm.com
License: Sarnia, ON held by Blackburn Radio Inc.
Group Owner: Blackburn Radio Inc.
Arbitron Metro Market: Sarnia, ON; *Format:* Rock/AOR
Jeff Telois, Sales Director
Dave Dentinger, News Director

Sault Ste. Marie

***CHAS-FM**
05-15-1964; 100.5 MHz FM; 13.9 kw
642 Great Northern Rd., Sault Ste. Marie, ON P6B 4Z9 Canada
(705) 759-9200; *Fax:* (705) 946-3575
www.kisssoo.com
License: Sault Ste. Marie, ON held by Rogers Broadcasting Ltd.
Group Owner: Rogers Broadcasting Ltd.; acq 4-19-2002; grpsl).
Format: Adult Contemp, Contemporary Hits/Top 40; *Special Programming:* Class 5 hrs, jazz 2 hrs, lt 2 hrs wkly; *No. News Employees:* 3; *Target Audience:* 25-54; adults
Scott Sexsmith, Programming Director
Craig Perdue, News Director
Derek Patterson, Multi Media Advertising

***CJQM-FM**
05-13-1964; 104.3 MHz FM; 100 kw
642 Great Northern Rd., Sault Ste. Marie, ON P6B 4Z9 Canada
(705) 759-9200; *Fax:* (705) 946-3575
www.country1043.com
License: Sault Ste. Marie, ON held by Rogers Broadcasting Ltd.
Group Owner: Rogers Broadcasting Ltd.; acq 4-19-2002; grpsl).
Format: Country; *Special Programming:* lt 4 hrs wkly; *Hrs. of News Programming:* News progmg 3 hrs wkly; *Target Audience:* 25-54; adults
Gary Creighton, Programming Director
Craig Perdue, News Director
Derek Patterson, Multi Media Advertising

Savant Lake

***CBQL-FM**
01-01-1977; 104.9 MHz FM; kw*Rebroadcasts:* Rebroadcasts CBQT-FM Thunder Bay
Canada
(807) 625-5000; *Fax:* (807) 625-5035
License: Savant Lake, ON held by CBC/Radio-Canada
Nat'l Network: CBC Radio One
Format: Public Affairs, News
Tom Grand, Station Manager

Scarborough

CJVF-FM
02-04-2012; 102.7 MHz FM; 45 watts; 63.4 meters
72-74 Dynamic Drive, Suite 10, Scarborough, ON M1V 3Z5 Canada
(416) 572-4040; *Fax:* (416) 572-4044
info@1059.fm
License: Scarborough, ON held by 105.9 FM Ltd.
Format: Ethnic
Subanasiri Vaithilingham, Owner/General Manager

Shelburne

CFDC-FM
104.9 MHz FM; 12.5 kw; N44 14 09 W80 17 19
270 9th St. E., Owen Sound, ON N4K 5P5 Canada
(519) 376-2030; *Fax:* (519) 371-4242
www.country105.ca
License: Shelburne, ON held by Bayshore Broadcasting Corp.
Group Owner: Bayshore Broadcasting Corp.
Format: Country
Ian Solecki, Operations Dir
Adam Ward, General Sales Mgr

Simcoe

***CHCD-FM**
01-01-1997; 98.9 MHz FM; *Hrs Open:* 24; kw
Mailing Address: Box 98, Simcoe, ON N3Y 4K8 Canada
Second Address: 55 Park Rd., Simcoe, ON N3Y 4J9
(519) 426-7700; *Fax:* (519) 426-8574
www.norfolktoday.ca
License: Simcoe, Norfolk County, ON held by My Broadcasting Corp.
Group Owner: My Broadcasting Corp.; (acq 2-26-01; C$1.05 million).
Nat'l Reps: Canadian Broadcast Sales
Format: Adult Contemp; *No. News Employees:* 3; *Target Audience:* Women; 25-54; *Adv. Rates:* 40; 30; 25; 10
Alan Duthie, General Manager
Alan Duthie, General Sales Mgr
D'Arcy Magee, Group Program Director
Cindy Clyne, News Director

Sioux Lookout

CKWT-FM
01-01-2007; 89.9 MHz FM; 224 w; N50 05 55 W91 55 08
Box 1180, 16 5th Avenue, Sioux Lookout, ON P8T 1B7 Canada
(807) 737-2951; *Fax:* (807) 737-3224
www.wawataynews.ca
License: Sioux Lookout, ON held by Wawatay Native Communications Society.
Population Served: 5,037; *Arbitron Metro Market:* Sioux Lookout, ON; *Format:* Native American
James Brohm, CEO
Lenny Carpenter, News Director
Roxy Shapwaykeesic, Art Director
James Brohm, Sales Administrator

CKDR-2-FM
01-01-2008; 97.1 MHz FM; *Hrs Open:* 24; 560 w; N50 06 07 W91 55 17*Rebroadcasts:* Rebroadcasts CKDR-FM Dryden 99%
122 King St., Dryden, ON P8N 1C2 Canada
(807) 223-2355; *Fax:* (807) 223-5090
www.ckdr.net
ckdr@radioabl.ca
License: Sioux Lookout, ON held by Acadia Broadcasting Ltd.
Group Owner: Acadia Broadcasting Ltd.; (acq 5-1-2007; grpsl)
Population Served: 7,617; *Arbitron Metro Market:* Dryden, ON; *Format:* Adult Contemp; *No. News Employees:* 1; *Target Audience:* 25-54.
Richard McCarthy, Operations Dir
Bruce Walchuck, Station Manager
Mike Ebbeling, News Director
Chris Pollard, Creative Director
Michelle Nault, Traffic Manager
Roxanne McGee, Sales
Val Artimowich, Sales

Sioux Narrows

***CBQS-FM**
05-01-1977; 95.7 MHz FM; kw*Rebroadcasts:* Rebroadcasts CBQT-FM Thunder Bay 100%
PO Box 3220, Station C, Ottawa, ON K1Y 1E4 Canada
(807) 625-5000; *Fax:* (807) 625-5035
www.cbc.ca/ottowa
License: Sioux Narrows, ON held by CBC/Radio-Canada
Special Programming: Canadian Indian one hr wkly
Tom Grand, General Manager

Smiths Falls

***CKBY-FM**
01-29-1969; 101.1 MHz FM; *Hrs Open:* 24; 100 kw
6A Beckwith St. N., Smiths Falls, ON K7A 4T4 Canada
(613) 283-4630
www.country1011.com
License: Smiths Falls, ON held by Rogers Broadcasting Ltd.
Group Owner: Rogers Broadcasting Ltd.; (acq 7-2-99; grpsl).
Format: Country; *Hrs. of News Programming:* news progmg 6 hrs wkly; *No. News Employees:* 2; *Target Audience:* 35-54; female
Mark Hunter, General Sales Mgr

CJET-FM
10-27-2000; 92.3 MHz FM; 17 kw
P.O. Box 340, Smiths Falls, ON K7A 4T4 Canada
(613) 283-4630; *Fax:* (613) 283-7243
www.923jackfm.com
License: Smiths Falls, ON held by Rogers Broadcasting Ltd.
Group Owner: Rogers Broadcasting Ltd.
Population Served: 8,978; *Arbitron Metro Market:* Smiths Falls, ON; *Format:* Adult Contemp, Contemporary Hits/Top 40
Mark Hunter, General Sales Mgr
Kalum Figura, Retail Sales Manager

St. Catharines

CHRE-FM
03-01-1967; 105.7 MHz FM; *Hrs Open:* 24; 50 kw
12 Yates St., St. Catherines, ON L2R 5R2 Canada
(905) 688-1057
www.1057ezrock.com
bob.harris@bellmedia.ca
License: St. Catharines, ON held by Bell Media Radio G.P.
Group Owner: Bell Media Inc.; (acq 10-29-2007; grpsl).
Format: Adult Contemp; *No. News Employees:* 4; *Target Audience:* 25-54.
Bob Harris, General Manager
Sarah Cummings, Programming Director
Lisa Peters, Promotions Manager
Mark Munroe, Music Director
Kristina Mantler-Arcand, General Sales Assistant
Brett Poole, Digital Account Manager

CHTZ-FM
02-01-1949; 97.7 MHz FM; 50 kw
12 Yates St., St. Catharines, ON L2R 5R2 Canada

(905) 688-0977; *Fax:* (905) 684-4800
www.htzfm.com
bob.harris@bellmedia.ca
License: St. Catharines, ON held by Bell Media Radio G.P.
Group Owner: Bell Media Inc.
Format: Rock/AOR
Bob Harris, General Manager
Jeff Winskell, Programming Director
Lisa Peters, Promotions Director
Paul Morris, Music Director

CKTB
01-01-1930; 610 kHz AM; 10 kw-D, 5 kw-N
Mailing Address: 12 Yates St., St. Catharines, ON L2R 5R2 Canada
Second Address: ON
(905) 684-1174; *Fax:* (905) 684-4800
www.610cktb.com
License: St. Catharines, ON held by Bell Media Radio G.P.
Group Owner: Bell Media Inc.; (acq 10-29-2007; grpsl).
Format: News/Talk; *Target Audience:* 35-65.
Bob Harris, General Manager
Sarah Cummings, Programming Director
Lisa Peters, Promotions and Marketing Director
Stephanie Sabourin, News Director

St. Thomas

CFHK-FM
06-20-1994; 103.1 MHz FM; *Hrs Open:* 24; 22 kw; 179.6 meters; N42 50 57 W81 08 52
380 Wellington St., Suite 222, London, ON N6A 5B5 Canada
(519) 931-6000; *Fax:* (519) 438-2415
www.1031freshradio.ca
brad.gibb@corusent.com
License: St. Thomas, ON held by Corus Radio Co.
Group Owner: Corus Entertainment Inc.; (acq 8-23-99; grpsl).
Population Served: 38,909; *Format:* Adult Contemp; *Target Audience:* 18-39.
Rob Chiaramida, Regional Manager
Kent Guy, Promotions & News Media Director
Chelsea Robinson, Marketing Promotions Coordinator
Toni Ross, Music Director

***CKZM-FM**
05-20-2011; 94.1 MHz FM; *Hrs Open:* 24
Mailing Address: 2-300 Tablot St., St. Thomas, ON N5P 4E2 Canada
Second Address: ON
(519) 633-6936; *Fax:* (519) 637-8410
www.stthomastoday.ca
License: St. Thomas, ON held by My Broadcasting Corp.
Group Owner: My Broadcasting Corp.
Format: Light Rock
Rob Mise, General Manager
Rob Mise, General Sales Mgr
D'Arcy Magee, Group Program Director
Cindy Clyne, Group News Director
Marg Tubman, Group Administrator

Stella

CJAI-FM
04-01-2006; 93.7 MHz FM; kw
5830 Front Road, Stella, ON K0H 2S0 Canada
(613) 384-8282
www.cjai.ca
air@cjai.ca
License: Stella, ON held by Amherst Island Radio Broadcasting Inc.
Arbitron Metro Market: Stella, ON; *Format:* Variety/Diverse
Rosemary Richmond, Station Manager

Stratford

CJCS-FM
08-03-2017; 107.1 MHz FM; 900 w; 32.6 meters
376 Romeo St. S., Stratford, ON N5A 4T9 Canada
(519) 271-2450; *Fax:* (519) 271-3102
www.mystratfordnow.com
acampagnola@vistaradio.ca
License: Stratford, ON held by Vista Radio Ltd.
Group Owner: Vista Radio Ltd.
Format: Oldies, Variety/Diverse; *Target Audience:* 25-54.
Wendy Gray, Regional Cluster Manager
Al Campagnola, Regional Cluster Program Director
Marie Cassidy, Regional News Director
Kapila Ratnayake, Chief Engineer
Gregory Rosser, News
Dave Elliott, Sr. Integrated Marketing Executive

CHGK-FM
09-02-2003; 107.7 MHz FM; 6 kw; 84.7 meters
376 Romeo St. S., Stratford, ON N5A 4T9 Canada
(519) 271-2450; *Fax:* (519) 271-3102
www.mystratfordnow.com
wgray@vistaradio.ca
License: Stratford, ON held by Vista Radio Ltd.
Group Owner: Vista Radio Ltd.
Population Served: 30,886; *Arbitron Metro Market:* Stratford, ON; *Format:* Adult Contemp
Wendy Gray, Regional Cluster Manager
Al Campagnola, Regional Cluster Program Director
Marie Cassidy, Regional News Director
Kapila Ratnayake, Chief Engineer
Dave Elliott, Sr. Integrated Marketing Executive
Gregory Rosser, News

Strathroy

CJMI-FM
02-06-2007; 105.7 MHz FM; 1.75 kw
85 Zimmerman St. S., Strathroy, ON N7G 0A3 Canada
(519) 246-6936; *Fax:* (519) 245-6670
www.strathroytoday.ca
License: Strathroy, ON held by My Broadcasting Corp.
Group Owner: My Broadcasting Corp.
Population Served: 20,978; *Arbitron Metro Market:* Strathroy, ON; *Format:* Adult Contemp
Kent Coleman, General Manager
Kent Coleman, General Sales Mgr
D'Arcy Magee, Group Program Director
Cindy Clyne, Group News Director

Sturgeon Falls

CFSF-FM
99.3 MHz FM; 1.35 kw; 48.5 meters
159 Main St., Unit 1, Sturgeon Falls, ON P2B 1P1 Canada
(705) 753-6776; *Fax:* (705) 753-6776
www.mywestnipissingnow.com
phobbs@vistaradio.ca
License: Sturgeon Falls, ON held by Vista Radio Ltd.
Group Owner: Vista Radio Ltd.
Arbitron Metro Market: Sturgeon Falls, ON; *Format:* Adult Contemp; *No. News Employees:* 4
Peter Hobbs, Regional Cluster Manager
Ryan Griffiths, Regional Cluster Program Director
Rocco Frangione, News
Nicholas Clement, Integrated Marketing Executive

Sudbury

***CBCSFM**
06-17-1978; 99.9 MHz FM; *Hrs Open:* 24; kw
15 Mackenzie Street, Sudbury, ON P3C 4Y1 Canada
(705) 688-3200
www.cbc.ca/news/canada/sudbury
License: Sudbury, ON held by Radio-Canada/CBC.
Group Owner: Canadian Broadcasting Corporation
Nat'l Network: CBC Radio One
Format: News, News/Talk, Talk; *Hrs. of News Programming:* news progmg 3 hrs wkly; *No. News Employees:* 4; *Target Audience:* 30 plus; College/university educated/professional
Fiona Christensen, Managing Editor

CIGM-FM
08-25-2009; 93.5 MHz FM; *Hrs Open:* 24; 100 kw
493-B Barrydowne Rd., Sudbury, ON P3A 3T4 Canada
(705) 560-8323; *Fax:* (705) 560-7765
www.hot935.ca
info@hot935.ca
License: Sudbury, ON held by NewCap Inc.
Group Owner: NewCap Inc.
Format: Contemporary Hits/Top 40; *No. News Employees:* 5; *Target Audience:* Adults 35+.
Mike Cameron, General Manager
Mike Cameron, General Sales Mgr
Karen Bass, Account Executive
Trinna Bertrand, Account Executive
Michelle Charbonneau, Account Executive
Marcelle Labelle, Account Executive
Denis Lanteigne, AccountExecutive

CJMX-FM
01-01-1980; 105.3 MHz FM; *Hrs Open:* 24; 100 kw; 285 meters; N46 30 02 W81 01 16
880 Lasalle Blvd., Sudbury, ON P3A 1X5 Canada
(705) 566-4480; *Fax:* (705) 560-7232
www.kisssudbury.com
License: Sudbury, ON held by Rogers Broadcasting Ltd.
Group Owner: Rogers Broadcasting Ltd.; (acq 4-19-2002; grpsl).
Nat'l Reps: Canadian Broadcast Sales
Population Served: 165,000; *Format:* Adult Contemp; *Hrs. of News Programming:* news progmg 1 hr wkly; *No. News Employees:* 6; *Target Audience:* Females 35-44.; *Adv. Rates:* 90; 80; 80; 70
Mike Allard, Programming Director
Mike Allard, Promotions Director

***CJRQ-FM**
09-01-1965; 92.7 MHz FM; *Hrs Open:* 24; 100 kw
880 Lasalle Blvd., Sudbury, ON P3A 1X5 Canada
(705) 566-4480; *Fax:* (705) 560-7232
www.q92rocks.com
License: Sudbury, ON held by Rogers Broadcasting Ltd.
Group Owner: Rogers Broadcasting Ltd.
Format: Rock/AOR; *Hrs. of News Programming:* news progmg one hr wkly; *No. News Employees:* 5
Mike Leclair, Market Sales Manager
Kevin Britton, Programming Director
Michelle Russell, Promotions

CJTK-FM
01-01-1998; 95.5 MHz FM; *Hrs Open:* 24; 1.4 kw
1720 Algonquin Avenue, North Bay, ON P1B 4Y9 Canada
(705) 472-2585; *Fax:* (705) 498-6949
www.kfmradio.ca
mail@kfmradio.ca
License: Sudbury, ON held by Eternacom Inc.
Population Served: 240,000; *Format:* Christian, Religious; *Hrs. of News Programming:* news progmg 2 hrs wkly; *No. News Employees:* 1; *Target Audience:* General.
Curtis Belcher, CEO
Louis Depatie, Operations Dir
Lou Dotta, Board of Directors

***CKLU-FM**
04-30-1997; 96.7 MHz FM; *Hrs Open:* 7:30 AM-2:30 AM; 1.3 kw; N46 25 29 W81 00 54
935 Ramsey Lake Rd., Sudbury, ON P3E 2C6 Canada
(705) 673-6538 ext. 1
www.cklu.ca
traffic@cklu.ca
License: Sudbury, ON held by Laurentian Student and Community Radio Corp.
Population Served: 150,000; *Format:* Jazz, News, News/Talk, Talk, Variety/Diverse; *Special Programming:* It one hr, Pol one hr, Fr 19 hrs, Sp one hr, Ger o; *Hrs. of News Programming:* News progmg 3 hrs wkly*TargetAudience:* General.; *Adv. Rates:* 26; 26; 26; 26
Dan Welch, President
Lindsey Chrysler, Operations Dir
Carl Jorgensen, Operations Manager

CHNO-FM
02-03-2000; 103.9 MHz FM; *Hrs Open:* 24; 100 kw; N46 30 14 W80 58 03
493-B Barrydowne Rd., Sudbury, ON P3A 3T4 Canada
(705) 560-8323; *Fax:* (705) 560-7765
www.rewind1039.ca
news@rewind1039.ca
License: Sudbury, ON held by NewCap Inc.
Group Owner: NewCap Inc.; (acq 11-9-01; C$2,843,000).
Nat'l Reps: CBS Radio
Population Served: 160,274; *Arbitron Metro Market:* Sudbury, ON; *Format:* Contemporary Hits/Top 40, Oldies; *Hrs. of News Programming:* news progmg 4 hrs wkly; *No. News Employees:* 25; *Target Audience:* 25-54;middle-income
Mike Cameron, General Manager
Mike Cameron, General Sales Mgr
Karen Bass, Account Executive
Michelle Carbonneau, Account Executive
Ann Connelly, Account Executive
Kristina Gervais, Account Executive
Marcelle Labelle, AccountExecutive
Denis Lanteigne, Account Executive

CHYC-FM
01-01-2000; 98.9 MHz FM; 1 kw
336 Pine Street, Suite 301, Sudbury, ON P3C 1X8 Canada
(705) 222-8306; *Fax:* (705) 222-2805
www.leloupfm.com
License: Sudbury, ON held by LE5 Communications Inc.
Population Served: 160,274; *Arbitron Metro Market:* Sudbury, ON; *Format:* Adult Contemp, Contemporary Hits/Top 40; *Target Audience:* General.; *Adv. Rates:* 18; 15; 12; 9
Christopher Grossman, General Manager
Sylvain Boucher, Programming/Engineering Director
Paul Lefebvre, Owner / Manager
Guy Rouleau, Billing and Routing
Lucie Boudreau, Sales Representative
Lise Beaulieu, Sales Representative
YvesNadeau, Sales Representative

CBBX-FM
03-29-2001; 90.9 MHz FM; 50 kw
PO Box 3220, Station C, Ottawa, ON K1Y 1E4 Canada
(514) 597-6000; (866) 306-4636
www.cbc.radio-canada.ca
auditoire@radio-canada.ca
License: Sudbury, ON held by CBC/Radio-Canada
Nat'l Network: Espace Musique
Population Served: 160,274; *Arbitron Metro Market:* Greater Sudbury, ON; *Format:* Variety/Diverse
R,mi Racine, Chairman
Hubert T. Lacroix, President & CEO
Sylvain LaFrance, Operations Dir
Maryse Bertrand, Vice-President, Real Estate, Legal Services and Ge
William B. Chambers, Vice-President, Brand, Communications and Corporat
Steven Guiton, Vice-President and Chief Regulatory Officer
Louis Lalande, Executive Vice-President French Services
Suzanne Morris, Vice-President and Chief Financial Officer
Roula Zaarour, Vice-President, People and Culture

***CBBS-FM**
03-29-2001; 90.1 MHz FM; kw
PO Box 500, Station A, Toronto, ON M5W 1E6 Canada
(866) 306-4636; *Fax:* (705) 688-3220
www.music.cbc.ca/#/radio2
License: Sudbury, ON held by CBC/Radio-Canada
Nat'l Network: CBC Radio Two
Arbitron Metro Market: Greater Sudbury, ON; *Format:* Adult Contemp, Triple A
R,mi Racine, Chairman
Hubert T. Lacroix, President & CEO
Heather Conway, Chief Engineer
Maryse Bertrand, Vice-President, Real Estate, Legal Services and Ge
William B. Chambers, Vice-President, Brand, Communications and Corporat
Steven Guiton, Vice-President, Tech/Chief Regulatory Officer
Louis Lalande, Executive Vice-President French Services
Suzanne Morris, Vice-President and Chief Financial Officer
Roula Zaarour, Vice-President, People and Culture

CKSO-FM
01-01-2002; 101.1 MHz FM; *Hrs Open:* 24; 50 w; N46 27 59 W80 58 23
Box 536, Greater Sudbury, ON P0N 1H0 Canada
(866) 799-3072; *Fax:* (705) 235-3921
License: Sudbury, ON held by David Jackson, on behalf of a corporation to be incorporated.
Population Served: 160,274; *Arbitron Metro Market:* Greater Sudbury, ON; *Format:* Christian
David Jackson, General Manager
Sarah Jackson, Programming Director

CICS-FM
08-18-2008; 91.7 MHz FM; 50 kw; N46 30 14 W80 58 03
60 Elm St., Sudbury, ON P3C 1R8 Canada
(705) 671-7330; *Fax:* (705) 671-7320
www.kicx917.com
License: Sudbury, ON held by Larche Communications Inc.
Group Owner: Larche Communications Inc.
Population Served: 164,000; *Format:* Country; *Target Audience:* 35-64.
Mick Weaver, General Manager
Mick Weaver, General Sales Mgr
Trinette Atkinson, Programming Director
Scott Ziliotto, Promotions Director
Brian Martin, News Director
Mora Austin, Vice President
Shelley Barry, Creative Director
Matt Mise, Director of Digital Media

Thamesville

CKBK-FM
07-27-2012; 104.3 MHz FM; 45 watts; 25 meters; N42 33 51 W82 52 28
14760 School House Lane, R R 3, Thamesville, ON N0P 2KO Canada
Fax: (519) 692-5522
firstnation.ca/moravian-thames
License: Thamesville, ON held by Delaware Nation Moravian Indian Reserve
Format: Ethnic
Gordon Peters, General Manager

Thunder Bay

***CBQ-FM**
07-05-1984; 101.7 MHz FM; *Hrs Open:* 24; 23.5 kw; 900 ft
213 Miles St. E., Thunder Bay, ON P7C 1J5 Canada
(807) 625-5000
www.cbc.ca/news/canada/thunder-bay
License: Thunder Bay, ON held by CBC/Radio-Canada
Nat'l Network: CBC Radio One
Format: News, Talk
Robert Rabinovitch, President
Tom Grand, General Manager

***CBQT-FM**
08-01-1990; 90.5 MHz FM; *Hrs Open:* 19; kw
PO Box 500, Station A, Toronto, ON M5W 1E6 Canada

www.cbc.ca
License: Thunder Bay, ON held by CBC/Radio Canada
Nat'l Network: CBC Radio One
Format: News; *Special Programming:* Canadian Indian one hr wkly; *Target Audience:* General; northwestern Ontario residents
Heather Conway, EVP, English Services
Louis Laland, EVP, French Services
Suzanne Moms, VP/CFO
Steven Guiton, VP, Technology
Maryse Bertrand, VP/General Counsel
Roula Zaarour, VP, People/Culture

CJSD-FM
10-01-1948; 94.3 MHz FM; *Hrs Open:* 24; kw
Canada
(807) 346-2600; *Fax:* (807) 345-9923
rock94.com
License: Thunder Bay, ON held by C.J.S.D. Inc.
Nat'l Reps: Target Broadcast Sales
Format: Rock/AOR; *Target Audience:* 18-44.
H.F. Dougall, President
K. Harris, General Sales Mgr
Brad Hilgers, Programming Director
Cora Cambly, Promotions Manager
Bryan Wyatt, News Director
D. Caron, Vice President

***CJOA-FM**
12-20-1998; 95.1 MHz FM; *Hrs Open:* 24; 50 w
42-63 Carrie Street, Thunder Bay, ON P7A 4J2 Canada
(807) 344-9525; *Fax:* (807) 344-9525
License: Thunder Bay, ON held by United Christian Broadcasters Canada
Population Served: 108,359; *Arbitron Metro Market:* Thunder Bay, ON; *Format:* Christian; *Target Audience:* All ages
Ray Gauthier, President
Bonnie Gauthier, General Manager

CJUK-FM
08-01-2001; 99.9 MHz FM; 37 w
200-180 Park Ave., Thunder Bay, ON P7B 6J4 Canada
(807) 344-2000
www.magic999.ca
magic@magic999.ca
License: Thunder Bay, ON held by Acadia Broadcasting Inc
Group Owner: Acadia Broadcasting Ltd.; (acq 5-10-2005; C$2.3 million).
Format: Adult Contemp
Dennis Landriault, President

CILU-FM
03-04-2005; 102.7 MHz FM; *Hrs Open:* 24; 100 w; N48 25 14 W89 15 37
Mailing Address: 955 Oliver Rd., Thunder Bay, ON P7B 5E1 Canada
Second Address: 707 Oliver Rd., Thunder Bay, ON P7B 2H8
(807) 343-8881
www.luradio.ca
info@luradio.ca
License: Thunder Bay, ON held by LU Campus Radio Inc.
Population Served: 108,359; *Arbitron Metro Market:* Thunder Bay, ON; *Format:* Talk
Jason Wellwood, Station Manager
Krista Harper, News Director
Shawn Hartriksen, Production Manager
David Ivany, Music Director

CKPR-FM
06-04-2007; 91.5 MHz FM; *Hrs Open:* 24; 100 kw; N48 31 27 W89 06 53
87 N. Hill St., Thunder Bay, ON P7A 5V6 Canada
(888) 218-1428; *Fax:* (807) 345-9923
ckpr.com
License: Thunder Bay, ON held by C.J.S.D. Inc.
Nat'l Reps: Target Broadcast Sales
Population Served: 108,359; *Arbitron Metro Market:* Thunder Bay, ON; *Format:* Adult Contemp; *Special Programming:* News/talk 10 hrs wkly; *Target Audience:* 25-54; families & office workers
H.F. Dougall, President
Cora Cambly, Operations, Marketing & Promotions Director
Kathy Harris, Local Sales Manager
Brad Hilgers, Programming Director
Bryan Wyatt, News Director
D. Caron, Vice President
Leslie Walker-Larson,National Sales Manager
Bill Hogan, Music Director

CKTG-FM
01-27-2005; 105.3 MHz FM; 100,000 kw
200-180 Park Ave., Thunder Bay, ON 97B 6J4 Canada
(807) 344-2000
www.country1053.ca
country@country1053.ca
License: Thunder Bay, ON held by Acadia Broadcasting Ltd.
Group Owner: Acadia Broadcasting Ltd.
Format: Country
Jim MacMullin, President

Tillsonburg

CKOT-FM
12-01-1965; 101.3 MHz FM; *Hrs Open:* 24; kw
Mailing Address: Canada
Second Address: 77 Broadway, Tillsonburg, ON N4G 4H3
(519) 842-4281; *Fax:* (519) 842-4284
www.easy101.com
info@easy101.com
License: Tillsonburg, ON held by Tillsonburg Broadcasting Co. Ltd.
Nat'l Reps: Target Broadcast Sales
Format: Easy Listening; *Special Programming:* Gospel one hr wkly; *Target Audience:* 30 plus; general
John Lamers, President
Robin Henry, General Sales Mgr

CJDL-FM
08-01-2007; 107.3 MHz FM; 4.5 kw; Ant 538 ft; N43 00 44 W80 50 10
Mailing Address: Box 10, Tillsonburg, ON N4G 4H3 Canada
Second Address: 77 Broadway, Tillsonburg, ON N4G 4H3
(519) 842-4281; *Fax:* (519) 842-4284
www.country1073.ca
info@easy101.com
License: Tillsonburg, ON held by Tillsonburg Broadcasting Co. Ltd.
Nat'l Reps: Target Broadcast Sales
Population Served: 2,000; *Arbitron Metro Market:* Tillsonburg, ON; *Format:* Country; *Special Programming:* Ger one hr, Hungarian one hr, Belgian one hr, Dutc; *Hrs. of News Programming:* news progmg 7 hrs wkly*No. NewsEmployees:* 5; *Target Audience:* 18-50; general
John Lamers, President
Robin Henry, General Sales Mgr

Timmins

CBON-FM
06-19-1978; 98.1 MHz FM; kw
Canada
(705) 688-3200; *Fax:* (705) 688-3220
www.radio-canada.ca
License: Timmins, ON held by Radio-Canada/CBC.
Nat'l Network: CBC Radio One
Format: French
Gui Babineau, General Manager

CJQQ-FM
09-06-1976; 92.1 MHz FM; *Hrs Open:* 24; 40 kw; Ant 400 ft
260 2nd Ave., Timmins, ON P4N 8A4 Canada
(705) 264-2351; *Fax:* (705) 264-2984
www.921rock.ca
License: Timmins, ON held by Rogers Broadcasting Ltd.
Group Owner: Rogers Broadcasting Ltd.; acq 4-19-02;. grpsl).
Format: Rock/AOR; *Target Audience:* 18-44.
Art Pultz, General Manager
Angelo Lia, Sales
Amanda Dyer, Marketing and Promotions

CHYK-FM
01-01-2000; 104.1 MHz FM; *Hrs Open:* 24; 3.5 kw
136 Third Avenue, Timmins, ON P4N 1C6 Canada
(705) 269-8307; *Fax:* (705) 269-8305
www.leloupfm.com
plefebvre@leloupfm.com
License: Timmins, ON held by LE5 Communications Inc.
Nat'l Reps: Canadian Broadcast Sales
Population Served: 42,997; *Arbitron Metro Market:* Timmins, ON; *Format:* Adult Contemp; *Hrs. of News Programming:* news progmg one hr wkly; *No. News Employees:* 1; *Target Audience:* 18-65.; *Adv. Rates:* 22.50;22.50; 22.50; 22.50

Paul Lefebvre, Owner
Kimberly Ward, Operations Dir
Christopher Grossman, General Manager
Sylvie Beaulieu, Sales Manager
Sylvain Boucher, Programming Director
Guy Rouleau, Billing/Routing
Penny Proulx, Traffic Manager
YvesNadeau, Director of Sales

CKGB-FM
08-01-2001; 99.3 MHz FM; 40 kw
260 2nd Ave., Timmins, ON P4N 8A4 Canada
(705) 264-2351; *Fax:* (705) 264-2984
License: Timmins, ON held by Rogers Broadcasting Ltd.
Group Owner: Rogers Broadcasting Ltd.; (acq 4-19-2002; grpsl).
Population Served: 42,997; *Arbitron Metro Market:* Timmins, ON;
Format: Adult Contemp; *Hrs. of News Programming:* news progmg 4 hrs wkly; *No. News Employees:* 2; *Target Audience:* 35-55.
Art Pultz, General Manager

CHMT-FM
93.1 MHz FM; *Hrs Open:* 24; 16.4 kw; 95 meters
49 Cedar St. S., Timmins, ON P4N 2G5 Canada
(705) 267-6070; *Fax:* (705) 267-6095
www.mytimminsnow.com
sarmstrong@vistaradio.ca
License: Timmins, ON held by Vista Radio Ltd.
Group Owner: Vista Radio Ltd.
Nat'l Network: CBS Radio
Format: Adult Contemp, Oldies; *Hrs. of News Programming:* news progmg 1.5 hrs wkly; *No. News Employees:* 2; *Target Audience:* 25-54.; *Adv. Rates:* 25; 25; 25; 25
Scott Armstrong, Regional Cluster Manager
Shane Button, Regional Cluster Program Director
Mackenzie Read, News Reporter

Toronto

CBL-FM
94.1 MHz FM; 38 kw; 420.5 meters
250 Front St. W, Toronto, ON M5W 1E6 Canada
(416) 205-3311
www.cbc.ca/toronto
torontotips@cbc.ca
License: Toronto, ON held by CBC
Group Owner: CBC
Nat'l Network: CBC Radio 2
Format: Public Affairs, News
Carly Klassen, Promo Producer and Director
Mark Steinmetz, Senior Music Director

CBLA-FM
99.1 MHz FM; 55.1 kw; 303.7 meters
250 Front St. W, Toronto, ON M5W 1E6 Canada
(416) 205-3311
www.cbc.ca/toronto
tonews@cbc.ca
License: Toronto, ON held by CBC
Group Owner: CBC
Nat'l Network: CBC Radio One
Format: Public Affairs, News
Carly Klassen, Promo Producer and Director
Mark Steinmetz, Senior Music Director

CFMZ-FM
01-01-1979; 96.3 MHz FM; *Hrs Open:* 24; 26 kw
70 Jefferson Ave., Toronto, ON M6K 1Y4 Canada
(416) 367-5353; *Fax:* (416) 367-1742
www.classical963fm.com
License: Toronto, ON held by MZ Media Inc.
Group Owner: ZoomerMedia Ltd.; (acq 8-31-2006; C$12 million with CFMX-FM Cobourg).
Nat'l Network: BN Audio *Nat'l Reps:* imsradio; *Wire Services:* Standard Broadcast News
Population Served: 4,800,000; *Format:* Classical; *Hrs. of News Programming:* news progmg 4 hrs wkly; *No. News Employees:* 3; *Target Audience:* 35 plus; well educated, upscale, owners/managers/professionals
Dan Hamilton, VP Sales, Broadcast and General Manager
John Van Driel, VP Programming/Operations
Libby Znaimer, VP of News and Information

CFRB
02-19-1927; 1010 kHz AM; *Hrs Open:* 24; 50 kw
250 Richmond St. W., Toronto, ON M5V 1W4 Canada
(416) 384-8000; *Fax:* (416) 872-8683
www.newstalk1010.com
mike.bendixen@newstalk1010.com
License: Toronto, ON held by Bell Media Radio G.P.
Group Owner: Bell Media Inc.; (acq 10-29-2007; grpsl).
Format: News/Talk; *Special Programming:* Class 7 hrs, farm 2 hrs wkly; *Hrs. of News Programming:* news progmg 40 hrs wkly; *No. News Employees:* 10; *Target Audience:* 25-64; general
Mike Bendixen, Programming Director
Nancy Ceneviva, National Promotions Manager

CFTR
08-08-1962; 680 kHz AM; *Hrs Open:* 24; 50 kw
1 Ted Rogers Way, 5th Fl., Toronto, ON M4Y 3B7 Canada
(416) 935-8468
www.680news.com
License: Toronto, ON held by Rogers Broadcasting Ltd.
Group Owner: Rogers Broadcasting Ltd.
Nat'l Network: ABC *Nat'l Reps:* Canadian Broadcast Sales; *Wire Services:* BN Wire; Bloomberg News
Format: News; *Hrs. of News Programming:* news progmg 168 hrs wkly; *No. News Employees:* 50; *Target Audience:* 25-54; owners, managers, professionals
Scott Metcalfe, News Director

CHFI-FM
02-08-1957; 98.1 MHz FM; *Hrs Open:* 24; 44 kw
1 Ted Rogers Way, Toronto, ON M4Y 3B7 Canada
(416) 935-8298; *Fax:* (416) 935-8480
www.chfi.com
License: Toronto, ON held by Rogers Broadcasting Ltd.
Group Owner: Rogers Broadcasting Ltd.
Format: Adult Contemp; *Target Audience:* 25-54.
Guy Laurence, President

CHIN
01-01-1966; 1540 kHz AM; *Hrs Open:* 24
622 College Street, Toronto, ON M6G 1B6 Canada
(416) 531-9991; *Fax:* (416) 531-5274
www.chinradio.com
sales@chinradio.com
License: Toronto, ON held by Radio 1540 Ltd.
Format: Ethnic; *Hrs. of News Programming:* news progmg 9 hrs wkly; *No. News Employees:* 4; *Target Audience:* 30 plus; immigrants in the Toronto census metropolitan area
Johnny Lombardi, CEO
Lenny Lombardi, President
Theresa Lombardi, Operations Dir
Joe Mulvihill, General Manager
Michael Evans, Engineering Dir
Donina Lombardi, Public Affairs Director

CHIN-FM
01-01-1967; 100.7 MHz FM; *Hrs Open:* 24; 8.5 kw; 1,700 ft; N48 38 33 W79 23 15
622 College St., Toronto, ON Canada
(416) 531-9991; *Fax:* (416) 531-5274
License: Toronto, ON held by Radio 1540 Ltd.
Hrs. of News Programming: News progmg 10 hrs wkly; *Target Audience:* 30 plus; multi-ethnic, first & second generation immigrants
Roger de Brabant, Chairman
Karen Turner, Station Manager

CHKT(AM)
1430 kHz AM; *Hrs Open:* 24; 50 kw-U, DA-2
151 Esna Park Drive, Markhan, ON L3R 3B1 Canada
(905) 415-1430; *Fax:* (905) 415-6292
www.fairchildradio.com
winniewong@am1430.com
License: Toronto, ON held by Fairchild Radio Group Ltd.
Format: Chinese; *Target Audience:* Chinese and other ethnic groups
Edmond Tse, General Manager
Jennifer Lo, Assistant GM
Winnie Wong, Sales & Marketing Director
River Lee, Programming Director
Louisa Lam, News Manager
Esther Kwong, Administration
David Choi, Assistant Operations Director

CHUM
10-01-1944; 1050 kHz AM; 50 kw-U, DA-2
250 Richmond St. W., Toronto, ON M5V 1W4 Canada
(416) 925-6666; *Fax:* (416) 926-4026
www.tsn.ca/radio/toronto-1050
live@tsn1050.ca
License: Toronto, ON held by Bell Media Toronto Radio 2013 Partnership
Group Owner: Bell Media Inc.; (acq 6-22-2007; grpsl).
Format: Sports; *No. News Employees:* 6
Loretta Tate, Promotions Director
Larry Keats, Chief Engineer

CHUM-FM
09-15-1963; 104.5 MHz FM; 40 kw; 1,380 ft
299 Queen St. W., Toronto, ON M5V 2Z5 Canada
(416) 925-6666
www.chumfm.com
License: Toronto, ON held by Bell Media Toronto Radio 2013 Partnership
Group Owner: Bell Media Inc.
Format: Adult Contemp; *Hrs. of News Programming:* News progmg 6 hrs wkly
David Corey, Programming Director
Loretta Tate, Promotions Manager

CFZM
01-08-1956; 740 kHz AM; *Hrs Open:* 24; 50 kw-U
70 Jefferson Ave., Toronto, ON M6K 1Y4 Canada
(416) 544-0740
www.zoomerradio.ca
License: Toronto, ON held by MZ Media Inc.
Group Owner: ZoomerMedia Ltd.; (acq 3-31-2008; C$7,320,433).
Population Served: 4,000,000; *Format:* Oldies; *Special Programming:* Scottish 2hrs, British 1hr, Irish 1hr; *Hrs. of News Programming:* News progmg 9 hrs wkly; *Target Audience:* 50 plus.; *Adv. Rates:* 120; 120; 120;60
Dan Hamilton, VP Sales, Broadcast and General Manager
John Van Driel, VP Programming/Operations
Libby Znaimer, VP of News and Information

CILQ-FM
05-22-1977; 107.1 MHz FM; *Hrs Open:* 24; 40 kw
Corus Quay, 25 Dockside Dr., Toronto, ON M5A 0B5 Canada
(416) 479-7000
www.q107.com
License: Toronto, ON held by Corus Premium Television Ltd.
Group Owner: Corus Entertainment Inc.; (acq 7-2000; grpsl).
Format: Classic Rock; *Hrs. of News Programming:* news progmg 15 hrs wkly; *No. News Employees:* 5; *Target Audience:* 18-44.
Matt Dawson, General Sales Mgr
Sarah Zinger, Promotions Coordinator
Blair Bartrem, Brand Director
Chris Santos, New Media Content Manager

CIRV-FM
01-01-1986; 88.9 MHz FM; *Hrs Open:* 24; 1.88 kw
1087 Dundas St. W., Toronto, ON M6J 1W9 Canada
(416) 537-1088; *Fax:* (416) 537-2463
www.cirvfm.com
info@cirvfm.com
License: Toronto, ON held by CIRC Radio Inc.
Format: Ethnic; *No. News Employees:* 5
Frank Alvarez, CEO
Alberto Elmir, Operations Dir

***CIUT-FM**
01-01-1986; 89.5 MHz FM; *Hrs Open:* 24; kw
Canada
(416) 978-0909; *Fax:* (416) 946-7004
www.ciut.fm
License: Toronto, ON held by University of Toronto Community Radio Inc.
Wire Services: Canadian Press
Format: Variety/Diverse; *Special Programming:* Fr 2 hrs, Sp 4 , Punjabi 5 hrs hrs wkly; *Hrs. of News Programming:* News progmg 3 hrs wkly; *Target Audience:* General.
Ken Stowar, Station Manager
Ken Stowar, Programming Director

CJBC
01-01-1947; 860 kHz AM; 50 kw-U
Box 500, Station A, Toronto, ON Canada
(416) 205-3311; *Fax:* (416) 205-5622
www.cbc.ca
License: Toronto, ON held by CBC.
Alain Dorion, General Manager

CJBC-FM
01-01-1993; 90.3 MHz FM; 5.73 kw; 1,414 ft; N43 38 33 W79 23 15
Box 500, Station A, Toronto, ON Canada
(416) 205-2522; *Fax:* (416) 205-7660
License: Toronto, ON held by CBC
Nat'l Network: Radio Canada
Manon Cote, General Manager

CJCL
02-21-1951; 590 kHz AM; *Hrs Open:* 24; 50 kw-U, DA-1
1 Ted Rogers Way, Toronto, ON M4Y 3B7 Canada
(416) 935-0590
www.sportsnet.ca
License: Toronto, ON held by Rogers Broadcasting Ltd.
Group Owner: Rogers Broadcasting Ltd.; acq 4-19-02; grpsl).
Population Served: 4,000,000; *Format:* Sports, Talk; *Target Audience:* 25-54; men
Dave Cadeau, Programming Director

CHBM-FM
05-24-1987; 97.3 MHz FM; 28.9 kw; Ant 1,500 ft
2 St. Clair Ave. W., 20th Floor, Toronto, ON M4V 1L5 Canada
(416) 482-0973
www.boom973.com
License: Toronto, ON held by 8504580 Canada Inc.
Group Owner: NewCap Inc.; (acq 03-19-2014; grpsl)
Population Served: 3,000,000; *Format:* Adult Contemp; *Target Audience:* 35-54.
Steve Parsons, Operations Manager
Lorie Russell, General Manager
Troy McCallum, Programming
John Downey, Marketing/Promotions
Wayne Webster, Music Director

***CJRT-FM**
01-01-1949; 91.1 MHz FM; *Hrs Open:* 24; kw
Canada
(416) 595-0404; *Fax:* (416) 595-9413
www.jazz.fm
info@jazz.fm
License: Toronto, ON held by CJRT-FM Inc.
Wire Services: Broadcast News Ltd.
Format: Jazz; *Target Audience:* 35 plus.
B. Webber, Chairman
Ross Porter, CEO
Brad Barker, Operations Dir
Vince De Lilla, General Sales Mgr
Stacy MacKenzie, News Director
Donnie Tong, Engineering Dir

CKFM-FM
07-01-1961; 99.9 MHz FM; 40 kw
299 Queen St. W., Toronto, ON M5V 2Z5 Canada
(416) 384-8000
toronto.virginradio.ca
License: Toronto, ON held by Bell Media Radio G.P.
Group Owner: Bell Media Inc.
Format: Contemporary Hits/Top 40
Taylor Jukes, Programming Director
Jennifer Collins, Promotions Manager
Bob Willette, Music Director

CKIS-FM
01-26-1993; 92.5 MHz FM; 4.7 kw
1 Ted Rogers Way, Toronto, ON M4Y 3B7 Canada
(416) 935-8392
www.kiss925.com
License: Toronto, ON held by Rogers Broadcasting Ltd.
Group Owner: Rogers Broadcasting Ltd.
Format: Contemporary Hits/Top 40
Karen Steele, Programming Director
David Lindores, Promotions Director

CFXJ-FM
02-09-2001; 93.5 MHz FM; *Hrs Open:* 9 AM-5:30 PM; 14 kw; Ant 980 ft
2 St. Clair Ave. W., 20th Fl., Toronto, ON M4V 1L5 Canada
(416) 482-0973
www.flow935.com
License: Toronto, ON held by 8384827 Canada Inc.
Group Owner: NewCap Inc.
Wire Services: BN Wire
Format: Urban Contemporary; *No. News Employees:* 1; *Target Audience:* 18-35.
Steve Parsons, Operations Manager
Lorie Russell, General Manager
Paul Parhar, Programming
John Downey, Promotions
Cory Balash, Music Director

CKAV-FM
12-13-2002; 106.5 MHz FM; 1.1 kw
PO Box 87, Station E, Toronto, ON M6H 4E1 Canada
(416) 703-1287; *Fax:* (416) 703-4328
aboriginalvoices.com
info@aboriginalvoices.com
License: Toronto, ON held by Voices Radio's broadcasting licenses have been revoked by the CRTC. All stations are now broadcasting solely on voicesradio.ca
Group Owner: Voices Radio Inc.
Population Served: 2,615,060; *Arbitron Metro Market:* Toronto, ON; *Format:* Ethnic
Mark MacLeod, Operations Dir
Patrice Mousseau, Programming Director
Roy Hennessy, Operations Manager

CHHA
11-21-2004; 1610 kHz AM; *Hrs Open:* 30; 6.2 kw-U; N43 42 40 W79 27 11
55 Bridesburg Drive, Suite 101, Toronto, ON M9R 2K7 Canada
(416) 694-1834
toronto.hispanocity.com
sales@torontohispano.com
License: Toronto, ON held by San Lorenzo Latin American Community Centre.
Hrs. of News Programming: News progmg 10 hrs wkly
Herman Astudillo, General Manager

CHOQ-FM
01-01-2005; 105.1 MHz FM; *Hrs Open:* 24; 188 w; 274.6 meters
425 W. Adelaide St., # 302, Toronto, ON M5V 3C1 Canada
(416) 599-2666; *Fax:* (416) 599-7639
www.choqfm.ca/accueil
info@choqfm.ca
License: Toronto, ON held by La Cooperative radiophonique de Toronto inc.
Population Served: 105,749; *Arbitron Metro Market:* Saint-Denis, RO; *Format:* French; *Adv. Rates:* 100; 100; 100; 100
Tonia Mori, General Manager

CJSA-FM
01-01-2004; 101.3 MHz FM; kw
Canada
(416) 292-4059; *Fax:* (416) 292-4574
License: Toronto, ON held by Canadian Multicultural Radio
Arbitron Metro Market: Tyler-Longview, TX; *Format:* Ethnic
Sivakumaran Sivapaphafundaram, General Manager

CKHC-FM
01-01-2007; 96.9 MHz FM; *Hrs Open:* 24; 60 w; N43 43 43 W79 36 30
Radio Humber 96.9fm, 205 Humber College Blvd., Toronto, ON M5W 5L7 Canada
(416) 675-6622; *Fax:* (416) 675-9730
radio.humber.ca
Dean.Sinclair@Humber.ca
License: Toronto, ON held by Humber Communications Community Corp.
Nat'l Reps: Target Broadcast Sales; *Wire Services:* Canadian Press
Population Served: 2,615,060; *Arbitron Metro Market:* Toronto, ON; *Format:* French, Country; *Special Programming:* All Canadian Music; *Hrs. of News Programming:* 9-Sep; *Target Audience:* College students*Adv. Rates:* $25/60 $15/30
Jerry Chomyn, Programming Director

CHTO
1690 kHz AM
437 Danforth Avenue, Suite 204, Toronto, ON M4K 1P1 Canada
(416) 465-1112; *Fax:* (416) 465-6592
www.am1690.ca
info@am1690.ca
License: Toronto, ON held by Canadian Hellenic Toronto Radio Inc.
Arbitron Metro Market: Toronto, ON; *Format:* Ethnic, Greek
Tom O'Brien, President
Sue O'Brien, General Manager
Dave Moore, General Sales Mgr
Tony Taylor, Programming Director
Don Barkman, Music Director

CIRR-FM
04-16-2007; 103.9 MHz FM; 225 w
5312 Dundas St. W., Toronto, ON M9B 1B3 Canada
(416) 922-1039; *Fax:* (416) 922-3692
www.proudfm.com
info@proudfm.com
License: Toronto, ON held by Dufferin Communications Inc.
Group Owner: Evanov Communications Inc.
Arbitron Metro Market: Toronto, ON; *Format:* Contemporary Hits/Top 40, Talk; *Special Programming:* LGBT Oriente Programming; *Target Audience:* LGBT Audience
Carmela Laurignano, President
Chris Edelman, General Sales Mgr
Jaret Sereda, Promotions Director
Jon Terminesi, Music Director
Sheila Koenig, Creative Director

CKFG-FM
11-28-2011; 98.7 MHz FM; 446 watts; 276.8 meters
34 Kern Road, Toronto, ON Canada
(416) 498-4987
www.g987fm.com
License: Toronto, ON held by Intercity Broadcasting Network Inc
Fitzroy Gordon, President

CIND-FM
88.1 MHz FM; 532 w; 328.4 meters
31R Atlantic Avenue, Toronto, ON M6K 3E7 Canada
(416) 588-7595
www.indie88.com
License: Toronto, ON held by Rock 95 Broadcasting Ltd.
Megan Bingley, General Manager

Trenton

CJTN-FM
01-01-1979; 107.1 MHz FM; *Hrs Open:* 24; 3.64 kw
10 S. Front St., Box 488, Belleville, ON K8N 5B2 Canada
(613) 969-5555; *Fax:* (613) 969-8122
www.rock107.ca
License: Trenton, ON held by Quinte Broadcasting Ltd.
Group Owner: Quinte Broadcasting Ltd.
Format: Classic Rock
Jody Brooker, General Sales Mgr
Sean Kelly, Programming Director
Lorne Brooker, Promotions Manager
John Spitters, News Director

Uxbridge

CIUX-FM
105.5 MHz FM; 372 w; 139.7 meters; N44 04 28 W79 09 53
380 Hunt Club Road, Suite 203, Ottawa, ON K1V 1C1 Canada
(613) 730-1019; *Fax:* (613) 730-1092
License: Uxbridge, ON held by Torres Media Ottawa Inc.

Vermilion Bay

CKQV-FM
11-22-2004; 103.3 MHz FM; 1.6 kw
619 Lakeview Dr., Kenora, ON P9N 3P6 Canada
(807) 468-1045
www.kenoraonline.com
License: Vermilion Bay, ON held by Golden West Broadcasting Ltd.
Group Owner: Golden West Broadcasting Ltd.
Population Served: 1,200; *Arbitron Metro Market:* Vermilion Bay, ON; *Format:* Contemporary Hits/Top 40
Shandis Duguay, Station Manager

Wahta Mohawk Territory near Bala

CFWP-FM
01-01-2003; 98.3 MHz FM; *Hrs Open:* 24; 1.06 kw; Ant 96 ft
Canada
(705) 762-1274; *Fax:* (705) 762-2045
License: Wahta Mohawk Territory near Bala, ON held by Wahta Communications Society.
Population Served: 716; *Arbitron Metro Market:* Wahta Mohawk Territory, ON; *Format:* Variety/Diverse; *Adv. Rates:* 5; 5; 5; 5
Cal White, General Manager

Walpole Island

CFRZ-FM
98.3 MHz FM; 50 w; 31 meters; N42 35 26 W82 28 38
R.R. 3, Walpole Island, ON N8A 4K9 Canada
(519) 627-1481; *Fax:* (519) 627-0440
License: Walpole Island, ON held by KIIG-DA WIN Media

Wasaga Beach

CHGB-FM
05-18-2007; 97.7 MHz FM; 200 w
9937 Hwy. 26, Collingwood, ON L9Y 0Y4 Canada
(705) 422-0970; *Fax:* (705) 422-0468
www.977thebeach.ca
info@977thebeach.ca
License: Wasaga Beach, ON held by Bayshore Broadcasting Corp.
Group Owner: Bayshore Broadcasting Corp.
Format: Adult Contemp
Kevin Brown, VP Sales and Marketing

Waterloo

CFCA-FM
04-03-1967; 105.3 MHz FM; *Hrs Open:* 24; 100 kw; 820 ft; N43 24 15 W80 38 05
255 King St. N., Suite 207, Waterloo, ON N2J 4V2 Canada

www.koolfm.com
websupport@koolfm.com
License: Waterloo, ON held by Bell Media Canada Radio 2013 Partnership
Group Owner: Bell Media Inc.
Format: Adult Contemp
Paul Fisher, General Manager
Tom Fits-Gerald, General Sales Mgr
Heidi Baiden, Programming Director
Steve Thompson, Creative Director
Kendra Roberts, Traffic Manager

CKMS-FM
10-16-1977; 100.3 MHz FM; *Hrs Open:* 6 AM-midnight; kw
Canada
(519) 886-2567; *Fax:* (519) 884-3530
www.soundfm.ca
ckmsfm@web.ca
License: Waterloo, ON held by Radio Waterloo Inc.
Format: Variety/Diverse; *No. News Employees:* 1; *Target Audience:* General.
Steve Krysak, President
promotion, General Sales Mgr
Mark Green, Programming Director
Carrie Humphries, Promotions Manager

CKWR-FM
03-23-1974; 98.5 MHz FM; *Hrs Open:* 24; kw
Canada
(519) 886-9870; *Fax:* (519) 886-0090
www.ckwr.com
general@ckwr.com
License: Waterloo, Waterloo County, ON held by Wired World Inc.
Nat'l Reps: CHUM Radio Sales; *Wire Services:* BN Wire
Format: Adult Contemp; *Special Programming:* Romanian 2 hrs, Ger 3 hrs, Greek 2 hrs, Serbian 2; *Hrs. of News Programming:* news progmg 8 hrs wkly; *No. News Employees:* 2; *Target Audience:* 35-64; mature audience*Adv.Rates:* 46; 40; 42; 24.
Clarence Mascoll, President
Clyde Ross, Station Manager
Marie Hurst, Programming Director

Wawa

CJWA-FM
01-01-1996; 107.1 MHz FM; 210 w
55 Broadway Ave., Wawa, ON P0S 1K0 Canada
(705) 856-4555; *Fax:* (705) 856-1520
License: Wawa, ON held by Labbe Media Incorporated
Nat'l Reps: Canadian Broadcast Sales
Format: Adult Contemp; *No. News Employees:* 1; *Target Audience:* 25-54.
Rick Labbe, President
Daniel Walker, News Director
Vern Valois, Chief Engineer

Welland

CIXL-FM
05-20-1999; 91.7 MHz FM; *Hrs Open:* 24; 50 kw; N52 42 56 W19 79 16
860 Forks Road West, Welland, ON L3B 5R6 Canada
(905) 732-4433; *Fax:* (905) 732-4780
www.giantfm.com
info@giantfm.com
License: Welland, Niagara County, ON held by R.B. Communications, LTD.
Nat'l Reps: Canadian Broadcast Sales
Population Served: 500,000; *Format:* Classic Rock; *Hrs. of News Programming:* news progmg 6 hrs wkly; *No. News Employees:* 20; *Target Audience:* 25-54; adults
Pat St. John, President
Peter Morena, Operations Dir
Brian Salmon, Programming Director
Susan Honsberger, News Director

Whitchurch-Stouffville

CIWS-FM
102.7 MHz FM; 50 w
Mailing Address: Box 59, Stouffville, ON L4A 7Z4 Canada
Second Address: 6379 Main St., Stouffville, ON L4A 7Z4
(905) 640-6429
www.whistleradio.com
License: Whitchurch-Stouffville, ON held by WhiStle Community Radio.
Population Served: 37,628; *Arbitron Metro Market:* Whitchurch-Stouffville, ON; *Format:* Talk
Jim Priebe, CEO

Windsor

***CBE-FM**
10-15-1978; 89.9 MHz FM; 100 kw; 164 metres
825 Riverside Dr. W, Windsor, ON N9A 5K9 Canada
(519) 255-3411; *Fax:* (519) 255-3443
www.cbc.ca/windsor
windsor@cbc.ca
License: Windsor, ON held by CBC
Group Owner: CBC
Nat'l Network: CBC Radio 2
Format: Public Affairs, News
Katia Augustin, Reporter

***CBEF**
1550 kHz AM; *Hrs Open:* 24; 10 kw
825 Riverside Dr. W, Windsor, ON N9A 5K9 Canada
(519) 255-3411
www.radio-canada.ca/regions/ontario
windsor@cbc.ca
License: Windsor, ON held by CBC
Group Owner: CBC
Nat'l Network: Radio-Canada's PremiŠre
Format: Public Affairs, News; *Hrs. of News Programming:* 15 hrs wkly
Katia Augustin, Reporter

CIDR-FM
01-01-1949; 93.9 MHz FM; *Hrs Open:* 24; 500 watts; Ant 700 ft
1640 Ouellette Ave., Windsor, ON N8X 1L1 Canada
(519) 258-8888
www.939theriverradio.com
License: Windsor, ON held by Bell Media Windsor Radio Partnership
Group Owner: Bell Media Inc.
Nat'l Reps: McGavren Guild
Arbitron Metro Market: Detroit; *Format:* Adult Contemp
Phat Matt, Programming Director
Amanda Wellinger, Promotions Director

CIMX-FM
07-10-1967; 88.7 MHz FM; 100 kw; 577 ft
1640 Ouellette Ave., Windsor, ON N8X 1L1 Canada
519-258-8888; *Fax:* 519-258-0182
www.89xradio.com
License: Windsor, ON held by Bell Media Windsor Radio Partnership
Group Owner: Bell Media Inc.
Format: Rock/AOR; *Target Audience:* 18-34.
Clare Baker, Promotions
Jamie Savalle, Promotions

CJAM-FM
11-01-1983; 99.1 MHz FM; kw
Canada
(519) 971-3606; *Fax:* (519) 971-3605
www.cjam.com
news@cjam.ca
License: Windsor, ON held by Student Media, University of Windsor.
Format: Ethnic; *Special Programming:* Black 10 hrs, class 4 hrs, folk 4 hrs, jazz 6 hrs,; *Target Audience:* General; listeners in Windsor/Detroit area
Josh Kolm, President
Vernon Smith, Station Manager
Sarah Morris, Programming Director

CKLW
06-01-1932; 800 kHz AM; *Hrs Open:* 24; 50 kw-U, DA-2
1640 Ouellette Ave., Windsor, ON N8X 1L1 Canada
(519) 258-8888; *Fax:* (519) 258-0182
www.am800cklw.com
contact@am800cklw.com
License: Windsor, Essex County, ON held by Bell Media Windsor Radio Partnership
Group Owner: Bell Media Inc.; (acq 6-22-2007; grpsl).
Nat'l Reps: McGavren Guild
Arbitron Metro Market: Detroit; *Format:* News/Talk; *Target Audience:* 25-54.
Eric Proksch, General Manager
Keith Chinnery, Programming Director
Melissa Hunter, Promotions Manager
Paul McDonald, News Director

CKWW
03-29-1964; 580 kHz AM; 500 w-U, DA-1
Mailing Address: 1640 Ouellette Ave., Windsor, ON N8X 1L1 Canada
Second Address: 30100 Telegraph Rd., Suite 460, Bingham Farms, MI 48025
(519) 258-8888
www.am580radio.com
info@am580radio.com
License: Windsor, ON held by Bell Media Windsor Radio Partnership
Group Owner: Bell Media Inc.; (acq 6-22-2007; grpsl).
Nat'l Reps: McGavren Guild
Arbitron Metro Market: Detroit; *Format:* Oldies; *Hrs. of News Programming:* News progmg 2 hrs wkly; *Target Audience:* 45 plus.
Eric Proksch, General Manager
Charlie O'Brien, Programming Director
Paul McMahon, Promotions Director
Steve Bell, Sports Director

CBEW-FM
03-04-2011; 97.5 MHz FM; kw
Canada
(519) 225-3411; *Fax:* (519) 255-3443
www.cbc.ca/windsor
License: Windsor, Essex County, ON held by CBC
Nat'l Network: CBC Radio One

CINA-FM
102.3 MHz FM; 1.9 kw; 55.5 meters
1515 Britannia Road East, Suite 315, Missisauga, ON L4W 4K1 Canada
neetiray@gmail.com
License: Windsor, Essex County, ON held by Neeti P Ray
Neeti P Ray, General Manager

CJWF-FM
11-16-2009; 95.9 MHz FM; 3.55 kw; N42 10 15 W82 59 29
2090 Wyandotte St. E., Windsor, ON N8Y 5B2 Canada
(519) 944-4400; *Fax:* (519) 944-3747
www.country959.com
License: Windsor, ON held by Blackburn Radio Inc.
Group Owner: Blackburn Radio Inc.
Format: Country; *Target Audience:* 25-64.
John Weese, General Manager

Wingham

CKNX
02-20-1926; 920 kHz AM; *Hrs Open:* 24
215 Carling Terrace, Box 300, Wingham, ON N0G 2W0 Canada
(519) 357-1310; *Fax:* (519) 357-1897
www.cknx.ca
License: Wingham, ON held by Blackburn Radio Inc.
Group Owner: Blackburn Radio Inc.
Format: Country; *Special Programming:* Relg 6 hrs wkly; *Hrs. of News Programming:* news progmg 10 hrs wkly; *No. News Employees:* 7; *Target Audience:* 35-54.
Duane Duck, General Manager

CKNX-FM
04-17-1977; 101.7 MHz FM; *Hrs Open:* 24; 100 kw
215 Carling Terrace, Wingham, ON N0G 2W0 Canada
(519) 357-1310; *Fax:* (519) 357-1897
www.1017theone.ca
License: Wingham, ON held by Blackburn Radio Inc.
Group Owner: Blackburn Radio Inc.
TV Affiliate: CKNX-TV affil.; *Format:* Adult Contemp; *Target Audience:* 25-49.
Kimberly Ward, Operations Dir
Duane Duck, General Manager

CIBU-FM
04-01-2005; 94.5 MHz FM; 75 kw*Rebroadcasts:* Rebroadcasts At 91.7 Under CIBU-FM-1 In Bluewater.
215 Carling Terrace, Wingham, ON N0G 2W0 Canada
(519) 357-1310; *Fax:* (519) 357-1897
www.945thebull.ca
License: Wingham, ON held by Blackburn Radio Inc.
Group Owner: Blackburn Radio Inc.
Format: Classic Rock
Duane Duck, General Manager

Woodstock

CKDK-FM
103.9 MHz FM; *Hrs Open:* 24; 51 kw
290 Dundas St., Woodstock, ON N4S 1B2 Canada
(519) 931-6000
www.country104.com
robc@corusent.com
License: Woodstock, ON held by Corus Radio Co.
Group Owner: Corus Entertainment Inc.; (acq 1991)
Nat'l Reps: Canadian Broadcast Sales
Format: Country; *Hrs. of News Programming:* news progmg 9 hrs wkly; *No. News Employees:* 3; *Target Audience:* 25-54, larger London market
Jessica Quackenbush, General Sales Mgr
Brad Gibb, Brand Director
Kent Guy, Promotions Director
Leigh Robert, Music Director
Tom Cooke, Local Sales Manager
Chelsea Robinson, Promotions Coordinator

CJFH-FM
01-01-2004; 94.3 MHz FM; *Hrs Open:* 24; 37 w
Hope FM 94.3, 1038 Parkinson Rd, Woodstock, ON N4S 7W3 Canada
(519) 539-2304; *Fax:* (519) 539-2011
www.hopefm.ca
info@hopefm.ca

License: Woodstock, ON held by Sound of Faith Broadcasting.
Population Served: 37,754; *Arbitron Metro Market:* Woodstock, ON; *Format:* Christian; *Adv. Rates:* 30, 30, 30, 20
Gary Hill, General Manager
Marci Fess, General Sales Mgr

CIHR-FM
04-10-2006; 104.7 MHz FM; *Hrs Open:* 24; 8.95 kw; Woodstock
223 Norwich Ave., Woodstock, ON Canada
(519) 537-8400; *Fax:* (519)537-8600
1047.ca
chris@1047.ca
License: Woodstock, Oxford County, ON held by Byrnes Communications Inc.
Nat'l Reps: Canadian Broadcast Sales
Population Served: 100,000; *No. News Employees:* 4; *Target Audience:* 25-54; adults; *Adv. Rates:* 66.50; 50; 61; 44
Chris Byrnes, President
Michael Jones, General Manager
Dan Henry, Programming Director
Adam Nyp, News Director

Pennsylvania

CMS Station Brokerage, Inc.
1439 Denniston St., Pittsburgh, PA 15217 USA
(412) 421-2600; *Fax:* (412) 421-6001
www.cmsstationbrokerage.com
roger.rafson@genmediapartners.com
Roger Rafson, President
Shirley Brown, Office Manager

Prince Edward Island

Charlottetown

CBCT-FM
01-01-1972; 96.1 MHz FM; *Hrs Open:* 24; kw
Canada
(902) 629-6400; *Fax:* (902) 629-6518
www.cbc.ca/pei
License: Charlottetown, PE held by CBC.
Group Owner: Canadian Broadcasting Corporation
Nat'l Network: CBC Radio One
Format: Talk; *Hrs. of News Programming:* News progmg 11 hrs wkly
Hank van Leeuwen, Operations Dir
Donna Allen, Programming Director
Mitch Cormier, News Director

***CHLQ-FM**
03-01-1982; 93.1 MHz FM
5 Prince St., Charlottetown, PE C1A 4P4 Canada
(902) 892-1066; *Fax:* (902) 566-1338
www.q93.fm
License: Charlottetown, Queens County, PE held by Maritime Broadcasting System Ltd.
Group Owner: Maritime Broadcasting
Format: Rock/AOR
Robert Pace, CEO/COO
Al Baldwin, Operations Manager

CHTN-FM
07-05-2006; 100.3 MHz FM; 33 kw; N46 11 22 W63 09 54
176 Great George St., Charlottetown, PE C1A 4K9 Canada
(902) 569-1003; *Fax:* (902) 569-8693
www.ocean100.com
License: Charlottetown, PE held by Newcap Inc.
Group Owner: NewCap Inc.
Nat'l Reps: Canadian Broadcast Sales
Population Served: 64,487; *Arbitron Metro Market:* Charlottetown, PE; *Format:* Adult Contemp, Contemporary Hits/Top 40; *Hrs. of News Programming:* news progmg 17 hrs wkly; *No. News Employees:* 2; *Target Audience:* 25-54.
Jennifer Evans, General Manager
Corey Tremere, Programming Director
Scott Chapman, News Director
Ron Gillespie, Production Director

CFCY-FM
01-01-2006; 95.1 MHz FM; 100 kw
5 Prince St., Charlottetown, PE C1A 4P4 Canada
(902) 892-1066; *Fax:* (902) 566-1338
www.cfcy.fm
License: Charlottetown, PE held by Maritime Broadcasting System Ltd.
Group Owner: Maritime Broadcasting
Population Served: 64,487; *Arbitron Metro Market:* Charlottetown, PE; *Format:* Country
Robert Pace, CEO/COO

CKQK-FM
07-25-2006; 105.5 MHz FM; 33 kw; N46 12 44 W63 20 32
176 Great George St., Charlottetown, PE C1A 4K9 Canada
(902) 569-1003; *Fax:* (902) 569-8693
www.hot1055fm.com
License: Charlottetown, PE held by Newcap Inc.
Group Owner: NewCap Inc.
Population Served: 64,487; *Arbitron Metro Market:* Charlottetown, PE; *Format:* Classic Rock, Contemporary Hits/Top 40; *Target Audience:* 25-44; male
Jennifer Evans, General Manager
Matt MacLeod, Programming Director
Stephanie Mueller, Promotions

CIOG-FM
01-01-2008; 91.3 MHz FM; 250 w; N46 17 14 W63 06 08
516 Pinewood Road, Unit Two, Riverview, NB E1B 5J9 Canada
(506) 872-2901; *Fax:* (506) 872-2234
www.ciogfm.com
License: Charlottetown, PE held by International Harvesters for Christ Evangelistic Association Inc.
Jeff Lutes, President

Summerside

CJRW-FM
01-01-2000; 102.1 MHz FM; *Hrs Open:* 5:57 AM-12:15 AM; 11 kw
763 Water St., Summerside, PE C1N 4J3 Canada
(902) 436-2202
www.spud.fm
License: Summerside, PE held by Maritime Broadcasting System Ltd.
Group Owner: Maritime Broadcasting; (acq 8-10-2000; C$650,000 for approximately 92.9% of the common shares).
Population Served: 14,751; *Arbitron Metro Market:* Summerside, PE; *Format:* Adult Contemp; *No. News Employees:* 1; *Target Audience:* General.
Robert Pace, CEO/COO

Québec

Acton Vale

CFID-FM
01-01-2004; 103.7 MHz FM; *Hrs Open:* 24; kw
Canada
(450) 546-1037; *Fax:* (450) 546-7521
www.radio-acton.com
info@radio-acton.com
License: Acton Vale, QC held by Radio-Acton inc.
Arbitron Metro Market: Acton Vale, QC; *Format:* Variety/Diverse, French
Gaetan Chevanelle, General Manager
Andr,e-Anne Dubois, General Sales Mgr
Pierre Brousseau, Programming Director
Marie-Pier Roy, Music Manager
Beatrice Trahan, Director General
Jean-Francois Fortier, Sales Representative
MichelMorin, Facilitator and copywriter
Eric Caron, Sales representative, bingo and Webmaster
Carole Chabot, Reception

Alma

CKYK-FM
01-01-1993; 95.7 MHz FM; 100 kw; N48 24 05 W72 05 23
345 rue des Saguen,ens, Office 160, Saguenay, QC G7H 6K9 Canada
(418) 543-8912; *Fax:* (418) 543-0225
License: Alma, QC held by Groupe Radio Antenne 6 Inc.
Group Owner: RNC Media Saguenay-Lac-Saint-Jean
Format: Rock/AOR, Classic Rock, French
Marc-Andre Levesque, President

CFGT-FM
10-13-2010; 104.5 MHz FM; 20 kw
460 Sacr,-Coeur Ouest, Alma, QC G8B 1L9 Canada
(418) 662-6888
www.alma.planeteradio.ca
License: Alma, QC held by Groupe Radio Antenne 6 Inc.
Group Owner: RNC Media Saguenay-Lac-Saint-Jean
Arbitron Metro Market: Alma, QC; *Format:* Adult Contemp, French
Marc-Andre Levesque, President

Amos

CHOW-FM
105.3 MHz FM; 5.376 kw; N48 34 25 W78 09 44
43, 1st Ave East, Bureau 100, Amos, QC J9T 1H2 Canada
(819) 732-6991; *Fax:* (819) 732-6988
www.radioboreale.com
License: Amos, QC held by Radio Boreale.
Population Served: 12,671; *Arbitron Metro Market:* Amos, QC; *Format:* Talk
Real Bordeleau, President
Jean Champagne, Vice President
Denis Germain, Administrator
Guylaine Belley, Coordinator

Amqui

CFVM-FM
01-01-2003; 99.9 MHz FM; 23.8 kw
111 rue de l'Hopital, Amqui, QC G5J 2K1 Canada
(418) 629-2025; *Fax:* (418) 629-2599
www.amqui.rougefm.ca
cfvm@globetrotter.net
License: Amqui, QC held by Astral Media Radio inc.
Group Owner: Bell Media Inc.
Population Served: 6,322; *Arbitron Metro Market:* Amqui, QC; *Format:* Adult Contemp, Classic Rock; *Hrs. of News Programming:* news progmg 6 hrs wkly; *No. News Employees:* 2; *Target Audience:* 18 plus.
Adalbert Levesque, General Manager
Jean Lemay, Programming Director
Jennifer Gravel, News Director
Jean Fournier, Engineering Dir
Alain Revard, Disc Jockey

Asbestos

CJAN-FM
01-01-2001; 99.3 MHz FM; kw
Canada
(819) 879-0993; *Fax:* (819) 879-7922
www.fm993.ca
info@fm993.ca
License: Asbestos, QC held by Radio Plus B.M.D. inc.
Nat'l Reps: Target Broadcast Sales
Arbitron Metro Market: Asbestos, QC; *Format:* Adult Contemp; *No. News Employees:* 1; *Target Audience:* 35-75; general
Marie-Paule Drouin, President
Marie-Paule G. Drouin, Owner, host
Denis Beaulieu, Aadvertising consultant
Sylvie Pion, Reporter, routing
Lydia Jacques, Moderator, production
Yvon Leblanc, Moderator, production
Jean-MathieuFontaine, Moderator

Baie St Paul

CIHO-FM
10-10-1986; 96.3 MHz FM; *Hrs Open:* 24; kw
Canada
(418) 457-3333; *Fax:* (418) 457-3518
www.cihofm.com
ciho@charlevoix.net
License: Baie St Paul, QC held by Radio MF Charlevoix Inc.
Format: Adult Contemp; *Special Programming:* Class 2 hrs, jazz 2 hrs wkly
Gervais Desbiens, General Manager
Rene Belanger, General Sales Mgr
Pierre Beauchesne, Programming Director
Dave Kid, News Director

Baie-Comeau

***CHLC-FM**
01-01-1996; 97.1 MHz FM; kw
Canada
(418) 589-3771; *Fax:* (418) 589-9086
www.chlc.com
info@chlc.com
License: Baie-Comeau, QC held by 9022-6242 Québec Inc.
Format: Adult Contemp; *Target Audience:* General.
Yvon Savoes, President
Francois Morache, Operations Dir
George Daviault, General Manager
Mike Mainville, Programming Director
Mark Andre Halle, News Director

Bathurst

CKLE-FM
03-29-1990; 92.9 MHz FM; *Hrs Open:* 24; kw
Canada
(506) 546-4600; *Fax:* (506) 546-6611
www.ckle.fm
superstation@ckle.fm

License: Bathurst, Gloucester County, NB held by Radio De LaBaie Ltd.
Format: Contemporary Hits/Top 40; *Special Programming:* Jazz 2 hrs wkly; *Adv. Rates:* 26; 23; 18; 14
Armand Roussy, General Manager

Becancour and Nicolet

CKBN-FM
01-01-2008; 90.5 MHz FM; 34 kw; Ant 118 ft; N46 17 04 W72 32 01
10275 Leblanc, Suite 127, Becancour, QC Canada
(819) 294-2526; *Fax:* (819) 294-2527
www.ckbn.ca
License: Becancour and Nicolet, QC held by Cooperative de solidarite radio communautaire Nicolet-Yamaska/Becancour.
Population Served: 25,000
Raymond Noel, President
Raymond Noel, General Manager
Elaine Bolove, Programming Director

Carleton

CIEU-FM
01-01-1983; 94.9 MHz FM; *Hrs Open:* 24; kw
Canada
(418) 364-7094; *Fax:* (418) 364-3150
www.cieufm.com
cieufm@cieufm.com
License: Carleton, Bonaventure County, QC held by Diffusion Communautaire Baie des Chaleurs Inc.
Group Owner: Cogeco Diffusion
Format: Adult Contemp, Contemporary Hits/Top 40; *Special Programming:* Blues 5 hrs, class 3 hrs, folk 3 hrs, jazz 3 hrs w; *Hrs. of News Programming:* news progmg 7 hrs wkly; *No. News Employees:* 2; *Target Audience:* General.
Jacques Veillette, President
Louis St-Laurent, General Manager
Carol Boudreau, Programming Director
Yues Sigouin, News Director
Claude Roy, Local News Editor

Chandler

CFMV-FM
06-08-2005; 96.3 MHz FM; 5.716 kw
Mailing Address: C.P. 99, Chandler, QC G0C 1K0 Canada
Second Address: 141 rue Commerciale Ouest, Chandler, PQ G0C 1K0
(418) 689-4921; *Fax:* (418) 689-3852
License: Chandler, QC held by Radio du Golfe inc.
Population Served: 7,703; *Arbitron Metro Market:* Chandler, QC; *Format:* French
Jacques Vallee, General Manager

Charlesbourg

CIMI-FM
08-10-2001; 103.7 MHz FM; 20 w
4500, Blvd. Henri-Bairassa bur. 103, Charlesbourg, QC G1H 3A5 Canada
(418) 841-4445; *Fax:* (418) 623-2538
www.cimifm.com
License: Charlesbourg, QC
Population Served: 516,622; *Arbitron Metro Market:* Québec City, QC; *Format:* Alternative
Gerald St. Arnaud, President
Francois Beaule, Operations Dir
Eric Veilleux, Programming Director

Chateauguay

CHAI-FM
01-01-1980; 101.9 MHz FM; 100 w
25 boul. St. Francis, Chateauguay, QC J6J 1Y2 Canada
(450) 698-3131; *Fax:* (450) 698-3339
www.101fm.net
License: Chateauguay, QC held by Radio Communautaires de Chateauguay Inc.
Population Served: 75,000; *Format:* Adult Contemp; *Hrs. of News Programming:* news progmg 4 hrs wkly; *No. News Employees:* 2; *Target Audience:* General; all ages
Christian Laberge, President
Sylvain Poirier, Operations Dir

Chibougamau

CKXO-FM
11-21-1969; 93.5 MHz FM; 75 kw; N49 56 46 W74 20 57
171A, rue Jean-Proulx, Gatineau, QC J8Z 1W5 Canada
(819) 770-9650
www.chibougamau.planeteradio.ca
License: Chibougamau, QC held by Groupe Radio Antenne 6 Inc.
Group Owner: RNC Media Saguenay-Lac-Saint-Jean
Population Served: 7,541; *Arbitron Metro Market:* Chibougamau, QC; *Format:* Adult Contemp, French
Robert Parent, Operations Dir

Chicoutimi

***CBJX-FM**
09-20-1933; 100.9 MHz FM; *Hrs Open:* 24; 98 kw; Ant 294 ft; N48 25 29 W71 06 32*Rebroadcasts:* Rebroadcasts CBF-FM Montreal 95%
500 rue Des Sagueneens, Chicoutimi, QC G7H 6N4 Canada
(418) 696-6600; *Fax:* (418) 696-6689
www.radio-canada.ca/espace_musique/
License: Chicoutimi, QC held by Canadian Broadcasting Corp.
Nat'l Network: Espace Musique
Population Served: 150,000; *Format:* Classical
Patrick Boie, Operations Dir

***CBJ-FM**
01-01-2001; 93.7 MHz FM; *Hrs Open:* 24; kw*Rebroadcasts:* Rebroadcasts CBF-FM Montreal, 70%
Canada
(418) 696-6600; *Fax:* (418) 696-6689
www.radio-canada.ca
License: Chicoutimi, QC held by Canadian Broadcasting Corp.
Nat'l Network: Premiere Chaine
Arbitron Metro Market: Chicoutimi, PQ; *Format:* Talk; *No. News Employees:* 7; *Target Audience:* 35 plus; adlut, news-oriented
Hubert T. Lacroix, President & CEO
Patrick Boie, General Manager
Maryse Bertrand, Vice-President, Real Estate, Legal Services and Ge
William B. Chambers, Vice-President, Brand, Communications and Corporat
Steven Guiton,Vice-President and Chief Regulatory Officer
Louis Lalande, Executive Vice-President, French Services
Kirstine Stewart, Executive Vice-President of CBC's English Services
Roula Zaar, Vice-President, People and Culture

Degelis

CFVD
01-01-1978; 95.5 MHz FM; *Hrs Open:* 24; 12.474 w; Vieux-Chemin
654 Rue East, Degelis, QC G5T1Y1 Canada
(418) 853-3370; *Fax:* (418) 853-3321
www.fm95.ca
horizon@fm95.ca
License: Degelis, QC held by Radio Degelis Inc.
Group Owner: Radio Degelis Inc.
Population Served: 23,000; *Format:* Adult Contemp, Country, Contemporary Hits/Top 40; *Hrs. of News Programming:* 24/24 7/7; *No. News Employees:* 10; *Target Audience:* General.; *Adv. Rates:* 24; 22; 20; 5
Gilles Caron, President/General Manager
Guylain Jean, News Director
Jacques Martin, Engineering Dir

Dolbeau-Mistassini

CHVD-FM
01-01-2002; 100.3 MHz FM; *Hrs Open:* 24; 50 kw
1975, boul Wallberg, Dolbeau, QC G8L 1J5 Canada
(418) 276-3333; *Fax:* (418) 276-6755
License: Dolbeau-Mistassini, QC held by Groupe Radio Antenne 6 Inc.
Group Owner: RNC Media Saguenay-Lac-Saint-Jean; (acq 5-2004).
Format: Adult Contemp, French
Marc-Andre Levesque, President
Marc Levesque, Operations Dir
Louis Arcand, Programming Director

CKII-FM
01-01-2004; 101.3 MHz FM; 250 w
1709 boul. Wallberg, Dolbeau-Mistassini, QC G8L 1H6 Canada
(418) 239-2544; *Fax:* (418) 239-0842
License: Dolbeau-Mistassini, QC held by L'Alliance Laurentienne des metis et indiens sans statut, Local 30 Mistassini inc.
Population Served: 12,125; *Arbitron Metro Market:* Dolbeau, QC; *Format:* French
Michel Bouchard, General Manager

Donnacona

CHXX-FM
01-01-1997; 100.9 MHz FM; 1.585 kw
#300, 1134 Grande-Allee ouest, Donnacona, QC G1S 1E5 Canada
(418) 687-9810; *Fax:* (418) 682-8427
www.rock1009.ca
License: Donnacona, QC held by RNC MEDIA Inc.
Group Owner: RNC MEDIA Inc.; (acq 12-23-2005)
Format: Rock/AOR
Raynald Briere, President

Drummondville

CHRD-FM
01-01-1997; 105.3 MHz FM; *Hrs Open:* 24; 2.9 kw
2070 rue St. Georges, Drummondville, QC J2C 5G6 Canada
(819) 475-1480; *Fax:* (819) 475-5180
www.drummondville.rougefm.ca
License: Drummondville, QC held by Astral Media Radio Inc.
Group Owner: Bell Media Inc.
Format: Adult Contemp, News; *Special Programming:* Relg one hr wkly; *Hrs. of News Programming:* news progmg 15 hrs wkly; *No. News Employees:* 3; *Target Audience:* 18 plus; general
Joel Rioux, President
Martin Tremblay, Programming Director
David Rivet, News Director
Michel Cournoyer, Chief Engineer
Robert Veilleux, Special Events Coordinator

CJDM-FM
08-15-1987; 92.1 MHz FM; *Hrs Open:* 24; kw
Canada
(819) 474-1892; *Fax:* (819) 474-6610
drummondville.radionrj.ca
License: Drummondville, QC held by Astral Media Radio inc.
Group Owner: Bell Media Inc.
Nat'l Reps: Canadian Broadcast Sales
Format: Adult Contemp; *Hrs. of News Programming:* news progmg 5 hrs wkly; *No. News Employees:* 2; *Target Audience:* 18-44.
Joel Rioux, General Manager
Claude Rene Piette, Programming Director
Martine Pichette, Promotions Manager
Claude Boucher, News Director
Daniel Pelletier, Engineering Dir
Alain Rivard, Music Director

CJRD-FM
12-27-2007; 88.9 MHz FM; 710 w; N45 53 00 W72 29 19
161 rue Marchand, Drummondville, QC J2B 4N3 Canada
(819) 474-2573; *Fax:* (819) 474-0296
www.cjrd.fm
License: Drummondville, QC held by Radio Drummond.
Population Served: 71,852; *Arbitron Metro Market:* Drummondville, QC; *Format:* News, Talk
Georges Masse, President
Jean-Pierre Charbonneau, General Manager

Fermont

CBMR-FM
01-01-1982; 105.1 MHz FM; 16 w
1400 Rene Levesque E., c/o CBM(AM) - A 4, Montr,al, QC H2L 8M2 Canada
(514) 597-4444; *Fax:* (514) 597-4416
www.cbc.ca
License: Fermont, QC held by Canadian Broadcasting Corp.
Format: News
Patricia Pleszczynska, Operations Dir
Judith Bleier, Operations Manager

CFMF-FM
01-01-1980; 103.1 MHz FM; 50 w; 100 ft
20 Daviault Place., Box 280, Fermont, QC G0G 1J0 Canada
(418) 287-5147; *Fax:* (418) 287-5776
www.cfmf.ca
License: Fermont, QC held by Radio Communautaire de Fermont Inc.
Format: Contemporary Hits/Top 40, Variety/Diverse; *Special Programming:* Jazz one hr, C&W 4 hrs wkly; *Target Audience:* 7-55.
Marc Poulin, President
Jocelyn Pelletier, Operations Dir
Nadia Larrivee, General Manager
Karl Gagne-Cote, Programming Director
Carl Champagne, News Director
Genevieve Richard, Music Director

Forestville

CFRP
01-01-1977; 620 kHz AM
Canada
(418) 589-3771; *Fax:* (418) 589-9086

License: Forestville, QC held by 9022-6242 Québec Inc.
Format: Adult Contemp
Yvon Savoie, President
George Baviauet, General Manager
Lynn Martin, News Director

Fort-Coulonge

*CHIPFM
05-02-1981; 101.5 MHz FM; *Hrs Open:* 24; kw
Mailing Address: Canada
Second Address: 138 Principal St., Fort Coulonge, PQ JOX 1VO
(819) 683-3155; *Fax:* (819) 683-3211
www.chipfm.com
radiopontiac@chipfm.com
License: Fort-Coulonge, QC held by La Radio du Pontiac Inc.
Format: Country; *Special Programming:* Oldies, rock, gospel 7 hrs, class 2 hrs wkly; *Hrs. of News Programming:* News progmg 5 hrs wkly; *Target Audience:* 35 yrs & up; rural people. farming communities, small towns
Chantele Legault, General Manager

Gaspe

CJRG-FM
12-01-1978; 103.1 MHz FM; kw
Canada
(418) 368-3511; *Fax:* (418) 368-1663
www.radiogaspesie.ca
License: Gaspe, QC held by Radio Gaspesie Inc.
Format: Adult Contemp; *Special Programming:* Class 2 hrs, jazz 2 hrs wkly
Jacques Chartier, General Manager
Paul Minville, General Sales Mgr
Richard O'Leary, News Director
Yvan DuPuis, Engineering Dir

Gatineau

CIMF-FM
01-01-1970; 94.9 MHz FM; kw
Canada
(819) 770-2463; *Fax:* (819) 770-9338
www.rockdetente.com
License: Gatineau, QC held by Astral Media Radio Inc.
Group Owner: Bell Media Inc.
Format: Classic Rock; *Hrs. of News Programming:* news progmg 3 hrs wkly; *No. News Employees:* 2; *Target Audience:* 18-45+
Ian Greenberg, President
Carmen Rodrigue, General Manager
Claude Raymond, General Sales Mgr
Patrice Croteau, Programming Director
Eric St-Louis, Promotions Manager
Mano Aube, News Director
Pierre Sylvestre, Chief Engineer
Jean-Guy Faucher, Music Director

CKTF-FM
03-11-1988; 104.1 MHz FM; *Hrs Open:* 24; kw
Canada
(819) 243-5555; *Fax:* (819) 243-6816
License: Gatineau, QC held by Astral Media Radio Inc.
Group Owner: Bell Media Inc.
Format: Contemporary Hits/Top 40, Rock/AOR
Carmen Rodrigue, General Manager
Vincent Pons, General Sales Mgr
Astral Musique, Programming Director
Melany Gauvin, Promotions Manager
Pierre Sylvestre, Engineering Dir

CHLX-FM
09-23-2002; 97.1 MHz FM; 12.6 kw
171-A, rue Jean-Proulx, Gatineau, QC J8Z 1W5 Canada
(819) 770-1040
www.rythmefm.com
License: Gatineau, QC held by RNC MEDIA Inc.
Group Owner: RNC MEDIA Inc.; (acq 8-25-2004)
Population Served: 66,246; *Arbitron Metro Market:* Hull, QC;
Format: Adult Contemp, Jazz
Amelie Gauvreau, Promotions Coordinator
Allen Vallieres, News Director
Etienne Gregoire, Musical Director

CKOF-FM
04-16-2007; 104.7 MHz FM; 36 kw; Ant 136 ft; N45 25 09 W75 42 18
150, rue d'Edmonton, Gatineau, QC J8Y 3S6 Canada
(819) 561-8801; *Fax:* (819) 561-3333
www.fm1047.ca
License: Gatineau, QC held by Cogeco Diffusion Inc.
Group Owner: Cogeco Diffusion Inc.
Population Served: 265,349; *Arbitron Metro Market:* Gatineau, QC; *Hrs. of News Programming:* news progmg 49 hrs wkly; *No. News Employees:* 3; *Target Audience:* 35-64; adult-babyboomers 50% males, 50% females*Adv. Rates:* 90; 75; 90; 50
Sylvie Charette, General Manager
Kathleen Michaud, General Sales Mgr
Louis-Philippe Bruce, News Director

CFTX-FM
04-13-2006; 96.5 MHz FM; 1.75 kw
171-A, rue Jean-Proulx, Gatineau, QC J8Z 1W5 Canada
(819) 770-1040
www.capitalerock.ca
License: Gatineau, QC held by RNC MEDIA Inc.
Group Owner: RNC MEDIA Inc.
Arbitron Metro Market: Gatineau, QC; *Format:* Rock/AOR
Raynald Briere, President

CKOF-FM
104.7 MHz FM
150 d'Edmonton, Gatineau, QC J8Y 3S6 Canada
(819) 561-8801; *Fax:* (819) 561-3333
www.fm1047.ca
License: Gatineau, La Vall,e-de-la-Gatineau County, QC
Group Owner: Cogeco Diffusion Inc.

Granby

CFXM
01-01-1997; 104.9 MHz FM; kw
Canada
(450) 372-5105; *Fax:* (450) 372-3105
www.m105.ca
License: Granby, QC held by Cooperative de travail de la radio de Granby.
Arbitron Metro Market: Granby, QC; *Format:* Adult Contemp
Stephan Roy, General Manager
Luc Normandin, General Sales Mgr
Guy Laporte, Promotions Manager

Harrington Harbour

*CFTH-FM-1
10-30-1991; 97.7 MHz FM; 180 w; N50 29 36 W59 28 50
Box 88, Harrington Harbour, Duplessis, QC G0G 1N0 Canada
(418) 795-3349; *Fax:* (418) 795-3200
License: Harrington Harbour, QC held by Radio Communautaire de Harrington Harbour.
Format: Adult Contemp, Country, Oldies; *Target Audience:* General; five fishing villages
Kate Nadeau, General Manager
Nancy Bobbitt, Programming Director
Lois Jones, Programming Director
Monica Anderson, Replacement Programming Director

CFTH-FM-2
01-01-1991; 98.5 MHz FM; 70 w
Box 88, Harrington Harbour, QC G0G 1N0 Canada
(418) 795-3349; *Fax:* (418) 795-3200
License: Harrington Harbour, QC held by Radio communautaire de Harrington Harbour.
Kate Nadeau, General Manager
Nancy Bobbitt, Programming Director
Lois Jones, Programming Director

Havre-Saint-Pierre

CILE-FM
01-01-1987; 95.1 MHz FM; *Hrs Open:* 24; 1.496 kw; Ant 201 ft
992 Rue du Bouleau, Havre-Saint-Pierre, QC G0G 1P0 Canada
(418) 538-2453; *Fax:* (418) 538-3870
www.cilemf.com
License: Havre-Saint-Pierre, QC held by Radio & Television Communautaire Havre-St. Pierre.
Format: Adult Contemp
Berchmens Boudreau, General Manager
Catherine Ramoisy, News Director
Gerald Gallant, Engineering Dir

Hudson/Saint-Lazare

CHSV-FM
11-04-2014; 106.7 MHz FM; 500 w; 94 meters
5312 Dundas St. W., Toronto, ON M9B 1B3 Canada
(416) 213-1035; *Fax:* (416) 233-8617
www.jewelradio.com/new/1067
info@jewel1067.com
License: Hudson/Saint-Lazare, QC held by Dufferin Communications Inc.
Group Owner: Evanov Communications Inc.
Format: Adult Contemp
Ky Joseph, General Sales Mgr
Vanessa Malloy, Promotions Coordinator

Iles-de-la-Madeleine

CFIM-FM
11-15-1981; 92.7 MHz FM; *Hrs Open:* 24; 6.3 kw
1172 chemin de La VerniŠRe, L'Etand du Nord, QC G4T 1R3 Canada
(418) 986-5233; *Fax:* (418) 986-5319
www.cfim.ca
administration@cfim.ca
License: Iles-de-la-Madeleine, QC held by Diffusion Communautaire des Iles Inc.
Group Owner: Cogeco Diffusion
Format: News, News/Talk, Talk, Variety/Diverse; *Target Audience:* General.
Charles-EugŠne Cyr, Director General
Huguette DŠraspe, Administrative Assistant

Joliette

CJLM-FM
01-01-1996; 103.5 MHz FM; *Hrs Open:* 24; 3 kw; N45 59 0 W73 25 52
540, rue St-Thomas, Joliette, QC J6E 3R4 Canada
(450) 756-1035; *Fax:* (450) 756-8097
www.m1035fm.com
radio@m1035fm.com
License: Joliette, QC held by 8470286 Canada Inc.
Group Owner: Attraction Radio Inc.
Format: Adult Contemp; *Special Programming:* Oldies 6 hrs wkly; *No. News Employees:* 4; *Target Audience:* 25-49.; *Adv. Rates:* 42; 42; 40; 39
Normand Masse, General Manager
Andre Giroux, Information
Jean Asselin, Sales
Alain Dansereau, Sales

Jonquiere

CKAJ-FM
04-11-1977; 92.5 MHz FM; *Hrs Open:* 6 AM-midnight; 14.164 kw
Mailing Address: 3877 Harvey Blvd, 2nd Fl., Jonquiere, QC G7X 0A6 Canada
Second Address: Pavillon Manicouagan, 3791, De La Fabrique, Jonquiere, PQ G7X 7W8
(418) 546-2525; *Fax:* (418) 546-2528
www.ckaj.org
ckaj@ckaj.org
License: Jonquiere, QC held by Radio Communautaire du Saguenay Inc.
Format: Country, Variety/Diverse; *Hrs. of News Programming:* news progmg 6 hrs wkly; *No. News Employees:* 1; *Target Audience:* 25-54.
Johanne Tremblay, President
Pierre Boivin, Programming Director
Henri Girard, Chief Engineer

Kahnawake

*CKRK-FM
03-30-1981; 103.7 MHz FM; *Hrs Open:* 24; kw
Canada
(450) 638-1313; *Fax:* (450) 638-4009
www.k103radio.com
info@k103radio.com
License: Kahnawake, QC held by Mohawk Radio Kahnawake Association.
Format: Adult Contemp, Country; *Special Programming:* Mohawk 10 wkly; *Hrs. of News Programming:* news progmg 3 hrs wkly; *No. News Employees:* 2; *Target Audience:* Native community in Kahawake; general audience Montrealregion
Lois Williams, General Sales Mgr
Vince Barrucco, Programming Director
Dino Sisto, News Director
Don Garrett, Disc Jockey
Lance Delisle, Disc Jockey
Thomasina Phillips, News Reporter
Marsha Dailleboust, Traffic Manager

CKKI-FM
06-12-2011; 89.9 MHz FM; kw
Canada
(450) 635-2099
License: Kahnawake, QC held by Brian Moon
Format: Country
Brian Moon, General Manager

Kuujjuaq

CKUJ-FM
01-01-1992; 97.3 MHz FM; *Hrs Open:* 10am-12pm; 2-5pm; 394 w
Box 1082, Kuujjuaq, QC J0M 1C0 Canada
(819) 964-2921; *Fax:* (819) 964-2229
License: Kuujjuaq, QC held by Minister Council of Kuujjuaq.
Population Served: 2,375; *Arbitron Metro Market:* Kuujjuaq, PQ; *Format:* Ethnic
Larry Watt, President
Mary Gordon, Operations Dir

La Baie

CKGS-FM
03-19-2009; 105.5 MHz FM; 2.93 kw; 32.87 meters; N48 21 08 W70 53 56
345, rue Racine, Chicoutimi, QC G7H 1S8 Canada
(418) 545-2577
www.rythmefm.com
License: La Baie, QC held by 9202-1617 Québec Inc.
Group Owner: Attraction Radio Inc.
Format: Adult Contemp
Sylvain Carbonneau, General Manager
Sylvain Carbonneau, General Sales Mgr
Pierre-Luc Desbiens, Promotions Director
Catherine Paquette, Promotions Coordinator

La Malbaie

***CBV-FM-6**
09-20-1979; 99.3 MHz FM; *Hrs Open:* 24; 820 w; Ant 108 ft; N47 41 02 W70 08 06*Rebroadcasts:* Rebroadcasts CBV-FM Québec 100%
888 Saint-Jean St., Québec, QC G1R 5H6 Canada
(418) 654-1341; *Fax:* (418) 656-8842
www.radio-canada.ca/Québec
License: La Malbaie, QC held by CBC.
Nat'l Network: Premiere Chaine
Format: News
Claude- Saindon, Operations Dir
Susan Campbell, General Manager
Sally Caldwell, News Director
Gaston LeBlanc, Engineering Dir

La Pocatiere

CHOX-FM
04-23-1992; 97.5 MHz FM; 25 kw
601 First St., Suite 50, La Pocatiere, QC G0R1Z0 Canada
(418) 856-1310; *Fax:* (418) 856-3747
www.chox97.com
chox@chox97.com
License: La Pocatiere, QC held by CHOX-FM Inc.
Group Owner: Groupe Radio Simard
Format: Adult Contemp
Guy Simard, President
Gilles Gosselin, Operations Dir
Diane Bouchard, General Sales Mgr
Renee Giard, Promotions Manager
Jacques Dufour, News Director
Clement Lavoie, Engineering Dir
Maxima Parabas, Music Director
Gabriel Hudon,Promotions Manager
Georgette Charent, Sales VP

La Sarre

CJGO-FM
01-01-1997; 102.1 MHz FM; 4.13 kw
380, rue Murdoch, Rouyn-Noranda, QC J9X 1G5 Canada
(819) 762-0741; *Fax:* (819) 762-2466
www.abitibi.capitalerock.ca
live@abitibi.capitalerock.ca
License: La Sarre, QC held by RNC MEDIA Inc.
Group Owner: RNC MEDIA Inc.
Arbitron Metro Market: Rouyn-Noranda, QC; *Format:* Rock/AOR
Nancy Deschenes, General Manager
Nancy Deschenes, General Sales Mgr
Francis Morin, Programming Director
Michelle Desjardins, Promotions Representative

La Tuque

CFLM-FM
01-01-2013; 97.1 MHz FM; 18.23 kw; 127.3 meters; N47 25 24 W72 45 49
C.P. 850, La Tuque, QC G9X 3P6 Canada
(819) 523-4575; *Fax:* (819) 676-8000
License: La Tuque, QC held by Radio Haute Mauricle Inc.
Rejean LeClerc, President

Lac Megantic

CJIT-FM
01-01-2000; 106.7 MHz FM; *Hrs Open:* 24; 4.25 kw
4766, rue Laval, Lac Megantic, QC G6B 1C7 Canada
(819) 583-0663
www.cjitfm.com
radiocjit@gmail.com
License: Lac Megantic, QC held by Les Productions du Temps Perdu Inc.
Group Owner: Attraction Radio Inc.; (acq 3-12-2007; C$200,000)
Nat'l Reps: Target Broadcast Sales
Population Served: 5,932; *Arbitron Metro Market:* Lac Megantic, QC; *Format:* Adult Contemp, Contemporary Hits/Top 40
Sylvain Chamberland, President
Michel Brochu, Account Manager

Lac-Brome

CIDI-FM
09-20-2007; 99.1 MHz FM; 1.45 kw; Ant 165 ft; N45 11 10 W72 35 20
Box 3611, 305B Knowlton Rd., Knowlton, QC J0E 1V0 Canada
(450) 243-6285; *Fax:* (450) 243-1041
www.sunnymead.org/cidi
deweydurrell@axion.ca
License: Lac-Brome, QC held by Radio Communautaire Missisquoi.
Population Served: 211,000; *Arbitron Metro Market:* Redding, CA; *Format:* Talk; *Hrs. of News Programming:* news progmg 21 hrs wkly; *No. News Employees:* 3; *Target Audience:* 18-60.; *Adv. Rates:* 160; 160; 160; 160
Lana Littlechief, General Manager

Lac-Etchemin

***CFIN-FM**
03-27-1992; 100.5 MHz FM; *Hrs Open:* 24; 6.7 kw; 676 ft; N46 24 41 W70 35 44
201 Claude-Bilodeau St., Lac-Etchemin, QC G0R 1S0 Canada
(418) 625-3737; *Fax:* (418) 625-3730
www.cfinfm.com
License: Lac-Etchemin, Bellechasse County, QC held by Radio Bellechasse.
Regional Reps: Target.
Population Served: 50,000; *Format:* Adult Contemp, Country; *Special Programming:* Class 4 hrs, jazz 6 hrs, relg one hr, country 6 hr; *Hrs. of News Programming:* news progmg 30 hrs wkly; *No. News Employees:* 2*TargetAudience:* 35-60.
Marcel Asselin, President
Raymond Boutin, Station Manager
Isabelle Giasson, Programming Director
Norman Poulin, News Director

Lac-Simon (Louvicourt)

CHUT-FM
01-01-2000; 95.3 MHz FM; 97.9 w
1016 rue Wabanonik, Lac-Simon, QC J0Y 3M0 Canada
(819) 736-4501; *Fax:* (819) 736-2333
License: Lac-Simon (Louvicourt), QC held by Radio communautaire MF Lac Simon inc.
Population Served: 984; *Arbitron Metro Market:* Lac-Simon, PQ; *Format:* Ethnic
Alain Flamand, General Manager

Lachute

***CJLA-FM**
12-01-1974; 104.9 MHz FM; *Hrs Open:* 24; 3 kw
11, av Argenteuil, Lachute, QC J8H 1X8 Canada
(450) 562-8862; *Fax:* (450) 562-1902
www.lachute.planeteradio.ca
License: Lachute, QC held by RNC MEDIA Inc.
Group Owner: RNC MEDIA Inc.; (acq 8-22-89)
Format: Adult Contemp; *Hrs. of News Programming:* news progmg 8 hrs wkly; *No. News Employees:* 1; *Target Audience:* 25-59.
Raynald Briere, President

Laval

CFGL-FM
09-01-1968; 105.7 MHz FM; *Hrs Open:* 24; kw Canada
(450) 664-1500; *Fax:* (450) 664-4138
www.rythmefm.com
License: Laval, QC held by Cogeco Diffusion inc.
Group Owner: Cogeco Diffusion Inc.
Format: Adult Contemp; *Hrs. of News Programming:* news progmg 2 hrs wkly; *No. News Employees:* 2; *Target Audience:* 25-54; those preferring soft & easy lstng hits
Sylvain Venne, Operations Dir
Richard LaChance, General Manager
Andre St-Amand, Programming Director
Daniel Brouilette, Promotions Manager
Jean Arcand, Engineering Dir
Lilianne Randall, Music Director

CJLV
01-01-2004; 1570 kHz AM; 10 kw-U
Radio Nostalgie, 2040 Autoroute Laval, Laval, QC Canada
(450) 680-1570
License: Laval, QC held by 759 474 Canada Inc
Colette Chabot, General Manager

Levis

CFEL-FM
12-01-1986; 102.1 MHz FM; *Hrs Open:* 24; 78 kw
#505, 815, boul Lebourgneuf, Québec, QC G2J 0C1 Canada
(418) 780-1021
www.blvd.fm
studio@blvd.fm
License: Levis, QC held by CFEL Inc.
Group Owner: Leclerc Communications Inc.
Format: Adult Contemp, Contemporary Hits/Top 40; *No. News Employees:* 1; *Target Audience:* 25-49.
Jean-Francois Leclerc, General Manager
Pierre-Luc Gilbert, Sales Manager
Dan Caron, Programming Director
Caroline Perron, Promotions
John Pedulla, Music Director

CFOM-FM
01-01-1992; 102.9 MHz FM; 16.8 kw
2136.ch.Ste-foy, Québec, QC G1V 1R8 Canada
(418) 694-1029; *Fax:* (418) 682-8430
radioflashback@cfom1029.com
License: Levis, QC held by Cogeco Diffusion Inc.
Group Owner: Cogeco Diffusion Inc.; (acq 1-21-2005; grpsl).
Target Audience: 25 plus.
Pierre DeMondehare, General Manager
Jean-Paul Lemire, General Sales Mgr
Mario Paquin, Programming Director
Annie Anglehart, Promotions Manager

Listuguj

CFIC-FM
01-01-2000; 105.1 MHz FM; 425 w
Mailing Address: Box 304, 44A Riverside East, Listuguj, QC G0C 2R0 Canada
Second Address: 44A Riverside E., Listuguj, PQ G0C 2R0
(418) 788-5166; *Fax:* (418) 788-3524
www.105hotcountry.com
Gerry@105hotcountry.com
License: Listuguj, QC held by Societe d'Art, de Culture et d'Histoire Micmacs.
Population Served: 399; *Arbitron Metro Market:* Lingwick, QC; *Format:* Country
Gerald Dedam, President
Jake Dedam, Manager
Linda Gilbert, General Sales Mgr

Longueuil

CHAA-FM
01-01-1987; 103.3 MHz FM; *Hrs Open:* 24; kw Canada
(450) 646-6800; *Fax:* (450) 646-7378
www.fm1033.ca
admin@fm1033.ca
License: Longueuil, QC held by Radio Communautaire de la Rive-Sud Inc.
Nat'l Reps: Target Broadcast Sales
Format: Adult Contemp; *Special Programming:* Fr 18 hrs, retro oldies 9 hrs, Greek 5 hrs, Vietna; *Hrs. of News Programming:* news progmg 5 hrs wkly; *No. News Employees:* 2; *Target Audience:* 24-54; general*Adv. Rates:* 34; 30; 34; 30
Eric Tetreault, Chairman
France Dube, Programming Director
Richard Boileau, Promotions Manager

CHMP-FM
04-09-1977; 98.5 MHz FM; 100 kw; 298.9 meters
211 avenue Gordon, Verdun, QC H4G 2R2 Canada
(514) 767-2435; *Fax:* (514) 761-0985
www.fm985.ca
License: Longueuil, QC held by Cogeco Diffusion Aquisition Inc
Group Owner: Cogeco Diffusion Inc.; (acq 2-01-2011; grpsl).

Nat'l Reps: Canadian Broadcast Sales
Hrs. of News Programming: News progmg 5 hrs wkly; *Target Audience:* 18-44.; *Adv. Rates:* 300; 250; 250; 200
Pierre Beland, President
Pierre Accand, Operations Dir
Jacques Papin, General Manager
David Therrien, General Sales Mgr
Denis Fortin, Programming Director
Pierre Tremblay, Promotions Manager
Real Terrault, Chief Engineer
MichelLacroix, General Sales Manager
Michel Belleau, Music Director
Maurice Tietolman, National Sales Manager

Louiseville

CHHO-FM
01-22-2007; 103.1 MHz FM; 1.52 kw
50-A de la Fabrique, Louiseville, QC J0K 2W0 Canada
(819) 228-1001; *Fax:* (819) 228-0330
info@ch2ofm.ca
License: Louiseville, QC held by Coop de solidarite radio communautaire de la MRC de Maskinonge.
Population Served: 7,517; *Arbitron Metro Market:* Louiseville, QC; *Format:* French
Stephane Carbonneau, General Manager

Lourdes-de-Blanc-Sablon

*CFBS-FM
01-01-1989; 89.9 MHz FM; *Hrs Open:* 7 AM-5 PM; 178 w; Blanc Sablon
C.P. 8, 1193 boul. Dr. Camille Marcoux, Lourdes-de-Blanc-Sablon, QC G0G 1W0 Canada
(418) 461-2445; *Fax:* (418) 461-2425
cfbs@globetrotter.net
License: Lourdes-de-Blanc-Sablon, QC held by Radio Blanc-Sablon Inc.
Population Served: 5,000; *No. News Employees:* 1
Vicki Driscoll, President
Janice Letemplier, Programming Director
Janice Letemplier, General Director

Magog

CIMO-FM
01-01-1979; 106.1 MHz FM; *Hrs Open:* 6 AM-8 PM; kw
Canada
(819) 347-1414; *Fax:* (819) 347-1061
www.radioenergie.com
License: Magog, QC held by Astral Media Radio Inc.
Group Owner: Bell Media Inc.
Format: Contemporary Hits/Top 40; *Target Audience:* 18-34.
Nathalie Johnson, General Manager
Isabelle Gagnon, General Sales Mgr
Anne-Marie Bercier, Promotions Manager
Marc Toussaint, News Director
J.P. Maheu, Chief Engineer

Maliotenam

CKAU-FM
01-01-1993; 104.5 MHz FM; 50 w
C.P. 338, Succ Bureau-chef, Sept-Îles, QC G4R 4K6 Canada
(418) 927-2476; *Fax:* (418) 927-2800
www.ckau.com
info@ckau.com
License: Maliotenam, QC held by Corporation de Radio Kushapetsheken Apetuamiss Uashat.
Population Served: 25,686; *Arbitron Metro Market:* Sept-Îles, PQ; *Format:* Variety/Diverse
Reginald Steering, CEO
Yves Rock, General Manager
Reginald Thomas, General Sales Mgr
Mathieu McKenzie, Engineering Dir
Guylaine St-Onge, Accounting
Marceline Ambrose, Secretariat
Popoye (George Eugene), Animation andadvertising
Alexander Aster, Animation and journalist

Maniwaki

CBOF-1(AM)
10-22-1973; 990 kHz AM; 40 w, DA-1*Rebroadcasts:* Rebroadcasts CBOF-FM Ottawa
Box 3220, Stn C, Ottawa, ON K1Y 1E4 Canada
(613) 288-6000; *Fax:* (613) 288-6560
cbc.ca
License: Maniwaki, QC held by Canadian Broadcasting Corp.
Format: Variety/Diverse
Robert Rabinowitz, CEO
Denis Simard, General Manager

CHGA-FM
11-01-1980; 97.3 MHz FM; *Hrs Open:* 24; kw
Canada
(819) 449-3959; *Fax:* (819) 449-7331
www.chga.fm
License: Maniwaki, QC held by Radio Communautaire FM de la Haute-Gatineau
Format: Adult Contemp, Variety/Diverse; *Special Programming:* Class one hr, jazz 3 hrs, country 8 hrs, folk 5 hr; *Hrs. of News Programming:* news progmg 15 hrs wkly; *No. News Employees:* 1
Hubert Tremblay, President
Lise Morisette, Operations Dir
Lise Morissette, General Manager
Gaitam Bussiere, General Sales Mgr
Gaetan Bussieres, Programming Director
Georges Vasiloff, Engineering Dir
Kim Lacaille, MusicDirector
Linda Lemieux, Regional Sales Manager

CFOR-FM
08-01-1994; 99.3 MHz FM; *Hrs Open:* 24; 2.4 kw
139 South Main, Maniwaki, QC J9E 1Z8 Canada
(819) 441-0993; *Fax:* (819) 441-3488
www.cforfm.com
cfor993@b2b2c.ca
License: Maniwaki, QC held by 9116-1299 Québec Inc.
Nat'l Reps: Radio Unie Target
Format: Rock/AOR; *No. News Employees:* 3; *Target Audience:* 15-45.
Rock Lepine, President
Laure Voilquin, General Sales Mgr

Maniwaki (Kitigan Zibi Anishinabeg

CKWE-FM
01-01-1987; 103.9 MHz FM; 50 w
River Desert Indian Band, Box 309, Maniwaki, QC J9E 3C9 Canada
(819) 449-5170; *Fax:* (819) 449-5673
www.tyendinaga.net
anita.tenasco@kza.qc.ca
License: Maniwaki (Kitigan Zibi Anishinabeg, QC held by Jean-Guy Whiteduck.
Population Served: 3,930; *Arbitron Metro Market:* Maniwaki, PQ; *Format:* News, Talk
Eleanor Whiteduck, Operations Dir
Anita Penasco, General Manager

Maria (Reserve)

CHRG-FM
01-01-1991; 101.7 MHz FM; *Hrs Open:* 24; 10 w
Mailing Address: Box 118, Maria (Reserve), QC G0C 1Y0 Canada
Second Address: 120 School St., Maria (Reserve), PQ G0C 1Y0
(418) 759-8196; *Fax:* (418) 759-8196
License: Maria (Reserve), QC held by Douglas Martin.
Population Served: 1,388; *Arbitron Metro Market:* Maria (Reserve), PQ; *Format:* Country, Oldies, Variety/Diverse
Douglas Martin, General Manager
Wes Jones, Programming Director

Mashteuiatsh (Pointe-Bleue)

CHUK-FM
01-01-1996; 107.3 MHz FM; *Hrs Open:* 24; 50 w
1491 rue Ouiatchouan, Mashteuiatsh, QC G0W 2H0 Canada
(418) 275-4684; *Fax:* (418) 275-7964
www.chukfm.ca
chuk@chukfm.ca
License: Mashteuiatsh (Pointe-Bleue), QC held by Corporation Mediatique Teuehikan.
Population Served: 2,213; *Arbitron Metro Market:* Mashteuiatsh, PQ; *Format:* French
Karl Clary, General Manager
Jean Denis Gill, Programming Director

Matagami

CHEF-FM
01-01-2001; 99.9 MHz FM; 36 w
110 boulevard Matagami, C.P. 39, Matagami, QC J0Y 2A0 Canada
(819) 739-9990; *Fax:* (819) 739-6003
www.chef99.ca
chef99fm@lino.com
License: Matagami, QC held by Radio Matagami.
Population Served: 1,526; *Arbitron Metro Market:* Matagami, PQ; *Format:* Adult Contemp
Daniel Clich,, Chairman
M. Constantineau, President
Marie-Eve Gallant, General Manager
Daniel Cliche, General Sales Mgr
David Chabot, News Director
Nathalie Poirier, Vice-Chair
Sylvain Cloutier, Secretary-Treasurer
Julie Flag,Director

Matane

CHOE-FM
05-01-1991; 95.3 MHz FM; *Hrs Open:* 24; 30 kw
800 Ouest du Phare, Matane, QC G4W 1V7 Canada
(418) 562-8181; *Fax:* (418) 562-0778
www.choefm.com
License: Matane, QC held by Les Communications Matane Inc.
Population Served: 20,000; *Format:* Light Rock; *Target Audience:* 18-34; young workers
Kenneth Gagne, President
Kenneth Gagne Jr., General Manager
Michel Desrosiers, General Sales Mgr
Carol St-Pierre, News Director
Jacques Tremblay, Chief Engineer

*CHRM-FM
04-01-2001; 105.3 MHz FM; *Hrs Open:* 24; kw
Canada
(418) 562-4141; *Fax:* (418) 562-0778
www.chrmfm.com
micheldesrosiers@choefm.com
License: Matane, QC held by Les Communications Matane inc.
Arbitron Metro Market: Matane, PQ; *Format:* Adult Contemp
Kenneth Gagne, President
Kenneth Gagne Jr., General Manager
Michel Desrosiers, General Sales Mgr
Carol St-Pierre, News Director
Michel Desrosiers, Commercial director
Carol St-Pierre, Advertising consultant
Romano Quagliano,Advertising consultant
Sylvain Caron, Advertising consultant
Denis L,vesque, Advertising consultant

CBGA-FM
01-01-2004; 102.1 MHz FM; *Hrs Open:* 5:30 AM-midnight; kw
Canada
(514) 597-6000; *Fax:* (418) 562-3555
radio-canada.ca/gaspesie
License: Matane, QC held by CBC.
Nat'l Network: Premiere Chaine
Arbitron Metro Market: Matane, QC; *Format:* Contemporary Hits/Top 40, Variety/Diverse, News/Talk; *Hrs. of News Programming:* news progmg 3 hrs wkly; *No. News Employees:* 5; *Target Audience:* General.
Louis Pelletier, General Manager
Richard Morisset, Programming Director
Johanne LaBrie, Promotions Manager

Mont-Laurier

CFLO-FM
01-01-1995; 104.7 MHz FM; 10.98 kw*Rebroadcasts:* Rebroadcasts CFLO FM-1 L'Annociation 100%.
332 de la Madone, Mont-Laurier, QC J9L 1R9 Canada
(819) 623-5610; *Fax:* (819) 623-7406
www.cflo.ca
cflofm@cflo.ca
License: Mont-Laurier, QC held by Soneme Inc.
Format: Adult Contemp; *Hrs. of News Programming:* News progmg 3 hrs wkly; *Target Audience:* 24-54.
Sylvain Lacasse, President
Dominic Bell, Programming Director

Montr,al

CBF-FM
01-01-1947; 95.1 MHz FM; 100 kw; 823 ft
Box 6000, Québec, QC H3C 3A8 Canada
(514) 597-6000
www.cbc.radio-canada.ca
License: Montr,al, QC held by CBC.
Group Owner: Canadian Broadcasting Corp
TV Affiliate: CBFT(TV) affil.; *Format:* Talk
Sylvain LaFrance, Operations Dir
Bertrand Emond, General Manager

CBFX-FM
01-01-1998; 100.7 MHz FM; 100 kw
Box 6000, Montr,al, QC H3C 3A8 Canada
(514) 597-6000; *Fax:* (416) 205-3714
www.cbc.radio-canada.ca
License: Montr,al, QC held by CBC.
Group Owner: Canadian Broadcasting Corp
Nat'l Network: Ici Musique

Format: Variety/Diverse
Sylvain LaFrance, Operations Dir
Bertrand Emond, Station Manager
Alain Saulnier, News Director

CBM-FM
01-01-1947; 93.5 MHz FM; 24.6 kw; 823 ft
Box 6000, Montr,al, QC H3C 3A8 Canada
(514) 597-6000; *Fax:* (514) 597-4416
www.music.cbc.ca
info@cbc.ca/montreal
License: Montr,al, QC held by Canadian Broadcasting Corp.
TV Affiliate: CBMT(TV) affil.; *Format:* Talk
Judith Bleier, Operations Dir
Patricia Pleszczynska, Station Manager
Patricia Plesczynska, Programming Director

CBME-FM
01-01-1998; 88.5 MHz FM; *Hrs Open:* 24; 16.9 kw
Box 6000, Montr,al, QC H3C 3A8 Canada
(514) 597-4444; *Fax:* (514) 597-4142
www.cbc.ca/montreal
License: Montr,al, QC held by Canadian Broadcasting Corp.
Nat'l Network: CBC Radio One
Format: News
Judith Bleier, Operations Dir
Patricia Pleszczynska, Station Manager
Sally Caldwell, Programming Director

CFMB
12-21-1962; 1280 kHz AM; *Hrs Open:* 24; 50 kw; N45 19 31 08 W73 32 53 16
5877 Avenue Papineau, Montr,Al, QC H2G 2W3 Canada
(514) 483-2362; *Fax:* (514) 483-1362
www.cfmbradio.com
info@cfmb.ca
License: Montr,al, QC held by CFMB Limited.
Group Owner: Evanov Communications Inc.
Regional Reps: Direct
Format: Ethnic; *Hrs. of News Programming:* news progmg 35 hrs wkly; *No. News Employees:* 7; *Adv. Rates:* 65; 60; 65; 50
Luigi Valente, Station Manager
Ivana Bombardieri, Promotions Manager
Nino Di Stefano, News Director
Tony Ferrara, Music Director
Walter Centa, National Sales Manager
Marcello Silveri, Regional Sales Manager

CKBE-FM
11-01-1966; 92.5 MHz FM; *Hrs Open:* 24; 100 kw; 298.9 meters
800 de la Gauchetiere West, Suite 1100, Montr,al, QC H5A 1M1 Canada
(514) 767-9250; *Fax:* (514) 787-7979
www.925thebeat.ca
License: Montr,al, QC held by Cogeco Diffusion Aquisitions Inc
Group Owner: Cogeco Diffusion Inc.
Target Audience: 25-54.
Ted Silver, Programming Director
Kathie Murphy, Promotions Manager

CHOM-FM
07-16-1963; 97.7 MHz FM; *Hrs Open:* 24; 41 kw
1717 boulevard Ren,-L,vesque Est., Montr,al, QC H2L 4T9 Canada
(514) 931-2466; *Fax:* (514) 989-3868
www.chom.com
License: Montr,al, QC held by Bell Media Radio G.P.
Group Owner: Bell Media Inc.
Format: Classic Rock
Andr, Lallier, Programming Director
Phil Vanden Brade, Promotions Manager

CIBL-FM
04-26-1980; 101.5 MHz FM; *Hrs Open:* 24; kw
Canada
(514) 526-2581; *Fax:* (514) 526-3583
www.cibl1015.com
administration@cibl1015.com
License: Montr,al, QU held by Radio Communautaire Francophone de Montreal Inc.
Format: Talk; *Special Programming:* Black 13 hrs, class 4 hrs, jazz 14 hrs, reggae 4 h; *Hrs. of News Programming:* news progmg 14 hrs wkly; *No. News Employees:* 4; *Target Audience:* General.; *Adv. Rates:* 35; 25;35; 20
Genevieve Dore, General Manager
Gilles Labelle, Programming Director
Eric Lefebvre, General Manager

CINQ-FM
01-27-1975; 102.3 MHz FM; *Hrs Open:* 24; 1.29 kw; Ant 180 ft
5212 Boul. St. Laurent, Montr,al, QC Canada
(514) 495-2597; *Fax:* (514) 495-2429
www.radiocentreville.com
License: Montr,al, QC held by Radio Centre-Ville Saint Louis Inc.
Special Programming: Sp 16, Portugese 13 hrs, Greek 13 hrs, Chinese 5 h; *No. News Employees:* 1; *Target Audience:* 25-54; Fr & multilingual
Rene Pluviose, President
Evan Kapetanakis, Station Manager
Daniel Moreau, General Sales Mgr
Miguel Greco (English), Programming Director
Robert Laplante, News Director
Marc Provencher, Chief Engineer
Suzanne Charland (Fr),Programming Director
Ricardo Costa, Programming Director

CIRA-FM
05-01-1995; 91.3 MHz FM; *Hrs Open:* 24; kw
Canada
(514) 382-3913; *Fax:* (514) 858-0965
www.radiovm.com
cira@radiovm.com
License: Montr,al, Québec County, QC held by Radio Ville-Marie.
Nat'l Reps: MPV Radio *Regional Reps:* Gaston Pearson
Format: Religious; *No. News Employees:* 15; *Target Audience:* Over 40; *Adv. Rates:* 50 to 90 $
Jean-Guy Roy, General Manager
Gaston Pearson, General Sales Mgr
Claudette Lambert, Programming Director
Philippe Vaillancourt, News Director
Joe Pacheco, Engineering Dir
Roger Landry, Chief Engineer

***CISM-FM**
03-01-1991; 89.3 MHz FM; 10 kw
Box 6128, C-1509, Montr,al, QC H3C 3J7 Canada
(514) 343-7511; *Fax:* (514) 343-2418
www.cism893.ca
License: Montr,al, QC held by Communications du Versant Nord.
Format: Alternative; *Target Audience:* 18-24 college students
Jules Hedert, General Manager
Guillaume Vincenot, Programming Director
Patrick Gelinas, Promotions Manager
Catherine Valois, Engineering Dir
Martin Roussy, Music Director

CITE-FM
05-20-1977; 107.3 MHz FM; *Hrs Open:* 24; kw
Canada
(514) 845-2483; *Fax:* (514) 288-1073
www.rock-detente.com
cite@rock-detente.com
License: Montr,al, QC held by Astral Media Radio Inc.
Group Owner: Bell Media Inc.
Format: Adult Contemp; *Target Audience:* 25-49.
Jacques Parisien, President
Sylvain Langlois, Operations Dir
Luc Tremblay, General Manager

CJAD
12-08-1945; 800 kHz AM; *Hrs Open:* 24; 50 kw-D, 10 kw-N
1717 boulevard Ren,-L,vedque Est., Montr,al, QC H2L 4T9 Canada
(514) 989-2523
www.cjad.com
cbury@cjad.com
License: Montr,al, QC held by Bell Media Radio G.P.
Group Owner: Bell Media Inc.
Format: News/Talk; *Hrs. of News Programming:* news progmg 14 hrs wkly; *No. News Employees:* 15
Phillip Dalp,, General Sales Mgr
Matthew Wood, Promotions Manager
Christopher Bury, News Director

CJFM-FM
10-01-1962; 95.9 MHz FM; 41 kw
1717 boulevard Ren,-L,vesque Est., Montr,al, QC H2L 4T9 Canada
(514) 989-2536
www.montreal.virginradio.ca
License: Montr,al, QC held by Bell Media Radio G.P.
Group Owner: Bell Media Inc.
Format: Adult Contemp
Mark Bergman, Programming Director
Matthew Wood, Promotions Manager

CJMS
05-01-1999; 1280 kHz AM; *Hrs Open:* 24
Canada
(514) 990-2567; *Fax:* (450) 632-0528
License: Montr,al, QC held by 3553230 Canada Inc.
Nat'l Network: Radio Unica
Format: Country; *No. News Employees:* 2
Dr. David Azoulay, CEO/COO
Alex Azoulay, President

CJPX-FM
06-25-1998; 99.5 MHz FM
124 Chemin du Chenal-Le-Moyne, Iles Notre Dame, Parc Jean-Drapeau, Montr,al, QC H3C 1A9 Canada
(514) 871-0995; *Fax:* (514) 871-0990
www.radioclassique.ca
License: Montr,al, QC held by Radio Classique Montreal Inc.
Format: Classical
Jean-Pierre Coallier, CEO
Pierre Barbeau, Operations Dir
Francois Pare, General Manager
Sebastian Beaulieu, General Sales Mgr

CKAC
09-22-1922; 730 kHz AM; *Hrs Open:* 24
Canada
(514) 845-5151; *Fax:* (514) 845-2229
www.ckac.com
License: Montr,al, QC held by 591991 B.C. Ltd.
Group Owner: Cogeco Diffusion Inc.; (acq 1-21-2005; grpsl)
Format: Sports; *Hrs. of News Programming:* News progmg 20 hrs wkly; *Target Audience:* 35-54.
Julie Gagnon, Operations Dir
Sylvain Chamberland, General Manager

CKGM
12-07-1959; 690 kHz AM; 50 kw-U; N45 17 43 W73 43 18
1717 boulevard Rene-Levesque Est., Montr,al, QC H2L 4T9 Canada
(514) 931-4487
www.tsn.ca/montreal-690
License: Montr,al, QC held by Bell Media Canada Radio 2013 Partnership
Group Owner: Bell Media Inc.; (acq 6-22-2007; grpsl).
Format: Sports
Lee Hambleton, General Manager
Wayne Bews, General Sales Mgr

CKMF-FM
05-11-1964; 94.3 MHz FM; *Hrs Open:* 24; kw
Canada
(514) 529-3229; *Fax:* (514) 529-9308
Lsabbatini@radio.astral.com
License: Montr,al, QC held by Astral Media Radio Inc.
Group Owner: Bell Media Inc.
Nat'l Network: Radiomutuel
Format: Contemporary Hits/Top 40; *Special Programming:* Disco; *Hrs. of News Programming:* News progmg one hr wkly; *Target Audience:* 18-34.
Jacques Parisien, Chairman
Ian Greenburg, CEO
Charles Benoit, Operations Dir
Luc Tremblay, General Manager
Marie Lefelbvre, General Sales Mgr
Andre Allara, Promotions Manager
Luc Sabbatini, Executive Vice President
MichelTartif, Regional Sales Manager

***CKUT-FM**
11-01-1987; 90.3 MHz FM; *Hrs Open:* 24; kw
Canada
(514) 448-4041; *Fax:* (514) 398-8261
www.ckut.ca
programming@ckut.ca
License: Montr,al, QC held by Radio McGill Inc.
Format: Variety/Diverse; *Special Programming:* Black 20 hrs, Fr 9 hrs, Sp 6 hrs, folk 3 hrs, gosp; *Hrs. of News Programming:* news progmg 6 hrs wkly; *No. News Employees:* 1
Louise Burns, General Sales Mgr
Kristiana Clemmens, Programming Director
Gretchen King, News Director
Marc Montanchez, Chief Engineer
Juliet Lammers, Promotions Director

CJWI
01-01-2002; 1610 kHz AM
Canada
(514) 287-1288; *Fax:* (514) 287-3299
License: Montr,al, QC held by CPAM Radio Union.com inc.
Format: Ethnic
Jean Pierre, General Manager

CKDG-FM
04-18-2004; 105.1 MHz FM; *Hrs Open:* 24; 224 w; Ant 722 ft; N45 30 10 W73 35 46
5899 Park Ave., Montr,al, QC Canada

(514) 273-2481; *Fax:* (514) 273-3707
www.mikefm.ca
info@mikefm.ca
License: Montr,al, Canada County, QC held by CHCR Ltd.
Wire Services: Catholic News Service
Population Served: 1,500,000; *Special Programming:* Multicultural; *Hrs. of News Programming:* 2 Hours/Day; *No. News Employees:* 3; *Target Audience:* 25-54; mostly trilingual
John Daperis, President
Pota Gotsis, Operations Dir
Marie Griffiths, General Manager
Geoffrey Marteng, Station Manager
Mandy Benoualid, Promotions Manager
Tony Choundalas, News Director
Jean Frechette, Engineering Dir
ChrisNucgaud, Music Director
Pota Gotsis, Traffic Manager

CKLX-FM
12-14-2004; 91.9 MHz FM; 1.9 kw; Ant 633 ft; N45 30 12 W73 35 49
#250, 200, av Laurier ouest, Montr,al, QC H2T 2N8 Canada
(514) 790-0919
www.919sport.ca
License: Montr,al, QC held by RNC MEDIA Inc.
Group Owner: RNC MEDIA Inc.
Format: Sports, Talk; *Target Audience:* 35-64.
Raynald Briere, President

CHOU
01-01-2007; 1450 kHz AM; *Hrs Open:* 24
Canada
(514) 790-0002; *Fax:* (514) 745-3475
www.1450am.ca
pdg@1450am.ca
License: Montr,al, QC held by 9015-2018 Québec inc.
Arbitron Metro Market: Montreal, QC; *Format:* Arabic, Ethnic
Antoine Karam, General Sales Manager
Zeina Karam, Programming Director

CJLO
01-01-2007; 1690 kHz AM
Canada
(514) 848-8663; *Fax:* (514) 848-7470
www.cjlo.com
feedback@cjlo.com
License: Montr,al, QC held by Concordia Student Broadcasting Corp.
Arbitron Metro Market: Montreal, QC; *Format:* Variety/Diverse
Stephanie Saretsky, Station Manager
Amrew Weekes, General Sales Mgr
Brian Joseph, Programming Director
Katie Seline, Promotions Manager
Hannah Besseau, News Director
Omar Husain, Music Director
Kayleigh Jordan-MacGregor,Volunteer Coordinator
Stephanie Doyle, Magazine Editor
Andrew Wieler, RPM Director/Interim Metal Director

CKIN-FM
04-15-2010; 106.3 MHz FM; 407 w
Canada
(514) 273-2481; *Fax:* (514) 273-3707
www.mikefm.ca
License: Montr,al, QC held by Canadian Hellenic Cable Radio Inc
Format: Ethnic

CKBE
92.5 MHz FM
Place Bonaventure, 800 De La GauchetiŠre West, Suite 1100, Montr,al, QC H51 1M1 Canada
(514) 767-9250; *Fax:* (514) 787-7979
www.925thebeat.ca
License: Montr,al, QC
Group Owner: Cogeco Diffusion Inc.
Mark Dickie, General Manager/General Sales Manager
Linda Jackson, Sales Coordinator
Leo Da Estrela, Program/Production Director
Linda Fraraccio, Promotions Director
Diane Lesser, Copywriter

CKOI
01-01-1953; 96.9 MHz FM; 307 kw; 712 feet; N45 29 54 W73 34 14
800 rue de la GauchetiŠre West, Suite 1100, Montreal, QC H5A 1M1 Canada
(514) 789-2564; *Fax:* (514) 789-7982
www.ckoi.com
License: Montr,al, QC held by Cogeco Diffusion Acquisitions Inc.
Group Owner: Cogeco Diffusion Inc.

CHRF
02-02-2015; 980 kHz AM; 50 kw-D, 10 kw-N
5877 avenue Papineau, Montr,al, QC H2G 2W3 Canada
(514) 483-2362; *Fax:* (514) 483-1362
License: Montr,al, QC held by Dufferin Communications Inc.
Group Owner: Evanov Communications Inc.
Format: Contemporary Hits/Top 40, Talk, Adult Contemp; *Target Audience:* LGBT Individuals
Ky Joseph, General Sales Mgr
Antoine de la Durantaye, Musical Director

Montr,al (zone LaSalle)

CKVL-FM
01-08-2008; 100.1 MHz FM; *Hrs Open:* 24; 250 w; N45 25 51 W73 35 37
55, ave. Dupras, 3rd Floor, LaSalle, QC H8R 4A8 Canada
(514) 360-2585; *Fax:* (514) 367-4471
www.100-1fm.com
License: Montr,al (zone LaSalle), QC held by La radio communautaire de LaSalle.
Population Served: 74,276; *Format:* Variety/Diverse
Patrick Coutu, General Manager
Marie-Eve ??Gaudreau, Programming Director
Claudia B,lair, Administrative Assistant

Natashquan

CKNA-FM
01-30-1983; 104.1 MHz FM; 6.56 kw
29 chemin d'en Haut, Natashquan, QC G0G 2E0 Canada
(418) 726-3284; *Fax:* (418) 726-3367
pages.globetrotter.net/ckna/
ckna@globetrotter.net
License: Natashquan, QC held by La Radio Communautaire CKNA Inc.
Population Served: 810; *Arbitron Metro Market:* Natashquan, QC; *Format:* Adult Contemp
Jean Jaques Landry, General Manager
Renee Lapierre, Promotions Manager

New Carlisle

CHNC-FM
12-23-2008; 107.1 MHz FM; *Hrs Open:* 24; 3.9 kw; 200 meters; N48 08 27 W65 14 35*Rebroadcasts:* Carleton, Chandler, PercÃ©, GaspÃ©
Mailing Address: 153 boulevard Gerard-D.-Levesque, New Carlisle, QC G0C 1Z0 Canada
Second Address: 153 boulevard Gerard-D.-Levesque, New Carlisle, PQ G0C 1Z0
(418) 752-2215; *Fax:* (418) 752-6939
www.radiochnc.com
radiochnc@globetrotter.net
License: New Carlisle, QC held by Cooperative des travailleurs CHNC.
Nat'l Reps: MPV Radio; *Wire Services:* Canada NewsWire
Population Served: 70,000; *No. News Employees:* 15; *Target Audience:* General; adult
Francis Remillard, General Manager
Michel Morin, News Director

Pikogan

CKAG-FM
01-01-1993; 100.1 MHz FM; 3.738 kw; Ant 126 ft; N48 35 48 W78 07 05
30 rue David Kistabish, Pikogan, QC J9T 3A3 Canada
(819) 727-3237; *Fax:* (819) 727-4432
www.ckagfm.com
ckagfm1001@hotmail.com
License: Pikogan, QC held by Societe de Communication Ikito Pikogan Ltee.
Population Served: 487; *Arbitron Metro Market:* Pikogan, PQ; *Format:* Variety/Diverse
Brenda Rankin, Operations Dir
Brenda Rankin, General Sales Mgr

Plessisville

CKYQ-FM
01-01-1996; 95.7 MHz FM; *Hrs Open:* 24; 1 kw
1646, av Saint-Laurent, Plessisville, QC G6L 2P6 Canada
(819) 362-3737; *Fax:* (819) 362-3414
www.kyqfm.com
programmation@kyqfm.com
License: Plessisville, QC held by 176100 Canada Inc.
Group Owner: Attraction Radio Inc.
Format: Adult Contemp
Stephane Dion, General Manager
Jean-Yves Gregoire, Account Manager
Lydia Jacques, Account Manager

Pohenegamook

CFVD-FM-2
09-10-1983; 92.1 MHz FM; 294 w*Rebroadcasts:* Rebroadcasts CFVD-FM Degelis
654 6th St. E., Degelis, QC G5T 1Y1 Canada
(418) 853-3370; *Fax:* (418) 853-3321
www.fm95.ca
cfvd@fm95.ca
License: Pohenegamook, QC held by Radio Degelis Inc.
Format: Variety/Diverse; *No. News Employees:* 10; *Target Audience:* General.
Gilles Caron, President

Port-Cartier

CIPC-FM
01-01-1995; 99.1 MHz FM; *Hrs Open:* 24; 10kw
Elijah 52-Rochefort, Port-Cartier, QC G5B 1N2 Canada
(418) 766-6868; *Fax:* (418) 766-6870
www.laradioactive.com
License: Port-Cartier, QC held by Radio Port-Cartier Inc.
Format: Contemporary Hits/Top 40
Yvan Beaulieu, General Manager
Luc Boucher, General Sales Mgr
Matthieu Pineau, Programming Director
Emie jane Dery, News Director
Elizabeth Chevalier, Music Director

Port-Menier

CJBE-FM
01-01-1988; 90.5 MHz FM; 88 w
C.P. 15, Port-Menier (Ile d'Anticosti), QC G0G 2Y0 Canada
(418) 535-0292; *Fax:* (418) 535-0497
info@radio-unie-target.com
License: Port-Menier, QC held by Radio Anticosti Inc.
Population Served: 281; *Arbitron Metro Market:* Anticosti, QC; *Format:* Public Affairs; *No. News Employees:* 1
Francine Ross, Chairman
Francine Ross, President
Julie Lavallee, General Manager
France Dub,, Programming Director
Gervais Desbiens, Vice President
Šric Lefebvre, Secretary-Treasurer
Lise Morissette, Administrative Director
Charles Eugene Cyr, Director General
Christian Roy, Member Support
Sylvie Vincent, Accounting Manager

Québec

***CBV-FM**
01-01-1974; 106.3 MHz FM; *Hrs Open:* 24; 100 kw; Ant 541 ft; N46 51 40 W71 04 46
888 Rue Saint-Jean, Québec, QC GIR 5H6 Canada
(418) 656-8235; *Fax:* (418) 656-8842
www.cbc.ca
License: Québec, QC held by Societe Radio Canada.
Nat'l Network: Premiere Chaine
Population Served: 500,000*TV Affiliate:* *CBVT-TV affil.; *Format:* News, News/Talk, Talk, Variety/Diverse; *Hrs. of News Programming:* News progmg 15 hrs wkly; *Target Audience:* General.
Robert Rabinovitch, President
Norman LaCombe, News Director
Robert Jacques, Engineering Dir

CBVE-FM
03-01-1979; 104.7 MHz FM; *Hrs Open:* 5:30-8:30 AM; 4-6 PM; kw
Canada
(418) 691-3613; *Fax:* (418) 691-3610
www.cbc.ca
License: Québec, QC held by Canadian Broadcasting Corp.
Nat'l Network: CBC Radio One
Format: News, News/Talk, Talk, Variety/Diverse
Judith Bleier, Operations Dir
Claude Saindon, General Manager
Peter Black, News Director

CBVX-FM
01-01-1998; 95.3 MHz FM; 100 kw; 541 ft; N46 51 40 W71 04 46
888 Saint-Jean St., Québec, QC G1R 5H6 Canada
(418) 654-1341; *Fax:* (418) 656-8212
www.cbc.ca
License: Québec, QC held by Societe Radio Canada.
Nat'l Network: Radio Canada
Format: Talk; *Special Programming:* Jazz 16 hrs, news 7 hrs wkly; *Target Audience:* General.

Real Jean, Operations Dir
Marleine Simard, General Manager
Clodine Dorval, News Director

CHIK-FM
08-01-1982; 98.9 MHz FM; kw
Canada
(418) 687-9900; *Fax:* (418) 687-3106
www.radioenergie.com
License: Québec, QC held by Astral Media Radio Inc.
Group Owner: Bell Media Inc.
Format: Adult Contemp
Daniel Tremblay, General Manager
Real Marcotte, General Sales Mgr
Jean Alexandre, Programming Director
Julie Durand, Promotions Manager
Rejean Bergeron, News Director
Michel Duval, Engineering Dir

CHRC
04-01-1926; 800 kHz AM; *Hrs Open:* 24
Canada
(418) 688-8080; *Fax:* (418) 670-1234
www.chrc.com
License: Québec, QC held by 9183-9084 Québec Inc.
Format: Sports; *Special Programming:* French; *Target Audience:* 35 plus.
Elmer Hildebrand, CEO
Lyndon Friesen, Operations Dir
Keith Leask, Station Manager
Menno Friesen, General Sales Mgr
Louis Painchaud, Programming Director
Don McCracken, News Director
Vern Moores, Chief Engineer

CION-FM
09-19-1995; 90.9 MHz FM; *Hrs Open:* 8 (M-S); 16 (Su); kw
Canada
(418) 659-9090; *Fax:* (418) 650-3306
www.radiogalilee.com
License: Québec, QC held by Radio Galilee.
Format: Adult Contemp, Religious; *Target Audience:* General.
Alexandre St. Hilaire, President
Denis Veilleux, General Manager
Berthold Bernier, Programming Director
Jacques Fortin, News Director
Daniel Coulombe, Engineering Dir
Mario Blouin, Music Director

CITF-FM
07-22-1982; 107.5 MHz FM; *Hrs Open:* 24; kw
Canada
(418) 527-3232; *Fax:* (418) 687-3106
www.rockdetente.com
License: Québec, QC held by Astral Media Radio Inc.
Group Owner: Bell Media Inc.; (acq 4-19-2002; grpsl).
Regional Reps: Radio Plus.
Format: Adult Contemp; *No. News Employees:* 2; *Target Audience:* 25-54.
Daniel Tremblay, General Manager
Suzie Baronet, General Sales Mgr
Marc Tanguay, Programming Director
Julie Durand, Promotions Manager
Michel Duval, Chief Engineer

CJMF-FM
09-15-1979; 93.3 MHz FM; *Hrs Open:* 24; kw
Canada
(418) 687-9330; *Fax:* (418) 687-0211
License: Québec, QC held by Cogeco Diffusion Inc.
Group Owner: Cogeco Diffusion Inc.; (acq 11-87; $8 million)
Format: Classic Rock, Talk; *Hrs. of News Programming:* news progmg 5 hrs wkly; *Target Audience:* 25-54; mostly males
Louis Audet, President
Jean-Paul Lemire, General Manager

CKIA-FM
10-31-1984; 88.3 MHz FM; *Hrs Open:* 24; 350 w; 700 ft; N46 48 28 W71 12 57
335 St. Joseph St., Suite 200, Québec, QC G1K 3B4 Canada
(418) 529-9026; *Fax:* (418) 529-4156
www.ckiafm.org
ckiafm@meduse.org
License: Québec, QC held by Radio Basse-Ville Inc.
Format: Classic Rock, Country, Variety/Diverse; *Special Programming:* Class 3 hrs, jazz 4 hrs, Sp 4 hrs, Haitian 2 hrs,; *Hrs. of News Programming:* news progmg 2 hrs wkly; *No. News Employees:* 1; *Target Audience:* 18-35; general
Bryan St. Louis, President
Ernst Caze, General Manager
Max Raneau, General Sales Mgr
Bryan St. Louis, Programming Director
Denis Roberge, Chief Engineer

CKRL-FM
02-15-1973; 89.1 MHz FM; *Hrs Open:* 24; kw
Canada
(418) 640-2575; *Fax:* (418) 640-1588
www.ckrl.qc.ca
License: Québec, QC held by CKRL MF 89.1 Inc.
Format: Adult Contemp, Jazz; *Special Programming:* Sp 2 hrs, It 2 hrs, Black 6 hrs, Arab 3 hrs wkly; *No. News Employees:* 1
Dany Fortin, General Manager
Bastien Gagnon La France, Programming Director
Daniel Deslauriers, Promotions Manager
Daniel Marcoux, Music Director

CJEC-FM
08-01-2003; 91.9 MHz FM; 31 kw
#505, 815, boul Lebourgneuf, Québec, QC G2J 0C1 Canada
(418) 781-9563
www.wknd.fm
License: Québec, QC held by CJEC Inc.
Group Owner: Leclerc Communications Inc.
Population Served: 516,622; *Arbitron Metro Market:* Québec City, QC; *Format:* Adult Contemp
Jean-Francois Leclerc, General Manager
Pierre-Luc Gilbert, Sales Manager
Dan Caron, Programming Director
Caroline Perron, Promotions
John Pedulla, Music Director

CJSQ-FM
07-25-2007; 92.7 MHz FM; 2.1 kw; N46 49 22 W71 29 41
Radio-Classique Québec, 2525 BLVD Laurier, Québec, QC G1V 2L2 Canada
(418) 650-9270; *Fax:* (418) 650-5735
www.radioclassique.ca
cjsq@radioclassique.ca
License: Québec, QC held by 9147-2605 Québec inc.
Population Served: 516,622; *Arbitron Metro Market:* Québec City, QC
Pierre Barbeau, General Manager
Bernard Poitras, General Sales Mgr

CHOI-FM
11-01-1949; 98.1 MHz FM; 40 kw
#300, 1134, Grande-Allee ouest, Québec, QC G1S 1E5 Canada
(418) 687-9810
License: Québec, QC held by RNC MEDIA Inc.
Group Owner: RNC MEDIA Inc.
Arbitron Metro Market: Québec City, QC; *Format:* Talk; *Target Audience:* 18-34; young adults
Philippe Lefebvre, General Manager

Radisson

CIAU-FM
01-01-1996; 103.1 MHz FM; 17 w
Mailing Address: PO Box 285, 143 rue Joliet, Radisson, QC J0Y 2X0 Canada
Second Address: 143 rue Jolliet, Radisson, PQ J0Y 2X0
(819) 638-7033; *Fax:* (819) 638-1031
www.ciaufm.ca
ciaufm@lino.com
License: Radisson, QC held by Radio communautaire de Radisson
Population Served: 1,303; *Arbitron Metro Market:* Baie-James, QC; *Format:* Variety/Diverse; *Special Programming:* Fr 8 hrs, Jazz 3 hrs wkly; *Hrs. of News Programming:* news progmg 3 hrs wkly; *No. News Employees:* 1; *Adv. Rates:* 5; 5; 5; 5
Eric Hamel, President
Patrice Maltais, Station Manager

Restigouche

CHRQ-FM
01-01-1991; 106.9 MHz FM; 31 w
Box 180, Restigouche, QC G0C 2R0 Canada
(418) 788-2449; *Fax:* (418) 788-2653
chrq1069@globetrotter.net
License: Restigouche, QC held by Gespegewag Communications Society.
Population Served: 157; *Arbitron Metro Market:* Restigouche, PQ; *Hrs. of News Programming:* news progmg one hr wkly; *No. News Employees:* 5; *Target Audience:* Community members all ages; *Adv. Rates:* 282; 282; 282;282
Sandra Bulmer, Station Manager
Chad Gedeon, General Sales Mgr
Steve Clement, Programming Director
Karen Duguay, Promotions Manager

Rimouski

CIKI-FM
02-14-1988; 104.5 MHz FM; *Hrs Open:* 24; kw
Canada
(418) 723-2323; *Fax:* (418) 722-7508
www.ciki.fm
License: Rimouski, QC held by Astral Media Radio inc.
Group Owner: Bell Media Inc.; (acq 5-30-2005; grpsl).
Format: Rock/AOR
Jean Fournier, Operations Dir
Bertrand Bellavance, General Manager
Ghislain Desgardins, General Sales Mgr
Francois La Fond, Programming Director
Martin Bressard, News Director
Alain Rivard, Music Director

***CBRXFM**
02-28-1959; 101.5 MHz FM; 50 kw; 931 ft
273 rue St-Jean Baptiste Ouest, Rimouski, QC Canada
(418) 723-2217; *Fax:* (418) 723-6126
www.radio-canada.ca/espace_musique/
License: Rimouski, QC held by Canadian Broadcasting Corp.
Nat'l Network: Espace Musique
Bernard Labarge, President
Bernard Lebarge, General Manager
Bernard Labarbe, Programming Director

CJOI-FM
10-22-2000; 102.9 MHz FM; *Hrs Open:* 24; 33.6 kw
287, rue Pierre Saindon, Suite 502, Rimouski, QC G5L9A7 Canada
(418) 723-2323; *Fax:* (418) 722-7508
www.rimouski.rougefm.ca
License: Rimouski, QC held by Astral Media Radio Inc.
Group Owner: Bell Media Inc.; (acq 5-30-2005; grpsl).
Population Served: 46,860; *Arbitron Metro Market:* Rimouski, PQ; *Format:* Adult Contemp
Mario Fournier, General Manager/Director of Sales
Francois La Fond, Programming Director
Martin Bressard, News Director
Cathy Pineault, Reception / Administrative Assistant
Guillaume Savard, Promotions and marketing coordinator
Jean Fournier, Technical Director
Bellavance, Webmaster / producer of digital content
Benoit Primeau, Facilitator

CJBR-FM
01-01-2000; 101.5 MHz FM; kw
Canada
(418) 696-6600; *Fax:* (418) 696-6689
www.radio-canada.ca
License: Rimouski, QC held by Canadian Broadcasting Corp.
Arbitron Metro Market: Chicoutimi, PQ; *Format:* Adult Contemp, News, News/Talk, Talk; *Special Programming:* Fr.; *Target Audience:* 35 plus; adlut, news-oriented
Hubert T. Lacroix, President & CEO
Bernard Labarge, General Manager
Maryse Bertrand, Vice-President, Real Estate, Legal Services and Ge
William B. Chambers, Vice-President, Brand, Communications and Corporat
Steven Guiton,Vice-President and Chief Regulatory Officer
Louis Lalande, Executive Vice-President, French Services
Kirstine Stewart, Executive Vice-President of CBC's English Services
Roula Zaar, Vice-President, People and Culture

CFYX-FM
10-01-2007; 93.3 MHz FM; 18.197 kw; N48 27 53 W68 12 32
158 Saint-Germain Ouest, Rimouski, QC G5L 4B7 Canada
(418) 722-2848
www.cfyx93.com
direction@cfyx93.com
License: Rimouski, QC held by Radio Rimouski Inc.
Population Served: 6,665; *Arbitron Metro Market:* Mont-Joli, QC; *Format:* Classic Rock
Pierre-Yves Renaud, General Manager
Rene Girard, General Sales Mgr

Rimouski-Mont Joli

CKMN-FM
06-04-1990; 96.5 MHz FM; *Hrs Open:* 24; 6.4 kw; N48 22 32 W68 35 43
323 Montee Industrielle, Rimouski, QC G5M 1A7 Canada
(418) 722-2566; *Fax:* (418) 724-7815
www.ckmn.fm
License: Rimouski-Mont Joli, Rimouski County, QC held by La Radio Communautaire du Comte.
Wire Services: CNW Broadcast

Format: Adult Contemp, Country; *Special Programming:* Oldies 3 hrs, classical 3 hrs wkly; *No. News Employees:* 5; *Target Audience:* 25-55; general; *Adv. Rates:* 18; 14; 18; 14
Line Meloche, CEO/COO
Daniel Menard, President
Renie Langlois, Programming Director
Reynald LaPierre, Promotions Manager
Michel Vallee, Chief Engineer
Gabriel Dumont, Executive Vice President

Riviere du Loup

CIBMFM
01-01-1966; 107.1 MHz FM; *Hrs Open:* 24; 100 kw; Ant 244 ft
64 Hotel de Ville, Riviere du Loup, QC Canada
(418) 867-1071; *Fax:* (418) 862-7704
www.cibm107.com
License: Riviere du Loup, QC held by CIBM Mont-Bleu.
Nat'l Network: Radiomedia
Guy Simard, General Manager
Renee Giard, General Sales Mgr
Daniel St. Pierre, Programming Director
Daniel St. Pierre, News Director
Clement LaVoie, Engineering Dir

CIEL-FM
12-15-1994; 103.7 MHz FM; kw
Canada
(418) 862-8241; *Fax:* (418) 867-4940
www.ciel103.com
clabrie@ciel103.com
License: Riviere du Loup, QC held by Radio CJFP (1986) Ltee.
Format: Adult Contemp
Guy Simard, President
Gilles Lamarre, General Sales Mgr
Daniel St. Pierre, Programming Director
Stephane Gemdrom, News Director
Christian Duchesne, Promotions Director

Roberval

CHRL-FM
03-01-2002; 99.5 MHz FM; *Hrs Open:* 24; 50 kw; N48 26 25 W72 06 47
568, boul Saint-Joseph, Roberval, QC G8H 2K6 Canada
(418) 275-1831; *Fax:* (418) 275-2475
www.roberval.planeteradio.ca
License: Roberval, QC held by Groupe Radio Antenne 6 inc.
Group Owner: RNC Media Saguenay-Lac-Saint-Jean
Population Served: 10,227; *Arbitron Metro Market:* Roberval, QC; *Format:* Adult Contemp, French; *Hrs. of News Programming:* news progmg 20 hrs wkly; *No. News Employees:* 1; *Target Audience:* General; mainly adults
Marc Levesque, General Manager
Lewis Gagnon, General Sales Mgr
Louis Arcand, Programming Director

Rouyn-Noranda

CHOA-FM
09-21-1990; 96.5 MHz FM; 61.1 kw; 600 ft
380, rue Murdoch, Rouyn-Noranda, QC J9X 1G5 Canada
(819) 762-0744
www.rythmefm.com
License: Rouyn-Noranda, QC held by RNC MEDIA Inc.
Group Owner: RNC MEDIA Inc.
TV Affiliate: CFEM-TV, CKRN-TV affils.; *Format:* Adult Contemp; *Target Audience:* 25-54.
Nancy Deschenes, General Manager
Nancy Deschenes, General Sales Mgr
Francis Morin, Programming Director
Karine Lapointe, Promotions Representative
Etienne Gregoire, Music Director

CJMM-FM
06-17-1988; 99.1 MHz FM; *Hrs Open:* 24; 3.5 kw; Ant 200 ft
191, avenue Murdoch, Rouyn-Noranda, QC J9X 1E3 Canada
(819) 797-2566; *Fax:* (819) 797-1664
www.radioenergie.com
mtrottier@radioenergie.astral.com
License: Rouyn-Noranda, QC held by Astral Media Radio Inc.
Group Owner: Bell Media Inc.; (acq 1-12-2000; grpsl).
Format: Contemporary Hits/Top 40; *Hrs. of News Programming:* news progmg 5 hrs wkly; *No. News Employees:* 1; *Target Audience:* 18-44.
Marlene Trottier, General Manager
Chantel Massicotte, General Sales Mgr
Ian Clermont, Promotions Manager
Fanny-Garance Carrier, News Director
Mathieu Barrette, Engineering Dir

CHIC-FM
01-01-2003; 88.7 MHz FM; 300 w
120 rue 9e, Rouyn-Noranda, QC J9X 2B6 Canada
(819) 797-4242; *Fax:* (819) 797-3803
www.chicfm.org
887@chicfm.org
License: Rouyn-Noranda, QC held by Communications CHIC (C.H.I.C.).
Population Served: 41,012; *Arbitron Metro Market:* Rouyn-Noranda, QC; *Format:* Christian
Andre Curadeau, General Manager
Vic Cimon, Station Manager
Jocelyn Cote, General Sales Mgr

CHUN-FM
01-01-2005; 98.3 MHz FM; 490 w; N48 18 05 W79 03 08
1016 rue Wabanonic, Lac Simon, QC J0Y 3M0 Canada
(819) 797-5316
www.chunfm.ca
chun98.3@tlb.sympatico.ca
License: Rouyn-Noranda, QC held by Radio communautaire MF Lac Simon Inc.
Population Served: 41,012; *Arbitron Metro Market:* Rouyn-Noranda, QC; *Format:* Country
Noe Mitchell, General Manager

Saguenay

CJAB-FN
05-25-1979; 94.5 MHz FM; *Hrs Open:* 24; kw
Canada
(418) 545-9450; *Fax:* (418) 543-7968
www.radioenergie.com
License: Saguenay, QC held by Astral Media Radio Inc.
Group Owner: Bell Media Inc.
Nat'l Network: Radiomutuel
Format: Contemporary Hits/Top 40
Richard Turcotte, General Manager
Carol Tremblay, General Sales Mgr
Katia Boivin, Programming Director
Jean-Francois Cote, News Director
Stephane Villeneuve, Engineering Dir

CFIX-FM
07-31-1987; 96.9 MHz FM; *Hrs Open:* 24; 43.8 kw
267 est, rue Racine, Chicoutimi, QC G7H 5K3 Canada
(418) 543-9797; *Fax:* (418) 543-7968
www.saguenay.rougefm.ca
cfix@rock-detente.com
License: Saguenay, QC held by Astral Media Radio inc.
Group Owner: Bell Media Inc.
Population Served: 60,008; *Arbitron Metro Market:* Chicoutimi, PQ; *Format:* Adult Contemp
Richard Durcotte, General Manager

CKRS-FM
01-01-2007; 98.3 MHz FM; 51 kw; N48 22 15 W71 10 20
345, rue Racine, Chicoutimi, QC G7H 1S8 Canada
(418) 545-2577
www.rythmefm.com
License: Saguenay, QC held by Radio Saguenay Inc.
Group Owner: Attraction Radio Inc.
Format: Adult Contemp; *No. News Employees:* 6; *Target Audience:* 25-54.
Sylvain Carbonneau, General Manager
Sylvain Carbonneau, General Sales Mgr
Pierre-Luc Desbiens, Promotions Director
Catherine Paquette, Promotions Coordinator

Saint Augustin

CJAS-FM
01-01-1992; 93.5 MHz FM; 100 w*Rebroadcasts:* Rebroadcasts VOCM(AM) St. John's, NF weekends
Box 100, 558 rue Principal, St. Augustine, QC G0G 2R0 Canada
(418) 947-2239; *Fax:* (418) 947-2664
www.cjasradio.piczo.com
cjasradio@gmail.com
License: Saint Augustin, QC held by La Radio Communautaire de Riviere St-Augustin Inc.
Population Served: 478; *Arbitron Metro Market:* Saint-Augustin, QC; *Format:* Adult Contemp
Laurette Gallibois, General Manager
Maria Shattler, Programming Director
Rachel Bilodeau, News Director
Lindsey Durepos, Music Director

Saint Georges-de-Beauce

CKRB-FM
10-01-1953; 103.5 MHz FM; *Hrs Open:* 24; 17 kw
Mailing Address: 11760, 3rd Ave., C.P. 100, Saint Georges-de-Beauce, QC G5Y 5C4 Canada
Second Address: 11760 Third Ave., Saint Georges-de-Beauce, PQ G5Y 5C4
(418) 227-0997; *Fax:* (418) 228-0096
www.mix997.com
adminrb@cgocable.ca
License: Saint Georges-de-Beauce, QC held by Radio Beauce Inc.
Format: Adult Contemp; *Hrs. of News Programming:* news progmg 11 hrs wkly; *No. News Employees:* 2; *Target Audience:* 35 plus.
Guy Simard, President
Maurice Marcotte, General Manager
Claude Girard, General Sales Mgr
Marcel Rancourt, Programming Director
Suzanne Bougie, News Director
Gaston Guay, Chief Engineer
Jacques Goulet, National Sales Manager

Saint Jean-Iberville

CFZZ-FM
01-01-1992; 104.1 MHz FM; *Hrs Open:* 24; 1.35 kw
104 rue Richelieu, St. Jean-Sur-Richelieu, QC J3B 6X3 Canada
(450) 346-0104; *Fax:* (450) 348-2274
www.boomfm.com
lstemarie@boomfm.astral.com
License: Saint Jean-Iberville, QC held by Astral Media Radio inc.
Group Owner: Bell Media Inc.; (acq 5-30-2005; grpsl).
Format: Oldies; *Adv. Rates:* 65; 65; 65; 65
Leopold Stemarie, General Manager
Ghislaine Plourde, Programming Director
Luc Lalonde, Promotions Manager

Saint Jerome

CIMEFM
03-25-1977; 103.9 MHz FM; *Hrs Open:* 24; 39.3 kw
120 Delagare St., Saint Jerome, QC Canada
(450) 431-2463; *Fax:* (450) 565-9755
ventes@cime.fm
License: Saint Jerome, QC held by Cogeco Diffusion Inc.
Group Owner: Cogeco Diffusion Inc.; (acq 2-01-2011; grpsl).
No. News Employees: 2; *Target Audience:* 25-54; Adult
John Cassidy, President
Gilbert Cerat, General Manager
Ghislaiu Plourde, Programming Director
Etienne Gregoire, Promotions Manager
Jean Rousseau, News Director

CFND-FM
12-29-2008; 101.9 MHz FM; 49 w; Ant 78 ft; N45 47 04 W73 59 21
Ecole Notre-Dame, 581 rue Ouimet, Saint Jerome, QC J5Z 1R3 Canada
(450) 432-4472; *Fax:* (450) 432-8694
radionotredame@edu.csrdn.qc.ca
License: Saint Jerome, QC held by Amie du Quartier.
Population Served: 68,456; *Arbitron Metro Market:* Saint Jerome, QC; *Format:* Talk
Marc Bourcier, General Manager

Saint Pamphile

CJDS-FM
12-07-2001; 94.7 MHz FM; 24 w
109 Route Eagles, Saint Pamphile, QC G0R 3X0 Canada
(418) 356-1303; *Fax:* (418) 356-2586
License: Saint Pamphile, QC held by 3819914 Canada inc.
Population Served: 2,685; *Arbitron Metro Market:* Saint-Pamphile, QC; *Format:* Adult Contemp
Jean-Claude Dignard, President
Claire Soulieres, Operations Dir
Ann Dignard, General Sales Mgr
J. Dignard, Public Affairs Director

Saint Remi

***CHOCFM**
01-01-1999; 104.9 MHz FM; 250 w
93 Ruelachapelle Est, Saint Remi, QC Canada
(450) 454-5500; *Fax:* (450) 454-9435
www.chocfm.com
studio@chocfm.com
License: Saint Remi, QC held by Radio Communautaire Intergeneration Jardin du Québec.
Hrs. of News Programming: news progmg 10 hrs wkly; *No. News Employees:* 1
Sylvain Remillard, President
Richard Vegneault, General Manager

Sainte Anne des Monts

CBGN(AM)
01-01-1972; 1340 kHz AM; 1 kw-D, 250 w-N
155 St. Sacrament St., Matane, QC G4W 1Y9 Canada
(418) 562-0290; *Fax:* (418) 566-6068
License: Sainte Anne des Monts, QC held by CBC.
Group Owner: Canadian Broadcasting Corp; (acq 9-1-72)
Format: News, Talk
Louis Pelletier, General Manager

CJMC-FM
03-01-1996; 100.3 MHz FM; *Hrs Open:* 24; 2.51 kw
170 Boul. Ste. Anne, Sainte Anne des Monts, QC G4V 1N1 Canada
(418) 763-5522; *Fax:* (418) 763-7211
License: Sainte Anne des Monts, QC held by Radio du Golfe Inc.
Format: Adult Contemp; *Special Programming:* Class 2 hrs, western 2 hrs wkly
Jacques Vallee, President
Stephane Cyr, Programming Director
Olivier Vallee, Promotions Director

Sainte Foy

***CHYZ-FM**
01-29-1997; 94.3 MHz FM; *Hrs Open:* 24; 6 kw
Local 0236, Pavillon Pollack, Cite Universitaire, Sainte Foy, QC G1K 7P4 Canada
(418) 656-2131; *Fax:* (418) 656-3660
www.chyz.ca
chyz@public.ulaval.ca
License: Sainte Foy, QC held by Radio Campus Laval.
Population Served: 600,000; *Format:* Variety/Diverse; *Special Programming:* Hip-hop/rap 15 hrs wkly; *Hrs. of News Programming:* news progmg 10 hrs wkly; *No. News Employees:* 4; *Target Audience:* 18-30; univ students
Jean-Philippe Lessard, General Manager
Sebastien Moffet, Programming Director

Sainte-Marie

***CHEQ-FM**
11-29-1998; 101.3 MHz FM; 26 kw
373, rte Cameron, Sainte-Marie-De-Beauce, QC G6E 3E2 Canada
(418) 387-1015; *Fax:* (418) 387-3757
www.fm1015.ca
studio@fm1015.ca
License: Sainte-Marie, QC held by 9174-8004 Québec Inc.
Group Owner: Attraction Radio Inc.; (acq 8-16-00).
Arbitron Metro Market: Sainte-Marie-de-Beauce, PQ; *Format:* Adult Contemp
Chantal Baribeau, General Manager
Nathalie Berthiaume, Sales Representative
Gilles Girard, Sales Representative
Mario Paquin, Sales Representative

Senneterre

CIBO-FM
01-01-1982; 100.5 MHz FM; *Hrs Open:* 24
C.P. 1150, Senneterre, QC J0Y 2M0 Canada
(819) 737-2222; *Fax:* (819) 737-8599
cibofm@yahoo.ca
License: Senneterre, QC held by Radio communautaire M.F. de Senneterre Inc.
Population Served: 5,600; *Format:* Talk
Guy Bilodeau, President

Sept-Îles

***CBSI-FM**
11-01-1982; 98.1 MHz FM; *Hrs Open:* 24; 96.7 kw; 350 ft
350 rue Smith, bur. 30, Sept-Îles, QC G4R 3X2 Canada
(418) 968-0720; *Fax:* (418) 968-9219
www.radio-canada.ca/cote-nord
cbsi@radio-canada.ca
License: Sept-Îles, QC held by CBC.
Population Served: 8,000; *Format:* Talk, Variety/Diverse; *Target Audience:* Over 30.
Pierre Lafreniere, Station Manager

CKCN-FM
12-01-1998; 94.1 MHz FM; 4.88 kw
365 Boul. Laure, Sept-Îles, QC G4R 3B3 Canada
(418) 962-3838; *Fax:* (418) 968-6662
License: Sept-Îles, QC held by Radio Sept-Îles Inc.
Population Served: 25,686; *Arbitron Metro Market:* Sept-Îles, PQ; *Format:* Adult Contemp, News, News/Talk, Talk; *Special Programming:* Country 8 hrs wkly; *Hrs. of News Programming:* News progmg 16 hrs wkly*TargetAudience:* 25-54.
Pierre Bergeron, President
Dominique Marquis, Station Manager

Shawinigan

CFUT-FM
02-07-2005; 91.1 MHz FM; 5 w
540 Avenue Broadway, Shawinigan, QC G9N 1M3 Canada
(819) 537-0911; *Fax:* (819) 537-6377
dg@radioshawinigan.com
License: Shawinigan, QC held by La radio campus communautaire francophone de Shawinigan inc.
Population Served: 50,060; *Arbitron Metro Market:* Shawinigan, QC; *Format:* French
Pierre-Yves Rousselle, Programming Director

Sherbrooke

CFLX-FM
01-01-1984; 95.5 MHz FM; *Hrs Open:* 24; kw
Canada
(819) 566-2787; *Fax:* (819) 566-7331
www.cflx.qc.ca
commentaire@cflx.qc.ca
License: Sherbrooke, QC held by Radio communautaire de l'Estrie.
Format: News, News/Talk, Talk, Variety/Diverse; *Special Programming:* Class 7 hrs, jazz 8 hrs, Sp 3 hrs wkly; *Hrs. of News Programming:* news progmg 10 hrs wkly; *No. News Employees:* 1; *Target Audience:* 18-35; collegedegree
Jean Comtois, President
Bruno Guillemette, General Manager

CITE-FM-1
09-01-1962; 102.7 MHz FM; 92.8 kw; Ant 1,851 ft
2145 King West, Suite 200, Sherbrooke, QC J1J 2E4 Canada
(819) 566-6655; *Fax:* (819) 566-1011
License: Sherbrooke, QC held by Astral Media Radio Inc.
Group Owner: Bell Media Inc.; (acq 4-19-2002; grpsl).
Natalie Johnson, General Manager

CJMQ-FM
01-01-2004; 88.9 MHz FM; *Hrs Open:* 6am-12am; 1.67 kw
184 Queen St., Sherbrooke, QC J1M 1J9 Canada
(819) 822-1838
www.cjmq.fm
cjmqnews@yahoo.ca
License: Sherbrooke, QC held by Radio Bishop's Inc.
Population Served: 170,000; *Format:* Talk; *Hrs. of News Programming:* News progmg 5 hrs wkly; *Target Audience:* General; campus & community
Maureen Dillon, Programming/Music Director
David Teasdale, News Director

CFAK-FM
01-01-2003; 88.3 MHz FM; 490 w
2500 University Boulevard, Sherbrooke, QC J1K 2R1 Canada
(819) 821-8000 ext. 62693; *Fax:* (819) 821-7930
dg.cfak883@usherbrooke.ca
License: Sherbrooke, QC held by Comite de la radio etudiante universitaire de Sherbrooke (CREUS).
Population Served: 154,601; *Arbitron Metro Market:* Sherbrooke, QC; *Format:* French
Serge Langlois, General Manager
Alexandre Desbiens-Brassard, Programming Director
Lucie Massinon, Director, Advertising and Marketing
Samuel Prefontaine, Music Director
Mary Jane Beaumier, Director of Information
CatherineBeaucage, Webmaster

CFGE-FM
07-01-2004; 93.7 MHz FM; kw
Canada
(819) 822-0937; *Fax:* (819) 562-1666
www.rythmefm.com/estrie
License: Sherbrooke, QC held by Cogeco Diffusion inc.
Group Owner: Cogeco Diffusion Inc.
Arbitron Metro Market: Sherbrooke, QC; *Format:* Adult Contemp; *No. News Employees:* 1; *Target Audience:* 25-54.
Michel Cloutier, General Manager
Marc Fabi, General Sales Mgr
Jocelyn Proulx, Programming Director
Julie Riendeau, Promotions Manager
Dany Lebeau, Engineering Dir
Lilianne Randall, Music Director
Dave Forest, Producer
NormandGagnon, Production Director
Andr, St-Amand, Vice President of Programming
Jean-Marc Allard, Music Librarian
Denis Desmarchais, Music Librarian

CKOY-FM
01-01-2004; 104.5 MHz FM; 1.3 kw; N45 23 48 W71 49 52
4020 Boul. Portland, Sherbrooke, QC J1L 2V6 Canada
(819) 563-6363; *Fax:* (819) 566-4222
www.fm1077.ca
info@grock.fm
License: Sherbrooke, QC held by Cogeco Diffusion Inc.
Group Owner: Cogeco Diffusion Inc.
Population Served: 154,601; *Arbitron Metro Market:* Sherbrooke, QC
Jocelyn Proulx, General Manager

CJRS
01-01-2007; 1510 kHz AM
Canada
(514) 738-4100
www.radio-shalom.ca
License: Sherbrooke, QC held by Radio Chalom.
Arbitron Metro Market: Montreal, QC; *Format:* Ethnic
Robert Levy, President
Greg McLachlan, General Sales Mgr
Jean-No‰l Guenot, Technical Director

CBFX-FM-2
90.7 MHz FM; 25 kw; 173 meters; N45 23 48 W71 49 52
Box 6000, Montr,al, QC H3C 38A Canada
(514) 597-6000; *Fax:* (514) 205-3714
www.espace.mu/espace-musique/
License: Sherbrooke, QC held by CBC
Nat'l Network: Espace Musique

Sorel

***CJSO-FM**
09-27-1989; 101.7 MHz FM; *Hrs Open:* 24; kw
52, Du Roi, Sorel-Tracy, QC J3P 4M7 Canada
(450) 743-2772; *Fax:* (450) 743-0293
www.fm1017.ca
jmbelzile@hotmail.fr
License: Sorel, QC held by Radio Diffusion Sorel-Tracy Inc.
Format: Classic Rock; *Special Programming:* Class 2 hrs wkly; *Hrs. of News Programming:* news progmg 5 hrs wkly; *No. News Employees:* 2; *Adv. Rates:* 30; 30; 30; 30
Jean-Marc Belzile, President/CEO
Jean Lemay, Production

St-Gabriel

CFNJ-FM
08-10-1985; 99.1 MHz FM; *Hrs Open:* 24; kw
Canada
(450) 835-3437; *Fax:* (450) 835-3581
www.cfnj.net
License: St-Gabriel, QC held by Radio Nord-Joli Inc.
Group Owner: Radio Nord-Joli Nc.
Format: Adult Contemp; *Special Programming:* Black one hr, class 2 hrs, C&W 4 hrs, jazz 2 hrs; *Hrs. of News Programming:* news progmg 14 hrs wkly; *No. News Employees:* 2
Denis Roch, General Manager
Denise LaVoie, General Sales Mgr
Nicolas Bellemare, Promotions Manager

St-George-Beauce

CHJM-FM
06-22-1987; 99.7 MHz FM; *Hrs Open:* 24; kw
Mailing Address: Canada
Second Address: 11760 Third Ave, Saint Georges-de-Beauce, PQ G5Y 5C4
(418) 227-0997; *Fax:* (418) 228-0096
www.mix997.com
adminrb@cgocable.ca
License: St-George-Beauce, QC held by Radio Beauce Inc.
Format: Contemporary Hits/Top 40; *Hrs. of News Programming:* news progmg 4 hrs wkly; *No. News Employees:* 1; *Target Audience:* 18-44.
Guy Simard, President
Maurice Marcotte, General Manager
Claude Girard, General Sales Mgr
Marcel Rancourt, Programming Director
Gaston Guay, Chief Engineer
Jacques Goulet, National Sales Manager

St-Hyacinthe

CFEI-FM
01-01-1988; 106.5 MHz FM; *Hrs Open:* 24; kw
Canada
(450) 774-6486; *Fax:* (450) 774-7785
www.boomfm.com
jhebert@boomfm.astral.com

License: St-Hyacinthe, QC held by Astral Media Radio Inc.
Group Owner: Bell Media Inc.; (acq 8-13-2001).
Format: News, Oldies
Jacques Parisien, President
Pierre Demondehare, General Manager
Leopold St. Marie, General Sales Mgr
Jean-Francois Hebert, Programming Director
Andre Lalier, Music Director

Tete-a-la-Baleine

CJTB-FM
01-01-2003; 93.1 MHz FM; 49 w; N50 42 12 W59 19 30
C.P. 138, Tete-a-la-Baleine, QC G0G 2W0 Canada
(418) 242-2974
License: Tete-a-la-Baleine, QC held by Radio Communautaire Tete-a-la-Baleine.
Population Served: 129; *Arbitron Metro Market:* T'te-...-la-Baleine, QC; *Format:* French
Bertha Monger, President
Mireille Monger, General Manager

Thetford Mines

CFJO-FM
07-15-1989; 97.3 MHz FM; *Hrs Open:* 24; 100 kw; Ant 270 ft
327, rue Labb,, Thetford Mines, QC G6G 1Z2 Canada
(418) 338-1009
www.o973.com
License: Thetford Mines, QC held by Reseau des Appalaches (FM) Ltee.
Group Owner: Attraction Radio Inc.
Nat'l Reps: Target Broadcast Sales
Population Served: 87,913; *Format:* Contemporary Hits/Top 40; *No. News Employees:* 15; *Target Audience:* 18-40.
Annie Labbe, General Manager

CKLD-FM
01-01-1999; 105.5 MHz FM; *Hrs Open:* 24; 6 kw
327, rue Labb,, Thetford Mines, QC G6G 4E1 Canada
(418) 335-7533
www.passionrock.com
License: Thetford Mines, QC held by Radio Megantic Ltee.
Group Owner: Attraction Radio Inc.
Nat'l Reps: Target Broadcast Sales
Population Served: 40,384; *Format:* Adult Contemp; *No. News Employees:* 5; *Target Audience:* 35-64.
Annie Labbe, General Manager

Trois-Rivières

CBF-FM-1
07-21-1977; 104.3 MHz FM; 100 kw; 1,000 ft; N46 29 27 W72 39 00
Box 6000, Montr,al, QC H3C 3A8 Canada
(514) 597-6000; *Fax:* (514) 597-4510
www.cbc.radio-canada.ca
License: Trois-Rivières, QC held by CBC French.
Group Owner: Canadian Broadcasting Corp
Nat'l Network: Radio Canada
Format: Talk
Sylvain La France, General Manager
Louise Carriere, Programming Director

CHEY-FM
08-22-1990; 94.7 MHz FM; 100 kw
1500 rue Royale, Bur 260, RockDetemte 94.7, Trois-Rivières, QC G9A 6J4 Canada
(819) 376-0947; *Fax:* (819) 373-5555
www.rockdetente.com
License: Trois-Rivières, QC held by Astral Media Radio Inc.
Group Owner: Bell Media Inc.
Format: Classic Rock; *Target Audience:* 30-40; women
Jean Martin, General Manager
Rene Rivard, General Sales Mgr
Eric Lachapelle, Programming Director
Damien Miville-Deschenes, Promotions Manager

CIGB-FM
08-27-1979; 102.3 MHz FM; *Hrs Open:* 24; kw
Canada
(819) 378-1023; *Fax:* (819) 378-1360
www.radioenergie.com
License: Trois-Rivières, QC held by Astral Media Radio Inc.
Group Owner: Bell Media Inc.
Format: Contemporary Hits/Top 40; *Hrs. of News Programming:* news progmg 3 hrs wkly; *No. News Employees:* 3; *Target Audience:* 18-30.
Jean Martin, General Manager
Mr. Danny Champagne, Programming Director
Mr. Damien Miville-Deschenes, Promotions Manager

CFOU-FM
09-07-1997; 89.1 MHz FM; *Hrs Open:* 24; 3 kw; Trois-Rivières, Québec, Canada
Universite du Québec a Trois-Rivieres, 3351, boul. des Forges, Pavilion N,r,e-Beauchemin, Trois-Rivières, QC G9A 5H7 Canada
(819) 376-5184; *Fax:* (819) 376-5239
www.cfou.ca
progcfou@uqtr.ca
License: Trois-Rivières, QC held by Radio campus des etudiants de lUniversite du Québec a Trois-Rivieres.
Nat'l Network: CBC Radio One
Population Served: 131,338; *Arbitron Metro Market:* Trois-RiviŠres, QC; *Format:* Variety/Diverse; *Hrs. of News Programming:* News progmg one hr wkly; *Target Audience:* 18-35.
Jean-Philippe Charbonneau, Director General
Alain Lefebvre, Programming Director
Mathieu Plante, Webmaster

CJEB-FM
06-08-2004; 100.1 MHz FM; 30.61 kw; Ant 1,177 ft
1350, rue Royale, Suite 1200, Trois-Rivières, QC G9A 4J4 Canada
(819) 691-1001; *Fax:* (819) 691-1002
www.rythmefm.com/mauricie
License: Trois-Rivières, QC held by Cogeco Diffusion Inc.
Group Owner: Cogeco Diffusion Inc.
Population Served: 131,338; *Arbitron Metro Market:* Trois-RiviŠres, QC; *Format:* Adult Contemp
Michel Cloutier, General Manager
Pierre Lamontagne, Programming Director
Pierre Lamontagne, Promotions Manager
Gerald Trives, Engineering Dir
Charles Romanos, Programmer/Integrator
Allen ValliŠres, News Media Coordinator
NormandGagnon, Production Director
Jean-Fran‡ois Filion, Producer
Jean-Marc Allard, Music Librarian
Denis Desmarchais, Music Librarian

CKOB-FM
08-20-2007; 106.9 MHz FM; 60 kw; Ant 285 ft; N46 14 21 W72 35 26
1350 rue Royale, Bureau 1200, Trois-Rivières, QC G9A 4J4 Canada
(819) 374-3556; *Fax:* (819) 374-3222
License: Trois-Rivières, QC held by Cogeco Diffusion Inc.
Group Owner: Cogeco Diffusion Inc.
Pierre Gaudreau, General Manager
Denis Pratte, Promotions Manager

CBFX-FM-1
104.3 MHz FM; 45.4 kw; 249.7 meters; N46 30 10 W72 38 13 0
Box 6000, Montr,al, QC H3C 3A8 Canada
(514) 597-6000; *Fax:* (514) 205-3714
www.espace.mu/espace-musique/
License: Trois-Rivières, QC held by CBC
Nat'l Network: Espace Musique

Val d'Or

CJMV-FM
06-17-1989; 102.7 MHz FM; *Hrs Open:* 24; 96 kw; 156.8 meters
173 Perreault St., Val d'Or, QC J9P 2H3 Canada
(819) 825-2568; *Fax:* (819) 825-2840
www.radioenergie.com
License: Val d'Or, Abitibi-est County, QC held by Astral Media Radio Inc.
Group Owner: Bell Media Inc.; (acq 1-12-2000; grpsl).
Population Served: 50,000; *Target Audience:* 18-49.
Ian Greenberg, President
Marlene Trottier, General Manager

CHGO-FM
01-01-2000; 104.3 MHz FM; 100 kw
380, rue Murdoch, Rouyn-Noranda, QC J9X 1G5 Canada
(819) 762-0741; *Fax:* (819) 762-2466
www.abitibi.capitalerock.ca
live@abitibi.capitalerock.ca
License: Val d'Or, QC held by RNC MEDIA Inc.
Group Owner: RNC MEDIA Inc.
Nat'l Network: Radiomedia
Population Served: 41,012; *Arbitron Metro Market:* Rouyn-Noranda, QC; *Format:* Classic Rock, Rock/AOR
Nancy Deschenes, General Manager
Nancy Deschenes, General Sales Mgr
Francis Morin, Programming Director
Michelle Desjardins, Promotions Representative

Val-des-Lacs

CHVL-FM
106.5 MHz FM; 5 w; -3.8 meters; N46 10 56 W74 20 32
348 Chemin Val des Lacs, Val-des-Lacs, QC J0T 2P0 Canada
(819) 321-1718
real.train@hotmail.com
License: Val-des-Lacs, QC held by Radio Vallacquoise Inc.
Real Terrault, President

Valleyfield

CKOD-FM
06-06-1994; 103.1 MHz FM; *Hrs Open:* 24; 3 kw; 167 ft; N45 16 08 W74 05 50
249 Victoria St., Suite 103, Salaberry-de-Valleyfield, QC J6T 1A9 Canada
(450) 373-0103; *Fax:* (450) 854-8103
License: Valleyfield, QC held by Radio Express Inc.
Nat'l Reps: Target Broadcast Sales
Format: Adult Contemp; *Hrs. of News Programming:* news progmg 7 hrs wkly; *No. News Employees:* 1; *Target Audience:* 18-54; general
Robert Brunet, President
Dean Nevins, General Sales Mgr
Martin Leblanc, Programming Director

Vaudreuil-Dorion

CJVD-FM
09-29-2008; 100.1 MHz FM; 550 w; N45 24 55 W74 02 45 Canada
(514) 790-1001
www.cjvd.ca
info@cjvd.ca
License: Vaudreuil-Dorion, QC held by Yves Sauve.
Population Served: 33,305; *Arbitron Metro Market:* Vaudreuil-Dorion, QC; *Format:* Oldies, French
Yves Sauve, President

Victoriaville

CFDA-FM
01-01-1999; 101.9 MHz FM; *Hrs Open:* 24; 1.35 kw
55, rue Saint-Jean-Baptiste, Victoriaville, QC G6P 4E1 Canada
(819) 752-5545
www.passionrock.com
License: Victoriaville, QC held by Radio Victoriaville Ltee.
Group Owner: Attraction Radio Inc.
Nat'l Reps: Target Broadcast Sales
Population Served: 43,462; *Arbitron Metro Market:* Victoriaville, PQ; *Format:* Adult Contemp; *Special Programming:* Country 3 hrs, retro/oldies 3 hrs wkly; *No. News Employees:* 7; *Target Audience:* 35-65.
Annie Labbe, General Manager

Ville-Marie

CKVM-FM
01-01-2004; 93.1 MHz FM; *Hrs Open:* 24; 18.4 kw; N47 19 57 W79 25 38
62, rue Ste-Anne, Ville-Marie, QC J9V 2B7 Canada
(819) 629-2710; *Fax:* (819) 622-0716
www.ckvmfm.com
License: Ville-Marie, QC held by Radio Temiscamingue Inc.
Group Owner: RNC MEDIA Inc.
Population Served: 2,595; *Arbitron Metro Market:* Ville-Marie, QC; *Format:* Adult Contemp; *Hrs. of News Programming:* news progmg 11 hrs wkly; *No. News Employees:* 1; *Target Audience:* General.
Francois Harrisson Gariepy, General Manager
Marilou Riopel, Sales Representative
Guy Bertrand, Sales Representative
Robert Guimond, Sales Representative

Windsor

CIAX-FM
01-01-2000; 98.3 MHz FM; 426 w
49 Sixth Ave., Windsor, QC J1S 1T2 Canada
(819) 845-2692
www.ciaxfm.net
unitewindsor@qc.aira.com
License: Windsor, QC held by La Radio communautaire de Windsor et region inc.
Population Served: 5,239; *Arbitron Metro Market:* Windsor, PQ; *Format:* Variety/Diverse
Patrick Levesque, President
Julie Lupien, Programming Director
Marc Savoy, Director of Sales and advertising

Saskatchewan

Blucher

CFAQ-FM
01-01-2006; 100.3 MHz FM; 36 w
2127 St. Andrews Ave., Saskatoon, SK S7M 0M2 Canada
(306) 290-7222
www.saskatoonchristianradio.com
orrrobert@gmail.com
License: Blucher, SK held by Bertor Communications Ltd.
Population Served: 234,200; *Arbitron Metro Market:* Saskatoon, SK; *Format:* Christian
Robert Orr, General Manager

Broadview

CKOO-FM
105.7 MHz FM; 50 watts; 22.7 meters
Box 609, Broadview, SK S0G 0K0 Canada
(306) 696-3291; *Fax:* (306) 696-3201
radio@kahkewistahaw.com
License: Broadview, SK held by Kahkewistahaw Radio Station
Monica Wasacase, General Manager

Cowessess

CIBC-FM
98.1 MHz FM; 49 watts; 25 meters
Box 100, Cowessess, SK S0G 5L0 Canada
(306) 696-2520; *Fax:* (306) 696-3237
License: Cowessess, SK held by Cowassess Community Projects Inc

Cumberland House

CJCF-FM
01-01-1990; 89.9 MHz FM; 30.5 w
Canada
(306) 888-4441; *Fax:* (306) 888-4444
www.cjcfradio.com
License: Cumberland House, SK held by Cumberland House Radio & Television Committee Inc.
Format: Ethnic
Ken Buck, Radio Manager

Estevan

CJSL
08-01-1961; 1280 kHz AM; *Hrs Open:* 24; 10 kw
1236 5th St., Suite 200, Estevan, SK S4A 0Z6 Canada
(306) 634-1280
www.discoverestevan.com
License: Estevan, SK held by Golden West Broadcasting Ltd.
Group Owner: Golden West Broadcasting Ltd.; (acq 3-95)
Nat'l Reps: Canadian Broadcast Sales; *Wire Services:* BN Wire
Format: Country; *Special Programming:* Farm 4 hrs, relg 10 hrs wkly; *Target Audience:* General.
Melissa Deitz, Station Manager
Melissa Deitz, General Sales Mgr

CHSN-FM
11-01-2001; 102.3 MHz FM; 100 kw
1236 5th St., Suite 200, Estevan, SK S4A 0Z6 Canada
(306) 634-1280
www.discoverestevan.com
License: Estevan, SK held by Golden West Broadcasting Ltd.
Group Owner: Golden West Broadcasting Ltd.
Format: Contemporary Hits/Top 40
Melissa Deitz, Station Manager
Lyle McGillivray, Programming Director

CKSE-FM
09-12-2012; 106.1 MHz FM; 100 kw; 70.85 meters
1236 5th St., Suite 200, Estevan, SK S4A 0Z6 Canada
(306) 634-1280
www.discoverestevan.com
License: Estevan, SK held by Golden West Broadcasting Ltd.
Group Owner: Golden West Broadcasting Ltd.
Format: Rock/AOR
Melissa Deitz, Station Manager
Lyle McGillivray, Programming Director

Gravelbourg

*CBKF-1(AM)
01-01-1952; 540 kHz AM; 5 kw-U, DA-2
2440 Broad St., Regina, SK S4P 4A1 Canada
(306) 347-9540; *Fax:* (306) 347-9635
www.cbc.ca
License: Gravelbourg, SK held by CBC French.
Format: Variety/Diverse
Robert Rabinowitz, CEO
Rikki Bote, General Manager

CFRG-FM
01-01-2003; 93.1 MHz FM; 48 w
133 5th Avenue East, BP / PO Box 176, Gravelbourg, SK S0H 1X0 Canada
(306) 648-2374; *Fax:* (306) 648-3258
www.cfrg.ca
License: Gravelbourg, SK held by Association communautaire fransaskoise de Gravelbourg Inc.
Population Served: 1,093; *Arbitron Metro Market:* Gravelbourg, SK; *Format:* French
Guylain Bergeron, Director/Station Manager

Hudson Bay

CFMQ-FM
09-15-1994; 98.1 MHz FM; *Hrs Open:* 24; kw
Canada
(306) 865-3065; *Fax:* (306) 865-2227
License: Hudson Bay, SK held by HB Communications Inc.
Format: Country, Variety/Diverse; *Hrs. of News Programming:* News progmg one hr wkly; *Target Audience:* General.
Mark Brann, President
Dan Brann, General Manager

Humboldt

CHBO-FM
107.5 MHz FM; 59 kw; 164.1 meters
640 10th St., P.O. Box 2888, Humboldt, SK S0K 2A0 Canada
(306) 682-2255
www.discoverhumboldt.com
License: Humboldt, SK held by Golden West Broadcasting Ltd.
Group Owner: Golden West Broadcasting Ltd.
Format: Contemporary Hits/Top 40
Brian Kusch, Station Manager
Brian Kusch, Sales Manager

Island Lake

CIFN-FM
106.5 MHz FM; 33 watts; 15 meters
Box 240, Island Lake, SK S0M 3G0 Canada
(306) 837-2188; *Fax:* (306) 837-2266
License: Island Lake, SK held by Island Lake First Nations Radio Inc

Kindersley

CFYM
07-29-1987; 1210 kHz AM*Rebroadcasts:* Rebroadcasts CJYM(AM) Rosetown 95%
404 12th Ave. E., P.O. Box 1330, Kindersley, SK S0L 1S0 Canada
(306) 882-2686
www.westcentralonline.com
cjymnews@goldenwestradio.com
License: Kindersley, SK held by Golden West Broadcasting Ltd.
Group Owner: Golden West Broadcasting Ltd.; (acq 10-21-99).
Nat'l Reps: Target Broadcast Sales
Format: Adult Contemp
Barbara G. Bell, Station Manager

La Ronge

*CBKA-FM
09-01-1979; 105.9 MHz FM; 80 w
Box 959, La Ronge, SK S0J 1L0 Canada
(306) 347-9540; *Fax:* (306) 425-2270
www.cbc.ca/news/canada/saskatchewan
License: La Ronge, SK held by CBC.
Nat'l Network: CBC Radio One
Format: Public Affairs; *Special Programming:* Cree & Dene 20 hrs wkly
David Kyle, General Manager

CJLR-FM
01-01-1990; 89.9 MHz FM; *Hrs Open:* 24; 216 w; Ant 151 ft
712 Finlayson Street, La Ronge, SK S0J 1L0 Canada
(306) 425-4003; *Fax:* (306) 425-3123
www.mbcradio.com
reception@mbcradio.com
License: La Ronge, SK held by Natotawin Broadcasting Inc.
Population Served: 50,000; *Format:* Country, Ethnic, Variety/Diverse; *Special Programming:* Cree & Dene languages; *Target Audience:* General.
Keith Kratchmer, CA, Controller
Dallas Hicks, Director of Operations
Deborah A. Charles, CEO
Kelly Provost, News Director

Marcelin

CICN-FM
01-26-2011; 104.3 MHz FM; 30 watts; 12.1 meters
Box 531, Leask, SK S0J 0M0 Canada
(306) 466-4959; *Fax:* (306) 466-2284
License: Marcelin, SK held by Muskeg Lake Cree Nation Radio Station Corp

Meadow Lake

CFDM-FM
01-01-2001; 105.7 MHz FM; 46.5 w
Box 8168, Flying Dust First Nation Reserve, Meadow Lake, SK S9X 1T8 Canada
(306) 236-1445; *Fax:* (306) 236-2861
cfdmradio@gmail.com
License: Meadow Lake, SK held by FDB Broadcasting Inc.
Population Served: 4,771; *Arbitron Metro Market:* Meadow Lake, SK; *Format:* Contemporary Hits/Top 40, Country
Duwayne Derocher, Station Manager
Josh Derocher, Broadcast Assistant

CJNS-FM
01-01-2004; 102.3 MHz FM; 50 kw
1711 100th St., North Battleford, SK S9A 0W7 Canada
(306) 445-2477; *Fax:* (306) 445-4599
www.cjnb.com
cjnbnews@jpbg.ca
License: Meadow Lake, SK held by Jim Pattison Broadcast Group Ltd. (the general partner) and Jim Pattison Industries Ltd. (the limited partner), carrying on business as Jim Pattison Broadcast Group L.P.
Group Owner: The Jim Pattison Broadcast Group
Population Served: 156,929; *Format:* Country
Garth Kalin, Operations Manager
Karl Johnston, General Manager
David Dekker, Station Manager
Betty Speed, Sales Manager
Doug Harrison, Programming Director
Nic Fransoo, Promotions Director

Melfort

CKJH(AM)
10-08-1966; 750 kHz AM; *Hrs Open:* 24; 25 kw-U, DA-N; N52 47 57 W104 35 25
Canada
(306) 752-2587
www.yourtownnews.ca/news/97
info@cjvr.com
License: Melfort, SK held by Radio CJVR Ltd.
Nat'l Reps: Target Broadcast Sales
Format: Contemporary Hits/Top 40; *Special Programming:* Relg 9 hrs wkly; *Hrs. of News Programming:* news progmg 15 hrs wkly; *No. News Employees:* 4; *Target Audience:* General.
Pat Brady, Promotions/New Media Manager
Royal Watson, Production Director
Karen Breiter, Creative Director
Ken Singer, VP, Broadcast Operations
Linda Rheaume, Station Manager
Dave Marcoux, General Sales Manager
Bill Wood, GroupProgram Director
Dave Baker, Music Director
Cam Lee, News/Sports

CJVR-FM
03-01-2002; 105.1 MHz FM; 100 kw
Canada
(306) 752-2587
www.yourtownnews.ca/news/97
License: Melfort, SK held by Radio CJVR Ltd.
Population Served: 5,576; *Arbitron Metro Market:* Melfort, SK; *Format:* Country
Ken Singer, VP, Broadcast Operations
Linda Rheaume, Station Manager
Dave Marcoux, General Sales Mgr
Bill Wood, Group Program Director
Pat Brady, Promotions/New Media Manager
Cam Lee, News/Sports Director
Karen Breiter, CreativeDirector
Cal Gratton, Music Director
Royal Watson, Production Director

Moose Jaw

CHAB
04-23-1922; 800 kHz AM; *Hrs Open:* 24; 10 kw
1704 Main St. N., Moose Jaw, SK S6J 1L4 Canada
(306) 694-0800
www.discovermoosejaw.com
License: Moose Jaw, SK held by 101142236 Saskatchewan Ltd.

Group Owner: Golden West Broadcasting Ltd.; (acq 8-20-92)
Nat'l Reps: Canadian Broadcast Sales
Format: Oldies; *No. News Employees:* 3; *Target Audience:* 25-54.
Darryl Pisio, Station Manager
Darryl Pisio, General Sales Mgr
Craig Hemingway, Programming Director

CILG-FM
07-23-2002; 100.7 MHz FM; 100 kw
1704 Main St. N., Moose Jaw, SK S6J 1L4 Canada
(306) 694-0800
www.discovermoosejaw.com
License: Moose Jaw, SK held by 101142236 Saskatchewan Ltd.
Group Owner: Golden West Broadcasting Ltd.
Population Served: 35,629; *Arbitron Metro Market:* Moose Jaw, SK; *Format:* Country
Darryl Pisio, Station Manager

CJAW-FM
04-22-2008; 103.9 MHz FM; 100 kw; N50 35 44 W105 04 09
1704 Main St. N., Moose Jaw, SK S6J 1L4 Canada
(306) 694-0800
www.discovermoosejaw.com
License: Moose Jaw, SK held by 101142236 Saskatchewan Ltd.
Group Owner: Golden West Broadcasting Ltd.
Population Served: 35,629; *Arbitron Metro Market:* Moose Jaw, SK; *Format:* Adult Contemp
Darryl Pisio, Station Manager
Craig Hemingway, Programming Director

Nipawin

CJNE-FM
06-01-2002; 94.7 MHz FM; 14.8 kw
PO Box 220, Nipawin, SK S0E 1E0 Canada
(306) 862-9478; *Fax:* (306) 862-2334
www.cjnefm.com
norm.cjne@sasktel.net
License: Nipawin, SK held by CJNE FM Radio Inc.
Population Served: 4,061; *Arbitron Metro Market:* Nipawin, SK; *Format:* Classic Rock, Oldies; *No. News Employees:* 1; *Target Audience:* 18-50.
Norm Rudock, General Manager
Treana Rudock, Station Manager
Les Blair, Promotions Manager

CIOT-FM
01-01-2005; 104.1 MHz FM; *Hrs Open:* 24; 200 w
Box 1240, Nipawin, SK S0E 1E0 Canada
(306) 862-2468; *Fax:* (306) 862-2660
www.lighthousefm.ca
License: Nipawin, SK held by Wilderness Ministries Inc.
Population Served: 17,000; *No. News Employees:* 1; *Target Audience:* 20-55.; *Adv. Rates:* 12; 12; 12; 12
Rod Petersen, Programming Director
Angela Petersen, News Director
Andrew Hildebrandt, Music Director
Andrew Clark, Programming Director

North Battleford

CJNB
01-28-1947; 1050 kHz AM; 10 kw
1711 100th St., North Battleford, SK S9A 0W7 Canada
(306) 445-2477; *Fax:* (306) 445-4599
www.cjnb.com
cjnbnews@jpbg.ca
License: North Battleford, SK held by Jim Pattison Broadcast Group Ltd. (the general partner) and Jim Pattison Industries Ltd. (the limited partner), carrying on business as Jim Pattison Broadcast Group L.P.
Group Owner: The Jim Pattison Broadcast Group
Format: Country
Garth Kalin, Operations Manager
Karl Johnston, General Manager
David Dekker, Station Manager
Betty Speed, Sales Manager
Doug Harrison, Programming Director
Nic Fransoo, Promotions Director

CJHD-FM
01-01-2008; 93.3 MHz FM; 100 kw; N52 48 15 W108 35 18
1711 100th St., North Battleford, SK S9A 0W7 Canada
(306) 445-2477; *Fax:* (306) 445-4599
www.933therock.ca
License: North Battleford, SK held by Jim Pattison Broadcast Group Ltd. (the general partner) and Jim Pattison Industries Ltd. (the limited partner), carrying on business as Jim Pattison Broadcast Group L.P.
Group Owner: The Jim Pattison Broadcast Group
Format: Rock/AOR
Garth Kalin, Operations Manager
Karl Johnston, General Manager
David Dekker, Station Manager
Jayna Hannah, Sales Manager
Nic Fransoo, Programming Director
Nic Fransoo, Promotions Director

CJCQ-FM
09-26-2001; 97.9 MHz FM; 100 kw
1711 100th St., North Battleford, SK S9A 0W7 Canada
(306) 445-2477; *Fax:* (306) 445-4599
www.q98.ca
cjnbnews@jpbg.ca
License: North Battleford, SK held by Jim Pattison Broadcast Group Ltd. (the general partner) and Jim Pattison Industries Ltd. (the limited partner), carrying on business as Jim Pattison Broadcast Group L.P.
Group Owner: The Jim Pattison Broadcast Group
Format: Adult Contemp
Garth Kalin, Operations Manager
Karl Johnston, General Manager
Karl Johnston, Station Manager
Mike Aimoe, Sales Manager
Nic Fransoo, Programming Director
Nic Fransoo, Promotions Director

Pinehouse Lake

CFNK-FM
01-01-1996; 89.9 MHz FM; 7 w
General Delivery, Box 370, Pinehouse Lake, SK S0J 2B0 Canada
(306) 884-2011; *Fax:* (306) 884-2365
License: Pinehouse Lake, SK held by Pinehouse Communications Society Inc.
Format: Adult Contemp
Peter Smith, General Manager
Vince Natomagan, Programming Director

Prince Albert

CFMM-FM
01-31-1982; 99.1 MHz FM; 100 kw; 606 ft
1316 Central Ave., Prince Albert, SK S6V 6P5 Canada
(306) 763-7421
www.power99fm.com
License: Prince Albert, SK held by Jim Pattison Broadcast Group Ltd. (the general partner) and Jim Pattison Industries Ltd. (the limited partner), carrying on business as Jim Pattison Broadcast Group L.P.
Group Owner: The Jim Pattison Broadcast Group
Format: Adult Contemp
Garth Kalin, Operations Manager
Karl Johnston, General Manager
Scott Anderson, Sales Manager
Garth Kalin, Programming Director
Garth Kalin, Promotions Director
Nigel Maxwell, News Director

CKBI
01-01-1934; 900 kHz AM; 10 kw
1316 Central Ave., Prince Albert, SK S6V 6P5 Canada
(306) 763-7421; *Fax:* (306) 764-1850
www.900ckbi.com
License: Prince Albert, SK held by Jim Pattison Broadcast Group Ltd. (the general partner) and Jim Pattison Industries Ltd. (the limited partner), carrying on business as Jim Pattison Broadcast Group L.P.
Group Owner: The Jim Pattison Broadcast Group; acq 1946).
Nat'l Reps: Canadian Broadcast Sales
Format: Country; *Special Programming:* Farm 2 hrs wkly; *Target Audience:* 34 plus; working women
Karl Johnston, General Manager
Tyler Kinash, Sales Manager
Garth Kalin, Programming Director
Garth Kalin, Promotions Director
Nigel Maxwell, News Director
Ken Landers, Music Director

CHQX-FM
06-18-2001; 101.5 MHz FM; *Hrs Open:* 24; 100 kw; Ant 606 ft
1316 Central Ave., Prince Albert, SK S6V 6P5 Canada
(306) 763-7421
www.mix101fm.com
License: Prince Albert, SK held by Jim Pattison Broadcast Group Ltd. (the general partner) and Jim Pattison Industries Ltd. (the limited partner), carrying on business as Jim Pattison Broadcast Group L.P.
Group Owner: The Jim Pattison Broadcast Group
Population Served: 35,129; *Arbitron Metro Market:* Prince Albert, SK; *Format:* Rock/AOR
Garth Kalin, Operations Manager
Karl Johnston, General Manager
Tyler Kinash, Sales Manager
Garth Kalin, Programming Director
Garth Kalin, Promotions Director
Nigel Maxwell, News Director

Regina

***CBK-FM**
05-01-1977; 96.9 MHz FM; 100 kw; Ant 501 ft
Canada
(360) 956-7400
www.cbc.ca/sask/
License: Regina, SK held by CBC
Nat'l Network: CBC Radio Two
TV Affiliate: *CBKT(TV) affil; *Format:* Classical, Jazz, Variety/Diverse
David Kyle, General Manager

CBKF-FM
09-01-1973; 97.7 MHz FM; *Hrs Open:* 24; 22.3 kw; 146.2 meters
Mailing Address: Canada
Second Address: 2440 Broad St., Regina, SK S4P-3Z4
(306) 347-9540; *Fax:* (306) 347-9493
www.cbc.ca
License: Regina, SK held by Radio Canada.
Nat'l Network: Premiere Chaine
TV Affiliate: CBKF(TV) affil.; *Format:* Variety/Diverse
Rene Fontaine, General Manager
Anne Brochu, News Director
Steve Tomchuk, Engineering Dir

CFWF-FM
04-15-1982; 104.9 MHz FM; 100 kw; 400 ft
1900 Rose St., Regina, SK S4P 0A9 Canada
(306) 546-6200
www.thewolfrocks.com
License: Regina, SK held by Harvard Broadcasting Inc.
Group Owner: Harvard Broadcasting Inc.; (Acq 8-25-95)
Nat'l Reps: Canadian Broadcast Sales
Format: Classic Rock, Rock/AOR
Jason Huschi, General Manager
Karen Broderick, General Sales Mgr
Tim Schutz, Programming Director
Megan Beatty, Promotions and Marketing
Trish Bezborotko, Retail Sales Manager

CHMX-FM
02-04-1966; 92.1 MHz FM; *Hrs Open:* 24; 100 kw; 499 ft
1900 Rose St., Regina, SK S4P 0A9 Canada
(306) 546-6200
www.my921.ca
License: Regina, SK held by Harvard Broadcasting Inc.
Group Owner: Harvard Broadcasting Inc.; (acq 3-1-81)
Format: Adult Contemp
Jason Huschi, General Manager
Karen Broderick, General Sales Mgr
Greg Morgan, Programming Director
Tom Staseson, Promotion and Marketing Director

CIZL-FM
06-01-1982; 98.9 MHz FM; 100 kw
210-2401 Saskatchewan Dr., Regina, SK S4P 4H8 Canada
(306) 525-0000
www.z99.com
License: Regina, SK held by Rawlco Radio Ltd.
Group Owner: Rawlco Radio Ltd.; (Acq 4-67).
Format: Adult Contemp; *Target Audience:* 18-49.
Tom Newton, General Manager
Russ Bryden, Sales Manager
Darren Robson, Programming Director
Amber Morse, Promotions Director

CKRM
07-27-1926; 620 kHz AM; 10 kw-U, DA-2
1900 Rose St., Regina, SK S4P 0A9 Canada
(306) 546-6200; *Fax:* (306) 781-7338
www.620ckrm.com
License: Regina, SK held by Harvard Broadcasting Inc.
Group Owner: Harvard Broadcasting Inc.; (acq 11-30-2001; C$4.2 million with co-located FM)
Format: Country
Jason Huschi, General Manager
Karen Broderick, General Sales Mgr
Grant Biebrick, Programming Director
Trish Bezborotko, Retail Sales Manager

CJME
11-24-1959; 980 kHz AM; *Hrs Open:* 24; 10 kw
210-2401 Saskatchewan Dr., Regina, SK S4P 4H8 Canada

(306) 525-0000
www.cjme.com
License: Regina, SK held by Rawlco Radio Ltd.
Group Owner: Rawlco Radio Ltd.; acq 11-30-2001).
Format: News, News/Talk, Talk
Tom Newton, General Manager
Kevin Antrobus, Sales Manager
Jay Stone, Programming Director

*CJTR-FM
11-01-2001; 91.3 MHz FM; *Hrs Open:* 24; 480 w; N50 27 18 W104 36 30
Mailing Address: #301-1102 8th Avenue, Regina, SK S4P 3A1 Canada
Second Address: PO Box 334, Station Main, Regina, SK S4P 3A1
(306) 525-7274; *Fax:* (306) 525-9741
www.cjtr.ca
radius@cjtr.ca
License: Regina, SK held by Radius Communications Inc.
Population Served: 200,000; *Arbitron Metro Market:* Regina, SK; *Format:* Variety/Diverse; *Special Programming:* American Indian 4 hrs, Black 2 hrs, Chinese one hr; *Hrs. of News Programming:* News progmg 10 hrs wkly*Adv.Rates:* 312; 276; 240; 204
Karl Valiaho, President
Norm Sacuta, Vice President
Tim Weisgarber, Secretary
Davin Stachoski, Treasurer
Norm Sacuta, Vice-President
Joan Beisel, Treasurer
Dave Morgan, Secretary
Brenda Tacik, Past President; co-chair ofFundraising Committee
Nadeem Naz, Member at Large
Callan David, Member at Large

CKCK-FM
08-09-2002; 94.5 MHz FM; *Hrs Open:* 24; 100 kw
210-2401 Saskatchewan Dr., Regina, SK S4P 4H8 Canada
(306) 525-0000; *Fax:* (306) 347-8557
www.jackfmregina.com
License: Regina, SK held by Rawlco Radio Ltd.
Group Owner: Rawlco Radio Ltd.
Population Served: 200,000; *Arbitron Metro Market:* Regina, SK; *Format:* Classic Rock, Oldies
Tom Newton, General Manager
Craig Romanyk, Sales Manager
Darren Robson, Programming Director
Amber Morse, Promotions Director

CHBD-FM
02-20-2008; 92.7 MHz FM; 100 kw; N50 28 58 W104 30 20
4303 Albert St., Suite 100, Regina, SK S4S 3R6 Canada
(306) 337-2850; *Fax:* (306) 359-0931
www.bigdog927.com
License: Regina, SK held by Bell Media Group G.P.
Group Owner: Bell Media Inc.
Population Served: 200,000; *Arbitron Metro Market:* Regina, SK; *Format:* Country; *Target Audience:* 25-64.
David Fisher, General Manager
Gary Wilson, General Sales Mgr
Tim Day, Program Director
Celeste Grebinski, Promotions Director
Luke Dickinson, Creative Director
Mike McGuire, Music Director

Rosetown

CJYM
08-08-1966; 1330 kHz AM; *Hrs Open:* 24; 10 kw
P.O. Box 490, 208 Hwy. #4, Rosetown, SK S0L 2V0 Canada
(306) 882-2686
www.westcentralonline.com
License: Rosetown, SK held by Golden West Broadcasting Ltd.
Group Owner: Golden West Broadcasting Ltd.; (acq 10-21-99)
Nat'l Reps: Target Broadcast Sales
Format: Adult Contemp, Contemporary Hits/Top 40; *No. News Employees:* 2; *Target Audience:* General.
Barbara G. Bell, Station Manager

Saskatoon

CBKF-2(AM)
11-06-1952; 860 kHz AM; 10 kw-U, DA-2
144 2nd Ave., Saskatoon, SK S7K 1K5 Canada
(306) 956-7400; *Fax:* (306) 956-7476
www.cbc.ca/news/canada/saskatchewan
License: Saskatoon, SK held by CBC French.
Format: Variety/Diverse; *Target Audience:* General.
David Kyle, General Manager
Robert Rabinowitz, Programming Director

*CBKS-FM
07-01-1978; 105.5 MHz FM; *Hrs Open:* 24; 98 kw; Ant 586 ft*Rebroadcasts:* Rebroadcasts CBK-FM Regina
144 2nd Ave. S., Saskatoon, SK S7K 1K5 Canada
(306) 956-7400; *Fax:* (306) 956-7417
www.cbc.ca/sask/
License: Saskatoon, SK held by CBC.
Nat'l Network: CBC Radio Two
Format: Classical, Jazz, Variety/Diverse
David Kyle, Station Manager

CFCR-FM
01-01-1991; 90.5 MHz FM; *Hrs Open:* 6 AM-1 AM; 1.48 kw
Mailing Address: 267 3rd Ave. S., Saskatoon, SK S7K 1M4 Canada
Second Address: PO Box 7544, Saskatoon, SK S7K 4L4
(306) 664-6678
www.cfcr.ca
cfcr@cfcr.ca
License: Saskatoon, SK held by Community Radio Society of Saskatoon Inc.
Population Served: 200,000; *Format:* Variety/Diverse; *Special Programming:* Fr one hr, Ger 2 hrs, It one hr, Pol one hr, Sp 2; *Hrs. of News Programming:* News progmg one hr wkly; *Target Audience:* General.*Adv.Rates:* 20; 20; 20; 15
Neil Bergen, Station Manager
Jay Allen, Programming Director
Arnold Van Lambalgen, Music/Promotions Director
Kira Yanko, Coordinator/Office Manager
Jordan Poniatowski, Production Manager/Copywriter

CFMC-FM
12-12-1964; 95.1 MHz FM; 100 kw; Ant 110 ft
715 Saskatchewan Cres. W., Saskatoon, SK S7M 5V7 Canada
(306) 934-2222; *Fax:* (306) 477-0002
www.c95.com
License: Saskatoon, SK held by Rawlco Radio Ltd.
Group Owner: Rawlco Radio Ltd.
Format: Adult Contemp, Contemporary Hits/Top 40
Kristy Werner, General Manager
Cliff Lesko, Sales Manager
Ryan Zimmerman, Programming Director
Nicole Kelly, Promotions Director
Wayne Balion, Website

CKBL-FM
02-06-1995; 92.9 MHz FM; 100 kw
366 3rd Ave. S., Saskatoon, SK S7K 1M5 Canada
(306) 244-1975; *Fax:* (306) 665-5501
www.929thebullrocks.com
thebull@929thebullrocks.com
License: Saskatoon, SK held by 629112 Saskatchewan Ltd.
Group Owner: Saskatoon Media Group
Nat'l Reps: Canadian Broadcast Sales
Format: Country; *No. News Employees:* 2; *Target Audience:* General.
Vic Dubois, General Manager
Myles Myrol, General Sales Mgr
Vic Dubois, Programming Director
Holly Robinson, Promotions Coordinator
Pat Dubois, Music Director

CKOM
06-08-1951; 650 kHz AM; 10 kw
715 Saskatchewan Cres. W., Saskatoon, SK S7M 5V7 Canada
(306) 934-2222
www.ckom.com
License: Saskatoon, SK held by Rawlco Radio Ltd.
Group Owner: Rawlco Radio Ltd.
Format: News, News/Talk, Talk; *Hrs. of News Programming:* 10
Kristy Werner, General Manager
Sandee Reed, Sales Manager
Angela Hill, Programming Director
Nicole Kelly, Promotions Director

CJWW
01-01-1976; 600 kHz AM; *Hrs Open:* 24
366 3rd Avenue S., Saskatoon, SK S7K 1M5 Canada
(306) 938-0600; *Fax:* (306) 665-5501
www.cjwwradio.com
License: Saskatoon, SK held by 629112 Saskatchewan Ltd.
Group Owner: Saskatoon Media Group; (acq 12-21-2000; C$7,450,000).
Nat'l Reps: Canadian Broadcast Sales
Format: Country; *Special Programming:* Gospel 3 hrs wkly; *No. News Employees:* 7; *Target Audience:* 35-64; central
Vic Dubois, General Manager
Myles Myrol, General Sales Mgr
Rod Kitter, Programming Director
Jay Richards, Community Relations Director
Tim Kostuik, Retail Sales Supervisor
Jason Lee, Music Director

CJDJ-FM
06-01-1990; 102.1 MHz FM; *Hrs Open:* 24; 100 kw
715 Saskatchewan Cres. W., Saskatoon, SK S7M 5V7 Canada
(306) 934-2222; *Fax:* (306) 477-0002
www.rock102rocks.com
License: Saskatoon, SK held by Rawlco Radio Ltd.
Group Owner: Rawlco Radio Ltd.; (acq 12-21-2000; C$870,000 for all the issued and outstanding shares).
Population Served: 200,000; *Format:* Rock/AOR; *Special Programming:* Relg 6 hrs wkly; *Hrs. of News Programming:* news progmg 4 hrs wkly; *No. News Employees:* 3; *Target Audience:* 25-49; well educated, well paidprofessionals
Kristy Werner, General Manager
Christine Thille, Sales Manager
Ryan Zimmerman, Programming Director
Nicole Kelly, Promotions Director

CJMK-FM
05-01-2001; 98.3 MHz FM; *Hrs Open:* 24; 100 kw
366 3rd Ave. S., Saskatoon, SK S7K 1M5 Canada
(306) 244-1975; *Fax:* (306) 665-5501
www.98cool.ca
License: Saskatoon, SK held by 629112 Saskatchewan Ltd.
Group Owner: Saskatoon Media Group
Population Served: 234,200; *Arbitron Metro Market:* Saskatoon, SK; *Format:* Adult Contemp
Vic Dubois, General Manager
Myles Myrol, General Sales Mgr
Steve Chisholm, Programming Director
Matt Bradley, Music Director
Tim Kostuik, Retail Sales Supervisor

CFWD-FM
04-01-2008; 96.3 MHz FM; 96 kw; N52 10 28 W106 26 04
105 21st St. E., Suite 200, Saskatoon, SK S7K 0B3 Canada
(306) 653-9630
www.cruzfm.com
heyyou@cruzfm.com
License: Saskatoon, SK held by Harvard Broadcasting Inc.
Group Owner: Harvard Broadcasting Inc.
Nat'l Reps: CHUM Radio Sales
Population Served: 234,200; *Arbitron Metro Market:* Saskatoon, SK; *Format:* Adult Contemp, Contemporary Hits/Top 40
Andy Ross, General Manager
Rob Lozinski, General Sales Mgr
Andy Ross, Programming Director
Zoe Vassos, Promotions and Marketing Director
Mel Kozun, Music Director

CBK-1-FM
09-26-2013; 94.1 MHz FM; 4.1 kw; 68.2 meters; N52 05 12 W106 40 12
100-128 4th Avenue South, Saskatoon, SK S7K 1M8 Canada
(306) 956-7414
www.cbc.ca/Saskatoon
License: Saskatoon, SK held by CBC
Nat'l Network: CBC Radio One
John Agnew, Managing Director

Shaunavon

CJSN
12-06-1966; 1490 kHz AM; 1 kw-U
134 Central Ave. N., Swift Current, SK S9H 0L1 Canada
(306) 773-4605
www.swiftcurrentonline.com
License: Shaunavon, SK held by Golden West Broadcasting Ltd.
Group Owner: Golden West Broadcasting Ltd.; (acq 1973)
Population Served: 1,200,000; *Format:* Country
Mike Saretsky, Station Manager
Mike Saretsky, General Sales Mgr

Swift Current

CIMG-FM
10-20-1979; 94.1 MHz FM; *Hrs Open:* 24; 100 kw; 400 ft
134 Central Ave. N., Swift Current, SK S9H 0L1 Canada
(306) 773-4605
www.swiftcurrentonline.com
License: Swift Current, SK held by Golden West Broadcasting Ltd.
Group Owner: Golden West Broadcasting Ltd.; (acq 11-8-95; C$97,500).
Nat'l Reps: Canadian Broadcast Sales
Population Served: 48,500; *Format:* Adult Contemp, Contemporary Hits/Top 40; *Hrs. of News Programming:* news progmg 4 hrs wkly; *No. News Employees:* 3; *Target Audience:* 18-35.

RADIO - CANADA

Mike Saretsky, General Manager
Mike Saretsky, Station Manager

CKSW
06-01-1956; 570 kHz AM; *Hrs Open:* 24; 10 kw
134 Central Ave. N., Swift Current, SK S9H 0L1 Canada
(306) 773-4605
www.swiftcurrentonline.com
License: Swift Current, SK held by Golden West Broadcasting Ltd.
Group Owner: Golden West Broadcasting Ltd.
Nat'l Reps: Canadian Broadcast Sales
Format: Country; *Special Programming:* Farm 5 hrs, Ger one hr wkly; *Hrs. of News Programming:* news progmg 9 hrs wkly; *No. News Employees:* 5; *Target Audience:* 25-54.
Mike Saretsky, Station Manager
Mike Saretsky, General Sales Mgr

CKFI-FM
11-05-2005; 97.1 MHz FM; 100 kw
134 Central Ave. N., Swift Current, SK S9H 0L1 Canada
(306) 773-4605
www.swiftcurrentonline.com
License: Swift Current, SK held by Golden West Broadcasting Ltd.
Group Owner: Golden West Broadcasting Ltd.
Population Served: 85,118; *Format:* Adult Contemp
Mike Saretsky, Station Manager
Mike Saretsky, General Sales Mgr

Watrous

***CBK**
07-29-1939; 540 kHz AM; *Hrs Open:* 24
Canada
(306) 347-9540; *Fax:* (306) 347-9524
www.cbc.ca/sask
License: Watrous, SK held by CBC.
Nat'l Network: CBC Radio One
Format: News, Talk, Variety/Diverse; *Special Programming:* Farm 5 hrs wkly
Debbie Carpentier, General Manager
David Kyle, Station Manager
Nigel Simms, News Director

Weyburn

CFSL
08-16-1957; 1190 kHz AM; *Hrs Open:* 24; 10 kw-D, 5 kw-N, DA-N
305 Souris Ave., Weyburn, SK S4H 0C6 Canada
(306) 848-1190
www.discoverweyburn.com
License: Weyburn, SK held by Golden West Broadcasting Ltd.
Group Owner: Golden West Broadcasting Ltd.; (acq 2-16-95)
Nat'l Reps: Canadian Broadcast Sales; *Wire Services:* BN Wire
Format: Country; *Special Programming:* Farm 3 hrs, relg 9 hrs wkly; *No. News Employees:* 3; *Target Audience:* 25 plus.
Cameron Birnie, Station Manager
Glenn Rogers, Programming Director

CKRC-FM
09-19-2006; 103.5 MHz FM; 100 kw
305 Souris Ave., Weyburn, SK S4H 0C6 Canada
(306) 848-1190
www.discoverweyburn.com
License: Weyburn, SK held by Golden West Broadcasting Ltd.
Group Owner: Golden West Broadcasting Ltd.
Format: Adult Contemp
Cameron Birnie, Station Manager
Glenn Rogers, Programming Director

CHWY-FM
12-10-2013; 106.7 MHz FM; 100 kw; 73.7 meters
305 Souris Ave., Weyburn, SK S4H 0C6 Canada
(306) 848-1190
License: Weyburn, SK held by Golden West Broadcasting Ltd.
Group Owner: Golden West Broadcasting Ltd.
Format: Rock/AOR
Cameron Birnie, Station Manager
Glenn Rogers, Programming Director

White Bear Lake Resort

CIDD-FM
01-01-2002; 97.7 MHz FM; 46.5 w
Box 875, Kenosee Lake, SK S0C 2S0 Canada
(306) 577-2450; *Fax:* (306) 577-4313
License: White Bear Lake Resort, SK held by White Bear Children's Charity Inc.
Population Served: 31,612,897; *Arbitron Metro Market:* Carlyle Lake, SK; *Format:* Variety/Diverse
Lana Littlechief, General Manager

Yorkton

CJGX
08-19-1927; 940 kHz AM
Canada
(306) 782-2256; *Fax:* (306) 783-4994
www.gx94radio.com
ykt-reception@harvardbroadcasting.com
License: Yorkton, SK held by Yorkton Broadcasting Ltd. and Walsh Investments Inc., partners of GX Radio, a gen partnership.
Nat'l Reps: CHUM Radio Sales; Target Broadcast Sales
Format: Country
Lyle Walsh, President
Chad Mikals, Operations Dir
Angie Norton, General Manager
Damon Kustra, General Sales Mgr
Brad Bazin, Programming Director
Gina Resler, Promotions Manager
Bryan Mireau, Engineering Dir

CFGW-FM
07-01-2001; 94.1 MHz FM; 100 kw
120 Smith St. E., Yorkton, SK S3N 3V3 Canada
(306) 782-9410; *Fax:* (306) 786-6805
www.941thefox.com
ykt-reception@harvardbroadcasting.com
License: Yorkton, SK held by Harvard Broadcasting
Population Served: 18,471; *Arbitron Metro Market:* Yorkton, SK; *Format:* Adult Contemp
Angie Norton, General Manager
Colin Laird, Sales Manager
Brad Bazin, Programming Director
Mike Wilson, Music Director
David Johnson, Production Manager
Kelsey Liebrecht, Promotions/Marketing Director

CJJC-FM
01-02-2006; 98.5 MHz FM; 50 kw; 118 meters
395 Riverview Rd., Yorkton, SK S3N 3V6 Canada
(306) 786-7625; *Fax:* (306) 782-4437
www.therock985.ca
License: Yorkton, SK held by 101056012 Saskatchewan Ltd
No. News Employees: 5
Dennis Dyck, Station Manager
Harry Ramsbottom, Sales
Christian McLeod, Production
Heidi Smithson, Office Administration/Traffic
Colleen Hoffort, Sales
Jack Dawes, Agricultural Programmer

CFGW-FM
07-01-2001; 94.1 MHz FM; 100 kw
120 Smith St. E., Yorkton, SK S3N 3V3 Canada
(306) 782-9410; *Fax:* (306) 783-4994
www.941thefox.com
ykt-reception@harvardbroadcasting.com
License: Yorkton, SK held by GX Radio Partnership
Group Owner: Harvard Broadcasting Inc.
Format: Adult Contemp
Angie Norton, General Manager
Colin Laird, Sales Manager
Brad Bazin, Programming Director
Kelsey Liebrecht, Promotions and Marketing Director
Mike Wilson, Music Director
David Johnson, Production Manager

CJGX
08-19-1927; 940 kHz AM; 50 kw
120 Smith St. E., Yorkton, SK S3N 3V3 Canada
(306) 782-2256; *Fax:* (306) 783-4994
www.gx94radio.com
ykt-reception@harvardbroadcasting.com
License: Yorkton, SK held by GX Radio Partnership
Group Owner: Harvard Broadcasting Inc.
Format: Country
Angie Norton, General Manager
Colin Laird, Sales Manager
Brad Bazin, Programming Director
Kelsey Liebrecht, Promotions and Marketing Director
Danny Ismond, Music Director
David Johnson, Production Manager

Zenon Park

CKZP-FM
01-01-2002; 102.7 MHz FM; 5.4 w
920 Park Road, Zenon Park, SK S0E 1W0 Canada
(306) 767-2000
License: Zenon Park, SK held by Radio Zenon Park Inc.
Population Served: 231; *Arbitron Metro Market:* Zenon Park, SK; *Format:* French
J. Ulysse Leger, General Manager

Yukon Territory

Dawson City

***CFYT-FM**
10-01-2006; 106.9 MHz FM; *Hrs Open:* Fri-Sun, noon to midnight; 5 w; N64 03 27 W139 24 36*Rebroadcasts:* CKRW-FM Whitehorse 86%
Box 689, Dawson City, YT Y0B 1G0 Canada
(867) 993-5152; *Fax:* (867) 993-6834
www.cfyt.ca
cfytradio@gmail.com
License: Dawson City, YT held by Dawson City Community Radio Society.
Population Served: 1,319; *Arbitron Metro Market:* Dawson City, YT; *Format:* Alternative
Georgia Hammond, President
John Watt, Vice President
Peter Menzies, Treasurer
Capri Simpson, Secretary
Jen Laliberte, Director
Brendan Reese, Director
Kyle Hammond, Director

Tagish

CFET-FM
06-01-2003; 106.7 MHz FM; 50 w
Mile 234, Tagish, YT Y0B 1T0 Canada
(867) 667-6397; *Fax:* (867) 668-2633
License: Tagish, YT held by Robert G. Hopkins.
Population Served: 206; *Arbitron Metro Market:* Tagish, YT; *Format:* Classic Rock
Robert Hopkins, General Manager

Whitehorse

***CFWH-FM**
06-01-2012; 94.5 MHz FM; *Hrs Open:* 24; 3.3 kw
3103 Third Ave., Whitehorse, YT Y1A 1E5 Canada
(867) 668-8400; *Fax:* (867) 668-8408
www.cbc.ca/north
License: Whitehorse, YT held by CBC
Nat'l Network: CBC Radio One
Special Programming: Fr one hr wkly
Frank Fry, Operations Dir

CHON-FM
02-01-1985; 98.1 MHz FM
Canada
(867) 668-6629; *Fax:* (867) 668-6612
nnby@nnby.net
License: Whitehorse, Canada County, YT held by Northern Native Broadcasting, YUKON
Format: Classic Rock, Country; *Special Programming:* Yukon native language 15 hrs wkly
Shirley Adamason, CEO
Sophie Green, General Manager
Manfred Janssen, General Sales Mgr
Dennis Gerard, Engineering Dir

CKRW-FM
11-17-1969; 96.1 MHz FM
203-4103 4th Ave., Suite 203, Whitehorse, YT Y1A 1H6 Canada
(867) 668-6100; *Fax:* (867) 668-4209
www.ckrw.com
admin@ckrw.com
License: Whitehorse, YT held by Klondike Broadcasting Co. Ltd.
Group Owner: Klondike Broadcasting Co
Nat'l Reps: Canadian Broadcast Sales
Rolf Hougen, CEO
Eva Bidrman, General Manager
Keith Ellert, Programming Director

CIAY-FM
01-01-2003; 100.7 MHz FM; *Hrs Open:* 24; 50 w
91806 Alaska Hwy., Whitehorse, YT Y1A 5B7 Canada
(867) 393-2429; *Fax:* (867) 393-2439
www.lifewhitehorse.com
info@lifewhitehorse.com
License: Whitehorse, YT held by Bethany Pentecostal Tabernacle.
Population Served: 23,276; *Arbitron Metro Market:* Whitehorse, YT; *Format:* Christian
Rod Carby, Station Manager
Theresa Aitcheson, General Sales Mgr
Ian McDonald, Programming Director

Canadian AM Radio Stations by Call Letters

CBEF Windsor, Ontario
CBG Gander, Newfoundland
CBGN(AM) Sainte Anne des Monts, Québec
CBGY Bonavista Bay, Newfoundland
CBI Sydney, Nova Scotia
CBK Watrous, Saskatchewan
CBKF-1(AM) Gravelbourg, Saskatchewan
CBKF-2(AM) Saskatoon, Saskatchewan
CBN St. John's, Newfoundland
CBOF-1(AM) Maniwaki, Québec
CBR Calgary, Alberta
CBT Grand Falls-Windsor, Newfoundland
CBU Vancouver, British Columbia
CBW Winnipeg, Manitoba
CBX Edmonton, Alberta
CBY Corner Brook, Newfoundland
CFAB Windsor, Nova Scotia
CFAC Calgary, Alberta
CFAM Altona, Manitoba
CFAR Flin Flon, Manitoba
CFAX Victoria, British Columbia
CFBC Saint John, New Brunswick
CFBV Smithers, British Columbia
CFCB Corner Brook, Newfoundland
CFCO Chatham, Ontario
CFCT Tuktoyaktuk, Northwest Territories
CFCW Camrose, Alberta
CFFB Iqaluit, Nunavut
CFFR Calgary, Alberta
CFGO Ottawa, Ontario
CFLD Burns Lake, British Columbia
CFMB Montréal, Québec
CFMJ Richmond Hill, Ontario
CFNC(AM) Cross Lake, Manitoba
CFNI Port Hardy, British Columbia
CFOS Owen Sound, Ontario
CFPL London, Ontario
CFPR Prince Rupert, British Columbia
CFRA Ottawa, Ontario
CFRB Toronto, Ontario
CFRN Edmonton, Alberta
CFRP Forestville, Québec
CFRW Winnipeg, Manitoba
CFRY Portage La Prairie, Manitoba
CFSL Weyburn, Saskatchewan
CFSX Stephenville, Newfoundland
CFTE Vancouver, British Columbia
CFTK Terrace, British Columbia
CFTR Toronto, Ontario
CFYM Kindersley, Saskatchewan
CFZM Toronto, Ontario
CHAB Moose Jaw, Saskatchewan
CHAK Inuvik, Northwest Territories
CHAM Hamilton, Ontario
CHCM Marystown, Newfoundland
CHED Edmonton, Alberta
CHHA Toronto, Ontario
CHIN Toronto, Ontario
CHKT(AM) Toronto, Ontario
CHMB Vancouver, British Columbia
CHMJ Vancouver, British Columbia
CHML Hamilton, Ontario
CHMO(AM) Moosonee, Ontario
CHNL Kamloops, British Columbia
CHOK Sarnia, Ontario
CHOU Montréal, Québec
CHQR Calgary, Alberta
CHQT Edmonton, Alberta
CHRB High River, Alberta
CHRC Québec, Québec
CHRF Montréal, Québec
CHSM Steinbach, Manitoba
CHTM Thompson, Manitoba
CHTO Toronto, Ontario
CHUM Toronto, Ontario
CIAO Brampton, Ontario
CINA Mississauga, Ontario
CISL Richmond, British Columbia
CIVH Vanderhoof, British Columbia
CIWW Ottawa, Ontario
CJAD Montréal, Québec
CJAR The Pas, Manitoba
CJBC Toronto, Ontario
CJBK London, Ontario
CJBQ Belleville, Ontario
CJCA Edmonton, Alberta
CJCB Sydney, Nova Scotia
CJCL Toronto, Ontario
CJCW Sussex, New Brunswick
CJDC Dawson Creek, British Columbia
CJGX Yorkton, Saskatchewan
CJGX Yorkton, Saskatchewan
CJLI Calgary, Alberta
CJLO Montréal, Québec
CJLV Laval, Québec
CJME Regina, Saskatchewan
CJMR Oakville, Ontario
CJMS Montréal, Québec
CJNB North Battleford, Saskatchewan
CJOB Winnipeg, Manitoba
CJOR Osoyoos, British Columbia
CJOY Guelph, Ontario
CJRB Boissevain, Manitoba
CJRJ Vancouver, British Columbia
CJRS Sherbrooke, Québec
CJSL Estevan, Saskatchewan
CJSN Shaunavon, Saskatchewan
CJVA Caraquet, New Brunswick
CJVB Vancouver, British Columbia
CJWI Montréal, Québec
CJWW Saskatoon, Saskatchewan
CJYE Oakville, Ontario
CJYM Rosetown, Saskatchewan
CJYQ St. John's, Newfoundland
CKAC Montréal, Québec
CKAD Middleton, Nova Scotia
CKAT North Bay, Ontario
CKBI Prince Albert, Saskatchewan
CKBX 100 Mile House, British Columbia
CKCM Grand Falls, Newfoundland
CKDM Dauphin, Manitoba
CKDO Oshawa, Ontario
CKDQ Drumheller, Alberta
CKDY Digby, Nova Scotia
CKFR Kelowna, British Columbia
CKGA Gander, Newfoundland
CKGL Kitchener, Ontario
CKGM Montréal, Québec
CKHJ Fredericton, New Brunswick
CKIM Baie Verte, Newfoundland
CKJH(AM) Melfort, Saskatchewan
CKJR Wetaskiwin, Alberta
CKJS Winnipeg, Manitoba
CKLQ Brandon, Manitoba
CKLW Windsor, Ontario
CKMX Calgary, Alberta
CKNB Campbellton, New Brunswick
CKNW New Westminster, British Columbia
CKNX Wingham, Ontario
CKOC Hamilton, Ontario
CKOM Saskatoon, Saskatchewan
CKOR Penticton, British Columbia
CKPC Brantford, Ontario
CKRM Regina, Saskatchewan
CKSL London, Ontario
CKST Vancouver, British Columbia
CKSW Swift Current, Saskatchewan
CKTB St. Catharines, Ontario
CKVO Clarenville, Newfoundland
CKWL Williams Lake, British Columbia
CKWW Windsor, Ontario
CKWX Vancouver, British Columbia
CKYL Peace River, Alberta
VOAR St. John's, Newfoundland
VOCM St. John's, Newfoundland
VOWR St. John's, Newfoundland

Canadian FM Radio Stations by Call Letters

CBA-FM Moncton, New Brunswick
CBAF-FM Moncton, New Brunswick
CBAF-FM-5 Halifax, Nova Scotia
CBAL-FM Moncton, New Brunswick
CBAM-FM Moncton, New Brunswick
CBAX-FM Halifax, Nova Scotia
CBBKFM Kingston, Ontario
CBBL-FM London, Ontario
CBBS-FM Sudbury, Ontario
CBBX-FM Sudbury, Ontario
CBCL-FM London, Ontario
CBCSFM Sudbury, Ontario
CBCT-FM Charlottetown, Prince Edward Island
CBCV-FM Victoria, British Columbia
CBCX-FM Calgary, Alberta
CBD-FM Saint John, New Brunswick
CBDQ-FM Labrador City, Newfoundland
CBE-FM Windsor, Ontario
CBEG-FM Sarnia, Ontario
CBEW-FM Windsor, Ontario
CBF-FM Montréal, Québec
CBF-FM-1 Trois-Rivières, Québec
CBFX-FM Montréal, Québec
CBFX-FM-1 Trois-Rivières, Québec
CBFX-FM-2 Sherbrooke, Québec
CBGA-FM Matane, Québec
CBH-FM Halifax, Nova Scotia
CBHA-FM Halifax, Nova Scotia
CBI-FM Sydney, Nova Scotia
CBJ-FM Chicoutimi, Québec
CBJX-FM Chicoutimi, Québec
CBK-1-FM Saskatoon, Saskatchewan
CBK-FM Regina, Saskatchewan
CBKA-FM La Ronge, Saskatchewan
CBKF-FM Regina, Saskatchewan
CBKS-FM Saskatoon, Saskatchewan
CBL-FM Toronto, Ontario
CBLA-FM Toronto, Ontario
CBLA-FM-2 Paris, Ontario
CBM-FM Montréal, Québec
CBME-FM Montréal, Québec
CBMR-FM Fermont, Québec
CBN-FM Saint John's, Newfoundland
CBO-FM Ottawa, Ontario
CBOFFM Ottawa, Ontario
CBON-FM Timmins, Ontario
CBOQ-FM Ottawa, Ontario
CBOX-FM Ottawa, Ontario
CBQ-FM Thunder Bay, Ontario
CBQL-FM Savant Lake, Ontario
CBQR-FM Rankin Inlet, Nunavut
CBQS-FM Sioux Narrows, Ontario
CBQT-FM Thunder Bay, Ontario
CBQX-FM Kenora, Ontario
CBR-FM Calgary, Alberta
CBRFFM Calgary, Alberta
CBRXFM Rimouski, Québec
CBSI-FM Sept-Îles, Québec
CBTEFM Crawford Bay, British Columbia
CBTK-FM Kelowna, British Columbia
CBTKFM Kelowna, British Columbia
CBU-FM Vancouver, British Columbia
CBUF-FM Vancouver, British Columbia
CBUFFM Vancouver, British Columbia
CBUX-FM Vancouver, British Columbia
CBV-FM Québec, Québec
CBV-FM-6 La Malbaie, Québec
CBVE-FM Québec, Québec
CBVX-FM Québec, Québec
CBW-FM Winnipeg, Manitoba
CBWK-FM Thompson, Manitoba
CBX-FM Edmonton, Alberta
CBYG-FM Prince George, British Columbia
CBYK-FM Kamloops, British Columbia
CBZ-FM Fredericton, New Brunswick
CBZF-FM Fredericton, New Brunswick
CFAD-FM Salmo, British Columbia
CFAI-FM Edmundston, New Brunswick
CFAK-FM Sherbrooke, Québec
CFAN-FM Miramichi, New Brunswick
CFAQ-FM Blucher, Saskatchewan
CFAR-FM Flin Flon, Manitoba
CFBG-FM Bracebridge, Ontario
CFBK-FM Huntsville, Ontario
CFBO-FM Moncton, New Brunswick
CFBR-FM Edmonton, Alberta
CFBS-FM Lourdes-de-Blanc-Sablon, Québec
CFBT-FM Vancouver, British Columbia
CFBU-FM Saint Catharines, Ontario
CFBW-FM Hanover, Ontario
CFBX-FM Kamloops, British Columbia
CFCA-FM Waterloo, Ontario
CFCH-FM Chase, British Columbia
CFCP-FM Comox Valley, British Columbia
CFCR-FM Saskatoon, Saskatchewan
CFCV-FM St. Andrew's, Newfoundland
CFCW-FM Camrose, Alberta
CFCY-FM Charlottetown, Prince Edward Island
CFDA-FM Victoriaville, Québec
CFDC-FM Shelburne, Ontario
CFDM-FM Meadow Lake, Saskatchewan
CFDV-FM Red Deer, Alberta
CFDY-FM Cochrane, Ontario
CFEI-FM St-Hyacinthe, Québec
CFEL-FM Levis, Québec
CFEP-FM Eastern Passage, Nova Scotia
CFET-FM Tagish, Yukon Territory
CFEX-FM Calgary, Alberta
CFFF-FM Peterborough, Ontario
CFFM-FM Williams Lake, British Columbia
CFFM-FM-2 Quesnel, British Columbia
CFGB-FM Happy Valley-Goose Bay, Newfoundland
CFGE-FM Sherbrooke, Québec
CFGI-FM Georgina Island, Ontario
CFGL-FM Laval, Québec
CFGM-FM Caledon, Ontario
CFGP-FM Grande Prairie, Alberta
CFGQ-FM Calgary, Alberta
CFGT-FM Alma, Québec
CFGW-FM Yorkton, Saskatchewan
CFGW-FM Yorkton, Saskatchewan
CFGX-FM Sarnia, Ontario
CFHK-FM St. Thomas, Ontario
CFIC-FM Listuguj, Québec
CFID-FM Acton Vale, Québec
CFIF-FM Iroquois Falls, Ontario
CFIM-FM Iles-de-la-Madeleine, Québec
CFIN-FM Lac-Etchemin, Québec
CFIS-FM Prince George, British Columbia
CFIT-FM Airdrie, Alberta
CFIX-FM Saguenay, Québec
CFJB-FM Barrie, Ontario
CFJL-FM Winnipeg, Manitoba
CFJO-FM Thetford Mines, Québec
CFJR-FM Brockville, Ontario
CFJU-FM Kedgwick, New Brunswick
CFLC-FM Churchill Falls, Newfoundland
CFLG-FM Cornwall, Ontario
CFLM-FM La Tuque, Québec
CFLN-FM Goose Bay, Newfoundland
CFLO-FM Mont-Laurier, Québec
CFLT-FM Dartmouth, Nova Scotia
CFLX-FM Sherbrooke, Québec
CFLY-FM Kingston, Ontario
CFLZ-FM Fort Erie, Ontario
CFMC-FM Saskatoon, Saskatchewan
CFMF-FM Fermont, Québec
CFMG-FM Edmonton, Alberta
CFMH-FM Saint John, New Brunswick
CFMI-FM New Westminster, British Columbia
CFMK-FM Kingston, Ontario
CFMM-FM Prince Albert, Saskatchewan
CFMO-FM Collingwood, Ontario
CFMQ-FM Hudson Bay, Saskatchewan
CFMS-FM Markham, Ontario
CFMU-FM Hamilton, Ontario
CFMV-FM Chandler, Québec
CFMX-FM Cobourg, Ontario
CFMY-FM Medicine Hat, Alberta
CFMZ-FM Toronto, Ontario
CFNA-FM Bonnyville, Alberta
CFND-FM Saint-Jérôme, Québec
CFNJ-FM St-Gabriel, Québec
CFNK-FM Pinehouse Lake, Saskatchewan
CFNO-FM Marathon, Ontario
CFNR-FM Terrace, British Columbia
CFNY-FM Brampton, Ontario
CFOB-FM Fort Frances, Ontario
CFOM-FM Levis, Québec
CFOR-FM Maniwaki, Québec
CFOU-FM Trois-Rivières, Québec
CFOX-FM Vancouver, British Columbia
CFOZ-FM Argentia, Newfoundland
CFPL-FM London, Ontario
CFPS-FM Port Elgin, Ontario
CFPV-FM Pemberton, British Columbia
CFPW-FM Powell River, British Columbia
CFPX-FM Pukatawagan, Manitoba
CFQK-FM Kaministiquia, Ontario
CFQM-FM Moncton, New Brunswick
CFQX-FM Selkirk, Manitoba
CFRC-FM Kingston, Ontario
CFRG-FM Gravelbourg, Saskatchewan
CFRH-FM Penetanguishene, Ontario
CFRI-FM Grande Prairie, Alberta
CFRK-FM Fredericton, New Brunswick
CFRM-FM Little Current, Manitoba
CFROFM Vancouver, British Columbia
CFRQ-FM Dartmouth, Nova Scotia
CFRT-FM Iqaluit, Nunavut
CFRU-FM Guelph, Ontario
CFRV-FM Lethbridge, Alberta
CFRZ-FM Walpole Island, Ontario
CFSF-FM Sturgeon Falls, Ontario
CFSH-FM Apsley, Ontario
CFSI-FM Salt Spring Island, British Columbia
CFSM-FM Cranbrook, British Columbia
CFSR-FM Hope, British Columbia
CFTA-FM Amherst, Nova Scotia
CFTH-FM-1 Harrington Harbour, Québec
CFTH-FM-2 Harrington Harbour, Québec
CFTX-FM Gatineau, Québec
CFUN-FM Sechelt, British Columbia
CFUR-FM Prince George, British Columbia
CFUT-FM Shawinigan, Québec
CFUV-FM Victoria, British Columbia
CFVD Degelis, Québec
CFVD-FM-2 Pohenegamook, Québec
CFVM-FM Amqui, Québec
CFVR-FM Fort McMurray, Alberta
CFWC-FM Brantford, Ontario
CFWD-FM Saskatoon, Saskatchewan
CFWE-FM Lac La Biche, Alberta
CFWF-FM Regina, Saskatchewan
CFWH-FM Whitehorse, Yukon Territory
CFWM-FM Winnipeg, Manitoba
CFWP-FM Wahta Mohawk Territory near Bala, Ontario
CFXE-FM Edson, Alberta
CFXH-FM Hinton, Alberta
CFXJ-FM Toronto, Ontario
CFXL-FM Calgary, Alberta
CFXM Granby, Québec
CFXN-FM North Bay, Ontario
CFXO-FM High River, Alberta
CFXU-FM Antigonish, Nova Scotia
CFXW-FM Whitecourt, Alberta
CFXX-FM Siksika, Alberta
CFXY-FM Fredericton, New Brunswick
CFYK-FM Yellowknife, Northwest Territories
CFYT-FM Dawson City, Yukon Territory
CFYX-FM Rimouski, Québec
CFZN-FM Haliburton, Ontario
CFZZ-FM Saint Jean-Iberville, Québec
CHAA-FM Longueuil, Québec
CHAD-FM Dawson Creek, British Columbia
CHAI-FM Chateauguay, Québec
CHAS-FM Sault Ste. Marie, Ontario
CHAT-FM Medicine Hat, Alberta
CHAY-FM Barrie, Ontario
CHBD-FM Regina, Saskatchewan
CHBE-FM Victoria, British Columbia
CHBI-FM Burnt Islands, Newfoundland
CHBM-FM Toronto, Ontario
CHBN-FM Edmonton, Alberta
CHBO-FM Humboldt, Saskatchewan
CHBW-FM Rocky Mountain House, Alberta
CHBY-FM Barry's Bay, Ontario
CHBZ-FM Cranbrook, British Columbia
CHCD-FM Simcoe, Ontario
CHCQ-FM Belleville, Ontario
CHCR-FM Killaloe, Ontario
CHDI-FM Edmonton, Alberta
CHDR-FM Cranbrook, British Columbia
CHEF-FM Matagami, Québec
CHEQ-FM Sainte-Marie, Québec
CHER-FM Sydney, Nova Scotia
CHES-FM Erin, Ontario
CHET-FM Chetwynd, British Columbia
CHEY-FM Trois-Rivières, Québec
CHEZ-FM Ottawa, Ontario
CHFA-10-FM Edmonton, Alberta
CHFI-FM Toronto, Ontario
CHFM-FM Calgary, Alberta
CHFN-FM Cape Croker (Neyaashiinigmiing), Ontario
CHFT-FM Fort McMurray, Alberta
CHFX-FM Halifax, Nova Scotia
CHGA-FM Maniwaki, Québec
CHGB-FM Wasaga Beach, Ontario
CHGK-FM Stratford, Ontario
CHGO-FM Val d'Or, Québec
CHHI-FM Miramichi, New Brunswick
CHHO-FM Louiseville, Québec
CHIC-FM Rouyn-Noranda, Québec
CHIK-FM Québec, Québec
CHIM-FM Kelowna, British Columbia
CHIN-FM Toronto, Ontario
CHIPFM Fort-Coulonge, Québec
CHIQ-FM Winnipeg, Manitoba
CHJM-FM St-George-Beauce, Québec
CHJX-FM London, Ontario
CHKF-FM Calgary, Alberta
CHKG-FM Richmond, British Columbia
CHKS-FM Sarnia, Ontario
CHKX-FM Hamilton, Ontario
CHLB-FM Lethbridge, Alberta
CHLC-FM Baie-Comeau, Québec
CHLG-FM Vancouver, British Columbia
CHLI-FM Rossland, British Columbia
CHLK-FM Perth, Ontario
CHLQ-FM Charlottetown, Prince Edward Island
CHLS-FM Lillooet, British Columbia
CHLX-FM Gatineau, Québec
CHLY-FM Nanaimo, British Columbia
CHMA-FM Sackville, New Brunswick
CHMM-FM MacKenzie, British Columbia
CHMN-FM Canmore, Alberta
CHMP-FM Longueuil, Québec
CHMR-FM Saint John's, Newfoundland
CHMS-FM Bancroft, Ontario
CHMT-FM Timmins, Ontario
CHMX-FM Regina, Saskatchewan
CHMY-FM Renfrew, Ontario
CHMY-FM-1 Arnprior, Ontario
CHMZ-FM Tofino, British Columbia
CHNC-FM New Carlisle, Québec
CHNI-FM Saint John, New Brunswick
CHNO-FM Sudbury, Ontario
CHNS-FM Halifax, Nova Scotia
CHNV-FM Nelson, British Columbia
CHOA-FM Rouyn-Noranda, Québec
CHOCFM Saint Remi, Québec
CHOD-FM Cornwall, Ontario
CHOE-FM Matane, Québec
CHOI-FM Québec, Québec
CHOM-FM Montréal, Québec
CHON-FM Whitehorse, Yukon Territory
CHOO-FM Drumheller, Alberta
CHOP-FM Newmarket, Ontario
CHOQ-FM Toronto, Ontario
CHOR-FM Summerland, British Columbia
CHOW-FM Amos, Québec
CHOX-FM La Pocatiere, Québec
CHOY-FM Moncton, New Brunswick
CHOZ-FM St. John's, Newfoundland
CHPB-FM Cochrane, Ontario
CHPD-FM Aylmer, Ontario
CHPK-FM Calgary, Alberta
CHPL-FM Plamondon, Alberta
CHPO-FM Portage La Prairie, Manitoba
CHPQ-FM Parksville, British Columbia
CHPR-FM Hawkesbury, Ontario
CHQC-FM Saint John, New Brunswick
CHQM-FM Vancouver, British Columbia
CHQX-FM Prince Albert, Saskatchewan
CHRC-FM Clarence-Rockland, Ontario
CHRD-FM Drummondville, Québec
CHRE-FM St. Catharines, Ontario
CHRG-FM Maria (Reserve), Québec
CHRI-FM Ottawa, Ontario
CHRK-FM Sydney, Nova Scotia
CHRL-FM Roberval, Québec
CHRM-FM Matane, Québec
CHRQ-FM Restigouche, Québec
CHRW-FM London, Ontario
CHRX-FM Fort St. John, British Columbia
CHRY-FM North York, Ontario
CHSB-FM Bedford, Nova Scotia
CHSJ-FM Saint John, New Brunswick
CHSL-FM Slave Lake, Alberta
CHSN-FM Estevan, Saskatchewan
CHSP-FM St. Paul, Alberta
CHSR-FM Fredericton, New Brunswick
CHST-FM London, Ontario
CHSU-FM Kelowna, British Columbia
CHSV-FM Hudson/Saint-Lazare, Québec
CHTD-FM Saint Stephen, New Brunswick
CHTK-FM Prince Rupert, British Columbia

CHTM-FM Thompson, Manitoba
CHTN-FM Charlottetown, Prince Edward Island
CHTT-FM Victoria, British Columbia
CHTZ-FM St. Catharines, Ontario
CHUB-FM Red Deer, Alberta
CHUC-FM Cobourg, Ontario
CHUK-FM Mashteuiatsh (Pointe-Bleue), Québec
CHUM-FM Toronto, Ontario
CHUN-FM Rouyn-Noranda, Québec
CHUO-FM Ottawa, Ontario
CHUP-FM Calgary, Alberta
CHUR-FM North Bay, Ontario
CHUT-FM Lac-Simon (Louvicourt), Québec
CHVD-FM Dolbeau-Mistassini, Québec
CHVL-FM Val-des-Lacs, Québec
CHVN-FM Winnipeg, Manitoba
CHVO-FM Carbonear, Newfoundland
CHVR-FM Pembroke, Ontario
CHWC-FM Goderich, Ontario
CHWE-FM Winnepeg, Manitoba
CHWF-FM Nanaimo, British Columbia
CHWK-FM Chilliwack, British Columbia
CHWN-FM Skownan, Manitoba
CHWV-FM Saint John, New Brunswick
CHWY-FM Weyburn, Saskatchewan
CHXL-FM Brockville, Ontario
CHXX-FM Donnacona, Québec
CHYC-FM Sudbury, Ontario
CHYK-FM Timmins, Ontario
CHYK-FM-3 Hearst, Ontario
CHYM-FM Kitchener, Ontario
CHYR-FM Leamington, Ontario
CHYZ-FM Sainte Foy, Québec
CIAJ-FM Prince Rupert, British Columbia
CIAM-FM Fort Vermilion, Alberta
CIAU-FM Radisson, Québec
CIAX-FM Windsor, Québec
CIAY-FM Whitehorse, Yukon Territory
CIBC-FM Cowessess, Saskatchewan
CIBH-FM Parksville, British Columbia
CIBK-FM Calgary, Alberta
CIBL-FM Montréal, Québec
CIBMFM Rivière-du-Loup, Québec
CIBO-FM Senneterre, Québec
CIBQ-FM Brooks, Alberta
CIBU-FM Wingham, Ontario
CIBW-FM Drayton Valley, Alberta
CIBX-FM Fredericton, New Brunswick
CICF-FM Vernon, British Columbia
CICK-FM Smithers, British Columbia
CICN-FM Marcelin, Saskatchewan
CICS-FM Sudbury, Ontario
CICU-FM Eskasoni Indian Reserve, Nova Scotia
CICV-FM Lake Cowichan, British Columbia
CICX-FM Orillia, Ontario
CICY-FM Selkirk, Manitoba
CICZ-FM Midland, Ontario
CIDC-FM Orangeville, Ontario
CIDD-FM White Bear Lake Resort, Saskatchewan
CIDG-FM Ottawa, Ontario
CIDI-FM Lac-Brome, Québec
CIDO-FM Creston, British Columbia
CIDR-FM Windsor, Ontario
CIEL-FM Rivière-du-Loup, Québec
CIEU-FM Carleton, Québec
CIFA-FM Comeauville, Nova Scotia
CIFM-FM Kamloops, British Columbia
CIFN-FM Island Lake, Saskatchewan
CIFX-FM Lewisporte, Newfoundland
CIGB-FM Trois-Rivières, Québec
CIGL-FM Belleville, Ontario
CIGM-FM Sudbury, Ontario
CIGO-FM Port Hawkesbury, Nova Scotia
CIGV-FM Penticton, British Columbia
CIHI-FM Fredericton, New Brunswick
CIHO-FM Baie St Paul, Québec
CIHR-FM Woodstock, Ontario
CIHS-FM Wetaskiwin, Alberta
CIHT-FM Ottawa, Ontario
CIJK-FM Kentville, Nova Scotia
CIKI-FM Rimouski, Québec
CIKR-FM Kingston, Ontario
CIKT-FM Grande Prairie, Alberta
CIKX-FM Grand Falls, New Brunswick
CIKZ-FM Kitchener, Ontario
CILB-FM Lac La Biche, Alberta
CILE-FM Havre-Saint-Pierre, Québec
CILG-FM Moose Jaw, Saskatchewan
CILK-FM Kelowna, British Columbia
CILQ-FM Toronto, Ontario
CILS-FM Victoria, British Columbia
CILT-FM Steinbach, Manitoba
CILU-FM Thunder Bay, Ontario
CILV-FM Ottawa, Ontario
CIMA-FM Alliston, Ontario
CIMEFM Saint-Jérôme, Québec
CIMF-FM Gatineau, Québec
CIMG-FM Swift Current, Saskatchewan
CIMI-FM Charlesbourg, Québec
CIMJ-FM Guelph, Ontario
CIMM-FM Ucluelet, British Columbia
CIMO-FM Magog, Québec
CIMS-FM Balmoral, New Brunswick
CIMX-FM Windsor, Ontario
CIMY-FM Pembroke, Ontario
CINA-FM Windsor, Ontario
CINB-FM Saint John, New Brunswick
CINC-FM Thompson, Manitoba
CIND-FM Toronto, Ontario
CING-FM Hamilton, Ontario
CINN-FM Hearst, Ontario
CINQ-FM Montréal, Québec
CINU-FM Truro, Nova Scotia
CIOC-FM Victoria, British Columbia
CIOG-FM Charlottetown, Prince Edward Island
CIOI-FM Hamilton, Ontario
CIOK-FM Saint John, New Brunswick
CION-FM Québec, Québec
CIOO-FM Halifax, Nova Scotia
CIOS-FM Stephenville, Newfoundland
CIOT-FM Nipawin, Saskatchewan
CIOZ-FM Marystown, Newfoundland
CIPC-FM Port-Cartier, Québec
CIPN-FM Pender Harbour, British Columbia
CIPU-FM Micmac, Nova Scotia
CIQB-FM Barrie, Ontario
CIQC-FM Campbell River, British Columbia
CIQM-FM London, Ontario
CIRA-FM Montréal, Québec
CIRK-FM Edmonton, Alberta
CIRP-FM Spryfield, Nova Scotia
CIRR-FM Toronto, Ontario
CIRV-FM Toronto, Ontario
CIRX-FM Prince George, British Columbia
CIRX-FM-1 Vanderhoof, British Columbia
CISB-FM Marius, Manitoba
CISC-FM Gibsons, British Columbia
CISM-FM Montréal, Québec
CISN-FM Edmonton, Alberta
CISO-FM Orillia, Ontario
CISP-FM Pemberton, British Columbia
CISQ-FM Squamish, British Columbia
CISS-FM Ottawa, Ontario
CISW-FM Whistler, British Columbia
CITA-FM Moncton, New Brunswick
CITE-FM Montréal, Québec
CITE-FM-1 Sherbrooke, Québec
CITF-FM Québec, Québec
CITI-FM Winnipeg, Manitoba
CITRFM Vancouver, British Columbia
CIUP-FM Edmonton, Alberta
CIUT-FM Toronto, Ontario
CIUX-FM Uxbridge, Ontario
CIVL-FM Abbotsford, British Columbia
CIWS-FM Whitchurch-Stouffville, Ontario
CIXF-FM Brooks, Alberta
CIXK-FM Owen Sound, Ontario
CIXL-FM Welland, Ontario
CIXM-FM Whitecourt, Alberta
CIXN-FM Fredericton, New Brunswick
CIXX-FM London, Ontario
CIYM-FM Brighton, Ontario
CIYN-FM Kincardine, Ontario
CIZL-FM Regina, Saskatchewan
CIZZ-FM Red Deer, Alberta
CJAB-FN Saguenay, Québec
CJAI-FM Stella, Ontario
CJAM-FM Windsor, Ontario
CJAN-FM Asbestos, Québec
CJAQ-FM Calgary, Alberta
CJAR-FM The Pas, Manitoba
CJAS-FM Saint Augustin, Québec
CJAT-FM Trail, British Columbia
CJAV-FM Port Alberni, British Columbia
CJAW-FM Moose Jaw, Saskatchewan
CJAX-FM Vancouver, British Columbia
CJAY-FM Calgary, Alberta
CJBB-FM Englehart, Ontario
CJBC-FM Toronto, Ontario
CJBE-FM Port-Menier, Québec
CJBI-FM Wabana, Newfoundland
CJBR-FM Rimouski, Québec
CJBX-FM London, Ontario
CJBZ-FM Taber, Alberta
CJCD-FM Yellowknife, Northwest Territories
CJCD-FM-1 Hay River, Northwest Territories
CJCF-FM Cumberland House, Saskatchewan
CJCH-FM Halifax, Nova Scotia
CJCI-FM Prince George, British Columbia
CJCJ-FM Woodstock, New Brunswick
CJCQ-FM North Battleford, Saskatchewan
CJCS-FM Stratford, Ontario
CJCY-FM Medicine Hat, Alberta
CJDJ-FM Saskatoon, Saskatchewan
CJDL-FM Tillsonburg, Ontario
CJDM-FM Drummondville, Québec
CJDR-FM Fernie, British Columbia
CJDS-FM Saint Pamphile, Québec
CJDV-FM Kitchener, Ontario
CJEB-FM Trois-Rivières, Québec
CJEC-FM Québec, Québec
CJED-FM Niagara Falls, Ontario
CJEF-FM Saint John, New Brunswick
CJEG-FM Bonnyville, Alberta
CJEL-FM Winkler, Manitoba
CJEM-FM Edmundston, New Brunswick
CJET-FM Smiths Falls, Ontario
CJFB-FM Bolton, Ontario
CJFH-FM Woodstock, Ontario
CJFM-FM Montréal, Québec
CJFO-FM Ottawa, Ontario
CJFW-FM Terrace, British Columbia
CJFX-FM Antigonish, Nova Scotia
CJFY-FM Miramichi, New Brunswick
CJGB-FM Meaford, Ontario
CJGM-FM Gananoque, Ontario
CJGO-FM La Sarre, Québec
CJGV-FM Winnipeg, Manitoba
CJGY-FM Grande Prairie, Alberta
CJHD-FM North Battleford, Saskatchewan
CJHK-FM Bridgewater, Nova Scotia
CJHR-FM Renfrew, Ontario
CJIE-FM Winnepeg Beach, Manitoba
CJIJ-FM Sydney, Nova Scotia
CJIQ-FM Paris, Ontario
CJIT-FM Lac Megantic, Québec
CJJC-FM Yorkton, Saskatchewan
CJJJ-FM Brandon, Manitoba
CJJM-FM Espanola, Ontario
CJJR-FM Vancouver, British Columbia
CJKC-FM Kamloops, British Columbia
CJKL-FM Kirkland Lake, Ontario
CJKR-FM Winnipeg, Manitoba
CJKX-FM Ajax, Ontario
CJLA-FM Lachute, Québec
CJLD-FM Leduc, Alberta
CJLF-FM Barrie, Ontario
CJLJ-FM Williams Lake, British Columbia
CJLL-FM Ottawa, Ontario
CJLM-FM Joliette, Québec
CJLR-FM La Ronge, Saskatchewan
CJLS-FM-1 Barrington, Nova Scotia
CJLS-FM-2 New Tusket, Nova Scotia
CJLSFM Barrington, Nova Scotia
CJLT-FM Medicine Hat, Alberta
CJLX-FM Belleville, Ontario
CJLY-FM Nelson, British Columbia
CJMB-FM Peterborough, Ontario
CJMC-FM Sainte Anne des Monts, Québec
CJMF-FM Québec, Québec
CJMG-FM Penticton, British Columbia
CJMI-FM Strathroy, Ontario
CJMJ-FM Ottawa, Ontario
CJMK-FM Saskatoon, Saskatchewan
CJMM-FM Rouyn-Noranda, Québec
CJMO-FM Moncton, New Brunswick
CJMP-FM Powell River, British Columbia
CJMQ-FM Sherbrooke, Québec
CJMV-FM Val d'Or, Québec
CJMX-FM Sudbury, Ontario
CJMY-FM Clarenville, Newfoundland
CJNE-FM Nipawin, Saskatchewan
CJNI-FM Halifax, Nova Scotia
CJNS-FM Meadow Lake, Saskatchewan
CJNU-FM Winnipeg, Manitoba
CJNW-FM Edmonton, Alberta
CJOA-FM Thunder Bay, Ontario
CJOC-FM Lethbridge, Alberta
CJOI-FM Rimouski, Québec
CJOJ-FM Belleville, Ontario
CJOK-FM Fort McMurray, Alberta
CJOS-FM Owen Sound, Ontario
CJOT-FM Ottawa, Ontario
CJOZ-FM Bonavista Bay, Newfoundland
CJPG-FM Portage la Prairie, Manitoba
CJPN-FM Fredericton, New Brunswick
CJPR-FM Blairmore, Alberta
CJPT-FM Brockville, Ontario
CJPX-FM Montréal, Québec
CJQM-FM Sault Ste. Marie, Ontario
CJQQ-FM Timmins, Ontario
CJRD-FM Drummondville, Québec
CJRG-FM Gaspe, Québec
CJRI-FM Fredericton, New Brunswick
CJRL-FM Kenora, Ontario
CJRM-FM Labrador City, Newfoundland
CJRQ-FM Sudbury, Ontario
CJRT-FM Toronto, Ontario
CJRW-FM Summerside, Prince Edward Island
CJRX-FM Lethbridge, Alberta
CJRY-FM Edmonton, Alberta
CJSA-FM Toronto, Ontario
CJSB-FM Swan River, Manitoba
CJSD-FM Thunder Bay, Ontario
CJSEFM Shediac, New Brunswick
CJSF-FM Burnaby, British Columbia
CJSI-FM Calgary, Alberta
CJSO-FM Sorel, Québec
CJSP-FM Leamington, Ontario
CJSQ-FM Québec, Québec
CJSR-FM Edmonton, Alberta
CJSS-FM Cornwall, Ontario
CJSU-FM Duncan, British Columbia
CJSW-FM Calgary, Alberta
CJTB-FM Tete-a-la-Baleine, Québec
CJTK-FM Sudbury, Ontario
CJTN-FM Trenton, Ontario
CJTR-FM Regina, Saskatchewan
CJTT-FM New Liskeard, Ontario
CJTW-FM Kitchener-Waterloo, Ontario
CJUK-FM Thunder Bay, Ontario
CJUM-FM Winnipeg, Manitoba
CJUV-FM Lacombe, Alberta
CJVD-FM Vaudreuil-Dorion, Québec
CJVF-FM Scarborough, Ontario
CJVR-FM Melfort, Saskatchewan
CJWA-FM Wawa, Ontario
CJWF-FM Windsor, Ontario
CJWL-FM Ottawa, Ontario
CJWV-FM Peterborough, Ontario
CJXB-FM Banff, Alberta
CJXK-FM Cold Lake, Alberta
CJXL-FM Moncton, New Brunswick
CJXR-FM Steinbach, Manitoba
CJXX-FM Grande Prairie, Alberta
CJXY-FM Burlington, Ontario
CJYC-FM Saint John, New Brunswick
CJZN-FM Victoria, British Columbia
CKAG-FM Pikogan, Québec
CKAJ-FM Jonquiere, Québec
CKAP-FM Kapuskasing, Ontario
CKAU-FM Maliotenam, Québec
CKAV-FM Toronto, Ontario
CKAV-FM-2 Vancouver, British Columbia
CKAV-FM-3 Calgary, Alberta
CKAV-FM-4 Edmonton, Alberta
CKAV-FM-9 Ottawa, Ontario
CKAY-FM Gibsons, British Columbia
CKBA-FM Athabasca, Alberta
CKBC-FM Bathurst, New Brunswick
CKBD-FM Lethbridge, Alberta
CKBE Montréal, Québec
CKBE-FM Montréal, Québec
CKBK-FM Thamesville, Ontario
CKBL-FM Saskatoon, Saskatchewan
CKBN-FM Becancour and Nicolet, Québec
CKBT-FM Kitchener-Waterloo, Ontario
CKBW-FM Bridgewater, Nova Scotia
CKBY-FM Smiths Falls, Ontario
CKBZ-FM Kamloops, British Columbia
CKCB-FM Collingwood, Ontario
CKCE-FM Calgary, Alberta
CKCH-FM Sydney, Nova Scotia
CKCK-FM Regina, Saskatchewan
CKCL-FM Winnipeg, Manitoba
CKCN-FM Sept-Iles, Québec
CKCQ-FM Quesnel, British Columbia
CKCR-FM Revelstoke, British Columbia
CKCUFM Ottawa, Ontario
CKCV-FM Creston, British Columbia
CKCW-FM Moncton, New Brunswick

RADIO - CANADA

CKDG-FM Montréal, Québec
CKDH-FM Amherst, Nova Scotia
CKDJ-FM Ottawa, Ontario
CKDK-FM Woodstock, Ontario
CKDR-2-FM Sioux Lookout, Ontario
CKDR-5-FM Red Lake, Ontario
CKDR-FM Dryden, Ontario
CKDU-FM Halifax, Nova Scotia
CKDV-FM Prince George, British Columbia
CKDX-FM Newmarket, Ontario
CKEA-FM Edmonton, Alberta
CKEB-FM Ebb and Flow, Manitoba
CKEC-FM New Glasgow, Nova Scotia
CKEE-FM Whistler, British Columbia
CKEN-FM Kentville, Nova Scotia
CKER-FM Edmonton, Alberta
CKEZ-FM Pictou, Nova Scotia
CKFG-FM Toronto, Ontario
CKFI-FM Swift Current, Saskatchewan
CKFM-FM Toronto, Ontario
CKFT-FM Fort Saskatchewan, Alberta
CKFU-FM Fort St. John, British Columbia
CKFX-FM North Bay, Ontario
CKGB-FM Timmins, Ontario
CKGE-FM Oshawa, Ontario
CKGF-FM Grand Forks, British Columbia
CKGN-FM Kapuskasing, Ontario
CKGR-FM Golden, British Columbia
CKGS-FM La Baie, Québec
CKGW-FM Chatham, Ontario
CKGY-FM Red Deer, Alberta
CKHA-FM Haliburton, Ontario
CKHC-FM Toronto, Ontario
CKHK-FM Hawkesbury, Ontario
CKHL-FM High Level, Alberta
CKHR-FM Hay River, Northwest Territories
CKHY-FM Halifax, Nova Scotia
CKHZ-FM Halifax, Nova Scotia
CKIA-FM Québec, Québec
CKII-FM Dolbeau-Mistassini, Québec
CKIN-FM Montréal, Québec
CKIQFM Big White Ski, British Columbia
CKIS-FM Toronto, Ontario
CKIX-FM St. John's, Newfoundland
CKIZ-FM Vernon, British Columbia
CKJJ-FM Belleville, Ontario
CKJM-FM Cheticamp, Nova Scotia
CKJX-FM Olds, Alberta
CKKC-FM Nelson, British Columbia
CKKI-FM Kahnawake, Québec
CKKL-FM Ottawa, Ontario
CKKN-FM Prince George, British Columbia
CKKO-FM Kelowna, British Columbia
CKKQ-FM Victoria, British Columbia
CKKS-FM Chilliwack, British Columbia
CKKW-FM Kitchener, Ontario
CKKX-FM Peace River, Alberta
CKKY-FM Wainwright, Alberta
CKLB-FM Yellowknife, Northwest Territories
CKLC-FM Kingston, Ontario
CKLD-FM Thetford Mines, Québec
CKLE-FM Bathurst, Québec
CKLF-FM Brandon, Manitoba
CKLH-FM Hamilton, Ontario
CKLJ-FM Olds, Alberta
CKLM-FM Lloydminster, Alberta
CKLO-FM London, Ontario
CKLP-FM Parry Sound, Ontario
CKLR-FM Courtenay, British Columbia
CKLU-FM Sudbury, Ontario
CKLX-FM Montréal, Québec
CKLY-FM Kawartha Lakes, Ontario
CKLZ-FM Kelowna, British Columbia
CKMA-FM Miramichi, New Brunswick
CKMB-FM Barrie, Ontario
CKMF-FM Montréal, Québec
CKMH-FM Medicine Hat, Alberta
CKMM-FM Winnipeg, Manitoba
CKMN-FM Rimouski-Mont Joli, Québec
CKMO-FM Orangeville, Ontario
CKMP-FM Calgary, Alberta
CKMQ-FM Merritt, British Columbia
CKMS-FM Waterloo, Ontario
CKMV-FM Grand Falls, New Brunswick
CKMW-FM Winkler-Morden, Manitoba
CKMY-FM Grand Falls, Newfoundland
CKNA-FM Natashquan, Québec
CKNG-FM Edmonton, Alberta
CKNI-FM Moncton, New Brunswick
CKNL-FM Fort St. John, British Columbia
CKNO-FM Edmonton, Alberta
CKNR-FM Elliot Lake, Ontario
CKNX-FM Wingham, Ontario
CKOA-FM Glace Bay, Nova Scotia
CKOB-FM Trois-Rivières, Québec
CKOD-FM Valleyfield, Québec
CKOE-FM Moncton, New Brunswick
CKOF-FM Gatineau, Québec
CKOF-FM Gatineau, Québec
CKOI Montréal, Québec
CKON-FM Akwesasne, Ontario
CKOO-FM Broadview, Saskatchewan
CKOS-FM Fort McMurray, Alberta
CKOT-FM Tillsonburg, Ontario
CKOY-FM Sherbrooke, Québec
CKOZ-FM Corner Brook, Newfoundland
CKPC-FM Brantford, Ontario
CKPE-FM Sydney, Nova Scotia
CKPK-FM Vancouver, British Columbia
CKPM-FM Port Moody, British Columbia
CKPP-FM Prescott, Ontario
CKPR-FM Thunder Bay, Ontario
CKPT-FM Peterborough, Ontario
CKQB-FM Ottawa, Ontario
CKQC-FM Abbotsford, British Columbia
CKQK-FM Charlottetown, Prince Edward Island
CKQM-FM Peterborough, Ontario
CKQN-FM Baker Lake, Nunavut
CKQQ-FM Kelowna, British Columbia
CKQR-FM Castlegar, British Columbia
CKQV-FM Vermilion Bay, Ontario
CKRA-FM Edmonton, Alberta
CKRB-FM Saint Georges-de-Beauce, Québec
CKRC-FM Weyburn, Saskatchewan
CKRD-FM Red Deer, Alberta
CKRH-FM Halifax, Nova Scotia
CKRI-FM Red Deer, Alberta
CKRK-FM Kahnawake, Québec
CKRL-FM Québec, Québec
CKRO-FM Inkerman, New Brunswick
CKRP-FM Falher, Alberta
CKRS-FM Saguenay, Québec
CKRU-FM Petersborough, Ontario
CKRV-FM Kamloops, British Columbia
CKRW-FM Whitehorse, Yukon Territory
CKRX-FM Fort Nelson, British Columbia
CKRY-FM Calgary, Alberta
CKRZ-FM Ohsweken, Ontario
CKSA-FM Lloydminster, Alberta
CKSB-10-FM Winnipeg, Manitoba
CKSB-FM St. Boniface, Manitoba
CKSE-FM Estevan, Saskatchewan
CKSG-FM Cobourg, Ontario
CKSJ-FM Saint John's, Newfoundland
CKSO-FM Sudbury, Ontario
CKSQ-FM Stettler, Alberta
CKSR-FM Chilliwack, British Columbia
CKSY-FM Chatham, Ontario
CKTF-FM Gatineau, Québec
CKTG-FM Thunder Bay, Ontario
CKTI-FM Kettle Point, Ontario
CKTK-FM Kitimat, British Columbia
CKTO-FM Truro, Nova Scotia
CKTP-FM Fredericton Centre, New Brunswick
CKTY-FM Truro, Nova Scotia
CKTZ-FM Cortes Island, British Columbia
CKUA-FM Edmonton, Alberta
CKUE-FM Chatham, Ontario
CKUJ-FM Kuujjuaq, Québec
CKUL-FM Halifax, Nova Scotia
CKUM-FM Moncton, New Brunswick
CKUN-FM Christian Island, Ontario
CKUT-FM Montréal, Québec
CKUV-FM High River, Alberta
CKUW-FM Winnipeg, Manitoba
CKVH-FM High Prairie, Alberta
CKVI-FM Kingston, Ontario
CKVL-FM Montréal (zone LaSalle), Québec
CKVM-FM Ville-Marie, Québec
CKVV-FM Kemptville, Ontario
CKVX-FM Kindersley, British Columbia
CKWB-FM Westlock, Alberta
CKWE-FM Maniwaki (Kitigan Zibi Anishinabeg, Québec
CKWF-FM Peterborough, Ontario
CKWM-FM Kentville, Nova Scotia
CKWR-FM Waterloo, Ontario
CKWS-FM Kingston, Ontario
CKWT-FM Sioux Lookout, Ontario
CKWV-FM Nanaimo, British Columbia
CKWY-FM Wainwright, Alberta
CKX-FM Brandon, Manitoba
CKXA-FM Brandon, Manitoba
CKXC-FM Kingston, Ontario
CKXD-FM Gander, Newfoundland
CKXG-FM Grand Falls, Newfoundland
CKXL-FM Saint Boniface, Manitoba
CKXM-FM Exeter, Ontario
CKXO-FM Chibougamau, Québec
CKXR-FM Salmon Arm, British Columbia
CKXU-FM Lethbridge, Alberta
CKXX-FM Corner Brook, Newfoundland
CKY-FM Winnipeg, Manitoba
CKYC-FM Owen Sound, Ontario
CKYE-FM Vancouver, British Columbia
CKYK-FM Alma, Québec
CKYM-FM Napanee, Ontario
CKYQ-FM Plessisville, Québec
CKYR-FM Calgary, Alberta
CKYX-FM Fort McMurray, Alberta
CKZM-FM St. Thomas, Ontario
CKZP-FM Zenon Park, Saskatchewan
CKZZ-FM Vancouver, British Columbia
VOCM-FM St. John's, Newfoundland

Canadian AM Stations by Frequency

1010 kHz
CBR Calgary, Alberta
CFRB Toronto, Ontario

1040 kHz
CKST Vancouver, British Columbia

1050 kHz
CHUM Toronto, Ontario
CJNB North Battleford, Saskatchewan

1060 kHz
CKMX Calgary, Alberta

1070 kHz
CFAX Victoria, British Columbia
CHOK Sarnia, Ontario

1130 kHz
CKWX Vancouver, British Columbia

1140 kHz
CBI Sydney, Nova Scotia
CHRB High River, Alberta

1150 kHz
CKFR Kelowna, British Columbia
CKOC Hamilton, Ontario

1190 kHz
CFSL Weyburn, Saskatchewan
CJMR Oakville, Ontario

1200 kHz
CFGO Ottawa, Ontario
CJRJ Vancouver, British Columbia

1210 kHz
CFYM Kindersley, Saskatchewan
VOAR St. John's, Newfoundland

1220 kHz
CJRB Boissevain, Manitoba

1230 kHz
CFFB Iqaluit, Nunavut

1240 kHz
CFNI Port Hardy, British Columbia
CJAR The Pas, Manitoba
CJOR Osoyoos, British Columbia
CKIM Baie Verte, Newfoundland

1250 kHz
CHSM Steinbach, Manitoba
CJYE Oakville, Ontario

1260 kHz
CFRN Edmonton, Alberta
CKHJ Fredericton, New Brunswick

1270 kHz
CJCB Sydney, Nova Scotia

1280 kHz
CFMB Montréal, Québec
CJMS Montréal, Québec
CJSL Estevan, Saskatchewan

1290 kHz
CFRW Winnipeg, Manitoba
CJBK London, Ontario

1310 kHz
CIWW Ottawa, Ontario

1320 kHz
CHMB Vancouver, British Columbia

1330 kHz
CJYM Rosetown, Saskatchewan

1340 kHz
CBGN(AM) Sainte Anne des Monts, Québec
CIVH Vanderhoof, British Columbia

1350 kHz
CKAD Middleton, Nova Scotia

1380 kHz
CKPC Brantford, Ontario

1400 kHz
CBG Gander, Newfoundland

1410 kHz
CFTE Vancouver, British Columbia
CKSL London, Ontario

1420 kHz
CKDY Digby, Nova Scotia

1430 kHz
CHKT(AM) Toronto, Ontario

1440 kHz
CKJR Wetaskiwin, Alberta

1450 kHz
CFAB Windsor, Nova Scotia
CHMO(AM) Moosonee, Ontario
CHOU Montréal, Québec

1460 kHz
CJOY Guelph, Ontario

1470 kHz
CJVB Vancouver, British Columbia

1490 kHz
CFNC(AM) Cross Lake, Manitoba
CJSN Shaunavon, Saskatchewan

1510 kHz
CJRS Sherbrooke, Québec

1540 kHz
CHIN Toronto, Ontario

1550 kHz
CBEF Windsor, Ontario

1570 kHz
CJLV Laval, Québec

1580 kHz
CKDO Oshawa, Ontario

1610 kHz
CJWI Montréal, Québec
CHHA Toronto, Ontario

1650 kHz
CINA Mississauga, Ontario

1690 kHz
CHTO Toronto, Ontario
CJLO Montréal, Québec

530 kHz
CIAO Brampton, Ontario

540 kHz
CBK Watrous, Saskatchewan
CBKF-1(AM) Gravelbourg, Saskatchewan
CBT Grand Falls-Windsor, Newfoundland

560 kHz
CFOS Owen Sound, Ontario

570 kHz
CFCB Corner Brook, Newfoundland
CKGL Kitchener, Ontario
CKSW Swift Current, Saskatchewan
CKWL Williams Lake, British Columbia

580 kHz
CFRA Ottawa, Ontario
CKWW Windsor, Ontario

590 kHz
CFAR Flin Flon, Manitoba
CFTK Terrace, British Columbia
CJCL Toronto, Ontario
CJCW Sussex, New Brunswick
VOCM St. John's, Newfoundland

600 kHz
CFCT Tuktoyaktuk, Northwest Territories
CJWW Saskatoon, Saskatchewan
CKAT North Bay, Ontario

610 kHz
CHNL Kamloops, British Columbia
CHTM Thompson, Manitoba
CKTB St. Catharines, Ontario
CKYL Peace River, Alberta

620 kHz
CFRP Forestville, Québec
CKRM Regina, Saskatchewan
CKCM Grand Falls, Newfoundland

630 kHz
CFCO Chatham, Ontario
CHED Edmonton, Alberta

640 kHz
CBN St. John's, Newfoundland
CFMJ Richmond Hill, Ontario

650 kHz
CKOM Saskatoon, Saskatchewan
CISL Richmond, British Columbia
CKGA Gander, Newfoundland

660 kHz
CFFR Calgary, Alberta

680 kHz
CFTR Toronto, Ontario
CJOB Winnipeg, Manitoba

690 kHz
CKGM Montréal, Québec

700 kHz
CJLI Calgary, Alberta

710 kHz
CKVO Clarenville, Newfoundland

730 kHz
CKAC Montréal, Québec
CKDM Dauphin, Manitoba
CHMJ Vancouver, British Columbia

740 kHz
CHCM Marystown, Newfoundland
CFZM Toronto, Ontario

750 kHz
CBGY Bonavista Bay, Newfoundland
CKJH(AM) Melfort, Saskatchewan

760 kHz
CFLD Burns Lake, British Columbia

770 kHz
CHQR Calgary, Alberta

800 kHz
CHAB Moose Jaw, Saskatchewan
CHRC Québec, Québec
CJAD Montréal, Québec
CJBQ Belleville, Ontario
CKLW Windsor, Ontario
CKOR Penticton, British Columbia
VOWR St. John's, Newfoundland

810 kHz
CJVA Caraquet, New Brunswick
CKJS Winnipeg, Manitoba

820 kHz
CHAM Hamilton, Ontario

840 kHz
CFCW Camrose, Alberta
CKBX 100 Mile House, British Columbia

860 kHz
CBKF-2(AM) Saskatoon, Saskatchewan

CHAK Inuvik, Northwest Territories
CJBC Toronto, Ontario

870 kHz

CFBV Smithers, British Columbia
CFSX Stephenville, Newfoundland

880 kHz

CHQT Edmonton, Alberta
CKLQ Brandon, Manitoba

890 kHz

CJDC Dawson Creek, British Columbia

900 kHz

CHML Hamilton, Ontario
CKBI Prince Albert, Saskatchewan

910 kHz

CKDQ Drumheller, Alberta

920 kHz

CFRY Portage La Prairie, Manitoba
CKNX Wingham, Ontario

930 kHz

CFBC Saint John, New Brunswick
CJCA Edmonton, Alberta
CJYQ St. John's, Newfoundland

940 kHz

CJGX Yorkton, Saskatchewan
CJGX Yorkton, Saskatchewan

950 kHz

CFAM Altona, Manitoba
CKNB Campbellton, New Brunswick

960 kHz

CFAC Calgary, Alberta

980 kHz

CFPL London, Ontario
CKNW New Westminster, British Columbia
CJME Regina, Saskatchewan
CHRF Montréal, Québec

990 kHz

CBOF-1(AM) Maniwaki, Québec
CBY Corner Brook, Newfoundland

Canadian FM Stations by Frequency

100.1 MHz
CIOO-FM Halifax, Nova Scotia
CJCD-FM Yellowknife, Northwest Territories
CJCD-FM-1 Hay River, Northwest Territories
CKAG-FM Pikogan, Québec
CHCQ-FM Belleville, Ontario
CKBZ-FM Kamloops, British Columbia
CHFN-FM Cape Croker (Neyaashiinigmiing), Ontario
CKFU-FM Fort St. John, British Columbia
CJEB-FM Trois-Rivières, Québec
CKVL-FM Montréal (zone LaSalle), Québec
CJVD-FM Vaudreuil-Dorion, Québec

100.3 MHz
CFBR-FM Edmonton, Alberta
CFOZ-FM Argentia, Newfoundland
CHVD-FM Dolbeau-Mistassini, Québec
CJLF-FM Barrie, Ontario
CJMC-FM Sainte Anne des Monts, Québec
CJMJ-FM Ottawa, Ontario
CKKQ-FM Victoria, British Columbia
CKMS-FM Waterloo, Ontario
CKRZ-FM Ohsweken, Ontario
CKCQ-FM Quesnel, British Columbia
CHTN-FM Charlottetown, Prince Edward Island
CFAQ-FM Blucher, Saskatchewan

100.5 MHz
CBBL-FM London, Ontario
CFIN-FM Lac-Etchemin, Québec
CFROFM Vancouver, British Columbia
CHAS-FM Sault Ste. Marie, Ontario
CHUR-FM North Bay, Ontario
CIBO-FM Senneterre, Québec
CIOK-FM Saint John, New Brunswick
CFSR-FM Hope, British Columbia
CHLS-FM Lillooet, British Columbia
CHFT-FM Fort McMurray, Alberta
CKRU-FM Petersborough, Ontario

100.7 MHz
CBFX-FM Montréal, Québec
CHIN-FM Toronto, Ontario
CIGV-FM Penticton, British Columbia
CIAJ-FM Prince Rupert, British Columbia
CFRM-FM Little Current, Manitoba
CILG-FM Moose Jaw, Saskatchewan
CFJL-FM Winnipeg, Manitoba
CIAY-FM Whitehorse, Yukon Territory
CKRI-FM Red Deer, Alberta
CJHK-FM Bridgewater, Nova Scotia
CJLJ-FM Williams Lake, British Columbia

100.9 MHz
CBJX-FM Chicoutimi, Québec
CHXX-FM Donnacona, Québec
CKTO-FM Truro, Nova Scotia
CKAP-FM Kapuskasing, Ontario
CKUV-FM High River, Alberta
CKHA-FM Haliburton, Ontario
CIYM-FM Brighton, Ontario

101.1 MHz
CFMI-FM New Westminster, British Columbia
CKBY-FM Smiths Falls, Ontario
CIQB-FM Barrie, Ontario
CFLZ-FM Fort Erie, Ontario
CKXA-FM Brandon, Manitoba
CFIF-FM Iroquois Falls, Ontario
CKSJ-FM Saint John's, Newfoundland
CIXF-FM Brooks, Alberta
CKSO-FM Sudbury, Ontario
CHLI-FM Rossland, British Columbia
CKMQ-FM Merritt, British Columbia
CKEE-FM Whistler, British Columbia

101.3 MHz
CKKN-FM Prince George, British Columbia
CKOT-FM Tillsonburg, Ontario
CHEQ-FM Sainte-Marie, Québec
CKUN-FM Christian Island, Ontario
CKII-FM Dolbeau-Mistassini, Québec
CJSA-FM Toronto, Ontario
CJEG-FM Bonnyville, Alberta
CJCH-FM Halifax, Nova Scotia
CKEB-FM Ebb and Flow, Manitoba

101.5 MHz
CBZ-FM Fredericton, New Brunswick
CHIPFM Fort-Coulonge, Québec
CIBL-FM Montréal, Québec
CILK-FM Kelowna, British Columbia
CIOI-FM Hamilton, Ontario
CBRXFM Rimouski, Québec
CJUM-FM Winnipeg, Manitoba
CKWF-FM Peterborough, Ontario
CJKL-FM Kirkland Lake, Ontario
CIGO-FM Port Hawkesbury, Nova Scotia
CJBR-FM Rimouski, Québec
CHQX-FM Prince Albert, Saskatchewan
CKNL-FM Fort St. John, British Columbia
CKCE-FM Calgary, Alberta
CKMO-FM Orangeville, Ontario

101.7 MHz
CBQ-FM Thunder Bay, Ontario
CJSO-FM Sorel, Québec
CKER-FM Edmonton, Alberta
CKNX-FM Wingham, Ontario
CHRG-FM Maria (Reserve), Québec
CHLY-FM Nanaimo, British Columbia
CKDH-FM Amherst, Nova Scotia

101.9 MHz
CFRC-FM Kingston, Ontario
CFUV-FM Victoria, British Columbia
CHAI-FM Chateauguay, Québec
CHFX-FM Halifax, Nova Scotia
CITRFM Vancouver, British Columbia
CJSS-FM Cornwall, Ontario
CKFX-FM North Bay, Ontario
CKKY-FM Wainwright, Alberta
CKLB-FM Yellowknife, Northwest Territories
CFDA-FM Victoriaville, Québec
CHRK-FM Sydney, Nova Scotia
CFND-FM Saint Jerome, Québec
CIDG-FM Ottawa, Ontario

102.1 MHz
CFEL-FM Levis, Québec
CFNY-FM Brampton, Ontario
CHPR-FM Hawkesbury, Ontario
CISW-FM Whistler, British Columbia
CJDJ-FM Saskatoon, Saskatchewan
CKHL-FM High Level, Alberta
CJRW-FM Summerside, Prince Edward Island
CBGA-FM Matane, Québec
CJCY-FM Medicine Hat, Alberta
CJGO-FM La Sarre, Québec

102.3 MHz
CIGB-FM Trois-Rivières, Québec
CINQ-FM Montréal, Québec
CKRX-FM Fort Nelson, British Columbia
CKWV-FM Nanaimo, British Columbia
CHST-FM London, Ontario
CKXG-FM Grand Falls, Newfoundland
CHSN-FM Estevan, Saskatchewan
CKY-FM Winnipeg, Manitoba
CKGF-FM Grand Forks, British Columbia
CKJJ-FM Belleville, Ontario
CJNS-FM Meadow Lake, Saskatchewan
CKNO-FM Edmonton, Alberta
CINA-FM Windsor, Ontario

102.5 MHz
CBOX-FM Ottawa, Ontario

102.7 MHz
CBH-FM Halifax, Nova Scotia
CITE-FM-1 Sherbrooke, Québec
CJMV-FM Val d'Or, Québec
CKZP-FM Zenon Park, Saskatchewan
CILU-FM Thunder Bay, Ontario
CIWS-FM Whitchurch-Stouffville, Ontario
CHOP-FM Newmarket, Ontario
CKPK-FM Vancouver, British Columbia
CJVF-FM Scarborough, Ontario
CFGM-FM Caledon, Ontario

102.9 MHz
CFOM-FM Levis, Québec
CKLH-FM Hamilton, Ontario
CJOI-FM Rimouski, Québec
CHCR-FM Killaloe, Ontario
CHDR-FM Cranbrook, British Columbia
CHDI-FM Edmonton, Alberta
CJAR-FM The Pas, Manitoba
CHTM-FM Thompson, Manitoba
CFMO-FM Collingwood, Ontario
CFAR-FM Flin Flon, Manitoba

103.1 MHz
CFHK-FM St. Thomas, Ontario
CFMF-FM Fermont, Québec
CFMX-FM Cobourg, Ontario
CJFW-FM Terrace, British Columbia
CJMO-FM Moncton, New Brunswick
CJRG-FM Gaspe, Québec
CKMM-FM Winnipeg, Manitoba
CHTT-FM Victoria, British Columbia
CKOD-FM Valleyfield, Québec
CJBB-FM Englehart, Ontario
CIAU-FM Radisson, Québec
CFXL-FM Calgary, Alberta
CJKC-FM Kamloops, British Columbia
CHHO-FM Louiseville, Québec
CKQQ-FM Kelowna, British Columbia

103.3 MHz
CBOQ-FM Ottawa, Ontario
CHAA-FM Longueuil, Québec
CKLP-FM Parry Sound, Ontario
CKQV-FM Vermilion Bay, Ontario

103.5 MHz
CHQM-FM Vancouver, British Columbia
CIDC-FM Orangeville, Ontario
CJLM-FM Joliette, Québec
CKRB-FM Saint Georges-de-Beauce, Québec
CJEF-FM Saint John, New Brunswick
CHMM-FM MacKenzie, British Columbia
CKHZ-FM Halifax, Nova Scotia
CHNV-FM Nelson, British Columbia
CKRC-FM Weyburn, Saskatchewan
CFCH-FM Chase, British Columbia
CKCH-FM Sydney, Nova Scotia
CILB-FM Lac La Biche, Alberta

103.7 MHz
CFBU-FM Saint Catharines, Ontario
CJPT-FM Brockville, Ontario
CIEL-FM Rivière-du-Loup, Québec
CKRK-FM Kahnawake, Québec
CIMI-FM Charlesbourg, Québec
CFID-FM Acton Vale, Québec
CFVR-FM Fort McMurray, Alberta

103.9 MHz
CFQM-FM Moncton, New Brunswick
CIMEFM Saint Jerome, Québec
CIMS-FM Balmoral, New Brunswick
CISN-FM Edmonton, Alberta
CKDK-FM Woodstock, Ontario
CKXX-FM Corner Brook, Newfoundland
CKWE-FM Maniwaki (Kitigan Zibi Anishinabeg, Québec
CHNO-FM Sudbury, Ontario
CBRFFM Calgary, Alberta
CIRR-FM Toronto, Ontario
CJAW-FM Moose Jaw, Saskatchewan
CHVO-FM Carbonear, Newfoundland

104.1 MHz
CFQX-FM Selkirk, Manitoba
CFZZ-FM Saint Jean-Iberville, Québec
CICZ-FM Midland, Ontario
CIFA-FM Comeauville, Nova Scotia
CKTF-FM Gatineau, Québec
CHYK-FM Timmins, Ontario
CKNA-FM Natashquan, Québec
CJCJ-FM Woodstock, New Brunswick
CHAD-FM Dawson Creek, British Columbia
CIOT-FM Nipawin, Saskatchewan

104.3 MHz
CBF-FM-1 Trois-Rivières, Québec
CFRQ-FM Dartmouth, Nova Scotia
CJQM-FM Sault Ste. Marie, Ontario
CHGO-FM Val d'Or, Québec
CKWS-FM Kingston, Ontario
CHLG-FM Vancouver, British Columbia
CKBK-FM Thamesville, Ontario
CICN-FM Marcelin, Saskatchewan
CBFX-FM-1 Trois-Rivières, Québec

104.5 MHz
CFLG-FM Cornwall, Ontario

CHUM-FM Toronto, Ontario
CIKI-FM Rimouski, Québec
CISP-FM Pemberton, British Columbia
CJTT-FM New Liskeard, Ontario
CKAU-FM Maliotenam, Québec
CFQK-FM Kaministiquia, Ontario
CKOY-FM Sherbrooke, Québec
CJRI-FM Fredericton, New Brunswick
CJSB-FM Swan River, Manitoba
CKJX-FM Olds, Alberta
CFGT-FM Alma, Québec

104.7 MHz

CBVE-FM Québec, Québec
CFLO-FM Mont-Laurier, Québec
CIPN-FM Pender Harbour, British Columbia
CHBZ-FM Cranbrook, British Columbia
CKLZ-FM Kelowna, British Columbia
CHIM-FM Kelowna, British Columbia
CIHR-FM Woodstock, Ontario
CKOF-FM Gatineau, Québec
CFRI-FM Grande Prairie, Alberta
CFDY-FM Cochrane, Ontario
CKOF-FM Gatineau, Québec

104.9 MHz

CBQL-FM Savant Lake, Ontario
CFMG-FM Edmonton, Alberta
CFWF-FM Regina, Saskatchewan
CJLA-FM Lachute, Québec
CHOCFM Saint Remi, Québec
CFJR-FM Brockville, Ontario
CKBC-FM Bathurst, New Brunswick
CKVX-FM Kindersley, British Columbia
CIMY-FM Pembroke, Ontario
CHWC-FM Goderich, Ontario
CFXM Granby, Québec
CFDC-FM Shelburne, Ontario

105.1 MHz

CBI-FM Sydney, Nova Scotia
CBMR-FM Fermont, Québec
CBQR-FM Rankin Inlet, Nunavut
CKQM-FM Peterborough, Ontario
CKRY-FM Calgary, Alberta
CITA-FM Moncton, New Brunswick
CFIC-FM Listuguj, Québec
CJVR-FM Melfort, Saskatchewan
CJED-FM Niagara Falls, Ontario
CKDG-FM Montréal, Québec
CHOQ-FM Toronto, Ontario
CKHY-FM Halifax, Nova Scotia

105.3 MHz

CFCA-FM Waterloo, Ontario
CHRD-FM Drummondville, Québec
CJMY-FM Clarenville, Newfoundland
CJMX-FM Sudbury, Ontario
CISS-FM Ottawa, Ontario
CFXY-FM Fredericton, New Brunswick
CHRM-FM Matane, Québec
CIXM-FM Whitecourt, Alberta
CKMH-FM Medicine Hat, Alberta
CHOW-FM Amos, Québec
CKTG-FM Thunder Bay, Ontario

105.5 MHz

CBKS-FM Saskatoon, Saskatchewan
CFBK-FM Huntsville, Ontario
CHRY-FM North York, Ontario
CKLD-FM Thetford Mines, Québec
CHUB-FM Red Deer, Alberta
CICY-FM Selkirk, Manitoba
CKQK-FM Charlottetown, Prince Edward Island
CJFB-FM Bolton, Ontario
CKGS-FM La Baie, Québec
CIUX-FM Uxbridge, Ontario

105.7 MHz

CFGL-FM Laval, Québec
CHRE-FM St. Catharines, Ontario
CIKR-FM Kingston, Ontario
CFDM-FM Meadow Lake, Saskatchewan
CICF-FM Vernon, British Columbia
CHQC-FM Saint John, New Brunswick
CJMI-FM Strathroy, Ontario
CIBQ-FM Brooks, Alberta
CKOO-FM Broadview, Saskatchewan

105.9 MHz

CBKA-FM La Ronge, Saskatchewan
CICX-FM Orillia, Ontario
CFEP-FM Eastern Passage, Nova Scotia
CHPD-FM Aylmer, Ontario
CJRY-FM Edmonton, Alberta
CFMS-FM Markham, Ontario

106.1 MHz

CHEZ-FM Ottawa, Ontario
CIMJ-FM Guelph, Ontario
CIMO-FM Magog, Québec
CKJM-FM Cheticamp, Nova Scotia
CKLM-FM Lloydminster, Alberta
CKKX-FM Peace River, Alberta
CFIT-FM Airdrie, Alberta
CBAM-FM Moncton, New Brunswick
CKCR-FM Revelstoke, British Columbia
CHWE-FM Winnepeg, Manitoba
CKSE-FM Estevan, Saskatchewan

106.3 MHz

CBV-FM Québec, Québec
CHKS-FM Sarnia, Ontario
CFXN-FM North Bay, Ontario
CKAV-FM-2 Vancouver, British Columbia
CKGR-FM Golden, British Columbia
CISB-FM Marius, Manitoba
CKIN-FM Montréal, Québec

106.5 MHz

CFEI-FM St-Hyacinthe, Québec
CIXK-FM Owen Sound, Ontario
CHMN-FM Canmore, Alberta
CKAV-FM Toronto, Ontario
CJJJ-FM Brandon, Manitoba
CIFN-FM Island Lake, Saskatchewan
CHBY-FM Barry's Bay, Ontario
CHVL-FM Val-des-Lacs, Québec

106.7 MHz

CJRX-FM Lethbridge, Alberta
CJIT-FM Lac Megantic, Québec
CIKZ-FM Kitchener, Ontario
CFET-FM Tagish, Yukon Territory
CFDV-FM Red Deer, Alberta
CHWY-FM Weyburn, Saskatchewan
CHSV-FM Hudson/Saint-Lazare, Québec
CKYR-FM Calgary, Alberta

106.9 MHz

CBN-FM Saint John's, Newfoundland
CHMA-FM Sackville, New Brunswick
CIBX-FM Fredericton, New Brunswick
CIXX-FM London, Ontario
CKKC-FM Nelson, British Columbia
CKQB-FM Ottawa, Ontario
CHRQ-FM Restigouche, Québec
CHWF-FM Nanaimo, British Columbia
CKOB-FM Trois-Rivières, Québec
CFYT-FM Dawson City, Yukon Territory

107.1 MHz

CIBMFM Rivière-du-Loup, Québec
CILQ-FM Toronto, Ontario
CISQ-FM Squamish, British Columbia
CJCS-FM Stratford, Ontario
CJWA-FM Wawa, Ontario
CKQC-FM Abbotsford, British Columbia
CKCL-FM Winnipeg, Manitoba
CJTN-FM Trenton, Ontario
CHNC-FM New Carlisle, Québec
CJNW-FM Edmonton, Alberta

107.3 MHz

CITE-FM Montréal, Québec
CKHR-FM Hay River, Northwest Territories
CFGQ-FM Calgary, Alberta
CHBE-FM Victoria, British Columbia
CFMH-FM Saint John, New Brunswick
CHUK-FM Mashteuiatsh (Pointe-Bleue), Québec
CFRT-FM Iqaluit, Nunavut
CKOE-FM Moncton, New Brunswick
CJDL-FM Tillsonburg, Ontario

107.5 MHz

CISC-FM Gibsons, British Columbia
CKKS-FM Chilliwack, British Columbia
CITF-FM Québec, Québec
CJDV-FM Kitchener, Ontario
CFUN-FM Sechelt, British Columbia
CKMB-FM Barrie, Ontario
CKIZ-FM Vernon, British Columbia
CJIE-FM Winnepeg Beach, Manitoba
CHBO-FM Humboldt, Saskatchewan
CFSM-FM Cranbrook, British Columbia

107.7 MHz

CFRV-FM Lethbridge, Alberta
CHGK-FM Stratford, Ontario
CKTI-FM Kettle Point, Ontario
CKHK-FM Hawkesbury, Ontario
CJXR-FM Steinbach, Manitoba
CHMY-FM-1 Arnprior, Ontario

107.9 MHz

CJXY-FM Burlington, Ontario
CKDJ-FM Ottawa, Ontario
CHUC-FM Cobourg, Ontario
CILS-FM Victoria, British Columbia
CFTA-FM Amherst, Nova Scotia
CKPP-FM Prescott, Ontario
CJXB-FM Banff, Alberta
CKFT-FM Fort Saskatchewan, Alberta
CFSI-FM Salt Spring Island, British Columbia

10MHz

CFAI-FM Edmundston, New Brunswick

88.1 MHz

CFRH-FM Penetanguishene, Ontario
CHES-FM Erin, Ontario
CKAV-FM-3 Calgary, Alberta
CHLK-FM Perth, Ontario
CIND-FM Toronto, Ontario

88.3 MHz

CKIA-FM Québec, Québec
CJIQ-FM Paris, Ontario
CFAK-FM Sherbrooke, Québec
CKXU-FM Lethbridge, Alberta

88.5 MHz

CBAF-FM Moncton, New Brunswick
CBME-FM Montréal, Québec
CJSR-FM Edmonton, Alberta
CKDX-FM Newmarket, Ontario
CIBH-FM Parksville, British Columbia
CILV-FM Ottawa, Ontario
CIVL-FM Abbotsford, British Columbia

88.7 MHz

CIMX-FM Windsor, Ontario
CFUR-FM Prince George, British Columbia
CHIC-FM Rouyn-Noranda, Québec
CKYM-FM Napanee, Ontario

88.9 MHz

CBTKFM Kelowna, British Columbia
CIRV-FM Toronto, Ontario
CJMQ-FM Sherbrooke, Québec
CJSI-FM Calgary, Alberta
CHNI-FM Saint John, New Brunswick
CJRD-FM Drummondville, Québec
CKMW-FM Winkler-Morden, Manitoba

89.1 MHz

CHUO-FM Ottawa, Ontario
CKRL-FM Québec, Québec
CFOU-FM Trois-Rivières, Québec
CBLA-FM-2 Paris, Ontario
CISO-FM Orillia, Ontario

89.3 MHz

CISM-FM Montréal, Québec
CKGW-FM Chatham, Ontario
CKAV-FM-4 Edmonton, Alberta
CIJK-FM Kentville, Nova Scotia

89.5 MHz

CFGB-FM Happy Valley-Goose Bay, Newfoundland
CIUT-FM Toronto, Ontario
CJSEFM Shediac, New Brunswick
CJRL-FM Kenora, Ontario
CHWK-FM Chilliwack, British Columbia
CKTZ-FM Cortes Island, British Columbia

89.7 MHz

CKGN-FM Kapuskasing, Ontario
CJSU-FM Duncan, British Columbia

CKOA-FM Glace Bay, Nova Scotia

89.9 MHz

CBE-FM Windsor, Ontario
CBTEFM Crawford Bay, British Columbia
CFNK-FM Pinehouse Lake, Saskatchewan
CFWE-FM Lac La Biche, Alberta
CJCF-FM Cumberland House, Saskatchewan
CJLR-FM La Ronge, Saskatchewan
CFBS-FM Lourdes-de-Blanc-Sablon, Québec
CIHT-FM Ottawa, Ontario
CHNS-FM Halifax, Nova Scotia
CKWT-FM Sioux Lookout, Ontario
CKKI-FM Kahnawake, Québec

90.1 MHz

CFJU-FM Kedgwick, New Brunswick
CBBS-FM Sudbury, Ontario
CJSF-FM Burnaby, British Columbia
CJMP-FM Powell River, British Columbia
CHMZ-FM Tofino, British Columbia

90.3 MHz

CBEG-FM Sarnia, Ontario
CJBC-FM Toronto, Ontario
CKUT-FM Montréal, Québec
CKMP-FM Calgary, Alberta

90.5 MHz

CBHA-FM Halifax, Nova Scotia
CBQT-FM Thunder Bay, Ontario
CFCR-FM Saskatoon, Saskatchewan
CJPN-FM Fredericton, New Brunswick
CJBE-FM Port-Menier, Québec
CJMB-FM Peterborough, Ontario
CKBN-FM Becancour and Nicolet, Québec
CKRD-FM Red Deer, Alberta
CKXM-FM Exeter, Ontario

90.7 MHz

CBOFFM Ottawa, Ontario
CFBO-FM Moncton, New Brunswick
CBFX-FM-2 Sherbrooke, Québec

90.9 MHz

CION-FM Québec, Québec
CJSW-FM Calgary, Alberta
CBBX-FM Sudbury, Ontario

91.1 MHz

CINN-FM Hearst, Ontario
CJRT-FM Toronto, Ontario
CKXL-FM Saint Boniface, Manitoba
CFUT-FM Shawinigan, Québec
CKOS-FM Fort McMurray, Alberta
CFAD-FM Salmo, British Columbia

91.3 MHz

CBD-FM Saint John, New Brunswick
CIRA-FM Montréal, Québec
CJLX-FM Belleville, Ontario
CJTR-FM Regina, Saskatchewan
CJZN-FM Victoria, British Columbia
CFBW-FM Hanover, Ontario
CIOG-FM Charlottetown, Prince Edward Island

91.5 MHz

CBO-FM Ottawa, Ontario
CBAX-FM Halifax, Nova Scotia
CKBT-FM Kitchener-Waterloo, Ontario
CKXR-FM Salmon Arm, British Columbia
CKPR-FM Thunder Bay, Ontario

91.7 MHz

CIXL-FM Welland, Ontario
CHBN-FM Edmonton, Alberta
CKAY-FM Gibsons, British Columbia
CICS-FM Sudbury, Ontario

91.9 MHz

CKLY-FM Kawartha Lakes, Ontario
CKVI-FM Kingston, Ontario
CJEC-FM Québec, Québec
CKLX-FM Montréal, Québec
CKNI-FM Moncton, New Brunswick

92.1 MHz

CFVD-FM-2 Pohenegamook, Québec
CHMX-FM Regina, Saskatchewan
CHOD-FM Cornwall, Ontario
CITI-FM Winnipeg, Manitoba
CJAY-FM Calgary, Alberta
CJDM-FM Drummondville, Québec
CJOZ-FM Bonavista Bay, Newfoundland
CJQQ-FM Timmins, Ontario
CKPC-FM Brantford, Ontario
CFNR-FM Terrace, British Columbia
CIMA-FM Alliston, Ontario
CHPL-FM Plamondon, Alberta

92.3 MHz

CKOZ-FM Corner Brook, Newfoundland
CJET-FM Smiths Falls, Ontario
CFGI-FM Georgina Island, Ontario
CFRK-FM Fredericton, New Brunswick
CJOS-FM Owen Sound, Ontario
CBAF-FM-5 Halifax, Nova Scotia

92.5 MHz

CKBE-FM Montréal, Québec
CKAJ-FM Jonquiere, Québec
CKIS-FM Toronto, Ontario
CKNG-FM Edmonton, Alberta
CFBX-FM Kamloops, British Columbia
CHRC-FM Clarence-Rockland, Ontario
CKBE Montréal, Québec

92.7 MHz

CFFF-FM Peterborough, Ontario
CFIM-FM Iles-de-la-Madeleine, Québec
CJBX-FM London, Ontario
CJEM-FM Edmundston, New Brunswick
CJRQ-FM Sudbury, Ontario
CIAM-FM Fort Vermilion, Alberta
CKDR-FM Dryden, Ontario
CHSL-FM Slave Lake, Alberta
CJSQ-FM Québec, Québec
CJSP-FM Leamington, Ontario
CHBD-FM Regina, Saskatchewan

92.9 MHz

CBBKFM Kingston, Ontario
CFLT-FM Dartmouth, Nova Scotia
CKBL-FM Saskatoon, Saskatchewan
CHYK-FM-3 Hearst, Ontario
CIBW-FM Drayton Valley, Alberta
CKLE-FM Bathurst, Québec
CFEX-FM Calgary, Alberta
CFSH-FM Apsley, Ontario

93.1 MHz

CFNO-FM Marathon, Ontario
CHAY-FM Barrie, Ontario
CHLQ-FM Charlottetown, Prince Edward Island
CKCUFM Ottawa, Ontario
CJXX-FM Grande Prairie, Alberta
CFOB-FM Fort Frances, Ontario
CHMT-FM Timmins, Ontario
CKVM-FM Ville-Marie, Québec
CFRG-FM Gravelbourg, Saskatchewan
CKYE-FM Vancouver, British Columbia
CJTB-FM Tete-a-la-Baleine, Québec
CFIS-FM Prince George, British Columbia
CJLD-FM Leduc, Alberta
CIHI-FM Fredericton, New Brunswick
CHPO-FM Portage La Prairie, Manitoba

93.3 MHz

CFMU-FM Hamilton, Ontario
CFRU-FM Guelph, Ontario
CJMF-FM Québec, Québec
CKSQ-FM Stettler, Alberta
CJOK-FM Fort McMurray, Alberta
CJBZ-FM Taber, Alberta
CKSG-FM Cobourg, Ontario
CJAV-FM Port Alberni, British Columbia
CFXU-FM Antigonish, Nova Scotia
CFYX-FM Rimouski, Québec
CJHD-FM North Battleford, Saskatchewan

93.5 MHz

CBCL-FM London, Ontario
CBM-FM Montréal, Québec
CHMR-FM Saint John's, Newfoundland
CIGM-FM Sudbury, Ontario
CJLS-FM-2 New Tusket, Nova Scotia
CKUM-FM Moncton, New Brunswick
CJEL-FM Winkler, Manitoba
CFXJ-FM Toronto, Ontario
CIKX-FM Grand Falls, New Brunswick
CJAS-FM Saint Augustin, Québec
CJLY-FM Nelson, British Columbia
CIHS-FM Wetaskiwin, Alberta
CKXO-FM Chibougamau, Québec
CHXL-FM Brockville, Ontario
CFZN-FM Haliburton, Ontario
CKXC-FM Kingston, Ontario
CKVH-FM High Prairie, Alberta

93.7 MHz

CJJR-FM Vancouver, British Columbia
CBJ-FM Chicoutimi, Québec
CKYC-FM Owen Sound, Ontario
CIFX-FM Lewisporte, Newfoundland
CFGE-FM Sherbrooke, Québec
CKWY-FM Wainwright, Alberta
CJLT-FM Medicine Hat, Alberta
CJAI-FM Stella, Ontario
CJNU-FM Winnipeg, Manitoba
CKMA-FM Miramichi, New Brunswick

93.9 MHz

CIDR-FM Windsor, Ontario
CKKL-FM Ottawa, Ontario
CFWC-FM Brantford, Ontario
CJBI-FM Wabana, Newfoundland
CICK-FM Smithers, British Columbia

94.1 MHz

CBL-FM Toronto, Ontario
CHSJ-FM Saint John, New Brunswick
CIMG-FM Swift Current, Saskatchewan
CKBA-FM Athabasca, Alberta
CKNR-FM Elliot Lake, Ontario
CKCN-FM Sept-Iles, Québec
CICU-FM Eskasoni Indian Reserve, Nova Scotia
CFGW-FM Yorkton, Saskatchewan
CJUV-FM Lacombe, Alberta
CJOC-FM Lethbridge, Alberta
CKEC-FM New Glasgow, Nova Scotia
CBK-1-FM Saskatoon, Saskatchewan
CKCV-FM Creston, British Columbia
CKZM-FM St. Thomas, Ontario
CFGW-FM Yorkton, Saskatchewan

94.3 MHz

CHIQ-FM Winnipeg, Manitoba
CHYZ-FM Sainte Foy, Québec
CIRX-FM Prince George, British Columbia
CJSD-FM Thunder Bay, Ontario
CKMF-FM Montréal, Québec
CKSY-FM Chatham, Ontario
CJTW-FM Kitchener-Waterloo, Ontario
CJFH-FM Woodstock, Ontario
CFXE-FM Edson, Alberta

94.5 MHz

CFWH-FM Whitehorse, Yukon Territory
CJAB-FN Saguenay, Québec
CKCW-FM Moncton, New Brunswick
CHBW-FM Rocky Mountain House, Alberta
CHET-FM Chetwynd, British Columbia
CFBT-FM Vancouver, British Columbia
CKCK-FM Regina, Saskatchewan
CIBU-FM Wingham, Ontario
CHAT-FM Medicine Hat, Alberta
CJFO-FM Ottawa, Ontario

94.7 MHz

CHEY-FM Trois-Rivières, Québec
CHKF-FM Calgary, Alberta
CHOZ-FM St. John's, Newfoundland
CHKX-FM Hamilton, Ontario
CKLF-FM Brandon, Manitoba
CJDS-FM Saint Pamphile, Québec
CJNE-FM Nipawin, Saskatchewan
CIRP-FM Spryfield, Nova Scotia

94.9 MHz

CHRW-FM London, Ontario
CIEU-FM Carleton, Québec
CIMF-FM Gatineau, Québec
CKGE-FM Oshawa, Ontario
CKPE-FM Sydney, Nova Scotia
CKUA-FM Edmonton, Alberta
CKWM-FM Kentville, Nova Scotia
CJPR-FM Blairmore, Alberta
CFFM-FM-2 Quesnel, British Columbia

RADIO - CANADA

95.1 MHz

CBF-FM Montréal, Québec
CFMC-FM Saskatoon, Saskatchewan
CILE-FM Havre-Saint-Pierre, Québec
CKCB-FM Collingwood, Ontario
CKUE-FM Chatham, Ontario
CHVN-FM Winnipeg, Manitoba
CJOA-FM Thunder Bay, Ontario
CKMV-FM Grand Falls, New Brunswick
CFCY-FM Charlottetown, Prince Edward Island

95.3 MHz

CBVX-FM Québec, Québec
CHOE-FM Matane, Québec
CING-FM Hamilton, Ontario
CKZZ-FM Vancouver, British Columbia
CHUT-FM Lac-Simon (Louvicourt), Québec
CJXK-FM Cold Lake, Alberta
CHPK-FM Calgary, Alberta

95.5 MHz

CBA-FM Moncton, New Brunswick
CFLX-FM Sherbrooke, Québec
CFVD Degelis, Québec
CHLB-FM Lethbridge, Alberta
CJOJ-FM Belleville, Ontario
CJTK-FM Sudbury, Ontario
CKGY-FM Red Deer, Alberta
CIYN-FM Kincardine, Ontario

95.7 MHz

CBQS-FM Sioux Narrows, Ontario
CFJB-FM Barrie, Ontario
CJAT-FM Trail, British Columbia
CKRP-FM Falher, Alberta
CKYK-FM Alma, Québec
CKYQ-FM Plessisville, Québec
CKTP-FM Fredericton Centre, New Brunswick
CJNI-FM Halifax, Nova Scotia
CKAV-FM-9 Ottawa, Ontario
CHBI-FM Burnt Islands, Newfoundland
CFPW-FM Powell River, British Columbia
CKEA-FM Edmonton, Alberta

95.9 MHz

CFPL-FM London, Ontario
CHFM-FM Calgary, Alberta
CKMY-FM Grand Falls, Newfoundland
CJFM-FM Montréal, Québec
CJKX-FM Ajax, Ontario
CKUW-FM Winnipeg, Manitoba
CKSA-FM Lloydminster, Alberta
CHHI-FM Miramichi, New Brunswick
CJWF-FM Windsor, Ontario
CIRX-FM-1 Vanderhoof, British Columbia

96.1 MHz

CBCT-FM Charlottetown, Prince Edward Island
CFMY-FM Medicine Hat, Alberta
CHKG-FM Richmond, British Columbia
CKRW-FM Whitehorse, Yukon Territory
CKX-FM Brandon, Manitoba
CINB-FM Saint John, New Brunswick
CHMY-FM Renfrew, Ontario

96.3 MHz

CBDQ-FM Labrador City, Newfoundland
CFMK-FM Kingston, Ontario
CFMZ-FM Toronto, Ontario
CIHO-FM Baie St Paul, Québec
CINC-FM Thompson, Manitoba
CIOZ-FM Marystown, Newfoundland
CJLS-FM-1 Barrington, Nova Scotia
CKRA-FM Edmonton, Alberta
CJLSFM Barrington, Nova Scotia
CFMV-FM Chandler, Québec
CFWD-FM Saskatoon, Saskatchewan
CJGY-FM Grande Prairie, Alberta
CKKO-FM Kelowna, British Columbia

96.5 MHz

CHOA-FM Rouyn-Noranda, Québec
CKUL-FM Halifax, Nova Scotia
CKMN-FM Rimouski-Mont Joli, Québec
CIXN-FM Fredericton, New Brunswick
CKLJ-FM Olds, Alberta
CJPG-FM Portage la Prairie, Manitoba
CJFY-FM Miramichi, New Brunswick
CFTX-FM Gatineau, Québec

96.7 MHz

CHVR-FM Pembroke, Ontario
CHYM-FM Kitchener, Ontario
CHYR-FM Leamington, Ontario
CILT-FM Steinbach, Manitoba
CKLU-FM Sudbury, Ontario
CFXW-FM Whitecourt, Alberta
CJWV-FM Peterborough, Ontario

96.9 MHz

CBK-FM Regina, Saskatchewan
CJAQ-FM Calgary, Alberta
CJAX-FM Vancouver, British Columbia
CJXL-FM Moncton, New Brunswick
CFIX-FM Saguenay, Québec
CKHC-FM Toronto, Ontario
CKOI Montréal, Québec

97.1 MHz

CHLC-FM Baie-Comeau, Québec
CIGL-FM Belleville, Ontario
CJMG-FM Penticton, British Columbia
CKRO-FM Inkerman, New Brunswick
CHLX-FM Gatineau, Québec
CKFI-FM Swift Current, Saskatchewan
CKDR-2-FM Sioux Lookout, Ontario
CKDR-5-FM Red Lake, Ontario
CIPU-FM Micmac, Nova Scotia
CFLM-FM La Tuque, Québec

97.3 MHz

CFJO-FM Thetford Mines, Québec
CHGA-FM Maniwaki, Québec
CIRK-FM Edmonton, Alberta
CHBM-FM Toronto, Ontario
CJRM-FM Labrador City, Newfoundland
CKLR-FM Courtenay, British Columbia
CKON-FM Akwesasne, Ontario
CHWV-FM Saint John, New Brunswick
CKUJ-FM Kuujjuaq, Québec
CJCI-FM Prince George, British Columbia

97.5 MHz

CFFM-FM Williams Lake, British Columbia
CHOX-FM La Pocatiere, Québec
CIQM-FM London, Ontario
CKDU-FM Halifax, Nova Scotia
CKRV-FM Kamloops, British Columbia
VOCM-FM St. John's, Newfoundland
CFXH-FM Hinton, Alberta
CKVV-FM Kemptville, Ontario
CBEW-FM Windsor, Ontario
CJKR-FM Winnipeg, Manitoba

97.7 MHz

CBKF-FM Regina, Saskatchewan
CBUFFM Vancouver, British Columbia
CFCV-FM St. Andrew's, Newfoundland
CFGP-FM Grande Prairie, Alberta
CFTH-FM-1 Harrington Harbour, Québec
CHOM-FM Montréal, Québec
CHTZ-FM St. Catharines, Ontario
CKEN-FM Kentville, Nova Scotia
CHMS-FM Bancroft, Ontario
CIDD-FM White Bear Lake Resort, Saskatchewan
CFXX-FM Siksika, Alberta
CKTK-FM Kitimat, British Columbia
CIDO-FM Creston, British Columbia
CHGB-FM Wasaga Beach, Ontario
CHUP-FM Calgary, Alberta
CHSP-FM St. Paul, Alberta

97.9 MHz

CFLC-FM Churchill Falls, Newfoundland
CFLN-FM Goose Bay, Newfoundland
CHSR-FM Fredericton, New Brunswick
CKYX-FM Fort McMurray, Alberta
CJLL-FM Ottawa, Ontario
CFPS-FM Port Elgin, Ontario
CKWB-FM Westlock, Alberta
CKEZ-FM Pictou, Nova Scotia
CJCQ-FM North Battleford, Saskatchewan

98.1 MHz

CBON-FM Timmins, Ontario
CBSI-FM Sept-Iles, Québec
CFMQ-FM Hudson Bay, Saskatchewan
CHFI-FM Toronto, Ontario
CHON-FM Whitehorse, Yukon Territory
CKBD-FM Lethbridge, Alberta
CHTD-FM Saint Stephen, New Brunswick
CKBW-FM Bridgewater, Nova Scotia
CHPB-FM Cochrane, Ontario
CKIQFM Big White Ski, British Columbia
CFCW-FM Camrose, Alberta
CHOI-FM Québec, Québec
CIBC-FM Cowessess, Saskatchewan
CKLO-FM London, Ontario

98.3 MHz

CBAL-FM Moncton, New Brunswick
CFLY-FM Kingston, Ontario
CKSR-FM Chilliwack, British Columbia
CIFM-FM Kamloops, British Columbia
CFPX-FM Pukatawagan, Manitoba
CIAX-FM Windsor, Québec
CJMK-FM Saskatoon, Saskatchewan
CFWP-FM Wahta Mohawk Territory near Bala, Ontario
CHER-FM Sydney, Nova Scotia
CKRS-FM Saguenay, Québec
CHUN-FM Rouyn-Noranda, Québec
CFRZ-FM Walpole Island, Ontario

98.5 MHz

CHRX-FM Fort St. John, British Columbia
CHMP-FM Longueuil, Québec
CIOC-FM Victoria, British Columbia
CKWR-FM Waterloo, Ontario
CFTH-FM-2 Harrington Harbour, Québec
CIBK-FM Calgary, Alberta
CINU-FM Truro, Nova Scotia
CJWL-FM Ottawa, Ontario
CJJC-FM Yorkton, Saskatchewan
CKRH-FM Halifax, Nova Scotia
CHOR-FM Summerland, British Columbia
CIOS-FM Stephenville, Newfoundland

98.7 MHz

CBQX-FM Kenora, Ontario
CKXD-FM Gander, Newfoundland
CJHR-FM Renfrew, Ontario
CKPM-FM Port Moody, British Columbia
CKFG-FM Toronto, Ontario
CHWN-FM Skownan, Manitoba
CICV-FM Lake Cowichan, British Columbia

98.9 MHz

CHCD-FM Simcoe, Ontario
CHIK-FM Québec, Québec
CIZL-FM Regina, Saskatchewan
CIZZ-FM Red Deer, Alberta
CJFX-FM Antigonish, Nova Scotia
CJYC-FM Saint John, New Brunswick
CHYC-FM Sudbury, Ontario
CFPV-FM Pemberton, British Columbia
CIKT-FM Grande Prairie, Alberta
CKLC-FM Kingston, Ontario
CFYK-FM Yellowknife, Northwest Territories

99.1 MHz

CBLA-FM Toronto, Ontario
CFMM-FM Prince Albert, Saskatchewan
CFNJ-FM St-Gabriel, Québec
CHRI-FM Ottawa, Ontario
CIPC-FM Port-Cartier, Québec
CJAM-FM Windsor, Ontario
CJMM-FM Rouyn-Noranda, Québec
CKIX-FM St. John's, Newfoundland
CJDR-FM Fernie, British Columbia
CJGV-FM Winnipeg, Manitoba
CIDI-FM Lac-Brome, Québec
CHTK-FM Prince Rupert, British Columbia

99.3 MHz

CBV-FM-6 La Malbaie, Québec
CFOX-FM Vancouver, British Columbia
CFOR-FM Maniwaki, Québec
CKQN-FM Baker Lake, Nunavut
CKQR-FM Castlegar, British Columbia
CJAN-FM Asbestos, Québec
CKGB-FM Timmins, Ontario
CFAN-FM Miramichi, New Brunswick
CKDV-FM Prince George, British Columbia
CFSF-FM Sturgeon Falls, Ontario
CIUP-FM Edmonton, Alberta
CHSB-FM Bedford, Nova Scotia
CJJM-FM Espanola, Ontario
CJGB-FM Meaford, Ontario

99.5 MHz

CBZF-FM Fredericton, New Brunswick
CFBG-FM Bracebridge, Ontario
CJPX-FM Montréal, Québec
CHRL-FM Roberval, Québec
CKTY-FM Truro, Nova Scotia
CIMM-FM Ucluelet, British Columbia
CKKW-FM Kitchener, Ontario
CHOO-FM Drumheller, Alberta

99.7 MHz

CFCP-FM Comox Valley, British Columbia
CHJM-FM St-George-Beauce, Québec
CFNA-FM Bonnyville, Alberta
CKPT-FM Peterborough, Ontario
CFXO-FM High River, Alberta
CIQC-FM Campbell River, British Columbia
CJOT-FM Ottawa, Ontario

99.9 MHz

CBCSFM Sudbury, Ontario
CFGX-FM Sarnia, Ontario
CFWM-FM Winnipeg, Manitoba
CHSU-FM Kelowna, British Columbia
CKFM-FM Toronto, Ontario
CHOY-FM Moncton, New Brunswick
CHEF-FM Matagami, Québec
CJUK-FM Thunder Bay, Ontario
CHJX-FM London, Ontario
CFVM-FM Amqui, Québec
CJIJ-FM Sydney, Nova Scotia
CHPQ-FM Parksville, British Columbia
CJGM-FM Gananoque, Ontario

Programming on Radio Stations in Canada

Adult Contemp

CFIT-FM Airdrie, Alberta
CIXF-FM Brooks, Alberta
CHFM-FM Calgary, Alberta
CHPK-FM Calgary, Alberta
CHUP-FM Calgary, Alberta
CKCE-FM Calgary, Alberta
CFCW-FM Camrose, Alberta
CHMN-FM Canmore, Alberta
CHOO-FM Drumheller, Alberta
CIUP-FM Edmonton, Alberta
CKNG-FM Edmonton, Alberta
CKNO-FM Edmonton, Alberta
CFXE-FM Edson, Alberta
CKRP-FM Falher, Alberta
CFVR-FM Fort McMurray, Alberta
CHFT-FM Fort McMurray, Alberta
CIKT-FM Grande Prairie, Alberta
CKUV-FM High River, Alberta
CJUV-FM Lacombe, Alberta
CFRV-FM Lethbridge, Alberta
CJOC-FM Lethbridge, Alberta
CFMY-FM Medicine Hat, Alberta
CJCY-FM Medicine Hat, Alberta
CHUB-FM Red Deer, Alberta
CKRI-FM Red Deer, Alberta
CJBZ-FM Taber, Alberta
CKWY-FM Wainwright, Alberta
CFLD Burns Lake, British Columbia
CIQC-FM Campbell River, British Columbia
CHET-FM Chetwynd, British Columbia
CKSR-FM Chilliwack, British Columbia
CKLR-FM Courtenay, British Columbia
CFSM-FM Cranbrook, British Columbia
CKCV-FM Creston, British Columbia
CHAD-FM Dawson Creek, British Columbia
CJSU-FM Duncan, British Columbia
CHRX-FM Fort St. John, British Columbia
CISC-FM Gibsons, British Columbia
CKAY-FM Gibsons, British Columbia
CKGR-FM Golden, British Columbia
CFSR-FM Hope, British Columbia
CKBZ-FM Kamloops, British Columbia
CKRV-FM Kamloops, British Columbia
CILK-FM Kelowna, British Columbia
CKQQ-FM Kelowna, British Columbia
CKWV-FM Nanaimo, British Columbia
CKKC-FM Nelson, British Columbia
CJOR Osoyoos, British Columbia
CHPQ-FM Parksville, British Columbia
CIBH-FM Parksville, British Columbia
CISP-FM Pemberton, British Columbia
CIPN-FM Pender Harbour, British Columbia
CKOR Penticton, British Columbia
CJAV-FM Port Alberni, British Columbia
CFNI Port Hardy, British Columbia
CFPW-FM Powell River, British Columbia
CKKN-FM Prince George, British Columbia
CKCR-FM Revelstoke, British Columbia
CISL Richmond, British Columbia
CKXR-FM Salmon Arm, British Columbia
CFBV Smithers, British Columbia
CISQ-FM Squamish, British Columbia
CFTK Terrace, British Columbia
CJAT-FM Trail, British Columbia
CHQM-FM Vancouver, British Columbia
CJAX-FM Vancouver, British Columbia
CKPK-FM Vancouver, British Columbia
CKZZ-FM Vancouver, British Columbia
CKIZ-FM Vernon, British Columbia
CHBE-FM Victoria, British Columbia
CHTT-FM Victoria, British Columbia
CIOC-FM Victoria, British Columbia
CISW-FM Whistler, British Columbia
CKLF-FM Brandon, Manitoba
CKX-FM Brandon, Manitoba
CJPG-FM Portage la Prairie, Manitoba
CILT-FM Steinbach, Manitoba
CJAR The Pas, Manitoba
CJEL-FM Winkler, Manitoba
CFJL-FM Winnipeg, Manitoba
CJGV-FM Winnipeg, Manitoba
CKY-FM Winnipeg, Manitoba
CKBC-FM Bathurst, New Brunswick
CKNB Campbellton, New Brunswick
CJVA Caraquet, New Brunswick
CJEM-FM Edmundston, New Brunswick
CIHI-FM Fredericton, New Brunswick
CJPN-FM Fredericton, New Brunswick
CIKX-FM Grand Falls, New Brunswick
CKRO-FM Inkerman, New Brunswick
CHHI-FM Miramichi, New Brunswick
CFBO-FM Moncton, New Brunswick
CKNI-FM Moncton, New Brunswick
CHWV-FM Saint John, New Brunswick
CIOK-FM Saint John, New Brunswick
CJCW Sussex, New Brunswick
CJCJ-FM Woodstock, New Brunswick
CFOZ-FM Argentia, Newfoundland
CJMY-FM Clarenville, Newfoundland
CKOZ-FM Corner Brook, Newfoundland
CIOZ-FM Marystown, Newfoundland
CHOZ-FM St. John's, Newfoundland
VOCM St. John's, Newfoundland
CIOS-FM Stephenville, Newfoundland
CJOZ-FM Bonavista Bay, Newfoundland
CKMY-FM Grand Falls, Newfoundland
CKSJ-FM Saint John's, Newfoundland
CJLS-FM-1 Barrington, Nova Scotia
CJLSFM Barrington, Nova Scotia
CKBW-FM Bridgewater, Nova Scotia
CFLT-FM Dartmouth, Nova Scotia
CIOO-FM Halifax, Nova Scotia
CKUL-FM Halifax, Nova Scotia
CKWM-FM Kentville, Nova Scotia
CKEC-FM New Glasgow, Nova Scotia
CJLS-FM-2 New Tusket, Nova Scotia
CIGO-FM Port Hawkesbury, Nova Scotia
CJIJ-FM Sydney, Nova Scotia
CKPE-FM Sydney, Nova Scotia
CJCD-FM-1 Hay River, Northwest Territories
CKHR-FM Hay River, Northwest Territories
CJCD-FM Yellowknife, Northwest Territories
CIMA-FM Alliston, Ontario
CHMY-FM-1 Arnprior, Ontario
CHMS-FM Bancroft, Ontario
CHAY-FM Barrie, Ontario
CHBY-FM Barry's Bay, Ontario
CIGL-FM Belleville, Ontario
CJOJ-FM Belleville, Ontario
CFBG-FM Bracebridge, Ontario
CKPC-FM Brantford, Ontario
CIYM-FM Brighton, Ontario
CFJR-FM Brockville, Ontario
CJPT-FM Brockville, Ontario
CFGM-FM Caledon, Ontario
CKSY-FM Chatham, Ontario
CHRC-FM Clarence-Rockland, Ontario
CKSG-FM Cobourg, Ontario
CHPB-FM Cochrane, Ontario
CKCB-FM Collingwood, Ontario
CFLG-FM Cornwall, Ontario
CKDR-FM Dryden, Ontario
CKNR-FM Elliot Lake, Ontario
CJBB-FM Englehart, Ontario
CJJM-FM Espanola, Ontario
CKXM-FM Exeter, Ontario
CFOB-FM Fort Frances, Ontario
CHWC-FM Goderich, Ontario
CIMJ-FM Guelph, Ontario
CJOY Guelph, Ontario
CFZN-FM Haliburton, Ontario
CING-FM Hamilton, Ontario
CKLH-FM Hamilton, Ontario
CHPR-FM Hawkesbury, Ontario
CKHK-FM Hawkesbury, Ontario
CHYK-FM-3 Hearst, Ontario
CINN-FM Hearst, Ontario
CFBK-FM Huntsville, Ontario
CFIF-FM Iroquois Falls, Ontario
CKAP-FM Kapuskasing, Ontario
CKLY-FM Kawartha Lakes, Ontario
CJRL-FM Kenora, Ontario
CFLY-FM Kingston, Ontario
CKWS-FM Kingston, Ontario
CJKL-FM Kirkland Lake, Ontario
CHYM-FM Kitchener, Ontario
CHYR-FM Leamington, Ontario
CIQM-FM London, Ontario
CFNO-FM Marathon, Ontario
CJGB-FM Meaford, Ontario
CKYM-FM Napanee, Ontario
CKDX-FM Newmarket, Ontario
CHUR-FM North Bay, Ontario
CKMO-FM Orangeville, Ontario
CISO-FM Orillia, Ontario
CISS-FM Ottawa, Ontario
CJMJ-FM Ottawa, Ontario
CJWL-FM Ottawa, Ontario
CIXK-FM Owen Sound, Ontario
CIMY-FM Pembroke, Ontario
CKPT-FM Peterborough, Ontario
CKRU-FM Petersborough, Ontario
CFPS-FM Port Elgin, Ontario
CKPP-FM Prescott, Ontario
CHMY-FM Renfrew, Ontario
CFGX-FM Sarnia, Ontario
CHOK Sarnia, Ontario
CHAS-FM Sault Ste. Marie, Ontario
CHCD-FM Simcoe, Ontario
CKDR-2-FM Sioux Lookout, Ontario
CJET-FM Smiths Falls, Ontario
CHRE-FM St. Catharines, Ontario
CFHK-FM St. Thomas, Ontario
CHGK-FM Stratford, Ontario
CJMI-FM Strathroy, Ontario
CFSF-FM Sturgeon Falls, Ontario
CBBS-FM Sudbury, Ontario
CHYC-FM Sudbury, Ontario
CJMX-FM Sudbury, Ontario
CJUK-FM Thunder Bay, Ontario
CKPR-FM Thunder Bay, Ontario
CHMT-FM Timmins, Ontario
CHYK-FM Timmins, Ontario
CKGB-FM Timmins, Ontario
CHBM-FM Toronto, Ontario
CHFI-FM Toronto, Ontario
CHUM-FM Toronto, Ontario
CHGB-FM Wasaga Beach, Ontario
CFCA-FM Waterloo, Ontario
CKWR-FM Waterloo, Ontario
CJWA-FM Wawa, Ontario
CIDR-FM Windsor, Ontario
CKNX-FM Wingham, Ontario
CHTN-FM Charlottetown, Prince Edward Island
CJRW-FM Summerside, Prince Edward Island
CFGT-FM Alma, Québec
CFVM-FM Amqui, Québec
CJAN-FM Asbestos, Québec
CIHO-FM Baie St Paul, Québec
CHLC-FM Baie-Comeau, Québec
CIEU-FM Carleton, Québec
CHAI-FM Chateauguay, Québec
CKXO-FM Chibougamau, Québec
CFVD Degelis, Québec
CHVD-FM Dolbeau-Mistassini, Québec
CHRD-FM Drummondville, Québec
CJDM-FM Drummondville, Québec
CFRP Forestville, Québec
CJRG-FM Gaspe, Québec
CHLX-FM Gatineau, Québec
CFXM Granby, Québec
CFTH-FM-1 Harrington Harbour, Québec
CILE-FM Havre-Saint-Pierre, Québec
CHSV-FM Hudson/Saint-Lazare, Québec
CJLM-FM Joliette, Québec
CKRK-FM Kahnawake, Québec
CKGS-FM La Baie, Québec
CHOX-FM La Pocatiere, Québec
CJIT-FM Lac Megantic, Québec
CFIN-FM Lac-Etchemin, Québec
CJLA-FM Lachute, Québec
CFGL-FM Laval, Québec
CFEL-FM Levis, Québec
CHAA-FM Longueuil, Québec
CHGA-FM Maniwaki, Québec
CHEF-FM Matagami, Québec
CHRM-FM Matane, Québec
CFLO-FM Mont-Laurier, Québec
CHRF Montréal, Québec
CITE-FM Montréal, Québec
CJFM-FM Montréal, Québec
CKNA-FM Natashquan, Québec
CKYQ-FM Plessisville, Québec
CHIK-FM Québec, Québec
CION-FM Québec, Québec
CITF-FM Québec, Québec
CJEC-FM Québec, Québec
CKRL-FM Québec, Québec
CJBR-FM Rimouski, Québec
CJOI-FM Rimouski, Québec
CKMN-FM Rimouski-Mont Joli, Québec
CIEL-FM Rivière-du-Loup, Québec
CHRL-FM Roberval, Québec
CHOA-FM Rouyn-Noranda, Québec
CFIX-FM Saguenay, Québec
CKRS-FM Saguenay, Québec
CJAS-FM Saint Augustin, Québec

CKRB-FM Saint Georges-de-Beauce, Québec
CJDS-FM Saint Pamphile, Québec
CJMC-FM Sainte Anne des Monts, Québec
CHEQ-FM Sainte-Marie, Québec
CKCN-FM Sept-Îles, Québec
CFGE-FM Sherbrooke, Québec
CFNJ-FM St-Gabriel, Québec
CKLD-FM Thetford Mines, Québec
CJEB-FM Trois Rivieres, Québec
CKOD-FM Valleyfield, Québec
CFDA-FM Victoriaville, Québec
CKVM-FM Ville-Marie, Québec
CFYM Kindersley, Saskatchewan
CKVX-FM Kindersley, British Columbia
CJAW-FM Moose Jaw, Saskatchewan
CJCQ-FM North Battleford, Saskatchewan
CFNK-FM Pinehouse Lake, Saskatchewan
CFMM-FM Prince Albert, Saskatchewan
CHMX-FM Regina, Saskatchewan
CIZL-FM Regina, Saskatchewan
CJYM Rosetown, Saskatchewan
CFMC-FM Saskatoon, Saskatchewan
CFWD-FM Saskatoon, Saskatchewan
CJMK-FM Saskatoon, Saskatchewan
CIMG-FM Swift Current, Saskatchewan
CKFI-FM Swift Current, Saskatchewan
CKRC-FM Weyburn, Saskatchewan
CFGW-FM Yorkton, Saskatchewan
CFGW-FM Yorkton, Saskatchewan

Agriculture

CFAM Altona, Manitoba

Alternative

CFEX-FM Calgary, Alberta
CHPK-FM Calgary, Alberta
CHDI-FM Edmonton, Alberta
CJSR-FM Edmonton, Alberta
CFOX-FM Vancouver, British Columbia
CKPK-FM Vancouver, British Columbia
CHSR-FM Fredericton, New Brunswick
CHMR-FM Saint John's, Newfoundland
CFNY-FM Brampton, Ontario
CIOI-FM Hamilton, Ontario
CFPL-FM London, Ontario
CHRW-FM London, Ontario
CILV-FM Ottawa, Ontario
CKDJ-FM Ottawa, Ontario
CIMI-FM Charlesbourg, Québec
CISM-FM Montréal, Québec
CFYT-FM Dawson City, Yukon Territory

Arabic

CHOU Montréal, Québec

Chinese

CHMB Vancouver, British Columbia
CHKT(AM) Toronto, Ontario

Christian

CJLI Calgary, Alberta
CJSI-FM Calgary, Alberta
CJCA Edmonton, Alberta
CJRY-FM Edmonton, Alberta
CKOS-FM Fort McMurray, Alberta
CHRB High River, Alberta
CJLT-FM Medicine Hat, Alberta
CKRD-FM Red Deer, Alberta
CHIM-FM Kelowna, British Columbia
CIAJ-FM Prince Rupert, British Columbia
CHVN-FM Winnipeg, Manitoba
CKJS Winnipeg, Manitoba
CITA-FM Moncton, New Brunswick
CKOE-FM Moncton, New Brunswick
CINB-FM Saint John, New Brunswick
CIRP-FM Spryfield, Nova Scotia
CINU-FM Truro, Nova Scotia
CFSH-FM Apsley, Ontario
CFWC-FM Brantford, Ontario
CKGW-FM Chatham, Ontario
CJGM-FM Gananoque, Ontario
CHJX-FM London, Ontario
CJYE Oakville, Ontario
CJTK-FM Sudbury, Ontario
CKSO-FM Sudbury, Ontario
CJOA-FM Thunder Bay, Ontario
CJFH-FM Woodstock, Ontario
CHIC-FM Rouyn-Noranda, Québec

CFAQ-FM Blucher, Saskatchewan
CIAY-FM Whitehorse, Yukon Territory

Classic Rock

CFGQ-FM Calgary, Alberta
CJXK-FM Cold Lake, Alberta
CIRK-FM Edmonton, Alberta
CKJX-FM Olds, Alberta
CFDV-FM Red Deer, Alberta
CIZZ-FM Red Deer, Alberta
CKIQFM Big White Ski, British Columbia
CKQR-FM Castlegar, British Columbia
CIFM-FM Kamloops, British Columbia
CKKO-FM Kelowna, British Columbia
CFMI-FM New Westminster, British Columbia
CFNR-FM Terrace, British Columbia
CKKQ-FM Victoria, British Columbia
CITI-FM Winnipeg, Manitoba
CJMO-FM Moncton, New Brunswick
CHNI-FM Saint John, New Brunswick
VOCM-FM St. John's, Newfoundland
CKXX-FM Corner Brook, Newfoundland
CKXD-FM Gander, Newfoundland
CKXG-FM Grand Falls, Newfoundland
CFRQ-FM Dartmouth, Nova Scotia
CIJK-FM Kentville, Nova Scotia
CHER-FM Sydney, Nova Scotia
CJIJ-FM Sydney, Nova Scotia
CFJB-FM Barrie, Ontario
CIQB-FM Barrie, Ontario
CHBY-FM Barry's Bay, Ontario
CKTI-FM Kettle Point, Ontario
CFMK-FM Kingston, Ontario
CICZ-FM Midland, Ontario
CILQ-FM Toronto, Ontario
CJTN-FM Trenton, Ontario
CIXL-FM Welland, Ontario
CIBU-FM Wingham, Ontario
CKQK-FM Charlottetown, Prince Edward Island
CKYK-FM Alma, Québec
CFVM-FM Amqui, Québec
CIMF-FM Gatineau, Québec
CHOM-FM Montréal, Québec
CJMF-FM Québec, Québec
CKIA-FM Québec, Québec
CFYX-FM Rimouski, Québec
CJSO-FM Sorel, Québec
CHEY-FM Trois Rivieres, Québec
CHGO-FM Val d'Or, Québec
CJNE-FM Nipawin, Saskatchewan
CFWF-FM Regina, Saskatchewan
CKCK-FM Regina, Saskatchewan
CFET-FM Tagish, Yukon Territory
CHON-FM Whitehorse, Yukon Territory

Classical

CBCX-FM Calgary, Alberta
CBUX-FM Vancouver, British Columbia
CKCL-FM Winnipeg, Manitoba
CBAL-FM Moncton, New Brunswick
CBAX-FM Halifax, Nova Scotia
CFMX-FM Cobourg, Ontario
CFMO-FM Collingwood, Ontario
CFMZ-FM Toronto, Ontario
CBJX-FM Chicoutimi, Québec
CJPX-FM Montréal, Québec
CBK-FM Regina, Saskatchewan
CBKS-FM Saskatoon, Saskatchewan

Comedy

CKMX Calgary, Alberta
CJEF-FM Saint John, New Brunswick
CHAM Hamilton, Ontario
CKSL London, Ontario

Contemporary Hits/Top 40

CJEG-FM Bonnyville, Alberta
CHFM-FM Calgary, Alberta
CIBK-FM Calgary, Alberta
CJAQ-FM Calgary, Alberta
CKMP-FM Calgary, Alberta
CFMG-FM Edmonton, Alberta
CHBN-FM Edmonton, Alberta
CJNW-FM Edmonton, Alberta
CKEA-FM Edmonton, Alberta
CKNO-FM Edmonton, Alberta
CFXE-FM Edson, Alberta
CFVR-FM Fort McMurray, Alberta
CHFT-FM Fort McMurray, Alberta
CKFT-FM Fort Saskatchewan, Alberta
CFRI-FM Grande Prairie, Alberta
CFXH-FM Hinton, Alberta
CILB-FM Lac La Biche, Alberta
CJUV-FM Lacombe, Alberta
CJOC-FM Lethbridge, Alberta
CJCY-FM Medicine Hat, Alberta
CKRI-FM Red Deer, Alberta
CJBZ-FM Taber, Alberta
CKKS-FM Chilliwack, British Columbia
CKAY-FM Gibsons, British Columbia
CKRV-FM Kamloops, British Columbia
CHSU-FM Kelowna, British Columbia
CKTK-FM Kitimat, British Columbia
CIPN-FM Pender Harbour, British Columbia
CJMG-FM Penticton, British Columbia
CJAV-FM Port Alberni, British Columbia
CHTK-FM Prince Rupert, British Columbia
CFUN-FM Sechelt, British Columbia
CFBT-FM Vancouver, British Columbia
CICF-FM Vernon, British Columbia
CHTT-FM Victoria, British Columbia
CJPG-FM Portage la Prairie, Manitoba
CJSB-FM Swan River, Manitoba
CHWE-FM Winnepeg, Manitoba
CKMM-FM Winnipeg, Manitoba
CKLE-FM Bathurst, Québec
CFAI-FM Edmundston, New Brunswick
CIBX-FM Fredericton, New Brunswick
CKTP-FM Fredericton Centre, New Brunswick
CKCW-FM Moncton, New Brunswick
CJYC-FM Saint John, New Brunswick
CKIX-FM St. John's, Newfoundland
CJFX-FM Antigonish, Nova Scotia
CFLT-FM Dartmouth, Nova Scotia
CHNS-FM Halifax, Nova Scotia
CJCH-FM Halifax, Nova Scotia
CHRK-FM Sydney, Nova Scotia
CKMB-FM Barrie, Ontario
CJOJ-FM Belleville, Ontario
CJSS-FM Cornwall, Ontario
CFLZ-FM Fort Erie, Ontario
CJOY Guelph, Ontario
CFBK-FM Huntsville, Ontario
CKVV-FM Kemptville, Ontario
CKBT-FM Kitchener-Waterloo, Ontario
CHST-FM London, Ontario
CJED-FM Niagara Falls, Ontario
CFXN-FM North Bay, Ontario
CIDC-FM Orangeville, Ontario
CIHT-FM Ottawa, Ontario
CISS-FM Ottawa, Ontario
CKQB-FM Ottawa, Ontario
CJOS-FM Owen Sound, Ontario
CKLP-FM Parry Sound, Ontario
CKDR-5-FM Red Lake, Ontario
CHAS-FM Sault Ste. Marie, Ontario
CJET-FM Smiths Falls, Ontario
CHNO-FM Sudbury, Ontario
CHYC-FM Sudbury, Ontario
CIGM-FM Sudbury, Ontario
CIRR-FM Toronto, Ontario
CKFM-FM Toronto, Ontario
CKIS-FM Toronto, Ontario
CKQV-FM Vermilion Bay, Ontario
CHTN-FM Charlottetown, Prince Edward Island
CKQK-FM Charlottetown, Prince Edward Island
CIEU-FM Carleton, Québec
CFVD Degelis, Québec
CFMF-FM Fermont, Québec
CKTF-FM Gatineau, Québec
CJIT-FM Lac Megantic, Québec
CFEL-FM Levis, Québec
CIMO-FM Magog, Québec
CBGA-FM Matane, Québec
CHRF Montréal, Québec
CKMF-FM Montréal, Québec
CIPC-FM Port-Cartier, Québec
CJMM-FM Rouyn-Noranda, Québec
CJAB-FN Saguenay, Québec
CHJM-FM St-George-Beauce, Québec
CFJO-FM Thetford Mines, Québec
CIGB-FM Trois Rivieres, Québec
CHSN-FM Estevan, Saskatchewan
CHBO-FM Humboldt, Saskatchewan
CFDM-FM Meadow Lake, Saskatchewan
CKJH(AM) Melfort, Saskatchewan
CJYM Rosetown, Saskatchewan
CFMC-FM Saskatoon, Saskatchewan
CFWD-FM Saskatoon, Saskatchewan
CIMG-FM Swift Current, Saskatchewan

Country

CJPR-FM Blairmore, Alberta
CFNA-FM Bonnyville, Alberta
CIBQ-FM Brooks, Alberta
CKRY-FM Calgary, Alberta
CFCW Camrose, Alberta
CIBW-FM Drayton Valley, Alberta
CKDQ Drumheller, Alberta
CISN-FM Edmonton, Alberta
CJOK-FM Fort McMurray, Alberta
CJXX-FM Grande Prairie, Alberta
CKHL-FM High Level, Alberta
CKVH-FM High Prairie, Alberta
CFXO-FM High River, Alberta
CFWE-FM Lac La Biche, Alberta
CJLD-FM Leduc, Alberta
CHLB-FM Lethbridge, Alberta
CKSA-FM Lloydminster, Alberta
CHAT-FM Medicine Hat, Alberta
CKLJ-FM Olds, Alberta
CKGY-FM Red Deer, Alberta
CHSP-FM St. Paul, Alberta
CKSQ-FM Stettler, Alberta
CKWB-FM Westlock, Alberta
CIXM-FM Whitecourt, Alberta
CKBX 100 Mile House, British Columbia
CKQC-FM Abbotsford, British Columbia
CHBZ-FM Cranbrook, British Columbia
CJDC Dawson Creek, British Columbia
CJKC-FM Kamloops, British Columbia
CIGV-FM Penticton, British Columbia
CJCI-FM Prince George, British Columbia
CKCQ-FM Quesnel, British Columbia
CJFW-FM Terrace, British Columbia
CHMZ-FM Tofino, British Columbia
CJJR-FM Vancouver, British Columbia
CIVH Vanderhoof, British Columbia
CKWL Williams Lake, British Columbia
CKLQ Brandon, Manitoba
CKXA-FM Brandon, Manitoba
CKDM Dauphin, Manitoba
CFRY Portage La Prairie, Manitoba
CHPO-FM Portage La Prairie, Manitoba
CFPX-FM Pukatawagan, Manitoba
CFQX-FM Selkirk, Manitoba
CJXR-FM Steinbach, Manitoba
CJAR The Pas, Manitoba
CKMW-FM Winkler-Morden, Manitoba
CFRK-FM Fredericton, New Brunswick
CJRI-FM Fredericton, New Brunswick
CKHJ Fredericton, New Brunswick
CFAN-FM Miramichi, New Brunswick
CHOY-FM Moncton, New Brunswick
CJXL-FM Moncton, New Brunswick
CFBC Saint John, New Brunswick
CHSJ-FM Saint John, New Brunswick
CHTD-FM Saint Stephen, New Brunswick
CKIM Baie Verte, Newfoundland
CKVO Clarenville, Newfoundland
CFCB Corner Brook, Newfoundland
CKGA Gander, Newfoundland
CKCM Grand Falls, Newfoundland
CHCM Marystown, Newfoundland
VOCM St. John's, Newfoundland
CFSX Stephenville, Newfoundland
CHVO-FM Carbonear, Newfoundland
CFLC-FM Churchill Falls, Newfoundland
CFCV-FM St. Andrew's, Newfoundland
CKDH-FM Amherst, Nova Scotia
CJHK-FM Bridgewater, Nova Scotia
CKJM-FM Cheticamp, Nova Scotia
CKDY Digby, Nova Scotia
CKOA-FM Glace Bay, Nova Scotia
CHFX-FM Halifax, Nova Scotia
CKHZ-FM Halifax, Nova Scotia
CKEN-FM Kentville, Nova Scotia
CKAD Middleton, Nova Scotia
CJCB Sydney, Nova Scotia
CKCH-FM Sydney, Nova Scotia
CKTY-FM Truro, Nova Scotia
CFAB Windsor, Nova Scotia
CKLB-FM Yellowknife, Northwest Territories
CJKX-FM Ajax, Ontario
CHCQ-FM Belleville, Ontario
CJBQ Belleville, Ontario
CKPC Brantford, Ontario
CFCO Chatham, Ontario
CHKX-FM Hamilton, Ontario
CFQK-FM Kaministiquia, Ontario
CKTI-FM Kettle Point, Ontario
CKXC-FM Kingston, Ontario
CIKZ-FM Kitchener, Ontario
CJSP-FM Leamington, Ontario
CFRM-FM Little Current, Manitoba
CJBX-FM London, Ontario
CHMO(AM) Moosonee, Ontario
CKAT North Bay, Ontario
CKRZ-FM Ohsweken, Ontario
CICX-FM Orillia, Ontario
CKKL-FM Ottawa, Ontario
CKYC-FM Owen Sound, Ontario
CHVR-FM Pembroke, Ontario
CJHR-FM Renfrew, Ontario
CJQM-FM Sault Ste. Marie, Ontario
CFDC-FM Shelburne, Ontario
CKBY-FM Smiths Falls, Ontario
CICS-FM Sudbury, Ontario
CKTG-FM Thunder Bay, Ontario
CJDL-FM Tillsonburg, Ontario
CKHC-FM Toronto, Ontario
CJWF-FM Windsor, Ontario
CKNX Wingham, Ontario
CKDK-FM Woodstock, Ontario
CFCY-FM Charlottetown, Prince Edward Island
CFVD Degelis, Québec
CHIPFM Fort-Coulonge, Québec
CFTH-FM-1 Harrington Harbour, Québec
CKAJ-FM Jonquiere, Québec
CKKI-FM Kahnawake, Québec
CKRK-FM Kahnawake, Québec
CFIN-FM Lac-Etchemin, Québec
CFIC-FM Listuguj, Québec
CHRG-FM Maria (Reserve), Québec
CJMS Montréal, Québec
CKIA-FM Québec, Québec
CKMN-FM Rimouski-Mont Joli, Québec
CHUN-FM Rouyn-Noranda, Québec
CJSL Estevan, Saskatchewan
CFMQ-FM Hudson Bay, Saskatchewan
CJLR-FM La Ronge, Saskatchewan
CFDM-FM Meadow Lake, Saskatchewan
CJNS-FM Meadow Lake, Saskatchewan
CJVR-FM Melfort, Saskatchewan
CILG-FM Moose Jaw, Saskatchewan
CJNB North Battleford, Saskatchewan
CKBI Prince Albert, Saskatchewan
CHBD-FM Regina, Saskatchewan
CKRM Regina, Saskatchewan
CJWW Saskatoon, Saskatchewan
CKBL-FM Saskatoon, Saskatchewan
CJSN Shaunavon, Saskatchewan
CKSW Swift Current, Saskatchewan
CFSL Weyburn, Saskatchewan
CJGX Yorkton, Saskatchewan
CJGX Yorkton, Saskatchewan
CHON-FM Whitehorse, Yukon Territory

Easy Listening

CJRB Boissevain, Manitoba
CKHK-FM Hawkesbury, Ontario
CJGB-FM Meaford, Ontario
CKOT-FM Tillsonburg, Ontario

Ethnic

CHKF-FM Calgary, Alberta
CKAV-FM-3 Calgary, Alberta
CKAV-FM-4 Edmonton, Alberta
CKER-FM Edmonton, Alberta
CHKG-FM Richmond, British Columbia
CJRJ Vancouver, British Columbia
CKAV-FM-2 Vancouver, British Columbia
CKYE-FM Vancouver, British Columbia
CKJS Winnipeg, Manitoba
CKQN-FM Baker Lake, Nunavut
CIAO Brampton, Ontario
CHFN-FM Cape Croker (Neyaashiinigmiing), Ontario
CJMR Oakville, Ontario
CJLL-FM Ottawa, Ontario
CKAV-FM-9 Ottawa, Ontario
CJVF-FM Scarborough, Ontario
CKBK-FM Thamesville, Ontario
CHIN Toronto, Ontario
CHTO Toronto, Ontario
CIRV-FM Toronto, Ontario
CJSA-FM Toronto, Ontario
CKAV-FM Toronto, Ontario
CJAM-FM Windsor, Ontario
CKUJ-FM Kuujjuaq, Québec
CHUT-FM Lac-Simon (Louvicourt), Québec
CFMB Montréal, Québec
CHOU Montréal, Québec
CJWI Montréal, Québec
CKIN-FM Montréal, Québec
CJRS Sherbrooke, Québec
CJCF-FM Cumberland House, Saskatchewan
CJLR-FM La Ronge, Saskatchewan

French

CBRFFM Calgary, Alberta
CKXU-FM Lethbridge, Alberta
CILS-FM Victoria, British Columbia
CBAF-FM Moncton, New Brunswick
CKRH-FM Halifax, Nova Scotia
CFRT-FM Iqaluit, Nunavut
CHUO-FM Ottawa, Ontario
CBON-FM Timmins, Ontario
CHOQ-FM Toronto, Ontario
CKHC-FM Toronto, Ontario
CFID-FM Acton Vale, Québec
CFGT-FM Alma, Québec
CKYK-FM Alma, Québec
CFMV-FM Chandler, Québec
CKXO-FM Chibougamau, Québec
CHVD-FM Dolbeau-Mistassini, Québec
CKII-FM Dolbeau-Mistassini, Québec
CHHO-FM Louiseville, Québec
CHUK-FM Mashteuiatsh (Pointe-Bleue), Québec
CHRL-FM Roberval, Québec
CFUT-FM Shawinigan, Québec
CFAK-FM Sherbrooke, Québec
CJTB-FM Tête-à-la-Baleine, Québec
CJVD-FM Vaudreuil-Dorion, Québec
CFRG-FM Gravelbourg, Saskatchewan
CKZP-FM Zenon Park, Saskatchewan

Gospel

CJRI-FM Fredericton, New Brunswick
VOAR St. John's, Newfoundland

Greek

CHTO Toronto, Ontario

Jazz

CBCX-FM Calgary, Alberta
CKUA-FM Edmonton, Alberta
CBUX-FM Vancouver, British Columbia
CKCL-FM Winnipeg, Manitoba
CBAL-FM Moncton, New Brunswick
CBAX-FM Halifax, Nova Scotia
CHRW-FM London, Ontario
CKLU-FM Sudbury, Ontario
CJRT-FM Toronto, Ontario
CHLX-FM Gatineau, Québec
CKRL-FM Québec, Québec
CBK-FM Regina, Saskatchewan
CBKS-FM Saskatoon, Saskatchewan

Light Rock

CJYQ St. John's, Newfoundland
CKZM-FM St. Thomas, Ontario
CHOE-FM Matane, Québec

Native American

CKWT-FM Sioux Lookout, Ontario

News

CBR Calgary, Alberta
CBR-FM Calgary, Alberta
CBRFFM Calgary, Alberta
CFFR Calgary, Alberta
CHQR Calgary, Alberta
CBX Edmonton, Alberta
CBX-FM Edmonton, Alberta
CHED Edmonton, Alberta
CHFA-10-FM Edmonton, Alberta
CHQT Edmonton, Alberta
CHRB High River, Alberta
CBTEFM Crawford Bay, British Columbia
CBYK-FM Kamloops, British Columbia
CBTK-FM Kelowna, British Columbia
CBTKFM Kelowna, British Columbia
CKNW New Westminster, British Columbia
CBYG-FM Prince George, British Columbia
CFPR Prince Rupert, British Columbia
CBU Vancouver, British Columbia
CBU-FM Vancouver, British Columbia
CBUF-FM Vancouver, British Columbia

CKWX Vancouver, British Columbia
CBCV-FM Victoria, British Columbia
CFAM Altona, Manitoba
CKSB-FM St. Boniface, Manitoba
CBWK-FM Thompson, Manitoba
CBW Winnipeg, Manitoba
CBW-FM Winnipeg, Manitoba
CJOB Winnipeg, Manitoba
CKSB-10-FM Winnipeg, Manitoba
CBZ-FM Fredericton, New Brunswick
CKIM Baie Verte, Newfoundland
CBGY Bonavista Bay, Newfoundland
CKVO Clarenville, Newfoundland
CBY Corner Brook, Newfoundland
CBG Gander, Newfoundland
CKGA Gander, Newfoundland
CBT Grand Falls-Windsor, Newfoundland
VOCM St. John's, Newfoundland
CFGB-FM Happy Valley-Goose Bay, Newfoundland
CBN-FM Saint John's, Newfoundland
CIFA-FM Comeauville, Nova Scotia
CBAF-FM-5 Halifax, Nova Scotia
CBH-FM Halifax, Nova Scotia
CBHA-FM Halifax, Nova Scotia
CJNI-FM Halifax, Nova Scotia
CBI Sydney, Nova Scotia
CBI-FM Sydney, Nova Scotia
CHAK Inuvik, Northwest Territories
CFYK-FM Yellowknife, Northwest Territories
CFFB Iqaluit, Nunavut
CBQR-FM Rankin Inlet, Nunavut
CJFB-FM Bolton, Ontario
CKPC Brantford, Ontario
CHFN-FM Cape Croker (Neyaashiinigmiing), Ontario
CFCO Chatham, Ontario
CHML Hamilton, Ontario
CBQX-FM Kenora, Ontario
CKGL Kitchener, Ontario
CFPL London, Ontario
CIWW Ottawa, Ontario
CFOS Owen Sound, Ontario
CBEG-FM Sarnia, Ontario
CBQL-FM Savant Lake, Ontario
CBCSFM Sudbury, Ontario
CKLU-FM Sudbury, Ontario
CBQ-FM Thunder Bay, Ontario
CBQT-FM Thunder Bay, Ontario
CBL-FM Toronto, Ontario
CBLA-FM Toronto, Ontario
CFTR Toronto, Ontario
CBE-FM Windsor, Ontario
CBEF Windsor, Ontario
CHRD-FM Drummondville, Québec
CJRD-FM Drummondville, Québec
CBMR-FM Fermont, Québec
CFIM-FM Iles-de-la-Madeleine, Québec
CBV-FM-6 La Malbaie, Québec
CKWE-FM Maniwaki (Kitigan Zibi Anishinabeg, Québec
CBME-FM Montréal, Québec
CBV-FM Québec, Québec
CBVE-FM Québec, Québec
CJBR-FM Rimouski, Québec
CBGN(AM) Sainte Anne des Monts, Québec
CKCN-FM Sept-Îles, Québec
CFLX-FM Sherbrooke, Québec
CFEI-FM St-Hyacinthe, Québec
CJME Regina, Saskatchewan
CKOM Saskatoon, Saskatchewan
CBK Watrous, Saskatchewan

News/Talk

CHQR Calgary, Alberta
CHED Edmonton, Alberta
CHNL Kamloops, British Columbia
CKFR Kelowna, British Columbia
CKNW New Westminster, British Columbia
CHMJ Vancouver, British Columbia
CFAX Victoria, British Columbia
CJOB Winnipeg, Manitoba
CBZ-FM Fredericton, New Brunswick
CBZF-FM Fredericton, New Brunswick
CBAF-FM Moncton, New Brunswick
CBAM-FM Moncton, New Brunswick
CBD-FM Saint John, New Brunswick
CKIM Baie Verte, Newfoundland
CKVO Clarenville, Newfoundland
CBY Corner Brook, Newfoundland
CBG Gander, Newfoundland
CFLN-FM Goose Bay, Newfoundland
CKCM Grand Falls, Newfoundland
CBT Grand Falls-Windsor, Newfoundland
VOCM St. John's, Newfoundland
CFSX Stephenville, Newfoundland
CFLC-FM Churchill Falls, Newfoundland
CFGB-FM Happy Valley-Goose Bay, Newfoundland
CBDQ-FM Labrador City, Newfoundland
CBN-FM Saint John's, Newfoundland
CFCV-FM St. Andrew's, Newfoundland
CBN St. John's, Newfoundland
CBHA-FM Halifax, Nova Scotia
CJNI-FM Halifax, Nova Scotia
CHML Hamilton, Ontario
CKGL Kitchener, Ontario
CFPL London, Ontario
CJBK London, Ontario
CIWW Ottawa, Ontario
CFOS Owen Sound, Ontario
CFMJ Richmond Hill, Ontario
CKTB St. Catharines, Ontario
CBCSFM Sudbury, Ontario
CKLU-FM Sudbury, Ontario
CFRB Toronto, Ontario
CKLW Windsor, Ontario
CFIM-FM Iles-de-la-Madeleine, Québec
CBGA-FM Matane, Québec
CJAD Montréal, Québec
CBV-FM Québec, Québec
CBVE-FM Québec, Québec
CJBR-FM Rimouski, Québec
CKCN-FM Sept-Îles, Québec
CFLX-FM Sherbrooke, Québec
CJME Regina, Saskatchewan
CKOM Saskatoon, Saskatchewan

Oldies

CKBA-FM Athabasca, Alberta
CFXL-FM Calgary, Alberta
CFCW-FM Camrose, Alberta
CKEA-FM Edmonton, Alberta
CKRA-FM Edmonton, Alberta
CFXH-FM Hinton, Alberta
CILB-FM Lac La Biche, Alberta
CHBW-FM Rocky Mountain House, Alberta
CHSL-FM Slave Lake, Alberta
CKJR Wetaskiwin, Alberta
CHAD-FM Dawson Creek, British Columbia
CHNL Kamloops, British Columbia
CKKC-FM Nelson, British Columbia
CIBH-FM Parksville, British Columbia
CKOR Penticton, British Columbia
CFNI Port Hardy, British Columbia
CKDV-FM Prince George, British Columbia
CISL Richmond, British Columbia
CHLG-FM Vancouver, British Columbia
CHIQ-FM Winnipeg, Manitoba
CJNU-FM Winnipeg, Manitoba
CFQM-FM Moncton, New Brunswick
VOWR St. John's, Newfoundland
CHNS-FM Halifax, Nova Scotia
CJBQ Belleville, Ontario
CJSS-FM Cornwall, Ontario
CFZN-FM Haliburton, Ontario
CIYN-FM Kincardine, Ontario
CKKW-FM Kitchener, Ontario
CKDO Oshawa, Ontario
CJOT-FM Ottawa, Ontario
CFOS Owen Sound, Ontario
CJCS-FM Stratford, Ontario
CHNO-FM Sudbury, Ontario
CHMT-FM Timmins, Ontario
CFZM Toronto, Ontario
CKWW Windsor, Ontario
CFTH-FM-1 Harrington Harbour, Québec
CHRG-FM Maria (Reserve), Québec
CFZZ-FM Saint Jean-Iberville, Québec
CFEI-FM St-Hyacinthe, Québec
CJVD-FM Vaudreuil-Dorion, Québec
CHAB Moose Jaw, Saskatchewan
CJNE-FM Nipawin, Saskatchewan
CKCK-FM Regina, Saskatchewan

Public Affairs

CBR Calgary, Alberta
CBR-FM Calgary, Alberta
CBX Edmonton, Alberta
CBX-FM Edmonton, Alberta
CHFA-10-FM Edmonton, Alberta
CBYK-FM Kamloops, British Columbia
CBTK-FM Kelowna, British Columbia
CBYG-FM Prince George, British Columbia
CFPR Prince Rupert, British Columbia
CBU Vancouver, British Columbia
CBU-FM Vancouver, British Columbia
CBUF-FM Vancouver, British Columbia
CBCV-FM Victoria, British Columbia
CKSB-FM St. Boniface, Manitoba
CBWK-FM Thompson, Manitoba
CBW Winnipeg, Manitoba
CBW-FM Winnipeg, Manitoba
CKSB-10-FM Winnipeg, Manitoba
CBN-FM Saint John's, Newfoundland
CBAF-FM-5 Halifax, Nova Scotia
CBH-FM Halifax, Nova Scotia
CBI Sydney, Nova Scotia
CBI-FM Sydney, Nova Scotia
CHAK Inuvik, Northwest Territories
CFYK-FM Yellowknife, Northwest Territories
CFFB Iqaluit, Nunavut
CBQR-FM Rankin Inlet, Nunavut
CJLX-FM Belleville, Ontario
CBQX-FM Kenora, Ontario
CBEG-FM Sarnia, Ontario
CBQL-FM Savant Lake, Ontario
CBL-FM Toronto, Ontario
CBLA-FM Toronto, Ontario
CBE-FM Windsor, Ontario
CBEF Windsor, Ontario
CJBE-FM Port-Menier, Québec
CBKA-FM La Ronge, Saskatchewan

Religious

VOAR St. John's, Newfoundland
CHSB-FM Bedford, Nova Scotia
CKPC Brantford, Ontario
CJTK-FM Sudbury, Ontario
CIRA-FM Montréal, Québec
CION-FM Québec, Québec

Rock/AOR

CJAY-FM Calgary, Alberta
CFBR-FM Edmonton, Alberta
CHDI-FM Edmonton, Alberta
CKYX-FM Fort McMurray, Alberta
CFGP-FM Grande Prairie, Alberta
CJRX-FM Lethbridge, Alberta
CKBD-FM Lethbridge, Alberta
CKLM-FM Lloydminster, Alberta
CKMH-FM Medicine Hat, Alberta
CFDV-FM Red Deer, Alberta
CKKY-FM Wainwright, Alberta
CFXW-FM Whitecourt, Alberta
CFCP-FM Comox Valley, British Columbia
CHDR-FM Cranbrook, British Columbia
CJDR-FM Fernie, British Columbia
CKRX-FM Fort Nelson, British Columbia
CKNL-FM Fort St. John, British Columbia
CKGF-FM Grand Forks, British Columbia
CIFM-FM Kamloops, British Columbia
CKLZ-FM Kelowna, British Columbia
CHWF-FM Nanaimo, British Columbia
CFMI-FM New Westminster, British Columbia
CIRX-FM Prince George, British Columbia
CFFM-FM-2 Quesnel, British Columbia
CFOX-FM Vancouver, British Columbia
CIRX-FM-1 Vanderhoof, British Columbia
CJZN-FM Victoria, British Columbia
CFFM-FM Williams Lake, British Columbia
CJAR The Pas, Manitoba
CITI-FM Winnipeg, Manitoba
CJKR-FM Winnipeg, Manitoba
CFXY-FM Fredericton, New Brunswick
CKXX-FM Corner Brook, Newfoundland
CFRQ-FM Dartmouth, Nova Scotia
CKHY-FM Halifax, Nova Scotia
CKTO-FM Truro, Nova Scotia
CJLX-FM Belleville, Ontario
CFNY-FM Brampton, Ontario
CJXY-FM Burlington, Ontario
CFZN-FM Haliburton, Ontario
CIKR-FM Kingston, Ontario
CKLC-FM Kingston, Ontario
CJDV-FM Kitchener, Ontario
CFPL-FM London, Ontario
CKFX-FM North Bay, Ontario
CKGE-FM Oshawa, Ontario
CHEZ-FM Ottawa, Ontario
CKWF-FM Peterborough, Ontario
CHKS-FM Sarnia, Ontario
CHTZ-FM St. Catharines, Ontario
CJRQ-FM Sudbury, Ontario

CJSD-FM Thunder Bay, Ontario
CJQQ-FM Timmins, Ontario
CIMX-FM Windsor, Ontario
CHLQ-FM Charlottetown, Prince Edward Island
CKYK-FM Alma, Québec
CHXX-FM Donnacona, Québec
CFTX-FM Gatineau, Québec
CKTF-FM Gatineau, Québec
CJGO-FM La Sarre, Québec
CFOR-FM Maniwaki, Québec
CIKI-FM Rimouski, Québec
CHGO-FM Val d'Or, Québec
CKSE-FM Estevan, Saskatchewan
CJHD-FM North Battleford, Saskatchewan
CHQX-FM Prince Albert, Saskatchewan
CFWF-FM Regina, Saskatchewan
CJDJ-FM Saskatoon, Saskatchewan
CHWY-FM Weyburn, Saskatchewan

Sports

CFAC Calgary, Alberta
CFRN Edmonton, Alberta
CHED Edmonton, Alberta
CHRB High River, Alberta
CHNL Kamloops, British Columbia
CKFR Kelowna, British Columbia
CFTE Vancouver, British Columbia
CKST Vancouver, British Columbia
CFRW Winnipeg, Manitoba
CJNI-FM Halifax, Nova Scotia
CKOC Hamilton, Ontario
CKGL Kitchener, Ontario
CFPL London, Ontario
CJBK London, Ontario
CHOP-FM Newmarket, Ontario
CFGO Ottawa, Ontario
CIWW Ottawa, Ontario
CJMB-FM Peterborough, Ontario
CFMJ Richmond Hill, Ontario
CHUM Toronto, Ontario
CJCL Toronto, Ontario
CKAC Montréal, Québec
CKGM Montréal, Québec
CKLX-FM Montréal, Québec
CHRC Québec, Québec

Talk

CBRFFM Calgary, Alberta
CHQR Calgary, Alberta
CHED Edmonton, Alberta
CFCH-FM Chase, British Columbia
CKNW New Westminster, British Columbia
CHMJ Vancouver, British Columbia
CFNC(AM) Cross Lake, Manitoba
CJOB Winnipeg, Manitoba
CBZ-FM Fredericton, New Brunswick
CBA-FM Moncton, New Brunswick
CKIM Baie Verte, Newfoundland
CKVO Clarenville, Newfoundland
CBY Corner Brook, Newfoundland
CKGA Gander, Newfoundland
VOCM St. John's, Newfoundland
CBDQ-FM Labrador City, Newfoundland
CIFX-FM Lewisporte, Newfoundland
CJNI-FM Halifax, Nova Scotia
CFMO-FM Collingwood, Ontario
CHML Hamilton, Ontario
CKGL Kitchener, Ontario
CFPL London, Ontario
CHOP-FM Newmarket, Ontario
CFRA Ottawa, Ontario
CIWW Ottawa, Ontario
CFOS Owen Sound, Ontario
CJMB-FM Peterborough, Ontario
CFMJ Richmond Hill, Ontario
CBCSFM Sudbury, Ontario

CKLU-FM Sudbury, Ontario
CBQ-FM Thunder Bay, Ontario
CILU-FM Thunder Bay, Ontario
CIRR-FM Toronto, Ontario
CJCL Toronto, Ontario
CIWS-FM Whitchurch-Stouffville, Ontario
CBCT-FM Charlottetown, Prince Edward Island
CHOW-FM Amos, Québec
CBJ-FM Chicoutimi, Québec
CJRD-FM Drummondville, Québec
CFIM-FM Iles-de-la-Madeleine, Québec
CIDI-FM Lac-Brome, Québec
CKWE-FM Maniwaki (Kitigan Zibi Anishinabeg, Québec
CBF-FM Montréal, Québec
CBM-FM Montréal, Québec
CHRF Montréal, Québec
CKLX-FM Montréal, Québec
CBV-FM Québec, Québec
CBVE-FM Québec, Québec
CBVX-FM Québec, Québec
CHOI-FM Québec, Québec
CJMF-FM Québec, Québec
CJBR-FM Rimouski, Québec
CFND-FM Saint Jerome, Québec
CBGN(AM) Sainte Anne des Monts, Québec
CIBO-FM Senneterre, Québec
CBSI-FM Sept-Îles, Québec
CKCN-FM Sept-Îles, Québec
CFLX-FM Sherbrooke, Québec
CJMQ-FM Sherbrooke, Québec
CBF-FM-1 Trois Rivieres, Québec
CIBL-FM Montréal, Québec
CJME Regina, Saskatchewan
CKOM Saskatoon, Saskatchewan
CBK Watrous, Saskatchewan

Triple A

CKUL-FM Halifax, Nova Scotia
CBBS-FM Sudbury, Ontario

Urban Contemporary

CIXX-FM London, Ontario
CFXJ-FM Toronto, Ontario

Variety/Diverse

CKUA-FM Edmonton, Alberta
CIAM-FM Fort Vermilion, Alberta
CKXU-FM Lethbridge, Alberta
CJSF-FM Burnaby, British Columbia
CHWK-FM Chilliwack, British Columbia
CIDO-FM Creston, British Columbia
CHAD-FM Dawson Creek, British Columbia
CFBX-FM Kamloops, British Columbia
CHLS-FM Lillooet, British Columbia
CHMM-FM MacKenzie, British Columbia
CHNV-FM Nelson, British Columbia
CJLY-FM Nelson, British Columbia
CJMP-FM Powell River, British Columbia
CFUR-FM Prince George, British Columbia
CIMM-FM Ucluelet, British Columbia
CITRFM Vancouver, British Columbia
CJAX-FM Vancouver, British Columbia
CFUV-FM Victoria, British Columbia
CFAM Altona, Manitoba
CJRB Boissevain, Manitoba
CJJJ-FM Brandon, Manitoba
CKXL-FM Saint Boniface, Manitoba
CICY-FM Selkirk, Manitoba
CHSM Steinbach, Manitoba
CINC-FM Thompson, Manitoba
CJUM-FM Winnipeg, Manitoba
CIMS-FM Balmoral, New Brunswick
CJVA Caraquet, New Brunswick
CHSR-FM Fredericton, New Brunswick
CFJU-FM Kedgwick, New Brunswick
CKMA-FM Miramichi, New Brunswick

CKUM-FM Moncton, New Brunswick
CFMH-FM Saint John, New Brunswick
CHQC-FM Saint John, New Brunswick
VOWR St. John's, Newfoundland
CHBI-FM Burnt Islands, Newfoundland
CJRM-FM Labrador City, Newfoundland
CHMR-FM Saint John's, Newfoundland
CFXU-FM Antigonish, Nova Scotia
CIFA-FM Comeauville, Nova Scotia
CKDU-FM Halifax, Nova Scotia
CFCT Tuktoyaktuk, Northwest Territories
CKON-FM Akwesasne, Ontario
CHXL-FM Brockville, Ontario
CKUE-FM Chatham, Ontario
CKUN-FM Christian Island, Ontario
CFDY-FM Cochrane, Ontario
CFGI-FM Georgina Island, Ontario
CFRU-FM Guelph, Ontario
CKHA-FM Haliburton, Ontario
CFMU-FM Hamilton, Ontario
CKGN-FM Kapuskasing, Ontario
CKVV-FM Kemptville, Ontario
CHCR-FM Killaloe, Ontario
CKVI-FM Kingston, Ontario
CHMO(AM) Moosonee, Ontario
CFXN-FM North Bay, Ontario
CHRY-FM North York, Ontario
CKRZ-FM Ohsweken, Ontario
CKCUFM Ottawa, Ontario
CJIQ-FM Paris, Ontario
CFBU-FM Saint Catharines, Ontario
CHOK Sarnia, Ontario
CJAI-FM Stella, Ontario
CJCS-FM Stratford, Ontario
CBBX-FM Sudbury, Ontario
CKLU-FM Sudbury, Ontario
CIUT-FM Toronto, Ontario
CFWP-FM Wahta Mohawk Territory near Bala, Ontario
CKMS-FM Waterloo, Ontario
CFID-FM Acton Vale, Québec
CFMF-FM Fermont, Québec
CFIM-FM Iles-de-la-Madeleine, Québec
CKAJ-FM Jonquiere, Québec
CKAU-FM Maliotenam, Québec
CBOF-1(AM) Maniwaki, Québec
CHGA-FM Maniwaki, Québec
CHRG-FM Maria (Reserve), Québec
CBGA-FM Matane, Québec
CBFX-FM Montréal, Québec
CJLO Montréal, Québec
CKUT-FM Montréal, Québec
CKVL-FM Montréal (zone LaSalle), Québec
CKAG-FM Pikogan, Québec
CFVD-FM-2 Pohenegamook, Québec
CBV-FM Québec, Québec
CBVE-FM Québec, Québec
CKIA-FM Québec, Québec
CIAU-FM Radisson, Québec
CHYZ-FM Sainte Foy, Québec
CBSI-FM Sept-Îles, Québec
CFLX-FM Sherbrooke, Québec
CFOU-FM Trois Rivieres, Québec
CIAX-FM Windsor, Québec
CBKF-1(AM) Gravelbourg, Saskatchewan
CFMQ-FM Hudson Bay, Saskatchewan
CJLR-FM La Ronge, Saskatchewan
CBK-FM Regina, Saskatchewan
CBKF-FM Regina, Saskatchewan
CJTR-FM Regina, Saskatchewan
CBKF-2(AM) Saskatoon, Saskatchewan
CBKS-FM Saskatoon, Saskatchewan
CFCR-FM Saskatoon, Saskatchewan
CBK Watrous, Saskatchewan
CIDD-FM White Bear Lake Resort, Saskatchewan

Special Programming on Radio Stations in Canada

Adult Contemp

CKXL-FM Saint Boniface, Manitoba
CFAN-FM Miramichi, New Brunswick
VOWR St. John's, Newfoundland
CFGX-FM Sarnia, Ontario
CKUT-FM Montréal, Québec

Agriculture

CFAC Calgary, Alberta
CFCW Camrose, Alberta
CKDQ Drumheller, Alberta
CFXE-FM Edson, Alberta
CHRB High River, Alberta
CKKY-FM Wainwright, Alberta
CKSR-FM Chilliwack, British Columbia
CIGV-FM Penticton, British Columbia
CKLQ Brandon, Manitoba
CFRY Portage La Prairie, Manitoba
CBN St. John's, Newfoundland
CKDY Digby, Nova Scotia
CKEN-FM Kentville, Nova Scotia
CKAD Middleton, Nova Scotia
CJBQ Belleville, Ontario
CFRB Toronto, Ontario
CJSL Estevan, Saskatchewan
CKBI Prince Albert, Saskatchewan
CKSW Swift Current, Saskatchewan
CBK Watrous, Saskatchewan
CFSL Weyburn, Saskatchewan

Big Band

CFBG-FM Bracebridge, Ontario

Black

CJSR-FM Edmonton, Alberta
CFROFM Vancouver, British Columbia
CKCUFM Ottawa, Ontario
CJAM-FM Windsor, Ontario
CKUT-FM Montréal, Québec
CKRL-FM Québec, Québec
CFNJ-FM St-Gabriel, Québec
CIBL-FM Montréal, Québec
CJTR-FM Regina, Saskatchewan

Blues

CKXL-FM Saint Boniface, Manitoba
CHMR-FM Saint John's, Newfoundland
CFMU-FM Hamilton, Ontario
CIEU-FM Carleton, Québec

Children

CHVN-FM Winnipeg, Manitoba
CKUW-FM Winnipeg, Manitoba
CHRI-FM Ottawa, Ontario

Chinese

CFROFM Vancouver, British Columbia
CINQ-FM Montréal, Québec
CJTR-FM Regina, Saskatchewan

Christian

CIXX-FM London, Ontario

Classical

CJSR-FM Edmonton, Alberta
CKBX 100 Mile House, British Columbia
CIGV-FM Penticton, British Columbia
CFAM Altona, Manitoba
CKUW-FM Winnipeg, Manitoba
CJLX-FM Belleville, Ontario
CHOD-FM Cornwall, Ontario
CFMU-FM Hamilton, Ontario
CHAS-FM Sault Ste. Marie, Ontario
CFRB Toronto, Ontario
CJAM-FM Windsor, Ontario
CIHO-FM Baie St Paul, Québec
CIEU-FM Carleton, Québec
CHIPFM Fort-Coulonge, Québec
CJRG-FM Gaspe, Québec
CHGA-FM Maniwaki, Québec
CKIA-FM Québec, Québec
CKMN-FM Rimouski-Mont Joli, Québec
CJMC-FM Sainte Anne des Monts, Québec
CFLX-FM Sherbrooke, Québec
CJSO-FM Sorel, Québec

Comedy

CFBW-FM Hanover, Ontario

Contemporary Hits/Top 40

CKHC-FM Toronto, Ontario

Country

CJVA Caraquet, New Brunswick
CFJU-FM Kedgwick, New Brunswick
CFNO-FM Marathon, Ontario
CFMF-FM Fermont, Québec
CFIN-FM Lac-Etchemin, Québec
CHGA-FM Maniwaki, Québec
CKCN-FM Sept-Îles, Québec
CFNJ-FM St-Gabriel, Québec
CFDA-FM Victoriaville, Québec

Disco

CKMF-FM Montréal, Québec

Ethnic

CJAR The Pas, Manitoba
CHSR-FM Fredericton, New Brunswick
CKXD-FM Gander, Newfoundland
CKJM-FM Cheticamp, Nova Scotia
CKEC-FM New Glasgow, Nova Scotia
CHAK Inuvik, Northwest Territories
CFCT Tuktoyaktuk, Northwest Territories
CBQR-FM Rankin Inlet, Nunavut
CBQS-FM Sioux Narrows, Ontario
CBQT-FM Thunder Bay, Ontario
CJDL-FM Tillsonburg, Ontario
CFZM Toronto, Ontario
CKWR-FM Waterloo, Ontario
CKDG-FM Montréal, Québec
CJBR-FM Rimouski, Québec
CBKA-FM La Ronge, Saskatchewan
CJLR-FM La Ronge, Saskatchewan
CHON-FM Whitehorse, Yukon Territory

French

CJSW-FM Calgary, Alberta
CFUV-FM Victoria, British Columbia
CKBC-FM Bathurst, New Brunswick
CKNB Campbellton, New Brunswick
CFDY-FM Cochrane, Ontario
CHRY-FM North York, Ontario
CKLU-FM Sudbury, Ontario
CIUT-FM Toronto, Ontario
CHRC Québec, Québec
CFCR-FM Saskatoon, Saskatchewan
CFWH-FM Whitehorse, Yukon Territory

Gospel

CILK-FM Kelowna, British Columbia
CHVN-FM Winnipeg, Manitoba
CFCO Chatham, Ontario
CKSY-FM Chatham, Ontario
CFBW-FM Hanover, Ontario
CKOT-FM Tillsonburg, Ontario
CHIPFM Fort-Coulonge, Québec
CJWW Saskatoon, Saskatchewan

Greek

CKJR Wetaskiwin, Alberta
CFROFM Vancouver, British Columbia
CJLX-FM Belleville, Ontario
CKWR-FM Waterloo, Ontario
CHAA-FM Longueuil, Québec
CINQ-FM Montréal, Québec

Italian

CJSW-FM Calgary, Alberta
CKER-FM Edmonton, Alberta
CFUV-FM Victoria, British Columbia
CKJS Winnipeg, Manitoba
CFRU-FM Guelph, Ontario
CJQM-FM Sault Ste. Marie, Ontario
CKLU-FM Sudbury, Ontario
CKRL-FM Québec, Québec
CFCR-FM Saskatoon, Saskatchewan

Japanese

CHMB Vancouver, British Columbia

Jazz

CKMX Calgary, Alberta
CKXL-FM Saint Boniface, Manitoba
CKUW-FM Winnipeg, Manitoba
CKLE-FM Bathurst, Québec
CJMO-FM Moncton, New Brunswick
CKUM-FM Moncton, New Brunswick
CHMR-FM Saint John's, Newfoundland
CKJM-FM Cheticamp, Nova Scotia
CJLX-FM Belleville, Ontario
CFBG-FM Bracebridge, Ontario
CHOD-FM Cornwall, Ontario
CHRY-FM North York, Ontario
CHUO-FM Ottawa, Ontario
CKCUFM Ottawa, Ontario
CFBU-FM Saint Catharines, Ontario
CHAS-FM Sault Ste. Marie, Ontario
CJAM-FM Windsor, Ontario
CIHO-FM Baie St Paul, Québec
CIEU-FM Carleton, Québec
CFMF-FM Fermont, Québec
CJRG-FM Gaspe, Québec
CFIN-FM Lac-Etchemin, Québec
CHGA-FM Maniwaki, Québec
CBVX-FM Québec, Québec
CKIA-FM Québec, Québec
CIAU-FM Radisson, Québec
CFLX-FM Sherbrooke, Québec
CFNJ-FM St-Gabriel, Québec
CIBL-FM Montréal, Québec

Native American

CJSR-FM Edmonton, Alberta
CHMB Vancouver, British Columbia
CFUV-FM Victoria, British Columbia
CHTM Thompson, Manitoba
CHSR-FM Fredericton, New Brunswick
CKON-FM Akwesasne, Ontario
CFBU-FM Saint Catharines, Ontario
CKRK-FM Kahnawake, Québec
CJTR-FM Regina, Saskatchewan

News

CKQR-FM Castlegar, British Columbia
CJSU-FM Duncan, British Columbia
CBZF-FM Fredericton, New Brunswick
CBCL-FM London, Ontario
CKPR-FM Thunder Bay, Ontario
CBVX-FM Québec, Québec

News/Talk

CKKS-FM Chilliwack, British Columbia
CISC-FM Gibsons, British Columbia
CIOK-FM Saint John, New Brunswick
CFBG-FM Bracebridge, Ontario
CHOK Sarnia, Ontario
CKPR-FM Thunder Bay, Ontario

Oldies

CJSU-FM Duncan, British Columbia
CKXX-FM Corner Brook, Newfoundland
CHIPFM Fort-Coulonge, Québec
CJLM-FM Joliette, Québec
CHAA-FM Longueuil, Québec
CKMN-FM Rimouski-Mont Joli, Québec
CFDA-FM Victoriaville, Québec

Polish

CKJS Winnipeg, Manitoba
CKLU-FM Sudbury, Ontario
CFCR-FM Saskatoon, Saskatchewan

Portugese

CJSF-FM Burnaby, British Columbia
CJOR Osoyoos, British Columbia
CJDV-FM Kitchener, Ontario
CINQ-FM Montréal, Québec

Reggae

CIBL-FM Montréal, Québec

Religious

CKDQ Drumheller, Alberta

CIVH Vanderhoof, British Columbia
CHTM Thompson, Manitoba
CFAN-FM Miramichi, New Brunswick
CJCW Sussex, New Brunswick
VOWR St. John's, Newfoundland
CFSX Stephenville, Newfoundland
CHMR-FM Saint John's, Newfoundland
CJSS-FM Cornwall, Ontario
CFRU-FM Guelph, Ontario
CJTW-FM Kitchener-Waterloo, Ontario
CKDO Oshawa, Ontario
CHUO-FM Ottawa, Ontario
CKNX Wingham, Ontario
CHRD-FM Drummondville, Québec
CFIN-FM Lac-Etchemin, Québec
CJSL Estevan, Saskatchewan
CKJH(AM) Melfort, Saskatchewan
CJDJ-FM Saskatoon, Saskatchewan
CFSL Weyburn, Saskatchewan

Spanish

CJSW-FM Calgary, Alberta
CKER-FM Edmonton, Alberta
CKJS Winnipeg, Manitoba
CFRU-FM Guelph, Ontario
CFMU-FM Hamilton, Ontario
CHUO-FM Ottawa, Ontario
CIUT-FM Toronto, Ontario
CKRL-FM Québec, Québec
CFLX-FM Sherbrooke, Québec

Sports

CFFR Calgary, Alberta
CHWK-FM Chilliwack, British Columbia
CFMJ Richmond Hill, Ontario
CHOK Sarnia, Ontario

Talk

CKFR Kelowna, British Columbia
CHLS-FM Lillooet, British Columbia
CISQ-FM Squamish, British Columbia
CFNR-FM Terrace, British Columbia
CIXX-FM London, Ontario
CKLP-FM Parry Sound, Ontario
CKPR-FM Thunder Bay, Ontario

Urban Contemporary

CHYZ-FM Sainte Foy, Québec

Vietnamese

CHMB Vancouver, British Columbia
CHAA-FM Longueuil, Québec

Most-Watched Shows of 2016-17
Michael Schneider

These Are the 100 Most-Watched TV Shows of the 2016-17 Season: Winners and Losers

It feels a bit antiquated to talk about ratings in 2017, when much of the television business remains transfixed on the streaming services – and it's become accepted that Netflix and its competitors are never going to share any viewership data.

As viewers migrate to other platforms, ratings just tell part of the story. The numbers have become so deflated that CBS felt the need to point out in January that if you looked at "Live + 35" data that included more than a month's worth of TV, DVR, VOD and streaming viewership, the network's primetime entertainment series average is actually up vs. 16 years ago (when only live viewing was measured).

"We really need to make sure that we are finding a way to capture all the views and the viewers of our programs in this multi-platform landscape," said ABC Entertainment president Channing Dungey. "There is, at this point, no truly effective system to really capture all the views that are happening in a timely manner. If we can't figure that out, particularly as a broadcast business, that's going to be a big issue for us."

For now, at least, this is what we have to go on, and last year's leaders – Football, "The Walking Dead" and "The Big Bang Theory" – remain this year's primetime winners. But they're all on the decline – which, of course, is the story of linear TV in general.

IndieWire looked at the Season-to-Date rankers for broadcast and cable, using the most recent Live+7 ratings (which include seven days' worth of DVR and video on-demand usage). Here's a final look at some of the hits and misses of 2016–2017, followed by our complete list of the most-watched shows of the season, according to both adults 18-49 and total viewers.

HIGHS

"This Is Us" and "Bull": NBC and CBS both get new series bragging rights, depending on which measurement you're looking at. NBC's "This Is Us" was the darling of the TV season, and for good reason: It's both the top-rated new series among adults 18-49 (4.8 rating – which in 2017 numbers, means it's a force) and is now the top-rated broadcast drama, edging out "Empire." CBS made sure to point out at its recent upfront presentation, however, that "Bull" is actually the year's most-watched new TV series among total viewers, with 15.5 million to "This Is Us" at 15.3 million.

"The Bachelor," "American Horror Story" and "South Park": Three veteran shows, late in their run, actually improving year-to-year in the adults 18-49 demo? Virtually impossible. But "The Bachelor" (3.1 rating, up from 3.0), "American Horror Story" (3.4, up from 3.3) and "South Park" (1.8, from 1.7) made it so. Of course, those gains were small, and the larger story remains how viewers are moving from their TV screens to other devices... but these three shows are bucking the trends.

"60 Minutes" and "The Simpsons": Sunday night stalwarts "60 Minutes" and "The Simpsons" also achieved virtually the impossible: They were flat year-to-year in the demo. And as we all know, "flat" is the new "up." Both shows had reason to stay relevant: "60 Minutes" had a presidential election to wrap itself around, while "The Simpsons" made headlines with its 600th episode (!) and cool events like a virtual reality couch gag.

LOWS

Football, "The Walking Dead" and "The Big Bang Theory": OK, hold on – don't cry for any of these series, as they're all still the most dominant programs on TV. But they're all still subject to gravity. AMC's "The Walking Dead" remains by far a dominant No. 1 among adults 18-49 (8.0 rating). No one comes close. "The Big Bang Theory" is the most-watched scripted show (19 million) and the top-rated scripted broadcast show among adults 18-49 (4.9 rating). And on the total viewers side, NBC's "Sunday Night Football" (20.1 million) towers over all. But when you're the biggest in the land, it also means the drop is more pronounced. And as great as those numbers are, they're substantial declines from last year. The NFL's drops were across the board, impacting "Thursday Night Football" and "Monday Night Football" as well.

"24: Legacy," "Hunted," "2 Broke Girls" and "The Great Indoors": One of these shows will ultimately be deemed the highest-rated series of the year to still be canceled. Fox hasn't yet announced the fate of "24: Legacy" (punting the decision while star Corey Hawkins appears on Broadway), while CBS also hasn't made a determination on reality series "Hunted." Should either "24: Legacy" (2.1 rating) or "Hunted" (2.0) be canned, they'll get the honors. But for now, that leaves the Joel McHale sitcom "The Great Indoors" and the long-running "2 Broke Girls," both of which have most definitely been canceled, as the top-rated (1.8) ax so far. (NBC's "Timeless" would have received these honors, until its two-days-later reprieve.)

"Crazy Ex-Girlfriend" and "No Tomorrow": You must be enjoying The CW's "Crazy Ex-Girlfriend" on other platforms, because for the second year in a row it was the lowest-rated broadcast network series (0.3 rating), tied with "No Tomorrow," which won't be having any more tomorrows. It's a reminder again that The CW isn't run based on ratings, given its output deals.

Here are the top series rankers according to adults 18-49 and total viewers, featuring seven days of time-shifted viewing. Most recent data is through May 14; these ratings will be updated as new numbers come in.

TOP 100 SHOWS, ADULTS 18-49

America's most-watched series of the 2016-2017 season in the key advertising demographic (measured in ratings points) are ...

1	**The Walking Dead** *AMC*	**8.0**
2	**NFL Sunday Night Football** *NBC*	**6.9**
3	**NFL Thursday Night Football** *NBC/NFL Network*	**5.2**
4	**NFL Thursday Night Football** *CBS/NFL Network*	**5.0**
5	**The Big Bang Theory** *CBS*	**4.9**
6	**This Is Us** *NBC*	**4.8**
7	**Empire** *Fox*	**4.3**
8	**NFL Monday Night Football** *ESPN*	**3.9**
9	**Modern Family** *ABC*	**3.7**
10	**Grey's Anatomy** *ABC*	**3.5**
11	**American Horror Story** *FX*	**3.4**
12	**The Bachelor** *ABC*	**3.1**
13	**The Voice (Monday + Tuesday)** *NBC*	**3.0**
14	**Designated Survivor** *ABC*	**2.9**
15	**How To Get Away With Murder** *ABC*	**2.6**

Rank	Show	Rating
	Scandal *ABC*	
	Survivor *CBS*	
	Talking Dead *AMC*	
	NCIS *CBS*	
	Chicago Fire *NBC*	
17	The Goldbergs *ABC*	2.5
	Law & Order: SVU *NBC*	
	Criminal Minds *CBS*	
	Black-ish *ABC*	
	Lethal Weapon *Fox*	
22	Chicago PD *NBC*	2.4
	Bull *CBS*	
	Kevin Can Wait *CBS*	
27	Speechless *ABC*	2.2
	The Simpsons *Fox*	
	American Housewife *ABC*	
	The Middle *ABC*	
	Dancing With the Stars *ABC*	
	The Blacklist *NBC*	
	Timeless *NBC*	
	Chicago Med *NBC*	
	24: Legacy *Fox*	
30	Love & Hip Hop Atlanta 6 *VH1*	2.1
	Scorpion *CBS*	
	Star *Fox*	
	Hunted *CBS*	
39	Family Guy *Fox*	2.0
	Life in Pieces *CBS*	
	Mom *CBS*	
	The Good Place *NBC*	
	NCIS: New Orleans *CBS*	
	The Flash *The CW*	
	Gotham *Fox*	
43	Saturday Night Football *ABC*	1.9
	Lucifer *Fox*	
	Blue Bloods *CBS*	
	The Great Indoors *CBS*	
	The Mick *Fox*	
	NCIS: Los Angeles *CBS*	
	Blindspot *NBC*	
	Hawaii Five-O *CBS*	
	60 Minutes *CBS*	
	South Park *Comedy Central*	
	Prison Break *Fox*	
50	Little Big Shots *NBC*	1.8
	Love and Hip Hop 7 *VH1*	
	Superstore *NBC*	
62	Last Man Standing *ABC*	1.7

Shark Tank *ABC*
Fresh off the Boat *ABC*
Code Black *CBS*
The Wall *NBC*
Thursday Night Football *NFL Network (without CBS or NBC)*
Marvel's Agents of S.H.I.E.L.D. *ABC*
MacGyver *CBS*
Hell's Kitchen *Fox*
Chicago Justice *NBC*
New Girl *Fox*
Real Housewives of Atlanta *Bravo*
Better Call Saul *AMC*
Gold Rush *Discovery*
Man With a Plan *CBS*
Teen Mom II (Season 7B) *MTV*
69 **Love & Hip Hop Hollywood 3** *VH1* **1.6**
Son of Zorn *Fox*
The Amazing Race *CBS*
Once Upon a Time *ABC*
81 **Westworld** *HBO* **1.5**
Masterchef Junior *Fox*
Superior Donuts *CBS*
Notorious *ABC*
The Last Man on Earth *Fox*
Bones *Fox*
Shades of Blue *NBC*
Street Outlaws *Discovery*
Grimm *NBC*
Pure Genius *CBS*
Brooklyn Nine-Nine *Fox*
Quantico *ABC*
Secrets and Lies *ABC*
Into the Badlands *AMC*
Teen Mom (Season 6+6B) *MTV*
85 **Pitch** *Fox* **1.4**
Bob's Burgers *Fox*
Madam Secretary *CBS*
Celebrity Apprentice *NBC*
Real Housewives of Beverly Hills *Bravo*
Taken *NBC*
Curse of Oak Island *History*
The Odd Couple *CBS*
Vikings *History*
Criminal Minds: Beyond Borders *CBS*
The Real O'Neals *ABC*
Chrisley Knows Best *USA*
WWE Raw *USA*
100 **Supergirl** *The CW* **1.3**

APB *Fox*

Source: Nielsen Media Research, 2016-2017 season to date through May 14, 2017, in ratings points. Nielsen prelim Live+7 Day, Prime, Originals only, Programs with majority of telecasts airing in season, Top 100 ranked on A18-49 rating. Excludes: Repeats, Specials, Post-Season Sports, Pre/Post Sports Commentary, Mini-Series (<5 telecasts in season) and News.

TOP 100 SHOWS, TOTAL VIEWERS

America's most-watched series of the 2016-2017 season are ...

Rank	Show	Viewers
1	**NFL Sunday Night Football** *NBC*	20.1
2	**The Big Bang Theory** *CBS*	19.0
3	**NCIS** *CBS*	18.4
4	**NFL Thursday Night Football** *NBC/NFL Network*	17.1
5	**The Walking Dead** *AMC*	16.4
6	**Bull** *CBS*	15.5
7	**This Is Us** *NBC*	15.3
8	**NFL Thursday Night Football** *CBS/NFL Network*	14.8
9	**Blue Bloods** *CBS*	14.1
10	**NCIS: New Orleans** *CBS*	13.4
	Dancing with the Stars *ABC*	
	The Voice (Monday) *NBC*	
11	**60 Minutes** *CBS*	12.6
	NCIS: Los Angeles *CBS*	
14	**The Voice (Tuesday)** *NBC*	12.5
16	**Hawaii Five-O** *CBS*	12.2
17	**Designated Survivor** *ABC*	12.1
18	**NFL Monday Night Football** *ESPN*	11.5
	Grey's Anatomy *ABC*	
19	**Empire** *Fox*	11.2
21	**Madam Secretary** *CBS*	11.1
22	**Criminal Minds** *CBS*	10.9
23	**Modern Family** *ABC*	10.8
	Chicago Fire *NBC*	
24	**Scorpion** *CBS*	10.7
26	**Survivor** *CBS*	10.5
27	**Little Big Shots** *NBC*	10.3
28	**Chicago PD** *NBC*	10.1
29	**Chicago Med** *NBC*	9.9
30	**MacGyver** *CBS*	9.8
31	**The Blacklist** *NBC*	9.7
32	**Mom** *CBS*	9.4
	Kevin Can Wait *CBS*	
	Code Black *CBS*	
33	**Lethal Weapon** *Fox*	9.2
36	**The Bachelor** *ABC*	9.0
37	**Law & Order: SVU** *NBC*	8.8

38	**Scandal** *ABC*	**8.6**
39	**Chicago Justice** *NBC*	**8.5**
40	**The Great Indoors** *CBS*	**8.4**
41	**Last Man Standing** *ABC*	**8.3**
42	**Life in Pieces** *CBS*	**8.2**
43	**Timeless** *NBC*	**8.0**
	Pure Genius *CBS*	
44	**How To Get Away With Murder** *ABC*	**7.9**
	The Middle *ABC*	
46	**The Goldbergs** *ABC*	**7.8**
48	**Elementary** *CBS*	**7.6**
49	**Man with a Plan** *CBS*	**7.5**
	Blindspot *NBC*	
50	**Black-ish** *ABC*	**7.4**
	24: Legacy *Fox*	
	Superior Donuts *CBS*	
51	**Hunted** *CBS*	**7.3**
	Criminal Minds: Beyond Borders *CBS*	
54	**Shades of Blue** *NBC*	**7.1**
	American Housewife *ABC*	
	2 Broke Girls *CBS*	
56	**Speechless** *ABC*	**7.0**
59	**Taken** *NBC*	**6.9**
60	**Doubt** *CBS*	**6.8**
	Shark Tank *ABC*	
61	**The Wall** *NBC*	**6.6**
63	**Undercover Boss** *CBS*	**6.5**
64	**The Amazing Race** *CBS*	**6.4**
65	**American Horror Story** *FX*	**6.3**
66	**Blacklist: Redemption** *NBC*	**6.2**
	Notorious *ABC*	
	Lucifer *Fox*	
67	**Grimm** *NBC*	**6.1**
	Saturday Night Football *ABC*	
	The Good Place *NBC*	
	The Odd Couple *CBS*	
70	**Star** *Fox*	**6.0**
74	**Dateline Friday** *NBC*	**5.9**
75	**Conviction** *ABC*	**5.7**
	Bones *Fox*	
	America's Funniest Home Videos *ABC*	
	Talking Dead *AMC*	
76	**Trial & Error** *NBC*	**5.5**
	20/20 *ABC*	
	Secrets and Lies *ABC*	
80	**Dr. Ken** *ABC*	**5.3**
	Gotham *Fox*	
83	**Superstore** *NBC*	**5.2**

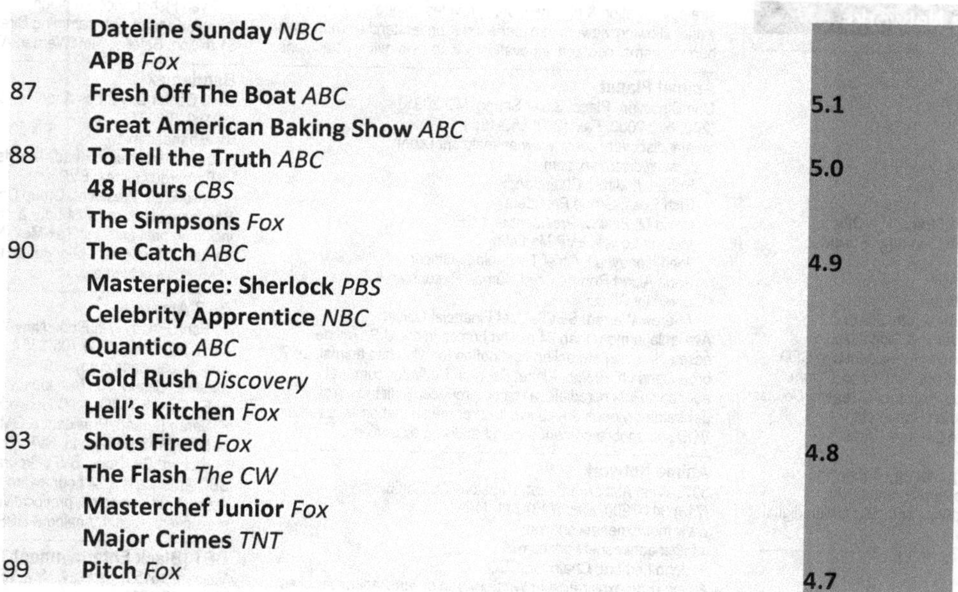

Dateline Sunday NBC
APB Fox
87 Fresh Off The Boat ABC
Great American Baking Show ABC
5.1
88 To Tell the Truth ABC
48 Hours CBS
The Simpsons Fox
5.0
90 The Catch ABC
Masterpiece: Sherlock PBS
Celebrity Apprentice NBC
Quantico ABC
Gold Rush Discovery
Hell's Kitchen Fox
4.9
93 Shots Fired Fox
The Flash The CW
Masterchef Junior Fox
Major Crimes TNT
4.8
99 Pitch Fox
4.7

Source: Nielsen Media Research, 2016-2017 season to date through May 14, 2017, in millions. Nielsen prelim Live+7 Day, Prime, Originals only, Programs with majority of telecasts airing in season, Top 100 ranked on P2+ rating. Excludes: Repeats, Specials, Post-Season Sports, Pre/Post Sports Commentary, Mini-Series (<5 telecasts in season) and News.

Michael Schneider, "These Are the 100 Most-Watched TV Shows of the 2016-17 Season: Winners and Losers," *IndieWire*, last modified May 26, 2017, http://www.indiewire.com/2017/05/most-watched-tv-show-2016-2017-season-the-walking-dead-this-is-us-football-1201832878/

National Cable Networks

A+E Network
on 10,000 Cable Systems
235 E 45th Street, New York, NY 10017
(212) 210-1400; *Fax:* (212) 210-9755
www.aetv.com
aefeedback@aenetworks.com
Satellite: Galaxy V; *Transponder:* 23
Abbe Raven, Chairman
Nancy Dubuc, President and Chief Executive Officer
Robert DeBitetto, President, Brand Strategy, Business Development
David Zagin, President, Distribution
Amanda Hill, Chief Marketing Officer
Melvin Berning,President, Chief Revenue Officer
Sean Cohan, President, International & Digital Media
David Granville-Smith, Executive Vice President and CFO
Michael Feeney, Executive Vice President, Corp. Comm.
Henry Hoberman, Executive Vice President &General Counsel
Stacy Green, Executive VP, Human Resources
Dan Suratt, President, Corporate Dvlpmnt, Strat. & Investments
Sola Winley, Executive VP, Corp Strategy & Planning
A+E Networks includes these six original brands: A&E, HISTORY, Lifetime, LMN, FYI, and Viceland. 500 million digital users worldwide.

ABS-CBN International
on 144 Cable Systems
Div/DBA: (formerly 14BS-CBN International)
150 Shoreline Drive, Redwood City, CA 94065-1400
(650) 508-6000, (800) 345-2465, (650) 394-8961; *Fax:* (650) 508-6001
www.abs-cbn.com/
Eugenio Lopez III, Chairman
Rafael Lopez, COO
Carlo L. Katigbak, President & Chief Executive Officer
Ma. Socorro Vidanes, COO, Broadcast
Martin L. Lopez, Chief Technology Officer
Mario Bautista, General Counsel
A 24-hour svc for Filipinos worldwide. Progmg originates at ABS-CBN, the Philippines top-rated net. Time-shifted for North America.
Satellite: Galaxy 11, PAS-2 for Pacific delivery, Telstar 5 (ku) transponder 22 for North America.

African Independent Television (AIT)
Mailing Address:
Second Address: Ladi Lawal Drive, Off. Gen. T.Y. Danjuma, Abuja, Nigeria
www.aitonline.tv
Satellite: Telstar 5; *Transponder:* 5
Aleogho A. Dokpesi, Founder
Paul Dokpesi Jr, Chairman
Dr. Oluwatosin Dokpesi, Managing Director, AIT
Faith Omokhosome Ikems, Executive Director, Marketing & Sales
Paulyn O. Ugbodaga, Executive Director, Admin./Human Resources
AIT is a Pan-African gen entertainment ch offering news, talk show, soap opera, sports, African culture & music 24 hours a day. Areas: United States & Africa.

AMC Networks, Inc.
11 Penn Plaza, 15th Floor, New York, NY 10001
(212) 324-8500
www.amcnetworks.com; www.amctv.com
info-amc@amc.com
Satellite: Satcom C-4; *Transponder:* 1
Charles Dolan, Executive Chairman
Josh Sapan, President & CEO
Ed Carroll, COO
Bob Broussard, President, AMC Networks Distribution
Charlie Collier, President & General Manager, AMC
John Barbieri, SVP/GM, Broadcasting & Technology
Distributes programming viewed by more than 85 million

American Heroes Channel
Div/DBA: (formerly Military Channel)
One Discovery Place, Silver Spring, MD 20910
(240) 662-2000; *Fax:* (240) 662-1854
www.ahctv.com; www.military.discovery.com
Henry S. Schleiff, Group President
Kevin Bennett, General Manager, ID & EVP, Programming
Sara Kozak, SVP, Production
Doug Seybert, SVP, Marketing
Real-world stories of heroism, military strategy, technological breakthroughs & turning points in history. Takes viewers 'behind the lines' to hear the personal stories of servicemen & women & offers in-depth explorations of militarytechnology, battlefield strategy, aviation & history. It also provides unique access to this world, allowing viewers to experience & understand a world full of human drama, courage, innovation & long-held military traditions.

Animal Planet
One Discovery Place, Silver Spring, MD 20910
(240) 662-2000; *Fax:* (240) 662-1854
animal.discovery.com/; www.animalplanet.com
first_last@discovery.com
Robert J. Miron, Chairman
Rich Ross, Group President
David M. Zaslav, President and CEO
Victoria Lowell, EVP Marketing
John Honeycutt, Chief Technology Officer
Adria Alpert Romm, Chief Human Resources & Global Diversity Officer
Andrew Warren, SEVP Chief Financial Officer
Available in more than 94 million homes in the U.S., online assets, the ultimate online destination for all things animal, 24/7 broadband ch, Animal Planet Beyond, Petfinder.com, pet adoption, PetsIncredible, a major producer & distributorof pet-training videos & web svc & other media platforms, a robust VOD svc, mobile content & merchandising extensions.

Anime Network
5373 West Alabama Street, Houston, TX 77056
(713) 341-7200; *Fax:* (713) 341-7199
www.theanimenetwork.com
info@theanimenetwork.com
John Ledford, Chairman/CEO
Anime is an exploration of Western pop culture. Anime reaches males 18-35 demographic with VOD genres, including martial arts, comedy, science fiction & drama on demand. Reaching 90 million homes with 22 million video subs.

Automotive Networks Corp.
Div/DBA: WheelsTV
Mailing Address: 289 Great Road, Suite 301, Acton, MA 01720
Second Address: 10642 Santa Monica Blvd, Suite 204, Los Angeles, CA 90025
(978) 264-4333; (310) 446-1960; *Fax:* (978) 264-9547
wheelstvnetwork.com
contact@wheelstv.net
Jim Barisano, Chairman & CEO
Lehel Reeves, President & Business Development
Collin Davis, CTO & Director of Operations
Theresa Carlo, CFO
Automotive entertainment & info via video on demand, worldwide web & dir mktg.
Serving 9.1 million subs.

AXS
Mailing Address: 8269 E 23rd Avenue, Denver, CO 80238
Second Address: 320 S Walton Street, Dallas, TX 75226
(303) 542-5600; (214) 698-3800; *Fax:* (303) 388-9600
www.axs.tv
mcuban@axs.tv
Mark Cuban, Chairman, President and CEO
Carol McDaniel, VP, Administration & Operations
Jeff Cuban, COO & General Manager
Michele Dix, SVP, Programming & Development
Rachael Weaver, GM, HDNET Movies
Robert Thoele, CFO & GeneralCounsel
Sue Hamilton, Exe VP, Distribution & Business Development
Colette Carey, VP of Marketing
Chris Markwell, Director, Live Event Operations
Bill Padalino, Director of Affiliate Sales
Robert H Ray, Advertising & Sponsorship Sales
HDNET, the leader in high-indefinition bcstg, produces & televises 24-hour a day. Satellite: Galaxy 9, transponder 19C. HDNET Movies is a 24-hour coml-free schedule of full-length feature films. Satellite: Galaxy 9, transponder 19C.

AYM Sports
Avenida Chapultepac 405, Colonia Juarez, Delegacion Cuauhtemoc, Mexico, 06600
Marco Polo Hinojosa Perez, Director General
Xavier Gonzalez, VP of Operations
Available 24 hours a day, 100% Mexican network consisting of soccer, basketball, rodeo charreadas, horse racing, boxing, kick boxing, jujitsu, karate, tae kwon do, swimming, driving, truck series, rallies and much more. Satellite: Telestar7, transponder 12.

BabyFirstTV
10390 Santa Monica Boulevard, Suite 310, Los Angeles, CA 90025
(888) 251-2229; (800) 251-2229; (310) 442-9853
www.babyfirsttv.com
Guy Oranim, CEO
Sharon Rechter, EVP Business Dvlpmt
Evan Fisher, Vice President
Arik Kerman, Programming Director
81 million. Satellie, TimeWarner, AT&T U-verse

Bandamax
5999 Center Drive, Los Angeles, CA 90045
(301) 348-3371
www.bandamax.tv/
Emilio Azcarraga, Head, Televisa
Bernardo Gomez, EVP
Jose Staff, President, Group Content
Bandamax features a 24-hour a day country music video, including best artists in Tex-Mex, Norteno, Banda & Manachi genres. De Pelicula Sp-language films, De Pelicula Clasico films of Mexico's golden era.

BBC America
11 Penn Plaza, 17th Floor, New York, NY 10001
(301) 347-2222, (212) 705-9387; (800) 216-1222
www.bbcamerica.com
Satellite: Galaxy VII; *Transponder:* 22
Ed Carroll, COO, AMC Networks
Sarah Barnett, President & GM, BBC America
Mary Pratt-Henaghan, SVP, Operations & Administration
Richard De Croce, SVP, Programming
BBC America is a 24 hour award-winning TV featuring razor-sharp comedies, provocative dramas & life changing makeovers. Digital, Analog & DBS. Satellite: Satcom C3.

BET (Black Entertainment Television)
Viacom, 1515 Broadway, New York, NY 10036
(212) 258-1000
www.bet.com
bet-tv_bizdev@bet.com
Satellite: Galaxy V; *Transponder:* 20
Debra Lee, Chairman & CEO
Scott Mills, COO
Maureen Guthman, Senior VP, Programming & Acquisition
78 million
BET/Los Angeles - Production
2801 W. Olive Ave, Burbank, CA 91505-4578
(818) 566-9940; *Fax:* (818) 566-1655
BET Film Production Facility
2000 West Pl. N.E., Washington, DC 20018-1226
(202) 608-2800; *Fax:* (202) 608-2629
BET/New York
380 Madison Ave, 20th Fl, New York, NY 10017-2513
(212) 716-5600; *Fax:* (212) 697-2050
Network Operations
1899 Ninth St. N.E., Washington, DC 20018-1001
(202) 608-2800
BET/Chicago
180 N. Stetson Ct, Suite 4350, Chicago, IL 60601-6710
(312) 819-8600

BET Networks (Black Entertainment Television)
Viacom, 1515 Broadway, New York, NY 10036
(212) 258-1000
www.bet.com
Satellite: Galaxy VII; *Transponder:* 21
Debra Lee, Chairman/CEO
Scott Mills, President & COO
Michael Pickrum, Chief Financial Officer
Denmark West, President, Digital Media
62.4 million

BLACK BELT TV/The Martial Arts Network
880 Calle Primavera, San Dimas, CA 91773
(213) 973-7381; *Fax:* (909) 854-9329
www.blackbelttv.com
info@blackbelttv.com
Erik D. Jones, Founder/CEO
A 24/7 cable TV net that targets demographics highly desired by advertisers and focuses on all income level individuals & families. Provides progmg for advertisers seeking to attract martial arts practitioners/enthusiasts,health/fitness-minded individuals, as well as sports enthusiasts, suppliers of exercise equipment, & other companies & product manufacturers that can directly reach their target audience. Programming includes martial arts movies, martial artstraining/self-defense, self-improvement programs, sports, women, & children-oriented programs, martial arts news, & much more.

Bloomberg Television
731 Lexington Avenue, New York, NY 10022
(212) 893-3331; (212) 318-2000; *Fax:* (202) 522-2400
www.bloomberg.com/live; www.bloomberg.tv
Kenneth Kohn, Operations Dir
Justin Smith, CEO, Media Group
Michael R Bloomberg, Co-Founder
Chuck Zegar, Co-Founder

Tom Secunda, Co-Founder
Duncan MacMillan, Co-Founder
A sophisticated 24-hour business & financial news ch. Serving over 310 million subs worldwide, United States, Canada, Central & South America, Europe,& Asia/Pacific. Satellite: Galaxy 11, HITS, C3.

BlueHighways TV
1242 Old Hillsboro Road, Franklin, TN 37069
(615) 264-3292; *Fax:* (615) 864-0674
www.bluehighwaystv.com
feedback@bluehighwaystv.com
Stan Hitchcock, Founder/Chairman
BlueHighways TV is a multi-platform progmg svc featuring roots music, American culture & back roads exploration. Satelite: AMC-10. Transponder 15.

Boston Kids & Family TV
Mailing Address: Boston City Hall, One City Hall Square, Boston, MA 02201
Second Address: 43 Hawkins Street, Boston, MA 02114
(617) 635-3112; *Fax:* (617) 635-4475
www.cityofboston.gov/cable
Michael Lynch, Director
David Burt, Station Manager
A partnership between the City of Boston & WGBH. Available 24 hour a day , edu TV progmg. PBS Kids from WGBH in Boston.

Bravo
Div/DBA: NBC Universal
3000 W Alameda Avenue, Suite 250, Burbank, CA 91523
(212) 664-4444
www.bravotv.com
bravositefeedback@nbcuni.com
Ryan Pinette, Senior VP, Production & Operations

Buzztime Entertainment, Inc.
2231 Rutherford Road, Suite 200, Carlsbad, CA 92008
(760) 438-7400; (800) 745-4686; *Fax:* (760) 438-3505
www.buzztime.com
Jeff Berg, Chairman
Ram Krishnan, CEO
Joe Adelizzi, Advertising Manager
Allen Wolff, CFO & Executive VP
Buzztime is the only 24-hour interactive entertainment bcst created exclusively for TV audiences. Featuring play-along trivia games for players of all interests & ability levels. 9 million registrations.

C-SPAN (Cable Satellite Public Affairs Network)
Mailing Address: 400 N Capitol Street NW, Suite 650, Washington, DC 20001
Second Address: PO Box 2909, West Lafayette, IN 47996
(202) 737-3220, (877) 662-7726; *Fax:* (202) 737-3323
www.c-span.org
journal@c-span.org
Satellite: AMC 10; *Transponder:* 19
Brian Lamb, Executive Chairman
Peter Kiley, VP Affiliate Relations & Communications
100 million

c/net: the computer network
235 Second Street, San Francisco, CA 94105
(415) 344-2000
www.cnet.com
Erica Argueta, Associate Producer/cNET in Espanol
Christine Cain, Social Media Manager
Donald Bell, Senior Editor
CNET news.com, airs weekly on CNBC & CNET tv.com airs on syndication.

The California Channel
on 114 Cable Systems
1121 L Street, Suite 110, Sacramento, CA 95814
(916) 444-9792; *Fax:* (916) 444-9812
www.calchannel.com
contact_us@calchannel.com
Transponder: 3 C
Sam Attisha, Chair
Walter Hughes, Vice-Chair
Del Heintz, Treasurer
Deane Leavenworth, Secretary
Carolyn McIntyre, State Association Rep
5.8 million

Canal 24 Horas
1100 Ponce de Leon Blvd, Coral Gables, FL 33134
(305) 444-4402; *Fax:* (305) 444-6301
www.rtve.es
Juanma Romero, Director
A 24 hour news network from TVE which offers a Headline News fromat with 30 minute blocks. The network also produces 17 different 30 minutes daily & wkly news magazines. Areas: United States, Mexico, Caribbean,

Cartoon Network
1050 Techwood Drive NW, Altanta, GA 30318
(404) 827-4700, (404) 827-1700
www.cartoonnetwork.com
pressroom@turner.com
Satellite: Galaxy IR; *Transponder:* 8 (East)
John Martin, Chairman And CEO
David Levy, President
Gary Albright, Operations Dir
James Anderson, SVP, Cartoon Network/Adult Swim
Joe Swaney, Director, Cartoon Network
Wendy Rutherford, Director, Cartoon Network/Adult Swim
KatieGordon, Manager, Cartoon Network
Elliott Niespodziani, Publicist, Adult Swim
Angie Weiss, Publicist, Cartoon Network
A Turner Broadcasting System. Inc.'s 24-hour Cartoon Network offers the best in animated entertainment. Drawing from the world's largest cartoon library, also showcases unique original ventures such as Johnny Bravo, Cow and Chicken, Dexter'sLaboratory, Ed, Edd n Eddy, and Cartoon Cartoon. Serving 94 million subs around the world. Satellite: Galaxy 1, transponder 15 (West).

Cartoon Network Latin America
1050 Techwood Drive NW, Atlanta, GA 30318
(404) 885-4398, (404) 827-1700; *Fax:* (404) 885-2157
www.cartoonnetworkla.com
larissa.pissarra@turner.com
Juan Carlos Urdaneta, President
Barry Koch, Senior VP & General Manager, Kids
Jim Samples, General Manager & Senior VP
The first global 24-hour cable ch programmed entirely with cartoons. Available in Sp, Portuguese or English. Serving more than 10.9 million subs. Satellite: PanAmSat 3R.

CBS Sports Network
28 East 28th Street, New York, NY 10016
www.cbssportsnetwork.com; www.cbsiam.com
Satellite: Galaxy IR; *Transponder:* 22
David Berson, President
Jen Sabatelle, SVP, Communications
Tiki Barber, Host
Dana Jacobson, Host
Boomer Esiason, Host
24 hour home of CBS Sports. 3,000+ hours of live programming including: Army & Navy, A-10, Patriot League, AAC, Big East, MW, C-USA.

centric
Div/DBA: BET Networks
Mailing Address: 1235 W Street NE, Washington, DC 20018-1211
Second Address: 1540 Broadway, New York, NY 10037
(202) 608-2000; (212) 258-1000
Network designed for black women.

CGTN (China Global Television Network)
Div/DBA: CCTV (China Central Television)
11B Fuxing Road, Beijing, 100038 China
(626) 912-3388; *Fax:* (310) 141-2101, 011-86-10-6-851-4993
english.cctv.com
cctv-4@cctv.com
Nie Chenxi, President
Zhang Jianfeng, Editor
China Central TV (CCTV) China's only national bcstg network. Provide Info about China's politics, economy, society, culture, science, edu & history, also Chinese viewers, living outside of China, 24 hours a day. Available in six languages.Serving more than 100 million subs. Satellite: Galaxy 11, transponder 24.

Cinemax
Div/DBA: (Home Box Office)
1100 Avenue Of the Americas, New York, NY 10036
(212) 512-1000; *Fax:* (212) 512-5637
www.cinemax.com
contactmax@hbo.com
Cinemax is a 24-hour digital pay-TV svc designed to provide viewers with the most movies & fewest repeats. Multiplex chs: Cinemax, MoreMAX, ActionMAX, ThrillerMAX, WMAX, @MAX, 5StarMAX, OuterMAX. Cinemax is seen in the U.S. & Puerto Rico.

Classic Arts Showcase
PO Box 828, Burbank, CA 91503-0828
(323) 878-0283; *Fax:* (323) 878-0329
www.classicartsshowcase.org
casmail@sbcglobal.net
James Rigler, President
Charlie Mount, General Manager
CAS is a non-profit arts progmg svc that include 16 art disciplines. The svc also features classic video from independent producers with the right to show clips. We require copies from masters on BetaCam-SP Tap. Available 24 hour. Serving50 million homes. Satellite: Galaxy 17, transponder 18C.

Cloo (Formerly Sleuth)
Div/DBA: NBC Universal Cable
Mailing Address: 900 Sylvan Avenue, 1 CNBC Plaza, Englewood Cliffs, NJ 07632
Second Address: 30 Rockefeller Plaza, 21st Floor, New York, NY 10112
(201) 735-3604; 212-664-4444
www.cloo.com
Mystery, crime dramas, 24/7.

CMT: Country Music Television
Div/DBA: Viacom
330 Commerce Street, Nashville, TN 37201
(615) 335-8400; *Fax:* (615) 335-8615
www.cmt.com
info@cmt.com
Brian Philips, President
Suzanne Norman, Senior VP, Operations
Quinn Brown, VP, Production
Jayson Dinsmore, EVP, Development & Programming
Shaleen Desai, VP, Scripted Programming
Rory Levine, Senior VP, Consumer Marketing
KurtPatat, Press Contact
CMT, America's # one country music network, 24 hours a day. Serving 87 million subs. Satellite: Satcom C-4, transponder 24, Satcom C3, transponder 18 west coast.

CNBC
900 Sylvan Avenue, Englewood Cliffs, NJ 07632
(201) 735-2622, (877) 280-4548
www.cnbc.com
Mark Hoffman, President & CEO
95 million homes in the U.S. 15 hours of live business programming during the week.

CNN en Espanol
One CNN Center, Atlanta, GA 30303
(404) 878-1555; *Fax:* (404) 878-0050
www.cnnespanol.cnn.com/
espanol.mesa@turner.com
SVP & General Manager, General Manager
A 24-hour Sp-language news network in the United States & Latin America. The network keeps its loyal viewers connected with the events, issues trends that matter most to them & their families.
Serving more than 24 million subs.

CNN-Cable News Network
One CNN Center, Atlanta, GA 30303
(404) 827-2300
www.cnn.com
Jeff Zucker, President, CNN Worldwide
Ken Jautz, Executive VP
Michael Bass, EVP, Programming
Allison Gollust, EVP & Chief Marketing Officer

CNNI (CNN International)
One CNN Center, 3rd Floor, Atlanta, GA 30348
(404) 827-1500; *Fax:* (404) 827-1995
edition.cnn.com
Jeff Zucker, President, CNN Worldwide
Tony Maddox, EVP & Managing Director, CNN International
A 24-hour global news & info, with live, breaking world news, sports, features & weather. Serving 170 million worldwide.

Comedy Central
345 Hudson Street, New York, NY 10014
(212) 767-8600; *Fax:* (212) 767-8592
www.cc.com
help@cc.com
Doug Herzog, President-Viacom Group
Kent Alterman, President
Debbie Beiter, SVP, Operations & Production
David Bernath, General Manager
Walter Levitt, Chief Marketing Officer
Steve Albani, Senior VP, Communications
Walter Levitt,Chief Marketing Officer
A 24-hour all comedy TV network that covers stand-up, sketch comedy, movies, talk shows, sitcoms, specials & classics TV shows. Serving 93.9 million subs. Satellites: Satcom C-3, transponder 21 (east), Galaxy 1R, transponder 1 (west).
2049 Century Park E, Suite 4250, Los Angeles, CA 90067-3101
(310) 201-9500; *Fax:* (310) 201-9488

The Crime Channel
310 West Bonita Avenue, #329, Claremont, CA 91711

(760) 360-6151; *Fax:* (760) 360-3258
www.thecrimechannel.com
crimechannel@dc.rr.com
Arnie Frank, President
The Crime Channel offers series, movies, documentaries, original productions, on the spot crime news & foreign programs. Satellite: Satcom C-1, transponder 11.

Daystar Television Network

Mailing Address: 3901 Hwy 121, Bedford, TX 76021
Second Address: PO Box 610546, Dallas, TX 75261
(817) 571-1229; (877) 805-2132; (800) 329-0029; *Fax:* (817) 571-7458
www.daystar.com
Marcus D Lamb, President & CEO
Our progmg is multi-ch & interdenominational. Christian TV net, is available from DirectTV, Dish Network 24-hours a day.

Deep Dish TV

16 Beaver Street, 4th Floor, New York, NY 10004
(212) 473-8933; *Fax:* (212) 420-8223
www.deepdishtv.org
deepdish@igc.org
Satellite: Galaxy IR; *Transponder:* 15
Ron Davis, Chairman
Brian Drolet, Executive Director
Julie Ludwig, Production Manager
Rebecca Centeno, Distribution & Outreach Manager
Educational progmg (one hour a wk) distributed to PBS & pub access chs.

Discovery Communications

One Discovery Place, Silver Springs, MD 20910
(240) 662-2000, (240) 662-3709; *Fax:* (240) 662-1854
privacy_policy@discovery.com
Satellite: Satcom C-4; *Transponder:* 13
Robert J. Miron, Chairman
David M. Zaslav, President /CEO
Joe Abruzzese, President, Advertising Sales
Billy Goodwyn, Pres/CEO Discovery Education
Adria Alpert Romm, Chief Human Resources & Global Diversity Officer
John Honeycutt,Chief Technology Officer
Andrew Warren, Senior Executive VP/CFO
David Leavy, Chief Comms Officer/Corporate Ops
The United States largest cable TV net, the nation's premier provider of real-world entertainment, offering a signature mix of compelling, high-end production values & vivid cinematography that consistently represents qulity for viewers.Primetime progmg features science & technology, exploration, adventure, history and in-depth, behind-the scenes glimpses at the people, places, organizations that shape, share our world & is dedicated to creating the highest quality TV & media toinspire audiences by delivering knowledge about the world in an energizing way; evolving a timeless brand for a changing world.

Discovery en Espanol

One Discovery Place, Silver Spring, MD 20910
(240) 662-2000; *Fax:* (240) 662-1854
www.dsc.discovery.com/
first_last@discovery.com
Robert J. Miron, Chairman
David M. Zaslav, President and CEO
Bill Goodwyn, Discovery Education
Robert R. Bennett, Managing Director
Paul A. Gould, Managing Director
M. LaVoy Robison, Director
John Honeycutt, Chief TechnologyOfficer
Adria Alpert Romm, Chief Human Resources & Global Diversity Officer
Andrew Warren, SEVP Chief Financial Officer
Provider of high quality nonfiction entertainment for Sp-speaking audiences in the United States. Offering original progmg, some of the best Discovery content from around the world, the portfolio includes Discovery en Espanol & DiscoveryFamilia.

Discovery HD Theater

One Discovery Place, Silver Spring, MD 20910
(240) 662-2000; *Fax:* (240) 662-1854
www.dsc.discovery.com/; www.discovery.com
first_last@discovery.com
Robert J. Miron, Chairman
David M. Zaslav, President and CEO
Bill Goodwyn, Discovery Education
Robert R. Bennett, Managing Director
Paul A. Gould, Managing Director
M. LaVoy Robison, Director
John Honeycutt, Chief TechnologyOfficer
Adria Alpert Romm, Chief Human Resources & Global Diversity Officer
Andrew Warren, SEVP Chief Financial Officer
Provide viewers with the hightest-quality TV experience available with spectacular images, dynamic sound & compelling stories from across the globe. A broad array of rich, original HD content across several progmg categories such as worldcultures, wildlife, high-end auto & adventure.

Discovery Kids Channel

Div/DBA: (Discovery Communications)
One Discovery Place, Silver Spring, MD 20910
(240) 662-2000; *Fax:* (240) 662-1854
first_last@discovery.com
Robert J Miron, Chairman
David M Zaslav, President & CEO
Bill Goodwyn, Discovery Education
John Honeycutt, Chief Technology Officer
Provides entertaining, engaging & high-quality real-world progmg that kids enjoy & parent trust. Kids can learn about science, adventure, exploration & natural history through documentaries, reality shows, scripted dramas & animated stories.

Discovery Kids en Espanol

One Discovery Place, Silver Spring, MD 20910
(240) 662-2000; *Fax:* (240) 662-1854
www.dsc.discovery.com/
first_last@discovery.com
Robert J. Miron, Chairman
David M. Zaslav, President and CEO
Bill Goodwyn, Discovery Education
Robert R. Bennett, Managing Director
Paul A. Gould, Managing Director
M. LaVoy Robison, Director
John Honeycutt, Chief TechnologyOfficer
Adria Alpert Romm, Chief Human Resources & Global Diversity Officer
Andrew Warren, SEVP Chief Financial Officer
Offering original progmg develop for Sp-speaking audiences, in addition to some of the best Discovery content from around the world, the portfolio includes Discovery en Espanol & Discovery Familia.

Discovery Life (formerly FitTV)

One Discovery Place, Silver Spring, MD 20910
(240) 662-2000; *Fax:* (240) 662-1854
www.dsc.discovery.com/; www.discovery.com
first_last@discovery.com
Robert J. Miron, Chairman
David M. Zaslav, President and CEO
Nancy Daniels, Group Manager
Howard Lee, EVP, Development & Production
John Honeycutt, Chief Technology Officer
Adria Alpert Romm, Chief Human Resources & GlobalDiversity Officer
Andrew Warren, SEVP & Chief Financial Officer
Reaches over 46 million households.

Disney Channel

500 S Buena Vista Street, Burbank, CA 91521-6066
(818) 569-7500; *Fax:* (818) 566-1358
www.disneyabctv.com
support@DisneyABC.tv
Ben Sherwood, Co-Chair
Gary Marsh, President & Chief Creative Officer Disney Channels
A 24-hour gen entertainment network for kids & families through original series, movies & contempary acquired progmg. Serving over 87 million subs. Satellite: Galaxy 5, transponder 1 east, Galaxy 1-R, transponder 7 west.

Disney XD (formerly Toon Disney)

500 South Buena Vista Street, Burbank, CA 91521
(818) 569-7500; (818) 460-7477; *Fax:* (818) 566-1358
disneyxd.disney.com
Eric Coleman, Senior VP & GM, Disney Television Animation
Gary Marsh, President & Chief Creative Officer
John Rood, Senior VP, Marketing
Adam Bonnett, Executive VP, Original Programming
Patti McTeague, Senior VP, Kid'sCommunications
Animated programming for ages 6-11. Basic cable channel.24-hours a day. Serving more than 74 million subs. Satellite: Galaxy 10R.

Ecology Global Network

9171 Victoria Drive, Ellicott City, MD 21042
(410) 465-0480; *Fax:* (410) 461-5152
www.ecology.com
Dr. David Nostbakken, Chairman
Annetta L. Hoagland, Chief Operating Officer
Eric McLamb, CEO & President
Bob Petz, News Director
David Beutel, Treasurer
Kevin F. Dages, Executive Vice President
Bobbie R. Crawford, ChiefDevelopment Officer & Sales
Rickey Green, VP Finance & Compliance
Jane Engelsiepen, Chief Web Officer & VP Content
Randy Weckerly, VP Ecology Enterprises
Ecology Communications focuse on ecology & enviroment in a var of entertainment-driven formats wkly.

Edmentum (formerly Plato Learning)

Mailing Address: 5600 W 83rd Street, Suite 300, 8200 Tower, Bloomington, MN 55437
Second Address: 2425 North Central Expressway, Suite 1000, Richardson, TX 75080
(800) 447-5286
www.edmentum.com
info@edmentum.com
Jamie Candee, President & CEO
Richard Whalley, Managing Director
Ryan Hagedorn, SVP, Sales & Marketing
Jim Stewart, CFO
Dave Adams, Chief Academic Officer
Stacey Herteux, VP, Human resources
Paul Johansen, Chief TechnologyOfficer
Interactive TV progmg for children.

Elation Media (formerly Oasis/OTV)

on 16 Cable Systems
Mailing Address: 2029 Century Park E, Suite 400, Los Angeles, CA 90067
Second Address: 2155 West Highway 89A, Suite 213, Sedona, AZ 86336
(310) 553-4300; (310) 553-3010; *Fax:* (310) 553-4300
www.oasistv.com
service@oasistv.com
Gerald Levin, Chairman
Robert Schnitzer, Founder/CEO
Independent content provider of branded Body-Mind-Spirit video progmg. Range of topics: Health, Healing, Metaphysics, Spirituality, Earth, Environment, World Peace, Visionary Arts & Personal Growth.

eSignal

3955 Point Eden Way, Hayward, CA 94545
(510) 266-6000; *Fax:* (510) 266-6100
www.esignal.com
Chuck Thompson, President
Grant Mader, Operations Dir

ESPN

ESPN Plaza, Bristol, CT 06010
(860) 766-2000; *Fax:* (860) 766-2400
www.espn.com
espnpr@espn.com
Satellite: Galaxy V; *Transponder:* 9
Chris Driessen, CFO
John Skipper, President
Ed Durso, Executive VP, Administration
Norby Williamson, EVP, Production
Stephanie Druley, SVP, Event & Studio Production
Rob King, SVP, News & Sports Center
Burke Magnus, EVP,Scheduling & Programming
John Kosner, Executive VP, Digital & Print Media
A 24-hour svc covering sports events, news, info, & lifestyle progmg.
ESPN CLASSIC is a 24-hour, all sports network devoted to telecasting the greatest games, stories, heroes & memories in the history of sports. ESPN DEPORTE offers a widevar of domestic & intl sports progmg 24-hours. ESPN HD offers a 24-hours high definition TV svc from ESPN, features high profile telecast. ESPNEWS, the nation's only 24-hours TV sports news svc, provides an expanded window for news & highlights,aswell as live coverage of beaking news.
605 3rd Ave, New York, NY 10158-0180
(212) 916-9200

ESPN2

ESPN Plaza, Bristol, CT 06010
(860) 766-2000; *Fax:* (860) 766-2400
www.espn.com
Satellite: Galaxy V; *Transponder:* 14
John Skipper, President
Rob King, SVP, News & Sports Center
Ed Durso, Executive VP, Administration
Norby Williamson, EVP, Production
Stephanie Druley, SVP, Event & Studio Production
Burke Magnus, EVP, Scheduling & Programming
John Kosner, Executive VP, Digital & Print Media
A 24-hour sports net features a progmg line-up on par with ESPN.

ESPNU

c/o ESPN Regional Television, 11001 Rushmore Drive, Charlotte, NC 28277

(704) 973-5000; *Fax:* (704) 973-5090
www.espn.com/college-sports
Rosalyn Durant, Senior Vice President
ESPNU is a TV ch that specializes in college sports & is produced by affil with & owned by parent Network ESPN.

Esquire Network (formerly The Style Network)
5750 Wilshire Blvd, Los Angeles, CA 90036-3709
(323) 954-2400; *Fax:* (323) 954-2500
tv.esquire.com
Style Network covers the gamut of the lifestyle genre.

Eurocinema
250 West 57th Street, Ste 2028, New York, NY 10107
www.eurocinema.com
contactus@eurocinema.com
Sebastien Perioche, Chairman & CEO
Ildemaro Martinez, Jr, Founder
Non-Hollywood movies service for Broadband & Digital TV. 36 million

EUROCINEMA
Div/DBA: European Movies on TV
Mailing Address: 387 Park Avenue, 3rd Floor, New York, NY 10016
Second Address: 250 West 57th St, Ste 2028, New York, NY 10107
(212) 763-5533
www.eurocinema.com/
contactus@eurocinema.com
Robert E. Richer, President
Iidemaro Martinez Jr
Broker specializing in the sale of overseas media properties.

Evine (formerly ShopNBC)
on 1900 Cable Systems
6740 Shady Oak Road, Eden Prairie, MN 55344
(952) 943-6000; (800) 676-5523; *Fax:* (952) 943-6011
www.shophq.com/; www.evine.com
Bob Rosenblatt, CEO
Dawn Zaremba, Media
Digital retailer, the television network provides entertainment shopping on popular categories. Reaches 87 million homes.

EWTN
Div/DBA: The Global Catholic Network
5817 Old Leeds Road, Irondale, AL 35210
(205) 271- 2900, (205) 271-2966; *Fax:* (205) 271-2957
www.ewtn.com
pilgrimages@ewtn.com
Satellite: Galaxy IR; *Transponder:* 11
Michael P. Warsaw, Chairman & CEO
Doug Keck, President & COO
Peter Gagnon, VP, Programming & Production
Michelle Laque Johnson, Director of Communications
Gerald Zukauckas, CFO
Len Marino, VP, Creative Services
America's largest relg cable network offers coml-free family-oriented progmg in English & Sp. EWTN features documentaries, music, drama, live talk shows, animated children shows & special church events from around the world.

FamilyNet
Div/DBA: Rural Media Group
Mailing Address: 49 Music Square West, Suite 301, Nashville, TN 37203 US
Second Address: , 921 Village Square, Gretna, NE 68028
(402) 289-2085
www.familynet.com
info@rfdtv.com
Patrick Gottsch, Founder
Steve Campione, CFO & COO
Gatsby Gottsch, EVP, Finance
Raquel Gottsch, EVP, Marketing
Gary Kanofsky, Chief Content Officer
Dane Randall, SVP, Advertising Sales
Mike Stodden, Director of SpecialProjects
Barry Kriha, Research Director
Mike Holland, Sales
Mike Hansen, Agriculture and Equine Division
Tim Moan, Midwest VP of Sales
FamilyNet TV is a full-time cable network, including original values-based programs & operates Christian talk ch 161 on sirius statellite radio. Reliable, safe TV for today's family. Reaches 25 million homes.

The Filipino Channel - TFC (ABS-CBN)
Sgt. E.A. Esguerra Avenue, Quezon City, 1103 Philppines
(650) 697-3700; (+632) 415-2272; *Fax:* (650) 697-3500
tfc.tv; www.tfc-usa.com; www.abs-cbn.com
web_feedback@abs-cbn.com
Eugenio Lopez III, Chairman
Rafael Lopez, COO
Carlo L. Katigbak, President & Chief Executive Officer
Ma. Socorro Vidanes, COO, Broadcast
Martin L. Lopez, Chief Technology Officer
Mario Bautista, General Counsel
A 24-hour all Filipino premium svc ch delivered via satellite from the Philippines. Serving 35,000 subs on 11 systems. Satellite: Galaxy 11, transponder 24.

FM (formerly NUVOtv)
Div/DBA: (FUSE Media)
Mailing Address: 700 N Central Avenue, Suite 600, Glendale, CA 91203 US
Second Address: 11 Penn Plaza, 11th Floor, New York, NY 10001
(323) 256-8900
www.fm.tv
Michael Schwimmer, President & CEO, Fuse Media
JT Ladt, Chief Content Officer
Jennifer McGovern, SVP, Current & Development
Diana Castro, Media
Multi-platform network for music lovers. 42 million subs.

Food Network
75 Ninth Avenue, New York, NY 10011
(212) 398-8836, (866) 587-4653; *Fax:* (212) 736-7716
www.foodnetwork.com
Satellite: Galaxy IR; *Transponder:* 4
Katherine Alford, Senior VP, Culinary
Mark Schuermann, Senior VP & Treasurer
Karen Grinthal, SVP, Ad Sales, Food Network & Cooking Channel
Courtney White, SVP, Programming, Food Network
Alaka Williams, SVP, Network Human Resources
A 24-hour net committed to exploring new, different & interesting ways to approach food. 100 million.

Fox Business Network
1211 Avenue of the Americas, 22nd Floor, New York, NY 10036
(888) 369-4762, (212) 301-5473; (212) 601-7000; *Fax:* (212) 601-7990
www.foxbusiness.com
Satellite: Galaxy 17; *Transponder:* 8, 2
Rupert Murdoch, Executive Chairman
Brian Jones, President
Tom Bowman, VP, Programming
Irena Briganti, Exec Vice President, Corporate Communications
Neil Cavuto, SVP/Managing Editor, Business News
Dianne Brandi, EVP, Legal &Business Affairs
Amy Listerman, Chief Financial Officer
Gary Schreier, Senior VP, Programming
Marianne Gambelli, President, Advertising Sales
Financial news channel

Fox Net
1440 S Sepulveda Ave, Los Angeles, CA 90025
(310) 369-1000
www.fox.com
Gail Berman, President
Steve Nazar, Operations Dir
Keith Goldberg, General Manager
Julie Allen, General Sales Mgr
Dwayne Bright, Programming Director
Betty Wang, Promotions Manager
A 24-hours basic cable affil to Fox Broadcasting Co.
FOX Broadcasting Co
10201 W. Pico Blvd., Los Angeles, CA 90064-2606
(310) 369-5153; *Fax:* (310) 969-0316
Susan Kiel, Vp, Network Distribution & Cable Operations

Fox News Channel: See listing in Major National TV News Organizations, this section.
1211 Ave of the Americas, New York City, NY 10036
(888) 369-4762
www.foxnews.com
yourcomments@foxnews.com
Irena Briganti, Executive Vice President, Corporate Communiations

Fox Sports 2 (formerly Fuel)
1440 S Sepulveda Blvd, Suite 1900, Los Angeles, CA 90025
Fax: (310) 444-8559
www.foxsports.com/ufc
hookup@fuel.tv
Nat'l Network: Fox Sports 2
Dana White, CEO/COO
A 24-hour sports network featuring snowboarding, wakeboarding, surfing, BMX, motorcross & skateboading. Serving 5 million subs. Satellite: Galaxy II, transponder 5.

Free Speech TV
Box 44099, Denver, CO 80201
(303) 442-8445; *Fax:* (303) 442-6472
www.freespeech.org
jon@freespeech.org
Nathanael Reeder, Operations Dir
Jon Stout, Chief of Staff/Co-Founder
Nina Henderson Moore, General Manager
Alexander Maness, Dir Brdcst Media
Ben Gass, Dir Ntl Partnerships
Ron Williams, Executive Dir.
Emma Lubitsch,Acquisitions Coordinator
Antoinette June, Web Dir.
Teo Lucero, Program Coordinator
Yolanda Williams, Controller
Valerie Appelbaum, Development Director
FSTV airs primarily social, political, cultural & environmental documentaries & news programs, 24-hours a day. Serving 40 million subs, on 180 cable systems & DISH Network.

Freeform TV (formerly ABC Family Channel)
Mailing Address: 3800 W Alameda Ave, Burbank, CA 91505
Second Address: PO Box 3000, Neenah, WI 54957
(818) 962-4096; *Fax:* (818) 450-0493
www.abcfamily.com
Satellite: Galaxy V; *Transponder:* 11
Anne Sweeney, Chairman
Paul Lee, President
Khai Tran, Digital Media
Basic cable network available in over 87 million homes nationwide 24 hours; delivers a dynamic mix of quality entertainment with original series & movies, classics from Disney.
1422 W. Main St, Suite 201, Lewisville, TX 75067-3388
(972) 436-2217; *Fax:* (972) 436-0209
Mark Solow, Dir Southwest Rgn
660 Newport Center Dr, Suite 770, Newport Beach, CA 92660-6401
(714) 759-7685; *Fax:* (714) 759-9491
Janice Slipp, Dir Western Rgn
5445 DCT Pkwy, Suite 525, Englewood, CO
(303) 220-8901; *Fax:* (303) 220-9102
Tracy Jenkins, J.D., Dir Rocky Mountain Rgn
1301 W. 22nd St, Suite 902, Oakbrook, IL 60523-2006
(630) 990-0437; *Fax:* (630) 990-0463
Ralph Trentadue, Natl Dir Lcl Adv Sls
Shirley Hill, Vp Western Division
Box 2050, 2877 Guardian Ln, Virginia Beach, VA
(757) 459-6281; *Fax:* (757) 459-6429
Craig Sherwood, Sr Vp/Mgng Dir
Box 492347, Atlanta, GA 30349-9338
(770) 461-4929; *Fax:* (770) 461-8678
Russell A. Breault, Vp Eastern Division
1133 Ave. of the Americas, 36th Fl, New York, NY 10036-6710
(212) 782-1860; *Fax:* (212) 782-1865
Steve Israelsky, Vp Northeast Rgn

Fuse
Madison Square Garden, 11 Pennsylvania Plaza, 17th Fl, New York, NY 10001
(212) 465-6741, (212) 465-MSG1, (212) 631-5422; *Fax:* (212) 324-3445
www.fuse.tv
James L. Dolan, Executive Chairman
Norman Schoenfeld, Programming Director
Diane Castro, Media
Timothy Dunn, Presenter
Robert Pollichino, EVP & CFO
Steve Collins, EVP, Facilities
Lawrence Burian, EVP, General Counsel &secretary
Fuse is the only all-music, viewer-influenced TV network, featuring music videos, exclusive artist interviews, live concerts & specials. Serving 35 million subs. NUVOtv merged with Fuse in September 2015. Satellite; Loral Skynet Telstar 7,transponder 14.
Chicago Office
205 N. Michigan, Suite 803A, Chicago, IL 60601-5927
(312) 938-4222
Joseph Glennon, Sr. Vp
The Water Garden
2425 W. Olympic Blvd., Suite 5050, Santa Monica, CA 90404-4030
(310) 998-9300
John Pezzini, Vp

FX Networks Inc.
Div/DBA: (A subsidiary of Fox, Inc.)
10201 W Pico Blvd, 1034th, Los Angeles, CA 90064
(310) 369-1000; *Fax:* (310) 444-8266
www.fxnetworks.com

Chuck Saftler, COO/President
John Landgraf, CEO
Barbara Crawford, VP, FX Current Productions
Dominic Pagone, SVP, Communications
An entertainment basic cable net from Fox Television involving hit series, daily films, original programs & sports.
Serving more than 53 million subs on 3,293 cable systems.
Satellite: Hughes Communications Galaxy 7, transponder 4 & 5.

FXM Retro (formerly Fox Movie Channel)
Div/DBA: (FX Networks Inc.)
10201 W Pico Blvd, Bldg 103, 4th Floor, Los Angeles, CA 90035
(310) 369-0586; *Fax:* (310) 969-4687
www.fxmretro.com; www.foxmoviechannel.com
Chuck Saftler, COO/President
Dominic Pagone, SVP, Communications
The network is dedicated to preserving Hollywood history through original series & specials.

Galavision
605 3rd Avenue, 12th Floor, New York, NY 10158
(212) 455-5330; *Fax:* (212) 867-6710
www.univision.com
Satellite: Satcom C-4; *Transponder:* 4
Ray Rodriguez, Communications President And COO
Joanne Lynch, President
Timothy Spillane, Operations Dir
A 24-hr Sp language cable network for United States Hispanics in distribution & viewership.
2323 Bryan St., Suite 1900, Dallas, TX 75201-2603
(214) 758-2300
6701 Center Dr. W, Suite 650, Los Angeles, CA 90045-1535
(310) 348-3600
541 N. Fairbanks Ct, Suite 1240, Chicago, IL 60611-3319
(312) 494-5101

Game Show Network
2150 Colorado Avenue, #100, Santa Monica, CA 90404
(310) 255-6933; *Fax:* (310) 255-6810
www.gsn.com
Mark Feldman, President & CEO
Steven Bunnell, EVP & COO
Amy Introcaso-Davis, EVP, Programming & Development
Alison Lazar, VP, Publicity & Corporate Communications
Game Show Network (GSN) is the only U.S. television network dedicated to game progmg and interactive game playing, featuring over 65 hours per week of original progmg & enhanced classics.
Reaching 50 million subs.
The Republic Center, 325 N. St. Paul St. Suite 1500, Dallas, TX 75201-3891
(214) 965-8500; *Fax:* (214) 965-8576
680 Fifth Ave. 11th Fl., New York, NY 10019-5429
(212) 333-2510; *Fax:* (646) 557-2996
515 N. State St. Suite 2120, Chicago, IL 60654-4864
(312) 261-4500; *Fax:* (312) 261-4521

The Golf Channel
7580 Golf Channel Drive, Orlando, FL 32819
(407) 355-4653; *Fax:* (407) 363-7976
www.golfchannel.com
Mike McCarley, President
Jay Madara, CFO
Regina O'Brien, SVP, Marketing
Phil Piazza, SVP, Programming
Tom Knapp, SVP, Golf Sponsorships
Christopher Murvin, SVP, Business Affairs & General Counsel
Will McIntosh, SVP, BusinessDevelopment & Strategy
David Schaefer, VP, Communications
Julie Lusk, VP, Human Resource
A 24-hour ch offering a blend of tournament coverage from the PGA, LPGA, Sr Tour, Nike, EPGA Tours, as well as instruction, interactive talk, news, profiles, classics, travel & more.
Serving 30 million subs on 2,200 cable systems.Satellite: Galaxy VI, Transponder 7.

Great American Country
9721 Sherrill Blvd., Knoxville, TN 37932
(615) 327-7525; *Fax:* (615) 329-8770
www.greatamericancountry.com; www.gactv.com
Satellite: Satcom C-3; *Transponder:* 20
Burton Jablin, COO, SNI
Vikki Neil, GM, Scripps Lifestyle Studios
John Feld, SVP, Programming
Dylan Jones, Chief Communications Officer
GAC is a country music and American lifestyle themed video net, features natl & loc adv, also featuring a broad var of videos programs.

Guthy-Renker Television
100 N Sepulveda Blvd, Suite 1600, El Segundo, CA 90245
(888) 651-6602, (888) 651-6607, (310) 581-6250; *Fax:* (310) 581-3232
www.guthy-renker.com
customerservice@guthy-renker.com
Greg Renker, Co-Chairman
Bill Guthy, Co-Chairman
Ben Van De Bunt, Board Member
Lenny Lieberman, Owner
Kendra Elliott, SVP, Media
Sam Sheard, SVP, Finance & Operations
Direct-response TV.

Hallmark Channel
12700 Ventura Blvd, Suite 200, Studio City, CA 91604-2463
(818) 755-2400; *Fax:* (818) 755-2564
www.hallmarkchannel.com
Satellite: Satcom C-3; *Transponder:* 5
Bill Abbott, President & CEO
Andrew Rooke, EVP, Operations & CFO
Michelle Vicary, EVP, Programming & Network Publicity
Susanne McAvoy, EVP, Marketing, Creative & Communications
A 24-hour basic cable ch that provides high quality entertainment progmg to a national audience. 88 million subs.

HBO (Home Box Office)
1100 Avenue of the Americas, New York, NY 10036
(212) 512-1000, (212) 512-1208
www.hbo.com
Richard Plepler, Chairman & CEO
Features 24-hour var progmg including theatrical films, original movies, specials, documentaries, sports, & series. Multiplex chs. HBO, HBO 2, HBO Latino, HBO Signature, HBO Family, HBO Comedy, HBO Zone - known collectively as HBO The Works.MoreMAX.

HLN
One CNN Center, Atlanta, GA 30348-5366
(404) 827-1500; *Fax:* (404) 827-1500
www.cnn.com/specials/videos/hln
Jeff Zucker, President, CNN Worldwide
Ken Jautz, Executive VP, HLN Operations
Provides viewers with a 30-minute news, 24-hours. Each half-hour covers major news stories as well as business, sports, medicine, entertainment, weather & human interest topics.
Areas: United States, Canada, Mexico & Caribbean.

Home & Garden Television Network (HGTV)
9721 Sherrill Blvd, Knoxville, TN 37932
(865) 694-2700, (800) 840-8056; *Fax:* (865) 531-1588
www.hgtv.com
Satellite: Galaxy IR; *Transponder:* 4
Kenneth W Lowe, Chairman, President & CEO
Lori A Hickok, Chief Financial Officer
Kathleen Finch, Chief Programming/Content/Brand Offcr-SNI
Vikki Neil, GM, Scripps Lifestyle Studios
John Feld, SVP, Programming
Donna Stephens, SVP,Ad Sales
Dylan Jones, Chief Communications Officer
HGTV is a 24-hour network that provides practical info & creative ideas to help the viewers to make the most of their lives at home & is designed to appeal to all ages & lifestyles.

HSN, The Home Shopping Network
1 HSN Drive, St Petersburg, FL 33729
(800) 933-2887, (800) 284-3900, (727) 872-1000; *Fax:* (727) 872-6559
www.hsn.com
Satellite: Satcom C-4; *Transponder:* 10
Rod Little, CFO & Office of the Chief Executive
Bill Brand, President & Chief Marketing Officer
Judy Schmeling, COO & Office of the Chief Executive
Jennifer Cotter, Executive VP, Television, Content & Programming
Maria Martinez,Chief Human Resources Officer
Rob Solomon, Executive VP, Customer Care & Operations Admin.
Karen Etzkorn, Chief Information Officer
Greg Henchel, Chief Legal Officer
HSN offers live, 24-hour video retailing.

IFC
Div/DBA: AMC Networks Inc
11 Penn Plaza, New York, NY 10001
(855) 879-3333; (212) 324-8500; *Fax:* (917) 542-6395
www.ifc.com www.ifcfilms.com
Satellite: Galaxy VII
Jonathan Sehring, President
Lisa Schwartz, EVP, Distribution, Operations&Business Development

iN DEMAND LLC
Mailing Address: 345 Hudson Street, 17th Floor, New York, NY 10014
Second Address: 4100 E Dry Creek Rd, Centennial, CO 80120
(646) 638-8200, (303) 712-3360; *Fax:* (646) 486-0854
www.indemand.com
Tom Montemagno, Chairman
Dale Hopkins, President & CEO
Michael Berman, EVP, Programming/General Counsel
Eric Petro, EVP, Business Development & CFO
Stacie Gray, Chief Creative Officer
John Vartanian, Chief Technology Officer
Claire Kostbar, Senior VP, Human Resources & Administration
Lauren LoFrisco, Executive VP, Distribution & Budiness Mgmt.
Pay-Per-View (PPV), Video-On-Demand (VOD) & high-definition (HD) progmg 24-hrs. National Cable Program Services.
Programming genres: gen entertainment.
1888 Century Park E, Los Angeles, CA 90067-1702
(310) 785-9094, (310) 785-9194; *Fax:* (310) 785-9195, (310) 785-9769
1117 Perimeter Ctr. W, Suite 500 E, Atlanta, GA 30338-5451
(404) 399-3119; *Fax:* (404) 399-3014
26677 W. Twelve Mile Rd, Southfield, MI
(810) 354-3375; *Fax:* (810) 358-9693

Independent Film Channel (IFC)
Div/DBA: AMC Networks
11 Penn Plaza, New York, NY 10001
(917) 542-6200, (855) 879-3333; (212) 324-8500; *Fax:* (917) 542-6395
www.ifc.com; www.ifcfilms.com
Bob Broussard, President, AMC Networks Distribution
Jennierf Caserta, President & GM, IFC
Jonathan Sehring, Co-President, IFC Films
Lisa Schwartz, Co-President, IFC Films
A 24-hour uncut coml-free ch, capturing the true spirit of ind film, original series, live events & enchanced new media progmg.
Offbeat and unexpected comedy. IFC Films.

INSP TV
Mailing Address: PO Box 7750, Charlotte, NC 28241 US
Second Address: , Indian Land, SC
(803) 578-1000; *Fax:* (803) 578-1735
www.insp.com
info@insp.com
Satellite: Galaxy 15; *Transponder:* 17
David Cerullo, CEO/COO
Dale Ardizzone, COO
Melissa Prince, VP, Corporate Communication
Tara Brown, Director, Media Relations
TV net which distributes life-enriching, edu entertainment progmg & digital, 24-hours.

The Inspirational Network INSP
Div/DBA: Inspiration TV
Box 7750, Charlotte, NC 28241
(803) 578-1000; *Fax:* (803) 578-1735
www.inspiration.org
Satellite: Galaxy IR; *Transponder:* 17
David Cerullo, Chairman & CEO
Ron Shuping, EVP, Programming
Inspiration TV blends ministry programs with family-oriented movies, dramas, music & children's programs along with concerts & specials.

Investigation Discovery
One Discovery Place, Silver Spring, MD 20910
(240) 662-2000; *Fax:* (240) 662-1854
www.investigation.discovery.com/
first_last@discovery.com
David M. Zaslav, President & CEO, Discovery Communications
Henry S. Schleiff, Group President
David C. Leavy, Chief Corporate Operations & Communications
Eric Phillips, President, Domestic Distribution
Provides the highest quality investigative progmg focused on dynamic stories of human nature from the past to the present.

Jewish Television Network
13743 Ventura Blvd, Suite 200, Sherman Oaks, CA 91423
(818) 789-5891; *Fax:* (818) 789-5892
chosen.tv
shalom@chosen.tv
Directors: Mike Wilson, Dennis Yocum, Garry Bowman, Harold Kimmel, Rick Smith, Harvey Oxner, Jay Butler, Doug Martin.

JLTV (Jewish Life Television)
Los Angeles, CA

(818) 786-4000; *Fax:* (818) 380-9232
www.jltv.tv
pblazer@jltv.tv
Phil Blazer, President & CEO
24/7 Jewish-theme tv station-comedy, entertainment, news, films, documentaries.

The Jones Companies
9697 E Mineral Avenue, Centennial, CO 80112
(303) 792-3111, (800) 525-7002; *Fax:* (303) 784-8454
www.jones.com
info@jones.com
Glenn R. Jones, Executive Chairman, President & CEO
Stacey Slaughter, CEO & CFO
Timothy J. Burke, Operations Dir
John Jennings, President, Interactive
Joseph Gregg, President, Library
Mary Bliss, VP, Real Estate & facilities
Vincent DiBiase, President, Jones/NCTI
A 24-hour revenue providing svc that features full-length product demonstrations & introduction of new products in a hands-on demonstration format.

JTV-Jewelry Television By ACN
9600 Parkside Drive, Knoxville, TN 37922
(865) 692-6000; (800) 550-8393; *Fax:* (865) 692-1346
www.jtv.com
F. Robert Hall, Chairman
Tim Matthews, President & CEO
Harry Bagley, Operations Dir
William C. Kouns, Chief Merchandising Officer
Crawford Wagner, CFO
Tim Engle, Chief Strategy Officer
Stephen E. Roth, General Counsel
CharlesA. Wagner, III, Vice Chairman
Gerald D. Sisk, Jr., G.G., Co-Founder, Deceased
Jewerly TV the only network that focuses exclusively on the sls of fine jewelry & gemstones, 24-hours a day. Satellite: Telstar 5. Serving 32 milion subs, on 11 million cable systems, transponder 19.

KTLA-TV
on 220 Cable Systems
5800 Sunset Blvd, Los Angeles, CA 90028
(323) 460-5500; *Fax:* (323) 460-5243
www.ktla.com
ktlacaptioning@tribune.com
Transponder: 15
David Cox, Chief Engineer
Los Angeles CW stn offers movies, news, specials & live sporting events, featuring the Los Angeles Clippers basketball. Services offered: Ind satellite carrier serving CATV, SMATV & MMDS distributing WGN, WPIX, KTLA & WFMT (FM) Networksvcs. Satellite: Spacenet 6E.

The Learning Channel (TLC)
Div/DBA: (Discovery Communications)
One Discovery Place, Silver Spring, MD 20910
(240) 662-2000; *Fax:* (240) 662-1854
www.tlc.com
first_last@discovery.com
David M. Zaslav, President & CEO, Disocvery Communications
Nancy Daniels, President & General Manager, TLC
Eric Phillips, President, Domestic Distribution
Bruce Campbell, Chief Development, Distribution & Legal Officer
Ben Price,President, National Advertising Sales
TLC's themed nights that focus on real families , relationship, careers & entertaining consist of perennial fashion favorite, makeover sensation, humorous & fun workplace competion. Real-life progmg portrays relatable people with compellingstories in the blockbuster hits Jon & Kate Plus 8, Little People, Big World & LA Ink.

Lifetime
Div/DBA: (A&E Television Networks)
235 East 45th Street, New York, NY 10017
(212) 424-7000; *Fax:* (212) 957-4264
www.mylifetime.com
Satellite: Satcom C-3; *Transponder:* 12
Nancy Dubuc, President/CEO, A+E Networks
Rob Sharenow, EVP & GM, Lifetime & A+E
Dan Suratt, President, Corporate Dvlpmnt, Strategy & Investmnt
Michael Feeney, Executive VP, Corporate Communications
Amanda Hill, Chief MarketingOfficer
Offering the highest quality entertainment, info progmg & advocating a wide range of issues affecting women & their families.

Lifetime Movies (LMN)
235 East 45th Street, New York, NY 10017
(212) 424-7000; *Fax:* (212) 957-4264
www.mylifetime.com/lifetime-movies
Nancy Dubuc, President/CEO, A+E Networks
Robert Sharenow, EVP & GM, Lifetime & A+E
Amanda Hill, Chief Marketing Officer
Offering the highest quality entertainment & info progmg 24-hours.

Lifetime Real Women (LRW)
235 East 45th Street, New York, NY 10017
(212) 424-7000; *Fax:* (212) 957-4264
www.mylifetime.com/lrw/
Nancy Dubuc, President/CEO, A+E Networks
Robert Sharenow, EVP & GM, Lifetime & A+E
Dan Suratt, President, Corporate Dvpmnt, Strategy & Investment
David Zagin, President, Distribution
Amanda Hill, Chief Marketing Officer
Programming geared toward the real contemporary woman including inspiring specials, scripted series, and real life experiences. 10 million.

MLB Network
One MLB Network Plaza, Secaucus, NJ 07094
(201) 520-6400
m.mlb.com/network/
mlbnviewerfeedback@mlb.com
Tony Petitti, COO
Rob McGlarry, President
Susan Stone, Senior VP, Operations & Engineering
Brent Fisher, VP, Distribution, Affiliate Sales & Marketing
Andy Butters, VP, Programming
Mary Beck, Senior VP, Marketing & Promotion
MarkHaden, VP, Engineering & IT
Joe Torre, Chief Baseball Officer
Bob Mincieli, Vice President, Studio & Broadcast Operations
Dave Patterson, Senior Vice President, Production
Bill Morningstar, Executive VP, Advertising Sales
Tony Santomauro,Senior Vice President, Finance & Administration
Chris Mallory, Vice President, Creative Services

Mother Nature Network
Div/DBA: Narrative Content Group
Mailing Address: 191 Peachtree Street NE, Ste 750, Atlanta, GA 30303
Second Address: One Discovery Place, Silver Spring, MD 20910
(404) 856-7021; (240) 662-2000; *Fax:* (240) 662-1854
www.mnn.com/
contact@mnn.com
Emily Murphy, President
Joel Babbit, Co-Founder & CEO
Dan Beeson, Director of Media Relations
Chuck Leavell, Co-Founder & Director of Environmental Affairs
Hope Dlugozima, VP & Director of Community & Social Networking
MichaelJacobson, Chief Financial Officer
Travis Bright, Vice President of Sponser Relations
Sarah Hicks, Managing Editor
Planet Green will provide entertaining, authentic & quality info for such categories as eco-design, organic food & green architecture, progmg for a green lifestyle.

The Movie Channel (TMC)
Div/DBA: (Showtime Networks Inc)
1633 Broadway, New York, NY 10019
(212) 708-1600; *Fax:* (212) 708-1212
www.sho.com
Matthew C. Blank, Chairman
David Nevins, President & CEO
TMC features daily movie marathons, overnight & double vision weekends & Movie Channel Xtra, offers more of viewers favorite movies, 24-hours a day. Serving 34.8 million subs. Satellites: Satcom C-3, transponder 19 east; Satcom G-9,transponder 5 west.

MSNBC
30 Rockefeller Plaza, New York, NY 10112
(212) 664-6605
www.msnbc.com
contact.nbcnews@nbcuni.com
Satellite: Galaxy IR; *Transponder:* 10
Andrew Lack, Chairman
Phil Griffin, President
John Reiss, Chief Engineer
Nick Ascheim, Senior VP, Digital
Errol Cockfield, Senior VP, Communications
Marc Greenstein, Creative Director
Jared DiPalma, CFO
Deb Finan, VP,Production & Programming
Bill Wolff, VP, Primetime Programming
MSNBC is an all news net 24-hours.

MTV Networks
1515 Broadway, New York, NY 10036
(212) 258-8000; *Fax:* (212) 258-8100
www.mtv.com/
Chris McCarthy, President
Tom Calderone, General Manager
Jacqueline Parkes, EVP, Marketing & Creative
MTV2 is the premier destination to find the hottest mix of music videos, long form music programs, exclusive access to their favorite bands, and ground-breaking music before it hits mainstream.

MTV Networks Latin America
Div/DBA: (formerly MTV Latino)
1111 Lincoln Road, 6th Floor, Miami Beach, FL 33139
(305) 535-3700; *Fax:* (305) 535-8388; (305) 535-5377
www.mtvla.com
Sarah Kirshbaum Levy, COO, Global Entertainment Group
David Lynn, President/CEO, Viacom International Media Networks
DeDe Lea, Executive VP, Government Affairs
Josh Greenberg, Sr VP, Programming & Creative Strategy
MTV's sixth global network, 24-hour progmg, advertiser supported & available in Latin America & the United States. Serving over 8.5 million subs. Satellite: Satcom C3, transponder 19 (USA); PanAm Sat 3, transponder 5C & 6C (Latin America).

MTV: Music Television
Div/DBA: MTV Networks Inc
1515 Broadway, New York, NY 10036
(212) 258-8000; *Fax:* (212) 258-8100
www.mtv.com
Robert Bakish, President & CEO, Viacom, Inc.
A 24-hrs music video ch in stereo, with 22 worldwide music on the web, original, innovative online music & entertainment progmg to each net. Also includes 14 international destinations throughout Europe, Asia, & Latin America.

National Geographic
1145 17th Street NW, Washington, DC 20090-8199
(202) 912-6770; *Fax:* (202) 912-6603
channel.nationalgeographic.com/
comments@natgeochannel.com; ngcpr@natgeotv.com
Satellite: Satcom C-3; *Transponder:* one
Declan Moore, CEO, National Geographic Partners
Laura Nichols, EVP, Communications & Chief Communications Officer
Rachel Webber, Executive VP, Digital Product
NGC provides the spectacular imagery that the National Geographic is know for in stunning high-dedinition.

NBC Sports Network (NBCSN)
on 4,893 Cable Systems
1 Blachley Road, Stamford, CT 06902
(203) 356-7000
www.nbcsports.com
Mike Lazarus, Chairman, NBC Sports Group
90 Park Ave., 2nd Fl., New York, NY 10016-1301
(212) 883-4000; *Fax:* (212) 687-1819
11835 W. Olympic Blvd., Suite 980, Los Angeles, CA 90064-5001
(310) 473-5404; *Fax:* (310) 473-6525

New Frontier Media
Mailing Address: 6000 Spine Road, Suite 100, Boulder, CO 80301
Second Address: 8484 Wilshire Blvd, Suite 850, Beverly Hills, CA 90211
(303) 444-0900, (888) 875-0632; *Fax:* (303) 938-8388
Larry Flynt, CEO
Michael Klein, President
William Mossa, Promotions Manager
Chris Woodward, Chief Financial Officer
TEN is a network that uses the 'un-inhibited' editing standard, 24-hours a day. Multiplex chs: TEN On Demand, TENBlox, TENBlue, TENClips & TENXtsy, PLEASURE. Serving 13.7 million subs. Satellite: Telstar 7-24, TUN, G10R-7.

Newsworld International
Div/DBA: (North American Television Inc.)
1230 Avenue of the Americas, New York, NY 10020
(212) 413-5000
John Bernbach, Chairman
Intl progmg covering top stories from around the world plus current affrs, documentaries, the latest business, financial & sports news, 24-hours.

CABLE - U.S.

NFL Network
10950 Washington Blvd, Culver City, CA 90232
(310) 840-4635; *Fax:* (310) 280-1132
www.nfl.com/nflnetwork/home
Hans Schroeder, President
Mark Quenzel, Senior VP, Programming & Production
Mike Muriano, Executive Producer, Studio & Remote Content
Michael Mandt, Executive Producer, Original Content
A national cable & satellite ch telecasting NFL content 24 hrs a day. Satellites: Galaxy 11, Transponder 9. Serving 30 million subs. On more than 60 cable systems.

NICK at NITE: See Nickelodeon.
1515 Broadway, New York, NY 10036-8901
(212) 258-8000; *Fax:* (212) 258-7676
www.nickatnite.com
Cyma Zarghami, President, Nickelodeon Group
Kim Rosenblum, EVP & Chief Creative Officer, Nickelodeon Group
Marva Smalls, EVP, Public Affairs & Chief of Staff

Nickelodeon
Div/DBA: Viacom Media Networks
1515 Broadway, New York, NY 10036
(212) 846-2543; *Fax:* (212) 258-6284
www.nickelodeon.com
nickprivacy@nickonline.com
Cyma Zarghami, President
Elizabeth Murray, EVP, Programming & Content Strategy
Matthew Evans, EVP, Strategy, New Business & Digital
Keith Dawkins, EVP, TeenNick and Nicktoons
Shelly Sumpter Gillyard, EVP, Talent, Music and Events
Kim Rosenblum, EVP & Chief Creative Officer
Chris Viscardi, Senior VP, Production, Development, Animation
Marva Smalls, Executive VP, Public Affairs & Chief of Staff
Nickelodeon cable net targets kids. NICK at NITE provides entertainment svc for the TV generation. NICKTOONS is the 24-hours digital destination for the next generation of animation. NICK2 gives viewers the convenience of watching theirfavorite Nickelodeon & NICK at NITE shows at different times of the day. NickJr, TeenNick, TV Land. 92 million.

The Outdoor Channel
1000 Chopper Circle, Denver, CO 80204
(800) 770-5750; *Fax:* (951) 719-8977
www.outdoorchannel.com
webmaster@outdoorchannel.com
Sean Luxton, VP & General Manager
Mitch Petrie, Vice President, Programming
Bill Osborn, Senior VP, Marketing
Jim Liberatore, President & CEO, Outdoor Sportsman Group
Bill Osborn, Executive VP, Networks Group
Tim Cremin, ExecutiveProducer
Outdoor Channel offers progmg such as fishing, hunting, hiking, competitive shooting & motor sports, 24-hours.

OVATION-The Arts Network
12910 Culver Blvd, Suite J, Los Angeles, CA 90066
(310) 430-7575; *Fax:* (703) 813-6336
www.ovationtv.com
info@ovationtv.com
Satellite: Galaxy VII; *Transponder:* 13
Ken Solomon, Chairman
Phil Gilligan, CFO
Scott Woodward, EVP, Programming & Production
John Malkin, EVP, Ontent Distribution
David Wideroe, SVP, Marketing & On Air Promotions
Liz Janneman, EVP, Network Strategy
Rob Rader, GeneralCounsel
The net covers arts news from around the world & children's arts programs, 20 hours a day. 50 million subs.

OWN: The Oprah Winfrey Network
5700 Wilshire Boulevard, Los Angeles, CA 90036
(424) 204-1800
www.oprah.com
Erik Logan, President
Neal Kirsch, COO/CFO
Mashawn Nix, Senior VP, Programming
Harriet Seitler, EVP/Chief Marketing Officer

Oxygen Media Inc.
Div/DBA: NBC Universal
30 Rockefeller Plaza, New York, NY 10112
(212) 651-2070; *Fax:* (212) 651-2099
www.oxygen.com
Shanon Smith, VP, Production & Operations
Oxygen Media is a 24-hour cable network for women and is available in 77 million homes in the U.S.

Pennsylvania Cable Network (PCN)
401 Fallowfield Road, Camp Hill, PA 17011
(717) 730-6000; *Fax:* (717) 730-6009, (717) 441-4540
www.pcntv.com
pcntv@pcntv.com
James J. Duratz, Chairman
Debra Kohr Sheppard, Sr VP & Chief Operating Officer
Brian Lockman, President & CEO
Shawn McLain, Director of Operations
Francine Schertzer, VP, Programming
Rick Cochran, Promotions Manager
John Fox,Chief Engineer
Melissa Hiler, VP & CFO
Mitzy Henry Jones, Director of Strategic Partnerships
Joel Bechtel, Director, Sports Fndrsg & Community Awareness
The nation's preeminent state pub affrs net, with live & same-day coverage of the Pennsylvania General Assembly. PCN also covers significant state events, such as high school sports finals. Serving 3.3 million subs on 150 cable systems,transponder 13C. Satellite: AMC-6.
400 N. Broad St., Philadelphia, PA 19130-4015
(215) 854-4455
Corey Clarke, Bureau Chief
Pittsburgh Post Gazette Bldg, 34 Blvd., Pittsburgh, PA
(412) 263-1300
Doug Sicchitano, Bureau Chief

Pennsylvania Cable Network (PCN)
401 Fallowfield Road, Camp Hill, PA 17011
(717) 730-6000; *Fax:* (717) 730-6009
www.pcntv.com
pcntv@pcntv.com
David R Breidinger, Chairman
Debra Kohr Sheppard, Senior VP, COO
Brian Lockman, President & CEO
Shawn McLain, Director of Operations
Francine Schertzer, VP, Programming
John Fox, Chief Engineer
Melissa Hiler, SVP & CFO
MitziHenry Jones, VP, Strategic Partnerships
Joel Bechtel, Vice President, Marketing and Brand Development
Larry Kaspar, Producer and Host
Matthew Hall, VP, Field Operations
PCN is the nation's pre-eminent state pub affrs network, with live & same day coverage of the Pennsylvania Senate/House & other govt activities. PCN televises significant state events (such as high school sports championships), toursmuseums & mfg facilities in the state & distributes educ progmg.

Pentagon Channel
601 North Fairfax Street, Alexandria, VA 22314
(301) 222-6780; *Fax:* (703) 428-0466
Gene Brink, General Manager
Pentagon Channel is a gov owned TV of the Department of Defense, providing internal communications to svc members, families, the National Guard, the Reserve & military retirees, available 24-hours.

Playboy TV
Div/DBA: (Playboy Entertainment Group)
2706 Media Center Drive, Los Angeles, CA 90065
(323) 276-4000, (877) 446-0771; *Fax:* (323) 276-4500
www.playboytv.com
Jeff Jenest, Sr VP And General Manager
Entertainment targeted to adults. Schedule consists of nearly 100% original Playboy programs with the balance comprised of acquired programs & feature films. Serving 4.5 under PPV svc. Satellite: Galaxy 5, transponder 2.
Hot Zone is a24-hour Pay-Per-View ch for adults. Satellite: Telstar 7, transponder 5.
Hot Networks is a 24-hour Pay-Per-View ch for adults. Satellite: Telstar 7, transponder 5.

POP (formerly TV Guide Channel)
5510 Lincoln Boulevard, Playa Vista, CA 90094
(323) 817-4600; (800) 866-1400; *Fax:* (323) 762-8815
www.poptv.com
Satellite: Satcom C-4
Brad Schwartz, President
David Mandell, COO
Kent Rees, Chief Marketing Officer
Jed Kapsos, CFO
70 million
708 Third Ave., 21st Fl., New York, NY 10017-4201
(212) 370-1799; *Fax:* (212) 370-7575
Chris Manning, Eastern Sls Mgr

Punch TV Network (Punch Animation)
Punch TV Studios, 11705 Willake Street, Santa Fe Springs, CA 90670
(310) 680-9245
www.ddgtv.com
ddgweb2011@ddgtv.com
Joseph Collins, CEO, Punch TV Studios
Floyd Norman, President, Creative Development
Leo Sullivan, COO
Rachel Ramos, VP, Broadcast Division

QVC
1200 Wilson Drive, West Chester, PA 19380
(484) 701-1000; 484-701-1647
www.qvc.com
Satellite: Satcom C-4; *Transponder:* 9
Michael A. George, President/CEO
Meade Rudasill, COO
Thaddeus J. Jastrzebski, EVP & CFO
Preeminent electronic retailer mktg a wide var of brand name products, categories as home furnishings, licensed products, fashions, beauty, electronics & fine jewelry.

Science Channel
One Discovery Place, Silver Spring, MD 20910
(240) 662-2000; *Fax:* (240) 662-1854
science.discovery.com/; www.sciencechannel.com
first_last@discovery.com
Robert J. Miron, Chairman, Discovery Communications
David C. Leavy, CCO and Communications Officer
Rich Ross, Group President
Bill Goodwyn, President/CEO, Discovery Education
John Honeycutt, Chief Technology Officer
Adria AlpertRomm, Chief Human Resources & Global Diversity Officer
Scientific topics ranging form string theory & futuristic cities to accidental discoveries & outrageous inventions. Reaching more than 50 million homes nationwide.

SCOLA
21557 270th Street, McClelland, IA 51548
(712) 566-2202; *Fax:* (712) 566-2502
www.scola.org
scola@scola.org
Satellite: Telstar 5
Francis Lajba, President/CEO
John Millar, Operations Dir
Foreign language news & educ progmg, 24-hours a day.

Scripps Networks
9721 Sherrill Blvd, Knoxville, TN 37932
(865) 694-2700; *Fax:* (865) 690-9281
www.scrippsnetworksinteractive.com
Satellite: Galaxy IR; *Transponder:* 4
Kenneth W. Lowe, Chairman, President & CEO
Burton Jablin, President
Mark S. Hale, Operations Dir
Allison Page, General Manager, U.S. Programming
Robyn Ulrich, Promotions Manager
Joseph G. Necastro, Chief Financial andAdministrative Officer
Henry Ahn, EVP, Content Distribution and Marketing
Jim Clayton, EVP, Corporate Giving and Community Relations
Cynthia Gibson, EVP, Chief Legal Officer & Corporate Secretary
NJ Pesci, Executive Vice President, HumanResources
Mark Schuermann, Senior Vice President and Treasurer
DIY cable TV net operated by Scripps Networks, providing in depth demonstrations & tips for categories such as home improvement, home bldg, tools, products, gardening, landscaping, automotive, boating, decorating, design, arts, crafts,cooking, hobby & recreations, 24-hours.

ShortsHD
Div/DBA: Shorts Entertainment Networks
2716 Ocean Park Boulevard, Suite 1091, Santa Monica, CA 90405
(310) 452-1400; *Fax:* (310) 288-6545
us.shorts.tv/
info@shorts.tv
Carter Pilcher, Chief Executive Officer
Marshall Nord, President
Leif Nelson, COO
Scott Parker, VP, Legal & Business Affairs
Bruce Rider, Head of Programming
Cathy Cassese Lingenfelser, VP, USA Marketing
T, Chief Engineer
Robert Barker, CFO
Stephanie Charmail, Head of Production
Short films, available 24-hours, ad-supported.

Showtime Networks Inc.
1633 Broadway, New York, NY 10019
(212) 708-1600; *Fax:* (212) 708-1212
www.sho.com
Satellite: Satcom C-3; *Transponder:* 19 (east)
Matthew C. Blank, Chairman
David Nevins, President & CEO
THE MOVIE CHANNEL & FLIX. SNI also operates & manages the premium TV net SUNDANCE CHANNEL, SHOWTIME on Espanol, a separate audio feed of SHOWTIME, available for the Sp-speaking audience. SNI also markets & distributes sports &entertainment events for exhibition to subscribers on a pay-per-view basis. Multiplex chs: SHOWTIME BEYOND, SHOWTIME PAY-PER-VIEW. SHOWTIME EXTREME, SHOWTIME FAMILY ZONE, SHOWTIME NEXT, targeting gen young adults 18-24, SHOWTIME SHOWCASE, SHOWTIMETOO, SHOWTIME WOMEN.

The Ski Channel
NSS Data: TV-CATV only
881 Alma Real Dr, Terrace 8, Pacific Palisades, CA 90272
(310) 230-2050
www.theskichannel.com
Steve Bellamy, Founder
Connie Lawn, Correspondent
Mtn sports tv network that covers major natl, international & specialty stories for radio & TV stns in the U.S. & around the world. Also do live talk-back features. Serves radio, TV & write ski reports.

Soapnet
3800 West Alameda Avenue, Burbank, CA 91505
(818) 569-7500; *Fax:* (818) 566-1358
www.soapnet.com
editor@sonuni.com
Mary Ellen DiPrisco, Programming Director
Sherri York, Promotions Manager
Errol Lewis, Editor In Chief And Publisher
Xavier Toups, Co-Founder
Soapnet features today's soaps tonight, classic soaps, news & info from the world of soaps, 24-hours. Serving 35.7 million subs.
Satellite: Galaxy 10 R.

SPEED Channel Inc
9711 Southern Pines Blvd, Charlotte, NC 28273
(704) 731-2222, (704) 731-2285; *Fax:* (704) 731-2197
www.speedtv.com
Nat'l Network: Fox Sports 1
Satellite: Satcom C-4; *Transponder:* 11
Hunter Nickell, President
Francois McGillicuddy, Vice President Of Finance
Patti Wheeler, Exec VP Of Programming & Production
Erik Arneson, Vice President Of Media Relations
Providing insight & action, number one authority for anything motorsports.

Spike (Paramount Network in 2018)
Div/DBA: (division of MTV Networks)
2600 Colorado Avenue, 37th Floor, Santa Monica, CA 90404
(310) 907-2400
www.spiketv.com
spike-feedback@spike.com
Satellite: Satcom C-3; *Transponder:* 18
Kevin Kay, President
Tom Zappala, EVP, Programming
Terry Minogue, SVP, Marketing & Brand Creative
Jonathan Ladd, SVP, Legal & Business Affairs
Jon Slusser, SVP, Sports & Specials
David Schwarz, SVP, Communications
Brian Dermody,Senior Sports Writer
Dana Flax, Social Media Editor
Network for men.
2806 Opryland Dr., Nashville, TN 37214-1209
(615) 457-7230

The Sportsman Channel
2855 S James Drive, Suite 101, New Berlin, WI 53151
(262) 432-9100; *Fax:* (262) 432-9101
www.thesportsmanchannel.com
viewerinfo@thesportsmanchannel.com
Satellite: Telstar 5; *Transponder:* 1
C. Michael Cooley, Founder
Jim Liberatore, President/CEO, Outdoor Sportsman Group
Todd D. Hansen, COO
Mitch Petrie, VP, Programming
Jeff Brown, Vice President Western Region
The Sportsman Channel provides continuous hunting & fishing progmg 24-hours a day.

Starz Entertainment LLC
Div/DBA: (formerly Encore Media Corp.)
8900 Liberty Circle, Englewood, CO 80112
(720) 852-7700; *Fax:* (720) 852-7710
www.starz.com
Chris Albrecht, CEO
Bill Myers, President
Jerry Maglio, Promotions Manager
Theano Apostolou, EVP, Communications
Offers 17 movie channels including the flagship Starz & Encore brands with approximately 24.5 million & 31.5 million subs. Advanced svcs including Starz HD, Encore HD, Starz On Demand, Encore On Demand, MoviePlex On Demand, Starz HD OnDemand, Encore On HD Demand, MoviePlex HD On Demand, Starz Play & Vongo.
southeast region
5775 Peachtree Dunwoody Rd, Suite D-620, Atlanta, GA 30342-1556
(404) 531-7060; *Fax:* (404) 531-7075
Cindy Feinberg, Rgnl Vp
Founders
5445 DTC Pkwy, Suite 600, Englewood, CO 80111-3045
(303) 771-7700; *Fax:* (303) 267-4001
Robin Feller, Rgnl Vp
eastern region
70 Hudson St, Hoboken, NJ 07030-5630
(201) 239-9020; *Fax:* (201) 239-2290
Shanita Evans, Rgnl Vp
central region
111 E. Wacker Dr., Suite 1300, Chicago, IL 60601-3713
(312) 938-8900; *Fax:* (312) 938-8902
Susan LeVarsky, Rgnl Vp
International Channel
11766 Wilshire Blvd, Suite 710, Los Angeles, CA 90025-6538
(310) 477-9922; *Fax:* (310) 477-4544
Victoria Kent, Rgnl Vp
New Media
5445 DTC Pkwy, Suite 600, Englewood, CO 80111-3045
(303) 771-7700; *Fax:* (303) 267-4098
Leslie Nittler, Vp Sls & Mktg
Time Warner & Central region office
2340 E. Trinity Mills Rd, Suite 300, Carrollton, TX 75006-1942
(972) 417-2866; *Fax:* (972) 417-2806
Paige Holmes, Chairman

Sundance Channel
Div/DBA: AMC Networks
11 Penn Plaza, New York, NY 10001
(212) 654-1500, (212) 708-8025
www.sundancechannel.com
feedback@sundancechannel.com
Satellite: Satcom C-4; *Transponder:* 20
Charles Collier, President & GM, SundanceTV
Jonathan Sehring, Co-President, Sundance Selects
Lisa Schwartz, Co-President, Sundance Selects
Sundance Channel is a 24-hours a day ch, featuring uncut coml-free programs, providing TV viewers daring & engaging feature films, short, documentaries, world cinema & animation.

Syfy
Div/DBA: (Entertainment Networks)
8800 W Sunset Blvd, 4th Floor, West Hollywood, CA 90069
(310) 360-2300; *Fax:* (212) 703-8533
www.syfy.com/scifi
feedback@syfy.com
Chris McCumber, President, Entertainment Networks
Alexandra Shapiro, EVP, Marketing
Rob Spodek, CFO
Katherine Nelson, SVP, Communications
David Giles, SVP, Research
Dedicated to a broad range of science fiction & fact, fantasy, & horror programs, 24-hours. 92 million.

Talkline Communications Network
Park West Station, PO Box 20108, New York, NY 10025
(212) 769-1925, (866) 4-TALKLINE,(866)JEWISH RADIO; *Fax:* (212) 799-4195
www.talklinecommunications.com
tcntalk@aol.com
Rabbi Zev J. Brenner, President, Executive Producer
Nationally acclaimed Jewish TV programs carried on NBC digital and cable systems in New York as well as nationwide and online.

TBN-Trinity Broadcasting Network
on 43.4 million Cable Systems
Div/DBA: (TBN Cable Network)
Mailing Address: 2823 W Irving Blvd, Irving, TX 75061
Second Address: PO Box A, Santa Ana, CA 92711
(972) 313-1333, (800) 735-5542, 888-731-1000, (714; *Fax:* (972) 313-1010
www.tbn.org
Satellite: Galaxy V; *Transponder:* 3
Matthew Crouch, Vice President
TBN is America's most watched relg network, offering 24-hours of coml-free inspiritional original programs, that appeal to viewers in many denominations. Progmg includes Nashville gospel concerts, health & fitness, talk shows & svcs fromAmerica's largest Churches. Multiplex ch: TBN Enlace USA is a 24-hour multi-faith Hispanic ch from Trinity Broadcasting Network. Hillsong Channel is the newest network. TBN reaches more than 100 million households in the U.S.

TBS
One CNN Center, Atlanta, GA 30303
(404) 885-4339; (404) 885-0758; *Fax:* (404) 885-4319
tbs.com
Satellite: Galaxy V; *Transponder:* 6
John Martin, Chairman & CEO, Turner
David Levy, President, Turner
Kevin Reilly, President, TBS/TNT & Chief Creative Officer,Turner
Louise Sam, EVP & General Counsel, Turner
Pascal Desroches, EVP/CFO, Turner
TBS is TV top-rated comedy network. It serves as home to such original comedy series as People of Earth, Wrecked, Full Frontal with Samantha Bee, American Dad, and Search party; blockbuster movies; & hosted movie showcases.

Telemundo
Mailing Address: 2290 W 8th Avenue, Hialeah, FL 33010
Second Address: 12200 NW 25th Street, Miami, FL
(305) 889-7200; (305) 884-8200; *Fax:* (305) 889-7205
www.telemundo.com
Cesar Conde, Chairman
Luis Silberwasser, President, Telemundo Network/Universo
Marcos Santana, President, Telemundo International
Ray Warren, President, Telemundo Deportes
Beau Ferrari, Executive VP
Michelle Alban, VP, CorporateCommunications & PR
Telemundo, a United States Sp-language TV network, available 24-hours. Multiplex ch: Telemundo Internacional. Serving 40 million subs. Satellite: Satcom, transponder 20 east, AMC-4, transponder 8 west.

The Tennis Channel
Mailing Address: 2850 Ocean Park Blvd, Suite 150, Santa Monica, CA 90405
Second Address: 250 Park Ave, Suite 825, New York, NY 10177
(310) 314-9400; (310) 392-1920; *Fax:* (310) 314-9433
www.tennischannel.com
Satellite: Telstar 5; *Transponder:* 15
Ken Solomon, Chairman & CEO
William Simon, EVP, Chief Operating Officer & CFO
Bob Whylevy, SVP, Production
Doug Martz, Senior Vice President, Advertising Sales
Jeremy M Langer, VP, Programming
John Iatesta, Public Relations
PeterSteckelman, Senior Vice President, Business and Legal Affairs
Steve Badeau, Senior Vice President, Research
Adam Ware, Senior Vice President, Head of Digital
The Tennis Channel is the 24-hour cable TV network devoted to professional tennis & tennis lifestyle.

The Theatre Channel
NSS Data: Radio Only
Box 2676, 21 South Venice Blvd #2, Venice, CA 90294
(310) 823-6508
www.dcski.com
connielawn@aol.com
Cheryl Beach, CEO/COO
Connie Lawn, President
Covers major natl, international & ski stories for radio & TV stns in the United States & around the world. Also live 'inserts' into radio & TV shows.

Time Warner Cable
One Time Warner Center, New York, NY 10019-8016
(212) 484-8000
www.timewarner.com
webmaster@timewarner.com
Jeff Bewkes, Chairman & CEO
Jeffrey L. Bewkes, President
John K. Martin, CFO & Administration Officer
Paul T. Cappuccio, EVP & General Counsel
Gary L. Ginsberg, EVP, Corporate Marketing & Communications
Carol A. Melton, EVP, GlobalPublic Policy
Olaf J. Olafsson, EVP, International & Corporate Strategy
Keith Cocozza, Senior VP Corporate Communications
Cable svc. Serving over 1.3 million subs.
41-61 Kissena Blvd, Flushing, NY 11355-3181

TNT (Turner Network Television)
One CNN Center, 13 North, Atlanta, GA 30303
(404) 885-4339; *Fax:* (404) 885-4319
www.tntdrama.com
privacy.tnt@turner.com
Satellite: Galaxy V; *Transponder:* 17
John Martin, Chairman & CEO, Turner
Kevin Reilly, President, TNT/TBS, Chief Creative Offcr, Turner
Sandra Dewey, Productions & Business Operations
Top-rated networks, offers original series, also home to powerful one-hr dramas, bcst premiere movies, compelling prime-time specials & championship sports coverage. Available in high definition.

TNT Latin America
One CNN Center, Atlanta, GA 30303
(404) 827-1700; *Fax:* (404) 575-5341
www.tntla.com
turner.info@turner.com
Joel Whitten Richardson III, President, Turner Latin America
Luis Esparza, VP, Technology & Operations
Sharon Zyman, VP, Ad Sales
Tomas Yankelevich, EVP & Chief Content Officer, General Entertainment
Caroline Rittenberry, VP,Marketing & Communications
Cable network bcst in Sp, Portuguese, English featuring contemp, original movies, NBA coverage & exclusive premieres, 24-hours a day. Serving more than 8.5 million subs in 39 countries in the rgn. Satellite: PanAmSat 1, transponder 3.

Travel Channel
9721 Sherrill Blvd, Knoxville, TN 37932
(865) 694-2700
www.travelchannel.com
Bob Madden, Senior VP, Network Creative Services & Operations
Greg Regis, Senior VP, Ad Sales
Courtney White, Senior VP, Programming
Bringing knowledge, insight & info to a community of people who want to experience their world & satisfy their curiosity.

truTV
One CNN Center, Atlanta, GA 30303
(404) 575-5577
www.trutv.com
privacy.truTV@turner.com
Chris Linn, President & Head of Programming
Court TV telecast trails day by day & high profile original programs 24-hours. Serving 80 million subs.

Turner Classic Movies (TCM)
One CNN Center, Atlanta, GA 30303
(404) 885-5535, (877) 826-5764
www.tcm.com
filmfestival@tcm.com
John Martin, Chairman & CEO, Turner
Jennifer Dorian, General Manager, TCM/EVP, Turner Portfolio 360
Features Hollywood's greatest movies of all time, presented 24-hours, coml-free.

TV Asia
Div/DBA: (Asian Star Broadcasting Network Inc.)
76 National Road, Edison, NJ 08817
(732) 650-1100; *Fax:* (732) 650-1112
www.tvasiausa.com
info@tvasiausa.com
Hasmukh R Shah, Chairman & CEO
Kavita T Asia, Regional Manager
Rohit Vyas, News Director
Rilesh Shah
TV Asia provides a wide range of prgmg produced for South Asian Americans, 24-hrs.

TV Japan
Div/DBA: (Japan Network Group Inc)
100 Broadway, 15th Floor, New York, NY 10005
(212) 262-3377; (877) 885-2726; *Fax:* (212) 262-5577
www.tvjapan.net/en
takeuchi@tvjapan.net
Koki Matsumoto, President
TV Japan is a Japanese language ch, available 24-hours a day. Satellite: Galaxy II, transponder 24. 80,000.

TV Land
1515 Broadway, New York, NY 10036
(212) 258-8000; *Fax:* (212) 846-1775
www.tvland.com
video.support@tvland.com
Satellite: Satcom C-3; *Transponder:* 18
Kevin Kay, President
Brad Gardner, SVP, Development & Original Programming
Keith Cox, President, Development & Production
Neil Schuurmans, Chief Marketing Officer
TV Land is the only network dedicated to the best of everything TV from the past 50 years, available 24-hours.

TVG Network
19545 NW Von Neumann Drive, Suite 210, Beaverton, OR 97006
(888) 752-9884
www.tvgnetwork.com; www.tvg.com
Satellite: GE-1; *Transponder:* 23
Kip Levin, CEO

Univision Communications Inc.
605 3rd Avenue, 12th Floor, New York, NY 10158
(212) 455-5200; *Fax:* (212) 867-6710
www.corporate.univision.com
Satellite: Galaxy IR
Francisco J. Lopez-Baloa, Executive VP & CFO
Randy Falco, President And CEO
John W. Eck, EVP, Technology, Ops & Eng/Chief Local Media Offcr
Jessica Rodriguez, Executive VP & CMO
Juan Carlos Rodriguez, President, Univision Sports
Keith Turner, President, Advertising Sales & Marketing
Isaac Lee, President, Univision News
Tonia O'Connor, President, Content Distribution & Chief Cmcl Offcr
Univision Network, the most-watched Spanish-language broadcast television network in the U.S. reaching 97% of U.S. Hispanic households.
Serving 34.5 million subs. Satellite: Galaxy 1R.
TeleFutura Network, a general-interestSpanish-language broadcast television network, which was launched in 2002 and now reaches 83 million U.S. Hispanic households. Serves 7.2 million subs. Satellite: Galaxy 1.
Central
2323 Bryan St., Suite 1900, Dallas, TX 75201-2603
(214) 758-2405; *Fax:* (214) 758-2395
Deanna Andaverde, Vp Affl Rel
East
605 Third Ave, 26 Fl., New York, NY 10158-0180
(212) 455-5342; *Fax:* (212) 986-4731
John Heffron, Vp Affl Rels

VH1 (Music First)
Div/DBA: (MTV Networks Inc)
1515 Broadway, 45th Floor, New York, NY 10036
(212) 846-8000; *Fax:* (212) 846-1804
www.vh1.com
velocityinfo@viacom.com
Satellite: Satcom C-4; *Transponder:* 23
Chris McCarthy, President
Laura Molen, SVP VH1 Ad Sales
Ellen Dominus, SVP VH1 Ad Sales
Jake Piasecki, SVP VH1 Ad Sales
Jim Balbirer, SVP VH1 New Business Development
Sarah Weir Looss, VP VH1 Digital Ad sales
Mark McIntire, SVPVH1 Integrated Marketing
VH1 is a 24-hours ch that features new, current & classic music video, for viewers ages 18-49 who grew up with music videos. Multiplex chs: VH1 Classic, VH1 Country, VH1 Megahits, VH1 Soul & VH Uno.

WE-Women's Entertainment
Div/DBA: AMC Networks
11 Pennsylvania Plaza, 19th Floor, New York, NY 10001
(212) 324-1300
www.wetv.com
Marc Juris, President & GM
A 24-hours cable net featuring classic movies & TV progmg devoted entirely to romance.

The Weather Channel
300 Interstate North Parkway SE, Atlanta, GA 30339
(866) 843-0392; *Fax:* (770) 226-2950
www.weather.com
Dave Shull, CEO/COO
Nora Zimmett, Senior VP, Programming
Stu Ostro, Senior Director, Weather Communications
All-weather progmg 24-hours a day; natl, international, rgnl & loc weather forecasts & features. Multiplex ch: WeatherScan. Serving 87.5 million subs. Satellite: GE Satcom C-3, transponder 13.
845 Third Ave., 11th Floor, New York, NY 10022-6601
(212) 893-2245
Lyn Andrews, Pres. Twc Media Solutions

WGN America
2501 West Bradley Place, Chicago, IL 60618-4718
(773) 528-2311, (773) 883-3241, (212) 210-5900; *Fax:* (773) 883-6299
WGNAmerica.com
WGNAmerica@tribunemedia.com
Gavin Harvey, Interim President
Rita Cooper Lee, EVP, Communications & Publicity
Broad scope entertainment network offering blockbuster movies & series, including regional Chicago sports. Total subscribers: 80 million. Satellite used and transponder: Galaxy 14. transponder 13C.

WNBC-TV
30 Rockefeller Plaza, 7th Floor, New York, NY 10012
(212) 664-4444 , (866) 639-7244; *Fax:* (212) 413-6509
www.nbcnewyork.com
Bob Greenblatt, Chairman, NBC Entertainment
Steve Burke, CEO
Noah Oppenheim, President, NBC News
Janice Huff, Chief Meteorologist
Lauren Scala, Reporter
Melissa Russo, Anchor/Government Affairs Reporter
Andrew Siff, GeneralAssignment Reporter
Network featuring 40 hours/week of locally produced newscasts, movies, original series, sports specials, teen & children's progmg, 24-hours.

Worship Network
PO Box 428, Safety Harbor, FL 34695
(800) 728-8723
www.worship.net
info@worship.net
Transponder: 7
Bruce Kobish, President
Worship Network features, scenery from around the world with words of wisdom from scriptures & inspirational music. Available 24 hours a day.

WSBK-TV
Div/DBA: (Boscom)
1170 Soldiers Field Road, Boston, MA 02134
(617) 787-7000; *Fax:* (617) 254-6383
www.boston.cbslocal.com/station/tv38/
Satellite: GE-3; *Transponder:* 3
Mark Lund, President and General Manager
Michael O'Grady, Sales Manager
WSBK-TV is a 24-hours ind ch from Boston featuring sports, movies, news & specials.

Youtoo America
Div/DBA: (formerly AmericanLife TV Network)
6565 North MacArthur Blvd, Suite 400, Las Colinas, TX 75039 US
(214) 444-7100; *Fax:* (469) 828-1745
www.youtoo.com; www.youtooamerica.com
Chris Wyatt, President

Regional Cable News Networks

ABC10
4600 Air Way, San Diego, CA 92102
(619) 237-1010; (619) 237-6285; *Fax:* (619) 527-0369
www.10news.com
kgtv_marketing@10news.com
Jeff Block, Vice President/General Manager
Joel Davis, Station Manager
Tiffani Lupenski, News Director
San Diego's Newchannel provides original newscasts, repeats of KGTV-10 newscasts & live break-ins 24 hours.

Allbritton Communications
1000 Wilson Blvd, Suite 2700, Arlington, VA 22209
(703) 647-8700; *Fax:* (703) 647-8746
www.allbritton.com/
James Killen, General Sales Mgr
There are 8 stns: WJLA. Newschannel 8. WHTM, WSET, WCIU, WBMA, KATV, KTUL.

The Arizona News Channel
5555 N 7th Avenue, Phoenix, AZ 85013
(602) 207-3333; *Fax:* (602) 207-3477
www.azfamily.com
Steve Rauscher, Sales Manager
Andy Lashbrooke, Local Sales Manager
Arizona's first & only 24-hour loc news svc built on a unique partnership; live loc breaking coverage gives viewers the latest news from around the Valley; NewsChannel 3's 'Good Morning Arizona,' 'Good Day Arizona,' 'Good Evening Arizona' &'The News Show' replay throughout the day on the AZ News Channel, Cox Cable Channel 14; progmg also includes loc productions exclusive to cable, such as 'Project Parenting.'

Bay News 9
Div/DBA: Bright House Networks
700 Carillon Pkwy, Suite 9, St. Petersburg, FL 33716
(727) 329-2400; (888) 437-1239; *Fax:* (727) 329-2434
www.baynews9.com
desk@charter.com
Mike Gautreau, Senior News Director
Bay News 9 is a 24-hour ch owned & operated by Bright House Network. The ch serves over 1 million cable customers in Tampa Bay. Also programs a 24-hour Sp & sports ch.

The California Channel
1121 L Street, Suite 110, Sacramento, CA 95814
(916) 444-9792; *Fax:* (916) 444-9812
www.calchannel.com
contact_us@calchannel.com
Sam Attisha, Chair
Walter Hughes, Vice Chair
Carolyn McIntyre, State Association Representative
Deane Leavenworth, Secretary
Del Heintz, Treasurer
The California Channel is an independent, nonprofit, public affairs cable television network. Programming includes coverage of California Assembly and Senate floor sessions and committee meetings, capitol press conferences, and proceedingsof regulatory boards and state commissions. 33.5 hours/week, serving 5,800,000 subs.

Central Florida News 13
Div/DBA: Bright House Networks
20 N Orange Avenue, Suite 13, Orlando, FL 32801
(407) 513-1300; *Fax:* (407) 513-1310
www.mynews13.com
newsdesk@mynews13.com
Robin A. Smythe, VP & General Manager
Tim Geraghty, Senior News Director
Central Florida News 13 is Orlando & the Central Florida Region's only 24-hour loc cable news ch seen only on Bright House Networks.

CLTV News (ChicagoLand Television News)
2501 West Bradley Place, Chicago, IL 60618-4718
(773) 528-2311; *Fax:* (630) 571-0489
www.cltv.com
Covers Chicago loc & rgnl news, sports, news, weather & traf info, serving 1.9 million subs.

The Comcast Network
3601 South Broad Street, Philadelphia, PA 19148
(215) 952-2200; *Fax:* (215) 981-8420
www.csnphilly.com
askcsn@comcastsportsnet.com
Brian Monihan, President & General Manager
Maureen Quilter, Senior Director of Communications
The Comcast Network, is an award-winning, 24-hours news, talk, sports & entertainment cable net created by Comcast Cable Communications, that has steadily won viewers, awards & accolades since its inception in 1996. It provides qualitylocally-produced progmg in four main areas-live, interactive television; rgnl news; entertainment; coverage of high school, college & professional sports. It continues to expand its compelling mix of news, talk, sports & entertainment progmg throughthe eastern seaboard, from Washington DC, to the new England area, broadcasting to 6.2 million viewers everyday.

County News Center
1600 Pacific Highway, Room 208, San Diego, CA 92101-2422
(619) 595-4633; *Fax:* (619)557-4027
www.countynewscenter.com/
communications@sdcounty.ca.gov
Michael Workman, Director
Tammy Glenn, Assistant Director
Tegan Glasheen, Communications Manager
Jose Alvarez, Communications Specialist
Craig Sturak, Health &ÿHuman Services Agency
Michael Clock, Public Safety
Country Television Network San Diego makes country govt more accessible & understandable to the citizens of San Diego County through informational progmg focusing on the svcs, programs & current issues of county gov, 24 hr a day, serving708,700 subs.

CP 24
299 Queen Street W, Toronto, ON M5V 2Z5 Canada
(416) 384-2400; *Fax:* (416) 384-6554
www.cp24.com
now@cp24.com
Lindsey Brodie, Advertising and Sales
Bianca Reino, Public Affairs Representative
Jeannette Rabito, Sponsorship & Community Relations
Rgnl 24-hour a day English language news & information channel.

8 Las Vegas News Now
Div/DBA: KLAS-TV
3228 Channel 8 Drive, Las Vegas, NV 89109
(702) 792-8888; *Fax:* (702) 792-2977
www.lasvegasnow.com
info@lasvegasnow.com
Lisa Howfield, President and General Manager
Eric Aegerter, Production Manager
Terri Foley, News Director
Joyce Kotnik, Assistant News Director
Irene Pengson, Programming Director
Misty Morgan-Yousfi, General Sales Manager
TimFoley, Director of Technical Services
Las Vegas Now is a 24-hours loc news ch serving the Las Vegas area.

Michigan Government Television
111 S Capitol Avenue, 4th Floor Romney Bldg, Lansing, MI 48933
(517) 373-4250; *Fax:* (517) 335-7342
www.mgtv.org
mgtv@mgtv.org
Bill Trevarthen, General Manager
Cable network covering all branches of Michigan's state government.

New England Cable News
160 Wells Avenue, Newton, MA 02459
(617) 630-5000; *Fax:* (617) 630-5055
www.necn.com
Bill McFarland, Managing Editor
Kenny Plotnik, VP, News
Brian Burnell, Evening Anchor
Latoyia Edwards, Anchor
Jackie Bruno, Entertainment Reporter
Pete Bouchard, Meteorologist
A 24-hour rgnl news net.

News 12 Bronx
930 Soundview Avenue, Bronx, NY 10473
(718) 861-6800
bronx.news12.com/
news12bx@news12.com
David Kirschner, General Manager
Pat O'Keefe, Sports Director
Lennaeia Batiste, Anchor/Reporter
J.T. Fetch, Anchor/Reporter
Darryl Green, Weather Anchor
A 24-hour regional news service.

News 12 Connecticut
28 Cross Street, Norwalk, CT 06851
(203) 849-1321; *Fax:* (203) 849-1327
connecticut.news12.com/
news12ct@news12.com
David Kirschner, General Manager
Tom Appleby, News Director
Damian Andrew, Sports Anchor/Reporter
Gwen Edwards, Reporter
Mike Rizzo, Meteorologist
Ted Koppy, Anchor/Reporter
Gillian Neff, Anchor/Reporter
24 hour, 7 day week reg news ch featuring hyper-loc news coverage including sports & weather.

News 12 Hudson Valley
235 West Nyack Road, West Nyack, NY 10994
(845) 624-8780; *Fax:* (845) 735-1601
hudsonvalley.news12.com
news12hv@news12.com
Neighborhood News 12 is a 24-hrs news ch for individual communities including: Bronx, Brooklyn, Connecticut, Hudson Valley, Long Island, New Jersey & Westchester.

News 12 Long Island
1 Media Crossways, Woodbury, NY 11797
(516) 393-1200; *Fax:* (516) 393-1456
longisland.news12.com
news12li@news12.com
David Kirschner, General Manager
Kevin Maher, Sports Director
Bob Wolff, Sports Correspondent
Danielle Campbell, Anchor
Rich Hoffman, Meteorologist
Doug Geed, Anchor
Stone Grissom, Anchor
Elizabeth Hashagen, Anchor
BillKorbel, Meteorologist
A 24-hours rgnl news svc.

News 12 New Jersey
450 Raritan Ctr Pkwy, Edison, NJ 08837-3994
(732) 346-3200; *Fax:* (732) 417-5155
newjersey.news12.com/
news12nj@news12.com
John Bathke, Anchor Reporter
Marisa Brahney, Anchor/Reporter
Kurt Siegelin, Anchor
Dave Curren, Meteorologist
Provides 24-hour coverage of breaking news & events throughout New Jersey, in addition to pub affrs, info & lifestyle progmg of loc interest. Serving 1.8 million households in 14 northern & central counties in New Jersey .

News 12 Westchester
6 Executive Plaza, Yonkers, NY 10701
(914) 378-8916; *Fax:* (914) 378-8938
wechester.news12.com/
news12wc@news12.com
Richard Giacovas, Reporter/Producer
Janine Rose, News Director
Lisa Salvadorini, Managing Editor
Walt Fowler, Sports Director
24-hour news organization covering Westchester County.

News 14 Carolina
316 East Morehead Street, Suite 100, Charlotte, NC 28202
(704) 973-5800; *Fax:* (704) 731-2760
www.twcnews.com/nc/
Caroline Blair, Anchor
Nick LaGrange, Anchor
New 14 Carolina offers 24-hours loc news & weather every ten minutes on the Ones.

News Channel 8
1100 Wilson Blvd, Arlington, VA 22209
(703) 236-9555; 703-236-9552; *Fax:* (703) 236-2331
www.wjla.com/newschannel-8/
apfenton@sbgtv.com
A 24-hour news svc offered in the Washington, DC metropolitan area over all cable svcs. It is available to cable subs in Alexandria, Arlington County, Fairfax City, Fairfax County & Loudoun County in Virginia, Montgomery & Prince George'sCounties in Maryland & Washington, DC. Reaches 1.2 million.

News On 6
303 N Boston Avenue, Tulsa, OK 74103
(918) 732-6000; *Fax:* (918) 732-6185
www.newson6.com/
Wade Deaver, Vice President of Sales
Derek Criss, Director of Local Sales
Jill Millaway, Digital Sales Manager
Lex Sehl, Local Sales Manager
Shawn Jordan, Director of National Sales
Jim Meek, Director of Key Accounts & New BusinessDevelopmnt
David Brace, Account Executive

NewsChannel 5+
474 James Robertson Pkwy, Nashville, TN 37219
(615) 248-5250; 615-244-5000; *Fax:* (615) 244-9883
www.newschannel5.com
Rick Casebeer, Executive Director
Mark Martin, News Operations Manager
Lyn Plantinga, General Manager
Lori Hinkle, Assignment Desk Manager
Natalie Ryman, Sales Manager
Mark Binda, Programming Director
Sandy Boonstra, NewsDirector
Gibson Prichard, Engineering Dir
Jared Turner, Director of New Media
Michelle Bonnett, Assistant News Director
Tommy Crouse, Executive Producer
Patsy Fowler, Executive Producer
NewsChannel 5+ is a loc news & info stn, serving 550,000 homes in Middle Tennessee & Southern Kentucky.

Pennsylvania Cable Network (PCN)
401 Fallowfield Road, Camp Hill, PA 17011
(717) 730-6000; *Fax:* (717) 730-6009
www.pcntv.com
pcntv@pcntv.com
David R Breidinger, Chairman
Debra Kohr Sheppard, Senior VP, COO
Brian Lockman, President & CEO
Shawn McLain, Director of Operations
Francine Schertzer, VP, Programming
John Fox, Chief Engineer
Melissa Hiler, SVP & CFO
MitziHenry Jones, VP, Strategic Partnerships
Joel Bechtel, Vice President, Marketing and Brand Development

Larry Kaspar, Producer and Host
Matthew Hall, VP, Field Operations
PCN is the nation's pre-eminent state pub affrs network, with live & same day coverage of the Pennsylvania Senate/House & other govt activities. PCN televises significant state events (such as high school sports championships), toursmuseums & mfg facilities in the state & distributes educ progmg.

Pittsburgh Cable News Channel (PCNC)
4145 Evergreen Road, Pittsburgh, PA 15214
(412) 237-1100; *Fax:* (412) 237-1286
www.wpxi.com/pcnc
Brian Abzanka, Operations Dir
Mark W. Barash, Station Manager
Paul Curran, General Sales Mgr
K Connolly, Programming Director
Otto Schellin, Director of Engineering
Loc & rgnl news, talk & info.

Radio Television Digital News Association
529 14th Street, NW, Suite 1240, Washington, DC 20045
(941) 896-4246; *Fax:* (202) 223-4007
www.rtdna.org
mikec@rtdna.org
Mike Cavender, Executive Director
Karen Hansen, Membership and Programs Manager
Kate Switchenko, Director, Events & Awards
Derrick Hinds, Communications, Marketing & Digital Media Manager
Jon Ebinger, International ProgramsConsultant
Holly Rose, Industry Relations and Sponsorship Manager
Orange County Newschannel features exclusive coverage of loc news, sports, weather & traf in southern California's Orange County, 24 hours serving over 575,000 subs.

Regional News Network (RNN)
800 Westchester Avenue, Suite S-640, Rye Brook, NY 10573
(914) 417-2700, (914) 417-2709
www.rnntv.com/
Christian J. French, Chief Operating Officer
Richard E. French, Jr., President & CEO
Richard French III, President of News & Programming
Marc Weiner, News Director
Tom O'Hara, Chief Financial Officer
RNN is a 24 hour provider of news & pub info targeted to suburban New York, Connecticut & and New Jersey reaching over 6.2 million homes.

Rhode Island News Channel
10 Orms Street, Providence, RI 02904
(401) 453-8000; *Fax:* (401) 331-4431
www.abc6.com
radeszkoza@abc6.com
John Methia, Director of Broadcast Operations & Engineering
Chris Tzianabos, Vice President/General Manager
Cindy Walsh, General Sales Manager
Elizabeth O'Brien, National Sales Manager
Don Curtin, Promotion Manager
Kelly Johnston,News Director
Ken Bell, Sports Director
Rhode Island News Channel is a simulcast & rebroadcast of WLNE newscasts for Rhode Island.

SNN News (WSNN-LD)
Div/DBA: Citadel Communications
1741 Main Street, Sarasota, FL 34236
(941) 953-7755, (941) 361-4880, (941) 361-4600; *Fax:* (941) 361-4699
www.snntv.com
news@snn6.com
Charles Cusimano, Station Manager & GSM
Valerie Rose Schmidt, Business Manager
Kelby Miller, Promotions Manager
Craig Burdick, News Director
Tony Fernandez, Chief Engineer
Allyson Henning, Anchor
Lynden Blake, Anchor
JustinMosely, Chief Meteorologist
A 24-hour cable news ch with focus on loc news & info.

Spectrum News Central NY (formerly TWC News)
Div/DBA: TWC
815 Erie Blvd E, Syracuse, NY 13210
(315) 234-1000; *Fax:* (315) 234-0635
www.twcnews.com/nys/central-ny
yournews@twcnews.com
Thomas Rutledge, CEO
Dinesh C. Jain, Chief Operating Officer
Ron Lombard, News Director
A 24-hour loc/rgnl news ch serving 560,000 Time Warner cable subscribers throughout central/upstate New York.

Spectrum News NY1 (formerly New York 1 News)
75 Ninth Avenue, New York, NY 10011
(212) 691-6397, (212) 379-3311, (212) 367-0600; *Fax:* (212) 379-3575
www.ny1.com
Pat Kiernan, Chief Engineer
John Davitt, Chief Meterologist
Roger Clark, General Assignment Reporter
Vivian Lee, Anchor/Reporter
Jamie Stelter, Traffic Reporter
Michael Herzenberg, General Assignment Reporter
A 24-hour, all-news cable ch devoted primarily to coverage of New York City, its burroughs and neighborhoods.

Spectrum News Rochester (formerly R News/TWC News)
71 Mt Hope Avenue, Rochester, NY 14620
(585) 756-2424; *Fax:* (585) 756-1673
www.twcnews.com/nys/rochester/
Thomas Rutledge, CEO
Dinesh C. Jain, COO
Loc news 24-hours 7 days per week. Interactive daily call-in show. Nightly loc Sp newscast.

WJLA-TV/Newschannel 8
1100 Wilson Blvd, Arlington, VA 22209
(703) 647-9552, (703) 236-9555; *Fax:* (703) 236-2345, (703) 236-2341
www.wjla.com
newsdesk@wjla.com
Scott Thuman, Chief Political Correspondent
Kellye Lynn, Anchor/Reporter
Steve Rudin, Meteorologist
Alex Parker, Sports Host
A 24-hours rgnl news svc for Washington, DC, suburban Maryland & northern Virginia. On 15 cable systems serving 1,125,000 subs.

WOWT 6 News
3501 Farnam Street, Omaha, NE 68131
(402) 346-6666; 402-233-7922; *Fax:* (402) 233-7888; 402-233-7881
www.wowt.com
sixonline@wowt.com
Matt Thompson, Programming Director & Community Affairs
Jeff Sabin, Director of Technology
Mary Beth Keating, National Sales Manager
Joel Helzer, General Sales Manager
Ross Jernstrom, Sports Producer

Regional Cable Sports Networks

AT&T Sportsnet (formerly Root Sports)
on 60 Cable Systems
323 North Shore Drive, Suite 200, Pittsburgh, PA 15212
(412) 316-3800; *Fax:* (412) 316-3892
www.attsportsnet.com
Ted Black, General Manager
Regional sports network serving the Pittsburgh, Rocky Mountain and Southwest Regions. Pittsburgh Pirates, Penguins. Colorado Rockies, Utah Jazz, Vegas Golden Knights, Big Sky Conference. Houston Rockets & Astros.

Big Ten Network
444 N Michigan Avenue, Suite 1200, Chicago, IL 60611
(312) 665-0700; *Fax:* (312) 665-0740
www.btn.com
btn2gosupport@btn.com
Mark Silverman, President
Kim Beauvais, VP, Human Resources & Business Operations
Mark Hulsey, Senior VP, Production & Executive Producer

CBS Sports Network
28 East 28th Street, New York, NY 10016 US
212-975-5100
www.cbssportsnetwork.com; www.cbsiam.com
David Berson, President
Jen Sabatelle, SVP, Communications
Tiki Barber, Host
Dana Jacobson, Host
Boomer Esiason, Host
24 hour home of CBS Sports. 3,000+ hours of live programming including: MW, C-USA, AAC, Big East, A-10, Patriot League, Army & Navy.

Cox Communications, Inc.
Mailing Address: 6205-B Peachtree Dunwoody Rd NE, Atlanta, GA 30328
Second Address: PO Box 78071, Phoenix, AZ 85062-8071
(623) 594-8759, (623) 594-1000, (888) 566-7751; *Fax:* (623) 322-7424
www.cox.com
Len Barlik, Executive VP & COO
Patrick J. Esser, President, Cox Communications
Stephen Rowley, Executive VP, Cox Business
Mark F. Bowser, Executive Vice President & Chief Financial Officer
Kevin Hart, Executive VP & Chief Product -Technology Officer
Sujata Gosalia, Executive Vice President & Chief Strategy Officer
Karen Bennett, Executive Vice President & Chief HR Officer
Phoenix Suns basketball, sports specials, high school sports & high school championships, etc. Phoenix metropolitan area serving over 500,000 subs. Loc microwave/fiber distributed regionally to additional operators.

Cox Sports Television
2121 Airline Drive, 3rd Floor, Metairie, LA 70001
(504) 304-2740; *Fax:* (504) 304-2243
www.coxsportstv.com
coxsportstv@cox.com
Rod Mickler, Vice President
Joe Pecoraro, Advertising Sales
Cox Sports TV is an innovated, 24 hours net providing compelling & rgnl sports progmg. Satellite: Galaxy 23. Serving 5.5 million sub, on 79 cable systems, transponder one.

CPTV Sports
1049 Asylum Avenue, Hartford, CT 06105-2411
(860) 278-5310; (860) 275-7550
http://cptvsports.org; cpbn.org/cptv-sports/
Thomas Barnes, Chairman
Gregory Butler, Vice Chairman
Jerry Franklin, President & CEO
Dean Orton, COO
Meg Sakellairdes, Chief Financial Officer

ESPN Chicago Radio
190 N State Street, 7th Floor, Chicago, IL 60601-3302
(312) 332-3776, (312) 980-1000; *Fax:* (860) 766-2400
www.espn.com
Jim Pastor, VP/General Manager
Adam Delevitt, Program Dir.
Randy Merkin, Asst. program Dir.
David Scharf, General Sales Manager
Keith Sgariglia, Managing Editor
Classic sporting events, sports series, documentaries & movies; home shopping for sports merchandise & interactive sports games.
Serving 20 million subs on 400 plus cable systems.
Satellite: Galaxy 7, transponder 13 (compressed).

ESPN Inc.
545 Middle Street, ESPN Plaza, Bristol, CT 06010
(860) 766-2000, (888) 549-3776; *Fax:* (860) 766-2400
www.espn.go.com
John Skipper, President
Ed Durso, Executive VP, Administration
Russell Wolff, Executive VP, Managing Director International
Seth Adler, VP, Sports Marketing
Norby Williamson, Executive VP, Programming
Aaron Laberge, Executive VP,Chief Technology Officer
Christine Driessen, Executive VP & CFO
Stacey Fitch, VP, Production Operations
Mary Byrne, Senior Deputy Editor
ESPN offers a var of professional & amateur sports, including NFL, college basketball, NHL major league baseball, the woman's NCAA tournament.
On 28,000 affiliating cable systems serving over 77 million subs.

ESPNews
ESPN Plaza, 545 Middle Street, Bristol, CT 06010-9454
(860) 585-2000; (888) 549-3776; *Fax:* (860) 766-2400
www.espn.com
John Skipper, President
Jill Frederickson, VP, News Editorial Operations
Elida Witthoeft, Senior Coordinating Producer, ESPNews
Chuck Salituro, Senior News Editor

Fox Deportes
1440 S Sepulveda Blvd, Los Angeles, CA 90025
(310) 444-8658; *Fax:* (310) 444-8445
www.foxdeportes.com
Carlos Sanchez, EVP & GM, Fox Deportes
Live, exclusive coverage in Sp of the Copa Toyota Libertadores & Major League Baseball's All-Star game & World Series postseason, boxing & nightly sports news. Serving 7.9 million subs on 1,321 cable systems. Satellite: Satcom C1,Transponder 1, ch 8 (SA Power VU IRD D9225).
1211 Ave. of the Americas, New York, NY 10036-8701
(212) 822-7000

Tom Maney, Vp Adv Sls

Fox Soccer
on 550+ Cable Systems
10201 West Pico Blvd, Los Angeles, CA 90035
(310) 444-8642; *Fax:* (310) 444-8445
www.foxsports.com/foxsoccer/
ben.alkaly@fox.com
Mike Petruzzi, VP, National Ad Sales
Robert Gottlieb, EVP, Marketing
George Greenberg, EVP, Content Integration & Presentation
Terri Hines, EVP, Communications
Larry Jones, EVP, Business
Jeff Krolik, President, Fox Sports RegionalNetworks
Fox Soccer Channel is the nation's leading TV destination for young, passionate & affluent soccer fans. The best in exclusive coverage of professional, college & youth soccer. Satellite: Galaxy 11, transponder 8.

Fox Sports
10201 W. Pico Boulevardard, Bld 103, Los Angeles, CA 90035
(310) 369-6000; (310) 369-1000; *Fax:* (310) 969-6700
www.foxsports.com
Eric Shanks, President , COO, Executive Producer
Bill Wanger, EVP, Programming, Research & Content Strategy
Robert Gottlieb, EVP, Marketing
Terri Hines, EVP, Communications
Larry Jones, EVP, Business
Neil Mulcahy, EVP, SportsSales
Jeff Krolik, President, Fox Sports Regional Networks
A natl, rgnl & loc supplier of sports progmg.
Serves 68 million subs through 22 rgnl sports nets.

Fox Sports Arizona
2 North Central Avenue, Suite 1700, One Renaissance Square, Phoenix, AZ 85004
(602) 257-9500; *Fax:* (602) 257-0848
www.foxsports.com/arizona
fsarizona.feedback@fox.com
Brian Hogan, SVP & General Manager
Brett Hansen, Senior Director, Communications & Marketing
Provides rgnl coverage of loc interest sports progmg. Serving 2.3 million subs in Arizona & Mexico. Satellite: C-1/16.

Fox Sports Florida
Div/DBA: Fox Sports Sun
500 East Broward Boulevard, Suite 1300, Fort Lauderdale, FL 33394 US
(954) 375-3634; *Fax:* (800) 369-0073
www.foxsports.com/florida
infoFL@foxsports.net
Steve Tello, SVP & General Manager
Marc LeSage, VP/General Sales Manager
Tim Ivy, VP, Marketing & Programming
Eric Esteban, Director of Media Relations
Ritchie Loerch, Director, Finance
Brett Opdyke, Executive Producer
Brian DeLos Santos, Digital Content Manager
Fos Sports Florida progmg includes Major League Baseball's Marlins, Tampa Bay Rays & National Hockey League's Florida Panthers, as well as Orlando Magic, Miami Heat, and Tampa Bay Lightning.

Fox Sports Midwest
700 St Louis Union Station, Suite 300, St. Louis, MO
(314) 206-7000; *Fax:* (314) 206-7070
www.foxsportsmidwest.com/
midwest@foxsports.net
Jack Donovan, General Manager
Fox Sports Net Midwest reaches more than 5.4 million cable & satellite TV homes in six Midwest states. It telecasts more that 2,000 hours of loc progmg each year, including coverage of St. Louis Cardinals baseball, St. Louis Blues hockey,Indiana Pacers basketball, Indiana Fever basketball, Kansas City Royals baseball, Cincinnati Reds baseball, Big 12: football, women's basketball & showcase, Univ. of Missouri athletics, Kansas State Univ. athletics, Univ. of Nebraska Basketball,Missouri Valley Conference basketball, championship events, Gateway Conference football, & loc high school sports programs, collegiate coaches shows.
FSN Indiana
135 N. Pennsylvania St., Suite 720, Indianapolis, IN 46204-2400

Fox Sports Net Bay Area
77 Geary Street, 5th Floor, San Francisco, CA 94108
(415) 296-8900; *Fax:* (415) 296-9198
Ted Griggs, General Manager
Michael McCright, General Sales Mgr
Programing: San Francisco Giants, Oakland Athletics, Golden State Warriors, San Jose Sharks, San Jose Saber Cats & San Jose Stealth.
Serving more than 4 million households in Northern California & Northern Nevada.
Satellite:Compressed, AMC 1, T 18 Channel 110.

Fox Sports Net Rocky Mountain
2399 Blake St, Suite 130, Denver, CO 80205
(720) 898-2700; *Fax:* (720) 898-2735
Amy Turner, VP Marketing & Communications
David Woodman, General Manager
David Belmonte, General Sales Mgr
Rgnl sports net serving 8 states. Progmg includes Denver Nuggets, Utah Jazz, Colorado Avalanche, Colorado Rockies, Univ of Denver & Big 12 conference. Serving 2.2 million subs on 300 cable systems.
Satellites: G7.

Fox Sports Networks Detroit
26555 Evergreen Road, Suite 90, Southfield, MI 48076-4206
(248) 226-9700; *Fax:* (248) 226-9725
www.foxsports.com/detroit
fsdetroit@foxsports.net
Jeff Krolik, President, Fox Sports Regional Networks
Greg Hammaren, SVP/GM
John Tuohey, Executive Producer
Marcia Turner, VP/General Sales Manager
Denise Bailey, Senior Director, Programming
Cable sports net featuring Detroit Pistons, Red Wings, Lions, Tigers, Fury, Shock, CCHA hockey & Michigan High School Association championship contests.
Serving 3.2 million subs on more than 70 cable systems.

Fox Sports Networks Southwest
100 E Royal Lane, Suite 200, Irving, TX 75039
(972) 868-1800; (972) 506-7709; *Fax:* (972) 868-1678
www.foxsportssouthwest.com
fssouthwest@foxsports.com
Jeff Krolik, President, Fox Sports Regional Networks
Mike Anastassiou, Senior Executive Producer
Rgnl sports net serving Texas, Oklahoma, Arkansas, Louisiana & parts of New Mexico. Serving 10 million subs on 1,300 cable and satellite systems. Satellite: Galaxy 11, transponder 4 (digitally compressed).

Fox Sports North
1 Main Street SE, Suite 600, Minneapolis, MN 55414-1036
(612) 330-2468, (612) 486-9500
www.foxsports.com/north
fsnnorthinfo@foxsports.net
Michael Dimond, Senior VP & General Manager
Rgnl Sports Network: Minnesota, Iowa, Wisconsin, South Dakota & North Dakota. MLB & Brewers, NBA Timberwolves & Bucks, University of Minnesota hockey, & women's athletics, University of Wisconsin men's & women's athletics, MarquetteUniversity athletics.
Serving 3 million subs.
Satellite: GE 3, transponder 6.

Fox Sports Ohio
Div/DBA: SportsTime Ohio
200 Public Square, 25th Floor, Cleveland, OH 44114
(216) 415-3300
www.foxsports.com/ohio
contactus-fso@foxsports.net
Tom Farmer, Executive Producer
Francois McGillicuddy, Senior VP & General Manager
Trey Dolle, VP & General Sales Manager
Mike Roche, Director, Programming
Alex Slemc, Director of Marketing & Communications
Kate Zelasko, PublicRelations Director
Connor Kiesel, Digital Content Manager
Live sports progmg: Cleveland Indians, Cleveland Cavaliers, Cincinnati Reds, Columbus Blue Jackets, college football, basketball & sports news.
Serving 4.5 million subs on 206 cable systems.
Satellite: Satcom GE1, transponder T4.Alternate: GE1 T17.
11311 Cornell Park Dr., Suite 406, Cincinnati, OH 45242-1889
(513) 469-2006; *Fax:* (513) 469-2007
www.foxsports.net

Fox Sports San Diego
350 Tenth Avenue, San Diego, CA 92101
(213) 743-7800; *Fax:* (213) 743-7841
www.foxsportsw.com/sandiego
Henry Ford, SVP & General Manager
Alex Tevlin, Director of Programming
Pete Stella, Digital Content Manager
Whitney Burak, Director of Communications
Rgnl sports net featuring the Los Angeles Angels, Los Angeles Clippers, Los Angeles Galaxy, Mighty Ducks of Anaheim, USC & UCLA athletic events & other sports.
Serving 3 million subs.
Satellite: G1, transponder 21.

Fox Sports South
1175 Peachtree Street NE, 100 Colony Square, Suite 200, Atlanta, GA 30361
(404) 230-7300; *Fax:* (404) 230-7399
www.foxsports.com/south
FSSouth@foxsports.net
Jeff Genthner, SVP & General Manager
Rosolyn Little, Client Service Manager
Cheryl Raiford, CFO
NCAA sports, Atlanta Hawks, Memphis Grizzlies basketball, Atlanta Braves, Baltimore Orioles, Cincinnati Reds, St. Louis Cardinals baseball, Carolina Hurricanes, Nashville Predators hockey, NASCAR, golf, tennis & much more.
Serving 11.3million subs on more than 1,100 cable systems.
Satellite: Galaxy 11, transponder 4, ch 2.

Fox Sports West & Prime Ticket
10201 W. Pico Blvd, Los Angeles, CA 90064
(213) 743-7800; *Fax:* (213) 743-7841
www.foxsports.com/west
Henry Ford, SVP & General Manager
Alex Tevlin, Director of Progamming
Whitney Burak, Director of Communication
Pete Stella, Digital Content Manager
Debbie Chavez, Director of Finance
Ian Lavallee, Director of Marketing
Kings hockey, Lazers indoor soccer, Strings tennis, San Diego Soccers soccer & collegiate sports, etc.

Fox Sports Wisconsin
200 N Harbor Drive, Milwaukee, WI 53202
(414) 224-5326
www.foxsports.com/wisconsin
Michael Dimond, Senior VP & General Manager

Madison Square Garden Network
11 Pennsylvania Plaza, 3rd Floor, New York, NY 10001
(212) 465-6741, (212) 465-6225; *Fax:* (212) 465-6024
www.msgnetworks.com
info@msgnetworks.com
James L. Dolan, Chairman
Bret Richter, EVP & Chief Financial Officer
Andrea Greenberg, President & CEO
Ryan O'Hara, President-Content, Distribution and Sales
Greg Seibert, Vice Chairman
Steve Collins, EVP, Facilities
LawrenceBurian, Executive Vice President/General Counsel/Secretary
Barry Watkins, EVP, Communications/Administration
Adam Levine, EVP, Business Affairs
New York Knicks and Rangers; WBNA Liberty; college football & basketball games; boxing. Exclusive Garden events as well as original series progmg.
Serving more than 6.1 million subs on more than 250 cable systems.
Satellite: Satcom 4,transponder 6.

Mid-Atlantic Sports Network
333 W Camden Street, Baltimore, MD 21201
(410) 625-7100
www.masnsports.com
Michael Haley, Executive VP, Chief Financial Officer
Chris Glass, VP/ Executive Producer, Director of Operations
John J. McGuinness, SVP General Sales Manager
Jim Cuddihy, EVP, Marketing/Programming/Affiliate Relations
Ken Stiver,Engineering, Operations
Rhonda Reives, Traffic Director
Available in 7 states.

MSG Plus
11 Pennsylvania Plaza, 3rd Floor, New York, NY 10001
(212) 465-6000; *Fax:* (212) 465-6024
www.msgnetworks.com
info@msgnetworks.com
Andrea Greenberg, President & CEO
Bret Richter, EVP & CFO
Lawrence Burian, EVP & General Counsel
A two-ch rgnl sports network that delivers live games of the New York Islanders, Lizards, Devils & Major League Lacrosse in addition to horse racing, college football, basketball & variety of sports specials.
On 128 affil cable systemsserving more than 2.7 million subs.
Satellite: GE SpaceNet 2, transponders 1.

NBC Sports Boston
42 3rd Avenue, Burlington, MA 01803-4414
(617) 933-9300; *Fax:* (617) 933-4677
www.csnne.com
Mark Lazarus, Chairman, NBC Broadcasting & Sports
David Preschlack, President, NBC Sports Regional Networks

Princell Hair, SVP & General Manager, NBC Sports New England
Boston Celtics basketball, New York Mets (Connecticut only), college basketball, golf, football, hockey, professional tennis, soccer & auto racing.
On 215 cable systems serving 2.9 million subs.
Satellite: GE1, transponder 14.

NBC Sports Philadelphia
3601 South Broad Street, Philadelphia, PA 19148
(215) 336-3500; *Fax:* (215) 952-5996
www.nbcsports.com/philadelphia
asknbcsportsphiladelphia@nbcuni.com
Mark Lazarus, Chairman, NBC Broadcasting & Sports
David Preschlack, President, NBC Sports Regional Networks
Brian Monihan, President & General Manager
Michelle Murray, VP, Content
Carol Ko, NBC Sports Group Communications
Rgnl TV progmg svcs includes live coverage of Philadelphia Flyers ice hockey, Philadelphia '76ers basketball, Philadelphia Phillies baseball, pro boxing, college basketball, football, indoor lacross, ABL, loc sports news & sports talkprograms.
Serving 3 million subs on MSOS(16).

NBC Sports Washington
7700 Wisconsin Ave, #200, Bethesda, MD 20814
(240) 223-6600
www.nbcsports.com/washington
nbcsportswashington@nbcuni.com
Mark Lazarus, Chairman, NBC Broadcasting & Sports
David Preschlack, President, NBC Sports Regional Networks
Rebecca Schulte, President, NBC Sports Mid-Atlantic
Rgnl sports net serving mid-Atlantic. Progmg includes Orioles baseball, Capitals, hockey, Wizards, basketball, ACC & CAA.
Serving 4.4 million subs on over 200 cable systems.
Satellite: Spacenet III, transponder 12-H, ch 23 (scrambled).

New England Sports Network (NESN)
480 Arsenal Street, Building #1, Watertown, MA 02472
(617) 536-9233; *Fax:* (617) 536-7814
www.nesn.com
sports@nesn.com
Sean McGrail, President/CEO
NESN is a cable sports svc that delivers Boston Bruins, Red Sox, New England college sports as well as boxing, tennis, fishing, bowling & wrestling.
Serving 3.5 million subs on 28 cable systems.
Satellites: Satcom F-4, transponder 13;GE C-3, transponder 14.

The Sports Network
2200 Byberry Road, Hatboro, PA 19040
(215) 441-8444; (800) 227-7249; *Fax:* (215) 441-5767
Ken Zajac, General Sales Mgr
Bernie Greenberg, Coordinator
Steve Cwitkowitz, Account Executive
International real-time sports wire svc providing content, branded web pages, satellite and/or computer feeds directly to broadcasters (radio & TV), print, Internet sites, wireless with state of the art technology.

SportsNet New York
75 Rockefeller Plaza, 29th Floor, New York, NY 10019
(212) 485-4800; *Fax:* (212) 485-4802
www.sny.tv
Steve Raab, President

Victory Sports One
60 S 6th Street, Suite 3900, Minneapolis, MN 55402
(612) 661-3778
Carl Pohlad, Owner
News 12 Bronx is a 24-hours rgnl news progmg svc (a News 12 Regional Network).

Yankees Entertainment and Sports Network LLC
The Chrysler Bldg, 405 Lexington Avenue, 36th Floor, New York, NY 10174-3699
(646) 487-3600; *Fax:* (646) 487-3612
web.yesnetwork.com
info@yesnetwork.com
John Litner, President
John Filippelli, President, Production & Programming

YurView California
Div/DBA: (formerly 4SD San Diego)
350 10th Avenue, Suite 500, San Diego, CA 92101
(619) 686-1900; *Fax:* (619) 876-4993
www.yurview.com
info@yurview.com
Sam Attisha, Region Manager, Cox Communications
No longer airs major live sports events, except for local highschool sports. Local stories from Cox.

Canadian Cable Networks

Aboriginal Peoples Television Network
339 Portage Avenue, Winnipeg, MB R3B 2C3 Canada
(204) 947-9331, (888) 330-2786; *Fax:* (204) 947-9307
www.aptn.ca
info@aptn.ca
Jean LaRose, CEO
Danielle Audette, Programming Director
Sherry Rasmussen, Manager Of On-Air Promotions
Lisa Dunsmore, Manager Of Purchasing
Sean Rickner, Senior Manager Of Marketing
Jacqueline Jubinville, Manager OfCommunications
Dave Prefontaine, Manager Of Facilities

AMI
Div/DBA: (A division of The National Broadcast Reading Serv
1090 Don Mills Road, Suite 200, Toronto, ON M3C 3R6 Canada
(416) 422-4222, (800) 567-6755; *Fax:* (416) 422-1633
www.ami.ca
info@ami.ca
Joe Tedesco, Chairman
David Errington, President & CEO
Mike Hanson, General Manager
Janis Davidson Pressick, Communications Manager
John Melville, VP, Programming & Production
Line Gendreau, VP, Finance
Terry Reid, VP, HumanResources
Peter Burke, VP, Marketing & Communications
Philippe Lapointe, VP, Programming & Production
Betty Nobel, Vice Chair
Read published news in audio format for blind, vision-restricted & sr Canadians.

ARTV
1400 boul. Rene-Levesque Est, Bureau A-53-1, Montreal, QC H2L 2M2 Canada
(514) 597-3636; *Fax:* (514) 597-3633
www.artv.ca
Catherine Dupont, Operations Dir
Marie Cote, General Manager
Marc Pichette, Promotions Manager
ARTV is a French-language channel dedicated entirely to arts and culture. Twenty-four hours a day of great performances, films, documentaries, dramas & design. The pleasure of capturing the art and culture of Quebec, Canada & the wholeworld.

Bell Media
1800 McGill College, Suite 1600, Montreal, QC H3A 3J6 Canada
(514) 939-5000; *Fax:* (514) 939-3151
www.bellmedia.ca/
bellmediacommunications@bellmedia.ca
Mary Ann Turcke, President
Johanne Saint-Laurent, Operations Dir
Stuart Garvie, President Bell Media Sales
Chris Gordon, President Bell Media Radio
Nikki Moffat, Sr VP Finance
Scott Henderson, VP Communications
Anne McNamara, VPHuman Resorces
Domenic Vivolo, Exec VP Content Sales&Distribution Mktg
Progmg includes Super Écran, the Fr pay-TV stn; Canal Famille, children's progmg stn devoted to children from ages 3 to 14; Canal D, a specialty ch featuring mainly documentaries.
Serving 245,000 subs (Super Ecran); 2,110,000 subs(Canal Famille), &1,705,000 subs (Canal D).
Serving 370 cable systems.
Satellite: Anik E-2, transponder 11-A.

BookTelevision: The Channel
Div/DBA: Bell Media
299 Queen Street West, Toronto, ON M5V 2Z5 Canada
(416) 384-8000; *Fax:* (416) 591-5117
www.booktelevision.com/
info@booktelevision.com
Mary Ann Turcke, President, Bell Media
Talent coaching.

Bravo!
Div/DBA: (div of Bell Media)
299 Queen Street W, Toronto, ON M5V 2Z5 Canada
(416) 591-5757; *Fax:* (416) 591-8497
www.bravo.ca
bravomail@bravo.ca
Bravo! NewStyle Arts Channel is dedicated to entertaining, stimulating & enlightening veiwers who have a taste for more complex TV. Bravo! delivers a wide array of fine arts progmg, balancing longer-form structured shows & shorter piecesthat appear in a more random way as 'flow' to create a fluid mix of distinctive music, dance, opera, drama, literature, cinema, visual art, the art of TV & the art of talk. Serving 5.8 million subs on 700 cable systems.

Business News Network
299 Queen Street West, Toronto, ON M5V 2z5 Canada
(416) 384-4511
www.bnn.ca
info@bnn.ca
Lesley Harmer, Executive Producer
Grant Ellis, General Manager
Susan Corey Ehrhardt, Traffic/Automation
Andrew Reddick, Advertising Sales
Jeremy Roach, Marketing
Derrick McElheron, News And Guest Information

CBC Newsworld
Authentic Relations, CBC, PO Box 500, Station A, Toronto, ON M5W 1E6 Canada
(416) 205-2409, (866) 306-4636; *Fax:* (416) 205-8684
www.cbc.ca/news
ombudsman@cbc.ca
Remi Racine, Chairman
Hubert T. Lacroix, President/CEO
Suzanne Morris, VP/CFO
Maria Mirowicz, Programming Director
Maryse Bertrand, VP, Real Estate, Legal Services & GC
Heather Conway, EVP, English Services
William B. Chambers,VP, Brand, Communications & Corp. Affairs
Steve Guiton, Technology & Chief Regulatory Officer
Roula Zaarour, VP, People & Culture
Louis Lalande, VP, French Services
Live 24-hours news & info net on basic cable, satellite & wireless in Canada.
On 1500 cable systems serving 8 million subs. Satellite: Anik E2 (Ku-band).

The Comedy Network
Box 1000, Station O, Toronto, ON M4A 2W3 Canada
(416) 332-5300; *Fax:* (416) 332-5283
mail@thecomedynetwork.ca
Rick Brace, President
Brent Haynes, Programming Director
A 24-hour service featuring Canadian & international programs devoted exclusively to comedy sketches, standup comedy, & ongoing comedy series. Coverage area: national.

Country Music Television (Canada)
64 Jefferson Ave, Unit 18, Toronto, ON M6K 3H4 Canada
(416) 534-1191; *Fax:* (416) 530-2215
www.cmt.ca
info@cmt.ca
Michael Harris, CEO
A 24-hour mus & entertainment net that combines mus videos with programs and features that focus on the artists and their mus.
Serving 7 million subs on 1,487 cable systems in Canada.
Satellite: Anik E2 (Ku-Band), transponder T4.

CPAC-Cable Public Affairs Channel
Div/DBA: (A subsidiary of Consortium of Canadian Cable Comp
PO Box 81099, Ottawa, ON K1P 1B1 Canada
(877) 287-2722; *Fax:* (613) 567-2741
www.cpac.ca
comments@cpac.ca
Uncut, unfiltered coverage of Canadian pub affrs issues including LIVE bcsts of the House of Commons & its Standing Committees. Serving 7.2 million subs.

CTV News Channel
Mailing Address: Box 9, Station O, Toronto, ON M4A 2M9 Canada
Second Address: 299 Queen Street West, Toronto, ON M1S 4B5
(416) 384-5000; *Fax:* (416) 291-5337
www.ctvnews.ca
news@ctv.ca
Jana Juginovic, Programming Director
Continually updated headline news, business, sports, weather & entertainment, every 15 minutes.

CTV Television Network
Mailing Address: PO Box 9, Station O, Toronto, Ca M4A 2M9 Canada
Second Address: 9 Channel Nine Court, Scarborough, ON M1S 4B5
(416) 384-5000, (866) 690-6179, (800) 668-0060; *Fax:* (902) 454-3302
www.ctv.ca
BellMediaPR@bellmedia.ca
Ivan Fecan, President/CEO
Phil King, President
L. Wartman, Operations Dir
Rich Marchand, General Sales Mgr
Movies & news, educ programs weekend mornings.
Serves 51 cable systems. Satellite: Anik C-1.

Discovery Channel
Div/DBA: CTV Television Network
Mailing Address: PO Box 9 Station O, Toronto, ON M4A 2M9 Canada
Second Address: 299 Queen Street West, Toronto, ON M5V 2Z5
(416) 384-5000; (866) 690-6179
www.ctv.ca
comments@discovery.ca
Ivan Fecan, President
Corrie Coe, Programming Director
Non-fiction documentary TV progmg focusing on the themes of nature, science & technology, adventure.
On 385 cable systems serving 5.6 million subs.
Satellite: Anik E2, Channel 210.

DMX Music-Canada
Mailing Address: 1703 West Fifth St, Suite 600, Austin, TX 78703 Canada
Second Address: 200 Evans, Toronto, ON M8Z 1J7
(512) 380-8500, (770) 225-2500; (416) 252-0477; *Fax:* (512) 380-8501, (770) 246-3941
www.dmx.com
brad.trumble@dmxmusic.com
John Cullen, CEO
Paul Stone, President
Brad Trumble, Operations Dir
Formerly a residential svc, now a coml svc exculsively.
Considering a return to the Canadian market. DMX commercial audio svc; 102 formats digital audio.
Serving 8000 subs. Satellites: C3 Bank, TBA (Ku-band) delivered by satellite ant.

Fairchild Television Ltd.
Mailing Address: #3300-4151, Hazelbridge Way, Aberdeen Centre, Richmond, BC V6X 4J7 Canada
Second Address: 35 East Beaver Creek Rd., Unit 8, Richmond Hill, ON L4B 1B3
(604) 295-1313, (905) 889-8090; *Fax:* (604) 295-1300, (905) 882-7140
www.fairchildtv.com/english/
info@fairchildtv.com
Joe Chan, President
The only Chinese language specialty TV across Canada. Serving 360,000 subs on 8 cable systems & DTH.

The Family Channel Inc.
181 Bay Street, PO Box 787, Toronto, ON M5J 2T3 Canada
(416) 956-2010, (800) 893-4862, (888) 835-7808; *Fax:* (416) 956-2035
www.family.ca
info@family.ca
Barbara Bailie, Director
Kevin Wright, Programming Director
Barbara Bailie, Director, Digital
Rebecca Hogg, Content Manager- Kids
Tom Szabla, Sales Coordinator
Niamh Marsh, Project Manager
Jason Yang, Developer
Rene Vega,Technical Lead
Premium TV net offering family entertainment based on 60% from the Disney Channel, 25% Canadian & 15% international progmg.
Serving 5.4 million subs, on 300 cable systems, transponder T20.

FashionTelevisionChannel
299 Queen Street W, Toronto, ON M5V 2Z5 Canada
(416) 384-7400; *Fax:* (416) 384-0080
Doug Holland, President
Turnkey opns, allocation studies, due diligence, transmitter installations, upgrades & coverage maps

Food Network Canada
Div/DBA: Shaw Media
121 Bloor St E #1500, Toronto, ON M4W 3M5 Canada
(416) 967-1174
www.foodnetwork.ca/
Barbara Williams, Exec VP, Broadcasting
Dervla Kelly, Sr VP, Marketing & Communications
Michael French, Vice President, Finance
Paul Cowling, Vice President, Regulatory Affairs
Promotional concepts, scripts & publications for the bcstg & entertainment industries.

Global Entertainment
121 Bloor Street, Toronto, ON M4W 3M5 Canada

(877) 307-1999; (416) 446-5460
www.globaltv.com www.globalnews.ca
viewercontacttoronto@globalnews.ca
Tim Schellenberg, General Manager
George Browne, Managing Editor
Ashley Applebaum, Publicity Manager
Anne Vranic, Senior Publicist
Rachelle Marion, Publicity Coordinator
The best of TV. Classy & classic entertainment & informational progmg for those moving on from youth-skewed traditional TV fare.

HGTV Canada
Div/DBA: Shaw Media
121 Bloor Street E, Suite 200, Toronto, ON M4W 3M5 Canada
(866) 967-4488, (416) 967-0022; *Fax:* (416) 960-0971
www.hgtv.ca
feedback@hgtv.ca
Norm Bolen, President
A 24-hour Canadian home & garden progmg resource.
Serving 5.2 million subs.
Satellite: F1, transponder T19.

Investigation Discovery
10212 Jasper Avenue, Edmonton, AB T5J 5A3 Canada
(780) 440-7777; *Fax:* (780) 440-8899
www.investigationdiscovery.ca/
info@courttvcanada.ca
Robert J Miron, Chairman
David M Zaslav, President & CEO
Jill Bonenfant, Programming Director
Court TV Canada, in partnership with the U.S. based Court TV, combines Court TV's compelling daytime live trial coverage, legal analysis from inside U.S. courts with legal & police dramas, movies, documentaries & series from Canada & abroad.

La Magnetotheque
1055 Rene Levesque E, Suite 501, Montreal, QC H2L 4S5 Canada
(800) 361-0635, (514) 282-1999; *Fax:* (514) 282-1676
www.lamagnetotheque.qc.ca
Majorie Theodore, President
Yvonne Senechal, VP, Operations
Majorie Theodore, General Manager
France Leduc, Communications
Yanick Plouffe, HR Director
French-language reading svc for persons who are blind, visually impaired, or print-handicapped.

Le Canal Nouvelles
1600 De Maisonneuve boulevard East, Montreal, QC H2L 4P2 Canada
(514) 598-2869; (514) 526-9251; *Fax:* (514) 598-6037; (514) 599-5502
www.tva.canoe.ca
Martin Cloutier, General Manager

Le Reseau des sports (RDS)
1755 Blvd. Rene-Levesque Est, Suite 300, Montreal, QC H2K 4P6 Canada
(514) 599-2244; *Fax:* (514) 599-2299
www.rds.ca
webmaster@rds.ca
Gerry Frappier, Chairman / managing director
Gerry Frappier, President/GM
Gerry Frappier, General Manager
Martin Cer, General Manager of Digital Media
Marie-Claude Girard, Senior Manager Human Resources
Johanne Provost, DirectorFinance Department
Robert Turcotte, Vice President of Programming
Charles Perreault, New Vice President, Information and RDS Info
Domenic Vannelli, Vice President Production
Patrick Jutras, Vice President Sales and Marketing
Provides 24-hour sports TV in Fr.
Satellite: ANIK E-2, transponder T-18.

Life Network
Mailing Address: 3700 Galley Road, Colorado Springs, CO 80909 Canada
Second Address: 3925 N Centennial Blvd, Colorado Springs, CO 80903
(719) 591-2609, (719) 591-2724; *Fax:* (719) 573-7960, (719) 623-2487
www.elifenetwork.com
info@lifenetwork.ca
Lawrence O'Connell MD, Chairman
Diane Foley MD, President/CEO
Laura Howe, VP Of Development And Operations
Luz Davidson, Administrative Manager
Brenda Shuler, VP Client Services
John Gore, Financial Manager

Offers lifestyle entertainment progmg about the people, places & experiences that make the journey of life worthwhile & interesting.
Serving 26 million English & Fr subs on 100 cable systems.
Satellite: Anik E2 (Ku-band), transponderT19 (horizontal).

Movie Central
Corus Quay, 25 Dockside Drive, Toronto, ON M5A 0B5 Canada
(416) 479-6784
www.moviecentral.ca
Coml-free premium pay TV svc including movies, mus & comedy specials, major sports events & boxing (Superchannel, Movie Max!, Viewers Choice, Pay-Per-View).
Serving 300,000 subs on 170 cable systems.
Satellite: Anik E2.

MuchLOUD
299 Queen Street W, Toronto, ON M5V 2Z5 Canada
(416) 340-7207; *Fax:* (416) 384-6824
www.much.com
Jay Sanderson, CEO
Production & cablecasting of net quality Jewish progmg in news, pub affrs, educ, arts, PBS & entertainment.

MuchMoreMusic
Div/DBA: M3 Bell Media
299 Queen Street West, Toronto, ON M5V 2Z5 Canada
(416) 591-5757; *Fax:* (416) 926-4026
www.m3tv.ca/
David Kines, General Manager
Brings music fans Hot AC MusicVideo, top international specials, documentaries, movies and a growing roster of exclusive, original programming they can't find anywhere else.

MuchMoreRetro
299 Queen Street West, Toronto, ON M5V 2Z5 Canada
(416) 591-5757; *Fax:* (416) 926-4026
www.m3tv.ca/; www.much.com
David Kines, General Manager
Source for 24/7 classic videoflow from artists including The Police, Madonna, Bon Jovi, Corey Hart, Prince, Aerosmith, Duran Duran, Janet Jackson, Rush, Nirvana and Alanis Morissette and more.

MuchMusic
299 Queen Street West, Toronto, ON M5V 2Z5 Canada
(416) 591-5757, (416) 340-7207; *Fax:* (416) 384-6824
www.much.com
contact@muchmusic.com
Jakob Nortman, President
Amanda Bino, Production Coordinator
For all your voice-over needs, including narration, corporate videos, on-hold telephone messages & announcements for GPS systems. Radio production facilities available.

MuchVibe
299 Queen Street W, Toronto, ON M5V 2Z5 Canada
(416) 591-5757
www.much.com
muchvibe@muchmusic.com
Joel Easton, General Manager
Virtual Radio is the oldest music website providing a new radio format, content & internet expertise to bcstrs world wide.

MusiMax & MusiquePlus
355, rue Sainte-Catherine Ouest, Montreal, QC H3B 1A5 Canada
(514) 284-7587; *Fax:* (514) 284-1889
www.musiqueplus.com
auditoire@musiqueplus.com
Pierre Marchand, General Manager
Musimax is a French-language speciality svc owned equally by Astral Media Inc. of Montreal and CHUM Ltd. of Toronto. MusiquePlus is MuchMusic's French-language counterpart in Quebec. Serving 2.078 million subs on approximately 120 cablesystems . Satellite: Anik F1, transponder 9B.

Outdoor Life Network (OLN)
Div/DBA: Rogers Digital Media Television
9 Channel Nine Court, Scarborough, ON M1S 4B5 Canada
(416) 332-5000; *Fax:* (416) 332-5861
www.oln.ca/
Anna Stamboic, General Manager
Canada's destination for adventurous entertainment. Going beyond the comforts of home, OLN's progmg reveals the onsatible human drive for adventure.

RDI-Le Reseau de l'information
Div/DBA: (Formerly RDI-Le Reseau de l'information de Radio
1400 Blvd Rene-Levesque E, Montreal, QC H2L 2M2 Canada
(514) 597-7224; *Fax:* (514) 597-5226
www.radio-canada.ca/rdi
Louis Lalande, Vice-President Principal
Michel Cormier, General Director
Guylaine Bergeron
Francois Messier, Productions
Jean Mongeau
Patricia Pleszczynska
Benoit Villeneuve
RDI-Le Reseau de l'information is Canada's French-language news network. RDI provide live of coverage major events, newscasts every 15 minutes, sports, financial news, as well as info programs on a wide range of topics.

Shaw Broadcast Services
2055 Flavelle Boulevard, Mississauga, ON L5K 1Z8 Canada
(905) 403-2020, (800) 268-2943; *Fax:* (905) 403-2022, (905) 403-2662
www.shawbroadcast.com
shawbroadcastsupport@sjrb.ca
Cam Kernahan, Vice President, IP And Video Technology
Karen Baglole, Manager/Director Of Sales
John Piercy, SR VP Business
Gary Pizante, Vice President of Business Development/Satellite
Expert in evaluating, selecting, integrating & implementing satellite-based solutions for business. Cancom operates in four main lines of business: broadcast solutions, tracking solutions, learning solutions & data solutions.

The Shopping Channel
59 Ambassador Drive, Mississauga, ON L5T 2P9 Canada
(800) 263-2900, (888) 202-0888; *Fax:* (877) 202-0877
www.theshoppingchannel.com
Steven Goldsmith, President
Ted Starkman, General Manager
Live, shop-at-home televised retail svc, offering a var of consumer products.
Serving 5.7 million subs across Canada via cable & satellite.
Satellite: Anik E2, transponder 5.

SPACE: The Imagination Station
299 Queen Street West, Toronto, ON M5V 2Z5 Canada
(416) 591-5757
www.space.ca/
Richard W. Burden, Engineering Dir
Bcst tech svcs, facilities design, Traveller's Information Service (TIS) & Educational FM (EDFM) FCC applications, Part 15 AM & FM bcst systems engrg.

Sportsnet 360
One Mount Pleasant Road, Toronto, ON M4Y 3A1 Canada
(888) 451-6363; (416) 764-2000
www.sportsnet.ca
feedback@sportsnet.rogers.com
Angela Reimer, Sales Manager
Kelly Kirch, Programming Director
John Flack, Publishing
Nancy Bevilacqua, Digital Sales
Delivers the most comprehensive svc of professional & amateur sports news & info from Canada & around the world & is in every major Canadian cable market.

Star! The Entertainment Information Station
299 Queen Street W, Toronto, ON M5V 2Z5 Canada
(416) 591-7400
www.cameraplanet.com
archive@cameraplanet.com
Steve Rosenbaum, President

TELETOON
on 1000 Cable Systems
Box 787, 181 Bay Street, Toronto, ON M5J 2T3 Canada
(416) 956-2060; *Fax:* (416) 956-2070
www.teletoon.com
info@teletoon.com
Heather Shaw, Executive Chair
Tom Peddie, Executive VP and Chief Financial Officer
Doug Murphy, President and Chief Executive Officer
Darrell Atherley, General Sales Mgr
Leslie Kruger, Promotions Manager
Judy Adam, Vice President,Finance
Scott Dyer, Executive VP, Strategic Planning/Chief Tech Offcr
This specialty net shows the best in animation from Canada & around the planet.
Serving 6 million subs on 1,000 cable systems.
Satellite: Anik E2, transponder 20.

TMN—The Movie Network/MOVIEPIX
Div/DBA: c/o Bell Media
Mailing Address: 299 Queen Street West, Toronto, ON M5V 2Z5 Canada
Second Address: PO Box 787 Suite 100, 181 Bay Street, Toronoto, ON M5J 2T3

(416) 956-2010, (800) 565-6684; *Fax:* (416) 956-2018
www.themovienetwork.ca
kwright@tv.astral.com
Kevin Wright, Programming Director
Aubie Greenberg, Director-Original Programming
Kathleen Meek, Manager-Original Programming
Lisa Gotlieb, Coordinator-Original Programming
Two English-language, gen interest, pay TV nets featuring recent movie titles on the multi-channeled TMN, & new classics on MOVIEPIX.
Serving 350,000 subs on 200 cable systems.
Satellite: Anik E1 (Ku-band), transponder T31 (TMN); AnikE2 (Ku-band), transponder T27 (MOVIEPIX).

Treehouse TV

64 Jefferson Avenue, Unit 18, Toronto, ON M6K-3H4 Canada
(416) 534-1191; (416) 479-6782
www.treehousetv.com/
info@treehousetv.com
Susan Ross, General Manager
Phil Piazza, Programming Director
Treehouse TV is a specialty net dedicated to providing a variety of imaginative, stimulating and coml-free progmg for preschoolers from morning until bedtime.
Serving 4 million subs on 180 cable systems.
Satellite: Anik E-2,transponder 5.

TSN—The Sports Network

9 Channel Nine Court City, Scarborough, ON M1S 4B5 Canada
(416) 332-5000; *Fax:* (416) 332-7656
www.tsn.ca
Stewart Johnson, President
Rick Chisholm, Operations Dir
Nikki Moffat, General Manager
Adam Ashton, Promotions Manager
TSN's flagship news program, SportsCentre, NHL & first three rounds of the Stanley Cups Playoffs, Toronto Maple Leafs hockey, International Hockey including the IIHF World Junior Championship, the Olympic Games through 2012. CFL, NFL, PGATour & all four golf Majors, Season of Champions Curling, NASCAR. A 24-hour sports ch distributed on cable in Canada. Covers all major professional & amateur sports.
Serving 8.8 million subs on more than 2,000 cable systems.
Satellite: Anik E1,transponder 18 KU-H.

TVOntario

Mailing Address: Box 200, Station Q, Toronto, ON M4T 2T1 Canada
Second Address: 2180 Yonge Street, Toronto, ON M4S 2B9
(416) 484-2665; (800) 613-0513; *Fax:* (416) 484-6285
www.tvo.org
jjavet@tvontario.org
Lisa De Wilde, CEO
Ray Newell, Operations Dir
Erika Kramer, VP, Production, Distribution & Administration
Clara Arnold, VP, Talent & Engagement
Paul Dancy, VP, Finance & Legal
John Ferri, VP, Current Affairs & Documentaries
KarenGrose, VP, Digital Education
Todd Slivinskas, Chief Technology Officer
Andrew Steele, VP, Strategy & Communications
Provides educ progmg in English & Fr off air & via cable systems throughout Ontario.
TVO network (English) serves 98% of Ontario households. (Fr) serves 75% of Ontario households & 300,000 households in Quebec. Together the nets are on327 cable systems.
Satellites: Anik F1, transponder 21.

Vision TV: (Canada's Multi Faith Network)

64 Jefferson Avenue, Toronto, ON M6K 1Y4 Canada
(416) 368-3194, (888) 321-2567; *Fax:* (416) 368-9774
www.visiontv.ca
estella@visiontv.ca
Cal Miller, President
Mark Prasuhn, VP And General Manager
Programs presented by 30 plus faith groups, British comedies, movies dramas, documentaries, pub affrs, music & performance.
Serving 7.8 million subs on 12 cable systems. Satellite: Anik F1, transponder 5.

W Network

Corus Quay, 25 Dockside Drive, Toronto, ON M5A 0B5 Canada
(416) 534-1191
www.wnetwork.com

The Weather Network/MeteoMedia Inc.

Div/DBA: (A division of Pelmorex Communications Inc.)
2655 Bristol Circle, Oakville, ON L6H 7W1 Canada
(514) 597-1700; *Fax:* (514) 597-2981
www.theweathernetwork.com
Pierre L. Morrissette, President
Luc Perreault, Operations Dir
Natl satellite-to-cable TV network bcstg in Fr (MétéoMédia) & English (The Weather Network) offering weather & environmental info 24-hours a day, 7 days a week.
Serving 8.2 million subs on 752 headends.
Satellite: Anik E2,transponder 1A.

YTV Canada Inc.

25 Dockside Drive, Toronto, ON M5A 0B5 Canada
(416) 479-6784; *Fax:* (416) 533-0346
www.ytv.ca
John M. Cassaday, President
Phil Piazza, Programming Director
Susan Schaefer, Promotions Manager
English language basic cable specialty svc dedicated to children, teens & their families.
On approximately 1,200 cable systems serving an estimated 8.1 million subs.
Satellite: ANIK E1 East/West-DVC, transponder 7 (nationwide), 111degrees (Ku-band), vert polarization, 11900 MHZ.

Major TV Program Syndicators/Distributors

CBS Television Distribution
Mailing Address: 2450 Colorado Avenue, Suite 500E, Santa Monica, CA 90404
Second Address: 825 Eighth Avenue, 30th Floor, New York, NY 10019
(310) 264-3300, (212) 315-4000; *Fax:* (310) 264-3301
www.cbstvd.com/
dtvwebmaster@cbsparamount.com
Paul Franklin, President, CBS Television Distribution
Steven LoCasio, COO & CFO, CBSTVD & Global
Stephen Hackett, President of Sales, CBSTVD
Paul Montoya, President, Media Sales, CBSTVD
New York Office
1700 Broadway, New York, NY 10019; Tel: 212-315-4000; Fax: 212-582-9255.
Major First-Run Programming
Judge Judy, Dr. Phil, Wheel of Fortune, Jeopardy!, Inside Edition, Judge Joe Brown, The Jeff Probst Show, Rachael Ray, Entertainment Tonight.
Major Off-Net Programming
Everybody Loves Raymond, CSI, Frazier, Criminal Minds, NCIS, NCIS: Los Angeles, The Good Wife, Blue Bloods, Hawaii Five-O, Hot in Cleveland.

Disney-ABC Home Entertainment & Television Distribution
500 South Buena Vista Street, FGW #3052, Burbank, CA 91521-6066
(818) 560-9300; *Fax:* (818) 560-5296
www.disneyabcpress.com
BVTV.Webmaster@disney.com
Ben Sherwood, Co-Chairman, Disney/ABC Television Group
Channing Dungey, President, ABC Entertainment
Bruce Rosenblum, President, Business Operations
Robert Langer, EVP/CFO Disney/ABC Television Group
Rita Ferro, President, AdSales
Gary Marsh, Pres. & Chief Creative Offcer, Disney Channels Ww
Rebecca Campbell, President, ABC Owned TV Stations Grp
Kevin Brockman, Exec VP, Global Communications, Disney/ABC TV Grp
Linda Bagley, Deputy General Counsel
New York Office
Advertising/Media Sales: 1133 Avenue of the Americas, 33rd floor, New York, NY 10036; Tel: 212-625-5100; Fax: 212-625-5140.
Major First Run Programming
Who Wants to be a Millionaire, Live! with Kelly and Michael, Katie.
Major Off-Net Comedies
According to Jim, Scrubs, Tyler Perry's Meet the Browns.

NBCUniversal Domestic Television Distribution
30 Rockefeller Plaza, 11th Floor West, New York, NY 10112
(212) 664-4444; (212) 664-3056
www.nbcumv.com/studios-distribution/nbcuniversal-domestic-television-distribution/
nbcucareers@nbcuni.com
Robert Greenblatt, Chairman, NBC Entertainment
Stephen B. Burke, CEO, NBCUniversal
Matt Bond, Chairman, Content Distribution
George Cheeks, President, Business Operations & Late Night Prgm
Sean O'Boyle, EVP & General SalesManager
Linda Finnell, Senior VP, Programming & Development
Tracie Wilson, Senior Vice President
Valerie Schaer, Executive VP, Creative Affairs
Domestic Syndication Programming
Access Hollywood, Access Hollywood Live, The Jerry Springer Show, Maury, The Steve Wilkos Show.
First-Run Syndicated Programming
The Chris Matthews Show, The Wall Street Journal Report with Maria Bartiromo.
Off-Network Distribution
30 Rock, Friday Night Lights, House, Law and Order, Monk, The Office, The Real Housewives franchise.

Sony Pictures Television
10202 West Washington Boulevard, Culver City, CA 90232
(310) 244-7737
www.sonypicturestelevision.com/us_dist.php
press@spe.sony.com
Jeff Frost, President, Sony Pictures Television
Jason Clodfelter, Co-President, Sony Pictures Television
Keith Le Goy, President, Distribution
John Weiser, President, US Distribution
Jeffrey Glaser, EVP, Current Programming
PhillipMartzolf, EVP, US Syndication Sales
Thanda Belker, EVP, Pay Television, US Distribution
Christopher L. Elwell, EVP, US Distribution Business Ops & Strategy
New York Office
550 Madison Avenue, New York, NY 10022; Tel: (212) 833-8500.
Daytime Dramas
The Young and the Restless, Days of Our Lives.
First-Run Syndication
The Dr. Oz Show, The Queen Latifah Show.
Off-Network Syndication
Rules of Engagement, Community, Seinfeld, The King of Queens.

Twentieth Television
2121 Avenue of the Stars, 21st Floor, Los Angeles, CA 90067
(310) 369-1000; *Fax:* (310) 369-3899
www.20thtv.com
Greg Meidel, President
First-Run Programming
The Ricki Lake Show, Dish Nation, The Wendy Williams Show, Family Feud, The Jeremy Kyle Show, Divorce Court, Judge Alex.
Major Off-Network Programming
Glee, Modern Family, Burn Notice, Family Guy, 24, Cops, The Simpsons, My Name is Earl, The Unit, How I met Your Mother, American Dad, The Cleveland Show.

Major National TV News Organizations

ABC News
47 West 66th Street, New York, NY 10023
(212) 456-2777; *Fax:* (212) 456-2795
abcnews.go.com
James Goldston, President, ABC News
Ben Sherwood, Co-Chair, Disney Media Networks
Barbara Fedida, Senior VP/Talent & Business Affairs
Al Prieto, Vice President, ABC News
Andrew Kubitz, EVP/Programming Strategy
Kevin Brockman,EVP/Global Communications
Robin Sproul, VP, Public Affairs
Tom Cibrowski, SVP, ABC News Programs
Ownership: Walt Disney Company
7 West 66th Street, New York, NY 10023; Tel: (212) 456-2777; Fax: (212) 456-2796; Executives: David Weston, President; Dave Davis, EVP; Paul Mason, SVP/Politics; Phyliis McGrady, vP/Creative Development.
Domestic Bureau: (Atlanta)
25810 Cumberland Parkway, SE, Suite 160, Atlanta, GA; Tel: (770) 431-2380.
Domestic Bureau: (Chicago)
190 North Sate Street, Chicago, IL 60601; Tel: (312) 899-4015; Suzanne Caraher, Assignment Editor.
Domestic Bureau: (Los Angeles)
4151 Prospect Ave., Los Angeles, CA 90027; Tel: (323) 671-5210; David Hernson, Bureau Chief; Mark Lima, Deputy Bureau Chief; Michael Ray Gammon, Assignment Editor; Roger Scott, Correspondent.
Domestic Bureau: (New York)
47 West 66th Street, 3rd Floor, New York, NY 10023; Tel: (212) 456-2700; Wendy Fisher, Director/Domestic News; John Berman, Correspondent.
Domestic Bureau: (Washington)
1717 DeSales Street, Washington, DC 20036; Tel: (202) 222-7777; Robin Sproul, VP/Bureau Chief; Jane Aylor, Director/Bureau Operations; David Chalian, Director/Political Unit.
Domestic Bureau: (Dallas)
606 Young Street, Dallat, TX 75202; Tel: (214) 749-7013.
Domestic Bureau: (Denver)
123 East Speer Blvd., Denver, CO 80203; Tel: (303) 832-7777.
Domestic Bureau: (Miami)
1320 South Dixie Highway, Coral Gables, FL 33146; Tel: (305) 662-2116.
Primetime Shows Exec. Producers:
20/20: David Sloan; Good Morning America: Tom Cibrowski; Nightline: Jeanmarie Condon; Primetime: Eric Strauss; World News Tonight with Diane Sawyer: Michael Corn.
Affiliate News Service:
ABSAT, 47 West 66th Street, 3rd Floor, Room 303, New York, NY 10023; Tel: (212) 456-1700; Mike Huitt, Director; Nac@abc.com

CBS News
51 W. 52nd Street, New York, NY 10019
(212) 975-4114
www.cbsnews.com
David Rhodes, President
Rick Jefferson, VP, News Operations
Christa Robinson, SVP/Communications
Ingrid Ciprian-Matthews, SVP, News Administration
Charles Palounis, Senior VP & CFO
Marsha Cooke, VP, News Services
Nancy Lane,Senior Executive Producer, CBS News Digital
Laurie Orlando, SVP, Talent Strategy
Domestic Bureau: (Atlanta)
260 14th Street NE, Atlanta, Ga 30309; Tel: (404) 685-2400.
Domestic Bureau: (Dallas)
10111 North Central Expressway, Dallas, TX 75231; Tel: (817) 451-1111.
Domestic Bureau: (Los Angeles)
7800 Beverly Blvd., Los Angeles, CA, 90036; Tel: (323) 575-2345.
Domestic Bureau: (Miami)
4700 Biscane Blvd., Suite 1170, Miami, FL 33101; Tel: (305) 571-4400.
Domestic Bureau: (San Francisco)
825 Battery Street, San Francisco, CA 94111; Tel: (415) 362-8177.
Domestic Bureau: (Washington)
2020 M Street NW, Washington, DC 20036; Tel: (202) 457-4444.
CBS News Programming:
The Early Show, Evening News, Up tot he Minute, Morning News, 60 Minutes, 48 Hours Mystery, Sunday Morning, The Saturday Early Show, Face the Nation.

CNBC Inc
900 Sylvan Avenue, Englewood Cliffs, NJ 07632
(201) 735-2622; *Fax:* (2012) 735-3200
www.cnbc.com
Mark Hoffman, Chairman
Trish Pomeroy, CFO
Thomas Clendenin, SVP/Marketing
Nikhil Deogun, SVP/Editor-in-Chief, Business News
Jennifer Dauble, VP, Public Relations
Jim Ackerman, EVP, Primetime Alternative CNBC
Domestic Bureau: (Washington)
1025 Connecticut Avenue NW, Suite 800, Washington, DC 20036; Tel: (202) 467-5400; Alan Murray, Bureau Chief/Anchor.
Domestic Bureau: (Los Angeles)
3000 West Almeda Avenue, Burbank, CA 91523; Tel: (818) 840-3214; Lacy O'Toole, Bureau Chief.
Programming:
Worldwide Exchange, Squawk Box, Squawk on the Street, Power Lunch, Street Signs, Closing Bell, Fast Money, The Kudlow Report.
Weekend Programming:
The Suze Orman Show, The Wall Street Journal Report.

CNN
One CNN Center, Atlanta, GA 30303
(404) 827-1700
www.cnn.com
Jeff Zucker, President, CNN Worldwide
Richard Davis, EVP/News Standards & Practices
Katrina Cukaj, EVP, Advertising Sales
Michael Bass, Executive VP, Programming CNN U.S.
Allison Gollust, Chief Marketing Officer
Domestic Bureau: (New York)
One Time Warner Center, New York, NY 10019; Tel: (212) 275-7800; Darius Walker, Bureau Chief.
Domestic Bureau: (Boston)
637 Washington Stree, Suite 200, Brookline, MA 02446; Tel: (617) 264-9905.
Domestic Bureau: (Chicago)
435 North Michigan Avenue, Chicago, IL 60611; Tel: (312) 645-8555.
Domestic Bureau: (Los Angeles)
6430 West Sunset Blvd., Los Angeles, CA 90028; Tel: (323) 993-5000.
Domestic Bureau: (Miami)
12000 Biscayne Blvd., Miami, FL 33181; Tel: (305) 892-5100; John Zarella, Bureau Chief.
Domestic Bureau: (Washington)
820 First Street NE, Washington, DC 20022; Tel: (202) 898-7900; Sam Feist, Bureau Chief.
Morning Programming:
Starting Point, Anderson Cooper 360, Early Start, CNN Newsroom, The Situation Room.
Evening Programming:
The Situation Room, Lou Dobbs, CNN Election Center, Piers Morgan, Anderson Cooper 360.
Overnight Programming:
Piers Morgan Tonight, Anderson Cooper 360.

Fox News Channel
1211 Avenue of the Americas, New York, NY 10036
(212) 301-3000
www.foxnews.com
Robert Murdoch, Executive Chairman
Jay Wallace, President, News
Sharri Berg, SVP, News Operations

Irena Briganti, Executive VP, Corporate Communications
Amy Listerman, CFO
Suzanne Scott, President, Programming & Development
90 million subs. Satellites: (SD) Galaxy 17, Transponder 6; (HD) Galaxy 15, Transponder 2
Ownership: News Corp.
Domestic Bureau: (Atlanta)
260 14th Street, Atlanta, GA 30318; Tel: (404) 685-2280; John Boswell, Bureau Chief.
Domestic Bureau: (Denver)
999 18th Street, Suite 1665, Denver, CO 80202; Tel: (303) 383-1170; Dennis King, Bureau Chief.
Domestic Bureau: (Dallas)
301 North Market Street, Suite 450, Dallas, TX 75202; Tel: (214) 742-5005; Russell Cosby, Bureau Chief.
Domestic Bureau: (Los Angeles)
2044 Armocast Avenue, Los Angeles, CA 90025; Tel: (310) 571-2000; Nancy Harmeyer, Bureau Chief.
Domestic Bureau: (Miami)
1440 79th St. Causeway, Suite 208, North Bay Village, FL 33141; Tel: (305) 866-8007.
Domestic Bureau: (Washington)
2201 C Street NW, Washington, DC 20520; Tel: (202) 496-0109.
Primetime Shows:
Fox and Friends, Special Report with Bret Baier, The O'Reilly Factor, Hannity; On Record with Greta Van Susteren, Your World with Cavuto.

MSNBC
30 Rockefeller Plaza, New York, NY 10112
(212) 664-6605
www.msnbc.com
Andrew Lack, Chairman
Phil Griffin, President
Nick Ascheim, Senior VP, Digital
Errol Cockfield, Senior VP, Communications
Deb Finan, VP, Production & Programming
Marc Greenstein, Creative Director
Programming:
Today Show, Nightly News, Dateline, Meet the Press, MSNBC TV.

NBC News
30 Rockefeller Plaza, New York, NY 10112
(212) 664-4444; *Fax:* (212) 664-4085
www.nbcnews.com
Andrew Lack, Chairman, NBC News & MSNBC
Noah Oppenheim, President, NBC News
Ownership: NBC Universal
Domestic Bureau: (Midwest)
454 North Columbus Drive, 1st Floor, Chicago, IL 60611.
Programming:
Nightly News, TODAY, Dateline NBC, Meet the Press, Weekend Today, Weekend Nightly News, NBC Sports.

TV News Services

AccuWeather Enterprise Solutions
385 Science Park Road, State College, PA 16803
(814) 235-8600; *Fax:* (316) 265-1949
enterprisesolutions.accuweather.com
salesmail@accuweather.com
Dr. Joel N. Myers, Founder, Chairman and President
Barry Lee Myers, CEO
Michael Smith, Senior VP and Chief Innovation Executive
Forecasts for radio & TV, meteorology training, slides & videotape of weather & related phenomena. Nexrad radar interpretation seminar; distributor of Nexrad weather display systems. Meteorologist 24/7, storm monitoring & customer svc.

AccuWeather Inc.
NSS Data: TV-CATV only
Mailing Address: 385 Science Park Road, State College, PA 16803
Second Address: 1270 Avenue of the Americas, Suite 1900, New York, NY 10020
(814) 237-0309; (212) 554-4750; *Fax:* (814) 235-8609
www.accuweather.com
sales@accuweather.com
Hoel N. Myers, Founder, President, Chairman
Barry Lee Myers, CEO
Evan Myers, COO
John Dokes, Chief Marketing Officer
Steven Hickson, CFO
TV, radio, weather progmg & systems, plus turnkey solutions to take your loc news to the mobile web.

Agence France-Presse
1500 K St NW, Suite 600, Washington, DC 20005
(202) 414-0600; *Fax:* (202) 414-0632
www.afp.com
afp-usa@afp.com
Emmanuel Hoog, Chairman & Chief Executive
Fabrice Lacroix, Managing Director
Stephane Marcovitch, Sales and Marketing Director
Michele Leridon, Global News Director
Sophie Huet-Trumpheme, Deputy News Director
Caroline Raveton,Chief Information Officer
Produces a variety of international news svcs for radio & TV, including text wires in six languages, photo wires, graphics & financial wires plus video svcs.

All Africa Global Media
922 M Street SE, Washington, DC 20003
(202) 546-0777; *Fax:* (202) 546-0676
www.allafrica.com
newsdesk@allafrica.com
Reed Kramer, Co-Founder & CEO
Amadou Mahtar Ba, Co-Founder & Executive Chairman
A news & info svc on African affrs for TV, radio & print news svcs.

American Academy of Dermatology
NSS Data: Radio Only
Div/DBA: American Academy of Dermatol
Mailing Address: Communications Department, Box 4014, Schaumburg, IL 60168
Second Address: 930 E. Woodfield Road, Schaumburg, IL 60173
(847) 240-1280, (866) 503-7546; *Fax:* (847) 240-1859
www.aad.org
mediarelations@aad.org
Henry W. Lim, President
Brian Berman, PhD, Vice President
Suzanne Olbricht, President Elect
Ted Rosen, VP Elect
Barbara Mathes, Secretary-Treasurer
Marta J. Van Beek, Assistant Secretary-Treasurer
Expert physicians available for TV & radio interviews, audio & video tapes on skin cancer pevention & detection, as well as info on skin, hair & nail conditions.

American Heart Association
7272 Greenville Avenue, Dallas, TX 75231
(888) 474-VIVE, (877) 242-4277; *Fax:* (214) 706-5243
www.americanheart.org
Nancy Brown, CEO
Suzie Upton, COO
Meighan Girgus, Chief Marketing & Programs Officer
Julie Del Barto, Multimedia Strategies
Periodic satellite news feeds of medical rsch stories.

APTN Productions
The Interchange, Oval Road,Camden Lock, London, NW1 7DZ United Kingdom
(0) 20 7482 7400; +44(0)20 7482 7600; *Fax:* (0) 20 7413 8312
www.aptn.com
aptninfo@ap.org
International TV svcs company, daily satellite news feeds to bcstrs worldwide, tech facilities, camera crew hire worldwide.
Serves TV.
1995 Broadway, New York, NY 10023-5882
(212) 362-4440

The Associated Press
NSS Data: TV-CATV only
AP Broadcast News Center, 1100 13th Street, Suite 500, Washington, DC 20005
(202) 641-9000; *Fax:* (202) 736-1124
www.ap.org
info@ap.org
Steven R. Swartz, Chairman
Gary Pruitt, President & CEO
Lauren Easton, Director, Media Relations
Jessica Bruce, SVP, Human Resources & Corporate Communications
Sally Buzbee, Senior Vice President - Executive Editor
Dave Gwizdowski,Senior Vice President - Revenue, Americas
Ken Dale, Senior Vice President - Chief Financial Officer
Jim Kennedy, Senior Vice President - Strategic Planning
AP Services for TV: Video: APTN Video News. Wires: APTV Wire, AP News Tickers, AP NewsPower, AP Data Stream. AP Alert Graphics: AP GraphicsBank. Software: AP NewsCenter; AP NewsDesk; AP NewsDesk (LAN), ENPS, SNAPfeed Satellite Delivery: APExpress. Elections: ENPS Stats, AP Politics, AP Election Wire. Online content: CustomNews, AP Online, Online Video Network, AP Spanish Online. Photos: Photo Archive, Photo Stream.

Bloomberg Finance LP
Div/DBA: (formerly Bloomberg LP
731 Lexington Avenue, New York, NY 10022
(212) 318-2300, EXT. 2201; (212) 318-2000; *Fax:* (212) 617-5999
www.bloomberg.com
inquiry1@bloomberg.net
John Meehan, Programming Director
Justin B. Smith, CEO, Bloomberg Media Group
John Micklethwait, Editor in Chief
Offers business & news reports for radio & TV stns. 24-hours a day. Full news svc.

Broadcast Interview Source
Div/DBA: Yearbook of Experts
2500 Wisconsin Avenue NW, Suite 949, Washington, DC 20007
(202) 333-5000; *Fax:* (202) 333-4904
www.expertclick.com
expertclick@gmail.com
Mitchell P. Davis, Editor & Publisher
Free source of interview contacts

The Canadian Press
36 King Street East, Toronto, ON M5C 2L9 Canada
(416) 364-0321; *Fax:* (416) 364-0207
www.thecanadianpress.com
broadcast@thecanadianpress.com
David Ross, CFO
Wayne Waldroff, General Manager
Terry Scott, News Director
Full wire & audio svcs (news agency), satellite delivery for radio program syndicators.
Serves radio & TV.

Capitol Television News Service (CTNS)
NSS Data: TV-CATV only
1629 S Street, Sacramento, CA 95811
(916) 446-7890, (800) 672-2728, (916) 335-1649; *Fax:* (916) 446-7893
www.pacsat.com
pacsat@pacsat.com
Steve Mallory, President
Marcia Calvin, VP Operations
Andrea Brooks, Controller
Video wire svc providing daily news coverage, via satellite, of California's capitol for subscribing TV stns throughout the state.

CBS News: See CBS listing in Major National TV News Organizations, this section.
51 W 52nd Street, New York, NY 10019-6188
(212) 975-4321, (877) 227-0787
www.cbscorporation.com
investorrelations@cbs.com
Sumner M. Redstone, Chairman Emeritus
Leslie Moonves, Chairman & CEO
Joseph Ianniello, Chief Operating Officer
Richard M. Jones, EVP, General Tax Counsel & Chief Veteran Officer
Gil Schwartz, SEVP & Chief Communications Officer
Larry Liding, EVP, Controller and Chief Accounting Officer
Jonathan H. Anschell, EVP, Deputy General Counsel and Secretary
Adam Townsend, EVP, Corporate Finance & Investor Relations
Anthony G. Ambrosio, EVP, CAO & Chief Human ResourcesOfficer

Cision / CNW
NSS Data: TV-CATV only
RBC WaterPark Place, 88 Qqueens Quay West, Ste 3000, Toronto, ON M5J 0B8 Canada
(877) 269-7890; *Fax:* (877) 269-5044
www.newswire.ca
info.ca@cision.com
Nicole Guillot, President
Elisa Schupp, VP, National Sales
Tim Griffin, VP, Product & Client Experience
David Furst, Senior Vice President, Technology
Laurie Smith, VP, Strategic Communications & Media
Offers a range of industry leading communication products & svcs for companies looking to maximize the strength of their news. Whether you are an investor rel off, or a specialist in PR, CNW offers the right tools for your communications.

CNN and CNN Headline News: See listing in Major National TV News Organizations, this section.
One CNN Center, Atlanta, GA 30303
(404) 827-1700
www.edition.cnn.com
Jeff Zucker, President, CNN Worldwide

Compu-Weather Inc.
NSS Data: TV-CATV only
2566 Route 52, Hopewell Junction, NY 12533
(800) 825-4445, (845) 227-8500; *Fax:* (845) 227-8400
www.compuweather.com
sales@compuweather.com
Jeff Wimmer, President
Steve Roberts, Director of Weather Operations
Tore Jakobsen, CFO
TV & radio svc providing weather forecasts, features, info & actualities.

Connecticut Weather Center Inc.
NSS Data: Radio Only
18 Woodside Avenue, Danbury, CT 06810-7123
(203) 730-2899; *Fax:* (203) 730-2839
www.ctweather.com
weatherlab@ctweather.com
William Jacquemin, President/Chief Meteorologist
Gregory Tulipani, Director of Advertising/Media
Jonathan Minovich, Media Representative
Weather forecasts for all media. Custom intros/outros/lives. Accurate forecasts. Barter or cash arrangement available.

CQ News
Div/DBA: CQ Roll Call
1625 Eye Street NW, Suite 200, Washington, DC 20006
(202) 650-6500; *Fax:* (202) 419-8760
www.cqrollcall.com
marketing@cq.com
Steve Komarow, Senior VP & Executive Editor
Meg Hargreaves, Senior VP & COO
Ann Dermody, Director, Content Marketing
CQ Roll Call & News, editorial rsch reports, newsletters, seminars, rsch, reference volumes, paperbacks; daily & wkly congressional info publications.

CW11.com WPIX-TV New York
220 E 42nd Street, New York, NY 10017
(212) 210-2411; *Fax:* (212) 210-2591
www.pix11.com/
Chris Wayland, Senior VP & General Manager
Debbie Presser, Director of Sales

Feature Story News
NSS Data: Radio Only
1730 Rhode Island Avenue NW, Suite 405, Washington, DC 20036
(202) 296-9012; *Fax:* (202) 296-9205
www.featurestorynews.com
info@featurestory.com
Simon Marks, President
Rob Flynn, Director of Business Development
Olly Barratt, Director of European News Coverage
Ind supplier of radio & TV news to English-language bcstrs worldwide. Bureaus in Washington, Moscow, London, New York, Orlando & San Francisco.

Fox News Channel: See listing in Major National TV News Organizations, this section.

Golden Lamb Productions
NSS Data: TV-CATV only
47 Schoolhouse Road, Nassau, NY 12123
(518) 766-4358
www.glpvideoproduction.com
Dow Haynor, President
ENG, EFP crews, HD & SD, SNG available. Serves the Northeast, 24-hour call, packages, live remotes, camera crane news & sports.

Hollywood News Service
Mailing Address: PO Box 55624, Sherman Oaks, CA 91413-0624
Second Address: 13636 Ventura Blvd, Suite 303, Sherman Oaks, CA 91423-0624
(818) 986-8168, (818) 990-5945; *Fax:* (818) 789-8047
www.newscalendar.com
editor@newscalendar.com
A wire svc to the entertainment media. Publisher of Hollywood News Calendar in Los Angeles; Entertainment News Calendar in New York.

Independent Television News of London Ltd.
200 Gray's Inn Road, London, UK WC1X 8XZ
+44(0)20 7833 3000; *Fax:* (202) 429-8948
www.itn.co.uk
michael.herrod@itn.co.uk
Geert Linnebank, Chairman
John Hardie, CEO
Geoff Hill, Editor, ITV News
Bryan Martin, Chief Financial Officer
James Scorer, Dir. of Buisness Affairs & Company Secretary
Melanie Tansey, Director of Human Resources
SarahVaughan-Brown, Dir. of Corporate Communications
Mark Browning, Managing Dir.,ITN Productions
Bevan Gibson, Chief Technology Officer
Other branches: South Africa, Moscow, London. Hong Kong. British TV news, Washington bureau.
ITN House, 200 Grays Inn Rd, London,
011-441-637-2424, 2017-833-3000
Stewart Purvis, Editor

Kyodo News International
780 Third Avenue, Suite 1103, New York, NY 10017
(212) 508-5440; *Fax:* (212) 508-5441
www.kyodonews.com
kni@kyodonews.com
Hajime Ozaki, New York Bureau Chief
Japan's leading newsgathering organization serving virtually all media in all parts of the world. The combined circulation of nwspr subscribers is about 50 million.

Medialink
1155 Avenue of the Americas, 8th Floor, New York, NY 10036
(646) 259-3001; *Fax:* (646) 259-3012
www.medialink.com
info@medialink.com, press@medialink.com
Michael E. Kassan, Chairman & CEO
Wenda Harris Millard, Vice Chairman
Dana Anderson, Chief Marketing Officer
Glenn Briffa, Executive VP
Angelo Dagostino, Head of Human Resources
International video & audio PR, satellite feed & news advisory service. Accessible by computer/newswire in U.S. & European newsrooms.
Serves radio & TV.
6430 Sunset Blvd, Suite 1100, Los Angeles, CA 90028-7901
(323) 465-0111; *Fax:* (323) 465-9230
One Maritime Plaza, Suite 1670, San Francisco, CA
(415) 296-8877; *Fax:* (415) 296-9929
The Time & Life Bldg, 541 N. Fairbanks Ct, Suite 1910, Chicago, IL 60611-3706
(312) 222-9850; *Fax:* (312) 222-9810
Natl. Press Bldg., 529 14th St. N.W., Suite 1230-A, Washington, DC 20045-2520
(202) 628-3800; *Fax:* (202) 628-2377
5000 Quorum, Suite 450, Dallas, TX 75254-7063
(972) 774-0200; *Fax:* (972) 774-0222
7 Fitzroy Sq., London,
44-207 554 2700; *Fax:* 44-207 554 2710

MediaOne Studios
NSS Data: TV-CATV only
333 Broadway, 3rd Floor, San Francisco, CA 94133
(415) 262-4222; *Fax:* (415) 693-5005
www.mediaoneservices.com
hi@mediaonestudios.com
Jim Miller, Chairman
Julia Miller, CEO
Benjamin Schick, President
Drew Norris, Studio Operations
Danny Skarka, General Manager/Director of Production
Rolf Kaiser, Chief Technology Officer
Karen Richer, Director, Finance
Full HD Studio and Remote Production for Broadcast and Web, Branded Spots, Conferences, Theatercasts. Two insert studios for news channel live shots. Media Training, Fiber transmission, and Satellite downlink.

Metro Weather Service Inc.
NSS Data: TV-CATV only
132 Franklin Place, PO Box 385, Woodmere, NY 11598
(516) 568-8844; *Fax:* (516) 568-8845
www.metroweather.com
contact@metroweather.com
Pat Pagano, President
Mike Merin, Senior Meterologist
Don McGrath, Part-time Weather Observer
Joseph Leonardi, Forecasting & Broadcasting Weather
John DiPasquale
Tailored weather forecasts for TV & briefings to weathercasters. Serves radio & TV.

Miami News Net
NSS Data: TV-CATV only
2641 SW 27th Street, Miami, FL 33133
(305) 285-0044; *Fax:* (305) 285-0074
www.miaminewsnet.com
mnn@bellsouth.net
Catherine Moghari, President
A 24-hour TV news, sports & entertainment svc that provides crews, video archive, avid, beta edit & feed facilities. Live talkback studio facilities, dual path digital KU uplink trunk.

Mountain News Corporation
Div/DBA: (OnTheSnow)
PO Box 17895, Boulder, CA 80308
(720) 887-7720; *Fax:* (720) 887-7730
www.mountainnews.com
info@mountainnews.com
Chad Dyer, Global Managing Director & COO
Mountain News Corporation, formally AMI News, is the largest & oldest producer of winter & summer progmg for media. We deliver the most accurate & timely news & info covering mountain activities.

The Nasdaq Stock Market
1 Liberty Plaza, 165 Broadway, New York, NY 10006
(212) 858-5211, (212) 401-8700; *Fax:* (646) 625-6548
www.nasdaq.com
Nelson Griggs, President
Customized loc data for the stock market.
Serves radio & TV.

NBC News: See NBC listing in Major National TV News Organizations, this section.
30 Rockefeller Plaza, New York, NY 10112
(212) 664-4444; *Fax:* (212) 664-4085
www.nbcnews.com
contact.nbcnews@nbcuni.com
Andrew Lack, Chairman, NBC News & MSNBC
Noah Oppenheim, President, NBC News

Nippon TV Network Corporation
645 5th Avenue, Suite 303, New York, NY 10022
(212) 660-6900; *Fax:* (212) 660-6998, (212) 265-8495
www.ntv.co.jp
motoko@ntvic.com
Jusaburo Hayashi, President
Motoko Hasegawa, Operations Dir
International media svcs.

NOAA/National Weather Service Headquarters
1325 East West Highway, Silver Spring, MD 20910
(301) 713-0700; *Fax:* (301) 713-1598
www.weather.gov
nws.answers@noaa.gov
Dr. Louis W. Uccellini, Director
Mary C. Erickson, Deputy Director
John Murphy, COO
Mike Sowko, NWS Operations Center
Susan Buchanan, Communications
Kevin Cooley, Director, Planning & Programming for Svc. Delivery
Weather & flood warnings, forecasts & related info for the media & gen public.
7220 N.W. 101 Terr., Kansas City, MO 64153-2371
(816) 891-8914
Sandy Boyse, Dir Central Rgn
630 Johnson Ave., Bohemia, NY 11716-2618
(516) 244-0101
Dean Gulezian, Dir Eastern Rgn
Grosvenor Ctr. Mauka Tower, 737 Bishop St., Suite 2200, Honolulu, HI 96813-3212
(808) 532-6416; *Fax:* (808) 532-5569
James Weyman, Dir Pacific Rgn
819 Taylor St., Rm. 10A06, Fort Worth, TX 76102-6124
(817) 978-1000
Erma Nations, Dir Southern Rgn
Federal Bldg., 125 S. State St., Rm. 1311, Salt Lake City, UT
(801) 524-5122
Vickie L. Nadolski, Dir Western Rgn
222 W. Seventh Ave, 23, Rm. 517, Anchorage, AK 99513-7500
(907) 271-5136

NorthStar Studios Inc.
NSS Data: TV-CATV only
3201 Dickerson Pike, Nashville, TN 37207
(615) 650-6000; (800) 605-3590; *Fax:* (615) 650-6300
realnetworksinc.com
info@NorthStarStudios.tv
Grant Barbre, President
Complete TV production svcs: 7 stages, mobile production/uplink trucks, network origination, transmissions, digital archiving, Avid/DS, linear editing, graphics/animations & ENG crews.

Skywatch Weather Center
NSS Data: TV-CATV only
347 Prestley Road, Bridgeville, PA 15017
(800) SKY-WATCH, (412) 221-6000, (800) 759-9282; *Fax:* (412) 221-3160
www.skywatchweather.com
airsci@skywatchweather.com
Dr.Stanley J. Penkala, PhD, President & Director of Air Programs

Stanley Bostjancic, Treasurer & Chief Meteorologist
Daniel Krzywiecki, Vice President
Harry Green, Secretary
Weather forecasts targeted to the viewing area, & comprehensive briefings for on-air talent. Serves radio & TV.

The Sports Network
2200 Byberry Road, Suite 200, Hatboro, PA 19040
(215) 441-8444; (800) 227-7249; *Fax:* (215) 441-5767
www.sportsnetwork.com
kzajac@sportsnetwork.com
Mickey Charles, CEO & President
Ken Zajac, General Sales Mgr
Ken Zajac, Sales Director
Bernie Greenberg, Client Relations Coordinator
Steve Cwitkowitz, Account Executive
International real-time sports wire svc providing content, branded web pages, satellite and/or computer feeds directly to broadcasters (radio & TV), print, Internet sites, wireless with state of the art technology.

Thomson Reuters
3 Times Square, New York, NY 10036
(646) 223-4000
www.thomsonreuters.com
David Thomson, Chairman
James C. Smith, President & CEO
Stephane Bello, EVP & CFO
David W. Craig, President, Financial & Risk
Richard King, EVP & CIO
Ganzalo Lissarrague, President, Global Growth Operation
Deirdre Stanley, EVP &General Counsel
Peter Warwick, Chief People Officer
Worldwide TV news production & transmission svcs for loc TV stns/producers. Camera crews, production facilities, news bureaus, satellite svcs, video/slide archives.

U.S. Conference of Catholic Bishops
NSS Data: TV-CATV only
Div/DBA: Department of Communication, Film/TV Review Svcs.
3211 Fourth Street NE, Washington, DC 20017
(202) 541-3000; *Fax:* (202) 541-3201
www.usccb.org
ofb@msn.com
Daniel N. DiNardo, President
Jose H. Gomez, Vice President
James Rogers, Chief Communications Officer
David Felber, Director, Creative Services
Mary McDonald, Director, Marketing & Episcopal Resources
Judy Keane, Director, PublicAffairs
Publishes wkly reviews of movies, TV with artistic & moral observations.

Washington News Bureau
NSS Data: TV-CATV only
969 National Press Building, Washington, DC 20045 US
(202) 783-1760; *Fax:* (202) 783-1955
STetreault@nationalpress.com
Edward B. Lasak, COO
Ed Moss, Chief Executive Officer and President
Mark Hinueber, Vice President And General Counsel
Mark Ficarra, Chief Revenue Officer
Mike Flanagan, Vice President of Sales
Ryan Christlansen, Vice President ofDigital Media
Steve Tetreault, Bureau Chief
Custom TV news coverage: ENG crews, producers & talent.
Prod svcs: editing, studio, remote & satellite capabilities. Two live studios. Teleconference capability. Fiber Optic connectivity with Capital, White House & other locations.

The Weather Company (formerly WSI)
Mailing Address: 400 Minuteman Road, Andover, MA 01810
Second Address: 401 Charmany Drive, Suite 200, Madison, WI 53719
(978) 983-6300, (608) 274-4789; *Fax:* (978) 983-6400, (608) 278-2746
business.weather.com
Mark Gildersleeve, VP & Head of Business Solutions
Jim Menard, Head of Travel, Transport, Energy & Utility
Bill Dow, Head of Media Solutions
Michelle Boockoff-Bajdek, Head of Global Marketing
Dr. Peter P. Neilley, Director, WeatherForecasting Sciences
Maia Sisk, Director, Office Mngmt, Location & New Markets
The leading source of professional on-air weather systems, solutions & forecasting svc for TV, including TrueView, the most innovative weather storytelling tool available.

Radio News Services

ABC News Radio
NSS Data: TV-CATV only
47 West 66th Street, New York, NY 10023
(212) 456-5100; *Fax:* (212) 456-5150
www.abcnewsradioonline.com
Jeff Fitzgerald, Executive Director Of Operations
Steve Jones, VP and General Manager
Andrew Kalb, Executive Director of Programming
Serves 2,500 affiliates & 92.5 million wkly listeners nationwide, with bcst facilities in New York City & Washington, DC.

AccuWeather Enterprise Solutions
385 Science Park Road, State College, PA 16803
(814) 235-8600; *Fax:* (316) 265-1949
enterprisesolutions.accuweather.com
Salesmail@AccuWeather.com
Dr. Joel N. Myers, Founder, Chairman and President
Barry Lee Myers, CEO
Michael Smith, Senior VP and Chief Innovation Executive
Weather radar, graphic & info display systems, training, on air forecast & storm warning svcs. Select Warn, Storm Hawk, 24/7 storm monitoring, & customer svc. Complete system integration & training.

AccuWeather Inc.
NSS Data: Radio Only
Mailing Address: 385 Science Park Road, State College, PA 16803
Second Address: Sales Office, 1270 Avenue of the Americas, New York, NY 10020
(814) 237-0309; (212) 554-4750; *Fax:* (814) 235-8609
www.accuweather.com/en/
CustomerService@accuweather.com
Barry Lee Myers, CEO
Dr. Joel N. Myers, Founder, President, Chairman
Evan Myers, COO
John Dokes, Chief Marketing Officer
Steven Hickson, CFO
World's most accurate svc provides products & svcs for TV, radio, internet, mobile web & all new media platforms.

Agence France-Presse
1500 K Street NW, Suite 600, Washington, DC 20005
(202) 414-0600; *Fax:* (202) 414-0525
www.afp.com
afp-usa@afp.com
Emmanuel Hoog, Chairman & Chief Executive
Michele Leridon, Global News Director
Fabrice Lacroix, Managing Director
Stephane Marcovitch, Sales and Marketing Director
Caroline Raveton, Chief Information Officer
JulietteHollier-Larousse, Video Director
Sylvie Vormus, Director Of Communications&Corp Brand
Christophe Walter Petit, General Counsel
Produces a var of international news svcs, including text wires in six languages, photo wires, graphics & financial wires.

Alaska Public Radio Network
3877 University Drive, Anchorage, AK 99508-4676
(907) 550-8400; *Fax:* (907) 550-8401
www.alaskapublic.org/
Ed Ulman, CEO/General Manager
Bernie Washington, CFO
Jessica Stugelmayer, Director of Marketing & Promotions
Lori Townsend, News Director
Bede Trantina, FM Program Director
Bob Wyatt, Chief Technology Officer
Satellite-delivered news/info programs to 26 member stn across Alaska from state-of-the-art studios, hqtr in Anchorage.

American Academy of Dermatology
NSS Data: Radio Only
Div/DBA: American Academy of Dermatol
Mailing Address: Communications Department, Box 4014, Schaumburg, IL 60168
Second Address: 930 E. Woodfield Road, Schaumburg, IL 60173
(847) 240-1280, (866) 503-7546; *Fax:* (847) 240-1859
www.aad.org
mediarelations@aad.org
Henry W. Lim, President
Brian Berman, PhD, Vice President
Suzanne Olbricht, President Elect
Ted Rosen, VP Elect
Barbara Mathes, Secretary-Treasurer
Marta J. Van Beek, Assistant Secretary-Treasurer
Expert physicians available for TV & radio interviews, audio & video tapes on skin cancer pevention & detection, as well as info on skin, hair & nail conditions.

1350 I Street NW, Suite 870, Washington, DC 20005-3305
(202) 842-3555; *Fax:* (202) 842-4355
1350 I Street NW, Suite 870, Washington, DC 20005-3305
(202) 842-3555; *Fax:* (202) 842-4355

American Heart Association
7272 Greenville Avenue, Dallas, TX 75231
(888) 474-VIVE, (800) 242-8721; *Fax:* (214) 706-5243
www.americanheart.org; www.heart.org
Nancy Brown, CEO
Suzie Upton, COO
Meighan Girgus, Chief Marketing & Programs Officer
Julie Del Barto, Multimedia Strategies
Rsch & lifestyle reports, distributed via podcast.

American Urban Radio Networks
938 Penn Avenue, Suite 701, Pittsburgh, PA 15222
(412) 456-4099; *Fax:* (412) 456-4077
www.aurn.com
jlopes@aurn.com
Jerry Lopes, President, Program Operations & Affiliations
Howard Eisen, President, Network Sales
Basil Murrain, VP, Marketing & Promotions
Carrie Cleary, Traffic Manager
Bob Sharkey, Chief Engineer
Info, news, sports & entertainment of special interest to Blacks & other minorities.
432 Park Ave. S., 14th Fl., New York, NY 10016-8013
(212) 883-2100; *Fax:* (212) 297-2571
jay@aurn.com
E.J. ""Jay"" Williams, Pres

Associated Press Broadcast Services
NSS Data: TV-CATV only
200 Liberty Street, New York, NY 10281
(212) 621-1500
www.ap.org
info@ap.org
Steven R. Swartz, Chairman
Gary Pruitt, President & CEO
Lauren Easton, Director, Media Relations
Jessica Bruce, SVP, Human Resources & Corporate Communications
Sally Buzbee, Senior Vice President - Executive Editor
Karen Kaiser,SVP, General Counsel & Corp. Secretary
Ken Dale, Senior Vice President - Chief Financial Officer
Jim Kennedy, SVP, Strategic Planning
Audio: PrimeCuts, Sound Bank. On Air: Radio News. On Line: News Tickers, Online Video Network; Custom News, Sp Online. Prep: Power Prep. Software: News Desk, APENPS. Sound Desk, News Center. Text Headlines, Sp, Sports Power, News Power,Images & Multimedia: asap, all AP.

Black Radio Network Inc. (BRN)
375 Fifth Avenue, New York, NY 10016 US
(212) 686-6850; *Fax:* (212) 686-7308
www.blackradionetwork.com
Roy Thompson, Operations Dir
Provides a daily actuality news service emphasizing minority-oriented items.

Cable Telecommunications Association
1410 Grant Street, Suite A-101, Denver, CO 80203
(720) 379-3623; *Fax:* (720) 379-3624
www.cocabletv.com
pboyle@rbwpolicy.com
Sean Hogue, President
Rich Jennings, Vice President
Jeff Weist, Executive Director
Patrick Boyle, Deputy Director

The Canadian Press
NSS Data: Radio Only
36 King St East, Toronto, ON M5C 2L9 Canada
(416) 364-0321; *Fax:* (416) 364-0207
www.thecanadianpress.com
broadcast@thecanadianpress.com
Guy Crevier, President, La Presse
Full wire & audio svcs (news agency), satellite delivery for radio program syndicators.

CBS News: See CBS listing in National Radio Programming Services, this section.
51 W 52nd Street, New York, NY 10019-6188
(212) 975-4321, (877) 227-0787
www.cbscorporation.com
investorrelations@cbs.com
Sumner M. Redstone, Chairman Emeritus
Leslie Moonves, Chairman & CEO
Joseph Ianniello, Chief Operating Officer
Richard M. Jones, EVP, General Tax Counsel & Chief Veteran Officer

PROGRAMMING & PRODUCTION SERVICES

Gil Schwartz, SEVP & Chief Communications Officer
Larry Liding, EVP, Controller and Chief Accounting Officer
Jonathan H. Anschell, EVP, Deputy General Counsel and Secretary
Adam Townsend, EVP, Corporate Finance & Investor Relations
Anthony G. Ambrosio, EVP, CAO & Chief Human ResourcesOfficer

Cision / CNW
NSS Data: TV-CATV only
RBC WaterPark Place, 88 Qqueens Quay West, Ste 3000, Toronto, ON M5J 0B8 Canada
(877) 269-7890; *Fax:* (877) 269-5044
www.newswire.ca
info.ca@cision.com
Nicole Guillot, President
Elisa Schupp, VP, National Sales
Tim Griffin, VP, Product & Client Experience
David Furst, Senior Vice President, Technology
Laurie Smith, VP, Strategic Communications & Media
Offers a range of industry leading communication products & svcs for companies looking to maximize the strength of their news. Whether you are an investor rel off, or a specialist in PR, CNW offers the right tools for your communications.
Gulf Canada Sq, 401 Ninth Ave. S.W., Suite 835, Calgary, AB Canada
(403) 269-7605; *Fax:* (403) 263-7888, TWX: 03-824872
Michle.dauphine@newswire.ca
Krista Wightman, Mgr
Gulf Canada Sq, 401 Ninth Ave. S.W., Suite 835, Calgary, AB Canada
(403) 269-7605; *Fax:* (403) 263-7888, TWX: 03-824872
Michle.dauphine@newswire.ca
Krista Wightman, Mgr
Sun Tower, 1550 Bedford Hwy., Suite 410, Halifax, NS Canada
(902) 422-1411; *Fax:* (902) 422-3507, TWX: 019-21534
jgallant@newswire.ca
Robert Moffatt, Mgr Atlantic Canada
Sun Tower, 1550 Bedford Hwy., Suite 410, Halifax, NS Canada
(902) 422-1411; *Fax:* (902) 422-3507, TWX: 019-21534
jgallant@newswire.ca
Robert Moffatt, Mgr Atlantic Canada
255 Albert St., Suite 460, Ottawa, ON Canada
(613) 563-4465; *Fax:* (613) 563-0548, TWX: 053-3292
Hugh Johnson, Vp Natl Capital Rgn
255 Albert St., Suite 460, Ottawa, ON Canada
(613) 563-4465; *Fax:* (613) 563-0548, TWX: 053-3292
Hugh Johnson, Vp Natl Capital Rgn
1155 Rene Levesque Blvd. W, Suite 3310, Montreal, PQ Canada
(514) 878-2520; *Fax:* (514) 878-4451, TWX: 055-60936
scmtl@newswire.ca
Elaire Carr, Vp Quebec
1155 Rene Levesque Blvd. W, Suite 3310, Montreal, PQ Canada
(514) 878-2520; *Fax:* (514) 878-4451, TWX: 055-60936
scmtl@newswire.ca
Elaire Carr, Vp Quebec
650 West Georgia St., Suite 1103, Vancouver, BC Canada
(604) 669-7764; *Fax:* (604) 669-4356, TWX: 04-508529
Larry Cardy, Vp Western Canada
650 West Georgia St., Suite 1103, Vancouver, BC Canada
(604) 669-7764; *Fax:* (604) 669-4356, TWX: 04-508529
Larry Cardy, Vp Western Canada

CNN Radio News
11330 Lakefield Drive, Building 2, Suite 200, Johns Creek, GA 30097
(770) 290-1338; *Fax:* (404) 827-5363
www.westwoodone.com
Fred Bennett, Operations Dir
Top- & bottom-of-the-hour radio newscasts 24-hours a day plus business, sports & lifestyle updates.

Compu-Weather Inc.
NSS Data: Radio Only
2566 Route 52, Forensic Services Division, Hopewell Junction, NY 12533
(800) 825-4445, (845) 227-8500; *Fax:* (845) 227-8400
www.compuweather.com
sales@compuweather.com
Jeff Wimmer, President
Steve Roberts, Director of Weather Operations
Jeff Hurwitz, EVP, Global Sales & Marketing
Tore Jakobsen, CFO
Patti Robertson, Forensic Account Executive/Forensic Order Sp.
Harold Schwan, MarketingAssociate
Kim Cuozzo, Marketing Associate
Eric DeRoche, Customer Service Manager
Weather forecasts, features, info & actualities for TV & radio.

Connecticut Weather Center Inc.
NSS Data: Radio Only
18 Woodside Avenue, Danbury, CT 06810-7123
(203) 730-2899; *Fax:* (203) 730-2839
www.ctweather.com
weatherlab@ctweather.com
William Jacquemin, President/Chief Meteorologist
Gregory Tulipani, Director of Advertising/Media
Jonathan Minovich, Media Representative
Weather forecasts for all media. Custom intros/outros/lives. Accurate forecasts. Barter or cash arrangement available.

Corus Radio Network
25 Dockside Drive, Corus Quay, Toronto, ON M5A 0B5 Canada
(416) 479-7078; (416) 479-7000; *Fax:* (416) 479-7002
www.corusent.com tunein.com
Doug Murphy, President & CEO
Barbara Williams, EVP & COO
Cheryl Fullerton, EVP, People & Communications
Live & pre-recorded info & entertainment program production & satellite delivery to rgnl & natl Canadian radio stns.

CQ News
Div/DBA: CQ Roll Call
1625 Eye Street NW, Suite 200, Washington, DC 20006
(202) 650-6500; (800) 432-2250; *Fax:* (202) 419-8760
www.cqrollcall.com/
Steve Komarow, Senior VP & Executive Editor
Meg Hargreaves, Senior VP & COO
Print & Web-based info products & svcs on govt, politics & current interest topics. Daily & wkly publications, reference books & newsletters.

Dairyline Radio
Div/DBA: DairyBusiness Communications
, Bend, OR
(360) 354-5596, EXT. 101; *Fax:* (360) 354-7517
cdn.dairybusiness.com
Scott A Smith, Chairman & Co-CEO
John L Montandon, President & Co-CEO
Joel P Hastings, President, DairyBusiness Communications
Five minute & 9 1/2 minute Dairy Report- weekdays. Daily updates of news affecting the dairy industry.
DairyBusiness Communications
7225 Wrightsville Ave, 204, Wilmington, NC 28403-7224
Lynden, WA

Entertainment News Calendar
NSS Data: Radio Only
Mailing Address: 13636 Ventura Blvd, Suite 303, Sherman Oaks, CA 91423
Second Address: PO Box 55624, Sherman Oaks, CA 91413-0624
(818) 986-8168, (818) 990-5945; *Fax:* (818) 789-8047
www.newscalendar.com
editor@newscalendar.com
Evelyn Heyward, Operations Dir
Daily entertainment news svc.
Hollywood News Calender
15030 Ventura Blvd., Ste 742, Sherman Oaks, CA 91403-5470
(818) 990-5945
Carolyn Fox, Publisher

Evan Weiner Productions
NSS Data: TV-CATV only
370 Claremont Avenue, Mount Vernon, NY 10552
(914) 667-9070, (203) 288-2597 (producer)
Evan Weiner, Programming Director
Sports commentaries & reporting. Current program: The Business of Sports, commentaries on Metro Source.

Fairchild Broadcast News
NSS Data: TV-CATV only
Box 535, Hewlett, NY 11557
(212) 686-6850; *Fax:* (212) 686-7308
www.fairchildgroup.com/news; www.fairchildtv.com
Thomas Fung, Chairman
Gathers & disseminates news around the world.

Feature Story News
NSS Data: Radio Only
1730 Rhode Island Avenue NW, Suite 405, Washington, DC 20036
(202) 296-9012; *Fax:* (202) 296-9205
www.featurestorynews.com
info@featurestory.com
Simon Marks, President
Rob Flynn, Director of Business Development
Olly Barratt, Director of European News Coverage
Ind supplier of radio & TV news to English-language bcstrs worldwide. Bureaus in Washington, Moscow, London, New York, Orlando & San Francisco.
1133 Broadway, Suite 1420, New York, NY 10010-7903
(917) 330-3806
Nathan King, Correspondent
1133 Broadway, Suite 1420, New York, NY 10010-7903
(917) 330-3806
Nathan King, Correspondent
1103 Palmer St., Orlando, FL 32801-4048
(407) 898-1929
Steve Mort, Correspondent
1103 Palmer St., Orlando, FL 32801-4048
(407) 898-1929
Steve Mort, Correspondent

Hollywood News Service
NSS Data: Radio Only
Mailing Address: 13636 Ventura Blvd, #303, Sherman Oaks, CA 91423
Second Address: PO Box 55624, Sherman Oaks, CA 91413-0624
(818) 986-8168, (818) 990-5945; *Fax:* (818) 789-8047
www.newscalendar.com
editor@newscalendar.com
Carolyn Fox, Publisher
Daily entertainment news svc. Publisher of Hollywood News Calendar in Los Angeles & Entertainment News Calendar in New York.
Entertainment News Calender
250 W. 57th St, #1431, New York, NY 10107-0001
(212) 421-1370; *Fax:* (212) 563-3488
Carolyn Fox, Publisher

Medialink
1155 Avenue of the Americas, 8th Floor, New York, NY 10036
(646) 259-3001; *Fax:* (646) 259-3012
www.medialink.com
Michael E. Kassan, Chairman & CEO
Wenda Harris Millard, Vice Chairman
Dana Anderson, Chief Marketing Officer
Glenn Briffa, Executive VP
Angelo Dagostino, Head of Human Resources
International video & audio PR, satellite feed & news advisory svc. Advisories accessible by computer/newswire in United States & Europe.
37/38 Golden Sq., London,
44-71-240-3923
Jim Gold, Chairman
One Maritime Plaza, San Francisco, CA
(415) 296-8877; *Fax:* (415) 296-9929
1401 New York Ave. N.W., Suite 520, Washington, DC 20005-2102
(202) 628-3800
6430 Sunset Blvd., Suite 1100, Los Angeles, CA 90028-7901
(323) 465-0111
The Time & Life Bldg., 541 N. Fairbanks Ct., Suite 1910, Chicago, IL 60611-3706
(312) 222-9850
3340 Peachtree Rd. N.E., Suite 1520, Atlanta, GA 30326-1000
(404) 848-7500
4851 LBJ Fwy., Suite 605, Dallas, TX 75244-6004
(972) 774-0200

Metro Weather Service Inc.
NSS Data: TV-CATV only
PO Box 255, Orangeburg, NY 10962
(516) 568-8844; *Fax:* (516) 568-8853
www.metroweather.com
Contact@MetroWeather.com
Pat Pagano, President
Mike Merin, Senior Meteorologist
Don McGrath
Tailored weather forecasts for radio & TV. Feature reports farming, marine, ski, long-range forecasts via phone, computer, fax, ISDN, MP3 & Skype.

News Broadcast Network
75 Broad Street, 15th Floor, New York, NY 10004
(212) 684-8910, (800) 920-6397, (646) 839-5128; *Fax:* (212) 684-9650
www.newsbroadcastnetwork.com
Michael J. Hill, President
Robert Hill, Programming Director
Production & distribution of electronic news releases, actualities & pub affrs programs distributed by satellite, telephone & tape.
Seattle, WA
(206) 624-7505; *Fax:* (206) 624-7556
Milwaukee, WI
(414) 321-6210; *Fax:* (414) 321-3608
Chicago, IL

(603) 963-4455; *Fax:* (603) 963-4487
Los Angeles, CA
(909) 621-6903; *Fax:* (909) 621-9492
Washington,
(703) 893-4577, (202) 638-1603; *Fax:* (703) 893-6967, (202) 638-1607

NOAA/National Weather Service
1325 East West Highway, Silver Spring, MD 20910
(301) 713-0622; *Fax:* (301) 713-1292
www.weather.gov
nws.answers@noaa.gov
Dr. Louis W. Uccellini, Director
Mary C. Erickson, Deputy Director
John Murphy, COO
Mike Sowko, NWS Operations Center
Susan Buchanan, Communications
Kevin Cooley, Director, Planning & Programming for Scv. Delivery
Weather & flood warnings, forecasts & related info for the media & general pub.

North American Network
5335 Wisconsin Avenue NW, #440, Washington, DC 20015
(202) 243-0592; *Fax:* (202) 243-0594
www.nanradio.com
info@nanradio.com
Tom Sweeney, President & Chief Client Advocate
Sherry Jones, Director, Station Services
Tammy Lemley, Vice President
Ryan McKenna, New Media & Client Svcs Mgr
Bob Tebo, Sr Producer
Tom Kajubi, Director, Finance & Administration
Audio news releases & talk show interviews. On-site coverage for corps, govt agencies & assns.

PA-SportsTicker
NSS Data: Radio Only
2775 Shermer Road, Stop 2, Northbrook, IL 60062
(847) 583-2100; *Fax:* (847) 583-2600
www.stats.com
sales@stats.com
Gary Walrath, CEO
Robert L. Schur, COO
Jim Morganthaler, General Manager
Jay Imus, General Sales Mgr
Gregory S. Kirkorsky, EVP
Ken Dale, Director
Brian Kopp, SVP, Sports Solutions
Nick Stamm, Director, Marketing &Communications
Eric Shanks, Director
Provides 24-hr sports news, info, instant scores & complete sports news coverage on all professional & major college events.
19 E 34th St., New York, NY 10016-4304
(212) 515-1000; *Fax:* (212) 515-1211
Boston Fish Pier, West Bldg. #1, Suite 302, Boston, MA
(617) 951-0070; *Fax:* (617) 737-9960

Radio America
NSS Data: TV-CATV only
1100 North Glebe Road, Suite 900, Arlington, VA 22201
(703) 302-1000, (800) 807-4703; *Fax:* (571) 480-4140
www.radioamerica.com
Michael Paradiso, COO
James C. Roberts, President
Rich McFadden, VP, Operations
Greg Corombos, News Director
Short & long-form programs, special series, documentaries, daily one hr news show & conservative talk radio.

RadioTour.com
NSS Data: TV-CATV only
2500 Wisconsin Avenue NW, Suite 949, Washington, DC 20007-4132 US
(202) 333-4904; (202) 333-5000
www.expertclick.com
expertclick@gmail.com
Mitchell P. Davis, Publisher/Editor
Publisher of free Yearbook of Experts, Authorities & Spokespersons.

Skywatch Weather Center
NSS Data: Radio Only
347 Prestley Road, Bridgeville, PA 15017
(800) SKY-WATCH, (412) 221-6000, (800) 759-9282; *Fax:* (412) 221-3160
www.skywatchweather.com
Dr.Stanley J. Penkala, PhD, President & Director of Air Programs
Stanley Bostjancic, Treasurer & Chief Meteorologist
Daniel Krzywiecki, Vice President
Harry Green, Secretary
Taped, live & MP3 weathercasts targeted to the listening area, in stn-specified formats. Featuring accuracy, clarity & mature voices.

The Sports Network
NSS Data: Radio Only
2200 Byberry Road, Hatboro, PA 19040
(215) 441-8444; *Fax:* (215) 441-5767
www.sportsnetwork.com
Mickey Charles, CEO & President
Ken Zajac, Director, Sales
Steve Cwitkowitz, Account Executive
Bernie Greenberg, Client Relations Coordinator
International real-time sports wire svc providing content, branded web pages, XML feeds directly to bcstrs (radio & TV), print, Internet sites, wireless with state of the art technology.

Texas State Networks
NSS Data: TV-CATV only
4131 N Central Expwy, Suite 1000, Dallas, TX 75204
(214) 525-7000; *Fax:* (214) 525-7372
www.tsnradio.com
Paul Davis, Sales & Marketing
Raul Jaurequi, Affiliate Relations
News svc of the Texas State Networks. Provides Texas news, sports, agriculture, business & weather, Texas Rangers Radio Network & special features & long form programs. Largest state network with 12 stations.
Austin News Bureau
502 E. 11th, Suite 320, Austin, TX 78701-2650
(512) 474-5264 (NEWS), (512) 474-5275 (SALES)
Robert Wood, Dir

Thomson Reuters
3 Times Square, New York, NY 10036 USA
(646) 223-4000; *Fax:* (202) 898-8383
www.thomsonreuters.com
David Thomson, Chairman
James C. Smith, President & CEO
Gonzalo Lissarrague, President, Global Growth Operation
Stephane Bello, EVP & CFO
David W. Craig, President, Fnancial & Risk
Richard King, EVP & CIO
Gus Carlson, EVP & ChiefCommunications Officer
Deirdre Stanley, EVP & General Counsel
Peter Warwick, Chief People Officer
Worldwide TV news production & transmission svcs for loc TV stns/producers. Camera crews, production facilities, news bureaus, satellite svcs, video/slide archives.

Total Traffic & Weather Network
Div/DBA: (Clear Channel Broadcasting)
Mailing Address: 8303 Southwest Fwy, Houston, TX 77074
Second Address: 13725 Montfort Drive, Dallas, TX 75240
(972) 406-6884; ((72) 991-9200; *Fax:* (713) 407-6849
www.ttwnetwork.com
Provider of traf reporting svcs & leading supplier of loc news, sports, weather & video news svcs to the TV & radio bcst industries.

United Press International Inc.
1133 19th Street NW, Washington, DC 20036
(202) 898-8000; *Fax:* (202) 898-8048
www.upi.com
Nicholas Chiaia, President
Michael J. Marshall, Editor Emeritus
Marc Oram, General Counsel
Full global text, audio, photo news , info svcs, morning drive progmg, world, natl news, sports, weather, features & financial reports 24 hours.

The Wall Street Journal Radio Network
1211 Avenue of the Americas, 7th Floor, New York, NY 10036
(203) 210-5703; *Fax:* (212) 659-1908
www.wsjradio.com
Ashley Huston, Head Of Corporate Communication
Nancy Abramson, General Manager
Patrice Sikora, Managing Editor
John Wordock, Executive Editor
Adam Wilbur, VP Affiliate Sales
Anthony Severino, Traffic & Affidavits
Mike Gavin,Producer
Hourly business & financial news reports transmitted live via satellite 18 times daily from the Journal's New York newsroom. Dow Jones Money Report also transmitted 18 times daily.

WINGS: Women's International News Gathering Service
Box 95090, Vancouver, BC V5T 4T8 Canada
(604) 876-6994
www.wings.org
wings@wings.org
Frieda Werden, Executive Producer
Syndicate audio news & current affrs program, both produced in-house & acquired, focus on women & hard news. Distribution CD, satellite, & FTP.
Box 33220, Austin, TX 78764-0220
Stacy Pettigrew, Bureau Mgr

World Radio Network
Div/DBA: Babcock Media
10 Wyvil Road, London, SW8 2TG United Kingdom
44-20-7896-9000; *Fax:* 44-20-7896- 9007
www.wrn.org
info@wrnbroadcast.com
Paul Firth, Director of Brodcast Operations
Dean Haddock, Director of Broadcast Services
World Radio Network (via Galaxy 25) was acquired by Babcock International Group and now focuses on national, regional, and international current affairs and news, coming directly from the countries of origin.

Radio Format Providers

ABC Radio
Div/DBA: Disney/ABC
47 West 66th Street, New York, NY 10023
(212) 456-5101
www.abcradio.com
Steve Jones, Vice President & General Manager
Andrew Kalb, Executive Director, Programming
Jeff Fitzgerald, Executive Director, Operations
Heidi Oringer, Affiliate Solutions
Abe Velez, Business Development

CRN International Inc.
One Circular Avenue, Hamden, CT 06514
(203) 407-3313; (203) 288-2002; *Fax:* (203) 281-3291
www.crnradio.com
Barry Berman, President/Founder
Peter H. Freiler, Director, IT & Operations
Rob O'Mara, Managing Director, Strategy & Development
Jim Alkon, Marketing Director
Dick Kalt, Executive Vice President
Cheryl Faught, Controller
Jennifer Anderson, VP, Human Resources
Christina Upton, Director of Client Services
Ron Pell, Director of Media Relations
Features include Ski Watch, a 60-second, daily ski conditions update. Summer-oriented progmg includes Beach Watch & Summer Watch. Small business programs include the Small Business Report & Small Business Profile. All programsavailable on a barter basis.

Dialogue
One Woodrow Wilson Plaza, 1300 Pennsylvania Avenue NW, Washington, DC 20004-3027
(202) 691-4000; *Fax:* (202) 691-4141
www.wilsoncenter.org/dialogue
wwics@wilsoncenter.org
Thomas R. Nides, Chairman
Jane Harman, President, Director & CEO
Blair A. Ruble, VP, Programs
Linda Roth, VP of External Relations
John Milewski, Director of Digital Programming
Meg King, Strategic & National Security Advisor
Wkly half-hour program of conversations on natl, internatl affrs, history & culture. Available to pub & coml stns free of charge on CD. Progmg produced by the Woodrow Wilson International Center for Scholars.

Hispanic Communications Network
50 F Street, NW, 8th Floor, Washington, DC 20001
(202) 360-4138; *Fax:* (202) 637-8801
www.hcnmedia.com
carlos.alcazar@hcnmedia.com
Jeff Kline, Founder & Chairman
Alison Rodden, CEO & Business Development
Mercy Padilla, VP, Affiliate & Media Relations
David Castro, Multimedia Producer & IT Director
Luisa Fernando Montero, Journalist
Cresta Archuletta, ClientEngagement Associate
Paul Castro, Director, Media Productions & Programming CS
Produces six daily Spanish radio programs & distributes them to Hispanic Radio net affiliates.

Miller Broadcast Management
616 W Fulton Street, Suite 516, Chicago, IL 60661
(312) 454-1111; *Fax:* (312) 454-0044
www.millerbroadcast.com/
info@millerbroadcast.com

Lisa Miller, President
Matt Miller, Vice President

MRN Radio (Motor Racing Network)
555 MRN Drive, Concord, NC 28027
(704) 262-6700; *Fax:* (704) 262-6811
www.mrn.com
David Hyatt, President
Frank Beers, Director, Operations
Doug Watson, Chief Engineer
Chris McKee, Director, Business Development
Tony Rizzuti, Director, New Media
John Younger, Director, Partnership Sales
Cheryl Knight, Director,Radio Partnerships
Ryan Horn, Live Event Program Director
Live bcsts of NASCAR stock car racing & related programs via satellite on over 700 radio stations.

Musical Starstreams
Box 12685, LaJolla, CA 92039-2685
(619) 276-8989
www.starstreams.com/
info@starstreams.com
Forest, Producer/Host/Programmer
Electronica mix from over 200 commercial radio stations, cable systems and the Internet.

Orange Productions
523 Righters Ferry Road, 2nd Floor, Bala Cynwyd, PA 19004
(610) 667-8620; *Fax:* (610) 667-8939
www.soundsofsinatra.com
Sid Mark, President
Production & distribution of a wkly two-hour program Sounds of Sinatra.

Premiere Networks Inc.
15260 Ventura Boulevard, Sherman Oaks, CA 91403
(818) 377-5300; *Fax:* (818) 377-5333
www.premierenetworks.com
feedback@premierenetworks.com;
akorowitz@premierenetworks.com
Julie Talbott, President
Alan Korowitz, EVP of Sales
Dan Metter, EVP/Director of Personality Sales
Premiere Radio features the following personalities: Rush Limbaugh, Delilah, Ryan Seacrest, Steve Harvey, Glenn Beck, George Noory, Sean Hannity, Elvis Duran, Dan Patrick, Nikki Sixx, Mario Lopez, Bobby Bones, Colin Cowherd, Big Boy, Brooke& Jubal, Doug Gottlieb, John Boy & Billy, Rich Eisen
1270 Ave. of the Americas, New York, NY 10020-1700
(212) 445-3900
Catherine Mongarella, Sr Vp/Eastern Sls
15260 Ventura Blvd., 5th Fl., Sherman Oaks, CA 91403-5307
(818) 377-5300
Theresa Gage, Sr Vp/Western Sls
875 N. Michigan Ave., Suite 1450, Chicago, IL 60611-1803
(312) 266-3870
Susan McDonald, Vp/Chicago Rgnl Sls Mgr
3405 Piedmont Rd., Suite 500, Atlanta, GA 30305-1745
(404) 870-5070
Alexandra Fenech, Vp/Southern Sls
14001 N. Dallas Pkwy., Suite 500, Dallas, TX 75240-4346
(972) 239-6220
Jeff Steele., Sr Vp/Natl Music Syndication
306 S. Washington Ave., Suite 214, Royal Oak, MI 48067-3845

Radio Center for People with Disabilities (RCPD)
230 East Ohio Street, Suite 101, Chicago, IL 60611
(312) 640-5000; *Fax:* (312) 640-5010
www.rcpd.org
Brad Saul, Executive Director
Jeffrey Smulyan, Chairman /CEO
Nancy Dussault, PR&Media Affairs Mgr, iRobot Corp
PCPD is a non-profit agency founded to recruit, train & place people with disabilities in paying, off-air jobs in the radio business.

Radio Express Inc.
1415 West Magnolia Blvd, Burbank, CA 91506
(818) 295-5800; *Fax:* (818) 295-5801
www.radioexpress.com
radioinfo@radioexpress.com
Barbara Maitland Rounds, CEO/President
Anita Rae Antonio, General Manager
Jessica D'Agostin, Senior VP, Sales & Marketing
Randy Massey, IT Director
Mark Brower, Music Director
Distributors outside the United States: The World Chart Show, Rick Dees Weekly Top 40, Retro Country USA, Hot Mix, Hitdisc, Golddisc, Supercharger Production tool kit & Production libraries by firstcom music. Programs available by cash orbarter, libraries & products cash only.

Radio Spirits
Mailing Address: PO Box 3107, Wallingford, CT 06492
Second Address: PO Box 1315, Little Falls, NJ 07424
(203) 265-8044; (800) 833-4248
www.radiospirits.com
Radio producers of the nationally-syndicated old time radio program When Radio Was. Complete digital recording studio features Sonic Solutions Digital Work Station with No-Noise.

RPM Radio Programming and Management Inc.
1133 West Long Lake Road, Suite 200, Bloomfield Hills, MI 48302
(800) 521-2537, (248) 647-1068; *Fax:* (248) 647-3936, (888) 776-0006
www.tophitsusa.com
info@tophitsusa.com
Thomas M. Krikorian, President
Top Hits USA wkly or monthly digital download or DVD Rom svc & libraries including Solid Gold, Spectrum A/C & Country One. Classic rock, Christmas library, and American Music Environments.

Salem Music Network Inc.
Div/DBA: (division of Salem Music Networks/Salem Radio Netw
402 BNA Drive, Suite 400, Nashville, TN 37217
(615) 367-2210; *Fax:* (615) 367-0758
www.salemmusicnetwork.com
vdillard@salemmusicnetwork.com
Michael S. Miller, VP & General Manager
Dave Santrella, President, Broadcast Media
Carl Campbell, Chief Engineer
Provider of three different 24-hour Christian music formats via digital satellite to 230 plus radio stns throughout the US, Canada & operator of two greater Nashville (TN) radio stns.

Sirius Satellite Radio
Mailing Address: 1221 Avenue of the Americas, 36th Floor, New York, NY 10020
Second Address: PO Box 33174, Detroit, MI 48232
(212) 584-5100; *Fax:* (212) 584-5200
www.siriusxm.com/
James E Meyer, CEO
Scott Greenstein, President & Chief Content Officer
Dara Altman, EVP & Chief Administrative Officer
Patrick L Donnelly, EVP & General Counsel
David Frear, EVP & CFO
Stephen Cook, EVP, Sales & Automotive
Samantha Bowman, Music & Entertainment Media Relations
30.6 million subs

Southcott Productions
Box 33185, Granada Hills, CA 91394 US
(818) 368-4938; *Fax:* (818) 368-4938
www.chucksouthcott.com
info@chucksouthcott.com
Chuck Southcott, President
Adult pop standards format; 'This is Music' fully hosted adult standards program available through mp3 or ftp for use from one hour per week to up to three hours daily, Monday through Friday.
4605 Lankershim Blvd., Suite 702, North Hollywood, CA 91602-1818
(818) 755-9952
Chuck Southcott, Program Dir

TAA Music / Toby Arnold Sound Studios
Mailing Address: 3234 Commander Drive, Carrollton, TX 75006-2507
Second Address: PO Box 828, Aubrey, TX 76227
(800) 527-5335; (972) 735-0641; *Fax:* (972) 248-8919
www.taamusic.com
Susan Bedwell, President/CEO
Troy Powers, Engineering Dir
Julie Simpson, Account Manager
Audio Production libraries for radio. Station Imaging, Morning show promo sweeper, stager packages for all formats. Cash or Barter.

Talkline Communications Network
PO Box 20108, Park West Station, New York, NY 10025
(212) 769-1925; (866) 4-talkline; (866)JewishRadio; *Fax:* (212) 799-4195
www.talklinecommunications.com/
tcntalk@aol.com
Rabbi Zev J. Brenner, President & Executive Producer
National Jewish radio net featuring news, interviews with newsmaker guests & celebrities; live call-in format; live segments from Israel; satellite delivered. Available on barter.

TM Studios
2002 Academy Ln, Ste #110, Dallas, TX 75234
(972) 406-6800; *Fax:* (972) 406-6890
www.tmstudios.com/
info@tmstudios.com
Greg Clancy, General Manager - VP/Creative
Jim Weisz, Music Sales
Lee Napier, Jingles & Production-East/Central
Mike Capozzoli, Jingles & Production-West/South
Lakeisha Black, Accounts Receivable
GoldDisc music libraries, HitDisc wkly mus svc, music on hard drive, jingles, mus libraries production, special programs, CD-ROM.

United Press International
Mailing Address: 1133 19th St NW, Washington, DC 20036
Second Address: , Boca Raton, FL
(202) 898-8111, (202) 898-8100; *Fax:* (202) 898-8057
www.upi.com
editorforms@upi.com
Nicholas Chiaia, President
Michael Marshall, Editor Emeritus
Marc Oram, General Counsel
Full-svc company offers a number of short-form info features to its affil radio stns.

WestWood One
Mailing Address: Candler Tower, 220 W 42nd Street, New York, NY 10036
Second Address: 4400 Jennifer St, NW, Ste 400, Washington, DC 20015
(212) 419-2926, (212) 967-2888, (888) HEL-P450; *Fax:* (212) 974-0615
www.westwoodone.com
barobinson@cbs.com
Charles Steinhauer, COO
Tim Seymour, Senior VP, Operations
Jana Polsky, Press Contact
245 million reached each week through 450 owned and operated stations in 90 US media markets. NFL Football, NCAA Basketball & College Football.

WFMT Fine Arts Radio
5400 N St Louis Avenue, Chicago, IL 60625-4698
(773) 279-2000; *Fax:* (773) 279-2199
www.wfmt.com
wfmtadsales@wfmt.com
James W. Mabie, Chairman
Reese Marcusson, COO & CFO
Daniel J. Schmidt, President & CEO
Jill Britton, Sr Vice President & Chief Development Officer
Anne Gleason, Senior Vice President of Marketing and Interactive
Classical, opera & folk mus, news & fine art progmg 24-hours per day through United Video Inc. Serving 200 cable systems in 30 states with 850,000 subs.

WFMT Radio Networks 98.7
Renee Crown Public Media Ctr, 5400 N St Louis Avenue, Chicago, IL 60625-4698
(773) 583-5000; *Fax:* (773) 583-3046
www.wfmt.com
wfmtadsales@wfmt.com
James W Mabie, Chairman
Daniel J. Schmidt, President & Chief Executive Officer
Jill Britton, Senior VP & Chief Development Officer
Reese Marcusson, COO & CFO
Anne Gleason, Senior VP Marketing & Interactive Media
Daniel Soles,Senior VP & Chief Television Content
Classical and fine arts music.

Cable Audio Services

The Classical Station, WCPE
; Raleigh
Box 897, Wake Forest, NC 27588
(800) 556-5178; *Fax:* (919) 556-9273
theclassicalstation.org
generalmanager@theclassicalstation.org
Deborah S. Proctor, General Manager/Chief Engineer
Dick Storck, Programming Director
Christina Romano, Chief Engineer
William Woltz, Music Director
John Graham, Engineering Services
Peter Blume, Business Development Director
EricMaynard, Webmaster
Robert Kennedy, Great Sacred Music Host
Curtis Brothers, Outreach Director & Media Liaison
Free 24-hour classical music progmg with live announcers for radio, cable, other distributors. Weekly request programs, opera and features. Satellite: AMC 1, Transponder 12 k, Vert, 1,1942 MHz.

CRN Digital Talk Radio
9135 Alabama Avenue, Ste A, Chatsworth, CA 91311
(818) 818-6400; *Fax:* (818) 352-3229
www.crntalk.com
info@crntalk.com
Michael Horn, President
Paul Stern, Vice-President of Operations
Jennifer Horn, VP of Sales & Marketing
Mathew Bissontz, Program Director
Tomas, Asst Operations Director
Nikki Barreras, Digital Media Coordinator
Courtney Kadera,Executive Producer

DMX, Inc.
Div/DBA: Mood Media
Mailing Address: 1703 West Fifth Street, Suite 600, Austin, TX 78703
Second Address: 3170 Reps Miller Road, Suite 100, Norcross, GA 30071
(512) 380-8500, (800) 345-5000, (770) 225-2500; *Fax:* (512) 380-8501
us.moodmedia.com
info@moodmedia.com
Steve Richards, President & CEO

Music Choice
Mailing Address: 650 Dresher Road, Horsham, PA 19044
Second Address: 328 W 34th Street, New York, NY 10001
(646) 459-3300; (215) 784-5870; (212) 563-0109; *Fax:* (215) 784-5869
www.musicchoice.com
David J. Del Beccaro, President
Damon Williams, Operations Dir
Steve Bolland, Mgr Programming Operations
Nolan Baynes, Senior Dir Marketing
Music Choice is the premier music television network, reaching U.S .households through digital cable and satellite television. Music Choice programs interruption-free music for homes and businesses and distributes televised concerts andmusic shows. The Music Choice music channels reach 33 million households and the Music Choice Concert Series airs in 44 million homes nationally. Music Choice is a partnership among subsidiaries of Microsoft Corporation, Motorola, Inc., SonyCorporation of America, Warner Music Group, Inc., EMI Music and several leading U.S. cable providers: Adelphia Cable Communications, Comcast Cable Communications, Cox Communications, and Time Warner Cable.

WFMT Radio Network
5400 N St Louis Avenue, Chicago, IL 60625-4698
(773) 279-2000; (773) 583-5000; (800) 872-9368; *Fax:* (773) 279-2199
www.wfmt.com
wfmtadsales@wfmt.com
James W Mabie, Chairman
Daniel J. Schmidt, President and Chief Executive Officer
Jill Britton, Senior VP & Chief Development Officer
Steve Robinson, Genral Manager/VP
Carol Martinez, Station Relations Manager
Tony Macaluso,Director/Syndication/Marketing
Reese Marcusson, COO & CFO
Steve Robinson, Executive Vice President for Radio and Project Dev
Anne Gleason, Senior VP of Marketing and Interactive
V. J. McAleer, Senior Vice President for Production andCommunity
Parke Richeson, Senior Vice President and Executive in Charge, WTT
Daniel Soles, Senior VP & Chief Television Content

Yesterday USA
2001 Plymouth Rock, Richardson, TX 75081
(972) 889-9872 (YUSA); *Fax:* (972) 889-2FAX
www.yesterdayusa.com
yesterdayusa@mail.com
William J. Bragg, Chairman
Mike Handy, Host
Walden Hughes, Host
Bobb Lynes, Host
A 24-hour natl radio voice of the National Museum of Communication of Irving, TX. Presenting public domain old-time radio shows & vintage music free of charge & without comls. Satellites: Galaxy 11, transponder 18, Ku verticel, frequency12060, audio PID 1620 left ch.

Producers, Distributors and Production Services Subject Index

PROGRAMMING & PRODUCTION SERVICES

Travelogues
Promark Television

Video Conferences
ComBridges
Communications III Inc.
Cornell University Broadcast Studios (Marketing Group)
Dome Productions
Educational Technologies Network (ETN)
Episcopal Church Center
Free To Choose Network
Gene Bayliss
John Driscoll Voice Over America
Level 3 Communications, LLC
Medialink
National Collegiate Athletic Association (NCAA)
PSSI Global Services-Strategic Television
Virginia Tech

Videotape Editing
Alan Weiss Productions
Broadview Media
Carpel Video Inc.
Diocese of Springfield
Encore Media
Fox 17 Studio Productions
GVI
Independent Edge Films
Limelight Communications Inc.
Montgomery Community Television Inc.
North by Northwest Productions
Palace Producers
PostWorks, New York
The History Makers
The Saturday Evening Post
Video Techniques Inc.
Vuolo Video Air-Chex
Wide Eye Productions, Inc.
Yada/Levine Video Productions

Voice-Overs
Ascent Capital Group
C 2 Productions Inc.
CA Media Development
Chinamerica Hit Radio
Continental Recordings Inc.
D-Squared Media
DaviSound
David Kaye Productions Inc.
Eurocine
Fischer Broadcast Services
GMI Media L.L.C.
Irving Productions Inc.
Jeff Davis Productions Inc.
John Driscoll Voice Over America
MSE
Magno Sound & Video
Maynard & Associates
N W Media
Perception Media Group
Primo Newservice Inc.
RDF Media
Sound of Birmingham Productions
Strand Media Group Inc.
Studio Center Total Production
Teen Kids News
The Image Generators
Time Capsule, Inc.
Work Edit
ZBS Foundation

Weather Programming
CompuWeather Inc.
Metro Weather Service Inc.
Skywatch Weather Center
System TV
The Weather Company (formerly WSI)

Weather Programming, Radio
CompuWeather Inc.
Ion Weather Network
Metro Weather Service Inc.
Sam Shad Productions
Skywatch Weather Center

Producers, Distributors & Production Services Alphabetical Index

A-1 Entertainment
611 Cedar Lane, Suite C-7, Teaneck, NJ 07666 USA
(201) 394-1849; *Fax:* (201) 357-8482
www.a-one-entertainment.com
alan@a-one-entertainment.com
Alan Miller, President
Distribution of film, TV & video progmg worldwide. Royalty-free classic prgmg.

Accuracy in Media Inc.
Div/DBA: American Journalsim Center
Mailing Address: 4350 East West Highway, Suite 555, Bethesda, MD 20814 USA
Second Address: 1717 K Street, NW, Ste 900, Washington, DC 20006
(202) 364-4401; *Fax:* (202) 364-4098
www.aim.org
Don Irvine, Chairman
Roger Aronoff, Editor
Cliff Kincaid, Director - AIM Center for Investigative Journalism
Deborah Lambert, Director of Special Projects
Nationwide media monitoring organization produces documentary TV films, radio and podcast commentaries, bi-monthly printed publications, daily website updates, and programs that critique media coverage.

Action Television
Div/DBA: Action Media, Inc.
10850 Dover Street, Suite 500, Westminster, CO 80021
(720) 443-1301
www.actiontelevision.com, www.golflife.com, www.golflifemedia.com
Michael Billingsley, President
Travis Harper, Post Production Supervisor
Stephanie Billingsley, Principal
Specializing in cable sports programming & distribution, extensive stock footage of golf, action sports, mountain lifestyle, skiing, family & travel. Full service crews, two Adobe Premiere edit suites, full graphics and animationcapabilities for 2D / 3D broadcast design.

Advanced Digital Services, Inc.
948 N. Cahuenga Blvd., Hollywood, CA 90038 USA
(323) 468-2200; *Fax:* (323) 468-2211
www.adshollywood.com
info@adshollywood.com
Andrew McIntyre, President
Brad Weyl, Chief Operating Officer
Russell Ruggieri, Vice President of Engineering
Valerie Kroll, Vice President, Client Services
Tom Sehenuk, Director of Technical Operations
Video duplication, standard conversion, digital post-production.

Adventist Media Center
11291 Pierce Street, Riverside, CA 92505 USA
(805) 955-7777; *Fax:* (805) 955-7701
www.adventistmediacenter.com
Warren Judd, General Manager
TV program production & distribution.

African Family Film Foundation
PO Box 630, Santa Cruz, CA 95061-0630 USA
(831) 426-3133
www.africanfamily.org
friends@africanfamily.org
Taale Rosellini, Founder & Executive Director
Yolisa Duley, Board of directors member
Ijeoma Iloputaife, Board of directors member
Lensa Gudina, Board of directors member
Gerard Kedrebeogo, Board of directors member
Taale LaafiRosellini, Board of directors member
David Anthony, Ph. D, Advisory Board member
Production & distribution of films & videotapes promoting African family life & culture.

Agency for Instructional Technology (AIT)
8111 N. Lee Paul Road, Bloomington, IN 47404-7916 USA
(800) 457-4509,(812) 339-2203; *Fax:* (812) 333-4218
www.ait.net
info@ait.net
Robert E. Yocum Jr., President/ CEO
Rolanda Kirkley, Operations/Facility Manager
Chuck Wilson, General Manager
Chuck Wilson, Executive Director
Cynthia M. Mosca, Director- Language Minority Services
Bernice Stafford, VicePresident- School Strategies and Evaluation
Barb Jackson, Controller
Dr. David Gudaitis, Executive Producer
Produces, acquires & distributes technology-based learning resources including video, videodisc, software & printfor all K-12 curricular areas, vocational educ/tech prep, early childhood, & professional dev.
1800 N. Stonelake Dr, Bloomington, IN 47404 United States

Agora TV
195 Hicks Dr. S.E., Marietta, GA 30060 US
(678) 581-3750
www.agoratv.tv
joe@agoratv.tv
Joseph Gora, CEO
TV production & equipment rental; Fly packages.

Agrinet News Network
176 Radio Rd., Powell's Point, NC 27966 USA
(252) 491-2249, (252) 491-2903, (252) 491-2908; *Fax:* (252) 491-2959
www.agrinet.com
info@agrinet.com
Tanya Gallop, Traffic Manager
Lisa Ray, Sales Manager
Bill Ray, News Host
John Bernier, Meteorologist
State, rgnl & natl agricultural news, mkts & weather.

Alan Weiss Productions
1243 California Road, Eastchester, NY 10709 USA
(212) 974-0606; *Fax:* (212) 974-0976
www.awptv.com
myacoub@awptv.com
Alan Weiss, President & Executive Producer
Marilou Yacoub, Project Manager
Fifteen Emmys for video production. We handle any broadcast, PR or corporate from concept to distribution.

Alden Films
PO Box 449, Clarksburg, NJ 08510 USA
(732) 462-3522; *Fax:* (732) 294-0330
www.aldenfilms.com
info@aldenfilms.com
Paul Weinberg, President
Fran Fried, Operations Dir
Distributes nearly 200 DVD's & CD's on Israel & Judaica. Official distributor for state of Israel.

Alden Films
PO Box 449, Clarksburg, NJ 08510 USA
(732) 462-3522, (800) 832-0980; *Fax:* (732) 294-0330
www.aldenfilms.com
info@aldenfilms.com
Paul Weinberg, President
TV program, promotion & educ film distribution.

Alfred Haber Distribution Inc.
111 Grand Ave., Suite 203, Palisades Park, NJ 07650 USA
(201) 224-8000; *Fax:* (201) 947-4500
www.alfredhaber.com
George Scanlon, COO
Alfred Haber, President
TV program distribution.

All Productions
PO Box19755, San Diego, CA 92159 USA
(619) 248-2566; *Fax:* (619) 460-6160
www.allproductions.com
allproductions1@sbcglobal.net
Michael All, CEO
Jean All, President
George Kay, Programming Director
Dr. Stephen A. All, Founder
Tony Stevens, Producer Director
TV & radio program production, distribution; cable-ready TV progmg; promotion film production, production svcs; TV, radio spots & coml announcers.
7025 Regner Rd, San Diego, CA 92119-1941 United States
(619) 460-4837 (619) 286-7733; *Fax:* (619) 460-6160

Allegro Productions Inc.
Div/DBA: Science Screen Report
347 Main Street, Chester, NJ 07930 USA
(800) 275-4636,800-ASK-INFO,800-232-2133; *Fax:* (888) 329-3737
www.ssrvideo.com
info@ssrvideo.com
Scott Forman, President
Educational & corporate progmg, including documentary/bcst. From concept to completion, offering full service video post production, CD-ROM/DVD authoring, multi-format duplication, 3D animation & effects.

Alliance for Christian Media / Day1
2715 Peachtree Rd NE, Atlanta, GA 30305 USA
(888) 411-DAY1, (404) 815-9110; *Fax:* (404) 815-0495
http://day1.org
info@day1.org
Rev. Peter Wallace, President and Executive Producer
Thomas Keuneke, Chief Financial Officer
Donal Jones, Production Coordinator/Audio Engineer
Ethel Ware Carter, Administrative Assistant
C. Patricia Reagan, Director ofPhilanthropy
Sherrie Miller, Announcer
Lydia Canales, Customer Service
Radio program production & distribution; relg ecumenical media.

Allumination FilmWorks, LLC
21250 Califa St., Suite 102, Woodland Hills, CA 91367 USA
(818) 712-9000; *Fax:* (818) 712-9074
Cheryl Freeman, CEO
Distribution, dev, production documentaries, TV series, kids, specials.

Altruist Media
2601A Wilson Blvd., Arlington, VA 22201 USA
(703) 812-8813; *Fax:* (703) 812-9710
Jan Dearth, President
A full-svc visual communications firm. Staff producers, writers & dirs provide full creative direction & project mgmt from concept dev, treatment, scripting & graphics design to production & delivery. Offers videotape, live eventproduction, consulting svcs for organizational communications. Provides comprehensive production svcs for videotape, special event & live business TV-video conference progmg. Also offers media training, VNR production, video press tours, consultingfor private networks, new media svcs including distributed multimedia, WWW design & CD-ROM dev.

Americ Disc
2525 Canadien, Drummondville, QC J2C 7W2 Canada
(819) 474-2655; (800) 263-0419; *Fax:* (819) 478-4575
info@americdisc.com
CD & DVD replication and fulfillment.

America ONE Television Network
6125 Airport Freeway, Suite 100, Ft. Worth, TX 76117 USA
(817) 546-1400; *Fax:* (682) 647-0756
lbowden@americaone.com
Matt Reiff, President
Preston Bornman, Operations Dir
LeAnn Bowden, Program Coordinator/ Traffic Manager
24 hour gen entertainment bcst network.

America's Most Wanted
2 Bethesda Metro Center, Suite 800, Bethesda, MD 20814 USA
(240) 482-1100; *Fax:* (240) 482-1181
feedback@amw.com
Marc Kaplan, President
Wkly reality-based program for Fox TV.

American Blues Network
PO Box 6216, Gulfport, MS 39506
(800) 896-5307; (228) 896-5307; *Fax:* (228) 896-5703
Stan Daniels, CEO
Thomas Bradley, Chief Engineer
Tabari Daniels, Affiliate Support
LaQueena Davis, Traffic/Website Manager
The only 24-hour blues syndication.

American Chiropractic Association Inc.
1701 Clarendon Blvd., Suite 200, Arlington, VA 22209 USA
(703) 276-8800; *Fax:* (703) 243-2593
www.acatoday.org
memberinfo@acatoday.org
N. Ray Tuck, Chairman
Jim Potter, CEO
David A. Herd, President
Karen Silberman, Executive VP
Amanda Donohue, Senior Associate, Communications
Professional membership organization. ACA Radio.

American Farm Bureau Inc.
600 Maryland Ave. SW, Suite 1000W, Washington, DC 20024 USA
(202) 406-3600; *Fax:* (202) 406-3602
www.fb.org
Zippy Duvall, President
Erin Anthony, Editor, Farm Bureau News
Christy Lilja, Executive Director, Administration
Julie Anna Potts, Executive Vice President
Brett Hom, CFO/Treasurer
Lynne Finnerty, Director, Project Management
SueDaoulas, Executive Assistant

Ellen Steen, General Counsel & Secretary
Mace Thornton, Executive Director, Communications
AGFeed, mthy video feed of news stories about food & agriculture, Newsline radio svc, Focus on Agriculture commentary, stock footage.

American Foundation for the Blind
2 Penn Plaza, Suite 1102, New York, NY 10121 USA
(212) 502-7600,(800) 232-5463; *Fax:* (888) 545-8331
www.afb.org
afbinfo@afb.net
Kirk Adams, President & CEO
Kelly Bleach, Chief Business Officer
Patsy Carvache, Finance Director
Adrianna Montague, Chief Community Engagement Officer
Alina Vayntrub, Executive Editor
Sonya Shiflet, Chief Human Resources &Planning Officer
Stacy Rollins, Executive Administrative Assistant
Provides consultation & referrals, social & technological rsch, publications, info svcs, public educ, govt rel & talking books.

American Heart Association
7272 Greenville Avenue, Dallas, TX 75231 USA
(800) 242-8721, 800-AHA-USA-1, 888-474-VIVE; *Fax:* (214) 706-5243
americanheart.org
Review.personal.info@heart.org
Nancy Brown, CEO
John Warner, President
Suzie Upton, COO
Meighan Girgus, Chief Marketing & Programs Officer
Julie Del Barto, Multimedia Strategies
Video news releases, podcasts, stock footage, limited animation related to heart & disease for news programs.

American Public Television
55 Summer St., Boston, MA 02110 USA
(617) 338-4455; *Fax:* (617) 338-5369
www.aptonline.org
info@aptonline.org
Cynthia A Fenneman, President & CEO
Judy Barlow, VP, Business Development & International Sales
Eric Luskin, Vice President, Premium Service and Syndication
Chris Funkhouser, VP, Exchange Programming and Multicast Services
JamieHaines, Vice President, Communications
Gerry Field, Vice President, Technology
David Fournier, Vice President, Finance and Administration
Major distributor of high quality TV programs to all U.S. public TV stns. Also distributor of programs to international media.

AmericaNurse TV Productions
Box 7717, Romeoville, IL 60446 USA
(815) 773-4497
www.americanurse.com
asktvnurse@yahoo.com
Karon Gibson, Programming Director
Consumer educ shows on health, safety & other self-help titles. Entertaining introduction to optional alternative & mainstream medicine & Rx. Travel, entertainment, legal, and reality tv. Also, internet programming on ustream.tv,'Outspoken' with Karon.

Anderson Productions Ltd. (APL)
51 West 81st Street, Suite 12L, New York, NY 10024 USA
(212) 414-9220; *Fax:* (212) 206-0279
www.apltv.com
steveanderson@apltv.com
Steven C.F. Anderson, President and Executive Producer
Sam Shinn, Cinematographer
Kevin Cloutier, Cinematographer
Agatha Malacos, Associate Producer
Joe Gentle, Content Correspondent
TV program production for bcst, cable TV & nonprofit orgs..

APM/Associated Production Music LLC
6255 W. Sunset Blvd., Suite 900, Hollywood, CA 90028 USA
(323) 461-3211,(800) 543-4276; *Fax:* (323) 461-9102
www.apmmusic.com
info@apmmusic.com
Adam Taylor, President
Sarah Konkoski, VP, Finance
Josh Roach, VP, Technology
Brian Stone, VP, Sales & Marketing
Keiko McNamara, Sales Coordinator
Jim Doane, Director of Marketing
David Tingley, Custom Music Administrator
Georgia Robertson, Music Director
Edwina Travis-Chin, Music Director
Sarah Ponder, Music Director
Mark Gracious, Music Director
50+ Libraries: KPM, Bruton, Sonoton, Cezame, Kosinus. Over 500,000 tracks, Personalized Packages, Music Search, 15-20 New CD releases mthy.
342 Madison Ave., Suite 1200, New York, NY 10173
(800) 276-6874
Craig Giummarra, Sls Mgr

Arab America
916 G Street NW, Washington, DC 20001 USA
(877) 272-2944, (877) ARAB-944; *Fax:* (718) 238-2465
www.arabamerica.com
Gamil M. Tawfik, President
Arabic language progmg bcst Time Warner Cable.

Archive Films/Archive Photos
Div/DBA: Getty Images
75 Varick St., New York, NY 10013 USA
(646) 613-4000,(800) 462-4379; *Fax:* (646) 613-4140
www.gettyimages.com
sales@gettyimages.com
Jonathan Klein, Co-Founder & Chairman
Dawn Airey, CEO
Craig Peters, EVP & COO
Jason Fischel, VP, Products & General Manager
Andrew Saunderse, Senior VP, Creative Content
Rik Powell, Interim CFO
Jennifer Ferguson, Senior VP,Global Communications
Yoko Miyashita, SVP, General Counsel
Gene Foca, Senior VP & Chief Marketing Officer
Leander LeSure, Chief Human Resources Officer
Stock footage/photo library providing all types of historical footage & photos for use in products for TV/CATV.
Archive Films/Archive Photos
17 Conway St, London W1P 6EE,
44 171 312 0300; *Fax:* 44 171 391 9123
Chris Blakeston, Contact
Archive Films GMBH
Bremstrasse 12, Cologne 50969,
49 221 936 4080; *Fax:* 49 221 360 4112
Craig Burns, Contact
Archive Films/Archive Photos
Italy Via Terraggio 17, Milan 20123,
39 2 874 693; *Fax:* 39 2 805 7739
Guido Rossi, Contact
Archive Films/Archive Photos
Scandinavia Birger Jarlsgatan 55, 111 45 Stockholm,
46 8 20 89 20; *Fax:* 46 8 20 89 33
Lennert Karlsson, Contact
Archive Films/Archive Photos
4 Boulevard Poissonniere, Paris Ducaud, 75009 France
33 1 55 77 00 00; *Fax:* 33 1 55 77 00 66
Sylvie Ducaud, Contact

Arkadia Entertainment Corp.
PO Box 77, Saugerties, NY 12477
(845) 246-9955; *Fax:* (845) 246-9966
www.view.com/
Bob Karcy, President & Founder
CD, DVD, video production & distribution worldwide. A broad range of exclusive progmg.

Artist View Entertainment Inc.
5775 E. Los Angeles Avenue, Suite 218, Los Angeles, CA 93063 USA
(818) 752-2480; *Fax:* (818) 301-3272
www.artistviewent.com
info@artistviewent.com
Scott Jones, President
Jay Joyce, Vice President
Jennifer Dillion, Director of Distribution Services
Lani Jones, Accounting
Worldwide distribution in all media specializing in feature films.

Ascent Capital Group
5251 DTC Parkway, Suite 1000, Greenwood Village, CO 80111-2755 USA
(203) 965-6000; *Fax:* (203) 965-6405
www.ascentmedia.com
William R. Fitzgerald, Chairman, Chief Executive Officer
Peter Brickman, General Manager
William E. Niles, Executive Vice President, General Counsel
John A. Orr, Senior Vice President
Mike A. Haislip, Executive Vice President
Michael R. Meyers, Senior Vice President, CFO
Carl E. Vogel, Director
Brian Deevy, Director
Video transmission, origination; tech consulting, new media products; private networks, post production, studio, graphics; bcst event svcs & satellite svcs.
GWNS Minneapolis
6845 20th Ave., Minneapolis, MN 55038
(612) 330-2639
Joel Helseth, Sls & Mktg
Asia Bcst Centre
Singapore,
(612) 330-2639
vhendra@abc.gwns.com
Vincent Helseth, Chairman

Ascent Capital Group
5251 DTC Parkway, Suite 1000, Greenwood Village, CO 80111 USA
(310) 434-7000
www.ascentmedia.com
William R. Fitzgerald, Chairman/ CEO
William E. Niles, EVP, General Counsel
Michael R. Myers, Senior Vice President/ CFO
Michael A. Haislip, Executive Vice President
Joh A. Orr, Senior Vice President
Carl E. Vogel, Board Member
Brain Deevy, Board Member
Network services, syndication, advertising solutions, satellite bcst distribution, & net construction & maintenance.

Asia Pacific Productions USA, Ltd.
19698 S.E. Cottonwood St., Portland, OR 97267 USA
(503) 723-6456
approd.com
info@approd.com
Tom Hopkins, Founder & President
Miyuki Shigeji, Operations Dir
Provides news, documentary & program production; coml production; business/promotional film & video production; production svcs for TV/CATV.
Asia-Pacific Productions
Japan - 3-17 Higashi Maruyama Cho, Kobe 653-086 Japan -,
81 78 691 2450

Associated Press Television News
The Interchange, Oval Road, Camden Lock, London, NW1 7DZ United Kingdom
+44(0)20 7482 7400; *Fax:* +44(0)20 7413 8302
www.aptn.com/
aptninfo@ap.org
TV news production, news library, video editing & ENG production.

Associated Television International
4401 Wilshire Blvd., Los Angeles, CA 90010 USA
(323) 556-5600; *Fax:* (323) 556-5610
www.associatedtelevision.com/
info@associatedtelevision.com
David McKenzie, President
Jim Romanovich, President, Worldwide Entertainment
Ron Braverman, Director of Marketing
Full-svc production, distribution & syndication company in business for over 30 years.

Association of Islamic Charitable Projects
4431 Walnut St., Philadelphia, PA 19104 USA
(215) 387-8888
www.aicp.org
Islamic services providing Education with a Full Time Elementary school for metro Philadelphia.

Auburn University
Broadcast Services/Communications & Marketing Office, 23 Sam Ford Hall, Auburn, AL 36849-5423 USA
(334) 844-9999; *Fax:* (334) 844-5708
www.auburn.edu
webmaster@auburn.edu
Jim Jackson, Producer/Director
Kevin Fitchner, Broadcast Associate
Keith Brewer, Supervisor, Audio-Visual Conference Center
Tape/CD/DVD Duplication, satellite uplink/downlink facilities, & CATV. Affiliate Studio production facilities (Broadview Media) are available in Montgomery Alabama via microwave link to the uplink.

The Audio Department Inc.
119 W. 57th Street, Suite 400, New York, NY 10019 USA
(212) 586-3503; *Fax:* (212) 245-1675
www.theaudiodepartment.com
Aimee Mitchaud, General Manager
Lola Norarevian, Manager
Audio & audio for video, adv & media promotion.

Audio Services, University of Colorado
College of Music, 301 UCB, Boulder, CO 80309 USA
(303) 492-5367; *Fax:* (303) 492-7017
www.colorado.edu/music/audio-services
kevin.harbison@colorado.edu

PROGRAMMING & PRODUCTION SERVICES

Kevin Harbison, Recording Engineer
Andrew Metzroth, Operations Director
Laima Haley, Director of Marketing & Public Relations
Radio program production.

Auritt Communications Group
315 West 36th Street, New York, NY 10018 USA
(212) 302-6230; *Fax:* (212) 302-2969
www.auritt.com
info@auritt.com
Joan Auritt, Founder & President
Anna Gartaganis, Senior Executive Project Manager & Producer
Laurie Doppman, Production & Project Manager
Paula Moskowitz, Operations Manager
Deirdre Reilly, Senior Executive Producer & Director
Satellite media tours, event coverage, video news releases, B-roll packages, radio tours, audio news releases, sls/corporate videos, web casting & print tours.

Avid
65-75 Network Drive, Burlington, MA 01803 USA
(800) 949-2843,(978) 640-6789; *Fax:* (978) 640-3366
www.avid.com
Louis Hernandez, Jr., Chairman & CEO
Jeff Rosica, President
John Frederick, EVP,CFO & Chief Administrative Officer
Brian E. Agle, Senior VP & CFO
Jason Duva, General Counsel & Senior VP, Strategic Initiatives
Rashid Desai, SeniorVP & Chief Technology Officer
Tom J.A. Cordiner, SVP, Global Sales
Jim Sheehan, Corporate Communications
Avid is a leading supplier of newsroom computer, editing, playback & effects systems. Implemented as stand-alone or networked systems, Avid solutions provide speed, creativity & operating efficiencies throughout the newsroom.

Bardel Entertainment Inc.
548 Beatty St., Vancouver, BC V6B 2L3 Canada
(604) 669-5589; *Fax:* (604) 669-9079
www.bardel.ca/
sales@bardel.ca
Delna Bhesania, CEO
Barry Ward, President
Sanja Zoric, Operations Dir
Florian Wagner, Studio Creative Director
High quality 3D, Maya, Flash, Harmony & hybrids of digital & traditional animation for feature film, television, interactive media, internet & commercials. Interactive and New Media services, specializing in virtual worlds and online casualgames.

Bavaria Film GmbH
Bavariafilmplatz 7, D-82031Geiselgasteig/Munich, GU Germany
49 (0) 89 - 64 99 -0; *Fax:* 49 (0) 89 - 64 92 507
www.bavaria-film.de
info@bavaria-film.de
Achim Rohnke, CEO
Dieter Frank, President
Dubbing, film laboratories, film & tape transfers, film & TV production, production svcs, multimedia svcs.

BBC Worldwide Americas Inc.
1120 Avenue of the Americas, New York, NY 10036 USA
(212) 705-9300; *Fax:* (212) 888-0576
www.bbc.co.uk/america
Radio & TV broadcaster, TV program production & distribution, home video, library sls, licensing.

BBC Worldwide Television Ltd.
Portland Place, London, UK W1A 1AA
Fax: (181) 749-0538,(181) 576-2000
www.bbc.co.uk
Program licensing to international bcstrs & generation of co-production business. Dev of BBC branded satellite & cable channels worldwide.

Beckmann International
Meadow Ct., West St., Ramsey, Isle of Man, AL IM8 1AE
4 401 624 816 585; *Fax:* 4 401 624 816 777
www.beckmann-international.de/
International sls distributor specializing in non-fiction progmg.

Bell Foto Art Productions
2577 S. Pennsylvania St., Denver, CO 80210-5722 USA
(303) 377-4606, (303) 478-3346; *Fax:* (303) 322-2443
bellfoto@att.net
Chris Bell, Director of Photography
Award winning High Definition video production: VNR, corporate, news, sports, medical, training & legal. Story tellers with AJ-HDX 900, HVX-200, Sony Z1-U, Sony EX-3 and now the Sony XD-HD. The future of HD production in the real world! Allowed and operated with the additional toys and hugely experienced crew. We want to work for you.

Bellon Entertainment Inc.
14 Vanderventer Ave, Suite L3A, Port Washington, NY 11050 USA
(516) 883-1810
www.bellonentertainment.com
webmail@bellonentertainment.com
Gregory Bellon, President
Represent and develop TV formats for worldwide distribution.

Ben Cromer Communications
PO Box 337, Stephenson, VA 22656 USA
(703) 819-0688
www.bencromer.com
ben@bencromer.com
Benjamin Cromer, President
Feature writing & script preparation for print & bcst media; specializing in the music & entertainment industry; telecommunications; business/economics & travel/history.

Ben Manilla Productions
66 Cleary Court, #801, San Francisco, CA 94109 USA
(415) 970-8020; *Fax:* (415) 970-8024
www.bmpaudio.com
Ben Manilla, President
Devon Strolovitch, Producer/Programming
Jennei Cataldo, Producer
Merle Kessler, Writer, Humorist & Performer
Andy Valvur, Writer, Journalist & Comedian
Audio production & progmg for a var of formats.

Bill Melendez Productions Inc.
13400 Riverside Dr., Suite 201, Sherman Oaks, CA 91423 USA
(818) 382-7382; *Fax:* (818) 382-7377
www.billmelendez.tv
Joanna Coletta, CEO/Producer-Los Angeles
Steven C. Melendez, President, Producer/Director
Bill Melendez, Founder
Warren Taylor, Producer-Los Angeles
Larry Leichliter, Animation Director-Los Angeles
Katie Perkins, Office Manager-LosAngeles
Kaj Melendez, Producer/ Euopean Rep.-London
Mirza-Javed Baig, Producer/ Euopean Rep.-London
TV program, coml animation production.

Billy Graham Evangelistic Association
1 Billy Graham Parkway, Charlotte, NC 28201 USA
(704) 401-2432, (877) 247-2426; *Fax:* (704) 401-3028
www.billygraham.org
had@bgea.org
Franklin Graham, Chairman, President & CEO
Steve McCay, COO
Ken Braun, EVP, Government & Partner Relations
David Beroth, Chief Financial Officer
Kathy Yokeley, VP, Communications
Bill Maupin, VP, Information Technology

Blackbird Productions
Courtwood House - 3 Courtlands, Southwater, Nr.Horsham, West Sussex, RH13 9AD GBR
+44 (0)1403 732 581; *Fax:* +44(0)20 7924 4778
www.blackbirdproductions.co.uk
enquiries@blackbirdproductions.co.uk
Program production & distribution.

Blackstone Stock Footage
509 Upsall Drive, Antioch, TN 37013 USA
(615) 731-5310; *Fax:* (615) 731-5232
g.clifford@worldnet.att.net
Glenda Clifford, President
We offer: Archival newsreel footage, medical, extreme sports, landmarks from around the world, food, people, animals, underwater, timelapse cities & nature.

Blaqk Audio
Box 106, Ventura, CA 93002-0106 USA
(805) 653-5557; *Fax:* (805) 653-5557
www.blaqkaudio.com

Blue Sky Studios
One American Lane, Greenwich, CT 06831 USA
(203) 992-6000; *Fax:* (203) 992-6001
www.blueskystudios.com
Brian Keane, COO & EVP
Chris Wedge, Creative Director
Dev & production of CG animated films.

Blue Star Media
Dallas Cowboys Football Club, One Cowboys Pkwy., Irving, TX 75063 USA
(972) 556-9345; *Fax:* (972) 556-9339
dallascowboys.com
Matt O'Neil, VP, Brand & Media
Scott Purcel, Director of Broadcasting
Radio play by play, wkly sports TV for NFL Dallas Cowboys & show for Dallas Cowboys.

BMG Production Music
6100 Wilshire Blvd., Ste 1600, Los Angeles, CA 90048 USA
(310) 201-0015, (323) 248-9527
www.bmgproductionmusic.com
Valentino@selectracks.com
Sinead Hartmann, Vice President, U.S.
Ryan Clodfelter Nielson, Manager, Production
Darrel Shirk, Senior Director, Operations
Amberly Crouse, Senior Director, Creative & Marketing
Valentino music and sound effect libraries/catalogs. Compact disc music & sound effects libraries.

Bonneville International
55 North 300 West, Salt Lake City, UT 84101-3502 USA
(801) 575-7500; *Fax:* (801) 575-5820
www.bonneville.com
bonneville@bonneville.com
Darrell Brown, President
Kent Nate, SVP & CFO
Mike Dowdle, SVP of Business Affairs & General Counsel
Bob Call, VP/ Market Manager, Denver
Carl Gardner, VP/ Market Manager, Seattle
Scott Sutherland, VP/ Market Manager, Phoenix
Tanya Vea, VP/ Market Manager, Salt Lake City
A values-driven adv agency engaged in communications for quality life.

Broadview Media
4455 W. 77th St., Edina, MN 55425 USA
(612) 280-6947; *Fax:* (952) 835-0971
www.broadviewmedia.com/
rwhite@globeuniversity.edu
Red White, President
Full-svc production.

Bruder Releasing Inc. (BRI)
2020 Broadway, 2nd Floor, Santa Monica, CA 90404 USA
(310) 829-2222, (800) 555-1212; *Fax:* (310) 829-0202
www.bruderreleasing.com/
info@brivideo.com
Marc Bruder, President
Celena Perkins, Director of Acquisitions
Studio, producer representative for worldwide broadcast distribution to IPTV platforms, pay-per-view channels, satellite netwroks, cable operators, lodging systems, internet streaming venues and mobile-cellular and hand-held-devicetransmission venues. CED is the leading broadcast program supplier of adult content worldwide. BRI is a major supplier of independent movies, specials, events and shows of all catagories.
BRI & CED headquarters
2020 Broadway-Santa Monica, CA 90404

Burrud Productions Inc.
468 N. Camden Drive, 2nd Floor, Beverly Hills, CA 90210 USA
(310) 860-5158; *Fax:* (562) 595-5986
www.burrud.com
info@burrud.com
John Burrud, President
Drew Horton, Operations Dir
Linda Karabin, Vice President
Feature film & TV production of reality, wildlife, oceanic, human adventure, documentary & world exploration progmg.

Buzzco Associates Inc.
33 Bleecker St., New York, NY 10012 USA
(212) 473-8800; *Fax:* (212) 473-8891
www.buzzzco.com
info@buzzzco.com
Candy Kugel, General Manager
A full range of animation from traditional to innovative computer 2-D.

C 2 Productions Inc.
15430 Catalpa Cove Ln., Fort Myers, FL 33908 USA
(212) 730-4500; *Fax:* (239) 437-2042
chriscorley.com
chris@chriscorley.com
Chris Corley, President
Voice-overs delivered digitally or in person.

C N R Radio
Box 27532, Minneapolis, MN 55427-0532 USA
(763) 537-5868
www.cnr-radio.com
CNRadio@comcast.net

George Carden, President
News interviews, soundbites & features with newsmakers for primarily Christian radio stns & nets.

CA Media Development
1415 Hooper Avenue, Suite 305, Toms River, NJ 08753 USA
(732) 797-1965; *Fax:* (732) 797-1260
www.camediadevelopment.com/
ca.media@comcast.net
Gregory Koziar, President
Full svc adv agency, as well as coml production, for radio & cable TV.

CABLEready Corp.
98 East Ave., Norwalk, CT 06851-5029 USA
(203) 855-7979; *Fax:* (203) 855-8370
www.cableready.net
info@cableready.net
Gary Lico, President
Lou Occhicone, Operations Dir
Liz Levenson, General Manager
Sabrina Toledo, General Sales Mgr
Dev & sls of programs to U.S. cable TV networks & systems & all international telecasters.

Call For Action Inc.
11820 Parklawn Drive, Suite 340, Rockville, MD 20852 USA
(240) 747-0229; *Fax:* (301) 657-2914
www.callforaction.org
Shirley Rooker, President
International hotline svc, affiliated with the bcst media, that provides info, assistance to individuals & small businesses with consumer problems.

Camera Group International
3920 N. 29th Ave., Hollywood, FL 33020 USA
(954) 925-3776; *Fax:* (954) 925-3760
www.cameragroupinternational.com
garcia2020@aol.com
Eileen B. Garcia, President
Greg Browning, Vice President
Rental, sls, svc & maintenance of motion picture, TV & video production equipment (16mm, 35mm & digital matte cameras).

CamMate Systems
425 E. Comstock, Chandler, AZ 85225 USA
(480) 813-9500; *Fax:* (480) 813-9292
www.cammate.com
Linda Mitchell, CEO
James Mitchell, Promotions Manager
Camera cranes, telescopic cranes & mini cranes.

Campbell-Ewald Advertising
2000 Brush Street, Suite 601, Detroit, MI 48226 USA
(586) 574-3400; *Fax:* (586) 558-5891
www.c-e.com
campbell.ewald@c-e.com
Anthony Hopp, Chairman
Kevin Wertz, CEO
Sal Taibi, President
Brian Phelps, COO & Managing Director
Jarilyn Auger, Chief Financial Officer
Jo Shoesmith, Chief Creative Officer
Chip Rich, Executive Creative Director
TV programs, TV radio coml, promotion film production.
One Dag Hammarskjold Plaza, New York, NY 10017 United States
(212) 605-8000
11100 Santa Monica Blvd, 6th Fl, Los Angeles, CA 90025 United States
(213) 914-2200
11444 W. Olympic Blvd, 11th Flr, Los Angeles, CA 90064-1549 United States
(310) 231 - 2900
One Magnificent Mile, 930 N. Michigan Ave, Suite 1060, Chicago, IL 60611 United States
(312) 587-2650

Canamedia Inc.
1540 Cornwall Rd., Suite 216, Oakville, ON L6J 7W5 Canada
(416) 363-6765, (866) 999-5292; *Fax:* (416) 483-7529
www.canamedia.com
Doug Connolly, President & Chief Operating Officer
Bill McGowan, VP Global Sales & Acquisitions
Dave Williams, Digital Content Manager
Brad Schroeder, Production Services, Business Development
Andrea Stokes, Managing Dir.,International Sales & Acquisitions
Daniel D'or, Senior Executive Producer, Content Development
Canamedia offers production & international distribution svcs. It also exclusively represents in Canada the ITN source Archive & Natural History New Zealand Archives as well as the PUMP audio music archive.

Cannell Studios
7083 Hollywood Blvd., Suite 600, Hollywood, CA 90028 USA
(323) 465-5800; *Fax:* (323) 856-7390
www.cannell.com
Stephen Cannell, Founder (deceased)

Capital Communications
2357-3 South Tamiami Trl., Venice, FL 34293 USA
(941) 492-4688; *Fax:* (941) 492-4923
www.isp.com
cap5678@isp.com
James Springer, CEO
International distributor of pre-packaged TV programs.

Careco TV LLC
5717 N.W. Pkwy., Suite 104, San Antonio, TX 78249 US
(210) 697-8081; *Fax:* (210) 697-0150
www.carecotv.com
Charles Goodloe, President
Producer of American Outdoors & Fishing Texas, weekly half hour series.

Carlton International Media Inc.
11145 N.W. 1st Pl., Coral Springs, FL 33071 USA
(954) 345-1620; *Fax:* (954) 345-1490
www.carltonint.co.uk
clarea@msn.com
Rupert Dillnot-Cooper, CEO
Claire Alter, Operations Dir
Louise Pedersen, General Manager
British TV distributor, licenses a wide range of programs worldwide.
Studio City, CA 91604 United States
(818) 753-6363
Jeri Sacks, Vp/Us Sls

Carpel Video Inc.
429 E. Patrick St., Frederick, MD 21701 USA
(800) 238-4300,(301) 694-3500; *Fax:* (301) 694-9510
www.carpelvideoonline.com
Acarpel@aol.com, Vfearnow@outlook.com
Andy Carpel, President
Videotape recyclers; production svcs, video tape to DVD duplication.

Carriage House Studios
119 Westhill Rd., Stamford, CT 06902 US
(203) 358-0065
carriagehousemusic.com/
johnny@carriagehousemusic.com
John Montagnese, Owner
Brendan Muldowney, Engineer
Phil Magnoti, Engineer/Mixer/Producer
Mikhail Pivovarov, Engineer/Mixer
Ian Callahan, Engineer/Producer
Recording studio.

Carsey-Werner Distribution
16027 Ventura Boulevard, Suite 600, Encino, CA 91436 USA
(818) 464-9618; (818) 464-9600; *Fax:* (818) 464-9650
www.carseywerner.com
jbonifer@carseywerner.com
Jim Kraus, President
Paul Schreiber, Executive VP
Bob Lloyd, VP, Sales
Janet Bonifer, VP, Marketing/Creative Services
TV program distribution.

Catholic Diocese of Youngstown
Div/DBA: Catholic Television Network of Youngstown
144 West Wood Street, Youngstown, OH 44503 USA
(330) 533-2243; *Fax:* (330) 533-2243
www.doy.org
chancery@youngstowndiocese.org
Bob Gavalier, General Manager
Patrick Kelly, Chief Financial Officer
John Zuraw, Chancellor
Trish Paulin, Financial Accountant
Robert Berry, Business Manager, Catholic Exponent
Pauli Butch, Secretary to the Bishop
Elena Brown,Administrative Assistant, Campus Ministry
24-hour ecumenical TV ch.

CBC International Sales
Audience Relations, CBC, Box 500, Stn. A, Toronto, ON M5W 1E6 Canada
(866) 306-4636; *Fax:* (416) 205-3482
www.cbc.ca/toronto
R,mi Racine, Chair
Hubert T. Lacroix, President and CEO
Judith Purves, EVP & Chief Financial Officer
Sylvie Gadoury, VP, Legal Services & General Counsel
Alex Johnston, VP, Strategy & Public Affairs
Steven Guiton, EVP, MediaTechnology & Infrastructure Services
Heather Conway, EVP, English Services
Monique Marcotte, Vice President, People & Culture
CBC is Canada's natl bcstr. Produces & distributes TV progmg in both English & French.
1950 Sawtelle Blvd, Suite 333, Los Angeles, CA 90025 United States
43/51 Great Titchfield St, London W1P 8DD,

CBS Studios International
7800 Beverly Blvd., Los Angeles, CA 90036 USA
(323) 575-5400; *Fax:* (323) 575-5469
www.cbssi.com
firstname.lastname@cbs.com
Armando Nunez, President & CEO
Barry Chamberlain, President, Sales
Meghan Lyvers, SVP, Co-Productions & Development
David Stapf, President, CBS Television Studios
International television distribution, co-production, local production formats, channel management.

CBS Television Distribution
2405 Colorado Avenue, Suite 500E, Santa Monica, CA 90404 USA
(310) 264-3300; *Fax:* (310) 264-3301
www.cbstvd.com
dtvlegal@cbsparamount.com
Paul Franklin, President, CBS Television Distribution
Steven LoCasio, COO & CFO, CBSTVD & Global
Stephen Hackett, President of Sales, CBSTVD
Paul Montoya, President, Media Sales, CBSTVD
TV program production, distribution, mktg to domestic syndication & other TV venues.

CBS Worldwide Distribution
524 West 57th Street, New York, NY 10019 USA
(212) 975-8139
http://cwd.cbs.com
Jaime Rockman, Vice President for Distribution & Operations
Larry Beirne, Director,International Distribution & Operations
Myra Cole, Director, Technical Operations
Karen Buck, Director, Domestic Distribution & Operations
Duplicate & distribute syndicated TV progmg via tape & satellite, coml integration, international standards conversion, uplink/downlink, tape duplication, space segment; high definition.
10877 Wilshire Blvd, Los Angeles, CA 90024 United States
(310) 446-6051; *Fax:* (310) 446-6066
Lee Salas, Vp & Natl Sls Mgr

CCI Entertainment Ltd.
210 St. Claire Avenue West, 4th Floor, Toronto, ON M4V 1R2 Canada
(416) 964-8750; *Fax:* (416) 964-1980
www.ccientertainment.com
info@ccientertainment.com
Arnie Zipursky, Co-Founder/ Executive Producer
Charles Falzon, Co-Founder/ Executive Producer
Marly Reed, Production & Development
Gary Yau, Controller
Dayna Zipursy, Business Affairs
Distributor & co-producer, producer

CDC United Network Brussels
350 Avenue Louise, Brussels, Be 1050 Belguim
32 2 502 66 40; *Fax:* 32 2 502 66 56
www.cdcun.com/en/home
alexandre@cdc.skynet.beMOBILE:3275713057
Alexandre Lippens, Chief Executive Officer
Erik Jensen, Managing Partner
Pieter Cosijn, Managing Partner
Jimmy van der Heyden, Sales Manager
Bartlomiej Falkowski, Chief Financial Officer
Silvia Benassi, Marketing Manager
JulienDandois, Traffic Coordinator
Aranzazu Iba¤ez Minteguiaga, Acquisitions Manager
Isabelle Pineau, Office Coordinator
TV distribution & merchandising in Latin America.

CDR Communications Inc.
9310-B Old Keene Mill Rd., Burke, VA 22015 USA
(703) 569-3400, (800) 729-2237; *Fax:* (703) 569-3448
www.cdrcommunications.com
info@cdrcommunications.com
Christopher Rogers, President
Nancy Rogers, VP, Media Placement

Anna Milograno, Producer & Editor
Josh Renkes, Producer & Editor
Film, TV, video & radio production: teleconferences, documentaries, adv campaigns, PSAs; graphics, animation, syndication, promotion, publishing, distribution, postproduction & mktg.
9302 C Old Keene Mill Rd., Burke, VA 22015

CelebrityFootage
320 South Almont Dr., Beverly Hills, CA 90211 USA
(310) 360-9600; *Fax:* (310) 360-9696
www.celebrityfootage.com
michael@celebrityfootage.com
Michael Goldberg, President
Provides media outlets with celebrity entertainment news from the Los Angeles area, including movie premieres, award shows & charity benefits.

Celluloid Dreams
2 Rue Turgot, Paris, 75009 France
(33) 1 49 70 03 70; *Fax:* (33) 1 49 70 03 71
www.celluloid-dreams.com
info@celluloid-dreams.com
Hengameh Panahi, President
Charlotte Mickie, VP
Frederique Rouault, Head of Sales
Nadine Rothschild, Marketing
Julien Herlory, Finance & Accounting
International distribution of ind features, documentaries & animation films.

Center City Film & Video
Mailing Address: 1501-1503 Walnut St., Philadelphia, PA 19102 USA
Second Address: 136 S. 15th Street, Philadelphia, PA 19102
(215) 568-4134; *Fax:* (215) 568-6011
www.ccfv.com
Jordan Schwartz, Chairman
Brian Isely, Executive VP
John Gillespie, General Manager & Senior Account Executive
Award winning production staff, video; film production, studio; remote camera packages including ultimatte, digital audio suite, flint, complete post production.

Central City Productions, Inc.
212 East Ohio Street, Suite 300, Chicago, IL 60611 USA
(312) 654-1100; *Fax:* (312) 654-0368
www.ccptv.com
info@ccptv.com
Don Jackson, Chairman & CEO
Erma Davis, President & COO
Rosemary Jackson, Operations Dir
Jennifer Jackson, General Manager
Production & mktg of bcst & cable TV progmg targeted towards minority viewers.

Channel Four Television
124 Horseferry Rd., London, AL SW1P 2TX
44 (0)845 076 0191
www.channel4.com
Lord Burns GCB, Chairman
Jonathan Allan, Sales Director
MT Rainey, Deputy Chairman
Stewart Purvis, Non-Executive Director
Dan Brooke, Director of Marketing & Communications
David Abraham, Chief Executive
UK bcstr.

Charles Morrow Productions, LLC
1961 Roaring Brook Road, Barton, VT 05822 USA
(212) 989-2400; *Fax:* (206) 222-2125
www.cmorrow.com
Jeff Aaron Bryant, Engineering Dir
Charlie Morrow, Founder & Creative Director
Robert I. Freedman, Business Manager/ Creative Associate
Maija-Leena Remes, Senior Editor/Writer/Supervisor of Translations
Marc Nasdor, IT & Head ofCommunications
Otto Romanowski, Marketing
Sound design, audio production, music production, audio/visual service, music composition, multimedia producers, surround sound studio, public service announcements.

Children's Media Productions
Box 40400, Pasadena, CA 91114-7400 USA
(626) 797-5462
www.childrensmedia.com
childrensmedia@yahoo.com
C. Carlson, President
Joy Carlson, Promotions Manager
Producer & distributor of children's progmg, dvds & feature films, worldwide.

Chinamerica Hit Radio
24-20 Jackson Avenue, Suite 209, Long Island City, NY 11101 US
(800) 827-1722, (718) 729-1962; *Fax:* (718) 729-1963
chinamericaradio.com
programming@chinamericaradio.com
Steve Warren, Executive Producer
Bo Qiao, Marketing Manager
Ethan Tsai, Promotions
Joan Chin, Public Affairs
24 Hour Pop-Contemporary Chinese hit music. Hosted in English
24-20 Jackson Ave., Suite 209, Long Island City, NY 11101

Christian Children's Associates Inc.
Div/DBA: Adventure Pals
PO Box 446, Toms River, NJ 08754 USA
(732) 240-3003; *Fax:* (732) 286-4244
www.adventurepals.com
adventurepals@juno.com
Rev. William H. Cook, President & Executive Director
Production, distribution of radio & TV progmg for children.

Christian Media Network
PO Box 448, Jacksonville, OR 97530 US
(541) 899-8888
www.christianmedianetwork.com
james@christianmedianetwork.com
James Lloyd, Host/Founder

The Christian Science Publishing Society
210 Massachusetts Ave., Boston, MA 02115-3122 USA
(617) 450-2000; *Fax:* (617) 450-2893
www.christianscience.com/prayer-and-health/more-inspiration/jsh-online-audio
info@ChristianScience.com
Ingrid Peschke, Church Media Contact
Religious radio programs.

Christian TV Services of Ellicottville Inc.
6490 Pine Tree Road, Apt 315, Bldg 5, Ellicottville, NY 14731-9603 USA
(716) 699-2549; *Fax:* (716) 397 - 9825
www.christiantvservices.us
geothayer@yahoo.com
Rev. George Allan Thayer, President & Chief Executive Officer
Roger A. Thayer, Manager
Randall A. Thayer, Production Director
Christian media consultants Ministering to ministries around the world; locally linked area worship places, internet listing places; svcs inc. since 1974.

The Christophers Inc.
5 Hanover Square, 22nd Floor, New York, NY 10004 USA
(212) 759-4050, (888) 298-4050; *Fax:* (212) 838-5073
www.christophers.org
mail@christophers.org
Mary Ellen Robinson, Vice President/COO
Robert V. Okulski, President/Treasurer
Yaneza Santos, Finance Manager
Tony Rossi, Director of Communications
We produce and distribute only our own media (radio, print)

Cinecraft Productions Inc.
2515 Franklin Blvd., Cleveland, OH 44113 USA
(216) 781-2300; *Fax:* (216) 781-1067
www.cinecraft.com
info@cinecraft.com
Neil McCormick, Chairman
Maria Keckan, President & CFO
Chris Karel, Creative Director/Business Development Manager
Betacam field production; 60' x 70' sound stage with hard cyc; AVID MC1000NT; Animation with Soft Image; interactive DVD & CD-R dev.

Cinema Concepts
2030 Powers Ferry Rd., #214, Atlanta, GA 30339 USA
(770) 956-7460, (800) 746-9237, (800) SHO-WADS; *Fax:* (770) 956-8358
www.cinemaconcepts.com
info@cinemaconcepts.com
Stewart Harnell, Owner/CEO
Sharron Harnell, Operations Dir
Theresa Dickey, VP/General Manager
John Price, VP/Studio Director
Animated corporate IDs, presentation/policy trailers for TV, cable & motion picture theatres, theatrical trailer fulfillment.

The Cinema Guild Inc.
115 West 30th Street, Suite 800, New York, NY 10001 USA
(800) 723-5522; (212) 685-6242; *Fax:* (212) 685-4717
www.cinemaguild.com
info@cinemaguild.com
Mary Hobel, Founder
Philip Hobel, Founder (deceased)
Film & video distribution to theatrical, non-theatrical, TV & home video mkts, worldwide.

Cisneros Media Distribution
Div/DBA: (formerly Venevision Int'l)
121 Alhambra Plaza, Suite 1400, Coral Gables, FL 33134 USA
(305) 442-3411; *Fax:* (305) 448-4762
info@venevisionintl.com
Jonathan Blum, President
Marcello Coltro, Executive VP, Content Distribution
Distribution of progmg.

The Classical Station, WCPE
Box 897, Wake Forest, NC 27588
(800) 556-5178; *Fax:* (919) 556-9273
www.theclassicalstation.org
Curtis Brothers, Outreach Director & Media Liaison
Deborah Proctor, General Manager & Chief Engineer
Peter Blume, General Sales Mgr
Dick Storck, Programming Director
William Woltz, Music Director
Betty Madren, Business DevelopmentDirector
John Graham, Engineering Services
Eric Maynard, Webmaster
Free 24-hour classical music progmg with live announcers for radio, cable, other distributors. Wkly request programs, opera & features.

Clayton-Davis & Associates Inc.
230 S. Bemiston Ave., Suite 1400, St. Louis, MO 63105 USA
(314) 862-7800; *Fax:* (314) 721-5171
Jennifer Jermak, President
Irving Davis, Operations Dir
Program production, syndication & barter.

Clever Cleaver Productions
4718 N. Placita Ventana Del Rio, Tucson, AZ 85750 USA
(520) 615-1582; *Fax:* (520) 615-1586
www.clevercleaver.com
clevercook@comcast.net
Lee Gerovitz, President
Steve Cassarino, Operations Dir
Offers 260 3-minute entertaining cooking vignettes; 27 30-minute entertaining cooking shows, 90-second high-definition cooking vignettes (cash or barter) & 2-minute tailgate cooking vignettes (free licensing fee).

CMT
330 Commerce St., Nashville, TN 37201 USA
(615) 335-8400; *Fax:* (615) 335-8615
www.cmt.com
info@cmt.com
Frank Tanki, General Manager, CMT & TV Land
Quinn Brown, VP, Production
Rory Levine, Senior VP, Consumer Marketing
Lucia Folk, VP, Public Affairs
Kurt Patat, Press Contact
America's #1 country music net, provides original progmg, live concerts, events, music videos by established & cutting edge artists, news & info.

CN8, The Comcast Network
3601 South Broad Street, Philadelphia, PA 19148 USA
(215) 468-2222; *Fax:* (215) 468-3812
www.csnphilly.com
askcsn@comcastsportsnet.com
Stephanie Millagranna, COO
Buck Dopp, Operations Dir
Brian McLendon, General Manager
Mark Dudzinski, Station Manager
Denise Pettyford, General Sales Mgr
Alex Soumbenioits, Promotions Manager
Rich Frantz, Engineering Dir
ScottClark, Chief Engineer
Larry Watzman, Creative Services Director
Jon Gurevitch, VP Sports
CN8, The Comcast Network, is a rgnl cable net offering news, sports, & entertainment progmg to 3.9 million cable homes.
New Castle Studio
2215 N. Dupont Hwy., New Castle, DE 19720
(302) 661-4202; *Fax:* (302) 661-4201

CNBC Syndication
900 Sylvan Ave., Englewood Cliffs, NJ 07632 USA
(201) 735-2622; *Fax:* (201) 585-3365
www.cnbc.com

KC Sullivan, President & Managing Director, CNBC International
Syndicated TV program, On The Money, business events.

CNN Newsource Sales Inc.
One CNN Center, 12 North, Atlanta, GA 30303 USA
(404) 926-6483, (404) 827-5475; *Fax:* (404) 827-4466
http://newsource.cnn.com
cnn.newsource@turner.com
Ed Stephen, Senior VP & General Manager
Taylor Fuller, General Sales Mgr
Provider of news & info content to the loc bcst news industry.

Coe Film Associates Inc.
70 E. 96th St., New York, NY 10128 USA
(212) 831-5355; *Fax:* (212) 996-6728
TV program distribution.

Colon & Associates Inc.
2914 Cashel Lane, Vienna, VA 22181 USA
(703) 281-2296; *Fax:* (703) 281-2299
www.colonassociates.com/
info@colonassociates.com
Eugenia Colon, Founder & President
Reinaldo Colon, CEO
Joann Gilbert, EVP, Marketing & Special Events
Patricia Cavallaro, Senior Vice President, Program Development
Program distribution, production, Sp language dubbing.

ComBridges
66 Via Holon, #11, Greenbrae, CA 94904 USA
(888) 530-5505
www.combridges.com
Jon Leland, President & Creative Director
Source of videos, seminars & interactive media. Producer, websites.

Combs Music
1325 Lewisville-Clemmons Road, Lewisville, NC 27023 USA
(800) 932-6627; *Fax:* (336) 723-1611
www.combsmusic.com
dave@combsmusic.com
Gary Prim, Arranger & Recoding Artist
Dave Combs, Composer / Publisher / Photographer
Composes, produces, publishes & distributes easy lstng instrumental music, e.g., Rachel's Song.

Command Productions
Mailing Address: Box 3000, Sausalito, CA 94966-3000 USA
Second Address: Industrial Center, 480 Gate Five Rd., Sausalito, CA 94965-1412
(415) 332-3161; *Fax:* (415) 332-1901
www.commandproductions.com
Warren Weagant, President
Kitt Weagant, Operations Dir
Radio-TV, CATV audio voice identification and promotion production.
480 Gate Five Rd., Suite 107, Sausalito, CA 94965

Communications III Inc.
1156 Dublin Road Ste. 101, Columbus, OH 43215 USA
(614) 485-4500; *Fax:* (614) 901-7721
www.comIII.com
Central Ohio C-band satellite & Teleport svc, with access to studio, edit suites, at Ohio State University & various downtown locations.

CompuWeather Inc.
2566 Rt. 52, Hopewell Junction, NY 12533 USA
(800) 825-4445, (845) 227-8500; *Fax:* (800) 825-4441
www.compuweather.com
Jeff Wimmer, CEO
Tore Jakobsen, CFO & Co-Founder
Steve Roberts, Director, Weather Operations
Eric DeRoche, CompuWeather Customer Service Manager
Patti Robertson, Forensic Account Executive
Weather, environmental features, actualities, forecasts, info, worldwide weather consulting svc, forecast, outcodes, studies, advice, site specific, 24/7 & 31 years experience.

Concept Videos
5371 Punta Alta, #1-E, Laguna Woods, CA 94637 US
(800) 333-8252; *Fax:* (877) 523-5592
wjconnell@preschoolpower.com
William Connell, President
Gold medal winning children's series, Pre-School Power, (13 x 30) recently telecast on 190 public TV stns.

Consolidated Film Industries (CFI)
959 N. Seward St., Hollywood, CA 90038 USA
(323) 960-7444; *Fax:* (323) 960-7573
www.technicolor.com
Didier Lombard, Chairman
Frederic Rose, CEO
Michel Rahier, EVP Operations Services & Transformation
Fabienne Brunet, EVP, Human Resources & CSR
Vince Pizzica, SEVP Corporate Development & Technology
Tim Sarnoff, EVP, President ofProduction Services
Sandra Carvalho, Chief Marketing Officer
St,phane Rougeot, Chief Financial Officer
Boris Teksler, SEVP Technicolor, Technology
Film processing; titles & opticals; videotape transfers; office rentals.

Continental Recordings Inc.
23 Mirimichi Street, Plainville, MA 02762-1710 USA
(508) 699- 0003; *Fax:* (617) 699-0005
danf31@earthlink.net
L. Daniel Flynn, President
Coml jingles, stn IDs, original music creation & production, cassette duplication & bcstg adv consultation, CD & DVD duplicator.

CONUS Archive
3415 University Ave., St. Paul, MN 55114 USA
(651) 642-4576; *Fax:* (651) 642-4669
www.conus.com
Jim Richter, Vice President
Chris Bridson, General Sales Mgr
Video archive svcs to natl & international program producers.

Cornell University Broadcast Studios (Marketing Group)
301 College Avenue, Ithaca, NY 14850 USA
(607) 255-8162; *Fax:* (607) 255-5373
http://univcomm.cornell.edu/videoprodgroup/stafflist.html
Glen Palmer, Director
Bert Odom-Reed, Chief Engineer
Micah Cormier, Producer/Director
Satellite uplinks, Betacam DvcPro video production & postproduction, audio production

Country Crossroads
PO Box 158, Dacula, GA 30019 USA
(678) 218-7253
www.countrycrossroadsradio.com
josh.tanner@countrycrossroadsradio.com
Josh Tanner, General Manager/Program Director
Chuck Ries, Programming Director
Jeff Hutch, On-Air Personality
Robie Longboat, On-Air Personality
Mike Matthews, On-Air Personality
Country music with interviews. Program hosted by Brother Jon Rivers, 30 minute wkly on CD or download.

Cramer
425 University Ave., Norwood, MA 02062 US
(781) 278-2300, (781) 278-8464; *Fax:* (781) 255-0721
www.cramer.com
info@crameronline.com
Tom Martin, Chairman
Rich Sturchio, President
Tim Martin, EVP, Operations
T.J. Martin, Executive Vice President
Mark Wilson, Executive Creative Director
Brent Turner, SVP, Solutions
Film & video production svcs from design to presentation; staging svcs; video duplications. Web-casting, interactive media.

Crawford Media Services
Div/DBA: (formerly Crawford Communications)
6 West Druid Hills Drive NE, Atlanta, GA 30329 USA
(404) 876-0333, (800) 831-8029; *Fax:* (678) 421-6717
www.crawford.com
info@crawford.com
Jesse Crawford, President & CEO
Emily Halevy, National Accounts Manager
Steve Davis, VP, Media Management
Jim Bowhall, Creative Director
Ron Heidt, Senior Editor & Technical Director
Computer graphics, animation, production & postproduction svcs domestic & international teleport.

The Crime Channel
310 West Bonita Avenue, #329, Claremont, CA 91711 USA
(760) 360-6151; *Fax:* (760) 360-3258
www.thecrimechannel.com/
crimechannel@dc.rr.com
Satellite: Satcom C-1*Transponder:* 11
Arnie Frank, President
The Crime Channel offers series, movies, documentaries, original productions, on the spot crime news & foreign programs.

Critical Information Network
17300 North Dallas Parkway, Suite 3010, Dallas, TX 75248 USA
(800) 294-1140, (866) 532-4866; *Fax:* (972) 309-5666
www.criticalinfonet.com/
Josh Karin, CEO
Gina Valencia, Promotions Manager
Video-based, interactive tech training programs for industry, utilities, govt relating to maintenance, opns & safety.

CRM Learning
Div/DBA: Media Partners
11400 SE 8th Street, Suite 210, Bellevue, WA 98004-0520 USA
(800) 421-0833, (760) 431-9800; *Fax:* (760) 931-5792
www.crmlearning.com
sales@crmlearning.com
John Hansen, CEO, Media Partners
Lyndi Calder, Marketing Manager
Production & distribution of business training films.

CRN International
One Circular Ave., Hamden, CT 06514 USA
(203) 288-2002; *Fax:* (203) 281-3291
www.crnradio.com
Barry Berman, President & Founder
Rob O'Mara, Managing Director, Strategy & Development
Jim Alkon, Marketing Director
Dick Kalt, Executive Vice President
Debra Berescik, SVP/ Director of Administration
Ron Pell, Director of MediaRelations
Jennifer Anderson, VP of Human Resources
Short-form customized radio progms & promotions; SkiWatch BeachWatch & small business reports.

Crossroads Christian Communications Inc.
PO Box 5100, 1295 North Service Road, Burlington, ON L7R 4M2 Canada
(905) 335-7100; *Fax:* (905) 332-6655
www.crossroads.ca
David Mainse, Founder
Lorna Dueck, CEO
Byron Winsor, Chief Operating Officer
Ken Pelissero, Chief Financial Officer
Carlo Espejo, Chief Marketing Officer
Steve Hubley, Chief Development Officer
Bruce Stacey, Chief ContentOfficer
Produces 100 Huntley Street program.

Crown International Pictures Inc.
301 N. Canon Drive, Suite 228, Beverly Hills, CA 90210 USA
(310) 657-6700; *Fax:* (310) 657-4489
www.crownintlpictures.com
crown@crownintlpictures.com
Mark Tenser, CEO
Scott Schwimer, Operations Dir
Lisa Agay, General Manager
Film production & distribution.

CTV Television Inc.
Mailing Address: PO Box 9, Station 'O', Toronto, ON M4A 2M9 Canada
Second Address: 9 Channel Nine Court, Scarborough, ON M1S 4B5
(416) 384-5000,(800)-668-0060,(866)-690-6179; *Fax:* (416) 332-5065
www.ctv.ca
BellMediaPR@bellmedia.ca
Randy Lennox, President, Bell Media
Wendy Freeman, President, CTV News
Laura Heath Potter, Director, Communications
TV bcstg, program production & distribution.

CTVC Hillside Studios
310 Goswell Road, McBeath House, First Floor, London, EC1V 7LW
44 (0)20 7940 8480; *Fax:* 44 (0)20 7940 8490
www.ctvc.co.uk
info@ctvc.co.uk
Caroline Matthews, Chief Executive Officer
Paul Connolly, Company Secretary & Head of Finance
Lareine Shea, Head of Production
Kristine Pommert, Executive Producer- Radio
Claire Faragher, Head of Television
Producers of programs with humanitarian values, especially relg. Also full bcst facilities available for hire.

Cube International
Box 307, Lehi, UT 84043-0307 USA
(801) 722-1000; *Fax:* (801) 722-1000
www.cubeinternational.com
info@cubeinternational.com
Olivier de Courson, General Manager
Phillip Catherall, Managing Director

Film & TV distribution to all worldwide markets & media.

Curb Entertainment International Corp.
3907 W. Alameda Ave., Burbank, CA 91505 USA
(818) 843-8580; *Fax:* (818) 566-1719
www.curbentertainment.com
ccurb@curb.com
Mike Curb, Chairman
Carole Curb Nemoy, President
Conor Barrett, Promotions Manager
Mona Kirton, Director/ Head of Distribution & Post Services
Eddie Francis, Worldwide Service Coordinator
International sales company.

Custom Productions Inc.
11845 W. Olympic Blvd., Suite 675 W, Los Angeles, CA 90064 USA
(310) 393-4144; *Fax:* (310) 393-1143
www.customproductions.TV
info@customproductions.tv
Steve Stockman, President
Creation & production of custom TV campaigns for radio stns and TV news stns in the top 25 markets.

D'Ocon Films Productions
C/Calaf.3 Bajos, Barcelona, 8021 ESP
34-93-240-41-22; *Fax:* 34-93-240-41-24
docon@docon.eu
Antoni D'Ocon, President
Principally an animation company offering full range of pre-production, production & postproduction svcs either developing our own concepts or co-producing.

D-Squared Media
330 E. 38th St., Suite 30Q, New York, NY 10016 USA
(212) 254-3489, (917) 705-3499; *Fax:* (212) 254-3489
www.dsquaredmedia.com
Adriana Davis, Producer/ Writer/ Editor
Andrew Blum, Public Relations Director
Film, video, & radio production svcs from script to screen.

The Daily Feed
1783 Lanier Pl. N.W., Suite B, Washington, DC 20009 USA
(202) 667-1234; *Fax:* (202) 667-5578
www.dailyfeed.com
dfeed@dailyfeed.com
John Dryden, President
Produces The Daily Feed, a 90-second political, social satire radio commentary. Markets cash and bartered radio inventory to 18 + demos.

Daniel Wilson Productions Inc.
265 East 66th Street, Suite 38F, New York, NY 10065 US
(212) 765-7148; *Fax:* (212) 765-7618
http://wilprod.com
info@wilprod.com
Daniel Wilson, President
Fran Sears, Executive in Charge of Production
Linda Kandel Kuehl, Content Executive
Mimi Goldman, Comptroller
Russel Schneider, Production Coordinator
TV & theatrical film production & distribution.

Daro Film Distribution
41 Avenue Hector Otto, Monaco, 98000
+3 (779) 797-1600; *Fax:* +3 (779) 797-1590
www.daro-films.mc/
daro@daro-films.mc
Monique Rochat, President
Nicole Fieschi, Chief Financial Officer
Pierre-Andre Rochat, President, Sales
Nadia Saidi, Finance
Sandy Crotty M'Sili, Head of Acquisitions
Patrice Aiello, Technical
Marilena Panighi, Sales Assistant/Shipping
International distribution, co-production, co-financing of TV programs & films.

David Finch Distribution Ltd.
6 Long Lodge Drive, Walton-on-Thames, Su KT12 3BY GBR
44-1932-882733; *Fax:* 44-1932-882108
www.david-finch.com/
sales@david-finch.com
David Finch, CEO/ Founder
Joseph Szew, Partner
Supply of programs for home video & TV worldwide. Acquisition for United Kingdom home video.

David Kaye Productions Inc.
Marks Talent Management, 6333 West 3rd Street, #918, Los Angeles, CA 90036 USA
(800) 843-3933,(323) 936-6040
www.davidkaye.com
David Kaye, President
Full svc voice-over production company, providing radio & TV imaging & branding around the world.

DaviSound
Box 521, 1504 Sunset Ave., Newberry, SC 29108-0521 USA
(803) 944-7972
www.davisound.com
davisound@davisound.com
Annette Davis, Operations Dir
Coml & promotional writing & producing for radio, jingles & program production & distribution. Also provides DaviSound Tool Boxes, custom fabricated pro audio equipment.

De Wolfe Music Library Inc.
37 West 17th Street, 7th Floor Suite E, New York, NY 10011 USA
(212) 259-0524; *Fax:* (212) 382-0278
www.dewolfemusic.com
info@dewolfemusicusa.com
Andrew Jacobs, President
Jamie Gillespie, General Sales Mgr
The largest independant production music library in the world!

DeLuxe Entertainment
1377 N. Serrano Ave., Hollywood, CA 90027 USA
(323) 462-6171; *Fax:* (323) 461-0608
www.bydeluxe.com
pr@bydeluxe.com
John Wallace, President & CEO
Walter Schonfeld, President, Deluxe Distribution
Allan Lamkin, CTO
Full svc motion picture processing lab with labs in Toronto, London, Rome.

Design Partners Inc.
5911 Lindenhurst Avenue, Los Angeles, CA 90036 USA
(818) 845-9191; *Fax:* (323) 938-1575
www.dpi-ld.com
Greg Brunton, President
Vicki Brenner, Resident Gaffer/ Partner
Jenny Bloom, Cinematographer
Marisa Davis, Lighting Designer
Lee Rose, Lighting Designer
Kim Killingsworth, Lighting Designer
Kirk Witherspoon, Lighting Consultant/Primary Lighting Designer
TV, lighting design, industrial production & TV production & tech supervision svcs.

Devlin Design Group Inc.
PO Box 3066, Crested Butte, CO 81224-3066 US
(970) 349-5836; *Fax:* (760) 634-6929
www.ddgtv.com
ddgweb2015@ddgtv.com
Mary Hofmockel, Office Manager
Dan Devlin, Owner/ Chief Creative Strategist
Kartik Dakshinamoorthy, Scenic Design Director
Bruce Aleksander, Lighting Director
Diane Fiolek, Creative Services Director
Hannes Kling, Director ofProduction
Laurel Lawrence, Scenic Projects Manager
Designs, builds & installs news sets & newsrooms. Facility planning, broadcast consulting, tech & lighting direction. Virtual Reality Rsch & Dev Ctr. Virtual sets, soft sets.

DG Systems
750 W. John Carpenter Fwy., Suite 700, Irving, TX 75039 USA
(972) 581-2000; *Fax:* (972) 581-2001
www.dgit.com/
Scott K Ginsburg, Executive Chairman of the Board of Directors
Neil Nguyen, President and Chief Executive Officer
Neil Nguyen, President and Chief Executive Officer
Andy Ellenthal, Executive Vice President of Sales and Ad Operation
Craig Holmes, Chief Financial Officer
Ricky Liversidge, Chief Marketing Officer
Duplication & distribution of corporate training & educ, TV & radio programs. Distribution of syndicated TV programs via satellite & videotape.

DHX Media Ltd
1478 Queen Street, Halifax, NS B3J 2H7 Canada
(902) 423-0260; *Fax:* (902) 422-0752
www.dhxmedia.com/
halifax@dhxmedia.com
Michael Patrick Donovan, Executive Chairman
Dana Sean Landry, CA, CEO
Steven Graham DeNure, President & Chief Operating Officer
Joe Tedesco, SVP & GM, DHX Television
Gary Finnegan, VP, Programming Strategy
Josh Scherba, ExecutiveVP, Content & Distribution
Keith Benjamin Abriel, CA, CFA, Chief Financial Officer
David Andrew Regan, Executive VP, Strategy & Corporate Development
Mark Gregory Gosine, EVP, Legal Affairs, General Counsel
DIC Entertainment, a leading children's entertainment company, is a full-service studio dedicated to creating, developing, producing, distributing, mktg & mdsg children's & family-based intellectual properties.

DHX Meida
1478 Queen Street, Halifax, NS B3J 2H7 Canada
(902) 423-0260; *Fax:* (902) 422-0752
www.dhxmedia.com/
halifax@dhxmedia.com
Katarina Dietrich, CEO
Kirk Bloomgarden, President
Michael Hirsh, CEO
Scott McCaw, CFO
Tom Mazza, EVP, Head of Worldwide Sales
Toper Taylor, President/COO
International dev, production, postproduction & distributer of live action, animated and educational programming. Worldwide consumer products and licensing division including ownership of CPLG.
Cookie Jar Entertainment
4100 W Alameda Ave, Burbank, CA 91505
818-955-5454
Cookie Jar Entertainment
11 Rue Torricelli - 75017 Paris, France
011 331 45 74 30 50
CPLG
3 Shortlands - London W6 8PP UK - 44 20 8563 6400,

The Dick Clark Productions
2900 Olympic Blvd., Santa Monica, CA 90404 USA
(310) 255- 4600; *Fax:* (310) 255- 4601
www.dickclark.com
generalinquiries@dickclark.com, gsorial@dickclark.com
Allen Shapiro, CEO
Michael Mahan, President
Amy Thurlow, COO & CFO
Mark Bracco, Executive VP of Programming & Development
Barry Adelman, Executive Vice President of Television
Kelly Striewski, SVP of Communications & Publicity
Linda Gierahn, SVP of Production
Michael Kohn, EVP of Business Operations and General Counsel
Mark Rafalowski, EVP International Distribution
TV production for networks, cable & syndication. Produces series, specials & movies for TV.

Dick Reizner Film and Video
801 Atherton Drive, Suite 120, Manteca, CA 95337 USA
(408) 828-3555, (408) 226-6339; *Fax:* (408) 226-6339
www.reizner.com
dick@reizner.com
Dick Reizner, President
Bcst & industrial production in all formats. Certified Legal Video Specialist. Gyrozoom rental.

Digital Brewery L.L.C.
3 West Main Street, Milan, MI 48160 USA
(734) 439-8501; *Fax:* (734) 975-8915
www.digitalbrewery.com
Sal Calabrese, Co-President
Terry Dollhoff, Co-President
Packaged animations include backgrounds, holidays, corporate, adv & globes, maps & flags.

Digital Force
149 Madison Ave., 12th Fl., New York, NY 10016 USA
(212) 252-9300, (877) DISC-USA; *Fax:* (212) 252-7377
www.digitalforce.com
Jerome Bunke, President
Arthur Crumlish, Operations Dir
Vanessa Towle-Mullin, Programming Director
Compact disc, CD-ROM & DVDproduction service to meet the needs of bcstrs, cable networks, & small labels/ind artists. Clients include the National Football League (NFL) & National Hockey League (NHL) on Fox TV as well as PSAs & promotionaldiscs from bcstrs nationwide, ABC-TV & NBC, Westwood One & CBS.

Diocese of Springfield
65 Elliot St., Springfield, MA 01105 USA
(413) 732-3175, (800) 854-0003; *Fax:* (413) 452-0647
www.diospringfield.org
m.dupont@diospringfield.org
Mark E. Dupont, Secretary for Communications
Rev. Mitchell T. Rozanski, Bishop
William LaBoard, Finance Officer
Peter Schmidt, Human Resources

Mark E. Dupont, Communications
Rev. Msgr. Daniel P. Liston, JCL, Canonical Affairs
TV & radio production svcs.

Disney Channel
3800 W. Alameda Ave., Burbank, CA 91505 USA
(818) 569-7700; *Fax:* (818) 845-8249
www.disneychannel.com
Gary Marsh, President/Chief Creative Officer, Disney Ch. WW
Original TV program production & distribution.

Diversified Communications Inc.
2000 M St. N.W., Suite 340, Washington, DC 20036 USA
(202) 775-4300; *Fax:* (202) 775-4363
www.dciteleport.com
Al Levin, President
Nelson Crumling, Operations Dir
Joe ConCaugh, General & Technical Inquires
Complete mobile facilities, Ku-band uplink trucks, extensive loc & global connectivity; internationally compliant, fully redundant Ku-band air transportable uplink.

DK
Div/DBA: Penguin Random House
345 Hudson Street, 4th Floor, New York, NY 10014 US
(646) 674-4000
www.dk.com/us/
customerservice@penguinrandomhouse.com
Michael Freeman, Library Sales
Jay Franco, Associate Sales Director
Produces programs for the international TV & video markets, incorporating visual design with universally appealing subjects.

DLT Entertainment Ltd.
124 E. 55th St., New York, NY 10022 USA
(212) 245-4680; *Fax:* (212) 315-1132
www.dltentertainment.com
Jeff Cotugno, COO
Donald Taffner, Jr, President
John Fitzgerald, Vice Chairman
Rohan Acharya, Producer
John Bartlett, Director of Comedy and Drama
Michaela Hennessy-Vass, Executive Producer
Simon Longden, Development Producer
TV program production & distribution.

DMX Music
Mailing Address: 411 1st Ave S.., Suite 501, Seattle, WA 98104 USA
Second Address: 77 Fourth Avenue, 5th Floor, Waltham, MA 2451
(800) 345-5000, (800) 525-6434; *Fax:* (206) 329-9952, (508) 393-5137
www.dmxmusic.com
dmx.canada@dmx.com
Liberty Media, President
Programmer & supplier of satellite-delivered music svcs for business & cable TV. Available satellite direct or through FM subcarrier.

Domain Communications L.L.C.
289 South Main Place, Carol Stream, IL 60188-2425 USA
(630) 668-5300, (800) DOMAIN.1; *Fax:* (630) 668-0158
www.domaincommunications.com
dmorris@domaincommunications.com
David Morris, Owner & President
Recording audio studios, production, CD replication, high-speed cassette duplicating, fulfillment.

Dome Productions
Mailing Address: 1 Blue Jays Way, Suite 3400, Toronto, ON M5V 1J3 Canada
Second Address: 5647 rue Ferrier, Mont-Royal, QC H4P 1N1
(416) 341-2001,(514) 731-3663; *Fax:* (416) 341-2020,(514) 731-4646
domeproductions.com/
Mary Carlyle, Senior VP & General Manager
Kate McClure, Senior Operations Manager
Mobile production trucks/airpacks (High Definition, Digital, Analog), telecommunications (Fibre/Satellite transmission, satellite media tours, playouts), Host bcst (Design, production, engrg, opons).
5647 Ferrier, Mont-Royal, PQ Canada

DreamWorks Classics (formerly Classic Media)
85 Fifth Avenue, 6th Floor, New York, NY 10003 USA
(212) 659-1959; *Fax:* (212) 659-1958
www.classics.dreamworksanimation.com
Eric Ellenbogen, Founder/President
John Engelman, CEO
Manages some of the most recognizable family oriented properties across all media including feature film, television, home video & consumer products.
8640 Wilshire Blvd., Beverly Hills, CA 90211
(310) 659-6004; *Fax:* (310) 659-4599
Leslie Levine, Dorothy Schecter

Duke Media Limited
Mailing Address: 19 Berkeley Street, London, UK W1J 8ED
Second Address: Champion House, Douglas, Isle of Man, IM99 1DD
(+44) 1624 640020; *Fax:* (+44) 1624 640001
www.dukesales.com
info@dukesales.com
Peter Duke, CEO/COO
Dave Bignell, Sales Manager
A large archive of motorsport programming, documentaries, clips for licensing; also production, aerial filming & editing facilities.

E! Entertainment Television
5750 Wilshire Boulevard, Los Angeles, CA 90036
(323) 954-2400; *Fax:* (323) 954-2500
www.eonline.com
Satellite: Satcom C-3 *Transponder:* 23
Adam Stotsky, President
A 24-hours progmg net covering celebrities, entertainment news, gossip & pop-culture, feature behind the scenes with today's biggest stars.
11 W. 42nd St, New York, NY 10036-8002
(212) 852-5100, (212) 852-5151
Dave Cassaro, Exec Vp
11 W. 42nd St, New York, NY 10036
(212) 852-5100 (212) 852-5151
Dave Cassaro, Exec Vp

Eagle Eye Film Company
824 North Victory Blvd., Burbank, CA 91502 USA
(818) 955-7662; *Fax:* (818) 955-7662
Chuck Spatariu, President
Editing facility, editing rentals & RAID storage solutions.

Eaton Films Ltd.
10 Holbein Mews, London, SW1W 8NN
(44) 207-823-6173; *Fax:* (44) 207-823-6017
www.eatonfilms.co.uk/
eaton.films@talk21.com
Judith Bland Gordon, Owner/General Manager
Louise Rimoldi
Carol Sinclair
Bill Treacy
TV & video distribution.

Echo Radio Productions Inc.
44895 Hwy. 82, Aspen, CO 81611 USA
(800) 385-4612,(970) 925-2640; *Fax:* (970) 925-9369
www.echoradio.com/echo3.html
kayla@echoradio.com
Rodney Jacobs, Chief Executive Officer
Kayla Hoffman-Cook, Chief Operating Officer
Chris Laursen, Staff Member
Glenda Summers, Technological Director
Syndicator & producer of radio vignette progmg.

Ecumenical Communications
Div/DBA: (Christian Podcasts Connection)
2914 42nd Street SW, Lehigh Acres, FL 33976 USA
(239) 491-5539, (203) 340-3121
www.ecucomm.ro
ecucomm@sbcglobal.net
Robert Geckler, President
Radio, podcast program production, distribution; production, restoration svcs, internet, website & podcast svcs.

Educational Technologies Network (ETN)
9300 Imperial Hwy., Los Angeles County Office of Education, Downey, CA 90242 USA
(562) 922-6111; *Fax:* (562) 922-8841
www.lacoe.edu
Debra Duardo, Superintendent
Manuel Sanchez, Production & Operations Engineer
Tyler Cook, Multimedia Production Manager
Mike McMahon, Multimedia Producer/Director/Editor
Jeffrey Reyna, Multimedia Producer/Director/Editor
ETN provides multimeda production svcs to LACOE division & school districts throughout Los Angeles county. Include: studio & remote video production, distance learning & vitual meetings, video streaming, videoconferencing, interactive CD-ROM& DVD authoring & live event video coverage,

Elation Media (formerly Oasis/OTV)
Mailing Address: 2155 West Highway 89A, Ste 213, Sedona, AZ 86336 USA
Second Address: 2029 Century Park East, Suite 400, Los Angeles, CA 90067
(928) 862-4110; (310) 553-4300
www.elationmedia.com
Gerald Levin, Chairman
Robert Schnitzer, Founder & CEO
24-hours cable/satellite net providing a broad, well-branded var of new age/human potential progmg.

Encore Media
1011 16th Avenue South, Nashville, TN 37212 US
(615) 256-1675, (615) 322-9927; *Fax:* (615) 322-9786
www.encorenashville.com
david@encorenashville.com
Scott Long, General Manager
David Deeb, Sales
Di Summitt, Scheduling
Offers a wide range of services including HD video, DVD authoring, post-production, closed captioning, music videos and national TV commercials

Encore Video Productions Inc.
811 Main St., Myrtle Beach, SC 29577 USA
(843) 448-7700, (843) 997-9900; *Fax:* (843) 448-9235
www.encorevideo.biz
frank@encorevideo.biz
Rik Dickinson, President
Frank Payne, VP
Location & studio production, specializing in EFP/ENG 1-Camera productions, full script to screen svc, VNR, EPK satellite media tours, teleconferences, & magazine TV production. Betagami SP, non-linear editing.

Envoy Productions
660 Mason Ridge Center Dr., St. Louis, MO 63141 USA
(888) 229-7743; *Fax:* (314) 317-4299
www.envoyproductions.com
contact@envoyproductions.com
Kurt Klaus, President
Sandi Clement, General Manager
TV, radio production, distribution (English & Sp). Syndicates 30-minute wkly radio shows, The Lutheran Hour & TV holiday specials.

Episcopal Church Center
815 2nd Ave., New York, NY 10017 USA
(212) 716-6000, (800) 334-7626; *Fax:* (212) 949-8059
www.episcopalchurch.org
Michael Collins, Manager, Multimedia Services
Lynette Wilson, Managing Editor, Episcopal News Service
Scott van Pletzen-Rands, Web Content & Digital Media Coordinator
Christopher Sikkema, Coordinator for Digital Evangelism
BerniceDavid, Communication Operations Manager
Olivia Green, Editor/Producer
Spokespersons for church & society issues.

ESPN / The SEC Network
11001 Rushmore Dr., Charlotte, NC 28277 USA
(704) 973-5000; *Fax:* (704) 973-5090
www.secsports.com
Rosalyn Durant, Senior VP, College Networks, Programming
Stephanie Druley, Senior VP, Event & Studio Production
Peter Burns, SEC Network Host
Jordan Rodgers, College Football Studio Analyst, SEC Network
Laura Rutledge, Reporter, ESPN& SEC Network
Producer & distributor of TV sports events including college & professional basketball, boxing & auto racing for over-the-air & cable.

ESPN Radio Network
ESPN Plaza, Bristol, CT 6010 USA
(860) 766-2661; *Fax:* (860) 860-5523
www.espnradio.com
Justin Craig, Senior Director, Programming & Operations
NBA On ESPN Radio; College Game Day (Sat); ESPN Radio weekends; Brent Musburger afternoon drive sportscasts; AM & PM drive commentaries; NFL Gameday (Sun)

Essence Television Productions Inc.
Div/DBA: TIME, Inc. Productions
225 Liberty Street, 9th Floor, New York, NY 10048 USA
(212) 522-1212, (800) 274-9398
www.essence.com
webmaster@essence.com
Edward Lewis, Founder
Bruce Gersh, SVP, Business Development & Strategy, TIME Inc.
Michelle Ebanks, President
TV program production.

EUE / Screen Gems Studios
603 Greenwich Street, New York, NY 10014 USA
(212) 450-1600; *Fax:* (212) 450-1610
www.euescreengems.com/
Chris Cooney, Chief Operating Officer, NYC
Chris Crowder, VP of Operations
Jeff Cooney, Senior VP & Creative Director
Sharon Cooney Shuttleworth, Senior VP / Director of Corporate Communications
TV program, coml production & distribution.
1223 N. 23rd St., Wilmington, NC 28405
(910) 343-3500

Euro Media France
29 avenue George Sand, Saint-Denis, Fr 93210 FRA
33 (0)1 83 72 66 00; *Fax:* 33 (0)1 49 83 43 06
www.euromedia-france.com
contact@euromediagroup.com
Patrick Van Den Berg, CEO, Euro Media Group
Gilles Chasson, Strategy & Business Development
Nathalie Gateau, Human Resources
Ronald Meyvisch, Innovation
Lucie Wibault, Communications & PR
Distribution worldwide rights (TV movies, series, mini-series documentaries).

Eurocine
4, impasse Morlet, Paris, 75011 FRA
33 (0)9.54.32.68.60; *Fax:* 33 (0)1.43.71.25.77
www.eurocine.net
eurocine@eurocine.net
Production & distribution in all media.

Evangelical Lutheran Church in America
8765 W. Higgins Rd., Chicago, IL 60631 USA
(773) 380-2700, (800) 638-3522; *Fax:* (773) 380-1465
www.elca.org
info@elca.org
Ava Martin, General Manager
Elizabeth A. Eaton, Presiding Bishop
Carlos E. Pena, Vice President
Chris Boerger, Secretary
Linda O. Norman, Treasurer
TV & radio progmg, promotional film production, distribution, production svcs & news.

Evergreen Entertainment Group
1825 Ponce De Leon Blvd., Suite 450, Coral Gables, FL 33134-3626 USA
(305) 460-4448
evergreenenter@juno.com
Migdalia Inocencio, President
Worldwide programs distribution; international co-production liaison; mktg & progmg cable/satellite.

Expand Images
7 Rue Taylor, Paris, 75010
(33) 4 78 66 47 30; *Fax:* (33) 0148-0345-04
www.expandmedia.com/fr
france@expandmedia.com
Production & distribution company.

Faith for Today
11291 Pierce Street, Riverside, CA 92505 USA
(805) 955-7700, (888) 940-0062; *Fax:* (805) 522-2114
www.faithfortoday.tv/
info@faithfortoday.tv
Mike Tucker, Speaker/Director
Gayle Tucker, Associate Speaker
Producer & distributor of Lifestyle Magazine, McDougall M.D. & The Evidence.

FaithAndReason
3000 Old Canton Road, Suite 505, Jackson, MS 39216 US
(601) 982-1020, (800) 882-7424; *Fax:* (601) 362-1040
www.faithandreason.org
davidd581@gmail.com
David Dykes, Executive Director
Clay Hardwick, Video Production
Debo Dykes, Director of Media & Readers' Guides
Jennifer Vail, Administrator
Christina Mattison, Special Promotions/ Designer
Darren Schwindaman, Graphic Designer/Brand Consultant

FamilyTalk Radio
1735 N. Lynn Street, Suite 500, Arlington, VA 22209 US
(703) 807-2266
familytalktoday.com
jerryh@salemmediadc.com
Gerald T. Halstead, Operations Dir
Tom Moyer, General Manager
FamilyTalk replaced FamilyNet Radio and is now on SIRIUS 131, Christian talk. We produce Mornings which airs only on SIRIUS .

Faraone Communications Inc.
75 West End Avenue, Suite R-9A, New York, NY 10023 USA
(212) 489-1313; *Fax:* (212) 489-8978
www.worldwidepublicrelations.com
ted.faraone@verizon.net
Ted Faraone, President
Randolph Nader, Operations Dir
Ted Farone, Principal
Media rel svcs to producers, distributors of radio, TV programs, talent & home video.
Valley Village
4804 Laurel Canyon Blvd., Ste 516, Valley Village, CA 91607

Festival de Television de Monte-Carlo
4, Boulevard du Jardin Exotique, Monte Carlo, 98000
377 93 10 40 60; *Fax:* 377 93 50 70 14
www.tvfestival.com
info@tvfestival.com
Competition of TV films & miniseries; news programs; producers. Conferences, panels & other market-related activities.

Film House Inc.
810 Dominican Dr., Nashville, TN 37228 USA
(615) 255-4000; *Fax:* (615) 255-4111
www.filmhouse.com/
davedonnelly@filmhouse.com
Andy Cohen, CFO
Ron Routson, President
Curt Hahn, CEO
David Donnelly, Director, Post Production
Creates & produces TV mktg campaigns for radio & TV stns worldwide.

Film Roman Inc.
6320 Canoga Avenue, Suite 490, Woodland Hills, CA 91367 USA
(818) 748-4056; *Fax:* (818) 985-2973
www.filmroman.com
info@filmroman.com
Steve Waterman, Chairman, Waterman Entertainment
Dana Booton, President of Production
Animation production studio.

Filmoption International Inc.
3401 St. Antoine St., Westmount, QC H3Z 1X1 Canada
(514) 931-6180; *Fax:* (514) 939-2034
www.filmoption.com
email@filmoption.com
Maryse Rouillard, President
Patricia Van de Weghe, International Sales Assistant
Lizanne Rouillard, Vice President
Carla Bruce, Director
Andrew Noble, Vice-President Theatrical and Homevideo Releasing
Marie-Pierre Rodier, VPAcquisitions
Susan Hewitt, Sales Consultant
International distribution of TV programs.
3401 St-Antoine, Westmount, PQ H3Z 1X1 Canada
(215) 931-6180; *Fax:* (514) 939-2034
mrouilla@filmoption.com
Maryse Rouillard, Pres
144 Front St. West, Suite 760, Toronto, ON M5J 2L7 Canada
(416) 598-1557; *Fax:* (416) 593-0013
mrosilio@filmoption.com
Muriel rosilio, Sr Exec Sls Co-Productions

Films Media Group
132 West 31st Street, 17th Floor, New York, NY 10001 USA
(800) 322-8755; *Fax:* (800) 678-3633
www.films.com
custserv@films.com
Amy Bevilacqua, President
Diane Bilello, General Sales Mgr
Distributes programs for bcst & cable industries to non-theatrical, educ, institutional, home video & business markets.

First Run/Icarus Films
32 Court St., 21st Fl., Brooklyn, NY 10201 USA
(718) 488-8900; *Fax:* (718) 488-8642
www.frif.com
info@frif.com
Jonathan Miller, President
International TV program distribution: documentaries, current affrs, music, arts, cultural programs.

FirstCom Music
1325 Capital Pkwy., Suite 109, Carrollton, TX 75006 USA
(800) 858-8880, (972) 446-8742; *Fax:* (972) 242-6526
www.firstcom.com
Carol Riffert, Vice President/ General Manager
Karen Helm, National Sales Manager
Ken Nelson, Programming Director
Ric Villa, Account Executive- Audio Post
IdaYarborough-Griffin, Account Executive- Radio
Linda Dillon, SeniorAccount Executive- Radio
Mike Lebolt, Account Executive- Television
Ian Parker, Account Executive- Corporate
Roger Kuehler, Account Executive- Audio Post
FirstCom's 18 spectacular libraries deliver the combined power of 186,000 compositions & growing by 6,000 new tracks a year. Delivery options include DVD, CD, Hard-drive & online. Guaranteed to add creativity to your production!
8750 Wilshire Blvd., 2nd Fl., Beverly Hills, CA 90211

Fischer Broadcast Services
10841 Bittersweet Lane, Fishers, IN 46038-2203
(317) 514-5757; *Fax:* (317) 578-3884
www.superfisch.com
superfisch@midspring.com
Scott Fischer, President
Jim Claussen, VP Promotion/Creative Services
SUPERFISCH—VOICE IMAGING & BRANDING. Scott Fischer voice artist for radio & TV loc, cable, Netw. Promax & Emmy award voice. A versitile-VO-value! Yes you CAN afford me-can you afford not to check me out?

Fox 17 Studio Productions
631 Mainstream Dr., Nashville, TN 37228 USA
(615) 244-1717; *Fax:* (615) 259-3962
www.fox17.com
production@fox17.com
Bill Zuckerman, Promotions Manager
Full range video & film production facility; 25 x 40 studio & 60 x 60 studio soundstage; betacams & a var of tape formats for TV/CATV.

Fox 29 WUTV Sinclair
699 Hertel Avenue, Suite 100, Buffalo, NY 14207 USA
(716) 447-3200; *Fax:* (716) 875-4919
www.wutv.com
closedcaptioning@mytvbuffalo.com
Jon May, COO
Don Moran, General Manager
Susan E. Domozych, Senior Paralegal
TV coml production; U.S. rep, Katz; Canadian rep, Airtime.

Fox Digital
Fox Network Ctr., 10201 W. Pico Blvd., Los Angeles, CA 90035 USA
(310) 369-6622; *Fax:* (310) 969-6125
www.fox.com
Videotape production facilities, stages & equipment.

Fox Sports West
1100 S. Flower St., Los Angeles, CA 90015 USA
(213) 743-7800; *Fax:* (213) 743-7835
www.foxsports.com
Dennis Johnson, Operations Dir
Steve Simpson, General Manager
TV program production & distribution.

France 2
1290 Ave. of the Americas, Suite 3410, New York, NY 10104 USA
(212) 581-1771; *Fax:* (212) 541-4309
www.france2.fr
TV program production.

Fred Wolf Films
4222 W. Burbank Blvd., Burbank, CA 91505 USA
(818) 846-0611; *Fax:* (818) 846-0979
www.fredwolffilms.com
administration@fredwolffilms.com
Fred Wolf, President
TV program production & distribution.

Free Speech TV (FSTV)
Box 44099, Denver, CO 80201 USA
(303) 442-8445; *Fax:* (303) 442-6472
www.freespeech.org
ron@freespeech.org
Ashindi Maxton, Chair
John Schwartz, President
Nathaniel Reeder, Operations Director
Jon Stout, General Manager & Co-Founder
Eric Galatas, Program Director
John Schwartz, Vice Chair
Ron Williams, Executive Director
JasonMcKain, Development Director
Ben Gass, Director of National Partnerships

Alexander Maness, Interim Program Director
Antoinette June, Web Director
Acquires works from activists, independent film/video artists & community based media; providing exposure to progressive ideas.

Free To Choose Network
2002 Filmore Ave., Erie, PA 16506 USA
(814) 833-7140, (800) 876-8930; *Fax:* (814) 833-7415
www.ideachannel.com
info@freetochoose.net
Brian Singer, Chairman
Tara L. Schupp, VP Production, COO
Bob Chitester, Presidentand CEO
Rick Platt, Operations Dir
Tom Skinner, Senior Executive Producer
Discussions 20-40 minutes in length, featuring two or three leading scholars on a wide variety of subjects. Internet offerings also.

Freeform
PO Box 3000, Neenah, WI 54957 USA
(818) 460-7477; *Fax:* (818) 840-1922
www.freeform.go.com
Freeform (formerly ABC Family), features quality, contemporary entertainment for all members of the family including original series, movies & specials. Available in over 97 million homes via basic cable.

Freewheelin' Films Ltd.
44895 Hwy. 82, Aspen, CO 81611 USA
(970) 925-2640; *Fax:* (970) 925-9369
www.fwf.com
kalyla@fwf.com
Rodney H. Jacobs, Principle/Executive Producer
Kayla B. Hoffman-Cook, Senior Vice President
Glenda Summers, Executive Assistant
Peter Sellers, Director
25-yr old production company specializing in entertainment, sports & lifestyle specials.

The Fremantle Corp.
25 Lesmill Road, #5, Toronto, ON M3B 2T3 Canada
(416) 443-9204; *Fax:* (416) 443-8685
www.fremantlecorp.com
Brad Pelman, CEO
Randall (Randy) H. Zalken, President
Diane Tripp, SVP International Sales
Arlene Hay, Director of Business Affairs & Client Services
Aliy Brown, Director
Wayne Broun, AAPS/ Fremantle Corp. Australia Sales
International TV program distribution & co-production.
New York Office
(212) 840-6269 LA Office: (310) 445-0700

Fremantle Media Ltd.
1 Stephen St., London, W1T 1AL GBR
44 (0)20 7691-6000; *Fax:* 44 (0)20 7691-6100
www.fremantlemedia.com/home.aspx
feedback@freemantlemedia.com
Cecile Frot-Coutazÿ, Chief Executive Officer
Tony Cohen, General Manager
Sangeeta Desai, Chief Operating Officer& Chief Financial Officer
Rob Clark, Director of Global Entertainment Development
Nicky Gray, Director of HumanResources
Ian Hogg, Chief Executive Officer, Asia Pacific
Keith Hindle, CEO of Digital & Branded Entertainment
Wolf Bauer, Chief Executive Officer, UFA Film & TV Production
TV production & distribution.

FremantleMedia North America Inc.
Mailing Address: 4000 West Alameda Avenue, 3rd Floor, Burbank, CA 91505 USA
Second Address: 435 Hudson Street, Suite 404, New York, NY 10014
(818) 748-1100; *Fax:* (310) 255-4800
www.fremantlemedia.com
Cecile Frot-Coutaz, CEO
David Lyle, President
Sangeeta Desai, COO/ CFO
Nicky Gray, Director of Human Resources
Rob Clark, Director of Global Entertainment Development
TV production.
1540 Broadway, New York, NY 10036 United States
Catherine V MacKay, Deputy Ceo

FTC/Orlando
503 W Robinson Street, Orlando, FL 32801 USA
(407) 422-8246; *Fax:* (407) 843-0738
www.ftcorlando.com
ftcorlando@aol.com
A.J. Foresta, President
Full-svc film & TV production company, specializing in coml & feature production. Area specialty: steadicam.

Galavision
605 Third Ave., 12th Fl., New York, NY 10158-0180 USA
(212) 455-5300; *Fax:* (212) 953-0198
www.univision.com
Ray Rodriguez, COO
Cesar Conde, Operations Dir
Joanne Lynch, General Manager
Spanish TV program distribution, cable.
541 N. Fairbanks Ct., 12th Fl., Suite 1240, Chicago, IL 60611
(312) 494-5100; *Fax:* (312) 494-5115
2323 Bryan St, Suite 1900, Dallas, TX 75201 United States
(214) 758-2420; *Fax:* (214) 758-2430
9405 N.W. 41st St., Miami, FL 33178
(305) 471-4022; *Fax:* (305) 471-3977
5999 Center Dr., Los Angeles, CA 90045 United States
(310) 348-3621; *Fax:* (310) 348-3619

Gedeon Programmes
155 rue de Charonne, Paris, Fr 75011
(33) 1 55 25 59 59ÿ; *Fax:* (33) 1 55 25 59 00
www.gedeonprogrammes.com
St,phane Milliere, President
Sonia Levine, Finance Director
Michael Liberman, Director-in-General
Noda Rungen, Assistant Director
Laurence Corre, Communication Director
Diane Riethof, Production Director
Thibaut Martin, Producerof documentaries & TV shows
Films, TV movies, TV series, interactive fiction.

Gene Bayliss
208 Good Hill Rd., Weston, CT 06883 USA
(203) 227-7521; *Fax:* (203) 454-1032
Gene Bayliss, Consultant
Produces, directs video conferences, videotapes for corporations & industries, meetings & special events.

General Broadcasting Co. Inc.
PO Box 279, Wauconda, IL 60084 US
(800) 323-2080
www.generalbroadcasting.com
Background music, environmental music progmg.

Georgia Film, Video & Music Office
Georgia Department of Economic Dev, 75 Fifth St. N.W., Atlanta, GA 30308
(404) 962-4000; *Fax:* (404) 962-4053
www.georgia.org
film@georgia.org
John Moffatt, Chief Financial Officer
Pat Wilson, Chief Operating Officer
Chris Carr, Commissioner
Nathan Deal, Governor
Karen Paty, ExecutiveÿDirector
Karen Hampton, Director Human Resources
Location scouting & preproduction svcs provided to feature film, TV movie, coml & multimedia production companies.

Getty Images
605 5th Ave South, Suite 400, Seattle, WA 98104 USA
(206) 925-5000, (888) 888-5889; *Fax:* (206) 925-5001
www.gettyimages.com
sales@gettyimages.com
Getty Images is an imagery company creating and providing still and moving images to communications professionals around the globe.

Ghostwriters/Radio Mall
2412 Unity Avenue N, Minneapolis, MN 55422-3450
(800) 759-4561, (763) 522-6256; *Fax:* (763) 522-6256
www.radio-mall.com
info@radio-mall.com
David Dworkin, President
Over 23 years experience with products sold to more than 7,300 radio stns worldwide as well as TV stns, audio-video producers & cable operators. If you have a product that you'd like to mkt to radio or TV stns, contact us.

Gibby Media Group
1213 S. Pines, Spokane Valley, WA 99206 US
(509) 467-1113,(800) 200-1113; *Fax:* (509) 467-4763
www.gibbymedia.com
info@gibbymedia.com
Lon Gibby, President and Chief Executive Officer
John Gibby, Operations Manager
Les Bohush, Senior Vice President, International Marketing
Michael Morgan, Multimedia Specialist
Beau Garner, Vice President, IT & SoftwareDevelopment
Loni Gibby, Office Manager
Greg Parch, Sales & Marketing Representative
Multimedia productions, video, CD-Rom, CD-I, producers of bcst TV programs, comls, infomercials, corporate videos & webcasting

Glenray Productions Inc.
Box 40400, Pasadena, CA 91114-7400 USA
(626) 797-5462
www.childrensmedia.com
2glenray@sbcglobal.net
C. Ray Carlson, President
Films, TV series, DVD distribution & production, primarily for family & children.

Global Entertainment Media
1200 N.W. 78th Ave., Suite 104, Miami, FL 33126 USA
(786) 206-4873; *Fax:* (786) 206-4889
www.globalentmedia.com/
Alexander A. Fiore, CEO
Mercedes M. Fiore, President
Production & distribution company.

Global Telemedia Inc.
PO Box 213, Boston, MA 02199 USA
(774) 203-3018; *Fax:* (781) 459-0279
www.globaltelemedia.com
gt@globaltelemedia.com
Greg Kimmelman, Founder/ Chief Executive Officer
Anne Corsak, Operations Dir
Production & distribution of broadcast TV & DVD programming worldwide.

GlobeCast
1270 Avenue of the Americas, Ste 2800, New York, NY 10020 USA
(212) 373-5140; *Fax:* (212) 399-1949
www.globecast.com
info@globecastna.com
Oliver Barberot, Chairman & Chief Executive Officer
Philippe Fort, Chief Operating Officer
Jonathan Feldman, Operations Dir
Mary Frost, General Sales Mgr
Keven Cahoon, Promotions Manager
Nathalie Krick, Chief Financial Officer
Darby Sanchez, CEO Globecast Asia
Christine Jecko, Vice President Marketing
Elisabeth Mazurie, Vice President General Counsel & Procurement
Didier Mainard, Global Account Manager
B,atrice de Lagrevol, Vice President Human Resources
GlobeCast Audio division supports a comprehensive package of audio transmission svcs:ABC/Keystone Ventures provides Satcom C5 DATS/SEDAT distribution svcs to 7,000 radio stns.3D2, a high-quality digital net designed to svc the entertainmentindustry, connections post-production facilities, recording studios & voice-over talent worldwide.A/FX Network utilizing Telos Zephyr code located at venues for sports backhauls & special events.Hybrid bridging svcs to simplify a digital world fullof different flavored audio codecs.Remote Production Packages for single or multi-stn remote bcsts.
GlobeCast Washington/DC
1120 G Street, NW - 2nd Floor, Washington, DC 20005 United States
1-202-383-2745; *Fax:* 1-202-393-4914
GlobeCast Miami Headquarters America/Florida
7291 NW 74th St., Miami, FL 33166 United States
1-310-687-1600; *Fax:* 1-305-341-4424
GlobeCast Los Angeles/California
10525 W. Washington Blvd., Culver City, CA 90232 United States
1-310-845-3900; *Fax:* 1-310-845-3904
GlobeCast Salt Lake City/Utah
1193 West 2400 South, Suite A, Salt Lake City, UT 84119 United States
1-801-908-1100; *Fax:* 1-801-954-0991

GlobeCast North America
; ? SUbscribers served
10525 W. Washington Blvd., Culver City, CA 90230 USA
(310) 845-3900; *Fax:* (310) 845-3904
www.globecast.com
Oliver Barberot, Chairman & Chief Executive Officer
Philippe Fort, Chief Executive Officer
Ken Drake, Operations Dir
Nathalie Krick, Chief Financial Officer
Darby Sanchez, CEO Globecast Asia
Christine Jecko, Vice PresidentMarketing
Elisabeth Mazurie, Vice President General Counsel &

Procurement
Didier Mainard, Global Account Manager
B,atrice de Lagrevol, Vice President Human Resources
In the center of Hollywood, GlobeCast North America's Sunset facility provides studio production second audio progmg (SAP), & related client facility svcs on an as-scheduled or contractual basis. GlobeCast's studio is completely integratedw/GlobeCast's network of global, end-to-end connectivity via satellite, fiber optics & microwave.GlobeCast North America, provides the bcstg industry with a unique combination of both recognized expertise & extensive inter-continental svcs. ThroughGlobeCast's vast global infrastructure of over 100 transponders, 30 teleports & interconnect facilities, the company provides instant access to the world's major media markets. GlobeCast North America is part of France Telecom, one of the worldslargest telecommunications companies.

GMI Media L.L.C.
325 Washington Ave S, #399, Kent, WA 98032 USA
(206) 374-8889; *Fax:* NA
www.gmimedia.com
Ron Erak, President
Richard Germaine, Operations Dir
Custom ID jingle packages for all radio & TV formats as well as commercial jingles for local adsales. CD production libraries. Voice overs & production for promotions & spots.

Golden Gate Studios
100 Pelican Way, Suite E, San Rafael, CA 94901 USA
(415) 485-5856; *Fax:* (415) 924-0264
www.goldengatestudios.com
lpeterson@tin.com
2 Studios, Green Screen Options, Full Production Packages

Good News Broadcasting Association Inc.
Mailing Address: 6400 Cornhusker Hwy., Lincoln, NE 68507-3123 USA
Second Address: PO Box 82808, Lincoln, NE 68501-2808
(800) 759-2425, (800) 759-6655; *Fax:* (402) 464-7474
www.backtothebible.org
info@backtothebible.org
Woodrow Kroll, President
Radio & TV program production & distribution.

Gordon Productions
1557 Pine St., San Francisco, CA 94109 USA
(415) 776-7484; *Fax:* (415) 776-7822
www.gpvideo.com
john@gpvideo.com
Jerry Gordon, CEO
John Gordon, President
Les Lieurance, Operations Dir
Broadcast pub rels svcs include: B-roll & VNR production & distribution, TV, radio PSA's & audio news releases. Corporate video production include: trade shows, patient educ, training & employee presentations.

The Gospel Greats
PO Box 1372, Lancaster, PA 17608-1372 USA
(717) 898-9100; *Fax:* (717) 898-6600
www.thegospelgreats.com
paul@thegospelgreats.com
Paul Heil, President
Shelia Heil, General Manager
Radio program (The Gospel Greats)

GPN Inc & Destination Education Inc.
4910 S 75th St, Lincoln, NE 68516 USA
(402) 435-0110; *Fax:* (402) 435-0119
www.shopdei.com
slenzen@shopdei.com
Stephen Lenzen, President and Co-Founder
Acquires, produces, promotes & distributes videotaped instructional videos for bcst, cablecast & audiovisual use.

GRB Entertainment
13400 Riverside Dr., Sherman Oaks, CA 91423 USA
(818) 728-7600; *Fax:* (818) 728-7601
www.grbtv.com
info@grbtv.com
Gary R. Benz, President & Chief Executive Officer
Karen M. Pinto, Senior Vice President, Production & Operations
Benn Watson, Vice President of International Sales
Michael Branton, Executive Vice President, Creative Affairs
StevenMontgomery, Senior Vice President, Business & Legal Affairs
Jean Shi, Vice President of Development
Michael Lolato, Senior Vice President, International Distribution
Joey Sabella, Senior Director of International Sales and Acquisi
Production & distribution (TV).

Great Chefs Television/Publishing
747 Magazine St., New Orleans, LA 70130 USA
(504) 581-5000, (800) 321-1499; *Fax:* (504) 581-1188
www.greatchefs.com
info@greatchefs.com
John Shoup, Chairman/ CEO
Production, distribution of cooking, jazz TV programs, videos, CDs, CD-ROMs & books.

Groove Addicts
3400 West Olive Avenue, Burbank, CA 91505 USA
(818) 238-6300; *Fax:* (818) 238-6330
www.grooveaddicts.com
info@grooveaddicts.com
Randy Wachtler, President & CEO
Randy Wachtler, President & CEO
Judd Maher, Studio Operations Manager/Senior Producer
Bryan Hofheins, Chief Creative Officer
Tom English, VP of Business Development
Marcia Kautz, Director ofOperations
Jennifer Stowe, Marketing Manager
Adward winning custom scoring & syndicated branding & ID packages for bcsts & entertainment projects worldwide.
Groove Addicts Chicago
108 W. Hubbard St., Chicago, IL 60610 United States
(312) 467-7047; *Fax:* (312) 467-7049

Groove Addicts Production Music Catalog
3400 West Olive Avenue, Burbank, CA 91505 USA
(818) 238-6300; *Fax:* (818) 238-6330
www.grooveaddicts.com
Randy Wachtler, President & CEO
Randy Wachtler, President & CEO
Judd Maher, Studio Operations Manager/Senior Producer
Bryan Hofheins, Chief Creative Officer
Tom English, VP of Business Development
Marcia Kautz, Director ofOperations
Jennifer Stowe, Marketing Manager
Continuously updated, sound design & SFX. Annual blanket license & custom music packages. 17 library collection with over 750 releases.

GVI
1775 K St. N.W., Suite 220, Washington, DC 20006 USA
(202) 293-4488; *Fax:* (202) 293-3293
www.g-v-i.com
Andy Hemmindinger, President
Bob Burnett, Operations Dir
Bob Burnett, VP & Creative Director
Curtis Croley, Producer
Michael Bartlett, Audio & Multimedia Designer
Full creative script-to-screen production, camera crews, Avid editing, DVD authoring & equipment rental.

Halland Broadcast Services
2412 Unity Ave N, Minneapolis, MN 55422 USA
(763) 522-6256, (800) 759-4561; *Fax:* (763) 522-6256, (800) 759-4561
www.h-b-s.com
info@radio-mall.com
Dave Dworkin, General Manager
Rock 'n' Roll Graffiti oldies library on compact disc, The Eighties Plus AC/CHR library on compact disc & The Seventies AC/CHR gold library on compact disc. Country music libraries on compact disc. Also available on hard drive. The Seventiesand Eighties Plus (1980-1995) are also available on Flash Drives of via Download with Cart Chunk metadata.

Harmony Gold U.S.A. Inc.
7655 Sunset Blvd., Los Angeles, CA 90046 USA
(323) 851-4900; *Fax:* (323) 851-5599
www.harmonygold.com
sales@harmonygold.com
Frank Agrama, Chairman
Frank Agrama, CEO
Melissa Wohl, General Sales Mgr
TV production, international TV distribution.

Harpo Productions
110 N. Carpenter St., Chicago, IL 60607 USA
(312) 633-1000
www.oprah.com
Produces The Oprah Winfrey Show.

Harvey Sheldon Productions
7855 E. Horizon View Dr., Anaheim Hills, CA 92808 US
(714) 281-5929
www.harveysheldontv.com
harveysheldontv@msn.com
Harvey Sheldon, President/ Founder
Daily or wkly classic rock/swing video format for TV & cable stns. On Century Cable available for syndication serving 150,000 TV/cable households in Los Angeles/Orange county.

HAVE Inc.
350 Power Ave., Hudson, NY 12534-2448 USA
(518) 828-2000,(888) 999-4283; *Fax:* (518) 828-2008
www.haveinc.com
ngordon@haveinc.com
Nancy Gordon, President/ CEO
Nancy Gordon, President
Paul Swedenburg, Operations Dir
Distribution of cable connected products, equipment, accessories & supplies, featuring BELDEN, CANARE, MOGAMI & GEPCO cable. Duplication, video/audio postproduction svcs & CD-Audio & CD-ROM, DVD & Blu-ray replication & duplication, DVD &Blu-ray authoring. Digital Archiving & file delivery & order fulfillment svcs.
HAVE, Inc.
Lancaster, CA 93536
phone 661-722-2957
email dherrera@haveinc.com

Hearst Entertainment, Inc.
300 W. 57th St., 15th Fl., New York, NY 10019 USA
(212) 969-7553; *Fax:* (646) 280-1553
www.hearstent.com
Bruce Paisner, President
Stacey Valenza, Senior VP Sales & Marketing
Nadine Rahiman, Assistant to SVP, Sales & Marketing
Michael Hausman, VP Technical Operations
Rob Angel, SVP, Business Development
Leading producer & distributor of made-for-television movies, first-run entertainment, animated series, reality & documentary progmg for the global marketplace.

Hearts of Space Inc.
454 Las Gallinas, #333, San Rafael, CA 94903 USA
(415) 499-9901; *Fax:* (415) 499-9903
www.hos.com
Stephen Hill, President/ Producer/ Art Director
Leyla Rael Hill, VP,Business Affairs
Joseph Jacobs, Director, Technology & Systems
Steve Davis, Radio Associate Producer
Sheila Gerzoff, Director, Stations Relations & Marketing
Slow Music for Fast Times. Syndicated one-hour progmg of ambient, electronic, multi-cultural & contemplative spacemusic via NPR satellite transmission & by direct subscription online at www.hos.com.

Henninger Media Services, Inc.
2601-A Wilson Blvd., Arlington, VA 22201 USA
(703) 243-3444,(888) 243-3444; *Fax:* (703) 243-5697
www.henninger.com
hmsquotes@henninger.com
Rob Henninger, CEO
TV postproduction, film & video, film processing, 2-D & 3-D graphics, TV progmg dev, distribution; multi-media & DVDs.
Henninger Media Services
1150 17th St, Suite 401, Washington, DC 20036 United States
(202) 833-3444; *Fax:* (202) 833-3995
Robert Anderson, Facility Mgr
Henninger Capitol
2121 Wisconsin Ave. N.W., Washington, DC 20007 United States
(202) 965-7800; *Fax:* (202) 965-7815
Bobby Wright, Gen Mgr
Commonwealth Film Labs
1500 Brook Rd, Richmond, VA 23220 United States
(804) 649-8611; *Fax:* (804) 648-7715
Roger Robison, Gen Mgr
Henninger Elite
Metro Center 50 Vantage Way, Suite 100, Nashville, TN 37228 United States
(615) 256-7678; *Fax:* (615) 255-7212
Roy Giorgio, Gen Mgr
Henninger Richmond
1901 E. Franklin St, Suite 103, Richmond, VA 23223 United States
(804) 644-5006; *Fax:* (804) 783-0820
Scott Witthaus, Gen Mgr

The History Makers
1900 S. Michigan Ave., Chicago, IL 60616 USA
(312) 674-1900; *Fax:* (312) 674-1915
www.thehistorymakers.com
Esther Franklin, Chair
Zhu Sun, Vice President, Business & Operations
Paul Mackey, Production Manager
Larry Crowe, Producer/Interviewer
Matthew Hickey, Videographer

Adam Manta, Researcher
Wade Ekstrom, Scheduler
Video production.

HIT Entertainment P.L.C.
Div/DBA: (Mattel)
Mailing Address: Maple House, 5th Floor, 149 Tottenham Court Rd., London, W1T 7NF GBR
Second Address: 675 Avenue of the Americas, 3rd Floor, New York, NY 10010
44 207 554 2500; *Fax:* (207) 388-9321
www.hitentertainment.com
contactus@hitentertainment.com
Catherine Balsam-Schwaber, Chief Content Officer
Distributor, co-producer & financier of quality animiation, children's & natural history progmg.
9300 Wilshire Blvd., 2nd Fl., Beverly Hills, CA 90212 United States
(301) 724-8979
830 Greenville Ave., Allen, TX 7500-3320 United States
(972) 390-6000

Home Improvement Television Network
Div/DBA: Lamb Production
3441 Baker Street, San Diego, CA 92117
(858) 273-0572; *Fax:* (858) 273-8410
www.hometvnet.com
homefix@hometvnet.com
Bruce Lamb, President
Providers of home improvement progmg & 90-second video vignettes.

Hometown Illinois Radio Network
Box 169, 918 E. Park, Taylorville, IL 62568-0169 USA
(217) 824-3395; *Fax:* (217) 824-3301
www.hometownillinoisradio.com
Randal Miller, President
Wired network providing loc reports & podcasts from Illinois State Fair, Illinois Farm Bureau Convention, Commodity Classic & Farm Progress Show.

Hope Channel
12501 Old Columbia Pike, Silver Spring, MD 20904 USA
(301) 680-6689, (888) 446-7388; *Fax:* (301) 680-6312
www.hopetv.org
info@hopetv.org
Gary Gibbs, Operations Dir
Brad Thorp, General Manager
Family friendly TV progmg, 24/7.

Horizons Television Inc.
9305 Monalaine Ct., Great Falls, VA 22066 USA
(703) 759-7500; *Fax:* (703) 759-1620
www.horizonstv.com
Leesa Kelly, President
Timothy Donner, Station Manager
Tim Donner, Executive Director
Leesa Kelly, Creative Director
Creative dev & full-svc production of reality-based TV programs & commissioned videos for diverse major & community-based organizations & assns. Avid media composer.

Huntridge Video Productions Inc.
Box 3813, Greenville, SC 29608 USA
(864) 271-3348; *Fax:* (864) 232-4462
www.huntridge.com
info@huntridge.com
TV production & postproduction.

iHeartMedia and Entertainment Inc.
200 E. Basse Rd., San Antonio, TX 78209 USA
(210) 822-2828
www.iheartmedia.com
Bob Pittman, Chairman & CEO
Richard J. Bressler, President & Chief Operating Officer
Wendy Goldberg, EVP & Chief Communications Officer
Robert H. Walls, Jr., EVP & General Counsel
Gayle Troberman, EVP & Chief Marketing Officer
Scott Wells, CEO, Clear Channel Outdoor
William Eccleshare, Chairman & CEO, Clear Channel International
Steven Cutler, EVP of Business Development & Corporate Strategy
State radio networking, collegiate radio & TV networking.

The Image Generators
18156 Darnell Dr., Olney, MD 20832 USA
(301) 924-5700; *Fax:* (301) 570-8916
www.imagegenerators.com
Michael Weiner, President/CEO
Howard Glassroth, Senior Consultant
Jack Palmer, Senior Consultant
Bill Holleran, Senior Consultant
Ann Quarzo, Senior Consultant
Jeff Porro, Senior Consultant
Voice-overs, radio spot & program production; media training, progmg concept to completion; ISDN-equipped (TELOS).

Imagers Inc.
1575 Northside Drive, Building 400, Suite 490, Atlanta, GA 30318-5411 USA
(404) 351-5800, (800) 232-5411; *Fax:* (404) 351-9020
www.imagers.com
Joe Edwards, Vice President for Sales
TV coml production & distribution; production svcs.

IMG College
540 North Trade Street, Winston-Salem, NC 27101 US
(336) 831-0700; *Fax:* (914) 334-9529
www.imgcollege.com
andrew.giangola@img.com
Tony Crispino, Senior Vice President/COO
Ben C. Sutton Jr., Chairman & President
Lou Doherty, SVP/General & Managing Counsel
Joe Weatherly, Vice President, Chief Financial Officer
Roger VanDerSnick, SVP, Chief Sales & MarketingOfficer
Mark Dyer, Senior Vice President, Chief Innovation Officer
Andrew Giangola, Vice President, Strategic Communications
Rick Barakat, VP,Sales Strategy & Operations
Matthew Carlomagno, Vice President, Human Resources
TV & radio production & syndication.

Impressions Media Group
Div/DBA: (formerly Video Enterprises Inc)
575 29th St., Manhattan Beach, CA 90266-3430 USA
(310) 220-0559
www.impressionsmediagroup.com
Heidi Lane-Ambrose, President
Natl placement of ten-second promotional spots on game shows, talk, var & sports programs.

In-Motion Pictures
5 Percy St., London, AL W1T 1DG GBR
(213) 232-9759; *Fax:* (207) 467-6890
www.inmotionpix.com
Dr. Hilmar Siebert, Chairman
Julian Freeston, CFO
Tom Shell, Director, President of Production
A.J. Draven, President of Development & Finance
Stephanie Lemelin, Actress/ Writer/ Producer
Nick Holmes, Shooter/ Editor/ VFX
RameshThadani, Writer/ Post Production Producer
Film & TV production & distribution.
412 S. Beverly Dr., 5th Fl., Beverly Hills, CA 90212 United States
(301) 789-4500

Independent Edge Films
112 West 6th Avenue, Vancouver, BC V5Y 1K6 USA
(604) 684-2203
www.iedgefilms.com/
Kyle Mann, President
Michael Fox, General Manager
Ind motion picture/TV/web production & distribution.

International Tele-Film
30 Macintosh Boulevard, Unit 7, Vaughan, ON L4K 4P1 Canada
(416) 252-1173; *Fax:* (416) 252-1676
www.itf.ca
Susan Walklate, Business Manager
Teresa Machado, Account Manager
Deb Fawcett, Manager Instructor Led Training
Distributor for documentaries, features, series & specials, in Canada & worldwide.

International Television Broadcasting Inc.
36-01 36th Ave., 2nd Fl., Long Island City, NY 11106 USA
(718) 784-8555; *Fax:* (718) 784-8901
www.itvgold.com
Dr. Sathya Viswanath, President
Full time Indian TV program for cable & bcst TV.

Ion Weather Network
PO Box 1223, Airport Road, Morristown, NJ 07960 USA
(973) 983-8222; *Fax:* (973) 983-1390
www.ionweather.com
sales@ionweather.com
Stephen Pellettiere, President
Stephen Pellettiere Jr., Consultant
Gen weather forecasts, science info.

Irving Productions Inc.
3202 E. 21st Street, Tulsa, OK 74114 USA
(918) 744-1221; *Fax:* (918) 744-1223
www.irvingproductions.com
Dick Schmitz, President
Audio recording & production svcs for all media.

It Is Written Television
Box O, Thousand Oaks, CA 91359 USA
(805) 433-0210; *Fax:* (805) 433-0218
www.itiswritten.com/
iiw@iiw.org
Mark Finley, General Manager
Pastor John Bradshaw, Speaker/Director
Shawn Boonstra, Associate Speaker
TV & radio program production & distribution; internet.

ITV1 Yorkshire (formerly Yorkshire Television)
Television Centre, 104 Kirkstall Rd., Leeds, LS3 IJS GBR
0113-243-8283; *Fax:* 0113-244-5107
www.itvplc.com
Julian Bellamy, Managing Director, ITV Studios
Kevin Lygo, Director of Television
Independent TV program maker & bcstr.

Ivanhoe Broadcast News Inc.
Mailing Address: 2745 W. Fairbanks Ave., Winter Park, FL 32789 USA
Second Address: PO Box 865, Orlando, FL 32802
(407) 740-0789; *Fax:* (407) 740-5320
www.ivanhoe.com
jcherry@ivanhoe.com
Majorie BeKaert Thomas, President/ Publisher
John Cherry, General Sales Mgr
Marsha Hitchcock, News Director
Producer & syndicator of targeted new series. Medical breakthroughs, Inside Science, Prescription Health & Smart Woman.

J. Arnold Productions
Mailing Address: 25 Stanley Avenue, Medford, MA 02155 USA
Second Address: 147 Cove Creek Loop, Mooresville, NC 28117
(704) 663-4444
www.jarnoldproductions.com
Lori@JArnoldProductions.com
James Arnold, President
Lori Arnold, Production Manager
Eric Fisher, Director of Photography
Full-svc on location video production. ENG-EFP crews & Betacam equipment packages.
147 Cove Creek Rd., Charlotte, NC 28117
(704) 663-4444; *Fax:* (704) 663-6696
James Arnold, Pres

JAM Creative Productions Inc.
5454 Parkdale Dr., Dallas, TX 75227-3202 USA
(214) 388-5454; *Fax:* (214) 381-4647
www.jingles.com
Jonathan Wolfert, President
Mary Lyn Wolfert, Operations Dir
Cary Bass, General Sales Mgr
Randy Bell, Sales
Tom Parma, Sales
ID jingle & coml production for radio & TV, custom music & production svcs.

Jameson Broadcast Inc.
1644 Hawthorne St., Sarasota, FL 34239 USA
(941) 906-8800; *Fax:* (941) 906-8801
www.jamesonbroadcast.com
jamie@jamesonbcast.com
Jamie Jameson, President
Trulee Jameson, Operations Dir
Radio program production, syndication & special projects.

Janson Media
88 Semmens Rd., Harrington Park, NJ 07640 USA
(201) 784-8488; *Fax:* (201) 784-3993
www.janson.com
info@janson.com
Stephen Janson, President
Anne Corsak, Vice President of Sales
Zara Janson, Vice-President
Jesse Janson, Director of Acquisitions
Betsy Van Ost, Art Director, Director of Distribution
Anne Corsak, Vice President of Sales
MikeMcdonnough, Publicity Associate
Natasha Kline, Director of Marketing
International TV & video/ DVD program distribution & production; video/DVD publishing.

JC Productions Inc.
49 Park Avenue, Suite PH, New York, NY 10016 USA
(212) 532-2820; *Fax:* (212) 532-2820
www.jc-productions.com

PROGRAMMING & PRODUCTION SERVICES

Joseph Conforti, President
Joe Conforti, General Manager
Joe Conforti, Director
Joan Fennell, Executive Producer
Live action coml production; CD-ROM multimedia production; 3D animation & graphic design.

Jeff Davis Productions Inc.
6166 Mulholland Hwy., Los Angeles, CA 90068 USA
(323) 464-3500; *Fax:* (323) 464-1414
www.jeffdavis.com
jeffdavis@jeffdavis.com
Jeff Davies, CEO
Voiceover, production, TV & radio.

Jim Owens Entertainment
1110 16th Avenue South, Nashville, TN 37212 USA
(615) 256-7700, (859) 492-4867; *Fax:* (615) 242-9735
www.crookandchase.com
jerryfox@aol.com
Jim Owens, President
Jerry Fox, Director of Sales
Jennifer Anderson, Programming Director
Lorianne Crook, Host
Charlie Chase, Host
Radio program production company for syndication. TV production for cable & home video.

Joe Jones Productions
10556 Arnwood Rd., Lake View Terrace, CA 91342 USA
(818) 899-4457; *Fax:* (818) 899-4457
www.joejonesproductions.wordpress.com/
Marion Jones, Operations Dir
Joe Jones, Programming Director
TV, radio coml & program production; jingle production & production svcs.

John Donnelly & Associates
9021 Shaughnessy Street, Vancouver, BC V6P 6R9 USA
(604) 654-2612; *Fax:* (323) 850-5866
www.donnellyevents.com
info@donnellyevents.com
John Donnelly, President
James Cowan, VP of Operations
Sarah Shandl, Artist & Production Manager
Shannon Durrant, Production Manager
Arlene Viccto, Office Manager & Event Supervisor
Mktg & licensing films to pay-TV, network & syndication packages.

John Driscoll Voice Over America
2358 University Ave., Suite 456, San Diego, CA 91614 USA
(888) 373-9849, (888) 766-2049
www.johndriscoll.com
johndriscoll@voiceoveramerica.com
John Moore, CEO
John Driscoll, Founder
Voice Over America, as heard on TNT,VH-1,NBC-TV,FOX-TV ,Spike TV,NBA,NFL,MLB and NHL affiliates. Comcast ,HBO/Cinemax, Global,Corus,Rogers,RTE, CBC, CTV. Direct TV.
Represented by AT&A
(818) 760-6688

John Lemmon Films
1325 Rock Point Rd., Charlotte, NC 28270 USA
(704) 532-1944; *Fax:* (704) 566-1984
www.jlf.com
jlemmon@jlf.com
John Lemmon, President/ Co-Owner
Mike Rosinski, Head Animator/ Co-Owner
Clay, cel & stop-motion animation for TV specials, comls, program openings & on-air IDs.

The Johnson Group
6800 Fleetwood Rd, Suite 100, McLean, VA 22101 USA
(703) 356-4004; *Fax:* (703) 356-6969
www.thejgroup.com
Robert M Johnson, Founder & President
Joe Fab, Operations Dir
Paula Sweeney, Marketing and Development Specialist
Nonie Steele, Accounting Manager
Video, film, multimedia & radio creative svcs & production.

Jordan Klein Film & Video
10197 S.E. 144th Pl., Summerfield, FL 34491 USA
(352) 288-3999, (352) 427-2560; *Fax:* (352) 288-5538
www.jordy.com
jordy@jordy.com
Jordan Klein, President & Owner
Underwater, on-the-water production; rental film, video housing & crews; Bahamas specialist.

Kazmark Entertainment Group
14320 Ventura Blvd., Suite 601, Sherman Oaks, CA 91423 USA
(818) 981-4410; *Fax:* (818) 501-2211
www.kazmarkentertainment.com/
info@kazmarkentertainment.com
Jeffrey Kazmark, President
Progmg distribution.

KCRA-TV
3 Television Cir., Sacramento, CA 95814-0794 USA
(916) 446-3333; *Fax:* (916) 325-3731
www.kcra.com
newstips@kcra.com
Elliott Troshinsky, General Manager
David Bienick, General Assignment Reporter
Brian Hickey, General Assignment Reporter
Claire Doan, General Assignment Reporter
Tom DuHain, General Assignment Reporter
Mallory Hoff, GeneralAssignment Reporter
Kevin Oliver, Journalist
TV program & coml production; production svcs.

KCSN 88.5 FM
18111 Nordhoff Street, Northridge, CA 91330-8312 USA
(818) 677-3090
www.kcsn.org
feedback@kcsn.org
Sky Daniels, General Manager & Program Director
Laura Kelly, General Sales Mgr
Martin Perlich, Programming Director
Keith Goldstein, News Director
Conor S. Watson, Chief Engineer
Yvonne Wolfe, Business Manager
David Kleinbart,Director of Underwriting
Meishel Menachekanian, Director of Broadcast Operations
Mark Shovel, Music Director
Laura Kelly, Director of Membership
Public radio serving parts of Los Angeles, CAclassical weekdays, eclectic weeknights & weekends. PRI, AP affil. The best of public radio.

The Kenwood Group
75 Varney Pl., San Francisco, CA 94107 USA
(415) 957-5333; *Fax:* (415) 957-5311
www.kenwoodgroup.com
info@kenwoodgroup.com
Christina Crowley, CEO
Daniel Pinkham, President/ Senior Creative Director
Nico Van Praag, VicePresident/ Chief Strategy Officer
Wayne Leonard, Vice President, Sr, Account Director
John Emmaneel, Director of Production
GaryGoodman, Business Manager
Melanie Goodwin, Associate Producer
Bill Goodale, Accountant
Creative svcs & production of comls & corporate communications, film, video, multimedia, meetings & events.

Killer Tracks
2110 Colorado Avenue, Suite 110, Santa Monica, CA 90404 USA
(310) 865-4455, (800) 454-5537; *Fax:* (310) 865-4470, (800) 787-2257
www.killertracks.com
Blaine McGovern, Operations Director
Anna Maria Hall, Vice President/Head, Music Licensing
Carl Peel, Vice President/Head, Music Production
Roxanna Brown, Music Director
Ryan Perez-Daple, Executive Producer
Andy Donohue, Directorof Marketing
Jason Bass, Music Licensing Executive
Provides production music library & sound effects.

Kipany Productions Ltd.
32 E. 39th St., New York, NY 10016 USA
(212) 883-8300; *Fax:* (212) 883-0409
www.kipany.com
info@kipany.com
Kip Colligan, Co-Founder & COO
Tiffany Hendry, Co-Founder & President
Michael Rupp, Senior VP, Operations
Andy Weinrich, Executive Vice President
Mario Marin, Senior Vice President, Marketing
Joseph Pennacchio, Chief TechnologyOfficer
Richard Brown, CFO
Video production, bcst progmg, mktg, sls & communications experts/web designers specializing in Telcom, event mgmt.

Knowledge In A Nutshell Inc.
1420 Centre Ave., Suite 2213, Pittsburgh, PA 15219 USA
(800) 688-7435,(412) 765-2020; *Fax:* (412) 765-3672
www.knowledgeinanutshell.com
sales@knowledgeinanutshell.com
Charles Reichblum, President
Syndicates radio/TV program, Knowledge in a Nutshell & Knowledge minute.

KodakFilm Lab Atlanta
2156 Faulkner Rd. N.E., Atlanta, GA 30324 USA
(404) 633-1449,(800) 633-1448; *Fax:* (404) 633-3867
www.kodak.com/us/en/motion/
jeremiah.drueke@kodak.com
Robert Wales, Lab Manager
Jeremiah Drueke, Sales & Booking
16mm, super 16mm, 35mm color negative processing & printing. Dailies thru release prints. State-of-the-art video dailies & scene-to-scene transfers. Spirit Data Cini, all HD Formats

KPTS-TV
320 West 21st St. N., Wichita, KS 67203-2499 USA
(316) 838-3090, (800) 794-8498; *Fax:* (316) 838-8586
www.kpts.org
tv8@kpts.org
Victor A. Hogstrom, President & CEO
Dave McClintock, Operations Dir
Steve Brosius, Community Pledge Coordinator/Producer
Jennifer Keller, Director, Marketing & Promotions
Phil Searle, Production Manager
Jime Grawe, ContentProducer
Richard Hess, Continuity Director
Jessica Rye, Broadcast Engineer
Industrial video production for corporate training & mktg communications.

KTOO-TV & Radio Station
360 Egan Drive, Juneau, AK 99801-1748 USA
(907) 586-1670; *Fax:* (907) 586-5692
www.ktoo.org
info@ktoo.org
Bill Legere, President & General Manager
David Waters, Operations Manager
Jeff Brown, Program Director
Tim Olson, Assistant GM, News & Public Affairs
Rich Parker, Director of Engineering
Sarah Schaefer, Development Director
Cheryl Levitt Snyder, Assistant GM for Arts & Culture
Jeremy Hsieh, News Director
Tripp Crouse, Digital Media Editor, Breaking News
David Jackson, Information Technology Manager
A radio program highlighting diversified music & stories for children.

Kultur International Films
PO Box 755, Forked River, NJ 08731 USA
(732) 229-2343, (888) 329-2580; *Fax:* (732) 229-0066
www.kulturvideo.com
info@kultur.com
Dennis M. Hedlund, Chairman
Pearl Lee, Operations Dir
Ronald Davis, General Manager
Suppliers of programs on DVD in North America. Selection includes documentaries, opera, ballet, classical music, profiles, theater, comedy, fitness, country music, rock & roll.

Lagardere Studios
7 rue du Dome, 92100 Boulogne Billancourt FRA
(33) 1 40 74 76 76; *Fax:* (33) 1 55 95 58 10
www.lagardere-studiosdistribution.com
Emmanuelle Bouilhaguet, Managing Director
Randall Broman, Senior Vice President
Catherine Couriat, Senior VP Sales & Acquisitions
Acquires, distributes & invests in international TV progmg. Catalog close to 5 hours broken into three categories, drama, children's documentaries.

Lambert Television
Div/DBA: Lambert Media Group
100 N. Crescent Drive, Suite 250, Beverly Hills, CA 90210 USA
(310) 385-4288; *Fax:* (310) 385-4004
www.lamberttv.com
Michael Lambert, Founder
Sam Altman, Managing Director
Taylor Rothchild, Director
Lambert Television owns and operates a television station group.

Lapco Communications
437 E. Beil Ave., Nazareth, PA 18064 USA
(610) 759-9444; *Fax:* (610) 759-8589
www.lapcocom.com
sales@lapcocom.com
P. Pagilaro, President
L. Van Winkle, Operations Dir

TV progmg & production, computer graphics, producers of original progmg, TV comls, TV promotion production, production mgmt, computer stock background library.

Larry Harmon Pictures Corp.
7080 Hollywood Blvd., Suite 202, Hollywood, CA 90028 USA
(818) 223-0230; *Fax:* (818) 223-0233
www.bozo.com
tellbozo@aol.com
Marci Breth, Operations Dir
Susan Harmon, Executive Vice President
Owner & distributor of Bozo cartoons & live show franchise, & Laurel & Hardy cartoons.

Larry John Wright Inc.
231 N. Alma School Road, Mesa, AZ 85201 USA
(480) 833-8111, (800) 821-5068; *Fax:* (480) 464-3032
www.larryjohnwright.com
jackson@larryjohnwright.com
JR Wright, CFO & Executive Director of Operations
Larry John, Co-Founder/Owner
John Wright, Co-Founder/Owner
Jackson Wright, Executive Director of New Account Sales
Jessica Stillwell, Executive Director of Media
Sam John, ExecutiveDirector of Account Services
Dave John, Creative Director
Own & operate production studios; produce film & video comls, radio comls & jingles, TV shows & industrial videos.

Lasgo Worldwide Media
Unit 1 Falcon Park, Neasden Lane, Neasden, London, NW10 1RZ UK
+44 (0)20 8459 8800; *Fax:* 44(0)20 8451 5555
lasgo.com
info@lasgo.com
Garry Elwood, Managing Director
Franco Pasaniti, Commercial Director
Steve Digby, Finance Director
Allan Macaskill, Buying Director
International sale of TV programs to all media worldwide.

LEG
6701 Center Dr. W., Suite 300, Los Angeles, CA 90045 USA
(310) 417-4800; *Fax:* (310) 410-1542
www.leg-corp.com/
info@leg-corp.com
Irving Azoff, Chairman
Robert Hartmann, CEO
Stu Schreiberg, COO
Judy Marmel, EVP, Management
Stephen Kroopnick, EVP, Production
Neil Sheridan, VP, Comedy Production & Distribution
Independent, full-svc production company with extensive experience in the production of TV & film; post-production facilities & motion control/graphics department.

Leo Productions
1 Rond Point Victor Hugo, 92130-Issy-Les-Moulineaux, FRA
(331) 55 95 57 00; *Fax:* (331) 55 95 57 01
www.leoproductions.com
info@leoproductions.com
Jean-Louis Brugat, General Manager
TV production, progmg consultants, live bcsts.

Leukemia & Lymphoma Society
3 International Drive, Suite 200, Rye Brook, NY 10573 USA
(914) 949-5213; *Fax:* (914) 949-6691
www.lls.org
Louis J. DeGennaro, Ph.D, President & CEO
Ingo Gefeke, COO
Andrew Coccari, Chief Product Officer
Danielle Gee, Chief of Staff
Marcie Klein, Chief Communications Officer
Aile Rodd O'Rourke, Chief Development Officer
Gwen Nichols,MD, Chief Medical Officer
Andrea Greif, Senior Director, Communications
Produces & distributes educational ideas to inform & educate viewers about leukemia & related diseases & available treatment.

Level 3 Communications, LLC
1025 Eldorado Boulevard, Broomfield, CO 80021 USA
720-888-2750, 855-381-0402; *Fax:* (918) 547-2989
www.level3.com/
Jeff Storey, President & CEO
Derek Smith, Operations Dir
Tiffany Thoms Osias, General Manager
Sunit Patel, Executive Vice President & Chief Financial Officer
Anthony Christie, Chief Marketing Officer
Laurinda Pang, RegionalPresident North America & Asia Pacific
Andrew Dugan, Chief Technology Officer
Atilla Tinic, Chief Information Officer
John Ryan, EVP, Chief Legal Officer & Secretary
Distributor of TV comls/traf via satellite by remote VTR control to 600 stns; radio coml distribution; production, postproduction. Multi-format duplication.

Liberty Studios Inc.
9948 Hibert Street, Suite 200, San Diego, CA 92131 USA
(858) 271-0695; *Fax:* (858) 271-0330
www.libertystudiosinc.com/
Mark Schmidt, President & Founder
John Sawyer, Operations Dir
Randy Williams, Producer & Founding Member
TV program, coml, film & video production.

Lifestyle Magazine
PO Box 7729, Riverside, CA 92513 USA
(888) 940-0062, (805) 955-7700; *Fax:* (805) 522-1082
www.lifestyle.org
info@lifestyle.org
Mike Tucker, Executive Producer
Chauncey Smith, Network & Station Director
Monique Roy, Associate Producer
TV program production & distribution.

Lighthouse Productions
1100 Chicago Avenue, Suite 2C, Goshen, IN 46528
(574) 533-1400, (574) 202-5502; *Fax:* (661) 760-8775
www.lighthousephotoandvideo.com/
lighthousevideo@gmail.com
Bill Landow, President
Audio, video full production svc, documentaries, training, audio & video recording svcs.

Lightyear Entertainment L.P.
4011 Alcove Avenue, Studio City, CA 91604 USA
(818) 855-1318; *Fax:* (818) 855-1320
www.lightyear.com
mail@lightyear.com
Arnold Holland, CEO
Sky Spooner, Vice President
TV program production & distribution. Audio & video distribution.

Limelight Communications Inc.
2812 Roesh Way, Vienna, VA 22181 USA
(703) 242-4596, (703) 626-3167; *Fax:* (703) 991-0616
www.limelightdc.com
moreinfo@limelightdc.com
Kenny Reff, President & Executive Producer
Writing, producing & editing svcs for bcst & industrial clients. Available as sub-contractors for specific svcs, or to fully produce complete shows.

Lindberg Productions Inc.
24 Mulford Ave., East Hampton, NY 11937 USA
(212) 599-1239,(917) 696-1826
ctimany@aol.com
Larry Lindberg, President
Erika Shapeero, Programming Director
Video production for business & industry.

Lion and Fox Recording, Inc.
9517 Baltimore Ave., College Park, MD 20740 USA
(301) 982-4431
www.lionfox.com
mail@lionfox.com
James Fox, President
Digital audio production for TV & radio; music & EFX libraries; CD and CD-ROM & cassette duplication; location audio.

Lions Gate Entertainment
2700 Colorado Ave., Suite 200, Santa Monica, CA 90404 USA
(310) 449-9200; *Fax:* (310) 392-0252
www.lionsgate.com/
Jon Feltheimer, Chief Executive Officer
Micheal Burns, Vice Chairman
Steve Beeks, Co-Chief Operating Officer
Brian Goldsmith, Co-Chief Operating Officer
James W. Barge, Chief Financial Officer
Wayne Levin, General Counsel, ChiefStrategic Officer
Peter Wilkes, SVP, Investor Relations & Executive Communications
Domestic & international TV, film, video distribution & adv sls firm. Builds, manages, invests in domestic & foreign bcst networks.

Litton Entertainment
884 Allbritton Blvd., Suite 200, Mount Pleasant, SC 29464 USA
(843) 883-5060; *Fax:* (843) 883-9957
www.litton.tv
sara@litton.tv
Dave Morgan, Chief Executive Officer
Nancy Smeltzer, VP of Operations
Mark Cooper, Director of Sales
Pete Sniderman, Chief Operating Officer
Dan Solomon, Managing Director
Andrew Tew, Business Development Associate
Meg LaVigne,President, Television
Pat Halsey, Account Receivable Manager
Rich Davis, Creative Services/Strategy
TV distribution (TV program sls & mktg).

London Weekend Television International
South Bank TV Ctr., Upper ground, London, SE1 9LT GBR
(020) 7620-1620
www.lwt.co.uk
Steve Morrison, Operations Dir
Charles Allen, General Manager
Bob Buhrman, Corporate Media Department
TV program production & distribution.
500 Fifth Ave, Suite 1710, New York, NY 10110 United States
(212) 682-3055; *Fax:* (212) 869-3693
Ellis Bell, Cpa

Longhorn Radio Network
300 W. DeanÿKeetonÿ(A0704), Austin, TX 78712-1061 USA
(512) 471-1631; *Fax:* (512) 471-3700, (512) 232-5441
www.kut.org
Scott O'Hare, Chair
Stewart Vanderwilt, Director & General Manager
Hawk Mendenhall, Programming Director
Emily Donahue, News Director, Executive Producer
Lynn Meredith, Vice Chair
Rodney Gibbs, Secretary
Matt Largey, NewsEditor
Rhonda Fanning, Producer
Jorge Sanhueza-Lyon, Senior Multimedia Producer
Bob Branson, Host

MacNeil/Lehrer Productions
2700 S. Quincy St., Arlington, VA 22206 USA
(703) 998-2170; *Fax:* (703) 998-5707
www.pbs.org/newshour
Dan Werner, President
David Sit, Operations Dir
Pam Wyatt, General Manager
Susan Mills, Programming Director
Harold Crawford, Controller
Travis Daub, Creative Director
Sara Just, Executive Producer
Gwen Ifill, Co-Anchor &Manging Editor
Judy Woodruff, Co-Anchor & Manging Editor
Fred de Sam Lazaro, Correspondent
Produces news & info programs for public TV & other coml & cable networks. Production of The News Hour with Jim Lehrer.

Madison Square Garden Network
11 Pennsylvania Plaza, 3rd Floor, New York, NY 10001 USA
(212) 465-6741; *Fax:* (212) 465-6024
www.msgnetworks.com
info@msgnetworks.com
James L. Dolan, Executive Chairman
Andrea Greenberg, President & CEO
Neil Davis, General Sales Mgr
Leon Schwier, Programming Director
Adam Levine, EVP, Business Affairs
NY Knicks, NY Rangers & NY Mets, NY MetroStars, NY Power, NY Islanders & NY Liberty; boxing, college football & basketball; exclusive Garden events; original series.

Magno Sound & Video
729 7th Ave., New York, NY 10019 USA
(212) 302-2505; *Fax:* (212) 819-1282
www.magnosound.com
staff@magnosound.com
Robert Friedman, President
David Friedman, Operations Dir
Complete film, TV & radio production & postproduction svcs for agency, feature, network, corporate & industrial clients.

Man From Mars Productions
159 Orange St., Manchester, NH 03104-4217 USA
(603) 668-0652; *Fax:* (603) 666-4878
www.manfrommars.com
brouder@juno.com
Ed Brouder, President
Aircheck sls for radio collectors; coml production.

Manhattan Production Music
1650 Broadway, Suite 900, New York, NY 10019 USA
(212) 333-5766,(800) 227-1954; *Fax:* (212) 262-0814
www.mpmmusic.com
info@mpmmusic.com

PROGRAMMING & PRODUCTION SERVICES

Norman Chesky, President
Five music libraries Apple Trax, Live Trax, MPM, AMM, BRg containing over 450 CDs, including the Audiophile Sound effects series & the Chesky Classical Library.

Mar Vista Entertainment
10277 W. Olympic Boulevard, Los Angeles, CA 90067 USA
(424) 274-3000; *Fax:* (424) 274-3050
www.marvista.net/
info@marvista.net
Ferdando Szew, Chief Executive Officer
George Port, President
Susan Young, Chief Financial Officer
Peggy Lisberger, SVP, Business Affairs
Venessa Shapiro, EVP, Distribution
Stephanie Slack, SVP, Acquisitions & Co-Productions
Sharon Bordas, EVP, Development and Production
Robyn Snyder, EVP Production & Development
Domestic & international distribution of children's animation & live action features & series, films & documentaries.
310 Grant Street, Suite 711, Pittsburgh, PA 15219

Marathon International
115-123 Avenue Charles de Gaulle, Neuilly-sur-Seine, Fr 92200
331-53-1091-00; *Fax:* 331-53-1091-49ÿ
marathon@marathon.fr
Philippe Alessandri, CEO
Yann Chassard, Producer
Jerome Vignac, Producer
Aude Albano, Development and Production Manager
Val,rie Tailland, Head of communication
Distributor of TV programs worldwide; series, documentaries, animation, wildlife, TV movies.

Maryknoll Productions
75 Ryder Rd., Maryknoll, NY 10545-0308 USA
Fax: (914) 762-6567
nkeel@maryknoll.com
Lawrence M. Rich, Programming Director
Offers a library of video & film productions featuring Third World countries; radio & TV programs also available.

Maryland Public Television
11767 Owings Mills Blvd., Owings Mills, MD 21117 USA
(410) 356-5600, (800) 223-3678; *Fax:* (410) 581-4338
www.mpt.org
comments@mpt.org
Robert Shuman, CEO
Larry D. Unger, President/ Chief Executive Officer
Eric Eggleton, Operations Dir
Martin G. Jacobs, Vice President, Chief Financial Officer
Colette Colclough, Vice President, Human Resources
George R. Beneman II,Vice President, Chief Technology Officer
Gail Porter Long, Senior Vice President, Chief Education Officer
Steven J. Schupak, Senior Vice President, Chief Content Officer
Andrew H. Levine, General Counsel
TV program production & distribution.

Maslow Media Group Inc.
2233 Wisconsin Ave. N.W., Suite 400, Washington, DC 20007-4104 USA
(202) 965-1100; *Fax:* (202) 965-6172
www.maslowmedia.com
sales@maslowmedia.com
Linda Maslow, Chief Executive Officer/ Founder
Harry Gorman, Chief Financial Officer
Mary Jane Boyle, Production Manager
Joan Fiddle-Ferder, Supervising Producer/Creative Division
Katy Maslow, Director, Online Services
DewieOppenheimer, Accounting Manager
Linda Bedell, Payroll Manager / Benefits Administrator
Video production, production support svcs, staffing (freelance & fulltime), factors, creative & tech people, camera crews anywhere in the world, cable, film, multimedia, animators, payroll & paymaster svcs nationwide for bcst studio, field &new media.

Mason Video
9632 N. 34th St., Omaha, NE 68112 USA
(402) 455-9422, (405) 680-5802; *Fax:* (402) 455-0707
www.masonvideo.com
MTMason@gmail.com
Mele Mason, President
Offers bcst video productions. Equipment includes Ikigami HLV55 Betacam, DVcam & HDV.

Maximum Marketing Services Inc.
833 West Jackson, Chicago, IL 60607 USA
(312) 226-4111; *Fax:* (312) 226-5765
www.maxmarketing.com
contact@maximummarketing.biz
John McGowan, President
TV & radio program, production & distribution; public relation services.

Maynard & Associates
1790 Bayshore Drive, Vancouver, BC V6G 3G5 Canada
604-331-0690
www.fmaynard.com
info@fmaynard.com
Jakob Nortman, President
Radio & TV engrg svcs & applications.

Maysles Films, Inc.
343 Lenox Avenue, New York, NY 10027 USA
(212) 582-6050; *Fax:* (212) 586-2057
www.mayslesfilms.com
info@mayslesfilms.com
Albert Maysles, President & Founder
Full production svcs for theatrical & TV non-fiction films; adv comls; industrial films, including pre- & postproduction.

Media Access Group at WGBH
One Guest St., Boston, MA 02135 USA
(617) 300-5400; *Fax:* (617) 300-1020
access.wgbh.org
access@wgbh.org
Richard M. Burnes, Jr., Chairman
Benjamin Godley, COO/EVP
Jonathan C. Abbott, President & CEO
Larry Goldberg, General Manager
John Bredar, Vice President for National Programming
Vinay Mehra, CFO, VP for Finance &Administration
David Bernstein, Vice President & General Manager
Stacey Decker, Chief Technology Officer
Jeanne M. Hopkins, VP, Communications & Government Relations
Susan L. Kantrowitz, Vice President & General Counsel
Liz Cheng, GeneralManager for Television
Provides real-time & off-line captioning, subtitling, descriptive narration & consulting.
Media Access Group West
300 E. Magnolia Blvd., 2nd Fl., Burbank, CA 91502 United States
(818) 562-3344

Media Planning Group (MPG)
195 Broadway, 12th Fl., New York, NY 10007 USA
(646) 587-5000; *Fax:* (646) 587-5005
Bob Riordan, General Manager
Producers, distributors & TV program packagers; videocassette producer/distributor. Full svc media buying & planning company.

Media Visions
424 W. 33rd St, St. 480, New York, NY 10001 USA
(877) 746-8375, (415) 391-9090; *Fax:* (415) 391-9192
www.media-vision.com/
info@media-vision.com
Fardad Zabetian, Chief Executive Officer
Kevin Stoner, Director of Operations
David Dunn, Sales Manager- Canada
Kyle Arizabal, Product Engineer
Ali Zabetian, Chief Financial Officer
Annabelle Gazzo, Director of Marketing
ZoeFournier, Marketing Manager
Oliver Blain, Product Manager
Patrick Herlihy, Director of Sales, North America
Alissa Massey, Customer Support Manager
Provides full-svc video duplication, packaging, warehousing & complete order fulfillment. CD, DVD.

Medialink
1155 Avenue of the Americas, 8th Floor, New York, NY 10036 USA
(646) 259-3001; *Fax:* (646) 259-3012
www.medialink.com
info@medialink.com, press@medialink.com
Michael E. Kassan, Chairman & CEO
Wenda Harris Millard, Vice Chairman
Dana Anderson, Chief Marketing Officer
Glenn Briffa, Executive VP
Angelo Dagostino, Head of Human Resources
Video & audio news release distributor & producer to TV & radio stns throughout the United States & Europe.

MediaTracks Communications
2250 E. Devon Ave., Suite 150, Des Plaines, IL 60018 USA
(847) 299-9500; *Fax:* (847) 299-9501
www.mediatracks.com
info@mediatracks.com
Shel Lustig, President
Erin Fleming, Director of Operations
Kim Sawyer, Sales Manager
Reed Pence, Vice President
Pat Reuter, Executive Producer
Sean Waldron, Production Director
Polly Hansen, Producer
Nancy Benson, Radio HealthJournal Host
Nick Hofstra, Audio Engineer
Produce, syndicate & distribute radio progmg, news, comls & PSAs. Specialists in health & medicine, news & pub affrs.

Megatrax Production Music Inc.
7629 Fulton Ave., North Hollywood, CA 91605 USA
(818) 255-7100,(888) 634-2555; *Fax:* (818) 255-7199
www.megatrax.com
Ron Mendelsohn, President, CEO & Executive Producer
Ron Mendelsohn, President, CEO & Executive Producer
Scott Linn, Office Manager
Philip Macko, Senior VP of Sales
JC Dwyer, CCO and Executive Producer
Steven Naugle, CFO
LeisaKorn, Vice President of Business Affairs
Marcia Kellogg, Associate Marketing Manager
Production music for bcst promotion & adv. Custom scoring & news music packages available.

Message on Hold
315 Arbor Ridge Ln, Conroe, TX 77384 USA
(800) 392-4664; *Fax:* (208) 978-9221
www.messageonholdservice.com/
J. Ellis Molton, President
Randy Molton, Operations Dir
Producers of high-quality comls for telephone hold lines. Specializing in automotive, financial, medical & pharmacies.

Metro Music Productions Inc.
155 S. Saint Andrew St., Dothan, AL 36301 USA
(334) 792-0883; *Fax:* (212) 229-9063
www.metromusicinc.com
greg@metromusicinc.net
Mitch Coodley, President
Katrina Haskell, General Manager
Original music scoring for TV progmg, prom, news, sports, comls. Production music library geared toward bcst.

Metro Weather Service Inc.
PO Box 255, Orangeburg, NY 10962 USA
(516) 568-8844,(800) 488-7866; *Fax:* (516) 568-8845
www.metroweather.com/
Contact@MetroWeather.com
Pat Pagano, President & Founder
Mike Merin, Senior Meteorologist & IT Worker
Don McGrath, Meteorologist
Provides accurate & understandable weather forecasts. Serves any part of the nation; live consultations.

MGC The Multimedia Group of Canada
415-A Mount Pleasant, Montreal Westmount, QC H3Y 3G9 Canada
(514) 844-3636; *Fax:* (514) 844-4990
mgc@the-mgc.com
Jacques Bouchard, CEO
David Seeler, General Sales Mgr
Roselyne Brovillet, Sales
Participates in the dev & distribution of progmg in the intl mkt.

MGM Studios Inc.
245 N Beverly Drive, Beverly Hills, CA 90210 USA
(310) 449-3000; *Fax:* (310) 264-1244
www.mgm.com
Gary Barber, Chairman & CEO
Ken Schapiro, COO
Jonathan Glickman, President, Motion Picture Group
Roma Khanna, President, Television Group and Digital
Dene B. Stratton, Chief Financial Officer
TV program distribution.

MGM TV Canada
20 Queen St. West #3500, Toronto, ON H5H 3R3 Canada
(416) 260-9680; *Fax:* (416) 260-9993
www.mgm.com
Gary Barber, Chairman & CEO
Ken Schapiro, COO
Jonathan Glickman, President, Motion Picture Group
Film distribution for all UA, Polygram & Orion film library (features, series & animated).

Miller Broadcast Management
616 W. Fulton St., Suite 516, Chicago, IL 60661 USA

(312) 454-1111; *Fax:* (312) 454-0044
www.millerbroadcast.com
info@millerbroadcast.com
Lisa Miller, President
Matt Miller, Vice President
Produces & syndicates natl progmg including KidsRadio.

The Miss Universe Organization
1370 Avenue of the Americas, 16th Floor, New York, NY 10019 USA
(212) 373-4999; *Fax:* (818) 972-9001
www.missuniverse.com
Paula M. Shugart, President
Tony Santomauro, Operations Dir
Larry Parra, VP of Fianance/ CFO
Andrea Chafouleas, Manager, Talent Development
Nicole Burke, Marketing Manager
Sam Alhante, Marketing Coordinator
Rachel Frimer, VicePresident, Production
Dara Busch, EVP, Managing Director
TV program production.

Mobile Video Services Ltd.
1620 I St. N.W., Washington, DC 20006 USA
(202) 331-8882; *Fax:* (202) 331-9064
www.mobilevideo.net
bookfeed@mobilevideo.net
Lawrence VanderVeen, President
Christine Baber, Operations Dir
Bcst production svcs, best Official Washington, live shot, remote crews, studio svcs, editing, graphics suites, satellite & fiber transmission svcs.

Modern Entertainment
Box 8075, Van Nuys, CA 91409-8075 USA
(231) 638-2032, (231) 215-3242; *Fax:* (231) 215-3242
www.modern-entertainment.com/
Michael Weiser, CEO
Allyson Hall, Operations Dir
Ken Du Bow, General Sales Mgr
Distribution of movies world wide, CD, DVD.

Modern Sound Pictures Inc.
1402 Howard St., Omaha, NE 68102 USA
(800) 228-9584; *Fax:* (402) 341-8487
www.modernsoundpictures.com
Sandra L. Smith, President
Non-theatrical 16mm film, video rental library & retail audiovisual equipment for rental & sls.

Mondo TV
Via G. Gatti 8/A, 00162 Rome, ITA
39 - 0774/573145-46; *Fax:* 39 - 0774/360029
www.mondotv.it/
mondotv@mondotv.it
Orlando Corradi, CEO
Gian Claudio Galatoli, General Manager
Roberto Farina, Head of International Sales
Animated TV series.

Montgomery Community Television Inc.
7548 Standish Pl., Rockville, MD 20855 USA
(301) 424-1730; *Fax:* (301) 294-7476
www.mymcmedia.org/
Nancy Poole, President
Stuart Garfinkle, Programming Manager
Don Katzen, Promotions Manager
Paul Silverman, Vice President
Merlyn Reineke, Executive Director
Debbie Billings, Director of Administration & Human Resources
TonyZucconi, Executive Producer & Production Manager
Tony Spearman-Leach, Communications & Development Director
Sonya Burke, Multimedia Manager/Producer
Full-svc video production & postproduction, 2,400 sq ft. studio including complete control room, GVG200 switcher, DVE, on- & off-line editing. Also, opn of two cable chs reaching 220,000 subs.

Moonstone Entertainment
PO Box 1599, Studio City, CA 91614-0599 USA
(818) 985-3003; *Fax:* (818) 985-3009
www.moonstonefilms.com
Ernst 'Etchie' Stroh, CEO
Yael Stroh, President
Shahar Stroh, Director Development & Acquisitions
Greg Majerus, Vice President of Finance
Luz Moretti, Executive Vice President
Michael Grant, Director Prod & Mark/ Int Sales &Distribution
International distribution and production.

MotorNet
57-7 Bridgewaters Drive, Oceanport, NJ 07757-1154 USA
(732) 935-1017; *Fax:* (866) 375-7497
www.motorsportsreport.com
motornet@exit109.com
Charlie Roberts, President
Ken Stout, Programming Director
Jack Schultz, Promotions Manager
Radio program production & distribution.

Mountain News Corporation
Div/DBA: (OnTheSnow)
PO Box 17895, Boulder, CO 80308 USA
(720) 887-7720, (720) 887-7727, (720) 887-7725; *Fax:* (720) 887-7730
www.mountainnews.com
info@mountainnews.com
Chad Dyer, Global Managing Director & COO
Produce & package outdoor recreation reports of 30, 60 & 90-seconds in length. Also deliver ski reports via phone, computer, facsimilie for on-air, phone lines & web sites.
Eastern Bureau
(800) 736-0370

MRN Radio
555 MRN Drive, Concord, NC 28027 USA
(704) 262-6700; *Fax:* (704) 262-6811
www.mrn.com/
David Hyatt, President
Frank Beers, Director of Operations
Steve Harrison, General Sales Mgr
Bob Wolfe, Engineer
Doug Watson, Engineer
Sharon Griffin, Executive Assistant
Stephanie Ellis, Traffic Manager
Chris McKee, Directorof Business Development
Tony Rizzuti, Director of New Media
Brian Nelson, Producer
Steve Tate, Senior Manager, Radio Partnerships
Live coverage of NASCAR stock car racing plus NASCAR LIVE wkly telephone talk, NASCAR Today daily news program, via satellite.

MSE
540 Toby Hill Rd., Westbrook, CT 06498 USA
(860) 399-0191; *Fax:* (860) 399-0196
www.mseusa.com
Marcia Simon, President & Founder
Alix Boyle, Writer, Media Relations
Christine Dunster, RN, MA, Writer, Preventive Health
Marcia Simon, APR, Strategist & Team Leader
Short form programs: Health/Medical, Green/Eco-Friendly, podcast production

Munhwa Broadcasting Corp. (MBC)
National Press Bldg., Suite 1131, Washington, DC 20045 USA
(202) 347-0078; *Fax:* (202) 347-0079
www.imbc.com
Ki-Young, Ohm, President & CEO
Chang-Young Choi, Station Manager
Se-Young Kim, Vice President
Seung-Han Kim, Auditor
Jae-Kap Lee, Executive Managing Director, Programming
Jeong-Soo Kim, Executive Managing Director, Radio
Jae-JongSong, Executive Managing Director, News & Sports
Young-Geun Choi, Executive Managing Director, TV Production
Korean natl TV net news.

Musical Starstreams
Box 12685, La Jolla, CA 92039-2685 USA
(619) 276-8989
www.starstreams.com
info@starstreams.com
Madison Cole, Host
Two-hour wkly or nightly syndicated exotic electronica music progmg also available as a full-time format; radio adv production.

Musivision Inc.
8 Deepwood Road, Weston, CT 06883 USA
(917) 601-2922
www.musivision.com/
alisa@musivision.com
Alisa Cohen, Executive Producer
Fred Kessler, Founding Partner & Editor/VFX

Muzak
3318 Lakemont Blvd., Fort Mill, SC 29708 USA
(803) 396-3000,(800) 331-3340; *Fax:* (803) 396-3136
www.muzak.com
info@moodmedia.com
Steve Richards, President & CEO
Tom Garrett, Executive Vice President & Chief Financial Officer
Jim McFelea, Executive Vice President, Global Operations
David Van Epps, Global Chief Product Officer/ EVP of Local Sales
RandalRudniski, EVP, Investor Relations & Cororate Development
John Miceli, President of Technomedia
CFO-North America
Bcsts 60 chs of business mus, adv parting audio messages, ZNET data bcstg & video via direct bcst satellite.

Myriad Pictures
3015 Main Street, Suite 400, Santa Monica, CA 90405 USA
(310) 279-4000; *Fax:* (310) 279-4001
www.myriadpictures.com
info@myriadpictures.com
Kirk D'Amico, President & Chief Executive Officer
Mark Padilla, VP, Sales & Distribution
Kevin Forester, Chief Financial Officer
Audrey Delaney, SVP, Marketing & Acquisitions
Thomas Loftus, SVP, Business Affairs & General Counsel
Christins Freberg, Executive Assistant to the President
Emily White, Director, Business Affairs & Sales Admin
Jason Weiss, SVP, Production
An ind TV co-production & distribution company specializing in music series, features, documentaries & drama for the international market.

N W Media
2117 NE Oregon Street, #702, Portland, OR 97232 USA
(503) 223-5010; *Fax:* (503) 223-4737
www.nwmedia.com
jeannea@nwmedia.com
Jeanne Alldredge, President
Mitchell Harris, General Sales Mgr
Audio/videotape duplication; CD/DVD Duplication, multimedia authoring, graphic design, mastering svcs & messaging.

NAHB Production Group
1201 15th St. N.W., Washington, DC 20005 USA
(202) 266-8090; *Fax:* (202) 266-8054
www.nahbprods.com/
Cary Goldweber, Programming Director
Complete video production/editing facility with large stock library. Productions include Scripps/DIY series, webisodes, political spots, PSA, & instructional/marketing programs.

National Collegiate Athletic Association (NCAA)
700 W. Washington Street, PO Box 6222, Indianapolis, IN 46206-6222 USA
(317) 917-6222; *Fax:* (317) 917-6888
www.NCAA.com
Mark Emmert, President
Greg Weitekamp, Programming Director
Chris Fitzpatrick, Chief Engineer
Televise and produce selected NCAA championships. Manage TV programming and production, including broadcast rights, for all 88 NCAA championships.

National Council of Churches Communications Unit
110 Maryland Avenue NE, Suite 108, Washington, DC 20002-5603 USA
(202) 544-2350; *Fax:* (202) 543-1297
www.nationalcouncilofchurches.us/
info@nationalcouncilofchurches.us
Rev. A. Roy Medley, Chair
Jim Winkler, General Secretary and President
Elspeth Cavert, Operations Manager/Executive Assistant
Carol Fouke, General Manager
Shirley Struchen, Programming Director
Wesley Pettillo, PromotionsManager
Rev. Dr. Sharon E. Watkins, Vice Chair
Bishop W. Darrin Moore, Treasurer
Rev. Geoffrey A. Black, Secretary
Dr. Joseph Crockett, Associate General Secretary
Dr. Tony Kireopoulos, Associate General Secretary
Philip E. Jenks,Information and Press Contact
Bcst production, distribution & assistance to reporters, networks, stns; prepared radio reports & actualities without charge from bcst news professionals.

National Film Board of Canada
PO Box 6100, Station Centre-ville, Montreal, QC H3C 3H5 USA
(800) 267-7710, (514) 283-9000; *Fax:* (212) 629-8502
www.nfb.ca
newyork@nfb.ca
Christina Rogers, Promotions Manager
TV program distribution.

National Public Radio
1111 North Capitol Street, NE, Washington, DC 20002 USA
(202) 513-2000; *Fax:* (513) 414-3329
www.npr.org
Howard Wollner, Chair
Jarl Mohn, President & CEO
Keith Woods, VP, Diversity in News & Operations
Barbara Hall, General Sales Mgr
Eric Nuzum, Vice President, Programming
Margaret Low Smith, Senior Vice President, News
MikeStarling, Chief Engineer
Zach Brand, Vice President, NPR Digital Media
Michael A. Beach, Vice President, Distribution
Emma Carrasco, Chief Marketing Officer
Deborah A. Cowan, Chief Financial Officer/ Vice President, Finance
Monique Hanson,Chief Development Officer
Robert Kempf, Vice President & General Manager, Digital Servic
Radio program production & distribution.

NBD Television Ltd.
2, Royalty Studios, 105 Lancaster Rd., London, W11 1QF GBR
44 (0) 20 7243 3646; *Fax:* 44 (0) 7243 3656
Nicky Williams, CEO
Andrew Winter, General Sales Mgr
International TV progmg sls distribution.

NCAA
700 W. Washington Street, PO Box 6222, Indianapolis, IN 46206-6222 USA
(317) 917-6222; *Fax:* (317) 917-6888
www.ncaa.org
jrinebold@ncaa.org
Mark Emmert, President
Chris Farrow, General Manager
Ron Schwartz, Director
Frank Rhodes, Manager
Greg Weitekamp, Manager
Jeramy Michiaels, Manager
NCAA championship progmg, distribution & footage requests.
19 West 57th St, New York, NY 10019 United States
(212) 541-8840; *Fax:* (212) 262-4647
Ron Schwartz, Dir Ncaa Tv New Svcs

NDR Media
Rothenbaumchaussee 159+161, Hamburg, 20149 DEU
(040) 44 1920
www.ndrtv.de
Horst Bennit, General Manager
Ulla Lamas-Torres, General Sales Mgr
Hans-Stefan Heyne, Head International A
Distribution of TV plays, dramas, wildlife, educ, children's & documentary programs.

NEP Studios
112 W. 34th Street, 21st Floor, Suite 2110, New York, NY 10120 USA
(212) 548-7727; *Fax:* (212) 355-0523
www.nepinc.com
wsheehy@nepstudios.com
Deb Honkus, Chairman
Kevin Rabbitt, Chief Executive Officer
William Sheehy, Operations Dir
Barry Katz, Senior Vice President/ General Manager
Gerry Delon, Chief Financial Officer
Stephen jenkins, Managing Director
Lynda Wilkes,SVP of Human Resources
George Hoover, CTO
Dean Naccarato, General Counsel
Tom McCracken, Sr. Board Member/ Director, Corporate Development
Shooting stage, Filmor tape, duplication all standards editing & DVD-R duplication.

New City Releasing Inc.
5959 Topanga Canyon Blvd, Suite 255, Woodland Hills, CA 91367 USA
(818) 348-2500; *Fax:* (818) 348-3022
www.newcityreleasing.com
info@newcityreleasing.com
Alan Burnsteen, President
Cathy Goodman-Robbins, Operations Dir
Producer & distributor of motion pictures to cable TV.

New Dimensions Radio
PO Box 7847, Santa Rosa, CA 95407 USA
(707) 468-5215
www.newdimensions.org
info@newdimensions.org
Michael Toms, President/ CEO
Justine Toms, Co-Founder/Managing Producer/ Host
Radio program production & distribution.

New Films International
14320 Ventura Boulevard, Suite 619, Sherman Oaks, CA 91423 USA
(818) 501-2720; *Fax:* (818) 501-2780
www.newfilmsint.com
info@newfilmsint.com
Amy Beecroft, Chief Executive Officer
Nesim Hason, President
Radu Nicolau, Vice President of Sales (Middle East, Asia & Afric
Gozde Sarilar, Chief Operating Officer
Douglas B. Mcclure, Senior Vice President, Legal & BusinessAffairs
Cachita Hynes, Vice President of Digital Distribution
Cigdem Tasgin, Information Services Manager
Eduardo Brandariz, Production Executive
Cetin Ortalan, Studio Manager
U.S.-based distribution company specialized in Romania, Bulgaria, & Turkey.

New Line Television
888 Seventh Ave., 20th Fl., New York, NY 10106 USA
(212) 649-4900; *Fax:* (212) 956-1936
www.warnerbros.com/
Kevin Tsujihara, Chairman and Chief Executive Officer
David Spiegelman, President
Robin Seidner, Operations Dir
Edward A. Romano, Executive Vice President & Chief Financial Officer
Thomas Gewecke, Chief Digital Officer/ EVP, Strategy& BD
Dee Dee Myers, EVP
John Rogovin, Executive Vice President & General Counsel
Richard J. Fox, Executive Vice President, International
Kiko Washington, EVP, Worldwide Human Resources
TV program production & distribution.
116 N. Robetson, Los Angeles, CA 90048 United States

New Visions Syndication Inc.
44895 Hwy. 82, Aspen, CO 81611 USA
(970) 366-2312; *Fax:* (970) 925-9369
www.newvisionssyndication.com
kayla@newvisionssyndication.com
Rodney Jacobs, Co-Partner
James Tusty, Co-Partner
Glenda Summers, Technological Development
Kayla B. Hoffman, Senior Vice President of Syndication
International & domestic syndicator of specials & series; sports, lifestyle & entertainment.

News Broadcast Network
75 Broad Street, 15th Floor, New York, NY 10004 USA
(212) 684-8910, (646)839-5128; *Fax:* (212) 684-9650
www.newsbroadcastnetwork.com
Jill Hill, Chairman
Mike Hill, President
Produce & distribute news & feature material to TV & radio stns.

NFL Films
One Sabol Way, Mt. Laurel, NJ 08054 USA
(856) 222-3500; *Fax:* (856) 638-0754
www.nflfilms.com
Rich Markowitz, Director, Audio Engeineering
Glenn Adamo, VP, Media Operations, NFL
Teleproduction facility: digital editing suites, 16mm & 35mm film processing, film-to-tape transfer, studio & remote production, sound studios, animation & flame.

NHK Japan Broadcasting Corp.
2030 M St. N.W., Suite 706, Washington, DC 20036 USA
(202) 828-5180; *Fax:* (202) 828-4571
www.nhk.or.jp/english/
Kenichiro Hamada, Chairman
Katsuto Momii, President
Ryuichi Teshima, Station Manager
Hiroyuki Tsukada, Executive Director
Hikaru Doumoto, Executive Vice-President
Yuji Itano, Executive Director
Yasuti Hamada, Senior Director
Yukinori klda, Senior Director
Tatsuhiko Inoue, Senior Director
TV & radio program distribution.

Nightingale-Conant Corp.
1400 South Wolf Road, Building 300, Suite 103, Wheeling, IL 60090 USA
(800) 560-6081, (800) 557-1660; *Fax:* (847) 647-7145
www.nightingale.com
Vic Conant, President
Radio program production & distribution.

Nine Network Australia
6255 Sunset Blvd., Suite 1500, Los Angeles, CA 90028 USA
(323) 461-3853; *Fax:* (323) 462-4849
www.channelnine.ninemsn.com.au/
Studio production facility, standard conversion & all format tape facilities.

No Soap Productions
936 Broadway, 4th Fl., New York, NY 10010 USA
(212) 581-5572, (877) NOS-OAP7; *Fax:* (212) 586-0045
www.nosoap.net
dan@nosoap.net
Dan Aron, President
Radio comls, sound design for radio & TV, voicecasting, production studio-digital.

North American Network, Inc.
5335 Wisconsin Ave. NW, #440, Washington, DC 20015 USA
(202) 243-0592; *Fax:* (202) 243-0594
www.radiospace.com/
info@nanradio.com
Thomas Sweeney, President
Tammy Lemley, Operations Dir
Tom Kajubi, Director of Finance and Administration
Full-svc radio P.R. providing progmg, news PSAs, promotional campaigns & sls opportunities to stns nationwide in English & Spanish.

North by Northwest Productions
Mailing Address: 903 W. Broadway Ave., Spokane, WA 99201 USA
Second Address: 601 W. Broad St., Boise, ID 83702
(509) 324-2949, (208) 345-7870; *Fax:* (509) 324-2959, (208) 345-7999
www.nxnw.net
contact@nxnw.net
Dave Tanner, CEO/ Partner
Marc Dahlstrom, President
Randy Kron, Producer/ Partner
Jason Miller, Interactive Director/ Partner
Matt Jaime, Producer/ Partner
Jason Payne, Post Production Suprvisor
Kimberly Hogberg, Producer
JoshSchlake, Producer
High end video & film production; D1/D2 postproduction; Paint/3D animation; sound design/production; HD ediiting.
601 W. Broad St, Boise, ID 83702 United States
(208) 345-7870
Shane Jibben, Opns Mgr

North Shore Productions
205 SE Grand Avenue, Ste 203, Portland, OR 97214 USA
(503) 225-0919; *Fax:* (503) 225-9948
www.northshorepro.com/
info@northshorepro.com
Rory Banyard, Founder
Produces & distributes The Career Clinic & the Successful Farming Radio Magazine, two-minute features with affil sharing natl revenues.

North Star Music
338 Compass Cir., Unit A1, North Kingstown, RI 2852 USA
(401) 886-8888; *Fax:* (401) 886-8886
www.northstarmusic.com
info@northstarmusic.com
Richard Waterman, President
Production, distribution, mktg & promotion of recorded music.

NTN Communications Inc.
2231 Rutherford Rd, Suite 200, Carlsbad, CA 92008 USA
(877) 963-9200, (800) 745-4686; *Fax:* (760) 438-3505
www.ntn.com
Jeff Berg, Chairman & interim CEO
James Frakes, CFO
Mark deGorter, President
Tyrone Lam, President, Buzztime Entertainment
Kendra Berger, CFO
Vladimir Edelman, Chief Product Officer
Barry Chandler, Chief Marketing Officer
KirkNagamine, Chief Revenue Offiver
NTN Communications, Inc., a leading producer & distributor of live interactive TV entertainment, bcsts exciting multi-player games to hospitality venues.

NTV International Corp.
645 Fifth Ave., Suite 303, New York, NY 10022 USA
(212) 660-6900; *Fax:* (212) 660-6998
www.ntvic.com
Jusaburo Hayashi, President

Complete video production & postproduction facility; satellite transmission capabilities worldwide; ENG package international TV coord, program sls & acquisitions.

NYSE Amex
11 Wall St., New York, NY 10005 USA
(212) 656-3000, (866) 873-7422
TV studio location on a trading floor, teleprompters, access to industry analysts, production and postproduction svcs.

OGM Production Music
6464 Sunset Blvd., Suite 770, Hollywood, CA 90028 USA
(323) 461-2701,(888) 359-9465; *Fax:* (323) 461-1543
www.ogmmusic.com
ogmmusic@gmail.com
Ole Georg, President
Video, cable, films, CD-ROM, bcst, multimedia, infomercials, satellite program, interactive TV, electronic publishing, theatrical features.

Omnimusic
52 Main St., Port Washington, NY 11050 USA
(800) 828-6664,(516) 883-0121; *Fax:* (516) 883-0271
www.omnimusic.com
Doug Wood, President & CEO
Shawn Green, VP, Operations & Technology
Dave Hab, VP, Production & Publishing
Patti Wood, Senior VP/Art Director
Christine Frankel, Accounting
Dom Dominick, Business Development
Allison Straub,Business Affairs Manager
Dynamic production music with four great libraries that deliver the sounds you need for maximum impact. Easy search and download on the web 24/7. We are always just a phone call or email away, ready to help you with your music needs.

Oppix Productions Inc
3531 Laurel Leaf Ln, Fairfax, VA 22031 USA
(703)280-8200; *Fax:* (703) 280-9292
www.oppix.com
info@oppix.com
James Oppenheimer, President
Denise Battistone, Operations Manager
David Weiner, Project Manager
Steve Weyrich, Editor
Michael Jennings-Offen, Producer/Editor
Juan Quiroga, Editor/Cameraman
Chris Arnold, Cinematographer
Full-svc video internet, DVD production & post, serving bcst, corporate assns, nonprofit & gov. All formats.

Orange Productions Inc.
523 Righters Ferry Road, 2nd Floor, Bala Cynwyd, PA 19004 USA
(610) 667-8620; *Fax:* (610) 667-8939
www.soundsofsinatra.com
Sid Mark, President
Brian Mark, Operations Dir
Production & distribution of a wkly two-hour program Sounds of Sinatra.

Outdoor Media Group
26602 Avenida Veronica, Mission Viejo, CA 92691 USA
(888) 589-9888, (949) 285-9044; *Fax:* (949) 916-8242
www.theoutdoormediagroup.com/
grant@theoutdoormediagroup.com
Russell Cameron, President
Diane Parterson, Vice President of Operations
Grant Bjorn, Project Manager/ Owner
Dave Boecker, Senior Graphic Artist
Carol Franzen, Accounts Coordinator
Sam Camm, Supervisor
Kevin Perkins, FieldInstallation Supervisor
Jose Rodriguez, Finish Department Technician
TV program, coml production & distribution; production svcs.

P. Allen Smith Gardens
Box 7347, Little Rock, AR 72217 USA
(501) 376-1894; *Fax:* (501) 376-1896
www.pallensmith.com
P. Allen Smith, President
Nationally syndicated gardening & lifestyle news inserts reported by professional garden designer Allen Smith.

PACSAT
1629 S St., Sacramento, CA 95811 USA
(916) 446-7890, (916) 335-1649; *Fax:* (916) 446-7893
www.pacsat.com
pacsat@pacsat.com
Steve Mallory, President
Marcia Calvin, Operations Dir
Video, audio & satellite professionals. Ku-HD satellite trucks. ENG crews. Fly pack with CCU'S. Post production & graphics.

Palace Producers
29 N. Main St., South Norwalk, CT 06854 USA
(203) 523-0602; *Fax:* (203) 855-9608
wendy@palacedigital.com
Chris Campbell, Chairman/ Creative Director
Wendy Lambert, President/Creative Director
Deb Weingrad, Vice President/ Editorial Director
Maureen Connelly, Managing Director
Soundstage w/Cyc; HD Production Services;HD Editorial;Broadcast Design & Animation;Audio Record & Mixing;DVD Authoring & Duplication

Parrot Communications International Inc.
2917 N. Ontario St., Burbank, CA 91504 USA
(818) 567-4700; *Fax:* (818) 567-4600
www.parrotmedia.com
info@parrotmedia.com
Rae Mertz, President
Blanca Pineda-Villanueva, Operations Dir
Karol L. Wagner Loy, Promotions Manager
Database mgmt, direct mail svcs, promotional fulfillment, warehousing, contest fulfillment, bcst faxing, high speed duplication & videotape duplication.

Pathe International
21 rue Francois 1 er, 75008 Paris, FRA
Fax: 33-1-40-76-9169,33-1-40-76-9194
www.pathe.fr
christine.hayet@pathe.com
Eduardo Malone, Chairman
Michel Crepon, COO
Emma Rami, Operations Dir
Production & distribution of TV films & documentaries. Production of multimedia programs.

Paulist Media Works
3055 4th St. N.E., Washington, DC 20017 USA
(202) 269-6064; *Fax:* (202) 269-4304
www.paulist.org/pmw
info@paulist.org
Sue Donovan, President
Support for non-profit organization in internet svcs/website/web design distribution of relg radio programs, video/documentary production

Paulist Productions
Mailing Address: Box 1057, 17575 Pacific Coast Highway, Pacific Palisades, CA 90272-1057 USA
Second Address: 17575 Pacific Coast Highway, Pacific Palisades, CA 90272
(310) 454-0688; *Fax:* (310) 459-6549
www.paulistproductions.org
paulistmail@paulistproductions.org
Eric Andrews, President
Barbara Gangi, Programming Director
Joseph Kim, Executive Vice President
Marybeth Sprows, Vice President, Development & Production
Mark Ortiz, Office Assistant
TV program production.

PBS Video
2100 Crystal Dr., Arlington, VA 22202 USA
(703) 739-5000; *Fax:* (703) 739-8487
www.pbs.org
Barbara Landes, CFO
Paula Kerger, President
John Boland, Programming Director
John McCoskey, Chief Engineer
Wayne Godwin, COO
Katherine Lauderdale, General Counsel
A trusted provider of classroom resources for more that 25 years, PBS Video extends the reach of public TV by distributing meda throughout the United States & Canada, making valuable resources available to educators, librarians & trainersthrough Shop PBS for Teacher.

Peckham Productions
50 S. Buckhout Street, Bedford, NY 10506 USA
(914) 591-4140; *Fax:* (914) 591-4149
www.peckhampix.com
info@peckhampix.com
Peter Peckham, President
Russell Peckham, General Manager
Waldine Peckham, Production Manager
Full-svc film & video producer of TV comls, TV programs & TV net promos.

Perception Media Group
5239 Challedon Drive, Virginia Beach, VA 23462 USA
(757) 270-1281; *Fax:* (540) 563-0117
www.perceptionmediagroup.com/
info@perceptionmediagroup.com
Ben Peyton, President
TV & radio coml program production, distribution & jingles. Religious programs & distribution.

PETER RODGERS ORGANIZATION
PO Box 2110, Hollywood, CA 90078 USA
(323) 962-1778; *Fax:* (323) 962-7174
www.profilms.com
info@profilms.com
Stephen Rodgers, Chief Executive Officer
Ron Adler, Director of Operations
Ron Adler, Chief Engineer
Arny Schorr, Vice President of Digital Entertainment
Pavel Miller, Primary Accountant/ Bookkeeper
Consultants, Distributors, Reps. Celebrating over 35 years representing productions, companies & independent producers with over 2,000 hours of progmg .

Philadelphia Flyers Hockey Club
3601 S. Broad St., Philadelphia, PA 19148 USA
(215) 465-4500; *Fax:* (215) 952-4103
www.philadelphiaflyers.com
Ed Snider, Chairman/ Founder/ Governor
Shawn Tilger, Chief Operating Officer, Alternate Governor
Paul Holmgren, President
Ron Hextall, General Manager
Bob Clarke, Senior Vice President
Phil Weinberg, Alternate Governor
CheriArnao, Executive Assistant
Ann Marie Nasuti, Executive Assistant
Sharon Allison, Executive Assistant
Barry Hanrahan, Assistant General Manager
TV & radio program production.

Phoenix Communications Group
3 Empire Blvd., South Hackensack, NJ 07606 USA
(201) 807-0888; *Fax:* (201) 807-0272
info@phoenixcomm.com
Joe Podesta, Chairman
Jim Holland, President
Trish Ferreri, General Manager
Geoff Belinfante, Programming Director
Rich Domich, Promotions Manager
Major League Sports Newsatellite; TV & video production & distribution; stock footage licensing.

Planet Pictures Ltd.
4222 Kingfisher Rd., Suite 208, Calabasas, CA 91302 USA
(818) 344-9100; *Fax:* (818) 344-4493
www.planetpictures.com
info@planetpictures.com
Jim Hayden, President
Peter Torvik, Operations Dir
Jenny Hayden, Managing Director
Production & distribution for documentary, informational, reality-based TV programs.

Playboy Entertainment Group Inc.
2706 Media Center Dr., Los Angeles, CA 90065 USA
(323) 276-4000; *Fax:* (323) 276-4500
Jim English, President
James Griffith, Operations Dir
TV program production, distribution & video.
Andrita Studios
3030 Andrita St., Los Angeles, CA 90065
Sol Weisel, Vp Production

Point 360
2701 Media Center Dr., Los Angeles, CA 90065 USA
(818) 565-1400, (866) 968-4336; *Fax:* (818) 847-2503
www.point360.com
careers@point360.com
Dennis Imbler, General Manager
Paul Ponzio, General Sales Mgr
Postproduction & duplication, film-to-tape transfers, audio svcs. Digital editing, distribution & syndication.
1220 N. Highland Ave, Hollywood, CA 90038 United States
(323) 957-5500
Rich Appel, Gen Mgr
VP business dev, President
12421 W. Olympic Blvd, Los Angeles, CA 90064 United States
(310) 207-7079
Carl Segal, Gen Mgr
Brian Grant, Vp Business Dev
1025 N. McCadden Pl, Hollywood, CA 90038 United States
(323) 461-8383
Fabian Sanchez, Gen Mgr
Brian Grant, Vp Business Dev
712 N. Seward St, Hollywood, CA 90038 United States
(323) 462-5330
Yvonne Parker, Gen Mgr
Brian Grant, Vp Business Dev

PorchLight Entertainment Inc.
14724 Ventura Boulevard, Suite 1105, Los Angeles, CA 91403 USA
(310) 477-8400; *Fax:* (310) 477-5555
www.porchlight.com
info@porchlight.com
William Baumann, CFO
Bruce Johnson, President
Produces & distributes family entertainment progmg including animation, TV movies & interactive multimedia progmg, licensing & merchandising.

Ports of Paradise
Box 33648, San Diego, CA 92163 USA
(619) 275-7357,(800) 223-2564; *Fax:* (619) 296-5909
aloharn@portparadise.com
J. Hal Hodgson, Programming Director
Hour-long radio program with Hawaiian music & info. Available on a barter basis.

PostWorks, New York
100 Ave. of the Americas, New York, NY 10013 USA
(212) 894-4000; *Fax:* (212) 983-4083
www.pwny.com
inquiry@postworks.com
Carol Jazwinski, Senior Vice President, Television Sales
Charles Herzfeld, Senior Vice President, Theatrical Sales
Jay Rubin, Senior Vice President, Feature Film and Sound Serv
Film-to-tape or data in standard or Hi-Definition; editing: digital, Hi-Definition, non-linear; duplication, conversion, satellite & fibre transmissions.

Powersports/Millenium International
14242 Ventura Boulevard, Penthouse, Sherman Oaks, CA 91423 USA
(818) 708-9995; *Fax:* (818) 708-0598
www.ps-mill.com
Jason Street, Operations Manager
Tal McAbian, Founder/ SVP, Worldwide Sales
William McAbian, Founder, Head of Middle East Sales
Viktoriya Khusit, Executive Assistant
Chris Eberlein, Executive Assistant
Micky McAbian, Tape andMaterials Trafficking
Production & distribution of special interest & documentaries for TV, cable & home video.

Prairie Dog Entertainment
PO Box 28700, San Diego, CA 92198 USA
(800) 448-7664
www.buckhowdy.com
Buck@BuckHowdy.com
Buck Howdy, Founder
Exclusively offering Buck Howdy's Cow Pie Radio, the fastest growing wkly kids radio program.

Premiere Networks Inc.
15260 Ventura Boulevard, Sherman Oaks, CA 91403 USA
(818) 377-5300; *Fax:* (818) 377-5333
www.premierenetworks.com
akorowitz@premierenetworks.com
Julie Talbott, President
Alan Korowitz, EVP of Sales
Dan Metter, EVP/Director of Personality Sales
Line-up includes Bcst Results Group (BRG) features, Olympia, Premiere Comedy Networks Formats, Long-form features, Mediabase rsch formats, music svcs, online, plain-wrap formats, prep & short-form. All features & svcs offered on a barterbasis are available via satellite, disc, tape, script or phone, depending on the program.

Presbyterian Church (U.S.A.)
100 Witherspoon St., Louisville, KY 40202 USA
(800) 728-7228; *Fax:* (502) 569-8845
www.pcusa.org/
info@pcusa.org
Jerry Marter, News Director
Radio & TV production, video, audio production, distribution, mktg & Internet svcs.

Prime Cut Productions Inc.
11909 E. Trail, San Fernando, CA 91342 USA
(310) 308-3584; *Fax:* (818) 834-9889
www.primecutproductions.com
vikkiberri@primecutproductions.com
Vikki Loh-Berri, CEO/Executive Producer
Jan Kaplan, President
Edward Flaherty, Operations Dir
NTSC Betacam European producers for American TV; bilingual location professionals; distribution, co-production, stock footage, TV script consultant/writer & editing.

Primo Newservice Inc.
Box 116, 182 Sound Beach Ave., Old Greenwich, CT 06870-0116 USA
(203) 637-0044; *Fax:* (203) 698-0812
www.teenkidsnews.com
primonews@aol.com
Albert Primo, CEO
TV news consulting, strategic news positioning talent & mgmt, coaching. Cable news training; Internet broadband svc.
355 W 52nd St. 3rd FL, New York, NY 10019

Producers Group, Ltd.
713 S. Pacific Coast Hwy., Suite B, Redondo Beach, CA 90277-4233 USA
(310) 316-0481; *Fax:* (310) 316-8905
www.producers-group.tv/
lee.gluckman@producers-group.tv
Lee Gluckman, Chairman
Lee Gluckman Jr., President
Dev & production of theatrical, TV films & series.

Production Garden Music
510 E. Ramsey, Suite 4, San Antonio, TX 78216 USA
(800) 247-5317, (210) 530-5200; *Fax:* (210) 530-5230
www.productiongarden.com
info@productiongarden.com
Mel Taylor, President
Ten distinct music libraries featuring production music, including production elements, sound effects; both lease & buy-out options available.

Productions La Fete
424, rue Guy, Suite 202, Montreal, QC H3J 1S6 Canada
(514) 848-0417; *Fax:* (514) 848-0064
www.lafete.com/
info@lafete.com
Rock Demers, President/ Producer/ Founder
Daniel Proulx, Operations Dir
Louise B,langer, Assistant to the President
M,lanie Bouchard, Accountant
St,phane Doyon, Assistant to the producers
Production of children/family feature films, drama series, documentaries, multimedia, etc.

The Program Exchange
299 W. Houston Street, New York, NY 10014 USA
(212) 859-1100; *Fax:* (212) 859-1150
info@programexchange.com
Allen Banks, President
Chris Hallowell, Operations Dir
TV program distribution.

Promark Television
500 South Palm Canyon, Suite 220, Palm Springs, CA 92264 USA
(760) 322-5149, (800) 266-6662; *Fax:* (760) 322-5149
www.promarktv.com
promarktv@promarktv.com
David Levine, CEO/ Founder
TV program production & distribution.

Promusic
941-A Clint Moore Rd., Boca Raton, FL 33487 USA
(561) 995-0331,(800) 322-7879; *Fax:* (561) 995-8434
www.pro-music.org/
mail@promusiclibrary.com
Alain Leroux, President
Mike Spitz, General Sales Mgr
Production music for film, TV & more. Vast CD catalog to choose from with extensive classical & opera.

PSSI Global Services-Strategic Television
7030 Hayvenhurst Ave., Van Nuys, CA 91406 USA
(310) 575-4400, (800) SAT-LINK; *Fax:* (310) 575-4451
www.pssiglobal.com
operations@pssiglobal.com
Robert C. Lamb, CEO, Global Services/Strategic Television
Matt Bridges, President, Startegic Television
Matt Scalici, General Manager
Clayton Packard, Promotions Manager
Brian Nelles, Senior Vice President
Jason Land, VicePresident, Strategic Television
Clayton Packard, VP Sales & Business Development
Joseph Kittrell, VP Flyaway & International Operations
Charles P. Storlie, Co-Founder/ Senior Consultant
Dianne Badoud, Co-Founder/ Senior Advisor, StrategicTelevision
Full service production & satellite transmission company with 25 fully redundant C- & Ku-band satellite trucks located nationwide. Available for news, sports, corporate, entertainment events, media tours, video conferencing, webcasting &downlinks. Additional svcs include Standard, High Definition digital transmission, encryption, multiple camera productions, event coordination & a C/Ku Flyaway system for international & domestic transmission. skIP Broadband also available forinternet, voice connectivity, & webcasting via satellite, ideal in remote areas with little or no connectivity.

The Pulse of Radio
Div/DBA: (a division of United Stations Radio Network)
Mailing Address: 485 Madison Avenue, 3rd Floor, New York, NY 10022
Second Address: 11400 W Olympic Blvd, Suite 200, Los Angeles, CA 90064
(212) 869-1111, (212) 536-3600, (310) 268-9292; *Fax:* (212) 536-3601; (212) 869-1115
www.unitedstations.com, www.pulseofradio.com
ccolombo@launchradionetworks.com
Nicholas J. Verbitsky, Chairman & CEO
James M Higgins, President & COO
Charlie Colombo, Executive Vice President
Richard Baum, Executive VP, Sales
Andy Denemark, Executive VP, Programming
Margaret Verghese, VP/Comedy & PrepServices
Stefan Jones, SVP, Content & Affiliation
Susan Moore, VP Research & Sales Support
Provides morning show radio prep; produces, distributes music, entertainment news & svcs for radio stns as well as other media worldwide.

Quality Film & Video
3321 Main Street, Suite B1, Manchester, MD 21102 USA
(410) 785-1920
www.qualityfilmvideo.com
Peter Garey, President
Guy Garey, Operations Dir
Video production, postproduction svcs, videotape, CD-ROM & DVD duplication.

Questar
307 N. Michigan Avenue, Suite 500, Chicago, IL 60601-5305 USA
(312) 266-9400; *Fax:* (312) 266-9523
www.questarentertainment.com
info@questarentertainment.com
Jason Nader, President
Producer, distributor of travel documentaries, children's cultural historical & natural history.

Radio Canada International
1400 Ren,-Levesque Boulevard East, Montreal, QC H2L 2M2 Canada
(514) 597-7461; *Fax:* (514) 597-6607
www.rcinet.ca
info@rcinet.ca
Jean Larin, Station Manager
Soleιman Mellali, Editor in Chief
Lynn Desjardins, Presenter-Produer
Gilda Salomone, Presenter-Produer
Terry Haig, Presenter-Produer
Ellis Quinn, Webmaster Commentator-Interviewer
Er Shen, Webmaster
Daily shortwave & internet, seven languages, 24-hour eutelsat F6 Europe, intelsat 707 Africa, asiasat 2. Recorded & live program placement on foreign stns.

Radio America
1100 North Glebe Road, Suite 900, Arlington, VA 22201 USA
(703) 302-1000; *Fax:* (571) 480-4141
www.radioamerica.com
affiliates@radioamerica.com
Mike Paradiso, COO
James C. Roberts, President
Rich McFadden, VP, Operations
Greg Corombos, News Director
News & feature svc providing daily, wkly & special programs (90 seconds to one hr) & multi-part documentaries.

Radio City Entertainmement
1260 Avenue of the Americas, New York, NY 10020 USA
(212) 465-6000,(212) 485-7000
www.radiocity.com/
Katie Schroeder, General Manager
TV program producers; production svcs.
2049 Century Park E, Suite 1200, Los Angeles, CA 90067 United States
(310) 551-2721

Radio Express Inc.
1415 W. Magnolia Blvd., Burbank, CA 91506 USA
(818) 295-5800; *Fax:* (818) 295-5801
www.radioexpress.com
radioinfo@radioexpress.com
Tom Rounds, CEO
Christian Jones, Operations Dir

Anita Antonio, General Manager
Jessica D'Agostin, General Sales Mgr
Christopher DiMatteo, Promotions Manager
Mark Brower, Music Director
Corina Camacho, Sales Staff
BarbaraRounds, Sales Staff
Jessica D'Agostin, Sales Staff
Chris Dimatteo, Sales Staff
Nadine Ellman, Sales Staff
Radio Express exports Radioplay, the best music svc for radio, production music & progmg to enhance any music format, worldwide.

Radio Spirits
PO Box 3107, Wallingford, CT 06492 USA
(203) 265-8044; *Fax:* (973) 539-1273
www.radiospirits.com
wholesale@radiospirits.com
Hakan Lindskog, President
David Carroll, General Sales Mgr
Syndicated radio production specializing in Golden Age of Radio. Production of When Radio Was with Stan Freberg, bartered to 300 affls.

Radio Television Espanola (RTVE)
Edificio Prado Del Rey/ Desp. 3/023, 28223 Pozuelo De Alarcon, Madrid, 28223
91 346 40 00; *Fax:* 91 346 30 55
www.rtve.es
Production & distribution of its own productions as well as some 250 feature films in co-production with independent Sp & Latin American film producers.

Radioguide People Inc.
Box 880, Novi, MI 48376 USA
(248) 926-1234
www.vuolovideo.com
artvuolo@aol.com
Arthur Vuolo Jr., President
Publishers of radio stn guides for the gen public, co-sponsored by loc stns & natl advertisers. Produces videos of radio stns, radio events for educational & entertainment purposes.

RadioOhio Incorporated
605 S. Front St., Columbus, OH 43215
(614) 460-3850; *Fax:* (614) 460-2831
Skip Mosic, Director of Programming & Affiliate Relations
Mike Hawkins, Morning Anchor & Reporter
Dave James, Afternoon Anchor & Reporter
Paul Keels, Sports
Milan Jordan, Sports
Chris Bradley, Meterologist
Mike Davis,Meterologist
Full-svc digital satellite audio & data distribution, including affil rel & net bldg. for new & existing sports, news/talk, music & specialty networks.

Rampion Visual Productions L.L.C.
225 Riverview Ave., Suite 101, Newton, MA 02466 USA
(617) 795-1900, (888) 49M-EDIA; *Fax:* (617) 795-1919
www.rampion.com
info@rampion.com
Michael Garneau, President
Steven Tringali, General Manager
Full Digital Component Editing (BetaSP & DigiBeta), Computer Graphics (2D & 3D), Green Screen Studio, Digital Compositing & DVD creation.

Raycom Sports
1900 W. Morehead St., Charlotte, NC 28208 USA
(704) 378-4400; *Fax:* (704) 374-3859
www.raycomsports.com
Jimmy Rayburn, COO
Ken Haines, President and CEO
Colin Smith, Operations Dir
Jim Ford, General Sales Mgr
George Johnson, SVP, Programming & Distribution
Charles Moye, Technical Operations Manager
Rob Reichley, ExecutiveProducer
Peter Rolfe, VP, Production
Jeff Tennant, SVP,Sales & Chief Revenue Offic
Becky Smith, Controller
Chad Swofford, Sr. Director,New Media & Business Development
Frank Kay, Director of Communications
TV, marketing, sports production & syndication.

Raycom Sports
1900 West Morehead Street, Charlotte, NC 28208 USA
(704) 378-4400; *Fax:* (704) 373-3324
www.raycomsports.com
khaines@raycomsports.com
Jimmy Rayburn, Chief Operating Officer
Ken Haines, President & CEO
Charles Moye, Technical Operations Manager
Jeff Tennant, Senior Vice President, Sales & Chief Revenue Offic
George Johnson, Senior Vice President, Programming &Distributio
Calan Canipe, Engineer-In-Charge
Peter Rolfe, VP Production
Jeff Tenant, SVP, Sales & Chief Revenue Officer
Rob Reichley, Executive Producer
Jim Brannon, Director of Sales
Chad Swofford, Senior Director, New Media & BusinessDevelopment
Frank Kay, Director of Communications
Production trucks and HD uplink, sls distribution, produce, market, distribute sports, entertainment progmg nationally & internationally.

RBC Ministries
Box 1622, Windsor, ON N9A 6Z7 USA
519-956-2400; *Fax:* 519-956-2449
www.rbc.net
canada@rbc.org
Martin De Haan II, President
TV & radio production & distribution. Programs: TV Day of Discovery, Radio-Discover the Word, Words To Live By, Our Daily Bread, Sports Spectrum, My Utmost for His Highest & Walk In The Wood.

RBC Ministries/Midwest Media Managers
PO Box 1622, Windsor, ON N9A 6Z7 USA
(519) 956 2400; *Fax:* (519) 956 2449
www.rbc.org
canada@rbc.org
Martin De Haan, President
John Nasby, General Manager
Rod McNany, Director
In-house agency for RBC Ministries; providing TV/Radio placement & promotional support of RBC resources including the devotional, Our Daily Bread.

RDF Media
The Gloucester Building, Kensington Village, Avonmore Road, London, W14 8RF GBR
44 (0)20 7 013 4000; *Fax:* 44 (0) 20 7013 4001
www.rdftelevision.com/
sales@rdfmedia.com
David Frank, CEO
Will Smith, Director of Programs
Jim Allen, Managing Director
Jane Wilson, Director of Production
Peter Usher, Head of Entertainment
Teresa Watkins, Creative Director- Development
Julia Waring, Head of ProductionTalent
Louise Dibley, Production Talent Executive
Production & distribution of TV & radio programs.

Reel Media International Inc.
7000 Independence Parkway, Suite 160-7, Plano, TX 75025 USA
(214) 521-3301; *Fax:* (214) 522-3448
www.reelmediaintl.com
reelmedia@aol.com
Tom T. Moore, President
Worldwide distributor of motion pictures, copyrighted documentaries, Public Domain Library of 2,000 movies, series & documentaries. Servicing all rights.

Reuters Media
3 Times Sq., 18th Fl., New York, NY 10036 USA
(646) 223-4300; *Fax:* (646) 223-4390,(646) 223-4370
www.reuters.com
David Thomson, Chairman
James C. Smith, President & CEO
Richard H. King, EVP/ Chief Operating Officer, Technology
Stephane Bello, Executive Vice President/ Chief Financial Officer
Gus Carlson, EVP/ Chief Communications Officer
Carla Jones, Chief of Staff
Andrew Rashbass, Chief Executive
James T. Powell, EVP/ Chief Technology Officer
Brian Scanlon, EVP & Chief Strategy Officer
International news for interactive multimedia news archive for CD-ROM & on-demand applications. Stock photos & film footage.

Reuters Television
1333 H St. N.W., Washington, DC 20005 USA
(202) 898-0056; *Fax:* (202) 898-1236
www.reuters.com
David Thomson, Chairman
James C. Smith, President & CEO
Richard H. King, EVP/ Chief Operating Officer, Technology
John Clarke, Programming Director
Stephane Bello, Executive Vice President/ Chief Financial Officer
Gus Carlson, EVP/Chief Communications Officer
Carla Jones, Chief of Staff
Andrew Rashbass, Chief Executive
James T. Powell, EVP/ Chief Technology Officer
Brian Scanlon, EVP & Chief Strategy Officer
Reuters news & sports svcs include 128 Reuters bureaus, camera crews & a comprehensive satellite network. It serves more than 200 bctrs & their affils in 84 countries. Satellite & news production svcs feature satellite delivery networks.International bcst centers in Moscow, Washington, DC & London. Offers live positions, studio facilities & direct access to the satellite network. Library & program packages cover major news & sporting events.

Rex Post
610 S.W. 17th Ave., Portland, OR 97205 USA
(503) 238-4525; *Fax:* (503) 236-8347
www.rexpost.com
info@rexpost.com
Tara Krick, General Manager/Chief Engineer
Russell Gorsline, Chief Engineer
Tara Krick, Producer, Business & Project Manager
Brent Rogers, Audio Production Specialist / Music Producer
Chris Borges-Silva, Video Editor / Engineer /Colorist
TV & radio production, audio recording, video production, CD-ROM & DVD, website. Audio/video production & post, ISDN &nSourceConnect digital patch, DVD authoring & web design.

Richter Productions Inc.
521 East 14th St./4F, New York, NY 10009 USA
(917) 608-7427; *Fax:* (212) 643-1208
www.richtervideos.com
Richter330@aol.com
Robert Richter, Founder
TV program, promo film production, distribution, film & video.

Riden International Inc.
6024 Paseo Palmilla, Goleta, CA 93117 USA
(805) 964-7041; *Fax:* (805) 964-1338
www.rideninc.com
rideninc@aol.com
Richard Dennison, President
Motion Picture , TV program production & distribution.

River City Video Productions
Box 310601, New Braunfels, TX 78131-0601 USA
(830) 625-3474; *Fax:* (830) 625-3710
www.highroadhunting.com/
Deborah Dougherty, President
Mktg, instructional & promotional videos & TV commercials.

Robert Michelson Inc.
932 Stanyan Street, San Francisco, CA 94117 USA
(415) 386-6862, (415) 793-5733; *Fax:* (415) 386-2714
www.rmitv.com
rm@rmitv.com
Robert Michelson, President & Owner
David Alexander, General Manager
TV coml production; custom & syndicated TV spots for radio stns. Leading producer of TV spots for rock radio.

Roberts Communications Network Inc.
4175 Cameron St., Suite 10, Las Vegas, NV 89103-3772 USA
(702) 227-7500
www.robertscomnet.com
Tommy Roberts, Chairman
Todd Roberts, CEO
C-Bond satellite transponder capacity, uplinking, encoding & decoding. 50 Ch Direct To Home Platform

Robin Miller, Filmaker Inc.
606 W. Broad St., Bethlehem, PA 18018 USA
(610) 691-0900; *Fax:* (610) 691-0952
www.filmaker.com
enquire@filmaker.com
Robin Miller, Founder
TV program, promotion film production; production svcs.

Rockwell Audio Media
56 W. 45th St., Suite 1503, New York, NY 10036 USA
(212)840-9200; *Fax:* (212)840-9203
www.rockwellaudiomedia.com
john@rockwellaudiomedia.com
John Rockwell, President
Audio editing & production-spoken word & educational.

PROGRAMMING & PRODUCTION SERVICES

Rose Entertainment
5529 McLennan Ave., Encino, CA 91436 USA
(818) 817-7554; *Fax:* (818) 817-7585
www.roseentertainment.com
Rosamaria Gonzalez, President
Flory Quiroa, Operations Dir
TV progmg distribution company for Latin America.

Rosler Creative
88 Howard St., #2307, San Francisco, CA 94105 USA
(415) 896-1414, (800) 707-1414; *Fax:* (415) 896-1616
www.roslercreative.com
rosler@sbcglobal.net
Peter Rosler, President/ Creative Director
TV comls, creative dev & production.TV-CATV only.

ROZON
2101 St. Laurent Boulevard, Montreal, QC H2X 2T5
(514) 845-3155; *Fax:* (514) 845-4140
www.hahaha.com
info@hahaha.com
Bruce Hills, COO
Gilbert Rozon, President
Christos Sourligas, General Sales Mgr
Producer/distributor of comedy programs, standup comedy & nonverbal light entertainment.

RPM Media Enterprises-The Relic Rack Review
108 Holmes Oval, New Providence, NJ 07974-1425 USA
(908) 464-2222
www.relic-rack.com
richardjlorenzo@relicrack.com
Richard J. Lorenzo, President
Margaret Lorenzo, Chief FinancialOfficer
Robert Longo, Lead Singer
Richard Dan Ingram, Music Programmer
Four-hour wkly rock & roll oldies syndicated entertainment program called the Relic Rack Review, that includes music, news & nostalgia entertainment. Prep svcs including Relic Rack Fast Facts. Multi format radio program consulting svcs.

Rukus
317 N. Eleventh Street, Suite 302, St. Louis, MO 63101 USA
(314) 621-2727; *Fax:* (314) 621-2732
www.rukuspost.com/
michael.hurst@rukuspost.com
Edgar Febus, Avid DS Senior Editor/Co-Founder
Nick Stroot, Avid Media Composer Editor/Co-Founder
Michael Hurst, Executive Producer/Co-Founder
16 & 35 mm film production, full-sound studios, video production, film & video editing.

Russ Reid Company
2 N. Lake Ave., Suite 600, Pasadena, CA 91101 USA
(626) 449-6100, (800) 275-4787; *Fax:* (626) 463-0028
www.russreid.com
mrhode@russreid.com
Chip Grizzard, Chairman
Alan Hall, President & CEO
Don Haggerstrom, COO
David DeBetta, Director of Broadcast
Lisa Scott Benson, EVP, Strategy, Insights & Integration
Roger Hiyama, SVP, Managing Director
Lori Burns, Senior VP,Client Services
Robbin Gehrke, SVP, Executive Creative Insights & Integration
Steve Harrison, Senior VP, Client Services
Holly Taylor, SVP of Marketing Operations
Full service agency specializing in fund-raising, govt rels, adv & PR for nonprofit organizations via mutiple chs, including: TV, radio, interactive/online, direct mail, nwspr, magazines, out-of-home & other media. Partners with loc & natlclients to help them thrive, supporting theirs efforts to change the world. Russ Reid merged with Grizzard in early 2017
Government Relations
2000 L St. N.W., Suiter 350, Washington, DC 20036
(202) 912-8600
Radio Division
25195 S.W. Parkway Ave., Suite 200, Wilsonville, OR 97070
(503) 682-7227

Sak Entertainment
29 S. Orange Avenue, Orlando, FL 32801 USA
(407) 648-0001; *Fax:* (407) 648-1333
www.sak.com
dave@sak.com
Dave Russell, President
Gina Hunter, Sales Director
Francie Moon, Finance Manager
Chris Dinger, Managing Director
John Valines, Production Manager & Technical Director
Brittany Wine, Production Assistant
John Hunter, VP/Education Director
Lindsay Taylor, Box Office Manager
Professional comedy actors, dirs, producers & writers. Entertainment consultants for WDW, Universal Studio, Harrahs Corp. & Busch Gardens.

Salem Publishing
750 Old Hickory Blvd Ste 150-1, Brentwood, TN 37027 USA
(615) 312-4244; *Fax:* (615) 312-4266
www.salempublishing.com
DeDe Donatelle-Tarrant, Senior Dircetor of Advertising
Publisher of Homecoming, Preaching, YouthWorker Journal, Singing News & Townhall magazines
Salem Communications
Santa Rosa Blvd, Camarillo, CA 93012

Sam Shad Productions
Box 10853, Reno, NV 89510 USA
(775) 857-2244, (775) 722-2442; *Fax:* (775) 857-2272
www.samshad.com/
sam@shad.reno.nv.us
Sam Shad, President
Bonnie McCorkle, Programming Director
Radio progmg & coml production, TV progmg & coml production, TV & radio progmg concepts dev from start to finish, internet design & adv, public relations.

The Samuel Goldwyn Films
9570 W. Pico Blvd., Suite 400, Los Angeles, CA 90035 USA
(310) 860-3100; *Fax:* (310) 860-3198
www.samuelgoldwynfilms.com/
info@samuelgoldwyn.com
Samuel Goldwyn Jr., Chairman
Samuel Goldwyn Jr., CEO
Meyer Gottlieb, President
Movie acquisition & distribution.

Sandra Carter Global, Inc.
230 W. 79th St., Suite 1C, New York, NY 10024 USA
(212) 875-1811; *Fax:* (212) 875-0088
www.sandra-carter.com
Sandra Carter, President
Nancy Ordonez Apolo, Sales
Distribution to all media, co-production deals, production, principle product in factual series.

Sandy Frank Entertainment Inc.
910 Fifth Avenue, New York, NY 10021 USA
(212) 772-1889; *Fax:* (212) 772-2297
www.sandyfrankentertainment.com
Sandy Frank, Chairman
Sandi Spidell, VP Operations and Publicity
Damaso Santana, Consultant
Barbara Kalicinska, Eastern European Sales Representative
Rosalie Perrone, VP Business Affairs/Comptroller
TV production & syndication.

The Saturday Evening Post
1100 Waterway Blvd., Indianapolis, IN 46202 USA
(317) 634-1100; *Fax:* (317) 637-0126
www.saturdayeveningpost.com/
editor@saturdayeveningpost.com
Quinton Lee, General Manager
Producers & distributors of health shows for radio & TV; coml production.

SCOLA
21557 270th Street, McClelland, IA 51548 USA
(712) 566-2202; *Fax:* (712) 566-2502
www.scola.org
scola@scola.org
Francis Lajba, President
John Millar, Operations Dir
SCOLA progmg from more than 100 countries in more than 90 languages. These programs are available via internet, satellite, cable to learners of languages study, ethnic communities & anyone seeking a global perspective. Mission is to helpthe people of the world learn about one another.

Seraphim Communications Inc.
1175 Winston Street, St. Paul, MN 55108 USA
(651) 645-9173; *Fax:* (651) 645-3515
www.seracomm.com
info@seracomm.com
Hal Dragseth, President
Kristin Wiersma, Principal
Hal Dragseth, Former President & Co-Founder
Kevin Dragseth, Media Producer
Full-svc video & AV capabilities. Emphasis on video production from concept through final product. In-house grahics, interactive Web, CD-ROM/DVD.

SESAC Inc.
55 Music Sq E, Nashville, TN 37203 USA
(615) 320-0055; *Fax:* (615) 329-9627
www.sesac.com
Pat Collins, COO
SESAC is a service organization created to assist both the creators & users of music through royalty collection & efficient music licensing.
152 W 57th St, 57th Fl, New York, NY 10019
(212) 484-0600; *Fax:* (212) 489-5699
Stephen Swid, Chairman
Freddie Gershon, CEO/COO
Ira Smith, Co-Chmn
67 Upper Berkeley St, London W1H 3FF,
020 7616 9284; *Fax:* 020 7563 7029
Dr. Wayne Bickerton, Chairman
420 Lincoln Rd, Ste 502, Miami, FL 33139
(305) 534-7500; *Fax:* (305) 534-7578
501 Santa Monica Blvd, Ste 450, Santa Monica, CA 90401
(310) 393-9671; *Fax:* (310) 393-6497
981 Joseph E Lowery Blvd NW, Ste 111, Atlanta, GA 30318
(404) 897-1330; *Fax:* (404) 897-1306

Sesame Workshop
One Lincoln Plaza, New York, NY 10023 USA
(212) 595-3456; *Fax:* (212) 875-6111
www.sesameworkshop.org
Joan Ganz Cooney, Co-Founder & Chairman
Gary Knell, President
TV program production.

Shark TV
14414 Blanco Road, Suite 320, San Antonio, TX 78216 USA
(210) 344-5982, (800) 798-5982; *Fax:* (210) 344-9910
www.sharktv.com
Thomas Horton, President
Jean Garner, Operations Dir
Garry R. Garner, Promotions Manager
TV program full-svc production, postproduction, international & domestic distribution, specializing in award-winning documentaries.

Shelly Palmer Productions
P. O. Box 1877, New York, NY 10156-1877 USA
(212) 532-3880
www.shellypalmer.com
info@shellypalmer.com
Shelly Palmer, Managing Director
Music, video, TV, film production & creative svcs. Adv & mktg. Music libraries, sound design, sls videos & post-production.

Silverline Pictures
22837 Ventura Blvd., Ste. 205, Woodland Hills, CA 91364 USA
(905) 870-5115; *Fax:* (818) 225-9053
www.silverlinepictures.ca/home.html
scott@silverlinepictures.ca
Leman Cetiner, CEO
Axel Munch, President
Scott C Newman, Writer/ Director/ Producer/ Editor
Full-svc production & distribution company producing theatrical, TV & kids series.

Silverman Stock Footage Inc.
750 Kappock St., #A-1, Bronx, NY 10463 USA
(347) 599-0363; *Fax:* (718) 764-4411
www.silvermanstockfootage.com
theotherdonald@gmail.com
Donald Silverman, President
Stock footage.

Sing For Joy
St. Olaf College, 1520 St. Olaf Avenue, Northfield, MN 55057-1098 USA
(507) 786-8596; *Fax:* (507) 786-3033
www.singforjoy.org
singforjoy@stolaf.edu
Miriam Mueller, COO
Jeffrey O'Donnell, Programming Director
Joshua Wyatt, Associate Producer
Dr. John Ferguson, Music Advisor
Pastor Bruce Benson, Program Host
Carolyn Pierson, Communications Coordinator
Jeffery O'Donnell,Executive Producer & Music Director
Rachel Brooks, Intern
Sacred choral works with host commentary relating the music to the scriptural lessons during each week of the church year.

Skywatch Weather Center
347 Prestley Rd., Bridgeville, PA 15017 USA
(412) 221-6000,(800)-759-9282, (800) SKY-WATCH; *Fax:* (412) 221-3160

www.skywatchweather.com
airsci@skywatchweather.com
Dr. Stanley J. Penkala, Ph.D., President & Director of Air Programs
Daniel Krzywiecki, Vice President
Stanley Bostjancic, Treasurer & Chief Meteorologist
Harry Green, Secretary
Specially formatted weathercasts produced in the Skywatch Weather Center.

Smith/Lee Productions, Inc.
7420 Manchester Boulevard, St. Louis, MO 63143 USA
(314) 647-3900, (877) 745-0900; *Fax:* (314) 647-3959
www.smithlee.com
sales@smithlee.com
David Smith, President
Barry Lee, Operations Dir
TV & radio coml promotional film production; production svcs; studio specializing in Audio Post; music production, voice recording & multimedia.

Soldiers Radio & Television, U.S. Army Public Affairs
Box 31, 2511 Jefferson Davis Hwy., Arlington, VA 22202 USA
(703) 602-4675; *Fax:* (703) 602-5220
www.army.mil/media/srtv/
armynewswatch@smc.army.mil
Jim Ryan, Operations Dir
George McNamara, General Manager
Melody Day, Promotions Manager
Gene Gunderson, Chief Engineer
Paul Schultz, Operations Manager
Radio, TV news bureau, soldiers radio network & Army Newswatch a biweekly TV newscast.

Solid Gospel Network (Reach Satellite Network, Inc.)
402 BNA Drive, Suite 400, Nashville, TN 37217 USA
(615) 367-2210, (800) 527-5226; *Fax:* (615) 367-0758
www.southerngospel.com/
Wade Schoenemann, Operations Dir
Jim Black, General Manager
Don Burns, Programming Director
Michael Miller, General Manager
Ed Evensen, Local Traffic Manager
Rick Shelton, Manager
24-hour, satellite delivered, Christian country & southern gospel network, featuring artists like Bill Gaither, The Isaacs, Gold City, Jeff & Sheri Easter & The Martins, live from Nashville, the Christian music capital of the world.

Sony Pictures
10202 West Washington Blvd., Culver City, CA 90232 USA
(310) 244-7737; *Fax:* (310) 244-2626
www.sonypictures.com
press@spe.sony.com
Tony Vinciquerra, Chairman & CEO
John Weiser, President, US Distribution, Sony Pictures TV
Jon Hookstratten, EVP, Administration & Operations
Keith Le Goy, President, Distribution
Leah Weil, Senior Executive Vice President & GeneralCounsel
Robert Lawson, EVP & Chief Communications Officer
Philip Rowley, Senior Executive Vice President & CFO
550 Madison Ave., New York, NY 10022 United States
(212) 883-8500
3500 Maple Ave., Suite 205, Dallas, TX 75219 United States
(214) 520-7070
455 N. Cityfront Plaza Dr., Suite 2520, Chicago, IL 60611 United States
(312) 644-0770
2859 Paces Ferry Rd., Suite 1130, Atlanta, GA 30339 United States
(770) 434-5400

Sound Ideas
105 W. Beaver Creek Rd., Suite 4, Richmond Hill, ON L4B 1C6 Canada
(905) 886-5000,(800) 387-3030, (800) 665-3000; *Fax:* (905) 886-6800
www.sound-ideas.com
wbc105@sound-ideas.com
Brian Nimens, President & CEO
Brian Nimens, President & CEO
Peter Alexander, Sales Manager
Marty Evans, Production Consultant
Ron Anthony, Production Consultant
Elliott Zimmerman, Production Consultant
Craig Nimens, ProductionConsultant
Royalty free sound effects, imaging elements, music for the professional audio industry; including bcst, cable, film, multimedia & internet applications.

Sound of Birmingham Productions
3625 5th Ave. S., Birmingham, AL 35222 USA
(205) 595-8497; *Fax:* (205) 595-0889
soundofbirmingham.com
don@soundofbirmingham.com
Don Mosley, President
Betty Mosley, Operations Dir
Radio & TV voice-overs, jingles, video sweetening, custom music, recording studios, full-svc studios, ISDN.

Sound*Bytes
1425 Hopkins St. N.W., Suite 401, Washington, DC 20036 USA
(202) 296-2022
www.soundbytesradio.com
press@soundbytesradio.com
Jan Ziff, President
Computer audio show production & syndication.

Soundshop Recording Studio LLC
1307 Division St., Nashville, TN 37203 US
(615) 244-4149; *Fax:* (615) 242-8759
Music production, recording studios, 2-48 track digital or 24 track analog studios.

Soundtrack Group
Mailing Address: 162 Columbus Ave., Boston, MA 02116 USA
Second Address: 936 Broadway, New York, NY 10010
(617) 303-7500, (212) 420-6010; *Fax:* (617) 303-7555
www.soundtrackgroup.com
Amy Blankenship, COO
Tony Prendatt, Producer / Executive
Jeanne Priest, General Manager
Terry Lockhart, Chief Engineer
Paul Cavicchio, CFO
Hillary Rider, Executice Producer
Mike Raneo, Dubroom Engineer
Mike Gros, Machine RoomEngineer
Hillary O'Rourke, Office Manager
Holly Miller, Producer
Production, postproduction & custom music of all kinds; specializing in sound designs.
936 Broadway, New York, NY 10010
(212) 420-6010
Chris Rich, Opns Mgr

Southcott Productions
Box 33185, Granada Hills, CA 91394 US
(818) 368-4938; *Fax:* (818) 368-4938
www.chucksouthcott.com
info@chucksouthcott.com
Chuck Southscott, President
Radio program, coml production & distribution.

Southern Star Entertainment
42-44 Victoria Street, McMahons Point 2060, NSW Australia, Australia
61 2 9202 8555; *Fax:* 61 2 9955 5759
www.southernstarentertainment.com.au
general@sstar.com.au
Janeen Faithfull, Chief Executive Officer
Peter Anderson, Director of Finance & Operations
Jason Franklin, General Manager - Brand Entertainment
Sarah Smith, Drama Producer
John Edwards, Producer
Noel Price, Children's TelevisionProducer
John Butt, Head of Legal and Business Affairs
Simon Nash, IT Manager
Lulu Wilkinson, Head of Digital
Deb Stewart, Executive Producer
Sam Pantos, Group Financial Controller
Julia Gretton-Roberts, Production Supervisor
Australia's largest independent television production group, it produces content for drama, entertainment, and children's programming.

Spanish Broadcasting System
26 W. 56th St., New York, NY 10019 USA
(212) 541-9200; *Fax:* (212) 541-6904
Raul Alarcon, Jr., Chairman/ President/ CEO
Albert Rodriguez, Chief Operating Officer
Joseph A. Garcia, Director/ SVP/ CFO/ CAO/ Secretary
Berry Jasin, VP of National Sales
Mitchell A. Yelen, Director
Donny Hudson, Vice Presidentof Consolidated Sales
Humberto Wispe, Digital Sales Manager
Elizabeth Paulino, Local Sales Manager
Spanish progmg syndication.

SPI International
55 White St., Suite 1A, New York, NY 10013 USA
(212) 673-5103; *Fax:* (212) 673-5183
www.spiintl.com
info@spiintl.com
Loni Farhi, President
Stacey Sobel, Operations Dir
For over nineteen years SPI International, Inc. has been a leading supplier of theatrical films and a wide variety of television programming to the international market. To further exploit its vast library SPI established its own cablestations on pay and basic cable level in Poland , Czech Republic ,Slovakia and Hungary. SPI will open additional channels throughout Eastern Europe during 2009.

Sports Byline U.S.A.
300 Broadway, Suite 8, San Francisco, CA 94133 USA
(415) 434-8300, (800) 878-PLAY, (800) 878-7529; *Fax:* (415) 391-2569
www.sportsbyline.com
Ron Barr, Chairman
Darren Peck, President
Satellite-delivered nationwide radio sports talk net, listener 800 number, 7days (West Coast), barter.

StarDate/Universo Productions
2609 University Ave., A2100, Austin, TX 78712 USA
(512) 471-5285; *Fax:* (512) 471-5060
www.stardate.org
perez@stardate.org
Damond Benningfield, Programming Director
Damond Benningfield, Executive Producer
Doug Addison, Producer
Dr. Taft Armandroff, Director
Sandra Preston, Asst. Director for Outreach & Education
Dr. Tom Barnes, Contributor
SuzanneGeiger, Contributor
Syndicated two-minute radio programs on stars & planets visible in the night sky. Each program is date-specific. English/Spanish.

Stellis Media
Div/DBA: (Ellis Library)
7B Pleasant Boulevard, Suite 960, Toronto, ON M4T 1K2 Canada
(416) 844-8650
www.sellismedia.com, www.ellisent.com
stephen.ellis@stellismedia.com
Stephen Ellis, President
Distributors of the 600 title Ellis Library: 1000+ hrs of non-fiction and family entertainment for TV and video for four decades.

Steve Rotfeld Productions Inc.
740 East Haverford Road, Bryn Mawr, PA 19010 USA
(610) 520-0671; *Fax:* (610) 520-0681
www.rotfeldproductions.com
fern@rotfeldproductions.com
Fern Rotfeld, Director of Sales
Steve Rotfeld, Programming Director
Carol Brooks, VP, Syndication Sales
Hope E. Kirschner, Regional Sales Director
A TV production company that produces & syndicates TV shows.

Strand Media Group Inc.
3955 Highway 17 Bypass, Suite D, Murrells Inlet, SC 29576 USA
(843) 626-8911; *Fax:* (310) 390-2857
strandmedia.com/
info@strandmedia.com
Mike Carruthers, President
Radio programs, coml production & distribution; media buying agent.

Studio Babelsberg GmbH
August-Bebel-St. 26-53, 14482 Potsdam, DEU
49 (0) 331-72 -13151; *Fax:* 49 (0) 331-72-12525
www.studiobabelsberg.com
info@studiobabelsberg.com
Christoph Fisser, Vice President/ Chief Operating Officer
Dr. Carl L. Woebcken, President/ Chief Executive Officer
Christoph Fisser, Vice President and COO
Marius Schwarz, Chief Financial Officer
Henning Molfenter, ManagingDirector
Dr. Carl L. Woebcken, Managing Director
Michael Düwel, Managing Director Art Department Studio Babelsberg
Studio area, studio technology, set design & construction, film laboratory, postproduction, dubbing theatres for films, TV & video.

Studio Center Total Production
161 Business Park Drive, Virginia Beach, VA 23462 USA
(866) 515-2111, (757) 286-3080; *Fax:* (757) 622-0583
www.studiocenter.com
info@studiocenter.com

William Prettyman, CEO
Radio & TV commmercials, station promotions, voice-over services, original music, copywriting, on hold & website audio.
3875 S. Jones Blvd., Las Vegas, CA 89103
(702) 248-2777; *Fax:* (702) 248-5400
2693 Union Ave. Ext., Memphis, TN 38112
(901)323-7060; *Fax:* (901) 320-0003
5245 Cleveland St., Ste. 204, Virginia Beach, VA 23462
(757)622-2111
315 Madison Ave., 11th Floor, New York, NY 10017
(212)986-1929
7033 W. Sunset Blvd., Suite 318, Los Angeles, CA 90028
(323)466-9673

Studio M Productions Unlimited
4032 Wilshire Blvd., Suite 403, Los Angeles, CA 90010 USA
(213) 389-7372, (888) 389-7372; *Fax:* (213) 389-3299
www.mandy.com/home.cfm?c=stu001
mixer@sound4film-tv.com
Mike Michaels, President
Robert Dickerson, Chief Engineer
TV & radio program production, tape, film & live production svcs. Live remotes for TV, radio, news & sports. (888) 389-7372.
Jim Walters Co
4224 Waialae #201, Honolulu, HI 96816-5330
808-373-2701

STV Central Ltd.
Pacific Quay, Glasgow, G51 1PQ Scotland
0141 300 3000
www.stv.tv/
viewerenquiries@stv.tv
Matt Roper, Online News Content
Bcstr & production company.

Suite Audio
21 Stone Wall Ln., Clinton, CT 06413 USA
(860) 664-9499
www.suiteaudio.com
info@suiteaudio.com
Bob Nary, President
Facility: ProTools HDII/TDM, Waves restoration & Platinum, Sonic Solutions. Commercial - Program - surround production. CD mastering - authoring - duplication. Cassette duplication.
Clinton
CT 21 Stonewall Ln, Clinton, CT 06413 United States
Bob Nary, Owner

Sullivan Entertainment Inc./Sullivan Entertainment International
110 Davenport Rd., Toronto, ON M5R 3R3 Canada
(416) 921-7177; *Fax:* (416) 921-7538
www.sullivanmovies.com/
Kevin Sullivan, President, Writer/Director, Executive Producer
Trudy Grant, President, Executive Producer
Dan Matthews, Studio Manager and Head of Post Production
Production, distribution, home video, dev series & feature film.
Sullivan Entertainment Europe Ltd
Savant House, 63-65 Camden High St., London United Kingdom, (207) 383-5192
Muriel Thomas, Sr Vp Intl Sls

SunGard Output Solutions
680 East Swedesford Road, Wayne, PA 19087 USA
(800) 825-2518; *Fax:* (205) 307-6813
www.sungard.com
getinfo@sungard.com
Marianne Brown, Chief Operating Officer, Financial Systems
Russ Fradin, President & Chief Executive Officer
Jamey Vella, General Sales Mgr
Mike Borman, Chief executive officer, Public Sector
Regina Brab, SVP, HR & Chief HumanResources Officer
Charles Neral, Chief Financial Officer
Vince Coppola, SVP, Global Business Services & Technology
Steven Silberstein, Chief Technology Officer
Victoria Silbey, Legal & Chief Legal Officer
SunGard's document distribution output channels include: paper, electronic (ebill/email), optical and/ or magnetic media.

Swell Pictures Inc.
455 N. City Front Plaza, 18th Fl., Chicago, IL 60611 USA
(805) 689-7367; *Fax:* (312) 464-8020
Brian Clark, President
Dave Mueller, Operations Dir
Joe Flores, Chief Engineer
Radi Akel, Operations Manager
Michael Topel, President
Film-to-tape transfer, videotape editing, digital sound editing & original music. Avid, 3-D graphics & compositing, audio & new media.

System TV
45/47 rue Paul Bert, Boulogne-Billancourt, Paris, 92100 FRA
(33)-1-55-38-20-20; *Fax:* (33)-1-55-38-20-30
www.systemtv.fr
Daniel Renouf, President
Hiam El Khoury, International Sales Manager
Sophie Montani, Executive Assistant
Roland Gouterman, Financial & Administrative Director
AgnŠs Brasselet, Production Manager
V‚ronique Laroulandrie, ProductionManager
Fran‡ois-Bernard Dauchy, Research and Development Manager
TV program production, press agency, produce weather & info svcs.

TAA Music / Toby Arnold Sound Studios
PO Box 828, Aubrey, TX 76227 USA
(800) 527-5335,(972) 661-8200; *Fax:* (972) 248-8919
www.taamusic.com
toby@taamusic.com
Susan Bedwell, President/CEO
Troy Powers, Engineering Dir
Julie Simpson, Account Manager
Audio production libraries for TV & radio. Station Imaging, Morning show promo sweeper, stager packages for all formats.

Talk Radio Network
Box 3755, Central Point, OR 97502 USA
(541) 664-6250
trncorporate.com
Mark Masters, President
Roy Masters, Host
Dr. Michio Kaku, Host
Dr. Bill Wattenburg, Host
Brian Oxman, Host
Jerry Doyle, Host
Monica Crowley, Host
Full-svc live talk radio format 24 hours daily. Serving more than 400 affils nationwide.

Talkline Communications Radio Network
Box 20108, Park West Station, New York, NY 10025 USA
(212) 769-1925, (866) JEWISH RADIO, (866) 4- TALKL; *Fax:* (212) 799-4195
www.talklinecommunications.com
tcntalk@aol.com
Rabbi Zev J. Brenner, President & Executive Producer
Zev J. Brenner, Programming Director
Natl Jewish radio net. Carried in over 2,500 markets. Contemp Jewish progmg; interview & call-in format with newsmaker guests from politics, entertainment & Israel. Live segments from Israel. Available on barter. Satellite delivered.

Tamouz Media
123 West 93rd Street, New York, NY 10025 USA
(212) 863-9954; *Fax:* (646) 568-5425
www.tamouzmedia.com/
tamouzmedia@aol.com
Ilan Ziv, Programming Director
TV program & documentary production.

Tankersley Productions, Inc., St. Louis
Mailing Address: 858 Hanley Industrial Court, St. Louis, MO 63144
Second Address: 120 N. Robinson, Suite 1600, Oklahoma City, OK 73102
(314) 570-0505
www.tankersleyproductions.com
randy@tankersleyproductions.com
Randy Tankersley, President
Susan Colman, Of Counsel
Neil S. Ende, Attorney
Craig Dindwall, Attorney
Greg Taylor, Of Counsel
Silsa Cabezas, Paralegal

Tapestry International
3 Church Street, Sea Bright, NJ 07760 USA
(732) 559-1300; *Fax:* (732) 559-1309
www.tapestry.tv/
Nancy Walzog, President/ Founder
Laura Ibanez, General Sales Mgr
Karen Carlson, Vice President
Production & distribution company working in the international TV marketplace.

Teen Kids News
182 Sound Beach Ave., Old Greenwich, CT 06870 US
(203) 637-0044; *Fax:* (203) 698-0812
www.teenkidsnews.com
info@teenkidsnews.com
Albert Primo, Executive Producer
Alan Weiss, Executive Producer
Coaching of TV news, program talent, strategic planning & production svcs.
355 W 52nd St, 3rd FL, New York, NY 10019

Tel-Air Interests Inc.
2040 Sherman St., Hollywood, FL 33020 USA
(954) 924-4949; *Fax:* (954) 924-4980
www.telairint.com
telair@aol.com
Grant Gravitt, President
M. Gravitt, Operations Dir
Syndicated TV specials (sports & music), contract production, theatrical short subjects & documentary TV & films, infomercials. Digital recording studio, digital & linear editing.

TeleCom Productions Inc.
5875 Peachtree Industrial Blvd., Suite 150, Norcross, GA 30092 USA
(770) 455-3569; *Fax:* (770) 455-3938
Roger Clark, Chairman
Budd O. Libby, President
Roger Clark, Co-Chairman
Production & syndicator of Let's Go to the Races, Free Cash Lotto, Daily Race Game & Post Time retail prize promotions; random animated digital drawing systems (RADDS).

Telepros
Box 1116, Belmont, CA 94002 USA
(650) 345-0505
www.telepros.org/
telepros@comcast.net
Niels Melo, President
Producers of live entertainment, sports, news, performing arts, corporate videos and webcasts.

The Television Syndication Company, Inc.
520 Sabal Lake Dr., Suite 108, Longwood, FL 32779 USA
(407) 788-6407; *Fax:* (407) 788-4397
www.tvsco.com
cassie@tvsco.com
Cassie M. Yde, President
Barbara DeMaio, Operations Manager
Mary Joyce, International Sales Executive & Acquisitions
Lisa Romine, Syndication Sales Executive, Domestic Markets
A full-svc TV syndication & distribution organization offering TV progmg to bcstrs worldwide.

Televix Entertainment Inc.
449 S. Beverly Drive, Penthouse Suite, Beverly Hills, CA 90212 USA
(310) 788-5500; *Fax:* (310) 286-0207
www.televix.com
Hugo Rose, CEO
Pamela Popp, Operations Dir
Distribution of TV programs in the Latin American & Spanish U.S. markets.

Thomas Craven Film Corp.
5 W. 19th St., 3rd Floor, New York, NY 10011-4216 USA
(212) 463-7190; *Fax:* (212) 627-4761
www.cravenfilms.com
info@cravenfilms.com
Michael Craven, President / Producer / Director
Ernest Barbieri, Vice President / Director / Writer
Penny Craven, Vice President/ Production Manager/ Writer
Ernest Barbieri, Vice President / Director / Writer
Complete film & video production svcs from scripting through shooting & editing to distribution.

Thompson Creative
4141 Office Parkway, Dallas, TX 75204 USA
(888) 976-9663; *Fax:* (214) 521-8578
www.thompsoncreative.com
bcupchurch@thompsoncreative.com
J. Larry Thompson, CEO
Susan Price Thompson, President
Contemp radio ID jingles for all formats.

Tim Cissell Music
1120 Grassmere Dr., Richardson, TX 75080-2909 USA
(972) 680-0817; *Fax:* (972) 680-0866
tcissell@wt.net
Tim Cissell, President
Offers music composition & production for all media (TV/CATV & radio)jingles, IDs, film & video.

Time Capsule, Inc.
124 Cottonwood Lane, Centerville, MA 02632-1911 USA

(800) 822-7785; *Fax:* (508) 637-3333
www.tcapsule.com/radio
tc@tcapsule.com
Richard Teimer, President
Bill Stephens, Operations Dir
Nancy Q. Proctor, VP/Affiliates Relations
Richard Teimer, Resident Sales Therapist
System to bring 1,000 more cash ads per year; daily quizzes fit all formats.

TM Studios
2002 Academy Ln., Suite 110, Dallas, TX 75234 USA
(972) 406-6800; *Fax:* (972) 406-6890
www.tmstudios.com
info@tmstudios.com
Chris Long, Operations Dir
TMC creates, produces & distributes music-based products for bcst, including compilation libraries, production music, I.D. packages & coml jingles.

Today Video
475 10th Ave. 10th Fl., New York, NY 11024 US
(212) 307-0707
www.todayvideo.com
todayvideo@aol.com
David Seeger, CEO
Production svcs.

Tomwil Inc.
4905 Gentry Ave., Valley Village, CA 91607 USA
(818) 769-0883; *Fax:* (818) 769-0887
www.tomwilinc.com/
tomwil@earthlink.net
James Rokos, President
Wilda Rokos, Operations Dir
Distributors of features, light entertainment, sports, series & documentaries to all media in the world market.

Top Hits U.S.A
1133 W. Long Lake Rd., Ste 200, Bloomfield Hills, MI 48302 USA
(248) 647-1068,(800) 521-2537; *Fax:* (888) RPM-0006
www.tophitsusa.com
info@tophitsusa.com
Thomas Kirkorian, President
Wkly CD svc top hits U.S. & CD music libraries. Full CD format svcs & progmg consultation.

Total Traffic & Weather Network
Div/DBA: (Clear Channel Broadcasting)
300 Bridge St., New Cumberland, PA 17070 USA
(717) 774-8150; *Fax:* (717) 774-8160
www.ttwnetwork.com
TV & radio net; radio production/distribution.

Tourism Australia
2029 Century Park E., Mailbox #358/Ste 3150, Los Angeles, CA 90067 USA
(310) 695-3200; *Fax:* (310) 695-3201
www.tourism.australia.com
John O' Sullivan, Managing Director
Lisa Ronson, Chief Marketing Officer
Mark Craig, Executive General Manager, Corporate Services
Penny Lion, Executive General Manager, Events
Karen Halbert, Executive GM, Corporate Affairs, Govt. &Industry
Various Marketing divisions.

TR Productions
2 Thirteenth Street, Floor 3, Charlestown, MA 2129 USA
(617) 241-5500; *Fax:* (508) 650-3455
www.trprod.com
info@trprod.com
Cary Benjamin, President
Production svcs.

The Transcription Company
4100 W. Burbank Blvd., 3rd Flr., Burbank, CA 91505 USA
(818) 848-6500; *Fax:* (818) 556-4150
www.transcripts.net
Michele Bartmon, General Manager
Samantha Somers, Manager, Entertainment
Transcribe all media: TV shows, films, news, sports, documentaries, meetings interviews. Provide closed captioning. Provide translations. Sell ABC News transcripts.
Rapidtext Inc.
1801 Dove St., Suite 101, Newport Beach, CA 92660
(949) 399-9200
Glory Johnson, Coo & Vp

TRF Production Music Libraries
106 Apple Street, Suite 302, Tinton Falls, NJ 07724 USA
(800) 899-MUSIC, (201) 335-0005; *Fax:* (201) 335-0004
www.trfmusic.com
info@trfmusic.com
Michael Nurko, CEO
Largest collection of contemporary, retro and traditional production music. Every category available including all types of ethnic and specialty music.

Troma Entertainment, Inc.
36-40 11th Street, Long Island City, NY 11106 USA
(212) 757-4555; *Fax:* (212) 399-9885
www.troma.com
Lloyd Kaufman, President
Troma is one of the oldest ind film companies in the world. We produce & distribute films & offer stock footage.

TVOntario
Box 200, Stn Q, Toronto, ON M4T 2T1 Canada
(416) 484-2600, (800) 613-0513; *Fax:* (416) 484-2662
ww3.tvo.org
asktvo@tvo.org
Peter O'Brian, Chair
Lisa de Wilde, Chief Executive Officer
Yuonne Carey-Le, General Manager
Clara Arnold, Vice President, Talent & Engagement
Paul Dancy, Vice President, Finance & Legal
John Ferri, Vice President, Current Affairs& Documentaries
Karen Grose, Vice President, Digital Education
Erika Kramer, VP, Production, Distribution & Administration
Todd Slivinskas, Chief Technology Officer
Educ production, educ bcst international program sls, coproduction.

Twentieth Century Fox Television Distribution
Box 900, Beverly Hills, CA 90213 USA
(310) 369-1000; *Fax:* (310) 369-8892
www.foxfast.com
Marion Edwards, President
Mark Kaner, President
Peter Levinshon, President
Production & distribution.
Fox Film Do Brasil Ltda.
Rua Dr. EDuardo De Souza Arrrrranha, 387-3o Andar, Sao Paulo, 04543-121 Brazil
5511-3365-5205; *Fax:* (5511) 3365-5177
Twentieth Century Fox France, Inc.
TV Division 21 bis rue Lord Byron, Paris, 75008 France
33-1-5393-9398; *Fax:* 33-1-5393-9397
Fox/Incendo
101 Bloor Street West, Suite #400, Toronto, ON M5S 2Z7 Canada
416-643-3897; *Fax:* 416-643-3907
Twentieth Century Fox Television Distribution
31-32 Soho Square..., London WID 3AP,
44-20-7437-7766; *Fax:* 44-20-7439-1806
Fox Studios Austrailia
Driver Avenue, Moore Park, 1363 Australia
61-8353-2200; *Fax:* 61-2-835-2205
Twentieth Century Fox Television Distribution
2000 N.W. 150th Avenue, Suite 1110, Pembroke Pines, FL 33028-2867 United States
954-322-5000; *Fax:* 954-322-5275

20th Century Fox/Incendo Television Distribution Ltd.
2 Bloor St. W., Suite 1700, Toronto, ON M4W 3E2 Canada
(416) 643-3897; *Fax:* (416) 643-3898
David Heath, General Sales Mgr
Kimberley Ball, Promotions Manager
Michael D. Murphy, Senior Vice President & Managing Director-Toronto
Michael McLaughlin, Vice-President, Program Sales-Toronto
Jean V,zina, Vice-President, ProgramSales-Montreal
TV program distribution.

Twentieth Television
2121 Ave. of the Stars, Suite 2100, Los Angeles, CA 90067 USA
(310) 369-1000; *Fax:* (310) 369-3898
www.20thtv.com
Greg Meidel, President
Jodi Chisarick, SVP & General Sales Manager
Michael Teicher, Executive Vice President
Richard DuMont, Senior VP, Marketing & Creative
Produces, distributes progmg for net TV, domestic & international TV markets.
Twentieth Television
1211 Avenue of the Americas, 16th Fl., New York, NY 10036 United States
Bob Cesa, Exec Vp Adv Sls & Cable Progmg Sls

TYG Media
PO Box 100120, Palm Bay, FL 32910 USA
(321) 725-0014; *Fax:* (321) 765-6420
www.tygmedia.com/
info@TYGMedia.com
Kerry Fink, CEO
Full Service Production Facility 30 ft Green Screen 3 High Def Cameras HD Edit Suite

U.S. Air Force Recruiting Service
Randolph AFB, 550 D Street W., Universal City, TX 78150-5421 USA
(210) 652-3937; *Fax:* (210) 652-4892
www.airforce.com
Ted Northrup, General Manager
Gary Quesenberry, Broadcasting
Custom production of radio & TV PSAs for Air Force recruiting for local communities.

U.S. Conference of Catholic Bishops
3211 4th St. N.E., Washington, DC 20017 USA
(202) 541-3000; *Fax:* (202) 541-3201
www.usccb.org/
pgarcia@usccb.org
Daniel N. DiNardo, President
Jose H. Gomez, Vice President
James Rogers, Chief Communications Officer
David Felber, Director, Creative Services
Mary McDonald, Director, Creative Services
Judy Keane, Director, Public Affairs
TV & radio pub svc programs.

U.S. Plan B Inc.
466 Orange St., Suite 280, Redlands, CA 92374 USA
(818) 998-8833; *Fax:* (702) 926-2532
www.usplanb.com
Marc Curtis, Programming Director
TV news gathering & production crews, stock footage, rsch.

United Methodist Communications
Mailing Address: 810 12th Avenue, S, Nashville, TN 37203 USA
Second Address: PO Box 320, Nashville, TN 37202
(888) 346-3862; *Fax:* (615) 742-5400
www.umcom.org
infoserv@umcom.org
Maldstone Mulenga, Director of Communications
TV & radio production & distribution.

United Stations Radio Network
25 W. 45 St., New York, NY 10036 USA
(212) 869-1111; *Fax:* (212) 869-1115
www.unitedstations.com
info@usrn.com
Nicholas J. Verbitsky, Chairman & CEO
James M. Higgins, President and COO
Andy Denemark, Executive Vice President, Programming
Charlie Colombo, Executive Vice President
Susan Moore, VP, Research & Sales Support
Richard Baum,Executive Vice President - Sales
Stefan Jones, SVP, Content & Affiliation
Entertainment & comedy. Progmg for radio stns, news, business & weather features.
11400 W. Olympic Blvd., # 200, Los Angeles, CA 90064 United States
(310) 914-0188
Anne Martinez, Mgr
Dallas, TX United States
(972) 506-8776
Rob Ellis, Mgr
333 W. Weeker Dr., # 700, Chicago, IL 60606 United States
(312) 444-2034
Rich Baum, Vp Midwest

University of Colorado Television
Campus Box 379, Boulder, CO 80309 USA
(303) 492-1857; *Fax:* (303) 492-7017
kathleen.albers@colorado.edu
Kate Albers, General Manager
TV & radio program production & distribution; production svcs.

University of Detroit Mercy
4001 W. McNichols, Detroit, MI 48221-3038 USA
(313) 993-1245, (800) 635-5020; *Fax:* (313) 993-1166
www.udmercy.edu
UDMgrad@udmercy.edu
John D. Lewis, Chairman
Antoine M. Garibaldi, PhD, President
Michael Jayson, Chief Engineer
M. Rosita Schiller, RSM, PhD, Vice Chairman
Pamela Zarkowski, MPH, JD, Provost and VP for Academic Affairs
Vincent Abatemarco, CPA, MBA, VPfor Business and Finance
Barbara S. Milbauer, VP for University Advancement

Lisa MacDonnell, M.A.L.S., Executive Assist. to the President
James Priskey, C.P.A., M.B.A., Associate VP for Finance
Radio program syndication.

University of Kentucky Public Relations & Radio-TV News Bureau
101 Main Building, Lexington, KY 40506-0032 USA
(859) 257-1754; *Fax:* (859) 257-4017
www.uky.edu/prmarketing
arl.nathe@uky.edu
Jay Blanton, Executive Director
Kathy Johnson, Director, Main Campus News Bureau
Carl Nathe, Marketing, News Bureau
Kristi Willett, Director, Medical Campus News Bureau
Chuck Ham, Technology & Web Administration
TV & radio program & coml, promotional film production & distribution.

Univision Communications Inc.
5999 Center Drive, Los Angeles, CA 90045 USA
(310) 556-7676; *Fax:* (310) 556-7615
corporate.univision.com/
Ownership: Broadcasting Media Partners Inc.
Randy Falco, President & CEO
John W. Eck, EVP, Technology/Operations/Engineering
Jessica Rodriguez, Executive VP & Chief Marketing Officer
Francisco J. Lopez-Balboa, Executive VP & CFO
Jonathan Schwartz, Chief Legal & CorporateAffairs Officer
Margaret Lazo, Chief Human Resources Officer
Tonia O'Connor, Chief Revenue Officer
Rosemary Mercedes, Executive VP & Chief Communications Officer
Sp language bcst & cable TV net radio stns, music record labels & an internet destination.

USAGov - Government Information & Services
Div/DBA: GSA
1800 F St. N.W., Washington, DC 20405 USA
(202) 501-1794; *Fax:* (202) 501-4281
www.gsa.gov/FCIC
nancy.tyler@gsa.gov
Timothy O. Horne, Acting Administrator, GSA
Alan Thomas, Federal Acquisition Service
Rob Cook, Director, Technology Transformation Services
TV & radio PSAs promoting USA.gov, the official web portal of the federal government.

Viacom Inc.
1515 Broadway, New York, NY 10036 USA
(212) 258-6000; *Fax:* (212) 258-6465
www.viacom.com
Robert Bakish, President & CEO
Tom Gorke, Executive VP/Head, Distribution & Business Dvlpmnt
Wade Davis, Executive VP & CFO
Christa A. D'Alimonte, EVP, General Counsel & Secretary
DeDe Lea, Executive VP, Global Government Affairs
Scott M. Mills, EVP & Chief Administrative Officer
TV program production & distribution, motion pictures production & distribution, book publishing, video production & distribution, theme parks.
Showtime Networks Inc.
1633 Broadway, New York, NY 10019 United States
Simon & Schuster
1230 Ave. of the Americas, New York, NY 10020 United States
MTV Networks
1515 Broadway, New York, NY 10036 United States
Paramount Parks
8720 Red Oak Blvd., Suite 375, Charlotte, NC 28217 United States
Blockbuster Entertainment
1201 Elm St., Dallas, TX 75270 United States
Paramount Pictures
5555 Melrose Ave., Hollywood, CA 90038 United States

Video I-D Teleproductions Inc.
105 Muller Rd., Washington, IL 61571 USA
(800) 333-9123, (309) 444-4323; *Fax:* (309) 444-4333
www.videoid.com
videoid@videoid.com
Sam Wagner, President
Larry Strantz, General Sales Mgr
Gwen Howarter, Promotions Manager
Full Teleproduction Svcs, Location Production, HD Editing, 3D graphics, Custom DVD Authoring, Branding Pkgs - Documentary, Corporate Image, Sales, Marketing, Safety, Training - Police Training - Turnkey Kiosks - Internet Streaming - Webbased instruction - Medical In Service Training

Video Techniques Inc.
1731 1st Street East, Bradenton, FL 34205 USA
(941) 758-3077; *Fax:* (941) 301-4696
www.videotechniques.com
vti1@videotechniques.com
Bob Lorentzen, President, CEO & Executive Producer
Beta SP & MII field & postproduction facilities. CD, DVD authoring & duplication, VHS duplication, streaming video hosting.

VideoActive Productions (VAP)
1560 Broadway, Suite 610, New York, NY 10036 USA
(212) 541-6592
www.videoactiveprod.com
Steven Garrin, President
Digital video, audio production & post production.

Videographic West
Box 1093, 30 Benchmark Rd., Avon, CO 81620 USA
(970) 949-5593; *Fax:* (970) 949-6331
skitv.com
video@colorado.net
Michael Billingsley, President
Stephanie Billingsley, Principal
Specializing in cable sports progmg & distribution, extensive stock footage of action sports, mountain lifestyle, skiing, golf, family & travel. Full-svc production house, field crews, two SD/component pinnacle Liquid uncompressed NLEworkstations, complete multimedia suite with DVD authoring/encoding, 2D animation suite with talented artists.

Videomedia
C/Jose Isbert, 2, Ciudad de la Imagen, Madrid, 28223 ESP
34-91-512.8000; *Fax:* 34-91-518.8017
Jorge Arque, CEO
Daniel Acuna, Programming Director
Mireia Acosta, Fiction manager
Fernanda Montoro, International Division
Independent production company. Entertainment formats & programs, documentaries, fiction.

Videosmith Inc.
200 Spring Garden Street, Suite C, Philadelphia, PA 19123 USA
(215) 238-5070; *Fax:* (215) 238-5075
www.videosmith.com
Steven Smith, President
Chris Cerasoli, General Manager
Helen Taylor, Controller
TV progmg, equipment rentals & production mgmt.

VIEW Video Inc. / Arkadia Entertainment Corp.
PO Box 77, Saugerties, NY 12477 USA
(845) 246-9955, (800) 843-9843; *Fax:* (845) 246-9966
www.view.com
info@view.com, jazz@view.com
Bob Karcy, President & Founder
Stephen Kates, Promotions Manager
International home video production & distribution of special interest progms in the areas of art, jazz, pop music, opera, dance, children's interactive sports & modern lifestyle progms.

Virginia Tech
Div/DBA: Digital Media Services
1185 Perry Street, Blacksburg, VA 24061 USA
(540) 231-8987; *Fax:* (540) 231-4622
www.dms.tlos.vt.edu/
Mark C Harden, Manager
Jeffery E. Dalton, Multimedia Producer Director Senior
David A Mattox Sr, Computer Systems Engineer
Christopher Thomas Valluzzo, Multimedia Producer/Director
Andy Parker, TV/Multimedia Systems Eng B
Taikara APeek, Distance Learning Technician
James J Murphy, Install & Repair Tech Sr
Complete video & audio production & postproduction svcs. Uplink, downlink & CATV opn. Telephone & data communication.

Virginia Tech, NI&S (Network Infrastructure & Services)
1770 Forecast Dr., Blacksburg, VA 24061 USA
(540) 231-6460; *Fax:* (540) 231-8418
www.nis.vt.edu
ask-nis@vt.edu
William C. Dougherty, Chair/ Executive Director
Joe Hutson, Deputy Executive Director & COO
Patricia L. Rodgers, CFO & CAO
Steve Lee, Director, Network Engineering Operations
Brian E. Jones, Director, Converged Network Operations
Data, Voice & Video networks to campus - faculty staff & students.

Vision Broadcasting - KVBA TV 19
1017 New York Ave., Alamogordo, NM 88310 US
(575) 437-1919; *Fax:* (575) 437-5353
www.kvbatv.com
bill@kvbatv.org
William Oechsner Jr., General Manager/Sales Manager
John Warren, Chief Engineer
Kelly Hargrove, Production Manager
Tom Lynch, Traffic & Computer Programmer
Zachary Stoll, Web Development
Bill Wittliff, Tiger Sports Director
Bcst of Christian, loc TV, sports & public interest TV.

Vision Maker Media
1800 North 33rd Street, Lincoln, NE 68503-1409 USA
(402) 472-3522; *Fax:* (402) 472-8675
www.visionmakermedia.org
visionmaker@unl.edu
Mark Trahant, Chairman
Maya Solis-Austin, Vice Chair
Shirley Sneve, Executive Director
Susan Hartmann, Director of Communications
Rebekka Herrera, Assistant Director
Mary Ann Koehler, Business & Projects Manager
Native stories for public broadcasting. Also, your premier source for quality Native American educational and home videos.

VRI (Video Rentals Inc.)
100 Stonehurst Ct., Northvale, NJ 7647 USA
(800) 255-2874,(201) 750-3200; *Fax:* (201) 784-2795
www.rentvri.com
Tom Canavan, Operations Dir
Full-svc rental facility with a complete inventory of bcst & industrial video equipment.

Vuolo Video Air-Chex
Box 880, Novi, MI 48376 USA
(248) 926-1234
www.vuolovideo.com
artvuolo@aol.com
Arthur Vuolo Jr., Founder
Video air checks of American radio stns & An Inside Look.

The Walt Disney Company
500 S. Buena Vista St., Burbank, CA 91521-0990 USA
(818) 560-1000; *Fax:* (818) 560-1930
www.thewaltdisneycompany.com
Robert A. Iger, Chairman & CEO
Christine M. McCarthy, Senior EVP, Chief Financial Officer
Alan Braverman, Senior EVP, General Counsel & Secretary
Ronald L. Iden, Senior VP, Global Security
Kevin Mayer, Senior EVP & Chief StrategyOfficer
Ben Sherwood, Co-Chair, Disney Media & President, Disney/ABC Grp
Zenia Mucha, Senior EVP & Chief Communications Officer
The Walt Disney Company subsidiary; devs & syndicates first-run adult & children's progmg, off-net progmg & feature film packages.

Warner Bros
4000 Warner Boulevard, Building 34R, Burbank, CA 91522 USA
(818) 977-7500; *Fax:* (818) 977-7510
www.hanna-barbera.com
William Hanna, Chairman
William Hanna, Co-Chairman
TV program production.

Warner Bros.
Bldg. 140, 300 Television Plaza, Burbank, CA 91505 USA
(818) 954-7500; *Fax:* (818) 954-7322
www.warnerbros.com/
Kevin Tsujihara, Chairman and Chief Executive Officer
Kim Williams, EVP & Chief Financial Officer
Thomas Gewecke, Chief Digital Officer/ EVP, Strategy & BD
Dee Dee Myers, EVP, Worldwide Communications & Public Affairs
John Rogovin,Executive Vice President & General Counsel
Blair Rich, President, Worldwide Marketing
Kiko Washington, EVP, Worldwide Human Resources
TV program production & distribution.

Warner Bros. Animation
15301 Ventura Blvd., Suite 115301, Unit E, Sherman Oaks, CA 91403 USA
(818) 977-8700; *Fax:* (818) 382-6056
www.warnerbros.com
Kevin Tsujihara, Chairman and Chief Executive Officer
Sam Register, President
Andy Lewis, Operations Dir
Kim Williams, EVP & Chief Financial Officer
Thomas Gewecke, Chief Digital Officer/ EVP, Strategy & BD
Dee Dee Myers, EVP,Worldwide Communications & Public Affairs

John Rogovin, Executive Vice President & General Counsel
Kiko Washington, EVP, Worldwide Human Resources
Dev & produces animated progmg for TV, video & other media.

Warner Bros. Domestic Television Distribution
4000 Warner Blvd., Burbank, CA 91522 USA
(818) 954-5877; *Fax:* (818) 954-5820
www.warnerbros.com
Kevin Tsujihara, Chairman and Chief Executive Officer
Jeffrey R. Schlesinger, President, Worldwide Television Distribution
Ken Werner, President
Kim Williams, Executive Vice President & Chief Financial Officer
Thomas Gewecke, ChjefDigital Officer/ EVP, Strategy & BD
Dee Dee Myers, EVP, Worldwide Communications & Public Affairs
John Rogovin, Executive Vice President & General Counsel
Richard J. Fox, Executive Vice President, International
Kiko Washington, EVP, WorldwideHuman Resources
Print DepartmentBurbank: Bud Rowe, foreign TV print administrator. (818) 954-3731.TV program syndication.

Warner Bros. International Distribution Inc. (Canada)
5000 Yonge St., Suite 1503, Toronto, ON M2N 6P1 Canada
(416) 250-8384; *Fax:* (416) 250-8598
www.wbtvd.com, www.warnerbros.com
Kevin Tsujihara, Chairman and Chief Executive Officer
Jeffrey R. Schlesinger, President, Worldwide Television Distribution
Mickie Steinmann, Senior VP/Managing Director
Kim Williams, Executive Vice President & Chief FinancialOfficer
Thomas Gewecke, Chief Digital Officer/ EVP, Strategy & BD
Dee Dee Myers, EVP, Worldwide Communications & Public Affairs
John Rogovin, Executive Vice President & General Counsel
Reg Harpur, EVP, International Warner Bros.Entertainment
Kiko Washington, EVP, Worldwide Human Resources
TV progm distribution & promotions for Canada.

Warner Bros. International Television Production
4000 Warner Blvd., Burbank, CA 91522 USA
(818) 954-6000; *Fax:* (818) 954-4040
www.warnerbros.com/studio/divisions/television/international-television-production.ht
Kevin Tsujihara, Chairman and Chief Executive Officer
Jeffrey Schlesinger, President, Worldwide Television Distribution
Kim Williams, Executive Vice President & Chief Financial Officer
Thomas Gewecke, Chief Digital Officer/ EVP,Strategy & BD
Dee Dee Myers, EVP, Worldwide Communications & Public Affairs
John Rogovin, Executive Vice President & General Counsel
Kiko Washington, EVP, Worldwide Human Resources
TV program production & distribution.
Warner Bros. PTY. Ltd.
8-20 Napier St, North Sydney, NSW 2060
011-61-2-9957-3899; *Fax:* 011-61-2-9956-7788
Wayne Broun, Vp Mgng Dir Australia, Asia Pacific
Greg Robertson, Vp Asia
Time Warner Entertainment Japan
1-2-4 Hamamatsu-cho, Minato-ku, Tokyo, 105 Japan
011-81-3-5472-8341; *Fax:* 011-81-3-5472-6343
Teruji Mochimaru, Mgng Dir Japan
Warner Bros. International TV
Artuto Soria, 336 1, Madrid 28033,
011-34-1-384-06-40; *Fax:* 011-34-1-384-06-41
Jose Abad, Sls Exec Sp Territories
Warner Bros. International TV
67 Avenue Dewagram, Paris, 75017 France
011-33-1-5537-5933; *Fax:* 011-33-1-5537-4968
Michel Lecourt, Vp Fr Territories
Warner Bros. (Mexico) S.A.
Colonea Codesa, Acapulco 37 06140,
011-525-211-3353-211-0293 211-0298-211-0466; *Fax:* 011-525-553-2822-553-2002
Jorge Sanchez, Vp Latin America
Warner Bros. International TV
135 Wardour St, London W1V 4AP,
011-44-171-494-3710; *Fax:* 011-44-171-287-9086
Richard Milnes, Vp Uk Territories, Turkey, Israel

Warner Bros. Television Production
4000 Warner Blvd., Burbank, CA 91522 USA
(818) 954-6000; *Fax:* (818) 954-7048
www.warnerbros.com
Kevin Tsujihara, Chairman and Chief Executive Officer
Kim Williams, Executive Vice President & Chief Financial Officer
Thomas Gewecke, Chief Digital Officer/ EVP, Strategy & BD
Dee Dee Myers, EVP, Worldwide Communications & PublicAffairs
John Rogovin, Executive Vice President & General Counsel
Kiko Washington, EVP, Worldwide Human Resources
TV program production.

Warren Miller Entertainment
Div/DBA: AIM-Active Interest Media
5720 Flatiron Parkway, Boulder, CO 80301 USA
(303) 253-6300; *Fax:* (303) 253-6380
www.warrenmillertv.com, www.aimstudios.tv, www.aimmedia.com
Andrew W. Clurman, President & CEO, AIM
Jeffrey Moore, Senior Executive Producer
Jonathan Dorn, Chief Innovation Officer / General Manager
Josh Haskins, Producer - Annual Warren Miller Feature Film
Second unit feature, coml, TV program, promotion; film production & distribution specializing in snow & outdoor adventure sports.

Wawatay Native Communications Society
Box 1180, 16 Fifth Ave., Sioux Lookout, ON P8T 1B7 Canada
(807) 737-2951, (800) 243-9059; *Fax:* (807) 737-3224
www.wawataynews.ca
John Gagnon, CEO & Publisher
Mike Metatawabin, President
Jeff Hindy, Head Technician/Audio Engineer
Adelaide Anderson, Office Manager/Finance Clerk
Tom Scura, Sales
Mark Kakekagumick, Radio Manager
Chris McKay, BusinessManager
Jerry Sawanas, Senior Broadcaster
Radio & TV (Cree, Ojibway & English) net, bilingual nwspr, aboriginal language translations, multi-track audio recording.

The Weather Company (formerly WSI)
400 Minuteman Rd., Andover, MA 01810 USA
(978) 983-6300; *Fax:* (978) 983-6400
business.weather.com
Mark Gildersleeve, VP & Head of Business Solutions
Bill Dow, Head of Media Solutions
Dr. Peter P. Neilley, Director, Weather Forecasting Sciences
Michelle Boockoff-Bajdek, Head of Global Marketing
World leader in providing real-time weather data, imagery, forecasting & weather progmg for bcst stns, cable operators & cable nets.

WeatherVision Inc.
NSS Data: TV-CATV only
916 Foley Street, Jackson, MS 39202
(601) 665-7737, (800) 353-9177; *Fax:* (601) 948-6052
www.weathervision.com
edward@weathervision.com
Edward Saint-Pe', President
Tracy Sandlin, General Sales Mgr
Brandon Bouche, Chief Meteorologist
Customized, localized TV weathercasts with or without meteorologists. Barter/cash via Ku-band satellite. Complete studio teleport for use by news media on site. Avid editing available on site. Serves radio, TV & 3-D branding animation svcs.

Webcasting Television, LLC
2500 E. Imperial Highway, Ste 201 #185, Brea, CA 92821 USA
(714) 782-7305, (866) 489-0643; *Fax:* (714) 693-5395
vbuttons.com
contact@webcastingtv.com
Burton Yale, CEO
Offers the latest in editing technology; from D-2 to Hi8.

WEP, Llc.
One Memorial Dr., St. Louis, MO 63102 USA
(314) 345-1000; *Fax:* (314) 345-1091
www.wep.com
Jeremy Corray, Creative Director
Tommy Yune, Robotech Creative Director
Bob Koplar, Vice President
Kevin McKeever, VP, Marketing for Robotech
Joseph Rybandt, Senior Editor-Dynamite Comics
TV program production & distribution.

Westar Music
105 West Beaver Creek Rd., Suite 4, Richmond Hill, ON L4B 1C6 Canada
(905) 886-3100, (866) 463-0100; *Fax:* (905) 886-6800
www.westarmusic.com
Peter Alexander, Sales Manager
Elliott Zimmerman, Music Consultant
Craig Nimens, Music Consultant
High caliber production music in a wide var of categories for bcst, cable, film, corporate video & multimedia applications.

Westwood One
Div/DBA: (Cumulus Media)
Candler Tower, 220 W. 42nd Street, New York, NY 10036 USA
(212) 967-2888, (888) HELP450
www.westwoodone.com/
Jana Polsky, Director, Communications
Independent, full-service radio network, offering formats, prep, programming, jingles & imaging as well as national advertising sales representation.

WestWorks Studios
4100 E. Dry Creek Rd., Centennial, CO 80122 USA
(800) 491-1947
www.westworksstudios.com
info@westworksstudios.com
Todd Smoots, Director of Production Operations
Robert Baker, Manager of Production Engineering
Network origination, production, postproduction, uplinking, compression, remote production, audio production.

WFMT Radio Network
5400 N. St. Louis Ave., Chicago, IL 60625-4698 USA
(773) 279-2000,(800) USA-WFMT; *Fax:* (773) 279-2199
www.wfmt.com
radionetwork@wfmt.com
James W. Mabie, Chairman
Daniel J. Schmidt, President & CEO
Reese Marcusson, COO & CFO
Tony Macaluso, Director, Network Syndication
Estlin Usher, Station Relations Manager
Joshua Sauvageau, Operations Manager
Jill Britton, SVP &Chief Development Officer
Anne Gleason, SVP of Marketing & Digital Media
Program production & distribution; 84 hour-a-week classical music format with program hosts in one-hour modules, loc sound included.

WGN Radio (Tribune Broadcasting)
435 N. Michigan Ave., Suite 720, Chicago, IL 60611 USA
(312) 222-4700; *Fax:* (312) 222-4180
www.wgnradio.com
aquigley@tribune.com
Jeff Hill, General Sales Manager
Tape & internet digital delivered talk, sports & specialty programs including: Chicago Blackhawks, WGN Radio Theater, Wintrust Business Lunch.

White Rabbit Productions
1587 S. Main St., Salt Lake City, UT 84115 USA
(800) 549-3115,(801) 463-9292; *Fax:* (801) 463-7226
www.whiterabbitproductions.com
diana@whiterabbitproductions.com
Sam Prigg, Photographer
Aron Prigg, Director, Photography
Diana Parsons, Production Manager
Complete film & video production svcs; two Ikegami HL-V55 Beta Sp camera packages, digital video point-of-view cam, non-linear editing.

Wide Eye Productions, Inc.
Mailing Address: 1018 W Hays Streetÿ, Boise, ID 83702 USA
Second Address: 10201 Roosevelt Way NE, Seattle, WA 98125
(208) 336-0391, (206) 999-2860; *Fax:* (208) 336-6644
www.wideeye.tv
info@wideeye.tv
Tom Hadzor, Director / Photographer
Jennifer Isenhart, Writer / Producer
David Didonato, Photographer/ Editor
Cheryl Reed, Book Keeper
Kevin Eslinger, Photographer/ Editor
Wolfgang Isenhart, Director/ Photographer/ Editor
SusieKoether, Writer/ Producer
Full-service bcst & industrial video production. ENG/EFP. High definition & Sony B-600.

William F. Cooke Television Programs
307-23 Lesmill Rd, Toronto, ON M3B 3P6 Canada
(416) 967-6141; *Fax:* (416) 967-5133
info@cooketv.com
William F. Cooke, CEO
Alex McWilliams, Promotions Manager
TV program production & distribution.

William Mauldin Productions Inc.
PO Box 39676, Greensboro, NC 27438 USA
(336) 299-2005; *Fax:* (540) 301-0399
www.mauldin.net
questions@mauldin.net
William Mauldin, CEO
Major market talent for narrations & voice overs, documentaries, stn IDs, program intros, comls for any media market. Let us provide the voice & production for your projects. We can offer

finished products via CD, MP3, or via the web. Checkour website for samples of our work!

WKMG Productions
4466 N. John Young Pkwy., Orlando, FL 32804 USA
(407) 521-1200; *Fax:* (407) 521-1204
www.clickorlando.com/
webstaff@clickorlando.com
Matt Austin, Anchor
Louis Bolden, Investigative Reporter
Tom Sorrells, Chief Meterologist
Jamie Seh, Sports Director
TV program, coml, promotional film production; production svcs, post production & field production. WKMG production resources primarily dedicated to stn use.

WMAQ-TV
Div/DBA: (NBC 5 Chicago)
454 N. Columbus Dr., Chicago, IL 60611 USA
(312) 836-5555, 800-CH5-NEWS; *Fax:* (312) 527-4290
www.nbcchicago.com/
Zoraida Sambolin, Weekday Edition Co-Anchor
TV program production; production svcs.

Work Edit
270 W. 39th St., 11th Floor, New York, NY 10018 USA
(212) 719-4577; *Fax:* (212) 719-4380
www.workedit.com
Dalton Helms, Producer/Cinematographer
Ken Sackheim, Director/Editor/Composer
Tom Viglietta, Project Manager
Marcus Bonilla, Editor
Post production svcs, DVD authoring.

World Radio Network
Div/DBA: Babcock Media
10 Wyvil Road, London, SW8 2TG United Kingdom
44-20-7896-9000; *Fax:* 44-20-7896- 9007
www.wrn.org
info@wrnbroadcast.com
Paul Firth, Director of Brodcast Operations
Dean Haddock, Director of Broadcast Services
World Radio Network (via Galaxy 25) was acquired by Babcock International Group and now focuses on national, regional, and international current affairs and news, coming directly from the countries of origin.

World Vision
Mailing Address: PO Box 9716, Federal Way, WA 98063 USA
Second Address: 34834 Weyerhaeuser Way South, Federal Way, WA 98001
(888) 511-6548
www.worldvision.org
Dr. Joan Singleton, Chair
Richard Stearns, President, U.S.
Edgar Sandoval, COO
Doug Treff, CFO
Christine Talbot, Senior Vice President, Human Resources
Chris Glynn, Senior VP, Transformational Engagement
TV program distribution for ind productions.

Worldvision Enterprises U.K. Ltd
54 Pont St, London SW1X OAE,
011-441-71-584-5357; *Fax:* 011-441-71-581-3483
Bill Peck, Chairman
Janice Wilson, CEO/COO
Zsuzsanna Jung, Operations Dir

Worldvision Enterprises S.A.R.L.
28, Rue Bayard, Paris, 75008 France
011-33-1-4723-3995; *Fax:* 011-33-1-4070-9269
Mary Jane Fourniel, Chairman
Catherine Molinier, CEO/COO
John Hernan, President

Worldvision Enterprises of Australia PTY Ltd.
5-13 Northcliff St, Sydney, Milsons Point, 02061
011-61-2-9922-4722; *Fax:* 011-61-2-9955-8207 TWX: (790) 70474
Brian Rhys-Jones, Chairman
Paul Stuart, CEO/COO
Karen Zylstra, President
22270 Rua Voluntarios Da Patria N, Gr.604, Rio de Janeiro, CEP 22270 Brazil
011-55-21-539-2992; *Fax:* 011-55-21-266-4737
Raymundo Rodriguez, Chairman
Maria Alice Freire, CEO/COO
Tsukiji Hamarikyu Bldg, 7th Fl, 5-3-3 Tsukiji, Chou-ku, Tokyo, 104 Japan
011-81-3-3545-3978; *Fax:* 011-81-3-5550-8316
Mie Horasawa, Chairman
Yukie Kumagai, CEO/COO

Adalia Anstalt
Via del Corso, 22/Int 10, 00186 Rome
011-39-6-322-5190; *Fax:* 011-39-6-322-6450
Michael Kiwe, Dorothy Shaw

Worldview Entertainment Inc.
1384 Broadway, 25th Floor, New York, NY 10018 US
(212) 431-3090; *Fax:* (212) 431-0390
http://worldviewent.com
info@worldviewent.com
Christopher Woodrow, Chairman/CEO
Molly Conners, COO
Archival stock footage library, distribution to international bcstrs.

The Worship Network
PO Box 428, Safety Harbor, FL 34695 USA
(800) 728-8723; *Fax:* (727) 530-0671
www.worship.net
info@worship.net
Bruce Koblish, President & CEO
Tim Brown, Operations Dir
Inspirational music set to nature scenes, overlaid with scripture 24 hours a day. Progmg is interspersed with short devotional teachings.

The WPA Film Library
16101 S. 108th Ave., Orland Park, IL 60467 USA
(708) 460-0555, (800) 323-0442; *Fax:* (708) 460-0187
www.wpafilmlibrary.com
sales@wpafilmlibrary.com
Diane Paradiso, Director of Sales
One of the largest stock footage libraries in the U.S. WPA offers holdings in newsreels, music, pop culture & stock shots. Archival & contemporary footage.

WQED Multimedia
4802 5th Ave., Pittsburgh, PA 15213 USA
(412) 622-1370; (412) 622-1300; *Fax:* (412) 622-1488
www.wqed.org
info@wqed.org
W. Thomas McGough, Chairman
Deborah L. Acklin, President & CEO
Mike Waruszewski, Finance Director
Jacqui Thomas, General Counsel
Lilli Mosco, General Sales Mgr
Darryl Ford Williams, Vice President of Content
Lilli Mosco, VicePresident of Development and Membership
TV & radio program/production, distribution; production svcs & web, publishing.

WQXR
C/O New York Public Radio, 160 Varick Street, 8th floor, New York, NY 10013 USA
(646) 829-4000; *Fax:* (212) 633-7666
www.wqxr.org
acohen@wqxr.org
Shannon Connolly, Senior VP & General Manager
Matt Abramovitz, Program Director
Michael Shobe, Assistant Program Director
Radio program production. The classical Radio Station of the New York Times.

WRS/Channel One
213 Tech Road, Pittsburgh, PA 15205 USA
(412) 937-1200; *Fax:* (412) 922-1200
jackn@wrslabs.com
F. Napor, President
Complete syndication & distribution svcs via satellite & tape. Integration, AMOL encoding, duplication, uplink/downlink fulfillment, audio, film-to-tape transfer; replication of CD/DVD.

WTOB—Community/Government Access TV
203 Washington Street, SW, Blacksburg, VA 24060 USA
(540) 443-1090; *Fax:* (540) 951-1875
www.blacksburg.gov
wtob@blacksburg.gov
Carlton Herman, Station Manager
Heather Browning, Community Relations Manager
Public interest video, live Town Council & Planning Commission meeting, live & archived streaming video.

WWE Media (World Wrestling Entertainment)
Titan Tower, 1241 E. Main St., Stamford, CT 6902 USA
(203) 352-8600; *Fax:* (203) 352-8699
www.wwe.com
Vincent McMahon, Chairman & CEO
George Barrios, CFO
Kevin Dunn, Executive VP, Television Production
Lance McConomy, Senior Director, Broadcast Operations
Michelle D. Wilson, Chief Revenue & Marketing Officer
Exclusive worldwide distributor of WWF events, TV programs (bcst network/syndication, PPV & basic cable) & other sports/entertainment properties.

The Wyland Group
Div/DBA: Lifestyle Magazine
PO Box 7729, Riverside, CA 92513 USA
(805) 955-7700, (888) 940-0062, (805) 955-7680; *Fax:* (805) 522-1082
www.lifestyle.org
Mike Tucker, Executive Producer
Jeff Wood, Producer
Chauncey Smith, Network & Station Director
Monique Roy, Associate Producer
Production of health related, family values progmg. 4 million viewers.

Yada/Levine Video Productions
135 N. Screenland Drive, Burbank, CA 91505 USA
(323) 461-1616; *Fax:* (323) 461-2288
www.yadalevine.com
Michael Yada, President
Full-service video productions. Crews & equipment including HD, DV & Betacam SP.

Youtoo America
Div/DBA: (formerly America ONE Network)
6565 North MacArthur Blvd, Suite 400, Las Colinas, TX 75039 US
(214) 444-7100; *Fax:* (469) 828-1745
www.youtoo.com; www.youtooamerica.com
Chris Wyatt, President

Zachry Associates
Mailing Address: 500 Chestnut Street, Suite 2000, Abilene, TX 79602 USA
Second Address: 6301 Gaston Avenue, Dallas, TX 75214
(325) 677-1342, (325) 829-1671; *Fax:* (325) 672-2001
www.zachryinc.com/
Paul Fulham, CFRE, President
Bob Nutt, Vice President
Produces & distributes TV & radio programs & comls as well as promotional films & production svcs.

ZBS Foundation
174 N. River Rd., Fort Edward, NY 12828 USA
(518) 695-6406, (800) 662-3345; *Fax:* (518) 695-4041
www.zbs.org
custserv@zbs.org, dave@davebush.com
Thomas Lopez, President
Producer of audio drama.

Equipment Manufacturers and Distributors Subject Index

Acoustic Equipment
Acoustic Systems/ETS-Lindgren HQ
Acoustical Solutions Inc.

Acoustical Panels and Treatment
Acoustical Solutions Inc.
Industrial Acoustics Co., Inc.
Noise Control Corp.
Pinta Acoustic Inc.
RAM SYSTEMS, LLC

Aerial Buckets
Equipment Technology LLC.
Time Manufacturing Co.

Amplifiers
Amplivox Portable Sound Systems
BEXT Inc.
Electroline Equipment Inc.
Emerson Network Power-Viewsonics
FitzCo. Inc.
Lindsay Broadband Inc.
M/A-COM Technology Solutions Inc.
Microsemi Corporation
Opamp Labs Inc.
Peavey Electronics Corporation
QSC Audio Products, LLC
Radio Design Labs. (RDL)
TOA Electronics Inc.
Whirlwind
e2v Inc.

Amplifiers, Audio
A R T Applied Research and Technology
ARRIS
Amplivox Portable Sound Systems
Audio Implements/GKC
BGW Systems, Amplifier Technologies, Inc.
Benchmark Media Systems Inc.
Bogen Communications Inc.
Bryston Ltd.
Cablynx, Inc.
DBX Professional Products
ESE
Galaxy Audio Inc.
Harman International
Henry Engineering
JBL Professional
LINK Electronics Inc.
Opamp Labs Inc.
Philip-Cooke Co.
RTS Systems Telex Communications Inc
Radio Engineering Industries Inc.
Sescom Inc.
TC Group Americas Inc.
Video Accessory Corp.
Yamaha Corp. of America

Amplifiers, RF
Andrew Corp.
Bauer Transmitters, Inc.
Blonder Tongue Laboratories Inc.
C-COR/ Arris
Channel Master
Communication & Power Industries
Crown Broadcast IREC
DMT USA, Inc.
Energy-Onix Broadcast Equipment Co. Inc.
LARCAN
Lindsay Broadband Inc.
MCL Inc.
North American Cable Equipment Inc.
North Hills Signal Processing Corp.
Qintar Technologies Inc.
Vertex Communications Corp.
e2v Inc.

Amplifiers, Video
Cablynx, Inc.
Comprehensive Cable and Connectivity Company
ESE
Interlogix
Intersil Corp.
LINK Electronics Inc.
Opamp Labs Inc.
Philip-Cooke Co.
Radio Engineering Industries Inc.
Video Accessory Corp.

Analyzers, Distortion, Intermodulation
Audio Precision Inc.
Boonton Electronics Corp.
Electro Rent Corp.
Potomac Instruments, Inc.
Radiodetection
Tektronix

Animation Systems
Autodesk
Autodesk, Inc.
Hotbox Digital

Announcement Systems
Bogen Communications Inc.
Interface Media Group
Talk-A-Phone Co.

Antennas and Accessories
ATCI/Antenna Technology Communications Inc.
American Antenna Inc.
California Amplifier
Channel Master
Cortland Cable Co. Inc.
Gorman-Redlich Manufacturing Co.
Harris Corp.
Jampro Antennas Inc.
Kathrein Inc., Scala Division
LBA Technology Inc.
Lindsay Broadband Inc.
M/A-COM Technology Solutions Inc.
Mega Hertz
NSI
Radio Engineering Industries Inc.
Radio Frequency Systems
S W R Inc.
Simplicity Tool Corp
Times Fiber Communications Inc.
Tyco Electronics

Antennas, Broadcast
ATCI/Antenna Technology Communications Inc.
Allen Osborne Associates Inc.
American Antenna Inc.
Andrew Corp.
BEXT Inc.
Comtech Antenna Systems Inc.
Continental Electronics Corporation
Crossed Field Antennas Inc.
DMT USA, Inc.
Dielectric Communications
ERI - Electronics Research, Inc.
Kathrein Inc., Scala Division
Kintronic Labs Inc.
LARCAN USA Inc
Lindsay Broadband Inc.
MYAT Inc.
Micro Communications Inc.
Phasetek Inc.
Pinzone Engineering Group Inc.
RF Specialties Group
Radio Frequency Systems
S W R Inc.
Scotts Valley Group Inc
Shively Labs
Superior Satellite Engineers Inc.
Tower Network Services
Transcom Corp.

Antennas, Earth Station
ATCI/Antenna Technology Communications Inc.
All Mobile Video Inc.
American Antenna Inc.
Andrew Corp.
Comtech Antenna Systems Inc.
D.H. Satellite
Mega Hertz
Pinzone Engineering Group Inc.
Radio Research Instrument Co. Inc.
Superior Satellite Engineers Inc.
Vertex Communications Corp.

Antennas, Installation
Abroyd Communications Ltd.
Connex Telecommunications Corporation
ERI - Electronics Research, Inc.
Fred A. Nudd Corp.
Mega Hertz
National Steel Erectors Corp.
S W R Inc.
Structural System Technology Inc.
Superior Satellite Engineers Inc.
Swager Communications Inc.
Tower Network Services

Antennas, Satellite
ATCI/Antenna Technology Communications Inc.
American Antenna Inc.
California Amplifier
Comtech Antenna Systems Inc.
D.H. Satellite
MRPP Inc.
Mega Hertz
North American Cable Equipment Inc.
Pinzone Engineering Group Inc.
Superior Satellite Engineers Inc.

Antennas, TVRO
American Antenna Inc.
California Amplifier
Comtech Antenna Systems Inc.
D.H. Satellite
Pinzone Engineering Group Inc.
Superior Satellite Engineers Inc.

Attenuators and Equalizers
ARRIS
Allen Avionics, Inc.
Emerson Network Power-Viewsonics
Lindsay Broadband Inc.
Narda Microwave-East L-3 Communications Co.
Penny + Giles
Shallco Inc.
Tech Laboratories Inc.

Audio Accessories
AKG Acoustics, U.S.
ATI-Audio Technologies Inc.
Allsop Inc.
Aphex Systems Ltd.
Audio Implements/GKC
HAVE Inc.
Henry Engineering
JOA Cartridge Service
Jensen Transformers Inc.
Peavey Electronics Corporation
Polyline Corp.
Professional Sound Corp.
Radio Design Labs. (RDL)
Sager Electronics
Sescom Inc.
Sprague Magnetics Inc.
Star Case Manufacturing Co. Inc.
TAI Audio
The J-Lab Co.
Trimm Inc.
Video Accessory Corp.
Westlake Audio
Wireworks Corporation
Zack Electronics Inc.

Audio Amps, AGC & Limiters
Professional Sound Corp.
Renkus-Heinz Inc.
Samson Technologies Corp.
Sescom Inc.

Audio Cartridges
Stanton Group, Inc.

Audio Compressors
Alesis
Furman
Orban Corporate
Sascom Marketing Group
Sescom Inc.
TC Electronic

Audio Consoles
Arrakis Systems Inc.
Euphonix Inc.
Henry Engineering
Imagine Communications Corp.
Logitek Electronic Systems Inc
Wheatstone Corp.

Audio Equipment
Audio Implements/GKC
Audio Precision Inc.
BBE Sound Inc.
Bexel
Bogen Communications Inc.
Broadcast Store Inc.
Burlington A/V Recording Media Inc.

EQUIPMENT MANUFACTURERS

Comprehensive Cable and Connectivity Company
Comrex Corp.
Countryman Associates Inc.
DBX Professional Products
EAGLE Avionics Systems
Film/Video Equipment Service Co. Inc.
FitzCo. Inc.
Full Compass Systems Ltd.
Galaxy Audio Inc.
Group One Ltd.
Intermed VideoTechnologies, Inc.
Jensen Transformers Inc.
Lectrosonics Inc.
Memorex Products Inc.
Nady Systems Inc.
Opamp Labs Inc.
Peavey Electronics Corporation
Photomart Cine-Video Inc.
ProAudio.com/Crouse-Kimzey Company
Professional Sound Corp.
Protech Audio Corp.
QSC Audio Products, LLC
Samson Technologies Corp.
Sascom Marketing Group
Sennheiser Electronic Corp.
Servoreeler Systems
Systems Wireless Ltd.
TAI Audio
TC Group Americas Inc.
TEAC America Inc.
Visual Sound Inc.
Whirlwind

Audio Jackfields, Pre-Wired
Audio Accessories Inc.
Furman
Glentronics Inc.
Miles Tek Corporation
Penny + Giles
Sager Electronics
Switchcraft Inc.

Audio Limiters
Harman International
Orban Corporate
Symetrix Inc.

Audio Mixers and Recorders
ATI-Audio Technologies Inc.
Alesis
Audio-Technica U.S., Inc.
Location Sound Corp.
Martinsound Inc.
Micro Technology Unlimited
Nady Systems Inc.
Otari USA Sales Inc.
Penny + Giles
Professional Sound Corp.
Professional Sound Services Inc.
Protech Audio Corp.
Radio Design Labs. (RDL)
Shure Inc.
Superscope Technologies
United States Broadcast
Yamaha Corp. of America

Audio Monitoring Systems
AKG Acoustics, U.S.
B&B Systems
Dorrough Electronics
Fostex USA
Furman
IRIS Technologies Inc.
Martinsound Inc.
McCurdy Radio Ltd.
Renkus-Heinz Inc.
Westlake Audio

Audio Noise Reduction Systems
Allen Avionics, Inc.
Avid : Digidesign
Dolby Laboratories Inc.
Image Video
Noise Control Corp.
Symetrix Inc.

Audio Processors
Audioarts Engineering
BBE Sound Inc.
Inovonics Inc.
Linear Acoustic Inc.
Modulation Sciences Inc.
Nady Systems Inc.
Peavey Electronics Corporation
Protech Audio Corp.
Samson Technologies Corp.
Sascom Marketing Group
Symetrix Inc.

Audio Replacement Heads
International Electro-Magnetics, Inc.
Sprague Magnetics Inc.

Audio Routing Switches
Burst Electronics Inc.
Logitek Electronic Systems Inc
NTV International Corporation
NVISION Products
Omicron Video
Radio Design Labs. (RDL)
Richmond Sound Design Ltd.
Sierra Automated Systems & Engineering Corp.
Sigma Electronics Inc.
The ISIS Group
Utah Scientific Inc.

Audio Signal Processing Systems
Alesis
Aphex Systems Ltd.
BBE Sound Inc.
Broadcasters General Store Inc.
Communications Specialties Inc.
Dolby Laboratories Inc.
Group One Ltd.
International Datacasting Corp.
Lectrosonics Inc.
Orban Corporate
Pixel Instruments Corp.
Sabine Inc.
Shure Inc.
Symetrix Inc.
TC Electronic

Audio Systems and Components
Audio Implements/GKC
Gefen Inc.
Parsons Audio LLC
Protech Audio Corp.
VidCAD LLC
Visual Sound Inc.

Audio Test Tapes, Gauges & Equipment
Audio Precision Inc.
Leader Instruments Corp.
Tentel

Audio Transmission Equipment
Artel Video Systems
Intelligent Media Technology
International Datacasting Corp.
MUSICAM U.S.A.
Neutrik U.S.A. Inc.
TFT Inc.

Audio/Video Cartridges
Memorex Products Inc.

Audiotape
Burlington A/V Recording Media Inc.
Intermed VideoTechnologies, Inc.
Maxell Corp. of America
Memorex Products Inc.
Moviola
Sony BMG Music Entertainment

Audiotape Cartridge Machines
A.C.C. Electronix, Inc.

Audiotape Duplicating Equipment
National Audio Co. Inc.

Automated Newsroom Systems
Avid Broadcast
Comprompter Inc.
Dalet Digital Media Systems
Harris Corporation
Thomson Reuters
WireReady NSI

Automated Radio
Dalet Digital Media Systems
ENCO Systems Inc.
Encoda Systems Inc.
Marketron Broadcast Solutions
Radio Computing Services (RCS)
Register Data Systems
WireReady NSI

Automated Tape Winders
Otari USA Sales Inc.

Automated Telephone & Voice Mail
Aspect Software
Microlog
TALX Corp.

Automatic Cassette Loaders
Otari USA Sales Inc.

Automatic Transmission Systems
Encoda Systems Inc.
Harris Corporation

Automation Systems
Adtec Digital
Arrakis Systems Inc.
Broadcast Electronics Inc.
ENCO Systems Inc.
Encoda Systems Inc.
Harris Corporation
Imagine Communications Corp.
Leightronix Inc.
Media Computing Inc.
Mediastar, Inc.
Orban
Radio Computing Services (RCS)
Register Data Systems
Sundance Digital Inc.
Technicolor SA
Time Logic Inc.
WireReady NSI

Automation, Switching and Control
Adtec Digital
Florical Systems
Harris Corporation
Leightronix Inc.
MATCO Inc.
Register Data Systems
Richmond Sound Design Ltd.
Sierra Automated Systems & Engineering Corp.
Sundance Digital Inc.
Technicolor SA
Texscan MSI

Automation, TV Station
Avid Broadcast
Dalet Digital Media Systems
Encoda Systems Inc.
Florical Systems
Harris Corporation
Leightronix Inc.
Media Computing Inc.
Sintec Media
Sundance Digital Inc.
Technicolor SA
Time Logic Inc.
Videotron Ltee
WireReady NSI

Batteries and Accessories
ADCOUR, Inc.
Acme Electric Corp., Aerospace Division
Alan Gordon Enterprises Inc.
Alexander Technologies
Alpha Technologies Inc.
Arri Canada Ltd.
Battery Pros Inc.
Burlington A/V Recording Media Inc.
Cine 60 Inc.
Frezzolini Electronics Inc.
Marathon Norco Aerospace, Inc.
The Tiffen Company

Blimps
Blimpy Floating Signs/Bend-A-Lite

Blowers and Fans
Allied Electronics Inc.
Bud Industries Inc.
Condux International, Inc.
Emcor Enclosures
Optima Electronic Packaging Systems
Sager Electronics

Booms and Cameras
Alan Gordon Enterprises Inc.

Boosters, TV
Axcera

Broadcast Audio Products
360 Systems
A.C.C. Electronix, Inc.
AKG Acoustics, U.S.
AheadTek
Aphex Systems Ltd.
Audio Implements/GKC
Belden
Benchmark Media Systems Inc.
Bradley Broadcast and Pro Audio
Comrex Corp.
DBX Professional Products
Dolby Laboratories Inc.
Ensemble Designs
FM SYSTEMS Inc.
Fostex USA
Full Compass Systems Ltd.
Furman
Gefen Inc.
JOA Cartridge Service
Lectrosonics Inc.
Logitek Electronic Systems Inc
MUSICAM U.S.A.
Marketron Broadcast Solutions
Orban
Parsons Audio LLC
Sennheiser Electronic Corp.
TAI Audio
Talk-A-Phone Co.
Telex Communications Inc.
WEGENER
Wheatstone Corp.
teletech.ca

Broadcast Equipment
Advanced Media Technologies, Inc.
Allen Osborne Associates Inc.
Allison Payments Systems L.L.C.
Analog Digital International Inc.
Audio Implements/GKC
Autodesk
BEXT Inc.
Bradley Broadcast and Pro Audio
Broadcast Store Inc.
Broadcast Supply Worldwide
C-COR/ Arris
Cisco Systems, Inc.
Energy-Onix Broadcast Equipment Co. Inc.
Ensemble Designs
FitzCo. Inc.
Ikegami Electronics (U.S.A.) Inc.
Inscriber Technology Corporation
Intermed VideoTechnologies, Inc.
J.A. Taylor & Associates
JVC Professional Products Company
Kathrein Inc., Scala Division
Kay Industries Inc.
Konica Minolta Business Solutions USA Inc
MRPP Inc.
MUSICAM U.S.A.
Marshall Electronics
Masterclock, Inc.
Merlin Engineering Works Inc.
Miranda Technologies Inc.
Modulation Sciences Inc.
NVISION Products
Nautel Ltd.
Panasonic Broadcast & Television Systems Co.
Phasetek Inc.
ProAudio.com/Crouse-Kimzey Company
RAM SYSTEMS, LLC
RF Specialties Group
Ross Video Ltd.
Sencore Inc.
Specialized Communications Corp.
Technet Systems Group
Thomson
Transcom Corp.
Westcott Co.

Broadcast RF Equipment
AVI Systems
Allen Avionics, Inc.
Bauer Transmitters, Inc.
Belar Electronics Laboratory Inc.
Bird Electronic Corp.
Bradley Broadcast and Pro Audio
Broadcast Microwave Services Inc.
Communication & Power Industries
Continental Electronics Corporation
Crown Broadcast IREC
DMT USA, Inc.
Delta Electronics Inc.
Dielectric Communications
EDX Wireless
Hitachi Kokusai Electric America, Ltd.
JSB Service Co.
Jampro Antennas Inc.
Kathrein Inc., Scala Division
Kintronic Labs Inc.
LARCAN USA Inc
Micro Communications Inc.
Narda Microwave-East L-3 Communications Co.
Nautel Ltd.
Shively Labs
Swintek Enterprises Inc.
TFT Inc.
V-Soft Communications
WILL-BURT Co.
e2v Inc.

Broadcast Radio Equipment
Arrakis Systems Inc.
BEXT Inc.
Belar Electronics Laboratory Inc.
Bradley Broadcast and Pro Audio
Broadcast Electronics Inc.
Broadcasters General Store Inc.
Comrex Corp.
Continental Electronics Corporation
DBX Professional Products
Dalet Digital Media Systems
Inovonics Inc.
Jampro Antennas Inc.
Marketron Broadcast Solutions
Nautel Ltd.
Shively Labs
Swintek Enterprises Inc.
TFT Inc.

Broadcast Studio Construction, Prefab
Devlin Design Group Inc.
Industrial Acoustics Co., Inc.
Northeastern Communications Concepts Inc.
RAM SYSTEMS, LLC

Broadcast Studio Equipment
A.C.C. Electronix, Inc.
AKG Acoustics, U.S.
Audioarts Engineering
Avid : Digidesign
Barco Inc.
Broadcasters General Store Inc.
Canon U.S.A. Inc.
ENCO Systems Inc.
Furman
Harris Corp.
Hitachi Kokusai Electric America, Ltd.
Inscriber Technology Corporation
MUSICAM U.S.A.
Marshall Electronics
Miranda USA
Mole-Richardson Co.
O'Connor Professional Camera Support Systems
Parsons Audio LLC
RAM SYSTEMS, LLC
Richardson Electronics
Rosco Laboratories Inc.
Theatre Service & Supply Corp.
Thomson
Transcom Corp.
United States Broadcast
Videotron Ltee
Vinten

Broadcast TV Equipment
AKG Acoustics, U.S.
AZCAR U.S.A. Inc.
Abekas, Incorporated
AccuWeather Inc.
All Mobile Video Inc.
Allen Osborne Associates Inc.
BEXT Inc.
Belar Electronics Laboratory Inc.
Bexel
Broadcast International Group
Canon U.S.A. Inc.
Comtech Antenna Systems Inc.
DMT USA, Inc.
Ensemble Designs
Full Compass Systems Ltd.
Hitachi Kokusai Electric America, Ltd.
J.A. Taylor & Associates
Jampro Antennas Inc.
LARCAN
Maze Corporation
Miranda USA
Mole-Richardson Co.
Snell & Wilcox Inc.
Specialized Communications Corp.
Standard Communications Corp.
Thomson
Toshiba America Consumer Products
WILL-BURT Co.
Wescam Inc.

Broadcast Video Products
360 Systems
Abekas, Incorporated
Analog Digital International Inc.
Battery Pros Inc.
Belden
Bitcentral Inc.
Canon U.S.A. Inc.
Fast Forward Video
Glentronics Inc.
Hitachi Kokusai Electric America, Ltd.
Hotronic Inc.
LINK Electronics Inc.
MATCO Inc.
Matrox Electronic Systems Ltd.
Maxell Corp. of America
Roscor Corp.
Sencore Inc.
Snell & Wilcox Inc.
Telemetrics Inc.
The Tiffen Company
Videomagnetics Inc.
WEGENER
Wiltronix Inc.
teletech.ca

Bulktape DeGausser
Audiolab Electronics Inc.
Data Security Inc.
Garner Products
Glentronics Inc.
Sprague Magnetics Inc.

Bulktape, Audio Cassette
National Audio Co. Inc.

CATV Equipment and Supplies
ADSCO Line Products Inc.
ARRIS
AVCOM of Virginia Inc.
Advanced Media Technologies, Inc.
Alpha Technologies Inc.
Andrew Corp.
Arista Information Systems
Benner-Nawman, Inc. and BN Products-USA, LLC.
Blonder Tongue Laboratories Inc.
C-COR/ Arris
CADCO SYSTEMS
CATV Services Inc.
Cable Prep
Cable Services Company Inc.
Cable Technologies International
Channell Commercial Corp.
Charles Industries Ltd.
Cisco Systems, Inc.
Comtech Antenna Systems Inc.
Condux International, Inc.
Convergys Inc.
Ditch Witch
Eagle Comtronics Inc.
Electroline Equipment Inc.
Emcore
Emerson Network Power-Viewsonics
FM SYSTEMS Inc.
Gefen Inc.
General Atomics Electronic Systems, Inc.
Harmonic Inc.
Hogg & Davis Inc.
ICM Corporation
JDS Uniphase Corp.
Kalun Communications Inc.
Kathrein Inc., Scala Division
Keywest Technology
Lemco Tool Corp.

EQUIPMENT MANUFACTURERS

Olesen
Theatre Service & Supply Corp.
Theatrical Services Inc.
UNISET Co., LLC

Data Communications Systems
Canon U.S.A. Inc.
EEG Enterprises Inc.
Entertainment Communications Network (ECN)
FM SYSTEMS Inc.
Great Lakes Data Systems, Inc.
Keywest Technology
MCG Surge Protection
MODCOMP Inc.
Microspace Communications Corp.
Milestone Technologies Inc.
Modulation Sciences Inc.
Norpak Corporation
Spacenet Services Inc.

Data Transmission Equipment
Broadcast Video Systems Corp.
Canon U.S.A. Inc.
Comtech EF Data
IPITEK
Inovonics Inc.
Intelligent Media Technology
International Datacasting Corp.
MCL Inc.
Moseley
Norpak Corporation
Spacenet Services Inc.
TELLABS
Vecima Networks Inc.
WEGENER

Dehydrators and Accessories
Dielectric Communications
Radio Frequency Systems
Shively Labs

Demodulators and Modulators
CADCO SYSTEMS
Cable Serv Inc.
FM SYSTEMS Inc.
General Atomics Electronic Systems, Inc.
Harris Broadcast
L-3 Communications Telemetry East
NUCOMM Inc.
North American Cable Equipment Inc.
Videotron Ltee

Descramblers, Pay TV
ARRIS
North American Cable Equipment Inc.

Design Services, Broadcast
Connex Telecommunications Corporation
Meridian Design Associates, Architects
Northeastern Communications Concepts Inc.
Quality Tower Erectors Inc.
Rees Associates Inc.
Studio Technology
VidCAD LLC
Yanchar Design & Consulting Group

Designers, Production Facilities
CBT Systems
Four Seasons Sunrooms, LLC
High Tech Furnishings Ltd.
Meridian Design Associates, Architects
Northeastern Communications Concepts Inc.
Rees Associates Inc.
Yanchar Design & Consulting Group

Digital Audio Processing Equipment
Airbus DS Communications
Aphex Systems Ltd.
Benchmark Media Systems Inc.
Broadcast Supply Worldwide
Eventide Inc.
Linear Acoustic Inc.
Logitek Electronic Systems Inc
Micro Technology Unlimited
NVISION Products
Orban
Orban Corporate
Penny + Giles
R.L. Drake Holdings LLC
Radio Computing Services (RCS)
Roland Corp. U.S.
Sabine Inc.
Sascom Marketing Group
Symetrix Inc.
TC Electronic
TC Group Americas Inc.
The ISIS Group
Ward-Beck Systems Ltd.

Digital Audio Recorders
360 Systems
Alesis
Fostex USA
Micro Technology Unlimited
Roland Corp. U.S.
Stancil Corp.
Superscope Technologies
Yamaha Corp. of America

Digital Audio Recording & Editing Station
360 Systems
Avid : Digidesign
Avid Broadcast
ENCO Systems Inc.
Micro Technology Unlimited
Orban
Parsons Audio LLC
Penny + Giles
Radio Computing Services (RCS)
Visual Sound Inc.
WireReady NSI

Digital Broadcast Equipment
ATCI/Antenna Technology Communications Inc.
ATI-Audio Technologies Inc.
Abekas, Incorporated
Adtec Digital
Arrakis Systems Inc.
Axcera
BEXT Inc.
Belar Electronics Laboratory Inc.
Bexel
Broadcast Electronics Inc.
Broadcast Store Inc.
Broadcast Supply Worldwide
Comtech EF Data
DMT USA, Inc.
Dalet Digital Media Systems
DiGi Co. Ltd.
Fast Forward Video
Fostex USA
General Atomics Electronic Systems, Inc.
Harris Corp.
Hitachi Kokusai Electric America, Ltd.
IPITEK
Imagine Communications Corp.
International Datacasting Corp.
JDS Uniphase Corp.
JVC Professional Products Company
MATCO Inc.
MUSICAM U.S.A.
Marshall Electronics
Mohawk
NEP
Panasonic Broadcast & Television Systems Co.
ProAudio.com/Crouse-Kimzey Company
R.L. Drake Holdings LLC
Register Data Systems
Talk-A-Phone Co.
Telos Systems
Utah Scientific Inc.
Visual Sound Inc.
WEGENER

Digital Image Processors
Barco Inc.
Eigen
Xintekvideo Inc.

Digital Special Effects Systems
AccuWeather Inc.
Autodesk
Autodesk, Inc.
Chyron Corp.
Cintel Inc.
Eastman Kodak Co.
FOR- A Corp. of America
Quantel Inc.
The Tiffen Company
Toshiba America Consumer Products

Digital Video Graphics and Animation
AccuWeather Inc.
Autodesk
Autodesk, Inc.
Keywest Technology
Quantel Inc.

Digital Video Processing Equipment
Cisco Systems, Inc.
Ensemble Designs
FOR- A Corp. of America
Hotronic Inc.
LINK Electronics Inc.
Leitch & Co.
NTV International Corporation
NVISION Products
Semtech
Television Equipment Assoc. Inc./Matthey
Video International Development Corp.
Visual Sound Inc.
Ward-Beck Systems Ltd.
Xintekvideo Inc.

Digital Video Production Systems
Bitcentral Inc.
Dalet Digital Media Systems
MAVRIC Media Inc.
NVISION Products
Specialized Communications Corp.
Thomson Broadcast & Media Solutions

Distortion Analyzers
Audio Precision Inc.
Boonton Electronics Corp.
Electro Rent Corp.
Tektronix

Distribution Amplifiers
Benchmark Media Systems Inc.
Burst Electronics Inc.
Cablynx, Inc.
ESE
Harris Broadcast
Horita
Intersil Corp.
Leitch & Co.
Microsemi Corporation
North American Cable Equipment Inc.
Omicron Video
Pesa Headquarters
Philip-Cooke Co.
Qintar Technologies Inc.
Radio Systems Inc.
Sigma Electronics Inc.
Studio Technologies Inc.
Symmetricom
Television Equipment Assoc. Inc./Matthey
Video Accessory Corp.
Ward-Beck Systems Ltd.

Distribution Systems
Aspera Inc.
Cisco Systems, Inc.
Enghouse Systems Limited
IPITEK
MAVRIC Media Inc.
North American Cable Equipment Inc.
Philip-Cooke Co.
WEGENER
Wiltronix Inc.

Dollies, Instrument Carts, Etc.
Ferno-Washington Inc.
Hogg & Davis Inc.
Matthews Studio Equipment Inc. (MSE)
Panavision New York

Dummy Loads
Altronic Research Inc.
Bird Electronic Corp.
Electro Impulse Laboratory Inc.
Kintronic Labs Inc.
Narda Microwave-East L-3 Communications Co.
Phasetek Inc.

Duplicators
Ascent Media Management Services
Interface Media Group
National Audio Co. Inc.
Newdoll Enterprises

EFP (Electronic Field Production)
Bexel
Mobile Video Services Ltd.
PMTV Producers Management Television

EQUIPMENT MANUFACTURERS

Arri Canada Ltd.
Automatic Devices Company
Band Pro Film & Digital Inc.
Bendalite
Camera Service Center
Colorado Video Inc.
Comprehensive Cable and Connectivity Company
DEDOTEC USA Inc.
Dove Systems
Electronic Theatre Controls Inc.
Emerson Network Power
Film/Video Equipment Service Co. Inc.
Flash Technology, An SPX Division
Frezzolini Electronics Inc.
Full Compass Systems Ltd.
GAMPRODUCTS Inc.
Group One Ltd.
Hughey & Philips
Illumination Dynamics Inc.
James Thomas Engineering Inc.
Leviton NSI Colortran
Lowel-Light Manufacturing Inc.
Matthews Studio Equipment Inc. (MSE)
Mole-Richardson Co.
Musco Mobile Lighting Ltd.
Neutrik U.S.A. Inc.
New York City Lites
Olesen
PC & E
Packaged Lighting Systems Inc.
Panavision New York
Photomart Cine-Video Inc.
Pro Video & Film Equipment Co. Inc.
Rosco Laboratories Inc.
ScreenLight & Grip
Sinar Bron Inc.
Skytec, Inc.
Stage Equipment & Lighting Inc.
Strand Lighting Inc.
Strong International
Teatronics/Entertainment Lighting Control
Theatre Service & Supply Corp.
Theatrical Services Inc.
Ultimate Support Systems Inc.
Vantage Lighting Inc.
Videssence L.L.C.
Vitec Videocom, Inc.
Westcott Co.

Lightning Protection Equip. & Systems
Abroyd Communications Ltd.
Emerson Network Power
LBA Technology Inc.
LEA International
Lightning Eliminators & Consultants Inc.
Lightning Master Corp.
Lightning Prevention Systems
MCG Surge Protection
Mole-Richardson Co.
North Hills Signal Processing Corp.
Transtector Systems Inc.
WILCAN Electronics Canada Ltd.
Windmade Products

Lights, On-Air
Electronic Theatre Controls Inc.
General Electric Co.
RAM SYSTEMS, LLC
Sinar Bron Inc.
Vitec Videocom, Inc.

Lights, Recording
Electronic Theatre Controls Inc.
General Electric Co.
Sinar Bron Inc.

Lights, Stage
AVAB America Inc.
Bendalite
Electronic Theatre Controls Inc.
GAMPRODUCTS Inc.
General Electric Co.
Hollywood Rentals Production Services
James Thomas Engineering Inc.
Mole-Richardson Co.
Olesen
Packaged Lighting Systems Inc.
Sacramento Theatrical Lighting (STL)
Stage Equipment & Lighting Inc.
Strong International
Theatre Service & Supply Corp.

Vantage Lighting Inc.

Line Conditioning
ADCOUR, Inc.
APC by Schneider Electric
Emerson Network Power
Emerson Network Power
Furman
LEA International
MCG Surge Protection
Newark Electronics
WILCAN Electronics Canada Ltd.

Line Surge Protectors
ADCOUR, Inc.
APC by Schneider Electric
Emerson Network Power
Emerson Network Power
LEA International
Lightning Master Corp.
MCG Surge Protection
Transtector Systems Inc.
WILCAN Electronics Canada Ltd.

Locks
CableTek Wiring Products Inc.
Penn Elcom Inc.

Logging System
Geac Libra
Horita
Image Logic Corp.
Imagine Products Inc.
Newdoll Enterprises
Telcom Research

Loudspeakers and Accessories
Amplivox Portable Sound Systems
Atlas Sound
Bogen Communications Inc.
JBL Professional
Sennheiser Electronic Corp.
Talk-A-Phone Co.
Ultimate Support Systems Inc.
Yanchar Design & Consulting Group

Machine Control Systems
Adtec Digital
General Electric Co.
Leightronix Inc.
MATCO Inc.
Mediastar, Inc.
Micro Technology Unlimited
Peter Albrecht Company Inc.
Philip-Cooke Co.
Tapeswitch Corp.

Master Control Switches
Evertz Microsystems Ltd.
Leitch & Co.
Miranda Technologies Inc.
Tapeswitch Corp.
Utah Scientific Inc.

Media Asset Management
Evertz Microsystems Ltd.

Meters
Aeroflex, Inc.
B&B Systems
Benchmark Media Systems Inc.
ComSonics Inc.
Dorrough Electronics
Electro Rent Corp.
Konica Minolta Business Solutions USA Inc
McCurdy Radio Ltd.
Photo Research, Inc.
Radiodetection
Techni-Tool Inc.
Tentel
Triplett Test Equipment & Tools
Weschler Instruments

Microphones and Accessories
AKG Acoustics, U.S.
Audio-Technica U.S., Inc.
Bogen Communications Inc.
COMTEK Inc.
Countryman Associates Inc.
DPA Microphones, Inc.
FitzCo. Inc.
Group One Ltd.
Location Sound Corp.
Marshall Electronics
Nady Systems Inc.
Professional Sound Corp.
RAM SYSTEMS, LLC
RTS Systems Telex Communications Inc
Sennheiser Electronic Corp.
Servoreeler Systems
Sescom Inc.
Shure Inc.
Systems Wireless Ltd.
Telex Communications Inc.
Ultimate Support Systems Inc.

Microwave
Ascent Media Services
Broadcast Microwave Services Inc.
Comsearch
Direct Broadcast Services Inc.
Harris Corp.
M/A-COM Technology Solutions Inc.
NSI
PMTV Producers Management Television
RF Specialties Group
Scotts Valley Group Inc
TFT Inc.
Tactical Communications and Surveillance - Cobham plc

Microwave Amplifiers
Harris Corp.
NUCOMM Inc.

Microwave Antennas
Broadcast Microwave Services Inc.
D.H. Satellite
NSI
NUCOMM Inc.
Radio Frequency Systems
Radio Research Instrument Co. Inc.

Microwave Equipment
AVCOM of Virginia Inc.
Blonder Tongue Laboratories Inc.
Broadcast Electronics
Broadcast Microwave Services Inc.
Dow-Key Microwave Corp.
E-N-G Mobile Systems Inc.
EAGLE Avionics Systems
Emcore
Frontline Communications
JSB Service Co.
Moseley
NUCOMM Inc.
Norsat International Inc.
Radio Research Instrument Co. Inc.
Radio Systems Inc.

Microwave Transmitters
Broadcast Microwave Services Inc.
JSB Service Co.
NUCOMM Inc.
Tactical Communications and Surveillance - Cobham plc
Windstream Communications

Mobile Communications
Aluma Tower Company Inc.
Amdocs
CSG Systems
EAGLE Avionics Systems
ICM (International Crystal Manufacturing)
MCL Inc.
Thermodyne International LTd

Mobile Studio Equipment
Calzone Case Co.
F&F Productions, L.L.C.
Ferno-Washington Inc.
Hollywood Rentals Production Services
Packaged Lighting Systems Inc.
Telos Systems
United States Broadcast

Mobile Units-Sales/Rental
All Mobile Video Inc.
Frontline Communications
J.A. Taylor & Associates
PMTV Producers Management Television

Mobile Vans
Alpha Video & Electronics (AVEC)
E-N-G Mobile Systems Inc.
Frontline Communications
Panavision New York

EQUIPMENT MANUFACTURERS

Broadcasters General Store Inc.
Cisco Systems, Inc.
Colorado Video Inc.
Continental Electronics Corporation
DMT USA, Inc.
Energy-Onix Broadcast Equipment Co. Inc.
Linear Acoustic Inc.
Nautel Ltd.
RF Specialties Group
Scotts Valley Group Inc
Siemens Dematic Limited
Swintek Enterprises Inc.
Technet Systems Group

Transmitters
Broadcast Supply Worldwide
Cisco Systems, Inc.
Colorado Video Inc.
Continental Electronics Corporation
Energy-Onix Broadcast Equipment Co. Inc.
L-3 Communications Telemetry East
Norsat International Inc.
OSI Laser Diode Inc.
Samson Technologies Corp.
Thomson

Transmitters, Radio
Bauer Transmitters, Inc.
Broadcast Electronics Inc.
Continental Electronics Corporation
Energy-Onix Broadcast Equipment Co. Inc.
Harris Corp.
Imagine Communications Corp.
Nautel Ltd.
Richardson Electronics
Scotts Valley Group Inc
TFT Inc.
Transcom Corp.

Transmitters, TV
Axcera
Cisco Systems, Inc.
DMT USA, Inc.
Harris Corp.
Imagine Communications Corp.
Kalun Communications Inc.
LARCAN
MRPP Inc.
Radian Communication Services Inc
Scotts Valley Group Inc
Transcom Corp.

Traveling Wave Tubes
Communication & Power Industries
Daily Electronics Corp.
Penta Laboratories
e2v Inc.

Tripods, Pedestals and Accessories
Argraph Corp.
Band Pro Film & Digital Inc.
Hoodman Corp.
Isaia & Co.
Manfrotto Distribution, Inc
Miller Camera Support, LLC USA
Moog QuickSet
O'Connor Professional Camera Support Systems
Photomart Cine-Video Inc.
Pro Video & Film Equipment Co. Inc.
Sinar Bron Inc.
Telemetrics Inc.
The Tiffen Company
The Tiffen Company
Thomas & Betts Corp.
Ultimate Support Systems Inc.
Vitec Videocom inc.
Vitec Videocom, Inc.

Tubes and Tube Rebuilding
Daily Electronics Corp.
General Electrodynamics Corp.
Narragansett Imaging
Penta Laboratories
Photonis USA Pennsylvania
Richardson Electronics

Tuning and Phasing Units
LBA Technology Inc.

Turnkey Studio Systems
Alpha Video & Electronics (AVEC)
CBT Systems
Connex Telecommunications Corporation
Imagine Communications Corp.
Peter Albrecht Company Inc.
RAM SYSTEMS, LLC
Technet Systems Group

Turntables
Audio-Technica U.S., Inc.

Used Broadcast Equipment
J.A. Taylor & Associates
Maze Corporation
Pro Video & Film Equipment Co. Inc.
System Associates
United States Broadcast

VBI Equipment
Broadcast Video Systems Corp.
Milestone Technologies Inc.
Norpak Corporation
Telestream East - USA

Vacuum Capacitors
Jennings Technology Co.
Penta Laboratories
Richardson Electronics

Vans and Mobile Units
Alpha Video & Electronics (AVEC)
CBT Systems
E-N-G Mobile Systems Inc.
F&F Productions, L.L.C.
Frontline Communications
J.A. Taylor & Associates
Maze Corporation
Panavision New York
Phoenix Engineering, Inc.
Shook Mobile Technology, LP

Video Accessories
ARRI Inc.
AVerMedia USA
Audiolab Electronics Inc.
Battery Pros Inc.
Bencher Inc.
Hoodman Corp.
Jensen Transformers Inc.
MAVRIC Media Inc.
North Hills Signal Processing Corp.
Peerless-AV
Research Technology International Inc.
Schneider Optics
Star Case Manufacturing Co. Inc.
Switchcraft Inc.
The J-Lab Co.
The Tiffen Company
Thermodyne International LTd
Video Accessory Corp.
Viking Cases
Westcott Co.
Winchester Electronics
Zack Electronics Inc.

Video Character Generators
Burst Electronics Inc.
Display Systems International Inc.
EEG Enterprises Inc.
FOR- A Corp. of America
Horita
Hotbox Digital
Inscriber Technology Corporation
Keywest Technology
Mediastar, Inc.
Wiltronix Inc.

Video Delay Lines
Allen Avionics, Inc.
Television Equipment Assoc. Inc./Matthey

Video Delay Subsystems
Abekas, Incorporated
Television Equipment Assoc. Inc./Matthey

Video Disc Recorders
Abekas, Incorporated
Leightronix Inc.
MATCO Inc.
Mediastar, Inc.
Optical Disc Corp.

Video Editing Equipment
Abekas, Incorporated
Avid Broadcast
Bitcentral Inc.
Imagine Products Inc.
MAVRIC Media Inc.
Matrox Electronic Systems Ltd.
NEC Corporation of America Inc.
NEP
Pinnacle Systems Inc.
Richardson Electronics
Tele-Measurements Inc.
United Media Inc.
United States Broadcast

Video Effects Generators and Accessories
Cintel Inc.
FOR- A Corp. of America
Utah Scientific Inc.

Video Equipment
AVI Systems
AVerMedia USA
All Mobile Video Inc.
Avtech Systems Inc.
Band Pro Film & Digital Inc.
Bencher Inc.
Broadcast Store Inc.
CamMate Systems
Dage-MTI Inc.
Dimension 3
EAGLE Avionics Systems
Ensemble Designs
Film/Video Equipment Service Co. Inc.
Full Compass Systems Ltd.
HAVE Inc.
Horita
Innovision Optics Inc.
MATCO Inc.
Maze Corporation
Mohawk
NEP
Photomart Cine-Video Inc.
Pro Video & Film Equipment Co. Inc.
Switchcraft Inc.
Telcom Research
Thermodyne International LTd
United Media Inc.
Vicon Industries Inc.
Westcott Co.

Video Graphics Systems
Autodesk, Inc.
Chyron Corp.
Hotbox Digital
Keywest Technology
Miranda Technologies Inc.

Video Processing Equipment
FM SYSTEMS Inc.
Thomson Broadcast & Media Solutions
Toner Cable Equipment Inc.
Xintekvideo Inc.

Video Production Switchers
FOR- A Corp. of America
Harris Broadcast
Thomson Broadcast & Media Solutions

Video Projection System, Large Screen
Barco Inc.
Sharp Electronics Corp.

Video Routing Switchers
Harris Broadcast
NTV International Corporation
Omicron Video
Pesa Headquarters
Sigma Electronics Inc.
The ISIS Group
Utah Scientific Inc.

Video Special Effects Systems
Abekas, Incorporated
Chyron Corp.
Image Logic Corp.
Ultimatte Corp.

Videotape Recorders
Fast Forward Video
Northrup Grumman Corp.
Sharp Electronics Corp.
Toshiba America Consumer Products

Videotape Recorders, Portable
Fast Forward Video

EQUIPMENT MANUFACTURERS

Equipment Manufacturers & Distributors

A & S Case Co. Inc.
5260 Vineland Ave., N. Hollywood, CA 91601 US
(818) 509-5920; *Fax:* (818) 509-1397
www.ascase.com
info@ascase.com
Bill Waskey, Sales/Operations Manager
Denise Berry, General Manager of Operations
Elden Boice, Purchasing

A R T Applied Research and Technology
4625 Witmer Industrial Estate, Niagara Falls, NY 14305 US
(585) 436-2720; *Fax:* (585) 436-3942
www.artproaudio.com
support@artproaudio.com
Philip Betette, President

A.C.C. Electronix, Inc.
420 Wylie Drive, Normal, IL 61761-4315 US
(309) 888-9990, (866) 458-7721; *Fax:* (309) 452-0893
www.accelectronix.com
acc@accelectronix.com
Andy Rector, Owner
John Franklin, Finance Executive
Repair cartridge tape recorders & reproducers.

Abekas, Incorporated
1090 O'Brien Drive, Menlo Park, CA 94025 US
(650) 470-0900; *Fax:* (650) 470-0913
www.abekas.com
info@abekas.com
Junaid Sheikh, President/CEO/Co-Founder
Phil Bennett, Co-founder/VP Engineering
Douglas Johnson, Chief Product Manager
Abekas, Incorporated is a privately-held company headquartered in Menlo Park, California. Abekas designs, manufactures, sells, and supports a complete line of digital video/audio delay devices, disk recorders, digital special effects andediting tools for use in the worldwide professional television marketplace encompassing the production, post production, broadcasting and computer video markets.

Abroyd Communications Ltd.
3-360 Montrose St.North, Cambridge, ON N3H 2H8 Canada
(519) 650-5093, (888) 658-5100; *Fax:* (519) 650-9546
www.abroyd.com
Ryan Schindler, President
Paul Firminger, Sales/Marketing
Designers, manufacturers & installers of communication towers; manufacturer for Lightning Dissipation Arrays Chem-Rod from LEC.

Access Intelligence LLC
4 Choke Cherry Rd., 2nd Fl., Rockville, MD 20850 US
(301) 354-2000; *Fax:* (301) 309-3847
www.accessintel.com
info@accessintel.com
Michael E W Jackson, Chairman
Don Pazour, President & CEO
Ed Pinedo, CFO
Macy Fecto, Executive Vice President
Michael Kraus, Advertising Inquiries
Macy Fecto, Hr & Corporate Communications
Diane Schwartz, Content Licensing &Syndication
Michael Kraus, Advertising Inquiries
Magazines, trade shows, seminars & cable publication.

AccuWeather Inc.
385 Science Park Rd., State College, PA 16803-2215 US
(814) 235-8500, (814) 235-8770; *Fax:* (814) 235-8639
www.accuweather.com
sales@accuweather.com
Barry Myers, CEO/COO
Dr. Joel Myers, President
Michael R. Smith, CEO/Weather Data Services
Elliot Abrams, SVP/Chief Meteorologist
Justin Robert, Communications Manager
Dr. R. Lee Rainy, VP of Marketing
Dr. Joe Sobel, SeniorVP/Director Forensics
AccuWeather, Inc. offers a broad new menu of powerful integrated, muturally supporting weather content & weather brand-building solutions.

Acme Electric Corp., Aerospace Division
528 W. 21st St., Suite 6, Tempe, AZ 85282 USA
(480) 894-6864; *Fax:* (480) 921-0470
John Gleason, General Manager
Gary Lesser, General Sales Mgr
Sealed fiber nickel-cadmium batteries, battery chargers, battery control units, & AC/DC & DC/OC converters.

Acoustic Systems/ETS-Lindgren HQ
1301 Arrow Point Dr., Cedar Park, TX 78613 US
(512) 531-6400, (512) 531-6498, (512) 531-2609; *Fax:* (512) 531-6500
www.ets-lindgren.com
Bruce Butler, CEO/COO
Glen Watkins, General Manager
Mark Mawdsley, General Sales Mgr

Acoustical Solutions Inc.
2420 Grenoble Rd., Richmond, VA 23294-3710 US
(800) 782-5742, (804) 346-8808; *Fax:* (804) 346-8808
www.acousticalsolutions.com
info@acousticalsolutions.com
David Ingersoll, General Sales Mgr
Michael Binns,
Architectural & Industrial Sales
Matt Boughan, Architectural Sales
Mark Brock, Architectural Sales
Ryan Colton, Architectural Sales
Kregg Hill, Outside Architectural Sales Rep
Gary Hudson, National Sales Manager
Sound & noise control materials including products for the bcst/recording industry, telecommunications industry, architectural acoustics & industrial noise control.

Adcom, LLC
8541 E Anderson Drive, Scottsdale, AZ 83225 US
(480) 607-2277; *Fax:* (480) 348-9876
www.adcom.com
Night Suite DI, non-linear editing systems, bcst control systems, video conferencing. Room control systems 1 room.

ADCOUR, Inc.
One Foxhill Drive, Suite 110, Walpole, MA 2081 US
(508) 921-3790; *Fax:* (508) 543-5489
www.adcourpower.com
info@adcourpower.com
Linda Jacobs Dangelo, President / CEO
Nicolo Miceli, Vice President /General Manager
Peter Dangelo, Director of Sales
Robert Lisi, Engineering / Quality Manager
Larry Shea, Inside Sales / Product Manager

Adrienne Electronics Corp.
901 American Pacific Driver, Suite 170, Henderson, NV 89014 US
(702) 896-1858, (800) 782-2321; *Fax:* (702) 896-3034
www.adrielec.com
info@adrielec.com
Tracey Ruesch, President
Time code reader/generator products with PCI, PCI Express, USB and serial interfaces

ADSCO Line Products Inc.
3500 Washington Ave., Houston, TX 77007 US
(713) 880-2424,(800) 247-6484; *Fax:* (713) 880-2456
www.adscoline.com
ajackd@adscoline.com
Linda Schmuck, President
Nancy Wallace, Marketing Manager

Adtec Digital
408 Russell St., Nashville, TN 37206 US
(615) 256-6619 ext. 113; *Fax:* (615) 256-6593
www.adtecdigital.com
sales@adtecinc.com
Ron Johnson, Operations Dir
Kevin Ancelin, General Sales Mgr
Amilcar Padilla, Director-Sales Engineering
Kevin Ancelin, SVP Sales - Co-Founder
Jonathan Redford, Sales Engineer US-EU
James Moore, Sales Engineer
Adriano Chagas,Support Engineer
Matt Lollar, Support Engineer
Travis Lowery, Support Engineer
2231 Corporate Square Blvd., Jacksonville, FL 32216 United States
(904) 720-2003
Kevin Ancelin, Pres

Advanced Designs Corp.
1169 W. 2nd St., Bloomington, IN 47403 US
(812) 333-1922; *Fax:* (812) 333-2030
www.doprad.com
Matt McGrath, President
Martin Riess, Owner
Advanced Designs Corporation, now twenty-five years in the weather radar and weather data display industry, continually adds features and options to enhance the capabilities of our products. ADC is committed to having the finest radar anddisplay products available.

Advanced Media Technologies, Inc.
3150 SW 15th Street, Suite G, Deerfield Beach, FL 33442 US
(888) 293-5856, (954) 427-5711; *Fax:* (954) 427-9688
www.amt.com
sales@amt.com
Ken Mosca, President
AMT offers a complete line of broadband products from the world's most recognized manufacturers. Products include CATV QAM IP set-tops, digital, analog & IP headend electronics, Digcipher receivers, off-air 8-vsb receivers, RF & fibertransport, digital encoders, ad insertion, line gear, modems & much more.

Advent Communications Ltd.
27 Maylands Avenue, Hemel Hempstead,Hertfordshire, HP5 3HE GBR
44 (144) 2 431300; *Fax:* 44 (149) 4 791127
advent.vislink.com
Stephen Rudd, General Manager
George Koumblis, General Sales Mgr
Provides satellite communication solutions for bcst, telecommunications, military & coml applications-design, manufacture & integrating a complete range of digital SNG flyaway & vehicle mounted terminals, a complete range of subsystemsupconverters, downconverters, DVB modulators, MPEG II Video Exciters, equalizers & remote control systems.

Aeroflex, Inc.
35 South Service Rd., P.O. Box 6022, Plainview, NY 11803-0622 US
(516) 694-6700, (800) 843-1553; *Fax:* (516) 694-0658
www.aeroflex.com
corporateinfo@aeroflex.com
Leonard Borow, CEO
Test & measurement instrumentation.
49 Trophy Club Rd., Trophy Club, TX 76262 United States
(817) 430-5842
Carlos Blanco, Sls Mgr - South America

AheadTek
6410 Via Del Oro, San Jose, CA 95119 USA
(408) 226-9800 (408) 226-9991 (800) 971-9191; *Fax:* (408) 226-9195
www.aheadtek.com
patj@aheadtek.com
Tim Higgins, President
Patrick Johnston, General Sales Mgr
Cost effective solutions for your specialty magnetic head applications.

Airbus DS Communications
Mailing Address: 117 Seaboard Lane, Suite D-100, Franklin, TN 37067 US
Second Address: 42505 Rio Nedo, Temecula, CA 92590
(615) 790-2882,(800) 723-3207; *Fax:* (615) 790-1329
airbus-dscomm.com
marketing@dccusa.com
Bob Freinberg, Chief Executive Officer
Gene Kirby, President
Mary Wathen, Chief Operating Officer,
Louis Albatro, CFO
FranØois Begaud, Chief Operating Officer-Land Mobile Radio
Becky Amantea, Vice President- Human Resources
Jeroen de Witte, Chief Technical Officer/Vice President-Research &
Jeff Wittek, Chief Strategic Officer
Paula Graham, General Counsel
Our solutions start from 9-1-1 call processing applications, through P25 land mobile radio, to emergency notification solutions and managed services. The breadth of our solutions is unmatched in the public safety, federal and corporateindustries.

Airlite Plastics Co.
Mailing Address: 2860 Bath Pike, Nazareth, PA 18064 USA
Second Address: 6110 Abbott Dr., Omaha, NE 68110
(610) 759-0280; *Fax:* (610) 759-0650
measurex@airliteplastics.com
John Bungert, President
Thermo plastic products.

AKG Acoustics, U.S.
8500 Balboa Blvd., Northridge, CA 91329 USA
(818) 920-3212; *Fax:* (818) 920-3208
www.akg.com
akgusamarketing@harman.com
Kim Temple Holmes, President
Doug Mac Callum, Operations Dir
Brendan Stead, Vice President
Microphones, headphones, wireless microphones, in-ear monitoring systems, wireless loudspeakers, conferencing products.

EQUIPMENT MANUFACTURERS

Alan Gordon Enterprises Inc.
5625 Melrose Ave., Hollywood, CA 90038 US
(323) 466-3561; *Fax:* (323) 871-2193
www.alangordon.com
info@alangordon.com
Don Sahlein, President
Wayne Loucks, General Manager
Tom Austin, Finance Director
Rental, Sale, Equipment Training and Repair Services for professional motion picture HD, film and video equipment.

Alesis
200 Scenic View Dr., Suite 201, Cumberland, RI 2864 US
(401) 658-5760
www.alesis.com
marketing@alesis.com
Digital tape recording system, mixing consoles, digital & analogue signal processing, amplification, drum machines, keyboards.

Alexander Technologies
1511 South Garfield Pl., Mason City, IA 50401 US
641) 423-8955; *Fax:* (641) 423-1644
www.alexandertechnologies.com
cservice@alexenergy.com
John Casey, CEO
Jay Miller, SVP
Rechargeable nicad in-board, on-board & battery belts; nicad battery chargers & analyzer/conditioners; portable radio & pager batteries.

All Mobile Video Inc.
221 W. 26th St., New York, NY 10001 US
(212) 727-1234; *Fax:* (212) 255-6644
www.allmobilevideo.com
contact@amvchelsea.com
Anton Duke, CEO
Eric Duke, President
Bcst video equipment rental including truck remotes & total carry-in packages, complete studio facilities.
10490 Gandy Blvd., Saint Petersburg, FL 33742 United States
(813) 579-8902
Bary Spencer, Dir Teleport Opns
9670 Aero Dr, San Diego, CA 92123 United States
(619) 569-8451
N. Tabkum, Dir West Coast Opns

Allen Avionics, Inc.
255 E. Second St., Mineola, NY 11501 US
(516) 248-8080; *Fax:* (516) 747-6724
www.allenavionics.com
Info@AllenAvionics.com
Jim Lyons, Operations Dir
Allen Avionics, Inc. is a major U.S. manufacturer of precision LC filters and electro-magnetic delay lines for the electronics industry. Video product engineers and OEM's have come to rely on Allen Avionics as the single source for acomplete line of standard and custom filters and delay lines. Our strong technical support team is an important part of our service to customers.

Allen Osborne Associates Inc.
756 Lakefield Rd., Westlake Village, CA 91361 USA
(805) 495-8420; *Fax:* (805) 373-6067
www.aoa-gps.com
Jim Osborne, Operations Dir
Pneumatic masts systems for remote E.N.G., fixed or mobile radio communications, etc.

Allied Electronics Inc.
7151 Jack Newell Blvd. S., Fort Worth, TX 76118 US
(401) 658-5760, (866) 433-5722; *Fax:* (817) 595-8530
ex-en.alliedelec.com
Lee Davidson, President
Broad line distributor of electronic components.

Allied Tower Co. Inc.
28805 South 563 Rd, Monkey Island, OK 74331 US
(918) 645-0902; *Fax:* (281) 331-9822
www.alliedtower.com
r.morrison@alliedtower.com
Max Bowen, CEO
Jeff Bowen, President
Doug Moore, Operations Dir
Jerry Moore, General Manager
Design, fabrication & erection of FM, AM, TV & communication towers.

Allison Payments Systems L.L.C.
2200 Production Dr., Indianapolis, IN 46241 US
(317) 808-2400,(800) 755-2440; *Fax:* (317) 808-2477
www.apsllc.com
sales@apsllc.com
Joseph H. Thomas, Chairman
Joseph P. Thomas, President/Chief Executive Officer
Robert V. Boles, Chief Engineer
Bradley E. Turner, Vice President Technical Services
Kevin W. Thomas, Vice President- Sales and Marketing
Dale J. Eland,Vice President Manufacturing Services
Jerry M. Mcnulty, Vice President
Allison Payment Systems, LLC, is a full service customer communication solutions provider specializing in digital transactional document presentment, print & mail services and a host of Electronic Document Delivery and Management (EDDM)tools.

Allsop Inc.
Mailing Address: 4201 Meridian Street, PO Box 23, Bellingham, WA 98227 US
Second Address: PO Box 4921, Ketchum, ID 83340-4921
(360) 734-9090, (360) 734-9858; *Fax:* (360) 733-4302
www.allsop.com
info@allsop.com
Jim Allsop, President
Brett Allsop, President
Ryan Allsop, Vice President
Linda Pilon, HR Executive
Cleaning accessories for audio & video, record care products & compact discs, computer accessories.

Allstate Tower Company Inc.
Div/DBA: (formerly Nationwide Tower Company Inc.)
232 Heilman Drive, P.O. Box 25, Henderson, KY 42419
(270) 830-8512; *Fax:* (270) 830-8475
www.allstatetower.com
kroth@allstatetower.com
William Johnston, CEO
Sam Dorris, Operations Dir
Andy Denton, CFO
Kevin Roth, General Sales Mgr
Von Hannah, Director of Inspections
Ben Johnston, Director
Wendy Mattingly, Agricultural Sales
Garrett Clark, V.P. of FabricatedProducts
Don McConnell, VP of Loss Prevention
Tower Manufacturing Co. including: Tower inspections, painting, repair re-guy, lighting, antennas, feedlines, analysis, erect, dismantle, line sweeping, site monitoring, & tower tracker svcs.

Alpack Associates, Inc.
141 Lanza Ave, Building 19, Garfield, NJ 7026 US
(973) 694-5510, (888) 225-7225; *Fax:* (973) 955-4750
www.alpack-pic.com
info@alpack-pic.com
Les Weinstock, President
Dante Cuoco, Manager
Standard & custom carrying & shipping cases for all bcst equipment. Both hard & soft case styles.

Alpha Technologies Inc.
3767 Alpha Way, Bellingham, WA 98226 US
(360) 647-2360; *Fax:* (360) 392-2144
www.alpha.com
alpha@alpha.com
Fred Kaiser, Chairman
Drew Zogby, President
Jeff Lechtanski, Chief Marketing Officer
Develops power conversion, protection and standby products for telecommunications and broadband cable industries, including custom, application-specific power solutions.

Alpha Video & Electronics (AVEC)
200 Mingo Church Rd., Finleyville, PA 15332 US
(412) 429-2000; *Fax:* (724) 348-8600
www.aveceng.com
henry@aveceng.com
Henry Lassige, Sr., President
O.B. vans, eng vans, DSNG vans, ENG mast safety device, turnkey systems, camera transporter.

Altronic Research Inc.
621 Highway 202 West, PO Box 249, Yellville, AR 72687 US
(800) 482-5623,(870) 449-4093; *Fax:* (870) 449-6000
www.altronic.com
info@altronic.com
John Dyess, President
Gary James, Engineering
Jim Keyes, Engineering
Billie Heenan, Finance
Omegaline RF coaxial load resistors (dummy loads).

Aluma Tower Company Inc.
Mailing Address: 1639 Old Dixie Hwy., Vero Beach, FL 32960 US
Second Address: PO Box 2806, Vero Beach, FL 32961-2806
(772) 567-3423; *Fax:* (772) 567-3432
www.alumatower.com
atc@alumatower.com
Robert Main, President
Theodore Gottry, Vice President
Aluminum telescoping towers combined with trailers & optional shelters provides mobile units. Vehicle mounted towers for installation on customer's vehicle.

AMCO Enclosures
1 Innovation Dr., Des Plaines, IL 60016 US
(847) 391-8100, (847) 391-8118, (847) 391-8200, (8; *Fax:* (847) 391-8354
www.amcoenclosures.com
customerservice@amcoenclosures.com
Thomas Anderson, CEO/President
Dave Presi, Chief Techinical Officer
Angela Oliver, Director Of Human Resources

Amdocs
1390 Timberlake Manor Pkwy., Chesterfield, MO 63017
(314) 212-7000; *Fax:* (314) 212 7500
www.amdocs.com
Eli Gelman, CEO
Guy Dubois, President
Amdocs is the market leader in customer experience systems innovation, enabling world-leading svc providers & integrated, innovative & intentional customer experience at every point of svc.

American Antenna Inc.
4707 Roosevelt St., Glen Park, IN 46408 US
(219) 985-4000; *Fax:* (219) 985-4001
www.americanantenna.com
Nick Michels, President
Rick Gard, Operations Dir
Chuck Forsyth, General Sales Mgr
Manufactuer, Distributor & installer of Earth Station Antennas up to 6.1m. Motorized, actuators, receivers, controllers, feeds, multi-beam feed system, LNB's & accessories.

American Eurocopter Corp.
2701 North Forum Drive, Grand Prairie, TX 75052 US
(972) 641-0000, (800) 873-0001; *Fax:* (972) 641-3419
airbushelicoptersinc.com
Marc Paganini, President/CEO
Brenda Revland, Promotions Manager
Servicing North American market; manufactures & sells complete line of single- & twin-engine turbine helicopters.

American Tower Corp.
116 Huntington Avenue, 11th Floor, Boston, MA 2116 US
(617) 375-7500, (877) 282-7483; *Fax:* (617) 375-7575
www.americantower.com
James Taillett Sr, President/Chairman
Tom Barlett, Chief Financial Officer
Matt Peterson, VP, Communications & Employee Development
Leah Stearns, VP, Investor Relations & Capital Markets
Owners & operators of TV, FM & other bcst towers & specialty structures.

Ampex Data Systems -America
500 Broadway, Redwood City, CA 94063-3199 US
(650) 367-3365; *Fax:* (650) 367-4669
www.ampex.com
info@ampexdata.com
Larry Chiarelli, CEO/President
Donald Downing, Business Dev Manager
John Hardy, Business Dev Manager
Data recorders, data systems, mass data storage, instrumentation recorder products; 19 mm scanning recorders, library systems (DST & DIS products), related tape, after-market parts & video recorder support.

Amplivox Portable Sound Systems
650 Anthony Trail, Suite D, Northbrook, IL 60062-2512 USA
(800) 267-5486; *Fax:* (800) 267-5489
www.ampli.com
droth@ampli.com
Don Roth, CEO
Ron Stelzer, Financial Executive
Jorelle Gates, Werehouse Staff
Jeremy Kowalewski, Warehouse Staff
Portable sound systems/lecterns/wireless/indoor-outdoor, made in USA, UL, CSA, CE, 6 years warranty.

Amtel Network
431 Myrtle St., Suite 6, Glendale, CA 91203 USA
(818) 842-8088, (800) 893-4509, (212) 832-3680; *Fax:* (818) 551-4999
www.amtelsystems.com

Mike Takamatsu, President
Text-visual intercom system.

Analog Digital International Inc.
20 E. 49th St., 2nd Fl., New York, NY 10017 USA
(212) 688-5110; *Fax:* (212) 688-5405
Ayres D'Cunha, Founder & President
Sls & rentals of professional /bcst-NTSC/PAL equipment. Post production svcs. DVD authoring replication. AVID/FCP editing.

Anchor Audio Portable Sound Systems
5931 Darwin Court, Carlsbad, CA 92008 US
(310) 784-2300,(800) 262-4671; *Fax:* (760) 827-7105
www.anchoraudio.com
sales@anchoraudio.com
Janet Jacobs, COO
David Jacobs, President
Alicia Gariby, Manufacturing Director
Anchor supplies products to sectors including education, commercial, hospitality, government, and military. Anchor manufactures its own products in its factory in Carlsbad, California and uses a total quality concept. As a result, thecompany can guarantee the quality of its products and deliver quickly.

Andrew Corp.
10500 W 153rd Street, Orlando, IL 60462 US
(779) 435-6500,(800) 255-1479; *Fax:* (779) 435-8579, (800) 349-5444
www.andrew.com
Frank M. Drendel, Chairman
Randall W. Crenshaw, EVP/COO
Marvin (Eddie) S. Edwards, Jr., President/CEO
Jonas Aleska, Manager
Nancy Lawrence, Manager
Philip M. Armstrong, Jr., SVP Corporate Finance
Michael Cross, SVP, Chieflnformation Officer
Peter U. Karlsson, Senior Vice President of Global Sales
Fiona Nolan, Senior Vice President of Global Marketing
VHF & UHF-TV transmitting, microwave & ESA's; coaxial cable; waveguides; towers; equipment shelters; instal svcs, combiners & pressurization equipment.
10500 W. 153rd St., Orland Park, IL 60462 United States
(708) 349-3300
Paul Cox, Group Pres
sls, President
George Tong, Govt Antennas & Esas

Anton/Bauer Inc.
14 Progress Drive, Shelton, CT 6484 US
(203) 929-1100, (800) 422-3473; *Fax:* (203) 929-9935, (800) 422-3473
www.antonbauer.com
americas@antonbauer.com
Michael Accardi, President
Pat Loch, Chief Administrative Officer
Shin Minowa, Chief Marketing Officer
NiCad, NIMH & Li-ion cameras batteries, chargers, lighting & diagnostic accessories for the professional video industry.

Anvil Cases
15730 Salt Lake Ave., City of Industry, CA 91745 US
(626) 968-4100, (800) 359-2684; *Fax:* (626) 968-1703
www.anvilcase.com
web.sales@anvilcase.com
Joseph Calzone, President
Deb Visckay, General Manager
Vince Calzone, Vice President
Heavy-duty reuseable, custom, standard shipping cases & containers for all bcst equipment.

APC by Schneider Electric
132 Fairgrounds Rd, West Kingston, RI 2892 US
(877) 272-2722, (800) 555-2725, (800) 788-2208; *Fax:* (401) 789-3710
www.apc.com
commercemaster@apcc.com
Laurent Vernerey, CEO
Daniel Doimo, President/CEO
Karen Miranda, Chief Financial Officer
Mike Maiello, Senior Vice President-Home and business networks
Neil Rasmussen, Senior Vice President of Innovation
Dave Johnson, Senior VicePresident Solutions
Leanne Cunnold, Senior Vice President-Strategy and Business Develo
Randy Amon, Senior Vice President-Customer Care, Quality & Pro
American Power Conversion provides protection against many of the primary causes of data loss, hardware damage and downtime. Founded in 1981, APC is a leading provider of global, end-to-end AC and DC-based back-up power products andservices, which include surge suppressors, uninterruptible power supplies (UPS), power conditioning equipment, power management software, and DC power systems as well as precision cooling equipment, and professional and consulting services forNonstop NetworkingT.
520 8th Ave., 21st Fl., New York, NY 10018 United States
(212) 594-9333; *Fax:* (212) 594-3691
2895 Greenspoint Pkwy. #350, Hoffman Estates, IL 60195 United States
(847) 585-1113; *Fax:* (847) 585 1125

Aphex Systems Ltd.
3500 N. San Fernando Blvd, Burbank, CA 91505 US
(801) 699-2272; *Fax:* (435) 604-7409
www.aphex.com
sales@aphex.com
David Wiener, CEO
Marvin Caesar, President
Jim Bailey, General Manager
Wayne La Farr, Programming Director
Michael Hurwitz, Director of Sales
Model 2020 MKIII, Compellor-intelligent AGC, Dominator II precision multi-band peak limiter, Aural Exciter, Expressor, remote controlled mic preams, TVGS MIC/instrument, preamplifiers, analog to digital converters.

APM Music
Mailing Address: 6255 Sunset Boulevard, Suite 820, Hollywood, CA 90028 US
Second Address: 381 Park Ave South, Suite 1101, New York, NY 10016
(323) 461-3211,(212) 856-9800; *Fax:* (323) 461-9102, (323) 856-9807
www.apmmusic.com
info@apmmusic.com
Adam Taylor, President
Colleen Oscarson, Vice President-Operations
George Macias, Sales Executive
Craig Giummarra, General Sales Mgr
Sharon Jennings, Promotions Manager
Johnnie Blankenship, Vice President- Sales
Jeannie Faller,Vice President- Finance
Sharon Jennings, Vice President-Music & Marketing
Steven Stern, Vice President- Custom Music
Craig Giummarra, Sales Director-Cable Division
Caron Nightingale, Director of Sales
Over 300,000 tracks, 30 production music libraries, over 4,000 CDs, personalized packages, music search svcs, 20-25 new CD releases mthy & fantastic music dir who can assist in searches for all productions.
381 Park Ave. S., Suite 1101, New York, NY 10016 United States

APT Technologies
111 E Illinois Street, Arthur, IL 61911 USA
(800) 278-2050, (217) 253-8292; *Fax:* (217) 258-5558
www.einc.com
webmaster@einc.com
Jay Martin, General Manager
Jim Remkel, Consultant
John Sullivan, President

Argraph Corp.
111 Asia Place, Carlstadt, NJ 7072 US
(201) 939-7722; *Fax:* (201) 939-7782
www.argraph.com
sales@argraph.com
Irvine Roth, CEO
Mark Roth, President
Martin Lipton, General Sales Mgr
Anti-stat cleaning cloths, samigron video tripods.

Argraph West
2710 McCone, Hayward, CA 94545 United States
(510) 298-0575

Aries Industries Inc.
Mailing Address: 550 Elizabeth St., Waukesha, WI 53186 US
Second Address: 5748 E. Shields Avenue, Suite 101, Fresno, CA 93727
(262) 896-7205,(800) 234-7205; *Fax:* (262) 246-7099
www.ariesindustries.com
James Lenahan, CEO
Claire Schaefier, Chief Technical Officer
Lisa Meissner, Chief Marketing Officer
Manufacture pipeline inspection televising test & seal equipment.
5748 E. Shields, Fresno, CA 93727 United States
(800) 671-0383; *Fax:* (559) 291-0463
J. Lenahan, Ceo

Arista Information Systems
Mailing Address: 2220 Northmont Parkway, Suite 100, Duluth, GA 30096 USA
Second Address: 1105 Fairchild Rd., Winston-Salem, NC 27105
(678) 473-1885, (336) 776-1105; *Fax:* (678) 473-1051, (336) 776-1202
www.aristainfo.com
Bob Greer, CEO
Tom Baglive, Manufacturing Executive
Cable TV subscriber & statement printing.

Arrakis Systems Inc.
6604 Powell St., Loveland, CO 80538-8714 US
(970) 461-0730; *Fax:* (970) 663-1010
www.arrakis-systems.com
arrakis@arrakis-systems.com
Michael Palmer, President
Roderic Graham, Operations Dir
Jon Young, General Sales Mgr
Audio consoles, digital audio, satellite, live-assist, hard drive automation & production systems, studio furniture.

Arri Canada Ltd.
Mailing Address: 1200 Aerowood Drive, Unit 29, Mississauga, ON L4W 2S7 Canada
Second Address: 2385 Stirling Road, Fort Lauderdale, FL 33312
(416) 255-3335, (954) 322-4545; *Fax:* (416) 255-3399, (954) 322-4188
www.arri.com
info@arri.com
Sebastien Laffoux, Programming Director
Hinwai Sheffield, Finance Manager
ARRI camera, lightning equipment & all professional accessories, sales & service.

ARRI Inc.
2385 Stirling Road, Fort Lauderdale, FL 33312 US
(954) 322-4545; *Fax:* (818) 848-4028, (954) 322-4188
www.arri.com
info@arri.com
Charles Davidson, COO
Volker Bahnemann, President
Bill Russell, Operations Dir
Juergen Schwinzer, VP, Camera Division
Glenn Kennel, VP, CTO
John Gresch, VP, Lighting Division
Ted Kampel, VP, Finance
Manufacturer of professional motion picture film cameras & accessories, lighting equipment & post-production tools.

ARRI Inc.
2385 Stirling Road Ft. Lauderdale, FL 33312
(954) 322-4545; *Fax:* (818) 954-4188

ARRI Inc.
617 Route 303, Blauvelt, CA 10913
(845) 353-1400; *Fax:* (845) 425-1250

Arris
Mailing Address: 3871 Lakefield Dr., Suwanee, GA 30024 US
Second Address: 1825 NW 167th Place, Beaverton, OR 97006
(866) 362-7747 (in US), (678) 473-5656, (678) 473-; *Fax:* (678) 473-8470
www.arris.com
Andrew T. Heler, Director
CMTS, cable modems, telephony voice ports & modems, oss/provisioning systems, HFC infrastructure products.

ARRIS
Mailing Address: 101 Tournament Dr., Horsham, PA 19044 US
Second Address: 3871 Lakefield Dr., Suwanee, GA 30024
(215) 323-1000, (866) 362-7747, (678) 473-2907; *Fax:* (678) 473-8470
www.arrisi.com/modems
broadband@motorola.com
Daniel M. Moloney, President
CATV headend & distribution equipment; sub terminals, addressable systems & interactive products.
1330 Capital Pkwy., Lewisville, TX 75057 United States
(972) 323-4100
Tim Roberti, Rgnl Mgr
6400 S. Fiddler-Green Cir., Englewood, CO 80111 United States
(303) 740-6118
Pete Wornski, Vp

Artel Video Systems
5B Lyberty Way, Westford, MA 1886 US
(978) 263-5775, (800) 225-0228; *Fax:* (978) 263-9755
www.artel.com
sales@artel.com
Richard Dellacanonica, President/CEO
Richard Lee Harrington, Vice President of Manufacturing
John Clark, Vice President of Product Development

EQUIPMENT MANUFACTURERS

Kevin Ancelin, Vice President of Sales and Business Development
Thomas Beardsley, Directorof International Sales and Marketing
Philip Dubs, Director of Broadcast Sales
Joanne Pederson, Inside Sales Manager
Artel Video Systems is a leading developer of media transport hardware. We offer solutions for transporting uncompressed and lightly compressed video, audio, and ancillary data across IP networks, fiber, and optical backbones.

Ascent Media Management Services
2901 W. Alameda Ave., Burbank, CA 91505 US
(818) 840-7000; *Fax:* (818) 840-7129
ascentcapitalgroupinc.com
William R. Fitzgerald, Chairman of the Board and CEO
William Humphrey, President
Andre Macaluso, Operations Dir
Chris Van Duyn, Director
Beth Simon, General Sales Mgr
William E. Niles, Executive Vice President, General Counsel
Michael A. Haislip, Executive Vice President
Michael R. Meyers, Senior Vice President and Chief Financial Officer
John A. Orr, Senior Vice President
Postproduction video & film svcs: editing, telecine, sound, duplication, satellite svcs, film lab, standard conversion tape to film transfers & digital asset mgmt.
235 Pegasus Ave., Northvale, NJ 07647
(201) 767-3800; *Fax:* (201) 767-4568
Beth Simon, Sr Vp Sls/Mktg

Ascent Media Services
5251 DTC Pkwy, Suite 1000, Greenwood Village, CA 80111-2755 USA
(310) 434-7000; *Fax:* (310) 434-7111
www.ascentmedia.com
William R. Fitzgerald, Chairman of the Board/Chief Executive Officer
William E. Niles, Executive Vice President/General Counsel
John Orr, Senior Vice President
Mike Meyers, Senior Vice President & Chief Financial Officer
Mike A.Haislip, Executive Vice President
Philip J. Holthouse, Chair of the Audit Committee
Michael J. Pohl, Member of the Audit Committee
A transmission company specializing in video switching, quality control, last mile connections, remote transmissions, production & audiovisual svcs to the bcst, cable & corporate TV industries.

Aspect Software
300 Apollo Dr., Chelmsford, MA 1824 US
(978) 250-7900,(888) 412-7728; *Fax:* (978) 244-7410
www.aspect.com
info@aspect.com
Stew Bloom, CEO
Mohammed Ali, President
Stephen Beaver, Senior Vice President and General Counsel
Automated telephone call processing products for inbound & outbound call centers.
3778 Realty Rd, Dallas, TX 75238 United States
(609) 235-1771
Randy Pugh, Natl Acct Exec
1010 Northern Blvd., Suite 208, Great Neck, NY 11021 United States
(516) 829-0390
Rich Bogner, Sls Rep
1300 Bristol St. N., Suite 100, Newport Beach, CA 92660 United States
(714) 261-9330
Roy Rich, Sls Rep
5001 LBJ Fwy., Suite 727, Dallas, TX 75244 United States
(214) 387-5210
Nick Pollard, Western Rgnl Sls Mgr

Aspera Inc.
5900 Hollis St., Suite E, Emeryville, CA 94608
(510) 849-2386; *Fax:* (510) 868-8392, (510) 578-1312
www.asperasoft.com
info@asperasoft.com
Michelle Munson, President, CEO & Co-Founder
Cary Capece, Operations Dir
Serban Simu, Engineering Dir
Mike Flathers, Chief Technologist
Richard Heitman, Vice President of Marketing
Steve Pollini, Vice President of TechnologySolutions
Cary Capece, Senior Vice President of Sales and Business Develo
Aspera's unwavering mission is to create the next-generation software technologies that move the world's large data at maximum speed, regardless of file size, transfer distance and network conditions.

Associated Press Broadcast Services
1100 13th St., Suite 700, Washington, DC 20005 USA
(800) 342-5127
www.ap.org
info@ap.org
Mary Junck, Chairman
Gary Pruitt, President and CEO
Jon Petrovich, Operations Dir
Lee Perryman, General Manager
Andy Wormser, Technical Operations
Greg Groce, Director/Business Operations
Jon Rust, Vice Chairman
Ken Dale,Senior Vice President and Chief Financial Officer
Jessica Bruce, Senior Vice President, Director of Human Resources
Kathleen Carroll, Senior Vice President and Executive Editor

Ellen Hale, Senior Vice President, Director of Corporate Commu
Karen Kaiser, Senior Vice President, General Counsel and Corpora
AP NewsDesk: Newsroom computer software program for mgng TV, radio news & info resources.

ATCI/Antenna Technology Communications Inc.
450 N. McKemy Ave., Chandler, AZ 85226 US
(480) 844-8501, (480) 308-4599; *Fax:* (480) 898-7667
www.atci.com
Gary Hatch, CEO
Ron Kahle, COO/CFO
Simulsat multibeam earth stns; parabolic antennas from 1.8 m to 32 m. Headend electronics, design & maintenance, used/refurbished equipment.

ATI-Audio Technologies Inc.
154 Cooper Road, Building 902, West Berlin, NJ 8091 US
(856) 719-9900; *Fax:* (856) 504-0220
www.atiaudio.com
sales@daysequerra.com
Contact Officer, Promotions Manager
Bcst audio, products: Mic, Line & Distribution Amps, AD/DA & Sample Rate Converters, AES Clock Generator, Portable Field Mixers & Audio Test Equipment.

Atlantic Inc.
10018 Santa Fe Springs Rd., PO Box 2399, Sante Fe Springs, CA 90670-2922 US
(562) 903-9550; *Fax:* (562) 903-9053
www.theatlanticstore.com
customer_relations@atlantic-inc.com
Leo Dardashti, President
Don Dolliver, General Sales Mgr
Mary Jo Schrader, Sales Executive
Brian Hilby, Purchasing Executive
Manufacturer of metal storage systems for DVDs, CDs, & VHS.

Atlas Case Corp.
1380 S. Cherokee St., Denver, CO 80223 USA
(888) 325-2199, (303) 778-7058; *Fax:* (877) 525-2329, (303) 778-7102
www.atlascases.com
sales@atlascases.com
Randy Sabey, President
Airline-approved shipping & carrying cases. Local transport cases, custom or from stock.

Atlas Sound
Mailing Address: 4545 E. Baseline Rd., Phoenix, AZ 85042 US
Second Address: 10972 West Cooper Dr, Littleton, CO 80127
(800) 876-3332,(602) 438-4545, (877) 689-8055, (30; *Fax:* (800) 765-3435
www.atlassound.com
atlascustser@atlassound.com
Lloyd Ivey, CEO
Ken Peck, General Sales Mgr
Steve Young, Promotions Manager
Manny Kitagawa, General Sales Manager
Atlas Sound brand microphone & equipment stands, accessories; equipment consoles, racks & cabinets; loudspeaker systems; a/v monitoring devices.
Atlas Sound Manufacturing
1601 Jack McKay, Ennis, TX 75119 United States

Audio Accessories Inc.
25 Mill St., PO Box 360, Marlow, NH 3456 US
(603) 446-3335; *Fax:* (603) 446-7543
www.patchbays.com
audioacc@patchbays.com
M.B. Hall, President
Michael Hart, Operations Executive
Jack panels, (audio & video patchbays) patch cords, telephone jacks & plugs, pre-wired jack panels (miniature & full-size) & video panels.

Audio Implements/GKC
1703 Pearl St., Waukesha, WI 53186-5626 US
(262) 524-2424; *Fax:* (262) 524-7898
www.audioimplements.com
info@audioimplements.com
Walter Kolb, President
Anita Kolb, Operations Dir
Acoustic coiled earpiece, receivers & cords, microphone line & monitor amplifiers, used in conjunction with IFB system.

Audio Precision Inc.
5750 S.W. Arctic Dr., Beaverton, OR 97005 US
(503) 627-0832, (800) 231-7350, (503) 643-3252, (5; *Fax:* (503) 641-8906
www.ap.com
sales@ap.com
David Schmoldt, President
John Scoles, General Sales Mgr
Tom Williams, Promotions Manager
2700 Series, Portable One & ATS-1, ATS-2 audio test sets for bcst & satellite use.

Audio-Technica U.S., Inc.
1221 Commerce Dr., Stow, OH 44224 US
(330) 686-2600; *Fax:* (330) 686-0719, (330) 688-3752
www.audio-technica.com
pro@atus.com
Tamara Hoffman, Chief Financial Officer
Greg Pinto, VP Marketing
Microphones, wireless microphones, headphones, automatic microphone mixers, phono cartridges, turntables, audio & video accessories.

Audio-Video Engineering Co.
One Pineapple Ln., Stuart, FL 34996 US
(772) 219-3623; *Fax:* (772) 219-3624
Olga Drucker, President/Chairman
Rolf Dracker, Director
Video hum stop coil (hum bucker).

Audioarts Engineering
600 Industrial Dr., New Bern, NC 28562 US
(252) 638-7000; *Fax:* (252) 635-4857
www.audioartsengineering.com
sales@wheatstone.com
Gary Snow, President
Andrew Calvanese, Operations Dir
Jay Tyler, General Sales Mgr
Manufacturer of digital & analog broadcast audio mixing consoles & processing equipment.

Audiolab Electronics Inc.
620 Commerce Street, Suite100, Roseville, CA 95678 US
(916) 784-0200, (800) 624-1903; *Fax:* (916) 784-1425
Ronald Stofan, CEO
Professional line of bulk tape degaussers for all formats of tape including: Beta SP, DAT 2 reels up to 16 diameters, hard drives, DLT media & degaussing svc.

Austin Insulators Inc.
7510 Airport Rd., Mississauga, ON L4T 2H5 Canada
(905) 405-1144; *Fax:* (905) 405-1150
www.austin-insulators.com
Beverly O'Brien, President
Patrick Warr, President
Arthur O. Austin, Founder
Base/guyline insulators, static drain devices, tower lighting transformers, replacements for obsolete insulators & LED lighting for AM(MW), LW antennas .

Autocue
Unit 3, Puma Trade Park, 145 Morden Rd., Mitcham, SY CR4 4DG USA
(208) 665-2992; *Fax:* (208) 687-4869
www.qtv.com
info@autocue.com
Aaron Brady, General Sales Mgr
Steven Carofone, Manager
Computer prompter software. 9, 12 & 15 on-camera prompters. Lightweight flat panel prompters.
19 W. 21st St., New York, NY 10010
(212) 929-7755; *Fax:* (212) 929-2105
Steve Carofalo, Gen Mgr
5919 W. 3rd St., Los Angeles, CA 90036 United States
(213) 936-6195
Steve Hulkower, Gen Mgr

Autodesk
111 McInnis Parkway, San Rafael, CA 94903 Canada
(415) 507-5000; *Fax:* (415) 507-5100
www.autodesk.com
med-ent@autodesk.com
Marc Petit, Operations Dir
Stig Gruman, VP, Digital Entertainment
Autodesk solutions for creating, mgng & distributing digital content, so artists can create once & use anywhere.

Autodesk, Inc.
11 McInnis Parkway, San Rafael, CA 94903
(415) 507-5000; *Fax:* (415) 507-5100
www.autodesk.ca
Carl Boss, CEO
Andrew Anagnost, SVP
Ken Bado, General Sales Mgr
2D & 3D computer graphic imaging & animation software for professionals in entertainment & industrial markets.

Automatic Devices Company
2121 S. 12th St., Allentown, PA 18103 US
(610) 797-6000, (800) 360-2321; *Fax:* (610) 797-4088
www.automaticdevices.com
info@automaticdevices.com
Dennis Lopez, COO
John Samuels, President
Robert Buchman, Purchasing Executive
Stan Nemeth, Customer Service Manager
Robert Jones, Technical Sales
Caryn Anderson, Sales
Barry Weirback, Technical support
Kathleen Schock,Controller
Cyclorama tracks, lighting tracks, lift & draw machines, electronic limit switches.

Autoscript
14 Progress Drive, Shelton, CT 06484-6219 US
(203) 929-1100; *Fax:* (203) 925-2684
www.autoscript.tv
support@autoscript.tv
Brian Larter, President
Joanne Pizzaferro, General Manager
Greg Prentiss, Sales Director
George Andros, Consultant
Charlotte Latham, Rental and Client Liaison Manager
Simon Clark, Head of Sales and Support EMEA
Robin Brown, SalesManager EMEA
Mark Washington, Sales and Aftersales support
Design & manufacture of digital teleprompting systems, maintain a high level of new product dev.

Autoscript (UK)
Unit 2, Heathlands Close., Twickenham, TW1 4BP United Kingdom
44 0 208 891 8900; *Fax:* 44 0 208 891 8901
b.larter@autoscript.tv
Brian Larter, Mgng Dir

AVAB America Inc.
434 Payran Street, Petaluma, CA 94952 US
(707)778-8990
www.avab.com
sales@avab.com
Frantz Lau, CEO/COO
Hans Lain, General Manager
Joe Dupre, Design Engineer, Tech Manager

AVCOM of Virginia Inc.
7729 Pocoshock Way, N Chesterfield, VA 23235 US
(804) 794-2500, (804) 794-2500, (804) 794-2500; *Fax:* (804) 794-8284
www.avcomofva.com
techsupport@avcomofva.com
Jay Evans, President
AVCOM of Virginia is a vertically integrated company with over 25 years of experience in designing and manufacturing high quality, low cost spectrum analyzers.

AVerMedia USA
47358 Fremont Blvd, Fremont, CA 94538 USA
(800) 863-2332,(408) 263-3828; *Fax:* 510) 403-0022
www.avermedia.com
avtsales.usa@avermedia.com
Michael Kuo, Co-founder, Chairman, and CEO
Sinar Pait, CEO
Arthur Pait, President
Julie Lange, Finance Executive
John Hall, Sales Executive
Ted Pepping, Executive Officer
Moses Lee, Chief Financial Officer
Aside from TV Turner/Desktop TV Personal Video Recorder products, AVerMeida also provides digital camera picture TV display devices, Document Camera & PC-to-TV Converters.

AVI Systems
Mailing Address: 7270 Trade St., Suite 102, San Diego, CA 92121 USA
Second Address: 9675 76th St., Suite 200, Eden Praire, MN 55344
(858) 653-4300, (800) 488-4954; *Fax:* (858) 695-7844
www.avisystems.com
info@avisystems.com
Joe Stoebner, Chairman
Jeff Stoebner, President & CEO
Bradley Sousa, Operations Dir
Randi Borth, CFO
Dealer & systems Integrator for video, audio, presentation distance learning & video conferencing, svc.

Avid : Digidesign
Mailing Address: 65-75 Network Drive, Burlington, MA 1803 US
Second Address: 101 South First Street, Suite 200, Burbank, CA 91502
(978) 640-6789, (818) 557-2520; *Fax:* (650) 731-6399, (818) 557-2558
www.avid.com
Louis Hernandez, Jr., President/Chief Executive Officer/Avid Board Membe
Jeff Rosica, Senior Vice President of Worldwide Field Operation
David Lebolt, General Manager
Christopher Bock, General Sales Mgr
John Frederick, Executive VicePresident/Chief Financial Officer/C
Chris Gahagan, Senior Vice President of Products and Services
W. Sean Ford, Vice President of Marketing
Jason Duva, Vice President/General Counsel/Corporate Secretary
Jodi Sweeney, Vice President ofServices and Customer Success
Bruce Yaung, Vice President of Supply and Hardware Technologies
Through Avid Everywhere, Avid delivers the industry's most open, innovative and comprehensive media platform connecting content creation with collaboration, asset protection, distribution and consumption for the most listened to, mostwatched and most loved media in the world-from the most prestigious and award-winning feature films, music recordings, and television shows, to live concerts and news broadcasts. Industry leading solutions include Pro Toolsr, Media Composerr, ISISr,Interplayr, and Sibeliusr.

France Office
44 Ave. Georges Pompidou, 92300 Levallois-Perret France
33 1 41 49 40 10; *Fax:* 33 1 47 49 40 10

UK Office West Complex Pinewood Studios
Pinewood Rd., Iver Heath, Bucks, SLO ONH United Kingdom
44 1753 653322; *Fax:* 44 1753 658501

Japan Office
4F ATT Bldg., 2-11-7 Akasaka, Minato-ku, Tokyo, 107-0052 Japan
81-3-3505-7963; *Fax:* 81-3-3505-3417

New York Office
1650 Broadway, Suite 1113, New York, NY 10019 United States
(212)664-7627

France Office
44 Ave. Georges Pompidou, 92300 Levallois-Perret France

Avid Broadcast
Mailing Address: 65-75, Network Drive, Burlington, MA 1803 US
Second Address: 90 Park Avenue, Suite 1700, New York, NY 10016
(978) 640-6789, (800) 949-2843, (212) 983-2424; *Fax:* (978) 640-1366, (978) 640-3366, (212) 983-9770
www.avid.com
Louis Hernandez, Jr., President/CEO
Jeff Rosica, Senior Vice President of Worldwide Field Operation
Glover Lawrence, VP/Corporate Development
W Sean Ford, VP/Marketing
John Frederick, Executive Vice President/Chief FinancialOfficer/C
Chris Gahagan, Senior Vice President of Products and Services
W. Sean Ford, Vice President of Marketing
Jason Duva, Vice President/General Counsel/Corporate Secretary
Jodi Sweeney, Vice President of Services/Customer Success
BruceYaung, Vice President of Supply and Hardware Technologies
Automated bcst newsroom systems. Non-linear video editing systems, media storage & networking systems, video server, content mgmt systems & asset mgmt systems.
6400 Enterprise Ln., Suite 200, Madison, WI 53719
(608) 274-8686; *Fax:* (608) 273-5876
Robert Long, Cto
115 N. First St., Burbank, CA 91502
(818) 557-2520; *Fax:* (818) 557-2558
John Steinhauer, Dir Bcst Group Sls
575 Lexington Ave., 14th Fl., New York, NY 10022
(212) 983-2424; *Fax:* (212) 983-8718
Michael Wright, Dir Sls

Avid Technology Inc.
Mailing Address: 65-75, Network Drive, Burlington, MA 1803 US
Second Address: 101 South First Street, Suite 200, Burbank, CA 91502
(800) 949-AVID,(978) 640-6789, (818) 557-2520; *Fax:* (978) 640-3366
www.avid.com
Louis Hernandez, Jr., President/CEO
Jeff Rosica, Senior Vice President of Worldwide Field Operation
Glover Lawrence, VP/Corporate Development
W Sean Ford, VP/Marketing
John Frederick, Executive Vice President/Chief FinancialOfficer/C
Chris Gahagan, Senior Vice President of Products and Services
W. Sean Ford, Vice President of Marketing
Jason Duva, Vice President/General Counsel/Corporate Secretary
Jodi Sweeney, Vice President of Services/Customer Success
BruceYaung, Vice President of Supply and Hardware Technologies
Avid's networked bcst news productions are designed to facilitate the process of digital news gathering (DNG).
317 Madison Ave., Suite 521, 5th Fl, New York, NY 10017 United States
(212) 983-2424
Michael Wright, Dir Strategic Sls
115 N. 1st St., Suite 100, Burbank, CA 91502 United States
(818) 557-2520
John Steinhauer, Dir Strategic Sls America

Avtech Systems Inc.
141 Ayers Ct., Suite 1B, Teaneck, NJ 7666 US
(201) 833-8777; *Fax:* (201) 833-4995
www.avtechsystems.com
Fred Samuel, President
David Samuel, General Sales Mgr
Founded in 1978, Avtech Systems has grown into a worldwide value-added reseller in the field of video surveillance and security solutions. Our systems have been installed in many countries around the world with particular emphasis on theUnited States and the Middle East. We represent most of the major manufacturers of video surveillance and access control equipment.

AVX Corp.
One Avx Blvd, Fountain Inn, SC 29644-9039 US
864-967-2150
www.avx.com
gib@avxcorp.com
John Gilbertson, CEO/COO
Kurt Cummings, VP/CFO/Secretary
Jimmy White, General Sales Mgr
Craig Hunter, Promotions Manager
Electronic component.

Axcera
103 Freedom Drive, PO Box 525, Lawrence, PA 15055 US
800-215-2614, (724) 873-8105; *Fax:* (724) 873-8105
Dave Neff, President
Richard Schwartz, Operations Dir
Mike Rosso, General Sales Mgr
Low Medium & High Power Solid State TV Transmitters, High Power Transmitters, Liquid-Cooled Solid State Transmitters, Mobile Multimedia Base Stations, MMDS/BRS/MDS & WCS Transmitters, DOCSIS(r) Based Broadband Wireless Access, Analog &Digital, UHF, VHF, L-Band & S-Band.

Aydin Displays Inc.
One Riga Lane, Birdsboro, PA 19508 USA
(610) 404-7400, (866) 367-2934; *Fax:* (610) 404-8190
www.aydindisplays.com
Ronald Ordway, CEO
Arthur Mengel, President
Clyde Mock, General Sales Mgr
Camera tubes for monochrome, color, special purpose applications & view finder CRTs.

AZCAR U.S.A. Inc.
121 Hillpointe Dr., Suite 700, Canonsburg, PA 15317 US
(724) 873-0800, (888) 873-0800; *Fax:* (724) 873-4770
www.azcar.com
Stephen Pumple, CEO
Gavin Schutz, President
Tom Deyo, Operations Dir
Karl Paulsen, Chief Engineer
Bcst engrg, systems integration.
3235 14th Ave., Markham, ON L3R 0H3 Canada
(905) 470-2545; *Fax:* (905)470-2556
S. Pumple, Pres/Ceo
#1 College Business Park, Coldhams Lane, Cambridge, CB1 3HD United Kingdom
44 1223 414101; *Fax:* 44 123 414102
F. Jarvis, Dir

B&B Systems
9420 Lurine Ave., Unit C, Chatsworth, CA 91311 US
(818) 998-9500; *Fax:* (818) 998-9106
www.bandbsystems.com
lou@broadcaststore.com
Design & instal of production & postproduction systems, vans & mobile units, manufacturer of audio monitoring products.

Band Pro Film & Digital Inc.
Mailing Address: 3403 W. Pacific Ave., Burbank, CA 91505 US
Second Address: 100 Hartsfield Center Parkway, Suite 508, Atlanta, GA 30354
(818) 841-9655, (404) 285-0179; *Fax:* (818) 841-7649
www.bandpro.com
sales@bandpro.com
Amnon Band, CEO
Renee Contreras, President
Band Pro Film and Digital, Home of HD, offers cinemtographers the highest level of expertise & finest equipment available.

Band Pro Munich GmbH
Karl-Hammerschmidt Str. 38, Dornach, 85909 Germany
49 89-945 48 490
Gerhard Baieir, Mgmg Dir

Band Pro Israel
Hasolelim 3, Tel Aviv 67897 Israel
(972) 3-562-1631; *Fax:* (972) 3-562-1632
Ofer Menashe, Mgng Dir

Barco Inc.
Mailing Address: 3078 Prospect Park Drive, Suite 100, Rancho Cordova, CA 95670 US
Second Address: 600 Bellbrook Avenue, Xenia, OH 45385
(678) 475-8000, (888) 414-7226, (937) 372-7579; *Fax:* (678) 475-8100
www.barco.com
bpsmarketing@barco.com
Herman Daems, Chairman
Filip Pintelon, Chief Operating Officer
Eric Van Zele, President/CEO
Dave Scott, General Manager- Defense, Aerospace & Training Div
Carl Peeters, Chief Financial Officer
Jan Van Acoleyen, Chief HumanResources Officer
Jacques Bertrand, Chief Sales Officer
Piet Candeel, General Manager-Healthcare Division
Wim Buyens, General Manager Projection Division
Steve Leyland, General Manager-Advanced Visualization Systems Div
Offers complete monitoring solutions for control rooms in telecom traf, surveillance, pub utilities, process control & financing.

Baron Group, Ltd
2355 Industrial Park Blvd., Cumming, GA 30041 USA
678) 455 1181; *Fax:* (678) 455 1153
www.barantelecom.com
Meir Dor, Founder, Chairman
Nahman Tsabar, Chief Executive Officer
Ross Kruchten, President
Sasson Shilo, Chief Financial Officer
Dan Shenbach, CEO Baran Israel
Steven Senter, CEO Baran International
Dan Ben Harosh, VP of HumanResources
Issac Friedman, Infrastructure & Construction Division GM, Founder
Arik Shaked, VP Business Development
Project mgmt & turn-key construction of communications towers, including erection, maintenance & inspection of tall towers.
10430 Rogers Rd., Houston, TX 77070 United States
(713) 973-6904; *Fax:* (713) 973-0205
Ross Kruchten, Chairman
11112 117th Pl. N.E., Kirkland, WA 98033 United States
(425) 739-9342; *Fax:* (425) 739-9314
Russ Stromberg, Chairman
4640 Wedgewood Blvd., Frederick, MD 21703 United States
(301) 663-9300; *Fax:* (301) 663-9584
Tom Cureton, Chairman

Battery Pros Inc.
30 Nashua St., Suite 3, Woburn, MA 1801 USA
(888) 399-8108, (781) 932-0076; *Fax:* (770) 498-2482
www.batteryproswoburn.net
batterypros@verizon.net
Patti Novak, President
Maria Arce, Operations Dir
Battery recelling/rebuilding for Bricks & Belts, primary & secondary batteries, custom battery pack design & manufacture.

Bauer Transmitters, Inc.
10870 Pellicano Drive, El Paso, TX 79935 US
(915) 595-1048; *Fax:* (915) 595-1840
www.bauertx.com
paul@bauertx.com
Paul Gregg, President
Remanufactured Bauer-Sparta & Elcom Bauer AM/FM transmitters, AM combining & antenna coupling equipment.

BBE Sound Inc.
2548 Fender Ave., Fullerton, CA 92831 US
(714) 897-6766, (800) 233-8346; *Fax:* (714) 895-6728
www.bbesound.com
info@bbesound.com
John McLaren, Chairman/CEO
Steve Hase, VP Licensing
David McLaren, Executive Vice President
Paul Gagon, Vice President-Technology
Audio/video signal processors to eliminate phase & amplitude distortion.

BEI Duncan Electronics
170 Technology Dr., Irvine, CA 92618-2401 US
(949) 341-9500; *Fax:* (949) 453-2700
Philippe Roux, General Manager
Manufacturer of motion & position sensors

Belar Electronics Laboratory Inc.
Mailing Address: 119 Lancaster Ave., Devon, PA 19333 US
Second Address: PO Box 76, Devon, PA 19333-0076
(610) 687-5550; *Fax:* (610) 687-2686
www.belar.com
sales@belar.com
Arno Meyer, President
AM, FM, FM stereo, SCA, RDS/RBDS, shortwave, TV, TV stereo modulation & frequency monitors.

Belden
Mailing Address: 2200 U.S. Hwy. 27 S., Richmond, IN 47374 US
Second Address: 401 Pennsylvania Parkway, Suite 200, Indianapolis, IN
(765) 983-5200, (800) BELDEN1, (317) 818-6300; *Fax:* (765) 983-5294, (317) 818-6382
www.belden.com
info@belden.com
Bryan C. Cressey, Chairman
David Aldrich, Director
Lance C. Balk, Director
Judy Brown, Director
Glenn Kalnasy, Director
George Minnich, Director
John M. Monter, Director
Precision video coaxial, triaxial cables, professional music cables, ENG cables, audio snakes, RGB cables & 50 ohm transmission cables.

Belden/ICM Corp.
6260 Downing St., Denver, CO 80216 US
(303) 288-8107,(800) 222-2142; *Fax:* (303) 288-4769
www.icmcorp.net
asutherland@icmcorp.net
Randy Holliday, President
Gary Williams, General Sales Mgr
Amanda Sutherland, Marketing
Painted galvolume molding with custom fittings backed by a 15-year warranty, U.L. listed and Class A fire rated.

Bencher Inc.
241 E. Depot St., Antioch, IL 60002 US
(847) 838-3195; *Fax:* (847) 838-3479
www.bencher.com
Tere Benedict, President
All products offered by Bencher are fabricated and assembled at our facilities in Antioch, Illinois, USA, by skilled professionals, using the finest materials available. Materials are supplied from American mills, foundries and componentsuppliers.

Benchmark Media Systems Inc.
203 East Hampton Pl., Suite 2, Syracuse, NY 13206-1707 US
(315) 437-6300,(800) 262-4675; *Fax:* (315) 437-8119
www.benchmarkmedia.com
sales@benchmarkmedia.com
Ruth Burdick, President
R. Rall, Sales Manager
Richard Kalinowski, Purchasing Manager
Audio processing & distribution systems, VU/PPM meters, interface/headphone amplifiers, microphone pre-amplifiers; digital to analog & analog to digital converters.

Bendalite
905 G St., Hampton, VA 23661 US
(757) 245-7675,(800) 236-3254; *Fax:* (757) 244-4819,(877) 445-7298
www.bendalite.com
cs@bendalite.com
Hugh Jones, President
Ron Koppel, Promotions Manager
Bendalite is the pioneer manufacturer of flexible neon specialty lighting product. We have added other specialty lighting products including disco lights, fiber optic lighting, border lighting and tree lighting. Browse our over 800 specialtylighting products, or call our customer service department to learn more

Benner-Nawman, Inc. and BN Products-USA, LLC.
3450 Sabin Brown Rd., Wickenburg, AZ 85390 US
(800) 992-3833,(928) 684-2813; *Fax:* (928) 684-7041
www.bnproducts.com
mail@bnproducts.com
Edward Kientz, President/CEO
Lon Brown, General Manager
Angel Bourne, Controller
Mel Kientz, Chief Marketing Officer
Daniel Sibiga, Business Development
Specialty tools for CATV, cable termination & distribution boxes (cabinets).

Bexel
Mailing Address: 2701 N. Ontario St., Burbank, CA 91504 US
Second Address: 1001 N Union Bower Road, Suite 130, Irving, TX 75061
(818) 841-5051 (818) 847-8670, (972) 870-2339; *Fax:* (818) 841-1572
www.bexel.com
Andy Crist, CEO
Halid Hatic, President/General Manager
Craig Schiller, Vice President Engineering & Operations
Scott Nardelli, Vice President/General Manager, Bexel ESS
Joyce Bente, General Sales Mgr
Kirsten Ballard, Vice Presidentof Administrations
Tom Dickinson, Chief Technology Officer
John Schrieber, Vice President of Finance

Joyce Bente, Director of Sales, Bexel TSS

Greg Bragg, Associate Director of Network Rentals
Lee Estroff, Vice President of AccountDevelopment
Bexel has delivered the finest customer svc & best audio/video production equipment rentals for over 30 years & remains the world leader. Real 24/7/365 emergency svc/tech natl offices/experts in solutions/custom engrg, systems design &application/sound tech advice, also used equipment sls.

Bexel Seattle Office
3314 Fourth Ave. South, Seattle, WA 98134 United States
(206) 628-7000
Chris Hunter, Account Executive

Bexel Miami Office.
20239 N.E. 15th Ct., Miami, FL 33179 United States
(305) 653-5051; *Fax:* (305) 655-6209
Andrea Rosenkrans, Accountant Exec

Bexel Atlanta Office
5555 Oak Brook Pkwy., Suite 160, Norcross, GA 30093 United States
(770) 448-3000; *Fax:* (770) 449-5747
Frank Zamor, Rental Mgr

Bexel Dallas Office
1001 N. Union Bower, Suite 130, Irving, TX 75061 United States
(214) 946-5051; *Fax:* (972) 831-9860
Jim Barrett, Rental Mgr

Bexel New York Office
625 W. 55th St., New York, NY 10019 United States
(212) 246-5051; *Fax:* (212) 246-6373
Mke King, Rental Mgr

Bexel DC Office
555 Herndon Pkwy., Suite 135, Herndon, VA 20170
(703) 437-5559; *Fax:* (703) 437-6931

Bexel Corporation
2701 N. Ontario St., Burbank, CA 91504 USA

818-565-4399
www.bexel.com
Halid Hatic, President & General Manager
Scott Nardelli, Vice President & General Manager
Craig Schiller, Vice President Engineering & Operations
Kirsten Ballard, Vice President of Administrations
Tom Dickinson, Chief TechnologyOfficer
Andrea Rosenkrans, Sales Coordination Manager
Lee Estroff, Vice President of Account Development
John Schrieber, Vice President of Finance
John Mills, Business Development Manager

BEXT Inc.
1045 10th Ave., San Diego, CA 92101 US
(619) 239-8462, (888) 239-8462; *Fax:* (619) 239-8474
www.bext.com
bext@bext.com
Dennis Pieri, CEO
Claudio Tilesi, CFO
Radio & Digital TV Transmitters, Antennas, Amplifiers, Receivers, Boosters, STLs, RF Combiners, RF Filters, Stereo Generators, FmExtra Digital Radio Encoders & Receivers.

Beyerdynamic
56 Central Ave., Farmingdale, NY 11735 US
(631) 293-3200,(800) 293-4463; *Fax:* (631) 293-3288
info@beyerdynamic.com
Nel Keinz, General Manager
Alan Feckanin, General Sales Mgr
Bob Lowig, Sales
Microphones, headsets, monitor headphones, studio & on-location UHF & VHF wireless systems.

Beyond Broadband Technology LLC
6125 Paluxy Dr., Tyler, TX 75703-5976 USA
(903) 561-4411; *Fax:* (903) 561-4031
www.bbtsolution.com
info@bbtsolution.com
Bennett Hooks, President
William Bauer, Partner/CEO
Tony Swain, Partner/COO
DCAS-open standard downloadable conditional access & MPEG 4 Transport.
8477 Trail Lake Dr., Powell, OH 43065 United States
1140 10th St., Gering, NE 69341

BGW Systems, Amplifier Technologies, Inc.
1749 Chapin Rd., Montebello, CA 90640 US
(323) 278-0001; *Fax:* (310) 323-0083
www.bgw.com
info@bgw.com
Morris Kessler, President
Angie Scott, Operations Dir
BGW is also an outstanding OEM supplier to many leading firms including NASA, the U.S. Navy and 3M Corporation, for whom we have designed and manufactured special audio amplifiers and customized computer systems.

Bird Electronic Corp.
Mailing Address: 30303 Aurora Rd., Solon, OH 44139 US
Second Address: 8625 Industrial Parkway, Angola, NY 14006
(866) 695-4569, (440) 248-1200; *Fax:* (866) 546-4306, (866) 546-4306
www.birdrf.com
David Hessler, Chairman
Mark Johnson, President
Edward J. Bratos. Jr., VP-Operations
Dennic Morgan, CFO
Terrence C. Grant, VP-Sales
Thomas L. Kuklo, VP-Buisness and Dvelopment
Micheal L. Fetto, VO-Engineering
W. StevenBeitscher, Director of Quality and Cstomer Service
Bird Technologies Group is a global, innovative supplier of RF products, systems, svcs & educ solutions.

Birns and Sawyer Inc.
5275 Craner Avenue, North Hollywood, CA 91601 US
(323) 466-8211; *Fax:* (323) 466-1868, (818) 358-4395
www.birnsandsawyer.com
rabed@birnsandsawyer.com
William Meurer, President
Jason Stuckey, General Manager
Kathie Dugan, Business Acct Manager
William Meurer, Owner/Cinematographer
Ramzi Abed, Director of Marketing and Sales
Jeff Jackson, Director of Rentals
Jason Stuckey,Controller
Camera and support, lighting, grip rental and sales

Bitcentral Inc.
4340 Von Karman Ave., Suite 410, Newport Beach, CA 92660 USA
(949) 253-9000, (800) 272-4004, (949) 417-4125; *Fax:* (949) 253-9027
www.bitcentral.com
Fred Fourcher, CEO/Owner
Rick Young, VP, Sales & Product Strategy
John King, VP, Prof. Engineering Services
Sameer Mohiuddin, VP, Support
Daniel Pugh, VP, Software Development
Bicentral is in the business of providing innovative solutions that transform the mgmt, production & distribution of the news.

Blimpy Floating Signs/Bend-A-Lite
905 G St., Hampton, VA 23661 US
(757) 245-7675,(800) 448-2014; *Fax:* (757) 244-4819
www.blimpy.com
cs@blimpy.com
Hugh Jones, President
Ron Koppel, Promotions Manager
Giant blimps, hot air balloons & rooftop balloons. Complete custom department for any shape or size, flexible neon in seven brilliant colors.

Blonder Tongue Laboratories Inc.
One Jake Brown Rd., PO Box 1000, Old Bridge, NJ 8857 US
(732) 679-4000,(800) 523-6049; *Fax:* (732) 679-4353
www.blondertongue.com
information@blondertongue.com
James Lukson, CEO/COO
John Lynon, Information Technology
Norman Westcott, General Sales Mgr
Lynne Russo, Director
Salim Chehade, Territory Manager
Tom Lowden, Territory Manager
Steve Hegge, Technical Solutions Director
SteveCimino, Director
Lauren Yesler, Marketing
Manufacturer of private cable equipment, including satellite receivers, modulators, processors, amplifiers, combiners & passives.

Bogen Communications Inc.
50 Spring Street, Suite 1, Ramsey, NJ 7446 US
(201) 934-8500,(800) 999-2809; *Fax:* (201) 934-9832
www.bogen.com
info@bogen.com
Jeffrey E. Schwarz, Co-Chairman
Jonathan Guss, CEO
Michael Fleischer, President
David Chambers, General Sales Mgr
Kasimir Arciszewski, Director
Maureen A. Flotard, Chief Financial Officer/Vice President Finance
David L.Delbrocco, Director
Audio amplifiers, mixer-preamplifiers, power amplifiers; FM/AM tuners & receivers; intercom systems; pub address & sound reinforcement systems; digital repeater products & speakers.

Boonton Electronics Corp.
25 Eastmans Rd., Parsippany, NJ 7054 US
(973) 386-9696; *Fax:* (973) 386-9191
www.boonton.com
info@boonton.com
Edward Garcia, CEO
John Kenneally, General Sales Mgr
Wolfgang Damm, Programming Director
Brent Hessen-Schmidt, Promotions Manager
Richard Blackwell, Chief Engineer
Monty Johnson, CEO
Marc Wolfsohn, CFO
Larry Henderson, CMO
Electronic test & measuring equipment: microwave/RF power, RF voltmeters, capacitance/inductance & modulation meters.

Bradley Broadcast and Pro Audio
Mailing Address: 7309-D Grove Rd., Frederick, MD 21704 US
Second Address: PO Box 756, New Market, MD 21774
(800) 732-7665,(301) 682-8700; *Fax:* (301) 263-7042
www.bradleybroadcast.com
info@bradleybroadcast.com
David Matthews, President
Art Reed, General Manager
Your source for all major brands of radio & professional audio equipment. The friendly personal svc of a family-owned company, the tech experience of many years in the business & very competeitive pricing too.

Broadcast Data Consultants
3980 E. State Rd. 64, Bradenton, FL 34208 US
(800) 275-6204, (941) 749-5566; *Fax:* (941) 749-5502
www.broadcastdata.com
sales@broadcastdata.com
Scott Wachtler, President
Neil Edwards, Operations Dir
Broadcast Data has been around since 1987. We were the first to develop music cataloguing and scheduling software for classical music radio stations. Today, this is still a very important part of our product mix. In 1992, we introducedTraffic C.O.P. 2 for DOS.

Broadcast Electronics
4100 N. 24th St., Quincy, IL 62305 US
(217) 224-9600; *Fax:* (217) 224-9607
bdcast.com/products/audio-data-links/marti
bdcast@bdcast.com
Tim Bealor, President
Brent Whelan, VP Operations & RF Technical Services
George Marti, General Manager
Tom Beck, Director, Sales & RF Products
Brian Lindemann, VP Engineering
Tim Bealor, Executive VP Product Development
BeckyKeck, CFO
Tina Zanger, HR Manager
Jim Roberts, Marketing Manager/ Sr. Product Manager
Composite, dual mono & digital STL systems, remote pickup systems, telemetry links, studio to transmitter links, FM exciters, transmitters & pots remote pickup systems.

Broadcast Electronics Inc.
4100 N. 24th St., Quincy, IL 62305 US
(217) 224-9600; *Fax:* (217) 224-9607
www.bdcast.com
bdcast@bdcast.com
Tim Bealor, President
Brent Whelan, Vice President Operations/RF Technical Services
Kevin Maider, General Sales Mgr
Ray Miklius, Vice President
Tim Bealor, Vice President
Brenne Ormone, Chief Marketing Officer
Tim Bealor,Executive Vice President Product Development
Brian Lindemann, Vice President Engineering
Tina Zanger, Human Resources Manager
Radio bcst equipment including digital studio systems, AM, FM transmitters, RPUs & STLs.

Broadcast Engineering
9800 Metcalf Ave., Overland Park, KS 66212 US
(913) 967-1737; *Fax:* (913) 967-1905
www.tvtechnology.com/index
brad.dick@penton.com
Jon Chalon, Operations Dir
Brad Dick, Programming Director
Broadcast Engineering: Published for mgmt & engrg personnel working in bcst, production, postproduction, cable facilities in North America.
335 Court St., 9, Brooklyn, NY 11231 United States
(718) 802-0488; *Fax:* (718) 522-4751
Josh Gordon, Chairman

Orient Echo Inc.
1101 Grand Maison, Shimomiyabi-cho 2-18, Shinjuku-ku, Tokyo, 162-0822
(03) 3235-5961; *Fax:* (03) 3235-5852
Mashy Yoshikawa, Chairman
Box 250, Banbury, Oxon, OX16 8YJ
+44-129-527-8407; *Fax:* +44-129-527-8408
Richard Woolley, Chairman

Broadcast International Group
10458 N.W. 31st Terr., Doral, FL 33172 US
(305) 599-2112; *Fax:* (305) 599-1133
www.bigmiami.com
sales@bigmiami.com
Ana Maria Sagastegui, President
BROADCAST INTERNATIONAL GROUP, has more than 25 years experience in the discipline of; analysis and consultation, design, engineering, documentation, project management, fabrication, construction, integration, installation, testing, trainingand service supporting a wide range of television production systems and facilities from Network Broadcast Studios to corporate production facilities.

Broadcast Microwave Services Inc.
12367 Crosthwaite Circle, Dock 10, Poway, CA 92064 US
(858) 391-3050,(800) 669-9667; *Fax:* (858) 391-3049
www.bms-inc.com
sales@bms-inc.com
Graham Bunney, President
Tim Macy, Contractor
COFDM wireless microwave, transmitters, receivers & antenna systems for ENG vehicles, helicopters, autotrackers, central receive sites.
293 Sycamore Grove, Los Angeles, CA 93065 United States

(805) 581-4566; *Fax:* (805) 527-8263
Jim Kubit, Sls Engr
105A Lew Dewitt Blvd., #278, Waynesboro, VA 22980 United States
(540) 932-3660; *Fax:* (858) 391-3049
Russell Murphy, Sls Engr

Broadcast Store Inc.
9420 Lurline Ave., Unit C, Chatsworth, CA 91311 US
(818) 998-9100; *Fax:* (818) 998-9106
www.broadcaststore.com
sales@broadcaststore.com
Lou Claude, President
Buy, sell, consign new & preowned Audio/Video bcst equiptment for production & post-production needs.
500 W. 37th St., New York, NY 10018
(212) 268-8800; *Fax:* (212) 268-1858
1031 Ives Dairy Rd., Miami, FL 33179
305-266-2112; *Fax:* 305-266-2113

Broadcast Supply Worldwide
2237 S. 19th St., Tacoma, WA 98405 US
(800) 426-8434, (800) 231-7055, (253) 565-2301; *Fax:* (800) 231-7055, (253) 565-8114
www.bswusa.com
sales@bswusa.com
Irv Law, Chairman
Tim Schwieger, President
Shannon Nichols, Sales Manager
Gary Beebe, Sales Engineer
Paul Schweiger, Senior Sales Representative
John Lynch, Senior Sales Representative
Jamie Singer, Senior SalesRepresentative
Adam Repp, Sales Representative
As one of the world's premiere broadcast equipment suppliers, BSW (Broadcast Supply Worldwide) is uniquely qualified to offer thousands of products at very competitive prices. For over 38 years, broadcast and audio professionals around theglobe trust BSW for all their equipment needs.

Broadcast Video Systems Corp.
25 Forest Ridge Rd., Richmond Hill, ON L4E 3L8 Canada
(905) 305-0565; *Fax:* (416) 946-1964
www.bvs.ca
broadcastvideosystems@gmail.com
Bert Verwey, President
SDI, analog video keyers, chroma keyers, closed captioning, encoders/decoders, positioner, bridge, V-chip, data transmission, encoders & transcoders.

Broadcasters General Store Inc.
2480 S.E. 52nd St., Ocala, FL 34480 US
(352) 622-7700; *Fax:* (352) 629-7000
www.bgs.cc
info@bgs.cc
David Kerstin, President
Lee Freshwater, Sales Executive
Cindy Edwards, Sales
Ricky Forguson, Sales
LeEwok Freshwater, Sales
Shannon Schneider, Support
Lorri Shute, Support
Professional audio, video & RF equipment, Telco interfaces, digital codecs, 400+ vendor line card. Axia Opx

BGS IN Office
765-935-6707
Gary Tibbot, Chairman

BGS NC Office
828-698-2893
Cindy Edwards, Chairman

BGS KY Office
Cecile Gibson - 270-928-1151

Bryston Ltd.
677 Neal Dr., PO Box 2170, Peterborough, ON K9J 6X7 Canada
(705) 742-5325, (800) 632-8217; *Fax:* (705) 742-0882
www.bryston.ca
contact@bryston.ca
Micah Sheveloff, General Manager
Bryston Ltd. has been designing and manufacturing state of the art specialty electronics to both the consumer and professional audio marketplaces for over 35 years.

Bud Industries Inc.
4605 E. 355 St., Willoughby, OH 44094 US
(440) 946-3200; *Fax:* (440) 951-4015
www.budind.com
saleseast@budind.com
Blair Haas, President
Josian Haas, General Sales Mgr
Open & welded racks; cabinets & accessories.

Box 41190, Phoenix, AZ 85080 United States
(623) 516-9494

Burk Technology
7 Beaver Brook Rd., Littleton, MA 1460 US
(978) 486-0086, (800) 255-8090; *Fax:* (978) 486-0081
www.burk.com
sales@burk.com
Peter Burk, President
Bill Irvine, Engineering Dir
Steve Danikel, Director of Sales
Nathan Burk, Marketing Executive
Bcst transmitter remote control & monitoring.

Burlington A/V Recording Media Inc.
106 Mott St., Oceanside, NY 11572-5823 US
(516) 678-4414,(800) 331-3191; *Fax:* (516) 678-8959
www.burlington-av.com
burlington@optonline.net
Jan Alan, President
Ruth Schwartz, Operations Dir
Burlington A/V Recording Media is the world's largest distributor of professional recording formats, equipment and accessories. For over four decades we've been serving the broadcast, audio, video and data industries.

Burst Electronics Inc.
Mailing Address: PO Box 65947, Albuquerque, NM 87193 US
Second Address: 6105 Coronado Ave NE, Suite E, Albuquerque, NM 87109
(505) 898-1455, (505) 890-8926; *Fax:* (505) 898-0159
www.burstelectronics.com
sales@burstelectronics.com
Brad Hamlin, President
CG, DA's, HD/analog video switchers, video mixers, decoders, logo generator, video generators, TBC & GPI converters.

C-COR/ Arris
60 Decibel Rd., State College, PA 16801 US
(814) 238-2461; *Fax:* (814) 238-4065
David Woodle, Chairman
David Woodle, CEO
Globally-tailored fiber optic, RF & digital video transport telecommunications products, OSS mgmt solutions & high-end tech field svcs for broadband networks.

Broadband Management Soultions Software Divison He
5673 Gibraltar Dr., Suite 100, Pleasanton, CA 94588 United States
(925) 251-3000; *Fax:* (925) 467-0600
Douglas W. Engerman, Chairman

Broadband Communication Products Product Division
999 Research Pkwy, Meriden, CT 06450 United States
(203) 630-5700; *Fax:* (203) 630-5701
John O. Caezza, Chairman

Broadband Network Services Services Division
300 Union Blvd., Suite 515, Lakewood, CO 80228 United States
(303) 980-8058
Paul E. Janson, Chairman

Cable Leakage Technologies
1211 Executive Dr. East, Richardson, TX 75081 US
(972) 907-8100,(800) 783-8878; *Fax:* (972) 907-2950
www.wavetracker.com
sales@wavetracker.com
Perry Havens, Sales Representative
Ed Harmon, Sales Representative
MJ Jackson, Sales Representative
Chris Davis, Team Sales
Digital RF tracking/mapping system used in CLI monitoring.

Cable Prep
207 Middlesex Ave, PO Box 373, Chester, CT 06412-0373 US
(860) 526-4337, (800) 394-4046; *Fax:* (860) 526-2291
www.cableprep.com
toolmaker@cableprep.com
Deborah Morrow, President
David Morrow, Operations Dir
Cable Prep TerminX, hex crimp, coring & stripping, drop wire stripping, jacket strippers, messenger removal & tools.

Cable Serv Inc.
4560 Eastgate Pkwy., Mississauga, ON L4W 3W6 Canada
(905) 629-1111, (800) 668-2033; *Fax:* (905) 629-1115
www.cableserv.com
Audley Alexander, President
TV Exciters, 5-10-20 watt LPTV trans & transmitters, TV modulators, demodulators, processors, & satellite receivers.

Cable Services Company Inc.
2113 Marydale Ave., Williamsport, PA 17701 US
(570) 323-8518,(800) 326-9444; *Fax:* (570) 322-5373
www.cable-services.com
Ken R. Michaels, CEO
John M. Roskowski, President
Eugene S. Welliver, Operations Dir
Harland W. Bergstrom, General Manager
Neal W. Kimberling, Vice President
Turnkey fiber-optic & coaxial construction; distributor of CATV products.

Cable Technologies International
Mailing Address: 460 Oakdale Ave., Hatboro, PA 19040 US
Second Address: 75 S. Central Avenue, Mechanicville, NY 12118
(215) 672-5400, (800) 378-8753; *Fax:* (215) 672-0440
www.cabletechnologies.com
sales@cabletechnologies.com
Paul E. Morse, Jr., CEO
Christopher Shirling, President
Joan Wixted, Director of Sales
Jo Ellington, Sales Coordinator/Account Executive
Joe Gabel, Sales Coordinator/Account Executive
Your #1 Co. for buying/selling/repairing/new/used/surplus-digital products-DCT's/parts/cables/universal remotes, advanced analog converters, headend/distribution equipment, test equipment including signal level meters, character generators,cables, HDTV/cables/modems/audio components/home theater/coax, remotes & batteries.
75 S. Central Ave., Mechanicville, NY 12118

Cable Yellow Pages
20917 Higgins Ct., Torrance, CA 90501 US
(800) 777-4320; *Fax:* (310) 212-5392
Neal Schnog, President
Glenn Schrader, Manager
Wade Pierce, VP/Associate Publisher
Phone directory for cable TV systems.

CableTek Wiring Products Inc.
1150 Taylor St., Elyria, OH 44035 US
(440) 365-3889,(800) 562-9378; *Fax:* (440) 322-0321
www.cable-tek.com
treilly@apk.net
Tim Reilly, General Manager
Interior & exterior surface wiring products; terminal enclosures, residential enclosures, security products.

Cablynx, Inc.
28 Tower Office Park, Woburn, MA 01801-6552 USA
(781) 933-2000, (877) 222-5969; *Fax:* (781) 933-4641
www.cablynx.com
sales@nova-sys.com
Shintaro Asano, President
Routing switchers, distribution amplifiers, time code, component video, PC accessories, compugraphics to video, frame synchronizer.

CADCO SYSTEMS
3401 Wynwood Dr., Plano, TX 75074 US
(972) 271-3651,(800) 877-2288; *Fax:* (972) 744-0753
howard.carmen@gmail.com
Steven Johnson, CEO
Carmen Howard, Contact
Manufacturer of CATV & broadband communication products such as modulators, demodulators, signal processors, ch converters, translators & special application headend equipment, fixed-channel & frequency agile.

Calculated Industries Inc.
4840 Hytech Dr., Carson City, NV 89706 US
(775) 885-4900,(800) 854-8075; *Fax:* (775) 885-4949
www.calculated.com
info@calculated.com
Steve Kennedy, President
Time code calculators work in & convert between all time formats; drop/non-drop, multiple EPS rates for all SMPTE/PAL equations.

California Amplifier
Mailing Address: 1401 N. Rice Ave., Oxnard, CA 93030 US
Second Address: 2231 Rutherford Rd., Suite 110, Carlsbad, CA 92008
(805) 987-9000, (760) 438-9010; *Fax:* (805) 987-8359, (760) 438-5835
www.calamp.com
Michael Burdiek, President & CEO
Rick Vitalle, Chief Financial Officer
Garo Sarkissian, Sr. VP of Corporate Development
Rick Vitelle, Executive VP, CFO & Secretary
Neil Friedlander, Vice President of Operations
Greg Gower, SeniorVice President and General Manager
Robert Hannah, Senior Vice President and General Manager
Manufacturer of mesh & offset satellite antennas ranging in size from 18 to 16'.

Calumet Photographic
Mailing Address: 819 W Eastman Street, Chicago, IL 60642 US
Second Address: 150 First Street, Cambridge, MA 2142
(312) 440-4920, (617) 576-2600; *Fax:* (800) 577-3686
www.calumetphoto.com
custserv@calumetphoto.com
Peter Biasotti, President
Don Ernest, Vice President

Calzone Case Co.
225 Black Rock Ave., Bridgeport, CT 6605 US
(800) 243-5152, (203) 367-5766; *Fax:* (203) 336-4406
www.calzonecase.com
vin.calzone@calzonecase.com
Joseph Calzone, President
Vincent Calzone, General Sales Mgr
Manufacturers of custom & standard shipping cases for all industries featuring Escort, LD-ATA, Military, X series, Titan
75006 Luna Rd., Suite 126, Carrollton, TX 75007 United States
(972) 241-3900; *Fax:* (972) 241-3998
Tom Mackno, Vp
15730 Salt Lake Ave., City of Industry, CA 91745 United States
(626) 968-4100; *Fax:* (626) 968-1703
Mike Herman, Vp Admin/Sls

Camera Service Center
25 Enterprise Ave. N., Secaucus, NJ 7094 USA
(212) 757-0906; *Fax:* (212) 713-0075
www.arricsc.com
Simon Broad, President and Vice President of Marketing
James Alexander, Operations Manger
Ed Stamm, Vice President and General Manager
David Lamadrio, Chief Financial Officer
Mark Machover, Vice President Finance
Hardwick Johnson,Senior Vice President Rental
Luciana Lenihan, Purchasing Department Manager
Lucy Dorta, Office Manager
Dennis Vermeal, Credit and Sales Manager
The largest full-svc film equipment rental company, carrying a complete line of camera & lighting products.
2385 Stirling Rd., Fort Lauderdale, FL 33312
(954) 322-4545; *Fax:* (954) 322-4188
Ed Stamm, Chairman

CamMate Systems
425 E. Comstock, Chandler, AZ 85225 US
(480) 813-9463; *Fax:* (480) 813-9292
www.cammate.com
cammate@cammate.com
Linda Mitchell, CEO
Exclusive sls & rental of the CamMate, a single operator remote camera crane in various configurations for video & film. Now offering Telescoping Jips.

Canare Corp.
45 Commerce Way, Unit C, Totowa, NJ 7512 US
973-837-0070; *Fax:* 973-837-0080
www.canare.com
sales@canare.com
Kazuo Urata, CEO
Larry Cano, General Sales Mgr
Canare manufactures the best in Pro Audio and Video Cable, 75 Ohm BNC, F and RCA Connectors, Patchbays, Cable Reels, Snake Systems, Assemblies, Crimp Tools and Cable Strippers. In 2004, we launched a full Optical Product Line for HD upgradesin the broadcast market. Professional broadcast engineers, sound technicians, A/V facility integrators, design consultants and many leading OEM's rely on Canare's product, proven reliability and top notch customer service. Optimize with Canare ...theProfessionals Choice!

Canon U.S.A. Inc.
65 Challenger Rd., Ridgefield Park, NJ 7660 US
(800) 321-4388; *Fax:* (201) 807-3333
www.usa.canon.com/cusa/professional
bctv@cusa.canon.com
Joe Adachi, President/Chief Executive Officer
John Rose, General Sales Mgr
Seymour Liebman, Executive Vice President, Chief Administrative Off
Yuichi Ishizuka, Executive Vice President-Imaging Technologies & Co
Kunihiko Tedo, SeniorVice President/Chief Financial Officer/Trea
Junichi Yoshitake, Senior Vice President-Business Imaging Solutions G
Eliott Peck, Senior Vice President-Imaging Technologies & Commu
Joseph G. Warren, Senior Vice President-Corporate HumanResources
The Canon Broadcast & Communications (BCTV) division a part of the larger Canon U.S.A. Inc. The BCTV lens products is squarely based on the highly advanced optical, mechanical & digital technologies for which Canon became legendary. Studio,field & ENG lenses & svc, (HDTV/SDTV) video, audio, data optical beam transmission, remote control P/T/Z camera system.
15955 Alton Pkwy., Irvine, CA 92618 United States
(949) 753-4330; *Fax:* (949) 753-4337
Tom Bender, Sls
Joe Patton, Sls
Stephanie Franz, Sls
100 Park Blvd., Itasca, IL 60143 United States
(630) 250-6236; *Fax:* (630) 250-0399
Dave Pavlik, Sls
5625 Oakbrook Pkwy., Norcross, GA 30093 United States
(770) 849-7890; *Fax:* (770) 849-7888
Jim Dobbins, Sls
3200 Regent Blvd., Irvine, TX 75063 United States
(972) 409-8871; *Fax:* (972) 409-8869
Mark Parks, Sls

Capacitor Industries
6455 N. Avondale Ave., Chicago, IL 60631 USA
(773) 774-6666; *Fax:* (773) 774-6690
www.capacitorindustries.com
liam.d@capacitorindustries.com
Terry Noone, President
High Voltage Filter Capacitors for radio & TV bcst transmission.

Capacitor Industries
6455 N. Avondale Ave., Chicago, IL 60631 USA
(773) 774-6666; *Fax:* (773) 774-6690
www.capacitorindustries.com
info@capacitorindustries.com
Terence Noone, President
Liam D, General Manager
Motor-run, motor-start, metalized, oil-filtered, high voltage, film, electrolytic & power capacitors, & R.C. networks. Our products are produced in modern, high-volume, state-of-the-art manufacturing facilities in Mainland China. Each ofthese factories is ISO Certified and operated by sophisticated management teams focused on worldwide growth.

Capstone Communications Group
15 Wilson St., Markham, ON L3P 1M9 US
(905) 472-2330
www.capstonecomm.com

Carpel Video Inc.
429 E. Patrick St., Frederick, MD 21701 US
(800) 238-4300,(301) 694-3500; *Fax:* (301) 694-9510
www.carpelvideoonline.com
Vfearnow@carpelvideo.com
Andy Carpel, President
Videotape wholesalers. Mail order post production in MD; store: DVD production and duplication. Lowest prices on 6 blank video tapes. 800-238-4300.

CATV Services Inc.
12099 N.W. 98th Ave., Hialeah Gardens, FL 33018 US
(305) 512-5601,(800) 227-1200; *Fax:* (305) 512-5606
www.catvservices.com
info@catvservices.com
Richard Richmond, President
CATV Services, Inc. was founded in 1975 by Richard C. Richmond. During its first two years of operation, it functioned primarily as a manufacturers representative organization. By the 1980's CATV Services had expanded in size, staff, andability, to handle our customers needs both in new and reconditioned equipment.

CBT Systems
12585 Kirkham Court, Poway, CA 92064 USA
(858) 536-2927; *Fax:* (858) 536-2354
www.cbt-net.com
info@cbt-net.com
Darrell Wendhardt, President
Rachel Barnes, CFO
TV bcst studio systems & mobile unit design, engrg & integration.

CCI Systems Inc.
105 Kent Street, Iron Mountain, MI 49801 US
800-338-9299, (855) 337-9299; *Fax:* (906) 774-6117
www.ccisystems.com
John Jamar, President
Lynn Hall, Sr. Account Manager
Jimmy Rigsby, Sr. Account Manager
Roy Mara, Sr. Account Manager
Terry Fletcher, Sr. Account Manager
Mike Falardeau, Sr. Account Manager
Keith Jones, Sr. Account Manager
CCI Systems designs, builds and integrates communication networks. With over 50 years of experience engineering, constructing, and integrating complex networks, CCI Systems has the unique expertise required to deliver carrier-class turnkeysolutions for all network platforms.

Celco
10291-A Trademark St., Rancho Cucamonga, CA 91730 USA
(909) 481-4648; *Fax:* (909) 481-6899
www.celco.com
info@celco.com
Michael Constantine, Financial Executive
Design & manufacture of motion picture film recorders.

Center City Film & Video
1701 JFK blvd, Suite 2400, Philadelphia, PA 19103 US
(267) 597-3500; *Fax:* (215) 568-6011
www.ccfv.com
info@ccfv.com
Jordan Schwartz, Chairman
Brian Tsely, Operations Dir
Studio/remote/postproduction D-2, D-3, 1 - Beta - 3/4 - ADO - Paint Box/Abekas 62/GV300 with E-Mem; film/tape DaVinci color correction, ADO repositioning & interactive motion control; D-s, D-3; AVID, Digital Betacam.

CGI
655 3rd Ave., Suite 2900, New York, NY 10017 US
(212) 682-7411; *Fax:* (212) 682-0715
www.cgi.com
Serge Godin, Founder and Executive Chairman
Michael E. Roach, President & CEO
R. David Anderson, EVP & CFO
Lorne Gorber, SVP Global Communications and Investor Relations
Benoit Dube, EVP & Chief Legal Officer
Julie Godin, EVP,Global HR & Strategic Planning
Jame Cofran, SVP & Chief Marketing Officer
Eva Maglis, EVP, Global Chief Information Officer
Consulting.

Channel Master
2065 W. Obispo Ave, Suite 102, Gilbert, AZ 85233 US
(919) 934-7078, (877) 746-7261; *Fax:* (919) 934-2809
www.channelmaster.com
sales@channelmaster.com
Coty Youtsey, President
Joe Bingochea, Programming Director
Manufacturer of TV Antennas and Accessories, Cable, Connectors and Amplifiers

Channell Commercial Corp.
26040 Ynez Rd., PO Box 9022, Temecula, CA 92589-9022 US
(951) 719-2600; *Fax:* (951) 296-2322
channellcorp.com
uscustsrv@channellcorp.com
William Channell, CEO
Gary Marge, President
John Kaiser, General Sales Mgr
Andrew Zogby, Chief Marketing Officer
Global designer & manufacturer of equipment, offers a complete line of enclosures for CATV & telecommunication

Charles Industries Ltd.
5600 Apollo Dr., Rolling Meadows, IL 60008 US
(847) 806-6300; *Fax:* (847) 806-6231
www.charlesindustries.com
Joseph Charles, President
Pedestals, custom security boxes, amplifier & TAP brackets-hardware, splicing vaults, taps, splitters & couplers.

Cheetah International
7050 120th Ave, Suite 14, Broomfield, CO 80020 USA
(720) 536-3618, (800) 869-6986, (888) 920-4587, (8; *Fax:* (720) 293-0017
www.cheetahinternational.com
support@cheetahinternational.com
Donald Miller, President/Chief Executive Officer
Laurie Wilson, National Sales Manager
Meredith Boyles, Helpdesk/Distance Training and Support Coordinator
Keanan Smith, Product Development
Closed captioning software on-line & postproduction & related hardware.

Chrono-Log Corp.
2 W. Park Rd., Havertown, PA 19083 US
(610) 853-1130, (800) 247-6665; *Fax:* (610) 853-3972
www.chronolog.com
webmail@chronolog.com
Paula Freilich, President

EQUIPMENT MANUFACTURERS

GPS Receiver (time only), WWV synchronizer, digital clocks & time display systems, time code generators.

Chyron Corp.
5 Hub Dr., Melville, NY 11747 USA
(631) 845-2000; *Fax:* (631) 845-2058
www.chyron.com
usa@chyronhego.com
Kevin Prince, COO
Michael Wellesley-Wesley, President
Mark Bachmore, Kathleen Pauger
SVP/Sales, Programming Director
Steve Papadakis, Key Accounts
Randy Dickerson, Sr. Account Executive, US
Brian Spears, Sr. National AccountExecutive USA & Canada
A leading provídor of broadcast hardware, software & services spanning television & the Internet. Provides a broad range of leading edge hardware & software products, including paint & animation systems, character generators, master controlswitches, & bcst, automation & media mgmt packages.
One CNN Ctr., South Towers, Suite 558, Atlanta, GA 30303 United States
(404) 880-9004; *Fax:* (404) 880-9104
Ryad Kahale, Chyron Rgnl Sls

Chryon Corp. West
10121 Miller Ave., Suite 201, Cupertino, CA 95014 United States
(408) 873-3800; *Fax:* (408) 986-0452
Denise Gallant, Product Mgr

Cine 60 Inc.
PO Box 770631, Woodside, NY 11377 US
(917) 239-8119
Paul Wildum, President
Richard Ortiz, General Manager
Vidal Ortiz, Station Manager
Nickel-Cadmium battery belts, battery packs, chargers, sun-guns, kits, dir chair, dir viewfinders, slates, cables & snaplocks.

Cintel Inc.
28910 Ave. Penn, Suite 202, Valencia, CA 91355-4184 USA
(661) 294-2310; *Fax:* (661) 294-1019
www.cintel.co.uk
Curtis Christianson, Operations Dir
Adam Welsh, General Manager
David Saville, General Sales Mgr
Flying spot telecines, DVE system, keycode system, high-resolution scanner, color correctors.
80 Red Schoolhouse Rd., Suite 103, Chestnut Ridge, NY 10977 United States
(914) 371-7220; *Fax:* (914) 371-6896
David Saville, Sls Dir

Cisco Systems, Inc.
170 W. Tasman Dr., San Jose, CA 95134 Canada
(416) 299-6888, (800) 553-6387; *Fax:* (416) 299-7145
www.scientificatlanta.com
Evan Sloves, President
Dwight Duke, Operations Dir
Dean Rockwell, General Manager
Patrick Tylka, Senior VP
Michael Harney, SVP, Sub Net
TV RF signal processing equipment, transmission products & cable TV amplifiers.

Cisco Systems, Inc.
170 West Tasman Dr., San Jose, CA 95134 USA
(770) 236-5000, (800) 553-6387; *Fax:* (770) 902-2591
www.cisco.com
gregg.echols@sciatl.com
James McDonald, Chairman & CEO
Dwight Duke, President
Michael Harney, President
Patrick Tylka, President
A complete line of cable TV & broadband communications systems, products. and professional services.

Clark Wire & Cable Co. Inc.
408 Washington Blvd., Mundelein, IL 60060 US
(847) 949-9944, (800) 222-5348, (800) 222-5348; *Fax:* (847) 949-9595
www.clarkwire.com
salesint@clarkwire.com
Shane Collins, President
Patti Stickler, Operations Dir
Javier Juarez, General Manager
Dan Collins, Promotions Manager
Audio, video, camera & speciality cable products for bcst industry, available in bulk or assembled harnesses, connectors, panels, reels, & boxes.

Clear-Com, LLC
Mailing Address: 1301 Marina Village Parkway, Suite 105, Alameda, CA 94501 US
Second Address: 1430 Hocquart, Suite 101, St-Bruno-de-Montarville, Qu J3V 6E1
(510) 337-6600, (800) 462-4357, (450) 653-9669; *Fax:* (510) 337-6699
www.clearcom.com
CustomerServicesUS@clearcom.com
Jake Dodson, Operations Dir
Matt Danilowicz, General Manager
Michael Shreve, Programming Director
Jiou-Pahn Lee, Chief Engineer
Single & multi-ch hardwire intercom systems for use in teleproduction. Wired & wireless partyline & digital matrix intercom systems.
Box 302, Walnut Creek, CA 94596 United States
(925) 932-8134
Peter Giddings, Asia/Pacific Dir of Sls

Eastleigh
England Eastleigh, England
44-23-8090-7000
Patrick Woolcocks, Emea Direct Sales

Clearone Communications Corp.
Edgewater Corporate Park South Tower, 5225 Wiley Post Way, Suite 500, Salt Lake City, UT 84116 US
(801) 975-7200,(800) 945-7730; *Fax:* (801) 977-0087
www.clearone.com
sales@clearone.com
Zee Hakimoglu, CEO/Chairman
Joe Sorrentino, Operations Dir
Tracy Bathurst, Chief Engineer
Narsi Narayanan, Vice President of Finance and Corporate Secretary
Michael Braithwaite, Chief Strategy Officer
Avishay Ben Natan, ChiefTechnical Officer
Professional audio & teleconferencing.

Coaxial Dynamics
6800 Lake Abram Dr., Middleburg Hts., OH 44130 US
(440) 243-1100, (800) COAXIAL; *Fax:* (440) 243-1101
www.coaxial.com
sales@coaxial.com
Joe Kluha, General Manager
RF wattmeters, terminations, RF load resistors, RF couplers & accessories.

CohuHD
12367 Crossthwaite Circle, Poway, CA 92064 US
(858) 277-6700, (800) 391-1800, (858) 391-1795; *Fax:* (858) 277-0221
www.cohuhd.com
info@cohu.com
Joe Olmstead, General Sales Mgr
Jeff Tyler, Promotions Manager
CCTV cameras & camera control systems, color, CCD, B/W.

Colorado Video Inc.
3335 Airport Rd, Suite E, Boulder, CO 80301 US
(303) 530-9580; *Fax:* (303) 530-9569
www.colorado-video.com
sales@colorado-video.com
Kirk Fowler, General Sales Mgr
Equipment manufacturer.

Commercial Electronics Ltd.
Mailing Address: 1565 W. 7th Avenue, Vancouver, BC V6J 1S1 Canada
Second Address: 405 Industrial Avenue, Vancouver, BC V6A 2P8
(604) 669-5525, (604) 669-5528; *Fax:* (604) 669-6347
www.commercialelectronics.ca
info@cemail.ca
H.H. von Tiesenhausen, President
Audio video equipment, systems designs.

Commercial Radio Monitoring Co.
103 S.W. Market St., Lee's Summit, MO 64063 US
(816) 524-3777; *Fax:* (816) 524-3777
W. R. Thorsen, Owner
Ronald Bruce Thorsen, Owner
Frequency measurements & equipment calibration.

CommScope Inc.
1100 CommScope Pl. S.E., Hickory, NC 28603 US
(800) 982-1708,(828) 324-2200; *Fax:* (828) 328-3400
www.commscope.com
communications@commscope.com
Randall W. Crenshaw, Executive Vice President/Chief Operating Officer
Marvin (Eddie) S. Edwards, Jr., President/Chief Executive Officer
Mark A. Olson, Executive Vice President/Chief Financial Officer
Frank (Burk) B. Wyatt, II, SeniorVice President/General Counsel/Secretary
Philip M. Armstrong, Jr., Senior Vice President of Corporate Finance
Michael Cross, Senior Vice President/Chief Information Officer
Robert Granow, Vice President/Corporate Controller/Principal Acco
Peter U. Karlsson, Senior Vice President of Global Sales
Coaxial & fiber-optic cables including CRD & NEC approved drop cables, QR, P3 & CableGuard.

Communication & Power Industries
607 Hansen Way, Palo Alto, CA 94304-1015 USA
(650) 846-2900; *Fax:* (650) 846-3276
www.cpii.com
cpi@airtelmail.in
O. Joe Caldarelli, CEO
Robert A. Fickett, President & COO
Andrew E. Tafler, Operations Dir
John R. Beighley, General Sales Mgr
Joel A. Littman, CFO
John R. Beighley, VP, Sales
Manufactures a complete line of power grid tubes, klystrons & klystrode IOTs, traveling wave tubes, satellite communication transmitters, microwave components.
811 Hansen Way, Palo Alto, CA 94304 United States
(415) 846-2800 (415) 846-3700
Armand Staprans, Pres Microwave Products
Jim Commendatore, Pres Satcom

Beverly Microwave Division
150 Sohier Rd, Beverly, MA 01915 United States
(978) 922-6000
Dennis Gleason, Division Pres
45 River Dr, Georgetown, ON L7G-2J4 Canada
(905) 877-0161
Joseph Caldarelli, Pres Communications & Medical Products
301 Industrial Way, San Carlos, CA 94070 United States
(415) 592-1221
H. Frederick Koehler, Pres Eimac Div
607 Hansen Way, Palo Alto, CA 94304 United States
(415) 846-2900
Al Ferriera, Pres Traveling Wave Tube Products

Communication Graphics, Inc.
1765 N. Juniper, Greenway Business Park, Broken Arrow, OK 74012 US
(800) 331-4438,(918) 258-6502; *Fax:* (918) 251-8223
www.cgilink.com
info@communicationgraphics.net
Choose the company MORE radio stations have selected for printing decals, event stickers, statics, concert patches, magnets, media kits and more!

Communications Specialties Inc.
125 Comac St., Ronkonkoma, NY 11779 US
(631) 273-0404; *Fax:* (631) 273-1638
www.commspecial.com
info@commspecial.com
John Lopinto, CEO & President
Larry Shulman, Chief Operating Officer
Michael Fazzi, Sales Manager
Paul Seiden, Director of Sales
Manufacturer of fiber-optic transmission sytems, including the Pure Digital Fiberlink line for professional quality video, audio and data.
100 Bencoolen Rd., # 22-09, Shaw Tower, 189702 Singapore
(+665) 656 391-8790; *Fax:* (+656) 656 396-0138
Jeohan Tohkingkeo, Rgnl Mgr Asia Pacific

Comprehensive Cable and Connectivity Company
80 Little Falls Road, Fairfield, NJ 7004 US
(800) 526-0242; *Fax:* (201) 814-0514
www.comprehensivecable.com
sales@comprehensivecable.com
Scott Schaefer, Operations Dir
Digital HDTV UpConverter, High Resolution bulk cable, Video/Audio Multi media & Data Cable assemblies (lifetime warranty), connectors, adaptors, wallplates, distribution amps, switches, convertors, etc.

Comprompter Inc.
1601 Caledonia St., Suite E, La Crosse, WI 54603 US
(800) 785-7766; *Fax:* (608) 784-5013
www.comprompter.com
sales@comprompter.com
Ralph King, President

The first COMPROMPTER ENR (Electronic NewsRoom) was installed and went into operation in August of 1982. The original system developer, Ralph King, organized a business partnership and in April of 1985, formed the present corporation andbecame its President. Comprompter was among the pioneers in electronic newsrooms and is the only independent company that still has the original developer as its president.

Comrex Corp.
19 Pine Rd., Devens, MA 1434 US
(978) 784-1776; *Fax:* (978) 784-1717
www.comrex.com
info@comrex.com
Kris Bobo, General Manager
Chris Crump, Director of Sales

Comsearch
19700 Janelia Farm Blvd., Ashburn, VA 20147 US
(703) 726-5500; (800) 318-1234; *Fax:* (703) 726-5595
www.comsearch.com
customersupport@comsearch.com
Chris Hardy, Vice President
Janeka Carlisle, Chief Marketing Officer
Melissa Wagner, Human Resources Director
Communication engrg svcs for mobile, microwave & satellite systems, including frequency, propagation & integrations svcs.

ComSonics Inc.
Mailing Address: 1350 Port Republic Rd., PO Box 1106, Harrisonburg, VA 22801 US
Second Address: 1350 Port Republic Rd., Harrisonburg, VA 22801
(540) 434-5965,(800) 336-9681; *Fax:* (540) 432-9794
www.comsonics.com
info@comsonics.com
Donn E. Meyerhoeffer, COO
Dennis A. Zimmerman, President
Donald J. Sommerville, General Sales Mgr
Dale Lann, CFO
Gary J. Tudor, Director of Product Sales
Bret Harrison, Director of Repair Services
Philip Bennett, National RepairServices Manager
Malcolm McIntyre, Calibration Services Manager
Bill Moore, National Accounts Manager
Manufacture RF signal level meter & RF leakage detector, CATV repair facility.

Comtech Antenna Systems Inc.
3100 Communications Rd., St. Cloud, FL 34769 US
(407) 892-6111; *Fax:* (407) 892-0994
www.comtechantenna.com
info@comtechantenna.com
Thomas Christy, President
Ronnie Hamilton, General Sales Mgr
Satellite antenna systems, sizes 1.8-7.3 meters; Offsat(tm), 2 degree spacing antenna; 3.8, 5.0m & Offsat(tm) transportables.

Comtech EF Data
Mailing Address: 2114 West 7th Street, Tempe, AZ 85281 US
Second Address: 3215 Skyway Court, Fremont, CA 94539
(480) 333-2200; *Fax:* (480) 333-2540
www.comtechefdata.com
sales@comtechefdata.com
Brenda Wyatt, General Manager
Robert McCollum, SVP
Larry Dumouchel, CFO/VP
Ted Binkowski, SVP-Operations
Bob Hansen, SVP-Global Sales
Daniel Enns, SVP- Marketing and Business Development
Jeffrey Harig, SVP-Engineering
Comtech EF Data Corp. manufactures a broad spectrum of satellite communications products, including Satellite Modems, Bandwidth & Capacity Management, TCP/IP Performance Enhancement Proxies, Encapsulators, Receivers, Converters, Amplifiers,Transceivers and Terminals.

COMTEK Inc.
357 West 2700 South, Salt Lake City, UT 84115 US
(801) 466-3463,(800) 496-3463; *Fax:* (801) 484-6906
www.comtek.com
service@comtek.com
Laurel Robertson, General Sales Mgr
Jon Belgique, Promotions Manager
Ralph Belgique, Chief Engineer
COMTEK manufactures synthesized & fixed frequency wireless communication equipment & accessories, including cuing systems (IFB) & wireless microphones.

Condor D C Power Supplies Inc.
Mailing Address: 6050 King Ddr., Ventura, CA 93003 USA
Second Address: 607 Neponset St., Canton, MA 2021
(800) 235-5929; *Fax:* (805) 832-6135
www.slpower.com
info@slpower.com
Jim Taylor, President
Mike Shaw, Promotions Manager
Multiple outlet strips, surge & noise suppressors, & uninterruptible power supplies.

Condux International, Inc.
Box 247, 145 Kingswood Rd., Mankato, MN 56002-0247 US
(800) 533-2077, (507) 387-6576; *Fax:* (507) 387-1442
www.condux.com
conduxinfo@condux.com
Eric Cope, CEO
Doug Mudler, Operations Manager
Tom Ortolano, Global Sales Manager
Tony Stockman, International Sales Manager
Josh Siebert, Engineering Manager
Jeanne Tolzman, Controller/HR Manager
Jason Hamond, MarketingManager
Tom Ortolano, VP, Global Sales
Tony Stockman, International Sales Manager
Sherman Kranz, Technical Sales Engineer
Joe Westphal, Product Specialist
Underground & aerial construction tools & equipment for coaxial cable, telephone & fiber.

Connectronics Corp.
2745 Avondale Ave., PO Box 3355, Toledo, OH 43607-3232 US
(419) 537-0020,(800) 965-0020; *Fax:* (419) 537-0007
www.connectronicscorp.com
info@connectronicscorp.com
Tom Ricketts, President
Al Mocek, Operations Dir
Audio wire & cable, special wire & cable assys. Interconnect products for audio, video, data & telephone.
California Box 2047, Morgan Hill, CA 95037
(408) 779-8888; *Fax:* (408) 778-0722

Connex Telecommunications Corporation
Mailing Address: 44 East Beaver Creek, Suite 16, Richmond Hill, ON L4B 1G8 Canada
Second Address: 121 Welham Rd., Units 6,7,8, Barrie, ON L4N 8Y3
(905) 944-6500, (866) 429-4625; *Fax:* (905) 944-6520
www.connexservice.ca
central@connexservice.ca
Jos Wintermans, Chairman
Brian Pedlar, CFO
John Challinor, Promotions Manager
Marianne Gracey, VP Marketing
Mgmt, instal & maintenance svcs for studios, radio-TV transmitters, satellite systems & CATV.

Conrac Inc.
Mailing Address: 5124 Commerce Dr., Baldwin Park, CA 91706 US
Second Address: 24 River Road, Suite 107, Bogota, NJ 7603
(626) 480-0095, (800) 451-5288; *Fax:* (626) 480-0077, (201) 883-1118
www.conrac.us
monitors@conrac.com
Bill Moeller, President
Manufacturer of a var of color & monochrome video monitors for bcst & computer graphic display.

Continental Electronics Corporation
4212 S. Buckner Blvd., Dallas, TX 75227 US
(214) 381-7161, (800) 733-5011; *Fax:* (214) 381-3250
www.contelec.com
sales@contelec.com
Adil Mina, Operations Dir
Michael Troje, General Sales Mgr
Continental is the premier manufacturer of radio frequency (RF) bcst transmission equipment. We specialize in the design, dev & manufacture of leading-edge digital & analog transmitter systems for the global market. We offer a full range ofproducts for high-power FM, HF, VHF, UHF, LF & VLP application including particle accelerators & fusion rsch, defense communications, radar & industrial heating.
2280 Rockcreek Tr., Birmingham, AL 35226 United States
(205) 822-1078
Dave Hultsman, Regional Sales Manager
1230 Rugged Oaks Rd., Glen Rose, TX 76043 United States
(254) 898-9200
Steve Schott, Rgnl Sls Mgr

Convergent Media Systems Corp.
190 Bluegrass Valley Pkwy., Alpharetta, GA 30005 US
(770) 369-9000; *Fax:* (770) 369-9100
www.convergent.com
convergent@convergent.com
Murray Holland, CEO
R. Bryan Allen, President/Chief Executive Officer
Greg Bloodworth, Senior Vice President of Operations
Frank Turner, Chief Financial Officer
Steve Dix, Chief Legal Counsel
Trevor Davies, Senior Vice President-Engineering
Gary Johns, Senior Vice President, Sales and Marketing
Transportable satellite uplinking & downlinking svcs. Includes facilities & transponder time for Ku- & C-band applications.

Convergys Inc.
Mailing Address: 201 E. 4th St., Cincinnati, OH 45202 US
Second Address: 3760 N. Commerce Dr., Suite 160, Tuscon, AZ 85705
(513) 723-7000, (888) 284-9900, (520) 407-7300; *Fax:* (513) 241-1543
www.convergys.com
Andrea J. Ayers, President/CEO
Erik Schumann, General Sales Mgr
David Stein, VP, Investor Relations
Andre S. Valentine, CFO
Claudia Cline, Sr. VP & General Counsel
Chandra Venkataramani, Chief Information Officer
Cablemaster/Icoms customer mgmt & billing system running on IBM as/400 platform; solution for the convergent cable TV/Telephone industry.
4170 Ashford Dunwoody Rd, Suite 525, Atlanta, GA 30319 United States
(404) 845-4400

Cooper Sound Systems Inc.
Mailing Address: 1241 Knollwood Dr., Suite 1365, Cambria, CA 93428-3343 US
Second Address: 1241 Knollwood Drive, PMB 106, Cambria, CA 93428-3343
(805) 772-1007; *Fax:* (805) 456-1631
www.coopersound.com
coopersoundsystems@gmail.com
Andrew Cooper, President
Janet Cooper, Operations Dir
Spare parts & tech asst.

Coptervision
7625 Hayvenhurst Ave., #36, Van Nuys, CA 91406 USA
(818) 782-6673; *Fax:* (818) 782-6636
www.coptervision.com
info@coptervision.com
Sarita Spiwak, CEO

Corning Cable Systems
P.O. Box 489, Hickory, NC 28603-0489 USA
(828) 901-5000, (800) 743-2671; *Fax:* (828) 325-5060
www.corning.com/cablesystems
Clark Kendall, President
Mike Genovese, Operations Dir
Manufacturer of optical fiber cables & accessories for video, data, voice communications applications.

Corning Incorporated
One Riverfront Plaza, Corning, NY 14831 US
(607) 974-9000; *Fax:* (623) 931-0684,(800) 334-6358
www.corning.com
Inquiries@corning.com
Wendell P. Weeks, Chairman/Chief Executive Officer
Kathy Murphy, CEO
Dr. Jeffrey Evenson, Senior Vice President/Operations Chief of Stafft
James B. Flaws, Vice Chairman and Chief Financial Officer
Kirk P. Gregg, Executive VicePresident and Chief Administrative
Lawrence D. McRae, Executive Vice President, Strategy and Corporate D
Dr. David L. Morse, Executive Vice President and Chief Technology Offi
Lewis A. Steverson, Senior Vice President and General Counsel
Trunk, distribution & F connectors for CATV.

Corning Incorporated
One Riverfront Plaza, Corning, NY 14831 US
(607) 248-2000
www.corning.com/opticalfiber
opticalfibcs@corning.com
Martin J. Curran, President
Single-mode & multimode optical fibers including: ClearCurve single-mode and multimode fibers, InfiniCor laser-optimized multimode fibers, SMF-28e fibers, LEAF fiber, & Vascade submarine fibers.

Cortland Cable Co. Inc.
Mailing Address: 44 River St., PO Box 330, Cortland, NY 13045 US

Second Address: 10333 Richmond Ave, Suite 1000, Houston, TX 77042-4128
(607) 753-8276, (832) 833-8000; *Fax:* (607) 753-3183, (832) 833-8002
www.cortlandcompany.com
cortland@cortlandcompany.com
John Stidd, President
Rick Nye, Operations Dir
Kevlar fiber antenna guys & ropes, including eye splice end terminations-potted sockets.

Costume Armour, Inc.
2 Mill St., Bldg 1 - Suite 101, Cornwall, NY 12518 US
(845) 534-9120; *Fax:* (845) 534-8602
www.costumearmour.com
info@costumearmour.com
Nino Novellino, President
Brian Wolfe, General Manager
Michelle Truncale, Chief Engineer
Susan Truncale, Administrative Assistant
Period armor & weapons, vacuum-formed background panels, custom made props & sculpture.

Countryman Associates Inc.
195 Constitution Dr., Menlo Park, CA 94025 US
(800) 669-1422,(650) 364-9988; *Fax:* (650) 364-2794
www.countryman.com
support@countryman.com
Carl Countryman, Chief Engineer
Very small precision electret condenser microphones for wide applications & the Type-85 Direct Box.

Crossed Field Antennas Inc.
48 Mountain Rd., Farmington, CT 60322 USA
(860) 676-0051; *Fax:* (860) 677-9639
cfaricher@snet.net
Robert Richer, President
Alec Thomas, Engineering Dir
Maurice Hately, Chief Engineer
Company mkts medium wave & long wave antennas.
97 Foxwood Close, Hansworth, Middlesex, NO TW13 7 United Kingdom
(1) 44 0797 085
Alex Thomas, Head Engrg

Crown Broadcast IREC
25166 Leer Dr., PO Box 2000, Elkhart, IN 46514-5425 US
(574) 262-8900, (877) 262-8900; *Fax:* (574) 262-5399
www.crownbroadcast.com
Clyde Moore, CEO/President
Kent Kaselle, General Sales Mgr
Alvaro Matina, Engineering Dir
Bcst RF equipment, FM radio transmitters. Supplier to the Natl weather svc for emergency weather radio transmitters.

CSG Systems
Mailing Address: 1000 Town Center Drive, Suite 300, Oxnard, CA 93036 US
Second Address: 509 Commerce Boulevard, Crawfordville, FL 32327
(303) 796-2850,(800) 366-2744, (888) 214-680; *Fax:* (303) 804-4088, (888) 214 -6643
www.csgi.com
sales@csgsystems.com
Bret C. Griess, Executive Vice President/Chief Operating Officer
Peter Kalan, Chief Executive Officer/President
Robert Scott, Operations Dir
Randy R. Wiese, Executive Vice President/Chief Financial Officer
Joseph T. Ruble, ExecutiveVice President/General Counsel/ Corporat
Michael Henderson, Executive Vice President/ Sales/ Marketing
Complete sub info mgmt & data processing systems for the cable TV & telephone industries.
6303 Blue Lagoon Dr., Miami, FL 33126 United States
(305) 421-8900 (305) 421-8934
1-11 John Adams St., London WC2N6HT United Kingdom
44 20 7004 1840 44 20 7004 1841
6 Temasek Blvd., 038986 Singapore
65 6883 1900 65 6883 1990

D.H. Satellite
600 N. Marquette Rd., PO Box 239, Prairie du Chien, WI 53821-0239 US
(608) 326-8406, (800) 627-9443; *Fax:* (608) 326-4233
www.dhsatellite.com
sales@dhsatellite.com
Mike Doll, Operations Dir
Manufacturer of solid spun aluminum antennas & mounts. Antennas range from .6m (24) to 5m (16') with various mounting options. Delivery & instal is available from DH for all of our antenna equipment.

Da-Lite Screen Company, Inc.
Mailing Address: 3100 N. Detroit St., PO Box 137, Warsaw, IN 46581-0137 US
Second Address: 11500 Williamson Road, Cincinnati, OH 45241
(574) 267-8101, (800) 622-3737, (513) 489-3222; *Fax:* (513)-489-4247, (877) 325-4832
www.da-lite.com
info@da-lite.com
Blake Brubaker, VP Sales
Collin Boggs, Sales Manager
Mobile projector, TV & video, tables & cabinets, wall & ceiling mount brackets.

Dage-MTI Inc.
701 N. Roeske Ave., Michigan City, IN 46360 US
(219) 872-5514; *Fax:* (219) 872-5559
www.dagemti.com
sales@dagemti.com
Arthur Sterling, President
Peggy Moore, Promotions Manager
Dage-MTI is an international leader in the design and manufacture of high performance digital Firewire cameras and analog video cameras and monitors. By supplying digital and analog products, Dage-MTI has separated itself from thecompetition as one of the only companies in the world to do so. All products are sold worldwide through a dealer network chosen for each application and geographic region. Biomedical research is one of the primary fields for Dage-MTI products.

Daily Electronics Corp.
Box 822437, 19311 NE 91st Street, Vancouver, WA 98682-0053 US
(360) 896-8856,(800) 346-6667; *Fax:* (360) 896-5476
www.dailyelectronics.net
daily@worldaccessnet.com
Jim Grimes, President
Produces vacuum tubes—transmitting, camera, industrial & receiving. Tube rebuilding.

Dalet Digital Media Systems
100 Wall Street, 15th floor, New York, NY 10005 US
(212) 269-6700; *Fax:* (212) 269-6709
www.dalet.com
Stephane Guez, COO
Fred Roux, Operations Dir
Benjamin Desbois, General Manager
Luc Comeau, General Sales Mgr
Software for radio & TV. Newsroom computer systems, acquisition, cataloging, producing, sharing, archiving, distribution of video & audio assets.

Data Security Inc.
300 S. 7th St., Lincoln, NE 68508 US
(800) 225-7554,(402) 434-5959, (877) 326-6630; *Fax:* (402) 434-3291
www.datasecurityinc.com
rschafer@telesis-inc.com
Brian Boles, CEO
Eric Schafer, Operations Dir
Renee Schafer, CSDS, Director of Sales and Marketing/Certified Secure D
Tape Enhancement Series features bulk tape deguassers & videotape cleaner/evaluators.

DBX Professional Products
10653 South River Front Parkway, Suite 300, South Jordan, UT 84095 US
(801) 566-8800; *Fax:* (801) 568-7662
www.dbxpro.com
support@dbxpro.com
Robert Benson, General Sales Mgr
Audio signal processing devices: compressor/limiters, De-essers, equalizers, gates & noise reduction.

DEDOTEC USA Inc.
48 Sheffield Business Park, Ashley Falls, MA 1222 US
(413) 229-2550; *Fax:* (413) 229-2556
www.dedolight.com
Paul Tepper, President
Dedolight precision lighting instruments for film, TV, ENG/EFP, still photo & architectural applications. Portable location lighting kits & studio equipment. Special effects attachments & accessories.

Delta Electronics Inc.
5730 General Washington Dr., PO Box 11268, Alexandria, VA 22312 US
(703) 354-3350, (800) 833-5828; *Fax:* (703) 354-0216
www.deltaelectronics.com
sales@deltaelectronics.com
William Fox, President
Joseph Novak, Operations Dir
Delta Electronics, Inc. is an employee-owned small business founded in 1962 to develop, manufacture and market professional quality electronic and electro-mechanical equipment for the broadcast and communications industries. In addition togeneral electronic circuit design and manufacturing capabilities, Delta has engineering experience in the areas of RF instrumentation, high power HF/VHF/UHF transmitter/antenna switching, HF receiver/antenna switching, HF receive signal distribution,and remote monitor/control systems.

Devlin Design Group Inc.
Mailing Address: 625 Broadway, Suite. 1101, PO Box 5208, Frisco, CO 80443-5208 US
Second Address: PO Box 3066, Crested Butte, CO 81224-3066
(970) 349-5836; *Fax:* (970) 688-2772
www.ddgtv.com
ddgweb2011@ddgtv.com
Kristina Jones, Programming Director
Judy Parker, Promotions Manager
Dan Devlin, Chief Creative Strategist
Kartik Dakshinamoorthy, Scenic Design Director
Julia Blair, Social Media Director
Mary B. Devlin, Office Manager
HannesKling, Director of Production
Laurel Lawrence, Scenic Projects Manager
Specializes in bcst news productions. News sets, newsrooms, turnkey & design only. Set design, virtual sets, hard set construction, consultation.

Dielectric Communications
22 Tower Rd., PO Box 949, Raymond, ME 4071 US
(207) 655-8100, (207) 655-8253; *Fax:* (207) 655-8177
www.dielectric.com
keith.pelletier@dielectric.com
Garrett VanAtta, President
Anna Morton, Operations Dir
Keith Pelletier, General Manager
Roger Cote, General Sales Mgr
Kim Savage, Director Business Services
Tammy White, Customer and Order Management
Cory Edwards, OEM SalesManager
Joe Zuba, National Sales
Federico D'Avis, International Sales
Antennas, inside equipment, waveguide, transmission line, switches, loads, filters, combiners, pressurization, lighting for TV, Radio, mobile media, mobile broadcasting.

DiGi Co. Ltd.
Unit 10 Silverglade Business Park, Leatherhead Rd.,Chessington, Surrey, UK KT9 2QL USA
(137) 284-5600; *Fax:* (137) 284-5656
www.digico.biz
info@digiconsoles.com
David Webster, Operations Dir
Taidus Vallandi, General Sales Mgr
James Gorden, Managing Director
John Stadius, Technical Director
Ian Staddon, VP of Sales
Tim Shaxson, Technical Sales Manager
Maria Fiorellino, MarketingCoordinator
Helen Culleton, Director
Digital audio mixing consoles

Dimension 3
5240 Medina Rd., Woodland Hills, CA 91364 USA
(818) 592-0999
www.d3.com
Daniel Symmes, CEO
Provides 3-D bcst TV processes. Supplies equipment, consultation & 3-D glasses.

Direct Broadcast Services Inc.
711 Executive Boulevard, Suite F, Valley Cottage, NY 10989 US
(845) 267-2800; *Fax:* (845) 267-2123
www.directbroadcast.com
Leo Rosenberg, President
Direct Broadcast Services, Inc. provides broadcast-quality transmission services using a variety of technologies including satellite uplinking, portable and newsvan microwave, portable fiber optics, and laser.

DISH Network Corp.
9601 S. Meridian Blvd., Englewood, CO 80112 USA
(888) 656-2461, (855) 318-0572; *Fax:* (303) 723-1046
www.dish.com
Charlie Ergen, Co-founder, Chairman
Bernie Han, Executive Vice President/ Chief Operating Officer

Joseph Clayton, President/Chief Executive Officer
W. Erik Carlson, Executive Vice President-Operations
Jim DeFranco, Co-founder, EVP,Special Advisor to the CEO
Tom Cullen, Executive Vice President-Corporate Development
R. Stanton Dodge, EVP-General Counsel and Secretary
Robert Olson, Executive Vice President
Dave Shull, Executive Vice President/Chief Commercial Officer
Roger Lynch, Executive Vice President, Advanced Technologies
Satellite TV reception systems.
5701 S. Santa Fe Rd, Littleton, CO 80120 United States
(303) 723-1000; *Fax:* (303) 723-1099
Charles Ergen, Ceo/Chman of Bd
Brent Gale, Dir Bcst Engrg

Display Devices Inc.
10828 Highway 93, Golden, CO 80403 US
(303) 412-0399; *Fax:* (303) 412-9346
www.displaydevices.com
sales@displaydevices.com
Merv Perkins, President
Ruth Perkins, Operations Dir
Eric Perkins, General Manager
Rich Nichols, Marketing Executive
CRT, LCD, slide projector motorized lifts & stationary mounts. Custom applications.

Display Systems International Inc.
2214 Hanselman Ave., Saskatoon, SK S7L 6A4 Canada
(306) 934-6884, (877) 934-6884; *Fax:* (306) 934-6447
www.displaysystemsintl.com
sales@displaysystemsintl.com
Dale Lemke, President
We provide cost-effective solutions, a variety of flexible payment options, and free technical support for all our products and services.

Ditch Witch
1959 W. Fir Ave., PO Box 66, Perry, OK 73077 US
(800) 654-6481; *Fax:* (580) 336-3458
www.ditchwitch.com
info@ditchwitch.com
Meg Whitman, President/Chief Executive Officer
John Hinshaw, Executive Vice President-Technology and Operations
Bill Veghte, Executive Vice President/General Manager, Enterpri
Tracy Keogh, Executive Vice President-Human Resources
Cathie Lesjak, Executive Vice President/Chief Financial Officer
Martin Fink, Executive Vice President/Chief Technology Officer
John Schultz, Executive Vice President/General Counsel
Henry Gomez, Executive Vice President/Chief Marketing andCommu
George Kadifa, Executive Vice President-HP Software
HP creates new possibilities for technology to have a meaningful impact on people, businesses, governments, and society. The world's largest technology company, HP brings together a portfolio that spans printing, personal computing,software, services and IT infrastructure to solve customer problems.

DMT USA, Inc.
109 Gibraltar Rd., Horsham, PA 19044 USA
(267) 961-USA1; *Fax:* (267) 961-1020
www.dmtonline.us
Alberto Giorgini, CEO
Stephen Blasetti, Enrinco Marantonio
SVP, Operations Dir
DMT USA specializes in digital television transmitters & Mobile TV. We manufacture UHF & VHF DTV transmitters, antennas & custom RF systems. All models are solid state & environmentally safe. Look to DMT USA for cutting edge technology &true customer service. We are your clear choice for turnkey DTV transmission equipment.

Dolby Laboratories Inc.
Mailing Address: 100 Potrero Ave., San Francisco, CA 94103-4813 US
Second Address: 99 Brannan Street, San Francisco, CA 94103-4938
(415) 558-0200; *Fax:* (415) 642-4000
www.dolby.com
Ray Dolby, Chairman
Bill Jasper, CEO
Kevin Yeaman, President/Chief Executive Officer
Mike Bergeron, Senior Vice President-orldwide Sales and Field Ope
Lewis Chew, Executive Vice President and Chief Financial Offic
Doug Darrow,Senior Vice President-Cinema Business Group
Andrew Dahlkemper, Senior Vice President- Human Resources
Michael Rockwell, Executive Vice President-Advanced Technology Group
Andy Sherman, Executive Vice President/General Counsel/Corporate
Michael Rockwell, Information Technology
Audio noise reduction & signal processing equipment; digital audio coding for ISDN, cable, satellite & other applications; dolby surround equipment.
Wootton Bassett, Wiltshire, SN4 8QJ
1793 842 100
Tony Spath, Bcst Projects Mgr

Dorrough Electronics
5221 Collier Pl., Woodland Hills, CA 91364 US
(818) 998-2824; *Fax:* (818) 998-1507
www.dorrough.com
dorroughel@aol.com
Mike Dorrough, President
Dorrough Electronics manufactures Audio Loudness Meters featuring Peak & Average signals ballistically set for a highly accurate reading.
20434 Corisco St, Chatsworth, CA 91311 United States
(818) 998-4886

Doty-Moore Tower Services LLC
1570 W. Beltline Rd., Cedar Hill, TX 75104 USA
(972) 637-5000, (800) 486-3333; *Fax:* (972) 293-1255
www.stainlessllc.com
Patrick Moore, President
Ed Deetscreek, VP Operations & Sales Acct Mgr.
Dave Bodossian, Sales Representative
Gregg Fehrman, Chief Engineer
Donald T. Doty, Sr. Vice President
Full spectrum of tower construction/installation, modifications, maintenance, repairs, inspections, complete RF mapping of tower and facilities, and 24-hour emergency services with our own safety trained and experienced crews.
Corp. Office - Stainless LLC
1140 Welsh Road, #250, North Wales, PA 19454
(800) 486-3333, (215) 631-1400; *Fax:* (215) 631-1425
www.stainlessllc.com
sales@stainlessllc.com
Ed Deetscreek, VP Operations & Sales Acct Mgr.

Dove Systems
3563 Sueldo St., Suite E, San Luis Obispo, CA 93401 US
(805) 541-8292; *Fax:* (805) 541-8293
www.dovesystems.com
Gary Dove, President
Denise Calder, Purchasing Executive
Brandon Dove, Sales Executive
Studio & stage lighting control equipment.

Dow-Key Microwave Corp.
4822 McGrath, Ventura, CA 93003 US
(805) 650-0260, (800) 266-3695; *Fax:* (805) 650-1734
www.dowkey.com
askdk@dowkey.com
Mark Mandrell, President
Dow-Key is specialized in a broad range of RF coaxial relays operating from DC to 40 GHZ, waveguide switches (operating up 70 GHz), electromechanical & solid state switch matrices, Fiber optics switching network, PXI moduless & CustomSolutions. Both 75 ohm & 50 ohm styles are available.

DPA Microphones, Inc.
1500 Kansas Avenue, Unit 3A, Longmont, CO 80501 USA
(303) 485-1025; *Fax:* (303) 485-6470
www.dpamicrophones.com
info-usa@dpamicrophones.com
Bruce Myers, President
Martin Stove, Director/Business Development
Paul Koza, Sales/Marketing Director
DPA Microphones features a complete line of cardioid & omnidirectional microphones & accessories for all applictions.

DRS Fermont
141 North Ave., Bridgeport, CT 6606 US
(203) 366-5211; *Fax:* (203) 367-3642
John Uvodich, Operations Dir
Michael D'Ottavio, Vice President, Business Development
Carl Geary, Director, Business Development
Ken Zurawski, Director, Business Development
Frank Pingelski, Business Development Manager
KeithMazurkowitz, Inside Sales Representative
Heidi Jantzen-Hubert, Manager, Marketing and Communications
Each of the DRS Power Solutions group has a history of providing quality products and services with a strong emphasis on customer satisfaction. We believe quality begins at first contact with you and continues throughout our businessrelationship.

DSC Laboratories
3565 Nashua Dr., Mississauga, ON L4V 1R1 Canada
(905) 673-3211; *Fax:* (905) 673-0929
www.dsclabs.com
dsc@dsclabs.com
D. Corley, President
S. Corley, Promotions Manager
Combi Optical Signal Generators (OSGs) & CamAlign chip charts for camera alignment & matching-deal for studio, shop & stadium.

Dubner International Inc.
13 Westervelt Pl., Westwood, NJ 07675-1921 USA
(201) 664-6434; *Fax:* (201) 358-9377
www.dubner.com
Robert Dubner, President
Frank Brescher, Vice President

E-N-G Mobile Systems Inc.
2245 Via De Mercados, Concord, CA 94520 US
(925) 798-4060; *Fax:* (925) 798-0152
www.e-n-g.com
info@e-n-g.com
Dick Glass, President
Rex Reed, General Manager
Bob Capps, Information Technology
Custom-designed ENG & DSNG vehicles, rack-ready & turnkey systems. Other mobile electronic systems & ENG system components.
119 Lloyd Rd., West Grove, PA 19390 United States
(610) 659-2640
John Watkins, Opns Mgr

E-Z Trench Manufacturing Co. Inc.
2315 S. Hwy. 701 S, Loris, SC 29569 US
(843) 756-6444; *Fax:* (843) 756-6442
www.eztrench.com
Gail Porter, President
Family owned and operated, E-Z TRENCHr has been manufacturing walk behind trenchers since 1982. Our mission has long been to provide innovative, quality equipment that lasts and provides you years of service. Our owner, Gail, and her sonsMonty & Scotty are involved in all facets of the business - See more at: http://www.eztrench.com/company-info/#sthash.815OB0yT.dpuf

E.F. Johnson Technologies
Mailing Address: 123 N. State St., Waseca, MN 56093 US
Second Address: 1440 Corporate Dr., Irving, TX 75038-2401
(800) 295-1773, (972) 819-0700, (800) 328-3911; *Fax:* (972) 819-0639
www.efjohnson.com
Andrew L. Adams, President & CEO
Jana Ahlfinger Bell, Executive VP & CFO
Jim Green, Chief Operating Officer
Karthik Rangarajan, VP, Marketing
Timi Jackson, VP & General Counsel
A leading provider of two way radios and communications systems.

e2v Inc.
Mailing Address: 520 White Plains Road, Suite 450, Tarrytown, NY 10591 US
Second Address: 765 Sycamore Drive, Milpitas, CA 95035
(914) 592-6050, (800) 342-5338; *Fax:* (914) 592-5148
www.e2v.com
enquiries@e2v.com
Neil Johnson, Chairman
Stephen Blair, CEO/COO
Vijay Patel, Operations Dir
Mark Strohecker, General Sales Mgr
Keith Atwood, Chief Financial Officer
Dr Krishnamurthy Rajagopal, Independent Non-Executive Director
Alison Wood,Independent Non-Executive Director
Kevin Dangerfield, Independent Non-Executive Director
Manufacturer of Digital & Analog IOTs, ESCiors, Klystrons for UHF TV transmitters, Stellar range of satellite uplink amplifiers.
Box 29667, Mississauga, ON L5A 4H2 Canada
(905) 848-6430; *Fax:* (905) 848-9343
Ann Au-Yong, Chairman

EAGLE Avionics Systems
823 McTavish Road NE, Calgary, AL T2E 7G9 USA
(403) 250 7370; *Fax:* (253) 395-9150
www.eaglecopters.com/
Jeff Shapiro, President
Steve Cudnosskey, Chief Engineer

Design, manufacture & instal of E.N.G. & microwave equipment for news helicopters.

Eagle Comtronics Inc.
Mailing Address: 7665 Henry Clay Blvd., Liverpool, NY 13008 US
Second Address: 7665 Henry Clay Blvd., Liverpool, NY 13088
(315) 622-3402,(800) 448-7474; *Fax:* (315) 622-3800
www.eaglecomtronics.com
info@eaglecomtronics.com
Alan Devendorf, Chairman
Timothy Devendorf, President
CATV manufacturer & designer of security traps, decoders, & tier traps. Custom OEM filter designs.

Eastman Kodak Co.
343 State St., Rochester, NY 14650 US
(800) 698-3324; *Fax:* (585) 724-0663
www.kodak.com
Antonio Perez, Chairman
Antonio Perez, CEO
Cameras, projectors, graphic & entertainment imaging products.

EDCOR Electronics Corp.
7130 National Parks Hwy., Carlsbad, NM 88220 US
(800) 854-0259, (575) 887-6790; *Fax:* (575) 887-6880
www.edcorusa.com
sales@edcorusa.com
Brian Weston, President
Phyllis Weston, Finance Executive
Audio mic/line, audio transformers, custom transformers & power transformers.

Eddie Egan & Associates
6138 West Washington Blvd, Culver City, CA 90232 US
(310) 278-0370, (310) 559-4341; *Fax:* (310) 559-4348
www.eddieegan.com
armand@eddieegan.com
Daniel Egan, President
Armand Egan, Operations Dir
Armand Egan, Vice President
Floor coverings for video stages including wood, vinyl & carpeting.

EDX Wireless
1400 Executive Parkway, Suite. 430, Eugene, OR 97401 US
(541) 345-0019; *Fax:* (541) 345-8145
www.edx.com
sales@edx.com
Mark Chapman, Chairman
Harry R. Anderson, Ph.D., P.E., CEO/President
Steve Webster, Director of Sales Engineering.
Ted G. Hicks, Vice President of Engineering.
Scott A. Blumberg, Ph.D., Executive Director of Software Development.
Greg Q. Leon, Director of Business Development.
Brian T. Cochran, Director of Support Services
RF Planning software for FM, TV & DTV.

EEG Enterprises Inc.
Mailing Address: 586 Main St., Farmingdale, NY 11735 US
Second Address: 20 Jay Street, Suite 736, Brooklyn, NY 11201
(516) 293-7472; *Fax:* (516) 293-7417
www.eegent.com
sales@eegent.com
Philip McLaughlin, CEO
Eric McErlain, General Sales Mgr
TV closed captioning technology; HDTV & SDTV, closes caption encoders, decoders; V-chip encoders, decoders & systems; affil communications.

EEG Enterprises
20 Jay Street, Suite 736, Brooklyn, NY 11201

Eigen
13366 Grass Valley Ave., Grass Valley, CA 95945 US
(530) 274-1240,(888) 924-2020; *Fax:* (530) 265-2792
www.eigen.com
Dr. Mahtab Damda, President
William Mandel, VP- Regulatory Affairs/ QA
Dr. Michael Ahmadi, VP- Global Marketing and Sales
Syed Zaid, CFO
Eigen provides reliable, competitive and quality products to satisfy our customers with optimum functionality relative to time and cost constraints. We dedicate ourselves to continuous improvement in performance, ease of installation,operation and maintenance.

Electro Impulse Laboratory Inc.
1805 Rt. 33, PO Box 278, Neptune, NJ 07754-0278 US
(732) 776-5800, (732) 741-0404; *Fax:* (732) 776-6793
www.electroimpulse.com
sales@electroimpulse.com
Mark Rubin, President/CEO
Peter Ferraro, Engineering
Manufacturer of dry, forced, air-cooled FM dummy loads & RF calorimeters.

Electro Rent Corp.
Mailing Address: 6060 Sepulveda Blvd., Van Nuys, CA 91411-2512 US
Second Address: 1770 Corporate Dr., Suite 550, Norcross, GA 30093
(818) 787-2100, (877) 581-3384; *Fax:* (818) 787-4354, (770) 813-6906
www.electrorent.com
Daniel Greenberg, President
Craig Birgi, General Sales Mgr
Test rental equipment including CATV sweep analyzers, signal level meters, video generators/monitors & cable fault locators, data equipment-desktops & laptops to rent, lease or purchase.
3500 Corporate Way, Duluth, GA 30096 United States
(770) 813-7000 (800) 688-1111
Rich Curry, Eastern Rgnl Sls Mgr

Electroline Equipment Inc.
395, Lebeau Blvd, Saint-Laurent, QC H4N 1S2 Canada
(514) 374-6335, (800) 461-3344; *Fax:* (514) 374-2257
www.electroline.com
info@electroline.com
John Vincent, CEO
Alain Servant, Operations Dir
Jay Staiger, VP of Product Management
Bernard Cadieux, VP of Sales and Business Development
Besnik Bashi, Director-Wireless Engineering & Network Architectu
Joseph Chen, SalesManager
Flavio Marcon, Sales Support Engineer
Mike Nicholson, Senior Technical Support
Since its inception in 1953, Electroline's mission has been to provide innovative products that both improve operations and meet the evolving requirements of the cable telecommunications marketplace.
Having emerged as a true leadingmanufacturer of integrated CATV service solutions, the Company currently offers six families of products which include the e-Optic line of products, broadband addressable tap systems, return path noise management tools , drop amplifiers, DOCSIS basednetwork status monitoring transponders and MPEG probes, and passive CATV devices. Renowned for its high caliber products, Electroline maintains that reputation by seeking out ideas and opportunities via its customers. Electroline's Customer KnowsBest approach brings forward the finest quality and the most practical solutions available on the market.

Electronic Script Prompting
6129 Western Ave., Willowbrook, IL 60527 US
(630) 887-0346; *Fax:* (630) 887-0389
www.prompting.com
support@prompting.com
Frank Warner, CEO
Electronic Script Prompting offers color LED & LCD teleprompter Camera Mounts for through the lens shooting. All our Teleprompters are available with mounts for ENG or DV and DSLR cameras. We also offer sales and rentals of PresidentialPublic Speaking teleprompters. Our PowerPrompter teleprompter software is a proven, easy to use, Windows based teleprompting software. Professionals around the world use our PowerPrompter teleprompter software for their prompting needs.

Electronic Theatre Controls Inc.
3031 Pleasant View Rd., PO Box 620979, Middleton, WI 53562-0979 US
(608) 831-4116, (800) 688-4116; *Fax:* (608) 836-1736
www.etcconnect.com
americas@etcconnect.com
Fred Foster, CEO
Dick Titus, President
Steve Downs, VP, Quality and International Operations.
Matthew Brookfield, General Manager
Julie Cymbalak, VP, Human Resources and IT
Sarah Danke, VP, Professional Services
BillGallinghouse, VP, Business Development and Marketing
Bill McGivern, VP, Manufacturing
Mark Vassallo, VP, World Sales
Steve Terry, VP, Research & Development
Entertainment & Architectural lighting systems, including control consoles, dimming equipment, interface products & elipsoidals.

Film Center Bldg.
630 Ninth Ave., Suite 1001, New York, NY 10036 United States
(212) 397-8080
Joe DiNardo, Northeast Rgnl Mgr
4201 Vineland Rd., Suite I-1, Orlando, FL 32811 United States
(407) 843-7770
Rob Raff, Southeast Rgnl Mgr

Emcor Enclosures
1600 4th Ave. N.W., Rochester, MN 55901 US
(507) 289-3371; *Fax:* (507) 287-3405
www.crenlo.com
Lance Fleming, President
Ed Doran, Vice President
Conventional & Flat Panel Display Consoles, modification/custom capabilities, EMI/RFI shielded & Seismic qualified enclosures, a full range of component accessories.

Emcore
Mailing Address: 2015 W. Chestnut St., Alhambra, CA 91803 USA
Second Address: 10420 Research Rd. SE., Bldg. 1, Albuquerque, NM 87123
(626) 293-3400, (505) 332-5000; *Fax:* (626) 293-3428, (505) 332-5100
www.emcore.com
Reuben F. Richards, Chairman
Hong Q. Hou, CEO & President
Brad Clevenger, EVP & General Manager
Gyo Shinozaki, Promotions Manager
John Ianelli, Chief Engineer
Christopher Larocca, COO
Mark B. Weinswing, CFO, VP
Monica VanBerkel, Chief Administration Officer
Alfredo Gomez, General Counsel & Corporate Secretary
Thomas J. Russell, Chaiman Emeritus
Charles Scott, Board Member
Signal transmission products, specializing in opto electronics & RF electronics technologies.

Emerson Network Power
1050 Dearborn Drive, Columbus, OH 43085 US
(614) 888-0246; *Fax:* (614) 841-6882
www.emersonnetworkpower.com
contact@emersonnetworkpower.com
Stephen Liang, President
Sarah Beadle, Promotions Manager
Scott Barbour, Business leader for Emerson Network Power Systems
Jay Geldmacher, Business leader for Emerson Network Power Embedded
Brian Mason, Business leader for EmersonNetwork Power Connecti
Hengke Fu, President- Emerson Network Power Systems in China
Sunil Khanna, President-Emerson Network Power Systems in India
Ken Poczekaj, President- Emerson Network Power Systems in EMEA
Power protection products for transmitters, studios, CATVs from transients & lightning induced voltages.

Emerson Network Power
Mailing Address: 1050 Dearborn Dr., Columbus, OH 43085 USA
Second Address: 3103 N. Andrews Ave. Extension, Pompano Beach, FL 33064
(614) 888-0246, (954) 984-3450; *Fax:* (614) 841-6882, (954) 984-3450
www.emersonnetworkpower.com
contact@emersonnetworkpower.com
David N. Farr, President
Craig W. Ashmore, Operations Dir
Scott Barbour EVP, Station Manager
Ed Feeney, Executive Vice President
Full line of transient control systems for AC, dataline & telephone, including UPS systems & regulators.

Emerson Network Power
1050 Dearborn Dr., Columbus, OH 43085 USA
(614) 888-0246; *Fax:* (614) 841-6882
www.emersonnetworkpower.com
Dusty Becker, Operations Dir
Scott Barbour, Business Leader
Brian Mason, Business Leader
Jay Geldmacher, Business Leader
34 Grosvenor, London WIK2HD United Kingdom
44 (0) 20 7493 8484; *Fax:* 44 (0) 20 7493 1974

Emerson Network Power-Viewsonics
3000 Lakeside Dr., Suite 308N, Bannockburn, IL 60015 USA
(847) 739-0300; *Fax:* (847) 739- 0301
www.emersonnetworkpower.com/connectivity
David N. Farr, CEO
Edward K. Feeney, President
Jay Goldmacher, EVP
Jerry Patton, General Sales Mgr

One GHz amplifiers, security systems, apartment boxes, combiners, LAN, CATV, one GHz splitters, taps, custom design systems & products, head end signal coupler/splitter system.

ENCO Systems Inc.
29444 Northwestern Hwy., Southfield, MI 48034 US
(248) 827-4440, (800) 362-6797; *Fax:* (248) 827-4441
www.enco.com
sales@enco.com
Neil Price, COO
Eugene Novacek, President
Ashwath K.M., Support & Operations Manager
Ken Frommert, General Manager
Ken Frommert, Director
Nick Mues, Executive VP
Dave Turner, Executive VP
Jerry Bufka, Sales Engineer
AaronJohnson, Domestic Sales Representative
Alexis Martin, International Sales Coordinator
DAD and Presenter digital audio delivery systems, custom software engineering for the broadcast industry.

Encoda Systems Inc.
525 Plymouth Rd., Suite 307, Plymouth Meeting, PA 19462 US
(610) 397-1632, (610) 397-1633, (610) 643-4995; *Fax:* (610) 672-9620
info@encodasystems.com
Wiliam Bronson Cox, CEO
Eileen Hardin, Director, Professional Services
John S. Sprankle, Sales Manager
Robert Lee, CFO
Rich Barlow, Development Manager
Eileen Harrow, Director of Professional Services
Encoda is the authority in seamless automation for the business of media. Encoda is the only company offering end-to-end technological solutions to buyers & sellers of adv time within the electronic media marketplace (bcst, cable, wireless,& DBS).

Encore Hollywood
Mailing Address: 6344 fountain avenue, Hollywood, CA 90028 USA
Second Address: 435 hudson street, 9th floor, New York, NY 10014
(323) 466-7663, (212) 444-5555; *Fax:* (323) 466-5539
www.encorepost.com
Steven Fuset, Creative Director
Bill Royeo, SVP
Josh Ouber, SVP/Technical
Robert Glass, Sales
Augie Melendez, Sales
Russ Robertson, Sales
Tom Kendall, VFX
Jennifer Tellefsen, VFX
Stephen Fleet, VFX
At Encore, we are committed to providing the highest quality of service and industry-leading technology while maintaining the integrity and creative tradition of the post production process. We aim to always meet or exceed our client'sexpectations through creative collaboration and the design of custom work flows for any situation.

Asia Broadcast Centre
(65) 548-0388
Jim Crowe, Mgng Dir

Energy-Onix Broadcast Equipment Co. Inc.
1306 River St., PO Box 801, Valatie, NY 12184 US
(518) 758-1690, (888) 324-6649; *Fax:* (518) 758-1476
www.energy-onix.com
energy-onix@energy-onix.com
Bernard Wise, President
Transmitters:AM solid state to 10 kw, ,grounded grid triode to 50 kw & AM & SW to 100 kw. STL, Translator & remote pick up. FM, Shortwave

Enghouse Systems Limited
80 Tiverton Ct., Suite 800, Markham, ON L3R 0G4 Canada
(905) 946-3200; *Fax:* (905) 946-3201
www.enghouse.com
info@enghouse.com
Stephen Sadler, CEO
Anthony Pearlman, President
Sunil Diaz, General Sales Mgr
Networks™—automated mapping/facilities mgmt software with integrated design capabilities for fiber, copper & coax solutions.

Ensemble Designs
Mailing Address: PO Box 993, Grass Valley, CA 95945 US
Second Address: 870 Gold Flat Road, Nevada City, CA 95959
(530) 478-1830; *Fax:* (530) 478-1832
www.ensembledesigns.com
info@ensembledesigns.com
David Wood, President
Mondae Hott, General Sales Mgr
Cindy Zuelsdorf, Promotions Manager
Video, audio conversion distribution, HD/down conversion, fiber satellite & desktop video applications.

Enterprise Electronics Corp.
Mailing Address: 128 S. Industrial Blvd., Enterprise, AL 36330 US
Second Address: PO Box 311270, Enterprise, AL 36331-1270
(334) 347-3478; *Fax:* (334) 393-4556
www.eecradar.com
accounting@eecradar.com
William Collins, CEO
Larry Sabourin, President
Gary Bruce, General Sales Mgr
Frank Sloan, Promotions Manager
Tim Thompson, Director
Chris Goode, Chief Marketing Officer
Doppler weather radar systems (rain & wind measurements) with PC-based graphics display & control.

Entertainment Communications Network (ECN)
4370 Tujunga Ave., Suite 210, Studio City, CA 91604 USA
(818) 752-1400, (877) 752-1400; *Fax:* (818) 752-1443
www.ecnmedia.com
Angela Tietze, President
Tom Skoblicki, Sales Director
Tom Skoblicki, Director of Sales
Gina Russo, Accounting Manager
DiAnne Charves, Media Services Manager
Deborah Washington, Client Services Manager
Gina Russo, AccountingManager
Tom Skoblicki, Director of Sales
Bcst faxing to entertainment data bases, online resources, E-mail networks, digital graphics-delivery.
1628 Dubac Rd., Wall, NJ 07719 United States
(732) 280-7107

EON Corporation
Mailing Address: 360 Herndon Pkwy., Herndon, VA 20170 US
Second Address: 301 Congress Ave., Suite 1250, Austin, TX
(703) 467-0230; *Fax:* (703) 467-0232
www.eoncorp.net
Alfonso J. Barragan, Chairman
Ted Tarr, Operations Dir
Tom Macleod, General Sales Mgr
Dev & mfg of wireless two-way interactive technology for consumers & businesses which operate via radio frequency.

Equipment Technology LLC.
341 NW 122nd Street, Oklahoma City, OK 73114 USA
(405) 748-3841, (888) 748-3841; *Fax:* (405) 755-6829
www.eti1.com
Chris Neuberger, President
Aerial buckets: articulating & telescoping; truck & van mounted; working height ranges 33 to 43 ft.
341 N.W. 122, Oklahoma City, OK 73114 United States
Glenn Smith, Vp Mktg/Sls

ERI - Electronics Research, Inc.
7777 Gardner Rd., Chandler, IN 47610-9219 US
(812) 925-6000, 877) ERI-LINE; *Fax:* (812) 925-4030
www.eriinc.com
sales@eriinc.com
Jim Meleski, COO
Thomas Silliman, President
Todd Forbes, CFO
RF and structural engineering, field, and installation services

ESE
142 Sierra St., El Segundo, CA 90245 US
(310) 322-2136; *Fax:* (310) 322-8127
www.ese-web.com
ese@ese-web.com
William Kaiser, President
Brian Way, Operations Dir
Teena Rael, Office Manager
Fernando Vallin, International Sales
Bill R, Sales & Technical Support
David Pitts, IT Product Specialist
Samantha Way, Customer Service
YvonneClarke, Customer Service
ESE was founded in 1971 in El Segundo, California. The co-founders' objective was two-fold; first to ESE's customers, ... to provide quality products, delivered on time along with excellent service and also first to ESE's employees, ... toprovide both a pleasant work environment and a stable company which can survive and grow as time marches on.

ETS-Lindgren
Mailing Address: 1301 Arrow Point Dr., Cedar Park, TX 78613 US
Second Address: 1360 N. Wood Dale Rd., Suite G, Wood Dale, IL 60191
(512) 531-6400, (512) 531-2609, (630) 307-7200; *Fax:* (512) 531-6500, (630) 307-7571
www.ets-lindgren.com
info@ets-lindgren.com
Bruce Butler, CEO
Dave Baron, General Sales Mgr
Glenn Warren, Chief Marketing Officer
Mark Mawdsley, VP Sales
Non-ionizing radiation test equipment; low frequency survey meters; RF/microwave broadband field strength meters; calibration svcs, software & training.

Euphonix Inc.
Mailing Address: 101 South First Street, Suite 200, Burbank, CA 91502 US
Second Address: 2001 Junipero Serra Blvd, Daly City, CA 94014-3886
(650) 855-0400, (818) 557-2520; *Fax:* (650) 855-0410, (818) 557-2558
www.avid.com
Louis Hernandez, Jr., President/CEO
Jeff Rosica, Senior Vice President of Worldwide Field Operation
Glover Lawrence, VP/Corporate Development
W Sean Ford, VP/Marketing
John Frederick, Executive Vice President/Chief FinancialOfficer/C
Chris Gahagan, Senior Vice President of Products and Services
W. Sean Ford, Vice President of Marketing
Jason Duva, Vice President/General Counsel/Corporate Secretary
Jodi Sweeney, Vice President of Services/Customer Success
BruceYaung, Vice President of Supply and Hardware Technologies
Manufactures the Euphonix CSII digitally-controlled analog audio mixing system.

Euphonix Sales & Marketing
11112 Ventura Blvd., #301, Studio City, CA 91604 United States
(818) 766-1666; *Fax:* (818) 766-3401

Euphonix NYC
424 West 33rd St., # 560, New York, NY 10001

Eventide Inc.
One Alsan Way, Little Ferry, NJ 7643 US
(201) 641-1200; *Fax:* (201) 641-1640
www.eventide.com
comm@eventide.com
Richard Factor, Chairman
Jason Beck, President
Gordon Moore, General Manager
Tony Agnello, Chief Engineer
Ray Maxwell, Chief Marketin Officer
Founded in 1971, Eventide is a leading developer and manufacturer of digital audio processing products for recording, broadcast, and live performance, as well as, digital communications products for public safety institutions. Headquarteredin Little Ferry, NJ, Eventide invented the first digital logging recorder in 1989, and introduced the H3000 Ultra-Harmonizer effects processor in 1987.

Evertz Microsystems Ltd.
Mailing Address: 5292 John Lucas Dr., Burlington, ON L7L 5Z9 Canada
Second Address: 100 Berkshire Place, Wharfedale Road, Winnersh Triangle, Be RG41 5RD
(905) 335-3700, (877) 995-3700; *Fax:* (905) 335-3573
www.evertz.com
sales@evertz.com
Joe Cirincione, General Manager
Orest Holyk, General Sales Mgr
Evertz provides the most comprehensive line of Fiber Optic Transport equipment, the most advanced line of Multi-Image Display, Monitoring Systems, SDTV & HDTV conversion, synchronization products for use in satellite, cable & bcstapplications.
9250 Mosby St., Suite 201, Manassas, VA 20110 United States
212 N. Evergreen St., Burbank, CA 91505 United States
59 Suttons Business Park, Reading, RG6 1AZ United Kingdom

The Express Group
3707 5th Avenue, Suite 624, San Diego, CA 92103 US
(619) 280-9061; *Fax:* (619) 280-9030
www.theexpressgroup.com
Byron Andrus, President
Robin Andrus, General Manager

EQUIPMENT MANUFACTURERS

George Andrus, Senior Design Consultant
Robin Andrus, Vice President/Art Director
Kim Booth, Marketing Director
Alan Calero, IT Manager
With 25 years experience and over 1,000 projects completed, The Express Group has a reputation for delivering the most beautiful Set Designs on time and on budget.

F&F Productions, L.L.C.
14333 Myerlake Cir., Clearwater, FL 33760 US
(727) 530-5000; *Fax:* (727) 535-6547
www.fandfhd.tv
kellyp@fandfhd.tv
George Orgera, President/CEO
Cheryl Wolcott, Operations Coordinator
Bill McKechney, Chief Engineer
Ryan Hatch, Executive Vice President
Bill McKechney, Vice President Engineering
Marc Orgera, Vice President of Sales & Marketing
Connie Vizaro, Director of Business Development & Marketing
Brian Hawley, Operations Coordinator
Remote production svcs & TV mobile units.

F-Conn Industries
6260 Downing St., Denver, CO 80216 USA
(303) 288-8107; *Fax:* (303) 288-4769
www.ppc-online.com/Solutions/AV_Security/
Randy Holliday, President
Susan Stockstill, General Sales Mgr

Faroudja Laboratories
180 Baytech Dr., Suite 110, San Jose, CA 95134 US
(408) 635-4200; *Fax:* (408) 957-0364
techsupport@lifestyleshomeentertainment.com
Eric Erdman, President
NTSC Encoder; NTSC & PAL/NTSC Decoder (RGB or D1 output); Bidirectional Transcoder; NTSC & PAL/NTSC Line Doublers & Line Quadruplers.

Fast Forward Video
1901 Carnegie Ave., Unit 1P, Santa Ana, CA 92705 US
(949) 852-8404; *Fax:* (949) 852-1226
www.ffv.com
support@ffv.com
Hal Reisiger, CEO
Paul Dekeyser, Chief Engineer
Dennis Mallon, COO
Kevin McNally, Sales Executive
Fast Forward Video is committed to providing cutting edge DVR technology in both award-winning finished goods & board-levl products along with engrg supports to a variety of industries including bcstg, sports, military, film production,surveillance & many more.

Feldmar Watch and Clock Center
9000 W. Pico Blvd., Los Angeles, CA 90035 US
(310) 274-8016; *Fax:* (310) 274-2081
www.feldmarwatch.com
sales@feldmarwatch.com
Sol Meller, President
Stopwatches, clocks, watches, timers, sls & repairs.

Ferno-Washington Inc.
70 Weil Way, Wilmington, OH 45177 US
(937) 382-1451, (800) 733-3766; *Fax:* (937) 382-6569
www.ferno.com
sales@ferno.com
Joe Bourgraf, CEO
Tim Schroeder, Promotions Manager
Tim Wells, Chief Marketing Officer
Paul Rankin, Chief Financial Officer
Carts designed to aid in the movement of heavy & bulky equipment.

Film/Video Equipment Service Co. Inc.
800 S. Jason St., Denver, CO 80223 US
(303) 619-6208; *Fax:* (303) 778-8657
www.fvesco.com
Dean D. Schneider, Rentals/Sales
Scott Schneider, eBay Sales
Film & video equipment rentals-cameras, lenses, lighting, grip, pro audio, camera support & specialty gear for quality production.

FitzCo. Inc.
4300 W. Wall, Bldg. B, PO Box 710, Midland, TX 79703 US
(432) 684-0861; *Fax:* (432) 682-9978
www.fitzcosound.com
fitzcosound@mac.com
Milt Hathaway, President
Speakers, recorders, amplifiers, mixers, tapes, microphones, & headphones; sound reinforcement & bcst equipment.

Flash Technology, An SPX Division
13320 Ballantyne Corporate Place, Charlotte, NC 28277 US
(615) 261-2000; *Fax:* (615) 261-2600
www.spx.com
Shannon Lyzckowski, Director of Operations
Klaus Thieme, General Manager
Doug Jones, Vice President of Sales
Chris Shumate, Vice President of Engineering
Brian Beck, Director of Business Development
Keri Cable, Director ofFinance
John Priest, Director of Human Resource
David Wise, Director of NOC Services
Our experience with the day-to-day realities of obstruction lighting systems operations also has made us a major supplier of remote asset monitoring solutions to manage critical applications. Flash Technology's remote Machine-to-Machinemonitoring solutions oversee critical assets across a wide range of applications, including solar, wind, telecommunications and broadcast, offering customers improved operating performance and reduced costs.
55 Lake St, Nashua, NH 03060 United States
(603) 883-6500

Florical Systems
4500 NW 27th Ave., Building B-1, Gainesville, FL 32606 US
(352) 372-8326; *Fax:* (352) 375-0859
www.florical.com
sales@florical.com
Shawn Maynard, VP/GM
Jim Berry, General Sales Mgr
Kim McKnight, Promotions Manager
TV Automation, complete on-air management and presentation systems include; asset mgmt, material acquisition, variable multi ch control systems, BXF traffic interface, e-mail reports, AssetDispatcher (HD central ingest tool) optional accessthrough web svcs. Dynamic, highly configurable, scalable & reliable.

Fluke Corp.
Mailing Address: PO Box 9090, Everett, WA 98206 US
Second Address: 6920 Seaway Blvd, Everett, WA 98203
(800) 443-5853, (425) 347-6100, (800) 443-5853); *Fax:* (206) 446-5116
www.fluke.com
fluke-info@fluke.com
H. Lawrence Culp, CEO
Wes Pringle, President
Andy Doppel, Vice President, Global Operations
Paul Heydron, Vice President/Chief Financial Officer
Paul Heydron, Vice President, Engineering
Salvatore Parlatore, Vice President,Worldwide Marketing
Ernie Lauber, Vice President, Americas
Herman Warnshuis, Vice President, Fluke EMEA
Paul de la Port, Vice President, Fluke Thermography
Electronic test, measurement & control instrumentation.

FM SYSTEMS Inc.
3877 South Main Street, Santa Ana, CA 92707 US
(714) 979-3355,(800) 235-6960; *Fax:* (714) 979-0913
www.fmsystems-inc.com
fmsystemsinc@sbcglobal.net
Don McClatchie, COO
Frank McClatchie, CEO
Our company designs and builds over 150 different products for the Broadcast Television, Cable Television, Terrestrial Microwave, Satellite communications, Security Industry and Professional Recording Industry.

FOR- A Corp. of America
11125 Knott Ave., Suite A, Cypress, CA 90630 US
(714) 894-3311; *Fax:* (714) 894-5399
Keizo Kiyohara, Chairman
Katsuaki Kiyohara, President/Representative Director
Chuck Bocan, General Sales Mgr
Video & audio bcst & postproduction equipment; TBCs, color correctors, production switchers, de/encoders, complete video editing systems, virtual studio & multiviewers.

Fostex USA
9 Mars Ct., Boonton, NJ 7005 US
(973) 394-0015; *Fax:* (973) 394-0800
www.fostex.com/usa
ed@fostexusa.com
Steven Savvides, President
Ed Alstrom, General Sales Mgr
Manufacturer & marketer of innovative digital recorders, field recorders, headphones & monitoring solutions for bcst environments, musicians, producers, personal & professional studios.

Four Seasons Sunrooms, LLC
5005 Veterans Memorial Hwy., Holbrook, NY 11741 US
(631) 563-4000, (800) 368-7732; *Fax:* (631) 563-4010
www.commercial.four-seasons-sunrooms.com
Patrick Marron, CEO
David Ewing, President
Peter Allen, Chief Marketing Officer
Four Seasons Solar Products was founded in 1975, and quickly became one of the largest manufacturers of sunrooms, enclosures and large-scale skylights in the world.

Fourth Wall Media
45925 Horseshoe Dr., Suite 100, Dulles, VA 20166 USA
(703) 406-2200; *Fax:* (703) 406-0402
www.fourthwallmedia.tv
mpruneau@fwm.tv
Winston Churchill, Chairman
Timothy Peters, Chief Executive Officer
John Gregoire, President
M. Ellen Dudar, Chief Product Officer, Co-Founder
Dr. Louis Slothouber, Chief Scientist, Co-Founder
Dr. Aaron Ye, Chief TechnologyOfficer
J. Lamont Hall, Chief Financial Officer
FourthWall Media's mission is to enable next-generation television that unlocks TV's Big Data opportunity and makes advertising more valuable. We do this through compelling products that deliver behavioral profiling for true one-to-onemessaging on TV. And we provide the data and insights to go head-to-head in today's fierce competition for attention.

Fred A. Nudd Corp.
Box 577, 1743, Rt. 104, Ontario, NY 14519 USA
(315) 524-2531; *Fax:* (315) 524-4249
www.nuddtowers.com
info@nuddtowers.com
Tom Nudd, President/Owner
Tim Wilson, Sales Executive
Design, manufacture, instal, maintenance & analysis of communication towers.

Frezzolini Electronics Inc.
5-7 Valley St., Hawthorne, NJ 7506 US
(973) 427-1160; *Fax:* (973) 427-0934
www.frezzi.com
info@frezzi.com
James Crawford, President
High-capacity NIMH, Lithium Ion & Nickel Zinc rechargeable batteries for professional cameras & camcorders; advanced charger & power supplies, location lighting with Frezzi Mini & Micro-fill tungsten quartz & Micro-Sun-Guns, LED MR-19replacement lamps for Mini & Micro fill lighting.

Frontline Communications
12770 44th St. N., Clearwater, FL 33762 USA
(727) 573-0400; *Fax:* (727) 571-3295
www.frontlinecomm.com
dmckay@frontlinecomm.com
John Sherk, SVP
Andy Callaway, General Manager
Steve Williamson, General Sales Mgr
Jonathan Sherr, VP-Sales
Stephen Williamson, Director of Sales
Paul Tanofsky, Regional Sales Manager
Bob King, International Sales Manager
TracyBrink, Sr. Sales Administrator
Our vehicles meet or exceed all applicable SAE standards, NEC Codes and FMVSS Standards 207, 210, 216, and 302.

FUJIFILM Recording Media U.S.A. Inc.
200 Summit Lake Dr., Valhalla, NY 10595-1356 US
(914) 789-8100; *Fax:* (914) 789-8530
www.fujifilmusa.com
Peter Faulhaber, Operations Dir
Gene Kern, General Manager
Professional recording media & data media for bcst, production, cinematography & industrial applications.
1100 King George Post Rd., Edison, NJ 08837 United States
(732) 857-3000
45 Crosby Drive, Bedford, MA 01730 United States
(781) 271-4400

Fujinon Inc.
10 High Point Dr., Wayne, NJ 7470 US
(973) 633-5600; *Fax:* (973) 633-5216
www.fujinon.com
lens.sales@fujinon.com
H. Hayashi, President
John Newton, Operations Dir
Tom Calabro, General Sales Mgr
HDTV, CTV, ENG, EFP lenses, optical systems, accessories.
4951 Airport Pkwy, Suite 802A, Addison, TX 75001 United States
(972) 385-8902
David Waddell, Mktg Mgr

4101 N. 48th Terr, Hollywood, FL 33021 United States
(954) 966-0484
Kelly Nelson, Southeast Rgnl Sls Mgr
West Bay Business Park, 2621A Manhattan Beach Blvd, Redondo, CA 90278 United States
(310) 536-0800
Miles Shozuya, West Coast Sls Mgr
Chuck Lee, Mktg Mgr

Full Compass Systems Ltd.
9770 Silicon Prarie Parkway, Madison, WI 53593-3194 US
(800) 356-5844,(608) 831-7330; *Fax:* (608) 831-6330
www.fullcompass.com
customerservice@fullcompass.com
Jonathan Lipp, CEO
Over 300 product lines for bcst recording, entertainment, video & sound reinforcement industries.

Fuller Manufacturing
315 South Flower Street, Suite 102, Burbank, CA 91502 USA
(818) 238-9911; *Fax:* (818) 238-9959
www.fullermanufacturing.com
fullermfg@hotmail.com
Ron Fuller, Chief Engineer
IFB for news & satellite trunks.

Furman
Mailing Address: 1730 Corporate Cir., Petaluma, CA 94954 US
Second Address: 1800 South McDowell Blvd, 2nd Floor, Petaluma, CA 94954
(707) 763-1010; *Fax:* (707) 763-1310
www.furmansound.com
info@furmansound.com
Dave Keller, General Sales Mgr
John Humphrey, CFO
Analog, digital, video monitor systems, power conditioning/distribution, mixers, equalizers, compressors, crossovers, patch bays, voltage regulators, headphone amplifliers & distribution systems.

Fusion Consoles
Mailing Address: 419 S. Flower Ave., Burbank, CA 91502 USA
Second Address: 928 N. San Fernando Blvd., Suite #J-15, Burbank, CA 91504
(818) 847-0200, (800) 557-8861; *Fax:* (888) 262-1726
www.fusionconsoles.com
info@marketec.com
Penny Russell, President
Penelope Russell, President/Sales
Suzi Russell, CFO
Patricia Cobilich, Inside Sales/Administrative Asst.
Laura Eisenbruch, Outside Sales/ Custom Furniture for Technology
Merlyn Morgan, Outside Sales/Electronics
Julio Ancheta, NO CA, OR, WA
Technical Furniture & Accessories including ready-to-assemble NLE console desks, racks & full custom tech furniture fabrication complete with CAD drawing for the bcst & cable, post production, audio & multimedia applications.

Future Productions Inc.
100 Industrial Ave., Little Ferry, NJ 07643-1913 US
(794) 993-3139; *Fax:* (201) 727-0908
future-productions.com
INFO@FUTURE-PRODUCTIONS.COM
Future Productions Films is a top UK media production company that blends the very finest in creative talent and originality with a hardworking dynamic approach to media production. We produce high-end film, photography and website designservices for everyone to enjoy!

FWT Inc.
Mailing Address: 5750 E Interstate 20, PO Box 8597, Fort Worth, TX 76119-7034 US
Second Address: 761 West High Street, Hicksville, OH 43526-1052
(817) 255-3060; *Fax:* (817) 255-2957
info@fwtllc.com
Fred Moore, CEO
David Savage, Chief Financial Officer
Bill Sales, Executive VP, Sales
Ashley Glenn, Merketing Manager
Lee Mitchell, Regional Sales Representative
Jared Orzolek, Regional Sales Representative
Monopoles, self supporting towers, guyed towers, communications bldgs, standby power systems, mobile communications bldgs, COWS, fiber optics, & splicing trailers.

Gala
3185 First Street, St. Hubert, QC J3Y 8Y6 Canada
(450) 678-7226; *Fax:* (450) 678-4060
galainfo.com
info@galasystems.com
Philippe Laforest, President
Philippe Desmarais, General Sales Mgr
Robert Heimbach, Vice President, Business Development
Theatrical rigging, revolving stages & orchestra lifts.
655 Calle Ladra, Es Condido, CA 92025 United States
(760) 738-5555
Richard R. Haller, Chairman

Galaxy Audio Inc.
PO Box 16285, Wichita, KS 67216-0285 USA
(316) 263-2852, (800) 369-7768; *Fax:* (316) 263-0642
www.galaxyaudio.com
Yule Jabara, CEO
Brock Jabara, Founder & President
Yule Jabara, General Sales Mgr
Bacheus, Marketing Director
Chris, Technical Resource Manager
Alison, Accounting & HR
Carlos, Service Tech
Grant Brewer, National SalesManager
Gerald, Purchasing Manager
Wireless speakers & microphones, headset mics, personal monitors power & unpowered, combiners, splitters SPL meters & audio test equipment.

GAMPRODUCTS Inc.
52 Harbor View, Stamford, CT 6902 US
(800) 767-2669, (203) 708-8900; *Fax:* (203) 708-8919
www.gamonline.com
info@rosco.com
Stan Miller, Chairman
Mark Engel, CEO
Ed Donohue, President
Heidi Vessels, Operations Dir
Jeff Davis, General Sales Mgr
Lighting equipment, portable, studio special effects, projections, control console, dimming, color, correction, diffusion filters & patterns (gobos).

Garner Products
10620 Industrial Avenue, Suite 100, Roseville, CA 95678
(916) 784-0200 (800) 624-1903; *Fax:* (916) 784-1425
www.garner-products.com
info@garner-products.com
Ronald Stofan, President
Professional line of bulk tape degaussers for all formats of tape including: Beta SP, DAT 2 reels up to 16 diameters, hard drives, DLT media & degaussing svc.

Geac Libra
9870 St. Vincent, Glasgow, DC 45 Fr 45. US
(800) 559-6580; *Fax:* (800) 889-9898
www.gcs.geac.com
Eric Schlor, General Sales Mgr
Accounting software for radio, including billing affidavits & sls analysis.

Gefen Inc.
20600 Nordhoff Street, Chatsworth, CA 91311 US
(800) 545-6900,(818) 772-9100; *Fax:* (818) 772-9120
www.gefen.com
gsinfo@gefen.com
Hagai Gefen, CEO
Robert Lemer, General Sales Mgr
Gefen supplies a wide selection of signal switchers,splitters, extenders, scalers, converters, and accessories that enable audio/video and computer systems to be easily integrated, extended, distributed, and optimized to maximizeperformance. The GefenPRO line suppies 24/7 technical support and valuable features for demanding broadcast industries.

General Atomics Electronic Systems, Inc.
3550 General Atomics Court, San Diego, CA 92121-1122 US
(858) 522-8300; *Fax:* (858) 522-8301
www.ga.com
epsales@ga-esi.com
Phil Arneson, President
Carol-Anne Mantz, Sales & Marketing Manager
Karen Anderson, Global Sales
Yulia Babushkina, System Integrator Business Manager
John Gilbert, Technical Sales
Ross Carlson, Technical Sales
Terminal automation products, radiation, monitoring system, triqq and manufacturer of Maxwell high voltage capactiors & power supplies.

General Cable
Mailing Address: 4 Tesseneer Dr., Highland Heights, KY 41076 US
Second Address: 3101 Pleasant Valley Blvd, Altoona, PA 16603
(859) 572-8000, (814) 944-5002; *Fax:* (859) 572-8458, (816) 944-5006
www.generalcable.com
info@generalcable.com
Greg Lampert, President/CEO
Copper, aluminum and fiberoptic wire, cable products for communications, energy & electrical markets.

General Electric Co.
3135 Easton Tpke., Fairfield, CT 06828 US
(800) 626-2004,(203)373-2211; *Fax:* (203) 373-3198
www.ge.com
Jeff Immelt, CEO
Ferdinando "Nani" Beccalli-Falco, Senior Vice President
Jeffrey S. Bornstein, Senior Vice President and Chief Financial Officer
Kathryn A. Cassidy, SVP and Treasurer
Beth Comstock, Chief Marketing Officer
MatthewG. Cribbins, Vice President
NBC bcstg; CNBC & MSNBC; lighting products; Americom satellite; electrical distribution & control; intercast; MSNBC desktop video.

CNBC & MSNBC
2200 Fletcher Ave, Fort Lee, NJ 07024 United States
Bill Bolste, Pres

NBC
30 Rockefeller Plaza, New York, NY 10020 United States
(212) 664-4444
Robert C. Wright, Pres
4338 Nela Park, Cleveland, OH 44112 United States
(216) 362-5600; *Fax:* (216) 266-2310
Keith T.S. Ward, Quartz-Stage Studio Production Mgr

General Electrodynamics Corp.
8000 Calendar Rd., P.O. Box 150089, Arlington, TX 76015-9967 US
(817) 572-0366,(800) 551-6038; *Fax:* (817) 572-0373
www.gecscales.com
Info@gecscales.com
Dick Davis, President
George Lindlonger, General Manager
Tubes, TV cameras, electronics, aircraft weighing equipment, contract weighing svcs, truck scales, load scales.

Gepco International Inc.
500 Thorndale Ave, Suite F, Wood Dale, IL 60191-1267 US
(847) 795-9555; *Fax:* (847) 795-8770
www.gepco.com
gepco@gepco.com
Gary Geppert, President
Jay Lahman, General Manager
Ken Bernd, General Sales Mgr
David Mecklenburger, CFO
Audio cable & video cable in bulk or cut to length. Assemblies, boxes, connectors, patchbays. ADC, Kings Neutrik & switchcraft
1000 N. Lake St, Burbank, CA 91502 United States
(818) 569-5222; *Fax:* (818) 569-5226

Glentronics Inc.
645 Heathrow Dr, Lincolnshire, IL 60069 Canada
(905) 475-8494, (800) 991-0466; *Fax:* (905) 475-0955
www.glentronics.com
mail@glentronics.com
Glentronics is a manufacturer of several consumer products including sump pumps, battery backup sump pumps, water alarms and plant lights. Our goal is to create products that solve the needs of our customers. We believe in designing highquality products that the homeowner can rely on.

Globecomm Systems Inc.
45 Oser Ave., Hauppauge, NY 11788-3816 USA
(866) 499-0223; *Fax:* (631) 231-1557
www.globecommsystems.com
info@globecomm.com
Keith A. Hall, Chief Executive Officer
Thomas C. Coyle, SVP/General Manager
Paul Scardino, Vice President, Sales and Marketing
Paul J. Johnson, Senior Vice President,Customer Relations& Contacts
Dwight R. Hunsicker, SVP & GeneralManager- Govt. Solutions
Paul J. Johnson, SVP, Strategic Marketing
Michelle P. Scotto di Ceasare, VP of Global Operations
Kristin S. Harrison, Vice President, Human Resources
Andrew Silberstein, SVP & General Manager, Services
Earth stn ground segements. Video Broadcasting Service & Content Delivery Service.

EQUIPMENT MANUFACTURERS

Gorman-Redlich Manufacturing Co.
257 W. Union St., Athens, OH 45701 US
(740) 593-3150; *Fax:* (740) 592-3898
www.gorman-redlich.com
jimg@gorman-redlich.com
James Gorman, President
EAS encoders & decoders, EAS with built-in character generator for TV; digital antennas monitors; NOAA weather radios with SAME decoding.

Grant Tower, Inc.
13064 Wisner Ave., Grant, MI 49327 US
(231) 834-5665; *Fax:* (231) 834-7870
Terry Sharp, President
Walter Knoch, General Manager
Bcst tower erection & maintenance svc.

Great Lakes Data Systems, Inc.
5954 Priestly Dr., Carlsbad, CA 92008 US
(760) 753-1024; *Fax:* (760) 753-2538
www.cablebilling.com www.glds.com
J. Alonzo Rosado, President
Garrick Russell, Vice President
Laura Rosado, General Sales Mgr
Affordable PC/Network billing & subscriber mgmt systems. Addressable interface, PPV, ARU, ANI, Hotel PPV. Training, data conversion & toll-free support.
Box 295, Beaver Dam, WI 53916 United States
(920) 887-7651; *Fax:* (920) 887-7653

Greenberg Teleprompting
115 S. Olive St., Orange, CA 92866 US
(818) 838-4437, (714) 288-8553; *Fax:* (818) 838-0447
www.greenprompt.com
info@greenprompt.com
Jim Estochin, President
Camera mounted teleprompting, speech prompting, nationwide clients.

Group One Ltd.
70 Sea Ln., Farmingdale, NY 11735 US
(631) 396-0195; *Fax:* (631) 396-0190
www.g1limited.com
sales@g1limited.com
Jack Kelly, President
Sue Adamson, Operations Manager
Chris Fichera, General Sales Mgr
Chris Fichera, Vice President, U.S. Sales
Norman Wright, Vice President, Technical Support
Vincent Finnegan, Vice President, U.S. Sales
Anne-Marie Zicari, Vice President, Admin./Operations
Tyler Wise, National Sales Manager
Brad White, National Sales Manager Avolites
Exclusive distributor for a number of prominent audio & lighting products including : BlueSky, Digico, Junger, MC, RTW, VanDamme, Elektalite, and Pulsar.

Harman International
400 Atlantic St., Stamford, CT 6901 USA
(203) 328-3500; *Fax:* (818) 892-9590
www.harman.com
Dinesh C. Paliwal, Chairman, President & CEO
Susan Bercovivi, General Manager
Herbert K. Parker, EVP & CFO
I.P. Park, EVP, Chief Technology Officer
Ralph Santana, EVP & Chief Marketing Officer
John Stacey, EVP & Chief HumanResource Officer
Todd A. Suko, EVP, General Counsel
Manufacturer of audio signal processing equipment designed for sound reinforcement, recording & bcstg.

Harmonic Inc.
4300 North First St., San Jose, CA 95134 US
(408) 542-2500, (800) 788-1330; *Fax:* (408) 542-2511
www.harmonicinc.com
Patrick Harshman, President & CEO
Charles Bonasera, Sr. VP, Operations
Nimrod Ben-Natan, Sr. VP & General Manager
Carolyn V. Aver, CFO
Paulien Ruijssenaars, Sr.Director, Corporate Communications
Peter Alexander, Sr. VP, CMO
Shahar Bar, Sr. VP, Corporate Development
Peter E. Hilliard, Sr. VP, Human Resources
Ron Howe, Sr. VP,Service & Support
Fiber-optic & digital transmission systems for cable TV, including transmitters, receivers, return path equipment & net mgmt hardware & software.

Harris Broadcast
Mailing Address: 5300 Kings Island Dr., Suite 101, Mason, OH 45040 USA
Second Address: 9800 S Meridian Blvd., Suite 300, Englewood, CO 80112
(800) 231-9673, (513) 459-3400, (303) 476-5000; *Fax:* (513) 459-3796, (303) 476-5004
www.broadcast.harris.com
Charlie Vogt, President & CEO
Richard Scott, Operations Dir
Bruce Allan, General Manager
Pablo Gargiulo, President, Global Sales
Mike Behling, CFO
Brian Cabeceiras, Chief Strategy Officer
Jeff Liening, EVP, Sales Operations
Steve Foreman, President, Global Operations & Serivces
Rick Thompson, Chief Information Officer
Manufacturer of test/measurement equipment, video demodulators, routing switchers, color correctors/processors, related equipment for professional video/TV bcst markets.

Harris Corp.
1025 W. NASA Blvd., Melbourne, FL 32919-0001 US
(321) 727-9100, (321) 727-9207, (800) 442-7747; *Fax:* (650) 594-3110
www.harris.com
webmaster@harris.com
Thomas A. Dattilo, Chairman
William M. (Bill) Brown, President & CEO
Gary L. McArthur, Sr. VP & CFO
Robert Duffy, Sr. VP, HR & Administration
Scott Mikuen, VP, General Counsel & Secretary
Dana A. Mehnert, Group President, RFCommunications
James Morris, Group President, Integrated Network Solutions
Sheldon J. Fox, Group President, Govt. Communications
Microwave for intercity relay & STLs.

Harris Corp.
1025 W. NASA Blvd., Melbourne, FL 32919-0001 US
(321) 727-9100, (321) 727-9207, (800) 442-7747; *Fax:* (650) 594-3110
www.harris.com
Thomas A. Dattilo, Chairman
William M. (Bill) Brown, President & CEO
Bob Weirather, Operations Dir
Jack O'Dear, General Sales Mgr
Gary L. McArthur, Sr. VP & CFO
Robert Duffy, Sr. VP, HR & Administration
Scott Mikuen, VP, GeneralCounsel & Secretary
Dana A. Mehnert, Group President, RF Communications
James Morris, Group President, Integrated Network Solutions
Sheldon J. Fox, Group President, Govt. Communications
Digital radio & TV transmission equipment, svc, tower studies, training, turnkey RF systems.
Box 1179, 10373 Saratoga Rd., South Glens Falls, NY 12803 United States
(518) 793-2181; *Fax:* (518) 793-7423
Rich Redmond, Sls Mgr
33430 13th Pl. S., Suite 205A, Federal Way, WA 98003 United States
(206) 874-7444; *Fax:* (206) 874-8866
Cal Vandegrift, Sls Rep

Harris Corporation
1025 West Nasa Blvd, Melbourne, FL 32919-0001 US
(321) 727-9100, (800) 442-7747, (321) 727-9207; *Fax:* (408) 990-8250
www.harris.com
webmaster@harris.com
Thomas A. Dattilo, Chairman
William Brown, CEO & President
Howard Lance, General Manager
Gary L. McArthur, Sr. VP & CFO
Robert Duffy, Sr. VP, HR & Administration
Scott Mikuen, VP, General Counsel & Secretary
James Morris, GroupPresident, Integrated Network Solutions
Dana A. Mehnert, Group President, Communications
Lewis Schwartz, VP, Principal Accounting Officer
Louth is a supplier of media mgmt, automation system: for bcst & cable TV.
700 NW Gilman Blvd, 133-227, Issaquah, WA 98027 United States
(425) 837-3799
Brian Lay, Dir Sls, Western & Central Rgn
Bos 3200, Wantagh, NY 11793 United States
(516) 783-6022
Martin Frange, Dir Sls

Harris Corporation
1025 W. NASA Blvd., Melbourne, FL 32919-0001 USA
(321) 727-9100
www.harris.com
Gary L. McArthur, CFO
Howard L. Lance, Chairman
R. Kent Buchanan, Chief Engineer
Robert K. Henry, EVP/COO
Provides a wide range of products & svcs for coml & govt communications markets such as wireless, bcst, & govt.
Box 867717, Plano, TX 75023 United States
(214) 612-2053 (800) 729-0494; *Fax:* (214) 612-2145
Doc Masoomian, Chairman

Harrison Consoles
1024 Firestone Pkwy., Nashville, TN 37086 US
(615) 641-7200; *Fax:* (615) 641-7224
www.harrisonconsoles.com
info@harrisonconsoles.com
Gary Thielman, Station Manager
Charley White, General Sales Mgr
Ben Loftis, Promotions Manager
David Ives, Contact
Analog & digital audio mixing consoles for on-air bcst, production, video, film sound postproduction, live sound & music recording.

HAVE Inc.
350 Power Ave., Hudson, NY 12534-2448 US
(518) 828-2000,(800) 999-4283; *Fax:* (518) 828-2008
www.haveinc.com
have@haveinc.com
Nancy Gordon, President
Paul Swedenburg, Operations Dir
Canare, Belden, Gepco, Flexygy, Mogami Cable; Network connectors & adaptors. Professional blank media, equipment & accessories. DVD, CD duplication & postproduction svcs.
HAVE, Inc.
West Coast Office - 661-722-2957

Henry Engineering
PO Box 3796, Sea Beach, CA 90740 US
(562) 493-3589; *Fax:* (626) 355-0077
www.henryeng.com
info@henryeng.com
Hank Landsberg, President
The Matchbox, and other digital and analog interface, distribution, mixing, control, and power conditioning products.

Hessler Enterprises Inc.
106 Susan Dr., Unit #1, Elkins Park, PA 19027 US
(800) 346-1304; *Fax:* (215) 663-8839
www.hessler.com
Ed Hessler, President
Brian Hessler, Operations Dir
Brian Hessler, Owner
Janis Navo, Sales Service Specialist
Bernice James, Sales Service Specialist
Ceil Whalen, Accounting Supervisor
Sharon Mancuso-Krolikowski, OfficeManager
Produces bcstg forms including script sets, contracts, program logs, invoices, labels, A/R statements & computer stock paper.

Hewlett Packard Co.
Mailing Address: 3000 Hanover St., Palo Alto, CA 94304-1185 US
Second Address: 5200 Blue Lagoon Drive, Waterford Building, 9th Floor, Miami, FL 33126
(650) 857-1501, (305) 267-4220; *Fax:* (650) 857-5518, (305) 265-5550
www.hp.com

High Tech Furnishings Ltd.
27636 Ynez Rd., Suite L7#209, Temecula, CA 92591-4645 US
(888) 747-9817; *Fax:* (951) 279-5773
www.customstudio.com
Douglas Kanczuzewski, General Manager
Audio & Radio rooms, AV Applications, Broadcast consoles, client tables, monitor walls, screening rooms, vertical racks

Hignite Tower Service
9945 Arkansas St., Bellflower, CA 90706 US
(562) 925-1951; *Fax:* (562) 925-6171
John Hignite, President
Jackie Hignite, General Manager
Tower erection, maintenance & painting.

Hipotronics Inc.
1650 Route 22 North, Brewster, NY 10509 US
(800) 727-4476; *Fax:* (845) 279-2467
www.hipotronics.com
sales@hipotronics.com
Richard Davies, Principal
Christopher Faust, Sales Executive
Michelle Gulkins, HR Executive
Melissa Fiorello, Marketing & Customer Service Manager
High-voltage DC power supplies & industrial grade voltage regulators for medium-to-high-power applications.

Hitachi Kokusai Electric America, Ltd.
150 Crossway Park Dr., Woodbury, NY 11797 US
(516) 921-7200; *Fax:* (516) 496-3718
www.hitachikokusai.us
info@hitachikokusai.us
Masahiko Momose, President
Bob Johnston, Operations Dir
Sean Moran, General Sales Mgr
Bob Johnston, VP of Sales, Board of Directors member
Sean Moran, VP of Sales, Broadcast & Professional Products
Kenneth Cyr, East Coast RegionalSales Manager of Broadcast & P
Danny Stephens, Southeast Regional Sales Manager of Broadcast & Pr
Larry Ottaviano, Crucial Imaging Division, National Sales Manager
Bcst, professional & industrial TV cameras, MPEG Codecs, microware links & RF telecommunication equipment.
371 Van Ness Way, Torrance, CA 90501 United States
(310) 328-6116
David Morris, Rgnl Sls Mgr

HME
Pro Audio Division, 14110 Stowe Dr., Poway, CA 92064-7147 US
(858) 535-6000; *Fax:* (858) 452-7207
www.hme.com
jkowalski@hme.com
John Kowalski, General Sales Mgr
Wireless Intercoms

Hoagland Instrument, Inc.
120 Eastern Ave., Unit #3, Chelsea, MA 2150 US
(617) 887-9492; *Fax:* (617) 887-9493
www.hoagland-instrument.com
info@hoagland-instrument.com
Jacob Burke, President
Machine automation, industrial controls, proto typing, welding, brazing, machining, turning, milling, drilling, grinding

Hogg & Davis Inc.
Box 405, 3800 Eagle Loop, Odell, OR 97044 US
(541) 354-1001; *Fax:* (541) 354-1080
www.hoggdavis.com
info@hoggdavis.com
F. Hogg, President
Fred G. Hogg, Founder
Willard W. Davis, Founder
Cable reels, cable reel trailers, pole tongs, cable sheaves, break-away reels, 36 & 52 tensioners underground puller, 4 drum puller.

Hollywood Rentals Production Services
22800 Foothill Road, Sylmar, CA 91342 US
(818) 407-7800, (800) 233-7830; *Fax:* (818) 407-7875
www.hollywoodrentals.com
Kelly Koskella, President
Production equipment & vehicles for film & video (rental); sale of new equipment & expendable items.
9100-C Perimeter Woods Dr, Charlotte, NC 28216 United States
(740) 597-1308
Jeff Pentek, Chairman

Hollywood Vaults Inc.
742 North Seward Street, Hollywood, CA 90038 US
(323) 461-6464, (800) 569-5336; *Fax:* (323) 461-6479
www.hollywoodvaults.com
vault@hollywoodvaults.com
David Wexler, President
Julianna Wexler, Operations Dir
State-of-the-art film & tape storage vault. Secure, climate-controlled, 24-hours self svc access.

Corporate office of Hollywood Vaults Inc.
1780 Prospect Ave., Santa Barbara, CA 93103 United States
(800) 569-5336

Homalite
11 Brookside Dr., Wilmington, DE 19804 US
(302) 652-3686, (800) 346-7802; *Fax:* (302) 652-4578, (800) 884-8777
www.homalite.com
samples@homalite.com
Robert Cahill, President
Manufactures low-reflectance, contrast enhancement filters for use on CRTs, LEDs & other forms of info display.

Hoodman Corp.
20445 Gramercy Pl., Suite #201, Torrance, CA 90501 US
(310) 222-8608, (800) 818-3946 (US); *Fax:* (310) 222-8623
www.hoodmanusa.com
info@hoodmanusa.com
Mike Schmidt, President
Louis Schmidt, Operations Dir
Bob Schmidt, General Sales Mgr
WristShot camcorder support systems, moniter hoods, RAW CF & SD memory cards.

Horita
Box 3993, Mission Viejo, CA 92690 US
(949) 489-0240; *Fax:* (949) 489-0242
www.horita.com
Gerald Hester, President
Christopher Lovallo, General Sales Mgr
SMPTE time code readers, generators, inserters, PC tape logging software; color bar, black, sync generators; titler, distribution amplifiers, audio meter & matte generator.

Hotbox Digital
367 N. Hwy. 101, Solana Beach, CA 92075 USA
(858) 292-8520; *Fax:* (858) 292-1812
www.hotboxdigital.com
info@hotboxdigital.com
Adam K, Creative Director/ President
Daniel Kershen, VP/ Artist Bookings
Andy Reid, Label Manager/ A&R
Design & production of bcst 3-D computer graphics. Logo animation, stn packages. All tape formats supported. Producers of Subito Studio Video Graphic Library.

Hotronic Inc.
1875 S. Winchester Blvd., Campbell, CA 95008 US
(408) 378-3883; *Fax:* (408) 378-3888
www.hotronics.com
sales@hotronics.com
Andy Ho, President
Linda Chang, General Sales Mgr
HD/SD/Analog Audio/Video delay from 1 video frame to 5 hrs. Test Signal Generator. HD/SD 8x2 or 4X1 Asynchronized Router with live quad, A/V Multiplexer/Demultiplexer, audio or video converter, Uncompressed digital video recorder/playerTBC/Frame Synchronizer etc.

Hughey & Philips
240 W. Twain Ave., Urbana, OH 43078 US
(877) 285-4466, (937) 652-3500; *Fax:* (937) 652-3508
www.hugheyandphillips.com
oblighting@honeywell.com
Steve Sortillion, Site Leader
Jim Sullivan, VP, Sales & Marketing
Jeff Jacobs, VP Technical Sales & Support
Julian Contreras, Technical Support
Daniel Jackson, Finance
Kay Nance, Customer Support
Tower, obstruction lighting & controls.

ICM (International Crystal Manufacturing)
10 N. Lee Ave., Oklahoma City, OK 73102 US
(405) 236-3741, (800) 725-1426; *Fax:* (405) 235-1904, (800) 322-9426
www.icmfg.com
customerservice@icmfg.com
Royden Freeland, CEO
Royden R. Freeland, Founder
Precision electronic crystals, crystal filters, clock oscillators, TCXO's, VCXO's.

ICM Corporation
6260 Downing St., Denver, CO 80216 USA
(303) 288-8107, (800) 222-2142; *Fax:* (303) 288-4769
www.icmcorp.net/
asutherland@icmcorp.net
Ramon Dempers, President/CEO
Doug Burgess, Co-Founder/CFO
Doug Marcotte, EVP/Sales/Marketing
CablePro's attention to design, material & workmanship produces the highest quality for instal tools.

ICX Global
8206 E. Park Meadows Dr., Lone Tree, CO 80134 USA
(720) 873-8400, (800) 777-2259
www.icxglobal.com
Matt Morgan, Operations Dir
Johhny Iverson, General Manager
Jerry Greenwald, Chief Engineer
Matt Morgan, VP Business Development
Jerry Greenwald, CTO
ICX Global designs, manufactures & markets a wide range of remote control products for bcst, satellite, cable, & consumer electronics devices.
3960 Harlem Rd., Amherst, NY 14226 United States
(716) 839-3803

Ikegami Electronics (U.S.A.) Inc.
Mailing Address: 37 Brook Ave., Maywood, NJ 7607 US
Second Address: 2633 Manhattan Beach Blvd., Redondo Beach, CA 90278
(201) 368-9171, (310) 297-1900; *Fax:* (201) 569-1626, (310) 536-9550
www.ikegami.com/index1.html
Akira Harada, President & CEO
Alan Keil, Chief Engineer
Bcst/professional video cameras, monitors, microwave equipment.
2631 Manhattan Beach Blvd., Manhattan Beach, CA 90273 United States
(310) 297-1900; *Fax:* (310) 536-9550
747 Church Rd., Unit C1, Elmhurst, IL 60126 United States
773 Bearden, Waxahachie, TX 75167 United States
5200 N.W. 33rd Ave., Suite 111, Ft. Lauderdale, FL 33309

Illumination Dynamics Inc.
Mailing Address: 13571 Vaughn Street, San Fernando, CA 91340 USA
Second Address: 3823 Barringer Drive, Charlotte, NC 28217
818-686-6400, (704) 679-9400, (866) 544-4843; *Fax:* 818-686-6776
www.illuminationdynamics.com
info@illuminationdynamics.com
Jeff Pentek, COO
Carly Barber, President
Craig Chiapuzio, Operations Dir
Maria Carpenter, Chief Marketing Officer
Complete line of lighting, grip, generators & power distribution for Feature Film, Television, Commercials, Broadcast & Special Events.
3823 Barringer Drive - Charlotte, NC 28217
704-679-9400

Image Logic Corp.
6807 Brennon Ln., Chevy Chase, MD 20815 US
(301) 907-8891; *Fax:* (301) 652-6584
www.imagelogic.com
Woodrow Landay, President/CEO
Alan Keil, Engineering Director
Rich Johnson, Sr. Field Engineer
Dennis Disinger, Field Engineer
Justin Chang, Field Engineer
Hiroaki Miyazaki, CCTV Engineer
AutoCaption desktop closed captioning & subtitling system for analog, DTV, HDTV, DVD & Web applications. Also Log Producer for video logging.

Image Video
1620 Midland Ave., Toronto, ON M1P 3C2 Canada
(416) 750-8872; *Fax:* (416) 750-8015
www.imagevideo.com
sales@imagevideo.com
Andy Vanags, President
Dave Russell, Operations Dir
Under monitor tally display systems, tally mappers, multi-video display systems & alarm systems..

Imagine Communications Corp.
3001 Dallas Parkway, Suite 300, Frisco, TX 75034 US
(469) 803-4900, (866) 446-2446; *Fax:* (469) 803-4899
www.imaginecommunications.com
insidesales@imaginecommunications.com
Charlie Vogt, President/CEO/Chief Product Officer
Jeff Liening, EVP of Sales Operations
L.R. Sorenson, CFO
Pablo Garguilo, President of Global Sales
Steve Foreman, President of Global Operations and Services
Brian Cabecerias, ChiefStrategy Officer
Sean Huurman, Chief People Officer
Rick Thompson, Chief Information Officer

Imagine Products Inc.
1052 Summit Dr., Carmel, IN 46032 US
(317) 843-0706; *Fax:* (317) 843-0807
www.imagineproducts.com
sales@imagineproducts.com
Dan Montgomery, CEO
M. Jane Montgomery, Operations Dir
Mac and Win software/hardware for logging and video libraries and web sharing. Offloading and proxy creation software.

IMS (Interactive Market Systems Inc.)
The Gig House, Oxford St., Malmesbury, WT SN16 9AX US
(166) 682-6065; *Fax:* (646) 654-5901
www.imsms.com
sales@imsusa.com

George Wishart, CEO
James O Hara, Chief Financial Officer
Barbara Kardas, VP/National Sales
IMS is the leading international provider of info systems & solutions for the media industry. IMS systems & software form an integral part of media & mktg decisions around the world. Media professionals trust IMS for innovative technologies,an unparalled global perspective & valuable insights.

Industrial Acoustics Co., Inc.
Mailing Address: 1160 Commerce Ave., Bronx, NY 10462-5599 US
Second Address: 10635 Brighton Lane, Stafford, TX 77477
(718) 931-8000, (832) 554-0980; *Fax:* (718) 863-1138, (832) 554-0990
www.iac-acoustics.com/us
Kenneth DeLasho, President
Martin Hirschorn, Founder
Complete accu-tone II acoustical environments for bcst industry plus noise-lock sound control doors, windows, walls & silencers.
Walton House, Central Trading Estate, Staines, Middlesex, TW18 4XB
Simon White, Dir Mktg

Hopewell Centre
183 Queen's Rd. E, Rm. 2501, 25/F, Wanchai
557-8633
Alvin Leung Jr, Chairman

Innovision Optics Inc.
1834 Broadway, Santa Monica, CA 90404 US
(310) 453-4866; *Fax:* (310) 453-4677
www.innovisionoptics.com
Mark Centkowski, President
Mark Centkowski, Sales
Randal Rausch, Rentals/ Webmaster
Eliot Hochberg, Webmaster
Remote-controlled Camera Tracking Systems, Specialized HD Lens, HD Cine SpeedCam. Remote controlled camera systems

Inovonics Inc.
5805 Hwy. 9, Felton, CA 95018 US
(831) 458-0552, (800) 733-0552; *Fax:* (831) 458-0554
www.inovonicsbroadcast.com
info@inovonicsbroadcast.com
Jim Wood, President/CEO
Lukas Hurwitz, Sales & Marketing Manager
Wolfgang Reitz, CFO
Jom Wood, Founder
Mark Drake, Founder
Manufacturers of bcst audio signal processing, encoding/decoding, sound recording & instrumentation equipment.

Inscriber Technology Corporation
26 Peppler St., Waterloo, ON N2J 3C4 Canada
(519) 570-9111; *Fax:* (519) 570-9140
Randy Fowlie, COO
Dan Mance, President
Mike Bernhardt, General Sales Mgr
Software for desktop & bcst video markets, including Character generators, digital stores & Video Server/Sequencers

Inscriber Technology-European Rep Office
Zijdsraat 72, 1431 EE Aalsmeer
+31-297-362030; *Fax:* +31-297-380939
David Hughes, Dir European Oper

Inscriber Technology-Asian Rep Office
Level 9, AIG Bldg, 1-1-3 Marunouchi, Chiyoda-ky, Tokyo, 100-0005 Japan
81-3-5288-5237; *Fax:* 81-3-5288-5111
Doug Strable, Dir Oper - Asia Pacific

Insulated Wire Inc. Microwave Products Division
20 E. Franklin St., Danbury, CT 6810 US
(203) 791-1999; *Fax:* (203) 748-5217
John Moredli, President
Ed Lagato, Sales Manager
High-frequency, low-loss microwave cable & cable assemblies featuring IW's Tuf-Flex Series to 60 GHz.

Intelligent Media Technology
4407 Vineland Rd., Suite D18, Orlando, FL 32811 US
(407) 428-1071; *Fax:* (407) 428-1075
Bob Proctor, Chief Engineer
We provide complete Concept-to-Production services for Audio-Video-Data products, including Regulatory Compliance, as an outsource option for clients who need fast Time-to-Market, earlier ROI, and the best in system performance andreliability. Our in-house engineering staff, and substantial cadre of consulting engineers are able to bring many years of experience, from many fields and disciplines, to bear on any given project. When combined with a tightly controlled andsupervised project management plan, IMT is able to offer on-time and in-budget performance. Beyond just product development, IMT also generates a Bill Of Materials very early in the project so that long lead items can be ordered and scheduled forinitial production as soon as the product is cleared from Regulatory Testing, avoiding any lag time in supplying products to the market.

Interface Media Group
1233 20th St. N.W., Washington, DC 20036 US
(202) 861-0500; *Fax:* (202) 296-4492
info@interfacevideo.com
Jeff Weingarten, President
Adam Hurst, EVP
Steve Yerman, Director, Client Services
FACILITY: film transfer/location/studio/motion control, Avid/interformat digital edit, audio, graphics, dubs, Vyvx/3D2/DGS/satellite, standards conversion.

Interlogix
280 Huyler St., South Hackensack, NJ 7606 US
(201) 489-9595; *Fax:* (201) 489-0111
Closed circuit TV cameras, monitors & accessories, specializing in covert surveillance cameras.

Intermed VideoTechnologies, Inc.
18 Commerce Rd., Newtown, CT 6470 USA
(203) 270-9100; *Fax:* (203) 270-9619
www.intermedvideo.com
support@intermedvideo.com
Harry Davies, President
Terry Cavalier, Purchasing Executive
Distribution of video equipment for corporate & industrial use; design & install of TV studios; mfg of video equipment; rsch & engrg.

International Datacasting Corp.
Mailing Address: 50 Frank Nighbor Pl., Kanata, ON K2V 1B9 Canada
Second Address: #100-6215 Ferris Square, San Diego, CA 92121
(613) 596-4120; *Fax:* (613) 596-4863
www.datacast.com
Del Lippert, Chairman
Doug Lowther, President/CEO/Director
Barry Grout, General Sales Mgr
Gary Carter, Chief Engineer
Gary Carter, VP & Chief Technology Officer
Rick Clements, CFO
Walter Capitani, VP of Product management
Virginia Lee Williams, VP of Sales& Marketing
Chris Barrett, VP of Research & Development
Peter Strom, Director
Rsch, dev, manufacture & mktg of value added high speed digital data transmission net & svcs.

International Electro-Magnetics, Inc.
1033A S. Noel Ave., Wheeling, IL 60090 US
(847) 358-4622; *Fax:* (847) 947-8239
www.iemmag.com
Anthony Pretto, President
Standard replacement & custom recording heads for audio, video & film.

Intersil Corp.
1001 Murphy Ranch Rd., Milpitas, CA 95035 US
(408) 432-8888; *Fax:* (408) 432-0640
www.intersil.com
Necip Sayiner, President/CEO
David Loftos, Chief Marketing Officer
Rick Crowley, Senior Vice President and Chief Financial Officer
Philip Chesley, Vice President, Precision Products
Vern Kelley, Senior Vice President, HumanResources
ICs for wireless networking, high performance analog-flat panel displays, optical storage (CD,DVD recordaable) & power mgmt.
2401 Palm Bay Rd., Palm Bay, FL 32905 United States
(321) 724-7000 (888) 486-3774
www.intersil.com
investor@intersil.com
Queen Tower A, 12F 2-3-1, Minato-Mirai, Nishi-ku, Yokohama, 220-5820 Japan
+81 45 682 5820; *Fax:* +81 45 682 5821
The Gateway, 9 Canton Rd., Suite 1506, 15F Tower 6, Tsimshatsui, Kowlon, Hong Kong
+852 2709 7600

IPITEK
2330 Faraday Ave., Carlsbad, CA 92008 US
(760) 438-1010, (888) 447-4835; *Fax:* (760) 438-2412
www.ipitek.com
Michael Salour, Chairman/CEO
Horace Tsiang, General Sales Mgr
Ralph Weeks, Tech Support
William J. Moore, Sr. VP, Corporate Development
Andrew Resnick, Controller

iPromptLA
1220 24th St. #6, Santa Monica, CA 90404 US
(310) 837-0389; *Fax:* (310) 837-0806
www.intelliprompltla.com
tony@iPromptLA.com
Tony Finetti, Owner
Computerized teleprompting svcs.
630 9th Ave., Suite. 907 (corner of 44th & 45th), New York, NY 10036
(212) 765-0555; *Fax:* (888) 504-5047
prompt@intelliprompt.com
Trish Devine, Chairman
44 Tecumseth St., Toronto, ON M5V 2R8 Canada
(888) 504-9535; *Fax:* (888) 504-5047
prompt@intelliprompt.com
Trish Devine, Chairman

IRIS Technologies Inc.
104 Industrial Park Rd., Greensburg, PA 15601 US
(724) 832-9855 (412) 867-1017; *Fax:* (724) 832-8999
www.iristech.com
Jerry Salandro, CEO
Video Commander icon based routing, iNED & SmartPort product lines which allow complete headend control from anywhere in the world.
563 W 500 South, Bountiful, VT 84010 United States
(801) 296-8250; *Fax:* (801) 296-8248

Isaia & Co.
PO Box 668, Hermosa Beach, CA 90254 US
(310) 466-9858; *Fax:* (310) 798-2146
www.isaia.com
matt@isaia.com
Matt Isaia, President
Angenieux Film & Digital Lenses, Runford Baker tripods & heads, Badger camera support, Tango & blue mod accessories.

The ISIS Group
119 E. McKnight Way, Unit A, Grass Valley, CA 95949-9503 US
(888) 622-4747,(530) 477-2984; *Fax:* (530) 477-2986
Bill Stillwaugh, CEO
Jerry Allgood, Test Technician and customer support
Bob Stillwaugh, Sales & Accounting
Jo Alsing, Accounting
Kay Stillwaugh, Office Manager
Mike Schatz, Purchasing
Manufacturer of routing switchers and signal processing equipment.

ITT Cannon Electric
Mailing Address: 666 East Dyer Road, Santa Ana, CA 92705 US
Second Address: 100 New Wood Rd., Watertown, CT 6795
(800) 854-3028, (860) 274-9681; *Fax:* (714) 628-2142, (860) 274-4963
www.ittcannon.com
William Taylor, President
Keith Teichmann, General Sales Mgr
Electronic connectors & interconnect systems & info card technology suppliers to a var of industries, including bcst & data communications companies.

J & R Film Co/Moviola Digital
1135 N. Mansfield Ave., Los Angeles, CA 90038-1109 US
(323) 467-3107; *Fax:* (213) 466-2201
www.moviola.com
Joe Paskal, CEO
Randy Paskal, Executive Vice President
Kathleen Savery, Executive Officer
Melissa Lichtle, CIO/CTO
Film editing equipment, film & video shipping & storage, film-to-video transfer machine.
8000 E. 40th Ave., Denver, CO 80238 United States
(303) 321-1099
Randy Urlik, Exec VP
636 11th Ave., New York, NY 10036 United States
(212) 247-0972
Bob Herman, VP
416 W. Ontario, Chicago, IL 60610 United States
(312) 787-0622
Jeff McNeir, VP

The J-Lab Co.
Box 6530, Malibu, CA 90264 US
(310) 457-4090; *Fax:* (310) 457-4494
www.j-lab.com
Jerry LaBarbera, President
Component accessories, battery-operated video, audio DAs, LCD monitors & portable switchers.

J.A. Taylor & Associates
PO Box 331, Boyertown, PA 19512-0331
(610) 754-6800; *Fax:* (610) 754-9766
www.broadcastassociates.com
info@broadcastassociates.com
John Taylor, President
John A. Taylor III, Associate
Harvey Caplan, Associate
Wes Dooley, AES, Associate
Dudley Freeman, Associate
Lloyd Smithson, Associate
Appraisers & brokers of TV production equipment. Serves video production companies, TV stns & financial institutions.

James Thomas Engineering Inc.
10240 Caneel Dr., Knoxville, TN 37931 USA
(865) 692-3060; *Fax:* (865) 692-9020
www.jthomaseng.com
salesus@jthomaseng.com
Mike Garl, President
Manufacturer of structural aluminum truss, towers & ground supported roof systems. Truss range includes: superlite, supertruss, gen purpose truss, ground support towers, speaker support towers, truss circles & custom fabricated structures.Also manufactures spun aluminum PAR fixtures, pre-wired lighting bars, spot baks & accessories. Distributor of CEEP Multipin connectors, Multicable, Kee Safety pipe fittings, CM Chain Hoists & rigging accessories.

Jampro Antennas Inc.
6340 Sky Creek Dr., Sacramento, CA 95828 US
(916) 383-1177; *Fax:* (916) 383-1182
www.jampro.com
jampro@jampro.com
Doug McCabe, COO
Alex Perchevitch, President
Cyndi Sanderson, Operations Dir
Dane Jubera, Engineering, Sr. Engineer
Doug McCabe, Chief Operations Officer
Cyndi Sanderson, VP (Accounting,Office Manager)
Sonia Del Castillo,Sales/Marketing Administrator
Greg Montano, US Sales
Manufacturers of TV & FM bcst antennas, combiners, filters & a complete line of rigid coaxial transmission line.

JBL Professional
8500 Balboa Blvd., Northridge, CA 91329 US
(818) 894-8850; *Fax:* (818) 830-7801, (818) 830-7865
www.jblpro.com
info@jblpro.com
Mark Terry, CEO
John Carpanini, President
Chief Marketing Officer, Operations Dir
John Sager, Operations
Ed Kamp, Director
Manufacturers of loudspeaker systems for bcstg, recording studios, theaters, concerts, stadiums & other applications.

JC Sound Stages
6670 Lexington Ave., Hollywood, CA 90038 US
(323) 467-7870; *Fax:* (323) 467-7832
www.jcband.com/jcsoundstages.html
jcinhollywood@hotmail.com
J.C. Belanger, President
Cable-controlled camera booms equipped for film or video, rehearsal pre-production recording all in classiest vibe avail anywhere.

JDS Uniphase Corp.
430 N. McCarthy Blvd., Milpitas, CA 95035 USA
(408) 546-5000; *Fax:* (408) 546-4300
www.jdsu.com
Richard E. Belluzzo, Chairman
Thomas Waechter, CEO & President
Rex Jackson, EVP & CFO
Brett Hooper, Human Resources
Judith Kay, Executive Operations & Corporate Strategy
David Heard, Network Service Enablement Business Segment
Andrew Pollack, General Counsel &Secretary
Alan Lowe, Communications & Commercial Optical Products Busin
Test equipment for video nets, including broadband RF & fiber optics. (SLMs, system analyzers, leakage, sweeps & OTDRs) software.

Jennings Technology Co.
1025 South Brown School Rd., Vandalia, OH 45377 US
(937) 415-0000; *Fax:* (937) 415-0600
www.jenningstech.com
sales@jenningstech.com
Steve Randazzo, President
Gary Marsh, Regional Sales Manager
Donna Laundrie, Customer Service Manager
Jeff Hilderbrand, Regional Sales Manager
Martin Bird, Global Sales Manager
High-voltage vacuum & gas capacitors; relays, switches, single- & three-phase contactors & instruments.

Jensen Transformers Inc.
9304 Deering Ave., Chatsworth, CA 91311 US
(818) 374-5857; *Fax:* (818) 374-5856
www.jensen-transformers.com
Bill Whitlock, President
Audio transformers, ISO-MAX audio & video ground isolation boxes

JNJ Industries Inc.
290 Beaver Street, Franklin, MA 2038 US
(508) 553-0529, (800) 554-9994; *Fax:* (508) 553-9973
www.jnj-industries.com
sales@jnj-industries.com
Jack Volpe, President
Gail Howe, Operations Dir
Bob Enterkin, Promotions Manager
CFC & HCFC free solvents, presaturated cloth wipes, spray bottles, dry cloth wipes, lens wipes; aqueous chemistries ; industrial & precision cleaning products.

JOA Cartridge Service
448 E. Hancock St., Lansdale, PA 19446 US
(215) 362-8796, (888) 562-8273; *Fax:* (215) 368-2336
www.joaonline.com
Mark Molyneaux, President
Bcst audiotape cartridges, audio, videotape, cassettes, tape accessories, DAT tape, cassettes, data storage diskettes, cassettes, optical disks, recordable CDs & reloading svc.

JSB Service Co.
204 S. Bayard Ave., Waynesboro, VA 22980 USA
(540) 949-5899, (877) 668-2634; *Fax:* (540) 949-5863
www.jsbservice.com
sale.jsb@cfw.com
Joseph Brumbelow, CEO
Paul Bosak, Operations Manager
Since 1977, JSB Service Company has been servicing most makes and models of microwave radio systems, modules and components. We repair all makes and models of major broadcast equipment that is no longer supported by the manufacturer or thatis out of warranty. We also repair new equipment. Cable, Satellite, Telephone and Television companies are among our customers. JSB Service Company also assists manufacturers in the service of their customers. Our goal to keep your present equipmenton-line! Rather than buy a new system, send JSB your equipment for service and save thousands of dollars.

JVC Professional Products Company
Mailing Address: 1700 Valley Road, Wayne, NJ 7470 US
Second Address: 2201 E. Dominguez St., Long Beach, CA 90810
(973) 317-5000, (800) 252-5722; *Fax:* (973) 317-5030
pro.jvc.com/splash.jsp
Bob Mueller, CEO
Kirk Hirota, President
Plasmas; full line of professional video equipment including digital VTRs cameras, monitors & projectors.
705 Enterprise St., Aurora, IL 60504-8149 United States
(630) 851-7809
Chris Dalaly, Branch Mgr
1700 Valley Rd., Wayne, NJ 07470 United States
(973) 317-5000
Paul Kasparian, Branch Mgr
5665 Corporate Ave., Cypress, CA 90630 United States
(714) 229-8024
Eric Rosenberg, Rgnl Sls Mgr

Kalun Communications Inc.
30 Todd Rd., Scarborough, ON M1S 2J9 Canada
(416) 410-4138; *Fax:* (416) 410-4138
Paul Wong, Chief Engineer
RF test equipment including wideband sweep generators, sweep comparator, switched attenuator, return loss bridge, detector & headend equipment for ATSC

Kangaroo Products Inc.
10845 Wheatlands Ave., Suite C, Santee, CA 92071-2856 US
(619) 562-9696; *Fax:* (619) 449-7244
www.kangarooproducts.com
sales@kangarooproducts.com
Steve Leiserson, President
Nancy Byrd, VP, Human Resources
Custom contract carrying cases.

Kathrein Inc., Scala Division
Mailing Address: 555 Airport Rd., Medford, OR 97504 USA
Second Address: PO Box 4580, Medford, OR 97501
(541) 779-6500; *Fax:* (541) 779-3991
www.kathrein-scala.com
Manfred Muenzel, President
Judy Young, General Sales Mgr
Michael Bach, Sales Engineer
Antennas & filters, low to full power, includes STL/TSL, LPTV, CATV, RPU, translator & FM/TV monitoring. Custom patterns our specialty.

Kay Industries Inc.
604 N. Hill St., South Bend, IN 46617 US
(574) 936-9374, (800) 348-5257; *Fax:* (574) 289-5932
www.kayind.com
phasemaster@kayind.com
John Colage, Managing Executive
Rotary phase converters for single phase to three phase power.

Keywest Technology
14563 W. 96th Terr., Lenexa, KS 66215 USA
(800) 331-2019, (913) 492-4666; *Fax:* (913) 322-1864
www.keywesttechnology.com
info@keywesttechnology.com
Wes Dixon, General Sales Mgr
Markus Lubick, Contact
Manufacturer of automated media servers, loc origination ch, LO ch, media player, CATV character generators, logo & ID inserters.

KFYR-TV
200 N. Fourth St., Bismarck, ND 58501 USA
(701) 255-5757, (701) 255-8105, (701) 255-8124, (7; *Fax:* (701) 255-8220
www.kfyrtv.com
Dick Heidt, General manager
Barry Schumaier, General Sales Manager
Jim Sande, Programming Director
Monica Hannan, News Director/ Anchor
Brian Funk, Chief Engineer
Kevin Lawrence, Chief Meterologist
Lisa Larson, MarketingConsultant
Angela Morrell, Projects & Sales Coordinator
Lee Ellison, Commercial Photographer
Wayne Wolff, Creative Services
Mary Cate Mannion, Anchor/ Reporter

Kidde-Fenwal Inc.
400 Main St., Ashland, MA 1721 US
(508) 881-2000; *Fax:* (508) 881-7619
www.kidde-fenwal.com
John Sullivan, President
Kevin Barron, Operations Dir
Kate Houghton, Chief Marketing Officer
Jim Livingstone, Chief Technical Officer
High-speed fire protection systems.

Kintronic Labs Inc.
Box 845, Bristol, TN 37621 US
(423) 878-3141; *Fax:* (423) 878-4224
www.kintronic.com
ktl@kintronic.com
Louis King, CEO
Tom King, President, General Manager
Gwen King, Operations Dir
Gwen King, Vice President
James R. Moser, Engineering
Larry Arnold, Engineering
Thomas F. King, Engineering
Robert A. Elder, Engineering
Bobby L.Cox, Engineering
AM matching & directional antenna phasing systems, AM multiplexers, transmitter combiners, AM dummy loads, isocouplers, passive RF components & transmission lines.

Knox Video
8547 Grovemont Cir., Gaithersburg, MD 20877 USA
(301) 840-5805; *Fax:* (301) 840-2946
sales@knoxvideo.com
Ted Neiman, President
Ken Nottingham, Promotions Manager
Electronic bulletin bd for video messages. VCR control units. Full matrix routing switches.

Konica Minolta Business Solutions USA Inc
100 Williams Drive, Ramsey, NJ 7446 USA
(201) 825-4000; *Fax:* (201) 529-6070
www.minoltausa.com
Masatoshi Matsuzaki, President & CEO
CRT & LCD color analyzing instrumentation.

EQUIPMENT MANUFACTURERS

L-3 Communications Telemetry East
Mailing Address: 1515 Grundy Lane, Bristol, PA 19007 US
Second Address: 600 Third Avenue, New York, NY 10016
(267) 545-7000, (212) 697-1111; *Fax:* (267) 545-0100, (212) 490-0731
www.l-3com.com
Michael T. Strianese, Chairman/President/Chief Executive Officer
Frank Lanza, CEO
Marc Lienard, President
Doug Crawford, Business Development
Todd Warton, Business Development
Robert Holland, Engineering/Technical
Lewis Kramer,Chairman of the Audit Committee
Alan H. Washkowitz, Chairman of the Nominating/Corporate Governance Co
Robert B. Millard, Lead Director
Claude R. Canizares, Member of the Audit Committee
Thomas A. Corcoran, Member of the Audit Committee
Lloyd W. Fig Newton, Member of the Compensation Committee
Manufacturer of satellite receiving systems, antennas, telemetry receiving systems, ancillary equipment, communications for aerospace & defense.

LARCAN
Mailing Address: 228 Ambassador Dr., Mississauga, ON L5T 2J2 Canada
Second Address: 1390 Overlook Dr., Lafayette, CO 80026
(905) 564-9222, (303) 665-8000; *Fax:* (905) 564-9244, (303) 673-9900
www.larcan.com
sales@larcan.com
Jim Adamson, General Sales Mgr
LARCAN is a full service Broadcast Solutions company. LARCAN innovates, designs, and manufactures superior Analog and Digital television transmitters for wireless and broadcast markets worldwide. We specialize in Custom Network Planning andRF Synergies for Broadcast and Mobile Video / DVB-H technologies. LARCAN offers 'End to End' engineering solutions in Solid State VHF, UHF, High Power IOT transmitters, as well as Low Power transmitters / translators and FM Solutions. We offer thebest in broadcast innovations and transmitters from 1W to 100kW strong, and provide a wealth of broadcast solutions and services designed with the right fit for you. Look to LARCAN for Truly Made to Measure Solutions.

LARCAN USA
1360 Overlook Dr., #2, Lafayette, CO 80026

LARCAN USA Inc
Mailing Address: 1390 Overlook Dr., Lafayette, CO 80026 USA
Second Address: 228 Ambassador Dr., Mississauga, ON L5T 2J2
(303) 665-8000, (905) 564-9222; *Fax:* (303) 673-9900, (905) 564-9244
www.larcan.com
sales@larcan.com
David Hale, Chairman
Jim Adamson, President
Repair & sls of high power UHF TV transmitters, low power TV transmitters & translators, FM transmitters & translators & AC line surge protectors.

LBA Technology Inc.
3400 Tupper Drive, Greenville, NC 27834 US
(800) 522-4464, (252) 757-0279; *Fax:* (252) 752-9155
www.lbagroup.com
lbatech@lbagroup.com
Lawrence Behr, CEO
Jerry Brown, President & COO
Javier Castillo, Operations Dir
Mark G. Fehlig, Sr. Engineer
Juliana A. Price, Controller- Business Manager
Chris K. Horne, Chief Technical Officer
Mike Britner, VP of Sales
Michael W. Hayden, Director of Site-Services
Byron Johnson, Business Developer
Betty Perez, Dir, of logistics & Resources
Design & manufacture medium wave antenna systems marketed worldwide, including folded unipole antennas, tuning units, transmitter combiners, diplexers, triplexers, RF components & collocation equiptment.

LEA International
4726 Eisenhower Blvd, Tampa, FL 33634 US
(813) 621-1324; *Fax:* (813) 621-8980
Shawn Thompson, President
Travis Coffey, General Manager
Dave Stimmel, Chief Financial Officer
Manufacturers of transient voltage surge suppression & power conditioning equipment.

10701 Airport Dr., Hayden Lake, ID 83835
(800) 881-8506; *Fax:* (208) 762-6099

Leader Instruments Corp.
1501 E. Orangethorpe Avenue, Suite 140, Fullerton, CA 92831-5252 US
(714) 527-9300, (800) 645-5104; *Fax:* (714) 527-7490
www.leaderamerica.com
sales@leaderamerica.com
Hiro Sawa, President
Maria Magbanua, Chief Administrative Officer
Electronic test equipment for video, audio, RF, microwave, oscilloscopes & gen use.
6484 Commerce Dr, Cypress, CA 90630 United States
(714) 527-9300

Lectrosonics Inc.
581 Laser Rd. NE, PO Box 15900, Rio Rancho, NM 87124 US
(505) 892-4501, (800) 821-1121; *Fax:* (505) 892-6243
www.lectrosonics.com
sales@lectrosonics.com
Larry Fisher, President
Wes Herron, Station Manager
Gordon Moore, General Sales Mgr
Bruce Jones, Promotions Manager
Bob Cunnings, Chief Engineer
Wireless microphone & IFB systems for bcst, motion picture & tele-product applications. Automatic sound mixers & audio signal processing equipment.

Leightronix Inc.
2330 Jarco Dr., Holt, MI 48842 US
(800) 243-5589, (517) 694-8000; *Fax:* (517) 694-1600
www.leightronix.com
David Leighton, President
Video Servers & TV Automation.

Leitch & Co.
1607 Abram Court, San Leandro, CA 94577 US
(800) 999-8485, (510) 483-2323; *Fax:* (510) 483-2366
mmalone@inter-tool.com
Paula Moore, General Manager
Tom Jordan, General Sales Mgr
Don Thompson, Promotions Manager
Audio & video distribution amplifiers, sync generators, clock systems & timers, synchronizers, test equipment, still storage, scramblers & descramblers. Audio, video, digital & data routing switchers, terminations, serial digital products.

Leitch Technology Corp.
150 Ferrand Dr., Suite 700, Toronto, ON M3C 3E5 Canada
(416) 445-9640 (800) 387-0233
John Nielson, South Central Rgnl Sls Mgr

Lemco Tool Corp.
1850 Metzger Ave., Cogan Station, PA 17728-8351 US
(570) 494-0620, (800) 233-8713; *Fax:* (570) 494-0860
toolinfo@lemco-tool.com
Mike Miller, President
Designers & manufacturers of mechanical tools, for the construction & maintenance of CATV systems. Also coaxial cables and cell tower networks.

LEMO USA Inc.
Mailing Address: 635 Park Court, Rohnert Park, CA 94928 US
Second Address: 44 East Beaver Creek Rd., Unit 20, Richmond Hill, ON L4B 1G8
(707) 578-8811, (905) 889-5678; *Fax:* (707) 578-0869, (905) 889-4970
www.lemo.com
Julie Carson, General Manager
Michael Greico, General Sales Mgr
Julie Carlson, Promotions Manager
LEMO designs & manufactures precision custom connection solutions. LEMO developed the 3K.93C series connector which is now the SMPTE standard for natl & international bcst companies.

Leviton NSI Colortran
Mailing Address: 20497 S.W. Teton, Tualatin, OR 97062 US
Second Address: 2222 - 222nd Street S.E., Bothell, WA 98021-4422
(503) 404-5500,(800) 576-6060, (800) 736-6682; *Fax:* (503) 404-5600, (503) 404-5594
www.leviton.com
pauls@leviton.com
Harold Leviton, President
Paul Sherbo, General Sales Mgr
Lighting fixtures & control devices for theater, TV & architectural applications.

Lightning Eliminators & Consultants Inc.
6687 Arapahoe Rd., Boulder, CO 80303 US
(303) 447-2828, (800) 521-6101; *Fax:* (303) 447-8122
www.lightningprotection.com
info@lecglobal.com
Avram Saunders, CEO
Peter Carpenter, President
Joanna Silberman, Marketing
Peter A. Carpenter, EVP, Director of Applied Engineering
Joe Lanzoni, V.P. of Operations
Lee B. Howard, Program Manager
Kirk S. Chynoweth, P.E., Directorof Engineering
Gary Williams, Controller
Designers & manufacturers of lightning strike prevention, grounding & power conditioning systems.

Lightning Master Corp.
1770 Calumet St., Clearwater, FL 33765 US
(877) 334-8006; *Fax:* (727) 499-0138
www.lightningmaster.com
Bruce A. Kaiser, Owner
Tom Lewellyn, Sales Executive
Richard Beatie, Chief Engineer
Structural lightning protection equipment, dissipator technology, transient voltage surge suppression, bonding & grounding products, consulting svcs; site survey, analysis & training.

Lightning Prevention Systems
154 Cooper Rd., Unit 1201, West Berlin, NJ 8091 US
(856) 767-7806, (888) 667-8745; *Fax:* (856) 767-7547
www.lpsnet.com
info@lpsnet.com
Pat McLaughlin, CEO
Ian E. Fawthrop, President
Manufactures equipment utilizing point discharge technology to remove the lightning attractive static charge on towers or structures that they're on, preventing lightning strikes.

Lindsay Broadband Inc.
2035-2 Fisher Dr. #5, Peterborough, ON K9J 6X6 Canada
(705) 742-1350, (800) 465-7046; *Fax:* (705) 742-7669
www.lindsaybroadbandinc.com
Linda Curtin, CFO
David Atman, President
David Hayford, Operations Dir
Jonathan Haight, General Sales Mgr
Laurie Matthews, Customer Support
A diverse range of last mile communication products, including Wi-Fi & mesh wireless systems, hard line passives, trunk, distribution amplifiers, free space optic systems, headend & subscriber passives, a range of MDU amplifers with UPSoptions, mini optical nodes, WDM fiber optic equipment & NRBS/MEF compliant media converters. Markets & sell to the worldwide telecommunications market.

Linear Acoustic Inc.
108 Foxshire Drive, Suite 110, Lancaster, PA 17603 USA
(717) 735-3611; *Fax:* (717) 735-3612, (201) 931-6687
www.linearacoustic.com
sales@linearacoustic.com
Tim Carroll, President
Christina Carroll, General Sales Mgr
Guy Huffard, Marketing Director

LINK Electronics Inc.
2137 Rust Ave., Cape Girardeau, MO 63703-7668 US
(573) 334-4433, (573) 382-2381; *Fax:* (573) 334-9255
www.linkelectronics.com
Bob Henson, President/CEO
Dave Aufdenberg, Operations Dir
Ellen Henson, Executive Vice President
James Timberlake, VP Operations
Manufacturer of Sync Generators, system timing, audio & video DAs, power amps, encoders, decoders, video processing, test equipment & video presence detectors, closed caption encoders, decoders, video switchers, routers for analog, SDI HD,digital distribution & conversion. Closed caption encoders for analog SD HD SDI, Up/Down/Cross Conversion, frame syncs.

LINK Electronics Inc.-Northeast & Southeast Rgnl S
2 W. Laurelwood Dr., Lawrenceville, NJ 08648 United States
(573) 257-9473
raybouchard@aol.com
Ray Bouchard, Rgnl Mgr-N.E. & S.W. Rgns

Lipsner-Smith
4700 Chase, Lincolnwood, IL 60712-1689 US
(847) 677-3000, (800) 323-7520; *Fax:* (847) 677-1311, (800) 784-6733
www.lipsner.com
sales@lipsner.com
Ray Short, CEO & President
Bill Wolavka, VP, RTI Sales
Jonathan Banks, President, RTI Film Group

Matthew Malone, CFO
Mark Trough, Traffic Manager
Kate Buzzell, Purchasing
Mike Swain, Service Manager
Jeff Kao, Technical SuportManager
Motion Picture Film Laboratory Equipment.

Location Sound Corp.
10639 Riverside Dr., North Hollywood, CA 91602 US
(818) 980-9891, (800) 228-4429; *Fax:* (818) 980-9911, (818) 980-7932
www.locationsound.com
salesdept@locationsound.com
Robert Noone, General Manager
Steve Joachim, General Sales Mgr
Angelica Dewlow, Marketing Director
Dealer of professional audio & communications solutions for film, video, broadcast, business, institutional & recording applications. Over 30 years experience.

Lockheed Martin Gyrocam Systems, LLC
7345 16th Street East, Suite 101, Sarasota, FL 34243 USA
(407) 356-6500, (800) 543-8947; *Fax:* (941) 355-3417
www.gyrocamsystems.com
Gyrocam.Info@lmco.com
Marillyn A. Hewson, President/CEO
Stefanie Kowitt, Station Manager
Joe Stark, General Sales Mgr
Bruce L. Tanner, Executive Vice President/Chief Financial Officer
Richard F. Ambrose, Executive Vice President-Space Systems
Sondra L.Barbour, Executive Vice President-Information Systems & Glo
Dale P. Bennett, Executive Vice President-Mission Systems and Train
Orlando P. Carvalho, Executive Vice President-Aeronautics
Patrick M. Dewar, Executive Vice President-Lockheed MartinInternati
Manufacturer of the Gyrocam-gyrostablized camera systems for aircraft, boats or vehicles. High Definition Cameras & V700 watt searchlight also available.

Logitek Electronic Systems Inc
5622 Edgemoor Dr., Houston, TX 77081 US
(713) 664-4470, (800) 231-5870, (877) 231-5870; *Fax:* (713) 664-4479
www.logitekaudio.com
Tag Borland, President
Frank Grundstein, General Sales Mgr
Digital audio consoles, digital audio routers & audio level indicators (meters).

Lowel-Light Manufacturing Inc.
90 Oser Avenue, Hauppauge, NY 11788 US
(631) 273-2500; *Fax:* (631) 273-2557
lowel.tiffen.com
info@lowel.com
Dale Marks, General Sales Mgr
Toni Pearl, Dealer Liaison
Eric Drucker, Eastern Sales Executive
Don Youngberg, Midwest Sales
Lights, controls, mounts & kits for imaging professionals, innovatively designed & built for rugged dependable use, ease of operation and portability.

Luxor
2245 Delany Rd., Waukegan, IL 60087 US
(800) 323-4656; *Fax:* (847) 244-1818
www.luxorfurn.com
Robert Raw, General Manager
Bill Gamber, General Sales Mgr
Randy Douglas, Director
Computer stands, A/V equipment stands, conference room furniture, TV stands, library, office furniture, ceiling, wall universal & projector mounts.

M/A-COM Technology Solutions Inc.
100 Chelmsford Street, Lowell, MA 1851 US
(978) 656-2500, (800) 366-2266; *Fax:* (978) 442-5350
www.macom.com
John Ocampo, Chairman & Director
John Croteau, CEO & President
Robert Dennehy, VP of Operations
Suja Ramnath, General Manager & VP
Jack Kennedy, VP of Sales
Michael Murphy, VP of Engineering
Conrad Gagnon, CFO
RF microwave & mm wave components & subsystems.

Magna-Tech Electronic Co
1998 N.E. 150th St., North Miami, FL 33181 US
(305) 573-7339; *Fax:* (305) 573-8101
www.myiceco.com
Steven H. Krams, President
Dara Reusch, Operations Dir
Julio Urbay, VP/International Sales
Julio Urbay, Sales & Marketing
Arturo Quintero, Architechtural Design & Development
Dara Reusch, Vice President
Roger Rodriguez,Crating
Francisco Blanco, VP of Tecnnical Services
Barnet (Barney) L. Kaufman, VP 21st Century Cinemas
Pablo Blanco Jr., Technician
Offered 16mm, 35mm, 70mm film projection equipment, film-to-tape transfer equipment, sound systems & editing equipment.

Magna-Tech Electronic Co. Inc.
1998 N.E. 150th St., North Miami, FL 33181 US
(305) 573-7339; *Fax:* (305) 573-8101
www.myiceco.com
Allen Lasky, CEO
Steven Krams, President
Barnet Kaufman, Operations Dir
Manufactures professional motion picture sound recording, reproducing & projection equipment, film recorders & reproducers; 16 & 35mm recorders, telecine followers, counters, pre amps, dubbers & looping systems.readers.

Magnum Towers Inc.
9370 Elder Creek Rd., Sacramento, CA 95829 US
(916) 381-5053; *Fax:* (916) 381-2144
magnumtowers.com
jeff@magnumtowers.com
Ron Craig Kardokus, President
Jeff Styler, Operations Dir
Lori Morris, General Manager
Pete Smith, Founder
Radio, TV & microwave towers.

Manfrotto Distribution, Inc
10 Mountainview Road, Suite 320 South, Upper Saddle River, NJ 7458 US
(201) 818-9500; *Fax:* (201) 818-9177
www.bogenimaging.us
info@manfrottodistribution.us
Stev Romanick, CEO/COO
Paul Wild, President
Kriss Brumgardener, General Manager
Mark Bender, General Sales Mgr
Paul Wagner, Sales Director
Manfrotto Distribution is a wholly owned subsidiary of the Vitec Group, headquartered and listed on the UK stock exchange. The primary mission of Manfrotto Distribution is to import and distribute the brands designed and manufactured by thePhotographic Division of Vitec; Gitzo, Manfrotto, Avenger, Kata and National Geographic as well as top brands of imaging-related products to our extensive Authorized Dealer network.

Marathon Norco Aerospace, Inc.
Div/DBA: Christie Electric Div.
8301 Imperial Drive, Waco, TX 76712 US
(254) 776-0650; *Fax:* (254) 776-6558
www.mnaerospace.com
marathon@mptc.com
Jack Stiffer, President
Clay Collins, General Manager
Deanne Hollenback, General Sales Mgr
CASP universal battery support systems & AC/DC power supplies.

Maritz Inc.
1375 North Highway Dr., Fenton, MO 63099 US
(877) 462-7489, (636) 827-4000, (636) 827-1000; *Fax:* (636) 827-8605
www.maritz.com
Steve Maritz, Chairman & CEO
Scott Wingenbach, Vice President
Steve Bowen, Operations Dir
Communications, film/video training, business meetings & mktg.

Marketron Broadcast Solutions
Mailing Address: 101 Empty Saddle Trail, Hailey, ID 83333 US
Second Address: 1624 Market, Suite 204, Denver, CO 80202
(208) 788-6800; *Fax:* (208) 788-6273
www.marketron.com
sales@marketron.com
Gary Coats, COO
Jeff Haley, President/CEO
Tony Gaughan, Chief Technical Officer
Jerome Hollus, Sales/Marketing
Deborah Esayian, Chief Revenue Officer/Co-President of Marketron In
Rey Mena, Co-President- Marketron Interactive
JeffLondon, Senior Vice President of Client Services
Tony Gaughan, Senior Vice President Products/Chief Technology Of
Martin Kristiseter, Vice President of Mobile Solutions
Walter Denekas, Chief Financial Officer
Marketron is the media industry's leading provider of business software solutions and services. Marketron develops and supports advanced software systems for radio operations, traffic, billing, and reporting functions.
Toronto, ON Canada
Opelika, AL
San Francisco, CA
Denver, CO

Marketron Broadcast Solutions
Mailing Address: 508 S. 7th St., Opelika, AL 36801 USA
Second Address: 101 Empty Saddle Trail, Hailey, ID 83333
(800) 476-7226, (208) 788-6800; *Fax:* (208) 788-6273
www.marketron.com
Jeff Haley, President & CEO
Bill Price, General Manager
Walt Denekas, CFO
Tony Gaughan, CTO & SVP Products
Deb Esayian, Chief Revenue Officer
Jeff London, SVP Client services
Emily Stephens, Director of Marketing
MartinKristiseter, VP Mobile Solutions

Marshall Electronics
1910 E. Maple Ave., El Segundo, CA 90245 US
(310) 333-0606, (800) 800-6608; *Fax:* (310) 333-0688
www.marshall-usa.com
support@marshall-usa.com
Leonard Marshall, CEO
Nathan Mordukhay, President
Rob Foster, Sales Director
Provides the hightest quality products to the bcst, video & music recording markets. Products include cable, connectors, Mogami superflex wire, cable, Tajimi connectors & LCD bcst monitors. Marshall also specializes in mfg optics microphones& multimedai devices.

Martinsound Inc.
1151 W. Valley Blvd., Alhambra, CA 91803-2493 USA
(626) 281-3555, (800) 582-3555; *Fax:* (626) 284-3092
www.martinsound.com
info@martinsound.com
Joe Martinson, President
Sharon Michael, Operations Dir
Doug Osborne, General Manager
Complete line of audio control consoles for music recording, bcst, & video postproduction applications. MultiMax surround monitor control system, flying faders console automation, Martech MSS-10 precision microphone preamplifier.

Masterclock, Inc.
2484 W. Clay St., St. Charles, MO 63301 US
(800) 940-2248, (636) 724-3666; *Fax:* (636) 724-3776
www.masterclock.com
sales@masterclock.com
William Clark, President
Masterclock systems! Accurate gps time! Network time, Power Over Ethernet & Time Code. Industrial grade generators, pci cards, analog & digital clocks. Extensive experience in the bcst industry. Designed & products in the U.S.A.

MATCO Inc.
Mailing Address: 100 Business Center Dr., Pittsburgh, PA 15205 US
Second Address: 7002 North 288th, Valley, NE 68064
(800) 221-9090, (412) 788-1263, (877) 359-6114; *Fax:* (408) 353-8781
info@matcoinc.com
David Harbert, President
Rita Harbert, General Manager
Playback automation, coml insertion, & machine control systems for bcst, cable & coml, industrial & medical. MPEG 2 video servers with automation software options.

Matrox Electronic Systems Ltd.
1055 St. Regis Blvd., Dorval, QC H9P 2T4 Canada
(514) 822-6364, (800) 361-4903, (514) 685-2036, (5; *Fax:* (514) 685-2853
www.matrox.com/video
video.info@matrox.com
Amantha Citia, Sales Director
Emmy award-winning technology & mktg leader in the field of digital video hardware for accelerated H.264 encoding, realtime editing, DVD/Blu-ray authoring & web streaming.

EQUIPMENT MANUFACTURERS

Matthews Studio Equipment Inc. (MSE)
4250 West Valerio Street, Burbank, CA 91505 US
(818) 843-6715, (800) CE-STAND; *Fax:* (323) 843-7419
www.msegrip.com
info@msegrip.com
Ed Phillips, President & Owner
Linda Swope, Sales Manager
Robert Kulesh, VP Sales & Marketing
Tyler Philips, Marketing
Daniel Flores, Sales Assistant
Pamela Hoffman, Account Manager
Sheira Whetstone, Account Manager Assistant
TV camera support dollies, land tripods, studio pedestals, pan/tilt heads, cases.

MAVRIC Media Inc.
117 Church St., Roseville, CA 95678
(800) 804-7756; *Fax:* (888) 453-8870
Garland Bell, Vice President/Chief Operating Officer
Don Smith, Founder & President
Garland Bell, VP/COO
Gene Marcucci, Chief Financial Officer
Ryan Sundberg, Director of Software Development and Support
Hosted, web-based asset mgmt & content delivery tools.

Maxell Corp. of America
3 Garret Mountain Plaza, 3rd Floor, Suite#300, Woodland Park, NJ 07424-3352 US
(800) 533-2836, (973) 653-2400, (800) 377-5887; *Fax:* (201) 796-8790
www.maxellpromedia.com
techsupp@maxell.com
Masaru Kanemoto, President
Blank audio & video recording tape for professional bcstrs & duplicators.

Maze Corporation
3867 Rock Ridge Rd., Irondale, AL 35210-3797 US
(205) 706-2080, (818) 237-5730; *Fax:* (205) 956-6328
Vira Maze, President
Tamara Syinn, Secretary
Remarketers of TV & video equipment.

McCurdy Radio Ltd.
75 First St., Suite 108, Orangeville, ON L9W 5B6 Canada
(416) 248-6155; *Fax:* (416) 248-6755
Paul Hudson, President
Bob Hudson, General Manager
Audio monitors & meters.
1051 Clinton St., Buffalo, NY 14206 United States

MCG Surge Protection
12 Burt Dr., Deer Park, NY 11729 US
(631) 586-5125, (800) 851-1508; *Fax:* (631) 586-5120
www.mcgsurge.com
info1@mcgsurge.com
Christine Jelley, CEO
Sue Baron, Sales Manager
Sue Baron, General Sales Mgr
Diane Lanciotti, CFO
Anthony Biondo, Sales Associate
Dion Neri, Engineering Design
Glenn Clifford, Engineering Design
Surge protectors for AC power lines, telephone/signal & data lines. Protecting industry since 1967.

MCL Inc.
501 S. Woodcreek Dr., Bolingbrook, IL 60440-4999 US
(630) 759-9500; *Fax:* (630) 759-5018
www.cpii.com
sales@mcl.com
David Krautheimer, President
John Harrington, Vice President
Satellite communication fixed & mobile High Power Amplifiers in C-band, X-Band, Ku-band, DBS, V-Band, Ka-Band & Multi-Band.

Media Computing Inc.
Box 4169, Cave Creek, AZ 85327-4169 US
(602) 614-2091
www.mediacomputing.com
MichaelRich@MediaComputing.comÿ
Michael Rich, CEO
Kathryn Hulka, Operations Dir
ANGIS-PC-based software automatically updates displays on characters generators & web pages with real-time data like elections, news tickers, closing.

Media Concepts Inc.
348 Elm St., Sudbury, ON P3C 1V8 US
(705) 688-1969; *Fax:* (705) 688-1901
www.mediaconcepts.ca
Leo Duquette, President/Owner
Jo-Ann Philipow, Vice-President/Owner
Chantal Muskovac, Designer
Video duplication, international video standards conversion, CD-Rom duplication, DVD duplication authoring. Macrovision copy-protection.

Mediasoft Inc.
7301 N. Broadway Ext., Suite 120, Oklahoma City, OK 73116-9038 US
(405) 607-2000; *Fax:* (405) 607-2071
www.mediasoftusa.com
Bob Alfson, CEO
Dave Easley, General Sales Mgr
Microcomputer products & svcs.

Mediastar, Inc.
702 Mangrove Ave., #221, Chico, CA 95926 USA
(530) 826-3342, (530) 82-MEDIA; *Fax:* (530) 898-9588
www.mediastar-sg.com
general@mediastar-sg.com
Ken Danner, Promotions Manager
Multimedia production systems for cable TV, bcst, PEG & corporate TV. Pre & post-launch consulting, training & sls seminars. Repair & support svcs for all competitors' products. Data recovery svcs.

Mega Hertz
4100 International Plaza, Suite 150, Fort Worth, TX 76109 USA
(800) 883-8839, (800) 628-0088, (817) 529-9898; *Fax:* (817) 529-0745
www.go2mhz.com
sales@go2mhz.com
Doug Sherar, Promotions Manager
Dave Adams, Regional Account Manager
Guy LeVassar, Director of Business Development
Steve Grossman, Product Manager
Doug Sherar, Marketing Manager
Robert Wilson, Integrated Services Group Manager
Jim Feola, Integrated Services Group Manager
Mega Hertz is a Value-Added-Reseller of Unique Multi-Vendor System Solutions that support the deployment of advanced technologies in hybrid Fiber/Coax Braodband Networks. MHz ƒ?oEngineering & Integration Groupƒ?? provides pre-saleEngineering, Design, Project Management, Installation, Activation & Training, as well, as Level 1 product support for MHz advanced video, voice and data end2end solutions.

Megastar Inc.
4709 Compass Bow Ln., Las Vegas, NV 89130 US
(702) 386-2844; *Fax:* (702) 388-1250
www.1megastar.com
Jim Foy, CEO
Nigel Macrae, President
Reseller, earth stations & all support equipment, c band transceivers.

MEGGER
2621 Van Buren Ave., Norristown, PA 19403 US
(610) 676-8500; *Fax:* (610) 676-8610
www.megger.com
sales@megger.com
Keiser Carvel, CEO/COO
Mark Snopek, President
Greame Thomson, Vice President
Cable fault-locating equipment & other electrical testing instruments.

Memorex Products Inc.
1 Imation Wayÿ, Oakdale, MN 55128-3414ÿ US
(888) 466-3456; *Fax:* (888) 704-4200
generaling@memorex.com
Michael Golacingki, CEO
Brad Yeager, Director, Product Marketing
Scott Stroup, Operations Dir
Brad Yeager, Director of Product Marketing
Adrian Degado, Director of Sales- Latin Sales
Nathan A. Cammack, Manager
Al Day,SalesDirector- US Eastern region
Memorex is a manufacturer, marketer of consumer media & computer products.

Meridian Design Associates, Architects
Mailing Address: 1140 Broadway, New York, NY 10001 USA
Second Address: 10630 NW 27 Street, Miami, FL 33172
(212) 431-8643, (305) 362-7663; *Fax:* (212) 431-8775
www.meridiandesign.com
info@meridiandesign.com
Antonio Argibay, Founder
Bice C Wilson, Founder
Luis Rogers, Principal
Robert Milkie, Principal
Antonio Argibay, AIA, LEED AP, Principal
Bice C. Wilson, AIA, Principal
Luis J. Roges, AAIA, Contact
Robert H. Milkie, Contact
Architectural firm specializing in the design of bcst & media facilities.
907 S.W. 79th Ave., Miami, FL 33144 United States
(305) 262-7663; *Fax:* (305) 262-7675
Antonio Argibay, Chairman

Merlin Engineering Works Inc.
1888 Embarcadero Rd., Palo Alto, CA 94303 USA
(650) 856-0900,(800) 227-1980; *Fax:* (650) 858-2302
Debbie Dirickson, General Manager
Bcst VTRs, custom VTRs & accessories, VTR automation systems, stereo audio encoders, standards converters.

Micro Communications Inc.
15 Caron St., Merrimack, NH 3054 USA
(603) 429-0800, (800) 545-0608; *Fax:* (603) 429-1633
www.mcibroadcast.com
frank.malanga@mcibroadcast.com
Paul D. Smith, Engineering Director/ CEO
Al Kula, General Sales Mgr
Sam Matthews, Promotions Manager
Kim Blackford, Branch Manager
Frank Malanga, Sales Director
Waveguide & coaxial transmission line; complete RF system packages for UHF, VHF, FM & LPTV panel antennas; antennas for UHF, VHF & FM.

Micro Technology Unlimited
PO Box 80124, Raleigh, NC 27623 USA
(919) 870-0344; *Fax:* (919) 870-7163
www.mtu.com
info@mtu.com
David B. Cox, President
Lynn Cox, Marketing
Howard (Hal) A. Chamberlin, Founder
David B. Cox, Founder
Karaoke software products & pro workstations.

Microlog
401 Professional Dr., Suite 125, Gaithersburg, MD 20879 USA
(301) 540-5500; *Fax:* (301) 330-2450
www.mlog.com
sales@mlog.com
Richard Meccarielli, CEO
Janet Turner, SVP Sales/Marketing
Call and contact Center Solutions, Speech Recognition, IVR, Outbound Marketing Solutions and custom application development.

Microsemi Corporation
One Enterprise, Aliso Viejo, CA 92656 US
(949) 380-6100, (800) 713-4113; *Fax:* (949) 215-4996
www.microsemi.com
Jim Peterson, Chairman of the Board and CEO
Paul Pickle, President and Chief Operating Officer
Bob Krist, Operations Dir
John Hohener, EVP, CFO, Secretary and Treasurer
Bill Minor, Executive Vice President-Global Human Resources
Phil Bourekas, Executive Vice President-Marketing
Juan Dewar, Executive Vice President-Global Sales & Services
Douglas J. Halbert, Jr., Executive Vice President-Global Operations & Quali
Jim Aralis, Chief Technology Officer
Time code generators, readers, displays, encoders, search systems, distribution amplifiers, transmitters & receivers; design & manufacture of precision frequency products & timing instruments.

Datum-Irvine
3 Parker, Irvine, CA 92718 United States
(714) 770-5000
Heinz Badura, Pres

Datum-Austin
Box 14766, Austin, TX 78761 United States
(512) 251-2341
Jack Rice, Pres

Microspace Communications Corp.
3100 Highwoods Blvd., Suite 120, Raleigh, NC 27604-1033 USA
(919) 850-4500; *Fax:* (919) 850-4518
www.microspace.com
uplink@microspace.com
Joseph Amor, Operations Dir
Joe Amor, VP & General Manager
Greg Hurt, Vice President of Sales & Marketing
Ron Burns, Chief Engineer

Megan Ely, Accountng Manager
Greg Hurt, VP of Sales & Marketing
Providing video, data & audio transmission svcs designed for antennas as small as 30 inches. Operates on domestic satellites for coverage of North America. Also providing fixed C- & Ku-band uplink svcs for video transmissions supportingapplications such as news, sports, program origination (live or taped); & business TV. Remote & studio production available. Turnaround svc to & from domestic & international satellites.

Microwave Filter Co. Inc.
6743 Kinne St., East Syracuse, NY 13057 USA
(315) 438-4700, (800) 448-1666, (888) 411-8860; *Fax:* (315) 463-1467
www.microwavefilter.com
mfcsales@microwavefilter.com
Carl Fahrenkrug, President
Scott Parsell, General Sales Mgr
Richard Jones, Chief Financial Officer
P. Scott, Director of Sales
N. Sandy, Customer Relations Manager
S. Jeff, Technical Sales Specialist
B. Sherry, Sr. SalesSpecialist
Y. Nancy, Sales Associate
Filters, traps, combiners & custom networks for TV, radio, CATV, wireless cable, LAN & mobile radio.

Miles Tek Corporation
1506 Interstate 35W, Denton, TX 76207-2402 USA
(940) 484-9400, (800) 958-5173, (866) 524-1553; *Fax:* (940) 566-1047
www.milestek.com
David McCarthy, President
Mike Guidry, General Manager
Leticia Hill, Finance
Lisa Daniels, Sales
Connectors including both 50 ohm & 75 ohm BNCs, cabling, patching & tools for coaxial cable.

Milestone Technologies Inc.
Software Division, PO Box 37145, Raleigh, NC 27627 USA
(919) 773 - 1772
www.milestonetechnologies.com
info@milestonetechnologies.com
Prem Chand, President/CEO
Tony Silveria, EVP
Jim Schultz, Chief Financial Officer
Data bcstg file transfer software (SATX). Bcst binary files over one-way data nets (DBS, VSAT, TV, FM, VBI, RDS, MPEG2, etc.). Consulting & system integration svcs.

Miller Camera Support, LLC USA
218 Little Falls Rd., Unit 15 & 16, Cedar Grove, NJ 7009 USA
(973) 857-8300; *Fax:* (973) 857-8188
www.millertripods.com
info@millertripods.us
Gus Harilaou, General Sales Mgr
Pan & tilt fluid heads, tripods & camera support systems & accessories for DV, ENG & EFP (OB).

Miranda Technologies Inc.
3499 Douglas B. Floreani, Montreal, QC H4S 2C6 Canada
(514) 333-1772, (800) 224-7882; *Fax:* (514) 333-9828
www.miranda.com
ussales@miranda.com
Strath Goodship, CEO
Spiro Plagakis, General Sales Mgr
David Cohen, Media Relations
Matthew Tractenberg, Financial Press
Roy Folkman, Miranda Canadian Sales Manager
Sean Murphy, Miranda Inside Sales Manager
Digital video interface products for bcstg & postproduction: serializers, digital-to-analog converters, NTSC encoders, computer video interfaces.

Miranda Asia
Unit 1706, Tai Tung Bldg., 8 Fleming Rd., Wanchai, Hong Kong
+852-2539-6987; *Fax:* +852-2539-0804
asiasales@miranda.com

Miranda China
Rm. 2402, Sichuan Bldg., E. Tower, 1 Fuchengmenwai St., Xicheng District, Beijing, 100037 China
+86 10-68364818; *Fax:* +81 10-68364817
chinasales@miranda.com

Miranda Europe
Hithercroft Rd., Wallingford, Oxfordshire, OX10 9DG United Kingdom
+44 (0) 1491 820 000; *Fax:* +44 (0) 1491 820 001
europesales@miranda.com

Miranda France
216 rue de Rosny, 931000 Montreuil, Montreuil, 93100 France
+33 (0) 1 55 86 87 88; *Fax:* +33 (0) 1 55 86 00 29
francesales@miranda.com

Miranda USA
195 Mountain Ave., Springfield, NJ 07081 United States
(973) 379-0089; *Fax:* (973) 379-1953
usssales@miranda.com

Miranda Japan
3-1-17 Nihombashi Ningyacho, Ishii Bldg. 2F, Cjuo-ku, Tokyo, 103-0013 Japan
+81 (0) 3-5644-7533; *Fax:* +81 (0) 3-3662-7555

Miranda USA
324 Clark St., Worcester, MA 1606 USA
(508) 754-4858; *Fax:* (508) 752-1520
www.telecast-fiber.com
salesamericas@miranda.com
Richard Cerny, President
Eugene Baker, Operations Dir
Joseph Commare, Promotions Manager
Mark Borezo, Financial Executive
Fiber-optic video & audio systems for TV bcst production.
3009 Bentwillow Dr., Fuquay-Varina, NC 27526
(919) 557-6059; *Fax:* (919) 557-5206
Bryan Keen, Southeast Sls
16 Rock River Ct., Naperville, IL 75231
(630) 717-9384; *Fax:* (630) 717-1844
Bill Hollis, Midwest Sls
280 Ferry Rd., Saco, ME 04072
(207) 282-9772; *Fax:* (207) 282-8666
Steve Nelson, Northeast & Gvt Sls
835 Autumn Ln., Mill Valley, CA 94941
(415) 383-5388; *Fax:* (650) 745-3711
James Hurwitz, Western U.S/Sls & Camera Systems

Mobile Video Services Ltd.
1620 I St. N.W., Suite 1000, Washington, DC 20006 USA
(202) 331-8882; *Fax:* (202) 331-9064
www.mobilevideo.net
bookfeed@mobilevideo.net
Lawrence VanderVeen, President
Christine Baber, Operations Dir
Complete EFP & ENG svcs, multi-camera remote packages, editing teleco & satellite transmission svcs available. CBS & CNN news feeds available.

MODCOMP Inc.
Mailing Address: 1500 S. Powerline Rd., Deerfield Beach, FL 33442 USA
Second Address: 9155 Dadeland Blvd., Suite 1112, Miami, FL 33156
(954) 571-4600, (800) 940-1111, (305) 670-4772; *Fax:* (954) 571-4700, (305) 670-4769
info@modcomp.com
Victor Dellovo, President & CEO
Ron Cook, Operations Dir
Christina Luis, Promotions Manager
Mike Newbanks, Division Controller
Minicomputer systems, hardware & software for ground stn monitoring & control. SCADA applications & website enabling software.

Modulation Sciences Inc.
14K World's Fair Dr., Somerset, NJ 8873 USA
(732) 302-3090, (800) 826-2603; *Fax:* (732) 302-0206
www.modsci.com
Eric Small, CEO
Judy Mueller, President
With 20+ years experience in the bcst industry, we manufacture full line of FM & TV equipment including: composite clipper, STL's distribution amplifiers, SteroMaxx—Spatial image englarger, modulation monitors, SCA & Data SCA equipment, TVstereo reference decoder, SAP & PRO generators, PRO ch receivers, SAP receivers, NTSC precision video demodulators.

Mohawk
324 Clark Street, Worcester, MA 1606 USA
(978) 537-9961, (800) 422-9961; *Fax:* (978) 537-4358
www.mohawk-cable.com
info@mohawk-cable.com
Jenna Desimone, General Sales Mgr
Joe Barry, Engineering Dir
Leslie Hicks, National Broadcast Sales
Mary Gozdur, Inside Sales Representative
Mohawk offers an end to end solution for your HDTV cabling needs. We use LEMO stainless connectors & have many varieties of SMPTE cable. Mohawk is the OEM for fiber & copper camera cable assemblies for all of the major camera manufacturers.

Mole-Richardson Co.
937 N. Sycamore Ave., Hollywood, CA 90038 USA
(323) 851-0111; *Fax:* (323) 851-5593
www.mole.com
info@mole.com
Larry Parker, President
Don Phillips, General Sales Mgr
Michael Parker, President/CEO
Peter Mole, Founder
Lighting equipment for the motion picture, TV, video & still photographic industries.

Moog QuickSet
Mailing Address: 3650 Woodhead Dr., Northbrook, IL 60062-1895 USA
Second Address: 2525 Park Central Blvd, Decatur, GA 30035
(847) 498-0700, (770) 987-7550, (716) 687-7157; *Fax:* (847) 498-3658
sales@quickset.com
Andy Lareau, President
Jim Fenning, General Sales Mgr
Dan Clove, Sales
Don Zeilenga, Finance Executive
Instrument positioning equipment. Tripods, pan & tilts.

Morpho Trust USA, Inc.
Mailing Address: 5705 W. Old Shakopee Rd., Suite 100, Bloomington, MN 55437 US
Second Address: 296 Concord Rd., Suite 300, Billerica, MA 1821
(952) 932-0888, (800) 932-0890, (978) 215-2400; *Fax:* (978) 215-2500
www.morphotrust.com
Robert Eckel, CEO
Robert Brigum, Principal
Nick Pattakos, Sr. VP of Enterprise Solutions
James Albers, Sr. VP of govt. Operations
Identix is a leading biometrics solutions provider with proven & cost-effective verification security for applications including banking, healthcare, government, & access control.

Moseley
82 Coromar Dr., Santa Barbara, CA 93117-3024 USA
(805) 968-9621; *Fax:* (805) 685-9638
www.moseleysb.com
info@moseleysb.com
Jamal Hamdani, President & CEO
Larry Sollecito, General Manager
Bruce Tarr, CMA & CFO
AM & FM stereo STLs, TV Digital STLs, data transmission systems & telecommunications, digital transmission systems.

Motion Picture Enterprises Inc.
Box 276, Tarrytown, NY 10591-0276 USA
(212) 245-0969; *Fax:* (212) 245-0974
www.mpe.net
mpeny@aol.com
Neal Pilzer, President
Shipping cases, cabinets & cans for film & tape; custom made fibre cases, film & video equipment, supplies, sls, rental & repairs.

Motorola Digital Media Systems
1303 E. Algonquin Rd., Schaumburg, 60196
(847) 576-5000
www.motorola.com/
Greg Brown, CEO
Patricia B Morrison, President
Karen P. Tandy, Operations Dir
Eduardo Courado, SVP/ Chief Marketing Officer
Gene Delaney, EVP
Mark Moon, EVP

Moviola
Mailing Address: 545 W. 45th St., New York, NY 10036 USA
Second Address: 1135 N Mansfield Ave, Hollywood, CA 90038
(323) 467-3107, (212) 247-0972 ,(800) 327-3724; *Fax:* (212) 581-7977
www.moviola.com
Joe Pascal, CEO
Robert Schoenberg, Operations Dir
Michael Blom Blakstad, Communications Director
Full-svc supplier of videotape, accessories & digital data storage products.

MRPP Inc.
201 W. Chatham St., Suite 202, Cary, NC 27511 USA
(919) 468-1000; *Fax:* (919) 468-1956
www.mrppinc.com
Sheila Ogle, CEO
Sue Toth, President
Procuring, servicing, instal, & sale of bcstg & satellite equipment. Leasing plans available.

EQUIPMENT MANUFACTURERS

Murray Company
Mailing Address: 7300 College Blvd, Suite 210, Overland Park, KS 66210 USA
Second Address: 1807 Park 270 Drive, Suite 460, St Louis, MS 63146
(888) 451-1884, (888) 323-5560; *Fax:* (913) 451-3761, (314) 434-5780
www.murray-company.com
Dick Arnold, Founder
John O'Hara, President
Gen construction, design, program mgmt, space planning, project budgeting & consolidation planning.
7300 College, Suite 210, Kansas City, KS 66210
(913) 451 1884; *Fax:* (913) 451-3761

Musco Mobile Lighting Ltd.
Box 808, 100 First Ave. W., Oskaloosa, IA 52577 USA
(641) 673-0411; *Fax:* (641) 673-4852
www.musco.com
lighting@musco.com
Joe Crookham, President
Jeff McNulty, Operations Dir
Jerome Fynaardt, General Sales Mgr
Leo Kirk, Manager
Jeff Rogers, Sales Executive
Mobile location lighting utilizing 6K HMIs; remote control of pan, tilt & focus.

MUSICAM U.S.A.
670 N. Beers St., Bldg. 4, Holmdel, NJ 7733 US
(732) 739-5600; *Fax:* (732) 739-1818
Cindy DeVito, Promotions Manager
We introduced the idea of intelligent audio codecs, with a wide range of programmable automatic features, and because innovation is ongoing at CCS MUSICAM USA, we make our products upgradeable through software that is easily available fromour website.

MYAT Inc.
360 Franklin Tpke., Mahwah, NJ 7430 US
(201) 684-0100; *Fax:* (201) 684-0104
www.myat.com
sales@myat.com
Philip Cindrich, President
Derek Small, General Manager
Dennis Heymans, General Sales Mgr
Transmision line systems, filters, combiners, UHF & L-band antenna.

Nady Systems Inc.
6701 Shellmound St., Emeryville, CA 94608 USA
(510) 652-2411; *Fax:* (510) 652-5075
www.nady.com
ussales@nady.com
John Nady, CEO & Founder
Scott Wunschel, General Sales Mgr
Wireless VMP & AMF products for bcst, film, video, stage, fixed instals. Consumer audio & communication equipment.

Nalpak
1267 Vernon Way, El Cajon, CA 92020 USA
(619) 258-1200, (888) 488-3372; *Fax:* (619) 258-0925
service@nalpak.com
Robert Kaplan, President
Debra Kaplan, Operations Dir
Packaging & Material Handling Products; teffpak,Torm, Magliner, Leatherman, Gerber, Buck, Surefire, Steamlight.

Narda Microwave-East L-3 Communications Co.
435 Moreland Rd., Hauppauge, NY 11788 US
(631) 231-1700; *Fax:* (631) 231-1711
nardamicrowave.com
Jihn Mega, President
Michael Sanator, Executive Vice President
Portable RF/microwave test instruments, power density meters, coaxial power monitors & meters.

Narda Satellite Networks
435 Moreland Road, Hauppauge, NY 11788 USA
(631) 231-1700, (800) 666-7060; *Fax:* (631) 272-5500
sn.mktg@l-3com.com
Frank C. Lanza, Chairman & CEO
Robert V. LaPenta, President & CFO
Ken Leighton, Operations Dir
Craig Meriam, General Sales
Margaret Pawetto, Administration
Jeff Okwit, Technical Inquiries
Turnkey satellite earth stns & networks, SNG & Fly Away electronics, ground communications equipment & M&C systems. Manufactures & implements a full line of earth stn network monitors & control systems.

Narragansett Imaging
51 Industrial Dr., North Smithfield, RI 2896 USA
(401) 762-3800; *Fax:* (401) 767-4407
www.nimaging.com
info@nimaging.com
Bill Ulmschneider, President
Keith Cowling, General Manager
Camera tubes, CCD camera modules.

National Audio Co. Inc.
309 E. Water Street, Springfield, MO 65806 USA
(417) 863-1925; *Fax:* (417) 863-7825
www.nationalaudiocompany.com
nac@nactape.com
Steve Stepp, President
Audio Pro-blank audio cassettes, Audio cassette custom duplication, printing & packaging, CDR & DVD blank media, CDR/DVD custom duplication, printing & packaging, CDR/DVD duplicating & printing equipment, CDR/DVD packing.

National Steel Erectors Corp.
Box 709, 3315 South Cherokee Drive, Muskogee, OK 74402-0709 USA
(918) 683-6511; *Fax:* (918) 683-0888
www.nsec.com
B.R. Bayless, President
Neal Bayless, Executive Vice President
Bob Scroggins, Contact
Erection of radio, TV & microwave towers, including turnkey construction, from design to completion.

National Video Tape Co. Inc.
Mailing Address: 845 N. Church Ct., Elmhurst, IL 60126 USA
Second Address: 4518 W. Vanowen St., Burbank, CA 91505
(800) 851-3113, (888) 277-6364, (818) 980-9916; *Fax:* (800) 258-0590, (818) 847-0543
nationalvideotape.com
Mike Cullen, President
Custom length VHS cassettes; Sony, Fuji, Maxell Panasonic video & data media products. CD/DVD printing & duplication.
1471 Elliott Ave. W., Seattle, WA 98199 United States
(206) 284-3340
Mari Scimeca, Chairman

Nautel Ltd.
10089 Peggy's Cove Rd., Hackett's Cove, NS B3Z 3J4 Canada
(902) 823-2900, (877) 662-8835; *Fax:* (902) 823-3183
www.nautel.com
info@nautel.com
Kevin Rodgers, President
Michael Morris, COO
Brian Irwin, General Manager
Blair Donovan, General Sales Mgr
Wendell Lonergan, Broadcast Sales Manager
John Whyte, Promotions Manager
John Wilton, Customer Service
Solid state AM/FM bcst transmitters.

Nautel Maine Inc.
201 Target Industrial Cir., Bangor, ME 04401 United States

Navitar Inc.
200 Commerce Dr., Rochester, NY 14623-3506 US
(585) 359-4000, (800) 828-6778; *Fax:* (585) 359-4999
www.navitar.com
info@navitar.com
Thomas McCune, COO
Julian Goldtein, Co-President
Jeremy Goldstein, Co-President
Mark Smith, Chief Financial Officer
Projection lenses, LCD, slide & overhead projectors.

NEC Corporation of America Inc.
6555 N. State Hwy. 161, Irving, TX 75039 USA
(214) 262-2000,(214) 262-6299; *Fax:* (214) 262-2586
www.necam.com
Bruce Blain, General Sales Mgr
VUES on-line digital editing system (video).

Nemal Electronics International Inc.
12240 N.E. 14th Ave., North Miami, FL 33161 USA
(305) 899-0900, (800) 522-2253; *Fax:* (305) 895-8178
www.nemal.com
info@nemal.com
Benjamin Nemser, President
Manufacturer of electronic cable, connectors, assemblies, & interconnect products for use in bcst applications.
Av. Morumbi 7948, Sao Paulo, Brazil
011-5535-2368
Carlos Heckmann Jr., Gen Mgr

NEP
Mailing Address: 915 Sherwood Dr., Lake Bluff, IL 60044 US
Second Address: 2 Beta Drive, Pittsburgh, PA 15238
(847) 582-8800,(888) 673-5400; *Fax:* (847) 582-8730
info@nepinc.com
Deb Honkus, Chairman
Kevin Rabbitt, CEO
Scott West, President
AJ Tozzi, Senior Vice President Operational Excellence
Barry Katz, Senior VP/General Manager
Mike Fernander, President/GM-US Mobile Units
Pittsburgh, PA
Tom McCracken,Senior Board Member/Director of Corporate Developm
Stephen Jenkins, Managing Director
Lynda Wilkes, Sr. VP of Human Resources
Glen Levine, VP Mobile Engineering and Operations, Supershooter
Scott Rothenberg, VP- Technology & AssetManagement
Video production equipment, postproduction equipment, rental & mobile TV.

Neutrik U.S.A. Inc.
4115 Taggart Creek Rd., Charlotte, NC 28208-5479 USA
(704) 972-3050; *Fax:* (704) 972-9202, (877) 220-4089
www.neutrikusa.com
info@neutrikusa.com
Pete Milbery, President
Julie Applegate, Station Manager
Audio connectors, plugs & jacks, patch panels, patch cord assemblies, circular, industrial connectors & accessories, knobs, BNC jacks & plugs, RJ45, 3-5 mm plugs.

New York City Lites
122 W. 27th St., 12th Floor, New York, NY 10001 USA
(212) 366-9800; *Fax:* (212) 366-5040
www.newyorkcitylites.tv
nycl@nycl.tv
Deke Hazirjian, President/CEo
Deke Hazirjian, Designer
Lighting design for video & TV.

Newark Electronics
300 S. Riverside Plaza, Suite 2200, Chicago, IL 60606 USA
(773) 784 - 5100; *Fax:* (888) 551-4801
www.newark.com
Peter Costello, Chairman
Mike Ruprich, CEO
Paul Buckley, Operations Dir
Barry Litwin, Promotions Manager
Distributor of bcst cable, assemblies, connectors voice/data networking & electronic component parts. Branches throughout the U.S., Canada, U.K. & Germany.

Newdoll Enterprises
3515- B Edison Way, Menlo Park, CA 94025 US
(650) 365-2843; *Fax:* (650) 365-3057
www.newdollenterprises.com
Ronald Newdoll, President
High-speed tape duplicating & recording equipment, digital audio logging recorders, audio & videotape conditioners, audio recorders. CD-R recorders for audio & ROM.

Noise Control Corp.
PO BOX 81774, Bakersfield, CA 93308 USA
(800) 606-6473; *Fax:* (661) 391-9999
Steve Anderson, President
Acoustical noise control products.

Norpak Corporation
10 Hearst Way, Kanata, ON K2L 2P4 Canada
(613) 592-4164; *Fax:* (613) 592-6560
www.norpak.ca
James Carruthers, President
Michael Dobson, Operations Dir
TV Data Broadcast; Interactive TV; Financial, News, Weather Radar Information Broadcast; HDTV Data Encoding; Closed Captioning; V-Chip; NABTS

Norsat International Inc.
110-4020 Viking Way, Richmond, BC V6V 2L4 Canada
(604) 821-2800, (855) 466-7728, (855) 4-NORSAT; *Fax:* (604) 821-2801
www.norsat.com
Fabio Doninelli, Director & Chairman of the Board
Aimee Chan, President & CEO
Frank So, Dir. Of Operations, Norsat Division
Ivan Gissing, General Manager, Norsat Power Solutuions Div.
Randy Witten, General Sales Mgr
MichaelSchefter, Dir. of Engineering, Norsat division
Arthur Chin, CFO
Brian Donnelly, VP, Sales & Marketing

Ken Broom, Dir. of Operations, Sinclair Division
Kang Lan, Director of R&D & Engineering, Sinclair Division
Joseph Caprio, Director & USChairman
High speed, reliable data transmission products & networks, microware products & worldwide installations of opns STDs, DVB & SAT networks.
The Old School, South Carlton, Lincoln, LN1 2RL
(011) 44 1522 730 800; *Fax:* 011- 44 1522 730 927
smullery@noisat.com
Stan Mullery, Chairman

Beijing Broadcasting Institute
1704-A Union Plaza, 20 Chao Wai Plaza, Beijing, 100029 China
(011) 86 10 65871281; *Fax:* (011) 86 10 65871081

North American Cable Equipment Inc.
1085 Andrew Dr., Suite A, West Chester, PA 19380 USA
(800) 688-9282; *Fax:* (800) 230-1793
www.northamericancable.com
sales@northamericancable.com
Aaron Starr, President
Kirk Davies, Sales Director
Thomas Knowles, Chief Financial Officer
Jennifer Kern, Sales Manager
Stuart Lindsay, Sales and Print Media
Doug Forward, Director Of Purchasing
Erika Forlino, AssistantPurchasing Manager
Nikki Owens, Controller
ACE has turned the specialty distribution of satellite downlink products, cable headend systems, fiber optics, wire, cable, and related connectivity products into a successful operational network.

North Hills Signal Processing Corp.
6851 Jericho Tpke., Suite 170, Syosset, NY 11791 USA
(516) 682-7700; *Fax:* (516) 682-7704
www.northhills-sp.com
Richard Schwarz, General Manager
Manufactures of MIL-STDT553 data bus products & wideband/video transformer. Our standard & custom product, offer unmatched performance & reliability for a wide range of applications in the military, aerospace & industrial OEM markets.

Northeast Towers Inc.
199 Brickyard Rd., Farmington, CT 6032 USA
(860) 677-1999; *Fax:* (860) 677-1300
info@northeasttowers.com
Stephen Savino Jr, President
HDTV, TV, Cellular, PCS, AM, FM, CATV & microwave towers; ground systems; maintenance, materials, turnkey instals, specialty coatings, & strobes.

Northeastern Communications Concepts Inc.
40 Benford Dr., Princeton Junction, NJ 8550 USA
(609) 936-0006
www.nccnewyork.com
webmaster@nccnewyork.com
Alfred D'Alessio, President
Bcst design svcs, studio furniture, custom audio equipment, custom data systems/components, cabinets, racks, panels, recording studios construction & prefab.

Northern Power Systems
Mailing Address: 29 Pitman Rd., Barre, VT 5641 USA
Second Address: 281 Winter St., Suite 120, Waltham, MA 2541
(802) 496-2955; *Fax:* (802) 496-2953
www.northernpower.com
info@northernpower.com
Troy Patton, CEO & President
Ciel Caldwell, CFO
Jonathan Lynch, Chief Technology Officer
Elliot Mark, VP & General Counsel
Reinout G. Oussoren, VP, Global Sales
Remote power systems based on renewable energy inputs (wind/solar); hybrid power systems.

Northrup Grumman Corp.
2980 Fairpark Park Dr., Falls church, VA 22042 USA
(703) 280-2900
www.northropgrumman.com
Wes Bush, Chairman, CEO & President
Linda A. Mills, Corporate VP, Operations
Sid Ashworth, Corporate VP, Govt. Relations
Sheila C. Cheston, Corporate VP & General Counsel
Darryl M. Fraser, Corporate VP, Communications
James F.Palmer, Corporate VP & CFO
Denise Peppard, Corporate VP & Chief Human Resources
David T. Perry, Corporate VP & Chie Global Business Development Of
Film & video cameras for military; video-to-film recorders; optics & optical systems.

Northwest Monitoring Service
Mailing Address: 2558 RW Johnson Blvd., J114, Eugene, WA 98512 USA
Second Address: 46 SW Chehalis Ave, Chehalis, WA 98532
(800) 916-4576
www.northwestmonitoring.com
office@northwestmonitoring.com
James Bradley, President
Mthy frequency measurements for AM-FM-TV. Mobile svc includes California, Oregon, Washington, Idaho & Nevada.

NSI
8265 Patuxent Range Rd., Jessup, MD 20794 USA
(410) 964-8400; *Fax:* (410) 964-9661
www.nsystems.com
Stephen Neuberth, President
Robert Boshka, Operations Dir
Microwave antennas & remote controls for ENG applications.

NTV International Corporation
645 5th Ave., Suite 303, New York, NY 10022 USA
(212) 660-6900; *Fax:* (212) 660-6998
www.ntvic.com
Jusaburo Hayahii, President
Leo Lahm, Engineering Dir
Yorihosha Kono, VP/Finance

NUCOMM Inc.
200 International Dr., Mt. Olive, NJ 7828 USA
(908) 852-3700, (800) 968-2666; *Fax:* (908) 813-0399
Dr. John Payne, CEO
Alan Conen, Sales Engineering Manager
Microwave transmitters, receivers including digital video microwave systems & accessories for both portable & fixed line of sight applications. Modulators/demodulators & color bar generators.

NVISION Products
125 Crown Point Ct., Grass Valley, CA 95945 USA
(530) 265-1000; *Fax:* (530) 265-1021
Charles Meyer, President
Jay Kuca, General Manager
Doug Buterbaugh, General Sales Mgr
Birney Dayton, Chief Engineer
Digital audio & data distribution, conversion, routing & transmission equipment for production/postproduction applications for bcstg industry.

NWL Capacitors
Mailing Address: 8550 Monetary Drive, Riviera Beach, FL 33419 USA
Second Address: 204 Carolina Dr., PO Box 97, Snow Hill, NC 28580
(561) 848-9009, (252) 747-5943; *Fax:* (561) 848-9011, (252) 747-8979
www.nwl.com
sales.caps@nwl.com
David Seitz, Owner
Robert Seitz, President
John Nothelfer, Founder
Manufacturers.

O'Connor Professional Camera Support Systems
2701 N. Ontario Street Burbank, Burbank, CA 91504 USA
(714) 979-3993; *Fax:* (714) 957-8138
www.ocon.com
sales@ocon.com
Joel Johnson, Operations Dir
Robert Low, General Sales Mgr
Jeannine McQuilliam, Chief Engineer
Manufacturer of camera support equipment including fluid heads, tripods & accessories.

Olesen
12800 Foothill Blvd, Sylmar, CA 91342 USA
(818) 407-7800, (800) 233-7830; *Fax:* (818) 407-7868
www.hollywoodrentals.com
info@hollywoodrentals.com
Kelly Koskella, President
Joe Dougherty, Operations Dir
Victor Duran, Chief Engineer
Steve Antman, Chief Marketing Executive
All production supplies, equipment for TV, theater, both live & taped.

Omicron Video
22251 Roscoe Blvd., West Hills, CA 91304 USA
(818) 704-0704; *Fax:* (818) 704-0475
Kimiharu Akiyama, Owner
Video/audio distribution equipment. Computer graphics/HDTV distribution equipment.

Omnimount Systems
3821 AH Amersfoort, Beeldschermweg 3, Netherlands, NT 85044 USA
+31 334545600; *Fax:* (480) 756-9000
www.omnimount.com
info@omnimount.com
Garrett Weyand, Chairman
Raymond Nakano, CEO
Geoff Miller, President
Mitch Jones, Chief Technical Officer
Loudspeaker mounts-omnidirectional adjustability supporting ounces to hundreds of pounds. Also, flexible, refined mounting systems for TV's/computer monitors & peripherals.

Opamp Labs Inc.
1033 N. Sycamore Ave., Los Angeles, CA 90038-2398 USA
(323) 934-3566; *Fax:* (323) 462-6490
www.opamplabs.com
opamplabs@gmail.com
B. Losmandy, President
Amplifiers: audio, video, microphone, line & power. Audio oscillators & transformers. Power supplies, network audio/video feed boxes, audio/video routing switches.

Open Text Digital Media Group
700 King Farm Blvd, Suite 600, Rockville, MD 20850 USA
(301) 548-7850; *Fax:* (301) 548-4015
www.opentext.com
P. Thomas Jenkins, Executive Chairman
Mark J. Barrenechea, President/Chief Executive Officer
John Schlipp, Vice President
Muhi Majzoub, Senior Vice President, Engineering
John Doolittle, Chief Financial Officer
Patrick A. Harper,Chief Information Officer
Jonathan Hunter, EVP, Worldwide Field Operations
Adam Howatson, Chief Marketing Officer
Manuel N. Sousa, Senior Vice President, Global Human Resources
Russ Stuebing, Vice President, Corporate Development

Optical Disc Corp.
490 E. Princeland Court, Suites 3 & 4, Corona, CA 92879 USA
(951) 372-9800, (951) 372-9803, (951) 372-9801; *Fax:* (951) 372-9119
www.optical-disc.com
sales@odc-nimbus.com
James Wu, President
John Brown, Operations Dir
Ken Shrimplin, Senior VP
Recordable laser video discs, videodisc recording systems & other auxiliary equipment. Compact disc & videodisc mastering systems.

Optima Electronic Packaging Systems
1775 MacLeod Dr., Lawrenceville, GA 30043 USA
(770) 496-4000; *Fax:* (770) 496-4041
www.apwmayville.com
Daniel Eder, President
Rich Runnels, General Sales Mgr
Ron Hall, National Sales manager
Robby Tavenier, Sr. Sales Application engineer
Tom Kennedy, Regional Sales Manager-South
Harold Kormos, Regional Sales Manager-North
RobertFleming, Sales Application engineer
Stantron racks, cabinets, enclosures, & related accessories for bcst integrators & professional audio video installations.

Orban
8350 E. Evans Rd., Suite C-4, Scottsdale, AZ 85260 USA
(480) 403-8300; *Fax:* (480) 403-8302
www.orban.com
info@orban.com
Charles Jayson Brentlinger, President
Bob Orban, Operations Dir
Bob Orban, Chief Engineer
Greg Ogonowski, VP of new Product Development
Roger Sales, CFO, VP
Keith Cheatem, Sales Support Manager
Dayton Winnie, Customer ServiceAdministrator
Robert Leembruggen, Service Technician
John F. Schaab, North American Sales manager
Orban manufacturers bcst audio equipment for radio & TV including processors for TV, FM, AM & HF & the Audicy digital audio workstation, & the Airtime digital audio delivery system.

Orban Corporate
Mailing Address: 8350 E. Evans Rd., Suite C-4, Scottsdale, AZ 85260 US
Second Address: 14798 Wicks Blvd, San Leandro, CA 94577

EQUIPMENT MANUFACTURERS

(480) 403-8300; *Fax:* (480) 403-8302
www.orban.com
sales@orban.com
Robert McMartin, CEO
Charles Jayson Brentlinger, President
Bob Orban, Chief Engineer
Greg Ogonowski, Vice President of New Product Development
Roger Sales, Chief Financial Officer, Vice President
Peter Lee, Vice President ofEuropean Operations
Keith Cheatem, Sales Support Manager
Terry Nall, Arkansas Office Manager
Scot McDougal, Customer Service Manager
From ESPN to the BBC, Orban products are at work in radio and television stations around the world. Designing audio products for the challenges of broadcasting has kept Orban busy, and successful, for over thirty years.
In fact, Bob Orbanfounded the company because he wasn't happy with the sound of albums being heard on the new stereo FM stations. So he developed the OPTIMOD solution that combines several processing structures into a single box to maximize loudness and still meetgovernment broadcast regulations.

OSI Laser Diode Inc.
4 Olsen Avenue, Edison, NJ 8820 US
(732) 549-9001; *Fax:* (732) 906-1559
www.laserdiode.com
Steve Lerner, Operations Dir
Rollin Ball, General Manager/Director
Peggy Scarillo, General Sales Mgr
George Minakas, Programming Director
Manufacture FP, high power pulsed & CW lasers along with high sensitivity detectors, FDDI/SONET modules for short/long haul transmission, test DWDM, military & coml fiber optic systems. Also offer Hi-Reliability custom packaging svcs.

Otari USA Sales Inc.
6410 Via Del Oro, San Jose, CA 95119 USA
(408) 226-9800; *Fax:* (408) 226-9195
www.otari.com
Nick Higashino, President
Tim Murray, General Sales Mgr
Patrick Johnston, VP- Sales
Manufacturer of audio & video cassette loaders & duplicators. Manufacturer of audio mixing consoles, hard disk audio recorders, tape recorders, DAT recorders, minidisc recorders & players, CD changers, digital audio format converters.

Pace Micro Technology P.L.C.
3701 FAU Blvd., Suite 200, Boca Raton, FL 33431 USA
(561) 995-6000; *Fax:* (561) 995-6001
www.pace.com
info@pace.com
Allan Leighton, Chairman
Mike Pulli, CEO
Tim O'Loughlin, President, Pace Americas,Inc.
Roddy Murray, CFO
Patricia Chapman-Pincher, Non-Executive Director
Amanda Mesler, Non-Executive Director
John Grant, Non-ExecutiveDirector
Shane McCarthy, President, Pace International
Anthony Dixon, General Counsel &Company Secretary
First DVB MPEG-2 set-top boxes, the first to integrate DOCSIS into a digital cable set-top box & launching the first ever H.264 DVB-S2 high definition set-top box.

Packaged Lighting Systems Inc.
Box 285, 29 Grant St., Walden, NY 12586 USA
(845) 778-3515,(800) 836-1024 (orders); *Fax:* (845) 778-1286
www.packagedlighting.com
Hy Hilzen, President
Factory prewired, self-contained TV studio systems complete with lighting/dimming/grid/power distribution.

Panasonic Broadcast & Television Systems Co.
3330 Cahuenga Blvd., Los Angeles, CA 90068 USA
(323) 436-3500; *Fax:* (201) 348-5318
www.panasonic.com
Shusaku Nagae, Chairman/CEO
Kazuhiro Tsuga, President
Steve Beck, Principal
Robert Harris, VP of Marketing & Product Development
MII VCR, D3 ½ digital VCRs, digital processed cameras, Carts (MARC) analog & digital, tapes, DVC pro, D5, Post Box, RAMJA products, monitors, projectors.
One Panasonic Way, 4E-7, Secaucus, NJ 07094 United States
(201) 348-7621
3330 Cahuenga Blvd. W., Los Angeles, CA 90068 United States
(323) 436-3500

Panavision New York
150 Varick St, Suite 2, New York, NY 10013 US
(212) 606-0700; *Fax:* (212) 244-4457
www.panavision.com
Peter Schnitzler, President
Ira Goodman, Operations Dir
16mm & 35mm motion picture & video equipment, lighting & grip equipment, generators, trucks, dollies & cranes.

Panel Authority Inc.
411 New Ave., Lockport, IL 60441 USA
(815) 838-0488; *Fax:* (815) 838-7852
www.panelauthority.com
preston@panelauthority.com
Preston Wakeland, President
Custom made engraved aluminum connector panels & enclosures.

Paragon Towers Inc.
Box 270655, 3820 North 8th Street, Oklahoma City, OK 73137 USA
(405) 948-3335; *Fax:* (405) 948-3358
Melvyn Lieberman, Chairman
Joe James, President
Competitively priced tower mfg, complete line of broadcasting, communications, cellular, microwave, turn-key, bundle package design, full range of tower accessories, guarantee of company's products.
3820 N.W. 8th St., Oklahoma City, OK 73107 United States

Parsons Audio LLC
192 Worcester St., Wellesley, MA 2481 USA
(781) 431-8708; *Fax:* (781) 431-8783
www.paudio.com
sales@paudio.com
Mark Parsons, CEO
Rick Scott, VP of Sales
Les Arnold, Sr. Sales Representative
Cat Reuthe, Sales Support
Lenore Fauliso, Sales Support
Roger Talkov, Managing VP
Rob Pemberton, VP of Service& Support
Dave Maclaughlin, VP ofSales
Equipment & courses for audio recording, production, broadcast, performance, etc. 200+ product lines: Yamaha, Dolby, Digidesign, Tascam, etc. Also, training courses for professionals, taught by masters.

PC & E
2235 Defoor Hills Rd., Atlanta, GA 30318 USA
(404) 609-9001; *Fax:* (404) 609-9926
www.pce-atlanta.com
Doug Smith, President
Randy Nappier, Operations Dir
Mark Wofford, Promotions Manager
Lighting, grip, camera, stage & generator rental. Full svc sls department with expendables.

Peavey Electronics Corporation
5022 Hartley Peavey Dr., Meridian, MS 39305 USA
(601) 483-5365, (800) 752-7896; *Fax:* (601) 486-1278
www.peavey.com
Courtland Gray, COO
Mary Peavey, President
Hartley D.Peavey, Founder & CEO
Recording & audio products, SMPTE/MIDI synchronization signal processing, reference monitors, microphones & production mixing consoles.

Peerless-AV
2300 White Oak Circle, Aurora, IL 60502 USA
(800) 865-2112, (630) 375-5100; *Fax:* (8000 359-6500, (630) 820-8537
www.peerlessindustries.com
info@peerless-av.com
Mike Campagna, President
John Potts, Vice President
Joe Mitchell, General Manager
Larry Zabinski, Finacial Executive
Adrian Czornik, Engineering Dir
Video Mounting hardware including stands, carts & brackets for floor, furniture, wall & ceiling applications.

Penn Elcom Inc.
Mailing Address: 12691 Monarch St., Garden Grove, CA 92841 USA
Second Address: 232 West Pky, Pompton Plains, NJ 7444
(714) 230-6200, (800) 228-9122, (973) 839-7777, (8; *Fax:* (714) 230-6222, (973) 839-2277
www.penn-elcom.com
Roger Williams, Chairman
Frank McCourt, President
Phil Stratford, General Manager
Zon Mendoza, HR Executive
Hardware & accessories for flightcases, racks, speaker cabinets, stagelights & trussing.

Penny + Giles
665 North Baldwin Park Blvd, City of Industry, CA 91746 USA
(626) 480-2150; *Fax:* (626) 369-6318
www.pgcontrols.com
u.s.sales@pennyandgiles.com
Chris Thomson, Operations Dir
Neil Parker, Principal
William A. Penny, Founder
James A. Giles, Founder
Studio faders; joystick controllers; T-Bar controllers for video effects generators; MIDI mgr & D.A.W. interface.
Cwmfelinfach, Gwent, NP1 7HZ
(44) 1495-202024

Penta Laboratories
9740 Cozycroft Ave., Chatsworth, CA 91311 USA
(818) 882-3872, (800) 421-4219; *Fax:* (818) 882-3968
www.pentalabs.com
info@pentlabs.com
Veronica Calderon, CFO
Steve Sanett, President
Marianne Griego, General Sales Mgr
Steve Sanett, Dir. Of Business Development & OEM Sales
Marianne Griego, Sales Coordinator
Veronica Urraca, Corporate Controller
Electron tubes distribution & mfg.

PENTA LABS OF BRASIL-NOVO ENDEREÇO
Av. Vicente Rao, 1636 -Jd Petrópolis - São Paulo - CEP 04636-001
Tel.: 55 11 5181-5555

Performance Products
Box 947, Roswell, GA 30077 USA
(770 887-4815
poweringcatv@yahoo.com
Jud Williams, President
Standby power supplies, AC power supplies & battery testers.

PerkinElmer
Mailing Address: 940 Winter Street, Waltham, MA 2451 US
Second Address: 2175 Mission College Boulevard, Santa Clara, CA 95054
(203) 925-4602, (800) 762-4000; *Fax:* (203) 944-4904
www.perkinelmer.com
customercareus@perkinelmer.com
Robert F. Friel, Chairman/CEO
John Pautler, Operations Dir
Jim Corbett, Senior Vice President & President- Diagnostics / L
Daniel R. Marshak, Ph.D., Senior Vice President/Chief Scientific Officer
Dusty Tenney, Senior VicePresident/President- Environmental
Joel S. Goldberg, Senior Vice President/General Counsel/Secretary
John Letcher, Senior Vice President/Human Resources
Andrew Okun, Vice President/Chief Accounting Officer
High-medium-intensity aviation obstruction lighting & beacons. FAA-approved; StrobeGuard & FlashGuard.

Pesa Headquarters
Mailing Address: 103 Quality Cir., Suite 210, Huntsville, AL 35806 USA
Second Address: 115 Apple Creek Blvd., Suite 204, Markham, ON LC4 6C9
(256) 726-9200, (800) 323-7372, (905) 752-3700; *Fax:* (256) 726-9271
www.pesa.com
sales@pesa.com
Howard G. Sutton, Executive Chairman
Chuck D. Tillett, President & COO
Ricky Ng, Chief Financial Officer
Ricky NG, CFO
Chris Thomas, SVP of Engineering & CTO
Dewaine McClellan, International Sales Manager
Seth Smith, Inside SalesManager
Randy Lloyd, Western Region Sales
Ray Lego, Eastern Region Sales
Manufacturer of HD/SD video/audio Routing switchers, signal processing & distribution.

Atlanta Branch
3305 Breckinridge Blvd., Suite 118, Duluth, GA 30096 United States
(770) 806-0234

Peter Albrecht Company Inc.
6250 Industrial Ct., Greendale, WI 53129-2432 US

(414) 421-6630; *Fax:* (414) 421-9091
www.peteralbrecht.com
sales@peteralbrecht.com
T.C. Ziolkowski, President/Owner
Don Lemoine, Engineering Tech
Motorized studio battens, plaks & other rigging systems. Tension Grids, Chandelier Hoist, Banner Hoists designed & installed.

Peter W. Dahl Co. Inc.
475 Cayuga Rd., Suite 100, Cheektowaga, NY 14225 US
(716) 630-7030; *Fax:* (716) 630-7042
www.pwdahl.com
mmercer@pwdahl.com
Peter Dahl, President
Gary Komassa, Operations Dir
Mark Mercer, Main Contact
Mark Mercer, Contact
Tom Ballou, Contact
Justin Pope, Contact
Ray Shatzel, Contact
Heavy duty plate, power, filament, modulation transformers & reactor; single- & three-phase rectifiers, vacuum & oil filled capacitors.

Phasetek Inc.
550 California Road, Unit 11, Quakertown, PA 18951 USA
(215) 536-6648, (800) PHASETEK; *Fax:* (215) 536-7180
www.phasetekinc.com
Kurl Gorman, President
Robin Nelson, Operations Dir
Matthew Nelson, Purchasing Executive
Matt Nelson, Plant manager
Robin Nelson, Office Manager
Manufactures AM/MW antenna, phasing equipment, antenna tuning units, diplexers, dummy loads, RF inducters & components.

Philip-Cooke Co.
132 N. 11th St., Allentown, PA 18102 US
(800) 887-0950,(610) 437-2251; *Fax:* (610) 437-1610
www.philipcooke.com
Kent Kjellgren, President
Distribute video cassette duplications equipment & CDs.

Phillystran Inc.
151 Commerce Dr., Montgomeryville, PA 18936-9628 USA
(215) 368-6611; *Fax:* (215) 362-7956
www.phillystran.com
information@phillystran.com
Wynne Wister III, President
Kenneth Knight, General Sales Mgr
Robert Lombardo, Managing Director
Phillystran HPTG; electrically transparent, maintenance free tower guy system; specially designed systems for high-power applications.

Phoenix Engineering, Inc.
3331 North Berkeley Lake Road, Suites 100 - 110, Berkeley Lake, GA 30096 USA
(404) 975-0795, (404) 975-0796, (770) 364-7240; *Fax:* (77) 783-8170
www.phxatl.net
reguest@phxatl.com
Kevin Jordan, President
Bob Braun, Operations Dir
One man band live trucks, vans, 4-wheel-drive. On-location radio vehicles & production trucks.

Photo Research, Inc.
9731 Topanga Canyon Pl., Chatsworth, CA 91311-4135 USA
(818) 725-9750; *Fax:* (818) 725-9770
www.photoresearch.com
Francis Dominic, President/CEO
Mike Klein, Chief Marketing Officer
George Ward, Engineering Tech
Brightness photometers, footcandle meters, telephotometers, spectroradiometers, spectral & spatial scanners.

Photomart Cine-Video Inc.
6869 Stapoint Court, Suite 112, Winter Park, FL 32792 USA
(407) 381-5606, (800) 443-2901, (888) 792-9283; *Fax:* (407) 381-5610
www.audiovideoelectrical.com
Jeffrey Bova, President
Sls, svc, of professional support equipment, supplies for video, film & still photography.

Photonis USA Pennsylvania
1000 New Holland Ave., Lancaster, PA 17601 US
(717) 295-6000, (800) 366-2875; *Fax:* (717) 295-6096
www.photonis.com/
info@photonisusa.com
E. Burlefinger, CEO
Carl Rintz, President
Kirk Jenne, General Counsel
VHF/FM power tubes, photomultipliers & imaging devices.

Pinnacle Systems Inc.
385 Rovendale Drive, Mountain View, CA 94043 USA
(800) 762-9741; *Fax:* (650) 526-1601
www.pinnaclesys.com
Sharad Rastogi, General Manager
Tanguy Leborgne, Promotions Manager
Manufacturer of a complete set of home video editing & PCTV viewing tools for the consumer market.

Pinta Acoustic Inc.
2601 49th Ave. N # 400, Minneapolis, MN 55430 USA
(612) 355-4200, (800) 662-0032; *Fax:* (612) 355-4299
www.pinta-acoustic.com
sales@pinta-acoustic.com
Mark Frederick, CFO
Sonex accoustical products including wall panels & ceiling tiles.

Pinzone Engineering Group Inc.
10142 Fairmount Rd., Newbury, OH 44065 USA
(304) 368-7950; *Fax:* (440) 729-5591
www.pinzone.com
systemsengineering@pinzone.com
Basil Pinzone, President
Bernadette Pinzone, Vice President
Satellite Uplinks Systems, Turnkey, Site Engineering, AM Broadcast Antenna- Anti-Skywave Antenna.

Pirod Inc.
1545 Pidco Drive, Plymouth, IN 46563-1354 USA
(574) 936-4221, (877) 467-4763; *Fax:* (574) 936-6796
www.valmont.com
pirod@pirod.com
Myron Noble, CEO
Hillary Asher, General Sales Mgr
Frank Epps, Engineering Dir
Solid-rod towers, monopoles & tower accessories for cellular, PCs, bdcst, microwave & two-way communication.

Pixel Instruments Corp.
20526 Prospect Road, Saratoga, CA 95032 USA
(408) 871-1975; *Fax:* (408) 871-1976
chris@pixelinstruments.tv
Mirko Vojnovic, President
Chris Smith, Director of Sales and Marketing
Chris Smith, Director of Sales and Marketing
Designs & manufactures innovative audio & video signals processing products with an emphasis on the measurement & correction of lips sync errors. These products are used in a wide range of bcst, cable TV, video production & relatedapplications. Current products include the LipTracker Lip Sync Analyer, Audio Delay Synchronizers for automatic lip sync correction & Tally/GPI Interfaces.

PMTV Producers Management Television
681 Moore Rd., Suite 100, King of Prussia, PA 19406
(877) 629-4122, (407) 629-4122; *Fax:* (610) 768-1773
www.productionhub.com/profile/pmtv-producers-management-television
mailto.pmtv@pmtv.com
Brian Powers, President
Danna Doo, Operations Dir
Rob Schmoll, SVP
Full-svc mobile TV production company, providing mobile units, crews, satellite svcs, lighting, staging, etc. for sports, entertainment & teleconferences worldwide.

Polyline Corp.
Mailing Address: 845 N Church Ct., Elmhurst, IL 60126 USA
Second Address: 4518 W. Vanowen St., Burbank, CA 91505
(800) 701-7689, (630) 993-2700; *Fax:* (800) 816-3330
www.polylinecorp.com
sales@polylinecorp.com
Edwin Kaiser, President
Ray Kaiser, Marketing Executive
Michael Sandborn, Manager
Stock media packaging for DVD, CD, VHS & audio plus bulk CD-R, DVD-R, Blu-ray media. Disc publishing equipment & supplies are also available.

Polyline West Coast Distribution Ctr.
4408 W. Vanowen St., Burbank, CA 91505 United States

PortaBrace
940 Water Street, PO Box 220, North Bennington, VT 5257 US
(802) 442-8171; *Fax:* (802) 442-9118
www.portabrace.com
info@portabrace.com
Gregg Haythorn, President
Mike D'Angelo, Station Manager
Willis Hunt, Audio/Video/Photography Sales
Mike D' Angelo, Custom Projects
Chris Miceli, Marketing-Related Inquiries
Nancy Briggs, Design-Related Inquiries
Craig O'Dell,Shipping
Tammy Roy, Accounting
Soft carrying cases for professional portable video/audio equipment.

Potomac Instruments, Inc.
7309 Grove Rd., Unit D, Fredrick, MD 21704 USA
(301) 696-5550; *Fax:* (301) 696-5553
www.pi-usa.com
sales@pi-usa.com
Chris Babendreier, COO
Zack Babendreier, President
Cliff Hall, Chief Engineer
Antenna monitors, field strength meters, repairs and calibration.

Power & Telephone Supply Co.
2673 Yale Ave., Memphis, TN 38112-3335 USA
(901) 324-6116, (800) 238-7514; *Fax:* (901) 320-3082
www.ptsupply.com
marketing@ptsupply.com
Jim Pentecost, Chairman
Jennifer Pentecost Sims, CEO
Jim Pentecost, President
Laburn Dye, Operations Dir
Don Pentecost, Vice-President, Contractors
Full-line supplier of communication products, including telecom, data & cable TV.
16666 S.W. 72nd, Bldg. 12, Tigard, OR 97224 United States
(503) 620-4909; *Fax:* (503) 620-9074
Andy Baker, Chairman
Box 244, Rt. 272, Reamstown, PA 17567 United States
(215) 267-4991; *Fax:* (215) 267-4367
Don Skinner, Chairman
Box 1856, 2950 Greensboro St., Lexington, NC 27292 United States
(704) 249-0256; *Fax:* (704) 249-7475
Don Skinner, Chairman
3107 S.W. 61st St., Bldg. D, Des Moines, IA 50321 United States
(515) 244-4375; *Fax:* (515) 244-4757
Doug McPhee, Chairman
12314 Bell Ranch Rd., Los Angeles, CA 90670 United States
(310) 903-1701; *Fax:* (310) 903-1705
Sonny Dickinson, Chairman
7535 N.W. 52nd St., Miami, FL 33166 United States
(305) 597-0091; 597-0262
Tommy Browder, Chairman

Powr-Ups Corp.
One Roned Rd., Brookhaven Red Plaza, Shirley, NY 11967 USA
(631) 345-5700; *Fax:* (631) 345-0060
www.powrupscorp.com
info@powrupscorp.com
Steven Summer, President
DC-motor controls.

Precision Microproducts of America
1 Comac Loop, Unit 13, Ronkonkoma, NY 11779 US
(631) 580-3456, (800) 932-9215; *Fax:* (631) 580-3003
www.p-m-a.com
sales@p-m-a.com
Carlos Fernades, President
Photographic processing machines & accessories.

Prime Image, Inc.
Mailing Address: 1415 Koll Circle, Suite 105, San Jose, CA 95112 USA
Second Address: 200 Highpoint Dr., Suite 215, Chalfont, PA 18914
(408) 452-7740, (215) 822-1561, (215) 817-2713; *Fax:* (408) 926-7294
www.primeimageinc.com
Bennett Lomax, Chairman
Dave Whalen, CEO
Rodney Hampton, Sales
Bob Waligunda, Promotions Manager
Keith Schindler, VP of Engineering
Jim Maury, Chief Technology Officer
Gary Gatchell, CFO
Al Snyder, Vice Chairman
Kevin Wagner,Core Development Officer & SVP, BD
Rodney Hampton, VP, Sales
Provides digital progmg time reduction/editingequipment; audio & video delays; transcoding time base correctors; synchronizers; digital standards converters; computer video products.

Prisma Packaging
2302 West Claibourn Street, Milwaukee, WI 53188 USA
(414) 342-6464; *Fax:* (414) 342-0932
www.prismapackaging.com
info@prismapackaging.com
Richard Schmaelzle, President
Printer manufacturer specializing in presentation folders, media kits, sls kits & videocassette packaging.

Pro Video & Film Equipment Co. Inc.
11425 Mathis Ave., Dallas, TX 75234 USA
(972) 869-9990, (888) 869-9998; *Fax:* (972) 869-0145
www.provideofilm.com
providfilm@aol.com
Bill Reiter, President & Founder
Stephanie Fox, Promotions Manager
Used equipment dealer specializing in video, bcst, film, lighting, audio. Consignment, sales, leasing & appraisal svcs available. Service & repairs.

ProAudio.com/Crouse-Kimzey Company
Mailing Address: 1320 Post & Paddock Rd, Suite 200, Grand Prairie, TX 75050 US
Second Address: PO Box 155999, Fort Worth, TX 76155
(800) 433-2105, (972) 660-6100; *Fax:* (972) 623-2800
www.proaudio.com
sales@proaudio.com
John Paul Kimzey, President/Chief Executive Officer
Stephanie Glockzin, Operations Manager
Mark Bradford, VP/GM
Lee Edwards, Chief Engineer
Barry Pike, Account Manager
Scott Price, Account Manager
Gary Mann, Account Manager
Kevin Lorensen, Account Manager
Matt Loria, Account Manager
Tim LaPrade, Account Manager
Founded in 1971 as Crouse-Kimzey Company, ProAudio.com is a Fort Worth, Texas based distributor and systems integrator for more than 400 professional audio, video, lighting and broadcast equipment lines. We are the supplier of choice forbusinesses large and small, individuals, churches, schools and contractors, in all 50 U.S. states and internationally.

Crouse Kimzey/Mid-America
9170 South U.S. Hwy. 27, Lynn, IN 47355 United States
(877) 223-2221; *Fax:* (765) 874-2540
Barry Pike, Acct Mgr

Crouse-Kimzey of Missouri
381 Molly Ln., Rockaway Beach, MO 65740
(417) 561-1050 (800) 955-6800; *Fax:* (417) 561-1052
Bill Wallace, Acct Mgr

Crouse-Kimzey of Colorado
4125 Novia Dr., Colorado Springs, CO 80911 United States
(800) 257-6233; *Fax:* (719) 392-8876
Lee Edwards, Acct Mgr

Production Intercom Inc./Technical Projects
Box 3247, Barrington, IL 60011-3247 USA
(800) 562-5872; *Fax:* (847) 381-4360
www.beltpack.com
info@beltpack.com
Glenn mullis, President
Sibbelina Mullis, Operations Dir
Unique talent receiver (IFB), small to large intercom systems, headsets for cameras & new half-duplex wireless system.

Professional Sound Corp.
28085 Smyth Dr., Valencia, CA 91355 USA
(661) 295-9395; *Fax:* (661) 295-8398
www.professionalsound.com
Ron Meyer, President
Debby Meyer, Promotions Manager
Design, manufacture of portable sound recording products for film & video industries

Professional Sound Services Inc.
Mailing Address: 311 W. 43rd St., Suite #200, New York, NY 10036 USA
Second Address: 1515 South Salcedo St., Suite 130, New Orleans, LA 70125
(212) 586-1033, (504) 309-7112, (800) 883-1033; *Fax:* (212) 586-0970, (504) 309-7138
www.pro-sound.com
Rich Topham, President
Wireless microphones, wireless, wired intercoms, IFB, telephone interfaces, analog, digital recorders, mixers, lavaliers, boompoles.Sls, rentals & svc.

Prophet Systems Innovations
214 Spruce Street, Ogallala, NE 69153 USA
(877) 774-1010; *Fax:* (308) 284-4181
www.prophetsys.com
prophetsales@prophetsys.com
Kevin Lockhart, President
Tim Gieschen, President/Operations
Tanya Gieschen, Director/Information Services

Protech Audio Corp.
192 Cedar River Rd., PO Box 597, Indian Lake, NY 12842 USA
(518) 648-6410; *Fax:* (518) 648-6395
www.protechaudio.com
Bill Murphy, President
Dugan Automatic Mixing Controllers, Audio Distribution Amplifiers, Dugan Automatic Mixers

Prysmian Communications Cables and Systems USA, LLC
700 Industrial Dr., Lexington, SC 29072 USA
(803) 951-4800; *Fax:* (803) 951-4898
energy.cables.na@prysmian.com
Martin Hanchard, CEO
Brian DiLascia, Operations Dir
ISO 9001-registered manufacturer of fiber-optic cables & Fiber to the Home (FTTH) solutions.

QEI Corporation
Box 805, One Airport Drive, Williamstown, NJ 8094 USA
(856) 728-2020, (800) 334-9154; *Fax:* (856) 629-1751
Bruce Sadzean, President
Rick Harvey, Vice President
John Turzanski, Purchasing Executive

Qintar Technologies Inc.
877 Daffodil Court, Simi Valley, CA 93065 USA
(818) 991-7300; *Fax:* (818) 889-7400
www.qintar.com
websales@qintar.com
Randy Tishkoff, Founder & CEO
Randall Tishkoff, President
Dave Richards, Product Manager
Active & passive devices for CATV, amplifiers, filters, connectors, wall plates & wiring products. We also make OEM and custom products.

QSC Audio Products, LLC
1675 MacArthur Blvd., Costa Mesa, CA 92626 USA
(714) 754-6175, (800) 854-4079; *Fax:* (714) 754-6174
www.qsc.com
info@qscaudio.com
Pat Quilter, Founder & Chairman
Barry Andrews, Founder & Co-CEO
Joe Pham, President and Chief Executive Officer
Ray Biba, Sales Director - Systems, US West
Jatan Shah, Executive Vice President/Chief Operating Officer
Barry Ferrell,Senior Vice President and Chief Strategy Officer
Ray van Straten, Vice President, Professional
John White, Vice President, Research & Development
Greg Wilson, Vice President, Quality and Service
Anna Csontos, Director of Strategic Programs
Professional power amplifiers, dual monaural power amplifiers, plug-in accessory products, integrated amplifiers, music & paging system.

Quality Tower Erectors Inc.
2280 10th St. S.E., Largo, FL 33771 USA
(727) 585-6176; *Fax:* (727) 581-3277
www.qualitytower.com
info@qualitytower.com
Robert Diamond, President/Owner
QTE offers a full line of tower services in addition to our other offerings. Now more than ever, QTE is the complete soloution for your communication site & asset needs. Tum Key civil services, erection, antenna systems, microwave,cellular, painting, turnkey service & tower site rental services included.

Quantel Inc.
Mailing Address: 1 Yonge St., Suite 1008, Toronto, ON M5E 1E5 USA
Second Address: 25 W. 43rd St., Suite 1118, New York, NY 10036-7406
(416) 362-9522, (212) 944-6820, (800) 331-8327; *Fax:* (416) 362-9215, (212) 944-6813
www.quantel.com
Tom McGowan, CEO
Steve Owen, Promotions Manager
Brad Wensley, District Sales Manager
Mark Northeast, VP Sales
Quantel is the world's leading designer & manufacturer of digital image processing & manipulation products for video, film & print.
5 Concourse Pkwy., Suite 330, Atlanta, GA 30338 United States
(770) 804-5470; *Fax:* (770) 804-5479
Dan Wingard, Chairman
111 W. 57th St., 10th Fl., New York, NY 10019 United States
(212) 977-4877; *Fax:* (212) 977-6539
Dave Saadatmandi, Chairman
8501 Wilshire Blvd., Suite 340, Los Angeles, CA 90212 United States
(310) 652-9227; *Fax:* (310) 657-8869
Mark Grasso, Chairman
1Yonge St., Suite 1100, Toronto, ON M5E 1E5 Canada
(416) 362-9522
Mark Northeast, Chairman
100 Bush St., Suite 1910, San Francisco, CA 94104 United States
(650) 225-9036 (415) 263-1300; *Fax:* (650) 225-9091
Tom McGowan, Chairman
541 N. Fairbanks, Suite 1225, Chicago, IL 60611 United States
(312) 755-1766; *Fax:* (312) 755-1767

R.L. Drake Holdings LLC
Mailing Address: 9900 Springboro Avenue, Miamisburg, OH 45342 US
Second Address: 655 The Queensway, Unit 16, Peterborough, ON K9J 7M1
(937) 746-4556, (937) 746-6990, (742) 742-3122; *Fax:* (937) 806-1510, (937) 806-1511, (742) 742-2838
www.rldrake.com
salesgroup@rldrake.net
Ron Wysong, CEO
Andy Ruffin, General Sales Mgr
Philip Hawkins, Sales
R.L. Drake designs and manufactures world-class systems for digital and analog cable, digital signage, and MPEG encoding. We're based in Miamisburg, Ohio, and have offices in the US and Canada. Our reputation for producing quality productsand providing exceptional customer service has been well earned and is respected internationally.
655 The Queensway, Peterborough, ON K9J 7M1 Canada
(705) 742-3122
Steve Roe, Sls Mgr

Radian Communication Services Inc
461 Cornwall Rd., Box 880, Oakville, ON L6J 5C5 Canada
(905) 844-1242; *Fax:* (905) 844-8837
www.radiancorp.com
info@radiancorp.com
H Douglas Tipple, President/CEO
David Hahn, Vice President
Design, supply, instal of bcst transmitters, antennas & towers.

Radio Computing Services (RCS)
445 Hamilton Ave., 7th Floor, White Plains, NY 10601 USA
(914) 428-4600, (914) 259-4900; *Fax:* (914) 428-5922, (914) 428-5923
www.rcsworks.com
info@rcsworks.com
Philippe Generali, President & CEO
Mike Powell, Operations Dir
Chip Jellison, EVP/ Technology & Development
Mike Powell, VP/ International
Dwight Douglas, VP/ Marketing
Neal Perchuk, VP/ Sales US
Ravish Bhattiprolu, VP/Finance
Dean Karounos, VP/ Information Technology
Digital studio automation & digital audio ripping/analysis, music scheduling, traf, sls, newsroom & talk show software/hardware, internet/streaming tools.
10 Anson Rd, 10-10 International Plaza, Singapore, 079903 Sin
+65 6324 6658; *Fax:* 65-6324-6659
cfawell@attglobel.net
Colin Fawell, Gen Mgr
Borsigallee 37, Frankfurt, 60388
49-610-973-4450; *Fax:* 49-610-973-4499
info@rcseurope.de
Karl Kessler, Gen Mgr
262 Hart Niwas, 30th Rd., Bandra Mumboi (West), 400050 India
+91 22 697 1600; *Fax:* +91 22 695 5760
Elliot Stechman, Chairman
83 Ave. Philippe Auguste, Paris, 75011 France
33-1-53-27-36-36; *Fax:* 33- 1-53- 27- 36-60
Eric Vanryckeghem, Chairman

RCS (NZ) Ltd.
33 Sir William Pickering Dr., Christchurch, 8005 New Zealand
+64.3.358.4333; *Fax:* +64.3.358.4330
info@rcs.co.nz www.rsc.co.nz
Ian Campbell, Chairman
Box 32060, 410 #5 Rd., Richmond, BC V6X 3R9 Canada
(604) 986-4468; *Fax:* (604) 986-4469
Ross Langbell, Chairman

Radio Design Labs. (RDL)
659 N. 6th St., Prescott, AZ 86301 USA
(928) 443-9391, (800) 281-2683; *Fax:* (928) 443-9392, (800) 289-7338

www.rdlnet.com
sales@rdlnet.com
Joel Bump, President
Daniel Bump, General Sales Mgr
Full line of microphone & line level amplifiers, mixers, DAs & processors.

Radio Engineering Industries Inc.
6534 L St., Omaha, NE 68117 USA
(402) 339-2200, (877) 726-4617, (800) 228-9275; *Fax:* (402) 339-1704
www.radioeng.com
info@radioeng.com
Terry Jukes, CEO
Dave Ruback, President
Gunnar Guenette, Promotions Manager
Sls, svc of bcst equipment, amplifiers, paging systems, SCA & coml sound equipment.

Radio Frequency Systems
200 Pondview Dr., Meriden, CT 6450-7195 US
(203) 630-3311, (800) 437-3045; *Fax:* (203) 634-2272
www.rfsworld.com
sales.americas@rfsworld.com
Bill Bayne, President
Bob Braun, Operations Dir
John Gu, Chief Technical Officer
Rick Kluesner, Controller
We provide RF Systems solutions for cell-based mobile communications, in-building, in-tunnels, television & radio, radio-link networks, LMR/PMR and HF & defense.

Radio Research Instrument Co. Inc.
584 N. Main St., Waterbury, CT 6704 USA
(203) 753-5840; *Fax:* (203) 754-2567
E. Doyle, President
Sy Chaimovich, Chief Engineer
P. Plishner, President
Provides radar systems, threat emitters & spare parts; complete maintenance facility for repair.

Radio Systems Inc.
601 Heron Dr., Logan Township, NJ 8085 USA
(856) 467-8000; *Fax:* (856) 467-3044
www.radiosystems.com
sales@radiosystems.com
Daniel Braverman, President
Gerrett Conover, Operations Dir
Analog, digital & Live-wire-compatible audio consoles, distribution amplifiers, low-power TIS/HAR AM transmitters, clock & timer systems, telephone hybrids, the StudioHub+wiring system & IP-Connect, a licensed 18 GHz digitalstudio-to-transmitter link.

Radiodetection
28 Tower Rd., Raymond, ME 4071 USA
(207) 655-8525, (877) 247-3797; *Fax:* (207) 655-8535
www.radiodetection.com
rd.sales.us@spx.com
Zenya Brackett, Operations Dir
Paul Sherman, General Sales Mgr
Electronic test equipment; cable fault locators; time domain reflectometer.

RAM SYSTEMS, LLC
Mailing Address: 27992 W. Rt. 120, Unit #138, Lakemoor, IL 60051 USA
Second Address: 92 Caplan Avenue, Suite #255, Barrie, ON L4N 0Z7
(815) 679-6574, (705) 487-2915; *Fax:* (815) 679-6634, (815) 679-6634
www.ramsystemsonline.com
Ron Mitchell, President
Switchers (audio & video) mixers, intercom systems, audio/video DAs, systems engrg & custom cabinetry.

Raven Screen Corp.
112-T Spring St., Monroe, NY 10950 USA
(800) 847-6906, (845) 782-1844; *Fax:* (845) 782-1840
www.ravenscreen.com
info@ravenscreen.com
Martin Soss, President
Manual, motorized & custom projection screens & materials.

Record/Play Tek Inc.
Box 790, 112 E. Vistula St., Bristol, IN 46507-0790 USA
(574) 848-5233, (800) 809-5233; *Fax:* (574) 848-5533
www.recordplaytek.com
info@recordplaytek.com
Michael Stoll, CEO
Voice logging recorders 911, cassette, reel-to-reel, VHS, computer CDR & DVD+ R.

Recortec Inc.
3329 Kifer Rd., Santa Clara, CA 95051-0719 USA
(408) 928-1480, (800) 729-7654; *Fax:* (408) 928-1489
www.recortec.com
George Walls, COO
Lester Lee, President
Manufacturer of coml disc players & LCD players.

Reel-O-Matic Inc.
6408 S. Eastern Ave., Oklahoma City, OK 73149 USA
(405) 672-0000, (888) 873-4000, (405) 672-7200; *Fax:* (405) 672-7200
sales@reelomatic.com
Terry Simmons, President
Mark Zercher, Operations Dir
Russell Maddox, Engineering Tech
Equipment to re-spool, coil, measure & distribute cable.

Rees Associates Inc.
1800 SW 2nd St., Des Moines, IA 50315-7147 USA
(515) 243-2127, (631) 292-2674; *Fax:* (515) 243-1026, (515) 246-0880
www.reesassociates.com
Quotes@reesassociates.com
C. Leroy James, COO
Frank Rees, President
Ralph S. Blackman, Operations Dir
William Yost, Vice President
Steven Lawson, Vice President
Dennis Hahn, National Accounts Manager
Scott Lundstrom, Account Executive Manager
PeterStein, Director of Business Development, New York
Bcst & production facility design; architectural svcs; studio design; equipment planning; facility business plans; interior design & consulting.
1801 N. Lamar St., Suite 600, Dallas, TX 75202 United States
(214) 522-7337
951 Peachtree St. N.E., Atlanta, GA 30309
(404) 351-6869
7810 N. Forker Rd., Spokane, WA 99217
(509) 921-1057

Register Data Systems
1691 Forsyth St., Macon, GA 31201 USA
(478) 745-5858; *Fax:* (478) 745-0500
www.registerdata.com
Lowell Register, President
Ricky Lockerman, General Sales Mgr
Digital audio automation systems for live assist, satellite, traf & billing software packages for radio & TV.

Renkus-Heinz Inc.
19201 Cook St., Foothill Ranch, CA 92610-3501 USA
(949) 588-9997; *Fax:* (949) 588-9514
www.renkus-heinz.com
sales@renkus-heinz.com
Harro K. Heinz, Chairman
Roscoe Anthony, President
Carl Dorwaldt, Promotions Manager
Tim Shuttleworth, Engineering Manager
Rik Kirby, VP Sales & Marketing
Karl Brunvoll, VP International Sales
Monika Smetona, Vice PresidentAdministration
Rik Kirby, Vice President Sales & Marketing
Margie Ulm, Marketing Manager
Karl Brunvoll, Vice President International Sales
Reference point arrays, powered network loudspeakers, R-control remote supervision network. Reference point arrays, powered network loudspeakers.

Research Technology International Inc.
4700 Chase Ave., Lincolnwood, IL 60712-1689 USA
(847) 677-3000, (800) 323-7520; *Fax:* (847) 677-1311, (800) 784-6733
www.rtico.com
sales@rtico.com
Ray Short, President & CEO
Thomas Boyle, Operations Dir
Bill Wolavka, General Sales Mgr
Matthew Malone, CFO
Tom Boyle, Sr. VP, RTI Sales
Cheryl Davis, Sales Administrator
Tany Enicinas, Administrative Asst.
Sherwin Berger,Sales & Advertising
William Deiker, Regional Sales Manager
Videotape evaluator/cleaners; degaussers; storage & care, supplies, film cleaners. CD/DVD cleaners-restorers inspectors.

RF Specialties Group
22406 N.E. 159th St., Kearney, MO 64060 USA
(800) 467-7373, (816) 628-5959; *Fax:* (816) 628-4508
www.rfspec.com
rfmo@uniteone.net
Patricia Kreger, Chairman
Chris Kreger, General Manager
John Sims, General Sales Mgr
John Sims, Sales Engineer, Raymore Office
Rick Funk, Sales Engineer, Indiana Slaes Office
Full-line radio bcst equipment suppliers. AM & FM transmitters, towers, lines, antenna systems, studios, microwave & digital systems.

RF Specialties of Missouri, Inc.
22406 N.E. 159th St., Kearney, MO 64060 United States
(800) 467-7373 (816) 628-5959; *Fax:* (816) 628-4508
rfmo@uniteone.net
Chris Kreger, Chairman
John Sims, CEO/COO

RF Specialties of Asia Corporation
4958 Guerrero St., Poblacion, Makati City, Metro Manila, 15239 Philippines
+63-2-412-4327; *Fax:* +63-2-895-6509
eedmiston@rfsasia.com
Ed Edmiston, Chairman

RF Specialties of Missouri, Inc.
1651 Capri Lane, Richmond, IN 47374-1501 United States
888-966-1990; *Fax:* 800-859-5481
rf@insightbb.com
Rick Funk, Chairman

RF Specialties of Pennsylvania, Inc.
40 Settlement Hill, New Ipswich, NH 03071 United States
(603) 878-0618 (800) 485-8684; *Fax:* (603) 878-1527
sam_on_the_hill@Monad.net
S.A. Matthews, Chairman

RF Specialties of California
3463 State St., Suite 229, Santa Barbara, CA 93105 United States
(805) 682-9429 (800) 346-6434; *Fax:* (805) 682-5170
rfsca@aol.com
Sam Lane, Chairman

RF Specialties of Florida
4706 Young Rd., Crestview, FL 32539 United States
(850) 423-7335 (800) 476-8943; *Fax:* (850) 423-7331
rfoffl@aol.com
William Hoisington, Chairman

RF Technologies Corp.
1 Gendron Dr., Lewiston, ME 4240 USA
(207) 777-7778; *Fax:* (207) 777-7784
George Harris, President
Peter Robicheau, Operations Dir
Bill Ammons, General Sales Mgr
Designs & manufactures high-power bcst RF nets, components for FM & TV bcstrs. Products include antennas, diplexers, combiners, filters, switches, coax, waveguides & coaxal.

Richardson Electronics
PO Box 393, 40W267 Keslinger Rd., LaFox, IL 60147-0393 USA
(630) 208-2200; *Fax:* (630) 208-2550
www.rell.com
broadcast@rell.com
Edward J. Richardson, CEO/ President/ Chairman/ COO
Robert Prince, Operations Dir
Kathleen S. Dvorak, EVP, CFO & Chief Strategy Officer
Kathleen M. McNally, SVP, Marketing Operations & Customer Support
Sandeep Beotra, EVP of Mergers& acquitions
James M. Dudek Jr., Controller & Chief Accounting Officer
Global provider of power tubes, TV, radio transmitters, IP, digital satellite systems, NLE video systems & studio pakages.
Box 393, 40W267 Keslinger Rd., LaFox, IL 60147-0393 United States
(630) 208-2200 (800) 882-3872; *Fax:* (630) 208-2550
broadcast@rell.com broadcast.rell.com

Richmond Sound Design Ltd.
5264 Ross Street, Vancouver, BC V5W 3K7 Canada
(604) 715-9441, (800) 664-5861; *Fax:* (604) 628-3391
www.richmondsounddesign.com
C.B. Richmond, President
M. Williams, General Manager
Charlie Richmond, Founder
Virtual Sound System & show control software.

RIO Steel & Tower, LTD
12017 Mitchell Drive, Alvarado, TX 76009 US
817-225-0890; *Fax:* 817-225-0895
www.riosteel.com
info@riosteel.com
Keith Cendrick, President
Vance Happerman, General Sales Mgr

EQUIPMENT MANUFACTURERS

Tower mf, Erection, maintenance, true turn-key installation, foundations, emergency svcs, antenna & transmission line replacement, site acquistion.

Ripley Company
46 Nooks Hill Rd., Cromwell, CT 6416 USA
(860) 635-2200, (800) 528-8665; *Fax:* (860) 635-3631
www.ripley-tools.com
info@ripley-tools.com
Kenneth McCormath, President
Tom Lindenmuth, General Manager
Keith D'Amato, General Sales Mgr
Annette Loomis, TechnicalCustomer Service Representative Team Lead
Sue Taylor, International Sales Coordinator
Christian Festa, Sr.Director of Sales & Marketing
Justin Rogers, Sales Trainer/ Applications Specialist
Geoff Kelly, Sales Manager Electrical & Utility
Julia Chen, Customer Service
Ripley's Cablematic, Miller & Utility tool lines offer manufacturers cable preparation tools for CATV telecomm data & electric utiliy.

Rodelco Electronics Corp.
111 Haynes Ct., Ronkonkoma, NY 11779 USA
(631) 981-0900; *Fax:* (631) 981-1792
www.rodelco-usa.com
Joseph Rodgers, President
John Mellon, Engineering Dir
Peter Nister, Chief Engineer
TV translators, VHF & UHF.

Rohn Products, LLC
Mailing Address: 6800 W. Plank Rd., Peoria, IL 61604 USA
Second Address: #1 Fairholm Ave., Peoria, IL 61603
(309) 566-3000, (800) 727-ROHN; *Fax:* (309) 566-3079
www.rohnnet.com
Horace Ward, CEO
Dave Ramsey, General Sales Mgr
Dave Brinker, VP of Engineering
Dan Ludolph, CFO
Mark Allen, VP of Sales/ Marketing
Chuck Hammond, Manufacturing Director
Ray Adams, Construction Manager
Chalmer Post,Documentation Control
Towers (up to 2,000 feet) monopoles, antenna mounts for communication industry. Turnkey construction & installation avaible worldwide.

Roland Corp. U.S.
5100 S. Eastern Ave., Los Angeles, CA 90040-2938 USA
(323) 890-3700, (323) 890-3700; *Fax:* (323) 890-3701
www.rolandus.com
Dennis Houlihan, CEO
Vince Landuca, Chief Marketing Executive
Mark Malbon, Executive Vice President
Electronic musical instruments, signal processors, sound reinforcement, hard disk editors, noise eliminators, bcst production equipment & post production equipment.

Rosco Laboratories Inc.
Mailing Address: 52 Harbor View Ave., Stamford, CT 6902 USA
Second Address: 9420 Chivers ave., Sun Valley, CA 91352
(203) 708-8900, (800) 767-2669, (818) 543-6700; *Fax:* (203) 708-8919, (818) 662-9470
www.rosco.com
info@rosco.com
Stan Miller, Chairman
Mark Engel, CEO
Ed Donohue, President
Tracey Cosgrove, Operations Director
Chad Tiller, Sales Manager
Pat Santarsiero, Director of Human Resources
Lauren Proud, Marketing Manager
Joshua Alemany, Directorof Global Marketing
Pat Santarsiero, Director of Human Resources
Ame Strong, Sales Director
Donna Nicol, Creative Director
Lighting filters & diffusers, studio floor covering, connectors & digital (or rental & custom) backdrops.
1120 N. Citrus Ave, Hollywood, CA 90038 United States
(323) 462-2233; *Fax:* (323) 462-3338
Jim Meyer, Mgr

Roscor Corp.
1061 Feehanville Dr., Mount Prospect, IL 60056 USA
(847) 299-8080; *Fax:* (847) 299-4206,(847) 803-8089
www.roscor.com
Mitch Roston, Vice President
Edward Jones, Operations Dir
Tom Voigts, General Sales Mgr
Paul Roston, President
Professional audio/video/RF/presentation equipment. Turnkey engrg & instal svcs.
27280 Haggerty Rd., Suite C2, Farmington Hills, MI 48331 United States
(248) 489-0090
Paul Niehaus, Branch Mgr
600 W. Virginia St., Milwaukee, WI 53204 United States
(414) 223-2600
Steve Olson, Branch Mgr
2868 E. Kemper Rd., Cincinnati, OH 45241
(513) 772-3393
Tim Navaro, Branch Mgr

Ross Video Ltd.
Mailing Address: Box 220, 8 John St., Iroquois, ON K0E 1K0 Canada
Second Address: 64 Auriga St., Ottawa, ON K2E 1B8
(613) 652-4886, (613) 228-0688; *Fax:* (613) 652-4425, (613) 228-0464
www.rossvideo.com
solutions@rossvideo.com
David Ross, CEO
Jeff Poapst, Operations Dir
Jeff Moore, General Sales Mgr
Joe Lalonde, CFO
Jeff Moore, EVP & Chief Marketing Officer
Darren Budrow, Sr. VP Worldwide Sales
Dae Choe, VP of Sales (Asia)
Jared Schartz, SalesDirector (USA-Central & Southern)
Pete Ross, Sales Director (USA-Northeast & Pacific)
Ross Video's product line includes Vision & Synergy Multi-Definition Video production switchers, openGear, RossGear & GearLite Terminal Equipment, SoftMetal Video Servers & the OverDrive Production Control System.

Royal Consumer Information Products
379 Campus Dr., Somerset, NJ 8875 USA
(732) 627-9977; *Fax:* (800) 232-4769
www.royal.com
Salomon Suwalsky, President
Todd Althoff, Operations Dir
Todd Althoff, VP of Marketing & New Development

RSD Consulting Services, LLC
208 Hamilton Rd., Ridgewood, NJ 7450 USA
(201) 389-3705; *Fax:* (201) 389-3705
www.rsdconsulting.com
postmaster@rsdconsulting.com
Bob Dietz, CEO
Walter Clarke, President
Esther McGinnis, Operations Dir
Richard Datz, Founder
Consulting engrs, tower engrg, design & construction mgmt.

RTI: BHP Inc.
4700 Chase Ave., Lincolnwood, IL 60712 US
(847) 677-3000, (800) 323-7520; *Fax:* (847) 677-1311, (800) 784-6733
www.rtico.com
sales@rtico.com
Ray Short, President/CEO
Chris Johnson, Export Sales Manager
Jonathan Banks, President-RTI Film Group
Tom Boyle, Senior Vice President
Bill Wolavka, Vice President
Matthew Malone, Chief Financial Officer
Scott Jahnke, RegionalSales Manager
Jeff Willour, Materials Manager
Motion picture laboratory equipment, film printers & accessories.

RTS Systems Telex Communications Inc
2550 N. Hollywood Way, Suite 207, Burbank, CA 91505-1055 USA
(818) 566-6700; *Fax:* (818) 843-7953
www.telex.com
Ralph Strader, Operations Dir
Britt Bowers, General Sales Mgr
Murray Porteous, National Sales Manager
Ken Smalley, Regional Sales Manager New York
Michael Brown, Regional Sales Manager NE
Rick Fisher, Regional Sales ManagerSouth
Dave Richardson, Regional Sales Manager West
Intercommunication systems, IFB systems, pro-audio amplifiers, microphones & phono preamplifiers.
10927 FM 1565, Terrell, TX 75160 United States
(972) 524-6047
Britt Bowers, Rgnl Sls
Box 866, 10 Park Pl. Bldg. 1, Butler, NJ 07405 United States
(973) 283-6200
Ken Smalley, Rgnl Sls
311 Stillwater Cove, Destin, FL 32541 United States
(850) 654-4058
Rick Fisher, Sls Regl Mgr
15463 Waters Creek, Centerville, VA 20120 United States
(703) 867-8333
Michael Brown, Sls Regnl
3807 Sunrise Lakes, Milford, PA 18337 United States
(570) 686-5444
Chuck Roberts, Tech Support/Engrg

Russ Bassett Corporation
8189 Byron Rd., Whittier, CA 90606 USA
(562) 945-2445, (800) 350-2445; *Fax:* (562) 698-8972
www.russbassett.com
info@russbassett.com
Ed Bassett, Owner
High density storage solutions for all media type.

S W R Inc.
619 Industrial Park Rd., Ebensburg, PA 15931 USA
(814) 472-5436, (800) 762-7743; *Fax:* (814) 472-5552
www.swr-rf.com
davide@swr-rf.com
David K Edmiston Sr., President & CEO
David Edmiston, General Sales Mgr
David K Edmiston Jr., Project Manager/ Field Engineer
Morgan James jr., Marketing/ Multi-media Director
Karen Edmiston, Accounts Manager
Becky McBreen,Logistics/ Purchasing Manager
Bob Campbell, CAD Designer
William T. Coyle, Supervisor, Production Dept.
Robert Laskowski Jr., Technical Dept.
Manufacturers of TV & FM transmit antennas, rigid coax, waveguide & associated accessories.
31-E Scout Bayoran, Timog, Quezon City
011-632-411-0068
Edward J. Edmiston, Pres

Sabine Inc.
13301 Hwy. 441, Alachua, FL 32615-8544 USA
(386) 418-2000; *Fax:* (386) 418-2001
www.sabine.com
Doran Oster, CEO
Kim Kelley, Finance Director
Manufacturers of digital signal processing equipment for sound systems. Makers of the patented FBX Feedback Exterminator & True MobilityTM wireless microphones.

Sacramento Theatrical Lighting (STL)
950 Richards Blvd., Sacramento, CA 95811 USA
(800) CUE-2STL, (916) 447-3258; *Fax:* (916) 447-5012
www.stlltd.com
saclight@aol.com
Steve Odehnal, General Manager
Bobbie Odehnal, Sales Dept./ Theatrical Manager
Marcus Daniel, Rental
Doug Van Zandt, Productions
Steve Odehnal, Special Projects
Dan Waters, Purchasing Dept.
Debbie Gunderson, Technical Services
Specialists in studio & location lighting, grip equipment, draperies, rigging & grid work. Consultation & production svcs. Sls, rentals & svcs.

Sadelco Inc.
75 W. Forest Ave., Englewood, NJ 7631 USA
(201) 569-3323, (800) 569-6299; *Fax:* (201) 569-6285
sadelco@aol.com
Les Kaplan, President
Robert Bradin, General Manager
Signal level meters, calibrators & leakage detectors.

Sager Electronics
97 Libbey Pkwy, Weymouth, MA 2189 US
(781) 682-4844
www.sager.com
Ray Norton, CEO
Frank Flynn, President
Merrill Mahoney, Vice President of Operations
Brian Flynn, Vice President of Sales East
Faris Aruri, Vice President of Corporate Marketing
Shannon Freise, Vice President of InformationTechnology
Craig Sanderson, Vice President of Product Marketing
Karen Renzi, Director of Human Resources
Paul Horgan, Corporate Controller
Grounded in 125 years of innovation and service, Sager Electronics is a North American electronic component distributor. Our Distributing Confidencer business model goes beyond fulfillment to provide our customers and suppliers a uniquecombination of operational excellence and innovative business solutions.

SAIC (Science Applications International Corp.)
1710 Saic Dr., Suite B, Mclean, VA 22102

(703) 676-4300
www.saic.com/
Edward Sanderson, Jr., Chairman of the Board, Director
Anthony J. Moraco, Chief Executive Officer
Deborah Lee James, Sector President
Thomas G. Baybrook, Executive VP & Operations Officer
Bob Bedingfield, Director
Jere Drummond,Director
Tommy Frist, Director
John Hamre, Director
Donna Morea, Director
Steven Shane, Director
Science Applications International Corporation (SAIC) is a leading technology integrator providing full lifecycle services and solutions in the technical, engineering, and enterprise IT markets. SAIC has approximately 14,000 employeesworldwide.

SAIC Inc.
10260 Campus Point Dr., San Diego, CA 92121 United States
(858) 826-6000 (800) 430-7629; *Fax:* (858) 826-6800

Samson Technologies Corp.
45 Gilpin Ave., Hauppauge, NY 11788 USA
(631) 784-2200; *Fax:* (631) 781-2201
www.samsontech.com
sales@samsontech.com
Scott Goodman, CEO
Douglas Bryant, Operations Dir
Mark Wilder, Promotions Manager
Jack Knight, VP Operations
Manufacturer of wireless microphones, mixing consoles, power amplifiers & audio products. Behringer audio processing, Hartke speakers & Zoom effects processors.

Sarnoff Corp.
Mailing Address: 201 Washington Rd., Princeton, NJ 8540 USA
Second Address: 333 Ravenswood Ave., Menlo Park, CA 94025-3493
(609) 734-2000, (650) 859-2000; *Fax:* (609) 734-2221
Curtis R. Carlson, President & CEO
John P. Riganati, Operations Dir
Jerry Harrison, VP & General Manager, Govt. Business Development
video, Promotions Manager
John W. Prausa, VP, Engineering & Systems Group
Peter J. Burt, VisionTechnologies
Thomas J. Furst, SVP & CFO
Mark Zaroogian, VP, Information Systems Division
Jean E. Tooker, VP, Human Resources
Alice R. Resnick, Corporate & Marketing Communications
William Mark, VP, Information & Computing Sciences
Contract rsch & dev facility for electronic, biomedical, & info technologies, specializing in digital video.

Sascom Marketing Group
34 Nelson St., Oakville, ON L6L 3H6 Canada
(905) 469-8080; *Fax:* (647) 439-1510
www.sascom.com
Curt Smith, President
Sascom Represents: Cube-Tec Plugins for Pro Tools, Nuendo and Sequoia, and Doremi Labs digital video products

Satellite Systems Corp.
101 Malibu Dr., Virginia Beach, VA 23452 USA
(757) 463-3553; *Fax:* (757) 463-3891
www.satsyscorp.com
jwilliams@satsyscorp.com
Bob Kite, President
SCPC & video subcarrier satellite systems for radio, SNG & data bcst networks.

Schneider Optics
Mailing Address: 7701 Haskell Ave., Van Nuys, CA 91406 US
Second Address: 285 Oser Ave, Hauppauge, NY 11788
(818) 766-3715, (800) 228-1254; *Fax:* (818) 505-9865
www.schneideroptics.com
info@schneideroptics.com
Bill Turner, Operations Dir
Wide angle & telephoto lens for video & motion picture cameras; lens accessories; lens service; schneider filters.

Schneider Optics Inc.
Mailing Address: 285 Oser Ave., Hauppauge, NY 11788 USA
Second Address: 7701 Haskell Ave., Van Nuys, CA 91406
(631) 761-5000, (800) 645-7239, (818)766-3715, (80; *Fax:* (631) 761-5090, (818) 505) 9865
www.schneideroptics.com
info@schneideroptics.com
Dwight Lindsay, CEO
Dawn Tenny, Manager
Manufacturer/distributor of high quality optical filters for video, still photography & motion picture. Product line also includes a wide range of lenses for CCTV, large format photography, darkroom enlarging, slide & film projection.
7701 Haskell Ave., Van Nuys, CA 91506
(818) 766-3715

Scotts Valley Group Inc
Div/DBA: MARCOM
540 Hauer Apple Way, Aptos, CA 95003-9315 US
(831) 768-8668; *Fax:* (831) 768-7810
www.mar-com.com
info@mar-com.com
Martin Jackson, President
FM, AM, TV & microwave transmitting equipment; sls engrg, instal & maintenance.

ScreenLight & Grip
502 Sprague St., Dedham, MA 2026 USA
(781) 326-5088; *Fax:* (781) 326-4751
www.screenlightandgrip.com
lightsne@aol.com
Guy Holt, President
Location lighting & production svcs, equipment rental, trucks, vans, etc.

Selco Products Co.
8780 Technology Way, Reno, NV 89521-5908 USA
(877) 807-5426; *Fax:* (775) 674-5111
www.selcoproducts.com
sales@selcoproducts.com
Tim Wilkinson, President
Michelle Blakeslee, Promotions Manager
A full range of product lines are offered by selco including thermal products, control knobs, electronic controls & digital panel meters.

Semtech
Mailing Address: 200 Flynn Road, Camarillo, CA 93012 Canada
Second Address: 4281 Harvester Rd., Burlington, ON L7L 5M4
(805) 498-2111, (905) 632-2996; *Fax:* (805) 498-3804,(905) 632-2055
www.semtech.com
Rockell N. Hankin, Chairman
Franz fINK, CEO
Mohan Maheswaran, President/CEO
Asaf Silberstein, Senior Vice President Operations
Gary Beauchamp, VP/GM
Emeka Chukwu, SVP/CFO
Jean-Paul Bardyn, Chief Technical Officer and VicePresident R&D, Wi
Alain Dantec, Senior Vice President and General Manager, Wireles
Sharon Faltemier, VP-Human Resources
Charles E. Harper, Senior Vice President, Strategy and Systems Innova
Jonathan Hahn, Chief Information Officer and VicePresident of In
High performance integrated circuits, including switches & processing functions, for analog & digital video applications.

Sencore Inc.
3200 W Sencore Dr., Sioux Falls, SD 57107 USA
(605) 339-0100; *Fax:* (605) 339-0317
sales@sencore.com
John Suranyi, CEO
Chuck Robertson, Operations Dir
Ken Christensen, Promotions Manager
Tom Stingley, EVP, Marketing & Sales
Dana Nachreiner, VP Operations
Electronic test equipment for servicing & performance testing of consumer electronics & CATV/MATV equipment.

Senior Aerospace
1075 Providence Hwy., Sharon, MA 2067 US
(781) 784-1400, (888) 235-5697; *Fax:* (7810 784-1405
www.metalbellows.com
Ron Case, General Manager
Scott Heather, Sales manager
Walid Boulos, Dir. of Sales & Marketing
John Meyer, Marketing & Business Development
Barry Ober, Regional Business Development Manager
Janice Costa, Account Manager
BradSimpson, Manufacturing Manager
Tom Nightingale, Account Manager
Design build-to-print aerospace products, cryogenic lines, valves, burst discs, electric motors, actuators.

Sennheiser Electronic Corp.
One Enterprise Dr., Old Lyme, CT 6371 USA
(860) 434-9190; *Fax:* (860) 434-1759
www.sennheiserusa.com
Daniel Sennheiser, CEO
Jeff Alexander, General Sales Mgr
Lachlan Brennan, Manager
Andreas Sennheiser, CEO
Volker Bartels, President, Research & Quality
Peter Claussen, President, Integrated Systems & Professional Syste
PaulWhiting, President, Global Sales
Thomas Weinzierl, President, Supply Chain
Microphones, headphones, boomsets, wireless microphones & infrared products as well as Neumann mucrophone, Klein+Hummel loudspeakers & HHB recorders.
Av. Xola No. 613 PH6, Col. Del Valle, 3100 D.F. Mexico
(525) 639-0956; *Fax:* (525) 639-9482

Servoreeler Systems
218-31 97th Ave., Queens Village, NY 11429 USA
(718) 464-9400, (800) 431-8900; *Fax:* (718) 464-9435
www.servoreelers.com
srsystems@servoreelers.com
Claude Karczmer, President
Eileen Karczmer, General Sales Mgr
SUSPENDED MICROPHONE SERVOREELERS - deploy, retract & position suspended microphones by remote pushbutton or computer control. They are used for Teleconferencing, Corporate board rooms, Houses of Worship, Concert halls, Sports arenas &Universities.

SES Americom Inc.
Mailing Address: 4 Research Way, Princeton, NJ 08540-6684 USA
Second Address: 1129 20th Street, N.W., Suite 1000, Washington, DC 20036
(609) 987-4000, (202) 478-7100; *Fax:* (609) 987-4517
www.ses-americom.com
Karim Michel Sabbagh, President and CEO/ Chairman
Karim Michel Sabbagh, CEO Designate
Padraig McCarthy, Chief Financial Officer
Martin Halliwell, Chief Technology Officer
Ferdinand Kayser, Chief Commercial Officer
Gerson Souto,Chief Development Officer
Satellite distribution svcs for coml bcst & cable TV; prog syndicators, SNG & bcst radio distribution svcs.

Sescom Inc.
PO Box 720, Mount Marion, NY 12456 USA
(845) 246-1915; *Fax:* (845) 246-0626
www.sescom.com
info@sescom.com
Bryan McGuirk, President
Jodi Morelli, Promotions Manager
John Fitzer, Director
Audio interfacing equipment, audio transformers & modules.

Setcom Corporation
3019 Alvin Devane Blvd., Suite 560, Austin, TX 78741 USA
(650) 965-8020; *Fax:* (650) 965-1193
www.setcomcorp.com
James Roberts, President
Police motorcycle communication equipment.

Seton Identification Products
20 Thompson Road, P.O. Box 819, Branford, CT 06405-0819 USA
(800) 571-2596, (203) 488-5973; *Fax:* (800) 345-7819, 9203) 571-2596
www.seton.com
help@seton.com
Richard Fisk, President
Tracy Carpenter, Manager
Signs, tags, labels, pipe markers, valve tags, & nameplates to meet OSHA/ANSI specifications.

Shallco Inc.
Box 1089, Smithfield, NC 27577 USA
(800) 876-3135, (919) 934-3298; *Fax:* (919) 934-3135 (outside USA only)
www.shallco.com
John Shallcross, President
Jason Shallcross, President
Mark Francis, Manager
John S. Shallcross, Founder
Variable & fixed audio attenuators.

Sharp Electronics Corp.
Sharp Plaza, Mahwah, NJ 07495-1163 USA
(201) 529-8200, (800) 303-9020; *Fax:* (201) 529-8425
www.sharpusa.com
ProLCD@SharpSEC.com
Doug Koshima, Chairmsn & CEO
Ron Colgan, Operations Dir
Fred Krazeisze, General Manager
Bob Soucy, General Sales Mgr

Bruce Pollack, Promotions Manager
Judah Zeilger, Associate VP, Marketing
Data/video projection systems for portable and permanent installation applications; LCD video monitors, TVs, VCRs, TV/VCRs and Viewcam Camcorders.

Shively Labs
Box 389, 188 Harrison Rd., Bridgton, ME 4009 USA
(207) 647-3327, (888) 744-8359, (888)-SHIVELY; *Fax:* (207) 647-8273
www.shively.com
sales@shively.com
David Allen, President
John Bliss, Director of Operations
Angela Gillespie, General Sales Mgr
Dale Ladner, Regional Sales Manager
Linda Rollins, Director of Human Resources
Bob Surette, Director of Sales engineering
Mark Cotton,Mechaical Designer
Martyn Gregory, Vice President
Jonathan Clark, Sales Manager
FM antennas, FM translators, branched & balanced combiners, coax, patch panels, filters, compressor dehydrators, & related RF equipment, pattern work & field svcs.

Shook Mobile Technology, LP
7451 FM 3009, Schertz, TX 78154 USA
(210) 651-5700, (888) 651-5775; *Fax:* (210) 651-5220
www.shook-usa.com
shook@shook-usa.com
John Heaney, CEO
Ronald Crockett, Promotions Manager
Ron Laurence, V.P. of Sales
Mobile TV production, ENG, SNV vehicles. Rack ready or turnkey delivery. HD/SD Systems integration.

Shure Inc.
5800 W. Touhy Ave., Niles, IL 60714-4608 USA
(847) 600-2000, (800) 25-SHURE, (800) 257-4873; *Fax:* (847) 600-1212
www.shure.com
info@shure.com
R.L. Shure, Chairman
S. LaMantia, President
World-standard microphones, wireless audio systems, phonograph cartridges, mixers, digital signal processors, & personal monitors.

Siemens Dematic Limited
167 Hunt St., Ajax, ON L1S 1P6 Canada
(905) 683-8200; *Fax:* (905) 683-0186
www.siemens.com

Sierra Automated Systems & Engineering Corp.
2821 Burton Ave., Burbank, CA 91504 USA
(818) 840-6749; *Fax:* (818) 840-6751
www.sasaudio.com
Ed Fritz, President
Al Salci, Operations Dir
Giovanni Morales, General Manager
Cam Eicher, General Sales Mgr
Mike Hagans, Engineering Dir
Al Salci, Vice President
Emilio Gomez, Sales Support
Audio switching & mixing systems maunufacturer. Mix-Minus/IFB, satellite distribution/switching, automated switching & distribution, studio intercom, on-air routing, teleconferencing.

Sigma Electronics Inc.
10830 Kinghurst Dr., Houston, TX 77099 USA
(281) 933-4700, (800) 874-7121; *Fax:* (281) 933-9067
Billy Swilley, CEO
Routing switchers for audio & video; distribution amplifiers; sync & test signal generators; encoders, decoders, transcoders, converters.

Western rgnl office
Santa Rosa, CA United States
(707)539-5314
Randy Smith, Western Rgnl Sls Mgr

Simplicity Tool Corp
10330 N.E. Marx St., Portland, OR 97220 USA
(503) 253-2000; *Fax:* (503) 253-2009
www.simplicitytool.com
Markus Burcker, President
CATV, MATV antennas.

Sinar Bron Inc.
17 Progress St., Edison, NJ 8820 USA
(908) 754-5800, (800) 456-0203; *Fax:* (908) 754-5807
www.sinarbron.com
Michael Hejtmanek, President
Gina Connor, Regional Sales Manager
Andrew Trumbach, Regional Sales Manager
Joe Boda, Regional Sales Manager
Pro-Cyc prefabricated coves for infiniti walls in video & photo studios; & studio lighting/HMI.

Sintec Media
Mailing Address: 1361 W. Towne Square Rd., Mequon, WI 53092 USA
Second Address: 2964 Peachtree Rd., Suite 400, Atlanta, GA 30305
(262) 241-9005, 9404) 869-4575; *Fax:* (262) 241-9036, (404) 869-9009
www.sintecmedia.com/
Amotz Yarden, CEO
Chanan Weiss, President
Adoram Yarden, Dir. Of Operations
Amos Simantov, EVP Sales
Shlomo Freidenreich, CFO
Dan Yuval, VP Product Management
Moses Zeliker, VP Marketing & Product Development
Dan Yuval, VPProduct Management
SIMS-Multi-Station/Network program rights, scheduling & finance system. Manages non-linear rights and scheduling as well.

Sintec Media
2964 Peachtree Rd., Suite 400, Atlanta, GA 30305
(917) 606-5310; *Fax:* (404) 844-9009
www.sintecmedia.com
info@argosys.com
Amotz Yarden, Chief Executive Officer
Chanan Weiss, President
Adoram Yarden, Director of Operations- Development
Amos Simantov, EVP Sales
Shlomo Freidenreich, Chief Financial Officer
Moses Zelniker, VP Marketing & ProductDevelopment
Dan Yuval, VP Product Management
Tanya Yankelevich, VP Operations- Customer
Eric Levitan, COO Americas & SIMS/Medea/Nestor Delivery
SintecMedia, the leading provider of media business management solutions, has over 300 client sites around the world. With the recent acquisitions of industry leaders Argo Systems and StorerTV, SintecMedia augmented its comprehensivesolutions for broadcasters, Pay TV networks, multichannel operators and station groups world-wide.

SiteSafe Inc.
Mailing Address: 200 N. Glebe Rd., Suite 1000, Arlington, VA 22203 US
Second Address: 2415 Campus Drive, Suite 200, Irvine, CA 92612
(703) 276-1100, (949) 809-4999; *Fax:* (703) 276-1169, (949) 553-3919
www.sitesafe.com
k.czosnowski@velocitel.com
Doug Hall, President
Tony DeMattia, Vice President of Operations
Phill Harris, Director of AM Engineering
Ed Katz, Chief Financial Officer
Ken Czosnowski, Sr VP, Business Development & Sales/Senior Account
Mike Chandler, AccountManager - Northeast Region
Michelle Calesini, Senior Account Manager - Midwest Region
Sara Dick, Senior Account Manager - West Region
Winston Smith, Information Technology
Engrg software & wireless telecom engrg consulting svcs.

Skytec, Inc.
23 Inland Farm Rd., Windham, ME 4062 USA
(207) 893-1700; *Fax:* (207) 893-1717
www.skytecinc.com
skytecinc@hotmail.com
Rick Sullivan, President
Manufacturer of skystrobe obstruction lighting systems - ETL certified, FAA approved. Parts, sls, svc & training seminars for obstruction lighting.

Snell & Wilcox Inc.
3519 Pacific Ave., Burbank, CA 91505 USA
(818) 556-2616; *Fax:* (818) 556-2626
www.snellwilcox.com
americas@snellwilcox.com
John Poulter, Chairman
Simon Derry, CEO
Jonathan Goldstein, President
Roderick Snell, General Sales Mgr
Peter Fredricks, Financial Director
Tim Banks, Global Sales director
Robert Rowe, Chief Technology Officer & ManagingDirector
Holly Walker, Marketing Group Manager
Jenny Carr, Head of HR
Paul Martin, President- Snell North America
Snell & Wilcox is one of the world's largest manufacturers of bcst electronics. The complete product family includes a full range of video & audio processing equipment consisting of Decoding, Encoding, High Definition Format Conversion, MPEGCompression & Pre-processing, Display, Noise Reduction, Post Production Switchers (both SDTV & HDTV), Standards Conversion, Synchronization, Test & Measurement & IQ Modular products.

Snell & Wilcox Ltd.
Durford Mill, Petersfield, Hampshire, GU33 5AZ
44-0-730-821-188 44-0-730-821-199
David Youlton, Chmn

Smith & Wilcox Ltd.
Southleigh Park House, Eastleigh Rd., Havant, Harts, P09 2PE

Solid State Logic Inc.
320 W. 46th St., New York, NY 10036 USA
(212) 315-1111; *Fax:* (212) 315-0251
www.solid-state-logic.com
nysales@solidstatelogic.com
Steve Zaretsky, President
Don Wershba, SVP
Bryon Engke, CFO
SSL is a leading manufacturer of digital audio broadcast consoles for on-air and live-to-tape production. New for 2009, the C10 brings a new level of price/performance to digital audio broadcast consoles
5757 Wilshire Blvd., Los Angeles, CA 90036 United States
(323) 549-9090
Phil Wagner, Pres

Sony BMG Music Entertainment
550 Madison Ave., New York, NY 10022 US
(212) 833-8000
www.sonymusic.com
Rolf Schmidt Hotz, Chairman
Doug Morris, CEO
Lauren Hubert, President/Creative Marketing
Kevin Kelleher, Executive Vice President and Chief Financial Offic
Produce, market & distribute recorded musics.

Sound Associates
424 W. 45th St., New York, NY 10036 USA
(212) 757-5679, (888) 772-7686, (914) 963-3452; *Fax:* (212) 265-1250, (914) 963-4236
www.soundassociates.com
newyork@soundassociates.com
T. Richard Fitzgerald, President
Domonic Sack, Operations Dir
Electronic equipment racking systems, console automation systems & digital recording facilities.

SOUND ASSOCIATES INC.
979 Saw Mill River Road, Yonkers, NY 10710
914-963-3452

Soundcraft U.S.A.
8500 Balboa Blvd., Northridge, CA 91329 USA
(818) 920-3212; *Fax:* (818) 920-3209
www.soundcraft.com
Tom Der, General Sales Mgr
Dave Neal, Promotions Manager
Kathy Templeman Holmes, US Sales/Marketing
Tom Der, US Sales
JP Espejo, Souncraft Sales Administrative
Marlene Lopez, Key Accounts Sales Administrative
Marlon Gonzalez,Parts Admin
Audio mixing consoles for recording, theater, concert sound reinforcement & bcstg.

Spacenet Services Inc.
Mailing Address: 1750 Old Meadow Rd., McLean, VA 22102 US
Second Address: 841 Livingston Court, Marietta, GA 30067
(703) 848-1000; *Fax:* (703) 848-1010
www.spacenet.com
info@spacenet.com
Glenn Katy, President
David Shiff, Operations Dir
Robert Turner, Business Development
Satellite-based interactive data, bcst data & bcst video for coml companies worldwide.

Specialized Communications Corp.
20940 Twin Springs Dr., Smithsburg, MD 21783 USA
(800) 359-1858, (301) 790-0103; *Fax:* (301) 790-0173
www.spec-comm.com
service@spec-comm.com
David Linetsky, President
Andrew Hoffman, Operations Dir

Judy Hoffman, Promotions Manager
Emily Hoffman, Service Coordinator
Andrew Hoffman, Vice President
Keith Wagaman, Service manager
Beth A. Linetsky, Office Manager
Factory Authorized Service Center providing repair & maintenance of bcst video equipment. Factory Integrator & Dealer for distinctive industry brands, such as Panasonic, Sony, JVS, Cannon. Also manufacturer of Digital Signage systems &provider of digital signage installation, integraton, content creation & content management.

Sprague Magnetics Inc.
12806 Bradley Ave., Sylmar, CA 91342 USA
(818) 364-1800, (800) 553-8712; *Fax:* (818) 364-1810
www.spraguemagnetics.com
smiav@spraguemagnetics.com
Dorothy Sprague, President/Finance Executive
Gary Moore, General Manager
Roger Emery, Data StorageSales & Service
John Austin, Pro Audio, Film/Video Srvices
Long-wearing cart, film, reel-to-reel tape heads, refurbishment svcs, replacement parts, alignment tapes, accessories.

Stage Equipment & Lighting Inc.
Mailing Address: 12250 N.E. 13th Ct., Miami, FL 33161 USA
Second Address: 4600 SW 36th St., Orlando, Fl 32811
(305) 891-2010, (407) 425-2010; *Fax:* (305) 893-2828, (800) 597-2010, (407) 648-2604
www.seal-fla.com
mail@seal-fla.com
Rick Rudolph, President
Michael Grosz, Operations Dir
Stephen Grieco, Engineering Dir
Vivian Gill, President
Film, video & theatrical lighting & grip, & related support equipment.
9207 Palm River Rd., Suite 108, Tampa, FL 33619 United States
(813) 626-8500; *Fax:* (813) 620-1404
Adam Vidaurri, Manager
4600 S.W. 36th St., Orlando, FL 32811 United States
(407) 425-2010; *Fax:* (407) 648-2604
Curt Contrata, Manager

Stahl, A Scott & Fetzer Co.
3201 Old Lincoln Way, Wooster, OH 44691 USA
(330) 264-7441, (800) 277-8245; *Fax:* (330) 264-3319
www.stahl.cc
Jim Kraschinsky, President
Brad Yocheim, General Sales Mgr
Cardington, OH 43315 United States
(419) 864-6871
Eric McNaly, Plant Mgr
Durant, OK 74701 United States
(405) 924-5575
Steve Shepard, Plant Mgr
Merced, CA 95340 United States
(209) 383-4336

Stainless LLC
1140 Welsh Rd., Suite 250, North Wales, PA 19454 USA
(215) 631-1400, (800) 486-3333; *Fax:* (215) 631-1425
www.stainlessllc.com
Donald T Doty, President
Ed Deetscreek, VP Operations & Sales Acct Manager
Gregg Fehrman, Chief Engineer
Patrick Moore, Sr. Vice President
Dave Bodossian, Sales Representative
Stainless provides design, engineering, fabrication, and installation of our complete line of guyed and self-support towers and monopole structures under the most extreme conditions. Stainless also offers analysis, modification, mapping andinspections, maintenance and repair, and installation to upgrade existing structures, as well as 24-hours emergency services with our own safety trained and experienced crews.
Doty Moore Stainless
1570 W. Beltline Rd., Cedar Hill, TX 75104
(972) 637-5000

Stancil Corp.
2644 S. Croddy Way, Santa Ana, CA 92704 USA
(714) 546-2002 ext. 4316,(800) 782-6245; *Fax:* (714) 546-2092
www.stancilcorp.com
guy.churchhouse@stancilcorp.com
Michael Custer, CEO
Sharon Stancil, President
Simon Farrow, Engineering Tech
Voice logging recorders, multichannel, 4-144 channels, 24-hour recording time; digital format, instant recall recorders, windows 2000 voiceXP.

Standard Communications Corp.
6260 Sequence Dr., San Diego, CA 92121 USA
(858) 546-5300, (800) 421-6511; *Fax:* (858) 546-5051, (858) 546-5055
www.standardcom.com
sales@picodigital.com
Ian A. Lerner, CEO/ Director
Carlos Shteremberg, President/ Director
Brian Trexel, VP of Engineering
Andrew Isherwood, Chief Technology Officer
Jose Rivero, VP of Network Technology/ Strategic Sales/ Directo
Dr. Josef Berger,Director
Jose Zyman, Director
Broadband TV receivers & cable headend products for broadcast and CATV.

Stanley Supply & Services
335 Willow St., North Andover, MA 01845-5995 US
(978) 682-9844, (888) 887-9473, (800) 225-5370; *Fax:* (800) 743-8141
www.stanleysupplyservices.com
sales@stanleyworks.com
Holly Tsourides, President
Electronic tool kits & cases, tools, test equipment.

Stanton Group, Inc.
Mailing Address: PO Box 993, Brentwood, TN 37024-0993 USA
Second Address: 5203 Maryland Way, Suite 100, Brentwood, TN 37027
(615) 373-9507; *Fax:* (615) 373-9516
www.stantonmagnetics.com
info@stantonmagnetics.com
Timothy Dorwart, CEO
Debra C. Viol, President
Louis M. Viol, General Manager
Jim Moore, Principal
Sharon Emerson, VP, Leasing & Management
Erin Bolton, Asst. Property Manager
Jo Craig, Property Manager
Michael Gordon, FacilityTechnician
Howard Wakefield, Maintainance
Turntables, professional cartridges, CD players, final scratch, monitors, speakers.
KRK
5242 Business Dr., Huntington, CA 92649 United States
(714) 373-4600 (714) 373-0421
Kerwin Vega
555 Fast Easy Street, Simi Valley, CA 93065 United States

Star Case Manufacturing Co. Inc.
648 Superior Ave., Munster, IN 46321 USA
(219) 922-4440, (800) 822-STAR, (800) 782-CASE; *Fax:* (219) 922-4442
www.starcase.com
star@starcase.com
Dennis Toma, President
Ralph Hoopes, Operations Dir
Flight cases (protective casement)—Carry Star, ATA Star, Super Star, Ultra Star, Star Light.

Strand Lighting Inc.
6603 Darin Way, Cypress, CA 90630 USA
(714) 230-8200; *Fax:* (714) 899-0042
www.strandlight.com
Peter Rogers, Sales Executive
Studio & remote lighting, & control equipment.
928 Broadway, New York, NY 10010-6008
(212) 242-1042

Strong International
13710 First National Bank Pkwy, Suite 400, Omaha, NE 68154 USA
(800) 722-4445, (8000 424-1215; *Fax:* (402) 453-7238
www.ballantyne-omaha.com
info@btn-inc.com
William F. Welsh II, Chairman
Chris D. Stark, Sr. VP & Chief Operating Officer
Gary L. Cavey, President & CEO
Mike Johnson, Dir. Of Operations
Francis Barrette, General manager
Rick Sanjurjo, VP of Engineering
Jake Fan, ManagingDirector
Lori Bruckner, HR Director
Andrew Harris, Dir. Of Information Technology
John Biegel, VP, Technical Services
Mary A.Carstens, Sr. VP, Treasurer & CFO
35/70mm projection equipment, Xenon lamphouse systems, platters, Xenon bulbs, follow spotlights.

Structural System Technology Inc.
6867 Elm Street, Suite 200, McLean, VA 22101 USA
(703) 356-9765; *Fax:* (703) 448-0979
Fred Purdy, CEO
Kaveh Mehrnama, President
Bryan Burton, Operations Dir
Monty Beck, Vice President
Mary Acker, Finance Executive
Structural engrg studies, analysis, design, modifications, inspections, fabrication, erection of towers & antenna.

Studio Technologies Inc.
5520 W. Touhy Ave., Suite 1, Skokie, IL 60077 USA
(847) 676-9177; *Fax:* (847) 982-0747
www.studio-tech.com
Gordon Kapes, President
Carrie Gage, Promotions Manager
Joe Urbanczyk, Sales Executive
Microphone pre-amplifiers, stereo simulators & recognition units, telephone & hard-wired IFB communications systems on-air announcer's consoles. Accessories for digital audio workstations.

Studio Technology
529 Rosedale Road, Number 103, Kennett Square, PA 19348 USA
(610) 925-2785; *Fax:* (610) 925-2787
www.studiotechnology.com
sales@studiotechnology.com
Vince Fiola, CEO
Vince Fiola, President
Bcst furniture, design & instal svcs.

Summit Software Systems Inc.
1891 N. Gaffey st., Suite I, San Pedro, CA 90731 USA
(800) 771-1824, (310) 831-2234
www.summitsoftware.com
Paul Adams, President
PC-based traf, sls, billing, accounts receivable, accounts payable, payroll & gen ledger for single or multi-stns & single or multi-users.

Sundance Digital Inc.
545 E. John Carpenter Fwy., Suite 200, Irving, TX 75062 USA
(972) 444-8442; *Fax:* (972) 444-8450
www.sundancedigital.com
Jacque Durocher, General Manager
Rick Stora, Promotions Manager
Eric Harrington, Engineering Dir
Sundance Digital a part of Avid is an award-winning leader in TV automation solutions for individual & multistation bcstrs. We are an innovative and dedicated software corporation. Your satisfaction is our goal!

Superior Satellite Engineers Inc.
1743 Middle Rd., Columbia Falls, MT 59912 USA
(406) 257-9590; *Fax:* (406) 257-9599
www.superiorsatelliteusa.com
Doyle Catlett, President
Jackie Williams, VP- Operations
Steve Catlett, VP of Engineering
Travis Lake, Plant manager
Connie Dalton, Treasurer
Navigator steerable & fixed antenna systems; multiple satellite feed systems & LNBs for cable bcst IPTV.

Superior Tower Services Inc.
5757 FM 1696, Iola, TX 77861 USA
(936) 394-9925 (800) 306-4504; *Fax:* (936) 394-4020
www.superiortowerservices.com/
Edward Carter, President/Owner
For all your tower & antenna needs: antenna, transmission line analysis, emergency repairs, two way, microwave, cellular, AM/FM, installations, tower erections, inspections, & maintenance.

Superscope Technologies
1508 Batavia Ave., Geneva, IL 60134 US
(800) 374-4118; *Fax:* (630) 232-8905
www.superscopetechnologies.com
Fred Hackendahl, President
Products include portable cassette recorders, single & dual cassette recorders, CD players, multi-track recorders, compact recorders, portable, & rackmount.

Swager Communications Inc.
Box 656, 501 E Swager Dr., Fremont, IN 46737 USA
(260) 495-2515, (800) 968-5601; *Fax:* (260) 495-4205
www.swager.com
tim@swager.com
Dan Swager, President
Lee Swager, Operations Dir
William E Swager, Founder

Designs, fabricates, installs & maintains AM/FM, TV/CATV & microwave communication towers.

Swintek Enterprises Inc.
Mailing Address: 7007-B6 Realm Dr., San Jose, CA 95119 USA
Second Address: 3422 Lake Lesina Dr., San Jose, CA 95135
(408) 727-4889; *Fax:* (408) 224-3869
www.swintek.com
sales@swintek.com
William Swintek, President
18 ch wireless intercom, 1 w IFB with wireless EAR piece receiver, complete linear headsets.

Switchcraft Inc.
5555 N. Elston Ave., Chicago, IL 60630 USA
(773) 792-2700; *Fax:* (773) 792-2129
www.switchcraft.com
sales@switchcraft.com
Keith Bandolik, CEO
Dave Dunmead, CFO
Jim Hoffman, Chief Marketing Executive
Judy Pulliam, Sales
Offers a variety of products including audio patchbays, connectors, adapters, jacks & plugs, and video patchbays.

Symetrix Inc.
6408 216th St. S.W., Mountlake Terrace, WA 98043 USA
(425) 778-7728; *Fax:* (425) 778-7727
www.symetrixaudio.com
Dane Butcher, Chairman/President/CEO
Jennifer Anderson, Financial Executive
Craig Richardson, VP of Global Sales
John Harris, Engineering Dir
Brooke Macomber, Dir. Of Marketing
Tim Murray, Western Region Sales Manager
JimLatimer, Mark Ullrich
International Sales Manager, Joe Bosslet
Ordering & Billing
Digital & analog audio signal processing.

Symmetricom
Mailing Address: 3750 Westwind Blvd, Santa Rosa, CA 95403 USA
Second Address: 2300 Orchard Parkway, San Jose, CA 95131
(707) 528-1230, (408) 428-7907; *Fax:* (707) 527-6640, (408) 428-6960
Elizabeth A. Fetter, CEO
Gurdip Jande, Operations Dir
Paul Chermak, General Sales Mgr
Doug Arnold, Chief Engineer
Justin Spencer, CFO
Bill Minor, EVP, Global Human Resources
Juan Dewar, EVP, Global Sales & Services
PhilBourekas, EVP, Marketing
Douglas J. Halbert, Jr., EVP, Global Opeartions & Quality
Time & frequency receivers traceable to NIST & USNO. Complete line of time code instrumentation.

Syntellect Inc.
Mailing Address: 2095 W Pinnacle Peak Road, Suite 110, Phoenix, AZ 85027 USA
Second Address: 700 Commerce Dr., Oak Brook, IL 60523
(800) 788-9733; *Fax:* (602) 789-2768
www.syntellect.com
info.ie@enghouse.com
Steve Dodenhoff, President
J.R. Sloan, Chief Marketing Officer
ARUs for automated customer svc, ANI svcs for PPV order processing, predictive dialing systems for telemarketing & collections.
20401 N. 29th Ave, Phoenix, AZ 85027 United States
(602) 789-2800
Scott Coleman, Pres

System Associates
4848 W Seldon Lane, Glendale, AZ 85312 USA
(866) 937-0209; *Fax:* (866) 435-0160
systemassociates.tv
michael@systemassociates.tv
Michael Ferguson, President
Used bcst TV equipment, to buy and sell, appraisals, auctions

Systems Wireless Ltd.
555 Herndon Pkwy., Ste. 135, Herndon, VA 20170 USA
(703) 471-7887; *Fax:* (703) 437-1107
Bill Sien, General Sales Mgr
Ron Gallihugh, Finance
Sls, service & rental of wireless microphones, wireless intercom, wireless listening devices, wireless video & Clear Com cabled intercom systems.

T-C Specialties Co.
Box 192, 17 S.Main St., Coudersport, PA 16915 USA
(814) 274-8060, (800) 458-6074; *Fax:* (814) 274-0690
www.tcspecialties.com
Daniel Major, President
Bill Crown, Operations Dir
Steve Astulfi, VP, Sales & Marketing
Judi Tucker, Secretary
Mike Harris, VP Operations
Tanja Marie Pino, Human Resources Manager
Bo Prum, Technical Support
Coupon billing systems & related forms; large volume dir mail inkjetting, presort/barcoding mailing

T.T. Technologies Inc.
2020 E. New York St., Aurora, IL 60502 USA
(800) 533-2078, (630) 851-8200; *Fax:* (630) 851-8299
www.tttechnologies.com
info@tttechnologies.com
Chris Brahler, President/CEO
Dave Holcomb, Operations Dir
Grundomat Pneumatic piercing tools, Grundoram pipe ramming system, Grundocrack Preumatic pipe bursting systems & Grundoburst Static Pipe Bursting.
3701 N.E. 36th Ave., Suite C, Ocala, FL 34479 United States
(352) 622-2077
Tom Garner, Gen Mgr

Tactical Communications and Surveillance - Cobham plc
1916 Palomar Oaks Way, Suite 100, Carlsbad, CA 92008-5523 USA
(760) 496-0055; *Fax:* (760) 496-0057
www.cobham.com
J Devaney, Chairman
R Murphy, CEO
Sam Nasiri, President
Ursula Meinhard, Operations Dir
Wayne Rogers, General Sales Mgr
James Henderson, Sales Executive
Simon Nicholls, Chief Financial Officer/Executive Director
M Wareing,Independent Non-executive Director
J Patterson, Independent Non-executive Director
M Ronald, Independent Non-executive Director
M Hagee, Independent Non-executive Director
A Wood, Independent Non-executive Director
The latest in microwave communications equipment.

TAI Audio
5828 Old Winter Garden Rd., Orlando, FL 32835 USA
(407) 296-9959, (800) 486-6444; *Fax:* (407) 648-1352
www.taiaudio.com
Joseph Guzzi, President
Rental, sls & svc of professional audio for film, video, TV & postproduction. Specializes in wireless communication equipment.

Talk-A-Phone Co.
7530 N. Natchez Ave., Niles, IL 60714 USA
(773) 539-1100; *Fax:* (773) 539-1241
www.talkaphone.com
info@talkaphone.com
S. Shanes, Chairman
Robert Shanes, Operations Dir
Bob Shanes, VP- Sales
Erez Sharoni, Eastern Regional Sales Manager
Don Strauch, Western Regional Sales manager
Jerry Nussbaum, Customer Service
Nicole Rivera, Inside Sales
Intercommunication systems, ADA compliant emergency phones, ADA areas of rescue, apartment access systems.

TALX Corp.
11342 Lackland, St. Louis, MO 63146 USA
(314) 214-7000; *Fax:* (314) 214-7588
www.talx.com
Michael Smith, Operations Dir
William Canfield, General Manager
Interactive communications; more specific svc; Interactive voice response, Interactive web, employment verification (work # for everyone) & Outsource svc.

Tamron U.S.A. Inc.
10 Austin Blvd., Commack, NY 11725 USA
(631) 858-8400, (800) 827-8880; *Fax:* (631) 543-5666
www.tamron.com
custserv@tamron.com
Morio Ono, President & CEO
Bert Krank, Operations Dir
Keiki Warashina, General Manager
John VanSteenberg, Station Manager
Gregg Maniaci, General Sales Mgr
Stacie Errera, Promotions Manager
Takeyuki Arai, Founder
Lenses for 35mm SLR digital & film cameras, & CCTV lenses.

Tapeswitch Corp.
100 Schmitt Blvd., Farmingdale, NY 11735 USA
(631) 630-0442, (800) 234-8273; *Fax:* (631) 630-0454
www.tapeswitch.com
sales@tapes.com
Michael Steele, President
Frank Pitrelli, Operations Manager
Barry Lipsman, Sales Manager
April Sabbatini, Promotions Manager
Al Russell, Engineering Manager
Patrick Falbo, Vice-President
Marie Collins, Dir. Of Finance
NicoleAllison, Marketing
Paul Dzialakiewicz, Applications Engineer/ Electronic Product manager
Bob Espionsa, Sales Supervisor
Safety light curtains, sensing mats, edges, ribbon switches, electronic zone controllers, sensing bumpers, safety & protection equipment.
Mission, CA 92692 United States
(949) 588-9387
Jeff Johnson, Rgnl Sls Mgr
Franklin, TN 37064 United States
(615) 591 7399
Tim DePeri, Rgnl Sls Mgr
Fishers, IN 46038 United States
(317) 570-6178
Tom Bertellotti, Rgnl Sls Mgr
New Bern, NC 28562 United States
(252) 637-7728
Vinnie Colucci, Rgnl Sls Mgr

TC Electronic
5706 Corsa Ave., Suite 107, Westlake Village, CA 91362 USA
(818) 665-4900; *Fax:* (818) 665-4901
www.tcbroadcast.com
info@tcus.com
Ed Simeone, Chairman
John Maier, CEO
Digital compressor/limiter expander, digital signal processors, DTV audio processors & high-resolution digital delays.

TC Group Americas Inc.
335 Gage Ave., Suite 1, Kitchener, ON N2M 5E1 Canada
(519) 745-1158; *Fax:* (519) 745-2364
www.tcgroup.tc
info@tcgroup.tc
Marc Bertrand, CEO
Brands offered: Tannoy, Lab.gruppen, tc electronic, TC Helicon, dynaudio acoustics, Linn

TC Group Americas

TDK Electronics Corp.
11070 Valley View St., Cypress, CA 90630 USA
(714) 934-1212; *Fax:* (714) 897-5894
www.tdk.com
Hajime Sawabe, Chairman & CEO
Takehiro Kamigama, President

TEAC America Inc.
7733 Telegraph Rd., Montebello, CA 90640 USA
(323) 726-0303; *Fax:* (323) 727-7652
www.teac.com
Koichiro Nakamura, President
Jim Savage, CFO
Les Luzar, General Sales Mgr
Hitomi Down, Controller
Consumer audio/video & professional recording equipment, airborne video recorder, instrumentation data recorders, computer peripherals/floppy disks, tape backup & industrial optical disk recorders & playback.

Teatronics/Entertainment Lighting Control
P.O. Box 508, Santa Mangarita, CA 93453 USA
(805) 438-4000; *Fax:* (805) 438-9000
www.teatronics.com
sales@teatronics.com
Gary Beckerman, President
Lighting control & power distribution systems for stage, studio & remote applications.

Tech Laboratories Inc.
955 Belmont Ave., North Haledon, NJ 7508 USA
(973) 427-5333; *Fax:* (973) 427-5455
www.techlabsinc.com
Bernard Ciongoli, President
Earl Bjorndal, Operations Dir

Rotary switches; electrical/electronic subcontract, attenuators, transformers, pcb assembly & infrared security systems.

TECH-SA-PORT
Box 5372, Pittsburgh, PA 15206-0372 USA
(412) 661-1620, (800) 543-2233; *Fax:* 412-774-2300
www.tech-sa-port.com
Lewis Scheinman, President
Computer & electronic equipment cleaning supplies, including lint-free wipers, contamination-free chemicals, & spray dusters. All types of wiping materials.

Technet Systems Group
PO Box 422, Auburn, NH 3032 USA
(603) 483-5365, (888) 832-4638, (888) TECHNET; *Fax:* (603) 483-0512, (800)-FAX-SOS, (800) 329-4767
sales@technetsystems.com
Steve Vanni, President
Bcst equipment supplier & distributor for radio & TV, specializing in complete turnkey packages including planning, design, equipment, instal, towers & FCC licensing.

Techni-Tool Inc.
1547 N. Trooper Rd., PO Box 1117, Worcester, PA 19490-1117 USA
(800) 832-4866, (610) 941-2400; *Fax:* (610) 828-5623, (800) 854-8665
www.techni-tool.com/comm
sales@techni-tool.com
Paul Weiss, President
Steve Porter, General Manager & VP
Michael Ryan, VP of Sales
David Weitner, Promotions Manager
Steven Weiss, Executive Vice President
Dave Deputy, Vpof Finance
Stuart Weiss, Executive Vice President
William Kushner, VP of Distribution Center Operations
Master distributor of hand tools, kits & cases, test equipment, supplies & safety products for the Communications Field Techician working with fiber optic, coaxial & twisted pair cabling. As well as for the bench tech working on electronicsproduction/repair & cable assemby.

Technicolor SA
2300 S. Decker Lake Blvd., Salt Lake City, UT 84119 US
(801) 972-8000; *Fax:* (801) 972-6304
www.technicolor.com
Frederic Rose, CEO
13 Kevin Ct, Wyomissing, PA 19610 United States
(215) 678-8711; *Fax:* (215) 678-8784
Jeff Rosica, Sls Mgr

Technologies for Worship
103 Niska Drive, Waterdown, ON L0R 2H3 Canada
(905) 690-4709; *Fax:* (905) 473-9928
www.tfwm.com
dk@tfwm.com
Shelagh Rogers, President
Barry Cobus, Operations Dir
Kevin Rogers-Cobus, Programming Director
Darryl Kirkland, Publisher/Sales and Marketing Director
Kim Hunt, Art Director/ Designer
Jean Anderson, Advertising SalesRepresentative
John Smale, Accounts Payable
Michelle Makariak, Editor

Tekskil Industries Inc.
102-998 Harbourside Dr., North Vancouver, BC V7P 3T2 Canada
(877) TEKSKIL, (877) 8357545, (604) 985-2248; *Fax:* (877) 576-8361
www.tekskil.com
tekskilprompters2008@tekskil.com
John Veenstra, President
Rick Anselmo, Operations & Technical Support
Howard Rothstein, National Sales & Marketing
Michelle Wehr, Senior Account Manager, Broadcast Sales
Mike McCollum, Account Manager, Broadcast Sales
PeteSchneider, Senior Account Manager
Manufacturer of video, speech & computer prompting equipment.

Tektronix
14150 SW Karl Braun Drive, PO Box 500, Beaverton, OR 97077 USA
(650) 364-1853, (800) 833-9200; *Fax:* (650) 364-5716
www.tek.com
info@synthesysresearch.com
Dr Lute Henckels, CEO
Jim Waschura, President
Bob Hayes, Founder
John Ryan, General Sales Mgr
Charlie Schaffer, VP Marketing

Our customers work in communications, computer, semiconductor, military/aerospace, consumer electronics, education, broadcast and other fields all over the globe. Their reputations and success depend on our passion for solving their mostcomplex measurement problems. We help them measure, analyze and test next generation devices to ensure accurate performance, reliability, and compatibility.

Tektronix Inc.
13975 SW Karl Braun Dr., PO Box 500, Beaverton, OR 97077 USA
(800) 833-9200, (503) 627-7111; *Fax:* (503) 627-6108
www.tek.com
Richard H Wills, CEO
Jim Lico, President
Arif Kareem, Operations Dir
Larry Brown, Information Tech
Jane Elliot, Information Tech
Tim Anderson, Information Tech
Howard Vollum, Founder

Telcom Research
15-850 Legion Rd., Burlington, ON L7S 1T5 Canada
(905) 336-2450; *Fax:* (647) 436-6954
www.telcomresearch.com
Douglas Finch, President
Brian Weppler, Operations Dir
SMPTE/EBU time code generators, readers; character inserters, LTC-VITC & VITC-LTC trans. Logging/offline/EDL software.

Tele-Measurements Inc.
145 Main Ave., Clifton, NJ 7014 USA
(973) 473-8822, (800) 223-0052; *Fax:* (973) 473-0521
www.tele-measurements.com
William Endres, President
W. Chris Endres, General Manager
Bcst video equipment, tapes TV systems, teleconferencing, maintenance support, CCTV & rentals, distance learning.

Telecrafter Products
12687 W. Cedar Dr., Suite 100, Lakewood, CO 80228 USA
(303) 986-0086, (800) 257-2448; *Fax:* (303) 986-1042
www.telecrafter.com
mail@telecrafter.com
Drop installation products for broadband telecommunications delivery svc, including cable clips, cablemakers, cable guard, house boxes, fitting savers, & more.

Telemetrics Inc.
6 Leighton Pl., Mahwah, NJ 7430 USA
(201) 848-9818, (201) 785-4450; *Fax:* (201) 848-9819
www.telemetricsinc.com
info@telemetricsinc.com
Anthony Cuomo, President
Anthony C. Cuomo, Founder
Camera pan, tilt systems & triax camera control systems.

Telescript Inc.
445 Livingston St., Norwood, NJ 7648 USA
(201) 767-6733, (888) 767-6713; *Fax:* (201) 784-0323
www.telescript.com
info@telescript.com
John McGrath, Station Manager
Andrew Wischmeyer, General Sales Mgr
IBM & compatibles prompting programs & equipment. Lightweight, high-resolution 12 & 17 monitor prompters. Flat panel prompters, window based prompting software for bcst & video productions applications, comprehensive line of LCD prompters.

Telescript West
7801 N. Lamar Blvd., Austin, TX 78752 United States
(512) 302-0766
Jim Stringer, Mgr

Telestream East - USA
21351 Ridgetop Circle, Suite 120, Sterling, VA 20166 US
(703) 964-8089; *Fax:* (703) 964-8090
www.telestream.net
Dilip Som, Co-Founder/President/CTO
Sidney Hoffman, Co-Founder/ Vice President
Closed captioning & subtitling systems & svc for HD, DVD, NLE, webcasts & ipod. Plus teleprompting systems.

teletech.ca
3A-820 Denison St., Markham, ON L3R 3K5 Canada
(905) 475-5646, (888) 353-8324; *Fax:* (905) 475-5684
www.teletech.ca
Jack Kirkpatrick, President
Total bcst, postproduction, audio & video sls, service, & rentals of equipment & supplies.

Television Equipment Assoc. Inc./Matthey
Box 404, Brewster, NY 10509-0404 USA
(310) 457-7401; *Fax:* (310) 457-0023
Bill Pegler, President
Joseph Tocidlowski, General Manager
Serial digital interface products, NTSC/PAL Decoders, analog & digital DAs, video & pulse delays, video filters, A/D & D/A converters, headsets, serial digital/Fiberoptic links, Routing switches for digital video and radio.

Telex Communications Inc.
12000 Portland Ave. S., Burnsville, MN 55337 USA
(952) 884-4051; *Fax:* (952) 884-0043
www.telex.com
prosound@telex.com
Ned Jackson, CEO
Wired & wireless microphones; headphones/headsets; wired & wireless intercoms; audio duplicators/copiers.
2550 Hollywood Way, Suite 207, Burbank, CA 91505 United States
(818) 566-6700

TELLABS
1415 W. Diehl Rd., Naperville, IL 60563 US
(630) 798-8800; *Fax:* (630) 798-2000
www.tellabs.com
Mike Dagenais, President/Chief Executive Officer
John M. Brots, Executive Vice President/Global Operations
Lawrence A. Rieger, Acting Chief Financial Officer
Roger J. Heinz, Executive Vice President/Global Sales and Services
James M.Sheehan, Executive Vice President/General Counsel/Chief Adm
Kenneth G. Craft, Executive Vice President-Product Development
Thomas Ruvarac, Vice President, Business Development
Teleconferencing systems, digital echo cancellers, data over voice multiplexers, signaling systems, video conferencing, audio systems.
60 Commerce Dr., Hauppauge, NY 11788 United States
(516) 231-1550
29 The Quandrant, Abingdon, Oxfordshire 0X14 3Y3
011-44-235-524-400

Telos Systems
1241 Superior Ave., Cleveland, OH 44114 USA
(216) 241-7225; *Fax:* (216) 241-4103
www.telos-systems.com
Frank Foti, Station Chief
Denny Sanders, Chief Engineer
Michael Dosch, President/Axia Audio
Steve Church, President/CEO/Founder
Telos Systems, is the leading global manufacturer of coded audio, ISDN, telephone interface and networked audio products for talk-shows, teleconferencing, audio production, remote broadcasts, and intercom applications. Omnia Audio, a Teloscompany, is world-renowned for its digital audio signal processing expertise. Omnia audio processors for FM, AM, TV, HD Radio & DAB, Internet, and audio production are setting new standards for professional audio quality. Axia Audio, a Telos company,builds Ethernet-based professional IP-Audio products for broadcast, production, sound-reinforcement and commercial audio applications. Products include digital audio routers, on-air control surfaces, DSP mixers and processors, audio logging devices,and software for configuring, managing, and interfacing networked audio systems.

Tentel
333 Industrial Drive #4, Placerville, CA 95667 USA
(530) 344-0183, (800) 538-6894, (530) 344-0183; *Fax:* (530) 344-0186
John Chavers, General Manager

Texas Electronics Inc.
Mailing Address: Box 7225, Dallas, TX 75209 USA
Second Address: 5529 Redfield St., Dallas, TX 75235
(214) 631-2490, (800) 424-5651; *Fax:* (214) 631-4218
www.texaselectronics.com
info@texaselectronics.com
Carol Westlund, President
Jane Hansen, Operations Dir
Jason Burson, General Sales Mgr
J.R. Tozer, Founder
Manufacturer of meteorological instruments & controls.

Texscan MSI
11800 Wills Rd., Suite 150, Alpharetta, GA 30009 USA
(678) 689-0146; *Fax:* (770) 664-8442
www.texscan.com
Leonard J. Fabiano, President & Founder

Character generators, digital, analog commercial insertion systems, audio/video playback systems, weather data svc, multimedia graphics production systems & VCR controllers.

TFT Inc.
1953 Concourse Dr., San Jose, CA 95131-1708 USA
(408) 943-9323; *Fax:* (408) 432-9218, (408) 432-9219
Darryl Parker, Operations Dir
Digital, analog STLs, Reciters, synchronous boosters, modulation monitors & emergency alert systems(EAS).

Thales Broadcast & Multimedia S.A.
1 rue de l'Hautil, Z.A. les Bountries, Conflans Sainte Honorine Cedex, 78702 FRA
(530) 265 1000; *Fax:* 1 34 90 30 00
www.grassvalley.com
Bill Patrizio, President
Jeff Rosica, Operations Dir
Handling everything from video, audio to data signals & control systems.

Theatre Service & Supply Corp.
1792 Union Ave., Baltimore, MD 21211 USA
(410) 467-1225; *Fax:* (410) 467-1289
www.stage-n-studio.com
sales@stage-n-studio.com
Richard Antisdel, President
Jacauelin Keleman, General Sales Mgr
Manufacturer of studio, theatrical curtains, track systems, distributor of lighting & theatrical hardware.

Theatrical Services Inc.
128 S. Washington, Wichita, KS 67202 USA
(316) 263-4415, (888) 874-2649; *Fax:* (316) 263-9927
www.theatricalservices.com
tsi@theatricalservices.com
Stephen Wolf, President
Manufacturers & distributors of studio lighting & control equipment, studio cycloramas, curtains & track.

Thermodyne International LTd
1841 Business Pkwy., Ontario, CA 91761 USA
(909) 923-9945, (877) 307-8425; *Fax:* (909) 923-7505
www.thermodyne-online.com
request@thermodyne.com
Gary Ackerman, President
Josh Ackerman, Chief Marketing Officer
Reusable shipping cases; rack-mounted operating cases. Provides protection for all electronic equipment during transit.

Thomas & Betts Corp.
8155 T&B Blvd., Memphis, TN 38125 US
(800) 816-7809,(901) 252-8000, (901) 252-5000; *Fax:* (800) 816-7810,(901) 252-1354
www.tnb.com
elec_custserv@tnb.com
Manufacturer of Poleline hardware aerial & drop systems, fiber-optic hand holes, MMDS antenna mounting hardware.

Thomas & Betts Ltd.
Mailing Address: 700 Thomas Ave., Saint-Jean-sur Richelieu, QC J2X 2M9 Canada
Second Address: 8155 T&B Blvd., Memphis, TN 38125
(450) 347-5318, (901) 252-5000, (800) 816-7809; *Fax:* (450) 347-1976, (800) 816-7810
www.tnb.com
Dominic Pileggi, Chairman & CEO
Michael Kenney, President
Manufacturer of quality products for aerial construction & subscriber instal hardware for the Cable TV & telephone industry.

Thomson
104 Feeding Hills Rd., Southwick, MA 1077 US
(413) 998-1100; *Fax:* (413) 569-0679
www.technicolor.com
joseph.turbolski@thomson.net
Joseph Turbolski, Operations Dir
Richard Fiore, Programming Director
Thomson manufuctures, markets equipment sytems & solutions in the fields of terrestrial transmission, digital videl processing & multimedia distribution.

Thomson Broadcast & Media Solutions
Box 599000, 400 Providence Mine Road, Nevada City, CA 95959-5900 USA
(800) 824-5127; *Fax:* (530) 478-3166
www.thomsongrassvalley.com
Tim Thorsteinson, CEO
Russ Johnson, General Sales Mgr
Stephen Wong, Pacific Region sales
Video servers/disk recorders, media platforms, video production centers (switchers), signal mgmt systems (routers, modular), DVEs & HDTV equipment.

Thomson Reuters
3 Times Square, New York, NY 10036 USA
(646) 223-4000
www.thomsonreuters.com
general.info@thomsonreuters.com
David Thomson, Chairman
James C. Smith, President & CEO
Stephane Bello, EVP & CFO
James T. Powell, EVP & Chief Technology Officer
Gonzalo Lissarrague, President Global Growth & Operations
Deirdre Stanley, EVP, General Counsel &Secretary
Carla Jones, Chief of Staff
Basil Moftah, President, Intellectual Property & Science
Supplier of natl, world, business news, info to media & professionals.
165 Sparks St., Booth Bldg., Ottawa, ON K1P 5P8 Canada
(613) 235-6745
Antony Parry, Financial Correspondent
John Rogers, Gen News
1333 H St. N.W., Suite 410, Washington, DC 20005 United States
(202) 898-8300
Bruce Russell, Chief
311 S. Wacker Dr., Suite 1100, Chicago, IL 60606 United States
(312) 922-6038
Geoffrey Atkins, Chief
445 S. Figueroa, Suite 2100, Los Angeles, CA 90071 United States
(213) 380-2014
Ronald Clarke, Chief

Standard Life Centre
121 King St. W., 20th Fl, Toronto, ON M5H 3T9 Canada
(416) 869-3600
Peter Thomas, Mgr Canada
2020 Rue Universite, Suite 1020, Montreal, PQ H3A 2A5 Canada
(514) 282-0705
William Miller, Chairman

360 Systems
3281 Grande Vista Dr., Newbury Park, CA 91320 USA
(818) 991-0360; *Fax:* (818) 991-1360
www.360systems.com
Robert Easton, President
Robert Nilo, Sales Manager
Daren Francom, Controller
Roxana Velteze, Sales Administrator
Image Server Maxx Video & Graphics servers in standard and High Defintion, Time Delay servers, DigiCart/E, Instant Replay2 and Short/Cut audio editors and players.

3M
3M Product Information Center, St. Paul, MN 55144-1000 USA
(651) 737-6501,(888) 3m-helps; *Fax:* (800) 713-6329,(651) 737-7117
www.3m.com
innovation@mmm.com
George Buckley, President
Robert MacDonald, Promotions Manager
Fault locators; cable & cabling equipment & supplies; Post-it notes & flags; Telephony: copper & fiber optic networks; Vikuiti display enhancement films; splicing kts; volition fiber optics; electrical tubing, tapes, terminations &connectors.

The Tiffen Company
90 Oser Avenue, Hauppauge, NY 11788 US
(631) 273-2500, (800) 645-2522; *Fax:* (631) 273-2557
www.tiffen.com
techsupport@tiffen.com
Joanne Camarda, President
Raymond Blumenthal, Operations Dir
Fully professional range of flat-panel, prompters for studio, field & conferencing applications complemented by Windows prompting software. PRO-Motion light & medium duty tripods. Brick House Video compact production switcher. USRepresentatives for IPV.
40-3 Oser Ave., Hauppauge, NY 11788 United States
(631) 273-3029; *Fax:* (631) 435-4544
Lisa Grunert, Sls & Product Support

The Tiffen Company
90 Oser Ave., Hauppauge, NY 11788 USA
(631) 273-2500, (800) 645-2522; *Fax:* (631) 273-2557
www.tiffen.com
steadicamprofessional@tiffen.com
Michael Cannatta, COO
Steve Tiffen, President
Jeff Cohen, Operations Dir
Hilary Araujo, Promotions Manager
Photographic filters, lens accessories for motion picture, still photography, digital video, Davis & Sanford tripods, Domke Bags, support systems; steadicam camera stabilizing systems..

Time Logic Inc.
1914 Palomar Oaks Way, Suite 150, Carlsbad, CA 92008 USA
(760) 517-0445, (877) 222-9543; *Fax:* (760) 431-1351
www.timelogic.com
Rick MacDonald, CEO
Automation systems for TV bcstrs & radio stns. Custom software dev for Tektronix Profile disks, HDTV time delay systems, using disk or tape.

Time Manufacturing Co.
7601 Imperial Dr., PO Box 20368, Waco, TX 76702-0368 USA
(254) 399-2100, (800) 825-1085; *Fax:* (254) 399-2651
www.timemfg.com
Charles Wiley, President
Amber Pierce, Promotions Manager
Truck mounted aerial lifts ranging from 29' to 210' in height.

Times Fiber Communications Inc.
358 Hall Ave., PO Box 384, Wallingford, CT 6492 USA
(203) 265-8500, (800) 677-2288; *Fax:* (203) 265-8422
www.timesfiber.com
Timothy Cohane, COO
Stan VonFeldt, General Sales Mgr
Chris Huffman, Promotions Manager
Diana Reardon, Chief Financial Officer
Coaxial, twisted pair composite cables for broadband, cellular/PCS applications, semiflex, svc entry, drop cables & connectors.
Box 14975, Phoenix, AZ 85063 United States
(602) 278-5576
Les Judd, Chairman
Box 430, Renfrew, ON Canada
(613) 432-8557
Box 119A, Rt. 2, Chatham, VA 24531 United States
(804) 432-1800

Tinsley Laboratory Inc.
4040 Lakeside Dr., Richmond, CA 94806-1963 USA
(510) 222-8110; *Fax:* (510) 223-4534
www.asphere.com
Daniel F. (Dan) Desmond, President
John Kincaid, General Manager
Gyrozoom image stabilizing lens, GX3 integrated CCD camera/stabilizing system.

TOA Electronics Inc.
Mailing Address: 1350 Bayshore Highway, Suite 270, Burlingame, CA 94010 USA
Second Address: 1 Harmon Plaza, Suite 602, Secaucus, NJ 7094
(650) 588-2538; *Fax:* (650) 588-3349
www.toaelectronics.com
info@toaelectronics.com
Hisayuki Okvoka, CEO
Allan Lamberti, General Sales Mgr
Sound, communication equipment for coml sound & audio/video industries. Manufacturer, distributor of high quality, reliable audio & security products.

Toner Cable Equipment Inc.
969 Horsham Rd., Horsham, PA 19044 USA
(215) 675-2053, (800) 523-5947; *Fax:* (215) 675-7543
www.tonercable.com
info@tonercable.com
Bob Toner, CEO/President
Steve Deasey, Sales Manager
Ted Tozzi, Director of Engineering
Mike Sheffer, Broadcast Sales Nationwide
Allen Morgan, Sales Manager
Courtney Cappa, Customer service
Bernie Petro, Purchasing Manager
TonyScarcelli, VP Administration
Karen Knight, Advertising/ Marketing Manager
International distributor & manufacturer of a complete line of cable TV & wireless cable equipment.

UK Ltd.
Unit 9 Berinsfield Business Park, Tower Industrial Estate, Fane Dr., Berinsfield, Oxfordshire, OX10 7LN United Kingdom
0186 534 1222

Torpey Time
580 Danforth Road, Toronto, ON M1K 1E3 Canada
(416) 298-7788, (800) 387-6141; *Fax:* (416) 267-4474
www.torpeytime.com
Bob Torpey, President
Master clock systems, digital & analog slave clocks, timers, video time & temperature equipment.

Toshiba America Consumer Products
1420 Toshiba Dr., Lebanon, TN 37087 USA
(615) 444-8501; *Fax:* (615) 443-3810
www.toshiba.com
Yoshirio Matsumoto, President
Jodi Sally, Operations Dir
Marcia Repole, VP/Communications
HDTV products: HD-VCR (Analog-UniHi), HD monitor (projection & CRT), NTSC to HDTV upconverter, HD-CCD color camera, HD horizon system.
82 Totowa Rd., Wayne, NJ 07470 United States
(973) 628-8000; *Fax:* (973) 628-1875

Tower Innovations
Mailing Address: 5688 Prospect Drive, Newburgh, IN 47630 US
Second Address: 3266 Tower Drive, Newburgh, IN 47630
(812) 853-0595,(800) 664-8222; *Fax:* (812) 853-6652
www.towerinnovations.net
towers@towerinnovations.net
David Nicholson, COO
Josh Bridgeman, General Manager
Melissa Nicholson, Promotions Manager
Manufacture towers for broadcast (up to 2000'), cellular & PCS Communications Innovative engrg solutions, fabrication, construction planning, tower erection & turnkey systems.
2855 Hwy 261, Newburgh, IN 47630

Tower Inspection Inc.
3317 S Cherokee Drive, PO Box 709, Muskogee, OK 74402-0709 USA
(918) 683-8915; *Fax:* (918) 683-0888
www.towerinspection.com
sales@towerinspection.com
Gary G. Lehman, President
Inspection svcs during construction; maintenance inspection, painting, repairs of radio, microwave & TV towers.

Tower Network Services
317 RR South, Suite 305, Austin, TX 78734 USA
(512) 266-6200; *Fax:* (512) 266-6210
www.towernetwork.com
info@towernetwork.com
Svc tower, antenna. RF testing & tower structural analysis. Tower elevator repair and upgrading.

Towers-R-Us
Box 1255, 3304 Wadley Road, Waycross, GA 31502 USA
(912) 283-6317; *Fax:* (912) 283-6318
towersrus2008@yahoo.com
Velvet Beard, CEO
Grant Balwanz, President
Design, engineer, fabricate, erect, maintain, and paint high radio towers

Transcom Corp.
PO Box 26744, Elkins Park, PA 19027 USA
(215) 938-7304, (800) 441-8454; *Fax:* (215) 938-7361
www.fmamtv.com
Martin Cooper, President
New digital (8VSB/DVB-T/H), angle TV transmitters, microwave links, antenna, cable & select used TV, AM, FM transmitters.
2655 Philmont Ave., Suite 200, Huntington Valley, PA 19006 United States
(215) 938-7304 (800) 441-8454; *Fax:* (215) 938-7361
Martin Cooper, Pres

Transcrypt International
3900 N.W. 12th St., Suite 200, Lincoln, NE 68521 USA
(800) 228-0226
Massoud Safavi, COO
Technological assst for installation, application in all types & brands of land mobile radios. Transcrypt ensures you the best value in the industry

Transtector Systems Inc.
10701 North Airport Drive, Hayden, ID 83835 USA
(800) 882-9110, (208) 772-8515; *Fax:* (208) 762-6133
www.transtector.com
sales@transtector.com
David Stimmel, CFO
Shawn Thompson, President/Director
James E. Harless, Operations Dir
Linda Johnson, Promotions Manager
Steve Pare, CFO
Transient overvoltage protective devices, power quality consulting svcs; college-accredited, power-quality assurance education courses.

Transvision International
550 Maulhardt Ave., Oxnard, CA 93030 USA
(805) 981-8740; *Fax:* (805) 981-8738
www.txvision.com
kvaughan@txvision.com
Maria Costa Husband, Traffic/Operations
Kimithy Vaughan, Sales/Marketing
Lisa Costa, Administration
Transportable, flyaway satellite transmission; mobile/TVROs; studio/remote production & transmission mgmt.

Tribune Media Services
40 Media Drive, Queensbury, NY 12801 USA
(800) 833-9581, (518) 792-9914; *Fax:* (518) 761-7118
John B. Kelleher, President/ COO
James McCormick, Operations Dir
Rebecca Baldwin, VP/General manager
Ken Carter, Station Manager
Kathy Tolstrup, SVP, Sales
Edwin Ong, EVP, Technology
Mark Yamada, Dir. Of Communications
SheelaChandrashekhera, Director, Business Development
Lanna Langlois, VP, Finance
Shannon Orborne, VP, Marketing
International source for TV info. Clients include interactive on-screen & on-line guides, nwsprs, print publications, cable companies, telephone companies, rsch organizations, producers, syndicators of TV programs & advertisers.

Trilogy Communications Inc.
2910 Highway 80 East, Pearl, MS 39208 USA
(601) 932-4461, (800) 874-5649, (800) TRILOGY; *Fax:* (601) 939-6637
www.trilogycoax.com
info@trilogycoax.com
John Kaye, Chairman
Grace Lee, President
Jim Oldham, General Sales Mgr
Fei Wei, Promotions Manager
Ryan Cole, SVP of Sales & Marketing
Edmund T. Lee, Sr. Business Development Manager
Angela Lourenco, Marketing & InternationalSales manger
Will Bodnar, Strategic Accounts Manager
World leading manufacturer of advanced technology coaxial cables for wireless networks for cellular, paging, PCS, SMR and in- building networking applications application, ISO-9001 certified.

Trimm Inc.
407 Railroad St., Butner, NC 27509 USA
(800) 298-7466, (919) 575-6100; *Fax:* 919) 575-6200
www.trimminc.com
trimminc@frontiernet.net
Will Newton, President
Ricky Brummet, General Sales Mgr
Manufacturer of fuse panel s& terminal blocks.

Triplett Test Equipment & Tools
850 Perimeter Rd., Manchester, NH 3103 USA
(800) 874-7538, (800) TRIPLETT; *Fax:* (603) 669-6400
www.triplett.com
Carlo Carluccio, President/CEO
Tim Cetto, General Manager
Panel instruments & test equipment. Electrical, electronic, telecommunication & railroad testers.

Trompeter Semflex
55550 E. McDowell Rd., Mesa, AZ 85215 USA
(480) 985-9000; *Fax:* (480) 985-0334
www.emerson.com
sales@trompeter.com
Joe Norwood, President
Dale Reed, Vice President
DS3 interconnection & DSX products for central office.

TTE Inc.
11652 W. Olympic Blvd., Los Angeles, CA 90064-1400 USA
(310) 478-8224; *Fax:* (310) 445-2791
www.tte.com
tte@tte.com
Stephen Sodaro, General Sales Mgr
Dave Zavac, Manager
LC filters to 18 GHz, balun, matching transformers, combiners, active filters to 1 MHz. RF, microwave filters DC-18ghz & video splitters.

Tulsat/An Addvantage Technologies Co.
1221 E. Houston St., Broken Arrow, OK 74012-4405 USA
(800) 331-5997, (918) 251-2887; *Fax:* (918) 258-7658
www.tulsat.com
tulsat@tulsat.com
David Chymiak, President/Sales
Ken Chymiak, President
Mark Schumacher, Sales Manager
Greg Harlan, Service Manager
Bruce Riggs, Sales Associate

TWR Lighting Inc.
4300 Windfern Rd., Suite 100, Houston, TX 77041-8943 USA
(713) 973-6905; *Fax:* (713) 973-9352
www.twrlighting.com
info@twrlighting.com
Edwin Wahler Jr, Chairman
Ray Kraemer, Vice President/Chief Operating Officer
Gavin Sebek, Director of Integrated Technology
Sandra Prewitt, Director of Marketing
Jeremy Lochner, Sales Director
Nathan Greene, Natl. Acc. Adm.
DanMonosn, Natl. Acc. Adm.
Raudel Barrerra, Wind Energy Specialist
Aviation obstruction lighting manufacturer, sls & svc of low, medium, LED products & High Intensity systems.

Tyco Electronics
Mailing Address: 1050 Westlakes Dr., Berwyn, PA 19312 USA
Second Address: PO Box 64874, St. Paul, MN 55164-0874
(610) 893-9800, (866) 258-4745, (651) 450-4064; *Fax:* (650) 361-2288
www.te.com
Tom Lynch, CEO & Chairman
Terrence Curtin, President, Industrial Solutions
Dennis Conway, General Sales Mgr
Robert (Bob) Hau, EVP & CFO
John Jenkins, EVP & General Counsel
Rob Shaddock, EVP & Chief Technology Officer
Joe Donahue,EVP & Chief Operating Officer
Brad Gambill, SVP, Strategy & Business Development
Jane Leipold, SVP, Global HR
Coaxial connectors, environmental sealing products & antenna de-icers.

U.S. Tape & Label Corp.
2092 Westport Ctr. Dr., St. Louis, MO 63146-3564 USA
(314) 824-4444, (800) 569-1906; *Fax:* (314) 824-4400
www.ustl.com
info@ustl.com
Jim Eiseman, President/Owner
Debbie Reed, Engineering
Bob Rubin, Finance
Don Johnstone, VP Production
Jamie Hatcher, Plant Manager
Dave Rosen, VP Sales & Marketing
Nicole Giraud, Regional Sales Manager
Doug Holtmeyer, VPLabeling Equipment
Milian Petrovic, Service Tech
Custom printed bumper strips & window labels for the bcst industry. Industrial labels, direct mail printing & label-aire equipment.

U.S. Traffic & Display Solutions
9603 John St., Santa Fe Springs, CA 90670 US
(562) 923-9600; *Fax:* (562) 923-7555
Glen Hirami, President
Changeable outdoor electronic adv displays.

Ultimate Precision/GKM
200 Finn Ct., Farmingdale, NY 11735 USA
(631) 249-7816; *Fax:* (631) 777-1828
www.gkmbroadcastracks.com
sales@afcosystems.com
Michael Mallia, CEO
Gerard Becker, President
GKM is the source for Bcst Racks & Communication Products featuring a comprehensive line of bcst racks, frames & enclosure solutions for the bcst industry. A division of Ultimate Precision Metal Products, Inc.-part of the AFCO Systems Group.Ultimate has been a recognized leader precision sheet metal mfg for over 30 years

Ultimate Support Systems Inc.
5836 Wright Dr., Loveland, CO 80538 USA
(800) 525-5628, (970) 776-1920; *Fax:* (970) 776-1941
www.ultimatesupport.com
info@ultimatesupport.com
Mike Belitz, CEO/President
Doug Towne, Manager
Jeff Moore, President
Dan Hoeye, Director of Marketing
Paul O'Brien, International Sales manager
Preston Clark, VP of Sales
Strong, lightweight speaker & lighting tripods. Microphone stands for nearly any application.

Ultimatte Corp.
20945 Plummer St., Chatsworth, CA 91311 USA

EQUIPMENT MANUFACTURERS

(818) 993-8007; *Fax:* (818) 993-3762
www.ultimatte.com
Lynne Sauve, President
Reid Baker, General Sales Mgr
Alan Dadourian, Chief Engineer
Max Portillo, Engineering
Video compositing devices for coms, live bcst, production, postproduction & computerized tripod head.

Union Connector Co.
8182Baymeadows Way West, Jacksonville, FL 32256 USA
(631) 753-9550; *Fax:* (631) 753-9560
www.unionconnector.com
Richard Wolpert, President
Alan Wolpert, Operations Dir
William J. Wolpert, Co-Founder
Electrical connectors, power distribution systems, portable power cabinets, custom switchgear, cases, carts & grip equipment.

Unique Business Systems
1100 Colorado Ave., Santa Monica, CA 90401 USA
(310) 396-3929; *Fax:* (310) 396-6114
www.unibiz.com
sales@unibiz.com
Pradeep Batra, President/Co-Founder
Stan Sugimoto, Co-Founder
Asset management software to track equipment sales and rentals, service and repair, and labor planning. Single system from quote to invoice. Two products: 'R2' software for Entertainment Rental companies and 'CR2' software for ConstructionEquipment Dealers.

UNISET Co., LLC
449 Ave. A, Rochester, NY 14621 USA
(585) 544-3820; *Fax:* (585) 544-1110
www.unisetcorp.com
info@unisetcorp.com
Ronald Kniffin, President
Sean Martin, Co-Owner
Brian McKinnon, Co-Owner
Modular studio staging systems for studio settings; news setting; 7 top talent tables, & UNI-CYC anywhere cyclorama.

Unisys Corp.
801 Lakeview Drive, Suite 100, Blue Bell, PA 19422 USA
(215) 986-4011
www.unisys.com
J. Edward Coleman, Chairman & CEO
Kevin Kern, Operations Dir
Barbara Harris, Programmer
Adam Brodman, Member
Nancy S. Sundheim, Senior VP & Gen Counsel
Quincy Allen, SVP/ Chief Marketing & Strategy Officer
Janet B. Haugen, SVP &CFO
David Loeser, SVP/ Worldwide Human Resources
Suresh Matthews, SVP / Chief Information Officer
M. Lazane Smith, SVP, Corporate Development
Cable info business systems. Unisys hardware: A1, A4, A6, A10, A12, A17 & IBM PC compatibles.

United Media Inc.
4771 E. Hunter, Anaheim, CA 92807 USA
(714) 227-7183; *Fax:* (714) 777-2434
United Media Inc is a developer & manufacturer which recognizes the ongoing need for high quality, affordable professional video equipment, developer of the On-Line Express non-linear editing system for Windows NT and multicom. The On-LineExpress offers uncompromised digital editing, compositing, digital audio editing, titling, 2D & 3D realtime effects & sophisticated media mgmt.

United States Broadcast
1371 Production Dr., Burlington, KY 41005 US
(859) 282-1802; *Fax:* (859) 282-1804
www.usbroadcast.com
Pete Beckett, President
New, used TV, audio equipment, bcst batteries & chargers.

UniVision Inc.
PO Box 4125, Missoula, MT 59806 USA
(406) 721-8876; *Fax:* (406) 721-0810
www.univision-computers.com
sales@univision-computers.com
Jim Green, President
Sell & repair computers. Program software, fiberoptics & wiring.

Utah Scientific Inc.
4750 Wiley Post Way, Suite 150, Salt Lake City, UT 84116 US
(800) 453-8782, (801) 575-8801; *Fax:* (801) 537-3099
www.utahscientific.com
David Burland, COO
Tom Harmon, CEO
Utah Scientific has operated for over thirty years with a single goal - to be the broadcast industry's leading supplier of routing switchers and associated products. The company is committed to maintaining the highest standards anduncompromised integrity, and continuing to earn customer satisfaction and loyalty by offering the best products and service in the business.

Utility Tower Company
Box 12369, 3200 N.W. 38th, Oklahoma City, OK 73157 USA
(405) 946-5551; *Fax:* (405) 947-8466
www.utilitytower.net
Gloria Nelson, President
Joe James, Operations Dir
Leo L. Roberts, Engineering Requirements & Drawings
Ron Nelson Jr., Vice President
Tower structures, accessories for bcstg & wireless applications; tower design, engrg analysis, turnkey instals; modifications, maintenance & inspections.

V-Soft Communications
401 Main Street, Suite 213, Cedar Falls, IA 50613 USA
(319) 266-8402, (800) 743-3684; *Fax:* (319) 432-7275
www.v-soft.com
info@v-soft.com
Doug Vernier, President & Senior Broadcast Engineer/Technical Co
Kate Michler, Engineering Dir
Kate English, Technical Consultant
John Gray, Director of Research and Development
Best engineering software for AM, FM, TV & general communications. Signal propagation, allocation work, path profiles, custom mapping & more.

Valmont Industries, Inc.
One Valmont Plaza, Omaha, NR 68154-5215 USA
(402) 963-1000; *Fax:* (402) 963-1198
www.valmont.com
custoinfo@microflect.com
Mogens C. Bay, Chairman & CEO
Aaron Schapper, VP & General Manager, International Irrigation
Bret Davis, Station Manager
Craig Malsam, VP, Engineering & Strategic Technology Development
Terry J. McClain, Executive VP & CFO
C. LeeAddams, VP, Strategy & Govt. Relations
Vanessa K. Brown, Vp, Human Resources
Brian J. Desigio, VP, Corporate Development
Stephen G. Kaniewski, VP, Information Development
Todd G. Atkinson, Executive VP & Corporate Secretary
Towers, microwave passive repeaters, waveguide support systems & tech svcs.

Vantage Lighting Inc.
175 Paul Dr., Suite E, San Rafael, CA 94903 USA
(800) 445-2677, (415) 507-0402; *Fax:* (415) 507-0502
www.vantagelighting.com
Arlene Allsman, President
Peter Allsman, General Manager
Replacement lamps including stage, studio, projection audiovisual, HMI, Xenon, 3D video & laser system. Electronic ballasts for HID lighting.

Vecima Networks Inc.
Mailing Address: 771 Vanalman Avenue, Victoria, BC V8Z 3B8 Canada
Second Address: 150 Cardinal Place, Saskatoon, SK S7L 6H7
(250) 881-1982; *Fax:* (250) 881-1982,(250) 881-1974
www.vecima.com
invest@vecima.com
Dr Surinder Kumar, Chairman
Marshall Sali, Senior Vice President of Operations
Sumit Kumar, President
John Hanna, Chief Financial Officer
Laird Froese, Senior Vice President of Research & Development
Mark Briggs, Senior VicePresident of Cable Sales
Designer, manufacturer & seller of products that enable broadband access to cable, wireless & telephony networks.
150 Cardinal Pl., Saskatoon, SK S7L 6H7 Canada
(306) 955-7075
Dr. Hugh Wood, COO

Veetronix Inc.
Box 480, 1311 W. Pacific, Lexington, NE 68850 USA
(308) 324-6661, (800) 445-0007; *Fax:* (308) 324-4985
www.veetronix.com
James Longley, President
Roger Teeters, General Sales Mgr
Ladonna Kwiatkowski, Purchasing Executive
Keyboard & panel reed switches & keycaps with in-house tooling.

Vega
18200 Olympic Ave. S., Tukwila, WA 98188 US
(425) 656-0683; *Fax:* (425) 656-0679
www.vegahelmet.com
OrderDesk@vegahelmet.com
Don Poysa, General Sales Mgr
Dispatch control consoles, amplifiers & monitoring products.

Vermeer Manufacturing Co.
1210 Vermeer Rd. E., PO Box 200, Pella, IA 50219 USA
(641) 628-3141; *Fax:* (641) 621-7773
www.vermeer.com
salesinfo@vermeermfg.com
Robert Vermeer, Chairman
Mary Andringa, CEO
Steve Heap, Sr Director/International Sales
Cable plows, trenchers, backhoes, stump cutters & hyraulic boring equipment.

Vertex Communications Corp.
Mailing Address: 274 West 5th St., Frederick, MD 21701 USA
Second Address: PO Box 384, Braddock Heights, MD 21714-0384
(240) 215-4915, (866) 384-9981; *Fax:* (240) 215-3781
www.vertexcommunication.com
Chris Marzizzi, President
Gary Kanipe, Operations Dir
Jeff Porter, General Manager
John Sciberras, Promotions Manager
Rob Davies, Co-Founder
Andy Roberts, Co-Founder
Jennifer Swafford, Senior Director, Sales
Patrick Quinn,Senior Director, Client Services
Antennas, control systems, passive microwave devices, field svcs, satcom net equipment, custom engrg solutions, SSPAs, LNAs, RF components/subsystems.

Vertex Beijing Office
COFCO Plaza, Suite 411, Tower B, N. 8 Jian Guo Men Nei Ave, Be, 100005
(+86-10) 6528-7258; *Fax:* (+86-10) 6528-7261
info@vertex.com.cn

Vertex Antennentechnik GmbH
Baumstr. 50, Duisburg, D-47198
49-2066-20960; *Fax:* 49-2066-209611
info@vertexant.com

Vertex International Ltd.
37 Kinghorn Rd., Burntisland, Fife, KY3 9EA
44-1592-873-956
vertes@mbox3.singnet.com.sg

Vertex Asia (Singapore Representative Office)
21-03 Suntec Tower One, 7 Temasek Blvd., 038987 Singapore
65-430-9524; *Fax:* 65-430-9516
vertex@pacific.net.sg

Vertex Antenna Systems LLC
2211 Lawson Ln., Santa Clara, CA 95054 United States
(408) 654-5600; *Fax:* (408) 654-5613/5614
bernard@tiw.com

Vertex Microwave Products Inc.
3111 Fujita St., Torrance, CA 90505 United States
(310) 539-6704; *Fax:* (310) 539-7463
info@vertexmpi.com

Vicon Industries Inc.
131 Heartland Blvd., Edgewood, NY 11717-8315 USA
(631) 952-2288, (800) 645-9116; *Fax:* (631) 951-9288
www.vicon-cctv.com
salse@vicon-security.com
John Badke, CFO
Larry Greenwald, President
Peter Horn, Operations Dir
Yacov Pshtissky, General Sales Mgr
Bret McGowan, Promotions Manager
Guy Arazi, Engineering Dir
Closed circuit TV equipment, systems for the security & surveillance industry.

VidCAD LLC
2010 E. Lohman Ave., Suite 2, Las Cruces, NM 88001 USA
(575) 522-0003, (800) VidCAD-6; *Fax:* (575) 635-4518
www.vidcad.com
sales@vidcad.com
Walter Black, CEO
John Weadock, Training Manager
VidCAD software connects your idea from diagram design & rack planning to installation, maintenance & rebuilds-on time & on budget.

Video Accessory Corp.
1243 Sherman Drive, Suite 8, Longmont, CO 80501 USA

(800) 821-0426, (303) 443-1319; *Fax:* (303) 440-8878
www.vac-brick.com
sales@vac-brick.net
Frank S. Barnes, President
Amy Barnes Frey, CEO
Bruce Wallingford, Promotions Manager
Richard Frey, Chief Engineer
Black Burst generators, video & audio distribution amplifiers, video line isolators, video & audio switches.

Video International Development Corp.
Box 349, 21 Winans Place, Locust Valley, NY 11560 USA
(516) 671-6765; *Fax:* (516) 730-5084
www.videointernational.com
Bernd Bressel, President/Broadcast Media Executive
Bernd Bressel, Director
Robert W. Smith, Itinerant Service Technician
Stan Paris, West Caoast Sales Manager
HD & SD Digital TV standards converters with motion compensated interpolation for bcst & industrial use as well as audio/video processores for production & post-production.

X-Form Systems-Spechtweg 1
Braunschweig, 38108 Germany
(0531) 30292890

Videomagnetics Inc.
3970 Clearview Frontage Rd., Colorado Springs, CO 80911 USA
(719) 390-1313, (800) 432-3887, (800) HEADVTR; *Fax:* (719) 390-1316
www.videomagnetics.com
Tony Korte, President/CEO
Jane Pennie, General Sales Mgr
Full service specialists in betacam camera & recorders. Refurbished video heads & scanners.

Videotron Ltee
300 Viger Avenue East, Montreal, QC H28 3W4 Canada
(514) 281-1711; *Fax:* (514) 985-8652
Robert Depatie, CEO
Manon Brouillette, Operations Dir
Saro Saroyan, General Manager
Bernard Bricallt, Vice President
Cable TV, digital TV, interactive TV and telecommunications.

LeGroupe Videotron Ltee.
300 ave Viger est, Montreal, PQ H2X 3W4 Canada

Videssence L.L.C.
10768 Lower Azusa Rd., El Monte, CA 91731 USA
(626) 579-0943; *Fax:* (626) 579-6803
www.videssence.tv
contact@videssence.tv
Toni Swarens, President
Lauri Maines, Operations Dir
Amanda McGinnis, International Account Manager
Gary Thomas, Technical Support & Design Layout:National Sales M
Stan Wong, Product Manager
Energy-efficient fluorescent and LED, studio lighting products for TV, film, stage, commercial broadcasting and communications applications.

Vidiom Systems Inc.
10901 W. 120th Ave., Suite 230, Broomfield, CO 80021 USA
(303) 604-0800; *Fax:* (303) 604-0080
www.vidiom.com
Timothy Wahlers, CEO
David Housman, Operations Dir
Michael Malcy, Promotions Manager
Travis Paranto, Finance Director
Software engrg & design, software testing, application development, technical writing, training for OCAP, ETV, headends.

Viking Cases
10480 Oak St. N.E., St. Petersburg, FL 33716 USA
(800) 237-8560, (727) 577-1216; *Fax:* (727) 577-2082
www.vikingcases.com
sales@vikingcases.com
Arthur Stemler, CEO
Bruce Stemler, President
Reese Autry, Operations Dir
Heavy-duty reusable shipping cases, lightweight carrying cases & EIA rack cases.

Vinten
Mailing Address: 709 Executive Blvd., Suite. A, Valley Cottage, NY 10989 USA
Second Address: 2701 N. Ontario St, Burbank, CA 91504
(845) 268 0100, (888) 284-6836, (818) 847-8666; *Fax:* (845) 268-9324, (818) 847-1205
www.vinten.com
info-cd-usa@vitecgroup.com
Bob Carr, President
Vinten's wide range of lightweight, studio and outside broadcast camera support equipment enables you to work the way you choose without compromise.

Vision Database Systems
1562 Park Lane South #500, Jupiter, FL 33458 USA
(561) 748-0711, (877) 727-4322; *Fax:* (561) 748-0712
www.visiondatabase.com
sales@visiondatabase.com
Emil Bonaduce, President
Photo image software.

Visual Sound Inc.
Mailing Address: 485 Park Way, Broomall, PA 19008 USA
Second Address: 1642 Sulphur Spring Rd., Baltimore, MD 21227-2539
(610) 544-8700, (410) 737-0130; *Fax:* (610) 544-3385, (410) 737-0188
www.visualsound.com
info@visualsound.com
Karen Bogosian, President
John Greene, General Sales Mgr
John S. Bogosian, Founder
Audio-video sls, svcs, installation, maintainance of teleconferencing rooms, interactive white boards, training rooms; ENG, production vans, studios, events production & rentals.
490 S. St. John's Church Rd., Camp Hill, PA 17011 United States
(717) 730-6651 (800) 382-1301; *Fax:* (717) 761-0874

Beltsville
3919 Vero Rd. # J, Halethorpe, MD 21227 United States
(410) 242-4216

VITEC
931 Benecia Avenue, Sunnydale, CA 94085 USA
(408) 739 1706, (800) 451-5101; *Fax:* (408) 739-1706
www.vitecmm.com
sunnyvale@vitec.com
Michael Conway, Chief Technical Officer
Tam Chiang, VP Marketing
Peter Mor, SVP
VITEC is also the only designer and manufacturer in the field of digital video that can respond fully to customer-specific needs, thanks to our custom development and production department.

Vitec Videocom Inc.
Mailing Address: 709 Executive Blvd., Valley Cottage, NY 10989 USA
Second Address: 2701 N. Ontario St., Burbank, CA 91504
(845) 268-0100, (818) 847-8666, 888 2 Vinten; *Fax:* (845) 268-9324, (818) 847-1205
www.vinten.com
info-cd-usa@vitecgroup.com
Bob Carr, President
Ali Ahmadi, Promotions Manager
Joan Frison, Financial Executive
Bob Jones, Regional Manager
Len Donovan, Key Account Manager
Michelle McCullough, Customer Service
Randy Frisch, Repair Service/ PartsIdentification
Remote control camera systems. Pneumatic studio pedestals, pan & tilt heads, lightweight tripods & heads.
50 Moberly Ave., Toronto, ON M4CC 2B1 Canada
(416) 693-8578; *Fax:* (416) 693-9489
Sam Duncan, Canadian Rgnl Sls Mgr
4 Birch Ct., Shamong, NJ 08088 United States
(609) 268-2405; *Fax:* 609-268-3204
Len Donovan, Northeast Rgnl Sls Mgr
10208 N.W. 47th St., Sunrise, FL 33351 United States
(945) 572-4344; *Fax:* (945) 572-4565
Joseph Lantowski, Southern Rgnl Sls Mgr
G 95 S. Glenwood, Suite B, Burbank, CA 91506 United States
(818) 843-5244; *Fax:* (818) 843-5176
Mark Playdon, West Rgn Sls Mgr

Vitec Videocom, Inc.
Mailing Address: 709 Executive Blvd., Valley Cottage, NY 10989 USA
Second Address: 2701 N. Ontario St., Burbank, CA 91504
(845) 268-0100, (818) 847-8666; *Fax:* (845) 268-0113, (818) 847 1205
www.sachtler.com
sales@sachtler.com
Bob Carr, President
Ali Ahmadi, Promotions Manager
Complete line of camera support equipment for ENG, EFP, O.B. & the new generation of studio cameras. Lighting for news, production & studio open-face technology & fresnel.
3316 W. Victory Blvd., Burbank, CA 91505 United States
(818) 854-4446

Vollmer-Gray Engineering Laboratories Inc.
2421 N. Palm Drive, Signal Hill, CA 90755 US
(562) 427-8435, (877) 885-6900; *Fax:* (562) 427-8434
www.vglabs.com
NewCase@VGLabs.com
Scott Gray, President
Vollmer-Gray Engineering Laboratories, Inc. is an independent engineering firm providing engineering consulting and expert witness services on accidents, incidents and other losses.

Vortek
7200 Rawson Road, Victor, NY 14564 US
(585) 924-5000; *Fax:* (585) 924-0545
www.etcconnect.com
Scott Seeman, President
David Ross, Operations Dir
Robin Allen, Purchasing Executive
Engineer manufacture rigging systems, motorized hoists & controls.

VSG Inc.
Mailing Address: 1033 Elm Hill Pike, Nashville, TN 37210 USA
Second Address: 11126 Lindbergh Business Ct., St. Louis, MO 63123
(615) 248-1010, (314) 487-8045; *Fax:* (615) 244-5712
www.vsginc.net
Chris Ramsey, President
Greg Shriner, General Sales Mgr
Philip Hullquist, Production
Mandy Rogers, Client Services
Rob Brown, Client Services
Greg Shriner, Regional Sales Manager
CD & DVD replication, CD DVD duplication, packaging & fulfillment.

VTECH Communications
9590 S.W. Gemini Drive, Suite 120, Beaverton, OR 97008-7109 USA
(503) 596-1200; *Fax:* (503) 644-9887
www.vtechphones.com
info@vtechphones.com
Bruce Garfield, CEO
Doug Vernier, President
Matt Ramage, Operations Dir
Tom Bacon, Marketing VP
Kate Michler, Engineering Dir
900 mhz cordless analog digital telephones.

Ward-Beck Systems Ltd.
945 Middlefield Road, Unit 9, Toronto, ON M1V 5E1 Canada
(416) 335-5999, (800) 771-2556; *Fax:* (416) 335-5202
ward-beck.com
Eugene Johnson, General Manager
Michael Jordan, General Sales Mgr
Gerald Bell, Manager
Doug Bascombe, Chief Engineer
In our forty plus years of operation, we have supplied high quality broadcast equipment to television and radio broadcasters worldwide for both fixed and mobile installations. We have an enviable track record in timely completion ofprojects and post installation support. In many instances, our clients have selected us to develop and supply products to address their specific operating requirements.

Wearguard
141 Longwater Dr., Norwell, MA 2061 USA
(781) 871-4100, (800) 388-3300; *Fax:* (800) 867-7160
www.wearguard.com
feedback@aramark-uniform.com
Joseph Neubauer, Chairman
Eric J. Foss, CEO & President
L. Frederick Sutherland, EVP, CFO & Group Executive
Lynn B. McKee, EVP, Human Resources &Communications
Stephen R. Reynolds, EVP, General Counsel, Secretary
Offers a comprehensive line of work clothing & identity apparel serving the cable industry.

WeatherBank Inc.
1015 Waterwood Pkwy., Suite J, Edmond, OK 73034 USA
(405) 359-0773, (800) 687-3562; *Fax:* (405) 341-0115
www.weatherbank.com
Steven A. Root, CEO & President
Michael R. Root, Operations Dir
Michael R. Root, EVP & CFO
Eric Freier, Consulting Division Manager
Satellite-delivered weather info, audio forecasting svcs & consulting to all industries.

WEGENER
11350 Technology Cir., Johns Creek, GA 30097 USA
(770) 814-4000, (800) 848-9467; *Fax:* (770) 623-0698
www.wegener.com
info@wegener.com
Robert Placek, Chairman
Troy Woodbury, CEO
Ned L. Mountain, President
Elias J. Livaditis, Chief Engineer
Elias J. Livaditis, CTO
Jim Traicoff, CFO
WEGENER is an international provider of digital video and audio solutions for broadcast television, radio, telco, private and cable networks. With over 30 years experience in optimizing point-to-multipoint multimedia distribution oversatellite, fiber, and IP networks, WEGENER offers a comprehensive product line that handles the scheduling, management and delivery of media rich content to multiple devices, including video screens, computers and audio devices. WEGENER focuses onlong- and short-term strategies for bandwidth savings, dynamic advertising, live events and affiliate management.

Wescam Inc.
Mailing Address: 649 N. Service Rd. W., Burlington, ON L7P 5B9 Canada
Second Address: 7455 Race Rd., Hanover, MD 21076
(905) 633-4000, (410) 564-2600; *Fax:* (905) 633-4100, (410) 564-2606
www.wescam.com
sales.wescam@L-3.com
Mark Chamberlain, CEO
John Dehne, President
Mario Grande, VP, Operations
Allan Bignell, VP & General Manager
Paul Jennison, VP, Govt Sales & New Business Development
Larry Spanier, VP & CFO
Roman Turchyn, VP, Human Resources
Steve Tritchew, CTO
Bruce Latimer, VP, General Counsel & Secretary
Rod Till, VP, Customer Service
Peter Larsson, GeneralManager, Broadcast Sports
Featuring Wescam Helicopter film, video, HD system, new & ultimately stable XR for all group applications.
7150 Hayvenhurst Ave., Van Nuys, CA 91406-3823 United States
(818) 785-9282; *Fax:* (818) 785-9787
Chris White, Chairman

Weschler Instruments
16900 Foltz Parkway, Cleveland, OH 44149 USA
(440) 238-2550, (800) 557-0064; *Fax:* (440) 238-0660
www.weschler.com
sales@weschler.com
David Hughes, President
Gary Lanham, Operations Dir
Michael Dorman, Executive Vice President
Mark Norquest, Manager
Mel Weschler, Founder
Digital & analog panel meters, RF ammeters, process indicators, digital multimeters, circuit tracers, power analyzers & test equipment.

Westcott Co.
1425-B Holland Rd., Toledo, OH 43537 USA
(419) 243-7311, (800) 886-1689; *Fax:* (419) 243-8401
www.fjwestcott.com
info@fjwestcott.com
Thomas Waltz, President
Robin Wilson, Manager
Kelly Mendora, Marketing Executive
Lightweight, portable & collapsible light control equipment: silks & solids, scrims, Illuminator™ reflectors, umbrellas, light modifiers, & Scrim Jim modular light panels.

Westlake Audio
2696 Lavery Ct., Unit 18, Newbury Park, CA 91320-1591 USA
(805) 499-3686; *Fax:* (805) 498-2571
www.westlakeaudio.com
westlakeaudio@gmail.com
Glenn Phoenix, President
Steve Burdick, Operations Dir
Deborah Rally, General Manager
Barbara Born, Sales Manager/Marketing
Ken Centrofante, Promotions Manager
Sherwood Davies, Finance
Audio monitors & accessories.

Westlake Audio
2696 Lavery Ct., Unit 18, Newbury Park, CA 91320-1591 USA
(805) 499-3686; *Fax:* (805) 498-2571
www.westlakeaudio.com
westlakeaudio@gmail.com
Glenn Phoenix, President
Steve Burdick, Operations Dir
Deborah Rally, General Manager
Barbara Born, Sales Manager/Marketing
Ken Centrofante, Promotions Manager
Professional audio equipment repairs, professional recording equipment sales, rentals, studio design. Westlake can provide all your Pro Audio needs, from Pro Audio equipment sls to full tracking & mixing.
2696 Lavery Ct., Unit 18, Newbury Park, CA 91320 United States
(805) 499-3686; *Fax:* (805) 498-2571
Glenn Phoenix, Pres
8447 Beverly Blvd., Los Angeles, CA 90048 United States
(323) 654-2155; *Fax:* (323) 655-0478

Wheatstone Corp.
600 Industrial Dr., New Bern, NC 28562 USA
(252) 638-7000; *Fax:* (252) 635-4857, (252) 637-1285
www.wheatstone.com
sales@wheatstone.com
Gary Snow, President
Andrew Calvanese, Operations Dir
Jay Tyler, General Sales Mgr
Dan Murdoch, Chief Technical Officer
Manufacturer of analog & digital bcst audio mixing consoles, processing equipment, radio & TV products since 1976.

Whirlwind
99 Ling Rd., Greece, NY 14612 USA
(585) 663-8820, (800) 733-9473; *Fax:* (585) 865-8930
www.whirlwindusa.com
Michael Laiacona, President
Al Keltz, GM/ Customer support
John Pape, Engineering
Carl Cornell, Engineering
Debbie Noble, Production Manager
Will Young, Marketing Director/ Artist Relations
Ray Bellizia, Export Sales
HollyBryan, Purchasing
Hector cruz, Building Supervisor
Janice Lewandowski, Credit/ Office Manager
Mix-6 audio mixers, presspower 2 active pressbox, active splitters; P-12 & power amplifiers, MD-1 MIC/line driver.

WILCAN Electronics Canada Ltd.
35-8560 Torbram Rd., Brampton, ON L6T 5C9 Canada
(905) 790-2711, (888) 596-2020; *Fax:* (905) 790-8861
www.powersurges.com
wilcan@lightningtvss.com
William Black, President
Gregory Black, VP/General Manager
Designers, manufacturers & consultants. Lightning & high energy transient control including protection for telephone, signal & data lines.
2316 Delaware Ave., Suite 285, Buffalo, NY 14216 United States
(888) 596-2020; *Fax:* (888) 866-7775
Gregory J. Black, Gen Mgr/Sec Treas

WILL-BURT Co.
169 S. Main St., Orrville, OH 44667 USA
(330) 682-7015, (330) 684-4000; *Fax:* (330) 684-1190
www.willburt.com
contact_us@willburt.com
Jeff Evans, CEO
Steven Pinkley, General Sales Mgr
John Mayles, Programming Director
Telescoping mast used to position antennas, lights & cameras to heights of 20 to 134 ft.

Wiltronix Inc.
Box 364, 16850 Oakmont Ave., Washington Grove, MD 20880 USA
(301) 258-7676; *Fax:* (301) 963-8624
www.wiltronix.com
equipsales@wiltronix.com
Dwight Wilcox, President
Ellen Packard, Operations Dir
Manufacturers rep for digital HD, SD, video, audio, signal processing, transmission for bcst production & govt video facilities.
6927R Mink Hollow Rd., Highland, MD 20777

Winchester Electronics
199 Park Rd.Extension, Suite 104, Middlebury, CT 6762 US
(203) 741-5400; *Fax:* (203) 741-5500
www.winchesterelectronics.com
info@winchesterelectronics.com
Robert Dock, President
Allen Trustman, Operations Dir
Holli Mills, Chief Marketing Officer
Virginia King, General Sales Mgr
Maria Berrellez, Customer Service- Connectors
Beth Beadle, Inside Sales Business Manager
Sandra Lopez,Customer Service- Cables
Dawn Bernard, Customer Service- Advanced Optical Fibre
Video patch panels, patch cords, coaxial connectors, triaxial connectors & twinaxial connectors.
62 Barnes Industrial Rd. N., Wallingford, CT 06492
(203) 741-5400 (203) 741-5500

Windmade Products
30 Pecks Lane, Newtown, CT 6470 USA
(203) 270-1100; *Fax:* (203) 270-7778
www.neumade.com
info@windmade-products.com
R.N. Jones, CEO
Gregory Jones, Operations Dir
Film handling & editing equipment; storage facilities for film, slides, videotape, overhead & opaque projectors, motion picture projection systems.

Windstream Communications
13935 Bishops Dr., Brookfield, WI 53005 USA
(262) 792-9700, (866) 445-5882; *Fax:* (262) 792-7276
www.windstreambusiness.com
Al Cinelli, Chairman
John Cinelli, CEO
John Iber, VP Operations
Robert Rogers SVP, Station Manager
Fiber-optic & microwave transmission of bcst level video.
3617 Oakton St., Skokie, IL 60076 United States
(847) 674-7476
Dave Pritchard, Dir

Winsted Corp.
10901 Hampshire Ave. S., Minneapolis, MN 55438 USA
(952) 944-9050, (800) 447-2257; *Fax:* (888) 995-7455
www.winsted.com
info@winsted.com
G.R. Hoska, Chairman
Stephen Hoska, CEO
Randy Smith, President
Editing, Production & Post production consoles, space saving tape & data storage systems. Multimedia & Lan/Wan server workstations. Console installations.

Winsted Technical Interiors
1750 Breckinridge Pwky., Suite 100, Duluth, GA 30096
Phone # 800-237-5606 or 770-840-0880

WIREMAX Ltd.
705 Wamba Ave., P.O. Box 3336, Toledo, OH 43607
(800) 843-9479, (419) 531-9500; *Fax:* (419) 531-9503
www.wiremax.com
info@wiremax.com
Al Mocek, President
Tom Ricketts, Operations Dir
Mark Robinson, General Manager
Manufacturer of high temp, wire, cable, high voltage wire & cable.

WireReady NSI
Mailing Address: PO Box 714, Eudora, KS 66025 USA
Second Address: 106 S 4th St., Lincoln, KS 67455
(800) 833-4459, (785) 542-2173; *Fax:* (508) 393-0255
www.wireready.com
sales@wireready.com
David Gerstmann, President/CEO
NewsReady 32, CartReady, ControlReady, NewsReady, StormReady & SalesReady software. Cart replacement, satellite, music on HD, newsrooms & sls automation. All windows/pc.

Wireworks Corporation
380 Hillside Avenue, Hillside, NJ 7205 USA
(908) 686-7400, (800) 642-9473; *Fax:* (908) 686-0483, (908) 686-0680
www.wireworks.com
Gerald Krulewicz, President
Larry Williams, Operations Dir
Susan Cochrane, Business Development
Audio, video, & audio/video combination cabling assemblies for bcst market; cable testers, transformer isolated mic splitters; multi-pin connectors & perfect custom panels.

Wohler Technologies Inc.
31055 Huntwood Ave., Hayward, CA 94544 USA
(510) 870-0810, (888) 596-4537; *Fax:* (510) 870-0811
www.wohler.com
Carl Dempsey, CEO
Dave Johnson, COO
Kim Templeman-Holmes, General Sales Mgr
Tom Belford, Director, Marketing

Wolf Coach Inc.
90 Nemco Way, Ayer, MA 1432 USA
(978) 568-5100; *Fax:* (978) 772-7581
Richard Wolf, Operations Dir
Emeric Feldmar, General Manager
Mark A. Leonard, General Sales Mgr
Thomas Jennings, National Sales Rep
News vans, satellite vehicles, production trailers, vehicle based microwave, satellite uplink, digital SNG, audio/video systems & turnkey systems.
2451 South 600 W., 200, Salt Lake City, UT 84115 United States
(801) 977-9533
Rex A. Reed, Systems Mgr/Engr
chief engr, President

World Tower Co. Inc.
Box 508, 1213 Compressor Dr., Mayfield, KY 42066 USA
(270) 247-3642, (888) 247-2580; *Fax:* (270) 247-0909
www.worldtower.com
worldtower@worldtower.com
Doug Walker, President/Owner
Brent Walker, Vice President
Keith Scoggins, Operations Executive
Keith Scoggins, Senior Operations Director
Doug Jones, Sales
Doug Moore, Sales
Manufactures & erects bcst & CATV towers, microwave & cellular.

Xintekvideo Inc.
56 W. Broad St., Stamford, CT 6902 US
(203) 348-9229; *Fax:* (203) 348-9266
www.xintekvideo.com
jrossi@xintekvideo.com
John Rossi, President
Video processing equipment, including transcoders, color correctors, image enhancers, noise reducers, co-channel filters, ghost removers & impulse noise eliminators.

Yamaha Corp. of America
6600 Orangethorpe Ave., Buena Park, CA 90620 USA
(714) 522-9011; *Fax:* (714) 522-9961
www.yamaha.com
Richard Hinsz, Chief Operating Officer
Takuya Nakata, President & Representative Director
Tom Sumner, Operations Dir
Paul Calvin, Chief Marketing Officer
Vomal Thomas, Chief Technical Officer
Hiroo Okabe, Managing ExecutiveOfficer
Masao Kondo, Senior Executive Officer
Wataru Miki, Executive Officer
Akira Iizuka, Executive Officer
Portable keyboards, synthesizers & drums. Manufactures a complete line of professional audio products targeted to the project studio, coml studio, postproduction, bcst & sound reinforcement markets.

Yanchar Design & Consulting Group
26741 Portola Pkwy., Suite 1E, Foothill Ranch, CA 92610 US
(949) 770-6601; *Fax:* (949) 770-6575
www.yanchardesign.com
info@yanchardesign.com
Carl J. Yanchar, President
Cesar Vergara, Designer
Acoustical design, facility design, consultation, systems design, studio construction & instal.

Zack Electronics Inc.
1075 Hamilton Rd., Duarte, CA 91010 USA
(626) 303-0655, (800) 466-0449; *Fax:* (626) 303-8694
www.zackelectronics.com
jlomas@zackelectronics.com
Dennis Awad, President
Judi Lomas, General Manager
Darren Godoy, Economic Manager
Victor Zacharia, Founder
Cable, connectors, & comprehensive core products for the bcst industry, custom audio/video/data cable assemblies. Featuring: Belden, Neutrik, Switchcraft, Pomona & avbcable.com.

Zenith Electronics LLC
2000 Millbrook Dr., Lincolnshire, IL 60069 USA
(847) 941-8000; *Fax:* (847) 941-9200
www.zenith.com
David Penski, CEO
T J Lee, President
Hyon Ick Jo, VP/Chief Financial Officer
Kathryn Wolfe, President/Sales
Michael Thomas, SVP
Richard Lewis, Business Development
Jack Kail, Licensing
Kim Regillio, Consumer Inquiries
WayneLuplow, Broadcasting Standards & Technologies
John Taylor, Media/Press Inquiries
Full line of CATV converters; MMDS systems; cable & pay TV systems for PAL & SECAM international markets; PC-based system controllers; accessories.

Zomax Inc.
7001 Discovery Blvd., Dublin, OH 43017 US
(888) 638-2832,(614) 761-2000; *Fax:* (614) 766-3176
www.zomax.com
Ellis Kern, Chairman
Arun Kurana, CEO/COO
Melodie Gee, COO
Vice President, General Manager
CD manufacturer specializing in printing fulfillment svcs, & custom work in CD entertainment & CD-ROM.

Satellite & Transmission Services

ABC Family Worldwide
Div/DBA: (a subsidiary of International Family Entertainmen
500 S. Buena Vista, Burbank, CA 91521-0001
(818) 560-1000
www.abcfamily.com
Haim Saban, Chairman
Basic cable net available in over 76 million homes nationwide; delivers a dynamic mix of quality entertainment with original movies, specials & series in prime time & a fun-filled daytime lineup of newly produced & classic series for kids.
12700 Ventura Blvd, Studio City, CA 91604-2469
(818) 755-2400
Tony Thomopoulos, Ceo Mtm Entertainment
1133 Ave. of the Americas, 37th Fl., New York, NY 10036-6710
(212) 782-0600
Rick Sirvaitis, Pres Adv Sls
Barbara Bekkedahl, Exec Vp/ Adv Sls

Agri Net Ray Communications Inc.
104 Radio Rd., Powells Point, NC 27966-9601
(252) 491-2414; *Fax:* (252) 491-2939
www.agrinetradio.com
William S. Ray, President
Bob Yanacek, Operations Dir
Lisa Ray, General Sales Mgr
Turnkey satellite transmission service for radio news, sports, syndicated program distribution, audio conferencing; transportable bcst studio/uplinks for remote bcsts & domestic back hauling; network coord svcs & space segment bookingsavailable.

American Microwave & Communications
Div/DBA: (A division of Western Tele-Communications)
4616 N. Grand River Ave., Suite D, Lansing, MI 48906-2576
(517) 327-3000, (517) 331-3719; *Fax:* (517) 327-4706
Microwave delivery of distant signals to cable systems; net TV & radio service to bcst stns; networking among TV stations.

AMV Gateway Teleport
Div/DBA: Williams Communications Group
27 Randolph St., Carteret, NJ 07008
(732) 969-3191; *Fax:* (732) 541-2007
www.allmobilevideo.com
info@amvchelsea.com
Michael Carberry, General Manager
Operates teleport facilities serving New York City. Videotape svcs; satellite transmission for the bcst, CATV & videoconferencing industries. International wideband voice, data & videoconferencing svcs overseas.

Arqiva Inc.
Div/DBA: (formerly BT North America, Broadcast Services)
2025 M St. N.W., Suite 450, Washington, DC 20036
(202) 721-8886; *Fax:* (202) 721-8595
www.arqiva.com
karen.foster@arqiva.com
Simon Thrush, Operations Dir
Operates international bcst center; 24-hour satellite rooftop teleport, digital compression & encryption svcs.
12950 Culver Blvd., Los Angeles, CA 90066-6781
(310) 577-6643

Arqiva Limited
Crawley Ct., Winchester, Hampshire, S021 2QA United Kingdom
01962 823434; *Fax:* 01962 822378
www.kingstoninmedia.com
Peter Douglas, Chairman
Satellite svcs company providing data bcst, business TV, international VSAT nets & uplink facilities.

Ascent Media
Div/DBA: (formerly Ascent Media Network Services)
250 Harbor Dr., Stamford, CT 06902
(203) 965-6000
www.ascentmedia.com
Peter Brickman, General Manager
C- & Ku-band domestic & international transmission service; fiber-optic connectivity to metropolitan New York. Cable origination, bcst, business TV, transponder availability, studio & postproduction.

Teleport Minnesota
90 S. 11th St, Minneapolis, MN 55403-2414
(612) 330-2645; *Fax:* (612) 330-2603
Kelly Gordon, Mgr

AT&T Alascom
505 E. Bluff Dr., Anchorage, AK 99501-1100
(907) 264-7274, (907) 223-7184; *Fax:* (907) 274-5029
www.attalascom.com
Mike Felix, President
Kay Witt, Operations Dir
Telecommunications, long-distance telephone carrier for the state of Alaska offering bcst, voice, data, WATS, Alaskanet & dedicated private line long-distance svcs.

BAF Satellite & Technology Corp.
200 S.harbor City Blvd., Suite 201, Melbourne, FL 32901
(800) 966-3822, (800) 223-1860 (24 hr); *Fax:* (800) 486-5983, (800) 223-1866 (24 hr)
www.bafsat.com
info@bafsat.com
Jim Vautrot, President
Long-term, short-term & occasional analog & digital KU & C band satellite space, full or partial transponder or transponders for domestic or international video, voice or data transmissions.

CATV Services Inc.
Div/DBA: (Penn Service Microwave Co. Inc.)
115 Mill St., Danville, PA 17821
(570) 275-1431, (570) 275-8410; *Fax:* (570) 275-3888
Video distribution of TV signals to various CATV companies in Pennsylvania.

Communications III
921 Eastwind Dr., Suite 104, Westerville, OH 43081
(614) 901-4420; *Fax:* (614) 901-7721
www.comiii.com
shalliday@comiii.com
Scott Halliday, President
Common carrier/C-band uplink svcs. ISDN, IP, & satellite videoconferencing, Polycom & First Virtual.

Crawford Communications
Div/DBA: (formerly Crawford Satellite Services)
3845 Pleasantdale Rd., Atlanta, GA 30340
(404) 876-7149; *Fax:* (678) 421-6717
www.crawford.com
info@crawford.com
Greg West, CFO
Jesse Crawford, President
Domestic/international satellite trasmission, net origination/playback, satellite uplink trucks, IP-media, fiber ooptics, studio & remote video production, HD/SD post production, DVD.

DCT Transmission L.L.C.
10040 E. Happy Valley Rd., Unit 454, Scottsdale, AR 85255
(480) 515-0913; *Fax:* (480) 515-4632
wiesenberg@spacedata.net
Jim Wiesenberg, General Manager
Broadband microwave provider.

Detroit Public Television
7441 Second Ave., Detroit, MI 48202
(313) 874-1801, (313) 873-7200
www.detroitpublictv.org
email@dptv.org
Daniel Alpert, General Manager
Detroit Public Television (WTVS-Analog 56 & Digital 43) offers Ku-band uplinking to any satellite; uplink, fiberlink, downlink, production, postproduction & teleconference svcs available.

DIRECTV Latin America
1211 Ave. of the Americas, 6th Fl., New York, NY 10036
(212) 462-5000; *Fax:* (212) 462-5081
www.directvla.com
webmaster@directvla.com
Bruce Churchill, President
Provides direct TV for Latin America.

GlobeCast America
10525 Washington Blvd., Culver City, CA 90232

(310) 845-3900; *Fax:* (310) 845-3904
Paul Rush, Operations Dir
GlobeCast America provides the bcstg industry with a unique combination of both recognized expertise & extensive inter-continental svcs. Through GlobeCast's vast global infrastructure of over 100 transponders, 30 teleports & interconnectfacilities, the company provides instant access to the world's major media markets. GlobeCast America is part of France Telecom, one of the world's largest telecommunications companies.

GlobeCast Hero Productions
7291 N.W. 74 St., Miami, FL 33166-2407
(305) 887-1600; *Fax:* (305) 391-4424

Home Shopping Network
1 HSN Dr., St. Petersburg, FL 33729
(727) 872-1000; *Fax:* (727) 872-6615
www.hsn.com
Mindy Grossman, CEO
Rob Solomon, Engineering Dir
Svcs include C- & Ku-band transmissions from Tampa, FL, C-band transmissions from New York, NY, & Los Angeles, CA, & postproduction.

International Telecommunications Satellite Organization (INTELSAT)
3400 International Dr. N.W., Washington, DC 20008-3098
(202) 944-6800; *Fax:* (202) 944-8125
www.intelsat.com
John Romm, President
Intelsat supplies video, data & voice connectivity in approximately 200 countries & territories for over 1,800 customers worldwide. Intelsat provides svcs on a global fleet of 53 satellites & 7 owned teleports & terrestrial facilities.

Kaufman Broadcast Services
3655 Olive St., St. Louis, MO 63108
(314) 533-6633; *Fax:* (314) 533-1113
www.kaufmanbroadcast.com
info@kaufmanbroadcast.com
Bill Kaufman, President
Transmission svcs via satellite or fiber optics, production & editing facilities.

MCI
500 Clinton Center Dr., Clinton, MS 39056
(601) 460-5600, (800) 644-news
www.mci.com
Tammy McLean, Promotions Manager
Data, internet, international long distance & telecom svcs throughout the United States.

MCI Tampa
3608 Queen Palm Dr., Tampa, FL 33619-1311
(813) 829-0011
www.mci.com
Michael Capellas, President
Serves Pennsylvania Public Television Network, Pennsylvania, Ohio, New Jersey, Vermont, New Hampshire, New York & Massachusetts. CATV systems with a variety of svcs.

Megastar Inc.
4709 Compass Bow Ln., Las Vegas, NV 89130
(702) 386-2844; *Fax:* (702) 388-1250
Nigel Macrae, President
Houston, TX Teleport svcs, C-band & Ku-band, fiber-optic & microwave interconnect. 11M Intelsat antenna, PanAmSat, etc. Other svcs available.

Microwave Networks Inc.
4000 Greenbriar St. #100A, Stafford, TX 77477
(281) 263-6500, (888) 225-6429; *Fax:* (281) 263-6400
www.microwavenetworks.com
Jim Gordon, General Manager

Microwave Service Co.
1359 Rd. 681, Saltillo, MS 38866
(662) 842-7620; *Fax:* (662) 844-7061
Jane Spain, CEO
Larry Harris, General Sales Mgr
Point-to-point transmission of video by microwave.

Multicomm Sciences International Inc. (MSI)
266 W. Main St., Denville, NJ 07834
(973) 627-7400; *Fax:* (973) 215-2168
www.multicommsciences.com
Victor J. Nexon Jr., President
Serves satellite, microwave, lightwave, radio & cable industries. Market info, field surveys, system design, feasibility studies, frequency coordination & project mgmt.

Norlight Telecommunications
13935 Bishops Drive, Brookfield, WI 53005
(888) 210-3100; *Fax:* (812) 759-1465
www.norlight.com
James Ditter, President
Michael J. Turnbull, General Manager
Design, installation & maintenance of custom network solutions, including HDTV transport, on-site data center - secure co-location svc, off-site video file servers & managed router svc.

Novanet Communications Ltd.
725 Westney Rd. S., Suite 4, Ajax, ON L1J 7J7 Canada
(905) 686-6666; *Fax:* (905) 619-1053
www.novanetcomm.com
getinfo@novanetcomm.com
Joseph Uyede, President
Stewart Sheriff, Operations Dir
Debbie MacLeod, General Sales Mgr
Provides info distribution svcs; audio svcs from 3.5 khz to 20 khz in analog or digital formats, also a line of data bcst offerings ranging in speed from 75 baud to T-1; & 'Satpac,' a packet-switched data net using receiver technology.

NPR Satellite Services
635 Massachusetts Ave. N.W., Washington, DC 20001
(202) 513-2626; *Fax:* (202) 513-3035
www.nprss.org
linkup@npr.org
George Gimourginas, General Manager
Comprehensive satellite solutions for audio & video distribution: space segment, equipment, systems design, engrg support 24-hrs customer svc.

PanAmSat
20 Westport Rd., Suite 270, Wilton, CT 06897
(203) 210-8000; *Fax:* (203) 210-8001
www.panamsat.com
Joseph R. Wright, Jr., CEO
Owns & operates private global network of communications satellites providing bcst, business communications, telephony & data svcs to customers worldwide.

Production & Satellite Services Inc. (PSSI)
11860 Mississippi Ave., Los Angeles, CA 90025
(310) 575-4400; *Fax:* (310) 575-4451
Robert Lamb, President
Joseph A. Kittrell, General Sales Mgr
Full service production & satellite transmission company specializing in coordination, production & transmission of international live-event progmg. Own & operate 12 fully redundant transportable upling/production trucks which are maintainedin Los Angeles, San Francisco, Seattle, Las Vegas, Denver, Phoenix & Chicago. Entire Western region of the United States is covered including Albuquerque, Salt Lake City & Portland. Also subcontract with vendors throughout U.S. to provide uplink,downlink & production svcs and production svcs for teleconferences & other events.

Reuters Television Internationale
3 Times Sq., 4th Fl., New York, NY 10036
(646) 223-6600; *Fax:* (646) 223-6615
www.reuters.com
Bob LaGrasso, General Sales Mgr
Satellite svcs for news departments. Satellite production & communication departments handle satellite feed requirements from anywhere in the world. Satellite coordinates, video crews & major studios on six continents. Standards conversion.

SES Americom
4 Research Way, Princeton, NJ 08540
(609) 987-4000; *Fax:* (609) 987-4517
www.ses-americom.com
Bryan A. McGuirk, President
Operates GE-1-3, SATCOM, GSTAR & SPACENET domestic satellites (C-band & six Ku-band). The fleet svcs the cable TV, bcst, radio & educ market & govt businesses. Supports net of earth stns, central terminal offices & TT&C facilities.

SpaceCom Systems
Div/DBA: A TV Guide Company
1950 E. 71st St., Tulsa, OK 74136
(800) 950-6690; *Fax:* (918) 477-6861
www.spacecom.com
David Pollack, President
Ruth Ann Odom, Promotions Manager
Satellite transmission svcs, equipment & space segment on C- & Ku-Band for point-to-multipoint applications. Also two-way high-speed Satellite Broadband for remote locations, quick connects, disaster recovery, Internet.

Spacenet Inc.
Div/DBA: (formerly Spacenet Services Inc.)
1750 Old Meadow Rd., McLean, VA 22102
(703) 848-1000; *Fax:* (703) 245-5426
www.spacenet.com
Glenn Katz, COO
Jim Norton, Operations Dir
Comprehensive range of satellite-based communication svcs for video & data; digital video networks for business applications.

Teleglobe
1555 Rue Carrie-Derick, Montr,al, QC H3C 6W2 Canada
(514) 868-7272; *Fax:* (514) 868-7234
Vinod Kumar, President
Jean-Louis Houde, Operations Dir
International satellite transmission svcs from Lawrentides/Lake Cowichan earth stns in Canada. Signatory on Intelsat, Immarsat. Full range of svcs to world satellite systems.
Two Pacifco Place, 88 Queensway, Hong Kong
852-2530-8500; *Fax:* 852-2-537-7417
Andrew Kwok, Dir

Telemundo Network
2470 W. 8th Ave, Hialeah, FL 33010
(305) 884-8200; *Fax:* (305) 882-8765
www.telemundo.com
James McNammara, President
Production capabilities & svcs. Uplink & video transmission. C- & Ku-band uplink & downlink. Fiber & microwave also available.

Telenor Satellite Services
1101 Wooton Pkwy, Rockville, MD 20852
(301) 838-7800; *Fax:* (301) 838-7801
www.telenor.com/satellite
customer.care@telenor.com
Bob Baker, President
Dave Farmer, Promotions Manager
Telenor is a global provider of satellite svcs, inmarsat, intelsat, new skies, satmex, digital networking svcs & technology.

Teleport Chicago
3617 Oakton St., Rear, Skokie, IL 60076
(847) 674-7476, (888) 255-8755; *Fax:* (847) 674-1991
www.norlight.com
sales@norlight.com
Dave Pritchard, General Manager
A full-svc teleport serving the upper Midwest via the Norlight Telecommunications microwave & fiber-optic transmission system.

Telesat
Div/DBA: (formerly Loral Skynet Inc.)
500 Hills Dr., Bedminster, NJ 07921
(908) 719-0094
www.telesat.ca
Daniel S. Goldberg, President

Telesat Canada
1601 Telesat Ct., Gloucester, ON K1B 5P4 Canada
(613) 748-0123; *Fax:* (613) 748-8712
www.telesat.ca
info@telesat.ca
Communications via satellite, consulting, & satellite earth stn nets.
1780 Centre Ave. N.E., Calgary, AB Canada
(403) 235-5751; *Fax:* (403) 273-3337
1200 Papineau Ave., Suite 140, Montreal, PQ Canada
(514) 521-7862; *Fax:* (514) 527-6429

Time Warner Cable
290 Harbor Dr., Stamford, CT 06902
(800) 479-0624
www.timewarnercable.com
Landel C. Hobbs, COO
Robert Marcus, President
Time Warner Cable is committed to in-home entertainment, communications, info, customer care & quality products that create the best possible customer experience.
75 Rockerfeller Plaza, New York, NY 10019-6908
(212) 484-8000

Transvision Inc.
550 Maulhardt Ave., Oxnard, CA 93030
(805) 981-8740; *Fax:* (805) 981-8738
www.txvision.com
info@txvision.com
Kimithy Vaughan, General Sales Mgr
Vince Waterson, Engineering Dir
Twelve transportable & satellite transmission facilities (video, audio, voice, data); flypack production & SNG svcs; digital compression; domestic & international. Facilities in Brazil, Australia, Phillipines & Western Europe.

TV Guide Inc.
7140 S. Lewis Ave., Tulsa, OK 74136
(918) 488-4000; *Fax:* (918) 488-4979
www.tvguide.com
Mike Burks, Operations Dir
Josh Axelrod, Programming Director
Diversified communications company serving cable, home satellite TV, radio/data networks, private businesses; operating companies: UVTV, Prevue Networks, Superstar Satellite Entertainment, SpaceCom Systems.

Verestar Inc.
3040 Williams Dr., Suite 600, Fairfax, VA 22031
(703) 206-9000; *Fax:* (703) 573-3522
www.verestar.com
info@verestar.com
Raymond J. O'Brien, President
Satellite svcs for bcstrs & communication net.

Videocom Media Services, LLC
Box 212, Boston, MA 02137
(781) 329-4080; *Fax:* (781) 329-8534
www.videocom.com
Ownership: Private.
Daniel V. Swartz, General Manager
Steerable C- & Ku-band antennas interconnected via private microwave & telco loops co-located with single- & multiple-camera program origination facility. Receives & transmits all formats of videotape; transportable uplinks; bcst newsdistribution; link with Canadian satellites. Digital video transmission & net mgmt svcs.

WGVU-TV
301 W. Fulton, Grand Rapids, MI 49504-6492
(616) 331-6666; *Fax:* (616) 331-6625
www.wgvu.org
wgvu@gvsu.edu
Michael Walenta, General Manager
Ken Kolbe, Station Manager
Bob Lumbert, Engineering Dir
Provides multiple studio post production, teleconferencing & satellite uplink svcs.

WHYY Inc.
Independence Mall W., 150 N. 6th St., Philadelphia, PA 19106
(215) 351-1200; *Fax:* (215) 351-0398
www.whyy.org
pgluck@whyy.org
Paul Gluck, Operations Dir
Occasional video, encryption svcs, transponder time available. Interconnect with Telco, on-site production facilities, & teleconferencing for up to 1,000 people. Transportable Ku-band earth stn; C- or Ku-band uplinking.

Williams Communications
111 E. 1st St., Vyvx Services, Tulsa, OK 74103
(918) 547-5760; *Fax:* (918) 547-5760
Jeff Storey, CEO
Provider of integrated fiber-optic, satellite, teleport multimedia, data gathering, mgmt & transmission svcs.
1802 Briarcliff Rd., Atlanta, GA 30329-4008
(800) 648-3333
One Maynard Dr., Park Ridge, NJ
(800) 746-3019
200 Oceangate, Suite 570, Long Beach, CA 90802-4302
(800) 747-7074

Teleports

Ascent Media
250 Harbor Dr., Stamford, CT 06902
(203) 965-6000
www.ascentmedia.com
Ownership: Stamford
Peter Brickman, General Manager
C- & Ku-band domestic & international transmission service; connectivity to metro New York via proprietary fiber origination, bcst, business TV, transponder availability; studio & postproduction svcs.

Atlanta International Teleport
3530 Bomar Rd., Douglasville, GA 30135
(770) 949-6600; *Fax:* (770) 942-6653
www.atlantateleport.com
Adam Grow, III, Chief Engineer
Internet, private business networks, VSAT Hub, C/Ku Up/down, audio, video, data, telephony, TDMA, SCPC, VCII+, fiber, standards conversion, Intelsat-B Station.

Crawford Communications Inc.
3845 Pleasantdale Rd., Atlanta, GA 30340
(404) 876-7149, (800) 831-8027; *Fax:* 678) 421-6717
www.crawford.com
info@crawford.com
Jesse Crawford, Chairman
Network origination & playback, domestic/international satellite transmissions, streaming media/webcasting, online svcs, fiber optics, satellite uplink trucks, studios, post production & DVD.

Echostar
6723 W. Steger Rd., Monee, IL 60449
(708) 534-2400; *Fax:* (708) 534-0060
www.echostar.com
lawrence.baer@echostar.com
Ownership: Chicago, IL.
Larry Baer, General Manager
C- & Ku-band satellite transmission svcs. Audio, video, data, uplink/downlink communication.

Edmonton Teleport. Telesat Canada
5311 Allard Way, Edmonton, AB T6H 5B8 Canada
(780) 437-6167; *Fax:* (780) 436-5667
www.telesat.ca
Major bcst teleport offering full North American arc at C-band, & Anik E1 & E2 at Ku-band for occasional use needs.

GlobeCast North America
10525 W. Washington Blvd., Culver City, CA 90232
(310) 845-3900 (sales), (310) 845-3939; *Fax:* (310) 845-3903
www.globecast.com
america.booking@globecast.com
Mary Frost, CEO

GlobeCast Hero Productions
7291 N.W. 74 St., Miami, FL 33166-2407
(305) 887-1600; *Fax:* (305) 887-7076
110 E. 42nd St., 11th Fl., New York, NY 10017-5611
(212) 885-8700; *Fax:* (212) 885-8701
400 North Capitol St. N.W, Suite 880, Washington, DC 20001-1511
(202) 737-4440; *Fax:* (202) 737-1476
1825 K St. N.W., 9th Fl., Washington, DC 20006-1202
(202) 861-0894; *Fax:* (202) 861-3107

GlobeCast North America
5 Teleport Dr., Staten Island, NY 10311
(718) 983-2600; *Fax:* (718) 983-2615
www.globecast.com
robert.marking@globecastna.com
Mary Frost, CEO
Offers a transmission network of leased domestic & international satellite transponders providing radio & TV origination svcs for more than 1,000 U.S. & international clients every year, including news, sports, program distribution &business TV clientele.

ICG Telecom Group
161 Inverness Dr., West Englewood, CO 80112
Alternative Access Carrier. Bay Area Teleport provides communications svcs at DS0, T1 or T3 levels for primary or alternative access applications. Bay Area Teleport's system connects 12 counties in northern California. Includes a fiber-opticnetwork in San Francisco, CA & across to Oakland, CA, as well as access to satellite svcs through its earth stn complex in Niles Canyon.

Jackson Teleport Inc.
916 Foley St., Jackson, MS 39202
(800) 353-9177, (601) 352-6673; *Fax:* (601) 948-6052
www.weathervision.com
edward@weathervision.com
Edward Saint Pe, President
Jason McCleave, Operations Dir
Fixed 7-meter earth stn on site. Video satellite transmission & reception. Videoconferencing, business TV, news, sports & weathercast feed, origination, program distribution & syndication svcs.

Megastar Inc.
4709 Compass Bow Ln., Las Vegas, NV 89130
(702) 386-2844; *Fax:* (702) 388-1250
www.1megastar.com
Nigel Macrae, President

Network Teleports Inc.
3200 Chartres St., New Orleans, LA 70117
(504) 942-9200; *Fax:* (504) 942-9204
Ownership: New Orleans.
C.E. Feltner, Chairman
C-band voice/video & data, Ku-band data/voice, B-MAC encryption, newsfeeds, production, fiber-optic links, audio-subcarrier & C- & Ku-band 5CPC, satellite telephones, IP multicasting, webcasting.

Norlight Teleport Chicago
3617 Oakton St., Skokie, IL 60076
(847) 674-7476; *Fax:* (847) 674-1991
www.norlight.com
Dave Pritchard, General Manager
Full-svc teleport, domestic & international, satellite uplink, downlink, turnaround, encryption, rgn access on Norlight Telecommunications Interstate Network, VYVX ant AT&T fiber access.
275 N. Corporate, Brookfield, WI 53045-5825

Pittsburgh International Telecommunications
Box 14070, Pittsburgh, PA 15239
(724) 337-1888; *Fax:* (724) 337-1754
www.pitcomm.com
info@pitcomm.com
Al Stem, President
Bill Sciolla, General Manager

Rainbow Network Communications
620 Hicksville Rd., Bethpage, NY 11714
(516) 803-0355, (516) 803-0300; *Fax:* (516) 918-6940
www.rncnetwork.com
togreco@rainbow-media.com
Steve Pontillo, President
Thomas A. Greco, Operations Dir
Multiple 11-meter & 9-meter uplinking antennas, multiple downlinking ants, both servicing the entire satellite arc. Connectivity in & out of New York & metropolitan area, Ku-band transportable, origination/editing svcs, & full, longterm &occasional transponder leasing. Compression svcs.

Telesat
1601 Telesat Ct., Gloucester, ON K1B 5P4 Canada
(613) 748-0123; *Fax:* (613) 748-8712
www.telesat.ca
info@telesat.ca
Ownership: Montreal.
Daniel Goldberg, President/CEO
Pat Enright, VP Network Operations
Paul Bush, VP Business Development
Access to all Telesat Anik and Nimiq satellites & most U.S. domestic satellites.

Toronto Teleport. Telesat Canada
1601 Telesat Ct., Gloucester, ON K1B 5P4 Canada
(613) 748-0123; *Fax:* (613) 748-8712
www.telesat.ca
info@telesat.ca
Ownership: Toronto.
Access to all Telesat Anik & Nimiq satellites & most united states domestic satellites.

Turner Teleport Inc.
Box 105366, One CNN Ctr, Atlanta, GA 30348-5366
(404) 827-1500
Satellite uplink & downlink svcs for Turner Broadcasting Services.

Vancouver Teleport. Telesat Canada
1601 Telesat Ct., Gloucester, ON K1B 5P4 Canada
(613) 748-0123; *Fax:* (613) 748-8712
www.telesat.ca
info@telesat.ca
Ownership: Vancouver.
Access to all Telesat Anik & Nimiq satellites & most North American satellites.

Verestar Inc.
3040 Williams Dr., Suite 600, Fairfax, VA 22031
(703) 206-9000; *Fax:* (703) 573-3522
www.verestar.com
info@verestar.com
Raymond J. O'Brien, President
Satellite svcs for bcstrs & communication net.

Videocom Media Services, LLC
Box 212, Boston, MA 02137
(781) 329-4080; *Fax:* (781) 329-8534
www.videocom.com
Ownership: Private.
Daniel V. Swartz, General Manager
Steerable C- & Ku-band antennas interconnected via private microwave & telco loops co-located with single- & multiple-camera program origination facility. Receives & transmits all formats of videotape; transportable uplinks; bcst newsdistribution; link with Canadian satellites. Digital video transmission & net mgmt svcs.

VYVX Level 3 Teleport Denver
9174 S. Jamaica St., Englewood, CO 80112
(303) 397-4100; *Fax:* (303) 799-8325

Ownership: Denver.
Theran Davis, Operations Dir
Domestic & international uplink, downlink & transponder service for video & date communications. Regional Fiber & microwave interconnectivity to broadcast affiliates, PoPs & sports venues

VYVX Teleport Atlanta
1802 Briarcliff Rd., Atlanta, GA 30329
(404) 325-0818
www.oabok.org
harrison@oabok.org
Vance Harrison, pres.

Willliams Services/VYVX Steele Valley Teleports
20021 Santa Rosa Mine Rd., Perris, CA 92570
(909) 943-5399; *Fax:* (909) 943-3459
gene.brookhart@wcg.com
Gene Brookhart, General Manager
Offers domestic U.S. & international uplink, downlink & transponder svc for video (analog or compressed), image, data & voice telecommunication. Fiber-optic & microwave links to points of presence for major bcst & telco locations in the LosAngeles metropolitan area. Direct access to all C- & Ku-band satellites in domestic U.S. arc & POR; include program origination; tape playback, recording & editing; standards conversion; encryption; & turnarounds.
58 Inverness Dr. E., Englewood, CO 80112-5104
(303) 397-4100, (800) 424-9757 (full-time svcs)

WLWT-TV
1700 Young St., Cincinnati, OH 45202
(513) 412-5000; *Fax:* (513) 412-6100
www.wlwt.com
rdyer@hearst.com
Richard Dyer, General Manager
Mark Diangelo, General Sales Mgr
On-line. Provides occasional C-band uplinking svcs.

Employment & Executive Search Services

Bishop Partners
28 W 44th Street, Suite 1120, New York, NY 10036
(212) 986-3419; *Fax:* (212) 575-1050
www.bishoppartners.com
info@bishoppartners.com
Susan K. Bishop, Founder/CEO
Sue Panzer, Business Development/Client Outreach
Alina Lee, VP-Client and Candidate Development
A retained exec search firm specializing in cable, bcst, telecommunications, wireless, entertainment, publishing & multimedia.

California Broadcasters Association
915 L St., Suite 1150, Sacramento, CA 95814
(916) 444-2237; *Fax:* (916) 444-2043
www.yourcba.com
SStatham@yourCBA.com
Stan Statham, President/CEO
Lobbyist for coml radio & TV for the state of California & other legal issues.

Entertainment Employment Journal (T.M.)
5632 Van Nuys Blvd., Suite 320, Van Nuys, CA 91401
(800) 335-4335, (818) 776-2800
Bimonthly magazine providing career information & job listings with major & independent motion picture, TV & cable companies.

Filcro Media Staffing
521 Fifth Ave., Suite 1801, New York, NY 10175
(212) 599-0909; *Fax:* (212) 599-1023
www.ExecutiveSearch.tv
mail@ExecutiveSearch.TV
Tony Filson, President & CEO
Helene Crocitto, Executive Vice President & CFO
Shannon Kay, Officer in Charge
Janice Miller, Senior Manager
Peter Santiago, National Director
Filcro Media Staffing has been providing specialized media recruitment services since 1985. The firm is a New York State Corporation with primary offices at 521 Fifth Avenue in New York City.

The Howard-Sloan-Koller Group
300 E. 42nd St., 15th Floor, New York, NY 10017
(212) 661-5250; *Fax:* (212) 557-9178
www.hsksearch.com
hsk@hsksearch.com
Edward R. Koller Jr., President/CEO
Edward R. Koller III, Partner
Dick Schenkel, Managing Director
Sharon Spielman, Managing Director
Thomas Culligan, Managing Director
Phil Growick, Managing Director
Mara Covell, ManagingDirector
Exec search & consulting in the cable, digital, entertainment & publishing industries.
9701 Wilshire Blvd., Beverly Hills, CA 90212-2020
(310) 601-7114; *Fax:* (310) 601-7110
Edward R. Koller Jr., President

Korn/Ferry International
Mailing Address: 1900 Avenue of the Stars, Suite 2600, Los Angeles, CA 90067
Second Address: 1201 West Peachtree Street, NW, Suite 2500, Atlanta, GA 30309
(310) 552-1834, (404) 577-7542
www.kornferry.com
Gary Burnison, CEO
Robert Rozek, CFO
Doug Charles, President,Americas
Worldwide sr level mgmt exec search firm servicing all sectors of the entertainment industry.

Lipson & Co.
10350 Santa Monica Blvd, Suite 205, Los Angeles, CA 90025
(310) 277-4646; *Fax:* (310) 277-8585
www.lipsonco.com
inquiries@lipsonco.com
Howard R. Lipson, Owner/Principal
Harriet Lipson, Marketing/Advertising
Specialists in international & domestic bcstg (TV & radio), cable & entertainment, & related financial, professional audio/video & electronic recruiting. Svcs also for TV & film production, merchandising, licensing, & computers.

Maslow Media Group Inc.
2233 Wisconsin Ave., Suite 400, Washington, DC 20007
(202) 965-1100; *Fax:* (202) 965-6172
www.maslowmedia.com
lmaslow@maslowmedia.com
Linda Maslow, CEO
Carl Neubecker, Operations Dir
Harry Gorman, Chief Financial Officer
Manish Sehgal, Director, Development, Sales, Marketing and Accoun
Jan Fiddle-Ferder, Supervising Producer/Creative Division
Beth Posada,Production Manager
Nevitt Greene, Manager, Payroll Client Services
Dewie Oppenheimer, Accounting Manager
Freelance & fulltime staffing, crewing & payroll svcs for bcst, corporate, & federal govt. Find a job @ www.tvgigsonline.com

Media Staffing Network
6518 East Shooting Star Way, Scottsdale, AZ 85266
(312) 944-9194; *Fax:* (312) 944-9195
www.mediastaffingnetwork.com
laurie@mediastaffingnetwork.com
Laurie Kahn, President
Patty Kincaid, Director New Business Development
Kate Glenn, VP/Senior Resource Manager & HR Director
Linda Tuttle, Account Manager
Shaylnn Totolo, Resource/Marketing Manager
Media Staffing Network the only full-service staffing company that specializes in media adv sls & associated departments, offering both temporary & full-time positions nationwide. Clients include radio & TV stns, rep firms, Internet, cablesystems, networks, syndication, magazines & adv agencies. Openings range from entry-level support to sr mgmt positions in sls, prom, buying, planning, traf, continuity, customer svc & rsch.

MediaLine
1209 Wood Valley Rd, Augusta, GA 30909
(706) 364-7564; *Fax:* (831) 648-5204
www.medialine.com
rich@medialine.com
Mark Shilstone, CEO
Job listings for TV news, production & promotions; streaming video of resume tapes on the Internet; daily eletronic newsletter.

Miller Broadcast Management Inc.
616 W. Fulton St., Suite 516, Chicago, IL 60661
(312) 454-1111; *Fax:* (312) 454-0044
info@millerbroadcast.com
Lisa Miller, President
For the past 27 years MBM has been dedicated to career development, planning, placement, syndication and contract negotiation for Talent and Management in the broadcast industry. Providing local and national representation, MBM forged newground in establishing the rights of Broadcasters and Broadcast Management to secure independent representation from a group of experienced broadcast professionals.

Ron Sunshine Associates
2404 Clear Field Dr., Plano, TX 75025
(214) 509-3778; *Fax:* (972) 599-9583
www.ronsunshineassociates.com
Ron Sunshine, President
Radio, TV & cable middle & upper mgmt.

RTNDA's Career Services
Div/DBA: (formerly RTNDA Job Services)
The National Press Building, 529 14th Street, NW, Suite 425, Washington, DC 20045
(202) 662-7257; *Fax:* (202) 223-4007
www.rtdna.org
rtnda@rtnda.org
Katie Switchenko, Programs, Awards & Membership Manager
Mike Cavender, Executive Director
Derrick Hinds, Communications, Marketing & Digital Media Manager
We offer current career opportuunties in electronic journalism, as well as a wealth of resources for job seekers. We also have the most accurate & current industry rsch on salaries, newsroom staffing, newsroom profitability & woman/minorityrepresentation in the newsroom.

Warren & Morris Ltd.
463 15th St., PO Box 1090, Del Mar, CA 92014-1090
(619) 520-9380; *Fax:* (858) 481-6221
www.warrenmorrisltd.com
cmorris@warrenmorrisltd.com
Chuck Morris, Senior Partner
Amy McCoy, Associate Partner
Natl & international exec/mgmt-level recruitment svcs in the cable TV, wireless communications & digital media industries.
132 Chapel St, Portsmouth, NH 03801-3848
(603) 431-7929; *Fax:* (603) 431-3460
Scott Warren., Sr Ptn
Arron Chaffee, Ptn

Youngs, Walker & Co.
266 Pebble Creek Dr., Tower Lakes, IL 60010
(847) 487-9500; *Fax:* (847) 934-6607
www.youngswalker.com
info@youngswalker.com
Carl Youngs, President
Exec recruitment on a retained basis for TV & radio stn mgmt levels & corporate positions.

Engineering & Technical Consultants

AF Associated Inc./Ascent Media
235 Pegasus Ave., Northvale, NJ 07647
(201) 767-3800; *Fax:* (201) 784-8637
www.afassoc.com
Tom Canavan, President
Chris Summey, Operations Dir
Andre Macaluso Sr., General Manager
Mgmt & distribution of content to major motion picture studios, ind producers, bcst networks, cable channels, adv agencies & other companies that produce, own/or distribute entertainment, adv, news, sports, corporate, educ & industrialcontent.

AZCAR U.S.A. Inc.
121 Hillpointe Dr., Suite 700, Canonsburg, PA 15317
(724) 873-0800; *Fax:* (724) 873-4770
www.azcar.com
info@azcar.com
Stephen Pumple, President
Bcst, video & audio system consultation, design, instal & training; serving cable systems, corporate & teleproduction facilities.

Broadcast Engineering & Equipment Maintenance Co.
Div/DBA: (BEEM Co.)
2322 S. 2nd Ave., Arcadia, CA 91006
(626) 446-3468; *Fax:* (626) 445-8028
www.beemco.com
joel@beemco.com
Joel T. Saxberg, Owner
Site studies, applications, AM directional arrays, allocation studies, field work, mobile signal analysis, bcst consulting & radiofrequency electromagnetic field measurements.

Bromo Communications Inc.
218 Tiger Connector, PO Box 191747, Tiger, GA 30576
(706) 782-7222, (404) 636-2257; *Fax:* (706) 782-0811
bill@bromocom.com
Consulting engrg for bcst stns. AM/FM & TV allocations, including field instals.
Washington, DC
(202) 429-0600

Carl T. Jones Corp.
7901 Yarnwood Ct., Springfield, VA 22153-2899
(703) 569-7704; *Fax:* (703) 569-6417
www.ctjc.com
info@ctjc.com
Carl T. (Tom) Jones, Jr., President
Herman E. Hurst, General Manager
John E. Hidle, P.E., Consulting Engineer
Cynthia M. Jacobson, P.E., Consulting Engineer
William J. Getz, Senior Engineer
Carl E. Gluck, Senior Engineer
James D.Sadler, Senior Engineer
Consulting engrs specializing in AM, FM & TV tech design & regulatory filings.

Cavell, Mertz & Associates, Inc.
7724 Donegan Drive, Manassas, VA 20109-2868
(703) 392-9090; *Fax:* (703) 392-9559
www.cavellmertz.com
gcavell@cavellmertz.com
Garrison C. Cavell, President
Michael D. Rhodes, Senior Engineer
Daniel G. Ryson, Senior Engineer
Robert M. Clinton, IT Resource & Principal Programmer
Broadcast & Communications Consulting Engineers located in suburban Washington, DC. Experts in radio/TV ch searches, upgrades, transmission, coverage studies, interference evaluation, RF safety, strategic planning, both bcst (AM/FM radio,TV, digital TV, microwave/satellite) & industrial.

Chenevert Architects LLC
Mailing Address:
Second Address: 8300 Earhart BLVD., Suite 101, New Orleans, LO 70118
(504) 314-1404; *Fax:* (504) 314-1406
www.chenevertarchitects.com
info@chenevertarchitects.com

Norman J. Chenevert, President
Architects, planners, & technical designers, specializing in new & renovated bcst/cable production facilities.

Cohen, Dippell and Everist, P.C.
1420 N Street, NW;, Suite One, Washington, DC 20005
(202) 898-0111; *Fax:* (202) 898-0895
www.broadcast-consulting-engineers.com
cdepc@comcast.net
Donald G. Everist, P.E., President
Professional engrg svcs to the bcstg industry, United States & worldwide.

Commercial Radio Co.
PO Box 43, Cavendish, VT 05142
(802) 226-7582; *Fax:* (802) 226-7738
www.commercialradiocompany.us
Daniel W. Churchill, PE, President
Centura L. Churchill, Operations Dir
Andre S. LaPlante, General Sales Mgr
William E. Ford, Engineering Dir
Custom bcst engrg; AM, FM & shortwave bcst equipment sls & svce, specializing in transmitting components.

Communications Design Associates Inc.
437 Turnpike St., Canton, MA 02021
(339) 502-6551, (413) 783-9200; *Fax:* (781) 502-6569, (413) 753-7300
www.cdaconsultants.com
Greg Vincent, Operations Dir
Stewart B. Randall, CTS-D, Chief Engineer
James C. Davis, Principal Consultant
Robert P. Hemenway, Principal Consultant
Scott P. MacLeod, CTS, Senior Design Consultant
Kristen M. Davis, Human FactorsSpecialist / Business Development Di
Ind consultants to radio, TV, corporate & govt clients. Designers of studios, production, presentation & multimedia facilities.

Communications Technologies Inc.
Mailing Address: PO Box 1130, Marlton, NJ 08053
Second Address: 65 Country Club Lane, Marlton, NJ 08053
(856) 985-0077; *Fax:* (856) 985-8124
www.commtechrf.com
Clarence M. Beverage, President
Laura M. Mizrahi, Vice President
Bcst engrg consulting svcs with emphasis on AM, FM & TV RF systems design & FCC application preparation consistent with FCC rules & policies.

Comsearch
19700 Janellia Farm Blvd., Ashburn, VA 20147
(703) 726-5500; *Fax:* (703) 726-5600
www.comsearch.com
Doug Hall, President
A complete communications engrg svc organization, specializing in frequency mgmt & propagation engrg.

ComSonics Inc.
1350 Port Republic Rd., PO Box 1106, Harrisonburg, VA 22801
(540) 434-5965, (800) 336-9681; *Fax:* (540) 432-9794
www.comsonics.com
info@comsonics.com
Gary J. Tudor, Director, Product Sales
Bret Harrison, Director Of Repair Services
ComSonics Test Equipment helps CATV providers with leakage detection, installation meters, and system integrity systems. Our leadership Snifferr leakage detectors provide a full range of solutions for every need, while the GPS-activeGenacisT and NexusT solutions enhance your ability to manage your cable plant efficiently and effectively. CompanionT and X-RayT make installation and ingress detection easier with less training so your team can make more tight installs in a singleday, and together the ComSonics product line makes you more efficient and profitable.

Crown Castle
2000 Corporate Dr., Cannonsburg, PA 15317
(724) 416-2000, (877) 486-9377; *Fax:* (724) 416-2200
www.crowncastle.com
James D. Young, COO
Benjamin W. Moreland, President\CEO
Brendan Walsh, Programming Director
Jay A. Brown, Chief Financial Officer And Treasurer
Blake Hawk, Executive Vice President
Laura Nichol, Senior Vice President, BusinessSupport
Communications engrg consultants & site/tower mgrs.

CSI Telecommunications Inc.
750 Battery St., Suite 350, San Francisco, CA 94111
(415) 751-8845; *Fax:* (415) 788-0791
www.csitele.com
info@csitele.com
Michael S. Newman, President
Tom Brinkoetter, Chief Engineer
Philip M. Kane, Esq./P.E., VP Regulatory Counsel & Engineering Manager
Catherine F. Newman, Vice President of Marketing & Sales
Alicia Charlberg, TelecommunicationsAnalyst
Stan Deller, Chief Electrical Engineer
Scott J. Mickelsen, Senior Project Manager
Steven J. Overacker, Project Manager
Telecommunications, radio & microwave engrg, feasibility studies, FCC applications, systems engrg; equipment specifications, project mgmt & lab measurements.

D.L. Markley & Associates Inc.
2104 W. Moss Ave., Peoria, IL 61604
(309) 673-7511; *Fax:* (309) 673-8128
www.dlmarkley.com
pom@dlmarkley.com
Phyllis O. Markley, President
Keith A. Turcot, Engineering Dir
AM/FM, TV, microwave applications, construction & measurements. Allocation studies, non-ionizing radiation measurements.

Devlin Design Group Inc.
P.O Box 3066, Crested Butte, CO 81224-3066 US
(970) 349-5836
www.ddgtv.com
Dan Devlin, Owner/Chief Creative Strategist
RF & frequency measurements for AM-FM-TV coml users via air or on location. Audio/video svc & instals.

Diversified Systems
Div/DBA: (formerly Diversified Systems Inc.)
363 Market St., Kenilworth, NJ 07033
(908) 245-4833; *Fax:* (908) 245-0011
www.divsysinc.com
kcollins@divsystems.com
Fred D'Alessandro, President/CEO / Founder
Full-svc engrg, specializing in video & RF systems.

Doug Vernier Telecom Consultants
401 Main St., Suite 213, Cedar Falls, IA 50613
(319) 266-8402; *Fax:* (319) 432-7275
www.v-soft.com
info@v-soft.com
Yonatan Stern, CEO
Doug Vernier, President
Mark Ruthfield, Vice President of Sales
Eugenia Gillan, Engineering Dir
Paul Boulanger, Chief Financial Officer
Santosh Sharan, Vice President of Product Mgmnt & Strategy
Don Wynns, VicePresident of Business Development
Hila Nir, Vice President of Marketing
Tech consulting for AM, FM, & TV. Coverage mapping, frequency searches, applications, site evaluations, stn watches, stn audits & more.

The Downtown Group
236 W. 27th St., #8RW, New York, NY 10001
(212) 675-9506; *Fax:* (212) 675-3276
www.downtowngroup.com
info@downtowngroup.com
Mark Winkleman, Operations Dir
Design of tech facilities: architecture, acoustics, engrg, testing. Typical projects include edit rooms, stages, recording studios & support facilities.

DSI RF Systems Inc.
26H World's Fair Dr., Somerset, NJ 08873
(732) 563-1144, (888) DSI-RFTV; *Fax:* (732) 563-1818
www.dsirf.com
info@dsirf.com
Tim Carroll, President
Herb Squire, Engineering Dir
Joseph Giardina, Chief Engineer
Radio & TV system design, transmitter & studio instal, microwave & satellite engrg & instal, remote control camera systems.

du Treil, Lundin & Rackley Inc.
201 Fletcher Ave., Sarasota, FL 34237
(941) 329-6000; *Fax:* (941) 329-6030
www.dlr.com
bobjr@dlr.com
Bob Du Treil Jr, President
Tech consulting for the communications industry.

ERI - Electronics Research Inc.
7777 Gardner Rd., Chandler, IN 47610-9219
(812) 925-6000, (877) ERI-LINE; *Fax:* (812) 925-4030
www.eriinc.com
sales@eriinc.com
Thomas B. Sillman, President
Antennas, transmission line, filters-combiners & towers for FM, AM TV BR'S-EBS, mobile media bcstrs, also related engng, field & installations svcs.

Evans Associates Consulting
210 S. Main St, Thiensville, WI 53092
(262) 242-6000; *Fax:* (262) 242-6045
B. Benjamin Evans, P.E., Operations Dir
Telecommunications consulting engrs, net design, FCC applications, digital bcstg strategic planning, fieldwork for AM, FM, TV, CATV, ITFS, microwave relay facilities & fiber, wireless, & PCS networks.

Federal Engineering Inc.
Redwood Plaza II, 10600 Arrowhead Dr., Fairfax, VA 22030
(703) 359-8200; *Fax:* (703) 359-8204
www.fedeng.com
info@fedeng.com
Ronald F. Brosco, President & CEO
John E. Murray, SVP
Strategic planning, coverage analysis, new product definition, market rsch, competitive analysis, rates & tariffs, bcst stn design, mergers & acquisitions, expert testimony, regulatory support.

GEI WideFormat
3874 Highland Park N.W., North Canton, OH 44720
(800) 842-8448, (888) 722-6434; *Fax:* (800) 358-7767
www.geiwideformat.com
sales@geiwideformat.com
Large-format digital printing systems.

GeoMart
516 Villanova Ct., Fort Collins, CO 80525
(970) 416-8340, (800) 248-6277; *Fax:* (970) 416-8345, (800) 321-6277
www.geomart.com
All USGS & DMA digital & paper maps. All NOS/NOAA charts, international topographic series, aerial photography, raised relief maps, digital products, business & mktg maps, travel maps, globes, etc.

George Jacobs & Associates Inc.
3210 N. Leisure World Blvd., Suite 1001, Silver Spring, MD 20906-7605
(301) 598-1282, (301) 587-8800; *Fax:* (301) 587-8801, (301) 598-7788
www.gjainc.com
gja@gjainc.com
George Jacobs, P.E., President
Bob German, Member
Anna L. Case, Member
Specialists in conceptional design, application filing & frequency mgmt for FCC-licensed International Broadcast Stations (shortwave). Consultative liaison with foreign bcst stns & organizations.

Hammett & Edison Inc.
470 Third St W, Sonoma, CA 95476-6509
(707) 996-5200, (202) 396-5200, (214) 559-5200; *Fax:* (707) 996-5280
www.h-e.com
engr@h-e.com
William F. Hammett, P.E., President
Rajat Mathur, P.E., Senior Engineer
Dane E. Ericksen, Senior Engineer
Design & FCC filings: AM, FM, TV, STL, wireless cable. Specialties: computerized coverage studies, AM directionals / diplexers, RF radiation predictions / measurements / mitigations, field strength measurements, due diligence technicalsurveys, FAA EMI analysis.

Hatfield & Dawson, Consulting Engineers L.L.C.
9500 Greenwood Ave. N., Seattle, WA 98103
(206) 783-9151; *Fax:* (206) 789-9834
www.hatdaw.com
hatdaw@hatdaw.com
Benjamin F. Dawson, President/CEO
Telecommunications, radio physics engrg, including bcst, electromagnetic compatibility, NIER measurement/analysis, antenna/propagation analysis & design.

HN Telecom Inc.
20130 Grade Cres, Langley, BC V3A 4J6 Canada
(604) 294-3401; *Fax:* (604) 299-6712
contact@hntelecom.com
Bruce W. Grantholm, President
Telecommunications tech consulting svcs for AM, FM, TV bcst & CATV systems, studio-to-transmitter links & studio systems.

iHeartCommunications Inc.
200 E. Basse Rd., San Antonio, TX 78209 USA
(210) 822-2828
www.iheartmedia.com
Bob Pittman, Chairman & CEO
Richard J. Bressler, President & Chief Operating Officer
Gayle Troberman, Executive Vice President
Wendy Goldberg, Executive Vice President
Robert H. Walls, Jr., Executive Vice President
iHeartCommunications Inc. was founded in San Antonio, TX with the purchase of a single radio station in 1972. After decades of growing media assets globally, the company has become one of the world's leading media and entertainmentcompanies. iHeartMedia consists of two main media businesses: Clear Channel Outdoor Holdings and the wholly owned iHeartMedia and Entertainment Inc. Between these divisions, iHeartMedia focuses on providing a spectrum of multi-platform advertisingand marketing opportunities for partners and world-class entertainment for listeners and users.

J. Boyd Ingram & Associates
PO Box 1528, Batesville, MS 38606
(662) 563-4007
www.radiobroker.com
garland@radiobroker.com
David Garland, President
Broker of radio stn properties in Texas & surrounding states.

J.M. Stitt & Associates Inc.
621 E. Mehring Way, Suite 2607, Cincinnati, OH 45202
(513) 621-9292; *Fax:* (513) 651-9622
www.jmstittassociates.com
solutions@jmstittassociates.com
James Stitt, President
Engrg consultants, facility design & instal, contract engrg svcs, acoustical consultants, tower site mgmt.

John F.X. Browne & Associates P.C.
38710 Woodward Ave., Suite 220, Bloomfield Hills, MI 48304
(248) 642-6226; *Fax:* (248) 642-6027
www.jfxb.com
John F.X. Browne, President
Bcst consulting AM/FM/TV/DTV, MMDS/ITFS, PCS & satellite systems. FCC/FAA applications, filings & studies. Field measurement vehicle AM/FM/TV/DTV.

KCI Technologies Inc.
936 Ridgebrook Road, Landmark Center II, Suite 220, Sparks, MD 21152
(410) 316-7800, (800) 572-7496; *Fax:* (410) 316-7885
www.kci.com
corpcom@kci.com
Terry F. Neimeyer, PE, BCEE, FACEC, ENV PL, Chief Executive Officer and Chairman
Nathan J. Beil, PE, President
Tom Donohue, P.E., Operations Dir
James Blake, Engineering Dir
Ken J. Harmel, Vice President
Christine Y. Koski, CPA,Vice President/Chief Financial Officer
Thomas G. Sprehe, PE, DEE, BCEE, Senior Vice President-Environmental Discipline Man
Harvey M. Floyd, PE, Executive Vice President-Transportation Discipline
Christopher J. Griffith, PE, CCM, Executive VicePresident-Telecom/Utilities Discipl
Harvey M. Floyd, PE, Executive Vice President-Transportation Disciplin
Full engrg svcs to the communications industry, including tower analysis & remediation, design of standard & non-standard sites, 'stealth' engrg, photo realistic renderings & turnkey construction.

Kessler & Gehman Associates Inc.
507 N.W. 60th St., Suite C, Gainesville, FL 32607
(352) 332-3157; *Fax:* (352) 332-6392
www.kesslerandgehman.com
info@kesslerandgehman.com
Beverly Gober, Office Manager
William T. Godfrey, P.E. Jr., Engineering Associate
Robert Gehman, Jr, Consulting Engineer
Jeffrey C. Gehman, Engineering Associate
Ryan Wilhour, Consulting Engineer
Carrie Lynn, Accounting Manager
Studies, system design, FCC applications, bidding documents & contract monitoring for bcst, ITFS, wireless cable, microwave & mobile communications systems & digital TV.

Lawrence Behr Associates Inc.
3400 Tupper Drive, Greenville, NC 27834
(252) 757-0279, (800) 522-4464; *Fax:* (252) 752-9155
www.lbagroup.com
lbagrp@lbagroup.com
Lawrence Behr, CEO
Mike Britner, COO, VP Sales
Kathryn Tesh, Senior Consultant
Juliana A. Price, Controller - Business Manager
Michael W. Hayden, CPBE, CBNT, AMD, Director of Site Services
Katie Sneed, Marketing Director
DavidHorn, Business Development
Jaiver Castillo, Broadcast Equipment Sales
Provides wireless svcs: site acquisition, construction mgmt, AM detuning, AM tower colocation, RF hazard mgmt, RF shielding, due diligence, facility mgmt, dev, maintenance, support svcs.

Lightning Eliminators & Consultants Inc.
6687 Arapahoe Rd., Boulder, CO 80303
(303) 447-2828 ext 107; *Fax:* (303) 447-8122
www.lightningprotection.com
info@lecglobal.com
Avram Saunders, President
Peter Carpenter, General Manager
JoOnna Silberman, Promotions Manager
JoOnna Silberman, News Director
Darwin Sletten, Engineering Dir
Kirk Chynoweth, Chief Engineer
Lightning protection, grounding solutions. protection consulting, design and installation, engineering and design.

Mahlum Architects
Mailing Address: 71 Columbia, Floor 4, Seattle, WA 98104
Second Address: 1231 NW Hoyt, Suite 102, Portland, OR 97209
(206) 441-4151, (503) 224-4032; *Fax:* (206) 441-0478, (503) 224-0918
www.mahlum.com
aschopf@mahlum.com
Diane Shiner AIA LEED AP, Operations Partner
Anne Schopf FAIA, Design Partner
Gerald Reifert FAIA, Managing Partner
Architect interiors & planning.

Marsand Inc.
Mailing Address: 6100 IH 35W, Alvarado, TX 76009
Second Address: PO Box 485, Alvarado, TX 76009-0485
(817) 783-5566; *Fax:* (817) 783-5577
tvcowboy@marsand.com
Matthew A. Sanderford, Jr., P.E., President
David Sanderford, Vice President
The facility is able to accommodate Digital Studio pre-assembly and is stocked with RF components and spectrum, network and DTV analyzers. A portable proof package is available to go on site and perform extensive troubleshooting andalignment besides the transmitter Proof of Performance for both NTSC and Digital systems. MARSAND, INC. owns and operates all of the required test .

Meintel, Sgrignoli, & Wallace
1282 Smallwood Dr., Suite 372, Waldorf, MD 20603
(202) 251-7589; *Fax:* (301) 645-1426
www.mswdtv.com
wallacedtv@aol.com
Gary Sgrignoli, Operations Dir
Specializing in digital & analog TV & Radio technical software, consumer electronics.

Morgan, Angel & Associates LLC
1601 Connecticut Ave. N.W., Suite 600, Washington, DC 20009-1035
(202) 265-1833; *Fax:* (202) 265-8022
www.morganangel.com
PubPol@morganangel.com
Luis A. Blandon Jr., Promotions Manager
Edward Angel, co-founder and partner
Kristen Autobee, objects curator
Robert Autobee
Jay Brigham, Partner
Consulting research firm specializing in Section 106 showings and environmental assessments for proposed towers and project sites.
3605 Nelson St., Wheat Ridge, CO 80033-5565
(303) 425-9170
Dr. Edward Angel, Principal Owner

Mueller Broadcast Design
613 S. La Grange Rd., La Grange, IL 60525
(708) 352-2166; *Fax:* (708) 352-2170
www.muellerbroadcastdesign.com
mark@muellerbroadcastdesign.com
Mark A. Mueller, President
Karen S. Mueller, Accounting/ Production/ Sales
AM/FM tech consultant, AM directional systems.

Mullaney Engineering Inc.
9049 Shady Grove Court, Gaithersburg, MD 20877
(301) 921-0115; *Fax:* (301) 590-9757
www.mullengr.com
mullaney@mullengr.com
John J. Mullaney, President
Mullaney Engineering, Inc., and its predecessor firms have been providing consulting engineering services to the radio and television industry since 1948. In the early 1970's, the firm pioneered the computer aided design and optimization ofAM directional arrays which minimizes construction costs through the elimination of unnecessary towers. The firm was also one of the first to provide a computer analysis of the allocation conditions for FM, TV, and MDS facilities. With theestablishment of its in-house computer facilities in 1974, the firm prides itself on remaining on the leading edge of technology. Mullaney Engineering, Inc., currently provides services in: AM, FM, TV, DTV, MDS/ITFS, LPTV, Cellular, and environmentalradiation analysis.

Multicomm Sciences International Inc.
266 W. Main St., Denville, NJ 07834
(973) 627-7400; *Fax:* (973) 215-2168
www.multicommsciences.com
victor@multicommsciences.com
Victor J. Nexon Jr., President
Frequency coord, site surveys, earth stn interference studies, FCC license, radiation hazard testing.

Munn-Reese Inc.
385 Airport Dr., PO Box 220, Coldwater, MI 49036
(517) 278-7339; *Fax:* (517) 278-6973
www.munn-reese.com
wayne@munn-reese.com
Wayne S. Reese, President
Chris Reese, Vice President
Don Baad, Staff Engineer
Ed Trombley, Field Engineer
Justin Asher, Spectrum Engineer
Rick Grzebik, Field Engineer /Frequency Coordinator
AM, FM, TV, low power TV & engrg consulting service, including applications, field tuning & problem solving.

Owl Engineering & EMC Test Labs, Inc.
5844 Avenue N., Shoreview, MN 55126
(651) 784-7445; *Fax:* (651) 784-7541
www.owleng.com
info@owleng.com
Garrett G. Lysiak, P.E., President
Telecommunications consulting engrg svcs, applications, facilities specifications svcs, field engrg svcs, maintenance & FCC compliance svcs, EMC testing.

Pacific Radio Electronics
3031 Thornton Ave, Burbank, CA 91504
(800) 634-9476, (818) 556-4177; *Fax:* (818) 556-4185
www.pacrad.com
sales@pacrad.com
Joseph Phillips, President
Distributor of racks, patch bays, cable, adaptors, connectors, handtools, outlet strips & many other products for the bcst industry.

Radiotechniques Engineering, LLC
402 10th Ave., PO Box 367, Haddon Heights, NJ 08035
(856) 546-8008, (202) 380-3222; *Fax:* (856) 546-1841
www.radiotechniques.com
sales@radiotechniques.com
Edward A. Schober, P.E., Operations Dir
AM, FM, TV, digital bcst, boosters, FCC, equipment, field, & systems engrg. RF, financial, opns, & acoustical design.

RF Technologies Corp.
1 Gendron Dr., Lewiston, ME 04240
(207) 777-7778; *Fax:* (207) 777-7784
Designs & manufactures high-power bcst RF networks & components for FM & TV bcstrs. Products include ants, diplexers, combiners, filters, switches, coaxial & waveguides.

Richard W. Burden Associates
20944 Sherman Way, Suite 213, Canoga Park, CA 91303
(818) 340-4590
rwburden@pacbell.net

RKF Engineering, LLC
1229 19th St., N.W., Washington, DC 20036-2413
(202) 463-1567; *Fax:* (202) 463-0344
www.rkf-eng.com
Philip A. Rubin, P.E., President/CEO
Ted M. Kaplan, COO
Jeffrey B. Freedman, CFO
Arnold L. Berman, Chief Scientist
MSS, FSS & BSS satellite experts, TV & radio cellular & other new media technologies. Experts in FCC rules & regulations.

International experience, experts in ITU regulation. Software developers, simulation & modeling. In business over 20years.

Rogers Cable Systems
35-73 Wolfdale, Mississauga, ON L5C 3T6 Canada
(905) 273-8000; *Fax:* (905) 273-9661
www.rogers.com
Consulting engrg svcs with emphasis on design, instal & testing of CATV systems, fiber-optic nets.

Salient Federal Solutions
Mailing Address: 4000 Legato Road, Suite 600, Fairfax, VA 22033-2893
Second Address: 10431 Wateridge Cir., Suite 210, San Diego, CA 92121
(703) 891-8200, (888) 789-6688; *Fax:* (703) 891-8201
www.salientfed.com
inquiries@salientfed.com
Bill Parker, COO
Brad Antle, CEO
Ted Dunn, EVP / Chief Financial Officer
Kay R. Curling, SVP / Chief Human Resources Officer
Tim May, SVP/Chief Marketing Officer
Software & systems dev, lifecycle mgmt, systems integration, testing IT, infrastructure outsourcing mgmt, business process improvement, info sharing, consulting, wireless svcs & specialized functional expertise.

Sellmeyer Engineering
2 Pecan Grove Circle, Lucas, TX 75002
(972) 542-2056; *Fax:* (214) 636-5940
www.sellmeyereng.com
Jack@SellmeyerEng.com
J.S. Sellmeyer, P.E., President
AM, FM, TV applications, hearing support, directional ant design & adjustment; facilities planning & specialized equipment design.

SiteSafe Inc.
200 N. Glebe Rd., Suite 1000, Arlington, VA 22203-3728
(703) 276-1100; *Fax:* (703) 276-1169
www.sitesafe.com
info@sitesafe.com
Doug Hall, President
Tony DeMattia, Vice President of Operations
Matt Butcher, P.E., VP- Engineering and Development
Sabrina Newson, Sr VP, Business Development & Sales & Senior Accou
Michelle Calesini, Senior Account Manager -Midwest Region
Bcst & land mobile & wireless engrg consulting svcs.

Smith and Fisher, LLC
2237 Tackett's Mill Dr., Suite A, Woodbridge, VA 22192
(703) 494-2101; *Fax:* (703) 494-2132
www.smithandfisher.com
kevin@smithandfisher.com
Kevin Fisher, President
Kyle Fisher, Associate Engineer
Engrg consultants to FM, TV, & LPTV stns, FCC applications, allocation studies, RFR measurements, coverage/ interference mapping & field studies.

T.Z. Sawyer Technical Consultants LLC
2130 Hutchison Grove Court, Falls Church, VA 22043
(703) 848-2130
www.tzsawyer.com
info@tzsawyer.com
Timothy Z. Sawyer, President
FCC applications for AM, FM, TV, LPTV & aux svcs; AM directional ant design; AM, FM, & TV ant measurements; allocation studies; site surveys & inspections.

Technet Systems Group
Div/DBA: (A division of Steve Vanni Associates Inc)
PO Box 422, Auburn, NH 03032
(603) 483-5365, (888) 832-4638; *Fax:* (603) 483-0512, (800) 329-4767
www.technetsystems.com
sales@technetsystems.com
Steve Vanni, President
Bcst equipment supplier/distributor for radio & TV, specializing in complete 'turnkeyed' packages including planning, design, equipment, instal, towers & FCC licensing.

TransVision
550 Maulhardt Ave., Oxnard, CA 93030
(805) 981-8740; *Fax:* (805) 981-8738
www.txvision.com
kvaughan@txvision.com
Maria Costa Husband, Traffic & Operations
Lisa Costa, Administration
Kimithy Vaughan, Sales & Marketing
Twelve transportable & satellite transmission facilities (video, audio, voice, data). Flypack production & SNG svcs. Facilities in Brazil, Australia, Phillipines & Western Europe.

W.L. Pritchard & Co. L.C.
2228 Q Street NW, Washington, DC 20008
(301) 654-1144; *Fax:* (301) 654-1814
www.wlpco.com
inquiries@wlpco.com
Ellen Hoff, President
Professional engrg, business problem solving in telecommunications, competitor analysis, satellite communications, earth stns, & launch vehicles.

Willoughby & Voss, LLC
2654 Pebble Breeze, San Antonio, TX 78270-1190
(210) 490-2778, (210) 525-1111; *Fax:* (210) 490-2779
willvoss@satx.rr.com
Lyndon H. Willoughby, President
AM, FM, TV, STL, trans applications, directional ant design, field svcs, allocations, site studies, system planning, frequency searches, facility inspection & non-ionized radiation studies.

Wireless Systems Engineering Inc./MLJ
Div/DBA: (formerly JMS/MLJ Worldwide Inc.)
15713 Crabbs Branch Way, Suite 140, Rockville, MD 20855
(301) 840-2030; *Fax:* (301) 840-2031
WSE-MLJ assists network development companies and wireless carriers in their efforts to design, build, and operate antenna sites and towers near AM broadcast stations without AM interference.

Legal Services

Akerman & Senterfitt
Mailing Address: 420 S Orange Ave., Suite 1200, Orlando, FL 32801
Second Address: 495 N Keller Rd., Suite 300, Maitland, FL 32751
(407) 423-4000; *Fax:* (407) 843-6610
www.akerman.com

Akin Gump Strauss Hauer & Feld LLP
Robert S. Strauss Bldg., 1333 New Hampshire Ave. N.W., Washington, DC 20036
(202) 887-4000; *Fax:* (202) 887-4288
www.akingump.com
Anthony T. Pierce, Partner

Anderson, Kill & Olick L.L.P.
1717 Pennsylvania Ave., NW, Suite 200, Washington, DC 20006
(202) 416-6500; *Fax:* (202) 416-6555
www.andersonkill.com
akoDC@andersonkill.com
Rhonda D. Orin, Partner

Arent & Fox, PLLC
1717 K St, NW, Washington, DC 20006
(202) 857-6000; *Fax:* (202) 857-6395
www.arentfox.com
delorey.denise@arentfox.com
Mathew J. Clark, Managing Partner

Arnold & Porter LLP
555 12th St. N.W., Washington, DC 20004-1206
(202) 942-5000; *Fax:* (202) 942-5999
www.arnoldporter.com
norman.sinel@aporter.com
Richard Alexander, Partner

Ausley & McMullen
123 S. Calhoun St., PO Box 391, Tallahassee, FL 32301
(850) 224-9115; *Fax:* (850) 222-7560
www.ausley.com
info@ausley.com
Ausley McMullen, President
Offers Strong legal knowledge & legal services acrossa Range of key practice disciplines, civil litiigation, regulatory issues, Government affairs & transactional matters

Baker & Hostetler LLP
Washington Sq., 1050 Connecticut Ave. N.W., Suite 1100, Washington, DC 20036-5304
(202) 861-1500; *Fax:* (202) 861-1783
www.bakerlaw.com
jparavano@bakerlaw.com
R. Steven Kestner, Chairman
Jeffery H. Paravano, Managing Partner
Kevin L. Cash, CFO
David D. Southern, Chief Marketing Officer
Lee Jensen, Director, Administration

Baker Botts L.L.P.
Mailing Address: 1299 Pennsylvania Ave. N.W., The Warner, Washington, DC 20004-2400
Second Address: 98 San Jacinto Boulevard, Suite 1500, Austin, TX 78701-4078
(202) 639-7700, (512) 322-2500; *Fax:* (202) 639-7890, (512) 322-2501
www.bakerbotts.com
john.taladay@bakerbotts.com
Lydia Companion, Chief Financial Officer
Mark White, Chief Administrative Officer
Tracy Hallenberger, Chief Knowledge Officer
Andrew M. Baker, Managing Partner
John Meuser, Director of Human Resources & Administrative Opera
Our Washington office provides a full range of legal services, including lobbying, advice on governmental affairs, appellate, antitrust, corporate and securities, energy, environmental, intellectual property and technology, international,litigation, project development, tax, telecommunications and white collar crime. Our lawyers represent foreign governments and private clients throughout the world.

Baker, Ravenel & Bender
3710 Landmark Dr., Suite 400, Columbia, SC 29204
(803) 799-9091, (888) 675-4538; *Fax:* (803) 779-3423
www.brblegal.com
Full service litigation Firm

Barron & Newburger, P.C.
Mailing Address: 1212 Guadalupe St., Suite 104, Austin, TX 78701
Second Address: 6300 West Loop South, Suite 341, Houston, TX 77041
(512) 476-9103, (713) 942-0808; *Fax:* (512) 279-0310, (713) 942-0449
www.bn-lawyers.com
hlenett@bn-lawyers.com
Howard Lenett, Operations Manager
Barbara Barron, Attorney
Kevin Crocker, Attorney

Bass, Berry & Sims
150 Third Ave S, Suite 2800, Nashville, TN 37201
(615) 742-6200; *Fax:* (615) 742-6293
www.bassberry.com
Bonna B. Canale, Office Administrator
Todd J. Rolapp, Managing Partner
Craig E. Bingham, Director Of Technology
Kimberley D. Bell, Managing Director, Litigation & Dispute Res.
Kimberley D. Cannon, Director Of Human Resources
J.David Evans, Executive Director

Berkowitz, Trager & Trager, P.C.
8 Wright St., Westport, CT 06880 US
(203) 226-1001; *Fax:* (203) 226-3801
www.bertralaw.com
Richard Berkowitz, Attorney
Paul Berg, Attorney
Anne E Crane, Attorney
Elizabeth A Brower, Attorney
Jeffrey J. Danile, Attorney

Best, Best & Krieger LLP
2000 Pennsylvania N.W., Suite 5300, Washington, DC 20006
(202) 785-0600; *Fax:* (202) 785-1234
www.bbklaw.com
Jamie B. Zamoff, COO
Gene Tanaka, Executive Committee
Eric L. Garner, Managing Partner
Cynthia M. Germano, Execuitve Committee
Shawn D. Hagerty, Execuitve Committee
Stacey Sheston, Execuitve Committee
A full-service law firm with nearly 200 attorneys in nine offices across California and in Washington, D.C., Best Best & Krieger LLP delivers effective, timely and service-oriented solutions to complex legal issues facing public agencies,businesses and individuals.

Bingham McCuthen, LLP
Mailing Address: 1111 Pennsylvania Ave. NW, Washington, DC 20004-2541
Second Address: One Federal Street, Boston, MA 02110-1726
(202) 739-3000, (617) 341-7700; *Fax:* (202) 739-3001, (617) 341-7701
www.morganlewis.com
andrew.lipman@bingham.com
Jay Zimmerman, Chairman
Kimiko Takeda Fields, Contract Attorney

Across our financial services practices, more than 300 Bingham lawyers guide clients through the global maze of markets, regulations and taxation with capabilities that span transactions, compliance, enforcement and litigation, winning theChambers USA Award for Excellence in Investment Funds in 2011 and Law Firm of the Year in Securitization and Structured Finance Law and Litigation - Securities according to Best Lawyers and U.S. News & World Report in 2012.

Birch, Horton, Bittner & Cherot
Mailing Address: 1156 15th St NW, Suite 1020, Washington, DC 20005
Second Address: 1127 W 7th Ave., Anchorage, AL 99501
(202) 659-5800, (888) 482-4724, (907) 276-1550, (8; *Fax:* (202) 659-1027, (907) 276-3680
www.birchhorton.com
Ronald G. Birch, VP/ Founder/ Attorney
Law Firm; dispute resolution activities,emphasis on preventative law

Blank, Rome, LLP
405 Lexington Ave., 23rd Floor, New York, NY 10174-0208
(212) 885-5000; *Fax:* (212) 885-5001
www.blankrome.com
Patrick O. Cavanaugh, Chief Operating Officer
Karen M. Jablonski, Senior Director of Operations
Allison V. Friend, Chief Human Resources Officer
Christopher A. Lewis, Partner & Chief Officer for Diversity and Inclusio
Laurence Liss,Chief Technology Officer
John Seifarth, Chief Financial Officer
Beatrice Seravello, Chief Strategy Officer
John M. Sperger, Secretary to the Firm
By listening to general counsel, business leaders and entrepreneurs, and anticipating their needs, Blank Rome has provided exceptional service to clients for more than 65 years. We have become one of America's largest law firms by addingleading talent and new practice areas to handle critical client matters. We invite you to explore this site to learn how our experience, depth, and diversity can enhance your business. At Blank Rome, we see the world through our clients' eyes.

Bleiweiss, Irene
U.S. FCC, Audio Services Division, 445 12th St. S.W., Washington, DC 20554
(202) 418-2700, (888) 225-5322, (888) 835-5322; *Fax:* (202) 418-1411, (866) 418-0232
www.fcc.gov/mb/audio
irene.bleiweiss@fcc.gov

Blooston, Mordkofsky, Dickens, Duffy & Prendergast, LLP
2120 L St. N.W., Suite 300, Washington, DC 20037
(202) 659-0830; *Fax:* (202) 828-5568
halmor@bloostonlaw.com
Harold Mordkofsky, Partner
Benjamin H. Dickens Jr., Partner
John A. Prendergast, Managing Partner
Gerard J. Duffy, Partner
Richard D. Rubino, Partner
Mary J. Sisak, Partner

Blumberg, Grace Ganz- UCLA School of Law
385 Charles E. Young Dr. East, 1242 Law Building, Los Angeles, CA 90095
(310) 267-4736; *Fax:* (310) 206-6489
Iman Anabtawi, Professor Of Law

BlumeLegal LLC
1001 Farmington Ave., Suite 302, West Hartford, CT 06107
(860) 521-3777; *Fax:* (860) 521-3778
www.blumelegal.net
db@blumelegal.net
Daniel Blume, Esq., Principal Owner & Manager
Law firm providing legal service related to communications, commercial real estate, business entities, and estate planning.

Boies, Schiller & Flexner, LLP
Mailing Address: 100 S.E. 2nd St., Suite 2800, Miami, FL 33131
Second Address: 1999 Harrison Stree, Suite 900, Oakland, CA 94612
(305) 539-8400, (510) 874-1000; *Fax:* (305) 539-1307, (510) 874-1460
www.bsfllp.com
dboies@bsfllp.com
David Boies, Chairman
Melissa Willett, Senior Attorney
Parker H. Bagley, Counsel
Hillel J. Bavli, Counsel
Rosanne C. Baxter, Counsel
Boies, Schiller & Flexner LLP, founded in 1997, has become one of the nation's premier law firms. Today, with over 200 lawyers practicing in offices across the country, we regularly serve as lead counsel in the most significant and highestprofile disputes in the world. While best known for landmark cases such as United States v. Microsoft, Bush v. Gore, and In re Vitamins, we represent some of the largest and most sophisticated organizations in the world when the results matter most.In less than a decade, we have won and saved our clients billions of dollars in trials, arbitrations, and settlements.

Bone McAllester Norton PLLC
Mailing Address: 511 Union St., Suite 1600, Nashville, TN 37219
Second Address: 131 Saundersville Rd., Suite 130, Hendersonville, TN 37075
(615) 238-6330, (615) 822-8822; *Fax:* (615) 238-6301,(615) 780-7979
www.bonelaw.com
mnorton@bonelaw.com
Vicki Scruggs, Chief Administrative Officer
Deron Peak, Director Of Technology
Ann Dee McClane, Director Of Marketing & Business Development

Borsari & Paxson
Div/DBA: Communications Law Firm
4000 Albemarle Street Northwest, Suite 100, Washington, DC 20016
(202) 296-4800; *Fax:* (202) 296-4460
www.baplaw.com
bap@baplaw.com
George Borsari, Partner
Anne Paxson, Partner

Borsari and Assoc., P.L.C.
Box 100009, Arlington, VA 22210
(703) 524-5800; *Fax:* (703) 524-4329
John@borsari.com

Bramson, Plutzik, Mahler, Birkhaeuser, LLP
2125 Oak Grove Rd., Suite 120, Walnut Creek, CA 94598
(925) 945-0200; *Fax:* (925) 945-8792
www.bramsonplutzik.com
info@bramsonplutzik.com
Robert M. Bramson, Attorney
Alan R. Plutzik, Attorney
Daniel E. Birkhaeuser, Attorney
Paul F. Mahler, Of Counsel
Michael S. Strimling, Attorney
Jennifer S. Rosenberg, Attorney

Brann & Isaacson
184 Main St., Fourth Floor, PO Box 3070, Lewiston, ME 04243-3070
(207) 786-3566; *Fax:* (207) 783-9325
www.brannlaw.com
DMcIntire@Brannlaw.com
Leon A. Gorman, Chairman of Board

Brickfield, Burchette, Ritts & Stone
1025 Thomas Jefferson St. N.W., West Tower, 8th Fl., Washington, DC 20007-5201
(202) 342-0800; *Fax:* (202) 342-0807
mail@bbrslaw.com
James W. Brew, Principal
Peter J. Brickfield, Principal
John H. Conway, Principal
Eric M. DeVito, Principal
Stephen J. Carina, Counsel
Eric J. Lacey, Principal
Michael K. Lavanga, Principal

Brighton , Runyon & Callahan
45 Main St., Suite 2B, Peterborough, NH 03458 -2447
(603) 924-3050; *Fax:* (603) 924-9764
Kenneth A.Bringhton, Of Counsel

Brooks, Pierce, McLendon, Humphrey & Leonard
Mailing Address: 1600 Wells Fargo Capitol Center, 150 Fayetteville St., Raleigh, NC 27601
Second Address: 230 North Elm Street, 2000 Renaissance Plaza, Greensboro, NC 27401
(919) 839-0300, (336) 373-8850; *Fax:* (919) 839-0304, (336) 378-1001
www.brookspierce.com
Elizabeth Biser, Govt. Relations & Policy Advisor
Brooks, Pierce, McLendon, Humphrey & Leonard, LLP is a business law firm providing comprehensive strategic counsel and innovative solutions to our clients. Our lawyers have expertise in all facets of business law. Brooks Pierce clients areleading organizations and successful individuals throughout the United States and the world. We are well known for our abiding commitment to clients and our service ethic, both on a professional and personal level.

Brown, Dean, Wiseman, Lisert, Proctor & Hart, L.L.P.
Mailing Address: 306 W. 7th St., Suite 200, Fort Worth, TX 76102
Second Address: 440 Louisana St., Suite 900, Houston, TX 77002
(817) 332-1391, (713) 275-2192; *Fax:* (817) 870-2427, (713) 236-7721
www.browndean.com
info@browndean.com
Alicia A. Wanker, Associates
John Proctor, Jr., Associates

Bryan Cave L.L.P.
1155 F St., NW, Washington, DC 20004
(202) 508-6000; *Fax:* (202) 508-6200
www.bryancave.com
mediainquiry@bryancave.com
LaDawn Naegle, Partner
Don G. Lents, Sr. Partner And Chair Emeritus
Rodney Page, Partner
1290 Ave. of the Americas, New York, NY 10104-0101
(212) 541-2000; *Fax:* (212) 541-4630
www.bryancave.com
Jerome S. Boros, Renee E. Frost
Andrew Irving, Alan Pearce
Michael Rosen, President
3500 One Kansas City Pl., Kansas City, MO 64105-2158
(816) 474-7400; *Fax:* (816) 374-3300
www.bryancave.com
John R. Wilner, Chairman

Bubar, James S., Attorney at Law
121 Chanlon Rd, Martindale-hubbell, New Providence, NJ 07974
(800) 526-4902, (908) 771-7777; *Fax:* (908) 771-8704
www.lawyers.com
info@martindale.com
James S.Bubar, Attorney at Law

Bullivant, Houser, & Bailey
888 S.W. 5th Ave., Suite 300, Portland, OR 97204-2017
(503) 228-6351, (800) 654-8972; *Fax:* (503) 295-0915
www.bullivant.com
John A. Bennet, Attorney
Matthew C. Casey, Attorney
Megan Cook, Attorney

Cades Schutte
1000 Bishop St., Suite 1200, Honolulu, HI 96813
(808) 521-9200, (808) 521-9200; *Fax:* (808) 521-9210
www.cades.com
cades@cades.com
Michi Momose, Associate
Calvert Chipchase, Partener

Cahill, Gordon & Reindel LLP
1990 K St. N.W., Suite 950, Washington, DC 20006
(202) 862-8900; *Fax:* (202) 862-8958
www.cahill.com
Michael Colpo, Executive Director
Verna Diaz, Dir. Of Administration
80 Pine St, New York, NY 10005-1702
(212) 701-3000
Floyd Abrams, Chairman

Calfee, Halter & Griswold
Mailing Address: 1405 East 6TH St., Cleveland, OH 44114
Second Address: 1200 Huntington Center, 41 South High Street, Columbus, OH 43215-3465
(216) 622-8200, (614) 621-1500; *Fax:* (216) 241-0816, (614) 621-0010
www.calfee.com
inf@calfee.com
Thomas F. McKee, Chairman
Philip M. Dawson, COO
Brent D. Ballard, Managing Partner
Donna Shurtleff, Dir. Of Human Resources & Benefits
Russell C. Mazzaro, Information Technology
Ronald R. Stupka, Office Services
Ellen M. Quinn,Research Services
Anne F. Cummings, Client Services/Film Sponsorships

Callister, Nebeker & McCullough
10 East South temple, Suite 900, Salt Lake City, UT 84133
(801) 530-7300; *Fax:* (801) 364-9127
www.cnmlaw.com
Louis H. Callister, Of Counsel, Chairman Emeritus
T. Richard Davis, President, Director, Shareholder
Jeffrey L. Shields, VP, Shareholder, Director
Cass C. Butler, Director, Shareholder, Construction Law
Brian W. Burnett, Director,Shareholder, Natural Resources
W. Jeffrey Filmore, Shareholder, Banking & Finance Section

Cameron & Mittleman LLP
301 Promenade St., Providence, RI 02908
(401) 331-5700; *Fax:* (401) 331-5787
www.cm-law.com
Richard S. Mittleman, Partner
Catherine T. Schneider, Associates
Justin T. Shay, Partners
Susan C. Kiernan, Associate

Carr, Morris & Graeff, P.C.
8300 Boone Blvd., Suite 250, Tyson's Corner, Vienna, VA 22182-2681
(703) 288-2900; *Fax:* (703) 288-9550
jbanford@cmgpc.com
Justin T. Banford, Attorney
Thomas K. Berger, Attorney
Nestor E. Cruz, Attorney
Roy R. Morris, Attorney
Lawrence E. Carr III, Attorney
Stephen D. Graeff, Attorney

Carter Ledyard & Milburn LLP
Mailing Address: 2 Wall St., New York, NY 10005
Second Address: 570 Lexington Ave., New York, NY 10022
212 732-3200, (212) 371-2720; *Fax:* (212) 732-3232, (212) 371-4234
www.clm.com
info@clm.com

Chadbourne & Parke
1200 New Hampshire Ave. N.W., Washington, DC 20036
(202) 974-5600; *Fax:* (202) 974-5602
www.chadbourne.com
washington@chadbourne.com
Keith Martin, Partner
John J. Marciano III, Partner
Kerrie L. Campbell, Partener
30 Rockefeller Plaza, New York, NY 10112-0015
(212) 408-5100
601 S. Figueroa St, Los Angeles, CA 90017-5704
(213) 892-1000

Chetkof, Gary H.
293 Tinker St., Woodstock, NY 12498
(845) 679-7600, (800) 679-9378; *Fax:* (845) 679-5395
www.wdst.com
live@radiowoodstock.com
Gary Chetkof, President
Mike Tuttle, Operations Manager
Richard Fusco, General Manager/ Digital Media Director
Ike Philips, VP, Sales & Marketing
Jimmy Buff, Program Director/ Morning Host
Katie DiMartile, Promotions Director
Justin Foy, Production Director
Cynthia Huggins, Business Manager/ Traffic
Abbie Alberto, Office & Property Manager/Receptionist
Valen Coscarella, Art Director: Graphics & Merchandise
Marisa Perez Rogers, Sr. Account Executive
Assa Sacko,Ecommerce Manager/Concerts & Festivals

Clark Hill P.L.C.
500 Woodward Ave., Suite 3500, Detroit, MI 48226
(313) 965-8300, (800) 949-3120; *Fax:* (313) 965-8252
www.clarkhill.com
email@clarkhill.com
Stephanie M. Anderson, Sr. Attorney
James Baiers, Counsel

Clifford, Chance, LLP
Mailing Address: 31 West 52 St., New York, NY 10019
Second Address: 2001 K Street NW, Washington, DC 20006
(212) 878-8000, (202) 912-5000; *Fax:* (212) 878-8375, (202) 912-6000
www.cliffordchance.com
Ira D. Frome, Regional COO/Director of Finance
Grace McLaughlin Rainey, Director of Operations
Gavin Goodwin, General Manager
Amy Flanagan Bogle, Director of Human Resources
Evette Pastoriza, Director of Information Technology
Clifford Chance's Americas practice offers clients outstanding legal advice on all aspects of corporate and finance law, with lawyers in our New York and Washington, D.C. offices combining pragmatism and creativity to address the day-to-daybusiness needs of our multinational and financial institution clients.

Cohn and Marks LLP
1920 N St. N.W., Suite 300, Washington, DC 20036-1622
(202) 293-3860; *Fax:* (202) 293-4827
www.cohnmarks.com
richard.helmick@cohnmarks.com
Robert B. Jacobi, Partner
Ronald A. Siegel, Partner
The business of communications law and policy today is to attempt to envision and help shape the social consequences of the current revolution in communications technology. To foster the benefits the new technology promises — and to avoidthe dangers it may pose — represents the greatest challenge ever to confront communications law and those who make and practice it.

Colby, Lauren A.
Box 113, 10 E. Fourth St., Frederick, MD 21705-0113
(301) 663-1086; *Fax:* (301) 695-8734

Cooley LLP
1299 Pennsylvania Ave. N.W., Suite 700, Washington, DC 20004
(202) 842-7800
www.cooley.com
Steve Neal, Chairman
Joe Conroy, CEO
One Ravinia Dr., Suite 1600, Atlanta, GA
(770) 901-8800

Cooper, White & Cooper, L.L.P.
Mailing Address: 201 California St., 17th Fl., San Francisco, CA 94111
Second Address: 1333 N California Blvd., Suite 450, Walnut Creek, CA 94596
(415) 433-1900, (925) 935-0700; *Fax:* (415) 433-5530, (925) 256-9428
www.cwclaw.com
whansell@cwclaw.com
Sarah J. Banola, Senior Counsel
David I. Blumenfeld, Associate
Peter C. Califano, Partner

Covington & Burling
One CityCenter, 850 Tenth Street, NW, Washington, DC 20004-2401
(202) 662-6000; *Fax:* (202) 662-6291
www.cov.com
Edward Yingling, Senior Counsel

Creative Industry Law Group
Div/DBA: (Formerly Hasse / Molesky P.C.)
155 Sansome St., Suite 500, San Francisco, CA 94104
(415) 433-4380; *Fax:* (415) 433-6580
info@cilawyers.com
Lizbeth Hasse, Attorney
Erin Harrison, Attorney
Shioun Lee, Attorney
Creative Industry Law Group provides high-quality, cost-effective legal services to clients with media, creative arts/entertainment and technology-oriented businesses and needs. We combine the attention and cost-consciousness of a small firmwith the quality and experience of a much larger one to give our domestic and international clients superior services. We have achieved the highest ratings for legal ability and ethics given by Martindale-Hubbell. We value community service andencourage sustainable practices.

Crowell & Moring
Mailing Address: 1001 Pennsylvania Ave. N.W., Washington, DC 20004-2595
Second Address: 590 Madison Ave., 20th Floor, New York, NY 10022-2544
(202) 624-2500, (212) 223-4000; *Fax:* (202) 628-5116, (212) 223-4134
www.crowell.com
sthomas@crowell.com
Kent Gardiner, Chairman
Kent Gardiner, Partener
Ellen Dwyer, Managing Partner, Executive Committee

Cuni, Ferguson, Levay & Bergmann
10655 Springfield Pike, Cincinnati, OH 45215
(513) 771-6768; *Fax:* (513) 771-6781
www.cfl-law.com
pmusgrove@cfl-law.com
Lisa M. Conn, Associate
Thomas L. Cuni, Esq., Partner
Amy S. Ferguson, Esq., Partner
Helen Fanz LeVay, Esq., Partner
Tony R. Martina, Associate
Cassaundra L. Edwards, Associate
Statement of Practice: Real Estate,Corporate,Community and Condominium Association,(including Foreclosure),Estate Planning and Probate,Civil Litigation

Davis Wright Tremaine LLP
Mailing Address: 1919 Pennsylvania Ave. N.W., Suite 800, Washington, DC 20006-3401
Second Address: 188 West Northern lights Blvd., Suite 1100, Anchorage, AK 99503-3985
(202) 973-4200, (907) 257-5300; *Fax:* (202) 973-4499, (907) 257-5399
www.dwt.com
bobcornrevere@dwt.com
Kelli Kohout, Chief Administrative Officer
John Reed, Partener
David C. Baca, Managing Partner
Rob O'Reilly, Chief Information Officer
Mark Usellis, Strategy Officer

Davis Wright Tremaine LLP
Mailing Address: 1919 Pennsylvania Ave. N.W., Suite 800, Washington, DC 20006-3401
Second Address: 188 West Northern lights Blvd., Suite 1100, Anchorage, AK 99503-3985
(202) 973-4200, (907) 257-5300; *Fax:* (202) 973-4499, (907) 257-5399
www.dwt.com
seattle@dwt.com
Keith Gorder, CFO
Kelli Kohout, Chief Administrative Officer
John Reed, General Counsel
David C. Baca, Managing Partner
Rob O'Reilly, Chief Information Officer
Mark Usellis, Strategy Officer
999 Main St, Suite 911, Boise, ID 83702-9000
(208) 338-8200; *Fax:* (208) 338-8299
Deborah Kristensen, Chairman
2300 First Interstate Tower, 1300 S.W. 5th Ave, Portland, OR 97201-5630
(503) 241-2300; *Fax:* (503) 778-5299
Duane A. Bosworth, Chairman
1000 Wilshire Blvd, Suite 600, Los Angeles, CA 90017-2457
(213) 633-6800; *Fax:* (213) 633-6899
Kelli L. Sager, Chairman
1155 Connecticut Ave. N.W., Washington, DC 20036-4306
(202) 508-6600; *Fax:* (202) 508-6699

Davis Wright Tremaine LLP
Mailing Address: 1919 Pennsylvania Ave. N.W., Suite 800, Washington, DC 20006-3401
Second Address: 865 S. Figueroa Street, Suite 2400, Los Angeles, CA 90017-2566
(202) 973-4200, (213) 633-6800; *Fax:* (202) 973-4499, (213) 633-6899
www.dwt.com
maryhaas@dwt.com
Keith Gorder, COO
Christopher Avery, Counsel
Steven J. Horvitz, Partner In Charge
Sally Linzau, Office Administrator
Elizabeth A. Drogula, Associate
Davis Wright Tremaine is dedicated to providing excellent legal services, and delivering them in a manner customized to each client's particular needs and preferences. This commitment has remained intact for decades as the firm has grownacross the nation and to China. Today, Davis Wright is a full-service firm with approximately 500 lawyers in nine offices on the east and west coasts of the United States and in Shanghai. We are recognized for excellence in a broad number of areas,with 89 of our attorneys across 32 practice areas cited as leaders in their fields in the most recent Chambers USA guide, and over 140 of our attorneys across 46 practice areas included in the 2013 edition of The Best Lawyers in America.

Day & Associates
577 Airport Blvd., Suite 130, Burlington, CA 94010
(650) 343-2660; *Fax:* (650) 344-8460
www.dayassociates.net
Kevin Day, Founder And Principal
Stephanie MacDonald, Search Consultant

Day Pitney LLP
Mailing Address: 242 Trumbull St., Hartford, CT 06103
Second Address: 24 Field Point Rd., Greenwich, CT 06830
(860) 275-0100, (203) 862-7800; *Fax:* (860) 275-0343, (203) 862-7801
www.daypitney.com
mwelsass@dbh.com
Nabil Mughal, Chief Information Officer
Stacy Smith Walsh, Dir. Of Human Resources
Mary Beth Donoghue, Dir. Of Administration
Joseph Barretti, Director of Finance
Lori Johnson, Dir. Of Professional Development
Paul P. Lach,Controller

Debevoise & Plimpton LLP
Mailing Address: 919 3rd Ave., New York, NY 10022
Second Address: 555 13th St., NW, Washington, DC 20004
(212) 909-6000, (202) 383-8000; *Fax:* (212) 909-6836, (202) 383-8118
www.debevoise.com

Jeffery P. Cunard, Managing Partner
21 Ave. George V, Paris
33-1-40-73-12-12
James A. Kiernan III, Chairman
Antoine F. Kirry, CEO/COO
Bolshoi Palashevsky Per 13/2, Moscow
7503-956-3858
Dmitri V. Nikiforov, Chairman
555 13th St. N.W., Suite 1100-E, Washington, DC 20004-1109
(202) 383-8000
Jeffrey P. Cunard, Chairman
13/F Entertainment Bldg, 30 Queen's Rd. Central, Hong Kong
852-2810-7918
Jeffrey S. Wood, Chairman
The International Financial Centre, 25 Old Broad St, London
44-171-786-9000
Robert R. Bruce, Chairman

Decker, Jones, McMackin, McClane, Hall & Bates
Burnett Plaza, 801 Cherry St., Suite 2000, Unit 46, Fort Worth, TX 76102-6838
(817) 336-2400, (817) 429-5260; *Fax:* (817) 332-3043
www.deckerjones.com
George Q. McGown, Founder
Daniel . Bates, Shareholder
Randy J. Hall, Shareholder
Elisa C. Fox, Associate
David L. Pratt II, Sr. Associate
Janet L. Hahn, Shareholder

Del, Shaw, Moonves, Tanaka, Finkelstein & Lezcano
2120 Colorado Ave., Suite 200, Santa Monica, CA 90404
(310) 979-7900; *Fax:* (310) 979-7999
www.dsmtfl.com

Dennis Ardi Attorney at Law Professional Corporation
Div/DBA: (formerly Ardi Dennis)
9595 Wilshire Blvd., Suite 410, Beverly Hills, CA 90210
(310) 271-6900; *Fax:* (310) 271-6963
www.dennisardi.com
da@dennisardi.com

Devine & Millimet
Mailing Address: 111 Amherst St., Manchester, NH 03101
Second Address: 43 N Main St., Concord, NH 3301
(603) 669-1000, (603) 226-1000; *Fax:* (603) 669-8547
www.devinemillimet.com
kmcginley@dm.com
Jon B. Sparkman, President & Shareholder
Sean P. Flanagan, Associate
Jonathan M. Eck, Shareholder
Maurice P. Gilbert, Director Of State Taxation

DeWitt, Ross & Stevens
Mailing Address: 2 E. Mifflin St., Suite 600, Madison, WI 53703
Second Address: 13935 Bishop's Drive, Suite 300, Brookfield, WI 53005
(608) 255-8891, (262) 754-2840; *Fax:* (608) 252-9243, (262) 754-2845
www.dewittross.com
Bradley W. Raaths, Attorney/Executive Committee Chairman
Stephen A. DiTullio, Attorney
Bradley W. Hauck, Attorney
William E. McCardell, Attorney
DeWitt Ross & Stevens S.C. understands that clients want attorneys who have a track record of success. The success of our clients is our ultimate and enduring goal. Our clients include large corporations and family owned businesses,employers, associations, individuals, municipalities and others who seek our advice in more than 30 different areas of the law. We are based in Wisconsin and proudly serve clients locally and beyond from our offices in Madison and Brookfield.

Dickstein Shapiro LLP
Div/DBA: (Formerly Dickstein Shapiro Morin and Oshinsky LLP
Mailing Address: 1825 Eye St., N.W., Washington, DC 20006-5403
Second Address: 1633 Broadway, New York, NY 10019-6708
(202) 420-2200, (212) 277-6500; *Fax:* (202) 420-2201, (212) 277-6501
www.dicksteinshapiro.com
info@dicksteinshapiro.com
James D. Kelly, Chairman
Kristan D. Morrell, COO
Elena R. Garcia, Chief Human Resources Officer
Donna B. Feeney, CFO
Richard J. Leveridge, Managing Partner
Deborah Skakel, Managing Partner
Paul A. Sicari, Chief AdministrativeOfficer
1177 Ave. of the Americas, 41st Fl, New York, NY 10036-2714

Dieguez, Richard P.
192 Garden St., Suite 2, Roslyn Heights, NY 11577
(516) 621-6424; *Fax:* (516) 621-6508
rpdieguez@rpdieguez.com

DLA Piper
Mailing Address: 500 Eighth Street, NW, Washington, DC 20004
Second Address: 1201 North Market Street, Suite 2100, Wilmington, DL 19801
(202) 799-4000, (302) 468 5700; *Fax:* (202) 799-5000, (302) 394-2341
www.dlapiper.com
juan.picon@dlapiper.com
Lee I. Miller, Global Co-Chairman
J. Terence O'Malley, CEO
Bob Bratt, Chief Operating Officer
Francis B. Burch Jr., Chairman Emeritus
Roger Meltzer, Partner
Peter S. Pantaleo, General Counsel
Michael S. Poulos, Co-ManagingPartners
DLA Piper became one of the largest business law firms in the world in 2005 through a merger of unprecedented scope in the legal sector. We were built to serve clients wherever in the world they do business - quickly, efficiently and withgenuine knowledge of both local and international considerations. Whether our clients require seamless coordination across multiple jurisdictions or delivery in a single location, they can count on us to deliver the right service and solutions.
1251 Ave. of the Americas, New York, NY 10020-1104
(212) 835-6000; *Fax:* (212) 835-6001
mmccabe@piperrudnick.com
Monica McCabe, Chairman

Don Buchwald & Associates
10 E. 44 St., New York, NY 10017
(212) 867-1200; *Fax:* (212) 972-3209
www.buchwald.com
info@buchwald.com
Don Buchwald, Owner/Founder
Ricki Olshan, EVP, Talent/Legit
Robyn Stecher, EVP, Commercial Dept.

Donald M. Craven P.C.
1005 N. 7th St., Springfield, IL 62702-3918
(217) 544-1777; *Fax:* (217) 544-0713
www.cravenlawoffice.com
don@cravenlawoffice.com
Donald M. Craven, Attorney
Esther J. Seitz, Attorney
The law firm serves as general counsel to the Illinois Press Association, the Illinois Broadcasters Association and the Illinois News Broadcasters Association. Attorney Donald M. Craven represents television and radio stations, newspapersand other media in an array of litigation.

Dorsey & Whitney, L L P
Mailing Address: 50 S. 6th St., Suite 1500, Minneapolis, MN 55402-1498
Second Address: 1031 W 4thAve., Suite 600, Anchorage, AK 99501-5907
(612) 340-2600, (907) 276-4557, (800) 759-4929; *Fax:* (612) 340-2868, (907) 276-4152
www.dorsey.com
Kevin Ha, Associate
Anne Marie Tavella, Associate
Gregory S. Tamkin, Partner
666 Burrard St., Suite 1300, Park Pl., Vancouver, BC Canada
(604) 687-5151; *Fax:* (604) 687-8504
1031 West 4th Ave., Suite 600, Anchorage, AK 99501-5900
(907) 276-4557; *Fax:* (907) 276-4152
Republic Plaza Bldg., Suite 4400, 370 Seventeenth St., Denver, CO 80202-5608
(303) 629-3400; *Fax:* (303) 629-3450
50 S. 6th St., Minneapolis, MN 55402-1540
(612) 340-2600; *Fax:* (612) 340-2868
Dakota Ctr., 51 N. Broadway, Suite 402, Fargo, ND
(701) 235-6000; *Fax:* (701) 235-9969
Veritas House, 125 Finsbury Pavement, London
011-44-171-588-0800; *Fax:* 011-44-171-588-0555
38 Technology Dr, Irvine, CA 92618-5310
(714) 424-5555; *Fax:* (714) 424-5554
1001 Pennsylvania Ave. N.W., Suite 200 South, Washington, DC 20004-2505
(202) 824-8800; *Fax:* (202) 824-8990
US Bank Building Ctr., 1420 5th Ave., Suite 400, Seattle, WA 98101-2613
(206) 654-5400; *Fax:* (206) 654-5500
250 Park Ave, New York, NY 10177-0001
(212) 415-9200; *Fax:* (212) 953-7201
125 Bank St., Suite 600, Missoula, MO
(406) 721-6025; *Fax:* (406) 543-0863
507 Davidson Bldg., 8 Third St., Great Falls, MO
(406) 727-3632; *Fax:* (406) 727-3638
Wells Fargo Plaza, 170 S. Main St., Suite 925, Salt Lake City, UT 84101-1666
(801) 350-3581; *Fax:* (801) 350-3585

Drinker Biddle & Reath L.L.P.
Mailing Address: 1500 K St. N.W., Washington, DC 20005-1209
Second Address: 222 Delaware Avenue, Suite 1410, Wilmington, DE 19801-1621
(202) 842-8800, (302) 467-4200; *Fax:* (202) 842-8465, (302) 467-4201
www.drinkerbiddle.com
Gary Rinkerman, Partner

Drinker Biddle & Reath L.L.P.
Mailing Address: 1500 K St. N.W., Washington, DC 20005-1209
Second Address: 222 Delaware Avenue, Suite 1410, Wilmington, DE 19801-1254
(202) 842-8800, 9302) 467-4200; *Fax:* (202) 842-8465, (302) 467-4201
Maureen Donahue Hardwick, Partner In Charge
Thomas P. McGonigle, Partner In Charge

Duane Morris LLP
30 S. 17th St., Philadelphia, PA 19103-4196
(215) 979-1000; *Fax:* (215) 979-1020
www.duanemorris.com

Eaton, Peabody
Mailing Address: 80 Exchange St., Bangor, ME 04401
Second Address: 77 Sewall St., Suite 3000, Augusta, ME 4330
(207) 947-0111, (207) 622-3747; *Fax:* (207) 942-3040, (207) 622-9732
www.eatonpeabody.com
eaton@eatonpeabody.com
David M. Austin, Managing Partner
Jason C. Barrett, Shareholder
Don Gerrish, Development Consultant
Shelley Doak, Management Consultant

Eckert, Seamans, Cherin & Mellott
50 S 16th St, Two Liberty Place, 22nd Flr., Philadelphia, PA 19102
(215) 851-8400; *Fax:* (215) 851-8383
www.escm.com
info@eckertseamans.com
Timothy P. Ryan, CEO

Edelstein, Laird & Sobel, L.L.P.
9255 Sunset Blvd., Suite 800, Los Angeles, CA 90069
(310) 274-6184; *Fax:* (310) 274-6185
www.elsentlaw.com
sobel@elsentlaw.com
Peter Laird, Partner
William R. Sobel, Partner

Edwards Angell Palmer & Dodge L.L.P.
111 Huntington Ave., Boston, MA 02199
(617) 951-2233; *Fax:* (888) 325-9120
www.eapdlaw.com
smeredith@eapdlaw.com
Paulette Brown, Partner

Edwards Wildman
Mailing Address: 111 S. Wacker Dr., Suite 3000, Chicago, IL 60606
Second Address: 111 Huntington Avenue, Boston, MA 02199-7613
(312) 443-0700, (617) 239-0100; *Fax:* (312) 443-0336, (617) 227-4420
www.edwardswildman.com
rnielsen@edwardswildman.com
Alan J. Levin, Chairman
John T. Gosnell, Director of Administration
Rita Nielsen, Office Administrator
William R. Andrichik, Associate
Frank Blechschmidt, Associate
Edwards Wildman has once again earned a spot in the BTI Client Service A-Team list. This ranking identifies the top law firms for client service through a national survey of corporate counsel. Published by The BTI Consulting Group, theA-Team recognizes the law firms providing excellent client service to Fortune 1000 companies.

Elam & Burke, P.A.
Mailing Address: 251 E. Front St., Suite 300, Boise, ID 83702
Second Address: PO Box 1539, Boise, ID 83701
(208) 343-5454; *Fax:* (208) 384-5844
www.elamburke.com
eblaw@elamburke.com
Ryan P. Armbruster, Shareholder

Faegre & Benson, L.L.P.
Mailing Address: 801 Grand Ave., 33rd floor, Des Moines, IA 50309
Second Address: 311 S. Wacker Dr., Suite 4300, Chicago, IL 60606
(515) 248-9000, (800) 228-0836, (312) 212-6500; *Fax:* (515) 248-9010, (312) 212-6501
www.faegrebd.com
Andrew Anderson, Partner
Michael B. Abbott, Partner
Stephen Bennett, Partner
Kirk B. Bainbridge, Associate
Deborah L. Cairns, Partner

Farmer, Shirley Stewart
22545 Pleasant Dr., Apt 1, Richton Park, IL 60471
(347) 216-0874; *Fax:* (212) 787-6567
www.shirleystewartfarmeronline.com
shirlstewfar@gmail.com

Farrand, Cooper P.C.
235 Montgomery St., Suite 905, San Francisco, CA 94104
(415) 399-0600; *Fax:* (415) 677-2950
www.fcblaw.com
Stephen R. Farrand, Partner
Nancy A. Jarvis, Partner
Wayne B. Cooper, Of Counsel

Federal Communications Comission Public Safety & Homeland Security Bureau Public Safe
445 12th St., S.W., Washington, DC 20554
(202) 418-0680
kba@kba.org
Gary White, pres; Patti L. Pollen, exec asst.

Ferris & Britton
501 W Broadway, Suite 1450, San Diego, CA 92101
(619) 233-3131; *Fax:* (619) 232-9316
www.ferrisbritton.com
info@ferrisbritton.com
Lee Biddle, Attorney
Christopher Q. Britton, Attorney

Fine & Block
2060 Mt. Paran Rd. N.W., Suite 106, Atlanta, GA 30327
(404) 261-6800; *Fax:* (404) 261-6960
www.fineandblock.com
A. J. Block Jr., Attorney
Bret L. Block, Attorney
BERTRAM LEVY, Attorney
James F. Brown Jr., Attorney

Finkelstein, Thompson & Loughran
1077 30th St., NW, Suite 150, Washington, DC 20007
(202) 337-8000, (877) 337-1050; *Fax:* (202) 337-8090
www.finkelsteinthompson.com
contact@finkelsteinthompson.com
Mila F. Bartos, Partner
Alyssa T. Dang, Associate
Burton H. Finkelstein, Partner
Rosalee B.C. Thomas, Associate
Yodit H. Haile, Paralegal

Fleischman & Walsh, L.L.P.
1919 Pennsylvania Avenue, N.W., Suite 600, Washington, DC 20006-3420
(202) 939-7900; *Fax:* (202) 745-0916
fw@fw-law.com

Fletcher, Heald & Hildreth, P.L.C.
1300 N. 17th St., 11th Fl., Arlington, VA 22209
(703) 812-0400; *Fax:* (703) 812-0486
www.fhhlaw.com
Kathleen Victory, Attorney
Robert M. Winteringham, Attorney
Thomas J. Dougherty, Jr., Attorney

Foley & Lardner
Mailing Address: 150 E. Gilman St., Suite 5000, Madison, WI 53703-1482
Second Address: 111 Huntington Ave., Suite 2600, Boston, MA 02199-7610
(608) 257-5035, (617) 342-4000; *Fax:* (608) 258-4258, (617) 342-4001
www.foley.com
dwalsh@foleylaw.com
William L. Abalona, Partner
William J. Abraham Jr., Partner
Carlos J. Abarca, Partner
Sharon Meit Abrahams, National Director, Professional Development
Archana R. Acharya, Associate

Fowler, Measle & Bell
300 W. Vine St., Suite 600, Lexington, KY 40507-1751
(859) 252-6700; *Fax:* (859) 255-3735
www.fowlerlaw.com
fmb@fmb.com
Curt Graham, Attorney
Tia J. Comb, Attorney
Susan S. Kennedy, Attorney
Christina L.Vessels, Attorney
Eric M. Case, Attorney
Christopher G. Colson, Attorney

Fox & Film Entertainment
10201 W. Pico Blvd., Los Angeles, CA 90035
(310) 369-1000; *Fax:* (310) 369-3333
www.fox.com

Gammon & Grange, P.C.
Mailing Address: 8280 Greensboro Dr., 7th Fl., McLean, VA 22102
Second Address: 161 Fort Evans Rd, NE, Suite 345, Leesburg, VA 20176-4420
(703) 873-7349, (866) 896-7682, (703) 478-1895; *Fax:* (703) 761-5023
www.gg-law.com
awf@gg-law.com
Robert B. Adams, Attorney
A. Wray Fitch III, Attorney
James A. Gammon, Attorney
Gerorge R Grange II, Attorney
Carol L. Browne, Attorney

Gardere Wynne Sewell LLP
Mailing Address: 1601 Elm St., Thanksgiving Tower, Suite 3000, Dallas, TX 75201
Second Address: One American Center, Suite 3000, 600 Congress Ave., Austin, TX 78701
(214) 999-3000, (512) 542-7000; *Fax:* (214) 999-4667, (512) 542-7100
www.gardere.com
mwebb@gardere.com
Holland N. O'Neil, Chairman
Claude R. Treece, Chief Operating Partner
Scott Fletcher, Chief Financial Officer
Judy Vetkoetter, Executive Director
Ken Orgeron, Chief Information Officer
Shawn L. Adams, Chief Strategy And MarketingOfficer

Garvey, Schubert & Barer
Mailing Address: 100 Wall St., 20th Fl., New York, NY 10005-3708
Second Address: Flour Mill Building, 1000 Potomac St NW,Suite 200, Washington, DC 20007-3501
(212) 431-8700, (202) 965-7880; *Fax:* (212) 334-1278, (202) 965-1729
www.gsblaw.com
kdavis@gsblaw.com
Anne F. Preston, Chair & Managing Director (Seattle)
Lucinda D. Fernald, Of Counsel
1000 Potomac St. N.W., 5th Fl., Washington, DC
(202) 965-7880; *Fax:* (202) 965-1729
www.gsblaw
jking@gsblaw.com
Matthew R. Schneider, D.C. Mgng Dir
John Wells King, Counsel
599 Broadway, 10th Fl., New York, NY
(212) 431-8700; *Fax:* (212) 334-1278
www.gsblaw.com
Matthew R. Schneider, Ny Mgng Dir
121 S. W. Morrison St., Portland, OR 97204-3117
(503) 228-3939; *Fax:* (503) 226-0259
www.gsblaw.com
Larry Brant, Steve Connolly
Bob Weaver, Portland Mgmt Comm

Gary P. Schonman
445 12th St. S.W., Federal Communications Commision, Washington, DC 20554-0004
(202) 418-1795; *Fax:* (202) 418-2080
www.fcc.gov

Gibbs & Associates
150 York St., Suite 1810, Toronto, ON M5H 3S5
(416) 361-0024; *Fax:* (416) 361-1992
www.gibbslaw.ca
bhg1cg2@aol.com
Gary Gibbs, Founding Partner
Michelle Gibbs, Partner

Gibson, Dunn & Crutcher
Mailing Address: 333 S. Grand Ave., Suite 4600, Los Angeles, CA 90071-3197
Second Address: 1050 Connecticut Ave, NW, Washington, DC 20036-5306
(213) 229-7000, (202) 955-8500; *Fax:* (213) 229-7520, (202) 467-0539
www.gibsondunn.com
William S. Scherman, Lawyer
Thomas G. Hungar, Lawyer
Robert F. Serio, Lawyer
Alexander H. Southwell, Lawyer
Judith A. Lee, Lawyer
1050 Connecticut Ave. N.W., Suite 900, Washington, DC 20036-5320
(202) 955-8500
Jill Sterner, Chairman

Gold & Pyle
526 Superior Ave. E., 720 Leader Bldg., Cleveland, OH. 44114-1498
(216) 225-5075, (216) 870-6282; *Fax:* (216) 619-9006
jpyle@gp-lpa.com
Gerald S. Gold, Lawyer
John S. Pyle, Lawyer

Goldberg, Godles, Wiener & Wright
1229 19th St. N.W., Washington, DC 20036-2413
(202) 429-4900; *Fax:* (202) 429-4912
www.g2w2.com
Henry Goldberg, Founder
Joseph A. Godles, Partner
Jonathan L. Wiener, Partner
Henrietta Wright, Of Counsel

Golden & Golden, P.C.
Div/DBA: Attorneys and Counsellors At Law
10627 Jones St., Suite 101B, Fairfax, VA 22030
(703) 691-0117; *Fax:* (703) 691-1367
www.gglawva.com
k8los@aol.com
Richard A. Golden, Attorney
Stephanie Golden, Attorney

Gray & Robinson
Mailing Address: 301 E. Pine St. (Suite 1400), P.O Box 3068 (32802-3068), Orlando, FL 32801
Second Address: 401 E. Las Olas Blvd., Suite 1000, Fort Lauderdale, FL 33301
(407) 843-8880, (954) 761-8111; *Fax:* (407) 244-5690, (954) 761-8112
www.gray-robinson.com
biff.marshall@gray-robinson.com
Byrd F. Marshall Jr., President/Managing Director
William G. McCormick, Shareholder
Michael J. Canan, Shareholder
William A. Grimm, Of Counsel
Evan Appell, Senior Associate

Greensfelder, Hemker & Gale, P.C.
Mailing Address: 10 S. Broadway, Suite 2000, St. Louis, MO 63102
Second Address: 12 Wolf Creek Dr., Suite 100, Belleville, IL 62226
(314) 241-9090, (618) 257-7308; *Fax:* (314) 241-8624, (618) 257-7353
www.greensfelder.com
mlw@greensfelder.com
Sarah Lund Allen, Dir. Of Administration & Human Resources
J. Danielle Carr, Dir. Of Professional Development & Inclusion
Michael T. Andrews, Chief Marketing Officer

Greiter, Pegger, Kofler & Partner
Maria Theresien-Strasse 24, A-6020, Innsbruck, AT
43 512-57-1811; *Fax:* 43 512-5849-25, 43 512-5711-52
www.lawfirm.at/en/
greiter@lawfirm.at
Dr. Ivo Greiter, Lawyer
Prof. Dr. Franz Pegger, Lawyer
Dr. Stefan Kofler, Lawyer

Groveman, Amy S.
Cablevision Systems Corp., 111 Stewart Ave., Bethpage, NY 11714
(516) 803-2300; *Fax:* (516) 803-2575
www.cablevision.com
agrovema@cablevision.com
Charles F. Dolan, Chairman
James L. Dolan, CEO
Brian Sweeney, President, CFO
Kristin Dolan, COO
Tom Montegamo, EVP Programming
Gregg Seibert, Vice Chairman
Sandra Kapell, EVP, Human Resources & Administration
David Ellen, EVP &General Counsel

Hank J. Ratner, Vice Chairman
Lisa Rosenblum, EVP, Govt. & Public Affairs
Wilt Hildenbrand, Senior Advisor

Gullett, Sanford, Robinson & Martin
150 3rd Ave. S., Suite 1700, Nashville, TN 37201
(615) 244-4994; *Fax:* (615) 256-6339
www.gsrm.com
info@gsrm.com
Kim Williams, Operations Manager
A. Scott Derrick, Partner
Maureen E. Wylie, COO
Janet L. Summey, Dir. Of Marketing
Penelope Wilburn, Billing Coordinator
Gareth S. Aden, Partner

Gust Rosenfeld P.L.C.
Mailing Address: One E. Washington, Suite 1600, Phoenix, AZ 85004-2553
Second Address: One S. Church Ave, Suite 1900, Tuscon, AZ 85701-1627
(602) 257-7422, (520) 628-7070, (800) 258-4878; *Fax:* (602) 254-4878, (520) 624-3849
www.gustlaw.com
chauncey@gustlaw.com
Raul Abad, Attorney
Laura S. Blanco, Attorney
Michael H. Bate, Attorney
Kyle B. Bate, Attorney

Handman, Stanley H.
10160 Cielo Dr., Beverly Hills, CA 90210-2037
(310) 276-7503; *Fax:* (310) 276-1559

Hansen, Jacobson, Teller, Hoberman, Newman, Warren & Sloan, L.L.P.
450 N. Roxbury Dr., 8th Fl., Beverly Hills, CA 90210-4222
(310 271-8777; *Fax:* (310) 726-8310
www.hjth.com
sdecker@hjth.com
Stewart Brookman, Attorney
Dan Fox, Attorney
Tom Hansen, Attorney
Jason Hendler, Attorney

Harvard & Kaitcer, LLP
1305 W Magnolia Ave, Suite A, Fort Worth, TX 76104
(817) 335-4911; *Fax:* (817) 870-2631
Michael Kaitcer, Partner

Head, Johnson & Kachigian
228 W. 17th Pl., Tulsa, OK 74119
(918) 587-2000, (800) 627-4323; *Fax:* (918) 584-1718
www.hjklaw.com
hjk@law.com
Donna Purdom-Hantwerker, Office Manager
Tammy Hamm, Sr. Paralegal
Steven R. Tollette, Of Counsel
Mark G. Kachigian, Managing Attorney
Shawn M. Dellegar, Shareholder

Hearn, Edward R. A Professional Law Corporation
Div/DBA: (formerly Hearn, Edward R)
111 N. Market St., Suite 300, San Jose, CA 95113-1116
(408) 418-4630; *Fax:* (408) 418-4631
www.internetmedialaw.com
nedhearnml@aol.com
Edward R. Hearn, Attorney

Heller Ehrman LLP
PO Box 351, Pinole, CA 94564-0351
(650) 324-7000; *Fax:* (650) 324-0638
www.hellerehrman.com
Shelley Salinero, Attorney

Hendrickson, Thomas
203 Alderwood Dr., Gaithersburg, MD 20878
(301) 519-0085
www.spacecast.com
space@spacecast.com
Cable-delivered, national, 24 hour, English-language Science Fiction, Science Fact, Speculation and Fantasy channel. The program mix includes memorable sci-fi classics and current popular series, plus feature films, documentaries, specialsand daily original productions with a tilt to information and new age speculation.

Hewitt Katz Stepp and Wright Attorney at Law
Mailing Address: 945 E. Paces Ferry Rd., Resurgens Plaza, Ste. 2230, Atlanta, GA 30326
Second Address: 1 decatur Town Center, Suite 300, 150 E. Ponce de Leon Ave., Decatur, GA 30030
(404) 240-0101, (877) 343-9598; *Fax:* (404) 240-0401
www.robertnkatz.com
katzleads@thekatzlawfirm.net
Robert N. Katz, Attorney
Lyn B. Dodson, Attorney
Briant G. Mildenhall, Attorney
Jennifer N. Cornelius, Attorney

Hinshaw & Culbertson
Mailing Address: 333 S. 7th St., Suite 2000, Minneapolis, MN 55402
Second Address: 2375 East Camelback Road, Suite 750, Phoenix, AZ 85016
(612) 333-3434, (602) 631-4400; *Fax:* (612) 334-8888
www.hinshawlaw.com
Kevin Joseph Burke, Chairman
Paul Boken, Executive Managing Director
Robert P. Johnson, Chief Financial Officer
Hinshaw & Culbertson LLP opened its office in Minneapolis in 1997. Attorneys here provide a full-service practice to businesses, banks, insurers, local government, nonprofit and for-profit corporations and individuals. The attorneys herehandle both litigation and corporate transactions.

Hogan Lovells US LLP
Mailing Address: Columbia Square, 555 13th St. N.W., Washington, DC 20004
Second Address: 875 3rd Ave., New York, NY 10022
(202) 637-5600, (212) 918-3000; *Fax:* (202) 637-5910, (212) 918-3100
www.hoganlovells.com
Jonathan L. Abram, Of Counsel
Ranee Adipat, Associate
Karla J. Aghedo, Associate
Stuart M. Altman, Partner
Tifarah Roberts Allen, Associate
1040 Brussels

Holland & Knight LLC
Mailing Address: 131 S. Dearborn St., 30th Flr., Chicago, IL 60603
Second Address: 1201 West Peachtree Street, One Atlantic Center, Suite 2000, Atlanta, GA 30309
(312) 263-3600, (404) 817-8500; *Fax:* (312) 578-6666, (404) 881-0470
www.hklaw.com
steven.elrod@hklaw.com
Steven M. Elrod, Executive Partner
Mary Ann Whitehall, Business Manager
J. Allen Maines, Executive Partner
Theresa C. Turner, Office Coordinator
Holland & Knight is a global law firm with more than 1,000 lawyers and other professionals in 18 U.S. offices, as well as Abu Dhabi, Beijing, Bogot and Mexico City. Our lawyers provide representation in litigation, business, real estate andgovernmental law. Interdisciplinary practice groups and industry-based teams provide clients with access to attorneys throughout the firm, regardless of location.

Holland & Knight LLP
Mailing Address: 800 17th St, NW, Suite 1100, Washington, DC 20006
Second Address: 1201 W. Peachtree St., One Atlantic center (suite 2000), Atlanta, GA 30309
(202) 955-3000, (404) 817-8500; *Fax:* (202) 955-5564, (404) 881-0470
www.hklaw.com
Paul J. Kiernan, Executive Partner
J. Allen Maines, Executive Partner

Ice Miller LLP
Mailing Address: One American Sq., Suite 2900, Indianapolis, IN 46282-0200
Second Address: 20 F St.,NW, Suite 850, Washington, DC 20001
(317) 236-2100, (202) 824-8666; *Fax:* (317) 236-2219, (202) 824-8667
www.icemiller.com
info@icemiller.com
Kris Dawley, Partner
John M. Daniels, Chief Financial Officer
Robert Gauss, Partner
Brenda Horn, Partner

Inghram & Inghram
529 Hampshire St., Suite 409, Quincy, IL 62301
(217) 222-7420; *Fax:* (217) 222-1653
www.inghramlaw.com
info@inghramlaw.com
John T. Inghram IV, Attorney
James R. Inghram, Attorney

Irwin, Campbell & Tannenwald, P.C.
1730 Rhode Island Ave. N.W. #200, Washington, DC 20036-3120
(202) 728-0400; *Fax:* (202) 728-0354
www.ictpc.com

Isaacman, Kaufman & Painter
10250 Constellation Boulevard, Suite 2900, Los Angeles, CA 90067
(310) 881-6800; *Fax:* (310) 881-6801
www.ikplaw.com
info@ikplaw.com
Alan Isaacman, Attorney
Michael Painter, Attorney
Chuck Hurewitz, Attorney
Anderw Zucker, Attorney
William S. Cohen, Attorney
Jack G. Cairl, Attorney
Founded in 1993, Isaacman, Kaufman & Painter PC ("IKP") is a law firm specializing in civil litigation, entertainment, business, real estate, intellectual property ("IP") and tax and estate planning. The attorneys of IKP have providedfirst-class legal services to its clients, including successfully arguing a landmark First Amendment case before the United States Supreme Court.

Jackson & Campbell, P.C.
Mailing Address: 1120 20th St. N.W., 1 Lafayette Centre, South Tower, Washington, DC 20036-3437
Second Address: 77 South Washington St., Suite 304, Rockville, MD 20850
(202) 457-1600, (800) 645-8498, (301) 340-0450; *Fax:* (202) 457-1678
www.jackscamp.com
jmatteo@jackscamp.com
John J. Matteo, Business Law Attorney
David H. Cox, Business Law Attorney
Michele L. Dearing, Employment Law Attorney
Robert N. Kelly, General Litigation & Trial Practice Attorney
Arthur D. Burger, General Litigation & Trial PracticeAttorney

Jacobs & Associates
The International Trade Center, 1300 Pennsylvania Ave NW Suite 700, Washington, DC 20004
(202) 204-3060; *Fax:* (202) 789-7349
www.regulatoryreform.com
janda@regulatoryreform.com
Fran Wall, Business Manager
Scott Jacobs, Managing Director
Michael Griffin, Senior Director
Dr. Cesar Cordova, senior director

Jeffer, Mangels, Butler & Marmaro LLP
Mailing Address: 1900 Ave. of the Stars, 7th Fl., Los Angeles, CA 90067
Second Address: 3 Park Plaza, #1100, Irvine, CA 92614
(310) 203-8080, (949) 623-7200; *Fax:* (310) 203-0567, (949) 623-7202
www.jmbm.com
Bruce P. Jeffer, Managing Partner
Burton A. Mitchell, Asst. Managing Partner
Joel J. Berman, Partner
William F. Capps, Chairman, Corporate Development
Rod S. Berman, Chairman, Intellectual Property Dept.
Robert E. Mangels,Chairman, Litigation Dept.

Jenner & Block
Mailing Address: 1099 New York Ave., NW, Suite 900, Washington, DC 20001-4412
Second Address: 353 N. Clark St., Chicago, IL 60654-3456
(202) 639-6000, (312) 222-9350; *Fax:* (202) 639-6066, (312) 527-0484
www.jenner.com
mstull@jenner.com
Philip L. Harris, Partner
Steven M. Siros, Attorney
Erica Ross, Associate
Colleen M. Reddan, Staff Attorney

John D. Pellegrin P.C.
10515 Dominion Valley Dr., Fairfax Station, VA 22039 US
(703) 250-1595; *Fax:* (703) 250-1597
www.lawpell.com
jp@lawpell.com
John D. Pellegrin, P.C., Attorney

Johnson, Andrea L.
225 Cedar St., California Western School of Law, San Diego, CA 92101
(619) 525-0391; *Fax:* (619) 696-9999
www.cwsl.edu
alj@cwsl.edu
Andrea L. Johnson, Director, I.P., Technology & Comm.

PROFESSIONAL SERVICES

Jones, Day
51 Louisiana Ave. N. W., Washington, DC 20001-2113
(202) 879-3939; *Fax:* (202) 626-1700
www.jonesday.com
Gregory M. Shumaker, Partner

K&L Gates LLP
Mailing Address: One Lincoln Street, State Street Financial Center, Boston, MA 02111-2950
Second Address: 599 Lexington Avenue, New York, NY 10022-6030
(617) 261-3100, (617) 951-9230 , (212) 536-3900; *Fax:* (617) 261-3175, (212) 536-3901
www.klgates.com
David M. Aceto, Of Counsel
Robert F. Ambrose, Of Counsel
George P. Barbatsuly, Of Counsel
C. Grainger Bowman, Of Counsel
K&L Gates LLP comprises more than 2,000 lawyers who practice in 48 offices located on five continents: Anchorage, Austin, Beijing, Berlin, Boston, Brisbane, Brussels, Charleston, Charlotte, Chicago, Dallas, Doha, Dubai, Fort Worth,Frankfurt, Harrisburg, Hong Kong, Houston, London, Los Angeles, Melbourne, Miami, Milan, Moscow, Newark, New York, Orange County, Palo Alto, Paris, Perth, Pittsburgh, Portland, Raleigh, Research Triangle Park, San Diego, San Francisco, Sao Paulo,Seattle, Seoul, Shanghai, Singapore, Spokane, Sydney, Taipei, Tokyo, Warsaw, Washington and Wilmington.

Kass, Mitek & Kass
1050 17th St. N.W., Suite 1100, Washington, DC 20036-5596
(202) 659-6500; *Fax:* (202) 293-2608
www.kmklawyers.com
John H. Brillian, Attorney
Anthony R. Champ, Attorney
Benny L. Kass, Attorney
Brian L. Kass, Attorney

Katten Muchin Rosenman LLP
2900 K Street, NW, North Tower - Suite 200, Washington, DC 20007-5118
(202) 625-3500; *Fax:* (202) 298-7570
www.kattenlaw.com
Katten is a firm of first choice for clients seeking sophisticated, high-value legal services in the United States and abroad.

Kay, Sheldon L.
30445 Northwestern Hwy., Suite 320, Farmington Hills, MI 48334
(248) 539-1111; *Fax:* (248) 539-1114
www.sheldonkaylaw.com
info@sheldonkaylaw.com
Sheldon kay, Attorney
Elizabeth Quinto, Associate Attorney
Lisa Mazur, Office Manager & Head Paralegal

Kaye, Scholer, L.L.P.
Mailing Address: 901 15th St. N.W., The McPherson Bldg, Washington, DC 20005-2327
Second Address: 3 First National Plaza, 70 W. Madison St., Suite 4200, Chicago, IL 60602-4231
(202) 682-3500, (312) 583-2300; *Fax:* (202) 682-3580, (312) 583-2360
www.kayescholer.com
jshrinsky@kayescholer.com
Claudia Higgins, Office Managing Partner
D. Tyler Nurnberg, Office Managing Partner

Keller & Heckman
Mailing Address: 1001 G St. N.W., Suite 500 W, Washington, DC 20001
Second Address: One Embarcadero Center, Suite 2110, San Francisco, CA 94111
(202) 434-4100, (415) 948-2800; *Fax:* (202) 434-4646, (415) 948-2808
www.khlaw.com
info@khlaw.com
Douglas J. Behr, Partner/ Advertising and Promotion
Melvin S. Drozen, Partner/ Advertising and Promotion
Leslie T. Krasny, Partner/ Advertising and Promotion

Kelley, Drye Collier Shannon
3050 K St. N.W., Suite 400, Washington, DC 20007
(202) 342-8400; *Fax:* (202) 342-8451
www.kelleydrye.com
Joan Galvin, Senior Advisor

Kilpatrick Townsend & Stockton LLP
Mailing Address: 1100 Peachtree Street NE, Suite 2800, Atlanta, GA 30309-4528
Second Address: 1450 Greene St Suite 230, Enterprise Mill, Augusta, GA 30901
(404) 815-6500, (706) 724-2622; *Fax:* (404) 815-6555, (706) 823-4204
www.kilpatricktownsend.com
Paguggia@kilpatricktownsend.com
Susan M. Spaeth, Managing Firm Partner
James G. Gilliland Jr., Litigation Dept. Chair
Wab P. Kadaba, I.P. Dept. Chair
Kilpatrick Townsend attorneys are fully engaged in the success of the firm's clients. We deliver results-oriented counsel for corporations at all stages of the growth cycle, from the challenging demands of financial transactions andsecurities to the disciplines of intellectual property management. A close collaboration between the firm's practice areas ensures that we are well-positioned to serve all of our clients' needs.

King & Ballow
Mailing Address: 315 Union St., Suite 1100, Nashville, TN 37201
Second Address: 6540 Lusk Boulevard, Suite 250, San Diego, CA 92121
(615) 259-3456, (858) 597-6000; *Fax:* (615) 254-7907
www.kingballow.com
Larry D. Crabtree, Partner
Robert L. Ballow, Partner
Richard C. Lowe, Partner
King & Ballow's attorneys counsel clients during administrative investigations, provide representation in administrative litigation before agency hearing offers and administrative law judges, including Postal rate proceedings, and seekjudicial review of administrative findings and orders.

Kleinberg Lange Cuddy & Klein LLP
11111 Santa Monica Blvd, Suite 1750, Los Angeles, CA 90025
(310) 286-9696; *Fax:* (310) 277-7145, (310) 286-6445
www.kleinberglange.com
Candace Carlo, Partner
Christine Cuddy, Partner
We provide advice and counsel to a broad range of clients who create, produce, finance, distribute and render services in the production, marketing and distribution of entertainment product.

Kraditor & Haber, P.C.
245 5th Ave, Suite 1001, New York, NY 10016
(212) 768-2100; *Fax:* (212) 768-2450
www.fcc.gov

Lang, Richert & Patch
5200 N. Palm Ave., Fourth Floor, Fresno, CA 93704
(559) 228-6700; *Fax:* (559) 228-6727
www.lrplaw.net
fhl@lrplaw.net
Frank H. Lang, Attorney
Robert L. Patch, II, Attorney
Victoria J. Salisch, Attorney
Rene Lastreto II, Attorney
Charles Trudrung Taylor, Attorney
Mark L. Creede, Attorney
Lang, Richert & Patch has developed an outstanding reputation in the community for high quality, results-oriented legal services. Lang, Richert & Patch has been recognized by Martindale-Hubbel as a "Firm of Distinction" the highest honorbestowed by the organization.

Latham & Watkins LLP
Mailing Address: 555 11th St. N.W., Suite 1000, Washington, DC 20004-1304
Second Address: 200 Clarendon Street, John Hancock Tower, 27th Floor, Boston, MA 2116
(202) 637-2200, (617) 948-6000; *Fax:* (202) 637-2201, (617) 948-6001
www.lw.com
alice.fisher@lw.com
LeeAnn Black, Chief Operating Officer
Kathryn A. Harrington, Associate
A client-first attitude backed by industry know-how, bet-the-company litigation strength, regulatory insights and powerhouse corporate capabilities - these are the hallmarks of Latham & Watkins' Washington, D.C. office.

Law Firm of Rosalind Lichter
375 Greenwich Street, # 712, New York, NY 10013
(212) 941-4075; *Fax:* (212) 941-4076
www.rlichterlaw.com
rl@rlichterlaw.com
Rosalind Lichter, Business Lawyer

Law Office of Dan J. Alpert
2120 N. 21st Rd., Arlington, VA 22201
(703) 243-8690; *Fax:* (703) 243-8692
www.commlaw.tv
dja@commlaw.tv

Law Offices of Edward L. Weidenfeld
888 17th St. N.W., Suite 1250, Washington, DC 20006
(202) 785-2143; *Fax:* (202) 452-8938
www.weidenfeldlaw.com
edward@weidenfeldlaw.com

Law Offices of George E. Darby
Box 893010, Mililani, HI 96789-3010
(808) 626-1300, (800) 583-3369; *Fax:* (808) 626-1350
George E. Darby, Patent Attorney

Law Offices of Jeff Berke
7236 Owensmouth Ave, Suite D, Canoga Park, CA 91303
(818) 804-5729
www.berkelawoffices.com
info@berkelawoffices.com
Robert G. Berke, Owner, Sr. Attorney

Law Offices of Jeffrey L. Graubart
800 East Colorado Boulevard, Suite 840, Pasadena, CA 91101-2173
(626) 304-2800; *Fax:* (626) 381-9601
www.entertainmentlaw.la
info@jlgraubart.com
Engrg svcs: AM, FM, TV, translators, LPTV.

Law Offices of Joel Weisman, P.C.
1901 Raymond Dr., Suite 6, Northbrook, IL 60062
(847) 400-5900; *Fax:* (847) 400-5534
www.weismanmedialaw.com
joel@weismanmedialaw.com
We're a full service law firm specializing in quality legal services to the Media (television anchors, reporters, and producers; radio personalities; columnists; and authors), as well as to individuals and businesses.

Law Offices of Lee Sacks
23852 Pacific Coast Hwy., Suite 157, Malibu, CA 90265-4879
(310) 451-3113; *Fax:* (310) 451-0089

Law Offices of Richard J. Hayes
27 Water's Edge Dr., Lincolnville, ME 04849
(207) 236-3333, (540) 270-9795; *Fax:* (202) 478-0048
www.rjhayes.com
mail@rjhayes.com
Richard J. Hayes, Jr., Attorney At Law

Law Offices of William D. Silva
, PO Box 1121, Stevensville, MD 21666
(443) 249-0109; *Fax:* (443) 249-0140
www.wmsilvalaw.com
bill@wmsilvalaw.com
William D. Silva, Attorney
This firm was established in 1993, in part the successor to the firm of Blair, Joyce & Silva. The founder, Bill Silva, has over thirty years experience both at the Federal Communications Commission and in private practice. While at theCommission, Mr. Silva served as Senior Trial Attorney and as Assistant Chief of the Enforcement Division of the Broadcast Bureau. In the private sector, Mr. Silva represents broadcasters, and wireless and satellite companies before the Commission andthe federal courts. This representation includes all aspects of licensing and enforcement matters, as well as business formation, acquisition of capital and the purchase and sale of assets.

Leibowitz & Associates, P.A.
2 S Biscayne Blvd., Suite 2460, Miami, FL 33137
(305) 530-1322; *Fax:* (305) 530-9417
ebuza@broadlaw.com
Matthew L. Leibowitz, Esq., Founder
Joseph A. Belisle, III, Esq, Attorney
Mark P. Lesniak, Attorney
Robert C. Allen, Esq., Attorney
Matthew L. Leibowitz, Founder and Principal
The Law Firm of Leibowitz & Associates was formed in 1979, originally called the Law Office of Matthew L. Leibowitz, PA. Since that time, it is the only full time law firm in the State of Florida that exclusively practices communications /telecommunications law.

Leopold, Petrich & Smith
2049 Century Park E., Suite 3110, Los Angeles, CA 90067
(310) 277-3333; *Fax:* (310) 277-7444
www.lpsla.com
vcox@lpsla.com
Vincent Cox, Member/Attorney
Jamie L. Frieden, Associate
Donald R. Gordon, Member/Attorney
Robert S. Gutierrez, Member/Attorney
Daniel M. Mayeda, Member
Eva Neuberg, Associate

Leopold, Petrich & Smith is a boutique Los Angeles law firm whose attorneys are leading experts in the fields of intellectual property, media and entertainment law.

Lerman Senter PLLC
Div/DBA: (Formerly Leventhal Senter & Lerman PLLC)
2000 K St. N.W., Suite 600, Washington, DC 20006
(202) 429-8970; *Fax:* (202) 293-7783
www.lermansenter.com
info@lermansenter.com
Philip A. Bonomo, Member/Attorney
Sally A. Buckman, Member/Attorney
Dennis P. Corbett, Member/Attorney
Laura M. Berman, Associate
Kevin M. Cookler, Of Counsel
Lerman Senter provides comprehensive, practical legal solutions to meet the diverse regulatory, transactional and business needs of communications and media businesses.

Levinsohn Associates, P.C.
1325 Ave. of the Americas, Floor 27, New York, NY 10019
(212) 262-1000; *Fax:* (212) 262-5022
www.entlawfirm.com

Lewis, Lewis & Ferraro
Mailing Address: 28 N. Main St., Suite 202, West Hartford, CT 06107
Second Address: 5 Maple Street, Bristol, CT 06010
(860) 881-2719, (866) 881-2719; *Fax:* (860) 521-4500
www.lewislewisferraro.com
attorney@lewislewisferraro.com
Scott F. Lewis, Attorney
Mark J. Ferraro, Attorney/Partner
With nearly 60 years of combined experience, the attorneys at Lewis, Lewis & Ferraro, L.L.C., provide knowledgeable and skilled representation to clients facing a range of legal issues. Attorneys Scott F. Lewis and Mark J. Ferraro, alongwith our legal staff, take a team approach to fight for your objectives, whether that involves a serious accident, ending a marriage, drafting a will or other legal issues.

Loeb & Loeb L.L.P.
Mailing Address: 345 Park Ave., New York, NY 10154
Second Address: 10100 Santa Monica Boulevard, Suite 2200, Los Angeles, CA 90067
(212) 407-4000, (310) 282-2000; *Fax:* (212) 407-4990, (310) 282-2200
www.loeb.com
jmanton@loeb.com
David P. Ansel, Partner
Kenneth A. Adler, Partner
Roger M. Arar, Partner
Norwood P. Beveridge Jr., Partner
Michael D. Beck, Partner
Loeb & Loeb LLP is a multi-service law firm with more than 300 attorneys and offices in Los Angeles, New York, Chicago, Nashville, Washington, DC, Beijing and Hong Kong. The firm focuses on select core industries and practice areas, ratherthan endeavoring to be all things to all clients.
10100 Santa Monica Blvd, Los Angeles, CA 90067-4003
(310) 282-2475; *Fax:* (310) 282-2192
Mickey Mayerson, Chairman
1000 Wilshire Blvd, Los Angeles, CA 90017-2457
(213) 688-3400; *Fax:* (213) 688-3460

Lommen Abdo, Cole, King & Stageberg, P. A.
Mailing Address: 1000 International Centre, 920 Second Ave. S., Minneapolis, MN 55402
Second Address: 210 Grandview Professional Building, 400 S. 2nd St., Hudson, WI 54016
(612) 339-8131, (800) 752-4297, (715) 386-8217; *Fax:* (612) 339-8064, (715) 386-8219
www.Lommen.com
Sandy Bassamore, Network Administrator
Jean Mykleby, Receptionist
Brad Wicklund, Office Administrator

Lowndes, Drosdick, Doster, Kantor & Reed, P.A.
Mailing Address: 215 North Eola Drive, Orlando, FL 32801
Second Address: 450 South Orange Avenue, Suite 200, Orlando, FL 32801-3344
(407) 843-4600, (800) 356-6818
www.lowndes-law.com
Info@lowndes-law.com
John F. Lowndes, Founding Partner
William T. Dymond Jr., CEO & President
William A. Beckett, Shareholder
Matthew G. Brenner, Shareholder
Crystal Espinosa Buit, Senior Associate
Dale A. Burket, Shareholder
Lyndon Carter,Associate
Founded in Orlando, Florida in 1969, Lowndes, Drosdick, Doster, Kantor & Reed, P.A. is, according to the Orlando Business Journal, the largest law firm in Central Florida currently with approximately 100 attorneys.

Lukas, Nace, Gutierrez & Sachs Chartered
8300 Greensboro Drive, Suite 1200, McLean, VA 22102
(703) 584-8678; *Fax:* (703) 584-8696
www.fcclaw.com
info@fcclaw.com
Russell D. Lukas, Partner
David L. Nace, Partner
Thomas Gutierrez, Partner
Elizabeth Sachs, Partner
David Lafuria, Partner
Pamela Gist, Principal
The attorneys and engineers of LNGS are tightly focused on the wireless industry, providing guidance in a complex and dynamic regulatory environment. Within those rules we identify opportunities to build innovative business models whileensuring compliance.

Madigan & Getzendanner
30 N. LaSalle St., Suite 3906, Chicago, IL 60602
(312) 346-4321; *Fax:* (312) 346-5619
www.madigetz.com
info@madigetz.com
Michael J. Madigan, Principal
Vincent J. Getzendanner, Principal
Harold J. Hicks, Attorney
Jeffrey A. Holland, Attorney
Michael C. Prinzi, Attorney
Robert E. Welsh, Attorney
Founded in 1972, Madigan & Getzendanner specializes in ad valorem real estate taxation. It is one of the premier firms in this practice, providing legal representation at every stage of the tax assessment appeal process to a wide spectrum ofsignificant properties situated in the Greater Chicagoland area.

Magee Law Firm, PLLC
6845 Elm St., Suite 515, McLean, VA 22101
(703) 356-7500; *Fax:* (703) 356-6863
www.mageelawfirm.com
jmagee@mageelawfirm.com
Corinne J. Magee, Attorney
James E. Magee, Attorney
Kathryn D. Leckey, Attorney
The Magee Law Firm was formed in 2003 with a commitment to its clients to provide hands-on, responsive and personalized services. It intentionally has remained small to assure that each client receives the individualized attention he or shedeserves. The firm's criminal practice lawyers offer years of experience trying cases throughout Northern Virginia, including Arlington, Fairfax, Loudoun and Prince William Counties, the Cities of Fairfax, Falls Church and Alexandria, and the Townsof Leesburg, Herndon and Vienna.

The Marshall Firm
302 N. Market, Suite #510, Dallas, TX 75202
(214) 742-4800; *Fax:* (214) 452-9064
www.marshall-firm.com
Richard Neely, CFO

Mary A. McReynolds, P.C.
1250 Connecticut Avenue N.W., Suite 200, Washington, DC 20036-1830
(202) 261-3547; *Fax:* (202) 261-3554
www.maryamcreynolds.com
Mary A. McReynolds, Attorney
The firm routinely addresses such matters as strategic planning; corporate governance, law and finance; taxation; labor; intellectual property; grant management and oversight; legislation; local, state and federal governmental regulation;and church canon law; and handles highly complex multi-jurisdictional litigation, including oversight of local counsel and of substantive and procedural matters. The firm is listed in the Martindale-Hubbell Bar Register of Preeminent Lawyers.

McDonald, Hopkins, L.P.A.
Mailing Address: 600 Superior Ave. E., Suite 2100, Cleveland, OH 44114
Second Address: 300 N. LaSalle Street, Suite 2100, Chicago, IL 60654
(216) 348-5400, (312) 280-0111; *Fax:* (216) 348-5474, (312) 280-8232
www.mcdonaldhopkins.com
Charles B. Zellmer, Chair, Buisness Law Service
Carl J. Grassi, President
Stephen M. Gross, Co-Chair, Buiness reconstruction service
Jeffrey P. Consolo, Member; Chair, Tax And Benefits Department
David B. Cupar, Member; Chair,Intellectual Property Department
John T. Metzger, Managing Member
Our comprehensive legal services are provided by teams of specialized attorneys and professionals who recognize that clients expect us to understand the complexities of their business or individual needs. Our service and industry specialtiesare designed to meet the growing challenges our clients face in an increasingly competitive environment. We approach every day with an entrepreneurial spirit and keen insight that enable us to furnish enhanced value.

Mensch, Linda Susan
161 N. Clark St., Suite 4300, Chicago, IL 60601-3315
(312) 602-5049; *Fax:* (312) 698 7449
Linda Mensch, Entertainment Lawyer
The Law Offices of Linda S. Mensch provides extensive services to individuals interested in the entertainment industry on multiple levels. Our offerings are as follows: Entertainment Law,Internet Law and Digital RightsManagement,Intellectual Property,Probate Contracts and Transactional Law

Messerli & Kramer
Mailing Address: 100 South Fifth Stree, 1400 Fifth Street Towers, Minneapolis, MN 55402-1217
Second Address: 525 Park Street, Suite 130, Saint Paul, MN 55103
(612) 672-3600, (651) 228-9757; *Fax:* (612) 672-3777, (651) 228-9787
www.messerlikramer.com
djohnson@mandklaw.com
Mary A. Anderson, Paralegal
Paul W. Anderson, Attorney
John F. Apitz, Attorney
Lisa M. Ashley, Attorney
John R. Beattie, Attorney
Messerli & Kramer consists of ten practice areas in three unique - yet complementary - divisions, including banking and finance, corporate and general business law, real estate, business litigation, collections, divorce and family law,employment, estate planning, government relations and intellectual property. We represent a variety of clients, from large corporations and banks, to closely-held entrepreneurial businesses, to individuals seeking divorce and family law or estateplanning services.

Miller, Balis and O'Neil
1015 15th St., NW, 12th Floor, Washington, DC 20005
202.753.3400; *Fax:* 202.296.0166
John Michael Adragna, Principals
Sean T. Beeny, Principals
Barry Cohen, Counsel
Kevin J. Conoscenti, Associates
Jeffrey K. Janicke, Associates

Miller, Canfield, Paddock & Stone, P.L.C.
Mailing Address: 150 W Jefferson Ave., Suite 2500, Detroit, MI 48226
Second Address: 101 North Main Street, 7th Floor, Ann Arbor, MI 48104
(313) 963-6420, (734) 663-2445; *Fax:* (313) 496-7500, (734) 747-7147
www.millercanfield.com
houser@millercanfield.com
David A. Robson, COO
Elizabeth K. Needleman, Director of Administrative/Human Resources
Gayla M. Houser, Director of Business Development
David R. Hoin, Director of Finance
N. Clark Campbell, Director of Information Technology
Catherine R. Mulla, Director of Library Services
Olivia Deng, Global Business Manager
Founded in 1852 in the United States, Miller Canfield was the first in Michigan to expand internationally by opening offices in Canada, Mexico, Poland and China. With a global presence and clients and connections around the world, we arewhere you are—and need to be to help you meet your goals.

Mintz, Levin, Cohn, Ferris, Glovsky & Popeo, P.C.
Mailing Address: 701 Pennsylvania Ave. N.W., Suite 900, Washington, DC 20004
Second Address: One Financial Center, Boston, MA 02111
(202) 434-7300, (617) 542-6000; *Fax:* (202) 434-7400, (617) 542-2241
www.mintzlevin.com
dlove@mintz.com
R. Robert Popeo, Chairman
David A. Ballinger, Chief Operating Officer
Alan M. Hertz, Director of Operations
Andrew R. Urban, Vice Chairman
Brian K. Mantarian, Director of Finance
Jon Hulak, Director Of Pricing & Client Service
Robert I. Bodian, Managing Member
Amy M. Fowler, Chief Marketing Officer

Our attorneys are no-nonsense, get-to-the-root-of-the-problem kind of people. If there's a faster way to get there, we'll find it. It's our job to give you clear answers and sound solutions.
One Financial Center, Boston, MA
(617) 542-6000; *Fax:* (617) 542-2241
Irwin Heller, Chairman

Mirowski & Associates
757 W. Ivy St., San Diego, CA 92101
(619) 702-5300; *Fax:* (619) 702-4666
www.mirlaw.com
pmirowski@mirlaw.com
Paul J. Mirowski, Attorney
Mirowski & Associates are committed to providing aggressive representation to businesses and residents of the San Diego and Southern California regions. For more than 20 years, Mirowski & Associates have assisted our clients in achievingoptimum results by goal oriented, cost effective planning & problem solving and tough-minded negotiation. However, when logic fails, we can back you up with 20 years of litigation experience.

Mitchell Silberberg & Knupp
Mailing Address: 11377 W. Olympic Blvd., Los Angeles, CA 90064
Second Address: 1818 N St., NW, 8th Floor, Washington, DC 20036
(310) 312-2000, (202) 355-7900; *Fax:* (310) 312-3100, (202) 355-7899
www.msk.com
info@msk.com
Kevin E. Gaut, Chairman
Dale Nohre, Dir. Of Operations & Facilities
Nimish Patel, Vice Chairman
Thomas Edwards, Executive Director
Won Me Park, Dir. Of hR & Attorney Recruiting
Jessica Pantukh, Dir. Of Marketing
Rebecca Sattin,Manager of Information Systems
Carolyn A. Pratt, Dir. Of Library Services

Mitchell, Charles D.
Mailing Address: 1601 N. Frontage Rd., Suite F, Vicksburg, MS 39180
Second Address: PO Box 821668, Vicksburg, MS 39182
(601) 636-4545, EXT. 123; *Fax:* (601) 634-0897
www.vicksburgpost.com
ads@vicksburgpost.com
Jimmy Clark, General manager
Becky Chandler, Director of sales & marketing
Paul Barry, Managing editor
Stacey Hartley, Circulation Manager
Linda Martin, Business Office
Angela Ross, Advertising
David Girard, Creative Services
The basic premise of this family newspaper is not lost in gigabytes and a tide of megahertz. Your life is molded by the environment you live in, and it has never been more important that you know what is happening in it ... that, dearreaders, is our commitment to you.

Morrison & Foerster L.L.P.
Mailing Address: 2000 Pennsylvania Ave. N.W., Suite 6000, Washington, DC 20006-1888
Second Address: 370 Seventeenth Street, 5200 Republic Plaza, Denver, CO 80202-5638
(202) 887-1500 / (303) 592-1500; *Fax:* (202) 887-0763, (202) 887-0764, (303) 592-1510, (3
www.mofo.com
lamii@mofo.com
Pat Cavaney, Chief Operating Officer
Kelly M. Brown, Director of Client Relations
Janet Stone Herman, Director of Professional Development
Eric R. Roberts, Director of Forensic Accounting Services
Tanisha M. Little, Senior Manager -Knowledge Management
With more than 1,000 lawyers in 16 offices in key technology and financial centers in the United States, Europe and Asia, our clients include some of the largest financial institutions, investment banks, and Fortune 100, technology and lifescience companies.

Moss & Barnett, A Professional Assn
150 S 5th Street, Suite 1200, Minneapolis, MN 55402
(612) 877-5000; *Fax:* (612) 877-5999
www.lawmoss.com
contact@lawmoss.com
Dave F. Senger, Chairman of the Board
Kevin M. Busch, Chief Operating Officer and Director
Thomas J. Shroyer, President and Chief Executive Officer
Richard J. Johnson, Atttorney
Brian T. Grogan, Attorney
Timothy L. Gustin,Attorney
James F. Baldwin, Attorney
Moss & Barnett has helped protect the intellectual property rights of entrepreneurs across the world. We provide forward-thinking and team-based custom counsel that keeps clients in business, financial, technology, and professional servicescompetitive in the digitally driven marketplace.

Myman, Abell, Fineman, Greenspan & Light
11601 Wilshire Blvd., Suite 2200, Los Angeles, CA 90025-1758
(310) 231-0800; *Fax:* (310) 207-2680
www.mymangreenspan.com
jbergman@mymangreenspan.com
Jessica Bergman, Contact
Eric Greenspan, Contact
David Fox, Contact
Tom Fineman, Contact
MYMAN GREENSPAN FINEMAN FOX ROSENBERG & LIGHT LLP, is a full service entertainment law firm specializing in the representation of clients in all areas of the film, television, music, internet and digital industries.

Nadel, Mark S.
U.S. Federal Communications Commission, 445 12th St. S.W., Rm. 5B 551, Washington, DC 20554
(202) 418-7385; *Fax:* (202) 418-7361
mnadel@fcc.gov

National Cable Telecommunications Association
25 Massachusetts Ave. N.W., Suite 100, Washington, DC 20001
(202) 222-2300; *Fax:* (202) 775-3603
www.ncta.com
webmaster@ncta.com
Michael Powell, President & CEO
James M. Assey, Executive Vice President
K. Dane Snowden, Chief Of Staff

National Exchange Carrier Association, N.E.C.A.
80 S. Jefferson Rd., Whippany, NJ 07981-1009
(973) 884-8000, (800) 228-8597; *Fax:* (973) 884-8469
www.neca.org
webmaster@neca.org
Ed Buchanan, Chairman
David L. Dunning, CEO & General Manager
Raymond Henagan, Vice Chairman

NBC Universal Television Group
10 Universal City Plaza, Universal City, CA 91608
(818) 777-1000
www.nbcuni.com
nbcucareers@nbcuni.com
Robert Greenblatt, Chairman
Stephen B. Burke, Chief Executive Officer
Kevin MacLellan, Chairman
Ted Harbert, Chairman- NBC Broadcasting
Bonnie Hammer, Chairman, NBCUniversal Cable Entertainment Group
Ron Meyer, Vice Chairman
The NBC Television Network's strength derives from combining NBC's strong national identity and programming with the local identity and programming of its affiliates in communities across America. The sale of advertising time enables the NBCTelevision Network to provide programming to the public free of charge.

Nemeth, Valerie A., Attorney at Law
191 Calle Magadalena, Suite 270, Encinitas, CA 92024
(760) 944-4130, (310) 471-7648 (L.A.); *Fax:* (760) 944-3325
www.entlawyer.com
vanemeth@entlawyer.com
Valerie Ann Nemeth, Attorney
Valerie has been in private practice since 1979, and as a sole practitioner since 1980. She has been active in the entertainment field since that time, forming a personal management company in 1981 for entertainment and sports personalities,for whom she remains an advisor.

Nilsson, Kent R.
1199 Prince Avenue, Athens, GA 30606
(706) 475-7000

Nixon Peabody L.L.P.
Mailing Address: 799 9th Street NW, Suite 500, Washington, DC 20001-4501
Second Address: 677 Broadway, 10th Floor, Albany, NY 12207
(202) 585-8000, (518) 427-2650; *Fax:* (202) 585-8080, (518) 427-2666
www.nixonpeabody.com
jlesk@nixonpeabody.com
John G. Roman, Jr., CISSP, Professional Staff
Christopher L. Melvin, Managing Director
Nixon Peabody LLP is a full-service law firm that helps clients navigate complex challenges in litigation, real estate, corporate law, and finance. With more than 600 attorneys throughout the U.S., Europe, and Asia, the firm has the abilityto handle matters anywhere in the world, ensuring that clients get the right attorneys, right where they need them.
Box 1051, Clinton Sq, Rochester, NY
(716) 263-1000
Richard D. Rochford Jr, Chairman

Nixon, Wilbert E. Jr.
7826 12th St NW, Washington, DC 20012-1323
(202) 882-3620

Nossaman, L.L.P.
Mailing Address: 50 California St., 34th Fl., San Francisco, CA 94111
Second Address: 777 S. Figueroa St., 34th Floor, Los Angeles, CA 90017
(415) 398-3600, (213) 612-7800; *Fax:* (415) 398-2438, (213) 612-7801
www.nossaman.com
mmattes@nossaman.com
Walter L. Nossaman, Founder
William E. Guthner II, Founder
Eric Miller, Communications Manager
Michelle Liffman, Chief Talent Management Officer

O'Connell & Aronowitz PC
Mailing Address: 54 State St., Albany, NY 12207
Second Address: 206 West Bay Plaza, Plattsburgh, NY 12901
(518) 462-5601, (518) 562-0600; *Fax:* (518) 462-2670, (518) 562.0657
www.oalaw.com
Benjamin Barry, Associate
Cristina Commisso, Associate
Danielle E. Holley, Associate
O'Connell and Aronowitz is one of the area's oldest law firms, having first opened our doors with two attorneys in 1925. Since that time, the firm has grown to over 35 attorneys and is one of the Capital Region's largest full service firms,with offices in Albany, Plattsburgh and Saratoga.

O'Melveny & Myers
Mailing Address: 1625 Eye St. N.W., Washington, DC 20006
Second Address: 7 Times Square, Times Square Tower, New York, NY 10036
(202) 383-5300, (212) 326-2000; *Fax:* (202) 383-5414, (212) 326-2061
www.omm.com
jbeisner@omm.com
Bradley J. Butwin, Chairman/Partner
George C. Demos, COO
Warren T. Lazarow, Partner
M. Randall Oppenheimer, Partner
Martin S. Checov, Partner
Allen Burton, Partner
Jonathan W. Kilduff, Partner
O'Melveny helps build and connect prosperous communities of law and business. Our public service and pro bono contributions strengthen the communities we serve. Because community building is a mutual effort, we receive as much as we give. Welearn from clients and industries that entrust us with their futures. We are reminded, often by those who most need our help, that the law respects and empowers all.

O'Neil, Cannon, Hollman, DeJong & Laing S.C
Mailing Address: Chase Tower, 111 E. Wisconsin Ave., Suite 1400, Milwaukee, WI 53202
Second Address: 1329 West Grand Ave., Suite 200, Port Washington, WI 53074
(414) 276-5000, (262) 284-3407; *Fax:* (414) 276-6581, (262) 284-0442
www.wilaw.com
Jean M. Ansay, Attorney
Melissa S. Blair, Attorney
Thomas G. Cannon, Attorney
Douglas P. Dehler, Attorney
The attorneys at O'Neil, Cannon, Hollman, DeJong & Laing S.C. focus on meeting the many needs of businesses and their owners. Our experienced attorneys work with businesses and their owners at all stages of the business life cycle, helpingthem start, grow, and transition their businesses from one generation to the next.

O'Neill, Athy & Casey
1310 19th St. N.W., Washington, DC 20036
(202) 466-6555; *Fax:* (202) 466-6596
www.oacpc.com
Christopher O'Neill, Partner
Andrew Athy, Partner
Martha Casey, Partner
Briana Nord Parish, Legislative Director
O'Neill, Athy & Casey, founded in 1977, is a Washington, D.C.-based law firm specializing in government relations and client

advocacy before the Legislative and Executive branches of the Federal government.

O'Reilly Rancilio P.C.
12900 Hall Rd., Suite 350, Sterling Heights, MI 48313
(586) 726-1000; *Fax:* (586) 726-1560
www.orlaw.com
paddis@orlaw.com
Nathan D. Petrusak, Associate
David K. Pontes, Associate
Eric C Turnbull, Associate
Albert B. Addis, Of Counsel
O'Reilly Rancilio P.C. is a diversified, full service law firm providing consulting, general counsel, and legal representation to businesses, financial institutions, governmental entities, and individuals. Located in Sterling Heights,Michigan, we serve a local, statewide, and nationwide clientele in business law, banking law and a wide range of legal matters.

Ogden Murphy Wallace, P.L.L.C.
Mailing Address: 901 5th Avenue, Suite 3500, Seattle, WA 98164
Second Address: One Fifth Street, Suite 200, Wenatchee, WA 98801
(206) 447-7000, (509) 662-1954; *Fax:* (206) 447-0215, (509) 663-1553
www.omwlaw.com
info@omwlaw.com
Douglas Albright, Attorney
Angela Summerfield, Attorney
Robert Andre, Attorney
Donald Black, Attorney
Ogden Murphy Wallace, P.L.L.C. is a leading multispecialty law firm committed to providing practical, cost-effective legal services to businesses, municipal entities, and individuals. We address each client's needs with the most appropriateexpertise available in our firm, using a team approach to draw on the specialized knowledge of attorneys best qualified to meet those needs.

OPASTCO
2020 K St NW #7, Washington, DC 20006
(202) 659-5990; *Fax:* (202) 659-4619
www.opastco.org
membership@ntca.org

Orr & Reno
Mailing Address: PO Box 3550, One Eagle Sq., Concord, NH 03302-3550
Second Address: 45 S. Main Street, Concord, NH 03301
(603) 224-2381; *Fax:* (603) 224-2318
www.orr-reno.com
mmclean@orr-reno.com
Peter F. Burger, President/Shareholder
Maureen McLean, Director of Administration and Finance
Maggie O Conway, Corp./Real Estate
Debra L. Silverstein, Paralegal
Caroline K. Brown, Associate
As one of New Hampshire's most respected law firms, Orr & Reno continues to redefine clients' notions of comprehensive and effective legal representation. Our lawyers and technical specialists guide clients toward their goals with insight,focus, and efficiency.

Patton Boggs L.L.P.
Mailing Address: 2550 M St. N.W., Washington, DC 20037
Second Address: 30 Rockefeller Plaza, New York, NY 10112
(202) 457-6000, (646) 557-5100; *Fax:* (202) 457-6315, (646) 557-5101
www.pattonboggs.com
Edward J. Newberry, Partner
Mitchell R. Berger, Partner
Jeff Cole, Partner
Donald V. Moorehead, Vice Chairman
Patton Boggs was founded as a small DC-based law firm focused primarily on international and trade law. Over the years, the firm's domestic practice also grew in stature and strength. Patton Boggs now offers legal services in every majorfacet of government advocacy, business law and litigation.

Paul Hastings
Mailing Address: 875 15th Street, N.W., Washington, DC 20005
Second Address: 71 S. Wacker Drive, 45th floor, Chicago, IL 60606
(202) 551-1700, (312) 499-6000; *Fax:* (202) 551-1705, (312) 499-6100
www.paulhastings.com
Scott Flicker, Office Chair
Greg Nitzkowski, Managing Partner
Barry G. Sher, Chair of Litigation Department
Philip N. Feder, Chair of Real Estate Department
Douglas A. Schaaf, Chair of Tax Dept.
Paul Hastings is a leading international law firm that provides innovative legal solutions to many of the world's top financial institutions and Fortune Global 500 companies. With a strong presence throughout Asia, Europe, Latin America, andthe U.S., we have the global reach and extensive capabilities to provide personalized service wherever our clients' needs take us.

Paul, Weiss, Rifkind, Wharton & Garrison, L.L.P.
1285 Avenue Of The Americas, New York, NY 10019-6064
(212) 373-3000; *Fax:* (212) 757-3990
www.paulweiss.com
esekler@paulweiss.com
Jill D. Berkowitz, Operations Chief
Mitchell E. Drucker, Associate
Matthew W. Abbott, Partner
Jessica S. Carey, Partner
Andrew L. Gaines, Partner
Jack Baughman, Partner
Paul, Weiss, Rifkind, Wharton & Garrison LLP is a firm of more than 700 lawyers, with diverse backgrounds, personalities, ideas and interests, who collaborate with clients to help them conquer their most critical legal challenges andbusiness goals.

Pearce & Durick
PO 400, 314 E. Thayer Ave., Bismarck, ND 58502
(701) 223-2890; *Fax:* (701) 223-7865
www.pearce-durick.com
law.office@pearce-durick.com
Christina A. Sambor, Associate
Benjamin W. Keup, Associate
An established and reputable firm since 1919, Pearce & Durick provides legal services to the corporate community throughout the United States, with specialty areas of practice in products liability law, oil and gas law, insurance defenselaw, and education law.

Pepper Hamilton LLP
Mailing Address: 3000 Two Logan Sq., Eighteenth & Arch St., Philadelphia, PA 19103-2799
Second Address: 400 Berwyn Park, 899 Cassatt Road, Berwyn, PA 19312-1183
(215) 981-4000, (610) 640-7800; *Fax:* (215) 981-4750, (610) 640-7835
www.pepperlaw.com
phinfo@pepperlaw.com
Julia D. Corelli, Partner
John P. Duke, Partner
Thomas M. Gallagher, Partner
Vincent V. Carissimi, Partner
Thomas J. Cole Jr., Partner
Pepper Hamilton LLP is a multi-practice law firm with more than 500 lawyers nationally. The firm provides corporate, litigation and regulatory legal services to leading businesses, governmental entities, nonprofit organizations andindividuals throughout the nation and the world.
600 14th St. N.W., Washington, DC 20005-2008
(202) 220-1200; *Fax:* (202) 220-1665
David A. Wormser, Chairman

Peter A. Casciato P.C.
335 Bryant St., Suite 410, San Francisco, CA 94107
(415) 291-8661; *Fax:* (415) 291-8165
pacasciato@gmail.com

Peter R. Meyers
360 E. Randolph St., Suite 3104, Chicago, IL 60601
(312) 616-1500; *Fax:* (312) 616-1737
peterarbme@aol.com
Peter R. Meyers, Arbitrator, Mediator & Attorney
Peter Meyers is available for arbitration, mediation, fact-finding, and other forms of alternative dispute resolution. Below are specific definitions for these processes, to help you in finding the one that best suits your needs.

Phillips Nizer LLP
Mailing Address: 666 5th Ave., 28th Fl., New York, NY 10103-0084
Second Address: 600 Old Country Rd., Suite 305, Citibank Building, Garden City, NY 11530-2011
(212) 977-9700, (516) 229-9400; *Fax:* (212) 262-5152, (516) 228-9612
www.phillipsnizer.com
hbindelglass@phillipsnizer.com
Robert L. Bachner, Senior Counsel
Elizabeth A. Adinolfi, Counsel
Phillips Nizer has been engaged in a wide-ranging domestic and international practice for over 85 years. Our size and the diversity of our practice enable us to be a full-service law firm in virtually all areas of law while affording clientsclose contact and working relationships with partners and associates.

Pierce & Robinson P A
Div/DBA: (Formerly Pierce, Robinson & Greene P A)
600 W. 4th St., North Little Rock, AR 72114-5360
(501) 372-3131; *Fax:* (501) 372-3825

Pillsbury Winthrop Shaw Pittman LLP
Mailing Address: 1200 Seventeenth Street, NW, Washington, DC 20036
Second Address: 333 Commerce St., Nashville, TN 37201
(202) 663-8000, (615) 622-3400; *Fax:* (202) 663-8007
www.pillsburylaw.com
Stephen S. Asay, Associate
James L. Alberg, Partner
Roland G. Backhaus, Associate
Kristen E. Baker, Senior Associate
Paul A. Cicelski, Counsel
Todd J. Canni, Partner

Pillsbury, Winthrop Shaw Pittman LLP
Mailing Address: 1540 Broadway, New York, NY 10036-4039
Second Address: 1650 Tysons Boulevard, 14th Floor, McLean, VA 22102-4856
(212) 858-1000, (877) 323-4171, (730) 770-7900; *Fax:* (415) 983-1200
www.pillsburylaw.com
erik.cummins@pillsburylaw.com
Pillsbury is a full-service law firm with an industry focus on energy & natural resources, financial services including financial institutions, real estate & construction, and technology.

Powell, Goldstein, Frazer & Murphy
1201 W. Peachtree St. N.W., Fl. 14, Atlanta, GA 30309
(404) 572-6600; *Fax:* (404) 572-6999
wmoeling@pgfm.com
1001 Pennsylvania Ave. N.W., 6th Fl, Washington, DC 20004-2505
(202) 347-0066; *Fax:* (202) 624-7222
Jerome S. Breed, Chairman

Proskauer Rose L.L.P.
Mailing Address: Eleven Times Square, Eighth Avenue & 41st Street, New York, NY 10036-8299
Second Address: One Newark Center, Newark, NJ 07102-5211
(212) 969-3000; *Fax:* (212) 969-2900
www.proskauer.com
info@proskauer.com
Sherrylynn Trotta, Director of Operations
James J. Barbaria, Chief Financial Officer
Elisabeth D. Bernard, Director of Human Resources
Lisa D. Cohen, Director of Business Development Information and T
Proskauer, founded in 1875, is a global law firm providing a wide variety of legal services to clients worldwide from offices in Beijing, Boca Raton, Boston, Chicago, Hong Kong, London, Los Angeles, New Orleans, New York, Newark, Paris, SaoPaulo, and Washington, DC.

Provosty, Sadler Delaunay, Fiorenza & Sobel
Mailing Address: 934 Third Street, Suite 800, PO Drawer 1791, Alexandria, LA 71309-1791
Second Address: 237 S Washington Street, Marksville, LO 71351
(318) 445-3631, (318) 253-4435; *Fax:* (318) 445-9377, (318) 253-6626
www.provosty.com
bsadler@provosty.com
David W. Lambert, Associate
Jeremy C. Cedars, Associate
David E. Boraks, Associate
Joseph R. Martin, Of Counsel
Provosty, Sadler, deLaunay, Fiorenza & Sobel, A Professional Corporation, founded in 1945, is the oldest business and defense oriented firm in central Louisiana serving local, statewide and national clients. The firm handles cases in allLouisiana State and Federal Courts and the United States Supreme Court. Three of its past members have served as President of the Louisiana State Bar Association.

Putbrese, Hunsaker & Trent, P.C.
200 S. Church St., Woodstock, VA 22664
(540) 459-7646; *Fax:* (540) 459-7656
www.phtpclaw.com
info@phtpclaw.com
John C. Trent, Attorney
The firm was originally founded by Keith E. Putbrese in 1962. Mr. Hunsaker joined the firm in 1977 and became a partner in 1981, when the firm name was changed to Putbrese & Hunsaker. Mr. Trent joined the firm as an Associate in 1990. In1996, when Mr. Putbrese retired from active practice, the firm name was reorganized as a professional corporation and Mr. Trent became a Member.

Reed Smith LLP
Mailing Address: 3110 Fairview Park Dr., Suite 1400, Falls Church, VA 22042

PROFESSIONAL SERVICES

Second Address: 1901 Ave. of the Stars, Suite 700, Los Angeles, CA 900067-6078
(703) 641-4200; *Fax:* (703) 641-4340
www.reedsmith.com
reedsmith@reedsmith.com
Gary A. Sokulski, COO
David Duckhouse, CFO
Michael C. Lynch, Chief HR Officer
Gary W. Becker, Chief Information Officer
Alexander Y. Thomas, Global Managing Partner
David S. Egan, Chief Marketing Officer
Nicholas Bagiatis, Chiefof Business & Finance Dept. Operations

Rees Broome, PC
Mailing Address: 1602 Village Market Blvd SE, Suite 270, Leesburg, VA 20175
Second Address: 7430 Heritage Village Plaza, Suite 202, Gainesville, VA 20155
(703) 790-6605, (571) 261-1970; *Fax:* (571) 261-5873
Steve Annino, Attorney/Shareholder
Joel M. Birken, Attorney/Founding Shareholder
Hillary Anne Collins, Associate
Rees Broome, PC has grown to forty attorneys and has honed its expertise in litigation, business, tax, estates, employment, construction defect liability, homeowners' and condominium associations, zoning, commercial real estate andcreditors' rights work.

Resnick, Bernard Max, Esq, P.C.
Two Bala Plaza, Suite 300, Bala Cynwyd, PA 19004
(610) 660-7774; *Fax:* (610) 668-0574
www.bernardresnick.com
bmresnick@gmail.com
Bernard M. Resnick, Attorney
Priscilla J. Sally Mattison, Attorney
Bernard M. Resnick, Esq., P.C. is a full-service entertainment and communications law firm headquartered in Philadelphia, Pennsylvania, USA. Our two attorneys, Bernard M. Bernie Resnick and Priscilla J. Sally Mattison, have combinedexperience of over thirty-five years in the entertainment industry. As a result of an extensive and confidential peer review by members of the Bar, our firm has been awarded the prestigious AV rating from LexisNexis Martindale-Hubbell.

Richard N. Clarvit, P.A.
1313 N.E. 125th St., Suite 200, North Miami, FL 33161
(305) 893-4135; *Fax:* (305) 893-4173
richsongs@aol.com
Richard Neal Clarvit, Member

Riezman & Berger
7700 Bonhomme Ave., 7th Fl., Clayton, MO 63105
(314) 727-0101; *Fax:* (314) 727-6458
www.riezmanberger.com
info@riezmanberger.com
Frederick J. Berger, Attorney
Suzanne M. Besnia, Attorney
Randall D. Grady, Attorney
Julie K. Graham, Attorney
Passionate, creative, resourceful, inquisitive, disciplined, honest, tenacious, insightful. These are just a few distinguishing traits of a Riezman Berger attorney. Together, these characteristics infuse everything we do, and the end resultis high quality legal counsel delivered by a strategic partner who acts with your best interests in mind.

Riker Danzig Scherer Hyland & Perretti LLP
One Speedwell Ave., Headquarters Plaza, Morristown, NJ 07962-1981
(973) 538-0800; *Fax:* (973) 538-1984
www.riker.com
info@riker.com
Dennis J. O'Grady, Chairman of Bankruptcy Dept
Marcia Miller Wefelmeier, Counsel
Laurie J. Sands, Counsel
Frank J. Vitolo, Counsel
With a rich history of New Jersey-focused litigation and business experience and a dedicated team that includes former key state government officials, our understanding of the intricacies in the state's legal system is second to none. Webelieve our role is to address our clients' legal needs in concert with their business goals, in the most cost-effective manner. Following the Riker Danzig tradition to always put the clients' needs first, we anticipate change, evaluate options andprovide solutions
50 W. State St, Suite 1010, Trenton, NJ 08608-1220

Riot Media Management
, PO Box 8553, Berkeley, CA 94707
(510) 763-7600; *Fax:* (510) 763-7894
joelturtle@yahoo.com
Joel S. Turtle, Contact
Cody Turtle, Contact
Riot Media (audio, video, digital, social media) is distributed worldwide both in physical and digital formats. We have complete digital distribution including but not limited to: iTunes, Rhapsody and Amazon.

Robert A. DePont, Attorney at Law
140 South St., PO Box 386, Annapolis, MD 21404
(410) 263-0632; *Fax:* (410) 990-9596
www.robertdepontlaw.com
robertade@msn.com
Robert DePont, Attorney
Chapter 13 bankruptcy is considered a wage earner bankruptcy, and may be advisable for people who do not qualify for Chapter 7 bankruptcy. Many people who are eligible for Chapter 13 bankruptcy have encountered temporary setbacks that resultin overwhelming debt.

Robins, Kaplan, Miller & Ciresi
Mailing Address: 800 LaSalle Ave., 2800 LaSalle Plaza, Minneapolis, MN 55402
Second Address: 1201 West Peachtree Street, One Atlantic Center, Suite 2200, Atlanta, GA 30309
(612) 349-8500, (404) 760-4300; *Fax:* (612) 339-4181, (404) 233-1267
www.rkmc.com
kamarron@rkmc.com
Ronald J. Schutz, Partner/ Chair
Steven A. Schumeister, Managing Partner
For 75 years, Robins, Kaplan, Miller & Ciresi L.L.P. has been advocating on behalf of our clients. From individuals to newly established businesses to the world's oldest and largest companies in a broad range of industries, we stand besideour clients to assess and manage risk through the life-cycle of their specific business goals and their most critical legal challenges-both in and out of the courtroom.

Rosenfeld, Meyer & Susman L.L.P.
232 North Canon Drive, Beverly Hills, CA 90210
(310) 858-7700; *Fax:* (310) 860-2430
www.rmslaw.com
info@rmslaw.com
W. Nathan Canby, Senior Attorney
Ron Dolecki, Senior Attorney
Todd W. Bonder, Partner
Rosenfeld, Meyer & Susman LLP is a full-service law firm, founded in 1957 and located in the heart of Beverly Hills. With deep roots in the entertainment industry and through a cadre of exceptional attorneys, Rosenfeld represents majorplayers in Hollywood and the greater business community, both domestically and abroad.

Rourke, Gerald S.
76 Northwood Rd., Madison, CT 06443
(203) 421-3424
wstacey@stacey.ca
Wayne A. Stacey, President
Govt rels, CRTC/IC applications, bcst rsch, bcst consulting, engrg svcs, demographic studies.

Rubin, Winston, Diercks, Harris & Cooke, L.L.P.
1201 Connecticut Ave. N.W., Washington, DC 20036
(202) 861-0870; *Fax:* (202) 429-0657
www.rwdhc.com
jwinston@rwdhc.com
Frederick D. Cooke, Jr., Attorney
Walter E. Diercks, Attorney
Jeffrey Harris, Attorney
Max Riederer von Paar, Attorney
We offer an unusually broad mix of practice areas for a firm of our size. Our diverse range of practice areas includes antitrust and trade regulation, business transactions, communications, corporate law, estate planning, litigation, media,outdoor advertising, and white collar criminal defense, among others. Our practice is both domestic and international in scope.

Ryan, Swanson & Cleveland P.L.L.C.
1201 3rd Ave., Suite 3400, Seattle, WA 98101-3034
(206) 464-4224, (800) 458-5973; *Fax:* (206) 583-0359
www.ryanlaw.com
collette@ryanlaw.com
John A. Bender, Attorney
Kari Brotherton, Attorney
Michael Jay Brown, Attorney
Daniel M. Caine, Attorney
Since the beginning, Ryan Swanson has always focused on helping businesses, small and large, privately-held and public, with legal counsel that helps them succeed. From business formation to employment contracts to licensing agreements, RyanSwanson lawyers are committed to providing clients with timely and practical advice. We emphasize service and responsiveness and take a practical, common-sense approach to our practice, making sure we do all we can to assist and protect our clients.

Sahl, Jack
School of Law, University of Akron, 150 University Ave, Akron, OH 44325-2901
(330) 972-7331; *Fax:* (330) 258-2343
www.uakron.edu/law
jps@uakron.edu
John P. Sahl, Professor Law

Sanchez Law Firm
13181 Crossroads Parkway N, Suite 460, City of Industry, CA 91746
(562) 692-6623; *Fax:* (562) 692-6624
www.sanchezlawcorp.com
esanchez@bellatlantic.net
Eduardo G. Sanchez, Attorney at Law
Recognises Business Law & Estate Planning needs

Sapronov & Associates, P. C.
Mailing Address: 1200 Abernathy Road, Suite 1700, Atlanta, GA 30328
Second Address: 1875 I St, NW, 5th Floor, Washington, DC 20006
(770) 399-9100, (202) 429-2055; *Fax:* (770) 395-0505
www.wstelecomlaw.com
info@wstelecomlaw.com
Kimberly Darmody, Attorney
Mike Zpevak, Advisors
Walt Sapronov, Attorney
Solves legal & regulatory telecommunication needs related to telecommunications transactions, regulatory compliance, broadband, finance, building access etc.

Schuster & Associates
3594 Armourdale Ave., Long Beach, CA 90808
(562) 596-5900; *Fax:* (562) 431-4540
www.flightlaw.com

Schwaninger and Associates Inc
6715 Little River Tnpk, Suite 204, Annandale, VA 22003
(703) 256-0637; *Fax:* (703) 256-3578
www.sa-lawyers.net
info@sa-lawyers.net
Robert H. Schwaninger, Attorney

Schwartz, Woods & Miller
2001 L Street, NW, Suite 900A, Washington, DC 20036-4940
(202) 833-1700; *Fax:* (202) 833-2351
www.swmlaw.com
Lawrence M. Miller, Attorney
Steven C. Schaffer, Attorney
Malcolm G. Stevenson, Attorney

Sell & Melton
577 Mulberry St., 14th Floor, Macon, GA 31201
(478) 207-6407, (800) 401-3194; *Fax:* (478) 745-6426
www.sell-melton.com
eds@sell-melton.com
Mitchel P. House, Jr., Attorney
John A. Draughon Sr., Attorney
R. Chix Miller, Attorney
With community roots dating back more than 70 years, Sell & Melton, L.L.P. has a long history of helping clients address complex legal matters. Today, we serve a wide range of business, government and individual clients, and practice in allof Georgia's federal and state courts.

Seyfarth Shaw
Mailing Address: One Century Plaza, 2029 Century Park East, Suite 3500, Los Angeles, CA 90067-3021
Second Address: 333 South Hope St., Suite 3900, Los Angeles, CA 90071-1406
(310) 277-7200, (213) 270-9600; *Fax:* (310) 201-5219, (213) 270-9601
www.seyfarth.com
Laura Wilson Shelby, Partner
Richard Mendelson, Partner
Raymond R. Kepner, Partner
Christopher J. Harney, Associate
Seyfarth Shaw LLP provides thoughtful, strategic, practical legal counsel to client companies and legal teams of all sizes.

Seyfarth Shaw LLP
Mailing Address: 131 S. Dearborn St., Suite 2400, Chicago, IL 60603-5577
Second Address: 1075 Peachtree St., NE, Atlanta, GA 30309-3962

(312) 460-5000, (404) 885-1500; *Fax:* (312) 460-7000, (404) 892-7056
www.seyfarth.com
Rita D. Abro, Associate
Victoria A. Bobryk, Senior Project Manager
Karl J. Haraldsson, Associate Data Solutions Architect
William Johnson, Data Analytics Specialist

Shapiro, Burton J.
2147 N. Beachwood Dr., Los Angeles, CA 90068
(323) 469-9452; *Fax:* (801) 653-6571
www.burtshapiro.com
burtjay@mail.com
Burt J. Sharpiro, esq., President

Shine and Hardin L.L.P.
2810 Beaver Ave., Fort Wayne, IN 46807
(260) 745-1970; *Fax:* (260) 744-5411
www.shineandhardinlaw.com
sshine@shineandhardin.com
Steven R. Shine, Attorney
Thomas A. Hardin, Attorney
Daniel P. Kensinger, Attorney
Shine & Hardin, LLP wants to be the only law firm you will ever need and we are prepared to earn your trust and confidence. Shine & Hardin offers its clients a variety of legal services, including family law, estate planning andadministration, real estate and zoning, trusts and trust administration, contracts, litigation, business and corporate law, and personal injury.

Shukat, Arrow, Hafer & Weber, L.L.P.
494 8th Ave, 6th Fl., New York, NY 10001
(212) 245-4580; *Fax:* (212) 956-6471
www.musiclaw.com
info@musiclaw.com
Peter S. Shukaat, Partner
Allen H. Arrow, Partner
J. Jeffrey Hafer, Partner
Dorothy M. Weber, Partner
Jonas E. Herbsman, Partner

Shulman, Rogers, Gandal, Pordy & Ecker, P.A.
12505 Park Potomac Avenue, 6th Fl., Potomac, MD 20854
(301) 230-5200; *Fax:* (301) 230-2891
www.shulmanrogers.com
info@shulmanrogers.com
Mortan A. Faller, Shareholder/Attorney
Focusing on solutions. Thinking creatively and tenaciously about outcomes. About what's in your best interests. Getting matters resolved, so you can get on with what matters to you. That's resolutionary thinking. And that's made Shulman,Rogers, Gandal, Pordy & Ecker, P.A., one of the largest, most respected law firms in the Washington Metropolitan Area.

Siegal, Joel H.
Mailing Address: 235 Montgomery, Suite 800, San Francisco, CA 94104
Second Address: 1800 Century Park East, Suite 600, Los Angeles, CA 90067
(415) 777-5547, (800) 425-5635; *Fax:* (415) 777-5247
www.litigateforjustice.com
joelsiegal@litigateforjustice.com
Joel H. Siegal, Attorney
For more than 25 years, I have represented people who don't always have the resources to take on litigation against the big powerful institutions of our society: big corporations, insurance companies and governments. I have the experience,the brains, the chutzpa, the resource and the desire to fight on your behalf. I have represented people in many of California's counties. I have spent my life in public service because I believe in it. I am passionate about it. - See more at:http://www.litigateforjustice.com/history-bio-joel-h-siegal.php#sthash.wHjRaQaB.dpuf

Silver, Garvett & Henkel P.A.
18001 Old Cutler Rd., Suite 600, Miami, FL 33157
(305) 377-8802; *Fax:* (305) 377-8804
www.sghpa.com
info@sghpa.com
Fredrick M. Garvett, Partner
Scott A. Silver, Partner

Skadden, Arps, Slate, Meagher & Flom L.L.P.
Mailing Address: 1440 New York Ave. N.W., Washington, DC 20005
Second Address: Four Times Square, New York, NY 10036
(202) 371-7000, (212) 735-3000; *Fax:* (202) 393-5760, (212) 735-2000/1
www.skadden.com
info@skadden.com
Maureen A. Donley, Of Counsel
Edmund C. Duffy, Of Counsel
Philippe Derouin, Of Counsel
With 23 offices, approximately 1,800 attorneys and more than 40 distinct areas of practice, Skadden, Arps, Slate, Meagher & Flom LLP and affiliates serves clients in every major international financial center, providing the specific legaladvice companies across a spectrum of industries need to compete most effectively in a global business environment. Our clients include approximately 50 percent of the Fortune 250 industrial and service corporations, as well as financial andgovernmental entities, small, entrepreneurial companies and nonprofits. Skadden's attorneys and staff share a commitment to providing our clients with the highest-quality and most cost-effective legal services in an atmosphere emphasizing teamwork,creativity, responsiveness and diversity.

Sommers, Schwartz, Silver & Schwartz, P.C.
One Towne Square, Suite 1700, Southfield, MI 48076
(248) 236-5753; *Fax:* (248) 746-4001
www.sommerspc.com
Joseph H. Bourgon, CEO/Shareholder
David M. Black, Of Counsel
Matthew G. Curtis, Senior Shareholder
Charles R. Ash III, Senior Shareholder
Michael J. Cunningham, Senior Shareholder
Andy Dragovic, Associate
Our lawyers have been recognized nationally in personal injury and medical malpractice, commercial and business law, intellectual property, employment and wage and hour laws, antitrust, and consumer protection. We try serious cases on behalfof people and families, businesses, and municipal entities seeking to enforce their rights. - See more at: http://www.sommerspc.com/en/the-firm/#sthash.rZCp2Pee.dpuf

Sonnenschein, Nath & Rosenthal LLP
Mailing Address: 233 S. Wacker Dr., Suite 5900, Chicago, IL 60606-6361
Second Address: 303 Peachtree Street, NE, Suite 5300, Atlanta, GA 30308
(312) 876-8000, (404) 527-4000; *Fax:* (312) 876-7934, (404) 527-4198
www.dentons.com
sfifer@sonnenschein.com
Dentons is the new global law firm created by international law firm Salans LLP, Canadian law firm Fraser Milner Casgrain LLP (FMC) and international law firm SNR Denton and is driven to provide you with the competitive edge in anincreasingly complex and interconnected marketplace.

Spiegel & McDiarmid, LLP
1875 Eye Street, NW, Suite 700, Washington, DC 20006
(202) 879-4000; *Fax:* (202) 393-2866
www.spiegelmcd.com
info@spiegelmcd.com
Carol Gloss, Executive Director
Lisa Jacobs, Human Resources Director
Jeff Berns, Librarian
Bryan Pigeon, Director Of Operations
Initially, the firm set out to apply these principles in the context of representing municipally owned and cooperative utility systems that found themselves at odds with private utility companies. In that arena, we found that therepresentation of municipal and cooperative systems - which are often subject to strict limitations on their legal budgets - required methods and approaches that would give clients the greatest return on their legal dollar. The firm has sincebroadened this approach to include representation in telecommunications and transportation.

Springman, Braden, Wilson & Pontius, P.C.
4175 Harlan Street, Suite 200, Wheat Ridge, CO 80033
(303) 685-4897/685-4633, (866) 685-4637; *Fax:* (303) 685-4627
www.sbwp-law.com
assoc@sbwp-law.com
Deborah L. Wilson, Attorney
Britten W. Hale, Attorney
Kristi Bunge, Attorney
Paul Farrer, Attorney
Our firm specializes in both EVICTION and COLLECTION services for landlords and property management companies. We also handle all forms of litigation for COMMUNITY ASSOCIATIONS, including foreclosures. The attorneys have over 50 years ofcombined experience in the apartment and community associations industry. The lawyers and staff of our firm are highly skilled and knowledgeable in these fields. Our firm's goal is to provide you with prompt, effective, professional and affordablerepresentation. This website is designed to inform you of our procedures. We hope that this information will help you to take full advantage of our legal services.

Squire, Sanders & Dempsey
Mailing Address: 1200 19th Street, N.W., Suite 300, Washington, DC 20036
Second Address: 30 Rockefeller Plaza, New York, NY 10112
(202) 626-6600, (212) 872-9800; *Fax:* (202) 626-6780, (212) 872-9815
john.burlingame@squiresanders.com
John A. Burlingame, Partner
Eric W. Cowan, Partner
Chris McLeod, Director of Trade Marks
Joe Abbott, Associate
We combine sound legal counsel with a deep knowledge of our clients' businesses to resolve their legal challenges. We care about the quality of our services, the success of our clients and the relationships that are forged through thosesuccesses.
4900 Key Tower, 127 Public Sq, Cleveland, OH 44114-1217
(216) 479-8500; *Fax:* (216) 479-8780
Terrence J. Clark, Ptnr

Stephens Media LLC
Mailing Address: 1111 W Bonanza Rd, Las Vegas, NV 89106
Second Address: PO Box 70 89125-0070
(702) 383-0211; *Fax:* (702) 383-0230
www.stephensmedia.com
Mark Ficarra, Chief Revenue Officer
Mark A. Hinueber, VP/ General Counsel
Ryan Christiansen, VP, Digital Media
Mike Flanagan, VP, Sales

Steptoe & Johnson
Mailing Address: 1330 Connecticut Ave. N.W., Washington, DC 20036
Second Address: 1114 Avenue of the Americas, New York, NY 10036
(202) 429-3000, (212) 506-3900; *Fax:* (202) 429-3902, (212) 506-3950
www.steptoe.com
information@steptoe.com
Elizabeth Hurley Burks, Managing Director, Government Affairs & Public Pol
Dr. Mitchell Cheeseman, Managing Director, Regulatory & Industry Affairs D
Rachel B. Peck, Associate
Over the past six decades, Steptoe has established a reputation for vigorous advocacy in complex litigation and arbitration, successful representation of clients before governmental agencies, and creative and practical advice in guidingbusiness transactions. The firm has more than 500 lawyers and other professionals in offices in Beijing, Brussels, Century City, Chicago, London, Los Angeles, New York, Phoenix, and Washington.

Stevens, Sally L.
, PO Box 41, Lumberville, PA 18933
(215) 297-8245; *Fax:* (215) 297-5106

Stewart & Irwin P.C.
251 E. Ohio St., Suite 1100, Indianapolis, IN 46204
(317) 639-5454; *Fax:* (317) 632-1319
Mary Schmid, Attorney
Suzanne Newcomb, Attorney
Ronald C. Smith, Attorney
Jeff Halbert, Attorney

Stroock, Stroock & Lavin
Mailing Address: 180 Maiden Lane, New York, NY 10038-4982
Second Address: 767 Third Avenue, New York, NY 10017-2023
(212) 806-5400, (212) 826-8853; *Fax:* (212) 806-6006
www.stroock.com
Elizabeth M. Akerman, Associate
Stroock was praised for its commitment to the [energy field], with particular commendation of its physical commodity focus.,Chambers Global: The World's Leading Lawyers for Business.over $12 billion in recent real estate financings.Listed asone of the top insurance law firms in the country, ReActions Magazine.The message from clients has been that Stroock [Intellectual Property] lawyers understand business.

Stryker, Tams & Dill LLP
2 Penn Plaza E., 12th Floor, Newark, NJ 07105
(973) 491-9500; *Fax:* (973) 491-9692
info@strykertams.com
John J. Rizzo, Partner
Charles H. Freidrich III, Partner
Dennis C. Linken, Partner
Martin G. Gilbert, Partner
Harold Freidman, Partner

Taylor, Jack
1289 Lincoln Rd., Yuba City, CA 95991
(530) 671-6800; *Fax:* (530) 671-6447
www.lawtaylor.yolasite.com

PROFESSIONAL SERVICES

Jack L. Taylor, Personal Injury Law
The Law Corporation of Jack Taylor represents those who have been injured. If you or a loved one has been injured it is important to act quickly. Cases can be won or lost on fleeting evidence. Moreover, there are strict legal deadlines forbringing personal injury claims. Unfortunately, delay benefits the insurance company, not you.

Technology Law Group L.L.C.
5335 Wisconsin Ave. N.W., Suite 440, Washington, DC 20015
(202) 895-1707, (405) 694-4747; *Fax:* (202) 478-5074, (800) 796-4732
www.tlgdc.com
info@tlgdc.com
Neil S. Ende, Managing Partner
Susan Colman, Of Counsel
Silsa Cabezas, Administrative Assistant
Matthew Friedman, Attorney

Thomas, Ballenger, Vogelman & Turner
124 S. Royal St., Alexandria, VA 22314
(703) 650-0367; *Fax:* (703) 836-3549
www.vogelmanturner.com
Matthew J. Ling, Associate
Ciara Ann Miller, Associate
Anders Thomas Sleight, Associate
Jeffrey A. Vogelman, Associate
Our attorneys and associates believe in the strength of numbers. We consistently work as a team as we collaborate to help our clients obtain outcomes that serve their best interests. Emotions often run high when facing a family law issue orbankruptcy. Our lawyers are committed to giving you the attention you need to make decisions that will foster a brighter future for you and your loved ones. By taking a tactical approach to our clients' situations, we are able to providestraightforward legal advice and support.

Thompson Hine LLP
1919 M Street, N.W., Suite 700, Washington, DC 20036-3537
(202) 331-8800; *Fax:* (202) 331-8330
www.thompsonhine.com
barry.friedman@thompsonhine.com
John C Allerding, Attorney
Jurgita Ashley, Partner
David A. Wilson, Partner
With the experience and resources to handle the most challenging legal issues, Thompson Hine strives to deliver consistently exceptional guidance, value and service, and to fulfill our Client Service Pledge from the inception of each matterto its close, and beyond. In fact, our goal is to be the best law firm our clients have ever dealt with.
10 W. Broad St., Suite 700, Columbus, OH 43215-3418
(614) 469-3200; *Fax:* (614) 469-3361
www.thompsonhine.com
tom.lodge@thompsonhine.com
Thomas E. Lodge, Chairman

Thrasher, Dinsmore & Dolan
Mailing Address: 100 7th Ave., Suite 150, Chardon, OH 44024
Second Address: 1400 W. Sixth Street, Suite 400, Cleveland, OH 44113
(440) 285-2242, (216) 255-5431; *Fax:* (440) 285-9423, (216) 255-5450
www.tddlaw.com
David E. Lowe, Principal
Dale H. Markowitz, Principal
Joseph R. Znidarsic, Principal
David M. Ondrey, Principal
Heidi M. Cisan, Principal
For 80 years, since our founding in 1931 we have upheld the same core principles as counselors at law: to provide exceptional service and effective legal representation to our clients. We are committed to the success of our clients and ofour community in Geauga and Cuyahoga County. Our advice is based upon experience and principles in legal counseling, not simply telling the client what they may want to hear from an attorney.

Troutman Sanders L.L.P.
Mailing Address: 600 Peachtree Street, NE, Suite 5200, Atlanta, GA 30308
Second Address: 100 SW Main Street, Portland, OR 97204
(404) 885-3000, (503) 290-2400; *Fax:* (404) 885-3900, (503) 290-2405
www.troutmansanders.com
Robert D. Seabolt, Partner
Stephen E. Lewis, Partner
Margaret Claiborne Campbell, Partner
Andrea M. Farley, Partner
Pete Robinson, Partner
Troutman Sanders LLP is an international law firm with more than 600 lawyers and offices located throughout the United States and China. Founded in 1897, the firm's heritage of extensive experience, exceptional responsiveness and anunwavering commitment to service has garnered strong, long-standing relationships with clients across the globe. These clients range from multinational corporations to individual entrepreneurs, federal and state agencies to foreign governments, andnon-profit organizations to businesses representing virtually every sector and industry.

Troy & Gould, PC
1801 Century Park E., Suite 1600, Los Angeles, CA 90067
(310) 553-4441; *Fax:* (310) 201-4746
www.troygould.com
lzamora@troygould.com
Sanford J. Hillsberg, Managing Members
William D. Gould, Managing Members
We have developed a reputation for excellence uncommon for a mid-size firm. U.S. News and World Report has recognized TroyGould as a premier corporate law firm, selecting us as a National Tier 1 "Best Law Firm" in Mergers and AcquisitionsLaw and one of only four Los Angeles Tier 1 law firms for Securities Regulation. Moreover, the firm authored Advising and Defending Corporate Directors and Officers, published by the Regents of the University of California, which has become astandard desk reference work reflecting the firm's extensive transactional and litigation expertise in the complex and challenging area of corporate governance.

Van Cott, Bagley, Cornwall & McCarthy
36 S. State St., Suite 1900, Salt Lake City, UT 84111
(801) 532-3333, (800) 540-4691; *Fax:* (801) 534-0058
info@vancott.com
Gregory P. Williams, President
Matthew S. Brahana, Associate
Timothy W. Blackburn, Shareholder
Joseph A. Cannon, Of Counsel
Robert S. Campbell, Of Counsel
Van Cott, Bagley, Cornwall & McCarthy is a nationally recognized law firm with a long record of excellence and professional leadership in the Intermountain West. Our attorneys offer comprehensive business, tax, litigation and naturalresource-related services to individual and corporate clients.

Varnum LLP
Div/DBA: (Formerly Varnum, Riddering, Schmidt & Howlett LL
Mailing Address: PO Box 352, Bridgewater Pl., Grand Rapids, MI 49501-0352
Second Address: 251 North Rose Street, Fourth Floor, Kalamazoo, MI 49007
(616) 336-6000, (269) 382-2300; *Fax:* (616) 336-7000, (269) 382-2382
www.varnumlaw.com
generalinfo@varnumlaw.com
Joan Andrew, Director
Bruce A. Barnhart, Of Counsel
Terrance R. Bacon, Of Counsel
Timothy J. Curtin, Of Counsel
Varnum clients represent a diverse range of business and legal interests: manufacturers, financial institutions, health care providers, professional groups, municipalities, colleges and universities, school districts, developers, publishers,retailers, governmental units, transportation, trade associations, charitable organizations, and utilities.

Venable LLP
Mailing Address: 750 E. Pratt Street, Suite 900, Baltimore, MD 21202
Second Address: 2049 Century Park East, Suite 2100, Los Angeles, CA 90067
(410) 244-7400, (310) 229-9900; *Fax:* (410) 244-7742, (310) 229-9901
www.venable.com
James L. Shea, Chairman
Brian L. Schwalb, Vice Chairman
Tamany Vinson Bentz, Partner
Paul S. Bernstein, Of Counsel
From its founding office in Baltimore, Venable has grown into a national Am Law 100 firm of more than 500 lawyers that today serves the needs of clients across the country and around the world. The Baltimore office is home to many of thefirm's top-ranked practices in business transactions and corporate law, bankruptcy and creditors' rights, commercial litigation, labor and employment law and tax law, as well as the country's foremost practice in the area of real estate investmenttrusts (REITs). The office also features a number of attorneys who have been ranked as among the top in their fields, and who represent clients in issues ranging from multi-billion dollar transactions, to complex commercial litigation mattersspanning a wide variety of industries, to Maryland corporate matters and local government issues.
1201 New York Ave. N.W, Suite 1000, Washington, DC 20005-3917
(202) 962-4800, (202) 962-8300

Veryl Miles/Professor at Law School
3600 John McCormack Rd., NE, Washington, DC 20064
(202) 319-5625; *Fax:* (202) 319-4459
www.law.edu
miles@law.edu
Daniel F. Attridge, Dean
Marin Scordato, Associate Dean for Academic Affairs and Research
Michelle Borda, Assistant Dean for Administration
Maura DeMouy, Assistant Dean for Student Support
Georgia A. Niedzielko, Assistant Dean forAcademic Affairs
Veryl Victoria Miles teaches consumer bankruptcy and several courses in commercial law. Much of her scholarship has been devoted to the subject of consumer bankruptcy law. She has also written and spoken about a range of issues regardinglegal education and admission to the bar.

Vorys, Sater, Seymour and Pease LLP
Mailing Address: 52 E. Gay St., Columbus, OH 43215
Second Address: 1909 K Street NW, Suite 900, Washington, DC 20006-1152
(614) 464-6400, (202) 467-8800; *Fax:* (614) 464-6350
www.vorys.com
bcschmidt@vorys.com
Rajeev K. Adlakha, Associate
Robin P. Amicon, Senior Attorney
Stephanie S. Angeloni, Associate
Vorys, Sater, Seymour and Pease LLP provides business and legal counsel to clients throughout the United States and around the world. Since its founding in 1909, our firm has grown into one of the largest law firms in the country, withnearly 375 attorneys who are located in six offices in Ohio, Texas, and Washington, D.C.
1828 L St. N.W, Suite 1111, Washington, DC 20036-5104
(202) 467-8800; *Fax:* (202) 467-8900
Mark J. Palchick, Robert E. Levine

Wagner, Michael Francis
Mass Media Bureau, 445 12th St. S.W., Rm. 2-A523, Washington, DC 20554
(202) 662-5496; *Fax:* (202) 778-5496

Waller Lansden Dortch & Davis, PLLC
Mailing Address: 511 Union St., Suite 2700, Nashville, TN 37219
Second Address: 1901 Sixth Avenue North, Suite 1400, Birmingham, AL 35203
(615) 244-6380, (205) 214-6380; *Fax:* (615) 244-6804, (205) 214-8787
www.wallerlaw.com
Lindsey R. Arnold, Associate
Bahar Azhdari, Associate
Mark M. Bell, Associate
Established in 1905, Waller is one of the oldest law firms in Tennessee. With more than 175 attorneys serving 10 core industries, we can quickly assemble a multi-dimensional team to address almost any matter. While we may begin by assistingwith one issue, clients come back for help in other areas as well.

Weil, Gotshal & Manges, L.L.P.
Mailing Address: 1300 Eye Street, NW, Suite 900, Washington, DC 20005
Second Address: 100 Federal Street, Floor 34, Boston, MA 02110-1800
(202) 682-7000, (617) 772-8300; *Fax:* (202) 857-0940, (617) 772-8333
www.weil.com
Steven A. Tyrrell, Partner
Kevin J. Sullivan, Partner
Our Washington office hosts many of the firm's regulatory lawyers and serves as a central hub for integrating the substantive skills of lawyers across the firm. From Washington, our lawyers advise clients in connection with numerousgovernment agencies, including the Securities and Exchange Commission, the Federal Deposit Insurance Corporation, the U.S. Patent and Trademark Office, the International Trade Commission, the Department of Justice, the Federal Trade Commission, andthe Committee on Foreign Investment in the United States, among others.

Weintraub Tobin
Mailing Address: 9665 Wilshire Blvd., Suite 900, Beverly Hills, CA 90212
Second Address: 400 Capitol Mall, 11th Floor, Sacramento, CA 95814
(310) 858-7888, (916) 558-6000; *Fax:* (310) 550-7191, (916) 446-1611
www.weintraub.com
seisner@wwllp.com

Eugene Payne III, Of Counsel
Jeffrey Pietsch, Shareholder
Mary Price, Of Counsel
On January 1, 2012, Sacramento's Weintraub Genshlea Chediak merged with San Francisco's Tobin & Tobin, the oldest practicing law firm in California. On July 1, 2012, they merged with highly-respected attorneys from the Los Angelesentertainment and business law firm of Weissmann Wolff Bergman Coleman & Grodin.

Westervelt, Johnson, Nicholl & Keller, LLC
411 Hamilton Boulevard, Suite 1400, Peoria, IL 61602
(309) 671-3550; *Fax:* (309) 671-3588
www.wjnklaw.com
wjnk@wjnklaw.com
Roger E. Holzgrafe, Attorney
Kevin D. Schneider, Attorney
Thomas A. McConnaughay, Attorney
Westervelt, Johnson, Nicoll & Keller LLC's roots date back to the Civil War when the firm was founded by Alexander McCoy and John S. Stevens in 1865. While serving as leader of the Illinois House of Representatives, Alexander McCoysuccessfully sponsored the motion that the 13th amendment to the U.S. Constitution, banning slavery, be ratified. His partner, John S. Stevens, was counsel for many prominent businesses and financial institutions in central Illinois.

WGBH Educational Foundation
1 Guest Street, Boston, MA 02135
(617) 300-2000; *Fax:* (617) 300-1014
www.wgbh.org
Johathan C. Abbott, President & CEO
Benjamin O. Godley, COO & EVP
David Bernstein, VP & General Manager,
John Bredar, VP, National Programming
Liz Cheng, General Manager, Television
Stacey Decker, CTO
Winifred Lenihan, VP forDevelopment
Jeanne M. Hopkins, VP, Communications & Govt. Relations
Vinay Mehra, CFO, VP for Finance & Administration
Susan L. Kantrowitz, VP & General Counsel

Wiley Rein LLP
Mailing Address: 1776 K St. N.W., Washington, DC 20006
Second Address: 7925 Jones Branch Dr., Suite 6200, McLean, VA 22102
(202) 719-7000, (703) 905.2800; *Fax:* (202) 719-7049, (703)905.2820
www.wileyrein.com
As a law firm, Wiley Rein LLP represents a diverse clientele of domestic and international corporations, associations and individuals in a wide array of industries. The list below contains links to valuable, industry-related resources suchas specialty areas of law, articles, emerging issues and news events.

Wilkinson Barker Knauer, L.L.P.
Mailing Address: 2300 N St. N.W., Suite 700, Washington, DC 20037
Second Address: 1755 Blake St, Suite 470, Denver, CO 80202
(202) 783-4141, (303) 626-2350; *Fax:* (202) 783-5851
www.wbklaw.com
Bryan N. Tramont, Managing Partner
Scott Blake Harris, Managing Partner
James D. Albright, Partner
Susan B. Bergles, Partner
Joshua M. Bercu, Partner
Patricia M. Chuh, Partner

Willcox & Savage, P.C.
Mailing Address: 440 Monticello Avenue, Suite 2200, Norfolk, VA 23510
Second Address: 222 Central Park Avenue, Suite 1500, Virginia Beach, VA 23462
(757) 628-5500, (757) 628-5600; *Fax:* (757) 628-5566
www.willcoxsavage.com
mshearon@wilsav.com
L. Lucy Brandon, Associate
J. David Crain, Associate
Willcox Savage is a full-service law firm with two offices located in Southeastern Virginia. While our roots have been deeply planted in this community since 1895, we enjoy relationships with local, regional, national and internationalclients.
Box 61888, One Columbus Ctr, Suite 1010, Virginia Beach, VA 23466-1888
Fax: (757) 628-5659
Jeffrey H. Gray, Chairman

William Morris Agency
Mailing Address: 9601 Wilshire Blvd., Beverly Hills, CA 90210
Second Address: 11 Madison Ave, New York, NY 10010
(310) 285-9000, (212) 586-5100; *Fax:* (310) 285-9010, (212) 246-3583
www.wma.com

Willkie Farr & Gallagher LLP
Mailing Address: 1875 K St. N.W., Washington, DC 20006-1238
Second Address: 787 Seventh Avenue, New York, NY 10019-6099
(202) 303-1000, (212) 728-8000; *Fax:* (202) 303-2000, (212) 728-8111
www.willkie.com
Dounia Ababou, Associate
Rajab S. Abbassi, Associate
Laura H. Acker, Associate
Willkie Farr & Gallagher LLP was founded more than 120 years ago upon principles that still characterize our practice today. Our founders and memorable colleagues, like Wendell Willkie and Felix Frankfurter, established a strong foundationof integrity, innovation, pragmatism, flexibility and intellectual agility designed to continually meet the ever-changing business needs of our clients. These values form our approach to providing legal and business advisory services today. Wecontinue our tradition of excellence by keeping nimble, working collaboratively together, with respect and professionalism, and by integrating this philosophy into our client relationships. Our clients not only rely on us for our creativity, skill,leadership, decisiveness and high-quality work, but because they know we are solution-oriented and we get the job done efficiently and effectively.

WilmerHale
Mailing Address: 1875 Pennsylvania Ave., N.W., Washington, DC 20006
Second Address: 950 Page Mill Road, Palo Alto, CA 94304
(202) 663-6000, (650) 858 6000; *Fax:* (202) 663-6363, (650) 858 6100
www.wilmerhale.com
James K. Dixon, Chief Operating Officer
Matthew Adams, Staff Attorney
Thomas M. Adams, Discovery Attorney
Natalie Achenbach, Senior Associate
Debo P. Adegbile, Partner
WilmerHale offers unparalleled legal representation across a comprehensive range of practice areas that are critical to the success of our clients. We practice at the very top of the legal profession and offer a cutting-edge blend ofcapabilities that enables us to handle deals and cases of any size and complexity. Today, businesses face greater scrutiny and more "bet the company" issues than ever before. With a practice unsurpassed in depth and scope by any other major firm, wehave the ability to anticipate obstacles, seize opportunities and get the case resolved or the deal done-and the experience and know-how to prevent it from being undone.

Wiltshire & Grannis, L.L.P.
1919ÿM Street, N.W., 8th Floor, Washington, DC 20036-3537
(202) 730-1300; *Fax:* (202) 730-1301
www.wiltshiregrannis.com
Walter E. Anderson, Associate
Cecil Hunt, Counsel
Anne K. Langer, Associate
Jared P. Marx, Associate
Danielle J. Pieres, Associate
Wiltshire & Grannis LLP is a boutique law firm with a simple yet ambitious purpose: To provide our clients with the best representation available at any price, and do it without either the wasteful overhead or the unrealistic billable hoursrequirements typical of our larger competitors. Since 1998, our distinctive blend of professionalism and parsimony has earned us a national reputation for excellence in communications and information technology regulation, civil and criminal triallitigation, appellate work, and international trade and national security matters.

Winston & Strawn
Mailing Address: 35 W. Wacker Dr., Chicago, IL 60601-9703
Second Address: 100 North Tryon Street, 29th floor, Charlotte, NC 28202-1078
(312) 558-5600, (704) 350-7700; *Fax:* (312) 558-5700, (704) 350-7800
www.winston.com
sfarrell@winston.com
Scot Farrell, Chief Operating Officer
Thomas J. Friedrick, Partner
John H. Cobb, Partner
Scott Cohen, Director
James Flynn, Director
Our firm serves the needs of enterprises of all types and sizes, in both the private and the public sector. The exceptional depth and geographic reach of our resources enable Winston & Strawn to manage virtually every type ofbusiness-related legal issue.
1400 L St. N.W., 8th Fl, Washington, DC
(202) 371-5700; *Fax:* (202) 371-5950
Deborah C. Costlow, Chairman

Womble Carlyle
Mailing Address: 1200 Nineteenth Street NW, Suite 500, Washington, DC 20036
Second Address: 222 Delaware Avenue, Suite 1501, Wilmington, DE 19801
(202) 467-6900, (302) 252-4320; *Fax:* (202) 467-6910, (302) 252-4330
www.wcsr.com
Keith W. Vaughan, Chairman/Managing Partner
Terry Wiley, Executive Director
William C. Raper, Partner
Keith W. Vaughan, Partner
A full-service business law firm, Womble Carlyle serves a wide range of regional, national and international clients in industries that include health care, life sciences, financial services, commercial real estate, intellectualproperty/patent, and telecommunications, as well as educational institutions and governmental bodies and agencies.

Wood, Maines & Nolan, Chartered
3300 Fairfax Dr., Suite 202, Arlingtron, VA 22201
(703) 650-5174; *Fax:* (703) 465-2365
wmb@legalcompass.com
Barry D. Wood, Attorney
Nathaniel J. Hardy, Attorney
Ronald D. Maines, Attorney

Wright Communications
1200 G St. N.W., Suite 600, Washington, DC 20005
(202) 393-1200; *Fax:* (202) 393-1240
www.wrightlaw.com
mail@wrightlaw.com
David S. Berman, Attorney
Carrie L. Bumgarner, Attorney
Matthew J. Binette, Attorney
Wendy N. Reed, Attorney
Wright Communications is a Colorado-based technology services company specializing in education, marketing and technical IT sales for UNIX computer systems, HPC clusters and data storage sys

WTTW Channel 11/Chicago
5400 N. St. Louis Ave., Chicago, IL 60625-4698
(773) 583-5000, (773) 279-2103, (773) 509-1111; *Fax:* (773) 583-3046
www.wttw.com
wttwadsales@wttw.com
Daniel J. Schmidt, President & CEO
Reese Marcusson, EVP & CFO
Daniel Soles, SVP & Chief Television Content Officer
Jill Britton, SVP & Chief Development Officer
Anne Gleason, SVP, Marketing & Interactive Media
Parke Richeson, SVP,WTTW National Products
V.J. McAleer, SVP for Production & Community partnerships

Young, Clement & Rivers L.L.P.
25 Calhoun Street, Suite 400, Charleston, SC 29401
(843) 577-4000, (803) 254-2238; *Fax:* (843) 724-6600
www.ycrlaw.com
tanderson@ycrlaw.com
Victoria L. Anderson, Associate
William J. Bates, Senior Counsel
Joshua Paul Cantwell, Associate
Our firm strives to consistently exceed our clients' expectations by delivering quality service, with integrity, at a value that recognizes the realities of today's marketplace.

Young, Williams, Kirk & Stone PC
Mailing Address: 800 South Gay Street, Suite 2021, Knoxville, TN 37929
Second Address: PO Box 550, Knoxville, TN 37929
(865) 637-1440; *Fax:* (865) 546-9808
www.ywlawfirm.com
chris@tn-attorneys.com
Walter T. Partain, Associate
Mark K. Williams, Attorney
Mindy L Nower, Attorney
Christopher J. Kirk, Attorney
Hugh B. Ward, Attorney
Young, Williams & Kirk, PC practices in the following areas of law: Business Law, Commercial Law, General Civil Practice, Civil Trials in all State and Federal Courts, Corporation, Professional Corporation, Banking, Partnership, Health Care,Employment, Estate Planning, Wills, Probate, Trust, Taxation, Securities, Real Estate

Management & Marketing Consultants

Abt Associates Inc.
Mailing Address: 55 Wheeler St., Cambridge, MA 02138-1168
Second Address: 4550 Montgomery Avenue, Suite 800 North, Bethesda, MD 20814-3343
(617) 492-7100, (301) 347-5000; *Fax:* (617) 492-5219, (301) 634-1801
www.abtassociates.com
Stanley J. Lukowski, Chairman
Kathleen L. Flanagan, President/CEO
Stephen Pellicca, Stephen Pelliccia Division Vice President,Interna
Jane Thomason, B.S.W., M.P.H., Ph.D., Chief Executive Officer, Abt JTA
Mauricio Poodts, VicePresident,Information Technology
Mark Spranca, Ph.D., Vice President-Reputational Capital & Technical Le
Patricia Shifflett, Vice President-U.S. Health
Mark A. Schulman, Founding Partner, Research Chief, & Chairman Emeri
Mktg rsch, strategic planning, mgmt consulting, audience rsch & segmentation; customer satisfaction programs, quality of svc programs, social science survey rsch, publ policy rsch, economical rsch.
4800 Montgomery Ln., Suite 600, Bethesda, MD 20814-3429
(301) 913-0500; *Fax:* (301) 652-3618
640 N. LaSalle, Chicago, IL 60654-3781
(312) 867-4000; *Fax:* (312) 867-4200
1110 Vermont Ave. N.W., Washington, DC 20005-3544
(202) 263-1800, (202) 263-1801

Alan Burns & Associates
27250 Perdido Beach Blvd, Suite G, Orange Beach, AL 36561
(251) 980-7070; *Fax:* (251) 980-7090
www.burnsradio.com
alan@burnsradio.com
Alan Burns, President/CEO
Donna Burns, Chief Of Operations
Jeff Johnson, Senior Vice President
Kelly Milowe, Executive Administrator & Marketing Assistant
Progmg & mktg consultants.

Anderson Productions Ltd.
51 West 81st Street, Suite 12L, New York, NY 10024
(212) 414-9220; *Fax:* (212) 206-0279
www.apltv.com
steveanderson@apltv.com
Steven C.F. Anderson, President, Executive Producer
Agatha Malacos, Associate Producer
Shane Stanfield, Sound Recordist, Audio Engineer
Joe Gentle, Content Correspondent
Alan McPheely, Cinematographer
Carly Freidman, Content &Social Media Associate
TV documentary, pub affrs production & short films for non-profits.

The Aspen Institute Communications & Society Program
One Dupont Circle, 7th Floor, Washington, DC 20036
202-736-5857; *Fax:* 202-862-8526
www.aspeninstitute.org
aspencs@aspeninstitute.org
Robert K. Steel, Chairman
Richard Braddock, Chairman And CEO
Walter Isaacson, President/CEO
Amy Margerum Berg, EVP, Development & Operations, Corp. Sec
Susan Sherwin, EVP, External Relations
James Schine Crown, vice-Chairman
Miguel (Mike) Bezos, vice President And Co-Founder
Cesar R. Conde, Executive Vice President
Pub policy seminars & reports.

Audience Research & Development (AR&D)
2440 Lofton Terr., Fort Worth, TX 76109
(817) 924-6922; *Fax:* (817) 924-7539
www.ar-d.com
info@ar-d.com
Jerry Gumbert, President/CEO
Jim Willi, Principal/Senior Vice President-Multimedia Innovat
Earle Jones, Senior Strategist/SVP, Research
Fred Ertz, Principal, Senior Station Strategist
Budd McEntee, Senior Station Strategist
HollisGrizzard Jr., Senior Station Strategist
Ken Elmore, Senior Station Strategist
Rsch-based, full-svc, new media consulting firm serving TV stns, cable systems, internet companies, nwsprs & program syndicators.

The Austin Company
Mailing Address: 6095 Parkland Blvd., Cleveland, OH 44124
Second Address: 9764 Portage Road, Portage, MI 49002
(440) 544-2600, (269) 329-1170; *Fax:* (440) 544-2690, (269) 329-1417
www.theaustin.com
Mike Pierce, President
Phil Todd, SVP, Operations & GM
Matt Edleman, SVP, Sales & Marketing
Mark Phillips, SVP, Finance
Ken Stone, VP & Project Executive
Jeff Deel, Director, Human Resources
Consulting, architectural design, engrg & construction svcs for TV, cable & radio bcstg facilities.
6410 Oak Canyon, #150, Irvine, CA 92618-5213
(949) 451-9000
Ken Stone, Chairman
3500 Piedmont N.E., #725, Atlanta, GA 30305-1507
(404) 564-3950
Matt Eddleman, Chairman

AVI Communications Inc.
517 Huffines Blvd., Lewisville, TX 75056
(972) 939-7135, (800) 221-2842; *Fax:* (972) 939-7139
www.avi-communications.com
Pat Shaughnessy, President/CEO
Annie Bendalin, SVP
Tommy Olcott, VP
Ron Edwards, Producer
TV sls training, new business dev svcs & Butch Harmon golf tips for TV & radio.

AZCAR
121 Hillpointe Dr., Suite 700, Canonsburg, PA 15317
(724) 873-0800; *Fax:* (724) 873-4770
www.azcar.com
info@azcar.com
Richard Bisignano, President
Mary Nahra, Operations Dir
Video & audio system consultation, systems integration, design, instal & training; serving cable systems, cable mfg, corporate, bcst & teleproduction facilities & engng.

Bayliss Broadcast Foundation
Box 51126, Pacific Grove, CA 93950
(831) 655-5229; *Fax:* (831) 655-5228
www.baylissfoundation.org
khfranke@baylissfoundation.org
Larry Patrick, Chairman
Carl Butrum, President
Kit Hunter Franke, General Manager
David Kennedy, Director & Treasurer
Bishop Cheen, Director & Secretary
Bayliss Radio Intern program & scholarships for college students studying for a career in radio are primary focus of Foundation.

The Benchmark Co.
907 S. Congress Ave., Suite 7, Austin, TX 78704
(512) 707-7500; *Fax:* (512) 707-7757
thebenc@earthlink.net
Dr. Robert E. Balon, President/CEO
Robert J. Gacutan, Director of Technology and Research
Joe Russell, VP of Research Services
Full-svc bcst consulting & rsch company featuring benchmark perceptual phone surveys & the Focus 100 system, which replaces focus groups.

The Benton Group
PO Box 5076, Vancouver, WA 98668
(360) 574-7369; *Fax:* (360) 576-6866
www.donbenton.com
Donald Benton, President
Yellow-page & nwspr experts, specialized sls training programs & seminars.

BIA Financial Network
15120 Enterprise Ct., Chantilly, VA 20151
(800) 331-5086; *Fax:* (703) 803-3299
www.bia.com
info@biakelsey.com
Tom Buono, Founder/CEO
Mark Giannini, COO/Senior Vice President
Rick Ducey, Managing Director
Woody Allen, CFO BIA Financial Network
Mark Fratrik, SVP and Chief Economist
Stacey Sedbrook, vP, Strategic Sales Consulting
GeoffPrice, VP Valuations and Financial Consulting
MacKenzie Lovings, VP Marketing
Financial & strategic consultants to communications industries offering fair market valuations, expert tax appraisals, due diligence, acquisition consulting, business plans, internal operational audits, litigation support, investmentbanking, venture funding, capital, industry rsch & analysis publications & software.

Big Blue Dot
124 Watertown St., Suite F, Watertown, MA 02472
(617) 600-1100; *Fax:* (617) 923-0002
Jan Craige Singer, President
Trend tracking resources for the kids' market, consulting, & newsletter via e-mail; creative svcs.

BillHennesMedia
605 S Riverside Dr., Suite 5, Pompano Beach, FL 28409
(954) 934-7814; *Fax:* (910) 313-0228
www.billhennesmedia.com
bhennes105@aol.com
Bill Hennes, President
Bill Hennes Media is a full service consulting company for radio station, Internet stations, Recording Artists and Music Companies.

Block Communications Group Inc.
2910 Neilson Way, Suite 503, Santa Monica, CA 90405-5368
(310) 452-3355; *Fax:* (310) 452-4077
www.blockcommunicationsgroup.com
dblock@earthlink.net
Dick Block, President
Consultants specializing in new cable svcs, bcstg stns, syndicated progmg, distribution & mktg serving U.S. & international clients since 1974.

Bond & Pecaro Inc.
1909 K Street, NW, Suite 320, Washington, DC 20006
(202) 775-8870; *Fax:* (202) 775-0175
www.bondpecaro.com
bp@bondpecaro.com
Timothy Pecaro, Operations Dir
Timothy S. Pecaro, Principal and Founder
John S. Sanders, Principal and Founder
Jeffrey P. Anderson, Principal
Andrew R. Gefen, Principal
Matthew H. Lochte, Principal
Benjamin K. Steinbock, SeniorAnalyst
Economic & financial consulting, valuation studies, asset allocations, appraisals, feasibility studies, fairness opinions, Internet valuations & expert testimony.

Bortz Media & Sports Group
5105 DTC Parkway, Suite 200, Greenwood Village, CO 80111
(303) 893-9902; *Fax:* (303) 893-9913
www.bortz.com
info@bortz.com
Arthur Steiker, Managing Director
Jim Trautman, Managing Director
Mark Wyche, Managing Director
TV stn mgmt consulting, cable financial & market analysis; corporate strategic planning.

Bowman Valuation Services
706 Duke St., 3rd Floor, Alexandria, VA 22314
(703) 549-5681; *Fax:* (703) 549-5682
www.bowmanvaluation.com
Peter Bowman, Principal
Peter Bowman, ASA, Principal
Chip Snyder, Principal
Appraisals, asset allocations, specialized studies.

Broadcast Media Associates
PO Box 1233, Santa Maria, CA 93456
(805) 937-1553; *Fax:* (805) 937-7212
Clifford M. Hunter, President
Mgmt consulting, mktg studies & bcst investment analysis.

BTMI (Broadcast Trustee Management Inc.)
111 South Calvert St, Suite 2700, Baltimore, MD 21202
(410) 385-5600; *Fax:* (410) 385-5601
www.ecrp.com
Robert E. Long, Chairman
Paul W. Robinson, CEO
Kent Burkhart, Senior Managing Partner
John P. Morgan, CFO
Financial-asset mgmt, valuation, mktg, restructuring & recovery consultation svcs.

Burkat Global LLC
16 Drake Rd., Scarsdale, NY 10583
(914) 231-9023; *Fax:* (914) 472-6225
www.burkatglobal.com
iburkat@burkatglobal.com
Iris Burkat, CEO/Managing Partner
Howard Burkat, Managing Partner/CEO & Director, Comm.
Iris Burkat, Burkat Company, President
David Zeitlin, Burkat Company Research Director

Alan Brooks, Burkat Company Creative Director
BridgetGibbons, Burkat Company Social Media Director
Sls, mktg & mgmt consulting for TV, cable, radio, domestic & international. Planning analysis, rsch & recruiting.

Carolina Media Professionals Inc.
2999 South Pine Street, Spartanburg, SC 29302
(864) 597-1301, (888) 368-4252; *Fax:* (864) 596-7539
www.carolinamedia.com
services@carolinamedia.com
Rachel Greene, CEO & President of Radio Airtime
Keli D. Carey, National Sales Manager

CEA Group
Mailing Address: 101 E. Kennedy Blvd., Suite 3300, Tampa, FL 33602
Second Address: 260 Madison Avenue, New York, NY 10016
(813) 226-8844; *Fax:* (813) 225-1513
www.ceaworldwide.com
RMichaels@ceaworldwide.com
J. Patrick (Rick) Michaels, Jr., Founder/Chairman/CEO
Ming Jung, Executive VP & COO
Brad Gordon, Executive VP & CFO
Dave Moyer, Senior Managing Director & President, CEA PAG
Beth Cahill, Senior Managing Director
Robert D. Berger,Managing Director
Michael Johnson, Vice President
Doris Rainey, Vice President
A leading provider of investment banking services and private equity to the global communications, media, entertainment, and information technology industries.
54 Thompson St., 4th Fl., New York, NY 10012-4308
(212) 218-5085

The Center for Sales Strategy, Inc.
6601 Memorial Highway, Tampa, FL 33615
(813) 254-2222, (800) 265-3276; *Fax:* (813) 254-9222
www.thecenterforsalesstrategy.com
TechSupport@CSScenter.com
Steve Marx, Chairman Emeritus
Jim Hopes, CEO
John Henley, Chief Operating Officer/Partner
Mike Anderson, Consumer Insights And Communication
Emily Estey, VP/Senior Consultant
Stephanie Downs, VP/Senior Consultant
Comprehensive consulting & training svcs for radio & TV, cable, and nwspr, in sls, mktg & mgmt, exclusively on a long-term, multi-year basis.

Chenevert Songy Rodi Soderberg
Div/DBA: (An Engrg/Architectural Corp.)
Mailing Address: 6767 Perkins Rd., Suite 200, Baton Rouge, LA 70808
Second Address: 550 Belle Terre Blvd., LaPlace, LO 70068
(225) 769-0546; *Fax:* (225) 767-0060
www.csrsonline.com
info@csrsonline.com
Michael B. Songy, P.E., P.L.S., CEO
Architects, planners & tech designers specializing in new & renovated bcst/cable production facilities.

Christian Television Services
9775 S.W. 87th Ave., Miami Beach, FL 33141
(305) 592-7642; *Fax:* (305) 596-4564
www.citv.com
webmaster@citv.com
Russell Thorne, CEO
Relg media buying.

Christian TV Services
Mailing Address: 6490 PineTree Rd, Apt. 315, Ellicottville, NY 14731
Second Address: PO Box 209, Ellicottville, NY 14731
(716) 699-2549; *Fax:* (716) 699-2590
George A. Thayer, President
Joyce E. Thayer, Operations Dir
Russell A. Thayer, General Manager
Roger A. Thayer, Programming Director
Randall A. Thayer, Promotions Manager
TVRO consultant for Christian media started: 1974; affil: TBN/TCT/CTS Ministering to Ministries, listing media organizations & Internet places of worship. (800) 982-8823.

Chubb Group of Insurance Companies
15 Mountain View Rd., Warren, NJ 07059
(908) 903-2000; *Fax:* (908) 903-2027
www.chubb.com
info@chubb.com
Endorsed multi-natl property/casualty carrier by the Bcst Financial Mgrs Assns.
Branches in more than 115 offices in 30 countries.

Claritas Inc.
Mailing Address: 5375 Mira Sorrento Place, Suite 400, San Diego, CA 92121-7703
Second Address: 1145 Sanctuary Parkway, Suite 355, Alpharetta, GE 30004
(858) 622-0800, (770) 77-4240; *Fax:* (703) 812-2701, (770) 777-4241
www.claritas.com
info@claritas.com
R. Bergh, Chairman
Peter Tordoir, Chief Executive Officer
Keith Peterson, Chief Operating Officer and President of Integras
Soren Lundgren, General Manager
Mark Patron, Vice President
Mike Mancini, Vice President of Data ProductManagement
Hugo Borda, Chief Technology Officer and Vice President
David Miller, SVP, Data Research & Development
Ben Tiesnitsch, Human Resources Director
Chris Smith, Director, Financial Services Group
Nielsen SiteReports is the most accurate online source for U.S. demographics and is the first to offer current year and five year demographic projections. SiteReports offers more than 50 reports and maps providing detailed informationhelping you analyze markets, select site locations and target your customers effectively.
332 S. Michigan Ave, Suite 200, Chicago, IL 60604-4434
(312) 986-2650
Margie Lymperis, Vp Electronic Media

Clifton Gardiner & Company, L.L.C.
24645 S. Augusta Court, Sun Lakes, AZ 85248
(623) 336-7272, (623) 337-3777; *Fax:* (623) 498-8310
www.cliftongardiner.com
cliff@cliftongardiner.com
Clifton H. Gardiner, President
Clifton Gardiner & Company, LLC provides experienced and professional brokerage representation to buyers and sellers of radio stations and other media properties. We represent our clients on an exclusive basis, and devote all of ourresources to achieving a successful completion of a transaction. We are known for the accuracy and completeness of our Memorandums and for our very thorough search for possible buyers. Marketing a "for sale" listing is not a "passive" activity. Wework hard from day one!

Colorado Springs Film Commission
515 S. Cascade Ave., Colorado Springs, CO 80903
(719) 685-7630, (800) 888-4748; *Fax:* (719) 635-4968
www.filmcoloradosprings.com
amy@visitcos.com
Amy Long, VP Marketing/ Membership
Chelsy Murphy, Director of Communications
Free location svcs, Production Resource Guide, location guide available for the Colorado Springs, CO area; help with crews, hotels & permits.

Coltrin & Associates Inc.
Mailing Address: 1212 Ave. of the Americas, New York, NY 10036
Second Address: 801 Floral Vale Blvd., Yardley, PA 19067
(212) 221-1616, (215) 497-3188; *Fax:* (212) 221-7718
www.coltrin.com
steve_coltrin@coltrin.com
Stephen H. Coltrin, Chairman /CEO
Jennifer Coltrin Webb, Senior Vice President of Operations
Susan Surillo Battafarano, Vice President-Human Resources & Executive Service
Consultant svcs to bcst mgmt, mktg sls, promotional rsch; New York, NY, & Washington, DC representation in corporate, govt & PR.
801 Floral Vale Blvd., Yardley, PA 19067-5513
(215) 497-3188
Gwen Coltrin, Coo
433 Airport Blvd, Suite 414, Burlingame, CA 94010-2017
(650) 373-2005
Benoit Rungeard, Dir
50 Raffles Pl., 37th Fl., Singapore, Indonesia
+65 6829 7149
Chan Chee Pong, Vp
215 Celebration Pl., Suite 500, Celebration, FL 34747-5400
(321) 559-1112
215 S. State St, Suite 675, Salt Lake City, UT 84111-2319
(801) 350-9412
35 Picadilly, 3rd Fl., London, United Kingdom
+44 20 7494 4748

Columbia Management Advisors
One S. Wacker Dr., Chicago, IL 60606
Fax: (312) 855-2552
William Rarkin, President
Investment counsel & mutual fund mgmt. Offices in Chicago, IL; Cleveland, OH; New York, NY; San Francisco, CA; & Puerto Rico.

ComBridges
66 Via Holon, #11, Greenbrae, CA 94904
(415) 454-5505, (888) 530-5505; *Fax:* (888) 530-5505
www.combridges.com
info@combridges.com
Jon Leland, President/Creative Director
Complete creative & production svcs including: animation, special effects, video production, video streaming, web site design, & computer-based production system design. Experience with creative svc departments & corporate communications.

Communication Trends Inc.
One Buckhead Plaza, 3060 Peachtree Road NW, Suite 350, Atlanta, GA 30305
(404) 843-8717; *Fax:* (404) 843-6869
www.ctimedia.com
info@ctimedia.com
Mktg & adv for cable, direct bcst, bcst communications industries & related technologies.

Communications Design Associates Inc.
437 Turnpike St., Canton, MA 02021
(339) 502-6551; *Fax:* (339) 502-6595
www.cdaconsultants.com
information@cdaconsultants.com
Stewart B. Randall, CTS-D, Principal Consultant
Greg T. Vincent, Principal Consultant
Jason Rogers, Project Design Manager
Nick McClelland, Project Design Manager
Scott MacLeod, Senior Designer
We service clients throughout the country, with a staff consisting of engineers with over 160 years combined experience in audio/video and telecommunications technologies. We are active members of the Audio Engineering Society, InfocommInternational (ICIA), Society of Motion Picture and Television Engineers and the National Systems Contractor Association. Many of our staff members hold Certified Technology Specialist (CTS) or higher designations. This industry standard forprofessional expertise is awarded by ICIA, the leading provider of certification and education for AV professionals. Additionally, we have earned certification from numerous manufacturers whose products are highly regarded in the industry.

Comsearch
19700 Janelia Farm Blvd., Ashburn, VA 20147
(703) 726-5500, (800) 318-1234; *Fax:* (703) 726-5600
www.comsearch.com
customersupport@comsearch.com
Douglass R. Hall, President
Since 1977, Comsearch has provided innovative spectrum management and wireless engineering solutions to the global market for fixed, mobile, and broadband wireless applications. Our experienced engineers, software products, and informationdatabases address the specific challenges of designing wireless networks while identifying, analyzing, and resolving radio frequency interference for wireless spectrum users worldwide.

Connecticut Film Video & Media Office
39 Woodland Street, 2nd Fl., Hartford, CT 06105
(800) 392-2122, (860) 256-2800, (860) 270-8000; *Fax:* (860) 256-2811
www.ct.gov
DECD@ct.gov
Karen Senich, General Manager
Catherine Smith, DECD Commissioner
George Norfleet, Director
Mark Dixon, Location Services
Ed Ruggiero, Film Tax Credit Administrator
Ellen Woolf, Production Services
Erika H. Steiner, ChiefFinancial Officer
A film commission eager to respond to any situation or need.

Convergent Media Systems
190 Bluegrass Valley Pky., Suite 800, Alpharetta, GA 30005
(770) 369-9000; *Fax:* (770) 369-9100
www.convergent.com
convergent@convergent.com
Gary L. Kavey, CEO/President & Director
R. Bryan Allen, President
Greg Bloodworth, Senior Vice President of Operations
Trevor Davies, Chief Engineer
Craig Leathers, Managing Director
Gary Johns, SVP, Sales & Marketing
Provider of video & data technologies to support the communication & training needs of companies. Svcs include consultation, design, instal, net & systems mgmt; systems

integration in the following areas: special event TV, business TV,desktop video, video production, videoconferencing, & interactive multimedia.

Cox & Cox, LLC
Mailing Address: 2454 Shiva Ct., St. Louis, MO 63011
Second Address: 4546 Sliver Bit Court, North Las Vegas, Las Vegas, Ne 89032
(702) 296-5814,(636) 458-4780; *Fax:* (702) 968-8618
Robert Cox, President
Linda Cox, Operations Dir
Media mergers & acquisitions, appraisals, consulting, expert testimony, receivership & workout.

Dave Gifford International
1142 Tano Del Este, Santa Fe, NM 87506
(505) 989-7007; *Fax:* (505) 988-1991
giff@talkgiff.com
Sls & sls management training, sls turnarounds & troubleshooting. Sls, mgmt & adv seminars. New account sls & client dev., creator of graduate school of sls.

DIS Consulting Corp.
PO Box 477, Woodstock, NY 12498-1101
(917) 692-0975
www.disresearch.com
dougsheer@gmail.com
Douglas I. Sheer, CEO & Chief Analyst
Regina C. Sheer, V. P./General Manager
Mktg consultants to 1,000 equipment manufacturers since 1982. Mktg consultation, business plan writing, financial & market rsch, mktg & distribution plans.

DME Holdings, LLC
2441 Bellevue Ave., Daytona Beach, FL 32114
(386) 257-2500, (877) 720-0082; *Fax:* (386) 271-3001
www.dmedelivers.com
info@dmedelivers.com
Mike Panaggio, CEO
Kathy Wise, President
Mike Dunn, COO
Terry Webber, EVP, Technology Solutions
Nancy Flint, CFO
Eric Remington, Chief Technology Officer
Rob Carll, Director, Sales & Marketing
High-impact, direct-mail campaigns, data base mgmt, audience rsch via cluster-targeted mktg, market exclusive.

Donna Halper & Associates
550 Adams St., Suite 3-365, Quincy, MA 02169
(617) 786-0666; *Fax:* (617) 786-1809
www.donnahalper.com
dlh@donnahalper.com
Donna L. Halper, President
Radio progmg & mgmt consulting, market studies, format changes, music library software. Staff training, motivation. Specialize in small & medium markets, new owners, turnarounds. Also bcst historian.

Electronicast Consultants
104 Hainline Road, Suite A, Aptos, CA 95003
(831) 708-2381; *Fax:* (707) 257-9502
www.electronicast.com
hans@electronicastconsultants.com
Jeff D. Montgomery, BSEE, MBA, Chairman
Stephen Montgomery, MBA/Technology Management, President
Theresa Hosking, BS, Vice President-Sales and Marketing
Hans van der Tang, Director Sales & Marketing - APAC Region.
Market forecast consulting concern for the fiber-optic, optoelectronic, telecommunication & CATV industries. Multi-client & custom reports available.

Enterprise Appraisal Co.
1450 E Boot Rd, West Chester, PA 19380
(610) 687-5855; *Fax:* (610) 971-0760
www.eacvaluations.com
info@eacvaluations.com
Frank L. Merenda, AVA, CMEA, MBA, MS, President/Ceo
Thomas H. Gudowicz, VP of Sales and Marketing
Chuck Bertsch, Senior Business Valuation Director
Francis ("Frank") J.X. Marcucci, Jr., National Director - Client Development
Evaluates communications-oriented assets, such as equipment & real estate, for TV, CATV, radio, cellular systems, & satellites.
Washington, DC
(202) 887-0948
New York, NY
(212) 517-8037

EnVest Media, LLC
6802 Patterson Ave., Richmond, VA 23226 23226
(804) 282-5561; *Fax:* (804) 282-5703
www.envest.biz
Mitt Younts, Managing Member
Nationwide radio, TV acquisition, valuation, financing & consulting firm. The company provides brokerage svcs to stn transaction, appraisal svcs to stn owners & financial institutions. The group secures debt & equity acquisition financing,offers consulting & asset mgmt svcs, acting as court appointed receivers or trustees for bcst stns.

Equidata
724 Thimble Shoals Blvd., Newport News, VA 23606
(757) 873-0519, (800) 288-9809; *Fax:* (757) 873-1224
Mary Emmett, President
Nationwide collection agency/credit reporting agency.

Evalueserve, Inc.
421 Fayetteville St., Suite 200, Raleigh, NC 27601
(919) 977-8200; *Fax:* (919) 977-3267
website.evalueserve.com
usa@evalueserve.com
Timo Vatto, Chairman
Marc Vollenweider, CEO
Nishant Jaiswal, Group Manager
Mariela Salisch, Group Manager
Nandlal Gangwani, CFO
Ashish Gupta, COO
Daniel Sadhu, Managing Director
Ashutosh Gupta, Co-BU Head Financial Services
After over a decade in operation, Evalueserve has grown to be one of the largest Knowledge Process Outsourcing (KPO) companies in the world. We help our clients by optimizing their existing knowledge processes using our experience from overten years of operation and over four million hours of services provided annually.

Executive Decision Systems Inc.
6421 W. Weaver Dr., Littleton, CO 80123
(303) 795-9090; *Fax:* (303) 795-1970
www.retailinsights.com
info@retailinsights.com
Provide sls & mgmt training, focusing on generating long-term, loc direct revenues. Provides academic approach to media mktg to stns around the United States & abroad. System 21 is guaranteed to return 12 times the revenues within 150 daysor your money is refunded.

The Exline Company
388 Lowell Avenue, Mill Valley, CA 94941
(415) 381-5473; *Fax:* (415) 381-5473
www.exlinecompany.com
exline@pacbell.net
Andrew P. McClure, President
Judi Lewis, Adminstrative Coordinator
Mgmt, financial rsch, appraisal, receiverships & bankruptcies. Station brokerage.

The Express Group
3360 Thorn St, San Diego, CA 92104
(619) 280-9061; *Fax:* (619) 280-9030
www.theexpressgroup.com
gandrus@theexpressgroup.com
Byron Andrus, President/Senior Designer
Roberta Andrus, Operations Dir
George Andrus, Senior Design Consultant
Robin Andrus, Vice President & Art Director
Tim Poremba, Designer/ Artist
Chris Andrus, Lighting Design
Kim Booth,Marketing Director
Alan Calero, IT Manager
Design, fabrication, instal & lighting of news environments, newsrooms, interview & talkshow sets.

Faraone Communications Inc./dba Worldwide Public Relations
75 West End Ave., Suite R-9A, New York, NY 10023
(212) 489-1313; *Fax:* (212) 489-8978
www.worldwidepublicrelations.com
ted.faraone@verizon.net
Ted Faraone, Chairman
Ted Farone, Principal
PR svc to bcst, cable, radio, TV & other entertainment properties & media companies.

Federal Engineering Inc.
Redwood Plaza II, 10600 Arrowhead Dr., Fairfax, VA 22030
(703) 359-8200; *Fax:* (703) 359-8204
www.fedeng.com
info@fedeng.com
Ronald F. Brosco, President & CEO
John E. Murray, SVP
Strategic planning, coverage analysis, new product definition, market rsch, competitive analysis, rates & tariffs, bcst stn design, mergers & acquisitions, expert testimony, regulatory support.

Ferraro Communications Inc.
39 Byron Rd., Weston, MA 02493
(781) 235-5556; *Fax:* (781) 235-5558
Tom Ferraro, President
Concept, script & production/direction for coml, radio, film & videotape productions.

Florical Systems
4500 NW 27th Ave., Bldg B-1, Gainesville, FL 32606
(352) 372-8326; *Fax:* (352) 375-0859
www.florical.com
support@florical.com
Philippe Generali, President/CEO
Shawn Maynard, VP & GM
Manufacturer of TV automations, controls & effects.

Focal Press
8th Floor, 711 3rd Ave, New York, NY 10017
(212) 216-7800, (800) 634-7064; *Fax:* (212) 564-7854
www.routledge.com
orders@taylorandfrancis.com
Joanne Tracy, General Manager
Chris Mebegon, Promotions Manager
Publishes professional tech books in bcstg, film, video, multimedia, theatre & photography.
Linacre House, Jordan Hill, Oxford
011-44-1-865-310366
Jennifer Welham, Chairman

Ford Foundation
320 East 43rd St., New York, NY 10017
(212) 573-5000; *Fax:* (212) 351-3677
www.fordfound.org
Kofi Appenteng, Chair
Ursula M. Burns, Chairman And CEO
Ddarren Walker, President
Tim Berners-Lee, Director
We work mainly by making grants or loans that build knowledge and strengthen organizations and networks. Since our financial resources are modest compared with societal needs, we focus on key problem areas and program strategies.

Franey, Muha & Alliant Inc.
9901 Business Pkwy., Suite B, Lanham, MD 20706
(301) 459-0055
William Franey, President
Insurance, bonding & benefits admin.
13921 Park Central Rd, Suite160, Herndon, VA
(703) 397-0977; *Fax:* (703) 397-0995
John Muha, Chairman

Frank Boyle & Co., L.L.C.
32 greystone, Shelton, CT 06484
(203)513-2402; *Fax:* (203)513-8189
Frank Boyle, President

Frank N. Magid Associates Inc.
Mailing Address: 8500 Normandale Lake Blvd, Suite 630, Minneapolis, MN 55437
Second Address: 15260 Ventura Blvd, Suite 1840, Sherman Oaks, CA 91403
(612) 216-0703, (818) 2630-300; *Fax:* (952) 835-3385, (818) 263-3311
www.magid.com
Brent Magid, CEO
Steve Ridge, President
Frank N. Magid, Founder
Specialists in rsch-driven consultation to traditional & new media firms; svcs include strategic planning, web site evaluation & dev, program evaluation, talent search, coaching, TMI, & the Magid Network.
15260 Ventura Blvd, Suite 2130, Sherman Oaks, CA 91403-5307
(818) 263-3300; *Fax:* (818) 263-3311
Jack MacKenzie, Exec Vp
1775 Broadway, Suite 1401, New York, NY 10019-1903
(212) 974-2310; *Fax:* (212) 515-4540
Vicki Cohen, Exec Vp

Frank N. Magid Associates Inc.
Div/DBA: (Division of Frank N. Magid Associates Inc.)
Mailing Address: One Research Ctr., Marion, IA 52302
Second Address: 15260 Ventura Blvd, Suite 1840, Sherman Oaks, CA 91403
(319) 377-7345, (818) 2630-300; *Fax:* (319) 377-5861, (818) 263-3311

www.magid.com
iowa@magid.com
Brent Magid, CEO
Steve Ridge, President
Bill Hague, Operations Dir
Frank N. Magid, Founder
Frank N. Magid Associates, Inc. helps our clients become more profitable by solving their business problems and helping them take advantage of opportunities
15260 Ventura Blvd., Suite 2130, Sherman Oaks, CA 91403-5307
(818) 263-3300; *Fax:* (818) 263-3311
Jack MacKenzie, Exec Vp
1775 Broadway, Suite 1401, New York, NY 10019-1903
(201) 974-2310; *Fax:* (212) 515-4540
Vicki Cohen, Exec Vp

George Moore & Associates Inc.
2046 John Rolfe Parkway, Richmond, VA 23238-8111
(214) 369-5665, (800) 220-3287; *Fax:* (214) 369-5667
W. James Moore, President
Brokerage of radio, TV & CATV properties; asset & market appraisals; introduction to institutional financing sources.

Getty Images
Peninsula Corporate Park, 7th floor, Tower A, Mumbai, In 400013
(+91)22 4063 4848; *Fax:* (+91)22 4063 4888
www.gettyimages.com
feedback@gettyimages.com
Jonathan Klein, CEO
Business & mgmt consulting, training, long-term strategic planning, organizations analysis, mktg positioning; seminars on goal setting, leadership, mgmt skills, sls training. Retail training.

Gilbert Communications
99 Colborne Street W, Brantford, ON N3T 1K8
(519) 756-2570; *Fax:* (865) 977-6633
www.gilbertcomm.com
rwgilbert@charter.com
Robert W. Gilbert, President
Gilbert Communications is the retail provider of Gilbert Communications and Security Services. Gilbert Security Services provides and installs high quality Fire, Burglar, Video and Outdoor perimeter detection systems, custom designed andmonitored to suit your specific needs. We service Southern Ontario customers in the 519 area code and have been doing so since 1976.

Greater Fort Lauderdale Alliance
110 E. Broward Blvd., Suite 1990, Fort Lauderdale, FL 33301-2248
(954) 524-3113 ext 220, (800) 741-1420; *Fax:* (954) 524-3167
www.gflalliance.org
info@browardalliance.org
Ben Wesley, Chairman
Bob Swindell, President/CEO
Jack Bennings, CAE, Director of Workforce Development
Gail Bulfin, Vice President - Membership Development
David Coddington, Vice President - Business Development
Ron Drew, VicePresident - Marketing and Communications
Maggie Gunther, Manager - Communications & Programs
Michelle Cook, Business Development Coordinator
Resource for film, TV & print industry production and business relocation.

Greenwood Performance Systems LLC
907 S. Detroit, Suite 720, Tulsa, OK 74120
(800) 331-9115, (918) 582-1713; *Fax:* (918) 665-7233
www.greenwoodperformance.com
info@greenwoodperformance.com
Jim Rhea, CEO
Dr. Jeanine Rhea, Managing Partner
Bcst-specific sls & mgmt training, seminars & courses including sls mgmt consultation, strategic planning, compensation, selection & evaluation.

Guidestar Corp.
1400 Clyde Ave, Suite 215, Ottawa, ON K2G 3J2
(613) 226-3018
www.guidestarrealty.com
guidestar@guidestarrealty.com
Ronald F. Bosco, General Manager
Mktg communications & PR specifically tailored to serve the telecommunications & info processing marketplaces.

Hoffman Schutz Media Capital Inc.
2044 West California St., San Diego, CA 92110
(206) 201-3822
www.hs-media.com
David Schutz, President
Strategic planning for lender & investor appraisals & litigation support.

The Howard-Sloan-Koller Group
Mailing Address: 300 E. 42nd St., 15th Floor, New York, NY 10017
Second Address: 9701 Wilshire Boulevard, Suite 1000, Beverly Hills, CA 90212
(212) 661-5250, (310) 601-7114; *Fax:* (212) 557-9178, (310) 601-7110
www.hsksearch.com
hsk@hsksearch.com
Edward R. Koller Jr., President/CEO
Mara Covell, Managing Director
Dick Schenkel, Managing Director
Sharon Spielman, Managing Director
Thomas Cullingan, Managing Director
Karen Shnek Lippman, Managing Director
ColletteRichardson, Director
Exec search & consulting in the cable, infotechnology, entertainment, new media & publishing industries.

The Image Generators
Div/DBA: (A division of Voicelines Inc.)
18156 Darnell Dr., Olney, MD 20832
(301) 924-5700; *Fax:* (301) 570-8916
www.imagegenerators.com
mike@imagegenerators.com
Michael J. Weiner, President/CEO
Mktg & mgmt issues; talent training workshops & coaching.

Inergize Digital Media
355 Randolph Ave, Suite 100, St. Paul, MN 55102
(952) 460-7600; *Fax:* (952) 460-7603
www.inergizedigital.com
Jason Gould, General Manager
Inergize Digital is the leader in fully integrated digital management solutions, and provides media companies with an integrated four-screen solution for content delivery in any format to meet the needs of today's digital consumer.

IPI Report
Div/DBA: The International Journalism Magazine
320 Lee Hills Hall, Columbia, MO 65211
(573) 884-6432; *Fax:* (573) 884-1870
www.voxmagazine.com
Shawn Donnelly, Operations Dir
IPI Report defends, celebrates, relects & explores the international media & freedom of expression.
132A Neff Annex, Columbia, MO
(573) 884-7542
Stuart H. Loory, Editor

J.M. Miller
Box 190, Ashburn, VA 20146
703-729-7745; *Fax:* 703-729-7745
broadcastappraisal@yahoo.com
Jan M. Miller, President
Bcst TV, DTV, AM, FM, production, satellite, microwave facility & equipment inspection, asset appraisal reports, engrg evaluation overviews & consulting svcs. For valuation, acquisition, finance, purchase price allocation, ad valorem tax,insurance, leasing, liquidation & litigation.

John P. Allen Airspace Consultants Inc.
290 Marsh Lakes Dr., Fernandina Beach, FL 32034
(904) 261-6523; *Fax:* (904) 277-3651
Mary C. Lowe, President
Conducts FAA aeronautical evaluations as specified in Subpart C of Part 77 of the Federal Aviation Regulations.

John R Ulmer, CPA, PC
2176 Highpoint Rd., Snellville, GA 30078
(770) 979-3031; *Fax:* (770) 979-3789
www.ulmercpa.com
john@ulmercpa.com
John R. Ulmer, President
Accounting, computer & financial mgmt consulting.

Kagan Media Appraisals, a division of Media Central/Primedia
Mailing Address: 40 Ragsdale Drive, Suite 250, Monterey, CA 93940
Second Address: 15 Broad Street, Suite 501, Boston, MA 2109
(831) 624-1536, (617) 371-3983; *Fax:* (831) 625-3225, (212) 542-8047
www.snl.com
kaganconsulting@snl.com
Nick Cafferillo, COO
Mike Chinn, President/CEO
Will Pappas, Managing Director, Sales
Adam Hall, CFO
Dan Oakey, Corporate Secretary/Chief Contracts Officer
Galen Warren, Chief Technology Officer
James Record, Managing Director ofProduct Research & Developmen
Nate Haskins, Managing Director of Content
Tom Corbitt, Chief Human Resources Officer
Specializes in the valuation & appraisal of media & communications properties. As part of the Media Central Group of Companies, we maintain the industry's most comprehensive data base of stn values, so we know what yesterday's stns sold for,what buyers are paying today & what they are likely to pay tomorrow. Svcs include: Fair market valuations, expert witness testimony, asset appraisals, ESOP valuations, fairness opinions, minority interest valuations, financial feasibility studies,strategic planning, custom rsch & reports & consulting.

Kagan World Media/Primedia, Inc.
Mailing Address: 40 Ragsdale Drive, Suite 250, Monterey, CA 93940
Second Address: 15 Broad Street, Suite 501, Boston, MA 2109
(831) 624-1536, (617) 371-3983; *Fax:* (831) 625-3225, (212) 542-8047
www.snl.com
Nick Cafferillo, COO
Mike Chinn, President/CEO
Will Pappas, Managing Director, Sales
Robin Flynn, Programming Director
Adam Hall, CFO
Dan Oakey, Corporate Secretary/Chief Contracts Officer
Galen Warren, Chief TechnologyOfficer
James Record, Managing Director of Product Research & Developmen
Nate Haskins, Managing Director of Content
Tom Corbitt, Chief Human Resources Officer
Strategic conferences on media & communications topics, including interactive, multimedia, telecommunications, entertainment deals & financing.

Kalba International Inc.
116 McKinley Ave., New Haven, CT 06515
(203) 397-2199; *Fax:* (781) 240-2657
www.kalbainternational.com
kalba@comcast.net
Kas Kalba, President/CEO
F. Roberts, Operations Dir
Brian Carvalho, Research Manager
Mouhamed Mahi Saikh SY, Senior Consultant
Guylaine Amyot, Managing Consultant
Paul Renaud, Managing Consultant
Avi Teitelman, ManagingConsultant
Susan Sweet, Managing Consultant
Consulting & advisory svcs on telecommunications, bcstg & cable TV, including international ventures, due diligence, litigation support.

Kozacko Media Services
6890 E Sunrise Dr., Suite 120-Box 40, Tucson, AZ 85750
(520) 299-4869, (520) 465-4302; *Fax:* (520) 844-8559
www.radioforsale.com
georgewkimble@aol.com
Dick Kozacko, President
Appraisals, current market evaluations of radio/TV stns & bcst acquisition planning.
6890 E. Sunrise Dr., Box 120-40, Tucson, AZ 85732-2040
(520) 299-4869; *Fax:* (520) 844-8559
George W. Kimble, Assoc
1071 Club Dr., Keswick, VA 22947-2613
(434) 244-2653; *Fax:* (434) 244-2666
W. Donald Roberts Jr., Assoc

KSL 5 Television
55 N. 3rd W., 5 Triad Center, Salt Lake City, UT 84180-1109
(801) 575-7601, (801) 575-5880; *Fax:* (801) 575-5560
www.ksl.com
support@ksl.com
Bruce Christensen, President
Greg James, Operations Dir
Tami Ostmark, Promotions Manager
John Dehnel, Chief Engineer
An advertiser-supported NABTS news & info svc available through TV decoders or personal computers equipped with modems. Modem number is (801) 575-5911.

Lawson & Associates Architects
7939 Norfolk Ave., Suite 200, Bethesda, MD 20814
(301) 654-1600; *Fax:* (301) 654-1601
www.lawsonarch.com
info1@lawsonarch.com
Bruce Lawson, Principal
James Ahn, Project Architect

PROFESSIONAL SERVICES

Consulting architectural design & construction mgmt svcs for the TV & cable industry; facility planning, design & coordination of construction svcs.

Lipson & Co.
10350 Santa Monica Blvd, Suite 205, Los Angeles, CA 90025
(310) 277-4646; *Fax:* (310) 277-8585
www.lipsonco.com
Howard R. Lipson, Owner/Principal
Harriet Lipson, Marketing/Advertising
Executive recruiting for international & domestic bcstg, cable, entertainment, adv, mktg, finance, mdse, licensing & digital medai.

Lund Consultants to Broadcast Management Inc.
840 Hinckley Rd., Suite 123, Burlingame, CA 94010
(650) 692-7777; *Fax:* (650) 692-7799
www.lundradio.com
lundradio@aol.com
John C. Lund, President
Dan R. Spice, Operations Dir
June H. Lund, Executive Vice President
Experts in progmg consulting; multiopoly strategy. Adult contemp, country, top 40, rock, classic rock, oldies, news-talk, music, formatics, proms, talent dev & perceptual rsch.

Mahlum Architects
Mailing Address: 71 Columbia, Floor 4, Seattle, WA 98104
Second Address: 1231 NW Hoyt, Suite 102, Portland, OR 97209
(206) 441-4151, (503) 224-4032; *Fax:* (206) 441-0478, (503) 224-0918
www.mahlum.com
Diane Shiner AIA LEED AP, Operations Partner
Anne Schopf FAIA, Design Partner
Gerald Reifert FAIA, Managing Partner
Design; tech consulting; feasibility & facilities studies; cost analysis & construction admin for TV/radio stns, production & equipment storage facilities, & film studios.

Marshall & Stevens Inc.
601 South Figueroa St, Suite 2301, Los Angeles, CA 90017
(213) 612-8000, (800) 950-9588; *Fax:* (213) 612-8010
www.marshall-stevens.com
info@marshall-stevens.com
Mark W. Santarsiero, President/CEO
John Spude, Executive Managing Director/Principal
Ralph J. Consola, Executive Managing Director/Principal
John F. Oates, Managing Director
Natl appraisal firm with extensive bcstg client base. Value real estate, equipment, intangible assets & overall business valuations. Assist in financing sls, purchase price allocation, & cast segregation.
701 Market Street, # 370, St. Louis, MO 63101-1830
(800) 325-7337, (800)-325-7337
Raymond Essma, Vp Central Div
1156 Ave. of the Americas, #703, New York, NY 10036-2702
(212) 425-4300
Wiley Scott, Vp Sls

Maxagrid
3939 Belt Line Rd., Suite 250, Addison, TX 75001
(972) 241-2110; *Fax:* (972) 241-2174
Jim Tiller, President
Karen Brian, General Manager
Yield mgmt systems for bcst in USA, Australia, & Canada. Systems & strategies that help mgrs improve yields on adv revenues.

McVay Media
2001 Crocker Rd., Suite 260, Cleveland, OH 44145
(440) 892-1910
www.mcvaymedia.com
Phil Hunt, President
Doris McVay, General Manager
Paige Nienaber, Promotions Specialist
Dave Lange, VP
Mike O'Malley, Associate Country Consultant
Specializes in short-form entertainment, info programs & promotions.

Media & Marketing
4245 Sarah St., Burbank, CA 91505-3815
(818) 558-3924
www.mediaandmarketing.com
mel.lambert@mediaandmarketing.com
Mel Lambert, General Sales Mgr
Consulting svc for the audio & multimedia industries.

Media Auditors International
5340 S. Quebec, Suite 100N, Greenwood Village, CO 80111
(303) 694-0444, (720) 407-7555; *Fax:* (303) 694-2559
www.mai-global.com
blazarus@mai-global.com
Tom Sassos, Chairman
Bruce Lazarus, CEO
Simon Pollock, SVP International
Raoul A. De Sota, SVP Strategic Development
Mitchell J. Walker, SVP Consulting and Technology Services
John Macdonald, Senior Vice President, AuditOperations
Mary Miller, Vice President- Client Relations & Contract Compli
Progmg license fee audits of cable operators, MMDS, SMATVs & TVRO middlemen.

Media Perspectives
127 Greensward Ln., Cherry Hill, NJ 08002
(856) 482-7979; *Fax:* (856) 482-0957
Steven G. Apel, President
Progmg & mktg counseling through applied audience & advertiser rsch.

The Mediacenter
7000 Kennedy Blvd. East, M-9, Guttenberg, NJ 07093
(866) 921-1026; *Fax:* (201) 210-4618
www.mediacenteronline.com
information@mediacenteronline.com
Barbara Zeiger, President
Russell Sands, General Manager
Promote increased mktg professionalism among TV execs & mgrs; provide sls support tools that identify & dev new adv budgets.

Mercer Capital Management Inc.
5100 Poplar Ave, Suite 2600, Memphis, TN 38137
(901) 685-2120; *Fax:* (901) 685-2199
www.mercercapital.com
mcm@mercercapital.com
Matthew R.Crow, Pesident
Lisa L. Doble, Sr Vice President
Jeff K. Davis, Managing Director
Mercer Capital provides high-quality independent business appraisals & other financial advisory svcs for all types of media including radio.
206 Kentuckey Towers, Louisville, KY
(502) 585-6340
James E. Graves, Vp

Metro Orlando Film & Television Commission
301 E. Pine St., Suite 900, Orlando, FL 32801
(407) 422-7159; *Fax:* (407) 425-6428
www.filmorlando.com
info@filmorlando.com
Suzy Allen, Operations Dir
Lindsey Fuller, Associate Director
Laura Kern, Media Inquires
Sheena Fowler, Film Commissioner
Christine Dellert, Media Inquiries
One stop permitting, locations library, location scouting, community familiarization tours, Filmbook with complete listings of crews, technicians & production support vendors.

Multimedia Research Group Inc. (MRG, Inc.)
7320 E. Butherus Dr., Suite 105, Scottsdale, AZ 85260
(888) 958-1472; *Fax:* (480) 685-4976
www.mrgco.com
Gary Schultz, President
Michael M. Murray, Co-Owner
Todd L. Marcelle, Co-Owner
Norm Bogen, Vice President Global Research
Waverly Deutsch, Advisor
Dan Mahoney, Advisor
Greg Nelson, Advisor
Provides strategic consulting & published market intelligence on content dev, content distribution, channels & networks.

Nashville Mayor's Office of Film
222 2nd Ave., Nashville, TN 37201
(615) 880-1827; *Fax:* (615) 862-6025
andyvr@nashville.org
Tessa Atkins, General Manager
Terry Cobb, Director of Development Services
Erik Cole, Director of Financial Empowerment
Laurel Creech, Chief Service Officer
Angie Goins, Executive Assistant to the Mayor
Tam Gordon, SpecialAssistant
Greg Hinote, Deputy Mayor
Location scouting, permits, produce annual production directory, assist with all logistics of TV/film/video projects, liaison to media & govt.

National Strategies Inc.
1400 Eye Street NW, Suite 900, Washington, DC 20005
(202) 349-7001; *Fax:* (202) 783-1041
www.nationalstrategies.com
info@nationalstrategies.com
Alfred Gordon, CEO
Timothy Onoff, President
Al Gordon, CFO
Pub policy strategies & implementation, business & investment dev.
Via San Senatore 10, Milan, Italy
+39 02 720 94266; *Fax:* +39 02 720 94759
14 E. 60th St., Suite 1002, New York, NY 10022-1006
(212) 758-0690, (212) 750-6518

Nick Anthony & Associates Inc.
Mailing Address: 1122 Partridge Drive, Wadsworth, OH 44281
Second Address: 1795 West Market Street, Akron, OH 44313
(330) 864-2268, (330) 969-9800; *Fax:* (330) 864-2261, (330) 864-6799
www.nickanthony.com
nick@nickanthony.com
Nick Anthony, President
Nick Anthony & Associates Inc. is an Akron, Ohio based media consulting firm, specializing in consulting programming, promotion and marketing for radio stations throughout North America.

Noll & Associates
Mailing Address: 20 Sunnyside Avenue, Suite I, Mill Valley, CA 94965
Second Address: 6841 E. Quail Hideaway Lane, Apache Junction, AZ 85219
(415) 888-8460; *Fax:* (415) 888-8462
www.nollmedia.com
Kennen Williams, President
Matt Chandler, Principal
Gary Greenway, Principal
Barbara Wilson, Principal
Bcst mktg/sls training, new business dev & organizational dev.

The Omnia Group
1501 W. Cleveland St, Suite. 300, Tampa, FL 33606
(800) 525-7117, (813) 254-9449; *Fax:* (813) 254-8558
www.omniagroup.com
Heather Caswell, CEO
Wendy Sheaffer, SVP-Operations
Carletta Clyatt, SVP-Sales
Steve Rorrer, Chief Financial Officer
Bob Hamilyon, Chief Technology Officer
Same-day response on best industry-validated selection tools that help hire the right person the first time.

Orbital Media Networks Inc.
76 Inverness Dr. E., Suite C, Englewood, CO 80112 USA
(303) 925-1708
www.orbitalmedianetworks.com
support@orbitalmedianetworks.com
Satellite: AMC1, AMC8, AMC9
Mike Hagans, President
Nathan Butler, Vice President of Operations
Orbital Media Networks Inc. provides satellite communication for some of the largest communications networks in the country.

Palazzo Intercreative
PO Box 2022, Vashon, WA 98070
(206) 328-5555; *Fax:* (206) 324-4348
www.palazzocreative.com
info@palazzocreative.com
Richard Roberts, President/CEO
Stn identity design & consultation svcs, including on-air, print, outdoor, graphics, syndicated animation packages, movie & news opns, & radio spots.

Paragon Advertising & Communications, Inc
Mailing Address: 73 Cavalier Blvd, Suite 217, Florence, KY 41042
Second Address: PO Box 335, Florence, KY 41022
(859) 647-2800, (888) 878-5646; *Fax:* (859) 647-2611
info@paragoncomm.com
Robin R. Webster, President/CEO
Rebecca Neal, Operations Dir
Jennie Searp, Director of Marketing/Promotions
Becky Grizovic, Executive Financial Officer
Tricia Burkhart, Vice President of Client Services
Gayril Gibson, Director(Non-profit Radio Division)
Paragon Advertising & Communications, Inc. has been in advertising for over 35 years. Through creativity, hard work, innovative thinking and an individual caring for each client that we represent, we have made it our business to knowadvertising and to know what works for our clients. In addition to our experience and dedication, you will not encounter a group that is more focused on your advertising efforts with the same compassion and passion for your cause.

Paragon Media Strategies
7550 W. Yale Avenue, Suite B-204, Denver, CO 80227
(303) 922-5600; *Fax:* (303) 922-1589
www.paragonmediastrategies.com
Mike Henry, CEO
John Stevens, COO
Sandy Chlumsky, CFO
Jay Randall, Music Director/Cloud Architect
Sara Schueller, Research Services Director
Cyndi Brassfield, Administrative Assistant
Larry Johnson, Senior Research Consultant
Dave Xaviers, Market Research Consultant
Media rsch & consulting.

Patrick Communications L.L.C.
6805 Douglas Legum Dr., Suite 100, Elkridge, MD 21075
(410) 799-1740; *Fax:* (410) 799-1705
www.patcomm.com
larry@patcomm.com
W. Lawrence Patrick, Managing Partner
Jason R. James, Vice President
Susan K. Patrick, Managing Partner
Gregory J. Guy, Managing Partner
DIANA WILKIN, Partner
Stn brokerage, investment banking, mgmt consulting svcs, appraisals & opns consulting.

PMA Marketing Inc./AMFMTV
4359 S. Howell Ave, Suite 105, Milwaukee, WI 53207
(414) 482-2638, (800) 678-4762; *Fax:* (414) 483-1980
Patrick Martin, President
Buy & sell new & used bcst equipment, radio stn start-ups & turnarounds, problem solving for difficult bcst situations.

Pollack Media Group Inc.
11777 San Vicente Blvd, Suite 790, Los Angeles, CA 90049
(310) 442-5544; *Fax:* (310) 454-5046
www.pollackmedia.com
hq@pollackmedia.com
Jeff Pollack, Chairman/CEO
Tommy Hadges, President
Tara Fortunato, VP/Operations
Candance Walheim, Financial Director/Business Manager
Dave Hill, Strategic Programming Advisor
Pat Welsh, SVP/Digital Content
Candace Walheim,Business Manager
Worldwide bcst progmg advisory firm, all facets of progmg, positioning, mktg, adv, rsch, music. All formats.

Poorman & Group
143-147 E. Main St., Suite 2D, Lock Haven, PA 17745
(570) 748-7000, (800) 532-1900; *Fax:* (570) 748-7700
www.poormangroup.com
Stephen P. Poorman, President
Pennsylvania & Texas-based mgmt consulting firm offers 'no-charge' interviews to radio & TV stns relating to business & real estate issues. Specializes in organizing & mgng financially distressed businesses.

PR/PR Public Relations
2301 Hickory Lane, Orlando, FL 32803
(407) 895-8800; *Fax:* (407) 299-2166
www.prpr.net
pam@prpr.net
Russell Trahan, Owner/President
Pam Lontos, Founder, Retired
Carter Breazeale, Agent/Communications Specialist
Publicity in Radio, TV, print for speakers & authors.

Price Waterhouse Coopers
1 North Wacker Drive, Chicago, IL 60606
(312) 298-2000; *Fax:* (312) 298-2001
www.pwc.com
Colm Kelly, Vice Chairman-Operations
Richard Collier-Keywood, Vice Chairman
Mike Burwell, Vice Chairman- Transformation
Javier H. Rubinstein, Vice Chairman- General Counsel
Richard Sexton, Vice Chairman- Global Assurance
JuanPujadas, Vice Chairman- Advisory
Robert Swaak, Vice Chairman- Clients & Markets
Provides valuation consulting svcs for acquisitions, swaps, estate planning & litigation.

RBC Capital Markets
Mailing Address: 3200 Cherry Creek S. Dr., Suite 500, Denver, CO 80209
Second Address: 1801 California Street, Suite 3850, Denver, CO 80202
(303) 778-5555, (303) 595-1100, (800) 234-3703; *Fax:* (303) 778-5599
www.rbccm.com
info@rbcdaniels.com
Doug McGregor, Chairman /CEO
Richard Talbot, COO
Troy Maxwell, CFO
Michael Bowick, Head, Global Markets
Blair Fleming, Head, RBC Capital Markets
Mark Hughes, Chief Risk Officer, RBC
Doug Guzman, Head, Global InvestmentBanking
Jonathan Hunter, Head, Fixed Income & Currencies
Clinton Lively, Global Head, Market Risk
Provides both mergers & acquisitions, corporate financial svcs to the cable telecommunications, media & technology industries.
711 5th Ave, Suite 405, New York, NY 10022-3111
(212) 935-5900; *Fax:* (212) 863-4859
Greg Ainsworth, Sr Mgng Dir
David Tolliver, Mgng Dir, Media Bcst Group

Rees Associates Inc.
9211 Lake Hefner Pkwy, Suite 300, Oklahoma City, OK 73120
(405) 942-7337, (888) 942-7337; *Fax:* (405) 948-1261
www.rees.com
rees@rees.com
Dr. Frank W. Rees, Jr, Founder/Chairman
Allan R. Parr AIA, LEED AP, BD+C, CEO
Robert W. Genter AIA, RID, LEED AP, Vice President & Director of Texas Operations
Kristina Dover Jr., Promotions Manager
C. Leroy James, AIA, IIDA, LEEDAP, Vice Chairman
Stephen E. Lawson AIA, LEED AP, Vice President / Client Development Leader
Melanie L. Compton AIA, LEED AP, Vice President and Practice Leader in Healthcare
Katheryn W. Potts LEED AP, Vice President
Farooq Karim AIA, RID,LEED AP, Vice President Practice Leader Design & Visualizat
Bcst & production facility design; architectural svcs; facility business plans; interior design; studio design; equipment planning, consulting.
1801 N. Lamar St., Suite 600, Dallas, TX 75202-1712
(214) 522-7337; *Fax:* (214) 522-0444
Frank Rees Jr., Pres
The Metropolis Bldg.
951 Peachtree St. N.E., Atlanta, GA 30309-3918 United Kingdom
(404) 351-6869; *Fax:* (404) 351-8343

Restivo Communications/Starstruck Entertainment Company
73 Widdicombe Hill Blvd., Suite 1515, Toronto, ON M9R 4B3 Canada
(416) 242-6146
www.prmediaconnection.com
Peter J. Restivo, President
Bcst & media consultants; media training, MOW development.

Richard A. Foreman Associates Inc.
330 Emery Dr. E., Stamford, CT 06902
(203) 327-2800; *Fax:* (203) 967-9393
www.rafamedia.com
raf@rafamedia.com
Dick Foreman, President
Fair market evaluations & asset appraisals, media brokerage, stn financing, & mgmt/production consultation.

Rick Ott
9225 Chatham Grove Ln., Suite D, Richmond, VA 23236
(804) 276-7202; *Fax:* (804) 745-7778
www.rickott.com
Sales@RickOtt.com
Rick Ott, President
Problem solving, consultation in complete confidentiality. Mgmt consulting.

Roehling Broadcast Services Ltd.
8563 E. Wilderness Trail, Unionville, IN 47468
(812) 988-6321, (317) 374-6906; *Fax:* (317) 870-8404
edradiobr@aol.com
Edward W. Roehling, President & Broker
Bcst appraisers, brokers, consultants, also financing, sls, mgmt consultation.

RPM Radio Programming & Management
1133 W. Longlake Rd., Suite 200, Bloomfield Hills, MI 48302
(888) 776-0006, (800) 521-2537, (248) 647-1068; *Fax:* (248) 647-2663
www.tophitsusa.com
Thomas M. Krikorian, President
Top Hits U.S. wkly CD svc & CD libraries including Solid Gold, Spectrum A/C & Country One; CD Christmas library.

Rumbaut & Co.
555 N.E. 34th St., Suite 2701, Miami, FL 33137-4060
(305) 868-0000, (305) 785-7000; *Fax:* (305) 571-0433
www.rumbaut.com
julio@rumbaut.com
Julio Rumbaut, Principal
Media brokers & consultants in all facets of the TV & radio industries.

San Antonio Convention & Visitors Bureau
203 S. St. Mary's St., Suite 200, San Antonio, TX 78205
(210) 207-6700, (800) 447-3372; *Fax:* (210) 207-6768
filmsa@filmsanantonio.com
Drew Mayer-Oakes, General Manager
City film commission. Photo Library. Liaison with all city offices. Filming permits. Parking assistance.

SATMAGAZINE.COM
800 Siesta Way, Sonoma, CA 95476
(707) 939-9306; *Fax:* (707) 939-9235
www.satnews.com
design@satnews.com
Jill Durfee, Sales Director
Don McGee, Production Manager
Hartley Lesser, Editorial Director
Simon Payne, Director MIS
Pattie Waldt, Associate Editor
Silvano Payne, Publisher
Publishers of the mthy Satmagazine online magazine on coml satellite systems. Also available on a CD-ROM & through the web at http://www.satnews.com.

Satterfield & Perry Inc.
7211 Fourth Ave. S., St. Petersburg, FL 33707
(727) 345-7338, (727) 439-4787; *Fax:* (727) 345-3809
www.satterfieldandperry.com
eraust@prodigy.net
Robert Austin, President
John Willis, Operations Dir
Bob Austin, Contact
Joe Benkert, Contact
Dick McMahon, Contact
Ken Hawkins, Contact
John Willis, Contact
Doug Stephens, Contact
Satterfield & Perry, Inc. is a nationwide media brokerage company specializing in radio and television. S&P has offices in Alabama, Colorado, Florida, Kansas, Oregon, and South Carolina.
2020 S. Monroe St., Suite 302, Denver, CO 80210-3700
Al Perry, Pres Emeritus
Joe Benkert, Vp
Jim Birschbach, Vp
Box 362, Coos Bay, OR 97420-0041
(541) 751-0043, (541) 256-5553
Dick McMahon, Vp
4918 W. 101st Terr., Overland Park, KS 66207-3431
(913) 649-5103; *Fax:* (913) 649-5103
Doug Stephens, Vp
131 Inwood Dr., Suite 302, Aiken, SC 29803-5613
(803) 649-0031, (803) 649-7786
John Willis, Vp
169 Mountain Meadows Ln., Wetumpa, AL 36093-3855
(334) 514-2241, (334) 514-2291
Ken Hawkins, Vp

SCRI International, Inc.
2023 N. Atlantic Avenue, Suite 310, Cocoa Beach, FL 32931
(321) 868-8273; *Fax:* (321) 799-3052
www.scri.com
Desmond C. Chaskelson, General Manager
Syndicated reports & custom rsch for manufacturers & investors in bcstg, professional video & audio; publishers of Broadcast Equipment Marketplace (BEM), Professional Video Marketplace (PFM), Professional Multi-Media Marketplace (PMM),European Telemedia Marketplace (ETM), Asian Telemedia Marketplace (ATM).

Shane Media Services
2500 Tanglewilde, Suite 106, Houston, TX 77063
(713) 952-9221; *Fax:* (713) 952-1207
www.shanemedia.com
smsofc@shanemedia.com
Ed Shane, CEO
Renee Revett, Programming Director
Radio progmg and mgmt consultation, custom designed perceptual and qualitative rsch for electronic media outlets.

Shotmakers, Inc.
One Horizon Rd., Fort Lee, NJ 07024
(201) 886-0287; *Fax:* (201) 886-0287
Dan Robinson, President
Media consultant, original film & TV productions; novelist. Represent historic photos & film of New York City & Atlanta.

SintecMedia
Div/DBA: (formerly Peter Storer & Associates Inc.)
Mailing Address: 1361 W. Towne Sq. Rd., Mequon, WI 53092
Second Address: 2964 Peachtree Rd, Suite 400, Atlanta, GA 30305
(262) 241-9005, (404) 869-4575; *Fax:* (262) 241-9036, (404) 844-9009
www.sintecmedia.com
doug@storertv.com
Amotz Yarden, CEO
Adoram Yarden, VP Operations - Development
Amir Lavi, EVP Enterprise Sales
Eric Levitan, COO
Shlomo Freidenreich, CFO
Amos Simantov, EVP Sales
Moses Zelniker, VP Marketing & Product Development
Dan Yuval, VPProduct Management
SintecMedia, the leading provider of media business management solutions, has over 300 client sites around the world. With the recent acquisitions of industry leaders Argo Systems and StorerTV, SintecMedia augmented its comprehensivesolutions for broadcasters, Pay TV networks, multichannel operators and station groups world-wide.

Skywatch Weather Center
347 Prestley Rd., Bridgeville, PA 15017
(412) 221-6000, (800) SKY-WATCH, (800) 759-9282; *Fax:* (412) 221-3160
www.skywatchweather.com
webmaster@skywatchweather.com
Dr. Stanley J. Penkala, Ph.D, President, Director - Air Programs
Stanley Bostjancic, Treasurer and Chief Meteorologist
Daniel Krzywiecki, Vice President
Harry Green, Secretary
Specially formatted weathercasts from the Skywatch Weather Center.

Smart Target Marketing
Mailing Address: 6800 Bird Rd, Suite 304, Miami, FL 33155
Second Address: 17 Old Colony Place, Falmouth, MA 02540
(305) 667-6665, (580) 540-8039, (800) 329-5478; *Fax:* (305) 667-3508
www.smarttargetlists.com
info@smarttargetlists.com
Custom strategic direct-mktg programs; complete promotional & adv svcs including direct mail/targeted mailing lists, telemarketing, data base, custom publishing, sls training, & interactive phone/prom, smart targets & prizm targeting svcs.

Soundtrack Group
162 Columbus Ave., Boston, MA 02116-5222
(617) 303-7500; *Fax:* (617) 303-7555
www.soundtrackgroup.com
ablankenship@soundtrackboston
Amy Blankenship, COO
Amy Blankenship, Operations Dir
Terry Lockhart, Chief Engineer
Paul Cavicchio, CFO
Mike Gross, Machine Room Engineer
Tim Movall, Accountant / Property Manager
Hillary Rider, Production Manager
Production, postproduction & custom music of all kinds; specializing in sound designs.
936 Broadway, New York, NY 10010-6013
(212) 420-6010
Chris Rich, Opns Mgr

Stonick Recruitment Inc.
1230 Lake Deeson Pointe, Lakeland, FL 33805
(863) 397-5615; *Fax:* (863) 680-1397
www.stonickrecruitment.com
stonick@gate.net
Chris Stonick, President
A natl radio sls consulting firm bringing 'recruitment adv' to radio (strictly new business dev).

Street Level Views
1551 Olde Mill Pl., Marietta, GA 30066
(678) 467-8650; *Fax:* (770) 924-3584
Rick Phillips, President
Natl qualitative moderator for one-on-one rsch. Nationwide recruiting for auditorium music tests since 1986. Video market rsch.

Structural System Technology Inc.
6867 Elm St., McLean, VA 22101 US
(703) 356-9765; *Fax:* (703) 448-0979
Fred W Purdy, Coo
Structural engrg studies, analysis, design, modifications, inspections, fabrication & erection of towers & antenna structures.

Szabo Associates Inc., Media Collection Professionals
3355 Lenox Rd. NE, Suite 945, Atlanta, GA 30326
(404) 266-2464; *Fax:* (404) 266-2165
www.szabo.com
info@szabo.com
Robin Szabo, President
Sandi Garris Henderson, Legal Services Manager
Nolan Childers, Manager Major Accounts
David Schimmack, Division Manager
Teri Louah, Business Manager
Kelly Chambers, Associate
Vernon Johnson, AdministrativeAssociate
Experts in creditor & debtor rights; consulting media properties in the accounts receivable process; domestic & international collections.

TalentTrainers
443 North Snowmass Circle, Superior, CO 80027
(303) 997-9164; *Fax:* 1-800-787-4284
www.talenttrainers.com
brice@talenttrainers.com
Shirley Brice, President
Talent coaching for TV stns & newspapers. Media trainer for corporate executives. One-on-one sessions, small workshops & individual critiques. Weekly 'live' coaching chat on www.talent trainers.com.

Tele-Measurements Inc.
145 Main Ave., Clifton, NJ 07014
(973) 473-8822, (800) 223-0052; *Fax:* (973) 473-0521
www.tele-measurements.com
contact@tele-measurements.com
William E. Endres, President
Douglas W. Cook, General Sales Mgr
Tele-Measurements is an innovative Telecommunications company speciallizing in Audio Visual Systems Design, Sales, Rentals and Service.

Television by Design Inc.
3277 Roswell Rd., Suite 714, Atlanta, GA 30305-1835
(404) 873-3277; *Fax:* (404) 873-7900
www.tvbd.com
jay@tvbd.com
Jay Antzakas, President
Creators of electronic graphic design; consultants on visual design, equipment & opns for TV stns.

Tenner & Associates Inc.
121 Quail Run Rd., Henderson, NV 89014
(702) 496-3286, (702) 454-9561; *Fax:* (702) 898-9938
www.tennerandassoc.com
Lisa Tenner, President
Event & conference producers for the entertainment industry.

TM Studios
2002 Academy Lane, Suite 110, Dallas, TX 75234
(972) 406-6800; *Fax:* (972) 406-6890
www.jonestm.com
info@tmstudios.com
David Graupner, CEO
Jay Noble, General Sales Mgr
The world's leading supplier of jingles, production & imaging libraries, wkly music svc & music libraries on hard drive.

Transcomm Inc.
3601 Pickett Road No. 2845, Fairfax, VA 22031
(703) 323-5150; *Fax:* (703) 426-4527
www.transcommusa.com
transcommUSA1@gmail.com
Dr. Norman C. Lerner, Founder And President
Norman C. Lerner, Engineer/Financial Economist
Financial/economic analysis, market rsch, pricing studies & regulatory economics.

Veronis, Suhler Stevenson
Park Avenue Plaza, 55 East 52nd Street, 33rd Floor, New York, NY 10055
(212) 935-4990; *Fax:* (212) 381-8168
www.vss.com
StevensonJ@vss.com
Jeffrey T. Stevenson, Investment Committee
Jack Hartfelder, Vice President/Director
Merchant bankers to media, communications & info industries, with focus on mergers & acquisitions, valuations, joint ventures & private equity.

VIP Research Inc.
5700 Broadmoor St., Suite 200, Mission, KS 66202
(913) 384-9494; *Fax:* (913) 677-2727
www.vipresearch.net
Valorie Heydman, CEO
Meloney Coons, Accounting/ Operations
Rich DePaoli, Project Consultant/ Sales
Matt Anzalone, Project Manager/ Client Services
Provides hook-tape production, listener screening, fielding & tabulation for all music testing, perceptual studies, focus groups & promotional telemarketing.

W.L. Pritchard & Co. L.C.
2228 Q Street NW, Washington, DC 20008
(301) 654-1144; *Fax:* (301) 654-1814
www.wlpco.com
inquiries@wlpco.com
Ellen Hoff, President
Professional engrg, business problem solving in telecommunications, competitor analysis, satellite communications, earth stns, & launch vehicles.

Wexler & Walker
1317 F St. N.W., Suite 800, Washington, DC 20004
(202) 638-2121; *Fax:* (202) 638-7045
www.wexlerwalker.com
healy@wexlerwalker.com
Robert Walker, Executive Chairman
George Robb Rogers, President
Tom Carpenter, Senior Vice President / Managing Director
Dale Snape, Vice Chairman
Jody Hoffman, SVP & Managing Director
Chad Wolf, Vice President & SeniorDirector
Rebecca K. Blood, VP
Consulting firm, specializing in govt rel & pub affrs with strong emphasis on mass media, telecommunications, copyright, trade.

Wind River Group, Inc.
117 E. 11th St., Loveland, CO 80537
(800) 669-3993, (970) 669-3442; *Fax:* (970) 663-6081
www.windriverbroadcast.com
jim@windriverbroadcast.com
Jim McDonald, CEO
Wind River Group, Inc. today continues to offer diverse engineering services for broadcasters. Preparation of FCC applications and the engineering services required to do so are chief among them, but systems design and regulatory technicalsupport for broadcasters, certain commercial and institutional clients remains a key part of our operation.

Wolfe Media
10755-F Scripps Poway Pkwy., Suite 612, San Diego, CA 92131
(858) 530-8787, (888) 965-3226; *Fax:* (858) 530-9974
www.wolfemedia.com
dw@wolfemedia.com
David Wolfe, President
David Wolfe, Contact
Wolfe Media offers years of experience creating custom marketing solutions for small business owners.

Music Licensing

American Society of Composers, Authors & Publishers (ASCAP)
1900 Broadway, New York, NY 10023
(212) 621-6000; *Fax:* (212) 621-8453
www.ascap.com
info@ascap.com
Paul Williams, President/Chairman of the Board
Jimmy Webb, Writer Vice Chairman
Irwin Robinson, Publisher Vice Chairman
James M. Kendrick, Treasurer
Fred Koenigsberg, Counsel
A membership assn of more than 275,000 composers, lyricists, & music publishers, ASCAP licenses the pub performances of its members' works. ASCAP has reciprocal agreements with foreign societies representing virtually every country that haslaws protecting copyright.

ASCAP - Atlanta
PMB 400, 541 Tenth St. N.W., Atlanta, GA 30318-5713
(404) 351-1224; *Fax:* (404) 351-1252

ASCAP - Los Angeles
7920 W. Sunset Blvd., 3rd Fl., Los Angeles, CA 90046-3300
(323) 883-1000; *Fax:* (323) 883-1049
Todd Brobeck, Sr Vp

ASCAP - Miami
420 Lincoln Rd., Suite 385, Miami Beach, FL 33139-3019
(305) 673-3446; *Fax:* (305) 673-2446

ASCAP - Midwest

1608 N. Milwaukee Ave., Suite 1007, Chicago, IL 60647-5456
(773) 394-4286; *Fax:* (773) 394-5639

ASCAP - Nashville
2 Music Sq. W., Nashville, TN 37203-3204
(615) 742-5000; *Fax:* (615) 742-5020

ASCAP - London
8 Cork St., London
01-44-207-439-0909; *Fax:* 001-44-207-434-0073

APM Music
Mailing Address: 6255 Sunset Blvd, Suite 900, Hollywood, CA 90028
Second Address: 381 Park Ave South, Suite 1101, New York, NY 10016
(323) 461-3211, (212) 856-9800; *Fax:* (323) 461-9102, (212) 856-9807
www.apmmusic.com
info@apmmusic.com
Adam Taylor, President
Colleen Oscarson, Operations Dir
George Mecias, General Sales Mgr
Sharon Jennings, Promotions Manager
Bruce Amdur, Key Account Director
David Begin, Account Director, Cable Team
April Flores, AccountManager, Studios Team
Lauren Bell, Key Account Director
Rob Cairns, Key Account Director, New Media & Games
Deborah Fisher, Key Account Director
Sixteen libraries: KPM, Bruton, Sonoton, Carlin, Castle, NFL. Over 3,000 CDs, personalized packages, music search, 15-20 new CD releases mthy.
381 Park Ave. S., Suite 1101, New York, NY 10016-8806
(212) 856-9800; *Fax:* (212) 856-9807
George Macisa, Natl Sls Mgr

BMI-Broadcast Music Inc.
Mailing Address: 7 World Trade Center, 250 Greenwich Street, New York, NY 10007-0030
Second Address: 10 Music Square East, Nashville, TN 37203-4399
(212) 220-3000, (615) 401-2000; *Fax:* (212) 582-5972
www.bmi.com
newyork@bmi.com
Bruce A. Esworthy, Chief Financial Officer
Michael O'Neill, President And CEO
Bruce A. Esworthy, SVP, Finance & Administration, CFO
Phillip R. Graham, SVP, Writer/Publisher Relations
Stuart Rosen, SVP, General Counsel
James A.King, SVP, Business Operations & Technology
Alison Smith, SVP, Distribution & Administrative Services
Michael Steinberg, SVP, Licensing
Licenses the pub performance rights of musical compositions for more than 300,000 songwriters, composers & music publishers; maintains reciprocal arrangements with more than 40 licensing organizations worldwide.
1691 Michigan Ave., Suite 350, Miami, FL
(305) 266-3636
Tower Pl. 100, 3340 Peachtree Rd. N.E., Suite 570, Atlanta, GA 30326-1059
(404) 261-5151
Bank Trust Plaza, 255 Ponce de leon Ave, East Wing, Suite A-262, Hato Rey, PR
(787) 754-6490
84 Harley House, Marlebone Rd., London, NO United Kingdom
0114420 7486 2036
8730 Sunset Blvd., Los Angeles, CA 90069-2210
(310) 659-9109
10 Music Sq. E., Nashville, TN 37203-4321
(615) 401-2000

European American Music Distributors L.L.C.
254 West 31st Street, Floor 15, New York, NY 10001
(212) 461-6940; *Fax:* (212) 810-4565
www.eamdc.com
info@eamdc.com
Jim Kendrick, President
Harry Searing, Head Of Sales
Chris Watford, Promotions Manager
Norman Ryan, Vice President - Composers and Repertoire
Caroline Kane, Vice President - Licensing and Administration
Scott Wollschleger, SeniorManager-Production
Cory Bracken, Promotion and Production Associate
Doriana Molla, Acting Head of Rental Services
Terri Raccioppi-McGann, Account Manager
Music publisher & distributor.

The Harry Fox Agency Inc.
40 Wall Street, 6th Floor, New York, NY 10005
(212) 922-3297, (212) 834-0100; *Fax:* (646) 487-6779
www.harryfox.com
press@harryfox.com
Patrick Clancy, Sr Vice President And Chief Financial Officer
Michael Simon, President/Chief Executive Officer
Michele Olton, Senior Vice President- Human Resources and Adminis
Patrick Clancy, Senior Vice President/ Chief FinancialOfficer
Maurice Russell, Senior Vice President- Client Services
Matthew Beekman, Chief Technology Officer
Mechanical licensing, mechanical royalty collection and distribution, rights management solutions.

SESAC Inc.
Mailing Address: 55 Music Square East, Nashville, TN 37203
Second Address: 152 West 57th St, 57th Floor, New York, NY 10019
(615) 320-0055, (212) 586-3450; *Fax:* (615) 329-9627, (212) 489-5699
www.sesac.com
Performing rights organization representing a diversity of copyrighted music.
420 Lincoln Rd., Suite 502, Miami, FL
(305) 534-7500; *Fax:* (305) 534-7578
501 Santa Monica Blvd., Suite 450, Santa Monica, CA 90401-2431
(310) 393-9671; *Fax:* (310) 393-6497
981 Joseph E. Lowery Blvd. N.W., Suite 11, Atlanta, GA 30318-5286
(404) 897-1330; *Fax:* (404) 897-1306
152 W. 57th St., 57th Fl., New York, NY 10019-3386
(212) 586-3450; *Fax:* (212) 489-5699
67 Upper Berkeley St., London, United Kingdom

Society of Composers, Authors & Music Publishers of Canada (SOCAN)
Div/DBA: Societe Canadienne des auteurs, compositeurs et ed
Mailing Address: 41 Valleybrook Drive, Toronto, ON M3B 2S6 Canada
Second Address: 600 de Maisonneuve Blvd. W, Suite 500, Montreal, QC H3A 3J2
(416) 445-8700, (866) 307-6226, (800) 557-6226, (8; *Fax:* (416) 445-7108
www.socan.ca
Eric Baptiste, CEO
Jeff King, Chief Operating Officer
David Wood, Chief Financial Officer
Andrew Berthoff, Chief Communications & Marketing Officer
Jennifer Brown, Vice President - Licensing
Gilles M. Daigle, General Counsel, LegalServices
David Wood, CFO
Janice Scott, Vice President - Information Technology
Randy Wark, Vice President - Human Resources & Chief Administr
SOCAN licenses the public performance of music in Canada & distributes performance royalties to copyright holders worldwide.
600, boul. de Maisonneuve Ouest, Bureau 500, Montreal
(514) 844-8377; *Fax:* (514) 849-8446
1201 W. Pender St., Suite 400, Vancouver
(604) 669-5569; *Fax:* (604) 688-1142
1145 Weber Centre, 5555 Calgary Tr., Edmonton
(780) 439-9049; *Fax:* (780) 432-1555
Queen Sq., 45 Alderney Dr., Suite 802, Dartmouth
(902) 464-7000; *Fax:* (902) 464-9696

Warner Bros. Publications
15800 NW 48th Avenue, Miami, FL 33014
(305) 620-1500, (800) 327-7643
www.warnerbros.com
Barry M. Meyer, Chairman
Kevin Tsujihara, Chairman And CEO
Kim Williams, Executive VP And CFO
Susan Nahley Fleishman, Executive Vice President - Worldwide Corporate Com
Richard J. Fox, Executive Vice President-International
ThomasGewecke, Chief Digital Officer/Executive Vice President-Str
John Rogovin, Executive Vice President/ General Counsel
Edward A. Romano, Executive Vice President /Chief Financial Officer,
Kiko Washington, Executive Vice President-Worldwide HumanResources
Full-line music publishers of popular, standard & educ music as well as instructional videos from influential musicians. International market.

Research Services

American Media Services L.L.C.
Mailing Address: PO Box 20696, Charleston, SC 29413
Second Address: 1311 Chuck Dawley Boulevard, Suite 202, Mt. Pleasant, SC 29464
(843) 972-2200; *Fax:* (843) 881-4436
www.americanmediaservices.com
eseeger@ams.fm
Edward F. Seeger, Chairman
Frank G. McCoy, President
Alesa I. Peace, Vice President - Finance & Station Operations
Laramie B. Guest, Vice President - Engineering & Research
Developers & brokers of radio properties. Also appraisals, search svcs (buyer's agent), upgrade studies.

Chicago office
24180 N. Forest Dr., Forest Lake, IL 60047-8825
(847) 540-5410
Frank McCoy, Exec Vp/Engrg

Dallas office
9208 Timbercreek Dr., Bonham, TX 75418-5134
(903) 640-5857; *Fax:* (903) 640-5859
David Reeder, Rgnl Broker

Austin office
303 Avenue Q, Marble Falls, TX 78654-5426
(877) 267-2636
Patrick McNamara, Rgnl Broker

Broadcast Media Associates
P.O. BOX 1233, Santa Maria, CA 93456 93456
(805) 937-1553; *Fax:* (805) 937 7212
Clifford M. Hunter, President
Radio/TV/cable brokerage in the western states. Confidential mktg for radio, TV & LPTV properties; valuation packages & financial analysis; consultants to sellers & buyers.

BroadcastStations4Sale.com
512 Jones St., Graham, NC 27253 27253
(336) 570-9133; *Fax:* (336) 570-3464
www.broadcaststations4sale.com
Ted J. Gray, President & Broker
Buy or sell radio stns or TV stns. List to sell yourself or let BroadcastStations4Sale.com sell it for you.

Bulkley Capital, L.P.
Mailing Address: 5949 Sherry Ln., Suite 1370, Dallas, TX 75225
Second Address: 3204 Huntersworth, Glenwood, MD 21738
(214) 692-5476, (410) 382-4622; *Fax:* (214) 692-9309
www.bulkleycapital.com
info@bulkleycapital.com
G. Bradford Bulkey, President
Oliver Cone, Operations Dir
Nancy Wallin, General Manager
Oliver Cone, Senior Vice President
William Herdrich, Director
Don Schmincke, Director
Richard Gilbert, Director & Advisory Board Member
Craig Lentzsch, Advisory Board Member
John McKay, Director
Investment banking: mergers, acquisitions, private placements of debt & equity capital.

Burt Sherwood & Associates Inc.
6415 Midnight Pass Rd., Apartment 206, Sarasota, FL 34242
(941) 349-2165; *Fax:* (941) 312-0974
bohica1@comcast.net
Burt Sherwood, Owner
Brokerage radio, TV & LPTV; appraisals.

CEA Group
Mailing Address: 101 E. Kennedy Blvd., Suite 3300, Tampa, FL 33602
Second Address: 260 Madison Avenue, New York, NY 10016
(813) 226-8844, 212-218-5085; *Fax:* (813) 225-1513, 212-957-0620
www.ceaworldwide.com
rmichaels@ceaworldwide.com
J. Patrick (Rick) Michaels, Jr., Founder/Chairman/CEO
Ming Jung, Executive VP & COO
Brad Gordon, Executive VP & CFO
Dave Moyer, Senior Managing Director & President, CEA PAG
Beth Cahill, Senior Managing Director
Robert D. Berger,Managing Director
Michael Johnson, Vice President
Doris Rainey, Vice President
A leading provider of investment banking services and private equity to the global communications, media, entertainment, and information technology industries.
1270 Avenue of the Americias, Suite 1818, New York, NY 10020-1700
(212) 218-5085; *Fax:* (212) 218-5099
Alexander Rossi, Mgng Director
Bob Ennis, Mgng Director
Waldo Glasman, Mgng Director
Paul Miller, Mgng Director

Evan Blum, Dir
Jason Donnell, Dir
191 Post Rd. W., Westport, CT 06880-4625
(203) 221-2662; *Fax:* (203) 221-2663
Dave Moyer, Pres

Chapin Enterprises
1248 O St., Suite 751, Lincoln, NE 68508 68508
(402) 475-5285; *Fax:* (402) 475-5293
dchapin@inetnebr.com
R.W. Chapin, President

Clifton Gardiner & Company, L.L.C.
24645 S. Augusta Court, Sun Lakes, AZ 85248
(623) 336-7272, (623) 337-3777; *Fax:* (623) 498-8310
www.cliftongardiner.com
cliff@cliftongardiner.com
Cliff Gardiner, Chairman
Clifton H. Gardiner, President
Brokerage & financial svcs for the bcst & cable industries.

CobbCorp, LLC
7400 Tamiami Trail North, Suite 102, Naples, FL 34108-2855 34108-2855
(212) 960-8468; *Fax:* (239) 596-0660
www.cobbcorp.com
briancobb@cobbcorp.com
Brian E. Cobb, President
Jeanette Kuszlyk, Controller
Dennis LeClair, Vice President
Mergers, acquisitions, investment & merchant banking.

Cox & Cox, LLC
Mailing Address: 2454 Shiva Ct., St. Louis, MO 63011
Second Address: 4546 Sliver Bit Court, North Las Vegas, Las Vegas, Ne 89032
(702) 296-5814,(636) 458-4780; *Fax:* (702) 968-8618
Robert Cox, President
Linda Cox, Operations Dir
Media mergers & acquisitions, appraisals, consulting, expert testimony, receivership & workout.

Dave Garland Media Brokerage
NSS Data: Radio Only
1007 Shadow Cir., League City, TX 77573 77573
(713) 882-2402
www.radiobroker.com
garland@radiobroker.com
David Garland, President
Robert Miles Master, Operations Dir
Broker of radio stn properties in Texas & surrounding states.

Diversified Investment Services, Inc.
7512 Dr. Phillips Blvd., Suite #50-250, Orlando, FL 32819
(407) 909-0825, (888) 999-7905; *Fax:* (407) 909-0826
diversifiedinvestment.com
a.stilli@yahoo.com
Nancy Hasselback, President/CEO
Armand J. Santilli, President
Media brokers/finders, real estate investment bankers & brokers.

Earl Reilly Enterprises
550 Aloha St., Suite 404, Seattle, WA 98019 98019
(206) 282-6914
Earl F. Reilly, President
Bcst rep, representing U.S. TV stns in Canada. Also licensed bcst stn brokers.
Box 1000, Freeland, WA
(206) 331-7223; *Fax:* (206) 331-7223

EnVest Media, LLC
6802 Patterson Ave., Richmond, VA 23226 23226
(804) 282-5561; *Fax:* (804) 282-5703
www.envest.biz
Mitt Younts, Managing Member
Nationwide radio, TV acquisition, valuation, financing & consulting firm. The company provides brokerage svcs to stn transaction, appraisal svcs to stn owners & financial institutions. The group secures debt & equity acquisition financing,offers consulting & asset mgmt svcs, acting as court appointed receivers or trustees for bcst stns.

The Exline Company
388 Lowell Ave, Mill Valley, CA 94941 94903
(415) 381-5473; *Fax:* (415) 479-1574
www.exlinecompany.com
exline@pacbell.net
Andrew P. McClure, President/Owner
Judi Lewis, Admin Coordinator
Judi Lewis, Administrative Coordinator
Complete brokerage, consulting & appraisal svcs for radio & TV properties.

Explorer Communications Inc.
4428 N. 12th Street, Phoenix, AZ 85014 34461
(602) 264-1721; *Fax:* (602) 798-8279
www.bbb.org
Brian Mohr, Chairman
Matthew M. Fehling, President
Brian Burt, Vice Chairÿ
Gary Sneed, Treasurer
David Lorenz, Secretary
Rick Dircks, Immediate Past Chairÿ
Bcst media brokerage svcs. Specialists in medium & small market entrepreneurial transactions.

Frank Boyle & Co., L.L.C.
32 greystone, Shelton, CT 06484
(203)513-2402; *Fax:* (203)513-8189
Frank Boyle, President

Fugatt Media Services
9214 Butternut Dr., Crystal Lake, IL 60014 60014
(815) 546-1470, (815) 788-7481
Michael L. Fugatt, President
Media brokerage firm specialing in radio & cable svcs including appraisals.

Gammon Miller L.L.C.
Div/DBA: (Formerly Gammon Media Brokers L.L.C.)
Mailing Address: 4806 Vue Du Lac Pl., Suite B, Manhattan, KS 66503
Second Address: 0123 Timber Trail, Cordillera, CO 81632
(785) 539-1700, (970) 926-3171; *Fax:* (785) 565-0437
www.gammonmiller.com
cmiller@gammonmiller.com
Christopher D. Miller, President/CEO
Brokerage & strategy advice to sellers, buyers of radio stns, TV stns, nwspr & cable TV systems. Gammon Miller Revenue Travel as a division Gammon Miller LLC, is a media based incentive travel provider for radio hstns, TV stns, nwspr andcable TV systems.

George Moore & Associates Inc.
2046 John Rolfe Parkway, Richmond, VA 23238-8111 75230
(804) 965-0550; *Fax:* 800-750-9059
www.manta.com
W. James Moore, President
Brokerage of radio, TV, asset & market appraisals prepared for owners, buyers & lenders.

Gordon Rice Associates
222 West Coleman Boulevard, Mount Pleasant, SC 29464 29413
(843) 884-3590; *Fax:* (843) 881-0358
Gordon Rice, Owner
Gordon Rice, Broker
Brokerage svcs, appraisals & investment analysis for radio & TV.

Hadden & Associates
Div/DBA: Media Brokers - Orlando
147 Eastpark Dr., Celebration, FL 34447 34447
(321) 939-3141; *Fax:* (321) 939-3142
www.haddenonline.com
hadden@haddenonline.com
Doyle Hadden, President
Ryan P. Hadden, Operations Dir
Communications broker, acquisitions, divestitures; financial assistance and appraisal to the broadcasting industry.

Henson Media Inc.
1930 Bishop Lane, Suite 1009, Louisville, KY 40218-1958 40202-2508
502-458-4222; *Fax:* 502-458-4999
www.hensonmedia.com
edhenson1@bellsouth.net
Edward Henson, President
Radio & TV brokers. Radio stations owned and operated.
7811 Saloma Rd., Campbellsville, KY 42718-8008
(270) 789-9513
Bryan McForland, Chairman

Holt Media Group
P. O. Box 21985, Lehigh Valley, PA 18002-1985 18017
(610) 814-2821; *Fax:* (610) 814-2826
www.holtmedia.com
Arthur Holt, President/CEO
Christine E.Borger, Executive Vice President
Brokerage, consulting, appraisals.

Howard E. Stark
53 North Park Avenue, Suite 50, Rockville Centre, NY 11570 10022
(516) 596-8929
www.howardstarkfoundation.com
starkfoundation@gmail.com
Howard E. Stark, Founder
Jennifer A. Franz, Executive Director
Media broker; mergers & acquisitions in the communications field.

HPC Puckett & Co.
Mailing Address: PO Box 9063, Rancho Santa Fe, CA 92067
Second Address: 5863 SW 29th St., Topeka, KS 66614
(858) 756-4915, (785) 273-0017; *Fax:* (858) 756-4534, (785) 273-5512
www.hpcpuckett.com
Thomas F. Puckett, Founder, Managing Director and Chief Executive Off
Hunter T. Puckett, Managing Director and General Counsel
Jason A. Meyer, Managing Director
Communications brokerage & investment banking.

John Pierce & Company L.L.C.
PO Box 863, Florence, KY 41022 41042
(859) 647-0101; *Fax:* (859) 647-2611
www.johnpierceco.com
John L. Perce, President
BECKY GRIZOVIC, Chief Financial Officer
Radio, TV, & cable sls & appraisals.

John W. Saunders, Media Broker
709 Rust St, Forney, TX 77057 77057
(713) 789-4222; *Fax:* (713) 789-4322
theradiobroker@aol.com
John W. Saunders, President
Nationwide radio brokerage & appraisals. Buyers or sellers represented on a confidential, professional & personal basis. Top 10 to small markets.

Jorgenson Broadcast Brokerage Inc.
Mailing Address: 426 S. River Rd., Tryon, NC 28782
Second Address: 6172 Bollinger Rd., Suite 108, San Jose, CA 95129
(828) 859-6982, (408) 255-7855; *Fax:* (828) 859-6831, (408) 228-1653
www.goradiotv.com
Mark Jorgenson, Owner
Mark W. Jorgenson, Vice President
Partner, Peter Mieuli
Partner
Confidential, nationwide brokerage of bcst properties.

Kalil & Co. Inc.
2960 N. Swan Rd., Suite 134, Tucson, AZ 85712
(520) 795-1050; *Fax:* (520) 322-0584
www.kalilco.com
kalil@kalilco.com
Frank Higney, Coo
Frank Kalil, Owner/President
Tom Zlaket, General Manager
Todd Hartman, VP
Media brokerage firm dealing in radio, TV & cable. Handles exclusive listings & confidential searches.

Kepper, Tupper & Company
2 Galleon, Suite 100, Hilton Head Island, SC 29928 6877
(203) 431-3366; *Fax:* (203) 431-3864
www.kepper-tupper.com
jtupper@kepper-tupper.com
John B. Tupper, President
Brokerage & investment banking svcs for the cable & bcst TV industries. Please visit our website kepper-tupper.com.

Knowles Media Brokerage Services
P.O. Box 9698, Bakersfield, CA 93389 93389
(661) 833-3834; *Fax:* (661) 833-3845
www.media-broker.com
gregg.knowles@netzero.com
Gregg K. Knowles, Broker
Knowles Media Brokerage Services is a full-service agency located in Bakersfield, California, offering sales, consultation, and appraisal services for print media owners nationwide.

Kozacko Media Services
Mailing Address: 800 S Salisbury St, Raleigh, NC 27602-2978
Second Address: P.O. Box 2978, Raleigh, NC 27601
(919) 664-7000; *Fax:* (919) 664-7097
www.raleighchamber.org
mail@raleighchamber.org
Richard Urquhart, Chairman
Tim Giuliani, President & CEO
Janet Carr, General Manager/SVP
Lisa Harris, Office Manager
Alice Avery, Communications Manager

Natalie Griffith, Operations Manager
Candice Coffey, Front OfficeCoordinator
Abbie Mahoney, Government Affairs Events Manager
Emily Atkinson, Vice President Of Government Affairs
Appraisals & current market evaluations of radio & TV stns; bcst stn acquisition brokers.
6890 E. Sunrise Dr., Box 120-40, Tucson, AZ 85732-2040
(520) 299-4869; *Fax:* (520) 844-8559
George W. Kimble, Assoc
1071 Club Dr., Keswick, VA 22947-2613
(434) 244-2653; *Fax:* (434) 244-2666
W. Donald Roberts Jr., Assoc

Lazard L.L.C.
Mailing Address: 30 rockefeller plaza, New York, NY 10112
Second Address: 600 Fifth Avenue, New York, NY 10020
(212) 632-6000
www.lazard.com
Kenneth M. Jacobs, Chairman and Chief Executive Officer
Alexander F. Stern, Chief Operating Officer
Robert Hougie, General Manager
Matthieu Bucaille, CFO
Ashish Bhutani, Vice Chairman
Scott D. Hoffman, General Counsel
Steven J.Heyer, Lead Director
Andrew Alper, Director
Sylvia Jay, Director
Lazard's broad range of svcs includes: gen financial advice; domestic, cross-border mergers & acquisitions; divestitures; privatizations; special committee assignments; takeover defenses; corporate restructurings; strategicpartnerships/joint ventures; & debt/equity underwriting.

Legacy Securities Corp.
PO Box 283, Gulf Breeze, FL 32562
(850) 677-1989
Christopher F. Battel, President/CEO
Henry J. Cardello, Advisory Member
John J. Huntz, Advisory Member
Ptrick E. Falcoio, Advisory Member

Media Services Group Inc.
Mailing Address: 3948 S. Third St. #191, Jacksonville Beach, FL 32250
Second Address: 149 South Roscoe Blvd., Ponte Vedra, FL 32082
(904) 285-3239, (904) 285-3239; *Fax:* (904) 285-5618, (904) 285-5618
www.mediaservicesgroup.com
George R. Reed, General Manager
One of the nation's leading full svc media brokerage, valuation & consulting firms with in-depth industry knowledge & market expertise.

Providence, RI
170 Westminster St., Suite 701, Providence, RI 02903-2101
(401) 454-3130; *Fax:* (401) 454-3131
rmaccini@ cox.net; scs@scsloan.com
Robert J. Maccini, Dir
Stephan Sloan, Assoc
Ted Clark, Analyst

Kansas City, KS
5225 W. 122nd Street, Overland Park, KS 66209-3547
(913) 498-0040; *Fax:* (913) 498-0041
75767.3151@compuserve.com
Bill Lytle, Dir
Mike Lytle, Assoc

Dallas, TX
1131 Rockingham Dr., Suite 209, Richardson, TX 75080-4354
(972) 231-4500; *Fax:* (972) 231-4509
whitelytx@cs.com
Bill Whitley, Dir

St. Simons Island, GA
205 Marina Dr., St. Simons Island, GA 31522-2243
(912) 634-6575; *Fax:* (912) 634-5770
edwesser@adlphia.net
Eddie Esserman, Dir

Salt Lake City
1289 North 1500 E., Logan, UT 84341-2848
(435) 753-8090; *Fax:* (435) 753-2980
ggm@cache.net
Greg Merrill, Dir

Colorado Springs, CO
2910 Electra Drive, Colorado Springs, CO 80906-1073
(719) 630-3111; *Fax:* (719) 630-1871
jbmccoy@adelphia.net
Jody McCoy, Dir

New York Metro
45 Park Pl. S. #146, Morristown, NJ 07960-3924
(973) 631-6612; *Fax:* (973) 631-6613
rtmck2515@aol.com
Tom McKinley, Dir
147 Oak Knoll Terr., Highland Park, IL 60035-5320
(847) 266-9822; *Fax:* (847) 266-9826
Robet L. Heymann, Dir

Media Venture Partners
Mailing Address: 244 Jackson St., 4th Fl., San Francisco, CA 94111
Second Address: 980-990 Washington St., Suite 200, Dedham, MA 02026
(415) 391-4877, (617) 345-7316; *Fax:* (415) 391-4912, (415) 549-0515
www.mediaventurepartners.com
pcanberryharris@mediaventurepartners.com
Brian Pryor, Managing Director
Tim Beach, Vice President
Renee Shaening, Vice President
Jason Nicolay, Vice President
Ari Cirtin, Vice President
Radio & TV brokerage svcs; mergers & acquisitions; telecom; investment banking.
75 State St., Suite 2500, Boston, MA 02109-1827
(617) 345-7316; *Fax:* (617) 507-5667
Jason Hill, Mgng Dir
6314 Brookside Plaza, Suite 203, Kansas City, MO 64113-1765
(816) 523-8566; *Fax:* (816) 817-0570
R. Clayton Funk, Mgng Dir

MyMediaBroker.com
407 Broadmoor Acres, Portales, NM 88130 88130
(575) 356-2000; *Fax:* (575) 356-2003
www.mymediabroker.com
sandibergman@mymediabroker.com
Sandi Usrey Bergman, President
Full svc media brokerage firm.

Nutmeg Broadcasting
Div/DBA: (formerly New England Media L.L.C.)
720 Main St., Willimantic, CT 06226
(860) 456-1111; *Fax:* (860) 456-9501
www.wili.com
Herbert C. Rice, Co-Founder
Ethel Rice, Co-Founder
Michael Rice, President
Andy Russell, Market Manager
Radio stn.

Patrick Communications L.L.C.
6805 Douglas Legum Dr., Suite 100, Elkridge, MD 21075
(410) 799-1740; *Fax:* (410) 799-1705
www.patcomm.com
larry@patcomm.com
W. Lawrence Patrick, Managing Partner
Jason R. James, Vice President
Susan K. Patrick, Managing Partner
Gregory J. Guy, Managing Partner
DIANA WILKIN, Partner
Stn brokerage, investment banking, mgmt consulting svcs, appraisals & opns consulting.

Questcom Media Services Inc.
4915 Crownvista Dr., Charlotte, NC 28269-0871
(704) 948-9800; *Fax:* (704) 948-9888
Donald R. Bussell, President
Radio & TV stn brokerage specialists concentrating in top 150 markets; offering asst with mergers & consolidations.

RadioStationsForSale.net
Div/DBA: (formerly SalesGroup)
41 Herbert Rd., Braintree, MA 02184 2184
(781) 848-4201; *Fax:* (781) 848-4715
www.radiostationsforsale.net
radio@beld.net
Harold Bausemer, President
Stn brokers, USA.

RBC Daniels
Div/DBA: (Formerly RBC Daniels, L.P.)
3200 Cherry Creek Dr. S., Suite 500, Denver, CO 80209
(303) 778-2329(800) 234-3703; *Fax:* (303) 778-5599
www.rbccm.com
info@rbcdaniels.com
Doug McGregor, Chairman and Co-CEO
Richard Talbot, Chief Operating Officer
Mark Standish, President and Co-CEO
Michael Bowick, Co-Head, Global Equities
Blair Fleming, Head, U.S. Investment Banking
Mark Hughes, Chief Risk Officer,RBC
Doug Guzman, Head, Global Investment Banking
Jonathan Hunter, Head, Fixed Income & Currencies
Clinton Lively, Global Head, Market Risk
Provides mergers, acquisitions, corporate finance & financial advisory svcs to the cable, telecommunications media & technology industries.
3 World Financial Center
200 Vesey St., 9th Fl., New York, NY 10285-0002
(212) 935-5900; *Fax:* (212) 863-4859
David Tolliver, Mgng Dir
11150 Santa Monica Blvd., Suite 1230, Los Angeles, CA 90025-3380
(310) 473-2300; *Fax:* (310) 943-2052

Richard A. Foreman Associates, Inc.
330 Emery Dr. E., Stamford, CT 06902 06902-2210
(203) 327-2800; *Fax:* (203) 967-9393
www.rafamedia.com
raf@rafamedia.com
Richard A. Foreman, President
Specializing in cash-positive radio & TV stns in major growth mkts.

Roehling Broadcast Services Ltd.
8563 E. Wilderness Trail, Unionville, IN 47468
(812) 988-6321, (317) 374-6906; *Fax:* (317) 870-8404
edradiobr@aol.com
Edward W. Roehling, President & Broker
Bcst appraisers, brokers, consultants, also financing, sls, mgmt consultation.

Rumbaut & Company
555 N.E. 34th St., Suite 2701, Miami, FL 33137-4060
(305) 868-0000, (305) 785-7000; *Fax:* (305) 571-0433
www.rumbaut.com
julio@rumbaut.com
Julio Rumbaut, President
Media brokers, advisors, and consultants in all sectors of the media industry including television, radio, and the new media.

S.R. Chanen & Co. Inc.
Div/DBA: (Media Technology Capital Corp.)
3300 N. 3rd Ave., Phoenix, AZ 85013
(602) 266-3600; *Fax:* (602) 285-9268
www.chanen.com
info@chanen.com
Herman Chanen, Founder And Chairman
Steven R. Chanen, Founder, Chief Executive Officer And Director
Steve Betts, President
Investment banking, brokerage & financial advisory svcs for the communications & entertainment industries.

Satterfield & Perry Inc.
7211 Fourth Ave. S., St. Petersburg, FL 33707 33707
(727) 345-7338; *Fax:* (727) 345-3809
www.satterfieldandperry.com
eraust@prodigy.net
Robert Austin, President
John Willis, Operations Dir
Radio & TV broker, mgmt & sls consultant, FDIC-approved appraiser & expert witness.
2020 S. Monroe St. #302, Denver, CO 80210-3767
(303) 758-1876; *Fax:* (303) 756-1865
Al Perry, Chmn Emeritus
4918 W. 101st Terr., Overland Park, KS 66207-3431
(913) 649-5103; *Fax:* (913) 649-5103
Douglas Stephens, Sr Vp
PO Box 362, Coos Bay, OR 97420-0041
(541) 751-0043; *Fax:* (541) 751-0043
Dick McMahon, Vp
20456 E. Orchard Pl., Centennial, CO 80016-3891
(303) 400-5150; *Fax:* (303) 400-5063
Jim Birschbach, Vp
Box 620308-B, Littleton, CO
(303) 948-2200; *Fax:* (303) 948-3468
Joe Benkert, Vp
131 Inwood Dr., Aiken, SC 29803-5613
(803) 270-5613; *Fax:* (803) 649-7786
John Willis, Vp
169 Mountain Meadows La., Wetumpka, AL
(334) 514-2241; *Fax:* (334) 514-2291
Ken Hawkins, Vp

Stan Raymond & Associates Inc.
3241 Bayoo Sound, Longboat Key, FL 34228 34228
(941) 383-9404; *Fax:* (941) 383-9132
stnray@aol.com
Stan Raymond, President
Financial svcs, media brokers, appraisers & consultants specializing in the Southeast.

The Thorburn Company
6625 Hwy. 53 E., Suite 410-72, Dawsonville, GA 30534 30534
(678) 513-1363; *Fax:* (678) 513-1615
www.thorburncompany.com
Robert M. Thorburn, President
Appraisals, brokerage, financial, mgmt consulting for radio, TV & cable.

Station & Cable System Brokers

American Media Services L.L.C.
Mailing Address: PO Box 20696, Charleston, SC 29413
Second Address: 1311 Chuck Dawley Boulevard, Suite 202, Mt. Pleasant, SC 29464
(843) 972-2200; *Fax:* (843) 881-4436
www.americanmediaservices.com
eseeger@ams.fm
Edward F. Seeger, Chairman
Frank G. McCoy, President
Alesa I. Peace, Vice President - Finance & Station Operations
Laramie B. Guest, Vice President - Engineering & Research
Developers & brokers of radio properties. Also appraisals, search svcs (buyer's agent), upgrade studies.

Broadcast Media Associates
P.O. BOX 1233, Santa Maria, CA 93456 93456
(805) 937-1553; *Fax:* (805) 937 7212
Clifford M. Hunter, President
Radio/TV/cable brokerage in the western states. Confidential mktg for radio, TV & LPTV properties; valuation packages & financial analysis; consultants to sellers & buyers.

BroadcastStations4Sale.com
512 Jones St., Graham, NC 27253 27253
(336) 570-9133; *Fax:* (336) 570-3464
www.broadcaststations4sale.com
Ted J. Gray, President & Broker
Buy or sell radio stns or TV stns. List to sell yourself or let BroadcastStations4Sale.com sell it for you.

Bulkley Capital, L.P.
Mailing Address: 5949 Sherry Ln., Suite 1370, Dallas, TX 75225
Second Address: 3204 Huntersworth, Glenwood, MD 21738
(214) 692-5476, (410) 382-4622; *Fax:* (214) 692-9309
www.bulkleycapital.com
info@bulkleycapital.com
G. Bradford Bulkey, President
Oliver Cone, Operations Dir
Nancy Wallin, General Manager
Oliver Cone, Senior Vice President
William Herdrich, Director
Don Schmincke, Director
Richard Gilbert, Director & Advisory Board Member
Craig Lentzsch, Advisory Board Member
John McKay, Director
Investment banking: mergers, acquisitions, private placements of debt & equity capital.

Burt Sherwood & Associates Inc.
6415 Midnight Pass Rd., Apartment 206, Sarasota, FL 34242
(941) 349-2165; *Fax:* (941) 312-0974
bohica1@comcast.net
Burt Sherwood, Owner
Brokerage radio, TV & LPTV; appraisals.

CEA Group
Mailing Address: 101 E. Kennedy Blvd., Suite 3300, Tampa, FL 33602
Second Address: 260 Madison Avenue, New York, NY 10016
(813) 226-8844, 212-218-5085; *Fax:* (813) 225-1513, 212-957-0620
www.ceaworldwide.com
rmichaels@ceaworldwide.com
J. Patrick (Rick) Michaels, Jr., Founder/Chairman/CEO
Ming Jung, Executive VP & COO
Brad Gordon, Executive VP & CFO
Dave Moyer, Senior Managing Director & President, CEA PAG
Beth Cahill, Senior Managing Director
Robert D. Berger,Managing Director
Michael Johnson, Vice President
Doris Rainey, Vice President
A leading provider of investment banking services and private equity to the global communications, media, entertainment, and information technology industries.

Chapin Enterprises
1248 O St., Suite 751, Lincoln, NE 68508 68508
(402) 475-5285; *Fax:* (402) 475-5293
dchapin@inetnebr.com
R.W. Chapin, President

Clifton Gardiner & Company, L.L.C.
24645 S. Augusta Court, Sun Lakes, AZ 85248
(623) 336-7272, (623) 337-3777; *Fax:* (623) 498-8310
www.cliftongardiner.com
cliff@cliftongardiner.com
Cliff Gardiner, Chairman
Clifton H. Gardiner, President
Brokerage & financial svcs for the bcst & cable industries.

CMS Station Brokerage, Inc.
1439 Denniston St., Pittsburgh, PA 15217 USA
(412) 421-2600; *Fax:* (412) 421-6001
www.cmsstationbrokerage.com
roger.rafson@genmediapartners.com
Roger Rafson, President
Shirley Brown, Office Manager
Offers media brokerage services. CMS Station Brokerage helps radio station owners sell their radio stations to qualified buyers and helps buyers find radio stations which make sense to meet their objectives. CMS Station Brokerage alsospecializes in providing radio brokerage services for broadcasters in small and medium sized markets across the United States and Canada.

CobbCorp, LLC
7400 Tamiami Trail North, Suite 102, Naples, FL 34108-2855 34108-2855
(212) 960-8468; *Fax:* (239) 596-0660
www.cobbcorp.com
briancobb@cobbcorp.com
Brian E. Cobb, President
Jeanette Kuszlyk, Controller
Dennis LeClair, Vice President
Mergers, acquisitions, investment & merchant banking.

Cox & Cox, LLC
Mailing Address: 2454 Shiva Ct., St. Louis, MO 63011
Second Address: 4546 Sliver Bit Court, North Las Vegas, Las Vegas, Ne 89032
(702) 296-5814,(636) 458-4780; *Fax:* (702) 968-8618
Robert Cox, President
Linda Cox, Operations Dir
Media mergers & acquisitions, appraisals, consulting, expert testimony, receivership & workout.

Dave Garland Media Brokerage
NSS Data: Radio Only
1007 Shadow Cir., League City, TX 77573 77573
(713) 882-2402
www.radiobroker.com
garland@radiobroker.com
David Garland, President
Robert Miles Master, Operations Dir
Broker of radio stn properties in Texas & surrounding states.

Diversified Investment Services, Inc.
7512 Dr. Phillips Blvd., Suite #50-250, Orlando, FL 32819
(407) 909-0825, (888) 999-7905; *Fax:* (407) 909-0826
diversifiedinvestment.com
a.stilli@yahoo.com
Nancy Hasselback, President/CEO
Armand J. Santilli, President
Media brokers/finders, real estate investment bankers & brokers.

Earl Reilly Enterprises
550 Aloha St., Suite 404, Seattle, WA 98019 98019
(206) 282-6914
Earl F. Reilly, President
Bcst rep, representing U.S. TV stns in Canada. Also licensed bcst stn brokers.

EnVest Media, LLC
6802 Patterson Ave., Richmond, VA 23226 23226
(804) 282-5561; *Fax:* (804) 282-5703
www.envest.biz
Mitt Younts, Managing Member
Nationwide radio, TV acquisition, valuation, financing & consulting firm. The company provides brokerage svcs to stn transaction, appraisal svcs to stn owners & financial institutions. The group secures debt & equity acquisition financing,offers consulting & asset mgmt svcs, acting as court appointed receivers or trustees for bcst stns.

The Exline Company
388 Lowell Ave, Mill Valley, CA 94941 94903
(415) 381-5473; *Fax:* (415) 479-1574
www.exlinecompany.com
exline@pacbell.net
Andrew P. McClure, President/Owner
Judi Lewis, Admin Coordinator
Judi Lewis, Administrative Coordinator
Complete brokerage, consulting & appraisal svcs for radio & TV properties.

Explorer Communications Inc.
4428 N. 12th Street, Phoenix, AZ 85014 34461
(602) 264-1721; *Fax:* (602) 798-8279
www.bbb.org
Brian Mohr, Chairman
Matthew M. Fehling, President
Brian Burt, Vice Chairÿ
Gary Sneed, Treasurer
David Lorenz, Secretary
Rick Dircks, Immediate Past Chairÿ
Bcst media brokerage svcs. Specialists in medium & small market entrepreneurial transactions.

Frank Boyle & Co., L.L.C.
32 greystone, Shelton, CT 06484
(203)513-2402; *Fax:* (203)513-8189
Frank Boyle, President

Fugatt Media Services
9214 Butternut Dr., Crystal Lake, IL 60014 60014
(815) 546-1470, (815) 788-7481
Michael L. Fugatt, President
Media brokerage firm specialing in radio & cable svcs including appraisals.

Gammon Miller L.L.C.
Div/DBA: (Formerly Gammon Media Brokers L.L.C.)
Mailing Address: 4806 Vue Du Lac Pl., Suite B, Manhattan, KS 66503
Second Address: 0123 Timber Trail, Cordillera, CO 81632
(785) 539-1700, (970) 926-3171; *Fax:* (785) 565-0437
www.gammonmiller.com
cmiller@gammonmiller.com
Christopher D. Miller, President/CEO
Brokerage & strategy advice to sellers, buyers of radio stns, TV stns, nwspr & cable TV systems. Gammon Miller Revenue Travel as a division Gammon Miller LLC, is a media based incentive travel provider for radio hstns, TV stns, nwspr andcable TV systems.

George Moore & Associates Inc.
2046 John Rolfe Parkway, Richmond, VA 23238-8111 75230
(804) 965-0550; *Fax:* 800-750-9059
www.manta.com
W. James Moore, President
Brokerage of radio, TV, asset & market appraisals prepared for owners, buyers & lenders.

Gordon Rice Associates
222 West Coleman Boulevard, Mount Pleasant, SC 29464 29413
(843) 884-3590; *Fax:* (843) 881-0358
Gordon Rice, Owner
Gordon Rice, Broker
Brokerage svcs, appraisals & investment analysis for radio & TV.

Hadden & Associates
Div/DBA: Media Brokers - Orlando
147 Eastpark Dr., Celebration, FL 34447 34447
(321) 939-3141; *Fax:* (321) 939-3142
www.haddenonline.com
hadden@haddenonline.com
Doyle Hadden, President
Ryan P. Hadden, Operations Dir
Communications broker, acquisitions, divestitures; financial assistance and appraisal to the broadcasting industry.

Henson Media Inc.
1930 Bishop Lane, Suite 1009, Louisville, KY 40218-1958 40202-2508
502-458-4222; *Fax:* 502-458-4999
www.hensonmedia.com
edhenson1@bellsouth.net
Edward Henson, President
Radio & TV brokers. Radio stations owned and operated.

Holt Media Group
P. O. Box 21985, Lehigh Valley, PA 18002-1985 18017
(610) 814-2821; *Fax:* (610) 814-2826
www.holtmedia.com
Arthur Holt, President/CEO
Christine E.Borger, Executive Vice President
Brokerage, consulting, appraisals.

Howard E. Stark
53 North Park Avenue, Suite 50, Rockville Centre, NY 11570 10022

(516) 596-8929
www.howardstarkfoundation.com
starkfoundation@gmail.com
Howard E. Stark, Founder
Jennifer A. Franz, Executive Director
Media broker; mergers & acquisitions in the communications field.

HPC Puckett & Co.
Mailing Address: PO Box 9063, Rancho Santa Fe, CA 92067
Second Address: 5863 SW 29th St., Topeka, KS 66614
(858) 756-4915, (785) 273-0017; *Fax:* (858) 756-4534, (785) 273-5512
www.hpcpuckett.com
Thomas F. Puckett, Founder, Managing Director and Chief Executive Off
Hunter T. Puckett, Managing Director and General Counsel
Jason A. Meyer, Managing Director
Communications brokerage & investment banking.

John Pierce & Company L.L.C.
PO Box 863, Florence, KY 41022 41042
(859) 647-0101; *Fax:* (859) 647-2611
www.johnpierceco.com
John L. Perce, President
BECKY GRIZOVIC, Chief Financial Officer
Radio, TV, & cable sls & appraisals.

John W. Saunders, Media Broker
709 Rust St, Forney, TX 77057 77057
(713) 789-4222; *Fax:* (713) 789-4322
theradiobroker@aol.com
John W. Saunders, President
Nationwide radio brokerage & appraisals. Buyers or sellers represented on a confidential, professional & personal basis. Top 10 to small markets.

Jorgenson Broadcast Brokerage Inc.
Mailing Address: 426 S. River Rd., Tryon, NC 28782
Second Address: 6172 Bollinger Rd., Suite 108, San Jose, CA 95129
(828) 859-6982, (408) 255-7855; *Fax:* (828) 859-6831, (408) 228-1653
www.goradiotv.com
Mark Jorgenson, Owner
Mark W. Jorgenson, Vice President
Partner, Peter Mieuli
Partner
Confidential, nationwide brokerage of bcst properties.

Kalil & Co. Inc.
2960 N. Swan Rd., Suite 134, Tucson, AZ 85712
(520) 795-1050; *Fax:* (520) 322-0584
www.kalilco.com
kalil@kalilco.com
Frank Higney, Coo
Frank Kalil, Owner/President
Tom Zlaket, General Manager
Todd Hartman, VP
Media brokerage firm dealing in radio, TV & cable. Handles exclusive listings & confidential searches.

Kepper, Tupper & Company
2 Galleon, Suite 100, Hilton Head Island, SC 29928 6877
(203) 431-3366; *Fax:* (203) 431-3864
www.kepper-tupper.com
jtupper@kepper-tupper.com
John B. Tupper, President
Brokerage & investment banking svcs for the cable & bcst TV industries. Please visit our website kepper-tupper.com.

Knowles Media Brokerage Services
P.O. Box 9698, Bakersfield, CA 93389 93389
(661) 833-3834; *Fax:* (661) 833-3845
www.media-broker.com
gregg.knowles@netzero.com
Gregg K. Knowles, Broker
Knowles Media Brokerage Services is a full-service agency located in Bakersfield, California, offering sales, consultation, and appraisal services for print media owners nationwide.

Kozacko Media Services
Mailing Address: 800 S Salisbury St, Raleigh, NC 27602-2978
Second Address: P.O. Box 2978, Raleigh, NC 27601
(919) 664-7000; *Fax:* (919) 664-7097
www.raleighchamber.org
mail@raleighchamber.org
Richard Urquhart, Chairman
Tim Giuliani, President & CEO
Janet Carr, General Manager/SVP
Lisa Harris, Office Manager
Alice Avery, Communications Manager
Natalie Griffith, Operations Manager
Candice Coffey, Front OfficeCoordinator
Abbie Mahoney, Government Affairs Events Manager
Emily Atkinson, Vice President Of Government Affairs
Appraisals & current market evaluations of radio & TV stns; bcst stn acquisition brokers.

Lazard L.L.C.
Mailing Address: 30 rockefeller plaza, New York, NY 10112
Second Address: 600 Fifth Avenue, New York, NY 10020
(212) 632-6000
www.lazard.com
Kenneth M. Jacobs, Chairman and Chief Executive Officer
Alexander F. Stern, Chief Operating Officer
Robert Hougie, General Manager
Matthieu Bucaille, CFO
Ashish Bhutani, Vice Chairman
Scott D. Hoffman, General Counsel
Steven J.Heyer, Lead Director
Andrew Alper, Director
Sylvia Jay, Director
Lazard's broad range of svcs includes: gen financial advice; domestic, cross-border mergers & acquisitions; divestitures; privatizations; special committee assignments; takeover defenses; corporate restructurings; strategicpartnerships/joint ventures; & debt/equity underwriting.

Legacy Securities Corp.
PO Box 283, Gulf Breeze, FL 32562
(850) 677-1989
Christopher F. Battel, President/CEO
Henry J. Cardello, Advisory Member
John J. Huntz, Advisory Member
Ptrick E. Falcoio, Advisory Member

Media Services Group Inc.
Mailing Address: 3948 S. Third St. #191, Jacksonville Beach, FL 32250
Second Address: 149 South Roscoe Blvd., Ponte Vedra, FL 32082
(904) 285-3239, (904) 285-3239; *Fax:* (904) 285-5618, (904) 285-5618
www.mediaservicesgroup.com
George R. Reed, General Manager
One of the nation's leading full svc media brokerage, valuation & consulting firms with in-depth industry knowledge & market expertise.

Media Venture Partners
Mailing Address: 244 Jackson St., 4th Fl., San Francisco, CA 94111
Second Address: 980-990 Washington St., Suite 200, Dedham, MA 02026
(415) 391-4877, (617) 345-7316; *Fax:* (415) 391-4912, (415) 549-0515
www.mediaventurepartners.com
pcanberryharris@mediaventurepartners.com
Brian Pryor, Managing Director
Tim Beach, Vice President
Renee Shaening, Vice President
Jason Nicolay, Vice President
Ari Cirtin, Vice President
Radio & TV brokerage svcs; mergers & acquisitions; telecom; investment banking.

MyMediaBroker.com
407 Broadmoor Acres, Portales, NM 88130 88130
(575) 356-2000; *Fax:* (575) 356-2003
www.mymediabroker.com
sandibergman@mymediabroker.com
Sandi Usrey Bergman, President
Full svc media brokerage firm.

Nutmeg Broadcasting
Div/DBA: (formerly New England Media L.L.C.)
720 Main St., Willimantic, CT 06226
(860) 456-1111; *Fax:* (860) 456-9501
www.wili.com
Herbert C. Rice, Co-Founder
Ethel Rice, Co-Founder
Michael Rice, President
Andy Russell, Market Manager
Radio stn.

Patrick Communications L.L.C.
6805 Douglas Legum Dr., Suite 100, Elkridge, MD 21075
(410) 799-1740; *Fax:* (410) 799-1705
www.patcomm.com
larry@patcomm.com
W. Lawrence Patrick, Managing Partner
Jason R. James, Vice President
Susan K. Patrick, Managing Partner
Gregory J. Guy, Managing Partner
DIANA WILKIN, Partner
Stn brokerage, investment banking, mgmt consulting svcs, appraisals & opns consulting.

Questcom Media Services Inc.
4915 Crownvista Dr., Charlotte, NC 28269-0871
(704) 948-9800; *Fax:* (704) 948-9888
Donald R. Bussell, President
Radio & TV stn brokerage specialists concentrating in top 150 markets; offering asst with mergers & consolidations.

RadioStationsForSale.net
Div/DBA: (formerly SalesGroup)
41 Herbert Rd., Braintree, MA 02184 2184
(781) 848-4201; *Fax:* (781) 848-4715
www.radiostationsforsale.net
radio@beld.net
Harold Bausemer, President
Stn brokers, USA.

RBC Daniels
Div/DBA: (Formerly RBC Daniels, L.P.)
3200 Cherry Creek Dr. S., Suite 500, Denver, CO 80209
(303) 778-2329(800) 234-3703; *Fax:* (303) 778-5599
www.rbccm.com
info@rbcdaniels.com
Doug McGregor, Chairman and Co-CEO
Richard Talbot, Chief Operating Officer
Mark Standish, President and Co-CEO
Michael Bowick, Co-Head, Global Equities
Blair Fleming, Head, U.S. Investment Banking
Mark Hughes, Chief Risk Officer,RBC
Doug Guzman, Head, Global Investment Banking
Jonathan Hunter, Head, Fixed Income & Currencies
Clinton Lively, Global Head, Market Risk
Provides mergers, acquisitions, corporate finance & financial advisory svcs to the cable, telecommunications media & technology industries.

Richard A. Foreman Associates, Inc.
330 Emery Dr. E., Stamford, CT 06902 06902-2210
(203) 327-2800; *Fax:* (203) 967-9393
www.rafamedia.com
raf@rafamedia.com
Richard A. Foreman, President
Specializing in cash-positive radio & TV stns in major growth mkts.

Roehling Broadcast Services Ltd.
8563 E. Wilderness Trail, Unionville, IN 47468
(812) 988-6321, (317) 374-6906; *Fax:* (317) 870-8404
edradiobr@aol.com
Edward W. Roehling, President & Broker
Bcst appraisers, brokers, consultants, also financing, sls, mgmt consultation.

Rumbaut & Company
555 N.E. 34th St., Suite 2701, Miami, FL 33137-4060
(305) 868-0000, (305) 785-7000; *Fax:* (305) 571-0433
www.rumbaut.com
julio@rumbaut.com
Julio Rumbaut, President
Media brokers, advisors, and consultants in all sectors of the media industry including television, radio, and the new media.

S.R. Chanen & Co. Inc.
Div/DBA: (Media Technology Capital Corp.)
3300 N. 3rd Ave., Phoenix, AZ 85013
(602) 266-3600; *Fax:* (602) 285-9268
www.chanen.com
info@chanen.com
Herman Chanen, Founder And Chairman
Steven R. Chanen, Founder, Chief Executive Officer And Director
Steve Betts, President
Investment banking, brokerage & financial advisory svcs for the communications & entertainment industries.

Satterfield & Perry Inc.
7211 Fourth Ave. S., St. Petersburg, FL 33707 33707
(727) 345-7338; *Fax:* (727) 345-3809
www.satterfieldandperry.com
eraust@prodigy.net
Robert Austin, President
John Willis, Operations Dir
Radio & TV broker, mgmt & sls consultant, FDIC-approved appraiser & expert witness.

Stan Raymond & Associates Inc.
3241 Bayoo Sound, Longboat Key, FL 34228 34228

PROFESSIONAL SERVICES

(941) 383-9404; *Fax:* (941) 383-9132
stnray@aol.com
Stan Raymond, President
Financial svcs, media brokers, appraisers & consultants specializing in the Southeast.

The Thorburn Company
6625 Hwy. 53 E., Suite 410-72, Dawsonville, GA 30534 30534
(678) 513-1363; *Fax:* (678) 513-1615
www.thorburncompany.com
Robert M. Thorburn, President
Appraisals, brokerage, financial, mgmt consulting for radio, TV & cable.

Station Financing Services

ABN AMRO
Mailing Address: 100 Park Avenue, 17th floor, New York, NY 10017
Second Address: 175 West Jackson Boulevard, Chicago, IL 60604
(917) 284-6814, (212) 251-3524, (312) 604-8000; *Fax:* (212) 409-7291
www.abnamro.com
Gerrit Zalm, Chairman
Johan van Hall, COO/Vice Chairman
Kees van Dijkhuizen, Chief Financial Officer
Caroline Princen, Integration, Communication & Compliance
Wietze Reehoorn, Chief Risk Officer and Strategy
Chris Vogelzang, Retail& Private Banking
Joop Wijn, Commercial & Merchant Banking
ABN AMRO serves retail, private and commercial banking customers in the Netherlands and across the globe. Along with a comprehensive range of products and services, we offer in-depth financial expertise, extensive knowledge of numeroussectors and an international network supporting our customers' domestic and international operations.

Alta Communications
1000 Winter Street, South Entrance, Suite 3500, Waltham, MA 02451
(617) 262-7770; *Fax:* (617) 262-9779
clarason@altacomm.com
Jessica Barry Reed, Vice President
Chris Dias, Vice President
Eileen McCarthy Toti, General Partner/CFO
Pam Hall, Controller
Provide equity & subordinated debt for acquisitions, buyouts, recapitalizations, etc. for companies in radio, TV, cable TV & related industries.

Ares Capital
Mailing Address: 2200 Pennsylvania Avenue, NW, Suite 600-W, Washington, DC 20037
Second Address: 2000 Avenue of the Stars, 12th Floor, Los Angeles, CA 90067
(202) 721-6100, (310) 201-4200; *Fax:* (202) 721-6101, (310) 432-8632
www.arescapitalcorp.com
Robert L. Rosen, Director
Michael Arougheti, Co-Chairman
Ann Torre Bates, Director
Frank E. O'Bryan, Director
Ares Capital Corporation (Ares Capital or ARCC) is a specialty finance company that provides one-stop solutions to meet the distinct and underserved financing needs of private middle-market companies across diverse industries. Ourflexibility, structuring expertise and self-origination capabilities enable us to invest across the capital structure and to meet the full spectrum of our clients' financing needs. As a patient, long-term investor with permanent capital, we havedeveloped a reputation for the flexibility of our approach, a willingness to hold large positions and the ability to offer sponsors and management teams increased certainty of execution. In addition to primarily providing debt financing tomiddle-market companies, we also provide, on a lesser scale, debt financing for power generation projects and financing to emerging growth companies typically backed by venture capital firms.

Bank of America Illinois
Mailing Address: 231 S. LaSalle St., Chicago, IL 60604
Second Address: 135 S. Lasalle Street, Chicago, IL 60603
(312) 828-2345, (312) 443-2000; *Fax:* (312) 828-7397
www.bankofamerica.com
John Brennan, President

The Barclays Group
745 Seventh Avenue, New York, NY 10019
(212) 526-7000
www.barcap.com
David Walker, Chairman
Dambisa Moyo, Non-Executive Director
Diane De Saint Victor, Non-Executive Director
Sir Michael Rake, Deputy Chairman And Senior Independent Director

Berkery, Noyes & Co.
165 Broadway, 13th Fl., New York, NY 10006
(212) 668-3022; *Fax:* (212) 747-9092
www.berkerynoyes.com
Berkery@berkerynoyes.com
Joseph Berkery, CEO
John T. Shea, Senior Advisor
Mary Jo Zandy, Managing Director
Jonathan Krieger, Managing Director
Jeffrey Smith, Managing Director
Peter Yoon, Managing Director
Assists with mergers, acquisitions, divestitures; financial analysis & counsel; debt or equity financing through private or pub chs, including LBOs, ESOPs & valuations.
40 Kirkstall Rd., Newton, MA 02460-2218
(617) 969-7935
Marlowe G. Teig, Mgng Dir
580 California St., 5th Fl., San Francisco, CA 94104-1000
(415) 440-5001

BIA Capital Strategies LLC
15120 Enterprise Ct., Suite 100, Chantilly, VA 20151
(703) 818-2425, (800) 331-5086; *Fax:* (703) 803-3299
www.bia.com
info@biakelsey.com
Tom Buono, Founder and CEO
Mark Giannini, COO and Senior Vice President
Rick Ducey, Managing Director
Woody Allen, CFO BIA Financial Network
Mark Fratrik, VP and Chief Economist
Steve Passwaiter, VP Business Development
WarrenKay, Executive in Residence
Geoff Price, VP Valuations and Financial Consulting
Investment banking svc, including placement of debt & equity, advice in capital structure & merger, & acquisition issues.

BIA Digital Partners, L.P.
15120 Enterprise Ct., Suite 200, Chantilly, VA 20151
(703) 227-9600; *Fax:* (703) 803-3299
www.biadigitalpartners.com
contactdp@bia.com
Thomas J. Buono, Principal
Gregg E. Johnson, Managing Principal
Charles A. Wiebe, Principal
Scott E. Chappell, Principal
Damien A. Dovi, Vice President
Lloyd R. Sams, Managing Principal
BIA Digital Partners is a private investment firm, making both debt and equity investments in middle market companies serving the media and entertainment, telecommunications, and information and business services industries. The firm wasoriginally formed in direct response to the lack of junior capital available for small to medium-sized communications companies. While larger companies can access the public markets, smaller firms have fewer options for a middle or junior layer ofcapital.

BIA Financial Network
14150 Parkeast Circle, Suite 110, Chantilly, VA 20151
(703) 818-2425; *Fax:* (703) 803-3299
www.bia.com
info@bia.com
Thomas J. Buono, Founder/ CEO
Neal Polacheck, President
Mark Giannini, COO
Rick Ducey, Managing Director
Woody A. Allen, CFO
Mark Fratrik, VP/Chief Economist
Steve Passwaiter, VP Business Development
Warren Kay, Executive inResidence
Geoff Price, VP Valuations and Financial Consulting
Financial consultants to the communications industry; fair market valuations, tax appraisals, acquisition consulting, business plans, internal operational audits, litigation support, investment, publications, & database software, venturefunding, capital.

BMO Nesbitt Burns (Bank of Montreal)
1 First Canadian Place, Toronto, ON M5X 1H3
(416) 359-4000 , (866) 797-8437; *Fax:* (212) 605-1648
www.bmo.com/nesbittburns?
yvonne.bos@bmo.com
Provides lending & other capital raising svcs, derivatives, & cash mgmt to the bcst & cable industries.

BNP Paribas
787 Seventh Avenue, The Equitable Tower, New York, NY 10019
(212) 841-3000; *Fax:* (212) 841-3251
www.usa.bnpparibas.com
BNP Paribas in the United States is part of a far-reaching global banking network, offering its clients a full range of services from investment and retail banking to asset management services. BNP Paribas has been present in the countrysince 1919 as the French American Banking Corporation and currently has over 14,000 employees in the US.

Bulkley Capital L.P.
Mailing Address: 5949 Sherry Ln., Suite 1616, Dallas, TX 75225
Second Address: 11276 Ridermark Row, Columbia, MD 21044
(214) 692-5476, (410) 382-4622; *Fax:* (214) 692-9309
www.bulkleycapital.com
info@bulkleycapital.com
G. Bradford Bulkley, President & Founder
Kristi Garrett, Office Manager
Nancy Wallin, General Manager
Oliver Cone, Senior Vice President
Kristi Garrett, Office Manager
Richard Gilbert, Director & Advisory Board Member
WilliamSkitbitsky, Director
Don Schmincke, Director
John McKay, Director
Investment banking; mergers, acquisitions, private placements of debt & equity capital.

CEA Group
Mailing Address: 101 E. Kennedy Blvd., Suite 3300, Tampa, FL 33602
Second Address: 260 Madison Avenue, New York, NY 10016
(813) 226-8844; *Fax:* (813) 225-1513
www.ceaworldwide.com
RMichaels@ceaworldwide.com
J. Patrick (Rick) Michaels, Jr., Founder/Chairman/CEO
Ming Jung, Executive VP & COO
Brad Gordon, Executive VP & CFO
Dave Moyer, Senior Managing Director & President, CEA PAG
Beth Cahill, Senior Managing Director
Robert D. Berger,Managing Director
Michael Johnson, Vice President
Doris Rainey, Vice President
A leading provider of investment banking services and private equity to the global communications, media, entertainment, and information technology industries.
101 Kennedy Blvd., #3300, Tampa, FL 33602-5151
(813) 226-8844

CEA Group
Mailing Address: 101 E. Kennedy Blvd., Suite 3300, Tampa, FL 33602
Second Address: 260 Madison Avenue, New York, NY 10016
(813) 226-8844; *Fax:* (813) 225-1513
www.ceaworldwide.com
rmichaels@ceaworldwide.com
J. Patrick (Rick) Michaels, Jr., Founder/Chairman/CEO
Ming Jung, Executive VP & COO
Brad Gordon, Executive VP & CFO
Dave Moyer, Senior Managing Director & President, CEA PAG
Beth Cahill, Senior Managing Director
Robert D. Berger,Managing Director
Michael Johnson, Vice President
Doris Rainey, Vice President
A leading provider of investment banking services and private equity to the global communications, media, entertainment, and information technology industries.
Prinzregentenstrasse 56, Muenchen
49-(0)89 290 7250; *Fax:* 49 (0)89 290 725 200
Dr. Stephan Goetz, Stefan Sanktjohanser
mgng ptnrs, Dr. Gemot Wunderle
mgng dir, President
1270 Avenue of the Americas, Suite 1818, New York, NY 10020-1700
(212) 218-5085; *Fax:* (212) 218-5099
Alexander Rossi, Mgng Director
Bob Ennis, Mgng Director
Waldo Glasman, Mgng Director
Paul Miller, Mgng Director
Evan Blum, Dir
Jason Donnell, Dir
191 Post Rd. W., Westport, CT 06880-4625
(203) 221-2662; *Fax:* (203) 221-2663
David Moyer, Mktg Dir

CIBC World Markets
300 Madison Ave., New York, NY 10017

(212) 856-4000; *Fax:* (212) 856-3996
www.cibcwm.com
Richard Nesbitt, COO
Gary W. Brown, President
Geoffrey Belsher, Managing Director
Harry Cullham, Managing Director
Scott Bere, Managing Director
Roman Dubczak, Managing Director
Christian Exshaw, Managing Director
MichaelHiggins, Managing Director
Investment banking & asset mgmt.

Clifton Gardiner & Company L.L.C.
24645 S. Augusta Court, Sun Lakes, AZ 85248
(623) 336-7272, (623) 337-3777; *Fax:* (623) 498-8310
www.cliftongardiner.com
cliff@cliftongardiner.com
Clifton Gardiner & Company, LLC provides experienced and professional brokerage representation to buyers and sellers of radio stations and other media properties. We represent our clients on an exclusive basis, and devote all of ourresources to achieving a successful completion of a transaction. We are known for the accuracy and completeness of our Memorandums and for our very thorough search for possible buyers. Marketing a "for sale" listing is not a "passive" activity. Wework hard from day one!

Cox & Cox, LLC
Mailing Address: 2454 Shiva Ct., St. Louis, MO 63011
Second Address: 4546 Sliver Bit Court, North Las Vegas, Las Vegas, Ne 89032
(702) 296-5814,(636) 458-4780; *Fax:* (702) 968-8618
Robert Cox, President
Linda Cox, Operations Dir
Media mergers & acquisitions, appraisals, consulting, expert testimony, receivership & workout.

EnVest Media, LLC
6802 Patterson Ave., Richmond, VA 23226 23226
(804) 282-5561; *Fax:* (804) 282-5703
www.envest.biz
Mitt Younts, Managing Member
Nationwide radio, TV acquisition, valuation, financing & consulting firm. The company provides brokerage svcs to stn transaction, appraisal svcs to stn owners & financial institutions. The group secures debt & equity acquisition financing,offers consulting & asset mgmt svcs, acting as court appointed receivers or trustees for bcst stns.

GE Capital Inc.
500 W. Monroe St., Chicago, IL 60661
(312) 463-2300; *Fax:* (312) 441-6728
www.gecapital.com
Keith S. Sherin, Chairman/CEO
Tom Gentile, President/COO
Robert Green, Chief Financial Officer
Aris Kekedjian, Vice-President/Managing Director
Michael Silva, Chief Regulatory Officer/Compliance Leader
Jack Ryan, Senior VicePresident Human Resources
Coml financial svcs.

Gleacher Partners
677 Broadway, 2nd Floor, Albany, NY 12207
(212) 273-7100; *Fax:* (212) 752-2711
www.gleacher.com
info@gleacher.com
William Payne, Chairman
Christopher J. Kearns, Chief Restructuring Officer and Chief Executive Of
Patricia Arciero-Craig, General Counsel and Secretary
Bryan Edminston, Controller
Provide advice & capital to companies in the media & telecommunications industries.

Great Hill Partners
One Liberty Sq., Boston, MA 02109
(617) 790-9400; *Fax:* (617) 790-9401
www.greathillpartners.com
Laurie Gerber, CEO
Private equity for media & communications companies.

Hoffman Schutz Media Capital Inc.
2044 W. California St., San Diego, CA 92110
(206) 201-3822
www.hs-media.com
We work extensively with financial institutions, equity sources, and owners engaged with the broadcast radio and television industries. The firm also provides specialized economic and market studies for use in regulatory proceedings,litigation support, and strategic planning.
Directors:
Lori Neeham, exec dir

HSBC
One HSBC Ctr., Buffalo, NY 14203
(716) 841-7855,(877) 472-2249; *Fax:* (716) 854-2751
www.us.hsbc.com
Postproduction & radio/TV equipment financing.

Hungerford, Aldrin, Nichols & Carter, CPAs
Mailing Address: 2910 Lucerne Dr. S.E., Grand Rapids, MI 49546
Second Address: 114 N. Lafayette St., Greenville, MI 48838
(616) 949-3200, (616) 754-8888; *Fax:* (616) 949-7720, (616)754-5281
www.hanc.com
charper@hanc.com
Tom Cripps, Firm Administrator
Sam DeMarco, Business Development Director
Sally Plachecki, Administrative Assistant
Dolly Savage-Lowe, Administrative Assistant
Joan Start, Administrative Assistant
Hungerford, Aldrin, Nichols & Carter, PC is a locally owned and controlled CPA firm, and has served West Michigan businesses since 1941. Our specialty is family owned and closely held companies. We've been recognized as a Small Business ofthe Year by the Greater Grand Rapids Chamber of Commerce and multiple times have been named one of West Michigan's "101 Best and Brightest Companies To Work For." These honors were presented, in part, due to the longevity of both our clients and ouremployees. That helps us provide continuity of service, something many of our clients have come to appreciate.

J P Morgan and Co. Inc.
60 Wall St., New York, NY 10260
(212) 483-2323
www.jpmorgan.com
Jamie Dimon, CEO
Mergers & acquisitions; debt & equity capital raising; swaps & derivatives; credit arrangement & loan syndication; securities sls & trading; asset mgmt.
333 S. Hope St, 35th Fl, Los Angeles, CA 90071-1406
(213) 437-9300
227 W. Monroe St, Suite 2800m, Chicago, IL 60606-5055
(312) 541-3300
101 California St, 38th Fl, San Francisco, CA 94111-5802
(415) 954-3200

KeyBanc Capital Markets
127 Public Sq., 6th Fl., Cleveland, OH 44114-1306
(216) 689-3000; *Fax:* (216) 689-4666
www.key.com/media
Beth E. Mooney, Chairman of the Board/Chief Executive Office
Kathleen Mayher, President
Financing for media—TV, radio, cable, nwsprs, bcstg & telecommunications.

M/C Venture Partners
Mailing Address: 75 State St., Suite 2500, Boston, MA 02109
Second Address: 3 Embarcadero Center, Suite 2360, San Francisco, CA 94111
(617) 345-7200, (415) 438-4875; *Fax:* (617) 345-7201, (415) 296-8901
www.mcpartners.com
mcp@mcpartners.com
David Ingraham, Vice President
Lydia Jett, Vice President
Edward J. Keefe, Chief Financial Officer/Chief Compliance Officer
Gillis S. Cashman, Managing Partner
David D. Croll, Managing Partner
M/C Partners is the quintessential lead investor, combining broad company building knowledge with deep domain expertise to guide companies from early stages to profitability and ultimately to successful exits. We take an active role in ourinvestments, working closely and effectively with management teams to deliver success and strong investment returns.

Nautic Partners
50 Kennedy Plaza, 12th Floor, Providence, RI 02903
(401) 278-6770; *Fax:* (401) 278-6387
www.nautic.com
bwheeler@nautic.com
Habib Gorgi, Managing Director
Bernie Buonanno, Managing Director
Scott Hilinski, Managing Director
Chris Crosby, Managing Director
Douglas Hill, Managing Director
Charles Bartolini, Chief Financial Officer
Founded in 1986, Nautic Partners is a middle-market private equity firm with over $2.5 billion of equity capital under management. Over three decades, we have completed more than 110 transactions, invested capital on behalf of our limitedpartners, and partnered with a wide array of talented management teams.

Patrick Communications L.L.C.
6805 Douglas Legum Dr., Suite 100, Elkridge, MD 21075
(410) 799-1740; *Fax:* (410) 799-1705
www.patcomm.com
larry@patcomm.com
W. Lawrence Patrick, Managing Partner
Jason R. James, Vice President
Susan K. Patrick, Managing Partner
Gregory J. Guy, Managing Partner
DIANA WILKIN, Partner
Stn brokerage, investment banking, mgmt consulting svcs, appraisals & opns consulting.

PK World Media
126 Clock Tower Pl., Suite 200, Carmel, CA 93923
(831) 624-5100; *Fax:* (831) 625-4417
info@pkworldmedia.com
Paul Kagan, Chairman/CEO
PK Worldmedia, Inc. is a forward-looking information provider with a strong foundation in industry history. Founder/CEO Paul Kagan, media industry investment analyst, consultant, commentator and investor, created the legendary Paul KaganAssociates, Inc. in 1969 and sold it, along with related companies, to Primedia, Inc. in 2000. The business he sold is now known as Kagan Research, a division of SNL Financial. Following the expiration of his five-year contract on Nov. 9, 2005, Kaganlaunched PK Worldmedia, Inc., to enable industry executives to continue to tap into his vast experience and unique new databases.

RBC Capital Markets
Div/DBA: (formerly Daniels & Associates)
Mailing Address: 3200 Cherry Creek S. Dr., Suite 500, Denver, CO 80209
Second Address: 1801 California Street, Suite 3850, Denver, CO 80202
(303) 778-5555, (303) 595-1200, (800) 234-3703; *Fax:* (303) 778-5599
www.rbccm.com
Doug McGregor, Chairman/Co-CEO
Richard Talbot, COO
Michael Bowick, Head-Global
Blair Fleming, Head- U.S. Investment Banking
Doug Guzman, Head-Global Investment Banking
Jonathan Hunter, Global Head Of Fixed Income And Currencies
Troy Maxwell, Chief Financial Officer
Provides mergers, acquisitions, corporate finance & financial advisory svcs to the tcable, telecom, media & internet industries.
711 5th Ave., Suite 405, New York, NY 10022-3111
(212) 935-5900; *Fax:* (212) 8634859
David Tolliver, Vp

Richard A. Foreman Associates Inc.
330 Emery Dr. E., Stamford, CT 06902
(203) 327-2800; *Fax:* (203) 967-9393
www.rafamedia.com
raf@rafamedia.com
Richard A. Foreman, President
Richard A. Foreman Associates is dedicated to providing transactional and consulting services to the broadcast, digital/interactive, entertainment and communications' industries, utilizing a forthright and highly focused approach. Our goalis the enhancement of our customer's needs. We commit our expertise and integrity to the goal of accomplishing a fair, balanced transaction between buyer and seller.

Schroder Investment Management North America Inc.
Div/DBA: (formerly Schroder Investment Management)
875 Third Ave., 22nd Fl., New York, NY 10022- 6225
(212) 632-2954, (212) 641-3830; *Fax:* (212) 641-3985
www.schroders.com/us
schroderfunds@schroders.com
Jamie Dorrien-Smith, CEO

Silicon Valley Bank
555 Mission Street, Suite 900, San Francisco, CA 94105
(415) 512-4227, (415) 764-3100; *Fax:* (415) 615-0076 , (415) 856-0810
www.svb.com
clientservice@svb.com
Ken Wilcox, Chairman
Greg W. Becker, President/CEO
Bruce Wallace, Chief Operations Officer/Principal Operating Offic
Harry Kellogg, Vice Chairman of Silicon Valley Bank
Head of Strat
Michael Descheneaux, Chief Financial Officer

PROFESSIONAL SERVICES

Michelle Draper, Chief Marketing Officer
Marc Verissimo, Chief Strategy and Risk Officer
Joan Parsons, Head of U.S. Banking
Chris Edmonds-Waters, Head of Human Resources
Comprehensive finance svcs for middle market bcst & cable operators.

Syndicated Communications Inc. (SYNCOM)
4800 Hampden Lane, Suite 200, Bethesda, MD 20814
(301) 608-3203; *Fax:* (301) 608-3307
www.syncom.com
info@syncom.com
Terry L. Jones, Managing Partner
Duane C. McKnight, Managing Member
April C. Floyd, Senior Accountant
Robert L. Greene, Principal
Kateri Jones, Analyst
Roy Kosuge, Principal
Syncom Venture Partners is aggressively focused on creating the next generation of market leaders within the rapidly growing sectors of digital media, mobile technology, and web based services. We bring the unique, hands on perspective thatcomes with witnessing the emergence, and now the transformation of traditional, distribution centric media to the digital, content and technology centric media we are presently experiencing. Syncom's deep domain experience transcends this evolutionand positions us to offer unparalleled guidance to our portfolio management teams as they navigate this complex environment.

Veronis Suhler Stevenson
55 East 52nd Street, 33rd Floor, New York, NY 10055
(212) 935-4990; *Fax:* (212) 381-8168
www.vss.com
StevensonJ@vss.com
James P. Rutherfurd, President
Jeffrey T. Stevenson, Operations Dir
John Sinatra, CFO
Bert Abrams, Senior Advisor
Randy Lehman, Tech. Director
Tanya Dessereau, Marketing & Communcations
Veronis Suhler Stevenson is a leading private investment firm that invests in the information, education, media, marketing and business services industries in North America and Europe.
London
St. James Square, Buchanan House, 8th Fl, London, United Kingdom
44-207-484-1440; *Fax:* 44-207-484-1415
Nigel Stapleton, Chmn Veloms Schler International

Waller Capital Corp.
One Rockefeller Plaza, 23rd Floor, New York, NY 10020
(212) 632-3600; *Fax:* (212) 632-3607
www.wallercapital.com
info@wallercapital.com
John W. Waller, III, Chairman
Garrett Baker, President
Jeffrey A. Brandon, Managing Director
Christine Frank, Managing Director
Financing & investment svcs to cable TV industry, specializing in cable TV mergers & acquisitions, buyout financing, raising debt & equity.

Wells Fargo
Wachovia Securities, 301 S. College St., Charlotte, NC 28288
(704) 348-9500; *Fax:* (704) 715-1997
www.wellsfargo.com
John G. Stumpf, Chairman/President/Chief Executive Officer
Patricia R. Callahan, Senior EVP/ Chief Administrative Officer
David M. Carroll, Senior EVP-Wealth, Brokerage and Retirement
Richard D. Levy, EVP- Controller
AvidModjtabai, Senior EVP, Consumer Lending
Timothy J. Sloan, Senior EVP- Chief Financial Officer
James M. Strother, Senior EVP-General Counsel
We believe in our vision and values just as strongly today as we did the first time we put them on paper more than 20 years ago. Staying true to them will guide us toward continued growth and success for decades to come. As you read moreabout our vision and values, you will learn about who we are, where we're headed and how every Wells Fargo team member can help us get there.

Wells Fargo Equipment Finance Inc.
530 Fifth Ave., 15th Fl., New York, NY 10036
(212) 805-1000; *Fax:* (212) 805-1050
www.wellsfargo.com
wfefi@wellsfargo.com
John Crum, President
Leading provider of equipment leasing & financing, intermediate term lending & specialty finance products to the bcst industry.
100 Mill Plain Rd., 3rd Fl., Danbury, CT 06811-5178
(203) 791-3944
Brian Rodden, Vp
14081 Yorba St., Suite 205, Tustin, CA 92780-2010
(714) 544-4190
Deborah Anderson, Vp

Talent Agents & Managers

Abrams Artists Agency
Mailing Address: 9200 Sunset Blvd., 11th Fl., Los Angeles, CA 90069
Second Address: 275 Seventh Ave, 26th floor, New York, NY 10001
(310) 859-0625, (646) 486-4600; *Fax:* (310) 276-6193
www.abramsartists.com
Performing artists rep talent agency.

Abrams Artists Agency
275 7th Ave, 26th Fl., New York, NY 10001-6708
(646) 486-4600; *Fax:* (646) 486-0100
Neal Altman, Sr Vp
Robert Attermann, Vp

Burt Shapiro Management
2147 N. Beachwood Dr., Los Angeles, CA 90068
(323) 469-9452; *Fax:* (801) 653-6571
home.mindspring.com
burtjay@mail.com
Burt J. Shapiro, President
Represents on-air talent including anchors, reporters, hosts, & sports anchor/reporters, as well as producers & news directors.

Ephraim & Associates, P.C.
108 W. Grand Ave., Chicago, IL 60654
(312) 321-9700; *Fax:* (312) 321-3655
www.ephraim.com
eliot@ephraim.com
Donald M. Ephraim, President
David M. Ephraim, Operations Dir
Talent representation, including contract negotiation, legal & career consulation, tax, estate & pension planning. Elliot Ephraim, atty/agent.

The Image Generators
18156 Darnell Dr., Olney, MD 20832
(301) 924-5700; *Fax:* (301) 570-8916
www.imagegenerators.com
Mike Weiner, President
Valle Bonhag, General Manager
Howard Glassroth, Senior Consultant
Jack Palmer, Senior Consultant
Bill Holleran, Senior Consultant
Ann Quarzo, Senior Consultant
Jeff Porro, Senior Consultant
Voiceover talent, audition svc, online demos of pro voices.

International Creative Management Inc.
730 Fifth Avenue, New York, NY 10019
(212) 556-5600; *Fax:* (212) 556-5665
www.ICMtalent.com
careersla@icmtalent.com
Jeff Berg, Chairman
ICM Partners is one of the world's largest talent and literary agencies with offices in New York, Los Angeles, and London. The agency represents creative and technical talent in the fields of motion picture, television, books, music, liveperformance, branded entertainment, and new media. ICM was formed in 1975 through the merger of Creative Management Associates and International Famous Agency. In 2005, the company raised equity financing from Rizvi Traverse and institutionalinvestors to fund strategic growth, and in 2006, ICM acquired the literary agency Broder Webb Chervin Silbermann. In 2012, the agency completed a management buyout and formed a partnership with the new name, ICM Partners.
10250 Constellation Blvd., Los Angeles, CA 90067-6200
(310) 550-4000
61 Frith Street, London
+44 207 851 4853

Miller Broadcast Management Inc.
616 W. Fulton St., Suite 516, Chicago, IL 60661
(312) 454-1111; *Fax:* (312) 454-0044
www.millerbroadcast.com
info@millerbroadcast.com
Lisa Miller, President
Matt Miller, Vice-President
For the past 27 years MBM has been dedicated to career development, planning, placement, syndication and contract negotiation for Talent and Management in the broadcast industry. Providing local and national representation, MBM forged newground in establishing the rights of Broadcasters and Broadcast Management to secure independent representation from a group of experienced broadcast professionals. MBM has successfully represented hundreds of broadcast performers and managementthroughout the United States, Canada, Mexico, Europe and Australia.

N S Bienstock Inc.
250 W. 57th St., Suite 333, New York, NY 10107
(212) 765-3040; *Fax:* (212) 757-6411
www.nsbtalent.com
nsb@nsbtalent.com
Jonathan Leibner, General Counsel
Jennifer Rohrer, Business Affairs Executive
Despina Beazoglou, Business Affairs Executive
Kari Boston, Business Affairs Executive
News & syndication talent specialists—loc & net—on & off camera. Packager of talk & reality progmg—MOWs.

Paradigm
360 N. Crescent Dr., N. Bldg., Beverly Hills, CA 90210
(310) 288-8000; *Fax:* (310) 288-2000
www.paradigmagency.com
info@paradigm-agency.com
Sam Gores, President
Paradigm's select yet diverse client list allows it to effectively compete with other large agencies while guaranteeing personalized attention to every client. With offices in Los Angeles, New York City, Monterey, California and Nashville,Tennessee, Paradigm provides representation to clients across its motion picture, television, music, comedy and personal appearances, theater, books, new media, commercial and physical production departments.
124 12th Ave. S., Suite 410, Nashville, TN 37203-3146
(831) 375-4889; *Fax:* (831) 375-2623
509 Hartnell St., Monterey, CA 93940-2825
(615) 251-4400; *Fax:* (615) 251-44001

Rebel Entertainment
5700 Wilshire Blvd., Los Angeles, CA 90036
(323) 935-1700; *Fax:* (323) 932-9901
inquiry@reptalent.com
Richard Lawrence, President
Joyce Goertzen, CFO
Philip Irven, Senior Vice President
Seth Lawrence, Senior Vice President
Matt Jackson, Vice President - Theatrical Divison
Denise Draper, Agent
Jared Thompson, Agent
Talent placement & TV show packaging.

Shirley Hamilton Inc.
333 E. Ontario, Suite 302, Chicago, IL 60611
(312) 787-4700; *Fax:* (312) 787-8456
www.shirleyhamiltontalent.com
shamilton@att.net
Lynne Hamilton, President/Director
Laurie Hamilton, Director Of Print
Representing talent for TV, PRINT, RADIO, ON CAMERA, FILM, LIVE, THEATRICAL, VOICEOVER, INDUSTRIALS. Audition facilities for OnCamera, Digital voiceover, Print.

The Voicecaster
1832 W. Burbank Blvd., Burbank, CA 91506
(818) 841-5300; *Fax:* (818) 841-2085
www.voicecaster.com
casting@voicecaster.com
Huck Liggett, President
Working with only the most experienced casting directors - and four state of the art audition studios - we get you the top talent at the best rate. And we do it quickly and without sacrificing quality or creativity.

Weisman, P.C., Law Offices of Joel
1901 Raymond Dr., Ste 6, Northbrook, IL 60062
(847) 400-5900; *Fax:* (847) 400-5534
www.weismanmedialaw.com
joel@weismanmedialaw.com
Joel Weisman, President
Scott A. Weisman, Of Counsel
Keith M. Kanter, Of Counsel
David S. Rosenberg, Attorney
We're a full service law firm specializing in quality legal services to the Media (television anchors, reporters, and producers; radio personalities; columnists; and authors), as well as to individuals and businesses

William Morris Agency Inc.
1325 Ave. of the Americas, New York, NY 10019
(212) 586-5100; *Fax:* (212) 246-3583
www.wma.com
Cara Stein, COO
Jim Griffin, Operations Dir

National Associations

Academy of Canadian Cinema & Television
49 Ontario Street, Suite 501, Toronto, ON M5A 2V1
416-366-2227, (800) 644-5194, (416) 586-1939; *Fax:* 416-366-8454
www.academy.ca
info@academy.ca
Beth Janson, Chief Executive Officer
Jennifer Stewart, VP, Partnerships & Communications
Jess Genevieve Brown, Manager, Communications
Alan Perris, COO
Ellen Benjamin, Director, Finance & Administration
Louis Calabro, VP,Programming
Karen Bruce, Director, Membership
Mission: A national, non-profit, professional association dedicated to the promotion, recognition, and celebration of exceptional achievements in Candian film, television, and digital media.

Academy of Television Arts and Sciences
5220 Lankershim Blvd, North Hollywood, CA 91601-3155
818-754-2800; *Fax:* 818-761-2827
www.emmys.com
Hayma Washington, Chairman & CEO
Jim Yeager, President
Founded: 1957 *Number of Members:* 22000 *Mission:* Nonprofit corporation devoted to the advancement of telecommunications arts and sciences and to fostering creative leadership in the telecommunications industry. In additionto recognizing outstanding programming and individual achivements for Primetime and Los Angeles area programming, ATAS sponsors meetings, conferences and activities for collaboration on a variety of topics involving traditional broadcast interests,new media and emerging digital technology.

Accrediting Council on Education in Journalism and Mass Communications
1435 Jayhawk Blvd, Stuart-Flint Hall, Lawrence, KS 66045-7594
785-864-3973; *Fax:* 785-864-5225
www.acejmc.org
Peter Bhatia, President
Paul Parsons, Vice President
Susanne Shaw, Executive Director
Founded: 1945 *Number of Members:* 113 *Mission:* ACEJMC members are journalism and media departments, education associations and professional organizations.

Accuracy in Media
Mailing Address: 1717 K Street NW, Suite 900, Washington, DC 20006
Second Address: American Journalism Center, 4350 East West Hwy, Ste 555, Bethesda, MD 20814
202-364-4401, 800-787-4567; *Fax:* 202-364-4098
www.aim.org
info@aim.org
Don Irvine, Chairman
Deborah Lambert, Director of Special Projects
Gene Schaerr, President
Mercedes Amaya, Mailroom Manager
Founded: 1969 *Number of Members:* 3500 *Mission:* Accuracy in Media is a non-profit, grassroots citizens watchdog of the news media that critiques botched and bungled news stories and sets the record straight on importantissues that have received slanted coverage.

Acoustical Society of America
1305 Walt Whitman Rd, Suite 300, Melville, NY 11747-4300
(516) 576-2360; *Fax:* (631) 923-2875
acousticalsociety.org
asa@acousticalsociety.org
Marcia J. Isakson, President
Lily M. Wang, President-Elect
Elaine Moran, Director of Operations
Susan E. Fox, Executive Director
James F. Lynch, Editor in chief
Since its organization in 1929, the Society has grown steadily in membership and stature. At this time about 7500 men and women who work in acoustics throughout the U.S. and abroad belong to this prestigious Society. A variety of fieldsrelated to sound are represented.

Ad Council
Div/DBA: (The Advertising Council)
Mailing Address: 815 2nd Ave, 9th Floor, New York, NY 10017-4503
Second Address: 1707 L Street, NW, Suite 600, Washington, DC 20036
212-922-1500, 202-331-9153; *Fax:* 212-962-1676
www.adcouncil.org
info@adcouncil.org
Lisa Sherman, President/CEO
Kate Emanuel, Business Operations & Strategy
Paula Veale, Marketing & Communications
Barbara Leshinsky, Development
Founded: 1941 *Number of Members:* 100 *Mission:* Our mission is to identify a select number of significant public issues and stimulate action on those issues through communications programs that make a measurable difference inour society.

Advanced Television Systems Committee
1776 K Street, 8th Floor, Washington, DC 20006-2304
202-872-9160; *Fax:* 202-872-9161
www.atsc.org
atsc@atsc.org
Mark Richer, President
Jerry Whitaker, VP, Standards Development
Daro Bruno, Director of Operations
Mission: ATSC is an international, non-profit organzation developing voluntary standards for digital television.

Advertising Council Inc
1707 L Street NW, Suite 600, Washington, DC 20036
202-331-9153; *Fax:* 202-331-9186
www.adcouncil.org
info@adcouncil.org
Peggy Conlon, President, CEO
John Fish, EVP, Chief Financial Officer
Barbara Leshinsky, EVP, Development
Priscilla Natkins, Director, Client Services
Paula Veale, Corporate Communications
Mission: The Ad Council marshals volunteer talent from the advertising and communications industries, the facilities of the media, and the resources of the business and non-profit communities to create awareness, foster understandingand motivate action.

Advertising Educational Foundation
708 Third Avenue, 23rd Floor, New York, NY 10017
212-986-8060; *Fax:* 212-986-8061
www.aef.com
pa@aef.com
Pat Lafferty, Chairman
Gordon McLean, President & CEO
Sharon Hudson, VP, Program Manager
Marcia Soling, VP, Content Manager
Founded: 1983 *Number of Members:* 48 *Mission:* The advertising industry's provider and distributor of educational content to enrich the understanding of advertising and its role in culture, society and the economy.

Advertising Research Foundation
432 Park Ave S, 4th Floor, New York, NY 10016
212-751-5656; *Fax:* 212-689-1859
www.thearf.org
help@thearf.org
Scott McDonald, President/CEO
Marc Rappin, Chief Marketing Officer
Thomas M. Higgins, COO & CFO
Paul Donato, Chief Research Officer
C, Engineering Dir
Founded: 1936 *Mission:* An open forum where the best and the brightest from every avenue of advertising can gather to exchange ideas and research strategies

Advertising Specialty Institute
4800 Street Rd, Langhorne, PA 19053-6698
215-953-4000, 800-546-1350; *Fax:* 215-953-3045
www.asicentral.com
info@asicentral.com
Norman Unger Cohn, Chairman
Timothy M. Andrews, President/CEO
Vince Bucolo, COO
Chris Lovell, Senior VP, Sales
Steve Bright, Executive VP/General Counsel
Andy Cohen, Editorial Director
Founded: 1950 *Number of Members:* 26000 *Mission:* Advertising Specialty Institute provides distributors, suppliers and decorators in the advertising specialty industry with catalogs, information directories, newsletters,magazines, web sites and databases, and offers interactive e-commerce, marketing and selling tools.

Alliance for Community Media
Mailing Address: 4248 Park Glen Road, Minneapolis, MN 55416
Second Address: 8817 2nd Avenue, Silver Spring, MD 20910
952-928-4643
www.allcommunitymedia.org
info@allcommunitymedia.org
Keith Thibault, Board Chair
Donna Keating, Chair-Elect
Mike Wassenaar, President & CEO
Melissa Place, COO
Katie Benson, Conference Manager
Angie Newgren, Marketing & Communications Coordinator
Clair Steil, MembershipCoordinator
Founded: 1976 *Number of Members:* 1000 *Mission:* Promotes civic engagement through community medias.

Alliance for Telecommunication Industry
1200 G St NW, Suite 500, Washington, DC 20005-6706
202-628-6380; *Fax:* 202-393-5453
www.atis.org
atispr@artis.org
Susan Miller, President/CEO
Kelly Weiss, VP, Finance & Operations
Lauren Layman, VP, Marketing & Public Relations
Mike Nawrocki, VP, Technology & Solutions
Rich Moran, Membership
Founded: 1983 *Number of Members:* 1400 *Mission:* Membership organization that provides the tools necessary for the industry to identify standards, guidelines and operating procedures that make the inoperability of existingand emerging telecommunications products and services possible.

Alliance for Women in Media
2365 Harrodsburg Road, #A325, Lexington, KY 40504
(202) 750-3664; *Fax:* (202) 750-3664
www.allwomeninmedia.org
info@allwomeninmedia.org
Sarah Foss, Chairman
Becky Brooks, Executive Director
Lori Weaver Hawkins, PR & Marketing Manager
LaTonya Jackson, Operations Manager
Lisa Stephenson, Events Director
Founded: 1951 *Mission:* Leverages the promise, passion, and power of women in all forms if media. One of the longest established professional association dedicated to advancing women in the media and entertainment. Still strongafter 60 years, carrying forth with its mission by educating, advocating, and acting as a resource to its members and the industry at large via inspired thought leadership that illuminates areas od social need.

Alliance of Motion Picture and Television Producers
15301 Ventura Boulevard, Building E, Sherman Oaks, CA 91403
818-995-3600; *Fax:* 818-382-1793
www.amptp.org
Carol Lombardini, President
Founded: 1982 *Number of Members:* 350 *Mission:* Trade association with respect to labor issues in the motion picture and television industry. We negotiate 80 industry wide collective bargaining agreements that cover actors,craftspersons, directors, musicians, technicians and writers — virtually all of the people who work on theatrical motion pictures and television programs. In these negotiations, the AMPTP represents over 350 production companies and studios.

America's Public Television Stations
2100 Crystal Drive, Suite 700, Arlington, VA 22202
202-654-4200; *Fax:* 202-654-4236
www.apts.org
Patrick Butler, President/CEO
Lonna Thompson, Executive VP/COO/General Counsel
Emil Mara, VP, Finance, Administration & Membership
Kate Riley, VP, Government & Public Affairs
Jennifer Kieley, Director, Government Relations
Founded: 1980 *Number of Members:* 153 *Mission:* Nonprofit membership organization that supports the continued growth and development of a strong and financially sound noncommercial television service for the American public.Provides advocacy for public television interests at the national level, as well as consistent leadership and information in marshaling grassroots and congressional support for its members: the nation's public television stations.

American Advertising Federation
1101 Vermont Ave NW, 5th Floor, Washington, DC 20005-6306
202-898-0089; *Fax:* 202-898-0159
www.aaf.org
aaf@aaf.org
Kim Kelleher, Chairman
Constance Cannon Frazier, COO
James Edmund Datri, President & CEO
Founded: 1905 *Number of Members:* 40000 *Mission:* The AAF is the oldest national advertising trade association, and protects and promotes the well-being of advertising. The AAF accomplishes this through a unique, nationallycoordinated grassroots network of advertisers, agencies, media companies, local advertising clubs and college chapters.

American Agricultural Editors' Association
251 SL White Blvd, PO Box 1444, LaGrange, GA 30241
706-407-2550; *Fax:* 706-883-8215
www.ageditors.com
skilgore@asginfo.net

Samantha Kilgore, Executive Director
Mike Wilson, President
Courtney Jackson, Member Service Coordinator
Mission: National professional development member association for agricultural communicators.

American Association of Advertising Agencies (AAAA)
Mailing Address: 1065 Avenue of the Americas, 16th Floor, New York, NY 10018
Second Address: 1707 L Street NW, Suite 600, Washington, DC 20036
(212) 682-2500, (202) 331-7345; *Fax:* (212) 682-8391
www.aaaa.org
membership@aaaa.org
Marla Kaplowitz, President & CEO
Todd Hittle, CFO/COO
Tina Allen, SVP, People & Culture
Alison Fahey, EVP, Chief Marketing Officer
Tom Finneran, EVP, Agency Management Services
Louis Jones, EVP, Media & Data

American Auto Racing Writers & Broadcasters Association
922 N Pass Ave, Burbank, CA 91505-2703
818-842-7005; *Fax:* 818-842-7020
www.aarwba.org
dusty@aarwba.org
Dusty Brandel, President/Executive Director
Kathy Seymour, National VP
Rhonda Williams, Treasurer
Nick Dettmann, Midwest VP
Joe Jennings, Southern VP
Founded: 1955 *Number of Members:* 400 *Mission:* Members are professional journalists who regularly cover auto racing and related sports events.

American Center for Children and Media
5400 North St Louis Avenue, Chicago, IL 60623
703-509-5510; *Fax:* 773-509-5303
info@centerforchildrenandmedia.org
James Fellows, Founder
David Kleeman, President
Mission: Mission is to support a vibrant children's media industry by convening key constituencies to develop, implement and promote policies and practices that respect young people's well being, and are sustainable.

American Cinema Editors Inc.
5555 Melrose Avenue, Marx Bldg, Rm 1084, Los Angeles, CA 90038
(323) 956-2900
www.americancinemaeditors.org
Stephen Rivkin, President
Alan Heim, Vice President
Lillian Bennson, Secretary
Stephen Lovejoy, Treasurer

American Composers Alliance (ACA)
PO Box 1108, New York, NY 10040
(212) 568-0036; *Fax:* (212) 925-6798
www.composers.com
info@composers.com
David Liptak, President
Gina Genova, Executive Director & General Manager
Eleanor Francis, Business Affairs Associate
ACA is a non-profit, alternative American concert music publisher in New York City (BMI affiliated). With a history dating to 1937, ACA distributes printed and electronic scores for orchestras, performing artists, chamber ensembles,libraries and other users of sheet music, as well as licenses its works for academic and commercial uses.

American Copy Editors Society (ACES)
Pulliam Journalism Center, 3909 N. Meridian Street, Indianapolis, IN 46208

www.aceseditors.org
info@aceseditors.org
Teresa Schmedding, President
David Sullivan, Vice President
Neil Holdway, Secretary
Sara Ziegler, Treasurer
Founded: 1997 *Mission:* ACES is a professional organization working toward the advancement of editors. Their aim is to provide opportunities through training, discussion and advocacy that promote the editing profession.

American Disc Jockey Association
20118 N 67th Avenue, Suite 300-605, Glendale, CA 85308
(888) 723-5776; *Fax:* (866) 310-4676
www.adja.org
office@adja.org
Rob Snyder, Director
Mission: An association of professional mobile entertainers. Encourages success for its members through continuous education, camaraderie, and networking. The primary goal is to educate Disc Jockeys so that each member acts ethicallyand responsibly.

American Electronics Association
Mailing Address: 3570 NE Ralph Powell Road, Suite 520, Lee's Summit, MO 64064
Second Address: 601 Pennsylvania Ave, Suite 900, South Bldg., Washington, DC 2004
(816) 347-8400, (202) 589-1144; *Fax:* (816) 347-8405, (202) 639-8238
www.aeanet.org
info@aea.net
David Loso, Chair
Paula Derks, President
Michael Kus, Vice Chairman
James Joubert, Treasurer
Kim Stephenson, Secretary
Rick Garcia, Director
Matthew Harrah, Director
Tom Harper, Director
601 Pennsylvania Ave, Washington, DC
(202) 682-9110; *Fax:* (202) 682-9111
William Archey, Pres

American Marketing Association
130 E. Randolph Street, 22nd Floor, Chicago, IL 60601
(312) 542-9000, (800) 262-1150; *Fax:* (312) 542-9001
www.ama.org; www.marketingpower.com
info@ama.org
Mary Garrett, Chair
Russ Klein, CEO
Andy Friedman, Chief Content Officer
Jeremy Van Eck, COO
Adara Bowen, Marketing
Molly Soat, Publications
Kim Williams, Customer Service
The American Marketing Association (AMA) was established in 1937 by visionaries in marketing and academia. Today, the AMA has grown to be one of the largest marketing associations in the world, with over 30,000 members who work, teach andstudy in the field of marketing across the globe.

American Medical Writers' Association
30 W Gude Dr, Suite 525, Rockville, MD 20850-4347
240-238-0940; *Fax:* 301-294-9006
www.amwa.org
amwa@amwa.org
Susan Krug, Executive Director
Shari Rager, Deputy Director
Rachel Spassiani, Manager, Communications & Resources
Katie Bergmann, Membership & Marketing Coordinator
Founded: 1940 *Number of Members:* 3.4M *Mission:* Concerned with the advancement and improvement of medical communications.

American Meteorological Society
Mailing Address: 45 Beacon St., Boston, MA 02108-3693
Second Address: 1200 New York Ave NW, Suites 450 & 500, Washington, DC 20005-3928
(617) 227-2425; *Fax:* (617) 742-8718
www.ametsoc.org/ams
amsinfo@ametsoc.org
Roger M. Wakimoto, President
Keith L. Seiter, Executive Director
William H. Hooke, Associate Executive Director
Tom Champoux, Director, Communications
Beth Farley, Director, Member Services
Joseph J. Boyd, Controller
The American Meteorological Society promotes the development and dissemination of information and education on the atmospheric and related oceanic and hydrologic sciences and the advancement of their professional applications. Founded in1919, AMS has a membership of more than 13,000 professionals, students, and weather enthusiasts. AMS publishes eleven atmospheric and related oceanic and hydrologic journals - in print and online - sponsors more than 12 conferences annually, andoffers numerous programs and services.

American Newspaper Representatives
2075 W Big Beaver Rd, Suite 310, Troy, MI 48084-3439
248-643-9910, 800-550-7557; *Fax:* 248-643-9914
gotoanr.com
Hilary Howe, President
Robert Sontag, Executive VP/COO
Mission: Supports newspaper representatives and distributors in the United States. Hosts annual trade show.

American Photographic Artists
5042 Wilshire Blvd., #321, Los Angeles, CA 90036
800-272-6264; *Fax:* 888-889-7190
www.apanational.com
members@apanational.com
Tony Gale, National Board President
RJ Muna, National Board Executive VP
Juliette Wolf-Robin, National Executive Director
Jeff Kausch, Membership Representative
Founded: 1981 *Mission:* Our goal is to establish, endorse and promote professional practices, standards and ethics in the photographic and advertising community.

American Press Institute (API)
4401 N. Fairfax Drive, Suite 300, Arlington, VA 22203
571-366-1200
www.americanpressinstitute.org
hello@pressinstitute.org
David Chavern, President & CEO
Tom Rosenstiel, Executive Director
Jeff Sonderman, Deputy Executive Director/Executive VP
Kevin Locker, Director, Program Operations & Partnerships
Founded: 1946 *Mission:* API is the trusted source for career leadership development for the newsmedia industry in North America and around the world. They help companies innovate and leaders realize their full potential.

American Private Radio Association (APRA)
PO Box 4221, Scottsdale, AZ 85261-4221
480-661-5000
Mission: Association members are from private radio stations.

American Radio Relay League (ARRL)
225 Main St., Newington, CT 06111-1494
(860) 594-0200; *Fax:* (860) 594-0259
www.arrl.org
Rick Roderick, President
Tom Gallagher, CEO
Barry J. Shelley, CFO
Noncommercial organization for radio amateurs.
Directors:
Joel Harrison, 1st VP

American Society of Composers, Authors & Publishers (ASCAP)
1900 Broadway, New York, NY 10023
(212) 621-6000; *Fax:* (212) 621-8453
www.ascap.com
cnevins@ascap.com
Paul Williams, President and Chairman of the Board
Irwin Z. Robinson, Vice Chairman, Publisher
Doug Wood, Vice Chairman, Writer
Elizabeth Matthews, CEO
Katherine Hinchey, Chief of Staff
Alison Toczylowski, Director, Marketing &Communications
(See listing under Music Licensing, Section G.)

ASCAP - Nashville
Two Music Square W., Nashville, TN
(615) 742-5000; *Fax:* (615) 742-5020

ASCAP - Miami
420 Lincoln Rd., Suite 385, Miami Beach, FL 33139-3036
(305) 673-3446; *Fax:* (305) 673-2446

ASAP - Los Angeles
7920 W. Sunset Blvd., 3rd Fl., Los Angeles, CA 90046-3300
(323) 883-1000; *Fax:* (323) 883-1049

ASCAP - Atlanta
541 Tenth St. N.W., PMB400, Atlanta, GA 30318-5713
(404) 351-1224; *Fax:* (404) 351-1252

ASCAP - Chicago
1608 N. Milwaukee, Suite 1007, Chicago, IL 60647-5456
(773) 394-4286; *Fax:* (773) 394-5639

ASCAP - Puerto Rico
654 Ave. Munoz Rivera, IBM Plaza Suite 1101 B, Hato Rey, PR
(787) 281-0782; *Fax:* (787) 767-2805

ASCAP - London
8 Cork St., London, United Kingdom
011 44-207-439-0909; *Fax:* 011 44-207-434-0073

American Society of Journalists and Authors
355 Lexington Avenue, 15th Floor, New York, NY 10017-6603
212-997-0947; *Fax:* 212-937-2315
www.asja.org
asjaoffice@asja.org
Holly Koenig, Interim Executive Director
Diane Jackson, Communications Director
Nora Keller, Membership

Gemma Rainer, General Manager
James Brannigan, Program Manager
Founded: 1948 *Number of Members:* 1000+ *Mission:* For freelance nonfiction writers whose bylines appear in periodicals and in books.

American Society of Magazine Editors
757 Third Avenue, 11th Floor, New York, NY 10017
212-872-3700; *Fax:* 212-906-0128
www.magazine.org/asme
asme@magazine.org
Sid Holt, Chief Executive
Nina Fortuna, Director
Christopher Keyes, President
Janice Min, Vice President
Founded: 1963 *Number of Members:* 700 *Mission:* ASME is the principal organization for magazine journalists in the United States. ASME works to defend the First Amendment, protect editorial independence and support thedevelopment of journalism.

American Society of Media Photographers
150 North 2nd Street, Philadelphia, PA 19108
215-451-2767, 877-771-2767; *Fax:* 231-946-6180
www.asmp.org
info@asmp.org
Luke Copping, Chairman
Marianne Lee, Vice Chair
Tom Kennedy, Executive Director
Founded: 1944 *Mission:* ASMP is the premier trade association for the world's most respectd photograhers. ASMP is the leader in promoting photographers' rights, providing education in better business practices, producing businesspublications for photographers, and helping to connect purchasers with professional photographers.

American Society of News Editors (ASNE)
209 Reynolds Journalism Institute, Missouri School of Journalism, Columbia, MO 65211
573-882-2430; *Fax:* 573-884-3824
www.asne.org
asne@asne.org
Teri Hayt, Executive Director
Arnie Robbins, Senior Adviser
Jiyoung Won, Communications Coordinator
Kevin Goldberg, Legal Counsel
Founded: 1922 *Mission:* ASNE is a membership organization for editors, producers or directors in charge of journalistic organizations or departments, deans or faculty at university journalism schools, and leaders and faculty ofmedia-related foundations and training organizations.

American Sportscasters Association Hall of Fame Trust
225 Broadway, Suite 2030, New York, NY 10007
(212) 227-8080; *Fax:* (212) 571-0556
americansportscastersonline.com
inquiry@americansportscastersonline.com
Dick Enberg, Chairman of the Board
Louis O. Schwartz, President
Paul R. Pops, Chief Financial Officer

American Sportscasters Association
225 Broadway, Suite 2030, New York, NY 10007
(212) 227-8080; *Fax:* (212) 571-0556
americansportscastersonline.com
inquiry@americansportscastersonline.com
Dick Enberg, Chairman of the Board
Louis O. Schwartz, President
Patrick Turturro, Associate Editor
Directors:
Lou Schwartz, Jon Miller, Jim Nantz, Dick Enberg & Bill Walton

American Sportscasters Association
225 Broadway, Suite 2030, New York, NY 10007-3742
212-227-8080; *Fax:* 212-571-0556
www.americansportscastersonline.com
lschwa8918@aol.com
Louis O Schwartz, President/Founder
Dick Enberg, Chairman
Founded: 1980 *Number of Members:* 500 *Mission:* National Association of Sportscasters, radio, television and cable covering the US, Puerto Rico and Canada. Very active web site. Offers seminars, compiles statistics andoperates a placement service, maintains a Hall of Fame and biographical archives and library.

American Women in Radio and Television Inc. Awards
8405 Greensboro Drive, Suite 800, McLean, VA 22102
(703) 506-3290; *Fax:* (703) 506-3266
www.awrt.org
info@awrt.org
Maria E. Brennan, President
Amy Lotz, Managing Director

Armed Forces Communications and Electronics Association
Div/DBA: AFCEA International
4400 Fair Lakes Ct., Fairfax, VA 22033-3899
(703) 631-6100, (800) 336-4583; *Fax:* (703) 631-6169
www.afcea.org
promo@afcea.org
Joe Sifer, Chair of the Board
Robert M. Shea, President/CEO
John R. Wood, Executive VP, Defense & National Security
Pat Moirin, EVP/Chief Financial Officer
Beverly Cooper, VP, Communications & Media
James L. Griggs Jr., VP/ChiefInformation Officer
Nancy Temple, International Secretary/VP, HR
AFCEA International, established in 1946, is a non-profit organization serving its members by providing a forum for the ethical exchange of information, and dedicated to increasing knowledge through the exploration of issues relevant to itsmembers in information technology, communications and electronics for the defense, homeland security and intelligence communities.

ASBPE (American Society of Business Publication Editors)
214 North Hale Street, Wheaton, IL 60187
630-510-4588; *Fax:* 630-510-4501
www.asbpe.org
info@asbpe.org
Jessi McCarthy, Coordinator
Founded: 1964 *Mission:* ASBPE is the professional association for full-time and freelance editors and writers employed in the business, trade, and specialty press. It is widely known for its annual Awards of Excellencecompetition, which recognizes the best editorial, design, and online achievement.

Asian American Journalists Association
5 Third Street, Suite 1108, San Francisco, CA 94103
415-346-2051; *Fax:* 415-346-6343
www.aaja.org
national@aaja.org
Kathy Chow, Executive Director
Justin Seiter, Program Coordinator
Yvonne Leow, National President
Founded: 1981 *Number of Members:* 1400 *Mission:* AAJA provides support among Asian American and Pacific Islander journalists. It provides encouragement, information, advice and scholarship assistance to Asian American andPacific Islander students who aspire to professional journalism careers.

The Associated Press
NSS Data: TV-CATV only
AP Broadcast News Center, 1100 13th Street, Suite 500, Washington, DC 20005
(202) 641-9000; *Fax:* (202) 736-1124
www.ap.org
info@ap.org
Steven R. Swartz, Chairman
Gary Pruitt, President & CEO
Lauren Easton, Director, Media Relations
Jessica Bruce, SVP, Human Resources & Corporate Communications
Sally Buzbee, Senior Vice President - Executive Editor
Dave Gwizdowski,Senior Vice President - Revenue, Americas
Ken Dale, Senior Vice President - Chief Financial Officer
Jim Kennedy, Senior Vice President - Strategic Planning
AP Services for TV: Video: APTN Video News. Wires: APTV Wire, AP News Tickers, AP NewsPower, AP Data Stream. AP Alert Graphics: AP GraphicsBank. Software: AP NewsCenter; AP NewsDesk; AP NewsDesk (LAN), ENPS, SNAPfeed Satellite Delivery: APExpress. Elections: ENPS Stats, AP Politics, AP Election Wire. Online content: CustomNews, AP Online, Online Video Network, AP Spanish Online. Photos: Photo Archive, Photo Stream.

Associated Press Broadcasters
1825 K Street NW, Suite 800, Washington, DC 20006-1202
202-968-8150; *Fax:* 202-736-1107
James R Williams III, VP Broadcast Services
Greg Groce, Director Business Operations
Brad Kalbfeld, Deputy Director\Managing Editor
Roger Lockhart, Director Marketing/Communications
George Galt, Director Business Affairs
Founded: 1941 *Number of Members:* 5.9m *Mission:* Seeks to advance journalism through radio and television, and cooperates with the AP to promote accurate and impartial news.

Associated Press Media Editors (APME)
450 W 33rd St, New York, NY 10001-2647
212-621-1849; *Fax:* 212-833-7574
www.apme.com
apme@ap.org
Jim Simon, Chairman
Angie Muhs, Vice President
Alison Gerber, Treasurer
Paula Froke, Executive Director
Founded: 1933 *Mission:* Members are managing editors or executives of Associated Press News Executives.

Associated Press Media Editors (APME)
450 West 33rd Street, New York, NY 10001
212-621-7007
www.apme.com
sjacobsen@ap.org
Jim Simon, President
Angie Muhs, Vice President
Michael Days, Secretary
Paula Froke, Executive Director
Michael Roberts, NewsTrain Project Director
Founded: 1933 *Mission:* APME is an association of U.S. and Canadian editors, broadcasters and educators whose entitites are members of The Associated Press.

Association for Communication Excellence
59 College Road, Taylor Hall, Durham, NH 03824
603-862-1564, 855-657-9544; *Fax:* 603-862-1585
www.aceweb.org
ace.info@unh.edu
Holly Young, Executive Director
Founded: 1970 *Number of Members:* 700+ *Mission:* Members are writers, editors, broadcasters and communicators who are involved in the dissemination of agricultural, food sciences and natural resource information in land-grantcolleges, federal and state agencies, international agencies and other private communications work.

Association for Education in Journalism & Mass Communication (AEJMC)
234 Outlet Pointe Blvd., Suite A, Columbia, SC 29210-5667
(803) 798-0271; *Fax:* (803) 772-3509
www.aejmc.org
aejmc@aejmc.org
Jeniffer D. Greer, AEJMC President
David Perlmutter, Vice-President
Marie Hardin, President-Elect
Jennifer McGill, Executive Director
Belinda Pearson, Association Business Manager
Janet Harley, Association Office Assistant
Samantha Higgins, Public Relations Manager

Association for Educational Communications & Technology
Mailing Address: 1800 N Stonelake Drive, Suite 2, Bloomington, IN 47404
Second Address: 320 W. 8th Street, Ste 101, Bloomington, IN 47404-3745
812-335-7675, 877-677-AECT; *Fax:* 812-335-7678
www.aect.org
aect@aect.org
Brad Hokanson, President
Michael Grant, Executive Secretary
Dr. Phillip Harris, Executive Director
Larry Vernon, Director, Electronic Services
Founded: 1923 *Number of Members:* 2200 *Mission:* For audiovisual and instructional materials specialists, educational technologists, audiovisual and television production personnel, school media specialists.

Association for Education in Journalism
234 Outlet Pointe Boulevard, Columbia, SC 29210-5667
803-798-0271; *Fax:* 803-798-3509
www.aejmc.org/
aejmchq@aol.com
Jennifer McGill, Executive Director
Felicia Greenlee Brown, Production Manager
Richard Burke, Business Manager
Mission: AEJMC promotes the highest possible standards for education in journalism and mass communication, encouraging the widest possible range of communication research and the implementation of a multi-cultural society in theclassroom and curriculum, defending and maintaining the freedom of expression in day-to-day living.

The Association for International Broadcasting
PO Box 141, Cranbrook, TN17 9AJ United Kingdom
+44 (0) 20 7993 2557; *Fax:* +44 (0) 20 7993 8043
www.aib.org.uk
contactaib@aib.org.uk

Simon Spanswick, Chief Executive
Tom Wragg, Business Development Director
Gunda Cannon, International Relations

Association for Interactive Marketing
1430 Broadway Avenue, 8th Floor, New York, NY 10018
Fax: 212-391-9233
www.interactivehq.org
Mission: AIM is a non-profit trade association for interactive marketers and service providers.

The Association for Maximum Service Television
4100 Wisconsin Avenue NW, PO Box 9897, Washington, DC 20016
202-966-1956; *Fax:* 202-966-9617
www.mstv.org
Craig Dubow, CEO
Mission: Formed in 1956, MSTV has endeavored to insure that American public receive the highest quality, interference free, over-the-air local television signals. Recognized as the industry leader in broadcasting technology andspectrum policy issues.

Association for Service Managers
11031 Via Frontera, Suite A, San Diego, CA 92127
239-275-7887; *Fax:* 239-275-0794
John Schoenewald, Executive Director
Jb Wood, President/Ceo
Founded: 1975 *Number of Members:* 3000+ *Mission:* A global organization dedicated to furthering the knowledge, understanding, and career development of executives, managers and professionals in the high technology serviceindustry.

Association for Women in Communications
1717 E. Republic Road, Suite A, Springfield, MO 65804
417-886-8606; *Fax:* 417-886-3685
www.womcom.org
info@womcom.org
Becky Lucas, National Office
Kristin E. Van Nort, Chair
Founded: 1909 *Number of Members:* 2500 (active) *Mission:* Supports all those professional women in the fields of journalism online media, public relations, advertising, marketing, educational communications, graphic and webdesign, photography and film. Hosts bi-annual conference.

Association of American Railroads
425 3rd Street, SW, Washington, DC 20024
(202) 639-2100, (202) 639-2345; *Fax:* (202) 639-2558
www.aar.org
jkahanek@aar.org
Edward R. Hamberger, President/CEO
Patricia M. Reilly, Senior VP, Communications

Association of Cable Communicators
25 Massachusetts Ave NW, Suite 100, Washington, DC 20013-5007
202-222-2370; *Fax:* 202-222-2371
www.cablecommunicators.org
Steven R Jones, Executive Director
Michelle L Butler, Associate Executive Director
Mission: ACC is the only national, professional organization specifically addressing the issues, needs and interests of the cable industry's communications and public affairs professionals.

Association of Cable Communicators: See listing for Cable & Telecommunications Association for Marketing (CTAM)
120 Waterfront Street, Suite 200, National Harbor, MD 20745
(301) 485-8900
www.ctam.com/strategic-collaboration/
The Association of Cable Communicators (ACC) has been integrated into Cable & Telecommunications Association for Marketing (CTAM). Executive leadership will form a CTAM Communications Steering Council.

Association of Canadian Advertisers
99 St Clair Avenue West, Suite 1103, Toronto, ON M4V 1N6
416-964-3805; *Fax:* 416-964-0771
www.acaweb.ca
rlund@acaweb.ca
Ron Lund, President, CEO
Susan Charles, Vice President, Member Services
Paul Hetu, Vice President, Montreal
Bob Reaume, Vice President, Policy and Research
Randy Scotland, Vice President, Communications
Mission: Industry organization exclusively dedicated to client-marketers, helping them maximize the full value of their investments in all forms of marketing communications.

Association of Federal Communications Consulting Engineers (AFCCE)
PO Box 19333, 20th Street Station, Washington, DC 20036-0333
941-329-6000; *Fax:* 703-591-0115
www.afcce.org
Thomas Silliman, President
Alan R Rosner, VP
Founded: 1948 *Number of Members:* 250 *Mission:* An organization of professional engineering consultants serving the telecommunications industry.

Association of Independent Commercial Producers
3 W 18th St, New York, NY 10011
212-929-3000; *Fax:* 212-929-3359
www.aicp.com
info@aicp.com
Matt Miller, President & CEO
Renee Paley, VP Communications
Founded: 1972 *Number of Members:* 500 *Mission:* The national trade association of television commercial producers who account for in excess of 80% of the commercial production done in the United States annually.

Association of Local Television Stations
1320 19th Street NW, Washington, DC 20036
202-887-1970
www.altv.com

Association of National Advertisers Inc. (ANA)
Mailing Address: 708 3rd Ave., 33rd Floor, New York, NY 10017
Second Address: 2020 K Street NW, Suite 660, Washington, D. 20006
(212) 697-5950, (202) 296-1883; *Fax:* (212) 687-7310, (202) 296-1430
www.ana.net
bliodice@ana.net
Bob Liodice, CEO
Christine Manna, President & COO
John Wolfe, Director, Public Relations
Duke Fanelli, Executive VP & CMO
Douglas Wood, Esq., General Counsel
Directors:
Donald F. Calhoon, Jocelyn Carter-Miller, J. Andrea Alstrup, Catherine D. Constable, Christopher Fraleigh, James J. Garrity, David B. Green, John D. Hayes, Stephen C. Jones, Dawn Hudson, David N. Iauco, Abby F. Kohnstamm, Ann Lewnes, Eric W.Leininger, Robert D. Liodice, Paula S. Sneed, Gary E. McCullough, James R. Stengel, James D. Speros, Allan H. Stefl, Stephen G. Sullivan, Joseph V. Tripodi, Rebecca Saeger, James L. McDowell, Nancy J. Wiese, Robert J. Gamgort & Robert C Lachky
Washington

Audio Engineering Society
60 E 42nd St, Room 2520, New York, NY 10165
212-661-8528; *Fax:* 212-682-0477
www.aes.org
HQ@aes.org
Roger Furness, Executive Director
Jim Anderson, President
Robert E Lee, Jr, Secretary
Louis Fielder, Treasurer
Mission: Professional society devoted to audio technology. Membership includes leading engineers, scientists and other authorities in the field. Serves its members, the industry and the public by stimulating and facilitating advancesin the constantly changing field of audio.

Baptist Communicators Association
PO Box 270187, Nashville, TN 37227
615-329-7543
baptistcommunicators.org
Jan Kelley, President
Teresa Dickens, Communications VP
Ele Clay, Missions VP
Jerilynn Armstrong, Treasurer
Founded: 1953 *Number of Members:* 300 *Mission:* PR and journalism profesionals.

BMI Broadcast Music Inc.
7 World Trade Center, 250 Greenwich Street, New York, NY 10007-0030
(212) 220-3000; *Fax:* (212) 246-2163
www.bmi.com
newyork@bmi.com
Michael O'Neill, President & CEO
Bruce A. Esworthy, Senior Vice President, Finance & Administration
Alison Smith, Executive VP, Distribution, PR & Administration
Eddie Gulley, SVP & Chief Information Officer
Stuart Rosen, Senior VicePresident and General Counsel
Founded: 1939. Supports the relationship between art and commerce, helping aspiring songwriters while also offering diverse content to licensees.
Directors:
Philip A. Jones, Frances W. Preston, James G. Babb, Harold C. Crump, N. John Douglas, Frank E. Melton, George V. Willoughby, K. James Yager, G. Neil Smith, David Sherman, Donald A. Thurston, Cecil L. Walker, Catherine L. Hughes, Craig A.Dubow, Amador Bustos & John L. Sander
8730 Sunset Blvd, 3rd Fl. W., West Hollywood, CA 90069-2210
(310) 659-9109
10 Music Sq. E, Nashville, TN 37203-4321
(615) 401-2000

Broadcast Cable Credit Association Inc. (BCCA)
Mailing Address: 550 W. Frontage Rd., Suite 3600, Northfield, IL 60093
Second Address: PO Box 1296, Bedford Park, IL 60499-1296
(847) 881-8757; *Fax:* (847) 784-8059
www.bccacredit.com
info@bccacredit.com
Mary Collins, President
Jamie Smith, Director of Operation

Broadcast Designers' Association
145 W 45th Street, Room 1100, New York, NY 10036-4008
212-376-6222; *Fax:* 212-376-6202
Mission: Association for manufacturers or suppliers of broadcast design equipment, supplies and services.

Broadcast Education Association
1771 N St. N.W., Washington, DC 20036-2891
(202) 429-5355; *Fax:* (202) 609-9940
www.beaweb.org
help@beaweb.org
Michael Bruce, President
Heather Birks, Executive Director
Traci Bailey, Manager, Business Operations
J-D Boyle, Director of Sales & Marketing
Directors:
Mary Alice Molgard, Thomas R. Berg, Rustin Greene, Joe Misiewicz, David Byland, Robert K. Avery, Gary Martin, Greg Luft, D'Artagnan Bebel, Stephen J. Cohen, Larry Patrick, Alan R. Albarran, Gary Corbitt, Steven Anderson, Norman Pattiz &Jannette L. Dates

Broadcast Education Association
1771 N St NW, Washington, DC 20036-2800
202-429-5355; *Fax:* 202-429-4199
www.beaweb.org
Heather Birks, Executive Director
Staven D. Anderson, VP Academic Relations
Gary Corbitt, VP Professional Relations
Founded: 1955 *Number of Members:* 1400 *Mission:* Serves as a higher education association of professors and industry professionals who teach college students worldwide and prepares them to go into the broadcasting and relatedemerging technologies professions upon graduation from college.

Broadcast Pioneers
320 W 57th St, Suite 3, New York, NY 10019-3705
212-586-2000; *Fax:* 212-246-2163
www.bmi.com
Del Bryant, President & CEO
Founded: 1942 *Number of Members:* 1.4M *Mission:* Honors radio or television stations for excellence in art and community service. Maintains library documents on television broadcasting history.

Broadcasters Foundation of America
125 West 55th Street, 4th Floor, New York, NY 10019
212-373-8250; *Fax:* 212-373-8254
www.broadcastersfoundation.org
info@thebfoa.org
James B. Thompson, President
Peter M. Doyle, Vice President
Frank Pesce, VP, Business Affairs
Mission: Provides financial assistance to radio and television broadcasters who are in financial need.

The Broadcasters Hall of Fame
1240 Ashford Lane, 1A, PO Box 8247, Akron, OH 44320
330-867-3779; *Fax:* 330-867-4907
C S (Doc) Williams, Founder, CEO
Henry Dunn, Chairman
Mission: A wealth of memorabilia from the early days of broadcasting, clippings from newspapers and magazines, taped recorded portions of early radio shows and other gems of broadcasting history.

Cable & Telecommunications Association
201 N Union Street, Suite 440, Alexandria, VA 22314-2642
703-549-4200; *Fax:* 703-684-1167
www.ctam.com
info@ctam.com
Char Beales, President/CEO
Daniel Cassidy, SVP/Finance/Administration

Founded: 1976 *Number of Members:* 5500 *Mission:* Dedicated to the discipline and development of consumer marketing excellence in cable television, new media and telecommunications services. As a member, you have the advantageof progressive research, insightful publications and forward thinking conferences all designed to help you and your company gain a competitive edge.

Cable & Television Association for Marketing (CTAM)
120 Waterfront Street, Suite 200, National Harbor, MD 20745
(301) 485-8900; *Fax:* (301) 560-4964
www.ctam.com
info@ctam.com
Vicki Lins, President/CEO
Angie Britt, SVP, Advanced Products
Todd Esenwein, Senior Director, Business Services
Anne Cowan, SVP/Chief Communications Officer
Mary Shaw, Director, Communications & Media Relations
Heather Baldino,Chair
Richard Lang, Vice Chair
CTAM unites leaders in entertainment, media and technology.

The Cable Center
2000 Buchtel Blvd., Denver, CO 80210
(720) 502-7500; *Fax:* (303) 871-4514
www.cablecenter.org
info@cablecenter.org
Jana Henthorn, President/Chief Executive Officer
Emily Gibson, Marketing & Communications Manager
Joyce Alden-Schuyler, Senior Executive Coordinator
Cassie Felix-Schoenfeld, Events Manager
Janice Silver, Director, Advancement &Outreach
Diane Christman, SVP, Programs & Development
The Cable Center's unique historical resources are a living, growing testament to the entrepreneurial spirit of cable's founders and to the innovative culture that drives the industry forward. Our programs help current professionals excel intheir roles, while our higher education programs introduce future generations to this dynamic industry. And our seminal customer care programs make a powerful contribution to the industry's collective efforts to improve customer relationships.

Cable in the Classroom
25 Massachussetts Ave NW, Suite 100, Washington, DC
202-222-2335; *Fax:* 202-222-2336
www.ciconline.org
help@ciconline.org
Frank Gallagher, Executive Director
Helen Dimsdale, Deputy Executive Director
Kat Stewart, Director, Strategic Initiatives
Beverly Hicks, Assistant Director
Mission: Promotes the visionary, sensible, responsible and effective use of cable's broaband technology, services, and content in teaching and learning. CIC also advocates digtial citizenship and supports the complimentary provision,by cable industry companies, of broadband and multichannel video services and educational content to the nation's schools.

Cable Television Laboratories Inc.
Div/DBA: (CableLabs)
Mailing Address: 858 Coal Creek Cir., Louisville, CO 80027-9750
Second Address: 400 California Avenue, Sunnyvale, CA 94086
(669) 777-9020; *Fax:* (303) 661-9199
www.cablelabs.com
info@cablelabs.com
Phil McKinney, President and Chief Executive Officer
Ike Elliott, Chief Strategy Officer
Christopher J. Lammers, Chief Operating Officer
Ralph W. Brown, Chief Technology Officer
Lee W. Zieroth, Senior Vice President & GeneralCounsel
Broadband dev for cable system operators.
Directors:
Brian L. Roberts, chmn

Canadian Association of Broadcast Consultants
130 Cree Crescent, Winnepeg, MB R3J 3W1
204-889-9202; *Fax:* 204-831-6650
www.cabc-accr.ca
jsadoun@yrh.com
Joseph Sadoun, Ing P Eng, President
Kerry Pelser, Secretary/Treasurer
Mission: Prepares technical briefs, coverage studies and frequencies.

Canadian Association of Broadcasters
770-45 O'Connor Street, PO Box 627, Station B, Ottawa, ON K1P 1A4
613-233-4035; *Fax:* 613-233-6961
www.cab-acr.ca
sbissonette@cab-acr.ca
Paul Ski, Chief Executive Officer
Rick Arnish, President
Charles Benoit, EVP
Sylvie Bissonette, VP, Finance & Administration & CFO
Mission: Serves as the eyes and ears of the private broadcasting community to advocate and lobby on its behalf and to act as a cebtral point on matters of joint interest.

Canadian Association of Ethnic Broadcaster
622 College Street, Toronto, ON M6G 1B6
416-531-9991; *Fax:* 416-531-5274
www.chinradio.com
info@chinradio.com
Johnny Lombardi, Founder, President
Mission: Pioneer in multicultural radio broadcasting and has lead the way for similar briadcast operations to be established.

Canadian Media Producers Association (CMPA)
Div/DBA: (formerly CFTPA)
160 John Street, 5th Floor, Toronto, ON M5V 2E5 Canada
(416) 304-0280; *Fax:* (416) 304-0499
www.cmpa.ca
toronto@cmpa.ca
Scott Garvie, Chairman
Reynolds Mastin, President & CEO
Marc Seguin, Senior VP, Policy
Liz Shorten, Senior VP, Operations & Member Services
Erin Finlay, Chief Legal Officer
Directors:
Cara Martin
151 Slater St., Suite 605, Ottawa, ON
(613)-233-1444; *Fax:* (613)-233-0073

CanWest Media Sales
121 Bloor Street East, Suite 1500, Toronto, ON M4W 3M5
416-967-1174; *Fax:* 416-967-1285
www.shawmedia.ca
Chris McDowell, Director, Publicity
Grace Park, Publicity Manager
Nick Porter, Publicist
Mission: Televison and newspaper advertising, marketing, and sales company.

Caribbean Broadcasting Union
Suite 1B, Building 6A, Harbor Industrial Estate, St Michael, BB 11145
246-430-1006; *Fax:* 242-228-9524
www.caribunion.com
patrick.cozier@caribsurf.com
Patrick Cozier, President
Mission: Stimulates the flow of broadcast material among the radio and television systems in the Caribbean region.

Catholic Academy for Communication Professionals
1645 Brook Lynn Dr., Suite 2, Dayton, OH 45432-1944
(937) 458-0265; *Fax:* (937) 458-0263
admin@catholicacademy.org
Sally Oberski, President
David Hains, First Vice President
Patricia Chivers, Second Vice President
Sean P. Dolan, Treasurer
Brian Finnerty, Secretary
Joseph Aponick, Representatives At-Large
Sue West, Administrator
CACP is the official and primary organization for diocesan Directors of Communication and communication professionals involved in the many ministries, offices, dioceses, archdioceses, religious orders and organizations serving the CatholicChurch.
Directors:
Jeanean Merkel, 1st VP; Vicki Bedard, 2nd VP

Center for Communication Inc.
110 East 23rd Street, Suite 900, New York, NY 10010
(212) 686-5005; *Fax:* (212) 504-2632
www.centerforcommunication.org
info@centerforcommunication.org
David J. Barrett, Chairman
Directors:
Edward Bleier, chmn; Frank Stanton, dir emeritus. Timothy Barry, William F. Baker, Robert M. Batscha, Patricia T. Carbine, Antoinette Cook Bush, John A. Dimling, David R. Drobis, Michael Eigner, Peter R. Ezersky, Charles B. Fruit, RalphGuild, Andrew Heyward, Peter Jennings, Gerald M. Levin, Kate McEnroe, Martin Nisenholtz, Herbert Scannell, Alan Siegel, Alfred C. Sikes, Kenneth Stoddard, Howard Stringer, Alberto Vitale, Stephen A. Weiswasser, David Westin, Bob Wright, Lois Wyse,Mortimer B. Zuckerman, Simon Michael Bessie, Louis D. Boccardi, David W. Burke, Henry A. Grunwald, Irwin Segelstein, Burton B. Staniar & Loet A. Velmans

Coalition Opposing Signal Theft
1724 Massachusetts Avenue NW, Washington, DC 20001
202-222-2300
www.ncta.com
webmaster@ncta.com
Nilda Cid Gumbs, Director
Mission: Acts as a clearinghouse of information regarding cable signal theft.

Collegiate Press Association
330 21st Avenue S, Minneapolis, MN 55455-0480
612-625-3500; *Fax:* 612-626-0720
Tom Rolnicki, Manager
Mission: Supports all those involved in the development and betterment of collegiate press. Hosts annual trade show.

Community Antenna Television Association
PO Box 1005, Fairfax, VA 22030-1005
202-775-3550
Number of Members: 3M *Mission:* An association of over 3,000 cable television systems serving over 30 million subscribers.

Cooperative Communicators Association
174 Crestview Dr, Bellefonte, PA 16823-8516
806-795-2783; *Fax:* 806-795-5289
www.communicators.coop
CCA@communicators.coop
Susie Bullock, Executive Director
Greg Brooks, Director Media/Public Relations
Chuck Lay, Board Member
Leta Mach, Board Member
Sheryl Meshke, Board Member
Founded: 1953 *Number of Members:* 350 *Mission:* A teaching and news tool for the Cooperative Communicators Association, CCA consists of 310 communicators, editors, photographers, graphics, designers, public relationsspecialists who work for cooperatives in 35 states, Canada and Poland.

Corporation for Public Broadcasting
401 9th Street, NW, Washington, DC 20004
202-879-9600; *Fax:* 202-879-9700
www.cpb.org
oigemail@cpb.org
Patricia de Stacy Harrison, President & CEO
Michael Levy, Executive VP & COO
Steven J. Altman, Executive VP/Chief Policy & Business Affrs Officer
William P. Tayman, Jr., CFO & Treasurer
Founded: 1967 *Mission:* A private, nonprofit corporation created by Congress in 1967. Its mission is to facilitate the development of, and ensure universal access to, non-commercial high-quality programming and telecommunicationsservices. It does this in conjunction with non-commercial educational telecommunications licensees across the country.

Council of Better Business Bureaus Inc.
Mailing Address: 3033 Wilson Blvd, Suite 600, Arlington, VA 22201
Second Address: 112 Madison Avenue, 3rd Floor, New York, NY 10016
(703) 276-0100; *Fax:* (703) 525-8277
www.bbb.org
BBB is an authority on trust in the marketplace. BBB sets and upholds high standards for ethical marketplace behavior. BBB accreditation is a coveted honor earned by elite businesses and charities. BBB is a valuable resource to turn tofor objective, unbiased information on businesses and charities. Our free BBB Business Reviews and BBB Wise Giving Reports help you make the right purchasing or donation decision. BBB is also a significant distributor of consumer and businesseducation information and tips and alerts about marketplace scams. And BBB offers dispute resolution programs for consumers and businesses when there is difference in viewpoints.
44 Byward Market Sq., Suite 220, Ottawa, ON Canada

Country Music Association Inc.
One Music Cir. S., Nashville, TN 37203
(615) 244-2840; *Fax:* (615) 726-0314
www.cmaworld.com
donations@cmaworld.com
Ed Hardy, Chairman
Frank Bumstea, President
John Esposito, President Elect
John Esposito, Secretary/Treasurer
Mike Dungan, Director
Kix Brooks, Director
Luke Bryan, Director
Steve Buchanan, Director
CMA is dedicated to bringing the poetry and emotion of Country Music to the world.
We will continue the tradition of leadership and professionalism, promoting the music, and recognizing excellence in all its forms. While fostering a spiritof community and sharing, we will respect and encourage creativity and the unique contributions of all.

CMA will be a place to have fun and celebrate success. We will take risks, embrace change, and always exceed the expectations of those we serve.

Country Radio Broadcasters
819 18th Ave S, Nashville, TN 37203-3218
615-327-4487; *Fax:* 615-329-4492
www.crb.org
info@crb.org
Ed Salamon, Executive Director
Chasity Crouch, Business Manager
Bill Mayne, VP
Gary Krantz, Secretary
Jeff Walker, Treasurer
Mission: Broadcasting forum.

Education Writers Association
3516 Connecticut Avenue NW, Washington, DC 20008
202-452-9830; *Fax:* 202-452-9837
www.ewa.org
ewa@ewa.org
Greg Toppo, President
Caroline W. Hendrie, Executive Director
Erik Robelen, Deputy Director
Lori Crouch, Assistant Director
George Dieter, COO
Tracee Eason, Administrative Coordinator/Events Assistant
Brooke Watson, EventsCoordinator
Founded: 1947 *Number of Members:* 800 *Mission:* The Education Writers Association is the national professional organization of education reporters and intent of improving education reporting to the public.

Educational Broadcasting Association
450 W 33rd St, New York, NY 10001-2605
212-560-3063; *Fax:* 212-560-3199
www.thirteen.org
programming@thirteen.org
William F. Bakerns, President & CEO
Stella Giammasi, VP Communication
Daisy Pommer, Manager
Number of Members: 500 *Mission:* Association members are producers and directors of public educational programming, channel 13, PBS.

Electro Federation Canada
180 Attwell Drive, Suite 320, Toronto, ON M9W 6A9 Canada
(866) 602-8877; *Fax:* (416) 679-9234
www.electrofed.com
info@electrofed.com
Jim Taggart, President/CEO
Bill Bryans, VP, Technical Services, Electrical
Wayne Edwards, VP, Sustainability & Electrical Safety
Anne Harrigan, VP, Marketing Resources
John Jefkins, VP, Marketing/Communications
Susan Winter, VP,Consumer Electronics Marketers of Canada
Philip Lefrancq, VP, Finance and Administration
EFC members contribute over $50B to the Canadian economy and employing more than 130,000 workers in more than 1,400 facilities across the country. EFC provides a powerful nucleus around which the Canadian electrical, consumer electronics andtelecommunications markets gain competitiveness in the global market through representation on issues and opportunities impacting electro-technical businesses.

Electronic Retailing Association (ERA)
607 14th Street, NW, Suite 530, Washington, DC 20005
(703) 841-1751, (800) 987-6462; *Fax:* (425) 977-1036
www.retailing.org
webadmin@retailing.org
Elliott Segal, Chairman
Kevin Kelly, COO/CFO
Julie Coons, President/CEO
Brian S. Archibald, Treasurer
Rich Yoegel, Secretary
Bill McClellan, Vice President, Government Affairs
Dave Martin, Vice President, Marketing andContent
Jennifer Williamson, Director, Membership Recruitment & Retention
Evan Shubin, Vice President, Sales and Group Show Director
ERA works hard to protect the regulatory and legislative climate of direct response while ensuring a favorable landscape that enhances direct response marketers' ability to bring quality products and services to the consumer. In addition,the association strives to promote thought leadership and the sharing of knowledge to advance the direct response industry, as well as to facilitate relationships that help members to drive their businesses' growth and profitability.
Directors:
Stephen F. Breimer, Esq.; Jeffrey Knowles, Esq.. Linda Goldstein, Mike Ackerman, Rick Cesari, Dan Danielson, Denise Dubarry Hay, Rollie Froehlig, Larry Jellen, Jack Kirby, Mark Lavin, Shigeru Ohashi, Rick Petry, Steve Pittenridgh, RichardProchnow, Randy Ronning, Robert Rosenblatt, Bret Saxton, Mark Thornton & Reiner Weihofen

Electronics Representatives Association
309 W. Washington St., Suite 500, Chicago, IL 60606
(312) 419-1432; *Fax:* (312) 419-1660
www.era.org
Mark Conley, Chairman
Thomas J. Shanahan, Executive VP/CEO
Paul C. Nielsen, CPMR, President
Dan Parks, CPMR, Senior Vice President/Fiscal & Legal
David Norris, Senior Vice President/Industry
Robert Logan, CPMR, Senior VicePresident/Membership
Kathie Cahill , CPMR, Senior Vice President/Education
Robert Terwall, Association President
William R. Warfield, Director of Finance
From ERA's Chicago headquarters flow the programs, publications and member benefits that respond to your multifaceted needs. A dedicated volunteer cadre of your peers and colleagues guides and oversees the operation of an outstandingprofessional staff, to respond to your multiple roles as entrepreneur, salesperson and employer while enhancing your well-being and that of the representative function.
Directors:
Tom Shanahan

FCBA (Federal Communications Bar Association)
1020 19th St. N.W., Suite 325, Washington, DC 20036-6101
(202) 293-4000; *Fax:* (202) 293-4317
www.fcba.org
fcba@fcba.org
Julie M. Kearney, President
Lee G. Petro, President-Elect
Joshua S. Tuner, Secretary
Ari Q. Fitzgerald, Assistant Secretary
Megan Anne Stull, Treasurer
Natalie G. Roisman, Assistant Treasurer
Through its many professional, social, and educational activities, the FCBA offers its members unique opportunities to interact with their peers and decision-makers in the communications and information technology field, and to keep abreastof significant developments relating to legal, engineering, and policy issues. Through its work with other specialized associations, the FCBA also affords its members opportunities to associate with a broad and diverse cross-section of otherprofessionals in related fields. Although the majority of FCBA members practice in the metropolitan Washington, D.C. area, the FCBA has 11 active regional chapters, including: Atlanta, Carolina, Florida, Midwest, New England, New York, NorthernCalifornia, Southern California, Pacific Northwest, Rocky Mountain, and Texas. The FCBA has members from across the U.S., its territories and several other countries.

Forest Industries Telecommunications
1565 Oak St, Eugene, OR 97401-4008
541-485-8441; *Fax:* 541-485-7556
www.landmobile.com
license@landmobile.com
Kevin Mc Carthy, President
Founded: 1947 *Number of Members:* 600 *Mission:* Organized to assist the forest industry in radio matters before the FCC.

Forestry Conservation Commuications
Po Box 3217, Gettysburg, PA 17325
717-338-1505; *Fax:* 717-334-5656
www.fcca-usa.org
nfc@fcca-usa.org
Ralph Haller, Executive Director
Paul Leary, President
Founded: 1944 *Number of Members:* 200 *Mission:* Certified by the FCC as the radio frequency coordinator for the Forestry Conservation Radio Service.

Foundation for American Communications
44 Avenue Road South, Suite 1200, Arlington, VA 22203
703-276-0100; *Fax:* 703-525-8277
www.facsnet.org
info@facsnet.org
John E Cox, CEO, President
Peter C McCarthy, Senior VP, COO
Paul Davis, Senior VP, Programs
Randy Reddick, Director
Christina Gardner, VP, Operations
Mission: A national non-profit educational organization with the mission of improving the quality of information reaching the public through the news.

Free TV Australia Ltd.
Div/DBA: (formerly Commercial Television Australia CTVA)
44 Avenue Rd., Mosman, N.S.W., 02088 Australia
61 2 8968 7100; *Fax:* 61 2 9969 3520
contact@freetv.com.au
Julie Flynnÿÿ, Chief Executive Officer
Roger Bunch, Director of Engineering
Rhonda Brown, Director of Marketing
Clare O'Neil, Director of Legal and Broadcasting Policy
Sarah Waladan, Manager of Media Policy and Regulatory Affairs
Sandra Slade, Director of Finance
RuthÿMcGuire, Director of Commercials Advice
Alison Lee, Lawyer, Commercials Advice
Provides a forum for discussion of industry matters by its members & is the pub voice of the industry on a wide range of issues & has represented the coml free-to-air TV industry for over 40 years.

Gay and Lesbian Press Association
PO Box 8185, Universal City, CA 91618-8185
Fax: 818-902-9576
Mission: Supports those gay and lesbian professionals in the field of journalism. Publishes quarterly newsletter.

Geospatial Information and Technology
14456 E Evans Ave, Aurora, CO 80014-1409
303-337-0513; *Fax:* 303-337-1001
www.gita.org
bsamborski@gita.org
Bob Samborski, Executive Director
Lisa Connor, Membership Services Manager
Wilma Kumar-Rubock, Secretary
Susan Ancel, Treasurer
Founded: 1960 *Number of Members:* 2200 *Mission:* Provides unbiased educational programs, forums and publications for professionals involved with geospatial information and technology.

Hollywood Foreign Press Association
646 N Robertson Blvd, West Hollywood, CA 90069-5022
310-657-1731; *Fax:* 310-939-9034
www.hfpa.org
info@hfpa.org
Phillip Berk, President
Mike Goodridge, VP
Lawrie Masterson, VP
Chantal Dinnage, Managing Director
Mission: Foreign correspondents covering Hollywood and the entertainment industry.

HRTS - Hollywood Radio and Television Society
16530 Ventura Blvd, Suite 411, Encino, CA 91436
818-789-1182; *Fax:* 818-789-1210
www.hrts.org
info@hrts.org
Melissa Grego, Executive Director
Jennie Nevin, Director of Operations
Ruzzo Martinelli, Events
Meshak Vallesillas, Marketing & Communications
Elvia Gonzalez, Member Services
Founded: 1947 *Number of Members:* 100 *Mission:* Sponsors monthly luncheons featuring top industry and government speakers and seminars about broadcasting, maintains film and audio library.

Independent Film & Television Alliance (IFTA)
10850 Wilshire Blvd., 9th Floor, Los Angeles, CA 90024-4311
(310) 446-1000; *Fax:* (310) 446-1600
www.ifta-online.org
info@ifta-online.org
Jean M. Prewitt, President & Chief Executive Officer
Robert Newman, Vice President & Chief Financial Officer
Jonathan Wolf, Executive Vice President and Managing Director of
Susan Cleary, Legal
Robin Burt, Marketing & Membership
Bill Anderson, Vice President, Research & Strategic Analysis
Directors:
Glen Basner, Steve Bickel, Alison Thompson, Nicolas Chartier, Roger Corman, Pierre David, Peter Elson, Kimberly Ferguson, Antony Ginnane, Peter Graham, Robert Hayward, Avi Lerner, Mark Lindsay, Nicole Mackey, Nicholas Meyer, Bobby Meyers,Michael Weiser, Kevin Williams & Andrew Stevens

Institute of Electrical and Electronics Engineers (IEEE)
3 Park Avenue, 17th Floor, New York, NY 10016-5997
(212) 419-7900; *Fax:* (212) 752-4929
www.ieee.org
executivedirector@ieee.org
Karen Bartleson, President & CEO
James A. Jefferies, President-Elect
Dr. E. James Prendergast, Executive Director

Donna Hourican, Staff Executive, Corporate Activities
Julie Eve Cozin, Staff Secretary
IEEE's core purpose is to foster technological innovation and excellence for the benefit of humanity.
3 Park Ave. 17th Fl., New York, NY 10016-5902
(212) 419-7900; *Fax:* (212) 752-4929

Interactive & Newsmedia Financial
14237 Bookcliff Ct, Purcellville, VA 20132-1771
703-421-4060; *Fax:* 703-421-4068
www.infe.org
Jeff Hood, President
Founded: 1947 *Number of Members:* 1000 *Mission:* Focuses on newspaper financial management, with members representing most North American newpaper companies, as well as many offshore. INFE's activities include publishing,conferences, workshops, industry surveys and studies, and offers members networking opportunities.

Intercollegiate Broadcasting Systems
367 Windsor Highway, New Windsor, NY 12553-7900
845-565-0003; *Fax:* 845-565-7446
www.ibsradio.org
ibs@ibsradio.org
Norman Prusslin, President
Fritz Kass, Chief Operating Officer
Founded: 1940 *Number of Members:* 800 *Mission:* Nonprofit association of student staffed radio stations based at schools and colleges across the country. Some 800 member stations operate all sizes and types of facilitiesincluding Internet-Webcasting, closed circuit, AM carrier-current, cable radio and FCC-licensed FM and AM stations.

International Academy of Television Arts and Sciences
25 West 52nd Street, New York, NY 10019
212-489-6969; *Fax:* 212-489-6557
www.iemmys.tv
membership@iemmys.tv
Camille Bidermann-Roizen, Senior VP & Executive Director
Nathaniel Brendel, Emmy Judging Director
Eva Obadia, Senior Director, Communications & Partnerships
Zoe Dyck, Marketing, Web & Design Manager
Jessica Franco, Emmy JudgingManager
Conor Hammonds, Entries Assistant
Erin Ferrell, Executive Assistant & Membership Coordinator
Mission: Member based organization comprised of leading media and entertainment figures from over 50 countries and 500 companies from all sectors of television including internet, mobile and technology.

International Advertising Association
Div/DBA: (The global partnership of advertisers, agencies &
747 Third Avenue, 2nd Floor, New York, NY 10017
(646) 722-2612; *Fax:* (646) 722-2501
www.iaaglobal.org
michael.lee@iaaglobal.org
Michael Lee, Managing Director
Marie Scotti, irector, Membership Services
Nubia Martinez, Education Coordinator
With members in 76 countries spanning six continents, we work together to: Promote freedom of commercial speech,Fight unwarranted regulation, Champion advertising as a growth engine of free market societies, Encourage the exchange ofknowledge and expertise amongst marketing peers around the world, Support self-regulation and provide an exchange of information and best practices, Provide professional development through education and training, Create industry forums that tackleissues with a single global voice
Directors:
Wendy Burrell, mgng dir. Richard Corner

International American Press Association
1801 Sw 3rd Ave, Miami, FL 33129-1487
305-634-2465; *Fax:* 305-635-2272
www.sipiapa.org
info@sipiapa.org
Julio Nunoz, Executive Director
Alejo Miro Cisneros, First VP
Diana Daniels, Second VP
Earl Maucker, Treasurer
Mission: Supports all those involved in the media and journalism industry. Hosts annual trade show.

International Animated Film Society
ASIFA-Hollywood, 2114 Burbank Blvd., Burbank, CA 91506
(818) 842-8330; *Fax:* (818) 842-5645
www.asifa-hollywood.org
info@asifa-hollywood.org
Jerry Beck, President
David Derks, VP
Jeff Wike, Treasurer
William C. Turner, Secretary
David Derks, Board of Director
Tom Sito, Board of Director
Danny Young, Board of Director
The International Animated Film Society, ASIFA-Hollywood is a California non profit organization established over thirty five years ago to promote and encourage the art and craft of animation.
Directors:
Jerry Beck, Stephen Worth, Bob Miller, Tom Knott, Frank Gladstone, David Derks, Margaret Kerry-Wilcox, Larry Loc & Will Ryan

International Association of Audio Information Services
1294 E 1600 Road, Lawrence, KS 60046
(800) 280-5325
www.iaais.org
iaaismember@gmail.com
Marjorie Moore, President
Maryfrances Evans, VP
Jennifer Nigro, Secretary
Amy Hatter, Treasurer
IAAIS is a volunteer-driven membership organization of services that turn text into speech for people who cannot see, hold or comprehend the printed word and who may be unable to access information due to a disability or health condition.

International Association of Broadcast Monitors
PO Box 986, Irmo, SC 29063
803-749-9833; *Fax:* 888-732-9004
Lisa Smith, Executive Director
Kevin Repka, President
Ron Coucil, VP International
John Croll, Secretary
Holly Wine, Treasurer
Founded: 1981 *Mission:* Worldwide trade association made up of news retrieval services which monitor television, radio, internet and print news mediums. It acts as a clearinghouse or forum for discussion on topics of collectiveconcerns and acts as a united voice for the news monitoring industry.

International Association of Audio Information
1090 Don Mills Road, Suite 303, Toronto, ON M3C 3R6
416-422-4222; *Fax:* 416-422-1622
www.iaais.org
Kim Walsh, President
Lori Kessinger, Chairperson
Stuart Holland, 1st Vice President
Mission: Encourages and supports the establishment and maintenance of audio information services that provide access to printed information for individuals who cannot read conventional print because of blindness or any other visual,physical, or learning disability.

International Association of Audio Visual
57 West Palo Verde Avenue, PO Box 250, Ocotillo, CA 92259-0250
760-358-7000; *Fax:* 760-358-7569
www.cindys.com
Sheemon Wolfe, Contact
Founded: 1957 *Number of Members:* 5200 *Mission:* Members are audio-visual professionals using the media of film, video, slides, filmstrips, multi-image and interactive media to communicate information

International Communication Agency Network (ICOM)
PO Box 490, Rollinsville, CO 80474-0490
(303) 258-9511; *Fax:* (303) 484-4087
www.icomagencies.com
info@icomagencies.com
Patrick Walhain, Chairman
Miguel dos Santos, Vice Chairman
Mr. Gary Burandt, Executive Director
Galina Epishkina, Director at Large
Patrick Gaulon, Director Finance
Rino Ferrari, Latin America Regional Director
Peter Jackson,Regional Director Africa
Our mission is:
To provide effective integrated communications resources to clients internationally
To provide a free exchange of ideas, information & support for members
Directors:
Frank G. Weyforth

International Communications Industry
11242 Waples Mill Road, Suite 200, Fairfax, VA 22030
703-273-7200; *Fax:* 703-278-8082
www.infocomm.org
customerservice@infocomm.org
Randy Pagnan, Chairman
Jay Armand, President
Randy Lemke, Executive Director
Mission: Centers on the technologies, products and systems for visual display, audio reproduction, video and audio production, interfacing and signal distribution, lighting, control systems, interactive display and audio presentationsystems, remote video and web conferencing.

International Communications Association
1500 21st St Nw, Washington, DC 20036-1000
202-955-1444; *Fax:* 202-530-9851
www.icahdq.org
icahdq@icahdq.org
M Haley, Executive Director
Founded: 1950 *Number of Members:* 3400 *Mission:* Supports all students and professionals in the international communications industry. Publishes bi-monthly newsletter.

International Institute of Communications
2 Printers Yard, 90a Broadway, London, UK SW19 1RD United Kingdom
(44) 020 8417 0600; *Fax:* (44) 207- 323- 9623
www.iicom.org
enquiries@iicom.org
Fabio Colasanti, President
Ann LaFrance, Treasurer
Andrew Barendse, Director
Andrea Millwood Hargrave, Director General
Amanda Crabbe, Director of Programmes
Dan Mygind, Programme Developer
Joanne Grimshaw, Projects Executive
The International Institute of Communications (IIC),established in 1969, provides senior professionals across the communications industry with the prospect of intellectually open and thought-provoking debate within a forum that analysesmarket and policy developments around the world. As a leading independent membership organisation focused on global telecommunications, media and digital media policy and regulation, and their impact on business and society, the IIC offers theopportunity to share experiences between practising communications professionals, policymakers, regulators and academics.

International Newspaper Marketing
10300 North Central Expressway, Suite 467, Dallas, TX 75231
214-373-9111; *Fax:* 214-373-9112
www.inma.org
inma@inma.org
Eivind Thomsen, President
Ross McPherson, VP
Scott C Schurz, Treasurer
Earl Wilkinson, Executive Director
Founded: 1930 *Number of Members:* 1100 *Mission:* Individuals in marketing, circulation, research and public relations of newspapers.

International Radio and Television Society Foundation Inc.
420 Lexington Ave, Suite 1601, New York, NY 10170
212-867-6650; *Fax:* 212-867-6653
www.irts.org
Joyce M. Tudrynff, President
Jim Cronin, Dir, Member Prgms & Development
Marilyn L. Ellis, Director, Program Administration
Lauren Kruk-Winokur, Dir, Academic Prgms & Communication
Tom Kane, Chairman
Founded: 1939 *Number of Members:* 750 *Mission:* The lines between broadcast televison and radio, cable, telephony and the computer industry may be blurring, but one thing remains clear, we all have an affinity for a businessthat entertains, informs, educates and serves the American public in a meaningful way. The foundation provides a unique common forum for all segments of the communication industry. Members can enjoy sharing insight and ideas with colleagues duringthe season's numerous events.

International Recording Media Association
182 Nassau Street, Suite 204, Princeton, NJ 08542
609-279-1700; *Fax:* 609-279-1999
Charles Van Horn, President
Thomas Van Sickle, Director
Mission: International trade association dealing with every facet of recording, media and related industries. Membership includes raw material providers, manufacturers, replicators, duplicators, packagers, and copyright holders.

Investigative Reporters and Editors
138 Neff Annex, Missouri School of Journalism, Columbia, MO 65211

573-882-2042; *Fax:* 573-882-5431
www.ire.org
info@ire.org
Brant Houston, Executive Director
Len Bruzzese, Deputy Director
John Green, Membership Coordinator
Evelyn Ruch-Graham, Conference Coordinator
Heather Feldman, Financial Officer
Founded: 1975 *Number of Members:* 3300 *Mission:* For individuals involved in investigative journalism.

Jones/NCTI-National Cable Television
Po Box 3309, Englewood, CO 80155
303-792-3111; *Fax:* 303-797-0829
www.jones.com
info@ncti.com
Glenn R Jones, CEO
Michael Guilfoyle, Director Market Strategy
Jerry Neese, Director Sales
Ken Ziel, VP/CFO
Mark Johnson, VP Business Development
Founded: 1968 *Number of Members:* 30 *Mission:* Workforce performance products, services and education.

Land Mobile Communications Council
8484 Westpark Drive, Suite 630, McLean, VA 22102-5117
703-528-5115; *Fax:* 703-524-1074
www.lmcc.org
donald.vasek@enterprisewireless.org
Alfred Ittner, President
Ralph Haller, VP
Donald Vasek, Secretary/Treasurer
Founded: 1967 *Mission:* A nonprofit association of organizations representing land mobile radio carriers and manufacturers equipment; LMCC membership represents diverse telecommunications sectors such as public safety,industrial/land transportation, private radio, specialized mobile radion and critical infrastructure.

League of Advertising Agencies
915 Clifton Avenue, Clifton, NJ 07013
973-473-6643; *Fax:* 973-473-0685
www.weinrichadv.com
info@weinrichadv.com
Andy Weinrich, Executive Vice President
Robert Weinrich, Marketing Director
Mission: Provides marketing solutions that maximize success.

Library of American Broadcasting Foundation Inc.
PO Box 2749, Alexandria, VA 22301
(703) 548-6090; *Fax:* (703) 549-4349
westsqn@aol.com
Kenneth Ray, General Manager
Pierre Bouvard, Senior Vice President of Sales at TRA
Eduardo Caballero, Director
Michael Carter, Director
Marc G. Guild, Director
Erwin G. Krasnow, Director
Dr. Judy Kuriansky, Director
Directors:
Donald H. Kirkley, Jr.. James L. Greenwald, Vincent Curtis, Arthur W. Carlson, Erwin Krasnow, Jerry Lee, Larry Taishoff, Jim Morley, Susan Ness, Don West, Richard Buckley, Perre Bouvard, Russ Withers, Carl Brazell, Michael Carter, TimCookerly, Sam Donaldson, James E. Duffy, Erica Farber, Skip Finley, Gary Fries, Marc Guild, Dr. Judy Kuriansky, David Kennedy, Dawson B. Nail, Allen Shaw, Ramsey Woodworth & Millard Younts
University of Maryland, College Park, Maryland, NO
(301) 405-9160; *Fax:* (301) 314-2634
www.lib.umd.edu/umcp/lab

Library of American Broadcasting
University of Maryland, College Park, MD 20742-7011
301-405-9160; *Fax:* 301-314-2634
www.lib.umd.edu
Founded: 1972 *Mission:* Holds a wide ranging collection of audio and video recordings, books, pamphlets, periodicals, personal collections, oral histories, photographs, scripts and vertical files devoted exclusively to the historyof broadcasting.

MAGNET: Marketing & Advertising Global
1017 Perry Hwy, Suite 5, Pittsburgh, PA 15237-2173
412-366-6850; *Fax:* 412-366-6840
www.magnetglobal.org
cheri@magnetglobal.org
Jim Nash, President
Cheri Gmiter, Executive Director
Founded: 1999 *Number of Members:* 40 *Mission:* A group of non-competing, independently owned advertising agenices in major markets throughout the world. Provides a way for member agencies to share their experience, knowledgeand ideas with other agencies in other parts of the world.

Manufacturers Radio Frequency Advisory
899-A Harrison St SE, Leesburg, VA 20175
703-669-0320
www.mrfac.com
Mary McKinley, President
Stan Jenkins, First VP
Clark Hart, Second VP
Dan Fiest, Secretary
Jim Pakla, Manager
Number of Members: 14000 *Mission:* Representing the voice of the manufacturing industry and private land mobile radio users before the Federal Communications Commision, the responsibe federal regulatory agency for the nation'sindustrial communications. The leaders of the manufacturing industry, individually and collectively, have an obligation to influence the policies, plans, and procedures which govern the growth, structure and use of our national radio spectrum andtelecommunications systems.

Media Access Group at WGBH
One Quest St., Boston, MA 02135
(617) 300-3600; *Fax:* (617) 300-1020
access.wgbh.org
access@wgbh.org
Jon Abbott, CEO, President, and member
Pat McDonald, Director
Lauren Madden, Business Manager
Ian McDonald, Business Manager
Ira Miller, Production Manager
Linda Idoni, Director
Kathy Kersey, Marketing Manager
36 million Americans who are deaf, hard of hearing, blind, or visually impaired rely on media access services provided by WGBH.

Media Alliance
1904 Franklin St, Suite 500, Oakland, CA 94612-2926
510-832-9000; *Fax:* 510-238-8557
www.media-alliance.org
Tracy Rosenberg, Executive Director
Eloise Rose Lee, Program Director
Mission: A nonprofit training and resource center for media workers, community organizations and political activists.

Media Communications Association
PO Box 5135, Madison, WI 53705-0135
608-836-0722; *Fax:* 888-899-6224
loiswei@aol.com
Gary Shifflet, President
Lois Weiland, Executive Director
Mike Brown, Treasurer
Jim Powell, Secretary
John Coleman, Board Member
Founded: 1968 *Mission:* Global community that provides its members opportunities for networking, learning and career advancement. Members work in video, film, collaborative communication, distance learning, web design andcreation, and all forms of interactive visual communication, along with associated crafts; serving businesses, nonprofit organizations, the government, educational institutions, the medical field, and electronic media. Chapters are throughout the US,with affiliates in Asia and Europe. It also provides professional development seminars and events, opportunities for networking, members-only benefits, forums for education and information resources for media communications professionals.

Media Financial Management Association (MFM)
550 W Frontage Road, Suite 3600, Northfield, IL 60093-1243
847-716-7000; *Fax:* 847-716-7004
www.mediafinance.org
info@mediafinance.org
Mary M Collins, President/CEO
Jamie L. Grande, Director of Operations
Arcelia Pimentel, Director of Sales
Founded: 1961 *Number of Members:* 1300 *Mission:* Professional society of more than 1,300 media's top financial, MIS Credit and HR executives, plus associates in auditing, data processing, software development, law, tax andcredit and collections. In 2009 MFM and Interactive & NewsMedia Financial Executives (INFE) combined under the leadership of MFM.

The Media Institute
2300 Clarendon Blvd, Suite 602, Arlington, VA 22201
703-243-5700; *Fax:* 703-243-8808
www.mediainstitute.org
info@mediainstitute.org
Patrick Maines, President
Richard Kaplar, Vice President
Susanna Coto, Director, Public Events
Mission: Non-profit research foundation specializing in communications policy isssues.

Minority Media and Telecommunications Council
3636 16th Street NW, Suite B 366, Washington, DC 20010
202-332-0500; *Fax:* 202-332-0503
www.mmtconline.org
info@mmtconline.org
Hon Julia L Johnson, Chairperson
Hon Deborah Taylor Tate, Vice Chair
Erwin Krasnow, Vice Chair
Ari Fitzgerald, Secretary
Ronald Johnson, Treasurer
Mission: national non-profit organization dedicated to promoting and oreserving equal opportunity and civil rights in the mass media, telecommunications and broadband industries, and closing the digital divide.

Motion Picture Association of America
Mailing Address: 1301 K Street, NW, Washington, DC 20005
Second Address: 15301 Ventura Blvd., Building E, Sherman Oaks, CA 91403
(202) 293-1966, (818) 995-6600; *Fax:* (202) 785-3026, (818) 285-4403
www.mpaa.org
contactus@mpaa.org
Christopher J. Dodd, Chairman
Charles H. Rivkin, Chief Executive Officer
Gail McKinnon, EVP, Government Affairs
Steve Fabrizio, Senior EVP & Global GC
David England, EVP & CFO
Matt Bennett, EVP, Global Communications
The MPAA continues to champion the creative and artistic freedoms of filmmakers, while working to rally public and private institutions around the world to the cause of safeguarding intellectual property rights, advancing technology-driveninnovation, and opening markets to the uniquely powerful and increasingly global medium of film.
15503 Ventura Blvd, Encino, CA 91436-3114
(818) 995-6600; *Fax:* (818) 382-1778

The Museum of Broadcast Communications
360 North State Street, Chicago, IL 60654-5411
312-245-8200; *Fax:* 312-245-8207
www.museum.tv
info@museum.tv
Bruce DuMont, President, CEO
Marc Glick, Executive Producer
Wally Podrazik, Consulting Curator
Adam Yenkin, Archives Clerk
Bert Gall, Project Manager
Mission: Collects, preserves, and presents historic and contemporary radio and television content as well as educate, inform , and entertain the public through its archives, public programs, screenings, exhibits, publications, andonline access to its resources.

MZTV Museum of Television
550 Queen St. E., Toronto, ON M5A 1V2 Canada
(416) 599-7339; *Fax:* (416) 599-3572
www.mztv.com
mztv@MZTV.com
Duane Parks, General Sales Mgr
Dan Hamilton, Vice President Broadcast

The National Academy of Television Arts & Sciences
1697 Broadway, Suite 404, New York, NY 10019
(212) 586-8424; *Fax:* (212) 246-8129
www.emmyonline.org
Chuck Dages, Chairman
Bob Mauro, President & CEO
Brent Stanton, Executive Director
Luke Smith, Awards Distribution Director
Alison Gibson, Treasurer
MaryEllen Eagelston, Secretary
Paul Pillitteri, SVP, PR & Communications
The National Academy of Television Arts and Sciences was founded in 1955. It is dedicated to the advancement of the arts and sciences of television and the promotion of creative leadership for artistic, educational and technical achievementswithin the television industry. It recognizes excellence in television with the coveted Emmyr Award for News, Sports, Daytime, Public Service and Technology.

National Academy of Television Arts and
111 W 57th St, Suite 600, New York, NY 10019-2271
212-586-8424; *Fax:* 212-246-8129
www.emmyonline.tv
Herb Granath, Chairperson
Darryl Cohen, 1st Vice Chair
Malachy Wienges, 2nd Vice Chair

Carolyn Grippi, COO/CFO
Paul Pillitteri, CAO
Founded: 1957 *Number of Members:* 12M *Mission:* Dedicated to the advancement of the arts and sciences of television and the promotion of creative leadership for artistic, educational and technical achievements within thetelevision industry. It recognizes excellence in television with the coveted Emmy Award.

National Association of Accredited Preventive Entities

Calle Castelb, 56, Madrid, 28001 Spain
915 75 04 04; *Fax:* 91 435 66 53
www.anepa.net
anepa@anepa.net
Juan Dancausa Roa, President/CEO
The National Association of Accredited Preventive Entities (ANEPA), founded in 1998, is a nonprofit organization that brings together major preventive accredited institutions of our country. It is a full member of the CEOE, being therepresentative of the business sector in the prevention of occupational hazards.occupational hazards .

National Association of Black Owned Broadcasters Inc. (NABOB)

1201 Connecticut Avenue NW, Suite 200, Washington, DC 20036
202-463-8970; *Fax:* 202-429-0657
www.nabob.org
nabobinfo@nabob.org
James L. Winston, President
Michael L. Carter, Vice President
Karen E. Slade, Treasurer
Mission: Largest trade organization representing the interests of African-American owners of radio and television stations across the country.

National Association of Broadcasters

1771 N St NW, Washington, DC 20036
202-429-5300; 800-622-3976
www.nab.org
nab@nab.org
Gordon H. Smith, President & CEO
Dennis Wharton, Executive VP, Communications
Ann Marie Cumming, Senior VP, Communications
Zamir Ahmed, Director, Media Relations
Founded: 1923 *Number of Members:* 7000 *Mission:* Full service trade association that represents the interests of free, over-the-air radio and television broadcasters. Offers seminars and workshops to members and holds localmeetings that offer support on legal and industry issues. Sponsors the National Association of Broadcasters Educational Foundation, dedicated to serving the public interest via education and training programs, strategies to increase diverseinitiatives, community support and philanthropy.

National Association of Black Journalists

8701-A Adelphi Rd, Adelphi, MD 20783-1716
301-445-7100; *Fax:* 301-445-7101
www.nabj.org
Karen Wynnfreeman, Executive Director
Ernie Suggs, Director
Stephanie Jones, Director
Elliott Lewis, Director
Marsha J. Eaglin, Director
Victor W. Vaughan, Director
Founded: 1975 *Number of Members:* 3300 *Mission:* An organization of journalists, students and media-related professionals that provides quality programs and services and advocates on behalf of black journalists worldwide.

National Association of College Radio/TV

71 George Street, Providence, RI 02912-1824
401-863-2225; *Fax:* 401-863-2221
nacb@aol.com
Founded: 1988 *Number of Members:* 1600 *Mission:* Members are student radio/TV stations and interested individuals. Has an annual budget of approximately $300,000.

National Association of Farm Broadcasters

PO Box 500, Platte City, MO 64079-2294
816-431-4032; *Fax:* 816-431-4087
www.nafb.com
info@nafb.com
Bill Oneill, Executive Director
Jeremy Povenmire, Member Service Manager
Rose Marie Lawrence, Secretary
Gene Millard, Director Marketing & Promotion
Founded: 1944 *Number of Members:* 600 *Mission:* Works to improve quantity and quality of farm programming and serves as a clearinghouse for new ideas in farm broadcasting.

National Association of Hispanic

1050 Connecticut Avenue NW, Washington, DC 20036
202-662-7145; *Fax:* 202-662-7144
www.nahj.org
nahj@nahj.org
Anna M. Lopez Buck, Interim Executive Director
Kevin Olivas, Recruitment and Guidance Manager
Founded: 1984 *Number of Members:* 2300 *Mission:* NAHJ is dedicated to the recognition and professional advancement of Hispanics in the news industry. NAHJ created a national voice and unified vision for all Hispanicjournalists.

National Association of Television Program Executives International

5757 Wilshire Blvd, Los Angeles, CA 90036
(310) 453-4440
www.yelp.com
See listing under Major National Associations, this section.

National Association of Telecommunications Officers and Advisors

3213 Duke Street, Suite 695, Alexandria, VA 22314
(703) 519-8035; *Fax:* (703) 997-7080
www.natoa.org
jharman@natoa.org
Tony Perez, President
Jennifer Harman, Manager of Operations
Keith Reeves, Station Manager
Jodie Miller, President-Elect
Joanne Hovis, Immediate Past President
Todd Barnes, Communications Director
Pam Berrian, Telecom. & CableProgram Manager
Steve Traylor, Executive Director
Tonya Rideout, Deputy Director
The National Association of Telecommunications Officers and Advisors is the premier local government professional association that provides support to our members on the many local, state, and federal communications laws, administrativerulings, judicial decisions, and technology issues impacting the interests of local governments. Founded in 1980, we offer a wide range of advocacy services to individual and agency members representing cities, towns, counties and commissions acrossthe country. NATOA actively analyzes and addresses emerging issues in areas such as local government communications and internet policy; broadband planning best practices; cable franchising; wireless zoning; new technology initiatives andadvancements; and operation of public, education and government (PEG) access channels.

National Association of Television

5757 Wilshire Blvd, Penthouse 10, Los Angeles, CA 90036-5810
323-937-4465; *Fax:* 310-453-5258
www.natpe.org
info@natpe.org
Rick Feldman, President/CEO
Wayneston Harbeson, Operations Manager
Jon Dobkin, CFO
Founded: 1963 *Number of Members:* 2800 *Mission:* A global, non-profit organization dedicated to the creation, development and distribution of televised programming in all forms across all mature and emerging media platforms.

National Cable and Telecommunications Association(NCTA)

25 Massachusetts Ave Nw, Suite 100, Washington, DC 20001-1434
202-222-2300; *Fax:* 202-775-3604
www.ncta.com
webmaster@ncta.com
Michael Powell, President & CEO
James Assey, Executive VP
K. Dane Snowden, COO
Brian Dietz, SVP, Strategic Communications
Bruce Carnes, SVP, Finance & Administration
David Pierce, VP, Public Affairs/NCTA Foundation
Founded: 1952 *Number of Members:* 3189 *Mission:* Members are cable TV systems; associate members are manufacturers, distributors, suppliers of hardware, programmers and other services. An association for those interested inprograms about cable television.

National Captioning Institute

3725 Concorde Parkway, Suite 100, Chantilly, VA 20151
703-917-7600; *Fax:* 703-917-9853
www.ncicap.org
tcalkins@ncicap.org
Gene Chao, CEO, President
Drake Smith, Chief Technology Officer
Marc Okrand, Director, Administration
Tony Calkins, Director, National Sales
Jay Feinberg, Director, Marketing
Mission: Non-profit organization whose primary purposes are to deliver effective captioning services and encourage, develop and fund the continuing development of captioning, subtitling, and other media access services for the benefitof peopl who require additional access to the auditory and visual information.

National Council for Families & TV

3801 Barham Boulevard, Los Angeles, CA 90068-1000
323-953-7300; *Fax:* 310-208-5984
www.salonprofessionals.org
Mission: Advances and promotes television awareness for family television shows.

National Education Association

1201 16th St. N.W., Washington, DC 20036-3290
(202) 833-4000; *Fax:* (202) 822-7974
www.nea.org
editorial@list.nea.org
Lily Eskelsen Garcia, President
Becky Pringle, Vice President
Princess R. Moss, Secretary-Treasurer
John C. Stocks, Executive Director
Barbara Davidson, Board of Directors
Susan Brown, Board of Directors
Timothy Parker, Board ofDirectors
The National Education Association (NEA), the nation's largest professional employee organization, is committed to advancing the cause of public education. NEA's 3 million members work at every level of education-from pre-school touniversity graduate programs. NEA has affiliate organizations in every state and in more than 14,000 communities across the United States.

National Federation of Community Broadcasters (NFCB)

1970 Broadway, Suite 1000, Oakland, CA 94612
510-451-8200; *Fax:* 510-451-8208
www.nfcb.org
comments@nfcb.org
Maxie C Jackson III, President/CEO
Brian Terhorst, Board Chair
Kim Bosler, Secretary
Peggy Berryhill, Treasurer
Mission: A national alliance of stations, producers, and others committed to community radio. NFCB advocates for national public policy, funding, recognition, and resources on behalf of its membership while providing services toempower and strengthen community broadcasters through the core values of localism, diversity, and public service.

National Federation of Press Women Inc.-NFPW

Mailing Address: PO Box 34798, Alexandria, VA 22334-0798
Second Address: PO Box 5556, Arlington, VA 22205
800-780-2715; *Fax:* 703-237-9808
www.nfpw.org
presswomen@aol.com
Ella Robinson, President
June Mathews, VP
Founded: 1937 *Number of Members:* 2000 *Mission:* Members are writers, editors and other communication professionals for newspapers, magazines, wire services, agencies and freelance.

National League of Cities

1301 Pennsylvania Ave. N.W., Suite 550, Washington, DC 20004
(202) 626-3000, (877) 827-2385; *Fax:* (202) 626-3043
www.nlc.org
info@nlc.org
Marie Lopez Rogers, President
Chris Coleman, First Vice President
Ralph Becker, Second Vice President
Clarence Anthony, Executive Director
Neil Bomberg, Program Director
Federal Advocacy
Human Dev & Pu
Julie Bosland, Director
James Brooks, Program Director
City Solutions and Applied Resea
The National League of Cities (NLC) is dedicated to helping city leaders build better communities. Working in partnership with the 49 state municipal leagues, NLC serves as a resource to and an advocate for the more than 19,000 cities,villages and towns it represents.
Directors:
James C. Hunt, pres; Bart Peterson, VP; Cynthia McCollum, 2nd VP. R. Michael Amyx, Tommy Baker & Vickie Barnett

National Lesbian and Gay Journalists

2120 L Street NW, Suite 850, Washington, DC 20037
202-588-9888
www.nlgja.org
info@nlgja.org
Bach Polakowski, National Office Administrator
Matthew Rose, Membership Coordinator

ASSOCIATIONS, EVENTS, EDUCATION & AWARDS

Michael Tune, Executive Director
David Steinberg, President
Jen Christensen, Vice President/Broadcast
Founded: 1990 *Number of Members:* 220 *Mission:* NLGJA is an organization of journalists, media professionals, educators and students working within the news industry to foster fair and accurate coverage of LGBT issues. NLGJAopposes all forms of workplace bias and provides professional development to its members.

National Newspaper Association
Mailing Address: PO Box 7540, Columbia, MO 65205-7540
Second Address: PO Box 5737, Arlington, VA 22205
800-829-4ANNA, 573-77-4890, 703-237-9802; *Fax:* 573-777-4985, 703-237-9808
www.nnaweb.org
lynn@nna.org
Lynn Edinger, Associate Director
Founded: 1885 *Number of Members:* 2000 *Mission:* To protect, promote and enhance America's community newspapers.

National Press Club
529 14th St NW, 13th Floor, Washington, DC 20045-2393
202-662-7500; *Fax:* 202-662-7512
www.press.org
Jeff Ballou, President
Andrea Edney, Vice President
Jen Judson, Secretary
Ferdous Al-Faruque, Treasurer
Michele Salcedo, Membership Secretary
Number of Members: 4.6M *Mission:* A private organization composed of professional journalists who are directly related to the media. Persons must qualify to be admitted.

National Press Foundation
1211 Connecticut Ave NW, Suite 310, Washington, DC 20036-2709
202-663-7280; *Fax:* 202-662-1232
www.nationalpress.org
jenny@nationalpress.org
Sandy Johnson, President & COO
Jenny Ash-Maher, Director of Operations
Chris Adams, Director, Training & Content
Tyler Mertins, Digital Media Manager
Jesse Schneider, Program Manager
Founded: 1976 *Mission:* Supports all those involved with national press and the media. Publishes bi-weekly newsletter.

National Public Radio Association
635 Massachusetts Ave Nw, Suite 1, Washington, DC 20001-3753
202-686-0516; *Fax:* 202-513-3329
www.npr.org
Gary E Knell, President/CEO
Joyce MacDonald, Chief of Staff/Vice President
Jeff Perkins, Chief People Officer
Robert Kempf, General Manager
Deborah Cowan, VP/Chief Financial Officer
Founded: 1970 *Number of Members:* 750 *Mission:* Works in partnership with member stations to create a more informed public, one challenged and invigorated by a deeper understanding and appreciation of events, ideas, andcultures.

National Religious Broadcasters
9510 Technology Dr, Manassas, VA 20110-4149
703-330-7000; *Fax:* 703-330-7100
www.nrb.org
info@nrb.org
Frank Wright, President
Linda Smith, President Assistant
David Keith, VP Operations
Number of Members: 1700 *Mission:* Represents more than 1500 evangelical Christian radio and television stations, program producers, multimedia developers and related organizations around the world. Members are responsible for muchof the world's Christian radio and television.

National Retail Federation
1101ÿNewÿYork Ave NW, Suite 1100, Washington, DC 20005
(202) 783-7971, (800) 673-4692; *Fax:* (202) 737-2849
www.nrf.com
Stephen I. Sadove, Chairman
Carleen Kohut, COO
Matthew Shay, President
Vicki Cantrell, Senior Vice President, Communities/Executive Direc
Ellen Davis, Senior Vice President/Executive Director
Mallory Duncan, Senior VicePresident/General Counsel
David French, Senior Vice President-Government Relations
Mike Gatti, Senior Vice President-Member Relations
Bill Thorne, Senior Vice President-Communications and Public Af
As the world's largest retail trade association and the voice of retail worldwide, NRF represents retailers of all types and sizes, including chain restaurants and industry partners, from the United States and more than 45 countries abroad.Retailers operate more than 3.6 million U.S. establishments that support one in four U.S. jobs - 42 million working Americans. Contributing $2.5 trillion to annual GDP, retail is a daily barometer for the nation's economy. NRF's This is Retailcampaign highlights the industry's opportunities for life-long careers, how retailers strengthen communities, and the critical role that retail plays in driving innovation.

National Scholastic Press Association
2221 University Ave SE, Suite 121, Minneapolis, MN 55414-3074
612-625-8335; *Fax:* 612-626-0720
www.studentpress.org
Logan Aimone, Executive Director
Ann Akers, Associate Director
Jesse Rinkenberger, Business Manager
Mission: Supports all those involved in yearbook printing and photographic services, college journalism departments and video yearbook production services. Hosts annual trade show.

National Sportscasters and Sportswriters
PO Box 1545, Salisbury, NC 28145-1545
704-633-4275; *Fax:* 704-633-2027
www.nssahalloffame.com
Bob Setzer, President
Dennis White, Vice President
Founded: 1959 *Number of Members:* 1000 *Mission:* Meet annually.

National Telemedia Council
1922 University Avenue, Madison, WI 53726
608-218-1182; *Fax:* 608-218-1183
www.nationaltelemediacouncil.org
ntelemedia@aol.com
Marieli Rowe, Editor of the Journal of Media Literacy
Karen Ambrosh, President
Mission: Promotes media literacy through workshops and telemediun.

National Translator Association
5611 Kendall Court, Suite 2, Arvada, CO 80002
303-378-8209; *Fax:* 303-940-8442
www.tvfmtranslators.com
stcl@comcast.net
Byron St. Clair, President
Arnold Cruze, VP
Paul Burkholder, Secretary/Treasurer
Arnold Cruze, Director
Dave Sunderman, Director
Founded: 1967 *Mission:* Dedicated to the preservation of free over-the-air TV in all geographical areas. It works to improve the technology of rebroadcast translators and regulatory climate which governs them. It continouslypromotes the concept of universal free over-the-air TV and reprsents the ineterests of translator operators before the FCC and other government agencies such as the Forest Service and the Bureau of Land Management. Membership is open to allindividuals and organizations that are interested.

Native American Journalists Association
University of Oaklahoma, Gaylor College, 395 W Lindsey Street, Norman, OK 73019-4201
405-325-9008; *Fax:* 405-325-6945
www.naja.com
Jeff Harjo, Executive Director
Heather Dutcher, Marketing Director
Rhonda LeValdo, President
Jolene Schonchin, Secretary
Founded: 1983 *Mission:* NAJA serves and empowers Native journalists through programs and actions designed to enrich journalism and promote Native cultures. NAJA educates and unifies its membership through journalism programs thatpromote diversity and defends challenges to free press.

New England Cable & Telecommunications
10 Forbes Road, Suite 440W, Braintree, MA 02184-2648
781-843-3418; *Fax:* 781-849-6267
www.necta.info
info@necta.info
Mission: NECTA is a six state regional trade association representing sbtstantially all private cable telecommunications companies in Connecticut, Maine, Massachusetts, New Hampshire, Rhode Island and Vermont.

New England Cable & Telecommunications Association Inc. (NECTA)
Mailing Address: Ten Forbes Road, Suite 440W, Braintree, MA 02184
Second Address: 21 Oak St, Suite 307, Capitol Place, Hartford, CT 6106
(781) 843-3418, (860) 524-5820; *Fax:* (781) 849-6267, (860) 728-1302
www.necta.info
info@necta.info
Mark Reilly, Chairman
Paul R. Cianelli, Presidentÿ
Timothy O. Wilkerson, VP & Policy Counsel
Carolyn Killian, Office Manager
John Sutich, Vice Chairman
Jay Allbaugh, Treasurer
Melinda Poore, Secretary
The New England Cable & Telecommunications Association, Inc. (NECTA) is a five state regional trade association representing substantially all private cable telecommunications companies in Connecticut, Massachusetts, New Hampshire, RhodeIsland and Vermont.

New England Press Association
360 Huntington Avenue 428CP, Boston, MA 02115
617-254-4880; *Fax:* 617-373-5615
www.nepa.org
Brenda Reedtani, Executive Director
Lynn Delaney, Second VP
Marlene Switzer, Secretary
Founded: 1950 *Number of Members:* 460 *Mission:* This organization offers a publication about the newspaper industry specifically focusing on New England newspapers and the issues that affect them, which goes to everynewspaper in New England.

New Jersey Collegiate Press Association
840 Bear Tavern Rd, Suite 305, Ewing, NJ 08628-1019
609-406-0600; *Fax:* 609-406-0300
www.njpa.org
foundation@njpa.org
John O'Brien, Executive Director
Founded: 1952 *Number of Members:* 49 *Mission:* Supports all those involved in the development and betterment of collegiate press. Hosts annual trade show.

Newseum
555 Pennsylvania Ave N.W., Washington, DC 20001
(703) 284-3544, (888) 639-7386
www.newseum.org
newseum@freedomforum.org
Peter S. Prichard, Chairman
James C. Duff, President/CEO
James Thompson, Senior vice president/operations
Cathy Trost, Vice president/exhibits and programs
Shelby Coffey, Vice chairman
Pam Galloway-Tabb, Senior vicepresident/conferences and special serv
Nicole F. Mandeville, Senior vice president/Finance and Treasurer
Paul Sparrow, Senior vice president/broadcasting
Courtney L. Surls, Senior Vice President/Development
Jim Updike, Senior VicePresident/Technology
The Newseum - a 250,000-square-foot museum of news - offers visitors an experience that blends five centuries of news history with up-to-the-second technology and hands-on exhibits.

Newspaper Association Managers
70 Washington Street, Salem, MA 01970-3518
978-744-8940; *Fax:* 978-744-0333
Bob New, Owner
Morley Piper, Executive Director
Founded: 1923 *Number of Members:* 65 *Mission:* Executives of state, regional, national and international newspaper associations.

Newspaper Association of America
4401 Wilson Blvd, Suite 900, Arlington, VA 22203-4195
571-366-1000; *Fax:* 571-366-1195
www.naa.org
Reggie Hall, Senior VP
Rebecca Albers, VP
Paula Hummel, Director
Joan Mills, Marketing Manager
Charles Pittman, Director
Donna Barrett, Director
Susan Clark-Johnson, Director
Paul Boyle, Director
Su Lin Nichols, Director
Randy Bennett, Director
Founded: 1992 *Number of Members:* 2000 *Mission:* Newspaper Association of America maintains close, cooperative relations with other newspaper and journalism organizations.

Newspaper Guild: CWA
501 3rd St Nw, 6th Floor, Washington, DC 20001-2760

202-434-1254; *Fax:* 202-434-1426
www.nabetcwa.org
guild@cwa-union.org
John Clark, President
Carol D Rothman, Secretary/Treasurer
Andy Zipser, Guild Reporter
Founded: 1937 *Mission:* Organization covering the newspaper industry, its employment practices, press freedom and labor movement.

North American Broadcasters Association (NABA)
Mailing Address: PO Box 500, Stn A, Rm. 6C 300, Toronto, ON M5W 1E6 Canada
Second Address: 205 Wellington Street, W., Suite 6C300, Toronto, ON M5V 3G7
(416) 598-9877; *Fax:* (416) 598-9774
www.nabanet.com
info@nabanet.com
Robert J. Ross, President
Michael McEwen, Director General
Anh Ngo, Director- Administration
Jason Paris, Senior Coordinator
Roxanne Riess, Executive Assistant
Vineet Mathur, IT & Web Administrator
Directors:
Joseph Flaherty, Felix Arauji Ramirez, Ignacio Suarez, Andy Setos & Peter Smith

North American Broadcasters Association (NABA)
25 John Street (205 Wellington St. W), Suite 6C300, Toronto, ON M5V 3G7
416-598-9877; *Fax:* 416-598-9774
www.nabanet.com
contact@nabanet.com
Richard Friedel, President
Michael McEwen, Director General
Anh Ngo, Director, Administration
Jenn Hadfield, Senior Coordinator, Committees
Ashley Lloyd Spanton, Executive Assistant
Mission: A non-profit association of broadcasting organizations in the United States, Mexico, and Canada committed to advancing the interests of broadcasters at home and internationally.

North American Network
3700 Crestwood Pkwy NW, Suite 350, Duluth, GA 30096-7154
770-279-4560; *Fax:* 770-279-4566
www.pkfnan.org
Terry Snyder, President
Mission: Radio broadcasting agency that provides news and programming services to radio stations and organizations. Programming is sponsored by the corporations, government angencies, associations and nonprofit organizations who areindentified in the program notes and scripts.

North American Retail Dealers Association
Mailing Address: 222 South Riverside Plaza, Suite #2100, Chicago, IL 60606 US
Second Address: P.O. Box 676, Downers Grove, IL 60515
(312) 648-0649, (800) 621-0298, (630) 435-6365; *Fax:* (866) 879-7505
www.kwmu.com
nardahdq@narda.com

Overseas Press Club of America
40 W. 45th St., New York, NY 10036
212-626-9220; *Fax:* 212-626-9210
www.opcofamerica.org
sonya@opcofamerica.org
Patricia Kranz, Executive Director
Deidre Depke, President
Abigail Pesta, Treasurer
Amy Russo, Office Manager
Founded: 1939 *Number of Members:* 450 *Mission:* OPC is a private non-profit membership organization of journalists engaged in international news.

Pacific Pioneer Broadcasters
PO Box 8673, Calabasas, CA 91372
(323) 461-2121; *Fax:* (818) 768-8251
www.ppbwebsite.org
Jeanne DeVivier Brown, Chairman
Chuck Street, President
Jeanne DeVivier Brown, Entertainment Chairman
Kay Henley, Membership and Friendship Chairman
Larry Vanderveen, Vice President & Diamond Circle Award
Bianca Pino, VicePresident
David Dow, Secretary
Ric Ross, Treasurer
Over the years, PPB has accumulated one of the largest collections of scripts, quality transcriptions of radio programs and broadcast equipment in existence. This irreplaceable material is now in the care of California's Thousand OaksLibrary in its future American Radio Archives Building. That ambitious project is seeking funding for what will be a beautiful new building housing America's most-extensive radio memorabilia.

The Paley Center for Media
Mailing Address: 25 West 52nd Street, New York, NY 10019
Second Address: 465 N. Beverly Dr., Beverly Hills, CA 90210
212-621-6800, 212-621-6600; 310-786-1000
www.paleycenter.org
coman@paleycenter.org
Pat Mitchell, President, CEO
John Wolters, Vice President, CFO
Jennifer Juzaitis, Vice President, Development
Diane Lewis, Vice President, Public Affairs
Mission: Leads the discussion about the cultural, creative, and social significance of television, radio, and emerging platforms for the professional community and media-interested public.

PCIA- The Wireless Industry Association
6355 Walker Ln, Suite 700, Alexandria, VA 22310-3247
703-971-7100; *Fax:* 703-922-5518
www.pcia.com
andrewd@pcia.com
Andrea Burns, Director Gov't Relations
Connie Durcksak, Sr Director Industry Relations
Rick Harris, Sr Director Press/Public Relations
Founded: 1949 *Number of Members:* 3000 *Mission:* Represents companies that develop, own, manage and operate towers, commercial rooftops and other facilities for the provision of all types of wireless, broadcasting andtelecommunications services.

PROMAX&BDA
5700 Wilshire Blvd, Suite 275, Los Angeles, CA 90036
(310) 788-7600, (800) 977-6629; *Fax:* (310) 788-7616
www.promaxbda.org
info@promaxbda.org
Steve Kazanjian, President & CEO
Lucian Cojescu, CIO
Stacey La Cotera, Senior VP, Global Awards Development
Christina Graziano, Director, Events & Global Conferences
Paul Lee, Awards Coordinator
PromaxBDA leads the global community of those passionately engaged in the marketing of television and video content on all platforms, inspiring creativity, driving innovation and honoring excellence. The association represents more than10,000 companies and individuals at every major media organization, marketing agency, research company, strategic and creative vendor and technology provider and is considered to be the leading global resource for education, community, creativeinspiration and career development in the media and media marketing sectors.
Directors:
David Snapp, George Pierson, Lisa Fengler, Leslie Celia, Jeannine Chanin, Tony Cleave, Ann Epstein-Cohen, Steve Delaney, Miguel Muelle, Karen Olcott, Jan Phillips, Abel Sanchez, Robin Skirboll, Anne White, Mark Stroman, Glynn Brailsford,Brian Blum, Judy Braune, Alan Cohen, Scott Danielson, C.J. Fredricksen, Lee Hunt, Kay Hutchison, Tony Lakin, Vince Manze, Brigitte McCray, Rob Middleton, Nick Miller, Michael Mischler, David Muscari, Billy Pittard, Sal Sardo, George Schweitzer,Curtis Symonds & Donna Weston

Synapse Pacific LTD
49 Hollywood Rd., 19th Fl., Hong Kong, China

Promax & BDA Europe
61 Webber St., London, NO United Kingdom

Public Media Alliance (formerly Commonwealth Broadcasting Assn)
Arts 1.80, DEV, University of East Anglia, Norwich, NR4 7TJ United Kingdom
(0)1603 592 335
www.publicmediaalliance.org
info@publicmediaalliance.org
Paul Thompson, President
Sally-Ann Wilson, CEO
Mervyn Warner, Finance Manager
Jasmine Chandler, Project & Membership Manager
Marta Catalano, Digital Author
The Public Media Alliance (formerly the Commonwealth Broadcasting Association [CBA]) is the largest global association of public service broadcasters. Its members are the broadcasters that communicate daily with the 2.5 billion citizens ofthe Commonwealth as well as a broader global focus, in the 54 member countries. It continues to support and facilitate high standards of media production and broadcasting, including the promotion of arts, science and diversity.
Directors:
George Valarino, Ronald Abraham, Roger Grant, Robert O'Rielly, Tombong Saidy, Sharon Crosbie & Cecilia Khuzwayo

Public Radio in Mid-America (PRIMA)
3651 Olive Street, St Louis, MO 63108
314-516-5968; *Fax:* 314-516-6397
Tim Eby, General Manager
Terrence Dupuis, Chief Engineer
Shelley Kerley, Director, Development
Mission: Trusted source of information and entertainment that opens minds and mourishes the spirit

Public Radio News Directors Incorporated
PO Box 838, Sturgis, SD 57785
(605) 490-3033; *Fax:* (608) 263-5838
www.prndi.org
walker@wpr.org
Terry Gildea, President
Christine Paige Diers, Business Manager
Rachel Osier Lindley, Treasurer
Johnathan Reaves, Small Station Representative
Teresa Collier, Large Station Representative
PRNDI is a non-profit professional association that exists to improve local news and information programming by serving public radio journalists. PRNDI educates, advocates and organizes to promote high standards, ethical principles, andsignificant public service.
Directors:
Dave Piznanelli, Martha Foley, Jonathan Ahl & Christine Paige-Diers

Public Relations Society of America
33 Maiden Ln., 11th Fl., New York, NY 10038-5150
(212) 460-1400; *Fax:* (212) 995-0757
www.prsa.org
William Murray, President/COO
Philip Bonaventura, Chief Financial Officer
Stephanie Cegielski, Vice President, Public Relations
Christina Darnowski, Vice President, Membership
Jeneen Garcia, Vice President, Education
John D.Robinson, Vice President, Corporate Development & Industry P
Karla Voth, Vice President, Special Events & Programs
PRSA is a community of more than 21,000 public relations and communications professionals across the United States, from recent college graduates to the leaders of the world's largest multinational firms. Our members represent nearly everypractice area and professional and academic setting within the public relations field. In addition, there are more than 10,000 students who are members of the Public Relations Student Society of America (PRSSA) at colleges and universities here andabroad.

Pulic Radio News Directors Incorporated
PO Box 838, Sturgis, SD 57785
605-490-3033; *Fax:* 605-490-3085
www.prndi.org
info@prndi.org
George Bodarky, President
Bob Beck, Treasurer
Naomi Starobin, Large Station Rep
Matt Schaffer, Medium Station Rep
Aaron Selbig, Small Station Rep
Mission: A non-profit professional association that exists to improve local news and information programming by serving public radio journalists.

Radio & Television News Directors Foundation
529 14th Street, NW, Suite 1240, Washington, DC 20045
(202) 659-6510; *Fax:* (202) 223-4007
www.rtndf.org
Amy Tardif, Chair
Mike Cavenderÿ, Executive Director
Derrick Hinds, Communications, Marketing & Digital Media Manager
Kate Switchenko, Director of Events and Awards
Karen Hansen, Membership and Programs Manager
Jon Ebinger,International Programs Consultant
Holly Rose, Industry Relations and Sponsorship Manager

Radio Advertising Bureau
1320 Greenway Dr, Suite 500, Irving, TX 75038-2547
972-753-6700; *Fax:* 972-753-6727
www.rab.com
jhaley@rab.com
Mike Mahone, VP
Leah Koman, SVP Marketing
Number of Members: 7000 *Mission:* Our mission is to lead industry initiatives and provide organizational, educational, research and advocacy programs and services that benefit the RAB membership and the Radio industry as a whole.

Radio and Television Museum
2608 Mitchellville Rd., Bowie, MD 20716

(301) 390-1020; *Fax:* (301)947-3338
www.radiohistory.org
info@ncrtv.org
Christopher Sterling, Chairman
Brian Belanger, Executive Director/Curator
Laurie Baty, Deputy Director
Ken Mellgren, Vice Chair
David Green, Treasurer
Angela Balsamo, Director
The National Capital Radio & Television Museum collects, preserves, and interprets artifacts, programming, and publications to educate the public about the development and impact of electronic media.
Directors:
Brian Belanger, exec dir. Kenneth Mellgren, Ed Walker, Peter Eldridge, William McMahon, William Goodwin, Tony Young, Rob Huddleston, Chris Sterling, Don Ross, Gerald Schneider, Paul Courson, Charles Grant & Michael Rubin

Radio and Television Research Council
245 5th Avenue, New York, NY 10016-8728
212-028-8933; *Fax:* 212-481-3071
Robert M Purcell, Executive Director
Founded: 1941 *Number of Members:* 200 *Mission:* Members are professionals actively engaged in radio/television research.

Radio Information Service
600 Forbes Ave, Suite 140, Pittsburgh, PA 15219-3016
412-488-3944; *Fax:* 412-488-3953
www.readingservice.org
info@readingservice.org
Andy Ai, President
Erica Hacker, Vice President
Number of Members: 10000 *Mission:* Membership is offered to radio reading and information services for the blind or print handicapped.

Radio Television Digital News Association
529 14th Street NW, Suite 425, Washington, DC 20045
Fax: 202-223-4007
www.rtdna.org
mikec@rtdna.org
Dan Shelley, Executive Director
Derrick Hinds, Communications
Katie Switchenko, Deputy Executive Director
Kate McGarrity, Awards & Programs Manager
Mission: An association dedicated to setting new standards for newsgathering and reporting.

Radio Television Digital News Association of Canada
1201 West Pender Street, #300, Vancouver, BC V6E 2V2
Canada
647-323-2152
www.rtdnacanada.com
info@rtdnacanada.com
Ian Koenigsfest, President
Joanne McPherson, Business Manager
Leya Duigu, Membership, Conference & Events
Jennifer Nguyen, Awards
Mission: Progressive organization offering a forum for open discussion and action in the broadcast news industry. Speaks for the leaders of Canada's radio and television news operations on the issues that impact the newsroom.

Radio Television News Directors
1025 Thomas Jefferson St, 7th Floor, Washington, DC 20007-5214
202-625-3500; *Fax:* 202-223-4007
www.rtnda.org
barbarac@rtnda.org
Barbara Cochran, President
Founded: 1946 *Number of Members:* 3000+ *Mission:* Largest professional organization exclusively serving the electronic news profession. Dedicated to setting standards for newsgathering and reporting. Represents electronicjournalists in radion, television and all digital media, as well as journalism educators and students.

Radio-Television Correspondents' Association
S-325, U.S. Capitol, Washington, DC 20510
(202) 224-6421; *Fax:* (202) 224-4882
www.rtcacaphill.org
lisa.desjardins@cnn.com
Frank Thorp, Chairman
Fred Haberstick, Vice Chair
The Radio-Television Correspondents Association is the major organization of broadcast journalists who report on the U.S. Congress in Washington, D.C. comprised of radio and television broadcasters from every part of the world. Its aim is tostrive to protect the rights and privileges of radio and television news reporters who are assigned to bring the news of the United States House of Representatives and the U.S. Senate to viewers and listeners across the globe, and assist in every waypossible to maintain the high standards of reporting news by its members.
Directors:
Jerry Bodlander, Bob Fuss, Edward O'Keefe, Dave McConnell, Richard Tillery & David Welna

Recording Industry Association of America Inc. (RIAA)
1025 F ST N.W., 10th Floor, Washington, DC 20004
(202) 775-0101; *Fax:* (202) 775-7253
www.riaa.com
Cary Sherman, President & CEO
Mitch Glazier, Senior Executive Vice President
Steven M. Marks, Chief, Digital Business and General Counsel
RIAA participates in technical standards work where creating a voluntary specification increases consumer confidence and reduces costs for its members. Some technical standards which RIAA has created or worked on include:

Royal Television Society, North America Inc.
Mailing Address: PO Box 870501, Arizona State University, Tempe, AZ 85287-0501
Second Address: 3 Dorset Rise, London, EC4Y 8EN
(480) 965-7661, (020) 7822-2810; *Fax:* (480) 965-1371, (020)7822-2811
www.rts.org.uk
info@rts.org.uk

Satellite Broadcasting & Communications Association
1100 17th St NW, Suite 1150, Washington, DC 20036
202-349-3620; *Fax:* 202-349-3621
www.sbca.com
info@sbca.org
Joseph Widoff, Executive Director
Benjamin Rowan, Education Manager
Joy O'Brien, Director Government Affairs
Pat Andrews, Senior VP
Brian Lynch, Director Program Development
Founded: 1986 *Number of Members:* 1000 *Mission:* National trade organization representing all segments of the satellite consumer services industry. The association is committed to expanding the utilization of satellitetechnology for the delivery of video, data, voice, interactive and broadband services.

Society for Features Journalism
1729 Grand Blvd, Kansas City, MO 64108
816-234-4394
featuresjournalism.org
Kathy Lu, President
Jim Haag, First Vice President
Margaret Myers, Second Vice President
Stephanie Allmon Merry, Secretary-Treasurer
Mission: An organization of editors dedicated to the quality of features in newspapers and the craft of feature writing.

Society for News Design
1130 Ten Rod Rd, Suite D-202, North Kingstown, RI 02852-4168
401-294-5233; *Fax:* 401-294-5238
www.snd.org
snd@snd.org
Scott Goldman, President
Gayle Grin, Vice President
Matt Mansfield, Secretary/Treasurer
Elise Burroughs, Executive Director
Founded: 1979 *Number of Members:* 2600 *Mission:* An international professional organization that encourage high standards of journalism through design. An international forum and resource for all those interested in newsdesign, SND works to recognize excellence and strengthen visual journalism as a profession.

Society of American Business Editors and Writers
ASU, Walter Cronkite School of Journalism, 555 North Central Ave, Suite 416, Phoenix, AZ 85004-1248
602-496-7862
www.sabew.org
sabew@sabew.org
Carrie Paden, Executive Director
Rex Seline, VP
Jon Lansner, Secretary/Treasurer
Brant Houston, Executive Director
Founded: 1964 *Number of Members:* 3200 *Mission:* Members are financial and economic news writers and editors for print and broadcast outlets.

Society of Broadcast Engineers
9102 N Meridian St, Suite 150, Indianapolis, IN 46260-1896
317-846-9000; *Fax:* 317-846-9120
www.sbe.org
mclappe@sbe.org
John Poray, Executive Director
Vincent A Lopez, VP
Founded: 1964 *Number of Members:* 5500 *Mission:* SBE provides members with the opportunity to network and share ideas and information in keeping current with the ongoing changes within the industry. Members can attend annualconferences and expositions, have access to educational opportunities and obtain professional certification.

Society of Cable Telecommunications Engineers Inc.
140 Philips Rd., Exton, PA 19341-1318
(610) 363-6888; *Fax:* (610) 363-5898
www.scte.org
scte@scte.org
Mark Dzuban, President & CEO
Lindsay Johnston, Senior Vice President, Operations
Kim Cooney, Executive Assistant to the President
Robin Fenton, Director, Chapter Support
Cathy Karch, Senior Director, Accounting
Heather Gosciniak,Director, Marketing and Business Development
Denise Beck, Manager, Facilities
Bill Schankel, Vice President, Marketing
Professional membership assn offering information, professional dev resources, standards to cable telecommunications engineers & other professional.
Directors:
Joel E. Welch, Thomas Russell & Joan Hagelin

The Society of Environmental Journalists
1629 K Street, NW, Suite 300, Washington, DC 20006
202-558-2300
www.sej.org
sej@sej.org
Beth Parke, Co-Executive Director
Chris Brugger, Co-Executive Director/Director, Awards & Programs
Lisa Cosgriff, Records & Administrative Manager
Mission: Mission is to strengthen the quality. reach and viability of journalism across all media to advance public understanding of environmental issues.

Society of Environmental Journalists(SEJ)
PO Box 2492, Jenkintown, PA 19046
215-884-8174; *Fax:* 215-884-8175
www.sej.org
bparke@sej.org
Beth Parke, Executive Director
Tim Wheeler, President
Linda Knouse, Records Manager
Jeanne Scanlon, Assistant
Founded: 1990 *Mission:* To advance public understanding of environmental issues by improving the quality, accuracy, and visibility of environmental reporting. To strengthenthe quality, reach and viability of journalism across allmedia to advance public understanding of environmental issues.

Society of Motion Picture & Television Engineers(SMPTE)
3 Barker Ave, 5th Floor, White Plains, NY 10601-1509
914-761-1100; *Fax:* 914-761-3115
www.smpte.org
contact through website
Barbara Lange, Executive Director
June M. Sobrito, Executive Assistant
Peter Symes, Engineering Director
Founded: 1916 *Number of Members:* 6000 *Mission:* More than 10,000 members are spread throughout 85 countries. Also, over 250 corporate members belong to SMPTE, allowing networking and contacts to occur on a larger scale.Touching on every discipline, our members include engineers, technical directors, cameramen, editors, technicians, manufacturers educators, and consultants.

Society of Professional Journalists
3909 N Meridian Street, Indianapolis, IN 46208
317-927-8000; *Fax:* 317-920-4789
www.spj.org
webmaster@spj.org
Gordon McKerral, President
David E Carlson, Secretary/Treasurer
James Highland, VP
Founded: 1909 *Number of Members:* 9000 *Mission:* Broad-based journalism organization, dedicated to encouraging the free practice of journalism and stimulating high standards of ethical behavior.12 regional directors, national officials elected annually, two students reps, two directors at-large and two campus advisors at-large

Society of Satellite Professionals International
New York Information Technology Center, 250 Parke Ave, 7th Floor, New York, NY 10004-2501

212-809-5199; *Fax:* 212-825-0075
www.sspi.org
Robert Bell, Executive Director
Louis Zacharilla, Director Development
Founded: 1983 *Number of Members:* 1700 *Mission:* Members are individuals in the fields of businesss, education, entertainment, media, science and industry who share common interests in satellite technology.

Society of Telecommunications Consultants
13275 State Highway 89, PO Box 70, Old Station, CA 96071
530-335-7313; *Fax:* 530-335-7360
Cathy Cimaglia, Administrative Manager
Founded: 1976 *Number of Members:* 180 *Mission:* The STC is an international organization of independent telecommunications and information technology consultants who serve clients in business and government

The Songwriters Guild of America
5120 Virginia Way, Suite C22, Brentwood, TN 37027
(615) 742-9945; *Fax:* (615) 630-7501
www.songwritersguild.com
corporate@songwritersguild.com
Rick Carnes, President
6430 Sunset Blvd, Hollywood, CA 90028-7901
(213) 462-1108
Aaron Meza, Rgnl Dir
1222 16th Ave. St, Suite 25, Nashville, TN
(615) 329-1782
Rondi Regan, Rgnl Dir
6430 Sunset Blvd., Los Angeles, CA 90028-7901

Special Industrial Radio Service
8484 Westpark Drive, # 630, Mc Lean, VA 22102-3590
703-528-5115
Mark Crosby, President/CEO
Founded: 1953 *Number of Members:* 15 *Mission:* Provides a license renewal reminder service. Maintains liaison with major radio manufacturers and mediates problems between licensees.

Statenets National Association of State Radio Networks Inc.
17911 Harwood Avenue, Homewood, IL 60430
708-799-6676; *Fax:* 708-799-6698
www.statenets.com
tdobrez@statenets.com
Tom Dobrez, Executive Director
Sharon Kitchell, Deputy Director
Mission: Works with hundreds of regional and national marketers and political campaigns solve marketing challenges.

Syndicated Network Television Association
One Penn Plaza, Suite 5310, New York, NY 10119
212-259-3740; *Fax:* 212-259-3770
www.snta.com
Mitch Burg, President
Jordan Harris, Director, Marketing
Hadassa Gerber, Director. Research
Mission: Communicates to advertisers, their agencies and media planners and buyers the benefits of syndication, from the wide range of programming choices to their high ratings and national reach, and the reliability and costeffectiveness of advertising in syndicated programming.

Telecommunications Industry Association
1320 N. Courthouse Rd., Suite 200, Arlington, VA 22201
(703) 907-7700; *Fax:* (703) 907-7727
www.tiaonline.org
jjacobs@tiaonline.org
Thomas Stanton, Chairman
Grant Seiffert, President
Mary Piper Waters, Senior Director of Operations
Cheryl Blum, Vice President
Danielle Coffey, Vice President- Government Affairs
John Jacobs, Senior Vice President-Membership,Marketing & Busi
Andrew Kurtzman, Vice President and Corporate Counsel
Taly Walsh, Vice President, Sustainability, Intelligence and N
David Gray, Associate, Government Affairs
The Telecommunications Industry Association (TIA) is the leading trade association representing the global information and communications technology (ICT) industries through standards development, policy initiatives, business opportunitiesand networking, market intelligence, and worldwide environmental regulatory compliance.
Directors:
Grant Seiffert, Bill Belt, John Derr, Derek Khlopin, Jason Leuck, Anna Amselle, Henry Wieland, Maryann Lesso, David Smith, Dan Bart & Henry Cuschieri

USITO
Rm. 332, 3/f Lido Office Tower, Lido Place, Jichang Rd., Jiang Tai Rd., Beijing 100004, China
(8610) 6430-1368/69/70/71/72; *Fax:* (8610) 6430-1367
www.usito.org
usito@usito.org
Anne Stevenson-Yang, Mgng Dir

Telecommunications Research and Action Center (TRAC)
PO Box 27279, Washington, DC 20005
(202) 263-2950; *Fax:* (202) 263-2960
www.trac.org
trac@trac.org

Television Bureau of Advertising
3 E 54th St, Suite 1000, New York, NY 10022-3139
212-486-1111; *Fax:* 212-935-5631
www.tvb.org
info@tvb.org
Steve Lanzano, President
Abby Auerbach, Executive VP/CMO
Scott Roskowski, SVP/Business Development
Stacey Lynn Schulman, SVP/Research
Founded: 1954 *Number of Members:* 600 *Mission:* Not-for-profit trade association of America's broadcast television industry. TVB provides a diverse variety of tools and resources to support its members and to help advertisersmake the best use of local television.

Television Bureau of Canada
160 Bloor St. E, Suite 1005, Toronto, ON M4W 1B9 Canada
(416) 923-8813; *Fax:* (416) 413-3879
www.tvb.ca
tvb@tvb.ca
Errol Da-Re, Chairman
Theresa Treutler, President & CEO
Monica Korry, Executive Assistant to the President
Kristene Howell, Office Assistant & Events/Telecaster Support
Sylvia Augaitis, Senior Communications Officer
DuncanRobertson, Director of Media Insights & Research
Alan Dark, Vice-Chairman
Darryl Coburn, Secretary
TVB of Canada Inc. is primarily a Resource Centre for our members - Canadian television stations, networks, specialty services and their sales representatives. TVB has over 150 members.

Television Critics Association
825 East Douglas Avenue, Witchita, KS 67202
316-268-6394; *Fax:* 316-288-6627
www.tvcritics.org
info@tvcritics.org
Candy Havens, President
Scott Pierce, Vice President
Amber Dowling, Secretary
Brian Gianelli, Treasurer
Mission: Represents more than 220 journalists writing about television for print and online outlets.

Television Operators Caucus
1176 K Street NW, 9th Floor, Washington, DC 20006
202-719-7090; *Fax:* 202-719-7548
Margita White, President
Mission: Non-profit group of memebers that support television issues and its impacts on the world today.

Think TV (Television Bureau of Canada-TVB)
160 Bloor Street East, Suite 1005, Toronto, ON M4W 1B9
416-923-8813; *Fax:* 416-413-3879
www.thinktv.ca
info@thinktv.ca
Catherine Macleod, President & CEO
Laura Baehr, VP, Marketing
Kathy Gardner, VP, Media Insights
Mission: TVB markets the benefits and effectiveness of the TV medium in all its forms to advertisers and agencies. TVB collects, interprets, develops, identifies, and communicates information and data to be used.

Trade Promotion Management Association
51 Cragwood Road, Suite 200, South Plainfield, NJ 07080
646-442-3703; *Fax:* 908-755-7451
www.tpmaww.com
Bob Houk, Executive Director
Susan Haupt, Operations Director
Founded: 1989 *Number of Members:* 90 *Mission:* Dedicated specifically to the practice of trade promotion marketing in all its forms. Serve as a resource for information and education on trade promotion programs as well asprovides strategies for developing, implementing and evaluating such programs.

Traffic Audit Bureau for Media Measurement
271 Madison Ave, Suite 1504, New York, NY 10016-1012
212-972-8075; *Fax:* 212-972-8928
www.tabonline.com
inquiry@tabonline.com
Joseph Philport, President
Sean McCarthy, VP Information Technology
Founded: 1933 *Number of Members:* 450 *Mission:* Acts as an independent third party provider of standardized and valid circulation measures for out of home media.

U.S. Conference of Catholic Bishops, Dept. of Communications
3211 4th St. N.E., Washington, DC 20017-1194
(202) 541-3000; *Fax:* (202) 541-3173
www.usccb.org
Joseph E. Kurtz, President
Daniel N. DiNardo, Vice President
Kevin J. Farrell, Treasurer
J. Peter Sartain, Secretary
To make the New Evangelization a reality is to become pilgrims on a journey or pilgrimage with Jesus Christ- much like the journey of Jesus meeting the disciples along the road to Emmaus. The journey or pilgrimage includes moments for adeepening of our faith, increasing our participation in the sacramental life of the Church, and leads finally to our destination of being Christian witnesses.

United Telecom Council
1901 Pennsylvania Ave Nw, 5th Floor, Washington, DC 20006-3406
202-872-0030; *Fax:* 202-872-1331
www.utc.org
William R Moroney, President/CEO
Jill Lyon, VP and General Counsel
Founded: 1948 *Number of Members:* 1500 *Mission:* Represents organizations using telecommunications in their operations before various federal and state legislative and regulatory agencies, particularly the FCC

Veteran Wireless Operators Association Inc.
PO Box 1003, Peck Slip, New York, NY 10272-1003
www.vwoa.org
Directors:
Richard T. Kenney & D. I. Temple

Veterans Bedside Network
Div/DBA: (The Veterans Hospital Radio & TV Guild.)
10 Fiske Pl., Rm. 328, Mount Vernon, NY 10550
(914) 699-6069; *Fax:* (914) 667-0405
www.veteransbedsidenetwork.org
contact@veteransbedsidenetwork.org
VBN is a 58-year-old 501(c)(3) not for profit organization of dedicated volunteers who conduct a program of therapeutic activities in veterans hospitals. If you believe our hospitalized veterans, men and women who defended our freedom,deserve your support please read more about how the VBN serves them.

Video Advertising Bureau (VAB)
830 3rd Avenue, 2nd Floor, New York, NY 10022 USA
(212) 508-1200; *Fax:* (212) 832-3268
www.thevab.com
evelyns@thevab.com
Sean Cunningham, President/CEO
Jim Spears, CFO/ SVP, Finance & Operations
Cynthia Perkins-Roberts, VP, Multicultural Marketing & Sales Development
Danielle DeLauro, Executive VP
Evelyn Skurkovich, VP, Strategic Research &Insights
Laura Valentin, Controller & Office Manager
VAB's member organizations include virtually all of the national and regional ad-supported cable networks; system operators and interconnects representing more than 90 percent of all U.S. cable subscribers; and suppliers to the cableadvertising business. All of these organizations actively work together through VAB to further increase awareness of the power of video as an advertising medium; and to make multiscreen video content an increasingly effective marketing environmentfor advertisers throughout the U.S.-nationally, regionally and locally.

WGBH Educational Foundation
One Guest Street, Boston, MA 2135
617-300-5400
www.wgbh.org
Jonathan Abbott, President/CEO
Benjamin Godley, Executive Vice President and Chief
David Bernstein, VP/Gneral Manager
Melinda Braithwate, VP for Human Resources
Margaret Drain, VP for National Programming

Founded: 1836 *Mission:* Make knowledge and the creative life of the arts, sciences, and humanities available to the widest possible public

Wireless Communications Association International, Inc.
1400 16th Street, NW, Suite 600, Washington, DC 20036
(202) 736-3200; *Fax:* (202) 785-0721
www.wcai.com
Dan Mead, Chairman
Patrick Riordan, Chairman Emeritus
Ronald Smith, Vice Chairman
Bret Comolli, Treasurer
Angel Ruiz, Secretary
CTIA-The Wireless Associationr is an international nonprofit membership organization that has represented the wireless communications industry since 1984. Membership in the association includes wireless carriers and their suppliers, as wellas providers and manufacturers of wireless data services and products.
Directors:
John T. von Harz III, William Andrle Jr., T. Lauriston Hardin III, Chris Farnworth & Patrick J. Gossman III

Women in Cable & Telecommunications
2000 K Street, NW, Suite 350, Washington, DC 20006
(202) 827-4794; *Fax:* (202)450-5596
www.wict.org
membership@wict.org
Mary Meduski, Chairman
Maria E. Brennan, CAE, President & CEO
Kathy Payne, Immediate Past Chair
Gail MacKinnon, Treasurer
Marva Johnson, Chapter Development Chair
Martha Soehren, Strategic Planning Committee Chair
Marc Aldrich,Director-At-Large
Monica Alexander, Director-At-Large
Developing women leaders is our mission. As the oldest and largest organization serving women professionals in cable and telecommunications, Women in Cable Telecommunications (WICT) is at the forefront of an industry undergoing constantchange. Since its founding in 1979, WICT has remained steadfast in its resolve to advance the position and influence of women through proven leadership programs and services at both the national and local level.
Directors:
Mary Busby, Robin Burke Zahory, Lisa McBee & Lisa Vega

Women In Film
6100 Wilshire Blvd, Suite 710, Los Angeles, CA 90048
(323) 935-2211; *Fax:* (323) 935-2212
www.wif.org
info@wif.org
Hannah Minghella, Chair
Cathy Schulman, President
Gayle Nachlis, Executive Director
David Kay, Controller
Pandora Kan, PSA/Production Manager
Maikiko James, Executive Assistant
Juliann Lee, Foundation Manager
Bill Harris, ChiefFinancial Officer

World Broadcasting Unions (WBU)
Mailing Address: PO Box 500, Stn. A, Rm. 6C 300, Toronto, ON M5W 1E6 Canada
Second Address: 205 Wellington Street West, Suite 6C300, Toronto, ON M5V 3G7
(416) 598-9877; *Fax:* (416) 598-9774
www.worldbroadcastingunions.org
Michael McEwen, Head-WBU Secretariat
Anh Ngo, Director-Administration
Jason Paris, Senior Coordinator
Vineet Mathur, IT /web Administrator
Roxanne Riess, Executive Assistant
Chew Yoong Lian, Finance Officer
The World Broadcasting Unions (WBU) is the coordinating body for broadcasting unions who represent broadcaster networks across the globe. It was established in 1992 as a coordinating body at the international broadcasting level. Since then,the WBU has provided global solutions on key issues for its member unions. The North American Broadcasters Association (NABA) acts as secretariat for the WBU.

World Teleport Association
55 Broad St., 14th Fl., New York, NY 10004
(212) 825-0218; *Fax:* (212) 825-0075
www.worldteleport.org
wta@worldteleport.org
M. Brett Belinsky, Chairman
Robert Kubbernus, CEO
Roger Franklin, President & CEO
Mark Rathert, General Manager, Ground Operations
Richard Hadsall, CTO
Kian Soon Lim, Head, Satellite, Business Group
Kurt Riegelman, Senior VicePresident, Global Sales
Scott Sprague, CCO
James Trevelyan, Sales Director
Robert Bell, Executive Director
Since 1985, the World Teleport Association (WTA) has been the only trade association that focuses on the business of satellite communications from the ground up. At the core of its membership are the world's most innovative operators ofteleports, from independents to multinationals, niche service providers to global hybrid carriers.
Directors:
Chris Russell, David Sprechman, Gary Hatch, Oliver Badard, Nick Thompson, Yoshihiro Yohoyama & tohm Tahahasin

State & Regional Broadcast Associations

Advertising Women of New York
25 W 45th St, Suite 1001, New York, NY 10036-4910
212-221-7969; *Fax:* 212-221-8296
www.awny.org
awny@awny.org
Liz Schroeder, Executive Director
Mary Morgan, President
Founded: 1912 *Number of Members:* 1300 *Mission:* AWNY is a professional organization comrising over 1,300 women and men in the advertising/communications industry. Its man focus is to provide a forum foe personal andfrofessional grouth; to serve as an catalyst for the advancement of women in the communications field; and to promote and support philanthropic endeavors through th AWNY foundation.

Alabama Broadcasters Association
2180 Pkwy. Lake Dr., Hoover, AL 35244
(205) 982-5001, (800) 211-5189; *Fax:* (205) 982-0015
www.al-ba.com
nmartin@bigriverbroadcasting.com
Nick Martin, Chairman
Sharon Tinsley, President
Rick Peters, Vice Chairman
Stan Pylan, Secretary/Treasurer
Al Stroh, Director
Lesa Rice, Business Manager
Larry Wilkins, Contract Engineer
Scott Johnson, Legal Counsel
The Alabama Broadcasters Association is the official voice of the broadcasting industry in Alabama. We are dedicated to protecting and enhancing broadcasting, and promoting the professional status of our members.

Alaska Broadcasters Association
700 W 41st Street, Suite 102, Anchorage, AK 99503
907-258-2424; *Fax:* 907-258-2414
www.alaskabroadcaster.org
akba@gci.net
Laurie Prax, President
Founded: 1964 *Mission:* To provide assistance, which enables members to serve their communities of license through education, representation and advocacy.

Arizona Broadcasters Association
426 N. 44th St., Suite 310, Phoenix, AZ 85008
(602) 252-4833; *Fax:* (602) 252-5265
www.azbroadcasters.org
info@azbroadcasters.org
Rich Howe, Chairman
Art Brooks, President/CEO
Michael Mallace, Vice Chairman
Debbie Bush, Secretary/Treasurer
Anita Helt, Board of Director
Stan Pierce, Board of director
Doug Martin, Board of director
Bill Shaw, Board ofdirector
The Arizona Broadcasters Association (ABA) is a 501-c(6) non-profit corporation founded in 1952. Membership includes radio stations, television stations and associate members. The ABA is managed by a full time President/CEO and ExecutiveAssistant and governed by a 10 member board of directors. The ABA is a member of the National Alliance of State Broadcast Associations and supports the programs of the National Association of Broadcasters.

Arkansas Broadcasters Association
2024 Arkansas Valley Dr., Suite 403, Little Rock, AR 72212 US
(501) 227-7564, (800) 844-3216; *Fax:* (501) 223-9798
www.arkbroadcasters.org
mail@arkbroadcasters.org
Steve Jonsson, President
Doug Krile, Executive Director
Steve Jonsson, Secretary-Treasurer
Dina Mason, Director-District 1
Bradford Caldwell, Director-District 1
Richard Nickols, Director-District 2
Rich Moellers,Director-District 3
Helen Aregood, Director-District 4

California Broadcasters Association
915 L St., Suite 1150, Sacramento, CA 95814
(916) 444-2237; *Fax:* (916) 444-2043
www.cabroadcasters.org
jberry@yourcba.com
Stan Statham, President/CEO
Directors:
Kathy Baker, chmn

Colorado Broadcasters Association
333 West Hampden Avenue, Suite 400, Englewood, CO 80110
(720) 536-5427; *Fax:* (720) 536-5259
www.coloradobroadcasters.org
cobroadcasters@earthlink.net
Wayne Johnson, Chairman
Justin Sasso, President/CEO
Evan Pappas, Vice Chair
Don Daboub, Secretary/Treasurer
Sarah Weber, Administrative Assistant
Pat Connor, Director
Mark Cornetta, Director
Byron Grandy, Director
Over the years the CBA has provided thousands of dollars for college scholarships, worked to provide public media access to the courts and fought to open public records. Among its many activities the CBA is probably best known for its annual"Awards Of Excellence," which honor broadcasters' service to their communities.
Directors:
Wick Rowland, sec/treas

Connecticut Broadcasters Association
Mailing Address: 90 South Park St., Willimantic, CT 6226
Second Address: PO Box 1785, Avon, CT 06001
(860) 633-5031, (860) 633-5031; *Fax:* (860) 456-5688, (860) 456-5688
www.ctba.org
mryan@ctba.org
Klarn DePalma, Chair
Michael Ryan, President
Kathy Browne, First Vice Chair
Steve Rabb, Second Vice Chair
Steve Honeycomb, Secretary
Andy Russell, Treasurer
Mike Rice, Vice President
Eric Kemmler, General Counsel/CorporateCompliance Officer
The Connecticut Broadcasters Association represents Connecticut's commercial, public, religious, college, and high school radio and TV stations. Members include more than 115 stations, as well as associates and individuals.

Festival of Nouveau Cinema Montreal
3805 Blvd. Saint-Lavrent, Montreal, QC H2W 7X9 Canada
(514) 282-0004; *Fax:* (514) 282-6664
www.nouveaucinema.ca
info@nouveaucinema.ca
Nicolas Girard Deltruc, Executive Director
Claude Chamberlan, Director of Programming
Katayoun Dibamehr, Financial and Institutional Relations Manager
Mackenson Rony, Head Accountant
Olivier Borzeix, Administrative Assistant

Florida Association of Broadcasters
201 S. Monroe St., Suite 201, Tallahassee, FL 32301 US
(850) 681-6444, (800) 825-5322; *Fax:* (850) 222-3957
www.fab.org
info@fab.org
Sherri Griswold, Chairman
Luis Fernandez-Rocha, Chariman-Elect
C. Patrick Roberts, President & CEO
Lindsay Varn, Vice President
Heather Smith, Director of Communications
Susan Larkin, Vice Chairman Radio
Mike Pumo, Vice ChairmanTV
Adib Eden, Vice Chairman Hispanic
Brooke Gray, Administrative Assistant

Georgia Association of Broadcasters Inc.
8046 Roswell Road, Suite 100A, Atlanta, GA 30350
(770) 395-7200; *Fax:* (770) 395-7235
www.gab.org
admin@gab.org

Drew Rhodes, Chairman
Bob Houghton, President
Tim Davies, Vice Chair Radio
John Deushane, Vice Chair TV
John Weatherfor, Secretary
Joseph Brannan, Treasurer
George Reed, Associates Chairmen
Paul Beliveau, Associates Chairmen

The Georgia Association of Broadcasters is the trade association representing the interests of Georgia's over-the-air radio and television licensees who reach over 90 percent of Georgia's population every week. GAB provides technical,regulatory and advocacy support to our members as well as offering continuing professional enrichment opportunities designed to keep Georgia broadcasters at the forefront of serving their communities. GAB and our member broadcasters also work withGeorgia's Department of Homeland Security and the National Weather Service via the Emergency Alert System to provide accurate and timely information before, during, and after emergencies and severe weather.

Idaho State Broadcasters Association
1674 W. Hill Rd, Suite 3, Boise, ID 83702
(208) 345-3072; *Fax:* (208) 343-8046
isba@qwestoffice.net
Brian Paul Lubanski, Chairman
Connie Searles, President/ CEO
Suzie Johnson, Administrative Assistant
Don Morin, Vice-Chairman
Marie McGlynn-Peach, Secretary / Treasurer
Jeff Nielsen, Associate Representative
Marie McGlynn-Peach,TV Representative
Ron Pisaneschi, PBS Liaison

Idaho's broadcasters are a vital part of every community in Idaho. Providing a free service to everyone is just the beginning. Local TV and radio stations donate immense resources - on and off air - to raise money for charities and helptheir neighbors.

Illinois Broadcasters Association
200 Missouri Ave., Carterville, IL 62918
(618) 985-5555; *Fax:* (618) 985-6070
www.ilba.org
iba@ilba.org
Sarah Hautala, Chairman
Dennis Lyle, President/CEO
Coby Cooper, Chairman Elect
Debra Gray, Marketing Director
Frank Whittaker, Vice-Chair TV
Doug Levy, Vice-Chair Radio
Drew Horowitz, Treasurer
Donna Bake, Director

IBA is the leading advocate for the broadcast industry in Illinois and is engaged in shaping public policy to create a positive legislative and regulatory environment for its members.

Indiana Broadcasters Association Inc.
14074 Trade Center Drive, Suite 141, Fishers, IN 46038
(317) 770-0970, (800) 342-6276; *Fax:* (317) 770-0972
www.indianabroadcasters.org
iba@indianabroadcasters.org
Chuck Williams, Chairman
Dr. Joe Misiewicz, President/CEO
Chuck Williams, Chairman Elect
Dave Crooks, Vice Chair - Radio
Alan Riebe, Vice Chair Television
Charlie Morgan, Secretary/Treasurer
John O'Brien, AssistantSecretary/Treasurer
Dan Byron, Legal Counsel

The Indiana Broadcasters Association (IBA) enters its 65th year representing the radio and television broadcasters of Indiana. Please browse the IBA web site and learn how Indiana Broadcasters are making a difference in our communities andmore. If your station or you are a dues paying member of IBA please click on 'REGISTER' in upper right and CREATE YOUR OWN USERNAME AND PASSWORD THEN SUBMIT. The IBA staff will approve or deny your request based on membership.

Iowa Broadcasters Association
PO Box 71186, Des Moines, IA 50325
(515) 224-7237; *Fax:* (515) 224-6560
www.iowabroadcasters.com
iowaiba@dwx.com
Jim Coloff, President
Sue Toma, Executive Director
Kevin Schrader, Vice President
Greg List, Treasurer
Bill Wells, Directors
Gene LaSuer, General Counsel

Kansas Association of Broadcasters
214 S.W. 6th St., # 300, Topeka, KS 66603
(785) 235-1307; *Fax:* (785) 233-3052
www.kab.net
info@kab.net
Jim Ogle, Chairman
Kent Cornish, President/Executive Director
Mark Trotman, Secretary-Treasurer
Bruce Dierking, Chair-Elect
Janet Campbell, Director
Ron Thomas, Director
Larry Calvery, Director
Mark Sullivan, Director

The mission of the Kansas Association of Broadcasters is to provide professional lobbying and governmental representation, efficient communication and effective recruiting, education and training for Kansas broadcasters, and to promote freeover-the-air broadcasting for the purpose of enhancing the success of Kansas broadcasters and helping them better serve the people of Kansas.

Kentucky Broadcasters Association
101 Enterprise Dr., Frankfort, KY 40601
(502) 682-2896 , (888) 843-5221
www.kba.org
kba@kba.org
Rick McCue, Chairman
Gary R. White, President/CEO
Chris Winkle, Chairman-Elect
Jim Moore, Radio Director, District 1
Bob Kelley, Radio Director, District 2
Bill Gentry, Radio Director, District 3
Ronna Corrente, TelevisionDirector
David Brinkley, Public Television Director

The Kentucky Broadcasters Association (KBA) unites public and commercial radio and television stations across the Commonwealth of Kentucky.
The purpose of the Kentucky Broadcasters Association is to represent and further the interest ofbroadcasters, communicate relevant information to broadcasters through meetings and publications, and provide educational services through conventions, workshops, or other appropriate means in order to better serve the public.

Louisiana Association of Broadcasters
660 Florida St., Baton Rouge, LA 70801
(225) 267-4522; *Fax:* (225) 267-4329
www.broadcasters.org
lab@broadcasters.org
Sandy Breland, Chairman
Polly Prince Johnson, President/CEO
Flynn Foster, Chairman Elect
Andrew D. Shenkan, TV Vice Chairman
Charlie Sporano, Radio Vice Chairman
Mike Grimsley, Secretary/Treasurer
Angelice F. Tyson, Manager ofBusiness Development
Suzette Daniel, Administrative Assistant

Founded in 1948, the Louisiana Association of Broadcasters is the only statewide organization dedicated, solely, to promoting and protecting the interests of Louisiana's Broadcast Industry. Our goal is to provide a stable governmental andcommunity environment in which Louisiana Radio and Television Stations may continue to fulfill the needs and desires of their listening and viewing audiences. Membership is open to Radio and Television stations licensed to and/or doing business inLouisiana. Business and Organizations with an interest in the broadcast industry are eligible for associate membership.

Maine Association of Broadcasters
69 Sewall St., Augusta, ME 04330
(207) 623-3870, (800) 664-6221; *Fax:* (207) 621-0585 (call first)
www.mab.org
info@mab.org
Michael Grant, Chairman
Suzanne Goucher, President/CEO
Irwin Gratz, First Vice Chair/Chair-Elect
Mark Nason, Second Vice Chair
Jonathan Shields, Secretary-Treasure
Heidi Shepard, Business Manager
Morgan Grumbach, Director
MikeMarshall, Director

The Maine Association of Broadcasters was formed in 1947 to cultivate a friendly spirit of cooperation in matters of common interest among Maine broadcasters.

Maryland-District of Columbia-Delaware Broadcasters Association
Mailing Address: 150 Fayetteville Street, Suite 1270, Raleigh, NC 27601
Second Address: PO Box 342, Raleigh, NC 27602
(410) 653-4122, (919) 839-0304, (888) FON-MDCD; *Fax:* (919) 834-8880
www.mdcd.com
info@mdcdbroadcasters.org
Dan Joerres, Chairman
Alan Sawyer, Vice Chairman
Jim Watkins, Secretary
Frank Jazzo, Legal Counsel
Craig Jahelka, Treasurer
Bob Philips, Director
Ed Kiernan, Director

The Maryland, DC, Delaware Broadcasters Association (MDCD) unites public and commercial radio and television across Maryland, DC, and Delaware. The main purpose of MDCD is to represent and further the interests of broadcasters, communicaterelevant information to broadcasters through meetings and publications, and provide educational services through webinars, workshops, or other appropriate means in order to better serve the public.

Massachusetts Broadcasters Association Inc.
43 Riverside Ave, PMB 401, Medford, MA 02155
(800) 471-1875; *Fax:* (800) 471-1876
www.massbroadcasters.org
info@massbroadcasters.org
Joe Flynn, Chairman
Alex Von Lichtenberg, Vice Chair, TV
Bill Macek, Vice Chair, Radio
Craig Swimm, Secretary
Merril Leferman, Treasurer
Jordan Walton, Executive Director
Bill Fine, Director

Founded in 1954, the Massachusetts Broadcasters Association (MBA) is a voluntary trade association representing over 200 over-the-air radio and television broadcasters in the Commonwealth of Massachusetts.

Michigan Association of Broadcasters
819 N. Washington Ave., Lansing, MI 48906-5815
(517) 484-7444, (800) 968-7622; *Fax:* (517) 484-5810
www.michmab.com
mab@michmab.com
Jill Saarela, Chairman
Karole L. White, President/CEO
Chris Warren, Vice-Chairman/Chairman-Elect
Ed Fernandez, Secretary/Treasurer
Tim Feagan, Immediate Past Chairman
Debbie Kenyon, At-Large Director
Tom Hahn, ExecutiveVice-President/Finance
Jennifer Preslar, Vice President, Programs

The Michigan Association of Broadcasters promotes the well being, cooperation, and prosperity of the owners, managers, employees, and specialists engaged in the business of broadcasting by helping members better serve their community,audience, advertisers, and staff through providing solutions to their problems and satisfying their needs.ski, Mario Iacbelli, Bart Brandmiller, Tom Mogush. Honorary Board Members: Ed Christian, Alan Frank, Bruce Goldsen. Legal/Legislative Counsel:Rob Elhenicky, John J. Ronayne III.

Minnesota Broadcasters Association
3033 Excelsior Blvd., Suite 440, Minneapolis, MN 55416
(612) 926-8123; *Fax:* (612) 926-9761
www.minnesotabroadcasters.com
jdubois@minnesotabroadcasters.com
Jim du Bois, President/CEO
Linda Lasere, Executive Assistant/Office Manager

The Minnesota Broadcasters Association (MBA) is a common voice that promotes and protects Minnesota broadcasting by representing radio and television broadcasters from across the state. We provide member stations with a wide variety ofservices, including lobbying at the state and federal levels, providing legal counsel, coordinating professional development seminars and producing high quality public affairs radio and TV programs..

Mississippi Association of Broadcasters
855 S. Pear Orchard Rd., Suite 403, Ridgeland, MS 39157
(601) 957-9121; *Fax:* (601) 957-9175
www.msbroadcasters.org
info@msbroadcasters.org
Bob Romine, Chairman
Scott Bebout, Vice Chairman
Margaret Perkins, Chair Elect
Larry Shirley, Immediate Past Chairman/Legislative Chairman
Bobby Edwards, Secretary/Treasurer
Reggie Bates, Radio Board Member
Ronnie Geiger, RadioBoard Member

The Mississippi Association of Broadcasters (MAB) is a nonprofit trade association for radio and television stations in Mississippi. Its purpose is to assist members with broadcast industry and general business related challenges. MABmembers are offered educational seminars, legal hotlines, lobbying representation, updates on industry trends, and opportunities to network with other broadcasters.

Missouri Broadcasters Association

1025 Northeast Dr., Jefferson City, MO 65109
(573) 636-6692; *Fax:* (573) 634-8258
www.mbaweb.org
dhicks@mbaweb.org

Danny Thomas, Chairman
Kevin Burge, Operations Manager
Mark Gordon, President/CEO
Victoria Sabatino, Business Manager
Dave Clemons, General Sales Manager
Jeff Elliott, News Director
Jerry Tibbitts, Chief Engineer
Donald J.Hicks, President Emeritus
Frank Forgey, Director of MO-PEP
Terry Harper, MO-PEP Coordinator
John Kijowski, Chairmain-Elect
Rick Lambert, Treasurer
John Beck Jr., District I - Radio

Directors: Rick McCoy, Dave Alpert, Gary Exline, Mike Smythe, Dennis Lamme, Craig Allison, Mike Mera, Mike Harbit, Richard Womack, Mark Gordon, Don Hicks, Mark Sableman, Spencer Koch, John Caran, Danny Thomas.

Montana Broadcasters Association

18 Ruby Mountain Road, Clancy, MT 59634
(406) 431-2139; *Fax:* (406) 244-5518
www.mtbroadcasters.org
mba@mtbroadcasters.org

Kevin Skaalure, Chairman
Pat Coone, Chair-Elect
Tim Keating, Vice-Chair
Susan Balding, Immediate Past Chair
Bob Breck, Director
Ron Davis, Director
Phyllis Hall, Director

The Montana Broadcasters Association is a membership organization dedicated to serving the needs of radio and television stations in Montana and educating the public on the value of free over-the-air broadcasting.

Nebraska Broadcasters Association

11414 West Center Road, Suite 324, Omaha, NE 68144
(402) 933-5995, (402) 474-6900, (402) 397-1700; *Fax:* (402) 933-0059
www.ne-ba.org
jim@ne-ba.org

Jason Effinger, Chairman
Jim Timm, President/Executive Director
Taylor Walet, Chairman-Elect
Joy Patten, Vice-Chairman
Patrick Maag, Secretary-Treasurer
Craig Eckert, Past-Chairperson
Dara Troutman, Associate Director
MartyRiemenschneider, President Emeritus

The Nebraska Broadcasters Association was formed in 1934, with the purposes of advancing the best interests of the free, local, over-the-air, full service radio and television broadcast industry in the State of Nebraska, and in that regard:to optimize the business and regulatory environment in which the broadcast industry operates on a state level, on a regional level, and on a federal level; to advance the state of the art of broadcasting; to increase respect for and the credibilityof broadcasting; to help each broadcast station to better serve the public interest; and to otherwise engage in activities an other undertakings, including but not limited to Noncommercial Sustaining Announcement Programs (NCSA), which serve thosepurposes.

Directors:
Marty Riemenschneider, pres; Marty Riemenschnieder, exec dir

Nevada Broadcasters Association

1050 E. Flamingo Rd., Suite S-102, Las Vegas, NV 89119
(702) 794-4994; *Fax:* (702) 794-4997
www.nevadabroadcasters.org
rdfnba@aol.com

Adrienne Abbott, Chairman
Bob Fisher, President
Adam Sandler, Vice-Pres
Eric Bonnici, Director of Sales and Marketing
Clay Giffin, Finance and Office Manager
Gary Campbell, Director of NCSA Production
Melanie Mueller, Director ofNCSA Reporting and Analysis

Directors:
Mary Ozer, chmn; Tony Bonnici, chmn elect

New Hampshire Association of Broadcasters

707 Chestnut St., Manchester, NH 03104
(603) 627-9600; *Fax:* (603) 627-9603
www.nhab.org
asprague@bggadvertising.com

Box Cox, Chairman
Peter Frid, Past Chair
Mark Ericson, Vice Chair Radio
Gerry McGavick, Vice Chair TV
Ray Garon, Secretary
Pete DeTone, Treasurer
Jordan Walton, Executive Director

New Jersey Broadcasters Association

348 Applegarth Rd., Monroe Twp., NJ 08831
(609) 860-0111, (888) 657-2346, (888) 652-2366; *Fax:* (609) 860-0110, (888) 652-2329
www.njba.com
njba@njba.com

Scott Taylor, Chairman
Paul S. Rotella, President/CEO
Richard K. Swetits, General Manager
Dave Coskey, 1st Vice Chair
Greg Janoff, 2nd Vice Chair
Phil Boyce, Secretary/Treasurer
Deon Levingston, Vice President/General Manager
Phil Boyce, VP/Director
Dan Spears, Vice President

Directors:
Arthur Camiolo, Josh Gertzog, Charles McCreery, Joseph M. Bilotta, Dan Spears, Richard Swetits, John F. Garziglia & Thomas R. Ray

New Mexico Broadcasters Association

2333 Wisconsin N.E., Albuquerque, NM 87110
(505) 881-4444, (800) 622-2414; *Fax:* (505) 881-5353
www.nmba.org
info@nmba.org

Steve Rooney, Chairman
Paula Maes, President/ CEO
Mike Langner, Chief Engineer
Chuck Hammond, Chair-Elect
Bill Kruger, Secretary
Mary Lynn Roper, Immediate Past-President
MaryAnn Morton, Resources Director
Gene Dow, Board ofDirector
Suzan Strong, Communications Director

New Mexico Broadcasters Association serves to promote cooperation and understanding among broadcasters, both radio and television, as well as among businesses and other organizations associated with the broadcast industry, in the service ofthe communities throughout the Land of Enchantment.

Directors:
Matt Martinez, Gene Dow & Milt McConnell

New York Market Radio Association

125 West 55th Street, 21st Floor, New York, NY 10019
(646) 254-4493; *Fax:* (646) 254-4498
www.nymrad.org
db@nymrad.org

Felix Perez, Chairman
Jennifer Donohue, Vice Chairman
Deon Levingston, Secretary
Deborah Beagan, Executive Director

New York Market Radio is a marketing association supported by the New York area Radio stations. Our mission is to raise the profile of Radio in the New York Market by providing information and research to companies that may be consideringadvertising on Radio, to advertising agencies that may be recommending Radio to new or existing clients, and to our member Radio stations in their pursuit of new business.

New York State Broadcasters Association Inc.

1805 Western Ave., Albany, NY 12203
(518) 456-8888; *Fax:* (518) 456-8943
www.nysbroadcasters.org
sandy@nysbroadcasters.org

Dave Davis, Chairman
David Donovan, President/Executive Director
Mary Anne Jacon, Vice President- Operations
Richard Novik, Senior Vice President, Member Services
Kristen Delaney, Vice Chair - Radio
Robert Krummenacker, Vice Chair- TV
Chuck Samuels, Secretary
Chuck Samuels, Treasurer
Carolyn Jung, Administrative Assistant

The New York State Broadcasters Association represents the interests of over 300 television and radio stations in the New York State Assembly, the United States Congress, and various other legislative bodies.

North Carolina Association of Broadcasters

Mailing Address: PO Box 627, Raleigh, NC 27602
Second Address: 150 Fayetteville Street, Suite 1270, Raleigh, NC 27601
(919) 821-7300; *Fax:* (919) 834-8880
www.ncbroadcast.com
info@ncbroadcast.comÿ

Steve Hammel, President
Gary McNair, President Elect
Joe Pomilla, Vice President for Television
Tiffany Hewitt, Vice President for Radio
Gary Weiss, Secretary-Treasurer
Lisa Reynolds, Executive Manager
Joanne Higgins, Director ofCommunications & Event Planning

NCAB is in business solely to protect and serve the interests of North Carolina broadcasters.For the past 61 years, NCAB has maintained a standard of excellence in services provided to members. NCAB is widely recognized as one of the topbroadcasters' associations in the nation in terms of legislative victories, education, education services, benefits and legal assistance.

North Dakota Broadcasters Association

PO Box 3178, Bismarck, ND 58502
(701) 258-1332; *Fax:* (701) 250-6372
www.ndba.org
bethh@ndba.org

Beth A. Helfrich, Executive Director

NDBA fosters and promotes the development of the art of broadcasting and encourages and promotes customs and practices which are in the best interest of the public and the broadcast industry. NDBA protects its members in every lawful andproper manner and acts as the contact with other broadcast associates across the nation.

Ohio Association of Broadcasters

17 South High Street, Suite 1010, Columbus, OH 43215
(614) 228-4052; *Fax:* (614) 228-8133
www.oab.org
oab@oab.org

David Glass, Chairman
Christine Merritt, President
Patricia Geary, Director of Operations
Richard Dyer, Vice Chair
Gary Mincer, Secretary/Treasurer
John Wharff, Past Chair
Lisa Barhorst, Vice President & General Manager
ThomasSzykowny, General Counsel
Katie Lovell, Director of Marketing and Communications

Ohio broadcasters know a simple fact: the Ohio Association of Broadcasters is here for them. No matter how times change, OAB works hard to protect the ability of the state's radio and TV stations to operate their businesses and serve theircommunity.

Oklahoma Association of Broadcasters

6520 N. Western, Suite 104, Oklahoma City, OK 73116
(405) 848-0771
www.oabok.org

David Griffin, Chairman
Vance Harrison, President/ CEO
Nancy Struby, Director of Operations
Gene Vidler, Chair-Elect
Wes Milbourn, Treasurer
Bill Hurley, Past Chair
Lee Anderson, Director
Pat Baldwin, Director
Brent Hensley,Director

The OAB is a non-profit organization of commercial radio and television stations organized to serve the public interest and promote the cooperation and prosperity of its members. A 12-member Board of Directors governs the OAB.A valuableresource for its members, the OAB provides information about regulation, advertising, employee recruitment, education and training, and the myriad of issues affecting our changing industry.

Oregon Association of Broadcasters

9020 SW Washington Square Road, Suite 140, Portland, OR 97223
(503) 443-2299; *Fax:* (503) 443-2488
www.theoab.org
theoab@theoab.org

Randy McKone, Chairman
Bill Johnstone, President
Keith Shipman, Vice-Chair / Secretary / Treasurer
John Rice, Ex-Officio Board Member
Tim Gleason, Ex-Officio Board Member
Robert Dove, Immediate Past-Chairman
Joe Costello, Boardof directors Member
J. Dominic Monahan, Legal Counsel

The mission of the Oregon Association of Broadcasters is to promote, enhance, strengthen and defend the broadcast industry. The OAB organizes programs and activities designed to encourage and promote sound broadcast customs and practices.The OAB serves as a clearinghouse to answer all public and member's questions about the broadcast industry. The OAB is the statewide organization dedicated to building Oregon citizens' perception of radio and television broadcasters.

Pennsylvania Association of Broadcasters
8501 Paxton St., Hummelstown, PA 17036
(717) 482-4820; *Fax:* (717) 482-1111
www.pab.org
gponti@pab.org, jconti@pab.org
Michael Young, Chairman
Richard Wyckoff, President
John Cadman, GM
Micheal Sherry, Director of Sales
Jeffery M. Androuloins, Vice Chairman Radio
Jon Hitchcock, Vice Chairman TV
Barry Fisher, Secretary
Jim Loftus, Treasurer
Bill Baldwin, Radio Director
Donald Fredeen, Radio Director

Rhode Island Broadcasters Association
11 S. Angell St., Providence, RI 02920
(401) 255-8200
www.ribroadcasters.com
georgeregis@yahoo.com
Barbara Haynes, President
Dave Piccerelli, Vice President
Tina Castano, Secretary
Vic Vetter, Treasurer

South Carolina Broadcasters Association
One Harbison Way, Suite 112, Columbia, SC 29212
(803) 732-1186; *Fax:* (803) 732-4085
www.scba.net
Clifton Metcalf, Chairman-Associate Membership
Suzanne Teagle, President
John George, Co-Chairman, Engineering Committee
Shani White, Executive Director
Jane Pigg, Chairman-Historical Development
Joy Henderson, ExecutiveAssistant
Bob Romine, Vice President-Television
Alex Snipe, Vice President-Radio

South Dakota Broadcasters Association
106 W. Capital Ave., PO Box 1037, Pierre, SD 57501
(605) 224-1034; *Fax:* (605) 224-7426
www.sdba.org
info@sdba.org
Cindy McNeill, Chairman
Steve Willard, President
Roger Currier, Chairman-Elect
Lia Green, Past Chairman
Dr. Michelle Van Maanen, Associate Board Member
Monte Loos, Director
Jack Caudill, Director
SDBA is affiliated with the National Association of Broadcasters (NAB) which conducts public service programs throughout the country, and supports a variety of community activities to promote the exciting field of radio/TV broadcasting.These PSA activities promote a drug-free society, the environment and education, among many others.Like its national counter-part, SDBA conducts a wide variety of programming to meet the needs of its myriad listeners. From the state-wide United Waytelevision marathons or local heart-fund broadcasts from shopping malls, to public affairs programming of candidates to state legislature or city-wide election results, are all part of the continuous broadcasts efforts of SDBA members to inform,educate and familiarize radio/TV listeners to current issues or pending legislation.
But radio/TV programming also entertains. SDBA is proud of its broadcasting efforts, and is pleased to have in it's membership the South Dakota Public TelevisionNetwork, along with dozens of FM radio stations which dedicate much of its broadcast schedule to music and entertainment.

Tennessee Association of Broadcasters
Two International Plaza Dr., Suite 507, Nashville, TN 37217
(615) 365-1840; *Fax:* (615) 365-1842
www.tabtn.org
info@tabtn.org
Phil Cox, Chairman
Whit Adamson, President
Brenda Heidt, Coordinator of Operations
Doug Combs, Vice President
Craig Jacobus, Past Chairman
Dan Barron, Chairman Elect
Dennis Banka, VP Radio
Stan Knott, VP TV
George DeVault,Sec/Treas
The TAB has helped enhance our educational and student scholarship responsibilities through the financial support of our membership, our non-commercial sustaining announcement program (NCSA) partners, our event sponsors, advertisers,exhibitors and many friendships.

Think LA
Div/DBA: (formerly Los Angeles Advertising Agencies Associa
3535 Hayden Ave, Suite 300, Culver City, CA 90232
(310) 876-0650; *Fax:* (310) 823-7325
www.thinkla.org
info@thinkla.org
Nick Bishop, President & CEO
Tim Hand, Vice-President
Barbara Overlie, Treasurer
Roger Van Remmen, Secretary
Eric Buchanan, Talent Manager
Nick Leal, Director of Sales
Wayne Aaronson, Senior Account Executive
The goal of thinkLA is to promote and support world class collaboration, innovation and creativity among the marketing, media, entertainment and advertising industries of Los Angeles. - See more at:http://thinkla.org/about/mission/#sthash.iv60LTG9.dpuf

Utah Broadcasters Association
1600 S. Main St., Salt Lake City, UT 84115
(801) 486-9521
www.utahbroadcasters.com
Providing Alerts, news and vital information to help keep you safe and informed.

Vermont Association of Broadcasters
500A Dalton Drive, PO Box 4489, Colchester, VT 05446
(802) 655-5764
www.vab.org
vab@vab.org
Eric Michaels, President
Alex Martin, Vice President
Wally Caswell, Secretary
Tom Beardsley, Treasurer
Ken Kasz, Past-President
Wendy Mays, Member-at-Large
Jim Condon, Executive Director
Since 1955, the VAB has helped promote over-the-air broadcasting in Vermont by protecting and assisting our member stations. Our services include: Regulatory Assistance and Advocacy, EEO and Jobs Assistance, ABIP subsidies, EAS assistance,etc.
Directors:
Jim Condon, exec dir

Virginia Association of Broadcasters
250 West Main Street, Suite 100, Charlottesville, VA 22902
(434) 977-3716; *Fax:* (434) 979-2439
www.vabonline.com
doug.easter@easterassociates.com
Brad Ramsey, President
Jack Dempsey, President- Elect
Charlie Russell, Secretary /Treasurer
Bob Willoughby, Past President
Doug Easter, CAE, Executive Director
Chris Manzella, Vice President
Bill Murrill, Controller/CFO
For over 50 years, the Virginia Association of Broadcasters has been dedicated to advancing broadcasting while providing valuable services for VAB members. Our areas of focus include consultant advice, education, government affairs, EEOrecruitment, and promoting radio & TV advertising to Virginia businesses.
Directors:
Michael Guild

Washington State Association of Broadcasters
724 Columbia St., Suite 310, Olympia, WA 98501-1249
(360) 705-0774; *Fax:* (360) 705-0873
www.wsab.org
wa-broadcasters@earthlink.net
David Praga, Chairman
Mark Allen, Esq., President/ CEO
Andy Skotdal, Vice Chair
Teddie Gibbon, Immediate Past Chairman
Professor Glenn A. Johnson, Secretary/Treasurer
Todd Ortloff, Director
Patricia McRae, Director
CarlGardner, Director
To promote and protect free, over-the-air, broadcasters' interests before Congress and Washington State Legislature; to facilitate additional contact between broadcasters and elected officials by providing them with opportunities to meet anddiscuss issues and build relationships.

West Virginia Broadcasters Association
140 7th Ave., South Charleston, WV 25303-1452
(304) 744-2143; *Fax:* (304) 744-1764
wvba@wvba.com
Roger Sheppard, Presidentÿ
Michele C. Crist, Executive Director
Bob Spencerÿ, Vice- President
Frank Brady, Secretary/Treasurer
Jay Philippone, Past President
Dave Barnette, Legal Counsel
The WVBA has served radio and television stations across the Mountain State since 1946. While the media landscape has changed dramatically over the last 67 years, one thing has not: The WVBA is here to serve West Virginia broadcasters!Whether your station needs to advertise a job opening or find training for your staff, the WVBA can help.

Wisconsin Broadcasters Association
44 E. Mifflin St., Suite 900, Madison, WI 53703
(608) 255-2600, (800) 236-1922; *Fax:* (608) 256-3986
www.wi-broadcasters.org
mendicott@wi-broadcasters.org
Kelly Radandt, Chairman
Michelle Vetterkind, President & CEO
Linda Baun, Vice President - Administration
Jeff Tyler, Vice Chair-Radio/Chair Elect
Scott Chorski, Vice Chair-Television
Tom Allen, Treasurer
Dick Record,Secretary
Dean Maytagÿ, Immediate Past Chair
The purpose of the Wisconsin Broadcasters Association shall be to foster and promote the development of the arts of aural and visual broadcastings in all its forms; to protect its members in every lawful and property manner from injusticesand unjust exactions; to do all things necessary and proper to encourage and promote customs and practices which will strengthen and maintain the broadcast industry to the end that it may best serve the public.
Box 2048, Wausau, WI 54402-2048
Bob Jung, Midwest Communications
1908 Grand Ave., Wausau, WI 54403-6870
Laurin Jorstad, Waow-Tv
Box 933, West Bend, WI 53095-0933
Jim Hodges, Wbkv/Wbwi

Wyoming Association of Broadcasters
7217 Hawthorne Dr., Cheyenne, WY 82003
(307) 632-7622; *Fax:* (307) 638-3469
www.wyomingbroadcasting.org
grottski@aol.com
Roger Gelder, Cody, Chairman
Laura Grott, Presidentÿ
Kent Smith, 1st Vice Chairman
Don Day, Cheyenne, 2nd Vice Chairman
Lee Wagner, Director
Dennis Switzer, Director
Bob Grammens, Director
Steve Core, Director
Mostly, the WAB is about working together as a group to keep the broadcast industry strong and viable. It's also about friendship and knowing each other personally as well as professionally. One of the highlights of the year is for allbroadcasters and their staffs to come together at the Annual Conference to renew old friendships and spend time talking about their livelihood.... the broadcast industry.

State & Regional Cable Associations

Alabama Cable Telecommunications Association
Mailing Address: 1333 Carmichael Way, Montgomery, AL 36106
Second Address: PO Box 230666, Montgomery, AL 36123
(334) 271-2281
www.alabamacable.org
jfrakes@alabamacable.org
Carrie Boggs, President
Brian Gregory, VP
Terry Womack, Secretary/Treasurer
Michelle Roth, Executive Director
Jennifer Frakes, Executive Assistant

Arkansas Cable Telecommunications Association
411 South Victory, Suite 201A, Little Rock, AR 72201
(501) 907-6440
arcta.org
joe@arcta.org
Joe Molinaro, Executive Director
Serving 140,000 subs on 2 cable systems.

Broadband Cable Association of Pennsylvania
127 State St., Harrisburg, PA 17101-1025
(717) 214-2000; *Fax:* (717) 214-2020
www.pcta.com

Joe Taylor, Chairman
Daniel R. Tunnell, President
Brian F. Barno, VP, Government Affairs
J. Brian Herrmann, Director of Communications
Suzette R. Riley, Office Manager
George H. Potter, IT Specialist
The Broadband Cable Association of Pennsylvania is an association of Pennsylvania cable operators, equipment suppliers, programmers and other allied companies that advocates, communicates and educates about industry positions to publicpolicy makers, opinion leaders and the general public in order to enhance member companies operations, competitiveness and profitability.

Broadband Communications Association of Washington
216 First Avenue S., Suite 435, Seattle, WA 98104
(206) 652-9303; *Fax:* (206) 652-8297
www.broadband4wa.com
Marian Jackson, President
Ron Main, Executive Director
Sena Krug, Association Manager
Directors:
Janet Turpen, Steve Kipp, Jerry Rotondo, Bob Lam, Matt Zavala, Bruce Gladner & Carlos Gutirrez

Broadband Innovation Group
150 W. Market Street, Suite 412, Indianapolis, IN 46204
(317) 237-2288; *Fax:* (317) 237-2290
www.broadbandig.org
info@broadbandig.org
Joni Hart, Executive Director
Christy Gormal, Media Contact
Founded as Indiana Cable Telecommunications Association (ICTA) in 1985, the Group represents cable operators and cable programmers, as well equipment suppliers and providers of other products to the cable industry, before the Indiana GeneralAssembly, the Indiana Utility Regulatory Commission, the Indiana Congressional Delegation, and in local, state, and federal matters.
Directors:
Rachel McKay & Nicole Roenl

Cable Television & Communications Association of Illinois
98 West Lawrence, Suite 317, Springfield, IL 62704
(217) 679-2978; *Fax:* (217) 679-2983
www.ctcil.com
ctcil@live.com
Joe Handley, President
Amy Alton, Executive Director
The Cable Television and Communications Association of Illinois serves as the trade association for the cable television industry in Illinois. Membership is divided into two categories: general members and associate members. Generalmembers are cable system operators, while associate members include programming services, equipment supply companies, and any other businesses that have an affiliation with the cable television industry.

California Cable & Telecommunications Association
1001 K Street, 2nd Floor, Sacramento, CA 95814
(916) 446-7732; *Fax:* (916) 446-1605
www.calcable.org
John Gauder, Chairman
Carolyn McIntyre, President
Richelle Orlando, Operations Manager
Lesla Lehtonen, Senior VP & General Counsel
Jessica Sullivan, Accounting Manager
The California Cable & Telecommunications Association (CCTA) is the industry's largest state cable and telecommunications association. CCTA is a leader in the development of video, broadband and communications policy in California, andrepresents the industry before the California Congressional Delegation, the State Legislature, state regulatory agencies and the state and federal courts. Paramount among the Association's goals is ensuring that the industry remains competitive inthe rapidly changing world of information and communication services that contribute significantly to California's economy.
1121 L St., Suite 400, Sacramento, CA 95814-3926
(916) 446-7732; *Fax:* (916) 446-1605

Colorado Telecommunications Association
1600 Broadway, Suite 1350, Denver, CO 80202
(303) 795-8080
www.colotelecom.com
petek@colotelecom.com
Gail Long, Board President
Terry Hendrickson, Board Vice President
Greg Grablander, Board Secretary-Treasurer
Pete Kirchhof, Executive VP

Georgia Cable Association
2300 Windy Ridge Parkwayў, Suite 205 South, Atlanta, GA 30339
(678) 540-7673; *Fax:* (404) 252-0215
www.gacable.com
information@gacable.com
Stephen Loftin, Executive Director
Leona Rittenhouse, Marketing & Membership Director
GCA has an 11 member board of directors with members representing large and small systems across the state. The board members are responsible for approving the organization's policies and legislative agenda, as well as setting the goals andbudget for the organization.

Idaho Cable Broadband Association
PO Box 2634, Boise, ID 83701
(208) 344-6633; *Fax:* (208) 344-0077
www.idahocable.com
info@idahocable.com
Ron Williams, Executive Director
JoAn Condie, Assistant
The mission of the association is to promote the well-being of the cable telecommunications industry through effective political, public relations, and educational activities.

Iowa Cable & Telecommunications Association
3737 Westown Parkway, Suite C, West Des Moines, IA 50266
(515) 697-6646; *Fax:* (515) 309-3779
www.iacable.com
info@iacable.com
Ed Pardini, President
William F. Peard, Executive Vice President
Steve Purcell, Director
Katelyn Hotle, Director
Tom Larsen, Director
John Renda, Director
Nick Paden, Director
Iowa's cable television operators provide informative, entertaining and reliable service throughout the state. Services include cable television, high-speed internet and telephone service to communities statewide through the use of fiberoptic technology and coaxial cable.

Kansas Cable Telecommunications Association
900 S. Kansas Avenue, Suite 300, Topeka, KS 66612
(785) 290-0018; *Fax:* (785) 232-1703
www.cableinkansas.org
staff@cableinkansas.org
Jarad Falk, Chairman
John J. Federico, J.D., President
Curt Stamp, Vice Chair
Megan Bottenberg, Secretary/Treasurer
Kurt David, Immediate Past Chair
Stephen P. Duerst, Associate
Lori Hogan, Associate
KCTA was founded in 1970 to represent the cable industry, which began as a way to bring television to homes in remote areas that were unable to receive conventional over-the-air broadcast signals. Over the years, KCTA has provided its membercompanies with a single, unified voice on issues affecting the cable and telecommunications industry in Kansas. KCTA is proud of the role the cable industry has played in development of competition for video, high-speed Internet and telephoneservices in Kansas.

Kentucky Cable Telecommunications Association
609 Chamberlin Ave., PO Box 415, Frankfort, KY 40601
(502) 226-5769; *Fax:* (502) 352-2489
www.cableconnectskentucky.com
rhollis@kycable.com
Jason Keller, President
Randy Hollis, Executive Director
Archie Everage, 1st Vice President
Joseph DiJulio, 2nd Vice President
Ronald Reimer, Secretary/Treasurer
Roy Baker, Board of Director
Paul Butcher, Board of Director
The Kentucky Cable Telecommunications Association (KCTA) is the trade association that represents Kentucky's investor owned cable companies. KCTA's member companies serve nearly 650,000 basic cable subscribers throughout the Commonwealth,providing a wide array of state-of-the-art broadband services including; analog and digital video services, high-speed Internet access and telephone service.
Directors:
Jim Finch, assoc dir; Jim Hays III, assoc dir; Robert Thacker III, assoc dir

LCTA - The Internet & Television Association
Div/DBA: Louisiana Cable & Telecommunications Association
763 North St., Baton Rouge, LA 70802
(225) 387-5960; *Fax:* (225) 383-6705
www.lacable.com
lcta@lacable.org
Cheryl P. McCormick, CEO
Shannon McCormick, Communications Director
Kim LaPoint, President
Mark Greene, Vice President
Fran Gladden, Treasurer
The mission of the Louisiana Cable & Telecommunications Association (LCTA) is to provide leadership, direction and a focal point for ideas of common interest so these ideas can grow into projects of benefit to the membership and generalpublic. This will be accomplished through coordinating and directing efforts in the following areas: effective representation within legislative and regulatory bodies at the state and federal levels; provision for ongoing education and exchange ofinformation/ideas to members regarding consumer and industry issues; and developing and maintaining key local, state and national relationships to further the mutual interest of members of LCTA.

Michigan Cable Telecommunications Association
412 W. Ionia St., Lansing, MI 48933
(517) 482-2622; *Fax:* (517) 482-1819
www.michcable.org
rtantraphol@mwadvocacy.com
Chris Horak, President
Marilyn Passmore, Vice President
Floyd Grocholski, Secretary/Treasurer
Matt Groen, Executive Director
Sherry Nelton, Office Administrator
David Waymire, Media Contact
The Michigan Cable Telecommunications Association was established in 1981 by a group of cable television companies in the state. The goal was to provide a united presence in the Michigan Legislature and before the Michigan Public ServiceCommission. Regular meetings also helped shape best practices in the industry, which deals with many levels of government - local, state and federal.

Minnesota Cable Communications Association (MCCA)
555 Park Street, Suite 200, St. Paul, MN 55103
(651) 641-0268; *Fax:* (651) 641-0319
www.mncca.com
info@mncca.com
Bill Jensen, President
Ron Orlando, Vice-President
David Pratt, Treasurer
Patrick Haggerty, Secretary
Anna Boroff, Executive Director
The Minnesota Cable Communications Association (MCCA) is a trade association of franchised cable television companies in Minnesota. All major companies are represented in its membership. Its 13-person board of directors governs the MCCA.Local communities regulate cable television and the state has a chapter of law governing the franchise process. At the federal level cable is regulated by the FCC. Despite the emergence of competition from both satellite and wire-based competitors,government closely regulates cable operations.

Minnesota Cable Communications Association
1885 University Ave., Suite 320, St. Paul, MN 55104
(651) 641-0268; *Fax:* (651) 641-0319
www.mncca.com
mncableassc@comcast.net
Bill Jensen, President
Emmett Coleman, Vice-President
David Pratt, Treasurer
Tom Bordwell, Secretary
John Gibbs, Director
Steve Miles, Director
Allyson Hartle, Director
The Minnesota Cable Communications Association (MCCA) is a trade association of franchised cable television companies in Minnesota. All major companies are represented in its membership. Its 13-person board of directors governs the MCCA.Local communities regulate cable television and the state has a chapter of law governing the franchise process. At the federal level cable is regulated by the FCC. Despite the emergence of competition from both satellite and wire-based competitors,government closely regulates cable operations.

Mississippi Cable Telecommunications Association
1501 Lakeland Dr., Suite 301, Jackson, MS 39216
(601) 981-3646; *Fax:* (601) 981-5547
www.mctaweb.net
mctams@comcast.net

Ronnie Colvin, Presidentÿ
Greg Capranica, Vice President/President-Elect
George King, Treasurer
Carrie Boggs, Secretary
Lisa Shoemakerÿ, Executive Director
Services the cable operators in the state for legislative representation and helps to maintain high levels of engagement in current industry issues.
Directors:
Lee Ann Hayes, exec dir

Missouri Cable Telecommunications Association
223 E. Capitol Ave., PO Box 1895, Jefferson City, MO 65102-1895
(573) 635-1915; *Fax:* (573) 635-1778
www.missouricable.tv
angie@statehouse-strategies.com
Andrew B. Blunt, Executive Director
Paul Berra, Chairman
Top Hopfinger, Vice Chair
Steve Bennett, Secretary
Don Vollmayer, Treasurer
We are the statewide organization representing the cable telecommunications industry within the State of Missouri
Directors:
Roger Ponder, chmn; Greg Harrison, pres

Nebraska Cable Communications Association
521 First Street, Milford, NE 68405 US
(402) 761-2216; *Fax:* (402) 310-1054
www.necable.org
aprenda@youraam.com
Amy Prenda, Executive Director
LeaAnn Quist, President
Rob Logsdon, Vice President
Mike Drahota, Secretary/Treasurer
The voice of the cable industry in Nebraska with 6 cable company members that serve more than 500,000 subscribers throughout the state.

New England Cable & Telecommunications Association Inc. (NECTA)
Mailing Address: Ten Forbes Road, Suite 440W, Braintree, MA 02184
Second Address: 21 Oak St, Suite 307, Capitol Place, Hartford, CT 6106
(781) 843-3418, (860) 524-5820; *Fax:* (781) 849-6267, (860) 728-1302
www.necta.info
info@necta.info
Mark Reilly, Chairman
Paul R. Cianelli, Presidentÿ
Timothy O. Wilkerson, VP & Policy Counsel
Carolyn Killian, Office Manager
John Sutich, Vice Chairman
Jay Allbaugh, Treasurer
Melinda Poore, Secretary
The New England Cable & Telecommunications Association, Inc. (NECTA) is a five state regional trade association representing substantially all private cable telecommunications companies in Connecticut, Massachusetts, New Hampshire, RhodeIsland and Vermont.
Directors:
Paul R. Cianelli, pres

New Jersey Cable Telecommunications Association
124 W. State St., Trenton, NJ 08608
(609) 392-3223; *Fax:* (609) 394-0074
www.cablenj.org
david_mayer@cable.comcast.com
Elizabeth Murray, Chairperson
Marilyn D. Davis, Vice Chairman
Camille C. Joseph, Secretary
David R. Mayer, Treasurer
NJCTA's mission is to help create a business environment that enables its member companies to invest in New Jersey communities, provide the best and most innovative service, technology, and programming for their customers, and connectfriends, families, and businesses in the state of New Jersey.

North Carolina Cable Telecommunications Association
Mailing Address: PO Box 1347, Raleigh, NC 27602
Second Address: 150 Fayetteville Street, Suite 1270, Raleigh, NC 27601
(919) 834-7113; *Fax:* (919) 834-8880
www.nccta.com
info@nccta.com
Mike Tanck, President
Bill Paramore, Vice President
Sammy Roberson, Secretary
Meredith Garwood, Treasurer
Lisa Reynolds, Executive Manager
Gail Summerville, Membership Manager
The NCCTA membership consists of cable systems located in the state, companies engaged in a business or activity related to the cable telecommunications industry and units and agencies of government. The Association offers a top-notchlegislative advocacy program, timely industry publications, educational and training workshops, annual meetings and industry-wide community service initiatives.

Ohio Cable Telecommunications Association
172 E. State Street, Suite 302, Columbus, OH 43215
(614) 461-4014; *Fax:* (614) 461-9326
www.associationdatabase.com/aws/OCTA/
Chris Thomas, President
Kelly Rehm, Vice President
Jim D'Innocenzo, Secretary
Rick Mlcek, Treasurer
Jonathon McGee, Executive Director
April Barrowman, Administration & Member Services Manager
Today, our members look to the Ohio Cable Telecommunications Association with confidence in its ability to represent the industry before the Ohio legislature, PUCO, Congress and the Courts. Through the work of the OCTA and the support of ourmembers we have been able to safeguard our industry's interests through the legislative process, including enactment of strong signal theft laws, legislation that places tough but necessary restrictions on government-run cable companies, and fair andreasonable right-of-way legislation.

Oklahoma Cable and Telecommunications Association
941 East Britton Rd, Suite 400, Oklahoma City, OK 73114
(405) 843-8855; *Fax:* (405) 843-8934
www.okcta.org
crystal@okcta.org
David Wall, Chairman
Len Pitcock, Vice Chairman
Jason Gebhart, Treasurer
Jim Walker, Executive Director & GC
Crystal Stromberg, Executive Assistant
The association represents over 700,000 cable households in the state. Cox Communications is the largest operator in the state, representing two-thirds of the cable subscriber households in Oklahoma.
Directors:
Dave Bialis, chmn; Andy Dearth, vice chmn; George Wilburn, sec/treas. Bill Drewry, Nicole Evans, Johnny Bowen, David Wall, Leon Pfeifer, Danny Thompson, Ed Perry, Holly Henderson & Tim Easley

Oregon Cable Telecommunications Association
1249 Commercial St. S.E., Salem, OR 97302
(503) 362-8838; *Fax:* (503) 399-1029
www.oregoncable.com
admin@oregoncable.com
Mike Dewey, Executive Director
Maggie Emery, Association Manager
The Oregon Cable Telecommunications Association (OCTA) is fully engaged in political advocacy on behalf of its members at the State Capitol in Salem, and within other governmental forums impacting cable regulations in Oregon. The Associationalso provides its members with valuable information and organizes and presents workshops and an annual convention that benefit member companies.

Southwest Cable Communications Association
4350 E. Camelback Rd, Suite G-200, Phoenix, AZ 85018
(602) 955-4122; *Fax:* (602) 955-4505
www.swcable.org
info@swcable.org
Susan Bitter Smith, Executive Director
John Schurz, President
Dan Spoelman, President-Elect
John Wolfe, Secretary/Treasurer
Susan Anable, Director-At-Large
Marla Bowen, Director-At-Large
John Christopher, Director-At-Large
Stephen Brideau, Director-At-Large
Serving the Cable Industry in Arizona and New Mexico.

Tennessee Cable Telecommunications Association
611 Commerce Street, Suite 2706, Nashville, TN 37203
(615) 256-7037; *Fax:* (615) 254-9710
www.tcta.net
info@tcta.net
Nick Pavlis, Chairman
Amy Martin, President
Curtis Person, Vice Chair
Gary Blount, Secretary/Treasurer
TCTA represents cable operators and cable programmers, as well as equipment suppliers and providers of other products to the cable industry, before the Tennessee General Assembly, the Tennessee Regulatory Authority, the TennesseeCongressional Delegation, and in local, state, and federal legal and public relations matters. TCTA also monitors legislation on the local, state, and national levels to keep our members informed of current developments.

Texas Cable Association
1350 Congress Avenue, Suite 1350, Austin, TX 78701
(512) 474-2082; *Fax:* (512) 474-0966
www.txcable.com
txcable@txcable.com
Velma Cruz, Vice President & General Counsel
Ryan Weiseman, Legislative Director
Kevin Jean, Government Relations Coordinator
Kirsten Voinis, Press Contact
Skip Ogle, Chairman
Jeff Burdett, Vice Chairman
Clem Maddox,Treasurer
Melinda Little, Secretary
Today, TCA also serves as an education forum, providing Texans with information about the complicated issues affecting the communications landscape in the state. Together, the industry and consumers play an important part in advancingtechnology policies that increase competition, encourage investment and innovation and provide real choices for Texas consumers.

Virginia Cable Telecommunications Association
1111 E. Main Street, Suite 802, Richmond, VA 23219
(804) 780-1776; *Fax:* (804) 225-8036
www.vcta.com
rlamura@vcta.com
Ray LaMura, President
Kimberly Voxland, Director of Public Relations & Office Operations
Heidi Schlicher Cook, VP of Government Affairs
Marie Schuler, Chair
Donna Rattley Washington, Vice Chair
Kevin Meek, Secretary
The mission of the Virginia Cable Telecommunications Association (VCTA) is to promote the cable television and telecommunications services of member companies in the Commonwealth of Virginia to the public, the business community and stateofficials.

West Virginia Cable Telecommunications Association
300 Summers St., Suite 700, Charleston, WV 25301
(304) 345-2000; *Fax:* (304) 342-1285
www.wvcta.org
Mark Polen, Executive Director
Chris Kyle, President
Gordon Waters, Vice President
Peter Brown, Treasurer
Paul Comes, Secretary
Chris Weikle, Assistant Executive Director
The West Virginia Cable Telecommunications Association (WVCTA), founded in 1978, represents cable television system operators and affiliated programming services and industry vendors in matters of public affairs and governmental relationsthroughout the state and in Washington, D.C.

Wisconsin Cable Communications Association
22 East Mifflin Street, Suite 1010, Madison, WI 53703
(608) 256-1683; *Fax:* (608) 256-6222
www.wicable.tv
info@wicable.tv
Celeste Flynn, President
Adam Raschka, Vice President
Gary Underwood, Treasurer
Thomas E. Moore, Executive Director
Laura Hanson, Office Administrator
WCCA provides a unified voice on issues affecting the cable and telecommunications industry at local, state, and federal levels in Wisconsin.

Wyoming Telecommunications Association
Mailing Address: PO Box 1052, Cheyenne, WY 82003
Second Address: 1825 Carey Avenue, Cheyenne, WY 82001
(307) 634-8816; *Fax:* (307) 632-0249
www.wyotelassn.org
christi@wywagan.org
Chris Brown, Administrator
Christi Anderson, Boards & Events Director
Kim Elder, Office Administrator

Provides representation, general assistance and information to its members in matters relating to the telecommunications industry.

Major Broadcasting & Cable Awards

AAAA Jay Chiat Awards
1065 Avenue of the Americas, 16th Floor, New York, NY 10018
212-682-2500; *Fax:* 212-682-8391
stratfest.aaaa.org/jaychiats/
awards@aaaa.org
Marla Kaplowitz, President & CEO
Alison Fahey, EVP, Chief Marketing Officer
Tom Finneran, EVP, Agency Management Services
Chick Foxgrover, EVP, Creative Technology & Innovation
Louis Jones, EVP, Media & Data
Mollie Rosen,Programming Director
Description: The Jay Chiat Award recognizes the best strategic thinking in the world of marketing communications.

AAAS Science Journalism Awards
1200 New York Ave. N.W., Washington, DC 20005
(202) 326-6440, (202) 326-6421; *Fax:* (202) 789-0455
www.sjawards.aaas.org
media@aaas.org
Barbara A. Schaal, Chair
Susan Hockfield, AAAS President
Margaret Hamburg, President-Elect
Rush D. Holt, Chief Executive Officer
Anne Hoy, Director, News & Information
Tiffany Lohwater, Chief Communications Officer
The AAAS Kavli Science Journalism Awards represent the pinnacle of achievement for professional journalists in the science writing field. The awards recognize outstanding reporting for a general audience and honor individuals (rather thaninstitutions, publishers or employers) for their coverage of the sciences, engineering and mathematics.
Award Description:
Awards of distinction for professional journalists in the science writing field.

Academy of Television Arts and Sciences Emmy Awards
5220 Lankershim Blvd, North Hollywood, CA 91601
(818) 754-2800; *Fax:* (818) 761-2827
www.emmys.org
whitcomb@televisionacademy.com
Laurel Whitcomb, Press Contact
Award Description:
Award for excellence in TV progmg.

Alfred I. duPont-Columbia University Awards
Div/DBA: duPont Center for Broadcast Journalism
Columbia Univ Graduate School of Journalism, 2950 Broadway, Pulitzer Hall, New York, NY 10027
(212) 854-5047; *Fax:* (212) 854-3148
www.dupontawards.org
dupontawards@jrn.columbia.edu
Steve Coll, Dean
Abi Wright, Executive Director, Professional Prizes
Lisa R. Cohen, Dir., Professional Prizes/Adjunct Assoc. Professor
Caroline Martinet, Program Manager
Lauren Meregildo-Santos, Program Coordinator
For over 70 years, the Alfred I. duPont-Columbia University Awards have recognized excellence in broadcast journalism. Regarded today as one of the most prestigious prizes in broadcast, documentary and digital news - the equivalent of thePulitzer Prizes - the duPont-Columbia Awards bring the best in broadcast, documentary and digital journalism to professional and public attention by honoring those who produce it.
Award Description:
These awards are now regarded as the most prestigious prizes in TV & radio news, the bcst equivalent of the Pulitzer Prizes.

Alliance for Community Media Hometown Media Awards
4248 Park Glen Road, Minneapolis, MN 55416
(952) 928-4643
www.allcommunitymedia.org/hometown-media-awards
info@allcommunitymedia.org
John Funfar, Vice Chair
Todd Thayer, Treasurer
John Donovan, Treasurer-Elect
Debra Rogers, Past Chair
Melissa Serres, Assistant Director
Michelle Herr, Hometown Media Awards and Conference
Award Description:
Award for excellence & innovation among original public access TV.

Alliance for Women in Media Gracie Awards
2365 Harrodsburg Road, #A325, Lexington, KY 40504
(202) 750-3664; *Fax:* (202) 750-3664
www.allwomeninmedia.org
info@allwomeninmedia.org
Becky Brooks, Executive Director
Lori Weaver Hawkins, PR & Marketing Manager
LaTonya Jackson, Operations Manager
Lisa Stephenson, Events Director
The Gracie Awards acknowledges individual achievement and outstanding programming created for, by and about women in all areas of media.

The American Legion Fourth Estate Award
Mailing Address: P.O. Box 1055, 700 N Pennslyvania St., Indianapolis, IN 46204
Second Address: 1608 K St. N.W., Washington, DC 20006
(317) 630-1200, (202) 861-2700; *Fax:* (317) 630-1223, (202) 861-2786
www.legion.org
pr@legion.org
Denise Rohan, National Commander
John Raughter, Media & Communications
Award Description:
The Fourth Estate Award is presented annually to an individual, publication or bcst organization for outstanding achievement in the field of journalism. A 2,000 dollar stipend accompanies the award to defray expenses of recipent acceptingaward.

American Women in Radio and Television Inc. Awards
8405 Greensboro Drive, Suite 800, McLean, VA 22102
(703) 506-3290; *Fax:* (703) 506-3266
www.awrt.org
info@awrt.org
Maria E. Brennan, President
Amy Lotz, Managing Director
Award Description:
Honors progmg & individuals of the highest caliber in all facets of radio, TV, cable & web-based media.

Armstrong Awards
Mailing Address: Armstrong Foundation, Columbia Univ., 2500 Columbia Avenue, Lancaster, PA 17603
Second Address: Armstrong Foundation, P.O. Box 3001, Lancaster, PA 17604-3001
(717) 396-5536; *Fax:* (717) 396-6055
www.armstrongfoundation.org
Foundation@armstrongfoundation.com
David S. Cookson, President
Leslie J. Kulis, Director General Manager
Christopher Parisi, Vice President
Michelle Trabosh, Assistant Secretary
Thomas J. Waters, Vice President and Treasurer
David S. Cookson, Senior VicePresident
Ellen R. Romano, Dir SVP HR & Government Relations
Stephen H. Poole, Director Vice President Business Development

Bart Richards Award for Media Criticism
302 James Bldg., Pennsylvania State Univ., University Park, PA 16801-3867
(814) 865-8801; *Fax:* (814) 863-6134
bellisario.psu.edu/news-events/awards/bart-richards-award-for-media-criticism
Gary Abdullah, Assistant Dean for Multicultural Affairs
Sandi Rockwell, Director, Finance & Administration
Steve Sampsell, Director, Strategic Communications
Jose Lugaro, Director of Development
The Bart Richards Award for Media Criticism honors work that evaluates news media coverage of significant subjects or issues. The award is intended to recognize constructively critical articles, books, and electronic media reports; academicand other research; and reports by media ombudsmen and journalism watchdog groups. Entrants are judged by professionals from journalism and journalism education. The winner receives $1,500 honorarium and is expected to attend the award ceremony andto talk on the subject for which he or she is being honored.
Award Description:
Recognnizes distinguished contributions to the improvement of print & bcst journalism through responsible journalism.

Batten Fellows Program
Mailing Address: 100 Darden Boulevard, The Darden School, University of Virginia, Charlottesville, VA 22903
Second Address: PO Box 6550, Charlottesville, VA 22906
(434) 924-1335; *Fax:* (434) 924-7104
www.darden.virginia.edu
batten@darden.virginia.edu
Sean Carr, Executive Director
Debbie White, Director of Operations
The Batten Fellows Program brings prominent and high-potential thought leaders to the Darden School of Business for short and long-term visits. The aims of the program are as follows:
Award Description:
Awarded to pursuants in areas of enterpreneurship & corporate innovation.

BDA International Design Award
1522e Cloverfield Blvd., Suite 900, Santa Monica, CA 90404
(310) 788-7600; *Fax:* (310) 788-7616
www.promax.tv
adrienne@promax.tv
Allen DeBevoise, Chairman
Jonathan Block-Verk, President/CEO
Joe Earley, COO
Jill Lindeman, General Manager
RANDY SMITH, CFO
Lucian Cojescu, Chief Information Officer
Neal Arthur, Managing Director
Alex Alonso, VP, Marketing
Award Description:
Presented for outstanding achievement in electronic & bcst media.

Christopher Video Contest for College Students
The Christophers, 5 Hanover Sq., 22nd Floor, New York, NY 10004
(212) 759-4050; *Fax:* (212) 838-5073
www.christophers.org/page.aspx?pid=273
s.holinski@christophers.org
Robert V. Okulski, President/Treasurer
Mary Ellen Robinson, VP/COO
Tony Rossi, Director of Communications
Yaneza Santos, Finance Manager
Award Description:
Awarded to 10 college students upon presentation of a short video depicting ways 'One Can Make a Difference'.

Cinema/Chicago
Div/DBA: Chicago International Film Festival
212 W Vam Buren Street, Suite 400, Chicago, IL 60607
(312) 683-0121; *Fax:* (312) 683-0122
www.chicagofilmfestival.com
info@chicagofilmfestival.com
Michael Kutza, Founder & CEO
Mimi Plauche, Artistic Director & Programming Director
Vivian Teng, Managing Director
Jesse Charbonier, Director, Corporate Giving & Sponsorship
Katie Abascal, Festival Marketing & Media RelationsDirector
Sam Flancher, Competitions Coordinator
Lauren Ponto, Education Manager
Award Description:
Gold HUGO to best overall production. Silver HUGO, Gold Plaque, Silver Plaque, certificate of Merit to best production with a specific category.

The CLIO Awards Ltd.
825 8th Avenue, 29th Floor, New York, NY 10019
(212) 683-4300; *Fax:* (212) 683-4796
www.clios.com/awards
Nicole Purcell, President
Brooke Levy, VP, Marketing
Steve Mergaman, Associate Director of Judging
Karon Cannon, Entries & Judging Coordinator
Alexa Martinelli, Entries & Judging Coordinator
Award Description:
Excellence awards for Advertising, Design & Interactive Media.

Corporation for Public Broadcasting
401 9th Street, NW, Washington, DC 20004
(202) 879-9600; *Fax:* (202) 879-9700
www.cpb.org
press@cpb.org
Patricia de Stacy Harrison, President & Chief Executive Officer
Michael Levy, EVP/COO
Westwood Smithers, Jr., Senior Vice President, General Counsel
William P. Tayman, Jr., Chief Financial Officer and Treasurer
Teresa Safon, SeniorVP, Corporate Secretary & Chief of Staff
Steven J. Altman, Executive VP & Chief Policy/Business Affrs Officer
Award Description:
Various grants throughout the year.

CTAM TAMI Award: See listing for Cable & Telecommunications Association for Marketing (CTAM)
Div/DBA: Cable & Telecommunications Assoc. for Marketing
120 Waterfront Street, Suite 200, National Harbor, MD 20745

(301) 485-8900; *Fax:* (301) 560-4964
www.ctam.com
info@ctam.com
Vivki Lins, President & CEO
Anne Cowan, SVP, Chief Communications Officer
Mary Shaw, Director, Communications & Media Relations
Members are honored for exceptional leadership in projects that benefit both CTAM and the industry at large.
Award Description:
Recognize individuals who have made outstanding contributions to cable communcations & pub affrs.

DGA Awards
Mailing Address: Directors Guild of America Inc., 7920 Sunset Blvd., Los Angeles, CA 90046
Second Address: 110 West 57th Street, New York, NY 10019
(310) 289-2000, (212) 258-0800; *Fax:* (310) 289-5384
www.dga.org
dgawebsupport@dga.org
Thomas Schlamme, DGA President
Russell Hollander, National Executive Director
Elisabeth Jones, Awards Administrator
Lily Bedrossian, Director, Media Relations
Award Description:
Adward for outstanding directorial achievement.

EDGE Awards - Entertainment Industries Council Inc.
Mailing Address: 12020 Sunrise Valley Drive, Suite 100, Reston, VA 20191
Second Address: GRB Entertainment, 13400 Riverside Dr., Ste 300, Sherman Oaks, CA 91423
(703) 481-1414, (818) 728-7600; *Fax:* (703) 481-1418
www.eiconline.org
eiceast@eiconline.org
Brian Dyak, Founder & Board Director
Marie Gallo Dyak, President/CEO
Award Description:
Recognizes feature films, TV movies, reality programs that effectively promote firearm safety & discourage gun violence.

Freedoms Foundation National Awards
Freedoms Foundation at Valley Forge, 1601 Valley Forge Rd., Valley Forge, PA 19482-0706
(610) 933-8825; *Fax:* (610) 935-0522
www.freedomsfoundation.org
info@ffvf.org
Wally Nunn, Interim President & CEO
Jason Raia, Executive VP
Maureen Troutman, Director, Comor Rltns/A A to the President
Eugene J. Halus, Jr., Director of Education
Shannon Sisson, Marketing & Development Coordinator
Teresa Erman,VP, Communications
Brett Wasdick, Maintenance Department
Deb Woolson, Director of Community Relations
This program was established as a way to say thank you to those citizens and organizations whose projects, words or deeds reflect the best of the American spirit of volunteerism and community service. We search for those doing good work intheir communities and bringing about the best in the spirit of America. Entries should focus on the themes of patriotism, responsible citizenship, values and community involvement.
Award Description:
Awarded to individuals or organizations which have made an impact on a loc, rgnl or natl level to teach, foster the principles & olbigations of freedom.

Gabriel Awards
205 West Monroe Street, Suite 470, Chicago, IL 60606
(312) 380-6789; *Fax:* (312) 361-0256
www.catholicpress.org
David Hains, President
Timothy M. Walter, Executive Director
Sue West, Gabriel Awards Adviser
The Catholic Academy of Communication Professionals has merged into the Catholic Press Association (CPA) in late 2017. Starting in 2018 the Gabriel Awards will be rolled into existing awards by CPA.
Award Description:
Honoring execellence in film, network & cable TV programs that uplift & enrich the human spirit.

George Foster Peabody Award
120 Hooper Street, University of Georgia, Room 320, Athens, GA 30602-3018
(706) 542-3787; *Fax:* (706) 542-9273
peabodyawards.com
peabody@uga.edu
Nate Kohn, Associate Academic Director
Margaret Blanchard, Communications Director
Molly Williams, Events & Sponsorship Coordinator
Lynh Tran, Associate Director, Strategy & Operations
Briana Kelly, Office Manager
Christine Drayer,Associate Director, Programming
The George Foster Peabody Awards recognize distinguished achievement and meritorious service by broadcasters, cable and Webcasters, producing organizations, and individuals.
Award Description:
Annual international awards for distinction & achievement within the fields of bcst journalism documentary film making & educ progmg .

George Polk Awards
Long Island Univ.,The English Dept, 1 University Plaza, Brooklyn, NY 11201-5372
(718) 488-1009; *Fax:* (718) 243-0766, (718) 246-6302
www.liu.edu/polk
polk.awards@liu.edu
Eric Krasnoff, Chairman
John Darnton, Curator
Ralph Engelman, Faculty Coordinator
Award Description:
A plaque.

Global Media Awards
Div/DBA: (For Excellence in Population Reporting)
The Population Institute, 105 2nd St. N.E., Washington, DC 20002
(202) 544-3300; *Fax:* (202) 544-0068
www.populationinstitute.org
info@populationinstitute.org
William Ryerson, Chairman & CEO
Robert Walker, President
Jennie Wetter, Director of Public Policy
Award Description:
Honors those who have contributed to creating awareness of population programs through their outstanding journalistic endeavors. Presented in developing countries.

Golden Mike Award
Broadcasters Foundation of America, 125 West 55th Street, 44th Floor, New York, NY 10019-5366
(212) 373-8250; *Fax:* (212) 373-8254
www.broadcastersfoundation.org
info@thebfoa.org
George G. Beasley, Chairman/CEO
Jim Thompson, President
Peter Doyle, Vice President
Emily Barratt, Office & Grant Manager
Award Description:
Broadcast industry excellent svc.

Heywood Broun Award
The Newspaper Guild-CWA, 501 Third St. N.W., 6th Fl., Washington, DC 20001-2797
(202) 434-7177; *Fax:* (202) 434-1472
www.newsguild.org
guild@cwa-union.org
Martha Waggoner, International Chairperson
Bernard J. Lunzer, President/CWA Vice President
Marian Needham, Executive Vice President
Sally Davidow, Communications Director
Kristina Harrison, Guild Coordinator
Marjolaine Botsford,Headquarters Contact
Joann Scheel, Headquarters Contact
Award Description:
Recognizes individual journalistic achievement by members of the working media in the advancement of social issues.

Ida B. Wells Award
Northwestern Univ., Medill School of Journalism, 1845 Sheridan Rd., Evanston, IL 60208
(847) 467-1882; *Fax:* (847) 491-2370
www.medill.northwestern.edu; www.nabj.org/?page=IdaBWells
m-awards@northwestern.edu
Award Description:
Presented annually to a media exec or mgr who has provided leadership in increasing access & opportunities to people of color in journalism. Sponsored jointly by the (NABJ) National Association of Black Journalists & the (NCEW) NationalConference of Editorial Writers.
Sam Adams (Curator)
Ida B.Wells Award, 1552 Alvamar Dr., Lawrence, KS 66047-1606

International Broadcasting Awards
HRTS, 16530 Ventura Blvd, Ste 411, Encino, CA 91436
(818) 789-1182; *Fax:* (818) 789-1210
www.hrts.org
info@hrts.org
Eric Schrier, Board President
Melissa Grego, Executive Director
Ruzzo Martinelli, Director of Events
Meshack Vallesillas, Marketing / Communications
Elvia Gonzalez, Executive Assistant / Member Services
Kira Hodge, OfficeManager
Adam Berkowitz, Vice President
Award Description:
Recognition for best radio & TV comls.

International Emmy Awards
The International Academy of Television Arts & Sciences, 25 West 52nd Street, New York, NY 10019
(212) 489-6969, (212) 489-1946; *Fax:* (212) 489-6557
www.iemmys.tv
iemmys@iemmys.tv
Ms. Camille Bidermann-Roizen, Senior Vice President & Executive Director
Tracy Oliver, General Manager
Ms. Gerry Brahney, Advertising Director
Mr. Nathaniel Brendel, Emmy Judging Director
Ms. Aurelie Dauphin-Fletcher, EventsDirector
Ms. Zoe Dyck, Marketing, Web & Design Manager
Ms. Jessica Franco, Emmy Judging Manager
Eva Obadia, Senior Director Communications & Partnership
The International Academy of Television Arts & Sciences is a membership based organization comprised of leading media and entertainment figures from over 50 countries and 500 companies from all sectors of television including internet,mobile and technology. The Academy's yearly schedule of events includes the prestigious International Emmyr Awards Ceremony held in New York, The International Digital Emmyr Awards at MIPTV and a series of industry events such as Academy Day, TheInternational Emmyr World Television Festival and Panels on substantive industry topics.
Award Description:
Awarded for excellence in TV programs produced & intially aired outside of the U.S.

International Radio & Television Society Foundation Gold Medal
1697 Broadway, 10th Floor, New York, NY 10019
(212) 867-6650 ext. 301; *Fax:* (212) 867-6653
www.irts.org
Stephen H. Coltrin, Chairman & CEO
Joyce M. Tudryn, President & CEO
Jennifer Webb, Senior Vice President of Operations
Kathleen Keefe, Vice Chairman
Henry Schleiff, Vice Chairman
Stuart Shorenstein, General Counsel & Secretary
Jed Kapsos, Treasurer
Susan Surillo Battafarano, VP Human Resources & Executive Services
Award Description:
Presented annually for significant career long contributions to the integrity, health & success of the electronic media industry.

IRE Annual Awards for Investigative Reporting
141 Neff Annex, Missouri School of Journalism, Columbia, MO 65211
(573) 882-2042; *Fax:* (573) 884-8151
www.ire.org
Sarah Cohen, President
Matt Goldberg, Vice President
Ellen Gabler, Secretary
Andrew Donohue, Treasurer
David Cay Johnston, Past President
Award Description:
The annual IRE Awards recognize outstanding investigative work across all media.

IRE Tom Renner Award for Crime Reporting
141 Neff Annex, UMC-Journalism, Columbia, MO 65211
(573) 882-2042; *Fax:* (573) 882-5431
www.ire.org
info@ire.org
Matt Goldberg, Vice President
Ellen Gabler, Secretary
Andrew Donohue, Treasurer
David Cay Johnston, Past President
The IRE Awards is the annual contest of Investigative Reporters and Editors Inc. recognizing the best in investigative reporting by print, broadcast and online media.
Award Description:
For outstanding crime reporting.

The John Bayliss Broadcast Foundation Internships, Scholarships Programs
Box 51126, Pacific Grove, CA 93950
(831) 655-5229; *Fax:* (831) 655-5228
Larry Patrick, Chairman
David Kennedy, Director & Treasurer
Bishop Cheen, Director & Secretary

Award Description:
Scholarships & internship opportunities for college students preparing for a career in radio bcstg.

John Chancellor Award
Columbia Univ Graduate School of Journalism, 2950 Broadway (at 116th Street), New York, NY 10027
(212) 854-8608; *Fax:* (212) 854-3148
www.journalism.columbia.edu
chancelloraward@jrn.columbia.edu
Sue Radmer, Operations Dir
Abi Wright, Director
Mike Pride, Administrator
Bud Kliment, Deputy Administrator
Lisa R. Cohen, Associate Director
Terri Thompson, Director
Gary Hill, Program Coordinator
The John Chancellor Award, founded in 1995, is presented each year to a reporter with courage and integrity for cumulative professional accomplishments. The prize honors the legacy of pioneering television correspondent and longtime NBC Newsanchor John Chancellor.
Award Description:
The $25,000 annual prize honors the legacy of John Chancellor. This award is intended to honor the sustained achievement of a single journalist, who may not be well-known nationally, but whose cumulative accomplishments are exemplary

Knight-Wallace Journalism Fellows
Wallace House, 620 Oxford Rd., Ann Arbor, MI 48104
(734) 998-7666; *Fax:* (734) 998-7979
www.kwfellows.org
kwfellows@umich.edu
Charles Eisendrath, Director
Birgit Rieck, Assistant Director
Melissa Riley, Special Projects Manager
Patty Meyers-Wilkens, Office Manager
Mary Ellen Doty, Finance Manager
A Knight-Wallace Fellowship is the rarest of opportunities: an academic year of study, reflection and growth at one of the world's finest universities, nestled in one of the nation's most livable cities. It is a time of expandingperspectives, intellectual growth and personal transformation.
Award Description:
Awarded to full-time journalists with a minimum of 5 years professional experience, $70,000.

The Livingston Awards for Young Journalists
Wallace House, 620 Oxford Rd., Ann Arbor, MI 48104
(734) 998-7575; *Fax:* (734) 998-7979
www.livawards.org
livawards@umich.edu
Charles R. Eisendrath, Director
Award Description:
For the best examples of print, online or bcst journalism, three $10,000 awards.

Mark of Excellence
3909 N. Meridian St., Society of Professional Journalists, Indianapolis, IN 46208-4011
(317) 927-8000; *Fax:* (317) 920-4789
www.spj.org
awards@spj.org
Dana Neuts, President
Paul Fletcher, President-Elect
Lynn Walsh, Secretary-Treasurer
David Cuillier, Immediate Past President
Sue Kopen Katcef, Vice President, Campus Chapter Affairs
Bill McCloskey, Directors At-Large
Joe Skeel,Executive Director
Annually, the Society of Professional Journalists presents the Mark of Excellence Awards, honoring the best in student journalism. The awards offer categories for print, radio, television and online collegiate journalism. Entries are firstjudged on the regional level. First place regional winners advance to the national competition and are recognized at SPJ spring conferences. National winners will be showcased on spj.org.
Award Description:
Awards honors the best in student journalism. Print, radio, TV & online collegiate journalism.

Missouri Honor Medal
Missouri School of Journalism, 120 Neff Hall, Columbia, MO 65211-1200
(573) 882-4821; *Fax:* (573) 884-5400
journalism.missouri.edu
journalism@missouri.edu
Medalists are selected by the faculty of the School on the basis of lifetime or superior achievement, for distinguished service performed in such lines of journalistic endeavor as shall be selected each year for consideration.
Award Description:
Awarded for distinguished svc in Journalism.

The Mobius Advertising Awards
713 S. Pacific Coast Hwy., Suite B, Redondo Beach, CA 90277-4233
(310) 540-0959; *Fax:* (310) 316-8905
www.mobiusawards.com
mobiusinfo@mobiusawards.com
Lee Gluckman, Chairman
Kristen Gluckman, Executive Director
Sandra Kelly, Media Relations
David Chan, Creative Director & Digital Coordinator
Each year, the competition recognizes outstanding work in Brochure/Book, Cinema-In-flight, Direct, Mixed Media Campaign, New Media, Online, Outdoor, Package Design, Photography, Point-of-Purchase, Print, Radio and Television mediums plusour Student competition.
Award Description:
Honoring creative excellence in mixed media.

NAB Crystal Radio Awards
NAB Radio, 1771 N St. N.W., Washington, DC 20036-2891
(202) 775-3511; *Fax:* (202) 775-3523
www.nab.org
nab@nab.org
W. Lawrence Patrick, Chairman
Gordon H. Smith, President & CEO
Joy Whitlow, CFO
Award Description:
Recognizes radio stns for outstanding year-round commitment to community svc.

NAB Marconi Radio Awards
NAB Radio, 1771 N St. N.W., Washington, DC 20036
(202) 775-3511; *Fax:* (202) 775-3523
www.nab.org
nab@nab.org
W. Lawrence Patrick, Chairman
Gordon H. Smith, President & CEO
Joy Whitlow, CFO
The NAB Marconi Radio Awards were established in 1989 and named after inventor and Nobel Prize winner Guglielmo Marconi. These prestigious awards recognize stations and individuals for their excellence and performance in 21 differentcategories.
Award Description:
Recognizes overall excellence in radio.

NAB National Radio Award
1771 N St. N.W., Washington, DC 20036-2891
(202) 775-3511; *Fax:* (202) 775-3523
www.nab.org
nab@nab.org
W. Lawrence Patrick, Chairman
Gordon H. Smith, President & CEO
Each year the National Radio Award honors an individual who is an outstanding leader in the radio industry. The NAB Radio Executive Committee selects the award recipient. Their decision is announced late spring/early summer. The award ispresented annually during the Radio Luncheon at the Radio Show.
Award Description:
Presented annually to an individual who is an outstanding leader in the radio industry.

The National Academy of Television Arts & Sciences Emmy Awards
1697 Broadway, Suite 404, New York, NY 10019
(212) 586-8424; *Fax:* (212) 246-8129
www.emmyonline.org
Chuck Dages, Chair
Bob Mauro, President & CEO
Paul Pillitteri, Senior VP, PR & Communicataions
Brent Stanton, Executive Director
Luke Smith, Awards Distribution Director
Steve Ulrich, Sports Emmy Awards & Events
David Wynn, News& Documentary Emmy Awards & Events
Award Description:
Recognizes outstanding achievements in all phases of TV, including progmg, directing, writing, performing, etc. The National Academy of TV Arts & Sciences also presents the Sports Emmy, The Technology, Engineering, New & Documentary, DayEntertainment, Humanitarian & Public Service Awards.

National Association of Broadcasters (NAB)
International Bcstg Excellence Award, 1771 N St., N.W., Washington, DC 20036
(202) 429-5300, (800) 622-3976
www.nab.org
nab@nab.org
W. Lawrence Patrick, Chairman
Gordon H. Smith, President & CEO
Joy Whitlow, CFO
Chris Ornelas, COO
The National Association of Broadcasters is the voice for the nation's radio and television broadcasters. As the premier trade association for broadcasters, NAB advances the interests of our members in federal government, industry and publicaffairs; improves the quality and profitability of broadcasting; encourages content and technology innovation; and spotlights the important and unique ways stations serve their communities.
Award Description:
Recognized international bcst organizations that have demonstrated exceptional leadership in advancing the bcst industry & svcs.

National Association of Broadcasters (NAB) Engineering Achievement Awards
1771 N St. N.W., Washington, DC 20036-2891
(202) 429-5300
www.nab.org
nab@nab.org
The National Association of Broadcasters is the voice for the nation's radio and television broadcasters. As the premier trade association for broadcasters, NAB advances the interests of our members in federal government, industry and publicaffairs; improves the quality and profitability of broadcasting; encourages content and technology innovation; and spotlights the important and unique ways stations serve their communities.
Award Description:
Awarded for individual outstanding achievement in significant contributions in advancement of the State of the Art of Broadcast Engineering.

National Awards for Education Reporting
Div/DBA: Education Writers Association (EWA)
3516 Connecticut Avenue NW, Washington, DC 20008
(202) 452-9830; *Fax:* (202) 452-9837
www.ewa.org
awards@ewa.org
Greg Toppo, President
Caroline W. Hendrie, Executive Director
Lori Crouch, Assistant Director
George Dieter, COO
Tracee Eason, Administrative Coordinator/Events Assistant
Brooke Watson, Events Coordinator
Award Description:
This prestigious contest awards prizes in 18 different categories & is the only independently judged educ writing competition of its kind in the United States.

National Headliner Awards
PO Box 239, 226 Mt. Vernon Ave., Northfield, NJ 08225
(609) 927-1850, (609) 350-3099; *Fax:* (609) 646-8826
www.headlinerawards.org
info@headlinerawards.org
Mark Melhorn, Program Chairman
Erika Melhorn, Contest Administrator
Diane D'Amico, Executive Director
Founded in 1934 by the Press Club of Atlantic City, the National Headliner Awards program is one of the oldest and largest annual contests recognizing journalistic merit in the communications industry.
Award Description:
Recognizes excellence in journalism.

The New York Festivals Advertising Awards
260 W. 39th St., 10th Fl., New York, NY 10018
(212) 643-4800; *Fax:* (212) 643-0170
www.nyfadvertising.com
nyfaprocessing@newyorkfestivals.com
Michael Demetriades, Executive Director
Susan Glass Ruse, Associate Executive Director
The New York Festivals Advertising Awards celebrates the best & most creative adv in the world. With entries and jury members from over 70 countries, it is the most diverse advertising awards competition in the world.
Award Description:
The New York Festivals Advertising Awards celebrates the best & most creative adv in the world.

The New York Festivals Radio Broadcasting Awards
260 W 39th St., 10th Fl., New York, NY 10018
(212) 643-4800; *Fax:* (212) 643-0170
www.newyorkfestivals.com/radio
info@newyorkfestivals.com
Gayle Mandel, Press Contact
Recognizes 'The World's Best Work' (TM) in radio bcstg. Entries are judged by a panel of radio experts from stns & companies throughout the world.
Award Description:
Recognizes 'The World's Best Work' (TM) in radio bcstg. Entries are judged by a panel of radio experts from stns & companies throughtout the world.

NPPA Annual TV News Photography & Editing Competitions
120 Hooper Street, Athens, GA 30602
(919) 237-1782
www.nppa.org
info@nppa.org
Melissa Lyttle, Board President
Akili Ramsess, Executive Director
Thomas Kenniff, Professional Services Director
Tom Barton, Editor - News Photographer Magazine
Mickey Osterreicher, General Counsel
Award Description:
Contest showcases the best news photography, editing in print, TV & on the website.

The Ollie Awards
American Center for Children and Media, 5400 N. Saint Louis Ave., Chicago, IL 60625
(773) 509-5510; *Fax:* (773) 509-5303
info@centerforchildrenandmedia.org
David Kleeman, President
Award Description:
Award for excellence in children's TV

Overseas Press Club of America Awards
40 W. 45th St., New York, NY 10036
(212) 626-9220; *Fax:* (212) 626-9210
www.opcofamerica.org
info@opcofamerica.org
Deidre Depke, President
Patricia Kranz, Executive Director
Amy Russo, Office Manager
The OPC seeks to maintain an international association of journalists working in the United States and abroad; to encourage the highest standards of professional integrity and skill in the reporting of news; to help educate a new generationof journalists; to contribute to the freedom and independence of journalists and the press throughout the world, and to work toward better communication and understanding among people.
Award Description:
Overseas Press Club of Americia has 20 awards for nwsprs, magazines, photography, cartoons, radio, TV, human rights & environment.

Paul Miller Washington Reporting Fellowships
National Press Foundation, 1211 Connecticut Ave. N.W., Suite 310, Washington, DC 20036
(202) 663-7280; *Fax:* (202) 530-2855
www.nationalpress.org
jschneider@nationalpress.org
Kevin M. Goldberg, Chair
Sandy Johnson, President & COO
Jenny Ash-Maher, Director of Operations
Tyler Mertins, Digital Media Manager
Jesse Schneider, Program Manager
Chris Adams, Director, Training & Content
Award Description:
Fellowship dedicated to itensive study sessions on subjects such as the Federal Budget, other Federal & Congressional matters.

PRISM Awards - Entertainment Industries Council Inc.
Mailing Address: 12020 Sunrise Valley Drive, Suite 100, Reston, VA 20191
Second Address: GBR Entertainment, 13400 Riverside Dr., Ste 300, Sherman Oaks, CA 91423
(703) 481-1414, (818) 728-7600; *Fax:* (703) 481-1418
www.prismawards.com
prism@eiconline.org
Brian Dyak, Founder & Board Director
Marie Gallo Dyak, EIC President & CEO
Tracy Thompson, Marketing, Publicity & PR
Award Description:
Recognize actors for outstanding performances in portrayal of substance abuse, addiction & mental illness onscreen, in TV & feature films.

PROMAXBDA Awards
5700 Wilshire Blvd, Suite 275, Los Angeles, CA 90036
(310) 788-7600; *Fax:* (310) 788-7616
www.promaxbda.org
awards@promaxbda.org
Steve Kazanjian, President & CEO
Stacey La Cotera, Senior VP, Global Awards Development
Lucian Cojescu, CIO
Christina Graziano, Director, Events & Global Conferences
Max Follmer, Manager, Marketing & Editorial
Award Description:
Recognizes the best in promotion & mktg.

Radio-Mercury Awards
22 Cortland St., 17th Fl., New York, NY 10001
(212) 681-7207; *Fax:* (212) 681-7223
www.radiomercuryawards.com
mercury@rab.com
Award Description:
Honors individuals, their employers who create, produce memorable, successful radio comls & pub svc announcements.

Robert F. Kennedy Journalism Awards
1300 19th Street, NW, Suite 750, Washington, DC 20036
(202) 463-7575; *Fax:* (202) 463-6606
www.rfkmemorial.org
info@rfkcenter.org
Robert Smith, Chairman
John Zurick, Chief Operating Officer
Kerry Kennedy, President
Terry Mazany, Vice Chairman
Anthony Williams, Treasurer/ Secretary
Anthony J. Cernera, Chief Institutional Advancement Officerÿ
Lynn Delaney,Executive Director
Brigette Vannall Wallace, Accountant
Saranah Holmes, Executive Assistant
Award Description:
Awarded for outstanding coverage of Social Justice issues.

RTNDA Edward R. Murrow Awards
529 14th Street, NW, Suite 1240, Washington, DC 20045
(202) 659-6510, 800-80-RTNDA; *Fax:* (202) 223-4007
www.rtnda.org
Amy Tardif, Chair
Loren Tobia, Treasurer
Mike Cavenderÿ, Executive Director
Derrick Hinds, Communications, Marketing & Digital Media Manager
Kate Switchenko, Director of Events and Awards
Karen Hansen, Membership and ProgramsManager
Jon Ebinger, International Programs Consultant
Award Description:
Awarded for outstanding achievement in electronic journalism.

Scripps Howard Foundation - National Journalism Awards
312 Walnut St., 28th Floor, Cincinnati, OH 45202-4067
(513) 977-3035; *Fax:* (513) 977-3800
www.scripps.com/foundation
sue.porter@scripps.com
Mike Philipps, President and CEO
Patty Cottingham, Vice President/Administration
Susan J. Porter, Vice President/Programs
Vickie Martin, Grants Administrator
Debbie L. Schneider, Executive Assistant
Jody Beck, Director
Award Description:
Since 1953 the Scripps Howard Foundation has recognized the best work in journalism through the National Journalism Awards. Cash prizes totaling $195,000 will be awarded in 19 categories for work January through December 2009. Most categoriesare open to staff and freelance journalists at radio, television and cable outlets. Online work also eligible. Entry deadline January 30; winners announced March 12; awards dinner April 23 in Tampa, FL. Review last year's winning entries and obtainofficial rules and entry form online after October 15:
www.scripps.com/foundation

Sigma Delta Chi Distinguished Service Awards Society of Professional Journalists
3909 N. Meridian St., Indianapolis, IN 46208
(317) 927-8000; *Fax:* (317) 920-4789
www.spj.org
awards@spj.org
Robert Leger, President
Dana Neuts, President-Elect
Paul Fletcher, Secretary-Treasurer
Sonny Albarado, Immediate Past President
Sue Kopen Katcef, Vice President, Campus Chapter Affairs
Al Cross, Director
David Cuillier,Director
Award Description:
Recognizes the best in professional journalism covering prints, radio, TV newsletters, photography online & rsch.

Silver Anvil Awards
Public Relations Society of America Inc., 33 Maiden Ln., 11th Fl., New York, NY 10038
(212) 460-1400; *Fax:* (212) 995-0757
www.prsa.org
awards@prsa.org
William Murray, President & COO
Philip Bonaventura, Chief Financial Officer
Stephanie Cegielski, Vice President, Public Relations
Christina Darnowski, Vice President, Membership
Jeneen Garcia, Vice President, Education
Alex Ortiz,Vice President, Information Technology
Nicole Zerillo, Vice President, Marketing
Award Description:
Recognizes excellence in PR, annually awarded to organization which have successfully addressed a contemporary issue.

Silver Gavel Awards
Mailing Address: American Bar Association, 321 North Clark Street, Chicago, IL 60654
Second Address: 1050 Connecticut Ave. N.W., Suite 400, Washington, DC 20036
(312) 988-5000, (202) 662-1000; *Fax:* (312) 988-5494
www.americanbar.org
howardkaplan@staff.abanet.org
Award Description:
Recognizes outstanding contributions to the pub info & understanding the roles of law & courts in our society.

Society of Motion Picture & Television Engineers Awards
3 Barker Ave., 5th Fl., White Plains, NY 10601
(914) 761-1100; *Fax:* (914) 761-3115
www.smpte.org
Wendy Aylsworth, President
Sally-Ann D'Amato, Director of Operations
Christopher Lennon, Engineering Dir
Barbara Lange, Executive Director
Joel E. Welch, Director of Professional Education
Roberta Gorman, Manager, MemberRelations
Aimee Ricca, Marketing & Communication
Mauricio Roldan, Manager of Engineering Services / Test Materials
June Marie Sobrito, Executive Assistant
The Society of Motion Picture and Television Engineers (SMPTE), is the leading technical society for the motion imaging industry.
Award Description:
Citation for Outstanding Svc to the Society recognizes individuals for dedicated svc to the society. The Presidential Proclamation recognizes individuals of established & outstanding status & reputation in the motion picture & TV industriesworldwide. Eastman Kodak Medal Award recognizes outstanding contributions that lead to new or unique educ programs using motion pictures, TV, high-speed & instrumental photography or other photographic sciences. The award recognizes dev in equipment,systems or instructional applications that advance the educ process at any or all levels. The John Grierson International Gold Medal Award recognizes significant tech achievements related to the production of documentary motion picture films.
Additional Awards
The Journal Award recognizes the outstanding paper originally published in the Journal of the Society during the previous calendar year. The Technicolor/Herbert T. Kalmus Gold medal Award recognizes outstanding contributions in the dev ofcolor films, processing, techniques or equipment useful in making color motion pictures for theater or TV use. The Fuji Gold Medal Award recognizes outstanding engrg achievements in the design & dev of new or enhanced techniques &/or equipment thathave contributed significantly to the advancement of photographic or electronic image origination.

Sunscan Award, Entertainment Industries Council Inc.
Mailing Address: 1856 Old Reston Avenue, Suite 215, Reston, VA 20190-3303
Second Address: 111 N First St, Suite 301, Burbank, CA 91502
(703) 481-1414, (818) 861-7782; *Fax:* (703) 481-1418, (818) 861-7186 (West Coast)
www.eiconline.org
eiceast@eiconline.org
John Landgraf, Chairman
Brian L. Dyak, President/CEO
David Goldsmith, Co-Chairman, Finance
Vice Treasurer
Award Description:
Recognition for entertainment production that address sun safety.

Voice of Democracy Scholarship Program
Mailing Address: VFW National Hqtrs., 406 W. 34th St., Kansas City, MO 64111
Second Address: 200 Maryland Ave., N.E., Washington, D. 20002
(816) 756-3390; *Fax:* (816) 968-1149
www.vfw.org
kharmer@vfw.org
Randi K. Law, Communications Manager
Joe Davis, Director of Public Affairs
Award Description:

Awarded to winner of audio essay competition based on their opinion of Civic Responsiblity, $30,000 scholarship. Open to high school students, ages 15-18.

Western Heritage Awards-The Wrangler
National Cowboy & Western Heritage Museum, 1700 N.E. 63rd St., Oklahoma City, OK 73111
(405) 478-2250; *Fax:* (405) 478-4714
www.nationalcowboymuseum.org
lyndahaller@nationalcowboymuseum.org
Award Description:
Honors works in Literature, Music Film & TV reflecting significant stories of the American West.

Trade Shows

AAF National Conference
1101 Vermont Avenue NW, Suite 500, Washington, DC 20005
202-898-0089; *Fax:* 202-898-0159
www.aaf.org
conference@aaf.org
James Edmund Datri, President & CEO
Number of Attendees: 807 *Description:* Provides a forum for all issues that concern constituents of the advertising industry. Share ideas and strategies for surviving and thriving, learn new strategies, network with clients,creatives, executives and students.

ADMERICA!
1101 Vermont Ave NW, Suite 500, Washington, DC 20005-6306
202-898-0089; *Fax:* 202-898-0159
www.aaf.org
aaf@aaf.org
James Edmund Datri, President & CEO
Constance Cannon Frazier, COO
Description: Connects all aspects of the advertising industry. Influential agencies, clients, media companies, suppliers, and colleges from across the country will address how to thrive in a recovering economy and how the changingculture of business and consumers is impacting our industry.

Advertising Law & Public Policy Conference
708 Third Avenue, 33 Floor, New York, NY 10017
212-697-5950; *Fax:* 212-661-8057
www.ana.net
info@ana.net
Bob Liodice, President & CEO
William Zengel, EVP, Member Relations
Duke Fanelli, SVP, Marketing & Communications
Description: Discuss new policy initiatives and how they will transform advertising; recent court decisions, regulatory changes reshaping the legal environment for advertising. Hear from FCC, FTC, and FDA experts and representatives.Registration begins at $795.

Advertising Media Credit Executives
PO Box 433, Louisville, KY 40201
502-582-4327; *Fax:* 502-582-4330
www.amcea.org
amcea@amcea.org
Cheryl E Szluzer, President
Sheila Wroten, Vice President
Number of Attendees: 400 *Description:* Media credit managers, editors, business mangers and other professionals gather for exhibits of advertising media such as newspapers, magazines, radio and television.

AES Convention
60 E 42nd Street, Room 2520, New York, NY 10165-2520
212-661-8528; *Fax:* 212-682-0477
www.aes.org
HQ@aes.org
Bob Moses, Executive Director
Roger Furness, Deputy Director
Jan Pederson, President
Frank Wells, President-Elect
Robert Breen, Vice President
Description: An international organization that unites audio engineers, creative artists, scientists and students worldwide by promoting advances in audio and dessiminating new knowledge and research.

Alaska Broadcasters Association Conference
700 W 41st Street, Suite 102, Anchorage, AK 99503
907-258-2424; *Fax:* 907-258-2414
akba@gci.net
Gary Donovan, President
Matt Wilson, Vice President
Charlie Ellis, Secretary/Treasurer
Chris Fry, Director

Number of Attendees: 225 *Description:* Provides assistance which enables members to serve their communities of license through educations, representation and advocacy.

American Public Communications Council
625 Slaters Lane, Suite 104, Alexandria, VA 22314
703-739-1322; *Fax:* 703-739-1324
Willard Nichols, President
Description: Conference, luncheon and 100 exhibits of public communications equipment and information including, pay phones, internet, atm, multimedia and more. Discussions include lobbying, the political climate, legal regulatory andlegislative updates.

American Society of Journalists and Authors
355 Lexington Avenue, 15th Floor, New York, NY 10017-6603
212-997-0947; *Fax:* 212-937-2315
www.asja.org
asjaoffice@asja.org
Holly Koenig, Interim Executive Director
Diane Jackson, Communications Director
Jennifer Murphy, Social Media Manager
Patrick Dougherty, Meetings Manager
Number of Attendees: 700 *Description:* A forum for the exchange of ideas between journalists.

American Society of News Editors (ASNE)
Washington Marriott Wardman Park, 2660 Woodley Road, NW, Washington, DC 20008
703-453-1122
www.asne.org/convention
jwon@asne.org
Jiyoung Won, Communications Coordinator
Teri Hayt, Executive Director
Description: ASNE's annual convention is the largest annual gathering of newsroom leaders from daily newspapers and other news organizations. Editors and leaders in the field of journalism education will gather to refresh their spiritsand create a roadmap to transform their newsrooms and shape the future of professional journalism.

ANA Annual Conference - The Masters of Marketing
708 Third Avenue, 33 Floor, New York, NY 10017
212-697-5950; *Fax:* 212-661-8057
www.ana.net
info@ana.net
Bob Liodice, President & CEO
William Zengel, EVP, Member Relations
Duke Fanelli, SVP, Marketing & Communications
Description: The conference offers an opportunity to learn from and engage with the leaders of the industry as they build brands, leverage the expanding array of media, make marketing more accountable and improve the quality of theirmarketing organizations.

ANA Digital & Social Media Conference
708 Third Avenue, 33 Floor, New York, NY 10017
212-697-5950; *Fax:* 212-661-8057
www.ana.net
info@ana.net
Robert Liodice, President & CEO
William Zengel, EVP, Member Relations
Duke Fanelli, SVP, Marketing & Communications
Description: Discussing how to use social media to impact the consumer decision journey and how to effectively partner with other companies to maximize social media reach and more.

ANA TV & Everything Video Forum
708 Third Avenue, 33 Floor, New York, NY 10017
212-697-5950; *Fax:* 212-661-8057
www.ana.net
info@ana.net
Bob Liodice, President & CEO
William Zengel, EVP, Member Relations
Duke Fanelli, SVP, Marketing & Communications
Description: The forum recognizes that the role of television in the media mix is being redefined and broadened. In addition to traditional television, the TV & Everything Video Forum will explore the use of video on any type of screenor device: the computer, Internet, mobile, point-of-purchase, gaming, and more. Registration starts at $595.

ANA/WFA Global Marketing Conference
708 Third Avenue, 33 Floor, New York, NY 10017
212-697-5950; *Fax:* 212-661-8057
www.ana.net
info@ana.net
Robert Liodice, President & CEO
William Zengell, EVP, Member Relations
Duke Fanelli, SVP, Marketing & Communications
Description: Offers tips on marketing on a worldwide scale.

Annual Community Radio Conference
1970 Broadway, Suite 1000, Oakland, CA 94612
510-451-8200; *Fax:* 510-451-8208
www.nfcb.org
Carol Pierson, President/CEO
Virginia Z Berson, VP Federation Services
Number of Attendees: 300 *Description:* National conference for public community radio stations offering opportunities for staff development, skill building, networking, affinity group, inspiration, new ideas, discussion andexchanges; exhibit area; programming awards. Business meetings for National Federation of Community Broadcasters.

Annual Conference for Catalog & Multichannel Merchants
1120 Avenue of Americas, New York, NY 10036
212-768-7277; *Fax:* 212-768-4547
www.the-dma.org
Julie Hogan, SVP Conference & Events
Number of Attendees: 10M *Description:* Adding all the best of digital and direct marketing, this even will provide a robust marketing tool box for attendees looking for innovative content that maximizes customer experience andROI.

Annual IBS Broadcasting & Webcasting
367 Windsor Highway, New Windsor, NY 12553-7900
845-565-0003; *Fax:* 845-565-7446
www.ibsradio.org
ibshq@aol.com
Norman Prusslin, President
Fritz Kass, Chief Operating Officer
Number of Attendees: 1.2M *Description:* Over 110 seminars, live music, over 250 top broadcasting professionals, and 1,200 student radio & webcasters from around the world. Live webstream during conference.

Annual Multimedia Convention & Career Expo
Disney's Coronado Spings Resort, 1000 W Buena Vista Drive, Lake Buena Vista, FL 32830

www.nahjconvention.org
Michele Salcedo, President
Manuel De La Rosa, Vice President/Broadcast
Russell Contreras, VP Print/Financial Officer
Description: NAHJ is dedicated to the recognition and professional advancement of Hispanics in the news industry. NAHJ created a national voice and unified vision for all Hispanic journalists.

Associated Press Media Editors (APME)
Washington Marriott Wardman Park, 2660 Woodley Road NW, Washington, DC 20008
212-621-1766
www.apme.com
apmeconference@ap.org; snordgren@ap.org
Jim Simon, President
Angie Muhs, Vice President
Paula Froke, Executive Director
Sarah Nordgren, Conference Contact
Description: APME is an association of U.S. and Canadian editors, broadcasters and educators whose entitites are members of The Associated Press.

Association for Education in Journalism & Mass Communication (AEJMC)
234 Outlet Pointe Boulevard, Suite A, Columbia, SC 29210-5667
803-798-0271; *Fax:* 803-772-3509
www.aejmc.org/
Jennifer D. Greer, President
Jennifer McGill, Executive Director
Belinda Pearson, Association Business Manager
Samantha Higgins, Public Relations Manager
Amanda Caldwell, Conference/Meetings Manager
Number of Attendees: 2000 *Description:* Annual show of publishers and educational groups. Exhibits include publications, information retrieval services and special programs.

Audio Engineering Society Meeting
60 E 42nd Street, Room 2520, New York, NY 10165-2520
212-661-8528; *Fax:* 212-682-0477
www.aes.org
Roger K Furness, Executive Director
Number of Attendees: 5M *Description:* 250 booths, held in the fall and spring of each year.

AWC National Conference
1717 E. Republic Road, Suite A, Springfield, MO 65804
417-886-8606; *Fax:* 417-886-3685
www.womcom.org
members@womcom.org

Becky Lucas, National Office
Kristin E. Van Nort, Chair
Description: Annual conference and exhibits of journalism, public relations, advertising, marketing, educational communications and film.

Broadcast Designers' Association
145 W 45th Street, Room 1100, New York, NY 10036-4008
212-376-6222; *Fax:* 212-376-6202
Description: Annual show and exhibits of broadcast design equipment, supplies and services.

Broadcast Engineering Conference (BEC)
9102 N Meridian Street, Suite 150, Indianapolis, IN 46260
317-846-9000; *Fax:* 317-846-9120
www.sbe.org
mclappe@sbe.org
John Poray, Executive Director
Vincent A Lopez, President
Number of Attendees: 500 *Description:* Offers broadcast engineers the opportunity to attend educational sessions, see the latest equipment and supplies, and meet with peers.

Cable Advertising Conference
830 3rd Avenue, 2nd Floor, New York, NY 10022
212-508-1200; *Fax:* 212-832-3268
www.thecab.tv
Sean Cunningham, President
Number of Attendees: 2000 *Description:* Annual conference and exhibits of advertising-supported cable television networks and services to support local advertising sales.

Cable and Satellite: European
255 Washington Street, Newton, MA 02458-1637
617-584-4900; *Fax:* 617-630-2222
Elizabeth Hitchcock, International Sales
Number of Attendees: 7.9M *Description:* Communications forum for professionals in the broadcasting industry.

Cable Television Trade Show and Convention: East
6175 Barfield Road NE, Suite 220, Atlanta, GA 30328-4327
404-252-2454; *Fax:* 404-252-0215
Nancy Horne, Show Manager
Number of Attendees: 6M *Description:* NCTA also hosts the industry's annual trade show, which serves as a national showcase for the cable industry's innovative services, including quality television programming, interactivetelevision services, high-speed Internet access, and competitive local telephone service.

Collegiate Press Association Trade Show
330 21st Avenue S, Minneapolis, MN 55455-0480
612-625-3500; *Fax:* 612-626-0720
Tom Rolnicki, Show Manager
Number of Attendees: 1.2M *Description:* 20 booths including learning sessions and press conferences.

Comprehensive CRM & Database Marketing
1120 Avenue of the Americas, New York, NY 10036-6700
212-768-7277; *Fax:* 212-302-6714
www.the-dma.org
customerservice@the-dma.org
Lawrence M Kimmel, CEO
Description: In an increasingly digital marketing landscape, metrics and ROI are being scrutinized and recalibrated like never before. Whether interested in classic database statistics or emerging trends in web analytics, the insightsgained in our classes will add up to success.

CreateTech
1065 Avenue of the Americas, 16th Floor, New York, NY 10018
212-682-2500; *Fax:* 212-682-8391
www.aaaa.org
kipp@aaaa.org
Marla Kaplowitz, President & CEO
Chick Fox Grover, EVP, Creative Technology & Innovation
Alison Fahey, EVP, Chief Marketing Officer
Louis Jones, EVP, Media & Data
Description: Ongoing initiative and annual conference that provides a forum for technologists and creatives working in advertising. The cutting edge of technology and its influence on the advertising world is explored.

CRS - Country Radio Show
819 18th Avenue South, Nashville, TN 37203
615-327-4487; *Fax:* 615-329-4492
www.crb.org
info@crb.org
Ed Salamon, Executive Director
Chasity Crouch, Business Manager
Number of Attendees: 2,000 *Description:* Jams, discussions, introduction of new comers, Hall of Fame presentations.

DMA Annual Conference & Exhibition
1120 Avenue of Americas, New York, NY 10036-6700
212-768-7277; *Fax:* 212-302-6714
www.the-dma.org
dmaconferences@the-dma.org
Lawrence M Kimmel, CEO
Julie A Hogan, SVP Conferences/Education Services
Number of Attendees: 12000 *Description:* Offers a progressive marketers to help better engage customers and improve bottom line results in all channels, including social, search, mobile, video and more.

IAB Annual Leadership Meeting
116 E 27th Street, 7th Floor, New York, NY 10016
212-380-4700
www.iab.net
Randall Rothenberg, President/CEO
Description: IAB Annual Leadership Meeting-three days of intense networking among the most influential brand marketers, agency executives, and publishers, paired with powerful debate and discussion. Focused on the theme 'Beyond Timeand Space,' the speakers and audience, together, tackled the most pressing challenges facing the advertising industry and addressed breaking down the complexity of the evolving marketplace in order to continue share shift.

INFE's Annual Conference
14237 Bookcliff Court, Suite 200, Purcellville, VA 20132
703-421-4060; *Fax:* 703-421-4068
Jeff Hood, President
Description: Offers attendees unparalleled opportunities to plug into their industry and profession. Exhibitors, networking sessions, and CPE classes.

Integrated Marketing Members Only
99 Bedford Street, Floor 5, Boston, MA 02111
617-457-3938
www.ana.net
ksweet@pohlyco.com
Kristina Sweet, Assoc Publisher, Dir Sales & Mktg
Description: The development of new communications and the evolution of traditional communications have shifted power from the marketer to the consumer, which created enormous opportunities, providing marketers with the ability tobetter target their customers. Discover how top marketers develop, execute, and evaluate their overall marketing communications strategy based on consumer insight.

International American Press Association
2911 NW 39th Street, Miami, FL 33142-5148
305-634-2465
Julio Munoz, Executive Director
Number of Attendees: 500 *Description:* 12 booths.

International Newspaper Marketing
World-Herald Square, Omaha, NE 68102
402-734-7632; *Fax:* 402-444-1370
Terry Ausenbaugh, Chairman
Number of Attendees: 100 *Description:* 20 booths.

Magazine Media Factbook
Div/DBA: MPA-Association of Magazine Media
757 Third Avenue, 11th Floor, New York, NY 10017
212-872-3700; *Fax:* 212-906-0128
www.magazine.org
info@magazine.org
Linda Thomas Brooks, President & CEO
Isadora Hicks, Executive Assistant
Susan Fraysse Russ, Senior VP, Communications
Patty Bogie, VP, Creative Services & Events
Glenn Spoto, Senior VP & CFO
Elizabeth Tighe, VP, Marketing
Description: A comprehensive guide of magazine media facts for advertisers, advertising agencies, media planners and consumer magazine marketers.

MFM & BCCA Annual Conference
Div/DBA: Media Finance Focus
550 W Frontage Road, Suite 3600, Northfield, IL 60093
847-716-7000; *Fax:* 847-716-7004
www.mediafinancefocus.org
info@mediafinance.org
Mary Collins, President/CEO
Jamie L. Grande, Director of Operations
Arcelia Pimentel, Director of Sales
Olivia Benish, Administrative Coordinator
Brendan Doyle, Membership Coordinator
Number of Attendees: 800 *Description:* Offers professional education targeting media financial and business executives; CPE opportunities; exhibitors; roundtables; and networking opportunities.

MIP-TV: International Television
255 Washington Street, Newton, MA 02458-1637
617-584-4900; *Fax:* 617-630-2222
Elizabeth Hitchcock, International Sales
Number of Attendees: 9M *Description:* Spring market for the television industry to buy, sell and distribute television programming.

MIXX Conference & Expo
116 E 27th Street, 7th Floor, New York, NY 10016
212-380-4700
www.iab.net
lisa@iab.net
Lisa Milgram, Events Director
Margaret Southwell, Events Coordinator
Description: The premiere event for marketing and agency professionals-and the publishers and technology firms who help drive their efforts. Brings together the industry's most prominent and influential figures to share insights on themost pressing topics in advertising.

NAB Radio Show
1771 N Street NW, Washington, DC 20036
202-429-5300; *Fax:* 202-429-4199
www.nabshow.com
NABSHOW@experient-inc.com
Ann Marie Cumming, Senior VP, Communications
Kim Broome, Director, Exhibitor Experience & Show Operations
Kelly Bryant, Manager, Convention Operations
Description: A unique networking opportunity for station professionals representing all format and market sizes, with exhibits showcasing technologies, tools and solutions for the industry.

NAB Show
1771 N Street NW, Washington, DC 20036
202-429-5300; *Fax:* 202-429-4199
www.nabshow.com
NABSHOW@experient-inc.com
Ann Marie Cumming, Senior VP, Communications
Dan Lemle, Communications Coordinator
Kim Broome, Director, Exhibitor Experience & Show Operations
Kelly Bryant, Manager, Convention Operations
Number of Attendees: 85M *Description:* A global event for broadcasting news, legislation, networking, education and technology. Over 160 countries represented by 102,000+ attendees and exhibitors; conferences, and trainingsessions, and over 1,700 exhibitors.

NAMIC Conference
320 West 37th Street, 8th Floor, New York, NY 10018
212-594-5985; *Fax:* 212-594-8391
www.namic.com
info@namic.com
Kathy A Johnson, President
James Jones, VP Programs
Number of Attendees: 700 *Description:* Educational forum focused on leadership development, corporate diversity and inclusion, digital media and multi-ethnic content and programming. Content emphasizes diversity as a strategicbusiness imperative

National Cable Television Association
25 Massachusetts Avenue NW, Suite 100, Washington, DC 20001
202-222-2300
www.ncta.com
webmaster@ncta.com
Robert Sachs, CEO
Number of Attendees: 14M *Description:* Convention newsletter and programs concerning cable television. 2,000 booths.

National Conference of the American Copy
Sheraton New Orleans Hotel, 500 Canal Street, Nw Orleans, LA 70130
504-525-2500; *Fax:* 504-595-5552
www.sheratonneworleans.com
Teresa Schmedding, President
Lisa McLendon, Vice President Conferences
Sara Hendricks, Vice President Membership
Rudy Bahr, Executive Director
Gerri Berendzen, Content Editor
Description: ACES is a professional organization working toward the advancement of editors. Their aim is to provide opportunities through training, discussion and advocacy that promote the editing profession.

National Convention & Annual LGBT Media
2120 L Street NW, Suite 850, Washington, DC 20037

202-588-9888
www.nlgja.org
info@nlgja.org
Bach Polakowski, National Office Administrator
Matthew Rose, Membership Coordinator
Michael Tune, Executive Director
David Steinberg, President
Jen Christensen, Vice President/Broadcast
Description: NLGJA is an organization of journalists, media professionals, educators and students working within the news industry to foster fair and accurate coverage of LGBT issues. NLGJA opposes all forms of workplace bias andprovides professional development to its members.

National Editorial Conference
The Gleacher Center, 450 N. Cityfront Plaza Drive, Chicago, IL 60611
312-464-8787; *Fax:* 312-464-8683
www.gleachercenter.com
info@asbpe.org
Amy Florence Fischbach, President
Erin Erickson, Vice President
Tina Grady Barbaccia, Secretary/Treasurer
Janet Svazas, Executive Director
Robin Sherman, Associate Dir. & Newsletter Editor
Description: The National Editorial Conference focuses on the skills and ideas you need to weather the down economy and thrive in the new B2B publishing landscape.

National Magazine Awards (Ellie Awards)
ASME, 757 Third Avenue, 11th Fl., New York, NY 10017
212-872-3737; *Fax:* 212-906-0128
www.ellieawards.org;
magazine.org/asme/national-magazine-awards
info@ellieawards.org
Sid Holt, Chief Executive
Nina Fortuna, Director
Description: The National Magazine Awards honor magazines, published in print and on digital platforms, that consistently demonstrate superior execution of editorial objectives, innovative techniques, noteworthy journalistic enterpriseand imaginative art direction.

National Public Radio Association
635 Massachusetts Avenue NW, Washington, DC 20001-3753
202-513-2000; *Fax:* 202-513-3329
www.npr.org
Vivian Schiller, President & CEO
Howard Stevenson, Chair of the Board of Directors
Mitch Praver, COO
Number of Attendees: 1.2M *Description:* Seventy five booths for public radio professionals and providers of resource materials for public radio.

National Religious Broadcasters Annual
9510 Technology Drive, Manassas, VA 20110
703-330-7000; *Fax:* 703-330-7100
www.nrb.org
info@nrb.org
Dr Frank Wright, President/CEO
Linda Smith, President Assistant
David Keith, VP Operations
Number of Attendees: 5,700 *Description:* Containing 280 exhibits. Broadcast and communications emphasis.

National Scholastic Press Association
330 21st Avenue S, Suite 620, Minneapolis, MN 55455-0479
612-625-8335; *Fax:* 612-626-0720
Tom Rolnicki, Executive Director
Number of Attendees: 1800 *Description:* Annual conference and exhibits of information on yearbook printing and photographic services, college journalism departments and video yearbook production services.

NATPE Market & Conference
5757 Wilshire Boulevard, Penthouse 10, Los Angeles, CA 90036-3681
310-453-4440; *Fax:* 310-453-5258
www.natpe.org
info@natpe.org
Nick Orfanopoulos, Senior VP Exhibitions
Beth Braen, Senior VP Marketing
Number of Attendees: 8000 *Description:* The National Association of Television Program Executives (NATPE) is a global alliance of business professionals engaged in the creation, development and distribution of content as well asadvertising and financial activities. NATPE is the world's largest non-profit association dedicated to facilitating the continued growth and convergence of all content across all distribution platforms.

NATPE: The Alliance of Media Content
6868 Wilshire Boulevard, Penthouse 10, Los Angeles, CA 90036-3681
310-453-4440; *Fax:* 310-453-5258
www.natpe.org
info@natpe.org
Pam Silverman, Exhibition & Advertising
Linda Nichols, Exhibitor Services
Eric Low, Registration & Membership
Number of Attendees: 1000 *Description:* The National Association of Television Program Executives (NATPE) is a global alliance of business professionals engaged in the creation, development and distribution of content as well asadvertising and financial activities. NATPE is the world's largest non-profit association dedicated to facilitating the continued growth and convergence of all content across all distribution platforms.

NECTA Convention & Exhibition
Ten Forbes Road, Suite 440W, Braintree, MA 02184-2648
781-843-3418; *Fax:* 781-849-6267
www.necta.info
info@necta.info, ckillian@necta.info
Paul Cianelli, President
Timothy O. Wilkeson, VP & Policy Counsel
Carolyn Killian, Office Manager
Number of Attendees: 1.1M *Description:* A five state regional trade association representing substantially all private cable telecommunications companies in Connecticut, Massachusetts, New Hampshire, Rhode Island, and Vermont.

Newspaper Association of America
1921 Gallows Road, Suite 600, Vienna, VA 22182-3995
703-902-1600; *Fax:* 703-902-1600
James Abbott, VP
Number of Attendees: 1M *Description:* NAA mediaXchange, the largest annual gathering of newspaper media industry executives in North America, offers unprecedented networking opportunities that combine an exchange of informationand ideas with programming designed to generate results. The conference is designed to provide valuable ideas and insights to help newspaper professionals grow audience and revenue for their print and digital products. Sessions highlight leading-edgethinking about media strategies, successes in product and revenue development, new ideas and innovation inside and outside the industry, and tactics and techniques to employ in print and digital.

NRF Annual Convention & EXPO
325 7th Street NW, Suite 1100, Washington, DC 20004
202-661-3052; *Fax:* 202-737-2849
www.rama-nrf.org
Mike Gatti, Executive Director
Megan Zatko, Marketing Manager
Number of Attendees: 400 *Description:* RAMA is undertaking in important transformation to become an organization that's representative of the changes that are affecting the retail marketing community with a strategic view thatincludes the integration of mobile, digital and traditional media.

OAB Broadcast Engineering Conference
9102 N Meridian Street, Suite 150, Indianapolis, IN 46260
317-846-9000; *Fax:* 317-846-9120
www.sbe.org
mclappe@sbe.org
Vincent A Lopez, President
John Poray, Executive Director
Description: Offers broadcast engineers the opportunity to attend educational sessions, see the latest equipment and supplies, and meet with peers.

RAB2009 Conference
1320 Greenway Drive, Suite 500, Irving, TX 75038
972-536-6700; *Fax:* 972-753-6727
www.rab.com
jhaley@rab.com
Jeff Haley, President
Leah Kamon, SVP Marketing
Number of Attendees: 1600 *Description:* Learn about new media opportunities from new digital platforms and monetizing streams to HD strategies that will empower you to compete at a new level and be an innovator at your station.

RAC: The Show
325 7th Street NW, Suite 1100, Washington, DC 20004
202-661-3052; *Fax:* 202-737-2849
www.rama-nrf.org
Mike Gatti, Executive Director
Megan Zatko, Marketing Manager
Number of Attendees: 700 *Description:* Event for advertising agencies, media partners, consultants and retailers seeking fresh ideas and lasting solutions to their marketing and advertising challenges.

Recruiting Conference and Expo
1 Phoenix Mill Lane, Floor 3, Peterborough, NH 03458
603-924-1006
www.recruiting2006.com
conferences@kennedyinfo.com
Matt Lyons, Director, Recruiting Group
Description: Learn about the winning strategies, best practices, and tools ou will need to succeed in a challenging talent market.

Response Expo
201 Sandpointe Ave, Suite 500, Santa Ana, CA 92707-8700
714-338-6700; *Fax:* 714-513-8482
www.responsemagazine.com
thaire@questex.com
Thomas Haire, Editor
Don Rosenberg, VP
Kristina Kronenberg, Marketing Director
Description: Focuses on the evolution of consumers from passive watchers to active and empowered brand evangelists. Technology and social media have enabled and encouraged consumers to engage and interact with content. Learn how totake DR marketing from traditional campaign management to the future of customer engagement.

SABEW Annual Conference
ASU, Walter Cronkite School of Journalism, 555 North Central Ave, Suite 416, Phoenix, AZ 85004-1248
602-496-7862
www.sabew.org
sabew@sabew.org
Warren Watson, Executive Director
Lacey Clements, Marketing Director
Mark Scarp, Membership Director
Brant Houston, Executive Director
Description: Defines and inspires excellence in business journalism.

Satellite Broadcasting and Communication
900 Jorie Boulevard, Suite 200, Oak Brook, IL 60523-3835
Fax: 630-990-2077
Diana Bubalo, Show Manager
Number of Attendees: 2.5M *Description:* Join thousands of communications professionals in the satellite community to explore next generation products and technology on the Exhibit Floor and discuss tomorrow's solutions for today'schallenges with experts, thought leaders and veterans from the field. Our mission is to keep you up-to-date on recent developments and challenges in the satellite community. The SATELLITE Conference and Exhibition is led by professionals in thecommunity who have their finger on the pulse of satellite-enabled communications to ensure you experience the most relevant topics and receive actionable solutions.

SCTE Cable-Tec EXPO
140 Philips Road, Exton, PA 19341-1318
610-363-6888; *Fax:* 610-363-5898
www.scte.org
scte@scte.org
Lori Bower, Director
John Clark, CEO
Number of Attendees: 12M *Description:* Five hundred booths and, exhibits featuring telecommunications and programming equipment; dozens of workshops, with new technologies showcased.

SMPTE Annual Tech Conference & EXPO
3 Barker Avenue, 5th Floor, White Plains, NY 10601
914-761-1100; *Fax:* 914-761-3115
www.smpte.org
Sally-Ann D'Amato, Director of Operations
Peter Symes, Director of Engineering & Standards
Joel Welch, Director, Professional Development
Description: SMPTE annual Technical Conference & Exhibition-THE premier annual event for motion imaging and media technology, production and operations. Join us and network with world-renowned technology thought-leaders in the motionpicture studios, broadcast and distribution networks, production and post-production community, software companies, systems integrators, manufacturers, display technologies and distribution providers. As an accredited industry standards-setting body,SMPTE is also the industry's leading nonprofit association providing technology education and information to the motion imaging industry. We're all about creation, management, distribution and display of the moving image. We offer three days ofhighly technical sessions, a high-tech exhibition hall and unparalleled networking opportunities.

Television Bureau of Advertising Annual
3 E 54th Street, New York, NY 10022

212-486-1111; *Fax:* 212-935-5631
www.tvb.org
info@tvb.org
Chris Rohrs, President
Abby Auerbach, EVP
Gary Bellis, VP/Communications
Description: Annual show of 20-25 exhibitors of services for television stations, including research, sales and management training programs, incentives, collection agencies, advertiser contests and computer software.

West Coast Practicum
550m Ritchie Highway #271, Severna Park, MD 21146
888-664-0428; *Fax:* 410-544-4640
aip@aipparl.org
Mary Remson, CP-T, President
Alison Wallis, Vice President
Sadie Boles, Treasurer
Jim Jones, CPP-T, Accrediting Director
Jeanette Williams, CP-T, Education Director
Description: Topics being covered are convention committees, boards and problems related to boards, reference committees and the parliamentarian's role in consulting with boards.

Western Cable Television Conference and
11820 Parklawn Drive, Suite 250, Rockville, MD 20852-2505
301-519-1610
Susan Rosenstock, Expo Director
Number of Attendees: 10M *Description:* One thousand three hundred booths featuring exhibits of programming, mobile aerial devices, video equipment and products and services for the communications and related industry fields.

Western Show
11820 Parklawn Drive, Suite 250, Rockville, MD 20852-2505
301-519-1610; *Fax:* 301-468-3662
Susan Rosenstock, Director
Number of Attendees: 10M *Description:* One thousand booths featuring exhibits from cable operators and suppliers to the cable industry. The California Cable Television Association and the Arizona Cable Television Associationsponsor this annual event.

Union/Labor Groups

Actors' Equity Association (AEA)
Div/DBA: (AFL-CIO)
Mailing Address: 165 W. 46th St., New York, NY 10036
Second Address: 557 West Randolph Street, Chicago, IL 60661
(212) 869-8530, (321) 641-0393; *Fax:* (212) 719-9815, (321) 641-6365
www.actorsequity.org
Kate Shindle, President
Mary McColl, Executive Director
Steve DiPaola, Assistant Exec. Dir., Finance & Administration
Thomas Carpenter, Assistant Exec. Dir./Eastern Regional Director
Gail E. Gabler, Assistant Exec. Dir./WesternRegional Director
Christian Hainds, Assistant Exec. Dir./Central Regional Director
Brandon Lorenz, National Director of Communications
Founded in 1913; represents more than 50,000 members. Labor Union for Theatrical Actors & Stage mgrs.
10319 Orangewood Blvd, Orlando, FL 32821-8239
(407) 345-8600; *Fax:* (407) 345-1522
Brian Spitler, Business Rep
350 Sansome St., Ste 900, San Francisco, CA 94104-1316
(415) 391-3838; *Fax:* (415) 391-0102
Joel Reamer, Business Rep
125 S. Clark St., Chicago, IL 60603-5200
(312) 641-0393; *Fax:* (312) 641-6365
Kathryn Lamkey, Central Rgnl Dir
5757 Wilshire Blvd, Suite 1, Los Angeles, CA 90036-5810
(323) 634-1750; *Fax:* (323) 634-1777

Affiliated Property Craftspersons (IATSE Local 44)
Div/DBA: (IATSE, AFL-CIO)
12021 Riverside Dr., North Hollywood, CA 91607
(818) 769-2500; *Fax:* (818) 769-1739
www.local44.org
callboard@local144.org
Affiliated Property Craftspersons Local 44 is a professional association of craft persons having specialized skills and talents within the entertainment industry.

American Federation of Labor-Congress of Industrial Organizations (AFL-CIO)
815 16th St. N.W., Washington, DC 20006
(202) 637-5000; *Fax:* (202) 637-5058
www.aflcio.org
Richard L. Trumka, President
Elizabeth Shuler, Secretary-Treasurer
Tefere Gebre, Executive Vice President
Carolyn Bob, Press Contact
The umbrella federation for 56 U.S. and international unions representing more than 12.5 million working men and women. They work to: ensure that all people who work receive the rewards of their work-decent paychecks and benefits, safe jobs,respect and fair treatment; to make the voices of working people heard in the White House, on Capitol Hill, in state capitals across the country and in corporate boardrooms;to provide an independent voice for working families and ways for workingpeople to be actively engaged in politics and legislation; to hold corporations accountable for their treatment of employees and ensure the voice of working people is heard in the financial system.

American Federation of Musicians, United States & Canada
Mailing Address: 1501 Broadway, Suite 600, New York, NY 10036
Second Address: Legislative Office, 5335 Wisconsin Ave., Ste 440, Washington, DC 20015
(212) 869-1330, (202) 274-4756; *Fax:* (212) 764-6134
www.afm.org
Ray Hair, International President
Bruce Fife, International Vice President
Everyday the American Federation of Musicians of the United States and Canada helps thousands of musicians just like you. We are the largest organization in the world representing the interests of professional musicians. Whether negotiatingfair agreements, protecting ownership of recorded music, securing benefits such as health care and pension, or lobbying our legislators, the AFM is committed to raising industry standards and placing the professional musician in the foreground of thecultural landscape.
75 The Donway W, Suite 1010, Don Mills, ON Canada
(416) 391-5161; *Fax:* (416) 391-5165
Bobby Herriot, Chairman
1717 K St. NW, Suite 500, Washington, DC 20036-5342
(202) 463-0772; *Fax:* (202) 466-9009
Hal Ponder, Chairman
Los Angeles
3550 Wilshire Blvd., Suite 1900, Los Angeles, CA 90010-2401
(213) 251-4510; *Fax:* (213) 251-4520

American Guild of Musical Artists
1430 Broadway, 14th Fl, New York, NY 10018-3308
(212) 265-3687; *Fax:* (212) 262-9088
www.musicalartists.org
agma@musicalartists.org
James Odom, President
Gerry Angel, Director of Operations
Leonard Egert, National Executive Director
Deborah Allton-Maher, Associate Executive Director
Griff Braun, New York Area Dance Executive
Eleni Kallas, National Director ofOrganizing and Training
Nora Heiber, National Dance Executive
John Ward, Midwest Counsel
Performing artists live to perform. But their talents, their skill and the beauty they create won't necessarily pay the rent, put food on the table or guarantee the necessities of life. Without forceful advocacy and defense of their rights,artists may be vulnerable to exploitation or illegal discrimination. They need protection. They can find it by joining AGMA, the American Guild of Musical Artists.

American Guild of Variety Artists
Div/DBA: (AFL-CIO)
Mailing Address: 363 Seventh Avenue, 17th Floor, New York, NY 10001-3904
Second Address: 11712 Moorpark Street, Suite 110, Studio City, CA 91604
(212) 675-1003, (818) 508-9984; *Fax:* (212) 633-0097, (818) 508-3029
Rod McKuen, President and CEO
David Cullum, Operations Dir
Judy Little, Vice President
Susanne K. Doris, Secretary-Treasurer
Labor Union for performers in live venues.
4741 Laurel Canyon Blvd, Los Angeles, CA
(818) 508-9984; *Fax:* (818) 508-3029

The Animation Guild (IATSE Local 839)
1105 N. Hollywood Way, Burbank, CA 91505
(818) 845-7500; *Fax:* (818) 843-0300
www.animationguild.org
info@animationguild.org
Steve Hulett, Business Representative
Steve Kaplan, Organizer
Lyn Mantta, Office Manager
Trell Jackson, Front Office
Ken Roskos, Computer Lab Administrator
Marta Strohi-Rowand, Plan Administrator
The labor union for animation & CG artists & technicians in southern CA.

Art Directors Guild & Scenic Title and Graphic Artists (IATSE Local 800)
11969 Ventura Blvd., 2nd Floor, Studio City, CA 91604
(818) 762-9995; *Fax:* (818) 762-9997
www.adg.org
scott@artdirectors.org
Mimi Gramatky, President
Cynthia Paskos, Operations Manager
Scott Roth, General Manager
Scott Roth, Executive Director
John Moffitt, Associate Executive Director
Alexandra Schaaf, Manager, Membership Department
Debbie Patton,Manager: ADG Awards, Events, and Gallery 800
Nicki La Rosa, Project Manager, Jurisdiction Info Management (JIM
Adrian Renteria, Manager, Mail Room
The ADG is comprised of Art Directors, Graphic Artists, Illustrators, Matte Artists, Model Makers, Scenic Artists, Set Designers and Title Artists.

Communications Workers of America (CWA)
Div/DBA: (AFL-CIO)
501 3rd St. N.W., Washington, DC 20001-2797
(202) 434-1100; *Fax:* (202) 434-1279
www.cwa-union.org
Larry Cohen, President
Jeff Miller, Promotions Manager
Annie Hill, Secretary-Treasurer
Chris Shelton, District 1 VP
Ed Mooney, District 2-13 VP
Judy Dennis, District 3 VP
Linda Hinton, District 4 VP

Directors Guild of America Inc. (DGA)
Mailing Address: 7920 Sunset Blvd., Los Angeles, CA 90046
Second Address: 110 West 57th Street, New York, NY 10019
(310) 289-2000, (212) 258-0800, (800) 421-4173; *Fax:* (310) 289-2029
www.dga.org
dgawebsupport@dga.org
Thomas Schlamme, President
Russell Hollander, National Executive Director
Through the collective voice of more than 15,000 members that the DGA represents, the Guild seeks to protect directorial teams' legal and artistic rights, contend for their creative freedom, and strengthen their ability to develop meaningfuland credible careers. On behalf of the DGA membership and staff, I hope you find our site useful and informative, and that you return often.
110 W. 57th St, New York, NY 10019-3319
(212) 581-0370; *Fax:* (212) 581-1441
Chris Lomdino, Eastern Exec Dir
400 N. Michigan Ave, Suite 307, Chicago, IL 60611-4130
(312) 644-5050; *Fax:* (312) 644-5775

International Alliance of Theatrical Stage Employees, Moving Picture (IATSE)
Mailing Address: 207 W. 25th St., 4th Fl., New York, NY 10001
Second Address: 10045 Riverside Drive, Toluca Lake, CA 91602
(212) 730-1770, (818) 980-3499; *Fax:* (212) 730-7809, (818) 980-3496
www.iatse-intl.org
iatsepac@iatse-intl.org
Matthew D. Loeb, President
James B. Wood, General Secretary-Treasurer
Michael J. Barnes, 1st International Vice President
J. Walter Cahill, 2nd International Vice President
Thomas Davis, 3rd International Vice President
AnthonyDePaulo, 4th Int'l Vice President / Co-Department Director,
Michael F. Miller, Jr., 6th Int'l Vice President / Dept. Director, Motion
The International Alliance of Theatrical Stage Employees, Moving Picture Technicians, Artists and Allied Crafts of the United States, Its Territories and Canada was founded in 1893 when representatives of stagehands working in eleven citiesmet in New York and pledged to support each others' efforts to establish fair wages and working conditions for their members. Our union has evolved over the succeeding 119 years to embrace the development of new entertainment mediums, craftexpansion, technological innovation and geographic growth.
10045 Riverside Dr., Toluca Lake, CA 91602-2543
(818) 980-3499; *Fax:* (818) 980-3496
Joseph Aredas, Chairman

ASSOCIATIONS, EVENTS, EDUCATION & AWARDS

258 Adelaide St E, Suite 403, Toronto, ON Canada
(416) 362-3569; *Fax:* (416) 362-3483

International Association of Machinists and Aerospace Workers (IAM)
9000 Machinists Pl, Upper Marlboro, MD 20772-2687
(301) 967-4500
R. Thomas Buffenbarger, President
Warren Mart, Operations Dir
Robert Roach, Jr., General Secretary/Treasurer
Dave Ritchie, General VP
Lynn D. Tucker, Jr., General Vice President
Robert Martinez, Jr., General Vice President
GaryR. Allen, General Vice President-Western Territory
Mark Blondin, General Vice President-Southern Territory

The International Brotherhood of Electrical Workers
6255 Sunset Blvd., Suite 721, Hollywood, CA 90028
(323) 851-5515; *Fax:* (323) 466-1793
www.ibew45.org
info@ibew45.org
The International Brotherhood of Electrical Workers is one of the most progressive unions in existence today representing some 750,000 members. Involved in the leading edge of technology, The IBEW represents more than 100,000 employees inthe telecommunications industry with over 400 collective bargaining agreements. Our members work in all phases of the industry-local and long distance telephone companies, cable television, wireless and communications systems.

International Brotherhood of Electrical Workers (IBEW)
Div/DBA: (AFL-CIO)
900 7th St. N.W., Washington, DC 20001
(202) 833-7000; *Fax:* (202) 728-7676
www.ibew.org
broadcasting@ibew.org
Edwin D. Hill, President
Peter Homes, General Manager
Salvatore J. Chilia, International Secretary-Treasurer
William F. Daniels, First District-International Vice-President
Frank J. Carroll, Second District-InternationalVice-President
Donald C. Siegel, Third District-International Vice-President
Kenneth W. Cooper, Fourth District-International Vice-President
Joseph S. Davis, Fifth District-International Vice-President
The International Brotherhood of Electrical Workers (IBEW) represents approximately 750,000 active members and retirees who work in a wide variety of fields, including utilities, construction, telecommunications, broadcasting, manufacturing,railroads and government. The IBEW has members in both the United States and Canada and stands out among the American unions in the AFL-CIO because it is among the largest and has members in so many skilled occupations.

International Cinematographers Guild
7755 Sunset Blvd., Suite 300, Hollywood, CA 90046
(323) 876-0160; *Fax:* (323) 876-6383
www.cameraguild.com
Steven Poster, President
Bruce C. Doering, General Manager
Lewis Rothenberg, National Vice President
Paul Varrieur, First National Vice President
John Toll, Second National Vice President
Alan M. Giltin, NationalSecretary-Treasurer
Bruce Maccallam, National Assistant Secretary-Treasurer
Michael St. Hilaire, National Sergeant-at-Arms
Represents our members' contracts & activities.
80 Either Ave, 14th Fl, New York, NY
(212) 647-7300; *Fax:* (212) 647-7317
1411 Peterson Ave, Suite 102, Park Ridge, IL 60068-5000
(847) 692-9900; *Fax:* (847-692-5607
7463 Conroy-Windermere Rd, Suite A, Orlando, FL 32835-2761
(407) 295-5577; *Fax:* (407) 295-5335

International Sound Technicians (IATSE Local 695)
Div/DBA: (IATSE, MPMO)
5439 Cahuenga Blvd., North Hollywood, CA 91601
(818) 985-9204, (323) 877-1052; *Fax:* (818) 760-4681
Mark Ulano, President
James Osburn, Operations Dir

International Union of Electronic & Communications Workers of America
Mailing Address: 501 3rd St. N.W., Washington, DC 20001
Second Address: 2701 Dryden Rd, Dayton, OH 45439
(202) 434-1100, (937) 298-9984; *Fax:* (937) 298-2636
www.iue-cwa.org
James D. Clark, President
Bill Gray, Operations Dir
Willie Thorpe, Asst to the President
Lela Klein, Staff Attorney
Laura Hagan, Administrative Director
Peter Mitchell, General Counsel
Heather Atkinson, Political ProgramsManager
Pamela Deer, Dues Specialist

Make-Up Artist & Hairstylists Guild (IATSE Local 706)
828 N. Hollywood Way, Burbank, CA 91505
(818) 295-3933; *Fax:* (818) 295-3930
www.local706.org
info@ialocal706.org
Susan Cabral-Ebert, President
Tommy Cole, Operations Dir
Union for make-up artists, hair stylist's in motion picture industry.

Motion Picture Costumers (IATSE Local 705)
4731 Laurel Canyon Blvd., Suite 201, Valley Village, CA 91607
(818) 487-5655; *Fax:* (818) 487-5663
www.motionpicturecostumers.org
mpc705@aol.com
Steve Ferry, President
Buffy Snyder, Operations Dir
Debby Curtis, Vice President
Wanda Leavey, Secretary-Treasurer/Assistant Business Representat
Bob Iannaccone, Business Representative
Sue Bub, Member-at-Large
The gathering (by rental or puchase) of costumes for film & TV. The construction of new costumes (wardrobe). The fitting & handling of costumes (wardrobe) during filming.

Motion Picture Editors Guild (IATSE Local 700)
Mailing Address: 7715 Sunset Blvd., Suite 200, Hollywood, CA 90046
Second Address: 145 Hudson Street, Suite 201, New York, NY 10013
(323) 876-4770, (212) 302-0700; *Fax:* (323) 876-0861
www.editorsguild.com
mail@editorsguild.com
Alan Heim, President
Gregg Rudloff, Vice President
Louis Bertini, 2nd Vice President
Diane Adler, Secretary
Rachel B. Igel, Treasurer
Bill Elias, Sergeant at Arms
Jay Palmer, Maintenance Engineer Representative
Labor union representin post-production employees.

New York
145 Hudson St., Suite 201, New York, NY 10013-2103
(212) 302-0700; *Fax:* (212) 302-1091
Paul Moore, Asst Exec Dir

Chicago
6317 N. Northwest Hwy, Chicago, IL 60631-1669
(773) 594-6598; *Fax:* (773) 594-6599

Motion Picture Set Painters & Sign Writers (IATSE Local 729)
1811 W. Burbank Blvd., Burbank, CA 91506
(818) 842-7729; *Fax:* (818) 846-3729
www.ialocal729.com
Kirk Hansen, President
George Palazzo, Operations Dir

National Association of Broadcast Employees & Technicians
Div/DBA: (Communications Workers of America, AFL-CIO)
501 3rd St. N.W., Washington, DC 20001
(202) 434-1254; *Fax:* (202) 434-1426
www.nabetcwa.org
nabet@cwa-union.org
James C. Joyce, President
Charles G. Braico, Sector Vice President
Rich Gelber, Region One-Vice President
Fred W. Saburro, Region Two-Vice President
Maurice Thomas, Region Three-Vice President
Don Farnham, Jr., Region Four-VicePresident
Leroy Jackson, Region Five-Vice President
Representing employees in the bcstg, cable TV & related industries.
Local 11, 888 7th Ave., Suite 4511, New York, NY 10106-0001
(212) 757-3065
John S. Clark, Pres Nabet-Cwa

The Newspaper Guild Communications Workers of America
Div/DBA: (CWA)
501 3rd St. N.W., Washington, DC 20001-2797
(202) 434-7177; *Fax:* (202) 434-1472
www.newsguild.org
guild@cwa-union.org
Linda K. Foley, President
Bernie Lunzer, Operations Dir
Represents newsroom & other media workers in U.S., Canada & Puerto Rico.
Baxter Centre, 1050 Baxter Rd, Unit 7B, Ottawa, ON Canada
(613) 820-9777
Arnold Amber, Canadian Dir

Office & Professional Employees International Union
80 Eighth Avenue, Sixth Floor, New York, NY 10011
(212) 367-0902
www.opeiu.org
Michael Goodwin, President
Mary Mahoney, Secretary-Treasurer
Nicole Korkolis, Director of Communications, Education and Research
Melvin Schwarald, General Counsel
Walter Allen Jr., VP
Dennis Arrington, VP
Greg Blackman, VP
Office and Professional Employees International Union was chartered in 1945 and with more than 110,000 members (representing 125,000 employees) strong, we're one of the larger unions of the AFL-CIO. OPEIU has locals in every state, PuertoRico and Canada. You are not alone when you join OPEIU.

Professional Musicians, Local 47, AFM
817 Vine St., Los Angeles, CA 90038-3779
(323) 462-2161; *Fax:* (323) 461-3090
www.promusic47.org
eb@promusic47.org
Vince Trombetta, President
Serena Kay Williams, Operations Dir
John Acosta, Vice President
Gary Lasley, Secretary/Treasurer
Pam Gates, Director
Greg Huckins, Director
John Lofton, Director
Andy Malloy, Director
Musicians, vocalists, orchestrators, copyists, composers, conductors, contractors & librarians, referral service & recording studio.

Screen Actors Guild
Mailing Address: 5757 Wilshire Blvd., 7th Floor, Los Angeles, CA 90036-3600
Second Address: 1900 Broadway, 5th Floor, New York, NY 10023
(323) 954-1600, (855) 724-2387, (212) 944-1030; *Fax:* (323) 549-6656
www.sag.org
Alan Rosenberg, President
David White, National Executive Director
Arianna Ozzanto, Chief Financial Officer
Martha Lomeli Holdridge, Chief Human Resources Officer
Daniel Inukai, Chief Information Officer
David Viviano, ChiefEconomist
John McGuire, Senior Advisor
Contract administration, negotiation & enforcement, residual payment processing, regulation franchising of talent agents, membership, record-keeping & communication.

Script Supervisors/Continuity & Allied Prodution Specialists Guild Local 871, IATSE
Div/DBA: (IATSE)
11519 Chandler Blvd., North Hollywood, CA 91601
(818) 509-7871; *Fax:* (818) 506-1555
www.sagaftra.org
We think for a living. Script Supervisors/Continuity. Telepromptor Operators, Production Office Coordinator, Art Department Coordinator, Production Accountants & Assistants.

Service Employees International Union (SEIU)
1800 Massachusetts Avenue NW, Washington, DC 20036
(202) 730-7000, (800) 424-8592; *Fax:* (202) 350-6614
www.seiu.org
burgera@seiu.org
Mary Kay Henry, President
Anna Burger, Operations Dir
Eliseo Medina, Intl. Secretary-Treasurer
Kirk Adams, International Executive Vice President
Mike Fishman, Intl. Executive VP
Gerald Hudson, Intl. Executive VP
Eileen Kirlin,Intl. Executive VP
Valarie Long, Executive Vice President
SEIU is the fastest-growing union in North America. Focused on uniting workers in three sectors to improve their lives.

Studio Electrical Lighting Technicians (IATSE Local 728)
1001 W. Magnolia Blvd., Burbank, CA 91506
(818) 954-0728, (800) 551-2158; *Fax:* (818) 891-5288, (818) 954-0732
www.iatse728.org
local728@iatse728.org
Greg Reeves, President
Karen Weilacher, Vice President
Patric J. Abaravich, Business Rep./ Secretary
Pascal M. Guillemard, Call Steward / Treasurer
Alan M. Rowe, Safety & Training Director
Branch M. Brunson, Executive BoardMember
Iain O'Higgins, Executive Board Member

United Electrical, Radio & Machine Workers of America (UE)
One Gateway Ctr., Suite 1400, Pittsburgh, PA 15222-1416
(412) 471-8919; *Fax:* (412) 471-8999
www.ueunion.org
ue@ranknfile-ue.org
John H. Hovis, President
Bruce Klipple, Operations Dir

United Scenic Artists (IATSE Local USA 829)
29 W. 38th St., 15th Fl., New York, NY 10018
(212) 581-0300, (877) 728-5635; *Fax:* (212) 977-2011
www.usa829.org
administrator@usa829.org
Beverly Miller, President
Michael McBride, Operations Dir
Cecilia A. Friederichs, National Business Agent
F. Mitchell Dana, Vice-President
Cathy Santucci-Keator, Financial Secretary
Carl Baldasso, Corresponding Secretary
MattWalters, Central Region Business Representative
Monique L'Heureux, Western Region Business Representative
Representing designers of set, costume, lighting, sound, scenic artists, computer arts and art dept coordinators in the entertainment industry.
5225 Wilshire Blvd, Suite 506, Los Angeles, CA 90036-4301
(323) 965-0957; *Fax:* (323) 965-0958
Charles Berliner, Rgnl Business Rep
203 N. Wabash, Suite 1210, Chicago, IL 60601-2406
(312) 857-0829; *Fax:* (312) 857-0819
Chris Phillips, Rgnl Business Rep
10459 SW 78th St, Miami, FL 33173-2908
(305) 596-4772; *Fax:* (305) 596-6095
David Goodman, Rgnl Business Rep

Writers Guild of America, East Inc. (WGAE)
250 Hudson Street, Suite 700, New York, NY 10013
(212) 767-7800; *Fax:* (212) 582-1909
www.wgaeast.org
strell@sunshinesachs.com
Michael Winship, President
Dana Weissman, Director of Programs
Lowell Peterson, Executive Director
Ruth Gallo, Assistant Executive Director
Marsha Seeman, Assistant Executive Director
Justin Molito, Director of Organizing
JeremyPikser, Vice President
Simon Maxwell Apter, Online Communications Manager

Writers Guild of America, West Inc. (WGAW)
7000 W. Third St., Los Angeles, CA 90048-4329
(323) 951-4000, (800) 548-4532; *Fax:* (323) 782-4800
www.wga.org
Chris Keyser, President
Gabriel Scott, Operations Dir
Howard A. Rodman, Vice President
Carl Gottlieb, Secretary-Treasurer
John Aboud, Board of Director
Scott Alexander, Board of Director
Alfredo Barrios, Jr., Board ofDirector
Marjorie David, Board of Director
WGAW represents writers primarily for the purpose of collective bargaining in the motion picture, bcst, cable & new technologies industries.

Vocational & Career Development Schools

The Art Institute of Pittsburgh
1400 Penn Avenue, Pittsburgh, PA 15222
(412) 291-6200, (800) 275-2470; *Fax:* (412) 263-6667
www.artinstitutes.edu
admissions-aip@aii.edu
George W. Sebolt, President
Courses offered include audio recording & production, engrg, EFP video production, bcst media, feature writing, scriptwriting, legal issues, non-linear editing, image manipulation, filmmaking & multicamera field production.

Broadcast Center
2360 Hampton Ave., St. Louis, MO 63139
(314) 647-8181, (877) 334-8429; *Fax:* (314) 647-1575
www.broadcastcenterinfo.com
jberry@yourcba.com
Douglas H. Huber, President
Linda Hoy, Operations Dir
Ralph Stanley, Executive Director
Brian J. Miller, Broadcasting Director
Don Golaszewski, Video Production Director
Tiana Davis, Admissions
John Aughey, Engineering
KaraSavio, Placement Director
Training in mktg & time sls, coml & program production, bcst journalism & bcst performance. Training includes voice training & dev for bcstg; announcing training including news, comls, DJ & sportscasting; news & coml copywriting.

Broadcasting Institute of Maryland
7200 Harford Rd., Baltimore, MD 21234
(410) 254-2770, (800) 942-9246; *Fax:* (410) 254-5357
www.bim.org
info@bim.org
John C. Jeppi Sr., President
John I. Perry Sr., Operations Dir
Lois Carringan Sr., General Manager
Courses offered include comprehensive course in radio & TV bcstg; majors available in radio, TV production, news & sports.

Brown College
1345 Mendota Heights Road, Mendota Heights, MN 55120
(651) 905-3401, (800) 456-7222; *Fax:* (651) 905-3550
www.browncollege.edu
lwright@browncollege.edu
Sheila Malewska, President
Lisa Wright, Dept Chair School Of
The Associate of Applied Science degree in Radio Broadcasting is designed to help develop an on-air presence as well as the technical-hands on, and writing skills needed for positions in this growing industry. The Associate of AppliedScience degree in Television Production is designed to prepare students for an entry level position in a number of areas including: broadcast TV stations, industrial video firms, cable companies and satellite operations.

Carolina School of Broadcasting
3435 Performance Rd., Charlotte, NC 28214
(704) 395-9272; *Fax:* (704) 395-9698
www.csbradiotv.edu
myfuture@csbradiotv.edu
Courses offered include a non-tech bcstg group session & an in-stn training lab course; announcing, production, copywriting, news, digital coml production, sls & administration. Day & night sessions. In-stn training, full- or part-time asdetermined by stn & student. TV facilities & stereo control room; resident training in studio & stn opns at coml radio & TV stns worldwide. Digital audio & non-linear editing for TV.

Cleveland Institute of Electronics
1776 E. 17th St., Cleveland, OH 44114
(216) 781-9400, (800) 243-6446; *Fax:* (216) 781-0331
www.cie-wc.edu
instruct@cie-wc.edu
Paul Valvoda, CFO
John R. Drinko, President
Scott D. Katzenmeyer, Operations Dir
Offers associate in applied science degree in electronics engrg technology, bsct engrg. FCC license preparation & cable technician training.

World College
5193 Shore Dr., Suite 105, Virginia Beach, VA 23455-2500
(757) 464-4600, (800) 696-7532; *Fax:* (757) 464-3687
www.worldcollege.edu
instruct@cie-wc.edu
John R. Drinko, Pres

Clover Park Technical College
Mailing Address: 4500 Steilacoom Blvd. S.W., Lakewood, WA 98499-4004
Second Address: 17214 110th Avenue E., Puyallup, WA 98374-9509
(253) 589-5800, (253) 583-8904; *Fax:* (253) 589-5797
www.cptc.edu
Lua Pritchard, Chair
Dr. Lonnie L. Howard, President
Joyce Loveday, Vice President for Instruction
Tawny Dotson, Chief Communications Officer
Linda Schoonmaker, Vice President for Finance and Administration
Mary Moss, ViceChair
Ted Broussard, Vice President for Student Services
Janet Holm, Marketing / Outreach Coordinator
Bcst training since 1954. Comprehensive Associate degree program in all aspects of radio stn opn prepares students for entry-level employment. Course includes staff experience at 51-kw *KVTI(FM). A two-year state college. Assoc of AppliedTechnology degree programs.

Columbia College Hollywood
18618 Oxnard St., Tarzana, CA 91356-1411
(818) 345-8414, (800) 785-0585; *Fax:* (818) 345-9053
www.columbiacollege.edu
info@columbiacollege.edu
Patrick W. Zilliacus, Chairman
Richard Kobritz, President/CEO
Mark J. Stratton, Operations Dir
Richard Crowe, MBA, Sr. Director of Finance, Administration and New Ve
Ronald Reeves, Director of I.T. and Production Services
BrucePostman, Director of Recruiting
TheodoreÿO'Karma, Secretary / Treasurer
Carmen Munoz, Director of Admissions
Megan Hughes, Admissions Coordinator
Courses offered in TV/video production & cinema; degree program includes classes in directing, studio lighting, camera opns, videotape editing, scriptwriting, film editing, sound mixing, asst camera & script supervision. A.A. degree inTV/video production; B.A. degree in TV/video, cinema, and cinema/TV combination.

Columbia School of Broadcasting
301 A Maple Ave West, Suite G, Vienna, VA 22180
(703) 591-6000, (800) 362-0660; *Fax:* (703) 591-6147
www.csbdream2destiny.com
Kevin Williams, Chairman
Marthalie Furber, President
Bryant Moore, Executive Vice President
Frank Simone, Senior Vice President of D2D Film School
Dr. Thomas Wade, Chief Technology Officer
Russ Ekanger, CPA Board Treasurer, ChiefFinancial Officer
Virginia E. Hayes, Williams-Board of Secretary
Dr. Thomas Wade, Director of Technology
The Columbia School of Broadcasting-Dream 2 Destiny Film School provides a caring environment for students to achieve excellence in broadcast and entertainment media by building a foundation in professional skills and creative explorationsin new media.

Columbia School of Broadcasting: Dream 2 Destiny Film School
Div/DBA: (Washington, DC Metro Area)
301 A Maple Ave West, Suite G, Vienna, VA 22180
(703) 591-6000; *Fax:* (703) 591-6147
www.columbiaschoolbroadcas.com
djtrain@columbiaschoolbroadcas.com
Kevin Williams, Chairman/CEO
Marthalie Furber, President
Bryant Moore, Executive Vice President
Frank Simone, Senior Vice President of D2D Film School
Dr. Thomas Wade, Chief Technology Officer
Russ Ekanger, CPA Board Treasurer,Chief Financial Officer
Virginia E. Hayes, Williams-Board of Secretary
Briana Barksdale, Administrative Assistant
Courses offered include English & Sp radio announcing (voice-over, newscaster, DJ, sportscaster, traffic/weather reporter & interviews/talk show host), TV announcing, radio play-by-play sportscasting & basic radio production. Distance educ &resident courses offer comprehensive training for entry-level bcstg positions. Founded in 1964.

Connecticut School of Broadcasting, Inc.
Mailing Address: 73 TV Place, Needham, MA 02494
Second Address: 130 Birdseye Rd., Farmington, CT 6032
(781) 559-0005; *Fax:* (617) 267-2004, (860) 677-7577
www.gocsb.com
Dick Robinson, Chairman
David Banner, COO
Scott Knight, President
Jason Muth, Operations Dir
Katie MacKay, Promotions Manager
Courses (day & evening): On-air performance: Radio, TV, Internet bcst. Production courses: Digital audio & video, linear & non-linear avid editing. Other communications courses: Sports, voice-overs, sls, proms, mktg, wireless & multi-mediatechnology.

GCP Pawcatuck LLC
185 S. Broad St., 3rd Fl. #303, Pawcatuck, CT

(860) 599-1108; *Fax:* (860) 599-5915
Mwlanie Mariano, Campus Coord

GCP Davie LLC
3538 S. University Dr., University Park Plaza, Davie, FL 33328-2003
(954) 474-3700; *Fax:* (954) 474-7404
Angie Lopez, Dir

GCP Hasbrouck Heights
377 Rt. 17 S., #140, Hasbrouck Heights, NJ
(201) 288-5800; *Fax:* (201) 288-7966
Janet Hutsebaut, Dir
Kevin Foley, Career Svcs, (Nyc Area)

GCP Cherry Hill LLC
One Cherry Hill, #201, Cherry Hill, NJ
(856) 755-1200; *Fax:* (856) 755-0865
Tom DeFranco, Dir
Nicole McClintock, Campus Coord, (Philadelphia Area)

GCP Atlanta LLC
1117 Perimeter Ctr W., Suite N-301, Atlanta, GA 30338-5451
(770) 522-8803; *Fax:* (770) 522-9876
Aarib Elya, Dir
Peter Bernier, Campus Coord

GCP Stratford LLC
80 Ferry Blvd., Stratford, CT 06615-6079
(203) 378-5155; *Fax:* (203) 378-4330
Joe LaChance, Dir

GCP Tampa LLC
3901 Coconut Palm Dr., Sabal Business Center II, Suite 105, Tampa, FL 33619-8362
(813) 740-0990; *Fax:* (813) 663-0085
Kelly Crain, Dir

GCP Westbury LLC
1400 Old Country Rd., Suite 211, Westbury, LI, NY
(516) 338-1000; *Fax:* (516) 338-1170
Marty Herstein, Dir

GCP Arlington
2170 Crystal Plaza Arcade, #38, Arlington, VA 22202-4601
(703) 415-7600; *Fax:* (703) 415-0238
R.J. Narsavage, Dir
Marcella Jones, Campus Coord

GCP CSB Austin LLC
9600 Great Hills Tr., Suite 200-E, Austin, TX 78759-6387
(512) 340-1420; *Fax:* (512) 340-1430
Randy Ahrens, Dir
Jason Seale, Campus Coord

GCP CSB Dallas LLC
5605 N. MacArthur Blvd., Suite 220, Irving, TX 75038-2617
(214) 441-9941; *Fax:* (214) 441-9942
Scott Powell, Dir
Kristin Tran, Campus Coord

GCP Farmington
Media Park, 130 Birdseye Rd., Farmington, CT
(860) 677-7577; *Fax:* (860) 677-1141
Stacey Buba, Dir

GCP Needham LLC
73 TV Pl., Needham, MA 02494-2302
(781) 235-2050; *Fax:* (781) 444-0406
Steve Williams, Dir
Matt Sawyer, Office Mgr

GCP Palm Beach Gardens LLC
3450 Northlake Blvd., Suite 110, FL
(561) 842-2000; *Fax:* (561) 775-8390
Dave Duran, Rgnl Dir
Skip Kelly, Campus Coord

Dunwoody College of Technology
818 Dunwoody Blvd., Minneapolis, MN 55403-1192
(612) 374-5800, (800) 292-4625; *Fax:* (612) 234-4346
www.dunwoody.edu
info@dunwoody.edu
Ted Ferrara, Chairman
Rich Wagner, President
Brian Seviola, Promotions Manager
Kay Phillips, Vice Chair
Charles B. Westling, Treasurer
James R. Fox, Secretary
Russell Becker, Member of the Board
Rick D. Clevette, VicePresident, Human Resources
Heidi M. Wilson, Vice President/General Counsel/Corporate Secretary
Courses offered include assoc in electronics tech degree, computer technician, radio-TV, industrial electronics technician, digital electronics specialists, electronics technician, TV specialists, certificate programs, aviation electronics,& info mgmt systems.

Grantham University
16025 W 113th Street, Lenexa, KS 66219
(913) 309-4800, (800) 955-2527; *Fax:* (816)-595-5757
www.grantham.edu
admissions@grantham.edu
Joseph McGrath, President
Steve Waldron, Chief OperatingÿOfficer
Joanna Boldt, General Manager
Dr. Jeff Cropsey, Vice President for Strategic Initiatives and Exter
Roman Yagnitinsky, Vice President of Financial Aid
Harry Dotson,Vice President of Compliance
Ed Sammarco, Chief Financial Officer
Jared Parlette, Vice President of Admissions
Alex Bach, Vice President of Marketing and Communications
Courses offered include computer science, electronics engrg tech & computer engrg tech by correspondence, leading to A.S. & B.S. degrees.

The Illinois Center for Broadcasting
455 Eisenhower Lane, Suite 200, Lombard, IL 60148
(630) 916-1700; *Fax:* (630) 916-1764
www.beonair.com
director.chicago@beonair.com
Patrick Johnson, School Dir
10-month, hands-on course in radio & TV bcstg procedures & techniques.

International College of Broadcasting
6 South Smithville Road, Dayton, OH 45431
(800) 517-7284 ,(937) 258-8251; *Fax:* (937) 258-8714
admissions@icb.edu
J Michael LeMaster, CEO/COO
J Michael LeMaster, President/ CEO
Eric Clark, Director of School & Director of Education
Kenny Pyles, Director of Placement & Student Services
James Stringfield, Director of Admissions
Joseph Bargdill,Production Manager and Media Instructor
Olivia LeMaster, Office Manager
Tommy Collins, Radio Department Head
Courses offered include radio, TV, cameraman, CATV, disc jockey, news, sports & audio/recording engrg. Assoc degree in communication arts available in radio/TV & video production/recording audio engrg. Diploma programs offered inaudio/recording engrg & bcstg.

Madison Media Institute-College of Media Arts
Mailing Address: 2702 Agriculture Dr., Madison, WI 53718
Second Address: 4100 West 76th St., Edina, MN 55435
(608) 663-2000, (800) 236-4997, (866) 701-1310; *Fax:* (608) 442-0141
www.mediainstitute.edu
swh@madisonmedia.com
Chris Hutchings, President
Steve Hutchings, Operations Dir
Courses offered include digital media design, production, video, motion graphics, recording & music technology. Accredited by Accrediting Commission of Career Schools & Colleges of Technology.

The New England Institute of Art
10 Brookline Pl. W., Brookline, MA 02445-7295
(617) 739-1700, (800) 903-4425; *Fax:* (617) 582-4500
www.artinstitutes.edu/boston
neiaadm@aii.edu
Christine Murphy, President
Fran Berger, Operations Dir
Debra Leahy, General Manager
Dennis Fantaski, Ph.D., Board of trustees
Dr. John W. Kraft, Board of trustees
Dr. Jo-Ann Merolla Sipple, Board of trustees
David Moulton, Boardof trustees
Joyce Mullen, Board of trustees
Programs offered: Bachelor's Degree in Graphic Design, Photography, Digital Film & Video Production, Interactive Media Design, Media Arts & Animation, Interior Design, Audio & Media Technology. Associate's Degrees in Audio Production,Broadcasting

New England School of Communications
1 College Circle, Bangor, ME 04401
(888) 877-1876, (207) 941-7176; *Fax:* (207) 947-3987
www.nescom.edu
Joe DiStefano, Partner/CEO
Thom Johnston, President
Rodney Verrill, Executive Director of Communications Technology Pr
Eric Ferguson, Interim Dir Audio Engineering
Jill McDonald, VP of Communications & Market Development
BillDevine, Director Career Services
Anne Reed, Director of Enrollment Management
James Ruksznis, Technical Director - Gracie Theatre
Ken Stack, Director of Entertainment Production
Nikki Vachon, Director of Financial Aid
Courses offered include announcing, bcst sls, writing for bcst, TV production, sound recording, voice/diction, news/sports reporting, adv & PR, pub speaking, video graphics, desktop publishing, print journalism & web design.

The New School
Mailing Address: 66 West 12th Street, New York, NY 10011
Second Address: 72 Fifth Avenue, New York, NY 10011
(212) 229-5150, (800) 292-3040, (212) 229-5600; *Fax:* (212) 229-5357
www.newschool.edu
admission@newschool.edu
Henry H. Arnhold, Chairman
David E. Van Zandt, President
Tokumbo Shobwale, Chief Operating Officer
Carol S. Cantrell, SVP for Human Resources and Labor Relations
Chris Ferguson, Vice President for Strategic Enrollment Management
Steve stabile, VP, Finance and Business and Treasurer
Kerry Kruckel, Chief Development Officer
Anne Adriance, Chief Marketing Officer
Martin Mueller, Executive Director
Courses offered include TV writing workshop; writing for TV, films & radio; TV production workshop; voice & speech for theater & TV; seminars on TV comls; writing TV comls. Offers certificate in film/TV studies, B.A., B.A./M.A., M.A. inmedia studies.

Northland Community & Technical College (KSRQ-FM)
Mailing Address: 1101 Hwy. One East, Thief River Falls, MN 56701
Second Address: 2022 Central Avenue NE, East Grand Forks, MN 56721
(218) 683-8800, (218) 793-2800, (800) 959-6282 (80; *Fax:* (218) 683-8980, (218) 793-2842
www.northlandcollege.edu
Dr. Anne K. Temte, President
Julie Olson, Operations Dir
MaryJo Bydal, Administrative Assistant - Vice President
Carey Castel, Vice President of Academic & Student Affairs
Justin Berry, Physical Therapist Assistant ProgramDirector
Michelle Bakken, Business Manager
Jonathan Beck, UAS Instructor/Program Manager
Michelle Benit, HRIS Manager
Courses offered include a diploma-earning program in radio bcstg working on a 24,000 kw educ FM stn.

The Ohio Center for Broadcasting-Cleveland
9000 Sweet Valley Drive, Valley View, OH 44125
(216) 447-9117; *Fax:* (216) 642-9232
www.beonair.com
Robert Mills, President
10-month, hands-on course on radio & TV bcstg & techniques. Fully accredited by ACCSCT. Graduates earn 36 quarter credit hrs with diploma. Instructors are professional bcstrs. Nationally accredited by ACCSCT. Full time placement assistance.
1310 Wadsworth Blvd., Denver, CO
(303) 937-7070

The Ohio Center for Broadcasting-Cincinnati
6703 Madison Rd., Cincinnati, OH 45227
(513) 271-6060; *Fax:* (513) 271-6135
www.beonair.com
Eric Armstrong, Operations Dir
10-month, hands-on course in Radio & TV procedures & techniques.

Penn Foster Career School
Mailing Address: 925 Oak St., Scranton, PA 18515
Second Address: 14300 N. Northsight Blvd, Suite 120, Scottsdale, AZ 85260
(888) 427-1000, (570) 343-9635, (570) 342-7701; *Fax:* (570) 961-4030
www.pennfoster.edu
info@educationdirect.com
Raymond McNulty, Chairman
Frank Britt, CEO
Joseph Gagnon, President/ COO
Dan Conrad, General Manager
Thomas Blesso, V.P. of Strategy and Finance
Robert Bruno, Chief Technology Officer
Peter Ockerbloom, Senior V.P. of GlobalClient Management
William Hollyer, Chief Financial Officer
Mark Slyaton, V.P. of Customer Relations Management
Dara Warn, Chief Marketing Officer
Diploma courses include basic electronics, electronics technology, basic computer progmg, TV/VCR repair or personal computer repair, Java progmg, internet web page design, electricians, telecommunications technician. Center for DegreeStudies: specialized assoc degree in electronics

technology & electrical, mechanical, civil & industrial engrg technology; specialized assoc degree in business mgmt, mktg, finance, accounting or applied computer science; Internet technology in webprogmg, Internet technology multimedia, Internet technology in e-commerce administration, graphic design, DC maintenance technology.

The Poynter Institute for Media Studies
801 3rd St. S., St. Petersburg, FL 33701
(727) 821-9494; *Fax:* (727) 821-0583
www.poynter.org
webstaff@poynter.org
Seminars & conferences for print & bcst & online journalists. Courses for TV/radio include stn leadership, new leaders in the newsroom, newsroom mgmt, ethical decision-making, anchors as newsroom leaders investigative reporting, powerreporting, computer-assisted journalism, visual storytelling & ethics, & producing newscasts.

Specs Howard School of Media Arts Inc.
Mailing Address: 19900 W. Nine Mile Rd., Southfield, MI 48075-3953
Second Address: 23801 Industrial Park Dr., Farmington Hills, MI 48335
(248) 358-9000, (866) 61-SPECS, (248) 427-1800; *Fax:* (248) 746-9772
www.specshoward.edu
Lisa Zahodne, President/COO
Dick Kernen, Operations Dir
Courses offered include Radio-TV-Film & video production graphic design. Accredited by ACCSCT.

Technical Career Institutes
320 W. 31st St., New York, NY 10001
(212) 594-4000; *Fax:* (212) 629-3937
www.tcicollege.edu
admissions@tcicollege.edu
Dr. John J. McGrath, Chairman/President
Bonnie Price, Operations Dir
Alberto Aponte, Chairperson of IET-NET
Miguel Arisa, Arts & Sciences Chair
Miguel Bustamante, Deputy Chairperson of the Electronic Security Syst
Jay RobertFrancisco, Director of Career Services
Lisa M. Sita, Assistant Director of Career Services
Shirley Erves, Director of the Human Resources
Tech courses offered include electronics engrg, EETT & IETC office technology, computerized accounting, bldg maintenance, air conditioning, heating & refrigeration technology. Assoc degree available.

Western Technical College
400 6th Street North, La Crosse, WI 54601
(608) 785-9140, (800) 322-9982; *Fax:* (608) 785-9407
www.westerntc.edu
bookstore@westerntc.edu
Daniel P. (Dan) Hanson, Chairman
Lee Rasch, President
Joan Pierce, Promotions Manager
David Laehn, Vice Chair
Edward J. Lukasek, Secretary
Dennis Treu, Treasurer
Wade Hackbarth, Assoc VP Accounting & Research
John Heath, HumanResources Director
Kimberly Hanson, Administrative Assistant - General Studies & Servi
Courses in the Visual Communications associates's degree include design fundamentals, audio production, media technologies, digital photography, Adobe Photoshop & illustrator, video production & web design.

Federal Communication Commission Executives & Staff

Federal Communications Commission (FCC)
445 12th Street, SW, Washington, DC 20554
(888) 225-5322; *Fax:* (866) 418-0232
www.fcc.gov
Ajit Pai, Chairman
Lori Alexiou, Confidential Assistant
Matthew Berry, Chief of Staff
Nicholas Degani, Senior Counsel
Nathan Leamer, Policy Advisor
Michael Carowitz, Special Counsel
Jay Schwarz, Wireline Advisor
Alison Nemeth,Media Advisor
Rachael Bender, Wireless & International Advisor
Zenji Nakazawa, Public Safety & Consumer Protection Advisor
Commissioner: Robert McDowell
Tel: (202) 418-2200; Angela Giancarlo, Chief of Staff; Christine Kurth, Policy Director; Erin McGGrath, Legal Advisor/Media; Brigid Calamis, Deputy Chief of Staff; Tasha Kinney, Staff Assistant.
Commissioner: Mignon Clyburn
Tel: (202) 418-2000; Dave Grimaldi, Chief of Staff; Drema Johnson, Deputy Chief of Staff; Rick Chessan, Legal Advisor; Angela Kronenberg, Legal Advisor; Louis Peraertz, Legal Advisor; DeeAnn Smith, Staff Assistant.
Commissioner: Jessica Rosenworcel
Tel: (202) 418-2300; Valarie Galasso, Confidential Assistant; David Goldman, Senior Legal Advisor; Priscilla Delgado, Legal Advisor; Alex Hoehn-Saric, Policy Director; Tajuana Dill, Staff Assistant.
Commissioner: Ajit Pai
Tel: (202) 418-2500; Lori Alexiou, Confidential Assistant; Matthew Berry, Legal Advisor; Nicholas Degani, Legal Advisor; Courtney Reinhard, Legal Advisor.
Office of Administrative Law Judges
Richard Sippel, Chief Administrative Law Judge; Mary Gosse, Administrative law Judge.
Office of the Secretary
Marlene Dortch, Secretary; William Caton, Deputy Secretary.
Office of Communications Business
Thomas Reed, Director
Office of Engineering Technology
Julius Knapp, Director; Ira Keltz, Deputy Chief; Jennifer Manner, Deputy Chief; Ron Repasi, Deputy Chief; Bruce Romano, Associate Chief (Legal).
Office of General Counsel
Matthew Berry, General Counsel; Paula Michelle Ellison, Deputy General Counsel; Ajit Pai, Deputy General Counsel; Jacob Lewis, Associate General Counsel.
Office of the Inpsector General
David Hunt, Inspector General.
Office of Legislative Affairs
Greg Guice, Director; Chris Lewis, Deputy Director; David Toomey, Deputy Director; Lori Holy Maarbjerg, Advisor.
Office of Managing Director
Anthony Dale, Managing Director; Mindy Ginsburg, Deputy Managing Director; Joseph Hall, Deputy Managing Director; Mark Stone, Deputy Managing Director.
Office of Media Relations
Tammy Sun, Director; Vacant, Deputy Director; Maribeth McCarrick, Associate Director; Neil Grace, Press Secretary.
Enforcement Bureau
Kris Monteith, Bureau Chief; Michael Carowitz, Chief of Staff; Ellen Conners, Senior Deputy Bureau Chief; Robert Ratcliffe, Deputy Bureau Chief; Susan McNeil, Deputy Bureau Chief; Gene Fullano, Deputy Bureau Chief; George Dillon, AssociateBureau Chief; William Davenport, Assistant Bureau Chief.
International Bureau
Mindel De La Torre, Bureau Chief; Roderick Porter, Deputy Bureau Chief; Troy Tanner, Deputy Bureau Chief; Tom Sullivan, Chief of Staff; Gardner Foster, Assistant Bureau Chief; Robert Somers, Outreach Coordinator.
Media Bureau
William Lake, Bureau Chief; Robert Ratcliffe, Sr Deputy Bureau Chief; Kris Monteith, Deputy Bureau Chief; Michelle Carey, Deputy Bureau Chief; Thomas Horan, Chief of Staff; Nancy Murphy, Associate Bureau Chief.
Wireline Competition Bureau
Julie Veach, Bureau Chief; Carol Mattey, Deputy Bureau Director; Kirk Burgee, Chief of Staff; Lisa Gelb, Deputy Bureau Chief; Deena Shelter, Associate Bureau Chief; Eric Ralph, Chief Economist.
Wireless Telecommunications Bureau
Ruth Milkman, Bureau Chief; James Schlichting, Sr Deputy Bureau Chief; Jane Jackson, Associate Bureau Chief; Jessica Almond, Chief of Staff; Tom Peters, Chief Engineer.

U.S. Government Agencies

Department of Agriculture
1400 Independence Ave. S.W., Washington, DC 20250
(202) 720-2791; *Fax:* (202) 720-5043
www.usda.gov
larry.quinn@usda.gov
Sonny Perdue, Secretary
Stephen Censky, Deputy Secretary Nominee
Diane L. Cullo, Public Affairs Contact
Gary Washington, Chief Information Officer
Garth Clark, Director, Creative Media & Broadcast Center
Wkly TV satellite newsfeed. Daily radio newsline. Wkly radio features on CD.

Department of Commerce
1401 Constitution Ave. N.W., Suite 5040, Washington, DC 20230
(202) 482-2000; *Fax:* (202) 482-2639
www.commerce.gov/opa
Vacant, Director, Office of Public Affairs
Wilbur Ross, Secretary

Department of Defense
1400 Defense Pentagon, Washington, DC 20301-1400
(703) 545-6700, (703) 571-3343; *Fax:* (703) 695-4299
www.defense.gov
Joseph F. Dunford, Jr., Chairman, JCS
Paul J. Selva, Vice Chairman, JCS
Jim Mattis, Secretary
Patrick Shanahan, Deputy Secretary
Dana W. White, Assistant Secretary for Public Affairs
Robert Manning, III, Director, Defense PressOperations

Department of Education
400 Maryland Ave. S.W., Washington, DC 20202
(202) 401-2000, (800) 872-5327
www.ed.gov
Betsey DeVos, Secretary of Education
Vacant, Asst. Secretary, Office of Communications/Outreach
The Office of Communications & Outreach includes the following units/teams: Digital Media, Studio Team, Press Office, Media & Customer Relations, and the Information Resource Center which is the national voice of the Department.

Department of Energy
1000 Independence Ave. S.W., Washington, DC 20585
(202) 586-5000; *Fax:* (202) 586-4403
www.energy.gov
Rick Perry, Secretary of Energy
Daniel Brouilette, Deputy Secretary of Energy
Five business lines encompass everything that DOE does: energy, resouces, natl security, environmental quality, science & technology, & economic productivity.

Department of Health and Human Services
200 Independence Ave. S.W., Washington, DC 20201
(877) 696-6775
www.hhs.gov
Eric D. Hargan, Secretary (Acting)
Vacant, Deputy Secretary
Charmaine Yoest, PhD, Assistant Secretary for Public Affairs
Lance Leggitt, Chief of Staff
John R. Graham, Assistant Secretary for Planning & Evaluation

Department of Justice, Office of Public Aff.
950 Pennsylvania Ave. N.W., Washington, DC 20530-0001
(202) 514-2007, (202) 514-2000
www.justice.gov
press@usdoj.gov.
Sara Hisgur Flores, Director
Ian Prior, Deputy Director
Wyn Hornbuckle, Deputy Director
Devin O'Malley, Media Affairs Coordinator

Department of Labor
200 Constitution Ave. N.W., Frances Perkins Bldg., Washington, DC 20210
(202) 693-6000, (866) 487-2365
www.dol.gov
R. Alexander Acosta, Secretary
Jeffrey Y. Grappone, Assistant Secretary, Public Affairs
Stephen Barr, Deputy Assistant Secretary, Public Affairs
Eric W. Holland, Deputy Assistant Secretary, Public Affairs
Fosters, promotes, & develops the welfare of working people.

Department of State
2201 C St. N.W., Washington, DC 20520
(202) 647-4000, (202) 647-6575
www.state.gov
Rex Tillerson, Secretary
John J. Sullivan, Deputy Secretary
Thomas Shannon, Political Affairs
Vacant, Under Secretary for Management
Vacant, Public Diplomacy and Public Affairs
Maliz E. Beams, Counselor of the Department

Department of the Treasury
1500 Pennsylvania Ave. N.W., Washington, DC 20220
(202) 622-2000, (202) 622-2960 (press off.); *Fax:* (202) 622-6415
www.treasury.gov
press@treasury.gov
Steven Terner Mnuchin, Secretary
Marisol Baribay, Press Contact, Domestic Finance
Jason Chung, Press Contact, International Affairs
Seth Unger, Press Contact, Terrorism/Financial Intelligance

Department of Transportation
1200 New Jersey St. S.E., Washington, DC 20590
(202) 366-4000, (855) 368-4200
www.transportation.gov
Elaine L. Chao, Secretary of Transportation
Jeffrey Rosen, Deputy Secretary of Transportation
Todd Inman, Operations Director
Judy Kaleta, Deputy General Counsel
Marianne McInerney, Director of Public Affairs
Geoff Burr, Chief ofStaff
Mission: To serve the United States by ensuring a fast, safe, efficient, accessible and convenient transportation system that meets our vital natl interests and enhances the quality of life of the American people, today & into the future.

Executive Office of the President
The White House, 1600 Pennsylvania Ave. N.W., Washington, DC 20500
(202) 456-1414; *Fax:* (202) 456-2461
www.whitehouse.gov
comments@whitehouse.gov
Donald J. Trump, President
Mike Pence, Vice President
John F. Kelly, Chief of Staff
Jeff Sessions, Attorney General
Mick Mulvaney, Director, Office of Management & Budget
Hope Hicks, Communications Director

Federal Communications Commission
445 12th Street, SW, Washington, DC 20554
(888) 225-5322; *Fax:* (866) 418-0232
www.fcc.gov
david.fiske@fcc.gov
Ajit Pai, Chairman
(For full listing of commissioners & staff, see FCC Executives & Staff.)

Federal Emergency Management Agency
Office of External Affairs, 500 C St. S.W., Washington, DC 20472
(800) 621-FEMA(3362), (202) 646-2500; *Fax:* (800) 827-8112
www.fema.gov
fema-news-desk@fema.dhs.gov
Brock Long, Administrator
Susan Phelan, Director, External Affairs
Stephanie Tennyson, Deputy Director
William Booher, Public Affairs Division
Vallee Bunting, Director, Coordination & Business Operations
Zachary Kittrie, Director,READY Campaign
Comprehensive info source on emergency preparedness, federal disaster response & recovery.

Federal Trade Commission
600 Pennsylvania Ave. N.W., Washington, DC 20580
(202) 326-2222, (202) 326-2334
www.ftc.gov
opa@ftc.gov
Maureen K. Ohlhausen, Chairman (Acting)
Peter Kaplan, Director, Office of Public Affairs

House Appropriations Committee
Capitol Bldg, Rm. H-305, Washington, DC 20515
(202) 225-2771
www.appropriations.house.gov
Rodney P. Frelinghuysen, Chairman
Funds government agencies.

House Committee on Energy and Commerce
2125 Rayburn House Office Bldg., Washington, DC 20515-6115
(202) 225-4972
www.energycommerce.house.gov
Greg Walden, Chairman
Laws to improve the quality of the air we breathe, to clean up toxic waste sites, to provide health care to senior citizens & children, to protect the safety of our food & drugs, to promote a

vibrant telecommunications industry, to preventfraud in our financial markets & much more.

House Committee on the Judiciary
2138 Rayburn House Office Bldg., Washington, DC 20515-6216
(202) 225-3951
www.judiciary.house.gov
judiciary@mail.house.gov
Bob Goodlatte, Chairman
Matters relating to the administration of justice in Federal courts, administrative bodies & law enforcement agencies. Its infrequent but important role in impeachment proceedings has also brought it much attention.

National Aeronautics & Space Administration (NASA)
300 E St. S.W., Suite 5R30, Washington, DC 20546
(202) 358-0001; *Fax:* (202) 358-4338
www.nasa.gov
public-inquiries@hq.nasa.gov
Robert N. Lightfoot, Jr., Administrator (Acting)
Renee Wynn, Chief Information Officer
Jenrae Wang, Assoc. Administrator, Office of Communications

National Labor Relations Board
1015 Half Street SE, Washington, DC 20570-0001
(202) 273-1000, (844) 762-6572; *Fax:* (202) 273-4483
www.nlrb.gov
EmergencyContact@NLRB.gov
Philip A. Miscimarra, Chairman
Gary Shinners, Executive Secretary
Carmen Torres, Director, Congressional & Public Affairs
The NLRB adjudicates unfair labor practice charges & conducts union representation elections under the Natl Labor Rel Act.

National Science Foundation
2415 Eisenhower Avenue, Alexandria, VA 22314
(703) 292-5111, (800) 877-8339; *Fax:* (703) 292-9087
www.nsf.gov
info@nsf.gov
Dr. France A. Cardova, Director
Amanda Hallberg Greenwell, Head, Legislative & Public Affairs

National Telecommunications and Information Administration
1401 Constitution Avenue, N.W., Washington, DC 20230
(202) 482-1840; *Fax:* (202) 219-2077
www.ntia.doc.gov
websitecomments@ntia.doc.gov
Vacant, Assistant Secretary/Administrator
Len Betchel, Performing tasks of the Asst. Sec./Administrator
Glenn Reynolds, Chief of Staff
Vacant, Public Affairs
NTIA serves as the principal advisor to the exec branch on domestic & international communication & info issues.

Senate Appropriations Committee
The Capitol, Room S-128, Washington, DC 20510
(202) 224-7257
www.appropriations.senate.gov
Thad Cochran, Chairman

Senate Committee on Commerce, Science, and Transportation
Dirksen Senate Office Bldg., Suite 512, Washington, DC 20510-6125
(202) 224-0411 (min.), (202) 224-1251 (maj.)
www.commerce.senate.gov
John Thune, Chairman
Jurisdiction includes communications, aviation, consumer affairs, foreign commerce & tourism, oceans & fisheries, science, technolgy & space, surface transportion & merchant marine, manufactruring & competiveness.

Senate Judiciary Committee
224 Dirksen Senate Office Bldg, Washington, DC 20510
(202) 224-5225 (R), (202) 224-7703 (D); *Fax:* (202) 224-9102
www.judiciary.senate.gov
Chuck Grassley, Chairman

U.S. Advisory Commission on Public Diplomacy
2200 C Street NW, C2CC17, Washington, DC 20520
(202) 647-4000; *Fax:* (202) 203-7886
www.state.gov/pdcommission/
Sim Farar, Chairman
Shawn Powers, Executive Director
Chris Hensman, Senior Advisor
Jennifer Rahimi, Senior Advisor
A bipartisan presidentially appointed panel created by Congress to oversee U.S. government activities intended to understand, inform & influence foreign publics.

U.S. Court of Appeals for the District of Columbia Circuit
333 Constitution Ave. N.W., Room 5205, Washington, DC 20001
(202) 216-7000; *Fax:* (202) 216-7200
www.cadc.uscourts.gov
Scott Atchue, Operations Manager
Mark Langer, Clerk
Appeals from District Court cases. Appeals from federal agency decisions.

U.S. District Court for the District of Columbia
333 Constitution Ave. N.W., Rm. 4826, Washington, DC 20001
(202) 354-3000
www.dcd.uscourts.gov
Angela D. Caesar, Clerk
Hears civil & criminal cases that arise under federal law, cases involving the U.S. Constitution, disputes between two states, or cases in which the United States is a party.

U.S. Securities and Exchange Commission
Mailing Address: 100 F St. N.E., Washington, DC 20549
Second Address: 950 East Paces Ferry, N.E., Ste 900, Atlanta, GA 30326-1382
(202) 942-8088, (202) 551-5400, (404) 842-7600; *Fax:* (202) 942-9628
www.sec.gov
Jay Clayton, Chair
Michael S. Piwowar, Commissioner
Kara M. Stein, Commissioner
John Nester, Director, Office of Public Affairs
Administers federal securities laws that protect investors. These laws ensure that securities markets are fair & provide sanctions for enforcement.

U.S. Supreme Court
One First St. N.E, Washington, DC 20543
(202) 479-3000,(202) 479-3011,(202) 479-3030 (VI)
www.supremecourt.gov/
pio@sc-us.gov
John G. Roberts, Jr., Chief Justice
Scott Harris, Clerk
Linda Maslow, Librarian
Kathleen L. Arberg, Public Information Officer
Robert J. Hawkins, Director, Information Technology
Catherine E. Fitts, Curator

U.S. State Cable Regulatory Agencies

Delaware Public Service Commission
861 Silver Lake Blvd. Cannon Bldg., Suite 100, Dover, DE 19904
(302) 736-7500; *Fax:* (302) 739-4849
depsc.delaware.gov/
matthew.hartigan@state.de.us
Dallas Winslow, Chair
Bruce Burcat, General Manager
Joann Conaway, Commissioner
Kim Drexler, Commissioner
Munabhai C. Karia, Commissioner
Harold Gray, Commissioner
Matthew Hartigan, Deputy Director
Created in 1949 to regulate investor-owned public utilities, the Delaware Public Service Commission (PSC) works to ensure safe, reliable and reasonably priced cable, electric, natural gas, wastewater, water and telecommunications servicesfor Delaware consumers. For those services that are moving toward competitive markets, the Commission makes rules to level the playing field between competing providers, and resolves disputes between these providers. The PSC also assists consumers inresolving disputes with their service providers.

Hawaii Cable Television Division
Mailing Address: PO Box 541, Dept. of Commerce & Consumer Affairs, Honolulu, HI 96809
Second Address: 335 Merchant Street, Rm 101, Honolulu, HI 96813
(808) 586-2620; *Fax:* (808) 586-2625
cca.hawaii.gov/catv/
cabletv@dcca.hawaii.gov
Catherine P. Awakuni Colon, Director, DCCA
Ji Sook Kim, Cable Television Administrator
The Cable Television Division regulates franchised wireline cable operators within the State of Hawaii. CATV determines whether the initial issuance, renewal or transfer of a cable franchise is in the public's best interest.

Massachusetts Department of Telecommunications and Cable
1000 Washington Street, Suite 820, Boston, MA 02118
(617) 305-3580, (800) 392-6066
www.mass.gov/ocabr/government/oca-agencies/dtc-lp/
Karen Charles Peterson, Commissioner
Sandra Merrick, General Counsel
Lindsay DeRoche, Director, Competition Division
Joslyn Day, Director, Consumer Division
Sara Clark, Dept. Secretary, Administration Division
The Department is responsible for regulating the telecommunications and cable industries of the state, ensuring: consumers receive high quality communications at reasonable rates; sustainable competition is promoted to increase consumerwelfare; and that consumer protections are enforced and maintained.

New Jersey Office of Cable Television
Div/DBA: NJ Board of Public Utilities
44 S. Clinton Avenue, Trenton, NJ 08625
(609) 341-9428, (800) 624-0331; *Fax:* (609) 777-3325
www.nj.gov/bpu/divisions/cable/
Richard Mroz, Board President
Dr. Lawanda Gilbert, Director
Renee Frierson, Assistant

New York State Department of Public Service
3 Empire State Plaza, Albany, NY 12223-1350
(518) 474-7080; *Fax:* (518) 474-0421
www.dps.ny.gov
secretary@dps.ny.gov
John B. Rhodes, Chairman
Debra LaBelle, Acting Director, Telecommunications
James Denn, Public Information Officer

The Public Utilities Regulatory Authority (PURA)
Ten Franklin Square, New Britain, CT 06051
(860) 827-1553; *Fax:* (860) 827-2822
www.ct.gov/pura
pura.information@ct.gov
Katie Scharf Dykes, Chair
John W. Betkoski III, Vice-Chairman
Michael Caron, Commissioner
The Public Utilities Regulatory Authority (PURA) is statutorily charged with regulating the rates and services of Connecticut's investor owned electricity, natural gas, water and telecommunication companies and is the franchising authorityfor the state's cable television companies. In the industries that are still wholly regulated, PURA balances the public's right to safe, adequate and reliable utility service at reasonable rates with the provider's right to a reasonable return onits investment. PURA also keeps watch over competitive utility services to promote equity among the competitors while customers reap the price and quality benefits of competition and are protected from unfair business practices.

Regulatory Commission of Alaska
701 W. Eigth Avenue, Suite 300, Anchorage, AK 99501-3469
(907) 276-6222, (800) 390-2782; *Fax:* (907) 276-0160
www.rca.alaska.gov
rca.mail@alaska.gov
Richard Gazaway, Administrative Law Judge
M. Grace Salazar, Chief, Media

Rhode Island Division of Public Utilities and Carriers
89 Jefferson Blvd., Warwick, RI 02888
(401) 941-4500; *Fax:* (401) 941-9248
www.ripuc.org
thomas.kogut@dpuc.ri.gov
Margaret Curran, Chair
Marion Gold, Commissioner
Abigail Anthony, Commissioner
Macky McCleary, Administrator
Kevin Lynch, Deputy Administartor
The Public Utilities Commission comprises two distinct regulatory bodies: a three-member Commission (Commission) and the Division of Public Utilities and Carriers (Division).

Vermont Public Service Board
112 State Street, Third Floor, Montpelier, VT 05620
(802) 828-2811, (800) 622-4496; *Fax:* (802) 828-2342
publicservice.vermont.gov/contact
psb.consumer@vermont.gov
June Tierney, Commissioner
Riley Allen, Deputy Commissioner
Audrey Fargo, Executive Assistant
Clay Purvis, Director, Telecommunications & Connectivity Div.

Canadian Government Agencies

Canadian Radio-Television and Telecommunications Commission

Les Terrasses de la Chaudiere, 1 Promenade du Portage, Gatineau, QC J8X 4B1 Canada
(819) 997-0313; *Fax:* (819) 994-0218
www.crtc.gc.ca

Ian Scott, Hhairman & Chief Executive Officer
Dr. Caroline J. Simard, Vice Chair, Broadcasting
Christianne Laizner, Vice Chair, Telecommunications
Claude Doucet, Executive Director, Communications/External Rltns
Scott Hutton,Executive Director, Broadcasting
Chris Seidl, Executive Director, Telecommunications
Amy Hanley, Chief of Staff

The Canadian Radio-television and Telecommunications Commission (CRTC) is an independent public organization that regulates and supervises the Canadian broadcasting and telecommunications systems.

Innovation, Science & Economic Development Canada (ISED)

C D Howe Building, 4th Fl, East Tower, 235 Queen Street, Ottawa, ON K1A 0H5 Canada
(800) 328-6189; *Fax:* (613) 954-2340
www.ic.gc.ca
info@ic.gc.ca

Hon. Navdeep Bains, Minister, ISED
Hon. Kirsty Duncan, Minister, Science
Hon. Bardish Chagger, Minister, Small Business & Tourism
John Knubley, Deputy Minister
David McGovern, Associate Deputy Minister
Kelly Acton, DirectorGeneral, Communications & Marketing

The mission of Innovation, Science & Economic Development Canada (ISED), (formerly Industry Canada is to help make Candians more productive and competitive in a global knowledge based economy. The departments policies, programs, and servicesassist in the creation of an economy that provides more and better paying jobs for Canadians; supports stronger buisness growth through sustained improvements in productivity and gives consumers, businesses, and investors confidence that themarketplace is fair, efficient, and competitive. To reach its clients, ISED collaborates extensively with partners at all levels of government and private sector.

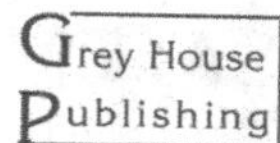

2018 Title List

Visit www.GreyHouse.com for Product Information, Table of Contents, and Sample Pages

General Reference
America's College Museums
American Environmental Leaders: From Colonial Times to the Present
Encyclopedia of African-American Writing
Encyclopedia of Constitutional Amendments
Encyclopedia of Human Rights and the United States
Encyclopedia of Invasions & Conquests
Encyclopedia of Prisoners of War & Internment
Encyclopedia of Religion & Law in America
Encyclopedia of Rural America
Encyclopedia of the Continental Congress
Encyclopedia of the United States Cabinet, 1789-2010
Encyclopedia of War Journalism
Encyclopedia of Warrior Peoples & Fighting Groups
The Environmental Debate: A Documentary History
The Evolution Wars: A Guide to the Debates
From Suffrage to the Senate: America's Political Women
Gun Debate: An Encyclopedia of Gun Rights & Gun Control in the U.S.
Opinions throughout History: National Security vs. Civil and Privacy Rights
Opinions throughout History: Immigration
Opinions throughout History: Drug Abuse & Drug Epidemics
Political Corruption in America
Privacy Rights in the Digital Era
The Religious Right: A Reference Handbook
Speakers of the House of Representatives, 1789-2009
This is Who We Were: 1880-1900
This is Who We Were: A Companion to the 1940 Census
This is Who We Were: In the 1900s
This is Who We Were: In the 1910s
This is Who We Were: In the 1920s
This is Who We Were: In the 1940s
This is Who We Were: In the 1950s
This is Who We Were: In the 1960s
This is Who We Were: In the 1970s
This is Who We Were: In the 1980s
This is Who We Were: In the 1990s
This is Who We Were: In the 2000s
U.S. Land & Natural Resource Policy
The Value of a Dollar 1600-1865: Colonial Era to the Civil War
The Value of a Dollar: 1860-2014
Working Americans 1770-1869 Vol. IX: Revolutionary War to the Civil War
Working Americans 1880-1999 Vol. I: The Working Class
Working Americans 1880-1999 Vol. II: The Middle Class
Working Americans 1880-1999 Vol. III: The Upper Class
Working Americans 1880-1999 Vol. IV: Their Children
Working Americans 1880-2015 Vol. V: Americans At War
Working Americans 1880-2005 Vol. VI: Women at Work
Working Americans 1880-2006 Vol. VII: Social Movements
Working Americans 1880-2007 Vol. VIII: Immigrants
Working Americans 1880-2009 Vol. X: Sports & Recreation
Working Americans 1880-2010 Vol. XI: Inventors & Entrepreneurs
Working Americans 1880-2011 Vol. XII: Our History through Music
Working Americans 1880-2012 Vol. XIII: Education & Educators
Working Americans 1880-2016 Vol. XIV: Industry Through the Ages
Working Americans 1880-2017 Vol. XV: Politics & Politicians
World Cultural Leaders of the 20th & 21st Centuries

Education Information
Charter School Movement
Comparative Guide to American Elementary & Secondary Schools
Complete Learning Disabilities Directory
Educators Resource Handbook
Special Education: Policy and Curriculum Development

Health Information
Comparative Guide to American Hospitals
Complete Directory for Pediatric Disorders
Complete Directory for People with Chronic Illness
Complete Directory for People with Disabilities
Complete Mental Health Directory
Diabetes in America: Analysis of an Epidemic
Guide to Health Care Group Purchasing Organizations
Guide to U.S. HMO's & PPO's
Medical Device Market Place
Older Americans Information Directory

Business Information
Complete Television, Radio & Cable Industry Directory
Directory of Business Information Resources
Directory of Mail Order Catalogs
Directory of Venture Capital & Private Equity Firms
Environmental Resource Handbook
Financial Literacy Starter Kit
Food & Beverage Market Place
Grey House Homeland Security Directory
Grey House Performing Arts Directory
Grey House Safety & Security Directory
Hudson's Washington News Media Contacts Directory
New York State Directory
Sports Market Place Directory

Statistics & Demographics
American Tally
America's Top-Rated Cities
America's Top-Rated Smaller Cities
Ancestry & Ethnicity in America
The Asian Databook
Comparative Guide to American Suburbs
The Hispanic Databook
Profiles of America
"Profiles of" Series - State Handbooks
Weather America

Financial Ratings Series
Financial Literacy Basics
TheStreet Ratings' Guide to Bond & Money Market Mutual Funds
TheStreet Ratings' Guide to Common Stocks
TheStreet Ratings' Guide to Exchange-Traded Funds
TheStreet Ratings' Guide to Stock Mutual Funds
TheStreet Ratings' Ultimate Guided Tour of Stock Investing
Weiss Ratings' Consumer Guides
Weiss Ratings' Financial Literary Basic Guides
Weiss Ratings' Guide to Banks
Weiss Ratings' Guide to Credit Unions
Weiss Ratings' Guide to Health Insurers
Weiss Ratings' Guide to Life & Annuity Insurers
Weiss Ratings' Guide to Property & Casualty Insurers

Bowker's Books In Print® Titles
American Book Publishing Record® Annual
American Book Publishing Record® Monthly
Books In Print®
Books In Print® Supplement
Books Out Loud™
Bowker's Complete Video Directory™
Children's Books In Print®
El-Hi Textbooks & Serials In Print®
Forthcoming Books®
Law Books & Serials In Print™
Medical & Health Care Books In Print™
Publishers, Distributors & Wholesalers of the US™
Subject Guide to Books In Print®
Subject Guide to Children's Books In Print®

Canadian General Reference
Associations Canada
Canadian Almanac & Directory
Canadian Environmental Resource Guide
Canadian Parliamentary Guide
Canadian Venture Capital & Private Equity Firms
Canadian Who's Who
Financial Post Directory of Directors
Financial Services Canada
Governments Canada
Health Guide Canada
The History of Canada
Libraries Canada
Major Canadian Cities

SALEM PRESS

SALEM PRESS

2018 Title List

Visit www.SalemPress.com for Product Information, Table of Contents, and Sample Pages

Science, Careers & Mathematics

Ancient Creatures
Applied Science
Applied Science: Engineering & Mathematics
Applied Science: Science & Medicine
Applied Science: Technology
Biomes and Ecosystems
Careers in the Arts: Fine, Performing & Visual
Careers in Building Construction
Careers in Business
Careers in Chemistry
Careers in Communications & Media
Careers in Environment & Conservation
Careers in Financial Services
Careers in Green Energy
Careers in Healthcare
Careers in Hospitality & Tourism
Careers in Human Services
Careers in Law, Criminal Justice & Emergency Services
Careers in Manufacturing
Careers in Outdoor Jobs
Careers in Overseas Jobs
Careers in Physics
Careers in Sales, Insurance & Real Estate
Careers in Science & Engineering
Careers in Sports & Fitness
Careers in Social Media
Careers in Sports Medicine & Training
Careers in Technology Services & Repair
Computer Technology Innovators
Contemporary Biographies in Business
Contemporary Biographies in Chemistry
Contemporary Biographies in Communications & Media
Contemporary Biographies in Environment & Conservation
Contemporary Biographies in Healthcare
Contemporary Biographies in Hospitality & Tourism
Contemporary Biographies in Law & Criminal Justice
Contemporary Biographies in Physics
Earth Science
Earth Science: Earth Materials & Resources
Earth Science: Earth's Surface and History
Earth Science: Physics & Chemistry of the Earth
Earth Science: Weather, Water & Atmosphere
Encyclopedia of Energy
Encyclopedia of Environmental Issues
Encyclopedia of Environmental Issues: Atmosphere and Air Pollution
Encyclopedia of Environmental Issues: Ecology and Ecosystems
Encyclopedia of Environmental Issues: Energy and Energy Use
Encyclopedia of Environmental Issues: Policy and Activism
Encyclopedia of Environmental Issues: Preservation/Wilderness Issues
Encyclopedia of Environmental Issues: Water and Water Pollution
Encyclopedia of Global Resources
Encyclopedia of Global Warming
Encyclopedia of Mathematics & Society
Encyclopedia of Mathematics & Society: Engineering, Tech, Medicine
Encyclopedia of Mathematics & Society: Great Mathematicians
Encyclopedia of Mathematics & Society: Math & Social Sciences
Encyclopedia of Mathematics & Society: Math Development/Concepts
Encyclopedia of Mathematics & Society: Math in Culture & Society
Encyclopedia of Mathematics & Society: Space, Science, Environment
Encyclopedia of the Ancient World
Forensic Science
Geography Basics
Internet Innovators
Inventions and Inventors
Magill's Encyclopedia of Science: Animal Life
Magill's Encyclopedia of Science: Plant life
Notable Natural Disasters
Principles of Artificial Intelligence & Robotics
Principles of Astronomy
Principles of Biology
Principles of Biotechnology
Principles of Chemistry
Principles of Climatology
Principles of Physical Science
Principles of Physics
Principles of Programming & Coding
Principles of Research Methods
Principles of Sustainability
Science and Scientists
Solar System
Solar System: Great Astronomers
Solar System: Study of the Universe
Solar System: The Inner Planets
Solar System: The Moon and Other Small Bodies
Solar System: The Outer Planets
Solar System: The Sun and Other Stars
World Geography

Literature

American Ethnic Writers
Classics of Science Fiction & Fantasy Literature
Critical Approaches: Feminist
Critical Approaches: Multicultural
Critical Approaches: Moral
Critical Approaches: Psychological
Critical Insights: Authors
Critical Insights: Film
Critical Insights: Literary Collection Bundles
Critical Insights: Themes
Critical Insights: Works
Critical Survey of American Literature
Critical Survey of Drama
Critical Survey of Graphic Novels: Heroes & Super Heroes
Critical Survey of Graphic Novels: History, Theme & Technique
Critical Survey of Graphic Novels: Independents/Underground Classics
Critical Survey of Graphic Novels: Manga
Critical Survey of Long Fiction
Critical Survey of Mystery & Detective Fiction
Critical Survey of Mythology and Folklore: Heroes and Heroines
Critical Survey of Mythology and Folklore: Love, Sexuality & Desire
Critical Survey of Mythology and Folklore: World Mythology
Critical Survey of Novels into Film
Critical Survey of Poetry
Critical Survey of Poetry: American Poets
Critical Survey of Poetry: British, Irish & Commonwealth Poets
Critical Survey of Poetry: Cumulative Index
Critical Survey of Poetry: European Poets
Critical Survey of Poetry: Topical Essays
Critical Survey of Poetry: World Poets
Critical Survey of Science Fiction & Fantasy
Critical Survey of Shakespeare's Plays
Critical Survey of Shakespeare's Sonnets
Critical Survey of Short Fiction
Critical Survey of Short Fiction: American Writers
Critical Survey of Short Fiction: British, Irish, Commonwealth Writers
Critical Survey of Short Fiction: Cumulative Index
Critical Survey of Short Fiction: European Writers
Critical Survey of Short Fiction: Topical Essays
Critical Survey of Short Fiction: World Writers
Critical Survey of World Literature
Critical Survey of Young Adult Literature
Cyclopedia of Literary Characters
Cyclopedia of Literary Places
Holocaust Literature
Introduction to Literary Context: American Poetry of the 20th Century
Introduction to Literary Context: American Post-Modernist Novels
Introduction to Literary Context: American Short Fiction
Introduction to Literary Context: English Literature
Introduction to Literary Context: Plays
Introduction to Literary Context: World Literature
Magill's Literary Annual 2018
Masterplots
Masterplots II: African American Literature
Masterplots II: American Fiction Series
Masterplots II: British & Commonwealth Fiction Series
Masterplots II: Christian Literature
Masterplots II: Drama Series
Masterplots II: Juvenile & Young Adult Literature, Supplement
Masterplots II: Nonfiction Series
Masterplots II: Poetry Series
Masterplots II: Short Story Series
Masterplots II: Women's Literature Series
Notable African American Writers
Notable American Novelists
Notable Playwrights
Notable Poets
Recommended Reading: 600 Classics Reviewed
Short Story Writers

2018 Title List

Visit www.SalemPress.com for Product Information, Table of Contents, and Sample Pages

History and Social Science

The 2000s in America
50 States
African American History
Agriculture in History
American First Ladies
American Heroes
American Indian Culture
American Indian History
American Indian Tribes
American Presidents
American Villains
America's Historic Sites
Ancient Greece
The Bill of Rights
The Civil Rights Movement
The Cold War
Countries, Peoples & Cultures
Countries, Peoples & Cultures: Central & South America
Countries, Peoples & Cultures: Central, South & Southeast Asia
Countries, Peoples & Cultures: East & South Africa
Countries, Peoples & Cultures: East Asia & the Pacific
Countries, Peoples & Cultures: Eastern Europe
Countries, Peoples & Cultures: Middle East & North Africa
Countries, Peoples & Cultures: North America & the Caribbean
Countries, Peoples & Cultures: West & Central Africa
Countries, Peoples & Cultures: Western Europe
Defining Documents: American Revolution
Defining Documents: American West
Defining Documents: Ancient World
Defining Documents: Asia
Defining Documents: Civil Rights
Defining Documents: Civil War
Defining Documents: Court Cases
Defining Documents: Dissent & Protest
Defining Documents: Emergence of Modern America
Defining Documents: Exploration & Colonial America
Defining Documents: Immigration & Immigrant Communities
Defining Documents: LGBTQ
Defining Documents: Manifest Destiny
Defining Documents: Middle Ages
Defining Documents: Middle East
Defining Documents: Nationalism & Populism
Defining Documents: Native Americans
Defining Documents: Political Campaigns, Candidates & Discourse
Defining Documents: Postwar 1940s
Defining Documents: Reconstruction
Defining Documents: Renaissance & Early Modern Era
Defining Documents: Secrets, Leaks & Scandals
Defining Documents: 1920s
Defining Documents: 1930s
Defining Documents: 1950s
Defining Documents: 1960s
Defining Documents: 1970s
Defining Documents: The 17th Century
Defining Documents: The 18th Century
Defining Documents: The 19th Century
Defining Documents: The 20th Century: 1900-1950
Defining Documents: Vietnam War
Defining Documents: Women
Defining Documents: World War I
Defining Documents: World War II
Education Today
The Eighties in America
Encyclopedia of American Immigration
Encyclopedia of Flight
Encyclopedia of the Ancient World
Fashion Innovators
The Fifties in America
The Forties in America
Great Athletes
Great Athletes: Baseball
Great Athletes: Basketball
Great Athletes: Boxing & Soccer
Great Athletes: Cumulative Index
Great Athletes: Football
Great Athletes: Golf & Tennis
Great Athletes: Olympics
Great Athletes: Racing & Individual Sports
Great Contemporary Athletes
Great Events from History: 17th Century
Great Events from History: 18th Century
Great Events from History: 19th Century
Great Events from History: 20th Century (1901-1940)
Great Events from History: 20th Century (1941-1970)
Great Events from History: 20th Century (1971-2000)
Great Events from History: 21st Century (2000-2016)
Great Events from History: African American History
Great Events from History: Cumulative Indexes
Great Events from History: LGBTG
Great Events from History: Middle Ages
Great Events from History: Secrets, Leaks & Scandals
Great Events from History: Renaissance & Early Modern Era
Great Lives from History: 17th Century
Great Lives from History: 18th Century
Great Lives from History: 19th Century
Great Lives from History: 20th Century
Great Lives from History: 21st Century (2000-2017)
Great Lives from History: American Women
Great Lives from History: Ancient World
Great Lives from History: Asian & Pacific Islander Americans
Great Lives from History: Cumulative Indexes
Great Lives from History: Incredibly Wealthy
Great Lives from History: Inventors & Inventions
Great Lives from History: Jewish Americans
Great Lives from History: Latinos
Great Lives from History: Notorious Lives
Great Lives from History: Renaissance & Early Modern Era
Great Lives from History: Scientists & Science
Historical Encyclopedia of American Business
Issues in U.S. Immigration
Magill's Guide to Military History
Milestone Documents in African American History
Milestone Documents in American History
Milestone Documents in World History
Milestone Documents of American Leaders
Milestone Documents of World Religions
Music Innovators
Musicians & Composers 20th Century
The Nineties in America
The Seventies in America
The Sixties in America
Sociology Today
Survey of American Industry and Careers
The Thirties in America
The Twenties in America
United States at War
U.S. Court Cases
U.S. Government Leaders
U.S. Laws, Acts, and Treaties
U.S. Legal System
U.S. Supreme Court
Weapons and Warfare
World Conflicts: Asia and the Middle East

Health

Addictions & Substance Abuse
Adolescent Health & Wellness
Cancer
Complementary & Alternative Medicine
Community & Family Health
Genetics & Inherited Conditions
Health Issues
Infectious Diseases & Conditions
Magill's Medical Guide
Nutrition
Nursing
Psychology & Behavioral Health
Psychology Basics

2018 Title List

Visit www.HWWilsonInPrint.com for Product Information, Table of Contents and Sample Pages

Current Biography
Current Biography Cumulative Index 1946-2013
Current Biography Monthly Magazine
Current Biography Yearbook: 2003
Current Biography Yearbook: 2004
Current Biography Yearbook: 2005
Current Biography Yearbook: 2006
Current Biography Yearbook: 2007
Current Biography Yearbook: 2008
Current Biography Yearbook: 2009
Current Biography Yearbook: 2010
Current Biography Yearbook: 2011
Current Biography Yearbook: 2012
Current Biography Yearbook: 2013
Current Biography Yearbook: 2014
Current Biography Yearbook: 2015
Current Biography Yearbook: 2016
Current Biography Yearbook: 2017

Core Collections
Children's Core Collection
Fiction Core Collection
Graphic Novels Core Collection
Middle & Junior High School Core
Public Library Core Collection: Nonfiction
Senior High Core Collection
Young Adult Fiction Core Collection

The Reference Shelf
Aging in America
Alternative Facts: Post Truth & the Information War
The American Dream
American Military Presence Overseas
The Arab Spring
Artificial Intelligence
The Brain
The Business of Food
Campaign Trends & Election Law
Conspiracy Theories
The Digital Age
Dinosaurs
Embracing New Paradigms in Education
Faith & Science
Families: Traditional and New Structures
The Future of U.S. Economic Relations: Mexico, Cuba, and Venezuela
Global Climate Change
Graphic Novels and Comic Books
Guns in America
Immigration
Immigration in the U.S.
Internet Abuses & Privacy Rights
Internet Safety
LGBTQ in the 21st Century
Marijuana Reform
The News and its Future
The Paranormal
Politics of the Ocean
Prescription Drug Abuse
Racial Tension in a "Postracial" Age
Reality Television
Representative American Speeches: 2008-2009
Representative American Speeches: 2009-2010
Representative American Speeches: 2010-2011
Representative American Speeches: 2011-2012
Representative American Speeches: 2012-2013
Representative American Speeches: 2013-2014
Representative American Speeches: 2014-2015
Representative American Speeches: 2015-2016
Representative American Speeches: 2016-2017
Representative American Speeches: 2017-2018
Rethinking Work
Revisiting Gender
Robotics
Russia
Social Networking
Social Services for the Poor
South China Seas Conflict
Space Exploration & Development
Sports in America
The Supreme Court
The Transformation of American Cities
U.S. Infrastructure
U.S. National Debate Topic: Educational Reform
U.S. National Debate Topic: Surveillance
U.S. National Debate Topic: The Ocean
U.S. National Debate Topic: Transportation Infrastructure
Whistleblowers

Readers' Guide
Abridged Readers' Guide to Periodical Literature
Readers' Guide to Periodical Literature

Indexes
Index to Legal Periodicals & Books
Short Story Index
Book Review Digest

Sears List
Sears List of Subject Headings
Sears: Lista de Encabezamientos de Materia

Facts About Series
Facts About American Immigration
Facts About China
Facts About the 20th Century
Facts About the Presidents
Facts About the World's Languages

Nobel Prize Winners
Nobel Prize Winners: 1901-1986
Nobel Prize Winners: 1987-1991
Nobel Prize Winners: 1992-1996
Nobel Prize Winners: 1997-2001

World Authors
World Authors: 1995-2000
World Authors: 2000-2005

Famous First Facts
Famous First Facts
Famous First Facts About American Politics
Famous First Facts About Sports
Famous First Facts About the Environment
Famous First Facts: International Edition

American Book of Days
The American Book of Days
The International Book of Days

Monographs
American Reformers
The Barnhart Dictionary of Etymology
Celebrate the World
Guide to the Ancient World
Indexing from A to Z
Nobel Prize Winners
The Poetry Break
Radical Change: Books for Youth in a Digital Age
Speeches of American Presidents

Wilson Chronology
Wilson Chronology of Asia and the Pacific
Wilson Chronology of Human Rights
Wilson Chronology of Ideas
Wilson Chronology of the Arts
Wilson Chronology of the World's Religions
Wilson Chronology of Women's Achievements